THE WORLD ALMANAC®

AND BOOK OF FACTS

2014

WORLD ALMANAC BOOKS

THE WORLD ALMANAC
AND BOOK OF FACTS

2014

Senior Editor: Sarah Janssen
Editor: M. L. Liu **Associate Editor:** Shmuel Ross
Index Editor: Nan Badgett
Contributors: Jeremy Eagle, Robert Famighetti, Marshall Gerometta, Jacqueline Laks Gorman, Richard Hantula, Sarah Hilliard, Michael J. Kaufman, Donhae Koo, John Mastroberardino, William A. McGeveran Jr., Lynn M. Messina, Janet M. Olson, Lisa Renaud, Albert Rolls, John Rosenthal, Helene Salmon, Peter J. Schmidtke, George W. Smith, Edward A. Thomas, Lori P. Wiesenfeld

Production: Newgen North America
Design and Production, Year in Pictures: Q2A/Bill Smith
Design, Cover: Takeshi Takahashi
Photo Research: Edward A. Thomas

For Infobase Learning:
Editorial Director: Laurie E. Likoff
Project Editor: Edward A. Thomas

Front cover: One World Trade Center, Timberlake, Williams: Shutterstock; LADEE spacecraft: NASA: Dana Berry/Ames; Obama inauguration: Newscom: Ron Sachs/dpa/picture-alliance. **Back cover:** Boston Marathon memorial: AP Images/Michael Dwyer; Pope Francis: Newscom/Massimiliano Migliorato/CPP/Polaris. **Tabs:** Shutterstock (unless otherwise noted); Star cluster: NASA: ESA/M. Livio (STScI); wedding rings: Thinkstock; football game: Wikipedia/Lpdrew. **Interior pages:** Photos are from **Getty Images** unless otherwise noted. **Alaska Resources Library and Information Services:** Exxon Valdez, 451. **ALMA Observatory:** telescope: Christoph Malin, 809. **AP Images:** King, 448; Brazil protests: Victor R. Caivano, 193, 198; Rodriguez: Charles Cherney, 812; train crash: Monica Ferreiros/La Voz de Galicia, 200; Hagman: Alan Greth, 815; Morsi coup: Khalil Hamra, 198; shutdown: Carolyn Kaster, 194; Havens: Peter Kramer, 815; Kim Jong Un: KRT via AP Video, 199; Kim Jong Il and Kim Jong Un: Kyodo News, 675; Moore, OK, tornado: Brennan Linsley, 197; El Reno, OK, tornado: Chris Machian/Omaha World-Herald, 313; Venezuela: Miraflores Press Office, 199; Jones: NFL Photos, 815; Detroit: Carlos Osorio, 196; popes: L' Osservatore Romano, HO, 193, 813; fertilizer plant: LM Otero, 197; Russian law: Lefteris Pitarakis, 199; meteoroid: Yekaterina Pustynnikova, Chelyabinsk.ru, 809; Hernandez: Rex Features, 813; Zimmerman: Craig Ruttle, 195; James: Lynne Sladky, 810; Vietnam War: Nick Ut, 669; Sandy Hook: Susan Walsh, 195. **Jimmy Carter Library & Museum:** Jimmy Carter, 506. **Federal Emergency Management Agency:** Hurricane Sandy: Jocelyn Augustino, 458; 9/11 attack: Andrea Booher, 453; Hurricane Katrina: Liz Roll, 454. **Gerald R. Ford Presidential Library and Museum:** Gerald R. Ford, 506. **iStockphoto:** Great Wall, 650. **Lyndon Baines Johnson Library and Museum:** Lyndon B. Johnson, 505. **Library of Congress:** 439, 440, 441 (Trail of Tears), 443-45, 447, 499-508 (U.S. presidents, unless otherwise noted), 662, 666. **NASA:** Moon landing, 668; Kepler: Ames/JPL-Caltech, 809. **Natl. Archives and Records Administration:** 446, 476, 478. **Newscom:** Mondale and Ferraro: Dennis Brack, 451; rubber duck: Archie Carpenter/UPI, 193, 814; 3D-printed ear: Lindsay France/AFP/Getty Images, 809. **Richard Nixon Library and Museum:** Richard Nixon, 450. **Public domain:** 437, 441 (gold discovery), 442, 656, 660. **Reuters:** Breaking Bad: Mario Anzuoni, 814; Grand Theft Auto V: Mike Blake, 814; Syria: Nour Fourat, 198; Sandy recovery: Shannon Stapleton, 197. **Shutterstock:** 315, 649, 652, 654, 657, 816 (Koch and Monteith). **Thinkstock:** spinning jenny, 659; Franklin: iStockphoto, 438; Aristotle: Photos.com, 651. **U.S. Army:** women in combat: Sgt. 1st Class John D. Brown, 196. **U.S. Dept. of Defense:** Oklahoma City bombing: Staff Sgt. Preston Chasteen, 452. **U.S. Marine Corps:** Iraq surge, 455; Iraq war: Lance Cpl. Kevin C. Quihuis Jr., 674. **U.S. Senate:** Inouye, 815. **USA Today Sports:** Wambach: Jim O'Connor, 812. **The White House:** George W. Bush: Eric Draper, 507; Obama inauguration: Sonya N. Hebert, 193, 194; bin Laden attack, 457, G. W. Bush library opening, 196, Obama, 508: Pete Souza. **Wikipedia Commons:** 488, 648.

Copyright © 2014 by Infobase Learning
The World Almanac® and The World Almanac and Book of Facts® are registered trademarks of Infobase Learning. All rights reserved. No part of this book may be reproduced or utilized in any form or by any means, electronic or mechanical, including photocopying, recording, or by any information storage or retrieval systems, without permission in writing from the publisher. For information, contact:

World Almanac® Books
An imprint of Infobase Learning
132 West 31st Street
New York, NY 10001

Hardcover	International Standard Serial Number	Paperback
ISBN-13: 978-1-60057-181-7	0084-1382	ISBN-13: 978-1-60057-182-4
ISBN-10: 1-60057-181-6		ISBN-10: 1-60057-182-4

The World Almanac® and Book of Facts is distributed to the trade by Simon & Schuster, and in paperback and hardcover to schools and libraries at special discounts by Infobase Learning. For further information, contact (800) 322-8755 or visit www.InfobaseLearning.com.

You can find The World Almanac® and Book of Facts on the Internet at www.worldalmanac.com.
Email: almanac@infobaselearning.com

The World Almanac® and Book of Facts 2014
Book printed and bound by RR Donnelly, Crawfordsville, IN
Date printed: November 2013
Printed in the United States of America
RRD 10 9 8 7 6 5 4 3 2 1

CONTENTS

2013: SPECIAL FEATURES AND YEAR IN REVIEW

2013: YEAR IN PICTURES 193, 809

ECONOMY, BUSINESS, & ENERGY

CRIME

MILITARY AFFAIRS

HEALTH & VITAL STATISTICS

PERSONALITIES, ARTS, & MEDIA

SCIENCE & TECHNOLOGY

CONSUMER INFORMATION

U.S. FACTS & HISTORY

WORLD MAPS & FLAGS

U.S. GOVERNMENT

U.S. CITIES, STATES, & POPULATION

WORLD HISTORY & CULTURE

NATIONS OF THE WORLD

SPORTS

GENERAL INDEX

THE WORLD ALMANAC
AND BOOK OF FACTS 2014

Top 10 News Topics of 2013

1. Budget Disputes Force a U.S. Government Shutdown. For the first time since 1995, large parts of the federal government were shut down, Oct. 1, when the new fiscal year began without budget legislation in place. A number of conservative congressional Republicans opposed any spending legislation unless the measure included a cutoff of funding to implement Obamacare. Key provisions of Obamacare, or the Patient Protection and Affordable Care Act, take effect Jan. 1, 2014; exchanges intended to help Americans buy health insurance began operating Oct. 1. With the government about to run out of authority to borrow money to pay its bills and creditors by Oct. 17, Congress passed legislation the night of Oct. 16 to fund government operations through Jan. 15, 2014, and to increase the debt ceiling to cover borrowing into early Feb. 2014. The legislation did not include the defunding of Obamacare.

2. Syria's Civil War Intensifies; Chemical Weapons Are Used. The civil war between the forces of Syrian Pres. Bashar al-Assad and a coalition of secular and Islamic-fundamentalist opposition groups entered its third year in Mar. 2013. The United Nations estimated in July that the war's death toll had passed 100,000, and reported in Sept. that more than 2 mil Syrians had fled the country, with many living in refugee camps in neighboring Jordan, Turkey, and Lebanon. An estimated 4.25 mil were displaced from their homes within Syria. A UN report in June found credible evidence that chemical weapons had been used by at least one side. After 1,400 people were killed Aug. 21 in a chemical weapons attack apparently by government forces, Pres. Barack Obama threatened U.S. military action against the Assad regime. U.S. strikes were put on hold when Assad agreed in Sept. to turn over his government's chemical weapons to international inspectors.

3. U.S. Supreme Court Rules on Voting Rights, Same-Sex Marriage. In a 5-4 decision June 25, the U.S. Supreme Court struck down a portion of the Voting Rights Act requiring certain states and localities (mainly in the South) to obtain prior federal approval for changes in their voting laws. The court invalidated the historic legislation's formula for determining what areas needed pre-clearance on the grounds that it was based on 40-year-old data. The ruling cleared the way for affected states to change their laws on voter ID requirements, electoral districts, and polling hours without consulting federal authorities. On June 26, in another 5-4 decision, the court struck down a provision of the federal Defense of Marriage Act (DOMA) that prohibited the federal government from recognizing legally performed same-sex marriages. The ruling made same-sex married couples eligible for a number of federal benefits and tax advantages. In another ruling the same day, the court dismissed on technical grounds a challenge to a lower court decision allowing same-sex marriages to be performed in California. New Jersey became the 14th state to perform same-sex marriages in Oct., after a ruling by the state's supreme court.

4. Leaked Documents Reveal Widespread U.S. Surveillance Program. Classified documents provided to journalists revealed a program by the U.S. National Security Agency to monitor phone calls, emails, and Internet activities of millions of Americans. NSA contractor Edward Snowden announced June 9 that he was the source of the leaked documents and maintained that he acted out of concern over violations of Americans' civil rights. The U.S. government charged Snowden with violating the Espionage Act, revoked his passport, and sought his extradition from Hong Kong. Snowden traveled to Russia, where (after spending weeks at the Moscow airport) he was granted temporary asylum Aug. 1. In Oct., U.S. relations with European allies were strained following reports that U.S. surveillance extended to foreign electronic communications, including those from a mobile phone of German Chancellor Angela Merkel. In another case in which the central figure claimed to be a whistleblower, Army Pfc. Bradley Manning pleaded guilty Feb. 28 to some of the lesser charges filed in connection with the 2010 release of thousands of classified documents to the website WikiLeaks. Manning was convicted on additional counts July 30 but found not guilty of aiding the enemy, the most serious charge. Sentenced to 35 years in prison Aug. 21, Manning came out as transgender the following day, taking the name Chelsea Manning.

5. Military Removes Egypt's President. Mohammed Morsi, who in 2012 had become Egypt's first democratically elected leader, was removed from office by the country's military leaders July 3. The action by the military, which placed Morsi under arrest, followed large-scale demonstrations in Cairo against what were characterized as authoritarian and pro-Islamist actions by the Morsi government. Demonstrations by Morsi supporters followed his ouster, and hundreds of protesters were killed in the succeeding weeks in clashes with security forces. A government prosecutor announced Sept. 1 that Morsi would be put on trial for inciting murder in connection with the deaths of anti-Morsi protesters outside the presidential palace in Dec. 2012.

6. Bombs Explode at the Boston Marathon. Two bombs exploded near the finish line of the Boston Marathon Apr. 15, killing three and injuring more than 200. Video footage led investigators to identify the bombers as two brothers of Chechen origin, Dzhokhar Tsarnaev and Tamerlan Tsarnaev. After the brothers apparently killed an MIT security officer Apr. 18, Tamerlan was killed in a shootout with police outside Boston. A daylong hunt for 19-year-old Dzhokhar followed, during which officials ordered a lockdown of the entire Boston area. Dzhokhar was captured in Watertown, MA, Apr. 19. At his arraignment July 10, he pleaded not guilty to 30 federal charges.

7. As Gun Violence Continues, Gun Control Legislation Fails. In a series of votes Apr. 17, the U.S. Senate failed to pass a number of gun control measures, including bills that would have mandated background checks for gun purchasers, banned some types of assault weapons, and limited the size of ammunition magazines. The measures had been introduced in the wake of a mass shooting at Sandy Hook Elementary School in Newtown, CT, on Dec. 14, 2012, in which 20 children and 6 staff members were killed. In another mass shooting, 12 people were killed Sept. 16, 2013, at the Washington Navy Yard in DC before police fatally shot the gunman. In a trial that drew wide media attention, neighborhood watch volunteer George Zimmerman was acquitted July 13 of murder and manslaughter charges arising from his 2012 shooting of unarmed black teenager Trayvon Martin.

8. New Leader of the Roman Catholic Church Is Elected. Cardinal Jorge Mario Bergoglio, archbishop of Buenos Aires, Argentina, was elected pope Mar. 13 by the Roman Catholic Church's College of Cardinals, meeting in Rome. He became the first Jesuit and first Latin American pope in the Church's history, as well as the first pope to take the name Francis. The election occurred soon after the resignation, effective Feb. 28, of Francis's predecessor, Benedict XVI, for health reasons. In his first international trip as pope, Francis traveled in July to Brazil, where he celebrated an outdoor mass before more than 1 mil people in Rio de Janeiro.

9. Athletes Make News Off the Field. On July 22 and Aug. 5, more than a dozen players, including former MVPs Ryan Braun and Alex Rodriguez, were suspended by Major League Baseball for their connection with a Florida clinic said to have supplied players with banned performance-enhancing drugs (PEDs). Rodriguez continued to play while appealing his suspension, which included all of the 2014 season; the other players accepted their suspensions, which were for the remainder of 2013 only. Reversing years of denials, cyclist Lance Armstrong, seven-time Tour de France winner, admitted in Jan. that he had used PEDs during his championship years. In South Africa, track star Oscar Pistorius was arrested in Feb. and later indicted for murder after he shot his girlfriend to death in their home; Pistorius said the death had been an accident. In June, NFL tight end Aaron Hernandez of the New England Patriots was arrested and charged with murdering a friend; he pleaded not guilty. The NFL reached a $765-mil settlement in Aug. with thousands of former players and players' families who had sued the league for allegedly concealing knowledge about serious health risks from head injuries; the league did not admit wrongdoing.

10. Heir to the British Throne Is Born. Catherine, Duchess of Cambridge and wife of Prince William, gave birth to their first child July 22, a son. Named George Alexander Louis, the child became third in line to the British throne, after his grandfather (Prince Charles) and his father. News media teams from around the world had been stationed for weeks outside St. Mary's Hospital in London, where the delivery occurred.

THE WORLD
AT A GLANCE

Surprising Facts

In 2009, the U.S. produced less than 10% of the world's new motor vehicles for the first time (9.5%, vs. 75.7% in 1950 and 21.5% in 2000). But American auto production's share of the world total was back up to 12.5% in 2012. *(p. 80)*

The number of U.S. households that owned televisions decreased for the second year in a row in 2013 to 114.2 million. TV-owning households peaked at 115.9 million in 2011. *(p. 257)*

Only 2% of American Internet users never check email. 87% of Americans check email at least once daily. *(p. 365)*

As recently as 2007, only 31% of Americans used their cell phones to send text messages. In 2012, 82% of people texted on their phones, and 59% used their cell phones to access the Internet (up from just 8% in 2007). *(p. 367)*

Sales of LP and EP records have steadily increased in recent years, from 1 million in 2005 to 7.1 million in 2012. However, that is a small share of music sales compared to the 116.7 million digital albums and 1.4 billion digital singles sold in 2012. *(p. 253)*

In 1990, the average U.S. movie ticket cost $4.23; the average ticket in 2012 cost $7.96. *(p. 245)*

Americans paid an average of 22.7% of their gross wage earnings in income tax and Social Security payments in 2012 (down from 24.7% in 2008); Belgians, who had some of the highest personal-income tax rates, paid 42.8%. *(p. 737)*

Since 2007, the percentage of children ages 2-17 diagnosed with attention deficit hyperactivity disorder (ADHD) has grown from 6.4% to 7.9% in 2012. *(p. 150)*

U.S. public debt has more than tripled since 2000, from $3.4 trillion to $12.4 trillion in 2013. As a percentage of the U.S. gross domestic product, debt has doubled from 34.7% to 76.6%. *(p. 60)*

Since 1975, the fuel efficiency of U.S. cars has more than doubled, from 13.5 miles per gallon to 27.3 miles per gallon in 2012. *(p. 83)*

In almost half (46.5%) of motor vehicle crashes in 2011, state traffic authorities did not report improper driving as a cause. *(p. 170)*

Nearly 30% of students ages 12-18 reported being bullied or cyberbullied in 2011. *(p. 386)*

In the 2010-11 school year, 82.3% of undergraduates received financial aid. *(p. 390)*

Number Ones

Most-visited social networking website . . . . Facebook, 144.7 million unique visitors in June 2013 *(p. 364)*

Most-used search engine . . . . Google, 12.8 billion searches in June 2013 *(p. 364)*

Airline that carried the most passengers . . . . Southwest/AirTran, 134.0 million in 2012 *(p. 89)*

Busiest U.S. airport by passenger traffic . . . . Hartsfield-Jackson Atlanta Intl. Airport, 95.5 million passengers in 2012 *(p. 89)*

Top U.S. state by traveler spending . . . . California, $105.3 billion in 2011 *(p. 87)*

Top-selling light truck in the U.S. . . . . Ford F-Series, 607,854 sold in 2012 *(p. 83)*

Most popular light truck color in the U.S. White/white pearl, 24% of 2012 model year light trucks *(p. 83)*

Top-selling passenger car in the U.S. . . . . Toyota Camry, 404,886 sold in 2012 *(p. 82)*

Most popular compact/sports car color in the U.S. . . . . . White/white pearl, 19% of 2012 model year compact/sports cars *(p. 83)*

Most popular luxury car color in the U.S. . . . . Black/black effect, 29% of 2012 model year luxury cars *(p. 83)*

Nations with the most paid days off of work per year . . . . Austria and Portugal, 35 paid days off *(p. 90)*

Americans: By the Numbers

49.5 million: number of students enrolled in U.S. public schools in 2010-11 school year *(p. 388)*

5.4 million: number of students enrolled in U.S. private schools in 2010-11 school year *(p. 388)*

1.8 million: number of students being homeschooled in 2011-12 school year *(p. 388)*

1.8 million: number of students enrolled in U.S. charter schools in 2010-11 school year *(p. 388)*

91.4%: public high school graduation rate in Vermont, the highest of any state in the U.S. *(p. 384)*

57.8%: public high school graduation rate in Nevada, the lowest of any state in the U.S. *(p. 384)*

76.3 years: average life expectancy for an American man in 2011, the highest ever *(p. 172)*

81.1 years: average life expectancy for an American woman in 2011, the highest ever *(p. 172)*

28.6: median age at first marriage for U.S. men in 2012 (the highest it has ever been) *(p. 164)*

26.6: median age at first marriage for U.S. women in 2012 (the highest it has ever been) *(p. 164)*

50: average total hours of TV viewed per week by U.S. women age 55 and over *(p. 255)*

45: average total hours of TV viewed per week by U.S. men age 55 and over *(p. 255)*

22: average total hours of TV viewed per week by young adults ages 12-17 *(p. 255)*

20.4: average total hours U.S. Internet users age 12 and older spent online per week *(p. 365)*

91%: percentage of U.S. households with at least one cell phone in 2012 *(p. 361)*

24.6%: percentage of the population of Texas without health insurance in 2012, higher than any other U.S. state *(p. 142)*

4.1%: percentage of the population of Massachusetts without health insurance in 2012, lower than any other U.S. state *(p. 142)*

23.7%: percentage of U.S. deaths in 2011 caused by heart disease, the leading cause of death *(p. 171)*

35.7%: percentage of U.S. population age 20 and over that was obese in 2009-10 *(p. 161)*

Money in America *(pp. 48-57)*

Median income for men in constant (2012) dollars . . . . in 2000: $37,791 . . . . .in 2005: $36,784 . . . . .in 2012: $33,904

Median income for women in constant (2012) dollars. . . . . in 2000: $21,417 . . . . .in 2005: $21,848 . . . . .in 2012: $21,520

Amount of money that Americans put in savings. . . . . in 2000: $297.9 bil . . .in 2005: $242.7 bil . . .in 2012: $687.4 bil

Percent of disposable income that Americans put in savings. . . in 2000: 4.0% . . . . . . .in 2005: 2.6% . . . . . . .in 2012: 5.6%

If all circulating U.S. dollars and coins were equally distributed among the nation's population in 2013, every American would receive $3,774.

Wealthiest American, 2013
Bill Gates, $72.0 billion net worth

Corporation With Largest Revenues, 2012
Wal-Mart Stores, Inc., $469.2 billion

Top of the World, 2012

Largest countries *(2013 population in millions, p. 735)*	**Largest urban areas** *(2011 population of metro area in millions, p. 735)*	**Per capita GDP** *(gross domestic product per capita, p. 736)*
1. China 1,349.6	1. Tokyo, Japan 37.2	1. Qatar $103,900
2. India 1,220.8	2. Delhi, India 22.7	2. Liechtenstein. 89,400
3. U.S. 316.7	3. Mexico City, Mexico 20.4	3. Luxembourg 81,100
4. Indonesia 251.2	4. New York-Newark, NY-NJ, U.S. 20.4	4. Monaco. 70,700
5. Brazil. 201.0	5. Shanghai, China 20.2	5. Singapore 61,400

Cell phone use *(millions of subscriptions, p. 366)*	**Personal computer use** *(millions in use, p. 360)*	**Internet users** *(millions, p. 363)*
1. China 1,100.0	1. U.S. 326.0	1. China 489.5
2. India 864.7	2. China 229.9	2. U.S. 271.4
3. U.S. 310.0	3. Japan 102.1	3. India 190.3
4. Indonesia 282.0	4. Germany. 74.6	4. Japan 108.1
5. Russia. 261.9	5. India 68.9	5. Brazil. 80.7

Health care spending *(per capita in 2010 among 50 most populous countries, p. 142)*	**Tourist destinations** *(millions of tourists, p. 86)*	**Winter Olympic medals** *(total medal count, 2010 Winter Games, p. 870)*
1. U.S. $8,233	1. France. 83.0	1. U.S. 37
2. Canada. 5,257	2. U.S. 67.0	2. Germany. 30
3. Australia 5,174	3. China 57.7	3. Canada 26
4. Germany 4,654	4. Spain. 57.7	4. Norway 23
5. France. 4,618	5. Italy 46.4	5. Austria. 16

World airports *(millions of passengers, p. 89)*	**Nuclear energy use** *(nuclear power as a percent of total electricity, p. 115)*	**Crude oil reserves** *(billions of barrels in 2013, p. 113)*
1. Hartsfield-Jackson Atlanta, GA, U.S. 95.5	1. France. 74.8%	1. Venezuela. 297.6
2. Beijing Capital, China 81.9	2. Slovakia 53.8	2. Saudi Arabia 267.9
3. London Heathrow, Eng., UK 70.0	3. Belgium. 51.0	3. Canada 173.1
4. Tokyo Haneda, Japan 66.8	4. Ukraine 46.2	4. Iran 154.6
5. Chicago O'Hare, IL, U.S. . . 66.6	5. Hungary 45.9	5. Iraq 141.4

Entertainment Award Winners, Then and Now (pp. 262-77)

Award	1963	2013
Academy Award: Best Picture[1]	Lawrence of Arabia	Argo
Emmy: Outstanding Comedy	Dick Van Dyke Show	Modern Family
Emmy: Outstanding Drama	The Defenders	Breaking Bad
Grammy: Album of the Year[1]	Vaughn Meader, The First Family	Mumford & Sons, Babel
Grammy: Record of the Year[1]	Tony Bennett, "I Left My Heart in San Francisco"	Gotye, "Somebody That I Used to Know"
Tony: Play	Who's Afraid of Virginia Woolf?	Vanya and Sonia and Masha and Spike
Tony: Musical	A Funny Thing Happened on the Way to the Forum	Kinky Boots
Pulitzer Prize: Fiction	William Faulkner, The Reivers	Adam Johnson, The Orphan Master's Son
Pulitzer Prize: Drama	No award	Ayad Akhtar, Disgraced

(1) Awarded in 2013 (now) or 1963 (then) for works released in 2012 or 1962.

Best Sellers, 2012 (pp. 245-50)

DVD . . . . Marvel's The Avengers
Video game . . . . Call of Duty: Black Ops II
Newspaper . . . . Wall Street Journal
Magazine . . . . AARP The Magazine
Fiction hardcover book . . . . The Casual Vacancy, J.K. Rowling
Nonfiction hardcover book . . . . Killing Kennedy: The End of Camelot, Bill O'Reilly and Martin Dugard
E-book . . . . Fifty Shades of Grey: Book One, E. L. James
Children's/YA hardcover book . . . . The Mark of Athena (Heroes of Olympus #3), Rick Riordan

More Entertainment Number Ones (pp. 243-56)

#1 top-grossing movie, 2012 . . . . Marvel's The Avengers, $622.7 mil
#1 top-grossing movie, all-time. . . . . Avatar, $760.5 mil
#1 prime-time TV program, 2012-13 . . . . NCIS, 11.4% of TV-owning households
#1 syndicated TV program, 2012-13 . . . . The Big Bang Theory, 7.1% of TV-owning households
#1 basic-cable TV program, 2012-13 . . . . Walking Dead, 1.6% of TV-owning households
#1 premium-cable TV program, 2012-13 . . . . Game of Thrones, 3.8% of TV-owning households
#1 most-watched TV program, all-time. Super Bowl XLVI, Feb. 5, 2012, 53.9 mil households
#1 commercial radio format, 2013 . . . . Country, 2,042 U.S. stations
#1 top-grossing North American concert tour, all-time . . . . Rolling Stones (2005), $162.0 mil
#1 top-selling albums, all-time . . . . Thriller, Michael Jackson, 29 mil copies
Eagles/Their Greatest Hits 1971-1975, Eagles, 29 mil copies
#1 top-selling music artist, all-time digital sales . . . . Taylor Swift, 45.0 mil digital units sold
#1 longest-running Broadway show . . . . The Phantom of the Opera (1988-), 10,353 performances (through May 26, 2013)

Milestone Birthdays, 2014 (pp. 173-234)

90	70	60	40
Doris Day, Apr. 3	Roger Daltrey, Mar. 1	Ang Lee, Oct. 23	Kate Moss, Jan. 16
George H.W. Bush, June 12	Diana Ross, Mar. 26	Condoleezza Rice, Nov. 14	Christian Bale, Jan. 30
Lauren Bacall, Sept. 16	George Lucas, May 14	Denzel Washington, Dec. 28	Steve Nash, Feb. 7
Jimmy Carter, Oct. 1	Patti LaBelle, May 24		Derek Jeter, June 26
Ruby Dee, Oct. 27	Rudy Giuliani, May 28	**50**	Hilary Swank, July 30
	Gladys Knight, May 28	Nicolas Cage, Jan. 7	Jimmy Fallon, Sept. 19
80	Michael Douglas, Sept. 25	Jeff Bezos, Jan. 12	Dale Earnhardt Jr., Oct. 10
Hank Aaron, Feb. 5	Danny DeVito, Nov. 17	Michelle Obama, Jan. 17	Joaquin Phoenix, Oct. 28
Bill Russell, Feb. 12	Lorne Michaels, Nov. 17	Mariska Hargitay, Jan. 23	Leonardo DiCaprio, Nov. 11
Gloria Steinem, Mar. 25	Tom Seaver, Nov. 17	Laura Linney, Feb. 5	Ryan Seacrest, Dec. 24
Jane Goodall, Apr. 3	Steve Carlton, Dec. 22	Glenn Beck, Feb. 10	
Donald Sutherland, July 17		Sarah Palin, Feb. 11	**30**
Sophia Loren, Sept. 20	**60**	Jonathan Lethem, Feb. 19	Mark Zuckerberg, May 14
Leonard Cohen, Sept. 21	Howard Stern, Jan. 12	Bret Easton Ellis, Mar. 7	Tim Lincecum, June 15
Joan Didion, Dec. 5	Oprah Winfrey, Jan. 29	Rob Lowe, Mar. 17	Prince Harry, Sept. 15
Judi Dench, Dec. 9	John Travolta, Feb. 18	Russell Crowe, Apr. 7	Lindsey Vonn, Oct. 18
Maggie Smith, Dec. 28	Ron Howard, Mar. 1	Stephen Colbert, May 13	Katy Perry, Oct. 25
	Jackie Chan, Apr. 7	Courteney Cox, June 15	Scarlett Johansson, Nov. 22
70	Jerry Seinfeld, Apr. 29	Dan Brown, June 22	LeBron James, Dec. 30
Jimmy Page, Jan. 9	James Cameron, Aug. 16	Barry Bonds, July 24	
Alice Walker, Feb. 9	Al Roker, Aug. 20	Sandra Bullock, July 26	**21**
Stockard Channing, Feb. 13	Elvis Costello, Aug. 25	Keanu Reeves, Sept. 2	Miranda Cosgrove, May 14
Jerry Springer, Feb. 13	Al Sharpton, Oct. 3	Trisha Yearwood, Sept. 19	Angus T. Jones, Oct. 8
		Don Cheadle, Nov. 29	
		Marisa Tomei, Dec. 4	

MARRIAGE IN THE U.S.:
A CHANGING PICTURE

At any period in U.S. history, the notion of a "typical" American family has been something of an overgeneralization. Households have always taken diverse forms—but perhaps never more so than today. In the mid-20th century, the image of a family consisting of a husband, a wife, and their children accurately portrayed far more households than it does now. In the 2010s, Americans are getting married later in life than ever before, and the portion of adult Americans who are married is at a historic low. The number of couples living together—and having children together—without getting married is increasing. The gender of married couples is changing as well.

Marriage by the Numbers

In 2012, according to U.S. Census Bureau estimates, the median age of Americans getting married for the first time was 28.6 years for men and 26.6 years for women. These figures were the highest since the Census Bureau began tracking marriage age in 1890, and they were about 6 years higher than the historic lows recorded in the mid-20th century. In both 1950 and 1960, the median marriage age was 22.8 years for men and 20.3 for women.

The percentage of American adults who were married in 2012 had dropped significantly from 1950. In 2012, only slightly more than half of Americans age 15 or over were married (54% of men and 52% of women, including people who were not living with their spouse). In 1950, the proportion was about two-thirds (68% of men and 66% of women age 14 or over). Almost one-third (31.2%) of all American adults in 2012 had never married. Among people in their 20s and 30s, more than one-half (50.9%) had never married.

Census Bureau data on U.S. households showed that fewer than half (48.7%) contained a married couple in 2012. In the same year, fewer than 6 out of 10 children (57.8%) under age 18 lived in a household with married biological parents. In 1960, three-quarters of American households (74.4%) contained a married couple, and about 85% of children lived in such households. The nuclear family is much less common in 21st-century America than it was in the mid-20th century. There are various possible reasons for this trend.

Attitudes About Marriage

Many unmarried people still appear to consider marriage desirable. For example, a June 2013 survey conducted by Gallup, Inc., found that, among never-married people questioned, about four out of five said they would like to marry. However, other survey data indicate that many people may not consider marriage essential to their lives—or essential for a couple desiring to live together or to have children together.

The U.S. Centers for Disease Control's 2006-10 National Survey of Family Growth (NSFG) questioned a nationally representative sample of more than 22,000 men and women ages 15-44 about their attitudes toward marriage and related topics. When asked to respond to this statement—"It is better to get married than to go through life being single."—48% of the women disagreed or strongly disagreed, as did 32% of the men.

Reacting to this statement—"A young couple should not live together unless they are married."—more than two-thirds of the survey participants disagreed or strongly disagreed (68% of women and 71% of men). In fact, 11% of the women in the 2006-10 NSFG were unmarried and cohabiting, up from 3% in the 1982 NSFG. And when the 2006-10 participants were asked to respond to "It is okay for an unmarried female to have a child," 78% of women and 70% of men agreed or strongly agreed.

In the June 2013 Gallup survey, 64% of participants considered it very or somewhat important that a couple marry when they plan to spend the rest of their lives together, down from 76% of participants in a 2006 Gallup poll. Asked how important it was for a couple to marry when they plan to have a child, again 64% said they thought it was very or somewhat important, but this was also down, from 73% in 2006.

Marriage appears to remain an important institution in American society, but the acceptability of unmarried couples living together and of unmarried women having children seems to be fairly widespread and on the increase, especially among younger adults.

Marriage and Money

Marriage rates increase as incomes go up, as illustrated by Census Bureau data for 2012. For men, the percentage never married is well above the overall national figure (31.2%) for people earning less than $25,000 a year; the percentage is about the same as the national figure for men in the $25,000-$39,999 income bracket, and it is well below the national figure for men earning $40,000 or above. Among women, the trend is similar. Women who had earned income but made less than $15,000 were less likely to be married than all adults. Among women earning $15,000-$24,999, the percentage never married was about the same as the overall national figure. Women with incomes of $25,000 or above were more likely to be married, compared to all adults. Some Americans with lower incomes may feel they have to forgo—or at least postpone—marriage because they cannot afford it.

A 2013 study titled "Knot Yet: The Benefits and Costs of Delayed Marriage in America" supports such a conclusion. Sponsored by the Univ. of Virginia's National Marriage Project, the National Campaign to Prevent Teen and

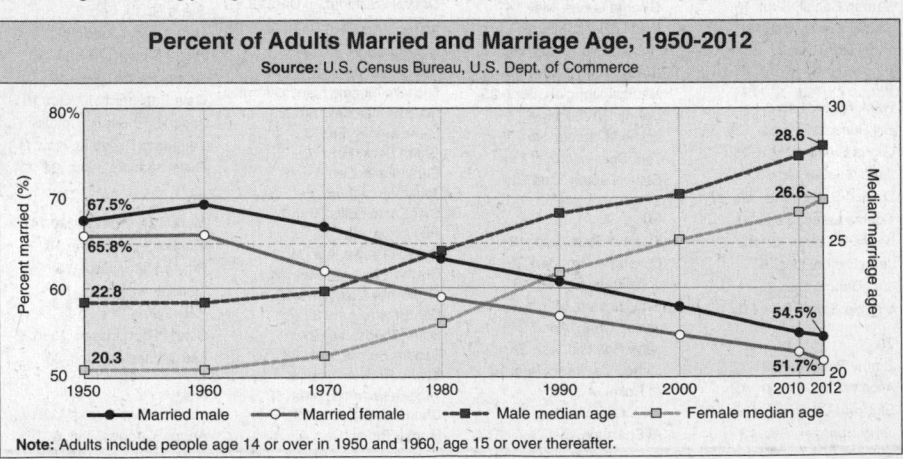

Percent of Adults Married and Marriage Age, 1950-2012

Source: U.S. Census Bureau, U.S. Dept. of Commerce

Married male • Married female • Male median age • Female median age

Note: Adults include people age 14 or over in 1950 and 1960, age 15 or over thereafter.

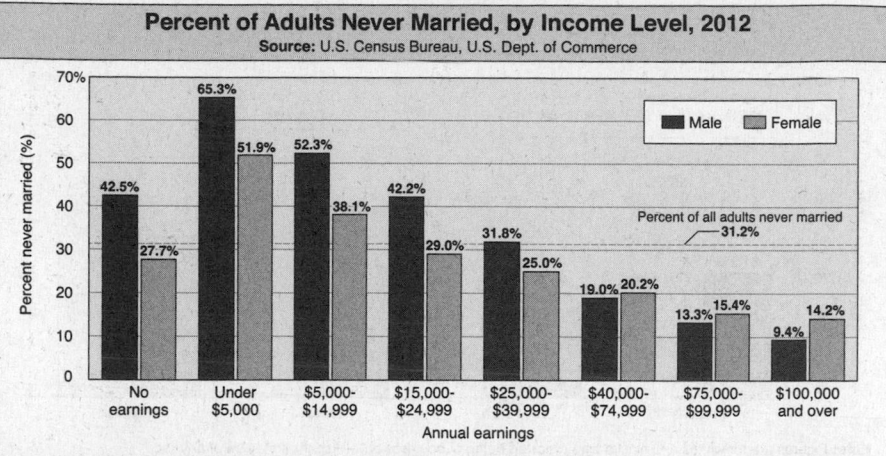

Percent of Adults Never Married, by Income Level, 2012
Source: U.S. Census Bureau, U.S. Dept. of Commerce

Unplanned Pregnancy, and the Relate Institute, the study looked for answers to this question (among others): "So why are young people putting off matrimony so much later than did previous generations?" It concluded, "One reason is money: the economic foundations that girded marriage in the mid-twentieth century have collapsed." At that time, the study notes, many men coming out of high school could readily find manufacturing or other unionized jobs that paid fairly high wages, offered reasonable job security, and provided benefit packages. Without needing to spend the time or money for a college education, many men in blue-collar jobs might well have felt, by their early 20s, that they were ready and able to support a family.

Now, says the Knot Yet study, "this world is all but gone," and data from the U.S. Bureau of Labor Statistics (BLS) seem to bear that out. According to the BLS, in 1950, 32% of all nonfarm workers in the U.S. were employed in manufacturing (14.8 mil out of 46.9 mil workers); by the end of 2012, that proportion had dropped to 9% (11.9 mil manufacturing workers out of 134.7 mil total nonfarm workers). The trend in unionization has been similar. In 1950, 32% of nonfarm wage and salary workers were in unions; by 2012, the proportion was 11%.

Adding to the financial challenges of young adults, this group of Americans has been hard hit by the economic recession that began in late 2007 and by the sluggish economy that has followed. A 2013 Pew Research Center study, based on Census Bureau data, found that a growing number of people in the so-called Millennial generation (ages 18-31 in 2012) were not living in their own households, suggesting they were perhaps not in a position to consider marriage. The study reported that 36% of 18-to-31-year-olds were living with their parents in 2012, the highest percentage in at least 40 years and 4 percentage points higher than before the start of the recession five years earlier. Although the overall figure for 2012 included college students, almost one in five Millennials living at home that year already had a bachelor's degree, and about one in six was at least 25 years old. The Pew study also noted that 63% of Millennials were employed in 2012, down from 70% of 18-to-31-year-olds in 2007, and that 23% were married and living in their own households in 2012, compared to 27% five years earlier and 56% in 1968. Among Americans ages 20-24 in the labor force, the BLS reported that the unemployment rate was 13.3% in 2012, well above the 8.1% rate for all people in the labor force.

At the same time that their financial prospects may be uncertain, at least in the near term, many of today's young adults are viewing marriage as a "capstone" event—something to consider after launching careers and gaining some level of economic security, according to the Knot Yet study. In contrast to earlier decades, when most young adults viewed marriage as a "cornerstone" event (a building block for one's career and adult life), young men and women today are more likely to defer marriage while they further their education and build a work history.

Certainly, more women are focusing on jobs and careers today than was typical in the mid-20th century. Statistics from the BLS show that, from 1950 to 2012, the portion of adult women in the labor force increased dramatically. In 1950, 34% of women were working or were looking for work. In 2012, the figure was 58%.

More young adults of both sexes are devoting years of their lives to higher education than was the case half a century ago. According to data from the U.S. Dept. of Education's National Center for Education Statistics, in Oct. 1960, 45% of students who had graduated from high school in the previous 12 months were enrolled in college. For Oct. 2011, the proportion was 68%.

Does delaying marriage for college and career actually produce financial rewards? Among women ages 33-35 in 2010, those who were never married or had married in their 30s had higher incomes than those who married earlier (the income difference was greatest for college-educated women). Among men ages 33-35, however, those who married in their 20s had higher incomes than the men who married later or had never married.

Racial and Ethnic Differences

Marriage rates vary by racial and ethnic group. For example, in 2012, a somewhat lower percentage of non-Hispanic white adults (26.1%), a somewhat higher percentage of Hispanics (39.9%), and a significantly higher percentage of African Americans (47.1%) were never married than the overall national figure of 31.2%. Among Americans in their 20s and 30s in 2012, more than two-thirds of blacks (67%), half (50%) of Hispanics, and a little less than half (47.5%) of non-Hispanic whites had never married, compared to the overall national figure of 50.9%.

Again, economics may play a role in the especially low marriage rates for African Americans. For example, the BLS reported that the 2012 black unemployment rate was 13.8%, versus 8.1% for all people in the labor force. Among 20-to-24-year-olds, the 2012 black unemployment rate was 23.1% (versus 13.3% overall). Census Bureau data show that median income in 2012 for all US households was $51,371; for African American households, however, it was less than two-thirds of that amount ($33,764).

Social Consequences of Delayed Marriage

Are the growing numbers of unmarried young adults content with their lives? There can be no single answer to such a question, but the Knot Yet report cited data from the federally

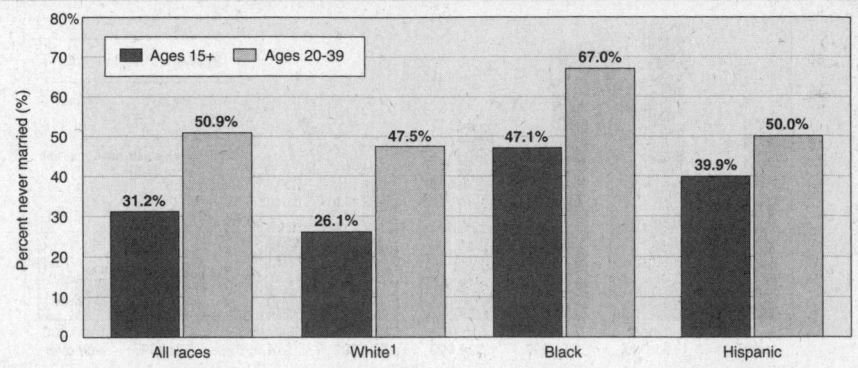

Percent of Adults Never Married, by Race and Ethnicity, 2012

Source: U.S. Census Bureau, U.S. Dept. of Commerce

Note: Figures are for whites and blacks who reported being of one race only. Hispanics may be of any race.
(1) Non-Hispanic whites only.

funded National Longitudinal Study of Adolescent Health indicating that unmarried people in their 20s were less likely to report being highly satisfied with their lives, more likely to report depression, and more likely to report alcohol abuse than their married peers. Slightly over one-fourth of married women ages 24-29 said they were "highly depressed," compared to more than one-third of unmarried women. One-fifth of married men ages 24-29 reported depression, compared to almost 30% of the unmarried men.

As more young adults remain unmarried, a growing proportion of children are being born out of wedlock. According to data from the National Center for Health Statistics, in 2010, four out of ten U.S. births (40.8%) were to an unmarried woman. This was an almost-fourfold increase since 1970, when the figure was 10.7%. (For African Americans, the proportion of out-of-wedlock births was 72.1% in 2010, up from 37.5% 40 years earlier.)

Based on an analysis of federal data, the Knot Yet study found that out-of-wedlock childbirth is especially common among women with less than a college education. Among women with at least a bachelor's degree, only 12% of first births in 2010 were to an unmarried mother. In contrast, among women who had graduated from high school but not college, a majority of first births—58%—occurred outside of marriage. And 83% of first births in 2010 to women with less than a high school education were out-of-wedlock births.

Overall, many Americans appear to be making decisions about childbirth independent of decisions about marriage.

Who Can Marry Whom?

Rules governing who is eligible to be married are largely set by state law. Historically, a number of states prohibited marriage between people of different races. It was only in 1967, less than half a century ago, that the U.S. Supreme Court struck down bans on interracial marriage, on the grounds that they violated the 14th Amendment guarantee of equal protection of the law. At the time of the decision, interracial marriage was illegal in almost one-third of all states (16 states). By the 21st century, both public attitudes toward and the frequency of interracial marriage appear to have changed. The Pew Research Center reported in 2012 that about 15% of new marriages in 2010 were between people of different races or different ethnicities. This was more than double the proportion in 1980 (6.7%). A 2012 Pew survey found that 43% of respondents considered the increase in interracial marriage "a change for the better in our society"; only 11% said they thought it was "a change for the worse." Positive attitudes toward interracial marriage were especially prevalent among younger people surveyed: 61% of respondents

ages 18-29 considered more interracial marriage in the U.S. a change for the better.

A controversial issue in the 21st century has been whether same-sex couples should have the same right to marriage as male-female couples. Until recent decades, same-sex marriage had not even been addressed in state law. In 1973, Maryland became the first state to define marriage as a union of one man and one woman. Several other states followed suit, and in 1995, Utah became the first state to enact a law refusing to recognize same-sex marriages performed in other states. Again, various states did the same. By late 2013, 35 states effectively prohibited same-sex marriages by either legislation or constitutional amendment. Because some state courts had ruled that statutes against same-sex marriage violated state constitutions, a number of states amended their constitutions to insulate same-sex marriage prohibitions from state court review.

Same-sex marriage has become legal in other states over the past decade. This occurred first in Massachusetts, where the state's highest court ruled in 2003 that the state constitution guaranteed marriage rights to gay and lesbian couples; the first marriages occurred in 2004. By Oct. 2013, 14 states and the District of Columbia had legalized same-sex marriage as a result of action by the legislature, a court decision, or action by the electorate voting on a ballot measure. About 33% of the U.S. population lived in states where same-sex marriage was legal. Six other states recognized civil unions or domestic partnerships between same-sex couples, giving them, to varying degrees, some of the rights and privileges of married couples.

Meanwhile, in 1996, Congress passed and Pres. Bill Clinton signed the federal Defense of Marriage Act (DOMA). A key provision of this law effectively meant that the federal government would not recognize same-sex marriages performed in states where they were legal. Legally married same-sex couples could not get such federal tax advantages as the ability to file joint returns or spousal exemption from estate taxes. People in same-sex marriages were not eligible for spousal Social Security payments, and same-sex spouses of federal employees could not get benefits, such as health insurance, that were available to opposite-sex spouses.

In a 5-4 decision in June 2013, the U.S. Supreme Court struck down that provision of DOMA. The majority opinion held that, by treating same-sex married couples differently—"as living in marriages less respected than others"—the provision was an unconstitutional "deprivation of the liberty of the person protected by the Fifth Amendment."

In another case the same day, the Supreme Court issued a narrow decision affecting same-sex marriage in California.

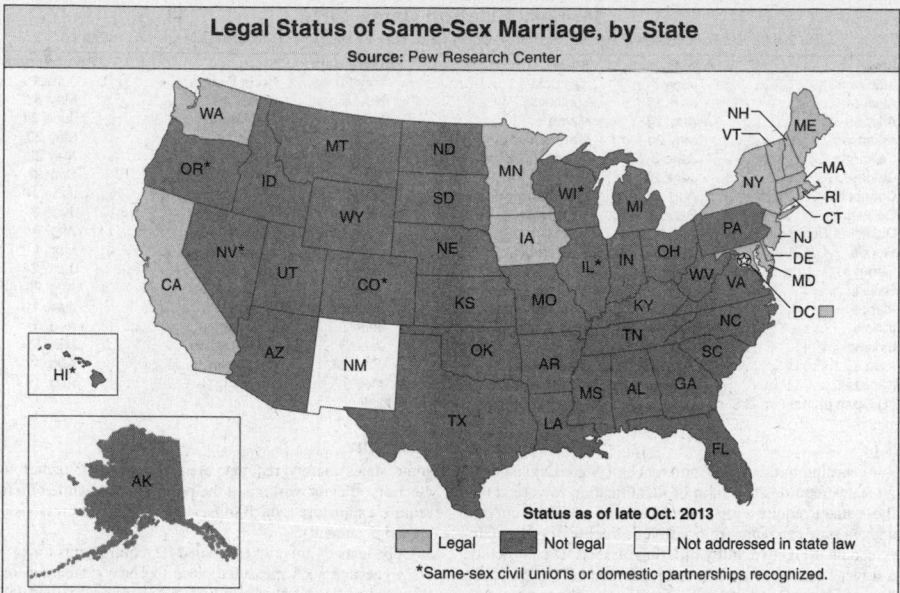

Legal Status of Same-Sex Marriage, by State

Source: Pew Research Center

Status as of late Oct. 2013

Legend: Legal | Not legal | Not addressed in state law

*Same-sex civil unions or domestic partnerships recognized.

California's supreme court had ruled in 2008 that the state constitution guaranteed same-sex couples the right to marry. However, later that year, California voters approved a constitutional amendment (Proposition 8 on the ballot) prohibiting same-sex marriage. In 2010, a federal district court struck down Proposition 8 as being in violation of the U.S. Constitution. The state government did not appeal that decision, but opponents of same-sex marriage did. In its June 2013 ruling, the U.S. Supreme Court dismissed the appeal on the grounds that the appellants did not have legal standing to appeal the case. The effect of that ruling was to restore the federal district court's decision striking down Proposition 8, allowing same-sex marriages to occur in California. But the Supreme Court action left unanswered the key questions of whether same-sex couples nationwide have a legal right to marry under the U.S. Constitution and whether states have the power to prohibit or not recognize same-sex marriage.

Amid the current patchwork of conflicting state laws, the Pew Research Center estimated, based largely on state records, that there were at least 71,165 same-sex married couples in the U.S. It noted, however, that the actual number was almost certainly higher, largely because of delays in reporting registered marriages and because some states no longer require people to indicate gender on marriage-license applications. (Census Bureau data indicated that, in 2012, almost 640,000 households were unmarried cohabiting same-sex couples.)

By a narrow margin, a majority of Americans appear to favor legalization of same-sex marriage. In a July 2013 Gallup poll, people were asked what they would do if, on Election Day, they could vote for or against legalizing same-sex marriage nationwide; 52% of respondents said they would vote for legalization. A Dec. 2012 NBC News/*Wall Street Journal* poll asked, "If a law passed that allowed same-sex marriages to become legal in your state, would you actively support such a law, be in favor but not actively support it, be opposed to it but not actively try to have it overturned, or be opposed to such a law and actively work to overturn it?" A total of 55% of respondents said they would actively support (25%) or at least favor (30%) such a law.

Support for same-sex marriage appears to vary by age and other factors. In the July 2013 Gallup poll about

nationwide legalization, 69% of 18-to-34-year-olds said they would vote in favor of legalization, compared to 52% of 35-to-54-year-olds (the same as the overall percentage) and 38% of respondents age 55 or over. Legalization was supported by 70% of Democrats, 53% of independents, and 30% of Republicans. Support for legalization was higher in the East and West (62% and 57%, respectively) and lower in the Midwest and South (51% and 43%).

Support for same-sex marriage has increased in recent years. Another 2013 Gallup survey asked, "Do you think marriage between same-sex couples should or should not be recognized by law as valid, with the same rights as traditional marriages?" A total of 54% of respondents said it should be recognized—double the proportion (27%) who had favored recognition when a similar question was asked in 1996. When a 2012 AP-National Constitution Center poll asked "Should the government give legal recognition to marriages between couples of the same sex, or not?" 53% of respondents said yes, up from 46% of those polled on an extremely similar question in 2009.

Many Types of Families

So what is the typical family in 21st-century America? Millions of households do contain a husband, a wife, and their children. But many more than in the past contain an unmarried adult or two cohabiting unmarried adults with and without children.

Young adults are putting off or forgoing marriage for a variety of reasons, some of them financial. Compared to half a century ago, many people are devoting more years to education and to trying to establish themselves in jobs and careers before considering marriage. A much higher proportion of women are seeking careers outside the home. Over the same time period, social acceptance of a variety of living arrangements outside conventional marriage has increased significantly.

Meantime, the right of same-sex couples to marry has not been settled nationwide. Legal in some states, not legal in others, same-sex marriage is the subject of much debate and a number of court cases, which may eventually lead to uniform status nationwide.

VOTER GUIDE, 2014

Primary Election Dates, 2014

The 2014 general election will be held Nov. 4. Primary dates vary by state. * = scheduled date not yet confirmed.

State	Primary date	State	Primary date	State	Primary date
Alabama	June 3	Kentucky	May 20	North Dakota	June 10
Alaska	Aug. 19	Louisiana	Nov. 4[1]	Ohio	May 6
Arizona	Aug. 26	Maine	June 10	Oklahoma	June 24
Arkansas	May 20	Maryland	June 24	Oregon	May 20
California	June 3	Massachusetts	Sept. 16*	Pennsylvania	May 20
Colorado	June 24	Michigan	Aug. 5	Rhode Island	Sept. 9
Connecticut	Aug. 12	Minnesota	Aug. 12	South Carolina	June 10
Delaware	Sept. 9	Mississippi	June 3	South Dakota	June 3
District of Columbia	Apr. 1	Missouri	Aug. 5	Tennessee	Aug. 7
Florida	Aug. 26	Montana	June 3	Texas	Mar. 4
Georgia	May 20*	Nebraska	May 13	Utah	June 24
Hawaii	Aug. 9	Nevada	June 10	Vermont	Aug. 26
Idaho	May 20	New Hampshire	Sept. 9	Virginia	June 10
Illinois	Mar. 18	New Jersey	June 3	Washington	Aug. 5
Indiana	May 6	New Mexico	June 3	West Virginia	May 13
Iowa	June 3	New York	June 24*	Wisconsin	Aug. 12
Kansas	Aug. 5	North Carolina	May 6	Wyoming	Aug. 19

(1) Open primary for U.S. congressional seats is on same day as general election.

Voter Identification

According to the Natl. Conference of State Legislatures, 30 states require some form of identification to vote; 11 of those states require a photo ID. The forms of ID required in a given state can range from a driver's license or other state-issued photo ID to a utility bill. State-issued ID can include a driver's license, a non-driver government ID, a passport, or a military ID, among other forms. Acquiring most government-issued ID requires a trip to a government office, usually the Dept. of Motor Vehicles (DMV), and a fee. Some voter ID laws require that the state provide free IDs to eligible voters if they do not already have one. Practices in the states that do not require identification vary widely; some states merely require voters to give their names to election officials working at the polling place, while others require a signature (which some states match to a previously signed document).

Opponents of government-issued ID requirements for voters argue that such measures place too heavy a burden on people who do not currently have a government-issued ID, particularly low-income, minority, and elderly voters. Supporters, however, have touted the requirement as a much-needed measure to improve election security and prevent voter fraud. The Census Bureau has estimated that 11% of eligible voters lack current government-issued IDs.

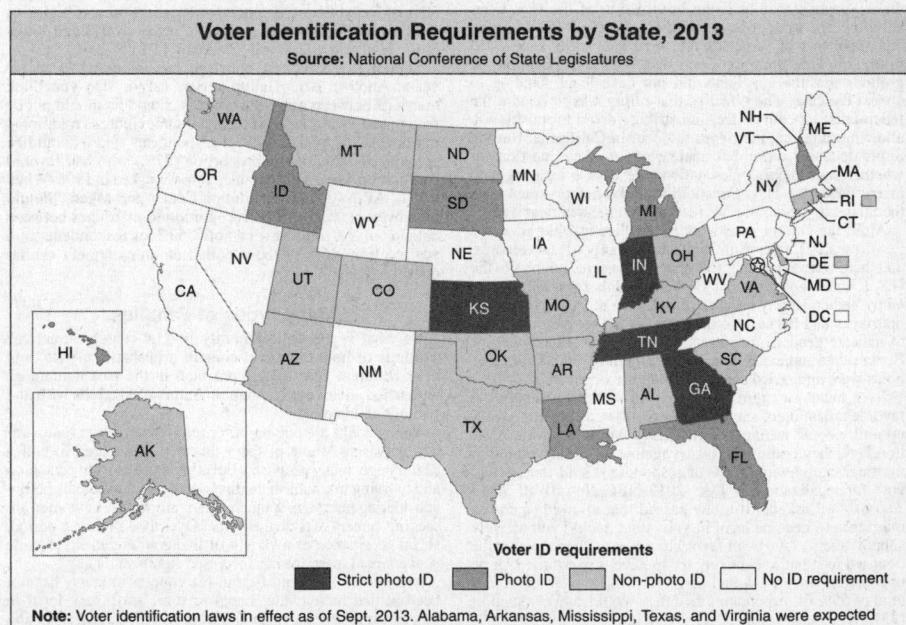

Voter Identification Requirements by State, 2013
Source: National Conference of State Legislatures

Voter ID requirements
Strict photo ID | Photo ID | Non-photo ID | No ID requirement

Note: Voter identification laws in effect as of Sept. 2013. Alabama, Arkansas, Mississippi, Texas, and Virginia were expected to require a photo ID by Election Day, 2014. Laws were pending in other state legislatures.

CHRONOLOGY OF EVENTS

Nov. 1, 2012, to Oct. 31, 2013

The Chronology of Events reports the top National, International, and General news stories, month by month.

November 2012

National

Obama Wins Reelection; Congress Still Split—Pres. Barack Obama and Vice Pres. Joe Biden emerged victorious in the presidential election Nov. 6, 2012, winning reelection over the Republican ticket of former Massachusetts Gov. Mitt Romney and U.S. Rep. Paul Ryan (WI). Shortly after Romney conceded, Obama delivered a victory speech in the early hours of Nov. 7, in which he offered to foster an environment of compromise in Washington during his second term and promised to meet with leaders of both parties, including Romney, to find a bipartisan approach to overcoming the nation's challenges.

When the 538 members of the Electoral College met in their respective states Dec. 17, Obama won 332 electoral votes to Romney's 206; the results were certified in a joint session of Congress Jan. 4, 2013. Official tabulations showed that Obama had won 65,899,660 popular votes, or 51.1% of the total, while Romney had received 60,932,152 votes, or 47.2%, making Obama the first president to receive more than 51% of the popular vote in two consecutive elections since Pres. Dwight D. Eisenhower.

Democrats gained two Senate seats, increasing their majority from 51 to 53 seats; two more seats were won by independents who caucused with Democrats, leaving Republicans with 45 seats. Democrats also picked up eight seats in the House of Representatives but fell short of the 25 seats needed to gain control of the House, leaving a divided government in place.

Republicans picked up one governorship, leaving them in control of 30 of 50 state governor's offices. Democrats saw modest gains in state legislatures, especially in California, where the party claimed a two-thirds supermajority of both chambers. Reflecting deep partisan divides, one party controlled both chambers of the state's legislative body in 46 states.

Same-Sex Marriage, Marijuana Find Success in Ballot Initiatives—Voters in Maine, Maryland, and Washington state, Nov. 6, approved measures that legalized same-sex marriage, making them the first states in which such marriages were approved by popular vote. More than 30 past ballot initiatives concerning same-sex marriage had been defeated, though six states and Washington, DC, approved such marriages through legislative action or court orders. Meanwhile, in Minnesota, voters rejected a measure to add a provision to the state constitution that would have defined marriage as between a man and a woman, though same-sex marriages remained illegal under state law.

Measures legalizing recreational use of marijuana were approved Nov. 6 in Colorado by a 55%-45% margin and in Washington state by a 56%-44% margin. A similar measure in Oregon was defeated. Meanwhile, Massachusetts—where penalties for recreational marijuana use had been substantially softened in 2009—became the 18th state to legalize medical marijuana. Not all such measures were successful: voters in Arkansas defeated a measure to legalize medical marijuana, and Montana voters approved more restrictive legislation, passed in 2011, to replace the state's 2004 law legalizing medical marijuana. Federal law still prohibits marijuana for any use in all states and territories of the U.S.

Petraeus Resigns as Director of the CIA—CIA Director David Petraeus, a retired four-star U.S. Army general, resigned his post Nov. 9 after an FBI investigation into potential cybercrime uncovered an extramarital affair between Petraeus and Paula Broadwell, a West Point graduate who cowrote Petraeus's official biography. The FBI investigation began over Broadwell's alleged cyberstalking of Jill Kelley, a Florida socialite. Broadwell admitted to the affair with Petraeus when the FBI questioned her regarding Kelley in the fall. The FBI told Director of Natl. Intelligence James Clapper Jr. what their investigation had revealed Nov. 6, and Clapper told Petraeus that he should resign. Pres. Barack Obama accepted Petraeus's letter of resignation three days later. Michael Morrell, the CIA deputy director, was named acting head of the agency. (Obama nominated CIA veteran John Brennan to the office Jan. 7, 2013; he was confirmed by the Senate Mar. 3.)

Unemployment Rate Rises, Stock Market Remains Steady—The Labor Dept. reported Nov. 2 that 171,000 jobs had been added to the U.S. economy, 46,000 more than had been expected. The unemployment rate nevertheless rose from 7.8% to 7.9%, an indication that more people were actively looking for work; thus, the rise in unemployment was seen as a positive sign by some analysts. Stock markets did not react with optimism, and were mostly flat for the month, with some pointing to the uncertainty surrounding ongoing fiscal-cliff negotiations as a cause of lackluster trading. For the month, the Dow Jones Industrial Average fell 0.54%, losing 70.88 points and closing at 13,025.58; the S&P 500 rose 0.28%, gaining 4.02 points and closing at 1,416.18; and the Nasdaq Composite Index rose 1.11%, gaining 33.01 points and closing at 3,010.24.

International

China's Five-Year Party Congress Concludes With New Leadership—More than 2,200 delegates met Nov. 8-14 for China's 18th Communist Party Congress, the nation's chief political assembly, held every five years to appoint new members to the governing Politburo Standing Committee and 25-member Politburo. Outgoing Pres. Hu Jintao opened the congress Nov. 8 with a speech extolling China's political system, although he favorably discussed community-level democracy, suggested the country's administrative system was in need of further reform, and warned against party corruption. Corruption had been a major topic of discussion in anticipation of the assembly and throughout the congress because of the corruption scandal around former party official Bo Xilai uncovered earlier in the year. On the closing day of the congress, Hu formally announced that he would be succeeded as Communist Party general secretary and as civilian chairman of the military by current Vice Pres. Xi Jinping, who was expected to assume the presidency Mar. 2013. Five more party officials entered the Politburo Standing Committee, as the group's size was reduced from nine to seven members. In spite of signs of party infighting leading up to the congress, the list of new leaders did not include any liberals, suggesting that political change would be unlikely in the coming years.

Israel Kills Hamas Military Leader, Deadly Clashes Follow—After a week of escalated fighting between Israel and Palestinian militant groups, Israeli air and naval strikes on the Gaza Strip Nov. 14 killed Ahmed al-Jabari—the commander of the military wing of Islamist group Hamas since at least 2006—and at least five other Palestinians. The violence continued for eight days, with Israeli strikes on more than 1,500 targets within Gaza and hundreds of Palestinian rocket attacks on Israeli cities. An estimated 160 Palestinians, two-thirds of whom were civilians, were killed, along with six Israelis, four of whom were civilians. International negotiators led by Egyptian Pres. Mohammed Morsi, who had condemned Israel's actions at the start of the violence, worked to end the conflict. Egyptian Foreign Min. Mohamed Kamel Amr, accompanied by U.S. Sec. of State Hillary Clinton, announced that a cease-fire agreement between Israel and Hamas had been reached from Egypt Nov. 21.

Egyptian President Sharply Limits the Judiciary—Claiming the need to end judicial obstructionism threatening democratic reform in Egypt, Pres. Mohammed Morsi Nov. 22 issued a decree that sharply restricted the courts' jurisdiction until a new constitution was approved. Earlier in the year, the courts had dissolved the lower chamber of parliament and an assembly tasked with drafting a constitution; they were now looking into dissolving the upper chamber and the new assembly, which liberals, secularists, and Christians had either boycotted or left. Morsi's decree barred them from dissolving either and from challenging his laws and decrees. It also gave the assembly an extra two months to work on the constitution, removed Egypt's top prosecutor from office, and reopened cases against ousted Pres. Hosni Mubarak and other officials from Mubarak's government. Mass protests followed—either supporting or condemning Morsi's power grab—leading to clashes of rival groups. The Islamist-dominated assembly rushed to finish a constitutional draft, doing so Nov. 30. Morsi annulled most of his decree Dec. 8, restoring court jurisdiction over everything except presidential declarations intended to shepherd the draft into enactment.

Syrian Opposition Forms New Coalition and Gains Strength—Activists involved in the fight to oust Syrian Pres. Bashar al-Assad announced Nov. 11 the formation of the Natl. Coalition for Syrian Revolutionary and Opposition Forces, uniting 90% of Syrian opposition groups. The new coalition displaced the Syrian Natl. Council (SNC), a group of Syrian exiles who claimed to represent the Syrian opposition but who had failed to gain sufficiently broad support and became increasingly ineffectual. Sheikh Ahmed Moaz al-Khatib—a former Damascus imam—was chosen as the group's president. The new group quickly gained international support. The Gulf Coalition Council (GCC), a group comprising Bahrain, Kuwait, Oman, Qatar, Saudi Arabia, and the United Arab Emirates (UAE), recognized the new organization as Syria's official government Nov. 12. France, Turkey, and the UK followed suit over the next several days. The U.S. voiced their support for the new coalition but withheld formal recognition until Dec. 11.

The opposition continued to gain military strength within Syria. Syrian rebels Nov. 27 downed an army helicopter using a surface-to-air missile at the government-held Sheikh Suleiman base about 16 mi west of Aleppo. Rebels had also captured air bases in the northern Aleppo and Idlib provinces, but the regime's air defenses remained a powerful obstacle in the way of rebel success. The UN High Commissioner for Human Rights announced Jan. 2 that nearly 60,000 people had died in Syria as a result of fighting between the Mar. 2011 beginning of the conflict and Nov. 20, 2012.

UN General Assembly Grants Palestine Observer State Status—In a move opposed by Israel and the U.S., the United Nations General Assembly Nov. 29 voted 138-9 (41 abstentions) to grant the Palestinian Authority the status of nonmember observer state, something that Palestinian Authority Pres. Mahmoud Abbas characterized as equal to recognizing Palestine as a nation. Israel had expected the outcome of the vote, which was supported by Russia and China, along with traditional U.S. allies such as France, Italy, Spain, and Switzerland. Israeli Prime Min. Benjamin Netanyahu characterized the change in status as "meaningless," noting that conditions in the region would not change. The next day, Israel announced that construction of 3,000 homes on contested land in the West Bank and East Jerusalem had been approved, a move believed to have been made to punish Palestine for seeking UN recognition.

General

Fort Larned wins Breeders' Cup Classic—Before a crowd of 55,123 Nov. 3 at Santa Anita Park in Arcadia, CA, 9-1 long shot Fort Larned took an early lead and held off Mucho Macho Man, who trailed closely throughout the race, to win the 29th Breeders' Cup Classic by a half-length. It was a first-time victory at the Breeders' Cup for jockey Brian Hernandez Jr. and trainer Ian Wilkes. The heavy favorite Game On Dude remained out of contention the entire race, placing seventh and ending his chances of being named Horse of the Year.

Coptic Christian Church Chooses New Pope—Egypt's Coptic Christian Church chose Bishop Tawadros of the Nile River delta region of El-Beheira to be its 118th pope Nov. 4. Approximately 2,400 electors narrowed the field to three candidates, and a blindfolded child picked Tawadros's name out of a chalice, according to traditional practice. Succeeding Pope Shenouda III, who died Mar. 17 after a 40-year tenure, Tawadros II was enthroned Nov. 18, when he pledged to follow integrationist policies in contrast with his predecessor. Shenouda had formed an alliance with Pres. Mubarak in exchange for state protection for the Copts, who make up 5% to 10% of Egypt's population; they suffered sectarian violence after Mubarak's fall in 2011.

BP Pleads Guilty, Agrees to Record Fine—More than two years after an explosion on the *Deepwater Horizon* oil rig killed 11 and caused millions of gallons of oil to spill into the Gulf of Mexico, BP Exploration and Production Inc. (BP) pleaded guilty Nov. 15 to manslaughter, obstruction of Congress, and violating the Clean Water and Migratory Bird Treaty Acts for its role in the disaster. The company agreed to pay $4.5 bil in fines and penalties, the largest-ever payment to resolve a U.S. criminal case. Approximately $2.4 bil will be used to restore and preserve the Gulf of Mexico's marine and coastal environment, including bird and wildlife habitats that were harmed in the spill. BP also agreed to hire monitors and auditors to oversee safety procedures and improve the company's code of conduct.

In a separate settlement announced Jan. 3, *Deepwater Horizon* rig owner Transocean Ltd. agreed to pay $1.4 bil over five years to settle charges against it. Both BP and Transocean are still liable to face civil charges.

Hostess Brands Inc. to Close—After a last ditch effort to mediate a dispute over pay and benefits between Hostess Brands Inc. and the Bakery Workers Union failed, a U.S. bankruptcy court approved, Nov. 21, 82-year-old Hostess's plan to close the company and sell its assets, including such iconic brands as Twinkies, Ding Dongs, and Wonder Bread. About 15,000 of the company's 18,500 employees were laid off immediately, and 3,200 were kept on to wind down operations.

December 2012
National

Congress Threatens to Send U.S. Over Fiscal Cliff—During the lame-duck session of Congress that followed Nov. elections, protracted partisan negotiations threatened to push the U.S. over a so-called fiscal cliff of some $500 bil in automatic budget cuts and expiring tax breaks set to go into effect Jan. 1, 2013. Pres. Barack Obama and House Speaker John Boehner (R, OH) met without other leaders Dec. 6 to negotiate a deal, which was stalled over Democrat unwillingness to make spending cuts and Republican unwillingness to allow tax rates to be raised. In an effort to get Democrats to agree to spending cuts—or shift public perception of fault if they did not do so—Boehner attempted to pass legislation, known as Plan B, that would have extended Bush-era tax cuts for incomes up to $1 mil, but he pulled the bill from consideration Dec. 20 after it became clear that it did not have the support of his own party.

In the face of the collapse of Plan B, Boehner said it was up to the president and the Senate to devise a solution. Vice Pres. Joe Biden and Senate Minority Leader Mitch McConnell (R, KY) negotiated an agreement Dec. 30-31, that made Bush-era tax cuts permanent for individuals earning up to $400,000 and couples earning up to $450,000, while allowing the tax cuts on incomes above those thresholds to expire. A 2% reduction on payroll taxes was also allowed to expire.

Amending the automatic budget and spending cuts, however, was deferred until Mar. 1, 2013, when the budget cuts would take effect in the absence of another agreement. Pres. Obama signed the legislation into law Jan. 2, 2013, the day after the Senate, 89-8, and House, 257-167, voted to pass the bill.

Supreme Court to Hear Same-Sex Marriage Cases—The U.S. Supreme Court Dec. 7 agreed to hear two cases on the constitutionality of same-sex marriage. The first case, *Hollingsworth v. Perry*, was filed in 2009 to challenge Proposition 8, a 2008 California ballot initiative that amended the state constitution to define marriage as a union between a man and a woman. The amendment was struck down in 2010 by U.S. District Judge Vaughn Walker, who argued the Constitution required the state to allow same-sex couples to marry; Walker's decision was upheld in a split vote Feb. 2012 by a three-judge panel of the U.S. Ninth Circuit Court of Appeals in San Francisco, CA.

The other case, *U.S. v. Windsor*, challenged the constitutionality of the federal Defense of Marriage Act (DOMA) passed in 1996. DOMA excluded same-sex couples from more than 1,000 marriage-related federal laws and programs, even if the couple was legally married in accordance with state law or the laws of another country. Edith Windsor filed the case following her receipt of a $363,053 estate-tax bill after she inherited the property of her wife, Thea Clara Spyer, whom she had married in Canada in 2007 after a 40-year partnership and who died in 2009. (Under federal tax codes, opposite-sex spouses are not required to pay estate tax.) A lower court determined June 6 that DOMA violated the 14th amendment guarantee of equal protection under the law, and that decision was upheld by a three-judge panel of the U.S. Second Circuit Court of Appeals in New York City Oct. 18.

Gunman Kills 26, Mostly Children, at Connecticut Elementary School—Armed with a semiautomatic rifle and two handguns, a gunman Dec. 14 entered Sandy Hook Elementary School in Newtown, CT, and shot to death 20 children, ages 6-7, as well as the school's principal, psychologist, two teachers, and two teacher's aides. It was the second-deadliest school shooting in U.S. history. (Thirty-two people were killed in the 2007 shooting at Virginia Tech in Blacksburg, VA.) As police arrived, the 20-year-old shooter, Adam Lanza, fatally shot himself; he had killed his mother in their home earlier that morning. The Newtown shooting reinvigorated the gun-control debate in ways that previous mass shootings had not, with some members of Congress pledging to revisit the assault-weapons ban that expired in 2004. At a memorial service held in Newtown Dec. 16, Pres. Barack Obama declared that the U.S. needed to do more to protect children from gun violence.

State Department Faulted in Benghazi Attack—An independent panel Dec. 18 made public the results of their investigation of the Sept. 11, 2012, attack on U.S. diplomatic facilities in Benghazi, Libya, that left four U.S. government employees dead, including U.S. ambassador to Libya J. Christopher Stevens. The panel, led by retired ambassador Thomas Pickering and Navy Adm. Mike Mullen, blamed failures in State Dept. management, not willful misconduct, for the facilities' "grossly inadequate" security. The next day, three State Dept. officials were placed on administrative leave, and a fourth resigned. Sec. of State Hillary Clinton, already preparing to leave her post, accepted the panel's 29 recommendations for improving diplomatic security in a letter to Congress.

Markets End Year on Upbeat Note, Despite Decline in Consumer Confidence—The Conference Board announced Dec. 27 that consumer confidence had fallen to its lowest level since Aug. as consumers worried about the so-called fiscal cliff and its impending tax increases and cuts in government spending. U.S. retailers reported lackluster holiday sales before an upswing at the end of Dec., but U.S. auto sales gained 13% over 2011. The Dow Jones Industrial

Average closed Dec. 31 at 13,104.14, up 7.26% for the calendar year—the fourth straight year it has seen an increase—while the S&P 500 closed at 1,426.19, a gain of 13.41% for the year, and the Nasdaq Composite Index (3,019.51) rose 15.91%. Gold, which surpassed $1,700 an ounce for several months during 2012, closed at $1,658, for the 12th consecutive year of gold price gains.

International

NATO Sending Patriot Missiles to Turkey—The North Atlantic Treaty Organization (NATO) Dec. 4 in Brussels, Belgium, authorized a plan to deploy Patriot missiles along the Turkish-Syrian border, demonstrating growing fears that the civil war in Syria was a threat to neighboring nations. Of particular concern was the fear among Western leaders that Syrian Pres. Bashar al-Assad would attack antigovernment forces or civilians with Syria's stockpile of chemical weapons, which reportedly included mustard gas and the nerve agent sarin. Israeli intelligence officials had noted activity in late Nov. that suggested Syria was mixing chemicals at storage sites and filling dozens of 500-lb bombs. The Syrian foreign ministry said Dec. 3 that they would not use chemical weapons on its own citizens, but concern remained.

Typhoon Kills More Than 1,000 in the Philippines—Typhoon Bopha, packing torrential rains and 109-mph winds with 130-mph gusts, made landfall Dec. 4 on the southern Philippine island of Mindanao. The storm took down trees and buildings and triggered landslides and flash floods, leaving more than 1,000 people dead and nearly 1 mil displaced. Relief centers were overwhelmed, and emergency agencies had difficulty reaching isolated areas and were obliged to use air drops to provide supplies. Philippines Pres. Benigno "NoyNoy" Aquino III declared a state of national calamity Dec. 8. Government troops and the Maoist rebel group New People's Army (NPA) agreed to a temporary cease-fire in the hardest hit regions. The government estimated the cost of the storm's damages would be more than $900 mil.

Multinational Banks Fined for Ignoring Sanctions, Other Illicit Financial Activities—Britain's Standard Chartered PLC bank Dec. 10 accepted a $327-mil fine levied by the U.S. for violating sanctions on Iran, Myanmar, Libya, and Sudan by facilitating the transfer of funds from those countries. Similarly, British-based international bank HSBC Dec. 11 agreed to forfeit $1.2 bil in assets and pay $700 mil in fines. HSBC was accused of violating U.S. money-laundering laws to benefit Mexican drug cartels and of ignoring U.S. sanctions. Swiss bank UBS AG announced Dec. 19 that it would pay $1.5 bil in fines to U.S., British, and Swiss authorities for manipulating benchmark interest rates such as the London interbank offered rate (Libor) to boost its trading profits and give the illusion that its financial health was stronger than it was in the fallout of the 2008 financial crisis.

In Poor Health, Chávez Names Successor in Venezuela—Just two months after he won reelection and claimed to be "totally free" of cancer, Venezuelan Pres. Hugo Chávez traveled to Cuba to undergo additional surgery Dec. 11 after tests found malignant cells. Chávez named Vice Pres. Nicolás Maduro Moros his successor Dec. 8 when he announced his plans. Concerns over Chávez's health called into question his ability to continue his presidential responsibilities or to be inaugurated as scheduled Jan. 10, 2013. Venezuela's Supreme Court Jan. 9 upheld the legislature's decision to postpone Chávez's inauguration to accommodate his recovery, but critics denounced the move as unconstitutional.

North Korea Launches First Satellite—North Korea successfully launched a satellite into orbit for the first time Dec. 12, employing a three-stage rocket comparable to the type used for intercontinental ballistic missiles. The launch provided Kim Jong Un, still establishing himself as North Korea's leader a year after the death of his father, with a public relations coup. The satellite, known as Kwangmyongsong-3,

achieved orbit but may have failed to function; by Dec. 17, it was apparently tumbling in space. Nevertheless, the rocket's successful launch troubled Western leaders, who regarded it as a violation of UN bans on North Korean development of missile technology.

Eurozone Finance Ministers Agree on Plan to Create Eurozone Bank Supervisor—During a Dec. 13 summit in Brussels, Belgium, finance ministers of the 17 countries in the eurozone—those that use the euro as currency—agreed on a roadmap to allow the European Central Bank (ECB) to supervise the operations of large eurozone banks. Under the plan, an administrative body within the ECB would supervise banks' decisions regarding lending and cash reserves and have the power to inject money from European bailout funds to save failing banks without adding to countries' sovereign debt. The agreement was hailed as an important step in establishing a centralized eurozone banking system and improving the overall stability of the eurozone's finances.

Japan's Ruling Party Loses Election in Landslide—In Dec. 16 elections for the lower house of Japan's parliament, the Liberal Democratic Party (LDP) and its coalition partner, the New Komeito party, took 325 of the 480 seats. The LDP coalition replaced the majority, held by the Democratic Party of Japan (DPJ) since 2009, with a supermajority that would allow the coalition to override vetoes from the upper house, where the DPJ still holds a majority. LDP leader Shinzo Abe, who had served previously as prime minister (2006-07), replaced Yoshihiko Noda as prime minister Dec. 26. With just 59% of the eligible electorate voting, the LDP victory was seen more as a repudiation of the DPJ than an embrace of the LDP.

South Korea Elects First Woman President—Park Geun Hye, the daughter of Park Chung Hee, South Korea's authoritarian leader from 1961 until his assassination in 1979, won South Korea's Dec. 19 presidential election with 51.6% of the vote. Park was set to become her country's first female president in Feb. 2013 and was expected to shift away from the hard-line stance toward North Korea of her predecessor, Pres. Lee Myung Bak.

Italian Prime Minister Monti Resigns, Parliament Dissolved—After parliament approved his government's 2013 budget, Italian Prime Min. Mario Monti resigned Dec. 21, fulfilling a promise he had made earlier in the month. Monti's government had lost the support of the People of Freedom (PDL), the center-right party of Silvio Berlusconi, who resigned amidst scandal in 2011 and whom Monti had been appointed to replace. After Monti's resignation, Pres. Giorgio Napolitano dissolved parliament, setting the stage for early elections in Feb. 2013. Monti, an economics professor and European Union commissioner, had succeeded in improving Italy's international fiscal credibility, but his methods, which included tax increases and budget cuts that contributed to Italy's recession, cost him popularity.

Egyptian Voters Approve New Constitution—After two rounds of voting Dec. 15 and Dec. 22, Egypt's new constitution, which was supported by Muslim Brotherhood leader and Pres. Mohammed Morsi, won approval with the support of 63.8% of those who went to the polls. Turnout was low: a mere 33% of eligible voters participated, and the Natl. Salvation Front, a coalition of opposition groups, alleged fraud. Critics believed the constitution failed to provide protection for the rights of women and non-Muslims, and left open the possibility that it could be used to impose sharia, or Islamic law. It nonetheless was ratified and went into effect Dec. 26.

General

British Royal Couple Announces Pregnancy—Buckingham Palace announced Dec. 3 that Prince William, second in line to the British throne, and his wife Catherine, Duchess of Cambridge, were expecting their first child. Catherine had been admitted to King Edward VII hospital, suffering from hyperemesis gravidarum, a condition characterized as severe morning sickness. The British Cabinet Office announced that the child will become third in line to the throne regardless of its gender; while the traditional rule that gives precedence to the eldest male child had yet to be formally changed, that change was planned and de facto in effect.

Galaxy Wins MLS Championship—In a repeat matchup of the previous year's final, the L.A. Galaxy defeated the Houston Dynamo, 3-1, before a sellout crowd Dec. 1 at the Home Depot Center in Carson, CA, to claim the MLS championship. The Dynamo captured the lead after Calen Carr scored in the 44th minute, but a header in the 60th minute by the Galaxy's Omar Gonzalez, who was named the match's MVP, tied the game. Forward and team captain Landon Donovan gave Los Angeles the lead, scoring a 65th minute penalty, and striker Robbie Keane put the game out of reach when he scored with another penalty in stoppage time. The Galaxy's high-priced midfielder David Beckham left his last game with the team a minute before the final whistle blew.

January 2013

National

Fiscal Cliff Deferred; 113th Congress Convenes—Pres. Barack Obama Jan. 2 signed a bill passed the day before by the House, 257-167, and Senate, 89-8, that temporarily averted the so-called "fiscal cliff," which would have triggered nearly $500 bil in automatic federal spending cuts and tax breaks. But it merely postponed for two months the sequestration, the across-the-board federal spending cuts that Congress imposed on itself in 2011 if it could not reach a broader budget agreement.

With a Republican majority in the House and a Democratic-controlled Senate, the 113th Congress convened Jan. 3, with 97 incoming freshman legislators. The incoming class included Tammy Baldwin (D, WI), the first openly gay member of the Senate, which had 20 women in its membership (the highest number of women ever concurrently serving).

House Speaker John Boehner (R, OH) was reelected to his post, but 12 fellow Republicans did not vote for him, a historically large number of defectors for House Speaker elections. The vote was thought to reflect Boehner's diminishing influence among conservative congressional Republicans. House Minority Leader Nancy Pelosi (D, CA), Senate Majority Leader Harry Reid (D, NV), and Senate Minority Leader McConnell (R, KY) all retained their leadership positions.

Economy Continues Slow Growth—The Labor Dept. reported Jan. 4 that the U.S. unemployment rate held steady at 7.8% for Dec. 2012. While 155,000 jobs were created, mostly in the construction, health care, and food-service industries, more government jobs were cut. The stock market continued its upward trend, with the Dow Jones Industrial Average closing at 13,860.58, up 5.8% for the month. The Standard & Poor's 500 Index closed at 1,498.11, up 5% over Dec. 2012. The Nasdaq Composite Index finished the month at 3,142.13, up 4.1% from the end of 2012.

Inaugurated for Second Term, Obama Proposes Stiffer Gun Control—In a private ceremony held Jan. 20 in the White House Blue Room, Supreme Court Chief Justice John Roberts swore in Pres. Barack Obama for a second term. Because Jan. 20 was a Sunday, the public ceremony was held the next day, which coincided with the Martin Luther King Jr. federal holiday. In his second inaugural address at the U.S. Capitol, in front of about 800,000 spectators, Obama exhorted the nation to act to halt climate change, defended social welfare programs like Social Security and Medicare, and became the first president to explicitly reference gay rights in an inaugural address.

Earlier in the month, Obama and Vice Pres. Joe Biden, the leader of Obama's gun task force, proposed a number of gun regulations Jan. 16, largely in response to the Newtown, CT, school shooting on Dec. 14, 2012. The most significant

proposal involved renewing the 1994 assault-weapons ban that was allowed to expire in 2004, a proposition that many in Congress were expected to oppose. Obama signed 23 executive orders that could be implemented without congressional approval, including strengthening enforcement of existing laws, and increasing information-sharing among state and local law-enforcement agencies.

Pentagon Lifts Ban on Women in Combat—At the Pentagon Jan. 24, Defense Sec. Leon Panetta reversed the Defense Dept.'s 1994 policy barring women from participating in combat missions. The Joint Chiefs of Staff and its chairman, Gen. Martin Dempsey, unanimously supported the decision. Women made up 14% of the 1.4 mil active-duty armed forces, and were already unofficially entering into combat in the wars in Iraq and Afghanistan, which lacked defined front lines. Nearly 300,000 women had been deployed to those two countries; more than 800 of them were wounded and 152 were killed. Women were still excluded from the Selective Service System, under which men ages 18-25 were compelled to register their draft eligibility.

Kerry Wins Confirmation as Secretary of State—With a vote of 94-3, the U.S. Senate approved Sen. John Kerry (D, MA) as secretary of state Jan. 29. The Senate vote followed a unanimous vote for Kerry's confirmation by the Senate Foreign Relations Committee, which Kerry had chaired for four years. A special election for Kerry's Senate seat was scheduled to be held June 25, following an Apr. 30 primary.

Pres. Barack Obama's first choice for the job, UN Ambassador Susan Rice, removed her name from consideration after congressional Republicans criticized her for reciting talking points alleging that the Sept. 11, 2012, attack on the U.S. embassy in Benghazi, Libya, had been a spontaneous response to an anti-Muslim film. U.S agencies later acknowledged that the incident, in which U.S. Ambassador to Libya J. Christopher Stevens and three other Americans died, was an orchestrated terrorist attack, prompting right-wing accusations of an Obama administration cover-up. In hearings before Congress Jan. 23, outgoing Sec. of State Hillary Clinton vigorously defended the administration's response while accepting responsibility for the security lapses that enabled the attack.

International

Syrian Civil War Continues as Death Toll Climbs—The United Nations' human rights commissioner reported Jan. 2 that more than 60,000 people had died in Syria's civil war since Mar. 2011. The conflict had also created a humanitarian crisis for some 4 mil people inside the country and produced about a million refugees. Both sides continued attacks throughout the month, using car bombs, air raids, and other types of assaults on forces and on armed and unarmed civilian populations, including children. On Jan. 6, Pres. Bashar al-Assad made his first public address since June 2012, appearing on TV denouncing the rebels and defiantly refusing to negotiate with them.

Opposition forces scored a major victory Jan. 11 when they captured the strategic Taftanaz air base in Idlib province. Israel entered the fray for the first time Jan. 30, bombing a target near Damascus that it believed was a convoy carrying missiles to Hezbollah forces in Lebanon. Syrian officials said the attack struck a scientific research facility—Western analysts had identified it as being involved in producing biological and chemical weapons—but did not vow retaliation.

Mali Regains Control of Key Cities With International Assistance—Malian soldiers fired on Islamist rebels Jan. 8 in the village of Gnimignama in the first fighting there since a military coup in Mar. 2012. The rebel groups, which included al-Qaeda in the Islamic Maghreb (AQIM), had taken over Northern Mali in the chaos surrounding the coup in hopes of forging their own homeland. Their Jan. 10 attack on the strategic town of Konna represented a foray south of the territory the insurgents had previously controlled, raising alarms

throughout the region. With the help of French troops and air support, Mali's military recovered Konna Jan. 18. West African nations also agreed to send 3,300 troops to aid the Malian government, and the European Union authorized 450-500 non-combat forces. French and Malian forces Jan. 28 liberated the city of Timbuktu, where Islamist rebels, during their occupation, had destroyed historic monuments and ancient texts as inconsistent with Islamic law. The Intl. Federation of Human Rights Leagues said Jan. 24 that Malian forces had summarily executed 11 people in the name of putting down the insurgency; Human Rights Watch announced investigations into similar executions of Arabs and ethnic Tuaregs.

U.S. Announces Accelerated Troop Withdrawal From Afghanistan—In a joint White House appearance with Afghan Pres. Hamid Karzai, Pres. Obama announced Jan. 11 that withdrawal of the 66,000 U.S. troops from Afghanistan would proceed sooner and faster than previously thought. Obama declined to specify a number of troops that would remain in Afghanistan after 2014 with the narrow mission of training Afghan security forces and conducting counterterrorism activities. Earlier predictions had placed the size of that U.S. presence at around 30,000 troops; revised estimates were closer to 9,000. Meanwhile, suicide attacks in Afghanistan continued throughout the month, including one at the Afghan Natl. Directorate of Security headquarters in Kabul Jan. 16 that killed six attackers and a security guard and injured 17. Another series of attacks Jan. 26-27 targeted the Afghan Natl. Police and killed more than 20 police officers.

North Korea Continues Nuclear Program Despite UN Condemnation—The UN Security Council voted unanimously Jan. 22 to condemn North Korea's Dec. 2012 rocket launch and tightened existing sanctions on the country. China, typically Pyongyang's staunchest ally, supported the Security Council decision and expressed "regret" that North Korea had gone through with the launch despite international opposition. As part of a compromise between the U.S. and China, rather than impose additional sanctions, North Korea's space agency and certain state officials were added to the list of those designated for sanctions. In a show of defiance, North Korea for the first time admitted its intention to develop weapons for military purposes (including missiles that could reach the U.S.) and announced that it was planning another underground nuclear weapons test.

Netanyahu Loses Strength But Retains Premiership in Israeli Elections—Israeli Prime Min. Benjamin Netanyahu's right-wing Likud-Yisrael Beiteinu political bloc won a narrow victory in parliamentary elections held Jan. 22. The 31 seats won by Likud Beiteinu represented a loss of 11 seats in the 120-seat Knesset. The centrist party Yesh Atid (There Is a Future), which was founded only a year earlier, had a surprisingly strong showing, winning 19 seats; the center-left Labor won 15. With a dozen different parties represented in parliament, assembling a new coalition government took nearly two months. Netanyahu finally brokered a deal with Yesh Atid and the religious and nationalist Jewish Home Party Mar. 15.

Brazil Nightclub Fire Kills 241 People—Fire broke out Jan. 27 during a concert by the band Gurizada Fandangueira at the Kiss nightclub in Santa Maria, Brazil, taking the lives of 241 patrons, most of them college students, and injuring more than 100 others. The fire was caused by an outdoor flare that the band set off inside during its performance. The flare ignited foam insulation in the club's ceiling. The crisis was exacerbated by a malfunctioning fire extinguisher and the absence of an alarm and sprinkler system. During the frantic exodus, many in the crowd, which was twice the club's legal capacity of 1,000, were overcome by toxic smoke. Two of the club's owners and two band members were subsequently charged with manslaughter; four others, including two firefighters, were charged for hiding evidence that the club's operating license had expired.

General

NHL Lockout Ends, Shortened Season Begins—The third lockout in the history of the Natl. Hockey League ended Jan. 6 after nearly four months of often-stagnant negotiations in which owners claimed that at least 10 of the league's 30 teams had been regularly losing money. The stoppage forced the cancellation of 510 games (nearly half the regular season), as well as the outdoor Winter Classic and the All-Star Game. The NHL's Board of Governors approved the new 10-year collective bargaining agreement Jan. 9, which the Players' Assn. signed Jan. 12, and teams began a 48-game season Jan. 19.

Crimson Tide Repeats as College Football Champion; Te'o Hoax Revealed—The Univ. of Alabama Crimson Tide won its second straight Bowl Championship Series title game and its third in four years when it scored a dominant 42-14 victory over the Fighting Irish of Notre Dame Jan. 7 in Miami Gardens, FL. The win gave the Southeastern Conference its seventh national championship title in a row. Running back Eddie Lacy, the game's offensive MVP, ran for a total of 140 yards, and quarterback A. J. McCarron completed 20 of 28 passes for four touchdowns and 264 yards. Alabama head coach Nick Saban claimed his fourth national title, placing him second on the all-time list behind Alabama's Bear Bryant, who won six.

The website Deadspin.com reported Jan. 16 that a much-circulated backstory about high-profile Notre Dame linebacker and Heisman Trophy finalist Manti Te'o was apparently a hoax. Te'o had told the media that his long-distance girlfriend—whom he had never met in person—had died of leukemia in Sept. 2012, inspiring him to work harder. According to school investigators, the woman with whom he thought he had conducted an online and phone relationship never existed; she was invented by Ronaiah Tuiasosopo, a young man infatuated with Te'o.

Baseball Writers Elect No Hall of Famers; New Steroid Scandal Emerges—For the first time since 1996, the Baseball Writers' Assn. of America failed to elect any players to the National Baseball Hall of Fame. It was the first year on the ballot for 14-time All-Star slugger Barry Bonds, who held the career and season home-run records, and 7-time Cy Young Award-winning pitcher Roger Clemens. Both Bonds and Clemens were widely suspected of using performance-enhancing drugs (PEDs). Candidates needed to be selected on 75% of the ballots in order to win election to the Hall, but Bonds received just 36.2% and Clemens 37.6%. Two other sluggers thought to be Hall of Fame contenders who played during the so-called steroid era were also denied election in their first year of eligibility: first baseman Jeff Bagwell, who received 59.6% of the vote, and catcher Mike Piazza, who earned 57.8%.

Several current players were caught up in a new PED scandal revealed Jan. 29 involving the Miami, FL, anti-aging clinic Biogenesis, which had abruptly closed in Dec. 2012. According to the *Miami New Times*, the clinic sold various PEDs, including human growth hormone (HGH), testosterone, and anabolic steroids to 13-time All-Star slugger Alex Rodriguez, 2011 Natl. League MVP Ryan Braun, and 18 other players.

Cyclist Armstrong Admits to Doping—In an interview with Oprah Winfrey broadcast Jan. 17-18, seven-time Tour de France winner Lance Armstrong, who had denied using PEDs throughout his career, admitted to doing just that. In Oct. 2012, the U.S. Anti-Doping Agency stripped Armstrong of all of his titles and banned him from future competition, but he had remained publicly defiant in the face of PED allegations until the interview. Armstrong said he had doped from the mid-1990s through 2005, when he won his last Tour, viewing the use as creating "a level playing field." Critics pointed out that Armstrong did not express remorse for denigrating his fellow cyclists and trainers who had told the truth when they testified to his PED use. Armstrong did express regret for the toll his admission was taking on his cancer-awareness-and-prevention foundation, Livestrong, with which he cut ties in Nov. 2012.

Azarenka, Djokovic Defend Australian Open Titles—Victoria Azarenka of Belarus successfully defended her Australian Open title against Li Na of China (4-6, 6-4, 6-3) in a grueling match that lasted almost three hours at Rod Laver Arena in Melbourne, Jan. 26. The match, in which Li was treated by a tournament doctor after twisting her ankle twice and hitting her head on the ground, was also interrupted by Australia Day fireworks. The following night, Serbian Novak Djokovic became the first man since Roy Emerson (1963-67) to win three consecutive Australian championships. He bested the UK's Andy Murray in a 3-hr., 40-min. match, 6-7 (2-7), 7-6 (7-3), 6-3, 6-2.

February 2013
National

Dow Closes at Five-Year High; Other Economic News—The Dow Jones Industrial Average Feb. 1 closed above 14,000 for the first time since Oct. 2007, just before the start of the recession. The Dow closed at 14,009.8, up 149 points, or 1.1%, from the previous day. The Standard & Poor's 500 also rose to its highest number since 2007, closing Feb. 1 at 1,513.17. The Dow and S&P 500 held onto their gains; the Dow finished the month at 14,054.49, up 1.4% from Jan., while the S&P 500 closed at 1,514.68, representing a 1.1% increase over the previous month. The Nasdaq Composite Index ended Feb. at 3,160.19, up 0.6% from Jan. Growth didn't extend to all segments of the economy, however. The Bureau of Economic Analysis's revised figures for the fourth quarter of 2012 showed that real GDP grew by only 0.1%. A 17.5% increase in residential investment wasn't enough to counteract a 22% decrease in spending on national defense as the U.S. began reducing its presence in Iraq and Afghanistan. The reductions in defense spending were the largest since the Vietnam War, and predated automatic cuts that would be dictated by the budget sequester. GDP growth for the entire year was 2.2%, up slightly from the 2011 level of 1.8%.

U.S. Airways agreed to merge with American Airlines Feb. 13 in an $11-bil agreement that would create the world's largest airline. The two would combine under the American Airlines name and would together serve about a quarter of all U.S. airline passengers. The merger would leave just four major airlines in the U.S. controlling more than 80% of the domestic market.

As part of a settlement for violating foreclosure-processing laws, five of the largest U.S. banks wrote off $45.8 bil in mortgage obligations for more than 550,000 homeowners in 2012, according to a report issued Feb. 21 by the overseer appointed by 49 states and the federal government. Of those, some 240,000 homeowners received permission from Ally, Bank of America, Citigroup, JPMorgan Chase, or Wells Fargo to conduct short sales (in which the sale price is lower than the outstanding mortgage) accounting for more than $19 bil in relief.

State of the Union Proposes Ambitious Agenda; Congress Passes Violence Against Women Act—In his Feb. 12 State of the Union Address, Pres. Barack Obama outlined a broad slate of measures designed to help the middle class. These included immigration reform, raising the minimum wage, passing a clean-energy climate bill, reducing pollution, dealing with the effects of climate change, making preschool mandatory for all 4-year-olds, closing corporate loopholes as the first step in tax-code reforms, investing in infrastructure, and helping homeowners refinance mortgages. He also pledged to find a bipartisan solution to the budget sequester that would begin Mar. 1 unless Congress found a way to prevent the automatic federal spending cuts and tax increases from going into effect. The speech included an emotional appeal to Congress to vote on several gun violence measures,

and announced that 34,000 troops (more than half the U.S. force in Afghanistan) would return home within a year.

Obama also endorsed renewal of the Violence Against Women Act, first passed in 1994. The Senate passed the bill, 78-22, on Feb. 12; after a sometimes contentious month-long debate, the House passed the Senate version, 286-138, Feb. 28, after voting down its own version hours earlier. The bill, signed into law by Obama Mar. 7, protects a wide range of abuse victims, including American Indians, LGBT (lesbian, gay, bisexual, and transgender) individuals, and immigrants.

Former L.A. Police Officer Tracked Down After Killing Spree—Christopher Dorner, a former member of the Los Angeles Police Department and a former U.S. Navy officer who was suspected of killing four people and wounding three others, died in a cabin in the San Bernardino Mountains Feb. 12 that caught fire during a shootout with police. Dorner had been the subject of a statewide manhunt since Feb. 3, when he shot and killed two people after posting an angry manifesto on Facebook decrying his 2008 termination from the LAPD.

Defense, Treasury Secretaries Confirmed; CIA Confirmation Hearings Held—The Senate Feb. 26 confirmed the nomination of former Sen. Chuck Hagel (R, NE) as Defense secretary by a vote of 58-41. All 41 opposition votes were cast by Republicans, who had filibustered his nomination earlier in the month, objecting to what they perceived as an anti-Israel stance and Hagel's stated opposition to the military surge in Afghanistan. Jacob Lew had an easier time with his confirmation as the new Treasury secretary, winning a 71-26 vote in the Senate Feb. 27.

The Obama administration's lead counterterrorism advisor John Brennan, nominated for director of the Central Intelligence Agency (CIA), faced tough questions in his Senate confirmation hearings Feb. 7 about an administration memo that legally justified using drones for targeted killings. The memo shed light on the administration's rationale behind the 2011 drone killing in Yemen, a country with which the U.S. is not at war, of Anwar al-Awlaki, a U.S. citizen who was an al-Qaeda leader. Brennan was ultimately confirmed on Mar. 7.

Private in WikiLeaks Scandal Pleads Guilty—A U.S. Army judge Feb. 28 accepted Pfc. Bradley Manning's guilty pleas to 10 counts in connection with sending classified military and State Dept. correspondence to the whistleblower website WikiLeaks in 2010. The 25-year-old Manning faced up to 20 years in prison on the charges, but prosecutors were still considering an additional 12 counts, including aiding the enemy, which could lead to a life sentence if convicted. Manning, who had served as an intelligence analyst in Baghdad, claimed not to have intended to harm U.S. military efforts by leaking the information, but rather meant to expose information on past acts by the armed forces—such as the 2007 Apache helicopter attack that killed a dozen civilians in Baghdad—to the general public.

International

Suicide Bomber Attacks U.S. Embassy in Turkey—A man detonated an explosive vest Feb. 1 at a side entrance of the U.S. embassy in Ankara, Turkey, killing himself and a guard and injuring a Turkish journalist. Coming just five months after the Sept. 11, 2012, attack on the U.S. consulate in Benghazi, Libya, that killed four U.S. government officials, including the U.S. ambassador, the incident raised new fears about the safety of American diplomats serving in the Middle East. The bomber was identified as Ecevit Sanli, a terrorist who had been convicted for attacking government buildings in Istanbul but released under a 2001 amnesty for ailments he incurred during a hunger strike. The anti-U.S. and anti-NATO Revolutionary People's Liberation Party claimed responsibility for the bombing, releasing a statement that called the U.S. "the murderer of the peoples of the world."

Amid Calls for Peace, Syrian Civil War Escalates—A week after Syria's main opposition leader called for peace talks with the government of Pres. Bashar al-Assad, both sides stepped up their attacks, making Feb. one of the deadliest months since the civil war began in 2011. Rebel groups Feb. 6 seized several suburbs of the capital, Damascus, but the government continued to hold the center of the capital city. Rebels also captured a military airfield—and, for the first time, usable warplanes—near Aleppo Feb. 12, a day after taking over the country's largest hydroelectric dam on the Euphrates River. The military launched several Scud missiles—not known for their precision accuracy—at rebel strongholds in Aleppo Feb. 21-22, killing at least 141 people according to Human Rights Watch, which estimated that about half of the victims were children. Both sides blamed the other for a car bomb that exploded near the headquarters of the ruling Baath Party Feb. 21, killing at least 53 people, and injuring hundreds of others. The UN High Commissioner for Human Rights Feb. 8 raised the conflict's death toll estimate to 70,000, and put the number of refugees to at nearly 800,000, with 5,000 people a day fleeing the country.

The U.S. government intervened in the conflict for the first time, announcing Feb. 28 that it would provide the rebel fighters with food and medical supplies, plus $60 mil for basic sanitation and education services in opposition-controlled areas.

Chinese Cyberattacks Revealed—U.S.-based security firm Mandiant issued a report Feb. 19 claiming that a unit of China's military had conducted a series of cyberattacks against 141 corporations and government agencies worldwide since 2006. Most of the attacks were on companies involved in critical U.S. infrastructure such as the electrical power grid, gas and water pipelines, and computer security technology. Mandiant traced the hacking operation to the Shanghai headquarters of Unit 61398 of the Chinese People's Liberation Army, a building with special fiber-optic communications infrastructure, and concluded that the attack was likely state-sponsored. The next day, China's government denied supporting any hacking, and said China was the victim of cyberattacks that originated in the U.S.

General

Ravens Defeat 49ers in Super Bowl XLVII—The Baltimore Ravens held off the San Francisco 49ers, 34-31, at the Mercedes-Benz Superdome in New Orleans, LA, Feb. 3 to win Super Bowl XLVII. When Jacoby Jones opened the third quarter with a 108-yard kickoff return for a touchdown—the longest in Super Bowl history—giving Baltimore a 22-point lead, it looked like the game might be a blowout. But a blackout—a power outage that affected half the stadium and delayed the game for 34 min.—appeared to allow San Francisco to regroup and score the next 17 points. The game marked the final contest in the career of Ravens veteran linebacker Ray Lewis, who was touted as a future Hall-of-Famer. It was also the first Super Bowl in which the two opposing head coaches were brothers: John Harbaugh led the victorious Ravens over his younger brother Jim Harbaugh, the 49ers head coach. Ravens quarterback Joe Flacco was the game's MVP, passing for 287 yards and three touchdowns.

Gotye and Black Keys Big Winners at the Grammy Awards—Belgian-Australian singer Gotye and U.S. rock band The Black Keys each won three Grammy Awards at the ceremony held in Los Angeles, CA, on Feb. 10. Gotye's "Somebody That I Used to Know," a duet with singer Kimbra, won Record of the Year, as well as Best Pop Duo/Group Performance, and his album *Making Mirrors* received Best Alternative Album. The Black Keys' song "Lonely Boy" won Best Rock Song and Best Rock Performance, and their *El Camino* was voted Best Rock Album. The Album of the Year was *Babel* by Mumford & Sons. The group fun. won Best New Artist.

Pope Benedict XVI Resigns; Scottish Archbishop Departs Over Sex Scandal—Pope Benedict XVI, the leader of the Roman Catholic Church since 2005, announced his resignation on Feb. 11, citing health issues. The last pope to have resigned was Gregory XII, who stepped down in 1415 to preserve the Church during the Great Western Schism, when three rival factions of the Church all chose different leaders. The 85-year-old Benedict, born Joseph Ratzinger, said his resignation would be effective Feb. 28. The decision shocked the College of Cardinals and much of the rest of the world, especially among the world's 1.2 bil Roman Catholics. Upon his departure, Benedict retired to Castel Gandolfo, the pope's summer residence southeast of Rome. An estimated 150,000 people crowded into St. Peter's Square for his final benediction Feb. 27.

Benedict's eight-year papacy was marred by sex-abuse scandals that continued to plague the Church, and his final days were no exception. On Feb. 25, Cardinal Keith O'Brien, Great Britain's highest-ranking Catholic, announced he would step down as Archbishop of St. Andrews and Edinburgh, Scotland, amid accusations of inappropriate relations with priests during the past 30 years. Although the 74-year-old cardinal was eligible for the conclave to appoint a new pope, he said he would not participate to avoid being a distraction during the process. O'Brien admitted to sexual misconduct Mar. 3.

Exploding Meteoroid Over Russia Injures Hundreds, Damages Property—A bright light flashed over central Russia Feb. 15, signaling the explosion of a meteoroid streaking across the sky. The sonic boom caused by the meteoroid's entrance into Earth's atmosphere shattered windows and injured about 1,200 people before it crashed in pieces in the Ural Mountains. It was the most powerful object to strike Earth in more than a century. No meteorites fell in populated areas; the largest piece found landed on the shore of a lake in the Chelyabinsk region, near the town of Chebarkul, home to 46,000 people. It created a 20-ft-wide crater. The Russian space agency Roscosmos estimated that the meteoroid, composed primarily of iron, was traveling 33,000 mph and weighed about 10,000 tons.

In an unrelated coincidence, the asteroid 2012 DA14 passed the Earth the same day, traveling from the opposite direction, just 17,200 mi from the planet—the closest ever for an asteroid.

South African "Blade Runner" Arrested for Murder—South African Olympic and Paralympic track star Oscar Pistorius was arrested Feb. 14 for the murder of his 29-year-old girlfriend, Reeva Steenkamp, at their home in Pretoria, South Africa. Neighbors reported hearing screams and shouting the night of the murder, when 26-year-old Pistorius allegedly shot Steenkamp through a closed bathroom door. He said that he thought the person in the bathroom was an intruder. Pistorius, who earned the nickname "Blade Runner" for the high-tech prosthetic blades that he wore when competing, won three medals in the Paralympic Games and was the first double-amputee to compete in the Olympic Games in 2012, when he reached the semifinals in the 400-m competition. He was released on $113,000 bail Feb. 22 and formally indicted Aug. 19. A trial was scheduled to be held in Mar. 2014.

***Argo* a Surprise Winner at the Oscars**—The Iran hostage-crisis film *Argo* received the Oscar for best picture at the Academy Awards ceremony held in Los Angeles, CA, Feb. 24, beating the Golden Globe-winning Steven Spielberg biopic *Lincoln*. Among other major awards, best director went to Ang Lee for *Life of Pi*. Daniel Day-Lewis's portrayal of America's 16th president in *Lincoln* won him a third Oscar for best actor in a leading role. The 22-year-old Jennifer Lawrence won best actress for *Silver Linings Playbook*, and Anne Hathaway received her first statuette as best supporting actress for *Les Miserables*. German actor Christoph Waltz, nominated for best supporting actor, and Quentin Tarantino, competing for best original screenplay, both won for the Civil War-era film *Django Unchained*. Despite critical pans for first-time host Seth MacFarlane, the broadcast drew its largest audience in three years, with 40.3 mil viewers tuned in.

March 2013
National

Sequestration Takes Effect; Impact Uncertain—Because Congress failed to pass a negotiated budget deal, the so-called sequestration went into effect Mar. 1, automatically triggering $1.2 tril in cuts to defense and domestic programs to be spread over 10 years. Pres. Barack Obama called Congress's self-imposed ultimatum on the budget process a "manufactured crisis." The first $85 bil in cuts (more than half of them to defense spending) took effect in fiscal 2013. They included an $11.4 bil decrease in Medicare payments to participating doctors and hospitals, and reductions in funding for unemployment, federally funded daycare, and Head Start. Many defense contracts were cancelled, and government employees were told to expect layoffs or furloughs. Tours of the White House were suspended Mar. 9 until further notice, and the U.S. Navy Apr. 9 announced it would cancel all remaining 2013 performances of the Blue Angels air shows.

Dow Exceeds Pre-Recession Levels; Other Economic News—The Dow Jones Industrial Average set an all-time closing record Mar. 5 at 14,253, surpassing its previous high close of 14,164, set Oct. 9, 2007. It took another three weeks for the S&P 500, which provides a broader measure of the economy, to surpass its pre-recession high, when it closed at a record 1,569.19 on the final day of Mar. (up 3.6% from Feb.). While some analysts attributed the Wall Street records to an improving economy, others credited the Federal Reserve, which continued to keep interest rates extremely low. The Labor Dept. reported Mar. 8 that the economy had added 236,000 jobs in Feb., more than analysts had predicted, and that the unemployment rate had fallen to 7.7%, down from 7.9% in Jan. The Dow closed the month higher still, reaching 14,578.54 for an increase of 3.7% over the previous month and 11.3% growth in the first quarter of 2013. The Nasdaq Composite Index, which closed the month at 3,267.52, showed slightly less improvement, rising 3.4% in Mar.

The European Union, Mar. 6, fined U.S. software giant Microsoft 561 mil euro ($731 mil) for failing to offer users of a Feb. 2011 Windows update a choice of Web browsers, as required in its settlement of a 2007 antitrust case. Upon its censure, Microsoft issued an apology, attributing the violation to a technical error.

Obama Makes First Presidential Visit to Israel—Pres. Barack Obama Mar. 20 traveled to Israel for the first time since becoming president in 2008. The trip was also his first outside the U.S. since his reelection. In a televised speech at the Jerusalem Convention Center Mar. 21, Obama called for renewed peace talks with Palestine, and urged a younger generation of Israelis and Palestinians to "create the change that you want to see." That same day, Obama visited the West Bank, where he urged Palestinian Pres. Mahmoud Abbas to drop his demand that Israel freeze construction of West Bank settlements before beginning peace talks, but Abbas refused. Obama also negotiated a Mar. 22 phone call between Netanyahu and Turkish Pres. Recep Tayyip Erdogan, in which Netanyahu apologized for the 2010 deaths of nine Turkish activists in an Israeli raid of a flotilla headed for Gaza. He then traveled to Jordan, where he met with King Abdullah II to discuss concerns over Syria and pledged $200 mil to care for refugees from Syria's civil war who had fled to Jordan.

International

Kenyans Elect Indicted Official—Despite facing charges for crimes against humanity from the last time Kenyans went to the polls, Deputy Prime Min. Uhuru Kenyatta won election as the nation's president Mar. 9. Kenyatta won 50.07% of

the vote over Prime Min. Raila Odinga's 43.31%, even as he faced a July 9 trial at the Intl. Criminal Court in The Hague, Netherlands, for his actions surrounding the 2007 election, when vote rigging set off widespread ethnic violence that killed 1,300 and displaced 300,000. Kenyans waited for up to 10 hours to vote in the 2013 elections, held Mar. 4. In anticipation of unrest, schools were closed and residents cleared out stores of flour, rice, bread, and other supplies, but violence was much less widespread. Odinga challenged the results with the country's Supreme Court, which upheld Kenyatta's victory Mar. 30. Violence and rioting were again feared in response, but Odinga pledged to respect the ruling and the country remained largely calm.

Venezuelan President Chávez Dies—Two years after a cancer diagnosis, 58-year-old Venezuelan Pres. Hugo Chávez died Mar. 5, marking the end of a 14-year rule. Chávez had been reelected in Oct. 2012, but he had not been seen publicly since Dec. 2012, when he departed for a Cuban hospital, failing to return to Venezuela even for his inauguration in Jan. 2013. Upon his death, Chávez's handpicked successor, Vice Pres. Nicolás Maduro Moros, became the nation's interim president. Chávez had been popular among the poor for his implementation of subsidized social services and other Socialist-inspired programs, but Venezuelan critics and international human-rights organizations questioned his efforts to consolidate power. Chávez returned to Venezuela from Cuba Feb. 18 but remained out of sight until his death.

North Korea's Saber-Rattling Spreads Fear—The government of 30-year-old North Korean leader Kim Jong Un made a series of public threats to South Korea and the U.S. throughout the month. According to a report on its state-run news agency Mar. 7, North Korea vowed to initiate preemptive nuclear strikes against the U.S. The threats coincided with the UN Security Council's newest sanctions against North Korea, which were designed to diminish Pyongyang's ability to fund its nuclear weapons program. North Korea announced Mar. 11 that it was negating the 1953 armistice that ended the Korean War. The government of Park Geun Hye, who was elected South Korea's first female president Feb. 25, dismissed the threat, saying the armistice could not be abandoned unilaterally, a position backed up by the UN.

North Korea performed short-range missile tests Mar. 15 in the Sea of Japan, and declared Mar. 30 that it was entering a "state of war" with South Korea. Photos published Mar. 29 in the state-run newspaper *Rodong Sinmun* showed Kim Jong Un planning nuclear strikes against Hawaii and the U.S. mainland. Most of the international community largely ignored Kim's latest provocations as propaganda efforts to raise his stature among his own people. But after conducting annual joint-military exercises throughout the month, the U.S. and South Korea announced Mar. 25 they had signed an agreement on how to conduct defense of South Korea in case of an attack. There are some 28,000 U.S. troops stationed in South Korea.

Karzai Accuses U.S. of Conspiring With Taliban—During Defense Sec. Chuck Hagel's first visit to Afghanistan since taking his post, Afghan Pres. Hamid Karzai Mar. 10 alleged that the U.S. was colluding with the Taliban to carry out random acts of violence in order to generate fear and insecurity among the Afghan people and discourage the U.S. military from withdrawing by 2014. Karzai made the accusation in a televised speech the day after a suicide bomber attacked the Afghan defense ministry in Kabul, killing at least 10 people. The Taliban claimed responsibility for the attack, saying it was intended to send Hagel a message.

Hagel had been negotiating the handover of a prison from U.S. to Afghan control, but the talks ended abruptly over a disagreement about how to handle prisoners the U.S. deemed "enduring security threats" even if they couldn't be prosecuted for specific offenses. The U.S. transferred control of the prison during an unscheduled visit by Sec. of State John Kerry Mar. 25, during which Karzai recanted his accusations of collusion between the U.S. and the Taliban. In the first three months of 2013, coalition fatalities in Afghanistan totaled 25, down from 98 the same period in 2012.

New Chinese President Selected—China's Natl. People's Congress elected Xi Jinping the nation's new president Mar. 14. The vote was largely ceremonial, as Xi had been already appointed Communist Party general secretary and chairman of the Central Military Commission in Nov. 2012. The new appointment made Xi head of the three most powerful Chinese institutions: the party, the army, and the state. A Xi ally, Li Yuanchao, was named vice president. Xi and Li advocated further economic reforms and spoke in favor of eliminating governmental corruption and permitting greater freedom to criticize the government.

Cyprus Agrees to $13-Bil Bailout—The European Union and officials in Cyprus agreed Mar. 25 to a 10 bil-euro ($13 bil) bailout of the island nation's banking system, which was on the verge of collapse, largely because of its close financial ties with Greece. Cyprus became the fifth European nation (following Greece, Ireland, Portugal and Spain) to receive emergency funds since the beginning of the global financial crisis in 2008. The deal guaranteed accounts of less than 100,000 euros ($130,000) but promised losses for bondholders and larger depositors, many of whom were foreign investors attracted by Cyprus's low corporate taxes and lax regulation. Approximately 30% of the assets in Cypriot banks were believed to be held by Russian depositors. The agreement downsized Cyprus's financial sector by restructuring the Bank of Cyprus, the nation's largest bank, and closing its second-largest bank, resulting in thousands of jobs lost. Banks remained closed Mar 16-28 to allow for the restructuring.

Fresh Violence Marks 10th Anniversary of Iraq War—Insurgents marked the 10th anniversary of the Iraq War with a series of coordinated bombings Mar. 19, killing at least 57 and wounding nearly 200. The Iraq Body Count project, which counts only documented violent civilian deaths, reported more than 112,000 civilian casualties during the 10-year period, in addition to the 4,800 deaths of U.S. service members and coalition forces.

General

Roman Catholics Select First Latin American Pope—After a two-day Papal Conclave in Vatican City, the College of Cardinals Mar. 13 chose Cardinal Jorge Mario Bergoglio, the 76-year-old head of the Argentinean diocese of Buenos Aires, as the Catholic Church's new pope and leader of the world's 1.2 bil Roman Catholics. He succeeded Pope Emeritus Benedict XVI, who had retired two weeks earlier. The new pontiff was not only the first pope from the Americas, but also the first Jesuit pope, the first non-European pope in more than a millennium, and the first to choose the name Francis, which he took for St. Francis of Assisi. Just as St. Francis championed the impoverished, Cardinal Bergoglio had a reputation as an advocate for the poor. Upon his introduction to a rain-soaked but ebullient crowd of tens of thousands in St. Peter's Square Mar. 13, the newly elected pontiff asked the people to pray for him and bless him, then offered his own blessing. Pope Francis conducted his inaugural Mass Mar. 19.

105th Archbishop of Canterbury Installed—The Most Reverend Justin Welby was sworn in as Archbishop of Canterbury Mar. 21 before an audience of 2,000 at Canterbury Cathedral in England. The 57-year-old Welby, who had worked in the oil industry before training in theology, became the leader of the Church of England and the world's 88 mil Anglicans. The ceremony featured the first woman to play a prominent role in an installation, as the Venerable

Sheila Watson, archdeacon of Canterbury, enthroned the archbishop as official head of the diocese and bishop of Canterbury. Welby favored ordination of women as bishops but opposed gay marriage.

Higgs Boson Particle Confirmed—European Organization for Nuclear Research (CERN) scientists at the Large Hadron Collider in Switzerland verified Mar. 14 that a particle first discovered in July 2012 was almost certainly a Higgs boson. The Higgs boson was sometimes called the "God particle" for its ability to demonstrate the means by which matter acquires mass. In their determination that the particle had the properties of a Higgs boson, scientists studied its spin and parity and decided that it appeared to provide long-sought evidence for the principles of particle theory. Physicists still didn't know whether there was only one kind of Higgs boson, or a variety of them.

Dominican Republic Goes Undefeated to Win World Baseball Classic—Led by All-Star second baseman Robinson Cano, shortstop Jose Reyes, and journeyman pitcher Samuel Deduno, the Dominican Republic team swept the 2013 World Baseball Classic, defeating Puerto Rico, 3-0, in the final game Mar. 19 at San Francisco's AT&T Park. Deduno finished the tournament with an 0.69 ERA, and Dominican relievers combined for a 25.2-inning scoreless streak. Cano was named the tournament's MVP with a .469 batting average, two home runs, and six RBIs. The U.S. team, plagued by injuries and low participation, were knocked out of the tournament by Puerto Rico Mar. 15.

April 2013
National

Bomb Blasts at Boston Marathon Injure Hundreds—The annual Patriots' Day running of the Boston Marathon was violently halted Apr. 15 at 2:50 PM by two consecutive explosions, 12 seconds apart, on sidewalks packed with spectators near the Boylston St. finish line. The explosions, which came at the race's 4:09 mark, killed three bystanders and injured 264 others, many of whom lost limbs. From video footage taken by surveillance cameras along Boylston St., the Boston Police Dept. and Federal Bureau of Investigation (FBI) identified the bombers as Dzhokhar Tsarnaev and Tamerlan Tsarnaev, Chechen brothers who had immigrated to the U.S. in 2002.

Authorities tracked down the brothers the night of Apr. 18, after the two allegedly shot and killed a Massachusetts Institute of Technology campus security officer and hijacked a car, withdrawing $800 from the driver's account at an ATM. A high-speed chase ensued, ending in a shootout between the brothers and police in Watertown, MA; 26-year-old Tamerlan was killed while 19-year-old Dzhokhar escaped. Authorities issued a day-long lockdown of the entire Boston area Apr. 19, during which schools were closed, public transportation was suspended, and residents were asked not to leave their homes. After authorities lifted the lockdown that evening, law enforcement officials captured Dzhokhar in a boat in a Watertown backyard just before 9:00 PM. He was hospitalized with a gunshot wound to the throat.

While Dzhokhar had become a naturalized U.S. citizen in 2012, the Dept. of Homeland Security had halted Tamerlan's citizenship application because of a 2011 warning from the Russian government that he might be engaged in terrorist activities. The FBI investigated Tamerlan in 2012 after he returned from a six-month trip to Russia but found no reason to include him on its watch list. Investigators questioned the hospitalized Dzhokhar for 16 hours before reading him his Miranda rights, at which point he stopped talking. During interrogation, Dzhokhar said that he and his brother were not sponsored by al-Qaeda or any other terrorist group. He claimed the original plan called for setting off the explosives on July 4, and that their next target was to have been New York City's Times Square.

Ricin-Laced Letters Sent to White House and Capitol Hill—Federal authorities Apr. 16 found large traces of the poisonous chemical ricin in letters addressed to Pres. Barack Obama, Sen. Roger Wicker (R, MS), and Judge Sadie Holland in Lee County, MS. All three letters included the salutation, "I am KC and I approve this message." When the substance was confirmed as ricin the next day, Senate office buildings were evacuated and quarantined for several hours while hazmat teams investigated. The FBI initially arrested Paul Kevin Curtis, an Elvis impersonator from Corinth, MS, who had been known for posting his outspoken views on the government on social media. But the FBI released Curtis Apr. 23, and three days later arrested 41-year-old Tupelo, MS, resident Everett Dutschke on charges of possessing a biological agent with the intent to use it as a weapon and for attempting to frame Curtis, a longtime enemy.

Texas Fertilizer Plant Explosion Leaves 14 Dead—An explosion that registered as strong as a magnitude-2.1 earthquake and could be felt up to 50 mi away occurred Apr. 17 at a fertilizer plant in West, TX, about 20 mi north of Waco. The blast killed 15 people, including 10 first responders, and injured more than 200. A fire began in the plant and combusted 20 minutes later, destroying 50 houses, a nursing home, and a middle school, necessitating the evacuation of half of the town's 2,700 residents. The plant, owned by West Chemical and Fertilizer Co., contained some 270 tons of ammonium nitrate, as well as about 54,000 lb of the highly combustible chemical anhydrous ammonia. The property damage was estimated at up to $100 mil, but the plant was only insured for $1 mil in liability insurance.

Congress Stalls on Gun Control, Acts to Ease Air Traffic Delays—Senate Republicans Apr. 17 blocked efforts to pass new gun control legislation. Among the defeated measures was a bipartisan effort sponsored by Sen. Joe Manchin (D, WV) and Sen. Patrick Toomey (R, PA) that would have mandated universal background checks prior to purchasing a gun. A majority (54-46) supported the amendment, but it fell short of the 60 votes required to overcome the Republican-led filibuster, as did an amendment supported by the Natl. Rifle Assn. that would have imposed stiff penalties on gun traffickers. Two other measures failed to win a simple majority: a ban on military-style assault weapons (defeated 60-40), and a limit on the size of ammunition magazines (54-46). An angry Pres. Barack Obama, who had called for Congress to act on gun control, called the legislative failure "a pretty shameful day for Washington." National polls showed broad popular support for many gun-control measures in the wake of the 2012 Newtown, CT, elementary school shootings.

Congress did, however, act to remedy the thousands of flight delays caused by furloughs of 10% of the nation's air traffic controllers, which were mandated by the Mar. 1 budget sequester. Legislators passed a bill Apr. 26 allowing the Dept. of Transportation to shift $253 mil to the Federal Aviation Admin., enabling controllers to return to work the following day. Pres. Obama signed the legislation May 1.

AP Hacker Causes Temporary Market Crash; Other Economic News—U.S. markets in Chicago and New York briefly fell 1% on Apr. 23 after the Associated Press (AP) Twitter feed was hacked and tweeted that the White House had been attacked and Pres. Obama was wounded. Traders at the Chicago Mercantile Exchange reacted by selling off S&P futures and picking up 10-year Treasury bonds, while the Dow Jones Industrial Average instantly fell more than140 points. The S&P 500 is estimated to have lost $136.5 bil in value but recovered six minutes later, when the AP tweeted a correction. The Syrian Electronic Army, a group that supports Pres. Bashar al-Assad, and which had previously claimed to have hacked the Twitter accounts of Natl. Public Radio, the BBC, and *60 Minutes*, took credit for the fraudulent tweet.

U.S. stock markets continued their generally strong performance in Apr., with the S&P 500 closing at a record high

of 1,597.57 and the Nasdaq Composite Index at 3,328.79, a 12-year-high. The Dow ended the month at 14,839.80, a 1.8% rise over Mar. The Labor Dept. reported Apr. 5 that the Mar. unemployment rate had dipped from 7.7% to 7.6%, but just 88,000 jobs were created, far fewer than the 200,000 that experts expected. The Bureau of Economic Analysis reported Apr. 26 that U.S. real gross domestic product in the first quarter of 2013 increased at an annual rate of 2.5%, crediting the growth to consumer spending, exports, and housing sales.

International

North Korea Continues to Escalate Nuclear Threat— The North Korean government, led by Kim Jong Un, announced Apr. 2 that it was resuming its nuclear program by restarting a reactor dormant since 2007 at the Yongbyon nuclear complex. That statement was followed by an Apr. 3 advisory that the government had approved plans for a nuclear strike on the U.S., and an Apr. 9 warning advising all foreigners to leave the Korean peninsula or else be caught up in a missile strike against South Korea. The threats were the latest episodes in a series of North Korean provocations since the UN imposed additional sanctions against Pyongyang in Mar. 2013. A North Korean official announced Apr. 8 that the country planned to withdraw its workers and suspend operations at the Kaesong industrial park, a complex in the North jointly operated by North and South Korea. The only symbol of economic cooperation between the two countries, Kaesong's 120 factories employed more than 50,000 North Korean workers (and about 850 from South Korea), and generated $2 bil dollars in trade annually for North Korea. South Korea withdrew its remaining workers from Kaesong Apr. 26.

As tensions rose, U.S. stealth fighters and B-52 bombers made several sorties over South Korea Apr. 3, while the destroyer USS *John McCain* was stationed off the coast of the southern peninsula. U.S. officials also announced the government's decision to establish a missile defense system in Guam. Chinese Pres. Xi Jinping weighed in on the controversy, saying a single country should not be allowed to break the peace. North Korea toned down its bluster following Sec. of State John Kerry's Apr. 12 visit to South Korea. But both sides held fast to preconditions that precluded any talks of a broader peace: North Korea's demand that the UN lift its sanctions for the most recent nuclear tests, and U.S.'s insistence that Pyongyang give up its nuclear program.

Maduro Declared Winner in Venezuela Elections—In Venezuelan presidential elections held Apr. 14, interim Pres. Nicolás Maduro Moros, the handpicked successor of late Pres. Hugo Chávez, received 50.6% of the vote. Henrique Capriles Radonski, the governor of Miranda state who had lost the previous election to Chávez in Oct. 2012, received 49.1% of votes. Capriles called for a recount, alleging that Maduro had broken campaign laws, that the election results indicated fraud, and that thousands of incidents of voting irregularities had taken place. The dispute prompted violent protests Apr. 15 in which nine people died. Maduro was inaugurated Apr. 19 to serve the remainder of Chávez's six-year term, which began in Jan. 2013, but Capriles refused to concede. The president of the Natl. Assembly banned Capriles's party from speaking during legislative sessions, which sparked an Apr. 30 melee that bloodied several lawmakers.

China Copes With Bird Flu, Sichuan Earthquake— The H7N9 strain of bird flu, described by the World Health Organization as "one of the most lethal influenza viruses," began affecting people in the eastern part of China in late Mar. and continued to spread throughout Apr., infecting more than 130 people and killing 36. Early cases appeared in the region around the coastal city of Shanghai before spreading to several nearby provinces. Health officials were unsure how the virus was transmitted between humans. Taiwanese officials reported the first case of the virus outside mainland China Apr. 24. Governments throughout Asia responded by stepping up precautions in anticipation of the summer travel season. China's health minister reported that the virus had been contained by mid-May.

In Lushan county, near Ya'an city in Sichuan province, an earthquake measuring 6.6-7.0 on the Richter scale struck Apr. 20 at 8:02 AM, killing more than 200 people and injuring nearly 12,000. Quick responses on the part of the Chinese government and emergency workers were believed to have kept the death and injury tolls from being much worse.

Bangladesh Factory Building Collapses, Killing 1,100 Workers—The worst garment-factory accident in history occurred Apr. 24, when an eight-story building in Savar, a suburb of Dhaka, Bangladesh, collapsed, killing more than 1,100 workers. Many were trapped in the rubble, including one woman who managed to survive in an air pocket for 17 days before being rescued. The illegally constructed and poorly maintained building, Rana Plaza, housed five garment factories employing more than 3,000 people and operated 24 hours a day. The day before the collapse, inspectors discovered cracks in the building's walls and support pillars. Shops and a bank on the lower floors of the building closed immediately, but the owners of the garment factories sent their employees back to work. The building's owner, Sohel Rana, and several garment factory owners were later arrested.

Coming on the heels of a Nov. 2012 fire that killed 112 workers at a different factory near Dhaka, the collapse intensified debate about working conditions, wages, and safety in Bangladesh's $20-bil garment industry, which employs more than 3 mil people, most of them women, who make as little as $40 per month.

Center-Right Parties Returned to Power in Iceland Elections—In parliamentary elections held Apr. 27, Iceland's center-right Independence Party and Progressive Party each won 19 seats in the 63-seat parliament. The results marked a return to power for the parties ousted in the aftermath of the 2008 economic crisis, which saw the collapse of Iceland's three major banks. A leftist coalition government responded to the crisis with austerity measures, which had become hugely unpopular, as was the coalition's support of a bid to join the European Union.

General

Louisville Men Win NCAA Basketball Tournament; Cardinal Women Fall to UConn—The top-seed Univ. of Louisville Cardinals defeated the Univ. of Michigan Wolverines 82-76 to win the school's third NCAA men's basketball championship Apr. 8 at the Georgia Dome in Atlanta, GA. The victory made Louisville coach Rick Pitino the first Division I head coach to win a national title with two different schools; he had a previous championship win with the Univ. of Kentucky in 1996. The Cardinals had to overcome the loss of one of their best players, Kevin Ware, during their Elite Eight matchup with Duke Univ. Mar. 31, when Ware suffered a gruesome compound fracture to his right leg and had to be carried off the court. Louisville's Luke Hancock came off the bench in the final game to score 22 points and became the first bench player to be named the most outstanding player of the Final Four. Before the game, Pitino learned that he would be inducted into the Basketball Hall of Fame Sept. 8.

In the women's tournament final Apr. 9, the Univ. of Connecticut Huskies defeated the Louisville Cardinals, 93-60, at New Orleans Arena in New Orleans, LA. UConn head coach Geno Auriemma claimed his eighth title, tying him with Tennessee's Pat Summitt for most women's college basketball championships. UConn freshman Breanna Stewart scored 23 points in the final game and was named the most outstanding player of the Final Four.

Masters Tournament Features First Aussie Winner and Youngest Player—Adam Scott became the first Australian

to win the Masters Tournament when he defeated Argentinian Angel Cabrera Apr. 14 in the second hole of a sudden-death finale at Augusta Natl. Golf Club in Augusta, GA. Both men finished the tournament at 9-under-279, forcing the play-off. The tournament featured an appearance by the youngest player ever to qualify for the Masters, 14-year-old Guan Tianlang from China, who finished 12-over-par. After leading early, Tiger Woods suffered a two-stroke penalty Apr. 13 for an error the previous day, when he made an improper drop after hitting a ball into the water. Woods finished the tournament 5-under-par.

NBA's First Openly Gay Active Player Comes Out—Jason Collins, a 34-year-old free-agent NBA center, became the first openly gay active male athlete in a major U.S. professional team sport, announcing his sexual orientation in an article posted on the *Sports Illustrated* website Apr. 29. In that article—the cover story of the magazine's May 6 print issue—Collins revealed his pain at hiding his homosexuality and explained his decision to go public. A number of fellow NBA players, other professional athletes, and public figures publicly expressed their support for Collins's decision to come out.

May 2013
National

Three More State Legislatures Legalize Same-Sex Marriage—Rhode Island, Delaware, and Minnesota all legalized same-sex marriage in May 2013, bringing the nation's count to twelve such states. In Rhode Island, the bill passed May 2 in a 56-15 vote in the state's House of Representatives and was slated to take effect Aug. 1. Delaware Gov. Jack Markell (D) May 7 signed legislation that had passed the state's Senate, 12-9, earlier in the day. The state said it would begin honoring marriages between same-sex couples July 1. Minnesota, which just six months earlier had voted down a constitutional amendment that would have declared marriage to be between one man and one woman, endorsed same-sex marriages May 14. Gov. Mark Dayton (D) signed a bill that the Senate had approved 37-30 the day before, enabling gay couples to marry legally as of Aug. 1. A total of 36 states still had laws forbidding same-sex marriage; 30 of them had written the ban into their state's constitution.

Dow Surpasses 15,000 for New Record; Other Economic News—The Dow Jones Industrial Average set a new record May 7, closing above 15,000 for the first time in its history. The index was up 87 points from the previous day and closed at 15,056.20. Analysts predicted that the milestone might prompt investors wary of the stock market since 2008 to shift more of their assets there. The Dow remained above 15,000 the rest of May, closing at 15,115.57 May 31, up 1.9% over Apr. The Nasdaq Composite Index closed the month at 3,455.91, up 3.8% in May, while the S&P 500 finished May at 1,630.74, up 2.1%.

The Apr. jobs report, released May 3 by the Labor Dept., showed that 165,000 jobs were added to the U.S. economy during the month—about 25,000 more than economists expected—bringing the unemployment rate down to 7.5%. Revisions to earlier figures also showed greater job growth during the first quarter of 2013 than originally thought, with about 114,000 more jobs added during Feb. and Mar. alone.

Internet services giant Yahoo! announced May 20 that it had acquired the microblogging site Tumblr for $1.1 bil in cash. Yahoo! CEO Marissa Mayer said the company would retain Tumblr's founder and CEO David Karp, and that Tumblr would continue operating independently.

New Benghazi Hearings Bring Much Criticism, Little Light—The House Committee on Oversight and Government Reform began new hearings May 8 into the Sept. 11, 2012, attack on the U.S. embassy in Benghazi, Libya, which killed four Americans, including Ambassador J. Christopher Stevens. The hearings followed an Apr. 23 report by Republican leaders of five House committees alleging that the Obama administration had covered up the truth about systemic failures in U.S. security preparations in Libya to deflect blame from the president. Testimony by two previously unheard-from State Dept. officials produced gripping accounts of the attack, but little evidence of malfeasance. Congressional Democrats criticized the hearings as a political attack on former Sec. of State Hillary Clinton (who was widely rumored to be seeking the presidency in 2016). The Obama administration May 15 released 100 pages of internal emails that showed disagreement between the State Dept. and the Central Intelligence Agency about the content of the talking points for the incident.

IRS Apologizes for Targeting Conservative Groups—Lois Lerner, director of the Internal Revenue Service (IRS) division that handles tax-exempt organizations, apologized May 10 for the agency's singling out for scrutiny about 300 groups with the terms "Tea Party" or "patriot" in their names. Lerner explained that the agents who targeted the groups in question were trying to streamline a process that was overwhelmed with applications for tax-exempt status under Section 501(c)(4) of the tax code. Those applications nearly doubled following the Supreme Court's Jan. 21, 2010, decision in *Citizens United v. FEC*, which allowed outside groups to spend unlimited amounts of money on political campaigns. The decision made 501(c)(4)s attractive to lobbying groups because unlike political action committees, 501(c)(4) organizations are not required to publicly disclose their donors. Lerner acknowledged that the screening was "absolutely inappropriate and not the way we should do things," but said it was not politically motivated. Pres. Barack Obama called the IRS actions "inexcusable," and forced acting IRS Commissioner Steven Miller to resign May 15. Lerner was suspended May 23 after invoking her Fifth Amendment rights against self-incrimination during a House Oversight Committee investigation into the matter.

Justice Dept. Admits to Secret Seizure of AP Phone Records—The U.S. Dept. of Justice notified the Associated Press (AP) May 10 that it had confiscated phone records—including home and cell phones—of more than 20 AP reporters after the news organization's May 7, 2012, report of a secret Central Intelligence Agency operation that broke up a Yemen-based terrorist plot. AP president and CEO Gary Pruitt, in a May 13 letter to Attorney Gen. Eric H. Holder Jr., called the actions a "massive and unprecedented intrusion" into its reporting efforts. The *Wall Street Journal*, the Newspaper Assn. of America, and other advocates for freedom of the press excoriated the Justice Dept. for failing to follow its own regulations, which require notifying journalists before seizing phone records so they may challenge a subpoena in court. Pres. Barack Obama May 16 defended the actions in the name of national security, saying "I make no apologies" for investigating leaks of information that might compromise the safety of U.S. troops or intelligence agents.

Deadly Tornadoes Devastate Oklahoma, Texas—A series of destructive tornadoes began in the central U.S. May 15, leveling neighborhoods and taking the lives of nearly 50 people. Ten tornadoes ripped through Northern Texas May 15, the most powerful of which—an EF-4 with speeds of 166-200 mph—struck the town of Granbury, killing six people and injuring 97. Tornado warnings continued throughout several states, before an EF-5 tornado 1.3-mi wide, with speeds of about 210 mph, touched down 2:45 PM May 20 in Moore, OK. The tornado, considered one of the most powerful on record, destroyed nearly everything in its path for about 20 mi, including schools and the town's major hospital. Twenty-four people died, including seven children at Plaza Towers Elementary School. Pres. Barack Obama pledged disaster relief May 21. Another EF-5 tornado touched down during rush hour in El Reno, OK, near Oklahoma City, May 31, claiming another 21 lives, including those of three experienced storm chasers. The tornado's

2.6-mi width was the largest on record, and its winds reached 296 mph. In addition, many commuters were trapped in their cars as eight inches of rain fell, causing major flooding on highways. Local hospitals reported treating more than 80 people for storm-related injuries.

International

Syrian Civil War Threatens to Spill Over Its Borders—

Mounting evidence that the government of Syrian Pres. Bashar al-Assad was using chemical weapons threatened to turn Syria's two-year-old civil war into a wider conflict. Israel reportedly conducted airstrikes on a warehouse at Damascus Intl. Airport May 2-3 out of fear that the Assad regime was preparing to ship missiles and chemical weapons to Hezbollah in Lebanon. Assad May 31 threatened to respond in kind to future air strikes by Israel. The two countries also engaged in ground skirmishes May 21 in the Golan Heights, an area Israel seized in the final days of the 1967 Six-Day War. After a Syrian rebel rocket attack on a Hezbollah stronghold in Beirut, Lebanon, May 26, Hezbollah leader Hassan Nasrallah publicly confirmed the group's involvement in the war on the side of the Syrian government, though it had been an open secret for months. Bolstered by fighters from Hezbollah and Iran, and arms from Russia and Iran, Assad's government forces stepped up attacks on the strategic rebel stronghold of Qusair.

Meanwhile, the United States inched closer to intervening after finding additional proof that Assad had killed more than 100 people with chemical weapons and might be planning further chemical attacks. U.S. voices for arming the rebels grew louder in Washington, especially from Sen. John McCain (R, AZ), who paid a surprise visit to a rebel camp in Syria May 27. The trip coincided with the European Union's announcement that it would end its arms embargo, allowing EU members to supply weapons to the rebels. The UN said more than 92,000 people had died in the civil war through the end of Apr.

Pakistanis Vote for Second Consecutive Civilian Government—

In the first peaceful transition of power between elected governments in Pakistani history, voters overwhelmingly chose former Prime Min. Nawaz Sharif May 11 for an unprecedented third term as prime minister. Sharif's center-right Pakistan Muslim League-Nawaz party won 126 seats in the 272-seat assembly. Pakistan's small independent parties customarily join the largest vote-getter, and Sharif easily formed a coalition government the following day. Voter turnout was estimated at 60%, the highest since 1977. Sharif previously had led Pakistan 1990-93 and again from Feb. 1997 until an Oct. 1999 coup, led by Gen. Pervez Musharraf, which forced him into exile in Saudi Arabia. Former Prime Min. Raja Pervez Ashraf, whose Pakistan People's Party (PPP) led the country from 2008-13, lost his seat in the rout, as the PPP captured just 33 seats. The Pakistan Tehreek-e-Insaf (Movement for Justice) party, led by popular former cricket player Imran Khan, generated excitement among younger voters, but came in a disappointing third with 28 seats. Election Day was marred by violence, as some 64 people died, including 11 in an explosion targeting an Awami Natl. Party candidate in Karachi.

British Soldier Brutally Attacked in So-Called Act of Terrorism—

A 25-year-old off-duty British soldier was killed by two British citizens of Nigerian descent in a startling daytime attack May 22. Lee Rigby had just left his barracks in London's Woolwich section when he was hit by a car. The men in the car then violently stabbed him with knives and meat cleavers. One of the attackers, 28-year-old Michael Adebolajo, encouraged witnesses to record him and his accomplice, 22-year-old Michael Adebowale, then launched into an anti-West tirade, claiming the murder was in retaliation for Western military operations in Muslim countries. Police shot and wounded the men at the scene and took them into custody. Britain's domestic intelligence agency, MI5, confirmed May 24 that it was aware of both men and of Adebolajo's attempts to join a group in Kenya that had links to al-Qaeda, which led to his deportation to Britain in 2010.

General

Orb Wins Kentucky Derby; Oxbow Takes Preakness—

Orb, a 3-year-old bay colt, won the 139th running of the Kentucky Derby May 4 at a muddy Churchill Downs in Louisville, KY. Ridden by jockey Joel Rosario, the favorite came from behind on the final turn and crossed the finish line at 2:02.89, two-and-a-half lengths ahead of second-place Golden Soul. It was the first Derby victory in the 34-year-long career of trainer Shug McGaughey, a Kentucky native inducted in the horse racing Hall of Fame in 2004. Jockey Rosie Napravnik, who rode Mylute, finished fifth, the highest place ever for a female jockey in the Kentucky Derby.

Orb was again the favorite at the May 18 Preakness Stakes at Pimlico Race Course in Baltimore, MD. But the Derby's sixth-place finisher, Oxbow, ridden by Hall-of-Fame jockey Gary Stevens, led the entire race and crossed the finish line first in 1:57.54, ensuring there would be no Triple Crown winner for the 36th consecutive year. The 138th running of the race saw Itsmyluckyday finish second, and Mylute place third with Napravnik achieving the best finish of any woman jockey in Preakness history. Derby champion Orb finished fourth.

Decade-Long Cleveland Kidnapping Ordeal Comes to an End—

Three women who went missing in 2002, 2003, and 2004 were found May 6 to have been held captive in a Cleveland home, less than five miles from where they disappeared. Michelle Knight was kidnapped in 2002 when she was 21, and Amanda Berry and Georgina DeJesus were teenagers when they were abducted in 2003 and 2004, respectively. The three women told police of extensive abuse by Ariel Castro, a 52-year-old unemployed bus driver, including rape, beatings, and being chained in a basement for months. Knight said Castro impregnated her several times but would starve and punch her to force a miscarriage. Castro was charged May 8 with the kidnapping and rape of all three women as well as the kidnapping of Berry's 6-year-old daughter, whom she gave birth to while in captivity. Berry was able to call police after Castro left the front door of the house unlocked, and neighbors helped her and her daughter crawl through a storm door.

Castro pleaded guilty July 27 to 937 counts of a 977-count indictment that included kidnapping, rape, and murder charges. He was sentenced Aug. 1 to life in prison plus 1,000 years, with no possibility of parole. On Sept. 3, he was found dead of an apparent suicide in his prison cell in Franklin County, OH.

Arias Convicted in Graphic Murder Trial—

After a five-month-long trial, Jodi Arias was found guilty of first-degree murder May 8, by a Phoenix, AZ, jury. The 32-year-old Arias had admitted to the 2008 killing of her boyfriend, Travis Alexander, but had claimed it was an act of self-defense. The trial, which was full of graphic testimony and salacious details, was covered extensively by cable-news media. The jury, however, failed to agree on a sentence during a separate trial phase.

One World Trade Center Reaches 1,776 Feet—

The top section of a 408-ft spire was lowered into place May 10 atop the building at 1 World Trade Center—formerly known as the Freedom Tower—in lower Manhattan, bringing the building to its full symbolic height of 1,776 ft. When completed, 1WTC will be the tallest building in the Western Hemisphere, and the third-tallest building in the world.

Human Embryo Successfully Produced Via Cloning—

Researchers led by Prof. Shoukhrat Mitalipov at Oregon Health and Science Univ. announced in a paper published May 13 in the journal Cell that they had succeeded

in extracting stem cells from a human embryo produced via cloning for therapeutic purposes. The procedure involved removing skin cells from an eight-month-old baby with a genetic disorder and injecting them into donated human eggs. From the embryos that resulted, stem cells were extracted and used to treat the baby's condition. Scientists said there was no intention to implant cloned embryos to create a human being, though critics, among them the Conference of Catholic Bishops, worried the development marked a significant step toward human cloning.

Boy Scouts Allow Gay Members, But Not Leaders—The Natl. Council of the Boy Scouts of America May 23 voted to permit openly gay youths to join its troops. A 61% majority cast votes in favor of lifting the ban on gays effective Jan. 2014. However, the national council left standing a ban on gay troop leaders. The Southern Baptist Convention, which sponsored nearly 4,000 Boy Scout troops in its churches, adopted a non-binding resolution opposing the decision, but said it would allow individual churches to decide whether to continue to sponsor scouting.

June 2013
National

Contractor Blows Whistle on Surveillance of Americans—The *Guardian* (UK) newspaper reported details June 5 of a highly classified U.S. Natl. Security Agency (NSA) surveillance program involving the monitoring of Verizon phone customers in the U.S., as well as the tracking of emails and Internet activities of Americans through central servers of Google, Apple, Microsoft, Facebook, YouTube, Skype, Yahoo, AOL, and Paltalk. Edward Snowden, a 29-year-old private contractor working for the Central Intelligence Agency (CIA), claimed responsibility for the leak June 9. Snowden had security clearance to work with the data at NSA offices in Hawaii. He said he revealed details on the program to reporters at the *Guardian* and *Washington Post* because he was disturbed at its violation of Americans' civil rights. U.S. officials claimed that the program, code-named PRISM, was operating within the bounds of the USA Patriot Act and that it did not allow the government to listen to individual phone conversations or read specific emails.

The U.S. June 14 charged Snowden with violating the Espionage Act and stealing government property, and submitted a warrant for his extradition from Hong Kong, where he had been since May 20. Snowden was not turned over to U.S. authorities there due to an alleged inadequacy in the extradition request, and he fled June 23 to Russia, where he stayed in Moscow's Sheremetyevo Intl. Airport while seeking political asylum in dozens of countries. (Because his passport was canceled by the U.S., he couldn't travel to several Latin American countries willing to grant asylum.)

Another Framing for Ricin-Laced Letters—Federal authorities June 7 arrested Shannon Guess Richardson for sending letters laced with deadly ricin to Pres. Barack Obama, New York Mayor Michael Bloomberg, and the office of a gun-control advocacy organization the mayor founded. All three letters, intercepted in late May, threatened death to any public official who might be responsible for taking away the writer's guns. Richardson originally tried to cast blame on her husband by placing castor beans (from which ricin can be made) in the trunk of his car and calling the police. After further investigation, authorities charged her with the crime, and she confessed June 6. It was the second time in two months that someone had tried to frame another person by sending ricin-laced letters to prominent politicians.

Stimulus Drawdown Outline Causes Markets to Plummet; More Economic News—The Dow Jones Industrial Average and S&P 500 suffered their most significant losses since Nov. 2011 on June 20, the day after Federal Reserve Chairman Ben Bernanke suggested that the central bank might begin scaling back its $85-bil monthly bond buying stimulus measure. The DJIA dropped 353 points—2.3% of its value—and the S&P fell by 2.5%. The losses were short-lived, however, as the markets rallied with three straight days of gains to end the month. The Dow closed the month at 14,909.60, while the S&P finished at 1,606.28 and the Nasdaq Composite Index at 3,403.25. All three were down about 1% from the previous month, but still up for 2013: the Dow had its strongest first half since 1999, with 13.8% growth. The S&P 500 and Nasdaq were each up more than 12% in the first six months of the year.

The Labor Dept. reported June 7 that 175,000 new jobs were added to payrolls in May, while unemployment inched up slightly to 7.6% from 7.5% in Apr.

Supreme Court Ends Term With Landmark Rulings in Civil Rights, Same-Sex Marriage—The U.S. Supreme Court June 26 concluded its 2012-13 term with two highly anticipated 5-4 decisions concerning same-sex couples. In *U.S. v. Windsor*, the Court struck down part of the 1996 Defense of Marriage Act (DOMA), which had denied federal benefits to same-sex couples. Writing for the majority, Associate Justice Anthony Kennedy said that DOMA attempted to "disparage and injure" a particular group of people, violating Fifth Amendment due-process rights. A different 5-4 majority let stand a lower court's ruling that had struck down California's Proposition 8, a ballot initiative that had outlawed same-sex marriage. Writing for the majority in *Hollingsworth v. Perry*, Chief Justice John Roberts said that Proposition 8's supporters did not have legal standing to represent the state's interests before the Court. California, which had declined to appeal the lower court's decision, resumed allowing same-sex couples to marry for the first time since 2008 later that same day. The federal government's Office of Personnel Management announced June 28 it would begin extending federal employee benefits, including health-care and retirement benefits, to eligible married same-sex couples and their families.

Earlier in the week, the Court addressed several other civil rights-related issues. A 5-4 decision June 25 in *Shelby County v. Holder* invalidated a key provision of the Voting Rights Act of 1965, which had required states (mostly in the South), counties, and municipalities with a history of discriminatory voting practices to obtain federal permission before changing voting procedures. Pointing out that the formula selecting the coverage areas used data that was more than 40 years old, the majority determined the law was outdated and thus invalid. Voters would be able to challenge discriminatory voting laws, but not until after they took effect. In a 7-1 ruling June 24, the Court sent the case of *Fisher v. Univ. of Texas at Austin et al.* back to a lower court, telling it to apply stricter standards for the use of affirmative action policies in higher education. The decision, written by Associate Justice Kennedy, cleared the way for more students to challenge race-based college admissions policies.

Senate Passes Immigration Reform Measure; Prospects Uncertain in House—By a 68-32 vote, the Senate June 27 passed the most significant immigration reform bill in decades. The legislation included a path to citizenship for 11 mil unauthorized immigrants already living in the U.S., and mandated stricter security along the U.S.-Mexico border. The bipartisan "gang of eight" senators that fashioned the legislation had hoped that the bill's fairly strong support among Republican senators (14 of whom voted for it), would propel the measure forward in the House. House Speaker John Boehner (R, OH) said the House would draft its own immigration bill.

Western Wildfires Bring Destruction and Tragedy—Nineteen members of the Granite Mountain Hotshots, an elite team of firefighters, died June 30 battling wildfires near the town of Yarnell, AZ, about 80 mi northwest of Phoenix. It was Arizona's worst loss of life battling wildfires since

1933. The blaze destroyed more than 100 homes and was not extinguished until July 10. Elsewhere, a wildfire that began at the end of May near a power station in California's Angeles Natl. Forest dramatically grew June 2, aided by strong winds and temperatures that sometimes hit 100 degrees. Despite the efforts of about 2,200 firefighters, the blaze burned more than 30,000 acres and claimed two dozen homes. A similar scenario played out June 12 in Colorado, where as many as four wildfires across the state burned out of control at once—in Royal Gorge, the Black Forest, Klikus, and Rocky Mountain Natl. Park. The Black Forest fire killed two people, destroyed nearly 500 homes, and burned 14,000 acres.

International

Floodwaters Sweep Through Europe, India, and Canada—Heavy rains produced record flooding throughout June in regions as disparate as Canada, India, and Central Europe. In the Czech Republic, the prime minister declared a state of emergency June 3, as 10 people died and more than 10,000 were evacuated when the Vitava River submerged parts of Prague. A state of emergency was also declared June 4 in Budapest, Hungary, though flood waters never reached the top of the city's 30-ft-high flood walls. In Germany, the Elbe flooded to its greatest height in four centuries, while the Danube crested more than 42 ft, a level not seen since 1501. Heavy rains that began June 14 in Uttarakhand, India, caused severe mudslides and flooding, killing more than 5,700 people. Heavy rains caused record levels of flooding in Calgary, AB, Canada, June 21, inundating Canada's third-largest city and forcing the evacuation of about 75,000 people.

Moderate Cleric Wins Iranian Election—Hassan Rouhani, a moderate cleric, won election June 14 as Iran's president. Rouhani defeated five other candidates by winning just over 50% of the vote, avoiding a run-off vote. Iran's Interior Ministry reported that voter turnout was 72%, much higher than expected. In his first comments as president-elect, Rouhani pledged to make the country less isolated than it had been under his predecessor, Mahmoud Ahmadinejad, although he added that Iran would not slow its nuclear program. Rouhani was sworn in Aug. 4.

Evidence Mounts for Syria's Use of Chemical Weapons—A United Nations report June 4 found "reasonable grounds to believe" chemical weapons had been used during Syria's ongoing civil war, though investigators did not determine which group was responsible. The Obama administration announced June 13 that its intelligence had concluded that the regime of Pres. Bashar al-Assad had used chemical weapons, causing the deaths of 100-150 people. Pres. Obama, who warned in 2012 that using chemical weapons would cross a "red line," announced June 14 that the U.S. would begin providing the rebels with military support; the European Union had allowed its own arms embargo to Syria's rebels to expire in May.

The UN June 7 asked the international community to contribute a total of $4.4 bil in humanitarian aid for Syrian refugees in 2013, the largest sum for which the UN has ever appealed. The UN estimated June 13 that at least 93,000 had died in the conflict so far, and that 1.6 mil had fled the country.

Popular Unrest Grips Turkey, Brazil, Egypt—Protests against the government of Turkish Prime Min. Recep Tayyip Erdogan that began May 28 continued throughout June and turned violent. Demonstrators were initially protesting redevelopment of one of Istanbul's few public parks. As the numbers of protesters swelled into the tens of thousands, the demonstration quickly evolved into a general antigovernment protest. Erdogan inflamed the situation by saying the demonstrators "walked arm in arm with terrorism" and repeatedly sent police in to clear the square with tear gas, water cannons, and rubber bullets, killing four. Turkey's largest labor union went on strike June 4-5, and 25 people were arrested June 5

for criticizing the government in social media. Protests had spread to 78 other cities across the country by June 11, and Erdogan began suggesting that he might use the army to end the protests.

Millions of Brazilians took to the streets in cities across Brazil throughout June to protest economic inequality in general and a 7% increase in public transportation fares in particular. Demonstrators expressed outrage that the government was spending billions on stadiums for the 2014 World Cup and the 2016 Olympic Games, while investing little in services and infrastructure for residents. Police responded to protests with tear gas and rubber bullets June 20, triggering a general unrest that fueled further demonstrations.

Antigovernment protests in Egypt grew throughout June against Pres. Mohammed Morsi, the Islamist leader and member of the Muslim Brotherhood who became the country's first democratically elected leader in 2012. Demonstrations reached a crescendo June 29-30, as millions gathered in Cairo—where protesters firebombed and looted the Muslim Brotherhood headquarters—and in Alexandria and other Egyptian cities, insisting on Morsi's resignation.

General

Palace Malice Wins Belmont Stakes—In the third event of horse racing's Triple Crown, Palace Malice, a 13-1 long-shot ridden by jockey Mike Smith, won the 145th Belmont Stakes June 8 at Belmont Park in Elmont, NY. The horse, which finished 12th in the previous month's Kentucky Derby, passed Preakness Stakes winner Oxbow on the final turn. Oxbow placed second; Derby winner Orb finished third.

Williams and Nadal Take French Open Titles—American Serena Williams defeated Russian Maria Sharapova (6-4, 6-4) June 8 to win her second French Open title and her first win at Roland Garros in Paris, France, in 11 years. The next day, Spaniard Rafael Nadal beat countryman David Ferrer (6-3, 6-2, 6-3) and became the first man to win eight titles at the same Grand Slam tournament. His record for match victories at the French Open improved to a nearly perfect 59-1. The Nadal-Ferrer match was briefly interrupted when a shirtless man ran onto the court with a lighted flare to protest France's new law legalizing same-sex marriages.

Justin Rose Takes U.S. Open—Justin Rose won the 113th U.S. Open golf tournament June 16 at a rain-soaked Merion Golf Club in Ardmore, PA. Rose, a South African-born Englishman, made five birdies in the final round to finish atop the leader board with a 1-over-par 281. American Phil Mickelson and Australia's Jason Day each finished two strokes back. The final day saw several lead changes among Rose, Mickelson, Day, and Hunter Mahan, who finished fourth. Rose was the first Englishman to win the tournament since 1970.

Wallenda Walks a High Wire Across Grand Canyon—Daredevil Nik Wallenda June 23 became the first person to cross a portion of the Grand Canyon on a 2-in.-wide tightrope suspended 1,500 ft above the Little Colorado River, outside the boundaries of the national park. With neither harness nor tether, Wallenda completed the 1,400-ft crossing in 22 min., 54 sec. Afterward, he expressed an interest in walking a high wire between New York City's Empire State and Chrysler Buildings, but the city was opposed to the stunt.

Chicago Blackhawks Hoist Stanley Cup—The Chicago Blackhawks defeated the Boston Bruins in six games to win the Natl. Hockey League's Stanley Cup Championship June 24 at Boston's TD Bank Garden. The series featured three overtime games and a tense final contest that Chicago won in the final minute by scoring two goals in 17 sec.; it was Chicago's second championship in four years. The Blackhawks did not lose during regulation in the first 24 games of the lockout-shortened 48-game season. Chicago forward Patrick Kane won the Conn Smythe Trophy as the most valuable player in the playoffs.

July 2013
National

Doubling of Student Loan Interest Rates Sparks Debate in Congress—Interest rates on subsidized student loans to low- and moderate-income undergraduates under the federal Stafford program doubled July 1, when Congress allowed the popular loan plan to expire. Interest rates for borrowers jumped from 3.4% to 6.8%. Three weeks later, the Senate, 81-18, passed a bill that tied student loan rates to the performance of financial markets, a provision that earned "no" votes from 17 Senate Democrats. It went on to pass the House 392-31 and Pres. Barack Obama signed the bill into law Aug. 9. For the school year beginning in 2013, the interest rate was 3.86% for undergraduates and 5.41% for graduate students. The rate for parents taking out loans was 6.41%.

Zimmerman Acquittal in Martin Killing Sparks Protests—A six-woman jury found George Zimmerman not guilty July 13 of second-degree murder and manslaughter in the Feb. 26, 2012, killing of Trayvon Martin, an unarmed black teenager, in a gated community in Sanford, FL. Zimmerman, a neighborhood-watch volunteer, claimed to have acted in self-defense under Florida's "stand your ground" law when he fatally shot the 17-year-old. Protests broke out almost immediately after the verdict was read; additional demonstrations were held the next day and were mainly peaceful. Pres. Barack Obama responded to the verdict by calling for calm and respect for the legal process, but in the White House briefing room July 19, he also gave an impromptu speech on his personal experiences with race relations in the U.S., noting the number of times he had been looked at with suspicion because of his skin color. A Justice Dept. civil rights investigation into Zimmerman's actions was ongoing.

Debt-Plagued Detroit Declares Bankruptcy; Other Economic News—The once-vibrant center of the American auto industry, Detroit, MI, filed for bankruptcy protection July 18, becoming the largest U.S. city ever to do so. With a population just over 700,000, the city was an estimated $18 to $20 bil in debt, far more than the next-largest municipal filing ($4.2 bil, claimed by Jefferson County, AL, in 2011). Observers speculated that many public services would need to be cut as a result of the filing, and that current and former city employees and retirees would likely see reductions in their benefits and pensions.

The Labor Dept. reported July 5 that the economy had added 195,000 jobs in June, and revised up its figures for the previous two months, claiming that 20,000 and 50,000 more jobs had been added in May and Apr., respectively, than initially reported. June's unemployment rate, however, held at 7.6%. The average hourly pay, which rose 10 cents to $24.01, was 2.2% higher than the same time in 2012. The financial markets continued to perform well during July. The Dow Jones Industrial Average set more records, reaching a new high of 15,567.74 on July 23 before closing the month at 15,499.54, up 4% from the end of June. The Nasdaq Composite Index also rose steadily, ending the month at 3,626.37, up 6.6%, while the S&P 500 closed at 1,685.73, up 4.9% in July.

Verdict in WikiLeaks Case Clears Accused of Aiding the Enemy, Finds Guilt on Other Charges—The military judge in Pfc. Bradley Manning's court-martial at Maryland's Ft. Meade July 30 pronounced the 25-year-old not guilty of aiding the enemy in violation of the Espionage Act but guilty of other charges that could carry a sentence of up to 136 years. Manning was charged in 2010 with leaking thousands of U.S. military and diplomatic documents to the WikiLeaks website. The judge, U.S. Army Col. Denise R. Lind, decided that Manning—while guilty of numerous counts of violating the Espionage Act, including stealing government property—did not willfully intend to help U.S. foes such as al-Qaeda. Journalists and civil libertarians had feared that if Manning had been found guilty of aiding the enemy, the verdict would have set a dangerous precedent for freedom of the press and deterred future whistleblowers.

International

Egyptian President Ousted in Military Coup—After days of sometimes violent protests calling for the resignation of Egypt's first democratically elected leader, the country's military forced matters by placing Pres. Mohammed Morsi under house arrest July 3. Adli Mansour, chief justice of the country's Supreme Constitutional Court, was installed as interim president. Protesters claimed Morsi had been hoarding power and had failed to address the country's major economic and security problems since his election in 2012. Secularists accused Morsi, the candidate of the Muslim Brotherhood, of imposing Islamist policies on the nation, while Egypt's Salafists, or fundamentalist Sunnis, said he had not done so enough.

The events plunged Egypt back into chaos reminiscent of the protests that led to the ouster of longtime Pres. Hosni Mubarak two years earlier. Morsi supporters and opponents clashed frequently, and police and armed forces joined the fray. More than 60 protesters were alleged to have been killed by armed forces and more than 2,000 were injured during protests over the course of several days. European Union representatives arrived in Cairo July 18 to advocate for Morsi's release, prompting tens of thousands to take to the streets in protest once again. A government crackdown in Cairo July 27 saw the armed forces fire live ammunition into the fracas, resulting in the deaths of as many as 100 Morsi supporters. Hazem el-Beblawi, a former finance minister, was sworn in as interim prime minister July 16; his cabinet included mostly liberals, but no members from either of Egypt's two biggest Islamist parties.

Québec Derailment and Explosion Kills Dozens—The derailment and subsequent explosion of a runaway train carrying crude oil killed 47 people and leveled a number of buildings in the small town of Lac-Mégantic, QC, Canada, July 6. When recovery teams concluded their search for bodies Aug. 1, as many as five people were still missing. At the time of the disaster, roughly 2,000 people in the community of 6,000 were forced to evacuate their homes. Investigators could not immediately determine the cause of the accident.

Syrian Rebels Choose a New Leader as Death Toll Climbs—The main group of Syrian exile opposition leaders (known as the Syrian Natl. Coalition) met July 6 in Istanbul, Turkey, and elected Ahmad al-Jarba, a tribal leader from the northeastern Hasakah province, their new president. Opposition forces hoped Jarba's election would unite the splintering rebel groups and gain the support of the international community, which was debating whether and how to get involved in the two-year-old civil war. Throughout July, the opposition lost ground to government forces, and Western countries, including the U.S. and UK, questioned the wisdom of providing anything more than small arms to rebel fighters.

UN Sec.-Gen. Ban Ki-moon announced July 26 that the conflict's death toll had passed 100,000 and called for peace talks in Geneva, Switzerland, a step supported by both the U.S. and Russia. Jarba, who had earlier said he was prepared to attend peace talks with representatives of Assad, said July 31 that he would not negotiate with Assad or "his clique" and would not begin talks until the rebels' military position had improved.

School Lunches Kill 23 Children in India—In the Indian village of Dharmasati Gandawa in Bihar's Saran district, 23 children died July 17 and many more had to be hospitalized after eating a school lunch. An investigation quickly found that the food had been cooked in oil stored in a container that once held insecticides, poisoning the children. The cooking oil had been bought from a store owned by the husband of the school's principal, who disappeared shortly after the tragedy unfolded but was arrested July 24.

Great Britain Legalizes Same-Sex Marriage—The British House of Commons July 16 voted 400-176 to legalize same-sex marriage in England and Wales. Queen Elizabeth II approved the bill the next day. The bill passed through the legislature despite opposition from nearly half the members of Prime Min. David Cameron's Conservative Party. The law recognizes civil marriage only; religious groups are not required to perform gay marriage ceremonies, and the Church of England and the Church in Wales were expressly forbidden from doing so. A similar bill was introduced in the Scottish parliament in June, with debate scheduled for Sept. 2013. Northern Ireland had no plans to legalize same-sex marriage.

Dozens Die, Hundreds Injured in China Earthquakes—A series of earthquakes, the most powerful reported to be magnitude 5.9, struck northwest China's Gansu province July 21-22. At least 89 people died and more than 600 were reported injured. The quakes triggered landslides in the poverty-stricken, mountainous region, as well as a number of building collapses.

High-Speed Train Derailment in Spain Kills Dozens—A train carrying 218 passengers through Spain's Galicia region derailed near Santiago de Compostela while taking a sharp turn July 24, killing 79 people and injuring 150 in one of the worst train disasters in European history. The high-speed locomotive, en route from Madrid to Ferrol, was moving at 119 mph through a curve with a 50-mph speed limit and flew off the tracks, crashing into a concrete barrier and bursting into flames. Many of those aboard were pilgrims on their way to Santiago de Compostela for an annual festival honoring St. James. The train's data recorder later showed that the driver, 30-year veteran Francisco Jose Garzon, took a phone call moments before the crash. In an emergency call to authorities immediately after the accident, Garzon admitted that he had been distracted and was going too fast. He was charged with 79 counts of homicide by professional recklessness.

The catastrophe overshadowed the July 12 derailment of a commuter train outside Paris, France, that killed seven and injured nearly 200. That disaster was caused by a faulty switch that led two cars to jump the tracks, bringing several others with them.

General

Bartoli and Murray Take Wimbledon Championships—In one of the more unexpected finals in recent memory, No. 15 seed Marion Bartoli of France defeated the No. 23 seed, Germany's Sabine Lisicki (6-1, 6-4), to win the women's final of the Wimbledon Championship at the All England Club in London July 6. The final match was noteworthy for who it did not include: top-ranked Serena Williams, who had lost in the fourth round to Lisicki. Bartoli finished off the 1-hr., 21-min. match with an ace to seal the tournament championship. The next day, Scotsman Andy Murray, the No. 2 seed, beat Serbia's Novak Djokovic, the No. 1 seed (6-4, 7-5, 6-4) to win the men's title. The match made Murray the first British man to win a Wimbledon final in 77 years.

Mickelson Wins His First British Open—Phil Mickelson shot three-under-281 to win the 142nd British Open Golf Championship July 21 at Muirfield Golf Links in Gullane, East Lothian, Scotland. It was the first British Open win and fifth major victory for the 43-year-old Mickelson. Swedish golfer Henrik Stenson finished in second place with an even-par-284. England's Lee Westwood, who started the final day of the four-day tournament atop the leader board, finished tied for third at one-over-285.

British Racer Froome Wins Tour de France—Chris Froome, a 28-year-old Briton born in Kenya, won the 100th Tour de France at the Arc de Triomphe in Paris July 21. It was Froome's first Tour win and the second consecutive victory by a British cyclist. While Froome received the yellow jersey as the Tour's winner, Slovakian Peter Sagan claimed the green jersey as the race's best sprinter for the second year in a row. Froome, who had placed second overall in 2012, finished the Tour in 83 hr., 56 min., 40 sec. In second place was Colombian Nairo Quintana, who finished 4 min., 20 sec. behind Froome, while Spaniard Joaquim Rodríguez finished in third, 5:04 out of first. The 23-year-old Quintana received the white jersey as the best rider 25 or younger and the polka dot jersey as the best climber.

British Royal Baby Born—England's Prince William and his wife Catherine (Kate), the Duke and Duchess of Cambridge, announced the birth of their first child July 22 at St. Mary's Hospital in London. They named the 8-lb, 6-oz boy George Alexander Louis two days later. The baby was third in line to the British throne after his grandfather (Prince Charles) and his father.

Pope Travels to Brazil for First Foreign Visit—In his first international visit since becoming the leader of the world's Roman Catholics in Mar. 2013, Pope Francis traveled to Brazil July 22 for a week-long visit. While there, he attended the World Youth Day festivities and celebrated mass before more than 1 mil people on Rio de Janeiro's Copacabana beach. Francis also encountered protests from Brazilians who objected to the estimated $52 mil spent on the visit. Some demonstrators complained that the money could have been put to better use on services for the nation's poor and on shoring up its economy—an ongoing argument in a country that was preparing to host soccer's World Cup in 2014 and the 2016 Olympic Games.

The pontiff also made news on the flight home July 29 when he told reporters, who asked for his comments on homosexuals, "Who am I to judge?" The expression of tolerance contrasted sharply with Francis's predecessor, Pope Benedict XVI, who called homosexuality "an intrinsic moral evil."

August 2013
National

NSA Leaker Granted Temporary Asylum in Russia; More Evidence of U.S. Spying Revealed—Former CIA and Natl. Security Agency employee Edward Snowden, living at Sheremetyevo Intl. Airport in Moscow after admitting to leaking classified information on the U.S.'s mass-surveillance programs in June, was granted temporary asylum by Russia Aug. 1. U.S. federal prosecutors had charged Snowden with espionage and Russian authorities had made the decision to grant asylum in the face of warnings from U.S. officials that it could damage U.S.-Russian relations. Pres. Barack Obama Aug. 7 canceled a meeting with Russian Pres. Vladimir Putin, scheduled to take place in Moscow during the upcoming G-20 summit.

The U.S. faced more diplomatic challenges due to Snowden's leaks, including further revelations in mid-Aug. that the NSA had been spying on South American countries and European allies as part of its antiterrorism activities. The *Washington Post* Aug. 15 reported that documents leaked by Snowden showed evidence that the NSA had violated privacy rules thousands of times since 2008.

U.S. Markets Hit All-Time Highs; New Ownership for *Washington Post* and *Boston Globe*—The Dow Jones Industrial Average and the S&P 500 both set records Aug. 1, closing the day at 15,628.02 and 1,706.87, respectively. Although both indexes were up 13%-15% for the year, by the end of the month both had lost between 3% and 4.5% from July. The Dow closed Aug. at 14,810.31, and the S&P was down to 1,632.97. The Nasdaq Composite Index finished Aug. at 3,589.87, down 1% from July. The Labor Dept. report Sept. 6 placed the unemployment rate at 7.3% for Aug., with 169,000 jobs created during the month.

Two of the nation's most prominent newspapers were sold in Aug., as the New York Times Co. sold the *Boston Globe* and the New England Media Group to billionaire John Henry, the principal owner of the Boston Red Sox, for

$70 mil Aug. 3. Washington Post Co. announced the sale of the *Washington Post* to Amazon.com founder Jeff Bezos for $250 mil Aug. 5. The *Globe* sale marked its return to ownership by a local entity but showed a huge loss in value over its last purchase price of $1.1 bil in 1993. The Graham family had owned the *Washington Post* since 1933.

State Department Closes Embassies Abroad on Terrorist Threat—The U.S. State Dept. closed more than 20 embassies and consulates in the Middle East and North Africa Aug. 1 and issued a travel alert for Americans abroad on what officials considered credible intelligence of an imminent terrorist attack. Authorities believed al-Qaeda was in the final stages of preparing a large-scale attack as the Islamic holy month of Ramadan was ending. The UK, France, and Germany followed suit Aug. 4-5, closing their embassies in Yemen. The State Dept. Aug. 4 extended the closures of 19 facilities through the week, while several others, including those in Kabul and Baghdad, reopened Aug. 5. The State Dept. added the U.S. consulate in Lahore, Pakistan, to the list of closures Aug. 9 and warned Americans not to travel there due to other intelligence. The U.S. reopened its facilities Aug. 11, except for the embassy in Yemen, where conditions were still considered unsafe.

California Rim Fire Threatens Yosemite—A wildfire that began in Stanislaus Natl. Forest in the San Francisco area Aug. 17 was only 32% contained by the end of the month and threatened neighboring Yosemite Natl. Park. The wildfire covered 199,237 acres—about 311 sq mi—Aug. 31, making it the sixth-largest fire in California history. Battling the blaze had cost the state $46.8 mil through the end of the month, with four people injured, 111 buildings damaged, and nearly 5,000 firefighters called into service. Eighty-percent containment of the blaze was reached the first week of Sept.

Manning Sentenced for Document Leaks—Pfc. Bradley Manning, who leaked more than 700,000 government documents and diplomatic cables to the whistleblower site WikiLeaks, was sentenced to 35 years in prison Aug. 21. The judge, U.S. Army Col. Denise R. Lind, also announced the 25-year-old Manning would be dishonorably discharged at the reduced rank of private. Col. Lind had found Manning guilty of most charges in July, including six counts of violating the Espionage Act. The case was next slated to undergo a mandatory review, followed by an automatic appeals process.

The day after the sentencing, Manning came out as transgender and asked to be known as Chelsea Manning.

Ft. Hood Shooter Sentenced to Death—Maj. Nidal Malik Hasan, the military psychiatrist who shot 45 people, killing 13, at the Ft. Hood Army base in Texas Nov. 5, 2009, was convicted by a 13-person military jury at his court-marshal Aug. 23. The same jury sentenced him to death Aug. 28. The 42-year-old Hasan had represented himself and admitted to the crime in his opening statement. After the prosecution rested, he offered no defense and made no closing statement, having stated years earlier that he wished to be "martyred" for the shooting, which he intended as an act of jihad for U.S. actions against Muslims in the Middle East. The case became one of the most expensive in U.S. military history, as the government paid more than $5 mil to court-martial and convict Hasan. The sentence will not be carried out for at least 10-15 years, due to the automatic appeals process.

International

Mugabe Declared Winner in Disputed Zimbabwe Election—Incumbent Pres. Robert Mugabe's ZANU-PF party Aug. 1 declared the 89-year-old Mugabe the victor of elections held July 31. The MDC party, backing Mugabe's opponent, Morgan Tsvangirai, immediately called the results fraudulent, an assertion echoed by the country's largest monitoring group, the Zimbabwe Election Support Network. Nevertheless, the Zimbabwe Electoral Commission said Aug. 3 that Mugabe had won 61% of the vote, compared to Tsvangirai's 34%, and that ZANU-PF had won more than two-thirds of the seats in

parliament, giving it a supermajority. Tsvangirai announced his official challenge of those results that same day, and an election commissioner, Mkhululi Nyathi, resigned in protest, claiming the election was conducted unfairly and unprofessionally. Many outside observers, including the African Union, said the elections were conducted mostly peacefully and largely without incident. Tsvangirai and the opposition party dropped the challenge Aug. 16.

Israeli-Palestinian Peace Talks Start—Palestinians and Israelis sat down in an undisclosed location to discuss potential terms for peace Aug. 14, hours after Israel released 26 Palestinian prisoners. The first direct negotiations between the two parties in five years were conducted by Israeli Justice Min. Tzipi Livni and Isaac Molho, a special envoy to Israeli Prime Min. Benjamin Netanyahu, who met Palestinian senior negotiators Saeb Erekat and Mohammed Shtayyeh. They were joined by senior American envoy Martin S. Indyk and deputy envoy Frank Lowenstein.

Hundreds Die in Violent Crackdown on Pro-Morsi Protesters by Egyptian Military—Egyptian security forces Aug. 14 cleared two camps near Cairo Univ. occupied by supporters of ousted Pres. Mohammed Morsi, killing hundreds of protesters in the process. Troops used armored vehicles, bulldozers, tear gas, snipers, and helicopters to carry out the operation. Protesters had been warned that a government crackdown was coming but had expected a gradual exertion of pressure instead of the level of violence that occurred. By the next day, the number of dead stood at 638, including 40 police officers, with nearly 4,000 injured.

A state of emergency was declared for the entire country within hours of the crackdown, and a 7 PM curfew was instated in most cities; it was later changed to 9 PM. The interim government, led by Egypt's military commander Gen. Abdul-Fattah el-Sisi, held the Muslim Brotherhood responsible for the violence and lauded the military, which it described as showing restraint. But Nobel Peace Prize-winner and interim Vice Pres. Mohamed ElBaradei resigned in protest, Turkey withdrew its ambassador, and Europe threatened to withhold economic aid. Saudi Arabia's King Abdullah praised the government for its response to the protesters, whom he called terrorists. At the Muslim Brotherhood-organized "Day of Rage" Aug. 16, as many as 100 protesters were reportedly killed by security forces firing live ammunition at demonstrators in Cairo's Ramses Square.

The day before the crackdown began, 25 new provincial governors were named, of which 19 were generals, raising concerns that Egypt was returning to an authoritarian state. A court ordered former Pres. Hosni Mubarak, ousted in 2011, released from prison Aug. 21. Members of the Muslim Brotherhood continued to demonstrate the rest of the month and violently targeted Christian communities, which they accused of supporting Morsi's removal.

Bomb Blasts Erupt in Beirut and Across Iraq, Killing Hundreds—A car bomb exploded Aug. 15 near a Hezbollah facility in Beirut, Lebanon, killing more than 20 people and injuring almost 300. The blast was understood to be in retaliation for Hezbollah's support of the regime of Syrian Pres. Bashar al-Assad, after a previously unknown Syrian Sunni group calling itself Aisha Umm-al Mouemeneen claimed responsibility for the attack.

Sectarian violence and a virulent insurgency also caused numerous deaths in Iraq throughout Aug., with the deadliest incident occurring Aug. 28 in Baghdad, where 68 people died and more than 200 were maimed in a series of coordinated attacks. After more than 1,000 were reported to have died in Iraq in July, more than 800 civilians were counted among the dead in Aug.

Soldier in Afghan Massacre Sentenced to Life Without Parole—Staff Sgt. Robert Bales, an Afghanistan and Iraq War veteran who killed 16 Afghan civilians in 2012, was sentenced to life without parole Aug. 23. The six-person jury deliberated for less than two hours before determining the

sentence; Bales had pleaded guilty in June. The day before his sentencing, Bales apologized for but did not explain his shooting spree, which took place while he was stationed in Kandahar province. Many witnesses and family members of the victims were flown in from Afghanistan for the trial but were not present when the sentence was rendered.

General

MLB Suspends Record Number of Players in Biogenesis Scandal—Major League Baseball suspended 13 players Aug. 5, including NY Yankees All-Star Alex Rodriguez, for their involvement with the Biogenesis clinic in Florida alleged to have supplied MLB players with a variety of performance-enhancing drugs (PEDs). Twelve of the 13 players received 50-game suspensions, but Alex Rodriguez received an unprecedented 211-game ban, encompassing the rest of the 2013 season and all of 2014. While the players receiving 50-game bans accepted them and offered statements of apology to their teammates and fans, Rodriguez appealed the decision. His appeal was not expected to be decided until Nov. or Dec., and until then, Rodriguez was permitted to play.

Milwaukee Brewers outfielder Ryan Braun, the 2011 National League MVP, had been suspended July 22 for the rest of the season (65 games). Braun first tested positive for elevated levels of testosterone in 2011 but had vehemently denied using PEDs and claimed his urine specimen had been tampered with. The 2011 suspension had been overturned on appeal, making Braun the first player to succeed in doing so since baseball's Joint Drug Agreement went into effect. Braun accepted the July 22 suspension and admitted to "mistakes" and the use of PEDs without giving specifics.

Federal Judge Finds New York's Stop-and-Frisk Unconstitutional—A federal judge in New York City Aug. 12 found in favor of plaintiffs claiming that the city's stop-and-frisk policy, a linchpin of the New York Police Dept.'s crime-fighting strategy, violated the civil rights of minorities and was a form of racial profiling. In her 195-page decision, Judge Shira A. Scheindlin asserted that the policy violated the Fourth Amendment's protection against unreasonable search and seizure and the Fourteenth Amendment's equal protection clause. A defiant Mayor Michael Bloomberg credited the stop-and-frisk policy with helping to make New York the nation's safest big city and his administration appealed the decision. Judge Scheindlin found that between 2004 and 2012, officers were too quick to suspect a person of color, as evidenced by the fact that 83% of those questioned in stop-and-frisk were black or Hispanic, and 90% of those singled out were found to be carrying no weapons.

Infamous Boston Mobster-Turned-Informant Convicted—The once-fugitive James "Whitey" Bulger was found guilty on 31 of 32 counts of racketeering, weapons possession, and murder Aug. 12 in Boston, MA. The trial exposed the corruption during the 1970s and 1980s of federal law enforcement officials, who protected Bulger from criminal prosecution in exchange for information. A tipoff from an FBI agent to his imminent arrest had enabled Bulger to flee to California in the mid-1990s and live as a fugitive for more than a decade; he was arrested in Santa Monica in 2011.

NFL Settles $765-Million Concussion Lawsuit—The Natl. Football League (NFL), accused by former players and family members of concealing knowledge of serious health risks brought on by severe head injuries, settled a lawsuit with retired players and their families Aug. 29 for $765 mil. The settlement allocated $675 mil to former players with cognitive injuries and their families, while $75 mil would pay for baseline medical examinations, and $10 mil would go toward research. The parties awaited approval of the deal by U.S. District Court in Philadelphia, at which time all retired players who met the medical requirements could start receiving money within six months. Among the plaintiffs in the case were retired players and families of retired players who displayed such brain disorders as chronic traumatic encephalopathy (CTE), which is caused by repeated head injury and can only be diagnosed after death; early-onset Alzheimer's; and ALS, or Lou Gehrig's disease.

September 2013
National

Heavy Rains Flood Colorado, Forcing Evacuations—Eight people died and thousands were displaced by torrential rains that turned north-central Colorado into a major flood zone Sept. 11-15. Six dams collapsed Sept. 12 and others were threatened by surging, swollen rivers. With more than 9 in. of rainfall in one 24-hr. period, the flood zone was estimated to be the size of the state of Connecticut. Rescuers struggled to reach stranded residents in especially hard-hit Larimer and Boulder Counties, as floodwaters washed away roads, created dangerous mudslides, and submerged houses. Pres. Barack Obama Sept. 14 signed a major disaster declaration, making federal funds available in the affected counties. By the end of the month, hundreds of residents were still living in shelters and the flood zone covered roughly 2,000 sq. mi.

Gunman Opens Fire at DC Navy Yard, Killing 12—A former U.S. Navy reservist and government subcontractor entered the Washington Navy Yard in southeast Washington, DC, and opened fire Sept. 16, killing 12 and wounding 8 before he was killed by police. Witnesses described the shooter, Aaron Alexis, as shooting indiscriminately. An investigation completed Sept. 25 found that the 34-year-old gunman had a troubled past that included mental health issues. Alexis had claimed to be hearing voices during the months before the shooting and believed his mind was being controlled by low-frequency radio waves. As a subcontractor servicing Navy Internet systems for a company affiliated with Hewlett-Packard, Alexis had access to the Navy Yard complex. Nevertheless, Pres. Barack Obama called for a review of security measures there and at other government facilities in the wake of the shooting.

Record Highs Recorded as Stock Markets React to Continuation of Fed Stimulus—The Federal Reserve announced Sept. 18 the continuation of its bond-buying stimulus program, surprising traders and causing U.S. stocks to soar. The Dow Jones Industrial Average gained 146.44 points, closing the day at a record 15,676.17, up 0.94%. The S&P 500 rose 1.21%, gaining 20.67 points to close at 1,725.43. The Nasdaq Composite Index, up 1.01%, closed at 3,783.64 and rose even higher the next day. Although all three indexes declined toward the end of the month in anticipation of a partial government shutdown starting Oct. 1, the S&P finished at 1,681.55, 3% higher for the month and up 4.7% for the quarter, while Nasdaq ended at 3,771.48, up 5.1% over Aug. and more than 10% for the quarter. The DJIA closed Sept. at 15,129.70, up 2.2% for the month and 1.5% for the quarter.

The U.S. Labor Dept. announced Sept. 6 that the unemployment rate fell to 7.3% for Aug., down from 7.4% in July, while 169,000 jobs were added for the month. The news was tempered by a decline in the labor force participation rate, which fell in Aug. to 63.2%, the lowest rate since 1978. The number of jobs created was also less than the 180,000 predicted by analysts. The number of jobs created for July was revised downward, from 162,000 to 104,000.

Contentious Congressional Debates Fail to Avert Government Shutdown—Members of Congress worked unsuccessfully in Sept. to pass legislation to fund the federal government for the fiscal year beginning Oct. 1. In the Republican-majority House, a group of conservatives sought to make passage of a new budget contingent upon the defunding of the Affordable Care Act (ACA), also known as Obamacare. Democratic leadership in the Senate pledged to reject any such bill, and Pres. Barack Obama said he would veto any legislation that defunded the ACA.

On Sept. 24, Sen. Ted Cruz (R, TX) began a 21 hr., 19-min. imitation filibuster, during which he had vowed to speak against Obamacare until no longer able to stand. Sen. John

McCain (R, AZ) chastised his freshman colleague for seeking to tie the budget to the defunding of the law, which had passed both chambers of Congress 2009-10 and was largely upheld by the U.S. Supreme Court in 2012.

The Senate's spending bill passed 54-44 with no policy attachments but was rejected by the House, which passed its own bill, 228-201, tying the funding of the government to a one-year delay in the ACA's individual mandate, which required that uninsured individuals buy health insurance or pay a small fine. The Senate rejected that bill, leaving the federal government without funding at midnight Sept. 30 for the first time in 17 years.

International

U.S. Threatens Force in Syria; Assad Agrees to Surrender Chemical Weapons—A few weeks after an estimated 1,400 Syrians were killed by Aug. 21 chemical weapons attacks in the Damascus suburbs, Syrian Pres. Bashar al-Assad agreed Sept. 12 to turn over those weapons to international weapons inspectors, as part of an agreement negotiated by Russia. The announcement of the agreement marked the first time Assad admitted to possessing chemical weapons. The agreement halted U.S. plans to take punitive military action in Syria, which Pres. Barack Obama had asked Congress to vote in favor of Aug. 31. While the Senate Foreign Relations Committee narrowly voted to back military strikes Sept. 4, a majority of Congress—along with many U.S. citizens—seemed opposed to U.S. involvement in another overseas conflict.

By the time Obama addressed the nation the night of Sept. 10 to make his case for military action, news of a potential agreement to surrender the weapons had emerged, causing Obama to temper the vehemence in his call for force against Assad. A United Nations report Sept. 16 confirmed that chemical weapons had been used in the Aug. 21 attack. In an address to the UN General Assembly Sept. 24, Obama reiterated that force was necessary at times to stop tyrants and defend their victims, suggesting that military action against Syria remained a possibility. The UN Security Council Sept. 27 passed a draft resolution on Syria, written by the U.S. and Russia, which directed the terms of Syria's surrender of its chemical weapons to inspectors.

Two Massive Storms Strike Mexico, Killing More Than 100—On Sept. 15, Tropical Storm Manuel, originating in the Pacific Ocean, made landfall on Mexico's west coast, as Hurricane Ingrid hit the east coast from the Gulf of Mexico. Manuel then developed into a hurricane and made second landfall Sept. 19. The impact of the storms caused more than 120 deaths. About 59,000 people were driven from their homes due to flooding and mudslides. Several crew members died when a Black Hawk helicopter crashed while trying to rescue victims. The town of Acapulco experienced major flooding, closing its airport for a week and necessitating the airlifting of thousands of tourists to Mexico City Sept. 17 as hotels rationed food and other supplies.

Radical Group Kills Dozens at Kenyan Shopping Mall—Members of the radical Somali group al-Shabab began a four-day assault on the Westgate shopping mall in Nairobi, Kenya, Sept. 21, killing 72 people, including Kofi Awoonor, a respected Ghanaian poet, diplomat, and scholar. More than 150 people were wounded, including five Americans, as masked gunmen opened fire and set off explosives throughout the mall. Many people escaped initially, and Kenyan security forces rescued more than 1,000 during the siege. The attack had been planned weeks in advance, and the gunmen had reportedly studied the building's blueprints, hid weapons in one of the mall's stores, and rehearsed the operation. Witnesses claimed that there were at least two women among the attackers, one of whom was believed to be Samantha Lewthwaite, a British woman who had been married to one of the suicide bombers in the 2005 London train bombing. While most of the attackers were thought to

have been killed or were in custody by the end of the siege, witnesses reported that some escaped by blending in with fleeing civilians, and at least one man—a British citizen of Somali origin—was detained under suspected involvement and prevented from leaving the country Sept. 23. Three days of mourning were observed in the country Sept. 25-27.

Pakistan Shaken by Powerful Earthquakes and Church Bombing—Worshippers at the Anglican All Saints Church in Peshawar, Pakistan, were the victims of a suicide bombing Sept. 22 that killed at least 85 people and injured more than 100. The two bombers belonged to a Taliban faction that targeted non-Muslims in an effort to force the U.S. to end its drone strikes in Pakistan. It was the deadliest-ever attack on Christians in Pakistan.

A magnitude 7.7 earthquake struck Balochistan province in western Pakistan, killing upwards of 500 people Sept. 24. Two hundred soldiers were dispatched for a rescue and recovery effort. Most affected people had been living in mud-walled homes in Awaran, a remote area and the poorest district in Balochistan, though the quake was felt across wide swaths of the country. The shifting of the land mass resulted in a rocky island about 100 ft wide, 250 ft long, and 60 ft high being raised out of the Arabian Sea half a mile off the Gwadar port. Almost a week later, on Sept. 28, another magnitude 6.8 earthquake struck 60 mi northeast of Awaran, killing at least a dozen more people and burying many under collapsed mud huts.

Historic Phone Call Renews Contact Between U.S. and Iran—For the first time since 1979, the leaders of the U.S. and Iran spoke directly Sept. 27. Iranian Pres. Hassan Rouhani, in office since Aug. 2013, accepted the 15 min. phone call from Pres. Barack Obama after spending the week in New York City attending the UN General Assembly. The phone call was said to be cordial and left both men feeling optimistic about future improvement in relations between the two countries. Earlier in the day, Rouhani had reiterated to reporters his confidence that the decade-long stalemate over Iran's nuclear efforts would soon be over, and he expressed his appreciation for the more open, positive tone Obama had used that week concerning a potential resolution of the dispute. Upon his return to Iran, Rouhani was greeted with protests and cheers, as supporters lauded what they saw as a step forward in international relations, while hard-liners expressed their displeasure by pelting his car with eggs.

General

Woman Is First to Swim From Cuba to Florida Without Shark Tank—Long-distance swimmer Diana Nyad Sept. 2 became the first person to swim the 103 mi from Cuba to Florida without a shark tank. During the nearly 53-hr. trip, which began at a Havana yacht club on Aug. 31, the 64-year-old Nyad was accompanied by several boats. It was her fifth attempt at the crossing, which she completed just before 2:00 PM when she landed on a Key West beach.

Williams and Nadal Victorious at U.S. Open—American tennis player Serena Williams, who at the age of 31 was the oldest woman ever to be ranked No. 1, won her fifth U.S. Open singles championship Sept. 8, beating No. 2-ranked Victoria Azarenka of Belarus (7-5, 6-7 (6), 6-1) at the Billy Jean King Natl. Tennis Center in Flushing Meadows Park in New York City. Williams struggled through parts of the match before winning her second Grand Slam tournament of the year. The next day, Spain's Rafael Nadal, the No. 2 seed, defeated top-seeded Novak Djokovic (6-2, 3-6, 6-4, 6-1), winning his 13th Grand Slam title. The victory placed Nadal just behind Pete Sampras (14) and Roger Federer (17) as all-time Grand Slam leaders.

Engineers Raise *Costa Concordia*; Salvage Operation Begins—The cruise ship *Costa Concordia*, which ran aground off Giglio, Italy, in Jan. 2012, was rotated and turned upright in a 19-hr. operation Sept. 17, enabling salvage teams to enter the wreckage to investigate. The 951-ft ship had been lodged against two large rocks and had to be slowly lifted by

cables onto an underwater platform. After the ship was turned upright, a search began for the remains of two passengers who were unaccounted for in the months after the disaster.

Breaking Bad, Modern Family Earn Top Emmy Awards—A week before its final episode was set to air, the AMC drama *Breaking Bad* won its first Emmy for outstanding drama at the Prime-Time Emmy Awards Sept. 22 at the Nokia Theater in Los Angeles, CA. ABC's *Modern Family* was named best comedy series for a fourth consecutive year. *Breaking Bad*'s Anna Gunn took home the Emmy for best supporting actress in a drama. In one of the biggest surprises of the evening, Jeff Daniels won the Emmy for best actor in a drama for his role in the HBO series *The Newsroom*. Claire Danes was awarded best actress in a drama for Showtime's *Homeland*. NBC's *The Voice* won its first award for best reality series, and *The Colbert Report* broke the *The Daily Show*'s 10-year winning streak by taking the Emmy for best variety series.

Oracle Catamaran Stages Record Comeback to Take America's Cup for U.S.—The 34th America's Cup yacht race, held in California's San Francisco Bay, was the site of a historic comeback by the Oracle Team USA crew Sept. 25. Behind 8-1 to Emirates Team New Zealand, the team continually modified several aspects of its boat to win eight races in a row and acquire the cup, the oldest trophy in international sports. Racing at more than 30 knots, the boats achieved some of the fastest speeds in the race's history.

UN Report Reinforces Evidence of Global Warming—The Intergovernmental Panel on Climate Change (IPCC) issued its fifth report Sept. 27, stating not only that the earth's atmosphere is warming, but also that human beings are probably to blame for the temperature increase. The scientific panel observed that the earth had warmed 0.5°C-1.3°C between 1951 and 2010 and stated with 95% confidence that much of the warming was due to greenhouse gas emissions generated by human beings.

October 2013
National

Budget Dispute Forces Government Shutdown—After weeks of wrangling between Republicans and Democrats in Congress, legislators failed to reach a new budget agreement, and the U.S. government partially shut down on Oct. 1. Roughly 800,000 employees were furloughed or working without pay. National parks, monuments, and museums were closed, and federal payments to government services deemed nonessential, such as Meals on Wheels and Head Start, were suspended. Just before the start of the 16-day shutdown, Congress passed, and Pres. Barack Obama signed, a bill to ensure active-duty members of the armed forces continued to be paid, and Congress ultimately voted to award back pay to all furloughed workers when the shutdown ended. Throughout the crisis, an Oct. 17 deadline to raise the debt ceiling loomed, with a lack of agreement on that matter threatening to send the country into default. Shortly before midnight Oct. 17, a compromise bill was passed to break the stalemate, as the House voted 285-144 in favor of a Senate bill approved earlier in the day, 81-18. The president signed the bill at about 12:30 AM Oct. 17. House Republicans failed to achieve their objective of defunding or postponing health care reform measures set to go into effect later in the year.

The legislation funded the government through Jan. 15, 2014, and raised the debt limit until Feb. 7, and the House and Senate were tasked with reaching a long-range agreement by Dec. 13. Economic fallout from the crisis was estimated at more than $3 bil in government services, and upwards of $23 bil of lost economic output.

Health Insurance Exchange Makes Glitch-Filled Debut—Healthcare.gov, the website of the new federal health insurance exchanges prescribed by the Patient Protection and Affordable Care Act (ACA, popularly referred to as Obamacare), opened for enrollment Oct. 1. An estimated 4.7 mil people tried to visit the website on its first day, but many users were met with slow response times, error messages, and disconnections. At hearings of the House Energy and Commerce Committee starting Oct. 24, executives from the contractors hired to create and maintain healthcare.gov spoke of being pressured to launch by Oct. 1 despite inadequate performance during a two-week testing phase. When Sec. of Health and Human Services Kathleen Sebelius testified before the committee Oct. 30, she apologized for the breakdown as Republican members of Congress called the rollout of the exchanges a "debacle." Sebelius estimated repairs on the website would continue until the end of Nov. Users would need to enroll by Dec. 15, 2013, in order to obtain coverage that starts on Jan. 1, 2014.

The rollout of health care reform measures was also troubled by reports of insured individuals receiving cancellation notices on their existing plans, belying Pres. Obama's 2012 pledge that individuals who were already insured could keep their plans after reforms took effect. In most cases, the canceled policies did not meet the minimum standards of insured care set by the ACA, and more expensive plans that did were being offered.

Woman Killed After Car Chase Around Capital—A Connecticut woman led the Metropolitan Police of Washington, DC, on a chase from the White House to the Capitol Oct. 3 before she was shot and killed. Miriam Carey, whose 1-year-old daughter was also in the car but was unharmed, was later described as mentally disturbed and possibly suffering from postpartum depression. The chase was initiated at 2:12 PM, when Carey tried to ram her car through barriers outside the White House. As Secret Service agents and police tried to stop her, she headed down Pennsylvania Ave. to the Capitol building at 80 mph, running several red lights. Police cornered Carey on Constitution Ave., where they fatally shot her. Aside from the car—with which she struck and injured a Secret Service member—she was unarmed. Two police officers were injured in the chase. The Capitol was on lockdown during the incident, which occurred as Congress negotiated the government shutdown.

"Prankster" Bomber Arrested at LAX—A contract employee at Los Angeles Intl. Airport (LAX) was arrested Oct. 15 for planting three dry-ice bombs at the airport Oct. 13-14. The first exploded Oct. 13 in an employee bathroom, briefly grounding all flights, and two unexploded devices were found the next day. Dicarlo Bennett, a 28-year-old Jamaican with U.S. citizenship, was arrested for what investigators called a horrible prank after ruling terrorism out as a motive.

Record Penalty Levied Against JPMorgan Chase; Other Economic News—Attorney Gen. Eric Holder and Jamie Dimon, head of JPMorgan Chase, the nation's largest bank, reached a tentative $13-bil deal Oct. 19 to settle charges that the bank engaged in questionable mortgage practices leading up to the financial crisis of 2008. The penalty, which would settle a civil suit against the bank, was the largest of its kind to date. Along with paying roughly $9 bil in fines and $4 bil to homeowners struggling with their mortgage payments, Chase would be required to cooperate with investigations of employees and former employees who had made reckless mortgage investments.

The Dept. of Labor released its Sept. jobs report Oct. 22, after an 18-day delay due to the government shutdown. While the month's 7.2% unemployment rate was the lowest since Nov. 2008, just 148,000 more people found work, significantly fewer than the 193,000 recorded in Aug.; 11.3 mil people were still jobless.

The Dow Jones Industrial Average hit an all-time high Oct. 29, finishing the day at 15,680.35. The Dow finished the month at 15,545.75, up 2.7% since Sept. 30. The Nasdaq Composite Index and S&P 500 also saw gains for the month, ending at 3,919.71 (up 3.9%) and 1,756.54 (4.5%), respectively.

New Jersey Allows First Same-Sex Marriages, Elects First Black Senator—New Jersey became the 14th U.S. state to marry same-sex couples Oct. 21. Republican New Jersey Gov. Chris Christie had sought to block the ceremonies while the state appealed a judge's ruling that the weddings could go forward, but the state supreme court ruled unanimously Oct. 18 that the governor's case had no merit. Christie formally dropped his legal opposition Oct. 21, ensuring that couples who got married in the state would remain legally married.

Newark, NJ, mayor Cory Booker (D) won a special election Oct. 16 against Steve Lonegan to fill the U.S. Senate seat vacated by Frank Lautenberg (D), who died in June 2013. Booker, the first black senator to be elected by the state, was sworn in by Vice Pres. Joe Biden Oct. 31.

Nevada Middle School Student Opens Fire, Killing Teacher—Just after school began Oct. 21, a 12-year-old student at Sparks Middle School in Sparks, NV, opened fire with a semiautomatic handgun, injuring two 12-year-old boys and killing math teacher Michael Landsberry. The shooter then killed himself. Landsberry, a veteran of the Afghanistan war, was hailed as a hero who had acted in defense of other students.

International

Boat Carrying African Migrants Capsizes off Sicilian Coast—Less than a quarter of a mile from the shore of Sicily, an autonomous region of Italy, an overcrowded boat carrying nearly 500 migrants from Eritrea and Somalia capsized, killing more than 350 people Oct. 3. The catastrophe was precipitated when the engine broke down and the ship began taking on water. Passengers set fire to a blanket in order to gain the attention of people on shore. The fire ignited gasoline, and passengers fleeing the blaze threw the boat off balance. At least 30 additional refugees were killed Oct. 11 in another shipwreck nearby.

Two U.S. Terror Raids Yield Opposite Results—U.S. Special Forces conducted simultaneous raids in Libya and Somalia Oct. 5. They captured one terror suspect but were forced to retreat in the other mission. Delta Force commandos captured Nazih Abdul-Hamed al-Ruqai in Tripoli, Libya, where he had settled with his wife and children after nearly 30 years as a fugitive. Al-Ruqai, also known as Abu Anas al-Libi, was suspected of participating in the 1998 bombings of the U.S. embassies in Nairobi and Dar es Salaam, Tanzania, which killed 234 people.

Navy SEALs in pursuit of al-Shabab operative Abdikadir Mohamed Abdikadir in Baraawe, Somalia, were turned away by forces firing on the squad. Abdikadir, also known as Ikrima, was believed to be a key planner of al-Shabab missions—including the four-day siege of a Nairobi shopping mall in Sept.—with strong connections to al-Qaeda and other Kenyan terrorists.

India Is Hit by Two Major Disasters in 24 Hours—A strong cyclone washed away mud houses and roads, downed power lines, and destroyed fishing boats and villages on India's east coast Oct. 12. Improved early warning systems had enabled more than 870,000 people to evacuate, saving thousands of lives while 53 people died. The storm, named Phailin, featured sustained winds of 124 mph and dropped about 10 in. of rain across several districts, causing severe flooding.

The next day, pilgrims in northern Madhya Pradesh state headed to a religious festival were involved in a stampede on a narrow bridge. At least 115 people were killed and more than 100 others injured. Daily newspaper *The Hindu* reported that as many as 25,000 people were crossing the bridge when a railing broke, prompting the belief that the bridge was collapsing. A number of people drowned after jumping into the river to escape the crush of people, while others were trampled underfoot.

Powerful Quake Kills Scores in the Philippines—A magnitude-7.2 earthquake struck the Philippines, Oct. 16,

killing at least 222 people on the islands of Bohol, Cebu, and Siquijor and injuring about 800. More than 10 of the country's landmark churches were severely damaged, including the Santo Niño de Cebu Basilica on Cebu, built in 1735, and the Church of San Pedro in Loboc on Bohol, dating to 1638.

European Allies Angered Over U.S. Spying—The governments of France, Germany, and Spain joined Mexico and Brazil in expressing outrage at the U.S. over a series of news reports, beginning Oct. 21, that the U.S. had spied on some of its closest European allies, according to documents leaked by former National Security Agency (NSA) contractor Edward Snowden. The French newspaper *Le Monde* reported that the U.S. had collected as many as 70 mil digital communications, including telephone calls and instant messages, inside France Dec. 10, 2012-Jan. 8, 2013. *Der Spiegel* reported Oct. 23 that there was evidence that the NSA had tapped German Chancellor Angela Merkel's cellphone. Spain also claimed to have been a victim of NSA spying programs, reporting Oct. 28 that the U.S. had collected data on phone calls and their locations.

At an Oct. 29 hearing of the House Intelligence Committee, NSA officials defended the agency's gathering of communications data among its allies, claiming that much of the data had been collected by European intelligence agencies and shared with the NSA as part of collective counterterrorism efforts. They also stated that spying on foreign leaders was a universal practice, and that allies of the U.S. no doubt did it as well. Many key members of Congress—even strong supporters of U.S. surveillance programs—expressed disapproval of eavesdropping on other world leaders' private cellphones. Pres. Barack Obama pledged to review the policies and cease conducting some of the more intrusive surveillance operations.

Six Die in Russian Suicide Bombing—A suicide bomber on a bus full of students in Volgograd, Russia, set off powerful explosives Oct. 21, killing six people and injuring 30. Authorities believed the perpetrator, one among a number of recent female suicide bombers, was married to an explosives expert who, as a member of a Dagestan-based insurgent group, may have prepared her for the attack. The bombing raised security concerns about the Winter Olympics, which were scheduled to be held in Sochi, Russia, in Feb. 2014.

General

Lynx Sweep to Win WNBA Championship—The Minnesota Lynx won Game 3 over the Atlanta Dream Oct. 10 at Gwinnett Center in Duluth, GA, to claim the Women's National Basketball Association championship. It was Minnesota's second WNBA title in three years and the third time in four years that Atlanta had been swept in the Finals. Minnesota forward Maya Moore was named MVP of the Finals, with 23 points scored in Game 3.

Boston Red Sox Win World Series—For the fourth time in their long franchise histories, the Boston Red Sox and St. Louis Cardinals met in the World Series, which the Red Sox won, four games to two, on Oct. 30 at Fenway Park in Boston, MA. It was the first time in 95 years that a Red Sox team had won the World Series at home and the third world title for the Sox in ten years. Both St. Louis and Boston had the best records in their respective leagues—an identical 97-65—but the 2013 Series demonstrated sloppy play as much as solid performances. Game 3 in St. Louis ended Oct. 26 with an obstruction call that advanced Cardinals baserunner Allen Craig to home plate. Game 4 ended Oct. 27 when Boston closer Koji Uehara picked off Cardinals pinch runner Kolten Wong at first base.

Young pitchers Michael Wacha, Joe Kelly, and Trevor Rosenthal turned in impressive postseason performances for St. Louis, and veteran Red Sox slugger David Ortiz, the World Series MVP, was Boston's hitting star, with 11 hits in 16 at-bats for a .688 batting average. Ortiz also had two home runs and six RBIs.

OBITUARIES

A

Achebe, Chinua, 82, Nigerian novelist best known for *Things Fall Apart* (1958); a pioneer of modern African literature; Boston, MA, Mar. 21, 2013.

Adams, Bud (Kenneth), 90, oil and gas exec. who owned the Houston Oilers/Tennessee Titans; Houston, TX, Oct. 21, 2013.

Anderson, Gerry, 83, British filmmaker known for work with marionettes, including the series *Thunderbirds* (1965-66); Henley-on-Thames, Eng., UK, Dec. 26, 2012.

Andreotti, Giulio, 94, Italian politician who served as prime min. of Italy seven times between 1972 and 1992; Rome, Italy, May 6, 2013.

Andrews, Patty, 94, singer who performed with her two siblings as the Andrews Sisters; Los Angeles, CA, Jan. 30, 2013.

Artschwager, Richard, 89, painter and sculptor who blended artistic styles; Albany, NY, Feb. 9, 2013.

Asawa, Ruth, 87, artist known for abstract wire sculptures who first learned to draw in an internment camp for Japanese-Americans during WWII; San Francisco, CA, Aug. 6, 2013.

B

Bain, Conrad, 89, Canadian-American actor best known for sitcoms *Maude* (1972-78) and *Diff'rent Strokes* (1978-86); Livermore, CA, Jan. 14, 2013.

Battelle, Kenneth, 86, hairdresser credited with creating Jacqueline Kennedy's bouffant hairstyle; Wappingers Falls, NY, May 12, 2013.

Bellah, Robert, 86, sociologist of religious and moral issues; Oakland, CA, July 30, 2013.

Bernstein, Sid, 95, music producer and promoter who brought The Beatles and Rolling Stones to the U.S.; New York, NY, Aug. 21, 2013.

Black, Karen, 74, character actress who appeared in iconic films *Easy Rider* (1969) and *Five Easy Pieces* (1970); Los Angeles, CA, Aug. 8, 2013.

Boggs, Lindy, 97, U.S. rep. (D, LA, 1973-91) who championed women's rights; Chevy Chase, MD, July 27, 2013.

Bork, Robert, 85, U.S. appellate judge (1982-88) and solicitor general (1973-77) whose Supreme Court nomination was rejected by Senate after an ideological battle (1987); Arlington, VA, Dec. 19, 2012.

Bose, Amar, 83, engineer who invented high-end audio speakers; an MIT professor for 45 years; Wayland, MA, July 12, 2013.

Brennan, Eileen, 80, actress best remembered for her role in *Private Benjamin* (1980); Burbank, CA, July 28, 2013.

Bromell, Henry, 65, writer, producer, and director of TV dramas including *Northern Exposure* (1990-95) and *Homeland* (2011-13); Santa Monica, CA, Mar. 18, 2013.

Brooks, Jack, 89, U.S. rep. (D, TX, 1953-95) known for support of civil rights and investigations into government waste; Beaumont, TX, Dec. 4, 2012.

Brothers, Joyce, 85, psychologist who was a columnist (1960-2013) and TV personality; Fort Lee, NJ, May 13, 2013.

Brown, Roy, Jr., 96, designer and engineer who created Ford Motor Co.'s Edsel model (1957); Ann Arbor, MI, Feb. 24, 2013.

Brubeck, Dave, 91, jazz pianist and composer best known for "Take Five" and *Time Out* (1959); Norwalk, CT, Dec. 5, 2012.

Buss, Jerry, 80, real estate investor and owner of the L.A. Lakers since 1979, as they won 10 NBA championships; Los Angeles, CA, Feb. 18, 2013.

Butler, Jack, 85, Hall of Fame defensive back for the Pittsburgh Steelers (1951-59); Pittsburgh, PA, May 11, 2013.

C

Byrd, Donald, 80, jazz and R&B trumpeter; Dover, DE, Feb. 4, 2013.

Byrd, Harry F., Jr., 98, newspaper publisher and U.S. sen. (D/I, VA, 1965-83); Winchester, VA, July 30, 2013.

Campbell, Will D., 88, Southern Baptist minister and author best known for civil rights work; Nashville, TN, June 3, 2013.

Carpenter, Scott, 88, one of seven original U.S. astronauts; circled Earth three times in the *Mercury* spacecraft (1962); Denver, CO, Oct. 10, 2013.

Carter, Elliott, 103, Pulitzer Prize-winning composer known for atonal, complex works; New York, NY, Nov. 5, 2012.

Casablancas, John, 70, founder of Elite Model Mgmt. (1972); Rio de Janeiro, Brazil, July 20, 2013.

Cassagnes, André, 86, French electrical technician who invented the Etch A Sketch drawing toy; Paris, France, Jan. 16, 2013.

Chambers, Julius L., 76, civil rights lawyer who won landmark Supreme Court case allowing forced busing (1971); Charlotte, NC, Aug. 2, 2013.

Chávez, Hugo, 58, socialist pres. of Venezuela (1999-2013) who consolidated power and often denounced the U.S.; Caracas, Venezuela, Mar. 5, 2013.

Clancy, Tom, 66, best-selling novelist known for military thrillers, including *The Hunt for Red October* (1984) and *Patriot Games* (1987); Baltimore, MD, Oct. 1, 2013.

Clark, William P., 81, national security adviser (1982-83) and interior sec. (1983-85); Shandon, CA, Aug. 10, 2013.

Clement, Jack, 82, producer and songwriter known for Johnny Cash's "Ring of Fire" (1963); Nashville, TN, Aug. 8, 2013.

Cliburn, Van, 78, pianist whose first-place award at the 1958 Intl. Tchaikovsky Competition in Moscow made him famous; Fort Worth, TX, Feb. 27, 2013.

Connors, "Stompin'" Tom, 77, Canadian singer-songwriter who wrote more than 300 songs; Halton Hills, Ontario, Can., Mar. 6, 2013.

Cooper, Jeanne, 84, actress who played matriarch on CBS's daytime soap opera *The Young and the Restless* (1973-2013); Los Angeles, CA, May 8, 2013.

D

Davis, Colin, 85, British conductor known for association with the London Symphony Orchestra (1995-2006); London, Eng., UK, Apr. 14, 2013.

Davis, Garry, 91, activist who renounced his U.S. citizenship to become a citizen of the world; Williston, VT, July 24, 2013.

Day, George "Bud," 88, Air Force fighter pilot who survived five years of torture in Hanoi and was awarded the Medal of Honor; Shalimar, FL, July 27, 2013.

De Maria, Walter, 77, sculptor best known for large-scale outdoor works; Los Angeles, CA, July 25, 2013.

DePreist, James, 76, conductor who was one of the first African-Americans to receive international acclaim in that role; Scottsdale, AZ, Feb. 8, 2013.

Dietzel, Paul, 89, football coach who led LSU to its first national championship (1958); Baton Rouge, LA, Sept. 24, 2013.

Dolby, Ray, 80, engineer and inventor of Dolby sound (1965), a system that removed the hiss associated with sound recordings; San Francisco, CA, Sept. 12, 2013.

Donovan, Art, 89, Hall of Fame defensive tackle for Baltimore Colts (1953-61); Baltimore, MD, Aug. 4, 2013.

Durbin, Deanna, 91, Canadian singer and actress in movie musicals of the 1930s and '40s; Neauphle-le-Château, Yvelines, France, Apr. 20, 2013.

Durning, Charles, 89, Tony Award-winning character actor known for the film *Tootsie* (1982) and play *Cat on a Hot Tin Roof* (1990); New York, NY, Dec. 24, 2012.

Dworkin, Ronald, 81, legal philosopher who developed the theory of "law as integrity"; London, Eng., UK, Feb. 14, 2013.

E

Ebert, Roger, 70, Pulitzer Prize-winning film critic for the *Chicago Sun-Times* (1967-2013) and several popular TV shows (1975-2006); Chicago, IL, Apr. 4, 2013.

Edwards, Robert G., 87, Nobel Prize-winning British physiologist who pioneered in vitro fertilization, leading to the first "test-tube baby" (1978); Cambridge, Eng., UK, Apr. 10, 2013.

Elshtain, Jean Bethke, 72, ethicist and philosopher who focused on the relationship between politics and ethics; Nashville, TN, Aug. 11, 2013.

Engelbart, Douglas, 88, computer scientist and engineer who invented the computer mouse and developed hypertext and networking; Atherton, CA, July 2, 2013.

Estes, Billie Sol, 88, con man imprisoned for a variety of crimes including looting a federal crop subsidy program; Granbury, TX, found dead May 14, 2013.

F

Farina, Dennis, 69, police officer turned actor best known for his roles on *Crime Story* (1986-88) and *Law and Order* (2004-06); Scottsdale, AZ, July 22, 2013.

Flynn, Vince, 47, best-selling author of thrillers; St. Paul, MN, June 19, 2013.

Foley, Charles "Chuck," 82, designer who co-developed the game Twister (1966); St. Louis Park, MN, July 1, 2013.

Foley, Thomas, 84, U.S. rep. (D, WA, 1965-95) who served as House speaker, 1989-95; Washington, DC, Oct. 18, 2013.

Ford, "T-Model" (James Lewis Clark Ford), 92?, blues singer and guitarist; Greenville, MS, July 16, 2013.

Franklin, Bonnie, 69, actress known for TV sitcom *One Day at a Time* (1975-84); Los Angeles, CA, Mar. 1, 2013.

Franklin, Frederic, 98, Britain-born dancer and director known for pairings with Russian ballerina Alexandra Danilova; New York, NY, May 4, 2013.

Fritz, Al, 88, engineer who invented the Sting-Ray bicycle (1963) for Schwinn Bicycle Co.; Barrington, IL, May 7, 2013.

Frost, David, 74, British journalist known for historic interviews, notably of former U.S. Pres. Richard Nixon (1977); at sea aboard HMS *Queen Elizabeth*, Aug. 31, 2013.

Funicello, Annette, 70, actress best known as a Mouseketeer on the *Mickey Mouse Club* (1955-57) and for 1960s "Beach Party" movies; Bakersfield, CA, Apr. 8, 2013.

G

Gandolfini, James, 51, Emmy Award-winning actor best known for playing mob boss Tony Soprano in *The Sopranos* (1999-2007); Rome, Italy, June 19, 2013.

Garment, Leonard, 89, lawyer who was counsel to Pres. Nixon during the Watergate crisis; New York, NY, July 13, 2013.

Germond, Jack, 85, syndicated political columnist; Charles Town, WV, Aug. 14, 2013.

Gilbert, Jack, 87, poet known for works about love and death; Berkeley, CA, Nov. 13, 2012.

Glaser, Donald, 86, Nobel Prize-winning physicist who invented a chamber used in subatomic particle physics; Berkeley, CA, Feb. 28, 2013.

Gold, Dave, 80, entrepreneur who debuted the 99 Cents Only store (1982); Los Angeles, CA, Apr. 22, 2013.

Gorme, Eydie, 84, singer who performed with husband Steve Lawrence; signature song was "Blame It on the Bossa Nova" (1963); Las Vegas, NV, Aug. 10, 2013.

Gray, William H., III, 71, Baptist minister and U.S. rep. (D, PA, 1979-91) who was House majority whip (1989-91); London, Eng., UK, July 1, 2013.

Greeley, Andrew, 85, Roman Catholic priest, sociologist, and novelist known for commentaries on religion and ethnicity; Chicago, IL, May 29, 2013.

Greenwood, L. C., 67, football defensive end for the Pittsburgh Steelers (1969-81); Pittsburgh, PA, Sept. 29, 2013.

Griffith, Émile, 75, Virgin Islands-born boxer best known for fatally beating opponent Benny Paret in a 1962 title match; Hempstead, NY, July 23, 2013.

Griffiths, Richard, 65, British stage and film actor known for Harry Potter films; Coventry, Eng., UK, Mar. 28, 2013.

Groening, Margaret, 94, model for son Matt Groening's character Marge Simpson on animated series *The Simpsons* (1989-); Portland, OR, Apr. 22, 2013.

H

Hagman, Larry, 81, TV actor best known for *I Dream of Jeannie* (1965-70) and *Dallas* (1978-91, 2012); Dallas, TX, Nov. 23, 2012.

Hanneman, Jeff, 49, guitarist and founding member of metal band Slayer; Los Angeles, CA, May 2, 2013.

Harris, Jean S., 89, private-school headmistress who was convicted of killing lover Dr. Herman Tarnower (1981); New Haven, CT, Dec. 23, 2012.

Harris, Julie, 87, Tony and Emmy Award-winning actress best known for her role as Emily Dickinson in *The Belle of Amherst* (1976); Chatham, MA, Aug. 24, 2013.

Harryhausen, Ray, 92, special-effects technician known for stop-motion animation in *Jason and the Argonauts* (1963); London, Eng., UK, May 7, 2013.

Hastings, Michael, 33, Polk Award-winning journalist for *Rolling Stone* and the website BuzzFeed; Los Angeles, CA, June 18, 2013.

Havens, Richie, 72, singer and guitarist best known for improvised song "Freedom" at Woodstock Festival (1969); Jersey City, NJ, Apr. 22, 2013.

Hazan, Marcella, 89, Italian-American cookbook author who evangelized simple Italian food; Longboat Key, FL, Sept. 29, 2013.

Heaney, Seamus, 74, Nobel Prize-winning Irish poet and playwright who wrote of violence and suffering related to Northern Ireland; Dublin, Ire., UK, Aug. 30, 2013.

Henson, Jane, 78, puppeteer who helped create the Muppets with husband Jim Henson; Greenwich, CT, Apr. 2, 2013.

Herbert, James, 69, British horror novelist known for *The Rats* (1974); Sussex, Eng., UK, Mar. 20, 2013.

Hessel, Stéphane, 95, French author and diplomat who served in the French Resistance during WWII; Paris, France, Feb. 26, 2013.

Hijuelos, Oscar, 62, Pulitzer Prize-winning novelist best known for *The Mambo Kings Play Songs of Love* (1989); New York, NY, Oct. 12, 2013.

Hollander, John, 83, scholar and writer of verse and prose; Branford, CT, Aug. 17, 2013.

Hood, James, 70, first African-American man to enroll at Univ. of Alabama (1963); Gadsden, AL, Jan. 17, 2013.

Houghton, Edith, 100, first woman MLB scout; Sarasota, FL, Feb. 2, 2013.

Huxtable, Ada Louise, 91, Pulitzer Prize-winning architecture critic for the *NY Times* (1963-82) and later the *Wall Street Journal*; New York, NY, Jan. 7, 2013.

I

Infantino, Carmine, 87, cartoonist who revived the Flash and Batman for DC Comics; New York, NY, Apr. 4, 2013.

Inouye, Daniel, 88, U.S. rep. (D, HI, 1959-63) and sen. (1963-2012) known for investigating Watergate and the Iran-contra scandal; received Medal of Honor for WWII service; Bethesda, MD, Dec. 17, 2012.

J

Jack, Barnaby, 36, New Zealand-born computer researcher and hacker; San Francisco, CA, July 25, 2013.

Jhabvala, Ruth Prawer, 85, German-born novelist and screenwriter; New York, NY, Apr. 3, 2013.

Johnson, Haynes, 81, Pulitzer Prize-winning journalist and TV analyst; Bethesda, MD, May 24, 2013.

Johnson, Virginia E., 88, sexologist who published *Human Sexual Response* (1966) with William H. Masters; St. Louis, MO, July 24, 2013.

Jones, David C., 92, U.S. Air Force general and chair of the Joint Chiefs of Staff (1978-82); Potomac Falls, VA, Aug. 10, 2013.

Jones, "Deacon" (David), 74, Hall of Fame football defensive end who popularized the term "sack" for his quarterback takedowns; Anaheim Hills, CA, June 3, 2013.

Jones, George, 81, country singer-songwriter known for songs that reflected private demons; Nashville, TN, Apr. 26, 2013.

Junior, Marvin, 77, baritone singer for the R&B group The Dells; Harvey, IL, May 29, 2013.

K

Kaplow, Herb, 86, Washington-based news correspondent (1951-86) for NBC and ABC; Arlington, VA, July 27, 2013.

Karlin, John E., 94, South Africa-born psychologist who designed the touchtone phone keypad; Little Silver, NJ, Jan. 28, 2013.

King, Marilyn, 82, singer who performed with siblings as The King Sisters; Laguna Niguel, CA, Aug. 7, 2013.

Klugman, Jack, 90, Emmy Award-winning actor best known for TV series *The Odd Couple* (1970-75) and *Quincy, M.E.* (1976-83); Los Angeles, CA, Dec. 24, 2012.

Koch, Edward, 88, brash politician who was mayor of New York City (1978-89); New York, NY, Feb. 1, 2013.

Konigsburg, E(laine) L(obl), 83, Newbery Medal-winning author known for *From the Mixed-Up Files of Mrs. Basil E. Frankweiler* (1967); Falls Church, VA, Apr. 19, 2013.

Koop, C(harles) Everett, 96, pediatric surgeon who served as outspoken U.S. surgeon general (1982-89); Hanover, NH, Feb. 25, 2013.

Koprowski, Hilary, 96, Poland-born virologist who created the first oral polio vaccine; Wynnewood, PA, Apr. 11, 2013.

L

Lance, Bert, 82, Office of Mgmt. and Budget director (1977) who resigned under suspicion of wrongdoing, of which he was later cleared; near Calhoun, GA, Aug. 15, 2013.

Lautenberg, Frank, 89, U.S. sen. (D, NJ, 1982-2001, 2003-13) who was known as an Amtrak champion and tobacco industry opponent; New York, NY, June 3, 2013.

Leonard, Elmore, 87, novelist and screenwriter whose best known works include *Freaky Deaky* (1988) and *Get Shorty* (1990); Bloomfield Hills, MI, Aug. 20, 2013.

Lewis, Anthony, 85, Pulitzer Prize-winning legal journalist; Cambridge, MA, Mar. 25, 2013.

Louis (Reed), Willie, 76, witness to the notorious 1955 murder of Emmett Till; Oak Lawn, IL, July 18, 2013.

Lowery, Evelyn G., 88, activist and wife of Joseph Lowery who founded the SCLC/Women's Organizational Movement for Equality Now; Atlanta, GA, Sept. 26, 2013.

M

MacPhail, Lee, 95, Hall of Fame baseball exec. who served as AL pres. (1974-83); general manager of the Baltimore Orioles and NY Yankees; Delray Beach, FL, Nov. 8, 2012.

Maier, Pauline, 75, historian of the American Revolution; Cambridge, MA, Aug. 12, 2013.

Mako, Gene, 97, Hungary-born tennis player who won four Grand Slam doubles titles in the 1930s; Los Angeles, CA, June 14, 2013.

Manford, Jeanne, 92, teacher and activist who helped found Parents, Families, and Friends of Lesbians and Gays (PFLAG); Daly City, CA, Jan. 8, 2013.

Manzarek, Ray, 74, keyboardist and founding member of The Doors; Rosenheim, Germany, May 20, 2013.

Marsh, Leonard, 80, businessman who cofounded Snapple Beverage Corp. (1972); Manhasset, NY, May 21, 2013.

McCready, Mindy, 37, country singer whose troubled life ended in suicide; Heber Springs, AR, Feb. 17, 2013.

McIlhenny, Paul, 68, chairman and CEO of McIlhenny Co., makers of Tabasco sauce; New Orleans, LA, Feb. 23, 2013.

McPartland, Marian, 95, Britain-born pianist who hosted long-running public radio show *Marian McPartland's Piano Jazz* (1978-2011); Port Washington, NY, Aug. 20, 2013.

Miller, Marvin, 95, labor leader who strengthened the MLB Players Assn. as its executive director (1966-82) and was instrumental in achieving free agency for players; New York, NY, Nov. 27, 2012.

Miller, Mulgrew, 57, jazz pianist considered one of the finest of his generation; Allentown, PA, May 29, 2013.

Misch, Rochus, 96, German SS officer who served as Adolf Hitler's bodyguard; last survivor of the Führer's bunker; Berlin, Germany, Sept. 5, 2013.

Missoni, Ottavio, 92, Yugoslavia-born fashion designer known for knitwear and use of zigzag patterns; Sumirago, Italy, May 9, 2013.

Mitchell, George P., 94, oilman who pioneered the use of hydraulic fracturing to extract natural gas from shale rock formations; Galveston, TX, July 26, 2013.

Monteith, Cory, 31, Canadian actor best known for his TV role on *Glee* (2009-13); Vancouver, BC, Can., July 13, 2013.

Moore, Caleb, 25, snowmobile athlete who died as a result of a crash at the X Games; Grand Junction, CO, Jan. 31, 2013.

Moran, Gussie, 89, tennis player whose short tennis dress scandalized Wimbledon in 1949; Los Angeles, CA, Jan. 16, 2013.

Morgan, Edmund S., 97, historian of best known for *The Puritan Dilemma* (1958); New Haven, CT, July 8, 2013.

Morrison, Tommy, 44, heavyweight boxer and actor who appeared in *Rocky V* (1990); Omaha, NE, Sept. 1, 2013.

Morton, George "Shadow," 72, producer and songwriter best known for co-writing the Shangri-Las' "Leader of the Pack" (1964); Laguna Beach, CA, Feb. 14, 2013.

Mrozek, Slawomir, 83, Polish dramatist who was the country's leading playwright; Nice, France, Aug. 15, 2013.

Murray, Albert, 97, scholar who interpreted the black experience; New York, NY, Aug. 18, 2013.

Murray, Joseph E., 93, Nobel Prize-winning surgeon who pioneered organ transplants and reconstructive plastic surgery; Boston, MA, Nov. 26, 2012.

Musial, Stan, 92, Hall of Fame outfielder and first baseman for the St. Louis Cardinals (1941-44, 1946-63); Ladue, MO, Jan. 19, 2013.

Mutis, Álvaro, 90, Colombian poet and novelist best known for *The Adventures and Misadventures of Maqroll* (1986); Mexico City, Mexico, Sept. 22, 2013.

N

Neuharth, Al(len), 89, newspaper columnist and author who founded *USA Today* (1982); Cocoa Beach, FL, Apr. 19, 2013.

Niemeyer, Oscar, 104, Brazilian architect known for Modernist buildings of Brazil's planned capital Brasília; Rio de Janeiro, Brazil, Dec. 5, 2012.

Norton, Ken, 70, heavyweight boxer best known for 12-round victory over Muhammad Ali in 1973, in which he broke Ali's jaw; Henderson, NV, Sept. 18, 2013.

O

O'Shea, Milo, 86, Irish actor known for Tony Award-nominated role in *Mass Appeal* (1981-82); New York, NY, Apr. 2, 2013.

P

Page, Patti, 85, singer best known for "Tennessee Waltz" (1950) and "(How Much Is) That Doggie in the Window" (1952); Encinitas, CA, Jan. 1, 2013.

Pardee, Jack, 76, Texas A&M fullback and linebacker who became an NFL player and coach; Denver, CO, Apr. 1, 2013.

Patrick, Ruth, 105, botanist and limnologist who was an authority on freshwater ecosystems; Lafayette Hill, PA, Sept. 23, 2013.

Pellegrini, Margaret, 89, one of the last surviving Munchkins from *The Wizard of Oz* (1939); Phoenix, AZ, Aug. 7, 2013.

Pohl, Frederik, 93, science-fiction writer known for anti-utopian novels; Palatine, IL, Sept. 2, 2013.

Priebke, Erich, 100, German SS officer convicted in 1996 of executing 335 men and boys in Italy in 1944; Rome, Italy, Oct. 11, 2013.

Pulitzer, Lilly, 81, socialite and fashion designer best known for bright shift dresses; West Palm Beach, FL, Apr. 7, 2013.

R

Ramirez, Richard, 53, serial killer dubbed the "Night Stalker" who killed at least 14 in California (1984-85); Greenbrae, CA, June 7, 2013.

Ramone, Phil, 79, South Africa-born music producer and engineer who co-founded A&R Recording Inc.; New York, NY, Mar. 30, 2013.

Reed, Lou, 71, singer, songwriter, and guitarist known as a member of the Velvet Underground and for solo work, including "Walk on the Wild Side" (1972); Amagansett, NY, Oct. 27, 2013.

Reems, Harry (Herbert Streicher), 65, actor who became famous for pornographic film *Deep Throat* (1972); Salt Lake City, UT, Mar. 19, 2013.

Reichmann, Paul, 83, Canadian real estate developer whose projects included London's Canary Wharf and New York's World Financial Center; Toronto, ON, Can., Oct. 25, 2013.

Remini, Robert, 91, historian known for works on Pres. Andrew Jackson; Evanston, IL, Mar. 28, 2013.

Resnik, Regina, 90, soprano turned mezzo-soprano at the Metropolitan Opera; New York, NY, Aug. 8, 2013.

Reynolds, Bruce, 81, British criminal who was mastermind of the 1963 Great Train Robbery; Croydon, London, Eng., UK, Feb. 28, 2013.

Rich, Marc, 78, Belgium-born financier who fled when indicted by the U.S. for tax evasion and illegal trade with Iran; pardoned by Pres. Bill Clinton (2001); Lucerne, Switzerland, June 26, 2013.

Rogers, Bobby, 73, singer who performed with the Motown group the Miracles (1956-2013); Southfield, MI, Mar. 3, 2013.

Rosen, Charles, 85, pianist known for award-winning book *The Classical Style* (1971); New York, NY, Dec. 9, 2012.

Royal, Darrell, 88, football coach (1957-76) who led the Texas Longhorns to three national championships; Austin, TX, Nov. 7, 2012.

Rudman, Warren, 82, U.S. sen. (R, NH, 1981-92) known for balanced-budget legislation and for breaking with party over Iran-contra scandal; Washington, DC, Nov. 19, 2012.

S

Sahlins, Bernard, 90, comedian and writer who cofounded the Second City improvisational comedy theater in Chicago (1959); Chicago, IL, June 16, 2013.

Sarria, José, 90, drag performer and activist; founder of gay-rights organization Imperial Court System (1965); Los Ranchos de Albuquerque, NM, Aug. 19, 2013.

Schwarzkopf, H(erbert) Norman, Jr., 78, U.S. Army general who commanded U.S.-led forces in Persian Gulf War (1991); Tampa, FL, Dec. 27, 2012.

Scranton, William, 96, Pennsylvania gov. (R, 1963-67) and U.S. amb. to the UN (1976-77); Montecito, CA, July 28, 2013.

Shankar, Ravi, 92, Indian sitar player and composer known for popularizing Indian music with Western audiences; San Diego, CA, Dec. 11, 2012.

Sharman, William "Bill," 87, Hall of Fame basketball player and coach; Redondo Beach, CA, Oct. 25, 2013.

Shea, George Beverly, 104, Canada-born gospel singer known for long-time association with Billy Graham's religious crusades; Asheville, NC, Apr. 16, 2013.

Sherr, Rubby, 99, nuclear physicist on the Manhattan Project who co-designed the plutonium-device trigger; Haverford, PA, July 8, 2013.

Siebert, Muriel, 84, stockbroker who was the first woman to hold a seat on the New York Stock Exchange (1967); New York, NY, Aug. 24, 2013.

Simont, Marc, 97, France-born Caldecott Medal-winning illustrator of children's books; Cornwall, CT, July 13, 2013.

Simpson, Vollis, 94, artist who used junkyard scrap to create windmill-like objects called whirligigs; Lucama, NC, May 31, 2013.

Springer, Ashton, 82, one of the first African-American producers to bring works by black artists to Broadway; Mamaroneck, NY, July 15, 2013.

Stanley, Allan, 87, Canadian Hall of Fame hockey player who helped the Toronto Maple Leafs win four Stanley Cups; Bobcaygeon, ON, Can., Oct. 18, 2013.

Stapleton, Jean, 90, Emmy Award-winning actress best known for role as Edith Bunker on sitcom *All in the Family* (1971-79); New York, NY, May 31, 2013.

Stevens, Risë, 99, mezzo-soprano celebrated for Bizet's *Carmen*; New York, NY, Mar. 20, 2013.

Summerall, Pat, 82, NFL football player who was later a TV sportscaster for football, golf, and tennis events, including 16 Super Bowls; Dallas, TX, Apr. 16, 2013.

Swartz, Aaron, 26, computer programmer and Internet activist; Brooklyn, NY, Jan. 11, 2013.

T

Tallchief, Maria, 88, first American Indian prima ballerina; well-known for roles husband George Balanchine developed for her; Chicago, IL, Apr. 11, 2013.

Thatcher, Margaret, 87, conservative politician who served as Britain's only female prime minister (1979-90); well-known for economic initiatives and firm leadership style; London, Eng., UK, Apr. 8, 2013.

Thomas, Helen, 92, White House correspondent for more than 50 years; Washington, DC, July 20, 2013.

Thorgerson, Storm, 69, British graphic designer best known for album-cover design for Pink Floyd's *The Dark Side of the Moon* (1973); Eng., UK, Apr. 18, 2013.

Toyoda, Eiji, 100, Japanese pres. of Toyota Motor Corp. who introduced the company to worldwide markets; Toyota City, Japan, Sept. 17, 2013.

Trickle, Dick, 71, NASCAR driver who was considered one of the best short-track drivers; Boger City, NC, May 16, 2013.

Turbeville, Deborah, 81, photographer who introduced new moods and settings to fashion photography; New York, NY, Oct. 24, 2013.

V

Valdés, Bebo, 94, Cuban pianist and composer during the big band era; Stockholm, Sweden, Mar. 22, 2013.

Van Buren, Abigail (Pauline Phillips), 94, "Dear Abby" advice columnist (1956-2002); Minneapolis, MN, Jan. 16, 2013.

Vance, Jack, 96, science-fiction and fantasy writer known for Dying Earth series; Oakland, CA, May 26, 2013.

Venturi, Ken, 82, golfer who won the U.S. Open (1964) and was a TV commentator (1968-2002); Rancho Mirage, CA, May 17, 2013.

Vishnevskaya, Galina, 86, Russian soprano who was also a prominent Soviet dissident; Moscow, Russia, Dec. 11, 2012.

W

Wallace, Marcia, 70, actress known for *The Bob Newhart Show* (1972-78) and for providing the voice of Edna Krabappel on *The Simpsons* (1990-2013); Los Angeles, CA, Oct. 25, 2013.

Ward, Michael Moses, a.k.a. Birdie Africa, 41, only child survivor of the MOVE bombing in Philadelphia (1985); at sea aboard *Carnival Queen*, Sept. 20, 2013.

Washington-Williams, Essie Mae, 87, teacher who became known as the daughter of segregationist U.S. Sen. Strom Thurmond and a black maid in his family's home; Columbia, SC, Feb. 4, 2013.

Weaver, Earl, 82, Hall of Fame manager for the Baltimore Orioles (1968-82, 1985-86); at sea, Jan. 19, 2013.

Whitman, Slim, 90, country singer-songwriter known for yodeling; Orange Park, FL, June 19, 2013.

Williams, Esther, 91, actress who performed synchronized-swimming routines in movie musicals; Los Angeles, June 6, 2013.

Williams, Paul, 64, journalist and critic who created the rock magazine *Crawdaddy!*; Encinitas, CA, Mar. 27, 2013.

Winner, Michael, 77, British film director known for *The Mechanic* (1972) and *Death Wish* (1974); London, Eng., UK, Jan. 21, 2013.

Winters, Jonathan, 87, comedian best known for characters such as Maude Frickert and film *It's a Mad, Mad, Mad, Mad World* (1963); Montecito, CA, Apr. 11, 2013.

Wolman, Jerry, 86, real estate developer and Philadelphia Eagles owner (1963-69); Potomac, MD, Aug. 6, 2013.

Woodland, N(orman) Joseph, 91, engineer known as co-inventor of the scannable bar code; Edgewater, NJ, Dec. 9, 2012.

Worthington, Cal, 92, car dealer who relentlessly ran offbeat TV commercials; Orland, CA, Sept. 8, 2013.

Y

Yamauchi, Hiroshi, 85, Japanese pres. of Nintendo (1949-2002) who transformed a playing-card company into the world's biggest video-game producer; Kyoto, Japan, Sept. 19, 2013.

Young, Lee Thompson, 29, child actor known for *The Famous Jett Jackson* (1998-2001) and *Rizzoli & Isles* (2010-13); Los Angeles, CA, Aug. 19, 2013.

Z

Ziglar, Zig, 86, salesman who became a best-selling author and motivational speaker; Plano, TX, Nov. 28, 2012.

STATE GOVERNMENT

Governors of the 50 States

Source: National Governors Association; Council of State Governments; World Almanac research
As of Oct. 2013, of the 50 state governors, 30 are Republicans and 20 are Democrats. Salary information is as of Apr. 2013.

State	Capital, ZIP code	Governor	Party	Term years	Term expires	Annual salary
Alabama	Montgomery, 36130	Robert Bentley	Rep.	4	Jan. 2015	$119,950[1]
Alaska	Juneau, 99811	Sean Parnell	Rep.	4	Dec. 2014	145,000
Arizona	Phoenix, 85007	Jan Brewer	Rep.	4	Jan. 2015	95,000
Arkansas	Little Rock, 72201	Mike Beebe	Dem.	4	Jan. 2015	86,890
California	Sacramento, 95814	Jerry Brown	Dem.	4	Jan. 2015	173,987
Colorado	Denver, 80203	John Hickenlooper	Dem.	4	Jan. 2015	90,000
Connecticut	Hartford, 06106	Dan Malloy	Dem.	4	Jan. 2015	150,000
Delaware	Dover, 19902	Jack A. Markell	Dem.	4	Jan. 2017	171,000
Florida	Tallahassee, 32399	Rick Scott	Rep.	4	Jan. 2015	130,273[1]
Georgia	Atlanta, 30334	Nathan Deal	Rep.	4	Jan. 2015	139,339
Hawaii	Honolulu, 96813	Neil Abercrombie	Dem.	4	Dec. 2014	117,312
Idaho	Boise, 83702	C. L. "Butch" Otter	Rep.	4	Jan. 2015	117,000
Illinois	Springfield, 62706	Patrick Quinn	Dem.	4	Jan. 2015	177,412
Indiana	Indianapolis, 46204	Mike Pence	Rep.	4	Jan. 2017	111,688
Iowa	Des Moines, 50319	Terry Branstad	Rep.	4	Jan. 2015	130,000
Kansas	Topeka, 66612	Sam Brownback	Rep.	4	Jan. 2015	99,636
Kentucky	Frankfort, 40601	Steven L. Beshear	Dem.	4	Dec. 2015	153,970[2]
Louisiana	Baton Rouge, 70804	Bobby Jindal	Rep.	4	Jan. 2016	130,000
Maine	Augusta, 04333	Paul LePage	Rep.	4	Jan. 2015	70,000
Maryland	Annapolis, 21401	Martin O'Malley	Dem.	4	Jan. 2015	150,000
Massachusetts	Boston, 02133	Deval Patrick	Dem.	4	Jan. 2015	139,832
Michigan	Lansing, 48909	Rick Snyder	Rep.	4	Jan. 2015	159,300[3]
Minnesota	St. Paul, 55155	Mark Dayton	Dem.	4	Jan. 2015	120,303
Mississippi	Jackson, 39205	Phil Bryant	Rep.	4	Jan. 2016	122,160
Missouri	Jefferson City, 65102	Jay Nixon	Dem.	4	Jan. 2017	133,821
Montana	Helena, 59620	Steve Bullock	Dem.	4	Jan. 2017	108,167
Nebraska	Lincoln, 68509	David Heineman	Rep.	4	Jan. 2015	105,000
Nevada	Carson City, 89701	Brian Sandoval	Rep.	4	Jan. 2015	149,573
New Hampshire	Concord, 03301	Maggie Hassan	Dem.	2	Jan. 2015	113,834
New Jersey	Trenton, 08625	Chris Christie	Rep.	4	Jan. 2014	175,000
New Mexico	Santa Fe, 87300	Susana Martinez	Rep.	4	Jan. 2015	110,000
New York	Albany, 12224	Andrew Cuomo	Dem.	4	Jan. 2015	179,000[4]
North Carolina	Raleigh, 27699	Pat McCrory	Rep.	4	Jan. 2017	141,265
North Dakota	Bismarck, 58505	Jack Dalrymple	Rep.	4	Dec. 2016	116,999
Ohio	Columbus, 43215	John Kasich	Rep.	4	Jan. 2015	148,886
Oklahoma	Oklahoma City, 73105	Mary Fallin	Rep.	4	Jan. 2015	147,000
Oregon	Salem, 97301	John Kitzhaber	Dem.	4	Jan. 2015	93,600
Pennsylvania	Harrisburg, 17120	Tom Corbett	Rep.	4	Jan. 2015	187,256[5]
Rhode Island	Providence, 02903	Lincoln Chafee	Dem.[6]	4	Jan. 2015	129,210
South Carolina	Columbia, 29201	Nikki R. Haley	Rep.	4	Jan. 2015	106,078
South Dakota	Pierre, 57501	Dennis Daugaard	Rep.	4	Jan. 2015	100,972
Tennessee	Nashville, 37243	Bill Haslam	Rep.	4	Jan. 2015	178,356[1]
Texas	Austin, 78711	Rick Perry	Rep.	4	Jan. 2015	150,000
Utah	Salt Lake City, 84114	Gary R. Herbert	Rep.	4	Jan. 2017	109,470
Vermont	Montpelier, 05609	Peter Shumlin	Dem.	2	Jan. 2015	142,542[4]
Virginia	Richmond, 23219	Bob McDonnell	Rep.	4	Jan. 2014	175,000
Washington	Olympia, 98504	Jay Inslee	Dem.	4	Jan. 2017	166,891
West Virginia	Charleston, 25305	Earl Ray Tomblin	Dem.	4	Jan. 2017	150,000
Wisconsin	Madison, 53707	Scott Walker	Rep.	4	Jan. 2015	144,423
Wyoming	Cheyenne, 82002	Matthew Mead	Rep.	4	Jan. 2015	105,000

Note: Kentucky, Massachusetts, Pennsylvania, and Virginia are self-designated commonwealths. (1) Does not accept salary. (2) Reflects a voluntary 10% salary reduction. (3) Accepts only $1. (4) Voluntary 5% salary reduction. (5) As part of management pay freeze, 1.7% of salary is being repaid. (6) Won election as an independent but registered as Democrat in May 2013.

Governors of Commonwealths and Territories

State	Capital, ZIP code	Governor	Party	Term years	Term expires	Annual salary
American Samoa	Pago Pago, 96799	Lolo Matalasi Moliga	Ind.	4	Jan. 2017	$50,000
Guam	Agana, 96932	Eddie Calvo	Rep.	4	Jan. 2015	90,000
Northern Mariana Islands	Saipan, 96950	Eloy S. Inos	Cov.[1]	4	Jan. 2015	70,000
Puerto Rico	San Juan, 00902	Alejandro García Padilla	PDP[2]	4	Jan. 2017	70,000
Virgin Islands	St. Thomas, 00802	John P. de Jongh Jr.	Dem.	4	Jan. 2015	80,000

(1) Covenant Party. (2) Popular Democratic Party.

U.S. SUPREME COURT

The U.S. Supreme Court's 2012-13 term began Oct. 1, 2012, and concluded June 26, 2013, for its summer recess. The justices decided 78 cases (73 of which carried signed opinions) and issued 23 rulings (29%) by a 5-4 majority.

Chief Justice John G. Roberts Jr. presided over his eighth full term. The eight associate justices, by order of seniority, were Antonin Scalia, Anthony M. Kennedy, Clarence Thomas, Ruth Bader Ginsburg, Stephen G. Breyer, Samuel A. Alito Jr., Sonia Sotomayor, and Elena Kagan.

In 2012-13, Roberts, Scalia, Thomas, and Alito tended to vote together as a conservative bloc, while Ginsburg, Breyer, Sotomayor, and Kagan composed the court's liberal wing. Kennedy was the swing vote on 16 out of 23, or 70% of, split decisions. Associate Justice Kennedy was in the majority 91% of the time; Chief Justice Roberts was in the majority 86% of the time.

Notable Supreme Court Decisions, 2012-13

Note: The columns on the right provide information on how each justice voted. Gray shading indicates a justice who was part of the majority; black indicates a justice recused himself or herself. MO = justice authored majority opinion; CO = justice authored concurring opinion; COJ = justice authored opinion concurring in judgment but not its reasoning; DO = justice authored dissenting opinion; CD in part = justice authored opinion containing both concurring and dissenting opinions.

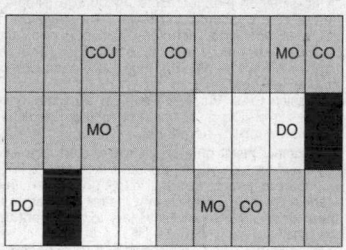

Affirmative Action

The Supreme Court June 24 ruled in *Fisher v. Univ. of Texas at Austin* that a case regarding the school's admissions policy—which took race and ethnicity into account, among other factors—be sent back to the lower court that had upheld the policy for reconsideration. The court held that the Univ. of Texas's admissions policy needed to be evaluated using a tougher constitutional standard.

Kagan	Sotomayor	Breyer	Ginsburg	Kennedy	Scalia	Thomas	Roberts	Alito
(recused)			DO	MO	CO	CO		

Biotechnology

The court June 13 unanimously held that human genetic material was a natural phenomenon that could not be patented, a ruling that was expected to usher in significant changes in the field of genetic research. However, the court said that a form of DNA that was fabricated in laboratories (complementary DNA, or cDNA) was not naturally occurring and thus not subject to the prohibition. The case was *Assn. for Molecular Pathology v. Myriad Genetics, Inc.*

Kagan	Sotomayor	Breyer	Ginsburg	Kennedy	Scalia	Thomas	Roberts	Alito
					COJ	MO		

Business

The Supreme Court Apr. 17 ruled in *Kiobel v. Royal Dutch Petroleum Co.* that a group of foreign nationals living in the U.S. could not sue Dutch, British, and Nigerian corporations in U.S. courts over alleged human rights abuses committed abroad. The justices were unanimous in saying U.S. courts did not have jurisdiction over the case but disagreed about the reasoning for the ruling.

Kagan	Sotomayor	Breyer	Ginsburg	Kennedy	Scalia	Thomas	Roberts	Alito
		COJ		CO			MO	CO

The court June 17 ruled, 5-3, that the Federal Trade Commission (FTC) could sue pharmaceutical companies that accepted settlement payments for keeping cheaper generic versions of patented drugs off the market. The Supreme Court vacated lower court rulings that had found such agreements to be legal though the court did not deem them to be presumptively illegal. The case was *FTC v. Actavis Inc.*

Kagan	Sotomayor	Breyer	Ginsburg	Kennedy	Scalia	Thomas	Roberts	Alito
		MO					DO	(recused)

The court June 20 ruled, 5-3, that when customers signed arbitration agreements with businesses that waived the customers' rights to participate in class-action arbitration, the waiver was binding even in cases where arbitration over a given issue would be too expensive or too difficult for one customer to undertake individually. The case was *American Express Co. v. Italian Colors Restaurant.*

Kagan	Sotomayor	Breyer	Ginsburg	Kennedy	Scalia	Thomas	Roberts	Alito
DO	(recused)				MO	CO		

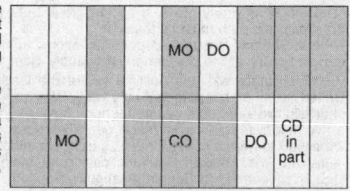

Criminal Justice

The Supreme Court June 3 ruled, 5-4, that law enforcement officials could take DNA samples via a cheek swab from people arrested for serious crimes and test the DNA in an effort to link the suspect to unrelated crimes. The court compared the practice to accepted identification procedures such as the routine fingerprinting and photographing of suspects. The case was *Maryland v. King.*

Kagan	Sotomayor	Breyer	Ginsburg	Kennedy	Scalia	Thomas	Roberts	Alito
				MO	DO			

In *Missouri v. McNeely*, the court Apr. 17 affirmed, 5-4, a verdict that the administration of a nonconsensual blood test without a warrant (to determine blood-alcohol level) violated an individual's rights. Thomas, dissenting, held that a warrant should never be required in such cases because the time taken to process one inevitably results in the destruction of evidence. The remaining eight justices differed as to whether a general rule could be made waiving the need for a warrant, and what that rule would be.

Kagan	Sotomayor	Breyer	Ginsburg	Kennedy	Scalia	Thomas	Roberts	Alito
	MO			CO		DO	CD in part	

Employment Discrimination

The court June 24 upheld, 5-4, a lower court's narrow definition of a workplace "supervisor" for the purposes of employment-discrimination lawsuits where the employer was liable for a supervisor's discriminatory actions. The case was *Vance v. Ball State Univ.*

Kagan	Sotomayor	Breyer	Ginsburg	Kennedy	Scalia	Thomas	Roberts	Alito
			DO			CO		MO

The court June 24 ruled, 5-4, that employees who said they had been the victims of discriminatory retaliation for prior claims of discrimination had to meet a higher standard of proof than the standard required for those who were claiming discrimination based on their race, ethnicity, skin color, religion, or sex. The case was *Univ. of Texas Southwestern Medical Center v. Nassar.*

Kagan	Sotomayor	Breyer	Ginsburg	Kennedy	Scalia	Thomas	Roberts	Alito
			DO	MO				

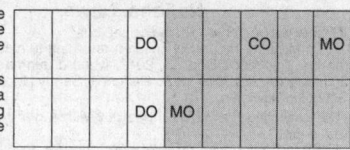

Same-Sex Marriage

In *U.S. v. Windsor*, the Supreme Court June 26 struck down, 5-4, the central provision of the 1996 federal Defense of Marriage Act (DOMA), which prohibited federal recognition of same-sex marriages. The ruling said that gay couples married in states that had legalized same-sex marriage were entitled to more than 1,000 federal rights and benefits granted to married couples.

Kagan	Sotomayor	Breyer	Ginsburg	Kennedy	Scalia	Thomas	Roberts	Alito
				MO	DO		DO	DO

The Supreme Court June 26 ruled, 5-4, that those appealing a 2010 federal district court ruling striking down Proposition 8—a 2008 California ballot initiative that had amended the state constitution to recognize only marriages between a man and a woman—had no standing to do so. The ruling had the effect of legalizing same-sex marriage in California. The case was *Hollingsworth v. Perry.*

Kagan	Sotomayor	Breyer	Ginsburg	Kennedy	Scalia	Thomas	Roberts	Alito
				DO			MO	

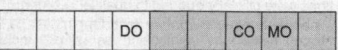

Voting Rights

The court June 25 ruled, 5-4, that a key provision of the 1965 Voting Rights Act was unconstitutional because it relied on outdated information to identify areas for additional scrutiny of voting procedures. The case was *Shelby County v. Holder.*

Kagan	Sotomayor	Breyer	Ginsburg	Kennedy	Scalia	Thomas	Roberts	Alito
			DO			CO	MO	

NOTABLE QUOTES, 2013

Around the World

"With all due respect, the fact is we had four dead Americans. Was it because of a protest or was it because of guys out for a walk one night who decided they'd go kill some Americans?"
—Sec. of State Hillary Clinton, testifying before Senate committee, Jan. 23, responding to criticism of the administration's initial explanation of the Sept. 11, 2012, attack on the U.S. consulate in Benghazi, Libya.

"After having repeatedly examined my conscience before God, I have come to the certainty that my strengths, due to an advanced age, are no longer suited to an adequate exercise of the Petrine ministry."
—Pope Benedict XVI, on Feb. 11, announcing his resignation, effective Feb. 28

"They thought that the bullets would silence us, but they failed."
—Pakistani teen Malala Yousafzai, in speech at UN Youth Assembly, July 12, referring to Taliban gunmen who had shot her for promoting girls' education in Pakistan.

"The indiscriminate slaughter of civilians, the killing of women and children and innocent bystanders by chemical weapons is a moral obscenity."
—Sec. of State John Kerry, Aug. 26, condemning Syrian regime's apparent massive use of chemical weapons against its people in civil war.

"Let me make something clear: The United States military doesn't do pinpricks. Even a limited strike will send a message to Assad that no other nation can deliver."
—Pres. Barack Obama in speech to nation on Syria, Sept. 10, in which he reiterated support for a possible punitive strike, for which he had been seeking congressional approval.

"It is extremely dangerous to encourage people to see themselves as exceptional, whatever the motivation. There are big countries and small countries, rich and poor, those with long democratic traditions and those still finding their way to democracy. ... We are all different, but ... we must not forget that God created us equal."
—Russian Pres. Vladimir Putin, in an often critical *NY Times* op-ed piece, Sept. 12, promoting the negotiated removal of chemical weapons from Syria.

"We cannot insist only on issues related to abortion, gay marriage and the use of contraceptive methods. ... [W]hen we speak about these issues, we have to talk about them in a context. The teaching of the church, for that matter, is clear and I am a son of the church, but it is not necessary to talk about these issues all the time."
—Pope Francis, from interviews in Aug. released Sept. 19 by 16 Jesuit journals around the world.

"The roadblocks may prove to be too great, but I firmly believe the diplomatic path must be tested."
—Pres. Obama, referring to possible efforts to negotiate with Iran, in speech at the UN General Assembly, Sept. 24.

"Commensurate with the political will of the leadership in the United States and hoping that they will refrain from following the short-sighted interest of warmongering pressure groups, we can arrive at a framework to manage our differences. ... Of course, we expect to hear a consistent voice from Washington."
—Iranian Pres. Hassan Rouhani, calling for dialogue with the U.S., in speech to UN General Assembly, Sept. 24.

National News

"[T]here will be some missing on the bus."
—Erin Milgram, mother of children returning to class Jan. 3, for the first time since Dec. 14, 2012, when a gunman massacred 20 first-grade students and 6 staffers at Sandy Hook Elementary School in Newtown, CT.

"The only thing that stops a bad guy with a gun is a good guy with a gun."
—NRA executive vice pres. Wayne LaPierre, Dec. 21, 2012, in response to calls for gun control after the Newtown, CT, school shootings.

"We, the people, declare today that the most evident of truths—that all of us are created equal—is the star that guides us still; just as it guided our forebears through Seneca Falls, and Selma, and Stonewall."
—Pres. Obama in his inauguration speech, Jan. 21, invoking milestones related to women's, civil, and gay rights movements.

"Not everyone is going to be able to be a combat soldier. But everyone is entitled to a chance."
—Defense Sec. Leon Panetta, Jan. 24, as military combat positions were officially opened to qualified women.

"There's no one reason we lost. Our message was weak; our ground game was insufficient; we weren't inclusive; we were behind in both data and digital; and our primary and debate process needed improvement."
—Republican Natl. Committee Chair Reince Priebus, on reasons for GOP losses in Nov. 2012 election, Mar. 18, after a months-long review.

"Marriage is different ... It's a magic word ... It is magic ... today is like a spectacular event for me."
—Edith Windsor, 83-year-old widow from a same-sex marriage, speaking to reporters, Mar. 27, as U.S. Supreme Court heard oral arguments in her case. The Supreme Court ruled that parts of the Defense of Marriage Act, challenged by Windsor's case, were unconstitutional in June.

"CAPTURED!!! The hunt is over. The search is done. The terror is over. And justice has won. Suspect in custody."
—Boston Police Dept., in a tweet, Apr. 19, announcing capture of the second of two suspects in the Apr. 15 Boston Marathon bombing.

"I'm not good at math."
—IRS official Lois Lerner, May 10, following reports agency personnel selectively targeted right-wing groups for audits.

"I couldn't hear anything but people screaming and crying. It felt like the school was just flying."
—Claire Gossett, 11, on the deadly tornado that struck her school in Moore, OK, May 20.

"Everyone everywhere now understands how bad things have gotten—and they're talking about it. They have the power to decide for themselves whether they are willing to sacrifice their privacy to the surveillance state."
—Edward Snowden, in Hong Kong, where he disclosed his identity June 9 as leaker of classified information about National Security Agency surveillance activities.

"I don't look at this as being a whistleblower. I think it's an act of treason ... He violated the oath, he violated the law. It's treason."
—Sen. Dianne Feinstein (D, CA), Senate Intelligence Committee chair, June 10, in reference to Snowden.

"You know, when Trayvon Martin was first shot, I said that this could have been my son. Another way of saying that is: Trayvon Martin could have been me 35 years ago."
—Pres. Obama, a few days after a jury, July 13, found neighborhood watch volunteer George Zimmerman not guilty in the shooting death of the African-American teenager.

"We can't get lower in the polls. We're down to blood relatives and paid staffers now."
—Sen. John McCain (R, AZ), on *Face the Nation*, Oct. 13, speaking of Congress's popularity, as talks stalemated over the government shutdown and possible default.

People

"In retrospect, I obviously should have been much more cautious."
—Notre Dame football star Manti Te'o, in statement issued Jan. 16, after learning that his highly publicized online relationship with a woman who died was in fact a hoax.

"I'm a flawed character."
—Disgraced cyclist Lance Armstrong, in interview with Oprah Winfrey, aired Jan. 17-18, in which he admitted use of performance-enhancing drugs.

"I don't condone what he does, but he's my friend."
—Former NBA star Dennis Rodman referring to North Korean leader Kim Jong Un, reported Mar. 11, following his trip to North Korea in late Feb.

"We've had enough Bushes."
—Former First Lady Barbara Bush, in a *Today* show interview, Apr. 25, after being asked whether her son, former Florida Gov. Jeb Bush, should try to follow his father and brother to the White House.

"Help me. I'm Amanda Berry. ... I've been kidnapped and I've been missing for ten years, and I'm, I'm here, I'm free now."
—Woman who had been kidnapped and held prisoner in a Cleveland home, to a 911 operator, May 6, after she escaped with the help of a neighbor.

"I'm a 34-year-old NBA center. I'm black. And I'm gay."
—Jason Collins, writing in May 6 *Sports Illustrated* issue, as the first active male athlete in one of the four major U.S. pro sports leagues to come out in public as gay.

"This is wonderful news that will make the whole country smile."
—British Deputy Prime Min. Nick Clegg, on announcement, July 22, that the Duchess of Cambridge had given birth to a baby boy, now third in line to the throne.

"These men didn't hunt animals, ladies and gentlemen, they hunted people."
—Prosecutor Fred Wyshak during the government's closing argument, Aug. 5, in trial of former Boston crime boss James "Whitey" Bulger.

Norwegian Wood

Canada's recently redesigned currency, printed on polymer, has a distinctive new anti-counterfeit feature: a frosted maple leaf window that reveals hidden numbers when held in front of a light. There are many species of maple trees native to Canada, but as botanist Sean Blaney pointed out, the leaf on the new bills wasn't one of them. The leaf on the bills was not from a North American sugar maple, or any other indigenous maple, but was instead from a Norway maple.

The Norway maple was brought across the Atlantic to Philadelphia in 1756 and made its way to Canada in 1778. A hardy and fertile species, with dense branches that limit light to other plants, it has rapidly supplanted native maples. Several U.S. states classify it as an invasive species.

A spokesperson for the Bank of Canada insisted in Jan. 2013 that this was mistaken identification. She said that they had combined the features of multiple native maples to get "a maple leaf that was not specific, so that Canadians from all the different regions could identify it." Blaney scoffed: "The maple that they've drawn is quite clearly a Norway maple."

My Kingdom for a Hearse

In 2009, screenwriter Philippa Langley was doing research on a screenplay about English King Richard III. After his death in 1485, his remains had been entombed in a Leicester monastery, which was demolished about a half century later. Richard's final resting place was lost. On a visit to the most likely site of the tomb, Langley "had the strongest sensation that [she] was walking on Richard's grave" while walking through a private parking lot nearby. She eventually convinced a reluctant team of archaeologists from the Univ. of Leicester to excavate the site. The lead archaeologist, who considered the project "a hare-brained scheme," applied for an exhumation license with the phrase "In the unlikely event that we find the remains of Richard III …" But in Aug. 2012, the archaeologists found a body which physical evidence suggested was that of Richard III, and in Feb. 2013, they announced that DNA evidence from a known descendant had confirmed it.

That left the question of what to do with the last Yorkist king's remains. The original license specified that they be reburied at Leiscester Cathedral, just a couple of blocks away from the parking lot. This drew protests from many Richard III fans and distant relatives, who claimed that a burial in York would be truer to the king's wishes. There was also debate on whether the planned "Christian-led but ecumenical service" was appropriate for a lifelong Catholic. Rival online petitions drew more than 30,000 signatures apiece. In Aug. 2013, a judge ruled that many people had a legitimate interest in determining the king's final resting place and strongly advised that an independent panel be appointed to consider the public's opinions, as "it would be unseemly, undignified and unedifying to have a legal tussle over these royal remains." As of Oct., however, that legal battle appeared likely.

Nutty Larceny

The *Columbia Daily Spectator* reported Mar. 5, 2013, that students at Columbia Univ. in New York, NY, were making off with up to 100 lb of Nutella from the dining halls per day, costing the school $5,000 a week. Columbia's executive director of Dining Services said that students had been filling up cups of the chocolate hazelnut spread and even taking away full jars. A spokesperson for the Ivy League school claimed that the figures given had been highly exaggerated, and that the costs claimed were "roughly 10 times greater than the actual figures."

All of this turned out to be penny-ante compared to a Nutella heist the following month. Thieves in the central German town of Bad Hersfeld stole 5½ tons of Nutella from a parked trailer in Apr. This was not the first food-related theft there; about $40,000 worth of coffee had been stolen two weeks earlier, not to mention a truckful of Red Bull energy drinks.

It's in the Cards

The distinctive smell of natural gas pervaded the town of Great Falls, MT, May 8, 2013. Several buildings were evacuated as emergency crews tried to pinpoint the source of the leak. It turned out that there was no leak, only a pile of scratch-and-sniff cards.

Natural gas is odorless. The smell associated with it comes from a chemical additive meant to alert bystanders to a leak. But for it to work, people need to know what the chemical additive smells like. Energy West in Great Falls had sent out scratch-and-sniff cards years earlier to that end. In spring 2013, workers cleaning out Energy West's storage areas found several boxes of old, expired scratch-and-sniff cards and threw them away. When a garbage truck crushed the scratch-and-sniff cards it released the odor of the chemical additive. It turns out that even expired scratch-and-sniff cards can be pretty smelly.

Stand-Up Cops

Everybody knows about scarecrows: life-sized dummies that look like human figures, set up to keep crows from stealing corn. Who knew the same tactic could work on people? The MBTA Transit Police placed two life-sized cardboard cutouts of a uniformed police officer next to the bike racks at the Alewife train station in Cambridge, MA, July 5, 2013. In the first month of the experiment, bike thefts were down 67%—two bikes were stolen compared with six in the same period in 2012. If the trend continued, they planned to try additional cutouts around the train system in order to reduce crime and to free cops to work on more serious cases.

Out of the Frying Pan …

Death Valley in California is the hottest place on Earth—it reached a world record 134°F in 1913, and temperatures weren't far off from that in the summer of 2013. To demonstrate how hot it gets, a park employee placed a skillet on the ground, let it warm up, then added an egg and a glass cover. A few minutes later, she had a fried egg. She then posted a video of the demonstration to YouTube.

Unfortunately, instead of getting the intended message of "It's really hot—stay hydrated!" some viewers got the message of "Bring eggs! This is so cool!" And many skipped the skillet. The park's Facebook page noted that the "maintenance crew has been busy cleaning up eggs cracked directly on the sidewalk, including egg cartons and shells strewn across the parking lot." They pleaded with visitors to at least use a pan and clean up afterward.

TV Goes to the Dogs

What does a dog do when its owner isn't home? Does it get bored? Does it feel lonely? On Aug. 1, 2013, DOGTV, the first-ever television channel for canine companions, debuted on DirecTV. The channel exclusively features programming for dogs. There's footage of dogs playing with Frisbees and running through woods, and shots of animals in zoos. Camera angles provide a dog's-eye view, and even the colors have been adjusted to better fit the spectrum that dogs can see.

Critics say that dogs care more about scents than other sensory input. Furthermore, dogs don't see images on older TV sets as continuous, though DOGTV claims that newer LCD screens negate that problem.

One challenge for the channel's producers is that they can't sell commercials. Currently, the programming costs $4.99-$9.99 per month depending on the provider. They're considering adding "evening shows for dog parents" to provide another revenue source.

Let Them Eat Wedding Cake

Willie and Carol Fowler of Atlanta, GA, had already arranged for a four-course reception at a very nice restaurant when their daughter Tamara's wedding was called off 40 days before the ceremony. Rather than try to get their money back, the couple called Hosea Feed the Hungry—a nonprofit organization for which Tamara had once volunteered—and said that they wanted to invite 200 homeless people to the reception. The charity thought the proposal was a prank at first. But once convinced that the offer was genuine, they called local shelters, invited guests, and arranged transportation. The reception, on Sept. 15, 2013, went off without a hitch. About 50 children enjoyed chicken fingers, fries, and fresh fruit while a clown and a juggler entertained them. The adults dined on salmon and chicken. Tamara, who attended the banquet, found it "surreal, but incredibly rewarding." The family now hopes to repeat the First Annual Fowler Family Celebration of Love and is looking into getting sponsors for next year.

HISTORICAL ANNIVERSARIES

1914 – 100 Years Ago

Ford Motor Co. raises basic wage rates from $2.40 for a nine-hour workday to $5 for eight-hour workday, Jan. 5.

U.S. sailors are arrested in Tampico, Mexico, Apr. 9; South Atlantic fleet is sent to Veracruz and occupies city Apr. 21; U.S. forces are withdrawn Nov. 23.

Canadian steamliner *Empress of Ireland* collides with Norwegian transporter *Storstad* and sinks in St. Lawrence River May 29; 1,014 killed.

Assassination of Austrian Archduke Franz Ferdinand by a Serbian nationalist, June 28, is impetus for World War I. Austria-Hungary declares war on Serbia July 28; Russia begins mobilizing in Serbia's defense. Germany declares war on Russia Aug. 1 and France Aug. 3; Germany invades Belgium, and Great Britain declares war on Germany Aug. 4. U.S. Pres. Woodrow Wilson proclaims U.S. neutrality Aug. 4.

The Panama Canal officially opens Aug. 15.

The Clayton Antitrust Act is signed into law Oct. 15, strengthening federal anti-monopoly powers.

U.S. Congress passes the Harrison Narcotics Tax Act to regulate opiates Dec. 17.

Art. David Bomberg's *The Mud Bath*; Giorgio de Chirico's *The Song of Love*; Marcel Duchamp's *Bottle Rack*; Raymond Duchamp-Villon's *The Horse*.

Film. Charlie Chaplin makes first film appearances, including in the first feature-length comedy, *Tillie's Punctured Romance*, with Marie Dressler. Cecil B. DeMille has first director's credit on *The Squaw Man*. *Gertie the Dinosaur*, *The Million Dollar Mystery*, *The Perils of Pauline*.

Health and medicine. Margaret Sanger is indicted on obscenity charges over her monthly newsletter *The Woman Rebel*, which advocates contraception.

Literature. Edgar Rice Burroughs's *Tarzan of the Apes*; James Joyce's *Dubliners*.

Music. American Society of Composers, Authors, and Publishers (ASCAP) is founded. John Alden Carpenter's *Adventures in a Perambulator*; Richard Strauss's *Josephslegende*.

Nonfiction. Arnold Bennett's *The Author's Craft*; Theodore Roosevelt's *Through the Brazilian Wilderness*.

Pop music. W. C. Handy's "St. Louis Blues"; "Keep the Home Fires Burning," by Ivor Novello and Lena Guilbert Ford.

Science and technology. New war technologies are introduced, including Germany's "Big Bertha" howitzers (capable of firing one-ton projectiles) and air bombing raids.

Sports. First U.S. championships in international style of figure skating are held in New Haven, CT. Future Hall-of-Famer Babe Ruth plays his first major league baseball game with the Boston Red Sox.

Theater. Irving Berlin's first show, *Watch Your Step*, debuts on Broadway starring Irene and Vernon Castle. First Broadway production of George Bernard Shaw's *Pygmalion*.

Miscellaneous. Congress passes resolution establishing Mother's Day. Mary Phelps Jacob patents the modern brassiere.

1964 – 50 Years Ago

Panama suspends relations with U.S. after Jan. 9 riots over the sovereignty of the Panama Canal Zone.

The 24th Amendment, which outlaws poll taxes as a prerequisite for voting, is ratified Jan. 23.

U.S. Supreme Court rules Feb. 17 in *Wesberry v. Sanders* that congressional districts "as nearly as is practicable" be equal in population.

Teamsters Union pres. James R. Hoffa is convicted Mar. 4 of jury tampering and Aug. 17 of fraud, receiving consecutive eight- and five-year sentences.

Good Friday earthquake off the Alaskan coast Mar. 27 causes tsunami that hits British Columbia, Canada, and the U.S. Pacific Coast, killing 131.

The Palestine Liberation Organization (PLO) is formed in the Jordan-held section of Jerusalem May 28.

South African anti-apartheid leader Nelson Mandela is sentenced to life imprisonment June 12.

Pres. Lyndon Johnson signs omnibus civil rights act July 2, which bans discrimination in voting, jobs, and public accommodations.

FBI investigation in Mississippi Aug. 4 uncovers the bodies of three civil-rights workers missing since June.

Congress Aug. 7 passes Tonkin Gulf Resolution, authorizing increased military involvement in Vietnam, after North Vietnamese gunboats reportedly attacked two U.S. destroyers Aug. 2-4.

Congress approves Economic Opportunity Act Aug. 11, providing for a domestic peace corps (VISTA), job corps, work training, and other antipoverty funding.

The Warren Commission Sept. 27 makes public its report on the Kennedy assassination, concluding that Lee Harvey Oswald acted alone.

China detonates its first nuclear device Oct. 16.

Pres. Johnson is elected to full term as president Nov. 3, defeating Sen. Barry Goldwater (R, AZ) in landslide.

Art. Jasper Johns's *Watchman*; Claes Oldenburg's *Giant Soft Toothpaste*; Gerhard Richter's *Christa and Wolfi*; George Segal's *Woman Standing in a Bathtub*; Andy Warhol's *Empire*.

Film. Stanley Kubrick's *Dr. Strangelove*; Sergio Leone's *A Fistful of Dollars* starring Clint Eastwood; *Goldfinger* starring Sean Connery; The Beatles in *A Hard Day's Night*; Alfred Hitchcock's *Marnie*; *Mary Poppins* starring Julie Andrews and Dick Van Dyke; *My Fair Lady* starring Audrey Hepburn and Rex Harrison; *Nothing But a Man*; *The Pink Panther* starring Peter Sellers; *Point of Order*; Michelangelo Antonioni's *Red Desert*.

Health and medicine. A U.S. Surgeon General report finds use of cigarettes "contributes substantially to mortality"; FTC rules that cigarette packages must carry warning labels beginning in 1965.

Literature. U.S. Supreme Court rules Henry Miller's *Tropic of Cancer* is not obscene and can be legally circulated. Saul Bellow's *Herzog*; John Berryman's *77 Dream Songs*; William Golding's *The Spire*; Ernest Hemingway's *A Moveable Feast*; Frank O'Hara's *Lunch Poems*; Shel Silverstein's *The Giving Tree*.

Music. Karlheinz Stockhausen's *Mixtur* uses live electronic sounds in an orchestral composition; Dmitri Shostakovich's *String Quartet No. 9* and *10*.

Nonfiction. John-Paul Sartre declines Nobel Prize. Eric Berne's *Games People Play*; Martin Luther King Jr.'s *Why We Can't Wait*; Herbert Marcuse's *One-Dimensional Man*; Marshall McLuhan's *Understanding Media*.

Pop music. The British Invasion begins: The Beatles hold the top five songs in Billboard's Hot 100 Apr. 4 ("Can't Buy Me Love," "Twist and Shout," "She Loves You," "I Want to Hold Your Hand," "Please Please Me") and the Rolling Stones release their eponymous first album. The Animals' "House of the Rising Sun"; Roy Orbison's "Oh, Pretty Woman"; The Supremes' "Where Did Our Love Go" and "Baby Love."

Science and technology. NASA's *Ranger 7* probe in July sends back the first close-up photographs of Moon's surface; Verrazano-Narrows Bridge opens in New York City, Nov. 21, with world's then-longest suspension span.

Sports. Cassius Clay defeats Sonny Liston in heavyweight title fight, then announces his conversion to Islam and changes name to Muhammad Ali. Winter Olympic Games are held in Innsbruck, Austria; Summer Games held in Tokyo, Japan.

Television. The Beatles appear Feb. 9 on *The Ed Sullivan Show* to record ratings. *The Beverly Hillbillies* and *Bonanza* are top-rated shows; *The Dick Van Dyke Show* and *The Defenders* win Emmy awards; *The Addams Family*, *Bewitched*, and *Peyton Place* premiere.

Theater. *Fiddler on the Roof* begins its record-setting, 8-year run on Broadway; also debuting: *Hello, Dolly!* starring Carol Channing and Charles Nelson Reilly, *Funny Girl* starring Barbra Streisand, Frank D. Gilroy's *The Subject Was Roses*, and Arthur Miller's *After the Fall*.

Miscellaneous. Martin Luther King Jr. wins the Nobel Peace Prize. The murder of Kitty Genovese in New York City—and exaggerated accounts of witnesses' lack of assistance—becomes a symbol of the perceived callousness of urban residents.

1989 – 25 Years Ago

Soviet military withdrawal from Afghanistan is completed Feb. 15, but fighting between Afghan rebels and government forces ensues.

The *Exxon Valdez* oil tanker strikes Bligh Reef in Alaska's Prince William Sound, Mar. 24, spilling at least 11 mil gallons of crude oil and causing massive ecological damages.

Soviet Union takes steps towards reform: first nationwide competitive election since 1917 to fill the new Congress of People's Deputies, Mar. 26; Soviet leadership does not interfere as communist governments are edged out across Eastern Europe.

Student-led protests begin Apr. 15 in Tiananmen Square, Beijing, China. By mid-May, over a million in Beijing demand democratic reforms, and protests spread to other Chinese cities. China imposes martial law in Beijing, May 20; army troops with tanks crush the demonstration June 3-4, killing hundreds and injuring thousands.

U.S. House Speaker Jim Wright (D, TX) resigns effective June 30 amid charges of ethics violations.

Myanmar (Burma) opposition leader Aung San Suu Kyi is placed under house arrest for first time July 20.

A measure to rescue the savings and loan industry is signed into law Aug. 9 by U.S. Pres. George H. W. Bush.

F. W. de Klerk is elected president of South Africa Sept. 14, promising "evolutionary" change to apartheid policies.

Hurricane Hugo sweeps through Caribbean islands Sept. 16-19 and the Carolinas Sept. 22, killing dozens.

An earthquake strikes the San Francisco Bay area in Northern California Oct. 17, causing 63 deaths.

After standing for nearly 30 years as a symbol of Cold War division, the Berlin Wall opens Nov. 9 and is partially dismantled by crowds of celebrating Germans.

Pres. Bush and Soviet Pres. Mikhail S. Gorbachev meet in shipboard summit; Gorbachev declares Cold War effectively over in closing statements Dec. 3.

U.S. troops invade Panama Dec. 20, overthrowing the government of former CIA operative Gen. Manuel Noriega, who had been indicted on U.S. drug charges.

Charged with genocide and abuse of power in a secret military trial, Romanian Pres. Nicolae Ceausescu is executed by a firing squad Dec. 25.

Art. Paris's landmark Louvre Museum opens new entrance, a glass-and-metal pyramid designed by I. M. Pei. Debate in Congress over public arts funding and censorship is sparked by Andres Serrano's *Piss Christ*; the Corcoran Gallery in Washington, DC, cancels Robert Mapplethorpe's solo show *The Perfect Moment*.

Film. *The Little Mermaid* launches the Disney Renaissance. Tim Burton's *Batman* starring Michael Keaton and Jack Nicholson; Oliver Stone's *Born on the Fourth of July*; *Dead Poets Society*; Spike Lee's *Do the Right Thing*; *Driving Miss Daisy* starring Morgan Freeman and Jessica Tandy; *Field of Dreams*; *Glory*; *Honey, I Shrunk the Kids*; *Indiana Jones and the Last Crusade*; *Lethal Weapon 2*; *Look Who's Talking*; *My Left Foot* starring Daniel Day-Lewis; *Parenthood*; Steven Soderbergh's *Sex, Lies, and Videotape*; *Steel Magnolias*; *When Harry Met Sally...*

Health and medicine. Univ. of Chicago Medical Center performs the first successful liver transplant from a living donor.

Literature. Iran's spiritual leader Ayatollah Ruhollah Khomeini issues a fatwa calling for the death of Salman Rushdie over his novel *The Satanic Verses*, published the previous year. Tom Clancy's *Clear and Present Danger*; Katherine Dunn's *Geek Love*; John Grisham's *A Time to Kill*; John Irving's *A Prayer for Owen Meany*; Kazuo Ishiguro's *The Remains of the Day*; Lois Lowry's *Number the Stars*; Amy Tan's *The Joy Luck Club*.

Music. John Tavener's *The Protecting Veil*.

Nonfiction. The New Revised Standard Version of the Christian Bible is released. The *Oxford English Dictionary* publishes its second edition, in 20 volumes. Stephen R. Covey's *The Seven Habits of Highly Effective People*.

Pop music. Paula Abdul's "Forever Your Girl" and "Cold Hearted"; The B-52's "Love Shack"; The Bangles' "Eternal Flame"; the Beastie Boys' *Paul's Boutique*; Garth Brooks's eponymous debut album; Bobby Brown's "My Prerogative," Phil Collins's "Another Day in Paradise"; Debbie Gibson's *Electric Youth*; Janet Jackson's *Rhythm Nation 1814*; Madonna's *Like a Prayer*; Bette Midler's "Wind Beneath My Wings"; Milli Vanilli's "Blame It on the Rain"; New Kids on the Block's "Hangin' Tough"; NWA's *Straight Outta Compton*; Tom Petty's *Full Moon Fever*; the Pixies' *Doolittle*; Bonnie Raitt's *Nick of Time*; Roxette's "The Look."

Science and technology. Stanley Pons and Martin Fleischmann announce they have achieved nuclear fusion at room temperature, but other scientists cannot reproduce the experiments. World Wide Web is conceptualized by Tim Berners-Lee.

Sports. The Detroit Pistons win franchise's first NBA championship. Baseball legend Pete Rose is banned from game for life Aug. 24 for involvement with gambling. The Oakland Athletics sweep the San Francisco Giants in Bay Area World Series; earthquake just before Game 3 causes 10-day delay.

Television. First episodes of *Saved by the Bell*, *The Simpsons*, and *Seinfeld*. *Cheers* and *L.A. Law* win Emmy Awards. *The Cosby Show* and *Roseanne* are highest-rated shows.

Theater. *The Heidi Chronicles* and *Jerome Robbins' Broadway* win Tony Awards. *City of Angels*, *Grand Hotel*, *Lend Me a Tenor*, and *Metamorphosis* starring Mikhail Baryshnikov debut on Broadway.

Miscellaneous. Sega Genesis and Game Boy video game devices are released in North America.

WORLD ALMANAC EDITORS' PICKS
2013 Time Capsule

The editors of *The World Almanac* have selected the following items as representative of the year 2013.

- Oprah Winfrey's Jan. 2013 interview with cyclist Lance Armstrong, in which he publicly admitted to doping for the first time, along with the July-Aug. suspension orders of 14 MLB players—including Ryan Braun and Alex Rodriguez—for allegedly using performance-enhancing drugs.

- A shard from the Chelyabinsk meteoroid that streaked across the Russian sky Feb. 15.

- Pope Benedict's fisherman's ring, the signet ring he used as pope to seal and authenticate documents, which was scored deeply so it could not be used following his Feb. 28 resignation.

- Sneakers and finishers' medals left as a makeshift memorial near the Boston Marathon finish line following the Apr. 15 bombings.

- Edward Snowden's hard drives, containing the top-secret NSA files that he leaked to reporters beginning in June.

- The federal tax-refund check for $363,053 plus interest expected by Edith Windsor, widow of a same-sex marriage, whose estate-tax challenge was ruled on by the U.S. Supreme Court June 26 in a landmark decision that struck down part of the Defense of Marriage Act.

- A selection of royal tchotchkes related to the July 22 birth of Prince George, the third-in-line heir to the British throne.

- Miley Cyrus's costume and props for her controversial VMA performance with Robin Thicke Aug. 25.

- A copy of the $765-mil settlement agreed to Aug. 29 by the NFL and former NFL players and family members, who had sued the league over its concealment of the health risks of head injuries.

- Syria's chemical-weapon stockpile, which Pres. Bashar al-Assad agreed in Sept. to turn over to international inspectors.

- *Grand Theft Auto V*, the video game that shattered sales records after its Sept. 17 release, with more than $1 bil in sales in only three days.

- Signs announcing the closure of Washington, DC, landmarks and monuments due to the partial government shutdown that began Oct. 1.

- The Walter White obituary that *Breaking Bad* fans published Oct. 4 in the *Albuquerque Journal* after the show's finale aired Sept. 29.

ECONOMICS

Index of Leading Economic Indicators
Source: The Conference Board

The Conference Board's index of leading economic indicators is used to project the U.S. economy's performance. The index is made up of 10 measurements of economic activity that tend to change direction in advance of the overall economy. The index has predicted economic downturns from 8 to 20 months in advance and recoveries from 1 to 10 months in advance. It can be inconsistent, however, and has occasionally shown false signals of recessions. In 2012, the Conference Board made significant changes to the composition of the Leading Economic Index for the first time since 1996. As a result, data from 2012 forward are not directly comparable with those from prior years. The components are listed below.

- Average weekly hours of production workers in manufacturing
- Institute for Supply Management index of new orders in manufacturing
- Consumer expectations for business conditions (surveys by The Conference Board and Reuters/Univ. of Michigan)
- Interest rate spread (10-yr Treasury bonds less federal funds)
- Building permits for new private housing units
- Manufacturers' new orders for consumer goods and materials, adjusted for inflation
- Leading Credit Index, a proprietary Conference Board measure of credit conditions
- Stock prices, 500 common stocks
- Manufacturers' new orders for nondefense capital goods, excluding aircraft, adjusted for inflation
- Average weekly initial claims for unemployment insurance

U.S. Gross Domestic Product, Gross National Product, Net National Product, National Income, and Personal Income, 1970-2012
Source: Bureau of Economic Analysis, U.S. Dept. of Commerce
(in billions of current dollars, revised)

	1970	1980	1990	2000	2005	2010	2011	2012
Gross domestic product	$1,075.9	$2,862.5	$5,979.6	$10,289.7	$13,095.4	$14,958.3	$15,533.8	$16,244.6
Gross national product	1,082.3	2,896.7	6,014.3	10,326.8	13,189.0	15,164.2	15,794.6	16,497.4
Less: Consumption of fixed capital...	136.8	426.0	886.8	1,514.2	1,982.0	2,381.6	2,452.6	2,542.9
Equals: Net national product.	945.5	2,470.7	5,127.4	8,812.5	11,207.0	12,782.6	13,342.0	13,954.6
Less: Statistical discrepancy	5.3	43.9	91.3	−94.5	−33.8	43.1	−53.7	−17.0
Equals: National income	940.1	2,426.8	5,036.1	8,907.0	11,240.8	12,739.5	13,395.7	13,971.6
Less: Corporate profits with inventory valuation and capital consumption adjustments	86.2	223.6	417.2	781.2	1,477.7	1,740.6	1,877.7	2,009.5
Taxes on production and imports less subsidies[1]	86.6	190.5	398.0	662.7	873.6	1,001.2	1,037.2	1,065.6
Contributions for government social insurance	46.4	166.2	410.1	705.8	873.3	984.1	918.2	950.7
Net interest and miscellaneous payments on assets	40.5	186.2	450.1	565.0	496.8	489.4	456.9	439.6
Business current transfer payments (net)	4.4	14.0	39.2	85.3	93.9	128.5	129.6	106.9
Current surplus of government enterprises	−1.2	−5.1	3.2	10.7	−6.4	−22.9	−23.8	−27.7
Plus: Personal income receipts on assets	112.7	386.0	991.2	1,453.5	1,666.5	1,739.6	1,884.6	1,958.5
Personal current transfer receipts	74.7	279.5	594.9	1,083.0	1,512.0	2,276.9	2,306.9	2,358.3
Equals: Personal income.	864.6	2,316.8	4,904.5	8,632.8	10,610.3	12,435.2	13,191.3	13,743.8
Addenda:								
Gross domestic income	1,070.5	2,818.6	5,888.2	10,384.3	13,129.2	14,915.2	15,587.5	16,261.6
Gross national income	1,076.9	2,852.8	5,922.9	10,421.3	13,222.7	15,121.1	15,848.3	16,514.5

Note: Numbers may not add up to totals due to rounding. (1) Subsidies are included net of the current surplus of government enterprises.

U.S. Gross Domestic Product, 2000-12
Source: Bureau of Economic Analysis, U.S. Dept. of Commerce

	Billions of current dollars				Billions of constant (2009) dollars			
	2000	2005	2011	2012	2000	2005	2011	2012
Gross domestic product	$10,289.7	$13,095.4	$15,533.8	$16,244.6	$12,565.2	$14,235.6	$15,052.4	$15,470.7
Personal consumption expenditures	6,801.6	8,790.3	10,711.8	11,149.6	8,182.1	9,527.8	10,291.3	10,517.6
Goods	2,452.9	3,080.3	3,602.7	3,769.7	2,588.3	3,177.2	3,419.9	3,534.1
Durable goods	912.6	1,127.2	1,129.9	1,202.7	758.3	1,046.9	1,157.1	1,246.7
Nondurable goods	1,540.3	1,953.1	2,472.8	2,567.0	1,863.6	2,132.3	2,266.0	2,296.8
Services	4,348.8	5,710.1	7,109.1	7,379.9	5,611.6	6,349.4	6,871.1	6,982.7
Gross private domestic investment	2,033.8	2,527.1	2,232.1	2,475.2	2,375.5	2,672.6	2,224.6	2,436.0
Fixed investment	1,979.2	2,467.5	2,195.6	2,409.1	2,316.2	2,611.0	2,184.6	2,365.3
Nonresidential	1,493.8	1,611.5	1,809.9	1,970.0	1,647.7	1,717.4	1,800.5	1,931.8
Structures	318.1	345.6	380.6	437.3	533.5	421.2	374.1	421.6
Equipment	766.1	790.7	832.7	907.6	726.9	801.6	841.7	905.9
Intellectual property products	409.5	475.1	596.6	625.0	426.1	495.0	586.1	605.8
Residential	485.4	856.1	385.8	439.2	637.9	872.6	384.3	433.7
Change in inventories	54.5	59.6	36.4	66.1	66.2	64.3	33.6	57.6
Net exports of goods and services	−380.1	−715.7	−568.7	−547.2	−482.7	−777.1	−445.9	−430.8
Exports	1,094.3	1,310.4	2,101.2	2,195.9	1,272.4	1,388.4	1,890.5	1,957.4
Goods	797.1	925.3	1,473.6	1,536.0	902.0	969.2	1,303.9	1,353.2
Services	297.2	385.1	627.6	659.9	368.2	418.4	586.3	603.7
Imports	1,474.4	2,026.1	2,669.9	2,743.1	1,755.1	2,165.5	2,336.4	2,388.2
Goods	1,250.4	1,716.2	2,234.6	2,295.4	1,454.4	1,814.7	1,923.4	1,964.3
Services	224.0	309.9	435.3	447.7	297.2	346.1	411.8	422.8
Government consumption expenditures and gross investment	1,834.4	2,493.7	3,158.7	3,167.0	2,498.2	2,826.2	2,992.3	2,963.1
Federal	632.4	946.3	1,304.1	1,295.7	817.7	1,034.8	1,237.9	1,220.3
National defense	391.7	608.3	835.8	817.1	512.3	665.5	794.6	769.1
Nondefense	240.7	338.1	468.2	478.6	305.4	369.4	443.3	451.2
State and local	1,202.0	1,547.4	1,854.7	1,871.3	1,689.1	1,792.3	1,754.5	1,742.8

U.S. Gross Domestic Product, 1930-2012

Source: Bureau of Economic Analysis, U.S. Dept. of Commerce
(in billions of current dollars)

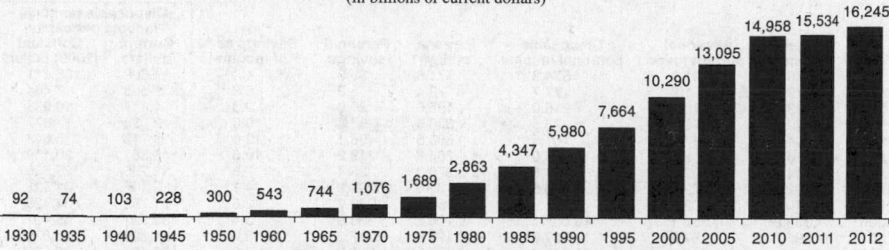

U.S. National Income by Type, 1930-2012

Source: Bureau of Economic Analysis, U.S. Dept. of Commerce
(in billions of current dollars)

	1930	1940	1950	1970	1980	1990	2000	2010	2011	2012
NATIONAL INCOME[1]	$83.1	$91.6	$267.0	$940.1	$2,426.8	$5,036.1	$8,907.0	$12,739.5	$13,395.7	$13,971.6
Employee compensation	47.2	52.8	158.5	625.1	1,626.2	3,342.7	5,856.6	7,967.3	8,278.5	8,611.6
Wages and salaries	46.2	49.9	147.3	551.6	1,373.4	2,741.2	4,825.9	6,377.5	6,638.7	6,926.8
Government	5.2	8.5	22.6	117.2	261.5	519.0	779.8	1,191.1	1,194.4	1,197.3
Other	41.0	41.4	124.6	434.3	1,112.0	2,222.2	4,046.1	5,186.4	5,444.3	5,729.4
Supplements to wages and salaries	1.0	2.9	11.2	73.6	252.8	601.5	1,030.7	1,589.8	1,639.8	1,684.9
Employer contributions for employee pension and insurance funds	1.0	1.6	7.8	49.7	163.9	395.0	685.5	1,120.4	1,145.4	1,170.6
Employer contributions for government social insurance	0.0	1.4	3.4	23.8	88.9	206.5	345.2	469.4	494.4	514.3
Proprietors' income with inventory valuation and capital consumption adjustments	10.9	12.2	37.5	77.8	171.6	354.4	757.8	1,032.7	1,155.1	1,224.9
Farm	3.9	4.1	12.9	12.9	11.7	32.2	31.5	46.0	72.6	75.4
Nonfarm	7.0	8.2	24.6	64.9	159.9	322.3	726.3	986.7	1,082.6	1,149.6
Rental income of persons with capital consumption adjustments	5.4	3.8	8.8	20.7	19.7	31.4	187.7	402.8	484.4	541.2
Corporate profits with inventory valuation and capital consumption adjustments	7.5	9.9	36.1	86.2	223.6	417.2	781.2	1,740.6	1,877.7	2,009.5
Taxes on corporate income	0.8	2.8	17.9	34.8	87.2	145.4	265.1	370.6	374.2	434.8
Profits after tax with inventory valuation and capital consumption adjustments	6.7	7.0	18.1	51.5	136.4	271.7	516.1	1,370.0	1,503.5	1,574.7
Net dividends	5.5	4.0	8.8	24.3	64.1	169.1	384.7	563.9	701.6	770.3
Undistributed profits with inventory valuation and capital consumption adjustments	1.2	3.0	9.3	27.2	72.3	102.7	131.4	806.0	801.9	804.3
Net interest and miscellaneous payments	4.8	3.3	3.2	40.5	186.2	450.1	565.0	489.4	456.9	439.6

Note: Numbers may not add up to totals because of rounding and incomplete enumeration. (1) National income is the aggregate of labor and property earnings that arise in the production of goods and services. It is the sum of employee compensation, proprietors' income, rental income, adjusted corporate profits, and net interest. It measures the total factor costs of goods and services produced by the economy. Income is measured before deduction of taxes. Total national income figures include adjustments not itemized.

U.S. National Income by Industry, 2000-12

Source: Bureau of Economic Analysis, U.S. Dept. of Commerce
(in billions of current dollars)

	2000	2005	2008	2009	2010	2011	2012
National income without capital consumption adjustment	$8,817.5	$11,339.8	$12,368.5	$12,088.3	$12,662.6	$13,130.0	$14,016.0
Domestic industries	8,780.5	11,246.3	12,195.5	11,941.1	12,456.7	12,869.2	13,763.2
Private industries	7,729.4	9,865.5	10,619.6	10,318.1	10,776.9	11,182.4	12,070.5
Agriculture, forestry, fishing, and hunting	73.8	94.0	114.6	104.4	120.9	150.1	159.4
Mining	90.7	175.0	260.1	149.2	185.3	233.0	254.5
Utilities	137.3	162.1	181.0	177.0	190.8	171.8	202.0
Construction	470.7	648.9	623.7	545.7	521.0	541.1	586.9
Manufacturing	1,243.1	1,326.7	1,385.6	1,216.5	1,356.9	1,412.0	1,561.5
Durable goods	758.2	753.2	770.3	651.3	757.1	785.7	879.7
Nondurable goods	485.0	573.5	615.3	565.2	599.8	626.3	681.8
Wholesale trade	570.6	685.2	756.2	704.6	737.9	772.0	852.8
Retail trade	666.7	857.0	840.5	840.0	872.2	898.6	959.0
Transportation and warehousing	268.5	333.4	361.7	342.3	369.0	380.6	423.7
Information	306.8	423.0	455.5	436.7	443.3	442.8	487.2
Finance, insurance, real estate, rental, and leasing	1,472.6	1,969.1	1,932.4	2,135.5	2,139.9	2,176.4	2,312.8
Professional and business services[1]	1,115.7	1,428.1	1,684.0	1,591.0	1,695.8	1,779.1	1,920.3
Educational services, health care, and social assistance	689.4	988.4	1,185.9	1,252.4	1,292.5	1,334.3	1,396.9
Arts, entertainment, recreation, accommodation, and food services	340.1	437.2	478.2	463.0	483.3	508.9	554.5
Other services, except government	283.3	337.4	360.1	359.8	368.0	381.8	399.0
Government	1,051.0	1,380.8	1,575.9	1,623.0	1,679.8	1,686.8	1,692.7
Rest of the world	37.0	93.5	173.0	147.2	206.0	260.8	252.8

Note: Estimates in this table are based on the 2002 North American Industry Classification System (NAICS). (1) Consists of professional, scientific, and technical services; management of companies and enterprises; and administrative and waste management services.

Distribution of U.S. Total Personal Income, 1930-2012

Source: Bureau of Economic Analysis, U.S. Dept. of Commerce
(in billions of current dollars, except for per capita figures)

Year	Personal income	Personal current taxes	Disposable personal income	Personal outlays	Personal savings	Savings as % of income[1]	Disposable personal income per capita Current dollars	Constant (2009) dollars
1930	$76.5	$1.6	$74.9	$71.6	$3.3	4.4%	$608	$6,411
1940	79.4	1.7	77.7	72.4	5.3	6.8	588	7,464
1950	233.9	18.9	215.0	195.0	20.0	9.3	1,417	10,033
1960	422.5	46.1	376.5	338.6	37.8	10.0	2,083	11,877
1970	864.6	103.1	761.5	665.5	96.1	12.6	3,713	16,643
1980	2,316.8	298.9	2,018.0	1,804.8	213.2	10.6	8,861	20,159
1990	4,904.5	592.7	4,311.8	3,976.3	335.4	7.8	17,235	25,556
2000	8,632.8	1,232.3	7,400.5	7,102.6	297.9	4.0	26,206	31,525
2005	10,610.3	1,208.5	9,401.8	9,159.1	242.7	2.6	31,763	34,428
2006	11,389.8	1,352.1	10,037.7	9,700.8	336.9	3.4	33,591	35,461
2007	11,995.7	1,487.9	10,507.9	10,190.6	317.2	3.0	34,829	35,870
2008	12,430.6	1,435.2	10,995.4	10,444.0	551.3	5.0	36,104	36,082
2009	12,082.1	1,144.9	10,937.2	10,266.5	670.7	6.1	35,598	35,598
2010	12,435.2	1,191.5	11,243.7	10,609.5	634.2	5.6	36,296	35,706
2011	13,191.3	1,404.0	11,787.4	11,119.1	668.2	5.7	37,776	36,293
2012	13,743.8	1,498.0	12,245.8	11,558.4	687.4	5.6	38,965	36,756

Note: Personal income minus current taxes equals disposable income; disposable income minus outlays equals savings. Figures may not add up to totals because of rounding. (1) Personal savings as a percentage of disposable personal income.

Consumer Price Index

The Consumer Price Index (CPI) is a measure of the change in prices over time of one or more kinds of basic consumer goods and services. Beginning in Jan. 1978, the Bureau of Labor Statistics began publishing CPIs for two population groups: (1) all urban consumers (CPI-U, which covers about 87% of the total U.S. population); and (2) urban wage earners and clerical workers (CPI-W, which covers about 32% of the U.S. population). The CPI-U also includes professional, managerial, and technical workers; the self-employed; short-term workers; the unemployed; retirees; and others not in the labor force.

The CPI is based on the price of food, clothing, shelter, and fuels; transportation fares; charges for doctors' and dentists' services; drug prices; and the cost of other goods and services bought for day-to-day living. The index currently measures price changes from a designated reference period, 1982-84, which equals 100.0. Use of this reference period began in Jan. 1988.

U.S. Consumer Price Index by Major Group, 1915-2012

Source: Bureau of Labor Statistics, U.S. Dept. of Labor
For all urban consumers. 1982-84 = 100, unless otherwise noted.

Year	All items	Apparel	Food & beverages	Housing	Transportation	Medical care	Entertainment & recreation[1]	Educ. & communication[1]	Other goods & services
1915	10.1	15.3	—	—	—	—	—	—	—
1920	20.0	43.1	—	—	—	—	—	—	—
1930	16.7	24.2	—	—	—	—	—	—	—
1940	14.0	21.8	—	—	14.2	10.4	—	—	—
1945	18.0	31.4	—	—	15.9	11.9	—	—	—
1950	24.1	40.3	—	—	22.7	15.1	—	—	—
1955	26.8	42.9	—	—	25.8	18.2	—	—	—
1960	29.6	45.7	—	—	29.8	22.3	—	—	—
1965	31.5	47.8	—	—	31.9	25.2	—	—	—
1970	38.8	59.2	40.1	36.4	37.5	34.0	—	—	40.9
1975	53.8	72.5	60.2	50.7	50.1	47.5	—	—	53.9
1980	82.4	90.9	86.7	81.1	83.1	74.9	—	—	75.2
1985	107.6	105.0	105.6	107.7	106.4	113.5	—	—	114.5
1990	130.7	124.1	132.1	128.5	120.5	162.8	—	—	159.0
1995	152.4	132.0	148.9	148.5	139.1	220.5	94.5	92.2	206.9
2000	172.2	129.6	168.4	169.6	153.3	260.8	103.3	102.5	271.1
2005	195.3	119.5	191.2	195.7	173.9	323.2	109.4	113.7	313.4
2008	215.3	118.9	214.2	216.2	195.5	364.1	113.3	123.6	345.4
2009	214.5	120.0	218.2	217.1	179.3	375.6	114.3	127.4	368.6
2010	218.1	119.5	220.0	216.3	193.4	388.4	113.3	129.9	381.3
2011	224.9	122.1	227.9	219.1	212.4	400.3	113.4	131.5	387.2
2012	229.6	126.3	233.7	222.7	217.3	414.9	114.7	133.8	394.4

— = Comparable data not available. (1) Dec. 1997 = 100. Entertainment was reclassified as Recreation in 1997. Data is not seasonally adjusted.

U.S. Consumer Price Index, 1915-2012

Source: Bureau of Labor Statistics, U.S. Dept. of Labor

Excluding 2009, prices as measured by the U.S. Consumer Price Index have risen steadily since World War II. What cost $1.00 in 1982-84 cost about $0.10 in 1913, $0.18 in 1945, and nearly $2.30 in 2012.

(Annual averages of monthly figures, for all urban consumers. 1982-84 = 100.)

U.S. Consumer Price Indexes for Selected Items and Groups, 1970-2012

Source: Bureau of Labor Statistics, U.S. Dept. of Labor

Annual averages of monthly figures, for all urban consumers. 1982-84 = 100, unless otherwise noted.

	1970	1975	1980	1985	1990	1995	2000	2005	2010	2011	2012
ALL ITEMS	38.8	53.8	82.4	107.6	130.7	152.4	172.2	195.3	218.1	224.9	229.6
Food and beverages	40.1	60.2	86.7	105.6	132.1	148.9	168.4	191.2	220.0	227.9	233.7
Food	39.2	59.8	86.8	105.6	132.4	148.4	167.8	190.7	219.6	227.8	233.8
Food at home	39.9	61.8	88.4	104.3	132.3	148.8	167.9	189.8	215.8	226.2	231.8
Cereals and bakery products	37.1	62.9	83.9	107.9	140.0	167.5	188.3	209.0	250.4	260.3	267.7
Meats, poultry, fish, eggs	44.6	67.0	92.0	100.1	130.0	138.8	154.5	184.7	207.7	223.2	231.0
Dairy products	44.7	62.6	90.9	103.2	126.5	132.8	160.7	182.4	199.2	212.7	217.3
Fruits and vegetables	37.8	56.9	82.1	108.4	149.0	177.7	204.6	241.4	273.5	284.7	282.8
Nonalcoholic beverages	27.1	41.3	91.4	104.3	113.5	131.7	137.8	144.4	161.6	166.8	168.6
Sugar and sweets	30.5	65.3	90.5	105.8	124.7	137.5	154.0	165.2	201.2	207.8	214.7
Fats and oils	39.2	73.5	89.3	108.9	126.3	137.3	147.4	167.7	200.6	219.2	232.6
Other foods	39.6	58.9	83.6	106.4	131.2	151.1	172.2	182.5	204.6	209.3	216.6
Food away from home	37.5	54.5	83.4	108.3	133.4	149.0	169.0	193.4	226.1	231.4	238.0
Alcoholic beverages	52.1	65.9	86.4	106.4	129.3	153.9	174.7	195.9	223.3	226.7	230.8
Housing	36.4	50.7	81.1	107.7	128.5	148.5	169.6	195.7	216.3	219.1	222.7
Shelter	35.5	48.8	81.0	109.8	140.0	165.7	193.4	224.4	248.4	251.6	257.1
Rent of primary residence	46.5	58.0	80.9	111.8	138.4	157.8	183.9	217.3	249.4	253.6	260.4
Fuels and utilities	29.1	45.4	75.4	106.5	111.6	123.7	137.9	179.0	214.2	220.4	219.0
Household furnishings and operations	46.8	63.4	86.3	103.8	113.3	123.0	128.2	126.1	125.5	124.9	125.7
Apparel	59.2	72.5	90.9	105.0	124.1	132.0	129.6	119.5	119.5	122.1	126.3
Men's and boys'	62.2	75.5	89.4	105.0	120.4	126.2	129.7	116.1	111.9	114.7	119.5
Women's and girls'	71.8	85.5	96.0	104.9	122.6	126.9	121.5	110.8	107.1	109.2	113.0
Footwear	56.8	69.6	91.8	102.3	117.4	125.4	123.8	122.6	128.0	128.5	131.8
Transportation	37.5	50.1	83.1	106.4	120.5	139.1	153.3	173.9	193.4	212.4	217.3
Private transportation	37.5	50.6	84.2	106.2	118.8	136.3	149.1	170.2	188.7	207.6	212.8
New vehicles	53.1	63.0	88.5	106.1	121.4	141.0	142.8	137.9	138.0	141.9	144.2
Used cars and trucks	31.2	43.8	62.3	113.7	117.6	156.5	155.8	139.4	143.1	149.0	150.3
Gasoline	27.9	45.1	97.5	98.6	101.0	99.8	128.6	194.7	238.6	301.7	311.5
Public transportation	35.2	43.5	69.0	110.5	142.6	175.9	209.6	217.3	251.4	269.4	271.4
Medical care	34.0	47.5	74.9	113.5	162.8	220.5	260.8	323.2	388.4	400.3	414.9
Recreation[1]	NA	NA	NA	NA	NA	94.5	103.3	109.4	113.3	113.4	114.7
Other goods and services	40.9	53.9	75.2	114.5	159.0	206.9	271.1	313.4	381.3	387.2	394.4
Tobacco products	43.1	54.7	72.0	116.7	181.5	225.7	394.9	502.8	807.3	834.8	853.5
Personal care	43.5	57.9	81.9	108.3	130.4	147.1	165.6	185.6	206.6	208.6	212.1
Personal care products	42.7	58.0	79.6	107.6	128.2	143.1	153.7	154.4	161.1	160.5	162.2
Personal care services	44.2	57.7	83.7	108.9	132.8	151.5	178.1	203.9	229.6	230.8	234.2

NA = Not available. **Note:** Data is not seasonally adjusted. (1) Dec. 1997 = 100.

Consumer Price Indexes by Region and Major Cities, 1990-2012

Source: Bureau of Labor Statistics, U.S. Dept. of Labor

For all urban consumers; % change not annualized. 1982-84 = 100, unless otherwise noted.

Region and city	1990	1995	2000	2005	2008	2009	2010	2011	2012
U.S. city average	130.7	152.4	172.2	195.3	215.3	214.5	218.1	224.9	229.6
Northeast urban	136.3	159.1	179.4	207.5	229.3	229.3	233.9	241.0	245.7
Boston-Brockton-Nashua, MA-NH-ME-CT	138.9	158.6	183.6	216.4	235.4	233.8	237.4	243.9	247.7
New York-Northern New Jersey-Long Island, NY-NJ-CT-PA	138.5	162.2	182.5	212.7	235.8	236.8	240.9	247.7	252.6
Philadelphia-Wilmington-Atlantic City, PA-NJ-DE-MD	135.8	158.7	176.5	204.2	224.1	223.3	227.7	233.8	238.1
Pittsburgh, PA	126.2	149.2	168.0	189.8	211.3	212.1	215.4	225.1	232.9
Midwest urban	127.4	148.4	168.3	188.4	205.4	204.1	208.0	214.7	219.1
Chicago-Gary-Kenosha, IL-IN-WI	131.7	153.3	173.8	194.3	212.5	210.0	212.9	218.7	222.0
Cincinnati-Hamilton, OH-KY-IN	126.5	146.2	164.8	181.6	201.5	200.6	204.7	211.1	216.3
Cleveland-Akron, OH	129.0	147.9	168.0	187.9	203.0	200.5	204.6	211.0	214.7
Detroit-Ann Arbor-Flint, MI	128.6	148.6	169.8	190.8	204.7	203.5	205.1	211.8	216.1
Kansas City, MO-KS	126.0	145.3	166.6	185.3	201.2	201.0	205.4	213.5	218.5
Milwaukee-Racine, WI	126.2	151.0	168.6	185.2	203.0	203.0	209.6	216.9	221.1
Minneapolis-St. Paul, MN-WI	127.0	147.0	170.1	193.1	209.0	207.9	211.7	219.3	224.5
St. Louis, MO-IL	128.1	145.2	163.1	186.2	198.7	198.5	203.2	209.8	214.8
South urban	127.9	149.0	167.2	188.3	208.7	207.8	211.3	218.6	223.2
Atlanta, GA	131.7	150.9	170.6	188.9	206.5	201.0	203.5	209.1	212.8
Dallas-Fort Worth, TX	125.1	144.9	164.7	184.7	201.8	200.5	201.6	207.9	212.2
Houston-Galveston-Brazoria, TX	120.6	139.8	154.2	175.6	190.0	190.5	194.2	200.5	204.2
Miami-Fort Lauderdale, FL	128.0	148.9	167.8	194.3	222.1	221.4	223.1	230.9	235.2
Tampa-St. Petersburg-Clearwater, FL[1]	111.7	129.7	145.7	168.5	190.1	189.9	193.5	198.9	203.6
Washington-Baltimore, DC-MD-VA-WV[2]	NA	NA	107.6	124.3	139.5	139.8	142.2	147.0	150.2
West urban	131.5	153.5	174.8	198.9	219.6	218.8	221.2	227.5	232.4
Anchorage, AK	118.6	138.9	150.9	171.8	189.5	191.7	195.1	201.4	205.9
Denver-Boulder-Greeley, CO	120.9	147.9	173.2	190.9	209.9	208.5	212.4	220.3	224.6
Honolulu, HI	138.1	168.1	176.3	197.8	228.9	230.0	234.9	243.6	249.5
Los Angeles-Riverside-Orange County, CA	135.9	154.6	171.6	201.8	225.0	223.2	225.9	231.9	236.6
Phoenix-Mesa, AZ[3]	NA	NA	NA	108.3	119.3	117.6	118.2	121.5	124.2
Portland-Salem, OR-WA	127.4	153.2	178.0	196.0	215.4	215.6	218.3	224.6	229.8
San Diego, CA	138.4	156.8	182.8	220.6	242.3	242.3	245.5	252.9	257.0
San Francisco-Oakland-San Jose, CA	132.1	151.6	180.2	202.7	222.8	224.4	227.5	233.4	239.6
Seattle-Tacoma-Bremerton, WA	126.8	152.3	179.2	200.2	224.7	226.0	226.7	232.8	238.7

NA = Not available. **Note:** Data is not seasonally adjusted. (1) 1987 = 100. (2) Nov. 1996 = 100. (3) Dec. 2001 = 100.

Median Income by Race, Hispanic Origin, and Sex, 1948-2012

Source: *Current Population Survey*, U.S. Census Bureau, U.S. Dept. of Commerce

Race, Hispanic origin, and year		Male			Female	
	Number with income (thous.)	Median income Current dollars	2012 dollars	Number with income (thous.)	Median income Current dollars	2012 dollars
All races 2012	107,534	$33,904	$33,904	109,383	$21,520	$21,520
2011	106,228	32,986	33,675	108,332	21,102	21,543
2010	105,191	32,205	33,915	107,220	20,775	21,878
2005	102,986	31,275	36,784	104,245	18,576	21,848
2000	98,504	28,343	37,791	101,704	16,063	21,417
1990	88,220	20,293	34,560	92,245	10,070	17,150
1980	78,661	12,530	33,242	80,826	4,920	13,053
1970	65,008	6,670	35,198	51,647	2,237	11,805
1960	55,172	4,080	27,682	36,526	1,261	8,556
1950	47,585	2,570	21,398	24,651	953	7,935
1948	47,370	2,396	19,949	22,725	1,009	8,401
White 2012	87,711	35,688	35,688	86,620	21,829	21,829
2011	87,083	35,344	36,082	85,993	21,379	21,826
2010	86,368	34,374	36,199	85,486	20,896	22,005
2005	85,996	32,179	37,847	84,768	18,669	21,957
2000	83,372	29,797	39,729	84,123	16,079	21,439
1990	76,480	21,170	36,053	78,566	10,317	17,570
1980	69,420	13,328	35,360	70,573	4,947	13,125
1970	58,447	7,011	36,997	45,288	2,266	11,958
1960	49,788	4,296	29,147	32,001	1,352	9,173
1950	NA	2,709	22,555	NA	1,060	8,825
1948	NA	2,510	20,898	NA	1,133	9,433
White, not Hispanic 2012	73,240	38,751	38,751	74,529	22,902	22,902
2011	72,902	38,148	38,945	74,206	22,226	22,690
2010	72,723	37,154	39,127	73,995	21,715	22,868
2005	73,219	35,345	41,571	75,014	19,451	22,877
2000	72,530	31,508	42,011	75,206	16,665	22,220
1990	69,987	21,958	37,395	72,939	10,581	18,020
1980	65,564	13,681	36,296	67,084	4,980	13,212
Black 2012	11,961	24,959	24,959	14,722	19,925	19,925
2011	11,562	23,584	24,077	14,411	19,561	19,970
2010	11,433	23,086	24,312	14,212	19,548	20,586
2005	10,651	22,609	26,591	13,237	17,595	20,694
2000	9,905	21,343	28,457	12,461	15,881	21,175
1990	8,820	12,868	21,915	10,687	8,328	14,183
1980	7,387	8,009	21,248	8,596	4,580	12,151
1970	5,844	4,157	21,936	5,844	2,063	10,886
1960	5,384	2,260	15,333	4,525	837	5,679
1950	NA	1,471	12,247	NA	474	3,946
1948	NA	1,363	11,348	NA	492	4,096
Asian 2012	5,810	39,606	39,606	5,972	23,290	23,290
2011	5,556	35,835	36,584	5,820	22,013	22,473
2010	5,406	35,121	36,986	5,604	23,552	24,802
2005	4,518	33,036	38,855	4,520	21,623	25,432
2000	4,303	30,833	41,111	4,192	17,356	23,141
1990	2,235	19,394	33,029	2,333	11,086	18,880
Hispanic 2012	16,005	24,592	24,592	13,689	16,725	16,725
2011	15,665	23,731	24,227	13,278	16,829	17,181
2010	15,106	22,420	23,610	12,947	16,292	17,157
2005	13,714	22,089	25,980	10,638	15,036	17,684
2000	11,343	19,498	25,997	9,431	12,248	16,331
1990	6,767	13,470	22,940	5,903	7,532	12,827
1980	3,996	9,659	25,626	3,617	4,405	11,687

NA = Not available. **Note:** Income for persons 15 years of age and over beginning in Mar. 1980; 14 years of age and over as of Mar. of the following year for previous years. Beginning in 2005, black and Asian numbers include those who identified themselves as being black or Asian in combination with some other race. Before 2005, Asian category includes Pacific Islanders. Hispanic persons may be of any race.

Consumer Credit Outstanding, 2010-12

Source: Federal Reserve System

(in billions of dollars as of Dec. of year shown, not seasonally adjusted)

	2010	2011	2012
TOTAL	$2,522.2	$2,615.7	$2,768.1
Major holders			
Depository institutions	1,185.5	1,192.6	1,218.6
Finance companies	705.0	688.0	680.7
Credit unions	226.5	223.0	243.6
Federal government[1]	308.8	417.4	526.8
Nonfinancial business	46.2	48.5	48.5
Pools of securitized assets[2]	50.3	46.2	49.9
Major types of credit, by holder			
Revolving	840.7	842.5	845.8
Depository institutions	664.7	663.9	676.5
Finance companies	81.5	82.9	71.4
Credit unions	36.3	37.9	38.9
Federal government[1]	—	—	—
Nonfinancial business	26.8	27.9	27.9
Pools of securitized assets[2]	31.4	29.8	31.2
Nonrevolving[3]	1,681.5	1,773.2	1,922.3
Depository institutions	520.8	528.7	542.2
Finance companies	623.5	605.0	609.3
Credit unions	190.1	185.1	204.8
Federal government[1]	308.8	417.4	526.8
Nonfinancial business	19.4	20.6	20.6
Pools of securitized assets[2]	19.0	16.4	18.7

— = Not available. (1) Includes loans originated by the Dept. of Education under the Federal Direct Loan Program, as well as Federal Family Education Loan Program loans that the government purchased from depository institutions and finance companies. (2) Outstanding balances of pools upon which securities have been issued; these balances are no longer carried on the balance sheets of the loan originators. (3) Includes estimates for holders that do not separately report consumer credit holding by type.

Financial Assets of U.S. Families, 1989-2010

Source: *Survey of Consumer Finances* (triennial), Federal Reserve System

Category	1989	1992	1995	1998	2001	2004	2007	2010
Median net worth (thous.)	$59.7	$56.5	$60.9	$71.6	$106.1	$107.2	$126.4	$77.3
Average net worth (thous.)	236.9	212.7	224.8	282.5	487.0	517.1	584.6	498.8
Financial assets				Percent of families holding asset				
Transaction accounts	19.1%	17.5%	14.0%	11.4%	11.4%	13.1%	10.9%	13.3%
Certificates of deposit...............	10.2	8.1	5.7	4.3	3.1	3.7	4.0	3.9
Savings bonds	1.5	1.1	1.3	0.7	0.7	0.5	0.4	0.3
Bonds.............................	10.2	8.4	6.3	4.3	4.5	5.3	4.1	4.4
Stocks............................	15.0	16.5	15.7	22.7	21.5	17.5	17.8	14.0
Mutual funds (excluding money market funds)	5.3	7.7	12.7	12.5	12.1	14.6	15.8	15.0
Retirement accounts.................	21.5	25.5	27.9	27.5	29.0	32.4	35.1	38.1
Cash value of life insurance	6.0	6.0	7.2	6.4	5.3	2.9	3.2	2.5
Other managed assets...............	6.6	5.4	5.9	8.6	10.5	7.9	6.5	6.2
Other.............................	4.8	3.8	3.4	1.7	1.9	2.1	2.1	2.3
Financial assets as % of total assets	30.4	31.5	36.6	40.6	42.2	35.8	34.0	37.9

Wealthiest Americans, 2011-13

Source: *Forbes* magazine
(as of Sept. 1, 2013; ranked by 2013 net worth)

The 20 wealthiest Americans saw their net worth increase by a combined $110.7 bil in 2013. The four biggest Wal-Mart heirs increased their wealth by at least $7 bil each, and Facebook founder Mark Zuckerberg doubled his net worth since 2012.

Rank	Name	Net worth (bil) 2011	2012	2013	% change, 2012-13	Age in 2013	Residence	Source of wealth
1.	Bill Gates	$59.0	$66.0	$72.0	9.1%	57	Medina, WA....	Microsoft
2.	Warren Buffett......	39.0	46.0	58.5	27.2	83	Omaha, NE.....	Berkshire Hathaway
3.	Lawrence Ellison	33.0	41.0	41.0	0.0	69	Woodside, CA ..	Oracle
4.	Charles Koch	25.0	31.0	36.0	16.1	77	Wichita, KS	Manufacturing, energy
	David Koch........	25.0	31.0	36.0	16.1	73	New York, NY ...	Manufacturing, energy
6.	Christy Walton	24.5	27.9	35.4	26.9	58	Jackson, WY	Wal-Mart
7.	Jim C. Walton	21.1	26.8	33.8	26.1	65	Bentonville, AR .	Wal-Mart
8.	Alice Walton	20.9	26.3	33.5	27.4	63	Fort Worth, TX..	Wal-Mart
9.	S. Robson Walton	20.5	26.1	33.3	27.6	69	Bentonville, AR .	Wal-Mart
10.	Michael Bloomberg .	19.5	25.0	31.0	24.0	71	New York, NY ...	Bloomberg LP
11.	Sheldon Adelson....	21.5	20.5	28.5	39.0	80	Las Vegas, NV..	Sands casinos
12.	Jeff Bezos	19.1	23.2	27.2	17.2	49	Seattle, WA	Amazon.com
13.	Larry Page	16.7	20.3	24.9	22.7	40	Palo Alto, CA ...	Google
14.	Sergey Brin........	16.7	20.3	24.4	20.2	40	Los Altos, CA...	Google
15.	Forrest Mars Jr.....	13.8	17.0	20.5	20.6	82	Big Horn, WY ...	Mars candy
	Jacqueline Mars	13.8	17.0	20.5	20.6	74	The Plains, VA..	Mars candy
	John Mars.........	13.8	17.0	20.5	20.6	77	Jackson, WY	Mars candy
18.	Carl Icahn.........	13.0	14.8	20.3	37.2	77	New York, NY ...	Investments
19.	George Soros	22.0	19.0	20.0	5.3	83	Katonah, NY	Hedge funds
20.	Mark Zuckerberg.....	17.5	9.4	19.0	102.1	29	Palo Alto, CA ...	Facebook

Poverty Rate

Source: U.S. Census Bureau, U.S. Dept. of Commerce

The poverty rate is the proportion of the population whose income falls below the government's official poverty level, which is adjusted each year for inflation. The national poverty rate held steady at 15.0% in 2012. More than 46 mil people in the U.S. were in poverty in 2012, up from 31.6 mil in 2000. More than one-third of families headed by a woman with no husband present were in poverty.

Persons Below Poverty Level, 1960-2012

Source: U.S. Census Bureau, U.S. Dept. of Commerce

Year	Number below poverty level (mil) All races[1]	Asian[2]	White	Black[2]	Hispanic[3]	% of subgroup below poverty level All races[1]	Asian[2]	White	Black[2]	Hispanic[3]	Avg. income cut-off, family of 4 at poverty level[4]
1960	39.9	NA	28.3	NA	NA	22.2%	NA	17.8%	NA	NA	$3,022
1970	25.4	NA	17.5	7.5	NA	12.6	NA	9.9	33.5%	NA	3,968
1980	29.3	NA	19.7	8.6	3.5	13.0	NA	10.2	32.5	25.7%	8,414
1990	33.6	0.9	22.3	9.8	6.0	13.5	12.2%	10.7	31.9	28.1	13,359
1995	36.4	1.4	24.4	9.9	8.6	13.8	14.6	11.2	29.3	30.3	15,569
2000	31.6	1.3	21.6	8.0	7.7	11.3	9.9	9.5	22.5	21.5	17,604
2001	32.9	1.3	22.7	8.1	8.0	11.7	10.2	9.9	22.7	21.4	18,104
2002	34.6	1.2	23.5	8.9	8.6	12.1	10.0	10.2	23.9	21.8	18,392
2003	35.9	1.4	24.3	9.1	9.1	12.5	11.8	10.5	24.3	22.5	18,810
2004	37.0	1.3	25.3	9.4	9.1	12.7	9.7	10.8	24.7	21.9	19,307
2005	37.0	1.5	24.9	9.5	9.4	12.6	10.9	10.6	24.7	21.8	19,971
2006	36.5	1.4	24.4	9.5	9.2	12.3	10.1	10.3	24.2	20.6	20,614
2007	37.3	1.5	25.1	9.7	9.9	12.5	10.2	10.5	24.4	21.5	21,203
2008	39.8	1.7	27.0	9.9	11.0	13.2	11.6	11.2	24.6	23.2	22,025
2009	43.6	1.9	29.8	10.6	12.4	14.3	12.4	12.3	25.9	25.3	21,954
2010	46.3	2.1	31.1	11.6	13.5	15.1	12.0	13.0	27.4	26.5	22,315
2011	46.2	2.2	30.8	11.7	13.2	15.0	12.3	12.8	27.5	25.3	23,021
2012	46.5	2.1	30.8	11.8	13.6	15.0	11.4	12.7	27.1	25.6	23,492

NA = Not available. **Note:** Because of a change in the definition of poverty, data prior to 1980 are not directly comparable to data since 1980. (1) Includes other races not shown separately. (2) Beginning in 2002, numbers include those who identified themselves as being Asian or black in combination with some other race. For 1990-2000, Asian includes Pacific Islanders. (3) Persons of Hispanic origin may be of any race. (4) Figures for 1960-80 for nonfarm families only.

Poverty Thresholds by Family Size, 1980-2012
Source: U.S. Census Bureau, U.S. Dept. of Commerce

	1980	1990	2000	2010	2012		1980	1990	2000	2010	2012
1 person	$4,190	$6,652	$8,791	$11,137	$11,720	3 people	$6,565	$10,419	$13,740	$17,373	$18,284
Under age 65. .	4,290	6,800	8,959	11,344	11,945	4 people	8,414	13,359	17,604	22,315	23,492
Age 65 or older . .	3,949	6,268	8,259	10,458	11,011	5 people	9,966	15,792	20,815	26,442	27,827
2 people	5,363	8,509	11,235	14,216	14,937	6 people	11,269	17,839	23,533	29,904	31,471
Householder						7 people	12,761	20,241	26,750	34,019	35,743
under age 65 . .	5,537	8,794	11,589	14,676	15,450	8 people	14,199	22,582	29,701	37,953	39,688
Householder age						9 or more people . .	16,896	26,848	35,150	45,224	47,297
65 or older.	4,983	7,905	10,418	13,194	13,892						

Note: Weighted averages; not used for computing poverty data.

Families Below Poverty Level by Status, Race, and Sex, 1990-2012
Source: U.S. Census Bureau, U.S. Dept. of Commerce
(numbers in thousands)

Year and race	All families		Below poverty level	Married-couple families		Below poverty level	Male householder, no wife present		Below poverty level	Female householder, no husband present		Below poverty level
	Total	Number	Percent	Total	Number	Percent	Total	Number	Percent	Total	Number	Percent
All races												
1990	66,322	7,098	10.7%	52,147	2,981	5.7%	2,907	349	12.0%	11,268	3,768	33.4%
1995	69,597	7,532	10.8	53,570	2,982	5.6	3,513	493	14.0	12,514	4,057	32.4
2000	73,778	6,400	8.7	56,598	2,637	4.7	4,277	485	11.3	12,903	3,278	25.4
2005	77,418	7,657	9.9	58,189	2,944	5.1	5,134	669	13.0	14,095	4,044	28.7
2010	79,559	9,400	11.8	58,667	3,681	6.3	5,649	892	15.8	15,243	4,827	31.7
2011	80,529	9,497	11.8	58,963	3,652	6.2	5,888	950	16.1	15,678	4,894	31.2
2012	80,944	9,520	11.8	59,224	3,705	6.3	6,231	1,023	16.4	15,489	4,793	30.9
White[1]												
1990	56,803	4,622	8.1	47,014	2,386	5.1	2,277	226	9.9	7,512	2,010	26.8
1995	58,872	4,994	8.5	47,877	2,443	5.1	2,711	351	12.9	8,284	2,200	26.6
2000	61,330	4,333	7.1	49,473	2,181	4.4	3,283	332	10.1	8,574	1,820	21.2
2005	63,414	5,068	8.0	50,369	2,317	4.6	3,906	439	11.2	9,139	2,312	25.3
2010	63,976	6,305	9.9	50,016	2,921	5.8	4,176	563	13.5	9,784	2,822	28.8
2011	64,625	6,334	9.8	50,061	2,863	5.7	4,348	614	14.1	10,216	2,857	28.0
2012	64,735	6,299	9.7	50,171	2,875	5.7	4,592	651	14.2	9,972	2,774	27.8
Black[1]												
1990	7,471	2,193	29.3	3,569	448	12.6	472	97	20.6	3,430	1,648	48.1
1995	8,055	2,127	26.4	3,713	314	8.5	573	112	19.5	3,769	1,701	45.1
2000	8,731	1,686	19.3	4,214	266	6.3	732	120	16.3	3,785	1,300	34.3
2005	9,051	1,997	22.1	4,128	341	8.3	806	170	21.1	4,117	1,486	36.1
2010	9,571	2,311	24.1	4,267	377	8.8	916	236	25.7	4,387	1,698	38.7
2011	9,656	2,334	24.2	4,362	408	9.4	956	234	24.4	4,338	1,693	39.0
2012	9,823	2,327	23.7	4,483	440	9.8	1,040	262	25.2	4,300	1,624	37.8

(1) Data are for one race only. The Census Bureau revised race categories in 2002, so data after 2002 are not directly comparable with data for previous years.

Poverty Rates by State, 1990-2012
Source: U.S. Census Bureau, U.S. Dept. of Commerce

State	1990	2000	2005	2010	2012	State	1990	2000	2005	2010	2012
Alabama	19.2%	13.3%	16.7%	17.2%	16.2%	Montana	16.3%	14.1%	13.8%	14.5%	13.4%
Alaska.	11.4	7.6	10.0	12.5	10.0	Nebraska	10.3	8.6	9.5	10.2	12.2
Arizona	13.7	11.7	15.2	18.8	19.0	Nevada	9.8	8.8	10.6	16.6	15.8
Arkansas.	19.6	16.5	13.8	15.3	20.1	New Hampshire . . .	6.3	4.5	5.6	6.5	8.1
California	13.9	12.7	13.2	16.3	15.9	New Jersey	9.2	7.3	6.8	11.1	9.3
Colorado.	13.7	9.8	11.4	12.3	11.9	New Mexico	20.9	17.5	17.9	18.3	20.4
Connecticut. . . .	6.0	7.7	9.3	8.6	10.3	New York	14.3	13.9	14.5	16.0	17.2
Delaware	6.9	8.4	9.2	12.2	13.5	North Carolina	13.0	12.5	13.1	17.4	17.2
Dist. of Columbia	21.1	15.2	21.3	19.5	18.4	North Dakota	13.7	10.4	11.2	12.6	11.4
Florida.	14.4	11.0	11.1	16.0	15.3	Ohio	11.5	10.0	12.3	15.4	15.4
Georgia.	15.8	12.1	14.4	18.8	18.1	Oklahoma	15.6	14.9	15.6	16.3	18.0
Hawaii.	11.0	8.9	8.6	12.4	13.8	Oregon	9.2	10.9	12.0	14.3	13.5
Idaho	14.9	12.5	9.9	13.8	14.4	Pennsylvania	11.0	8.6	11.2	12.2	13.9
Illinois	13.7	10.7	11.5	14.1	12.6	Rhode Island . . .	7.5	10.2	12.1	14.0	13.6
Indiana	13.0	8.5	12.6	16.3	15.2	South Carolina . . .	16.2	11.1	15.0	16.9	16.7
Iowa	10.4	8.3	11.3	10.3	10.3	South Dakota	13.3	10.7	11.8	13.6	12.8
Kansas	10.3	8.0	12.5	14.5	14.0	Tennessee	16.9	13.5	14.9	16.7	18.6
Kentucky	17.3	12.6	14.8	17.7	17.9	Texas	15.9	15.5	16.2	18.4	17.0
Louisiana	23.6	17.2	18.3	21.5	21.1	Utah	8.2	7.6	9.2	10.0	11.0
Maine	13.1	10.1	12.6	12.6	12.8	Vermont	10.9	10.0	7.6	10.9	11.2
Maryland	9.9	7.4	9.7	10.9	9.9	Virginia	11.1	8.3	9.2	10.7	10.6
Massachusetts . .	10.7	9.8	10.1	10.9	11.3	Washington.	8.9	10.8	10.2	11.6	11.6
Michigan	14.3	9.9	12.0	15.7	13.7	West Virginia	18.1	14.7	15.4	16.8	16.7
Minnesota	12.0	5.7	8.1	10.8	10.0	Wisconsin	9.3	9.3	10.2	10.1	11.4
Mississippi	25.7	14.9	20.1	22.5	22.0	Wyoming	11.0	10.8	10.6	9.6	9.6
Missouri	13.4	9.2	11.6	15.0	15.2	**United States . .**	13.5	11.3	12.6	15.1	15.0

Selected Personal Consumption Expenditures in the U.S., 1990-2012

Source: Bureau of Economic Analysis, U.S. Dept. of Commerce
(in billions of dollars)

	1990	1995	2000	2005	2010	2011	2012
Personal consumption expenditures	$3,825.6	$4,984.2	$6,801.6	$8,790.3	$10,201.9	$10,711.8	$11,149.6
Goods	1,491.3	1,815.5	2,452.9	3,080.1	3,362.8	3,602.7	3,769.7
Durable goods	497.1	635.7	912.6	1,127.2	1,070.7	1,129.9	1,202.7
Motor vehicles and parts	205.1	255.7	363.2	410.0	342.0	368.7	401.7
New motor vehicles	134.7	147.5	210.7	248.9	182.3	207.8	236.8
Motor vehicle parts and accessories	28.3	35.4	41.8	50.6	55.5	59.6	61.8
Furnishings and durable household equipment	120.9	146.7	208.1	271.3	250.4	260.1	275.1
Furniture and furnishings	69.2	83.4	121.7	160.6	148.4	153.7	164.1
Household appliances	23.7	26.6	34.1	45.1	41.7	42.9	43.9
Recreational goods and vehicles	105.6	153.7	230.9	305	312.7	321.1	334.5
Video, audio, photographic, and information processing equipment and media	56.1	84.7	127.7	172.7	194.1	198.3	205.0
Sporting equipment, guns, ammunition	19.9	27.2	39.1	50.9	51.3	54.1	57.3
Sports and recreational vehicles	16.6	22.5	34.9	49.1	35.6	37.1	39.3
Recreational books	10.9	16.4	24.4	27.0	27.1	27.0	27.8
Other durable goods	65.5	79.6	110.4	141.0	165.6	179.9	191.3
Jewelry and watches	30.3	37.8	49.1	59.8	62.6	69.4	73.7
Therapeutic appliances and equipment	18.4	21.0	32.2	43.2	55.6	58.8	62.0
Nondurable goods	994.2	1,179.8	1,540.3	1,953.1	2,292.1	2,472.8	2,567.0
Food and beverages purchased for off-premises consumption	391.2	443.7	540.6	668.2	788.9	833.0	863.3
Food and nonalcoholic beverages	341.2	388.3	463.1	575.3	675.9	715.4	740.9
Alcoholic beverages	49.3	55.0	77.1	92.6	112.6	117.2	121.8
Clothing and footwear	195.2	231.2	280.8	310.7	320.6	338.3	354.6
Women's and girls' clothing	94.5	108.9	132.7	149.6	152.8	161.1	169.5
Men's and boys' clothing	57.4	72.2	85.9	86.3	84.9	89.7	93.5
Children's and infants' clothing	8.1	9.0	11.4	15.4	17.7	18.5	19.2
Other clothing materials and footwear	35.3	41.2	50.8	59.3	65.2	69.0	72.5
Gasoline and other energy goods	124.2	133.4	184.5	283.8	333.4	408.9	417.0
Motor vehicle fuels, lubricants, and fluids	111.4	120.4	168.6	261.4	307.3	379.5	390.4
Other nondurable goods	283.6	371.4	534.4	690.4	849.2	892.6	932.1
Pharmaceutical and other medical products	59.1	85.1	159.0	248.5	334.1	353.2	370.0
Recreational items	50.9	68.9	91.9	112.6	127.7	133.2	142.0
Household supplies	54.2	70.4	86.7	102.0	108.3	112.9	117.3
Personal care products	39.3	50.2	68.5	88.0	104.7	110.0	114.6
Tobacco	41.0	49.2	68.5	76.7	106.3	108.3	108.8
Magazines, newspapers, and stationery	36.5	46.1	56.6	58.0	62.8	68.1	73.1
Services	2,334.3	3,168.6	4,348.8	5,710.1	6,839.1	7,109.1	7,379.9
Housing and utilities	696.5	913.7	1,198.6	1,583.6	1,909.0	1,960.9	2,013.9
Housing	570.6	756.1	1,010.5	1,332.5	1,609.7	1660.0	1719.9
Rental of tenant-occupied nonfarm housing	150.8	186.6	227.9	268.3	372.6	402.3	430.4
Imputed rental of owner-occupied nonfarm housing	412.8	559.4	768.9	1,044.3	1,214.5	1,233.8	1,263.7
Household utilities	125.9	157.6	188.1	251.1	299.3	300.9	294.0
Water supply and sanitation	27.1	39.3	50.4	61.3	78.0	82.1	85.9
Electricity and gas	98.8	118.3	137.6	189.9	221.4	218.8	208.1
Electricity	71.8	87.6	98.4	128.5	166.8	166.7	163.4
Natural gas	27.0	30.7	39.3	61.3	54.6	52.1	44.7
Health care	506.2	719.9	918.4	1,322.3	1,690.7	1,767.8	1,847.6
Outpatient services	232.1	336.6	436.6	626.2	767.9	797.2	827.5
Physician services	134.8	177.8	229.2	333.9	402.8	418.4	433.9
Dental services	32.4	45.4	63.6	87.9	104.5	106.8	109.4
Paramedical services	64.9	113.4	143.8	204.4	260.6	272.1	284.2
Hospital and nursing home services	274.1	383.3	481.8	696.1	922.8	970.6	1020.2
Hospitals	228.8	318.4	393.9	577.2	770.5	811.4	861.2
Nursing homes	45.3	64.8	87.9	119.0	152.3	159.2	159.0
Transportation services	126.4	177.9	263.5	289.4	292.9	308.2	318.1
Motor vehicle services	87.2	129.1	189.3	211.8	211.9	223.0	230.6
Public transportation	39.2	48.8	74.3	77.6	81.0	85.2	87.5
Ground transportation	12.9	16.7	22.9	29.6	35.6	38.0	37.1
Air transportation	25.9	31.1	49.2	45.4	42.7	44.3	47.3
Recreation services	121.8	181.1	254.4	328.9	385.1	399.7	416.6
Clubs, sports centers, parks, theaters, museums	49.7	69.5	91.9	117.9	141.8	147.6	153.7
Audio-video, photographic, and information processing equipment services	37.9	50.0	70.1	81.5	96.1	99.8	104.2
Gambling	23.7	45.4	67.6	96.5	105.6	108.9	112.5
Food services and accommodations	262.7	316.1	408.8	530.6	617.7	658.7	701.7
Food services	235.1	279.6	353.8	458.1	532.2	567.6	604.2
Accommodations	27.6	36.6	55.0	72.5	85.5	91.1	97.5
Financial services and insurance	247.4	366.4	566.3	689.6	763.2	801.1	821.0
Financial services	135.7	212.9	360.0	417.4	473.3	490.3	496.1
Insurance	111.7	153.5	206.3	272.2	290.0	310.7	325.0
Other services	297.5	391.2	580.7	755.3	905.1	934.8	970.4
Communication	68.3	95.9	152.7	177.8	226.8	238.1	251.7
Telecommunication services	60.7	85.2	126.4	137.7	152.1	156.0	160.6
Postal and delivery services	7.5	9.2	9.9	10.4	11.7	10.8	10.4
Internet access	0.1	1.6	16.4	29.7	63.0	71.3	80.7
Education services	60.7	85.5	125.2	170.7	235.5	250.9	264.9
Higher education	34.7	51.9	76.8	110.9	158.3	170.6	182.4
Nursery, elementary, and secondary schools	14.8	19.2	24.1	29.6	35.3	37.0	37.8
Commercial and vocational schools	11.1	14.4	24.3	30.3	42.0	43.3	44.7
Professional and other services	67.7	82.8	113.0	148.4	163.3	165.9	169.4
Personal care and clothing services	44.5	57.1	80.4	103.3	114.9	119.6	124.8
Social services and religious activities	41.2	58.1	81.1	110.2	138.9	143.7	147.3
Household maintenance	25.4	34.5	48.6	57.9	58.6	61.5	65.9
Net foreign travel	-10.3	-22.8	-20.4	-13.0	-32.9	-44.8	-53.6
Foreign travel by U.S. residents	42.7	54.9	81.8	94.9	103.4	105.8	110.0
Less: Expenditures in the U.S. by nonresidents	53.0	77.7	102.2	108.0	136.4	150.5	163.6

Note: Subtotals may not add up to totals due to rounding or incomplete enumeration.

Leading U.S. Businesses, 2012

Source: *Fortune* magazine

(in millions of revenue-dollars; rank among all businesses by revenue)

Company (rank)	Revenue
Advertising, Marketing	
Omnicom Group (191)	$14,200
Interpublic Group (366)	7,000
Aerospace and Defense	
Boeing (30)	$81,700
United Technologies (50)	59,800
Lockheed Martin (59)	47,200
Honeywell International (78)	37,700
General Dynamics (98)	31,500
Northrop Grumman (120)	25,200
Raytheon (124)	24,400
L-3 Communications (197)	14,100
Textron (225)	12,200
Precision Castparts (355)	7,300
Huntington Ingalls Indus. (380)	6,700
Airlines	
United Continental Holdings (79)	$37,200
Delta Air Lines (83)	36,700
AMR (121)	24,900
Southwest Airlines (164)	17,100
US Airways Group (199)	13,800
Apparel	
Nike (126)	$24,100
VF (250)	10,900
Ralph Lauren (370)	6,900
PVH (422)	6,000
Automotive Retailing, Services	
AutoNation (177)	$15,700
Penske Automotive Group (203)	13,600
CarMax (190)	10,500
Hertz Global Holdings (293)	9,000
Sonic Automotive (307)	8,500
Group 1 Automotive (343)	7,500
Avis Budget Group (350)	7,400
Beverages	
Coca-Cola (57)	$48,000
Coca-Cola Enterprises (339)	7,600
Dr Pepper Snapple Group (427)	6,000
Chemicals	
Dow Chemical (52)	$56,800
DuPont (72)	39,500
PPG Industries (182)	15,200
Monsanto (206)	13,500
Ecolab (229)	11,800
Huntsman (241)	11,200
Praxair (241)	11,200
Mosaic (246)	11,100
Air Products & Chemicals (273)	9,900
Sherwin-Williams (282)	9,500
Ashland (321)	8,200
Eastman Chemical (324)	8,100
Avery Dennison (375)	6,800
Celanese (396)	6,400
CF Industries Holdings (419)	6,100
Commercial Banks	
J.P. Morgan Chase & Co. (18)	$108,200
Bank of America Corp. (21)	100,100
Wells Fargo (25)	91,200
Citigroup (26)	90,800
Goldman Sachs Group (68)	41,700
American Express (90)	33,800
Morgan Stanley (96)	32,400
Capital One Financial (127)	23,800
U.S. Bancorp (132)	22,200
PNC Fin. Services Group (170)	16,600
Bank of New York Mellon Corp. (180)	15,500
Ally Financial (221)	12,600
SunTrust Banks (239)	11,200
BB&T Corp. (251)	10,700
State Street Corp. (268)	10,100
Discover Fin. Services (294)	9,000
Fifth Third Bancorp (361)	7,100
Regions Financial (401)	6,300
Computer Peripherals	
EMC (133)	$21,700
Western Digital (222)	12,500
NetApp (408)	6,200
Computer Software	
Microsoft (35)	$73,700
Oracle (80)	37,100
Symantec (379)	6,700
CA (499)	4,800
Computers, Office Equipment	
Apple (6)	$156,500
Hewlett-Packard (15)	120,400
Dell (51)	56,900
NCR (441)	5,800

Company (rank)	Revenue
Construction and Farm Machinery	
Caterpillar (42)	$65,900
Deere (85)	36,200
Cummins (160)	17,300
AGCO (272)	10,000
Terex (351)	7,300
Joy Global (446)	5,700
Diversified Financials	
General Electric (8)	$146,900
Fannie Mae (12)	127,200
Freddie Mac (31)	80,600
INTL FCStone (39)	69,300
Marsh & McLennan (228)	11,900
Ameriprise Financial (263)	10,300
SLM (418)	6,100
Diversified Outsourcing	
Aramark (205)	$13,500
Automatic Data Processing (255)	10,700
Electronics, Electrical Equipment	
Emerson Electric (123)	$24,500
Whirlpool (154)	18,100
Rockwell Automation (403)	6,300
General Cable (425)	6,000
Energy	
NRG Energy (314)	$8,400
Williams (342)	7,500
UGI (388)	6,500
Energy Future Holdings (447)	5,600
Engineering, Construction	
Fluor (110)	$27,600
Peter Kiewit Sons' (243)	11,200
URS (248)	11,000
Jacobs Engineering Group (249)	10,900
AECOM Technology (320)	8,200
KBR (334)	7,900
Quanta Services (397)	6,400
EMCORGroup (399)	6,300
CH2M Hill (415)	6,200
Shaw Group (426)	6,000
Entertainment	
Walt Disney (66)	$42,300
News Corp. (91)	33,700
Time Warner (105)	28,700
CBS (186)	14,700
Viacom (198)	13,900
CC Media Holdings (407)	6,200
Live Nation Entertainment (439)	5,800
Financial Data Services	
First Data (254)	$10,700
Visa (260)	10,400
MasterCard (348)	7,400
Fidelity Natl. Info. Services (434)	5,900
Western Union (445)	5,700
Food Consumer Products	
PepsiCo (43)	$65,500
Mondelēz International (88)	35,000
Kraft Foods Group (151)	18,300
General Mills (169)	16,700
Kellogg (192)	14,200
Land O'Lakes (194)	14,100
ConAgra Foods (209)	13,300
Dean Foods (217)	12,900
H.J. Heinz (234)	11,600
Hillshire Brands (288)	9,300
Hormel Foods (319)	8,200
Campbell Soup (338)	7,700
Dole Food (372)	6,800
Hershey (384)	6,600
Food and Drug Stores	
CVS Caremark (13)	$123,100
Kroger (23)	96,800
Walgreen (37)	71,600
Safeway (62)	44,200
Supervalu (86)	36,100
Publix Super Markets (108)	27,700
Rite Aid (113)	26,100
Whole Foods Market (232)	11,700
Food Production	
Archer Daniels Midland (27)	$89,000
Tyson Foods (93)	33,300
Smithfield Foods (213)	13,100
Leucadia National (289)	9,300
Ingredion (386)	6,500
Seaboard (411)	6,200
Food Services	
McDonald's (111)	$27,600
Yum Brands (201)	13,600
Starbucks (208)	13,300
Darden Restaurants (328)	8,000

Company (rank)	Revenue
Forest and Paper Products	
International Paper (107)	$27,800
Weyerhaeuser (363)	7,100
General Merchandisers	
Wal-Mart Stores (1)	$469,200
Target (36)	73,300
Sears Holdings (71)	39,900
Macy's (109)	27,700
Kohl's (148)	19,300
Dollar General (175)	16,000
J.C. Penney (215)	13,000
Nordstrom (227)	12,100
Family Dollar Stores (287)	9,300
Dillard's (378)	6,800
Health Care: Insurance and Managed Care	
UnitedHealth Group (17)	$110,600
WellPoint (47)	61,700
Humana (73)	39,100
Aetna (84)	36,600
Cigna (103)	29,100
Coventry Health Care (195)	14,100
Health Net (236)	11,500
Centene (303)	8,700
WellCare Health Plans (345)	7,400
Molina Healthcare (423)	6,000
Health Care: Medical Facilities	
HCA Holdings (82)	$36,800
Community Health Sys. (184)	15,000
Tenet Healthcare (269)	10,100
DaVita HealthCare Partners (311)	8,500
Universal Health Services (337)	7,800
Health Management Assoc. (376)	6,800
Vanguard Health Systems (391)	6,500
Kindred Healthcare (410)	6,200
Health Care: Pharmacy and Other Services	
Express Scripts Holding (24)	$94,400
Quest Diagnostics (341)	7,500
Omnicare (416)	6,200
Laboratory Corp. of Amer. (444)	5,700
Home Equipment, Furnishings	
Stanley Black & Decker (245)	$11,100
Masco (336)	7,800
Jarden (383)	6,700
Newell Rubbermaid (433)	5,900
Hotels, Casinos, Resorts	
Marriott International (230)	$11,800
Las Vegas Sands (244)	11,100
MGM Resorts Intl. (292)	9,200
Caesars Entertainment (300)	8,800
Starwood Hotels & Resorts (400)	6,300
Household and Personal Products	
Procter & Gamble (28)	$85,100
Kimberly-Clark (136)	21,100
Colgate-Palmolive (165)	17,100
Avon Products (252)	10,700
Estée Lauder (279)	9,700
Industrial Machinery	
Illinois Tool Works (155)	$18,100
Parker Hannifin (211)	13,100
Dover (308)	8,500
SPX (431)	5,900
Information Technology Services	
IBM (20)	$104,500
Xerox (131)	22,400
Computer Sciences (176)	15,900
SAIC (240)	11,200
CDW (267)	10,100
Cognizant Tech. Solutions (352)	7,300
Booz Allen Hamilton Holding (436)	5,900
Insurance: Life, Health (Mutual)	
New York Life Insurance (89)	$34,300
Massachusetts Mutual Life Insurance (94)	32,900
TIAA-CREF (97)	32,200
Northwestern Mutual (114)	26,000
Guardian Life Ins. Co. of America (238)	11,300
Thrivent Financial for Lutherans (335)	8,000
Insurance: Life, Health (Stock)	
Prudential Financial (29)	$84,500
MetLife (40)	68,200
Aflac (118)	25,400
Lincoln National (235)	11,500
Unum Group (257)	10,500
Genworth Financial (271)	10,000

Company (rank)	Revenue
Reinsurance Group of America (275)	$9,800
Principal Financial (290)	9,200
Pacific Life (369)	6,900
Mutual of Omaha (394)	6,400
Insurance: Property and Casualty (Mutual)	
State Farm Insurance Cos. (44)	$65,300
Nationwide (100)	30,400
Auto-Owners Insurance (443)	5,700
Insurance: Property and Casualty (Stock)	
Berkshire Hathaway (5)	$162,500
American Intl. Group (38)	70,100
Liberty Mutual (81)	36,900
Allstate (92)	33,300
Hartford Financial Services Group (112)	26,400
Travelers Cos. (116)	25,700
United Services Auto. Assn. (139)	20,700
Progressive (166)	17,100
Loews (188)	14,600
Chubb (202)	13,600
Assurant (309)	8,500
Fidelity National Financial (353)	7,300
American Family (393)	6,500
W.R. Berkeley (438)	5,800
Internet Services and Retailing	
Amazon.com (49)	$61,100
Google (55)	52,200
eBay (196)	14,100
Liberty Interactive (270)	10,700
Priceline.com (473)	5,300
Facebook (482)	5,100
Yahoo (494)	5,000
Mail, Package, Freight Delivery	
United Parcel Service (53)	$54,100
FedEx (63)	42,700
Medical Products and Equipment	
Medtronic (172)	$16,500
Baxter International (193)	14,200
Stryker (305)	8,700
Becton Dickinson (332)	7,900
Boston Scientific (357)	7,200
Metals	
Alcoa (128)	$23,700
Nucor (146)	19,400
United States Steel (147)	19,300
Reliance Steel & Aluminum (313)	8,400
Commercial Metals (335)	7,900
Steel Dynamics (354)	7,300
AK Steel Holding (430)	5,900
Mining, Crude Oil Production	
ConocoPhillips (45)	$63,400
Occidental Petroleum (125)	24,300
Freeport-McMoRan Copper & Gold (156)	18,000
Apache (167)	17,100
Marathon Oil (174)	16,200
Anadarko Petroleum (207)	13,400
Chesapeake Energy (223)	12,300
EOG Resources (233)	11,700
Newmont Mining (274)	9,900
Devon Energy (284)	9,500
Peabody Energy (315)	8,300
Alpha Natural Resources (365)	7,000
Cliffs Natural Resources (424)	6,000
Miscellaneous	
3M (101)	$29,900
Spectrum Group Intl. (331)	8,000
Mohawk Industries (442)	5,800
Motor Vehicles and Parts	
General Motors (7)	$152,300
Ford Motor (10)	134,300
Johnson Controls (67)	42,000
Goodyear Tire & Rubber (137)	21,000
Paccar (168)	17,100
TRW Automotive Holdings (173)	16,400
Icahn Enterprises (178)	15,700
Lear (187)	14,600
Navistar International (216)	12,900
Autoliv (317)	8,300
Oshkosh (322)	8,200
Tenneco (349)	7,400
Dana Holding (356)	7,300
BorgWarner (358)	7,200
Visteon (359)	7,200
Network and Other Communications Equipment	
Cisco Systems (60)	$46,100
Qualcomm (149)	19,100
Motorola Solutions (304)	8,700
Corning (326)	8,000
Harris (429)	6,000

Company (rank)	Revenue
Oil and Gas Equipment, Services	
Halliburton (106)	$28,500
Baker Hughes (135)	21,400
National Oilwell Varco (144)	20,000
Cameron International (310)	8,500
FMC Technologies (417)	6,200
Packaging, Containers	
Rock-Tenn (291)	$9,200
Ball (301)	8,700
Crown Holdings (312)	8,500
Sealed Air (333)	7,900
Owens-Illinois (364)	7,000
MeadWestvaco (448)	5,600
Petroleum Refining	
Exxon Mobil (2)	$449,900
Chevron (3)	233,900
Phillips 66 (4)	169,600
Valero Energy (9)	138,300
Marathon Petroleum (33)	76,800
Hess (75)	38,400
Tesoro (95)	32,500
Murphy Oil (104)	28,800
PBF Energy (142)	20,100
HollyFrontier (143)	20,100
Western Refining (283)	9,500
Pharmaceuticals	
Johnson & Johnson (41)	$67,200
Pfizer (48)	61,200
Merck (58)	47,300
Abbott Laboratories (70)	39,900
Eli Lilly (130)	22,600
Bristol-Myers Squibb (158)	17,600
Amgen (162)	17,300
Gilead Sciences (280)	9,700
Mylan (374)	6,800
Actavis (432)	5,900
Allergan (440)	5,800
Pipelines	
Enterprise Products Partners (64)	$42,600
Plains All American Pipeline (77)	37,800
Energy Transfer Equity (161)	17,300
Onook (219)	12,700
Kinder Morgan (265)	10,200
Enbridge Energy Partners (381)	6,700
NuStar Energy (389)	6,500
Targa Resources (435)	5,900
Publishing, Printing	
R.R. Donnelley & Sons (264)	$10,200
McGraw-Hill (390)	6,500
Railroads	
Union Pacific (138)	$20,900
CSX (231)	11,800
Norfolk Southern (247)	11,000
Real Estate	
CBRE Group (387)	$6,500
Scientific, Photo, Control Equipment	
Danaher (152)	$18,300
Thermo Fisher Scientific (220)	12,700
Agilent Technologies (371)	6,900
Securities	
KKR (277)	$9,700
BlackRock (286)	9,300
Franklin Resources (362)	7,100
Semiconductors and Other Electronic Components	
Intel (54)	$53,300
Jabil Circuit (163)	17,200
Texas Instruments (218)	12,800
Applied Materials (302)	8,700
Micron Technology (318)	8,200
Broadcom (327)	8,000
Sanmina (420)	6,100
Specialty Retailers: Apparel	
TJX (115)	$25,900
Gap (179)	15,700
L Brands (258)	10,500
Ross Stores (278)	9,700
Foot Locker (413)	6,200
Specialty Retailers: Other	
Costco Wholesale (22)	$99,100
Home Depot (34)	74,800
Lowe's (56)	50,500
Best Buy (61)	45,100
Staples (122)	24,700
Toys "R" Us (204)	13,500
Office Depot (253)	10,700
Bed Bath & Beyond (285)	9,500
GameStop (298)	8,900
AutoZone (306)	8,600
TravelCenters of America (329)	8,000
Dollar Tree (346)	7,400

Company (rank)	Revenue
Pantry (347)	$7,400
Barnes & Noble (360)	7,100
OfficeMax (367)	6,900
PetSmart (377)	6,800
Casey's General Stores (392)	6,500
Advance Auto Parts (409)	6,200
O'Reilly Automotive (412)	6,200
Dick's Sporting Goods (437)	5,800
Telecommunications	
AT&T (11)	$127,400
Verizon Communications (16)	115,800
Comcast (46)	62,600
Sprint Nextel (87)	35,300
DirecTV (102)	29,700
Time Warner Cable (134)	21,400
CenturyLink (150)	18,400
DISH Network (189)	14,300
Liberty Global (256)	10,600
Charter Communications (340)	7,500
Cablevision Systems (382)	6,700
Level 3 Communications (398)	6,400
Windstream (414)	6,200
NII Holdings (421)	6,100
Temporary Help	
Manpower (140)	$20,700
Tobacco	
Philip Morris International (99)	$31,400
Altria Group (159)	17,500
Reynolds American (316)	8,300
Toys	
Mattel (395)	$6,400
Transportation and Logistics	
C.H. Robinson Worldwide (237)	$11,400
Expeditors Intl. of Washington (428)	6,000
Con-way (450)	5,600
Transportation Equipment	
Harley-Davidson (449)	$5,600
Trucking	
Ryder System (404)	$6,300
Utilities: Gas and Electric	
Exelon (129)	$23,500
Duke Energy (145)	19,600
AES (153)	18,200
Southern (171)	16,500
FirstEnergy (181)	15,300
PG&E Corp. (183)	15,000
American Electric Power (185)	14,900
NextEra Energy (190)	14,300
Dominion Resources (210)	13,200
Edison International (212)	13,100
PPL (224)	12,300
Consolidated Edison (226)	12,200
Entergy (261)	10,300
Xcel Energy (266)	10,100
Public Service Enterprise Group (276)	9,800
Sempra Energy (281)	9,600
DTE Energy (299)	8,800
CenterPoint Energy (344)	7,500
Ameren (373)	6,800
Northeast Utilities (402)	6,300
CMS Energy (406)	6,300
Waste Management	
Waste Management (200)	$13,600
Republic Services (323)	8,100
Wholesalers: Diversified	
World Fuel Services (74)	$38,800
Global Partners (157)	17,600
Genuine Parts (214)	13,000
W. W. Grainger (295)	9,000
HD Supply (330)	8,000
WESCO International (385)	6,600
Anixter International (405)	6,300
Wholesalers: Electronics and Office Equipment	
Ingram Micro (76)	$37,800
Avnet (117)	25,700
Tech Data (119)	25,400
Arrow Electronics (141)	20,400
Synnex (262)	10,300
Wholesalers: Food and Grocery	
Sysco (65)	$42,400
CHS (69)	40,600
Core-Mark Holding (368)	6,900
Andersons (472)	5,300
Wholesalers: Health Care	
McKesson (14)	$122,700
Cardinal Health (19)	107,600
AmerisourceBergen (32)	79,700
Henry Schein (296)	8,900
Owens & Minor (297)	8,900

100 U.S. Corporations With Largest Revenues, 2012

Source: *Fortune* magazine

(in millions of dollars; ranked by 2012 revenues)

Rank	Company (2011 rank)	Revenues	Profits	Rank	Company (2011 rank)	Revenues	Profits
1.	Wal-Mart Stores (2)	$469,200	$16,999	51.	Dell (44)	$56,900	$2,372
2.	Exxon Mobil (1)	449,900	44,880	52.	Dow Chemical (47)	56,800	1,182
3.	Chevron (3)	233,900	26,179	53.	United Parcel Service (52)	54,100	807
4.	Phillips 66 (4)	169,600	4,124	54.	Intel (51)	53,300	11,005
5.	Berkshire Hathaway (7)	162,500	14,824	55.	Google (73)	52,200	10,737
6.	Apple (17)	156,500	41,733	56.	Lowe's (54)	50,500	1,959
7.	General Motors (5)	152,300	6,188	57.	Coca-Cola (59)	48,000	9,019
8.	General Electric (6)	146,900	13,641	58.	Merck (57)	47,300	6,168
9.	Valero Energy (12)	138,300	2,083	59.	Lockheed Martin (58)	47,200	2,745
10.	Ford Motor (9)	134,300	5,665	60.	Cisco Systems (64)	46,100	8,041
11.	AT&T (11)	127,400	7,264	61.	Best Buy (53)	45,100	−441
12.	Fannie Mae (8)	127,200	17,220	62.	Safeway (63)	44,200	597
13.	CVS Caremark (18)	123,100	3,877	63.	FedEx (70)	42,700	2,032
14.	McKesson (14)	122,700	1,403	64.	Enterprise Products Partners (62)	42,600	2,420
15.	Hewlett-Packard (10)	120,400	−12,650	65.	Sysco (69)	42,400	1,122
16.	Verizon Communications (15)	115,800	875	66.	Walt Disney (66)	42,300	5,682
17.	UnitedHealth Group (22)	110,600	5,526	67.	Johnson Controls (67)	42,000	1,226
18.	J.P. Morgan Chase & Co. (16)	108,200	21,284	68.	Goldman Sachs Group (80)	41,700	7,475
19.	Cardinal Health (21)	107,600	1,069	69.	CHS (78)	40,600	1,261
20.	International Business Machines (19)	104,500	16,604	70.	Abbott Laboratories (71)	39,900	5,963
21.	Bank of America Corp. (13)	100,100	4,188	71.	Sears Holdings (65)	39,900	−930
22.	Costco Wholesale (24)	99,100	1,709	72.	DuPont (72)	39,500	2,788
23.	Kroger (23)	96,800	1,496	73.	Humana (79)	39,100	1,222
24.	Express Scripts Holding (60)	94,400	1,313	74.	World Fuel Services (85)	38,900	189
25.	Wells Fargo (26)	91,200	18,897	75.	Hess (77)	38,400	2,025
26.	Citigroup (20)	90,800	7,541	76.	Ingram Micro (81)	37,800	306
27.	Archer Daniels Midland (28)	89,000	1,223	77.	Plains All American Pipeline (87)	37,800	1,094
28.	Procter & Gamble (27)	85,100	10,756	78.	Honeywell International (77)	37,700	2,926
29.	Prudential Financial (55)	84,800	469	79.	United Continental Holdings (76)	37,200	−723
30.	Boeing (39)	81,700	3,900	80.	Oracle (82)	37,100	9,981
31.	Freddie Mac (25)	80,600	10,982	81.	Liberty Mutual Insurance Group (84)	36,900	829
32.	AmerisourceBergen (29)	79,700	719	82.	HCA Holdings (94)	36,800	1,605
33.	Marathon Petroleum (31)	76,800	3,389	83.	Delta Air Lines (83)	36,700	1,009
34.	Home Depot (35)	74,800	4,535	84.	Aetna (89)	36,600	1,658
35.	Microsoft (37)	73,700	16,978	85.	Deere (97)	36,200	3,065
36.	Target (38)	73,300	2,999	86.	Supervalu (75)	36,100	−1,040
37.	Walgreen (32)	71,600	2,127	87.	Sprint Nextel (90)	35,300	−4,326
38.	American International Group (33)	70,100	3,438	88.	Mondelēz International (50)	35,000	3,028
39.	INTL FCStone (30)	69,300	15	89.	New York Life Insurance (86)	34,300	1,333
40.	MetLife (34)	68,200	1,324	90.	American Express (95)	33,800	4,482
41.	Johnson & Johnson (42)	67,200	10,853	91.	News Corp. (91)	33,700	1,179
42.	Caterpillar (46)	65,900	5,681	92.	Allstate (93)	33,300	2,306
43.	PepsiCo (41)	65,500	6,178	93.	Tyson Foods (96)	33,300	583
44.	State Farm Insurance Cos. (43)	65,300	3,159	94.	Massachusetts Mutual Life Insurance (121)	32,900	1,115
45.	ConocoPhillips (4)	63,400	8,428	95.	Tesoro (101)	32,500	743
46.	Comcast (49)	62,600	6,203	96.	Morgan Stanley (68)	32,400	68
47.	WellPoint (45)	61,700	2,656	97.	TIAA-CREF (81)	32,200	2,060
48.	Pfizer (40)	61,200	14,570	98.	General Dynamics (92)	31,500	−332
49.	Amazon.com (56)	61,100	−39	99.	Philip Morris International (99)	31,400	8,800
50.	United Technologies (48)	59,800	5,130	100.	Nationwide (100)	30,400	749

Note: Revenue figures rounded at source.

Top U.S. Franchises, 2013

Source: *Entrepreneur* magazine

Rank	Company (2012 rank)	Type of business	Locations	Startup costs[1]
1.	Hampton Hotels (1)	Mid-priced hotels	1,917	$3.7 mil-$13.52 mil
2.	Subway (2)	Submarine sandwiches & salads	39,447	$85,200-$260,350
3.	Jiffy Lube Intl. Inc. (15)	Fast oil change	2,086	$196,500-$304,000
4.	7-Eleven Inc. (3)	Convenience stores	47,298	$30,800-$1.5 mil
5.	Supercuts (14)	Hair salons	2,316	$103,550-$196,500
6.	Anytime Fitness (11)	Fitness centers	2,169	$56,300-$353,900
7.	Servpro (4)	Insurance/disaster restoration & cleaning	1,626	$134,800-$183,450
8.	Denny's Inc. (7)	Full-service family restaurants	1,688	$1.18 mil-$2.4 mil
9.	McDonald's (6)	Hamburgers, chicken, salads	34,565	$1.03 mil-$2.18 mil
10.	Pizza Hut Inc. (9)	Pizza, pasta, wings	13,747	$295,000-$2.15 mil
11.	H&R Block (8)	Tax preparation & electronic filing	11,671	$31,510-$138,700
12.	Jimmy John's Gourmet Sandwich Shops (22)	Gourmet sandwiches	1,638	$300,500-$489,500
13.	Dunkin' Donuts (10)	Coffee, doughnuts, baked goods	10,464	$310,250-$1.77 mil
14.	Hardee's (32)	Burgers, chicken, biscuits	1,956	$1.15 mil-$1.54 mil
15.	KFC Corp. (17)	Chicken	17,401	$1.31 mil-$2.47 mil
16.	Kumon Math & Reading Centers (18)	Supplemental education	25,443	$66,510-$140,620
17.	Days Inn (5)	Hotels	1,828	$200,670-$7.13 mil
18.	Aaron's (21)	Furniture, electronics, computer, appliance leasing & sales	3,088	$263,870-$692,580
19.	Jan-Pro Franchising Intl. Inc. (NA)	Commercial cleaning	11,146	$3,150-$50,410
20.	System4 (38)	Commercial cleaning	1,197	$6,160-$37,750

NA = Not available. **Note:** Franchises are ranked by a combination of factors, including financial strength and stability, growth rate, number of locations, startup costs, and whether the company provides financing. (1) Does not include franchise fee, which varies.

United States Mint

Source: United States Mint, U.S. Dept. of the Treasury

The United States Mint was created on Apr. 2, 1792, by an act of Congress, which established the U.S. national coinage system. In 1799, the mint became an independent agency reporting directly to the president. It was made a statutory bureau of the Treasury Department in 1873, with a director appointed by the president. The mint manufactures and ships all U.S. coins for circulation to Federal Reserve banks and branches, which in turn issue coins to the public and business community through depository institutions. The mint also safeguards the Treasury Department's stored gold and silver, as well as other monetary assets.

The composition of dimes, quarters, and half dollars, traditionally produced from silver, was changed by the Coinage Act of 1965, which mandated that these coins from then on be minted from a cupronickel-clad alloy and reduced the silver content of the half dollar to 40%. In 1970, legislative action mandated that the half dollar and a dollar coin be minted from the same alloy.

Mint headquarters are in Washington, DC. Mint production facilities are in Philadelphia, Denver, San Francisco, and West Point, NY. In addition, the mint is responsible for the U.S. Bullion Depository at Fort Knox, KY.

The mint offers free public tours and operates sales centers at the U.S. mints in Denver and Philadelphia. Further information is available from the U.S. Mint, Customer Care Center, 801 9th St. NW, Washington, DC 20220; (800) USA-MINT. **Website:** www.usmint.gov.

New Circulating and Commemorative Coins

Source: United States Mint, U.S. Dept. of the Treasury

Dollar coins. A large, unwieldy dollar coin featuring the likeness of Pres. Dwight D. Eisenhower was minted 1971-78. The smaller Susan B. Anthony dollar, minted 1979-81, marked the first time that a woman other than a mythical figure appeared on a generally circulated U.S. coin. A golden dollar coin was first minted in 2000. It depicts Sacagawea, a Shoshone woman who helped guide explorers Lewis and Clark, on the obverse. The reverse shows an eagle and 17 stars, one for each of the states at the time of the Lewis and Clark expedition. In 2007, the mint began issuing a series of golden dollar coins featuring U.S. presidents on the front and the Statue of Liberty on the back. Each includes the president's name, likeness, and years of service. Four are to be issued each year in the order in which the presidents served. William McKinley, Theodore Roosevelt, William Howard Taft, and Woodrow Wilson were honored in 2013. The 2014 set features Warren G. Harding, Calvin Coolidge, Herbert Hoover, and Franklin D. Roosevelt. Only presidents deceased more than two years will be honored, so the program is currently slated to end in 2016 with coins commemorating Richard Nixon, Gerald Ford, and Ronald Reagan. The mint also issues golden dollar coins whose reverse sides celebrate the important contributions made by American Indian tribes to the development of the U.S. The 2011 coin celebrated the Wampanoag Treaty of 1621; the 2012 coin commemorates trade routes of the 17th century; and the 2013 coin celebrates the 1778 treaty with the Delaware tribe of Native Americans.

America the Beautiful quarters. In 2010, the U.S. Mint began an initiative to honor 56 national parks and other sites of national importance. Five new reverse designs appear on the quarter-dollar each year in 2010-21; the order of issuance corresponds to the order in which the featured site was first established. The 2012 coins commemorated El Yunque Natl. Forest, PR; Chaco Culture Natl. Historical Park, NM; Acadia Natl. Park, ME; Hawai'i Volcanoes Natl. Park, HI; and Denali Natl. Park, AK. The 2013 coins commemorate White Mountain Natl. Forest, NH; Perry's Victory and Intl. Peace Memorial, OH; Great Basin Natl. Park, NV; Fort McHenry Natl. Monument and Historic Shrine, MD; and Mount Rushmore Natl. Memorial, SD. The 2014 coins will commemorate Great Smoky Mountains Natl. Park, TN; Shenandoah Natl. Park, VA; Arches Natl. Park, UT; Great Sand Dunes Natl. Park, CO; and Everglades Natl. Park, FL.

Commemorative coins. From 1892 to 1954, and again since 1982, Congress has authorized the mint to produce more than 50 different commemorative coins. Recent issues include the 2007 Little Rock Central High School Desegregation silver dollar coin; the 2009 Louis Braille Bicentennial-Braille Literacy silver dollar; the 2013 Girl Scouts of the USA silver dollar coin; and the 2014 National Baseball Hall of Fame coins.

Bureau of Engraving and Printing

Source: Bureau of Engraving and Printing, U.S. Dept. of the Treasury

The Bureau of Engraving and Printing manufactures the financial and other securities of the United States. It designs and prints a variety of products, including Federal Reserve notes (bills in various denominations), Treasury securities, identification cards, naturalization certificates, and other special security documents. Denominations of the various types of printings produced by the bureau range from a 1/5-cent wine stamp to a $100,000,000 International Monetary Fund special note. Among its products are all hand-engraved invitations issued by the White House.

The first general circulation of paper money by the federal government dates back to 1861, prior to the establishment of the bureau, when Congress authorized the U.S. Treasury to issue non-interest-bearing demand notes, nicknamed "greenbacks" because of their color, to finance the Civil War. A portrait of Pres. Abraham Lincoln appeared on the face of the first $10 notes. By 1862, the design of U.S. currency incorporated fine-line engraving, intricate geometric lathe work patterns, a Treasury seal, and engraved signatures to aid in counterfeit deterrence. All U.S. currency issued since 1861 remain valid and redeemable at full face value.

The Bureau of Engraving and Printing began operations by 1862, originally separating and sealing bank notes that were printed by private companies. In 1877, the bureau became the sole producer of U.S. currency. In 1894, it also began producing postage stamps. On June 10, 2005, the bureau printed its last stamps, a roll of 37-cent flag stamps; stamps are now produced by private printers.

The Federal Reserve Act of 1913 created the Federal Reserve as the nation's central bank and provided for currency called Federal Reserve notes. The first notes, issued the following year, were $10 notes bearing a portrait of Pres. Andrew Jackson. In 1929, the look of U.S. currency was standardized. The national motto, "In God We Trust," was added to paper money in 1957.

The Bureau of Engraving and Printing currently operates two facilities, one in Washington, DC, opened in 1914, and one in Fort Worth, TX, which began operations in 1991.

Denominations of U.S. Currency

Since 1969 the largest denomination of U.S. currency that has been issued is the $100 bill. As larger-denomination bills reach the Federal Reserve Bank, they are removed from circulation. Because some discontinued currency is expected to be in the hands of holders for many years, the description of the various denominations below is continued.

Note	Portrait	Embellishment on back	Note	Portrait	Embellishment on back
$1	George Washington	Great Seal of U.S.	$500	William McKinley	Ornate denominational marking
2	Thomas Jefferson	Signers of Declaration	1,000	Grover Cleveland	Ornate denominational marking
5	Abraham Lincoln	Lincoln Memorial	5,000	James Madison	Washington resigning as Army commander
10	Alexander Hamilton	U.S. Treasury			
20	Andrew Jackson	White House	10,000	Salmon Chase	Embarkation of the Pilgrims
50	Ulysses S. Grant	U.S. Capitol	100,000*	Woodrow Wilson	Ornate denominational marking
100	Benjamin Franklin	Independence Hall			

*For use only in transactions between Federal Reserve System and Treasury Department.

Portraits on U.S. Treasury Bills, Bonds, Notes, and Savings Bonds

The U.S. Treasury discontinued the issuing of Treasury bill, bond, and note certificates in 1986. Since then, all issues of marketable Treasury securities have been available only in book-entry form, although some certificates remain in circulation.

Denomination	EE savings bonds	Treasury bills	Treasury bonds	Treasury notes
$50	George Washington		Thomas Jefferson	
75	John Adams			
100	Thomas Jefferson		Andrew Jackson	
200	James Madison			
500	Alexander Hamilton (Treasury Sec., 1789-95)		George Washington	
1,000	Benjamin Franklin	Hugh McCulloch (Treasury Sec., 1865-69, 1884-85)	Abraham Lincoln	Abraham Lincoln
5,000	Paul Revere	John G. Carlisle (Treasury Sec., 1893-97)	James Monroe	James Monroe
10,000	James Wilson (Supreme Court Justice, 1789-98)	John Sherman (Treasury Sec., 1877-81)	Grover Cleveland	Grover Cleveland
50,000	Carter Glass (Treasury Sec., 1918-20)			
100,000		Albert Gallatin (Treasury Sec., 1801-14)	Ulysses S. Grant	Ulysses S. Grant
1,000,000		Oliver Wolcott (Treasury Sec., 1795-1800)	Theodore Roosevelt	Theodore Roosevelt
100,000,000				James Madison
500,000,000				William McKinley

U.S. Currency Designs

After production delays, redesigned $100 notes were introduced into circulation Oct. 8, 2013. The new bills feature a number of new security and anti-counterfeiting features, including a blue 3-D security ribbon and the image of a bell in an inkwell on the front of the note. The security ribbon contains images of bells and the numeral 100 that change as the note is tilted. The bell in the copper-colored inkwell changes color from copper to green when the note is tilted. The new notes were initially scheduled for release in Feb. 2011, but problems in the printing process postponed the release. Older $100 notes remain legal tender but will gradually be withdrawn from circulation.

The new $100 bill is the last denomination of the major currency redesign that the Treasury launched Oct. 9, 2003, with the introduction of the new $20 note, which used background colors for the first time since 1905. The notes have a vertical security thread on one side, with "USA TWENTY" and a small U.S. flag; the thread glows green under UV light. Other security features include color-shifting ink in the number 20 in the lower right corner on the note's face. A new $50 note with similar security features was released Sept. 28, 2004, followed by a $10 note on Mar. 2, 2006, and a $5 note Mar. 13, 2008.

Website: www.newmoney.gov.

The U.S. $1 Bill

Plate position: Shows where on the 32-note plate this bill was printed.

Serial number: Each bill has its own.

Federal Reserve District number: Shows which district issued the bill.

Federal Reserve District seal: The name of the Federal Reserve Bank that issued the bill is printed in the seal. The letter tells you where the bill is from. Here are the letter codes for the 12 Federal Reserve Districts:

A: Boston
B: New York
C: Philadelphia
D: Cleveland
E: Richmond
F: Atlanta
G: Chicago
H: St. Louis
I: Minneapolis
J: Kansas City
K: Dallas
L: San Francisco

Treasury Department seal: The balancing scales represent justice. The pointed stripe across the middle has 13 stars for the original 13 colonies. The key represents authority.

Plate serial number: Shows which printing plate was used for the face of the bill.

Treasurer of the U.S. signature

Series indicator: Year note's design was first used.

Secretary of the Treasury signature

Plate serial number: Shows which plate was used for the back.

Front of the Great Seal of the United States: The bald eagle is the national bird. The shield has 13 stripes for the 13 original colonies. The eagle holds 13 arrows (symbol of war) and an olive branch (symbol of peace). Above the eagle is the motto "E Pluribus Unum," Latin for "out of many, one," and a constellation of 13 stars.

Reverse of the Great Seal of the United States: The pyramid symbolizes something that endures for ages. The eye, known as the Eye of Providence, probably comes from an ancient Egyptian symbol. The pyramid has 13 levels; at its base are the Roman numerals for 1776, the year of American independence. "Annuit Coeptis" is Latin for "God has favored our undertaking." "Novus Ordo Seclorum" is Latin for "a new order of the ages." Both phrases are from the works of the Roman poet Virgil.

U.S. Currency and Coin

Source: Financial Management Service, U.S. Dept. of the Treasury

Total Money in Circulation, 1955-2013

Date	Dollars (mil)	Per capita[1]	Date	Dollars (mil)	Per capita[1]	Date	Dollars (mil)	Per capita[1]
June 30, 1955.	$30,229	$183	Sept. 30, 1985	$187,337	$782	June 30, 2009.	$909,697	$2,963
June 30, 1960.	32,064	177	Sept. 30, 1990	278,903	1,105	June 30, 2010.	945,138	3,051
June 30, 1965.	39,719	204	Sept. 30, 1995	409,272	1,553	June 30, 2011.	1,028,910	3,302
June 30, 1970.	54,351	265	Sept. 30, 2000	568,614	2,061	June 30, 2012.	1,111,901	3,540
June 30, 1975.	81,196	380	Sept. 30, 2005	766,487	2,578	June 30, 2013.	1,193,771	3,774
Sept. 30, 1980	129,916	581	June 30, 2008	826,314	2,676			

Note: As of June 30, 2013. (1) Based on U.S. Census Bureau population estimates.

Currency in Circulation by Denomination, 2013

(in millions of dollars)

Denomination	$1	$2	$5	$10	$20	$50	$100	$500	$1,000	$5,000	$10,000	Total currency[2]
Total currency in circulation	$10,334	$2,009	$12,025	$17,332	$148,219	$71,751	$889,207	$142	$165	$2	$3	$1,151,191
Federal Reserve notes[1]	10,192	1,877	11,892	17,312	148,199	71,740	889,185	142	165	2	3	1,150,710
U.S. notes	—	132	108	—	—	—	NA	—	—	NA	NA	240
Currency no longer issued	141	—	25	20	20	11	22	—	—	—	—	241

NA = Not applicable. — = Less than $1 million. (1) Issued on or after July 1, 1929. (2) Includes fractional notes and the value of partial denominations not presented for redemption.

Budget Receipts and Outlays, 1789-1940

Source: U.S. Dept. of the Treasury

(in thousands of dollars; annual statements for years ending June 30, unless otherwise noted)

Yearly average	Receipts	Outlays	Yearly average	Receipts	Outlays	Yearly average	Receipts	Outlays
1789-1800[1]	$5,717	$5,776	1866-1870	$447,301	$377,642	1906-1910	$628,507	$639,178
1801-1810[2]	13,056	9,086	1871-1875	336,830	287,460	1911-1915	710,227	720,252
1811-1820[2]	21,032	23,943	1876-1880	288,124	255,598	1916-1920	3,483,652	8,065,333
1821-1830[2]	21,928	16,162	1881-1885	366,961	257,691	1921-1925	4,306,673	3,578,989
1831-1840[2]	30,461	24,495	1886-1890	375,448	279,134	1926-1930	4,069,138	3,182,807
1841-1850[2]	28,545	34,097	1891-1895	352,801	363,599	1931-1935	2,770,973	5,214,874
1851-1860	60,237	60,163	1896-1900	434,877	457,451	1936-1940	4,960,614	10,192,367
1861-1865	160,907	683,785	1901-1905	559,481	535,559			

(1) Average for period Mar. 4, 1789, to Dec. 31, 1800. (2) Years 1801-42 end Dec. 31; average for 1841-50 is for the period Jan. 1, 1841, to June 30, 1850.

U.S. Budget Receipts and Outlays, Fiscal Years 2000-12

Source: Congressional Budget Office; *Budget of the U.S. Government*, Office of Mgmt. and Budget, Exec. Office of the President

A $236 bil surplus in 2000 turned into a $1.4 tril deficit by 2009; estimates for 2014 show the deficit reduced by half. Over the past decade, the total amount of money the government receives in taxes has varied little, while outlays have more than doubled for national defense, Medicare, and other health and income security programs.

(in millions of current dollars; numbers may not add up to totals because of independent rounding or omitted subcategories, including some subcategories with negative values)

Function and subfunction	2000	2005	2009	2010	2011	2012
NET RECEIPTS	$2,025,191	$2,153,611	$2,104,989	$2,162,706	$2,303,466	$2,450,164
Individual income taxes	1,004,462	927,222	915,308	898,549	1,091,473	1,132,206
Corporation income taxes	207,289	278,282	138,229	191,437	181,085	242,289
Social insurance and retirement receipts	652,852	794,125	890,917	864,814	818,792	845,314
Employment and general retirement	620,451	747,664	848,885	815,894	758,516	774,927
Old-age and survivors insurance (off-budget)	411,677	493,646	559,067	539,996	483,683	486,783
Disability insurance (off-budget)	68,907	83,830	94,942	91,691	82,105	82,718
Hospital insurance	135,529	166,068	190,663	180,068	188,490	201,143
Railroad retirement/pension fund	2,688	2,284	2,301	2,285	2,415	2,519
Railroad social security equivalent account	1,650	1,836	1,912	1,854	1,823	1,764
Unemployment insurance	27,640	42,002	37,889	44,823	56,241	66,647
Other retirement	4,761	4,459	4,143	4,097	4,035	3,740
Excise taxes	68,865	73,094	62,483	66,909	72,381	79,061
Federal funds	22,692	22,547	13,854	18,256	18,904	20,359
Alcohol	8,140	8,111	9,903	9,229	9,294	9,765
Tobacco	7,221	7,920	12,841	17,160	16,685	16,351
Telephone	5,670	6,047	1,115	993	930	757
Transportation fuels	819	−770	−10,324	−11,030	−8,644	−5,751
Trust funds	46,173	50,547	48,629	48,653	53,477	58,702
Transportation	34,972	37,892	34,961	34,992	36,906	40,169
Airport and airway	9,739	10,314	10,569	10,612	11,532	12,532
Black lung disability	518	610	645	595	623	629
Inland waterway	101	91	76	74	84	90
Oil spill liability	182	—	447	476	501	497
Aquatic resources	342	429	576	580	593	614
Leaking underground storage tank	184	189	169	169	152	170
Tobacco assessments	—	899	951	937	932	939
Vaccine injury compensation	133	123	235	218	278	254
Other receipts	91,723	80,888	98,052	140,997	139,735	151,294

Function and subfunction	2000	2005	2009	2010	2011	2012
OUTLAYS	$1,788,950	$2,471,957	$3,517,677	$3,457,079	$3,603,059	$3,537,127
National defense	294,363	495,308	661,023	693,498	705,557	677,856
Department of Defense—Military	281,029	474,071	636,742	666,703	678,064	650,851
Military personnel	75,950	127,463	147,348	155,690	161,608	152,266
Operation and maintenance	105,812	188,118	259,312	275,968	291,038	282,297
Procurement	51,696	82,294	129,218	133,603	128,003	124,712
Research, development, test, and evaluation	37,602	65,694	79,030	76,990	74,871	70,396
Military construction	5,109	5,331	17,614	21,169	19,917	14,553
Family housing	3,413	3,720	2,721	3,173	3,432	2,331
Atomic energy defense activities	12,138	18,042	17,552	19,315	20,410	19,247
Defense-related activities	1,196	3,195	6,729	7,480	7,083	7,758
International affairs	17,213	34,565	37,529	45,195	45,685	47,189
International development and humanitarian assistance	6,516	17,696	22,095	19,014	21,255	21,882
International security assistance	6,387	7,895	6,247	11,363	12,042	11,464
Conduct of foreign affairs	4,708	9,148	12,152	13,557	12,486	13,553
Foreign information and exchange activities	817	1,129	1,330	1,485	1,575	1,556
International financial programs	−1,215	−1,303	−4,295	−224	−1,673	−1,266
General science, space, and technology	18,594	23,597	28,417	30,100	29,466	29,060
General science and basic research	6,167	8,819	10,020	11,730	12,434	12,458
Space flight, research, and supporting activities	12,427	14,778	18,397	18,370	17,032	16,602
Energy	−761	429	4,749	11,611	12,174	14,857
Energy supply	−1,818	−940	2,045	5,794	8,084	9,016
Energy conservation	666	883	1,432	4,997	6,736	4,941
Emergency energy preparedness	162	162	754	199	−3,263	375
Energy information, policy, and regulation	229	324	518	621	617	525
Natural resources and environment	25,003	27,980	35,568	43,661	45,470	41,628
Water resources	5,078	5,723	8,063	11,656	11,618	9,175
Conservation and land management	6,762	6,226	9,813	10,783	11,955	11,101
Recreational resources	2,540	2,990	3,550	3,911	4,157	3,752
Pollution control and abatement	7,395	8,065	8,270	10,841	10,946	10,813
Agriculture	36,458	26,565	22,237	21,356	20,662	17,791
Farm income stabilization	33,446	22,048	17,635	16,604	16,017	13,173
Agricultural research and services	3,012	4,517	4,602	4,752	4,645	4,618
Commerce and housing credit	3,207	7,566	291,535	−82,316	−12,573	40,823
Mortgage credit	−3,335	−862	99,760	35,804	14,158	−8,143
Postal Service	2,129	−1,223	−978	−682	909	2,744
Deposit insurance	−3,053	−1,371	22,573	−32,033	−8,697	6,666
Transportation	46,853	67,894	84,289	91,972	92,966	93,019
Ground transportation	31,697	42,317	54,103	60,784	60,902	61,308
Air transportation	10,571	18,807	20,799	21,431	21,353	21,725
Water transportation	4,394	6,439	9,093	9,351	10,359	9,650
Community and regional development	10,623	26,262	27,676	23,894	23,883	25,132
Community development	5,480	5,861	7,719	9,901	9,605	8,769
Area and regional development	2,538	2,745	3,221	3,249	4,050	4,424
Disaster relief and insurance	2,605	17,656	16,736	10,744	10,228	11,939
Education, training, employment, and social services	53,764	97,555	79,749	128,598	101,233	90,823
Elementary, secondary, and vocational education	20,578	38,271	53,206	73,261	66,476	47,492
Higher education	10,115	31,442	−3,258	20,908	1,108	12,113
Research and general education aids	2,543	3,124	3,456	3,631	3,710	3,704
Training and employment	6,777	6,852	7,652	9,854	9,139	7,779
Social services	12,557	16,251	17,047	19,179	18,931	17,867
Health	154,504	250,548	334,335	369,068	372,504	346,742
Health care services	136,201	219,559	300,013	330,710	332,210	308,160
Health research and training	15,979	28,050	30,570	34,214	36,198	34,502
Consumer and occupational health and safety	2,324	2,939	3,752	4,144	4,096	4,080
Medicare	197,113	298,638	430,093	451,636	485,653	471,793
Income security	253,724	345,847	533,224	622,210	597,352	541,344
Retirement and disability insurance (excl. social security)	5,189	6,976	8,218	6,564	6,697	7,760
Federal employee retirement and disability	77,152	93,351	118,119	119,867	124,450	122,388
Unemployment compensation	23,012	35,435	122,537	160,145	120,556	93,771
Housing assistance	28,949	37,899	50,913	58,651	55,440	47,948
Food and nutrition assistance	32,483	50,833	79,080	95,110	103,199	106,871
Social security	409,423	523,305	682,963	706,737	730,811	773,290
Veterans benefits and services	46,989	70,120	95,429	108,384	127,189	124,595
Income security for veterans	24,907	35,767	45,952	49,163	58,747	55,899
Veterans education, training, and rehabilitation	1,285	2,790	3,495	8,089	10,683	10,402
Hospital and medical care for veterans	19,516	28,754	41,882	45,714	50,062	50,588
Veterans housing	364	860	−578	540	1,262	1,413
Administration of justice	28,499	40,019	52,581	54,383	56,056	56,277
Federal law enforcement activities	12,121	19,912	28,584	28,713	29,802	28,977
Federal litigative and judicial activities	7,762	9,641	12,083	13,073	13,565	14,670
Federal correctional activities	3,707	5,862	7,298	7,748	8,057	8,294
Criminal justice assistance	4,909	4,604	4,616	4,849	4,632	4,336
General government	13,013	16,997	22,017	23,014	27,476	28,036
Legislative functions	2,227	3,460	3,823	4,100	3,974	3,908
Executive direction and management	456	569	535	528	446	628
Central fiscal operations	8,285	9,515	10,752	11,906	11,631	11,985
General property and records management	−32	472	554	1,194	2,304	2,247
Central personnel management	184	101	102	338	124	67
General purpose fiscal assistance	2,084	3,333	4,097	5,082	7,475	7,787
Deductions for offsetting receipts	−2,383	−2,841	−1,012	−1,721	−1,479	−2,011
Net interest	222,949	183,986	186,902	196,194	229,962	220,408
Undistributed offsetting receipts	−42,581	−65,224	−92,639	−82,116	−88,467	−103,536
Employer share, employee retirement (on-budget)	−30,214	−47,977	−56,431	−62,100	−64,581	−68,347
TOTAL SURPLUS/DEFICIT	236,241	−318,346	−1,412,688	−1,294,373	−1,299,593	−1,086,963

Federal Receipts, Outlays, and Surpluses or Deficits, 1901-2014

Source: *Budget of the U.S. Government, Fiscal Year 2014,* Office of Management and Budget, Exec. Office of the President
(in millions of current dollars)

Fiscal year	Receipts	Outlays	Surplus or deficit (–)
1901	$588	$525	$63
1902	562	485	77
1903	562	517	45
1904	541	584	–43
1905	544	567	–23
1906	595	570	25
1907	666	579	87
1908	602	659	–57
1909	604	694	–89
1910	676	694	–18
1911	702	691	11
1912	693	690	3
1913	714	715	—
1914	725	726	—
1915	683	746	–63
1916	761	713	48
1917	1,101	1,954	–853
1918	3,645	12,677	–9,032
1919	5,130	18,493	–13,363
1920	6,649	6,358	291
1921	5,571	5,062	509
1922	4,026	3,289	736
1923	3,853	3,140	713
1924	3,871	2,908	963
1925	3,641	2,924	717
1926	3,795	2,930	865
1927	4,013	2,857	1,155
1928	3,900	2,961	939
1929	3,862	3,127	734
1930	4,058	3,320	738
1931	3,116	3,577	–462
1932	1,924	4,659	–2,735
1933	1,997	4,598	–2,602
1934	2,955	6,541	–3,586
1935	3,609	6,412	–2,803
1936	3,923	8,228	–4,304
1937	5,387	7,580	–2,193
1938	6,751	6,840	–89
1939	$6,295	$9,141	–$2,846
1940	6,548	9,468	–2,920
1941	8,712	13,653	–4,941
1942	14,634	35,137	–20,503
1943	24,001	78,555	–54,554
1944	43,747	91,304	–47,557
1945	45,159	92,712	–47,553
1946	39,296	55,232	–15,936
1947	38,514	34,496	**4,018**
1948	41,560	29,764	**11,796**
1949	39,415	38,835	**580**
1950	39,443	42,562	–3,119
1951	51,616	45,514	**6,102**
1952	66,167	67,686	–1,519
1953	69,608	76,101	–6,493
1954	69,701	70,855	–1,154
1955	65,451	68,444	–2,993
1956	74,587	70,640	**3,947**
1957	79,990	76,578	**3,412**
1958	79,636	82,405	–2,769
1959	79,249	92,098	–12,849
1960	92,492	92,191	**301**
1961	94,388	97,723	–3,335
1962	99,676	106,821	–7,146
1963	106,560	111,316	–4,756
1964	112,613	118,528	–5,915
1965	116,817	118,228	–1,411
1966	130,835	134,532	–3,698
1967	148,822	157,464	–8,643
1968	152,973	178,134	–25,161
1969	186,882	183,640	**3,242**
1970	192,807	195,649	–2,842
1971	187,139	210,172	–23,033
1972	207,309	230,681	–23,373
1973	230,799	245,707	–14,908
1974	263,224	269,359	–6,135
1975	279,090	332,332	–53,242
1976	298,060	371,792	–73,732
1977	$355,559	$409,218	–$53,659
1978	399,561	458,746	–59,185
1979	463,302	504,028	–40,726
1980	517,112	590,941	–73,830
1981	599,272	678,241	–78,968
1982	617,766	745,743	–127,977
1983	600,562	808,364	–207,802
1984	666,438	851,805	–185,367
1985	734,037	946,344	–212,308
1986	769,155	990,382	–221,227
1987	854,288	1,004,017	–149,730
1988	909,238	1,064,416	–155,178
1989	991,105	1,143,744	–152,639
1990	1,031,958	1,252,994	–221,036
1991	1,054,988	1,324,226	–269,238
1992	1,091,208	1,381,529	–290,321
1993	1,154,335	1,409,386	–255,051
1994	1,258,566	1,461,753	–203,186
1995	1,351,790	1,515,742	–163,952
1996	1,453,053	1,560,484	–107,431
1997	1,579,232	1,601,116	–21,884
1998	1,721,728	1,652,458	**69,270**
1999	1,827,452	1,701,842	**125,610**
2000	2,025,191	1,788,950	**236,241**
2001	1,991,082	1,862,846	**128,236**
2002	1,853,136	2,010,894	–157,758
2003	1,782,314	2,159,899	–377,585
2004	1,880,114	2,292,841	–412,727
2005	2,153,611	2,471,957	–318,346
2006	2,406,869	2,655,050	–248,181
2007	2,567,985	2,728,686	–160,701
2008	2,523,991	2,982,544	–458,553
2009	2,104,989	3,517,677	–1,412,688
2010	2,162,706	3,457,079	–1,294,373
2011	2,303,466	3,603,059	–1,299,593
2012	2,450,164	3,537,127	–1,086,963
2013[1]	2,712,045	3,684,947	–972,902
2014[1]	3,033,618	3,777,807	–744,189

— = $500,000 or less. Figures in **bold** denote annual surplus. **Note:** Budget figures prior to 1933 are based on "Administrative Budget" concepts rather than "Unified Budget" concepts. Through 1976, fiscal year ends June 30; after 1976, fiscal year ends Sept. 30. Surplus or deficit column may not equal difference between figures because of rounding. (1) Estimate as of Feb. 1, 2012.

Budget Deficits as Percent of GDP in Selected Countries, 1995-2014

Source: *OECD Economic Outlook,* Organization for Economic Cooperation and Development (OECD)

Country/area	1995	2000	2005	2008	2009	2010	2011	2012	2013	2014
Australia	–3.9%	0.4%	1.2%	–0.7%	–5.0%	–5.2%	–3.6%	–3.3%	–1.8%	–0.7%
Austria	–5.9	–1.9	–1.8	–1.0	–4.1	–4.5	–2.4	–2.5	–2.3	–1.7
Belgium	–4.5	–0.1	–2.8	–1.1	–5.6	–3.9	–3.9	–4.0	–2.6	–2.3
Canada	–5.3	2.9	1.5	–0.3	–4.8	–5.2	–4.0	–3.2	–2.9	–2.1
Czech Republic	–13.4	–3.7	–3.6	–2.2	–5.8	–4.8	–3.3	–4.4	–3.3	–3.0
Denmark	–2.9	2.2	5.0	3.3	–2.8	–2.7	–2.0	–4.1	–1.8	–1.8
Estonia	1.1	–0.2	1.6	–2.9	–2.0	0.2	1.2	–0.3	0.0	0.3
Finland	–6.2	6.8	2.5	4.3	–2.7	–2.8	–1.1	–2.3	–2.3	–1.8
France	–5.5	–1.5	–3.0	–3.3	–7.6	–7.1	–5.3	–4.9	–4.0	–3.5
Germany	–9.7	1.3	–3.3	–0.1	–3.1	–4.2	–0.8	0.2	–0.2	0.0
Greece	–9.1	–3.7	–5.3	–9.9	–15.6	–10.8	–9.6	–10.0	–4.1	–3.5
Hungary	–8.7	–3.0	–7.9	–3.7	–4.5	–4.4	4.2	–2.0	–2.8	–3.2
Iceland	–3.0	1.7	4.9	–13.5	–9.9	–10.1	–5.6	–3.4	–0.2	0.8
Ireland	–2.1	4.8	1.6	–7.4	–13.9	–30.8	–13.3	–7.5	–7.5	–4.6
Israel	NA	–4.0	–4.9	–4.0	–6.7	–4.8	–4.4	–5.1	–5.7	–4.2
Italy	–7.4	–0.9	–4.4	–2.7	–5.4	–4.3	–3.7	–2.9	–3.0	–2.3
Japan	–4.7	–7.6	–6.7	–1.9	–8.8	–8.3	–8.9	–9.9	–10.3	–8.0
Korea, South	3.5	5.4	3.4	3.0	–1.1	1.3	2.0	2.1	1.4	2.0
Luxembourg	2.4	6.0	0.0	3.2	–0.8	–0.9	–0.2	–0.8	–0.7	–0.6
Netherlands	–9.2	2.0	–0.3	0.5	–5.6	–5.0	–4.4	–4.0	–3.7	–3.6
New Zealand	2.5	1.8	4.7	0.4	–2.7	–7.5	–5.3	–3.9	–2.4	–1.1
Norway	3.2	15.4	15.1	18.8	10.5	11.1	13.4	13.9	12.3	11.8
Poland	–4.4	–3.0	–4.1	–3.7	–7.4	–7.9	–5.0	–3.9	–3.4	–2.7
Portugal	–5.0	–2.9	–5.9	–3.7	–10.2	–9.9	–4.4	–6.4	–6.4	–5.6
Spain	–6.5	–1.0	1.0	–4.5	–11.2	–9.7	–9.4	–10.6	–6.9	–6.4
Sweden	–7.3	3.6	1.9	2.2	–1.0	0.0	0.0	–0.7	–1.6	–1.1
Switzerland	–2.0	0.1	–0.7	2.0	0.8	0.3	0.5	0.7	0.7	0.6
United Kingdom	–5.8	3.7	–3.3	–4.9	–10.8	–10.0	–7.9	–6.5	–7.1	–6.5
United States	–3.3	1.5	–3.3	–6.6	–11.9	–11.4	–10.2	–8.7	–5.4	–5.3
Euro area	–7.5	–0.1	–2.6	–2.1	–6.4	–6.2	–4.1	–3.7	–3.0	–2.5
Total OECD	**–4.8**	**0.1**	**–2.8**	**–3.4**	**–8.2**	**–7.7**	**–6.4**	**–5.7**	**–4.3**	**–3.8**
Brazil	NA	NA	NA	–2.0	–3.3	–2.5	–2.6	–2.5	–2.4	–2.2
China	NA	NA	NA	0.9	–1.1	–0.7	0.1	–0.4	–1.4	–1.5
India	NA	NA	NA	–7.1	–9.6	–7.3	–7.8	–7.6	–7.0	–6.6
Indonesia	NA	NA	NA	–0.1	–1.6	–0.7	–1.1	–2.0	–2.1	–1.9
Russia	NA	NA	NA	7.3	–4.0	–1.0	1.5	0.4	–0.6	–0.5
South Africa	NA	NA	NA	–1.4	–5.2	–6.0	–5.6	–5.6	–5.2	–4.4

NA = Not available.

Public Debt of the U.S., 1946-2014

Source: *Budget of the U.S. Government*, Office of Management and Budget, Exec. Office of the President

Year	Debt held by public — Current dollars (bil)	FY 2012 dollars (bil)	As % of GDP	Interest on public debt as % of — Total federal outlays	GDP	Year	Debt held by public — Current dollars (bil)	FY 2012 dollars (bil)	As % of GDP	Interest on public debt as % of — Total federal outlays	GDP
1946	$241.9	$2,368.9	108.7%	7.4%	1.8%	2002	$3,540.4	$4,432.1	33.6%	8.9%	1.7%
1950	219.0	1,745.4	80.2	11.4	1.8	2003	3,913.4	4,801.0	35.6	7.5	1.5
1955	226.6	1,586.9	57.2	7.6	1.3	2004	4,295.5	5,139.5	36.8	7.3	1.4
1960	236.8	1,472.4	45.6	8.5	1.5	2005	4,592.2	5,321.5	36.9	7.7	1.5
1965	260.8	1,516.0	37.9	8.1	1.4	2006	4,829.0	5,412.0	36.6	8.9	1.8
1970	283.2	1,368.9	28.0	7.9	1.5	2007	5,035.1	5,480.9	36.3	9.2	1.8
1975	394.7	1,404.0	25.3	7.5	1.6	2008	5,803.1	6,173.6	40.5	8.7	1.8
1980	711.9	1,751.3	26.1	10.6	2.3	2009	7,544.7	7,924.1	54.0	5.7	1.4
1985	1,507.3	2,826.5	36.4	16.2	3.7	2010	9,018.9	9,377.3	62.9	6.6	1.6
1990	2,411.6	3,873.0	42.1	16.2	3.5	2011	10,128.2	10,314.0	67.8	7.4	1.8
1995	3,604.4	5,099.7	49.1	15.8	3.3	2012	11,281.1	11,281.1	72.6	6.6	1.5
2000	3,409.8	4,441.4	34.7	13.0	2.4	2013¹	12,403.5	12,149.9	76.6	7.2	1.6
2001	3,319.6	4,224.3	32.5	11.6	2.1	2014¹	13,295.9	12,781.7	78.2	7.1	1.6

Note: As of end of fiscal year. Through 1976, the fiscal year ended June 30. For 1977 on, the fiscal year ended Sept. 30. (1) Estimate.

State Finances: Revenues, Taxes, Expenditures, and Debt, 2011

Source: U.S. Census Bureau, U.S. Dept. of Commerce

(in thousands of dollars)

State	Revenues — Total revenue	General revenues	Intergovt. revenue	Taxes	Total expenditures	Debt at end of fiscal year
Alabama	$26,305,162	$23,276,781	$8,881,520	$8,635,527	$28,061,237	$9,067,280
Alaska	14,920,900	12,665,675	3,040,677	5,537,679	11,320,127	6,417,682
Arizona	36,611,494	27,048,737	12,360,358	10,848,179	32,875,412	14,163,076
Arkansas	22,807,859	17,453,870	6,313,263	7,975,526	18,861,507	3,748,749
California	334,233,317	211,358,143	68,430,680	116,695,284	280,212,581	149,670,954
Colorado	30,248,080	21,864,224	7,007,888	9,467,684	29,169,425	16,335,260
Connecticut	28,927,902	23,508,277	6,561,366	13,432,252	28,094,106	30,523,708
Delaware	9,105,971	7,309,677	1,890,925	3,017,837	7,936,467	5,807,957
Florida	106,165,531	75,290,282	27,804,346	32,557,946	84,633,065	43,471,755
Georgia	52,294,783	37,167,825	15,266,487	16,003,250	44,750,297	13,402,568
Hawaii	12,931,811	10,203,676	2,918,445	4,857,729	11,475,771	7,912,833
Idaho	10,776,454	7,344,101	2,804,663	3,261,722	8,733,485	3,928,080
Illinois	79,512,457	58,202,342	19,586,991	29,433,475	74,655,351	64,801,423
Indiana	38,894,976	31,449,911	10,858,319	14,909,416	35,261,522	22,144,251
Iowa	24,088,747	18,097,362	7,043,992	7,236,476	19,937,080	7,573,811
Kansas	18,613,184	15,019,196	4,940,903	6,828,477	16,686,643	6,893,030
Kentucky	31,056,300	23,572,816	9,025,194	10,203,241	29,369,940	14,522,026
Louisiana	33,974,652	26,939,024	12,532,918	8,865,421	33,396,449	18,447,200
Maine	10,611,116	8,249,133	3,241,435	3,675,810	9,099,085	5,904,221
Maryland	41,716,504	32,998,746	11,335,533	16,002,529	37,672,576	25,250,138
Massachusetts	56,636,798	44,897,892	14,136,989	22,089,530	52,550,586	74,315,823
Michigan	64,440,454	54,727,497	19,914,367	23,540,253	63,108,508	30,975,273
Minnesota	45,684,189	33,451,689	9,819,493	18,952,919	38,488,350	12,896,921
Mississippi	23,606,197	17,807,309	8,726,548	6,714,180	20,157,417	6,768,371
Missouri	38,606,945	27,082,904	12,015,114	10,109,918	30,646,880	20,682,303
Montana	7,950,510	5,768,585	2,414,552	2,303,516	7,105,366	4,266,731
Nebraska	11,523,401	9,389,153	3,401,587	4,153,113	9,356,473	2,345,750
Nevada	17,597,124	10,443,848	2,826,846	6,332,128	13,203,265	4,201,115
New Hampshire	8,521,161	6,252,239	2,158,531	2,320,014	7,638,166	8,450,218
New Jersey	70,798,018	51,676,400	14,792,596	27,182,753	67,114,331	64,004,651
New Mexico	19,866,682	14,949,450	6,364,080	4,980,115	17,865,171	8,118,832
New York	205,546,377	148,840,822	60,200,009	67,945,152	184,009,243	134,928,505
North Carolina	63,199,284	45,857,925	16,048,794	22,405,841	53,088,745	18,556,175
North Dakota	7,805,674	6,683,088	1,737,078	3,822,347	5,515,725	2,060,516
Ohio	98,560,223	61,983,770	24,133,257	25,176,562	79,153,495	30,926,386
Oklahoma	26,224,924	20,189,621	7,873,706	7,766,332	22,377,598	10,254,716
Oregon	34,991,146	20,816,600	7,608,740	8,112,049	27,334,818	14,069,253
Pennsylvania	91,705,305	69,499,280	23,842,639	32,352,286	90,791,525	45,267,281
Rhode Island	9,371,534	7,140,710	2,731,772	2,737,952	8,270,898	9,173,572
South Carolina	31,733,200	22,791,506	8,689,743	7,687,496	29,352,302	15,341,040
South Dakota	6,017,179	4,124,318	1,878,950	1,379,607	4,498,447	3,544,772
Tennessee	34,680,853	27,520,317	12,116,843	11,235,404	30,841,226	5,899,369
Texas	134,344,602	107,189,851	42,858,907	43,188,251	125,939,778	38,530,338
Utah	16,984,797	13,834,601	4,364,882	5,475,904	16,682,581	7,205,779
Vermont	6,506,203	5,627,897	2,035,378	2,687,926	5,853,842	3,485,346
Virginia	50,781,571	39,194,046	10,512,522	17,409,072	45,544,347	26,479,450
Washington	50,420,289	34,993,013	10,944,017	17,411,033	45,999,749	28,153,562
West Virginia	15,329,476	12,646,080	4,748,528	5,142,771	13,000,033	7,406,254
Wisconsin	44,807,389	32,132,862	10,535,845	15,347,327	39,349,832	22,878,524
Wyoming	7,494,341	6,056,459	2,400,542	2,461,977	5,673,561	1,364,404
United States	**2,265,533,046**	**1,652,589,530**	**593,678,758**	**757,869,188**	**2,002,719,384**	**1,132,537,232**

Note: Figures may not add up to totals because of rounding.

State and Local Government Receipts and Current Expenditures, 1960-2012

Source: Bureau of Economic Analysis, U.S. Dept. of Commerce

(in billions of current dollars; as of Aug. 2013)

	1960	1970	1980	1990	2000	2005	2010	2011	2012
Receipts	$44.2	$118.9	$335.3	$729.6	$1,303.1	$1,708.8	$1,998.5	$2,029.9	$2,039.4
Current tax receipts	37.0	91.3	230.0	519.1	893.2	1,166.5	1,305.6	1,366.3	1,405.2
Personal current taxes	4.2	14.2	48.9	122.6	236.7	276.4	297.6	327.0	348.8
Income taxes	2.5	10.9	42.6	109.6	217.4	251.5	267.1	296.1	317.3
Other	1.7	3.3	6.3	13.0	19.4	24.9	30.5	30.9	31.6
Taxes on production and imports	31.5	73.3	166.7	374.1	621.3	835.1	960.4	988.5	1,004.9
Sales taxes	12.2	31.6	82.9	184.3	316.8	402.5	446.0	463.7	474.9
Property taxes	16.2	36.7	68.8	161.5	254.7	351.3	435.0	436.9	440.0
Other	3.1	5.0	15.0	28.3	49.8	81.4	79.4	87.9	90.0
Taxes on corporate income	1.2	3.7	14.5	22.5	35.2	54.9	47.7	50.7	51.4
Contributions for government social insurance	0.5	1.1	3.6	10.0	10.8	24.6	18.1	18.3	17.5
Income receipts on assets	1.3	5.2	26.3	68.5	93.9	88.6	82.6	80.0	78.5
Interest receipts	1.0	4.3	23.1	64.1	86.3	76.8	69.1	66.3	64.2
Dividends	—	—	0.1	0.2	1.4	2.0	2.3	2.3	2.4
Rents and royalties	0.3	0.8	3.1	4.2	6.3	9.8	11.2	11.4	11.9
Current transfer receipts	4.3	20.1	76.9	126.4	299.7	436.4	612.0	581.8	552.6
Federal grants-in-aid	3.8	18.3	69.7	104.4	233.1	343.4	505.3	472.5	443.2
From business (net)	0.2	0.6	2.5	7.1	28.6	36.5	43.4	44.2	41.9
From persons	0.3	1.2	4.7	14.9	38.0	56.5	63.2	65.2	67.5
Current surplus of government enterprises	1.2	1.3	-1.4	5.6	5.4	-7.3	-19.8	-16.5	-14.3
Expenditures	41.6	115.9	329.9	736.0	1,293.2	1,775.4	2,235.8	2,243.0	2,292.1
Consumption expenditures	34.1	92.1	252.8	546.2	969.1	1,256.6	1,518.3	1517.4	1,536.4
Government social benefit payments to persons	4.6	16.1	51.2	127.7	271.4	406.6	523.8	532.0	544.3
Interest payments	3.0	7.7	25.6	61.8	52.1	111.8	192.1	192.9	211.0
Subsidies	0.0	0.0	0.4	0.4	0.5	0.4	1.6	0.5	0.5
Net state and local government saving	2.6	3.0	5.4	-6.5	9.9	-66.6	-237.3	-213.1	-252.7
Social insurance funds	0.0	0.2	1.3	2.0	2.0	7.2	3.2	4.2	3.9
Other	2.5	2.8	4.1	-8.4	7.9	-73.8	-240.5	-217.3	-256.6
Addenda:									
Total receipts	47.2	125.1	353.9	754.6	1,347.3	1,765.6	2,075.2	2,103.8	2,113.5
Current receipts	44.2	118.9	335.3	729.6	1,303.1	1,708.8	1,998.5	2,029.9	2,039.4
Capital transfer receipts	3.0	6.2	18.6	25.0	44.2	56.8	76.7	73.9	74.1
Total expenditures	52.0	135.4	364.7	807.2	1,418.5	1,925.3	2,385.5	2,368.6	2,405.9
Current expenditures	41.6	115.9	329.9	736	1,293.2	1,775.4	2,235.8	2,243.0	2,292.1
Gross government investment	14.1	29.3	65.7	132.2	232.9	290.8	351.9	337.2	334.9
Capital transfer payments	—	—	—	—	0.0	6.4	0.0	0.0	0.0
Net purchases of nonproduced assets	0.9	1.1	2.2	5.7	8.6	10.0	10.6	10.1	10.2
Less: Consumption of fixed capital	4.5	10.9	33.1	66.7	116.2	157.3	212.7	221.7	231.4
Net lending or net borrowing (-)	-4.8	-10.3	-10.8	-52.7	-71.2	-159.7	-310.3	-264.8	-292.4

Federal Deposit Insurance Corporation (FDIC)

The Federal Deposit Insurance Corporation (FDIC) was created by Congress during the height of the Depression to maintain stability and public confidence in the nation's banking system. It covered depositors for up to $2,500 in case of bank failure in 1934; the limit today is 100 times that much, or $250,000. In its unique role as deposit insurer of banks and savings associations, and in cooperation with other federal and state regulatory agencies, the FDIC seeks to promote the safety and soundness of insured depository institutions in the U.S. financial system.

The quarterly premiums on deposit insurance are paid by the banks rather than by consumers. The amount of the premium is based on the institution's balance of insured deposits for the preceding quarter and the institution's risk to the insurance fund. In 2009, Congress permanently increased the limit that the FDIC may borrow from the U.S. Treasury from $30 bil to $100 bil.

U.S. Banks, 1935-2013

Source: *Summary of Deposits*, Federal Deposit Insurance Corp.

Comprises all FDIC-insured commercial and savings banks, including savings and loan institutions (S&Ls).

	Number of banks				Deposits (in mil dollars)				
		Commercial banks[1]		Savings banks, total		Commercial banks[1]			Savings banks, total
Year	All banks[2]	National charter	State charter	Non-members		All deposits[2]	National charter	State charter	Non-members	
1935[3]	15,295	5,386	1,001	7,735	1,173	$45,102	$24,802	$13,653	$5,669	$978
1940	15,772	5,144	1,342	6,956	2,330	67,494	35,787	20,642	7,040	4,025
1950	16,500	4,958	1,912	6,576	3,054	171,963	84,941	41,602	19,726	25,694
1960	17,549	4,530	1,641	6,955	4,423	310,262	120,242	65,487	34,369	90,164
1970	18,205	4,621	1,147	7,743	4,694	686,901	285,436	101,512	95,566	204,367
1980	18,763	4,425	997	9,013	4,328	1,832,716	656,752	191,183	344,311	640,470
1990	15,158	3,979	1,009	7,355	2,815	3,637,292	1,558,915	397,797	693,438	987,142
1995	12,289	2,941	995	6,230	2,082	3,214,678	1,337,105	439,430	696,108	735,856
2000	10,119	2,302	996	5,180	1,622	4,003,744	1,792,773	707,562	793,275	706,461
2005	8,855	1,864	906	4,779	1,293	5,933,742	2,946,589	765,673	1,191,977	1,023,620
2007	8,605	1,676	888	4,786	1,244	6,702,053	3,273,531	831,116	1,425,412	1,165,119
2008	8,441	1,585	874	4,744	1,227	7,025,791	3,596,712	857,003	1,432,614	1,132,356
2009	8,185	1,505	858	4,632	1,180	7,559,590	4,141,792	962,232	1,512,677	936,101
2010	7,821	1,427	836	4,413	1,135	7,676,878	4,305,697	1,002,425	1,464,022	891,159
2011	7,523	1,349	824	4,240	1,100	8,249,233	4,708,210	1,120,747	1,491,112	909,912
2012	7,255	1,285	836	4,101	1,023	8,947,239	5,250,842	1,220,930	1,576,616	874,850
2013	6,950	1,194	849	3,937	960	9,433,525	5,667,790	1,281,662	1,648,153	806,933

Note: Figures are for the end of the year shown through 1990 and for June 30 thereafter. (1) Nonmembers are banks that are not members of the Federal Reserve System; national charter and state charter institutions are Federal Reserve members. (2) Includes U.S. branches of foreign banks not listed separately. (3) Figures for 1935 do not include S&Ls, the data for which are not available.

U.S. Bank Failures, 1934-2013

Source: Federal Deposit Insurance Corp.

Covers all FDIC-insured commercial and savings banks, including savings and loan institutions (S&Ls) 1980 and after. As of Sept. 11, 2013.

Year	Closed or assisted	Year	Closed or assisted	Year	Closed or assisted	Year	Closed or assisted	Year	Closed or assisted
1934....	9	1960-69 ..	44	1988.....	470	1998.....	3	2007.....	3
1935....	25	1970-79 ..	79	1989.....	534	1999.....	8	2008.....	30
1936....	69	1980.....	22	1990.....	382	2000.....	7	2009.....	148
1937....	75	1981.....	40	1991.....	271	2001.........	4	2010.....	157
1938....	74	1982.....	119	1992.....	181	2002.....	11	2011.....	92
1939....	60	1983.....	99	1993.....	50	2003.....	3	2012.....	51
1940....	43	1984.....	106	1994.....	15	2004.....	4	2013.....	20
1941....	15	1985.....	180	1995.....	8	2005.....	0	**Total,**	
1942....	20	1986.....	204	1996.....	6	2006.....	0	**1934-2013**	**4,053**
1950-59 ..	28	1987.....	262	1997.....	1				

Largest U.S. Bank Holding Companies, 2013

Source: National Information Center, Federal Financial Institutions Examination Council
(ranked by total assets, in billions of dollars; as of June 30, 2013)

Rank	Institution name, location	Total assets	Rank	Institution name, location	Total assets
1.	JPMorgan Chase & Co., New York, NY ..	$2,439.5	21.	Charles Schwab Corp., San Francisco, CA	$135.9
2.	Bank of America Corp., Charlotte, NC ...	2,125.7	22.	Fifth Third Bancorp, Cincinnati, OH	123.4
3.	Citigroup Inc., New York, NY...........	1,884.0	23.	U.S. Automobile Assn., San Antonio, TX..	120.3
4.	Wells Fargo & Co., San Francisco, CA ..	1,440.6	24.	Regions Financial Corp., Birmingham, AL	118.8
5.	Goldman Sachs Group, Inc., New York, NY	938.6	25.	RBS Citizens Financial Group, Inc.,	
6.	Morgan Stanley, New York, NY	802.7		Providence, RI	118.1
7.	American Intl. Group, Inc., New York, NY	537.4	26.	BMO Financial Corp., Wilmington, DE ...	112.3
8.	General Electric Capital Corp., Norwalk, CT	529.0	27.	UnionBanCal Corp., San Francisco, CA ..	102.3
9.	Bank of New York Mellon Corp., New York,		28.	Northern Trust Corp., Chicago, IL.......	97.2
	NY...............................	360.5	29.	KeyCorp, Cleveland, OH.	90.9
10.	U.S. Bancorp, Minneapolis, MN	353.4	30.	M&T Bank Corp., Buffalo, NY	83.2
11.	HSBC North America Holdings Inc., New		31.	BancWest Corp., Honolulu, HI	80.1
	York, NY	322.0	32.	Santander Holdings USA, Inc., Boston, MA	79.2
12.	PNC Financial Services Group, Inc.,		33.	Discover Financial Services, Riverwoods,	
	Pittsburgh, PA	304.5		IL................................	74.9
13.	Capital One Financial Corp., McLean, VA	296.7	34.	Deutsche Bank Trust Corp., New York, NY	72.0
14.	TD Bank U.S. Holding Co., Portland, ME	228.9	35.	BBVA USA Bancshares, Inc., Houston, TX	69.7
15.	State Street Corp., Boston, MA	227.0	36.	Comerica Inc., Dallas, TX.............	63.0
16.	Principal Financial Group, Inc.,		37.	Huntington Bancshares Inc., Columbus,	
	Des Moines, IA	196.5		OH	56.1
17.	BB&T Corp., Winston-Salem, NC	182.7	38.	Zions BanCorp., Salt Lake City, UT	54.9
18.	SunTrust Banks, Inc., Atlanta, GA	171.6	39.	Utrecht-America Holdings, Inc., New York,	
19.	American Express Co., New York, NY ...	152.0		NY................................	48.7
20.	Ally Financial Inc., Detroit, MI.........	150.6	40.	E*Trade Financial Corp., New York, NY ..	45.0

Note: Includes foreign-owned banks with a strong presence in the U.S.

Status of Top Recipients of Treasury Department "Bailout" Funds, 2013

Source: ProPublica

Since Oct. 2008, the federal government has spent more than $600 bil to bail out more than 900 institutions severely affected by the financial crisis. As of Aug. 2013, the government had recouped more than 90% of those funds. Companies that have failed to repay the government, resulting in a loss to the taxpayers, are listed in bold italics.

(in billions of dollars; as of Aug. 9, 2013)

Recipient	Disbursed	Repaid[1]	Net profit or amount still outstanding[2]	Recipient	Disbursed	Repaid[1]	Net profit or amount still outstanding[2]
Fannie Mae	*$116.1*	*$95.0*	*−$21.2*	AllianceBernstein Legacy			
Freddie Mac............	*71.3*	*36.6*	*−34.8*	Securities Master Fund, L.P.	$3.2	$3.8	$0.6
AIG Insurance	67.8	72.9	5.0	BB&T	3.1	3.3	0.2
General Motors	*50.7*	*31.7*	*−19.0*	Bank of New York Mellon ..	3.0	3.2	0.2
Bank of America	45.0	49.6	4.6	KeyCorp	2.5	2.9	0.4
Citigroup..............	45.0	58.4	13.4	*CIT Group*	*2.3*	*—*	*−2.3*
JPMorgan Chase	25.0	26.7	1.7	Comerica Incorporated....	2.3	2.6	0.3
Wells Fargo............	25.0	27.3	2.3	State Street.............	2.0	2.1	0.1
GMAC (now Ally Financial)	*16.3*	*6.1*	*−10.2*	RLJ Western Asset Public/			
Chrysler	*10.7*	*9.4*	*−1.3*	Private Master Fund, L.P.	1.9	2.3	0.5
Goldman Sachs	10.0	11.4	1.4	Invesco Legacy Securities			
Morgan Stanley.........	10.0	11.3	1.3	Master Fund, L.P.	1.7	2.3	0.6
PNC Financial Services ...	7.6	8.3	0.7	Marshall & Ilsley	1.7	1.9	0.2
U.S. Bancorp	6.6	6.9	0.3	Oaktree PPIP Fund, L.P. ..	1.7	2.0	0.3
SunTrust	4.9	5.4	0.5	Blackrock PPIF, L.P.	1.6	2.0	0.4
Capital One Financial Corp.	3.6	3.8	0.3	Northern Trust..........	1.6	1.7	0.1
Regions Financial Corp. ...	3.5	4.1	0.6	Chrysler Financial Services	1.5	1.5	—
Wellington Management				Marathon Legacy Securities			
Legacy Securities PPIF				Public-Private Investment			
Master Fund, LP	3.4	4.2	0.7	Partnership, L.P.	1.4	1.8	0.4
Fifth Third Bancorp	3.4	4.0	0.6	Zions Bancorp	1.4	1.7	0.3
Hartford Financial Services				Huntington Bancshares ...	1.4	1.6	0.2
Insurance	3.4	4.2	0.8	Discover Financial Services	1.2	1.5	0.2
American Express Financial				*JPMorgan Chase*			
Services	3.4	3.8	0.4	*subsidiaries*	*1.2*	*0.0*	*−1.2*
AG GECC PPIF Master				*Bank of America subsidiaries*			
Fund, L.P.	3.4	4.3	0.9	*(incl. Countrywide)*	*1.2*	*0.0*	*−1.2*
				Total	**608.0**	**549.9**	**−58.1**

— = less than $0.1 bil. **Note:** Total includes other disbursements not shown. Figures may not add up to totals due to rounding. (1) Amounts repaid include principal, dividends, interest, warrants, and other proceeds. (2) Negative number represents outstanding debt.

Federal Reserve System

The Federal Reserve System is the central bank for the U.S. The system was established on Dec. 23, 1913, originally to give the country an elastic currency, provide facilities for discounting commercial paper, and improve the supervision of banking. Since then, the system's responsibilities have been broadened. Over the years, stability and growth of the economy, a high level of employment, stability in the purchasing power of the dollar, and reasonable balance in transactions with other countries have come to be recognized as primary objectives of governmental economic policy.

The Federal Reserve System consists of the Board of Governors, the 12 District Reserve Banks and their branch offices, and the Federal Open Market Committee. Several advisory councils help the board meet its varied responsibilities.

The hub of the system is the 7-member Board of Governors in Washington, DC. The members of the board are appointed by the president and confirmed by the Senate to 14-year terms. The president also appoints the chairman and vice chairman of the board from among the board members for 4-year terms. As of Sept. 2013, the board members were Ben S. Bernanke, chair; Janet L. Yellen, vice-chair; Daniel K. Tarullo; Sarah Bloom Raskin; Jeremy C. Stein; and Jerome H. Powell, with one vacancy. Powell's term ends Jan. 31, 2014; Bernanke's second term as chair concludes the same day, though he will remain a board member through 2020.

The 12 **District Reserve Banks** and their branch offices serve as the decentralized portion of the system, carrying out day-to-day operations such as circulating currency and coin and providing fiscal agency functions and payments mechanism services. The 12 are in Boston, New York, Philadelphia, Cleveland, Richmond, Atlanta, Chicago, St. Louis, Minneapolis, Kansas City, Dallas, and San Francisco.

The system's principal function is monetary policy, which it controls using three tools: reserve requirements, the discount rate, and open market operations.

Uniform **reserve requirements**, set by the board, are applied to the transaction accounts and nonpersonal time deposits of all depository institutions. Responsibility for setting the **discount rate** (the interest rate at which depository institutions can borrow money from the Reserve Banks) is shared by the Board of Governors and the Reserve Banks. Changes in the discount rate are recommended by the individual boards of directors of the Reserve Banks and are subject to approval by the Board of Governors.

The most important tool of monetary policy is **open market operations**, or the purchase and sale of government securities. Responsibility for influencing the cost and availability of money and credit through the purchase and sale of government securities lies with the **Federal Open Market Committee** (FOMC), which is composed of the seven members of the Board of Governors, the president of the Federal Reserve Bank of New York, and four other Federal Reserve Bank presidents, who each serve 1-year terms on a rotating basis. The committee bases its decisions on economic and financial developments and outlook, setting yearly growth objectives for key measures of money supply and credit. The decisions of the committee are carried out by the domestic trading desk of the Federal Reserve Bank of New York.

A Federal Advisory Council meets with the Federal Reserve Board four times a year to discuss business and financial conditions, as well as to make recommendations.

Website: www.federalreserve.gov.

Federal Reserve Board Discount Rates, 1955-2013

The interest rate that the Federal Reserve charges its member banks to borrow money overnight is often referred to as the discount rate. On Jan. 9, 2003, the Fed divided the discount window into two categories: primary credit, for banks in sound financial condition, and secondary credit, for banks that do not qualify for primary credit. The secondary credit rate is ½ a percentage point higher than the primary credit rate. Banks typically raise or lower the rates they extend to their customers to track changes in the discount rate.

Effective date	Rate	Effective date	Rate	Effective date	Rate	Effective date	Rate	Effective date	Rate
1955:		**1970:**		**1979:**		**1990:**		**2003:**	
Jan. 3	1½	Nov. 13	5¾	July 20	10	Dec. 18	6½	Jan. 9	2¼ [1]
Apr. 15	1¾	Dec. 4	5½	Aug. 17	10½	**1991:**		June 25	2
Aug. 5	2	**1971:**		Sept. 19	11	Apr. 30	5½	**2004:**	
Sept. 9	2¼	Jan. 8	5¼	Oct. 8	12	Sept. 13	5	June 30	2¼
Nov. 18	2½	Jan. 22	5	**1980:**		Nov. 6	4½	Aug. 10	2½
1956:		Feb. 19	4¾	Feb. 15	13	Dec. 20	3½	Sept. 21	2¾
Apr. 13	2¾	July 16	5	May 30	12	**1992:**		Nov. 10	3
Aug. 24	3	Nov. 19	4¾	June 13	11	July 2	3	Dec. 14	3¼
1957:		Dec. 17	4½	July 28	10	**1994:**		**2005:**	
Aug. 23	3½	**1973:**		Sept. 26	11	May 17	3½	Feb. 2	3½
Nov. 15	3	Jan. 15	5	Nov. 17	12	Aug. 16	4	Mar. 22	3¾
1958:		Feb. 26	5½	Dec. 5	13	Nov. 15	4¾	May 3	4
Jan. 24	2¾	May 4	5¾	**1981:**		**1995:**		June 30	4¼
Mar. 7	2¼	May 11	6	May 5	14	Feb. 1	5	Aug. 9	4½
Apr. 18	1¾	June 11	6½	Nov. 2	13	**1996:**		Sept. 20	4¾
Sept. 12	2	July 2	7	Dec. 4	12	Jan. 31	5	Nov. 1	5
Nov. 7	2½	Aug. 14	7½	**1982:**		**1998:**		Dec. 13	5¼
1959:		**1974:**		July 20	11½	Oct. 15	4¾	**2006:**	
Mar. 6	3	Apr. 25	8	Aug. 2	11	Nov. 17	4½	Jan. 31	5½
May 29	3½	Dec. 9	7¾	Aug. 16	10	**1999:**		Mar. 28	5¾
Sept. 11	4	**1975:**		Aug. 27	10	Aug. 24	4¾	May 10	6
1960:		Jan. 10	7¼	Oct. 12	9½	Nov. 16	5	June 29	6¼
June 10	3½	Feb. 5	6¾	Dec. 15	8½	**2000:**		**2007:**	
Aug. 12	3	Mar. 19	6¼	**1984:**		Feb. 2	5¼	Aug. 17	5¾
1963:		May 16	6	Apr. 9	9	Mar. 21	5½	Sept.18	5¼
July 17	3½	**1976:**		Nov. 21	8½	May 16	6	Nov. 1	5
1964:		Jan. 19	5½	Dec. 24	8	**2001:**		Dec. 12	4¾
Nov. 24	4	Nov. 22	5¼	**1985:**		Jan. 3	5¾	**2008:**	
1965:		**1977:**		May 20	7½	Jan. 31	5	Jan. 22	4
Dec. 6	4½	Aug. 31	5¾	**1986:**		Mar. 20	4½	Jan. 30	3½
1967:		Oct. 26	6	Mar. 7	7	Apr. 18	4	Mar. 17	3¼
Apr. 7	4	**1978:**		Apr. 21	6½	May 15	3½	Mar. 18	2½
Nov. 20	4½	Jan. 9	6½	July 11	6	June 27	3¼	Apr. 30	2¼
1968:		May 11	7	Aug. 21	5½	Aug. 21	3	Oct. 8	1¾
Mar. 22	5	July 3	7¼	**1987:**		Sept. 17	2½	Oct. 29	1¼
Apr. 19	5½	Aug. 21	7¾	Sept. 4	6	Oct. 2	2	Dec. 16	½
Aug. 30	5¼	Sept. 22	8	**1988:**		Dec. 11	1¼	**2010:**	
Dec. 18	5½	Oct. 16	8½	Aug. 9	6½	**2002:**		Feb. 19	¾
1969:		Nov. 1	9½	**1989:**		Nov. 6	¾		
Apr. 4	6			Feb. 24	7				

Note: As of Sept. 11, 2013, rate effective Feb. 19, 2010, was unchanged. (1) Adjustment credit rate replaced with primary credit rate. See note above.

Standard & Poor's 500 Index, 1997-2013

Monthly closing levels beginning with Oct. 1997; record high daily closing was 1,725.52 on Sept. 18, 2013.

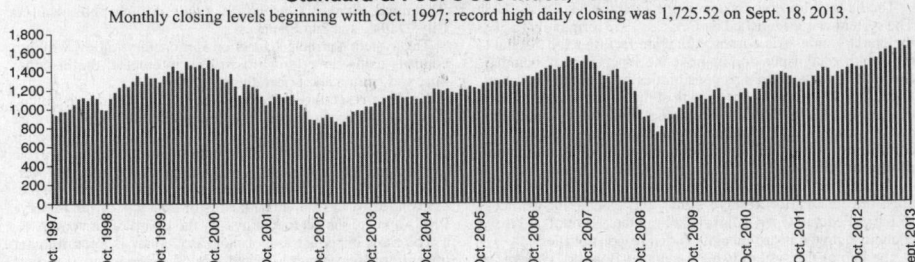

U.S. Holdings of Foreign Securities, 2006-12

Source: *U.S. Portfolio Holdings of Foreign Securities*, U.S. Dept. of the Treasury
(in billions of dollars)

	2006	2008	2010	2011	2012[1]		2006	2008	2010	2011	2012[1]
Europe	$3,129	$2,172	$3,154	$2,978	$3,562	**Latin America and**					
United						**Caribbean**	$946	$733	$1,064	$1,393	$1,598
Kingdom	1,076	647	1,001	989	1,129	Cayman Islands . .	376	315	366	709	784
France	402	285	366	306	375	Brazil	110	91	235	196	216
Switzerland	264	218	327	292	333	Bermuda	208	163	159	161	178
Germany	292	255	299	266	330	Mexico	108	65	109	108	157
Netherlands	234	169	233	242	286	Netherlands					
Ireland	121	63	132	149	181	Antilles	58	38	83	70	70
Sweden	102	59	122	115	122	**Asia**	**1,166**	**775**	**1,342**	**1,232**	**1,426**
Italy	106	62	66	62	110	Japan	596	403	519	509	521
Luxembourg	60	60	100	93	105	South Korea	124	56	148	146	175
Spain	111	93	87	76	99	Hong Kong	88	65	135	116	145
Canada.	**478**	**378**	**695**	**736**	**808**	China, mainland	75	55	102	77	120
Africa	**57**	**43**	**99**	**88**	**110**	Taiwan	74	41	95	72	88
South Africa	43	32	78	71	86	India	49	32	91	59	79
Australia	**173**	**146**	**323**	**334**	**351**	**Total holdings**	**5,991**	**4,291**	**6,763**	**6,841**	**7,941**

(1) Preliminary.

Record One-Day Gains and Losses of the Dow Jones Industrial Average

Source: Dow Jones & Co., Inc.

(ranked by largest one-day losses and gains for two terms; as of Oct. 10, 2013)

Greatest % losses

Rank	Date	Close	Net chg.	% chg.
1.	10/19/1987	1,738.74	−508.00	−22.61%
2.	10/28/1929	260.64	−38.33	−12.82
3.	10/29/1929	230.07	−30.57	−11.73
4.	11/6/1929	232.13	−25.55	−9.92
5.	12/18/1899	58.27	−5.57	−8.72

Greatest point losses

Rank	Date	Close	Net chg.	% chg.
1.	9/29/2008	10,365.45	−777.68	−6.98%
2.	10/15/2008	8,577.91	−733.08	−7.87
3.	9/17/2001	8,920.70	−684.81	−7.13
4.	12/1/2008	8,149.09	−679.95	−7.70
5.	10/9/2008	8,579.19	−678.92	−7.33

Greatest % gains

Rank	Date	Close	Net chg.	% chg.
1.	3/15/1933	62.10	8.26	15.34%
2.	10/6/1931	99.34	12.86	14.87
3.	10/30/1929	258.47	28.40	12.34
4.	9/21/1932	75.16	7.67	11.36
5.	10/13/2008	9,387.61	936.42	11.08

Greatest point gains

Rank	Date	Close	Net chg.	% chg.
1.	10/13/2008	9,387.61	936.42	11.08%
2.	10/28/2008	9,065.12	889.35	10.88
3.	3/11/2008	8,835.25	552.60	6.67
4.	3/16/2000	10,630.61	499.19	4.93
5.	3/23/2009	7,775.86	497.48	6.84

Dow Jones Industrial Average, 1965-2013

Source: Dow Jones & Co., Inc.

(as of Oct. 10, 2013)

Year	Highest close		Lowest close		Year	Highest close		Lowest close	
1965	Dec. 31	969.26	June 28	840.59	**2000**	Jan. 14	11,722.98	Mar. 7	9,796.03
1970	Dec. 29	842.00	May 6	631.16	**2001**	May 21	11,337.92	Sept. 21	8,235.81
1975	July 15	881.81	Jan. 2	632.04	**2002**	Mar. 19	10,635.25	Oct. 9	7,286.27
1980	Nov. 20	1,000.17	Apr. 21	759.13	**2003**	Dec. 31	10,453.90	Mar. 11	7,524.06
1985	Dec. 16	1,553.10	Jan. 4	1,184.96	**2004**	Dec. 28	10,854.54	Oct. 25	9,749.99
1990	July 16	2,999.75	Oct. 11	2,365.10	**2005**	Mar. 4	10,940.50	Apr. 20	10,012.36
1991	Dec. 31	3,168.83	Jan. 9	2,470.30	**2006**	Dec. 27	12,510.57	Jan. 20	10,667.39
1992	June 1	3,413.21	Oct. 9	3,136.58	**2007**	Oct. 9	14,164.53	Mar. 5	12,050.41
1993	Dec. 29	3,794.33	Jan. 20	3,241.95	**2008**	Jan. 3	13,056.72	Nov. 20	7,552.29
1994	Jan. 31	3,978.36	Apr. 4	3,593.35	**2009**	Dec. 30	10,548.51	Mar. 9	6,547.05
1995	Dec. 13	5,216.47	Jan. 30	3,832.08	**2010**	Dec. 29	11,585.38	July 2	9,686.48
1996	Dec. 27	6,560.91	Jan. 10	5,032.94	**2011**	Apr. 29	12,810.54	Oct. 3	10,655.30
1997	Aug. 6	8,259.31	Apr. 11	6,391.69	**2012**	Oct. 5	13,610.15	June 4	12,101.46
1998	Nov. 23	9,374.27	Aug. 31	7,539.07	**2013**	Sept. 18	15,676.94*	Jan. 8	13,328.85
1999	Dec. 31	11,497.12	Jan. 22	9,120.67					

*Record high closing.

Milestones of the Dow Jones Industrial Average
(as of Oct. 10, 2013)

First close over—		First close over—		First close over—		First close over—		First close over—	
100	Jan. 12, 1906	3,000	Apr. 17, 1991	6,000	Oct. 14, 1996	9,000	Apr. 6, 1998	12,000	Oct. 19, 2006
500	Mar. 12, 1956	3,500	May 19, 1993	6,500	Nov. 25, 1996	9,500	Jan. 6, 1999	12,500	Dec. 27, 2006
1,000	Nov. 14, 1972	4,000	Feb. 23, 1995	7,000	Feb. 13, 1997	10,000	Mar. 29, 1999	13,000	Apr. 25, 2007
1,500	Dec. 11, 1985	4,500	June 16, 1995	7,500	June 10, 1997	10,500	Apr. 21, 1999	13,500	May 18, 2007
2,000	Jan. 8, 1987	5,000	Nov. 21, 1995	8,000	July 16, 1997	11,000	May 3, 1999	14,000	July 19, 2007
2,500	July 17, 1987	5,500	Feb. 8, 1996	8,500	Feb. 27, 1998	11,500	Jan. 7, 2000	15,000	July 19, 2007

Components of the Dow Jones Averages
(as of Oct. 10, 2013)

Dow Jones Industrial Average

Company name (ticker symbol)
American Express Co. (AXP)
AT&T Inc. (T)
Boeing Co. (BA)
Caterpillar Inc. (CAT)
Chevron Corp. (CVX)
Cisco Systems, Inc. (CSCO)
Coca-Cola Co. (KO)
E. I. DuPont de Nemours & Co. (DD)
Exxon Mobil Corp. (XOM)
General Electric Co. (GE)
Goldman Sachs Group (GS)

Company name (ticker symbol)
Home Depot Inc. (HD)
Intel Corp. (INTC)
International Business Machines
   Corp. (IBM)
Johnson & Johnson (JNJ)
JPMorgan Chase & Co. (JPM)
McDonald's Corp. (MCD)
Merck & Co., Inc. (MRK)
Microsoft Corp. (MSFT)
Nike (NKE)

Company name (ticker symbol)
Pfizer Inc. (PFE)
Procter & Gamble Co. (PG)
3M Co. (MMM)
Travelers Companies, Inc. (TRV)
United Technologies Corp. (UTX)
UnitedHealth Group Inc. (UNH)
Verizon Communications Inc. (VZ)
Visa Inc. (V)
Wal-Mart Stores Inc. (WMT)
Walt Disney Co. (DIS)

Dow Jones Utility Average

Company name (ticker symbol)
AES Corp. (AES)
American Electric Power Co.
   Inc. (AEP)
CenterPoint Energy (CNP)
Consolidated Edison Inc. (ED)
Dominion Resources Inc. (Virginia) (D)

Company name (ticker symbol)
Duke Energy Corp. (DUK)
Edison International (EIX)
Exelon Corp. (EXC)
FirstEnergy Corp. (FE)
NextEra Energy, Inc. (NEE)
NiSource Inc. (NI)

Company name (ticker symbol)
PG&E Corp. (PCG)
Public Service Enterprise Group
   Inc. (PEG)
Southern Co. (SO)
Williams Cos. (WMB)

Dow Jones Transportation Average

Company name (ticker symbol)
Alaska Air Group, Inc. (ALK)
C.H. Robinson Worldwide Inc.
   (CHRW)
Con-way Inc. (CNW)
CSX Corp. (CSX)
Delta Air Lines, Inc. (DAL)
Expeditors Intl. of Washington
   Inc. (EXPD)

Company name (ticker symbol)
FedEx Corp. (FDX)
GATX Corp. (GMT)
J.B. Hunt Transport Services Inc.
   (JBHT)
JetBlue Airways Corp. (JBLU)
Kansas City Southern (KSU)
Kirby Corp. (KEX)
Landstar System Inc. (LSTR)

Company name (ticker symbol)
Matson Inc. (MATX)
Norfolk Southern Corp. (NSC)
Ryder System Inc. (R)
Southwest Airlines Co. (LUV)
Union Pacific Corp. (UNP)
United Continental Holdings (UAL)
United Parcel Service Inc. CIB (UPS)

Record One-Day Gains and Losses on the Nasdaq Stock Market
Source: Nasdaq Stock Market
(ranked by largest one-day losses and gains for two terms; as of Oct. 10, 2013)

	Greatest point gains			Greatest % gains			Greatest point losses			Greatest % losses	
Rank	Date	Change	Rank	Date	% change	Rank	Date	Change	Rank	Date	% change
1.	1/3/2001	324.83	1.	1/3/2001	14.17%	1.	4/14/2000	−355.49	1.	10/19/1987	−11.35%
2.	12/5/2000	274.05	2.	10/13/2008	11.81	2.	4/3/2000	−349.15	2.	4/14/2000	−9.67
3.	4/18/2000	254.41	3.	12/5/2000	10.48	3.	4/12/2000	−286.27	3.	9/29/2008	−9.14
4.	5/30/2000	254.37	4.	10/28/2008	9.53	4.	4/10/2000	−258.25	4.	10/20/1987	−9.00
5.	10/19/2000	247.04	5.	4/5/2001	8.92	5.	1/4/2000	−229.46	5.	10/26/1987	−9.00
6.	10/13/2000	242.09	6.	4/18/2001	8.12	6.	3/14/2000	−200.61	6.	12/1/2008	−8.95
7.	6/2/2000	230.88	7.	5/30/2000	7.94	7.	5/10/2000	−200.28	7.	8/31/1998	−8.56
8.	4/25/2000	228.75	8.	10/13/2000	7.87	8.	5/23/2000	−199.66	8.	10/15/2008	−8.47
9.	4/17/2000	217.87	9.	10/19/2000	7.79	9.	9/28/2000	−199.61	9.	4/3/2000	−7.64
10.	10/13/2008	194.74	10.	5/8/2002	7.78	10.	10/25/2000	−190.22	10.	1/2/2001	−7.23

Nasdaq Stock Market Closing Prices, 1971-2013
Source: Nasdaq Stock Market

Year	High	Low	Year	High	Low	Year	High	Low	Year	High	Low
1971	114.12	99.68	1982	241.63	158.92	1993	790.56	645.02	2004	2,178.00	1,752.00
1972	135.15	113.65	1983	329.11	229.88	1994	803.93	691.23	2005	2,273.37	1,904.18
1973	136.84	88.67	1984	288.41	223.91	1995	1,072.82	740.53	2006	2,465.98	2,020.39
1974	96.53	54.87	1985	325.53	245.82	1996	1,328.45	978.17	2007	2,811.61	2,340.68
1975	88.00	60.70	1986	411.21	322.14	1997	1,748.62	1,194.39	2008	2,609.63	1,505.90
1976	97.88	78.06	1987	456.27	288.49	1998	2,200.63	1,357.09	2009	2,167.70	1,265.52
1977	105.05	93.66	1988	397.54	329.00	1999	4,090.61	2,193.13	2010	2,671.48	2,091.79
1978	139.25	99.09	1989	487.60	376.87	2000	5,048.62*	2,332.78	2011	2,873.54	2,335.83
1979	152.29	117.84	1990	470.30	322.93	2001	2,892.36	1,387.06	2012	3,183.95	2,648.36
1980	208.29	124.09	1991	586.35	352.85	2002	2,059.38	1,114.11	2013	3,817.98	3,091.81
1981	223.96	170.80	1992	676.95	545.85	2003	2,009.88	1,271.47			

*Record high closing, Mar. 10, 2000; as of Oct. 10, 2013.

Average Yields of Treasury, Corporate, and State and Local Bonds, 1986-2013

Source: Office of Market Finance, U.S. Dept. of the Treasury; Federal Reserve System

Period	Treasury 30-year bonds[1]	New Aa corporate bonds[2]	New Aa municipal bonds[3]	Period	Treasury 30-year bonds[1]	New Aa corporate bonds[2]	New Aa municipal bonds[3]	Period	Treasury 30-year bonds[1]	New Aa corporate bonds[2]	New Aa municipal bonds[3]
1986				**1995**				**2004**			
June	7.57%	9.39%	7.87%	June	6.57%	7.42%	5.84%	June	5.45%	6.01%	5.05%
Dec.	7.37	8.87	6.87	Dec.	6.06	7.02	5.45	Dec.	4.88	5.47	4.49
1987				**1996**				**2005**			
June	8.57	9.64	7.79	June	7.06	8.00	6.02	June	4.35	4.96	4.23
Dec.	9.12	10.22	7.96	Dec.	6.55	7.45	5.64	Dec.	4.73	5.37	4.46
1988				**1997**				**2006**			
June	9.00	10.08	7.78	June	6.77	7.71	5.53	June	5.15	5.89	4.60
Dec.	9.01	10.05	7.61	Dec.	5.99	6.68	5.19	Dec.	4.68	5.32	4.11
1989				**1998**				**2007**			
June	8.27	9.24	7.02	June	5.70	6.43	5.12	June	5.20	5.79	4.60
Dec.	7.90	9.23	6.98	Dec.	5.06	6.13	4.98	Dec.	4.53	5.49	4.42
1990				**1999**				**2008**			
June	8.46	9.69	7.24	June	6.04	7.21	5.37	June	4.69	5.68	4.69
Dec.	8.24	9.55	7.09	Dec.	6.35	7.55	5.95	Dec.	2.87	5.05	5.56
1991				**2000**				**2009**			
June	8.47	9.37	7.13	June	5.93	7.75	5.80	June	4.52	5.61	4.81
Dec.	7.70	8.55	6.69	Dec.	5.49	7.21	5.22	Dec.	4.49	5.26	4.21
1992				**2001**				**2010**			
June	7.84	8.45	6.49	June	5.67	7.11	5.20	June	4.13	4.88	4.36
Dec.	7.44	8.12	6.22	Dec.	5.48	6.80	5.25	Dec.	4.42	5.02	4.92
1993				**2002**				**2011**			
June	6.81	7.48	5.63	June	5.65	6.57	5.09	June	4.23	4.99	4.51
Dec.	6.25	7.22	5.35	Dec.	5.01	5.93	4.85	Dec.	2.98	3.93	3.95
1994				**2003**				**2012**			
June	7.40	8.16	6.11	June	4.34	4.97	4.33	June	2.70	3.64	3.94
Dec.	7.87	8.66	6.80	Dec.	5.11	5.62	4.65	Dec	2.88	3.65	3.48
								2013			
								June	3.40	4.27	4.27

(1) On Feb. 18, 2002, the U.S. treasury discontinued the 30-year constant maturity yield and reintroduced it on Feb. 9, 2006; rates in the interim are for 20-year yields. (2) Treasury series based on 3-week moving average of reoffering yields of new corporate bonds rated Aa by Moody's Investors Service with an original maturity of at least 20 years. Treasury discontinued yield index after Jan. 31, 2003. Rates thereafter are for Moody's seasoned Aaa corporate bonds as listed by Federal Reserve. (3) Index of new reoffering yields on 20-year general obligations rated Aa by Moody's Investors Service; discontinued by Treasury Jan. 31, 2003; rates thereafter are from Bond Buyer Index of general obligation, 20-year-to-maturity, mixed quality state and local bonds.

Ownership of U.S. Treasury Securities, 2001-12

Source: *Treasury Bulletin, June 2013*, Financial Management Service, U.S. Dept. of the Treasury

In 2001, just over 17% of U.S. treasury securities were held by foreign and international investors. By 2013, the total public debt had nearly tripled, while the portion held by investors outside the U.S. had nearly doubled, to 33.9%.

(in billions of dollars)

	2001	2004	2005	2006	2007	2008	2009	2010	2011	2012
Total public debt	$5,943.4	$7,596.1	$8,170.4	$8,680.2	$9,229.2	$10,699.8	$12,311.3	$14,025.2	$15,222.8	$16,432.7
Federal Reserve and intra-governmental holdings ..	3,123.9	3,905.6	4,199.8	4,558.1	4,833.5	4,806.4	5,276.9	5,656.2	6,439.6	6,523.7
Total privately held	2,819.5	3,690.5	3,970.6	4,122.1	4,395.7	5,893.4	7,034.4	8,368.9	8,783.3	9,909.1
Depository institutions	181.5	125.0	117.1	114.8	129.8	105.0	202.4	319.1	279.7	352.9
U.S. savings bonds.	190.3	204.5	205.2	202.4	196.5	194.1	191.3	187.9	185.2	182.5
Private pension funds[1]	145.8	173.7	184.9	207.2	257.2	297.3	432.8	524.4	589.6	635.8
Pension funds of state and local governments.	155.1	151.0	153.8	153.4	144.2	129.9	151.9	160.0	173.8	215.3
Insurance companies	105.7	188.5	202.3	197.9	141.9	171.4	222.0	248.4	260.7	270.2
Mutual funds.	261.9	254.1	251.3	250.6	362.4	758.3	658.2	631.2	809.6	880.3
State and local governments.	328.4	389.1	475.0	551.7	588.1	526.7	547.2	538.7	485.2	476.9
Foreign and international ..	1,040.1	1,849.3	2,033.9	2,103.1	2,353.2	3,077.2	3,685.1	4,435.6	5,006.9	5,573.8
Other investors[2]	410.7	355.4	347.0	341.0	222.5	633.6	943.6	1,323.8	992.6	1,321.5

(1) Includes securities held by the Federal Employees Retirement System Thrift Savings Plan "G Fund." (2) Includes individuals, government-sponsored enterprises, brokers and dealers, bank personal trusts and estates, corporate and noncorporate businesses, and other investors.

Federal Corporate Tax Rates, 2013

Personal service corporations (used by incorporated professionals such as attorneys and doctors) pay a flat rate of 35%.

Taxable income amount	Tax rate	Taxable income amount	Tax rate
Not more than $50,000.	15%	$335,001 to $10,000,000	34%
$50,001 to $75,000.	25	$10,000,001 to $15,000,000	35
$75,001 to $100,000.	34	$15,000,001 to $18,333,333	38
$100,001 to $335,000	39	More than $18,333,333	35

Characteristics of Mutual Fund Investors, 2012

Source: *The Investment Company Fact Book 2013*, Investment Company Institute

Median age	51	Employed.	72%
Median annual household income	$80,000	Married or living with a partner	75
Median household financial assets.	$190,000	Four-year college degree or more	48
Median mutual fund assets	$100,000	Investing to save for retirement	93
Median number of funds owned	4	Own Individual Retirement Accounts (IRAs)	68

Performance of Mutual Funds by Type, 2013

Source: *Kiplinger Personal Finance* magazine
(as of Aug. 31, 2013)

Fund type/fund objective	1-year	3-year	5-year	Fund type/fund objective	1-year	3-year	5-year
Large-Company				**Sector**			
Growth	17.53%	17.31%	6.80%	Financial	27.03%	13.80%	4.63%
Blend	19.22	16.78	6.41	Health	32.58	24.78	12.20
Value	20.93	16.69	6.42	Natural Resources	3.84	6.47	−1.44
Midsize-Company				Real Estate	−0.45	11.66	4.86
Growth	22.01	18.21	7.75	Technology	15.76	14.89	8.24
Blend	24.47	17.94	7.51	Utilities	12.28	12.67	4.86
Value	25.74	18.08	8.44	**Multialternative**			
Small-Company				Multialternative Funds	1.53	2.60	1.27
Growth	26.18	21.21	9.35	**International**			
Blend	25.04	19.29	8.00	Diversified Emerging Markets	1.69	0.99	1.26
Value	26.33	18.23	8.70	World Stock	17.50	12.10	4.69
Taxable Government Bond				**Corporate Bond**			
Short-Term	−1.19	0.65	2.18	High Yield	7.16	8.84	9.22
Intermediate-Term	−3.22	1.63	4.08	Short-Term	0.30	1.76	3.22
Long-Term	−13.50	2.67	6.99	Intermediate-Term	−1.34	3.29	5.68
Tax-Free Government Bond				Long-Term	−1.94	5.73	8.42
Short-Term	−0.60	1.12	2.13				
Intermediate-Term	−3.18	1.98	3.78				
Long-Term Municipal	−5.37	2.21	3.92				

Mutual Fund Ownership, 1940-2012

Source: *The Investment Company Fact Book 2013*, Investment Company Institute

Year	Mutual funds	Mutual fund accounts (thous.)	Households owning mutual funds — Number (thous.)	Households owning mutual funds — Percent of all households	Total net assets (bil)	Exchange-traded funds (ETFs) — Number of funds	Exchange-traded funds (ETFs) — Total net assets (bil)
1940	68	296	NA	NA	$0.45	NA	NA
1950	98	939	NA	NA	2.53	NA	NA
1960	161	4,898	NA	NA	17.03	NA	NA
1970	361	10,690	NA	NA	47.62	NA	NA
1980	564	12,088	4,600	5.7%	134.76	NA	NA
1990	3,079	61,948	23,400	25.1	1,065.19	NA	NA
2000	8,155	244,705	48,600	45.7	6,964.63	80	$65.58
2005	7,974	275,479	50,300	44.4	8,891.11	204	300.82
2007	8,026	292,555	51,600	43.6	12,001.46	629	608.42
2008	8,022	264,599	55,000	45.0	9,603.65	728	531.29
2009	7,663	269,450	52,600	43.0	11,112.97	797	777.13
2010	7,555	291,299	53,200	45.3	11,831.88	923	991.99
2011	7,591	275,024	52,900	44.1	11,627.36	1,134	1,048.13
2012	7,596	264,131	53,800	44.4	13,045.22	1,194	1,337.11

NA = Not available. **Note:** Does not include data for funds that invest primarily in other mutual funds. Mutual fund accounts data include both individual and omnibus accounts.

Chicago Futures and Options, 2011-12

Source: Chicago Mercantile Exchange Group, Inc.

Futures group	2011	2012	% change, 2011-12	Futures group	2011	2012	% change, 2011-12
Futures	2,900,914,065	2,451,973,414	−15.5%	FX products	9,866,679	10,458,884	6.0%
Commodities & alternative investments	218,156,249	228,866,989	4.9	Interest rate	274,011,450	227,833,251	−16.9
Equity index	755,636,901	588,508,170	−22.1	Metals–CMX	12,351,645	11,393,005	−7.8
FX products	222,467,404	203,302,545	−8.6	Energy	74,176,489	69,401,374	−6.4
Interest rate	1,245,645,034	995,269,254	−20.1	**Combined futures and options**	3,386,986,678	2,890,036,506	−14.7
Metals–CMX	85,240,389	77,580,193	−9.0	Commodities & alternative investments	273,197,405	288,701,777	5.7
Energy	373,768,088	358,446,263	−4.1	Equity index	816,262,095	647,649,960	−20.7
Options	486,072,613	438,063,092	−9.9	FX products	232,334,083	213,761,429	−8.0
Commodities & alternative investments	55,041,156	59,834,788	8.7	Interest rate	1,519,656,484	1,223,102,505	−19.5
Equity index	60,625,194	59,141,790	−2.4	Metals–CMX	97,592,034	88,973,198	−8.8
				Energy	447,944,577	427,847,637	−4.5

Gold Owned by the U.S, 2013

Source: *Status Report of U.S. Treasury-Owned Gold*, Financial Management Service, U.S. Dept. of the Treasury
(as of July 30, 2013)

	Fine troy ounces	Book value		Fine troy ounces	Book value
Total Treasury-owned gold	261,498,926	$11,041,059,958	**Held by the Federal Reserve Bank**	13,452,811	$568,007,258
Gold bullion	258,641,878	10,920,429,099	Gold bullion	13,378,981	564,890,013
Gold coins, blanks, miscellaneous	2,857,048	120,630,859	Federal Reserve Banks– NY vault	13,376,988	564,805,851
Held by the U.S. Mint	248,046,116	10,473,042,701	Federal Reserve Banks–display	1,993	84,162
Denver, CO, deep storage	43,853,707	1,851,599,996	Gold coins	73,830	3,117,245
Fort Knox, KY, deep storage	147,341,858	6,221,097,413	Federal Reserve Banks– NY vault	73,452	3,101,308
West Point, NY, deep storage	54,067,331	2,282,841,677	Federal Reserve Banks–display	377	15,937
Gold coins, blanks, miscellaneous	2,783,219	117,513,615			

World's Leading Gold Producers, 1980-2012

Source: *Minerals Yearbook*, U.S. Geological Survey, U.S. Dept. of the Interior
(in thousands of troy ounces; ranked by 2012 production)

Country	1980	1990	2000	2005	2007	2008	2009	2010	2011	2012[1]
China[1]	225	3,215	5,787	7,234	8,841	9,163	10,288	11,092	11,639	11,896
Australia	548	7,845	9,530	8,423	7,941	6,912	7,202	8,391	8,295	8,038
United States	970	9,452	11,349	8,231	7,652	7,491	7,170	7,427	7,523	7,395
Russia[2]	8,300	9,710	4,598	5,279	5,047	5,531	6,200	6,173	6,430	6,591
South Africa	21,669	19,451	13,767	9,474	8,121	6,840	6,354	6,076	5,819	5,466
Peru[3]	134	293	4,263	6,682	5,473	5,783	5,864	5,273	5,273	5,305
Canada	1,627	5,433	5,022	3,844	3,286	3,054	3,130	2,926	3,119	3,279
Indonesia[4]	60	360	4,006	4,200	3,789	2,070	4,180	3,858	3,086	3,054
Uzbekistan	NA	NA	2,733	2,894	2,733	2,733	2,894	2,894	2,926	2,894
Ghana	353	540	2,318	2,149	2,322	2,346	2,568	2,637	2,572	2,861
Mexico	196	311	848	976	1,265	1,619	1,652	2,347	2,701	2,797
World total	39,197	70,089	82,949	79,412	75,554	73,304	79,091	82,306	85,521	86,807

NA = Not available. **Note:** One kg is equal to 32.1507 troy oz. (1) Estimated. (2) Russia figures for 1980-90 refer to the former USSR. Includes gold recovered as a byproduct, but excludes secondary production. (3) Includes documented production from placer artisanal production. (4) Excludes production from "people's mines," which may add more than 600,000 troy oz. to the total.

Prices of Precious Metals, 1990-2012

Source: *Minerals Yearbook* and *Mineral Industry Surveys*, U.S. Geological Survey, U.S. Dept. of the Interior

Year	Dollars per troy ounce			Dollars per pound			
	Platinum[1]	Gold	Silver	Copper[2]	Lead	Tin[3]	Zinc[4]
1990	$467	$385	$4.82	$1.23	$0.46	$3.86	$0.75
1995	425	386	5.15	1.38	0.42	4.16	0.56
1997	397	332	4.89	1.07	0.47	3.81	0.65
1998	375	295	5.54	0.79	0.45	3.73	0.51
1999	379	280	5.25	0.76	0.44	3.66	0.53
2000	549	280	5.00	0.88	0.44	3.70	0.56
2001	533	272	4.39	0.77	0.44	3.15	0.44
2002	543	311	4.62	0.76	0.44	2.92	0.39
2003	694	365	4.91	0.85	0.44	3.40	0.41
2004	849	411	6.69	1.34	0.55	5.47	0.52
2005	900	446	7.34	1.74	0.61	4.83	0.67
2006	1,144	606	11.57	3.15	0.77	5.65	1.59
2007	1,308	699	13.41	3.28	1.24	8.99	1.54
2008	1,578	874	15.00	3.19	1.20	11.29	0.89
2009	1,208	975	14.69	2.41	0.87	8.37	0.78
2010	1,616	1,228	20.20	3.48	1.09	12.40	1.02
2011	1,725	1,571	35.12	4.06	1.22	15.75	1.06
2012	1,555	1,672	31.23	3.67[P]	1.22	12.83[P]	0.96[P]

P = Preliminary. (1) Average annual dealer prices. (2) U.S. producer price for cathode copper. (3) Platt's Metals Week price. (4) Platt's Metals Week price for North American special high grade zinc except for 1990, which shows average prices for high grade zinc.

Economic and Financial Glossary

Reviewed by William M. Gentry, Graduate School of Business, Columbia University.

Annuity contract: An investment vehicle sold by insurance companies. Annuity buyers can elect to receive periodic payments for the rest of their lives. Annuities provide insurance against outliving one's wealth.

Arbitrage: A form of hedged investment meant to capture slight differences in the prices of two related securities—for example, buying gold in London and selling it at a higher price in New York.

Balance of payments: The difference between all payments, for some categories of transactions, made to and from foreign countries over a set period of time. A favorable balance of payments exists when more payments are coming in than going out; an unfavorable balance of payments obtains when the reverse is true. Payments may include gold, the cost of merchandise and services, interest and dividend payments, money spent by travelers, and repayment of principal on loans.

Balance of trade (trade gap): The difference between exports and imports, in both actual funds and credit. A nation's balance of trade is favorable when exports exceed imports and unfavorable when the reverse is true.

Balanced budget: A budget is balanced when receipts equal expenditures. When receipts exceed expenditures, there is a **surplus;** when they fall short of expenditures, there is a **deficit.**

Bear market: A market in which prices are falling.

Bearer bond: A bond issued in bearer form rather than being registered in a specific owner's name. Ownership is determined by possession.

Bond: A written promise, or IOU, by the issuer to repay a fixed amount of borrowed money on a specified date and generally to pay interest at regular intervals in the interim.

Bull market: A market in which prices are on the rise.

Capital gain (loss): An increase (decrease) in the market value of an asset over some period of time. For tax purposes, capital gains are typically calculated from when an asset is bought to when it is sold.

Commercial paper: An extremely short-term corporate IOU, generally due in 270 days or less.

Consumer price index (CPI): A statistical measure of the change in the price of consumer goods.

Convertible bond: A corporate bond (see below) that may be converted into a stated number of shares of common stock. Its price tends to fluctuate along with fluctuations in the price of the stock and with changes in interest rates.

Corporate bond: A bond issued by a corporation. The bond normally has a stated life and pays a fixed rate of interest. Considered safer than the common or preferred stock of the same company.

Cost of living: The cost of maintaining a standard of living measured in terms of purchased goods and services. Inflation typically measures changes in the cost of living.

Cost-of-living adjustments: Changes in promised payments, such as retirement benefits, to account for changes in the cost of living.

Credit crunch (liquidity crisis): A situation in which cash for lending is in short supply.

Debenture: An unsecured bond backed only by the general credit of the issuing corporation.

Deficit spending: Government spending in excess of revenues, generally financed with the sale of bonds. A deficit increases the government debt.

Deflation: A decrease in the level of prices.

Depression: A long period of economic decline marked by low prices, high unemployment, and many business failures.

Derivatives: Financial contracts, such as options, whose values are based on, or derived from, the price of an underlying financial asset or indicator such as a stock or an interest rate.

Devaluation: The official lowering of a nation's currency, decreasing its value in relation to foreign currencies.

Discount rate: The rate of interest set by the Federal Reserve that member banks are charged when borrowing money through the Federal Reserve System.

Disposable income: Income after taxes that is available to persons for spending and saving.

Diversification: Investing in more than one asset in order to reduce the riskiness of the overall asset portfolio. By holding more than one asset, losses on some assets may be offset by gains realized on other assets.

Dividend: Discretionary payment by a corporation to its shareholders, usually in the form of cash or stock shares.

Dow Jones Industrial Average: An index of stock market prices, based on the prices of 30 companies, 27 of which are on the New York Stock Exchange.

Econometrics: The use of statistical methods to study economic and financial data.

Federal Deposit Insurance Corp. (FDIC): A U.S. government-sponsored corporation that insures accounts in national banks and other qualified institutions against bank failures.

Federal Reserve System: The entire banking system of the U.S., incorporating 12 Federal Reserve banks (one in each of 12 Federal Reserve districts), 25 Federal Reserve branch banks, all national banks, and state-chartered commercial banks and trust companies that have been admitted to its membership. The governors of the system greatly influence the nation's monetary and credit policies.

Full employment: The economy is said to be at full employment when everyone who wishes to work at the going wage-rate for his or her type of labor is employed, save only for the small amount of unemployment due to the time it takes to switch from one job to another.

Futures: A futures contract is an agreement to buy or sell a specific amount of a commodity or financial instrument at a particular price at a set date in the future. For example, futures based on a stock index (such as the Dow Jones Industrial Average) are bets on the future price of that group of stocks.

Golden parachute: Provisions in contracts of some high-level executives guaranteeing substantial severance benefits if they lose their position in a corporate takeover.

Government bond: A bond issued by the U.S. Treasury, considered a safe investment. These are divided into 2 categories—marketable and not marketable. Savings bonds cannot be bought and sold once the original purchase is made. Marketable bonds fall into several categories. Treasury bills are short-term U.S. obligations, maturing in 3, 6, or 12 months. Treasury notes mature in up to 10 years. Treasury bonds mature in 10 to 30 years. Indexed bonds are adjusted for inflation.

Greenmail: A company buying back its own shares for more than the going market price to avoid a threatened hostile takeover.

Gross domestic product (GDP): The market value of all goods and services that have been bought for final use during a period of time. It became the official measure of the size of the U.S. economy in 1991, replacing **gross national product (GNP)**, in use since 1941. GDP covers workers and capital employed within the nation's borders. GNP covers production by U.S. residents regardless of where it takes place. The switch aligned U.S. terminology with that of most other industrialized countries.

Hedge fund: A flexible investment fund for a limited number of large investors (the minimum investment is typically $1 mil). Hedge funds use a variety of investment techniques, including those forbidden to mutual funds, such as short-selling and heavy leveraging.

Hedging: Taking two positions whose gains and losses will offset each other if prices change, in order to limit risk.

Individual retirement account (IRA): A self-funded tax-advantaged retirement plan that allows employed individuals to contribute up to a maximum yearly sum. With a traditional IRA, individuals contribute pre-tax earnings and defer income taxes until retirement. With a Roth IRA, individuals contribute after-tax earnings but do not pay taxes on future withdrawals (the interest is never taxed). **401(k) plans** are employer-sponsored plans similar to traditional IRAs but having higher contribution limits.

Inflation: An increase in the level of prices.

Insider information: Important facts about the condition or plans of a corporation that have not been released to the general public.

Interest: The cost of borrowing money.

Investment bank: A financial institution that arranges the initial issuance of stocks and bonds and offers companies advice about acquisitions and divestitures.

Junk bonds: Bonds issued by companies with low credit ratings. They typically pay relatively high interest rates because of the fear of default.

Leading indicators: A series of 11 indicators from different segments of the economy used by the U.S. Commerce Dept. to predict when changes in the level of economic activity might occur.

Leverage: The extent to which a purchase was paid for with borrowed money. Amplifies the potential gain or loss for the purchaser.

Leveraged buyout (LBO): An acquisition of a company in which much of the purchase price is borrowed, with the debt to be repaid from future profits or by subsequently selling off company assets. A leveraged buyout is typically carried out by a small group of investors, often including incumbent management.

Liquid assets: Assets consisting of cash and/or items that are easily converted into cash.

Margin account: A brokerage account that allows a person to trade securities on credit. A **margin call** is a demand for more collateral on the account.

Money supply: The currency held by the public, plus checking accounts in commercial banks and savings institutions.

Mortgage-backed securities: Created when a bank, builder, or government agency gathers a group of mortgages and then sells bonds to other institutions and the public. The investors receive their proportionate share of the interest payments on the loans as well as the principal payments. Usually, the mortgages in question are guaranteed by the government.

Municipal bond: Issued by governmental units such as states, cities, local taxing authorities, and other agencies. Interest is exempt from U.S.—and sometimes state and local—income tax. Municipal bond unit investment trusts offer a portfolio of many different municipal bonds chosen by professionals. The income is exempt from federal income taxes.

Mutual fund: A portfolio of professionally bought and managed financial assets in which one pools one's money along with that of many other people. A share price is based on net asset value, or the value of all the investments owned by the funds, less any debt, and divided by the total number of shares. The major advantage, relative to investing individually in only a small number of stocks, is less risk—the holdings are spread out over many assets, and if one or two do badly the remainder may shield one from the losses. **Bond funds** are mutual funds that deal in the bond market exclusively. Money market mutual funds buy in the so-called **money market**—institutions that need to borrow large sums of money for short terms. These funds often offer special checking account advantages.

National debt: The debt of the national government, as distinguished from the debts of political subdivisions of the nation and of private business and individuals.

National debt ceiling: Total borrowing limit set by Congress beyond which the U.S. national debt cannot rise. This limit is periodically raised by congressional vote.

Option: A type of contractual agreement between a buyer and a seller to buy or sell shares of a security. A **call** option contract gives one the right to purchase shares of a specific stock at a stated price within a given period of time. A **put** option contract gives the buyer the right to sell shares of a specific stock at a stated price within a given period of time.

Per capita income: The total income of a group divided by the number of people in the group.

Prime interest rate: The rate charged by banks on short-term loans to large commercial customers with the highest credit rating.

Producer price index: A statistical measure of the change in the price of wholesale goods. It is reported for 3 different stages of the production chain: crude, intermediate, and finished goods.

Program trading: Trading techniques involving large numbers and large blocks of stocks, usually used in conjunction with computer programs. Techniques include index arbitrage, in which traders profit from price differences between stocks and futures contracts on stock indexes, and portfolio insurance, which is the use of stock-index futures to protect stock investors from potentially large losses when the market drops.

Public debt: The total of a nation's debts owed by state, local, and national government. Increases in this sum, reflected in public-sector deficits, indicate how much of the nation's spending is being financed by borrowing rather than by taxation.

Recession: A mild decrease in economic activity marked by a decline in real (inflation-adjusted) GDP, employment, and trade, usually lasting from six months to a year, and marked by widespread decline in many sectors of the economy.

Savings Association Insurance Fund (SAIF): Created in 1989 to insure accounts in savings and loan associations up to $100,000.

Seasonal adjustment: Statistical changes made to compensate for regular fluctuations in data that are so great they tend to distort data and make comparisons meaningless. For instance, seasonal adjustments are made for a slowdown in housing construction in midwinter and for the rise in farm income in the fall after summer crops are harvested.

Short-selling: Borrowing shares of stock from a brokerage firm and selling them, hoping to buy the shares back at a lower price, return them, and realize a profit from the decline in prices.

Stagnation: Economic slowdown in which there is little growth in the GDP, capital investment, and real income.

Stock: Common stocks are shares of ownership in a corporation. For publicly held firms, the stock typically trades on an exchange, such as the New York Stock Exchange; for closely held firms, the founders and managers own most of the stock. There can be wide swings in the prices of this kind of stock. **Preferred** stock is a type of stock on which a fixed dividend must be paid before holders of common stock are issued their share of the issuing corporation's earnings. Preferred stock is less risky than common stock. **Convertible preferred** stock can be converted into the common stock of the company that issued the preferred. **Over-the-counter** stock is not traded on the major or regional exchanges but bought directly from dealers. **Blue-chip** stocks are so called because they have been leading stocks for a long time. **Growth** stocks are from companies that reinvest their earnings, rather than pay dividends, with the expectation of future stock price appreciation.

Supply-side economics: A school of thinking about economic policy holding that lowering income tax rates will inevitably lead to enhanced economic growth and general revitalization of the economy.

Takeover: Acquisition of one company by another company or group by sale or merger. A friendly takeover occurs when the acquired company's management is agreeable to the merger; when management is opposed to the merger, it is a hostile takeover.

Tender offer: A public offer to buy a company's stock; usually priced at a premium above the market.

Zero coupon bond: A corporate or government bond that is issued at a deep discount from the maturity value and pays no interest during the life of the bond. It is redeemable at face value.

Top Brands in Selected Categories, 2012-13

Source: Information Resources, Inc., a Chicago-based marketing research company

Figures for 52-week period ending Aug. 11, 2013. Percent change represents dollar sales change in 2012-13 over same period in 2011-12.

Product	Sales (mil)	% change	Market share	Product	Sales (mil)	% change	Market share
Baby food, total	$971.8	4.5%		Coffee (ground decaffeinated), total	$241.2	−5.2%	
Gerber Second Foods Nature Select	130.2	16.1	13.4%	Folger's	55.4	−9.3	23.0%
Gerber Second Foods	78.5	−21.9	8.1	Private label	39.8	−9.6	16.5
Gerber	78.4	−8.6	8.1	Starbucks	22.6	1.1	9.4
Gerber Graduates	62.0	−8.2	6.4	Dunkin' Donuts	21.5	1.9	8.9
Plum Organics Yum	42.2	128.3	4.3	Maxwell House	20.2	−13.1	8.4
Batteries (alkaline), total	$1,137.6	0.6%		Cookies, total	$4,484.9	3.1%	
Duracell Coppertop	471.2	−1.9	41.4%	Private label	661.6	2.6	14.8%
Energizer Max	347.2	6.6	30.5	Nabisco Oreo	381.5	11.9	8.5
Private label	216.8	−0.5	19.1	Nabisco Chips Ahoy	364.2	10.3	8.1
Duracell	23.6	11.7	2.1	Nabisco Oreo Double Stuf	173.7	13.4	3.9
Ray O Vac	18.9	−25.7	1.7	Lofthouse	128.4	−2.3	2.9
Beer, domestic, total	$8,226.3	3.0%		Dog food (dry), total	$2,135.0	1.6%	
Bud Light	1,424.1	−0.7	17.3%	Private label	184.7	0.8	8.7%
Coors Light	788.7	3.1	9.6	Pedigree	159.0	6.4	7.5
Miller Lite	636.5	−3.5	7.7	Purina One Smart Blend	149.9	19.7	7.0
Budweiser	559.9	−4.8	6.8	Purina Dog Chow	146.9	295.6	6.9
Michelob Ultra	258.8	6.3	3.1	Purina Beneful	124.3	−3.1	5.8
Beer, imported, total	$2,053.8	2.1%		Ice cream, total	$4,131.3	−0.6%	
Corona Extra	428.8	1.4	20.9%	Private label	1,014.0	−4.9	24.5%
Heineken	269.5	−1.2	13.1	Blue Bell	370.2	4.0	9.0
Modelo Especial	154.8	23.1	7.5	Breyer's	349.5	−6.4	8.5
Corona Light	133.3	1.5	6.5	Häagen Dazs	312.2	14.5	7.6
Stella Artois Lager	119.1	13.5	5.8	Ben & Jerry's	277.6	4.0	6.7
Bottled water, total	$4,021.3	−0.4%		Pizza (frozen), total	$2,969.5	−2.0%	
Private label	1,053.8	9.4	26.2%	DiGiorno	663.2	−6.0	22.3%
Dasani	352.4	5.6	8.8	Private label	324.0	−4.3	10.9
Aquafina	302.7	−6.5	7.5	Red Baron	245.0	−0.2	8.3
Poland Spring	263.1	−0.4	6.5	Tombstone	201.3	−6.9	6.8
Nestle Pure Life	229.5	2.0	5.7	Totino's Party Pizza	184.2	1.8	6.2
Cat food (dry), total	$1,095.3	1.6%		Potato chips, total	$3,755.8	1.5%	
Meow Mix Original Choice	79.3	46.3	7.2%	Lay's	1,059.6	4.2	28.2%
Private label	73.5	−3.0	6.7	Wavy Lay's	324.1	10.6	8.6
Purina Kit & Kaboodle	72.2	14.8	6.6	Ruffles	309.4	−10.1	8.2
Iams Proactive Health	66.0	36.0	6.0	Private label	277.0	1.5	7.4
Friskies Seafood Sensations	44.5	−2.0	4.1	Pringles	259.5	11.3	6.9
Cereal (ready-to-eat), total	$6,211.8	−2.7%		Salad dressing, total	$1,368.0	−2.6%	
Private label	621.4	−7.4	10.0%	Kraft	264.1	−10.1	19.3%
General Mills Honey Nut Cheerios	347.8	2.2	5.6	Hidden Valley Ranch	238.3	1.0	17.4
Kellogg's Frosted Flakes	257.4	1.2	4.1	Private label	208.2	0.9	15.2
Post Honey Bunches Of Oats	256.8	−10.1	4.1	Wishbone	174.1	0.1	12.7
General Mills Cheerios	253.9	−3.6	4.1	Ken's Steak House	160.2	−0.2	11.7
Chocolate candy, total	$2,398.3	6.6%		Soft drinks (regular), total	$8,054.8	−2.4%	
M&M's	318.5	−0.5	13.3%	Coca Cola	1,861.9	0.1	23.1%
Hershey's	167.7	3.0	7.0	Pepsi	1,186.5	−4.7	14.7
Reese's	125.2	3.9	5.2	Mountain Dew	784.4	−0.9	9.7
Dove Promises	109.4	9.0	4.6	Dr Pepper	631.6	−0.3	7.8
Hershey's Kisses	104.8	10.5	4.4	Sprite	556.9	0.1	6.9
Coffee (ground), total	$2,758.8	−4.7%		Soft drinks (low-calorie), total	$4,474.4	−4.4%	
Folger's	750.8	−8.4	27.2%	Diet Coke	1,097.4	−3.7	24.5%
Maxwell House	424.2	−7.5	15.4	Diet Pepsi	607.8	−5.3	13.6
Private label	289.1	−1.5	10.5	Diet Mountain Dew	329.7	−0.8	7.4
Starbucks	265.0	3.1	9.6	Diet Dr Pepper	283.4	−3.0	6.3
Dunkin' Donuts	185.0	−2.7	6.7	Caffeine Free Diet Coke	248.6	−6.9	5.6

Note: For all categories, brands are ranked by dollar sales at supermarkets, drugstores, and mass merchandisers, excluding Walmart. "Private label" represents the aggregated sales figures for store-branded products in that category. Total category sales include other brands not listed here.

Who Owns What: Familiar Consumer Products and Services

The following is a partial list of well-known consumer brands with their (U.S.) parent companies as of Sept. 2013. Among brands not listed are many whose parent companies have the same or a similar name (e.g., Colgate is owned by Colgate-Palmolive Co.).

ABC broadcasting: Walt Disney
Advil: Pfizer
Ajax cleanser: Colgate-Palmolive
Altoids mints: Mars
Amana appliances: Whirlpool
American Girl: Mattel
Aquafina water: PepsiCo
Arm & Hammer: Church & Dwight
Band-Aid bandages: Johnson & Johnson
Barbie dolls: Mattel
Ben & Jerry's ice cream: Unilever
Betty Crocker prods.: General Mills
Bounty paper towels: Procter & Gamble
Braun appliances: Procter & Gamble
Brillo soap pads: Armaly Brands
Brita water systems: Clorox
Calphalon cookware: Newell Rubbermaid
Canada Dry ginger ale: Dr Pepper Snapple Group
Cap'n Crunch cereal: PepsiCo
ChapStick: Pfizer
Charmin toilet tissue: Procter & Gamble
Cheer detergent: Procter & Gamble
Cheerios cereal: General Mills
Cheez Whiz: Kraft Foods
Chips Ahoy!: Mondelēz International
Clairol hair products: Procter & Gamble
Claritin allergy products: Merck
Coppertone sunscreen: Merck
Crest toothpaste: Procter & Gamble
Crisco shortening: J.M. Smucker
Dasani water: Coca-Cola
Doritos chips: PepsiCo
Dove soap: Unilever
Dreyer's ice cream: Nestlé
Duracell batteries: Procter & Gamble
Fantastik: S.C. Johnson
Febreze: Procter & Gamble
Fisher-Price toys: Mattel
Folger's coffee: J.M. Smucker
Formula 409 spray cleaner: Clorox
Friskies cat food: Nestlé
Frito-Lay's snacks: PepsiCo
Fruit of the Loom apparel: Berkshire Hathaway
Gatorade: PepsiCo
Gerber baby food: Nestlé
Gillette razors: Procter & Gamble
Glad products: Clorox
Glade air fresheners: S.C. Johnson
Green Giant vegetables: General Mills

Häagen-Dazs: General Mills
Halls cough drops: Mondelēz International
Head & Shoulders shampoo: Procter & Gamble
Healthy Choice meals: ConAgra
Hebrew National meats: ConAgra
Hellmann's mayonnaise: Unilever
Hot Wheels/Matchbox cars: Mattel
Huggies diapers: Kimberly-Clark
Hunt's tomatoes: ConAgra
Iams pet food: Procter & Gamble
Irish Spring soap: Colgate-Palmolive
Ivory soap: Procter & Gamble
Jell-O: Kraft Foods
Jennie-O turkey: Hormel
Jif peanut butter: J.M. Smucker
Jimmy Dean sausages: Hillshire Brands
Keebler cookies: Kellogg Co.
KFC restaurants: Yum! Brands
Kibbles 'n Bits pet food: Del Monte
Kingsford charcoal: Clorox
Kit Kat candy: Hershey
KitchenAid appliances: Whirlpool
Kleenex: Kimberly-Clark
Knorr soups: Unilever
Kool-Aid: Kraft Foods
Lipton tea: Unilever
Listerine mouthwash: Johnson & Johnson
Maxwell House coffee: Kraft Foods
Maytag appliances: Whirlpool
Minute Maid juices: Coca-Cola
Mr. Clean: Procter & Gamble
Mountain Dew soda: PepsiCo
Neosporin: Johnson & Johnson
Neutrogena soap: Johnson & Johnson
9 Lives cat food: Del Monte
OFF! insect repellents: S.C. Johnson
Olay: Procter & Gamble
Old Navy clothing: Gap
Oreo cookies: Mondelēz International
Oscar Mayer meats: Kraft Foods
Pampers: Procter & Gamble
Pantene shampoo: Procter & Gamble
Paper Mate pens: Newell Rubbermaid
Parker Bros. games: Hasbro
Pedigree pet food: Mars
Pepperidge Farm prods.: Campbell Soup
Pepto-Bismol: Procter & Gamble
Perrier water: Nestlé
Pillsbury: General Mills
Pine-Sol cleaner: Clorox

Pizza Hut restaurants: Yum! Brands
Planters nuts: Kraft Foods
Prego pasta sauce: Campbell Soup
Pringles snacks: Kellogg Co.
Purina pet foods: Nestlé
Q-Tips: Unilever
Ragu sauce: Unilever
Raid insecticide: S.C. Johnson
Reese's candy: Hershey
Rice-A-Roni: PepsiCo
Right Guard deodorant: Henkel
Ritz crackers: Mondelēz International
Robitussin: Pfizer
Rogaine hair-growth aide: Johnson & Johnson
Saran wrap: S.C. Johnson
Schick razors: Energizer
Scope mouthwash: Procter & Gamble
Scotch tape: 3M
Scott tissue: Kimberly-Clark
Skippy peanut butter: Hormel
SlimFast: Unilever
S.O.S. soap pads: Clorox
Splenda sweetener: Johnson & Johnson
Sprite soda: Coca-Cola
Sudafed: Johnson & Johnson
Swanson broth: Campbell Soup
Taco Bell restaurants: Yum! Brands
Tampax tampons: Procter & Gamble
Tide detergent: Procter & Gamble
Timberland apparel: V.F. Corp.
Trident gum: Mondelēz International
Triscuit crackers: Mondelēz International
Trojan condoms: Church & Dwight
Tropicana juice: PepsiCo
Twizzlers candy: Hershey
Tylenol: Johnson & Johnson
V8 vegetable juice: Campbell Soup
Vans apparel: V.F. Corp.
Vaseline: Unilever
Velveeta cheese products: Kraft Foods
Viagra: Pfizer
Vicks cold medicines: Procter & Gamble
Visine eye drops: Johnson & Johnson
Wheaties cereal: General Mills
Windex: S.C. Johnson
Wrigley's candy and gum: Mars
Xanax: Pfizer
Yoplait yogurt : General Mills
Ziploc storage bags: S.C. Johnson

U.S. Home Ownership Rates, by Selected Characteristics, 2005, 2013
Source: U.S. Census Bureau, U.S. Dept. of Commerce

Region	2005	2013	Age	2005	2013	Race/ethnicity[1]	2005	2013	Income	2005	2013
Northeast	64.7%	63.2%	Under 35	42.8%	36.7%	White, non-Hispanic	75.6%	73.3%	Median family income or more	84.0%	79.7%
Midwest	73.4	69.4	35-44	68.7	60.3	Black	48.0	42.9	Below median family income	52.7	50.3
South	70.4	66.5	45-54	76.3	70.9	Hispanic	49.2	45.9	Total U.S.	68.6	65.0%
West	63.8	59.4	55-64	81.3	76.7	Other	58.0	54.5			
			65+	80.3	80.9						

Note: Figures are for 2nd quarter of the year shown. Not seasonally adjusted. (1) Hispanic households may be of any race. "Other" includes householders self-identifying as Asian, Native Hawaiian/Pacific Islander, and Native American/Alaska Native, as well as combinations of two or more races/ethnicities.

U.S. Housing Affordability, 1990-2013
Source: National Association of REALTORS®

Year	Median-priced existing home	Avg. mortgage rate[1]	Monthly principal & interest payment	Payment as % of median monthly income	Year	Median-priced existing home	Avg. mortgage rate[1]	Monthly principal & interest payment	Payment as % of median monthly income
1990	$92,000	10.04%	$648	22.0%	2006	$221,900	6.58%	$1,131	23.2%
1995	110,500	7.85	639	18.9	2007	217,900	6.52	1,104	21.7
2000	139,000	8.03	818	19.3	2008	196,600	6.15	958	18.1
2001	147,800	7.03	789	18.4	2009	172,100	5.14	751	14.8
2002	158,100	6.55	804	18.3	2010	173,100	4.89	734	14.5
2003	180,200	5.74	840	19.1	2011	166,200	4.67	687	13.4
2004	195,200	5.73	909	20.2	2012	177,200	3.83	663	12.9
2005	219,000	5.91	1,040	22.4	2013[2]	214,000	4.13	830	15.8

(1) All figures assume a down payment of 20% of the home price. Based on effective rate on loans closed on existing homes for the period shown. (2) Preliminary figures, as of July 2013.

Median Price of Existing Single-Family Homes, by Metropolitan Area, 2010-13

Source: National Association of REALTORS®

Median prices are in thousands of dollars and based on all transactions within time period shown. 2nd qtr. 2013 figures are preliminary.

Metropolitan area	2010	2012	2013
Akron, OH	$108.9	$109.5	$126.7
Albany-Schenectady-Troy, NY	195.7	200.3	208.6
Albuquerque, NM	178.7	170.3	171.6
Allentown-Bethlehem-Easton, PA-NJ	224.0	189.6	228.5
Amarillo, TX	124.7	133.8	140.3
Anaheim-Santa Ana-Irvine, CA	546.4	542.7	657.1
Atlanta-Sandy Springs-Marietta, GA	114.8	101.4	143.3
Atlantic City, NJ	226.4	220.4	226.5
Austin-Round Rock, TX	193.6	206.0	231.3
Baltimore-Towson, MD	246.1	206.0	262.7
Barnstable Town, MA	326.0	320.5	335.6
Baton Rouge, LA	169.6	164.3	173.9
Beaumont-Port Arthur, TX	125.1	127.8	136.3
Birmingham-Hoover, AL	143.0	151.1	173.7
Bismarck, ND	163.4	193.0	217.5
Bloomington-Normal, IL	157.9	156.4	165.6
Boise City-Nampa, ID	136.2	138.7	168.5
Boston-Cambridge-Quincy, MA-NH	357.3	351.2	382.2
Boulder, CO	358.1	383.7	431.2
Bridgeport-Stamford-Norwalk, CT	408.6	390.5	425.9
Buffalo-Niagara Falls, NY	121.2	126.9	132.0
Burlington-South Burlington, VT	261.2	270.6	280.9
Canton-Massillon, OH	90.9	NA	NA
Cape Coral-Fort Myers, FL	88.9	128.1	177.9
Cedar Rapids, IA	144.7	145.2	164.8
Champaign-Urbana, IL	141.9	149.1	149.2
Charleston-North Charleston, SC	200.5	207.5	224.1
Charleston, WV	129.1	132.3	135.6
Charlotte-Gastonia-Concord, NC-SC	143.3	156.6	180.1
Chattanooga, TN-GA	121.4	129.1	135.2
Chicago-Naperville-Joliet, IL	191.4	175.3	201.3
Cincinnati-Middletown, OH-KY-IN	128.0	128.3	143.8
Cleveland-Elyria-Mentor, OH	114.5	110.0	122.7
Colorado Springs, CO	195.5	201.6	219.4
Columbia, MO	146.3	153.7	155.6
Columbia, SC	142.6	142.0	148.2
Columbus, OH	136.4	136.5	151.1
Corpus Christi, TX	135.1	142.7	153.4
Cumberland, MD-WV	100.3	96.2	102.7
Dallas-Fort Worth-Arlington, TX	143.8	159.3	181.8
Davenport-Moline-Rock Island, IA-IL	112.2	114.6	124.6
Dayton, OH	103.6	103.5	113.8
Deltona-Daytona Beach-Ormond Beach, FL	115.6	109.5	118.7
Denver-Aurora, CO	232.4	252.4	286.5
Des Moines, IA	150.9	158.6	172.7
Detroit-Warren-Livonia, MI[1]	NA	NA	NA
Dover, DE	193.3	175.3	180.7
Durham, NC	158.3	185.7	205.7
El Paso, TX	134.3	138.6	138.6
Erie, PA	107.7	114.9	112.8
Eugene-Springfield, OR	196.3	NA	NA
Ft. Wayne, IN	97.4	106.2	109.5
Gainesville, FL	161.6	145.6	172.3
Gary-Hammond, IN	122.9	126.1	134.4
Glens Falls, NY	147.5	164.4	166.1
Grand Rapids, MI	91.5	112.3	131.4
Green Bay, WI	130.4	134.7	135.5
Greensboro-High Point, NC	129.8	124.8	135.9
Greenville, SC	145.3	152.0	159.6
Gulfport-Biloxi, MS	125.0	101.0	113.3
Hagerstown-Martinsburg, MD-WV	144.4	134.7	147.6
Hartford-West Hartford-East Hartford, CT	235.8	222.8	234.2
Honolulu, HI	607.6	628.8	660.1
Houston-Baytown-Sugar Land, TX	155.0	164.8	189.0
Indianapolis, IN	123.3	129.6	139.7
Jackson, MS	133.2	143.7	149.6
Jacksonville, FL	137.7	128.2	166.5
Kansas City, MO-KS	141.6	142.6	159.6
Knoxville, TN	140.9	141.3	152.6
Lansing-East Lansing, MI	84.4	87.2	103.2
Las Vegas-Paradise, NV	138.0	134.1	171.8
Lexington-Fayette, KY	143.2	143.2	148.0
Lincoln, NE	133.6	139.6	145.3
Little Rock-North Little Rock, AR	$132.5	$138.2	$144.2
Los Angeles-Long Beach-Santa Ana, CA	323.3	327.5	378.4
Louisville, KY-IN	134.6	137.1	146.2
Madison, WI	217.7	210.6	222.9
Manchester-Nashua, NH	232.0	212.8	233.2
Memphis, TN-MS-AR	120.2	117.2	136.2
Miami-Fort Lauderdale-Miami Beach, FL	201.9	203.1	251.0
Milwaukee-Waukesha-West Allis, WI	205.9	187.4	208.7
Minneapolis-St. Paul-Bloomington, MN-WI	170.6	171.8	199.6
Mobile, AL	121.0	105.0	114.6
Montgomery, AL	129.0	128.3	138.5
Nashville-Davidson–Murfreesboro, TN	153.8	151.9	175.5
New Haven-Milford, CT	231.0	220.6	228.4
New Orleans-Metairie-Kenner, LA	159.7	156.2	176.9
New York-Northern New Jersey-Long Island, NY-NJ-PA	393.7	379.3	399.9
New York-Wayne-White Plains, NY-NJ	450.0	444.9	472.3
New York: Edison, NJ	345.4	298.2	299.8
New York: Nassau-Suffolk, NY	387.0	382.7	406.3
New York: Newark-Union, NJ-PA	379.2	369.7	398.1
Norwich-New London, CT	204.7	186.9	179.7
Oklahoma City, OK	145.7	145.0	149.1
Omaha, NE-IA	137.3	139.2	151.3
Orlando, FL	134.7	134.0	161.1
Palm Bay-Melbourne-Titusville, FL	103.0	116.5	131.7
Pensacola-Ferry Pass-Brent, FL	141.0	135.9	153.7
Peoria, IL	116.9	130.3	117.0
Philadelphia-Camden-Wilmington, PA-NJ-DE-MD	214.9	213.4	227.2
Phoenix-Mesa-Scottsdale, AZ	139.2	147.6	183.3
Pittsfield, MA	195.5	183.1	173.0
Portland-South Portland-Biddeford, ME	218.0	219.5	233.4
Portland-Vancouver-Beaverton, OR-WA	237.3	232.9	264.2
Providence-New Bedford-Fall River, RI-MA	228.5	214.7	233.9
Raleigh-Cary, NC	190.4	188.5	198.8
Reading, PA	153.3	146.0	150.4
Reno-Sparks, NV	179.5	169.7	219.3
Riverside-San Bernardino-Ontario, CA	179.9	189.3	239.6
Rochester, NY	118.9	124.2	126.8
Sacramento–Arden-Arcade–Roseville, CA	184.2	176.8	237.0
Saint Louis, MO-IL	131.1	123.9	136.6
Salem, OR	173.5	147.7	160.5
Salt Lake City, UT	206.5	NA	NA
San Antonio, TX	151.0	159.5	175.5
San Diego-Carlsbad-San Marcos, CA	385.7	385.5	469.0
San Francisco-Oakland-Fremont, CA	525.6	543.8	706.3
San Jose-Sunnyvale-Santa Clara, CA	595.0	645.0	808.5
Sarasota-Bradenton-Venice, FL	164.6	171.9	204.9
Seattle-Tacoma-Bellevue, WA	295.7	300.4	347.4
Shreveport-Bossier City, LA	156.6	156.6	159.7
Sioux Falls, SD	143.3	149.2	158.3
Spartanburg, SC	118.2	122.7	127.0
Spokane, WA	172.2	169.5	174.8
Springfield, IL	124.0	121.0	120.0
Springfield, MA	190.0	178.9	195.2
Springfield, MO	109.1	108.4	NA
Syracuse, NY	125.1	124.8	126.1
Tallahassee, FL	152.8	144.9	172.7
Tampa-St. Petersburg-Clearwater, FL	134.2	133.9	145.7
Toledo, OH	81.5	80.4	92.9
Topeka, KS	107.2	106.2	117.4
Trenton-Ewing, NJ	250.7	247.6	278.1
Tucson, AZ	156.6	149.9	171.7
Tulsa, OK	132.3	136.3	146.9
Virginia Beach-Norfolk-Newport News, VA-NC	205.0	187.5	200.0
Washington-Arlington-Alexandria, DC-VA-MD-WV	325.3	352.0	403.0
Wichita, KS	118.7	116.9	127.8
Worcester, MA	223.3	206.0	238.0

NA = Not available. (1) $53,800 in 2011, and $66,700 in the fourth quarter of 2012.

Characteristics of American Housing Units, 2011

Source: *American Housing Survey, 2011*, U.S. Dept. of Housing and Urban Development

Characteristic	Number of homes (thous.)	% of all homes
Total units	132,419	100.0%
Units in structure		
1, detached	82,974	62.7
1, attached	7,768	5.9
2-4	10,678	8.1
5-9	6,354	4.8
10-19	6,028	4.6
20-49	4,474	3.4
50 or more	5,096	3.8
Manufactured/mobile home or trailer	9,049	6.8
Cooperatives	896	0.7
Condominiums	9,363	7.1
Year built		
2010-14	720	0.5
2005-09	8,267	6.2
2000-04	9,250	7.0
1995-99	8,948	6.8
1990-94	7,206	5.4
1985-89	9,014	6.8
1980-84	7,715	5.8
1975-79	13,579	10.3
1970-74	11,176	8.4
1960-69	15,405	11.6
1950-59	13,455	10.2
1940-49	7,836	5.9
1930-39	5,536	4.2
1920-29	5,323	4.0
1919 or earlier	8,989	6.8
Median year built	1974	—
Location		
Inside metropolitan statistical areas	104,017	78.6
In central cities	38,599	29.1
Not in central cities	65,418	49.4
Outside metropolitan statistical areas	28,402	21.4
Northeast	23,717	17.9
Midwest	29,545	22.3
South	50,381	38.0
West	28,776	21.7
Number of bedrooms		
None	1,413	1.1
1	14,924	11.3
2	35,083	26.5
3	54,245	41.0
4 or more	26,755	20.2

Characteristic	Number of homes (thous.)	% of all homes
Number of complete bathrooms		
None	1,808	1.4%
1	46,800	35.3
1-1/2	16,666	12.6
2 or more	67,145	50.7
Square footage of unit[1]		
Less than 500	973	1.1
500-749	2,678	2.9
750-999	6,529	7.1
1,000-1,499	20,919	22.7
1,500-1,999	20,560	22.3
2,000-2,499	14,343	15.6
2,500-2,999	7,553	8.2
3,000-3,999	7,225	7.9
4,000 or more	4,479	4.9
Not reported/Don't know	6,762	7.3
Median square footage	1,700	—
Lot size[2]		
Less than 1/8 acre	15,638	16.2
1/8-1/4 acre	25,011	25.9
1/4-1/2 acre	17,705	18.4
1/2-1 acre	11,321	11.7
1-5 acres	19,076	19.8
5-10 acres	3,037	3.2
10+ acres	4,599	4.8
Median lot size (acres)	0.25	—
Equipment		
Dishwasher	85,831	64.8
Kitchen sink disposal	65,976	49.8
Trash compactor	4,349	3.3
Washing machine	103,435	78.1
Clothes dryer	100,642	76.0
Lacking full kitchen facilities	5,875	4.4
Air conditioning	113,558	85.8
Central air	85,251	64.4
1 room unit	13,379	10.1
2 room units	9,069	6.8
3 room units or more	5,859	4.4
Main heating source[3]		
Piped gas	63,791	48.6
Electricity	48,330	36.8
Fuel oil	8,867	6.7
Bottled gas	6,780	5.2
Wood	2,442	1.9

(1) Percentages based on 92,023 single detached homes and trailers. (2) Percentages based on 96,386 total single-unit structures. (3) Percentages based on 131,368 homes with heat.

Fair Market Rents for Select Metropolitan Areas, 2014

Source: *Fair Market Rents 2014*, U.S. Dept. of Housing and Urban Development

Metropolitan area	0	1	2	3	4
Atlanta-Sandy Springs-Marietta, GA	$693	$756	$896	$1,187	$1,442
Austin-Round Rock-San Marcos, TX	696	853	1,074	1,454	1,762
Baltimore-Towson, MD	847	1,001	1,252	1,599	1,741
Birmingham-Hoover, AL	524	627	743	976	1,098
Boston-Cambridge-Quincy, MA-NH	1,042	1,164	1,454	1,811	1,969
Buffalo-Niagara Falls, NY	537	570	710	908	1,027
Charlotte, NC-SC	622	686	813	1,096	1,359
Chicago-Joliet-Naperville, IL	727	826	979	1,248	1,455
Cincinnati, OH-KY-IN	442	554	735	1,018	1,121
Cleveland-Elyria-Mentor, OH	493	592	750	1,005	1,037
Columbus, OH	498	620	806	1,039	1,202
Dallas, TX	602	722	913	1,218	1,471
Denver-Aurora, CO	600	742	960	1,409	1,633
Detroit-Warren-Livonia, MI	508	646	843	1,124	1,228
Hartford-West Hartford-East Hartford, CT	749	939	1,170	1,457	1,693
Honolulu, HI	1,267	1,382	1,820	2,682	3,078
Houston-Sugar Land, TX	623	750	926	1,264	1,563
Indianapolis, IN	506	625	777	1,036	1,209
Jacksonville, FL	631	778	935	1,233	1,509
Kansas City, MO-KS	534	687	852	1,168	1,300
Las Vegas-Paradise, NV	675	843	1,038	1,530	1,816
Los Angeles-Long Beach, CA	896	1,083	1,398	1,890	2,106
Louisville, KY-IN	485	567	705	976	1,104
Memphis, TN-MS-AR	576	658	780	1,066	1,188
Miami-Miami Beach, FL	747	910	1,166	1,600	1,869
Milwaukee-Waukesha, WI	$524	$646	$812	$1,036	$1,120
Minneapolis-St. Paul, MN-WI	608	756	946	1,332	1,573
Nashville-Davidson, TN	616	711	851	1,131	1,214
New Orleans-Metairie, LA	646	765	948	1,190	1,440
New York, NY	1,163	1,215	1,440	1,852	2,075
Oklahoma City, OK	486	565	723	989	1,188
Orlando-Kissimmee, FL	697	825	983	1,311	1,586
Philadelphia-Camden-Wilmington, PA-NJ-DE-MD	799	942	1,135	1,414	1,518
Phoenix-Mesa-Glendale, AZ	614	774	957	1,410	1,647
Pittsburgh, PA	551	633	789	991	1,054
Portland-Vancouver, OR-WA	666	774	922	1,359	1,633
Providence-Fall River, RI-MA	663	748	913	1,137	1,361
Richmond, VA	790	830	984	1,294	1,568
Riverside-San Bernardino-Ontario, CA	766	882	1,120	1,582	1,930
Sacramento, CA	717	854	1,072	1,580	1,899
St. Louis, MO-IL	532	631	814	1,061	1,203
Salt Lake City, UT	589	707	876	1,249	1,471
San Antonio, TX	542	683	857	1,117	1,226
San Diego, CA	939	1,032	1,354	1,969	2,398
San Francisco, CA	1,191	1,551	1,956	2,657	3,212
San Jose-Sunnyvale-Santa Clara, CA	1,105	1,293	1,649	2,325	2,636
San Juan-Guaynabo, PR	435	468	555	755	907
Seattle-Bellevue, WA	771	913	1,123	1,655	1,899
Tampa-St. Petersburg, FL	605	758	951	1,269	1,520
Washington-Arlington-Alexandria, DC-VA-MD	1,176	1,239	1,469	1,966	2,470

Note: Figures are projections made in the previous year. Metropolitan area may include individual cities not shown.

TRADE

U.S. Trade With Selected Countries and Major Areas, 2012

Source: U.S. Census Bureau, U.S. Bureau of Economic Analysis, U.S. Dept. of Commerce

(in millions of dollars; top 25 countries as ranked by amount of total trade with U.S.)

Rank	Country	Total trade with U.S.	U.S. exports to	Rank[1]	U.S. imports from	Rank[1]	U.S. trade balance with	Rank[2]
1.	Canada	$616,476.2	$292,539.7	1	$323,936.5	2	–$31,396.8	6
2.	China[3]	536,062.5	110,483.6	3	425,578.9	1	–315,095.3	1
3.	Mexico	493,501.0	215,931.2	2	277,569.8	3	–61,638.6	3
4.	Japan	216,347.2	69,955.0	4	146,392.2	4	–76,437.2	2
5.	Germany	157,505.2	48,797.1	6	108,708.1	5	–59,911.0	4
6.	United Kingdom	109,812.9	54,850.5	5	54,962.4	8	–111.9	73
7.	South Korea	101,179.2	42,283.5	8	58,895.7	6	–16,612.2	13
8.	Brazil	75,929.0	43,806.0	7	32,123.0	15	11,682.9	229
9.	Saudi Arabia	73,638.9	17,972.0	20	55,666.9	7	–37,694.9	5
10.	France	72,555.8	30,806.0	12	41,749.8	9	–10,943.8	19
11.	Taiwan	63,206.3	24,348.7	16	38,857.6	11	–14,509.0	16
12.	Netherlands	62,884.7	40,627.2	9	22,257.5	21	18,369.8	231
13.	India	62,619.6	22,105.5	18	40,514.1	10	–18,408.7	11
14.	Venezuela	56,240.0	17,516.2	21	38,723.8	12	–21,207.6	8
15.	Italy	53,036.4	16,097.8	23	36,938.6	13	–20,840.7	9
16.	Switzerland	52,063.1	26,390.4	15	25,672.7	19	717.6	206
17.	Singapore	50,757.1	30,525.2	13	20,231.9	24	10,293.4	228
18.	Belgium	46,812.3	29,448.5	12	17,363.8	27	12,468.0	232
19.	Hong Kong	42,916.8	37,461.3	10	5,455.5	46	32,005.8	234
20.	Colombia	40,974.7	16,354.9	22	24,619.8	20	–8,264.9	24
21.	Ireland	40,718.6	7,391.8	36	33,326.8	14	–25,934.9	7
22.	Australia	40,700.4	31,151.2	11	9,549.2	36	21,602.0	233
23.	Russia	40,080.3	10,699.5	28	29,380.8	16	–18,681.3	10
24.	Malaysia	38,774.1	12,840.9	25	25,933.2	18	–13,092.4	18
25.	Thailand	36,996.0	10,888.0	27	26,108.0	17	–15,220.0	15

Major area/group

North America		$1,109,977.2	$508,470.9		$601,506.3		–$93,035.4
Europe		784,505.8	329,204.7		455,301.1		–126,096.3
Euro Area		487,896.2	193,945.9		293,950.3		–100,004.5
EU		646,567.2	265,359.6		381,207.6		–115,848.0
Africa		99,554.6	32,737.5		66,817.1		–34,079.6
OECD		2,194,675.7	959,776.8		1,234,898.9		–275,122.1
Pacific Rim Countries		1,141,435.1	379,228.3		762,206.8		–382,978.5
Asia-Near East		186,375.3	69,605.1		116,770.2		–47,165.1
Asia-Newly Industrialized Countries		258,059.4	134,618.7		123,440.7		11,178.0
Asia-South		77,331.2	25,895.3		51,435.9		–25,540.5
ASEAN		198,338.3	75,419.0		122,919.3		–47,500.3
APEC		2,396,838.6	941,676.4		1,455,162.2		–513,485.8
South/Central America		354,968.3	183,187.8		171,780.5		11,407.3
Twenty Latin American Republics		820,885.2	383,793.6		437,091.6		–53,298.0
CAFTA-DR		60,780.3	29,900.6		30,879.7		–979.2
Central American Common Market		49,441.6	22,926.9		26,514.7		–3,587.8
Latin American Free Trade Area		747,440.3	342,543.7		404,896.6		–62,352.9
NATO Allies		1,215,006.6	555,108.1		659,898.5		–104,790.4
OPEC		262,492.1	81,722.1		180,770.0		–99,047.9
WORLD TOTAL		**$3,821,028.3**	**$1,545,708.5**		**$2,275,319.8**		**–$729,611.3**

Note: Figures shown are on Census Bureau basis. Figures may not equal totals due to rounding. Country grouping data reflect the groups as they were at the time of reporting. (1) Rank shown is for column to the left. Ranking includes territories as well as nations. (2) Rank by decreasing size of U.S. trade deficit. Ranking includes territories as well as nations. (3) Not including Hong Kong, Macao, and Taiwan. **Definitions of major areas/groups used in table, as provided by source: North America**—Canada, Mexico. **Europe**—Albania, Andorra, Armenia, Austria, Azerbaijan, Belarus, Belgium, Bosnia-Herzegovina, Bulgaria, Croatia, Cyprus, Czech Republic, Denmark, Estonia, Faroe Isls., Finland, France, Georgia, Germany, Gibraltar, Greece, Hungary, Iceland, Ireland, Italy, Kazakhstan, Kosovo, Kyrgyzstan, Latvia, Liechtenstein, Lithuania, Luxembourg, Macedonia, Malta, Moldova, Monaco, Montenegro, Netherlands, Norway, Poland, Portugal, Romania, Russia, San Marino, Serbia, Slovakia, Slovenia, Spain, Svalbard, Jan Mayen Isl., Sweden, Switzerland, Tajikistan, Turkey, Turkmenistan, Ukraine, United Kingdom, Uzbekistan, Vatican City. **Euro Area**—Austria, Belgium, Cyprus, Estonia, Finland, France, Germany, Greece, Ireland, Italy, Luxembourg, Malta, Netherlands, Portugal, Slovakia, Slovenia, Spain. **EU (European Union)**—Euro Area plus Bulgaria, Czech Republic, Denmark, Hungary, Latvia, Lithuania, Poland, Romania, Sweden, United Kingdom. **Africa**—Algeria, Angola, Benin, Botswana, British Indian Ocean Territories, Burkina Faso, Burundi, Cameroon, Cape Verde, Central African Republic, Chad, Comoros, Congo (Brazzaville), Congo (Kinshasa), Côte d'Ivoire, Djibouti, Egypt, Equatorial Guinea, Eritrea, Ethiopia, French Southern and Antarctic Lands, Gabon, The Gambia, Ghana, Guinea, Guinea-Bissau, Kenya, Lesotho, Liberia, Libya, Madagascar, Malawi, Mali, Mauritania, Mauritius, Mayotte, Morocco, Mozambique, Namibia, Niger, Nigeria, Réunion, Rwanda, St. Helena, São Tomé and Príncipe, Senegal, Seychelles, Sierra Leone, Somalia, South Africa, South Sudan, Sudan, Swaziland, Tanzania, Togo, Tunisia, Uganda, Western Sahara, Zambia, Zimbabwe. **OECD (Org. for Economic Cooperation and Development)**—Australia, Austria, Belgium, Canada, Chile, Czech Republic, Denmark, Estonia, Finland, France, Germany, Greece, Hungary, Iceland, Ireland, Israel, Italy, Japan, Korea (South), Luxembourg, Mexico, Netherlands, New Zealand, Norway, Poland, Portugal, Slovakia, Slovenia, Spain, Sweden, Switzerland, Turkey, United Kingdom. **Pacific Rim Countries**—Australia, Brunei, China, Hong Kong, Indonesia, Japan, Korea (South), Macao, Malaysia, New Zealand, Papua New Guinea, Philippines, Singapore, Taiwan. **Asia-Near East**—Bahrain, Gaza Strip Administered by Israel, Iran, Iraq, Israel, Jordan, Kuwait, Lebanon, Oman, Qatar, Saudi Arabia, Syria, United Arab Emirates, West Bank Administered by Israel, Yemen. **Asia-Newly Industrialized Countries**—Hong Kong, Korea (South), Singapore, Taiwan. **Asia-South**—Afghanistan, Bangladesh, India, Nepal, Pakistan, Sri Lanka. **ASEAN (Assn. of Southeast Asia Nations)**—Brunei, Cambodia, Indonesia, Laos, Malaysia, Myanmar (Burma), Philippines, Singapore, Thailand, Vietnam. **APEC (Asia-Pacific Economic Cooperation)**—Australia, Brunei, Canada, Chile, China, Hong Kong, Indonesia, Japan, Korea (South), Malaysia, Mexico, New Zealand, Papua New Guinea, Peru, Philippines, Russia, Singapore, Taiwan, Thailand, Vietnam. **South/Central America**—Anguilla, Antigua and Barbuda, Argentina, Aruba, The Bahamas, Barbados, Belize, Bermuda, Bolivia, Brazil, British Virgin Isls., Cayman Isls., Chile, Colombia, Costa Rica, Cuba, Dominica, Dominican Republic, Ecuador, El Salvador, Falkland Isls., French Guiana, Grenada, Guadeloupe, Guatemala, Guyana, Haiti, Honduras, Jamaica, Martinique, Montserrat, Netherlands Antilles, Nicaragua, Panama, Paraguay, Peru, St. Kitts and Nevis, St. Lucia, St. Vincent and the Grenadines, Sint Maarten, Suriname, Trinidad and Tobago, Turks and Caicos Isls., Uruguay, Venezuela. **Twenty Latin American Republics**—Argentina, Bolivia, Brazil, Chile, Colombia, Costa Rica, Cuba, Dominican Republic, Ecuador, El Salvador, Guatemala, Haiti, Honduras, Mexico, Nicaragua, Panama, Paraguay, Peru, Uruguay, Venezuela. **CAFTA-DR (Dominican Republic-Central America-United States Free Trade Agreement)**—Costa Rica, Dominican Republic, El Salvador, Guatemala, Honduras, Nicaragua. **Central American Common Market**—Costa Rica, El Salvador, Guatemala, Honduras, Nicaragua. **Latin American Free Trade Area**—Argentina, Bolivia, Brazil, Chile, Colombia, Ecuador, Mexico, Paraguay, Peru, Uruguay, Venezuela. **NATO (North Atlantic Treaty Org.) Allies**—Belgium, Bulgaria, Canada, Czech Republic, Denmark, Estonia, France, Germany, Greece, Hungary, Iceland, Italy, Latvia, Lithuania, Luxembourg, Netherlands, Norway, Poland, Portugal, Romania, Slovakia, Slovenia, Spain, Turkey, United Kingdom. **OPEC (Org. of the Petroleum Exporting Countries)**—Algeria, Angola, Ecuador, Iran, Iraq, Kuwait, Libya, Nigeria, Qatar, Saudi Arabia, United Arab Emirates, Venezuela.

U.S. Exports and Imports by Principal Commodity Groupings, 2012

Source: U.S. Census Bureau, U.S. Bureau of Economic Analysis, U.S. Dept. of Commerce

(in millions of dollars)

Item	Exports	Imports	Item	Exports	Imports
TOTAL[1]	$1,545,709	$2,275,320	Liquefied propane and butane	$3,390	$2,072
Manufactured goods[2]	1,019,084	1,705,052	Live animals	1,174	2,611
Agricultural commodities[2]	141,252	103,230	Meat and preparations	17,482	6,226
Mineral fuels[2]	136,023	423,591	Metal manufactures[3]	21,938	33,464
			Metal ores; scrap	28,063	9,103
Selected commodities[2]			Metalworking machines	6,250	10,325
ADP equipment; office machinery	22,620	118,853	Mineral fuels, other	8,351	3,942
Airplanes, engines, and parts	95,899	29,147	Natural gas	4,827	8,742
Alcoholic beverages, distilled	1,418	6,504	Nickel	1,572	2,943
Aluminum	6,588	11,310	Oils and fats of vegetable	2,598	5,447
Animal feeds	10,764	2,522	Optical goods	3,404	6,082
Artwork/antiques	3,132	7,825	Paper and paperboard	15,854	15,621
Basketware, etc.	9,104	14,808	Petroleum preparations	101,687	89,950
Cereal flour	3,785	5,333	Photographic equipment	3,011	2,164
Chemicals[3]	28,813	13,950	Plastic articles[3]	11,130	18,979
Chemicals-cosmetics	14,213	11,379	Platinum	924	4,376
Chemicals-dyeing	7,882	3,763	Pottery	107	1,519
Chemicals-fertilizers	4,497	8,759	Power generating machines	39,162	57,819
Chemicals-inorganic	12,282	15,501	Printed materials	5,853	4,521
Chemicals-medicinal	42,662	68,325	Pulp and waste paper	8,951	3,354
Chemicals-organic	42,363	52,241	Records and magnetic media	4,517	5,870
Chemicals-plastics	45,426	21,719	Rice	2,050	659
Cigarettes	317	188	Rubber articles[3]	2,613	4,127
Clothing	3,455	84,916	Rubber tires and tubes	5,595	14,654
Coal	15,048	1,508	Scientific instruments	50,214	45,870
Coffee	8	5,808	Ships and boats	3,359	1,865
Copper	4,217	8,945	Silver and bullion	2,500	6,628
Cork, wood, and lumber	5,504	5,172	Soybeans	24,639	328
Corn	9,816	948	Spacecraft	613	120
Cotton, raw and linters	6,255	8	Specialized industrial machines	53,753	44,989
Crude fertilizers and minerals	2,584	2,839	Sugar	58	1,339
Crude oil	2,420	315,445	Televisions, VCRs, etc.	23,080	143,845
Electrical machinery	77,783	144,305	Textile yarn, fabric	12,532	24,750
Fish and preparations	5,165	16,564	Tobacco, unmanufactured	1,101	958
Footwear	825	23,886	Toys, games, and sporting goods	4,469	28,038
Furniture and bedding	5,755	35,610	Travel goods	541	9,996
Gem diamonds	3,122	20,196	Vegetables and fruits	19,897	24,594
General industrial machines	64,451	81,640	Vehicles	116,883	235,338
Glass[3]	3,623	2,731	Watches, clocks, and parts	397	4,836
Glassware	1,027	2,704	Wheat	8,161	832
Gold, nonmonetary	36,421	17,830	Wood manufactures	2,106	7,724
Hides and skins	2,249	52	Re-exports	193,507	NA
Iron and steel mill products	18,934	36,756	Agricultural commodities	4,073	NA
Jewelry	5,293	10,496	Manufactured goods	186,761	NA
Lighting and plumbing	3,011	9,309	Mineral fuels	1,058	NA

NA = Not available. **Note:** Commodity group totals include products not listed here. Figures may not equal totals due to rounding. (1) Both domestic and foreign exports (re-exports); total census basis. (2) Domestic exports. (3) Not specified elsewhere.

Trends in U.S. Foreign Trade, 1790-2012

Source: U.S. Census Bureau, U.S. Bureau of Economic Analysis, U.S. Dept. of Commerce

In 1790, U.S. exports and imports combined came to $43 mil, and there was a $3 mil trade deficit. The global recession caused total U.S. trade and the overall trade deficit to fall in 2009, but they then resumed the ever-upward path they had been following since the last recorded surplus in 1975.

(in millions of dollars)

Year	Exports	Imports	Trade balance	Year	Exports	Imports	Trade balance	Year	Exports	Imports	Trade balance
1790	$20	$23	-$3	1890	$858	$789	$69	1990	$535,233	$616,097	-$80,864
1795	48	70	-22	1895	808	732	76	1995	794,387	890,771	-96,384
1800	71	91	-20	1900	1,394	850	545	1996	851,602	955,667	-104,065
1805	96	121	-25	1905	1,519	1,118	401	1997	934,453	1,042,726	-108,273
1810	67	85	-19	1910	1,745	1,557	188	1998	933,174	1,099,314	-166,140
1815	53	113	-60	1915	2,769	1,674	1,094	1999	967,008	1,230,764	-263,755
1820	70	74	-5	1920	8,228	5,278	2,950	2000	1,072,782	1,450,119	-377,337
1825	91	90	1	1925	4,910	4,227	683	2001	1,007,725	1,370,065	-362,339
1830	72	63	9	1930	3,843	3,061	782	2002	980,879	1,399,044	-418,165
1835	115	137	-22	1935	2,283	2,047	235	2003	1,023,937	1,514,482	-490,545
1840	124	98	25	1940	4,021	2,625	1,396	2004	1,163,724	1,768,622	-604,897
1845	106	113	-7	1945	9,806	4,159	5,646	2005	1,288,257	1,996,171	-707,914
1850	144	174	-29	1950	9,997	8,954	1,043	2006	1,460,792	2,213,191	-752,399
1855	219	258	-39	1955	14,298	11,566	2,732	2007	1,652,859	2,351,925	-699,065
1860	334	354	-20	1960	25,940	22,432	3,508	2008	1,840,332	2,542,634	-702,302
1865	166	239	-73	1965	35,285	30,621	4,664	2009	1,578,187	1,961,844	-383,657
1870	393	436	-43	1970	56,640	54,386	2,254	2010	1,844,468	2,343,847	-499,379
1875	513	533	-20	1975	132,585	120,181	12,404	2011	2,112,825	2,669,663	-556,838
1880	836	668	168	1980	271,834	291,241	-19,407	2012	2,210,585	2,745,240	-534,656
1885	742	578	165	1985	289,070	410,950	-121,880				

Note: Figures shown using balance of payments basis.

World Trade Organization (WTO)

The World Trade Organization is an international body that seeks to promote free trade by eliminating barriers to trade. Founded in 1995, the WTO had grown to 159 member countries as of Mar. 2013, with 25 others granted observer status. International inter-governmental organizations, such as the International Monetary Fund and the World Bank, may also be granted observer status. With the exception of Vatican City, observers must start accession negotiations within five years of becoming observers.

U.S. Trade in Goods and Services, 2012

Source: U.S. Census Bureau, U.S. Bureau of Economic Analysis, U.S. Dept. of Commerce
(in millions of dollars; top five trade partners as ranked by amount of total trade with U.S.)

Country/ category	Food and live animals	Beverages and tobacco	Crude materials, except fuels	Mineral fuels, lubricants	Chemicals[1]	Manufactured goods	Machinery and transport equipment	Misc. manufactured	Commodities and transactions[1]	Total
Canada										
U.S. exports to	$20,999	$1,542	$7,591	$18,286	$32,258	$39,817	$130,138	$30,697	$9,752	$291,758
U.S. imports fr.	19,135	928	12,064	105,596	27,287	39,841	92,835	13,230	15,724	328,720
Trade balance	1,864	614	−4,472	−87,309	4,971	−24	37,303	17,467	−5,971	−36,962
China										
U.S. exports to	6,372	217	35,584	2,519	13,284	5,635	37,684	8,107	842	110,590
U.S. imports fr.	6,268	75	2,253	310	14,915	49,240	225,430	141,380	4,539	444,469
Trade balance	103	142	33,330	2,208	−1,631	−43,604	−187,746	−133,273	−3,696	−333,879
Mexico										
U.S. exports to	14,254	592	7,375	23,726	25,955	28,008	93,900	14,970	6,690	216,331
U.S. imports fr.	14,892	3,012	1,695	40,304	5,233	20,026	154,548	27,439	12,787	280,025
Trade balance	−638	−2,420	5,680	−16,578	20,722	7,982	−60,648	−12,469	−6,097	−63,694
Japan										
U.S. exports to	12,517	647	3,715	2,627	12,868	3,710	22,316	10,546	1,040	70,046
U.S. imports fr.	648	93	661	639	9,497	11,786	112,435	10,835	3,764	150,401
Trade balance	11,869	554	3,054	1,988	3,371	−8,076	−90,119	−289	−2,724	−80,355
Germany										
U.S. exports to	1,035	257	2,509	1,054	7,546	3,667	24,024	6,516	2,096	48,786
U.S. imports fr.	1,063	508	941	336	19,638	10,185	64,261	10,152	3,511	110,612
Trade balance	−28	−251	1,568	718	−12,092	−6,518	−40,237	−3,636	−1,415	−61,826

Note: Figures for exports are "free alongside ship" values; figures for imports are "cost, insurance, and freight" values. Neither is directly comparable with the Census Bureau basis shown in other tables in this section. Trade balance is with U.S. Total includes categories not shown. (1) Not classified elsewhere.

Foreign Exchange Rates, 1970-2012

Source: Federal Reserve Board

One U.S. dollar was worth the following amounts in each country's national currency; exchange rates are annual averages.

Year	Australia (dollar)	Austria (schilling; euro)	Belgium (franc; euro)	Canada (dollar)	China (yuan)	Denmark (krone)	France (franc; euro)	Germany[1] (deutsche mark; euro)	Greece (drachma; euro)
1970	0.8980	25.8800	49.6800	1.0103	NA	7.4890	5.5200	3.6480	30.0000
1980	0.8772	12.9450	29.2370	1.1693	NA	5.6340	4.2250	1.8175	42.6200
1990	1.2799	11.3700	33.4180	1.1668	NA	6.1890	5.4453	1.6157	158.5100
1995	1.3486	10.0810	29.4800	1.3724	8.3700	5.6020	4.9915	1.4331	231.6600
2000	1.7197	1.0832	1.0832	1.4855	8.2784	8.0950	1.0832	1.0832	365.9200
2005	1.3111	0.8033	0.8033	1.2115	8.1936	5.9953	0.8033	0.8033	0.8033
2007	1.1918	0.7293	0.7293	1.0734	7.6058	5.4413	0.7293	0.7293	0.7293
2008	1.1714	0.6791	0.6791	1.0660	6.9477	5.0885	0.6791	0.6791	0.6791
2009	1.2615	0.7176	0.7176	1.1412	6.8307	5.3574	0.7176	0.7176	0.7176
2010	1.0870	0.7541	0.7541	1.0298	6.7696	5.6266	0.7541	0.7541	0.7541
2011	0.9679	0.7178	0.7178	0.9887	6.4630	5.3535	0.7178	0.7178	0.7178
2012	0.9653	0.7777	0.7777	0.9995	6.3093	5.7922	0.7777	0.7777	0.7777

Year	Hong Kong (dollar)	India (rupee)	Ireland (pound; euro)	Italy (lira; euro)	Japan (yen)	Malaysia (ringgit)	Mexico (new peso)	Netherlands (guilder; euro)	Norway (krone)
1970	NA	7.576	2.3959	623.0000	357.60	3.0900	NA	3.5970	7.1400
1980	NA	7.887	2.0577	856.0000	226.63	2.1767	NA	1.9875	4.9381
1990	NA	17.504	1.6585	1,198.0000	144.79	2.7049	2.812	1.8209	6.2597
1995	7.7357	32.427	1.6038	1,628.9000	94.06	2.5044	6.419	1.6057	6.3352
2000	7.7925	45.000	1.0832	1.0832	107.80	3.8000	9.459	1.0832	8.8131
2005	7.7775	44.000	0.8033	0.8033	110.11	3.7869	10.894	0.8033	6.4412
2007	7.8016	41.180	0.7293	0.7293	117.76	3.4354	10.928	0.7293	5.8557
2008	7.7862	43.390	0.6791	0.6791	103.39	3.3292	11.143	0.6791	5.6365
2009	7.7514	48.330	0.7176	0.7176	93.68	3.5231	13.498	0.7176	6.2908
2010	7.7687	45.65	0.7541	0.7541	87.78	3.2175	12.623	0.7541	6.0451
2011	7.7841	46.58	0.7178	0.7178	79.70	3.0564	12.427	0.7178	5.6022
2012	7.7569	53.37	0.7777	0.7777	79.82	3.0862	13.154	0.7777	5.8181

Year	Portugal (escudo; euro)	Singapore (dollar)	South Korea (won)	Spain (peseta; euro)	Sweden (krona)	Switzerland (franc)	Taiwan (dollar)	Thailand (baht)	UK (pound)
1970	28.7500	3.0800	310.57	69.7200	5.1700	4.3160	NA	21.000	0.4174
1980	50.0800	2.1412	607.43	71.7600	4.2309	1.6772	NA	20.476	0.4302
1990	142.5500	1.8125	707.76	101.9300	5.9188	1.3892	NA	25.585	0.5603
1995	151.1100	1.4174	771.27	124.6900	7.1333	1.1825	26.495	24.915	0.6335
2000	1.0832	1.7250	1,130.90	1.0832	9.1735	1.6904	31.260	40.210	0.6598
2005	0.8033	1.6639	1,023.75	0.8033	7.4710	1.2459	32.131	40.252	0.5493
2007	0.7293	1.5065	928.97	0.7293	6.7550	1.1999	32.852	32.203	0.4995
2008	0.6791	1.4140	1,098.71	0.6791	6.5846	1.0816	31.521	32.962	0.5392
2009	0.7176	1.4543	1,274.63	0.7176	7.6539	1.0860	33.020	34.310	0.6385
2010	0.7541	1.3629	1,155.74	0.7541	7.2053	1.0432	31.498	31.700	0.6472
2011	0.7178	1.2565	1,106.94	0.7178	6.4878	0.8862	29.382	30.462	0.6233
2012	0.7777	1.2492	1,126.16	0.7777	6.7721	0.9377	29.558	31.055	0.6308

NA = Not available. **Note:** The euro, the European Union's single currency, replaced the national currencies in the EU nations shown above. Since 1999 (2001 in the case of Greece), the euro has been fixed at the following conversion rates: 13.7603 Austrian schillings, 40.3399 Belgian francs, 6.55957 French francs, 1.95583 German marks, 340.750 Greek drachmas, 0.787564 Irish pounds, 1,936.27 Italian lire, 2.20371 Netherlands guilders, 200.482 Portuguese escudos, and 166.386 Spanish pesetas. (1) West Germany before 1991.

Top U.S. Trading Partners, 1995-2012

Source: U.S. Census Bureau, U.S. Dept. of Commerce
(in millions of dollars; top five trade partners as ranked by amount of total trade with U.S. in 2012)

Country/category	1995	2000	2005	2008	2009	2010	2011	2012
Canada								
U.S. exports	$127,226.0	$178,940.9	$211,898.7	$261,149.8	$204,658.0	$249,256.5	$281,291.5	$292,539.7
U.S. imports from	144,369.9	230,838.3	290,384.3	339,491.4	226,248.4	277,636.7	315,366.5	323,936.5
Trade balance	−17,143.9	−51,897.4	−78,485.6	−78,341.6	−21,590.5	−28,380.3	−34,075.0	−31,396.8
China								
U.S. exports to	11,753.7	16,185.2	41,192.0	69,732.8	69,496.7	91,911.1	103,986.5	110,483.6
U.S. imports from	45,543.2	100,018.2	243,470.1	337,772.6	296,373.9	364,952.6	399,378.9	425,578.9
Trade balance	−33,789.5	−83,833.0	−202,278.1	−268,039.8	−226,877.2	−273,041.6	−295,392.4	−315,095.3
Mexico								
U.S. exports to	46,292.1	111,349.0	120,247.6	151,220.1	128,892.1	163,664.6	198,068.6	215,931.2
U.S. imports from	62,100.4	135,926.3	170,108.6	215,941.6	176,654.4	229,985.6	262,873.9	277,569.8
Trade balance	−15,808.3	−24,577.3	−49,861.0	−64,721.6	−47,762.2	−66,321.0	−64,805.3	−61,638.6
Japan								
U.S. exports to	64,342.7	64,924.4	54,680.6	65,141.8	51,134.2	60,471.9	65,686.4	69,955.0
U.S. imports from	123,479.3	146,479.4	138,003.7	139,262.2	95,803.7	120,552.1	128,927.9	146,392.2
Trade balance	−59,136.6	−81,555.0	−83,323.1	−74,120.4	−44,669.5	−60,080.3	−63,241.5	−76,437.2
Germany								
U.S. exports to	22,394.3	29,448.4	34,183.7	54,505.3	43,306.3	48,155.3	49,146.8	48,797.1
U.S. imports from	36,843.9	58,512.9	84,750.9	97,496.6	71,498.2	82,450.4	98,687.9	108,708.1
Trade balance	−14,449.6	−29,064.5	−50,567.2	−42,991.3	−28,191.9	−34,295.1	−49,541.1	−59,911.0

Note: Trade balance is with U.S. Figures shown are on Census Bureau basis.

Busiest U.S. Ports, 2011

Source: U.S. Army Corps of Engineers, Dept. of the Army, U.S. Dept. of Defense
(figures in tons; ranked by total tonnage handled)

Rank	Port	Total	Domestic	Foreign	Imports	Exports
1.	South Louisiana, LA	246,508,817	125,663,604	120,845,213	39,711,125	81,134,088
2.	Houston, TX	237,798,639	70,721,272	167,077,367	88,889,008	78,188,359
3.	New York, NY and NJ	139,172,674	49,678,657	89,494,017	65,406,950	24,087,067
4.	Long Beach, CA	80,276,183	13,226,534	67,049,649	42,695,705	24,353,944
5.	New Orleans, LA	77,174,712	38,940,698	38,234,014	18,486,234	19,747,780
6.	Beaumont, TX.	73,672,069	25,841,403	47,830,666	38,854,187	8,976,479
7.	Corpus Christi, TX	70,537,732	17,603,975	52,933,757	36,354,382	16,579,375
8.	Los Angeles, CA	64,991,842	6,880,071	58,111,771	34,434,974	23,676,797
9.	Huntington-Tristate, WV	58,551,459	58,551,459	0	0	0
10.	Baton Rouge, LA	57,871,900	35,820,864	22,051,036	15,066,060	6,984,976
11.	Texas City, TX.	57,757,532	18,867,032	38,890,500	30,510,237	8,380,263
12.	Mobile, AL.	55,552,383	25,906,034	29,646,349	14,709,539	14,936,810
13.	Lake Charles, LA	54,246,843	21,336,332	32,910,511	25,800,022	7,110,489
14.	Plaquemines, LA	54,093,006	33,882,225	20,210,781	2,555,469	17,655,312
15.	Norfolk Harbor, VA	47,352,771	6,491,011	40,861,760	9,385,884	31,475,876
16.	Baltimore, MD.	44,865,703	8,100,274	36,765,429	13,222,656	23,542,773
17.	Pascagoula, MS	36,862,791	8,819,822	28,042,969	20,804,368	7,238,601
18.	St. Louis, MO and IL	36,486,870	36,486,870	0	0	0
19.	Savannah, GA	35,459,297	2,351,500	33,107,797	16,720,274	16,387,523
20.	Duluth-Superior, MN and WI.	35,081,473	27,985,393	7,096,080	603,595	6,492,485
21.	Pittsburgh, PA	33,819,097	33,819,097	0	0	0
22.	Tampa, FL.	31,407,913	20,956,104	10,451,809	4,851,071	5,600,738
23.	Philadelphia, PA	30,631,987	11,010,701	19,621,286	18,867,225	754,061
24.	Port Arthur, TX	30,274,736	10,205,058	20,069,678	11,936,521	8,133,157
25.	Valdez, AK	29,838,038	29,838,028	10	10	0
26.	Seattle, WA.	26,610,253	4,872,566	21,737,687	8,524,287	13,213,400
27.	Portland, OR.	25,479,035	8,010,660	17,468,375	3,092,054	14,376,321
28.	Newport News, VA	25,200,668	3,423,639	21,777,029	286,555	21,490,474
29.	Richmond, CA	24,256,158	10,474,730	13,781,428	11,402,869	2,378,559
30.	Tacoma, WA.	24,151,452	6,030,044	18,121,408	5,335,417	12,785,991
31.	Freeport, TX	23,311,868	4,734,136	18,577,732	16,291,250	2,286,482
32.	Port Everglades, FL	20,955,921	10,580,678	10,375,243	6,891,615	3,483,628
33.	Chicago, IL	20,351,240	16,814,077	3,537,163	2,428,057	1,109,106
34.	Marcus Hook, PA	18,826,013	7,685,396	11,140,617	10,474,234	666,383
35.	Oakland, CA.	18,494,837	2,655,048	15,839,789	5,886,207	9,953,582
36.	Boston, MA.	18,407,118	6,035,639	12,371,479	10,760,202	1,611,277
37.	Charleston, SC.	17,916,618	2,422,591	15,494,027	9,477,707	6,016,320
38.	Paulsboro, NJ	17,582,921	5,702,890	11,880,031	10,395,077	1,484,954
39.	Jacksonville, FL	16,827,591	6,824,886	10,002,705	7,513,504	2,489,201
40.	Two Harbors, MN	15,630,264	15,461,804	168,460	0	168,460
41.	Galveston, TX.	13,743,671	6,472,905	7,270,766	1,927,537	5,343,229
42.	Detroit, MI.	13,738,737	11,003,976	2,734,761	2,495,505	239,256
43.	Portland, ME.	13,177,968	1,415,707	11,762,261	11,738,281	23,980
44.	Honolulu, HI	12,657,699	11,576,697	1,081,002	718,641	362,361
45.	Memphis, TN	12,611,541	12,611,541	0	0	0
46.	Kalama, WA	12,234,007	788,048	11,445,959	528,271	10,917,688
47.	Indiana Harbor, IN	11,977,265	11,646,000	331,265	146,022	185,243
48.	Anacortes, WA	11,975,902	7,206,761	4,769,141	2,278,248	2,490,893
49.	Cincinnati, OH	11,733,363	11,733,363	0	0	0
50.	Cleveland, OH	11,573,531	10,185,645	1,387,886	1,282,844	105,042

U.S. Railroad Freight and Miles, 1890-2012

Source: Assn. of American Railroads; Bureau of Transportation Statistics, Research and Innovative Technology Admin., U.S. Dept. of Transportation

(in billion ton-miles)

Year	Class I freight[1]	All freight	Miles[2]	Year	Class I freight[1]	All freight	Miles[2]	Year	Class I freight[1]	All freight	Miles[2]
1890 ...	NA	76	163,597	1960 ...	572	575	217,552	2007 ...	1,771	1,820	140,695
1900 ...	NA	142	193,346	1970 ...	765	771	205,782	2008 ...	1,777	1,730	139,326
1910 ...	NA	255	240,293	1980 ...	919	932	178,056	2009 ...	1,532	NA	139,118
1920 ...	410	414	252,845	1990 ...	1,034	1,064	145,979	2010 ...	1,691	NA	138,623
1930 ...	383	386	249,052	2000 ...	1,466	1,546	144,473	2011 ...	1,729	NA	138,565
1940 ...	373	375	233,670	2005 ...	1,696	1,733	140,810	2012 ...	1,712	NA	NA
1950 ...	589	592	223,779	2006 ...	1,772	1,856	140,490				

NA = Not available. **Note:** A ton-mile equals one ton of freight transported one statute mile. (1) Largest class of freight railroad companies, determined by annual operating revenue. (2) Aggregate length of operating roadway in U.S., excluding yard tracks, sidings, and parallel tracks.

Merchant Fleets of the World, 2013

Source: Maritime Administration, U.S. Dept. of Transportation

(tonnage in thousands; self-propelled oceangoing vessels of 10,000 gross deadweight tons or more, ranked by total tons, all vessels)

By flag of registry	Total[1] No.	Total[1] Tons (thous.)	Dry bulk No.	Dry bulk Tons (thous.)	Container No.	Container Tons (thous.)	General cargo No.	General cargo Tons (thous.)	Tanker No.	Tanker Tons (thous.)
Panama	6,158	328,206	2,604	199,557	706	38,105	1,103	10,846	1,331	73,728
Liberia...............	2,974	193,408	785	63,205	1,010	47,839	235	3,779	910	78,132
Marshall Islands	1,876	136,328	753	59,229	237	8,700	92	1,894	772	66,196
Hong Kong	1,855	127,077	930	76,864	330	17,910	219	4,476	362	27,668
Singapore	1,776	92,513	349	31,191	378	15,451	121	2,473	852	42,156
Bahamas, The	1,029	63,125	256	14,794	57	1,748	247	4,245	394	41,072
Malta................	1,587	69,065	549	34,527	130	6,015	321	2,356	537	25,503
Greece	704	72,480	250	24,289	33	2,392	28	65	383	45,655
China[2]...............	1,416	49,384	553	27,898	160	5,985	286	2,662	389	12,707
Cyprus	788	31,438	290	18,781	208	4,894	153	1,344	123	6,335
Japan	577	22,696	183	12,988	2	101	37	243	247	8,480
United Kingdom	397	17,661	37	4,219	153	9,842	75	580	80	2,277
Isle of Man	332	23,343	80	9,947	8	743	56	540	177	12,067
Italy.................	483	20,254	111	8,624	15	820	45	502	242	8,980
Norway (NIS)[3]........	383	17,657	66	4,358	0	0	59	1,634	210	10,600
Germany.............	288	14,622	2	326	218	13,518	41	269	24	487
Antigua and Barbuda	1,221	13,798	40	1,534	390	6,723	751	5,241	21	169
South Korea	764	17,232	180	12,475	82	1,053	259	1,576	221	1,897
Denmark (DIS)[4]	307	13,373	4	401	90	7,430	34	82	167	5,328
Indonesia	1,396	12,856	120	2,894	156	1,461	671	2,770	398	5,597
Bermuda	118	10,874	26	3,986	17	745	4	56	71	6,086
U.S.	185	7,887	6	260	75	3,357	22	238	48	3,340
Malaysia	269	8,188	8	258	23	225	66	316	159	7,315
Turkey..............	546	9,388	105	4,978	44	747	261	1,419	112	2,003
Netherlands	749	7,171	9	693	57	1,084	575	4,353	89	812
Top 25 registries........	**28,178**	**1,380,025**	**8,296**	**618,276**	**4,579**	**196,889**	**5,761**	**53,959**	**8,319**	**494,591**
Total.................	**36,307**	**1,508,939**	**9,307**	**654,966**	**4,909**	**206,547**	**9,908**	**74,617**	**10,499**	**552,645**

Note: As of Jan. 31, 2013. (1) Includes roll-on/roll-off cargo not shown separately. (2) Excludes Hong Kong. (3) Norwegian Intl. Shipping Registry. (4) Danish Intl. Shipping Registry.

U.S. International Transactions, 1970-2012

Source: U.S. Bureau of Economic Analysis, U.S. Dept. of Commerce

(in millions of dollars; revised as of June 2013)

CURRENT ACCT.	1970	1980	1990	2000	2005	2010	2011	2012
Exports of goods and services								
and income receipts	$68,387	$344,440	$706,975	$1,425,260	$1,825,596	$2,522,520	$2,873,654	$2,986,949
Goods, BOP basis[1]	42,469	224,250	387,401	784,781	911,686	1,288,882	1,495,853	1,561,239
Services	14,171	47,584	147,832	288,002	375,755	553,603	616,973	649,346
Income receipts on U.S.-owned								
assets abroad	11,748	72,606	170,570	348,083	532,542	670,641	754,724	770,079
Imports of goods and services								
and income payments	−59,901	−333,774	−759,290	−1,783,419	−2,465,880	−2,844,240	−3,197,844	−3,297,677
Goods, BOP basis[1]	−39,866	−249,750	−498,438	−1,230,568	−1,692,416	−1,934,006	−2,239,991	−2,302,714
Services	−14,520	−41,491	−117,659	−218,964	−303,649	−403,216	−429,672	−442,527
Income payments on foreign-owned								
assets in U.S.	−5,515	−42,532	−139,728	−322,345	−453,800	−479,624	−513,997	−537,815
Unilateral current transfers, net	−6,156	−8,349	−26,654	−58,159	−99,512	−127,751	−133,535	−129,688
CAPITAL ACCT.: Transactions, net ...	NA	NA	−7,220	−1	13,116	−157	−1,212	6,956
FINANCIAL ACCT.								
U.S.-owned assets abroad								
(decrease/financial outflow [−])[2]	−9,337	−86,967	−81,234	−560,523	−546,631	−939,484	−452,304	−97,469
U.S. official reserve assets........	2,481	−8,155	−2,158	−290	14,096	−1,834	−15,877	−4,460
U.S. govt. assets, other than official								
reserve assets	−1,589	−5,162	2,317	−941	5,539	7,540	−103,666	85,331
U.S. private assets..................	−10,229	−73,651	−81,393	−559,292	−566,266	−945,189	−332,761	−178,341
Foreign-owned assets in U.S.								
(increase/financial inflow [+])[2]	7,226	62,037	139,357	1,038,224	1,247,347	1,308,279	969,006	543,884
Statistical discrepancy (sum of								
above with sign reversed)	−219	22,613	28,066	−61,361	31,942	59,237	−92,771	−5,891
BALANCE ON CURRENT ACCT. ...	**2,331**	**2,317**	**−78,968**	**−416,317**	**−739,796**	**−449,471**	**−457,725**	**−440,416**

NA = Not available or applicable. (1) BOP = Balance of payments. Excl. exports of goods under U.S. military agency sales contracts identified in Census Bureau export documents as well as imports of goods under direct defense expenditures identified in Census import documents, and reflects various other adjustments. (2) Excl. financial derivatives.

U.S. International Direct Investments, 1990-2012

Source: U.S. Bureau of Economic Analysis, U.S. Dept. of Commerce
(in millions of dollars)

	U.S. direct investment abroad					Foreign direct investment in U.S.				
	1990	2000	2005	2010	2012	1990	2000	2005	2010	2012
All countries	$430,521	$1,316,247	$2,241,656	$3,741,910	$4,453,307	$394,911	$1,256,867	$1,634,121	$2,280,044	$2,650,832
Canada	69,508	132,472	231,836	295,206	351,460	29,544	114,309	165,667	192,463	225,331
Europe	**214,739**	**687,320**	**1,210,679**	**2,034,559**	**2,477,040**	**247,320**	**887,014**	**1,154,048**	**1,659,774**	**1,876,240**
Austria	1,113	2,872	11,236	11,485	15,591	625	3,007	2,425	4,532	5,206
Belgium	9,464	17,973	49,306	43,975	53,769	3,900	14,787	10,024	69,565	88,697
Czech Rep.	NA	1,228	2,729	5,268	6,389	NA	NA	NA	NA	NA
Denmark	1,726	5,270	6,914	11,802	15,092	819	4,025	6,117	7,772	8,807
Finland	544	1,342	1,950	1,597	2,013	1,504	8,875	5,938	4,943	7,162
France	19,164	42,628	60,526	78,320	82,596	18,650	125,740	114,260	189,763	209,121
Germany	27,609	55,508	100,473	103,319	121,184	28,232	122,412	177,176	203,077	199,006
Greece	282	795	1,884	1,775	969	NA	NA	NA	NA	NA
Hungary	NA	1,920	2,795	4,237	6,014	NA	NA	NA	NA	NA
Ireland	5,894	35,903	55,173	158,851	203,779	1,340	25,523	17,465	24,097	24,917
Italy	14,063	23,484	24,528	27,137	26,754	1,524	6,576	7,725	20,142	23,260
Luxembourg	1,697	27,849	79,937	272,206	383,603	2,195	58,930	79,680	170,309	202,338
Netherlands	19,120	115,429	240,205	514,689	645,098	64,671	138,894	156,602	234,408	274,904
Norway	4,209	4,379	8,533	28,541	38,803	773	2,665	9,810	10,478	16,432
Poland	NA	3,884	5,575	13,152	14,178	NA	NA	NA	NA	NA
Portugal	897	2,664	2,138	2,612	2,383	NA	NA	NA	NA	NA
Russia	NA	1,147	9,363	10,040	14,066	NA	NA	NA	NA	NA
Spain	7,868	21,236	50,197	52,390	31,377	792	5,068	7,472	43,095	47,352
Sweden	1,787	25,959	30,153	23,275	24,532	5,484	21,991	22,269	38,780	42,387
Switzerland	25,099	55,377	100,692	119,891	130,315	17,674	64,719	133,387	180,642	203,954
Turkey	522	1,826	2,563	4,155	6,028	NA	NA	NA	NA	NA
UK	72,707	230,762	351,513	501,247	597,813	98,676	277,613	371,350	400,435	486,833
Latin America[1]	**71,413**	**266,576**	**379,582**	**752,788**	**869,268**	**20,168**	**53,691**	**57,175**	**62,130**	**95,642**
Argentina	2,531	17,488	10,103	11,747	14,396	NA	NA	NA	NA	NA
Bahamas	NA	NA	NA	NA	NA	1,535	1,254	650	1,753	2,876
Barbados	252	2,141	3,881	7,524	13,082	NA	NA	NA	NA	NA
Bermuda	20,169	60,114	113,222	265,524	304,524	1,550	18,336	2,147	365	2,324
Brazil	14,384	36,717	30,882	66,963	79,394	377	882	2,051	1,357	3,590
Chile	1,896	10,052	11,127	30,747	39,870	NA	NA	NA	NA	NA
Colombia	1,677	3,693	4,292	6,181	8,434	NA	NA	NA	NA	NA
Costa Rica	251	1,716	1,598	1,827	1,681	NA	NA	NA	NA	NA
Curaçao[2]	NA	NA	NA	NA	NA	12,974	3,807	5,531	2,819	4,904
Dominican Rep.	529	1,143	815	1,432	1,655	NA	NA	NA	NA	NA
Ecuador	280	832	941	1,283	851	NA	NA	NA	NA	NA
Honduras	262	399	821	936	881	NA	NA	NA	NA	NA
Mexico	10,313	39,352	73,687	85,751	101,030	575	7,462	3,595	10,970	14,883
Panama	9,289	30,758	4,826	5,156	5,113	4,188	3,819	10,983	952	1,003
Peru	599	3,130	5,542	7,196	10,918	NA	NA	NA	NA	NA
UK isls. in Caribbean	5,929	33,451	83,164	191,680	219,851	-2,979	15,191	23,063	38,477	58,584
Venezuela	1,087	10,531	8,934	10,255	15,034	496	792	5,292	3,122	4,638
Africa	**3,650**	**11,891**	**22,756**	**54,816**	**61,381**	**505**	**2,700**	**2,341**	**2,265**	**5,338**
Egypt	1,231	1,998	5,475	12,599	17,134	NA	NA	NA	NA	NA
Nigeria	-401	470	1,105	5,058	8,152	NA	NA	NA	NA	NA
South Africa	775	3,562	3,969	6,017	5,502	10	704	493	699	1,465
Middle East	**3,959**	**10,863**	**21,115**	**34,431**	**42,853**	**4,425**	**6,506**	**8,306**	**16,808**	**20,603**
Israel	746	3,735	7,978	9,464	10,208	640	3,012	4,231	8,714	9,821
Saudi Arabia	1,899	3,661	3,830	7,436	9,692	NA	NA	NA	NA	NA
UAE	409	683	2,285	4,935	7,826	99	64	NA	747	1,340
Asia and Pacific	**64,718**	**207,125**	**375,689**	**570,111**	**651,305**	**92,948**	**192,647**	**246,585**	**346,605**	**427,679**
Australia	15,110	34,838	75,669	125,421	132,825	6,542	18,775	36,392	35,632	42,685
China	354	11,140	19,016	58,996	51,363	NA	NA	574	3,300	5,154
Hong Kong	6,055	27,447	36,415	41,264	47,767	1,511	1,493	3,467	4,440	6,283
India	372	2,379	7,162	24,666	28,385	NA	NA	1,497	4,102	5,158
Indonesia	3,207	8,904	8,603	10,558	13,480	NA	NA	NA	NA	NA
Japan	22,599	57,091	81,175	113,523	133,967	83,091	159,690	189,851	255,012	308,253
Malaysia	1,466	7,910	11,097	11,791	15,001	56	310	420	338	662
New Zealand	3,156	4,271	5,191	6,724	9,466	157	395	690	584	1,663
Philippines	1,355	3,638	6,522	5,399	4,591	77	47	NA	NA	NA
Singapore	3,975	24,133	76,390	102,778	138,603	1,289	5,087	3,338	21,517	26,244
South Korea	2,695	8,968	19,760	26,233	35,125	-1,009	3,110	6,077	15,746	24,467
Taiwan	2,226	7,836	14,356	22,188	16,482	836	3,174	3,731	4,642	5,454
Thailand	1,790	5,824	10,252	12,999	16,882	NA	NA	NA	NA	NA
EU[3]	**180,491**	**609,674**	**1,078,384**	**1,834,559**	**2,239,580**	**220,874**	**814,033**	**999,276**	**1,457,842**	**1,647,567**
OPEC[4]	**7,145**	**28,545**	**35,720**	**51,499**	**63,369**	**4,216**	**4,330**	**9,286**	**11,282**	**15,487**

NA = Not available. **Note:** On a historical cost basis for comparison purposes. Direct investment in all industries. Book value of foreign direct investors' equity in, and net outstanding loans to, their U.S. affiliates. A U.S. affiliate is a U.S. business enterprise in which a single foreign direct investor owns at least 10% of the voting securities or the equivalent. Regional totals include counties or territories not shown. (1) Latin America region incl. the Caribbean and other Western Hemisphere. (2) Figures before 2010 are for the entire Netherlands Antilles, a confederation that ended in 2010. (3) European Union members in 2012: Austria, Belgium, Bulgaria, Cyprus, Czech Rep., Denmark, Estonia, Finland, France, Germany, Greece, Hungary, Ireland, Italy, Latvia, Lithuania, Luxembourg, Malta, Netherlands, Poland, Portugal, Romania, Slovakia, Slovenia, Spain, Sweden, and the UK. (4) Org. of Petroleum Exporting Countries in 2012: Algeria, Angola, Ecuador, Iran, Iraq, Kuwait, Libya, Nigeria, Qatar, Saudi Arabia, United Arab Emirates, and Venezuela.

TRANSPORTATION AND TRAVEL

Top Motor Vehicle Producing Nations, 2012

Source: R.L. Polk
(in thousands of units; ranked by total production)

Nation	Total motor vehicles	Cars	Trucks[1]	% change, 2011-12[2]
China[3]	17,611	13,297	4,314	6.67%
U.S.	10,142	4,264	5,878	19.85
Japan	9,448	8,554	894	19.58
Germany	5,601	5,388	212	-8.31
South Korea	4,472	4,167	305	-2.00
India	3,748	3,304	444	6.76
Brazil	3,138	2,531	607	0.87
Mexico	2,878	1,811	1,066	12.82
Canada	2,454	1,040	1,414	15.36
Thailand	2,410	958	1,452	67.68
Russia	2,121	1,969	152	11.85
France	1,966	1,674	292	-12.25
Spain	1,946	1,528	418	-16.47
UK	1,559	1,465	94	7.75
Iran	1,352	1,171	181	-13.47
Czech Republic	1,177	1,175	2	-1.81
Turkey	1,012	557	455	-11.63
Indonesia	916	757	159	38.68
Slovakia	844	844	0	46.02
Argentina	757	497	260	-7.73
Italy	637	397	241	-13.15
Poland	636	550	86	-23.13
Malaysia	549	400	149	6.79

Nation	Total motor vehicles	Cars	Trucks[1]	% change, 2011-12[2]
South Africa	530	298	231	0.57%
Belgium	505	505	0	-10.21
Romania	338	327	11	0.77
Taiwan	332	280	52	-0.97
Uzbekistan	236	236	0	6.39
Hungary	225	225	0	3.35
Australia	219	190	29	-4.12
Sweden	169	169	0	-17.73
Portugal	160	116	44	-15.20
Colombia	133	94	39	-2.68
Slovenia	131	125	6	-24.84
Austria	124	124	0	-5.17
Morocco	109	100	9	NA
Philippines	103	50	53	5.08
Asia-Pacific/ Middle East	41,161	33,128	8,033	10.29
Western Europe	15,474	7,116	8,358	10.59
NAFTA	12,693	11,392	1,301	-3.40
Central & Eastern Europe	6,850	6,138	712	1.98
South America	4,199	3,215	984	-0.09
Africa	706	466	240	8.03
World total	81,082	19,628	61,454	6.65

NA = Not available. **Note:** Regional and world totals include countries or territories not listed here. Numbers may not add up to totals due to rounding. (1) Light commercial vehicles (pickup trucks and vans). (2) Percent change in number of total motor vehicles. (3) Not including Taiwan.

World Motor Vehicle Production, 1950-2012

Source: For 1950-97, American Automobile Manufacturers Assn.; for 2000 and on, Automotive News Data Center and R.L. Polk
(in thousands of units)

Year	United States	Canada	Europe[1]	Japan	Other	World total	U.S. % of world total
1950	8,006	388	1,991	32	160	10,577	75.7%
1960	7,905	398	6,837	482	866	16,488	47.9
1970	8,284	1,160	13,049	5,289	1,637	29,419	28.2
1980	8,010	1,324	15,496	11,043	2,692	38,565	20.8
1990	9,783	1,928	18,866	13,487	4,496	48,554	20.1
1995	11,985	2,408	17,045	10,196	8,349	49,983	24.0
2000	12,832	2,952	17,678	10,145	16,098	59,704	21.5
2001	11,518	2,535	17,825	9,777	16,170	57,705	19.7
2002	12,328	2,624	17,419	10,240	16,975	59,587	20.7
2003	12,145	2,547	16,943	10,286	19,641	61,562	19.7
2004	12,021	2,698	20,850	10,512	16,573	65,654	18.3
2005	12,018	2,665	20,855	10,800	20,691	67,892	17.7
2006	11,351	2,545	21,490	11,486	23,180	70,992	16.0
2007	10,611	2,602	22,858	11,596	26,019	74,647	14.2
2008	8,503	2,046	21,608	10,969	31,224	67,602	12.6
2009	5,591	1,476	17,075	7,648	32,374	59,096	9.5
2010	7,632	2,074	19,371	9,197	35,036	73,311	10.4
2011	8,462	2,127	20,709	7,901	36,828	76,027	11.1
2012	10,142	2,454	22,324	9,448	36,714	81,082	12.5

Note: Data for 2000 and on are not fully comparable with earlier years because they are derived from different sources. Number of units may not add up to totals due to rounding. (1) Prior to 2004, numbers exclude Eastern European production.

New and Used Passenger Cars Imported Into the U.S. by Country of Origin, 1970-2012

Source: Foreign Trade Division, U.S. Census Bureau
(in number of units)

Year	Japan	Germany[1]	Italy	UK	Sweden	France	S. Korea	Mexico	Canada	Total[2]
1970	381,338	674,945	42,523	76,257	57,844	37,114	NA	NA	692,783	2,013,420
1975	695,573	370,012	102,344	67,106	51,993	15,647	NA	0	733,766	2,074,653
1980	1,991,502	338,711	46,899	32,517	61,496	47,386	NA	1	594,770	3,116,448
1985	2,527,467	473,110	8,689	24,474	142,640	42,882	NA	13,647	1,144,805	4,397,679
1990	1,867,794	245,286	11,045	27,271	93,084	1,976	201,475	215,986	1,220,221	3,944,602
1995	1,114,360	204,932	1,031	42,450	82,593	14	131,718	462,800	1,552,691	3,624,428
2000	1,839,093	488,323	3,125	81,196	86,707	134	568,121	934,000	2,138,811	6,324,284
2001	1,790,346	494,131	2,580	82,487	92,439	92	633,769	861,853	1,855,789	6,065,138
2002	2,046,902	574,455	3,504	157,633	87,709	150	627,881	845,181	1,882,660	6,477,659
2003	1,770,355	561,482	2,943	207,158	119,773	298	692,863	680,214	1,811,892	6,127,485
2004	1,727,065	547,008	3,373	185,621	98,131	2,417	860,424	652,509	2,035,345	6,521,248
2005	1,832,534	547,191	5,377	184,716	93,736	412	730,500	693,149	1,967,985	6,564,844
2006	2,347,532	532,022	5,469	148,014	81,008	567	697,061	947,824	1,963,922	7,380,077
2007	2,300,913	466,458	5,650	108,576	92,600	1,746	676,594	889,474	1,912,744	7,220,792
2008	2,190,013	502,971	5,783	110,737	59,638	28,198	612,300	928,273	1,609,005	6,525,836
2009	1,238,773	348,093	3,067	78,999	27,017	16,909	476,912	649,740	1,164,849	4,276,163
2010	1,569,220	506,053	4,298	96,689	38,749	4,153	515,601	902,565	1,741,493	5,668,111
2011	1,436,515	537,178	5,390	95,759	26,884	5,018	587,574	968,413	1,836,166	5,819,877
2012	1,735,564	629,490	11,800	114,097	24,625	10,988	705,089	1,067,358	2,094,951	6,759,734

NA = Not available. **Note:** Excludes cars assembled in U.S. foreign trade zones. (1) Figures prior to 1991 are for West Germany. (2) Includes units imported from countries not shown in table.

Passenger Car Production in U.S. Plants, 2011-12

Source: WardsAuto InfoBank
(in number of units)

	2012	2011	2010		2012	2011	2010
AAI/FLAT ROCK ASSEMBLY[1]				**HONDA TOTAL**	639,108	349,969	426,119
TOTAL	133,004	117,836	122,754	Acura ILX............	30,244	—	—
Ford Mustang..........	95,438	78,286	77,586	Acura TL	39,421	35,763	35,294
Mazda6..............	37,566	39,550	45,168	**Acura total**	69,665	35,763	35,294
				Honda Accord	400,143	229,439	295,709
CHRYSLER TOTAL	334,825	250,417	169,398	Honda Civic	169,300	84,767	95,116
Chrysler Sebring.......	—	—	39,986	**Honda total**	569,443	314,206	390,825
Chrysler 200 Series.....	150,321	122,625	2,197				
Chrysler total	150,321	122,625	42,183	**HYUNDAI TOTAL**	361,348	338,127	238,387
Dodge Avenger	113,541	75,951	59,170	Hyundai Elantra	138,997	112,665	19,780
Dodge Caliber	—	51,841	67,586	Hyundai Sonata	222,351	225,462	218,607
Dodge Dart...........	69,645	—	—				
Dodge Viper...........	—	—	459	**KIA MOTORS TOTAL**	128,536	35,132	—
Dodge total	183,186	127,792	127,215	Kia Optima..........	128,536	35,132	—
Lancia Flavia	1,318	—	—				
				MITSUBISHI TOTAL........	13,716	26,583	22,969
FORD TOTAL	419,907	311,814	298,639	Mitsubishi Eclipse	—	7,142	6,424
Ford C-Max	19,890	—	—	Mitsubishi Galant......	13,716	19,441	16,545
Ford Focus............	283,447	221,514	199,502				
Ford Taurus...........	101,875	77,664	83,052	**NISSAN TOTAL**	406,782	385,109	346,891
Total Ford	405,212	299,178	282,554	Nissan Altima........	334,710	319,203	275,115
Lincoln MKS...........	14,695	12,636	16,085	Nissan Leaf	192	—	—
				Nissan Maxima	71,877	65,906	71,776
GENERAL MOTORS TOTAL...	840,700	721,501	600,703[2]	Nissan Sentra	3	—	—
Buick LaCrosse	56,561	64,729	73,480				
Buick Lucerne	—	15,882	29,654	**NUMMI[3] TOTAL**	—	—	63,319
Buick Verano	57,435	4,471	—	Toyota Corolla	—	—	63,319
Buick total...........	113,996	85,082	103,134				
Cadillac ATS..........	26,278	—	—	**SUBARU[4] TOTAL**.........	143,529	125,738	131,522
Cadillac CTS..........	48,247	64,935	60,688	Subaru Legacy	50,403	46,568	43,791
Cadillac DTS	—	6,515	21,023	Toyota Camry	93,126	79,170	87,731
Cadillac STS	—	1,907	4,792				
Cadillac total	74,525	73,357	86,503	**TOYOTA TOTAL**	531,876	268,314	310,404
Chevrolet Cobalt	—	—	91,796	Toyota Avalon	42,442	38,684	40,155
Chevrolet Corvette.....	14,960	13,222	15,791	Toyota Camry	359,832	227,663	270,249
Chevrolet Cruze.......	279,382	281,810	66,303	Toyota Corolla	129,602	1,967	—
Chevrolet Malibu	229,170	214,388	235,956				
Chevrolet Sonic	97,840	36,527	—	**VOLKSWAGEN TOTAL**	152,543	46,451	—
Chevrolet Volt........	24,196	14,510	1,219	Volkswagen Passat	152,543	46,451	—
Chevrolet total	645,548	560,457	411,065				
Opel Ampera	6,631	2,605	—	**TOTAL CARS**	4,105,874	2,976,991	2,731,105

— = No production. (1) AutoAlliance Intl., a joint venture between Ford and Mazda, produced cars for both automakers (1992-2012). The joint agreement changed in Sept. 2012, after which Ford renamed the operation Flat Rock Assembly. (2) Incl. a single Pontiac G6 produced in 2010. (3) NUMMI (New United Motor Manufacturing, Inc.) was a joint venture between GM and Toyota (1984-2010). (4) SIA (Subaru of Indiana Automotive) also builds the Toyota Camry in collaboration with Toyota.

Domestic and Imported Retail Car Sales in the U.S., 1980-2012

Source: WardsAuto Group, a division of Penton Media Inc.
(in number of units)

	Cars			Light trucks			All vehicles		
Year	Domestic[1]	Imports	Total cars	Domestic[1]	Imports	Total light trucks	Domestic[1]	Imports	Total vehicles
1980	6,579,778	2,369,457	8,949,235	1,750,735	478,887	2,229,622	8,330,513	2,848,344	11,178,857
1981	6,180,784	2,308,418	8,409,202	1,591,575	461,975	2,053,550	7,772,369	2,770,393	10,542,752
1982	5,756,658	2,199,802	7,956,460	1,968,534	430,330	2,398,864	7,725,192	2,630,132	10,355,324
1983	6,795,299	2,352,739	9,148,038	2,477,259	496,969	2,974,228	9,272,558	2,849,708	12,122,266
1984	7,951,523	2,372,172	10,323,695	3,208,371	674,153	3,882,524	11,159,894	3,046,325	14,206,219
1985	8,204,670	2,774,517	10,979,187	3,629,080	832,186	4,461,266	11,833,750	3,606,703	15,440,453
1986	8,215,017	3,189,222	11,404,239	3,675,914	977,920	4,653,834	11,890,931	4,167,142	16,058,073
1987	7,085,279	3,106,598	10,191,877	3,791,882	921,698	4,713,580	10,877,161	4,028,296	14,905,457
1988	7,543,116	3,003,692	10,546,808	4,199,643	710,661	4,910,304	11,742,759	3,714,353	15,457,112
1989	7,098,098	2,680,419	9,778,517	4,113,441	641,387	4,754,828	11,211,539	3,321,806	14,533,345
1990	6,918,869	2,384,346	9,303,215	3,956,756	611,941	4,568,697	10,875,625	2,996,287	13,871,912
1991	6,161,573	2,023,406	8,184,979	3,605,633	538,008	4,143,641	9,767,206	2,561,414	12,328,620
1992	6,285,916	1,927,197	8,213,113	4,247,097	408,003	4,655,100	10,533,013	2,335,200	12,868,213
1993	6,741,667	1,776,192	8,517,859	5,000,482	377,639	5,378,121	11,742,149	2,153,831	13,895,980
1994	7,255,303	1,735,214	8,990,517	5,658,302	409,759	6,068,061	12,913,605	2,144,973	15,058,578
1995	7,113,902	1,506,257	8,620,159	5,705,708	402,181	6,107,889	12,819,610	1,908,438	14,728,048
1996	7,206,349	1,272,196	8,478,545	6,179,881	438,757	6,618,638	13,386,230	1,710,953	15,097,183
1997	6,862,175	1,355,305	8,217,480	6,324,758	579,483	6,904,241	13,186,933	1,934,788	15,121,721
1998	6,705,208	1,379,781	8,084,989	6,802,016	656,002	7,458,018	13,507,224	2,035,783	15,543,007
1999	6,918,781	1,718,927	8,637,708	7,480,607	775,223	8,255,830	14,399,388	2,494,150	16,893,538
2000	6,761,603	2,016,120	8,777,723	7,719,707	852,325	8,572,032	14,481,310	2,868,445	17,349,755
2001	6,254,371	2,097,629	8,352,000	7,789,089	981,280	8,770,369	14,043,460	3,078,909	17,122,369
2002	5,816,671	2,225,584	8,042,255	7,707,738	1,066,375	8,774,113	13,524,409	3,291,959	16,816,368
2003	5,472,500	2,083,051	7,555,551	7,856,322	1,227,180	9,083,502	13,328,822	3,310,231	16,639,053
2004	5,333,496	2,149,059	7,482,555	8,138,107	1,246,258	9,384,365	13,471,603	3,395,317	16,866,920
2005	5,473,450	2,186,533	7,659,983	8,072,456	1,215,315	9,287,771	13,545,906	3,401,848	16,947,754
2006	5,416,828	2,344,764	7,761,592	7,396,058	1,346,750	8,742,808	12,812,886	3,691,514	16,504,400
2007	5,197,271	2,365,063	7,562,334	7,138,803	1,388,085	8,526,888	12,336,074	3,753,148	16,089,222
2008	4,490,836	2,278,271	6,769,107	5,329,165	1,096,469	6,425,634	9,820,001	3,374,740	13,194,741
2009	3,557,608	1,843,282	5,400,890	4,116,550	884,242	5,000,792	7,674,158	2,727,524	10,401,682
2010	3,791,192	1,844,240	5,635,432	5,020,441	898,644	5,919,085	8,811,633	2,742,884	11,554,517
2011	4,142,506	1,946,897	6,089,403	5,662,578	982,443	6,645,021	9,805,084	2,929,340	12,734,424
2012	5,116,425	2,125,325	7,241,900	6,137,440	1,060,720	7,198,160	11,254,015	3,186,045	14,440,060

Note: Vehicles are cars and light trucks belonging to gross vehicle weight (GVW) classes 1-3 (under 14,001 lbs). (1) Includes the U.S., Canada, and Mexico.

U.S. Vehicle Sales, 2000-12

Source: WardsAuto Group, a division of Penton Media Inc.

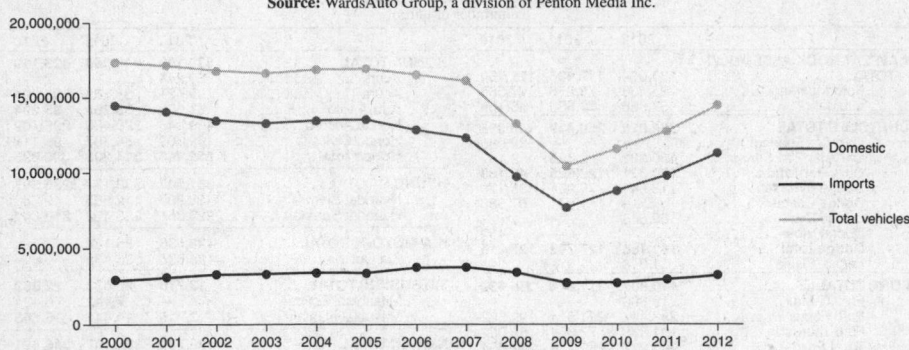

Note: Vehicles are cars and light trucks belonging to gross vehicle weight (GWV) classes 1-3 (under 14,001 lbs). Domestic sales include the U.S., Canada, and Mexico.

U.S. Sales of Hybrid and Electric Vehicles, 2000-12

Source: WardsAuto Group, a division of Penton Media Inc; in number of units.

Power type	2000	2005	2006	2007	2008	2009	2010	2011	2012
Hybrid car	9,350	151,253	177,674	282,790	250,462	237,263	231,819	231,075	407,628
Hybrid light truck	0	54,575	75,844	70,072	65,226	53,477	42,286	30,432	24,170
Total hybrid	**9,350**	**205,828**	**253,518**	**352,862**	**315,688**	**290,740**	**274,105**	**261,507**	**431,798**
Electric car	463	0	0	0	27	675	326	10,447	13,749
Electric light truck	0	0	0	0	0	0	0	0	192
Total electric	**463**	**0**	**0**	**0**	**27**	**675**	**326**	**10,447**	**13,941**
Plug-in hybrid car	0	0	0	0	0	0	326	7,671	38,585

U.S. Sales of Hybrid and Electric Vehicles, 2000-12

Source: WardsAuto Group, a division of Penton Media Inc.

Top-Selling Passenger Cars in the U.S., 2009-12

Source: WardsAuto Group, a division of Penton Media Inc; in number of units.
(ranked by number of vehicles sold)

Rank, car	2012 sales	Rank, car	2012 sales	Rank, car	2012 sales
1. Toyota Camry	404,886	8. Chevrolet Cruze	237,758	15. Kia Optima	152,399
2. Honda Accord	331,872	9. Hyundai Sonata	230,605	16. Chrysler 200	125,476
3. Honda Civic	317,909	10. Chevrolet Malibu	210,951	17. Mazda3	123,361
4. Nissan Altima	302,934	11. Hyundai Elantra	202,034	18. Volkswagen Passat	117,023
5. Toyota Corolla/Matrix	286,473	12. Toyota Prius	200,926	19. Kia Soul	115,778
6. Ford Focus	245,922	13. Volkswagen Jetta	170,424	20. Nissan Versa	113,327
7. Ford Fusion	241,263	14. Chevrolet Impala	169,351		

Rank, car	2011 sales	Rank, car	2010 sales	Rank, car	2009 sales
1. Toyota Camry	308,510	1. Toyota Camry	327,804	1. Toyota Camry	356,824
2. Nissan Altima	268,981	2. Honda Accord	282,530	2. Toyota Corolla/Matrix	296,874
3. Ford Fusion	248,067	3. Toyota Corolla/Matrix	266,082	3. Honda Accord	287,492
4. Toyota Corolla	240,259	4. Honda Civic	260,218	4. Honda Civic	259,722
5. Honda Accord	235,625	5. Nissan Altima	229,263	5. Nissan Altima	203,568
6. Chevrolet Cruze	231,732	6. Ford Fusion	219,219	6. Ford Fusion	180,671
7. Hyundai Sonata	225,961	7. Chevrolet Malibu	198,770	7. Chevrolet Impala	165,565
8. Honda Civic	221,235	8. Hyundai Sonata	196,623	8. Chevrolet Malibu	161,568
9. Chevrolet Malibu	204,808	9. Ford Focus	172,421	9. Ford Focus	160,433
10. Hyundai Elantra	186,361	10. Chevrolet Impala	172,078	10. Toyota Prius	139,682

U.S. Retail Car Sales by Vehicle Size, 1985-2012

Source: WardsAuto Group, a division of Penton Media Inc.
(as percent of total U.S. sales)

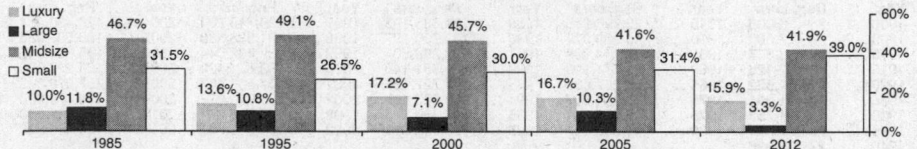

U.S. Light Truck Sales by Type, 1985-2012

Source: WardsAuto Group, a division of Penton Media Inc.
(as percent of total U.S. sales)

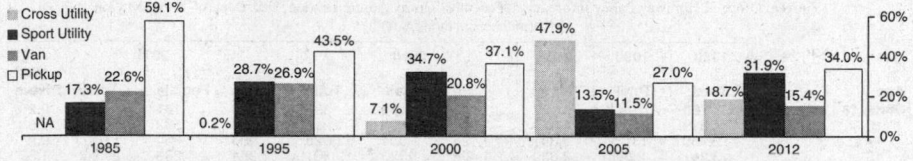

NA = Not available. **Note:** Comm. chassis sales (not shown) were 1.0% (for 1985), 0.7% (1995), 0.2% (2000), 0.1% (2005), 0.1% (2012).

Top-Selling Light Trucks in the U.S., 2010-12

Source: WardsAuto Group, a division of Penton Media Inc.
(ranked by number of vehicles sold)

Rank, truck	2012 sales	Rank, truck	2011 sales	Rank, truck	2010 sales
1. Ford F-Series	607,854	1. Ford F-Series	552,647	1. Ford F-Series	502,125
2. Chevrolet Silverado	418,312	2. Chevrolet Silverado	415,130	2. Chevrolet Silverado	370,135
3. Ram Pickup	283,056	3. Ford Escape	254,293	3. Honda CR-V	203,714
4. Honda CR-V	281,652	4. Ram Pickup	237,236	4. Ram Pickup	194,175
5. Ford Escape	261,008	5. Honda CR-V	218,373	5. Ford Escape	191,026
6. Chevrolet Equinox	218,621	6. Chevrolet Equinox	193,274	6. Toyota RAV4	170,877
7. Toyota RAV4	171,877	7. GMC Sierra	149,170	7. Chevrolet Equinox	149,979
8. Ford Explorer	164,207	8. Ford Explorer	135,704	8. GMC Sierra	129,794
9. GMC Sierra	157,185	9. Toyota RAV4	132,237	9. Ford Edge	118,637
10. Jeep Grand Cherokee	154,734	10. Kia Sorento	130,235	10. Chrysler Town & Country	112,275

Most Popular Colors, by Vehicle Type, 2012

Source: WardsAuto Group, a division of Penton Media Inc.; DuPont Automotive Products; for 2012 model year

Luxury cars/SUVs		Intermediate cars/CUVs		Compact/sports cars		Light trucks	
Color	Percent	Color	Percent	Color	Percent	Color	Percent
Black/black effect	29%	Black/black effect	19%	White/white pearl	19%	White/white pearl	24%
White/white pearl	19	Silver	18	Black/black effect	18	Black/black effect	19
Gray	16	Gray	17	Silver	18	Silver	16
Silver	15	White/white pearl	17	Gray	17	Gray	15
Red	8	Red	10	Red	12	Red	10
Beige/brown	5	Blue	8	Blue	9	Blue	7
Yellow/gold	3	Beige/brown	7	Beige/brown	3	Beige/brown	5
Blue	3	Green	2	Yellow/gold	2	Green	2
Green	2	Yellow/gold	1	Green	1	Yellow/gold	2
Other	<1	Other	1	Other	1	Other	<1

U.S. Light-Duty Vehicle Fuel Efficiency, 1975-2012

Source: Natl. Vehicle and Fuel Emissions Laboratory, Office of Transportation and Air Quality, U.S. Environmental Protection Agency

Cars and light-duty trucks (SUVs, minivans, passenger vans, and pickup trucks) showed significant fuel-efficiency improvements from 1975 through 1987, when the fuel economy for both reached a high of 22 miles per gallon (mpg). The fuel economy value declined steadily, 1988-2004, but since 2005, fuel economy has generally increased. Most of this increase has been due to higher truck fuel economy.

Year[1]	Cars (mpg)	Light-duty trucks (mpg)	All light-duty vehicles (mpg)	Year[1]	Cars (mpg)	Light-duty trucks (mpg)	All light-duty vehicles (mpg)
1975	13.5	11.6	13.1	2002	22.8	16.5	19.5
1980	20.0	15.8	19.2	2003	23.0	16.7	19.6
1985	23.0	17.5	21.3	2004	22.9	16.5	19.3
1990	23.3	17.4	21.2	2005	23.1	16.9	19.9
1995	23.3	17.0	20.5	2006	23.0	17.2	20.1
1996	23.1	17.2	20.4	2007	23.7	17.4	20.6
1997	23.2	16.8	20.2	2008	23.9	17.8	21.0
1998	23.0	17.1	20.1	2009	25.0	18.5	22.4
1999	22.7	16.6	19.7	2010	25.7	18.8	22.6
2000	22.5	16.8	19.8	2011	25.6	19.1	22.4
2001	22.6	16.5	19.6	2012	27.3	19.4	23.8

Note: Adjusted mpg composite values (city and highway fuel efficiency combined in a 55%/45% ratio) are used for all vehicles and are intended to reflect real-world use. (1) Because of changes in methodology, mpg figures prior to 1986 are not entirely comparable with later values.

Registered Cars in the U.S., 1900-2011

Source: Office of Highway Policy Information, Federal Highway Administration, U.S. Dept. of Transportation

(number of automobiles for public and private use)

Year	Reg. cars	Year	Reg. cars	Year	Reg. cars	Year	Reg. cars	Year	Reg. cars
1900	8,000	1945	25,796,985	1985	127,885,193	1997	129,748,704	2004	136,430,651
1905	77,400	1950	40,339,077	1990	133,700,497	1998	131,838,538	2005	136,568,083
1910	458,377	1955	52,144,739	1991	128,299,601	1999	132,432,044	2006	135,399,945
1915	2,332,426	1960	61,671,390	1992	126,581,148	2000	133,621,420	2007	135,932,930
1920	8,131,522	1965	75,257,588	1993	127,327,189	2001	137,633,467	2008	137,079,843
1925	17,481,001	1970	89,243,557	1994	127,883,469	2002	135,920,677	2009	134,879,600
1930	23,034,753	1975	106,705,934	1995	128,386,775	2002	135,920,677	2010	130,892,240
1935	22,567,827	1980	121,600,843	1996	129,728,311	2003	135,669,897	2011	125,656,528
1940	27,465,826								

Note: There were no publicly owned vehicles before 1925; statistics also exclude military vehicles for all years. Alaska and Hawaii data included since 1960.

Licensed Drivers, by Age and Sex, 1980-2011

Source: Office of Highway Policy Information, Federal Highway Administration, U.S. Dept. of Transportation

(numbers in thousands)

Age	1980 Total	1990 Total	2000 Total[1]	2010 Male	2010 Female	2010 Total[1]	2011 Male	2011 Female	2011 Total[1]	% total drivers
Under 16	93	43	27	199	198	398	180	181	361	0.2%
16	1,823	1,443	1,470	608	605	1,213	585	582	1,168	0.6
17	2,790	2,132	2,331	1,025	1,004	2,028	986	964	1,950	0.9
18	3,247	2,595	2,839	1,408	1,323	2,731	1,364	1,286	2,650	1.3
19	3,542	3,037	3,077	1,641	1,546	3,187	1,605	1,525	3,130	1.5
19 and under.......	11,496	9,249	9,744	4,880	4,676	9,556	4,721	4,538	9,258	4.4
20	3,636	3,229	3,140	1,744	1,682	3,426	1,724	1,660	3,384	1.6
21	3,733	3,249	3,172	1,756	1,717	3,474	1,787	1,745	3,531	1.7
22	3,811	3,262	3,182	1,757	1,725	3,483	1,790	1,760	3,551	1.7
23	3,938	3,398	3,247	1,767	1,748	3,515	1,793	1,779	3,572	1.7
24	3,915	3,758	3,225	1,792	1,779	3,571	1,806	1,806	3,612	1.7
20-24	19,032	16,897	15,966	8,817	8,651	17,469	8,899	8,750	17,649	8.3
25-29	18,925	19,895	17,586	9,179	9,253	18,431	9,252	9,364	18,616	8.8
30-34	17,369	20,578	19,155	8,934	8,915	17,849	9,052	9,225	18,277	8.6
35-39	13,696	19,055	21,059	9,079	9,082	18,161	8,787	8,892	17,679	8.3
40-44	11,134	16,905	21,093	9,613	9,565	19,178	9,599	9,661	19,260	9.1
45-49	10,076	13,020	19,154	10,381	10,433	20,814	10,130	10,241	20,372	9.6
50-54	10,090	10,484	16,868	10,241	10,388	20,628	10,292	10,508	20,801	9.8
55-59	9,770	9,438	12,760	9,127	9,313	18,440	9,313	9,574	18,888	8.9
60-64	8,232	9,235	9,915	7,847	8,011	15,858	8,132	8,378	16,510	7.8
65-69	6,580	8,375	8,386	5,652	5,816	11,468	5,895	6,079	11,974	5.7
70-74	NA	NA	7,468	4,029	4,202	8,231	4,176	4,362	8,538	4.0
75-79	NA	NA	5,911	2,966	3,192	6,158	3,005	3,221	6,225	2.9
80-84	NA	NA	3,511	2,090	2,373	4,464	2,092	2,341	4,433	2.1
85 and over	NA	NA	2,050	1,541	1,870	3,411	1,554	1,841	3,395	1.6
Total	145,295	167,015	190,625	104,374	105,740	210,115	104,900	106,975	211,875	100.0

NA = Not available. (1) Numbers may not add up to totals due to rounding.

Handheld Phone and Texting Device Laws for Drivers, 2013

Source: Insurance Institute for Highway Safety; as of July 2013

State	Handheld ban	Texting ban	Enforcement	State	Handheld ban	Texting ban	Enforcement	State	Handheld ban	Texting ban	Enforcement
AL	(1)	Yes	(2)	KY	No	Yes	P	ND	No	Yes	P
AK	No	Yes	P	LA	(6)	Yes	P[6]	OH	No	Yes	(9)
AZ	No	No	NA	ME	No	Yes	P	OK	(7)	(7)	P
AR	(3)	Yes	(2)	MD	Yes	Yes	P	OR	Yes	Yes	P
CA	Yes	Yes	P[4]	MA	No	Yes	P	PA	No	Yes	P
CO	No	Yes	P	MI	No	Yes	P	RI	No	Yes	P
CT	Yes	Yes	P	MN	No	Yes	P	SC	No	No	NA
DE	Yes	Yes	P	MS	No	(7)	P	SD	No	(8)	S
DC	Yes	Yes	P	MO	No	(8)	P	TN	No	Yes	P
FL	No	Yes	S	MT	No	No	NA	TX	No	(10)	P
GA	No	Yes	P	NE	No	Yes	S	UT	No	Yes	P
HI	Yes	Yes	P	NV	Yes	Yes	P	VT	No	Yes	P
ID	No	Yes	P	NH	No	Yes	P	VA	No	Yes	P[11]
IL	No	Yes	P	NJ	Yes	Yes	P	WA	Yes	Yes	P
IN	No	Yes	P	NM	No	(7)	P	WV	No	Yes	P
IA	No	Yes	(5)	NY	Yes	Yes	P	WI	No	Yes	P
KS	No	Yes	P	NC	No	Yes	P	WY	No	Yes	P

NA = Not applicable. P = Officer may stop vehicle for violation (primary); S = officer may issue citation only when vehicle is stopped for another moving violation (secondary). **Note:** Laws shown for licensed passenger car drivers. Different laws and regulations apply to school bus, municipal transit, and other mass transit operators. Different laws may apply in school zones, construction zones, or other such areas. (1) All drivers age 16 and drivers age 17 who have held an intermediate license for fewer than 6 months. (2) Primary for texting by all drivers; secondary for cell phone use by young drivers. (3) Drivers younger than 21. (4) Secondary for cell phone use by young drivers. (5) Primary for learner's permit and intermediate license holders; secondary for texting. (6) All learner's permit holders and all intermediate license holders are prohibited from driving while using a handheld cell phone, and all drivers younger than 18 are prohibited from using any cell phone. All drivers issued a first driver's license are prohibited from using a cell phone for one year. The cell phone ban is secondary for novice drivers age 18 and older. (7) Learner's permit and intermediate license holders. (8) Drivers 21 and younger. (9) Primary for drivers younger than 18; secondary for texting. (10) Drivers younger than 18. (11) Secondary for drivers younger than 18.

Selected Motor Vehicle Statistics

Source: Federal Highway Admin., U.S. Dept. of Transportation; Insurance Inst. for Highway Safety; American Petroleum Inst.
Driver's license age requirements, state gas tax, and safety belt use laws (incl. laws passed, but not in effect) as of 2013. Other figures are for 2011.

STATE	Driver's license age requirements — Learner's permit	Driver's license age requirements — Regular[1]	Gas taxes (cents/gal)[4]	Safety belt use law[5]	Licensed drivers — Per 1,000 resident pop.	Licensed drivers — Per reg. motor vehicle	Reg. motor vehicles per 1,000 pop.	Fuel use per reg. motor vehicle (gal)	Annual miles driven — Per gal used	Annual miles driven — Per reg. vehicle	Annual miles driven — Per lic. driver
Alabama	15	17	39.3	P	791	0.82	1,002	695	19.40	13,490	17,089
Alaska	14	16y, 6m	26.4	P	721	0.73	1,049	671	9.03	6,060	8,811
Arizona	15y, 6m	16y, 6m	37.4	S	708	0.95	788	667	17.47	11,660	12,972
Arkansas	14	18	40.2	P	666	0.84	833	830	16.22	13,459	16,846
California	15y, 6m	17	71.9	P	633	0.85	774	596	18.45	10,995	13,446
Colorado	15	17	40.4	S	717	0.90	847	616	17.46	10,758	12,700
Connecticut	16	18[2]	67.7	P	834	1.11	790	616	17.92	11,028	10,447
Delaware	16	17[2]	41.4	P	789	0.81	1,025	538	18.06	9,714	12,607
Dist. of Columbia	16	18[3]	41.9	P	640	1.37	512	405	27.87	11,283	9,023
Florida	15	18	53.8	P	728	0.94	812	614	20.19	12,402	13,820
Georgia	15	18[2]	46.9	P	663	0.90	768	785	18.34	14,396	16,671
Hawaii	15y, 6m	17[2]	69.0	P	663	0.83	835	454	19.33	8,768	11,042
Idaho	14y, 6m	16[2]	43.4	S	684	0.70	1,025	576	17.04	9,806	14,702
Illinois	15	18[2]	57.5	P	651	0.84	812	594	16.63	9,883	12,328
Indiana	15	18[2]	57.3	P	1,008	1.12	941	698	17.87	12,472	11,642
Iowa	14	17[2]	40.4	P	716	0.67	1,142	679	13.18	8,944	14,269
Kansas	14	16y, 6m	43.4	P(a)	705	0.87	852	692	17.73	12,274	14,821
Kentucky	16	17[2]	50.7	P	677	0.82	861	781	16.35	12,772	16,238
Louisiana	15	17[2]	38.4	P	696	0.81	886	756	15.19	11,477	14,598
Maine	15	16y, 9m[2]	49.9	P	764	0.92	882	750	16.21	12,165	14,040
Maryland	15y, 9m	18	48.9	P(a)	662	1.04	670	817	17.62	14,395	14,578
Massachusetts	16	18[2]	41.9	S	711	0.86	865	562	17.10	9,620	11,699
Michigan	14y, 9m	17[2]	57.9	P	715	0.81	930	579	17.82	10,319	13,422
Minnesota	15	17[2]	47.0	P	619	0.72	919	641	18.01	11,546	17,145
Mississippi	15	16y, 6m	37.2	P	647	0.98	684	1,056	18.07	19,077	20,165
Missouri	15	17y, 11m	35.7	S(b)	712	0.86	860	794	16.76	13,305	16,083
Montana	14y, 6m	16[2]	46.2	S	754	0.65	1,221	614	15.57	9,564	15,495
Nebraska	15	17	45.6	S	736	0.75	1,024	668	15.15	10,119	14,077
Nevada	15y, 6m	18[2]	51.5	S	625	0.83	790	642	17.50	11,238	14,222
New Hampshire	15y, 6m	18[2]	38.0	None	802	0.89	970	625	15.93	9,949	12,035
New Jersey	16	18	32.9	P(a)	678	0.80	900	629	14.64	9,206	12,228
New Mexico	15	16y, 6m[2]	37.3	P	681	0.85	851	834	17.28	14,409	17,998
New York	16	17[2]	68.2	P	576	1.14	536	661	18.51	12,245	11,393
North Carolina	15	16y, 6m[2]	56.3	P(a)	680	1.11	647	861	19.29	16,605	15,796
North Dakota	14	16	41.4	S	717	0.66	1,149	932	12.47	11,619	18,628
Ohio	15y, 6m	18[2]	46.4	P	691	0.82	885	632	17.35	10,961	14,030
Oklahoma	15y, 6m	16y, 6m[2]	35.4	P	625	0.73	904	763	18.15	13,843	20,021
Oregon	15	17[2]	49.5	P	716	0.93	808	642	16.61	10,669	12,031
Pennsylvania	16	17	50.7	S(b)	690	0.90	809	626	15.38	9,629	11,277
Rhode Island	16	17y, 6m[2]	51.4	P	713	0.86	874	477	18.04	8,600	10,539
South Carolina	15	16y, 6m	35.2	P	728	0.93	818	869	14.65	12,733	14,297
South Dakota	14	16	40.4	S	732	0.66	1,208	660	13.69	9,043	14,922
Tennessee	15	17	39.8	P	710	0.90	828	771	17.30	13,343	15,571
Texas	15	18	38.4	P	589	0.80	764	838	14.45	12,104	15,701
Utah	15	17[2]	42.9	S(b)	620	0.98	669	837	16.64	13,922	15,005
Vermont	15	16y, 6m[2]	50.6	S	833	0.92	966	631	18.72	11,802	13,689
Virginia	15y, 6m	18[2]	35.7	S	675	0.82	864	682	16.97	11,570	14,811
Washington	15	17[2]	55.9	P	758	0.93	861	564	17.19	9,685	10,998
West Virginia	15	17	53.1	P	646	0.87	786	756	17.20	13,004	15,818
Wisconsin	15y, 6m	16y, 9m[2]	51.3	P	726	0.85	918	612	16.96	10,374	13,117
Wyoming	15	16y, 6m[2]	42.4	S	743	0.56	1,405	832	13.91	11,581	21,911
U.S. AVERAGE			49.4		680	0.88	813	680	17.10	11,635	13,905

Note: Most states have graduated licensing systems that phase in full driving privileges. During the learner's stage, driving generally is not permitted without adult supervision. In an intermediate stage, young licensees may be allowed to drive unsupervised only under certain conditions. (1) Min. age at which all restrictions may be lifted on private passenger car operation. (2) Applicants under a specified age (typically between 17 and 19) must complete driver education. Some states allow applicants to substitute home training, state-sponsored traffic school, or a number of hours of supervised driving for driver ed. (3) Learner's stage mandatory for all license applicants regardless of age. (4) Includes 18.4 cents per gallon in federal excise taxes. (5) P = officer may stop vehicle for violation (primary); S = officer may issue seat belt citation only when vehicle is stopped for another moving violation (secondary). (a) Secondary enforcement for rear seat occupants; (b) Primary enforcement for children under a specified age.

Tourism Trends

World tourist arrivals increased 6.4% between 2009 and 2010 and increased 4.8% between 2010 and 2011, according to the World Tourism Organization's (UNWTO) *Barometer* publication. The number of international tourist arrivals in 2012 was an estimated 1.035 bil, an increase of 4.0% over the previous year. Worldwide tourism receipts, as measured in constant U.S. dollars, increased 1.1% from 2011 to 2012, to a value of $1.075 tril. Europe as a region again commanded the largest share of international tourist arrivals (52%) and receipts (43%) in 2012. Asia and the Pacific posted the second-largest share in each category, with 23% of international tourist arrivals and 30% of receipts worldwide. With 163 mil arrivals, the Americas held a 16% share of the world total. All regions showed an increase in the number of international tourist arrivals in 2012 compared to 2011 except for the Middle East, which had a decrease of 5.4%.

The International Air Transport Association (IATA) reported a 5.3% increase in international passenger traffic (as measured in revenue passenger kilometers) in 2012. It expected an increase in the global airline industry's net profits in 2013. The price of fuel remains a challenge, having risen from 14% of airline operating costs in 2003 to 32% in 2012, although this is lower than the high of 33% four years earlier. IATA forecasted that fuel will account for 31% of operating costs in 2013.

World Tourism Receipts, 1990-2012
Source: World Tourism Organization (UNWTO), © UNWTO
(in billions of U.S. dollars)

Year	Receipts[1]	Year	Receipts[1]	Year	Receipts[1]	Year	Receipts[1]	Year	Receipts[1]	Year	Receipts[1]
1990	$262	1994	$356	1998	$443	2002	$485	2006	$745	2010	$930
1991	278	1995	403	1999	457	2003	532	2007	860	2011	1,042
1992	317	1996	436	2000	475	2004	634	2008	944	2012	1,075*
1993	323	1997	436	2001	466	2005	680	2009	855		

*Preliminary. (1) Total of all transactions made by or on behalf of visitors for the duration of their visit. Does not include receipts from international passenger transport contracted from companies outside a traveler's country of residence.

Top 10 Countries in Tourism Earnings, 2011-12
Source: World Tourism Organization (UNWTO), © UNWTO
(in billions of U.S. dollars; ranked by receipts from most recent year)

Rank	Country	Receipts[1] 2012*	2011	% change, 2011-12	Rank	Country	Receipts[1] 2012*	2011	% change, 2011-12
1.	United States	$126.2	$115.6	9.2%	6.	Italy	$41.2	$43.0	−4.2%
2.	Spain	55.9	59.9	−6.6	7.	Germany	38.1	38.9	−1.9
3.	France	53.7	54.5	−1.5	8.	United Kingdom	36.4	35.1	3.7
4.	China[2]	50.0	48.5	3.2	9.	Hong Kong	32.1	27.7	16.0
5.	Macao	43.7	38.5	13.7	10.	Australia	31.5	31.5	0.2

*Preliminary. (1) Excluding receipts from international passenger transport contracted from companies outside a traveler's country of residence. (2) Not including Hong Kong, Macao, and Taiwan.

World's Top 10 Tourist Destinations, 2012
Source: World Tourism Organization (UNWTO), © UNWTO
(ranked by number of arrivals in millions; preliminary)

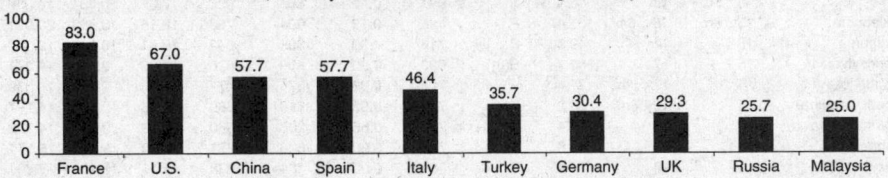

International Travel to the U.S., 1990-2012
Source: Office of Travel and Tourism Industries, Intl. Trade Admin., U.S. Dept. of Commerce; World Tourism Organization
(number of visitors in millions)

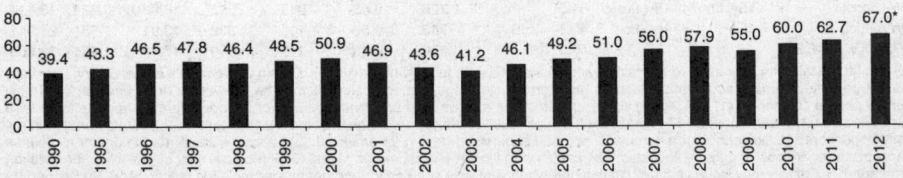

*Preliminary figure.

U.S. Domestic Leisure Travel Volume, 1995-2012

Source: U.S. Travel Assn.

(in billions of person-trips of 50 mi or more, one-way)

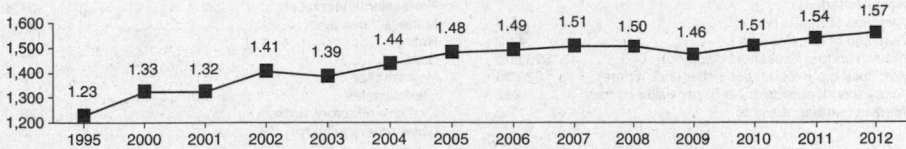

Note: Method of collecting travel data has been revised; data for earlier years have been adjusted to maintain comparability.

Top 10 U.S. States by Traveler Spending, 2011

Source: U.S. Travel Assn.

(domestic and international traveler spending within state, in billions of dollars)

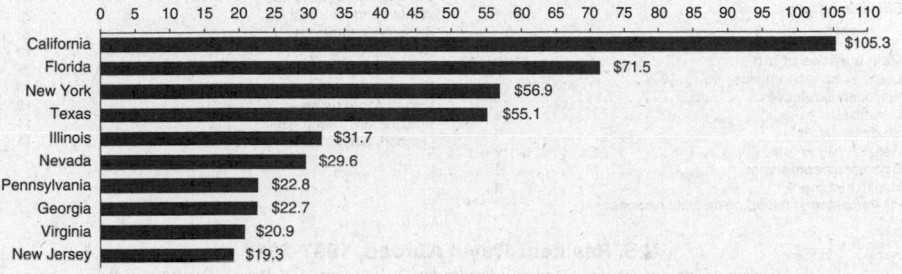

International Visitors to the U.S. by Top Countries of Origin, 2012

Source: Office of Travel and Tourism Industries, Intl. Trade Admin., U.S. Dept. of Commerce

(ranked by number of visitors)

Country of origin	Visitors	Expenditures (mil)	Expenditures per visitor	Country of origin	Visitors	Expenditures (mil)	Expenditures per visitor
1. Canada........	22,699,000	$25,542	$1,125.25	12. India..........	724,433	$4,852	$6,697.65
2. Mexico	14,509,000	9,962	686.61	13. Venezuela......	674,754	3,284	4,866.96
3. UK.............	3,763,381	12,644	3,359.74	14. Argentina	614,504	3,160	5,142.36
4. Japan	3,698,073	16,527	4,469.08	15. Spain	607,273	NA	NA
5. Germany.......	1,875,952	6,940	3,699.45	16. Colombia	602,338	NA	NA
6. Brazil.........	1,791,103	9,305	5,195.12	17. Netherlands	591,746	2,259	3,817.52
7. China[1]........	1,474,408	8,770	5,948.15	18. Switzerland.....	476,637	NA	NA
8. France.........	1,455,720	5,307	3,645.62	19. Sweden........	442,013	NA	NA
9. South Korea	1,251,432	4,154	3,319.40	20. Ireland........	331,850	NA	NA
10. Australia	1,122,180	5,428	4,837.01	All countries.......	66,969,038	165,574	2,472.40
11. Italy...........	831,343	3,848	4,628.66				

NA = Not available. **Note:** Expenditures include passenger fares. (1) Not including Hong Kong, Macao, and Taiwan.

Traveler Spending in the U.S., 1987-2012

Source: Office of Travel and Tourism Industries, Intl. Trade Admin., U.S. Dept. of Commerce; U.S. Travel Assn.

(in billions of dollars)

Year	Traveler spending Domestic	International	Year	Traveler spending Domestic	International	Year	Traveler spending Domestic	International
1987....	$235	$31	1996....	$385	$70	2005....	572	$82
1988....	258	38	1997....	406	73	2006....	610	86
1989....	273	47	1998....	425	71	2007....	641	97
1990....	291	43	1999....	458	75	2008....	662	110
1991....	296	48	2000....	503	82	2009....	606	94
1992....	306	55	2001....	484	72	2010....	644	103
1993....	323	58	2002....	478	67	2011....	697	116
1994....	340	58	2003....	496	65	2012....	727	126
1995....	360	63	2004....	532	75			

Characteristics of U.S. Travelers Visiting Overseas Destinations, 2011

Source: Survey of Intl. Air Travelers, Office of Travel and Tourism Industries, Intl. Trade Admin., U.S. Dept. of Commerce

Total U.S. resident travelers	27,023,000
Males (adults)	49%
Females (adults)	51%
Avg. age of males (yrs.)	45.9
Avg. age of females (yrs.)	44.2
Median annual household income	$96,500
Avg. total trip expend. per visitor (incl. airfare)	$2,936
Avg. expend. outside the U.S. per visitor per day	$67
Median number of nights	11.0

Region of residence	% of travelers
Middle Atlantic	27%
South Atlantic (incl. Florida, DC metro area)	23
Pacific (incl. California, Washington)	13
East North Central (incl. Illinois, Ohio)	8
West South Central (incl. Texas)	8
New England	7
Mountain	5
West North Central	5
East South Central	2

Main purpose of trip	% of travelers
Leisure/recreation/holiday	39%
Visit friends/relatives	35
Business	18
Study/teaching	4
Religion/pilgrimage	2
Convention/conference	1
Health treatment	1

Occupation	% of travelers
Professional/technical	37%
Manager/executive	21
Retired	14
Student	11
Homemaker	6
Clerical/sales	4
Craftsman/factory worker	3
Government/military	3

Leisure/recreational activities[1]	% of travelers
Dining in restaurants	82%
Shopping	70
Visit historical places	50
Visit small towns/villages	43
Sightseeing in cities	40
Touring the countryside	34
Cultural heritage sights	33
Water sports/sunbathing	25
Art gallery, museum	22
Nightclub/dancing	19
Guided tours	17
Ethnic heritage sites	13
Visit national parks	12
Amusement/theme parks	11
Concert, play, musical	11

(1) Percentages based on multiple responses.

U.S. Resident Travel Abroad, 1997-2011

Source: Office of Travel and Tourism Industries, Intl. Trade Admin., U.S. Dept. of Commerce

(numbers in thousands; regions ranked by most recent numbers)

Region/country[1]	2011	2000	1997	Region/country[1]	2011	2000	1997
Total outbound[2]	58,702	61,327	52,735	Caribbean	6,134	3,867	NA
Mexico	20,084	19,285	17,909	Jamaica	1,486	886	1,341
Canada	11,595	15,189	13,401	Asia	5,107	4,914	NA
Overseas subtotal[3]	27,023	26,853	21,634	China[4]	1,108	644	476
Europe	9,674	13,373	NA	South America	1,973	2,095	NA
Western Europe	9,053	12,916	NA	Central America	1,946	886	NA
United Kingdom	2,405	4,189	3,570	Middle East	1,756	1,370	NA
France	1,756	2,927	2,098	Eastern Europe	1,054	806	NA
Italy	1,702	2,148	1,471	Africa	892	483	NA
Germany	1,594	2,309	1,796	Oceania	486	1,047	NA
Spain	1,081	1,262	714				

NA = Not available. **Note:** Visits of one or more nights. Visitation estimates for Canada and Mexico include all modes of transportation used. Estimates for all other countries are available only for air travel to that country and are based upon data from the airlines that voluntarily provided it. (1) Only individual countries that received more than 1 mil visitors in 2011 are shown. Region figures include U.S. resident travelers to all countries in region. (2) To Canada, Mexico, and overseas. (3) To all countries except Canada and Mexico. (4) Not including Hong Kong, Macao, and Taiwan.

Airline Safety, U.S. Scheduled Commercial Carriers, 1985-2012

Source: National Transportation Safety Board; Federal Aviation Administration, U.S. Dept. of Transportation

Year	Departures (mil)	Fatal accidents	Fatalities[1]	Rate of fatal accidents[2]	Year	Departures (mil)	Fatal accidents	Fatalities[1]	Rate of fatal accidents[2]
1985	6.1	4	197	0.066	2003	10.2	2	22	0.020
1990	7.8	6	39	0.077	2004	10.8	1	13	0.009
1995	8.1	1	160	0.012	2005	10.9	3	22	0.027
1996	7.9	3	342	0.038	2006	10.6	2	50	0.019
1997	9.9	3	3	0.030	2007	10.7	0	0	—
1998	10.5	1	1	0.009	2008	10.3	0	0	—
1999	10.9	2	12	0.018	2009	9.6	1	50	0.010
2000	11.1	2	89	0.018	2010	9.5	0	0	—
2001[3]	10.6	6	531	0.019	2011	9.4	0	0	—
2002	10.3	0	0	—	2012*	9.3	0	0	—

— = Not applicable. *Preliminary. (1) Includes deaths that occurred on the ground as a result of an accident, except for fatalities resulting from the Sept. 11, 2001, terrorist attacks. (2) Per 100,000 departures. (3) The Sept. 11, 2001, terrorist attacks have been included among the number of fatal accidents but have been excluded when calculating the accident rate.

U.S. Airline Statistics, 2000-12

Source: Airlines for America
(in millions, except where otherwise noted)

	2000	2005	2006	2007	2008	2009	2010	2011	2012
Passengers enplaned[1]	666.1	738.6	744.7	769.6	743.3	703.9	720.5	730.8	736.6
Revenue passenger miles[1,2]	692,757	779,035	797,434	829,441	812,377	769,412	798,043	814,354	823,184
Available seat miles[1,3]	956,950	1,003,364	1,006,351	1,037,691	1,021,330	957,105	972,601	992,672	994,548
Cargo revenue ton miles[1,2]	23,888	28,039	29,340	29,571	28,119	24,970	27,885	28,123	27,790
% of seating utilized[1]	72.4	77.6	79.2	79.9	79.5	80.4	82.1	82.0	82.8
Passenger revenue	$93,639	$93,633	$101,968	$107,678	$111,511	$91,443	$103,978	$114,299	$115,653
Net profit[4]	$2,238	−$28,647	$16,527	$6,306	−$24,500	−$2,905	$2,245	$541	$264
Total employment[4,5]	520.6	421.2	404.3	413.1	407.6	385.9	378.1	386.0	387.7

(1) Schedule service only. (2) One fare-paying passenger or one ton of revenue cargo transported one mile. (3) One seat transported one mile. (4) Passenger carriers only. (5) Figures are of avg. full-time equivalents (FTE), i.e., the number of full-time employees that could have been employed if the reported number of hours worked by part-time employees had been worked by full-time employees. In this table, part-time employees are treated as 0.5 FTEs.

Top 25 U.S. Passenger Airlines, 2012

Source: Airlines for America
(in millions; ranked by number of passengers enplaned in scheduled service)

Airline	Passengers		Airline	Passengers		Airline	Passengers		Airline	Passengers
1. Southwest/			6. ExpressJet	32.4		13. Spirit	10.2		20. Air Wisconsin . . .	6.1
AirTran	134.0		7. JetBlue	28.9		14. Republic	9.5		21. Shuttle America . .	5.8
2. Delta	116.4		8. SkyWest	26.2		15. Hawaiian	9.5		22. PSA	5.0
3. United/			9. American Eagle . .	18.7		16. Mesa	7.6		23. Chautauqua	4.6
Continental . .	92.4		10. Alaska	18.5		17. Horizon	6.8		24. Compass	4.0
4. American	86.3		11. Pinnacle	14.6		18. Allegiant	6.6		25. GoJet	3.5
5. US Airways . . .	54.2		12. Frontier	10.3		19. Virgin America . . .	6.2			

Note: Includes domestic and international passengers on U.S. airlines.

Top North American Airports by Passenger Traffic, 2012

Source: *2012 World Annual Traffic Report*, Airports Council Intl.

City/airport name (airport code)	Total passengers[1]
1. Hartsfield-Jackson Atlanta Intl. (ATL)	95,513,828
2. Chicago O'Hare Intl. (ORD)	66,633,503
3. Los Angeles Intl. (LAX)	63,688,121
4. Dallas/Ft. Worth Intl. (DFW)	58,621,369
5. Denver Intl. (DEN)	53,156,278
6. New York John F. Kennedy Intl. (JFK)	49,291,765
7. San Francisco Intl. (SFO)	44,399,885
8. Charlotte Douglas Intl. (CLT)	41,228,372
9. Las Vegas McCarran Intl. (LAS)	40,799,830
10. Phoenix Sky Harbor Intl. (PHX)	40,421,611
11. Houston George Bush Intercontinental (IAH)	39,891,444
12. Miami Intl. (MIA)	39,467,444
13. Orlando Intl. (MCO)	35,288,887
14. Toronto Pearson Intl. (YYZ)	34,912,029
15. Newark Liberty Intl. (EWR)	34,014,027
16. Seattle-Tacoma Intl. (SEA)	33,223,111
17. Minneapolis-St. Paul Intl. (MSP)	33,170,960
18. Detroit Metro Wayne County (DTW)	32,241,731
19. Philadelphia Intl. (PHL)	30,252,816
20. Boston Logan Intl. (BOS)	29,349,759
21. New York LaGuardia (LGA)	25,707,784
22. Fort Lauderdale-Hollywood Intl. (FLL)	23,569,103
23. Baltimore/Wash. Intl. Thurgood Marshall (BWI) . .	22,679,887
24. Washington Dulles Intl. (IAD)	22,408,105
25. Salt Lake City Intl. (SLC)	20,102,078

Note: World list excludes North American airports and airports that do not participate in Airports Council Intl.'s Airport Traffic Statistics collection. (1) Arriving and departing passengers and direct transit passengers counted once.

Top World Airports by Passenger Traffic, 2012

Source: *2012 World Annual Traffic Report*, Airports Council Intl.

City/airport name (country; airport code)	Total passengers[1]
1. Beijing Capital Intl. (China; PEK)	81,929,359
2. London Heathrow Intl. (UK; LHR)	70,038,804
3. Tokyo Haneda Intl. (Japan; HND)	66,795,178
4. Paris Charles de Gaulle (France; CDG)	61,611,934
5. Jakarta Soekarno-Hatta Intl. (Indonesia; CGK) . .	57,772,762
6. Dubai Intl. (United Arab Emirates; DXB)	57,684,550
7. Frankfurt Intl. (Germany; FRA)	57,520,001
8. Hong Kong Intl. (China; HKG)	56,061,595
9. Bangkok Intl. Suvarnabhumi (Thailand; BKK)	53,002,328
10. Singapore Changi (Singapore; SIN)	51,181,804
11. Amsterdam Schiphol (Netherlands; AMS)	51,035,590
12. Guangzhou Baiyun Intl. (China; CAN)	48,309,410
13. Madrid-Barajas (Spain; MAD)	45,176,978
14. Istanbul Atatürk Intl. (Turkey; IST)	45,124,831
15. Shanghai Pudong Intl. (China; PVG)	44,880,164
16. Kuala Lumpur Intl. (Malaysia; KUL)	39,887,866
17. Seoul Incheon Intl. (South Korea; ICN)	39,154,375
18. Munich (Germany; MUC)	38,360,604
19. Sydney Intl. (Australia; SYD)	37,311,536
20. Rome Leonardo Da Vinci-Fiumicino (Italy; FCO) .	36,980,157
21. Barcelona El Prat (Spain; BCN)	35,132,303
22. London Gatwick (UK; LGW)	34,235,982
23. Delhi Indira Gandhi Intl. (India; DEL)	34,211,608
24. Shanghai Hongqiao Intl. (China; SHA)	33,828,726
25. Tokyo Narita Intl. (Japan; NRT)	32,864,912

Busiest Amtrak Stations, 2012

Source: Amtrak National Fact Sheet, Amtrak; ranked by total ridership

Station	Tickets from	Tickets to	Total ridership	Station	Tickets from	Tickets to	Total ridership
New York, NY	4,767,849	4,725,565	9,493,414	BWI Airport, MD	343,393	360,211	703,604
Washington, DC	2,527,155	2,486,836	5,013,991	Newark, NJ	342,706	338,097	680,803
Philadelphia, PA	2,031,158	2,037,382	4,068,540	Seattle, WA	339,156	333,195	672,351
Chicago, IL	1,744,354	1,738,959	3,483,313	Providence, RI	330,654	338,922	669,576
Los Angeles, CA	829,553	827,893	1,657,446	Portland, OR	333,630	335,193	668,823
Boston South Station,				Milwaukee, WI	318,377	313,701	632,078
MA	727,170	720,331	1,447,501	Emeryville, CA	296,689	290,187	586,876
Sacramento, CA	601,031	585,927	1,186,958	Harrisburg, PA	285,212	286,005	571,217
Baltimore, MD	514,019	514,890	1,028,909	Lancaster, PA	279,810	279,554	559,364
Albany-Rensselaer,				Boston Back Bay, MA	272,711	255,329	528,040
NY	385,547	383,866	769,413	Bakersfield, CA	253,457	253,601	507,058
New Haven, CT	379,846	375,823	755,669	Martinez, CA	236,644	239,265	475,909
Wilmington, DE	367,373	370,473	737,846	Boston North Station,			
San Diego, CA	358,185	350,749	708,934	MA	237,603	236,309	473,912

Top Travel Websites, 2013
Source: comScore Media Metrix, Inc.; ranked by number of visitors

Rank	Website	Visitors (thous.)[1]	% of all travel websites	Rank	Website	Visitors (thous.)[1]	% of all travel websites
1.	Expedia Inc.	21,091	21.9%	10.	Delta Airlines.	6,479	6.7%
2.	TripAdvisor Inc.	20,800	21.6	11.	Kayak.com Network	5,708	5.9
3.	Priceline.com Inc.	17,939	18.6	12.	Marriott.	5,668	5.9
4.	Southwest Airlines Co.	10,691	11.1	13.	United Airlines.	5,360	5.6
5.	Travora Media	10,118	10.5	14.	Hilton Worldwide.	5,261	5.5
6.	Yahoo! Travel	9,311	9.7	15.	USATODAY Travel.	5,149	5.3
7.	Orbitz Worldwide	8,892	9.2	Total travel audience[2].		96,470	100.0
8.	Travelocity.	7,108	7.4	Total Internet audience[2]		224,318	—
9.	Fareportal Media Group	6,828	7.1				

(1) Number of unique visitors, in thousands, who visited website at least once in June 2013. (2) Audience comprises all persons older than two years of age, at U.S. home/work locations.

Number of Paid Days Off Per Year in Selected Countries
Source: 2011 Worldwide Benefit and Employment Guidelines, Mercer

The figures are based on statutory entitlements for an employee working five days a week, with 10 years' service. Ranked by total paid days off.

Country	Paid vacation days	Paid holidays	Total paid days off	Country	Paid vacation days	Paid holidays	Total paid days off	Country	Paid vacation days	Paid holidays	Total paid days off
Austria	22	13	35	New Zealand	20	10	30	Finland	25	0	25
Portugal	22	13	35	Ireland.	20	9	29	Sweden.	25	0	25
Germany.	24	10	34	UK.	28	0	28	Netherlands	20	0	20
Spain	22	12	34	Australia	20	8	28	Switzerland.	20	0	20
France.	30	1	31	Norway.	25	2	27	Canada.	10	9	19
Italy.	20	11	31	Greece	20	6	26	Japan.	10	0	10
Belgium.	20	10	30	Denmark.	25	0	25	U.S.	0	0	0

Note: The U.S. has no nationwide statutory entitlement that mandates paid days off.

Record-Breaking Roller Coasters
Source: UltimateRollerCoaster.com; speed measured in mph, length and height in ft

Steel-Tracked Roller Coasters

Fastest	Roller coaster	Theme park, location
149.1 mph	Formula Rossa	Ferrari World Abu Dhabi, United Arab Emirates
128	Kingda Ka	Six Flags Great Adventure, Jackson, NJ
120	Top Thrill Dragster	Cedar Point, Sandusky, OH
106.8	Dodonpa	Fuji-Q High Land, Fujiyoshida-shi, Japan
100	Tower of Terror.	Dreamworld, Gold Coast, Australia
100	Superman the Escape	Six Flags Magic Mountain, Valencia, CA

Tallest

456 ft	Kingda Ka	Six Flags Great Adventure, Jackson, NJ
420	Top Thrill Dragster	Cedar Point, Sandusky, OH
415	Superman the Escape	Six Flags Magic Mountain, Valencia, CA
377	Tower of Terror.	Dreamworld, Gold Coast, Australia
318	Steel Dragon 2000	Nagashima Spa Land, Mie, Japan

Largest drop

418 ft	Kingda Ka	Six Flags Great Adventure, Jackson, NJ
400	Top Thrill Dragster	Cedar Point, Sandusky, OH
306	Steel Dragon 2000	Nagashima Spa Land, Mie, Japan
300	Millennium Force	Cedar Point, Sandusky, OH
300	Intimidator 305	Kings Dominion, Doswell, VA

Longest

8,133 ft	Steel Dragon 2000	Nagashima Spa Land, Mie, Japan
7,450	The Ultimate	Lightwater Valley, UK
6,709	Fujiyama	Fuji-Q High Land, Fujiyoshida-shi, Japan
6,595	Millennium Force	Cedar Point, Sandusky, OH
6,562	Formula Rossa	Ferrari World Abu Dhabi, United Arab Emirates

Wood-Tracked Roller Coasters

Fastest	Roller coaster	Theme park, location
70 mph	El Toro	Six Flags Great Adventure, Jackson, NJ
68.4	Colossos	Heide Park, Soltau, Germany
68	Outlaw Run	Silver Dollar City, Branson, MO
67.4	The Voyage	Holiday World & Splashin' Safari, Santa Claus, IN
66.3	The Boss	Six Flags St. Louis, Eureka, MO

Tallest

197 ft	Colossos	Heide Park, Soltau, Germany
183	T Express	Everland, Yongin, S. Korea
181	El Toro	Six Flags Great Adventure, Jackson, NJ
179	The Rattler	Six Flags Fiesta Texas, San Antonio, TX
173	The Voyage	Holiday World & Splashin' Safari, Santa Claus, IN

Largest drop

176 ft	El Toro.	Six Flags Great Adventure, Jackson, NJ
159	Colossos	Heide Park, Soltau, Germany
155	Mean Streak	Cedar Point, Sandusky, OH
154	The Voyage	Holiday World & Splashin' Safari, Santa Claus, IN
151	T Express	Everland, Yongin, S. Korea

Longest

7,400 ft	The Beast	Kings Island, Cincinnati, OH
6,442	The Voyage	Holiday World & Splashin' Safari, Santa Claus, IN
5,578	White Cyclone	Nagashima Spa Land, Mie, Japan
5,427	Mean Streak	Cedar Point, Sandusky, OH
5,384	Shivering Timbers	Michigan's Adventure, Muskegon, MI

Passports, Health Regulations, and Travel Warnings for Foreign Travel

Source: Bureau of Consular Affairs, U.S. Dept. of State; Centers for Disease Control and Prevention (CDC), U.S. Dept. of Health and Human Services; World Health Organization (WHO); Transportation Security Administration (TSA), U.S. Dept. of Homeland Security

Passports, Visas

Passports are issued by the Dept. of State to U.S. citizens and nationals to provide documentation for foreign travel. As of Sept. 2013, the fees for a new passport book and passport card for persons ages 16 and over total $165; provided certain criteria are met, these can be renewed for $140. For a passport book alone, fees are $135 for a new passport and $110 for passport renewal.

In July 2008, the U.S. government began issuing passport cards. Travelers arriving by land or sea from Canada, Mexico, the Caribbean, and Bermuda may present a passport card to enter the U.S. Passport cards may not be used for air travel, however. The fees for a new passport card for persons ages 16 and over total $55.

A U.S. passport is often sufficient for U.S. citizens to gain admission for a limited stay in another country. Some countries also require an entry visa. Each country has its own specific guidelines concerning length and purpose of visit, among other considerations. Visitors may need to provide proof of sufficient funds for their intended stay, onward/return tickets, and/or at least six months remaining validity on their U.S. passports.

All persons traveling by air outside of the U.S. (excluding direct travel to and from a U.S. territory) are required to present a passport or other valid document upon reentering the U.S.

For up-to-date passport and international travel information, visit the Consular Affairs website (travel.state. gov) or call the National Passport Information Center at 1-877-4USA-PPT (1-877-487-2778).

Health Regulations

Under WHO regulations, first instituted in 1969, member countries agree to abide by resolutions meant to contain the spread of disease. For example, some countries require travelers to provide proof of vaccination against yellow fever before entering.

Detailed information can be found in *Health Information for International Travel*, or the "yellow book," published every two years by the CDC. The book is written primarily for health care providers but may be of use to other travelers. The CDC also issues travel notices on outbreaks, health precautions, and health warnings. For current notices and more on travelers' health, visit wwwnc. cdc.gov/travel/.

WHO publishes a more technical guide, *International Travel and Health*, which can be found online at www. who.int/ith/.

Travel Warnings and Alerts

The State Dept. issues travel warnings as recommendations that Americans avoid travel to certain countries. Long-term conditions in such countries may be dangerous or unstable; because of an embassy closure or limited personnel, the U.S. government's ability to assist U.S. citizens may be reduced. As of Sept. 2013, travel warnings were in effect for the following countries: Afghanistan, Algeria, Burundi, Central African Republic, Chad, Colombia, Côte d'Ivoire, Dem. Rep. of the Congo, Egypt, El Salvador, Eritrea, Guinea, Haiti, Honduras, Iran, Iraq, Israel (incl. West Bank and Gaza), Kenya, Lebanon, Libya, Mali, Mauritania, Mexico, Niger, Nigeria, North Korea, Pakistan, Philippines, Saudi Arabia, Somalia, South Sudan, Sudan, Syria, Tunisia, Turkey, and Yemen.

The department issues travel alerts when it has concerns about short-term conditions—natural disasters, terrorist attacks, anniversaries of attacks, election-related demonstrations, and regional sporting events, among others. For the latest travel warnings and alerts, see travel. state.gov.

Summary of TSA Regulations

Airplane carry-ons. TSA promotes the "3-1-1" rule regarding carry-on items. Containers with liquids, gels, or aerosols may hold only 3.4 oz or less; these containers should be packed inside a single 1-quart, clear plastic, zip-top bag; and this 1 bag must be X-rayed when going through security. Exceptions to the 3-1-1 rule include medication, baby formula and food, and breast milk. Travelers must declare any exceptions at security.

Security checkpoint identification. Adult travelers (18 years of age and over) must present a photo ID. Acceptable documents include a U.S. passport or passport card; foreign government-issued passport; state-issued driver's license; permanent resident card; or U.S. military ID, among others.

Screening process. Travelers may wear loose fitting or religious garments (incl. head coverings) through security. They may be subject to additional screening if clothing could conceal prohibited items. Travelers may request a private area if selected for personal screening. Travelers will be screened by someone of the same gender.

Disability-related permitted carry-on items:

- Wheelchairs
- Crutches, canes, and walkers
- Personal supplemental oxygen (though not permitted by all airlines)
- Slate and stylus
- Medications and associated supplies
- Service animals

Permitted carry-on items:

- Safety razors (incl. disposable razors)
- Eye drops and saline solution (amounts greater than 3.4 oz must be declared)
- Nail clippers, tweezers
- Metal scissors with pointed tips and blades shorter than 4 inches
- Mobile phones
- Umbrellas (must be inspected at security)
- Common lighters
- Beverages (any size) purchased after security screening
- Musical instruments (one per traveler going through security, though some airlines prohibit musical instruments as carry-ons)

Prohibited carry-on items:

- Knives (except for plastic or round-bladed butter knives), incl. knives that are religious objects
- Baseball bats, golf clubs
- Flares
- Firearms or realistic firearm replicas, ammunition, firearm parts
- Hammers, screwdrivers, wrenches, pliers, and other tools more than 7 in. in length
- Brass knuckles
- Lighter fluid
- Liquid bleach, turpentine, paint thinner
- Spray paint
- Self-defense sprays

For complete travel information, visit www.tsa.gov/traveler-information.

Air Distances Between Selected World Cities

Point-to-point measurements, in miles, are usually from City Hall or its equivalent.

	Bangkok	Beijing	Berlin	Cairo	Cape Town	Caracas	Chicago	Hong Kong	Honolulu	Lima
Bangkok	...	2,046	5,352	4,523	6,300	10,555	8,570	1,077	6,609	12,244
Beijing	2,046	...	4,584	4,698	8,044	8,950	6,604	1,217	5,077	10,349
Berlin	5,352	4,584	...	1,797	5,961	5,238	4,414	5,443	7,320	6,896
Cairo	4,523	4,698	1,797	...	4,480	6,342	6,141	5,066	8,848	7,726
Cape Town	6,300	8,044	5,961	4,480	...	6,366	8,491	7,376	11,535	6,072
Caracas	10,555	8,950	5,238	6,342	6,366	...	2,495	10,165	6,021	1,707
Chicago	8,570	6,604	4,414	6,141	8,491	2,495	...	7,797	4,256	3,775
Hong Kong	1,077	1,217	5,443	5,066	7,376	10,165	7,797	...	5,556	11,418
Honolulu	6,609	5,077	7,320	8,848	11,535	6,021	4,256	5,556	...	5,947
London	5,944	5,074	583	2,185	5,989	4,655	3,958	5,990	7,240	6,316
Los Angeles	7,637	6,250	5,782	7,520	9,969	3,632	1,745	7,240	2,557	4,171
Madrid	6,337	5,745	1,165	2,087	5,308	4,346	4,189	6,558	7,872	5,907
Melbourne	4,568	5,643	9,918	8,675	6,425	9,717	9,673	4,595	5,505	8,059
Mexico City	9,793	7,753	6,056	7,700	8,519	2,234	1,690	8,788	3,789	2,639
Montreal	8,338	6,519	3,740	5,427	7,922	2,438	745	7,736	4,918	3,970
Moscow	4,389	3,607	1,006	1,803	6,279	6,177	4,987	4,437	7,047	7,862
New York, NY	8,669	6,844	3,979	5,619	7,803	2,120	714	8,060	4,969	3,639
Paris	5,877	5,120	548	1,998	5,786	4,732	4,143	5,990	7,449	6,370
Rio de Janeiro	9,994	10,768	6,209	6,143	3,781	2,804	5,282	11,009	8,288	2,342
Rome	5,494	5,063	737	1,326	5,231	5,195	4,824	5,774	8,040	6,750
San Francisco	7,931	5,918	5,672	7,466	10,248	3,902	1,859	6,905	2,398	4,518
Singapore	883	2,771	6,164	5,137	6,008	11,402	9,372	1,605	6,726	11,689
Stockholm	5,089	4,133	528	2,096	6,423	5,471	4,331	5,063	6,875	7,166
Tokyo	2,865	1,307	5,557	5,958	9,154	8,808	6,314	1,791	3,859	9,631
Warsaw	5,033	4,325	322	1,619	5,935	5,559	4,679	5,147	7,366	7,215
Washington, DC	8,807	6,942	4,181	5,822	7,895	2,047	596	8,155	4,838	3,509

	London	Los Angeles	Madrid	Melbourne	Mexico City	Montreal	Moscow	New Delhi	New York, NY	Paris
Bangkok	5,944	7,637	6,337	4,568	9,793	8,338	4,389	1,813	8,669	5,877
Beijing	5,074	6,250	5,745	5,643	7,753	6,519	3,607	2,353	6,844	5,120
Berlin	583	5,782	1,165	9,918	6,056	3,740	1,006	3,598	3,979	548
Cairo	2,185	7,520	2,087	8,675	7,700	5,427	1,803	2,758	5,619	1,998
Cape Town	5,989	9,969	5,308	6,425	8,519	7,922	6,279	5,769	7,803	5,786
Caracas	4,655	3,632	4,346	9,717	2,234	2,438	6,177	8,833	2,120	4,732
Chicago	3,958	1,745	4,189	9,673	1,690	745	4,987	7,486	714	4,143
Hong Kong	5,990	7,240	6,558	4,595	8,788	7,736	4,437	2,339	8,060	5,990
Honolulu	7,240	2,557	7,872	5,505	3,789	4,918	7,047	7,412	4,969	7,449
London	...	5,439	785	10,500	5,558	3,254	1,564	4,181	3,469	214
Los Angeles	5,439	...	5,848	7,931	1,542	2,427	6,068	7,011	2,451	5,601
Madrid	785	5,848	...	10,758	5,643	3,448	2,147	4,530	3,593	655
Melbourne	10,500	7,931	10,758	...	8,426	10,395	8,950	6,329	10,359	10,430
Mexico City	5,558	1,542	5,643	8,426	...	2,317	6,676	9,120	2,090	5,725
Montreal	3,254	2,427	3,448	10,395	2,317	...	4,401	7,012	331	3,432
Moscow	1,564	6,068	2,147	8,950	6,676	4,401	...	2,698	4,683	1,554
New York, NY	3,469	2,451	3,593	10,359	2,090	331	4,683	7,318	...	3,636
Paris	214	5,601	655	10,430	5,725	3,432	1,554	4,102	3,636	...
Rio de Janeiro	5,750	6,330	5,045	8,226	4,764	5,078	7,170	8,753	4,801	5,684
Rome	895	6,326	851	9,929	6,377	4,104	1,483	3,684	4,293	690
San Francisco	5,367	347	5,803	7,856	1,887	2,543	5,885	7,691	2,572	5,577
Singapore	6,747	8,767	7,080	3,759	10,327	9,203	5,228	2,571	9,534	6,673
Stockholm	942	5,454	1,653	9,630	6,012	3,714	716	3,414	3,986	1,003
Tokyo	5,959	5,470	6,706	5,062	7,035	6,471	4,660	3,638	6,757	6,053
Warsaw	905	5,922	1,427	9,598	6,337	4,022	721	3,277	4,270	852
Washington, DC	3,674	2,300	3,792	10,180	1,885	489	4,876	7,500	205	3,840

	Rio de Janeiro	Rome	San Francisco	Singapore	Stockholm	Tehran	Tokyo	Vienna	Warsaw	Wash., DC
Bangkok	9,994	5,494	7,931	883	5,089	3,391	2,865	5,252	5,033	8,807
Beijing	10,768	5,063	5,918	2,771	4,133	3,490	1,307	4,648	4,325	6,942
Berlin	6,209	737	5,672	6,164	528	2,185	5,557	326	322	4,181
Cairo	6,143	1,326	7,466	5,137	2,096	1,234	5,958	1,481	1,619	5,822
Cape Town	3,781	5,231	10,248	6,008	6,423	5,241	9,154	5,656	5,935	7,895
Caracas	2,804	5,195	3,902	11,402	5,471	7,320	8,808	5,372	5,559	2,047
Chicago	5,282	4,824	1,859	9,372	4,331	6,502	6,314	4,698	4,679	596
Hong Kong	11,009	5,774	6,905	1,605	5,063	3,843	1,791	5,431	5,147	8,155
Honolulu	8,288	8,040	2,398	6,726	6,875	8,070	3,859	7,632	7,366	4,838
London	5,750	895	5,367	6,747	942	2,743	5,959	771	905	3,674
Los Angeles	6,330	6,326	347	8,767	5,454	7,682	5,470	6,108	5,922	2,300
Madrid	5,045	851	5,803	7,080	1,653	2,978	6,706	1,128	1,427	3,792
Melbourne	8,226	9,929	7,856	3,759	9,630	7,826	5,062	9,790	9,598	10,180
Mexico City	4,764	6,377	1,887	10,327	6,012	8,184	7,035	6,320	6,337	1,885
Montreal	5,078	4,104	2,543	9,203	3,714	5,880	6,471	4,009	4,022	489
Moscow	7,170	1,483	5,885	5,228	716	1,532	4,660	1,043	721	4,876
New York, NY	4,801	4,293	2,572	9,534	3,986	6,141	6,757	4,234	4,270	205
Paris	5,684	690	5,577	6,673	1,003	2,625	6,053	645	852	3,840
Rio de Janeiro	...	5,707	6,613	9,785	6,683	7,374	11,532	6,127	6,455	4,779
Rome	5,707	...	6,259	6,229	1,245	2,127	6,142	477	820	4,497
San Francisco	6,613	6,259	...	8,448	5,399	7,362	5,150	5,994	5,854	2,441
Singapore	9,785	6,229	8,448	...	5,936	4,103	3,300	6,035	5,843	9,662
Stockholm	6,683	1,245	5,399	5,936	...	2,173	5,053	780	494	4,183
Tokyo	11,532	6,142	5,150	3,300	5,053	4,775	...	5,689	5,347	6,791
Warsaw	6,455	820	5,854	5,843	494	1,879	5,689	347	...	4,472
Washington, DC	4,779	4,497	2,441	9,662	4,183	6,341	6,791	4,438	4,472	...

AGRICULTURE

Number and Acreage of Farms by State, 2000, 2012

Source: National Agricultural Statistics Service, U.S. Dept. of Agriculture

State	No. of farms (thous.) 2012	2000	Acreage in farms (mil) 2012	2000	Acreage per farm 2012	2000
AL.....	46.5	47.0	8.9	9.0	190	191
AK.....	0.7	0.6	0.9	0.9	1,294	1,569
AZ.....	15.5	10.7	26.1	26.9	1,684	2,518
AR.....	47.8	48.0	13.5	14.6	282	304
CA.....	80.5	83.1	25.4	28.0	316	337
CO.....	36.3	30.0	31.3	31.6	862	1,060
CT.....	4.9	4.2	0.4	0.4	82	86
DE.....	2.5	2.6	0.5	0.6	196	215
FL.....	47.5	44.0	9.3	10.4	195	238
GA.....	47.0	49.1	10.4	10.9	221	223
HI	7.5	5.5	1.1	1.4	148	251
ID	24.5	24.5	11.4	11.9	465	486
IL	74.3	77.0	26.6	27.5	358	357
IN	60.0	63.4	14.7	15.2	245	240
IA	92.2	94.0	30.7	32.5	333	346
KS.....	65.5	64.5	46.0	47.5	702	736
KY.....	85.5	90.0	14.0	13.7	164	152
LA.....	29.0	29.0	8.0	8.0	274	277
ME	8.1	7.1	1.4	1.4	167	190
MD	12.8	12.4	2.1	2.1	160	172
MA	7.7	6.1	0.5	0.5	68	89
MI	54.7	53.0	9.9	10.2	181	192
MN	79.4	81.0	26.8	27.9	338	344
MS	42.3	42.0	11.2	11.2	264	266
MO	106.0	109.0	29.0	30.2	274	277
MT	28.6	27.8	58.8	59.3	2,056	2,133

State	No. of farms (thous.) 2012	2000	Acreage in farms (mil) 2012	2000	Acreage per farm 2012	2000
NE.....	46.7	46.1	45.5	46.1	974	887
NV.....	3.0	3.1	5.8	6.4	1,980	2,065
NH	4.2	3.3	0.5	0.4	113	133
NJ	10.2	9.7	0.7	0.8	72	86
NM	23.8	18.0	43.9	44.9	1,845	2,494
NY.....	36.0	37.5	7.0	7.7	194	205
NC	50.0	55.5	8.5	9.2	170	166
ND	31.6	30.8	39.6	39.4	1,253	1,279
OH	73.4	79.0	13.6	14.8	185	187
OK	85.5	84.5	34.8	33.8	407	401
OR	38.1	40.0	16.5	17.3	433	433
PA	62.1	59.0	7.7	7.7	124	130
RI	1.2	0.8	0.1	0.1	57	75
SC	26.7	24.2	4.8	4.9	180	203
SD	31.0	32.4	43.7	44.0	1,408	1,358
TN	76.0	88.0	10.8	11.8	142	134
TX	244.7	228.3	128.0	130.9	523	573
UT	16.4	15.5	11.1	11.6	677	747
VT	7.0	6.6	1.2	1.3	174	192
VA	46.2	48.5	8.1	8.7	174	180
WA	39.3	37.0	14.8	15.6	377	420
WV	22.1	20.8	3.6	3.6	164	173
WI	76.8	77.5	15.0	16.0	195	206
WY	10.8	9.2	30.2	34.5	2,796	3,750
U.S. ...	2,170.0	2,166.8	914.0	945.1	421	436

Number and Average Size of U.S. Farms, 1940-2012

Source: National Agricultural Statistics Service, U.S. Dept. of Agriculture

The number of farms in the United States in 2012 was estimated at 2.2 mil, about 11,600 fewer than in 2011. Total land in farms decreased 3 mil acres between 2011 and 2012 to 914 mil acres. The average farm size in 2012 was 421 acres, a slight increase from the previous year.

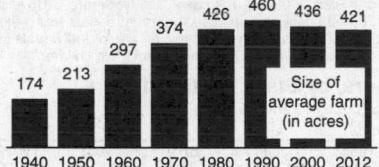

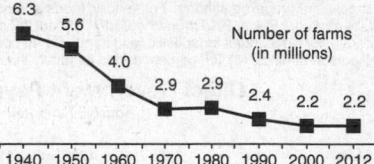

U.S. Federal Food Assistance Programs, 1990-2012

Source: Food and Nutrition Service (FNS), U.S. Dept. of Agriculture
(in millions of dollars; for fiscal years ending on Sept. 30)

Program	1990	1995	2000	2005	2008	2009	2010	2011	2012
Supplemental Nutrition Assistance Program (SNAP)[1]	$15,491	$24,620	$17,054	$31,073	$37,642	$53,621	$68,313	$75,716	$78,437
Puerto Rico nutrition assistance[2]	937	1,131	1,268	1,495	1,623	2,001	2,001	2,001	2,001
Natl. school lunch[3]	3,834	5,160	6,149	8,031	9,318	9,994	10,880	11,301	11,578
School breakfast[3,4]	596	1,048	1,393	1,927	2,366	2,583	2,859	3,035	3,277
WIC (Women, Infants, and Children)[5]...	2,122	3,440	3,982	4,994	6,189	6,472	6,683	7,169	6,799
Summer food service[6]	164	237	267	267	326	348	359	373	398
Child and adult care[7]	813	1,464	1,683	2,111	2,403	2,534	2,639	2,724	2,855
Special milk[4]..................	19	17	15	16	15	14	12	12	12
Nutrition for the elderly (NSIP)[8]	142	148	137	4	2	2	3	2	3
Food distrib. to Indian reserv.[9]	66	65	76	76	96	100	95	94	97
Commodity supplemental food prog.[9] ...	85	99	98	156	161	155	165	198	209
Food distrib. to charitable inst.[10]	104	64	2	4	0	0	1	1	0
Emergency food assistance (TEFAP)[11]..	334	135	225	373	283	617	631	532	444
Total............................	24,707	37,628	32,317	50,673	60,424	78,441	94,641	103,158	106,110

Note: 2012 data are preliminary. All data subject to revision by the FNS. Figures may not add up to totals because of rounding and administrative costs not shown. (1) Formerly known as the Food Stamp Program. Includes benefits and admin. expenses. (2) Provides benefits analogous to SNAP. (3) Data are nine-month averages (summer months excluded). (4) Cash payments or federal reimbursements to states. (5) Includes food benefits, nutrition services and admin. funds, Farmers' Market Nutrition Program, infrastructure, breastfeeding promotion and peer counseling, program evaluation, and technical assistance. (6) Includes cash payments, commodity costs, and admin. expenditures. Similar services provided by natl. school lunch and breakfast programs. (7) Includes cash payments, entitlement and bonus commodities, cash-in-lieu of commodities, sponsor admin. costs, start-up costs, and audits. (8) For 2003 and on, program was administered by the Agency on Aging (Dept. of Health and Human Services); FNS costs limited to value of commodities distributed. (9) Includes commodity distribution costs and admin. expenses. (10) Includes summer camps. (11) Food made available to hunger relief orgs. such as food banks and soup kitchens.

U.S. Cost of Food, 2013

Source: Center for Nutrition Policy and Promotion (CNPP), U.S. Dept. of Agriculture (USDA)

Age-gender group	Weekly cost[1]				Monthly cost[1]			
	Thrifty plan	Low-cost plan	Mod.-cost plan	Liberal plan	Thrifty plan	Low-cost plan	Mod.-cost plan	Liberal plan
Individual child[2]								
1 year	$21.50	$28.50	$32.40	$39.30	$93.30	$123.50	$140.40	$170.40
2-3 years	23.40	29.60	35.80	43.50	101.50	128.40	155.20	188.40
4-5 years	24.40	30.80	38.00	46.20	105.80	133.40	164.80	200.40
6-8 years	31.10	42.70	52.00	61.10	134.70	185.00	225.20	264.80
9-11 years	35.30	46.70	60.10	70.00	152.90	202.40	260.30	303.20
Individual male[2]								
12-13 years	38.00	53.60	67.00	78.40	164.60	232.20	290.20	339.80
14-18 years	39.00	54.60	69.00	79.10	169.10	236.50	299.10	342.90
19-50 years	42.00	54.10	68.00	83.30	182.00	234.60	294.80	360.70
51-70 years	38.40	51.20	63.60	76.50	166.20	221.70	275.60	331.40
71+ years	38.70	50.80	62.90	77.30	167.80	220.20	272.40	335.10
Individual female[2]								
12-13 years	38.10	46.20	55.40	67.90	165.10	200.30	240.10	294.20
14-18 years	37.40	46.30	56.00	68.90	162.10	200.80	242.80	298.40
19-50 years	37.50	47.00	58.10	74.10	162.40	203.70	251.70	321.20
51-70 years	36.90	46.00	57.20	68.40	160.10	199.10	247.70	296.40
71+ years	36.10	45.70	56.60	68.00	156.30	198.10	245.10	294.70
2-person family[3]								
19-50 years	87.40	111.30	138.70	173.10	378.90	482.10	601.10	750.20
51-70 years	82.80	106.80	132.80	159.40	358.90	462.90	575.60	690.50
4-person family[4] with 2 children ages—								
2-3 and 4-5 years	127.30	161.60	200.00	247.10	551.70	700.10	866.40	1,070.80
6-8 and 9-11 years	145.90	190.60	238.20	288.50	632.00	825.70	1,031.90	1,250.00

Note: The official USDA food plans represent a nutritious diet at four different cost levels. The nutritional bases are the 1997-2005 Dietary Reference Intakes, 2005 Dietary Guidelines for Americans, and 2005 MyPyramid food intake recommendations. In addition to cost, differences among plans are in specific foods and quantities of foods. Another basis of the food plans is that all meals and snacks are prepared at home. For specific foods and quantities, see Thrifty Food Plan, 2006 and The Low-Cost, Moderate-Cost, and Liberal Food Plans, 2007 from the CNPP. All four food plans are based on 2001-02 data and updated to current dollars using the consumer price index for specific food items. (1) All costs are rounded to nearest 10 cents. (2) The costs given are for individuals in 4-person families. (3) Ten percent added for family size adjustment. (4) Defined as a couple, 19-50 years old, and two children.

Direct Government Payments to Farmers, by State, 1950-2012

Source: Economic Research Service, U.S. Dept. of Agriculture

(in millions of dollars)

State	1950	1960	1970	1980	1990	2000	2010	2011	2012
Alabama	$8.1	$13.0	$79.5	$23.0	$82.2	$171.0	$134.6	$115.8	$118.0
Alaska	NA	0.1	0.1	0.2	1.1	1.7	9.6	11.3	12.4
Arizona	1.7	2.2	52.0	5.1	43.3	107.2	70.2	58.1	50.2
Arkansas	5.7	13.4	87.7	34.5	312.7	976.8	389.4	364.8	365.1
California	13.6	21.9	131.9	14.1	252.3	689.0	363.7	259.1	287.5
Colorado	11.9	24.8	68.0	18.0	236.7	351.4	271.6	235.4	215.7
Connecticut	0.5	0.6	0.8	0.9	2.1	18.1	15.5	10.5	8.9
Delaware	0.4	0.6	1.7	1.0	3.2	25.1	24.3	21.0	15.4
Florida	3.2	7.1	18.5	7.0	37.2	114.1	93.0	175.1	69.1
Georgia	10.6	22.9	83.6	28.9	130.6	385.1	262.3	222.3	256.7
Hawaii	NA	9.2	11.1	0.7	0.5	11.9	16.2	16.9	11.4
Idaho	3.5	13.3	48.0	7.9	133.4	264.1	163.6	113.4	126.7
Illinois	10.1	17.9	166.6	35.7	506.6	2,010.4	697.9	627.4	630.8
Indiana	5.7	16.8	111.0	15.0	244.2	939.9	372.5	300.5	323.0
Iowa	10.9	20.8	235.8	44.6	753.7	2,303.2	1,024.8	811.8	855.4
Kansas	9.1	28.5	227.6	93.3	834.7	1,233.9	631.8	542.8	518.6
Kentucky	7.4	15.8	45.8	10.0	81.6	449.5	319.6	273.8	303.4
Louisiana	11.4	15.1	55.1	20.0	154.6	471.0	209.7	209.8	219.1
Maine	1.0	2.7	1.7	3.4	7.0	13.9	48.8	17.4	21.9
Maryland	1.3	2.8	8.0	3.5	17.4	104.4	54.3	41.1	56.2
Massachusetts	0.6	0.7	0.6	0.7	3.0	11.0	20.1	20.9	17.0
Michigan	7.2	18.0	65.7	10.7	168.8	381.3	184.6	156.6	175.4
Minnesota	8.2	31.7	151.8	69.6	511.8	1,504.4	566.1	487.9	534.7
Mississippi	9.9	12.5	146.5	18.8	186.0	464.9	251.2	245.6	219.1
Missouri	10.4	23.7	153.9	78.9	299.1	872.3	435.6	367.1	396.0
Montana	6.1	15.6	85.4	58.5	299.6	490.4	327.1	298.6	239.3
Nebraska	8.8	22.1	203.0	82.9	624.6	1,407.8	509.4	470.3	480.3
Nevada	0.2	0.9	2.1	1.3	5.3	9.3	9.8	10.4	12.9
New Hampshire	0.6	0.7	0.5	0.7	1.9	4.8	20.1	12.9	14.9
New Jersey	0.9	1.8	4.3	0.9	15.7	22.5	22.0	17.1	11.9
New Mexico	2.4	11.2	43.1	20.9	63.8	79.8	91.5	88.1	97.7
New York	5.7	12.7	22.0	5.8	59.3	160.2	66.0	57.4	104.3
North Carolina	8.8	12.8	59.7	13.2	73.3	449.1	438.4	401.1	430.4
North Dakota	5.9	38.6	167.2	116.6	545.4	1,178.0	844.8	460.8	409.1
Ohio	7.3	19.2	89.6	9.4	197.0	678.3	373.2	256.7	279.8
Oklahoma	8.8	24.9	118.0	34.9	319.0	440.1	318.7	341.8	295.6

State	1950	1960	1970	1980	1990	2000	2010	2011	2012
Oregon	$3.4	$8.7	$23.1	$5.9	$89.1	$137.6	$150.4	$110.8	$118.0
Pennsylvania	6.3	11.8	25.2	8.3	41.4	147.9	81.3	73.8	119.3
Rhode Island	0.1	0.1	0.1	0.1	0.2	1.2	6.4	3.9	3.9
South Carolina	3.8	14.2	54.4	13.4	62.6	144.9	125.5	113.6	110.2
South Dakota	5.4	28.9	91.7	65.3	332.9	795.7	401.0	303.4	330.8
Tennessee	6.7	14.9	71.0	18.7	91.0	300.8	153.3	140.2	176.2
Texas	24.9	72.5	543.2	231.8	974.7	1,670.4	1,018.3	917.4	838.1
Utah	2.4	6.6	11.1	5.1	34.9	36.3	39.2	35.1	39.5
Vermont	1.3	1.6	1.4	1.3	5.8	26.1	21.1	17.8	22.2
Virginia	5.0	7.1	20.0	13.3	32.4	153.0	110.9	100.4	139.9
Washington	3.3	9.7	57.9	9.5	205.4	352.8	313.8	231.1	203.7
West Virginia	2.1	3.0	3.6	2.5	6.0	23.5	16.5	14.3	25.2
Wisconsin	7.7	16.9	51.7	12.4	181.2	603.8	259.3	196.0	281.8
Wyoming	3.0	9.9	15.2	7.3	31.3	37.3	42.7	41.3	42.6
U.S.	283.5	702.4	3,717.4	1,285.7	9,298.0	23,221.6	12,391.7	10,420.5	10,635.1

NA = Not available. **Note:** Direct federal government payments to farmers are for eligible historic production of wheat, corn, barley, grain sorghum, oats, upland cotton, long/medium grain rice, soybeans, other oilseeds, and peanuts. Producers enroll annually to receive payments based on rates specified in the Farm Act and their historic program payment acres and yields.

U.S. Annual Per Capita Consumption of Selected Foods, 1970-2011

Source: Economic Research Service, U.S. Dept. of Agriculture; Distilled Spirits Council of the U.S., Inc.; Beer Institute; Wine Institute
(fruits and vegetables in pounds, beverages in gallons)

	1970	1990	2011	% change, 1970-2011		1970	1990	2011	% change, 1970-2011
Fresh fruit	96.3	111.4	123.3	28.0%	**Fresh vegetables**	144.4	163.9	172.2	19.3%
Apples	16.5	19.0	14.8	–10.3	Bell peppers	2.0	5.4	9.7	385.0
Avocados	0.4	1.3	4.4	1,000.0	Broccoli	0.5	3.1	6.4	1,180.0
Bananas	17.4	24.3	25.5	46.6	Cabbage	8.1	7.8	6.4	–21.0
Grapes	2.7	7.2	7.0	159.3	Carrots	5.8	8.0	7.3	25.9
Melons	19.4	22.3	22.7	17.0	Celery	6.8	6.7	5.5	–19.1
Oranges	15.7	12.0	9.7	–38.2	Cucumbers	2.6	4.3	5.8	123.1
Peaches/nectarines	5.5	5.3	4.3	–21.8	Garlic	0.4	1.1	1.9	375.0
Pears	1.8	3.1	3.1	72.2	Head lettuce	20.8	25.8	14.4	–30.8
Pineapples	0.7	1.9	5.4	671.4	Onions	9.5	14.2	17.9	88.4
Strawberries	1.6	3.0	6.8	325.0	Potatoes	59.3	44.9	32.7	–44.9
Canned vegetables	93.0	110.3	91.1	–2.0	Sweet corn	7.2	6.2	8.0	11.1
Green peas	0.9	2.0	0.8	–11.1	Tomatoes	10.3	13.2	17.9	73.8
Snap beans	1.1	3.7	3.2	190.9	**Beverages**				
Sweet corn	14.3	11.0	5.8	–59.4	Bottled water	NA	8.8	NA	NA
Tomatoes	62.1	75.3	65.2	5.0	Carbonated soft drinks	24.3	46.2	NA	NA
Frozen vegetables	43.7	66.7	70.0	60.2	Regular	22.2	35.6	NA	NA
Broccoli	1.0	2.2	2.7	170.0	Diet	2.1	10.7	NA	NA
Carrots	1.4	2.3	1.5	7.1	Coffee	33.4	26.8	24.7	–26.0
Green peas	1.9	2.2	1.5	–21.1	Fruit juice	5.5	7.0	6.8	23.6
Potatoes	28.5	46.4	48.2	69.1	Beer	18.5	23.9	20.3	9.7
Sweet corn	5.7	8.6	9.5	66.7	Wine	1.3	2.1	2.7	107.7
NA = Not available.					Distilled spirits	1.8	1.5	1.5	–16.7

U.S. Meat Production and Consumption, 1940-2013

Source: Economic Research Service, U.S. Dept. of Agriculture
(in millions of pounds)

Year	Beef Prod.	Beef Cons.	Veal Prod.	Veal Cons.	Lamb and mutton Prod.	Lamb and mutton Cons.	Pork Prod.	Pork Cons.	All red meats[1] Prod.	All red meats[1] Cons.	All poultry Prod.	All poultry Cons.
1940	7,175	7,257	981	981	876	873	10,044	9,701	19,076	18,812	NA	NA
1950	9,534	9,529	1,230	1,206	597	596	10,714	10,390	22,075	21,721	3,174	3,097
1960	14,728	15,465	1,109	1,118	769	857	13,905	14,057	30,511	31,497	6,310	6,168
1970	21,684	23,451	588	613	551	669	14,699	14,957	37,522	39,689	10,193	9,981
1980	21,643	23,560	400	420	318	351	16,617	16,838	38,978	41,170	14,173	13,525
1990	22,743	24,030	327	325	363	397	15,354	16,025	38,787	40,778	23,468	22,152
1995	25,222	25,534	319	319	285	346	17,849	17,768	43,675	43,967	30,393	25,944
2000	26,888	27,338	225	225	234	354	18,952	18,643	46,299	46,560	36,073	30,508
2007	26,523	28,144	145	144	188	384	21,962	19,763	48,817	48,435	42,117	35,667
2008	26,663	27,302	152	150	180	343	23,367	19,415	50,361	47,210	43,235	35,379
2009	25,965	26,904	147	147	177	338	22,999	19,839	49,274	47,227	41,673	34,116
2010	26,304	26,392	145	150	168	317	22,437	19,072	49,039	45,931	43,058	35,201
2011	26,195	25,545	138	139	153	295	22,758	18,384	49,222	44,363	43,513	35,548
2012	25,913	25,752	126	124	161	299	23,253	18,604	49,439	44,779	43,523	34,870
2013*	25,337	24,713	126	127	159	306	23,402	19,183	49,005	45,185	44,201	35,561

*Preliminary. NA = Not available. (1) Numbers may not add up to totals because of rounding.

U.S. Per Capita Consumption of Meat and Dairy, 1910-2011

Source: Economic Research Service, U.S. Dept. of Agriculture

(in pounds per capita, unless otherwise noted)

	1910	1930	1950	1970	1990	2000	2010	2011	% change, 1910-2011
Meat									
Beef	48.5	33.7	44.6	79.6	63.9	64.5	56.7	54.5	12.4%
Chicken	11.0	11.1	14.3	27.4	42.4	54.2	58.0	58.4	430.9
Fish/shellfish	11.2	10.2	11.9	11.7	14.9	15.2	15.8	14.9	33.0
Pork	38.2	41.1	43.0	48.1	46.4	47.8	44.3	42.4	11.0
Red meat	96.0	83.6	95.8	131.9	112.2	113.7	102.1	97.8	1.9
Dairy									
Butter	18.4	17.6	10.9	5.4	4.4	4.5	4.9	5.4	-70.7
Cheese, American	2.8	3.2	5.5	7.0	11.1	12.7	13.4	13.2	371.4
Cheese, other	1.5	1.5	2.2	4.4	13.5	17.2	19.5	20.2	1,246.7
Ice cream	1.9	9.3	16.4	16.7	14.8	15.6	13.5	13.0	584.2
Milk, skim/lower fat (gallons)	7.1	5.0	2.9	5.8	15.2	14.4	14.7	14.2	100.0
Milk, whole (gallons)	25.2	28.2	34.2	25.3	10.5	8.0	5.6	5.5	-78.2

U.S. Organic Farmland and Animals, 1995-2011

Source: Economic Research Service, U.S. Dept. of Agriculture

Crop	1995	2000	Organic acreage[1] 2004	2005	2008	2011	% change, 1995-2011	% change, 2005-11	Total U.S. farmland[2]
Grains									
Corn	32,650	77,912	99,111	130,672	194,637	234,470	618.1%	79.4%	93,600,000
Wheat	120,820	206,474	214,244	293,824	415,902	344,644	185.3	17.3	60,433,000
Oats	13,250	29,771	42,616	46,465	57,374	62,015	368.0	33.5	3,760,000
Barley	17,150	41,904	26,629	39,271	46,954	63,903	272.6	62.7	4,020,000
Rice	8,400	26,870	22,173	26,428	49,638	48,533	477.8	83.6	2,761,000
Beans									
Soybeans	47,200	136,071	114,239	122,217	125,621	132,411	180.5	8.3	63,631,000
Dry beans	NA	14,010	7,642	10,561	16,465	28,656	NA	171.3	1,526,900
Dry peas & lentils	5,900	10,144	15,893	17,757	16,987	17,887	203.2	0.7	571,000
Hay & silage	84,100	231,207	356,590	411,342	793,442	785,970	834.6	91.1	61,625,000
All vegetables	NA	62,342	86,822	98,525	177,049	147,446	NA	49.7	2,045,000
All fruits	NA	43,481	80,707	97,277	121,066	131,498	NA	35.2	3,839,300
Other crops									
Cotton	32,850	15,027	9,213	9,537	15,377	12,030	-63.4	26.1	10,830,300
Peanuts	NA	2,085	9,514	11,940	16,776	13,258	NA	11.0	1,230,000
Potatoes	NA	5,433	7,300	6,581	8,273	13,258	NA	101.5	1,148,800
Trees for maple syrup	10,200	11,965	13,357	12,247	31,340	43,831	329.7	257.9	NA
Fallow land	NA	57,688	116,582	198,650	194,428	271,644	NA	36.7	37,968,749
Total cropland	638,500	1,218,905	1,452,353	1,723,271	2,655,382	3,084,989	383.2	79.0	370,653,755
Total pasture & rangeland	276,300	557,167	1,592,756	2,331,158	2,160,577	2,298,130	731.8	-1.4	473,212,960
Total farmland	914,800	1,776,073	3,045,109	4,054,429	4,815,959	5,383,119	488.4	32.8	843,866,715

Animal	1995	2000	Number of organic animals[1] 2004	2005	2008	2011	% change, 2000-11	% change, 2005-11	Total U.S. animals
Total livestock	NA	56,028	157,253	196,506	475,829	492,353	778.8%	150.6%	167,512,858
Beef cows	NA	13,829	36,662	36,113	63,680	106,181	667.8	194.0	32,834,801
Milk cows	NA	38,196	74,840	87,082	249,766	254,771	567.0	192.6	9,266,574
Other cows[3]	NA	NA	36,598	58,822	144,817	113,114	NA	92.3	54,246,483
Hogs & pigs	NA	1,724	4,883	10,018	10,111	12,373	617.7	23.5	65,110,000
Sheep & lambs	NA	2,279	4,270	4,471	7,455	5,914	159.5	32.3	6,055,000
Total poultry	NA	3,159,050	7,304,566	13,757,270	15,518,075	37,028,242	1,072.1	169.2	9,632,362,000
Layer hens	NA	1,113,746	1,787,901	2,415,056	5,538,011	6,663,278	498.3	175.9	377,492,000
Broilers	NA	1,924,807	4,769,104	10,405,879	9,015,984	28,644,354	1,388.2	175.3	8,882,000,000
Turkeys	NA	9,138	164,292	144,086	398,531	504,315	5,418.9	250.0	262,460,000
Other/ unclassified	NA	111,359	583,269	792,249	565,549	1,216,295	992.2	53.5	110,410,000

NA = Not available. (1) Based on information from USDA-accredited state and private organic certifiers. (2) Total acreage of organic and nonorganic land used for agricultural purposes. (3) Includes breeding stock, replacement heifers, and unclassified cows.

Livestock on Farms in the U.S., 1900-2013

Source: National Agricultural Statistics Service, U.S. Dept. of Agriculture

(in thousands)

Year (on Jan. 1)	All cattle[1]	Milk cows	Sheep and lambs	Hogs and pigs[2]	Year (on Jan. 1)	All cattle[1]	Milk cows	Sheep and lambs	Hogs and pigs[2]
1900	59,739	16,544	48,105	51,055	1995	102,755	9,487	8,886	57,150
1910	58,993	19,450	50,239	48,072	2000	98,199	9,183	7,036	59,335
1920	70,400	21,455	40,743	60,159	2002	96,723	9,106	6,623	59,722
1930	61,003	23,032	51,565	55,705	2003	96,100	9,142	6,321	59,554
1940	68,309	24,940	52,107	61,165	2004	94,888	8,990	6,105	60,444
1950	77,963	23,853	29,826	58,937	2005	95,838	9,005	6,135	60,975
1955	96,592	23,462	31,582	50,474	2006	96,702	9,063	6,230	61,449
1960	96,236	19,527	33,170	59,026	2007	97,003	9,132	6,165	62,490
1965	109,000	16,981	25,127	56,106	2008	96,035	9,257	5,950	66,963
1970	112,369	12,091	20,423	57,046	2009	94,521	9,333	5,747	66,768
1975	132,028	11,220	14,515	54,693	2010	93,881	9,086	5,620	65,327
1980	111,242	10,758	12,699	67,318	2011	100,000	9,200	5,480	64,625
1985	109,582	10,777	10,716	54,073	2012	90,769	9,230	5,365	66,361
1990	95,816	10,015	11,358	53,788	2013	89,300	9,220	5,335	66,373

(1) For 1970 and on, includes milk cows and heifers that have calved. (2) As of Dec. 1 of preceding year.

Production of Principal U.S. Crops, 1990-2012

Source: National Agricultural Statistics Service, U.S. Dept. of Agriculture

Year	Corn for grain (1,000 bu)	Oats (1,000 bu)	Barley (1,000 bu)	Sorghum for grain (1,000 bu)	All wheat (1,000 bu)	Rye (1,000 bu)	Flaxseed (1,000 bu)	Cotton (upland) (1,000 b)	Cottonseed (1,000 t)
1990	7,934,028	357,654	422,196	573,303	2,729,778	10,176	3,812	15,505.4	5,968.5
1995	7,373,876	162,027	359,562	460,373	2,182,591	10,064	2,211	17,532.2	6,848.7
2000	9,915,051	149,545	318,728	470,526	2,232,460	8,386	10,730	16,799.2	6,435.6
2001	9,506,840	117,024	249,420	514,524	1,957,043	6,971	11,455	19,602.4	7,452.2
2002	8,966,787	116,002	226,906	360,713	1,605,878	6,488	11,863	16,530.3	6,183.9
2003	10,089,222	144,383	278,283	411,237	2,344,760	8,634	10,516	17,822.9	6,664.6
2004	11,807,086	115,695	279,743	453,654	2,158,245	8,255	10,368	22,505.1	8,242.1
2005	11,114,082	114,878	211,896	392,933	2,104,690	7,537	19,695	23,259.7	8,172.1
2006	10,534,868	93,638	180,165	277,538	1,812,036	7,193	11,019	20,822.4	7,347.9
2007	13,037,875	90,430	210,110	497,445	2,051,088	6,311	5,896	18,355.1	6,588.7
2008	12,091,648	89,135	240,193	472,342	2,499,164	7,979	5,716	12,384.5	4,300.3
2009	13,091,862	93,081	227,323	382,983	2,218,061	6,993	7,423	11,787.6	4,148.8
2010	12,446,865	81,190	180,268	345,625	2,206,916	7,431	9,056	17,600.0	6,098.1
2011	12,359,612	53,649	155,780	214,443	1,999,347	6,326	2,791	14,722.0	5,370.0
2012	10,780,296	64,024	220,284	246,932	2,269,117	6,944	5,762	16,250.0	5,759.0

Year	Tobacco (1,000 lb)	All hay (1,000 t)	Beans, dry edible (1,000 cwt)	Peas, dry edible (1,000 cwt)	Peanuts[1] (1,000 lb)	Soybeans[2] (1,000 bu)	Potatoes (1,000 cwt)	Sweet potatoes (1,000 cwt)
1990	1,626,380	146,212	32,379	2,372	3,602,770	1,925,947	402,110	12,594
1995	1,268,538	154,166	30,812	4,765	4,247,455	2,176,814	443,606	12,906
2000	1,052,999	151,921	26,409	3,474	3,265,505	2,757,810	513,621	13,794
2001	991,223	156,764	19,583	3,763	4,276,704	2,890,682	437,888	14,637
2002	871,122	149,467	30,312	4,727	3,321,040	2,756,147	458,171	12,799
2003	802,560	157,585	22,492	5,202	4,144,150	2,453,665	457,814	15,891
2004	881,973	158,247	17,788	11,419	4,288,200	3,123,686	456,041	16,112
2005	645,015	151,017	26,772	14,003	4,869,860	3,063,237	423,926	15,730
2006	727,347	142,336	24,247	13,203	3,464,250	3,188,247	441,348	16,248
2007	787,653	146,901	25,586	16,287	3,672,250	2,667,117	444,875	18,070
2008	800,504	146,270	25,558	12,270	5,162,400	2,967,007	415,055	18,443
2009	822,581	147,700	25,427	17,137	3,691,650	3,359,011	432,601	19,469
2010	718,190	145,624	31,801	14,221	4,156,840	3,329,181	404,273	23,845
2011	598,252	131,216	19,890	5,625	3,658,590	3,093,524	429,647	26,964
2012	762,441	119,878	31,925	10,872	6,741,440	3,014,998	467,126	26,482

Year	Rice (1,000 cwt)	Sugarcane (1,000 t)	Sugar beets (1,000 t)	Pecans[3] (1,000 lb)	Apples (1,000 t)	Grapes (1,000 t)	Peaches (1,000 t)	Oranges[4] (1,000 bx)	Grapefruit[4] (1,000 bx)
1990	156,088	28,136	27,513	205,000	4,828	5,660	1,121	184,415	49,300
1995	173,871	30,944	27,954	268,000	5,293	5,922	1,150	263,605	71,050
2000	190,872	36,114	32,541	209,850	5,291	7,688	1,276	299,760	66,980
2001	215,270	34,587	25,764	338,500	4,712	6,569	1,204	280,935	59,750
2002	210,960	35,553	27,707	172,900	4,262	7,339	1,268	283,760	58,660
2003	199,897	33,858	30,710	282,100	4,397	6,664	1,260	267,040	50,080
2004	232,362	29,013	30,021	185,800	5,220	6,240	1,307	294,620	52,540
2005	223,235	26,606	27,433	280,250	4,853	7,814	1,185	216,500	25,640
2006	193,736	29,564	34,064	207,300	4,912	6,378	1,010	210,750	30,600
2007	198,388	29,969	31,834	387,305	4,545	7,057	1,127	177,280	39,900
2008	203,733	27,603	26,881	202,080	4,817	7,319	1,135	234,376	37,900
2009	219,850	30,432	29,783	302,020	4,853	7,307	1,104	210,709	32,025
2010	243,104	27,360	32,034	293,740	4,646	7,471	1,150	192,835	30,400
2011	184,941	29,224	28,896	269,700	4,713	7,448	1,072	204,949	30,360
2012	199,479	32,637	35,236	302,800	4,531	7,343	978	207,019	28,050

b = bale; bu = bushel; bx = box; cwt = hundred weight. **Note:** Some 2012 figures are preliminary estimates. (1) Harvested for nuts. (2) Harvested for beans. (3) Utilized production only. (4) Crop year ending in year cited.

Animal Products: Average Prices Received by U.S. Farmers, 1940-2012

Source: National Agricultural Statistics Service, U.S. Dept. of Agriculture

Figures represent dollars per 100 lb for beef cattle, veal calves, hogs, lambs, milk (wholesale), and sheep; dollars per head for milk cows; cents per lb for broilers, chickens, turkeys, and wool; and cents per dozen for eggs. Weighted calendar year prices for livestock and livestock products other than wool. For 1943-63, wool prices were weighted on marketing year basis. The marketing year was changed in 1964 from a calendar year to a Dec.-Nov. basis for broilers, chickens, eggs, and hogs.

Year	Broilers	Calves (veal)	Cattle (beef)	Chickens (excl. broilers)	Eggs	Hogs	Lambs	Milk cows	Milk	Sheep	Turkeys	Wool
1940	17.3	8.83	7.56	13.0	18.0	5.39	8.10	61	1.82	3.95	15.2	28.4
1950	27.4	26.30	23.30	22.2	36.3	18.00	25.10	198	3.89	11.60	32.8	62.1
1960	16.9	22.90	20.40	12.2	36.1	15.30	17.90	223	4.21	5.61	25.4	42.0
1970	13.6	34.50	27.10	9.1	39.1	22.70	26.40	332	5.71	7.51	22.6	35.4
1980	27.7	76.80	62.40	11.0	56.3	38.00	63.60	1,190	13.05	21.30	41.3	88.1
1990	32.6	95.60	74.60	9.3	70.9	53.70	55.50	1,160	13.74	23.20	39.4	80.0
1995	34.4	73.10	61.80	6.5	62.4	40.50	78.20	1,130	12.78	28.00	41.6	104.0
2000	33.6	104.00	68.60	5.7	61.8	42.30	79.80	1,340	12.40	34.30	40.7	33.0
2001	39.3	106.00	71.30	4.5	62.2	44.30	66.90	1,500	15.04	34.60	39.0	36.0
2002	30.5	96.40	66.50	4.8	58.9	33.40	73.80	1,600	12.18	27.90	36.5	53.0
2003	34.6	102.00	79.70	4.9	73.2	37.20	94.40	1,340	12.55	34.90	36.1	73.0
2004	44.6	119.00	85.80	5.8	71.4	49.30	101.00	1,580	16.13	38.80	42.0	80.0
2005	43.6	135.00	89.70	6.5	54.0	50.20	110.00	1,770	15.19	45.10	44.9	71.0
2006	36.3	133.00	87.20	5.8	58.2	46.00	95.50	1,730	12.96	35.20	47.9	68.0

Year	Broilers	Calves (veal)	Cattle (beef)	Chickens (excl. broilers)	Eggs	Hogs	Lambs	Milk cows	Milk	Sheep	Turkeys	Wool
2007	43.6	119.00	89.90	5.6	88.5	46.60	98.50	1,830	19.21	31.00	52.3	87.0
2008	45.8	110.00	89.10	6.6	109.00	47.00	99.60	1,950	18.45	27.20	56.5	99.0
2009	45.7	105.00	80.30	7.2	81.7	41.60	99.60	1,390	12.93	32.50	50.0	79.0
2010	48.2	117.00	92.20	8.1	85.7	54.10	125.00	1,330	16.35	49.70	61.5	115.0
2011	46.6	142.00	113.00	8.7	95.6	65.30	NA	1,420	20.25	NA	68.2	167.0
2012	50.0	168.00	122.00	8.8	101.1	64.20	NA	1,430	18.56	NA	72.1	153.0

NA = Not available.

Crops: Average Prices Received by U.S. Farmers, 1940-2012

Source: National Agricultural Statistics Service, U.S. Dept. of Agriculture

Figures represent cents per lb for apples, cotton, and peanuts; dollars per bushel for barley, corn, oats, soybeans, and wheat; dollars per 100 lb for potatoes, rice, and sorghum; and dollars per ton for cottonseed and baled hay. Weighted crop year prices. The marketing year is described as follows: apples, June-May; barley, hay, oats, potatoes, and wheat, July-June; cotton, cottonseed, peanuts, and rice, Aug.-July; soybeans, Sept.-Aug.; and corn and sorghum grain, Oct.-Sept.

Year	Apples	Barley	Corn	Cotton-seed	Cotton (upland)*	Hay	Oats	Peanuts	Pota-toes	Rice	Sor-ghum	Soy-beans	Wheat
1940	NA	0.39	0.62	21.70	9.8	9.78	0.30	3.7	0.85	1.80	0.87	0.89	0.67
1950	NA	1.19	1.52	86.60	39.9	21.10	0.79	10.9	1.50	5.09	1.88	2.47	2.00
1960	2.7	0.84	1.00	42.50	30.1	21.70	0.60	10.0	2.00	4.55	1.49	2.13	1.74
1970	6.5	0.97	1.33	56.40	21.9	26.10	0.62	12.8	2.21	5.17	2.04	2.85	1.33
1980	12.1	2.86	3.11	129.00	74.4	71.00	1.79	25.1	6.55	12.80	5.25	7.57	3.91
1990	20.9	2.14	2.28	121.00	67.1	80.60	1.14	34.7	6.08	6.68	3.79	5.74	2.61
1995	24.0	2.89	3.24	106.00	75.4	82.20	1.67	29.3	6.77	9.15	5.69	6.72	4.55
2000	17.8	2.11	1.85	105.00	49.8	84.60	1.10	27.4	5.08	5.61	3.37	4.54	2.62
2001	22.9	2.22	1.97	90.50	29.8	96.50	1.59	23.4	6.99	4.25	4.25	4.38	2.78
2002	25.6	2.72	2.32	101.00	44.5	92.40	1.81	18.2	6.69	4.49	4.14	5.53	3.56
2003	29.4	2.83	2.42	117.00	61.8	85.50	1.48	19.3	5.89	8.08	4.26	7.34	3.40
2004	21.8	2.48	2.06	107.00	41.6	92.00	1.48	18.9	5.67	7.33	3.19	5.74	3.40
2005	24.4	2.53	2.00	96.00	47.7	98.20	1.63	17.3	7.06	7.65	3.33	5.66	3.42
2006	31.7	2.85	3.04	111.00	46.5	110.00	1.87	17.7	7.33	9.96	5.88	6.43	4.26
2007	28.8	4.02	4.20	162.00	59.3	128.00	2.63	20.5	7.51	12.80	7.28	10.10	6.48
2008	23.2	5.37	4.06	223.00	47.8	152.00	3.15	23.0	9.09	16.80	5.72	9.97	6.78
2009	23.1	4.66	3.55	158.00	62.9	108.00	2.02	21.7	8.25	14.40	5.75	9.59	4.87
2010	25.1	3.86	5.18	161.00	81.5	114.00	2.52	22.5	9.20	12.70	8.96	11.30	5.70
2011	30.3	5.35	6.22	260.00	88.3	178.00	3.49	31.8	9.41	14.50	10.70	12.50	7.24
2012[1]	34.3	6.40	7.20	256.00	69.9	191.00	3.80	34.5	8.39	14.90	12.80	14.30	7.90

*Beginning in 1964, 480-lb net weight bales. NA = Not available. (1) Preliminary data.

World Meat Production, 2000, 2011

Source: UN Food and Agriculture Organization; in thousands of metric tons; ranked by top producers in 2011

	Top beef producers				Top pork producers				Top poultry producers		
Rank	Country	2000	2011	Rank	Country	2000	2011	Rank	Country	2000	2011
1.	U.S.	12,298	11,988	1.	China	40,752	51,535	1.	U.S.	16,416	19,791
2.	Brazil	6,579	9,030	2.	U.S.	8,597	10,331	2.	China	12,689	17,443
3.	China	5,156	6,491	3.	Germany	3,982	5,616	3.	Brazil	6,125	11,497
4.	India	2,237	2,589	4.	Spain	2,905	3,469	4.	Russia	775	2,956
5.	Argentina	2,718	2,420	5.	Brazil	2,600	3,227	5.	Mexico	1,868	2,807
6.	Australia	1,988	2,110	6.	Vietnam	1,409	3,099	6.	India	904	2,245
7.	Mexico	1,409	1,804	7.	Russia	1,569	2,428	7.	France	2,220	1,805
8.	Russia	1,894	1,625	8.	France	2,312	2,157	8.	Iran	815	1,698
9.	Pakistan	886	1,536	9.	Canada	1,640	1,954	9.	Argentina	1,000	1,695
10.	France	1,528	1,502	10.	Poland	1,923	1,935	10.	Indonesia	818	1,643
11.	Germany	1,304	1,170	11.	Denmark	1,625	1,720	11.	Turkey	661	1,626
12.	Canada	1,263	1,154	12.	Philippines	1,213	1,649	12.	UK.	1,513	1,561
13.	Italy	1,153	1,011	13.	Italy	1,479	1,602	13.	South Africa	821	1,492
14.	Colombia	745	940	14.	Netherlands	1,623	1,347	14.	Malaysia	714	1,428
15.	UK.	705	936	15.	Japan	1,256	1,267	15.	Germany	790	1,423
16.	Egypt	544	850	16.	Mexico	1,030	1,202	16.	Japan	1,195	1,382
17.	South Africa	625	829	17.	Belgium	1,042	1,108	17.	Thailand	1,149	1,340
18.	Uzbekistan	390	763	18.	Thailand	693	867	18.	Poland	5,899	1,285
19.	Turkey	359	647	19.	South Korea	916	837	19.	Spain	987	1,233
20.	New Zealand	572	623	20.	UK.	899	806	20.	Canada	1,065	1,222
21.	Spain	651	604	21.	Indonesia	413	721	21.	Italy	1,092	1,216
22.	Ireland	577	546	22.	Ukraine	676	704	22.	Myanmar	248	1,114
23.	Indonesia	386	503	23.	Myanmar	123	585	23.	Colombia	504	1,086
24.	Japan	530	500	24.	Austria	502	544	24.	Peru	542	1,085
25.	Venezuela	429	495	25.	Chile	261	528	25.	Australia	643	1,055
	Africa	4,327	5,481		Africa	767	1,282		Africa	2,972	4,874
	Asia	13,001	16,844		Asia	48,007	61,801		Asia	22,898	35,690
	Central America	1,766	2,279		Central America	1,140	1,374		Central America	2,371	3,627
	Europe	11,768	10,697		Europe	25,258	27,436		Europe	11,864	16,932
	North America	13,561	13,143		North America	10,237	12,284		North America	17,480	21,013
	Oceania	2,581	2,753		Oceania	489	483		Oceania	767	1,242
	South America	11,846	14,621		South America	3,774	5,003		South America	9,741	17,739
	World total	**59,075**	**66,055**		**World total**	**89,882**	**110,012**		**World total**	**68,585**	**101,739**

World Corn, Rice, and Wheat Production, 2000, 2011

Source: UN Food and Agriculture Organization; in millions of metric tons; ranked by top producers in 2011

	Top corn producers				Top rice producers				Top wheat producers		
Rank	Country	2000	2011	Rank	Country	2000	2011	Rank	Country	2000	2011
1.	U.S.	251.9	313.9	1.	China	189.8	202.7	1.	China	99.6	117.4
2.	China	106.2	192.9	2.	India	127.5	155.7	2.	India	76.4	86.9
3.	Brazil	31.9	55.7	3.	Indonesia	51.9	65.7	3.	Russia	34.5	56.2
4.	Argentina	16.8	23.8	4.	Bangladesh	37.6	50.6	4.	U.S.	60.6	54.4
5.	Ukraine	3.8	22.8	5.	Vietnam	32.5	42.3	5.	France	37.4	38.0
6.	India	12.0	21.6	6.	Thailand	25.8	34.6	6.	Australia	22.1	27.4
7.	Mexico	17.6	17.6	7.	Myanmar	21.3	32.8	7.	Canada	26.5	25.3
8.	Indonesia	9.7	17.6	8.	Philippines	12.4	16.7	8.	Pakistan	21.1	25.2
9.	France	16.0	15.7	9.	Brazil	11.1	13.5	9.	Germany	21.6	22.8
10.	Romania	4.9	11.7	10.	Cambodia	4.0	8.8	10.	Kazakhstan	9.1	22.7
11.	Canada	7.0	10.7	11.	Japan	11.9	8.4	11.	Ukraine	10.2	22.3
12.	South Africa	11.4	10.4	12.	U.S.	8.7	8.4	12.	Turkey	21.0	21.8
13.	Italy	10.1	9.8	13.	South Korea	7.2	6.3	13.	Argentina	16.1	16.4
14.	Nigeria	4.1	9.2	14.	Pakistan	7.2	6.2	14.	UK	16.7	15.3
15.	Hungary	5.0	8.0	15.	Egypt	6.0	5.7	15.	Iran	8.1	14.4
16.	Philippines	4.5	7.0	16.	Madagascar	2.5	5.1	16.	Poland	8.5	9.3
17.	Russia	1.5	7.0	17.	Nigeria	3.3	4.6	17.	Egypt	6.6	8.4
18.	Egypt	6.5	6.9	18.	Nepal	4.2	4.5	18.	Romania	4.5	7.1
19.	Serbia	NA	6.5	19.	Sri Lanka	2.9	3.9	19.	Spain	7.3	6.9
20.	Germany	3.3	5.2	20.	Iran	2.0	3.2	20.	Italy	7.5	6.6
21.	Ethiopia	2.7	5.0	21.	Laos	2.2	3.1	21.	Uzbekistan	3.5	6.5
22.	Thailand	4.5	4.8	22.	Malaysia	2.1	2.7	22.	Brazil	1.7	5.7
23.	Vietnam	2.0	4.7	23.	Peru	1.9	2.6	23.	Czech Republic	4.1	4.9
24.	Tanzania	2.0	4.3	24.	Colombia	2.7	2.5	24.	Denmark	4.7	4.8
25.	Pakistan	1.6	4.3	25.	North Korea	1.7	2.5	25.	Bulgaria	2.8	4.5
	Africa	44.3	65.1		Africa	17.5	26.5		Africa	14.3	22.1
	Asia	149.1	270.9		Asia	545.5	653.2		Asia	254.5	317.9
	Central America	20.3	21.3		Central America	1.2	1.4		Central America	3.5	3.6
	Europe	63.5	108.6		Europe	3.2	4.4		Europe	183.6	226.0
	North America	258.8	324.6		North America	8.7	8.4		North America	87.2	79.7
	Oceania	0.6	0.6		Oceania	1.1	0.7		Oceania	22.4	27.8
	South America	55.4	91.8		South America	20.9	26.8		South America	20.2	27.0
	World total	592.5	883.5		World total	599.4	722.8		World total	585.7	704.1

NA = Not available.

Value of U.S. Agricultural Exports and Imports, 1978-2012

Source: Economic Research Service, U.S. Dept. of Agriculture
(in billions of dollars, unless otherwise noted)

Year[1]	Agric. trade surplus	Agric. exports	% of all exports	Agric. imports	% of all imports	Year[1]	Agric. trade surplus	Agric. exports	% of all exports	Agric. imports	% of all imports
1978	$13.4	$27.3	21%	$13.9	8%	1996	$26.8	$60.3	10%	$33.5	4%
1980	23.2	40.5	19	17.3	7	1997	21.7	57.3	9	35.7	4
1981	26.4	43.8	19	17.3	7	1998	16.8	53.7	8	36.8	4
1982	23.6	39.1	18	15.5	6	1999	11.8	49.1	8	37.3	4
1983	18.5	34.8	18	16.3	7	2000	11.9	50.8	7	38.9	3
1984	19.1	38.0	18	18.9	6	2001	13.7	52.7	8	39.0	3
1985	11.5	31.2	15	19.7	6	2002	12.4	53.3	8	41.0	4
1986	5.4	26.3	13	20.9	6	2003	10.3	56.0	9	45.7	4
1987	7.2	27.9	12	20.7	5	2004	9.7	62.4	9	52.7	4
1988	14.3	35.3	12	21.0	5	2005	4.8	62.5	8	57.7	4
1989	18.1	39.7	12	21.6	5	2006	4.6	68.6	8	64.0	4
1990	16.6	39.5	11	22.9	5	2007	12.2	82.2	8	70.1	4
1991	16.4	39.3	10	22.9	5	2008	35.6	114.9	10	79.3	4
1992	18.3	43.1	10	24.8	5	2009	22.9	96.3	10	73.4	5
1993	17.7	42.9	10	25.1	4	2010	29.6	108.6	10	79.0	4
1994	19.2	46.2	10	27.0	4	2011	42.9	137.4	10	94.5	4
1995	26.0	56.3	10	30.3	4	2012	32.4	135.8	10	103.4	5

(1) Fiscal year (Oct.-Sept.).

Crop Consumption Per Capita in Selected Nations, 1980-2009

Source: UN Food and Agriculture Organization
(in kg per capita per year)

	Corn				Rice				Wheat			
Country	1980	1990	2009	% change, 1980-2009	1980	1990	2009	% change, 1980-2009	1980	1990	2009	% change, 1980-2009
Australia	2	4	5	121.7%	8	8	12	51.3%	81	70	79	-1.9%
Bangladesh	0	0	8	NA	148	163	173	17.4	29	22	16	-45.4
Brazil	22	22	25	10.4	39	41	35	-12.0	50	44	54	7.9
Cambodia	11	8	17	46.5	138	158	160	16.3	4	0	2	-60.5
Canada	4	3	20	429.7	3	5	10	185.3	76	78	86	12.2
Chad	5	4	11	130.6	7	11	7	9.1	2	4	11	378.3
China	5	4	7	38.8	76	83	76	0.7	59	79	66	13.5
Congo Republic	5	3	3	-44.7	2	5	8	382.4	33	33	51	55.0
Cuba	0	0	NA		51	48	62	22.2	78	74	49	-36.8
Egypt	49	57	60	24.1	26	31	39	46.2	129	149	145	12.4
France	2	13	12	572.2	4	4	5	31.4	96	92	102	6.8
Germany	3	7	15	374.2	2	2	5	152.6	69	68	78	11.7
India	8	8	5	-36.3	64	78	68	7.1	45	41	58	28.8
Indonesia	23	28	38	68.0	121	127	127	5.6	9	9	21	123.4
Iran	1	1	2	266.7	30	31	23	-23.1	155	169	157	1.2
Israel	12	23	30	164.3	6	8	10	58.3	138	124	108	-21.7
Italy	5	3	4	-20.0	5	5	6	28.3	174	149	144	-17.0

Country	Corn 1980	1990	2009	% change, 1980-2009	Rice 1980	1990	2009	% change, 1980-2009	Wheat 1980	1990	2009	% change, 1980-2009
Japan	15	19	11	−22.6%	73	65	54	−26.4%	44	44	48	9.6%
Kenya	114	88	77	−32.3	2	1	8	233.3	20	18	25	23.2
Korea, North	43	56	44	2.1	72	70	76	6.3	32	22	18	−44.0
Korea, South	2	13	14	768.8	138	97	81	−40.9	49	48	50	0.6
Mexico	121	127	121	−0.1	5	4	6	20.8	43	43	32	−25.3
New Zealand	1	3	3	153.8	2	4	10	295.8	78	69	76	−3.3
Nigeria	6	32	29	398.3	14	20	21	46.2	15	3	21	36.2
Pakistan	7	6	8	20.9	22	14	17	−24.1	113	127	110	−2.6
Philippines	22	19	7	−70.3	98	94	123	26.5	17	20	24	39.1
Rwanda	14	15	17	16.0	2	1	10	464.7	2	3	10	363.6
Saudi Arabia	12	13	23	97.4	33	18	36	6.6	88	105	89	1.5
South Africa	120	108	104	−13.7	4	8	15	236.4	56	57	61	8.4
Spain	1	1	2	150.0	6	7	12	101.8	98	93	86	−12.5
Thailand	0	1	4	1,950.0	132	104	133	1.1	4	6	17	312.5
Turkey	8	21	16	86.9	3	7	9	173.5	209	222	200	−4.4
United Arab Emirates	1	1	1	12.5	34	41	47	38.0	86	127	123	42.8
United Kingdom	3	3	3	−6.3	2	3	6	221.1	82	82	99	19.8
United States	8	13	13	60.8	4	7	8	112.8	70	81	81	15.4
Uruguay	23	28	29	28.3	8	10	19	146.2	105	96	124	18.2
Venezuela	76	54	64	−14.8	21	13	32	53.6	51	51	49	−3.4
Vietnam	7	7	11	60.3	131	132	141	8.2	17	3	14	−16.5
Africa	37	41	42	13.8	15	17	21	44.5	47	47	50	6.0
Asia	8	9	9	17.9	78	83	77	−1.2	53	60	63	20.0
Central America	109	115	106	−3.2	8	7	10	31.6	38	39	33	−14.8
Europe	4	5	7	97.3	5	4	5	4.0	118	118	108	−8.4
North America	8	12	13	78.7	4	7	9	123.7	71	81	82	15.1
Oceania	2	4	4	131.6	9	10	14	61.2	79	69	78	−1.6
South America	23	23	27	19.7	30	32	31	6.4	58	53	57	−2.7
World per capita consumption	13	15	17	31.5	50	54	53	6.4	64	68	66	2.5

NA = Not applicable. **Note:** All figures are rounded. Percent change based on unrounded raw data.

Meat Consumption Per Capita in Selected Nations, 1980-2009

Source: UN Food and Agriculture Organization
(in kg per capita per year)

Country	Beef 1980	1990	2009	% change, 1980-2009	Pork 1980	1990	2009	% change, 1980-2009	Poultry 1980	1990	2009	% change, 1980-2009
Australia	53	47	39	−26.4%	15	18	22	48.6%	21	24	38	84.6%
Bangladesh	2	1	1	−13.3	0	0	0	NA	1	1	1	85.7
Brazil	23	28	38	68.4	8	7	12	46.3	10	14	35	247.5
Cambodia	2	4	5	157.1	1	6	9	1,012.5	1	2	2	155.6
Canada	40	36	31	−23.3	35	28	26	−25.7	22	28	37	65.6
Chad	7	12	8	13.7	0	0	0	NA	1	1	1	−28.6
China	0	1	5	1,100.0	12	20	37	209.2	2	3	13	641.2
Congo Republic	4	1	1	−75.0	1	2	1	42.9	2	5	3	55.0
Cuba	15	13	7	−55.7	5	10	22	363.8	10	12	20	108.4
Egypt	7	8	12	75.7	0	0	0	−100.0	4	5	10	163.2
France	33	33	26	−22.0	38	34	31	−17.3	16	21	22	38.5
Germany	23	22	13	−45.1	61	61	55	−10.0	10	11	17	76.5
India	2	2	2	−30.4	0	1	0	−25.0	0	1	2	750.0
Indonesia	2	2	2	29.4	1	3	3	125.0	1	3	6	400.0
Iran	6	6	7	14.5	0	0	0	NA	6	7	22	282.8
Israel	13	14	25	91.6	3	2	3	8.0	35	39	67	89.0
Italy	26	27	24	−9.9	25	32	43	71.9	18	20	17	−4.4
Japan	5	8	9	76.0	14	15	20	47.4	10	14	17	67.3
Kenya	12	9	12	3.4	0	0	0	NA	2	1	1	−70.0
Korea, North	2	2	1	−50.0	10	11	5	−52.1	2	3	2	−14.3
Korea, South	3	6	12	376.0	8	13	29	273.1	3	6	13	412.0
Mexico	11	14	17	61.1	18	10	15	−17.0	7	10	30	353.8
New Zealand	57	39	28	−51.9	12	14	22	89.6	10	17	30	216.7
Nigeria	5	2	2	−63.5	1	1	2	200.0	2	2	2	−5.6
Pakistan	5	6	8	76.6	0	0	0	NA	1	1	4	533.3
Philippines	3	2	4	57.1	9	12	18	108.0	5	4	10	108.3
Rwanda	2	2	3	41.7	1	0	1	40.0	0	0	0	0.0
Saudi Arabia	6	5	6	−4.8	0	0	0	NA	24	29	42	75.0
South Africa	20	17	15	−21.8	3	4	7	126.7	8	15	32	310.3
Spain	11	13	14	25.4	31	48	49	57.2	21	23	28	33.5
Thailand	6	6	3	−50.0	6	6	11	100.0	7	9	12	68.1
Turkey	3	7	5	40.6	0	0	0	NA	6	8	17	191.2
United Arab Emirates	14	13	9	−35.5	0	0	0	NA	43	39	49	13.2
United Kingdom	23	21	20	−12.8	26	25	26	−0.8	14	19	32	136.8
United States	47	44	40	−16.0	33	29	30	−8.8	26	40	49	85.6
Uruguay	76	47	18	−76.9	9	7	16	82.6	5	7	19	310.9
Venezuela	22	18	24	10.4	6	5	8	26.7	18	13	36	106.9
Vietnam	2	2	4	126.3	5	11	35	546.3	2	3	10	466.7
Africa	7	6	6	−9.9	1	1	1	100.0	2	3	6	200.0
Asia	2	3	4	121.1	6	10	15	146.8	2	3	9	319.0
Central America	11	13	15	43.8	15	8	13	−13.8	6	9	27	355.9
Europe	23	25	16	−30.9	32	35	34	5.9	12	15	22	87.2
North America	47	43	39	−16.7	33	28	30	−10.8	26	38	48	83.8
Oceania	50	43	35	−31.0	14	17	21	53.3	18	22	36	98.3
South America	28	27	31	11.0	7	6	10	41.7	9	12	30	228.3
World per capita consumption	11	10	10	−9.4	12	13	16	32.8	6	8	14	134.5

NA = Not applicable. **Note:** All figures are rounded. Percent change based on unrounded raw data.

World Capture of Fish, Crustaceans, and Mollusks, 2002-11

Source: UN Food and Agriculture Organization
(in thousands of metric tons; ranked by 2011 captures; total includes nations not shown)

Country	2002	2005	2009	2010	2011	Country	2002	2005	2009	2010	2011
China	14,174	14,589	14,920	15,417	15,772	Norway	2,740	2,393	2,524	2,680	2,281
Peru	8,765	9,388	6,914	4,261	8,248	Thailand	2,842	2,814	1,871	1,811	1,862
Indonesia	4,323	4,696	5,104	5,380	5,708	South Korea	1,694	1,647	1,859	1,733	1,747
U.S.	4,937	4,893	4,222	4,426	5,153	Bangladesh.	1,104	1,334	1,822	1,727	1,601
India	3,737	3,691	4,067	4,689	4,302	Mexico	1,451	1,320	1,613	1,529	1,566
Russia	3,232	3,198	3,826	4,070	4,255	Malaysia	1,276	1,214	1,398	1,433	1,379
Japan	4,374	4,313	4,091	4,069	3,761	Iceland	2,135	1,665	1,142	1,061	1,138
Myanmar	1,284	1,732	2,767	3,063	3,333	Spain	881	853	920	972	993
Chile	4,271	4,328	3,454	2,680	3,063	Morocco	962	1,026	1,165	1,136	959
Vietnam	1,803	1,988	2,281	2,414	2,503	World total	91,044	92,478	90,019	88,970	93,494
Philippines	2,030	2,270	2,603	2,612	2,363						

World Aquaculture Production, 2001-10

Source: UN Food and Agriculture Organization; ranked by 2010 production

Country	Metric tons (thous.)					Value (mil)				
	2001	2005	2008	2009	2010	2001	2005	2008	2009	2010
China	22,702	28,121	32,731	34,780	36,734	$23,050	$30,509	$51,346	$55,142	$59,142
India	2,120	2,967	3,851	3,792	4,649	2,393	3,763	6,240	5,648	9,085
Vietnam	588	1,437	2,462	2,556	2,672	1,346	2,931	4,606	4,803	5,150
Indonesia	864	1,197	1,690	1,733	2,305	2,397	1,999	2,814	3,206	4,895
Bangladesh	713	882	1,006	1,064	1,309	1,065	1,246	1,766	2,351	2,840
Thailand	814	1,304	1,331	1,417	1,286	1,752	1,741	2,346	2,623	2,817
Norway	511	662	848	962	1,008	1,020	2,136	3,139	3,590	5,020
Egypt	343	540	694	705	920	757	792	1,251	1,356	1,546
Myanmar (Burma)	121	485	675	778	851	320	959	817	912	956
Philippines	435	557	741	737	745	661	794	1,576	1,486	1,563
Japan	800	746	730	787	718	2,846	2,892	3,149	3,601	3,532
Chile	566	724	843	793	701	1,725	3,229	4,503	4,668	3,753
U.S.	480	514	500	480	495	804	896	976	953	1,016
Brazil	206	258	365	416	479	325	445	737	806	949
South Korea	294	437	474	473	476	484	1,195	1,287	1,361	1,482
Malaysia	158	176	243	333	373	318	339	564	676	839
Taiwan	297	305	324	286	310	895	969	1,069	910	1,116
Ecuador	58	139	172	218	272	272	610	765	1,010	1,247
Spain	309	219	250	267	252	339	308	557	519	520
France	252	245	238	234	224	454	674	1,018	959	871
World total[1]	34,614	44,296	52,946	55,714	59,873	48,554	65,933	100,693	106,498	119,444

Note: Does not include production of aquatic plants or marine mammals. (1) Includes nations not shown.

U.S. Commercial Landings of Fish and Shellfish, 1990-2011

Source: Natl. Marine Fisheries Service, Natl. Oceanic and Atmospheric Admin., U.S. Dept. of Commerce

Year	Landings for human food		Landings for industrial purposes[1]		Total	
	Weight (mil lbs)	Value (mil)	Weight (mil lbs)	Value (mil)	Weight (mil lbs)	Value (mil)
1990	7,041	$3,366	2,363	$156	9,404	$3,522
1995	7,667	3,625	2,121	145	9,788	3,770
1996	7,474	3,355	2,091	132	9,565	3,487
1997	7,244	3,285	2,598	163	9,842	3,448
1998	7,173	3,009	2,021	119	9,194	3,128
1999	6,832	3,265	2,507	202	9,339	3,467
2000	6,912	3,398	2,157	152	9,069	3,550
2001	7,311	3,064	2,178	154	9,489	3,218
2002	7,205	2,940	2,192	152	9,397	3,092
2003	7,521	3,185	1,986	157	9,507	3,347
2004	7,794	3,611	1,889	145	9,683	3,756
2005	7,997	3,825	1,710	117	9,707	3,942
2006	7,842	3,911	1,641	113	9,483	4,024
2007	7,490	4,015	1,819	177	9,309	4,192
2008	6,633	4,231	1,692	152	8,325	4,383
2009	6,198	3,733	1,833	158	8,031	3,891
2010	6,526	4,356	1,705	164	8,231	4,520
2011[2]	7,911	5,116	2,179	187	10,090	5,303

Note: Does not include products of aquaculture, except oysters and clams. Landings reported in round (live) weight for all items except univalve and bivalve mollusks (e.g., clams, oysters, and scallops), which are reported in weight of meats (excluding the shell). (1) Processed into meal, oil, solubles, and shell products or used as bait or animal food. (2) Preliminary.

U.S. Domestic Landings by Region, 2005, 2011

Source: Natl. Marine Fisheries Service, Natl. Oceanic and Atmospheric Admin., U.S. Dept. of Commerce

Region	2005		2011[1]	
	Weight (thous. lbs)	Value (thous.)	Weight (thous. lbs)	Value (thous.)
New England	684,090	$971,663	623,606	$1,117,048
Middle Atlantic	199,937	221,505	207,572	256,659
Chesapeake	508,953	218,933	571,564	268,386
South Atlantic	122,422	125,117	124,582	176,477
Gulf	1,196,355	620,987	1,984,244	797,000
Pacific Coast incl. Alaska	6,950,647	1,700,927	6,530,947	2,579,607
Great Lakes[2]	16,732	12,434	17,811	17,241
Hawaii	28,139	70,811	29,289	91,565
Total	9,707,275	3,942,376	10,089,615	5,303,983

Note: Landings reported in round (live) weight for all items except univalve and bivalve mollusks (e.g., clams, oysters, scallops), which are reported in weight of meats (excluding the shell). (1) Preliminary. (2) Data for the Great Lakes states lag by one year.

EMPLOYMENT

Employment and Unemployment in the U.S., 1900-2012

Source: Bureau of Labor Statistics, U.S. Dept. of Labor

(civilian labor force, persons 16 years of age and older unless otherwise noted; annual averages, in thousands)

Year	Employed	Unemployed Number	Rate	Year	Employed	Unemployed Number	Rate	Year	Employed	Unemployed Number	Rate
1900[1] ...	26,956	1,420	5.0%	1987	112,440	7,425	6.2%	1999	133,488	5,880	4.2%
1910[1] ...	34,599	2,150	5.9	1988	114,968	6,701	5.5	2001	136,933	6,801	4.7
1920[1] ...	39,208	2,132	5.2	1989	117,342	6,528	5.3	2002	136,485	8,378	5.8
1930[1] ...	44,183	4,340	8.9	1990	118,793	7,047	5.6	2003	137,736	8,774	6.0
1940[1] ...	47,520	8,120	14.6	1991	117,718	8,628	6.8	2004	139,252	8,149	5.5
1950	58,918	3,288	5.0	1992	118,492	9,613	7.5	2005	141,730	7,591	5.1
1955	62,170	2,852	4.4	1993	120,259	8,940	6.9	2006	144,427	7,001	4.6
1960	65,778	3,852	5.5	1994	123,060	7,996	6.1	2007	146,047	7,078	4.6
1965	71,088	3,366	4.5	1995	124,900	7,404	5.6	2008	145,362	8,924	5.8
1970	78,678	4,093	4.9	1996	126,708	7,236	5.4	2009	139,877	14,265	9.3
1975	85,846	7,929	8.5	1997	129,558	6,739	4.9	2010	139,064	14,825	9.6
1980	99,303	7,637	7.1	1998	131,463	6,210	4.5	2011	139,869	13,747	8.9
1985	107,150	8,312	7.2	2000	136,891	5,692	4.0	2012	142,469	12,506	8.1
1986	109,597	8,237	7.0								

Note: Because of revisions in population controls, data for a given year may not be strictly comparable to other years. Other unemployment rates (1905-45), 14 years of age and older: 1905, 4.3; 1915, 8.5; 1925, 3.2; 1935, 20.3; 1936, 16.9; 1937, 14.3; 1938, 19.0; 1939, 17.2; 1945, 1.9. (1) Persons 14 years of age and older.

Unemployment Insurance Data by State, 2012

Source: Employment and Training Admin., U.S. Dept. of Labor; state programs only

State/ terr.	Unemployment rate	Monetarily eligible claimants	Number of first payments	Number of final payments	Initial claims	Benefits paid	Average weekly benefit	Employers subject to state law
AL	7.3%	153,538	102,277	41,564	275,594	$299,300,944	$204	85,396
AK	7.0	54,128	33,633	20,771	78,649	142,389,425	245	17,737
AZ	8.3	176,149	127,183	69,237	273,105	424,508,787	212	122,204
AR	7.3	122,856	83,513	35,195	199,667	313,938,816	289	67,051
CA	10.5	1,614,564	1,248,618	696,740	3,015,698	5,981,643,607	295	1,286,230
CO	8.0	142,664	114,811	65,346	178,876	594,383,516	347	148,806
CT	8.4	172,513	146,518	64,459	264,798	785,895,658	337	96,814
DE	7.1	34,868	22,372	13,026	54,516	113,030,538	245	25,644
DC	8.9	27,416	26,109	15,767	21,399	138,809,077	296	29,232
FL	8.6	516,634	271,595	204,669	794,350	1,193,945,899	232	469,200
GA	9.0	341,387	238,525	125,130	601,428	774,081,007	272	204,638
HI	5.8	42,431	33,074	14,243	92,767	225,039,034	421	30,472
ID	7.1	72,438	53,983	24,015	121,137	162,493,861	253	46,791
IL	8.9	412,488	414,266	185,528	754,644	2,095,603,061	314	301,127
IN	8.4	230,738	180,558	81,173	357,404	648,564,525	284	129,826
IA	5.2	122,066	99,107	35,193	177,138	401,346,564	325	74,847
KS	5.7	93,988	78,252	35,316	159,627	273,937,546	329	69,055
KY	8.2	162,643	85,673	38,145	269,651	443,308,022	290	86,538
LA	6.4	134,351	80,333	35,838	177,715	269,422,190	199	103,592
ME	7.3	55,880	42,050	17,444	87,447	163,455,226	279	41,758
MD	6.8	174,249	136,554	65,271	321,652	730,774,398	327	137,445
MA	6.7	154,373	259,341	122,716	415,479	1,582,700,522	392	195,589
MI	9.1	386,665	321,939	154,222	709,182	1,281,481,968	292	198,128
MN	5.6	202,181	144,931	64,240	285,358	752,210,797	361	128,006
MS	9.2	99,478	67,527	27,818	149,801	174,840,762	193	53,431
MO	6.9	225,327	149,970	75,571	395,226	490,687,061	239	138,732
MT	6.0	43,884	28,285	14,368	70,601	119,113,033	270	36,636
NE	3.9	58,268	39,668	20,222	92,603	126,468,207	265	53,391
NV	11.1	120,705	98,107	50,913	218,835	493,414,764	304	57,278
NH	5.5	45,516	29,371	8,635	69,357	113,979,654	280	40,205
NJ	9.5	444,647	386,591	186,893	690,800	2,324,269,370	396	227,529
NM	6.9	89,673	44,635	25,030	87,111	229,740,189	301	43,728
NY	8.5	841,532	635,600	289,772	1,363,220	3,043,106,216	305	505,473
NC	9.5	413,864	284,522	159,973	676,248	1,222,949,516	298	196,604
ND	3.1	22,912	16,563	6,119	26,466	70,119,777	354	23,411
OH	7.2	327,576	249,906	92,946	627,063	1,132,412,029	305	218,324
OK	5.2	97,891	60,636	31,906	138,064	252,861,928	274	83,642
OR	8.7	194,372	139,239	67,667	405,684	704,649,511	302	110,830
PA	7.9	595,357	502,609	204,218	1,293,047	2,882,033,942	348	314,065
PR	14.5	100,910	84,139	48,714	140,011	196,463,073	118	47,390
RI	10.4	50,012	42,126	21,778	88,104	250,018,596	377	32,807
SC	9.1	168,667	104,714	55,534	274,678	304,324,206	242	96,591
SD	4.4	12,964	7,691	1,906	19,333	33,340,436	264	25,807
TN	8.0	187,325	146,946	75,328	315,020	494,190,579	235	113,135
TX	6.8	649,783	459,806	240,709	887,714	2,101,331,838	325	472,079
UT	5.7	75,364	53,687	22,095	101,482	207,499,106	326	69,396
VT	5.0	29,352	23,619	5,603	46,603	87,591,223	306	21,648
VA	5.9	223,350	132,668	67,952	313,953	586,948,635	290	195,515
VI	NA	4,631	4,282	2,097	5,222	20,721,851	355	3,404
WA	8.2	280,298	217,523	86,188	511,680	1,195,750,860	378	216,139
WV	7.3	73,913	56,193	17,360	90,987	220,195,185	273	36,086
WI	6.9	302,109	232,949	88,685	618,738	869,050,459	271	131,527
WY	5.4	23,639	16,790	6,643	28,087	77,512,786	347	21,977
U.S.	8.1	11,404,527	8,661,577	4,227,891	19,433,019	43,107,603,742	303	7,682,900

NA = Not available.

Unemployed Persons in the U.S. by Industry and Duration of Unemployment, 2012

Source: Bureau of Labor Statistics, U.S. Dept. of Labor

Occupation	Total	Number of unemployed persons (thous.)				Weeks of unemployment	
		Less than 5 weeks	5 to 14 weeks	15 to 26 weeks	27 weeks and over	Average (mean) duration	Median duration
Management, professional, and related	2,318	445	511	340	1,022	42.6	21.5
Management, business, and financial operations	935	146	189	144	456	46.9	26.0
Professional and related	1,383	299	322	196	566	39.7	18.7
Service	2,540	584	600	386	971	35.9	17.2
Sales and office	2,775	534	618	411	1,211	41.8	21.4
Sales and related	1,318	276	304	191	547	39.7	19.3
Office and administrative support	1,457	258	314	220	664	43.6	23.4
Natural resources, construction, and maintenance	1,668	381	373	238	676	39.3	18.3
Farming, fishing, and forestry	167	46	54	31	37	22.9	11.6
Construction and extraction	1,181	272	252	173	484	39.5	18.9
Installation, maintenance, and repair	320	64	67	34	155	46.9	24.8
Production, transportation, and material moving	1,845	392	413	268	773	39.7	19.8
Production	865	168	190	127	379	43.0	21.7
Transportation and material moving	980	224	223	140	394	36.7	18.2
Industry[1]							
Agriculture and related industries	194	49	63	34	48	25.3	12.4
Mining, quarrying, and oil and gas extraction	60	18	17	8	17	26.8	10.9
Construction	1,152	262	247	179	464	38.4	18.7
Manufacturing	1,134	185	246	169	533	46.8	24.4
Durable goods	701	113	145	103	341	48.5	26.2
Nondurable goods	433	72	102	66	192	44.2	21.7
Wholesale and retail trade	1,684	339	375	240	731	40.7	20.8
Transportation and utilities	449	96	91	65	198	39.6	21.3
Information	225	41	42	35	107	46.2	25.9
Financial activities	482	72	98	67	245	48.1	28.3
Professional and business services	1,394	280	321	214	580	39.4	19.8
Education and health services	1,642	358	376	239	668	38.0	18.9
Leisure and hospitality	1,462	349	374	220	519	34.6	15.0
Other services	475	107	107	69	192	39.6	18.5
Public administration	246	48	54	31	112	39.9	23.1
No previous work experience	1,316	302	341	209	464	35.6	15.5

(1) Includes wage and salary workers only.

Persons Not in the U.S. Labor Force, 2012

Source: Bureau of Labor Statistics, U.S. Dept. of Labor

The Labor Dept.'s unemployment rate, based on its household survey, shows the number of people out of work as a percentage of U.S. adults age 16 and older in the labor force. That rate excludes, however, the millions of adults considered not to be in the labor force.

(in thousands)

	Number	Age in years			Sex	
		16 to 24	25 to 54	55 and over	Men	Women
Total not in the labor force	88,310	17,499	23,061	47,750	35,017	53,293
Do not want a job now[1]	81,752	15,383	20,248	46,120	31,989	49,763
Want a job[1]	6,558	2,115	2,813	1,630	3,028	3,530
Did not search for work in previous year	3,390	1,064	1,328	998	1,490	1,900
Searched in previous year but not previous 4 weeks.[2]	3,168	1,052	1,484	632	1,537	1,630
Not available to work now	651	282	288	82	253	399
Available to work now	2,516	770	1,196	550	1,285	1,232
Reason not currently looking[3]						
Discouragement over job prospects[4]	909	217	451	241	541	368
Reasons other than discouragement	1,608	553	746	309	743	864
Family responsibilities	229	33	147	49	61	168
In school or training	339	257	73	9	175	164
Ill health or disability	168	18	83	66	80	87
Other[5]	871	245	442	185	427	444

(1) Includes some persons who are not asked if they want a job. (2) Persons who had a job in the prior 12 months must have searched since the end of that job to be considered unemployed. (3) Of those available to work now. (4) Includes believing no work is available, not being able to find work, lacking necessary schooling or training, thought of as too young or old by employers, and other types of discrimination. (5) Includes those who did not actively look for work in the prior four weeks for such reasons as child care and transportation problems, as well as a small number for which reason for nonparticipation was not ascertained.

U.S. Displaced Workers, 2012

Source: Bureau of Labor Statistics, U.S. Dept. of Labor

	Number (thous.)	Reason for job loss		
		Plant or company closed down or moved	Insufficient work	Position or shift abolished
Total displaced workers	6,121	30.8%	39.5%	29.7%
Age: 20 to 24 years	128	40.5	39.3	20.3
25 to 54 years	4,268	31.8	40.2	28.0
55 to 64 years	1,338	27.8	37.0	35.2
65 years and over	386	26.7	40.8	32.5
Sex: Men	3,440	31.1	43.2	25.7
Women	2,681	30.4	34.8	34.8
Race: White	5,027	30.2	38.9	30.9
Black	662	33.5	41.0	25.5
Asian	230	30.5	46.9	22.7
Hispanic or Latino	901	35.9	50.1	14.0

Note: As of Jan. 2012. Displaced workers are persons age 20 or older who lost or left jobs they had held for at least three years. Workers in this table were displaced between Jan. 2009 and Dec. 2011. Hispanic or Latino persons may be of any race.

U.S. Unemployment Rates by Selected Characteristics, 1995-2013

Source: Bureau of Labor Statistics, U.S. Dept. of Labor

	1995	2000	2005	2008	2009	2010	2011	2012 Jan.	2012 June	2012 Yr.	2013 Jan.	2013 June
Total (all civilian workers)	**5.6%**	**4.0%**	**5.1%**	**5.8%**	**9.3%**	**9.6%**	**8.9%**	**8.8%**	**8.4%**	**8.1%**	**8.5%**	**7.8%**
Men, 20 years and older	4.8	3.3	4.4	5.4	9.6	9.8	8.7	8.7	7.5	7.5	8.4	6.8
Women, 20 years and older	4.9	3.6	4.6	4.9	7.5	8.0	7.9	7.8	7.6	7.3	7.4	7.0
Both sexes, 16 to 19 years	17.3	13.1	16.6	18.7	24.3	25.9	24.4	24.2	26.5	24.0	24.2	26.6
White	4.9	3.5	4.4	5.2	8.5	8.7	7.9	8.0	7.5	7.2	7.6	6.8
Black	10.4	7.6	10.0	10.1	14.8	16.0	15.8	14.2	14.8	13.8	14.3	14.3
Asian	—	3.6	4.0	4.0	7.3	7.5	7.0	6.7	6.3	5.9	6.5	5.0
Hispanic or Latino (of any race)	9.3	5.7	6.0	7.6	12.1	12.5	11.5	11.5	11.0	10.3	10.5	9.1
Married men, spouse present	3.3	—	—	3.4	6.6	6.8	5.8	5.1	4.9	4.9	4.6	4.3
Married women, spouse present	3.9	—	—	3.6	5.5	5.9	5.6	5.6	5.4	5.3	5.2	4.6
Women who maintain families, spouse absent	8.0	5.9	7.8	8.0	11.5	12.3	12.4	12.0	11.8	11.4	11.3	10.7
Occupation												
Management, professional, and related	2.4	1.8	2.3	2.7	4.6	4.7	4.5	4.3	4.4	4.1	3.9	4.2
Service	7.5	5.2	6.4	6.7	9.6	10.3	9.9	10.6	9.0	9.1	10.0	9.3
Sales and office	5.0	3.8	4.8	5.3	8.5	9.0	8.7	8.2	8.1	7.7	8.5	6.9
Nat. resources, constr., and maintenance	—	5.3	6.5	8.8	15.6	16.1	13.3	14.6	10.0	11.5	13.3	8.9
Prod., transp., and material moving	—	5.1	6.5	7.6	13.3	12.8	11.3	10.8	9.8	9.8	11.1	8.7
Industry												
Nonagricultural, private wage, and salary workers	5.8	4.1	5.2	5.9	9.8	9.9	9.0	9.0	7.9	7.9	8.6	7.2
Mining	5.2	4.4	3.1	3.1	11.6	9.4	6.1	9.4	4.8	6.0	9.6	6.4
Construction	11.5	6.2	7.4	10.6	19.0	20.6	16.4	17.7	12.8	13.9	16.1	9.8
Manufacturing	4.9	3.5	4.9	5.8	12.1	10.6	9.0	8.4	6.9	7.3	7.9	6.4
Durable goods	4.4	3.2	4.6	5.6	12.9	11.2	9.2	8.3	6.8	7.2	7.1	5.9
Nondurable goods	5.7	4.0	5.3	6.0	10.6	9.6	8.5	8.6	7.0	7.5	9.1	7.1
Wholesale and retail trade	6.5	4.3	5.4	5.9	9.0	9.5	8.9	9.3	8.3	8.1	8.2	7.0
Transportation and utilities	4.5	3.4	4.1	5.1	8.9	8.4	8.2	7.0	7.2	6.9	7.7	6.3
Information	—	3.2	5.0	5.0	9.2	9.7	7.3	7.9	7.1	7.6	8.2	5.6
Financial activities	3.3	2.4	2.9	3.9	6.4	6.9	6.4	4.9	5.6	5.1	5.5	4.7
Professional and business services	—	4.8	6.2	6.5	10.8	10.8	9.7	9.5	8.9	8.9	10.4	8.2
Education and health services	—	2.5	3.4	3.5	5.3	5.8	5.6	5.5	6.2	5.5	5.4	5.6
Leisure and hospitality	—	6.6	7.8	8.6	11.7	12.2	11.6	12.6	9.8	10.4	12.0	10.7
Other services	8.4	3.9	4.8	5.3	7.5	8.5	8.8	9.3	7.5	7.2	7.9	6.3
Agriculture and related	11.1	9.0	8.3	9.2	14.3	13.9	12.5	17.6	8.4	12.4	13.1	8.2
Government	2.9	2.1	2.6	2.4	3.6	4.4	4.7	4.2	5.2	4.3	4.2	5.2
Self-employed and unpaid family workers	—	2.1	2.7	3.6	5.5	5.9	6.0	5.8	5.0	5.4	5.8	5.0

— = Not available. **Note:** All monthly rates are unadjusted, except for married men and women, which are seasonally adjusted.

Employed Persons in the U.S. by Occupation and Sex, 2011-12

Source: Bureau of Labor Statistics, U.S. Dept. of Labor

(persons 16 years of age and older; numbers in thousands)

	Total 2011	Total 2012	Men 2011	Men 2012	Women 2011	Women 2012
Total	139,869	142,469	74,290	75,555	65,579	66,914
Management, professional, and related occupations	52,547	54,043	25,552	26,208	26,995	27,834
Management, business, and financial operations	21,589	22,678	12,275	12,779	9,314	9,899
Management	15,250	16,042	9,439	9,849	5,812	6,194
Business and financial operations	6,339	6,636	2,837	2,931	3,503	3,705
Professional and related	30,957	31,365	13,277	13,429	17,681	17,936
Computer and mathematical	3,608	3,816	2,705	2,841	903	976
Architecture and engineering	2,785	2,846	2,406	2,457	379	390
Life, physical, and social science	1,303	1,316	687	720	616	596
Community and social services	2,352	2,265	835	819	1,518	1,446
Legal	1,770	1,786	889	885	881	901
Education, training, and library	8,619	8,543	2,274	2,253	6,345	6,290
Arts, design, entertainment, sports, and media	2,779	2,814	1,499	1,456	1,281	1,358
Healthcare practitioner and technical	7,740	7,977	1,982	1,998	5,758	5,979
Service occupations	24,787	25,459	10,929	11,135	13,858	14,324
Healthcare support	3,359	3,496	413	434	2,945	3,062
Protective service	3,210	3,096	2,546	2,449	664	647
Food preparation and serving related	7,747	8,018	3,534	3,648	4,213	4,370
Building and grounds cleaning and maintenance	5,492	5,591	3,359	3,430	2,133	2,160
Personal care and service	4,979	5,258	1,077	1,173	3,902	4,085
Sales and office occupations	33,066	33,152	12,450	12,653	20,616	20,500
Sales and related	15,330	15,457	7,733	7,922	7,597	7,535
Office and administrative support	17,736	17,695	4,717	4,730	13,019	12,965
Natural resources, construction, and maintenance occupations	13,009	12,821	12,457	12,266	552	554
Farming, fishing, and forestry	1,001	994	785	768	216	226
Construction and extraction	7,125	7,005	6,962	6,832	163	173
Installation, maintenance, and repair	4,883	4,821	4,710	4,666	173	156
Production, transportation, and material moving occupations	16,461	16,994	12,902	13,294	3,558	3,701
Production	8,142	8,455	5,826	6,109	2,316	2,346
Transportation and material moving	8,318	8,540	7,076	7,185	1,242	1,355

Note: Numbers may not add up to totals because of independent rounding.

Projected Openings for Selected High-Paying Occupations, 2010-20

Source: Employment Projections Program, Bureau of Labor Statistics, U.S. Dept. of Labor

Job openings shown below represent the average number expected each year, from 2010 to 2020, for workers in the U.S. who are entering these occupations for the first time.

Occupation	Annual avg. job openings[1]	Median annual earnings[2]	Occupation	Annual avg. job openings[1]	Median annual earnings[2]
Registered nurses	1,207,400	$64,690	Accountants and auditors	452,100	$61,690
Truck drivers, heavy and tractor-trailer	649,400	37,770	Gen. and operations mgrs.	410,100	94,400
Postsecondary teachers	586,100	62,050	Carpenters	408,300	39,530
First-line office and admin. support supvrs.	584,400	47,460	Gen. maintenance and repair workers	379,100	34,730
Elementary school teachers[3]	573,200	51,660	Lic. practical and voc. nurses	369,200	40,380
Sales representatives[4]	559,900	52,440	Secondary school teachers[3]	355,600	53,230
First-line retail supvrs.	513,700	35,820	Business operations specialists[5]	327,200	62,450
Bookkeeping, accounting, auditing clerks	467,800	34,030			

(1) As a result of growth and net replacement needs. (2) For 2010. (3) Except special and vocation education. (4) Wholesale and manufacturing, except technical and scientific products. (5) Except agents, business mgrs. of artists, performers, and athletes; buyers and purchasing agents; claims adjusters, appraisers, examiners, and investigators; compliance officers; cost estimators; human resource workers; logisticians; management analysts; meeting, convention, and event planners; compensation, benefits, and job analysis specialists; training and development specialists; and market research analysts and specialists.

Highest Average Weekly Wages by County, 2012

Source: Bureau of Labor Statistics, U.S. Dept. of Labor

County	Avg. weekly wage	% change, 2011-12	County	Avg. weekly wage	% change, 2011-12
San Mateo, CA	$3,240	107.3%	Douglas, CO	$1,591	48.0%
New York, NY	2,107	11.5	Fairfax, VA	1,588	4.3
Santa Clara, CA	1,906	5.0	Morris, NJ	1,476	5.4
Suffolk, MA	1,724	8.0	Alexandria City, VA	1,460	2.5
Fairfield, CT	1,704	6.8	Middlesex, MA	1,434	4.5
Washington, DC	1,703	2.2	Somerset, NJ	1,429	2.2
San Francisco, CA	1,694	7.6	Westchester, NY	1,346	5.4
Arlington, VA	1,625	2.1	United States	1,000	4.7

Note: Figures shown are for 4th quarter, from among the 329 largest U.S. counties, which comprise 71.3% of total covered workers. Horry County, SC, recorded the lowest average weekly earnings among the largest counties, with an average weekly wage of $576 in the 4th quarter of 2012. It was followed by Cameron County, TX ($609); Hidalgo County, TX ($612); Lake County, FL ($653); Yakima County, WA ($679); and Pasco County, FL ($681). Data include all workers covered by state and federal unemployment insurance programs.

Federal Minimum Hourly Wage Rates

Source: Bureau of Labor Statistics, U.S. Dept. of Labor

Effective date	Minimum wage	% avg. earnings[1]	In 2013 dollars	Effective date	Minimum wage	% avg. earnings[1]	In 2013 dollars
Oct. 24, 1938	$0.25	40%	$4.13	Jan. 1, 1978	$2.65	43%	$9.46
Oct. 24, 1939	0.30	48	5.02	Jan. 1, 1979	2.90	43	9.30
Oct. 24, 1945	0.40	39	5.17	Jan. 1, 1980	3.10	43	8.76
Jan. 25, 1950	0.75	52	7.24	Jan. 1, 1981	3.35	42	8.58
Mar. 1, 1956	1.00	51	8.56	Apr. 1, 1990	3.80	35	6.77
Sept. 3, 1961	1.15	50	8.95	Apr. 1, 1991	4.25	38	7.26
Sept. 3, 1963	1.25	51	9.51	Oct. 1, 1996	4.75	37	7.05
Feb. 1, 1967	1.40	49	9.76	Sept. 1, 1997	5.15	39	7.47
Feb. 1, 1968	1.60	53	10.70	July 24, 2007	5.85	34	6.57
May 1, 1974	2.00	45	9.44	July 24, 2008	6.55	37	7.08
Jan. 1, 1975	2.10	43	9.09	July 24, 2009	7.25	40	7.87
Jan. 1, 1976	2.30	44	9.41				

Note: Before 1961, the minimum wage applied primarily to employees engaged in, or producing goods for, interstate commerce. Coverage was added 1961-64 primarily to employees in large retail and service enterprises and to local transit, construction, and gas station employees. Coverage was added 1966-77 (at reduced rates) to farm workers; federal, state, and local government employees; workers in various retail and service trades; and certain domestic workers. Starting in 1978, the minimum wage applied equally to all covered, nonexempt workers. At present, exceptions apply under specific circumstances to workers with disabilities, full-time students, youths under age 20 in their first 90 consecutive calendar days of employment, tipped employees, and student-learners. (1) Percent of gross hourly earnings of production workers in manufacturing.

Fatal Occupational Injuries, 2012

Source: Census of Fatal Occupational Injuries, Bureau of Labor Statistics, U.S. Dept. of Labor, in cooperation with other agencies

Event or exposure	Number	%	Event or exposure	Number	%
Total	4,383	100%	Contact with objects and equipment	712	16%
			Struck by object or equipment	509	12
Transportation incidents	1,789	41	Struck by falling object or equipment	233	5
Roadway, involving motorized land vehicles	1,044	24	Struck by flying object or equipment	27	1
Collision between vehicles	512	12	Caught in or compressed by equipment or objects	122	3
Vehicle struck object on side of road	282	6	Caught in running equipment or machinery	92	2
Noncollision	228	5	Caught in or crushed in collapsing materials	74	2
Jackknifed or overturned	187	4			
Nonroadway	227	5	Falls, slips, trips	668	15
Jackknifed or overturned	111	3	Falls to lower level	544	12
Pedestrian vehicular incident	283	6	Fall on same level	108	2
Railway vehicle incident	33	1			
Water vehicle incident	64	1	Exposure to harmful substances or environments	320	7
Aircraft incident	125	3	Contact with electric current	156	4
			Contact with temperature extremes	40	1
Violence by persons or animals	767	17	Exposure to other harmful substances	94	2
Homicides	463	11	Inhalation of harmful substance	40	1
Shooting	375	9			
Stabbing	32	1	Fires and explosions	116	3
Self-inflicted injuries	225	5			

Note: Totals for categories may include subcategories not shown separately. Percentages show incidence rate per total fatalities. Numbers are preliminary.

U.S. Occupational Injuries and Illnesses Involving Days Away From Work, 2011

Source: Bureau of Labor Statistics, U.S. Dept. of Labor

Characteristic	Illnesses/ injuries[2]	Days-away-from-work cases[1] involving—							Median days away from work
		1 day	2 days	3-5 days	6-10 days	11-20 days	21-30 days	31 days or more	
Total	908,310	13.9%	10.8%	17.8%	11.8%	11.3%	6.5%	27.9%	8
Gender									
Male	559,740	13.3	10.2	17.3	11.7	11.3	6.9	29.3	9
Female	344,730	14.9	11.8	18.6	12.0	11.1	6.0	25.5	7
Age[3]									
14-15.	200	10.0	80.0	NA	NA	NA	NA	NA	2
16-19.	20,030	25.2	14.9	22.5	11.7	9.1	4.2	12.6	3
20-24.	85,940	19.7	13.7	21.8	13.3	11.1	5.1	15.3	5
25-34.	198,660	16.4	12.5	20.2	12.1	11.0	5.9	22.0	6
35-44.	202,270	13.3	11.0	17.0	11.8	10.6	6.4	29.8	9
45-54.	225,680	11.5	9.5	16.2	11.3	11.6	7.4	32.6	12
55-64.	133,740	10.7	8.6	15.2	11.9	11.7	7.3	34.7	14
65 and over	26,670	7.9	7.2	16.6	11.1	13.8	7.0	36.3	14
Occupation(s)									
Management.	21,910	14.3	12.7	23.1	10.9	10.9	3.8	24.4	5
Business, financial operations	5,780	14.5	11.1	17.0	8.7	11.1	5.2	32.5	10
Computer and mathematical.	2,180	16.1	18.8	16.5	11.9	7.8	15.1	14.2	5
Architecture, engineering	2,860	24.8	7.7	15.4	11.9	11.5	4.2	24.8	7
Life, physical, social science	1,530	18.3	13.7	15.0	17.6	11.8	3.9	19.6	6
Community, social services.	6,560	14.8	12.2	23.6	17.8	10.2	5.3	16.0	5
Legal	970	9.3	5.2	10.3	6.2	4.1	58.8	6.2	22
Education, training, library	7,960	19.7	13.6	22.5	10.7	10.4	3.6	19.5	4
Arts, design, entertainment, sports, media.	5,760	11.6	9.5	14.1	8.3	21.0	7.3	28.1	14
Health care practitioners	49,910	15.0	12.6	19.6	13.8	11.3	6.1	21.6	6
Health care support	61,640	15.4	12.4	20.4	13.3	10.6	6.5	21.5	6
Protective service	9,580	13.0	12.9	17.2	11.1	11.0	6.7	28.0	8
Food preparation, serving	66,980	16.1	13.2	20.5	12.8	11.1	5.2	21.0	6
Building and grounds cleaning, maintenance	59,440	14.9	11.1	20.8	12.8	9.7	5.9	24.8	7
Personal care, service.	22,450	17.1	11.8	19.5	12.2	10.1	6.6	22.5	6
Sales.	57,220	14.0	12.0	18.3	11.0	11.1	6.1	27.6	8
Office administrative support.	72,250	14.5	10.9	17.3	12.6	11.7	5.9	27.1	8
Farming, fishing, forestry.	13,910	14.2	9.4	20.7	12.9	13.0	7.3	22.4	7
Construction, extraction	73,000	11.8	9.1	14.1	10.8	11.8	7.0	35.4	14
Installation, maintenance, repair . . .	85,570	13.4	9.3	16.5	11.9	11.7	7.5	29.8	10
Production.	109,960	14.9	11.0	16.4	11.3	12.1	6.5	27.9	9
Transportation, material moving.	168,980	11.0	9.0	16.1	10.8	11.0	7.3	34.8	13
Length of service with employer									
Less than 3 months.	88,540	17.1	13.0	18.8	12.0	9.7	6.2	23.1	6
3-11 months	163,570	16.2	11.9	19.2	12.1	11.0	5.4	24.2	6
1-5 years	315,900	14.4	11.6	19.0	11.7	10.8	6.3	26.3	7
More than 5 years	325,090	11.5	9.0	15.7	11.8	12.0	7.5	32.4	12
Race or ethnic origin[4]									
White only	377,530	15.6	11.6	18.0	11.3	11.0	6.9	25.6	7
Hispanic or Latino only	117,210	13.6	11.6	17.0	12.6	11.1	6.4	27.8	8
Black only	70,290	14.1	11.6	19.4	11.8	11.0	5.7	26.5	7
Asian only	12,070	13.5	11.3	18.6	15.1	11.3	8.3	21.9	7
American Indian or Alaskan Native only	4,350	20.7	9.9	19.8	14.0	9.2	4.8	21.4	5
Native Hawaiian or Pacific Islander only	2,880	14.6	7.6	17.4	10.1	10.8	5.2	34.4	11
More than one race	660	16.7	4.5	25.8	7.6	15.2	10.6	21.2	7
Hispanic or Latino and other race . .	500	6.0	8.0	18.0	12.0	12.0	10.0	34.0	14
Not reported	322,840	11.9	9.5	17.5	12.1	11.6	6.4	31.1	10

NA = Not available. (1) Cases include those that resulted in days away from work, some of which also included job transfers or restrictions. (2) Number of nonfatal occupational injuries and illnesses involving days away from work for private industry workers; excludes farms with fewer than 11 employees. (3) Information is not shown separately for injured workers under age 14; they accounted for fewer than 50 cases. (4) Some cases may be counted as "More than one race" and another category.

Civilian Employment of the Executive Branch, 1940-2011

Source: U.S. Office of Personnel Management

(numbers in thousands)

Year	Total executive branch	Dept. of Defense	Civilian agencies/depts.									
			Total employees	Agriculture	HHS, Education, Social Sec.[1]	Homeland Sec.	Interior	Justice	Transportation	Treasury	Veterans Affairs	Other
1940	699	256	443	98	9	18	46	11	NA	45	40	176
1945	3,370	2,635	736	82	11	20	45	19	NA	84	65	409
1950	1,439	753	686	84	13	20	66	20	NA	76	188	219
1955	1,860	1,187	673	86	40	21	54	24	NA	65	178	206
1960	1,808	1,047	761	99	62	21	56	24	NA	62	172	265
1965	1,901	1,034	867	113	87	21	71	27	NA	74	167	307
1970	2,203	1,219	983	118	112	23	75	33	62	84	169	308
1975	2,149	1,042	1,107	121	147	31	80	47	69	101	213	297
1980	2,161	960	1,201	129	163	40	77	48	66	102	228	346
1985	2,252	1,107	1,145	122	147	40	80	55	56	110	247	286
1990	2,250	1,034	1,216	123	129	49	78	71	61	132	248	326
1991	2,243	1,013	1,230	126	135	50	82	77	64	139	256	302
1992	2,225	952	1,274	128	136	56	85	82	64	133	260	329
1993	2,157	891	1,266	124	135	56	85	82	63	127	268	326
1994	2,085	850	1,235	120	133	55	81	83	59	128	262	315
1995	2,012	802	1,210	113	132	56	76	87	58	128	264	297
2000	1,778	651	1,127	104	126	70	74	98	58	113	220	265
2001	1,792	647	1,145	109	129	73	76	99	59	117	226	258
2002	1,818	645	1,173	98	130	76	77	96	96	118	223	258
2003	1,867	636	1,231	100	131	153	72	102	58	132	226	257
2004	1,882	644	1,238	111	130	153	77	104	57	111	236	257
2005	1,872	649	1,224	108	131	147	76	105	56	108	235	258
2006	1,880	653	1,227	105	129	154	72	107	54	107	239	260
2007	1,888	651	1,237	103	129	159	72	107	54	104	254	254
2008	1,960	670	1,289	104	132	172	76	109	55	106	274	261
2009	2,094	737	1,357	104	139	180	75	113	57	109	297	283
2010	2,133	773	1,360	107	144	183	70	118	58	110	305	265
2011	2,146	774	1,372	104	143	194	77	117	58	108	314	257

NA = Not available. **Note:** End-of-fiscal-year count; U.S. Postal Service excluded. (1) Estimated, 1940-50.

Median Earnings by Industry and Sex, 2011

Source: 2011 American Community Survey, U.S. Census Bureau, U.S. Dept. of Commerce

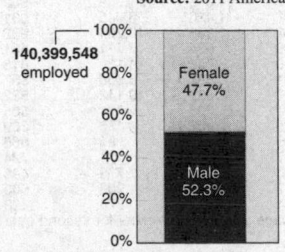

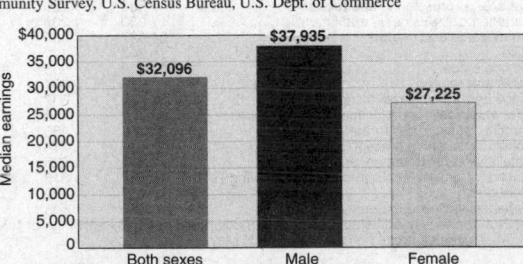

Industry	Number employed	Male (%)	Female (%)	Median earnings	Median earnings (male)	Median earnings (female)
Agriculture; forestry; fishing, hunting; mining	2,720,289	81.7%	18.3%	$29,931	$31,610	$18,997
Arts, entertainment, recreation; accommodation, food services	13,210,187	48.4	51.6	15,149	17,665	12,471
Construction	8,563,737	91.1	8.9	32,417	32,446	32,107
Educational services; health care, social assistance	32,601,321	25.5	74.5	33,384	42,335	31,165
Finance, insurance; real estate, rental, leasing	9,233,893	45.3	54.7	42,119	54,178	36,814
Information	2,950,890	57.8	42.2	44,919	51,705	36,653
Manufacturing	14,665,712	71.0	29.0	40,675	44,596	31,718
Other services, except public administration	7,056,697	46.8	53.2	21,745	29,628	16,691
Professional, scientific, management; administrative, waste management services	15,079,731	58.4	41.6	39,893	46,276	32,366
Public administration	7,098,715	56.0	44.0	50,283	56,692	42,011
Retail trade	16,335,831	50.6	49.4	21,182	26,077	17,090
Transportation, warehousing; utilities	6,987,923	76.0	24.0	41,617	44,312	34,819
Wholesale trade	3,894,622	70.3	29.7	40,121	42,217	32,925

Note: For the civilian employed population 16 years of age and over includes workers not employed full-time.

U.S. Median Weekly Earnings, 2013
Source: Bureau of Labor Statistics, U.S. Dept. of Labor

AGE, RACE, AND ETHNICITY	Total Number of workers (thous.)	Total Median weekly earnings	Men Number of workers (thous.)	Men Median weekly earnings	Women Number of workers (thous.)	Women Median weekly earnings
All workers, by age						
16 years and over	104,194	$776	58,164	$860	46,030	$707
16 to 24 years	9,373	452	5,304	479	4,069	422
16 to 19 years	1,068	362	619	373	449	326
20 to 24 years	8,305	472	4,685	492	3,620	440
25 years and over	94,821	828	52,859	913	41,961	743
25 to 54 years	74,384	810	41,936	890	32,449	735
25 to 34 years	25,031	706	14,193	731	10,838	670
35 to 44 years	24,149	868	13,888	956	10,262	760
45 to 54 years	25,204	892	13,855	1,007	11,348	767
55 years and over	20,436	893	10,924	1,018	9,513	769
55 to 64 years	17,007	907	8,993	1,023	8,013	789
65 years and over	3,429	825	1,930	987	1,499	682
White						
16 years and over	82,612	799	47,223	885	35,390	718
16 to 24 years	7,464	471	4,324	492	3,140	426
25 years and over	75,148	851	42,899	936	32,249	753
25 to 54 years	58,203	831	33,670	907	24,533	743
55 years and over	16,945	924	9,229	1,061	7,717	783
Black						
16 years and over	12,353	634	5,876	666	6,476	610
16 to 24 years	1,110	392	532	383	578	400
25 years and over	11,243	667	5,344	695	5,899	639
25 to 54 years	9,105	657	4,362	695	4,743	623
55 years and over	2,138	727	982	702	1,156	738
Asian						
16 years and over	6,085	973	3,356	1,117	2,729	861
16 to 24 years	365	495	209	518	155	487
25 years and over	5,721	1,019	3,147	1,155	2,574	896
25 to 54 years	4,718	1,058	2,621	1,166	2,097	926
55 years and over	1,002	898	526	1,095	477	768
Hispanic[1]						
16 years and over	16,990	572	10,478	583	6,512	549
16 to 24 years	2,103	415	1,334	422	769	406
25 years and over	14,887	598	9,144	607	5,743	583
25 to 54 years	12,916	594	8,022	604	4,894	579
55 years and over	1,971	635	1,122	651	849	619
OCCUPATION						
Managerial, professional, and related	41,607	1,126	20,298	1,345	21,309	962
Management, business, and financial	17,080	1,205	9,036	1,428	8,045	1,031
Professional and related	24,527	1,060	11,262	1,268	13,264	932
Service	15,203	493	7,793	534	7,411	461
Sales and office	23,349	658	9,219	750	14,130	615
Sales and related	9,279	704	5,291	897	3,988	557
Office and administrative support	14,070	637	3,928	658	10,142	632
Natural resources, construction, and maintenance	10,272	759	9,871	766	401	565
Farming, fishing, and forestry	665	460	529	488	136	369
Construction and extraction	5,289	744	5,195	747	95	668
Installation, maintenance, and repair	4,318	826	4,147	828	171	724
Production, transportation, and material moving	13,762	616	10,983	657	2,779	498
Production	7,188	622	5,279	685	1,909	503
Transportation and material moving	6,574	608	5,704	625	870	488

Note: Not seasonally adjusted; figures are median usual weekly earnings of full-time wage and salary workers for second quarter 2013. Total includes races not shown here. (1) May be of any race.

Average Hours and Earnings of U.S. Production Workers, 1969-2012
Source: Bureau of Labor Statistics, U.S. Dept. of Labor
(annual averages)

Year	Weekly hours	Hourly earnings	Weekly earnings	Year	Weekly hours	Hourly earnings	Weekly earnings	Year	Weekly hours	Hourly earnings	Weekly earnings
1969	37.5	$3.22	$120.70	1984	35.1	$8.49	$298.26	1999	34.3	$13.49	$463.35
1970	37.0	3.40	125.79	1985	34.9	8.74	304.62	2000	34.3	14.02	481.36
1971	36.7	3.63	133.22	1986	34.7	8.93	309.78	2001	34.0	14.55	494.05
1972	36.9	3.90	143.87	1987	34.7	9.14	317.39	2002	33.9	14.97	507.03
1973	36.9	4.14	152.59	1988	34.6	9.44	326.48	2003	33.7	15.38	518.41
1974	36.4	4.43	161.61	1989	34.5	9.80	338.34	2004	33.7	15.70	529.23
1975	36.0	4.73	170.29	1990	34.3	10.20	349.72	2005	33.8	16.13	544.44
1976	36.1	5.06	182.65	1991	34.1	10.52	358.51	2006	33.9	16.76	567.89
1977	35.9	5.44	195.58	1992	34.2	10.77	368.25	2007	33.9	17.44	590.24
1978	35.8	5.88	210.29	1993	34.3	11.05	378.94	2008	33.6	18.08	608.11
1979	35.6	6.34	225.69	1994	34.5	11.34	391.28	2009	33.1	18.63	617.50
1980	35.2	6.85	241.07	1995	34.3	11.66	400.22	2010	33.4	19.07	637.18
1981	35.2	7.44	261.53	1996	34.3	12.05	413.47	2011	33.6	19.46	654.73
1982	34.7	7.87	273.10	1997	34.5	12.51	432.05	2012	33.7	19.77	666.99
1983	34.9	8.20	286.43	1998	34.5	13.02	448.76				

Note: Data refer to production workers in natural resources, mining, and manufacturing; construction workers; and non-supervisory workers in the service industries.

Elderly in U.S. Labor Force, 1890-2012

Source: U.S. Census Bureau, U.S. Dept. of Commerce
(labor force participation rate of persons age 65 and older; 1910 figures not available)

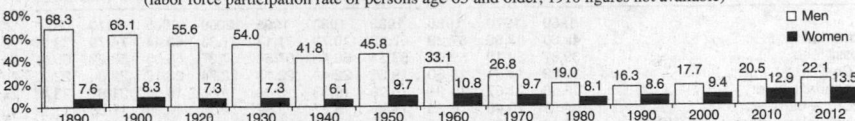

□ Men
■ Women

Year	Men	Women
1890	68.3	7.6
1900	63.1	8.3
1920	55.6	7.3
1930	54.0	7.3
1940	41.8	6.1
1950	45.8	9.7
1960	33.1	10.8
1970	26.8	9.7
1980	19.0	8.1
1990	16.3	8.6
2000	17.7	9.4
2010	20.5	12.9
2012	22.1	13.5

Median Weekly Earnings of U.S. Wage and Salary Workers by Union Affiliation, 2000, 2012

Source: Bureau of Labor Statistics, U.S. Dept. of Labor

Sex and age	Total (2000)	Union member[1]	Represented by unions[2]	Non-union	Total (2012)	Union member[1]	Represented by unions[2]	Non-union
Total, 16 years and older	$576	$696	$691	$542	$768	$943	$933	$742
16 to 24 years	361	437	436	355	444	545	551	434
25 years and older	611	709	705	592	815	960	950	786
25 to 34 years	550	627	624	529	707	871	863	686
35 to 44 years	631	716	712	614	858	983	974	831
45 to 54 years	671	755	752	639	878	997	985	850
55 to 64 years	617	727	723	592	897	1,005	997	870
65 years and older	442	577	565	422	757	839	832	748
Men, 16 years and older	646	739	737	620	854	997	990	821
16 to 24 years	376	458	457	370	468	572	576	459
25 years and older	700	753	752	682	910	1,015	1,010	887
25 to 34 years	603	678	675	591	738	910	903	718
35 to 44 years	731	776	774	718	957	1,035	1,029	941
45 to 54 years	777	801	799	769	994	1,061	1,055	979
55 to 64 years	738	755	757	729	1,005	1,049	1,044	994
65 years and older	537	613	613	514	860	911	926	849
Women, 16 years and older	491	616	613	472	691	877	865	663
16 to 24 years	342	406	405	339	416	510	513	412
25 years and older	515	627	623	497	727	891	880	701
25 to 34 years	493	579	578	483	666	817	809	647
35 to 44 years	520	605	604	506	747	915	906	722
45 to 54 years	565	697	692	522	746	913	900	719
55 to 64 years	505	659	647	481	766	938	918	743
65 years and older	378	485	484	365	667	766	735	653

Note: Data refer to the sole or principal job of full- and part-time workers. Excluded are self-employed workers regardless of whether or not their businesses are incorporated. (1) Including members of an employee association similar to a union. (2) Including members of a labor union or employee association similar to a union, and others whose jobs are covered by a union or an employee-association contract.

Work Stoppages (Strikes and Lockouts) in the U.S., 1950-2012

Source: Bureau of Labor Statistics, U.S. Dept. of Labor; involving 1,000 workers or more

Year	No.	Workers (thous.)	Days idle (thous.)	Year	No.	Workers (thous.)	Days idle (thous.)	Year	No.	Workers (thous.)	Days idle (thous.)
1950	424	1,698	30,390	1985	54	324	7,079	1999	17	73	1,996
1955	363	2,055	21,180	1986	69	533	11,861	2000	39	394	20,419
1960	222	896	13,260	1987	46	174	4,481	2001	29	99	1,151
1965	268	999	15,140	1988	40	118	4,381	2002	19	46	660
1970	381	2,468	52,761	1989	51	452	16,996	2003	14	129	4,091
1975	235	965	17,563	1990	44	185	5,926	2004	17	171	3,344
1976	231	1,519	23,962	1991	40	392	4,584	2005	22	100	1,736
1977	298	1,212	21,258	1992	35	364	3,989	2006	20	70	2,688
1978	219	1,006	23,774	1993	35	182	3,981	2007	21	189	1,265
1979	235	1,021	20,409	1994	45	322	5,020	2008	15	72	1,954
1980	187	795	20,844	1995	31	192	5,771	2009	5	13	124
1981	145	729	16,908	1996	37	273	4,889	2010	11	45	302
1982	96	656	9,061	1997	29	339	4,497	2011	19	113	1,020
1983	81	909	17,461	1998	34	387	5,116	2012	19	148	1,131
1984	62	376	8,499								

Note: Numbers cover stoppages that began in the year indicated. Workers are counted more than once if they are involved in more than one stoppage during the year. For work stoppages ongoing at the end of a calendar year, days idle include only the days for the calendar year.

U.S. Union Membership, 1930-2012

Source: Bureau of Labor Statistics, U.S. Dept. of Labor
(numbers in thousands)

Year	Total employed[1]	% in union	Union members[2]	Year	Total employed[1]	% in union	Union members[2]	Year	Total employed[1]	% in union	Union members[2]
1930	29,424	11.6%	3,401	1970	70,920	27.3%	19,381	2006	128,237	12.0%	15,359
1935	27,053	13.2	3,584	1975	76,945	25.5	19,611	2007	129,767	12.1	15,670
1940	32,376	26.9	8,717	1980	90,564	21.9	19,843	2008	129,377	12.4	16,098
1945	40,394	35.5	14,322	1985	94,521	18.0	16,996	2009	124,490	12.3	15,327
1950	45,222	31.5	14,267	1990	103,905	16.1	16,740	2010	124,073	11.9	14,715
1955	50,675	33.2	16,802	1995	110,038	14.9	16,360	2011	125,187	11.8	14,764
1960	54,234	31.4	17,049	2000	120,786	13.5	16,258	2012	127,577	11.3	14,366
1965	60,815	28.4	17,299	2005	125,889	12.5	15,685				

(1) Does not include agricultural employment; from 1985 on, does not include self-employed or unemployed persons. (2) From 1930 to 1980, includes dues-paying members of traditional trade unions, regardless of employment status; after 1980, includes employed only. From 1985 on, includes members of employee associations that engage in collective bargaining with employers.

ENERGY

U.S. Energy Overview, 1960-2012

Source: *Monthly Energy Review*, Aug. 2013, Energy Information Administration (EIA), U.S. Dept. of Energy; in quadrillion Btu

	1960	1970	1980	1985	1990	1995	2000	2005	2010	2011	2012
Production	42.80	63.50	67.23	67.80	70.70	71.17	71.33	69.44	74.79	78.00	79.13
Fossil fuels	39.87	59.19	59.01	57.54	58.56	57.54	57.37	55.05	58.22	60.56	62.21
Coal[1]	10.82	14.61	18.60	19.33	22.49	22.13	22.74	23.19	22.04	22.22	20.60
Natural gas (dry)	12.66	21.67	19.91	16.98	18.33	19.08	19.66	18.56	21.81	23.41	24.59
Crude oil[2]	14.93	20.40	18.25	18.99	15.57	13.89	12.36	10.98	11.60	11.97	13.78
Natural gas plant liquids (NGPL)	1.46	2.51	2.25	2.24	2.17	2.44	2.61	2.33	2.78	2.97	3.24
Nuclear electric power	0.01	0.24	2.74	4.08	6.10	7.08	7.86	8.16	8.43	8.27	8.05
Renewable energy	2.93	4.08	5.49	6.18	6.04	6.56	6.10	6.23	8.13	9.17	8.87
Conventional hydroelectric power[3]	1.61	2.63	2.90	2.97	3.05	3.21	2.81	2.70	2.54	3.10	2.69
Biomass[4]	1.32	1.43	2.48	3.02	2.74	3.10	3.01	3.10	4.33	4.52	4.36
Geothermal energy	(*)	0.01	0.11	0.20	0.17	0.15	0.16	0.18	0.21	0.21	0.23
Solar	NA	NA	NA	(*)	0.06	0.07	0.07	0.06	0.13	0.17	0.24
Wind	NA	NA	NA	(*)	0.03	0.03	0.06	0.18	0.92	1.17	1.36
Imports	4.19	8.34	15.80	11.78	18.82	22.26	28.97	34.71	29.88	28.86	26.61
Coal	0.01	(*)	0.03	0.05	0.07	0.24	0.31	0.76	0.48	0.33	0.23
Natural gas	0.16	0.85	1.01	0.95	1.55	2.90	3.87	4.45	3.83	3.56	3.22
All petroleum prods.[5]	4.00	7.47	14.66	10.61	17.12	18.88	24.53	29.25	25.37	24.74	22.89
Electricity[6]	0.02	0.02	0.09	0.16	0.06	0.15	0.17	0.15	0.15	0.18	0.20
Exports	1.48	2.63	3.69	4.20	4.75	4.51	4.01	4.56	8.23	10.46	11.45
Coal	1.02	1.94	2.42	2.44	2.77	2.32	1.53	1.27	2.10	2.75	3.22
Natural gas	0.01	0.07	0.05	0.06	0.09	0.16	0.25	0.74	1.15	1.52	1.63
All petroleum prods.[5]	0.43	0.55	1.16	1.66	1.82	1.99	2.15	2.44	4.84	6.00	6.45
Electricity[6]	(*)	0.01	0.01	0.02	0.06	0.01	0.05	0.07	0.07	0.05	0.04
Consumption	45.09	67.84	78.12	76.49	84.49	91.03	98.81	100.24	97.97	97.47	95.10
Fossil fuels	42.14	63.52	69.83	66.09	72.33	77.26	84.73	85.79	81.37	80.00	78.06
Coal	9.84	12.26	15.42	17.48	19.17	20.09	22.58	22.80	20.79	19.66	17.37
Natural gas[7]	12.39	21.80	20.24	17.70	19.60	22.67	23.82	22.57	24.57	24.86	26.00
Petroleum[8]	19.92	29.52	34.20	30.92	33.55	34.44	38.26	40.39	36.01	35.47	34.69
Nuclear electric power	0.01	0.24	2.74	4.08	6.10	7.08	7.86	8.16	8.43	8.27	8.05
Renewable energy	2.93	4.08	5.49	6.18	6.04	6.56	6.11	6.24	8.08	9.07	8.83
Conventional hydroelectric power[3]	1.61	2.63	2.90	2.97	3.05	3.21	2.81	2.70	2.54	3.10	2.69
Biomass[4]	1.32	1.43	2.48	3.02	2.74	3.10	3.01	3.12	4.29	4.42	4.32
Geothermal energy	(*)	0.01	0.11	0.20	0.17	0.15	0.16	0.18	0.21	0.21	0.23
Solar	NA	NA	NA	(*)	0.06	0.07	0.07	0.06	0.13	0.17	0.24
Wind	NA	NA	NA	(*)	0.03	0.03	0.06	0.18	0.92	1.17	1.36

NA = Not available. (*) = Less than 0.005 quadrillion Btu. **Note:** Numbers may not add up to totals because of rounding. (1) Incl. waste coal supplied beginning in 1989 and refuse recovery beginning in 2001. (2) Incl. lease condensate. (3) Starting in 2000, pumped storage was removed and expanded coverage of industrial use of hydroelectric power was included. (4) Category known as "wood, waste, and alcohol" for years prior to 2000. Includes wood, waste, and alcohol fuels (ethanol blended into motor gasoline). Ethanol is included in both Petroleum and Biomass categories but is only counted once in totals. (5) Incl. imports of crude oil for the Strategic Petroleum Reserve, which began in 1977; excl. biofuels. (6) Small amts. transmitted across borders with Canada and Mexico. (7) Incl. supplemental gaseous fuels. (8) Petroleum products supplied, incl. natural gas plant liquids and crude oil burned as fuel.

U.S. Energy Flow, 2012

Source: *Monthly Energy Review*, Aug. 2013, Energy Information Administration (EIA), U.S. Dept. of Energy; in quadrillion Btu

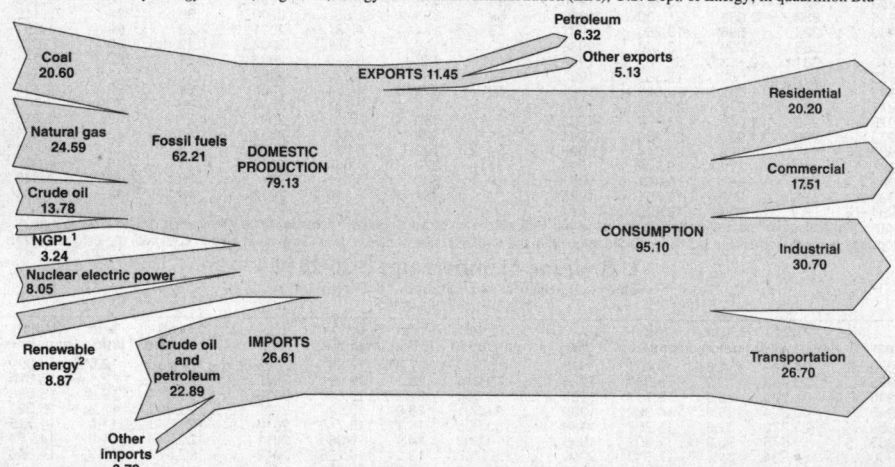

Note: Preliminary figures. Some numbers may not add up to totals because of rounding. (1) Natural gas plant liquids. (2) Conventional hydroelectric power, biomass, geothermal, solar thermal and photovoltaic, and wind.

U.S. Energy Consumption by Source, 1949-2012

Source: *Monthly Energy Review*, Aug. 2013, Energy Information Administration (EIA), U.S. Dept. of Energy

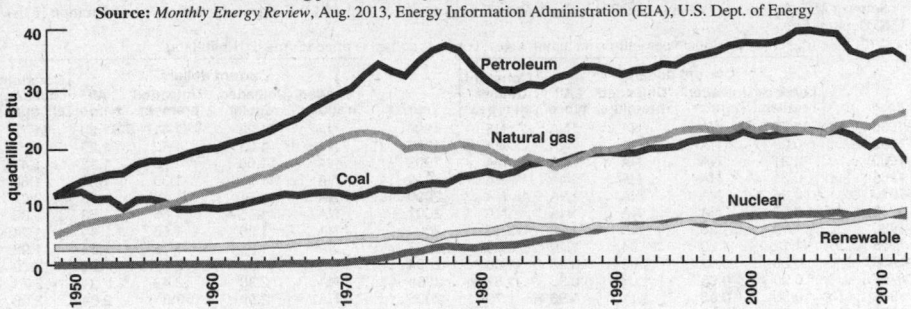

World's Largest Energy Producers and Consumers, 1980-2011

Source: Energy Information Administration (EIA), U.S. Dept. of Energy

(primary energy in quadrillion Btu; ranked by top producers/consumers in 2011)

Production	1980	1985	1990	1995	2000	2005	2009	2010	2011
1. China	18.12	23.31	28.39	33.54	38.78	63.95	84.06	90.39	97.83
2. United States	67.18	67.70	70.71	71.17	71.33	69.44	72.64	74.80	78.00
3. Russia	NA	NA	NA	41.42	41.70	51.08	50.43	53.22	54.89
4. Saudi Arabia	22.43	8.64	15.92	20.66	21.59	25.44	22.84	24.74	26.23
5. Canada	10.28	12.02	13.41	16.83	18.13	18.89	18.32	18.36	18.83
6. India	3.10	5.27	6.82	9.48	9.83	11.74	14.57	15.29	16.01
7. Indonesia	4.23	4.20	5.30	6.95	7.69	9.06	12.58	13.78	14.84
8. Iran	3.94	5.59	7.67	9.35	10.40	13.12	14.26	14.61	14.80
9. Australia	3.25	5.00	6.16	7.43	9.66	11.21	12.38	12.92	12.85
10. Brazil	1.90	3.38	3.76	4.47	6.36	7.67	8.93	9.47	9.93
Consumption	**1980**	**1985**	**1990**	**1995**	**2000**	**2005**	**2009**	**2010**	**2011**
1. China	17.29	21.01	26.00	33.25	40.94	67.92	94.37	100.88	109.62
2. United States	78.07	76.39	84.49	91.03	98.81	100.28	94.56	98.04	97.47
3. Russia	NA	NA	NA	27.94	26.14	27.92	27.69	29.32	32.77
4. India	4.04	5.91	7.88	11.44	13.33	16.33	21.42	21.92	23.61
5. Japan	15.20	15.69	18.77	20.94	22.41	23.13	20.70	21.77	20.86
6. Canada	9.80	10.15	10.98	12.21	13.30	14.17	13.10	13.00	13.50
7. Germany[1]	14.86	14.83	14.86	14.39	14.41	14.42	13.52	13.94	13.08
8. Brazil	4.02	4.59	5.75	7.02	8.53	9.36	10.43	11.30	11.66
9. South Korea	1.76	2.31	3.84	6.36	7.83	9.33	9.97	10.78	11.16
10. France	8.39	8.35	9.13	10.05	10.96	11.36	10.73	11.03	10.78

NA = Not available. (1) Data for 1980-90 represents sum of figures for East and West Germany and may not be comparable with other years.

Gasoline Retail Prices in Selected Countries, 1990-2012

Source: *Energy Prices and Taxes*, International Energy Agency

(average price in dollars per gallon, including taxes)

Country	Regular unleaded													
Country	1990	1995	2000	2001	2002	2003	2004	2005	2006	2007	2008	2009	2010	2011	2012
Australia	NA	$1.93	$1.93	$1.70	$1.78	$2.20	$2.73	$3.22	$3.52	$3.86	$4.47	$3.79	$4.35	$5.56	$5.60
Canada	$1.85	1.51	1.85	1.70	1.70	2.01	2.35	2.88	3.26	3.60	4.09	3.14	3.79	4.77	4.81
China	NA	NA	NA	1.21	1.21	1.32	1.48	1.70	2.12	2.31	3.10	3.26	3.71	NA	NA
Germany	2.65	3.97	3.44	3.41	3.67	4.58	5.26	5.64	6.02	6.89	7.76	6.81	7.12	NA	NA
Japan	3.14	4.43	3.63	3.26	3.14	3.48	3.94	4.28	4.47	4.50	5.75	4.85	5.72	6.93	6.97
Korea, South	2.04	2.95	4.16	3.75	3.82	4.13	4.50	5.26	5.91	6.21	5.83	4.69	5.60	6.59	6.66
Mexico	1.02	1.10	2.01	2.20	2.23	2.04	2.04	2.23	2.31	2.42	2.46	2.12	2.46	2.80	2.95
Taiwan	2.46	2.23	2.16	2.01	1.93	2.16	2.46	2.76	3.07	3.22	3.52	3.03	3.56	4.05	NA
United States	1.17	1.10	1.48	1.44	1.36	1.55	1.85	2.27	2.57	2.80	3.26	2.35	2.76	3.52	3.63

Country	Premium unleaded													
Country	1990	1995	2000	2001	2002	2003	2004	2005	2006	2007	2008	2009	2010	2011	2012
France	$3.63	$4.28	$3.79	$3.52	$3.63	$4.35	$5.00	$5.45	$5.87	$6.59	$7.50	$6.36	$6.74	$7.91	$7.61
Germany	2.76	4.09	3.56	3.48	3.75	4.69	5.34	5.75	6.13	6.97	7.76	6.81	7.12	8.21	8.03
Italy	4.58	4.01	3.79	3.56	3.75	4.54	5.30	5.75	6.09	6.74	7.65	6.47	6.85	8.18	8.71
Mexico	NA	NA	2.23	2.46	2.50	2.31	2.38	2.57	2.73	2.95	3.03	2.65	2.95	3.14	3.14
South Africa	NA	NA	1.78	1.59	1.40	1.93	2.57	3.07	3.41	3.63	4.13	3.22	4.09	NA	NA
Spain	NA	3.26	2.84	2.73	2.91	3.48	4.09	4.50	4.85	5.38	6.13	5.26	5.83	6.97	6.93
Thailand	NA	1.25	1.36	1.32	1.36	1.51	1.78	2.23	2.76	3.22	4.01	4.13	4.85	NA	NA
United Kingdom	2.84	3.22	4.58	4.13	4.16	4.69	5.56	5.98	6.36	7.15	7.42	5.87	6.85	8.10	8.10
United States	NA	1.21	1.59	1.51	1.44	1.67	1.97	2.38	2.69	2.91	3.37	2.46	2.91	3.63	3.75

NA = Not available. **Note:** Premium unleaded refers to fuels with a research octane number of 95.

Average U.S. Gasoline Prices, 1950-2012

Source: *Monthly Energy Review*, Aug. 2013; *Short-Term Energy Outlook*, Aug. 2013; Energy Information Administration (EIA), U.S. Dept. of Energy

(in dollars per gallon, including taxes; constant dollars is price in Aug. 2013 dollars)

Year	Current dollars Leaded regular	Current dollars Unleaded regular	Current dollars Unleaded premium	All types[1]	Constant dollars, all types[1]	Year	Current dollars Leaded regular	Current dollars Unleaded regular	Current dollars Unleaded premium	All types[1]	Constant dollars, all types[1]
1950	$0.27	NA	NA	NA	NA	1996	NA	$1.23	$1.41	$1.29	$1.79
1955	0.29	NA	NA	NA	NA	1997	NA	1.23	1.42	1.29	1.74
1960	0.31	NA	NA	NA	NA	1998	NA	1.06	1.25	1.12	1.47
1965	0.31	NA	NA	NA	NA	1999	NA	1.17	1.36	1.22	1.60
1970	0.36	NA	NA	NA	NA	2000	NA	1.51	1.69	1.56	2.01
1975	0.57	NA	NA	NA	NA	2001	NA	1.46	1.66	1.53	1.88
1980	1.19	$1.25	NA	$1.22	$3.53	2002	NA	1.36	1.56	1.44	1.74
1985	1.12	1.20	$1.34	1.20	2.53	2003	NA	1.59	1.78	1.64	1.98
1986	0.86	0.93	1.09	0.93	1.88	2004	NA	1.88	2.07	1.92	2.29
1987	0.90	0.95	1.09	0.96	1.87	2005	NA	2.30	2.49	2.34	2.71
1988	0.90	0.95	1.11	0.96	1.79	2006	NA	2.59	2.81	2.64	2.98
1989	1.00	1.02	1.20	1.06	1.86	2007	NA	2.80	3.03	2.85	3.16
1990	1.15	1.16	1.35	1.22	2.01	2008	NA	3.27	3.52	3.32	3.53
1991	NA	1.14	1.32	1.20	1.89	2009	NA	2.35	2.61	2.40	2.55
1992	NA	1.13	1.32	1.19	1.81	2010	NA	2.79	3.05	2.84	2.97
1993	NA	1.11	1.30	1.17	1.72	2011	NA	3.53	3.79	3.58	3.66
1994	NA	1.11	1.31	1.17	1.69	2012	NA	3.64	3.92	3.70	3.68
1995	NA	1.15	1.34	1.21	1.70						

NA = Not applicable. **Note:** Until unleaded gas became available in 1976, leaded was the only type used in automobiles. (1) Also includes types of motor gasoline not shown separately. Starting in Sept. 1981, the Bureau of Labor Statistics included gasohol in the average for all types, and unleaded premium is weighted more heavily.

Energy Consumption, Total and Per Capita, by State, 2011

Source: State Energy Data System, Energy Information Administration (EIA), U.S. Dept. of Energy

Total Consumption

Rank, state	Btu (tril)	Rank, state	Btu (tril)
1. Texas	12,206.6	27. Maryland	1,426.4
2. California	7,858.4	28. Massachusetts	1,395.1
3. Florida	4,217.1	29. Mississippi	1,163.4
4. Louisiana	4,055.3	30. Kansas	1,162.5
5. Illinois	3,977.8	31. Arkansas	1,117.1
6. Ohio	3,827.6	32. Oregon	1,014.2
7. Pennsylvania	3,725.3	33. Nebraska	871.4
8. New York	3,614.8	34. Utah	797.2
9. Georgia	3,002.1	35. Connecticut	741.6
10. Indiana	2,869.2	36. West Virginia	724.3
11. Michigan	2,802.7	37. New Mexico	688.0
12. North Carolina	2,572.7	38. Alaska	637.9
13. New Jersey	2,438.5	39. Nevada	632.5
14. Virginia	2,388.5	40. Wyoming	553.0
15. Tennessee	2,201.1	41. North Dakota	526.2
16. Washington	2,080.2	42. Idaho	525.6
17. Alabama	1,931.3	43. Maine	412.5
18. Kentucky	1,911.4	44. Montana	397.5
19. Missouri	1,878.1	45. South Carolina	382.4
20. Minnesota	1,866.6	46. New Hampshire	292.1
21. Wisconsin	1,789.2	47. Hawaii	286.0
22. South Carolina	1,610.3	48. Delaware	271.6
23. Oklahoma	1,594.6	49. Rhode Island	183.9
24. Iowa	1,512.6	50. District of Columbia	180.3
25. Colorado	1,480.8	51. Vermont	149.3
26. Arizona	1,431.5	**United States**	**97,387.3**

Note: U.S. total includes 11.1 tril Btu in coal coke imports not allocated to states.

Consumption per Capita

Rank, state	Btu (mil)	Rank, state	Btu (mil)
1. Wyoming	975	27. Illinois	309
2. Louisiana	886	28. Georgia	306
3. Alaska	881	29. Washington	305
4. North Dakota	768	30. Delaware	299
5. Iowa	494	31. Virginia	295
6. Texas	476	32. Pennsylvania	292
7. Nebraska	473	33. District of Columbia	291
8. South Dakota	464	34. Colorado	289
9. Indiana	440	35. Michigan	284
10. Kentucky	438	36. Utah	283
11. Oklahoma	421	37. New Jersey	276
12. Kansas	405	38. North Carolina	267
13. Alabama	402	39. Oregon	262
14. Montana	398	40. Maryland	244
15. Mississippi	391	41. Vermont	238
16. West Virginia	390	42. Nevada	233
17. Arkansas	380	43. New Hampshire	222
18. Minnesota	349	44. Arizona	221
19. South Carolina	345	45. Florida	221
20. Tennessee	344	46. Massachusetts	211
21. Ohio	332	47. California	209
22. Idaho	332	48. Hawaii	208
23. New Mexico	331	49. Connecticut	207
24. Wisconsin	313	50. New York	185
25. Missouri	313	51. Rhode Island	175
26. Maine	311	**United States**	**313**

U.S. Production of Crude Oil by State, 2012

Source: *Petroleum Supply Annual 2012*, Energy Information Administration (EIA), U.S. Dept. of Energy

Oil production in North Dakota more than doubled between 2010 and 2012 through the use of hydraulic fracturing, or fracking, a process by which water, sand, and chemicals are injected at high pressure to create fractures in shale rock, releasing the oil within.

(in thousands of barrels)

Rank, state	Total	Rank, state	Total	Rank, state	Total	Rank, state	Total
1. Texas	729,474	9. Colorado	49,352	17. Arkansas	6,536	25. South Dakota	1,754
2. North Dakota	242,486	10. Kansas	43,734	18. Ohio	4,877	26. Nevada	368
3. California	196,324	11. Utah	30,271	19. Pennsylvania	4,348	27. New York	353
4. Alaska	192,368	12. Montana	26,492	20. Kentucky	3,198	28. Tennessee	288
5. Oklahoma	89,300	13. Mississippi	24,154	21. West Virginia	2,573	29. Missouri	173
6. New Mexico	84,657	14. Illinois	9,792	22. Nebraska	2,513	30. Arizona	52
7. Louisiana	70,654	15. Alabama	9,516	23. Indiana	2,350	31. Virginia	9
8. Wyoming	57,681	16. Michigan	7,366	24. Florida	2,147	**U.S. total**	**2,374,021**

Note: One barrel is equal to 42 U.S. gallons. U.S. total includes 478,859 thousand barrels of federal offshore oil production.

U.S. Petroleum Trade, 1976-2013

Source: *Monthly Energy Review*, Aug. 2013, Energy Information Administration (EIA), U.S. Dept. of Energy
(in thousands of barrels per day; average for the year)

Year	Imports from Persian Gulf[1]	Total imports	Total exports	Net imports[2]	Petroleum products supplied[3]	Year	Imports from Persian Gulf[1]	Total imports	Total exports	Net imports[2]	Petroleum products supplied[3]
1976	1,840	7,313	223	7,090	17,461	2001	2,761	11,871	971	10,900	19,649
1980	1,519	6,909	544	6,365	17,056	2002	2,269	11,530	984	10,546	19,761
1985	311	5,067	781	4,286	15,726	2003	2,501	12,264	1,027	11,238	20,034
1990	1,966	8,018	857	7,161	16,988	2004	2,493	13,145	1,048	12,097	20,731
1991	1,845	7,627	1,001	6,626	16,714	2005	2,334	13,714	1,165	12,549	20,802
1992	1,778	7,888	950	6,938	17,033	2006	2,211	13,707	1,317	12,390	20,687
1993	1,782	8,620	1,003	7,618	17,237	2007	2,163	13,468	1,433	12,036	20,680
1994	1,728	8,996	942	8,054	17,718	2008	2,370	12,915	1,802	11,114	19,498
1995	1,573	8,835	949	7,886	17,725	2009	1,689	11,691	2,024	9,667	18,771
1996	1,604	9,478	981	8,498	18,309	2010	1,711	11,793	2,353	9,441	19,180
1997	1,755	10,162	1,003	9,158	18,620	2011	1,861	11,504	2,986	8,518	18,949
1998	2,136	10,708	945	9,764	18,917	2012	2,151	10,596	3,184	7,412	18,555
1999	2,464	10,852	940	9,912	19,519	2013[4]	NA	9,831	3,089	6,742	18,783
2000	2,488	11,459	1,040	10,419	19,701						

NA = Not available. **Note:** U.S. exports include shipments to U.S. territories; imports include receipts from U.S. territories. Numbers may not add up to totals because of rounding. (1) Bahrain, Iran, Iraq, Kuwait, Qatar, Saudi Arabia, United Arab Emirates, and the Neutral Zone between Kuwait and Saudi Arabia. (2) Total imports minus total exports. (3) Includes domestic production and imports minus change in stocks, refinery imports, and exports. (4) Estimated annualized 7-month average, for Jan.-July.

World Fossil Fuel Reserves

Source: International Energy Statistics Database, Energy Information Administration (EIA), U.S. Dept. of Energy

	Crude oil (bil barrels), 2013	Natural gas (tril cu ft), 2013	Coal (mil short tons), 2008		Crude oil (bil barrels), 2013	Natural gas (tril cu ft), 2013	Coal (mil short tons), 2008
North America[1]	**208.9**	**378.5**	**269,343**	**Middle East**	**802.2**	**2,823.2**	**1,326**
Canada	173.1	68.2	7,255	Bahrain	0.1	3.3	NA
Greenland	0.0	0.0	202	Iran	154.6	1,187.0	1,326
Mexico	10.3	17.2	1,335	Iraq	141.4	111.5	NA
United States[1]	23.3	304.6	260,551	Israel	0.0	9.5	NA
Central & South America	**325.9**	**268.9**	**13,788**	Kuwait	104.0	63.5	NA
				Oman	5.5	30.0	NA
Argentina	2.8	11.7	551	Qatar	25.4	890.0	NA
Bolivia	0.2	9.9	1	Saudi Arabia	267.9	287.8	NA
Brazil	13.2	14.0	5,025	Syria	2.5	8.5	NA
Chile	0.2	3.5	171	United Arab			
Colombia	2.2	6.0	7,436	Emirates	97.8	215.0	NA
Cuba	0.1	2.5	NA	Yemen	3.0	16.9	NA
Ecuador	8.2	0.2	26	**Africa**	**127.6**	**514.8**	**34,934**
Peru	0.6	12.7	49	Algeria	12.2	159.1	65
Trinidad and				Angola	10.5	12.9	NA
Tobago	0.7	13.3	NA	Congo	0.2	0.0	97
Venezuela	297.6	195.1	528	Egypt	4.4	77.2	18
Europe	**12.0**	**145.5**	**84,202**	Libya	48.0	54.6	NA
Albania	0.2	0.0	875	Mozambique	0.0	4.5	234
Bosnia and				Namibia	0.0	2.2	NA
Herzegovina	0.0	0.0	3,145	Niger	NA	0.0	77
Bulgaria	0.0	0.2	2,608	Nigeria	37.2	182.0	209
Czech Republic	0.0	0.1	1,213	South Africa	0.0	NA	33,241
Germany	0.3	4.4	44,863	Sudan[2]	5.0	3.0	NA
Greece	0.0	0.0	3,329	Swaziland	0.0	0.0	159
Hungary	0.0	0.3	1,830	Tanzania	0.0	0.2	220
Italy	0.5	2.2	11	Zimbabwe	0.0	0.0	553
Macedonia	0.0	0.0	366	**Asia & Oceania**	**47.2**	**504.4**	**293,042**
Montenegro	0.0	0.0	157	Afghanistan	0.0	1.8	73
Norway	5.4	73.1	6	Australia	1.4	43.0	84,217
Poland	0.2	3.2	6,293	Bangladesh	0.0	6.5	323
Romania	0.6	3.7	321	Brunei	1.1	13.8	NA
Serbia	0.1	1.7	15,179	China	25.6	124.2	126,215
Slovakia	0.0	0.5	289	India	5.5	43.8	66,800
Slovenia	0.0	0.0	246	Indonesia	4.0	108.4	6,095
Spain	0.2	0.1	584	Japan	0.0	0.7	386
Turkey	0.3	0.2	2,583	Korea, North	0.0	0.0	661
United Kingdom	3.1	8.7	251	Korea, South	NA	0.2	139
Eurasia	**118.9**	**2,177.8**	**251,364**	Laos	0.0	0.0	554
Armenia	0.0	0.0	180	Malaysia	4.0	83.0	4
Azerbaijan	7.0	35.0	NA	Mongolia	NA	0.0	2,778
Belarus	0.2	0.1	110	Myanmar			
Georgia	0.0	0.3	222	(Burma)	0.1	10.0	2
Kazakhstan	30.0	85.0	37,038	New Zealand	0.1	1.0	629
Kyrgyzstan	0.0	0.2	895	Pakistan	0.2	24.0	2,282
Russia	80.0	1,688.0	173,074	Philippines	0.1	3.5	348
Tajikistan	0.0	0.2	413	Thailand	0.5	10.1	1,366
Turkmenistan	0.6	265.0	NA	Vietnam	4.4	24.7	165
Ukraine	0.4	39.0	37,339	**World[1]**	**1,473.8**	**6,707.3**	**948,000**
Uzbekistan	0.6	65.0	2,094				

NA = Not reported separately but included in regional and world totals. **Note:** Regional and world totals may include countries not shown here. Proved reserves only. Some countries omitted for lack of appreciable reserves. (1) Figures for crude oil and natural gas are from 2011, the latest year available. (2) Includes South Sudan.

U.S. Crude Oil Imports by Selected Countries, 1975-2012

Source: *Petroleum Supply Annual*, Energy Information Administration (EIA), U.S. Dept. of Energy

The United States' dependence on foreign oil continues to decline, thanks to increased production of crude oil, natural gas, and domestic biofuels like ethanol and biodiesel. Imports fell to fewer than 8,500 barrels a day, down from a peak of more than 10,000 barrels a day less than a decade ago. Since 2005, Canada has been the largest supplier of U.S. oil, responsible for more than a quarter of all U.S. imports. Western Hemisphere nations provide more than half of the oil that the U.S. imports. Sanctions do not permit the U.S. to import oil from Iran.

(in thousands of barrels per day; ranked by 2012 imports)

Country	1975	1980	1985	1990	1995	2000	2005	2010	2011	2012
Canada..............	600	199	468	643	1,040	1,348	1,633	1,970	2,225	2,408
Saudi Arabia#.........	701	1,250	132	1,195	1,260	1,523	1,445	1,082	1,186	1,356
Mexico.............	70	507	715	689	1,027	1,313	1,556	1,152	1,102	972
Venezuela#...........	395	156	306	666	1,151	1,223	1,241	912	868	906
Iraq#................	2	28	46	514	0	620	527	415	459	474
Nigeria#.............	746	841	280	784	621	875	1,077	983	767	405
Colombia	0	0	0	140	207	318	156	338	397	401
Kuwait#.............	4	27	4	79	213	263	227	195	191	306
Angola#[1]...........	71	37	104	236	360	295	456	383	335	221
Brazil..............	0	1	0	0	0	5	94	255	232	187
Ecuador[2]..........	0	0	0	0	96	125	276	210	203	174
Algeria#............	264	456	84	63	27	1	228	328	178	120
Russia[3]............	0	0	0	1	14	7	199	269	223	101
Libya#.............	223	548	0	0	0	0	44	43	9	56
Gabon[4]...........	NA	NA	NA	NA	229	143	127	47	34	42
Equatorial Guinea.......	NA	NA	NA	NA	NA	6	68	50	19	41
Cameroon...........	NA	NA	NA	NA	2	4	3	50	36	31
Egypt	NA	NA	NA	NA	32	4	4	7	4	31
Congo Republic	NA	NA	NA	NA	20	42	25	70	53	29
Chad...............	NA	NA	NA	NA	NA	NA	74	18	49	28
Norway	12	144	31	96	258	302	119	25	53	26
Trinidad and Tobago.....	115	115	98	76	62	56	64	45	33	26
Azerbaijan...........	NA	NA	NA	NA	NA	NA	NA	55	36	24
Argentina	NA	NA	NA	NA	44	53	56	29	28	21
Thailand	NA	NA	NA	NA	1	3	2	13	17	20
United Kingdom	0	173	278	155	341	291	224	120	36	18
Oman	NA	NA	NA	NA	20	2	22	12	41	10
Non-OPEC countries ...	**NA**	**NA**	**NA**	**NA**	**3,660**	**4,526**	**5,310**	**4,661**	**4,727**	**4,473**
OPEC countries[1,2,4].....	**3,211**	**3,864**	**1,312**	**3,514**	**3,570**	**4,544**	**4,816**	**4,553**	**4,209**	**4,019**
Persian Gulf countries ..	**1,121**	**1,508**	**244**	**1,801**	**1,479**	**2,409**	**2,207**	**1,694**	**1,849**	**2,136**
TOTAL	**4,105**	**5,263**	**3,201**	**5,894**	**7,230**	**9,071**	**10,126**	**9,213**	**8,935**	**8,491**

= OPEC member. NA = Not available. **Note:** Totals and subtotals include countries not shown. (1) Angola became an OPEC member Jan. 1, 2007, and is not included in OPEC totals from before that year. (2) Ecuador suspended its OPEC membership Dec. 1992-Nov. 2007. Ecuador's imports in 1993-2007 appear in non-OPEC totals. (3) May include oil from USSR states before 1992. (4) Gabon withdrew from OPEC Dec. 31, 1994. Imports after Jan. 1, 1995, appear in non-OPEC totals.

U.S. Coal Production and Consumption, 1950-2012

Source: *Monthly Energy Review*, Aug. 2013; *Annual Coal Report, 2012*; Energy Information Administration (EIA), U.S. Dept. of Energy

(in thousand short tons)

Year	Coal production[1]			Coal consumption				
	Surface mining	Underground mining	Total production	Residential	Commercial	Industrial	Electric power[2]	Total consumption
1950....	139,388	421,000	560,388	51,562	63,021	224,637	91,871	494,102
1960....	141,745	292,584	434,329	24,159	16,789	177,402	176,685	398,081
1970....	272,131	340,530	612,661	9,024	7,090	186,637	320,182	523,231
1975....	361,174	293,467	654,641	2,823	6,587	147,244	405,962	562,640
1980....	492,192	337,508	829,700	1,355	5,097	127,004	569,274	702,730
1985....	532,838	350,800	883,638	1,711	6,068	116,429	693,841	818,049
1990....	604,529	424,546	1,029,076	1,345	5,379	115,207	782,567	904,498
1995....	636,725	396,249	1,032,974	755	5,052	106,067	850,230	962,104
2000....	699,953	373,659	1,073,612	454	3,673	94,147	985,821	1,084,095
2005....	762,887	368,612	1,131,498	378	4,342	83,774	1,037,485	1,125,978
2006....	803,728	359,022	1,162,750	290	2,936	82,429	1,026,636	1,112,292
2007....	794,845	351,790	1,146,635	353	3,173	79,331	1,045,141	1,127,998
2008....	814,729	357,079	1,171,809	351	3,506	76,463	1,040,580	1,120,548
2009....	742,862	332,062	1,074,923	353	3,210	60,641	933,627	997,478
2010....	745,357	337,155	1,084,368	339	3,081	70,381	975,052	1,048,514
2011....	748,372	345,606	1,095,628	307	2,793	67,671	932,484	1,002,948
2012....	NA	NA	1,016,822	NA	2,045	63,681	824,758	890,483

NA = Not available. (1) A small amount of refuse recovery has been included in coal production figures since 2001. (2) Electricity-only and combined-heat-and-power (CHP) plants whose primary business is to sell electricity or electricity and heat to the public. Through 1988, data are for electric utilities only; beginning in 1989, data are for electric utilities and independent power producers.

World Nuclear Power Summary, 2013

Source: *Nuclear Power Reactors in the World*, International Atomic Energy Agency; as of Sept. 2013 except where noted

Country	Reactors in operation No. of units	Reactors in operation Total MW(e)	Reactors under construction No. of units	Reactors under construction Total MW(e)	Nuclear electricity supplied in 2012 TW(e).h[1]	Nuclear electricity supplied in 2012 % of nation's total	Total operating experience[2] Years	Total operating experience[2] Months
Argentina	2	935	1	692	5.9	4.7	68	7
Armenia	1	375	—	—	2.1	26.6	38	4
Belgium	7	5,927	—	—	38.5	51.0	254	7
Brazil	2	1,884	1	1,245	15.2	3.1	43	3
Bulgaria	2	1,906	—	—	14.9	31.6	153	3
Canada	19	13,500	—	—	89.1	15.3	634	5
China	18	13,860	28	27,784	92.7	2.0	141	10
Czech Republic	6	3,804	—	—	28.6	35.3	128	10
Finland	4	2,752	1	1,600	22.1	32.6	135	4
France	58	63,130	1	1,600	407.4	74.8	1,874	4
Germany	9	12,068	—	—	94.1	16.1	790	2
Hungary	4	1,889	—	—	14.8	45.9	110	2
India	20	4,391	7	4,824	29.7	3.6	377	3
Iran	1	915	—	—	1.3	0.6	1	4
Japan	50	44,215	2	2,650	17.2	2.1	1,596	2
Korea, South	23	20,739	5	6,320	143.5	30.4	404	1
Mexico	2	1,530	—	—	8.4	4.7	41	11
Netherlands	1	482	—	—	3.7	4.4	68	0
Pakistan	3	725	2	630	5.3	5.3	55	8
Romania	2	1,300	—	—	10.6	19.4	21	11
Russia	33	23,643	10	8,382	166.3	17.8	1,091	4
Slovakia	4	1,816	2	880	14.4	53.8	144	7
Slovenia	1	688	—	—	5.2	36.0	31	3
South Africa	2	1,860	—	—	12.4	5.1	56	3
Spain	8	7,567	—	—	58.7	20.5	293	6
Sweden	10	9,408	—	—	61.5	38.1	402	6
Switzerland	5	3,308	—	—	24.4	35.9	189	11
Taiwan	6	5,028	2	2,600	38.7	18.4	188	1
Ukraine	15	13,107	2	1,900	84.9	46.2	413	6
United Kingdom	16	9,231	—	—	64.0	18.1	1,511	8
United States	100	98,560	3	3,399	770.7	19.0	3,835	1
Total	**434**	**370,543**	**69**	**67,196**	**2,346.2**	**—**	**15,247**	**5**

MW(e) = Megawatt electricity. (1) 1 terawatt-hour [TW(e).h] = 1 mil megawatt-hours [MW(e).h]. For an average power plant, 1 TW(e).h = 0.39 megaton of coal equivalent (input) and 0.23 megaton of oil equivalent (input). (2) As of Dec. 31, 2012. Total includes shutdown plants for countries not listed here: Italy (81 years), Kazakhstan (25 years, 10 months), and Lithuania (43 years, 6 months).

Nations Most Reliant on Nuclear Energy, 2012

Source: *Nuclear Share in Electricity Generation*, International Atomic Energy Agency (IAEA)
(nuclear electricity generation as % of total electricity generated within country)

Rank	Country	Nuclear share	Rank	Country	Nuclear share	Rank	Country	Nuclear share	Rank	Country	Nuclear share
1.	France	74.8%	8.	Switzerland	35.9%	15.	Romania	19.4%	22.	Pakistan	5.3%
2.	Slovakia	53.8	9.	Czech Republic	35.3	16.	United States	19.0	23.	South Africa	5.1
3.	Belgium	51.0	10.	Finland	32.6	17.	Taiwan	18.4	24.	Argentina	4.7
4.	Ukraine	46.2	11.	Bulgaria	31.6	18.	United Kingdom	18.1		Mexico	4.7
5.	Hungary	45.9	12.	Korea, South	30.4	19.	Russia	17.8	26.	Netherlands	4.4
6.	Sweden	38.1	13.	Armenia	26.6	20.	Germany	16.1	27.	India	3.6
7.	Slovenia	36.0	14.	Spain	20.5	21.	Canada	15.3	28.	Brazil	3.1

U.S. Nuclear Reactors and Power Plant Operations, 1953-2012

Source: *Monthly Energy Review*, Aug. 2013, Energy Information Administration (EIA), U.S. Dept. of Energy

Years	Number of reactor units Ordered[1]	Number of reactor units Cancelled	Number of reactor units Construction permits issued[2]	Number of reactor units Low-power licenses issued[3]	Number of reactor units Full-power licenses issued[4]	Number of reactor units Shutdown[5]	Operable units[6]	Capacity factor[6,7]	Nuclear electricity generation (bil net kWh)[6]	Nuclear share of domestic electricity generation[6]
1953-59	15	0	8	2	2	0	2	NA	0.2	—
1960-64	7	0	12	13	12	2	13	NA	3.3	0.3%
1965-69	81	0	50	8	9	4	17	NA	13.9	1.0
1970-74	143	16	59	41	41	5	55	47.8%	114.0	6.1
1975-79	13	43	48	17	17	3	69	58.4	255.2	11.3
1980-84	0	54	0	24	19	1	87	56.3	327.6	13.5
1985-89	0	7	0	24	28	4	111	62.2	529.4	17.8
1990-94	0	2	0	2	3	3	109	73.8	640.4	19.7
1995-99	0	2	0	1	1	6	104	85.3	728.3	19.7
2000-04	0	0	0	0	0	0	104	90.1	788.5	19.9
2005-09	0	0	0	0	0	0	104	90.3	798.9	20.2
2010-12	0	0	0	0	0	0	104	86.2	769.3	19.0
Total	**259**	**124**	**177**	**132**	**132**	**28**	**NA**	**NA**	**NA**	**NA**

— = less than 0.05%. NA = Not applicable. **Note:** The permit/license categories shown here are historic. The Nuclear Regulatory Commission anticipates 16 or more new combined license applications under current regulations over the next few years (the first of which was submitted in Sept. 2007) may amount to 25 or more new reactor units. (1) Order placed by a utility or government agency for a nuclear steam supply system. (2) Permits issued in a given period, not extant permits. (3) Permission to conduct testing but not operate at full power. (4) Permission to operate at full power. (5) Permanently ceased operation. (6) As of the last year of given period. (7) The ratio of electric energy produced to the amount that could be produced at continuous full-power operation.

U.S. Nuclear Reactors Generating the Most Electricity, 2010

Source: U.S. Nuclear Statistics Database, Energy Information Administration (EIA), U.S. Dept. of Energy
(in thousand net megawatt-hours)

Rank	Reactor, location	Electricity generated	Capacity[1]	Rank	Reactor, location	Electricity generated	Capacity[1]
1.	Palo Verde-2, Wintersburg, AZ	11,652,972	101%	14.	LaSalle-2, Seneca, IL.........	9,925,542	101%
2.	South Texas-1, Bay City, TX ...	11,304,107	101	15.	Catawba-1, Lake Wylie, SC ...	9,889,074	100
3.	Seabrook-1, Portsmouth, NH ..	10,910,055	100	16.	Limerick-2, Pottstown, PA	9,879,131	99
4.	Perry-1, Dothan, OH.........	10,619,711	98	17.	South Texas-2, Bay City, TX ...	9,822,674	88
5.	Comanche Peak-2, Glen Rose, TX	10,531,748	104	18.	Peach Bottom-3, Lancaster, PA...........	9,759,275	100
6.	Byron-1, Byron, IL...........	10,337,288	101	19.	Diablo Canyon-2, San Luis Obispo, CA	9,752,476	100
7.	Waterford-3, Taft, LA.........	10,276,184	100	20.	Watts Bar-1, Spring City, TN...	9,738,457	99
8.	Vogtle-1, Waynesboro, GA	10,247,423	102	21.	Comanche Peak-1, Glen Rose, TX	9,676,719	91
9.	Palo Verde-3, Wintersburg, AZ	10,238,992	89	22.	Grand Gulf-1, Port Gibson, MS	9,643,241	88
10.	Susquehanna-2, Berwick, PA..	10,221,221	98	23.	Wolf Creek-1, Burlington, KS ..	9,555,712	94
11.	McGuire-2, Cowens Ford Dam, NC............	10,014,695	104	24.	Sequoyah-2, Chattanooga, TN	9,536,672	97
12.	Braidwood-2, Braidwood, IL	10,003,246	99	25.	Byron-2, Byron, IL............	9,518,424	96
13.	Salem-2, Salem, NJ	9,954,772	98				

(1) The ratio of power generated to the maximum potential generation expressed as a percentage.

Renewable Energy Sources

Source: U.S. Dept. of Energy

Concern over the environmental impact of burning fossil fuels has helped spur interest in alternative fuels that are less polluting. And because the supply of fossil fuels is finite and diminishing, there is interest in "renewable" sources that do not deplete existing supplies. However, renewable energy sources still make up only a small share of U.S. domestic energy production (about 11% in 2012). The main reason for this is their relatively higher cost (in some cases two to four times that of power obtained from traditional fuels). The following are the major renewable energy sources available.

Biomass is plant-derived material usable as an energy source. It includes wood energy crops such as hybrid poplars and willow trees, agricultural crops including soybeans and corn, and animal and other wastes. Biomass is one of the two most common renewable energy sources in the U.S. today, along with hydropower. Biomass such as wood can be burned to produce heat and generate electricity. Agricultural crops can be chemically converted into fuels such as ethanol and biodiesel; these are the only known renewable liquid energy sources and may one day replace petroleum and fossil-fuel-produced diesel. But bringing ethanol and biodiesel into wide use would require more energy-efficient methods of production and transportation. Overall, biomass fuels burn much cleaner than fossil fuels, though biomass fuels still produce carbon dioxide and other pollutants.

Geothermal energy is generated from heat inside of the Earth. This form of energy is both clean and renewable. The technology has caught on in countries with substantial geothermal activity such as Iceland, where it accounted for 66% of primary energy use in 2011. In the U.S., the best sources for geothermal power are in the West, where there are many heated underground lakes. Large-scale access would require drilling. A major goal in this field is to find a way to harness energy directly from magma (molten rock material), which has great potential because of its high temperatures.

Hydrogen is the third most abundant element on Earth. It does not naturally occur on Earth as a pure gas or liquid but is always combined with other elements (such as oxygen, to form water, or carbon, to form methane). If hydrogen is to be used for energy, it must be separated from these other elements. That can be achieved through methods involving heat, photosynthesis, sunlight, or electricity.

Hydrogen batteries, or fuel cells, were used by NASA's space shuttles. Within a fuel cell, a chemical reaction occurs in which electrons are released from hydrogen atoms. These electrons flow through an external circuit as electricity. The hydrogen atoms' protons combine with oxygen (and some of the electrons in the electric current) to produce heat and water suitable for drinking. Fuel cells do not run down but work as long as hydrogen is supplied. Some experts think hydrogen will be the power source of the future. An infrastructure would need to be created for safe and cost-effective transportation and storage of hydrogen.

Hydropower, or hydroelectric power, is generated by water flowing through turbines. Along with biomass fuels, it is one of the two most common renewable energy sources in the U.S. today. A dam on a river is a common hydropower producer. No harmful greenhouse gases are produced, but the dams needed to generate power can harm river ecosystems. Researchers are working on turbine technologies to maximize use of hydropower and reduce adverse environmental effects.

Ocean energy can be generated in two ways. Thermal ocean energy uses heat that the ocean absorbs from the sun to power generators, sometimes producing drinkable desalinated water as a byproduct. Mechanical ocean energy is generated by the movement of tides and waves through turbines. In both cases, power generation is not very efficient with current technology. Much more research is needed. Mechanical ocean energy requires the building of large dams or breakwater-type structures called tidal barrages, which could harm coastal ecosystems.

Solar energy is generated using heat and light from the sun. Solar energy is an increasingly common source of electricity. Photovoltaic (PV) solar cells are made of semiconducting materials that can directly convert sunlight to electricity without producing any harmful waste. Arrays of mirrors can concentrate the sun's rays onto PV panels, making solar collectors more efficient. Sunlight can also be used to heat water directly. According to the Dept. of Energy, homes incorporating solar heating designs can save as much as 50% on heating bills. The downside to solar energy is that it depends heavily on a range of factors including location, time of year, and weather.

Wind energy uses wind turbines to produce energy. They are perched on high towers, usually 100 ft tall or higher, and often placed in large groups ("farms"). Farmers and homeowners sometimes use stand-alone turbines to generate supplemental electricity. Tax credits for wind energy producers and government incentives for homeowners have significantly lowered the price of wind power. But some object to wind farms because of their appearance or the noise the turbines make. Wind power raises few other environmental problems, but the turbines can pose a danger to birds. In addition, because weather is involved, consistent energy generation can be a challenge.

CRIME

Measuring Crime

Source: Federal Bureau of Investigation (FBI) and Bureau of Justice Statistics (BJS), U.S. Dept. of Justice

The U.S. Dept. of Justice administers two statistical programs to measure trends in crime in the U.S. Because of differences in focus and methodology, their results are not strictly comparable.

The Federal Bureau of Investigation (FBI) conducts the **Uniform Crime Report (UCR)** program, which aims to provide statistics for law enforcement administration, operation, and management. It collects actual counts on the crimes of homicide, forcible rape, robbery, aggravated assault, burglary, larceny-theft, motor vehicle theft, and arson as they are reported to law enforcement agencies. Each year, the program releases a preliminary report in the spring, followed by a more detailed, final report in the fall.

The **National Crime Victimization Survey (NCVS)** is conducted annually by the Bureau of Justice Statistics through interviews with members of a nationally representative sample of households about their experiences with crime. The survey complements the UCR by providing alternative and previously unavailable data, including details about the victims of crime and their offenders (e.g., age, sex, ethnicity, victim-offender relationship) and information on crimes not reported to law enforcement. In contrast to the UCR, the NCVS does not cover homicide, arson, commercial crimes, or crimes against children under age 12.

Further explanation of the UCR and NCVS is available at www.bjs.gov/content/pub/html/ntcm.cfm.

Uniform Crime Report, 2011

Source: *Crime in the United States, 2011*, Federal Bureau of Investigation, U.S. Dept. of Justice

In 2011, more than 18,000 city, county, college and university, state, tribal, and federal agencies—representing more than 304 mil people—voluntarily participated in the Uniform Crime Report (UCR) program.

Although crime tends to rise in hard economic times, the number of reported violent crimes dropped 3.8% between 2010 and 2011, marking the fifth straight year violent crime declined. The number of property crimes reported was also down, by 0.5% from 2010, making it the ninth year in a row property crime reports fell.

Between 2002 and 2011, the total number of violent crimes decreased 15.5%, while property crimes dropped 13.3%. The decline in the crime rate, i.e. the number of crimes per 100,000 residents, was even more precipitous. The violent crime rate fell by 21.9% over the past decade, while the property crime rate decreased by 19.9%.

Additional details from the 2011 report:

- The South accounted for 41.3% of all violent crime in the U.S., and almost half of all murders (43.6%). The Northeast had the lowest portion of the nation's violent crime (16.2% of the total), murder (14.8%), and property crime (13.0%).
- Men committed 89% of the murders in which the offender's gender was known, and accounted for 78% of all murder victims. Half of all murder victims were black.
- Firearms were used in 68% of all murders and 41% of all robberies.
- Husbands killed wives 552 times, compared with 108 wives who killed husbands; 474 men killed their girlfriends, while 161 women killed boyfriends.

National Crime Victimization Survey, 2011

Source: *Criminal Victimization, 2011*, Bureau of Justice Statistics (BJS), U.S. Dept. of Justice

The National Crime Victimization Survey (NCVS) paints a slightly different picture from the Uniform Crime Report of crime in the U.S. It shows an increase in victimizations of U.S. residents age 12 and over, from 4.9 mil in 2010 to 5.8 mil. Simple and aggravated assaults were responsible for the increase, while rape/sexual assaults and robberies continued their decade-long decline. The violent crime rate decreased by 30% between 2002 and 2011, from 32.1 victimizations per 100,000 people to 22.5. The property crime

rate increased 11% between 2010 and 2011 but was still down 18% from the levels set in 2002.

The Bureau of Justice Statistics cautions that rape and sexual assault statistics are based on a small number of incidents. The NCVS does not include figures for murders because published data are based on victim interviews. The 2011 survey used a different methodology than in previous years, so data from earlier surveys may not be directly comparable.

Criminal Victimization, 2002-11

Source: *Criminal Victimization, 2011*, Bureau of Justice Statistics, U.S. Dept. of Justice

A crime committed against an individual or single household counts as one **victimization**. Because a personal crime may involve more than one victim, the number of victimizations may be greater than the number of personal crime incidents. In property crimes, the affected household is considered one victim.

Type of crime	Number of victimizations			Percent change, 2002-11	Percent change, 2010-11	Avg. annual change, 2002-11
	2002	2010	2011			
All violent crimes[1]	7,424,550	4,935,980	5,805,430	−21.8%	17.6%	−5%
Rape/sexual assault	349,810	268,570	243,800	−30.3	−9.2	−3
Robbery	624,390	568,510	556,760	−10.8	−2.1	−1
Assault	6,450,350	4,098,900	5,004,860	−22.4	22.1	−5
Aggravated assault	1,332,520	857,750	1,052,080	−21.0	22.7	−5
Simple assault	5,117,840	3,241,150	3,952,780	−22.8	22.0	−5
Domestic violence[2]	1,308,320	1,129,560	1,353,340	3.4	19.8	−2
Intimate partner violence[3]	929,760	773,430	851,340	−8.4	10.1	−2
All property crimes	18,554,320	15,411,610	17,066,780	−8.0	10.7	−2
Household burglary	3,251,810	3,176,180	3,613,190	11.1	13.8	NA
Motor vehicle theft	1,018,680	606,990	628,070	−38.3	3.5	−6
Theft	14,283,820	11,628,440	12,825,510	−10.2	10.3	−2

NA = Not applicable. **Note:** Details may not add up to totals due to rounding. (1) Excludes murder because the National Crime Victimization Survey (NCVS) is based on interviews with victims. (2) Victimization by intimate partners and family members. (3) Victimization by current or former spouses, boyfriends, or girlfriends.

Crime in the U.S., 1989-2011

Source: *Crime in the United States, 2011*, Federal Bureau of Investigation (FBI), U.S. Dept. of Justice

In the FBI's Uniform Crime Report (UCR) Program, offenses are classified as **violent crimes** if they involve force or the threat of force: murder and nonnegligent manslaughter, forcible rape, robbery, and aggravated assault. The following offenses are considered **property crimes**: burglary, larceny-theft, motor vehicle theft, and arson. Arson data is excluded from this table because of variations in the level of participation by reporting agencies. That data is presented separately online at www.fbi.gov/about-us/cjis/ucr/.

		Violent crime					Property crime			
Year(s)	Population[1]	All violent crimes	Murder and nonnegligent manslaughter	Forcible rape[2]	Robbery	Aggravated assault[3]	All property crimes	Burglary	Larceny-theft[4]	Motor vehicle theft
NUMBER OF OFFENSES										
1989	246,819,230	1,646,037	21,500	94,504	578,326	951,707	12,605,412	3,168,170	7,705,872	7,872,442
1990	249,464,396	1,820,127	23,438	102,555	639,271	1,054,863	12,655,486	3,073,909	7,945,670	1,635,907
1995	262,803,276	1,798,792	21,606	97,470	580,509	1,099,207	12,063,935	2,593,784	7,997,710	1,472,441
1999	272,690,813	1,426,044	15,522	89,411	409,371	911,740	10,208,334	2,100,739	6,955,520	1,152,075
2000	281,421,906	1,425,486	15,586	90,178	408,016	911,706	10,182,584	2,050,992	6,971,590	1,160,002
2001[5]	285,317,559	1,439,480	16,037	90,863	423,557	909,023	10,437,189	2,116,531	7,092,267	1,228,391
2002	287,973,924	1,423,677	16,229	95,235	420,806	891,407	10,455,277	2,151,252	7,057,379	1,246,646
2003	290,788,976	1,383,676	16,528	93,883	414,235	859,030	10,442,862	2,154,834	7,026,802	1,261,226
2004	293,656,842	1,360,088	16,148	95,089	401,470	847,381	10,319,386	2,144,446	6,937,089	1,237,851
2005	296,507,061	1,390,745	16,740	94,347	417,438	862,220	10,174,754	2,155,448	6,783,447	1,235,859
2006	299,398,484	1,435,123	17,309	94,472	449,246	874,096	10,019,601	2,194,993	6,626,363	1,198,245
2007	301,621,157	1,422,970	17,128	92,160	447,324	866,358	9,882,212	2,190,198	6,591,542	1,100,472
2008	304,059,724	1,394,461	16,465	90,750	443,563	843,683	9,774,152	2,228,887	6,586,206	959,059
2009	307,006,550	1,325,896	15,399	89,241	408,742	812,514	9,337,060	2,203,313	6,338,095	795,652
2010	309,330,219	1,251,248	14,722	85,593	369,089	781,844	9,112,625	2,168,459	6,204,601	739,565
2011	311,591,917	1,203,564	14,612	83,425	354,396	751,131	9,063,173	2,188,005	6,159,795	715,373
PERCENT CHANGE: NUMBER OF OFFENSES										
2011/2010........		−3.8%	−0.7%	−2.5%	−4.0%	−3.9%	−0.5%	0.9%	−0.7%	−3.3%
2011/2007........		−15.4	−14.7	−9.5	−20.8	−13.3	−8.3	−0.1	−6.6	−35.0
2011/2002........		−15.5	−10.0	−12.4	−15.8	−15.7	−13.3	1.7	−12.7	−42.6
RATE PER 100,000 RESIDENTS										
1989		666.9	8.7	38.3	234.3	385.6	5,107.1	1,283.6	3,189.6	634.0
1990		729.6	9.4	41.1	256.3	422.9	5,073.1	1,232.2	3,185.1	655.8
1995		684.5	8.2	37.1	220.9	418.3	4,590.5	987.0	3,043.2	560.3
1999		523.0	5.7	32.8	150.1	334.3	3,743.6	770.4	2,550.7	422.5
2000		506.5	5.5	32.0	145.0	324.0	3,618.3	728.8	2,477.3	412.2
2001		504.5	5.6[5]	31.8	148.5	318.6	3,658.1	741.8	2,485.7	430.5
2002		494.4	5.6	33.1	146.1	309.5	3,630.6	747.0	2,450.7	432.9
2003		475.8	5.7	32.3	142.5	295.4	3,591.2	741.0	2,416.5	433.7
2004		463.2	5.5	32.4	136.7	288.6	3,514.1	730.3	2,362.3	421.5
2005		469.0	5.6	31.8	140.8	290.8	3,431.5	726.9	2,287.8	416.8
2006		479.3	5.8	31.6	150.0	292.0	3,346.6	733.1	2,213.2	400.2
2007		471.8	5.7	30.6	148.3	287.2	3,276.4	726.1	2,185.4	364.9
2008		458.6	5.4	29.8	145.9	277.5	3,214.6	733.0	2,166.1	315.4
2009		431.9	5.0	29.1	133.1	264.7	3,041.3	717.7	2,064.5	259.2
2010		404.5	4.8	27.7	119.3	252.8	2,945.9	701.0	2,005.8	239.1
2011		386.3	4.7	26.8	113.7	241.1	2,908.7	702.2	1,976.9	229.6
PERCENT CHANGE: RATE PER 100,000 RESIDENTS										
2011/2010........		−4.5%	−1.5%	−3.2%	−4.7%	−4.6%	−1.3%	0.2%	−1.4%	−4.0%
2011/2007........		−18.1	−17.4	−12.4	−23.3	−16.1	−11.2	−3.3	−9.5	−37.1
2011/2002........		−21.9	−16.8	−19.0	−22.2	−22.1	−19.9	−6.0	−19.3	−47.0

Note: Figures for 2010 have been revised from previous reports. (1) U.S. Census Bureau estimates for July 1 of each year except for 1990, 2000, and 2010, which show Apr. 1 decennial census counts. (2) Does not include statutory rape (i.e., rape not involving force) and other offenses of a sexual nature. Also does not include sexual attacks on males, which are considered aggravated assaults or sex offenses, depending on circumstances and extent of injuries. (The FBI revised its definition of rape in 2012 to be more inclusive.) (3) Attack upon another with the intent of doing serious bodily harm; usually accompanied by the use of a weapon or other means likely to produce death or great bodily harm. (4) The unlawful taking of another's property not involving force or fraud (e.g., theft of motor vehicle parts, shoplifting). Excludes crimes such as embezzlement and check fraud. (5) The murder and nonnegligent homicides that occurred as a result of the Sept. 11, 2001, terrorist attacks are not included.

Law Enforcement Officers and Civilian Employees, 2011

Source: *Crime in the United States, 2011*; *Law Enforcement Officers Killed and Assaulted, 2011*; Federal Bureau of Investigation (FBI), U.S. Dept. of Justice

As of Oct. 31, 2011, 14,633 city, county, state, college and university, and tribal agencies around the country collectively employed 1,001,984 full-time law enforcement workers. About 69.7% of employees were sworn officers. The FBI's Uniform Crime Report (UCR) program defines a sworn law enforcement officer as a person who ordinarily carries a firearm and badge, has full arrest powers, and is paid from government funds specifically dedicated to law enforcement. Civilians (e.g., clerks, radio dispatchers, correctional officers) made up the remaining 30.3% of law enforcement employees.

Altogether, they provided service to an estimated 293.1 mil people around the country, meaning there were 3.4 full-time law enforcement employees (sworn officers and civilians) and 2.4 sworn officers per 1,000 residents.

The great majority of sworn officers (88.2%) were male, but females made up 60.8% of civilian employees. Not surprisingly, the most populous state, California, employed the greatest number of full-time law enforcement workers (116,797). The nation's capital, Washington, DC, had the highest rate, with 8.0 full-time law enforcement employees (and 7.0 sworn officers) for every 1,000 residents in its population.

Nationwide, 72 law enforcement officers were killed in the line of duty in 2011, up dramatically from 56 in 2010. Of that number, 23 died while attempting to make arrests, 15 in ambush situations, 11 while performing traffic stops, 9 were killed during tactical situations, and 7 were killed answering disturbance calls. Five died while investigating suspicious persons or circumstances. Almost all (63 of the 72 officers) were killed with firearms, even though 51 of those officers were wearing body armor. Handguns were responsible for the majority (50) of officer murders.

U.S. Crime Rates by Region, Geographic Division, and State, 2011
Source: *Crime in the United States, 2011*, Federal Bureau of Investigation (FBI), U.S. Dept. of Justice
(per 100,000 residents, as estimated by U.S. Census Bureau for July 1 of year)

	Violent crime					Property crime[1]			
	All violent crimes	Murder and nonnegligent manslaughter	Forcible rape[2]	Robbery	Aggravated assault[3]	All property crimes	Burglary	Larceny-theft[4]	Motor vehicle theft
Total U.S.[5]	**386.3**	**4.7**	**26.8**	**113.7**	**241.1**	**2,908.7**	**702.2**	**1,976.9**	**229.6**
Northeast	**352.1**	**3.9**	**19.2**	**124.0**	**205.0**	**2,121.8**	**437.5**	**1,547.6**	**136.7**
New England	**314.3**	**2.6**	**24.6**	**83.6**	**203.5**	**2,297.2**	**527.3**	**1,615.8**	**154.1**
Connecticut.	272.8	3.6	19.2	102.7	147.3	2,167.4	437.9	1,542.1	187.4
Maine	123.2	2.0	29.6	27.8	63.8	2,545.5	591.3	1,873.0	81.2
Massachusetts	428.4	2.8	24.7	102.7	298.1	2,258.7	554.6	1,540.3	163.7
New Hampshire	188.0	1.3	32.5	36.0	118.2	2,283.9	436.1	1,773.9	73.9
Rhode Island.	247.5	1.3	28.9	71.0	146.3	2,676.8	662.4	1,796.8	217.5
Vermont	135.2	1.3	19.0	13.6	101.4	2,309.0	581.5	1,647.7	79.7
Middle Atlantic	**365.4**	**4.4**	**17.3**	**138.3**	**205.5**	**2,059.9**	**405.8**	**1,523.5**	**130.6**
New Jersey.	308.4	4.3	11.4	138.4	154.3	2,150.7	490.2	1,463.1	197.4
New York	398.1	4.0	14.1	145.9	234.1	1,912.4	336.0	1,477.2	99.2
Pennsylvania.	355.0	5.0	26.1	126.6	197.3	2,222.3	454.0	1,636.1	132.2
Midwest	**349.9**	**4.5**	**31.4**	**106.2**	**207.8**	**2,844.3**	**685.0**	**1,953.0**	**206.3**
East North Central	**365.2**	**4.9**	**31.4**	**125.0**	**203.8**	**2,872.6**	**729.3**	**1,931.8**	**211.5**
Illinois	429.3	5.6	28.8	157.4	237.5	2,688.8	604.1	1,861.1	223.5
Indiana	331.8	4.8	27.0	107.1	193.0	3,161.8	775.7	2,158.8	227.3
Michigan	445.3	6.2	44.0	105.2	289.9	2,612.1	724.9	1,629.0	258.2
Ohio	307.4	4.4	31.5	139.1	132.4	3,354.7	976.3	2,195.9	182.5
Wisconsin	236.9	2.4	20.4	78.2	135.9	2,432.7	466.7	1,821.9	144.1
West North Central	**315.7**	**3.4**	**31.4**	**63.9**	**216.8**	**2,780.5**	**585.2**	**2,000.9**	**194.5**
Iowa	255.6	1.5	27.2	26.9	199.9	2,330.3	568.2	1,633.6	128.5
Kansas	353.9	3.8	37.8	50.8	261.5	3,080.1	654.4	2,193.2	232.5
Minnesota	221.2	1.4	31.1	63.4	125.4	2,549.4	481.3	1,915.1	153.1
Missouri.	447.4	6.1	24.3	104.3	312.7	3,308.8	745.7	2,308.3	254.8
Nebraska.	253.2	3.6	37.7	54.1	157.7	2,752.9	472.9	2,057.3	222.7
North Dakota.	247.0	3.5	37.9	13.3	192.3	1,936.7	355.7	1,437.7	143.3
South Dakota	254.1	2.5	60.2	20.3	171.1	1,817.7	351.8	1,351.1	114.8
South[5]	**428.8**	**5.5**	**27.2**	**114.1**	**282.0**	**3,370.8**	**876.8**	**2,270.4**	**223.6**
South Atlantic[5]	**427.1**	**5.4**	**24.0**	**122.2**	**275.5**	**3,308.3**	**839.2**	**2,248.0**	**221.1**
Delaware.	559.5	4.5	31.9	169.5	353.5	3,410.6	830.2	2,411.8	168.7
District of Columbia[5]	1,202.1	17.5	28.0	662.3	494.3	4,795.5	623.0	3,451.5	721.0
Florida.	515.3	5.2	27.7	134.4	348.0	3,522.0	892.9	2,421.1	207.9
Georgia.	373.2	5.6	20.9	123.8	222.9	3,626.5	974.6	2,351.7	300.3
Maryland.	494.1	6.8	20.5	177.5	289.3	2,860.2	614.0	1,970.5	275.7
North Carolina.	349.8	5.3	20.7	98.9	224.9	3,526.8	1,099.2	2,251.2	176.4
South Carolina	571.9	6.8	34.5	92.2	438.4	3,904.2	1,002.8	2,609.4	292.0
Virginia.	196.7	3.7	19.0	67.1	106.9	2,249.6	377.9	1,751.6	120.1
West Virginia.	315.9	4.3	20.9	49.0	241.6	2,273.9	603.2	1,549.2	121.5
East South Central	**418.0**	**5.7**	**30.8**	**103.4**	**278.1**	**3,298.1**	**955.7**	**2,146.7**	**195.6**
Alabama	420.1	6.3	28.5	102.2	283.0	3,606.1	1,064.3	2,319.7	222.0
Kentucky.	238.2	3.5	33.5	84.5	116.7	2,708.8	745.0	1,811.1	152.7
Mississippi.	269.8	8.0	29.0	83.7	149.1	3,025.5	1,037.7	1,822.5	165.4
Tennessee	608.2	5.8	31.6	126.2	444.5	3,595.9	979.9	2,396.8	219.2
West South Central	**437.1**	**5.4**	**30.6**	**106.4**	**294.7**	**3,509.5**	**898.8**	**2,369.3**	**241.5**
Arkansas	480.9	5.5	41.3	82.6	351.5	3,754.1	1,173.3	2,383.0	197.8
Louisiana.	555.3	11.2	27.7	114.5	401.9	3,688.5	1,012.5	2,476.6	199.4
Oklahoma	454.8	5.5	37.0	86.6	325.7	3,356.2	958.5	2,106.8	290.9
Texas	408.5	4.4	29.0	110.6	264.5	3,472.3	838.3	2,387.3	246.7
West	**378.0**	**4.2**	**27.6**	**112.2**	**234.0**	**2,831.5**	**641.6**	**1,858.4**	**331.5**
Mountain	**368.4**	**4.4**	**36.2**	**80.3**	**247.5**	**2,948.3**	**659.8**	**2,041.4**	**247.0**
Arizona	405.9	6.2	34.9	109.9	254.8	3,554.5	847.3	2,401.3	305.9
Colorado	320.2	2.9	44.5	64.6	208.1	2,606.3	503.6	1,886.8	215.9
Idaho.	200.9	2.3	27.4	11.6	159.6	2,068.6	436.6	1,547.9	84.1
Montana	267.5	2.8	35.8	16.9	212.0	2,319.7	339.6	1,834.0	146.1
Nevada	562.1	5.2	33.5	157.9	365.6	2,560.5	742.3	1,470.0	348.3
New Mexico	567.5	7.5	41.2	82.7	436.2	3,531.5	1,028.9	2,242.9	259.7
Utah	195.0	1.9	30.3	38.4	124.4	2,973.1	465.8	2,287.8	219.5
Wyoming.	219.3	3.2	25.7	12.5	177.9	2,266.4	327.9	1,846.8	91.7
Pacific	**382.2**	**4.1**	**23.8**	**126.3**	**228.0**	**2,779.8**	**633.6**	**1,777.3**	**368.9**
Alaska.	606.5	4.0	58.1	79.7	464.6	2,632.8	391.0	2,056.0	185.8
California.	411.1	4.8	20.3	144.0	242.0	2,583.8	610.4	1,583.8	389.6
Hawaii	287.2	1.2	31.6	75.8	178.6	3,337.8	728.0	2,305.6	304.3
Oregon	247.6	2.1	31.4	57.4	156.6	3,114.6	528.1	2,352.8	233.7
Washington.	294.6	2.4	33.5	82.5	176.1	3,574.6	827.7	2,383.3	363.6
Puerto Rico	**284.4**	**1.2**	**30.6**	**174.4**	**78.1**	**1,395.2**	**447.6**	**789.7**	**157.9**

Note: Offense totals are based on all reporting agencies and estimates for unreported areas. Figures may not add up to totals due to rounding. U.S. total excludes Puerto Rico. (1) Data for arson, considered a property crime, are not included in this table. (2) Does not include statutory rape (i.e., rape not involving force) and other offenses of a sexual nature. Also does not include sexual attacks on males, which are considered aggravated assaults or sex offenses, depending on circumstances and extent of injuries. (The FBI revised its definition of rape in 2012 to be more inclusive.) (3) Attack upon another with the intent of doing serious bodily harm; usually accompanied by the use of a weapon or other means likely to produce death or great bodily harm. (4) The unlawful taking of another's property not involving force or fraud (e.g., theft of motor vehicle parts, shoplifting). Excludes crimes such as embezzlement and check fraud. (5) Includes offenses reported by National Zoological Park Police and Washington Metro Transit Police.

State and Federal Prison Population; Death Penalty, 2000-11

Source: *Prisoners in 2011*; *Capital Punishment, 2011*; Bureau of Justice Statistics, U.S. Dept. of Justice

After rising for four decades, the prison population declined in 2011 for the second straight year. As of Dec. 31, 2011, 1,598,780 prisoners were under the jurisdiction, or legal authority, of state (86.5%) or federal (13.5%) correctional authorities. Under orders from the U.S. Supreme Court to reduce inmate overcrowding to 137.5% of the state's prison capacity, California decreased its prison population to 15,493, which accounts for more than half of the U.S. decline. New Jersey and Connecticut also saw their prison populations drop more than 4.5%, while Kentucky's inmates increased by 4.9%. The federal prison population increased by 3.1%. Jails, which are locally operated, typically hold persons awaiting trial or sentencing as well as those sentenced to one year or less.

The imprisonment rate, or number of prisoners per 100,000 U.S. residents, also declined in 2011, from 500 to 492. The rate is still significantly higher than the rate of 470 at year-end 2001. Black males were incarcerated at 6.3 times the rate of white males (3,023 per 100,000 U.S. residents for black males vs. 478 per 100,000 for white males) and more than twice as often as Hispanic males (1,238 per 100,000).

There were 3,082 persons under sentence of death at year-end 2011; 13 states executed a total of 43 inmates (13 in Texas alone). Twenty-four inmates died of other causes, and 70 were removed from death row. A total of 80 inmates were received on death row in 2011, the lowest number since 1973. Since 2000, the death row population has decreased every year, but the composition has changed little: 98% were male, 55% were white, and 42% were black. This population continues to linger longer on death row: the average time between sentencing and execution leapt from 14 years, 10 months to 16 years, 6 months.

Illinois repealed the death penalty July 1, 2011; New Mexico repealed its death penalty law for crimes committed after July 1, 2009, but the repeal was not retroactive. All 35 death penalty states authorize lethal injection as a method of execution; 8 also permit electrocution, 3 permit the gas chamber, 3 hanging, and 2 (Oklahoma and Utah) authorize firing squads.

	Prisoners				Death penalty[1]			Executed, as of 2011[2]—	
Region/jurisdiction	Year-end 2000	Year-end 2010	Year-end 2011	% change, 2010-11	Death penalty statute?	Under sentence of death, year-end 2011	Executed in 2011	Since 1930	Since 1977
U.S. total	1,391,261	1,613,803	1,598,780	-0.9%	—	3,082	43	5,136[3]	1,277[3]
Federal[4]	145,416	209,771	216,362	3.1	Y	56	0	36	3
State	1,245,845	1,404,032	1,382,418	-1.5	35[5]	3,026	43	5,100	1,274
Alabama	26,332	31,764	32,270	1.6	Y	196	6	190	55
Alaska[6]	4,173	5,391	5,412	0.4	N	—	—	—	—
Arizona[7]	26,510	40,209	40,020	-0.5	Y	130	4	66	28
Arkansas	11,915	16,204	16,108	-0.6	Y	39	0	145	27
California	163,001	165,062	149,569	-9.4	Y	705	0	305	13
Colorado	16,833	22,815	21,978	-3.7	Y	3	0	48	1
Connecticut[8]	18,355	19,321	18,324	-5.2	Y	10	0	22	1
Delaware[6,7]	6,921	6,615	6,739	1.9	Y	18	1	27	15
Florida	71,319	104,306	103,055	-1.2	Y	393	2	241	71
Georgia	44,232	56,432	55,944	-0.9	Y	96	4	418	52
Hawaii[6,8]	5,053	5,912	6,037	2.1	N	—	—	—	—
Idaho	5,535	7,431	7,739	4.1	Y	13	1	5	2
Illinois	45,281	48,418	48,427	0.0	Y	—	0	102	12
Indiana	20,125	28,028	28,906	3.1	Y	12	0	61	20
Iowa	7,955	9,455	9,116	-3.6	N	—	—	18	—
Kansas	8,344	9,051	9,327	3.0	Y	9	0	15	0
Kentucky	14,919	20,544	21,545	4.9	Y	34	0	106	3
Louisiana	35,207	39,445	39,710	0.7	Y	87	0	161	28
Maine	1,679	2,154	2,145	-0.4	N	—	—	—	—
Maryland	23,538	22,645	22,558	-0.4	Y	5	0	73	5
Massachusetts	10,722	11,313	11,623	2.7	N	—	—	27	—
Michigan	47,718	44,165	42,940	-2.8	N	—	—	—	—
Minnesota	6,238	9,796	9,800	0.0	N	—	—	—	—
Mississippi	20,241	21,067	21,386	1.5	Y	57	2	169	15
Missouri	27,543	30,623	30,833	0.7	Y	46	1	130	68
Montana	3,105	3,716	3,678	-1.0	Y	2	0	9	3
Nebraska	3,895	4,587	4,616	0.6	Y	11	0	7	3
Nevada	10,063	12,653	12,778	1.0	Y	81	0	41	12
New Hampshire	2,257	2,761	2,614	-5.3	Y	1	0	1	0
New Jersey	29,784	25,007	23,834	-4.7	N	—	—	74	0
New Mexico	5,342	6,763	6,998	3.5	N	2	0	9	1
New York	70,199	56,656	55,436	-2.2	Y	0	0	329	0
North Carolina	31,266	40,382	39,440	-2.3	Y	158	0	306	43
North Dakota	1,076	1,487	1,423	-4.3	N	—	—	—	—
Ohio	45,833	51,712	50,964	-1.4	Y	142	5	218	46
Oklahoma	23,181	26,252	25,977	-1.0	Y	63	2	156	96
Oregon	10,580	14,876	14,510	-2.5	Y	36	0	20	2
Pennsylvania	36,847	51,264	51,578	0.6	Y	207	0	155	3
Rhode Island[6,8]	3,286	3,357	3,337	-0.6	N	—	—	—	—
South Carolina	21,778	23,578	22,914	-2.8	Y	52	1	205	43
South Dakota	2,616	3,434	3,535	2.9	Y	4	0	2	1
Tennessee	22,166	27,451	28,479	3.7	Y	87	0	99	6
Texas	166,719	173,649	172,224	-0.8	Y	301	13	774	477
Utah	5,637	6,807	6,879	1.1	Y	8	0	21	7
Vermont[6]	1,697	2,079	2,053	-1.3	N	—	—	4	—
Virginia	30,168	37,638	38,130	1.3	Y	9	1	201	109
Washington	14,915	18,235	17,847	-2.1	Y	8	0	52	5
West Virginia	3,856	6,681	6,826	2.2	N	—	—	40	0
Wisconsin	20,754	22,729	22,654	-0.3	N	—	—	—	—
Wyoming	1,680	2,112	2,183	3.4	Y	1	0	8	1

— = Not available or applicable. (1) Figures do not include persons held under Armed Forces jurisdiction with a military death sentence for murder. (2) Military authorities carried out an additional 160 executions between 1930 and 1961. (3) Total executed includes 40 executions performed under the District of Columbia's jurisdiction since 1849. (4) Prisoners sentenced under DC's criminal code are housed in federal facilities. (5) The death penalty is legally authorized by 35 states. (6) Prisons and jails form one integrated system. Data includes total jail and prison population. (7) Prisoner population based on custody counts. (8) Counts include dual jurisdiction cases where the inmate is currently housed in another jurisdiction's facilities.

Prison Situation Under Correctional Authorities' Jurisdiction, 2011

Source: *Prisoners in 2011*, Bureau of Justice Statistics, U.S. Dept. of Justice

Largest prison populations		Imprisonment rate of sentenced prisoners		% change in prison population, 2010-11		Avg. annual % change in prison population, 2000-10	
Jurisdiction	Number	Jurisdiction	Rate[1]	Jurisdiction	% change	Jurisdiction	% change
U.S. total	1,598,780	U.S. total	492	U.S. total	−1.0%	U.S. total	1.4%
Federal[2]	216,362	Federal[2]	63	Federal[2]	3.4%	Federal[2]	3.8%
State	1,382,418	State	430	State	−1.6	State	1.1
1. Texas	172,224	1. Louisiana	865	1. Kentucky	5.1	1. West Virginia . .	5.1
2. California	149,569	2. Mississippi	690	2. Alaska[4]	4.5	2. Minnesota	4.1
3. Florida.	103,055	3. Alabama	650	3. Idaho	4.1	3. Arizona[3]	3.8
4. Georgia.	55,944	4. Texas	632	4. Tennessee	3.7	4. North Dakota . .	3.7
5. New York	55,436	5. Oklahoma	631	5. New Mexico . . .	3.6	5. Florida	3.5
6. Pennsylvania . .	51,578	6. Arizona[3]	589	6. Wyoming.	3.4	6. New Mexico . . .	3.2
7. Ohio	50,964	7. Georgia.	547	7. Indiana	3.1	7. Indiana	3.1
8. Illinois	48,427	8. Arkansas	544	8. Kansas	3.0	8. Oregon	3.1
9. Michigan	42,940	9. Florida.	538	9. Massachusetts	2.9	9. Pennsylvania . .	3.0
10. Arizona[3]	40,020	10. Missouri	512	10. South Dakota . .	2.9	10. Arkansas.	2.8

Note: Excludes jail population unless otherwise noted. (1) Prisoners sentenced to more than one year. Rates are per 100,000 population, based upon U.S. Census Bureau population estimates for Jan. 1, 2012. (2) Federal totals include prisoners sentenced under DC's criminal code. (3) Population based on custody count (number of prisoners held in its facilities) as opposed to jurisdiction count (number of prisoners under its legal authority). Some states are unable to provide both counts. (4) Prisons and jails form one integrated system. Data includes total jail and prison population.

Imprisonment Rate by Gender, Race, Hispanic Origin, and Age, 2011

Source: *Prisoners in 2011*, Bureau of Justice Statistics, U.S. Dept. of Justice

(number of prisoners sentenced to more than one year per 100,000 of each group in the U.S. resident population)

Age	Male				Age	Female			
	All races[1]	White	Black	Hispanic		All races[1]	White	Black	Hispanic
18-19	475	166	1,544	574	18-19	21	14	41	25
20-24	1,561	712	4,702	1,898	20-24	106	85	183	114
25-29	2,169	1,074	6,883	2,666	25-29	171	144	300	177
30-34	2,278	1,115	7,517	2,762	30-34	175	151	313	169
35-39	2,029	1,049	6,603	2,460	35-39	156	136	286	142
40-44	1,707	949	5,450	2,084	40-44	138	110	274	138
45-49	1,459	834	4,604	1,830	45-49	110	85	226	107
50-54	999	565	3,257	1,402	50-54	64	46	143	74
55-59	601	345	1,999	990	55-59	31	22	66	44
60-64	364	230	1,125	685	60-64	15	12	30	23
65 or older	137	95	409	286	65 or older	4	3	7	7
Total[2]	932	478	3,023	1,238	Total[2]	65	51	129	71

Note: Rates are based on U.S. Census Bureau population estimates for Jan. 1, 2012. Hispanics may be of any race but are not included in white and black populations here. (1) Includes races not shown and persons who reported being of two or more races. (2) Includes persons under age 18.

Crime Rates in the 10 Largest U.S. Metropolitan Areas, 2011

Source: *Crime in the United States, 2011*, Federal Bureau of Investigation, U.S. Dept. of Justice

(per 100,000 population, as estimated by U.S. Census Bureau for July 1 of year)

	Population	Violent crime					Property crime			
		All violent crimes	Murder and nonnegligent manslaughter	Forcible rape	Robbery	Aggravated assault	All property crimes	Burglary	Larceny-theft	Motor vehicle theft
Atlanta-Sandy Springs-Marietta, GA	5,338,234	400.9	6.0	20.6	152.6	221.8	3,552.0	973.7	2,201.4	376.9
Boston-Cambridge-Quincy, MA-NH	4,578,146	374.7	2.8	22.4	100.1	249.3	2,109.0	437.6	1,512.8	158.6
Chicago-Joliet-Naperville, IL-IN-WI	9,491,301	NA	6.4	NA	190.7	205.2	2,791.5	592.2	1,913.4	285.9
Dallas-Fort Worth-Arlington, TX	6,505,848	358.4	4.5	26.9	124.3	202.6	3,498.5	922.8	2,280.5	295.3
Houston-Sugar Land-Baytown, TX	6,071,933	550.8	5.4	26.8	189.9	328.7	3,576.9	900.8	2,336.7	339.4
Los Angeles-Long Beach-Santa Ana, CA	12,979,653	405.4	4.9	17.8	170.6	212.0	2,232.7	462.6	1,413.2	356.9
Miami-Ft. Lauderdale-Pompano Beach, FL	5,640,473	596.7	6.1	25.7	204.1	360.7	4,193.3	963.9	2,907.1	322.3
New York-Northern New Jersey-Long Island, NY-NJ-PA	18,974,419	406.0	4.5	10.0	166.7	224.8	1,744.1	297.8	1,305.5	140.8
Philadelphia-Camden-Wilmington, PA-NJ-DE-MD	5,988,988	532.3	8.1	27.2	218.0	279.0	2,747.3	557.9	1,973.0	216.4
Washington-Arlington-Alexandria, DC-VA-MD-WV	5,651,690	334.6	4.4	16.1	159.3	154.7	2,386.0	355.9	1,769.6	260.5

NA = Not available.

Arrests by Race, 2011

Source: *Crime in the United States, 2011*, Federal Bureau of Investigation, U.S. Dept. of Justice

Each instance in which a person is arrested, cited, or summoned for an offense is counted as one arrest. The figures below therefore do not represent the number of individuals arrested but the number of times persons were arrested, as an individual may be arrested multiple times in one year. Arrest estimates are based on statistics from law enforcement agencies that reported 12 months of arrest data.

Offense charged	Total	Number of arrests where arrestee was—				% distrib. for offense charged[1]			
		White	Black	Amer. Indian/ Alaska Native	Asian/ Pacific Islander	White	Black	Amer. Indian/ Alaska Native	Asian/ Pacific Islander
Violent crime.............	410,608	243,928	157,384	5,434	3,862	59.4%	38.3%	1.3%	0.9%
Murder and nonnegligent manslaughter.........	8,341	4,000	4,149	105	87	48.0	49.7	1.3	1.0
Forcible rape............	14,611	9,504	4,811	170	126	65.0	32.9	1.2	0.9
Robbery	82,436	35,443	45,827	619	547	43.0	55.6	0.8	0.7
Aggravated assault........	305,220	194,981	102,597	4,540	3,102	63.9	33.6	1.5	1.0
Property crime	1,265,509	861,756	372,993	17,982	12,778	68.1	29.5	1.4	1.0
Burglary	227,899	151,934	72,244	2,095	1,626	66.7	31.7	0.9	0.7
Larceny-theft...........	977,743	670,768	281,197	15,122	10,656	68.6	28.8	1.5	1.1
Motor vehicle theft	50,902	32,575	17,250	658	419	64.0	33.9	1.3	0.8
Arson	8,965	6,479	2,302	107	77	72.3	25.7	1.2	0.9
Other assaults[2]...........	952,421	625,330	304,083	14,875	8,133	65.7	31.9	1.6	0.9
Forgery and counterfeiting	53,791	35,239	17,695	295	562	65.5	32.9	0.5	1.0
Fraud	127,664	84,919	40,621	1,140	984	66.5	31.8	0.9	0.8
Embezzlement	12,454	8,155	4,032	65	202	65.5	32.4	0.5	1.6
Stolen property: buying, receiving, possessing......	71,727	47,434	23,191	542	560	66.1	32.3	0.8	0.8
Vandalism................	182,482	132,850	45,055	3,029	1,548	72.8	24.7	1.7	0.8
Weapons: carrying, possessing, etc...........	117,820	68,453	47,515	859	993	58.1	40.3	0.7	0.8
Prostitution and commercialized vice.......	44,090	23,555	19,227	255	1,053	53.4	43.6	0.6	2.4
Sex offenses (except forcible rape and prostitution)	52,891	38,422	13,189	729	551	72.6	24.9	1.4	1.0
Drug abuse violations........	1,171,866	783,564	371,248	8,275	8,779	66.9	31.7	0.7	0.7
Gambling	6,507	1,937	4,351	40	179	29.8	66.9	0.6	2.8
Offenses against the family and children	87,586	56,973	28,183	1,848	582	65.0	32.2	2.1	0.7
Driving under the influence....	924,210	788,175	111,480	13,618	10,937	85.3	12.1	1.5	1.2
Liquor laws	380,663	312,106	51,446	12,896	4,215	82.0	13.5	3.4	1.1
Drunkenness	413,723	339,019	64,268	7,619	2,817	81.9	15.5	1.8	0.7
Disorderly conduct	447,201	281,531	153,840	8,771	3,059	63.0	34.4	2.0	0.7
Vagrancy	22,375	12,989	8,794	447	145	58.1	39.3	2.0	0.6
All other offenses (except traffic violations)...........	2,693,823	1,794,893	837,095	42,869	18,966	66.6	31.1	1.6	0.7
Suspicion[3]................	1,150	634	506	5	5	55.1	44.0	0.4	0.4
Curfew and loitering law violations................	59,164	36,271	21,343	829	721	61.3	36.1	1.4	1.2
Total arrests	9,499,725	6,578,133	2,697,539	142,422	81,631	69.2	28.4	1.5	0.9

(1) Percentages may not add up to 100 due to rounding. (2) Simple assaults, where no weapons were used and where the victim did not sustain serious injury (e.g., stalking). (3) Arrested for no specific offense and released without formal charges being placed against a person.

Sentenced Prisoners by Offense, Race, and Hispanic Origin, 2010

Source: *Prisoners in 2011*, Bureau of Justice Statistics, U.S. Dept. of Justice

Offense	All inmates		White[1]		Black[1]		Hispanic	
	Number	% of total	Number	% of total	Number	% of total	Number	% of total
Total...................	1,362,028	100.0%	468,528	100.0%	518,763	100.0%	289,429	100.0%
All violent crimes	725,000	53.2	231,800	49.5	286,400	55.2	164,200	56.7
Murder[2].............	166,700	12.2	47,200	10.1	70,100	13.5	38,900	13.4
Manslaughter	21,500	1.6	8,600	1.8	7,800	1.5	3,300	1.1
Rape	70,200	5.2	32,500	6.9	22,200	4.3	8,600	3.0
Other sexual assault	90,600	6.7	44,100	9.4	17,200	3.3	26,200	9.1
Robbery	185,800	13.6	40,400	8.6	96,600	18.6	38,000	13.1
Assault	146,800	10.8	44,300	9.5	57,200	11.0	38,500	13.3
Other violent crimes	43,400	3.2	14,900	3.2	15,400	3.0	10,700	3.7
All property crimes........	249,500	18.3	110,800	23.6	76,300	14.7	41,900	14.5
Burglary...............	130,000	9.5	54,400	11.6	43,000	8.3	22,600	7.8
Larceny	45,900	3.4	20,500	4.4	14,600	2.8	6,700	2.3
Motor vehicle theft........	15,000	1.1	6,000	1.3	3,100	0.6	5,700	2.0
Fraud.................	30,800	2.3	15,900	3.4	8,400	1.6	2,800	1.0
Other property crimes.....	27,700	2.0	14,000	3.0	7,200	1.4	4,000	1.4
Drug offenses[3]	237,000	17.4	69,500	14.8	105,600	20.4	47,800	16.5
Public-order offenses[4].....	142,500	10.5	53,100	11.3	47,800	9.2	34,400	11.9
Other/unspecified[5]........	7,900	0.6	3,300	0.7	2,700	0.5	1,200	0.4

Note: Counts based on state prisoners with a sentence of more than one year. Details may not add up to total due to rounding and missing offense data. (1) White and black totals exclude Hispanics and persons of two or more races. (2) Includes non-negligent manslaughter. (3) Includes trafficking, possession, and other drug offenses. (4) Includes weapons, drunk driving, court offenses, commercialized vice, morals and decency offenses, liquor law violations, and other public-order offenses. (5) Includes juvenile offenses and other unspecified offense categories.

Firearm Violence, 1993-2011

Source: *Firearm Violence, 1993-2011*, Bureau of Justice Statistics, U.S. Dept. of Justice

The number of homicides due to firearms has declined by nearly 40% since 1993, the year Congress passed the Brady Handgun Violence Prevention Act. The Brady Act required licensed dealers to conduct background checks on individuals seeking to purchase firearms. As of Dec. 31, 2009, federal, state, and local authorities had denied more than 1.9 mil of 108 mil applications to purchase firearms; the most common reason for denial was a previous felony conviction or indictment. (The Federal Assault Weapons Ban, which Congress passed in 1994 to prohibit the manufacture of certain semi-automatic weapons, expired in 2004.)

Year	Homicides By handgun	By other type of firearm	Total	Rate[1]	Nonfatal victimizations By handgun	By other type of firearm	Total	Rate[2]
1993	NA	NA	18,253	7.0	NA	NA	1,529,700	730
1994	13,510	2,830	17,527	6.7	1,387,100	150,200	1,568,200	740
1995	12,090	2,670	15,551	5.8	1,240,200	132,800	1,193,200	550
1996	10,800	2,510	14,037	5.2	999,600	141,000	1,100,800	510
1997	9,750	2,630	13,252	4.9	894,200	159,800	1,024,100	470
1998	8,870	2,160	11,798	4.3	783,400	141,100	835,400	380
1999	8,010	2,150	10,828	3.9	659,600	74,100	640,900	290
2000	8,020	2,190	10,801	3.8	555,800	65,300	610,200	270
2001	7,820	2,220	11,348	4.0	506,600	65,900	563,100	250
2002	8,230	2,620	11,829	4.1	471,600	63,200	540,000	230
2003	8,890	2,180	11,920	4.1	436,100	53,200	467,300	200
2004	8,330	2,350	11,624	4.0	391,700	53,400	456,500	190
2005	8,550	2,840	12,352	4.2	410,600	56,200	503,500	210
2006	9,060	2,700	12,791	4.3	497,400	47,600	614,400	250
2007	8,570	3,080	12,632	4.2	509,700	65,600	554,800	220
2008	7,930	3,120	12,179	4.0	400,700	57,400	371,300	150
2009	7,370	2,970	11,493	3.8	348,700	37,600	410,100	160
2010	6,920	3,030	11,078	3.6	382,100	26,700	415,000	160
2011	7,230	2,690	11,101	3.6	389,400	49,700	467,300	180

NA = Not available. **Note:** Numbers may not add up to totals because of small differences in sample sizes. (1) Per 100,000 persons. (2) Per 100,000 persons age 12 or older.

Hate Crimes by Offense Type, Bias Motivation, 2011

Source: *Hate Crime Statistics, 2011*, Federal Bureau of Investigation (FBI), U.S. Dept. of Justice

Hate crimes are defined as crimes in which victims are chosen because of one or more personal characteristics, such as race, ethnicity, or religion. Congress enacted the Hate Crime Statistics Act of 1990, which led to the collection of hate crime data as part of the FBI's Uniform Crime Report (UCR) program beginning in 1992. Not all agencies that participate in the UCR program submit hate crime data, so the data presented is not representative of the nation as a whole.

Bias motivation	Incidents	Crimes against persons[1] Aggravated assault	Simple assault	Intimidation	Other	Total crimes against persons	Crimes against property[2] Robbery	Burglary	Larceny-theft	Destruction/ damage/vandalism	Other	Total crimes against property	Total crimes against society[3]
SINGLE-BIAS INCIDENTS	7,240	893	1,593	2,101	27	4,614	131	124	152	2,121	78	2,606	20
Race	3,465	470	752	1,135	8	2,365	50	52	76	868	39	1,085	15
Anti-white	577	91	171	147	2	411	24	9	41	77	14	165	1
Anti-black	2,494	347	500	897	5	1,749	21	34	19	647	12	733	12
Anti-American Indian/ Alaskan Native	67	12	20	4	0	36	1	0	11	10	7	29	2
Anti-Asian/Pacific Islander	165	9	45	56	1	111	1	3	5	42	3	54	0
Anti-multiple races, group	162	11	16	31	0	58	3	6	0	92	3	104	0
Religion	1,318	36	108	291	3	438	5	29	49	780	17	880	0
Anti-Jewish	820	15	43	187	0	245	3	7	13	549	3	575	0
Anti-Catholic	68	0	3	3	0	6	0	4	11	46	1	62	0
Anti-Protestant	49	4	4	1	0	9	0	6	2	30	2	40	0
Anti-Islamic	175	14	41	70	0	125	1	1	7	39	2	50	0
Anti-other religion	139	3	8	23	3	37	1	8	3	84	6	102	0
Anti-multiple religions, group	63	0	9	7	0	16	0	3	11	31	2	47	0
Anti-atheism/ agnosticism/etc.	4	0	0	0	0	0	0	0	2	1	1	4	0
Sexual orientation	1,508	252	491	380	11	1,134	54	17	17	275	10	373	1
Anti-male homosexual	871	162	291	218	8	679	33	9	6	138	5	191	1
Anti-female homosexual	168	28	42	56	2	128	3	1	1	35	0	40	0
Anti-homosexual	429	60	142	99	1	302	17	5	7	96	2	127	0
Anti-heterosexual	17	2	5	3	0	10	1	2	0	3	1	7	0
Anti-bisexual	23	0	11	4	0	15	0	0	3	3	2	8	0
Ethnicity/national origin	891	128	226	280	1	635	22	25	8	190	8	253	3
Anti-Hispanic	506	82	144	153	1	380	17	11	4	87	5	124	2
Anti-other ethnicity/ national origin	385	46	82	127	0	255	5	14	4	103	3	129	1
Disability	58	7	16	15	4	42	0	1	2	8	4	15	1
Anti-physical	23	0	7	5	2	14	0	0	1	4	4	9	0
Anti-mental	35	7	9	10	2	28	0	1	1	4	0	6	1
MULTIPLE-BIAS INCIDENTS[4]	14	2	2	5	0	9	0	0	0	4	1	5	0
TOTAL OFFENSES	7,254	895	1,595	2,106	27	4,623	131	124	152	2,125	79	2,611	20

(1) Includes murder and non-negligent manslaughter, forcible rape, and additional offenses not shown here in detail. (2) Includes arson, motor vehicle theft, and additional offenses not shown here in detail. (3) Includes drug or narcotic offenses, gambling and prostitution offenses, and weapon law violations where society as a whole is considered the victim. (4) Where more than one offense type occurs and at least two offense types are motivated by different biases.

Notable Assassinations Since 1865

1865—Apr. 14: U.S. Pres. Abraham Lincoln shot by John Wilkes Booth, well-known actor with Confederate sympathies, at Ford's Theater in Washington, DC; died Apr. 15.
1881—Mar. 13: Alexander II of Russia. **July 2:** U.S. Pres. James A. Garfield shot by Charles J. Guiteau, disappointed office seeker, in Washington, DC; died Sept. 19.
1894—June 24: French Pres. Sadi Carnot by Sante Caserio, Italian anarchist, in Lyon.
1898—Sept. 10: Empress Elizabeth of Austria stabbed by Luigi Lucchesi, Italian anarchist.
1900—July 29: Umberto I, king of Italy, by an anarchist.
1901—Sept. 6: U.S. Pres. William McKinley shot by Leon Czolgosz, anarchist, in Buffalo, NY; died Sept. 14.
1908—Feb. 1: King Carlos I of Portugal and his son Luís Filipe in Lisbon.
1913—Feb. 23: Mexican Pres. Francisco I. Madero and Vice Pres. José María Pino Suárez. **Mar. 18:** King George of Greece.
1914—June 28: Archduke Francis Ferdinand of Austria-Hungary and his wife shot by Gavrilo Princip, Serb nationalist, in Sarajevo, Bosnia.
1916—Dec. 30: Grigory Rasputin, Russian mystic and court figure, by group of aristocrats.
1918—July 12: Grand Duke Michael of Russia, at Perm. **July 16:** Nicholas II, former (abdicated) czar of Russia; his wife, Czarina Alexandra; their son, Czarevitch Alexis; their daughters, Grand Duchesses Olga, Tatiana, Marie, Anastasia; and 4 members of household executed by Bolsheviks at Ekaterinburg.
1920—May 20: Mexican Pres. Gen. Venustiano Carranza, in Tlaxcalantongo.
1922—Aug. 22: Michael Collins, Irish revolutionary, in West Cork. **Dec. 16:** Polish Pres. Gabriel Narutowicz in Warsaw.
1923—July 20: Gen. Francisco "Pancho" Villa, ex-rebel leader, in Parral, Mexico.
1928—July 17: Gen. Alvaro Obregon, president-elect of Mexico, in San Angel.
1932—May 6: French Pres. Paul Doumer shot by Russian émigré, Pavel Gorgulov, in Paris.
1934—July 25: Austrian Chancellor Engelbert Dollfuss by Nazis, in Vienna.
1935—Sept. 8: Sen. Huey P. Long, former Louisiana governor, shot by Dr. Carl Austin Weiss, son-in-law of political opponent, in Baton Rouge; died Sept. 10.
1940—Aug. 20: Leon Trotsky (Lev Bronstein), exiled Soviet commissar of war, fatally wounded with ice ax by Soviet agent nr. Mexico City.
1948—Jan. 30: Leader of movement for Indian independence Mohandas K. Gandhi (Mahatma) shot by Hindu fanatic in New Delhi. **Sept. 17:** Count Folke Bernadotte, UN mediator for Palestine, by Jewish extremists in Jerusalem.
1951—July 20: Jordanian King Abdullah ibn Hussein. **Oct. 16:** Prime Min. Liaquat Ali Khan of Pakistan shot, in Rawalpindi.
1956—Sept. 21: Pres. Anastasio Somoza of Nicaragua shot in Leon; died Sept. 29.
1957—July 26: Guatemalan Pres. Carlos Castillo Armas, in Guatemala City by one of his guards.
1958—July 14: King Faisal of Iraq, Crown Prince Abdullah, and **July 15,** Prem. Nuri as-Said, by rebels in Baghdad.
1959—Sept. 25: Prime Min. Solomon Bandaranaike of Ceylon (Sri Lanka), by Buddhist monk in Colombo.
1961—Jan. 17: First elected prime min. of the Congo, Patrice Lumumba, in Katanga Prov. by political rivals. **May 30:** Dominican dictator Rafael Leónidas Trujillo Molina, nr. Ciudad Trujillo.
1963—June 12: Medgar Evers, NAACP's Mississippi field secretary, shot by Byron De La Beckwith in Jackson, MS. **Nov. 2:** Pres. Ngo Dinh Diem of South Vietnam and his brother, Ngo Dinh Nhu, in military coup. **Nov. 22:** U.S. Pres. John F. Kennedy shot while riding in motorcade through downtown Dallas, TX; accused assailant Lee Harvey Oswald murdered by nightclub owner Jack Ruby while awaiting trial.
1965—Jan. 21: Iranian Prem. Hassan Ali Mansour, in Tehran. **Feb. 21:** Malcolm X, black nationalist leader, shot by 3 men linked to Nation of Islam at New York City rally.
1966—Sept. 6: Prime Min. Hendrik F. Verwoerd of South Africa stabbed to death in parliament at Cape Town.
1968—Apr. 4: Rev. Martin Luther King Jr. fatally shot in Memphis, TN; James Earl Ray convicted of crime. **June 5:** Sen. Robert F. Kennedy (D, NY) shot in Los Angeles; died June 6. Sirhan Sirhan convicted of crime.
1971—Nov. 28: Jordanian Prime Min. Wasfi Tal by Palestinian guerrillas, in Cairo, Egypt.
1973—Mar. 2: U.S. Amb. Cleo A. Noel Jr., U.S. Charge d'Affaires George C. Moore, and Belgian Charge d'Affaires Guy Eid by Palestinian guerrillas in Khartoum, Sudan. **Dec. 20:** Spanish Prem. Luis Carrero Blanco in car bombing by Basque separatist group ETA, in Madrid.
1974—Aug. 19: U.S. Amb. to Cyprus, Rodger P. Davies, by sniper's bullet in Nicosia.

1975—Feb. 11: Pres. Richard Ratsimandrava of Madagascar shot in Tananarive. **Mar. 25:** Saudi Arabian King Faisal shot by nephew Prince Musad Abdel Aziz, in Riyadh. **Aug. 15:** Bangladesh Pres. Sheik Mujibur Rahman killed in coup.
1976—Feb. 13: Nigerian head of state, Gen. Murtala Ramat Mohammed, by self-styled young revolutionaries.
1977—Mar. 16: Kamal Jumblat, Lebanese Druse chieftain, shot nr. Beirut. **Mar. 18:** Rep. of the Congo Pres. Marien Ngouabi shot in Brazzaville.
1978—May 9: Former Italian Prem. Aldo Moro killed by Red Brigades terrorists who had abducted him Mar. 16 in Rome and held him hostage. **July 9:** Former Iraqi Prem. Abdul Razak Al-Naif shot in London.
1979—Feb. 14: U.S. Amb. Adolph Dubs shot by Afghan Muslim extremists in Kabul. **Aug. 27:** Lord Mountbatten, WWII hero, and 2 others killed when a bomb exploded on his fishing boat off coast of Co. Sligo, Ireland. IRA claimed responsibility. **Oct. 26:** S. Korean Pres. Park Chung Hee and 6 bodyguards fatally shot by Kim Jae Kyu, head of S. Korean intelligence agency.
1980—Apr. 12: Liberian Pres. William R. Tolbert in military coup. **Sept. 17:** Former Nicaraguan Pres. Anastasio Somoza Debayle shot in Paraguay.
1981—Oct. 6: Egyptian Pres. Anwar al-Sadat shot by commandos while reviewing military parade in Cairo; 7 others killed, 28 wounded.
1982—Sept. 14: Lebanese Pres.-elect Bashir Gemayel killed by bomb in east Beirut.
1983—Aug. 21: Philippine opposition leader Benigno Aquino Jr. shot by gunman at Manila Intl. Airport.
1984—Oct. 31: Indian Prime Min. Indira Gandhi shot by 2 Sikh bodyguards in New Delhi.
1986—Feb. 28: Swedish Prime Min. Olof Palme shot by gunman on Stockholm street for unknown reasons.
1987—June 1: Lebanese Prem. Rashid Karami killed when bomb exploded aboard helicopter.
1988—Apr. 16: PLO military chief Khalil Wazir (Abu Jihad) gunned down by Israeli commandos in Tunisia.
1989—Aug. 18: Colombian pres. candidate Luis Carlos Galán killed by Medellín cartel drug traffickers at campaign rally in Bogotá. **Nov. 22:** Lebanese Pres. Rene Moawad killed when bomb exploded next to his motorcade.
1990—Mar. 22: Colombian pres. candidate Bernardo Jaramillo Ossa shot by gunman at airport in Bogotá.
1991—May 21: Former Indian Prime Min. Rajiv Gandhi killed by bomb during election rally in Madras.
1992—June 29: Algerian Pres. Mohammed Boudiaf shot by gunman in Annaba.
1993—May 1: Sri Lankan Pres. Ranasinghe Premadasa killed by bomb in Colombo.
1994—Mar. 23: Mexican pres. candidate Luis Donaldo Colosio shot by gunman Mario Aburto Martinez. **Apr. 6:** Burundian Pres. Cyprien Ntaryamira and Rwandan Pres. Juvénal Habyarimana killed with 8 others when their plane was shot down.
1995—Nov. 4: Israeli Prime Min. Yitzhak Rabin shot by Yigal Amir, Jewish extremist, at peace rally in Tel Aviv.
1996—Oct. 2: Andrei Lukanov, former Bulgarian prime min., shot outside home by unidentified gunman.
1998—Feb. 6: Prefect of Corsica, Claude Erigmac, shot in back by 2 unidentified gunmen while walking to concert. **Apr. 26:** Guatemalan Roman Catholic Bishop Juan Gerardi Conedera, human rights champion, found beaten to death in Guatemala City.
1999—Mar. 23: Paraguayan Vice Pres. Luis María Argaña, ambushed and shot to death along with his driver, by 4 unidentified assailants, in Asunción. **Apr. 9:** Niger Pres. Ibrahim Bare Mainassara ambushed and killed by dissident soldiers. **Oct. 27:** Armenian Prime Min. Vazgen Sarkissian, along with 7 others, shot during session of parliament.
2000—Jan. 15: Serbian paramilitary leader Zeljko Raznjatovic (Arkan), with 2 others, shot by unidentified gunman in Belgrade. **June 8:** Brig. Gen. Stephen Saunders, Britain's senior military rep. in Greece, fatally shot by 2 men on motorcycle, while driving car in Athens suburb.
2001—Jan. 16: Dem. Rep. of the Congo Pres. Laurent Kabila shot to death by bodyguard at pres. palace in Kinshasa. **June 1:** Nepal's King Birendra, Queen Aiswarya, and 7 other royals fatally shot by Crown Prince Dipendra, who also killed himself. **Oct. 14:** Abdel Rahman Hamad, a leader of Palestinian militant group Hamas, shot by Israeli military snipers. **Oct. 17:** Israeli tourism min. Rehavam Zeevifatally shot; Popular Front for the Liberation of Palestine claimed responsibility.
2002—Mar. 16: Colombian cleric Isaías Duarte Cancino, critic of Colombian guerrillas and drug traffickers, shot by unidentified gunmen outside of church in Cali. **May 6:** Dutch right-wing politician Pim Fortuyn shot outside radio station in Hilversum. **July 6:** Afghan Vice Pres. Haji Abdul Qadir shot outside his office in Kabul.
2003—Mar. 12: Serbian Prime Min. Zoran Djindjic shot by paramilitary snipers outside govt. headquarters in Belgrade.

Apr. 10: Shiite Muslim cleric Abdul Majid al-Khoei attacked by crowd, hacked to death at Imam Ali mosque, Najaf, Iraq. **Apr. 17:** Sergei Yushenkov, former Russian legislator and Liberal Party head, shot outside apartment in Moscow. **Sept. 10:** Swedish Foreign Min. Anna Lindh stabbed in Stockholm dept. store by mentally ill man; died Sept. 11.

2004—Feb. 13: Former Chechen Pres. Zelimkhan Yandarbiyev killed after car exploded in Qatar. **Mar. 22:** Sheik Ahmed Yassin, spiritual leader of Hamas, by Israeli missile attack in Gaza City. **Apr. 17:** Hamas leader Abdel Aziz Rantisi by Israeli missile strike, in Gaza City. **May 9:** Chechen Pres. Akhmad Kadyrov by bomb at WWII memorial service in Grozny. **May 17:** Iraqi Gov. Council Pres. Ezzedine Salim, by car bomb at Green Zone checkpoint in Baghdad. **Nov. 2:** Filmmaker Theo van Gogh, critic of Islam and great-grandnephew of painter Vincent van Gogh, shot and stabbed by Muslim militant in Amsterdam.

2005—Jan. 4: Baghdad Gov. Ali al-Haidari gunned down by insurgents in Baghdad, Iraq. **Feb. 14:** Former Lebanese Prime Min. Rafik al-Hariri killed when motorcade bombed in Beirut. **Mar. 8:** Former Chechen pres. Aslan Maskhadov killed in raid by Russian special forces, in village outside Grozny.

2006—Feb. 11: Leading Kazakhstan opposition politician Altynbek Sarsenbayev (Sarsenbaiuly) kidnapped, found murdered outside Almaty. **Sept. 14:** Andrei Kozlov, Russian central banker active in reforming industry, shot by unidentified gunmen in Moscow. **Oct. 7:** Anna Politkovskaya, reporter critical of Kremlin's Chechnya policies, fatally shot by unidentified gunman in apartment building in Moscow.

2007—June 13: Walid Eido, Lebanese parliament member who was part of anti-Syria coalition, killed by car bomb in Beirut. **Aug. 2:** *Oakland Post* editor Chauncey Bailey, who was investigating financial status of black Muslim organization, shot in Oakland, CA. **Dec. 27:** Benazir Bhutto, former Pakistani prime min. and first female elected leader of a Muslim state, by gunfire and/or bomb as she was leaving political rally for Pakistan People's Party.

2008—Feb. 12: Imad Mughniyeh, top Hezbollah commander and reputed mastermind of the 1983 bombing of U.S. embassy in Beirut, by car bomb in Damascus, Syria. Mughniyeh had been on FBI's Most Wanted Terrorist list. **May 8:** Edgar Eusebio Millán

Gómez, Mexico's acting national police chief, by gunmen outside his Mexico City home. **Aug. 1:** Syrian brig. gen. and top presidential aide Mohammed Suleiman reportedly shot by sniper nr. Tartus. **Oct. 23:** Ivo Pukanic, editor-in-chief of Croatian political newspaper *Nacional*, killed in Zagreb when bomb exploded nr. his car.

2009—Mar. 2: Guinea-Bissau's longtime Pres. João Bernardo Vieira shot and killed by army troops outside his home in Bissau. **Mar. 31:** Sulim Yamadayev, former Chechen general and enemy of the Kremlin-installed president, killed by gunmen in Dubai, UAE. **May 31:** Dr. George Tiller, one of the few doctors in the U.S. to perform abortions late in pregnancy, shot to death in his Wichita, KS, church by anti-abortion activist. **June 12:** Harith al-Obaidi, Sunni member of Iraq's parliament, shot at a Baghdad mosque. **Sept. 27:** Two officials from the Russian republic of Dagestan, Alim-Sultan Alkhamatov and Alim-Sultan Atuyev, shot dead in separate incidents.

2010—Jan. 19: Mahmoud al-Mabhouh, a senior commander for Hamas, found drugged and suffocated in his Dubai, UAE, hotel room; Israel's Mossad spy agency suspected. **Aug. 2:** Raza Haider, member of Pakistan's parliament, shot by 4 gunmen in a mosque in Karachi.

2011—July 12: Ahmed Wali Karzai, power-wielding half-brother of Afghan Pres. Hamid Karzai, shot dead in his Kandahar home by a longtime confidant. Two other Karzai allies, including Kandahar mayor Ghulam Hamidi, assassinated over the next 2 weeks. **July 28:** Gen. Abdul Fattah Younes, Libya's rebel commander, and 2 officers killed in Benghazi. **Sept. 20:** Burhanuddin Rabbani, leader of Afghanistan's High Peace Council and a former pres., killed in his Kabul home by assassin with explosives hidden in his turban.

2012—Jan. 11: Iranian nuclear scientist Mostafa Ahmadi Roshan killed by car bomb. **July 18:** Three senior Syrian officials, including Defense Min. Dawoud Rajiha and Assef Shawkat, brother-in-law to Pres. Bashar al-Assad, killed by bomb.

2013—Feb. 6: Chokri Belaid, vocal critic of Tunisian Prime Min. Hamadi Jobali, shot in front of his home, sparking violent demonstrations against the Islamist govt. **May 3:** Gunmen on motorbikes killed Sadiq Zaman Khattak, an anti-Taliban candidate for Pakistan's National Assembly, and his 4-year-old son in Karachi.

Notable Assassination Attempts Since 1912

1912—Oct. 14: Former U.S. Pres. Theodore Roosevelt shot and wounded by mentally ill man in Milwaukee, WI.

1933—Feb. 15: In Miami, FL, anarchist Joseph Zangara shot at Pres.-elect Franklin D. Roosevelt, but a woman seized his arm; bullet fatally wounded Chicago Mayor Anton J. Cermak, who died Mar. 6.

1944—July 20: Adolf Hitler injured when bomb, planted by German officer, exploded in his headquarters; one aide killed,12 injured.

1950—Nov. 1: In attempt to assassinate Pres. Harry Truman, 2 members of Puerto Rican nationalist movement—Griselio Torresola and Oscar Collazo—tried to shoot their way into Blair House, across the street from White House. Torresola killed. Pvt. Leslie Coffelt, White House policeman, fatally shot.

1970—Nov. 27: Pope Paul VI unharmed by knife-wielding assailant who attempted to attack him in airport in Manila, Philippines.

1972—May 15: Alabama Gov. George Wallace seriously wounded when shot in Laurel, MD, by fame-seeking Arthur Bremer.

1975—Sept. 5: Pres. Gerald R. Ford unharmed when Secret Service agent grabbed pistol aimed at him by Lynette "Squeaky" Fromme, follower of cult leader Charles Manson, in Sacramento, CA. **Sept. 22:** Pres. Ford unharmed when bystander grabbed arm of Sara Jane Moore as she fired upon Ford in San Francisco.

1980—May 29: Civil rights leader Vernon E. Jordan Jr. shot and wounded in Ft. Wayne, IN.

1981—Mar. 30: Pres. Ronald Reagan, along with Press Sec. James Brady, Secret Service agent Timothy J. McCarthy, and Washington, DC, policeman Thomas Delahanty shot and seriously wounded by John W. Hinckley Jr. in DC. **May 13:** Pope John Paul II and 2 bystanders shot and wounded by Mehmet Ali Agca, an escaped Turkish prisoner, in St. Peter's Square, Rome.

1982—May 12: Pope John Paul II wounded by ultra-conservative priest wielding bayonet, in Fatima, Portugal.

1984—Oct. 12: British Prime Min. Margaret Thatcher unharmed when a bomb, said to have been planted by the IRA, exploded at the Grand Hotel in Brighton, England, during a Party conference; 4 died, incl. a member of Parliament.

1986—Sept. 7: Chilean Pres. Gen. Augusto Pinochet Ugarte unharmed after motorcade was attacked by rebels.

1995—June 26: Egyptian Pres. Hosni Mubarak unharmed when gunmen fired on his motorcade in Addis Ababa, Ethiopia; 4 died, incl. 2 Ethiopian police officers.

1997—Feb. 12: Colombian Pres. Ernesto Samper Pizano unharmed when bomb exploded on runway in Barranquilla as his plane was preparing to land. **Apr. 30:** Tajik Pres. Imamali Rakhmanov injured when a grenade was thrown at him.

1998—Feb. 9: Georgian Pres. Eduard A. Shevardnadze unharmed when gunmen fired on his motorcade in Tbilisi.

2002—Apr. 14: Leading Colombian pres. candidate Álvaro Uribe Vélez unharmed after bomb exploded under parked bus as his motorcade passed in Barranquilla; 3 bystanders killed. **July 14:** French Pres. Jacques Chirac unharmed after Maxime Brunerie, gunman with ties to neo-Nazi groups, fired at his open-top jeep during Bastille Day parade in Paris. **Sept. 5:** Afghan Pres. Hamid Karzai unharmed after militant shot at car in Kandahar. **Nov. 25:** Turkmenistan Pres. Saparmurat Niyazov unharmed after gunmen opened fire on his motorcade in Ashgabat.

2003—Dec. 14: Pakistani Pres. Pervez Musharraf unharmed after bomb detonated on bridge in Rawalpindi seconds after his motorcade crossed.

2004—Mar. 19: Taiwanese Pres. Chen Shui-bian shot while campaigning in motorcade; minor injuries. **July 13:** Separatists bombed motorcade of Sergei Abramov, Chechnya's acting pres. **Sept. 5:** Ukrainian opposition presidential candidate Viktor Yushchenko, who later won office, fell ill after meeting; diagnosed with dioxin poisoning. **Sept. 16:** Rocket fired at helicopter carrying Afghan Pres. Hamid Karzai, nr. Gardez.

2005—Mar. 15: Kosovo Pres. Ibrahim Rugova survived bombing of his motorcade as it traveled through Pristina.

2007—June 29: Rockets hit plane carrying former rebel chief and Côte d'Ivoire Prime Min. Guillaume Soro, shortly after plane landed in Bouake; Soro unhurt.

2008—Feb. 11: Pres. José Ramos-Horta shot in attack led by fugitive former army official in Dili, Timor-Leste. Ambush of Prime Min. Xanana Gusmão's motorcade a short time later unsuccessful. **Apr. 27:** Afghan Pres. Hamid Karzai unharmed after Taliban gunmen fired on military parade in Kabul where Karzai was in attendance.

2009—June 22: Yunus-Bek Yevkurov, president of Ingushetia region of Russia, seriously wounded when suicide bomber in car packed with explosives crashed into his motorcade.

2010—Sept. 23: Alexander Ankvab, vice pres. of Georgian region of Abkhazia, survived 4th assassination attempt in 5 years, a grenade fired into his Gudauta home.

2011—Jan. 8: U.S. Rep. Gabrielle Giffords (D, AZ) severely wounded by lone gunman at public meeting nr. an Arizona supermarket; 6 others killed, including a federal judge. **June 3:** Yemeni Pres. Ali Abdullah Saleh survived bombing of presidential palace.

2012—May 18: Taliban soldiers killed 7 in attempt to kill governor of the Afghanistan prov. of Farah. **Sept. 12:** Hassan Sheik Mohamud survived suicide bombing attack on his home 2 days after being elected Somalia's president.

Notable U.S. Kidnappings Since 1924

Bobby Franks, 14, in Chicago, May 21, 1924, by 2 youths from wealthy families—Richard Loeb, 18, and Nathan Leopold, 19—who killed boy. Demand for $10,000 ignored. Loeb killed in prison; Leopold paroled 1958.

Charles A. Lindbergh Jr., 20 months old, nr. Hopewell, NJ, Mar. 1, 1932; found dead May 12. Ransom of $50,000 paid to man identified as Bruno Richard Hauptmann, 35, paroled German convict who entered U.S. illegally. Hauptmann convicted, electrocuted in Trenton, NJ, prison, Apr. 3, 1936.

William A. Hamm Jr., 39, brewing company pres. in St. Paul, MN, June 15, 1933, by Karpis-Barker gang. $100,000 paid. Alvin Karpis given life, paroled in 1969.

Charles F. Urschel, in Oklahoma City, July 22, 1933. Released July 31 after $200,000 paid. George "Machine Gun" Kelly and 5 others sentenced to life.

Brooke L. Hart, 22, in San Jose, CA. Thomas Thurmond and John Holmes arrested after demanding $40,000. When Hart's body was found in San Francisco Bay, Nov. 26, 1933, a mob forced its way into jail and lynched the 2 kidnappers.

June Robles, 6, abducted in Tucson, AZ, Apr. 25, 1934. Missing for 19 days after ransom note sent to parents. Found alive in iron cage buried in desert. No arrests ever made.

George Weyerhaeuser, 9, of Weyerhaeuser lumber company, in Tacoma, WA, May 24, 1935. Returned home June 1 after $200,000 paid. Kidnappers given 20 to 60 years.

Robert C. Greenlease, 6, son of wealthy car dealer, taken from Kansas City, MO, school Sept. 28, 1953; held for $600,000. Body found Oct. 7. Bonnie Brown Heady and Carl A. Hall pleaded guilty, were executed.

Lee Crary, 8, in Everett, WA, Sept. 22, 1957; $10,000 ransom not paid. Crary escaped after 3 days and led police to George E. Collins, who was convicted.

Frank Sinatra Jr., 19, from hotel room in Lake Tahoe, CA, Dec. 8, 1963. Released Dec. 11 after his father paid $240,000 ransom. Three men sentenced to prison.

Barbara Jane Mackle, 20, abducted Dec. 17, 1968, from Atlanta, GA, motel; found unharmed 3 days later, buried in coffin-like box 18 in. underground, after her father paid $500,000 ransom. Gary Steven Krist sentenced to life, Ruth Eisenmann-Schier to 7 years.

Virginia Piper, 49, abducted July 27, 1972, from her home in suburban Minneapolis, MN; found unharmed nr. Duluth 2 days later after husband, retired banker, paid $1 mil ransom.

J. Paul Getty III, 17, grandson of the oil billionaire, disappeared July 10, 1973, in Rome, Italy. Ransom of $2.8 mil paid after abductors sent one of Getty's ears to an Italian newspaper with a warning that other parts of his body would be mutilated.

Patricia "Patty" Hearst, 19, taken from her Berkeley, CA, apartment Feb. 4, 1974; "Symbionese Liberation Army" captors demanded her father, publisher Randolph Hearst, give millions to area poor. Patty implicated in San Francisco bank holdup, Apr. 15. The FBI, Sept. 18, 1975, captured her and others. She was convicted of bank robbery, Mar. 20, 1976; released from prison under executive clemency, Feb. 1, 1979. In 1978, William and Emily Harris were sentenced to 10 years to life for the kidnapping; both were paroled in 1983.

J. Reginald Murphy, 40, an editor of *Atlanta Constitution* (GA), kidnapped Feb. 20, 1974; freed Feb. 22 after newspaper paid $700,000 ransom. William A. H. Williams later convicted.

Jack Teich, Kings Point, NY, steel executive, seized Nov. 12, 1974; released Nov. 19 after payment of $750,000.

Adam Walsh, 6, abducted from Hollywood, FL, dept. store, July 27, 1981. Severed head found 2 weeks later. John Walsh, Adam's father, became active in raising awareness about missing children.

Terry Anderson, 37, Middle East bureau chief for Associated Press, in Beirut, Lebanon, by members of Islamic fundamentalist group Hezbollah on Mar. 16, 1985. Freed Dec. 4, 1991. Anderson had been held hostage with **William Buckley**, 55, CIA station chief in Beirut who was kidnapped Mar. 16, 1984, and died in captivity.

Jaycee Dugard, 11, kidnapped nr. her home in South Lake Tahoe, CA, June 10, 1991; held for 18 years by Nancy and Philip Garrido, who fathered 2 girls with Dugard during her captivity. Dugard, along with her 11- and 15-year-old daughters, was reunited with her family Aug. 27, 2009, after police arrested the Garridos.

Sidney J. Reso, oil company exec., seized Apr. 29, 1992; died May 3. Arthur D. Seale—former security official at oil company—and his wife, Irene, arrested June 19. Arthur sentenced to life in prison; Irene sentenced to 20-year prison term.

Polly Klaas, 12, Petaluma, CA, abducted at knife point, Oct. 1, 1993, during slumber party at her home. Police arrested Richard Allen Davis on Nov. 30; he led them to her body, found Dec. 4 in wooded area of Cloverdale, CA. Davis found guilty June 18, 1996, and sentenced to death Sept. 26.

Tionda Z. Bradley, 10, and sister **Diamond Yvette Bradley**, 3, went missing July 6, 2001, in Chicago. Note left by Tionda at home stated the 2 girls were going to the store and playground. Disappearance still unsolved.

Daniel Pearl, 38, reporter for *Wall Street Journal*, disappeared Jan. 23, 2002, while researching story in Karachi, Pakistan. British-born militant Ahmad Omar Saeed Sheikh Feb. 14 admitted to organizing the kidnapping and said Pearl was dead. Sheikh and 3 others convicted July 15 of kidnapping and murder by judge in Hyderabad.

Elizabeth Smart, 14, abducted from her home in Salt Lake City, UT, June 5, 2002, by Brian D. Mitchell, and forced to live with Mitchell and wife Wanda for 9 months in various U.S. cities; found walking down street with captors in Sandy, UT, 15 mi from Smart family home, Mar. 12, 2003.

Michelle Knight, 21, abducted Aug. 23, 2002; **Amanda Berry**, 17, seized Apr. 21, 2003; and **Gina DeJesus**, 14, kidnapped Apr. 2, 2004. All 3 women escaped from the Cleveland, OH, home of Ariel Castro, May 6, 2013, after a decade in captivity during which Berry gave birth to a daughter.

Jill Carroll, 28, freelance journalist on assignment for *Christian Science Monitor*, seized in Baghdad by group called the Revenge Brigade, Jan. 7, 2006. She was released Mar. 30; 4 Iraqis arrested in connection with her kidnapping.

Steve Centanni, 60, Fox News reporter released Aug. 26, 2006 (along with a colleague), after being held hostage for 13 days by Palestinian militant group Holy Jihad Brigades. The group had demanded U.S. release of all Muslims in its prisons.

Reigh Storrow Mills, 7, abducted July 27, 2008, by her father, Christian Gerhartsreiter (alias Clark Rockefeller); reunited with her mother Aug. 2, 2008, by FBI agents who took Gerhartsreiter into custody.

Felix Batista, 55, Cuban-American security expert who negotiated the release of numerous kidnapping victims in Latin America, abducted in Mexico Dec. 10, 2008.

David Rohde, 41, *NY Times* reporter captured by the Taliban in Afghanistan Nov. 10, 2008; escaped June 19, 2009.

Jessica Buchanan, 32, aid worker for Danish Refugee Council, taken hostage by Somali pirates Oct. 25, 2011; rescued by U.S. Navy SEALs Jan. 25, 2012.

James Foley, 39, freelance journalist, taken hostage by gunmen during civil war in Syria's Idlib province, Nov. 22, 2012.

Richard Engel, 39, NBC News foreign correspondent in Syria, and his crew held captive by gunmen, Dec. 13, 2012; freed by rebel militia 5 days later.

Hannah Anderson, 16, abducted Aug. 3, 2013, by James DiMaggio, a family friend who killed her mother and brother at his California home before fleeing with her to Idaho; freed Aug. 10 when FBI agents shot and killed DiMaggio.

Notable Terrorist Incidents Worldwide Since 1971

Source: U.S. Dept. of State; *Facts On File World News Digest*; World Almanac research

Selected noteworthy incidents, excluding most assassinations, kidnappings, and military targets. Does not include all incidents in Iraq or Afghanistan, 2001-present; see also Chronology of the Year's Events.

1971—Mar. 1: Senate wing of U.S. Capitol Building in Wash., DC, bombed by Weather Underground; no deaths.

1972—July 21: "Bloody Friday." Provisional IRA exploded 20+ bombs across Belfast, N. Ireland; 9 killed, hundreds injured.
Sept. 5: Palestinian group Black September killed 2 Israeli athletes and seized 9 others at Olympic Village in Munich, W. Germany, during Summer Olympics; 9 hostages, 5 militants, 1 Ger. officer died in botched rescue.

1973—Dec. 17: Palestinian gunmen attacked Rome airport and bombed plane on tarmac; hijacked Lufthansa plane with 5 Italian hostages to Athens, Greece, then to Kuwait; 31 killed in all.

1974—June 17: Houses of Parliament in London, England, bombed by Provisional IRA; 11 injured.

1975—Jan. 27: Puerto Rican FALN nationalists bombed Fraunces Tavern in New York City; 4 killed, 53 injured. **Jan. 29:** U.S. State Dept. building in Wash., DC, bombed by Weather Underground; no deaths.

1976—June 27: Palestinian and Baader-Meinhof militants forced Air France jet to land in Entebbe, Uganda. Israeli army rescued 103 hostages from airport terminal in battle with terrorists and Ugandan troops, July 3-4; 32 killed in all.

1978—Mar. 11: Palestinian militants shot civilians and hijacked bus with hostages from Haifa to Tel Aviv, Israel. Bus exploded during firefight with police at a roadblock; 38 killed.

1979—Nov. 4: Iranian radicals seized U.S. embassy in Tehran, taking 66 Americans hostage. 52 were held until Jan. 20, 1981.

Nov. 20: 200 Islamic terrorists seized Grand Mosque in Mecca, Saudi Arabia, and held hundreds of pilgrims hostage. Saudi forces retook mosque Dec. 4; about 250 died.
1980—Feb. 27: Members of leftist guerrilla group April 19 Movement (M-19) seized Dominican Republic embassy in Bogota, Colombia; 80 hostages taken, 18 held until Apr. 27.
1983—Apr. 18: Hezbollah suicide truck bomb at U.S. embassy in Beirut, Lebanon, killed 63. **Oct. 9:** N. Korean agents ambushed a S. Korean govt. delegation in Rangoon, Burma, killing 21. **Oct. 23:** Hezbollah suicide truck bombings of U.S. and French military bases, Beirut, Lebanon; 242 Americans, 58 French killed.
1984—Sept. 20: U.S. embassy annex nr. Beirut, Lebanon, bombed, killing approx. 20.
1985—June 14: Hezbollah members hijacked TWA Flight 847 with 153 passengers and crew to Beirut, Lebanon; 39 held for 17 days, 1 U.S. Navy sailor killed. **June 23:** Air India Flight 182 destroyed by bomb off coast of Ireland; 329 killed. Blamed on Sikh terrorists. **Apr. 12:** Bomb blast at restaurant nr. U.S. air base in Torrejon, Spain; 18 killed. **Oct. 7:** Four Palestinians hijacked Italian cruise ship *Achille Lauro*; 1 passenger killed. **Nov. 23:** EgyptAir Flight 648 from Athens, Greece, to Cairo hijacked to Malta by Palestinian group Abu Nidal; 60 killed in rescue. **Dec. 27:** Palestinian militants opened fire at El-Al airline counters at Rome and Vienna airports; 19 killed.
1986—Apr. 5: Nightclub in Berlin, W. Germany, bombed; 3 killed, incl. 2 U.S. service personnel, 200+ hurt. 3 Libyan embassy workers in Germany convicted.
1987—Apr. 17: Bomb in Sri Lankan capital killed 100+; blamed on Tamil rebels who, 4 days later, attacked Sinhalese travelers on highway, killing 127. **June 19:** Basque group ETA bombed supermarket garage in Barcelona, Spain; 21 killed, 45 injured. **Nov. 29:** Bomb planted by N. Korean agents exploded on Korean Air Lines Flight 858 over Indian Ocean; 115 killed.
1988—Dec. 21: Pan Am Flight 103 exploded over Lockerbie, Scotland, killing all 259 aboard and 11 on ground; Libya took responsibility for bombing in Aug. 2003.
1989—Sept. 19: French UTA Flight 722 from Congo Republic to Paris destroyed by bomb in midair over Niger; 171 killed.
1992—Mar. 17: Israeli embassy in Buenos Aires, Argentina, bombed; 28 killed, 200+ injured. Hezbollah suspected.
1993—Feb. 26: Truck bomb exploded in World Trade Center garage in New York City; 6 killed. Blast later linked to al- Qaeda. **Mar. 12-19:** At least 11 bombs ripped through Bombay and Calcutta, India; 300+ killed.
1994—Feb. 25: U.S.-born Israeli settler Baruch Goldstein opened fire in mosque in Hebron, West Bank; about 30 Muslim worshippers killed. **July 18:** Buenos Aires, Argentina, Jewish center bombed; 87 killed. Blamed on Hezbollah.
1995—Mar. 20: Twelve killed and over 5,000 injured when Japanese Aum Shinri-kyu cult members released Sarin nerve gas in several Tokyo subway cars. **Apr. 19:** Murrah Federal Building in Oklahoma City bombed, killing 168 and injuring 500+. Timothy McVeigh and Terry Nichols convicted. McVeigh executed in 2001; Nichols sentenced to life in prison. **Nov. 13:** U.S. military compound in Riyadh, Saudi Arabia, bombed by Islamic Movement of Change; 7 killed.
1996—Jan. 31: Tamil Tigers drove explosives-laden truck into Central Bank in Colombo, Sri Lanka; 90 killed. **June 25:** Bomb-laden fuel truck exploded outside Khobar Towers, a U.S. military complex in Dhahran, Saudi Arabia; killed 19. **July 27:** Bomb exploded at Centennial Olympic Park in Atlanta, GA, during Summer Games; killed 2, injured 100+. Eric Robert Rudolph sentenced to life in prison, 2005. **Dec. 3:** Bomb exploded on subway train in Paris; 4 killed, 86 injured. Blamed on Algerian extremists.
1997—Nov. 17: Gamaa al-Islamiya gunmen killed 58 tourists and 4 Egyptians in Valley of the Kings nr. Luxor, Egypt.
1998—Aug. 7: U.S. embassies in Nairobi, Kenya, and Dar-es-Salaam, Tanzania, bombed; 257 people killed. Al-Qaeda blamed. **Aug. 15:** IRA car bomb exploded outside courthouse in Omagh, N. Ireland; killed 29, injured 300+. **Oct. 18:** National Liberation Army of Colombia blew up Ocensa oil pipeline; about 71 killed, 100+ injured.
1999—Sept. 9-16: Three buildings bombed in Moscow and Volgodonsk, Russia; about 300 killed. Chechen rebels blamed.
2000—Oct. 12: Small boat assisting in docking of U.S.S. *Cole* exploded while alongside it in Aden, Yemen; 17 U.S. sailors killed, 39 injured. Blamed on al-Qaeda.
2001—Sept. 11: 19 al-Qaeda terrorists hijacked 4 U.S. domestic flights, including 2 planes that crashed into New York City's World Trade Center towers and 1 into Pentagon. Total dead minus hijackers: 2,973; deadliest terrorist attack yet on U.S. soil. **Sept.-Nov. 7:** Letters tainted with deadly anthrax bacteria mailed through U.S. postal system killed 5.
2002—Mar. 27: Suicide bombing at hotel in Netanya, Israel, during Passover celebration; 27 killed. **Oct 12:** Resort in Bali,

Indonesia, bombed; 202 dead. Jemaah Islamiah blamed. **Oct. 23:** Chechen guerrillas seized theater in Moscow, held 700+ hostages. Russian authorities gassed theater; most guerrillas and about 128 hostages killed. **Dec. 27:** Chechen rebels plowed truck bomb into pro-Russian govt. headquarters in Grozny, Chechnya; 80 killed, 152 injured.
2003—May 12-13: Al-Qaeda militants detonated car bombs at 3 residential complexes used by Westerners in Riyadh, Saudi Arabia; 34 killed. **May 16:** Five explosions in Casablanca, Morocco; 44 killed, 100+ wounded. Blamed on al-Qaeda. **Aug. 19:** UN headquarters in Baghdad bombed by truck; 22 killed, incl. UN envoy to Iraq. **Aug. 25:** 2 bombs exploded in taxis in Mumbai, India; 46 killed, 100+ injured. Islamic militants suspected. **Nov. 15:** Two synagogues in Istanbul, Turkey, bombed; 25 killed. **Nov. 20:** British consulate and offices of British bank HSBC bombed in Istanbul, Turkey; 27 killed. Blamed on al-Qaeda. **Dec. 5:** Suicide bombing on commuter train in Yessentuki, Russia; 44 killed, 150 injured. Blamed on Chechen rebels.
2004—Feb. 6: Bomb exploded in Moscow subway; 39 killed, 130 injured. Chechen rebels blamed. **Mar. 11:** Al-Qaeda cell bombed 4 commuter trains during morning rush hour in Madrid, Spain; 191 killed, about 1,200 injured. **May 29:** Al-Qaeda militants stormed foreigner compound in Khobar, Saudi Arabia, taking hostages; 22 killed. **Aug. 24:** Two Russian passenger planes crashed nearly simultaneously in diff. parts of Russia; 90 killed. Blamed on Chechen rebels. **Sept. 1:** Chechen militants seized school in Beslan, in North Ossetia, Russia; held 1,000+ hostage for 3 days before Russian troops stormed school. About 330 killed, incl. 27 hostage-takers.
2005—July 7: Four bombs exploded on 3 separate subways and 1 bus in central London, Eng., UK; 52 killed, about 700 injured. **July 21:** Four bombs placed on 3 subways and 1 bus in London malfunction. No deaths reported. **July 23:** Three car bombs explode nr. resorts at Sharm el Sheik, Egypt; about 90 killed. **Nov. 9:** 3 suicide bombings targeting hotels in Amman, Jordan; killed 56+, injured about 100. Al-Qaeda in Iraq took responsibility.
2006—July 11: 8 explosions struck 7 different trains and 1 station of public commuter rail system in Mumbai, India; 207 killed, 700+ wounded. Lashkar-e-Qahhar (Army of Terror) claimed responsibility.
2007—July 19: Train traveling between New Delhi and border with Pakistan caught fire, 68 killed; Indian ministers blamed Muslim militants for trying to disrupt peace talks between India and Pakistan. **Dec. 11:** Two coordinated car bombs went off outside govt. building and UN office building in Algiers, Algeria; 41 killed, incl.17 UN employees, 170 wounded.
2008—Sept. 20: Suicide bomber in truck set off explosion outside of Marriott Hotel in Islamabad, Pakistan. Hotel was popular among foreigners and wealthy residents and was located nr. prime min.'s house and parliament building; 53 killed, 271 wounded. **Nov. 26-29:** Series of attacks and bombings on luxury hotels and high-profile targets in Mumbai, India; 171 killed, 300 injured.
2009—Feb. 20: Suicide bomber targeted Shiite funeral in Dera Ismail Khan, Pakistan; 30 killed, 50+ wounded. **Dec. 25:** Umar Farouk Abdulmutallab, 23-year-old Nigerian, failed in his attempt to blow up a Northwest Airlines flight from Amsterdam to Detroit with a bomb hidden in his underpants.
2010—Jan. 1: Taliban suicide bomber killed more than 100 on a playground in NW Pakistan. **Mar. 29:** Two female Chechen separatists detonated suicide bombs at two landmark subway stations in Moscow, killing at least 40. **July 9:** Suicide bombers attacked tribal elders in Mohmand, Pakistan, killing more than 100. **July 11:** Several bombs exploded simultaneously in Kampala, Uganda, killing more than 70 people who had gathered to watch the broadcast of the World Cup final.
2011—Jan. 24: Suicide bomber killed 35 in Moscow's Domodedovo Airport, a location chosen to maximize deaths of foreigners. **July 22:** Anders Behring Breivik, a right-wing Norwegian extremist, set off car bomb outside govt. buildings in Oslo, then massacred dozens of young people at a summer camp on Tyrifjorden Lake, bringing death toll to 77.
2012—May 21: Suicide bomber claimed by al-Qaeda in the Arabian Peninsula killed more than 100 soldiers and wounded 200 during military parade rehearsal nr. Yemeni presidential palace. **Sept. 11:** Terrorists stormed the U.S. diplomatic mission in Benghazi, Libya, killing 4 Americans, including U.S. Amb. J. Christopher Stevens.
2013—Apr. 15: Two bombs exploded nr. Boston Marathon finish line, killing 3 and injuring 264 others; 4-day search ended in death of 1 bomber, Tamerlan Tsarnaev, and capture of the other, his brother Dzhokhar, a naturalized Chechen immigrant. **May 22:** Off-duty soldier Lee Rigby fatally stabbed to death in London by 2 British citizens of Nigerian descent.

MILITARY AFFAIRS

Chief Commanding Officers of the U.S. Military

Chairman, Joint Chiefs of Staff: Gen. Martin E. Dempsey (U.S. Army)
Vice Chairman: Adm. James A. Winnefeld Jr. (U.S. Navy)

Date of rank is date when the individual achieved his or her current rank. While serving in any of these positions, or as commander of a unified or specified combatant command, basic pay is $20,937.90 per month. Officers hold positions listed as of Oct. 2, 2013.

Army

Chief of Staff (CSA)	Date of rank
Odierno, Raymond T.	Sept. 16, 2008

Other Generals

Alexander, Keith B.	May 7, 2010
Allyn, Daniel	May 10, 2013
Austin, Lloyd J., III.	July 29, 2010
Brooks, Vincent K.	July 2, 2013
Campbell, John F.	Mar. 8, 2013
Cone, Robert W.	Apr. 14, 2011
Dempsey, Martin E.	Dec. 8, 2008
Grass, Frank J.	Sept. 7, 2012
Jacoby, Charles H., Jr.	Aug. 2, 2011
Rodriguez, David M.	Apr. 14, 2011
Scaparrotti, Curtis M.	Oct. 2, 2013
Thurman, James D.	Mar. 19, 2010
Via, Dennis L.	Aug. 7, 2012

Air Force

Chief of Staff (CSAF or AF/CC)	Date of rank
Welsh III, Mark A.	Dec. 13, 2010

Other Generals

Breedlove, Philip M.	Jan. 14, 2011
Carlisle, Herbert J.	Aug. 3, 2012
Fraser, William M., III.	Oct. 8, 2008
Gorenc, Frank	Aug. 2, 2013
Hostage, Gilmary M., III.	Sept. 13, 2011
Kehler, C. Robert "Bob"	Oct. 12, 2007
Rice, Edward A., Jr.	Nov. 17, 2010
Selva, Paul J.	Nov. 30, 2012
Shelton, William L.	Jan. 5, 2011

Air Force

Spencer, Larry O.	July 27, 2012
Wolfenbarger, Janet C.	June 5, 2012

Navy

Chief of Naval Operations (CNO)	Date of rank
Greenert, Jonathan W. (submariner)	Sept. 29, 2007

Other Admirals

Clingan, Bruce W. (aviator)	Feb. 24, 2012
Ferguson, Mark E., III (surface warfare)	Aug. 2, 2011
Gortney, William E. (aviator)	May 24, 2012
Haney, Cecil D. (surface warfare)	Jan. 20, 2012
Locklear, Samuel J., III (surface warfare)	Mar. 9, 2012
McRaven, William H. (special operations)	June 30, 2011
Richardson, John M. (submariner)	July 26, 2012
Winnefeld, James A. "Sandy," Jr. (aviator)	May 7, 2010

Marine Corps

Commandant of the Marine Corps (CMC)	Date of rank
Amos, James F.	July 2, 2008

Other Generals

Dunford, Joseph F., Jr.	Aug. 4, 2010
Kelly, John F.	July 26, 2012
Paxton, John M., Jr.	Dec. 15, 2012

Coast Guard

Commandant, with rank of Admiral	Date of rank
Papp, Robert Jr.	May 25, 2010
Vice Commandant, with rank of Vice Admiral	
Currier, John P.	May 18, 2012

Unified Combatant Commands Commanders-in-Chief

U.S. European Command, Stuttgart-Vaihingen, Germany:
Gen. Philip M. Breedlove (USAF)
U.S. Pacific Command, Honolulu, Hawaii:
Adm. Samuel J. Locklear III (USN)
U.S. Special Operations Command, MacDill AFB, Florida:
Adm. William H. McRaven (USN)
U.S. Transportation Command, Scott AFB, Illinois:
Gen. William M. Fraser III (USAF)
U.S. Central Command, MacDill AFB, Florida:
Gen. Lloyd J. Austin III (U.S. Army)

U.S. Southern Command, Miami, Florida:
Gen. John F. Kelly (USMC)
U.S. Northern Command, Peterson AFB, Colorado:
Gen. Charles H. Jacoby Jr. (U.S. Army)
U.S. Strategic Command, Offutt AFB, Nebraska:
Gen. C. Robert "Bob" Kehler (USAF)
U.S. Africa Command, Kelley Barracks, Stuttgart, Germany:
Gen. David M. Rodriguez (U.S. Army)

North Atlantic Treaty Organization (NATO) International Commands

NATO Headquarters: Chairman, NATO Military Committee:
Gen. Knud Bartels (Danish Army)
Strategic Commands:
Allied Command Operations (ACO): Gen. Philip M. Breedlove (USAF), Supreme Allied Commander, Europe
Allied Command Transformation (ACT): Gen. Jean-Paul Paloméros (French Air Force), Supreme Allied Commander Transformation

ACO Subordinate Commands:
Joint Force Command Brunssum (JFC Brunssum): Gen. Hans-Lothar Domröse (German Army), Commander
Joint Force Command Naples (JFC Naples): Adm. Bruce W. Clingan (USN), Commander
Joint Force Command Lisbon (JHQ Lisbon): Lt. Gen. Manuel Mestre (Spanish Air Force), Commander

Chairmen of the Joint Chiefs of Staff, 1949-2013

Gen. of the Army Omar N. Bradley, USA	8/16/1949-8/15/1953	Gen. John W. Vessey Jr., USA	6/18/1982-9/30/1985
Adm. Arthur W. Radford, USN	8/15/1953-8/15/1957	Adm. William J. Crowe Jr., USN	10/1/1985-9/30/1989
Gen. Nathan F. Twining, USAF	8/15/1957-9/30/1960	Gen. Colin L. Powell, USA	10/1/1989-9/30/1993
Gen. Lyman L. Lemnitzer, USA	10/1/1960-9/30/1962	Gen. John M. Shalikashvili, USA	10/25/1993-9/30/1997
Gen. Maxwell D. Taylor, USA	10/1/1962-7/1/1964	Gen. Henry H. Shelton, USA	9/30/1997-9/30/2001
Gen. Earle G. Wheeler, USA	7/3/1964-7/2/1970	Gen. Richard B. Myers, USAF	10/1/2001-9/30/2005
Adm. Thomas H. Moorer, USN	7/2/1970-7/1/1974	Gen. Peter Pace, USMC	9/30/2005-9/30/2007
Gen. George S. Brown, USAF	7/1/1974-6/20/1978	Adm. Michael G. Mullen, USN	10/1/2007-9/30/2011
Gen. David C. Jones, USAF	6/21/1978-6/18/1982	Gen. Martin E. Dempsey, USA	10/1/2011-

Directors of the Central Intelligence Agency, 1946-2013

In 1942, Pres. Franklin D. Roosevelt established the Office of Strategic Services (OSS); it was disbanded in 1945. In 1946, Pres. Harry Truman established the Central Intelligence Group (CIG) to operate under the National Intelligence Authority (NIA). A 1947 law replaced the NIA with the National Security Council (NSC) and the CIG with the Central Intelligence Agency (CIA).

Director	Served	Appointed by President	Director	Served	Appointed by President
Adm. Sidney W. Souers	1946	Truman	William J. Casey	1981-1987	Reagan
Gen. Hoyt S. Vandenberg	1946-1947	Truman	William H. Webster	1987-1991	Reagan
Adm. Roscoe H. Hillenkoetter	1947-1950	Truman	Robert M. Gates	1991-1993	Bush, G. H. W.
Gen. Walter Bedell Smith	1950-1953	Truman	R. James Woolsey	1993-1995	Clinton
Allen W. Dulles	1953-1961	Eisenhower	John M. Deutch	1995-1997	Clinton
John A. McCone	1961-1965	Kennedy	George J. Tenet	1997-2004	Clinton
Adm. William F. Raborn Jr.	1965-1966	Johnson, L. B.	Porter Goss	2004-2006	Bush, G. W.
Richard Helms	1966-1973	Johnson, L. B.	Gen. Michael V. Hayden	2006-2009	Bush, G. W.
James R. Schlesinger	1973	Nixon	Leon E. Panetta	2009-2011	Obama
William E. Colby	1973-1976	Nixon	Gen. David H. Petraeus	2011-2012	Obama
George H. W. Bush	1976-1977	Ford	John O. Brennan	2013-	Obama
Adm. Stansfield Turner	1977-1981	Carter			

U.S. Army and Air Force Units

Army Units. Squad: In infantry, usually 8-16 enlisted personnel under a staff sergeant. **Platoon:** In infantry, 2-4 squads under a lieutenant. **Company:** Headquarters and 3-5 platoons under a captain. (Company-size unit in the artillery is a battery; in the cavalry, a troop.) **Battalion:** Hdqts. and 4-6 companies under a lieutenant colonel. (In cavalry, battalion-size unit is a squadron.) **Brigade:** Hdqts. and 2-5 battalions under a colonel. (Brigade-size unit in the cavalry and rangers is a regiment; in the special forces, a group.) **Division:** Hdqts. and 3 brigades with artillery, combat support, and combat service support units under a major general. **Corps:** Two or more divisions with corps troops under a lieutenant general. **Army:** Hdqts. and 2 or more corps with operational and support responsibilities under a general.

Air Force Units. Flight: Numerically designated flights are the lowest level unit. They are used primarily where there is a need for small mission elements to be incorporated into an organized unit. **Squadron:** The basic unit. Designates specific operational or support capability like mission units in operational commands. **Group:** Flexible unit composed of 2 or more squadrons whose functions may be operational, support, or administrative in nature. **Wing:** Primary group with supporting groups on a distinct mission with significant scope such as combat, flying training, or airlift. **Numbered Air Force (NAF):** Normally operationally oriented, the numbered air force is designed for the control of subordinate units with the same mission and/or geographical location. **Major Command (MAJCOM):** A major subdivision with full staff that manages a major segment of the USAF mission. Major command is composed of 3 or more numbered air forces.

Active Duty U.S. Military Personnel Strength Worldwide, 2012
Source: U.S. Dept. of Defense
(as of Dec. 31, 2012)

TOTAL WORLDWIDE[1] 1,372,522

U.S. TERRITORIES AND SPEC. LOCATIONS
U.S., 48 contiguous states.	1,123,219
Alaska.	21,280
Hawaii.	49,242
Guam.	5,646
Puerto Rico	162
Regional total[2]	**1,199,556**

OTHER WESTERN HEMISPHERE
Canada	146
Colombia	64
Cuba (Guantánamo)	988
Haiti.	14
Honduras.	388
Regional total[2]	**2,105**

EUROPE
Belgium	1,165
Germany	45,596
Greece.	361
Greenland	138
Italy	10,916
Netherlands.	374
Portugal.	713
Spain	1,600
Turkey	1,491
United Kingdom.	9,310
Regional total[2].	**72,198**

SUB-SAHARAN AFRICA
Djibouti.	139
Regional total[2].	**489**

FORMER SOVIET UNION
Total	**187**

EAST ASIA AND PACIFIC
Australia	183
Japan.	52,692
Korea, South	NA
Philippines.	131
Singapore	180
Thailand.	114
Regional total[2]	**54,025**

NORTH AFRICA, NEAR EAST, AND SOUTH ASIA*
Afghanistan[3]	76,818
Bahrain	2,902
Diego Garcia	516
Egypt.	292
Iraq[3].	1,101
Qatar.	800
Saudi Arabia	278
United Arab Emirates	193
Regional total[2,4].	**4,805**

NA = Not available. *Special Forces personnel involved in Operation Enduring Freedom (OEF) in Afghanistan were not reported by Dept. of Defense. (1) Includes undistributed personnel. (2) Most countries and areas with fewer than 100 assigned U.S. military members not listed; regional totals include personnel stationed in those countries and areas not shown. (3) Includes troops in surrounding areas and deployed Reserve/National Guard. (4) Excludes troops deployed for OEF/Operation New Dawn.

U.S. Army Personnel on Active Duty
Source: Dept. of the Army, U.S. Dept. of Defense

(as of midyear, except where noted)

Date	Total strength[1]	Commissioned officers Total	Male	Female[2]	Warrant officers[3] Male	Female	Enlisted personnel Total	Male	Female
1940	267,767	17,563	16,624	939	763	—	249,441	249,441	—
1942	3,074,184	203,137	190,662	12,475	3,285	—	2,867,762	2,867,762	—
1943	6,993,102	557,657	521,435	36,222	21,919	—	6,413,526	6,358,200	55,325
1944	7,992,868	740,077	692,351	47,726	36,893	10	7,215,888	7,144,601	71,287
1945	8,266,373	835,403	772,511	62,892	56,216	44	7,374,710	7,283,930	90,780
1946	1,889,690	257,300	240,658	16,642	9,826	18	1,622,546	1,605,847	16,699
1950	591,487	67,784	63,375	4,409	4,760	22	518,921	512,370	6,551
1955	1,107,606	111,347	106,196	5,151	10,552	48	985,659	977,943	7,716
1960	871,348	91,056	86,832	4,224	10,141	39	770,112	761,833	8,279
1965	967,049	101,812	98,029	3,783	10,285	23	854,929	846,409	8,520
1970	1,319,735	143,704	138,469	5,235	23,005	13	1,153,013	1,141,537	11,476
1975	781,316	89,756	85,184	4,572	13,214	22	678,324	640,621	37,703
1980 (Sept. 30) . . .	772,661	85,339	77,843	7,496	13,265	113	673,944	612,593	61,351
1985 (Sept. 30) . . .	776,244	94,103	83,563	10,540	15,296	288	666,557	598,639	67,918
1990 (Mar. 31). . .	746,220	91,330	79,520	11,810	15,177	470	639,713	567,015	72,698
1995	521,036	72,646	62,250	10,396	12,053	599	435,807	377,832	57,975
2000	471,633	66,344	56,391	9,953	10,608	781	393,900	333,947	59,953
2002	485,536	66,446	55,715	10,731	10,900	812	404,363	341,794	62,569
2003 (Sept. 30) . . .	499,301	68,198	56,980	11,218	11,273	854	414,769	351,921	62,848
2004 (Sept. 30) . . .	499,543	68,640	57,245	11,395	11,414	914	414,438	354,043	60,395
2005 (Sept. 30) . . .	492,728	69,174	57,675	11,499	11,506	976	406,923	346,194	57,354
2006 (Sept. 30) . . .	505,402	68,742	57,318	11,424	11,931	1,035	419,353	361,528	57,825
2007 (Sept. 30) . . .	522,017	70,657	58,854	11,803	13,844	1,160	433,109	374,989	58,120
2008 (Sept. 30) . . .	539,170	72,650	60,357	12,293	13,428	1,246	451,846	392,163	59,683
2009 (Sept. 30) . . .	553,044	75,337	63,146	12,191	13,815	1,348	457,980	398,579	59,401
2010 (Sept. 30) . . .	566,045	78,588	64,952	13,636	14,106	1,434	467,248	406,871	60,377
2011 (Sept. 30) . . .	565,463	81,395	67,140	14,255	14,373	1,472	463,605	403,381	60,224
2012 (Sept. 30) . . .	550,064	82,538	68,021	14,517	14,401	1,484	447,075	389,646	57,429
2013 (Feb. 28) . .	540,743	82,265	NA	NA	15,686*	NA	438,347	NA	NA

NA = Not available. *2013 figure for male warrant officers includes female officers. **Note:** Represents strength of active Army, including Philippine Scouts (1940-46), ret. Regular Army personnel on extended active duty, and National Guard and Reserve personnel on extended active duty; excl. U.S. Military Academy cadets, contract surgeons, and National Guard and Reserve personnel not on extended active duty. (1) Includes categories not listed, e.g., West Point cadets. Data for 1940-46 include personnel in the Army Air Forces and its predecessors (Air Service and Air Corps). (2) Includes Army Nurse Corps for all years, Women's Army Corps (1942-78), and Medical Specialists Corps (1949 and after). (3) Act of Congress approved Apr. 27, 1926, directed the appointment as warrant officers of field clerks still in active service. Includes flight officers as follows: 1943, 5,700; 1944, 13,615; 1945, 31,117; 1946, 2,580.

U.S. Navy Personnel on Active Duty
Source: U.S. Dept. of Defense
(as of midyear, except where noted)

Year	Officers	Nurses[1]	Enlisted	Officer candidates[1]	Total[2]	Year	Officers	Nurses[1]	Enlisted	Officer candidates[1]	Total[2]
1940	13,162	442	144,824	2,569	160,997	1999	55,726	—	322,372	—	378,098
1945	320,293	11,086	2,988,207	61,231	3,380,817	2000 (Oct.)	53,698	—	320,212	—	373,910
1950	42,687	1,964	331,860	5,037	381,538	2005	54,039	—	305,368	—	363,858
1960	67,456	2,103	544,040	4,385	617,984	2006	53,209	—	295,773	—	353,496
1970	78,488	2,273	605,899	6,000	692,660	2007 (Sept.)	51,385	—	281,772	—	337,547
1980	63,100	—	464,100	—	527,200	2008	52,184	—	276,346	—	331,785
1990 (Sept.)	74,429	—	530,133	—	604,562	2009	52,233	—	274,858	—	331,637
1995 (May)	61,075	—	402,626	—	463,701	2010	53,071	—	273,609	—	330,065
1996	60,013	—	376,595	—	436,608	2011	53,620	—	270,425	—	328,648
1997	57,341	—	340,616	—	397,957	2012 (Mar.)	52,558	—	263,928	—	320,961
1998 (Sept.)	55,007	—	326,196	—	381,203	2013 (Feb.)	52,450	—	260,581	—	317,464

(1) Starting in 1980, "Nurses" are included with "Officers," and "Officer candidates" are included with "Enlisted." (2) May include categories not shown, e.g., midshipmen.

U.S. Air Force Personnel on Active Duty
Source: U.S. Dept. of Defense
(as of midyear, except where noted)

Year[1]	Strength	Year[1]	Strength	Year[1]	Strength	Year[1]	Strength	Year[1]	Strength	Year[1]	Strength
1918	195,023	1943	2,197,114	1980	557,969	1994	426,327	2000	357,777	2009	334,009
1920	9,050	1944	2,372,292	1986	608,200	1995	400,051	2005	358,705	2010	337,505
1930	13,531	1945	2,282,259	1990	535,233	1996	389,400	2006	352,620	2011	333,729
1940	51,165	1950	411,277	1991	510,432	1997	378,681	2007	340,596	2012[2]	332,709
1941	152,125	1960	814,213	1992	470,315	1998	363,479	2008	328,771	2013[3]	334,157
1942	764,415	1970	791,078	1993	444,351	1999	357,929				

(1) Prior to 1947, data are for U.S. Army Air Corps and Air Service of the Signal Corps. (2) In Mar. (3) In Feb.

U.S. Marine Corps Personnel on Active Duty
Source: U.S. Dept. of Defense
(as of midyear, except where noted)

Year	Officers	Enlisted	Total	Year	Officers	Enlisted	Total	Year	Officers	Enlisted	Total
1940	1,800	26,545	28,345	1994	18,430	159,949	178,379	2006	19,218	159,705	178,923
1945	37,067	437,613	474,680	1995	18,017	153,929	171,946	2007	19,456	162,085	181,541
1950	7,254	67,025	74,279	1996	18,146	154,141	172,287	2008	20,137	172,903	193,040
1960	16,203	154,418	170,621	1997	18,089	154,240	172,329	2009	21,031	183,243	204,274
1970	24,941	234,796	259,737	1998	17,984	154,648	172,632	2010	21,680	179,446	201,126
1980	18,198	170,271	188,469	1999	17,892	155,250	173,142	2011	22,281	178,546	200,827
1990	19,958	176,694	196,652	2000	17,897	154,744	172,641	2012 (Mar.)	22,253	176,174	198,427
1993	18,878	161,205	180,083	2005	19,118	159,113	178,231	2013 (Feb.)	21,907	173,222	195,129

U.S. Coast Guard Personnel on Active Duty
Source: U.S. Dept. of Defense
(as of midyear, except where noted)

Year	Officers	Cadets	Enlisted	Total	Year	Officers	Cadets	Enlisted	Total
1970	5,512	653	31,524	37,689	2007	8,231	720	32,314	41,265
1980	6,463	877	32,041	39,381	2008	8,282	1,005	33,137	42,424
1985	6,775	733	31,087	38,595	2009	8,497	993	34,024	43,514
1990	6,475	820	29,860	37,308	2010	8,678	744	33,713	43,135
1995	7,489	841	28,401	36,731	2011	8,659	1,053	33,615	43,327
2000	7,154	863	27,695	35,712	2012 (Mar.)	8,316	988	33,758	43,062
2005	7,908	1,006	31,900	40,814	2013 (Jan.)	8,376	1,010	32,971	42,357
2006	8,032	1,004	32,001	40,639					

Women in the U.S. Armed Forces
Source: U.S. Dept. of Defense; U.S. Census Bureau, U.S. Dept. of Commerce; U.S. Coast Guard, U.S. Dept. of Homeland Security
Women in the Army, Navy, Air Force, Marines, and Coast Guard are fully integrated with male personnel. All enlisted jobs were open to women when the draft ended June 30, 1973. Admission to service academies began in 1976. Under rules instituted in 1993, women were allowed to fly combat aircraft and serve aboard warships. By the mid-1990s, 80% of all jobs and more than 90% of all career fields had been opened to women. The first woman achieved the rank of four-star general in 2009. In Apr. 2010, the Navy announced that women would be placed on submarine crews by Jan. 2012. The Pentagon in 2013 lifted its ban on women serving in direct ground combat units.

(on active duty as of Sept. 30 in year shown)

Women Active Duty Troops, 2012
Service	% women
Army	13.5%
Navy	16.7
Marines	7.0
Air Force	19.0
Coast Guard	14.4

Women on Active Duty, All Services, 1973-2012
Year	% women	Year	% women
1973	2.5%	1997	13.6%
1975	4.6	2000	14.4
1981	8.9	2005	14.6
1987	10.2	2011	14.6
1993	11.6	2012	14.6

Women Veterans by Period of Service, 2011
Period of service	% women vets
Gulf War era (post-9/11)	27.7%
Gulf War era (pre-9/11)	23.7
Vietnam era	12.7
Korean War	3.3
World War II	5.0
Peacetime only	27.6

Average Age and Length of Service of Active Enlisted Personnel, 1973-2011
Source: U.S. Dept. of Defense

Year	Avg. age	Avg. months of service	Year	Avg. age	Avg. months of service	Year	Avg. age	Avg. months of service
1973	25.0	69.8	1987	26.1	74.8	1999	27.3	87.3
1974	25.0	69.6	1988	26.3	76.7	2000	27.1	85.5
1975	24.9	68.2	1989	26.4	78.0	2001	27.0	84.4
1976	24.9	67.6	1990	26.7	81.8	2002	27.1	84.1
1977	24.9	66.5	1991	27.0	84.8	2003	27.0	83.3
1978	25.0	67.3	1992	27.1	86.4	2004	27.0	82.6
1979	25.1	67.7	1992	27.1	86.4	2005	27.1	83.2
1980	25.0	66.5	1993	27.2	87.7	2006	27.1	82.0
1981	25.1	67.1	1994	27.3	89.6	2007	27.1	81.0
1982	25.4	68.6	1995	27.4	89.3	2008	27.1	80.3
1983	25.6	70.0	1996	27.4	89.6	2009	27.2	80.4
1984	25.7	71.1	1997	27.4	89.2	2010	27.3	80.9
1985	25.8	72.3	1998	27.3	88.4	2011	27.4	81.1
1986	25.9	73.1						

Monthly Military Pay Scale
Source: U.S. Dept. of Defense

(effective Jan. 1, 2013; salaries rounded to nearest dollar)

	<2	2	3	4	6	8	10	12	14	16	18	20	22	24	26
Commissioned officers															
O-10	NA	NA	NA	NA	NA	NA	NA	NA	NA	NA	NA	15,913	15,991	16,324	16,903
O-9	NA	NA	NA	NA	NA	NA	NA	NA	NA	NA	NA	13,918	14,119	14,408	14,913
O-8	9,848	10,170	10,385	10,444	10,712	11,158	11,261	11,685	11,807	12,172	12,700	13,187	13,512	13,512	13,512
O-7	8,183	8,563	8,739	8,879	9,132	9,382	9,671	9,959	10,249	11,158	11,925	11,925	11,925	11,925	11,986
O-6	6,065	6,663	7,100	7,100	7,127	7,433	7,473	7,473	7,898	8,649	9,089	9,530	9,781	10,034	10,527
O-5	5,056	5,696	6,090	6,164	6,410	6,557	6,881	7,118	7,425	7,895	8,118	8,339	8,590	8,590	8,590
O-4	4,362	5,050	5,387	5,462	5,775	6,110	6,528	6,853	7,079	7,209	7,284	7,284	7,284	7,284	7,284
O-3	3,836	4,348	4,693	5,117	5,362	5,631	5,805	6,091	6,240	6,240	6,240	6,240	6,240	6,240	6,240
O-2	3,314	3,774	4,347	4,494	4,586	4,586	4,586	4,586	4,586	4,586	4,586	4,586	4,586	4,586	4,586
O-1	2,876	2,994	3,619	3,619	3,619	3,619	3,619	3,619	3,619	3,619	3,619	3,619	3,619	3,619	3,619
Commissioned officers with over 4 years of active duty service as enlisted member or warrant officer															
O-3	NA	NA	NA	5,117	5,362	5,631	5,805	6,091	6,332	6,471	6,659	6,659	6,659	6,659	6,659
O-2	NA	NA	NA	4,494	4,586	4,733	4,979	5,169	5,311	5,311	5,311	5,311	5,311	5,311	5,311
O-1	NA	NA	NA	3,619	3,865	4,008	4,154	4,297	4,494	4,494	4,494	4,494	4,494	4,494	4,494
Warrant officers															
W-5	NA	NA	NA	NA	NA	NA	NA	NA	NA	NA	NA	7,048	7,406	7,672	7,967
W-4	3,964	4,264	4,386	4,507	4,714	4,919	5,127	5,440	5,714	5,974	6,188	6,395	6,701	6,952	7,239
W-3	3,620	3,770	3,925	3,976	4,138	4,457	4,789	4,946	5,126	5,313	5,648	5,874	6,010	6,154	6,350
W-2	3,203	3,506	3,599	3,663	3,871	4,194	4,354	4,511	4,704	4,854	4,991	5,154	5,261	5,346	5,346
W-1	2,812	3,114	3,195	3,368	3,571	3,871	4,010	4,206	4,398	4,550	4,689	4,858	4,858	4,858	4,858
Enlisted members															
E-9	NA	NA	NA	NA	NA	NA	4,789	4,898	5,034	5,195	5,357	5,618	5,837	6,069	6,423
E-8	NA	NA	NA	NA	NA	3,920	4,094	4,201	4,330	4,469	4,721	4,848	5,065	5,185	5,481
E-7	2,725	2,975	3,088	3,239	3,357	3,559	3,673	3,876	4,044	4,159	4,281	4,328	4,487	4,573	4,898
E-6	2,357	2,594	2,708	2,819	2,936	3,197	3,299	3,495	3,556	3,600	3,651	3,651	3,651	3,651	3,651
E-5	2,159	2,304	2,416	2,530	2,708	2,894	3,046	3,064	3,064	3,064	3,064	3,064	3,064	3,064	3,064
E-4	1,980	2,081	2,194	2,305	2,403	2,403	2,403	2,403	2,403	2,403	2,403	2,403	2,403	2,403	2,403
E-3	1,787	1,900	2,015	2,015	2,015	2,015	2,015	2,015	2,015	2,015	2,015	2,015	2,015	2,015	2,015
E-2	1,700	1,700	1,700	1,700	1,700	1,700	1,700	1,700	1,700	1,700	1,700	1,700	1,700	1,700	1,700
E-1[1]	1,516	NA	NA	NA	NA	NA	NA	NA	NA	NA	NA	NA	NA	NA	NA

NA = Not applicable. **Note:** Basic pay rate for Academy cadets/midshipmen and ROTC members/applicants is $1,007.80. See Dept. of Defense Financial Management Regulations for details on payscale limitations and eligibility requirements. **Over 30 years**—O-10: 17,748; O-9: 15,659; O-8: 13,850; O-7: 12,225; O-6: 10,737; W-5: 8,365; W-4: 7,383; E-9: 6,743 ; E-8: 5,591. **Over 34 years**—O-10: 18,635; O-9: 16,442; O-8: 14,197; W-5: 8,783; E-9: 7,081. **Over 38 years**—O-10: 19,567; O-9: 17,264; W-5: 9,223; E-9: 7,435. (1) Applicable to E-1 with 4 months or more of active duty. Basic pay for an E-1 with less than 4 months of active duty is $1,402.20.

U.S. Veteran Population, 2013
Source: U.S. Dept. of Veterans Affairs
(population projection, in thousands, as of Sept. 30)

Period of service	Vet. pop.	Period of service	Vet. pop.
Total peacetime veterans[1]	5,497.7	Total Vietnam era[3]	7,330.0
Service between Vietnam era and Gulf War era	3,312.4	Vietnam era with no prior wartime service	6,787.9
Service between Korean War and Vietnam era	2,073.4	Vietnam era with service in Korea	178.9
Service between WWII and Korean War	95.1	Vietnam era with service in Korea and WWII	31.9
Pre WWII service	16.8	Total Gulf War era[3]	6,484.9
Total wartime veterans[2]	16,475.3	Gulf War era pre-9/11 with service in Vietnam era	288.1
Total World War II[3]	1,245.7	Gulf War era pre-9/11, post-9/11, and with service	
WWII only	1,128.9	in Vietnam era	43.2
Total Korean War[3]	2,073.6	Gulf War era pre-9/11	2,717.5
Korean War with no prior wartime service	1,777.9	Gulf War era pre-9/11 and post-9/11	1,256.3
Korean War with service in WWII	84.9	Gulf War era post-9/11	2,179.7
		TOTAL VETERANS IN CIVILIAN LIFE	21,973.0

Note: Figures are for U.S. veterans worldwide. Includes those who served on active duty in Army, Navy, Air Force, Marines, Coast Guard, uniformed Public Health Service and NOAA, and reservists called to federal active duty. Excludes those dishonorably discharged, those whose only active duty was training, and those currently on active duty. (1) Veterans with both wartime and peacetime service are counted only as "wartime veterans." (2) Veterans serving in more than one period are counted only once in total. (3) Total includes veterans who also served in previous periods."

African American Service in U.S. Wars
Source: U.S. Dept. of Defense; U.S. Census Bureau

American Revolution. About 5,000 served in the Continental Army, mostly in integrated units, some in all-black combat units.
Civil War. Some 180,000 served in 163 units of the Union Army's U.S. Colored Troops, and 200,000 worked in service units—10% of the Union Army in all; about 37,000 died, 31,000 wounded.
World War I. 350,000-400,000 served in the armed forces, 100,000 in France. Some 40,000 fought.
World War II. Some 1 mil served in the armed forces—8% of all troops—mostly in Army service units; all-black fighter and bomber Army Air Force units and infantry divisions gave distinguished service.

Korean War. More than 600,000 served in the military; 3,075 lost their lives in combat. By 1954, armed forces were completely desegregated.
Vietnam War. 274,937 served in the armed forces (1965-74)— 9.8% of all troops; 7,243 were killed in combat.
Persian Gulf War. About 104,000 served in the Kuwaiti theater—20% of all U.S. troops; 66 died in combat.
Operation Enduring Freedom. 182 military deaths and 1,340 wounded in Afghanistan and elsewhere (as of Sept. 20, 2013).
Operation Iraqi Freedom/Operation New Dawn. 444 military deaths and 2,766 wounded (as of Sept. 20, 2013).

Outlays for Individual Payments to Veterans, 1940-2014
Source: White House Office of Management and Budget
(in millions of dollars)

Year	Total	Compensation	Pensions	Hospital, medical	Education	Insurance & burial	Year	Total	Compensation	Pensions	Hospital, medical	Education	Insurance & burial
1940	$578	$244	$185	$69	—	$80	2004	$55,021	$26,297	$3,334	$21,590	$2,408	$1,392
1950	8,827	1,533	476	764	$2,739	3,315	2005	62,206	30,877	3,663	23,073	3,224	1,369
1960	5,355	2,049	1,263	931	392	720	2006	63,658	30,991	3,547	24,445	3,325	1,350
1970	8,808	2,980	2,255	1,723	1,002	848	2007	69,740	31,055	3,376	30,537	3,427	1,345
1980	20,927	7,446	3,585	6,290	2,418	1,188	2008	76,113	36,256	3,790	31,096	3,607	1,364
1990	28,545	10,735	3,594	12,021	795	1,400	2009	85,501	40,399	4,161	35,264	4,308	1,369
1995	36,822	14,842	3,024	16,196	1,386	1,374	2010	95,997	43,377	4,359	38,216	8,727	1,318
2000	46,086	20,775	2,969	19,343	1,636	1,363	2011	111,100	52,762	4,664	41,299	11,088	1,287
2001	45,435	18,579	2,760	20,966	1,783	1,347	2012	108,214	50,050	4,537	41,688	10,696	1,243
2002	50,969	22,418	3,166	22,384	1,681	1,320	2013*	125,529	60,772	5,220	44,816	13,446	1,275
2003	55,792	24,696	3,229	24,487	2,049	1,331	2014*	133,121	65,215	5,565	47,146	13,989	1,206

— = Not available *Estimate. **Note:** Compensation is service-connected; pension is not.

Veterans Health Administration Characteristics, 2002-12
Source: U.S. Dept. of Veterans Affairs

Fiscal year	Total enrollees[1] (mil)	Outpatient visits[2] (mil)	Inpatient admissions (thous.)	Fiscal year	Total enrollees[1] (mil)	Outpatient visits[2] (mil)	Inpatient admissions (thous.)
2002	6.8	46.5	564.7	2008	7.8	67.7	641.4
2003	7.1	49.8	567.3	2009	8.1	74.9	662.0
2004	7.3	54.0	589.8	2010	8.3	80.2	682.3
2005	7.7	57.5	585.8	2011	8.6	79.8	692.1
2006	7.9	59.1	568.9	2012	8.8	83.6	703.5
2007	7.8	62.3	589.0				

(1) Includes non-enrolled veteran patients. Enrollment encouraged but not required for veterans with a service-connected disability rating of 50% or more; veterans seeking a registry exam for chemical/radiation exposure; veterans seeking care for a service-connected disability only; and veterans who, within 12 months of discharge, seek care for a disability that the military determined was incurred/aggravated in active duty but which has not yet been rated by the VA. (2) Includes fee visits.

Employment Status of Veterans With Service-Connected Disabilities, 2012
Source: Burea of Labor Statistics, U.S. Dept. of Labor
(employment is as of Aug. 2012; unemployment is based on annual average for 2012)

Veteran status, presence of disability, and period of service	Total employed (thous.)	Employment distribution percentage						Unemployed (thous.)	Unemployment rate	Not in labor force
		Private sector	Fed. govt.	State/ local govt.	Self-employed[1]	Agr. and related industries				
Total veterans[2]	10,228	70.3%	8.3%	12.1%	7.5%	1.7%		773	7.0%	10,177
With service-connected disability	1,301	59.0	19.4	15.1	5.8	0.7		—	—	—
Without service-connected disability	7,123	71.8	6.6	12.6	7.3	1.8		—	—	—
Gulf War era, total[2]	4,258	71.5	12.4	11.7	3.4	0.9		335	7.7	977
With service-connected disability	827	58.5	24.5	14.1	2.8	0.1		—	—	—
Without service-connected disability	2,722	75.2	8.7	12.2	3.0	0.9		—	—	—
Gulf War era II[2]	1,854	72.3	15.3	9.5	2.4	0.6		205	9.9	496
With service-connected disability	460	62.3	24.4	12.2	1.1	0.0		—	—	—
Without service-connected disability	1,086	75.5	11.4	10.0	2.2	0.9		—	—	—
Gulf War era I[2]	2,043	71.0	10.1	13.5	4.3	1.2		150	5.9	501
With service-connected disability	367	53.7	24.7	16.4	5.0	0.3		—	—	—
Without service-connected disability	1,636	75.1	7.0	13.6	3.5	0.9		—	—	—
WWII, Korean War, and Vietnam era[2]	2,939	69.8	4.0	10.8	12.1	3.3		201	6.4	6,707
With service-connected disability	257	61.9	4.6	16.1	14.2	3.1		—	—	—
Without service-connected disability	2,127	71.1	4.4	10.4	10.8	3.3		—	—	—
Other service periods[2]	3,031	68.9	6.9	14.0	8.8	1.3		217	6.7	2,473
With service-connected disability	216	57.8	17.1	17.5	7.5	0.1		—	—	—
Without service-connected disability	2,274	68.3	6.1	15.1	9.1	1.4		—	—	—
Nonveteran population	130,730	78.7	2.1	11.5	6.2	1.6		11,200	7.9	71,194

— = Not available. **Note:** Veterans in survey were on active duty in the U.S. Armed Forces during these periods of service: Gulf War era II (Sept. 2001-present), Gulf War era I (Aug. 1990-Aug. 2001), Vietnam era (Aug.1964-Apr. 1975), Korean War (July 1950-Jan. 1955), World War II (Dec. 1941-Dec. 1946), and other service periods. Veterans who served in more than one wartime period are classified in the most recent period only. A service-connected disability is a health condition or impairment caused or made worse by military service. (1) Includes unpaid family workers. (2) Includes veterans who did not report presence of disability.

Nations With Largest Armed Forces, by Active-Duty Troop Strength

Source: *The Military Balance 2013*, International Institute for Strategic Studies, published by Routledge Journals, Taylor & Francis, UK
(as of Nov. 2012 except troop strength data, which is as of 2013)

Rank	Country	Troop strength Active troops	Reserve troops (thous.)	Defense expend. ($ mil)	Tanks (MBT) (army only)	Navy Cruisers/ frigates/ destroyers	Sub-marines	Combat aircraft FGA	FTR (air force only)
1.	China	2,285	510	$102,436	7,430+	62F/14D*	65	543+	842
2.	United States	1,520	810	645,700	5,838	22C/17F/62D*	72	826	279
3.	India	1,325	1,155	38,538	3,274+	12F/11D*	15	736	63
4.	Korea, North	1,190	600	—	3,500+	3F	72	48	441+
5.	Russia	845	20,000	59,851	2,800+	5C/9F/18D*	64	323	630
6.	Korea, South	655	4,500	28,978	2,414	2C/12F/6D	23	294	174
7.	Pakistan	642	0	5,878	2,411+	10F	8	174	200
8.	Iran	523	350	23,932	1,663+	0	29	111	184+
9.	Turkey	511	379	16,954	2,494	18F	14	301	53
10.	Vietnam	482	5,000	3,330	1,315	2F	2	97	0
11.	Egypt	439	479	5,510	2,497	8F	4	310	82
12.	Myanmar	406	0	2,273	160	3F	0	0	69
13.	Indonesia	396	400	7,741	0	11F	2	10	22
14.	Thailand	361	200	5,503	283	10F*	0	6	88
15.	Brazil	318	1,340	35,266	439	11F/3D*	5	61	57
16.	Taiwan	290	1,657	10,316	565	4C/22F	4	128	290
17.	Colombia	281	62	6,164	0	4F	4	23	0
18.	Iraq	271	0	14,727	336+	0	0	0	0
19.	Mexico	270	87	5,119	0	7F	0	0	10
20.	Japan	247	56	59,443	777	2C/13F/30D*	18	139	201
21.	Sudan	244	0	—	390	0	0	0	22
22.	Saudi Arabia	234	0	52,510	600	4F/3D	0	165	81
23.	France	229	30	48,121	254	11F/12D*	10	143	73
24.	South Sudan	210	0	537	110+	0	0	0	0
25.	Eritrea	202	120	80[1]	270	0	0	10	6
26.	Germany	196	40	40,356	322	12F/7D	4	69	119
27.	Morocco	196	150	3,374	380	5F	0	51	22
28.	Afghanistan	191	0	2,092	0	0	0	0	0
29.	Italy	181	18	23,631	320	12F/4D*	6	127	64
30.	Syria	178	314	2,296[1]	4,950	0	0	240	85

— = Not available. Note: MBT = Main battle tank. FGA = Fighter, ground attack. FTR = Fighter. * = Navy with aircraft carrier(s), as follows: Brazil 1, China 1, France 1, India 1, Italy 2, Japan 2, Russia 1, Thailand 1, U.S. 11. (1) As of 2010.

Budget for Global War on Terror Operations, 2001-11

Source: Congressional Research Service, Library of Congress
(in billions of dollars)

	2001/02[1]	2003	2004	2005	2006	2007	2008	2009	2010	2011[2]	Total
Total: All missions	$33.8	$81.1	$94.1	$107.6	$121.5	$170.9	$185.6	$155.1	$165.3	$168.1	$1,283.3
Dept. of Defense.	33.0	77.4	72.4	102.6	116.8	164.9	179.2	148.3	154.3	159.1	1,208.1
Foreign aid and diplomacy[3]	0.8	3.7	21.7	4.8	4.3	5.0	5.4	5.4	9.1	6.5	66.7
Veterans Affairs medical. . . .	0.0	0.0	0.0	0.2	0.4	1.0	1.0	1.5	1.9	2.4	8.4
Op. Iraqi Freedom/New Dawn[4]	0.0	53.0	75.9	85.6	101.7	131.3	142.1	95.5	71.3	49.3	805.5
Dept. of Defense.	0.0	50.0	56.4	83.4	98.1	127.2	138.5	92.0	66.5	45.7	757.8
Foreign aid and diplomacy[3]	0.0	3.0	19.5	2.0	3.2	3.2	2.7	2.2	3.3	2.3	41.4
Veterans Affairs medical. . . .	0.0	0.0	0.0	0.2	0.4	0.9	0.9	1.2	1.5	1.3	6.3
Op. Enduring Freedom[5]	20.8	14.7	14.6	20.0	19.0	39.2	43.4	59.5	93.8	118.6	443.5
Dept. of Defense.	20.0	14.0	12.4	17.2	17.9	37.2	40.6	56.1	87.7	113.3	416.2
Foreign aid and diplomacy[3]	0.8	0.7	2.2	2.8	1.1	1.9	2.7	3.1	5.7	4.1	25.1
Veterans Affairs medical. . . .	0.0	0.0	0.0	0.0	0.0	0.1	0.1	0.2	0.5	1.1	2.1
Op. Noble Eagle[6].	13.0	8.0	3.7	2.1	0.8	0.5	0.1	0.1	0.1	0.1	28.6
Dept. of Defense unallocated	0.0	5.5	0.0	0.0	0.0	0.0	0.0	0.0	0.0	0.0	5.5

(1) Fiscal year (FY) 2001 and FY2002 funds combined because most were obligated in FY2002 after the Sept. 11, 2001, attacks at the end of FY2001, on Sept. 30, 2001. (2) FY2011 Continuing Resolution, signed by Pres. Obama Mar. 18, 2011, extended funding for all agencies through Apr. 8, 2011. (3) Includes monies for reconstruction, development and humanitarian aid, embassy operations, counternarcotics, initial training of the Afghan and Iraqi armies, foreign military sales credits, and Economic Support Funds. (4) Began in fall 2002 with the buildup of troops for the Mar. 2003 invasion of Iraq and continued with counterinsurgency and stability operations. (5) Covers Afghanistan and other ongoing Global War on Terror operations, ranging from the Philippines to Djibouti, that began immediately after the Sept. 11, 2001, attacks. (6) Dept. of Defense funds that rebuilt the Pentagon and provided higher security at U.S. military bases and other homeland security, including combat air patrol.

Leading Purchasers of U.S. Defense Articles and Services

Source: Congressional Research Service, Library of Congress
(in current U.S. dollars)

	Worldwide deliveries, 2004-07					Worldwide deliveries, 2008-11				
Rank	Country	Value	Rank	Country	Value	Rank	Country	Value	Rank	Country	Value
1.	Israel.	$5.7 bil	6.	South Korea . . .	$2.5 bil	1.	Saudi Arabia. . .	$5.9 bil	6.	Iraq	$2.6 bil
2.	Egypt	5.2 bil	7.	Japan	2.4 bil	2.	Egypt	3.9 bil	7.	Japan	2.5 bil
3.	Saudi Arabia. .	4.3 bil	8.	Poland	1.9 bil	3.	Israel.	3.8 bil	8.	South Korea . . .	2.5 bil
4.	Taiwan	4.3 bil	9.	Australia	1.7 bil	4.	Australia	2.9 bil	9.	Greece	2.1 bil
5.	Greece	2.8 bil	10.	UK.	1.6 bil	5.	Taiwan	2.9 bil	10.	Turkey.	2.0 bil

Note: Total dollar value of all U.S. defense articles and services actually delivered to top 10 purchasers worldwide. Figures include government-to-government sales through the Foreign Military Sales system (which accounts for the overwhelming majority of U.S. conventional arms deliveries) concluded in calendar years listed, as well as commercially licensed exports concluded in pertinent fiscal years.

U.S. Foreign Military Financing, 2005-12

Source: Defense Security Cooperation Agency, U.S. Dept. of Defense
(in thousands of U.S. dollars)

	2005	2010	2012		2005	2010	2012
Western Hemisphere	$108,155	$89,720	$64,435	**Europe**	$220,274	$151,696	$113,850
Colombia	99,200	55,000	40,000	Bosnia and			
El Salvador.......	1,488	1,000	1,250	Herzegovina	8,480	4,000	4,500
Mexico	0	5,250	7,000	Bulgaria	6,944	9,000	8,647
Near East and				Czech Republic ...	5,952	6,000	5,000
South Asia	4,541,843	4,666,797	5,642,340	Georgia..........	11,904	16,000	14,400
Afghanistan.......	396,800	0	0	Macedonia	5,208	4,000	3,600
Bahrain..........	18,847	19,000	10,000	Poland	76,470	47,000	24,165
Egypt	1,289,600	1,300,000	1,300,000	Romania	13,412	12,999	12,000
Israel............	2,202,240	2,775,000	3,075,000	Turkey...........	33,728	0	0
Jordan...........	304,352	300,000	300,000	Ukraine..........	2,976	11,000	7,000
Lebanon	0	0	75,000	**Africa**	49,453	45,370	54,318
Oman	19,840	8,847	8,000	Djibouti	4,468	2,000	1,500
Pakistan	298,000	248,000	0	Morocco	15,128	9,000	8,000
Yemen	10,420	12,500	20,000	Liberia	2,976	6,000	6,500
East Asia and				Tunisia	10,407	18,000	29,500
Pacific	36,537	59,100	48,302	**World total**........	4,956,262	5,015,952	5,929,245
Indonesia	0	20,000	14,000				
Mongolia.........	2,778	4,500	3,000				
Philippines	29,760	29,000	27,000				

Note: Regional subtotals include countries not listed. Grants extended to foreign governments in a fiscal year to pay for military equipment and services. May be from U.S. Dept. of Defense (DOD) or, for specific countries, negotiated directly with U.S. commercial suppliers with DOD approval.

Defense Contracts, 2013

Source: U.S. Dept. of Defense
(in millions of U.S. dollars)

Listed are the 50 companies or organizations receiving the largest dollar volume of prime contract awards from the U.S. Dept. of Defense during fiscal year 2013 (Oct. 1, 2012-Sept. 30, 2013).

Rank Contractor	Contracts awarded[1]	% of total	Rank Contractor	Contracts awarded[1]	% of total
1. Lockheed Martin Corp.............	$21,178.7	10.11%	27. Computer Sciences Corp.	$1,335.2	0.64%
2. The Boeing Co.....................	13,648.8	6.51	28. Oshkosh Corp...................	1,227.7	0.59
3. Raytheon Co.	9,189.1	4.39	29. Sierra Nevada Corp...............	1,157.0	0.55
4. General Dynamics Corp.	8,904.8	4.25	30. General Atomic Technologies Corp. ..	1,149.2	0.55
5. United Technologies Corp.	4,436.1	2.12	31. Fluor Corp.	1,052.5	0.50
6. Humana Inc.	3,185.8	1.52	32. AmerisourceBergen Corp.	989.7	0.47
7. BAE Systems PLC	2,965.4	1.42	33. Booz Allen Hamilton Holding Corp. ..	953.2	0.45
8. Northrup Grumman Corp.	2,868.5	1.37	34. Miscellaneous foreign contractors ...	930.2	0.44
9. SAIC Inc.	2,647.6	1.26	35. ManTech International Corp.	908.8	0.43
10. Huntington Ingalls Inc.	2,612.3	1.25	36. Harris Corp.	886.7	0.42
11. Health Net Inc.	2,612.1	1.25	37. Honeywell International Inc.	865.5	0.41
12. Northrup Grumman Shipbuilding Inc...	2,608.1	1.24	38. CACI International Inc.	841.6	0.40
13. Bechtel Group Inc.	2,378.4	1.14	39. URS Corp.	839.6	0.40
14. United Launch Alliance LLC	2,370.1	1.13	40. ITT Corp.	828.7	0.40
15. L-3 Communications Holdings Inc.....	2,073.3	0.99	41. Lockheed Martin Corp.	825.3	0.39
16. L-3 Communications Corp.	2,028.9	0.97	42. UnitedHealth Group Inc...........	789.0	0.38
17. Bell Boeing Joint Project Office	1,907.4	0.91	43. FedEx Corp.	772.1	0.37
18. Textron Inc.....................	1,815.5	0.87	44. Total SA	752.7	0.36
19. TriWest Healthcare Alliance Corp.	1,793.8	0.86	45. Chevron Corp.	742.5	0.35
20. General Electric Co.	1,747.5	0.83	46. McKesson Corp..................	716.0	0.34
21. Northrup Grumman Corp.	1,746.2	0.83	47. Austal USA LLC	714.6	0.34
22. Veritas Capital Fund II LP	1,626.3	0.78	48. Compañía Española de Petróleos SA	709.4	0.34
23. Northrup Grumman Systems Corp. ...	1,521.8	0.73	49. Valero Energy Corp..............	704.3	0.34
24. Supreme Group Holding SARL.......	1,511.4	0.72	50. A.P. Moller-Maersk A/S	696.3	0.33
25. Hewlett-Packard Co.	1,367.6	0.65	Other..........................	87,481.9	
26. Refinery Associates of Texas Inc. ...	1,340.1	0.64	**Total**..........................	**210,955.4**	

Note: Contractors listed more than once represent different company locations or facilities. Amounts given are as reported by Sept. 30, 2013. Total is sum of all contracts to top 50,000 contractors. (1) Amounts include contracts awarded to subsidiaries of each company.

Arms Transfer Agreements With the World by Supplier, 2004-11

Source: Congressional Research Service, Library of Congress
(in millions of current U.S. dollars)

Supplier	2004	2005	2006	2007	2008	2009	2010	2011	2004-11
United States	$12,368	$12,099	$15,435	$23,691	$36,323	$22,002	$21,103	$66,274	$209,295
Russia................	8,800	8,400	15,400	10,400	6,600	13,300	8,800	4,800	76,500
France	2,900	6,300	7,700	2,200	3,800	9,600	1,800	4,400	38,700
United Kingdom	4,200	2,900	4,100	9,500	300	1,400	1,500	400	24,300
China	1,000	2,700	2,000	2,500	2,100	2,500	1,600	2,100	16,500
Germany..............	4,100	2,000	2,800	1,800	5,500	3,600	100	100	20,000
Italy..................	400	1,500	1,200	1,400	4,100	1,600	1,900	1,200	13,300
All other European	5,200	7,400	5,600	6,700	5,300	6,500	4,200	3,300	44,200
All others..............	3,300	1,900	3,400	2,800	3,100	5,000	2,900	2,700	25,100
Total................	**42,268**	**45,199**	**57,635**	**60,991**	**67,123**	**65,502**	**43,903**	**85,274**	**467,895**

Note: All data are for the calendar year given except for U.S. MAP (Military Assistance Program), IMET (International Military Education, and Training), and Excess Defense Article data, which are included for the particular fiscal year. All amounts given include the values of all categories of weapons, spare parts, construction, all associated services, military assistance, excess defense articles, and training programs. Statistics for foreign countries are based upon estimated selling prices. All foreign data are rounded to the nearest $100 mil.

Personal Salutes and Honors

The U.S. **national salute**, 21 guns, is also the salute to a national flag. U.S. independence is commemorated by the salute to the Union—one gun for each state—fired at noon July 4, at all military posts provided with suitable artillery.

A 21-gun salute on arrival and departure, with 4 ruffles and flourishes, is rendered to the **president**, to a former president, and to a president-elect. The national anthem or "Hail to the Chief," as appropriate, is played for the president, and the national anthem for the others. A 21-gun salute on arrival and departure, with 4 ruffles and flourishes, also is rendered to the **sovereign or chief of state of a foreign country** or a member of a reigning royal family, and the national anthem of his or her country is played. The music is considered an inseparable part of the salute and immediately follows the ruffles and flourishes without pause. For the Honors March, generals receive the "General's March," admirals receive the "Flag Officer's March," and all others receive the 32-bar medley of "The Stars and Stripes Forever."

| | SALUTE (IN GUNS) | | Ruffles and | |
GRADE, TITLE, OR OFFICE	Arriving	Leaving	flourishes	Music
Vice President of U.S.	19	—	4	Hail, Columbia
Speaker of the House.	19	—	4	Honors March
U.S. or foreign ambassador in country to which accredited	19	—	4	Natl. anthem of official
Premier or prime minister.	19	—	4	Natl. anthem of official
Secretary of Defense, Army, Navy, or Air Force	19	19	4	Honors March
Other cabinet members, Senate president pro tempore, governor, or chief justice of U.S.	19	—	4	Honors March
Chairman, Joint Chiefs of Staff.	19	19	4	Honors March
Army chief of staff, chief of naval operations, Air Force chief of staff, Marine commandant.	19	19	4	Honors March
General of the Army, general of the Air Force, fleet admiral	19	19	4	Honors March
Generals, admirals.	17	17	4	Honors March
Assistant secretaries of Defense, Army, Navy, or Air Force.	17	17	4	Honors March
Chair of a committee of Congress	17	—	4	Honors March

Medal of Honor

Source: Congressional Medal of Honor Society; U.S. Army, U.S. Dept. of Defense

(as of Oct. 15, 2013)

The Medal of Honor is the highest military award for bravery that can be given to any individual in the U.S. The first Army Medals of Honor were awarded on Mar. 25, 1863; the first Navy medals went to sailors and Marines on Apr. 3, 1863.

On Dec. 21, 1861, Pres. Abraham Lincoln signed a bill to create the Navy Medal of Honor. Lincoln, on July 14, 1862, approved a resolution providing for the presentation of Medals of Honor to enlisted men of the Army and Voluntary Forces. The law was amended on Mar. 3, 1863, so that officers as well as enlisted men were eligible.

The Medal of Honor is awarded in the name of Congress to a person who, while a member of the armed forces, distinguishes himself or herself conspicuously by gallantry and intrepidity at the risk of life above and beyond the call of duty while engaged in an action against any enemy of the U.S.; while engaged in military operations involving conflict with an opposing foreign force; or while serving with friendly foreign forces engaged in an armed conflict against an opposing armed force in which the U.S. is not a belligerent party.

The deed performed must have been one of personal bravery or self-sacrifice so conspicuous as to clearly distinguish the individual above his or her comrades and must have involved risk of life. Incontestable proof of the performance of service is required, and each recommendation for award of this decoration is considered on the standard of extraordinary merit.

Prior to World War I, the 2,625 Army Medal of Honor awards up to that time were reviewed to determine which met new stringent criteria. The Army removed 911 names from the list, most of them former members of a Civil War volunteer infantry group who had been induced to extend their enlistments when they were promised the medal. However, the medal was restored to Dr. Mary Walker in 1977 and to Buffalo Bill Cody and seven other Indian scouts in 1989.

The Medal of Honor was awarded posthumously to Army Master Sgt. Gary I. Gordon and to Sgt. First Class Randall D. Shughart, the only recipients for actions occurring in the 1990s. During the Battle of Mogadishu (Somalia), Oct. 3, 1993, they voluntarily guarded a helicopter crash site and its downed crew while under heavy enemy fire.

Seven African American soldiers were awarded Medals of Honor for service in World War II (six of them posthumously) in Jan. 1997. Previously, no black soldier had received the medal for World War II service; an Army inquiry begun in 1993 concluded that the prevailing political climate and Army practices of the time had prevented proper recognition of heroism on the part of black soldiers in that war. In 1996, Congress authorized a review of Asian American and Pacific Islander recipients of the Distinguished Service Cross whose award should be upgraded.

Twenty-two Asian Americans received the Medal of Honor for World War II service in June 2000.

Iraq. Four Medals of Honor have been awarded for actions in Operation Iraqi Freedom. On Apr. 4, 2003, Army Sgt. First Class Paul R. Smith was mortally wounded while holding an exposed position, near Baghdad Intl. Airport, against enemy attack. On Apr. 14, 2004, Marine Cpl. Jason L. Dunham was mortally wounded at Karbala when he covered a live grenade with his helmet and body to protect his fellow Marines. On Sept. 29, 2006, Navy Petty Officer Second Class (SEAL) Michael A. Monsoor was mortally wounded at Ar Ramadi when he threw himself onto a grenade, saving the lives of two teammates. Army Pvt. First Class Ross A. McGinnis was posthumously honored after he covered a grenade with his body, saving his four Humvee crew members from serious injury, on Dec. 4, 2006.

Afghanistan. Nine Medals of Honor have been awarded for actions in Afghanistan. The medal was awarded posthumously to Navy Lt. Michael P. Murphy, whose SEAL team came under attack by Taliban fighters June 28, 2005. Heavily outnumbered and with all four team members wounded, Lt. Murphy left cover to radio for help and was shot in the back. On June 21, 2006, Army Sgt. First Class Jared C. Monti and his patrol were ambushed. Monti repeatedly tried to rescue a wounded soldier despite overwhelming gunfire. Monti was killed by a grenade on his third attempt and received the Medal of Honor posthumously. Special Forces Staff Sgt. Robert Miller received the medal after dying to save the lives of 7 U.S. and 15 Afghan Army soldiers during a battle against more than 100 insurgents on Jan. 25, 2008.

Army Staff Sgt. Salvatore Giunta on Oct. 25, 2007, advanced in the face of persistent Taliban fire to give aid to comrades injured in an ambush; he became the first surviving Medal of Honor recipient since the Vietnam War Nov. 16, 2010. A wounded Staff Sgt. Leroy Petry, May 26, 2008, protected fellow injured rangers by throwing a live enemy grenade, losing his right hand as it detonated. On Sept. 8, 2009, Marine Corps Cpl. Dakota Meyer helped rescue 13 American and 23 Afghan soldiers from an ambush, manning a Humvee gun turret on five trips into enemy fire over six hours. In the same six-hour battle, Army Capt. William D. Swenson on multiple occasions put himself in harm's way to evacuate wounded U.S. and Afghan soldiers and played a key role in coordinating airstrikes.

Army Staff Sgt. Clinton L. Romesha, Oct. 3, 2009, carried out reconnaissance activities under intense gunfire and continued to mobilize troops after sustaining shrapnel wounds. Heavily outnumbered, Army Spc. Ty M. Carter in the same battle defended key positions and repeatedly exposed himself to enemy gunfire to rescue a wounded solider.

Other Selected Awards

Source: U.S. Army Institute of Heraldry, Navy Department Awards Web Service, Air Force Personnel Center

Distinguished Service Cross

Established in Congress July 9, 1918, on recommendation of Gen. John J. "Black Jack" Pershing, and awarded for extraordinary heroism not justifying the award of a Medal of Honor. The act or acts of heroism must have been so notable and have involved risk of life so extraordinary as to set the individual apart from his or her comrades.

Silver Star

An earlier version of this award, the Citation Star, was established by Congress on July 19, 1918, and retroactively awarded to soldiers for "gallantry in action," back to the Spanish-American War. The Silver Star medal replaced the Citation Star in 1932 and is awarded for gallantry in action which, while of a lesser degree than that required for award of the Distinguished Service Cross, must nevertheless have been performed with marked distinction.

Legion of Merit

Established by Congress on July 20, 1942, and awarded to individuals who have distinguished themselves by exceptionally meritorious conduct in the performance of outstanding services. There are different designs depending on the level of command of the award recipient.

Distinguished Flying Cross

Established by Congress July 2, 1926, and awarded for heroism or extraordinary achievement while participating in aerial flight. Awards are made only to recognize single acts of heroism or extraordinary achievement, not sustained operational activities against an armed enemy. Initial awards were given to persons who made record-breaking long-distance and endurance flights or who set altitude records. The first DFC was awarded to Cpt. Charles A. Lindbergh on May 31, 1927. DFCs were awarded retroactively to Orville and Wilbur Wright.

Soldier's Medal

Established by Congress July 2, 1926, to recognize acts of heroism not involving actual conflict with an enemy. The same degree of heroism is required as for the award of the Distinguished Flying Cross. The performance must have involved personal hazard or danger and the voluntary risk of life under conditions not involving conflict with an armed enemy. Awards are not made solely on the basis of having saved a life.

Bronze Star

Established by Executive Order Feb. 4, 1944, largely to raise the morale of ground troops in WWII, on the recommendation of Gen. George C. Marshall. It is awarded to any person who, while serving in any capacity in or with the U.S. military, distinguishes himself or herself by heroic or meritorious achievement or service not involving participation in aerial flight.

Purple Heart

The original Purple Heart, designated as the Badge of Military Merit, was established by Gen. George Washington on Aug. 7, 1782. Following the American Revolution, the badge fell into disuse until 1932, the 200th anniversary of Washington's birth. During WWII, the Order of the Purple Heart was awarded for both wounds received in action and for meritorious service. Following the introduction of the Legion of Merit, the Purple Heart was awarded only for combat wounds. Today, it is awarded to any armed forces member who, while serving with the U.S. Armed Services, has been wounded or killed, or who has died or may hereafter die after being wounded in action against an enemy of the U.S. or in an armed conflict in which the U.S. or friendly foreign forces are engaged; as the result of an act of any hostile foreign force; as a result of an international terrorist attack against the U.S. or a friendly foreign nation; or as a result of military operations outside the U.S. as part of a peacekeeping force. Wounds must be inflicted by weapon fire while directly engaged in armed conflict, regardless of the fire causing the wound, or while held as a prisoner of war or while being taken captive.

Air Medal

Authorized by Pres. Franklin D. Roosevelt on May 11, 1942, and awarded for heroism or meritorious achievement while participating in aerial flight. Awards may be made to recognize single acts of merit or heroism or for meritorious service. Awards are not made to individuals who use air transportation solely for the purpose of moving between points in a combat zone.

Army Commendation

Established Dec. 18, 1945, and awarded for heroism, meritorious achievement, or meritorious service. It may also be awarded to a member of the armed forces of a friendly foreign nation who distinguishes him- or herself by an act of heroism, extraordinary achievement, or meritorious service which has been of mutual benefit to a friendly nation and the U.S.

U.S. Military Awards in Selected Wars and Conflicts

Source: U.S. Army Human Resources Command, U.S. Dept. of Defense; Congressional Medal of Honor Society

Award	Civil War	WWI	WWII	Korea	Vietnam	Gulf War	OEF[1]	Iraq[2]
Medal of Honor	1,522	119	467	137	249	0	9	4
Distinguished Service Cross....	NA	6,430	4,434	724	848	0	13	15
Silver Star	NA	NA	73,654	10,061	21,634	75	342	355
Legion of Merit	NA	NA	20,273	NA	10,356	158	136	133
Distinguished Flying Cross.....	NA	NA	126,318	NA	21,697	108	207	118
Soldier's Medal	NA	NA	12,485	581	5,402	43	39	111
Bronze Star (total)[3]	NA	NA	395,380	30,359	719,968	27,967	59,896	111,460
Purple Heart	NA	NA	NA	NA	220,516	504	8,526	22,101
Air Medal (total)[3]	NA	NA	1,166,471	0	1,039,124	6,399	15,938	21,880
Army Commendation (total)[3] ...	NA	NA	0	0	837,037	81,979	156,364	388,205

NA = Not available or applicable. **Note:** Numbers for the individual decorations shown here represent only those awards that were properly processed and reported to Dept. of the Army Headquarters. The actual number of individual decorations awarded under combat conditions, when award approval authority is delegated to field commanders, cannot be stated with absolute certainty. Numbers here reflect the current statistics recorded by the Military Awards Branch, as of July 17, 2013, except for MOH, which is as reported by the Congressional Medal of Honor Society as of Oct. 15, 2013. (1) Operation Enduring Freedom (primarily Afghanistan). (2) Operation Iraqi Freedom and Operation New Dawn. (3) Includes awards for valor/heroism and for meritorious service or achievement.

Federal Service Academies

U.S. Military Academy, West Point, NY. Founded 1802. Awards BS degree and Army commission for a 5-year service obligation. **Website:** www.usma.edu

U.S. Naval Academy, Annapolis, MD. Founded 1845. Awards BS degree and Navy or Marine Corps commission for a 5-year service obligation. **Website:** www.usna.edu

U.S. Air Force Academy, Colorado Springs, CO. Founded 1954. Awards BS degree and Air Force commission for a 6-year service obligation. **Website:** www.usafa.edu

U.S. Coast Guard Academy, New London, CT. Founded 1876. Awards BS degree and Coast Guard commission for a 5-year service obligation. **Website:** www.cga.edu

U.S. Merchant Marine Academy, Kings Point, NY. Founded 1943. Awards BS degree; a license as a deck, engineer, or dual officer; and a U.S. Naval Reserve commission. Service obligations vary according to options taken by the graduate. **Website:** www.usmma.edu

U.S. Army, Navy, Air Force, Marine Corps, and Coast Guard Insignia

Source: Dept. of the Army, Dept. of the Navy, Dept. of the Air Force, U.S. Dept. of Defense; U.S. Coast Guard, U.S. Dept. of Homeland Security

Army

General of the Armies—Gen. John J. Pershing (1860-1948), the only person to have held this rank while living, was authorized to prescribe his own insignia but never wore in excess of four stars. Congress established the rank in 1799 to be bestowed posthumously on George Washington; Washington was finally promoted to the rank by joint resolution of Congress, approved by Pres. Gerald Ford, Oct. 19, 1976.

General of the Army—Five silver stars fastened together in a circle and the coat of arms of the U.S. in gold color metal with shield and crest enameled. Reserved for wartime use only.

Rank	Insignia
General of the Army*	Five silver stars
General	Four silver stars
Lieutenant General	Three silver stars
Major General	Two silver stars
Brigadier General	One silver star
Colonel	Silver eagle
Lieutenant Colonel	Silver oak leaf
Major	Gold oak leaf
Captain	Two silver bars
First Lieutenant	One silver bar
Second Lieutenant	One gold bar

Warrant Officers

Grade Five—Silver bar with enamel black line.
Grade Four—Silver bar with 4 enamel black squares.
Grade Three—Silver bar with 3 enamel black squares.
Grade Two—Silver bar with 2 enamel black squares.
Grade One—Silver bar with 1 enamel black square.

Noncommissioned Officers

Sergeant Major of the Army (E-9)—Three chevrons above 3 arcs, with a U.S. coat of arms centered on the chevrons, flanked by 2 stars—1 star on each side of the eagle. Also distinctive red-and-white shield collar insignia.

Command Sergeant Major (E-9)—Three chevrons above 3 arcs with a 5-pointed star with a wreath around the star between the chevrons and arcs.

Sergeant Major (E-9)—Three chevrons above 3 arcs with a 5-pointed star between the chevrons and arcs.

First Sergeant (E-8)—Three chevrons above 3 arcs with a lozenge between the chevrons and arcs.

Master Sergeant (E-8)—Three chevrons above 3 arcs.
Sergeant First Class (E-7)—Three chevrons above 2 arcs.
Staff Sergeant (E-6)—Three chevrons above 1 arc.
Sergeant (E-5)—Three chevrons.
Corporal (E-4)—Two chevrons.

Specialists

Specialist (E-4)—Eagle device only.

Other Enlisted

Private First Class (E-3)—One chevron above 1 arc.
Private (E-2)—One chevron.
Private (E-1)—None.
*Rank reserved for wartime use only.

Air Force

Insignia for Air Force officers are identical to those of the Army. Insignia for enlisted personnel are worn on both sleeves and consist of 1 star and an appropriate number of rockers. Chevrons appear above 5 rockers for the top three noncommissioned officer ranks, as follows (in ascending order): Master Sergeant, 1 chevron; Senior Master Sergeant, 2 chevrons; Chief Master Sergeant, 3 chevrons. The insignia of the Chief Master Sergeant of the Air Force has 3 chevrons and a wreath around the star design. General of the Air Force is reserved for wartime use only.

Navy

The following stripes are worn on the lower sleeves of the Service Dress Blue uniform. They are of gold embroidery.

Rank	Insignia
Fleet Admiral*	1 two inch with 4 one-half inch
Admiral	1 two inch with 3 one-half inch
Vice Admiral	1 two inch with 2 one-half inch
Rear Admiral (upper half)	1 two inch with 1 one-half inch
Rear Admiral (lower half)	1 two inch
Captain	4 one-half inch
Commander	3 one-half inch
Lieutenant Commander	2 one-half inch with 1 one-quarter inch between
Lieutenant	2 one-half inch
Lieutenant (jr. grade)	1 one-half inch with 1 one-quarter inch above
Ensign	1 one-half inch
Warrant Officer W-4	½" stripe with 1 break
Warrant Officer W-3	½" stripe with 2 breaks, 2" apart
Warrant Officer W-2	½" stripe with 3 breaks, 2" apart

Enlisted personnel (noncommissioned petty officers)—A rating badge worn on the upper left sleeve consisting of a spread eagle, appropriate number of chevrons, and centered specialty mark.

*Rank reserved for wartime use only.

Marine Corps

Marine Corps' distinctive cap and collar ornament is the Marine Corps emblem—a combination of the American eagle, a globe, and an anchor. Marine Corps and Army officer insignia are similar. Marine Corps enlisted insignia, although basically similar to the Army's, feature crossed rifles beneath the chevrons. Marine Corps enlisted rank insignia are as follows:

Sergeant Major of the Marine Corps (E-9)—Same as Sergeant Major (below) but with Marine Corps emblem in the center with a 5-pointed star on both sides of the emblem.

Sergeant Major (E-9)—Three chevrons above 4 rockers with a 5-pointed star in the center.

Master Gunnery Sergeant (E-9)—Three chevrons above 4 rockers with a bursting bomb insignia in the center.

First Sergeant (E-8)—Three chevrons above 3 rockers with a diamond in the middle.

Master Sergeant (E-8)—Three chevrons above 3 rockers with crossed rifles in the middle.

Gunnery Sergeant (E-7)—Three chevrons above 2 rockers with crossed rifles in the middle.

Staff Sergeant (E-6)—Three chevrons above 1 rocker with crossed rifles in the middle.

Sergeant (E-5)—Three chevrons above crossed rifles.
Corporal (E-4)—Two chevrons above crossed rifles.
Lance Corporal (E-3)—One chevron above crossed rifles.
Private First Class (E-2)—One chevron.
Private (E-1)—None.

Coast Guard

Coast Guard insignia follow Navy custom, with certain minor changes such as the officer cap insignia. The Coast Guard shield is worn on both sleeves of officers and on the right sleeve of all enlisted personnel.

For Further Information on the U.S. Armed Forces

Additional information on all the U.S. Armed Forces branches, as well as many other related organizations, can be accessed through the official website of the Dept. of Defense: www.defense.gov.

Army—Office of the Chief of Public Affairs, Media Relations Division—MRD, 1500 Army Pentagon, Washington, DC 20310-1500. **Website:** www.army.mil

Navy—Chief of Information, 1200 Navy Pentagon, Washington, DC 20350-1200. **Website:** www.navy.mil

Air Force—Office of Public Affairs, 1690 Air Force Pentagon, Washington, DC 20330-1690. **Website:** www.af.mil

Marine Corps—Marine Corps Headquarters, Division of Public Affairs, 3000 Marine Corps, Pentagon, Washington, DC 20350-3000. **Website:** www.usmc.mil

Coast Guard—Commandant (CG-09222), Attn: Chief of Media Relations, U.S. Coast Guard, 2100 2nd St. SW, Stop 7362, Washington, DC 20593-7362. **Website:** www.uscg.mil

Casualties in Principal Wars of the U.S.
Source: U.S. Dept. of Defense; U.S. Coast Guard, U.S. Dept. of Homeland Security

Data prior to World War I are based on incomplete records in many cases. Casualty data are confined to dead and wounded personnel and, therefore, exclude personnel captured or missing in action who were subsequently returned to military control.

	Branch of service	Number serving	CASUALTIES Battle deaths	Other deaths	Wounds not mortal[1]	Total[2]
Revolutionary War	**Total**	—	**4,435**	**—**	**6,188**	**10,623**
1775-83	Army	184,000	4,044	—	6,004	10,048
	Navy	to	342	—	114	456
	Marines	250,000[13]	49	—	70	119
War of 1812	**Total**	**286,730[14]**	**2,260**	**—**	**4,505**	**6,765**
1812-15	Army	—	1,950	—	4,000	5,950
	Navy	—	265	—	439	704
	Marines	—	45	—	66	111
Mexican War	**Total**	**78,718[14]**	**1,733**	**11,550**	**4,152**	**17,435**
1846-48	Army	—	1,721	11,550	4,102	17,373
	Navy	—	1	—	3	4
	Marines	—	11	—	47	58
	Coast Guard[8]	71 off.	—	—	—	—
Civil War						
1861-65						
Union forces[3]	**Total**	**2,213,363**	**140,414**	**224,097**	**281,881**	**646,392**
	Army	2,128,948[14]	138,154	221,374	280,040	639,568
	Navy	84,415	2,112	2,411	1,710	6,233
	Marines	(in Navy total)	148	312	131	591
	Coast Guard[8]	219 off.	1	—	—	1
Confederate forces (estimate)[3]	**Total**	—	**74,524**	**59,297**	**—**	**133,821**
	Army	600,000	—	—	—	—
	Navy	to	—	—	—	—
	Marines	1,500,000	—	—	—	—
Spanish-American War	**Total**	**306,760**	**385**	**2,061**	**1,662**	**4,108**
1898	Army[9]	280,564	369	2,061	1,594	4,024
	Navy	22,875	10	—	47	57
	Marines	3,321	6	—	21	27
	Coast Guard[8]	660	0	—	—	—
World War I	**Total**	**4,734,991**	**53,402**	**63,114**	**204,002**	**320,518**
Apr. 6, 1917-Nov. 11, 1918	Army[10]	4,057,101	50,510	55,868	193,663	300,041
	Navy	599,051	431	6,856	819	8,106
	Marines	78,839	2,461	390	9,520	12,371
	Coast Guard	8,835	111	81	—	192
World War II[4]	**Total**	**16,112,566**	**291,557**	**113,842**	**670,846**	**1,076,245**
Dec. 7, 1941-Dec. 31, 1946	Army[11]	11,260,000	234,874	83,400	565,861	884,135
	Navy[12]	4,183,466	36,950	25,664	37,778	100,392
	Marines	669,100	19,733	4,778	67,207	91,718
	Coast Guard	241,093	574	1,343	—	1,917
Korean War[5]	**Total**	**5,720,000**	**33,739**	**2,835**	**103,284**	**139,858**
June 25, 1950-July 27, 1953	Army	2,834,000	27,731	2,125	77,596	107,452
	Navy	1,177,000	503	154	1,576	2,233
	Marines	424,000	4,267	242	23,744	28,253
	Air Force	1,285,000	1,238	314	368	1,920
	Coast Guard	44,143	—	—	—	—
Vietnam War[6]	**Total**	**8,744,000**	**47,434**	**10,786**	**153,303**	**211,523**
Aug. 4, 1964-Jan. 27, 1973	Army	4,368,000	30,963	7,261	96,802	135,026
	Navy	1,842,000	1,631	935	4,178	6,744
	Marines	794,000	13,095	1,749	51,392	66,236
	Air Force	1,740,000	1,745	841	931	3,517
	Coast Guard	8,000	7	2	60	69
Persian Gulf War	**Total**	**2,225,000**	**148**	**235**	**467**	**850**
1991	Army	782,000	98	126	354	578
	Navy	669,000	6	50	12	68
	Marines	213,000	24	44	92	160
	Air Force	561,000	20	15	9	44
	Coast Guard	400	—	—	—	—
Iraq War[7]	**Total**	**269,363[15]**	**3,519**	**957**	**32,230**	**36,706**
Mar. 19, 2003-Dec. 15, 2011	Army	99,664[15]	2,574	719	22,518	25,811
	Navy	61,018[15]	63	41	635	739
	Marines	66,166[15]	852	171	8,626	9,649
	Air Force	42,515[15]	29	26	451	506
	Coast Guard	1,250[15]	1	—	—	1

— = Not available. Off. = Officers. **Note:** As of Aug. 27, 2013, there have been 1,778 battle deaths, 482 non-hostile deaths, and 19,204 wounded in Op. Enduring Freedom, mostly in Afghanistan and the Persian Gulf area. (1) Marine Corps data for Iraq War, World War II, the Spanish-American War, and prior wars represent the number of individuals wounded, whereas all other data in this column represent the total number (incidence) of wounds. (2) Totals for all branches do not include categories for which no data are listed. (3) From the final report of the Provost Marshal General, 1863-66. Authoritative statistics for the Confederate forces are not available. In addition, an estimated 26,000-31,000 Confederate personnel died in Union prisons. New estimates published in *Civil War History* in 2012 recalculated the death toll for both sides and determined that it was 20% higher than previously thought, at 750,000. (4) Data are for Dec. 1, 1941, through Dec. 31, 1946, when hostilities were officially terminated by presidential proclamation; few battle deaths or wounds not mortal were incurred after Japanese acceptance of Allied peace terms on Aug. 14, 1945. Numbers serving Dec. 1, 1941-Aug. 31, 1945: Total—14,903,213; Army—10,420,000; Navy—3,883,520; Marine Corps—599,693. (5) As a result of an ongoing Dept. of Defense review of available Korean War casualty record information, updates have been made to previously reported figures for battle deaths and other deaths. (6) Number serving Aug. 5, 1964-Jan. 27, 1973 (date of cease-fire). Includes casualties incurred in Mayaguez incident. Wounds not exclude 150,341 persons not requiring hospital care. (7) Military deaths during the invasion phase, which ended Apr. 30, 2003, totaled 115 combat-related and 23 other. (8) Then known as the U.S. Revenue Cutter Services, predecessor to the U.S. Coast Guard. (9) Number serving Apr. 21-Aug. 13, 1898, while dead and wounded data are for May 1-Aug. 31, 1898. Active hostilities ceased on Aug. 13, 1898, but the U.S. and Spain did not exchange ratifications of the treaty of peace until Apr. 11, 1899. (10) Includes Army Air Forces battle deaths and wounds not mortal, as well as casualties suffered by American forces in northern Russia to Aug. 25, 1919, and in Siberia to Apr. 1, 1920. Other deaths cover Apr. 1, 1917-Dec. 31, 1918. (11) Includes Army Air Forces. (12) Battle deaths and wounds not mortal include casualties incurred in Oct. 1941 due to hostile action. (13) Estimated. (14) As reported by Commissioner of Pensions in his Annual Report for Fiscal Year 1903. (15) Number serving as of Mar. 31, 2003, i.e., does not include numbers of troops deployed since then.

Timeline of Major Wars Since 1066

Norman Conquest 1066-71	William I, duke of Normandy, landed on the English coast near Hastings on Sept. 28, 1066, and defeated Harold II, Saxon king of England, at Battle of Hastings Oct. 14. William crowned king Dec. 25 in Westminster Abbey. Most revolts were suppressed by 1071. **Conquest linked England's interests with those of the continent and led to its rise as a powerful monarchy.**
Crusades 1095-1270/1291	Military expeditions undertaken by **Western European Christians**, usually at the behest of the **papacy**, to recover **Jerusalem** and other Biblical places of pilgrimage from **Muslim** control; in the long term, stimulated trade and flow of ideas between East and West. Pope Urban II called Nov. 27, 1095, for the **First Crusade**; Crusaders took Jerusalem on July 15, 1099, massacred inhabitants, and founded four temporary states: Antioch, Edessa, Jerusalem, and Tripoli. The failed **Second Crusade** was prompted by Muslims' capture of Edessa in 1144. Jerusalem was captured by Ayyubid sultan Saladin on Oct. 2, 1187, leading to the **Third Crusade**, which involved the Holy Roman emperor, Frederick I (Barbarossa); the French king, Philip II (Augustus); and the English king, Richard I (Lion-Heart) but did not lead to a Crusader victory. The **Fourth Crusade** sacked Constantinople on Apr. 13, 1204. The **Fifth Crusade** began with capture of Damietta in Egypt (1219) but failed at Cairo. A **Sixth Crusade** led to the Treaty of Jaffa in 1229, giving Jerusalem to the Crusaders until 1244, when its seizure by the Khwarezmians led to the launch of a **Seventh Crusade**. The last crusade abruptly ended when its leader, French King Louis IX, died in 1270. The last major Crusader stronghold, Acre, was lost on May 18, 1291.
Hundred Years War 1337-1453	Series of armed conflicts over rival claims to the French throne, broken by a number of truces and peace treaties. Edward III declared self king of France in 1338 and invaded, with victories at Crécy in 1346 and Poitiers in 1356. **Treaty of Brétigny** signed May 8, 1360, but French king Charles V renewed fighting in 1369. Truce from 1396 until **Henry V** of England invaded in 1415 and **defeated French army at Agincourt**, capturing land north of Loire River including Paris. **Treaty of Troyes** in 1420 made Henry VI heir of both thrones. The siege of French stronghold Orléans, lifted in 1429 with help from **Joan of Arc**, turned the tide in favor of French. **War ended English claims to France, paved way for French absolute monarchy.**
Wars of the Roses 1455-85	Series of dynastic civil wars for the throne in England fought by the **rival houses of Lancaster and York**. Richard, third duke of York, in conflict with the Lancastrian King **Henry VI**, won victories at St. Albans (1455) and Northampton (1460); Richard died at battle of Wakefield on Dec. 30, 1460, before coronation, leaving his son to become King Edward IV. Henry VI imprisoned in Tower of London, 1465. Edward died in 1483; his brother became **Richard III** after usurping throne from Edward V. Henry Tudor defeated Richard III at the Battle of Bosworth Field (1485). As Henry VII, he married Edward's daughter Elizabeth, 1486, finally **uniting the houses**.
Thirty Years' War 1618-48	A series of religious and political conflicts involving **most countries of western Europe**; majority of fighting in Germany, devastating it. Protestants stormed Hapsburg palace in the "Defenestration of Prague" (May 23, 1618). Major conflicts included defeat of King Christian IV of Denmark and Norway by Catholic League (1626); victories by Lutheran King Gustav II Adolph of Sweden at Breitenfeld (1631) and Lützen (1632). France, under cardinal and statesman **Richelieu**, chief minister of King Louis XIII, declared war on the Hapsburgs in May 1635; defeated Austro-Bavarian army (Aug. 3, 1645), leading to Truce of Ulm. **Peace of Westphalia** signed at Münster on Oct. 24, 1648, bringing peace by recognizing the rulers' sovereignty within their lands and their right to determine the religious beliefs of their subjects.
English Civil Wars 1638-60	Series of conflicts between followers of King Charles (Cavaliers) and Parliament (Roundheads), over divine right of king versus Parliament's right to control national finances. Presbyterian Scots, allied with Parliament, rioted and in 1640 occupied the northern counties of England. Oliver Cromwell, second in command of Parliament's New Model Army, destroyed the king's army at Battle of Naseby (June 14, 1645); first civil war ended May 1646 when Charles surrendered to the Scots. Charles later allied with Scots but was defeated by Cromwell at Preston Aug. 17-19, 1648, and executed Jan. 30, 1649. Parliament abolished monarchy and House of Lords. Cromwell suppressed Irish and Scottish rebellions, was briefly succeeded by son Richard after death (1658); **Charles II restored to the throne** by the "Long Parliament," May 1660.
War of the Spanish Succession 1701-14	War fought by the Grand Alliance (originally England, Netherlands, Denmark, and Austria; later also Portugal), against coalition of France, Spain, and a number of small Italian and German principalities to preserve balance of power after death of Spanish king Charles II. Opened with invasion of Italy, via Venice, by an Austrian army under Prince Eugène of Savoy in May 1701. French forced to withdraw from Netherlands and Italy in 1706 and were finally defeated in 1709 in bloodiest battle of the war at French village of Malplaquet. Treaty of Rastatt and Baden signed in 1714; **Austria given control of Spanish Netherlands, and peace settled between Austria and France.**
War of the Austrian Succession 1740-48	Conflict over rival claims for the **hereditary dominions of the Habsburg family**, following death (1740) of Charles VI, Holy Roman emperor and archduke of Austria. An alliance of Bavaria, France, Spain, Sardinia, Prussia, and Saxony fought against Austria, allied with Holland and Great Britain. King Frederick the Great of Prussia captured Silesia from Austria in the First (1740-42) and Second (1744-45) Silesian Wars. British king George II defeated French army at Battle of Dettingen am Main (June 27, 1743). French conquered Austrian Netherlands (1745-46). Treaty of Aix-la-Chapelle Oct. 18, 1748, **restored most original borders; Prussia became significant force.**
Seven Years' War 1756-63	Worldwide conflicts fought for the **control of Germany** and for **supremacy in colonial N America and India**. French defeated British Gen. Edward Braddock in Battle of Monongahela in 1754, leading to formal declaration of **French-Indian War**, May 1756. Frederick II of Prussia invaded Saxony on Aug. 29, 1756; defeated French at Rossbach (1757), Austrians at Leuthen (1757), Russians at Zorndorf (1758). By 1760, British conquered French Canada. Peter III of Russia signed armistice with Prussia, 1762. Treaty of Paris signed Feb. 10, 1763; Peace of Hubertusburg Feb. 15, 1763, between Prussia and Austria. **England emerged as leading world naval power.**
American Revolution 1775-83	Conflict between Great Britain and 13 British colonies in eastern N America. George Washington took command of the Continental Army, July 2, 1775, and King George III declared colonies traitors on Aug. 23. **Declaration of Independence of colonies adopted July 4, 1776.** France recognized the colonies' independence Feb. 6, 1778, followed by Spain on June 21, 1779; both pledged support. French fleet drove British fleet under Adm. Thomas Graves from Chesapeake Bay on Sept. 5, 1781. French and Americans laid siege to Yorktown, VA, Sept. 28-Oct. 19, forcing British Gen. Cornwallis to surrender. **Treaty of Paris** (Sept. 3, 1783) recognized U.S. independence.
Wars of French Revolution and Napoleonic Wars 1792-1815	Large-scale wars fought between France and two multinational coalitions. France declared war on the Austrian part of the Holy Roman Empire, Apr. 20, 1792, for aiding King Louis XVI. Newly created French Republic declared war on monarchs of Britain and Holland, Feb. 1, 1793, and of Spain, Mar. 7. **Napoleon Bonaparte** defeated Austria in N Italy (1796-97), captured Egypt from Britain (1798-99; Battle of the Pyramids, July 21, 1798), and became First Consul after coup d'état of Nov. 9-10, 1799. French Grande Armée later swept through Europe using innovative and aggressive tactics. French navy defeated by British under Adm. Horatio Nelson at **Trafalgar** (Oct. 21, 1805), but Napoleon defeated Austro-Russian forces at Austerlitz (Dec. 2) and controlled most of Europe except Russia and Great Britain by 1808. France suffered its first major defeat by Austria at Aspern-Essling, May 21-22, 1809. **Napoleon invaded Russia**, captured Moscow Sept. 14, 1812, but was forced to flee the bitter Russian winter and abandoned German army after defeat at Leipzig, Oct. 16-19, 1813. Paris captured by Allied armies Mar. 30-31, 1814. Napoleon exiled to Elba May 4 but returned for "Hundred Days" reign, Mar. 20-June 28, 1815; **final defeat at Waterloo** by British and Prussian troops (June 18). The **Bourbon monarchy was restored under Louis XVIII**, and Britain, Prussia, Russia, and Austria maintained European peace.

Crimean War
1853-56

Conflict between **Russia** and coalition of **Great Britain, France, Sardinia, and Turkey for influence over Balkans** and the straits between the Black Sea and Mediterranean. Russia destroyed Turkish fleet at Sinope on Nov. 30, 1853. Britain and France declared war in Mar. 1854 and with Turkish troops defeated Russians at Battle of Alma River, Sept. 20. Lord Lucan of Britain prevented Russia from capturing Balaklava on Oct. 25 ("Charge of the Light Brigade" led by Lord Cardigan). Siege of Sevastopol ended when Russia evacuated Sept. 8, 1855. Treaty of Paris signed Mar. 30, 1856; **curbed Russian expansion and loosened European power alignments.**

American Civil War
1861-65

Conflict between the U.S. (the Union) and 11 secessionist Southern states, organized as the Confederate States of America. Union garrison at Fort Sumter in harbor of Charleston, SC, surrendered to Brig. Gen. Pierre Beauregard (Apr. 12-13, 1861). 22,000 Confederates under Beauregard repelled 35,000 Union troops under Gen. Irvin McDowell along Bull Run stream near Manassas, VA (July 21). The *Merrimack* (renamed the *Virginia*) battled the *Monitor* Mar. 9, 1862. In **Battle of Antietam** (Sept. 17), some 12,000 Northerners and 12,700 Southerners were killed or wounded. Pres. Abraham Lincoln announced **Emancipation Proclamation** on Sept. 22. Confederate Gen. Robert E. Lee's forces numbering 75,000 battled 88,000 Union troops under Gen. George Meade at **Gettysburg** July 1-3, 1863; Lee's army forced back across the Potomac River. Lee surrendered to Ulysses S. Grant at **Appomattox Court House** (Apr. 9, 1865). **The Union was preserved and slavery abolished.**

Franco-Prussian War
1870-71

German states led by Prussia defeated France, seizing Alsace and part of Lorraine. French defeated in several major battles, culminating at **Sedan** Sept. 1, 1870, when Prussian forces decisively defeated the French army and captured emperor Napoleon III. Prussian king crowned William I, emperor of unified Germany, Jan 18, 1871. **France surrendered** Jan. 28. Final treaty signed May 10; set the stage for later **German imperialistic expansion.**

Spanish-American War
1898

War waged by the U.S. to **liberate Cuba from Spanish rule.** A mysterious explosion, blamed on Spain by American newspapers, sank the U.S. battleship *Maine* in Havana's harbor (Feb. 15, 1898), killing 260. The U.S. called for Spain's withdrawal from Cuba, and Spain declared war (Apr. 24). Rufus Shafter led 17,000 U.S. troops from Daiquirí to Santiago de Cuba, taking **San Juan Hill** with help of the Rough Riders under Teddy Roosevelt. Santiago de Cuba surrendered July 17. The Treaty of Paris (Dec. 10, 1898) provided for the **independence of Cuba** and the cession by Spain to the U.S. of **Puerto Rico, Guam, and for a $20 mil payment, the Philippine Islands.**

World War I
1914-18

Local European war that grew into a global war involving 32 nations: the Allies and the Associated Powers—28 nations including Great Britain, France, Russia, Italy, and the U.S.—versus the Central Powers of Germany, Austria-Hungary, Turkey, and Bulgaria. Archduke Francis Ferdinand of Austria assassinated in Sarajevo, Bosnia (June 28, 1914). Germany invaded France through Belgium; advance on Paris halted by the French under Gen. Joseph Jacques Césaire Joffre at the **First Battle of the Marne**, Sept. 5-12. Germany checked the Russian army at the Battle of Tannenberg, Aug. 26-30. The British suffered 57,470 casualties (19,240 dead) in the opening day of the **First Battle of the Somme** (July 1-Nov. 18, 1916), first of 12 battles that forced Germany back to Hindenburg Line. **U.S. declared war on Germany Apr. 6, 1917.** Russian involvement ended when Bolshevik party seized power on Nov. 7; signed armistice Dec. 15. German offensive halted by U.S. and French troops at **Second Battle of the Marne** (July 15-Aug. 5, 1918), turning point of the war. Allied counteroffensive broke the Hindenburg Line, and an armistice was signed Nov. 11.

World War II
1939-45

Global military conflict stemming from European unrest after World War I and Japan's aggressive expansion into Asia and the Pacific. **War in Europe:** Nazi-Soviet nonaggression pact (Aug. 23, 1939) freed Germany and the Soviet Union to attack Poland in Sept. **Britain and France declared war on Germany** Sept. 3. German forces raced through Europe (Apr.-June 1940), captured Paris June 14. **Italy declared war on France and Britain** June 10; German-Italian campaigns won the Balkans and N Africa by June 1941. U.S. entered war Dec. 1941. Three million Axis troops invaded Russia June 22, 1941, but Russian counterthrusts stopped the German advance (**Stalingrad**, Aug. 20, 1942-Feb. 2, 1943), and Allies took N Africa (Nov. 8, 1942-May 13, 1943), Italy (July 10, 1943-May 2, 1945). Normandy invaded on **D-Day**, June 6, 1944; Paris liberated Aug. 25. Leaders at Yalta Conference (Feb. 4-11, 1945) discussed defeat and division of Germany into four. Adolf Hitler committed suicide Apr. 30. **Germany surrendered unconditionally** May 7. **War in the Pacific:** Japan invaded China (July 7, 1937), joined alliance with Germany and Italy (Sept. 27, 1940), and signed nonaggression pact with Russia (Apr. 13, 1941); attacked Hawaii's Pearl Harbor, Dec. 7, 1941; U.S. declared war on Japan Dec. 8. **Battle of Midway** (June 4-7, 1942) repulsed Japanese advance. Marines landed on Guadalcanal Aug. 7. Navy defeated Japanese fleet at **Leyte Gulf**, Oct. 23-26, 1944. B-29 bombing raids on Japan began in Nov. Marines invaded Iwo Jima (Feb. 19-Mar. 16, 1945) with heavy casualties, then Okinawa (Apr. 1-June 21). **U.S. atom bombs dropped** on Hiroshima (Aug. 6) and Nagasaki (Aug. 9) and Soviet invasion of Manchuria (Aug. 8) **forced Japan to agree, on Aug. 14, to surrender**; formal surrender on Sept. 2.

Korean War
1950-53

Military struggle fought on the Korean Peninsula between the Democratic Peoples' Republic of Korea (N Korea) and the Republic of Korea (S Korea) that developed into an international war involving China allied with N Korea against the U.S. and other nations under the UN flag. DPRK army crossed the 38th parallel and invaded S Korea (June 25, 1950), entering Seoul (June 26). Amphibious assault launched at **Inchon** by Gen. Douglas MacArthur (Sept. 15) helped U.S. forces rout DPRK close to Yalu River by Nov. 24. Chinese counterattack retook Seoul (Jan. 4, 1951) but were forced back to the 38th parallel by Apr. 22. Armistice was signed (July 27, 1953) by the UN, DPRK, and China, but not ROK, **leaving the peninsula partitioned at the 38th parallel.**

Vietnam War
1959-75

Struggle primarily in S Vietnam that widened into a war between S Vietnam supported mainly by the U.S. and N Vietnam supported by the USSR and China. Viet Minh, led by Communist leader Ho Chi Minh, formed the Democratic Republic of Vietnam (Sept. 2, 1945). Colonial power France withdrew after fortress at Dien Bien Phu fell (May 8, 1954). Pres. John F. Kennedy pledged U.S. commitment to S Vietnamese independence Dec. 14, 1961. USS *Maddox* destroyer damaged in **Gulf of Tonkin** (Aug. 2, 1964), prompting Congress to increase involvement. Regular bombing of N Vietnam began (Feb. 24, 1965), and the first U.S. combat ground forces arrived (Mar. 6). N Vietnamese Army siege of **Khe Sanh** (Jan. 21-Apr. 7, 1968) and the **"Tet" offensive** (Jan. 30) aimed to cause insurrection in the S. **My Lai Massacre** by U.S. soldiers of civilians (Mar. 16, 1968) created scandal, fueled U.S. disaffection with war. U.S. forces peaked at 543,400 in Apr. 1969. NVA **"Easter Offensive"** (Mar. 30, 1972) rebuffed, and U.S. responded with aerial bombings in May and Dec. U.S. withdrew after ceasefire, Jan. 1973. **NVA offensive captured Saigon, Apr. 30, 1975, and unified Vietnam under Communist rule.**

Persian Gulf Wars
1991, 2003-10

Conflicts fought principally between Iraq and the U.S. concerning Iraq's influence in the Middle East and its development of weapons of mass destruction. **First Gulf War:** Iraq under dictator Saddam Hussein invaded Kuwait Aug 2, 1990, and annexed it; UN Security Council ordered Iraqi forces to withdraw by Jan. 15, 1991. Beginning Jan. 17, a U.S.-led multinational force (**Operation Desert Storm**) bombed military targets in Iraq and Kuwait. A coordinated air-land offensive (**Operation Desert Sabre**, begun Feb. 24) retook Kuwait City Feb. 26, and permanent ceasefire was signed on Apr. 6. Iraq was ordered to pay reparations to Kuwait, reveal locations of biological and chemical weapons, and eliminate weapons of mass destruction. **Second Gulf War:** The U.S. and UK mistakenly asserted that Iraq was still producing WMDs and posed an imminent threat. The UN passed Resolution 1441, Nov. 8, 2002, warning Iraq of "serious consequences" if it failed to cooperate fully and unconditionally with UN weapons inspectors. Iraq rejected a Mar. 17, 2003, U.S. ultimatum demanding Hussein and his sons leave Iraq; U.S. launched **Operation Iraqi Freedom** Mar. 19, 2003, with support from UK and other allies, but without full UN Security Council support. Baghdad fell Apr. 9, and major combat operations declared over May 1. Hussein was captured Dec. 13, but guerrilla opposition to U.S. troops and insurgent violence continued. U.S. combat operations in Iraq formally ended Aug. 31, 2010.

HEALTH

U.S. Health Expenditures, 1960-2010

Source: *Health, United States, 2012*, National Center for Health Statistics, Centers for Disease Control and Prevention

	1960	1970	1980	1990	2000	2005	2008	2009	2010
					Amount in billions				
National health expenditures	$27.4	$74.9	$255.8	$724.3	$1,377.2	$2,029.1	$2,403.9	$2,495.8	$2,593.6
					Percent distribution				
Health consumption expenditures	90.6%	89.6%	92.1%	93.3%	93.6%	93.8%	93.6%	94.1%	94.3%
Personal health care	85.4	84.3	84.9	85.2	84.6	83.6	83.6	84.5	84.3
Hospital care	32.8	36.3	39.3	34.6	30.2	30.0	30.3	31.1	31.4
Professional services	29.3	26.4	25.3	28.7	28.3	27.4	27.1	26.9	26.6
Physician and clinical services	20.6	19.1	18.7	21.9	21.1	20.5	20.2	20.1	19.9
Other professional services	1.4	1.0	1.4	2.4	2.7	2.6	2.6	2.6	2.6
Dental services	7.3	6.3	5.2	4.4	4.5	4.3	4.3	4.1	4.0
Other personal care	1.6	1.8	3.3	3.4	4.7	4.8	4.7	4.9	5.0
Home health care[1]	0.2	0.3	0.9	1.7	2.4	2.4	2.6	2.6	2.7
Nursing care facilities and retirement communities[1]	3.0	5.4	6.0	6.2	6.2	5.5	5.5	5.6	5.5
Retail outlet sales of medical products	18.4	14.1	10.1	10.6	12.9	13.5	13.4	13.4	13.2
Prescription drugs	9.8	7.3	4.7	5.6	8.8	10.1	10.1	10.3	10.0
Durable medical equipment	2.7	2.3	1.6	1.9	1.8	1.5	1.5	1.4	1.5
Nondurable medical products	5.9	4.4	3.8	3.1	2.3	1.8	1.8	1.7	1.7
Government administration[2]	0.2	1.0	1.1	1.0	1.2	1.4	1.2	1.2	1.2
Net cost of health insurance	3.7	2.5	3.6	4.4	4.7	6.0	5.7	5.4	5.6
Government public health activities	1.4	1.8	2.5	2.8	3.1	2.8	3.0	3.1	3.2
Investment	9.4	10.4	7.9	6.7	6.4	6.2	6.4	5.9	5.7
Research[3]	2.5	2.6	2.1	1.8	1.8	2.0	1.8	1.8	1.9
Structures and equipment	6.8	7.8	5.7	5.0	4.5	4.2	4.6	4.0	3.8
				Average annual percent change from previous year shown					
National health expenditures	—	10.6%	13.1%	11.0%	6.6%	8.1%	5.8%	3.8%	3.9%
Health consumption expenditures	—	10.5	13.4	11.1	6.7	8.1	5.8	4.4	4.0
Personal health care	—	10.4	13.2	11.0	6.6	7.8	5.8	4.9	3.7
Hospital care	—	11.7	14.0	9.6	5.2	8.0	6.2	6.4	4.9
Professional services	—	9.5	12.6	12.4	6.5	7.4	5.4	2.9	2.6
Physician and clinical services	—	9.8	12.8	12.8	6.2	7.5	5.3	3.3	2.5
Other professional services	—	5.8	17.5	17.4	7.8	7.5	6.3	3.8	3.6
Dental services	—	8.9	11.0	9.0	7.0	6.9	5.6	0.1	2.2
Other personal care	—	10.0	20.7	11.1	10.3	8.4	5.5	7.7	5.3
Home health care[1]	—	7.2	28.2	18.0	9.9	8.5	8.1	7.5	6.2
Nursing care facilities and retirement communities[1]	—	17.5	14.4	11.4	6.6	5.7	5.7	4.5	3.2
Retail outlet sales of medical products	—	7.7	9.4	11.4	8.8	9.0	5.5	4.3	2.0
Prescription drugs	—	7.4	8.1	12.9	11.6	11.1	6.0	5.1	1.2
Durable medical equipment	—	9.3	9.2	12.9	6.2	4.4	3.8	0.9	7.1
Nondurable medical products	—	7.5	11.5	8.6	3.5	3.3	4.5	2.6	2.8
Government administration[2]	—	30.0	14.1	10.0	9.1	10.4	1.6	0.4	1.7
Net cost of health insurance	—	6.4	17.3	13.1	7.3	13.6	4.4	-2.2	8.4
Government public health activities	—	13.8	16.9	12.0	8.0	5.5	9.0	4.9	8.2
Investment	—	11.7	10.0	9.2	6.0	7.6	6.7	-4.9	1.9
Research[3]	—	10.9	10.8	8.9	7.2	9.6	2.5	5.3	7.9
Structures and equipment	—	12.0	9.7	9.4	5.6	6.8	8.6	-8.9	-0.8

— = Not applicable. **Note:** Numbers may not add up to totals because of rounding. (1) Freestanding facilities only. Additional services of this type provided in hospital-based facilities are counted as hospital care. (2) Includes personal care services delivered by government public health agencies. (3) Excludes research and development expenditures of drug companies, other mfrs. and providers of medical equipment, and supplies. They are included in the expenditure class in which a product falls.

Health Coverage for Persons Under 65, 1984-2011

Source: *Health, United States, 2012*, National Center for Health Statistics, Centers for Disease Control and Prevention

	Private insurance				Medicaid[1]				Not covered[2]			
	1984[3]	1995[3]	2000	2011	1984[3]	1995[3]	2000	2011	1984[3]	1995[3]	2000	2011
					Percent of each population group							
Total	76.8%	71.3%	71.5%	61.8%	6.8%	11.5%	9.5%	17.8%	14.5%	16.1%	17.0%	17.2%
Age												
Under 18 years	72.6	65.2	66.6	53.7	11.9	21.5	19.6	38.2	13.9	13.4	12.6	7.0
18-44 years	76.5	70.9	70.5	60.9	5.1	7.8	5.6	11.6	17.1	20.4	22.4	25.4
45-64 years	83.3	80.1	78.7	70.6	3.4	5.6	4.5	7.5	9.6	10.9	12.6	15.4
Race and Hispanic origin[4,5]												
White, non-Hispanic	82.4	78.6	79.5	72.2	3.7	7.1	6.1	11.8	11.9	13.0	12.5	12.9
Black, non-Hispanic	58.2	53.4	56.0	46.5	20.7	28.1	21.0	30.5	19.7	17.9	19.5	18.8
Hispanic, any race	55.7	46.4	47.8	36.4	13.3	21.9	15.5	30.1	29.5	31.4	35.6	31.1
Percent of poverty level[4]												
Below 100%	32.2	22.6	25.2	17.2	33.0	48.4	38.4	51.4	33.9	29.6	34.2	28.4
100%-199%	70.3	55.3	50.1	35.1	5.3	14.4	16.2	30.6	21.8	28.3	31.0	30.0
200%-399%	89.3	86.4	78.1	71.1	0.8	2.3	4.0	8.9	7.6	10.0	15.4	16.5
400% or more	95.4	93.2	91.9	90.7	0.2	0.4	0.9	1.7	3.2	5.4	5.9	5.2
Geographic region[4]												
Northeast	80.5	75.4	76.3	66.8	8.6	11.7	10.6	19.6	10.2	13.3	12.2	11.8
Midwest	80.6	77.3	78.8	67.9	7.4	10.5	8.0	16.7	11.3	12.2	12.3	13.4
South	74.3	66.9	66.8	57.8	5.1	11.3	9.4	17.3	17.7	19.4	20.5	20.4
West	71.9	67.5	66.5	58.4	7.0	12.9	10.4	18.4	18.2	17.9	20.7	20.0

Note: Data based on household interviews of a sample of the civilian noninstitutionalized population. Percents may not add up to 100 because other types of health insurance (e.g., Medicare, military) are not shown, and persons with both private insurance and Medicaid appear in both sections. (1) Includes Medicaid and other public assistance. (2) Includes persons not covered by private insurance, Medicaid or other public assistance, Medicare, or military plans. (3) A change in the questionnaire in 1997 prevents direct comparison with later years. (4) Age adjusted. (5) Changed reporting methods make race percentages before 1999 not strictly comparable with those from 1999 on.

Spending on Health in the 50 Most Populous Countries, 2010

Source: *World Health Statistics 2013*, World Health Organization

Country	As % of GDP	Per capita[1]	Country	As % of GDP	Per capita[1]	Country	As % of GDP	Per capita[1]	Country	As % of GDP	Per capita[1]
Afghanistan...	10.4%	$44	Germany.....	11.5%	$4,654	Myanmar			Tanzania.....	7.2%	$37
Algeria	4.3	198	Ghana.......	5.2	69	(Burma)....	2.0%	$17	Thailand	3.9	179
Argentina	8.3	759	India........	3.7	51	Nepal	5.1	28	Turkey.......	6.7	668
Australia	9.0	5,174	Indonesia	2.8	84	Nigeria	5.4	67	Uganda......	9.2	44
Bangladesh..	3.7	25	Iran	5.3	302	Pakistan	1.0	10	Ukraine......	7.8	234
Brazil.......	9.0	990	Iraq[2]	8.5	247	Peru	4.9	258	United		
Canada......	11.4	5,257	Italy........	9.5	3,247	Philippines ...	4.1	89	Kingdom	9.6	3,495
China.......	5.0	219	Japan.......	9.2	3,958	Poland.......	7.0	851	United States	17.6	8,233
Colombia	6.5	407	Kenya	4.4	35	Russia.......	6.5	670	Uzbekistan ...	5.6	80
Congo, Dem.			Korea, South.	7.1	1,452	Saudi Arabia..	4.0	659	Venezuela ...	5.3	720
Rep. of..	7.5	15	Malaysia	4.4	368	South Africa ..	8.7	631	Vietnam	6.8	83
Egypt	4.7	125	Mexico	6.3	603	Spain	9.6	2,896	Yemen.......	5.6	80
Ethiopia.....	4.8	15	Morocco	5.4	153	Sudan.......	7.2	111	World[3]	9.2	941
France......	11.7	4,618	Mozambique..	6.3	25						

(1) At average exchange rate. (2) Not including expenditures for Northern Iraq. (3) Includes other nations not shown.

Population Not Covered by Health Insurance, by State, 1990-2012

Source: Annual Social and Economic Supplements, Current Population Survey, U.S. Census Bureau, U.S. Dept. of Commerce
(numbers in thousands)

	1990 No. not covered	1990 % pop. not covered	2000 No. not covered	2000 % pop. not covered	2012 No. not covered	2012 % pop. not covered		1990 No. not covered	1990 % pop. not covered	2000 No. not covered	2000 % pop. not covered	2012 No. not covered	2012 % pop. not covered
AL	710	17.4%	557	12.7%	711	14.8%	MT	115	14.0%	146	16.4%	181	18.1%
AK	77	15.4	114	18.3	134	19.0	NE	138	8.5	140	8.3	245	13.3
AZ	547	15.5	834	16.0	1,198	18.0	NV	201	16.5	336	16.4	642	23.5
AR	421	17.4	367	13.8	535	18.4	NH	107	9.9	99	8.0	157	12.0
CA	5,683	19.1	6,154	18.1	6,787	17.9	NJ	773	10.0	985	11.7	1,223	14.0
CO	495	14.7	598	13.8	705	13.7	NM	339	22.2	426	23.7	453	21.9
CT	226	6.9	313	9.3	284	8.1	NY	2,176	12.1	3,001	16.0	2,185	11.3
DE	96	13.9	69	8.9	97	10.8	NC	883	13.8	1,046	13.1	1,658	17.2
DC	109	19.2	75	13.6	50	7.9	ND	40	6.3	66	10.7	80	11.5
FL	2,376	18.0	2,727	17.0	4,116	21.5	OH	1,123	10.3	1,191	10.7	1,402	12.3
GA	971	15.3	1,145	14.1	1,856	19.2	OK	574	18.6	624	18.4	640	17.2
HI	81	7.3	110	9.1	105	7.7	OR	360	12.4	417	12.2	597	15.4
ID	159	15.2	194	15.0	253	15.9	PA	1,218	10.1	963	8.0	1,521	12.0
IL	1,272	10.9	1,632	13.3	1,732	13.6	RI	105	11.1	74	7.1	128	12.3
IN	587	10.7	650	10.8	849	13.4	SC	550	16.2	473	11.9	665	14.3
IA	225	8.1	239	8.4	306	10.1	SD	81	11.6	77	10.5	119	14.4
KS	272	10.8	274	10.3	358	12.6	TN	673	13.7	585	10.4	892	13.9
KY	480	13.2	521	13.0	682	15.7	TX	3,569	21.1	4,650	22.4	6,426	24.6
LA	797	19.7	755	17.3	819	18.3	UT	156	9.0	259	11.5	411	14.4
ME	139	11.2	135	10.6	126	9.5	VT	54	9.5	50	8.3	43	7.0
MD	601	12.7	511	9.7	733	12.4	VA	996	15.7	747	10.7	998	12.5
MA	530	9.1	527	8.4	272	4.1	WA	557	11.4	772	13.2	933	13.6
MI	865	9.4	838	8.5	1,060	10.9	WV	249	13.8	247	13.9	264	14.6
MN	389	8.9	368	7.5	443	8.3	WI	321	6.7	398	7.5	550	9.7
MS	531	19.9	361	12.9	444	15.3	WY	58	12.5	74	15.3	89	15.4
MO	665	12.7	511	9.3	794	13.3	U.S.	34,719	13.9	38,426	13.7	47,951	15.4

Persons Not Covered by Health Insurance, by Selected Characteristics, 2012

Source: Annual Social and Economic Supplements, Current Population Survey, U.S. Census Bureau, U.S. Dept. of Commerce
(numbers in thousands)

Race and Hispanic origin[1]	Number not covered	% of pop. specified at left	Region	Number not covered	% of pop. specified at left
White	35,625	14.7%	Northeast	5,939	10.8%
Non-Hispanic................	21,585	11.1	Midwest	7,937	11.9
Black.......................	7,629	19.0	South	21,587	18.6
Asian	2,477	15.1	West	12,488	17.0
Hispanic	15,500	29.1	**Household income**		
Nativity			Less than $25,000	14,512	24.9
Native born	35,127	13.0	$25,000 to $49,999...........	14,962	21.4
Foreign born	12,824	32.0	$50,000 to $74,999...........	8,526	15.0
Naturalized citizen...........	3,322	18.3	$75,000 or more.............	9,951	7.9
Not a citizen................	9,502	43.4	**Work experience[2]**		
Age			Worked at least one week	28,378	19.5
Under 65 years..............	47,312	17.7	Worked full-time year-round ...	15,309	15.5
Under 18 years	6,586	8.9	Worked less than full-time		
18 to 24 years	7,605	25.3	year-round	13,069	27.7
25 to 34 years	11,435	27.4	Did not work	12,348	25.8
35 to 44 years	8,428	21.1	**Total**	47,951	15.4
45 to 54 years	7,887	18.2			
55 to 64 years	5,370	14.0			
65 years and over............	639	1.5			

(1) Persons of Hispanic origin may be of any race. (2) Persons 18 to 64 years of age only.

Provisions of the Patient Protection and Affordable Care Act (PPACA)

Source: U.S. Dept. of Health and Human Services

On Mar. 23, 2010, Pres. Barack Obama signed a sweeping health care reform measure into law that would extend medical insurance to more than 30 mil uninsured people. The legislation—the Patient Protection and Affordable Care Act (PPACA)—is projected to still leave some 23 mil people in the U.S., one-third of whom are undocumented immigrants, without insurance in 2019. The Congressional Budget Office released a Mar. 2010 report which projected that the final reform package would cost $938 bil over 10 years and reduce the budget deficit by $138 bil during the same period.

Upon signing, the PPACA activated provisions allowing health insurance tax credits to small businesses; a $15-bil fund invested in prevention and public health programs; increased payments to rural health care providers; and efforts to crack down on health care fraud, expand primary care, and hold insurance companies accountable for rate hikes. Beginning Apr. 1, 2010, more people were covered under state Medicaid programs. Beginning June 2010, coverage to early retirees was expanded, and seniors who reached the gap in Medicare prescription drug coverage known as the "donut hole" received a $250 rebate check from Medicare to pay for prescriptions. Beginning July 2010, new health insurance options were made available online, and access to insurance was extended for uninsured individuals with pre-existing conditions.

For health plan years beginning on or after Sept. 23, 2010: Insurance companies were prevented from denying coverage to children under age 19 due to a pre-existing condition and from rescinding coverage. Lifetime dollar limits on insurance coverage were eliminated, annual dollar limits on coverage were regulated, and insurance company decisions could be appealed by consumers. Insurance companies were required to cover certain preventive services for free, and young adults could stay on their parents' plan until age 26. Beginning Oct. 2010, grants were awarded to states to fund consumer assistance programs.

After the PPACA was challenged by 26 states, the U.S. Supreme Court on June 28, 2012, upheld most parts of the law.

Note: Provisions go into effect Jan. 1 of year shown, unless otherwise noted.

2011
- Prescription drug discounts offered.
- Senior citizens: free preventive care; improved care after they leave the hospital.
- At least 85% of all premium dollars collected by insurance companies for large employer plans must be spent on health care services and health care quality improvement.
- The new Community First Choice Option allows states to offer home and community-based services to disabled individuals through Medicaid rather than institutional care in nursing homes. (Oct. 1)

2012
- Incentives for physicians to join together to form integrated health systems.
- Federal health programs required to collect and report racial, ethnic, and language data to help reduce health disparities. (Mar.)
- Financial incentives to hospitals to improve quality of care. (Oct. 1)
- Health plans required to use electronic records. (Oct. 1)

2013
- New funding to state Medicaid programs that choose to cover preventive services for patients at little or no cost.

- Authority expanded to bundle payments to hospitals, doctors, and other providers.
- Medicaid payments increased for primary care doctors.
- Individuals and small businesses can buy qualified health benefit plans in the Health Insurance Marketplace. (Oct. 1)

2014
- Most individuals who can afford it will be required to obtain basic health insurance coverage or pay a fine.
- Strong reforms prohibiting discrimination due to pre-existing conditions or gender.
- Annual limits on insurance coverage eliminated.
- Coverage ensured for people in clinical trials.
- Tax credits to help those in the middle class not eligible for other affordable coverage.
- Option of buying affordable insurance directly through the Health Insurance Marketplace for those whose employers do not offer insurance.
- Small-business tax credit increased.
- Access to Medicaid for those who earn less than 133% of the poverty level.

2015
- Physicians to be paid based on value, not volume.

Health Care Visits by Selected Characteristics, 1997-2011

Source: National Health Interview Survey; *Health, United States*; National Center for Health Statistics; Centers for Disease Control and Prevention; U.S. Dept. of Health and Human Services

Characteristic	Zero visits			1-3 visits			4-9 visits			10 or more visits		
	1997	2000	2011	1997	2000	2011	1997	2000	2011	1997	2000	2011
						Percent distribution						
All persons	16.5%	16.7%	15.5%	46.2%	45.4%	46.8%	23.6%	24.6%	24.7%	13.7%	13.3%	13.0%
Age												
Under 6 years	5.0	6.3	4.5	44.9	44.5	50.1	37.0	38.1	36.3	13.0	11.1	9.1
6-17 years	15.3	15.2	10.3	58.7	58.2	61.0	19.3	20.6	22.1	6.8	6.0	6.5
18-44 years	21.7	23.5	23.7	46.7	45.2	45.5	19.0	19.1	19.2	12.6	12.2	11.6
45-64 years	16.9	15.0	14.6	42.9	43.4	44.0	24.7	25.7	26.0	15.5	15.9	15.3
65-74 years	9.8	9.0	6.2	36.9	34.5	36.0	31.6	34.5	34.9	21.6	22.1	22.9
75 years and over	7.7	5.8	4.7	31.8	29.3	31.5	33.8	39.3	37.0	26.6	25.6	26.8
Sex												
Male	21.3	21.7	20.0	47.1	45.9	47.8	20.6	22.3	21.9	11.0	10.1	10.3
Female	11.8	11.9	11.0	45.4	44.8	45.9	26.5	27.0	27.6	16.3	16.3	15.5
Race and Hispanic origin												
White, not Hispanic	14.7	14.5	13.1	46.6	45.4	47.1	24.4	25.9	25.9	14.3	14.1	13.9
Black, not Hispanic	16.9	17.1	14.8	46.1	46.8	47.9	23.1	23.5	24.3	13.8	12.6	13.0
Hispanic[1]	24.9	26.8	23.3	42.3	41.8	43.7	20.3	19.8	22.6	12.5	11.6	10.4
Health insurance status[2]												
Insured continuously	14.1	14.0	12.2	49.2	48.8	50.5	23.6	24.6	25.0	13.0	12.6	12.3
Uninsured for any period	18.9	20.6	19.0	46.0	44.5	47.3	20.8	20.8	21.5	14.4	14.1	12.2
Uninsured	39.0	43.2	43.0	41.4	39.6	41.7	13.2	12.1	11.2	6.4	5.1	4.1

Note: Covers visits to doctor's offices, emergency departments, and home visits in the 12-month period prior to interview. Estimates are age-adjusted to the year 2000 standard population. Totals include persons of races not shown separately and of unknown health insurance status. (1) Persons of Hispanic origin may be of any race. (2) In 12 months prior to interview, for under-65 population only; persons having both Medicaid and private coverage are classified as having private coverage.

Reasons Given by Patients for Outpatient Visits, 2010

Source: National Hospital Ambulatory Medical Care Survey, National Center for Health Statistics, Centers for Disease Control and Prevention, U.S. Dept. of Health and Human Services

Rank	Reason	Number of visits (thous.)	% of all visits	Rank	Reason	Number of visits (thous.)	% of all visits
1.	Progress visit, not otherwise specified	11,960	11.9%	11.	Well-baby examination	1,226	1.2%
2.	General medical examination	5,275	5.2	12.	Earache or ear infection	1,164	1.2
3.	Prenatal examination, routine	3,015	3.0	13.	Knee symptoms	1,151	1.1
4.	Diabetes mellitus	2,831	2.8	14.	Hypertension	1,146	1.1
5.	Medication, other and unspecified kinds	2,436	2.4	15.	Other special examination	1,126	1.1
				16.	Back symptoms	1,002	1.0
6.	Cough	2,253	2.2	17.	Gynecological examination	942	0.9
7.	Counseling, not otherwise specified	2,235	2.2	18.	Skin rash	940	0.9
8.	Postoperative visit	2,233	2.2	19.	Headache, pain in head	927	0.9
9.	Stomach pain, cramps, and spasms	1,655	1.6	20.	Fever	915	0.9
10.	Symptoms referable to throat	1,585	1.6		All other reasons	54,725	54.3
					All visits	100,742	100.0

Emergency Room Visits by Diagnosis, 2010

Source: National Hospital Ambulatory Medical Care Survey, National Center for Health Statistics, Centers for Disease Control and Prevention, U.S. Dept. of Health and Human Services

Rank	Principal diagnosis group	Number of visits (thous.)	% of all visits	Rank	Principal diagnosis group	Number of visits (thous.)	% of all visits
1.	Heart disease, excluding ischemic	1,100	6.4%	11.	Chronic and unspecified bronchitis	294	1.7%
2.	Chest pain	1,001	5.8	12.	Fractures, excluding lower limb	287	1.7
3.	Pneumonia	784	4.5	13.	Fracture of the lower limb	264	1.5
4.	Ischemic heart disease	505	2.9	14.	Asthma	260	1.5
5.	Cerebrovascular disease	457	2.7	15.	Disorder of gallbladder and biliary tract	236	1.4
6.	Psychoses, excluding major depressive disorder	455	2.6	16.	Malignant neoplasms	230	1.3
				17.	Diabetes mellitus	225	1.3
7.	Cellulitis and abscess	368	2.1	18.	Noninfectious enteritis and colitis	210	1.2
8.	Abdominal pain	344	2.0	19.	Anemias	209	1.2
9.	Syncope and collapse	308	1.8	20.	Gastrointestinal hemmorhage	186	1.1
10.	Urinary tract infection, site not specified	299	1.7		All other diagnoses[1]	9,217	53.5
					All visits	17,239	100.0

(1) Includes blanks and discharges in which diagnosis was unknown.

Most Frequently Mentioned Drugs at Outpatient Department Visits, 2010

Source: National Hospital Ambulatory Medical Care Survey, National Center for Health Statistics, Centers for Disease Control and Prevention, U.S. Dept. of Health and Human Services

Rank	Therapeutic drug category[1]	No. of mentions (thous.)	% of total[2]	Rank	Therapeutic drug category[1]	No. of mentions (thous.)	% of total[2]
1.	Analgesics	31,287	11.0%	11.	Diuretics	8,817	3.1%
2.	Antidiabetic agents	14,549	5.1	12.	ACE[3] inhibitors	8,144	2.9
3.	Antihyperlipidemic agents	13,380	4.7	13.	Proton pump inhibitors	7,826	2.7
4.	Antidepressants	12,828	4.5	14.	Dermatological agents	7,736	2.7
5.	Anxiolytics, sedatives, and hypnotics	11,233	3.9	15.	Vitamins	7,576	2.7
6.	Immunostimulants	9,996	3.5	16.	Antihistamines	6,917	2.4
7.	Bronchodilators	9,978	3.5	17.	Antiemetic/antivertigo agents	6,206	2.2
8.	Antiplatelet agents	9,726	3.4	18.	Vitamin and mineral combinations	5,695	2.0
9.	Beta-adrenergic blocking agents	9,710	3.4	19.	Calcium channel blocking agents	5,645	2.0
10.	Anticonvulsants	9,695	3.4	20.	Thyroid hormones	4,936	1.7

Note: A mention is a documentation in a patient's record of a drug provided, prescribed, or continued. (1) Based on the Multum Lexicon second-level therapeutic drug category. (2) Based on an estimated 285,056,000 drugs provided, prescribed, or continued at outpatient department visits in 2010. (3) Angiotensin-converting enzyme.

U.S. Organ Transplants

Source: Organ Procurement and Transplantation Network (OPTN), United Network for Organ Sharing (UNOS)

Waiting List, June 2013

Type of transplant	Patients waiting	% of total
Any organ[1]	128,648	100.0%
Kidney	103,312	80.3
Liver	16,483	12.8
Heart	3,520	2.7
Kidney-pancreas	2,147	1.7
Lung	1,684	1.3
Pancreas	1,186	0.9
Intestine	268	0.2
Heart-lung	48	0.0

Transplants Performed, 2012

Type of transplant	Number	% of total
Any organ	28,051	100.0%
Kidney	16,485	58.8
Liver	6,256	22.3
Heart	2,378	8.5
Lung	1,754	6.3
Kidney-pancreas	801	2.9
Pancreas	242	0.9
Intestine	106	0.4
Heart-lung	29	0.1

Note: Waiting list as of June 7, 2013. (1) Figures may not add up to total because patients waiting for more than one organ are included in multiple categories.

Drug Use in the General U.S. Population, 2011

Source: Substance Abuse and Mental Health Services Administration (SAMHSA), U.S. Dept. of Health and Human Services

According to the 2011 results of SAMHSA's annual survey, an estimated 121.1 mil Americans 12 years of age and older (or 47.0% of that population) had used an illicit drug at least once in their lifetimes. Of that number, an estimated 75.4 mil (29.3% of persons 12 or older) had used an illicit drug other than marijuana at least once in their lives. About 14.9% of the 12-and-older population had used an illicit drug in the previous year; 8.7% had used one in the month prior to their participation in the survey.

The rate of current illicit drug use (i.e., within the past month) in 2011 was 11.1% for men and 6.5% for women.

SAMHSA's Drug Abuse Warning Network (DAWN) reported 2.5 mil drug abuse or misuse-related visits to hospital emergency departments in 2011. Just over half (51%) of all visits involved illicit drugs, with the highest rates for cocaine and marijuana. About 25% of all visits associated with drug misuse or abuse also involved alcohol.

Illicit Drug Use Among Persons 12 or Older, 2005-11

Source: National Survey on Drug Use and Health, Substance Abuse and Mental Health Services Admin. (SAMHSA), U.S. Dept. of Health and Human Services

(numbers in thousands)

	2005 No.	%	2007 No.	%	2008 No.	%	2009 No.	%	2010 No.	%	2011 No.	%
Used in lifetime												
Illicit drugs[1]	112,085	46.1	114,275	46.1	117,325	47.0	118,705	47.1	119,508	47.1	121,078	47.0
Illicit drugs other than marijuana[1]	71,822	29.5	73,494	29.7	75,573	30.3	75,780	30.1	76,203	30.0	75,447	29.3
Used in past month												
Illicit drugs[1]	19,720	8.1	19,857	8.0	20,077	8.0	21,813	8.7	22,622	8.9	22,454	8.7
Illicit drugs other than marijuana[1]	8,963	3.7	9,270	3.7	8,565	3.4	9,157	3.6	9,017	3.6	8,020	3.1
Used in past year												
Illicit drugs[1]	35,041	14.4	35,692	14.4	35,525	14.2	37,954	15.1	38,806	15.3	38,287	14.9
Marijuana and hashish	25,375	10.4	25,085	10.1	25,768	10.3	28,521	11.3	29,206	11.5	29,739	11.5
Illicit drugs other than marijuana[1]	20,109	8.3	21,144	8.5	19,990	8.0	21,000	8.3	20,576	8.1	18,959	7.4
Cocaine	5,523	2.3	5,738	2.3	5,255	2.1	4,797	1.9	4,499	1.8	3,857	1.5
Crack	1,381	0.6	1,451	0.6	1,109	0.4	1,016	0.4	871	0.3	625	0.2
Heroin	379	0.2	366	0.1	453	0.2	605	0.2	618	0.2	620	0.2
Hallucinogens	3,809	1.6	3,762	1.5	3,678	1.5	4,509	1.8	4,517	1.8	4,069	1.6
LSD	563	0.2	620	0.3	802	0.3	779	0.3	874	0.3	880	0.3
PCP	164	0.1	137	0.1	99	0.0	122	0.0	95	0.0	119	0.0
Ecstasy	1,960	0.8	2,132	0.9	2,139	0.9	2,799	1.1	2,645	1.0	2,422	0.9
Inhalants	2,187	0.9	2,080	0.8	2,047	0.8	2,090	0.8	2,030	0.8	1,861	0.7
Nonmedical use of psychotherapeutics[2]	15,346	6.3	16,280	6.6	15,166	6.1	16,006	6.4	16,031	6.3	14,657	5.7
Pain relievers	11,815	4.9	12,466	5.0	11,885	4.8	12,405	4.9	12,213	4.8	11,143	4.3
OxyContin®	1,226	0.5	1,422	0.6	1,459	0.6	1,677	0.7	1,869	0.7	1,623	0.6
Tranquilizers	5,249	2.2	5,282	2.1	5,103	2.0	5,460	2.2	5,581	2.2	5,109	2.0
Stimulants	3,088	1.3	2,998	1.2	2,639	1.1	3,060	1.2	2,887	1.1	2,700	1.0
Sedatives	750	0.3	864	0.3	621	0.2	811	0.3	907	0.4	526	0.2

(1) Includes marijuana/hashish, cocaine (including crack), heroin, hallucinogens, inhalants, or prescription-type psychotherapeutics used nonmedically. (2) Includes the nonmedical use of pain relievers, tranquilizers, stimulants, or sedatives but not over-the-counter drugs.

Lifetime Prevalence of Drug Use in 12th Graders, 1975-2012

Source: Monitoring the Future study, Univ. of Michigan Inst. for Social Research; National Institute on Drug Abuse

(percent who have ever used)

Drug	1975	1980	1985	1990	1995	2000	2005	2008	2009	2010	2011	2012	2011-12 change
Any illicit drug[1,2]	55.2%	65.4%	60.6%	47.9%	48.4%	54.0%	50.4%	47.4%	46.7%	48.2%	49.9%	49.1%	−0.8%
Marijuana/hashish	47.3	60.3	54.2	40.7	41.7	48.8	44.8	42.6	42.0	43.8	45.5	45.2	−0.3
Inhalants[3]	—	17.3	18.1	18.5	17.8	14.6	11.9	10.1	10.2	9.0	8.1	7.9	−0.2
Amyl/butyl nitrites[4]	—	11.1	7.9	2.1	1.5	0.8	1.1	0.6	1.1	—	—	—	—
Hallucinogens[5,6]	—	15.6	12.1	9.7	13.1	13.6	9.3	9.0	8.0	8.6	8.3	7.5	−0.8
LSD	11.3	9.3	7.5	8.7	11.7	11.1	3.5	4.0	3.1	4.0	4.0	3.8	−0.2
PCP[4]	—	9.6	4.9	2.8	2.7	3.4	2.4	1.8	1.7	1.8	2.3	1.6	−0.7
Ecstasy (MDMA)	—	—	—	—	—	11.0	5.4	6.2	6.5	7.3	8.0	7.2	−0.9
Cocaine	9.0	15.7	17.3	9.4	6.0	8.6	8.0	7.2	6.0	5.5	5.2	4.9	−0.3
Crack	—	—	—	3.5	3.0	3.9	3.5	2.8	2.4	2.4	1.9	2.1	0.2
Heroin (with and without a needle)	2.2	1.1	1.2	1.3	1.6	2.4	1.5	1.3	1.2	1.6	1.4	1.1	−0.3
Narcotics other than heroin[7,8]	9.0	9.8	10.2	8.3	7.2	10.6	12.8	13.2	13.2	13.0	13.0	12.2	−0.8
Amphetamines[2,7]	22.3	26.4	26.2	17.5	15.3	15.6	13.1	10.5	9.9	11.1	12.2	12.0	−0.2
Methamphetamine	—	—	—	—	—	7.9	4.5	2.8	2.4	2.3	2.1	1.7	−0.3
Crystal meth. (ice)	—	—	—	2.7	3.9	4.0	4.0	2.8	2.1	1.8	2.1	1.7	−0.4
Sedatives (barbiturates)[7]	18.2	14.9	11.8	7.5	7.6	9.3	11.0	8.9	8.4	7.5	7.0	6.9	−0.1
Methaqualone[7]	8.1	9.5	6.7	2.3	1.2	0.8	1.3	0.8	0.7	0.4	0.6	0.8	0.2
Tranquilizers[5,7]	17.0	15.2	11.9	7.2	7.1	8.9	9.9	8.9	9.3	8.5	8.7	8.5	−0.2
Alcohol[9]	90.4	93.2	92.2	89.5	80.7	80.3	75.1	71.9	72.3	71.0	70.0	69.4	−0.6
Cigarettes	73.6	71.0	68.8	64.4	64.2	62.5	50.0	44.7	43.6	42.2	40.0	39.5	−0.5
Smokeless tobacco	—	—	—	—	30.9	23.1	17.5	15.6	16.3	17.6	16.9	17.4	0.5
Steroids[7]	—	—	—	2.9	2.3	2.5	2.6	2.2	2.2	2.0	1.8	1.8	0.0

— = Not available. (1) Includes marijuana, LSD, other hallucinogens, crack, other cocaine, or heroin; or any use of narcotics other than heroin, amphetamines, sedatives (barbiturates), methaqualone (excluded since 1990), or tranquilizers not under a doctor's orders. (2) Because of changes to question wording, data from 1982 on are not directly comparable to data from prior years. (3) Not adjusted for underreporting of amyl and butyl nitrites. (4) Because of changes to question wording, data from 1987 on are not directly comparable to data from prior years. (5) Because of changes to question wording, data from 2001 on are not directly comparable to data from prior years. (6) Not adjusted for underreporting of PCP. (7) Includes only drug use not under a doctor's orders. (8) Because of changes to question wording, data from 2002 on are not directly comparable to data from prior years. (9) Because of changes to question wording, data from 1993 on are not directly comparable to data from prior years.

Cigarette Use in the U.S., 1985-2011

Source: National Survey on Drug Use and Health, Substance Abuse and Mental Health Services Admin. (SAMHSA), U.S. Dept. of Health and Human Services

(percentage reporting use in the month prior to the survey)

	1985	2000	2005	2009	2010	2011		1985	2000	2005	2009	2010	2011
Total[1]	38.7	24.9	24.9	23.3	23.0	22.1	**Race/ethnicity**						
							White, not Hispanic	38.9	25.9	26.0	24.5	24.3	24.7
Sex							Black, not Hispanic	38.0	23.3	24.5	22.8	22.6	23.6
Male	43.4	26.9	27.4	25.3	25.4	24.3	Hispanic	40.0	20.7	22.1	21.2	20.1	20.5
Female	34.5	23.1	22.5	21.4	20.7	19.9	**Education[2]**						
Age group							Non-high school graduate	37.3	32.4	34.8	35.4	34.3	33.7
12-17 years	29.4	13.4	10.8	8.9	8.3	7.8	High school graduate	37.0	31.1	31.8	30.0	29.6	28.3
18-25 years	47.4	38.3	39.0	35.8	34.2	33.5	Some college	32.6	27.7	28.1	25.4	25.8	25.9
26 years and older	45.7[3]	24.2	24.3	23.0	22.8	21.9	College graduate	23.0	13.9	13.8	13.1	12.8	11.7

(1) Persons 12 years of age and older. (2) Persons aged 18 and older. (3) Persons aged 26 to 34 only.

Daily Use of Cigarettes by 8th, 10th, and 12th Graders, 1995-2012

Source: Monitoring the Future study, Univ. of Michigan Inst. for Social Research; National Inst. on Drug Abuse

(percent who smoked daily in last 30 days)

	8th grade						10th grade						12th grade					
	1995	2000	2005	2010	2012	% change, 2010-12	1995	2000	2005	2010	2012	% change, 2010-12	1995	2000	2005	2010	2012	% change, 2010-12
Total	9.3	7.4	4.0	2.9	1.9	−34.5	16.3	14.0	7.5	6.6	5.0	−24.2	21.6	20.6	13.6	10.7	9.3	−13.1
Sex																		
Male	9.2	7.0	3.9	3.5	2.0	−42.9	16.3	13.7	7.2	7.2	5.6	−22.2	21.7	20.9	14.6	12.3	10.9	−11.4
Female	9.2	7.5	4.0	2.3	1.6	−30.4	16.1	14.1	7.7	5.9	4.4	−25.4	20.8	19.7	11.9	8.7	7.3	−16.1
College plans																		
None or under 4 yrs.	22.5	21.7	14.4	12.8	8.0	−37.5	32.7	28.8	19.2	19.1	17.0	−11.0	33.7	31.7	24.9	21.6	18.4	−14.8
Complete 4 yrs.	7.5	5.6	2.9	2.0	1.4	−30.0	13.3	11.6	5.9	5.0	3.7	−26.0	17.4	16.6	10.5	8.2	7.0	−14.6
Region																		
Northeast	9.2	6.9	3.2	2.4	1.8	−25.0	15.8	14.1	7.6	5.7	5.1	−10.5	22.5	22.8	13.3	10.3	11.3	9.7
Midwest	11.0	9.0	4.8	3.3	1.3	−60.6	17.6	16.3	8.6	7.3	4.4	−39.7	25.7	23.6	16.3	12.5	11.6	−7.2
South	9.4	7.8	5.0	3.8	2.9	−23.7	19.3	15.7	8.8	7.9	6.9	−12.7	21.7	19.4	15.4	12.3	9.0	−26.8
West	7.0	4.9	2.4	1.4	0.8	−42.9	9.4	7.8	4.0	4.4	2.6	−40.9	14.5	16.9	7.6	6.7	5.8	−13.4
Race/ethnicity[1]																		
White	10.5	9.0	4.6	3.2	2.4	−25.0	23.9	25.7	17.1	7.4	6.2	−16.2	23.9	25.7	17.1	13.5	12.1	−10.4
Black	2.8	3.2	2.1	1.9	1.6	−15.8	6.1	8.0	5.6	3.5	2.9	−17.1	6.1	8.0	5.6	5.3	4.7	−11.3
Hispanic	9.2	7.1	3.1	2.3	1.8	−21.7	11.6	15.7	7.7	4.4	3.0	−31.8	11.6	15.7	7.7	5.7	4.9	−14.0

Note: Figures may not add up to totals because of rounding. (1) For each of these groups, data for the specified year and previous year have been combined to increase sample size and thus provide a more reliable estimate.

Alcohol Use by 8th and 12th Graders, 1980-2012

Source: Monitoring the Future study, Univ. of Michigan Inst. for Social Research; National Inst. on Drug Abuse

	1980	1990	1995	2000	2005	2008	2009	2010	2011	2012	2011-12 change
Alcohol use[1]				Percent using in the month before the survey							
All 12th graders	72.0%	57.1%	51.3%	50.0%	47.0%	43.1%	43.5%	41.2%	40.0%	41.5%	1.5%
Male	77.4	61.3	55.7	54.0	50.7	45.8	47.8	44.2	42.1	43.8	1.7
Female	66.8	52.3	47.0	46.1	43.3	40.9	38.9	37.9	37.5	38.8	1.3
White	75.4	63.8	54.5	55.1	52.3	48.6	47.2	45.4	43.8	43.8	0.1
Black	47.6	35.8	35.2	30.0	29.0	28.6	30.5	31.4	30.1	29.6	−0.5
Hispanic	63.6	49.1	48.7	51.2	43.3	38.9	40.1	40.1	39.7	39.8	0.1
All 8th graders	—	—	24.6	22.4	17.1	15.9	14.9	13.8	12.7	11.0	−1.7
Male	—	—	25.0	22.5	16.2	15.4	14.7	13.2	12.1	10.3	−1.8
Female	—	—	24.0	22.0	17.9	16.4	14.9	14.3	12.8	11.6	−1.3
White	—	—	25.4	24.7	17.9	15.2	15.4	13.9	12.3	10.7	−1.5
Black	—	—	18.7	16.0	14.9	12.9	12.3	11.8	11.6	10.0	−1.6
Hispanic	—	—	32.4	26.7	20.6	21.5	19.2	18.1	18.0	17.5	−0.5
Heavy alcohol use[2]				Percent heavily using in the two weeks before the survey							
All 12th graders	41.2%	32.2%	29.8%	30.0%	27.1%	24.6%	25.2%	23.2%	21.6%	23.7%	2.0%
Male	52.1	39.1	36.9	36.7	32.6	28.4	30.5	28.0	25.5	27.2	1.7
Female	30.5	24.4	23.0	23.5	21.6	21.3	20.2	18.4	17.6	19.7	2.1
White	44.3	36.6	32.3	34.6	32.5	29.9	29.0	27.6	25.9	25.7	−0.2
Black	17.7	14.4	14.9	11.5	11.3	10.9	12.0	13.1	11.3	11.3	0.0
Hispanic	33.1	25.6	26.6	31.0	23.9	21.5	22.6	22.1	20.8	21.8	0.9
All 8th graders	—	—	12.3	11.7	8.4	8.1	7.8	7.2	6.4	5.1	−1.3
Male	—	—	12.5	11.7	8.2	8.1	7.8	6.5	6.1	4.6	−1.4
Female	—	—	12.1	11.3	8.6	8.0	7.7	7.8	6.5	5.5	−1.0
White	—	—	12.1	13.0	9.0	7.8	7.7	7.1	6.2	4.9	−1.4
Black	—	—	8.3	7.3	6.1	5.7	5.2	5.3	5.1	4.3	−0.8
Hispanic	—	—	18.4	16.0	12.1	12.3	11.5	10.8	10.4	9.9	−0.5

— = Data not available. **Note:** Monitoring the Future study excludes high school dropouts (about 3%-6% of the class group) and absentees (about 16%-17% of 12th graders and 9%-10% of 8th graders). These pops. have higher alcohol usage than those surveyed. (1) Since 1993 the alcohol question has indicated that a "drink" is defined as "more than a few sips." (2) Five or more drinks in a row.

Acquired Immune Deficiency Syndrome (AIDS)

Source: Centers for Disease Control and Prevention

AIDS (Acquired Immune Deficiency Syndrome) is caused by the human immunodeficiency virus (**HIV**). HIV kills or disables crucial immune cells, progressively destroying the body's ability to fight disease.

HIV is commonly **spread** through unprotected sexual contact with an infected partner's semen or vaginal fluids. It is also spread through contact with infected blood. Where modern screening techniques are used, it is rare to contract HIV from transfusion or organ/tissue transplants. But it can be contracted when intravenous drug users share syringes and similar equipment with others. A woman can also transmit HIV to her child during pregnancy or delivery or through breastfeeding. With treatment, a woman can reduce her transmission rate from about 25% to less than 1%. There is no evidence HIV can spread through saliva or casual contact such as in the sharing of food utensils, towels and bedding, telephones, or toilet seats.

Some people experience flu-like symptoms within a few weeks of being infected with HIV. Even when symptoms are not present, HIV is active in the body, multiplying, infecting, and killing crucial CD4+ T cells, also known as T-lymphocytes or T-helper cells, which signal other immune cells to perform their functions.

The term AIDS applies to the most advanced stages of HIV infection. According to the official case definition issued by the Centers for Disease Control and Prevention (CDC), an HIV-infected person with fewer than 200 CD4+ T cells per cubic millimeter of blood can be said to have AIDS. (Healthy adults usually have 500-1,600 per cubic millimeter.) An HIV-infected person, regardless of T cell count, is diagnosed with AIDS if he or she develops one of 20+ conditions that typically affect people with advanced HIV. Most of these conditions are opportunistic infections that occur when the immune system is so ravaged by HIV that the body cannot fight off certain bacteria, viruses, and microbes.

Months or years prior to the onset of AIDS, people may experience such **symptoms** as swollen glands, lack of energy, fevers and sweats, and skin rashes. People diagnosed with AIDS may develop infections of the intestinal tract, lungs, brain, eyes, and other organs and become severely debilitated. They also are prone to developing certain cancers, especially those caused by viruses, such as Kaposi's sarcoma, cervical cancer, and lymphoma. Children with AIDS may have delayed development or fail to thrive.

HIV is primarily **detected** by testing a person's blood for the presence of antibodies (disease-fighting proteins of the immune system) to HIV. In very rare cases, HIV antibodies may take more than six months after exposure to reach detectable levels. But in 97% of infected individuals, the antibodies are detectable in the first three months. HIV testing may also be performed on oral fluid and urine samples. Rapid HIV tests can provide preliminary results in about 20 minutes.

Patients are typically given a combination of different **drugs**, because no single drug will stop HIV from harming patients, and taking more than one drug prevents the HIV virus from becoming resistant to any single one. While these drugs extend the period of time between HIV infection and the development of serious illness, they do not prevent the spread of the disease to others and can have severe side effects.

In 1987, a drug called zidovudine (commonly known as AZT) became the first approved treatment for HIV disease. Since then, the U.S. Food and Drug Administration has approved approximately 30 drugs to treat people living with HIV/AIDS, and more are under development.

There are currently five different classes of HIV drugs. Each class of drug attacks the virus at different points in its life cycle. Patients taking HIV medications will generally take three different antiretrovirals (ARVs) from two different classes. The five classes are Nucleoside/Nucleotide Reverse Transcriptase Inhibitors (NRTIs), Non-Nucleoside Reverse Transcriptase Inhibitors (NNRTIs), Protease Inhibitors (PIs), Entry/Fusion Inhibitors, and Integrase Inhibitors.

There are also fixed-dose combinations of drugs. These are not a separate class of HIV medications but combinations of two or more medications, with specific fixed doses, from one or more different classes. These ARVs are combined into a single pill.

Since there is no vaccine or cure for AIDS, the only **protection** is to avoid activities that carry a risk. The CDC recommends abstinence (the only certain protection) if a potential partner's HIV status is unknown, mutual monogamy with an uninfected partner, or correct and consistent use of male latex condoms.

New AIDS Diagnoses in the U.S., by Transmission Category, 1985-2011

Source: *HIV Surveillance Report, 2011*; National Center for HIV/AIDS, Viral Hepatitis, STD, and TB Prevention; Centers for Disease Control and Prevention

Transmission category	All years[1]	1985	1990	2000	2005	2008	2009	2010	2011
All males 13 years of age and older	913,368	7,504	36,193	30,251	27,436	24,015	23,226	22,030	24,088
Male-to-male sexual contact	555,032	5,348	23,658	13,648	16,824	15,427	15,458	14,934	16,694
Injection drug use	187,938	1,103	6,923	5,554	4,350	2,985	2,563	2,323	2,346
Male-to-male sexual contact and injection drug use	80,902	661	2,943	1,587	2,085	1,714	1,491	1,393	1,392
Heterosexual contact[2]	77,521	32	715	2,537	3,920	3,724	3,581	3,256	3,526
Other[3]	11,975	—	—	—	256	165	134	123	131
All females 13 years of age and older	228,541	524	4,547	9,979	9,799	8,593	7,971	7,410	7,949
Injection drug use	73,382	287	2,347	2,545	2,724	2,041	1,776	1,582	1,615
Heterosexual contact[2]	104,037	119	1,538	4,025	6,856	6,432	6,073	5,697	6,206
Other[3]	51,122	—	—	—	219	119	122	130	129
All children, under 13 years of age	9,483	—	—	—	55	37	14	24	15
Perinatal	8,623	—	—	—	50	32	13	19	12
Other[4]	860	—	—	—	5	5	1	5	2

Note: The definition of AIDS cases for reporting purposes was expanded in 1985, 1987, and 1993, as more was learned about the spectrum of human immunodeficiency virus-associated diseases. (1) Includes number of diagnoses for years not shown, from the beginning of the epidemic (1981) through 2011. (2) Heterosexual contact with a person known to have or be at high risk for HIV infection. (3) Includes hemophilia, blood transfusion, perinatal exposure, and risk factors not reported or not identified. (4) Includes hemophilia, blood transfusion, and risk factors not reported or not identified.

AIDS Deaths and New AIDS Diagnoses in the U.S., 1981-2010

Source: HIV/AIDS Surveillance Supplemental Report; *Health, United States*; Office of Analysis and Epidemiology, National Center for Health Statistics, Centers for Disease Control and Prevention

	% of total, all years	All years[1]	2007	2008	2009	2010
DEATHS OF PERSONS DIAGNOSED WITH AIDS, BY YEAR[2]	—	620,048	NA	14,980	14,087	12,158
CASES, BY YEAR AIDS FIRST DIAGNOSED						
All persons[3]	100.0%	1,129,127	34,319	33,613	32,942	33,015
All males, 13 years of age and older	79.1%	893,058	24,979	24,735	24,507	24,749
Race/origin						
Not of Hispanic origin						
White	43.1	385,023	8,196	7,886	7,683	7,596
Black	36.7	327,877	10,450	10,497	10,319	10,754
Asian[4]	0.8	7,436	360	399	358	408
Native Hawaiian or other Pacific Islander[4]	0.1	723	39	37	46	34
American Indian or Alaska Native	0.3	2,881	86	132	108	126
Hispanic[5]	17.7	157,853	5,295	5,268	5,449	5,406
Age diagnosed						
13-14 years	0.1	745	28	27	22	20
15-24 years	4.1	36,920	1,686	1,756	2,000	2,250
25-34 years	30.9	275,806	5,222	5,304	5,454	5,641
35-44 years	39.1	349,525	8,803	8,219	7,430	7,110
45-54 years	18.6	165,995	6,631	6,548	6,723	6,750
55-64 years	5.6	49,926	2,065	2,278	2,287	2,329
65 years and over	1.6	14,140	544	603	591	650
All females, 13 years of age and older	20.1%	226,593	9,304	8,839	8,421	8,242
Race/origin						
Not of Hispanic origin						
White	19.1	43,182	1,474	1,353	1,291	1,275
Black	61.6	139,621	5,981	5,783	5,468	5,422
Asian[4]	0.6	1,274	85	84	87	70
Native Hawaiian or other Pacific Islander[4]	0.1	140	8	4	6	10
American Indian or Alaska Native	0.4	809	41	35	28	44
Hispanic[5]	16.6	37,667	1,490	1,371	1,349	1,224
Age diagnosed						
13-14 years	0.3	653	51	33	30	31
15-24 years	6.9	15,611	590	536	547	541
25-34 years	32.3	72,469	2,060	2,062	1,834	1,746
35-44 years	36.7	82,599	3,168	2,930	2,676	2,552
45-54 years	16.8	38,745	2,385	2,295	2,300	2,269
55-64 years	5.2	12,226	835	802	805	864
65 years and over	1.9	4,291	215	181	229	239
All children, under 13 years of age	0.8%	9,475	36	39	14	23
Race/origin						
Not of Hispanic origin						
White	16.9	1,599	4	5	1	4
Black	60.5	5,731	27	25	8	12
Asian[4]	0.5	49	0	2	0	1
Native Hawaiian or other Pacific Islander[4]	0.1	7	0	0	0	0
American Indian or Alaska Native	0.3	31	0	0	0	0
Hispanic[5]	20.4	1,929	4	3	4	6

NA = Not available. **Note:** Data are for the 50 states and DC and are based on reporting by state and DC health departments. (1) Based on cases reported to the CDC from the beginning of the epidemic (1981) through June 30, 2011. (2) Deaths may be due to any cause. (3) Total for all years includes 170 persons of unknown races. (4) The "Asian" category includes persons formerly classified as "Asian or Pacific Islander," before new race categories were implemented in 2003. (5) May be of any race.

Allergies and Asthma

Source: Asthma and Allergy Foundation of America

An estimated one in five Americans suffers from **allergies**. People with allergies have immune systems that overreact to a foreign protein substance ("allergen") that is eaten, breathed into the lungs, injected, or touched. Common allergens include plant pollens, dust mites, or animal dander; plants such as poison ivy; certain drugs, such as penicillin; and foods such as eggs, milk, wheat, nuts, or seafood.

The **tendency to develop allergies** is usually inherited. While allergies typically manifest in childhood, they can show up at any age. Food allergies and eczema (patches of dry skin) are common allergies among infants. Older children and adults may develop allergic rhinitis, or hay fever, in reaction to an inhaled allergen. Allergic rhinitis symptoms include nasal congestion, runny nose, and sneezing.

People with allergies should avoid contact with an allergen, if feasible. **Medications**, such as antihistamines and nasal steroids, may be used to decrease an allergic reaction. Other effective allergy treatments include decongestants, eye drops, and ointments. There are also treatments aimed at gradually desensitizing a patient to an allergen.

Some allergy sufferers also have **asthma**. Asthma, which can develop at any age, is a chronic inflammation disease affecting the passageways that carry air into and out of the lungs. About 20 mil Americans have asthma. During what is known as an asthma attack, these inflamed, supersensitive airways tighten and fill with mucus. A person may experience wheezing, difficulty breathing, tightening of the chest, and coughing. Exposure to an allergen can set off an attack. Asthma can become life-threatening if not controlled in its early stages. The following **symptoms** may be indicative of an emergency: the patient shows no improvement minutes after initial treatment; struggles to breathe while hunched over with his or her chest and neck pulled in; has trouble walking or talking; and develops gray or blue lips or fingernails.

Besides common allergens, tobacco smoke, cold air, and anxiety can trigger an asthma attack, as can viral infections or physical exercise. An accurate diagnosis by a physician is important. Although there is no cure for asthma or allergies, they can be controlled through lifestyle changes and medications.

Website: www.aafa.org

Alzheimer's Disease

Source: Alzheimer's Association

Alzheimer's disease, the most common form of dementia, is a progressive, degenerative brain disease in which nerve cells deteriorate and die. Its first symptoms usually involve impaired memory and confusion about recent events. As the disease advances, it results in greater impairment of memory, thinking, judgment, language, behavior, and physical health.

The **rate of progression** of Alzheimer's varies, ranging from 4 to 20 years. The average length of time from onset of symptoms until death is eight years. As they become progressively debilitated, affected individuals grow increasingly susceptible to infections of the lungs, urinary tract, and other organs.

Alzheimer's disease affects an estimated 5.2 mil Americans, striking men and women of all races and ethnicities. Almost two-thirds of all Americans living with Alzheimer's are women. Although most people are older than age 65 when diagnosed with Alzheimer's, younger-onset, or early-onset, cases occur in people in their 40s and 50s. An estimated 11% of the U.S. population over age 65 has Alzheimer's.

Diagnosis involves a comprehensive evaluation that may include a complete health history, physical examination, neurological and mental status assessments, and other tests. Skilled health care professionals can generally diagnose Alzheimer's with more than 90% accuracy. Depression, drug interactions, nutritional imbalances, and infections such as AIDS, meningitis, and syphilis can cause similar symptoms. Other forms of dementia, such as those associated with stroke, Huntington's disease, Parkinson's disease, frontotemporal dementia, and vascular disease, can also appear to be Alzheimer's. Absolute confirmation of a diagnosis requires a brain biopsy or autopsy.

Treatments for cognitive and behavioral symptoms are available, but no intervention has yet been developed to prevent Alzheimer's or reverse its course. The U.S. Food and Drug Administration has approved five drugs that temporarily slow worsening of symptoms for about six to twelve months. They are effective for only about half of the individuals who take them. Some research suggests that risk factors for heart disease, such as high blood pressure, elevated cholesterol, diabetes, and excess body weight, may increase a person's risk of developing Alzheimer's. Staying physically and mentally active and socially connected may be associated with a lower risk for the disease.

Providing **care** for people with Alzheimer's is physically and psychologically demanding. About 60%-70% of affected individuals live at home, where family or friends tend to them without pay. In the disease's advanced stages, many individuals require long-term residential care. Nearly half of all nursing home residents in the U.S. have Alzheimer's.

The costs of diagnosing, treating, and providing long-term care in this country for Alzheimer's patients are estimated to be $203 bil in 2013. People with Alzheimer's need a safe, stable environment and a regular daily schedule offering appropriate stimulation. Physical exercise and social interaction are important, as are proper nutrition and adequate pain management. Security is also a consideration, because many people with Alzheimer's tend to wander. An identification bracelet with the person's name, address, and condition can help ensure the safe return of an individual who wanders.

Website: www.alz.org

Warning Signs of Alzheimer's Disease

- Memory loss that disrupts daily life
- Challenges in planning or solving problems
- Difficulty completing familiar tasks at home, at work, or at leisure
- Confusion with time or place
- Trouble understanding visual images and spatial relationships
- New problems with words in speaking or writing
- Misplacing things and losing the ability to retrace steps
- Decreased or poor judgment
- Withdrawal from work or social activities
- Changes in mood and personality

Arthritis

Source: Arthritis Foundation; Centers for Disease Control and Prevention

The term arthritis refers to more than 100 different diseases that cause pain, aching, stiffness, and swelling in or around the joints. The condition is usually chronic. The CDC estimates that 50 mil adults in the United States report being told by a doctor that they had arthritis. Arthritis annually results in 44.2 mil ambulatory care visits and an estimated 992,000 hospitalizations. The **cause** for most types of arthritis is unknown; scientists are studying the roles played by genetics, lifestyle, and environment.

Symptoms may develop slowly or suddenly. A visit to the doctor is indicated when pain, stiffness, swelling in a joint, or difficulty in moving a joint persists for three days or more. To **diagnose** arthritis, the doctor records the patient's symptoms and examines his or her joints, looking for any swelling or limited movement. In addition, the doctor checks for other signs often seen with arthritis, such as rashes, mouth sores, or eye involvement. The doctor may test blood, urine, or joint fluid, or take X-rays of the joints.

Of the three most prevalent forms of arthritis, **osteoarthritis** is the most common, affecting approximately 27 mil Americans. It usually occurs after age 40. In patients with osteoarthritis, also called degenerative arthritis, the protective cartilage of joints is lost and changes occur in the bone, leading to pain and stiffness. The joints most commonly affected are the knees, hips, and those in the hands and spine.

Fibromyalgia, another common arthritis condition, affects about 5 mil Americans. People suffering from fibromyalgia experience widespread pain and tenderness in muscles and their attachments to bone. Common symptoms include fatigue, disturbed sleep, stiffness, and psychological distress. More women than men are afflicted with this type of arthritis.

Rheumatoid arthritis, which affects an estimated 1.5 mil in the U.S., is one of the most serious and disabling forms of the disease. In this type—which is also more common and more degenerative in women—inflammation of the joints leads to cartilage and bone damage. The areas of the body that can be affected are the hands, wrists, feet, knees, ankles, and elbows.

Other forms of arthritis and related conditions include lupus, gout, psoriatic arthritis, and Sjögren's syndrome. Bursitis and tendinitis, which may result from injuring or overusing a joint, are also related.

Medications that relieve pain and swelling, such as analgesics, anti-inflammatory drugs, biologic response modifiers, glucocorticoids, and antirheumatic drugs, can be used to treat arthritis. They also tend to slow the disease process. Most treatment programs call for exercise, use of heat or cold, and joint-protection techniques, such as avoidance of excess stress on the joints, the use of assistive devices, and weight loss and control. In some cases, surgery may help.

Website: www.arthritis.org

Attention Deficit Hyperactivity Disorder (ADHD)

Source: Centers for Disease Control and Prevention; Natl. Institute of Mental Health

Attention deficit hyperactivity disorder, or ADHD, is one of the most common neurobehavioral disorders of childhood. It is usually first diagnosed in childhood and often lasts into adulthood. Children with ADHD may have trouble paying attention, controlling impulsive behaviors, or be overly active.

Signs and Symptoms of ADHD

- Daydreaming a lot
- Forgetting or losing things a lot
- Squirming or fidgeting
- Talking too much
- Making careless mistakes or taking unnecessary risks
- Having a hard time resisting temptation or taking turns
- Having difficulty getting along with others

There are three different types of ADHD, depending on which types of symptoms are strongest in the individual. A person who is **predominantly inattentive** is easily distracted or forgets details of daily routines. Someone who is **predominantly hyperactive-impulsive** may fidget and talk a lot and find it hard to sit still for long. In the third type, **combined presentation**, the individual displays symptoms of the first two types equally. The cause of ADHD is unknown, but current research shows that genetics plays an important role.

The average age of onset is 7 years old. ADHD affects about 4.1% of American adults age 18 years and older in a given year. The disorder affects 9.0% of American children age 13 to 18 years. Boys are four times more at risk than girls. Studies show that the number of children being diagnosed with ADHD is increasing, but it is unclear why. Rates of ADHD diagnosis increased an average of 3% per year from 1997 to 2006 and an average of 5.5% per year from 2003 to 2007. In addition, a 2007 survey found an estimated 6.4% of children aged 2-17 years in the U.S. currently had ADHD; this rose to 7.9% in the 2011-12 survey.

In most cases, ADHD is treated with a combination of medication and behavior therapy. Stimulants are the most widely used medication. Nonstimulants, approved for treating ADHD in 2003, have fewer side effects than stimulants and can last up to 24 hours.

Breast Cancer

Source: American Cancer Society, Inc.

In 2013, an estimated 232,340 women and 2,240 men in the U.S. will be newly diagnosed with breast cancer, and about 39,620 women and 410 men will die from it. Currently, nearly 3.0 mil women are living with a history of breast cancer, the second biggest cause of cancer death for women in the U.S. (lung cancer ranks first). But mortality rates have been declining, especially among younger women, probably because of earlier detection and improved treatment.

The **risk** for breast cancer increases with age. It is higher for women with a personal or family history of cancer (particularly breast cancer), a long menstrual history (menstrual periods that started early and ended later in life), recent use of birth control pills, use of menopausal hormone therapy containing estrogen and progestin, and in those who have no children or had no live birth until age 30 or older. Other risk factors include alcohol consumption and being overweight or obese. Inherited mutations such as in the BRCA1 and BRCA2 genes greatly increase risk, but these probably account for 5% to 10% of all breast cancers. By far the majority of women who develop breast cancer have no family history of it.

Breast cancer often manifests first as an abnormality on a mammogram X-ray. Physical symptoms that show up later, which may be detectable by a woman or her doctor, include a breast lump and, less commonly, persistent changes to the breast, such as thickening, swelling, distortion, tenderness, skin irritation, redness, scaliness, or nipple abnormalities, such as ulceration, retraction, or spontaneous discharge. Breast pain is more likely to be caused by benign conditions and is not a common early symptom of breast cancer.

Studies show that early detection increases survival and treatment options. Although most detected breast lumps are noncancerous, any suspicious lump should be biopsied.

Treatment for breast cancer may involve lumpectomy (local removal of a tumor), mastectomy (surgical removal of the breast), radiation therapy, targeted therapy, chemotherapy, and/or hormone therapy. The five-year survival rate for female invasive breast cancer patients has improved from 75% in the mid-1970s to 90% today. The five-year survival for women diagnosed with localized breast cancer (cancer that has not spread to lymph nodes or other locations outside the breast) is 98%.

Website: www.cancer.org

Prostate Cancer

Source: Prostate Cancer Foundation; American Cancer Society, Inc.

The prostate is a male gland located between the bladder and scrotum that secretes seminal fluid. Prostate cancer is the most common non-skin cancer in the U.S., and the second-most common cause, after lung cancer, of cancer deaths in American men. In 2013, an estimated 238,590 men will be diagnosed with prostate cancer, and about 29,720 will die from the disease. Currently, more than 2.7 mil men in the U.S. are living with a history of prostate cancer.

The exact cause of prostate cancer is unknown. The most identifiable **risk factors** are age, family history, and race. About 60% of all prostate cancers are diagnosed in men over the age of 65, and the chances of developing the disease rise dramatically with age. Having a single first-degree relative with a history of prostate cancer more than doubles a man's risk of developing the disease, and those with several affected relatives have a much higher risk. African-American men are much more likely to develop prostate cancer than non-Hispanic white men and are more than twice as likely to die from it. The cause for this disparity remains unclear.

Usually, the disease has no **symptoms** in its early stages. As the disease advances, a man may experience weak or interrupted urine flow; inability to urinate or difficulty starting or stopping the urine flow; the need to urinate frequently, especially at night; blood in the urine; or pain or burning with urination. Advanced prostate cancer commonly spreads to the bones, which can cause pain in the hips, spine, ribs, or other areas.

The American Cancer Society recommends that once they reach 50, men at average risk of prostate cancer should speak with their health care provider about the benefits and risks of being screened through a prostate-specific antigen (PSA) blood test or digital rectal exam (DRE). African-American men or those with a family history of the disease should be aware of their screening options beginning at age 40 or 45. Men under 40 seldom get prostate cancer.

Prostate cancer **treatment** may include surgery, radiation, hormonal therapy, chemotherapy, or some combination. If caught early on, while tumor cells are localized within the prostate, the five-year relative survival rate approaches 100%.

Websites: www.pcf.org; www.cancer.org

Cancer Risk Factors

Source: American Cancer Society, Inc., www.cancer.org

Alcohol: Alcohol consumption increases the risk of cancers of the mouth, pharynx, larynx, esophagus, liver, colorectum, and breast. Alcohol consumption combined with tobacco use increases the risk of cancers of the mouth, larynx, and esophagus far more than either drinking or smoking alone.

Diet and physical activity: Overweight and obesity are associated with increased risk for developing many cancers, including cancers of the breast in postmenopausal women, colon and rectum, endometrium, kidney, pancreas, and adenocarcinoma of the esophagus. Overweight and obesity may also be associated with increased risk of cancers of the liver, non-Hodgkin lymphoma, multiple myeloma, cervix, ovary, and aggressive prostate cancer. Obesity likely increases the risk of cancer of the gallbladder. It's not yet known for certain how diet, nutrition intake, and the amount and distribution of body fat factor into the development of certain cancers.

Environmental hazards: Exposure to various chemicals (including benzene, asbestos, vinyl chloride, arsenic, and aflatoxin) increases risk of various cancers. Risk of lung cancer from asbestos is greatly increased among smokers.

Estrogen: Menopausal hormone therapy (MHT, formerly called hormone replacement therapy) without the use of progestin can increase the risk of endometrial and ovarian cancer. Combining progestin with estrogen MHT may help minimize that risk. Studies, however, suggest that use of MHT increases the risk of breast cancer. The benefits and risks of the use of estrogen should be discussed carefully with one's doctor.

HPV infection: There are two vaccines (Gardasil and Cervarix) approved for use in females ages 9-26 for the prevention of the most common types of HPV infection that cause cervical cancer. Gardasil is also approved for use in males ages 9-26 for the prevention of anal and penile cancers, and the prevention of anal, vaginal, and vulvar cancers (and precancers) in women.

Radiation: Excessive exposure to ionizing radiation can increase cancer risk. Medical and dental X-rays are adjusted to deliver the lowest dose possible without sacrificing image quality. Excessive radon exposure in the home may increase lung cancer risk, especially in cigarette smokers.

Smokeless tobacco: Use of chewing tobacco, snuff, and other tobacco products that are not smoked causes oral, esophageal, and pancreatic cancers. The excess risk of cancer of the cheek and gum is especially high among long-term snuff users.

Smoking: The risk of developing lung cancer is about 23 times higher for current male smokers and 13 times higher for current female smokers than for those who have never smoked. Smoking accounts for at least 30% of all U.S. cancer deaths. Tobacco use is responsible for nearly 1 in 5 deaths in the U.S. Smoking increases the risk of the following types of cancer: nasopharynx, nasal cavity and paranasal sinuses, lip, oral cavity (mouth, tongue, lips), pharynx, larynx, lung, esophagus, pancreas, cervix, ovary (mucinous), kidney, bladder, stomach, colorectum, and acute myeloid leukemia.

Sunlight: Many of the more than 2 mil skin cancers diagnosed annually in the U.S. could have been prevented by protection from the sun's rays and avoiding indoor tanning. Epidemiological evidence shows that sun exposure is a major factor in the development of melanoma and that incidence rates are increasing worldwide.

Screening Guidelines for Early Detection of Cancer

Cancer site	Population	Test or procedure	Frequency
Breast	Women, age 20+	Breast self-examination (BSE)	Beginning in their early 20s: women should be told about BSE. Reporting any new breast symptoms to a health professional should be emphasized. Women should receive instruction and have their technique reviewed at a periodic health exam.
		Clinical breast examination (CBE)	Women in their 20s and 30s: CBE should be part of a periodic health exam, preferably at least every 3 years. Asymptomatic women aged 40+ should continue to receive a CBE as part of a periodic health exam, preferably annually.
		Mammography	At age 40: begin annual mammography. A clinical breast examination should be performed prior to mammography.
Cervix	Women, age 21-65	Pap test, HPV DNA test	All women should begin screening by age 21. Women ages 21-29 should have a Pap test every 3 years. From ages 30-65, the preferred way to screen is with a Pap test combined with an HPV test every 5 years. Another option is to get tested every 3 years with just the Pap test. Some women age 65 or over who have had a certain number of negative consecutive tests in the previous 10 years should consult a physician; health history may allow them to stop cervical cancer screening. Women who have had a total hysterectomy may stop screening. Women should not be screened annually by any method at any age.
Colorectal	Men and women, age 50+	Fecal occult blood test (FOBT) with at least 50% test sensitivity for cancer, or fecal immunochemical test (FIT) with at least 50% test sensitivity for cancer, **or**	Annual, starting at age 50. Testing at home with adherence to manufacturer's recommendation for collection techniques and number of samples is recommended. FOBT with the single stool sample collected on the clinician's fingertip during a digital rectal examination in a health care setting is not recommended. Guaiac-based toilet bowl FOBT tests also are not recommended. In comparison with guaiac-based tests for the detection of occult blood, immunochemical tests are more patient-friendly and are likely to be equal or better in sensitivity and specificity. There is no need to repeat an FOBT in response to an initial positive finding.
		Stool DNA test, **or**	Interval uncertain, starting at age 50. The stool DNA test approved for colorectal cancer screening in 2008 is no longer commercially available. New stool DNA tests are in development and may be available at some future time.
		Flexible sigmoidoscopy (FSIG), **or**	Every 5 years, starting at age 50. FSIG can be performed alone, or consideration can be given to combining FSIG performed every 5 years with a highly sensitive guaiac FOBT or FIT performed annually.
		Double contrast barium enema (DCBE), **or**	Every 5 years, starting at age 50
		Colonoscopy	Every 10 years, starting at age 50
		CT Colonography	Every 5 years, starting at age 50
Endometrial	Women, at menopause		Women at average risk should be informed about risks and symptoms of endometrial cancer and strongly encouraged to report any unexpected bleeding or spotting to their physicians.
Lung	Current or former smokers, age 55-74	Low dose helical CT (LDCT)	Apparently healthy patients who currently smoke or have quit within the past 15 years should discuss lung-cancer screening with a clinician. Informed and shared decision making related to the potential benefits, limitations, and harms associated with screening for lung cancer with LDCT should occur before any decision is made.
Prostate	Men, age 50+	Digital rectal examination (DRE) and prostate-specific antigen test (PSA)	Men who have at least a 10-year life expectancy should make an informed decision with their health care provider about whether to be screened for prostate cancer after receiving information about the potential benefits, risks, and uncertainties associated with prostate cancer screening. Screening should not occur without an informed decision-making process.

Estimated New U.S. Cancer Cases and Deaths for Leading Sites, 2013

Source: *Cancer Facts & Figures 2013*, American Cancer Society, Inc.

The following estimates exclude basal and squamous cell skin cancers and in situ carcinomas (i.e., noninvasive cancers), except of the urinary bladder. In 2013, an estimated 64,640 new cases of carcinoma in situ of the breast and 61,300 cases of melanoma in situ are expected to be diagnosed. More than 3 mil cases of basal cell and squamous cell cancer are diagnosed yearly. They are highly curable forms of skin cancer.

Estimated New Cases

Both sexes		Male		Female	
Prostate	238,590	Prostate	238,590	Breast	232,340
Breast	234,580	Lung and bronchus	118,080	Lung and bronchus	110,110
Lung and bronchus	228,190	Urinary bladder	54,610	Colon	52,390
Colon	102,480	Colon	50,090	Uterine corpus	49,560
Melanoma—skin	76,690	Melanoma—skin	45,060	Thyroid	45,310
Urinary bladder	72,570	Kidney and renal pelvis	40,430	Melanoma—skin	31,630
Non-Hodgkin lymphoma	69,740	Non-Hodgkin lymphoma	37,600	Non-Hodgkin lymphoma	32,140
Kidney and renal pelvis	65,150	Rectum	23,590	Kidney and renal pelvis	24,720
Thyroid	60,220	Pancreas	22,740	Pancreas	22,480
Uterine corpus	49,560	Liver and intrahepatic bile duct	22,720	Ovary	22,240
All sites	**1,660,290**	**All sites**	**854,790**	**All sites**	**805,500**

Estimated Deaths

Both sexes		Male		Female	
Lung and bronchus	159,480	Lung and bronchus	87,260	Lung and bronchus	72,220
Colon and rectum	50,830	Prostate	29,720	Breast	39,620
Breast	40,030	Colon and rectum	26,300	Colon and rectum	24,530
Pancreas	38,460	Pancreas	19,480	Pancreas	18,980
Prostate	29,720	Liver and intrahepatic bile duct	14,890	Ovary	14,030
Liver and intrahepatic bile duct	21,670	Esophagus	12,220	Non-Hodgkin lymphoma	8,430
Non-Hodgkin lymphoma	19,020	Urinary bladder	10,820	Uterine corpus	8,190
Esophagus	15,210	Non-Hodgkin lymphoma	10,590	Liver and intrahepatic bile duct	6,780
Urinary bladder	15,210	Kidney and renal pelvis	8,780	Brain and other nervous system	6,150
Brain and other nervous system	14,080	Brain and other nervous system	7,930	Kidney and renal pelvis	4,900
All sites	**580,350**	**All sites**	**306,920**	**All sites**	**273,430**

U.S. Cancer Survival Rates by Year of Diagnosis, 1960-2009

Source: SEER (Surveillance, Epidemiology, and End Results) Cancer Statistics Review, 1975-2010, National Cancer Institute, National Institutes of Health

Year of diagnosis	All races % total	% male	% female	White % total	% male	% female	Black % total	% male	% female
1960-63	—	—	—	39.0%	—	—	27.0%	—	—
1970-73	—	—	—	43.0	—	—	31.0	—	—
1975-77	48.9%	41.7%	55.8%	49.8	42.7%	56.5%	39.0	32.7%	46.2%
1978-80	49.0	43.1	54.9	50.0	44.3	55.6	38.9	33.3	45.5
1981-83	50.2	45.2	55.1	51.3	46.5	56.0	38.8	34.1	44.3
1984-86	52.4	47.1	57.6	53.6	48.6	58.5	40.1	35.4	45.4
1987-89	55.3	51.1	59.6	56.6	52.8	60.6	42.9	38.8	47.7
1990-92	59.9	59.1	60.9	61.3	60.8	62.0	47.7	47.5	48.1
1993-95	61.2	60.8	61.7	62.4	62.0	62.8	52.6	54.3	50.5
1996-98	63.3	63.0	63.6	64.3	64.0	64.7	55.0	57.7	51.9
1999-2001	66.3	66.7	65.9	67.5	67.9	67.1	58.1	61.7	54.0
2003-09	68.1	68.8	67.3	69.2	69.9	68.4	60.8	64.4	56.9

— = Statistic could not be calculated. **Note:** The geographic areas of surveillance may vary for different years. Rates are five-year relative (estimated) survival rates for all invasive cancer sites; based on follow-up of patients into 2010.

U.S. Cancer Survival Rates by Age at Diagnosis, 2003-09

Source: SEER (Surveillance, Epidemiology, and End Results) Cancer Statistics Review, 1975-2010, National Cancer Institute, National Institutes of Health

Age at diagnosis	All races % total	% male	% female	White % total	% male	% female	Black % total	% male	% female
Under age 45	80.6%	75.7%	83.8%	82.2%	77.7%	85.2%	69.0%	62.2%	73.0%
Ages 45-54	72.5	67.0	77.1	74.0	68.3	78.8	61.6	59.9	63.3
Ages 55-64	69.4	69.4	69.4	70.3	70.0	70.6	62.3	65.6	57.4
Under age 65	72.7	69.8	75.7	73.9	70.8	77.0	63.4	63.3	63.6
Ages 65-74	65.2	68.5	60.4	65.7	68.7	61.5	60.0	66.5	50.5
Ages 65 and older	58.7	63.2	53.3	59.2	63.3	54.3	53.1	60.9	43.8
Ages 75 and older	52.1	56.7	47.6	52.8	56.9	48.8	43.2	50.7	36.9

Note: Rates are five-year relative (estimated) survival rates for all invasive cancer sites; based on follow-up of patients into 2010.

Skin Cancer

Source: American Cancer Society, Inc.

Skin cancer is generally divided into two main classes, **nonmelanomas** and **melanomas**, both types affecting different types of skin cells. Melanoma develops in skin cells called melanocytes, which produce melanin, a pigment that gives skin a tan or brown color and helps to protect the deeper layers of skin from some of the harmful effects of the sun.

Melanoma is the most dangerous type of skin cancer because it can easily spread to other parts of the body.

Although skin cancer is the most common type of cancer diagnosed in the U.S., melanoma accounts for less than 5% of all skin cancers. The American Cancer Society estimates that in 2013, 76,690 new cases of melanoma will be diagnosed in

the U.S., and about 9,480 people will die from melanoma, while 12,650 will die from any skin cancer.

The exact causes of melanoma are unclear, but there are several **risk factors** that have been associated with the disease:

- Overexposure to UV light (sunlight or tanning booths)
- Multiple or unusual moles
- Fair skin, freckling, and light hair
- Family history or personal history of skin cancers
- Occupational exposure to coal tar, pitch, creosote, arsenic compounds, or radium
- Past history of severe sunburns

Melanomas generally look like abnormal moles on the surface of the skin. Normal moles are most often an evenly colored brown, tan, or black spot on the skin that can be flat or raised. They normally have a distinct border that separates them from normal skin cells. Moles can be present at birth, form over time, or even disappear. Abnormal moles differ from regular skin cells and may be a sign of skin cancer. An irregular mole should be examined as soon as possible. Irregular moles generally have the following characteristics:

- Asymmetry: one half does not match the other half.
- Border: edges are irregular, ragged, notched, or blurred.
- Color: not uniform; may be shades of brown or black, and patches of pink, red, blue, or white.
- Diameter: moles wider than ¼ inch are abnormal (however, melanomas can be smaller).
- Evolving: mole is changing in size, shape, or color

If a melanoma is suspected, the doctor will perform a biopsy using cells extracted from the suspected cancer or by removing the whole mass and examining it. If a melanoma is found, doctors will often check to see if the cancer has spread to other parts of the body. This is called staging and is represented by Roman numerals I through IV (1-4). The lower the number, the less the cancer has spread. This will determine what course of treatment is necessary.

If caught early, melanoma is highly curable. The overall five-year survival rate for melanoma is 91%. For localized melanoma, the five-year survival rate is 98%; survival rates for regional and distant stage diseases are 62% and 15%, respectively. About 84% of melanomas are diagnosed at a localized stage.

Treatment may include simple removal of the melanoma; amputation if the cancer is found on a finger or toe; or chemotherapy, immunotherapy, and/or radiation if the melanoma has spread to other parts of the body.

Website: www.cancer.org

Depression

Source: National Institute of Mental Health, National Institutes of Health, U.S. Dept. of Health and Human Services

Depression is a serious illness that affects thoughts, feelings, and the ability to function in everyday life. It strikes all age groups and often goes unrecognized or is inadequately treated. The National Institute of Mental Health (NIMH) estimates that about 20.9 mil American adults age 18 and older suffer from depression or some other mood or depressive disorder in any given year; more than 16% of all Americans will have had depression at some point in life. Young people are at particular risk; in a one-year period, persons aged 18 to 29 years were 200% more likely to have experienced depression than those who were 60 or older.

Nearly twice as many women as men suffer from a depressive illness in a given year. Although conventional wisdom holds that depression is most closely associated with menopause, the childbearing years, followed by the years prior to menopause, are marked by the highest rates of depression. The influence of hormones on depression in women has been an active area of NIMH research.

Available **treatments** can alleviate symptoms, and with awareness growing, more people with depression are seeking help. But many depressed people—and those around them—still fail to realize that they have an illness or could benefit from medical help.

Symptoms and Types of Depression

- Persistent sad, anxious, or "empty" feelings
- Feelings of hopelessness or pessimism
- Feelings of guilt, worthlessness, or helplessness
- Irritability, restlessness
- Loss of interest in activities or hobbies once pleasurable, including sex
- Fatigue and decreased energy
- Difficulty concentrating, remembering details, and making decisions
- Insomnia, early-morning wakefulness, or excessive sleeping
- Overeating, or appetite loss
- Thoughts of suicide, suicide attempts
- Aches or pains, headaches, cramps, or digestive problems that do not ease even with treatment

A diagnosis of **major depressive disorder** (or **major depression**) is made if an individual reports experiencing five or more of these symptoms in the same two-week period.

Bipolar disorder (or **manic-depressive illness**) is characterized by episodes of major depression alternating with periods of mania, when a person experiences a persistent, abnormally elevated mood or irritability, accompanied by feelings of inflated self-esteem, less need for sleep, increased talkativeness, racing thoughts, distractibility, agitation, and excessive involvement in pleasurable activities that have a high potential for painful consequences. While it shares some of the features of major depression, bipolar disorder is a distinct illness.

Treatments for Depression

A variety of **medicines** are used to treat depression. These drugs influence the functioning of certain neurotransmitters in the brain, primarily serotonin and norepinephrine, known as monoamines. Older drugs—tricyclic antidepressants (TCAs) and monoamine oxidase inhibitors (MAOIs)—affect the functioning of both of these neurotransmitters. But they can have strong side effects or, in the case of MAOIs, require dietary restrictions. Newer medications, such as selective serotonin reuptake inhibitors (SSRIs), have fewer side effects. All of these medications can be effective, but some people respond to one type and not another.

NIMH research has shown that certain types of **psychotherapy**, particularly cognitive-behavioral therapy (CBT) and interpersonal therapy (IPT), can help relieve depression. CBT helps patients change the negative thinking and behaving patterns often associated with depression. IPT focuses patients on working through personal relationships that may contribute to depression. Studies of adults have shown that a combination of psychotherapy and antidepressant medication is most effective in treating moderate-to-severe depression.

Electroconvulsive therapy (ECT) has been found effective in treating some cases of severe depression, particularly those that have not responded to other forms of treatment. ECT involves producing a seizure in the brain of a patient under general anesthesia by applying electrical stimulation through electrodes placed on the scalp. Memory loss and other cognitive problems, though common side effects, are typically short-lived.

Website: www.nimh.nih.gov

Diabetes

Source: American Diabetes Association; Centers for Disease Control and Prevention

Diabetes is a chronic disease in which the body does not produce or properly use the hormone **insulin.** Insulin is needed to convert sugar, starches, and other foods into energy. Both genetics and environment appear to play roles in the onset of diabetes. This disease, which has no cure, is the seventh leading cause of death by disease in the U.S. According to death certificate data, 73,282 people in the U.S. died as a result of diabetes in 2011. In 2011, an estimated 25.8 mil Americans had diabetes, 7 mil of whom were undiagnosed.

The American Diabetes Association supports studies proving that detection at an earlier stage and modest lifestyle changes, such as eating better and exercising more, will help prevent or delay complications.

There are two major types of diabetes:

Type 1 (formerly known as insulin dependent, or juvenile diabetes). The body does not produce insulin; the disease is usually diagnosed in children and young adults. People with type 1 diabetes must take daily insulin to stay alive.

Type 2 (formerly known as non-insulin dependent, or adult-onset diabetes). The body does not produce enough or cannot properly use insulin. It is the most common form of the disease (90%-95% of diabetes cases in people over age 20) and often begins later in life.

Prediabetes

There are 79 mil people in the U.S. who have prediabetes, the state that occurs when a person's blood glucose levels are higher than normal but not high enough for a diagnosis of diabetes. One study indicated that about 11% of people with prediabetes developed type 2 diabetes each year during the average three-year study follow-up period. Other studies showed that most people with prediabetes develop type 2 diabetes within 10 years.

Complications From Diabetes

People often have diabetes for many years before it is diagnosed. During that time, serious complications may develop. Potential complications include the following:

Blindness. Diabetes is the leading cause of new cases of blindness in people ages 20-74. Each year, 12,000 to 24,000 people lose their eyesight because of diabetes.

Kidney disease. 10% to 21% of all people with diabetes develop kidney disease. In 2008, a total of 48,374 people in the U.S. initiated treatment for end-stage renal disease (kidney failure) because of diabetes.

Amputations. Diabetes is the most frequent cause for nontraumatic lower limb amputations. The risk of a leg amputation is 15 to 40 times greater for a person with diabetes than for the average American. In 2006, approximately 65,700 lower-limb amputations were performed as a result of complications brought on by diabetes.

Heart disease and stroke. People with diabetes are two to four times more likely to have heart disease. They are also two to four times more likely to suffer a stroke.

Warning Signs of Diabetes

Type 1 diabetes (signs usually occur suddenly):
- frequent urination
- unusual thirst
- extreme hunger
- unusual weight loss
- extreme fatigue
- irritability

Type 2 diabetes (signs occur less suddenly):
- any type 1 symptoms
- frequent infections
- blurred vision
- cuts/bruises slow to heal
- tingling/numbness in hands or feet
- recurring skin, gum, or bladder infections

Gestational Diabetes

Gestational diabetes is a form of diabetes that affects about 18% of pregnant women. Usually there are no symptoms, or the symptoms are mild. Because the condition usually appears around the 24th week, it is recommended that all pregnant women receive a glucose tolerance test between the 24th and 28th week. Pregnancy hormones can cause insulin resistance, making blood glucose levels rise. The goal of treatment is to keep blood glucose levels within normal limits, mainly through diet and exercise; treatment may also include daily blood glucose testing and insulin injections. Women with gestational diabetes tend to have larger babies at birth, which can increase the chance of problems at the time of delivery. Glucose levels usually return to normal after delivery, but odds of recurrence in future pregnancies are two-in-three.

Website: www.diabetes.org

Eating Disorders

Source: National Institute of Mental Health, National Institutes of Health, U.S. Dept. of Health and Human Services

Eating disorders involve serious disturbances in eating behavior, usually in the forms of extreme and unhealthy reduction of food intake or severe overeating. They are not due to a failure of will; rather, they are real and treatable medical illnesses in which certain behavior patterns get out of control. The main types are anorexia nervosa, bulimia nervosa, and binge-eating disorder (technically categorized with "eating disorders not otherwise specified"). These disorders usually develop in adolescence or early adulthood and often occur with other illnesses such as depression, substance abuse, and anxiety disorders. They are much more common among females; only about 5% to 15% of anorexia or bulimia patients and 35% of binge eaters are male.

If not treated, eating disorders can lead to serious complications, including heart conditions and kidney failure, which may result in death.

Anorexia nervosa affects an estimated 0.9% of all females. Symptoms include resistance to maintaining weight at minimally healthy levels, intense fear of gaining weight, exaggerated importance of body weight or shape in one's self image, and infrequent or absent menstrual periods. Anorexics see themselves as overweight even when they are dangerously thin. In response, they avoid food and take other extreme measures to lose weight, such as exercising compulsively or purging by means of vomiting or laxatives and enemas. While some anorexics fully recover after a single episode, others may relapse frequently or experience chronic deterioration.

Bulimia nervosa affects an estimated 0.5% of females. It is characterized by recurrent uncontrolled binge-eating episodes followed by what is believed to be compensatory behavior to prevent weight gain, such as self-induced vomiting, exercising excessively, or fasting. Persons with bulimia can weigh within the normal range for their age and height, but they still fear gaining weight and are intensely dissatisfied with their bodies. They often perform their behaviors in secret, feeling shame when they binge and relief when they purge.

Binge-eating disorder affects an estimated 2% to 3.5% of males and females in the U.S. As with bulimia, a binge-eating disorder involves episodes of excessive eating during which the sufferer may feel a complete lack of control. But individuals with this disorder do not compensate by purging, exercising, or fasting. Many are thus overweight or obese, and the shame they feel can lead to further binge-eating.

Eating disorder sufferers may not admit they are ill. Early diagnosis and a comprehensive **treatment** program are essential to recovery. Some patients may need immediate hospitalization. For anorexia, treatment usually follows three established steps: weight restoration, usually in an inpatient hospital setting; treatment of any accompanying psychological disturbances, including the use of medications; and achieving long-term remission or recovery by reducing or eliminating negative thoughts and behaviors.

Heart and Blood Vessel Disease

Source: American Heart Association; National Center for Chronic Disease Prevention and Health Promotion, Centers for Disease Control and Prevention; National Heart, Blood, and Lung Institute, National Institutes of Health, U.S. Dept. of Health and Human Services

Warning Signs of Heart Attack

- Chest discomfort. Most heart attacks involve discomfort in the center of the chest that lasts more than a few minutes or that goes away and then returns. It can feel like uncomfortable pressure, squeezing, fullness, or pain.
- Discomfort in other areas of the upper body. Symptoms can include pain or discomfort in one or both arms, the back, neck, jaw, or stomach.
- Shortness of breath. This feeling may occur with or without chest discomfort.
- Other signs may include breaking out in a cold sweat, nausea, or lightheadedness.

The American Heart Association advises immediate action at onset of symptoms, as more than half of heart attack victims die within an hour of symptoms first manifesting. Call 9-1-1. Get to a hospital right away.

Warning Signs of Stroke

- Sudden numbness or weakness of the face, arm, or leg, especially on one side of the body.
- Sudden confusion, trouble speaking, or understanding.
- Sudden trouble seeing in one or both eyes.
- Sudden trouble walking, dizziness, loss of balance or coordination.
- Sudden severe headache with no known cause.

Prompt treatment of a stroke can be a major factor in controlling the effects. If you have one or more stroke symptoms that last more than a few minutes, call 9-1-1 or the emergency medical service number immediately so an ambulance, ideally one with advanced life support, can be sent for you quickly.

Major Modifiable Risk Factors

High blood pressure. High blood pressure, or hypertension, increases the risk of stroke, heart attack, kidney failure, and congestive heart failure. It affects men and women of all races, ethnic origins, and ages. Obesity, physical inactivity, and an unhealthy diet can contribute to this often symptomless disease. Individuals should have a blood pressure reading at least once every two years or more often if advised by a physician.

A blood pressure reading consists of two measurements, with one value written above the other, such as 122/78 mmHg. The upper number (systolic pressure) represents the amount of pressure in the arteries when the heart contracts (beats) and pushes blood through the circulatory system. The lower number (diastolic pressure) represents the pressure in the arteries between beats, when the heart is resting. According to National Institutes of Health (NIH) guidelines, a blood pressure reading below 120/80 is considered normal, while readings from 120/80 to 139/89 are considered prehypertension.

There are two stages of high blood pressure:
Stage 1 is 140-159 (systolic) over 90-99 (diastolic);
Stage 2 is 160+ (systolic) over 100+ (diastolic).
The diagnosis can be based on either the systolic or the diastolic reading.

High blood pressure usually cannot be cured, but it can be controlled in a variety of ways, including lifestyle modifications and medication. **Treatment** always should be at the direction and under the supervision of a physician. The treatment goal for patients with hypertension is blood pressure below 140/90. Individuals with hypertension and diabetes or chronic kidney disease should aim for blood pressure lower than 130/80.

High blood cholesterol. Cholesterol is a waxy fat-like substance found in all cells of the body. It is produced by the body and also comes in some foods. The body needs some cholesterol, but excess levels increase the risk of heart disease. High cholesterol in itself usually does not cause **symptoms**, so many people are unaware that they have a problem.

There are two major kinds of cholesterol: LDL (low-density lipoprotein), often called "bad" cholesterol, leads to narrowing of the arteries. HDL (high-density lipoprotein), known as "good" cholesterol, helps reduce that risk.

NIH guidelines classify total cholesterol levels (determined by a blood test) of less than 200 mg/dl as desirable, 200-239 as borderline high, and 240 and higher as high. About 14% of Americans have a cholesterol level of 240 mg/dl or higher. LDL levels of less than 100 are considered optimal, 130-159 as borderline high, 160-189 as high, and 190 and higher as very high. For HDL, levels of 60 mg/dl and higher are considered protective against heart disease, while levels under 40 mg/dl are considered a risk factor.

As with high blood pressure, high blood cholesterol can be controlled by lifestyle changes and medication and should be treated by a physician.

Triglycerides, another form of fat in the blood, can also raise the risk of heart disease. Levels that are borderline high (150-199) or high (200 or more) may need treatment.

Diabetes. Diabetes is a major risk factor for heart disease; at least 65% of people with diabetes mellitus die of some form of heart or blood vessel disease.

Smoking. Cigarette smokers are two to four times more likely to develop coronary heart disease (CHD). Smoking is also associated with the risk of sudden cardiac death.

Obesity. Using a body mass index (BMI) of 25 and higher for overweight and 30 and higher for obesity, about 65% of Americans are either overweight or obese. Of these, more than 78 mil are obese.

Physical inactivity. A sedentary lifestyle is a risk factor for CHD. The risk increase is comparable to that observed for high blood cholesterol, high blood pressure, or cigarette smoking.

Women and Cardiovascular Disease

The American Heart Association reports that heart disease, stroke, and other cardiovascular diseases are the number one cause of death in American women. (Cancer is the second leading cause.) One in three women died of some form of cardiovascular disease in 2009. Because heart disease was long viewed as a "man's" disease, many of the major cardiovascular studies were conducted only on men. Recent attention has been directed toward understanding the influence of gender on cardiovascular disease risk and prevention, but important gaps in knowledge remain.

Women often present some of the same classic symptoms of heart attack as men, such as chest pain that spreads to the shoulders and arms. But women may more often report atypical chest pain or complain of abdominal pain, difficulty breathing (dyspnea), and nausea. Another problem in **diagnosis** is that women tend to have heart attacks later in life than men, so symptoms may be masked by other age-related diseases such as arthritis or osteoporosis. Even certain diagnostic tests and procedures such as the exercise stress test may not be as accurate in women, with the result that the disease process leading to heart attack or stroke may not be detected early on, with potentially serious consequences.
Website: www.heart.org

Irritable Bowel Syndrome

Source: National Institute of Diabetes and Digestive and Kidney Diseases, National Institutes of Health

Irritable bowel syndrome (IBS)—a functional disorder, not a disease, in the gastrointestinal tract—is one of the most common disorders diagnosed by physicians. An estimated 10%-15% of Americans have IBS symptoms; however, less than one-third of people with the condition see a health care provider for diagnosis. IBS occurs more frequently in women than in men, and it is most often found in people younger than 45 years. Though IBS causes discomfort and may even be painful, it does not damage the bowel.

Many people are uncomfortable discussing IBS because of its embarrassing **symptoms**. They may include the following:

- Bowel movements occurring more or less often than usual
- Abdominal pain
- Bloating
- Discomfort
- Constipation
- Mucus in the stool
- Diarrhea

For most people, IBS is a chronic condition, and there will likely be times when the symptoms may worsen or disappear altogether only to reappear in the future. Most **complications** are derived from the symptoms, such as hemorrhoids, which may form as a result of diarrhea and constipation. People with chronic IBS may also go through periods of depression because of the constant discomfort and the symptoms' interference in work and personal relationships.

The specific **causes** for IBS are unknown. The walls of the intestines are lined with layers of muscle that contract and relax in a coordinated manner as they move food through the digestive system. When a person has IBS, the contractions cause food to either speed up or slow down as it moves though the bowel, subsequently causing gas, bloating, diarrhea, or constipation. Some researchers believe that people who suffer from IBS have a colon that is particularly sensitive to certain foods. Foods rich in carbohydrates, spicy or fatty foods, coffee, and alcohol in particular can trigger IBS symptoms. Another common factor is a low tolerance for stretching of the large intestine. Women tend to have more severe symptoms during menstrual periods, leading researchers to believe that IBS may have a hormonal trigger. Recent research has shown that serotonin, a neurotransmitter hormone, may be linked with gastrointestinal functioning.

IBS can sometimes result from infection or other problems in the body. Researchers have found that people who have had gastroenteritis later develop IBS. But because IBS symptoms can match those of many serious diseases, it is important for chronic sufferers to consult their doctors. If symptoms began early in life and have remained stable, one may need to get a colonoscopy to rule out inflammatory bowel disease, such as Crohn's disease or ulcerative colitis or even colon cancer. Those with IBS over 50 years of age should be regularly screened for colon cancer.

Despite the uncertainty over what causes IBS, there are known **precautionary measures** that people with sensitive digestive systems can take. Keeping a well-balanced diet is the best possible preventive. Eating foods with dietary fiber, such as whole-grain bread and cereal, as well as vegetables and beans as part of a daily diet can reduce IBS symptoms, although high-fiber diets may cause gas and bloating. Eating large meals has been shown to worsen the condition, so IBS sufferers may want to eat several smaller meals.

There is no cure for IBS. **Treatment** usually involves lessening the symptoms so that they don't interfere as much in a person's life.

Common Infectious Diseases

Source: National Institutes of Health, Centers for Disease Control and Prevention, U.S. Dept. of Health and Human Services; World Health Organization

The following is a list of major infectious diseases. It is meant to be used for reference purposes only and not as a tool for diagnosis. Statistics may appear uneven because of the different reporting methods used by the various agencies and because not all diseases are surveyed in the same year.

Chicken pox

(*Varicella simplex*) Usually nonthreatening viral disease commonly associated with children. In adults, the disease can be serious. **Transmission:** highly contagious. Transmitted by direct contact with rash, coughing, or sneezing of infected persons. **Symptoms:** blister-like rash, discomfort, high fever. Infected people may develop shingles later in life. **Vaccine:** available since 1995. **Treatment:** none; antibiotics in some severe cases. **Annual U.S. cases:** before 1995, about 4 mil, mostly children; 14,513 reported in 2011.

Chlamydia

(*Chlamydia trachomatis*) One of the most widely spread sexually transmitted diseases (STDs). **Transmission:** sexually transmitted. **Symptoms:** about 70% of those infected show no symptoms. In women, vaginal discharge, infection of the cervix and urinary tract, can cause pelvic inflammatory disease. In men, infection of urinary tract and epididymitis (inflammation of testicular duct); can also infect the throat, rectum, and eyes. **Treatment:** curable with antibiotics. **Annual U.S. cases:** 1,412,791 in 2011.

Common cold

(More than 200 different viruses) An upper respiratory viral infection. **Transmission:** touching one's nose, eyes, or mouth after touching something contaminated by the virus; inhalation of airborne virus. **Symptoms:** irritated nose or scratchy throat, sneezing and watery green or yellow nasal discharge, coughing, muscle aches, headaches, postnasal drip, decreased appetite. **Treatment:** no cure. Over-the-counter remedies can relieve symptoms; effectiveness of antiviral drugs uncertain. **Est. annual U.S. cases:** about 1 bil.

Gonorrhea

(*Neisseria gonorrhoeae*) Common bacterial STD. **Transmission:** sexually transmitted. **Symptoms:** in men, discomfort in urethra, yellow or green discharge, burning during urination. In women, pelvic pain, bleeding associated with intercourse, burning during urination, yellow or bloody discharge. **Treatment:** highly curable with antibiotics. **Annual U.S. cases:** 321,849 in 2011.

Hepatitis

A viral disease that causes inflammation of the liver. In the U.S., five forms are endemic: A, B, C, D, and E. Forms A, B, and C are the most common. **Symptoms:** all forms have generally similar symptoms including jaundice, fatigue, abdominal pain, loss of appetite, nausea, mild flu-like symptoms. Many cases cause no symptoms. In extreme cases, liver transplants may be necessary.

Hepatitis A (*Hepatovirus picornaviridae*). **Transmission:** consuming food or water contaminated with feces from infected persons. **Vaccine:** effective; travelers are advised to not drink tap water in countries where disease is common. **Treatment:** disease usually resolves on its own; alcohol consumption should be avoided. **Est. annual U.S. cases:** 17,000 infections in 2010; 1,398 acute lab-confirmed cases reported in 2011.

Hepatitis B (*Orthohepadnavirus hepadnaviridae*). **Transmission:** unsterilized needle sharing; contaminated blood transfusions; sexual contact. **Vaccine:** highly effective. **Treatment:** for chronic cases, drug treatment is necessary. For acute cases, disease usually resolves itself. Severe cases treated with lamivudine. **Est. annual U.S. cases:** 38,000 infections in 2011; 2,903 acute lab-confirmed cases reported in 2011.

Hepatitis C (*Hepacivirus flavinviridae*). **Transmission:** unsterilized needle sharing; contaminated blood transfusions; sexual contact. **Vaccine:** none. **Treatment:** chronic cases treated with drugs, which eliminates virus in about 50% of patients. For acute cases, treatment recommended if disease present after two to three months. **Est. annual U.S. cases:** 17,000 infections in 2010; 1,229 acute lab-confirmed cases reported in 2011.

HPV infection

(More than 100 strains of human papillomavirus) Common viral infection; leading cause of cervical cancer. **Transmission:** sexually transmitted. **Symptoms:** most of those infected have no symptoms but can still transmit virus. In some cases, genital warts and precancerous bumps on anus, cervix or vulva, or penis. **Vaccine:** Gardasil and Cervarix. **Treatment:** while there is no cure, a healthy immune system can usually fight off HPV naturally. Women with HPV should have a Pap smear and pelvic exam every six months. **Est. annual U.S. cases:** 14 mil new cases; approximately 79 mil currently infected with HPV.

Influenza

(Various influenza viruses) Highly contagious viral respiratory infection. **Transmission:** airborne; contact with face after touching infected surface. **Symptoms:** chills, fatigue, fever, headaches, sore throat, sinus congestion, coughing. ("Stomach flu" is not influenza.) **Vaccine:** yearly vaccinations recommended; available as injection or nasal spray. **Treatment:** antiviral drugs; disease normally runs its course in a matter of days. **Est. annual U.S. cases:** 5%-20% of population; more than 200,000 flu-related hospitalizations, 36,000 flu-related deaths.

Lyme disease

(*Borrelia burgdorferi*) Bacterial inflammatory disease, first identified 1975 in Old Lyme, CT. Found across the U.S., usually in areas with large deer populations. **Transmission:** bite from infected deer ticks. Mice and deer are most common tick hosts. **Symptoms:** mimic those of other diseases. Flu-like symptoms: fatigue, stiff neck, joint inflammation; skin rash may appear at site of tick bite. **Treatment:** antibiotics in early stages; anti-inflammatory drugs to relieve symptoms. Without treatment, long-term complications (some fatal) involving joints, heart, and nervous system. **Annual U.S. cases:** from 9,895 reported cases in 1992 to 33,097 confirmed and probable cases in 2011.

Malaria

(*Plasmodium* parasite) Infectious disease known from as early as 2700 BCE. Virtually eradicated in developed countries; still a major killer in tropical regions. **Transmission:** bite from infected mosquito. **Symptoms:** high fever, shaking chills, heavy sweating, headaches, fatigue, enlarged spleen. If left untreated, organ damage and death. **Treatment:** antimalarial drugs, including chloroquine, for treatment and prevention. **Annual cases:** 1,724 in the U.S. in 2011; worldwide, an estimated 219 mil cases and 660,000 deaths, most young children in sub-Saharan Africa, in 2010.

Measles

(*Rubeola* virus) Once-common viral infection; today almost nonexistent in U.S. and Canada. **Transmission:** airborne transmission by infected persons. **Symptoms:** itchy and raised rash, sore throat, cough, pink eye, high fever. In rare cases, encephalitis, seizures, permanent deafness, death. **Vaccine:** highly effective. **Treatment:** no specific treatment; symptoms relieved with bed rest, acetaminophen, humidified air. **Annual U.S. cases:** 220 in 2011.

Mumps

(Mumps virus) Acute and contagious viral infection. **Transmission:** direct contact with mucus or saliva of infected persons. **Symptoms:** painful, visible swelling of the salivary or parotid glands in the face. Chills, headaches, fever, painful swallowing. In some cases, inflammation of testes, pancreas, ovaries. In severe cases, brain swelling and symptoms ranging from nausea and drowsiness to seizures and permanent deafness. **Vaccine:** MMR (measles, mumps, and rubella) vaccine is effective. **Treatment:** no specific treatment; symptoms may be relieved by applying ice or heat to swollen glands. **Annual U.S. cases:** 404 in 2011.

Peptic ulcer

(Most from *Helicobacter pylori* [*H. pylori*] bacteria; also overuse of aspirin or other anti-inflammatory drugs) Weakening of the stomach's protective mucous coating, allowing stomach acid and bacteria to irritate stomach lining. **Transmission:** *H. pylori* may be transmitted through food and water. **Symptoms:** indigestion; bloating; dull, transient abdominal pain or discomfort; nausea; vomiting. **Treatment:** antibiotics, acid-suppressing drugs. **Est. annual U.S. cases:** about 20% of the population under 40 years of age and half of those over 60 may be infected with *H. pylori*. An estimated 500,000 to 850,000 develop peptic ulcers each year.

Pertussis or Whooping cough

(*Bordetella pertussis* or *B. parepertussis*) Upper respiratory bacterial infection. **Transmission:** airborne transmission by infected persons; highly contagious. **Symptoms:** initially, mild cold-like symptoms, fever, diarrhea, difficulty breathing; later, violent coughing with characteristic "whooping" sound when patient tries to breathe between coughs, vomiting. In severe cases, apnea, pneumonia, seizures, encephalopathy. **Vaccine:** available as part of combination vaccine that also prevents diphtheria and tetanus. **Treatment:** antibiotics in early cases; otherwise, disease must run its course. **Annual U.S. cases:** 18,719 in 2011.

Salmonella or Salmonellosis

(*Salmonella enteritidis*) Bacterial infection. **Transmission:** eating foods contaminated by feces carrying the bacteria or eating undercooked meats or raw eggs contaminated by bacteria. Contact with feces of infected animal or pet. **Symptoms:** fever, diarrhea, abdominal cramps 12 to 72 hours after infection. **Treatment:** no standard treatment. Runs its course in four to seven days. Antibiotics in severe cases. **Annual U.S. cases:** 51,887 in 2011.

Shigellosis

(Four species of *Shigella*: *boydii*, *dysenteriae*, *flexneri*, and *sonnei*) Bacterial infection and a form of dysentery, an intestinal disease. **Transmission:** consuming food contaminated by infected feces or eating vegetables grown in fields containing contaminated sewage. Swimming in contaminated water. **Symptoms:** watery or bloody diarrhea one to four days after infection, high fever, vomiting, painful bowel movements. In extreme cases, seizures in children, intestinal perforation. **Treatment:** mild infection allowed to run its course; replacement of fluids and salts lost through excessive diarrhea. Antibiotics in severe cases. Although severe diarrhea is symptomatic, antidiarrheal medicines may make illness worse. **Annual U.S. cases:** 13,352 in 2011.

Syphilis

(*Treponema pallidum*) Bacterial infection known since ancient times that spread rampantly throughout Europe in the Middle Ages. **Transmission:** sexually transmitted. **Symptoms:** primary stage: painless sore, called a chancre, where bacteria enters the body; usually heals in 3 to 12 weeks with or without treatment. Without treatment, disease enters secondary stage: skin rash as chancre is healing or weeks after it is healed. Without treatment, enters tertiary stage: mouth sores, fever, fatigue, loss of appetite, weight loss, hair loss, jaundice, syphilitic meningitis, aortal aneurysms, lesions, damage to nervous system, heart, and eyes. Most infected do not progress beyond primary or secondary stage. **Treatment:** curable with antibiotics (mostly penicillin). **Annual U.S. cases:** 46,042 in 2011; 13,970 primary and secondary.

Tetanus or Lockjaw

(*Clostridium tetani*) Bacterial infection. **Transmission:** bacteria, found in soil, entering body through broken skin. **Symptoms:** muscle stiffness and spasms or "locking" of muscles of the jaw, neck, and limbs. **Vaccine:** four forms of immunization. **Treatment:** tetanus immune globulin to fight infection. With treatment, less than 10% of cases are fatal. **Annual U.S. cases:** 36 in 2011.

Tuberculosis

(*Mycobacterium tuberculosis*) Bacterial infection that primarily affects the lungs. **Transmission:** airborne transmission by persons with active TB infection. **Symptoms:** weight loss, fever, cough with discharge (sometimes with bloody sputum), night sweats, growing shortness of breath over time, chest pains. **Vaccine/treatment:** BCG (Bacille Calmette Guerin) vaccine only effective in protecting young children and used where TB is prevalent. Not recommended by health experts for use in the U.S. because of the low risk of infection and its variable effectiveness. **Annual U.S. cases:** 10,528 in 2011.

Yellow fever

(Yellow fever virus, in *flavivirus* group) Viral infection that has caused large epidemics in South America, the Caribbean, and Africa. **Transmission:** bite from mosquitoes carrying the virus. **Symptoms:** headaches, muscle aches, fever, jaundice (yellowing skin), nausea and vomiting, kidney failure, severe generalized pain. In severe cases, shock, coma, and death. **Vaccine:** available, safe, and effective. **Treatment:** symptoms treated until disease runs its course. **Annual cases:** none in the U.S.; an estimated 200,000 new cases, 30,000 deaths worldwide.

Dietary Guidelines for Americans, 2010: Key Recommendations

Source: *Dietary Guidelines for Americans, 2010*, U.S. Dept. of Agriculture; U.S. Dept. of Health and Human Services

Balancing Calories to Manage Weight

- Prevent and/or reduce overweight and obesity through improved eating and physical activity behaviors.
- Control total calorie intake to manage body weight.
- Increase physical activity and reduce time spent in sedentary behaviors.
- Maintain appropriate calorie balance during each stage of life.

Foods and Food Components to Reduce

- Reduce daily sodium intake to less than 2,300 mg. Further reduce intake to 1,500 mg among persons who are 51 and older and those of any age who are African American or have hypertension, diabetes, or chronic kidney disease.
- Consume less than 10% of calories from saturated fatty acids by replacing them with monounsaturated and polyunsaturated fatty acids.
- Consume less than 300 mg per day of dietary cholesterol.
- Keep trans fatty acid consumption as low as possible by limiting foods that contain synthetic sources of trans fats, such as partially hydrogenated oils.
- Reduce the intake of calories from solid fats and added sugars.
- Limit the consumption of foods that contain refined grains, especially refined grain foods that contain solid fats, added sugars, and sodium.
- If alcohol is consumed, it should be consumed in moderation—up to one drink per day for women and two drinks per day for men.

Foods and Nutrients to Increase

- Increase vegetable and fruit intake.
- Eat a variety of vegetables (especially dark-green, red, and orange vegetables), beans, and peas.
- Consume at least half of all grains as whole grains. Replace refined grains with whole grains.
- Increase intake of fat-free or low-fat milk and milk products, such as milk, yogurt, cheese, or fortified soy beverages.
- Choose a variety of protein foods, which include seafood, lean meat/poultry, eggs, beans and peas, soy products, and unsalted nuts and seeds.
- Increase seafood consumed by choosing seafood in place of some meat and poultry.
- Replace protein foods that are higher in solid fats with choices that are lower in solid fats and calories and/or are sources of oils.
- Use oils to replace solid fats where possible.
- Choose foods that provide more potassium, dietary fiber, calcium, and vitamin D, which are nutrients of concern in American diets. These foods include vegetables, fruits, whole grains, and milk and milk products.

Building Healthy Eating Patterns

- Select an eating pattern that meets nutrient needs over time at an appropriate calorie level.
- Account for all foods and beverages consumed and assess how they fit within a total healthy eating pattern.
- Follow food safety recommendations when preparing and eating foods to reduce the risk of foodborne illnesses.

Website: www.health.gov/dietaryguidelines/

Dietary Requirements

The Food and Nutrition Board of the National Academy of Sciences' Institute of Medicine, in reports published between 1997 and 2005, established **Dietary Reference Intakes (DRIs)**. DRIs establish daily consumption values for vitamins and elements (often called minerals) that aim to optimize health, not just guard against nutritional deficiencies, at all stages of life.

There are four DRI categories. The **Recommended Dietary Allowance (RDA)** gives intake values that meet the nutrient requirements of almost all (97%-98%) healthy individuals in a specified group. The **Estimated Average Requirement (EAR)** specifies the average daily nutrient intake level

estimated to meet the requirement of half the healthy individuals in a specified group. **Adequate Intake (AI)** values are given when there's inadequate scientific evidence to calculate an RDA. For healthy breastfed infants, the AI is the mean intake; for other life stage groups, the AI is thought to cover the needs of all group individuals, but lack of data or uncertainty in the data prevents the percentage of individuals covered from being specified with confidence. The **Tolerable Upper Intake Level (UL)** designates the maximum intake amount that is unlikely to pose a risk of adverse health effects in almost all healthy individuals in a group. RDAs and AIs may both be used as individual intake goals.

Estimated Calorie Requirements

Source: *Dietary Guidelines for Americans, 2010*, U.S. Dept. of Agriculture; U.S. Dept. of Health and Human Services
Estimated amount of calories, rounded to the nearest 200, needed to maintain energy balance by sex, for various age groups and levels of physical activity.

	Age (years)	Sedentary[1]	Moderately active[2]	Active[3]		Age (years)	Sedentary[1]	Moderately active[2]	Active[3]
Child	2-3	1,000-1,200	1,000-1,400	1,000-1,400					
Female[4]	4-8	1,200-1,400	1,400-1,600	1,400-1,800	Male	4-8	1,200-1,400	1,400-1,600	1,600-2,000
	9-13	1,400-1,600	1,600-2,000	1,800-2,200		9-13	1,600-2,000	1,800-2,200	2,000-2,600
	14-18	1,800	2,000	2,400		14-18	2,000-2,400	2,400-2,800	2,800-3,200
	19-30	1,800-2,000	2,000-2,200	2,400		19-30	2,400-2,600	2,600-2,800	3,000
	31-50	1,800	2,000	2,200		31-50	2,200-2,400	2,400-2,600	2,800-3,000
	51+	1,600	1,800	2,000-2,200		51+	2,000-2,200	2,200-2,400	2,400-2,800

Note: Based on Estimated Energy Requirements (EER) equations, using reference heights (average) and reference weights (healthy) for each age/gender group. For children and adolescents, reference height and weight vary. For adults, the reference man is 5 ft 10 in. tall and weighs 154 lbs. The reference woman is 5 ft 4 in. tall and weighs 126 lbs. (1) Engaging only in the light activities associated with ordinary day-to-day life. (2) Includes physical activity equivalent to walking 1.5 to 3 miles per day at 3-4 mph. (3) Includes physical activity equivalent to walking more than 3 miles per day at 3-4 mph. (4) Excludes women who are pregnant or breastfeeding.

Understanding Food Components

Protein

Proteins, composed of amino acids, are essential to good nutrition. They build, maintain, and repair the body. Best sources: eggs, milk, fish, meat, poultry, soybeans, nuts. High-quality proteins such as eggs, meat, or fish supply all eight amino acids needed in a diet. Plant-sourced foods can be combined to meet protein needs as well.

Fats

Fats provide energy by furnishing calories to the body. They also help the body absorb vitamins A, D, E, and K. Best sources of polyunsaturated and monounsaturated fats: vegetable/plant oils, nuts. Concentrated sources of saturated fats: meats, cheeses, butter, cream, egg yolks, lard.

Carbohydrates

Carbohydrates are the most important source of energy for the body. The digestive system changes carbohydrates into glucose, which the body uses for energy for cells, tissues, and organs. The body stores extra sugar in the liver and muscles. Best sources: grains, legumes, potatoes, vegetables, fruits.

Fiber

The portion of plant foods that our bodies cannot digest is known as fiber. There are two basic types: insoluble and soluble. Insoluble fibers help move food materials through the digestive tract; soluble fibers tend to slow them down. Both types absorb water, thus preventing and treating constipation. Soluble fibers may also be helpful in reducing blood cholesterol levels. Best sources: beans, bran, fruits, whole grains, vegetables.

Water

Water dissolves and transports other nutrients throughout the body, aiding in the processes of digestion, absorption, circulation, and excretion. It helps regulate body temperature.

Vitamins

Vitamin A—promotes good eyesight; helps keep skin and mucous membranes resistant to infection. Best sources: liver, sweet potatoes, carrots, kale, cantaloupe, turnip greens, collard greens, broccoli, fortified milk.

Vitamin B_1 (thiamine)—prevents beriberi. Essential to carbohydrate metabolism and nervous system health. Best sources: eggs, enriched bread and flour, nuts, seeds, organ meats, whole grains.

Vitamin B_2 (riboflavin)—protects the skin, mouth, eyes, and mucous membranes. Essential to growth, red blood cell production, and energy metabolism. Best sources: dairy products, meat, poultry, broccoli, spinach, eggs, nuts.

Vitamin B_6 (pyridoxine)—important in the regulation of the central nervous system and in protein metabolism. Best sources: whole grains, meat, fish, nuts, avocado, bananas.

Vitamin B_{12} (cobalamin)—needed to form red blood cells. Best sources: meat, shellfish, poultry, eggs, dairy products.

Niacin—maintains health of skin, nerves, and the digestive system. Best sources: poultry, nuts, fish, eggs.

Folic acid (folacin)—required for new cell formation, growth, and reproduction and for important chemical reactions in body cells. Best sources: leafy green vegetables, fruits, dried beans, peas, nuts, enriched bread, cereals.

Other B vitamins—biotin, pantothenic acid.

Vitamin C (ascorbic acid)—maintains collagen, a protein necessary for the formation of skin, ligaments, and bones. Helps heal wounds and mend fractures. Best sources: citrus fruits and juices, cantaloupe, broccoli, Brussels sprouts, potatoes and sweet potatoes, tomatoes, cabbage.

Vitamin D—important for bone development. Best sources: sunlight, milk products, tuna, salmon, oysters.

Vitamin E (tocopherol)—helps protect red blood cells. Best sources: vegetable oils, wheat germ, whole grains, eggs, peanuts, margarine, green leafy vegetables.

Vitamin K—necessary for formation of prothrombin, which helps blood to clot. Also made by intestinal bacteria. Best dietary sources: green leafy vegetables, tomatoes.

Minerals

Calcium—works with phosphorus to build and maintain bones and teeth. Best sources: dairy, leafy green vegetables.

Phosphorus—main function is in the formation of bones and teeth; performs more functions than any other mineral and plays a part in nearly every chemical reaction in the body. Best sources: cheese, milk, meats, poultry, fish, tofu.

Iron—necessary for the formation of myoglobin, a reservoir of oxygen for muscle tissue, and hemoglobin, which transports oxygen within blood. Best sources: lean meats, beans, green leafy vegetables, shellfish, whole grains.

Other minerals—chloride, chromium, cobalt, copper, fluoride, iodine, magnesium, manganese, molybdenum, potassium, selenium, sodium, sulfur, zinc.

Understanding Food Label Claims

Source: Center for Food Safety and Applied Nutrition, Food and Drug Admin., U.S. Dept. of Health and Human Services

Manufacturers can make certain claims on processed food labels only if they meet the definitions specified here.

Sugar

Sugar free: less than 0.5 g per serving

No added sugars; Without added sugars: no sugars or sugar-containing ingredients added during processing; must state if food is not "low calorie" or "reduced calorie"

Unsweetened; No added sweeteners: remain as factual statements

Reduced sugar: at least 25% less sugar than reference food

Fat

Fat free: less than 0.5 g of fat per serving

Saturated fat free: less than 0.5 g of saturated fat and less than 0.5 g of trans fatty acids per serving

Low fat: 3 g or less per serving and, if the serving is 30 g or less or 2 tbs or less, per 50 g of the food

Low saturated fat: 1 g or less per serving and not more than 15% of calories from saturated fat

Reduced fat; Less fat: at least 25% less per serving than reference food

Fiber

High fiber: 5 g or more per serving (must also meet low-fat definition or state level of total fat)

Good source of fiber: 2.5 g to 4.9 g per serving

More fiber; Added fiber: at least 2.5 g more per serving than reference food

Sodium

Sodium free: less than 5 mg per serving

Low sodium: 140 mg or less per serving and, if the serving is 30 g or less or 2 tbs or less, per 50 g of the food

Very low sodium: 35 mg or less per serving and, if the serving is 30 g or less or 2 tbs or less, per 50 g of the food

Reduced sodium; Less sodium: at least 25% less per serving than reference food

Calories

Calorie free: less than 5 calories per serving

Low calorie: 40 calories or less per serving; if the serving is 30 g or less or 2 tbs or less, 40 calories or less per 50 g of food

Reduced calories; Fewer calories: at least 25% less calories than reference food

Cholesterol

Cholesterol free: less than 2 mg of cholesterol and 2 g or less of saturated fat per serving

Low cholesterol: 20 mg or less and 2 g or less of saturated fat per serving and, if the serving is 30 g or less or 2 tbs or less, per 50 g of the food

Reduced cholesterol; Less cholesterol: at least 25% less than reference food

Other Food Label Claims

Source: Food Safety and Inspection Service, Agricultural Marketing Service, U.S. Dept. of Agriculture

The FDA allows food producers and marketers to use language on their packaging that advertises the health benefits and production methods of their products. Products marked *certified* have been formally evaluated for class, grade, or other quality characteristics by the U.S. Dept. of Agriculture's (USDA) Food Safety and Inspection Service. Below are some common packaging terms and their meanings.

Organic: Produced by farmers who use environmentally friendly methods to raise their crops or animals. Before a product can be labeled organic, the farm where the food is grown must pass a special inspection by a USDA official. Organic foods must be produced without conventional pesticides; fertilizers made with synthetic ingredients or sewage sludge; bioengineering; or ionizing radiation.

The official *USDA organic* label may appear on vegetables, fruit, packages of meat, cartons of milk, eggs, cheese, and other single-ingredient foods. Foods with more than one ingredient can place the official seal on their packaging if at least 95% of the ingredients are organic. Products with at least 70% organic ingredients may advertise prominently on the front of the package that the item contains organic ingredients. Products with less than 70% organic ingredients may not make any organic claims on the front of the package but may list organic ingredients on the side panel. Foods that contain 100% organic ingredients may advertise that fact on the front of the packaging along with the organic seal.

Natural: A minimally processed product that does not contain any artificial ingredient or added color. The label must explain the specific use of the term *natural* with regard to the product, such as "no added colorings," "no artificial ingredients," or "minimally processed."

Free range or **free roaming:** Producers must demonstrate to the USDA that the poultry has been allowed access to the outside. There are no specifications on the quality or size of outdoor range or on duration of access.

Fresh poultry: Whole poultry and cuts that have never been below 26°F.

Frozen poultry: Temperature of raw, frozen poultry is 0°F or below.

Gluten free: Products with a gluten limit of 20 parts per million.

Halal and **Zabiah Halal:** Produced in federally inspected meat packing plants and handled in accordance with Islamic law and under Islamic authority.

Kosher: Meat and poultry products prepared under Rabbinical supervision.

No hormones administered: Hormones are not approved for use in the raising of hogs, poultry, and veal calves, so those products may not make this claim. If sufficient documentation is provided to the USDA, this term may appear on packages of beef.

No antibiotics added: Claim may be made on a package (red meat and poultry) if sufficient documentation is provided to the USDA showing that the animals were raised without antibiotics.

Recommended Levels for Elements (Minerals)

Source: Food and Nutrition Board, Institute of Medicine, National Academy of Sciences, 2010

(in milligrams per day (mg/d) or micrograms per day (μg/d); asterisk denotes level defined as "adequate intake" (AI))

Life stage group		Calcium (mg/d)	Chromium (μg/d)	Copper (μg/d)	Fluoride (mg/d)	Iodine (μg/d)	Iron (mg/d)	Magnesium (mg/d)	Manganese (mg/d)	Molybdenum (μg/d)	Phosphorus (mg/d)	Selenium (μg/d)	Zinc (mg/d)
Infants	0-6 mos.	200*	0.2*	200*	0.01*	110*	0.27*	30*	0.003*	2*	100*	15*	2*
	6-12 mos.	260*	5.5*	220*	0.5*	130*	11	75*	0.6*	3*	275*	20*	3
Children	1-3 yrs.	700	11*	340	0.7*	90	7	80	1.2*	17	460	20	3
	4-8 yrs.	1,000	15*	440	1*	90	10	130	1.5*	22	500	30	5
Males	9-13 yrs.	1,300	25*	700	2*	120	8	240	1.9*	34	1,250	40	8
	14-18 yrs.	1,300	35*	890	3*	150	11	410	2.2*	43	1,250	55	11
	19-30 yrs.	1,000	35*	900	4*	150	8	400	2.3*	45	700	55	11
	31-50 yrs.	1,000	35*	900	4*	150	8	420	2.3*	45	700	55	11
	51-70 yrs.	1,000	30*	900	4*	150	8	420	2.3*	45	700	55	11
	over 70 yrs.	1,200	30*	900	4*	150	8	420	2.3*	45	700	55	11
Females	9-13 yrs.	1,300	21*	700	2*	120	8	240	1.6*	34	1,250	40	8
	14-18 yrs.	1,300	24*	890	3*	150	15	360	1.6*	43	1,250	55	9
	19-30 yrs.	1,000	25*	900	3*	150	18	310	1.8*	45	700	55	8
	31-50 yrs.	1,000	25*	900	3*	150	18	320	1.8*	45	700	55	8
	51-70 yrs.	1,200	20*	900	3*	150	8	320	1.8*	45	700	55	8
	over 70 yrs.	1,200	20*	900	3*	150	8	320	1.8*	45	700	55	8
Pregnancy	14-18 yrs.	1,300	29*	1,000	3*	220	27	400	2.0*	50	1,250	60	12
	19-30 yrs.	1,000	30*	1,000	3*	220	27	350	2.0*	50	700	60	11
	31-50 yrs.	1,000	30*	1,000	3*	220	27	360	2.0*	50	700	60	11
Lactation	14-18 yrs.	1,300	44*	1,300	3*	290	10	360	2.6*	50	1,250	70	13
	19-30 yrs.	1,000	45*	1,300	3*	290	9	310	2.6*	50	700	70	12
	31-50 yrs.	1,000	45*	1,300	3*	290	9	320	2.6*	50	700	70	12

Note: For healthy breastfed infants, the AI is the mean intake. The AI for other life stage and gender groups is believed to cover needs of all healthy individuals in the group, but lack of data or uncertainty in the data prevent being able to specify with confidence the percentage of individuals covered by this intake.

Recommended Levels for Vitamins

Source: Food and Nutrition Board, Institute of Medicine, National Academy of Sciences, 2010

(in milligrams per day (mg/d) or micrograms per day (µg/d); asterisk denotes level defined as "adequate intake" (AI))

Life stage group		Vitamin A (µg/d)	Vitamin C (mg/d)	Vitamin D (µg/d)	Vitamin E (mg/d)	Vitamin K (µg/d)	Thiamin (mg/d)	Riboflavin (mg/d)	Niacin (mg/d)	Vitamin B_6 (mg/d)	Folate (µg/d)	Vitamin B_{12} (µg/d)	Pantothenic acid (mg/d)	Biotin (µg/d)	Choline (mg/d)
Infants	0-6 mos.	400*	40*	10	4*	2.0*	0.2*	0.3*	2*	0.1*	65*	0.4*	1.7*	5*	125*
	6-12 mos.	500*	50*	10	5*	2.5*	0.3*	0.4*	4*	0.3*	80*	0.5*	1.8*	6*	150*
Children	1-3 yrs.	300	15	15	6	30*	0.5	0.5	6	0.5	150	0.9	2*	8*	200*
	4-8 yrs.	400	25	15	7	55*	0.6	0.6	8	0.6	200	1.2	3*	12*	250*
Males	9-13 yrs.	600	45	15	11	60*	0.9	0.9	12	1.0	300	1.8	4*	20*	375*
	14-18 yrs.	900	75	15	15	75*	1.2	1.3	16	1.3	400	2.4	5*	25*	550*
	19-30 yrs.	900	90	15	15	120*	1.2	1.3	16	1.3	400	2.4	5*	30*	550*
	31-50 yrs.	900	90	15	15	120*	1.2	1.3	16	1.3	400	2.4	5*	30*	550*
	51-70 yrs.	900	90	15	15	120*	1.2	1.3	16	1.7	400	2.4	5*	30*	550*
	over 70 yrs.	900	90	20	15	120*	1.2	1.3	16	1.7	400	2.4	5*	30*	550*
Females	9-13 yrs.	600	45	15	11	60*	0.9	0.9	12	1.0	300	1.8	4*	20*	375*
	14-18 yrs.	700	65	15	15	75*	1.0	1.0	14	1.2	400	2.4	5*	25*	400*
	19-30 yrs.	700	75	15	15	90*	1.1	1.1	14	1.3	400	2.4	5*	30*	425*
	31-50 yrs.	700	75	15	15	90*	1.1	1.1	14	1.3	400	2.4	5*	30*	425*
	51-70 yrs.	700	75	15	15	90*	1.1	1.1	14	1.5	400	2.4	5*	30*	425*
	over 70 yrs.	700	75	20	15	90*	1.1	1.1	14	1.5	400	2.4	5*	30*	425*
Pregnancy	14-18 yrs.	750	80	15	15	75*	1.4	1.4	18	1.9	600	2.6	6*	30*	450*
	19-30 yrs.	770	85	15	15	90*	1.4	1.4	18	1.9	600	2.6	6*	30*	450*
	31-50 yrs.	770	85	15	15	90*	1.4	1.4	18	1.9	600	2.6	6*	30*	450*
Lactation	14-18 yrs.	1,200	115	15	19	75*	1.4	1.6	17	2.0	500	2.8	7*	35*	550*
	19-30 yrs.	1,300	120	15	19	90*	1.4	1.6	17	2.0	500	2.8	7*	35*	550*
	31-50 yrs.	1,300	120	15	19	90*	1.4	1.6	17	2.0	500	2.8	7*	35*	550*

Note: For healthy breastfed infants, the AI is the mean intake. The AI for other life stage and gender groups is believed to cover the needs of all healthy individuals in the group, but lack of data or uncertainty in the data prevent being able to specify with confidence the percentage of individuals covered by this intake.

Top 10 Calorie Sources in American Diets

Source: *Dietary Guidelines for Americans, 2010*, U.S. Dept. of Agriculture

Rank	All Americans (ages 2+)	Children and adolescents (ages 2-18)	All adults (ages 19+)
1.	Grain-based desserts	Grain-based desserts	Grain-based desserts
2.	Yeast breads	Pizza	Yeast breads
3.	Chicken dishes	Soda/energy/sports drinks	Chicken dishes
4.	Soda/energy/sports drinks	Yeast breads	Soda/energy/sports drinks
5.	Pizza	Chicken dishes	Alcoholic beverages
6.	Alcoholic beverages	Pasta dishes	Pizza
7.	Pasta dishes	Reduced-fat milk	Tortillas, burritos, tacos
8.	Tortillas, burritos, tacos	Dairy desserts	Pasta dishes
9.	Beef dishes	Potato/corn/other chips	Beef dishes
10.	Dairy desserts	Ready-to-eat cereals	Dairy desserts

Note: Data are drawn from analyses of usual dietary intakes conducted by the Natl. Cancer Institute. Foods and beverages consumed were divided into 97 categories and ranked according to calorie contribution to the diet. Average total daily calorie intake was 2,157 overall, 2,027 for children and adolescents (ages 2-18), and 2,199 for adults ages 19+.

Weight Guidelines for Adults

Source: *Dietary Guidelines for Americans, 2010*, U.S. Dept. of Agriculture; National Center for Health Statistics, CDC

Guidelines on identification, evaluation, and treatment of overweight and obesity in adults were released in June 1998 by the National Heart, Lung, and Blood Institute (NHLBI), in cooperation with the National Institute of Diabetes and Digestive and Kidney Diseases (NIDDK). The guidelines, based on research into risk factors contributing to heart disease, stroke, and other conditions, define overweight and obesity in terms of **body mass index (BMI)**. BMI is based on a person's weight and height and is strongly correlated with total body fat content. A BMI of 25-29 is said to indicate **overweight**; a BMI of 30 or higher indicates **obesity**. Weight reduction is advised for persons with a BMI of 25 or higher. Factors such as a large waist circumference, high blood pressure or cholesterol, and family medical history may increase a person's risk of developing an obesity-related disease.

The National Center for Health Statistics notes that in 2009-10, 35.7% of American adults were obese. Over the past three decades, childhood obesity rates in America have almost tripled, and in 2009-10, 16.9% of children (ages 2-19) were obese. Based on directly measured weight and height, between 1988-94 and 2009-10, the proportion of adults ages 20 years and over who were obese rose by 55.9%, from 22.9%. During the same period, obesity increased by 59.3% in children ages 6-11, from 11.3% to 18.0%, and by 75.2% in adolescents ages 12-19, from 10.5% to 18.4%.

A high prevalence of overweight and obesity is a public health concern because excess body fat has been associated with type 2 diabetes, hypertension, dyslipidemia, cardiovascular disease, stroke, gall bladder disease, respiratory dysfunction, gout, osteoarthritis, and certain kinds of cancers.

Body Mass Index (BMI) by Height and Weight

Weight (lbs)

Height	HEALTHY						OVERWEIGHT					OBESE									
4'10"	91	96	100	105	110	115	119	124	129	134	138	143	148	153	158	162	167	172	177	181	186
4'11"	94	99	104	109	114	119	124	128	133	138	143	148	153	158	163	168	173	178	183	188	193
5'0"	97	102	107	112	118	123	128	133	138	143	148	153	158	163	168	174	179	184	189	194	199
5'1"	100	106	111	116	122	127	132	137	143	148	153	158	164	169	174	180	185	190	195	201	206
5'2"	104	109	115	120	126	131	136	142	147	153	158	164	169	175	180	186	191	196	202	207	213
5'3"	107	113	118	124	130	135	141	146	152	158	163	169	175	180	186	191	197	203	208	214	220
5'4"	110	116	122	128	134	140	145	151	157	163	169	174	180	186	192	197	204	209	215	221	227
5'5"	114	120	126	132	138	144	150	156	162	168	174	180	186	192	198	204	210	216	222	228	234
5'6"	118	124	130	136	142	148	155	161	167	173	179	186	192	198	204	210	216	223	229	235	241
5'7"	121	127	134	140	146	153	159	166	172	178	185	191	198	204	211	217	223	230	236	242	249
5'8"	125	131	138	144	151	158	164	171	177	184	190	197	203	210	216	223	230	236	243	249	256
5'9"	128	135	142	149	155	162	169	176	182	189	196	203	209	216	223	230	236	243	250	257	263
5'10"	132	139	146	153	160	167	174	181	188	195	202	209	216	222	229	236	243	250	257	264	271
5'11"	136	143	150	157	165	172	179	186	193	200	208	215	222	229	236	243	250	257	265	272	279
6'0"	140	147	154	162	169	177	184	191	199	206	213	221	228	235	242	250	258	265	272	279	287
6'1"	144	151	159	166	174	182	189	197	204	212	219	227	235	242	250	257	265	272	280	288	295
6'2"	148	155	163	171	179	186	194	202	210	218	225	233	241	249	256	264	272	280	287	295	303
6'3"	152	160	168	176	184	192	200	208	216	224	232	240	248	256	264	272	279	287	295	303	311
6'4"	156	164	172	180	189	197	205	213	221	230	238	246	254	263	271	279	287	295	304	312	320
BMI[1]	19	20	21	22	23	24	25	26	27	28	29	30	31	32	33	34	35	36	37	38	39

(1) The BMI numbers apply to both men and women. Some very muscular people may have a high BMI without health risks.

Calories Used During Physical Activity

Source: Center for Nutrition Policy and Promotion, U.S. Dept. of Agriculture

Amount of calories burned during physical activities are estimates for a man who is 5 ft 10 in. tall and weighs 154 lbs. The more an individual weighs, the more calories he or she will burn by exercising at the same intensity.

Moderate physical activities	In 1 hr.	In 30 min.	Vigorous physical activities	In 1 hr.	In 30 min.
Hiking............................	370	185	Running/jogging (5 miles per hour)	590	295
Light gardening/yard work	330	165	Bicycling (more than 10 miles per hour)	590	295
Dancing	330	165	Swimming (slow freestyle laps)	510	255
Golf (walking and carrying clubs)......	330	165	Aerobics	480	240
Bicycling (less than 10 miles per hour)..	290	145	Walking (4½ miles per hour)	460	230
Walking (3½ miles per hour)	280	140	Heavy yard work (e.g., chopping wood)	440	220
Weight training (general light workout)..	220	110	Weight lifting (vigorous effort).........	440	220
Stretching........................	180	90	Basketball (vigorous)	440	220

Obesity Among Adults in the U.S., 2009-10

Source: National Health and Nutrition Examination Survey, National Center for Health Statistics, CDC

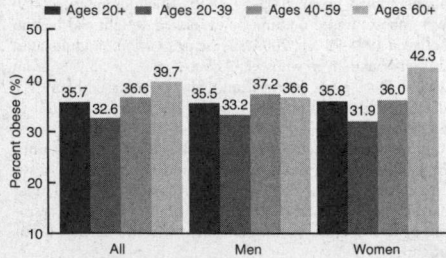

Obesity Among Children and Adolescents in the U.S., 2009-10

Source: National Health and Nutrition Examination Survey, National Center for Health Statistics, CDC

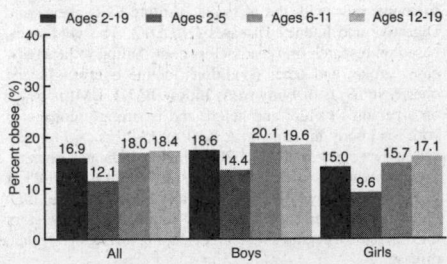

Basic First Aid

Source: Courtesy of the American National Red Cross, www.redcross.org. All rights reserved in all countries.

Note: This information is not intended to be a substitute for formal training. It is recommended that you contact your local American Red Cross chapter to sign up for a First Aid/CPR/AED (automated external defibrillator) course.

In an emergency, it is important to get medical assistance as soon as possible, but knowing what to do until a doctor or other trained person gets to the scene can save a life, especially in cases of severe bleeding, choking, poisoning, and shock.

People with special medical problems, such as diabetes, cardiovascular disease, epilepsy, or allergies, are urged to wear some sort of emblem identifying the problem as a safeguard against receiving medication that might be harmful or even fatal. Emblems may be obtained from Medic Alert Foundation, 2323 Colorado Ave., Turlock, CA 95382; (888) 633-4298; www.medicalert.org.

Animal bite: Call 9-1-1 or the local emergency number if the wound is bleeding seriously or if you suspect the animal might have rabies. Control any bleeding. Wash minor wounds with soap under running water and apply antibiotic ointment and a dressing. When possible, proper authorities should test the animal for rabies.

Asphyxiation: Call 9-1-1 or the local emergency number.

Bleeding: Use a barrier between your hand and the wound to help prevent infection. Cover wound with a sterile dressing. Apply direct pressure until bleeding stops. Cover compress with a bandage. Call 9-1-1 or the local emergency number if bleeding is severe.

Burn: Check for life-threatening conditions. If the burn is mild, with skin unbroken and no blisters, flush with cold running water for at least 20 minutes. Gently wash with soap and water and pat dry. Apply a thin layer of antibiotic ointment. Apply a loose, sterile dry dressing to prevent infection. If the burn is severe, call 9-1-1 or the local emergency number. Care for shock (see separate entry). Keep the person from getting chilled or overheated until advanced medical assistance arrives. Do not try to clean a severe burn or break blisters.

Chemical in eye: Call 9-1-1 or the local emergency number. Turn the person's head to the side so that the affected eye is lower than the unaffected eye. Flush the affected eye with large amounts of water for at least 20 minutes.

Choking: See **First Aid for Choking** below.

Convulsions (seizures): Remove nearby objects that might cause injury. Protect the person's head by placing a thin folded towel or item of clothing under it. Roll him or her on one side to drain fluids from the mouth. Do not place anything between the person's teeth. Stay with the person until he or she is fully conscious. If convulsions do not stop, get medical attention immediately.

Cut (minor): Use a clean barrier between your hand and the wound to prevent infection. Apply direct pressure for a few minutes to control any bleeding. Wash the wound thoroughly with soap and water and apply a thin layer of antibiotic ointment or a microthin film dressing. Cover the wound with a sterile dressing and a bandage.

Foreign object in eye: If an object is impaled in someone's eye, do not remove it. If not impaled, try to remove the object by having the person blink several times. If the object doesn't come out, gently flush the eye with saline solution or water. Do not rub the eye. If the object still doesn't come out, the person should receive professional medical attention.

Frostbite: Handle the frostbitten area gently. Do not rub. If there is no danger of the affected area refreezing, soak it in warm water (not warmer than 105°F). Do not allow the frostbitten area to touch the side of the water container. Keep the frostbitten part in the water until normal color returns and it feels warm. Loosely bandage the area with dry, sterile dressings. If fingers or toes are frostbitten, put cotton or gauze between them. Do not break any blisters. Call 9-1-1 or seek emergency help as soon as possible.

Heart attack and stroke: See **Heart and Blood Vessel Disease** earlier in chapter.

Heat stroke: Remove the person from the heat. Loosen any tight clothing. Immerse person in cold water until he or she becomes alert. If a large enough source of water is not available, drench the person with cold water and fan constantly. If the person is conscious, have him or her slowly drink some cool water. Call 9-1-1 if the person's condition does not improve.

Hypothermia: Call 9-1-1 or the local emergency number. For mild hypothermia, cover all exposed skin. Replace wet clothes with something dry. If the person is alert, give him or her simple carbohydrates to eat and warm, nonalcoholic and decaffeinated liquids to drink. Apply heat pads or other heat sources if available but do not place against bare skin.

Loss of limb: Call 9-1-1 or the local emergency number and care for any life-threatening conditions. If a limb is severed, it is important to properly protect the limb so that it can possibly be reattached. After the victim is cared for, the limb should be wrapped in sterile gauze and placed in a plastic bag. Place bag in a larger bag or container of an ice and water slurry, not ice alone. Be sure the limb is taken to the hospital with the person.

Poisoning: Care for any life-threatening conditions. Call the National Capital Poison Center (800-222-1222), 9-1-1, or the local emergency number and follow their directions. Do not give the person any food or drink or induce vomiting unless specified to do so by medical professionals.

Shock (injury-related): Monitor breathing and consciousness. Have the person lie down and keep him or her as comfortable as possible. Maintain an open airway. Give sips of cool water if he or she tolerates fluids. Elevate his or her legs about 12 inches unless you suspect injuries to the head or lower extremities. Maintain normal body temperature. If the weather is cold or damp, place blankets or extra clothing over and under the person; if the weather is hot, provide shade.

Snakebite: Call 9-1-1 or the local emergency number. Gently wash the injury. Splint bitten extremities, and keep the area at approximately the level of the heart. Keep the person calm. Do not cut, suck, apply a constricting band, or apply cold to a bite from a pit viper (such as a rattlesnake, copperhead, or cottonmouth). For a bite from an elapid snake, such as a coral snake, apply an elastic roller bandage after washing the wound.

Sprains and strains: Splint any injured bone or joint that the person cannot use.

Sting from bee or wasp: If possible, remove the stinger by scraping it away with your finger or a plastic card (like a credit card) or using tweezers. If you use tweezers, grasp the stinger, not the venom sac. Wash the area with soap and water. Cover it to keep it clean. Apply cold to the area. Call 9-1-1 or the local emergency number immediately if the wound does not stop swelling, the person collapses, or he or she is known to be allergic to the sting.

Unconsciousness: Call 9-1-1 or the local emergency number immediately. Do not move the person if a spinal injury is suspected.

First Aid for Choking

The recommended first aid for a conscious choking victim who is unable to speak, cough, or breathe is to deliver a series of five blows to the back and five thrusts to the abdomen. Have another person call 9-1-1 or the local emergency number. Obtain consent from the victim to treat him or her. Lean the victim forward and apply five blows to his or her back with the heel of your hand. Then stand or kneel behind the victim and wrap your arms around his or her waist. Make a fist with one hand and place the thumb side against the middle of the person's abdomen, just above the navel and well below the lower tip of the breastbone. Grasp your fist in your other hand and quickly thrust upwards into the abdomen five times. Continue back blows and abdominal thrusts until the object is dislodged, and the person can breathe or cough forcefully, or the person loses consciousness.

VITAL STATISTICS

Recent Trends in Vital Statistics

Source: National Center for Health Statistics (NCHS), U.S. Dept. of Health and Human Services

Births

An estimated 3,958,000 babies were born in the U.S. in 2012, a slight decrease from 3,961,000 in 2011. The birth rate decreased to 12.6 per 1,000 total population, a new record low.

The fertility rate (number of live births per 1,000 women aged 15-44 years) decreased to an estimated 63.2 for 2012, down from the 2011 rate of 63.4.

Deaths

The number of deaths during 2012 was estimated at 2,539,000 according to provisional data, up from 2,508,000 in 2011. The death rate in 2012 increased to 8.1 deaths per 1,000 population, up from 8.0 in 2011. The death rate for infants under 1 year of age was 5.9 deaths per 1,000 live births in 2012, a decrease from 6.0 in 2011.

Natural Increase

As a result of natural increase (the excess of births over deaths), an estimated 1,419,000 persons were added to the population in 2012.

Marriages

An estimated 2,118,000 marriages were performed in 2011, compared to 2,096,000 in 2010. The provisional marriage rate for 2011 (6.8 per 1,000 population) remained the same as in 2010.

Divorces

The divorce rate was 3.6 per 1,000 population in 2011, the same as in 2010, according to provisional data. However, the rate is incomplete because the NCHS does not include divorce data for California, Georgia, Hawaii, Indiana, Louisiana, and Minnesota.

Births and Deaths in the U.S., 1960-2012

Source: National Center for Health Statistics (NCHS), U.S. Dept. of Health and Human Services

Year	BIRTHS Total number	Rate	DEATHS Total number	Rate	Year	BIRTHS Total number	Rate	DEATHS Total number	Rate
1960	4,257,850	23.7	1,711,982	9.5	2001	4,025,933	14.1	2,416,425	8.5
1970	3,731,386	18.4	1,921,031	9.5	2002	4,021,726	13.9	2,443,387	8.5
1980	3,612,258	15.9	1,989,841	8.8	2003	4,089,950	14.1	2,448,288	8.4
1990	4,092,994	16.7	2,148,463	8.6	2004	4,112,052	14.0	2,397,615	8.2
1993	4,000,240	15.4	2,268,553	8.7	2005	4,138,349	14.0	2,448,017	8.3
1994	3,952,767	15.0	2,278,994	8.7	2006	4,265,555	14.2	2,426,264	8.1
1995	3,899,589	14.6	2,312,132	8.7	2007	4,316,233	14.3	2,423,712	8.0
1996	3,891,494	14.4	2,314,690	8.6	2008	4,247,604	14.0	2,471,984	8.1
1997	3,880,894	14.2	2,314,245	8.5	2009	4,130,665	13.5	2,437,163	7.9
1998	3,941,553	14.3	2,337,256	8.5	2010	3,999,386	13.0	2,468,435	8.0
1999	3,959,417	14.2	2,391,399	8.6	2011[1]	3,961,000	12.7	2,508,000	8.0
2000	4,058,814	14.4	2,403,351	8.5	2012[1]	3,958,000	12.6	2,539,000	8.1

Note: Statistics cover only events occurring within the U.S. and exclude fetal deaths. Rates per 1,000 population; enumerated as of Apr. 1 for decennial census years; estimated as of July 1 for all other years. Beginning 1970, statistics exclude births and deaths occurring among nonresidents of the U.S. (1) Provisional.

Marriage and Divorce Rates in the U.S., 1920-2011

Source: National Center for Health Statistics (NCHS), U.S. Dept. of Health and Human Services

(Divorce rates for 2005-11 were calculated excluding data and populations from the nonreporting states California, Georgia, Hawaii, Indiana, Louisiana, and Minnesota. Some data are provisional.)

The U.S. marriage rate dipped during the Depression and peaked sharply just after World War II; the trend after that has been more gradual. The divorce rate generally rose from the 1920s through 1981, when it peaked at 5.3 per 1,000 population, before declining somewhat. The graph below shows marriage and divorce rates since 1920.

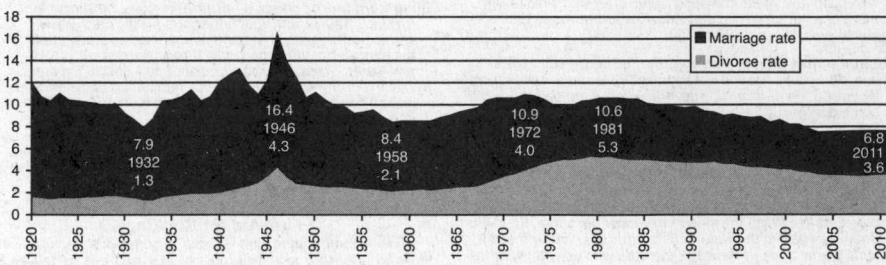

U.S. Median Age at First Marriage, 1890-2012

Source: U.S. Census Bureau, U.S. Dept. of Commerce

Year[1]	Men	Women	Year[1]	Men	Women	Year[1]	Men	Women	Year[1]	Men	Women	Year[1]	Men	Women
1890	26.1	22.0	1950	22.8	20.3	1985	25.5	23.3	2003	27.1	25.3	2008	27.6	25.9
1900	25.9	21.9	1960	22.8	20.3	1990	26.1	23.9	2004	27.4	25.3	2009	28.1	25.9
1910	25.1	21.6	1965	22.8	20.6	1995	26.9	24.5	2005	27.1	25.3	2010	28.2	26.1
1920	24.6	21.2	1970	23.2	20.8	2000	26.8	25.1	2006	27.5	25.5	2011	28.4	26.4
1930	24.3	21.3	1975	23.5	21.1	2001	26.9	25.1	2007	27.5	25.6	2012	28.6	26.6
1940	24.3	21.5	1980	24.7	22.0	2002	26.9	25.3						

(1) Figures after 1947 based on Current Population Survey data; earlier figures based on decennial censuses.

Divorce Rates by State, 2011

Source: National Center for Health Statistics (NCHS), U.S. Dept. of Health and Human Services

State	Divorce rate	State	Divorce rate	State	Divorce rate
Alabama	4.3	Louisiana	NA	Ohio	3.4
Alaska	4.8	Maine	4.2	Oklahoma	5.2
Arizona	3.9	Maryland	2.9	Oregon	3.8
Arkansas	5.3	Massachusetts	2.7	Pennsylvania	2.8
California	NA	Michigan	3.4	Rhode Island	3.2
Colorado	4.4	Minnesota	NA	South Carolina	3.2
Connecticut	3.1	Mississippi	4.0	South Dakota	3.3
Delaware	3.6	Missouri	3.9	Tennessee	4.3
District of Columbia	2.9	Montana	4.0	Texas	3.2
Florida	4.5	Nebraska	3.5	Utah	3.7
Georgia	NA	Nevada	5.6	Vermont	3.6
Hawaii	NA	New Hampshire	3.8	Virginia	3.8
Idaho	4.9	New Jersey	2.9	Washington	4.1
Illinois	2.6	New Mexico	3.3	West Virginia	5.2
Indiana	NA	New York	2.9	Wisconsin	2.9
Iowa	2.4	North Carolina	3.7	Wyoming	4.8
Kansas	3.9	North Dakota	2.7	**United States**	**3.6**
Kentucky	4.4				

NA = Not available. **Note:** Rate per 1,000 population. Rate includes annulments and may also include divorce petitions filed and legal separations for some counties and states.

Birth Rates and Fertility Rates by Age of Mother, 1950-2011

Source: National Center for Health Statistics (NCHS), U.S. Dept. of Health and Human Services

Live births per 1,000 women by age of mother

Year	Birth rate[1]	Fertility rate[2]	10-14 years	15-19 years	15-17 years	18-19 years	20-24 years	25-29 years	30-34 years	35-39 years	40-44 years	45-49 years
1950	24.1	106.2	1.0	81.6	40.7	132.7	196.6	166.1	103.7	52.9	15.1	1.2
1960	23.7	118.0	0.8	89.1	43.9	166.7	258.1	197.4	112.7	56.2	15.5	0.9
1970	18.4	87.9	1.2	68.3	38.8	114.7	167.8	145.1	73.3	31.7	8.1	0.5
1980	15.9	68.4	1.1	53.0	32.5	82.1	115.1	112.9	61.9	19.8	3.9	0.2
1990	16.7	70.9	1.4	59.9	37.5	88.6	116.5	120.2	80.8	31.7	5.5	0.2
1993	15.4	67.0	1.4	59.0	37.5	91.1	111.3	113.2	79.9	32.7	6.1	0.3
1994	15.0	65.9	1.4	58.2	37.2	90.2	109.2	111.0	80.4	33.4	6.4	0.3
1995	14.6	64.6	1.3	56.0	35.5	87.7	107.5	108.8	81.1	34.0	6.6	0.3
1996	14.4	64.1	1.2	53.5	33.3	84.7	107.8	108.6	82.1	34.9	6.8	0.3
1997	14.2	63.6	1.1	51.3	31.4	82.1	107.3	108.3	83.0	35.7	7.1	0.4
1998	14.3	64.3	1.0	50.3	29.9	80.9	108.4	110.2	85.2	36.9	7.4	0.4
1999	14.2	64.4	0.9	48.8	28.2	79.1	107.9	111.2	87.1	37.8	7.4	0.4
2000	14.4	65.9	0.9	47.7	26.9	78.1	109.7	113.5	91.2	39.7	8.0	0.5
2001	14.1	65.3	0.8	45.3	24.7	76.1	106.2	113.4	91.9	40.6	8.1	0.5
2002	13.9	64.8	0.7	43.0	23.2	72.8	103.6	113.6	91.5	41.4	8.3	0.5
2003	14.1	66.1	0.6	41.6	22.4	70.7	102.6	115.6	95.1	43.8	8.7	0.5
2004	14.0	66.3	0.7	41.1	22.1	70.0	101.7	115.5	95.3	45.4	8.9	0.5
2005	14.0	66.7	0.7	40.5	21.4	69.9	102.2	115.5	95.8	46.3	9.1	0.6
2006	14.2	68.5	0.6	41.9	22.0	73.0	105.9	116.7	97.7	47.3	9.4	0.6
2007	14.3	69.5	0.6	42.5	22.1	73.9	106.3	117.5	99.9	47.5	9.5	0.6
2008	14.0	68.6	0.6	41.5	21.7	70.6	103.0	115.1	99.3	46.9	9.8	0.7
2009	13.5	66.2	0.5	37.9	19.6	64.0	96.2	111.5	97.5	46.1	10.0	0.7[4]
2010	13.0	64.1	0.4	34.2	17.3	58.2	90.0	108.3	96.5	45.9	10.2	0.7[4]
2011[3]	12.7	63.2	0.4	31.3	15.4	54.1	85.3	107.2	96.5	47.2	10.3	0.7[4]

(1) Live births per 1,000 population. (2) Live births per 1,000 women 15-44 years of age. (3) Preliminary. (4) Women 45-54 years of age.

Cesarean Delivery Rates by State, 1990-2010

Source: National Center for Health Statistics (NCHS), U.S. Dept. of Health and Human Services

State	1990	2000	2010	Percent change, 1990-2010	State	1990	2000	2010	Percent change, 1990-2010
Alabama	25.9%	26.3%	35.3%	36.3%	Missouri	22.8%	22.3%	31.9%	39.9%
Alaska	15.1	17.0	21.5	42.4	Montana	20.5	19.0	30.3	47.8
Arizona	18.3	18.6	27.0	47.5	Nebraska	19.1	22.5	31.1	62.8
Arkansas	27.6	26.3	34.8	26.1	Nevada	19.6	21.7	34.8	77.6
California	22.3	23.4	33.0	48.0	New Hampshire	21.8	21.0	30.4	39.4
Colorado	17.0	18.3	25.9	52.4	New Jersey	24.7	27.3	38.4	55.5
Connecticut	17.4	21.6	35.1	101.7	New Mexico	18.3	17.1	22.8	24.6
Delaware	24.9	24.8	33.9	36.1	New York	23.1	24.6	34.5	49.4
District of Columbia	25.9	22.6	33.0	27.4	North Carolina	22.7	23.0	30.8	35.7
Florida	25.2	24.9	37.8	50.0	North Dakota	19.3	20.6	27.7	43.5
Georgia	22.5	22.5	33.8	50.2	Ohio	23.7	20.0	30.7	29.5
Hawaii	20.2	14.6	27.2	34.7	Oklahoma	0.9	21.0	34.7	3,755.6
Idaho	18.8	18.3	24.8	31.9	Oregon	19.0	19.4	29.4	54.7
Illinois	22.2	20.9	31.1	40.1	Pennsylvania	22.2	21.7	31.3	41.0
Indiana	21.3	21.5	30.3	42.3	Rhode Island	18.4	21.9	33.0	79.3
Iowa	20.6	20.8	30.3	47.1	South Carolina	22.4	25.2	35.0	56.3
Kansas	23.1	22.2	30.5	32.0	South Dakota	19.6	22.8	26.6	35.7
Kentucky	23.7	23.6	35.4	49.4	Tennessee	24.3	24.8	34.2	40.7
Louisiana	27.0	26.6	39.6	46.7	Texas	22.3	24.7	35.1	57.4
Maine	21.2	22.8	29.8	40.6	Utah	17.7	16.8	23.1	30.5
Maryland	21.1	24.1	34.5	63.5	Vermont	19.3	17.3	27.5	42.5
Massachusetts	22.2	23.3	33.0	48.6	Virginia	23.4	23.1	34.3	46.6
Michigan	21.8	21.9	32.6	49.5	Washington	17.8	20.6	29.5	65.7
Minnesota	17.5	19.4	27.1	54.9	West Virginia	26.7	25.4	36.0	34.8
Mississippi	26.6	28.2	37.0	39.1	Wisconsin	17.6	17.5	26.0	47.7
					Wyoming	19.8	19.4	27.9	40.9
					United States	**22.0**	**22.8**	**32.7**	**48.6**

Note: The cesarean rate is the percentage of all live births by cesarean delivery.

Assisted Reproductive Technology (ART) Pregnancy Success Rates, 2010

Source: Centers for Disease Control and Prevention (CDC), U.S. Dept. of Health and Human Services

Type of cycle	Under 35	35-37	Age of woman[1] 38-40	41-42	43-44
			Number		
Fresh embryos from nondonor eggs	41,741	21,366	21,739	10,120	4,501
Average number of embryos transferred	2.0	2.2	2.6	3.0	3.2
Frozen embryos from nondonor eggs	12,631	6,195	4,682	1,591	710
Average number of embryos transferred	2.0	1.9	2.1	2.2	2.2
Fresh embryos from nondonor eggs			**Percent distribution**		
Cycles resulting in pregnancies	47.6%	38.8%	29.9%	19.9%	10.6%
Cycles resulting in live births[2]	41.5	31.9	22.1	12.4	5.0
Retrievals resulting in live births[2]	44.4	35.4	25.3	14.8	6.3
Transfers resulting in live births[2]	47.6	38.3	28.1	16.7	7.4
Transfers resulting in singleton live births	31.4	27.3	21.5	13.7	6.6
Pregnancies with twins	32.9	27.3	21.6	15.0	8.1
Pregnancies with triplets or more.	2.6	3.1	3.7	3.0	0.6
Live births having multiple infants[2]	34.0	28.7	23.3	18.0	10.2
Cancellations	6.6	9.9	12.8	16.4	20.6
Frozen embryos from nondonor eggs					
Transfers resulting in live births[2]	38.4%	34.7%	28.4%	21.5%	16.8%

Donor eggs (all ages)	Fresh embryos[3]	Frozen embryos[3]
Number of transfers	9,866	6,665
Average number of embryos transferred	2.0	2.0
Percentage of transfers resulting in live births[2]	55.8%	34.9%

Note: Data are preliminary. 443 ART clinics in the U.S. submitted data in 2010. A total of 154,417 cycles were reported. There were 47,102 live-birth deliveries and 61,561 infants born resulting from ART cycles in 2010. (1) Clinic-specific outcome rates are unreliable for women older than 44 undergoing ART cycles using fresh or frozen embryos with nondonor eggs. (2) A multiple-infant birth is counted as one live birth. (3) Data for women of all ages (including ages over 44) are reported together because previous data show that patient age does not materially affect success with donor eggs.

Numbers of Multiple Births in the U.S., 1990-2010

Source: National Center for Health Statistics (NCHS), U.S. Dept. of Health and Human Services

The general upward trend in multiple births reflects greater numbers of births to older women and increased use of fertility drugs.

Year	Twins	Triplets	Quadruplets	Quintuplets[1]	Year	Twins	Triplets	Quadruplets	Quintuplets[1]
1990	93,865	2,830	185	13	2003	128,665	7,110	468	85
1995	96,736	4,551	365	57	2004	132,219	6,750	439	86
1997	104,137	6,148	510	79	2005	133,122	6,208	418	68
1998	110,670	6,919	627	79	2006	137,085	6,118	355	67
1999	114,307	6,742	512	67	2007	138,961	5,967	369	91
2000	118,916	6,742	506	77	2008	138,660	5,877	345	46
2001	121,246	6,885	501	85	2009	137,217	5,905	355	80
2002	125,134	6,898	434	69	2010	132,562	5,153	313	37

(1) Quintuplets and other multiple births of five or more.

Origin Countries for U.S. Foreign Adoptions, 2000-12

Source: Office of Immigration Statistics, U.S. Dept. of Homeland Security
(ranked by 2012 adoptions)

Country	2012	2011	2010	2009	2008	2007	2006	2005	2002	2001	2000
China	2,697	2,589	3,401	2,990	3,852	5,453	6,493	7,906	6,119	4,681	5,053
Ethiopia	1,568	1,727	2,513	2,221	1,666	1,255	732	441	105	158	95
Russia	748	970	1,082	1,580	1,859	2,310	3,706	4,639	4,939	4,279	4,269
South Korea	627	736	863	1,106	1,038	939	1,376	1,630	1,779	1,870	1,794
Ukraine	395	632	445	605	487	606	460	821	1,106	1,246	659
Congo, Dem. Rep. of the	240	133	41	21	9	10	4	11	0	6	1
Uganda	238	207	62	69	55	54	12	17	18	3	1
Nigeria	197	149	189	109	148	33	62	65	45	33	4
Colombia	195	216	235	237	308	310	344	291	334	407	246
Taiwan	177	205	285	254	262	184	187	141	41	44	24
Total[1]	**8,668**	**9,320**	**11,059**	**12,782**	**17,229**	**19,741**	**20,705**	**22,710**	**20,100**	**19,087**	**18,120**

(1) Includes countries not shown.

Leading Causes of Infant Death in the U.S., 2011

Source: National Center for Health Statistics (NCHS), U.S. Dept. of Health and Human Services

Cause	Number	Percent of total deaths	Mortality rate[1]
Congenital malformations, deformations, and chromosomal abnormalities	4,984	20.8%	126.1
Disorders related to short gestation and low birth weight, not elsewhere classified	4,116	17.2	104.1
Sudden infant death syndrome	1,711	7.2	43.3
Newborn affected by maternal complications of pregnancy	1,578	6.6	39.9
Accidents (unintentional injuries)	1,089	4.6	27.5
Newborn affected by complications of placenta, cord, and membranes	992	4.1	25.1
Bacterial sepsis[2] of newborn	526	2.2	13.3
Respiratory distress of newborn	514	2.1	13.0
Diseases of the circulatory system	496	2.1	12.5
Neonatal hemorrhage	444	1.9	11.2
All other causes	7,457	31.2	188.6
All causes	**23,907**	**100.0**	**604.7**

(1) Infant deaths during the first year of life per 100,000 live births. (2) Toxic condition resulting from the spread of bacteria.

Nonmarital Childbearing in the U.S., 1970-2010

Source: National Center for Health Statistics (NCHS), U.S. Dept. of Health and Human Services

	1970	1975	1980	1985	1990	1995	2000	2005	2007	2008	2009	2010
Births to unmarried mothers (thous.) . . .	399	448	666	828	1,165	1,254	1,347	1,527	1,715	1,727	1,694	1,633
Race/Hispanic origin of mother					*Percent of live births to unmarried mothers*							
All races and origins.	10.7%	14.3%	18.4%	22.0%	28.0%	32.2%	33.2%	36.9%	39.7%	40.6%	41.0%	40.8%
White	5.5	7.1	11.2	14.7	20.4	25.3	27.1	31.7	34.8	35.7	36.0	35.9
Black	37.5	49.5	56.1	61.2	66.5	69.9	68.5	69.3	71.2	71.8	72.3	72.1
American Indian or Alaska Native	22.4	32.7	39.2	46.8	53.6	57.2	58.4	63.5	65.3	65.8	65.4	65.6
Asian or Pacific Islander	—	—	7.3	9.5	13.2	16.3	14.8	16.2	16.6	16.9	17.2	17.0
Hispanic origin (selected states)[1,2]	—	—	23.6	29.5	36.7	40.8	42.7	48.0	51.3	52.6	53.2	53.4
Maternal age					*Percent distribution of live births to unmarried mothers*							
Under 20 years	50.1%	52.1%	40.8%	33.8%	30.9%	30.9%	28.0%	23.1%	22.5%	22.2%	21.4%	20.1%
20-24 years.	31.8	29.9	35.6	36.3	34.7	34.5	37.4	38.3	37.6	37.1	36.9	36.8
25 years and over.	18.1	18.0	23.5	29.9	34.4	34.7	34.6	38.6	39.9	40.7	41.7	43.1
Race/Hispanic origin of mother					*Live births per 1,000 unmarried women 15-44 years of age[3]*							
All races and origins.	26.4	24.5	29.4	32.8	43.8	44.3	44.0	47.5	52.3	52.5	50.5	47.6
White[4]	13.9	12.4	18.1	22.5	32.9	37.0	38.2	43.0	48.1	48.2	46.3	44.5
Black[4]	95.5	84.2	81.1	77.0	90.5	74.5	70.5	67.8	72.6	72.5	69.9	65.3
Hispanic origin (selected states)[1,2]	—	—	—	—	89.6	88.7	87.2	100.3	108.4	105.1	96.8	80.6

— = Not available. (1) Hispanic origin data prior to 1995 is not directly comparable to data for more recent years due to differences in reporting area. (2) Hispanics may be of any race. (3) Rates computed by relating births to unmarried mothers, regardless of mother's age, to unmarried women 15-44 years of age. (4) For 1970 and 1975, birth rates are by race of child.

Number, Ratio, and Rate of Legal Abortions in U.S., 1970-2009

Source: *Abortion Surveillance—United States, 2009*, Centers for Disease Control and Prevention, U.S. Dept. of Health and Human Services

Year	Legal abortions	Ratio[1]	Rate[2]	Year	Legal abortions	Ratio[1]	Rate[2]	Year	Legal abortions	Ratio[1]	Rate[2]
1970	193,491	52	5	1992	1,359,146	334	23	2001	853,485	251	16
1971	485,816	137	11	1993	1,330,414	333	23	2002	854,122	252	16
1972	586,760	180	13	1994	1,267,415	321	21	2003	848,163	247	16
1973	615,831	196	14	1995	1,210,883	311	20	2004	839,226	243	16
1974	763,476	242	17	1996	1,225,937	315	21	2005	820,151	238	16
1975	854,853	272	18	1997	1,186,039	306	20	2006	852,385	238	16
1980	1,297,606	359	25	1998	884,273	270	17	2007	827,609	231	16
1990	1,429,247	344	24	1999	861,789	261	17	2008	825,564	234	16
1991	1,388,937	338	24	2000	857,475	251	16	2009	784,507	227	15

Note: After 1998, reporting area varies. (1) Number of abortions per 1,000 live births. (2) Number of abortions per 1,000 women aged 15-44 years.

Reported Abortions by Age, Race, and Marital Status, 2009

Source: *Abortion Surveillance—United States, 2009*, Centers for Disease Control and Prevention, U.S. Dept. of Health and Human Services

	White		Race Black		Other		Total, all races	
Characteristic Age[1]	No.	%	No.	%	No.	%	No.	%
Under 15 years	645	0.4%	779	0.7%	81	0.3%	1,505	0.5%
15-19 years.	24,523	15.7	18,635	16.2	2,913	11.7	46,071	15.6
20-24 years.	52,792	33.8	38,391	33.3	7,190	28.9	98,373	33.2
25-29 years.	36,574	23.4	29,358	25.5	6,239	25.1	72,171	24.4
30-34 years.	21,725	13.9	17,083	14.8	4,414	17.8	43,222	14.6
35-39 years.	14,403	9.2	8,679	7.5	2,808	11.3	25,890	8.7
40 years and over	5,480	3.5	2,295	2.0	1,210	4.9	8,985	3.0
Total	**156,142**	**100.0**	**115,220**	**100.0**	**24,855**	**100.0**	**296,217**	**100.0**
Marital status[2]								
Married	24,518	16.9	8,255	8.7	6,536	28.1	39,309	14.9
Unmarried	120,957	83.1	86,382	91.3	16,716	71.9	224,055	85.1
Total	**145,475**	**100.0**	**94,637**	**100.0**	**23,252**	**100.0**	**263,364**	**100.0**

(1) Data from 28 reporting areas; excludes 23 areas (CA, CT, DE, FL, HI, IL, KY, LA, MD, MA, NE, NV, NH, NM, NY, PA, RI, TX, UT, VT, WA, WI, WY) that did not report, did not report by race or age, or did not meet reporting standards for race or for age. (2) Data from 27 reporting areas; excludes 24 areas (CA, CT, DE, FL, GA, HI, IL, KY, LA, MD, MA, NE, NV, NH, NM, NY, PA, RI, TX, UT, VT, WA, WI, WY) that did not report, did not report by race or marital status, or did not meet reporting standards for race or marital status.

Lifetime and Median Number of Sexual Partners by Age and Race, 2008

Source: *Sexual Behavior, Sexual Attraction, and Sexual Identity in the United States*, National Center for Health Statistics (NCHS), U.S. Dept. of Health and Human Services

	No. of opposite-sex partners in lifetime, % distrib.						Median		No. of opposite-sex partners in lifetime, % distrib.						Median
	0	1	2	3-6	7-14	15+	no.[2]		0	1	2	3-6	7-14	15+	no.[2]
Male, 15-44 years[1]	11.4	15.0	7.6	26.5	18.1	21.4	5.1	**Female, 15-44 years[1]**	11.3	22.2	10.7	31.6	16.0	8.3	3.2
Age								**Age**							
15-19 years	43.3	21.2	9.4	17.6	5.4	3.1	1.8	15-19 years.	48.1	22.7	8.2	15.7	4.1	1.1	1.4
20-24 years	14.4	19.1	8.0	26.1	18.1	14.2	4.1	20-24 years.	12.6	24.5	12.5	31.6	11.7	7.2	2.6
25-44 years	2.4	12.3	7.0	28.9	21.5	27.9	6.1	25-44 years.	1.6	21.4	10.9	35.6	20.1	10.4	3.6
Race/ethnicity[3]								**Race/ethnicity[3]**							
White	11.6	16.1	7.3	25.7	18.4	20.9	5.1	White	11.7	19.2	9.7	31.4	18.9	8.9	3.7
Black	9.6	8.3	5.0	25.6	21.6	30.0	6.9	Black	10.5	12.3	8.3	40.9	16.7	11.3	4.4
Hispanic	7.9	12.5	10.2	32.6	17.8	19.1	4.6	Hispanic	10.7	35.0	16.7	26.6	6.6	4.4	1.6

(1) Includes people of other or multiple races and origin groups, not shown separately. (2) Excludes people who have never had sex with a partner. (3) Figures are for whites and blacks who are not Hispanic. Hispanics may be of any race.

Number of Opposite-Sex Partners in Past Year, 2008

Source: *Sexual Behavior, Sexual Attraction, and Sexual Identity in the United States*, National Center for Health Statistics, USDHHS (U.S. males and females 15-44 years of age)

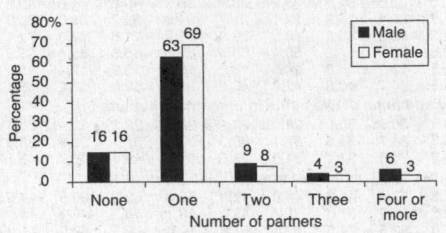

Number of Opposite-Sex Partners in Lifetime by Age, 2008

Source: *Sexual Behavior, Sexual Attraction, and Sexual Identity in the United States*, National Center for Health Statistics, USDHSS (U.S. males and females 15-44 years of age)

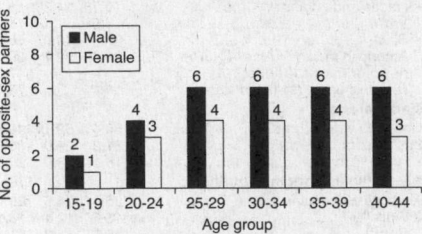

Contraceptive Use in the U.S. by Age and Race, 2006-10

Source: National Survey of Family Growth, National Center for Health Statistics (NCHS), U.S. Dept. of Health and Human Services

| | All women | Age in years | | | | | | Race and ethnicity[1] | | | |
		15-19	20-24	25-29	30-34	35-39	40-44	White	Black	Asian	Hispanic
All women (thous.)	61,755	10,478	10,365	10,535	9,188	10,538	10,652	37,384	8,451	2,456	10,474
Contraceptive status and method					**Percent distribution**						
Using contraception	62.2	30.5	58.3	65.3	69.7	74.6	75.3	65.6	54.2	58.5	59.7
Female sterilization	16.5	—	1.5	10.7	20.9	27.9	38.1	15.5	20.2	6.6	18.9
Male sterilization	6.2	—	0.5	2.7	6.6	12.4	15.1	8.7	0.9	4.0	3.3
Pill	17.1	16.2	27.4	21.5	17.7	12.7	7.4	21.0	9.9	12.3	11.8
Other hormonal methods	4.5	4.9	7.1	7.4	3.9	2.0	1.4	3.5	7.2	2.2	5.5
Implant, Lunelle™, or patch	0.9	0.7	1.1	1.5	0.9	0.5	—	0.5	1.0	—	1.5
3-month injectable (Depo-Provera™)	2.3	3.5	3.3	3.4	1.7	1.0	0.6	1.6	4.6	—	2.9
Contraceptive ring	1.3	0.7	2.7	2.4	1.4	0.5	0.4	1.4	1.6	—	1.0
Intrauterine device (IUD)	3.5	0.8	3.3	4.7	4.9	4.8	2.4	3.6	2.6	2.7	4.0
Condom	10.2	6.1	14.9	13.6	10.8	9.0	6.8	9.2	10.5	23.6	10.8
Periodic abstinence, calendar rhythm	0.6	—	0.2	0.5	0.8	1.0	1.1	0.6	0.2	1.8	0.8
Periodic abstinence, natural family planning	0.1	0.0	0.0	0.0	0.4	—	—	0.1	—	—	—
Withdrawal	3.2	2.1	3.3	4.1	3.2	4.1	2.6	3.1	2.4	4.9	3.4
Other methods[2]	0.3	0.2	—	0.3	0.5	0.6	0.4	0.3	0.1	—	0.7
Not using contraception[3]	37.8	69.5	41.7	34.7	30.3	25.4	24.7	34.4	45.8	41.6	40.3
Surgically sterile, female (noncontraceptive)	—	—	—	0.2	—	0.4	1.5	0.3	0.4	0.0	0.7
Nonsurgically sterile, female or male	1.7	0.5	1.4	1.4	1.8	2.0	3.1	1.5	2.3	1.5	1.6
Pregnant or postpartum	5.0	3.2	8.1	8.4	7.2	2.3	1.4	4.5	6.1	3.6	6.7
Seeking pregnancy	4.0	0.6	4.0	6.3	6.0	4.8	2.4	3.6	4.7	3.4	4.5
Never had intercourse	11.8	51.4	11.6	3.1	1.9	1.1	0.6	11.3	11.8	17.6	12.4
No intercourse in 3 months before interview	7.3	7.1	7.9	7.0	6.6	6.5	8.6	6.4	9.2	8.8	7.5
Had intercourse in 3 months before interview	7.7	6.7	8.7	8.4	6.7	8.4	7.1	6.9	11.2	6.7	7.0

— = Figure does not meet standard of reliability or precision. **Note:** Data was collected in interviews with women aged 15-44, 2006-10. For all methods shown, the reported standard error was less than 3.9%. (1) Hispanics may be of any race. Other columns below are for non-Hispanic persons. (2) Includes diaphragm (with or without jelly or cream), emergency contraception, female condom or vaginal pouch, foam, cervical cap, Today™ sponge, suppository or insert, jelly or cream (without diaphragm), and other methods. (3) Includes male sterilization unknown reason and male surgical sterilization for noncontraceptive reasons, not shown separately.

Sexual Activity of Older Adults, 1999-2009

Source: *Sex, Romance, and Relationships–AARP Survey of Midlife and Older Adults*, Apr. 2010

| | Total | | | Men | | | Women | | |
Sexual activity[1]	1999	2004	2009	1999	2004	2009	1999	2004	2009
Kissing and hugging	65%	69%	58%	74%	76%	67%	58%	62%	49%
Sexual touching or caressing	55	53	44	63	61	54	47	46	35
Sexual intercourse	38	36	28	42	41	33	35	31	23
Oral sex	13	14	16	14	19	20	11	10	12
Anal sex	—	—	3	—	—	4	—	—	2
Self stimulation	12	20	22	23	34	34	3	8	12

(1) Sexual activities engaged in at least once a week by persons ages 45 and older in the six months prior to the survey.

Sexual Activity of High School Students, 2011

Source: *Youth Risk Behavior Surveillance—United States, 2011*, Centers for Disease Control and Prevention, U.S. Dept. of Health and Human Services

Race/ethnicity	Ever had sexual intercourse			First sexual intercourse before age 13			Currently sexually active[1]			Condom use during last sexual intercourse[2]		
	Female	Male	Total	Female	Male	Total	Female	Male	Total	Female	Male	Total
White[3]	44.5%	44.0%	44.3%	2.6%	5.2%	3.9%	35.0%	30.0%	32.4%	53.4%	66.3%	59.5%
Black[3]	53.6	66.9	60.0	7.0	21.2	13.9	36.9	46.0	41.3	53.8	75.4	65.3
Hispanic.........	43.9	53.0	48.6	2.9	11.1	7.1	31.6	35.3	33.5	53.0	63.4	58.4
Grade												
9	27.8	37.8	32.9	4.1	13.3	8.8	19.0	23.6	21.3	56.3	67.0	62.2
10	43.0	44.5	43.8	3.9	8.6	6.3	31.4	29.1	30.3	56.7	69.9	63.3
11	51.9	54.5	53.2	3.0	6.8	4.9	38.9	38.5	38.7	55.5	67.0	61.1
12	63.6	62.6	63.1	2.2	6.2	4.2	50.7	44.4	47.5	48.9	64.7	56.3
Total..............	**45.6**	**49.2**	**47.4**	**3.4**	**9.0**	**6.2**	**34.2**	**33.3**	**33.7**	**53.6**	**67.0**	**60.2**

(1) Sexual intercourse during the 3 months preceding the survey. (2) Among the 33.7% who were sexually active. (3) Non-Hispanic.

Risk Behaviors in High School Students, 2011

Source: *Youth Risk Behavior Surveillance—United States, 2011*, Centers for Disease Control and Prevention, U.S. Dept. of Health and Human Services

		Percent rarely or never wore seat belts[1]			Percent rarely or never wore bicycle helmets[2]			Percent who rode with a driver who had been drinking alcohol[3]		
		Female	Male	Total	Female	Male	Total	Female	Male	Total
Race/	White, non-Hispanic	5.1%	7.3%	6.3%	83.9%	87.1%	85.7%	23.8%	20.5%	22.1%
ethnicity	Black, non-Hispanic	8.0	12.6	10.3	89.4	94.4	92.3	23.2	22.5	22.8
	Hispanic	8.4	10.1	9.3	92.0	92.2	92.1	30.7	30.7	30.7
Grade	9	8.4	10.3	9.5	85.8	87.2	86.6	22.9	20.7	21.8
	10	5.9	9.0	7.5	85.2	87.9	86.7	23.5	23.1	23.3
	11	4.9	7.0	6.0	85.7	89.2	87.7	25.2	22.4	23.8
	12	5.5	8.5	7.1	87.3	92.0	89.9	28.0	27.4	27.7
Total............................		**6.3**	**8.9**	**7.7**	**85.9**	**88.8**	**87.5**	**24.9**	**23.3**	**24.1**

(1) When riding in a car driven by someone else. (2) Among the 70.2% of students who rode a bicycle during the 12 months preceding the survey. (3) In a car or other vehicle one or more times in the 30 days preceding the survey.

Risky Driving Behaviors by High School Students, 2011

Source: *Youth Risk Behavior Surveillance–United States, 2011*, Centers for Disease Control and Prevention, U.S. Dept. of Health and Human Services

		Percent who drove when drinking alcohol[1]			Percent who texted or emailed while driving[2]		
		Female	Male	Total	Female	Male	Total
Race/	White, non-Hispanic	7.0%	8.9%	8.0%	35.4%	36.9%	36.2%
ethnicity	Black, non-Hispanic	4.0	7.8	5.9	19.0	29.3	24.1
	Hispanic	7.8	11.5	9.7	26.3	35.2	30.9
Grade	9	3.3	6.1	4.7	9.4	13.9	11.7
	10	5.2	6.0	5.6	20.6	25.6	23.2
	11	7.8	10.4	9.1	40.6	45.0	42.9
	12	11.2	16.0	13.6	55.9	60.0	58.0
Total......................................		**6.7**	**9.5**	**8.2**	**30.4**	**34.9**	**32.8**

(1) One or more times during the 30 days before the survey. (2) On at least one day during the 30 days before the survey.

U.S. Motor Vehicle Crashes, 2011

Source: National Safety Council (NSC); Natl. Highway Traffic Safety Admin. (NHTSA)

An estimated 34,600 people in the U.S. were killed in motor vehicle crashes in 2011, down 2% from the total for 2010. Although the number of drivers (212 mil) increased in 2011, the vehicle miles driven (2.9 tril) decreased; the death rate per 100 mil vehicle miles decreased 1% to 1.18, the lowest on record.

Motor vehicle deaths per 10,000 registered vehicles dropped from 1.41 in 2010 to 1.39 in 2011 and were down from 1.93 in 2002, a decrease of 28% over nine years. The rate of fatalities per 100,000 population declined 30% between 2002 and 2011 and 3% between 2010 and 2011.

Male drivers were involved in about 5.2 mil crashes, whereas female drivers were in 4.2 mil. Male drivers were also involved in 74% of fatal crashes, or about 31,809, compared with 11,209 accidents involving female drivers.

In 2011, 9,878 traffic fatalities, or 31%, involved an intoxicated (blood alcohol concentration of 0.08 or greater) driver or motorcycle operator, a decline of 2.5% from 2010.

Seat belt use was 86% in 2012. In 2011, safety belts and child restraints saved an estimated 12,212 lives. Another 2,204 lives were saved by frontal air bags. Women used safety belts (86%) more often than men (81%). In 2012, the least likely safety belt users were rural drivers (84%) and drivers of pickup trucks (77%).

Crashes	Deaths	Injuries
All motor vehicle crashes	34,600	3,700,000
Collision between motor vehicles	12,800	2,750,000
Collision with fixed object	11,100	510,000
Collision with pedestrian	5,700	160,000
Noncollision accidents (e.g., rollovers)	3,900	160,000
Collision with pedalcycle	900	110,000
Collision with railroad train	100	1,000
Other (mostly collisions with animals)..	100	9,000

Note: NSC numbers are rounded and preliminary.

Improper Driving Reported in Crashes, 2000-11
Source: National Safety Council

Type	Percentage of fatal crashes			Percentage of injury crashes			Percentage of all crashes		
	2011	2005	2000	2011	2005	2000	2011	2005	2000
Improper driving................	54.6%	62.7%	61.6%	57.0%	62.7%	60.3%	53.5%	58.5%	57.8%
Speed too fast or unsafe............	13.6	18.1	23.7	12.0	15.0	16.3	9.6	12.7	13.6
Right of way.....................	10.6	12.2	18.6	15.2	17.5	19.9	12.6	14.3	20.1
Failed to yield..............	6.9	8.0	10.1	10.3	12.5	12.5	9.3	10.8	12.7
Disregarded signal.............	1.7	1.4	4.6	2.4	2.5	3.6	1.7	1.7	5.3
Passed stop sign..............	2.0	2.8	3.8	2.6	2.5	1.3	1.6	1.8	2.2
Drove left of center..............	4.6	8.0	8.2	0.9	2.2	1.1	0.7	1.6	1.0
Made improper turn.............	4.6	4.5	0.7	3.3	4.2	2.0	2.8	4.5	2.4
Improper overtaking.............	1.1	1.4	0.9	0.8	0.6	0.6	0.9	0.8	0.9
Followed too closely..............	1.2	1.0	0.5	6.5	6.8	4.3	7.8	8.7	5.7
Other improper driving............	18.9	17.5	9.0	18.5	16.4	16.1	19.1	15.9	14.1
No improper driving stated........	45.4	37.3	38.4	43.0	37.3	39.7	46.5	41.5	42.2

Note: Based on reports from state traffic authorities. When a driver was under the influence of alcohol or drugs, the crash was considered a result of the driver's physical condition—not a driving error.

U.S. Passenger Deaths and Death Rates, 1999-2010
Source: National Safety Council

Year	Passenger automobiles[1]		Vans, SUVs, pickup trucks[1]		Buses[2]		Railroad passenger trains		Scheduled airlines[3]	
	Deaths	Rate[4]	Deaths	Rate[4]	Deaths	Rate[4]	Deaths	Rate[4]	Deaths	Rate[4]
1999...........	20,851	0.84	11,295	0.76	40	0.07	14	0.10	24	0.005
2000...........	20,689	0.81	11,545	0.76	3	0.01	4	0.03	94	0.02
2001...........	20,310	0.78	11,736	0.76	11	0.02	3	0.02	279	0.06
2002...........	20,564	0.78	12,278	0.78	36	0.06	7	0.05	0	0.00
2003...........	19,723	0.74	12,551	0.78	30	0.05	3	0.02	24	0.005
2004...........	19,183	0.71	12,678	0.75	27	0.05	3	0.02	13	0.002
2005...........	18,509	0.68	13,043	0.76	43	0.07	16	0.10	22	0.004
2006...........	17,792	0.66	12,723	0.72	15	0.02	2	0.01	52	0.01
2007...........	29,075	0.66	NA	NA	18	0.03	5	0.03	0	0.00
2008...........	25,344	0.59	NA	NA	50	0.08	24	0.13	0	0.00
2009...........	23,376	0.53	NA	NA	21	0.04	3	0.02	49	0.01
2010...........	22,185	0.50	NA	NA	28	0.05	3	0.02	0	0.00

NA = Not available. (1) Drivers of passenger automobiles are considered passengers. Includes taxi passengers. Starting in 2007, passenger automobiles includes vans, SUVs, and pickup trucks. (2) Excludes school buses. (3) Excludes charter, cargo, and on-demand service and deaths due to suicide/sabotage. (4) Deaths per 100 mil passenger miles.

Death Rates for Suicide at Selected Ages, 1960-2010
Source: *Health, United States, 2012*, National Center for Health Statistics (NCHS), U.S. Dept. of Health and Human Services

Age	2010			2000			1980			1960		
	Both sexes	Male	Female	Both sexes	Male	Female	Both sexes	Male	Female	Both sexes	Male	Female
15-24 years..................	10.5	16.9	3.9	10.2	17.1	3.0	12.3	20.2	4.3	5.2	8.2	2.2
25-44 years..................	15.0	23.6	6.4	13.4	21.3	5.4	15.6	24.0	7.7	12.2	17.9	6.6
45-64 years..................	18.6	29.2	8.6	13.5	21.3	6.2	15.9	23.7	8.9	22.0	34.4	10.2
65 years and older	14.9	29.0	4.2	15.2	31.1	4.0	17.6	35.0	6.1	24.5	44.0	8.4
All ages	12.1	19.8	5.0	10.4	17.7	4.0	12.2	19.9	5.7	12.5	20.0	5.6

Note: Rate is per 100,000 population. Rates for all ages include ages not shown here.

U.S. Fires, 2012
Source: National Fire Protection Association

Fires

- Public fire departments responded to 1,375,000 fires in 2012, a slight decrease of 1.0% from 2011.

- Every 23 seconds, a fire department responds to a fire somewhere in the United States.

- There were 480,500 structure fires in 2012, a very slight decrease of 0.8% from 2011. Of those fires, 76% (365,000 fires) occurred in homes.

- Fires in highway vehicles decreased 8.0% from the previous year, totaling 172,500 in 2012.

- There were 692,000 fires in outside properties, a slight increase of 0.9% from 2011.

Intentionally set fires

- There were an estimated 26,000 intentionally set structure fires in 2012, a decrease of 1.9% from 2011.

- Intentionally set structure fires are believed to have resulted in 180 civilian deaths in 2012, a decrease of 5.3% from the year before. Property damage from intentionally set structure fires totaled $581 mil, a decrease of 3.3% from the 2011 figure.

Civilian deaths

- There were an estimated 2,855 civilian fire deaths in 2012. This was a 5.0% decrease from the year before.

- The number of civilian fire deaths that occurred in home structure fires decreased 5.6% to 2,380, and fires in the home caused 83% of all fire deaths.

- Fires caused an average of one civilian death every 184 minutes.

Civilian injuries

- There were an estimated 16,500 civilian fire injuries reported in 2012, a 5.7% decrease from 2011. Nationwide, a civilian was injured in a fire every 32 minutes; a civilian fire injury occurred in a home fire every 41 minutes.

- Home structure fires were the site of 12,875 civilian fire injuries in 2012. Non-home structure fires accounted for 3,625 civilian injuries.

Property damage

- Direct property damage from fires amounted to an estimated $12.4 bil in 2012, an increase of 5.9% from 2011. Structure fires accounted for $9.7 bil of property damage.

- Property loss associated with home fires came to $7.0 bil for 2012.

Leading Causes of Death in the U.S., 2011

Source: National Center for Health Statistics (NCHS), U.S. Dept. of Health and Human Services

	Number	% of total deaths	Death rate[1]		Number	% of total deaths	Death rate[1]
All causes	2,512,873	100.0%	806.5	10. Intentional self-harm (suicide)...	38,285	1.5%	12.3
1. Diseases of the heart	596,339	23.7	191.4	11. Septicemia	35,539	1.4	11.4
2. Cancer	575,313	22.9	184.6	12. Chronic liver disease and cirrhosis	33,539	1.3	10.8
3. Chronic lower respiratory diseases	143,382	5.7	46.0	13. Hypertension and hypertensive			
4. Stroke	128,931	5.1	41.4	renal disease	27,477	1.1	8.8
5. Accidents (unintentional injuries)	122,777	4.9	39.4	14. Parkinson's disease	23,107	0.9	7.4
6. Alzheimer's diseases	84,691	3.4	27.2	15. Pneumonitis due to solids			
7. Diabetes	73,282	2.9	23.5	and liquids	18,090	0.7	5.8
8. Influenza and pneumonia	53,667	2.1	17.2	All other causes (residual)	512,723	20.4	164.6
9. Kidney disease	45,731	1.8	14.7				

(1) Per 100,000 population.

Principal Types of Accidental Deaths in the U.S., 1970-2011

Source: National Safety Council

Year[1]	Total	Motor vehicle	Falls	Poisoning	Drowning	Fires, flames, smoke	Suffocation: ingestion of food, object	Firearms	Mechanical suffocation
1970	NA	54,633	16,926	5,299	7,860	6,718	2,753	2,406	NA
1980	105,718	53,172	13,294	4,331	7,257	5,822	3,249	1,955	NA
1985	93,457	45,901	12,001	5,170	5,316	4,938	3,551	1,649	NA
1990	91,983	46,814	12,313	5,803	4,685	4,175	3,303	1,416	NA
1995	93,320	43,363	13,986	9,072	4,350	3,761	3,185	1,225	NA
2000	97,900	43,354	13,322	12,757	3,482	3,377	4,313	776	1,335
2002	106,742	45,380	16,257	17,550	3,447	3,159	4,128	762	1,389
2003	109,277	44,757	17,229	19,457	3,306	3,369	4,272	730	1,309
2004	112,012	44,933	18,807	20,950	3,308	3,229	4,470	649	1,421
2005	117,809	45,343	19,656	23,617	3,582	3,197	4,386	789	1,514
2006	121,599	45,316	20,823	27,531	3,579	3,109	4,332	642	1,580
2007	123,706	43,945	22,631	29,846	3,443	3,286	4,344	613	1,653
2008	121,902	39,790	24,013	31,116	3,548	2,912	4,366	592	1,759
2009	118,046	36,216	24,792	31,758	3,517	2,756	4,370	554	1,569
2010	120,834	35,332	26,009	33,041	3,782	2,782	4,570	606	1,595
2011[2]	122,900	34,600	27,500	34,900	3,600	2,800	4,600	600	1,600
Death rates per 100,000 population									
1970	NA	26.8	8.3	2.6	3.9	3.3	1.4	1.2	NA
1980	47.8	23.4	5.9	1.9	3.2	2.6	1.4	0.9	NA
1985	39.3	19.3	5.0	2.2	2.2	2.1	1.5	0.7	NA
1990	36.9	18.8	4.9	2.3	1.9	1.7	1.3	0.6	NA
1995	35.5	16.5	5.3	3.4	1.7	1.4	1.2	0.5	NA
2000	35.6	15.7	4.8	4.6	1.3	1.2	1.6	0.3	0.5
2002	37.1	15.8	5.6	6.4	1.2	1.1	1.4	0.3	0.5
2003	37.6	15.4	5.9	6.7	1.1	1.2	1.5	0.3	0.4
2004	38.1	15.3	6.4	7.1	1.1	1.1	1.5	0.2	0.5
2005	39.7	15.3	6.6	8.0	1.2	1.1	1.5	0.3	0.5
2006	40.8	15.2	7.0	9.2	1.2	1.0	1.5	0.2	0.5
2007	41.1	14.6	7.5	9.9	1.1	1.1	1.4	0.2	0.5
2008	40.0	13.1	7.9	10.2	1.2	1.0	1.4	0.2	0.6
2009	38.5	11.8	8.1	10.3	1.1	0.9	1.4	0.2	0.5
2010	39.0	11.4	8.4	10.7	1.2	0.9	1.5	0.2	0.5
2011[2]	39.4	11.1	8.8	11.2	1.2	0.9	1.5	0.2	0.5

NA = Not available. **Note:** All figures include on-the-job deaths. (1) Data after 1999 are not comparable with earlier data because of classification changes. (2) Preliminary. Totals include 12,700 other accidental deaths in 2011.

Deaths in the U.S. Involving Firearms by Age and Sex, 2009

Source: National Safety Council

Type and sex	All ages	Under 5	5-14	15-19	20-24	25-44	45-64	65-74	75 & older
Total firearms deaths	31,347	86	269	2,456	3,840	10,838	9,127	2,320	2,411
Male	26,921	50	207	2,194	3,451	9,226	7,572	2,029	2,192
Female	4,426	36	62	262	389	1,612	1,555	291	219
Unintentional	554	16	32	66	66	175	121	46	32
Male	497	11	31	64	59	159	102	40	31
Female	57	5	1	2	7	16	19	6	1
Suicide	18,735	—	64	736	1,266	5,253	7,166	2,035	2,215
Male	16,307	—	53	655	1,142	4,461	6,075	1,834	2,087
Female	2,428	—	11	81	124	792	1,091	201	128
Homicide	11,493	66	168	1,621	2,430	5,169	1,672	215	152
Male	9,615	36	119	1,446	2,175	4,391	1,252	134	62
Female	1,878	30	49	175	255	778	420	81	90
Legal intervention	333	1	0	17	52	163	87	11	2
Male	311	1	0	16	52	154	77	9	2
Female	22	0	0	1	0	9	10	2	0
Undetermined[1]	232	3	5	16	26	78	81	13	10
Male	191	2	4	13	23	61	66	12	10
Female	41	1	1	3	3	17	15	1	0

— = Not applicable. (1) The intention involved (whether accident, suicide, or homicide) could not be determined.

U.S. Infant Mortality Rates by Race and Sex, 1960-2011

Source: National Center for Health Statistics (NCHS), U.S. Dept. of Health and Human Services

Year	All races[1] Both sexes	Male	Female	White Both sexes	Male	Female	Black Both sexes	Male	Female
1960	26.0	29.3	22.6	22.9	26.0	19.6	44.3	49.1	39.4
1970	20.0	22.4	17.5	17.8	20.0	15.4	32.6	36.2	29.0
1980	12.6	13.9	11.2	11.0	12.3	9.6	21.4	23.3	19.4
1990	9.2	10.3	8.1	7.6	8.5	6.6	18.0	19.6	16.2
1995	7.6	8.3	6.8	6.3	7.0	5.6	15.1	16.3	13.9
1996	7.3	8.0	6.6	6.1	6.7	5.4	14.7	16.0	13.3
1997	7.2	8.0	6.5	6.0	6.7	5.4	14.2	15.5	12.8
1998	7.2	7.8	6.5	6.0	6.5	5.4	14.3	15.7	12.8
1999	7.1	7.7	6.4	5.8	6.4	5.2	14.6	15.9	13.2
2000	6.9	7.6	6.2	5.7	6.2	5.1	14.1	15.5	12.6
2001	6.8	7.5	6.1	5.7	6.2	5.1	14.0	15.5	12.5
2002	7.0	7.6	6.3	5.8	6.4	5.1	14.4	15.4	13.3
2003	6.9	7.6	6.1	5.7	6.3	5.0	14.0	15.5	12.4
2004	6.8	7.5	6.1	5.7	6.2	5.1	13.8	15.2	12.3
2005	6.9	7.6	6.2	5.7	6.3	5.1	13.7	15.2	12.3
2006	6.7	7.3	6.0	5.6	6.1	5.0	13.3	14.4	12.2
2007	6.8	7.4	6.1	5.6	6.2	5.1	13.2	14.5	11.9
2008	6.6	7.2	6.0	5.6	6.1	5.0	12.7	13.9	11.5
2009	6.4	7.0	5.8	5.3	5.8	4.8	12.6	14.1	11.2
2010	6.2	6.7	5.6	5.2	5.7	4.7	11.6	12.7	10.5
2011[2]	6.1	NA	NA	5.1	NA	NA	11.4	NA	NA

NA = Not available. **Note:** Rates per 1,000 live births in specified group. (1) Includes races other than white and black. (2) Preliminary.

Years of Life Expected at Birth in U.S., 1900-2011

Source: National Center for Health Statistics (NCHS), U.S. Dept. of Health and Human Services

Year[2]	All races[1] Both sexes	Male	Female	White Both sexes	Male	Female	Black Both sexes	Male	Female
1900	47.3	46.3	48.3	47.6	46.6	48.7	NA	NA	NA
1910	50.0	48.4	51.8	50.3	48.6	52.0	NA	NA	NA
1920	54.1	53.6	54.6	54.9	54.4	55.6	NA	NA	NA
1930	59.7	58.1	61.6	61.4	59.7	63.5	NA	NA	NA
1940	62.9	60.8	65.2	64.2	62.1	66.6	NA	NA	NA
1950	68.2	65.6	71.1	69.1	66.5	72.2	NA	NA	NA
1960	69.7	66.6	73.1	70.6	67.4	74.1	NA	NA	NA
1970	70.8	67.1	74.7	71.7	68.0	75.6	64.1	60.0	68.3
1980	73.7	70.0	77.5	74.4	70.7	78.1	68.1	63.8	72.5
1985	74.7	71.2	78.2	75.3	71.9	78.7	69.3	65.0	73.4
1990	75.4	71.8	78.8	76.1	72.7	79.4	69.1	64.5	73.6
1995	75.8	72.5	78.9	76.5	73.4	79.6	69.6	65.2	73.9
1996	76.1	73.1	79.1	76.8	73.9	79.7	70.2	66.1	74.2
1997	76.5	73.6	79.4	77.1	74.3	79.9	71.1	67.2	74.7
1998	76.7	73.8	79.5	77.3	74.5	80.0	71.3	67.6	74.8
1999	76.7	73.9	79.4	77.3	74.6	79.9	71.4	67.8	74.7
2000	76.8	74.1	79.3	77.3	74.7	79.9	71.8	68.2	75.1
2001	76.9	74.2	79.4	77.4	74.8	79.9	72.0	68.4	75.2
2002	76.9	74.3	79.5	77.4	74.9	79.9	72.1	68.6	75.4
2003	77.1	74.5	79.6	77.6	75.0	80.0	72.3	68.8	75.6
2004	77.5	74.9	79.9	77.9	75.4	80.4	72.8	69.3	76.0
2005	77.4	74.9	79.9	77.9	75.4	80.4	72.8	69.3	76.1
2006	77.7	75.1	80.2	78.2	75.7	80.6	73.2	69.7	76.5
2007	77.9	75.4	80.4	78.4	75.9	80.8	73.6	70.0	76.8
2008	78.1	75.6	80.6	78.5	76.1	80.9	74.0	70.6	77.2
2009	78.6	76.0	80.9	78.8	76.4	81.2	74.7	71.4	77.7
2010	78.7	76.2	81.0	78.9	76.5	81.3	75.1	71.8	78.0
2011[3]	78.7	76.3	81.1	79.0	76.6	81.3	75.3	72.1	78.2

NA = Not available. (1) Includes races other than white and black. (2) Data prior to 1940 does not include all states. (3) Preliminary.

U.S. Life Expectancy at Selected Ages, 2011

Source: National Center for Health Statistics (NCHS), U.S. Dept. of Health and Human Services

Exact age in years	All races[1] Both sexes	Male	Female	White Both sexes	Male	Female	Black Both sexes	Male	Female
0	78.7	76.3	81.1	79.0	76.6	81.3	75.3	72.1	78.2
1	78.2	75.8	80.5	78.4	76.0	80.7	75.2	72.0	78.0
5	74.3	71.9	76.6	74.4	72.1	76.7	71.3	68.2	74.1
10	69.3	66.9	71.6	69.5	67.1	71.8	66.3	63.2	69.1
15	64.4	62.0	66.7	64.5	62.2	66.8	61.4	58.3	64.2
20	59.5	57.2	61.8	59.7	57.4	61.9	56.6	53.6	59.3
25	54.8	52.5	56.9	54.9	52.7	57.0	51.9	49.0	54.4
30	50.0	47.9	52.0	50.2	48.0	52.2	47.3	44.5	49.6
35	45.3	43.2	47.2	45.4	43.4	47.4	42.6	40.0	44.9
40	40.6	38.6	42.5	40.7	38.7	42.6	38.0	35.5	40.2
45	36.0	34.0	37.8	36.1	34.2	37.9	33.6	31.0	35.7
50	31.5	29.6	33.2	31.6	29.8	33.3	29.3	26.8	31.3
55	27.2	25.5	28.8	27.3	25.6	28.9	25.2	22.9	27.1
60	23.1	21.5	24.5	23.2	21.6	24.5	21.5	19.3	23.2
65	19.2	17.8	20.4	19.2	17.8	20.4	18.0	16.1	19.4
70	15.5	14.3	16.5	15.5	14.3	16.5	14.7	13.1	15.8
75	12.1	11.0	12.9	12.1	11.0	12.9	11.7	10.3	12.5
80	9.1	8.2	9.7	9.1	8.2	9.6	9.0	7.9	9.6
85	6.5	5.9	6.9	6.5	5.8	6.9	6.8	5.9	7.2
90	4.6	4.1	4.8	4.5	4.0	4.8	5.0	4.4	5.3
95	3.2	2.9	3.3	3.2	2.8	3.3	3.7	3.3	3.8
100	2.3	2.1	2.3	2.3	2.0	2.3	2.8	2.5	2.8

Note: Data is preliminary. (1) Includes races other than white and black.

NOTED PERSONALITIES

Widely Known Americans of the Present

Political leaders, journalists, other prominent living persons. As of Oct. 2013. Excludes most who fall in categories listed elsewhere in Noted Personalities, such as Writers of the Present and Entertainment Personalities of the Present. Includes some figures who are active in American life but are not U.S. citizens.

Roger Ailes, b 5/15/40 (Warren, OH), TV exec.

Madeleine K. Albright, b 5/15/37 (Prague, Czech.), former sec. of state.

Edwin "Buzz" Aldrin, b 1/20/30 (Montclair, NJ), former astronaut, second person to walk on the Moon.

Samuel A. Alito Jr., b 4/1/50 (Trenton, NJ), Supreme Court justice.

Paul Allen, b 1/21/53 (Seattle, WA), co-founder of Microsoft.

Christiane Amanpour, b 1/12/58 (London, Eng., UK), TV journalist.

Marc Andreessen, b 1971 (New Lisbon, IA), co-author of web browser Mosaic, cofounder of Netscape.

Richard K. Armey, b 7/7/40 (Cando, ND), former U.S. rep. (R, TX), House majority leader.

John Ashcroft, b 5/9/42 (Chicago, IL), former MO gov., U.S. attorney gen.

David Axelrod, b 2/22/55 (New York, NY), sr. adviser to Pres. Obama, political strategist.

Michele Bachmann, b 4/6/56 (Waterloo, IA), U.S. rep (R, MN), former 2012 pres. contender.

F. Lee Bailey, b 6/10/33 (Waltham, MA), attorney.

Russell Baker, b 8/14/25 (Morrisonville, VA), columnist.

Dave Barry, b 7/3/47 (Armonk, NY), humorist.

Marion Barry, b 3/6/36 (Itta Bena, MS), DC city council member; former Wash., DC, mayor.

Max Baucus, b 12/11/41 (Helena, MT), senator (D, MT), Finance Committee chair.

Gary Bauer, b 5/4/46 (Covington, KY), domestic policy adviser to Pres. Reagan; founder, Campaign for Working Families.

Glenn Beck, b 2/10/64 (Mount Vernon, WA), political commentator.

William Bennett, b 7/31/43 (Brooklyn, NY), author, former education secretary.

Chris Berman, b 5/10/55 (Greenwich, CT), sportscaster.

Ben Bernanke, b 12/13/53 (Augusta, GA), Federal Reserve Chairman.

Carl Bernstein, b 2/14/44 (Washington, DC), journalist; with Bob Woodward cracked Watergate scandal.

Jeff Bezos, b 1/12/64 (Albuquerque, NM), founder and CEO of Amazon.com.

Jill Biden, b 6/5/51 (Hammonton, NJ), English college professor, wife of vice pres. Joe Biden.

Joseph R. Biden Jr., b 11/20/42 (Scranton, PA), U.S. vice pres.; former sen. (D, DE).

James H. Billington, b 6/1/29 (Bryn Mawr, PA), librarian of U.S. Congress.

Rod Blagojevich, b 12/10/56 (Chicago, IL), former IL governor (D).

Lloyd Blankfein, b 9/20/54 (Bronx, NY), CEO and chairman of Goldman Sachs.

Wolf Blitzer, b 3/22/48 (Augsburg, Germany), TV journalist.

Harold Bloom, b 7/11/30 (New York, NY), literary critic.

Michael R. Bloomberg, b 2/14/42 (Brighton, MA), NYC mayor, financial information/media entrepreneur.

Roy Blunt, b 1/10/50 (Niangua, MO), senator (R, MO); former U.S. rep., House minority whip.

John Boehner, b 11/17/49 (Cincinnati, OH), U.S. rep. (R, OH), speaker of the House.

Charles F. Bolden, b 8/19/46 (Columbia, SC), NASA head.

Julian Bond, b 1/14/40 (Nashville, TN), civil rights leader, former NAACP chairman.

Cory Booker, b 4/27/69 (Washington, DC), Newark, NJ, mayor; 2013 sen. nominee (D, NJ).

Barbara Boxer, b 11/11/40 (Brooklyn, NY), senator (D, CA).

Bill Bradley, b 7/28/43 (Crystal City, MO), former senator (D, NJ), basketball player, pres. candidate.

James Brady, b 8/29/40 (Centralia, IL), gun control advocate; former pres. press sec.

L. Paul Bremer III, b 9/30/41 (Hartford, CT), diplomat, former top U.S. civilian administrator in Iraq.

John O. Brennan, b 9/22/55 (North Bergen, NJ), CIA director.

Jimmy Breslin, b 10/17/30 (Jamaica, Queens, NY), columnist, author.

Stephen Breyer, b 8/15/38 (San Francisco, CA), Supreme Court justice.

Sergey Brin, b 8/21/73 (Moscow, Russia), cofounder of Google.

Roslyn M. Brock, b 5/30/65 (Fort Pierce, FL), NAACP chair.

Tom Brokaw, b 2/6/40 (Webster, SD), TV journalist, retired NBC anchor.

David Brooks, b 8/11/61 (Toronto, ON, Can.), columnist, political commentator.

Aaron Brown, b 11/10/48 (Hopkins, MN), broadcast journalist.

Jerry (Edmund G.) Brown Jr., b 4/7/38 (San Francisco, CA), CA gov (1975-83, 2011-), former atty. gen. (CA), pres. candidate.

Scott Brown, b 9/12/59 (Wakefield, MA), former senator (R, MA).

Pat Buchanan, b 11/2/38 (Washington, DC), journalist, former pres. candidate.

Warren Buffett, b 8/30/30 (Omaha, NE), investor, leading philanthropist.

Barbara Bush, b 6/8/25 (Flushing, NY), former first lady.

Barbara Bush, b 11/25/81 (Dallas, TX), daughter of former Pres. George W. Bush.

George H. W. Bush, b 6/12/24 (Milton, MA), former U.S. president.

George W. Bush, b 7/6/46 (New Haven, CT), former U.S. president.

Laura Bush, b 11/4/46 (Midland, TX), former first lady.

Herman Cain, b 12/13/45 (Memphis, TN), former chairman and CEO of Godfather's Pizza; former 2012 pres. contender.

Eric Cantor, b 6/6/63 (Richmond, VA), U.S. rep. (R, VA), House majority leader.

Tucker Carlson, b 5/16/69 (San Francisco, CA), journalist, TV commentator.

Jay Carney, b 5/22/65 (Washington, DC), White House press secretary.

Jimmy Carter, b 10/1/24 (Plains, GA), former U.S. president; 2002 Nobel Peace Prize winner.

Rosalynn Carter, b 8/18/27 (Plains, GA), former first lady.

James Carville Jr., b 10/25/44 (Fort Benning, GA), TV political commentator.

Steve Case, b 8/21/58 (Honolulu, HI), former AOL Time Warner chairman.

Julie Chen, b 1/6/70 (New York, NY), host of *The Talk* and *Big Brother.*

Dick Cheney, b 1/30/41 (Lincoln, NE), former U.S. vice president.

Lynne Cheney, b 8/14/41 (Casper, WY), political commentator, wife of Dick Cheney.

Noam Chomsky, b 12/7/28 (Philadelphia, PA), linguist; activist.

Chris Christie, b 9/6/62 (Newark, NJ), NJ governor (R).

Steven Chu, b 2/28/48 (St. Louis, MO), physicist; former energy secretary.

Connie Chung, b 8/20/46 (Washington, DC), TV journalist.

James R. Clapper Jr., b 1941, director of national intelligence.

Bill Clinton, b 8/19/46 (Hope, AR), former U.S. president.

Chelsea Clinton, b 2/27/80 (Little Rock, AR), daughter of former pres. Bill Clinton and Hillary Rodham Clinton.

Hillary Rodham Clinton, b 10/26/47 (Chicago, IL), former sec. of state, senator (D, NY), and first lady, 2008 pres. contender.

James Clyburn, b 7/21/40 (Sumter, SC), U.S. rep. (D, SC), former House majority whip.

Kenneth Cole, b 3/23/54 (Brooklyn, NY), fashion designer.

Gail Collins, b 11/25/45 (Cincinnati, OH), newspaper columnist, writer.

James Comey, b 12/14/60 (Yonkers, NY), FBI director.

Tim Cook, b 11/1/60 (Robertdale, AZ), CEO of Apple, Inc.

Anderson Cooper, b 6/3/67 (New York, NY), CNN anchor.

John Cornyn, b 2/2/52 (Houston, TX), senator (R, TX); majority whip.

Jon Corzine, b 1/1/47 (Willey's Station, IL), former sen. (D, NJ) and NJ governor.

Bob Costas, b 3/22/52 (Queens, NY), TV sports journalist.

Ann Coulter, b 12/8/61 (New Canaan, CT), political commentator, author.

Katie Couric, b 1/7/57 (Arlington, VA), TV journalist, host of *Katie,* former *Today* show news anchor, former anchor of *CBS Evening News.*

Candy Crowley, b 12/12/48 (Kalamazoo, MI), CNN senior political correspondent.

Ted Cruz, b 12/22/70 (Calgary, AB, Canada), senator (R, TX).

Mark Cuban, b 7/31/58 (Pittsburgh, PA), entrepreneur, Dallas Mavericks (NBA) owner.

Andrew Cuomo, b 12/6/57 (New York, NY), NY governor (D), former state atty. gen.

Mario Cuomo, b 6/15/32 (Jamaica, Queens, NY), former NY governor.

Ann Curry, b 11/19/56 (Guam), former *Today* show news anchor.

Richard M. Daley, b 4/24/42 (Chicago, IL), former Chicago mayor.

William Daley, b 8/9/48 (Chicago, IL), former White House chief of staff.

Thomas Daschle, b 12/9/47 (Aberdeen, SD), former senator (D, SD) and Senate minority leader.

Howard Dean, b 11/17/48 (New York, NY), former VT gov., former Dem. Natl. Committee chair.

Oscar de la Renta, b 7/22/36 (Santo Domingo, Dominican Rep.), fashion designer.

Tom DeLay, b 4/8/47 (Laredo, TX), former U.S. rep. (R, TX), House Majority leader.

Michael Dell, b 2/23/65 (Houston, TX), founder, chairman, and CEO of Dell computers.

Martin Dempsey, b 3/14/52 (Bayonne, NJ) chairman, Joint Chiefs of Staff.

Alan Dershowitz, b 9/1/38 (Brooklyn, NY), attorney.

Barry Diller, b 2/2/42 (San Francisco, CA), media exec.

John Dingell, b 7/8/26 (Colorado Springs, CO), U.S. rep. (D, MI), Dean of the House.

Lou Dobbs, b 9/24/45 (Childress, TX), TV journalist.

James Dobson, b 4/21/36 (Shreveport, LA), evangelical Christian leader, chairman of Focus on the Family.

Christopher Dodd, b 5/27/44 (Willimantic, CT), Motion Picture Assn. of America chair/CEO; former senator (D, CT), 2008 pres. contender.

Timothy Dolan, b 2/6/50 (St. Louis, MO), Rom. Cath. cardinal.

Elizabeth Hanford Dole, b 7/29/36 (Salisbury, NC), former senator (R, NC), Red Cross pres., cabinet member.

Robert Dole, b 7/22/23 (Russell, KS), former Senate majority leader (R, KS), 1996 pres. nominee.

Sam Donaldson, b 3/11/34 (El Paso, TX), TV journalist.

Elizabeth Drew, b 11/16/35 (Cincinnati, OH), journalist.

Matt Drudge, b 10/27/66 (Takoma Park, MD), Internet journalist.

Michael S. Dukakis, b 11/3/33 (Brookline, MA), former MA gov. (D), 1988 pres. nominee.

Arne Duncan, b 11/6/64 (Chicago, IL), education secretary.

Dick Durbin, b 11/21/44 (East St. Louis, IL), Senate majority whip (D, IL).

Bernard Ebbers, b 8/27/41 (Edmonton, AB, Can.), former WorldCom CEO; jailed for fraud.

Marian Wright Edelman, b 6/6/39 (Bennettsville, SC), pres. and founder of Children's Defense Fund.

John Edwards, b 6/10/53 (Seneca, SC), former senator (D, NC), 2004 vice-pres. candidate, 2008 pres. contender.

Edward Egan, b 4/2/32 (Oak Park, IL), Rom. Cath. cardinal, archbishop emeritus of New York.

Michael Eisner, b 3/7/42 (Mt. Kisco, NY), former Disney Co. CEO.

Lawrence J. Ellison, b 8/17/44 (New York, NY), Oracle Corp. founder, CEO.

Rahm Emanuel, b 11/29/59 (Chicago, IL), Chicago mayor; former White House chief of staff, U.S. rep. (D, IL).

Myrlie Evers-Williams, b 3/17/33 (Vicksburg, MS), civil rights activist.

Louis Farrakhan, b 5/11/33 (Roxbury, MA), Nation of Islam leader.

Russell Feingold, b 3/2/53 (Janesville, WI), former senator (D, WI).

Dianne Feinstein, b 6/22/33 (San Francisco, CA), senator (D, CA).

Carly (Carleton) S. Fiorina, b 9/6/54 (Austin, TX), former CEO of Hewlett-Packard, 2010 Senate candidate (R, CA).

Larry Flynt, b 11/1/42 (Lakeville, KY), publisher.

Steve (Malcolm) Forbes Jr., b 7/18/47 (Morristown, NJ), publisher, former pres. contender.

Tom Ford, b 8/27/61 (Austin, TX), fashion designer.

Barney Frank, b 3/31/40 (Bayonne, NJ), attorney, former U.S. rep. (D, MA).

Al Franken, b 5/21/51 (New York, NY), senator (D, MN); humorist, political writer, radio host.

Thomas Friedman, b 7/20/53 (Minneapolis, MN), columnist, author.

Bill Gates, b 10/28/55 (Seattle, WA), software pioneer; Microsoft exec.

Henry Louis Gates Jr., b 9/16/50 (Keyser, WV), African American studies scholar.

Robert M. Gates, b 9/25/43 (Wichita, KS), former sec. of defense.

David Geffen, b 2/21/43 (Brooklyn, NY), entertainment exec.

Timothy Geithner, b 8/18/61 (New York, NY), former Treasury secretary.

Robert Gibbs, b 3/29/71 (Auburn, AL), former White House press secretary.

Charles Gibson, b 3/4/43 (Evanston, IL), TV journalist, former host of ABC's *World News*.

Gabrielle Giffords, b 8/8/70 (Tucson, AZ), former U.S. rep. (D, AZ), shot in 2011 assassination attempt.

Kirsten Gillibrand, b 12/9/66 (Albany, NY), senator (D, NY), attorney.

Newt Gingrich, b 6/17/43 (Harrisburg, PA), former House speaker (R, GA), former 2012 pres. contender.

Ruth Bader Ginsburg, b 3/15/33 (Brooklyn, NY), Supreme Court justice.

Rudolph Giuliani, b 5/28/44 (Brooklyn, NY), former NYC mayor.

John Glenn, b 7/18/21 (Cambridge, OH), former senator (D, OH), astronaut.

Alberto Gonzales, b 8/4/55 (San Antonio, TX), former U.S. attorney general.

Roger Goodell, b 2/19/59 (Jamestown, NY), NFL commissioner.

Ellen Goodman, b 4/11/41 (Newton, MA), columnist.

Doris Kearns Goodwin, b 1/4/43 (Brooklyn, NY), historian, TV commentator.

Berry Gordy, b 11/28/29 (Detroit, MI), Motown record label founder.

Al Gore Jr., b 3/31/48 (Washington, DC), former sen. (D, TN), U.S. vice pres., 2000 pres. nominee; 2007 Nobel Peace Prize winner.

Tipper Gore, b 8/19/48 (Washington, DC), former wife of Al Gore.

Rev. Billy Graham, b 11/7/18 (Charlotte, NC), evangelist.

(William) Franklin Graham III, b 7/14/52 (Asheville, NC), evangelist, son of Billy Graham.

Temple Grandin, b 8/29/47 (Boston, MA), animal behavioral scientist, autism activist.

Jeff Greenfield, b 6/10/43 (New York, NY), TV journalist.

Alan Greenspan, b 3/6/26 (New York, NY), former Federal Reserve chairman.

Chuck Hagel, b 10/4/46 (North Platte, NE), defense sec., former senator (R, NE).

Jenna Bush Hager, b 11/25/81 (Dallas, TX), daughter of former Pres. George W. Bush.

Pete Hamill, b 6/24/35 (Brooklyn, NY), journalist, author.

Lee Hamilton, b 4/20/31 (Daytona Beach, FL), 9/11 commission vice-chair, former U.S. rep. (D, IN).

Sean Hannity, b 12/30/61 (New York, NY), radio and TV host, author, political commentator.

J. Dennis Hastert, b 1/2/42 (Aurora, IL), former House speaker, U.S. rep. (R, IL).

Reed Hastings, b 10/8/60 (Boston, MA), founder, pres., CEO and board chair, Netflix, Inc.

Orrin Hatch, b 3/22/34 (Homestead Park, PA), senator (R, UT).

Hugh Hefner, b 4/9/26 (Chicago, IL), publisher.

Tommy Hilfiger, b 3/24/51 (Elmira, NY), fashion designer.

Anita Hill, b 7/30/56 (Morris, OK), legal scholar; complainant against Clarence Thomas.

Paris Hilton, b 2/17/81 (New York, NY), heiress; actress.

Perez Hilton, b 3/23/78 (Miami, FL), gossip columnist.

James P. Hoffa, b 5/19/41 (Detroit, MI), Teamsters Union head.

Eric Holder Jr., b 1/21/51 (Bronx, NY), first African American U.S. atty. gen.

David Horowitz, b 1/10/39 (New York, NY), consumer advocate, columnist, author.

Steny H. Hoyer, b 6/14/39 (New York, NY), House minority whip, former majority leader (D, MD).

Mike Huckabee, b 8/24/55 (Hope, AR), former gov. (R, AR), minister, 2008 pres. contender, TV host.

Arianna Huffington, b 7/15/50 (Athens, Greece), political commentator.

H. Wayne Huizenga, b 12/29/39 (Evergreen Park, IL), entrepreneur, sports exec.

Brit Hume, b 6/22/43 (Washington, DC), TV journalist on FOX.

Jon Huntsman Jr., b 3/26/60 (Palo Alto, CA), former UT gov. (R), ambassador to China, 2012 pres. contender.

Kay Bailey Hutchison, b 7/22/43 (Galveston, TX), former senator (R, TX).

Lee Iacocca, b 10/15/24 (Allentown, PA), former auto exec.

Carl Icahn, b 2/16/36 (Queens, NY), financier.

Gwen Ifill, b 9/29/55 (Queens, NY), TV journalist, moderator on PBS.

Don Imus, b 7/23/40 (Riverside, CA), talk-show host.

Patricia Ireland, b 10/19/45 (Oak Park, IL), feminist leader.

Rev. Jesse Jackson, b 10/8/41 (Greenville, SC), civil rights leader, former pres. contender.

Marc Jacobs, b 4/9/64 (New York, NY), fashion designer.

Valerie Jarrett, b 11/14/56 (Shiraz, Iran), sr. adviser to Pres. Obama.

Bobby Jindal, b 6/10/71 (Baton Rouge, LA), LA governor (R), first elected Indian American governor.

Jasper Johns, b 5/15/30 (Augusta, GA), artist.

Gary Johnson, b 1/1/53 (Minot, ND), former NM governor (R); 2012 Libertarian pres. nominee.

Robert L. Johnson, b 4/8/46 (Hickory, MS), Black Entertainment Television founder.

Vernon E. Jordan Jr., b 8/15/35 (Atlanta, GA), attorney, former pres. adviser, civil rights leader.

Elena Kagan, b 4/28/60 (New York, NY), Supreme Court justice.

Tim Kaine, b 2/26/58 (St. Paul, MN), former Dem Natl. Committee chair, VA governor.

Donna Karan, b 10/2/48 (Forest Hills, Queens, NY), fashion designer.

Jeffrey Katzenberg, b 12/21/50 (New York, NY), entertainment exec.

Thomas Kean, b 4/21/35 (New York, NY), 9/11 commission chair, former Drew Univ. pres., former NJ gov.

Garrison Keillor, b 8/7/42 (Anoka, MN), author, broadcaster.

Mark Kelly, b 2/21/64 (Orange, NJ), U.S. Navy capt., former NASA shuttle commander.

Anthony M. Kennedy, b 7/23/36 (Sacramento, CA), Supreme Court justice.

Kirk Kerkorian, b 6/6/17 (Fresno, CA), pres. and CEO of investment firm Tracinda Corp.

John Kerry, b 12/11/43 (Aurora, CO), sec. of state, former senator (D, MA), 2004 pres. nominee.

Larry King, b 11/19/33 (Brooklyn, NY), TV talk show host.

Michael Kinsley, b 3/9/51 (Detroit, MI), editor, political commentator.

Calvin Klein, b 11/19/42 (Bronx, NY), fashion designer.

Philip H. Knight, b 2/24/38 (Portland, OR), founder and chairman of the board of Nike.

Charles G. Koch, b 5/3/40 (Wichita, KS), Koch Industries executive; philanthropist.

David H. Koch, b 11/1/35 (Wichita, KS), Koch Industries executive; philanthropist.

Ted Koppel, b 2/8/40 (Lancashire, Eng., UK), former ABC network TV journalist; former anchor of *Nightline*.

Larry Kramer, b 6/25/35 (Bridgeport, CT), AIDS activist, writer.

Nicholas D. Kristof, b 4/27/59 (Chicago, IL), Pulitzer Prize winning columnist, author.

William Kristol, b 12/23/52 (New York, NY), editor, columnist.

Steve Kroft, b 8/22/45 (Kokomo, IN), TV journalist.

Paul Krugman, b 2/28/53 (Long Island, NY), economist, columnist.

Dennis Kucinich, b 10/8/46 (Cleveland, OH), U.S. rep. (D, OH), pres. contender.

Brian Lamb, b 10/9/41 (Lafayette, IN), cable TV exec., journalist.

Wayne LaPierre Jr., b 11/8/49 (NY), National Rifle Assn. exec. VP.

Matt Lauer, b 12/30/57 (New York, NY), TV journalist; NBC *Today* show co-host.

Ralph Lauren, b 10/14/39 (Bronx, NY), fashion designer.

Bernard F. Law, b 11/4/31 (Torreon, Mexico), cardinal archbishop emeritus of Boston.

Patrick Leahy, b 3/31/40 (Montpelier, VT), senator (D, VT), president pro tempore.

Norman Lear, b 7/27/22 (New Haven, CT), TV producer, political activist.

Jim Lehrer, b 5/19/34 (Wichita, KS), TV journalist, author.

Carl Levin, b 6/28/34 (Detroit, MI), senator (D, MI), Armed Services Committee chair.

Jacob Lew, b 8/29/55 (New York, NY), sec. of treasury, former White House chief of staff.

Monica Lewinsky, b 7/23/73 (San Francisco, CA), former White House intern.

Joseph Lieberman, b 2/24/42 (Stamford, CT), former senator (ind., CT), 2000 vice pres. nominee.

Rush Limbaugh, b 1/12/51 (Cape Girardeau, MO), radio talk-show host.

Gary Locke, b 1/21/50 (Seattle, WA), U.S. ambassador to China, former commerce sec., WA governor (D).

Trent Lott, b 10/9/41 (Grenada, MS), former senator (R, MS) and majority leader.

Shannon Lucid, b 1/14/43 (Shanghai, China), NASA scientist, astronaut.

Richard Lugar, b 4/4/32 (Indianapolis, IN), senator (R, IN).

Rachel Maddow, b 4/1/73 (Castro Valley, CA), TV/radio host, political commentator.

Bernie Madoff, b 4/29/38 (Queens, NY), financier who swindled investors; sentenced to 150 years in prison.

Chelsea (fmr. Bradley) Manning, b 12/17/87 (Crescent, OK), Army pvt. convicted on espionage charges for providing classified information to WikiLeaks.

Mary Matalin, b 8/19/53 (Chicago, IL), political commentator.

Chris Matthews, b 12/18/45 (Philadelphia, PA), TV journalist.

John McCain, b 8/29/36 (Panama Canal Zone), senator (R, AZ), 2008 Republican presidential candidate.

Kevin McCarthy, b 1/26/65 (Bakersfield, CA), U.S. rep. (R, CA), House majority whip.

Mitch McConnell, b 2/20/42 (Tuscumbia, AL), senator (R, KY), Senate minority leader.

David McCullough, b 7/7/33 (Pittsburgh, PA), historian, biographer.

Denis McDonough, b 12/2/69 (Stillwater, MN), White House chief of staff.

Dr. Phil McGraw, b 9/1/50 (Vinita, OK), talk-show host, motivational speaker, author.

James McGreevey, b 8/6/57 (Jersey City, NJ), former NJ governor (D); resigned amid allegations of sexual harassment.

John McLaughlin, b 3/29/27 (Providence, RI), TV journalist.

Kate Michelman, b 8/4/42 (NJ), abortion-rights activist.

Kate Millett, b 9/14/34 (St. Paul, MN), author, feminist.

George Mitchell, b 8/20/33, (Waterville, ME), former spec. envoy for Middle East peace, Senate majority leader (D, ME), diplomat, Disney Co. chair.

Walter Mondale, b 1/5/28 (Ceylon, MN), former vice pres., senator (D, MN), 1984 pres. nominee.

Ernest Moniz, b 12/22/44 (Fall River, MA), energy sec., nuclear physicist.

Michael Moore, b 4/23/54 (Davison, MI), activist, documentary filmmaker, author.

Bill Moyers, b 6/5/34 (Hugo, OK), TV journalist, author.

Robert S. Mueller III, b 8/7/44 (New York, NY), former FBI director.

Michael Mullen, b 10/4/46 (Los Angeles, CA), former chairman of Joint Chiefs of Staff.

Rupert Murdoch, b 3/11/31 (Melbourne, Aust.), media exec.

Ralph Nader, b 2/27/34 (Winsted, CT), consumer advocate, independent pres. cand. in 1996, 2000, 2004, and 2008.

Janet Napolitano, b 11/29/57 (New York, NY), homeland security sec., former AZ governor.

Craig Newmark, b 12/6/52 (Morristown, NY), founder of Craigslist.com.

Peggy Noonan, b 9/7/50 (Brooklyn, NY), columnist, speechwriter.

Oliver North, b 10/7/43 (San Antonio, TX), talk-show host, former Natl. Sec. Council aide, figure in Iran-contra scandal.

Eleanor Holmes Norton, b 6/13/37 (Washington, DC), U.S. House delegate for Washington, DC (D).

Sam Nunn, b 9/8/38 (Perry, GA), former senator (D, GA).

Barack Obama, b 8/4/61 (Honolulu, HI), U.S. president, former senator (D, IL).

Michelle Obama, b 1/17/64 (Chicago, IL), first lady, lawyer.

Soledad O'Brien, b 9/19/66 (Smithtown, NY), TV journalist.

Sandra Day O'Connor, b 3/26/30 (El Paso, TX), former Supreme Court justice.

Keith Olbermann, b 1/27/59 (New York, NY), political commentator, former ESPN/MSNBC host.

Todd Oldham, b 11/22/61 (Corpus Christi, TX), fashion designer.

Bill O'Reilly, b 9/10/49 (New York, NY), TV commentator, host.

Joel Osteen, b 3/5/63 (Houston, TX), televangelist, author.

Michael Ovitz, b 12/14/46 (Encino, CA), entertainment exec.

Clarence Page, b 6/2/47 (Dayton, OH), journalist, TV commentator.

Lawrence Page, b 3/26/73 (East Lansing, MI), cofounder of Google.

Camille Paglia, b 4/2/47 (Endicott, NY), scholar, author.

Sarah Palin, b 2/11/64 (Sandpoint, ID), former AK governor (R), 2008 vice-pres. nominee.

Leon E. Panetta, b 6/28/38 (Monterey, CA), former sec. of defense; former CIA director, White House chief of staff, U.S. rep. (D, CA).

Sean Parker, b 12/3/79 (Herndon, VA), cofounder of Napster, Facebook.

Richard Parsons, b 4/4/48 (Brooklyn, NY), former Citigroup chairman, Time Warner CEO.

David Paterson, b 5/20/54 (Brooklyn, NY), attorney, former NY governor (D).

Rand Paul, b 1/7/63 (Pittsburgh, PA), senator (R, KY).

Ron Paul, b 8/20/35 (Pittsburgh, PA), physician, former U.S. rep. (R, TX), pres. contender (2008, 2012).

Jane Pauley, b 10/31/50 (Indianapolis, IN), TV journalist.

Henry Paulson, b 3/28/46 (Palm Beach, FL), former sec. of treasury, former CEO/chairman of Goldman Sachs.

Nancy Pelosi, b 3/26/40 (Baltimore, MD), U.S. rep. (D, CA); House minority leader; former House speaker.

Ross Perot, b 6/27/30 (Texarkana, TX), entrepreneur, former pres. nominee.

Rick Perry, b 3/4/50 (Paint Creek, TX), TX governor (R), former 2012 pres. contender.

David Petraeus, b 11/7/52 (Cornwall-on-Hudson, NY), former CIA director, U.S. Forces Afghanistan cmdr., CENTCOM cmdr.

Fred Phelps Sr., b 11/13/29 (Meridan, MS), pastor and activist.

Colin Powell, b 4/5/37 (New York, NY), former sec. of state, natl. security adviser, Joint Chiefs of Staff chairman.

Samantha Power, b 9/21/70 (Dublin, Ireland), U.S. ambassador to UN.

Reince Priebus, b 3/18/72 (Kenosha, WI), Rep. Natl. Committee chair.

Dan Quayle, b 2/4/47 (Indianapolis, IN), former U.S. vice pres., senator (R, IN).

Anna Quindlen, b 7/8/53 (Philadelphia, PA), author, columnist.

Martha Raddatz, b 1953 (Idaho Falls, ID), ABC news correspondent.

Dan Rather, b 10/31/31 (Wharton, TX), TV journalist, retired CBS anchor.

Nancy Reagan, b 7/6/21 (Flushing, Queens, NY), former first lady.

Sumner Redstone, b 5/27/23 (Boston, MA), Viacom/CBS chairman.

Ralph Reed Jr., b 6/24/61 (Portsmouth, VA), political adviser.

Robert B. Reich, b 6/24/46 (Scranton, PA), economist, author, former labor sec.

Harry Reid, b 12/2/39 (Searchlight, NV), Senate majority leader (D, NV).

Janet Reno, b 7/21/38 (Miami, FL), former U.S. attorney gen.

Condoleezza Rice, b 11/14/54 (Birmingham, AL), former sec. of state, former natl. security adviser.

Susan Rice, b 11/17/64 (Washington, DC), national security adviser, former U.S. ambassador to UN.

Frank Rich, b 6/2/49 (Washington, DC), essayist, columnist.

Cecile Richards, b 1957 (Waco, TX), pres. of Planned Parenthood.

Bill Richardson, b 11/15/47 (Pasadena, CA), former energy sec., UN rep., U.S. rep. (D, NM), NM gov.; 2008 pres. contender.

Tom Ridge, b 8/26/45 (Munhall, PA), former sec. of homeland security, former PA gov.

Geraldo Rivera, b 7/4/43 (New York, NY), TV journalist.

Cokie Roberts, b 12/27/43 (New Orleans, LA), TV journalist.

John G. Roberts, b 1/27/55 (Buffalo, NY), Supreme Court chief justice.

Robin Roberts, b 11/23/60 (Tuskegee, AL), *Good Morning America* co-host.

Rev. Pat Robertson, b 3/22/30 (Lexington, VA), religious broadcasting exec., former pres. contender.

V. Gene Robinson, b 5/29/47 (Lexington, KY), first openly gay Episcopal bishop.

David Rockefeller, b 6/12/15 (New York, NY), banker.

Buddy Roemer, b 10/4/43 (Shreveport, LA), former LA governor, U.S. rep (D); former 2012 pres. contender.

Al Roker, b 8/20/54 (Queens, NY), TV weather person.

Mitt Romney, b 3/12/47 (Detroit, MI), 2012 pres. nominee; former MA governor.

Charlie Rose, b 1/5/42 (Henderson, NC), TV journalist.

Karl Rove, b 12/25/50 (Denver, CO), former adviser to Pres. G. W. Bush, political commentator.

Marco Rubio, b 5/28/71 (Miami, FL), senator (R, FL).

Donald Rumsfeld, b 7/9/32 (Chicago, IL), former sec. of defense.

Paul Ryan, b 1/29/70 (Janesville, WI), 2012 vice pres. nominee; U.S. rep. (R, WI).

Morley Safer, b 11/8/31 (Toronto, ON, Can.), TV journalist.

Rick Santorum, b 5/10/58 (Winchester, VA), former sen. (R, PA), U.S. rep; 2012 pres. contender.

Diane Sawyer, b 12/22/45 (Glasgow, KY), TV journalist, anchor of ABC *World News With Diane Sawyer.*

Antonin Scalia, b 3/11/36 (Trenton, NJ), Supreme Court justice.

Bob Schieffer, b 2/25/37 (Austin, TX), CBS TV news anchor.

Phyllis Schlafly, b 8/15/24 (St. Louis, MO), political activist.

Caroline Kennedy Schlossberg, b 11/27/57 (New York, NY), ambassador to Japan, author, daughter of Pres. Kennedy.

Eric Schmidt, b 4/27/55 (Washington, DC), former Google CEO.

Rev. Robert Schuller, b 9/16/26 (Alton, IA), TV evangelist.

Charles Schumer, b 11/23/50 (Brooklyn, NY), senator (D, NY).

Arnold Schwarzenegger, b 7/30/47 (Thal, Styria, Austria), actor, former CA governor.

Willard Scott, b 3/7/34 (Alexandria, VA), former TV weather person.

Kathleen Sebelius, b 5/15/58 (Cincinnati, OH), health and human services sec., former KS governor.

Allan H. (Bud) Selig, b 7/30/34 (Milwaukee, WI), MLB commissioner.

Richard Serra, b 11/2/39 (San Francisco, CA), sculptor.

Rev. Al Sharpton, b 10/3/54 (Brooklyn, NY), activist, civil rights leader, TV personality.

Eric Shinseki, b 11/28/42 (Lihue, HI), veterans affairs sec., former Army chief of staff.

Will Shortz, b 8/26/52 (Crawfordsville, IN), puzzle editor.

Maria Shriver, b 11/6/55 (Chicago, IL), TV journalist, former CA first lady.

George P. Shultz, b 12/13/20 (New York, NY), former sec. of state, other cabinet posts.

Nate Silver, b 1/13/78 (E. Lansing, MI), statistician.

Russell Simmons, b 10/4/57 (Queens, NY), music producer.

Bob Simon, b 5/29/41 (Bronx, NY), TV journalist.

O. J. Simpson, b 7/9/47 (San Francisco, CA), former football star, murder defendant.

Harry Smith, b 8/21/51 (Lansing, IL), NBC TV journalist, former CBS morning anchor.

Liz Smith, b 2/2/23 (Ft. Worth, TX), gossip columnist.

Edward Snowden, b 6/21/83 (Elizabeth City, NC), computer specialist accused of leaking classified information about U.S. and UK govt. surveillance.

Hilda Solis, b 10/20/57 (Los Angeles, CA), labor sec., former U.S. rep. (D, CA).

George Soros, b 8/12/30 (Budapest, Hungary), financier, philanthropist.

Sonia Sotomayor, b 6/25/54 (Bronx, NY), Supreme Court justice.

David H. Souter, b 9/17/39 (Melrose, MA), former Supreme Court justice.

Kate Spade, b 1962 (Kansas City, MO), fashion designer.

Steven Spielberg, b 12/18/46 (Cincinnati, OH), movie director, producer.

Eliot Spitzer, b 6/10/59 (Bronx, NY), former NY gov. (D); resigned after involvement with prostitutes exposed.

Lesley Stahl, b 12/16/41 (Swampscott, MA), TV journalist.

Michael Steele, b 10/19/58 (Prince George's Co., MD), former Rep. Natl. Committee chair, MD lt. gov.

Shelby Steele, b 1/1/46 (Chicago, IL), scholar, critic.

Ben Stein, b 11/25/44 (Washington, DC), attorney, columnist, former speechwriter, actor, TV personality.

Gloria Steinem, b 3/25/34 (Toledo, OH), author, feminist.

Frank Stella, b 5/12/36 (Malden, MA), painter.

George Stephanopoulos, b 2/10/61 (Fall River, MA), TV journalist, former pres. adviser; *Good Morning America* co-host.

David J. Stern, b 9/22/42 (New York, NY), NBA commissioner.

Howard Stern, b 1/12/54 (Roosevelt, NY), radio talk show host.

John Paul Stevens, b 4/20/20 (Chicago, IL), former Supreme Court justice.

Martha Stewart, b 8/3/41 (Nutley, NJ), homemaking adviser, entrepreneur, TV personality.

Biz Stone, b 3/10/74 (Boston, MA), cofounder of Twitter.

Chesley Sullenberger III, b 1/23/51 (Denison, TX), US Airways pilot who safely landed a jet in the Hudson River.

Andrew Sullivan, b 8/10/63 (Eng., UK), political commentator and blogger.

Arthur Ochs Sulzberger Jr., b 9/22/51 (Mt. Kisco, NY), newspaper publisher.

Lawrence H. Summers, b 11/30/54 (New Haven, CT), economist; former Natl. Economic Council dir., Harvard Univ. pres., sec. of treasury.

George Tenet, b 1/5/53 (Flushing, Queens, NY), former CIA director.

Clarence Thomas, b 6/23/48 (Savannah, GA), Supreme Court justice.

Richard Trumka, b 7/24/49 (Waynesburg, PA), pres. of AFL-CIO.

Donald Trump, b 6/14/46 (Jamaica, Queens, NY), real estate exec., TV personality.

Ted Turner, b 11/19/38 (Cincinnati, OH), TV exec., philanthropist.

Neil deGrasse Tyson, b 10/5/58 (New York, NY), astrophysicist, director of NYC's Hayden Planetarium, author, TV host.

Gloria Vanderbilt, b 2/20/24 (New York, NY), fashion designer, heiress.

Greta Van Susteren, b 6/11/54 (Appleton, WI), attorney, TV journalist.

Jesse Ventura, b 7/15/51 (Minneapolis, MN), former wrestler, former MN governor; radio talk show host.

Meredith Vieira, b 12/30/53 (Providence, RI), former *Today* show co-host.

Antonio Villaraigosa, b 1/23/53 (East Los Angeles, CA), first Hispanic mayor of L.A. since 1870s.

Paul Volcker, b 9/5/27 (Cape May, NJ), economist, former Federal Reserve chairman.

Jimmy Wales, b 8/8/66 (Huntsville, AL), co founder of Wikipedia.

Barbara Walters, b 9/25/31 (Boston, MA), TV journalist.

Vera Wang, b 6/27/49 (New York, NY), fashion designer.

Rick Warren, b 1/28/54 (San Jose, CA), evangelical Christian pastor, founder of Saddleback Church, author.

Debbie Wasserman Schultz, b 9/27/66 (Forest Hills, NY), U.S. rep. (D, FL), Dem. Natl. Committee chair.

James Watson, b 4/6/28 (Chicago, IL), biochemist, DNA pioneer, co-winner of the 1962 Nobel Prize.

Dr. Andrew Weil, b 6/8/42 (Philadelphia, PA), health adviser.

Anthony Weiner, b 9/4/64 (Brooklyn, NY), former U.S. rep. (D, NY); resigned after 2011 scandal.

Harvey Weinstein, b 3/19/52 (Flushing, Queens, NY), movie exec.

Jack Welch, b 11/19/35 (Peabody, MA), former General Electric CEO.

Jann Wenner, b 1/7/46 (New York, NY), publisher, founder of *Rolling Stone*.

Cornel West, b 6/23/53 (Tulsa, OK), African American scholar, critic.

Ruth Westheimer, b 6/4/28 (Frankfurt am Main, Germany), human sexuality expert.

Meg Whitman, b 8/4/56 (Cold Spring Harbor, NY), 2010 CA gubernatorial candidate (R), former eBay CEO; HP CEO.

Elie Wiesel, b 9/30/28 (Sighet, Romania), scholar, author, 1986 Nobel Peace Prize winner.

George Will, b 5/4/41 (Champaign, IL), journalist, author.

Brian Williams, b 5/5/59 (Ridgewood, NJ), NBC TV news anchor.

Evan Williams, b 3/31/72 (Clarks, NE), cofounder and CEO of Twitter.

Jody Williams, b 10/9/50 (Brattleboro, VT), peace activist, 1997 Nobel Peace Prize winner.

Oprah Winfrey, b 1/29/54 (Kosciusko, MS), TV and media personality, businesswoman, actress.

Bob Woodward, b 3/26/43 (Geneva, IL), journalist; with Bernstein cracked Watergate scandal.

Steve Wozniak, b 8/11/50 (Sunnyvale, CA), inventor, cofounder of Apple Computer.

Steve Wynn, b 1/27/42 (New Haven, CT), casino developer.

Chuck Yeager, b 2/13/23 (Myra, WV), test pilot, first man to break sound barrier.

Paula Zahn, b 2/24/56 (Omaha, NE), TV journalist.

Mark Zuckerberg, b 5/14/84 (Dobbs Ferry, NY), founder of Facebook.

Mortimer Zuckerman, b 6/4/37 (Montreal, QC, Can.), publisher, columnist.

Widely Known World Personalities of the Present

Living non-Americans only. Generally excludes current heads of state or government (see Nations chapter) and excludes most others covered elsewhere, such as in Widely Known Americans, Writers, and Entertainment or Sports Personalities.

Mahmoud Abbas (Abu Mazen), b 3/26/35 (Safed, Palestine [now Israel]), president of the Palestinian National Authority.

Gerry Adams, b 10/6/48 (Belfast, N. Ireland, UK), Sinn Féin leader.

Mahmoud Ahmadinejad, b 10/28/56 (Garmsar, Iran), former Iranian pres.

Albert II, b 6/6/34 (Brussels, Belgium), former king (1993-2013).

Viswanathan Anand, b 12/11/69 (Chennai, Madras, India), world chess champion.

Prince Andrew, b 2/19/60 (London, Eng., UK), Duke of York (second son of Queen Elizabeth II).

Kofi Annan, b 4/8/38 (Kumasi, Ghana), former UN sec.-gen.; 2001 Nobel laureate.

Princess Anne, b 8/15/50 (London, Eng., UK), Princess Royal (daughter of Queen Elizabeth II).

Michael Arad, b 1969 (London, Eng., UK), designer of the Natl. 9/11 Memorial in NYC.

Oscar Arias Sánchez, b 9/13/41 (Heredia, Costa Rica), former Costa Rican pres., peace negotiator, 1987 Nobel laureate.

Giorgio Armani, b 7/30/34 (Piacenza, Italy), fashion designer.

Julian Assange, b 7/3/71 (Townsville, Queensland, Australia), founder of WikiLeaks media org.

Michelle Bachelet, b 9/29/51 (Santiago, Chile), former Chilean pres.

Ban Ki-moon, b 6/13/44 (Umsong, [now] South Korea), UN sec.-gen.

Ehud Barak, b 2/12/42 (Mishmar Ha-Sharon Kibbutz, Israel), former Israeli minister of defense, former Israeli prime min.

Beatrix, b 1/31/38 (Netherlands), former queen (1980-2013).

Benedict XVI (Joseph Ratzinger), b 4/16/27 (Marktl am Inn, Germany), pope emeritus of Rom. Cath. Church, elected 2005.

Boris Berezovsky, b 1/23/46 (Moscow, USSR), businessman, politician.

Tim Berners-Lee, b 6/8/55 (London, Eng., UK), World Wide Web inventor.

Tony Blair, b 5/6/53 (Edinburgh, Scot., UK), former British prime min.

Hans Blix, b 6/28/28 (Uppsala, Swed.), former UN weapons inspector.

Bono (Paul David Hewson), b 5/20/60 (Glasnevin, Dublin, Ire., UK), musician, social activist, philanthropist.

Fernando Botero, b 4/19/32 (Medellín, Col.), Colombian artist.

Boutros Boutros-Ghali, b 11/14/22 (Cairo, Egypt), former UN sec.-gen.

Richard Branson, b 7/18/50 (S. London, Eng., UK), British Virgin Records and Airways founder.

Gordon Brown, b 2/20/51 (Glasgow, Scot., UK), former British prime min.

Tina Brown, b 11/21/53 (Maidenhead, Eng., UK), journalist, TV talk show host, author.

Carla Bruni, b 12/23/67 (Turin, Italy), former first lady of France, musician, actress, model.

Mark Burnett, b 7/17/60 (Myland, Eng., UK), reality TV producer.

Rhonda Byrne, b 3/12/51 (Australia), author, TV writer and producer.

Kim Campbell, b 3/10/47 (Port Alberni, BC, Can.), former Canadian prime min.

Pierre Cardin, b 7/7/22 (San Biaggio di Callalta, Italy), fashion designer.

Princess Caroline, b 1/23/57 (Monte Carlo, Monaco), Monaco royal (eldest daughter of Prince Rainier and Princess Grace).

Fidel Castro, b 8/13/26 (Birán, Cuba), former prime min., pres. of Cuba.

Prince Charles, b 11/14/48 (London, Eng., UK), Prince of Wales (eldest son of Queen Elizabeth II); heir to British throne.

Chen Guangcheng, b 11/12/71 (Dongshigu, China), civil rights activist.

Jacques Chirac, b 11/29/32 (Paris, France), former French pres.

Deepak Chopra, b 1946 (New Delhi, India), new age writer.

Jean Chrétien, b 1/11/34 (Shawinigan, QC, Can.), former Canadian prime min.

Christo (Javacheff), b 6/13/35 (Gabrovo, Bulg.), artist.

Joe (Charles Joseph) Clark, b 6/5/39 (High River, AB, Can.), former Canadian prime min.

King Constantine II, b 6/2/40 (Psychiko, Greece), former king of Greece.

Simon Cowell, b 10/7/59 (Brighton, East Sussex, Eng., UK), music exec., TV producer, former *American Idol* host.

Dalai Lama, 14th (Tenzin Gyatso), b 7/6/35 (Taktser, Amdo, Tibet), Buddhist leader; 1989 Nobel Peace Prize laureate.

Richard Dawkins, b 3/26/41 (Nairobi, Kenya), ethologist, evolutionary biologist, author.

F. W. (Frederik Willem) de Klerk, b 3/18/36 (Johannesburg, S. Africa), former S. African pres.; 1993 Nobel Peace Prize winner.

Mario Draghi, b 9/3/47 (Rome, Italy), European Central Bank pres.

Shirin Ebadi, b 6/21/47 (Hamadan, Iran), human rights activist, 2003 Nobel Peace Prize winner.

Prince Edward, b 3/10/64 (London, Eng., UK), Earl of Essex (third son of Queen Elizabeth II).

Mohamed ElBaradei, b 6/17/42 (Cairo, Egypt), former director general of the International Atomic Energy Agency (IAEA); 2005 Nobel Peace Prize winner.

Prince Felipe, b 1/30/68 (Madrid, Spain), heir to Spanish throne.

Sarah Ferguson, b 10/15/58 (London, Eng., UK), Duchess of York, ex-wife of Prince Andrew.

Francis (Jorge Mario Bergoglio) b 12/17/36 (Buenos Aires, Argentina), pope of Rom. Cath. Church.

John Galliano, b 11/28/60 (Gibraltar, UK terr.), fashion designer.

Prince George Alexander Louis (of Cambridge), b 7/22/13 (London, Eng., UK), third in line to British throne, prince of Cambridge.

Wael Ghonim, b 12/23/80 (Cairo, Egypt), computer engineer and Internet activist.

Valery Giscard d'Estaing, b 2/2/26 (Koblenz, Ger.), former French pres.

Jane Goodall, b 4/3/34 (London, Eng., UK), anthropologist, primatologist.

Mikhail Gorbachev, b 3/2/31 (Privolnoye, USSR), former Soviet pres.; 1990 Nobel Peace Prize winner.

Jürgen Habermas, b 6/18/29 (Dusseldorf, Ger.), philosopher.

Stephen Hawking, b 1/8/42 (Oxford, Eng., UK), physicist, author.

Prince Henry (Harry) (of Wales), b 9/15/84 (London, Eng., UK), son of Prince Charles.

Damien Hirst, b 6/7/65 (Bristol, Eng., UK), artist.

David Hockney, b 7/9/37 (Bradford, Eng., UK), artist.

Hu Jintao, b 12/21/42 (Shanghai, China), former pres. of China.

Jiang Zemin, b 8/17/26 (Yangzhou, Jiangsu Prov., China), former pres. of China.

Garry Kasparov, b 4/13/63 (Baku, Azerbaijan, USSR), former world chess champion; Russian pro-democracy leader.

Ayatollah Ali Khamenei, b 7/17/39 (Mashhad, Iran), Supreme Leader and former president of Iran, cleric, author.

Helmut Kohl, b 4/3/30 (Ludwigshafen, Ger.), former German chancellor.

Hans Kung, b 3/19/28 (Sursee, Switz.), Rom. Cath. theologian.

Christine Lagarde, b 1/1/56 (Paris, France), Intl. Monetary Fund managing dir.

Karl Lagerfeld, b 9/10/38 (Hamburg, Germany), fashion designer.

Richard Leakey, b 12/19/44 (Nairobi, Kenya), anthropologist, paleontologist, conservationist.

Jean-Marie Le Pen, b 6/20/28 (La Trinitesur-Mer, Fr.), French right-wing politician.

Marine Le Pen, b 8/5/68 (Neuilly-sur-Seine, France), head of France's National Front Party.

Tzipi Livni, b 7/5/58 (Tel Aviv, Israel), attorney, former head of Israeli Kadima party, foreign affairs minister of Israel.

John Major, b 3/29/43 (Wimbledon, Eng., UK), former British prime min.

Nelson Mandela, b 7/18/18 (Transkei, S. Africa), former pres. of S. Africa; 1993 Nobel Peace Prize winner.

Imelda Marcos, b 7/2/29 (Manila, Philip.), former first lady of Philippines; Philip. House of Rep. member.

Paul Martin, b 8/28/38 (Windsor, ON, Can.), former prime min. of Canada.

Peter Max, b 10/19/37 (Berlin, Ger.), artist, designer.

Stella McCartney, b 9/13/71 (London, Eng., UK), fashion designer.

Angela Merkel, b 7/17/54 (Hamburg, Ger.), first woman chancellor of Germany.

Jean-Marie Messier, b 12/13/56 (Grenoble, Fr.), former CEO of Vivendi Universal.

Empress Michiko, b 10/20/34 (Tokyo, Japan), empress of Japan.

Kate Middleton (Catherine, Duchess of Cambridge), b 1/9/82 (Reading, UK), wife of Prince William.

Mohammed Morsi, b 8/8/51 (Edwa, Egypt), first democratically elected pres. of Egypt; deposed July 2013.

Kate Moss, b 1/16/74 (Addiscombe, Surrey, Eng., UK), model.

Hosni Mubarak, b 5/4/28 (Kafre al-Musailha, Egypt), deposed Egyptian president.

Brian Mulroney, b 3/20/39 (Baie-Corneau, QC, Can.), former Canadian prime min.

Prince Naruhito, b 2/23/60 (Tokyo, Japan), crown prince of Japan.

Hassan Nasrallah, b 8/31/60 (Qarantina, Lebanon), leader of the Hezbollah in Lebanon.

Queen Noor (Lisa Halaby), b 8/23/51 (Washington, DC), American-born widow of Jordan's King Hussein.

Ehud Olmert, b 9/30/45 (Binyamina, Palestine), former prime min. of Israel.

Daniel Ortega Saavedra, b 11/11/45 (La Libertad, Nicar.), Nicaraguan pres., Sandinista leader.

Camilla Parker-Bowles, Duchess of Cornwall, b 7/17/47 (London, Eng., UK), wife of Prince Charles.

Javier Perez de Cuellar, b 1/19/20 (Lima, Peru), former UN sec.-gen.

Prince Philip, b 6/10/21 (Corfu, Greece), Duke of Edinburgh (husband of Queen Elizabeth II).

Gerhard Richter, b 2/9/32 (Dresden, Ger.), artist.

Mary Robinson, b 5/21/44 (Ballina, Co. Mayo, Ireland), former Irish pres., former UN High Commissioner for Human Rights.

Ségolène Royal, b 9/22/53 (Dakar, Senegal), French socialist politician.

Muqtada al-Sadr, b 8/12/73? (Najaf, Iraq), extremist Shiite cleric.

Carlos Salinas de Gortari, b 4/3/48 (Mexico City, Mex.), former Mexican pres.

Nicolas Sarkozy, b 1/28/55 (Paris, France), former French pres.

Helmut Schmidt, b 12/23/18 (Hamburg, Germany), former German chancellor.

Gerhard Schröder, b 4/7/44 (Mossenburg, Germany), former German chancellor.

Ariel Sharon, b 2/26/28 (Kfar Malal, Palestine), former Israeli prime min.

Eduard Shevardnadze, b 1/25/28 (Mamati, Georgia, USSR), former Georgian pres.

Ayatollah Ali al-Sistani, b 8/4/30 (Mashhad, Iran), major Iraqi Shiite religious leader.

Carlos Slim Helú, b 1/28/40 (Mexico City, Mexico), chairman and CEO of Telmex, Telcel and América Móvil.

Princess Stephanie, b 2/1/65 (Monte Carlo, Monaco), youngest child of Prince Rainier and Princess Grace.

Dominique Strauss-Kahn, b 4/25/49 (Neuilly-sur-Seine, France), former Intl. Monetary Fund managing dir.

Aung San Suu Kyi, b 6/19/45 (Rangoon, Myanmar), member of parliament, pro-democracy political activist, 1991 Nobel Peace Prize winner.

Valentina Tereshkova, b 3/6/37 (Maslennikovo, Russia, USSR), first woman in space.

John Napier Turner, b 6/7/29 (Richmond, Surrey, Eng., UK), former Canadian prime min.

Desmond Tutu, b 10/7/31 (Klerksdorp, Transvaal, S. Africa), former S. African archbishop; 1984 Nobel Peace Prize winner.

Lech Walesa, b 9/29/43 (Popowo, Pol.), Solidarity leader; 1983 Nobel Peace Prize winner; former president of Poland.

Prince William (Duke of Cambridge), b 6/21/82 (London, Eng., UK), son of Prince Charles; 2nd in line to British throne.

Rowan Williams, b 6/14/50 (Ystradgynlais, Wales, UK), Archbishop of Canterbury.

Malala Yousafzai, b 7/12/97 (Mingora, Pakistan), education activist.

Muhammad Yunus, b 6/28/40 (Chittagong, India), economist, 2006 Nobel Peace Prize winner.

Mohammad Javad Zarif, b 1/8/60 (Tehran, Iran), Irani minister of foreign affairs.

Ayman al-Zawahiri, b 6/19/51 (Cairo, Egypt), reputed high-ranking al-Qaeda leader.

Architects

Alvar Aalto, 1898-1976, Säynätsalo, Jyväskylä, Finland; Vuoksenniska Church, Vuoksenniska, Finland.

Max Abramovitz, 1908-2004, Avery Fisher Hall, New York, NY; U.S. Steel Bldg. (now USX Towers), Pittsburgh, PA.

Tadao Ando, b 1941, Modern Art Museum, Ft. Worth, TX; Stone Hill Center, MA.

Michael Arad, b 1969, World Trade Center Memorial, New York, NY.

Henry Bacon, 1866-1924, Lincoln Memorial, Washington, DC.

Benjamin Banneker, 1731-1806, African American inventor, astronomer, mathematician; helped design and lay out Washington, DC.

Pietro Belluschi, 1899-1994, Juilliard School, Lincoln Center, Pan Am Bldg.

(now MetLife Bldg.) with Walter Gropius, New York, NY.

Marcel Breuer, 1902-81, Whitney Museum of American Art (with Hamilton Smith), New York, NY.

Charles Bulfinch, 1763-1844, State House, Boston, MA; Capitol (part), Wash., DC.

Gordon Bunshaft, 1909-90, Lever House, Park Ave., New York, NY; Hirshhorn Museum, Washington, DC.

Daniel H. Burnham, 1846-1912, Union Station, Washington, DC; Flatiron Bldg., New York, NY.

Irwin Chanin, 1892-1988, theaters, skyscrapers, New York, NY.

David Childs, b 1941, Washington Mall Master Plan/Constitution Gardens,

Washington, DC; One World Trade Center, New York, NY.

Lucio Costa, 1902-98, master plan for city of Brasilia, Brazil (with Oscar Niemeyer).

Ralph Adams Cram, 1863-1942, Cath. of St. John the Divine, New York, NY; U.S. Military Acad. (part), West Point, NY.

Norman Foster, b 1935, Commerzbank Headquarters, Frankfurt-am-Main, Ger.; London Millennium Bridge, Eng., UK; 30 St. Mary Axe, Eng., UK.

James Ingo Freed, 1930-2005, Holocaust Memorial Museum, Washington, DC; Jacob K. Javits Center, New York, NY.

R. Buckminster Fuller, 1895-1983, U.S. Pavilion (geodesic domes), Expo 67, Montreal, QC, Can.

Frank O. Gehry, b 1929, Guggenheim Museum, Bilbao, Spain; Experience Music Project, Seattle, WA; Walt Disney Concert Hall, Los Angeles, CA.

Cass Gilbert, 1859-1934, Custom House, Woolworth Bldg., New York, NY; Supreme Court Bldg., Washington, DC.

Bertram G. Goodhue, 1869-1924, Capitol, Lincoln, NE; St. Thomas's Church, St. Bartholomew's Church, New York, NY.

Michael Graves, b 1934, Portland Bldg., Portland, OR; Humana Bldg., Louisville, KY.

Walter Gropius, 1883-1969, Pan Am Bldg. (now MetLife Bldg.) (with Pietro Belluschi), New York, NY.

Zaha Hadid, b 1950, Rosenthal Center for Contemporary Art, Cincinnati, OH; London Aquatics Centre, Eng., UK.

Lawrence Halprin, 1916-2009, Ghirardelli Sq., San Francisco, CA; Nicollet Mall, Minneapolis, MN; FDR Memorial, Washington, DC.

Peter Harrison, 1716-75, Touro Synagogue, Redwood Library, Newport, RI.

Wallace K. Harrison, 1895-1981, Metropolitan Opera House, Lincoln Center, New York, NY.

Thomas Hastings, 1860-1929, NY Public Library (with John Carrère), Frick Mansion, New York, NY.

James Hoban, 1762-1831, White House, Washington, DC.

Raymond Hood, 1881-1934, Rockefeller Center (part), Daily News Bldg., New York, NY; Tribune Tower, Chicago, IL.

Richard M. Hunt, 1827-95, Metropolitan Museum (part), New York, NY; Biltmore Estate, Asheville, NC.

Helmut Jahn, b 1940, United Airlines Terminal, O'Hare Airport, Chicago, IL.

William Le Baron Jenney, 1832-1907, Home Insurance Bldg. (demolished 1931), Chicago, IL.

Philip C. Johnson, 1906-2005, AT&T headquarters (now 550 Madison Ave.), New York, NY; Transco (now Williams) Tower, Houston, TX.

Albert Kahn, 1869-1942, General Motors Bldg., Detroit, MI.

Louis Kahn, 1901-74, Salk Laboratory, La Jolla, CA; Yale Art Gallery, New Haven, CT.

Rem Koolhaas, b 1944, Seattle Central Library, Seattle, WA.

Christopher Grant LaFarge, 1862-1938, Roman Catholic Chapel, West Point, NY.

Benjamin H. Latrobe, 1764-1820, Capitol (part), Washington, DC; State Capitol Bldg., Richmond, VA.

Le Corbusier (Charles-Edouard Jeanneret), 1887-1965, Salvation Army Hostel, Swiss Dormitory, Paris, France; master plan for cities of Algiers and Buenos Aires.

William Lescaze, 1896-1969, Philadelphia Savings Fund Society, PA; Borg-Warner Bldg., Chicago, IL.

Daniel Libeskind, b 1946, primary architect for the rebuilding World Trade Center site, New York, NY.

Maya Lin, b 1959, Vietnam Veterans Mem., Washington, DC.

Charles Rennie Mackintosh, 1868-1928, Glasgow School of Art; Hill House, Helensburgh, Scot., UK.

Bernard R. Maybeck, 1862-1957, Hearst Hall, Univ. of CA, Berkeley; First Church of Christ Scientist, Berkeley, CA.

Charles F. McKim, 1847-1909, Boston Public Library; Columbia Univ. (part), New York, NY.

Charles M. McKim, b 1920, KUHT-TV Transmitter Bldg., Lutheran Church of the Redeemer, Houston, TX.

Richard Meier, b 1934, Getty Center Museum, Los Angeles, CA; High Museum of Art, Atlanta, GA.

Ludwig Mies van der Rohe, 1886-1969, Seagram Bldg. (with Philip C. Johnson), New York, NY; National Gallery, Berlin, Ger.

Robert Mills, 1781-1855, Washington Monument, Washington, DC.

Charles Moore, 1925-93, Sea Ranch, nr. San Francisco, CA; Piazza d'Italia, New Orleans, LA.

Julia Morgan, 1872-1957, San Simeon, CA.

John Nash, 1752-1835, Buckingham Palace, London, Eng., UK.

Richard J. Neutra, 1892-1970, Mathematics Park, Princeton, NJ; Orange Co. Courthouse, Santa Ana, CA.

Oscar Niemeyer, 1907-2012, government buildings, Brasilia Palace Hotel, all Brasilia, Braz.

Gyo Obata, b 1923, Natl. Air and Space Museum, Smithsonian Inst., Washington, DC; Dallas-Ft. Worth Airport, TX.

Frederick L. Olmsted, 1822-1903, Central Park, New York, NY; Fairmount Park, Philadelphia, PA.

I(eoh) M(ing) Pei, b 1917, East Wing, Natl. Gallery of Art, Washington, DC; Pyramid, The Louvre, Paris, Fr.; Rock & Roll Hall of Fame and Museum, Cleveland, OH.

Cesar Pelli, b 1926, World Financial Center, Carnegie Hall Tower, New York, NY; Petronas Twin Towers, Malaysia.

William Pereira, 1909-85, Cape Canaveral, FL; Transamerica Bldg., San Francisco, CA.

Renzo Piano, b 1937, Pompidou Centre, Paris, Fr.; New York Times Bldg., New York, NY; The Shard, London.

John Russell Pope, 1874-1937, National Gallery, Jefferson Memorial, Wash., DC.

John Portman, b 1924, Peachtree Center, Atlanta, GA.

George Browne Post, 1837-1913, NY Stock Exchange, New York, NY; Capitol, Madison, WI.

James Renwick Jr., 1818-95, Grace Church, St. Patrick's Cathedral, New York, NY; Smithsonian Institution (Castle), Washington, DC.

Henry H. Richardson, 1838-86, Trinity Church, Boston, MA.

Kevin Roche, b 1922, Oakland Museum, Oakland, CA; Fine Arts Center, University of Massachusetts, Amherst, MA.

James Gamble Rogers, 1867-1947, Columbia-Presbyterian Medical Ctr., New York, NY; Northwestern Univ., Evanston, IL.

John Wellborn Root, 1887-1963, Palmolive Bldg., Chicago, IL; Hotel Statler, Washington, DC.

Paul Rudolph, 1918-97, Jewitt Art Center, Wellesley College, MA; Art & Architecture Bldg., Yale Univ., New Haven, CT.

Eero Saarinen, 1910-61, Gateway to the West Arch, St. Louis, MO; Trans World Airlines Flight Center, New York, NY.

Kazuyo Sejima, b 1956, 21st Century Museum of Contemporary Art, Kanazawa, Japan (with Ryue Nishizawa).

Louis Skidmore, 1897-1962, Atomic Energy Commission town site, Oak Ridge, TN; Terrace Plaza Hotel, Cincinnati, OH.

Norma Merrick Sklarek, 1928-2012, Terminal One at Los Angeles International Airport, CA.

Clarence S. Stein, 1882-1975, Temple Emanu-El, New York, NY.

Edward Durell Stone, 1902-78, interior of Radio City Music Hall, Museum of Modern Art, New York, NY.

Louis H. Sullivan, 1856-1924, Auditorium Bldg., Chicago, IL.

Kenzo Tange, 1913-2005, Hiroshima Peace Park, 1964 Tokyo Olympics twin stadiums, Japan.

Richard Upjohn, 1802-78, Trinity Church, New York, NY.

Max O. Urbahn, 1912-95, Vehicle Assembly Bldg., Cape Canaveral, FL.

Joern Utzon, 1918-2008, Sydney Opera House, Australia.

William Van Alen, 1883-1954, Chrysler Building, New York, NY.

Robert Venturi, b 1925, Gordon Wu Hall, Princeton, NJ; Mielparque Nikko Kirifuri Resort, Japan.

Ralph T. Walker, 1889-1973, NY Telephone Bldg., New York, NY; IBM Research Lab, Poughkeepsie, NY.

Roland A. Wank, 1898-1970, Cincinnati Union Terminal, OH; head architect, 1933-44, Tennessee Valley Authority.

Stanford White, 1853-1906, Washington Arch in Washington Square Park, first Madison Square Garden, New York, NY.

Christopher Wren, 1632-1723, St. Paul's Cathedral, London, Eng., UK.

Frank Lloyd Wright, 1867-1959, Imperial Hotel, Tokyo, Jpn.; Guggenheim Museum, New York, NY; Kaufmann "Fallingwater" house, Bear Run, PA; Taliesin West, Scottsdale, AZ.

Thomas Wright, b 1957, Burj Al Arab hotel, Dubai.

William Wurster, 1895-1973, Ghirardelli Sq., San Francisco, CA.

Minoru Yamasaki, 1912-86, World Trade Center (destroyed 2001), New York, NY.

Artists, Photographers, and Sculptors of the Past

Artists are painters unless otherwise indicated.

Berenice Abbott, 1898-1991, (U.S.) photographer. Documentary of New York City, *Changing New York* (1939).

Ansel Easton Adams, 1902-84, (U.S.) photographer. Landscapes of the American Southwest.

Washington Allston, 1779-1843, (U.S.) landscapist. *Belshazzar's Feast.*

Albrecht Altdorfer, 1480-1538, (Ger.) landscapist.

Fra Angelico, c. 1400-55, (It.) Renaissance muralist. *Madonna of the Linen Drapers' Guild.*

Diane Arbus, 1923-71, (U.S.) photographer. Disturbing images.

Alexsandr Archipenko, 1887-1964, (U.S.) sculptor. *Boxing Match*, *Medrano.*

Jean Arp, 1887-1966, (Fr.) sculptor and painter, founder of Dada movement.

Richard Artschwager, 1923-2013, (U.S.) painter and sculptor. *Table With Pink Tablecloth.*

Eugène Atget, 1856-1927, (Fr.) photographer. Paris life.

John James Audubon, 1785-1851, (U.S.) *Birds of America.*

Richard Avedon, 1923-2004, (U.S.) fashion and celebrity photographer.

Hans Baldung-Grien, 1484-1545, (Ger.) *Todentanz.*

Ernst Barlach, 1870-1938, (Ger.) Expressionist sculptor. *Man Drawing a Sword.*

Frédéric-Auguste Bartholdi, 1834-1904, (Fr.) sculptor. *Liberty Enlightening the World* (Statue of Liberty).

Fra Bartolommeo, 1472-1517, (It.) *Vision of St. Bernard.*

Romare Bearden, 1911-88, (U.S.) collage and other media. *The Visitation.*

Aubrey Beardsley, 1872-98, (Br.) illustrator. *Salome, Lysistrata, Morte d'Arthur, Volpone.*

Cecil Beaton, 1904-80, (Br.) fashion and celebrity photographer.

Max Beckmann, 1884-1950, (Ger.) Expressionist. *The Descent From the Cross.*

Gentile Bellini, 1426-1507, (It.) Renaissance. *Procession in St. Mark's Square.*

Giovanni Bellini, 1428-1516, (It.) Renaissance. *St. Francis in Ecstasy.*

Jacopo Bellini, 1400-70, (It.) Renaissance. *Crucifixion.*

George Wesley Bellows, 1882-1925, (U.S.) sports artist, portraitist, landscapist. *Stag at Sharkey's*, *Edith Clavell.*

Thomas Hart Benton, 1889-1975, (U.S.) American regionalist. *Threshing Wheat, Arts of the West.*

Ruth Bernhard, 1905-2006, (Ger.-U.S.) photographer. Black-and-white studies of female nudes.

Gianlorenzo Bernini, 1598-1680, (It.) Baroque sculptor. *The Assumption.*

Albert Bierstadt, 1830-1902, (U.S.) landscapist. *The Rocky Mountains, Mount Corcoran.*

George Caleb Bingham, 1811-79, (U.S.) American frontier. *Fur Traders Descending the Missouri.*

William Blake, 1757-1827, (Br.) engraver. *Book of Job, Songs of Innocence, Songs of Experience.*

Rosa Bonheur, 1822-99, (Fr.) Realist. *The Horse Fair.*

Pierre Bonnard, 1867-1947, (Fr.) Intimist. *The Breakfast Room, Girl in a Straw Hat.*

Gutzon Borglum, 1867-1941, (U.S.) sculptor. Mt. Rushmore Memorial.

Hieronymus Bosch, 1450-1516, (Flem.) religious allegories. *The Crowning With Thorns.*

Sandro Botticelli, 1444-1510, (It.) Renaissance. *Birth of Venus, Adoration of the Magi, Guiliano de'Medici.*

Louise Bourgeois, 1911-2010, (Fr.) sculptor. *Maman.*

Margaret Bourke-White, 1904-71, (U.S.) photographer, photojournalist. WWII, USSR, rural South during the Depression.

Mathew Brady, c. 1823-96, (U.S.) official photographer of the Civil War.

Constantin Brancusi, 1876-1957, (Romania-Fr.) Nonobjective sculptor. *Flying Turtle, The Kiss.*

Georges Braque, 1882-1963, (Fr.) Cubist. *Violin and Palette.*

Pieter Bruegel the Elder, c. 1525-69, (Flem.) Renaissance. *The Peasant Dance, Hunters in the Snow, Magpie on the Gallows.*

Pieter Bruegel the Younger, 1564-1638, (Flem.) Baroque. *Village Fair, The Crucifixion.*

Edward Burne-Jones, 1833-98, (Br.) Pre-Raphaelite artist-craftsman. *The Mirror of Venus.*

Alexander Calder, 1898-1976, (U.S.) sculptor. *Lobster Trap and Fish Tail.*

Julia Margaret Cameron, 1815-79, (Br.) photographer, prominent portraitist.

Robert Capa (Endre Friedmann), 1913-54, (Hung.-U.S.) photographer, war photojournalist. Invasion of Normandy.

Michelangelo Merisi da Caravaggio, 1573-1610, (It.) Baroque. *The Supper at Emmaus.*

Emily Carr, 1871-1945, (Can.) landscapist. *Blunden Harbour, Big Raven, Rushing Sea of Undergrowth.*

Carlo Carrà, 1881-1966, (It.) Metaphysical school. *Lot's Daughters, The Enchanted Room.*

Leonora Carrington, 1917-2011, (Br.) Surrealist. *The Inn of the Dawn Horse (Self-Portrait).*

Henri Cartier-Bresson, 1908-2004, (Fr.) photographer. *Imagenes à la sauvette.*

Mary Cassatt, 1844-1926, (U.S.) Impressionist. *The Cup of Tea, Woman Bathing, The Boating Party.*

George Catlin, 1796-1872, (U.S.) American Indian life. *Gallery of Indians, Buffalo Dance.*

Benvenuto Cellini, 1500-71, (It.) Mannerist sculptor, goldsmith. *Perseus and Medusa.*

Paul Cézanne, 1839-1906, (Fr.) Post-Impressionist. *Card Players, Mont-Sainte-Victoire With Large Pine Trees.*

Marc Chagall, 1887-1985, (Russ.) Jewish life and folklore. *I and the Village, The Praying Jew.*

John Chamberlain, 1927-2011, (U.S.) sculptor of automobile metal.

Jean Simeon Chardin, 1699-1779, (Fr.) still lifes. *The Kiss, The Grace.*

Giorgio de Chirico, 1888-1978, (It.) founded the Metaphysical school. *Enigma of an Autumn Night.*

Frederick Church, 1826-1900, (U.S.) Hudson River school. *Niagara, Andes of Ecuador.*

Giovanni Cimabue, 1240-1302, (It.) Byzantine mosaicist. *Madonna Enthroned With St. Francis.*

Claude (Lorrain) (Claude Gellée), 1600-82, (Fr.) Ideal-landscapist. *The Enchanted Castle.*

Thomas Cole, 1801-48, (U.S.) Hudson River school. *The Ox-Bow, In the Catskills.*

John Constable, 1776-1837, (Br.) landscapist. *Salisbury Cathedral From the Bishop's Grounds.*

John Singleton Copley, 1738-1815, (U.S.) portraitist. *Samuel Adams, Watson and the Shark.*

Lovis Corinth, 1858-1925, (Ger.) Expressionist. *Apocalypse.*

Jean-Baptiste-Camille Corot, 1796-1875, (Fr.) landscapist. *Souvenir de Mortefontaine, Pastorale.*

Correggio, 1494-1534, (It.) Renaissance muralist. *Mystic Marriages of St. Catherine.*

Gustave Courbet, 1819-77, (Fr.) Realist. *The Artist's Studio.*

Lucas Cranach the Elder, 1472-1553, (Ger.) Protestant Reformation portraitist. *Luther.*

Imogen Cunningham, 1883-1976, (U.S.) photographer, portraitist. Plants.

Nathaniel Currier, 1813-88, and **James M. Ives**, 1824-95, (both U.S.) lithographers. *A Midnight Race on the Mississippi, American Forest Scene—Maple Sugaring.*

John Steuart Curry, 1897-1946, (U.S.) Americana, murals. *Baptism in Kansas.*

Edward S. Curtis, 1868-1952, (U.S.) photographer. *The Native American Indian.*

Salvador Dalí, 1904-89, (Sp.) Surrealist. *Persistence of Memory, The Crucifixion.*

Honoré Daumier, 1808-79, (Fr.) caricaturist. *The Third-Class Carriage.*

Jacques-Louis David, 1748-1825, (Fr.) Neoclassicist. *The Oath of the Horatii.*

Arthur Davies, 1862-1928, (U.S.) Romantic landscapist. *Unicorns, Leda and the Dioscuri.*

Edgar Degas, 1834-1917, (Fr.) Realist/Impressionist. *The Ballet Class.*

Willem de Kooning, 1904-97, (Neth.-U.S.) Abstract Expressionist. *Excavation, Woman I, Door to the River.*

Eugène Delacroix, 1798-1863, (Fr.) Romantic. *Massacre at Chios, Liberty Leading the People.*

Paul Delaroche, 1797-1856, (Fr.) historical themes. *Children of Edward IV.*

Luca Della Robbia, 1400-82, (It.) Renaissance terra-cotta. *Cantoria* (singing gallery), Florence cathedral.

Donatello, 1386-1466, (It.) Renaissance sculptor. *David, Gattamelata.*

Aaron Douglas, 1899-79, (U.S.) Harlem Renaissance illustrator and muralist.

Jean Dubuffet, 1902-85, (Fr.) painter, sculptor, printmaker. *Group of Four Trees.*

Marcel Duchamp, 1887-1968, (Fr.) Dadaist. *Nude Descending a Staircase, No. 2.*

Raoul Dufy, 1877-1953, (Fr.) Fauvist. *Chateau and Horses.*

Asher Brown Durand, 1796-1886, (U.S.) Hudson River school. *Kindred Spirits.*

Albrecht Dürer, 1471-1528, (Ger.) Renaissance painter, engraver, woodcuts. *St. Jerome in His Study, Melencolia I.*

Anthony van Dyck, 1599-1641, (Flem.) Baroque portraitist. *Portrait of Charles I Hunting.*

Thomas Eakins, 1844-1916, (U.S.) Realist. *The Gross Clinic.*

Alfred Eisenstaedt, 1898-1995, (Ger.-U.S.) photographer, photojournalist. Famous photo, V-J Day, Aug. 14, 1945.

Peter Henry Emerson, 1856-1936, (Br.) photographer. Promoted photography as an independent art form.

Jacob Epstein, 1880-1959, (Br.) religious and allegorical sculptor. *Genesis, Ecce Homo.*

Erté (Romain de Tiertoff), 1892-1990, (Fr.) painter, fashion and stage designer.

Walker Evans, 1903-75, (U.S.) photographer. Documented Great Depression.

Jan van Eyck, c. 1390-1441, (Flem.) naturalistic panels. *Adoration of the Lamb.*

Horst Faas, 1933-2012, (Ger.) Vietnam War photographer.

Roger Fenton, 1819-69, (Br.) photographer. Crimean War.

Anselm Feuerbach, 1829-80, (Ger.) Romantic Classicist. *Judgment of Paris, Iphigenia.*

John Bernard Flannagan, 1895-1942, (U.S.) animal sculptor. *Triumph of the Egg.*

Jean-Honoré Fragonard, 1732-1806, (Fr.) Rococo. *The Swing.*

Helen Frankenthaler, 1928-2011, (U.S.) Abstract Expressionist. *Mountains and Sea.*

Daniel Chester French, 1850-1931, (U.S.) sculptor. *The Minute Man of Concord;*

seated *Lincoln*, Lincoln Memorial, Washington, DC.

Lucian Freud, 1922-2011, (Ger.-Br.) portraitist. *Girl With Roses.*

Caspar David Friedrich, 1774-1840, (Ger.) Romantic landscapist. *Man and Woman Gazing at the Moon.*

Thomas Gainsborough, 1727-88, (Br.) portraitist. *The Blue Boy, The Watering Place, Orpin the Parish Clerk.*

Alexander Gardner, 1821-82, (U.S.) photographer. Civil War, railroad construction, Great Plains Indians.

Paul Gauguin, 1848-1903, (Fr.) Post-Impressionist. *The Tahitians, Spirit of the Dead Watching.*

Lorenzo Ghiberti, 1378-1455, (It.) Renaissance sculptor. "Gates of Paradise" baptistery doors, Florence, It.

Alberto Giacometti, 1901-66, (Switz.) attenuated sculptures of solitary figures. *Man Pointing.*

Giorgione, c. 1477-1510, (It.) Renaissance. *The Tempest.*

Giotto di Bondone, 1267-1337, (It.) Renaissance. *Presentation of Christ in the Temple.*

François Girardon, 1628-1715, (Fr.) Baroque sculptor of classical themes. *Apollo Tended by the Nymphs.*

Edward Gorey, 1925-2000, (U.S.) illustrator. *The Doubtful Guest.*

Arshile Gorky, 1905-48, (U.S.) Surrealist. *The Liver Is the Cock's Comb.*

Francisco de Goya y Lucientes, 1746-1828, (Sp.) painter, printmaker. *The Naked Maja, The Disasters of War* (etchings).

El Greco (Domenikos Theotokopoulos), 1541-1614, (Gr.-Sp.) painter, sculptor. *View of Toledo, Assumption of the Virgin.*

Horatio Greenough, 1805-52, (U.S.) Neoclassical sculptor.

Matthias Grünewald, 1480-1528, (Ger.) mystical religious themes. *The Resurrection.*

Frans Hals, c. 1580-1666, (Neth.) portraitist. *Laughing Cavalier, Gypsy Girl.*

Richard Hamilton, 1922-2011, (Br.) Pop Art. *Just What Is It That Makes Today's Homes So Different, So Appealing?*

Austin Hansen, 1910-96, (U.S.) photographer. Harlem, NY, life.

Childe Hassam, 1859-1935, (U.S.) Impressionist. *Southwest Wind, July 14 Rue Daunon.*

Edward Hicks, 1780-1849, (U.S.) folk. *The Peaceable Kingdom.*

Lewis Wickes Hine, 1874-1940, (U.S.) photographer. Studies of immigrants, children in industry.

Hans Hofmann, 1880-1966, (U.S.) early Abstract Expressionist. *Spring, The Gate.*

William Hogarth, 1697-1764, (Br.) caricaturist. *The Rake's Progress.*

Katsushika Hokusai, 1760-1849, (Jpn.) printmaker. *Crabs.*

Hans Holbein the Elder, 1460-1524, (Ger.) late Gothic. *Presentation of Christ in the Temple.*

Hans Holbein the Younger, 1497-1543, (Ger.) portraitist. *Henry VIII, The French Ambassadors.*

Winslow Homer, 1836-1910, (U.S.) naturalist, marine themes. *Marine Coast, High Cliff.*

Edward Hopper, 1882-1967, (U.S.) realistic urban scenes. *Nighthawks, House by the Railroad.*

Horst P. Horst, 1906-99, (Ger.) fashion, celebrity photographer.

Jean-Auguste-Dominique Ingres, 1780-1867, (Fr.) Classicist. *Valpincon Bather.*

George Inness, 1825-94, (U.S.) luminous landscapist. *Delaware Water Gap.*

William Henry Jackson, 1843-1942, (U.S.) photographer. American West, building of Union Pacific Railroad.

Jeanne-Claude (Javacheff), 1935-2009, (Moroc.), created large-scale, temporary installations in public places with her husband, Christo.

Donald Judd, 1928-94, (U.S.) sculptor, major Minimalist.

Frida Kahlo, 1907-54, (Mex.) folkloric stylist. *Self-Portrait With Monkey.*

Wassily Kandinsky, 1866-1944, (Russ.) Abstractionist. *Capricious Forms, Improvisation 28 (second version)*.

Paul Klee, 1879-1940, (Switz.) Abstractionist. *Twittering Machine, Pastoral, Death and Fire*.

Gustav Kilmt, 1862-1918, (Austria) cofounder of Vienna Secession Movement. *The Kiss*.

Oscar Kokoschka, 1886-1980, (Austria) Expressionism. *View of Prague, Harbor of Marseilles*.

Kathe Kollwitz, 1867-1945, (Ger.) printmaker, social justice themes. *The Peasant War*.

Gaston Lachaise, 1882-1935, (U.S.) figurative sculptor. *Standing Woman*.

John La Farge, 1835-1910, (U.S.) muralist. *Red and White Peonies, The Ascension*.

Sir Edwin (Henry) Landseer, 1802-73, (Br.) painter, sculptor. *Shoeing, Rout of Comus*.

Dorothea Lange, 1895-1965, (U.S.) photographer. Great Depression, migrant farm workers.

Fernand Léger, 1881-1955, (Fr.) Machine art. *The Cyclists*.

Leonardo da Vinci, 1452-1519, (It.) Renaissance. *Mona Lisa, Last Supper, The Annunciation*.

Emanuel Leutze, 1816-68, (U.S.) historical themes. *Washington Crossing the Delaware*.

Roy Lichtenstein, 1923-97, (U.S.) Pop Art.

Jacques Lipchitz, 1891-1973, (Fr.) Cubist sculptor. *Harpist*.

Filippino Lippi, 1457-1504, (It.) Renaissance. *Adoration of the Magi*.

Fra Filippo Lippi, 1406-69, (It.) Renaissance. *Coronation of the Virgin, Madonna and Child With Angels*.

Morris Louis, 1912-62, (U.S.) Abstract Expressionism. *Signa, Stripes, Alpha-Phi*.

René Magritte, 1898-1967, (Belg.) Surrealist. *The Descent of Man, The Betrayal of Images*.

Aristide Maillol, 1861-1944, (Fr.) sculptor. *L'Harmonie*.

Édouard Manet, 1832-83, (Fr.) forerunner of Impressionism. *Luncheon on the Grass, Olympia*.

Andrea Mantegna, 1431-1506, (It.) Renaissance frescoes. *Triumph of Caesar*.

Robert Mapplethorpe, 1946-89, (U.S.) photographer.

Franz Marc, 1880-1916, (Ger.) Expressionist. *Blue Horses*.

John Marin, 1870-1953, (U.S.) Expressionist seascapes. *Maine Island*.

Reginald Marsh, 1898-1954, (U.S.) satire. *Tattoo and Haircut*.

Agnes Martin, 1912-2004, (U.S.) abstract artist. *Night Sea*.

Masaccio, 1401-28, (It.) Renaissance. *The Tribute Money*.

Henri Matisse, 1869-1954, (Fr.) Fauvist. *Woman With the Hat*.

John McCracken, 1934-2011, (U.S.) minimalist sculptor.

Michelangelo Buonarroti, 1475-1564, (It.) Renaissance. *Pietà, David, Moses, The Last Judgment*, Sistine Chapel ceiling.

Jean-Francois Millet, 1814-75, (Fr.) peasants. *The Gleaners, The Man With a Hoe*.

Joan Miró, 1893-1983, (Sp.) exuberant colors, playful images. Catalan landscape, *Dutch Interior*.

Amedeo Modigliani, 1884-1920, (It.) figurative works. *Reclining Nude*.

Piet Mondrian, 1872-1944, (Neth.) Abstractionist. *Composition With Red, Yellow and Blue*.

Claude Monet, 1840-1926, (Fr.) Impressionist. *The Bridge at Argenteuil, Haystacks, Bridge Over a Pond of Water Lillies*.

Henry Moore, 1898-1986, (Br.) sculptor of large-scale, abstract works. *Reclining Figure* (several).

Gustave Moreau, 1826-98, (Fr.) Symbolist. *The Apparition, Dance of Salome*.

James Wilson Morrice, 1865-1924, (Can.) landscapist. *The Ferry, Quebec, Venice, Looking Over the Lagoon*.

William Morris, 1834-96, (Br.) decorative artist, leader of Arts and Crafts movement.

Grandma Moses (Anna Mary Robertson Moses), 1860-1961, (U.S.) folk. *Out for the*

Christmas Tree, Catching the Thanksgiving Turkey.

Edvard Munch, 1863-1944, (Nor.) Expressionist. *The Cry*.

Bartolome Murillo, 1618-82, (Sp.) Baroque religious artist. *Vision of St. Anthony, The Two Trinities*.

Elizabeth Murray, 1940-2007, (U.S.) abstract colors. *Kitchen Party*.

Eadweard Muybridge, 1830-1904, (Br.-U.S.) photographer. Studies of motion, *Animal Locomotion*.

Nadar (Gaspar-Félix Tournachon), 1820-1910, (Fr.) photographer, caricaturist, portraitist. Invented photo-essay.

LeRoy Neiman, 1921-2012, (U.S.) sports expressionist painter.

Arnold Newman, 1918-2006, (U.S.) portrait photographer.

Barnett Newman, 1905-70, (U.S.) Abstract Expressionism. *Stations of the Cross*.

Isamu Noguchi, 1904-88, (U.S.) abstract sculptor, designer. *Kouros, BirdC(MU)*, sculptural gardens.

Kenneth Noland, 1924-2010, (U.S.) Color Field, abstract.

Georgia O'Keeffe, 1887-1986, (U.S.) southwest motifs. *Cow's Skull: Red, White, and Blue; The Shelton With Sunspots*.

José Clemente Orozco, 1883-1949, (Mex.) frescoes. *House of Tears, Pre-Columbian Golden Age*.

Timothy H. O'Sullivan, 1840-82, (U.S.) Civil War photographer.

Gordon Parks, 1912-2006, (U.S.) African American photographer, filmmaker. *Life* photographer, 1948-68.

Charles Willson Peale, 1741-1827, (U.S.) Amer. Revolutionary portraitist. *The Staircase Group*, U.S. presidents.

Rembrandt Peale, 1778-1860, (U.S.) portraitist. *Thomas Jefferson*.

Irving Penn, 1917-2009, (U.S.) portraitist, fashion photographer.

Pietro Perugino, 1446-1523, (It.) Renaissance. *Delivery of the Keys to St. Peter*.

Pablo Picasso, 1881-1973, (Sp.) painter, sculptor. *Guernica; Dove; Head of a Woman; Head of a Bull, Metamorphosis*.

Piero della Francesca, c. 1415-92, (It.) Renaissance. *Duke of Urbino, Flagellation of Christ*.

Camille Pissarro, 1830-1903, (Fr.) Impressionist. *Boulevard des Italiens, Morning, Sunlight; Bather in the Woods*.

Jackson Pollock, 1912-56, (U.S.) Abstract Expressionist. *Autumn Rhythm*.

Nicolas Poussin, 1594-1665, (Fr.) Baroque pictorial classicism. *St. John on Patmos*.

Maurice B. Prendergast, c. 1860-1924, (U.S.) Postimpressionist watercolorist. *Umbrellas in the Rain*.

Pierre-Paul Prud'hon, 1758-1823, (Fr.) Romanticist. *Crime Pursued by Vengeance and Justice*.

Pierre Cecile Puvis de Chavannes, 1824-98, (Fr.) muralist. *The Poor Fisherman*.

Raphael Sanzio, 1483-1520, (It.) Renaissance. *Disputa, School of Athens, Sistine Madonna*.

Robert Rauschenberg, 1925-2008, (U.S.) printmaker. *Combine, Bed, Revolvers, Outpost*.

Man Ray (Emmanuel Radnitsky), 1890-1976, (U.S.) Dadaist and Surrealist. *Observing Time, The Lovers, Marquis de Sade*.

Odilon Redon, 1840-1916, (Fr.) Symbolist painter, lithographer. *In the Dream, Vase of Flowers*.

Rembrandt van Rijn, 1606-69, (Neth.) painter, printmaker. *The Bridal Couple, The Night Watch*.

Frederic Remington, 1861-1909, (U.S.) painter, sculptor. Portrayer of the American West, *Bronco Buster*.

Pierre-Auguste Renoir, 1841-1919, (Fr.) Impressionist. *The Luncheon of the Boating Party, Dance in the Country*.

Joshua Reynolds, 1723-92, (Br.) portraitist. *Mrs. Siddons as the Tragic Muse*.

Herb Ritts, 1952-2002, (U.S.) photographer. Nudes, celebrities.

Diego Rivera, 1886-1957, (Mex.) frescoes. *The Flowered Earth*.

Larry Rivers, 1923-2002, (U.S.) painter, sculptor, often realistic. Dutch Masters series.

Henry Peach Robinson, 1830-1901, (Br.) photographer. A leader of "high art" photography.

Norman Rockwell, 1894-1978, (U.S.) painter, illustrator. *Saturday Evening Post* covers.

Auguste Rodin, 1840-1917, (Fr.) sculptor. *The Thinker*.

Milton Rogovin, 1909-2011, (U.S.) documentary photographer.

Willy Ronis, 1910-2009, (Fr.) photographer. Post-war Paris.

Joe Rosenthal, 1911-2006, (U.S.) photojournalist; photographed six marines raising the U.S. flag over Iwo Jima in WWII.

Mark Rothko, 1903-70, (U.S.) Abstract Expressionism. *Light, Earth and Blue*.

Georges Rouault, 1871-1958, (Fr.) Expressionist. *Three Judges*.

Henri Rousseau, 1844-1910, (Fr.) primitive exotic themes. *The Snake Charmer*.

Theodore Rousseau, 1812-67, (Switz.-Fr.) landscapist. *Under the Birches, Evening*.

Peter Paul Rubens, 1577-1640, (Flem.) Baroque. *Mystic Marriage of St. Catherine*.

Jacob van Ruisdael, c. 1628-82, (Neth.) landscapist. *Jewish Cemetery*.

Charles M. Russell, 1866-1926, (U.S.) Western life.

Salomon van Ruysdael, c. 1600-70, (Neth.) landscapist. *River With Ferry-Boat*.

Albert Pinkham Ryder, 1847-1917, (U.S.) seascapes, allegories. *Toilers of the Sea*.

Augustus Saint-Gaudens, 1848-1907, (U.S.) memorial statues. *Farragut, Mrs. Henry Adams (Grief)*.

Niki de Saint Phalle, 1930-2002, (Fr.) paintings, sculptures, prints, large public installations.

Andrea Sansovino, 1460-1529, (It.) Renaissance sculptor. *Baptism of Christ*.

Jacopo Sansovino, 1486-1570, (It.) Renaissance sculptor. *St. John the Baptist*.

John Singer Sargent, 1856-1925, (U.S.) Edwardian society portraitist. *The Wyndham Sisters, Madam X*.

Andrea del Sarto, 1486-1530, (It.) frescoes. *Madonna of the Harpies*.

George Segal, 1924-2000, (U.S.) sculptor. Life-sized figures realistically depicting daily life.

Georges Seurat, 1859-91, (Fr.) Pointillist. *Sunday Afternoon on the Island of La Grande Jatte*.

Gino Severini, 1883-1966, (It.) Futurist and Cubist. *Dynamic Hieroglyph of the Bal Tabarin*.

Ben Shahn, 1898-1969, (U.S.) social and political themes. *Sacco and Vanzetti* series, *Seurat's Lunch, Handball*.

Charles Sheeler, 1883-1965, (U.S.) abstractionist.

David Alfaro Siqueiros, 1896-1974, (Mex.) political muralist. *March of Humanity*.

David Smith, 1906-65, (U.S.) welded metal sculpture. *Hudson River Landscape, Zig, Cubi* series.

Edward Steichen, 1879-1973, (U.S.) photographer. Credited with transforming photography into an art form.

Alfred Stieglitz, 1864-1946, (U.S.) photographer, editor. Helped create acceptance of photography as art.

Paul Strand, 1890-1976, (U.S.) photographer. People, nature, landscapes.

Gilbert Stuart, 1755-1828, (U.S.) portraitist. George Washington, Thomas Jefferson, James Madison.

Thomas Sully, 1783-1872, (U.S.) portraitist. *Col. Thomas Handasyd Perkins, The Passage of the Delaware*.

William Henry Fox Talbot, 1800-77, (Br.) photographer. *Pencil of Nature*, early photographically illustrated book.

George Tames, 1919-94, (U.S.) photographer. Presidents, political leaders.

Yves Tanguy, 1900-55, (Fr.) Surrealist. *Rose of the Four Winds; Mama, Papa Is Wounded!*

Giovanni Battista Tiepolo, 1696-1770, (It.) Rococo frescoes. *The Crucifixion*.

Jacopo Tintoretto, 1518-94, (It.) Mannerist. *The Last Supper*.

Titian (Tiziano Vecellio), c. 1488-1576, (It.) Renaissance. *Venus and the Lute Player, The Bacchanal*.

Jose Rey Toledo, 1916-94, (U.S.) Native American life. Tribal dances.

George Tooker, 1920-2011, (U.S.) Magic Realist. *Subway.*

Henri de Toulouse-Lautrec, 1864-1901, (Fr.) Postimpressionist. *At the Moulin Rouge.*

John Trumbull, 1756-1843, (U.S.) historical themes. *The Declaration of Independence.*

J(oseph) M(allord) W(illiam) Turner, 1775-1851, (Br.) Romantic landscapist. *Snow Storm.*

Cy Twombly, 1928-2011, (U.S.) painter and sculptor. *Leda and the Swan.*

Paolo Uccello, 1397-1475, (It.) Gothic-Renaissance. *The Rout of San Romano.*

Maurice Utrillo, 1883-1955, (Fr.) Impressionist. *Sacre-Coeur de Montmartre.*

Vincent van Gogh, 1853-90, (Neth.) *The Starry Night, L'Arlesienne, Bedroom at Arles, Self-Portrait.*

John Vanderlyn, 1775-1852, (U.S.) Neo-classicist. *Ariadne Asleep on the Island of Naxos.*

Diego Velázquez, 1599-1660, (Sp.) Baroque. *Las Meninas, Portrait of Juan de Pareja.*

Jan Vermeer, 1632-75, (Neth.) interior genre subjects. *Young Woman With a Water Jug.*

Paolo Veronese, 1528-88, (It.) devotional themes, vastly peopled canvases. *The Temptation of St. Anthony.*

Andrea del Verrocchio, 1435-88, (It.) sculptor. *Colleoni.*

Maurice de Vlaminck, 1876-1958, (Fr.) Fauvist landscapist. *Red Trees.*

Andy Warhol, 1928-87, (U.S.) Pop Art. *Campbell's Soup Cans, Marilyn Diptych.*

Antoine Watteau, 1684-1721, (Fr.) Rococo "scenes of gallantry." *The Embarkation for Cythera.*

George Frederic Watts, 1817-1904, (Br.) painter and sculptor. Grandiose allegorical themes. *Hope.*

Benjamin West, 1738-1820, (U.S.) realistic historical themes. *Death of General Wolfe.*

Edward Weston, 1886-1958, (U.S.) photographer. Landscapes of American West.

James Abbott McNeill Whistler, 1834-1903, (U.S.) *Arrangement in Grey and Black, No. 1: The Artist's Mother.*

Archibald M. Willard, 1836-1918, (U.S.) murals. *The Spirit of '76.*

Grant Wood, 1891-1942, (U.S.) Midwestern regionalist. *American Gothic, Daughters of Revolution.*

Andrew Wyeth, 1917-2009, (U.S.), regionalist. *Christina's World.*

Ossip Zadkine, 1890-1967, (Russ.) School of Paris sculptor. *The Destroyed City, Musicians, Christ.*

Business Leaders and Philanthropists of the Past

Giovanni Agnelli, 1921-2003, (It.) industrialist; principal shareholder of Fiat.

Walter Annenberg, 1908-2002, (U.S.) publisher, founder of *TV Guide*, philanthropist.

Elizabeth Arden (F. N. Graham), 1884-1966, (U.S.) Canadian-born founder of cosmetics empire.

Philip D. Armour, 1832-1901, (U.S.) industrialist; streamlined meatpacking.

Brooke Astor, 1902-2007, (U.S.) philanthropist; president of Vincent Astor Foundation.

John Jacob Astor, 1763-1848, (U.S.) German-born fur trader, banker, real estate magnate; at death, richest in U.S.

Francis W. Ayer, 1848-1923, (U.S.) ad industry pioneer.

August Belmont, 1816-90, (U.S.) German-born financier.

James B. (Diamond Jim) Brady, 1856-1917, (U.S.) financier, philanthropist; legendary bon vivant.

Adolphus Busch, 1839-1913, (U.S.) German-born businessman; established brewery empire.

Asa Candler, 1851-1929, (U.S.) founded Coca-Cola Co.

Andrew Carnegie, 1835-1919, (U.S.) Scottish-born industrialist, philanthropist; founded Carnegie Steel Co.

Tom Carvel, 1908-89, (Gr.-U.S.) founded ice cream chain.

William Colgate, 1783-1857, (Br.-U.S.) businessman, philanthropist; founded soap-making empire.

Jay Cooke, 1821-1905, (U.S.) financier; sold $1 billion in Union bonds during Civil War.

Peter Cooper, 1791-1883, (U.S.) industrialist, inventor, philanthropist; founded Cooper Union (1859).

Ezra Cornell, 1807-74, (U.S.) businessman, philanthropist; headed Western Union, established university.

Erastus Corning, 1794-1872, (U.S.) financier; headed New York Central Railroad.

Charles Crocker, 1822-88, (U.S.) railroad builder, financier.

Samuel Cunard, 1787-1865, (Can.) pioneered transatlantic steam navigation.

Marcus Daly, 1841-1900, (U.S.) Irish-born copper magnate.

W. Edwards Deming, 1900-93, (U.S.) quality-control expert who revolutionized Japanese manufacturing.

Walt Disney, 1901-66, (U.S.) pioneer in cinema animation; built entertainment empire.

Herbert H. Dow, 1866-1930, (U.S.) founder of chemical co.

Anthony Drexel, 1826-93, (U.S.) banker, philanthropist, university founder.

James Duke, 1856-1925, (U.S.) founded American Tobacco, Duke Univ.

Eleuthere I. du Pont, 1771-1834, (Fr.-U.S.) gunpowder manufacturer; founded one of the largest business empires.

Thomas C. Durant, 1820-85, (U.S.) railroad official, financier.

William C. Durant, 1861-1947, (U.S.) industrialist; formed General Motors.

George Eastman, 1854-1932, (U.S.) inventor; manufacturer of photographic equipment.

Marshall Field, 1834-1906, (U.S.) merchant; founded Chicago's largest department store.

Harvey Firestone, 1868-1938, (U.S.) founded tire company.

Avery Fisher, 1906-94, (U.S.) industrialist, philanthropist; founded Fisher Electronics.

Henry M. Flagler, 1830-1913, (U.S.) financier; helped form Standard Oil, developed FL as resort state.

Malcolm Forbes, 1919-90, (U.S.) magazine publisher.

Henry Ford, 1863-1947, (U.S.) automaker; developed first popular low-priced car.

Henry Ford II, 1917-87, (U.S.) headed auto company founded by grandfather.

Henry C. Frick, 1849-1919, (U.S.) steel and coke magnate; had prominent role in development of U.S. Steel.

Jakob Fugger (Jakob the Rich), 1459-1525, (Ger.) headed leading banking, trading house, in 16th cent. Europe.

Alfred C. Fuller, 1885-1973, (U.S.) Canadian-born businessman; founded brush company.

Elbert H. Gary, 1846-1927, (U.S.) one of the organizers of U.S. Steel; chaired board of directors, 1903-27.

Jean Paul Getty, 1892-1976, (U.S.) founded oil empire.

Amadeo Giannini, 1870-1949, (U.S.) founded Bank of America.

Stephen Girard, 1750-1831, (U.S.) French-born financier, philanthropist; richest man in U.S. at time of death.

Leonard H. Goldenson, 1905-99, (U.S.) turned ABC into major TV network.

Jay Gould, 1836-92, (U.S.) railroad magnate, financier.

Hetty Green, 1834-1916, (U.S.) financier, the "witch of Wall St."; richest woman in U.S. in her day.

William Gregg, 1800-67, (U.S.) launched textile industry in the South.

Meyer Guggenheim, 1828-1905, (U.S.) Swiss-born merchant, philanthropist; built merchandising, mining empires.

Armand Hammer, 1898-1990, (U.S.) headed Occidental Petroleum, promoted U.S.-Soviet ties.

Elliot Handler, 1916-2011, (U.S.) cofounder of Mattel; introduced the Barbie doll.

Edward H. Harriman, 1848-1909, (U.S.) railroad financier, administrator; headed Union Pacific.

Henry J. Heinz, 1844-1919, (U.S.) founded food empire.

Leona Helmsley, 1920-2007, (U.S.) real estate magnate, philanthropist.

Milton Snavely Hershey, 1857-1945, (U.S.) chocolate co. founder, philanthropist.

James J. Hill, 1838-1916, (U.S.) Canadian-born railroad magnate, financier; founded Great Northern Railway.

Conrad N. Hilton, 1888-1979, (U.S.) hotel chain founder.

Howard Hughes, 1905-76, (U.S.) industrialist, aviator, filmmaker.

H. L. Hunt, 1889-1974, (U.S.) oil magnate.

Collis P. Huntington, 1821-1900, (U.S.) railroad magnate.

Henry E. Huntington, 1850-1927, (U.S.) railroad builder, philanthropist.

Walter L. Jacobs, 1898-1985, (U.S.) founder of the first rental car agency, which later became Hertz.

Steve Jobs, 1955-2011, (U.S.) Apple cofounder and exec.; Pixar exec.

Howard Johnson, 1896-1972, (U.S.) founded restaurants.

John H. Johnson, 1918-2005, (U.S.) built publishing empire based on *Ebony* and *Jet.*

Samuel Curtis Johnson, 1928-2004, (U.S.) headed S.C. Johnson & Sons.

Henry J. Kaiser, 1882-1967, (U.S.) industrialist; built empire in steel, aluminum.

Minor C. Keith, 1848-1929, (U.S.) railroad magnate; founded United Fruit Co.

Will K. Kellogg, 1860-1951, (U.S.) businessman, philanthropist; founded breakfast food co.

Richard King, 1825-85, (U.S.) cattleman; founded half-million-acre King Ranch in Texas.

John W. Kluge, 1914-2010, (Ger.-U.S.) Metromedia chair; philanthropist.

William S. Knudsen, 1879-1948, (U.S.) Danish-born auto industry executive.

Samuel H. Kress, 1863-1955, (U.S.) businessman, art collector, philanthropist; founded "dime store" chain.

Ray A. Kroc, 1902-84, (U.S.) original CEO of McDonald's Corp.; oversaw company's vast expansion.

Alfred Krupp, 1812-87, (Ger.) armaments magnate.

Estée Lauder, 1908-2004, (U.S.) cofounder of Estée Lauder companies.

Kenneth L. Lay, 1942-2006, (U.S.), former CEO of Enron; indicted on fraud charges.

William Levitt, 1907-94, (U.S.) industrialist; "suburb maker."

Thomas Lipton, 1850-1931, (Scot.) merchant; tea empire.

James McGill, 1744-1813, (Scot.-Can.) founded university.

Andrew W. Mellon, 1855-1937, (U.S.) financier, industrialist; benefactor of National Gallery of Art.

Charles E. Merrill, 1885-1956, (U.S.) financier; developed firm of Merrill Lynch.

J(ohn) P(ierpont) Morgan, 1837-1913, (U.S.) most powerful figure in finance and industry at turn of 20th cent.

Akio Morita, 1921-99, (Jpn.) cofounded Sony Corp.

Malcolm Muir, 1885-1979, (U.S.) created *Business Week* magazine; headed *Newsweek,* 1937-61.

Roy Neuberger, 1903-2010, (U.S.) financier and art patron.

Samuel Newhouse, 1895-1979, (U.S.) publishing and broadcasting magnate; built communications empire.

Aristotle Onassis, 1906-75, (Gr.) shipping magnate.

William S. Paley, 1901-90, (U.S.) built CBS communications empire.

Frederick D. Patterson, 1901-88, (U.S.) founder of United Negro College Fund, 1944.

George Peabody, 1795-1869, (U.S.) merchant, financier, philanthropist.
James C. Penney, 1875-1971, (U.S.) businessman; developed department store chain.
Frank Perdue, 1920-2005, (U.S.) founder of Perdue Farms, chicken-processing company.
William C. Procter, 1862-1934, (U.S.) headed soap co.
John D. Rockefeller, 1839-1937, (U.S.) industrialist; established Standard Oil.
John D. Rockefeller Jr., 1874-1960, (U.S.) philanthropist; established foundation, provided land for UN.
Laurance S. Rockefeller, 1910-2004, (U.S.) philanthropist, conservationist.
Meyer A. Rothschild, 1743-1812, (Ger.) founded international banking house.
Thomas Fortune Ryan, 1851-1928, (U.S.) financier; a founder of American Tobacco.
Edmond J. Safra, 1932-99, (U.S.) banker.
David Sarnoff, 1891-1971, (U.S.) broadcasting pioneer; established first radio network, NBC.
Richard Sears, 1863-1914, (U.S.) founded mail-order co.
Werner von Siemens, 1816-92, (Ger.) industrialist, inventor.

Alfred P. Sloan, 1875-1966, (U.S.) industrialist, philanthropist; headed General Motors.
A. Leland Stanford, 1824-93, (U.S.) railroad official, philanthropist; founded university.
Frank Stanton, 1908-2006, (U.S.) president of CBS network, 1946-71.
Larry Stewart, 1948-2007, (U.S.) "Kansas City's Secret Santa."
Nathan Straus, 1848-1931, (U.S.) German-born merchant, philanthropist; headed Macy's dept. stores.
Levi Strauss, c. 1829-1902, (U.S.) pants manufacturer.
Clement Studebaker, 1831-1901, (U.S.) wagon, carriage maker.
Gustavus Swift, 1839-1903, (U.S.) pioneer meatpacker.
Gerard Swope, 1872-1957, (U.S.) industrialist, economist; headed General Electric.
Dave Thomas, 1932-2002, (U.S.) Wendy's founder.
James Walter Thompson, 1847-1928, (U.S.) ad executive, founder of ad agency.
Alice Tully, 1902-93, (U.S.) philanthropist, arts patron.
Theodore N. Vail, 1845-1920, (U.S.) organized Bell Telephone system, headed AT&T.
Cornelius Vanderbilt, 1794-1877, (U.S.) financier; established steamship, railroad empires.

Henry Villard, 1835-1900, (U.S.) German-born railroad executive, financier.
Charles R. Walgreen, 1873-1939, (U.S.) founded drugstore chain.
Madame C. J. Walker, 1867-1919, (U.S.) African-American hair care entrepreneur and philanthropist.
DeWitt Wallace, 1889-1981, (U.S.) and **Lila Wallace**, 1889-1984, (U.S.) cofounders of *Reader's Digest* magazine.
Sam Walton, 1918-92, (U.S.) founder of Wal-Mart stores.
John Wanamaker, 1838-1922, (U.S.) department-store merchandising pioneer.
Aaron Montgomery Ward, 1843-1913, (U.S.) established first mail-order firm.
Thomas J. Watson, 1874-1956, (U.S.) IBM head, 1914-56.
George Westinghouse, 1846-1914, (U.S) inventor, manufacturer; organized Westinghouse Electric Co., 1886.
John Hay Whitney, 1905-82, (U.S.) publisher, sportsman, philanthropist.
Charles E. Wilson, 1890-1961, (U.S.) auto exec., public official.
Frank W. Woolworth, 1852-1919, (U.S.) created five and dime chain.
William Wrigley Jr., 1861-1932, (U.S.) founded Wrigley chewing gum company.

American Cartoonists

Reviewed by Lucy Shelton Caswell, Professor and Curator, Cartoon Research Library, Ohio State University.

Scott Adams, b 1957, Dilbert.
Charles Addams, 1912-88, macabre cartoons.
Brad Anderson, b 1924, Marmaduke.
Sergio Aragones, b 1937, *MAD* magazine.
Peter Arno, 1904-68, *The New Yorker*.
Tex Avery, 1908-80, animator; Bugs Bunny, Porky Pig.
George Baker, 1915-75, The Sad Sack.
Carl Barks, 1901-2000, Donald Duck comic books.
C. C. Beck, 1910-89, Captain Marvel.
Dave Berg, 1920-2002, *Mad* magazine.
Jim Berry, b 1932, Berry's World.
Herb Block (Herblock), 1909-2001, political cartoonist.
George Booth, b 1926, *The New Yorker*.
Berkeley Breathed, b 1957, Bloom County.
Dik Browne, 1917-89, Hi & Lois, Hagar the Horrible.
Marjorie Buell, 1904-93, Little Lulu.
Ernie Bushmiller, 1905-82, Nancy.
Milton Caniff, 1907-88, Terry & the Pirates, Steve Canyon.
Al Capp, 1909-79, Li'l Abner.
Roz Chast, b 1954, *The New Yorker*.
Gene Colan, 1926-2011, *Daredevil*.
Paul Conrad, 1924-2010, political cartoonist.
Roy Crane, 1901-77, Captain Easy, Buz Sawyer.
R(obert) Crumb, b 1943, underground cartoonist.
Shamus Culhane, 1908-96, animator.
Jay N. "Ding" Darling, 1876-1962, political cartoonist.
Jack Davis, b 1924, *MAD* magazine.
Jim Davis, b 1945, Garfield.
Billy DeBeck, 1890-1942, Barney Google.
Rudolph Dirks, 1877-1968, The Katzenjammer Kids.
Walt Disney, 1901-66, produced animated cartoons; created Mickey Mouse, Donald Duck.
Steve Ditko, b 1927, Spider-Man.
Mort Drucker, b 1929, *MAD* magazine.
Will Eisner, 1917-2005, the Spirit.
Jules Feiffer, b 1929, political cartoonist.
Bud Fisher, 1884-1954, Mutt & Jeff.
Ham Fisher, 1900-55, Joe Palooka.
Max Fleischer, 1883-1972, Betty Boop.
Hal Foster, 1892-1982, Tarzan, Prince Valiant.
Fontaine Fox, 1884-1964, Toonerville Folks.
Isadore "Friz" Freleng, 1905-95, animator; Yosemite Sam, Porky Pig, Sylvester and Tweety Bird.
Rube Goldberg, 1883-1970, Boob McNutt.
Chester Gould, 1900-85, Dick Tracy.
Harold Gray, 1894-1968, Little Orphan Annie.
Matt Groening, b 1954, Life in Hell, The Simpsons.

Cathy Guisewite, b 1950, Cathy.
Bill Hanna, 1910-2001, and **Joe Barbera**, 1911-2006, animators; Tom & Jerry, Yogi Bear, Flintstones.
Oliver Harrington, 1912-95, Bootsie.
Johnny Hart, 1931-2007, BC, Wizard of Id.
Alfred Harvey, 1913-94, created Casper the Friendly Ghost.
Jimmy Hatlo, 1898-1963, Little Iodine.
John Held Jr., 1889-1958, Jazz Age.
George Herriman, 1881-1944, Krazy Kat.
Harry Hershfield, 1885-1974, Abie the Agent.
Stephen Hillenburg, b 1961, SpongeBob SquarePants.
Al Hirschfeld, 1903-2003, *NY Times* theater caricaturist.
Burne Hogarth, 1911-96, Tarzan.
Helen Hokinson, 1900-49, *The New Yorker*.
Nicole Hollander, b 1939, Sylvia.
Lynn Johnston, b 1947 (Can.), For Better or For Worse.
Oliver Johnston, 1912-2008, Disney animator.
Chuck Jones, 1912-2002, animator; Bugs Bunny, Porky Pig.
Mike Judge, b 1962, Beavis and Butt-head, King of the Hill.
Bob Kane, 1916-98, Batman.
Bil Keane, 1922-2011, The Family Circus.
Walt Kelly, 1913-73, Pogo.
Hank Ketcham, 1920-2001, Dennis the Menace.
Ted Key, 1912-2008, Hazel.
Frank King, 1883-1969, Gasoline Alley.
Jack Kirby, 1917-94, Fantastic Four, The Incredible Hulk.
Rollin Kirby, 1875-1952, political cartoonist.
B(ernard) Kliban, 1935-90, cat books.
Edward Koren, b 1935, *The New Yorker*.
John Kricfalusi, b 1955, Ren & Stimpy.
Joe Kubert, 1926-2012, Sgt. Rock.
Harvey Kurtzman, 1921-93, *MAD* magazine.
Walter Lantz, 1900-94, Woody Woodpecker.
Gary Larson, b 1950, The Far Side.
Mell Lazarus, b 1927, Momma, Miss Peach.
Stan Lee, b 1922, Marvel Comics.
David Levine, 1926-2009, *NY Review of Books* caricatures.
Seth MacFarlane, b 1973, Family Guy.
Jeff MacNelly, 1947-2000, political cartoonist; Shoe.
Doug Marlette, 1949-2007, political cartoonist; Kudzu.
Don Martin, 1931-2000, *MAD* magazine.
Bill Mauldin, 1921-2003, political cartoonist.
Winsor McCay, 1872-1934, Little Nemo.
John T. McCutcheon, 1870-1949, political cartoonist.
Dwayne McDuffie, 1962-2011, *Justice League*.

Aaron McGruder, b 1974, The Boondocks.
George McManus, 1884-1954, Bringing Up Father.
Dale Messick, 1906-2005, Brenda Starr.
Norman Mingo, 1896-1980, Alfred E. Neuman.
Bob Montana, 1920-75, Archie.
Dick Moores, 1909-86, Gasoline Alley.
Willard Mullin, 1902-78, sports cartoonist; Dodgers "Bum," Mets "Kid."
Russell Myers, b 1938, Broom Hilda.
Thomas Nast, 1840-1902, political cartoonist; Republican elephant, Democratic donkey.
Pat Oliphant, b 1935, political cartoonist.
Frederick Burr Opper, 1857-1937, Happy Hooligan.
Richard Outcault, 1863-1928, Yellow Kid, Buster Brown.
Brant Parker, 1920-2007, Wizard of Id.
Trey Parker, b 1969, animator, co-creator of South Park.
Harvey Pekar, 1939-2010, American Splendor.
Mike Peters, b 1943, cartoonist; Mother Goose & Grimm.
George Price, 1901-95, *The New Yorker*.
Antonio Prohias, 1921-98, Spy vs. Spy.
Alex Raymond, 1909-56, Flash Gordon, Jungle Jim.
Forrest (Bud) Sagendorf, 1915-94, Popeye.
Art Sansom, 1920-91, The Born Loser.
Charles Schulz, 1922-2000, Peanuts.
Elzie C. Segar, 1894-1938, Popeye.
Joe Shuster, 1914-92, and **Jerry Siegel**, 1914-96, Superman.
Sidney Smith, 1887-1935, The Gumps.
Otto Soglow, 1900-75, Little King.
Art Spiegelman, b 1948, Raw, Maus.
William Steig, 1907-2003, *The New Yorker*.
Matt Stone, b 1971, animator, co-creator of South Park.
James Swinnerton, 1875-1974, Little Jimmy, Canyon Kiddies.
Paul Szep, b 1941, political cartoonist.
Paul Terry, 1887-1971, animator of Mighty Mouse.
Bob Thaves, 1924-2006, Frank and Ernest.
James Thurber, 1894-61, *The New Yorker*.
Garry Trudeau, b 1948, Doonesbury.
Jim Unger, 1937-2012, Herman.
Mort Walker, b 1923, Beetle Bailey.
Bill Watterson, b 1958, Calvin and Hobbes.
Russ Westover, 1887-1966, Tillie the Toiler.
Signe Wilkinson, b 1950, political cartoonist.
Frank Willard, 1893-1958, Moon Mullins.
J. R. Williams, 1888-1957, The Willets Family, Out Our Way.
Gahan Wilson, b 1930, *The New Yorker*.
Tom Wilson, 1931-2011, Ziggy.
Art Young, 1866-1943, political cartoonist.
Chic Young, 1901-73, Blondie.

Economists, Educators, Historians, and Social Scientists of the Past

For psychologists, see Scientists of the Past.

Brooks Adams, 1848-1927, (U.S.) historian, political theoretician; *The Law of Civilization and Decay.*

Henry Adams, 1838-1918, (U.S.) historian, autobiographer; *The Education of Henry Adams.*

Stephen Ambrose, 1936-2002, (U.S.) historian; *Eisenhower.*

Francis Bacon, 1561-1626, (Eng.) philosopher, essayist, statesman; championed observation and induction.

George Bancroft, 1800-91, (U.S.) historian; 10-volume *History of the United States.*

Jack Barbash, 1910-94, (U.S.) labor economist; helped create the AFL-CIO.

Henry Barnard, 1811-1900, (U.S.) public school reformer.

Charles A. Beard, 1874-1948, (U.S.) historian; *The Economic Basis of Politics.*

(St.) Bede (the Venerable), c. 673-735, (Br.) scholar, historian; *Ecclesiastical History of the English People.*

Daniel Bell, 1919-2011, (U.S.) sociologist; *The End of Ideology.*

Ruth Benedict, 1887-1948, (U.S.) anthropologist; studied Indian tribes of the Southwest.

Sir Isaiah Berlin, 1909-97, (Br.) philosopher, historian; *The Age of Enlightenment.*

Leonard Bloomfield, 1887-1949, (U.S.) linguist; *Language.*

Franz Boas, 1858-1942, (U.S.) Germanborn anthropologist; studied American Indians.

Van Wyck Brooks, 1886-1963, (U.S.) historian; critic of New England culture, especially literature.

Edmund Burke, 1729-97, (Ire.) British parliamentarian and political philosopher; *Reflections on the Revolution in France.*

Nicholas Murray Butler, 1862-1947, (U.S.) educator; headed Columbia Univ., 1902-45; Nobel Peace Prize, 1931.

Joseph Campbell, 1904-87, (U.S.) author, editor, teacher; wrote books on mythology, folklore.

Thomas Carlyle, 1795-1881, (Scot.) historian, critic; *Sartor Resartus, Past and Present, The French Revolution.*

(Charles) Bruce Catton, 1899-1978, (U.S.) historian; *A Stillness at Appomattox.*

Edward Channing, 1856-1931, (U.S.) historian; 6-volume *History of the United States.*

Henry Steele Commager, 1902-98, (U.S.) historian, educator; *The Growth of the American Republic.*

John R. Commons, 1862-1945, (U.S.) economist, labor historian; *Legal Foundations of Capitalism.*

James B. Conant, 1893-1978, (U.S.) educator, diplomat; *The American High School Today.*

Benedetto Croce, 1866-1952, (It.) philosopher, statesman, historian; *Philosophy of the Spirit.*

Bernard A. De Voto, 1897-1955, (U.S.) historian; wrote trilogy on American West, edited Mark Twain manuscripts.

Melvil Dewey, 1851-1931, (U.S.) devised decimal system of library-book classification.

Donald Herbert Donald, 1920-2009, (U.S.) Pulitzer Prize-winning Civil War and Lincoln historian.

St. Clair Drake, 1911-90, (U.S.) sociologist, black studies pioneer; *Black Metropolis* (1945), with Horace R. Cayton.

W(illiam) E(dward) B(urghardt) Du Bois, 1868-1963, (U.S.) historian, sociologist; NAACP founder, 1909.

Will(iam), 1885-1981, (U.S.) and **Ariel Durant,** 1898-1981, (Ukraine), historians; *The Story of Civilization.*

Emile Durkheim, 1858-1917, (Fr.) a founder of modern sociology; *The Rules of Sociological Method.*

Jean Baptiste Point du Sable, c. 1750-1818, (U.S.) pioneer trader and first settler of Chicago, 1779.

Charles Eliot, 1834-1926, (U.S.) educator, Harvard president.

Friedrich Engels, 1820-95, (Ger.) political writer; with Marx wrote the *Communist Manifesto.*

Irving Fisher, 1867-1947, (U.S.) economist; contributed to the development of modern monetary theory.

John Fiske, 1842-1901, (U.S.) historian and lecturer; popularized Darwinian theory of evolution.

Charles Fourier, 1772-1837, (Fr.) utopian socialist.

John Hope Franklin, 1915-2009, (U.S.) historian; *From Slavery to Freedom: A History of African Americans.*

Sir James George Frazer, 1854-1941, (Br.) anthropologist; studied myth in religion; *The Golden Bough.*

Milton Friedman, 1912-2006, (U.S.) economist.

Paul Fussell, 1924-2012, (U.S.) literary historian; *The Great War and Modern Memory.*

John Kenneth Galbraith, 1908-2006, (Can.-U.S.) economist, author, professor, former amb. to India.

Giovanni Gentile, 1875-1944, (It.) philosopher, educator; reformed Italian educational system.

Henry George, 1839-97, (U.S.) economist, reformer; led single-tax movement.

Edward Gibbon, 1737-94, (Br.) historian; *The History of the Decline and Fall of the Roman Empire.*

Andrew Greeley, 1928-2013, (U.S.) Rom. Cath priest; sociologist.

Francesco Guicciardini, 1483-1540, (It.) historian; *Storia d'Italia,* principal historical work of the 16th cent.

Thomas Hobbes, 1588-1679, (Eng.) philosopher, political theorist; *Leviathan.*

Richard Hofstadter, 1916-70, (U.S.) historian; *The Age of Reform.*

Charles Hamilton Houston, 1895-1950, (U.S.) African American lawyer, Howard University instructor; champion of minority rights.

Samuel Huntington, 1927-2008, (U.S.), political scientist, Harvard University professor; *The Clash of Civilizations.*

Alfred Kahn, 1917-2010, (U.S.) economist; deregulated the U.S. airline industry.

John Keegan, 1934-2012, (Br.) war historian; *The Face of Battle.*

George F. Kennan, 1904-2005, (U.S.) diplomat, historian; main architect of U.S. Cold War "containment" strategy.

John Maynard Keynes, 1883-1946, (Br.) economist; principal advocate of deficit spending.

Alfred Kinsey, 1894-1956, (U.S.) zoologist; pioneering human sex researcher.

Russell Kirk, 1918-94, (U.S.) social philosopher; *The Conservative Mind.*

Alfred L. Kroeber, 1876-1960, (U.S.) cultural anthropologist; studied Indians of North and South America.

Elisabeth Kubler-Ross, 1926-2004, (Switz.) psychiatrist, author; *On Death and Dying.*

Christopher Lasch, 1932-94, (U.S.) social critic, historian; *The Culture of Narcissism.*

James L. Laughlin, 1850-1933, (U.S.) economist; helped establish Federal Reserve System.

Margaret Leech, 1893-1974, (U.S.) historian; *Reveille in Washington, 1860-1865.*

Lucien Lévy-Bruhl, 1857-1939, (Fr.) philosopher; studied the psychology of primitive societies; *Primitive Mentality.*

John Locke, 1632-1704, (Eng.) philosopher, political theorist; *Two Treatises of Government.*

Thomas B. Macaulay, 1800-59, (Br.) historian, statesman.

Niccolò Machiavelli, 1469-1527, (It.) writer, statesman; *The Prince.*

Bronislaw Malinowski, 1884-1942, (Pol.) considered the father of social anthropology.

Thomas R. Malthus, 1766-1834, (Br.) economist; *Essay on the Principle of Population.*

Horace Mann, 1796-1859, (U.S.) pioneered modern public school system.

Karl Mannheim, 1893-1947, (Hung.) sociologist, historian; *Ideology and Utopia.*

Harriet Martineau, 1802-76, (Eng.) writer, feminist; *Society in America.*

Karl Marx, 1818-83, (Ger.) political theorist, proponent of Communism; *Communist Manifesto, Das Kapital.*

Benjamin Mays, 1895-1984, (U.S.) minister, educator, civil rights leader; headed Morehouse College, 1940-67.

Giuseppe Mazzini, 1805-72, (It.) political philosopher.

William H. McGuffey, 1800-73, (U.S.) his *Reader* was a mainstay of 19th-cent. U.S. public education.

George H. Mead, 1863-1931, (U.S.) philosopher, social psychologist.

Margaret Mead, 1901-78, (U.S.) cultural anthropologist; popularized field; *Coming of Age in Samoa.*

Alexander Meiklejohn, 1872-1964, (U.S.) Br.-born educator; championed academic freedom and experimental curricula.

James Mill, 1773-1836, (Scot.) philosopher, historian, economist; a proponent of utilitarianism.

John Stuart Mill, 1806-73, (Eng.) philosopher, economist; *Utilitarianism;* eldest son of James Mill.

Perry G. Miller, 1905-63, (U.S.) historian; interpreted 17th-cent. New England.

Theodor Mommsen, 1817-1903, (Ger.) historian; *The History of Rome.*

Ashley Montagu, 1905-99, (Eng.) anthropologist; *The Natural Superiority of Women.*

Charles-Louis Montesquieu, 1689-1755, (Fr.) social philosopher; *The Spirit of Laws.*

Maria Montessori, 1870-1952, (It.) educator, physician; started Montessori method of student self-motivation.

Samuel Eliot Morison, 1887-1976, (U.S.) historian; chronicled voyages of early explorers.

Lewis Mumford, 1895-1990, (U.S.) sociologist, critic; *The Culture of Cities.*

Gunnar Myrdal, 1898-1987, (Swed.) economist, social scientist; *Asian Drama: An Inquiry Into the Poverty of Nations.*

Allan Nevins, 1890-1971, (U.S.) historian, biographer; *The Ordeal of the Union.*

José Ortega y Gasset, 1883-1955, (Sp.) philosopher; advocated control by elite; *The Revolt of the Masses.*

Elinor Ostrom, 1933-2012, (U.S.) political economist.

Robert Owen, 1771-1858, (Br.) political philosopher, reformer; pioneer in cooperative movement.

Thomas Paine, 1737-1809, (Br.-U.S.) political theorist, writer; *Common Sense.*

Vilfredo Pareto, 1848-1923, (It.) economist, sociologist.

Francis Parkman, 1823-93, (U.S.) historian; *France and England in North America.*

Elizabeth P. Peabody, 1804-94, (U.S.) education pioneer; founded first kindergarten in U.S., 1860.

William Prescott, 1796-1859, (U.S.) early American historian; *The Conquest of Peru.*

Pierre Joseph Proudhon, 1809-65, (Fr.) social theorist; father of anarchism; *The Philosophy of Property.*

François Quesnay, 1694-1774, (Fr.) economic theorist.

Robert V. Remini, 1921-2013, (U.S.) historian; *The Life of Andrew Jackson.*

David Ricardo, 1772-1823, (Br.) economic theorist; advocated free international trade.

David Riesman, 1909-2002, (U.S.) sociologist; co-author, *The Lonely Crowd*.

Jacqueline de Romilly, 1913-2010, (Fr.) scholar of Greek civilization and language.

Theodore Roszak, 1933-2011, (U.S.) historian; *The Making of a Counter Culture*.

Jean-Jacques Rousseau, 1712-78, (Fr.) social philosopher; the father of romantic sensibility; *Confessions*.

Paul Samuelson, 1915-2009, (U.S.) economist, famed for modern mathematical approach to economics.

Edward Sapir, 1884-1939, (Ger.-U.S.) anthropologist; studied ethnology and linguistics of U.S. Indian groups.

Ferdinand de Saussure, 1857-1913, (Switz.) a founder of modern linguistics.

Arthur Schlesinger Jr., 1917-2007, (U.S.) historian, author; *The Imperial Presidency*.

Joseph Schumpeter, 1883-1950, (Czech.-U.S.) economist, sociologist.

Elizabeth Seton, 1774-1821, (U.S.) nun; est. parochial school education in U.S., first native-born American saint.

Georg Simmel, 1858-1918, (Ger.) sociologist, philosopher; helped establish German sociology.

Robert Sklar, 1936-2011, (U.S.) film scholar.

Adam Smith, 1723-90, (Br.) economist; advocated laissez-faire economy, free trade; *The Wealth of Nations*.

Jared Sparks, 1789-1866, (U.S.) historian, educator, editor; *The Library of American Biography*.

Oswald Spengler, 1880-1936, (Ger.) philosopher, historian; *The Decline of the West*.

Leo Steinberg, 1920-2011, (Rus.-Am.) art historian.

William G. Sumner, 1840-1910, (U.S.) social scientist, economist; laissez-faire economy, Social Darwinism.

Hippolyte Taine, 1828-93, (Fr.) historian; basis of naturalistic school; *The Origins of Contemporary France*.

A(lan) J(ohn) P(ercivale) Taylor, 1906-90, (Br.) historian; *The Origins of the Second World War*.

Nikolaas Tinbergen, 1907-88, (Neth.-Br.) ethologist; pioneer in study of animal behavior.

Alexis de Tocqueville, 1805-59, (Fr.) political scientist, historian; *Democracy in America*.

Francis E. Townsend, 1867-1960, (U.S.) led old-age pension movement, 1933.

Arnold Toynbee, 1889-1975, (Br.) historian; *A Study of History*, sweeping analysis of hist. of civilizations.

George Trevelyan, 1876-1962, (Br.) historian, statesman; favored "literary" over "scientific" history; *History of England*.

Henri Troyat, 1911-2007, (Russ.-Fr.), biographies of major figures in Russian history.

Frederick J. Turner, 1861-1932, (U.S.) historian, educator; *The Frontier in American History*.

Thorstein B. Veblen, 1857-1929, (U.S.) economist, social philosopher; *The Theory of the Leisure Class*.

Giovanni Vico, 1668-1744, (It.) historian, biographer; regarded by many as first modern historian; *New Science*.

Izaak Walton, 1593-1683, (Eng.) biographer; political-philosophical study of fishing, *The Compleat Angler*.

Booker T. Washington, 1856-1915, (U.S.) founder, 1881, and first pres. of Tuskegee Institute; *Up From Slavery*.

Sidney J., 1859-1947, and **Beatrice Webb**, 1858-1943, (Br.) leading figures in Fabian Society and Labor Party.

Max Weber, 1864-1920, (Ger.) sociologist; *The Protestant Ethic and the Spirit of Capitalism*.

Walter White, 1893-1955, (U.S.) exec. sec., NAACP, 1931-55.

Roy Wilkins, 1901-81, (U.S.) exec. director, NAACP, 1955-77.

Emma Hart Willard, 1787-1870, (U.S.) pioneered higher education for women.

James Q. Wilson, 1931-2012, (U.S.) political scientist; co-authored broken windows theory.

Carter G. Woodson, 1875-1950, (U.S.) historian; founded Assn. for the Study of Negro Life and History.

C. Vann Woodward, 1908-99, (U.S.) historian; *The Strange Career of Jim Crow*.

American Journalists of the Past

Reviewed by Dean Mills, Dean, Missouri School of Journalism.
See also Business Leaders and Philanthropists, American Cartoonists, and Writers of the Past.

Franklin P. Adams (F.P.A.), 1881-1960, humorist; wrote column "The Conning Tower."

Joseph W. Alsop, 1910-89, and **Stewart Alsop**, 1914-74, Washington-based political analysts, columnists.

Jack Anderson, 1922-2006, muckraking Washington, DC, syndicated columnist.

Brooks Atkinson, 1894-1984, theater critic.

Robert L. Bartley, 1937-2003, editorial-page editor for *Wall Street Journal*.

James Gordon Bennett, 1795-1872, editor and publisher; founded *NY Herald*.

James Gordon Bennett, 1841-1918, succeeded father, financed expeditions, founded afternoon paper.

Nellie Bly (Elizabeth Cochrane), 1867-1922, pioneer woman journalist, investigative reporter; noted for series on trip around the world.

Elias Boudinot, c. 1803-39, founding editor of first Native American newspaper in U.S., *Cherokee Phoenix* (1828-34).

Ed Bradley, 1941-2006, TV journalist (*60 Minutes*); one of the first African American journalists to report on the Vietnam War.

Andrew Breitbart, 1969-2012, conservative commentator and blogger.

David Brinkley, 1920-2003, co-anchor of NBC's *Huntley-Brinkley Report*, host of ABC's *This Week With David Brinkley*.

Arthur Brisbane, 1864-1936, editor; helped introduce "yellow journalism" with sensational, simply written articles.

David Broder, 1929-2011, political journalist for *The Washington Post*.

Joyce Brothers, 1927-2013, psychologist, columnist.

Heywood Broun, 1888-1939, author, columnist; founded American Newspaper Guild.

Helen Gurley Brown, 1922-2012, author; editor-in-chief of *Cosmopolitan* magazine (1965-97).

Art Buchwald, 1925-2007, journalist, humorist, syndicated columnist.

William F. Buckley Jr., 1925-2008, columnist and commentator; founder of *National Review*.

Herb Caen, 1916-97, longtime columnist for *San Francisco Chronicle* and *Examiner*.

John Campbell, 1653-1728, published *Boston News-Letter*, first continuing newspaper in the American colonies.

Jimmy Cannon, 1909-73, syndicated sports columnist.

John Chancellor, 1927-96, NBC reporter, anchor.

Harry Chandler, 1864-1944, *Los Angeles Times* publisher (1917-41); made it a dominant force.

Otis Chandler, 1928-2006, *Los Angeles Times* publisher (1960-80).

Marquis Childs, 1903-90, reporter and columnist for *St. Louis Post-Dispatch* and United Feature syndicate.

Craig Claiborne, 1920-2000, *NY Times* food editor and critic; key in internationalizing American tastes.

Alexander Cockburn, 1941-2012, left-wing journalist.

Charles Collingwood, 1917-85, CBS news correspondent.

Alistair Cooke, 1908-2004, journalist, TV narrator; naturalized American citizen, "Letter From America" series.

Howard Cosell, 1920-95, TV and radio sportscaster.

Gardner Cowles, 1861-1946, founded newspaper chain.

Judith Crist, 1922-2012, film critic.

Walter Cronkite, 1916-2009, CBS evening news anchor, TV journalist.

Evelyn Cunningham, 1916-2010, African American civil rights reporter.

Cyrus Curtis, 1850-1933, publisher of *Saturday Evening Post*, *Ladies' Home Journal*, *Country Gentleman*.

John Charles Daly, 1914-91, war correspondent, TV journalist; Voice of America head.

Charles Anderson Dana, 1819-97, editor, publisher; made *NY Sun* famous for its news reporting.

Elmer (Holmes) Davis, 1890-1958, *NY Times* editorial writer, radio commentator.

Richard Harding Davis, 1864-1916, war correspondent, travel writer, fiction writer.

Benjamin Day, 1810-89, published *NY Sun* beginning in 1833, introducing penny press to the U.S.

Dorothy Dix (Elizabeth Meriwether Gilmer), 1861-1951, reporter; pioneer of the advice column genre.

Finley Peter Dunne, 1867-1936, humorist, social critic; wrote "Mr. Dooley" columns.

Roger Ebert, 1942-2013, film critic.

Mary Baker Eddy, 1821-1910, founded Christian Science movement and *Christian Science Monitor*.

Rowland Evans Jr., 1921-2001, Washington columnist.

Fanny Fern (Sara Willis Parton), 1811-72, newspaper columnist, author.

Marshall Field III, 1893-1956, retail magnate, *Chicago Sun* founder.

Doris Fleeson, 1901-70, war correspondent, columnist.

Benjamin Franklin, 1706-90, publisher of *Poor Richard's Almanack*.

James Franklin, 1697-1735, printer, pioneer journalist; publisher of *New England Courant* and *Rhode Island Gazette*.

Fred W. Friendly, 1915-98, radio, TV reporter, producer, executive; collaborator with Edward R. Murrow.

Margaret Fuller, 1810-50, social reformer, transcendentalist, critic and foreign correspondent for *NY Tribune*.

Frank E. Gannett, 1876-1957, founded newspaper chain.

Mary Ellen Garber, 1916-2008, sports journalist.

William Lloyd Garrison, 1805-79, abolitionist; publisher of *The Liberator*.

Jack Germond, 1928-2013, political reporter.

Jack Germond, 1928-2013, political reporter.

Edwin Lawrence Godkin, 1831-1902, founder of *The Nation*, editor of *NY Evening Post*.

Katharine Graham, 1917-2001, *Washington Post* publisher.

Sheilah Graham, 1904-89, Hollywood gossip columnist.

Horace Greeley, 1811-72, editor, politician; founded *NY Tribune*.

Meg Greenfield, 1930-99, *Newsweek* columnist, *Washington Post* editorial page editor.

Gilbert Hovey Grosvenor, 1875-1966, longtime editor of *National Geographic* magazine.

John Gunther, 1901-70, *Chicago Daily News* foreign correspondent, author.

David Halberstam, 1934-2007, journalist, sports reporter, author; *The Best and the Brightest*, *Summer of '49*.

Sarah Josepha Buell Hale, 1788-1879, first female magazine editor; *Ladies' Magazine*, later *Godey's Lady's Book*.

Paul Harvey, 1918-2009, radio broadcaster and commentator.

William Randolph Hearst, 1863-1951, founder of Hearst newspaper chain, one of the pioneers of yellow journalism.

Gabriel Heatter, 1890-1972, radio commentator.

John Hersey, 1914-98, foreign correspondent for *Time*, *Life*, and *The New Yorker*; author.

Marguerite Higgins, 1920-66, reporter, war correspondent.

Christopher Hitchens, 1949-2011, columnist and literary critic.

Hedda Hopper, 1885-1966, Hollywood gossip columnist.

Roy Howard, 1883-1964, editor, executive; Scripps-Howard papers and United Press (later United Press International).

Chet (Chester Robert) Huntley, 1911-74, co-anchor of NBC's *Huntley-Brinkley Report*.

Ada Louise Huxtable, 1921-2013, architecture critic.

Ralph Ingersoll, 1900-85, editor; *Fortune*, *Time*, *Life* exec.

Molly Ivins, 1944-2007, author, syndicated political columnist.

Peter Jennings, 1938-2005, ABC correspondent, anchor.

Pauline Kael, 1919-2001, film critic.

H. V. (Hans von) Kaltenborn, 1878-1965, radio commentator, reporter.

Murray Kempton, 1917-97, reporter, columnist for magazines and newspapers, including *NY Post*.

Dorothy Kilgallen, 1913-65, crime reporter, columnist.

James J. Kilpatrick, 1920-2010, political columnist, author and television personality.

John S. Knight, 1894-1981, editor, publisher; founded Knight newspaper group, which merged into Knight-Ridder.

Joseph Kraft, 1942-86, foreign policy columnist.

Irving Kristol, 1920-2009, columnist, commentator.

Arthur Krock, 1886-1974, *NY Times* political writer, Washington bureau chief.

Charles Kuralt, 1934-97, TV anchor; host of CBS "On the Road" featuring stories about life in the U.S.

Ann Landers (Eppie Lederer), 1918-2002, advice columnist.

David Lawrence, 1888-1973, reporter, columnist, publisher; founded *U.S. News & World Report*.

Frank Leslie, 1821-80, engraver, publisher of newspapers and magazines, notably *Leslie's Illustrated Newspaper*.

Anthony Lewis, 1927-2013, legal journalist.

Alexander Liberman, 1912-99, editorial director for Condé Nast magazines.

A(bbott) J(oseph) Liebling, 1904-63, foreign correspondent, critic; principally with *The New Yorker*.

Walter Lippmann, 1889-1974, political analyst, social critic, columnist, author.

Peter Lisagor, 1915-76, Washington bureau chief, *Chicago Daily News*; broadcast commentator.

David Ross Locke, 1833-88, humorist, satirist under pseudonym P.V. Nasby; owned *Toledo (Ohio) Blade*.

Elijah Parish Lovejoy, 1802-37, abolitionist editor in St. Louis and in Alton, IL; killed by proslavery mob.

Clare Booth Luce, 1903-87, war correspondent for *Life*, diplomat, playwright.

Henry R. Luce, 1898-1967, founded *Time*, *Fortune*, *Life*, *Sports Illustrated*.

Dwight Macdonald, 1906-82, reporter, social critic.

Don Marquis, 1878-1937, humor columnist for *NY Sun* and *NY Tribune*; wrote "Archy and Mehitabel" stories.

Nancy Hicks Maynard, 1946-2008, African American publisher, journalist.

Robert Maynard, 1937-93, first African American editor and then owner of major U.S. paper, the *Oakland Tribune*.

C(harles) K(enny) McClatchy, 1858-1936, founder of McClatchy newspaper chain.

Sarah McClendon, 1910-2003, veteran White House correspondent.

Samuel McClure, 1857-1949, founder (1893) of *McClure's Magazine*, famous for its investigative reporting.

Anne O'Hare McCormick, 1889-1954, foreign correspondent; first woman on *NY Times* editorial board.

Robert R. McCormick, 1880-1955, editor, publisher, executive of *Chicago Tribune* and *NY Daily News*.

Ralph McGill, 1893-1969, crusading editor, publisher of *Atlanta Constitution*.

Mary McGrory, 1918-2004, Washington columnist.

O(scar) O(dd) McIntyre, 1884-1938, feature writer, syndicated columnist on everyday life in New York City.

Joseph Medill, 1823-99, longtime editor of the *Chicago Tribune*.

H(enry) L(ouis) Mencken, 1880-1956, reporter, editor, columnist with *Baltimore Sun* papers; anti-establishment viewpoint.

Edwin Meredith, 1876-1928, founder of magazine company.

Frank A. Munsey, 1854-1925, owner, editor, and publisher of newspapers and magazines, including *Munsey's Magazine*.

Edward R. Murrow, 1908-65, broadcast reporter, executive; reported from Britain in WWII; hosted *See It Now*, *Person to Person*.

Allen Neuharth, 1924-2013, *USA Today* founder.

Edwin Newman, 1919-2010, NBC news correspondent.

Louella Parsons, 1881-1972, Hollywood gossip columnist.

Ethel L. Payne, 1911-91, African American civil rights reporter.

Daniel Pearl, 1963-2002, American journalist; kidnapped and murdered in Pakistan.

Drew (Andrew Russell) Pearson, 1897-1969, investigative reporter, columnist.

(James) Westbrook Pegler, 1894-1969, reporter, columnist.

Shirley Povich, 1905-98, sports columnist.

Joseph Pulitzer, 1847-1911, *NY World* publisher; founded Columbia Journalism School, Pulitzer Prizes.

Joseph Pulitzer II, 1885-1955, longtime *St. Louis Post-Dispatch* editor, publisher; built it into major paper.

Ernie Pyle, 1900-45, reporter, war correspondent; killed in WWII.

William Raspberry, 1935-2012, public affairs columnist.

Henry Raymond, 1820-69, cofounder, editor, *NY Times*.

Harry Reasoner, 1923-91, ABC and CBS news reporter, anchor.

John Reed, 1887-1920, reporter; foreign correspondent famous for coverage of Bolshevik Revolution; buried at the Kremlin.

Whitelaw Reid, 1837-1912, longtime editor, *NY Tribune*.

James Reston, 1909-95, *NY Times* political reporter, columnist.

Frank Reynolds, 1923-83, ABC reporter, anchor.

(Henry) Grantland Rice, 1880-1954, sportswriter.

Jacob Riis, 1849-1914, reporter, photographer; exposed slum conditions in *How the Other Half Lives*.

Max Robinson, 1939-88, first African American to anchor network news (ABC), 1978.

Andy Rooney, 1919-2011, radio and TV commentator (*60 Minutes*).

A. M. Rosenthal, 1922-2006, editor for *NY Times* (1943-99).

Harold Ross, 1892-1951, founder, editor, *The New Yorker*.

Carl T. Rowan, 1925-2000, reporter, columnist, author.

Mike Royko, 1932-97, Chicago newspaper columnist; wrote *Boss*, biography of Mayor Richard J. Daley (1902-76).

Louis Rukeyser, 1933-2006, TV journalist, financial analyst; hosted *Wall Street Week* on public television.

(Alfred) Damon Runyon, 1884-1946, sportswriter, columnist; stories collected in *Guys and Dolls*.

Tim Russert, 1950-2008, TV journalist; moderator of *Meet the Press* (NBC).

John B. Russwurm, 1799-1851, cofounded (1827) nation's first black newspaper, *Freedom's Journal*, in New York, NY.

William Safire, 1929-2009, Pulitzer Prize-winning columnist, *NY Times*.

Adela Rogers St. Johns, 1894-1988, reporter, sportswriter for Hearst newspapers.

Pierre Salinger, 1925-2004, press sec. under Pres. Kennedy and Johnson, foreign correspondent.

Harrison Salisbury, 1908-93, reporter, foreign correspondent; a Soviet specialist.

Andrew Sarris, 1928-2012, film critic, *Village Voice*.

Daniel Schorr, 1916-2010, broadcast and print journalist.

E(dward) W(illis) Scripps, 1854-1926, founded first large U.S. newspaper chain, pioneered syndication.

Eric Sevareid, 1912-92, war correspondent, radio newscaster, CBS commentator.

Anthony Shadid, 1968-2012, foreign correspondent.

Randy Shilts, 1951-94, journalist; author of *And the Band Played On*.

William L. Shirer, 1904-93, broadcaster, foreign correspondent; wrote *The Rise and Fall of the Third Reich*.

Howard K. Smith, 1914-2002, ABC news reporter, anchor.

Red (Walter) Smith, 1905-82, sportswriter.

Edgar P. Snow, 1905-71, correspondent; expert on Chinese Communist movement.

Tony Snow, 1955-2008, columnist, radio/TV journalist, White House press sec.

Tom Snyder, 1936-2007, television journalist.

Lawrence Spivak, 1900-94, co-creator, moderator, producer of *Meet the Press*.

(Joseph) Lincoln Steffens, 1866-1936, muckraking journalist.

I(sidor) F(einstein) Stone, 1907-89, one-man editor of *I. F. Stone's Weekly*.

Arthur Hays Sulzberger, 1891-1968, long-time publisher of *NY Times* (1935-61).

Arthur Ochs "Punch" Sulzberger, 1926-2012, long-time publisher of *NY Times* (1963-92).

C(yrus) L(eo) Sulzberger, 1912-93, *NY Times* foreign correspondent, columnist.

David Susskind, 1920-87, TV producer, public affairs talk-show host (*Open End*).

John Cameron Swayze, 1906-95, early TV newscaster (NBC).

Herbert Bayard Swope, 1882-1958, war correspondent, editor of *NY World*.

Ida Tarbell, 1857-1944, muckraking journalist.

Helen Thomas, 1920-2013, White House correspondent, 1959-2010.

Isaiah Thomas, 1750-1831, printer, publisher; cofounder of revolutionary journal, *Massachusetts Spy*.

Lowell Thomas, 1892-1981, radio newscaster, world traveler.

Dorothy Thompson, 1894-1961, foreign correspondent, columnist, radio commentator.

Hunter S. Thompson, 1937-2005, political journalist, author; *Fear and Loathing on the Campaign Trail* (1972).

Kenneth Thompson, 1923-2006, Canadian media magnate; owned Toronto *Globe and Mail* newspaper.

Abigail Van Buren (Pauline Phlips), 1918-2013, advice columnist.

Mike Wallace, 1918-2012, TV journalist (*60 Minutes*).

Ida Bell Wells-Barnett, 1862-1931, African American reporter, editor, anti-lynching crusader.

William Allen White, 1868-1944, newspaper editor, publisher.

Tom Wicker, 1926-2011, *NY Times* political reporter, columnist.

Walter Winchell, 1897-1972, reporter, columnist, broadcaster of celebrity news.

John Peter Zenger, 1697-1746, printer, journalist; acquitted in precedent-setting libel suit (1735).

Military and Naval Leaders of the Past

Reviewed by Alan C. Aimone, USMA Library.

Alexander the Great, 356-323 BCE, (Maced.) conquered Persia and much of the world known to Europeans.

Harold Alexander, 1891-1969, (Br.) led Allied invasion of Italy, 1943, WWII.

Ethan Allen, 1738-89, (U.S.) headed Green Mountain Boys; captured Ft. Ticonderoga, 1775, Amer. Rev.

Edmund Allenby, 1861-1936, (Br.) in Boer War, WWI; led Egyptian expeditionary force, 1917-18.

Benedict Arnold, 1741-1801, (U.S.) victorious at Saratoga; tried to betray West Point to British, Amer. Rev.

Henry "Hap" Arnold, 1886-1950, (U.S.) commanded Army Air Force in WWII.

Ashurnasirpal II, 884-859 BCE, (Assyria) king; began Assyrian conquest of Middle East.

John Barry, 1745-1803, (U.S.) won numerous sea battles during Amer. Rev.

Pierre Beauregard, 1818-93, (U.S.) Confed. general; ordered bombardment of Ft. Sumter that began Civil War.

Belisarius, c. 505-565, (Byzant.) won remarkable victories for Byzantine emperor Justinian I.

Gebhard von Blücher, 1742-1819, (Ger.) helped defeat Napoleon at Waterloo.

Simón Bolívar, 1783-1830, (Venez.) S. Amer. revolutionary who liberated much of the continent from Spanish rule.

Napoleon Bonaparte, 1769-1821, (Fr.) defeated Russia and Austria at Austerlitz, 1805; invaded Russia, 1812; defeated at Waterloo, 1815.

Edward Braddock, 1695-1755, (Br.) commanded forces in French and Indian War.

Omar N. Bradley, 1893-1981, (U.S.) headed U.S. ground troops in Normandy invasion, 1944, WWII.

John Burgoyne, 1722-92, (Br.) general; defeated at Saratoga, Amer. Rev.

Julius Caesar, 100-44 BCE, (Rom.) general and politician; conquered northern Gaul, overthrew Roman Republic.

Charlemagne, 742-814, (Fr.) king of the Franks, Holy Roman Emperor; conquered most of Western Europe.

Claire Lee Chennault, 1893-1958, (U.S.) headed Flying Tigers in WWII.

El Cid (Rodrigo Diaz de Vivar), 1040-99, (Sp.) renowned knight; captured Valencia (1094), hero of "Song of Cid" epic.

Mark W. Clark, 1896-1984, (U.S.) helped plan N African invasion in WWII; commander of UN forces, Korean War.

Karl von Clausewitz, 1780-1831, (Prus.) military theorist.

Lucius D. Clay, 1897-1978, (U.S.) led Berlin airlift, 1948-49.

Henry Clinton, 1738-95, (Br.) commander of forces in Amer. Rev., 1778-81.

Cochise, c. 1815-74, (Amer. Ind.) chief of Chiricahua band of Apache Indians in Southwest U.S.

Charles Cornwallis, 1738-1805, (Br.) victorious at Brandywine, 1777; surrendered at Yorktown, Amer. Rev.

Hernán Cortés, 1485-1547, (Sp.) led Spanish conquistadors in the defeat of the Aztec empire, 1519-28.

Crazy Horse, 1849-77, (Amer. Ind.) Sioux war chief victorious at Battle of Little Bighorn.

George Armstrong Custer, 1839-76, (U.S.) army officer defeated and killed at Battle of Little Bighorn.

Benjamin O. Davis Jr., 1912-2002, (U.S.) leader of WWII black aviators; first African American general in U.S. Air Force.

Benjamin O. Davis Sr., 1877-1970, (U.S.) first African American general in U.S. Army, 1940.

Moshe Dayan, 1915-81, (Isr.) directed campaigns in the 1967, 1973 Arab-Israeli wars.

Stephen Decatur, 1779-1820, (U.S.) naval hero of Barbary wars, War of 1812.

Anton Denikin, 1872-1947, (Russ.) led White forces in Russian civil war.

George Dewey, 1837-1917, (U.S.) destroyed Spanish fleet at Manila, 1898, Span.-Amer. War.

Karl Doenitz, 1891-1980, (Ger.) submarine cmdr. in chief and naval cmdr., WWII; last pres. of Third Reich.

Jimmy Doolittle, 1896-1993, (U.S.) led 1942 air raid on Tokyo and other Japanese cities in WWII.

Hugh Dowding, 1882-1970, (Br.) headed RAF Fighter Command, 1936-40, WWII.

Jubal Early, 1816-94, (U.S.) Confed. general; led raid on Washington, 1864, Civil War.

Dwight D. Eisenhower, 1890-1969, (U.S.) commanded Allied forces in Europe, WWII.

Erich von Falkenhayn, 1861-1922, (Ger.) minister of war, general, commander at Verdun in WWI.

David Farragut, 1801-70, (U.S.) Union admiral; captured New Orleans, Mobile Bay, Civil War.

John Arbuthnot Fisher, 1841-1920, (Br.) WWI admiral; naval reformer.

Ferdinand Foch, 1851-1929, (Fr.) headed victorious Allied armies, 1918, WWI.

Nathan Bedford Forrest, 1821-77, (U.S.) Confed. general; led raids against Union supply lines, Civil War.

Frederick the Great, 1712-86, (Prus.) led Prussia in Seven Years War.

Horatio Gates, 1728-1806, (U.S.) commanded army at Saratoga, Amer. Rev.

Genghis Khan, 1162-1227, (Mongol) unified Mongol tribes, subjugated much of Asia, 1206-21.

Geronimo, 1829-1909, (Amer. Ind.) leader of Chiricahua band of Apache Indians.

Charles G. Gordon, 1833-85, (Br.) led forces in China, Crimean War; killed at Khartoum.

Ulysses S. Grant, 1822-85, (U.S.) headed Union army, Civil War, 1864-65; forced Robert E. Lee's surrender, 1865.

Nathanael Greene, 1742-86, (U.S.) defeated British in Southern campaign, 1780-81, Amer. Rev.

Heinz Guderian, 1888-1954, (Ger.) tank theorist; led panzer forces in Poland, France, Russia, WWII.

Gustavus Adolphus, 1594-1632, (Swed.) king, military tactician, reformer; led forces in Thirty Years' War.

Douglas Haig, 1861-1928, (Br.) led British armies in France, 1915-18, WWI.

William F. Halsey, 1882-1959, (U.S.) defeated Japanese fleet at Leyte Gulf, 1944, WWII.

Hannibal, 247-183 BCE, (Carthage) invaded Rome, crossing Alps, in Second Punic War, 218-201 BCE.

Sir Arthur Travers Harris, 1895-1984, (Br.) led Britain's WWII bomber command.

Paul von Hindenburg, 1847-1934, (Ger.) chief of general staff, WWI; second pres. of Weimar Republic.

Richard Howe, 1726-99, (Br.) commanded navy in Amer. Rev., 1776-78; June 1 victory against French, 1794.

William Howe, 1729-1814, (Br.) commanded forces in Amer. Rev., 1776-78.

Isaac Hull, 1773-1843, (U.S.) sunk British frigate *Guerriere*, War of 1812.

Thomas "Stonewall" Jackson, 1824-63, (U.S.) Confed. general; led Shenandoah Valley campaign, Civil War.

Daniel James Jr., 1920-78, (U.S.) first black 4-star general, 1975; commander, N. American Air Defense Command.

Joseph Joffre, 1852-1931, (Fr.) headed Allied armies; won Battle of the Marne, 1914, WWI.

John Paul Jones, 1747-92, (U.S.) commanded *Bonhomme Richard* in victory over *Serapis*, Amer. Rev., 1779.

Chief Joseph, c. 1840-1904, (Amer. Ind.) chief of the Nez Percé; forced by army to retreat and surrender.

Stephen Kearny, 1794-1848, (U.S.) headed Army of the West in Mexican War.

Albert Kesselring, 1885-1960, (Ger.) field marshal who led the defense of Italy in WWII.

Ernest J. King, 1878-1956, (U.S.) key WWII naval strategist.

Horatio H. Kitchener, 1850-1916, (Br.) led forces in Boer War, victorious at Khartoum, organized army in WWI.

Henry Knox, 1750-1806, (U.S.) general in Amer. Rev.; first sec. of war under U.S. Constitution.

Lavrenti Kornilov, 1870-1918, (Russ.) commander-in-chief, 1917; led counterrevolutionary march on Petrograd.

Thaddeus Kosciusko, 1746-1817, (Pol.) aided Amer. Rev.

Walter Krueger, 1881-1967, (U.S.) led Sixth Army in WWII in Southwest Pacific.

Mikhail Kutuzov, 1745-1813, (Russ.) fought at Borodino, Napol. Wars, 1812; abandoned Moscow, forced French retreat.

Marquis de Lafayette, 1757-1834, (Fr.) fought in, secured French aid for Amer. Rev.

T(homas) E. Lawrence (of Arabia), 1888-1935, (Br.) organized revolt of Arabs against Turks in WWI.

William Daniel Leahy, 1875-1959, (U.S.) chief of staff to Pres. Roosevelt in WWII, Fleet Admiral.

Henry (Light-Horse Harry) Lee, 1756-1818, (U.S.) cavalry officer in Amer. Rev.

Robert E. Lee, 1807-70, (U.S.) Confed. general; defeated at Gettysburg, Civil War; surrendered to Grant, 1865.

Curtis LeMay, 1906-90, (U.S.) Air Force cmdr. in WWII, Korean War, Vietnam War.

Lyman Lemnitzer, 1899-1988, (U.S.) WWII hero; later general, chairman of Joint Chiefs of Staff.

James Longstreet, 1821-1904, (U.S.) aided Lee at Gettysburg, Civil War.

Erich Ludendorff, 1865-1937, (Ger.) general; victor at Tannenberg, WWI.

Douglas MacArthur, 1880-1964, (U.S.) commanded forces in SW Pacific in WWII; headed occupation forces in Japan, 1945-51; UN commander in Korean War.

Carl Gustaf Mannerheim, 1867-1951, (Fin.) army officer and pres. of Finland, 1944-46.

Erich von Manstein, 1887-1973, (Ger.) served WWI, WWII; planned inv. of France (1940); convicted of war crimes.

Francis Marion, 1733-95, (U.S.) led guerrilla actions in South Carolina during Amer. Rev.

Duke of Marlborough, 1650-1722, (Br.) led forces against Louis XIV in War of the Spanish Succession.

George C. Marshall, 1880-1959, (U.S.) chief of staff in WWII; authored Marshall Plan.

Maurice, Count of Nassau, 1567-1625, (Neth.) military innovator; led forces in Thirty Years' War.

George B. McClellan, 1826-85, (U.S.) Union general; commanded Army of the Potomac, 1861-62, Civil War.

George Meade, 1815-72, (U.S.) commanded Union forces at Gettysburg, Civil War.

Doris "Dorie" Miller, 1919-43, (U.S.) Navy hero of Pearl Harbor attack; first African American awarded Navy Cross.

Billy Mitchell, 1879-1936, (U.S.) WWI air-power advocate; court-martialed for insubordination, later vindicated.

Helmuth von Moltke, 1800-91, (Ger.) victorious in Austro-Prussian, Franco-Prussian wars.

Louis de Montcalm, 1712-59, (Fr.) headed troops in Canada, French and Indian War; defeated at Quebec, 1759.

Bernard Law Montgomery, 1887-1976, (Br.) stopped German offensive at Alamein, 1942, WWII; helped plan Normandy invasion.

Daniel Morgan, 1736-1802, (U.S.) victorious at Cowpens, 1781, Amer. Rev.

Louis Mountbatten, 1900-79, (Br.) Supreme Allied Commander of SE Asia, 1943-46, WWII.

Joachim Murat, 1767-1815, (Fr.) led cavalry at Marengo, Austerlitz, and Jena, Napoleonic Wars.

Horatio Nelson, 1758-1805, (Br.) naval commander; destroyed French fleet at Trafalgar.

Michel Ney, 1769-1815, (Fr.) commanded forces in Switz., Austria, Russ., Napoleonic Wars; defeated at Waterloo.

Chester Nimitz, 1885-1966, (U.S.) cmdr. of naval forces in Pacific in WWII.

George S. Patton, 1885-1945, (U.S.) led assault on Sicily, 1943, Third Army invasion of Europe, WWII.

Oliver Perry, 1785-1819, (U.S.) won Battle of Lake Erie in War of 1812.

John Pershing, 1860-1948, (U.S.) commanded Mexican border campaign, 1916; Amer. Expeditionary Force, WWI.

Henri Philippe Pétain, 1856-1951, (Fr.) defended Verdun, 1916; headed Vichy government in WWII.

George E. Pickett, 1825-75, (U.S.) Confed. general famed for "charge" at Gettysburg, Civil War.

Charles Portal, 1893-1971, (Br.) chief of staff, Royal Air Force, 1940-45; led in Battle of Britain.

Manfred Frieherr von Richthofen (Red Baron), 1892-1918, (Ger.) WWI flying ace, led elite fighter squadron.

Hyman Rickover, 1900-86, (U.S.) father of nuclear navy.

Matthew Bunker Ridgway, 1895-1993, (U.S.) commanded Allied ground forces in Korean War.

Erwin Rommel, 1891-1944, (Ger.) headed Afrika Korps, WWII.

Gerd von Rundstedt, 1875-1953, (Ger.) supreme cmdr. in West, 1942-45, WWII.

Saladin, 1138-93, (Kurdish Muslim) recaptured Jerusalem from Crusaders.

Aleksandr Samsonov, 1859-1914, (Russ.) led invasion of E Prussia, WWI; defeated at Tannenberg, 1914.

Antonio Lopez de Santa Anna, 1794-1876, (Mex.) defeated Texans at the Alamo; defeated in Mexican War.

Maurice, Count of Saxe, 1696-1750, (Fr.) general, noted tactician; War of Austrian Succession, War of Pol. Succession.

H. Norman Schwarzkopf, 1934-2012, (U.S.) army general; led Persian Gulf War, 1991.

Scipio Africanus the Elder, 234?-183 BCE, (Rom.) hero of Second Punic War; defeated Hannibal, invaded N Africa.

Winfield Scott, 1786-1866, (U.S.) hero of War of 1812; headed forces in Mexican War, took Mexico City.

Philip Sheridan, 1831-88, (U.S.) Union cavalry officer; headed Army of the Shenandoah, 1864-65, Civil War.

William T. Sherman, 1820-91, (U.S.) Union general; sacked Atlanta during "march to the sea," 1864, Civil War.

Sitting Bull, c. 1831-90, (Amer. Ind.) Hunkpapa Sioux chief; victorious at Battle of the Little Big Horn.

Carl Spaatz, 1891-1974, (U.S.) directed strategic bombing against Germany, later Japan, in WWII.

Raymond Spruance, 1886-1969, (U.S.) victorious at Midway Island, 1942, WWII.

Joseph W. Stilwell, 1883-1946, (U.S.) headed forces in the China, Burma, India theater in WWII.

J.E.B. Stuart, 1833-64, (U.S.) Confed. cavalry commander, Civil War.

Sun Tzu, 6th? cent. BCE, (China) general; author of *The Art of War*.

Aleksandr Suvorov, 1729-1800, (Russ.) commanded Allied Russian and Austrian armies, Russo-Turkish War.

Tamerlane, 1336-1405, (Turkoman Mongol) conqueror; established empire from India to Mediterranean Sea.

Tecumseh, 1768-1813, (Amer. Ind.) Shawnee chief; led Indian confederation opposing colonists.

George H. Thomas, 1816-70, (U.S.) saved Union army at Chattanooga, 1863; won at Nashville, 1864, Civil War.

Semyon Timoshenko, 1895-1970, (USSR) defended Moscow, Stalingrad, WWII; led winter offensive, 1942-43.

Alfred von Tirpitz, 1849-1930, (Ger.) responsible for submarine blockade in WWI.

Henri de la Tour d'Auvergne, Viscount of Turenne, 1611-75, (Fr.) marshal; Thirty Years' War, Fronde, War of Devolution.

Sebastien Le Prestre de Vauban, 1633-1707, (Fr.) innovative military engineer, theorist.

Jonathan M. Wainwright, 1883-1953, (U.S.) forced to surrender on Corregidor, Philippines, 1942, WWII.

George Washington, 1732-99, (U.S.) led Continental army, 1775-83, Amer. Rev.

Archibald Wavell, 1883-1950, (Br.) commanded forces in N and E Africa, SE Asia in WWII.

Anthony Wayne, 1745-96, (U.S.) captured Stony Point, NY, 1779, Amer. Rev.

Duke of Wellington, 1769-1852, (Br.) defeated Napoleon at Waterloo, 1815.

William Westmoreland, 1914-2005, (U.S.) commanded forces in Vietnam, 1964-68.

William I (The Conqueror), 1027-87, (Br.) victor, Battle of Hastings, 1066; became first Norman king of England.

James Wolfe, 1727-59, (Br.) captured Quebec from French, 1759, French and Indian War.

Isoroku Yamamoto, 1884-1943, (Jpn.) cmdr. in chief of Japanese fleet, naval planner before and during WWII.

Georgi Zhukov, 1895-1974, (Russ.) defended Moscow, 1941; led assault on Berlin, 1945, WWII.

Philosophers and Religious Figures of the Past

Excludes most biblical figures and popes (see Religion chapter). For Greeks and Romans, see also Historical Figures chapter.

Lyman Abbott, 1835-1922, (U.S.) clergyman, reformer; advocate of Christian Socialism.

Pierre Abelard, 1079-1142, (Fr.) philosopher, theologian, teacher; used dialectic method to support Christian beliefs.

Felix Adler, 1851-1933, (U.S.) German-born founder of the Ethical Culture Soc.

Mortimer Adler, 1902-2001, (U.S.) philosopher; helped create "Great Books" program.

(St.) Anselm, c. 1033-1109, (It.) philosopher-theologian, church leader; "ontological argument" for God's existence.

(St.) Thomas Aquinas, 1225-74, (It.) pre-eminent medieval philosopher-theologian; *Summa Theologica*.

Aristotle, 384-322 BCE, (Gr.) pioneering wide-ranging philosopher, logician, ethician, naturalist.

(St.) Augustine, 354-430, (N Africa) philosopher, theologian, bishop; *Confessions*, *City of God*, *On the Trinity*.

J. L. Austin, 1911-60, (Br.) ordinary-language philosopher.

Averroes (Ibn Rushd), 1126-98, (Sp.) Islamic philosopher, physician.

Avicenna (Ibn Sina), 980-1037, (Iran) Islamic philosopher, scientist.

A(lfred) J(ules) Ayer, 1910-89, (Br.) philosopher, logical positivist; *Language, Truth, and Logic*.

Roger Bacon, c. 1214-94, (Eng.) philosopher, scientist.

Bahá'u'lláh (Mirza Husayn Ali), 1817-92, (Pers.) founder of Bahá'í faith.

Karl Barth, 1886-1968, (Swiss) theologian; a leading force in 20th-cent. Protestantism.

Thomas à Becket, 1118-70, (Eng.) archbishop of Canterbury; opposed Henry II, murdered by King's men.

(St.) Benedict, c. 480-547, (It.) founded the Benedictines.

Jeremy Bentham, 1748-1832, (Br.) philosopher, reformer; enunciated utilitarianism.

Henri Bergson, 1859-1941, (Fr.) philosopher of evolution.

George Berkeley, 1685-1753, (Ire.) idealist philosopher, bishop.

John Biddle, 1615-62, (Eng.) founder of English Unitarianism.

Jakob Boehme, 1575-1624, (Ger.) theosophist, mystic.

Dietrich Bonhoeffer, 1906-45, (Ger.) Lutheran theologian, pastor; executed as opponent of Nazis.

William Brewster, 1567-1644, (Eng.) led Pilgrims.

Emil Brunner, 1889-1966, (Switz.) Protestant theologian.

Giordano Bruno, 1548-1600, (It.) philosopher, pantheist.

Martin Buber, 1878-1965, (Ger.) Jewish philosopher, theologian; *I and Thou*.

Buddha (Siddhartha Gautama), c. 563-c. 483 BCE, (India) philosopher; founded Buddhism.

John Calvin, 1509-64, (Fr.) theologian; a key figure in the Protestant Reformation.

Rudolph Carnap, 1891-1970, (U.S.) German-born analytic philosopher; a founder of logical positivism.

William Ellery Channing, 1780-1842, (U.S.) clergyman; early spokesman for Unitarianism.

Auguste Comte, 1798-1857, (Fr.) philosopher; originated positivism.

Confucius, 551-479 BCE, (China) founder of Confucianism.

John Cotton, 1584-1652, (Eng.) Puritan theologian.

Thomas Cranmer, 1489-1556, (Eng.) Anglican churchman; wrote much of *Book of Common Prayer*.

Jacques Derrida, 1930-2004, (Fr.) deconstructionist philosopher.

René Descartes, 1596-1650, (Fr.) philosopher, mathematician; "father of modern philosophy"; *Discourse on Method*, *Meditations on First Philosophy*.

John Dewey, 1859-1952, (U.S.) philosopher, educator; instrumentalist theory of knowledge, progressive education.

Denis Diderot, 1713-84, (Fr.) philosopher, encyclopedist.

John Duns Scotus, c. 1266-1308, (Sc.) Franciscan philosopher, theologian.

Mary Baker Eddy, 1821-1910, (U.S.) founder of Christian Science; *Science and Health*.

Jonathan Edwards, 1703-58, (U.S.) preacher, theologian; "Sinners in the Hands of an Angry God."

(Desiderius) Erasmus, c. 1466-1536, (Neth.) Renaissance humanist; *On the Freedom of the Will*.

Jerry Falwell, 1933-2007, (U.S.) TV evangelist, religious commentator.

Johann Fichte, 1762-1814, (Ger.) idealist philosopher.

Michel Foucault, 1926-84, (Fr.) structuralist philosopher, historian.

George Fox, 1624-91, (Br.) founder of Society of Friends (Quakers).

(St.) Francis of Assisi, 1182-1226, (It.) espoused voluntary poverty, founded Franciscans.

al-Ghazali, 1058-1111, ([now] Iran) Islamic philosopher.

Billy James Hargis, 1925-2004, (U.S.) anti-Communist televangelist; founder of the Church of the Christian Crusade.

Georg W. F. Hegel, 1770-1831, (Ger.) idealist philosopher; *Phenomenology of Mind*.

Martin Heidegger, 1889-1976, (Ger.) existentialist philosopher; affected many fields; *Being and Time*.

Johann G. Herder, 1744-1803, (Ger.) philosopher, cultural historian; a founder of German Romanticism.

Thomas Hobbes, 1588-1679, (Eng.) philosopher, political theorist; *Leviathan*.

David Hume, 1711-76, (Scot.) empiricist philosopher; *Enquiry Concerning Human Understanding*.

Jan Hus, 1369-1415, (Czech.) religious reformer.

Edmund Husserl, 1859-1938, (Ger.) philosopher; founded the phenomenological movement.

Thomas Huxley, 1825-95, (Br.) philosopher, educator.

William Ralph Inge, 1860-1954, (Br.) theologian; explored mystic aspects of Christianity.

William James, 1842-1910, (U.S.) philosopher, psychologist, pragmatist; studied religious experience.

Karl Jaspers, 1883-1969, (Ger.) existentialist philosopher.

Joan of Arc, 1412-31, (Fr.) national heroine, a patron saint of France; key figure in the Hundred Years' War.

Immanuel Kant, 1724-1804, (Ger.) philosopher; founder of modern critical philosophy; *Critique of Pure Reason*.

Thomas à Kempis, c. 1380-1471, (Ger.) monk, devotional writer; *Imitation of Christ* attributed to him.

Soren Kierkegaard, 1813-55, (Den.) religious philosopher, pre-existentialist; *Either/Or*, *The Sickness Unto Death*.

John Knox, 1505-72, (Scot.) leader of Protestant Reformation in Scotland.

Lao-Tzu, 604-531 BCE, (China) philosopher; considered the founder of the Taoist religion.

Gottfried von Leibniz, 1646-1716, (Ger.) rationalist philosopher, logician, mathematician.

John Locke, 1632-1704, (Eng.) political theorist, empiricist philosopher; *Essay Concerning Human Understanding*.

(St.) Ignatius Loyola, 1491-1556, (Sp.) founder of the Jesuits; *Spiritual Exercises*.

Martin Luther, 1483-1546, (Ger.) leader of the Protestant Reformation; founded Lutheran church.

Jean-Francois Lyotard, 1924-98, (Fr.) postmodern philosopher, lecturer; *The Post-Modern Condition*.

Maimonides, 1135-1204, (Sp.) major Jewish philosopher.

Gabriel Marcel, 1889-1973, (Fr.) Rom. Cath. existentialist philosopher, dramatist.

Jacques Maritain, 1882-1973, (Fr.) neoThomist philosopher.

Cotton Mather, 1663-1728, (U.S.) defender of orthodox Puritanism; founded Yale, 1701.

Aimee Semple McPherson, 1890-1944, (Can.) Pentecostal evangelist.

Philipp Melanchthon, 1497-1560, (Ger.) theologian, humanist; an important voice in the Reformation.

Maurice Merleau-Ponty, 1908-61, (Fr.) existentialist philosopher; *Phenomenology of Perception*.

Thomas Merton, 1915-68, (U.S.) Trappist monk, spiritual writer; *The Seven Storey Mountain*.

Dwight Moody, 1837-99, (U.S.) evangelist.

Rev. Sun Myung Moon, 1920-2012, (N. Kor.) Unification Church founder.

G(eorge) E(dward) Moore, 1873-1958, (Br.) philosopher; *Principia Ethica*, "A Defense of Common Sense."

Muhammad, c. 570-632, (Arab.) prophet of Islam.

Elijah Muhammad, 1897-1975, (U.S.) founder of Black Muslim group, Nation of Islam.

Heinrich Muhlenberg, 1711-87, (Ger.) organized the Lutheran Church in America.

John H. Newman, 1801-90, (Br.) Rom. Cath. convert, cardinal; led Oxford Movement; *Apologia pro Vita Sua*.

Reinhold Niebuhr, 1892-1971, (U.S.) Protestant theologian.

Richard Niebuhr, 1894-1962, (U.S.) Protestant theologian.

Friedrich Nietzsche, 1844-1900, (Ger.) philosopher; *The Birth of Tragedy*, *Beyond Good and Evil*, *Thus Spake Zarathustra*.

Robert Nozick, 1938-2002, (U.S.) political philosopher; *Anarchy, State, and Utopia*.

Blaise Pascal, 1623-62, (Fr.) philosopher, mathematician; *Pensées*.

(St.) Patrick, c. 389-c. 461, (Br.) brought Christianity to Ireland.

Norman Vincent Peale, 1898-1993, (U.S.) minister, author; *The Power of Positive Thinking*.

C(harles) S. Peirce, 1839-1914, (U.S.) philosopher, logician; originated concept of pragmatism, 1878.

Plato, c. 428-347 BCE, (Gr.) philosopher; wrote Socratic dialogues; argued for immortality of soul, indep. reality of ideas or forms; *Republic*, *Meno*, *Phaedo*, *Apology*.

Plotinus, 205-70, (Rom.) a founder of neo-Platonism; *Enneads*.

W(illard) V(an) O(rman) Quine, 1908-2001, (U.S.) philosopher, logician; "On What There Is."

John Rawls, 1922-2002, (U.S.) political philosopher; *A Theory of Justice*.

Oral Roberts, 1918-2009, (U.S.) televangelist, university founder.

Moishe Rosen, 1932-2010, (U.S.) Jews for Jesus founder.

Josiah Royce, 1855-1916, (U.S.) idealist philosopher.

Bertrand Russell, 1872-1970, (Br.) philosopher, logician; one of the founders of modern logic; a prolific popular writer.

Charles T. Russell, 1852-1916, (U.S.) founder of Jehovah's Witnesses.

Gilbert Ryle, 1900-76, (Br.) analytic philosopher; *The Concept of Mind*.

George Santayana, 1863-1952, (U.S.) philosopher, writer, critic; *The Sense of Beauty*, *The Realms of Being*.

Jean-Paul Sartre, 1905-80, (Fr.) philosopher, novelist, playwright; *Nausea*, *No Exit*, *Being and Nothingness*.

Friedrich von Schelling, 1775-1854, (Ger.) philosopher of romantic movement.

Friedrich Schleiermacher, 1768-1834, (Ger.) theologian; a founder of modern Protestant theology.

Arthur Schopenhauer, 1788-1860, (Ger.) philosopher; *The World as Will and Idea*.

Albert Schweitzer, 1875-1965, (Ger.) theologian, social philosopher, medical missionary.

Joseph Smith, 1805-44, (U.S.) founded Latter-Day Saints (Mormon) movement, 1830.

Socrates, 469-399 BCE, (Gr.) philosopher immortalized by Plato.

Herbert Spencer, 1820-1903, (Br.) philosopher of evolution.

Herbert Spiegel, 1914-2009, (U.S.) psychiatrist who popularized hypnosis.

Baruch de Spinoza, 1632-77, (Neth.) rationalist philosopher; *Ethics*.

John Stott, 1921-2011, (Br.) evangelical Anglican cleric.

Billy Sunday, 1862-1935, (U.S.) evangelist.

Emanuel Swedenborg, 1688-1772, (Swed.) philosopher, mystic; *Principia*.

Pierre Teilhard de Chardin, 1881-1955, (Fr.) Jesuit priest, paleontologist, philosopher-theologian; *The Divine Milieu*.

Daisetz Teitaro Suzuki, 1870-1966, (Jpn.) Buddhist scholar.

(St.) Therese of Lisieux, 1873-97, (Fr.) Carmelite nun ("Little Flower"), revered for everyday sanctity; *The Story of a Soul*.

Paul Tillich, 1886-1965, (U.S.) German-born philosopher, theologian; brought depth psychology to Protestantism.

John Wesley, 1703-91, (Br.) theologian, evangelist; founded Methodism.

Alfred North Whitehead, 1861-1947, (Br.) philosopher, mathematician; *Process and Reality*.

William of Occam, c. 1285-c. 1349, (Eng.) medieval scholastic philosopher, nominalist.

Roger Williams, c. 1603-83, (U.S.) clergyman; championed religious freedom and separation of church and state.

Ludwig Wittgenstein, 1889-1951, (Austria) philosopher; major influence on contemporary language philosophy; *Tractatus Logico-Philosophicus*, *Philosophical Investigations*.

John Woolman, 1720-72, (U.S.) Quaker social reformer, abolitionist, writer; *The Journal*.

John Wycliffe, 1320-84, (Eng.) theologian, reformer.

(St.) Francis Xavier, 1506-52, (Sp.) Jesuit missionary; "Apostle of the Indies."

Brigham Young, 1801-77, (U.S.) Mormon leader after Joseph Smith's assassination; colonized Utah.

Huldrych Zwingli, 1484-1531, (Switz.) theologian; led Swiss Protestant Reformation.

Political Leaders of the Past

U.S. presidents, vice presidents, Supreme Court justices, and signers of the Declaration of Independence listed elsewhere.

Abu Bakr, 573-634, (Arab.) Muslim leader, first caliph, chosen successor to Muhammad.

Dean Acheson, 1893-1971, (U.S.) sec. of state; architect of Cold War foreign policy.

Samuel Adams, 1722-1803, (U.S.) patriot; Boston Tea Party firebrand.

Konrad Adenauer, 1876-1967, (Ger.) first West German chancellor.

Emilio Aguinaldo, 1869-1964, (Philip.) revolutionary; fought against Spain and the U.S.

Corazon Aquino, 1933-2009, (Philip.) pres. of the Philippines, 1986-92.

Akbar, 1542-1605, Mogul emperor of India.

Carl Albert, 1908-2000, (U.S.) House rep. (D, OK), Speaker, 1971-76.

Salvador Allende Gossens, 1908-73, (Chile) Marxist pres., 1970-73; ousted and died in coup.

Idi Amin, 1925-2003, (Uganda) Ugandan ruler, 1971-79; blamed for hundreds of thousands of deaths.

Yasir Arafat, 1929-2004, (Egypt) leader of the Palestine Liberation Organization (PLO).

Herbert H. Asquith, 1852-1928, (Br.) Liberal prime min.; instituted major social reforms.

Hafez al Assad, 1930-2000, (Syr.) Syrian ruler from 1970.

Atahualpa, 1500?-1533, (Inca) ruling chief of Peru.

Kemal Ataturk, 1881-1938, (Turk.) founded modern Turkey.

Clement Attlee, 1883-1967, (Br.) Labour party leader, prime min.; enacted natl. health care system, nationalized many industries.

Stephen F. Austin, 1793-1836, (U.S.) led Texas colonization.

Mikhail Bakunin, 1814-76, (Russ.) revolutionary; leading exponent of anarchism.

Arthur J. Balfour, 1848-1930, (Br.) foreign sec. under Lloyd George; issued Balfour Declaration backing Zionism.

Bernard M. Baruch, 1870-1965, (U.S.) financier, govt. adviser.

Fulgencio Batista y Zaldívar, 1901-73, (Cub.) Cuban pres., 1940-44, 1952-59; overthrown by Castro.

Lord Beaverbrook, 1879-1964, (Br.) financier, statesman, newspaper owner.

Menachem Begin, 1913-92, (Isr.) Israeli prime min.; shared 1978 Nobel Peace Prize.

Ahmed Ben Bella, 1918-2012, (Alg.) first Algerian pres., 1963-65.

Eduard Benes, 1884-1948, (Czech.) pres. during interwar and post-WWII eras.

David Ben-Gurion, 1886-1973, (Isr.) first prime min. of Israel, 1948-53, 1955-63.

Thomas Hart Benton, 1782-1858, (U.S.) MO senator; championed agrarian interests and westward expansion.

Aneurin Bevan, 1897-1960, (Br.) Labour party leader.

Ernest Bevin, 1881-1951, (Br.) Labour party leader, foreign minister; helped lay foundation for NATO.

Benazir Bhutto, 1953-2007, (Pak.) former prime min. of Pakistan.

Otto von Bismarck, 1815-98, (Ger.) statesman known as the Iron Chancellor; uniter of Germany, 1870.

James G. Blaine, 1830-93, (U.S.) Republican politician, diplomat; influential in Pan-American movement.

Léon Blum, 1872-1950, (Fr.) socialist leader, writer; headed first Popular Front government.

William E. Borah, 1865-1940, (U.S.) isolationist senator; helped block U.S. membership in League of Nations.

Cesare Borgia, 1476-1507, (It.) soldier, politician; an outstanding figure of the Italian Renaissance.

P. W. Botha, 1916-2006, (S. Africa) S. African president, prime min.

Tom Bradley, 1917-98, (U.S.) first African American mayor of L.A.

Willy Brandt, 1913-92, (Ger.) statesman, chancellor of West Germany, 1969-74; promoted East/West peace, *Ostpolitik*.

Leonid Brezhnev, 1906-82, (USSR) Soviet leader, 1964-82.

Aristide Briand, 1862-1932, (Fr.) foreign min.; chief architect of Locarno Pact and anti-war Kellogg-Briand Pact.

William Jennings Bryan, 1860-1925, (U.S.) Democratic, populist leader, orator; 3 times lost race for presidency.

Ralph Bunche, 1904-71, (U.S.) first black person to win the Nobel Peace Prize, 1950; undersecretary of the UN, 1950.

Robert Byrd, 1917-2010, (U.S.) longest serving senator (D, WV).

John C. Calhoun, 1782-1850, (U.S.) political leader; champion of states' rights and a symbol of the Old South.

James Callaghan (Baron Callaghan), 1912-2005, (Br.) Labour party politician, prime min., 1976-79.

Robert Castlereagh, 1769-1822, (Br.) foreign sec.; guided Grand Alliance against Napoleon.

Camillo Benso Cavour, 1810-61, (It.) statesman; largely responsible for uniting Italy under the House of Savoy.

Nicolae Ceausescu, 1918-89, (Roman.) Communist leader, head of state, 1967-89; executed.

Austen Chamberlain, 1863-1937, (Br.) statesman; helped finalize Locarno Treaties, both 1925.

Neville Chamberlain, 1869-1940, (Br.) Conservative prime min. whose appeasement of Hitler led to Munich Pact.

Hugo Chávez, 1954-2013, (Venez.) socialist Venezuelan pres., 1999-2013.

Chiang Kai-shek, 1887-1975, (China) Nationalist Chinese pres. whose government was driven from mainland to Taiwan.

Madame Chiang Kai-shek (Mayling Soong), 1898-2003, (China) highly influential wife of Nationalist Chinese leader Chiang Kai-shek.

Shirley Chisholm, 1924-2005, (U.S.) first black woman elected to U.S. House (1968, D, NY); pres. contender, 1972.

Warren Christopher, 1925-2011, (U.S.) secretary of state, diplomat.

Winston Churchill, 1874-1965, (Br.) prime min., soldier, author; guided Britain through WWII.

Galeazzo Ciano, 1903-44, (It.) Fascist foreign minister; helped create Rome-Berlin Axis; executed by Benito Mussolini.

Henry Clay, 1777-1852, (U.S.) "The Great Compromiser"; one of the most influential pre-Civil War political leaders.

Georges Clemenceau, 1841-1929, (Fr.) twice prem.; Woodrow Wilson's antagonist at Paris Peace Conference after WWI.

DeWitt Clinton, 1769-1828, (U.S.) political leader; responsible for promoting the Erie Canal.

Robert Clive, 1725-74, (Br.) first administrator of Bengal; laid foundation for British Empire in India.

Jean Baptiste Colbert, 1619-83, (Fr.) statesman; influential under Louis XIV; created the French navy.

Bettino Craxi, 1934-2000, (It.) Italy's first post-WWII Socialist premier.

David Crockett, 1786-1836, (Fr.) frontiersman, congressman; died defending the Alamo.

Oliver Cromwell, 1599-1658, (Br.) Lord Protector of England; led parliamentary forces during Civil War.

Curzon of Kedleston, 1859-1925, (Br.) viceroy of India, foreign sec.; major force in post-WWI world.

Édouard Daladier, 1884-1970, (Fr.) Radical Socialist politician, arrested by Vichy, interned by Germans until 1945.

Richard J. Daley, 1902-76, (U.S.) Chicago mayor.

Georges Danton, 1759-94, (Fr.) leading French Rev. figure.

Jefferson Davis, 1808-89, (U.S.) pres. of the Confederacy.

Charles G. Dawes, 1865-1951, (U.S.) statesman, banker; advanced plan to stabilize post-WWI German finances.

William L. Dawson, 1886-1970, (U.S.) IL congressman; first black chairman of a major U.S. House committee.

Alcide De Gasperi, 1881-1954, (It.) prime min.; founder of Christian Democratic party.

Charles De Gaulle, 1890-1970, (Fr.) general, statesman; first pres. of the Fifth Republic.

Deng Xiaoping, 1904-97, (China) "paramount leader" of China; backed economic modernization.

Eamon De Valera, 1882-1975, (Ire.-U.S.) statesman; led fight for Irish independence.

Thomas E. Dewey, 1902-71, (U.S.) NY governor (R); twice lost in try for presidency.

Ngo Dinh Diem, 1901-63, (Viet.) South Vietnamese pres.; assassinated in government takeover.

Everett M. Dirksen, 1896-1969, (U.S.) Senate Republican minority leader, orator.

Benjamin Disraeli, 1804-81, (Br.) prime min.; considered founder of modern Conservative party.

Anatoly Dobrynin, 1919-2010, (Russ.) diplomat and Soviet amb. to U.S. (1962-86).

Engelbert Dollfuss, 1892-1934, (Austria) chancellor; assassinated by Austrian Nazis.

Andrea Doria, 1466-1560, (It.) Genoese admiral, statesman; called "Father of Peace" and "Liberator of Genoa."

Stephen A. Douglas, 1813-61, (U.S.) Democratic leader, orator; ran against Lincoln for IL sen. seat, presidency.

Alexander Dubcek, 1921-92, (Czech.) statesman whose attempted liberalization was crushed, 1968.

John Foster Dulles, 1888-1959, (U.S.) sec. of state under Eisenhower; Cold War policy maker.

Lawrence Eagleburger, 1930-2011, (U.S.) diplomat and foreign policy advisor.

Abba Eban, 1915-2002, (Isr.) diplomat; foreign min., 1966-74.

Friedrich Ebert, 1871-1925, (Ger.) Social Democratic movement leader; first pres., Weimar Republic, 1919-25.

Sir Anthony Eden, 1897-1977, (Br.) foreign sec., prime min. during Suez invasion of 1956.

Ludwig Erhard, 1897-1977, (Ger.) economist, West German chancellor; led nation's economic rise after WWII.

King Fahd, 1923-2005, (Saudi Arabia) monarch from 1982 but inactive after 1995 stroke; encouraged U.S. relations.

Geraldine Ferraro, 1935-2011, (U.S.) former U.S. rep. (D, NY), vice-pres. nominee.

Joao Baptista de Figueiredo, 1918-99, (Braz.) president of Brazil; restored the nation's democracy.

Hamilton Fish, 1808-93, (U.S.) sec. of state; successfully mediated disputes with Great Britain, Latin America.

James V. Forrestal, 1892-1949, (U.S.) sec. of navy, first sec. of defense.

Francisco Franco, 1892-1975, (Sp.) leader of rebel forces during Spanish Civil War, longtime ruler of Spain.

Benjamin Franklin, 1706-90, (U.S.) printer, publisher, author, inventor, scientist, diplomat.

Louis de Frontenac, 1620-98, (Fr.) governor of New France (Canada); encouraged explorations, fought Iroquois.

J. William Fulbright, 1905-95, (U.S.) senator (D, AR); leading figure in U.S. foreign policy during Cold War years.

Hugh Gaitskell, 1906-63, (Br.) Labour party leader; major force in reversing its stand for unilateral disarmament.

Albert Gallatin, 1761-1849, (U.S.) sec. of treasury; instrumental in negotiating end of War of 1812.

Léon Gambetta, 1838-82, (Fr.) statesman, politician; one of the founders of the Third Republic.

Indira Gandhi, 1917-84, (In.) daughter of Jawaharlal Nehru; prime min. of India, 1966-77, 1980-84; assassinated.

Mohandas K. Gandhi, 1869-1948, (In.) political leader, ascetic; led movement against British rule; assassinated.

Giuseppe Garibaldi, 1807-82, (It.) patriot, soldier; a leader in the Risorgimento, Italian unification movement.

William E. Gladstone, 1809-98, (Br.) prime min. dominant force of Liberal party 1868-94.

Paul Joseph Goebbels, 1897-1945, (Ger.) Nazi propagandist; master of mass psychology.

Barry Goldwater, 1909-98, (U.S.) conservative U.S. senator (R, AZ), 1964 pres. nominee.

Klement Gottwald, 1896-1953, (Czech.) Communist leader; ushered Communism into his country.

Alexander Hamilton, 1755-1804, (U.S.) first treasury sec.; champion of strong central government.

Dag Hammarskjold, 1905-61, (Swed.) statesman; UN sec.-general.

King Hassan II, 1929-99, (Moroc.) ruler of Morocco, 1962-99.

Vaclav Havel, 1936-2011, (Czech.) first president of Czech Republic, 1989-92.

John Hay, 1838-1905, (U.S.) sec. of state; primarily associated with Open Door Policy toward China.

Sir Edward Heath, 1916-2005, (Br.) Conservative prime min., 1970-74; promoted European unity.

Jesse Helms, 1921-2008, (U.S.) conservative senator (R, NC).

Patrick Henry, 1736-99, (U.S.) major Revolutionary War figure, orator.

Édouard Herriot, 1872-1957, (Fr.) Radical Socialist leader; twice prem., pres. of National Assembly.

Theodor Herzl, 1860-1904, (Hung.) founded modern Zionism.

Heinrich Himmler, 1900-45, (Ger.) head of Nazi SS and Gestapo.

Paul von Hindenburg, 1847-1934, (Ger.) field marshal, WWI; second pres. of Weimar Republic, 1925-34.

Adolf Hitler, 1889-1945, (Ger.) dictator; built Nazism, launched WWII, presided over the Holocaust.

Ho Chi Minh, 1890-1969, (Viet.) N. Vietnamese pres., Vietnamese Communist leader.

Harry L. Hopkins, 1890-1946, (U.S.) New Deal administrator; closest adviser to Franklin D. Roosevelt during WWII.

Edward M. House, 1858-1938, (U.S.) diplomat; confidential adviser to Woodrow Wilson.

Samuel Houston, 1793-1863, (U.S.) leader of struggle for Texas independence.

Cordell Hull, 1871-1955, (U.S.) sec. of state, 1933-44; initiated reciprocal trade to lower tariffs, helped organize UN.

Hubert H. Humphrey, 1911-78, (U.S.) senator (D, MN), vice pres., pres. candidate.

King Hussein, 1935-99, (Jordan) peacemaker; ruler of Jordan, 1952-99.

Saddam Hussein, 1937-2006, (Iraq) Iraqi ruler; put to death for crimes against humanity.

Muhammad Ali Jinnah, 1876-1948, (Pak.) founder, first gov.-gen. of Pakistan.

Barbara Jordan, 1936-96, (U.S.) congresswoman, orator, educator; first black woman to win a seat in the TX senate, 1966.

Benito Juarez, 1806-72, (Mex.) rallied his country against foreign threats; sought to create democratic, federal republic.

Constantine Karamanlis, 1907-98, (Gr.) Greek prime min.; restored democracy, later president.

Frank B. Kellogg, 1856-1937, (U.S.) sec. of state; negotiated Kellogg-Briand Pact to outlaw war.

Jack Kemp, 1935-2009, (U.S.) sec. of HUD, U.S. rep. (R, NY), football player.

Edward M. Kennedy, 1932-2009, (U.S.) senator (D, MA); championed progressive causes.

Robert F. Kennedy, 1925-68, (U.S.) attorney general, sen. (D, NY); assassinated while seeking presidency.

Aleksandr Kerensky, 1881-1970, (Russ.) headed provisional government after Feb. 1917 revolution.

Ayatollah Ruhollah Khomeini, 1900-89, (Iran), religious-political leader; spearheaded overthrow of Shah, 1979.

Nikita Khrushchev, 1894-1971, (USSR) prem., first sec. of Communist party; initiated de-Stalinization.

Kim Dae Jung, 1925-2009, (Korea) S. Korean dissident, opposition leader, pres.; 2000 Nobel Peace Prize winner.

Kim Il Sung, 1912-94, (Korea) N. Korean dictator, 1948-94.

Kim Jong Il, 1942-2011, (Korea) N. Korean dictator, 1994-2011.

Edward I. Koch, 1924-2013, (U.S.) New York City mayor, 1978-89.

Lajos Kossuth, 1802-94, (Hung.) principal figure in 1848 Hungarian revolution.

Pyotr Kropotkin, 1842-1921, (Russ.) anarchist; championed the peasants but opposed Bolshevism.

Kublai Khan, c. 1215-94, (Mongol) emperor; founder of Yüan dynasty in China.

Béla Kun, 1886-c. 1939, (Hung.) member of 3rd Communist International; tried to foment worldwide revolution.

Robert M. LaFollette, 1855-1925, (U.S.) WI public official; leader of progressive movement.

Fiorello La Guardia, 1882-1947, (U.S.) New York City reform mayor, 1933-45.

Pierre Laval, 1883-1945, (Fr.) politician, Vichy foreign min.; executed for treason.

Andrew Bonar Law, 1858-1923, (Br.) Conservative party politician; led opposition to Irish home rule.

Vladimir Ilyich Lenin (Ulyanov), 1870-1924, (Russ.) revolutionary; founded Bolshevism; Soviet leader, 1917-24.

Ferdinand de Lesseps, 1805-94, (Fr.) diplomat, engineer; conceived idea of Suez Canal.

Rene Levesque, 1922-87, (Can.) prem. of Quebec, 1976-85; led unsuccessful separatist campaign.

Trygve Lie, 1896-1968, (Nor.) first UN sec.-gen.

Maxim Litvinov, 1876-1951, (Pol.-Russ.) revolutionary, commissar of foreign affairs; favored cooperation with West.

Liu Shaoqi, c. 1898-1969, (China) Communist leader; fell from grace during Cultural Revolution.

David Lloyd George, 1863-1945, (Br.) Liberal party prime min.; laid foundations for modern welfare state.

Henry Cabot Lodge, 1850-1924, (U.S.) Republican senator; led opposition to participation in League of Nations.

Huey P. Long, 1893-1935, (U.S.) Louisiana political demagogue, governor, U.S. senator; assassinated.

Rosa Luxemburg, 1871-1919, (Ger.) revolutionary; leader of the German Social Democratic party and Spartacus party.

J. Ramsay MacDonald, 1866-1937, (Br.) first Labour party prime min. of Great Britain.

Harold Macmillan, 1895-1986, (Br.) prime min. of Great Britain, 1957-63.

Makarios III, 1913-77, (Cyprus) Greek Orthodox archbishop; first pres. of Cyprus.

Wilma Mankiller, 1945-2010, (U.S.) first female Chief of the Cherokee Nation.

Mao Zedong, 1893-1976, (China) chief Chinese Marxist theorist, revolutionary, political leader; led revolution establishing his nation as Communist state.

Jean Paul Marat, 1743-93, (Fr.) revolutionary, politician; identified with radical Jacobins; assassinated.

Thurgood Marshall, 1908-93, (U.S.) first black U.S. solicitor general, 1965; first black justice of U.S. Supreme Court, 1967-91.

José Martí, 1853-95, (Cub.) patriot, poet; leader of Cuban struggle for independence.

Jan Masaryk, 1886-1948, (Czech.) foreign min.; died under mysterious circumstances, allegedly committed suicide following Communist coup.

Thomas G. Masaryk, 1850-1937, (Czech.) statesman, philosopher; first pres. of Czechoslovakia.

Jules Mazarin, 1602-61, (Fr.) cardinal, statesman; prime min. under Louis XIII and queen regent Anne of Austria.

Giuseppe Mazzini, 1805-72, (It.) reformer dedicated to Risorgimento movement for renewal of Italy.

Tom Mboya, 1930-69, (Kenya) political leader; instrumental in securing independence for Kenya.

Eugene McCarthy, 1916-2005, (U.S.) political leader, author; 1968 Dem. presidential contender.

Joseph R. McCarthy, 1908-57, (U.S.) senator (R, WI); extremist in searching out alleged Communists and pro-Communists.

George McGovern, 1922-2012, (U.S.) liberal senator (D, SD), 1972 pres. nominee.

Cosimo I de' Medici, 1519-74, (It.) Duke of Florence, grand duke of Tuscany.

Lorenzo de' Medici, the Magnificent, 1449-92, (It.) merchant prince; a towering figure in Italian Renaissance.

Catherine de Médicis, 1519-89, (Fr.) queen consort of Henry II, regent of France; influential in Catholic-Huguenot wars.

Golda Meir, 1898-1978, (Isr.) a founder of the state of Israel; prime min., 1969-74.

Klemens W. N. L. Metternich, 1773-1859, (Austria) statesman; arbiter of post-Napoleonic Europe.

Slobodan Milosevic, 1941-2006, (Serbia/Yugoslavia) former Yugoslav pres.; tried for war crimes.

François Mitterrand, 1916-96, (Fr.) pres. of France, 1981-95.

Mobutu Sese Seko, 1930-97, (Zaire) longtime ruler of Zaire (now Dem. Rep. of Congo), 1965-97; exiled after rebellion.

Guy Mollet, 1905-75, (Fr.) socialist politician, resistance leader.

Henry Morgenthau Jr., 1891-1967, (U.S.) sec. of treasury; fundraiser for New Deal and U.S. WWII activities.

Gouverneur Morris, 1752-1816, (U.S.) statesman, diplomat, financial expert; helped plan decimal coinage.

Daniel Patrick Moynihan, 1927-2003, (U.S.) senator (D, NY), diplomat, social scientist, author.

Benito Mussolini, 1883-1945, (It.) leader of the Italian fascist state; assassinated.

Imre Nagy, c. 1896-1958, (Hung.) Communist prem.; assassinated after Soviets crushed 1956 uprising.

Gamal Abdel Nasser, 1918-70, (Egypt) leader of Arab unification, second Egyptian pres.

Jawaharlal Nehru, 1889-1964, (In.) prime min.; guided India through its early years of independence.

Kwame Nkrumah, 1909-72, (Ghana) first prime min., 1957-60; pres., 1960-66, of Ghana.

Frederick North, 1732-92, (Br.) prime min.; his policies led to loss of American colonies.

Julius K. Nyerere, 1922-99, (Tanz.) founding father; first pres., 1962-85, of Tanzania.

Daniel O'Connell, 1775-1847, (Ire.) nationalist political leader; known as The Liberator.

Omar, c. 581-644, (Arab.) Muslim leader; second caliph, led Islam to become an imperial power.

Thomas P. (Tip) O'Neill Jr., 1912-94, (U.S.) U.S. rep. (D, MA), Speaker of the House, 1977-86.

Ignace Paderewski, 1860-1941, (Pol.) statesman, pianist, composer, briefly prime min.; ardent patriot.

Viscount Palmerston, 1784-1865, (Br.) Whig-Liberal prime min., foreign min.; embodied British nationalism.

Andreas George Papandreou, 1919-96, (Gr.) leftist politician; served twice as prem., 1981-89, 1993-96.

Georgios Papandreou, 1888-1968, (Gr.) Republican politician; served 3 times as prime min.

Franz von Papen, 1879-1969, (Ger.) politician; major role in overthrow of Weimar Republic and rise of Hitler.

Charles Stewart Parnell, 1846-1891, (Ire.) nationalist leader; "uncrowned king of Ireland."

Lester Pearson, 1897-1972, (Can.) diplomat, Liberal party leader, prime min.

Robert Peel, 1788-1850, (Br.) reformist prime min.; founder of Conservative party.

Frances Perkins, 1882-1965, (U.S.) first female cabinet member (sec. of labor).

Eva (Evita) Perón, 1919-52, (Arg.) highly influential second wife of Juan Perón.

Juan Perón, 1895-1974, (Arg.) dynamic pres. of Argentina, 1946-55, 1973-74.

Joseph Pilsudski, 1867-1935, (Pol.) statesman; instrumental in reestablishing Polish state in the 20th cent.

Charles Pinckney, 1757-1824, (U.S.) founding father; his Pinckney plan largely incorporated into Constitution.

Christian Pineau, 1905-95, (Fr.) leader of French Resistance during WWII; French foreign min., 1956-58.

Augusto Pinochet (Ugarte), 1915-2006, (Chile) former Chilean ruler; indicted for human rights abuses while in office.

William Pitt the Elder, 1708-78, (Br.) statesman; the "Great Commoner," transformed Britain into imperial power.

William Pitt the Younger, 1759-1806, (Br.) prime min. during French Revolutionary wars.

Georgi Plekhanov, 1857-1918, (Russ.) revolutionary, social philosopher; called "father of Russian Marxism."

Raymond Poincaré, 1860-1934, (Fr.) French pres.; advocated harsh punishment of Germany after WWI.

Pol Pot, 1925-98, (Camb.) leader of Khmer Rouge; ruled Cambodia, 1975-79; responsible for mass deaths.

Georges Pompidou, 1911-74, (Fr.) Gaullist political leader; pres., 1969-74.

Grigori Potemkin, 1739-91, (Russ.) field marshal; favorite of empress Catherine II.

Adam Clayton Powell Jr., 1908-72, (U.S.) civil rights leader; U.S. rep. (D, NY), 1945-69.

Muammar al-Qaddafi, 1942-2011, (Libya) Libyan ruler, 1969-2011.

Yitzhak Rabin, 1922-95, (Isr.) military, political leader; prime min. of Israel, 1974-77, 1992-95; assassinated.

Joseph H. Rainey, 1832-87, (U.S.) first black person elected to U.S. House (1869), from SC.

Edmund Randolph, 1753-1813, (U.S.) attorney; prominent in drafting, ratification of Constitution.

John Randolph, 1773-1833, (U.S.) southern planter; strong advocate of states' rights.

Jeannette Rankin, 1880-1973, (U.S.) pacifist; first woman member of U.S. Congress (R, MT).

Walter Rathenau, 1867-1922, (Ger.) industrialist, statesman.

Sam Rayburn, 1882-1961, (U.S.) U.S. rep. (D, TX) for 47 years, House Speaker for 17.

Hiram R. Revels, 1822-1901, (U.S.) first African American U.S. senator; elected in MS, served 1870-71.

Paul Reynaud, 1878-1966, (Fr.) statesman; prem. in 1940 at time of France's defeat by Germany.

Syngman Rhee, 1875-1965, (Korea) first pres. of S. Korea.

Cecil Rhodes, 1853-1902, (Br.) imperialist, industrial magnate; established Rhodes scholarships in his will.

Ann Richards, 1933-2006, (U.S.) former TX gov.

Cardinal de Richelieu, 1585-1642, (Fr.) statesman, known as "red eminence"; chief minister to Louis XIII.

Maximilien Robespierre, 1758-94, (Fr.) leading figure in French Revolution and Reign of Terror.

Nelson Rockefeller, 1908-79, (U.S.) Republican governor of NY, 1959-73; U.S. vice pres., 1974-77.

Eleanor Roosevelt, 1884-1962, (U.S.) influential first lady, humanitarian, UN diplomat.

Elihu Root, 1845-1937, (U.S.) lawyer, statesman, diplomat; leading Republican supporter of the League of Nations.

Dean Rusk, 1909-95, (U.S.) statesman; sec. of state, 1961-69.

John Russell, 1792-1878, (Br.) Liberal prime min. during the Irish potato famine.

Anwar al-Sadat, 1918-81, (Egypt) pres., 1970-81; promoted peace with Israel; Nobel laureate; assassinated.

António de Oliveira Salazar, 1889-1970, (Port.) longtime dictator.

José de San Martín, 1778-1850, S. Amer. revolutionary; protector of Peru.

Eisaku Sato, 1901-75, (Jpn.) prime min.; presided over Japan's post-WWII emergence as major world power.

Abdul Aziz Ibn Saud, c.1880-1953, (Saudi Arabia) king of Saudi Arabia, 1932-53.

Robert Schuman, 1886-1963, (Fr.) statesman; founded European Coal and Steel Community.

Carl Schurz, 1829-1906, (U.S.) German-American political leader, journalist, orator, dedicated reformer.

Kurt Schuschnigg, 1897-1977, (Austria) chancellor; unsuccessful in stopping Austria's annexation by Germany.

William H. Seward, 1801-72, (U.S.) antislavery activist; as U.S. sec. of state purchased Alaska.

Carlo Sforza, 1872-1952, (It.) foreign min., anti-Fascist.

Yitzhak Shamir, 1915-2012, (Isr.) prime min. of Israel, 1983-84, 1986-92.

Norodom Sihanouk, 1922-2012, (Camb.) King of Cambodia (1941-55, 1993-2004).

Sitting Bull, c.1831-90, (Amer. Ind.) Sioux leader in Battle of Little Bighorn against George A. Custer, 1876.

Alfred E. Smith, 1873-1944, (U.S.) NY Democratic governor; first Roman Catholic to run for president.

Margaret Chase Smith, 1897-1995, (U.S.) congresswoman, senator (R, ME); first woman elected to both houses of Congress.

Jan C. Smuts, 1870-1950, (S. Africa) statesman, philosopher, soldier, prime min.

Paul Henri Spaak, 1899-1972, (Belg.) statesman, socialist leader.

Joseph Stalin, 1879-1953, (USSR) Soviet dictator, 1924-53; instituted forced collectivization, massive purges, and labor camps, causing millions of deaths.

Edwin M. Stanton, 1814-69, (U.S.) sec. of war, 1862-68.

Alexander Stephens, 1812-1883, (U.S.) vice pres. of the Confederacy.

Edward R. Stettinius Jr., 1900-49, (U.S.) industrialist; sec. of state who coordinated aid to WWII allies.

Adlai E. Stevenson, 1900-65, (U.S.) Democratic leader, diplomat, governor (IL), presidential candidate.

Henry L. Stimson, 1867-1950, (U.S.) statesman; served in 5 administrations, foreign policy adviser in 1930s and 1940s.

Carl Stokes, 1927-96, (U.S.) first black mayor of a major American city (Cleveland, 1967-72).

Suharto, 1921-2008, (Indon.) former longtime Indonesian ruler.

Sukarno, 1901-70, (Indon.) dictatorial first pres. of the Indonesian republic.

Sun Yat-sen, 1866-1925, (China) revolutionary; leader of Kuomintang pol. party, regarded as father of modern China.

Robert A. Taft, 1889-1953, (U.S.) conservative Senate leader (OH); called "Mr. Republican."

Charles de Talleyrand, 1754-1838, (Fr.) statesman, diplomat; the major force of the Congress of Vienna of 1814-15.

U Thant, 1909-74, (Burma) statesman, UN sec.-general.

Margaret Thatcher, 1925-2013, (Br.) conservative British prime min., 1979-90; first woman UK prime min.

Norman M. Thomas, 1884-1968, (U.S.) social reformer; 6 times Socialist party presidential candidate.

Josip Broz Tito, 1892-1980, (Yug.) pres. of Yugoslavia from 1953; WWII guerrilla chief, postwar rival of Stalin.

Palmiro Togliatti, 1893-1964, (It.) major Italian Communist leader.

Hideki Tojo, 1885-1948, (Jpn.) statesman, soldier; prime min. during most of WWII.

François Toussaint L'Ouverture, c.1744-1803, (Haiti) patriot, martyr; thwarted French colonial aims.

Leon Trotsky, 1879-1940, (Russ.) revolutionary; founded Red Army, expelled from party in conflict with Stalin; assassinated.

Pierre Elliott Trudeau, 1919-2000, (Can.) longtime liberal prime min. of Canada, 1968-79, 1980-84; achieved native Canadian constitution.

Rafael L. Trujillo Molina, 1891-1961, (Dominican) dictator of Dominican Republic, 1930-61; assassinated.

Moise K. Tshombe, 1919-69, (Congo) pres. of secessionist Katanga prov., prem. of Congo (now Dem. Rep. of the Congo).

William M. Tweed, 1823-78, (U.S.) political boss of Tammany Hall, New York City's Democratic political machine.

Walter Ulbricht, 1893-1973, (Ger.) Communist leader of German Democratic Republic.

Arthur H. Vandenberg, 1884-1951, (U.S.) senator (R, MI); proponent of bipartisan anti-Communist foreign policy.

Eleutherios Venizelos, 1864-1936, (Gr.) most prominent Greek statesman of early 20th cent.

Hendrik F. Verwoerd, 1901-66, (S. Africa) prime min.; rigorously applied apartheid policy despite protest.

Kurt Waldheim, 1918-2007, (Austria) UN sec.-gen., Austrian pres.

George Wallace, 1919-98, (U.S.) former segregationist governor of Alabama, pres. candidate.

Robert Walpole, 1676-1745, (Br.) statesman; generally considered Britain's first prime min.

Harold Washington, 1922-87, (U.S.) first black mayor of Chicago.

Robert C. Weaver, 1907-97, (U.S.) first African American appointed to cabinet; sec. of Housing and Urban Development.

Daniel Webster, 1782-1852, (U.S.) orator, politician; advocate of business interests during Jacksonian agrarianism.

Caspar Weinberger, 1917-2006, (U.S.) business exec., former defense sec., other cabinet posts.

Chaim Weizmann, 1874-1952, (Russ.-Isr.) Zionist leader, scientist; first Israeli pres.

Kevin White, 1929-2012, (U.S.) Boston mayor, 1967-84.

Wendell L. Willkie, 1892-1944, (U.S.) Republican who tried to unseat Franklin D. Roosevelt when he ran for his third term.

Harold Wilson, 1916-95, (Br.) Labour party leader; prime min., 1964-70, 1974-76.

Boris Yeltsin, 1931-2007, (USSR-Russia) first freely elected president of post-Soviet Union.

Coleman A. Young, 1918-97, (U.S.) first African-American mayor of Detroit, 1974-93.

Emiliano Zapata, c.1879-1919, (Mex.) revolutionary; major influence on modern Mexico.

Todor Zhivkov, 1911-98, (Bulg.) Communist ruler of Bulgaria from 1954 until ousted in a 1989 coup.

Zhou Enlai, 1898-1976, (China) diplomat, prime min.; a leading figure of the Chinese Communist party.

Scientists of the Past

Revised by Peter Barker, Prof. and Chair, Dept. of the History of Science, Univ. of Oklahoma.

For pre-modern scientists, see also Philosophers and Religious Figures of the Past and the Historical Figures chapter.

Albertus Magnus, c.1200-80, (Ger.) theologian, philosopher; helped found medieval study of natural science.

Alhazen (Ibn al-Haytham), c. 965-c. 1040, mathematician, astronomer, optical theorist.

Andre-Marie Ampère, 1775-1836, (Fr.) mathematician, chemist; founder of electrodynamics.

Neil Armstrong, 1930-2012, (U.S.) astronaut, first man to walk on the Moon.

John V. Atanasoff, 1903-95, (U.S.) physicist; co-invented Atanasoff-Berry Computer (1939-41).

Amedeo Avogadro, 1776-1856, (It.) chemist, physicist; proposed that equal volumes of gas contain equal numbers of molecules, permitting determination of molecular weights.

John Bardeen, 1908-91, (U.S.) double Nobel laureate in physics (transistor, 1956; superconductivity, 1972).

A. H. Becquerel, 1852-1908, (Fr.) physicist; discovered radioactivity in uranium (1896).

Alexander Graham Bell, 1847-1922, (U.S.) inventor; first to patent and commercially exploit the telephone (1876).

Daniel Bernoulli, 1700-82, (Switz.) mathematician; developed fluid dynamics and kinetic theory of gases.

Clifford Berry, 1918-63, (U.S.) collaborated with John V. Atanasoff on the ABC computer (1939-41).

Jöns Jakob Berzelius, 1779-1848, (Swed.) chemist; developed modern chemical symbols and formulas.

Henry Bessemer, 1813-98, (Br.) engineer; invented Bessemer steel-making process.

Hans Bethe, 1906-2005, (Ger.-U.S.) physicist; won Nobel Prize in 1967 for describing how stars generate energy.

Bruno Bettelheim, 1903-90, (Austria-U.S.) psychoanalyst; studied disturbed children; Uses of Enchantment (1976).

Louis Blériot, 1872-1936, (Fr.) engineer; monoplane pioneer, first Channel flight (1909).

Franz Boas, 1858-1942, (Ger.-U.S.) founded modern anthropology; studied Pacific Coast tribes.

Niels Bohr, 1885-1962, (Den.) atomic and nuclear physicist; founded quantum mechanics.

Norman Borlaug, 1914-2009, (U.S.) plant pathologist and geneticist; father of "green" (agricultural) revolution.

Max Born, 1882-1970, (Ger.) atomic and nuclear physicist; helped develop quantum mechanics.

Satyendranath Bose, 1894-1974, (India) physicist; forerunner of modern quantum theory for integral-spin particles.

Louis de Broglie, 1892-1987, (Fr.) physicist; proposed quantum wave-particle duality.

Robert Bunsen, 1811-99, (Ger.) chemist; pioneered spectroscopic analysis; discovered rubidium, caesium.

Luther Burbank, 1849-1926, (U.S.) naturalist; developed plant breeding into a modern science.

Vannevar Bush, 1890-1974, (U.S.) electrical engineer; developed differential analyzer, an early analogue computer; headed WWII Office of Scientific Res. and Dev.

Marvin Camras, 1916-95, (U.S.) inventor, electrical engineer; invented magnetic tape recording.

Alexis Carrel, 1873-1944, (Fr.) surgeon, biologist; developed methods of suturing blood vessels, transplanting organs.

Rachel Carson, 1907-64, (U.S.) marine biologist, environmentalist; Silent Spring (1962).

James Chadwick, 1891-1974, (Br.) physicist; discovered the neutron (1932); led Brit. Manhattan Project group in U.S.

Albert Claude, 1898-1983, (Belg.-U.S.) a founder of modern cell biology; determined role of mitochondria.

Samuel Cohen, 1921-2010, (U.S.) physicist who invented the neutron bomb.

Barry Commoner, 1917-2012, biologist; noted environmentalist.

Nicolaus Copernicus, 1473-1543, (Pol.) first modern astronomer to propose Sun as center of the planets' motions.

Jacques Yves Cousteau, 1910-97, (Fr.) oceanographer; co-inventor, with Emile Gagnan, of the Aqualung (1943).

Seymour Cray, 1925-96, (U.S.) computer industry pioneer; developed supercomputers.

Francis Crick, 1916-2004, (Br.) biophysicist; co-discoverer of genetic code; shared 1962 Nobel Prize.

Marie, 1867-1934, (Pol.-Fr.) and **Pierre Curie**, 1859-1906, (Fr.) physical chemists; pioneer investigators of radioactivity; discovered radium and polonium (1898).

Gottlieb Daimler, 1834-1900, (Ger.) engineer, inventor; pioneer automobile manufacturer.

John Dalton, 1766-1844, (Br.) chemist, physicist; formulated atomic theory, made first table of atomic weights.

Charles Darwin, 1809-82, (Br.) naturalist; established theory of organic evolution; Origin of Species (1859).

Lee De Forest, 1873-1961, (U.S.) inventor of triode; pioneer in wireless telegraphy, sound pictures, television.

Pierre-Gilles de Gennes, 1932-2007, (Fr.) physicist whose research aided development of liquid-crystal-display (LCD), awarded Nobel Prize for Physics, 1991.

Max Delbrück, 1906-81, (Ger.-U.S.) founded molecular biology.

Rudolf Diesel, 1858-1913, (Ger.) mechanical engineer; patented Diesel engine (1892).

Theodosius Dobzhansky, 1900-75, (Russ.-U.S.) biologist; reconciled genetics and natural selection.

Christian Doppler, 1803-53, (Austria) physicist; showed change in wave frequency caused by motion of source, now known as Doppler effect.

J. Presper Eckert Jr., 1919-95, (U.S.) co-inventor, with John W. Mauchly, of the ENIAC computer (1943-45).

Thomas A. Edison, 1847-1931, (U.S.) inventor; held more than 1,000 patents, including incandescent electric lamp.

Robert Edwards, 1925-2013, (Br.) physiologist; pioneered in vitro fertilization.

Paul Ehrlich, 1854-1915, (Ger.) medical researcher in immunology and bacteriology; pioneered antitoxin production.

Albert Einstein, 1879-1955, (Ger.-U.S.) theoretical physicist; founded relativity theory.

John F. Enders, 1897-1985, (U.S.) virologist; helped discover vaccines against polio, measles, mumps and chicken pox.

Erik Erikson, 1902-94, (U.S.) psychoanalyst, author; theory of developmental stages of life; Childhood and Society (1950).

Leonhard Euler, 1707-83, (Switz.) mathematician, physicist; pioneer of calculus, revived ideas of Fermat.

Gabriel Fahrenheit, 1686-1736, (Ger.) physicist; improved thermometers and introduced Fahrenheit temperature scale.

Michael Faraday, 1791-1867, (Br.) chemist, physicist; discovered electrical induction and invented dynamo (1831).

Philo T. Farnsworth, 1906-71, (U.S.) inventor; built first television system (San Francisco, 1928).

Pierre de Fermat, 1601-65, (Fr.) mathematician; founded modern theory of numbers.

Enrico Fermi, 1901-54, (It.-U.S.) nuclear physicist; demonstrated first controlled chain reaction (Chicago, 1942).

Richard Feynman, 1918-88, (U.S.) theoretical physicist, author; founder of Quantum Electrodynamics (QED).

Alexander Fleming, 1881-1955, (Br.) bacteriologist; discovered penicillin (1928).

Jean B. J. Fourier, 1768-1830, (Fr.) introduced Fourier Series, method of analysis in math and physics.

Sigmund Freud, 1856-1939, (Austria) psychiatrist; founder of psychoanalysis; Interpretation of Dreams (1901).

Erich Fromm, 1900-80, (U.S.) psychoanalyst; Man for Himself (1947).

Galileo Galilei, 1564-1642, (It.) physicist; used telescope to vindicate Copernicus, founded modern science of motion.

Carl Friedrich Gauss, 1777-1855, (Ger.) math. physicist; completed work of Fermat and Euler in number theory.

Josiah W. Gibbs, 1839-1903, (U.S.) theoretical physicist, chemist; founded chemical thermodynamics.

Robert H. Goddard, 1882-1945, (U.S.) physicist; invented liquid fuel rocket (1926).

George W. Goethals, 1858-1928, (U.S.) chief engineer who completed Panama Canal (1907-14).

William C. Gorgas, 1854-1920, (U.S.) physician; pioneer in prevention of yellow fever and malaria.

Stephen Jay Gould, 1941-2002, (U.S.) paleontologist, evolutionary biologist, writer.

Ernst Haeckel, 1834-1919, (Ger.) zoologist, evolutionist; early Darwinist, introduced concept of "ecology."

Otto Hahn, 1879-1968, (Ger.) chemist; with Lise Meitner discovered nuclear fission (1938).

Edmund Halley, 1656-1742, (Br.) astronomer; predicted return of 1682 comet (Halley's Comet) in 1759.

William Harvey, 1578-1657, (Br.) physician, anatomist; discovered circulation of the blood (1628).

Werner Heisenberg, 1901-76, (Ger.) physicist; developed matrix mechanics and uncertainty principle (1927).

Hermann von Helmholtz, 1821-94, (Ger.) physicist, physiologist; formulated principle of conservation of energy.

William Herschel, 1738-1822, (Ger.-Br.) astronomer; discovered Uranus (1781).

Heinrich Hertz, 1857-94, (Ger.) physicist; discovered radio waves and photo-electric effect (1886-87).

David Hilbert, 1862-1943, (Ger.) mathematician; contributed to algebra, calculus, and foundational studies (formalism).

Albert Hofmann, 1906-2008, (U.S.) father of LSD.

Edwin P. Hubble, 1889-1953, (U.S.) astronomer; discovered observational evidence of expanding universe.

Alexander von Humboldt, 1769-1859, (Ger.) naturalist, author; explored S. America, created ecology.

Edward Jenner, 1749-1823, (Br.) physician; pioneered vaccination, introduced term "virus."

James Joule, 1818-89, (Br.) physicist; found relation between heat and mechanical energy (conservation of energy).

Carl Jung, 1875-1961, (Switz.) psychiatrist; founder of analytical psychology.

Ernest Everett Just, 1883-1941, (U.S.) marine biologist; studied egg development; Biology of Cell Surfaces (1941).

Johannes Kepler, 1571-1630, (Ger.) astronomer; discovered laws of planetary motion.

Al-Khawarizmi, early 9th cent., (Arab.) mathematician; regarded as founder of algebra.

Robert Koch, 1843-1910, (Ger.) bacteriologist; isolated bacterial causes of tuberculosis and other diseases.

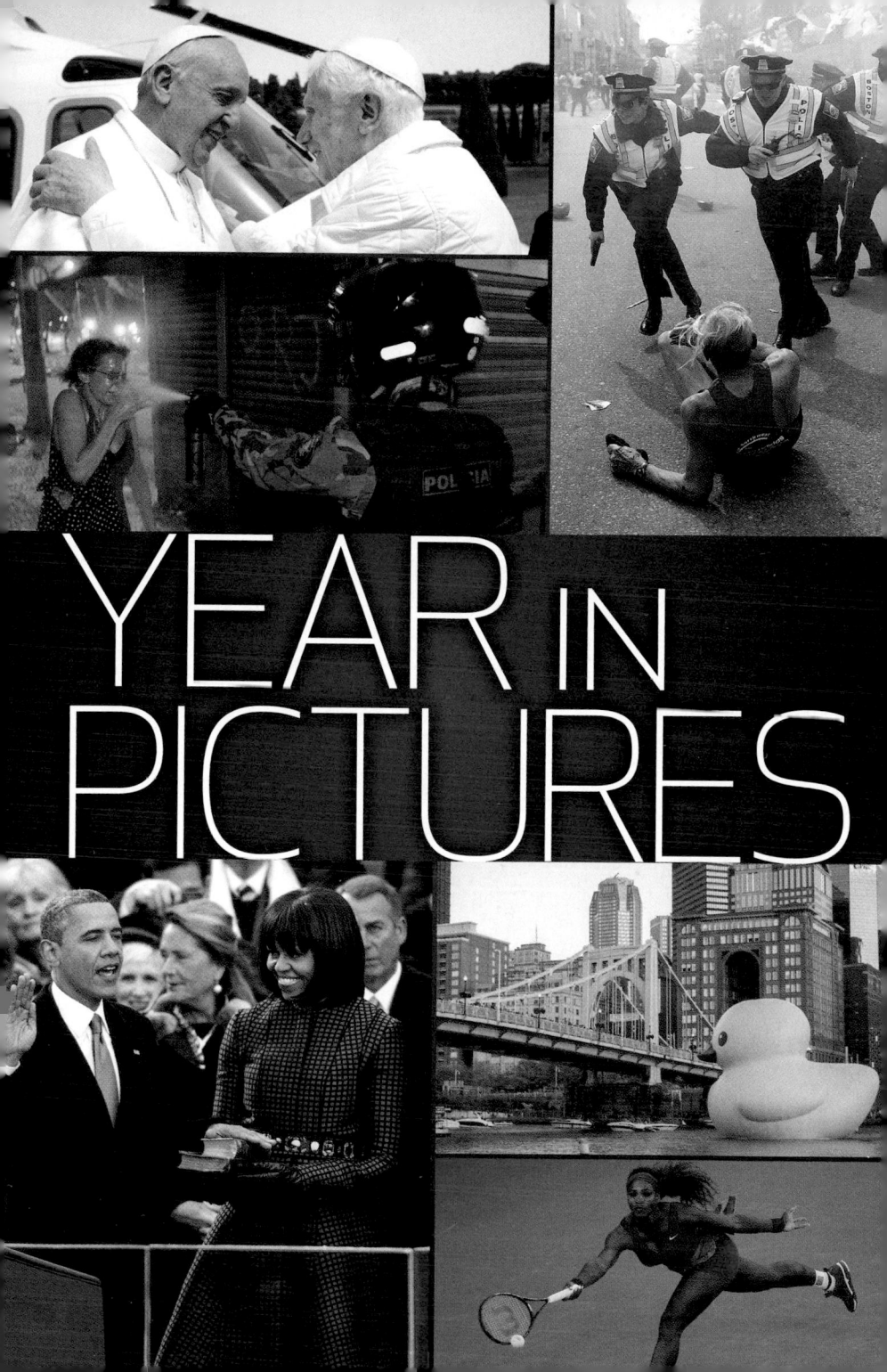

YEAR IN PICTURES

NATIONAL

A Second Term Barack Obama was inaugurated for his second term as president Jan. 21, 2013.

Soldier Sentenced Chelsea Manning (formerly known as Army Pfc. Bradley Manning) was sentenced Aug. 21, 2013, to 35 years in prison for providing classified material to WikiLeaks.

Shutdown A budget stalemate in Congress forced the U.S. federal government to shut down many facilities and operations nationwide Oct. 1, 2013, for the first time in nearly two decades.

National Park Service
U.S. Department of the Interior

Because of the
Federal Government SHUTDOWN,
**All National Parks
Are CLOSED.**

Benghazi Hearings Sec. of State Hillary Clinton appeared Jan. 23, 2013, at Senate hearings investigating the 2012 attack on the American consulate in Benghazi, Libya.

Hero or Traitor? Natl. Security Agency contractor Edward Snowden touched off a firestorm beginning in June 2013 by revealing details of several top-secret mass surveillance government programs; he was charged with espionage June 14.

In Memoriam Families of victims of the Dec. 2012 shooting at Sandy Hook Elementary School in Newtown, CT, joined Apr. 2013 efforts to lobby for new gun control legislation.

Boston Bombing Two bombs exploded near the finish line of the Boston Marathon Apr. 15, 2013, killing three and injuring more than 260; after a citywide search, police killed one suspect and arrested another Apr. 19.

Another Mass Shooting A shooting rampage at the Navy Yard in Washington, DC, left 13 people dead, including the gunman, Sept. 16, 2013.

Verdict Protested George Zimmerman was acquitted July 13, 2013, in the 2012 shooting death of unarmed 17-year-old Trayvon Martin; demonstrations erupted around the country in protest.

Deadly Blaze Nineteen firefighters were killed June 30, 2013, battling a fast-moving wildfire outside Prescott, AZ.

NATIONAL

Marriage Rights The Supreme Court June 26, 2013, struck down part of the Defense of Marriage Act, which had denied same-sex married couples the rights and benefits of straight married couples, after the law was challenged by plaintiff Edith Windsor.

Fighting Women In a sharp reversal, the Pentagon announced Jan. 24, 2013, that women would no longer officially be barred from front-line combat roles.

GEORGE W. BUSH PRESIDENTIAL LIBRARY AND MUSEUM

Exclusive Club Pres. Barack Obama and former Pres. George W. Bush, Bill Clinton, George H.W. Bush, and Jimmy Carter attended the dedication of the George W. Bush Presidential Library and Museum in Dallas, TX, Apr. 25, 2013.

Struggles in Detroit Once flourishing on the strength of the American auto industry, Detroit, MI, became the largest U.S. city ever to declare bankruptcy July 18, 2013, with debt estimated at around $18 bil.

Disaster Strikes A massive tornado struck Moore, OK, May 23, 2013, destroying hundreds of buildings, including Plaza Towers Elementary School, where seven children died.

Devastating Explosion A fertilizer plant explosion Apr. 17, 2013, in the town of West, TX, killed 15 people and destroyed a 37-block swath of the town.

Plane Crash Horror An Asiana Airlines plane crashed at San Francisco Intl. Airport July 6, 2013, killing three and injuring dozens; it was the first notable airline crash in the U.S. in more than four years.

Lingering Damage Recovery efforts continued throughout 2013 as devastated communities in New Jersey, New York, and other coastal states sought to rebuild what was lost in Hurricane Sandy.

WORLD

Egypt in Crisis Just a year after Egypt's first free presidential elections in decades, demonstrators demanded Pres. Mohammed Morsi's ouster; the military removed him from office, leading to further unrest.

War in Syria The crisis in Syria escalated with airstrikes and the use of chemical weapons, which in one incident Aug. 21, 2013, killed more than 1,400 in the Damascus suburbs.

Brazil Protests Police responded with tear gas and rubber bullets as demonstrators in more than 100 Brazilian cities in June 2013 voiced dissatisfaction over a wide range of issues.

Unrest in Turkey Antigovernment protesters were forcibly dispersed by police from demonstrations nationwide in early June 2013.

New Leadership The People's National Congress appointed Xi Jinping president of China Mar. 14, 2013.

Venezuela Transition Longtime Venezuelan Pres. Hugo Chávez died Mar. 5, 2013, and was succeeded by Vice Pres. Nicolás Maduro.

Empty Threats? The government of North Korean leader Kim Jong Un escalated tensions with new threats against the U.S. and its allies in early 2013, but signalled a willingness, June 16, to resume high-level talks on the future of its nuclear program.

Iran Election Voters in Iran selected moderate cleric Hassan Rouhani (left) as the nation's new president June 14, 2013; he was sworn in Aug. 4, succeeding Mahmoud Ahmadinejad (right).

Repression in Russia Demonstrators in London Aug. 10, 2013, protested a new Russian law banning "propaganda of nontraditional sexual relations" as anti-gay as Russia prepared to host the Winter Olympic Games in 2014.

WORLD

Last Days of War After more than a decade of war, U.S. soldiers prepared to withdraw from Afghanistan by the end of 2014, winding down operations and training Afghan forces to take over security in the country.

Fatal Crash Nearly 80 people died in Galicia, Spain, July 24, 2013, when a train traveling at twice the legal speed crashed.

International Assistance France sent troops to Mali in Jan. 2013 to assist forces there in their fight against Islamist rebels linked to al-Qaeda.

Factory Collapse An eight-story building housing garment factories collapsed Apr. 24, 2013, outside of Dhaka, Bangladesh, killing more than 1,100 people.

Deadly Mall Siege More than 60 people died when Somali Islamist group al-Shabab launched an attack at the Westgate Mall in Nairobi, Kenya, Sept. 21-24, 2013.

Georges Köhler, 1946-95, (Ger.) immunologist; with Cesar Milstein, developed monoclonal antibody technique.

Willem Kolff, 1911-2009, (Neth.-U.S.) physician, biomedical engineer; developed first practical kidney dialysis machine; considered the "father of artificial organs."

Jacques Lacan, 1901-81, (Fr.) influential psychoanalyst.

Joseph Lagrange, 1736-1813, (Fr.) geometer, astronomer; showed that gravity of Earth and Moon cancel, creating stable points in space around them.

Jean B. Lamarck, 1744-1829, (Fr.) naturalist; forerunner of Darwin in evolutionary theory.

Pierre Simon de Laplace, 1749-1827, (Fr.) astronomer, physicist; proposed nebular origin for solar system.

Lewis H. Latimer, 1848-1928, (U.S.) African American scientist; associate of Edison; supervised installation of first electric street lighting in New York City.

Antoine Lavoisier, 1743-94, (Fr.) a founder of modern chemistry.

Ernest O. Lawrence, 1901-58, (U.S.) physicist; invented the cyclotron.

Louis, 1903-72, and **Mary Leakey**, 1913-96, (Br.) early hominid paleoanthropologists; discovered remains in Africa.

Anton van Leeuwenhoek, 1632-1723, (Neth.) founder of microscopy.

Jerome Lejeune, 1927-94, (Fr.) geneticist; discovered chromosomal cause of Down syndrome (1959).

Claude Levi-Strauss, 1908-2009, (Belg.-Fr.) cultural anthropologist, sociologist, philosopher.

Kurt Lewin, 1890-1947, (Ger.-U.S.) social psychologist; studied human motivation and group dynamics.

Justus von Liebig, 1803-73, (Ger.) founded quantitative organic chemistry.

Joseph Lister, 1827-1912, (Br.) physician; pioneered antiseptic surgery.

Hendrik Lorentz, 1853-1928, (Neth.) physicist; developed electron theory of matter, contrib. to relativity theory.

Konrad Lorenz, 1903-89, (Austria) ethologist; pioneer in study of animal behavior.

Bernard Lovell, 1913-2012, (Br.) physicist and radio astronomer.

Percival Lowell, 1855-1916, (U.S.) astronomer; predicted the existence of Pluto.

Louis, 1864-1948, and **Auguste Lumière**, 1862-1954, (Fr.) invented cinematograph, made first motion picture (1895).

Theodore H. Maiman, 1927-2007, (U.S.) physicist; invented the first workable laser, which he displayed in 1960.

Guglielmo Marconi, 1874-1937, (It.) physicist; developed wireless telegraphy.

John W. Mauchly, 1907-80, (U.S.) co-inventor, with J. Presper Eckert Jr., of computer ENIAC (1943-45).

James Clerk Maxwell, 1831-79, (Br.) physicist; unified electricity and magnetism, electromagnetic theory of light.

Maria Goeppert Mayer, 1906-72, (Ger.-U.S.) physicist; developed shell model of atomic nuclei.

Barbara McClintock, 1902-92, (U.S.) geneticist; showed that some genetic elements are mobile.

Lise Meitner, 1878-1968, (Austria) co-discoverer, with Otto Hahn, of nuclear fission (1938).

Gregor J. Mendel, 1822-84, (Austria) botanist, monk; his experiments became the foundation of modern genetics.

Dmitri Mendeleyev, 1834-1907, (Russ.) chemist; established Periodic Table of the Elements.

Bruce R. Merrifield, 1921-2006, (U.S.) chemist; discovered how to synthesize proteins quickly and efficiently.

Franz Mesmer, 1734-1815, (Ger.) physician; introduced hypnotherapy.

Albert A. Michelson, 1852-1931, (U.S.) physicist; invented interferometer.

Robert A. Millikan, 1868-1953, (U.S.) physicist; measured electronic charge.

Thomas Hunt Morgan, 1866-1945, (U.S.) geneticist, embryologist; established role of chromosomes in heredity.

Isaac Newton, 1642-1727, (Br.) natural philosopher; discovered laws of gravitation, motion; with Gottfried Wilhelm Leibniz, founded calculus.

Robert N. Noyce, 1927-90, (U.S.) invented microchip.

J. Robert Oppenheimer, 1904-67, (U.S.) physicist; scientific director of Manhattan Project.

Wilhelm Ostwald, 1853-1932, (Ger.) chemist, philosopher; main founder of modern physical chemistry.

Louis Pasteur, 1822-95, (Fr.) chemist; showed that germs cause disease and fermentation; originated pasteurization.

Linus C. Pauling, 1901-94, (U.S.) chemist; studied chemical bonds; campaigned for nuclear disarmament.

Jean Piaget, 1896-1980, (Switz.) psychologist; four-stage theory of intellectual development in children.

Max Planck, 1858-1947, (Ger.) physicist; introduced quantum hypothesis (1900).

Jules Henri Poincaré, 1854-1912, (Fr.) mathematician; founded algebraic topology, many other discoveries.

Walter S. Reed, 1851-1902, (U.S.) Army physician; proved mosquitoes transmit yellow fever.

Theodor Reik, 1888-1969, (Austria-U.S.) psychoanalyst; major Freudian disciple.

Sally Ride, 1951-2012, (U.S.) astronaut; 1st U.S. woman in space.

Bernhard Riemann, 1826-66, (Ger.) mathematician; developed non-Euclidean geometry used by Einstein.

Norbert Rillieux, 1806-94, (U.S.) African American inventor of a vacuum pan evaporator (1846); revolutionized sugar-refining industry.

Wilhelm Roentgen, 1845-1923, (Ger.) physicist; discovered X-rays (1895).

Carl Rogers, 1902-87, (U.S.) psychotherapist, author; originated nondirective therapy.

Ernest Rutherford, 1871-1937, (Br.) physicist; pioneer investigator of radioactivity, identified the atomic nucleus.

Albert B. Sabin, 1906-93, (Russ.-U.S.) developed oral polio live-virus vaccine.

Carl Sagan, 1934-96, (U.S.) astronomer, author.

Jonas Salk, 1914-95, (U.S.) developed first successful polio vaccine, widely used in U.S. after 1955.

Allan Sandage, 1926-2010, (U.S.) astronomer; refined the Hubble Constant, a measure of the universe's expansion.

Giovanni Schiaparelli, 1835-1910, (It.) astronomer; reported canals on Mars.

Erwin Schrödinger, 1887-1961, (Austria) physicist; developed wave equation for quantum systems.

Glenn T. Seaborg, 1912-99, (U.S.) chemist; Nobel Prize winner (1951); co-discoverer of plutonium.

Harlow Shapley, 1885-1972, (U.S.) astronomer; mapped galactic clusters and position of Sun in our galaxy.

Norman E. Shumway, 1923-2006, (U.S.) surgeon; performed world's first successful heart-lung transplant.

B. F. Skinner, 1904-90, (U.S.) psychologist; leading advocate of behaviorism.

Richard E. Smalley, 1943-2005, (U.S.) chemist; with three other scientists, discovered buckminsterfullerenes, a previously unknown class of carbon molecules.

Roger W. Sperry, 1913-94, (U.S.) neurobiologist; established different functions of right and left sides of brain.

Benjamin Spock, 1903-98, (U.S.) pediatrician, child care expert; *Common Sense Book of Baby and Child Care*.

Charles P. Steinmetz, 1865-1923, (Ger.-U.S.) electrical engineer; developed basic ideas in alternating current.

Ernst Stuhlinger, 1913-2008, (Ger.) rocket scientist; electric propulsion for NASA in early space age.

Leo Szilard, 1898-1964, (Hung.-U.S.) physicist; helped on Manhattan Project, later opposed nuclear weapons.

Edward Teller, 1908-2003, (Hung.-U.S.) physicist; aided on Manhattan Project, had key role in development of H-bomb.

Nikola Tesla, 1856-1943, (Serb.-U.S.) invented electrical devices including AC dynamos, transformers, and motors.

William Thomson (Lord Kelvin), 1824-1907, (Br.) physicist; aided in success of transatlantic telegraph cable (1865); proposed Kelvin absolute temperature scale.

Alan Turing, 1912-54, (Br.) mathematician; helped develop basis for computers.

James Van Allen, 1914-2006, (U.S.) physicist; discovered the presence of radiation belts around Earth (Van Allen belts).

Rudolf Virchow, 1821-1902, (Ger.) pathologist; pioneered the modern theory that diseases affect the body through cells.

Alessandro Volta, 1745-1827, (It.) physicist; electricity pioneer.

Wernher von Braun, 1912-77, (Ger.-U.S.) developed rockets for warfare and space exploration.

John von Neumann, 1903-57, (Hung.-U.S.) mathematician; originated game theory; basic design for modern computers.

Alfred Russell Wallace, 1823-1913, (Br.) naturalist; proposed concept of evolution independently of Darwin.

John B. Watson, 1878-1958, (U.S.) psychologist; a founder of behaviorism.

James E. Watt, 1736-1819, (Br.) mechanical engineer, inventor; invented modern steam engine (1765).

Alfred L. Wegener, 1880-1930, (Ger.) meteorologist, geophysicist; postulated continental drift.

Norbert Wiener, 1894-1964, (U.S.) mathematician; founder of cybernetics.

Daniel Hale Williams, 1858-1931, (U.S.) African American surgeon; performed one of first two open-heart operations (1893).

Sewall Wright, 1889-1988, (U.S.) evolutionary theorist; helped found population genetics.

Wilhelm Wundt, 1832-1920, (Ger.) founder of experimental psychology.

Qian Xuesen (Tsien Hsue-shen), 1911-2009, (China) rocket scientist; father of China's space program.

Rosalyn Yalow, 1921-2011, (U.S.), physicist; co-developer of radioimmunoassay.

Ferdinand von Zeppelin, 1838-1917, (Ger.) soldier, aeronaut, airship designer.

Social Reformers, Activists, and Humanitarians of the Past

Ralph David Abernathy, 1926-90, (U.S.) black civil rights activist; pres., 1968, Southern Christian Leadership Conf.

Jane Addams, 1860-1935, (U.S.) cofounder of Hull House; won Nobel Peace Prize, 1931.

Susan B. Anthony, 1820-1906, (U.S.) a leader in temperance, antislavery, and woman suffrage movements.

Thomas Barnardo, 1845-1905, (Br.) social reformer; pioneer in care of destitute children.

Clara Barton, 1821-1912, (U.S.) organized American Red Cross.

Daisy Bates, 1914-99, (U.S.) black civil rights leader who fought for integration; advocate for the "Little Rock 9" during Arkansas desegregation crisis in 1957.

Henry Ward Beecher, 1813-87, (U.S.) clergyman, abolitionist.

Peter Benenson, 1921-2005, (Br.) activist; founded Amnesty International, 1961.

Mary McLeod Bethune, 1875-1955, (U.S.) black educator, civil rights activist; adviser to FDR and Truman; founder, pres., Bethune-Cookman College.

Amelia Bloomer, 1818-94, (U.S.) suffragette, social reformer.

Yelena Bonner, 1923-2011, (Russ.) human rights activist in former Soviet Union.

William Booth, 1829-1912, (Br.) founded Salvation Army.

John Brown, 1800-59, (U.S.) abolitionist who led murder of 5 pro-slavery men; hanged.

Frances Xavier (Mother) Cabrini, 1850-1917, (It.-U.S.) Italian-born nun; founded charitable institutions; first American canonized as a saint, 1946.

Stokely Carmichael (Kwame Toure), 1941-98, (U.S.) black power activist; major proponent of Pan-Africanism; prime min. Black Panthers.

Carrie Chapman Catt, 1859-1947, (U.S.) suffragette.

Cesar Chavez, 1927-93, (U.S.) labor leader; helped establish United Farm Workers of America.

Eldridge Cleaver, 1935-98, (U.S.) revolutionary social critic; former minister of information for Black Panthers; *Soul on Ice*.

Clarence Darrow, 1857-1938, (U.S.) lawyer; defender of underdog, opponent of capital punishment.

Ossie Davis, 1917-2005, (U.S.) black civil rights activist, actor, director.

Dorothy Day, 1897-1980, (U.S.) founder of Catholic Worker movement.

Eugene V. Debs, 1855-1926, (U.S.) labor leader; led Pullman strike, 1894; 4-time Socialist presidential candidate.

Vine Deloria Jr., 1933-2005, (U.S.) Native American activist, author; *Custer Died for Your Sins*.

Dorothea Dix, 1802-87, (U.S.) crusader for mentally ill.

Thomas Dooley, 1927-61, (U.S.) "jungle doctor"; noted for efforts to supply medical aid to developing countries.

Marjory Stoneman Douglas, 1890-1998, (U.S.) writer, environmentalist; campaigned to save Florida Everglades.

Frederick Douglass, 1817-95, (U.S.) slave, author, editor, orator, diplomat; edited abolitionist weekly *The North Star*.

Andrea Dworkin, 1946-2005, (U.S.) radical feminist, antipornography crusader.

Medgar Evers, 1925-63, (U.S.) black civil rights leader; campaigned to register black voters; assassinated.

James Farmer, 1920-99, (U.S.) black civil rights leader; founded Congress of Racial Equality (CORE).

Betty Friedan, 1921-2006, (U.S.) author, feminist; *The Feminine Mystique*.

Millard Fuller, 1935-2009, (U.S.) founder of Habitat for Humanity.

William Lloyd Garrison, 1805-79, (U.S.) abolitionist.

Miep Gies, 1909-2010, (Neth.) protector of Anne Frank and her family during WWII.

Emma Goldman, 1869-1940, (Russ.-U.S.) published anarchist *Mother Earth*; birth-control advocate.

Samuel Gompers, 1850-1924, (U.S.) labor leader; first president of the American Federation of Labor (AFL).

Prince Hall, 1735-1807, (U.S.) activist; founded black Freemasonry; served in American Revolutionary war.

Michael Harrington, 1928-89, (U.S.) exposed poverty in affluent U.S. in *The Other America*, 1963.

Dorothy Height, 1912-2010, (U.S.) civil rights activist; pres. of the National Council of Negro Women, 1957-97.

Sidney Hillman, 1887-1946, (U.S.) labor leader; helped organize CIO.

Benjamin Hooks, 1925-2010, (U.S.) civil rights activist; exec. dir. NAACP, 1977-92.

Samuel G. Howe, 1801-76, (U.S.) social reformer; changed public attitudes toward the handicapped.

Franklin Kameny, 1925-2011, (U.S.) gay rights activist.

Helen Keller, 1880-1968, (U.S.) crusader for better treatment for the handicapped; deaf and blind herself.

Jack Kevorkian 1928-2011, (U.S.) pathologist; assisted-suicide activist.

Coretta Scott King, 1927-2006, (U.S.) black civil rights leader; wife of Rev. Martin Luther King Jr.

Rev. Martin Luther King Jr., 1929-68, (U.S.) civil rights leader; led 1955-56 Montgomery, AL, boycott; founder, pres., Southern Christian Leadership Conference, 1957; Nobel peace laureate, 1964; assassinated.

Maggie Kuhn, 1905-95, (U.S.) founded Gray Panthers, 1970.

William Kunstler, 1919-95, (U.S.) civil liberties attorney.

John L. Lewis, 1880-1969, (U.S.) labor leader; headed United Mine Workers, 1920-60.

Almena Lomax, 1915-2011, (U.S.) civil rights activist; journalist who founded *The Los Angeles Tribune*.

Clara Luper, 1923-2011, (U.S.) civil rights activist.

Wangari Maathai, 1940-2011, (Kenya), environmental activist; 2004 Nobel Peace Prize winner.

Robert Macauley, 1923-2010, (U.S.) founder of AmeriCares.

Malcolm X (Little), 1925-65, (U.S.) Black Muslim, black nationalist leader; promoted black pride; assassinated.

Russell Means, 1939-2012, (U.S.) American Indian activist.

Karl Menninger, 1893-1990, (U.S.) with brother William, founded Menninger Clinic and Menninger Foundation.

Lucretia Mott, 1793-1880, (U.S.) reformer, pioneer feminist.

Philip Murray, 1886-1952, (U.S.) Scottish-born labor leader.

Huey P. Newton, 1942-89, (U.S.) co-founded Black Panther Party, 1966.

Florence Nightingale, 1820-1910, (Br.) founder of modern nursing.

Emmeline Pankhurst, 1858-1928, (Br.) woman suffragist.

Rosa Parks,1913-2005, (U.S.) black civil rights activist; her actions sparked 1955-56 Montgomery, AL, bus boycott.

A. Philip Randolph, 1889-1979, (U.S.) organized Brotherhood of Sleeping Car Porters, 1925; an organizer of 1941 and 1963 March on Washington movements.

Walter Reuther, 1907-70, (U.S.) labor leader; headed UAW.

Jacob Riis, 1849-1914, (U.S.) crusader for urban reforms.

Paul Robeson, 1898-1976, (U.S.) actor, singer, black civil rights activist.

Bayard Rustin, 1910-87, (U.S.) an organizer of the 1963 March on Washington; exec. director, A. Philip Randolph Institute.

Margaret Sanger, 1883-1966, (U.S.) social reformer; pioneered the birth-control movement.

Earl of Shaftesbury (A. A. Cooper), 1801-85, (Br.) social reformer.

Eunice Kennedy Shriver, 1921-2009, (U.S.) cofounder of Special Olympics for mentally challenged athletes.

Sargent Shriver, 1915-2011, (U.S.) founding director of Peace Corps; founder of Job Corps, Head Start.

Fred Shuttlesworth, 1922-2011, (U.S.) civil rights activist.

Albertina Sisulu, 1918-2011, (S. Africa), anti-apartheid activist.

Elizabeth Cady Stanton, 1815-1902, (U.S.) woman suffrage pioneer.

Lucy Stone, 1818-93, (U.S.) feminist, abolitionist.

Mother Teresa of Calcutta, 1910-97, (Alban.) nun; founded order to care for sick, dying poor; 1979 Nobel Peace Prize.

Willard Townsend, 1895-1957, (U.S.) organized the United Transport Service Employees (Red Caps), 1935.

Sojourner Truth (Isabella Baumfree), 1797-1883, (U.S.) preacher, abolitionist; worked for black educ. opportunity.

Harriet Tubman, 1823-1913, (U.S.) prominent figure in the Underground Railroad, which helped runaway slaves in the South reach safety in the North; nurse, spy for Union Army in the Civil War.

Nat Turner, 1800-31, (U.S.) slave who led the most significant of more than 200 slave revolts in U.S., in Southampton, VA; hanged.

Philip Vera Cruz, 1905-94, (Philip.-U.S.) helped found the United Farm Workers Union.

Edgar Wayburn, 1906-2010, (U.S.) conservationist; Sierra Club pres.

William Wilberforce, 1759-1833, (Br.) social reformer; prominent in struggle to abolish slave trade.

Frances E. Willard, 1839-98, (U.S.) temperance, women's rights leader.

Mary Wollstonecraft, 1759-97, (Br.) *Vindication of the Rights of Women*.

Sports Personalities of the Past and Present

Henry (Hank) Aaron, b 1934, Milwaukee-Atlanta outfielder; hit record 755 home runs, led NL 4 times; record 2,297 RBI.

Kareem Abdul-Jabbar, b 1947, Milwaukee, L.A. Lakers center; MVP 6 times; all-time leading NBA scorer, 38,387 points.

Andre Agassi, b 1970, won Wimbledon (1992); U.S. Open ('94, '99), Austral. Open ('95, 2000-01, '03), French Open ('99).

Troy Aikman, b 1966, quarterback; led Dallas Cowboys to Super Bowl wins in 1993-94, '96; Super Bowl MVP, 1993.

Ben Ainslie, b 1977, (Br.) most decorated Olympic sailor; gold, 2000, '04, '08, '12, silver, 1996.

Amy Alcott, b 1956, golfer; 33 career wins (5 majors); inducted into Hall of Fame, 1999.

Grover Cleveland "Pete" Alexander, 1887-1950, pitcher; won 373 NL games; pitched 16 shutouts, 1916.

Muhammad Ali, b 1942, 3-time heavyweight champion.

Fernando Alonso, b 1981, (Sp.) Formula 1 racer; youngest ever to win a World Grand Prix championship, 2005; defended title, 2006.

Morten Andersen, b 1960, (Den.) kicker; NFL's career points leader, with 2,544 (1982-2007).

Gary Anderson, b 1959, (S. Afr.) kicker; NFL's 2nd in career points, with 2,434.

Sparky Anderson, 1934-2010, first manager to win World Series in the NL (Cincinnati, 1975-76) and AL (Detroit, 1984).

Mario Andretti, b 1940, (Ital.) race-car driver; won Daytona 500 (1967), Indy 500 (1969); Formula 1 world title (1978).

Earl Anthony, 1938-2001, bowler; won record 6 PBA Championships (1973-75, 1981-83), 43 career PBA tournaments.

Eddie Arcaro, 1916-97, only jockey to win racing's Triple Crown twice, 1941, '48; rode to 4,779 wins in his career.

Lance Armstrong, b 1971, cyclist; record 7-time winner of Tour de France (1999-2005); stripped of victories in 2012 for use of performance-enhancing drugs.

Arthur Ashe, 1943-93, tennis player; won U.S. Open (1968); Wimbledon (1975).

Evelyn Ashford, b 1957, sprinter; won 100m gold (1984) and silver (1988); member of 5 U.S. Olympic teams.

Red Auerbach, 1917-2006, coached Boston to 9 NBA titles.

Tracy Austin, b 1962, youngest player to win U.S. Open tennis title (age 16 in 1979).

Victoria Azarenka, b 1989, (Belarus) tennis player; won Australian Open (2012-13).

Ernie Banks, b 1931, Chicago Cubs slugger; hit 512 NL homers; twice MVP.

Roger Bannister, b 1929, (Br.) physician; ran 1st sub-4-min. mile, May 6, 1954 (3 min. 59.4 sec.).

Charles Barkley, b 1963, NBA MVP, 1993; 4th player ever to surpass 20,000 points, 10,000 rebounds, 4,000 assists.

Rick Barry, b 1944, NBA scoring leader, 1967; ABA scoring leader, 1969.

Sammy Baugh, 1914-2008, Washington Redskins quarterback; held numerous records upon retirement after 16 seasons.

Elgin Baylor, b 1934, L.A. Lakers forward; 11-time all-star.

Bob Beamon, b 1946, Olympic long jump gold medalist, 1968; world record jump of 29 ft 2½ in. stood until 1991.

Boris Becker, b 1967, (Ger.) tennis star; won U.S. Open 1989; Wimbledon champ 1985-86, '89.

David Beckham, b 1975, (Br.) soccer star; joined L.A. Galaxy, 2007-12, with record-breaking $250-mil contract.

Bill Belichick, b 1952, NFL coach; led New England Patriots to 3 Super Bowl wins (2001, '03-'04); best all-time post-season coaching record.

Jean Béliveau, b 1931, (Can.) Montréal Canadiens center; scored 507 goals; twice MVP.

Johnny Bench, b 1947, Cincinnati Reds catcher; twice MVP; led league in home runs twice, RBIs 3 times.

Patty Berg, 1918-2006, 80+ golf tournament wins; AP Woman Athlete of the Year 3 times.

Chris Berman, b 1955, sportscaster, anchor for ESPN and ABC Sports.

Yogi Berra, b 1925, Yankee catcher (1946-63); 3-time MVP.

Abebe Bikila, 1932-73, (Eth.) runner; won consecutive Olympic marathon gold medals in 1960 (barefoot), 1964.

Matt Biondi, b 1965, swimmer; won 5 golds, 1988 Olympics.

Larry Bird, b 1956, Boston Celtics forward (1979-92); NBA MVP, 1984-86; 1998 coach of the year with Indiana Pacers.

Bonnie Blair, b 1964, speed skater; won 5 individual gold medals in 3 Olympics (1988, '92, '94).

George Blanda, 1927-2010, quarterback, kicker; 26 years as active player, scored 2,002 career points.

Fanny Blankers-Koen, 1918-2004, (Neth.) track star; won 4 golds in 1948 Olympics.

Wade Boggs, b 1958, AL batting champ, 1983, 1985-88; reached 3,000 career hits, 1999 (3,010).

Usain Bolt, b 1986, (Jam.) Olympic sprinter, gold medalist, 2008, '12; world record for men's 100m, 200m runs.

Barry Bonds, b 1964, outfielder; hit record 73 homers, 2001; NL MVP, 1990, 1992-93, 2001-04; 1st all-time in HRs (762); indicted in steroid scandal, 2007; convicted of obstruction of justice, 2011.

Björn Borg, b 1956, (Swed.) led Sweden to first Davis Cup, 1975; 6-time French Open, 5-time Wimbledon champion.

Ray Bourque, b 1960, (Can.) Boston defenseman,1979-2000; 5-time Norris Trophy winner; won Stanley Cup with Colorado, 2001.

Bill Bradley, b 1943, All-American at Princeton; led NY Knicks to 2 NBA titles (1970, '73); U.S. senator, 1979-97.

Donald Bradman, 1908-2001, (Austral.) widely regarded as greatest cricketer ever; set several batting records.

Terry Bradshaw, b 1948, quarterback; led Pittsburgh to 4 Super Bowl wins, 1975-76, 1979-80; NFL MVP, 1978.

Tom Brady, b 1977, quarterback; led New England Patriots to 3 Super Bowl titles, 2002, '04-'05; Super Bowl MVP, 2002, '04; NFL MVP, 2007, '11; most single-season TD passes (50), 2007.

Ryan Braun, b 1983, Milwaukee Brewers left fielder; NL MVP, 2011.

Drew Brees, b 1979, New Orleans Saints quarterback; Super Bowl MVP, 2010; single-season record-holder for passing yards (5,476), 2011.

Christine Brennan, b 1958, sports journalist for USA Today, radio and TV commentator specializing in figure skating.

George Brett, b 1953, Kansas City Royals infielder; led AL in batting, 1976, '80, '90; MVP, 1980.

Lou Brock, b 1939, St. Louis Cardinals outfielder; stole NL single-season record 118 bases, 1974; led NL 8 times.

Jim Brown, b 1936, Cleveland fullback; 12,312 career yds.; NFL MVP 1957-58, '65.

Paul Brown, 1908-91, football team-owner, coach; led eponymous Cleveland Browns to 3 NFL championships.

Bob Bryan and **Mike Bryan**, b 1978, doubles tennis players; won French Open (2003, '13); U.S. Open, (2005, '08, '10, '12); Wimbledon, (2006, '11, '13); Austral. Open (2006-07, '09-'12); Olympic gold, 2012.

Kobe Bryant, b 1978, NBA guard; won 3 straight titles with Lakers (2000-02); leading NBA scorer, 2005-06 and 2006-07; 2007-08 NBA MVP; NBA Finals MVP 2009-10; member of U.S. Olympic gold medal teams (2008, '12).

Paul "Bear" Bryant, 1913-83, college football coach with 323 wins; led Alabama to 6 national titles (1961, '64-'65, '73, '78-'79).

Sergei Bubka, b 1963, (Ukr.) pole vaulter; first to clear 20 ft; gold medal, 1988 Olympics.

Don Budge, 1915-2000, won numerous amateur and pro tennis titles; Grand Slam, 1938.

Reggie Bush, b 1985, NFL running back; helped USC to 2 national titles (2003-04; '04 vacated).

Dick Butkus, b 1942, Chicago Bears linebacker; NFL defensive player of the year (1969-70).

Dick Button, b 1929, figure skater; won 1948, 1952 Olympic gold medals; world titleholder, 1948-52.

Miguel Cabrera, b 1983, (Venez.) 8-time All-Star; won AL triple crown (2012).

Walter Camp, 1859-1925, Yale football player, coach, athletic director; established many rules for modern football.

Roy Campanella, 1921-93, Hall of Fame catcher for the Brooklyn Dodgers (1948-57); 3-time NL MVP.

Earl Campbell, b 1955, NFL running back; MVP 1978-79.

Jose Canseco, b 1964, outfielder; led Oakland A's to the World Series, 1988; wrote book about steroids in baseball, 2005.

Eric Cantona, b 1966, (Fr.) soccer star; Manchester United (1992-97).

Rod Carew, b 1945, AL infielder; 7 batting titles, 1977 MVP.

Steve Carlton, b 1944, NL pitcher; won 20 games 6 times, Cy Young award 4 times; 4,136 career strikeouts.

Pete Carroll, b 1951, college and pro football coach; coached the USC Trojans to 2 championships (2003-04).

Billy Casper, b 1931, PGA Player of the Year 2 times; U.S. Open champ twice.

Tamika Catchings, b 1979, Indiana Fever forward; 3-time Olympic gold medalist (2004, '08, '12); WNBA MVP, 2011.

Wilt Chamberlain, 1936-99, center; NBA leading scorer 7 times, MVP 4 times; scored 100 pts. in a game, 1962.

Bobby Clarke, b 1949, (Can.) Philadelphia Flyers center; led team to 2 Stanley Cup championships; MVP 3 times.

Roger Clemens, b 1962, pitcher; 1986 AL MVP; only 7-time Cy Young winner (1986-87, '91, '97-'98, 2001, '04); twice recorded record 20 Ks in a game; 354 wins, 4,672 Ks (3rd all-time); indicted, accused of lying to Congress about using steroids, 2010.

Roberto Clemente, 1934-72, Pittsburgh Pirates outfielder; won 4 batting titles; MVP, 1966; 3,000 career hits; killed in plane crash.

Kim Clijsters, b 1983, (Belg.) tennis player; U.S. Open winner (2005, '09-'10); Austral. Open (2011).

Ty Cobb, 1886-1961, Detroit Tigers outfielder; record .367 lifetime batting average, 12 batting titles.

Sebastian Coe, b 1956, (Br.) runner; won Olympic 1,500m gold medal and 800m silver medal in 1980 and '84.

Nadia Comaneci, b 1961, (Rom.) gymnast; won 3 gold medals, achieved 7 perfect scores, 1976 Olympics; 9 Olympic medals overall.

Maureen Connolly, 1934-69, won tennis Grand Slam, 1953; AP Woman Athlete of the Year 3 times.

Jimmy Connors, b 1952, tennis player; 5 U.S. Open, 2 Wimbledon titles.

Alberto Contador, b 1982, (Sp.) cyclist; won Tour de France 2007, '09; stripped of '10 title because of doping offense.

Cynthia Cooper, b 1963, basketball; 4-time MVP of WNBA finals; 2-time league MVP for the Houston Comets.

James J. Corbett, 1866-1933, heavyweight champion, 1892-97; credited with being the first "scientific" boxer.

Angel Cordero Jr., b 1942, jockey; leading money winner, 1976, 1982-83; rode 3 Kentucky Derby winners.

Margaret Smith Court, b 1942, (Austral.) tennis great; won 24 Grand Slam events.

Bob Cousy, b 1928, Boston guard; 6 NBA titles, 1957 MVP.

Sidney Crosby, b 1987, (Can.) hockey player; Art Ross Trophy (2007), Olympic gold medal (2010).

Mark Cuban, b 1958, Dallas Mavericks owner; known for criticism of NBA.

Bjoern Daehlie, b 1967, (Nor.) cross-country skier; won record 8 Winter Olympic gold medals.

Lindsay Davenport, b 1976, tennis player; won Olympic gold, 1996; U.S. Open, 1998; Wimbledon, 1999; Austral. Open, 2000.

Al Davis, 1929-2011, Oakland Raiders owner, former coach.

Oscar De La Hoya, b 1973, won IBF lightweight (1995); WBC super lightweight (1996); welterweight (1997-99, 2000) titles.

Donna de Varona, b 1947, swimmer; won 2 Olympic golds, 1964; 1st female sportscaster at a major network, 1965.

Dizzy Dean, 1910-74, pitcher; St. Louis Cardinals' "Gashouse Gang" in the '30s.

Mary Decker Slaney, b 1958, runner; has held 6 separate American records from the 800m to 10,000m.

Frank Deford, b 1938, sr. contributing writer for Sports Illustrated; author, commentator.

Juan Martin del Potro, b 1988, (Arg.) tennis player; won U.S. Open, 2009.

Jack Dempsey, 1895-1983, heavyweight champ, 1919-26.

Gail Devers, b 1966, Olympic 100m gold medalist (1992, '96).

Joe DiMaggio, 1914-99, NY Yankees outfielder; hit safely in record 56 consecutive games, 1941; AL MVP 3 times.

Novak Djokovic, b 1987, (Serb.) tennis player; won Austral. Open (2008, '11-'13), Wimbledon (2011), U.S. Open (2011).

Landon Donovan, b 1982, forward for L.A. Galaxy; all-time leading U.S. international goal scorer with 56; MLS MVP, 2009.

Tony Dorsett, b 1954, Heisman winner who led the Dallas Cowboys to an NFL title in his rookie year, 1977.

Gabrielle Douglas, b 1995, first African-American gymnast to win Olympic gold in all-around (2012).

Tim Duncan, b 1976, San Antonio center; 3-time NBA Finals MVP, 1999, 2003, '05; NBA MVP, 2002-03.

Roberto Duran, b 1951, (Pan.) boxer; held titles at 5 weights; lost 1980 "no mas" fight to Sugar Ray Leonard.

Leo Durocher, 1905-91, manager; won 3 NL pennants (Brooklyn, 1941; NY Giants, 1951, '54), 1954 World Series.

Dale Earnhardt Jr., b 1974, stock car racer; 2004 Daytona 500 winner.

Dale Earnhardt Sr., 1951-2001, 7-time NASCAR Winston Cup champ; died in a last-lap crash at 2001 Daytona 500.

Stefan Edberg, b 1966, (Swed.) tennis player; U.S. Open (1991-92), Wimbledon (1988, '90), Austral. Open (1985, '87).

Gertrude Ederle, 1905-2003, first woman to swim English Channel; broke existing men's record, 1926.

Teresa Edwards, b 1964, 5-time basketball Olympian; gold medalist, 1984, '88, '96, 2000; bronze medalist, 1992.

Hicham El Guerrouj, b 1974, (Morocco) runner; holds world records in mile (3:43.13) and 1,500m (3:26); won gold medals in 1,500m and 5,000m, 2004 Olympics.

John Elway, b 1960, quarterback; led Denver Broncos to 2 Super Bowl wins, 1998-99; NFL MVP, 1987; Super Bowl MVP, 1999.

Julius "Dr. J" Erving, b 1950, 3-time ABA MVP, 1981 NBA MVP.

Phil Esposito, b 1942, (Can.) NHL scoring leader 5 times.

Janet Evans, b 1971, 4 Olympic swimming golds, 1988, '92.

Lee Evans, b 1947, Olympic 400m gold medalist in 1968 with 43.86-sec. world record not broken until 1988.

Chris Evert, b 1954, 6-time U.S. Open tennis champ, 3-time Wimbledon champ.

Ray Ewry, 1873-1937, track-and-field star; won 8 Olympics gold medals (1900, '04, '08).

Nick Faldo, b 1957, (Br.) golfer; won Masters, British Open 3 times each.

Juan Manuel Fangio, 1911-95 (Arg.), 5-time World Grand Prix driving champ (1951, 1954-57).

Marshall Faulk, b 1973, 2000 NFL MVP; scored then-record 26 TDs, 2001; 3-time Off. Player of the Year (1999-2001).

Brett Favre, b 1969, quarterback; led Green Bay to Super Bowl win, 1997; NFL MVP, 1995-96; co-MVP, 1997; left retirement to play for NY Jets, 2008; Minnesota Vikings, 2009-10.

Roger Federer, b 1981, (Switz.) tennis star; won Austral. Open (2004, '06-'07, '10), Wimbledon (2003-07, '09, '12), U.S. Open (2004-08), French Open (2009).

Bob Feller, 1918-2010, Cleveland Indians pitcher; won 266 games; pitched 3 no-hitters, 12 one-hitters.

Rollie Fingers, b 1946, pitcher; 341 career saves; AL MVP, Cy Young Award, 1981; World Series MVP, 1974.

Peggy Fleming, b 1948, world figure skating champion, 1966-68; gold medalist, 1968 Olympics.

Whitey Ford, b 1928, NY Yankees pitcher; won record 10 World Series games.

George Foreman, b 1949, heavyweight champion, 1973-74, 1994-95; at 45, oldest to win a heavyweight title; gold medalist, 1968 Olympics.

Dick Fosbury, b 1947, high jumper; won 1968 Olympic gold medal; developed the "Fosbury Flop."

Jimmie Foxx, 1907-67, Red Sox, Athletics slugger; MVP 3 times; triple crown, 1933.

A. J. Foyt, b 1935, won Indy 500 4 times; U.S. Auto Club champ 7 times.

Dario Franchitti, b 1973, (Scot.) 3-time Indy 500 winner, 2007, '10, '12.

Missy Franklin, b 1995, won 4 Olympic swimming golds, 2012.

Joe Frazier, 1944-2011, heavyweight champion, 1970-73; gold medalist, 1964 Olympics.

Walt Frazier, b 1945, Hall of Fame guard for NY Knicks' NBA championship teams (1970, '73).

Peter Gammons, b 1945, sportswriter, broadcaster; named to Baseball Hall of Fame.

Lou Gehrig, 1903-41, NY Yankees 1st baseman; MVP, 1927, '36; triple crown, 1934; AL record 184 RBIs, 1931; played in 2,130 straight games (1925-39), a record that stood until 1995.

Althea Gibson, 1927-2003, 2-time U.S. and Wimbledon champ.

Bob Gibson, b 1935, St. Louis Cardinals pitcher; won Cy Young award twice; struck out 3,117 batters.

Josh Gibson, 1911-47, Hall of Fame catcher; known as "Babe Ruth of the Negro Leagues"; credited with as many as 84 homers in 1 season, about 800 in his career.

Marc Girardelli, b 1963, (Lux.) skier; won 5 World Cup titles.

Raul Gonzalez, b 1977, (Sp.) soccer player; led Real Madrid to 3 Champions League titles (1998, 2000, '02); all-time top UEFA goal scorer (71).

Jeff Gordon, b 1971, race-car driver; youngest to win NASCAR title 4 times (1995, '97-'98, 2001).

Steffi Graf, b 1969, (Ger.) won tennis Grand Slam 1988; U.S. Open champ 5 times; Wimbledon, 7 times; Austral. 4 times; French 6 times.

Otto Graham, 1921-2003, Cleveland quarterback; 4-time all-pro.

Red Grange, 1903-91, All-American at Univ. of Illinois, 1923-25; played for Chicago Bears, 1925-35.

"Mean" Joe Greene, b 1946, Pittsburgh Steelers lineman; twice NFL outstanding defensive player.

Wayne Gretzky, b 1961, (Can.) top scorer in NHL history with record 894 goals, 1,963 assists, 2,857 points; MVP, 1980-87, '89.

Bob Griese, b 1945, All-Pro quarterback; led Miami Dolphins to 17-0 season, 1972, 2 Super Bowl titles, 1973-74.

Ken Griffey Jr., b 1969, outfielder; led AL in homers 1994, '97-'99; 1997 AL MVP; 10 gold gloves.

Archie Griffin, b 1954, Ohio State running back; only 2-time winner of the Heisman Trophy (1974-75).

Florence Griffith Joyner, 1959-98, sprinter; won 3 gold medals at 1988 Olympics; world and Olympic record for 100m.

Lefty Grove, 1900-75, pitcher; won 300 AL games.

Vladimir Guerrero, b 1975, (Dom. Rep.) right fielder; 2004 AL MVP award.

Janet Guthrie, b 1938, 1st woman driver in Indy 500 (1977).

Tony Gwynn, b 1960, 8-time NL batting champ (1984, '87-'89, '94-'97); 3,141 career hits.

Walter Hagen, 1892-1969, golfer; 5 PGA, 4 British Open titles.

Mika Hakkinen, b 1968, (Fin.) Formula One racing driver; Formula One champion, 1998-99.

George Halas, 1895-1983, founder/player/coach of Chicago Bears; won 6 NFL championships as coach.

Roy Halladay, b 1977, pitcher; Cy Young Award, 2003, '10; pitched perfect game, 2010.

Dorothy Hamill, b 1956, figure skater; gold medalist at the Olympics and World championships, 1976.

Josh Hamilton, b 1981, Texas Rangers outfielder; AL MVP, 2010.

Scott Hamilton, b 1958, U.S. and world figure skating champion, 1981-84; Olympic gold medalist, 1984.

Mia Hamm, b 1972, soccer player; led U.S. teams to World Cup victories (1991, '99) and Olympic gold (1996, 2004).

Franco Harris, b 1950, running back; 4 Super Bowls with Steelers (1975-76, '79-'80); 1,000+ yds. in a season 8 times.

Marvin Harrison, b 1972, Indianapolis Colts wide receiver; NFL record for single-season receptions (143), 2002.

Bill Hartack, 1932-2007, jockey; rode 5 Kentucky Derby winners.

Dominik Hasek, b 1965, (Czech.) NHL goaltender; won Vezina Trophy, 1994-95, '97-'99, 2001; NHL MVP, 1997-98.

John Havlicek, b 1940, Boston Celtics forward; scored 26,395 career pts.

Eric Heiden, b 1958, speed skater; won 5 Olympic golds, 1980.

Rickey Henderson, b 1958, outfielder; 1990 AL MVP; record 130 stolen bases, 1982; all-time leader in steals, runs.

Sonja Henie, 1912-69, (Nor.) world champion figure skater, 1927-36; Olympic gold medalist, 1928, '32, '36.

Martina Hingis, b 1980, (Switz.) won Austral. and U.S. Opens, Wimbledon; youngest number one player (16 yrs., 6 mos.), 1997.

Ben Hogan, 1912-97, golfer; won 4 U.S. Open titles, 2 PGA Championships, 2 Masters.

Santonio Holmes, b 1984, wide receiver; Super Bowl MVP, 2009.

Evander Holyfield, b 1962, 4-time heavyweight champion.

Rogers Hornsby, 1896-1963, NL 2nd baseman; batted record .424, 1924; twice won triple crown.

Paul Hornung, b 1935, Green Bay Packers running back, placekicker; scored record 176 points, 1960.

Ryan Howard, b 1979, first baseman for Philadelphia Phillies; known for his hitting; 2006 NL MVP.

Gordie Howe, b 1928, (Can.) hockey forward; NHL MVP 6 times; scored 801 goals in 26 NHL seasons.

Carl Hubbell, 1903-88, NY Giants pitcher; 20-game winner 5 consecutive years, 1933-37.

Bobby Hull, b 1939, (Can.) NHL all-star 10 times; MVP, 1965-66.

Brett Hull, b 1964, (Can.) St. Louis Blues forward; led NHL in goals, 1990-92; MVP, 1991.

Catfish Hunter, 1946-99, pitched perfect game, 1968; 20-game winner 5 times.

Don Hutson, 1913-97, Packers receiver; caught 99 TD passes; 2-time NFL MVP.

Juli Inkster, b 1960, Hall of Fame golfer; 2nd to win all 4 of LPGA's modern majors; won 7 career major titles.

Bo Jackson, b 1962, NFL running back (1987-90) and MLB outfielder (1986-91, '93-'94); 1985 Heisman Trophy winner.

Phil Jackson, b 1945, won 11 NBA titles as coach of Bulls and Lakers; 1970, '73 title as player with NY Knicks.

Reggie Jackson, b 1946, slugger; led AL in home runs 4 times; MVP, 1973; hit 5 World Series home runs, 1977.

"Shoeless" Joe Jackson, 1889-1951, outfielder; 3rd highest career batting average (.356); one of the "Black Sox" banned for allegedly throwing 1919 World Series.

Jaromir Jagr, b 1972, (Czech.) hockey player; NHL MVP, 1999; Art Ross Trophy (leading scorer), 1995, 1998-2001.

LeBron James, b 1984, NBA forward; Rookie of the Year, 2004; member of 2008, '12 U.S. Olympic gold medal teams; NBA MVP, 2009, '10, '12, '13.

Ron Jaworski, b 1951, former NFL quarterback (1974-89); NFL analyst on ESPN.

Sally Jenkins, b 1960, sports journalist and writer for *Washington Post*.

Bruce Jenner, b 1949, Olympic decathlon gold medalist, 1976.

Lynn Jennings, b 1960, runner; 3-time World, 9-time U.S. cross country champ; bronze (10,000m), 1992 Olympics.

Derek Jeter, b 1974, shortstop; led NY Yankees to 5 World Series titles; World Series MVP, 2000; 1st Yankee to reach 3,000 hits, 2011.

Earvin "Magic" Johnson, b 1959, NBA MVP, 1987, '89, '90; playoff MVP, 1980, '82, '87; 4th in career assists.

Jack Johnson, 1878-1946, heavyweight champion, 1908-15.

Jimmie Johnson, b 1975, 5-time NASCAR Sprint Cup Series champ, 2006-10; Daytona 500 winner, 2006.

Michael Johnson, b 1967, 4-time Olympic gold medalist (1992, '96, 2000); world and Olympic record, 400m and 4 × 400m.

Randy Johnson, b 1963, 5-time Cy Young winner; strikeout leader, 1992-95, 1999-2002, '04; 4,875 strikeouts (2nd all-time); pitched perfect game, 2004.

Walter Johnson, 1887-1946, Washington Senators pitcher; won 417 games; record 110 shutouts.

Bobby Jones, 1902-71, won golf's Grand Slam, 1930; U.S. amateur champ 5 times, U.S. Open champ 4 times.

Cobi Jones, b 1970, soccer player; most U.S. national team appearances with 164.

David "Deacon" Jones, 1938-2013, 5-time All-Pro with L.A. Rams (1965-69); "sack" specialist credited with inventing the term.

Marion Jones, b 1975, 2000 Olympic 100m, 200m, 1,600m relay gold medalist, bronze in long jump and 400m relay; stripped of medals in 2007 after admitting use of performance-enhancing drugs.

Roy Jones Jr., b 1969, light heavyweight champ, 1999-2004.

Michael Jordan, b 1963, guard; leading NBA scorer, 1987-93, '96-'98; MVP, 1988, 1991-92, '96, '98; playoff MVP, 1991-93, '96-'98; ESPN Athlete of the Century.

Dorothy Kamenshek, 1925-2010, led Rockford (IL) Peaches to 4 All-American Girls Baseball League titles in the 1940s.

Jackie Joyner-Kersee, b 1962, Olympic gold medalist in heptathlon (1988, '92), long jump (1988).

Clayton Kershaw, b 1988, pitcher; NL Cy Young Award (2011).

Harmon Killebrew, 1936-2011, Minnesota Twins slugger; led AL in home runs 6 times; 573 lifetime.

Jean Claude Killy, b 1943, (Fr.) skier; 3 Olympic golds, 1968.

Kim Yu-Na, b 1990, (S. Kor.) figure skater; Olympic gold medal winner, 2010; world champion, 2009.

Ralph Kiner, b 1922, Pittsburgh Pirates slugger; led NL in home runs 7 consecutive years, 1946-52.

Billie Jean King, b 1943, U.S. singles champ 4 times; Wimbledon champ 6 times; beat Bobby Riggs, 1973.

Peter King, b 1957, senior writer for *Sports Illustrated*.

Bob Knight, b 1940, ESPN studio analyst, ret. basketball coach; led Indiana U. to NCAA title in 1976, '81, '87; winningest men's college basketball coach (902).

Olga Korbut, b 1955, (Belarus) gymnast; 3 Olympic golds, 1972.

Sandy Koufax, b 1935, 3-time Cy Young winner; lowest ERA in NL, 1962-66; pitched 4 no-hitters, 1 perfect game.

Jack Kramer, 1921-2009, world's number one tennis player, 1946-53; first at Wimbledon to compete in shorts.

Ingrid Kristiansen, b 1956, (Nor.) only runner to have held world records in 5,000m, 10,000m, and marathon.

Julie Krone, b 1963, winningest female jockey; only woman to ride a winner in a Triple Crown race (Belmont, 1993).

Michelle Kwan, b 1980, figure skater; 9 U.S., 5 World titles; silver medalist at 1998 Olympics, bronze in 2002.

Guy Lafleur, b 1951, (Can.) 3-time NHL scoring leader; 1977-78 MVP.

Alexi Lalas, b 1970, soccer player; first modern-era American to play in Italian League Serie A.

Kenesaw Mountain Landis, 1866-1944, 1st commissioner of baseball (1920-44); banned the 8 "Black Sox" involved in fixing 1919 World Series.

Tom Landry, 1924-2000, Dallas Cowboys head coach, 1960-88; won 2 Super Bowls (1972, '78); 3rd in career wins (270).

Dick "Night Train" Lane, 1928-2002, Hall of Fame defensive back; intercepted an NFL season record 14 passes (1952).

Don Larsen, b 1929, as NY Yankee, pitched only World Series perfect game, Oct. 8, 1956—2-0 win over Brooklyn.

Rod Laver, b 1938, (Austral.) won tennis Grand Slam, 1962, 1969; Wimbledon champ 4 times.

Mario Lemieux, b 1965, (Can.) 6-time NHL leading scorer; MVP, 1988, '93, '96; playoff MVP, 1991-92.

Greg Lemond, b 1961, cyclist; 3-time Tour de France winner (1986, '89-'90); first American to win the event.

Ivan Lendl, b 1960, (Czech.) 8 Grand Slam tennis titles, including U.S. Open, 1985-87.

Sugar Ray Leonard, b 1956, boxer; held titles in 5 different weight classes.

Lisa Leslie, b 1972, L.A. Sparks center; 3-time WNBA MVP (2001, '04, '06).

Carl Lewis, b 1961, track-and-field star; won 9 Olympic gold medals in sprinting and long jump.

Lennox Lewis, b 1965, (Br.) heavyweight champ, 1994, 1997-2004, retired undefeated; gold medalist, 1998 Olympics.

Ray Lewis, b 1975, linebacker for the Baltimore Ravens; Super Bowl MVP, 2001.

Tim Lincecum, b 1984, S.F. Giants pitcher; NL Cy Young Award, 2008-09.

Tara Lipinski, b 1982, youngest figure skater to win U.S., world championships, 1997, and Winter Olympic gold, 1998.

Ryan Lochte, b 1984, swimmer; 11-time Olympic medalist, incl. 5 gold (2004, '08, '12).

Vince Lombardi, 1913-70, Green Bay Packers coach; led team to 5 NFL championships, 2 Super Bowl victories.

Nancy Lopez, b 1957, Hall of Fame golfer; 4-time LPGA Player of the Year, 3-time winner of the LPGA Championship.

Greg Louganis, b 1960, won Olympic gold medals in both springboard and platform diving, 1984, '88.

Joe Louis, 1914-81, heavyweight champion, 1937-49.

Sid Luckman, 1916-98, Chicago Bears quarterback; led team to 4 NFL championships; MVP, 1943.

Evan Lysacek, b 1985, figure skater; world champion, 2009, Olympic gold winner, 2010.

Connie Mack, 1862-1956, Philadelphia Athletics manager, 1901-50; won 9 pennants, 5 championships.

John Madden, b 1936, won Super Bowl as coach of Oakland Raiders (1977); former NFL TV analyst.

Greg Maddux, b 1966, NL pitcher; won 4 consecutive Cy Young awards, 1992-95; 355 career wins.

Karl Malone, b 1963, Utah Jazz, L.A. Lakers forward; MVP, 1997, '99; 14-time All-Star; 36,928 career points (2nd all-time).

Moses Malone, b 1955, NBA center; MVP, 1979, '82-'83.

Eli Manning, b 1981, NY Giants quarterback; Super Bowl MVP, 2008, '12.

Peyton Manning, b 1976, quarterback; most NFL MVP awards, 2003-04, '08-'09; Super Bowl MVP, 2007; highest single-season passer rating (121.1), 2004.

Mickey Mantle, 1931-95, NY Yankees outfielder; triple crown, 1956; 18 World Series home runs; MVP 3 times.

Diego Maradona, b 1960, (Arg.) soccer player; led Argentina to World Cup, 1986.

"Pistol" Pete Maravich, 1947-88, guard; scored NCAA record 44.2 ppg during collegiate career; led NBA in scoring, 1977.

Rocky Marciano, 1923-69, heavyweight champion, 1952-56; retired undefeated.

Dan Marino, b 1961, Miami quarterback; NFL record single-season yards passing (5,084), 1984.

Roger Maris, 1934-85, NY Yankees outfielder; hit AL record 61 home runs, 1961, record held 37 years; MVP, 1960-61.

Marta (Marta Vieira da Silva), b 1986, (Braz.) soccer forward; FIFA World Player of the Year, 2006-10.

Curtis Martin, b 1973, Jets running back; 5-time Pro-Bowler; 4th in all-time rushing yards with 14,101.

Eddie Mathews, 1931-2001, Milwaukee-Atlanta Braves 3rd baseman; hit 512 career home runs.

Christy Mathewson, 1880-1925, pitcher; won 373 games.

Bob Mathias, 1930-2006, decathlon gold, 1948, '52 Olympics.

Misty May-Treanor, b 1977, beach volleyball player; 3-time Olympic gold medalist with Kerri Walsh Jennings (2004, '08, '12).

Willie Mays, b 1931, NY-S.F. Giants center fielder; hit 660 home runs, led NL 4 times; had 3,283 hits; twice MVP.

Willie McCovey, b 1938, S.F. Giants slugger; hit 521 home runs; led NL 3 times; MVP, 1969.

John McEnroe, b 1959, U.S. Open tennis champ (1979-81, '84); Wimbledon champ (1981, '83-'84).

John McGraw, 1873-1934, NY Giants manager; led team to 10 pennants, 3 championships.

Mark McGwire, b 1963, hit then-record 70 home runs in 1998; 583 career home runs (10th); admitted career steroid use, 2010.

Rory McIlroy, b 1989, (N. Ire.) golfer; won U.S. Open 16 under par, 2011; won PGA Championship, 2012.

Tamara McKinney, b 1962, 1st U.S. skier to win overall Alpine World Cup championship (1983).

Andrea Mead Lawrence, 1932-2009, skier; first woman to win 2 gold medals in alpine skiing at one Olympics (1952).

Lionel Messi, b 1987, (Arg.) forward for FC Barcelona; FIFA World Player of the Year, 2009-10.

Mark Messier, b 1961, (Can.) center; NHL MVP, 1990, '92; Conn Smythe Trophy, 1984.

Debbie Meyer, b 1952, 1st swimmer to win 3 individual Olympic golds (1968).

Al Michaels, b 1944, *NBC Sunday Night Football* announcer; 5-time Outstanding Sports Personality Emmy winner.

Phil Mickelson, b 1970, golfer; 5 career major titles.

George Mikan, 1924-2005, Minn. Lakers center; considered the best basketball player of first half of 20th cent.

Stan Mikita, b 1940, (Czech.) Chicago Blackhawks center; led NHL in scoring 4 times; MVP twice.

Billy Mills, b 1938, runner; upset winner of the 1964 Olympic 10,000m; only American man ever to win the event.

Joe Montana, b 1956, S.F. 49ers quarterback; Super Bowl MVP, 1982, '85, '90.

Archie Moore, 1913-98, light-heavyweight champ, 1952-62.

Howie Morenz, 1902-37, (Can.) Montréal Canadiens forward; considered best hockey player of first half of 20th cent.

Edwin Moses, b 1955, undefeated in 122 consecutive 400m hurdles races, 1977-87; Olympic gold medalist, 1976, '84.

Shirley Muldowney, b 1940, 1st woman to race Natl. Hot Rod Assn. Top Fuel dragsters; 3-time NHRA points champ.

Eddie Murray, b 1956, 3rd player with both 3,000+ hits and 500+ home runs.

Stan Musial, 1920-2013, St. Louis Cardinals star; won 7 NL batting titles; MVP 3 times.

Rafael Nadal, b 1986, (Sp.) tennis player; won French Open (2005-08, '10-'13), Wimbledon (2008, '10), Australian Open (2009), U.S. Open (2010, '13); Olympic gold medal in men's singles (2008).

Bronko Nagurski, 1908-90, (Can.) Chicago Bears fullback and tackle; gained more than 4,000 yds. rushing.

Joe Namath, b 1943, Jets quarterback; 1969 Super Bowl MVP.

Steve Nash, b 1974, (Can.) Phoenix Suns point guard; NBA MVP, 2005, '06.

Martina Navratilova, b 1956, (Czech.) Wimbledon champ 9 times; U.S. Open champ (1983-84, '86-'87); Austral. 3 times, French 2 times.

Byron Nelson, 1912-2006, won 11 consecutive golf tournaments in 1945; twice Masters and PGA titlist.

Ernie Nevers, 1903-76, Stanford football star; selected as best college fullback to play between 1919 and 1969.

Paula Newby-Fraser, b 1962, ([now] Zimbabwe) 8-time Ironman Triathlon world champ; holds women's course record.

John Newcombe, b 1944, (Austral.) twice U.S. Open tennis champ; Wimbledon champ 3 times.

Jack Nicklaus, b 1940, PGA Player of the Year, 1967, '72; leading money winner 8 times; won 18 majors (6 Masters).

Chuck Noll, b 1932, Pittsburgh coach; won 4 Super Bowls.

Dirk Nowitzki, b 1978, (Ger.) NBA forward; led Mavericks to NBA title, 2011; NBA MVP, 2007.

Paavo Nurmi, 1897-1973, (Fin.) distance runner; won 9 Olympic gold medals, 1920, '24, '28.

Lorena Ochoa, b 1981, (Mex.) LPGA Player of the Year, 2006-09, money leader 2006-08.

Al Oerter, 1936-2007, discus thrower; won gold medal at 4 consecutive Olympics, 1956, '60, '64, '68.

Apolo Ohno, b 1982, speed skater; most decorated American Winter Olympic athlete with 2 gold, 2 silver, 4 bronze (2002, '06, '10).

Hakeem Olajuwon, b 1963, (Nigeria) Houston center; NBA MVP, 1994, playoff MVP, 1994-95; career blocked shots leader (3,830).

Barney Oldfield, 1878-1946, pioneer auto racer; was first to drive a car 60 mph, 1903.

Shaquille O'Neal, b 1972, center; led L.A. Lakers to NBA titles, 2000-02, and Miami Heat to NBA title, 2006; Finals MVP 2000-02; NBA MVP 2000.

Bobby Orr, b 1948, (Can.) Boston Bruins defenseman; 8-time Norris Trophy winner; led NHL in scoring twice, assists 5 times.

Mel Ott, 1909-58, NY Giants right fielder; hit 511 home runs; led NL 6 times.

Jesse Owens, 1913-80, track and field; 4 1936 Olympic golds.

Terrell Owens, b 1973, wide receiver.

Satchel Paige, 1906-82, pitcher; starred in Negro leagues, 1924-48; entered major leagues at age 42.

Arnold Palmer, b 1929, golf's first $1 mil winner; won 4 Masters, 2 British Opens.

Jim Palmer, b 1945, Baltimore Orioles pitcher; won Cy Young award 3 times; 20-game winner 8 times.

Inbee Park, b 7/12/88, (S. Kor.) golfer; U.S. Women's Open winner 2008, '13; 2nd player to win first 3 majors (2013).

Candace Parker, b 1986, L.A. Sparks forward; first woman to dunk in an NCAA tournament game; 2008 WNBA MVP award, Rookie of the Year.

Joe Paterno, 1926-2012, Penn St. football coach; national title-winner 1982, '86; had most wins in NCAA Div. I coaching history until 111 Penn St. wins (1998-2011) were vacated as penalty for the child sex abuse scandal.

Danica Patrick, b 1982, race car driver; 4th woman to race at Indy 500, 1st to lead, 2005, 1st to win NASCAR Sprint Cup series pole, 2013.

Floyd Patterson, 1935-2006, 2-time heavyweight champion; first to ever regain the title after losing it.

Walter Payton, 1954-99, Chicago Bears running back; 2nd most rushing yards in NFL history; top NFC rusher, 1976-80.

Pelé (Edson Arantes do Nascimento), b 1940, (Braz.) soccer player; led Brazil to 3 World Cups (1958, '62, '70); scored 1,281 goals.

Bob Pettit, b 1932, first NBA player to score 20,000 points; twice NBA scoring leader.

Richard Petty, b 1937, NASCAR national champ 7 times; 7-time Daytona 500 winner.

Michael Phelps, b 1985, swimmer; holds record for most Olympic medals (22) and gold medals (18) won by single athlete; won 8 medals at 2004 Olympics; 8 gold in 2008; 6 medals in 2012.

Laffit Pincay Jr., b 1946, (Pan.) jockey; leading money-winner, 1970-74, '79, '85.

Oscar Pistorius, b 1986, (S. Afr.) sprinter; 1st double-leg amputee to compete in Olympics, 2012; charged with murder in the death of his girlfriend, 2013.

Jacques Plante, 1929-86, (Can.) NHL goaltender; 7 Vezina trophies; first goalie to wear mask in a game.

Gary Player, b 1935, (S. Afr.) golfer; won 3 Masters, 3 British Opens, 2 PGA Championships, and U.S. Open.

Mike Powell, b 1963, track and field athlete; holds world record for long jump (29 ft 4.5 in.).

Steve Prefontaine, 1951-75, runner; 1st to win 4 NCAA titles in same event (5,000m, 1970-73).

Kirby Puckett, 1960-2006, Minnesota Twins center fielder (1984-95); led team to World Series titles in 1987, '91.

Albert Pujols, b 1980, St. Louis first baseman; NL MVP, 2005, '08-'09.

Paula Radcliffe, b 1973, British runner; set marathon world record of 2:15:25 in London, 2003.

Kimi Räikkönen, b 1979, (Fin.) Formula One race car driver; 2007 Formula One World Drivers' Champion.

Manny Ramirez, b 1972, (Dom. Rep.) outfielder; 2004 World Series MVP; suspended for violating MLB performance-enhancing drug policy, 2009; retired after testing positive for P.E.D.s, 2011.

Willis Reed, b 1942, NY Knicks center; MVP, 1970; playoff MVP, 1970, '73.

Mary Lou Retton, b 1968, gymnast; won all-around gold medal at 1984 Olympics; also won 2 silvers, 2 bronzes.

Claudio Reyna, b 1973, midfielder; U.S. National Team; named to the FIFA World Cup All-Star team, 2002.

Jerry Rice, b 1962, receiver; 1989 Super Bowl MVP; NFL record for career touchdowns (208), receptions (1,549).

Maurice Richard, 1921-2000, (Can.) Montréal Canadiens forward; scored 544 regular season goals, 82 playoff goals.

Branch Rickey, 1881-1965, MLB exec. helped break baseball's color barrier, 1947; initiated farm system, 1919.

Cal Ripken Jr., b 1960, Baltimore shortstop; AL MVP, 1983, '91; most consecutive games played (2,632).

Mariano Rivera, b 1969, (Pan.) relief pitcher; helped NY Yankees to 5 World Series titles; World Series MVP, 1999; all-time MLB leader in regular season and postseason saves.

Oscar Robertson, b 1938, NBA guard; averaged career 25.7 points per game; 5th in career assists (9,887); MVP, 1964.

Brooks Robinson, b 1937, Baltimore Orioles 3rd baseman; played in 4 World Series; MVP, 1964; 16 gold gloves.

Frank Robinson, b 1935, MVP in both NL and AL; triple crown, 1966; 586 career home runs; first black manager in majors.

Jackie Robinson, 1919-72, broke baseball's color barrier with Brooklyn Dodgers, 1947; NL MVP, 1949.

Sugar Ray Robinson, 1921-89, boxer; middleweight champion 5 times; welterweight champion, 1946-51.

Knute Rockne, 1888-1931, Notre Dame football coach, 1918-31; revolutionized game by stressing forward pass.

Aaron Rodgers, b 1983, Green Bay quarterback; led Packers to victory in Super

Bowl XLV; Super Bowl MVP, 2011; NFL MVP, 2011, highest single-season passer rating (122.5), 2011.

Bill Rodgers, b 1947, runner; won Boston and New York City marathons 4 times each between 1975 and 1980.

Alex Rodriguez, b 1975, NY Yankees third baseman; AL MVP in 2003, '05, '07; 14-time All Star; youngest player to ever hit 500 HRs; admitted steroid use 2001-03; appealed 211-game suspension for P.E.D. use, 2013.

Juan "Chi Chi" Rodriguez, b 1935, champion golfer; 8 PGA tour wins, 22 Champions tour wins.

Ben Roethlisberger, b 1982, Pittsburgh Steelers quarterback; youngest to win Super Bowl, 2005.

Ronaldinho, b 1980, (Braz.) soccer midfielder; led Brazil to World Cup Finals in 2006; FIFA World Player of the Year, 2004, '05.

Ronaldo (Ronaldo Luiz Nazario de Lima), b 1976, (Braz.) soccer forward; led Brazil to 2002 World Cup title; 3-time FIFA world player of the year, 1996-97, 2002; most World Cup goals, 15.

Cristiano Ronaldo, b 1985, (Port.) soccer forward; FIFA player of the year, 2008.

Art Rooney, 1901-88, NFL owner; bought Pittsburgh Pirates in 1933, renamed Steelers, 1940.

Pete Rose, b 1941, won 3 NL batting titles; hit in 44 consecutive games, 1978; most career hits, 4,256; banned for gambling, 1989; admitted betting on his team, 2004.

Ken Rosewall, b 1934, (Austral.) tennis player; 2-time U.S. champ; 8 Grand Slam singles titles.

Patrick Roy, b 1965, (Can.) Montréal-Colorado goalie; only 3-time NHL playoffs MVP (Conn Smythe Trophy), 1986, '93, 2001.

Wilma Rudolph, 1940-94, sprinter; won 3 1960 Olympic golds.

Adolph Rupp, 1901-77, NCAA basketball coach; led Kentucky to 4 national titles, 1948-49, '51, '58.

Bill Russell, b 1934, Boston Celtics center; led team to 11 NBA titles; MVP 5 times; first black coach of major pro sports team.

Babe Ruth, 1895-1948, NY Yankees outfielder; hit 60 home runs, 1927, 714 lifetime (3rd all-time); led AL 12 times.

Johnny Rutherford, b 1938, auto racer; won 3 Indy 500s.

Nolan Ryan, b 1947, pitcher; holds season (383), career (5,714) strikeout records; won 324 games (7 no-hitters).

Pete Sampras, b 1971, tennis star; 1st man in Open era to win 7 Wimbledons; 2nd-most career Grand Slam wins (14).

Joan Benoit Samuelson, b 1957, won 1st Olympic women's marathon (1984), Boston Marathon (1979, '83).

Barry Sanders, b 1968, rushed for 2,053 yards in 1997; led NFL in rushing, 1990, '94, '96-'97.

Deion Sanders, b 1967, NFL cornerback (1989-2000, '04-'05) and MLB outfielder (1989-95, '97, 2005).

Gale Sayers, b 1943, Chicago running back; twice led NFL in rushing.

Mike Schmidt, b 1949, Phillies 3rd baseman; led NL in home runs 8 times; 548 lifetime; NL MVP, 1980-81, '86.

Michael Schumacher, b 1969, (Ger.) race-car driver; 7-time Formula 1 world champ (1994-95, 2000-04).

Tom Seaver, b 1944, pitcher; won NL Cy Young award 3 times; won 311 major league games.

Monica Seles, b 1973, (Yug.) tennis player; won U.S. (1991-92), Austral. (1991-93, '96), French (1990-92) Opens; stabbed on court by spectator, 1993.

Maria Sharapova, b 1987, (Russ.) tennis star; won Wimbledon (2004), U.S. Open (2006), Australian Open (2008), French Open (2012); Olympic silver, 2012.

Patty Sheehan, b 1956, Hall of Fame golfer; 3 LPGA Championships (1983-84, '93).

Willie Shoemaker, 1931-2003, jockey; rode 4 Kentucky Derby, 5 Belmont Stakes winners.

Frank Shorter, b 1947, runner; only American to win men's Olympic marathon (1972) since 1908; silver medalist (1976).

Don Shula, b 1930, all-time winningest NFL coach (347 games).

Bill Simmons, b 1969, columnist known as "The Sports Guy."

O. J. Simpson, b 1947, running back; rushed for 2,003 yds., 1973; AFC leading rusher 4 times; acquitted of murder, 1995; jailed after being found guilty of robbery and kidnapping, 2008.

Webb Simpson, b 1985, golfer; won U.S. Open, 2012.

Dean Smith, b 1931, retired basketball coach; 879 Division I wins; led North Carolina to 2 NCAA titles (1982, '93).

Emmitt Smith, b 1969, running back; NFL and Super Bowl MVP, 1993; rushed for career record 18,355 yds.

Conn Smythe, 1895-1980, (Can.) won 7 Stanley Cups as Toronto GM (1929-61); playoff MVP award named in his honor.

Sam Snead, 1912-2002, PGA and Masters champ 3 times each; record 82 PGA tournament victories.

Annika Sorenstam, b 1970, (Swed.) golfer; set LPGA 18-hole record of 59 (−13), 72-hole record of 27-under-par, 2001; won 10 LPGA majors, including career Grand Slam.

Sammy Sosa, b 1968, (Dom. Rep.) right fielder; 66 homers, NL MVP, 1998; 1st to hit 60+ homers 3 times (1998-99, 2001).

Warren Spahn, 1921-2003, pitcher; won 363 NL games; 20-game winner 13 times; Cy Young award, 1957.

Tris Speaker, 1888-1958, AL outfielder; batted .345 over 22 seasons; hit record 792 career doubles.

Mark Spitz, b 1950, swimmer; won 7 golds at 1972 Olympics.

Amos Alonzo Stagg, 1862-1965, football innovator; Univ. of Chicago football coach for 41 years, 5 undefeated seasons.

Bart Starr, b 1934, Green Bay Packers quarterback; led team to 5 NFL titles, 2 Super Bowl victories.

Roger Staubach, b 1942, Dallas Cowboys quarterback; leading NFC passer 5 times.

George Steinbrenner, 1930-2010, NY Yankees owner.

Casey Stengel, 1890-1975, managed Yankees to 10 pennants, 7 World Series wins between 1949 and 1960.

Jackie Stewart, b 1939, (Scot.) auto racer; 27 Grand Prix wins.

John Stockton, b 1962, Utah Jazz guard; NBA career leader in assists, steals; NBA assists leader, 1988-96.

Samantha Stosur, b 1984, (Austral.) tennis player; won U.S. Open, 2011; French Open, 2012.

Picabo Street, b 1971, skier; 2-time World Cup downhill champion (1995-96); Olympic super G gold medalist, 1998.

Louise Suggs, b 1923, golfer; U.S. Women's Open champ, 1949, '52; 11 major victories, ranks 3rd all-time.

John L. Sullivan, 1858-1918, last bare-knuckle heavyweight champion, 1882-92.

Pat Summerall, 1930-2013, NFL kicker, radio and TV sportscaster who announced 26 Super Bowls.

Pat Summitt, b 1952, women's basketball coach; led Tennessee Lady Vols to 8 NCAA titles (1987, '89, '91, '96-'98, 2007-08); all-time winningest NCAA coach.

Ichiro Suzuki, b 1973, (Japan) center fielder; AL MVP, 2001; single-season hits record (262), 2004; 4,000th career (Japan/U.S.) hit (2013).

Sheryl Swoopes, b 1971, guard/forward; 1st player named WNBA MVP 3 times (2000, '02, '05).

Fran Tarkenton, b 1940, Minnesota, NY Giants quarterback; 4th in career TD passes (342); 1975 Player of the Year.

Diana Taurasi, b 1982, WNBA shooting guard, Phoenix Mercury; Olympic gold medalist, 2008, '12; WNBA MVP, 2009.

Lawrence Taylor, b 1959, linebacker; led NY Giants to 2 Super Bowl titles; played in 10 Pro Bowls.

Daley Thompson, b 1958, (Br.) decathlete; Olympic gold medalist in 1980, '84.

Jenny Thompson, b 1973, swimmer; most decorated U.S. female Olympian; 12 medals (8 gold) in 1992, '96, 2000, '04.

Bobby Thomson, 1923-2010, outfielder/3B; known for pennant-clinching "Shot Heard 'Round the World" for the NY Giants, 1951.

Jim Thorpe, 1888-1953, football All-American, 1911-12; won pentathlon and decathlon, 1912 Olympics.

Bill Tilden, 1893-1953, won 7 U.S. tennis titles, 3 Wimbledon.

Y. A. Tittle, b 1926, NY Giants quarterback; MVP, 1961, '63.

Alberto Tomba "La Bomba," b 1966, (It.) skier; 5 Olympic alpine medals (3 golds, 2 silver) in 1988, '92, '94.

LaDainian "L.T." Tomlinson, b 1979, running back; NFL records for single season touchdowns (31), rushing touchdowns (28), most points scored in a single season (186).

Joe Torre, b 1940, former MLB player; managed L.A. Dodgers, NY Yankees, St. Louis Cardinals, Atlanta Braves, and NY Mets.

Lee Trevino, b 1939, golfer; won U.S., British Open twice.

Bryan Trottier, b 1956, (Can.) Islanders, Penguins center for 6 Stanley Cup champs.

Gene Tunney, 1897-1978, heavyweight champion, 1926-28.

Mike Tyson, b 1966, undisputed heavyweight champ, 1987-90; at 20, youngest to win a heavyweight title (WBC, 1986).

Wyomia Tyus, b 1945, Olympic 100m gold medalist, 1964, '68.

Johnny Unitas, 1933-2002, Baltimore Colts quarterback; passed for more than 40,000 yds., MVP, 1957, '67.

Al Unser, b 1939, Indy 500 winner 4 times.

Bobby Unser, b 1934, Indy 500 winner 3 times.

Brian Urlacher, b 1978, Chicago Bears linebacker; Defensive Rookie of the Year, 2000; 7-time Pro Bowler.

Norm Van Brocklin, 1926-83, quarterback; passed for game record 554 yds., 1951; MVP, 1960.

Amy Van Dyken, b 1973, swimmer; first American woman to win 4 gold medals in one Olympics (1996).

Justin Verlander, b 1983, pitcher; won AL MVP and Cy Young, 2011.

Michael Vick, b 1980, quarterback; suspended and convicted (2007) of illegal dog fighting, gambling activities.

Lasse Viren, b 1949, (Fin.) runner; Olympic 5,000m and 10,000m gold medalist in 1972, '76.

Lindsey Vonn, b 1984; 1st U.S. woman to win the world super-G championship, gold medal in downhill, 2010 Olympics; 4 World Cup titles 2008-10, '12.

Joey Votto, b 1983, (Can.) Cincinnati Reds 1st baseman; NL MVP, 2010.

Dwyane Wade, b 1982, guard; led Miami Heat to NBA title, 2006, '12-'13; finals MVP, 2006; NBA scoring title, 2009.

Honus Wagner, 1874-1955, Pittsburgh Pirates shortstop; 8 NL batting titles.

Grete Waitz, 1953-2011, (Nor.) 9-time winner of the New York City Marathon (1978-80, '82-'86, '88).

"Jersey" Joe Walcott, 1914-94, boxer; became heavyweight champion at age 37, 1951-52.

Kerri Walsh Jennings, b 1978, beach volleyball player; 3-time Olympic gold medalist with Misty May-Treanor (2004, '08, '12).

Bill Walton, b 1952, center; led Portland Trail Blazers to 1977 NBA title; MVP, 1978; NBA TV commentator.

Abby Wambach, b 1980, soccer; 2 gold medals in Olympics (2004, '12); all-time world-competition goal scorer (161).

Kurt Warner, b 1971, Rams, Giants, Cardinals quarterback; NFL MVP, 1999, 2001; Super Bowl MVP, 2000.

Tom Watson, b 1949, golfer; 6-time PGA Player of the Year; won 5 British Opens, 2 Masters, U.S. Open.

Karrie Webb, b 1974, (Austral.) golfer; youngest woman (26 yrs., 6 mos.) to win career Grand Slam, 1999-2001.

Johnny Weissmuller, 1903-84, swimmer; won 52 national championships, 5 Olympic gold medals; set 67 world records.

Jerry West, b 1938, L.A. Lakers guard; had career average 27 pts. per game; first team all-star 10 times.

Dan Wheldon, 1978-2011, (Br.) race-car driver; 2-time Indy 500 winner (2005, '11).

Byron "Whizzer" White, 1917-2002, running back; led NCAA in scoring and rushing at Colorado, 1937; led NFL in rushing twice, 1938, '40; Supreme Court justice, 1962-93.

Shaun White, b 1986, snowboarder/skateboarder, Olympic gold medalist in half-pipe (2006, '10).

Kathy Whitworth, b 1939, 7-time LPGA Player of the Year (1966-69, '71-'73); 88 tour wins, most on LPGA or PGA tour.

Michelle Wie, b 1989, golfer; in 2002 became youngest-ever qualifier for LPGA event; turned pro at age 15.

Bradley Wiggins, b 1980, (Br.) cyclist; Tour de France winner, 2012; 4-time Olympic gold medalist (2004, '08, '12).

Michael Wilbon, b 1958, commentator/analyst for ESPN and ABC.

Lenny Wilkens, b 1937, 2nd winningest coach in NBA history; Hall of Fame player and coach.

Serena Williams, b 1981, tennis champ; won at Wimbledon (2002-03, '09-'10, '12), U.S. Open (1999, 2002, '08, '12-'13); Australian Open (2003, '05, '07, '09-'10); French Open (2002, '13); Olympic gold medals in singles (2012) and doubles (2000, '08, '12) with sister Venus.

Ted Williams, 1918-2002, Boston Red Sox outfielder; won 6 batting titles, 2 triple crowns; hit .406 in 1941.

Venus Williams, b 1980, tennis champ at Wimbledon (2000-01, '05, '07-'08), U.S. Open (2000-01); Olympic gold medals in singles (2000) and doubles with sister Serena (2000, '08, '12).

Helen Wills Moody, 1905-98, tennis star; won U.S. Open 7 times, Wimbledon 8 times.

Katarina Witt, b 1965, (Ger.) figure skater; won Olympic gold medal, 1984, '88; world champ, 1984-85, '87-'88.

John Wooden, 1910-2010, UCLA basketball coach; 10 NCAA titles.

Tiger Woods, b 1975, golfer; youngest to win career Grand Slam, at age 24 (1997-2000); 14 career major titles.

Mickey Wright, b 1935, golfer; won LPGA and U.S. Open championship 4 times; 82 career wins, including 13 majors.

Eric Wynalda, b 1969, soccer; scored 1st goal in major league soccer history (1996).

Kristi Yamaguchi, b 1971, figure skater; won national, world, Olympic titles, in 1992.

Yao Ming, b 1980, (China) center for Houston Rockets; 8-time NBA All-Star.

Carl Yastrzemski, b 1939, Boston Red Sox slugger; won 3 batting titles; triple crown, 1967.

Cy Young, 1867-1955, pitcher; won record 511 games.

Steve Young, b 1961, 49ers quarterback; led NFL in passing, 1991-94, '96-'97; NFL MVP, 1992, '94; Super Bowl MVP, 1995.

Babe Didrikson Zaharias, 1911-56, all-around athlete; 3 track-and-field medals (2 golds), 1932 Olympics; won 10 golf majors; also played baseball; 6-time AP Female Athlete of the Year.

Emil Zátopek, 1922-2000, (Czech.) runner; won 3 gold medals at 1952 Olympics (5,000m, 10,000m, marathon).

Zinedine Zidane, b 1972, (Fr.) soccer midfielder; led France to 1998 World Cup title; named top player in 2006; 3-time FIFA world player of the year (1998, 2000, '03).

Writers of the Present

Name	Birthplace	Birthdate
Richard Adams	Newbury, England, UK	5/9/20
Edward Albee	Washington, DC	3/12/28
Mitch Albom	Passaic, NJ	5/23/58
Elizabeth Alexander	New York, NY	5/30/62
Isabel Allende	Lima, Peru	8/2/42
Dorothy Allison	Greenville, SC.	4/11/49
Martin Amis	Oxford, England, UK.	8/25/49
Maya Angelou	St. Louis, MO	4/4/28
Piers Anthony	Oxford, England, UK.	8/6/34
Jeffrey Archer	Somerset, England, UK	4/15/40
John Ashbery	Rochester, NY	7/28/27
Margaret Atwood	Ottawa, ON, Canada.	11/18/39
David Auburn	Chicago, IL	1969
Jean Auel	Chicago, IL	2/18/36
Paul Auster	Newark, NJ.	2/3/47
Alan Ayckbourn	Hampstead, England, UK.	4/12/39
Nicholson Baker	New York, NY	1/7/57
David Baldacci	Richmond, VA.	8/5/60
Russell Banks	Newton, MA	3/28/40
John Barth	Cambridge, MD	5/27/30
Ann Beattie	Washington, DC	9/8/47
Alan Bennett	Leeds, UK.	5/9/34
John Berendt	Syracuse, NY	12/5/39
Elizabeth Berg	St. Paul, MN	12/2/48
Thomas Berger	Cincinnati, OH	7/20/24
Judy Blume	Elizabeth, NJ	2/12/38
T. Coraghessan Boyle	Peekskill, NY.	12/2/48
Barbara Taylor Bradford	Leeds, England, UK	5/10/33
Christopher Bram	Buffalo, NY	2/22/52
Geraldine Brooks	Sydney, Australia	9/14/55
Dan Brown	Exeter, NH	6/22/64
Rita Mae Brown	Hanover, PA	11/28/44
Christopher Buckley	New York, NY	5/5/05
James Lee Burke	Houston, TX	12/5/36
Augusten Burroughs	Pittsburgh, PA	10/23/65
Robert Olen Butler	Granite City, IL	1/20/45
A. S. Byatt	Sheffield, England, UK	8/24/36
Ethan Canin	Ann Arbor, MI	7/19/60
Peter Carey	Bacchus-Marsh, Victoria, Australia	5/7/43
Robert A. Caro	New York, NY	10/30/35
Caleb Carr	New York, NY	8/2/55
Michael Chabon	Washington, DC	5/24/63
Tracy Chevalier	Washington, DC	10/19/62
Sandra Cisneros	Chicago, IL	12/20/54
Mary Higgins Clark	Bronx, NY	12/24/27
Beverly Cleary	McMinnville, OR	4/12/16
Harlan Coben	Newark, NJ.	1/4/62
Paulo Coelho	Rio de Janeiro, Brazil	8/24/47
J(ohn) M(axwell) Coetzee	Capetown, S. Africa	2/9/40
Billy Collins	New York, NY	3/22/41
Jackie Collins	London, England, UK	10/4/41
Suzanne Collins	Hartford, CT	8/10/62
Pat Conroy	Atlanta, GA	10/26/45
Robin Cook	New York, NY	5/4/40
Patricia Cornwell	Miami, FL	6/9/56
Michael Cunningham	Cincinnati, OH	11/6/52
Clive Cussler	Aurora, IL	7/15/31
Don DeLillo	Bronx, NY	11/20/36
Nelson DeMille	New York, NY	8/23/43
Junot Díaz	Santo Domingo, Dominican Republic	12/31/68
Joan Didion	Sacramento, CA	12/5/34
Annie Dillard	Pittsburgh, PA	4/30/45
E. L. Doctorow	Bronx, NY	1/6/31
Emma Donoghue	Dublin, Ireland.	10/24/69
Rita Dove	Akron, OH.	8/28/52
Roddy Doyle	Dublin, Ireland.	5/8/58
Carol Ann Duffy	Glasgow, Scotland, UK.	12/23/55
Umberto Eco	Alessandria, Italy	1/5/32
Jennifer Egan	Chicago, IL	9/7/62
Dave Eggers	Boston, MA.	3/12/70
Bret Easton Ellis	Los Angeles, CA.	3/7/64
James Ellroy	Los Angeles, CA.	3/4/48
Louise Erdrich	Little Falls, MN	6/7/54
Laura Esquivel	Mexico City, Mexico	9/30/50
Jeffrey Eugenides	Detroit, MI.	3/8/60
Janet Evanovich	South River, NJ.	4/22/43
Lawrence Ferlinghetti	Yonkers, NY	3/24/19
Helen Fielding	Morley, Yorkshire, England, UK	2/19/58
Fannie Flagg	Birmingham, AL	9/21/44
Gillian Flynn	Kansas City, MO.	2/24/71
Dario Fo	San Giano, Italy	3/26/26
Ken Follett	Cardiff, Wales, UK.	6/5/49
Richard Ford	Jackson, MS	2/16/44
Frederick Forsyth	Ashford, England, UK	8/25/38
Paula Fox	New York, NY	4/22/23
Jonathan Franzen	Western Springs, IL	8/17/59
Michael Frayn	London, England, UK	9/8/33
Charles Frazier	Asheville, NC	11/4/50
Brian Friel	Killyclogher, N. Ireland, UK	1/9/29
Ernest J. Gaines	Oscar, LA	1/15/33
Gabriel García Márquez	Aracataca, Colombia	3/6/27
Frank Gilroy	Bronx, NY	10/13/25
Malcolm Gladwell	Fareham, Hampshire, Eng., UK	9/3/63
Robert Goddard	Fareham, Hampshire, Eng., UK	11/13/54
Gail Godwin	Birmingham, AL	6/18/37
William Goldman	Highland Park, IL	8/12/31
Nadine Gordimer	Springs, S. Africa	11/20/23
Mary Gordon	Far Rockaway, NY.	12/8/49
Sue Grafton	Louisville, KY	4/24/40
Günter Grass	Danzig [now Gdansk], Poland	10/16/27
Shirley Ann Grau	New Orleans, LA	7/8/29
John Grisham	Jonesboro, AR	2/8/55
John Guare	New York, NY	2/5/38
Pete Hamill	Brooklyn, NY.	6/24/35
David Handler	Los Angeles, CA.	9/14/52
Paul Harding	Wenham, MA	12/19/67
David Hare	St. Leonards, Sussex, England, UK.	6/5/47
Jim Harrison	Grayling, MI	12/11/37
Robert Hass	San Francisco, CA	3/1/41
Mark Helprin	New York, NY	6/28/47
Carl Hiaasen	Plantation, FL	3/12/53
Laura Hillenbrand	Fairfax, VA.	5/15/67
S. E. Hinton	Tulsa, OK	7/22/48
Alice Hoffman	New York, NY	3/16/52
Alan Hollinghurst	Stroud, Gloucestershire, UK.	5/26/54
Khaled Hosseini	Kabul, Afghanistan	3/4/65
John Irving	Exeter, NH	3/2/42
Walter Isaacson	New Orleans, LA	5/20/52
Kazuo Ishiguro	Nagasaki, Japan.	11/8/54
John Jakes	Chicago, IL	3/31/32
E. L. James	London, England, UK.	1963
P. D. James	Oxford, England, UK.	8/3/20
Elfriede Jelinek	Müzzuschlag, Austria	10/20/46
Ha Jin	Liaoning, China.	2/21/56
Edward P. Jones	Washington, DC	10/5/50
Erica Jong	New York, NY	3/26/42
Sebastian Junger	Boston, MA.	1/17/62
Jan Karon	Lenoir, NC.	3/14/37
Garrison Keillor	Anoka, MN	8/7/42
Thomas Keneally	Sydney, Australia	10/7/35
William Kennedy	Albany, NY	1/16/28
Sue Monk Kidd	Sylvester, GA	8/12/48
Jamaica Kincaid	St. John's, Antigua	5/25/49
Stephen King	Portland, ME.	9/21/47
Barbara Kingsolver	Annapolis, MD	4/8/55
Maxine Hong Kingston	Stockton, CA.	10/27/40
Galway Kinnell	Providence, RI	2/1/27
Dean Koontz	Everett, PA	7/9/45
Ted Kooser	Ames, IA.	4/25/39
Jon Krakauer	Brookline, MA.	4/12/54
Judith Krantz	New York, NY	1/9/28
Maxine Kumin	Philadelphia, PA	6/6/25
Milan Kundera	Brno, Czechoslovakia.	4/1/29
Tony Kushner	New York, NY	7/16/56
Jhumpa Lahiri	London, England, UK	1967
Erik Larson	Brooklyn, NY.	1/3/54
John Le Carré	Poole, England, UK	10/19/31
Jean Marie Gustave Le Clézio	Nice, France.	4/13/40
Ursula K. Le Guin	Berkeley, CA.	10/21/29
David Leavitt	Pittsburgh, PA.	6/23/61
Harper Lee	Monroeville, AL.	4/28/26
Doris Lessing	Kermanshah, Persia	10/22/19
Jonathan Lethem	Brooklyn, NY.	2/19/64
David Lodge	South London, England, UK.	1/28/35
Alison Lurie	Chicago, IL	9/3/26
Gregory Maguire	Albany, NY	6/9/54
David Malouf	Brisbane, Queensland, Australia	3/20/34
Thomas Mallon	Glen Cove, NY.	11/2/51
David Mamet	Chicago, IL.	11/30/47
Hilary Mantel	Derbyshire, England, UK	7/6/52
Yann Martel	Salamanca, Spain	6/25/63
George R.R. Martin	Bayonne, NJ.	9/20/48
Bobbie Ann Mason	nr. Mayfield, KY.	5/1/40
Peter Matthiessen	New York, NY	5/22/27
Armistead Maupin	Washington, DC	4/13/44
Cormac McCarthy	Providence, RI	7/20/33
Colleen McCullough	Wellington, NSW, Australia.	6/1/37
David McCullough	Pittsburgh, PA	7/7/33
Alice McDermott	Brooklyn, NY.	6/27/53
Ian McEwan	Aldershot, England, UK	6/21/48
Thomas McGuane	Wyandotte, MI	12/11/39
Terry McMillan	Port Huron, MI	10/18/51
Larry McMurtry	Wichita Falls, TX.	6/3/36

Name	Birthplace	Birthdate
Terrence McNally	St. Petersburg, FL	11/3/39
John McPhee	Princeton, NJ	3/8/31
W(illiam) S(tanley) Merwin	New York, NY	9/30/27
Stephenie Meyer	Hartford, CT	12/24/73
Steven Millhauser	New York, NY	8/3/43
Toni Morrison	Lorain, OH	2/18/31
Walter Mosley	Los Angeles, CA	1/12/52
Andrew Motion	London, England, UK	10/26/52
Bharati Mukherjee	Calcutta, India	7/27/40
Herta Müller	Nitzkydorf, Banat, Romania	8/17/53
Alice Munro	Wingham, ON, Canada	7/10/31
Haruki Murakami	Kyoto, Japan	1/12/49
V. S. Naipaul	Chaguanas, Trinidad	8/17/32
Joyce Carol Oates	Lockport, NY	6/16/38
Edna O'Brien	Tuamgraney, Ireland	12/15/32
Tim O'Brien	Austin, MN	10/1/46
Kenzaburo Oe	Uchiko, Japan	1/31/35
Michael Ondaatje	Colombo, Sri Lanka	9/12/43
Cynthia Ozick	New York, NY	4/17/28
Orhan Pamuk	Istanbul, Turkey	6/7/52
Suzan-Lori Parks	Fort Knox, KY	5/10/63
Ann Patchett	Los Angeles, CA	12/2/63
James Patterson	Newburgh, NY	3/22/47
Jodi Picoult	New York, NY	5/19/66
Marge Piercy	Detroit, MI	3/31/36
Robert Pinsky	Long Branch, NJ	10/20/40
Michael Pollan	New York, NY	2/6/55
Richard Powers	Evanston, IL	6/18/57
Richard Price	Bronx, NY	10/12/49
E. Annie Proulx	Norwich, CT	8/22/35
Philip Pullman	Norwich, England, UK	10/19/46
Thomas Pynchon	Glen Cove, NY	5/8/37
David Rabe	Dubuque, IA	3/10/40
Ishmael Reed	Chattanooga, TN	2/22/38
Ruth Rendell	London, England, UK	2/17/30
Anne Rice	New Orleans, LA	10/4/41
Mary Roach	Etna, NH	3/20/59
Nora Roberts	Silver Spring, MD	10/10/50
Marilynne Robinson	Sandpoint, IL	11/26/43
Philip Roth	Newark, NJ	3/19/33

Name	Birthplace	Birthdate
J. K. Rowling	Chipping Sodbury, Eng., UK	7/31/65
Norman Rush	Oakland, CA	10/24/33
Salman Rushdie	Bombay, India	6/19/47
Richard Russo	Johnstown, NY	7/15/49
Alice Sebold	Madison, WI	9/6/63
David Sedaris	Johnson City, NY	12/26/56
Vikram Seth	Calcutta, India	6/20/52
John Patrick Shanley	New York, NY	10/13/50
Sam Shepard	Ft. Sheridan, IL	11/5/43
Anne Rivers Siddons	Atlanta, GA	1/9/36
Neil Simon	Bronx, NY	7/4/27
Jane Smiley	Los Angeles, CA	9/26/49
Wole Soyinka	Abeokuta, Nigeria	7/13/34
Nicholas Sparks	Omaha, NE	12/31/65
Danielle Steel	New York, NY	8/14/47
Mary Stewart	Sunderland, England, UK	9/17/16
R(obert) L(awrence) Stine	Columbus, OH	10/8/43
Kathryn Stockett	Jackson, MS	1969
Tom Stoppard	Zlin, Czechoslovakia	7/3/37
Mark Strand	Summerside, PE, Canada	4/11/34
Elizabeth Strout	Portland, ME	1/6/56
Amy Tan	Oakland, CA	2/19/52
Donna Tartt	Greenwood, MS	12/23/63
Paul Theroux	Medford, MA	4/10/41
Calvin Trillin	Kansas City, MO	12/5/35
Scott F. Turow	Chicago, IL	4/12/49
Anne Tyler	Minneapolis, MN	10/25/41
Mario Vargas Llosa	Arequipa, Peru	3/28/36
Paula Vogel	Washington, DC	11/16/51
Sarah Vowell	Muskogee, OK	12/27/69
Derek Walcott	Castries, Saint Lucia	1/23/30
Alice Walker	Eatonton, GA	2/9/44
Joseph Wambaugh	East Pittsburgh, PA	1/22/37
Edmund White	Cincinnati, OH	1/13/40
Elie Wiesel	Sighet, Romania	9/30/28
Tom Wolfe	Richmond, VA	3/2/31
Tobias Wolff	Birmingham, AL	6/19/45
Herman Wouk	New York, NY	5/27/15
Yevgeny Yevtushenko	Zima, Russia	7/18/33

Writers of the Past

See also Journalists, and Greeks and Romans in Historical Figures chapter.

Chinua Achebe, 1930-2013, (Nigeria) novelist. *Things Fall Apart.*

Alice Adams, 1926-99, (U.S.) novelist, short-story writer. *Superior Woman.*

James Agee, 1909-55, (U.S.) novelist. *A Death in the Family.*

S(hmuel) Y(osef) Agnon, 1888-1970, (Isr.) Hebrew novelist. *Only Yesterday.*

Conrad Aiken, 1889-1973, (U.S.) poet, critic. *Ushant.*

Anna Akhmatova, 1889-1966, (Russ.) poet. *Requiem.*

Louisa May Alcott, 1832-88, (U.S.) novelist. *Little Women.*

Sholom Aleichem, 1859-1916, (Russ.) Yiddish novelist. *Tevye's Daughters, The Old Country.*

Vicente Aleixandre, 1898-1984, (Sp.) poet. *La destrucción o el amor, Dialogolos del conocimiento.*

Horatio Alger, 1832-99, (U.S.) "rags-to-riches" books.

Jorge Amado, 1912-2001, (Brazil) novelist. *Dona Flor and Her Two Husbands, The Violent Land.*

Eric Ambler, 1909-98, (Br.) suspense novelist. *A Coffin for Dimitrios.*

Kingsley Amis, 1922-95, (Br.) novelist, critic. *Lucky Jim.*

Hans Christian Andersen, 1805-75, (Den.) author of fairy tales. *The Ugly Duckling.*

Maxwell Anderson, 1888-1959, (U.S.) playwright. *What Price Glory?, High Tor, Winterset, Key Largo.*

Sherwood Anderson, 1876-1941, (U.S.) short-story writer. "Death in the Woods," *Winesburg, Ohio.*

Reinaldo Arenas, 1943-90, (Cuba) short-story writer, novelist. *Before Night Falls.*

Ludovico Ariosto, 1474-1533, (It.) poet. *Orlando Furioso.*

Matthew Arnold, 1822-88, (Br.) poet, critic. "Thrysis," "Dover Beach," "Culture and Anarchy."

Isaac Asimov, 1920-92, (U.S.) versatile writer, espec. of science-fiction. *I Robot.*

Miguel Angel Asturias, 1899-1974, (Guatemala) novelist. *El Señor Presidente.*

Louis Auchincloss, 1917-2010, (U.S.) novelist, memoirist, short-story writer. *The Rector of Justin.*

W(ystan) H(ugh) Auden, 1907-73, (Br.) poet, playwright, literary critic. "The Age of Anxiety."

Jane Austen, 1775-1817, (Br.) novelist. *Pride and Prejudice, Sense and Sensibility, Emma, Mansfield Park.*

Isaac Babel, 1894-1941, (Russ.) short-story writer, playwright. *Odessa Tales, Red Cavalry.*

James Baldwin, 1924-87, (U.S.) author, playwright. *The Fire Next Time, Blues for Mister Charlie.*

Honoré de Balzac, 1799-1850, (Fr.) novelist. *Le Père Goriot, Cousine Bette, Eugénie Grandet.*

James M. Barrie, 1860-1937, (Br.) playwright, novelist. *Peter Pan, Dear Brutus, What Every Woman Knows.*

Charles Baudelaire, 1821-67, (Fr.) poet. *Les Fleurs du Mal.*

L(yman) Frank Baum, 1856-1919, (U.S.) *Wizard of Oz* series.

Simone de Beauvoir, 1908-86, (Fr.) novelist, essayist. *The Second Sex, Memoirs of a Dutiful Daughter.*

Samuel Beckett, 1906-89, (Ire.) novelist, playwright. *Waiting for Godot, Endgame* (plays); *Murphy, Watt, Molloy* (novels).

Brendan Behan, 1923-64, (Ire.) playwright. *The Quare Fellow, The Hostage, Borstal Boy.*

Saul Bellow, 1915-2005, (U.S.) novelist. *The Adventures of Augie March, Humboldt's Gift.*

Robert Benchley, 1889-1945, (U.S.) humorist.

Stephen Vincent Benét, 1898-1943, (U.S.) poet, novelist. *John Brown's Body.*

Jan Berenstain, 1923-2012, and **Stan Berenstain**, 1923-2005, (U.S.) co-writers and illustrators of *Berenstain Bears* series of children's books.

John Berryman, 1914-72, (U.S.) poet. *Homage to Mistress Bradstreet.*

Ambrose Bierce, 1842-1914, (U.S.) short-story writer, journalist. *In the Midst of Life, The Devil's Dictionary.*

Maeve Binchy, 1940-2012, (Ire.) novelist, short-story writer, *Circle of Friends, Tara Road.*

Elizabeth Bishop, 1911-79, (U.S.) poet. *North and South—A Cold Spring.*

William Blake, 1757-1827, (Br.) poet, artist. *Songs of Innocence, Songs of Experience.*

Aleksandr Blok, 1880-1921, (Russ.) poet. "The Twelve," "The Scythians."

Giovanni Boccaccio, 1313-75, (It.) poet. *Decameron.*

Heinrich Böll, 1917-85, (Ger.) novelist, short-story writer. *Group Portrait With Lady.*

Jorge Luis Borges, 1900-86, (Arg.) short-story writer, poet, essayist. *Labyrinths.*

James Boswell, 1740-95, (Scot.) biographer. *The Life of Samuel Johnson.*

Pierre Boulle, 1913-94, (Fr.) novelist. *The Bridge Over the River Kwai, Planet of the Apes.*

Paul Bowles, 1910-99, (U.S.) novelist, short-story writer. *The Sheltering Sky.*

Ray Bradbury, 1920-2012, (U.S.) novelist, short-story writer. *Fahrenheit 451, The Martian Chronicles.*

Anne Bradstreet, c. 1612-72, (U.S.) poet. *The Tenth Muse Lately Sprung Up in America.*

Bertolt Brecht, 1898-1956, (Ger.) dramatist, poet. *The Threepenny Opera, Mother Courage and Her Children*.

Joseph Brodsky, 1940-96, (Russ.-U.S.) poet. *A Part of Speech, Less Than One, To Urania*.

Charlotte Brontë, 1816-55, (Br.) novelist. *Jane Eyre*.

Emily Brontë, 1818-48, (Br.) novelist. *Wuthering Heights*.

Sterling A. Brown, 1901-89, (U.S.) poet, literature professor. *Southern Road*.

William Wells Brown, 1815-84, (U.S.) writer, memoirist; first African American to publish a novel, *Clotel*, 1853.

Elizabeth Barrett Browning, 1806-61, (Br.) poet. *Sonnets From the Portuguese, Aurora Leigh*.

Robert Browning, 1812-89, (Br.) poet. "My Last Duchess," "Fra Lippo Lippi," *The Ring and the Book*.

Pearl S. Buck, 1892-1973, (U.S.) novelist. *The Good Earth*.

Charles Bukowski, 1920-94, (U.S.) novelist, poet. *Ham on Rye, Women*.

Mikhail Bulgakov, 1891-1940, (Russ.) novelist, playwright. *The Heart of a Dog, The Master and Margarita*.

John Bunyan, 1628-88, (Br.) writer. *Pilgrim's Progress*.

Anthony Burgess, 1917-93, (Br.) author. *A Clockwork Orange*.

Frances Hodgson Burnett, 1849-1924, (Br.-U.S.) novelist. *The Secret Garden*.

Robert Burns, 1759-96, (Scot.) poet. "Flow Gently, Sweet Afton," "My Heart's in the Highlands," "Auld Lang Syne."

Edgar Rice Burroughs, 1875-1950, (U.S.) "Tarzan" books.

William S. Burroughs, 1914-97, (U.S.) novelist. *Naked Lunch*.

George Gordon, Lord Byron, 1788-1824, (Br.) poet. *Don Juan, Childe Harold, Manfred, Cain*.

Pedro Calderon de la Barca, 1600-81, (Sp.) playwright. *Life Is a Dream*.

Hortense Calisher, 1911-2009, (U.S.) novelist, short-story writer. *False Entry*.

Italo Calvino, 1923-85, (It.) novelist, short-story writer. *If on a Winter's Night a Traveler*.

Luis Vaz de Camoes, 1524?-80 (Port.) poet. *The Lusiads*.

Albert Camus, 1913-60, (Fr.) writer. *The Stranger, The Fall*.

Elias Canetti, 1905-94, (Bulg.) novelist, essayist. *Auto-Da-Fe*.

Karel Capek, 1890-1938, (Czech.) playwright, novelist, essayist. *R.U.R. (Rossum's Universal Robots)*.

Truman Capote, 1924-84, (U.S.) author. *Other Voices, Other Rooms; Breakfast at Tiffany's; In Cold Blood*.

Lewis Carroll (Charles Dodgson), 1832-98, (Br.) writer, mathematician. *Alice's Adventures in Wonderland*.

Barbara Cartland 1901-2000, (Br.) romance novelist.

Giacomo Casanova, 1725-98, (It.) adventurer, memoirist.

Willa Cather, 1873-1947, (U.S.) novelist. *O Pioneers!, My Ántonia, Death Comes for the Archbishop*.

Constantine Cavafy, 1863-1933, (Gr.) poet. "Ithaka," "Sensual Pleasures."

Camilo Jose Cela, 1916-2001, (Sp.) novelist. *The Family of Pascual Duarte, The Hive*.

Miguel de Cervantes Saavedra, 1547-1616, (Sp.) novelist, dramatist, poet. *Don Quixote*.

Raymond Chandler, 1888-1959, (U.S.) writer of detective fiction. Philip Marlowe series.

Geoffrey Chaucer, c. 1340-1400, (Br.) poet. *The Canterbury Tales, Troilus and Criseyde*.

John Cheever, 1912-82, (U.S.) novelist, short-story writer. *The Wapshot Scandal*, "The Country Husband."

Anton Chekhov, 1860-1904, (Russ.) short-story writer, dramatist. *Uncle Vanya, The Cherry Orchard, The Three Sisters*.

Charles Waddell Chesnutt, 1858-1932, (U.S.) author known for his short stories. *The Conjure Woman*.

G(ilbert) K(eith) Chesterton, 1874-1936, (Br.) critic, novelist, relig. apologist. Father Brown series of mysteries.

Kate Chopin, 1851-1904, (U.S.) writer. *The Awakening*.

Agatha Christie, 1890-1976, (Br.) mystery writer; created Miss Marple, Hercule Poirot. *And Then There Were None, Murder on the Orient Express, Murder of Roger Ackroyd*.

Tom Clancy, 1947-2013, novelist. *The Hunt for Red October*.

Arthur C. Clarke, 1917-2008, (Br.) science fiction writer. *2001: A Space Odyssey*.

James Clavell, 1924-94, (Br.-U.S.) novelist. *Shogun, King Rat*.

Jean Cocteau, 1889-1963, (Fr.) writer, visual artist, filmmaker. *The Beauty and the Beast, Les Enfants Terribles*.

Samuel Taylor Coleridge, 1772-1834, (Br.) poet, critic. "Kubla Khan," "The Rime of the Ancient Mariner."

(Sidonie) Colette, 1873-1954, (Fr.) novelist. *Claudine, Gigi*.

Wilkie Collins, 1824-89, (Br.) novelist. *The Moonstone*.

Evan S. Connell, 1924-2013, (Br.) novelist, short-story writer. *Mrs. Bridge*.

Joseph Conrad, 1857-1924, (Br.) novelist. *Lord Jim, Heart of Darkness, The Secret Agent*.

James Fenimore Cooper, 1789-1851, (U.S.) novelist. *Leatherstocking Tales, The Last of the Mohicans*.

Pierre Corneille, 1606-84, (Fr.) dramatist. *Medeé, Le Cid*.

Hart Crane, 1899-1932, (U.S.) poet. "The Bridge."

Stephen Crane, 1871-1900, (U.S.) novelist, short-story writer. *The Red Badge of Courage*, "The Open Boat."

Harry Crews, 1935-2012, (U.S.) novelist. *A Feast of Snakes*.

Michael Crichton, 1942-2008, (U.S.) writer. *The Andromeda Strain, Jurassic Park*.

Countee Cullen, 1903-46, (U.S.) poet, prominent in the Harlem Renaissance of the 1920s. *The Black Christ*.

E. E. Cummings, 1894-1962, (U.S.) poet. *Tulips and Chimneys*.

Roald Dahl, 1916-90, (Br.-U.S.) writer. *Charlie and the Chocolate Factory, James and the Giant Peach*.

Gabriele D'Annunzio, 1863-1938, (It.) poet, novelist, dramatist. *The Child of Pleasure, The Intruder, The Victim*.

Dante Alighieri, 1265-1321, (It.) poet. *The Divine Comedy*.

Robertson Davies, 1913-95, (Can.) novelist, playwright, essayist. Salterton, Deptford, and Cornish trilogies.

Daniel Defoe, 1660-1731, (Br.) writer. *Robinson Crusoe, Moll Flanders, Journal of the Plague Year*.

Philip K. Dick, 1928-82, (U.S.) science fiction writer. *Do Androids Dream of Electric Sheep?*

Charles Dickens, 1812-70, (Br.) novelist. *David Copperfield, Oliver Twist, Great Expectations, A Tale of Two Cities*.

James Dickey, 1923-97, (U.S.) poet, novelist. *Deliverance*.

Emily Dickinson, 1830-86, (U.S.) lyric poet. "Because I could not stop for Death . . .," "Success is counted sweetest . . ."

Isak Dinesen (Karen Blixen), 1885-1962, (Den.) author. *Out of Africa, Seven Gothic Tales, Winter's Tales*.

John Donne, 1573-1631, (Br.) poet. *Songs and Sonnets*.

José Donoso, 1924-96, (Chile) surreal novelist and short-story writer. *The Obscene Bird of Night*.

John Dos Passos, 1896-1970, (U.S.) novelist. *U.S.A.*

Fyodor Dostoyevsky, 1821-81, (Russ.) novelist. *Crime and Punishment, The Brothers Karamazov, The Possessed*.

Arthur Conan Doyle, 1859-1930, (Br.) novelist. Sherlock Holmes mystery stories.

Theodore Dreiser, 1871-1945, (U.S.) novelist. *An American Tragedy, Sister Carrie*.

John Dryden, 1631-1700, (Br.) poet, dramatist, critic. *All for Love, Mac Flecknoe, Absalom and Achitophel*.

Alexandre Dumas (père), 1802-70, (Fr.) novelist, dramatist. *The Three Musketeers, The Count of Monte Cristo*.

Alexandre Dumas (fils), 1824-95, (Fr.) dramatist, novelist. *La Dame aux Camélias, Le Demi-Monde*.

Paul Laurence Dunbar, 1872-1906, (U.S.) poet, novelist. *Lyrics of Lowly Life*.

Lawrence Durrell, 1912-90, (Br.) novelist, poet. *Alexandria Quartet*.

Ilya G. Ehrenburg, 1891-1967, (Russ.) writer. *The Thaw*.

George Eliot (Mary Ann or Marian Evans), 1819-80, (Br.) novelist. *Silas Marner, Middlemarch*.

T(homas) S(tearns) Eliot, 1888-1965, (Br.) poet, critic. *The Waste Land*, "The Love Song of J. Alfred Prufrock."

Stanley Elkin, 1930-95, (U.S.) novelist, short-story writer. *George Mills*.

Ralph Ellison, 1914-94, (U.S.) writer. *Invisible Man*.

Ralph Waldo Emerson, 1803-82, (U.S.) poet, essayist. "Brahma," "Nature," "The Over-Soul," "Self-Reliance."

James T. Farrell, 1904-79, (U.S.) novelist. *Studs Lonigan*.

Howard Fast, 1914-2003, (U.S.) novelist. *Spartacus, The Immigrants*.

William Faulkner, 1897-1962, (U.S.) novelist. *Sanctuary; Light in August; The Sound and the Fury; Absalom, Absalom!*

Edna Ferber, 1887-1968, (U.S.) novelist, short-story writer, playwright. *So Big, Cimarron, Show Boat*.

Henry Fielding, 1707-54, (Br.) novelist. *Tom Jones*.

F(rancis) Scott Fitzgerald, 1896-1940, (U.S.) short-story writer, novelist. *The Great Gatsby, Tender Is the Night*.

Gustave Flaubert, 1821-80, (Fr.) novelist. *Madame Bovary*.

Ian Fleming, 1908-64, (Br.) novelist; James Bond spy thrillers. *Dr. No, Goldfinger*.

Horton Foote, 1916-2009, (U.S.) playwright, screenwriter. *The Trip to Bountiful*.

Ford Madox Ford, 1873-1939, (Br.) novelist, critic, poet. *The Good Soldier*.

C(ecil) S(cott) Forester, 1899-1966, (Br.) writer. Horatio Hornblower books.

E(dward) M(organ) Forster, 1879-1970, (Br.) novelist. *A Passage to India, Howards End*.

Anatole France, 1844-1924, (Fr.) writer. *Penguin Island, My Friend's Book, The Crime of Sylvestre Bonnard*.

Dick Francis, 1920-2010, (Br.) crime novelist.

Marilyn French, 1929-2009, (U.S.) novelist. *The Women's Room*.

Robert Frost, 1874-1963, (U.S.) poet. "Birches," "Fire and Ice," "Stopping by Woods on a Snowy Evening."

Carlos Fuentes, 1928-2012, (Pan.) novelist, essayist. *The Old Gringo*.

William Gaddis, 1922-98, (U.S.) novelist. *The Recognitions*.

John Galsworthy, 1867-1933, (Br.) novelist, dramatist. *The Forsyte Saga*.

Federico García Lorca, 1898-1936, (Sp.) poet, dramatist. *Blood Wedding*.

Erle Stanley Gardner, 1889-1970, (U.S.) mystery writer; created Perry Mason.

Jean Genet, 1911-86, (Fr.) playwright, novelist. *The Maids*.

Kahlil Gibran, 1883-1931, (Leban.-U.S.) mystical novelist, essayist, poet. *The Prophet*.

André Gide, 1869-1951, (Fr.) writer. *The Immoralist*, *The Pastoral Symphony*, *Strait Is the Gate*.

Allen Ginsberg, 1926-97, (U.S.) Beat poet. "Howl."

Jean Giraudoux, 1882-1944, (Fr.) novelist, dramatist. *Electra*, *The Madwoman of Chaillot*, *Ondine*, *Tiger at the Gate*.

Johann Wolfgang von Goethe, 1749-1832, (Ger.) poet, dramatist, novelist. *Faust*, *Sorrows of Young Werther*.

Nikolai Gogol, 1809-52, (Russ.) short-story writer, dramatist, novelist. *Dead Souls*, *The Inspector General*.

William Golding, 1911-93, (Br.) novelist. *Lord of the Flies*.

Oliver Goldsmith, 1728-74, (Br.-Ire.) dramatist, novelist. *The Vicar of Wakefield*, *She Stoops to Conquer*.

Maxim Gorky, 1868-1936, (Russ.) dramatist, novelist. *The Lower Depths*.

Robert Graves, 1895-1985, (Br.) poet, classical scholar, novelist. *I, Claudius*; *The White Goddess*.

Thomas Gray, 1716-71, (Br.) poet. "Elegy Written in a Country Churchyard," "The Progress of Poesy."

Julien Green, 1900-98, (U.S.-Fr.) expatriate American, French novelist. *Moira*, *Each Man in His Darkness*.

Graham Greene, 1904-91, (Br.) novelist. *The Power and the Glory*, *The Heart of the Matter*, *The Ministry of Fear*.

Zane Grey, 1872-1939, (U.S.) writer of Western stories.

Jakob Grimm, 1785-1863, (Ger.) philologist, folklorist; with brother **Wilhelm Grimm**, 1786-1859, collected *Grimm's Fairy Tales*.

Alex Haley, 1921-92, (U.S.) author. *Roots*.

Dashiell Hammett, 1894-1961, (U.S.) detective-story writer; created Sam Spade. *The Maltese Falcon*.

Jupiter Hammon, c. 1720-1800, (U.S.) poet; first African American to have his works published, 1761.

Knut Hamsun, 1859-1952, (Nor.) novelist. *Hunger*.

Lorraine Hansberry, 1930-65, (U.S.) playwright. *A Raisin in the Sun*.

Thomas Hardy, 1840-1928, (Br.) novelist, poet. *The Return of the Native*, *Tess of the D'Urbervilles*, *Jude the Obscure*.

E. Lynn Harris, 1955-2009, (U.S.) novelist. *Invisible Life*, *Basketball Jones*.

Joel Chandler Harris, 1848-1908, (U.S.) writer. Uncle Remus stories.

Moss Hart, 1904-61, (U.S.) playwright. *Once in a Lifetime*, *You Can't Take It With You*, *The Man Who Came to Dinner*.

Bret Harte, 1836-1902, (U.S.) short-story writer, poet. *The Luck of Roaring Camp*.

Jaroslav Hasek, 1883-1923, (Czech.) writer, playwright. *The Good Soldier Schweik*.

Vaclav Havel, 1936-2011, (Czech.) essayist, poet, playwright. *The Power of the Powerless*.

John Hawkes, 1925-98, (U.S.) experimental fiction writer. *The Goose on the Grave*, *Blood Oranges*.

Nathaniel Hawthorne, 1804-64, (U.S.) novelist, short-story writer. *The Scarlet Letter*, "Young Goodman Brown."

Seamus Heaney, 1939-2013, (Ire.) poet. *Death of a Naturalist*.

Heinrich Heine, 1797-1856, (Ger.) poet. *Book of Songs*.

Robert Heinlein, 1907-88, (U.S.) science-fiction writer. *Stranger in a Strange Land*.

Joseph Heller, 1923-99, (U.S.) novelist. *Catch-22*.

Lillian Hellman, 1905-84, (U.S.) playwright, memoirist. *The Little Foxes*, *An Unfinished Woman*, *Pentimento*.

Ernest Hemingway, 1899-1961, (U.S.) novelist, short-story writer. *A Farewell to Arms*, *For Whom the Bell Tolls*.

O. Henry (W. S. Porter), 1862-1910, (U.S.) short-story writer. "The Gift of the Magi."

George Herbert, 1593-1633, (Br.) poet. "The Altar," "Easter Wings."

Zbigniew Herbert, 1924-98, (Pol.) poet. "Apollo and Marsyas."

Robert Herrick, 1591-1674, (Br.) poet. "To the Virgins to Make Much of Time."

John Hersey, 1914-93, (U.S.) novelist, journalist. *Hiroshima*, *A Bell for Adano*.

Hermann Hesse, 1877-1962, (Ger.) novelist, poet. *Death and the Lover*, *Steppenwolf*, *Siddhartha*.

Oscar Hijuelos, 1951-2013, (U.S.) novelist. *The Mambo Kings Play Songs of Love*.

Tony Hillerman, 1925-2008, (U.S.) novelist. *Dance Hall of the Dead*.

James Hilton, 1900-54, (Br.) novelist. *Lost Horizon*.

Chester Himes, 1909-84, (U.S.) novelist. *Cotton Comes to Harlem*.

Oliver Wendell Holmes, 1809-94, (U.S.) poet, novelist. *The Autocrat of the Breakfast-Table*.

Gerard Manley Hopkins, 1844-89, (Br.) poet. "Pied Beauty," "God's Grandeur."

A(lfred) E. Housman, 1859-1936, (Br.) poet. *A Shropshire Lad*.

William Dean Howells, 1837-1920, (U.S.) novelist, critic. *The Rise of Silas Lapham*.

Langston Hughes, 1902-67, (U.S.) poet, lyric writer, author; a major influence in 1920s Harlem Renaissance.

Ted Hughes, 1930-98, (Br.) British poet laureate, 1984-98. *Crow*, *The Hawk in the Rain*.

Victor Hugo, 1802-85, (Fr.) poet, dramatist, novelist. *Notre Dame de Paris*, *Les Misérables*.

Zora Neale Hurston, 1903-60, (U.S.) novelist, folklorist. *Their Eyes Were Watching God*, *Mules and Men*.

Aldous Huxley, 1894-1963, (Br.) writer. *Brave New World*.

Henrik Ibsen, 1828-1906, (Nor.) dramatist, poet. *A Doll's House*, *Ghosts*, *The Wild Duck*, *Hedda Gabler*.

William Inge, 1913-73, (U.S.) playwright. *Picnic*; *Come Back, Little Sheba*; *Bus Stop*.

Eugene Ionesco, 1910-94, (Fr.) surrealist dramatist. *The Bald Soprano*, *The Chairs*.

Washington Irving, 1783-1859, (U.S.) writer. "Rip Van Winkle," "The Legend of Sleepy Hollow."

Christopher Isherwood, 1904-86, (Br.) novelist, playwright. *The Berlin Stories*.

Shirley Jackson, 1919-65, (U.S.) short-story writer. "The Lottery."

Henry James, 1843-1916, (U.S.) novelist, short-story writer, critic. *The Portrait of a Lady*, *The Ambassadors*, *Daisy Miller*.

Robinson Jeffers, 1887-1962, (U.S.) poet, dramatist. *Tamar and Other Poems*, *Medea*.

James Weldon Johnson, 1871-1938, (U.S.) poet, novelist, diplomat; lyricist for *Lift Every Voice and Sing*.

Samuel Johnson, 1709-84, (Br.) author, scholar, critic. *Dictionary of the English Language*, *Vanity of Human Wishes*.

Ben Jonson, 1572-1637, (Br.) dramatist, poet. *Volpone*.

James Joyce, 1882-1941, (Ire.) writer. *Ulysses*, *Dubliners*, *A Portrait of the Artist as a Young Man*, *Finnegans Wake*.

Ernst Junger, 1895-1998, (Ger.) novelist, essayist. *The Peace*, *On the Marble Cliff*.

Franz Kafka, 1883-1924, (Austria-Hung./Czech.) novelist, short-story writer. *The Trial*, *The Castle*, "The Metamorphosis."

George S. Kaufman, 1889-1961, (U.S.) playwright. *The Man Who Came to Dinner*, *You Can't Take It With You*.

Yasunari Kawabata, 1899-1972, (Jpn.) novelist. *The Sound of the Mountains*.

Nikos Kazantzakis, 1883-1957, (Gr.) novelist. *Zorba the Greek*, *A Greek Passion*.

Alfred Kazin, 1915-98 (U.S.) author, critic, teacher. *On Native Grounds*.

John Keats, 1795-1821, (Br.) poet. "Ode on a Grecian Urn," "Ode to a Nightingale," "La Belle Dame Sans Merci."

Jack Kerouac, 1922-69, (U.S.) author, Beat poet. *On the Road*, *The Dharma Bums*, "Mexico City Blues."

Joyce Kilmer, 1886-1918, (U.S.) poet. "Trees."

Rudyard Kipling, 1865-1936, (Br.) author, poet. "The White Man's Burden," "Gunga Din," *The Jungle Book*.

Jean de la Fontaine, 1621-95, (Fr.) poet. *Fables choisies*.

Pär Lagerkvist, 1891-1974, (Swed.) poet, dramatist, novelist. *Barabbas*, *The Sybil*.

Selma Lagerlöf, 1858-1940, (Swed.) novelist. *Jerusalem*, *The Ring of the Lowen-skolds*.

Alphonse de Lamartine, 1790-1869, (Fr.) poet, novelist, statesman. *Méditations poétiques*.

Charles Lamb, 1775-1834, (Br.) essayist. *Specimens of English Dramatic Poets*, *Essays of Elia*.

Louis L'Amour, 1908-88, (U.S.) Western author, screenwriter. *Hondo*, *The Cherokee Trail*.

Giuseppe di Lampedusa, 1896-1957, (It.) novelist. *The Leopard*.

William Langland, c. 1332-1400, (Br.) poet. *Piers Plowman*.

Ring Lardner, 1885-1933, (U.S.) short-story writer, humorist.

Stieg Larsson, 1954-2004, (Swed.) novelist. *The Girl With the Dragon Tattoo*.

Arthur Laurents, 1917-2011, (U.S.) playwright and director. *West Side Story*.

D(avid) H(erbert) Lawrence, 1885-1930, (Br.) novelist. *Sons and Lovers*, *Women in Love*, *Lady Chatterley's Lover*.

Halldór Laxness, 1902-98, (Iceland) novelist. *Iceland's Bell*.

Madeleine L'Engle, 1918-2007, (U.S.) novelist of young adult fiction. *A Wrinkle in Time*.

Elmore Leonard, 1925-2013, (U.S.) novelist. *Get Shorty*.

Mikhail Lermontov, 1814-41, (Russ.) novelist, poet. "Demon," *Hero of Our Time*.

Alain-René Lesage, 1668-1747, (Fr.) novelist. *Gil Blas de Santillane*.

Gotthold Lessing, 1729-81, (Ger.) dramatist, philosopher, critic. *Miss Sara Sampson*, *Minna von Barnhelm*.

Ira Levin, 1929-2007, (U.S.) novelist, playwright. *Deathtrap*.

C(live) S(taples) Lewis, 1898-1963, (Br.) critic, novelist, religious writer. *Allegory of Love*; *The Lion, the Witch and the Wardrobe*; *Out of the Silent Planet*.

Sinclair Lewis, 1885-1951, (U.S.) novelist. *Babbitt*, *Main Street*, *Arrowsmith*, *Dodsworth*.

Li Po, 701-762, (China) poet. "Song Before Drinking," "She Spins Silk."

Vachel Lindsay, 1879-1931, (U.S.) poet. *General William Booth Enters Into Heaven*, *The Congo*.

Hugh Lofting, 1886-1947, (Br.) writer. Dr. Doolittle series.

Jack London, 1876-1916, (U.S.) novelist, journalist. *Call of the Wild*, *The Sea-Wolf*, *White Fang*.

Henry Wadsworth Longfellow, 1807-82, (U.S.) poet. *Evangeline*, *The Song of Hiawatha*.

Lope de Vega, 1562-1635, (Sp.) playwright. *Noche de San Juan*, *Maestro de Danzar*.

H(oward) P(hillips) Lovecraft, 1890-1937, (U.S.) novelist, short-story writer. "At the Mountains of Madness."

Amy Lowell, 1874-1925, (U.S.) poet, critic. "Lilacs."

James Russell Lowell, 1819-91, (U.S.) poet, editor. *Poems*, *The Biglow Papers*.

Robert Lowell, 1917-77, (U.S.) poet. "Lord Weary's Castle."

Joaquim Maria Machado de Assis, 1839-1908, (Brazil) novelist, poet. *The Posthumous Memoirs of Bras Cubas.*

Archibald MacLeish, 1892-1982, (U.S.) poet. *Conquistador.*

Naguib Mahfouz, 1911-2006, (Egypt) novelist; first Arabic-language writer to win the Nobel Prize for Literature. *Cairo Trilogy.*

Norman Mailer, 1923-2007, (U.S.) novelist, essayist, journalist. *The Naked and the Dead.*

Bernard Malamud, 1914-86, (U.S.) short-story writer, novelist. "The Magic Barrel," *The Assistant, The Fixer.*

Stéphane Mallarmé, 1842-98, (Fr.) poet. *Poésies.*

Sir Thomas Malory, c. 1410-71, (Br.) writer. *Morte d'Arthur.*

Andre Malraux, 1901-76, (Fr.) novelist. *Man's Fate.*

Osip Mandelstam, 1891-1938, (Russ.) poet. *Stone, Tristia.*

Thomas Mann, 1875-1955, (Ger.) novelist, essayist. *Buddenbrooks, The Magic Mountain*, "Death in Venice."

Katherine Mansfield, 1888-1923, (Br.) short-story writer. "Bliss."

Christopher Marlowe, 1564-93, (Br.) dramatist, poet. *Tamburlaine the Great, Dr. Faustus, The Jew of Malta.*

Andrew Marvell, 1621-78, (Br.) poet. "To His Coy Mistress."

John Masefield, 1878-1967, (Br.) poet. "Sea Fever," "Cargoes," *Salt Water Ballads.*

Edgar Lee Masters, 1869-1950, (U.S.) poet, biographer. *Spoon River Anthology.*

W(illiam) Somerset Maugham, 1874-1965, (Br.) author. *Of Human Bondage, The Moon and Sixpence.*

Guy de Maupassant, 1850-93, (Fr.) novelist, short-story writer. "A Life," "Bel-Ami," "The Necklace."

François Mauriac, 1885-1970, (Fr.) novelist, dramatist. *Viper's Tangle, The Kiss to the Leper.*

Vladimir Mayakovsky, 1893-1930, (Russ.) poet, dramatist. *The Cloud in Trousers.*

Mary McCarthy, 1912-89, (U.S.) critic, novelist, memoirist. *Memories of a Catholic Girlhood.*

Frank McCourt, 1930-2009, (U.S.) memoirist. *Angela's Ashes, 'Tis, Teacher Man.*

Carson McCullers, 1917-67, (U.S.) novelist. *The Heart Is a Lonely Hunter, Member of the Wedding.*

Herman Melville, 1819-91, (U.S.) novelist, poet. *Moby-Dick, Typee, Billy Budd, Omoo.*

George Meredith, 1828-1909, (Br.) novelist, poet. *The Ordeal of Richard Feverel, The Egoist.*

Prosper Mérimée, 1803-70, (Fr.) author. *Carmen.*

James Merrill, 1926-95, (U.S.) poet. *Divine Comedies.*

James Michener, 1907-97, (U.S.) novelist. *Tales of the South Pacific.*

Edna St. Vincent Millay, 1892-1950, (U.S.) poet. *The Harp Weaver and Other Poems.*

Arthur Miller,1915-2005, (U.S.) playwright. *The Crucible, After the Fall, Death of a Salesman.*

Henry Miller, 1891-1980, (U.S.) erotic novelist. *Tropic of Cancer.*

A(lan) A(lexander) Milne, 1882-1956, (Br.) author. *Winnie-the-Pooh.*

Czesław Milosz, 1911-2004, (Pol.) essayist, poet. "Esse," "Encounter."

John Milton, 1608-74, (Br.) poet, writer. *Paradise Lost, Comus, Lycidas, Areopagitica.*

Mishima Yukio (Hiraoka Kimitake) 1925-70, (Jpn.) writer. *Confessions of a Mask.*

Gabriela Mistral, 1889-1957, (Chile) poet. *Sonnets of Death.*

Margaret Mitchell, 1900-49, (U.S.) novelist. *Gone With the Wind.*

Jean Baptiste Molière, 1622-73, (Fr.) dramatist. *Tartuffe, Le Misanthrope, Le Bourgeois Gentilhomme.*

Ferenc Molnár, 1878-1952, (Hung.) dramatist, novelist. *Liliom, The Guardsman, The Swan.*

Michel de Montaigne, 1533-92, (Fr.) essayist. *Essais.*

Eugenio Montale, 1896-1981, (It.) poet.

Brian Moore, 1921-99, (Ire.-U.S.) novelist. *The Lonely Passion of Judith Hearne.*

Clement C. Moore, 1779-1863, (U.S.) poet, educator. "A Visit From Saint Nicholas."

Marianne Moore, 1887-1972, (U.S.) poet.

Alberto Moravia, 1907-90, (It.) novelist, short-story writer. *The Time of Indifference.*

Sir Thomas More, 1478-1535, (Br.) writer, statesman, saint. *Utopia.*

Wright Morris, 1910-98, (U.S.) novelist. *My Uncle Dudley.*

Murasaki Shikibu, c. 978-1026, (Jpn.) novelist. *The Tale of Genji.*

Iris Murdoch, 1919-99, (Br.) novelist, philosopher. *The Sea, The Sea.*

Alfred de Musset, 1810-57, (Fr.) poet, dramatist. *La Confession d'un Enfant du Siècle.*

Vladimir Nabokov, 1899-1977, (Russ.-U.S.) novelist. *Lolita, Pale Fire.*

R. K. Narayan, 1906-2001, (India) novelist. *The Guide.*

Ogden Nash, 1902-71, (U.S.) poet of light verse.

Irène Némirovsky, 1903-42, (Ukraine) novelist. *David Golder, Suite Française.*

Pablo Neruda, 1904-73, (Chile) poet. *Twenty Love Poems and One Song of Despair, Toward the Splendid City.*

Patrick O'Brian, 1914-2000, (Br.) historical novelist. *Master and Commander, Blue at the Mizzen.*

Sean O'Casey, 1884-1964, (Ire.) dramatist. *Juno and the Paycock, The Plough and the Stars.*

Flannery O'Connor, 1925-64, (U.S.) novelist, short-story writer. *Wise Blood*, "A Good Man Is Hard to Find."

Frank O'Connor (Michael Donovan), 1903-66, (Ire.) short-story writer. "Guests of a Nation."

Clifford Odets, 1906-63, (U.S.) playwright. *Waiting for Lefty, Awake and Sing, Golden Boy, The Country Girl.*

John O'Hara, 1905-70, (U.S.) novelist, short-story writer. *From the Terrace, Appointment in Samarra, Pal Joey.*

Omar Khayyam, c. 1028-1122, (Per.) poet. *Rubaiyat.*

Eugene O'Neill, 1888-1953, (U.S.) playwright. *Emperor Jones, Anna Christie, Long Day's Journey Into Night.*

George Orwell (Eric Arthur Blair), 1903-50, (Br.) novelist, essayist. *Animal Farm, Nineteen Eighty-Four.*

John Osborne, 1929-95, (Br.) dramatist, novelist. *Look Back in Anger, The Entertainer.*

Wilfred Owen, 1893-1918, (Br.) poet. "Dulce et Décorum Est."

Grace Paley, 1922-2007, (U.S.) short-story writer, poet. *The Little Disturbances of Man.*

Dorothy Parker, 1893-1967, (U.S.) poet, short-story writer. *Enough Rope, Laments for the Living.*

Robert B. Parker, 1932-2010, (U.S.) crime novelist. "Spenser" novels.

Boris Pasternak, 1890-1960, (Russ.) poet, novelist. *Doctor Zhivago.*

Alan Paton, 1903-88, (S. Africa) novelist. *Cry, the Beloved Country.*

Octavio Paz, 1914-98, (Mex.) poet, essayist. *The Labyrinth of Solitude, They Shall Not Pass!, The Sun Stone.*

Samuel Pepys, 1633-1703, (Br.) public official, diarist.

S(idney) J(oseph) Perelman, 1904-79, (U.S.) humorist. *The Road to Miltown, Under the Spreading Atrophy.*

Charles Perrault, 1628-1703, (Fr.) writer. *Tales From Mother Goose (Sleeping Beauty, Cinderella).*

Petrarch (Francesco Petrarca), 1304-74, (It.) poet. *Africa, Trionfi, Canzoniere.*

Harold Pinter, 1930-2008, (Br.) playwright. *The Birthday Party, The Caretaker, The Homecoming.*

Luigi Pirandello, 1867-1936, (It.) novelist, dramatist. *Six Characters in Search of an Author.*

Sylvia Plath, 1932-63, (U.S.) author, poet. *The Bell Jar.*

Edgar Allan Poe, 1809-49, (U.S.) poet, short-story writer, critic. "Annabel Lee," "The Raven," "The Purloined Letter."

Alexander Pope, 1688-1744, (Br.) poet. *The Rape of the Lock, The Dunciad, An Essay on Man.*

Katherine Anne Porter, 1890-1980, (U.S.) novelist, short-story writer. *Ship of Fools.*

Chaim Potok, 1929-2002, (U.S.) novelist. *The Chosen.*

Ezra Pound, 1885-1972, (U.S.) poet. *Cantos.*

Anthony Powell, 1905-2000, (Br.) novelist. *A Dance to the Music of Time* series.

Reynolds Price, 1933-2011, (U.S.) novelist, short-story writer, poet. *A Long and Happy Life.*

J(ohn) B(oynton) Priestley, 1894-1984, (Br.) novelist, dramatist. *The Good Companions.*

Marcel Proust, 1871-1922, (Fr.) novelist. *Remembrance of Things Past.*

Aleksandr Pushkin, 1799-1837, (Russ.) poet, novelist. *Boris Godunov, Eugene Onegin.*

Mario Puzo, 1920-99, (U.S.) novelist. *The Godfather.*

François Rabelais, 1495-1553, (Fr.) writer. *Gargantua.*

Jean Racine, 1639-99, (Fr.) dramatist. *Andromaque, Phèdre, Bérénice, Britannicus.*

David Rakoff, 1964-2012, (Can.-U.S.) essayist. *Fraud, Don't Get Too Comfortable.*

Ayn Rand, 1905-82, (Russ.-U.S.) novelist, moral theorist. *The Fountainhead, Atlas Shrugged.*

Terence Rattigan, 1911-77, (Br.) playwright. *Separate Tables, The Browning Version.*

Erich Maria Remarque, 1898-1970, (Ger.-U.S.) novelist. *All Quiet on the Western Front.*

Mary Renault, 1905-83, (Br.) novelist. *The Last of the Wine.*

Adrienne Rich, 1929-2012, (U.S.) poet. *Diving Into the Wreck: Poems, 1971-1972.*

Samuel Richardson, 1689-1761, (Br.) novelist. *Pamela; or Virtue Rewarded.*

Rainer Maria Rilke, 1875-1926, (Ger.) poet. *Life and Songs, Duino Elegies, Poems From the Book of Hours.*

Arthur Rimbaud, 1854-91, (Fr.) poet. *A Season in Hell.*

Harold Robbins, 1916-97, (U.S.) novelist. *The Carpetbaggers.*

Edwin Arlington Robinson, 1869-1935, (U.S.) poet. "Richard Cory," "Miniver Cheevy," *Merlin.*

Theodore Roethke, 1908-63, (U.S.) poet. *Open House, The Waking, The Far Field.*

Romain Rolland, 1866-1944, (Fr.) novelist, biographer. *Jean-Christophe.*

Pierre de Ronsard, 1524-85, (Fr.) poet. *Sonnets pour Hélène, La Franciade.*

Christina Rossetti, 1830-94, (Br.) poet. "When I Am Dead, My Dearest."

Dante Gabriel Rossetti, 1828-82, (Br.) poet, painter. "The Blessed Damozel."

Edmond Rostand, 1868-1918, (Fr.) poet, dramatist. *Cyrano de Bergerac.*

Damon Runyon, 1880-1946, (U.S.) short-story writer, journalist. *Guys and Dolls, Blue Plate Special.*

John Ruskin, 1819-1900, (Br.) critic, social theorist. *Modern Painters, The Seven Lamps of Architecture.*

François Sagan (Françoise Quoirez), 1935-2004, (Fr.) novelist. *Bonjour Tristesse.*

Antoine de Saint-Exupéry, 1900-44, (Fr.) writer. *Wind, Sand and Stars; The Little Prince.*

Saki (or H[ector] H[ugh] Munro), 1870-1916, (Br.) writer. *The Chronicles of Clovis.*

J. D. Salinger, 1919-2010, (U.S.) novelist. *The Catcher in the Rye.*

George Sand (Amandine Lucie Aurore Dupin), 1804-76, (Fr.) novelist. *Indiana, Consuelo.*

Carl Sandburg, 1878-1967, (U.S.) poet. *The People, Yes; Chicago Poems; Smoke and Steel; Harvest Poems.*

Jose Saramago, 1922-2010, (Port.) novelist. *Blindness.*

William Saroyan, 1908-81, (U.S.) playwright, novelist. *The Time of Your Life, The Human Comedy.*

Nathalie Sarraute, 1900-99, (Fr.) Nouveau Roman novelist. *Tropismes.*

May Sarton, 1914-95, (Belg.-U.S.) poet, novelist. *Encounter in April, Anger.*

Dorothy L. Sayers, 1893-1957, (Br.) mystery writer; created Lord Peter Wimsey.

Richard Scarry, 1920-94, (U.S.) author of children's books. *Richard Scarry's Best Story Book Ever.*

Friedrich von Schiller, 1759-1805, (Ger.) dramatist, poet, historian. *Don Carlos, Maria Stuart, Wilhelm Tell.*

Sir Walter Scott, 1771-1832, (Scot.) novelist, poet. *Ivanhoe.*

Gil Scott-Heron, 1949-2011, (U.S.) poet. "The Revolution Will Not Be Televised."

Jaroslav Seifert, 1902-86, (Czech.) poet.

Maurice Sendak, 1928-2012, (U.S.) children's book author and illustrator. *Where the Wild Things Are.*

Dr. Seuss (Theodor Seuss Geisel), 1904-91, (U.S.) children's book author and illustrator. *The Cat in the Hat.*

William Shakespeare, 1564-1616, (Br.) dramatist, poet. *Romeo and Juliet, Hamlet, King Lear, Julius Caesar,* sonnets.

Karl Shapiro, 1913-2000, (U.S.) poet. "Elegy for a Dead Soldier."

George Bernard Shaw, 1856-1950, (Ire.-Br.) playwright, critic. *St. Joan, Pygmalion, Major Barbara, Man and Superman.*

Sidney Sheldon, 1917-2007, (U.S.) screenwriter, novelist. *Rage of Angels, Memories of Midnight.*

Mary Wollstonecraft Shelley, 1797-1851, (Br.) novelist, feminist. *Frankenstein, The Last Man.*

Percy Bysshe Shelley, 1792-1822, (Br.) poet. *Prometheus Unbound, Adonais,* "Ode to the West Wind," "To a Skylark."

Richard B. Sheridan, 1751-1816, (Br.) dramatist. *The Rivals, School for Scandal.*

Robert Sherwood, 1896-1955, (U.S.) playwright, biographer. *The Petrified Forest, Abe Lincoln in Illinois.*

Mikhail Sholokhov, 1906-84, (Russ.) writer. *The Silent Don.*

Shel Silverstein, 1932-99, (U.S.) poet, writer. *The Giving Tree, Where the Sidewalk Ends.*

Georges Simenon (Georges Sims), 1903-89, (Belg.-Fr.) mystery writer; created Inspector Maigret.

Upton Sinclair, 1878-1968, (U.S.) novelist. *The Jungle.*

Isaac Bashevis Singer, 1904-91, (Pol.-U.S.) novelist, short-story writer, in Yiddish. *The Magician of Lublin.*

C(harles) P(ercy) Snow, 1905-80, (Br.) novelist, scientist. *Strangers and Brothers, Corridors of Power.*

Aleksandr Solzhenitsyn, 1918-2008, (Russ.) novelist, dramatist. *One Day in the Life of Ivan Denisovich.*

Susan Sontag, 1933-2004, (U.S.) critic, essayist, novelist. *Notes on Camp, The Volcano Lover, In America.*

Stephen Spender, 1909-95, (Br.) poet, critic, novelist. *Twenty Poems,* "Elegy for Margaret."

Edmund Spenser, 1552-99, (Br.) poet. *The Faerie Queen.*

Mickey Spillane, 1918-2006, (U.S.) novelist; series of novels with the character detective Mike Hammer. *The Killing Man.*

Johanna Spyri, 1827-1901, (Switz.) children's author. *Heidi.*

Christina Stead, 1903-83, (Austral.) novelist, short-story writer. *The Man Who Loved Children.*

Richard Steele, 1672-1729, (Br.) essayist, playwright; began the *Tatler* and *Spectator. The Conscious Lovers.*

Gertrude Stein, 1874-1946, (U.S.) writer. *Three Lives.*

John Steinbeck, 1902-68, (U.S.) novelist. *The Grapes of Wrath, Of Mice and Men, The Winter of Our Discontent.*

Stendhal (Marie Henri Beyle), 1783-1842, (Fr.) novelist. *The Red and the Black, The Charterhouse of Parma.*

Laurence Sterne, 1713-68, (Br.) novelist. *Tristram Shandy.*

Wallace Stevens, 1879-1955, (U.S.) poet. *Harmonium, The Man With the Blue Guitar, Notes Toward a Supreme Fiction.*

Robert Louis Stevenson, 1850-94, (Br.) novelist, poet, essayist. *Treasure Island, A Child's Garden of Verses.*

Bram Stoker, 1847-1912, (Br.) writer. *Dracula.*

Rex Stout, 1886-1975, (U.S.) mystery writer; created Nero Wolfe.

Harriet Beecher Stowe, 1811-96, (U.S.) novelist. *Uncle Tom's Cabin.*

Lytton Strachey, 1880-1932, (Br.) biographer, critic. *Eminent Victorians, Queen Victoria, Elizabeth and Essex.*

August Strindberg, 1849-1912, (Swed.) dramatist, novelist. *The Father, Miss Julie, The Creditors.*

William Styron, 1925-2006, (U.S.) novelist, essayist. *The Confessions of Nat Turner, Sophie's Choice, Darkness Visible: A Memoir of Madness.*

Jonathan Swift, 1667-1745, (Br.) satirist, poet. *Gulliver's Travels,* "A Modest Proposal."

Algernon C. Swinburne, 1837-1909, (Br.) poet, dramatist. *Atalanta in Calydon.*

John M. Synge, 1871-1909, (Ire.) poet, dramatist. *Riders to the Sea, The Playboy of the Western World.*

Wislawa Szymborska, 1923-2012, (Pol.) poet. "Cat in an Empty Apartment."

Rabindranath Tagore, 1861-1941, (India) author, poet. *Sadhana, The Realization of Life, Gitanjali.*

Booth Tarkington, 1869-1946, (U.S.) novelist. *Seventeen.*

Peter Taylor, 1917-94, (U.S.) novelist. *A Summons to Memphis.*

Sara Teasdale, 1884-1933, (U.S.) poet. *Helen of Troy and Other Poems, Rivers to the Sea.*

Alfred, Lord Tennyson, 1809-92, (Br.) poet. *Idylls of the King, In Memoriam,* "The Charge of the Light Brigade."

William Makepeace Thackeray, 1811-63, (Br.) novelist. *Vanity Fair, Henry Esmond, Pendennis.*

Dylan Thomas, 1914-53, (Wales) poet. *Under Milk Wood, A Child's Christmas in Wales.*

Hunter S. Thompson, 1937-2005, (U.S.) author, journalist. *Hell's Angels, Fear and Loathing in Las Vegas.*

Henry David Thoreau, 1817-62, (U.S.) writer, philosopher, naturalist. *Walden,* "Civil Disobedience."

James Thurber, 1894-1961, (U.S.) humorist. "The Secret Life of Walter Mitty," *My Life and Hard Times.*

J(ohn) R(onald) R(euel) Tolkien, 1892-1973, (Br.) writer. *The Hobbit, Lord of the Rings* trilogy.

Leo Tolstoy, 1828-1910, (Russ.) novelist, short-story writer. *War and Peace, Anna Karenina,* "The Death of Ivan Ilyich."

Lionel Trilling, 1905-75, (U.S.) critic, author, teacher. *The Liberal Imagination.*

Anthony Trollope, 1815-82, (Br.) novelist. *The Warden, Barchester Towers,* the Palliser novels.

Ivan Turgenev, 1818-83, (Russ.) novelist, short-story writer. *Fathers and Sons, First Love, A Month in the Country.*

Amos Tutuola, 1920-97, (Nigeria) novelist. *The Palm-Wine Drunkard, My Life in the Bush of Ghosts.*

Mark Twain (Samuel Clemens), 1835-1910, (U.S.) novelist, humorist. *The Adventures of Huckleberry Finn.*

Sigrid Undset, 1881-1949, (Nor.) novelist. *Kristin Lavransdatter.*

John Updike, 1932-2009, (U.S.) novelist, literary critic. *Rabbit Is Rich, The Witches of Eastwick.*

Paul Valéry, 1871-1945, (Fr.) poet, critic. *La Jeune Parque, The Graveyard by the Sea.*

Paul Verlaine, 1844-96, (Fr.) Symbolist poet. *Songs Without Words.*

Jules Verne, 1828-1905, (Fr.) novelist. *Twenty Thousand Leagues Under the Sea.*

Gore Vidal, 1925-2012, (U.S.) novelist. *The City and the Pillar.*

François Villon, 1431-c. 1463, (Fr.) poet. *The Lays, The Grand Testament.*

Voltaire (F. M. Arouet), 1694-1778, (Fr.) writer of "philosophical romances"; philosopher, historian. *Candide.*

Kurt Vonnegut Jr., 1922-2007, (U.S.) novelist, essayist. *Cat's Cradle, Slaughterhouse-Five, Breakfast of Champions.*

David Foster Wallace, 1962-2008, (U.S.) novelist, essayist. *Infinite Jest, A Supposedly Fun Thing I'll Never Do Again.*

Robert Penn Warren, 1905-89, (U.S.) novelist, poet, critic. *All the King's Men.*

Wendy Wasserstein, 1950-2006, (U.S.) playwright. *The Heidi Chronicles.*

Evelyn Waugh, 1903-66, (Br.) novelist. *The Loved One, Brideshead Revisited, A Handful of Dust.*

H(erbert) G(eorge) Wells, 1866-1946, (Br.) novelist. *The Time Machine, The Invisible Man, The War of the Worlds.*

Eudora Welty, 1909-2001, (U.S.) Southern short-story writer, novelist. "Why I Live at the P.O.," "The Ponder Heart."

Rebecca West, 1893-1983, (Br.) novelist, critic, journalist. *Black Lamb and Grey Falcon.*

Edith Wharton, 1862-1937, (U.S.) novelist. *The Age of Innocence, The House of Mirth, Ethan Frome.*

Phillis Wheatley, c. 1753-84, (U.S.) poet; 2nd American woman and first black woman to be published, 1770.

E(lwyn) B(rooks) White, 1899-1985, (U.S.) essayist, novelist. *Charlotte's Web, Stuart Little.*

Patrick White, 1912-90, (Austral.) novelist. *The Tree of Man.*

T(erence) H(anbury) White, 1906-64, (Br.) author. *The Once and Future King, A Book of Beasts.*

Walt Whitman, 1819-92, (U.S.) poet. *Leaves of Grass.*

John Greenleaf Whittier, 1807-92, (U.S.) poet, journalist. *Snow-Bound.*

Oscar Wilde, 1854-1900, (Ire.) novelist, playwright. *The Picture of Dorian Gray, The Importance of Being Earnest.*

Laura Ingalls Wilder, 1867-1957, (U.S.) novelist. Little House on the Prairie series of children's books.

Thornton Wilder, 1897-1975, (U.S.) playwright. *Our Town, The Skin of Our Teeth, The Matchmaker.*

Tennessee Williams, 1911-83, (U.S.) playwright. *A Streetcar Named Desire, Cat on a Hot Tin Roof, The Glass Menagerie.*

William Carlos Williams, 1883-1963, (U.S.) poet, physician. *Tempers, Al Que Quiere! Paterson,* "This Is Just to Say."

Edmund Wilson, 1895-1972, (U.S.) critic, novelist. *Axel's Castle, To the Finland Station.*

Lanford Wilson, 1937-2011, (U.S.) playwright. *Talley's Folly, Fifth of July.*

P(elham) G(renville) Wodehouse, 1881-1975, (Br.-U.S.) humorist. "Jeeves" novels, *Anything Goes.*

Thomas Wolfe, 1900-38, (U.S.) novelist. *Look Homeward, Angel; You Can't Go Home Again.*

Virginia Woolf, 1882-1941, (Br.) novelist, essayist. *Mrs. Dalloway, To the Lighthouse, A Room of One's Own.*

William Wordsworth, 1770-1850, (Br.) poet. "Tintern Abbey," "Ode: Intimations of Immortality," *The Prelude.*

Richard Wright, 1908-60, (U.S.) novelist, short-story writer. *Native Son, Black Boy, Uncle Tom's Children.*

Elinor Wylie, 1885-1928, (U.S.) poet. *Nets to Catch the Wind.*

William Butler Yeats, 1865-1939, (Ire.) poet, playwright. "The Second Coming," *The Wild Swans at Coole.*

Frank Yerby, 1916-91, (U.S.) first bestselling African American novelist. *The Foxes of Harrow.*

Émile Zola, 1840-1902, (Fr.) novelist. *Nana, Thérèsè Raquin.*

Poets Laureate

There is no record of the origin of the office of Poet Laureate of England. Henry III (1216-72) reportedly had a Versificator Regis, or King's Poet, paid 100 shillings per year. Other poets said to have filled the role include Geoffrey Chaucer (d 1400), Edmund Spenser (d 1599), Ben Jonson (d 1637), and Sir William d'Avenant (d 1668). The first official English poet laureate was John Dryden, appointed 1668, for life (as was customary). Then came Thomas Shadwell, in 1689; Nahum Tate, 1692; Nicholas Rowe, 1715; Rev. Laurence Eusden, 1718; Colley Cibber, 1730; William Whitehead, 1757; Rev. Thomas Warton, 1785; Henry James Pye, 1790; Robert Southey, 1813; William Wordsworth, 1843; Alfred, Lord Tennyson, 1850; Alfred Austin, 1896; Robert Bridges, 1913; John Masefield, 1930; C. Day Lewis, 1968; Sir John Betjeman, 1972; Ted Hughes, 1984; Andrew Motion, 1999; and Carol Ann Duffy, 2009.

In the U.S., appointment is by the Librarian of Congress and is not for life: Robert Penn Warren, appointed 1986; Richard Wilbur, 1987; Howard Nemerov, 1988; Mark Strand, 1990; Joseph Brodsky, 1991; Mona Van Duyn, 1992; Rita Dove, 1993; Robert Hass, 1995; Robert Pinsky, 1997; Stanley Kunitz, 2000; Billy Collins, 2001; Louise Gluck, 2003; Ted Kooser, 2004; Donald Hall, 2006; Charles Simic, 2007; Kay Ryan, 2008; W. S. Merwin, 2010; Philip Levine, 2011; Natasha Trethewey, 2012.

Composers of Classical and Avant Garde Music

John Adams, b 1947, (U.S.) *Nixon in China, The Death of Klinghoffer.*

Milton Babbitt, 1916-2011, (U.S.) serial and electronic music.

Carl Philipp Emanuel Bach, 1714-88, (Ger.) cantatas, passions, numerous keyboard and instrumental works.

Johann Christian Bach, 1735-82, (Ger.) concertos, operas, sonatas. Known as the "English" Bach.

Johann Sebastian Bach, 1685-1750, (Ger.) *St. Matthew Passion, The Well-Tempered Clavier.*

Samuel Barber, 1910-81, (U.S.) *Adagio for Strings, Vanessa.*

Béla Bartók, 1881-1945, (Hung.) *Concerto for Orchestra, The Miraculous Mandarin.*

Amy Beach (Mrs. H. H. A. Beach), 1867-1944, (U.S.) *The Year's at the Spring, Fireflies, The Chambered Nautilus.*

Ludwig van Beethoven, 1770-1827, (Ger.) concertos (*Emperor*), sonatas (*Moonlight, Pathétique*), 9 symphonies.

Vincenzo Bellini, 1801-35, (It.) *I Puritani, La Sonnambula, Norma.*

Alban Berg, 1885-1935, (Austria) *Wozzeck, Lulu.*

Hector Berlioz, 1803-69, (Fr.) *Damnation of Faust, Symphonie Fantastique, Requiem.*

Leonard Bernstein, 1918-90, (U.S.) *Chichester Psalms, Jeremiah Symphony, Mass.*

Georges Bizet, 1838-75, (Fr.) *Carmen, Pearl Fishers.*

Ernest Bloch, 1880-1959, (Switz.-U.S.) *Macbeth* (opera), *Schelomo, Voice in the Wilderness.*

Luigi Boccherini, 1743-1805, (It.) chamber music and guitar pieces.

Alexander Borodin, 1833-87, (Russ.) *Prince Igor, In the Steppes of Central Asia, Polovtzian Dances.*

Pierre Boulez, b 1925, (Fr.) *Le Visage nuptial, Edats/Multiple, Domaines.*

Johannes Brahms, 1833-97, (Ger.) *Liebeslieder Waltzes, Acad. Festival Overture,* chamber music, 4 symphonies.

Henry Brant, 1913-2008, (Can.) spatial music.

Benjamin Britten, 1913-76, (Br.) *Peter Grimes, Turn of the Screw, A Ceremony of Carols, War Requiem.*

Anton Bruckner, 1824-96, (Austria) 9 symphonies.

Dietrich Buxtehude, 1637-1707, (Den.) organ works, vocal music.

William Byrd, 1543-1623, (Br.) masses, motets.

John Cage, 1912-92, (U.S.) *Winter Music, Fontana Mix.*

Elliott Carter, 1908-2012, (U.S.) *Second String Quartet, Third String Quartet.*

Emmanuel Chabrier, 1841-94, (Fr.) *Le Roi Malgré Lui, España.*

Gustave Charpentier, 1860-1956, (Fr.) *Louise.*

Frédéric Chopin, 1810-49, (Pol.) mazurkas, waltzes, etudes, nocturnes, polonaises, sonatas.

Aaron Copland, 1900-90, (U.S.) *Appalachian Spring, Fanfare for the Common Man, Lincoln Portrait.*

John Corigliano, b 1938, (U.S.) *Symphony No. 2.*

Paul Creston, 1906-1985, (U.S.) *Walt Whitman.*

Claude Debussy, 1862-1918, (Fr.) *Pelleas et Melisande, La Mer, Prelude to the Afternoon of a Faun.*

David Del Tredici, b 1937, (U.S.) *Child Alice, In Memory of a Summer Day.*

Gaetano Donizetti, 1797-1848, (It.) *Elixir of Love, Lucia di Lammermoor, Daughter of the Regiment.*

Paul Dukas, 1865-1935, (Fr.) *Sorcerer's Apprentice.*

Antonín Dvořák, 1841-1904, (Czech.) *Songs My Mother Taught Me, Symphony in E Minor (From the New World).*

Edward Elgar, 1857-1934, (Br.) *Enigma Variations, Pomp and Circumstance.*

Manuel de Falla, 1876-1946, (Sp.) *El Amor Brujo, La Vida Breve, The Three-Cornered Hat.*

Gabriel Fauré, 1845-1924, (Fr.) *Requiem, Elègie for Cello and Piano.*

Cesar Franck, 1822-90, (Belg.) *Symphony in D minor, Violin Sonata.*

George Gershwin, 1898-1937, (U.S.) *Rhapsody in Blue, An American in Paris, Porgy and Bess.*

Philip Glass, b 1937, (U.S.) *Einstein on the Beach, The Voyage.*

Mikhail Glinka, 1804-57, (Russ.) *A Life for the Tsar, Ruslan and Ludmilla.*

Christoph W. Gluck, 1714-87, (Ger.) *Alceste, Iphigénie en Tauride.*

Henryk Gorecki, 1933-2010, (Pol.) Symphony no. 3 (*Symphony of Sorrowing Songs*).

Charles Gounod, 1818-93, (Fr.) *Faust, Romeo and Juliet.*

Percy Grainger, 1882-1961, (Austral.) *Country Gardens.*

Edvard Grieg, 1843-1907, (Nor.) *Peer Gynt Suite, Concerto in A minor for piano.*

George Frideric Handel, 1685-1759, (Ger.-Br.) *Messiah, Water Music.*

Howard Hanson, 1896-1981, (U.S.) Symphonies No. 1 (Nordic) and No. 2 (Romantic).

Roy Harris, 1898-1979, (U.S.) symphonies.

(Franz) Joseph Haydn, 1732-1809, (Austria) symphonies (*Clock, London, Toy*), chamber music, oratorios.

Hildegard von Bingen, 1098-1179, (Ger.) *Ordo virtutum.*

Paul Hindemith, 1895-1963, (U.S.) *Mathis der Maler.*

Gustav Holst, 1874-1934, (Br.) *The Planets.*

Arthur Honegger, 1892-1955, (Fr.) *Judith, Le Roi David, Pacific 231.*

Alan Hovhaness, 1911-2000, (U.S.) symphonies, *Magnificat.*

Engelbert Humperdinck, 1854-1921, (Ger.) *Hansel and Gretel.*

Charles Ives, 1874-1954, (U.S.) *Concord Sonata,* symphonies.

Aram Khachaturian, 1903-78, (Russ.) ballets, piano pieces, *Sabre Dance.*

Zoltán Kodaly, 1882-1967, (Hung.) *Háry János, Psalmus Hungaricus.*

Fritz Kreisler, 1875-1962, (Austria) *Caprice Viennois, Tambourin Chinois.*

Edouard Lalo, 1823-92, (Fr.) *Symphonie Espagnole.*

David Lang, b 1957, (U.S.) *The Little Match Girl Passion.*

Morten Lauridsen, 1943 (U.S.) *Lux Aeterna.*

Ruggero Leoncavallo, 1857-1919, (It.) *Pagliacci.*

György Ligeti, 1923-2006, (Rom.) *Atmosphères, Requiem.*

Franz Liszt, 1811-86, (Hung.) 20 Hungarian rhapsodies, symphonic poems.

Edward MacDowell, 1861-1908, (U.S.) *To a Wild Rose.*

Gustav Mahler, 1860-1911, (Austria) *Das Lied von der Erde;* 9 complete symphonies.

Pietro Mascagni, 1863-1945, (It.) *Cavalleria Rusticana.*

Jules Massenet, 1842-1912, (Fr.) *Manon, Le Cid, Thaïs.*

Felix Mendelssohn, 1809-47, (Ger.) *A Midsummer Night's Dream, Songs Without Words*, violin concerto.

Gian Carlo Menotti, 1911-2007, (It.-U.S.) *The Medium, The Consul, Amahl and the Night Visitors.*

Olivier Messiaen, 1908-1992, (Fr.) *Apparition de l'Église Éternelle.*

Claudio Monteverdi, 1567-1643, (It.) opera, masses, madrigals.

Wolfgang Amadeus Mozart, 1756-91, (Austria) chamber music, concertos, operas (*Magic Flute, Marriage of Figaro*), 41 symphonies.

Modest Mussorgsky, 1839-81, (Russ.) *Boris Godunov, Pictures at an Exhibition.*

Carl Nielsen, 1865-1931, (Den.) *Saul og David.*

Jacques Offenbach, 1819-80, (Fr.) *Tales of Hoffmann.*

Carl Orff, 1895-1982, (Ger.) *Carmina Burana.*

Johann Pachelbel, 1653-1706, (Ger.) Canon and Fugue in D major.

Ignacy Paderewski, 1860-1941, (Pol.) Minuet in G.

Niccolò Paganini, 1782-1840, (It.) Caprices for violin solo.

Giovanni Palestrina, c. 1525-94, (It.) masses, madrigals.

Arvo Pärt, b 1935, (Eston.) sacred music. *Fratres, Cantus in memoriam Benjamin Britten, Tabula Rasa.*

Krzysztof Penderecki, b 1933, (Pol.) *Psalmus, Polymorphia, De natura sonoris.*

Francis Poulenc, 1899-1963, (Fr.) *Dialogues des Carmèlites.*

Mel Powell, 1923-98, (U.S.) *Duplicates: A Concerto for Two Pianos and Orchestra, Cantilena Concertante.*

Sergei Prokofiev, 1891-1953, (Russ.) *Classical Symphony, Love for Three Oranges, Peter and the Wolf.*

Giacomo Puccini, 1858-1924, (It.) *La Boheme, Manon Lescaut, Tosca, Madama Butterfly.*

Henry Purcell, 1659-95, (Eng.) *Dido and Aeneas.*

Sergei Rachmaninoff, 1873-1943, (Russ.) concertos, preludes (Prelude in C sharp minor), symphonies.

Maurice Ravel, 1875-1937, (Fr.) *Bolèro, Daphnis et Chloè*, Piano Concerto in D for Left Hand Alone.

Steve Reich, b 1936, (U.S.) *Double Sextet, Three Tales.*

Nikolai Rimsky-Korsakov, 1844-1908, (Russ.) *Golden Cockerel, Scheherazade, Flight of the Bumblebee.*

Gioacchino Rossini, 1792-1868, (It.) *Barber of Seville, Otello, William Tell.*

John Rutter, b 1945, (Br.) *Magnificat, Requiem.*

Camille Saint-Saëns, 1835-1921, (Fr.) *Carnival of Animals (The Swan), Samson and Delilah, Danse Macabre.*

Alessandro Scarlatti, 1660-1725, (It.) cantatas, oratorios, operas.

Domenico Scarlatti, 1685-1757, (It.) harpsichord works.

Alfred Schnittke, 1934-98, (Sov.-Ger.) *Life With an Idiot.*

Arnold Schoenberg, 1874-1951, (Austria) *Pelleas and Melisande, Pierrot Lunaire, Verklärte Nacht.*

Franz Schubert, 1797-1828, (Austria) chamber music (*Trout Quintet*), lieder, symphonies ("Unfinished").

Robert Schumann, 1810-56, (Ger.) *Die Frauenliebe und Leben, Träumerei.*

Dmitri Shostakovich, 1906-75, (Russ.) symphonies, *Lady Macbeth of the District Mzensk.*

Jean Sibelius, 1865-1957, (Fin.) *Finlandia.*

Bedrich Smetana, 1824-84, (Czech.) *The Bartered Bride.*

Karlheinz Stockhausen, 1928-2008, (Ger.) *Kontra-Punkte, Kontakte for Electronic Instruments.*

Richard Strauss, 1864-1949, (Ger.) *Salome, Elektra, Der Rosenkavalier, Thus Spake Zarathustra.*

Igor Stravinsky, 1882-1971, (Russ.) *Noah and the Flood, The Rake's Progress, The Rite of Spring.*

Toru Takemitsu, 1930-96, (Jpn.) *Requiem for Strings, Dorian Horizon.*

Thomas Tallis, 1515?-85, (Br.) anthems, motets.

Peter I. Tchaikovsky, 1840-93, (Russ.) *Nutcracker, Swan Lake, The Sleeping Beauty.*

Georg Philipp Telemann, 1681-1767, (Ger.) church music, orchestral suites, chamber music.

Virgil Thomson, 1896-1989, (U.S.) opera, film music, *Four Saints in Three Acts.*

Dmitri Tiomkin, 1894-1979, (Russ.-U.S.) film scores, including *High Noon.*

Sir Michael Tippett, 1905-98, (Br.) *A Child of Our Time, The Midsummer Marriage, The Knot Garden.*

Michael Torke, b 1961, (U.S.) *Bright Blue Music, Ecstatic Orange.*

Eric Whitacre, b 1970, (U.S.) *Cloudburst.*

Ralph Vaughan Williams, 1872-1958, (Br.) *Fantasia on a Theme by Thomas Tallis*, symphonies, vocal music.

Giuseppe Verdi, 1813-1901, (It.) *Aida, Rigoletto, Don Carlo, Il Trovatore, La Traviata, Falstaff, Macbeth.*

Heitor Villa-Lobos, 1887-1959, (Braz.) *Bachianas Brasileiras.*

Antonio Vivaldi, 1678-1741, (It.) Concerto grossos (*The Four Seasons*).

Richard Wagner, 1813-83, (Ger.) *Rienzi, Tannhäuser, Lohengrin, Tristan und Isolde.*

William Walton, 1902-83, (Br.) *Façade, Belshazzar's Feast.*

Carl Maria von Weber, 1786-1826, (Ger.) *Der Freischutz.*

Composers of Operettas, Musicals, and Popular Music

Richard Adler, 1921-2012, (U.S.) *Pajama Game; Damn Yankees.*

Milton Ager, 1893-1979, (U.S.) "I Wonder What's Become of Sally;" "Hard-Hearted Hannah;" "Ain't She Sweet?"

Leroy Anderson, 1908-75, (U.S.) "Sleigh Ride"; "Blue Tango"; "Syncopated Clock."

Paul Anka, b 1941, (Can.) "My Way"; *Tonight Show* theme.

Harold Arlen, 1905-86, (U.S.) "Stormy Weather"; "Over the Rainbow"; "Blues in the Night"; "That Old Black Magic."

Burt Bacharach, b 1928, (U.S.) "Raindrops Keep Fallin' on My Head"; "Walk on By"; "What the World Needs Now Is Love."

Ernest Ball, 1878-1927, (U.S.) "Mother Machree"; "When Irish Eyes Are Smiling."

John Barry, 1933-2011, (U.S.) *Born Free; Lion in Winter; Out of Africa.*

Irving Berlin, 1888-1989, (U.S.) *Annie Get Your Gun; Call Me Madam;* "God Bless America"; "White Christmas."

Leonard Bernstein, 1918-90, (U.S.) *On the Town; Wonderful Town; Candide; West Side Story.*

Eubie Blake, 1883-1983, (U.S.) *Shuffle Along;* "I'm Just Wild About Harry."

Jerry Bock, 1928-2010, (U.S.) *Mr. Wonderful; Fiorello; Fiddler on the Roof; The Rothschilds.*

Carrie Jacobs Bond, 1862-1946, (U.S.) "I Love You Truly."

Nacio Herb Brown, 1896-1964, (U.S.) "Singing in the Rain"; "You Were Meant for Me"; "All I Do Is Dream of You."

Hoagy Carmichael, 1899-1981, (U.S.) "Stardust"; "Georgia on My Mind"; "Old Buttermilk Sky."

James Cleveland, 1931-91, (U.S.) composer, musician, singer; first black gospel artist to appear at Carnegie Hall.

George M. Cohan, 1878-1942, (U.S.) "Give My Regards to Broadway"; "You're a Grand Old Flag"; "Over There."

Cy Coleman, 1929-2004, (U.S.) *Sweet Charity;* "Witchcraft."

John Frederick Coots, 1895-1985, (U.S.) "Santa Claus Is Coming to Town"; "You Go to My Head"; "For All We Know."

Noël Coward, 1899-1973, (Br.) *Bitter Sweet;* "Mad Dogs and Englishmen"; "Mad About the Boy."

Neil Diamond, b 1941, (U.S.) "I'm a Believer"; "Sweet Caroline."

Walter Donaldson, 1893-1947, (U.S.) "My Buddy"; "Carolina in the Morning"; "Makin' Whoopee."

Vernon Duke, 1903-69, (U.S.) "April in Paris."

Bob Dylan, b 1941, (U.S.) "Blowin' in the Wind"; "Like a Rolling Stone."

Gus Edwards, 1879-1945, (U.S.) "School Days"; "By the Light of the Silvery Moon"; "In My Merry Oldsmobile."

Sherman Edwards, 1919-81, (U.S.) *See You in September;* "Wonderful! Wonderful!"

Duke Ellington, 1899-1974, (U.S.) "Sophisticated Lady"; "Satin Doll"; "It Don't Mean a Thing"; "Solitude."

Sammy Fain, 1902-89, (U.S.) "I'll Be Seeing You"; "Love Is a Many-Splendored Thing."

Fred Fisher, 1875-1942, (U.S.) "Peg O' My Heart"; "Chicago."

Stephen Collins Foster, 1826-64, (U.S.) "My Old Kentucky Home"; "Old Folks at Home"; "Beautiful Dreamer."

Rudolf Friml, 1879-1972, (Czech.-U.S.) *The Firefly; Rose Marie; Vagabond King; Bird of Paradise.*

John Gay, 1685-1732, (Br.) *The Beggar's Opera.*

George Gershwin, 1898-1937, (U.S.) "Someone to Watch Over Me"; "I've Got a Crush on You"; "Embraceable You."

Morton Gould, 1913-96, (U.S.) "Fall River Suite"; "Holocaust Suite"; "Spirituals for Orchestra"; "Stringmusic."

Ferde Grofe, 1892-1972, (U.S.) "Grand Canyon Suite."

Marvin Hamlisch, 1944-2012, (U.S.) "The Way We Were"; "Nobody Does It Better"; *A Chorus Line.*

Ray Henderson, 1896-1970, (U.S.) *George White's Scandals;* "That Old Gang of Mine"; "Five Foot Two, Eyes of Blue."

Victor Herbert, 1859-1924, (Ire.-U.S.) *Mlle. Modiste; Babes in Toyland; The Red Mill; Naughty Marietta; Sweethearts.*

Jerry Herman, b 1931, (U.S.) *Hello Dolly; Mame.*

Brian Holland, b 1941, **Lamont Dozier**, b 1941, **Eddie Holland**, b 1939, (all U.S.) "Heat Wave"; "Stop! In the Name of Love"; "Baby, I Need Your Loving."

Rupert Holmes, b 1947, (Eng.-U.S.) *The Mystery of Edwin Drood; Curtains.*

Antonio Carlos Jobim, 1927-94, (Brazil) "The Girl From Ipanema"; "Desafinado"; "One Note Samba."

Billy Joel (William Martin), b 1949, (U.S.) "Just the Way You Are"; "Honesty"; "Piano Man."

Elton John, b 1947, (Br.) *The Lion King;* "Candle in the Wind"; "Your Song."

Scott Joplin, 1868-1917, (U.S.) Maple Leaf Rag; *Treemonisha.*

John Kander, b 1927, (U.S.) *Cabaret; Chicago; Funny Lady.*

Jerome Kern, 1885-1945, (U.S.) *Sally; Sunny; Show Boat.*

Carole King, b 1942, (U.S.) "Will You Love Me Tomorrow?"; "Natural Woman"; "One Fine Day"; "Up on the Roof."

Burton Lane, 1912-97, (U.S.) *Finian's Rainbow.*

Jonathan Larson, 1960-96, (U.S.) *tick, tick... BOOM!; Rent.*

Franz Lehar, 1870-1948, (Hung.) *Merry Widow.*

Jerry Leiber (1933-2011) and **Mike Stoller**, b 1933, (both U.S.) "Hound Dog"; "Searchin'"; "Yakety Yak"; "Love Me Tender."

Mitch Leigh, b 1928, (U.S.) *Man of La Mancha.*

John Lennon, 1940-80, and **Paul McCartney**, b 1942, (both Br.) "I Want to Hold Your Hand"; "She Loves You."

Jay Livingston, 1915-2001, (U.S.) "Mona Lisa"; "Que Sera, Sera."

Andrew Lloyd Webber, b 1948, (Br.) *Jesus Christ Superstar; Evita; Cats; The Phantom of the Opera.*

Frank Loesser, 1910-69, (U.S.) *Guys and Dolls; Where's Charley?; The Most Happy Fella; How to Succeed in Business....*

Frederick Loewe, 1901-88, (Austria-U.S.) *Brigadoon; Paint Your Wagon; My Fair Lady; Camelot.*

Henry Mancini, 1924-94, (U.S.) "Moon River"; "Days of Wine and Roses"; "Pink Panther Theme."

Barry Mann, b 1939, and **Cynthia Weil**, b 1937, (both U.S.) "You've Lost That Loving Feeling."

Hugh Martin, 1914-2011, (U.S.) "Have Yourself a Merry Little Christmas"; "The Trolley Song."

Jimmy McHugh, 1894-1969, (U.S.) "Don't Blame Me"; "I'm in the Mood for Love"; "I Feel a Song Coming On."

Alan Menken, b 1949, (U.S.) *Little Shop of Horrors; Beauty and the Beast.*

Joseph Meyer, 1894-1987, (U.S.) "If You Knew Susie"; "California, Here I Come"; "Crazy Rhythm."

Chauncey Olcott, 1858-1932, (U.S.) "Mother Machree."

Jerome "Doc" Pomus, 1925-91, (U.S.) "Save the Last Dance for Me"; "A Teenager in Love."

Cole Porter, 1891-1964, (U.S.) *Anything Goes; Kiss Me Kate; Can Can; Silk Stockings.*

Smokey Robinson, b 1940, (U.S.) "Shop Around"; "My Guy"; "My Girl"; "Get Ready."

Richard Rodgers, 1902-79, (U.S.) *Oklahoma!; Carousel; South Pacific; The King and I; The Sound of Music.*

Sigmund Romberg, 1887-1951, (Hung.) *Maytime; The Student Prince; Desert Song; Blossom Time.*

Harold Rome, 1908-93, (U.S.) *Pins and Needles; Call Me Mister; Wish You Were Here; Fanny; Destry Rides Again.*

Vincent Rose, 1880-1944, (U.S.) "Avalon"; "Whispering"; "Blueberry Hill."

Harry Ruby, 1895-1974, (U.S.) "Three Little Words"; "Who's Sorry Now?"

Arthur Schwartz, 1900-84, (U.S.) *The Band Wagon;* "Dancing in the Dark"; "By Myself"; "That's Entertainment."

Steven Schwartz, b 1948, (U.S.) *Godspell; Pippin; Wicked.*

Neil Sedaka, b 1939, (U.S.) "Breaking Up Is Hard to Do."

Marc Shaiman, b 1959, (U.S.) *Hairspray.*

Paul Simon, b 1942, (U.S.) "Sounds of Silence"; "I Am a Rock"; "Mrs. Robinson"; "Bridge Over Troubled Waters."

Stephen Sondheim, b 1930, (U.S.) *A Little Night Music; Company; Sweeney Todd; Sunday in the Park With George.*

John Philip Sousa, 1854-1932, (U.S.) *El Capitan;* "Stars and Stripes Forever."

Oskar Straus, 1870-1954, (Austrian) *Chocolate Soldier.*

Johann Strauss, 1825-99, (Austrian) *Gypsy Baron; Die Fledermaus;* waltzes: Blue Danube; Artist's Life.

Charles Strouse, b 1928, (U.S.) *Bye Bye, Birdie; Annie.*

Jule Styne, 1905-94, (Br.-U.S.) *Gentlemen Prefer Blondes; Bells Are Ringing; Gypsy; Funny Girl.*

Arthur S. Sullivan, 1842-1900, (Br.) *H.M.S. Pinafore; Pirates of Penzance; The Mikado.*

Deems Taylor, 1885-1966, (U.S.) *Peter Ibbetson.*

Harry Tobias, 1905-94, (U.S.) *I'll Keep the Lovelight Burning.*

Egbert van Alstyne, 1882-1951, (U.S.) "In the Shade of the Old Apple Tree"; "Memories"; "Pretty Baby."

Jimmy Van Heusen, 1913-90, (U.S.) "Moonlight Becomes You"; "Swinging on a Star"; "All the Way"; "Love and Marriage."

Albert von Tilzer, 1878-1956, (U.S.) "I'll Be With You in Apple Blossom Time"; "Take Me Out to the Ball Game."

Harry von Tilzer, 1872-1946, (U.S.) "Only a Bird in a Gilded Cage"; "Wait 'til the Sun Shines, Nellie."

Fats Waller, 1904-43, (U.S.) "Honeysuckle Rose"; "Ain't Misbehavin."

Harry Warren, 1893-1981, (U.S.) "You're My Everything"; "We're in the Money"; "I Only Have Eyes for You."

Jimmy Webb, b 1946, (U.S.) "Up, Up and Away"; "By the Time I Get to Phoenix"; "Didn't We?"; "Wichita Lineman."

Kurt Weill, 1900-50, (Ger.-U.S.) *Threepenny Opera; Lady in the Dark; Knickerbocker Holiday; One Touch of Venus.*

Percy Wenrich, 1887-1952, (U.S.) "When You Wore a Tulip"; "Moonlight Bay"; "Put On Your Old Gray Bonnet."

Richard A. Whiting, 1891-1938, (U.S.) "Till We Meet Again"; "Sleepytime Gal"; "Beyond the Blue Horizon"; "My Ideal."

Fred Wildhorn, b 1959, (U.S.) *Jekyll and Hyde; Victor/Victoria; The Civil War.*

John Williams, b 1932, (U.S.) *Jaws; E.T.; Star Wars* series; *Raiders of the Lost Ark* series.

Meredith Willson, 1902-84, (U.S.) *The Music Man.*

Stevie Wonder, b 1950, (U.S.) "You Are the Sunshine of My Life"; "Signed, Sealed, Delivered, I'm Yours."

Vincent Youmans, 1898-1946, (U.S.) *Two Little Girls in Blue; Wildflower; No, No, Nanette; Hit the Deck; Rainbow; Smiles.*

Lyricists

Howard Ashman, 1950-91, (U.S.) *Little Shop of Horrors; The Little Mermaid.*

Johnny Burke, 1908-84, (U.S.) "Misty"; "Imagination."

Irving Caesar, 1895-1996, (U.S.) "Swanee"; "Tea for Two"; "Just a Gigolo."

Sammy Cahn, 1913-93, (U.S.) "High Hopes"; "Love and Marriage"; "The Second Time Around"; "It's Magic."

Leonard Cohen, b 1934, (Can.) "Suzanne"; "Stranger Song."

Betty Comden, 1917-2006, (U.S.) and **Adolph Green**, 1915-2002, (U.S.) "The Party's Over"; "New York, New York."

Hal David, 1921-2012, (U.S.) "What the World Needs Now Is Love."

Buddy De Sylva, 1895-1950, (U.S.) "When Day Is Done"; "Look for the Silver Lining"; "April Showers."

Howard Dietz, 1896-1983, (U.S.) "Dancing in the Dark"; "That's Entertainment."

Al Dubin, 1891-1945, (U.S.) "Tiptoe Through the Tulips"; "Lullaby of Broadway."

Fred Ebb, 1936-2004, (U.S.) *Cabaret; Zorba; Woman of the Year; Chicago.*

Ray Evans, 1915-2007, (U.S.) "Mona Lisa"; "Que Sera, Sera."

Dorothy Fields, 1905-74, (U.S.) "On the Sunny Side of the Street"; "Don't Blame Me"; "The Way You Look Tonight."

Ira Gershwin, 1896-1983, (U.S.) "The Man I Love"; "S'Wonderful"; "Embraceable You."

William S. Gilbert, 1836-1911, (Br.) *H.M.S. Pinafore; Pirates of Penzance.*

Gerry Goffin, b 1939, (U.S.) "Will You Love Me Tomorrow"; "Take Good Care of My Baby"; "Up on the Roof."

Mack Gordon, 1905-59, (Pol.-U.S.) "You'll Never Know"; "The More I See You"; "Chattanooga Choo-Choo."

Oscar Hammerstein II, 1895-1960, (U.S.) *Ol' Man River; Oklahoma!; Carousel.*

E.Y. (Yip) Harburg, 1898-1981, (U.S.) "Brother, Can You Spare a Dime"; "April in Paris"; "Over the Rainbow."

Sheldon Harnick, b 1924, (U.S.) *Fiddler on the Roof; She Loves Me.*

Lorenz Hart, 1895-1943, (U.S.) "Isn't It Romantic"; "Blue Moon"; "Lover"; "Manhattan"; "My Funny Valentine."

DuBose Heyward, 1885-1940, (U.S.) "Summertime."

Gus Kahn, 1886-1941, (U.S.) "Memories"; "Ain't We Got Fun."

Alan J. Lerner, 1918-86, (U.S.) *Brigadoon; My Fair Lady; Camelot; Gigi; On a Clear Day You Can See Forever.*

Johnny Mercer, 1909-76, (U.S.) "Blues in the Night"; "Come Rain or Come Shine"; "Laura"; "That Old Black Magic."

Bob Merrill, 1921-98, (U.S.) "People"; "(How Much Is That) Doggie in the Window."

Jack Norworth, 1879-1959, (U.S.) "Take Me Out to the Ball Game"; "Shine On Harvest Moon."

Mitchell Parish, 1901-93, (U.S.) "Stardust"; "Stairway to the Stars."

Andy Razaf, 1895-1973, (U.S.) "Honeysuckle Rose"; "Ain't Misbehavin."

Leo Robin, 1900-84, (U.S.) "Thanks for the Memory"; "Diamonds Are a Girl's Best Friend."

Robert Sherman, 1925-2012, (U.S.) *Mary Poppins, The Jungle Book.*

Bernie Taupin, b 1947 (Br.) "Rocket Man"; "Your Song."

Paul Francis Webster, 1907-84, (U.S.) "Secret Love"; "The Shadow of Your Smile"; "Love Is a Many-Splendored Thing."

Jack Yellen, 1892-1991, (U.S.) "Ain't She Sweet"; "Happy Days Are Here Again."

Blues and Jazz Artists of the Past

Julian "Cannonball" Adderley, 1928-75, alto sax.

Nat Adderley, 1931-2000, cornet.

Henry "Red" Allen, 1908-67, trumpet.

Louis "Satchmo" Armstrong, 1901-71, trumpet, singer, bandleader.

Albert Ayler, 1936-70, tenor sax, alto sax.

Mildred Bailey, 1907-51, singer.

Chet Baker, 1929-88, trumpet, singer.

Ray Barretto, 1930-2006, conga drummer.

William "Count" Basie, 1904-84, bandleader, piano, composer.

Sidney Bechet, 1897-1959, soprano sax, clarinet.

Bix Beiderbecke, 1903-31, cornet, composer, piano.

Rowland "Bunny" Berigan, 1908-42, trumpet.

Barney Bigard, 1906-80, clarinet.

Eubie Blake, 1883-1983, composer, piano.

Art Blakey, 1919-90, drums, bandleader.

Jimmy Blanton, 1921-42, bass.

Charles "Buddy" Bolden, 1877-1931, cornet, pioneer bandleader.

Lester Bowie, 1941-99, trumpet, composer, bandleader.

Michael Brecker, 1949-2007, saxophone.

Big Bill Broonzy, 1893-1958, blues singer, guitar.

Clarence "Gatemouth" Brown, 1924-2005, guitar, singer.

Clifford Brown, 1930-56, trumpet.

Ray Brown, 1926-2002, bass.

Don Byas, 1912-72, tenor sax.

Charlie Byrd, 1925-99, guitar; popularized bossa nova.

Cab Calloway, 1907-94, bandleader, singer.

Harry Carney, 1910-74, baritone sax, clarinet.

Benny Carter, 1907-2003, alto sax.
Betty Carter, 1930-98, jazz singer.
Sidney "Big Sid" Catlett, 1910-51, drums.
Adolphus Anthony "Doc" Cheatham, 1905-97, trumpet.
Don Cherry, 1936-95, trumpet.
Charlie Christian, 1916-42, guitar.
Kenny "Klook" Clarke, 1914-85, drums.
Buck Clayton, 1911-91, trumpet.
Al Cohn, 1925-88, tenor sax.
Nat "King" Cole, 1919-65, piano, singer.
William "Cozy" Cole, 1909-81, drums.
Alice Coltrane, 1937-2007, piano, composer.
John Coltrane, 1926-67, tenor sax, soprano sax, composer.
Eddie Condon, 1905-73, guitar, bandleader.
Tadd Dameron, 1917-65, piano, composer.
Eddie "Lockjaw" Davis, 1921-86, tenor sax.
Miles Davis, 1926-91, trumpet, composer.
Wild Bill Davison, 1906-89, cornet.
Blossom Dearie, 1924-2009, singer.
Paul Desmond, 1924-77, alto sax.
Vic Dickenson, 1906-84, trombone.
Willie Dixon, 1915-92, composer, bass.
Johnny Dodds, 1892-1940, clarinet.
Warren "Baby" Dodds, 1898-1959, drums.
Eric Dolphy, 1928-64, alto sax, bass clarinet, flute.
Jimmy Dorsey, 1904-57, alto sax, bandleader.
Tommy Dorsey, 1905-56, trombone, bandleader.
Billy Eckstine, 1914-93, singer, bandleader.
Harry "Sweets" Edison, 1915-99, trumpet.
David "Honeyboy" Edwards, 1915-2011, guitar, singer.
Roy Eldridge, 1911-89, trumpet, singer.
Duke Ellington, 1899-1974, piano, bandleader, composer.
Bill Evans, 1929-80, piano.
Gil Evans, 1912-88, composer, arranger, piano.
Art Farmer, 1928-99, trumpet, flugelhorn.
Maynard Ferguson, 1926-2006, trumpet, bandleader.
Ella Fitzgerald, 1917-96, singer.
Tommy Flanagan, 1930-2001, piano.
Erroll Garner, 1921-77, piano, composer.
Stan Getz, 1927-91, tenor sax.
Dizzy Gillespie, 1917-93, trumpet, composer, singer.
Benny Goodman, 1909-86, clarinet, bandleader.
Dexter Gordon, 1923-90, tenor sax.
Stéphane Grappelli, 1908-97, violin.
Bobby Hackett, 1915-76, trumpet, cornet.
Lionel Hampton, 1908-2002, vibraphone, bandleader.
W. C. Handy, 1873-1958, composer.
Jimmy Harrison, 1900-31, trombone.
Coleman Hawkins, 1904-69, tenor sax.
Percy Heath, 1923-2005, bass.
Fletcher Henderson, 1898-1952, bandleader, arranger.
Woody Herman, 1913-87, clarinet, alto sax, bandleader.
Jay C. Higginbotham, 1906-73, trombone.
Ruiz Hilton, 1952-2006, piano, composer.
Earl "Fatha" Hines, 1903-83, piano.
Milt Hinton, 1910-2000, bass.
Al Hirt, 1922-99, trumpet.
Johnny Hodges, 1906-70, alto sax.
Billie Holiday, 1915-59, singer.
John Lee Hooker, 1917-2001, blues guitar, singer.
Sam "Lightnin'" Hopkins, 1912-82, blues singer, guitar.
Shirley Horn, 1934-2005, piano, singer.
Howlin' Wolf (Chester Burnett), 1910-76, blues singer, harmonica, guitar.
Alberta Hunter, 1895-1984, singer.
Mahalia Jackson, 1911-72, gospel singer.
Milt Jackson, 1923-99, vibraphone.

Elmore James, 1918-63, blues singer, guitar.
Etta James, 1938-2012, blues singer.
"Blind" Lemon Jefferson, 1897-1929, blues singer, guitar.
J. J. Johnson, 1924-2001, trombone.
James P. Johnson, 1891-1955, piano, composer.
Robert Johnson, 1912-38, blues singer, guitar.
William "Bunk" Johnson, 1879-1949, trumpet.
Elvin Jones, 1927-2004, drums.
Jo Jones, 1911-85, drums.
Philly Joe Jones, 1923-85, drums.
Thad Jones, 1923-86, cornet, bandleader, composer.
Scott Joplin, 1868-1917, ragtime composer.
Louis Jordan, 1908-75, singer, alto sax.
Stan Kenton, 1911-79, bandleader, composer, piano.
Barney Kessel, 1923-2004, guitar.
Albert King, 1923-92, blues guitar.
John Kirby, 1908-52, bandleader, bass.
Rahsaan Roland Kirk, 1936-77, saxophone, composer.
Gene Krupa, 1909-73, drums, bandleader.
Scott LaFaro, 1936-61, bass.
Lead Belly (Huddie Ledbetter), 1888-1949, folk and blues singer, guitar.
Peggy Lee, 1920-2002, singer.
John Lewis, 1920-2001, piano, Modern Jazz Quartet founder.
Mel Lewis, 1929-90, drums, bandleader.
Jimmie Lunceford, 1902-47, bandleader.
Machito (Frank Grillo), 1908-84, Latin percussion, singer, bandleader.
Shelly Manne, 1920-84, drums, bandleader.
Jackie McLean, 1931-2006, saxophone, composer.
Jimmy McPartland, 1907-91, trumpet.
Marian McPartland, 1918-2013, jazz pianist.
Carmen McRae, 1920-94, singer.
Glenn Miller, 1904-44, trombone, bandleader.
Charles Mingus, 1922-79, bass, composer, bandleader.
Thelonious Monk, 1917-82, piano, composer.
Wes Montgomery, 1925-68, guitar.
James Moody, 1925-2010, saxophone.
Ferdinand "Jelly Roll" Morton, 1885-1941, composer, piano.
Bennie Moten, 1894-1935, piano, bandleader.
Gerry Mulligan, 1927-96, baritone sax, composer.
Theodore "Fats" Navarro, 1923-50, trumpet.
Red Nichols, 1905-65, cornet, bandleader.
Red Norvo, 1908-99, vibraphone, xylophone, bandleader.
Anita O'Day, 1919-2006, singer.
Arturo "Chico" O'Farrill, 1921-2001, Latin composer, arranger.
King Oliver, 1885-1938, cornet, band-leader.
Sy Oliver, 1910-88, arranger, composer.
Edward "Kid" Ory, 1886-1973, trombone, bandleader.
Johnny Otis, 1921-2012, blues singer.
Oran "Hot Lips" Page, 1908-54, trumpet, singer.
Charlie "Bird" Parker, 1920-55, alto sax, composer.
Joe Pass, 1929-94, guitar.
Art Pepper, 1925-82, alto sax.
Pinetop Perkins, 1913-2011, piano.
Oscar Peterson, 1925-2007, piano.
Oscar Pettiford, 1922-60, bass.
Earl "Bud" Powell, 1924-66, piano.
Chano Pozo, 1915-48, Cuban percussion, singer.
Louis Prima, 1911-78, singer, bandleader.

Tito Puente, 1923-2000, Latin percussion, bandleader.
Gertrude "Ma" Rainey, 1886-1939, blues singer.
Lou Rawls, 1933-2006, singer.
Dewey Redman, 1931-2006, tenor sax.
Don Redman (Robert Rodney Chudnick), 1900-64, composer, arranger.
Django Reinhardt, 1910-53, guitar.
Buddy Rich, 1917-87, drums.
Max Roach, 1924-2007, drums, composer.
Red Rodney (Robert Chudnick), 1927-94, trumpet.
Jimmy Rowles, 1918-96, piano.
Jimmy Rushing, 1903-72, blues and jazz singer.
Charles "Pee Wee" Russell, 1906-69, clarinet.
Artie Shaw, 1910-2004, swing-era bandleader, clarinet.
George Shearing, 1919-2011, piano.
Nina Simone (Eunice Waymon), 1933-2003, singer.
John "Zoot" Sims, 1925-85, tenor sax.
Zutty Singleton, 1898-1975, drums.
Bessie Smith, 1894-1937, blues singer.
Clarence "Pinetop" Smith, 1904-29, piano, singer, boogie woogie pioneer.
Willie "The Lion" Smith, 1897-1973, piano, composer.
Francis "Muggsy" Spanier, 1906-67, cornet.
Edward "Sonny" Stitt, 1924-82, tenor sax, alto sax.
Billy Strayhorn, 1915-67, composer, piano, Duke Ellington collaborator.
Sun Ra (Herman Blount), 1915?-93, bandleader, piano, composer.
Art Tatum, 1910-56, piano.
Art Taylor, 1929-95, drums.
Billy Taylor, 1921-2010, piano.
Jack Teagarden, 1905-64, trombone, singer.
Mel Tormé, 1925-99, singer ("The Velvet Fog").
Dave Tough, 1908-48, drums.
Lennie Tristano, 1919-78, piano, composer.
Joe Turner, 1911-85, blues singer.
Sarah Vaughan, 1924-90, singer.
Joe Venuti, 1903-78, violin.
Aaron "T-Bone" Walker, 1910-75, blues guitar.
Thomas "Fats" Waller, 1904-43, piano, singer, composer.
Dinah Washington (Ruth Jones), 1924-63, singer.
Grover Washington Jr., 1943-99, pop-jazz sax, composer.
Ethel Waters, 1896-1977, jazz and blues singer.
Muddy Waters (McKinley Morganfield), 1915-83, blues singer, songwriter.
Julius Watkins, 1921-77, French horn.
William "Chick" Webb, 1902-39, bandleader, drums.
Ben Webster, 1909-73, tenor sax.
Junior Wells (Amos Blackmore), 1934-98, blues singer, harmonica.
Paul Whiteman, 1890-1967, bandleader.
Margaret Whiting, 1924-2011, singer.
Charles "Cootie" Williams, 1910-85, trumpet, bandleader.
Joe Williams, 1918-99, singer.
Mary Lou Williams, 1910-81, piano, composer.
Tony Williams, 1945-97, drums.
John Lee "Sonny Boy" Williamson, 1914-48, blues singer, harmonica.
Sonny Boy Williamson (Aleck "Rice" Miller), 1900?-65, blues singer, harmonica.
Teddy Wilson, 1912-86, piano.
Kai Winding, 1922-83, trombone.
Jimmy Yancey, 1894-1951, piano.
Lester "Pres" Young, 1909-59, tenor sax.

Country Music Artists of the Past and Present

Roy Acuff, 1903-92, fiddler, singer, songwriter; "Wabash Cannon Ball."

Alabama (Jeff Cook, b 1949; Teddy Gentry, b 1952; Mark Herndon, b 1955; Randy Owen, b 1949); "Feels So Right."

Jason Aldean, b 1977, singer; "Don't You Wanna Stay."

James "Whispering Bill" Anderson, b 1937, singer, songwriter; "Make Mine Night Time."

Eddy Arnold, 1918-2008, singer, guitarist, known as the "Tennessee Plowboy."

Chet Atkins, 1924-2001, guitarist, composer, producer; helped create the "Nashville sound."

Gene Autry, 1907-98, first great singing movie cowboy; "Back in the Saddle Again."

Clint Black, b 1962, singer, songwriter; "Killin' Time."

Garth Brooks, b 1962, singer, songwriter; "Friends in Low Places."

Brooks & Dunn (Kix Brooks, b 1955; Ronnie Dunn, b 1953); "Hard Workin' Man."

Luke Bryan, b 1976, singer; "Someone Else Calling You Baby."

Boudleaux, 1920-87, and **Felice Bryant**, 1925-2003, songwriting team; "Hey Joe."

Glen Campbell, b 1936, singer, guitarist; "Gentle on My Mind."

Mary Chapin Carpenter, b 1958, singer, songwriter; "I Feel Lucky."

Carter Family (original members A. P., 1891-1960; "Mother" Maybelle, 1909-78, Sara, 1898-1979); "Wildwood Flower."

Johnny Cash, 1932-2003, singer, songwriter; "I Walk the Line," "Ring of Fire," "Folsom Prison Blues."

Kenny Chesney, b 1968, guitarist, singer, songwriter; "You Had Me From Hello."

Roy Clark, b 1933, guitarist, banjoist, singer, co-host of *Hee Haw*; "Yesterday, When I Was Young."

Patsy Cline, 1932-63, singer; "Walkin' After Midnight," "Crazy," "Sweet Dreams."

Billy Ray Cyrus, b 1961, singer, songwriter; "Achy Breaky Heart."

Charlie Daniels, b 1936, guitarist, fiddler; "The Devil Went Down to Georgia."

Jimmy Dean, 1928-2010, singer; "Big Bad John."

John Denver, 1943-97, singer, songwriter; "Rocky Mountain High."

Dixie Chicks (Natalie Maines, b 1974; Emily Erwin Robison, b 1972; Martie Seidel, b 1969); "Wide Open Spaces."

Dale Evans, 1912-2001, singer, actress, married Roy Rogers.

Sara Evans, b 1971, singer, songwriter; "Born to Fly."

Flatt & Scruggs (Lester Flatt, 1914-79; Earl Scruggs, 1924-2012), guitar-banjo duo and soloists; "Foggy Mountain Breakdown."

Red Foley, 1910-68, singer; "Chattanoogie Shoe Shine Boy."

Tennessee Ernie Ford, 1919-91, singer, TV host; "Sixteen Tons."

William "Lefty" Frizzell, 1928-75, singer, guitarist; "Long Black Veil."

Vince Gill, b 1957, singer, songwriter; "When I Call Your Name."

Merle Haggard, b 1937, singer, songwriter; "Okie From Muskogee."

Emmylou Harris, b 1947, singer, songwriter, folk-country crossover artist; "If I Could Only Win Your Love."

Hunter Hayes, b 1991, singer; "Wanted."

Faith Hill, b 1967, singer, songwriter; "Breathe."

Alan Jackson, b 1958, singer, songwriter; "Where Were You (When the World Stopped Turning)."

Waylon Jennings, 1937-2002, singer, songwriter, "outlaw country" pioneer; "Luckenbach, Texas."

George Jones, 1931-2013, singer; "He Stopped Loving Her Today."

The Judds (Naomi, b 1946; Wynonna, b 1964), mother-daughter duo; Wynonna also a solo act.

Toby Keith, b 1961, singer, songwriter; guitarist; "Should've Been a Cowboy."

Alison Krauss, b 1971, bluegrass fiddler, singer, bandleader; "When You Say Nothing at All."

Kris Kristofferson, b 1936, singer, songwriter, actor; "Me and Bobby McGee."

Lady Antebellum (Dave Haywood, b 1982; Charles Kelley, b 1981; Hillary Scott, b 1984); "I Run to You."

Miranda Lambert, b 1983, singer, guitarist; "The House That Built Me."

Louvin Brothers (Charlie, 1927-2011; Ira, 1924-65), singers; "If I Could Only Win Your Love."

Patty Loveless, b 1957, singer, songwriter; "How Can I Help You Say Goodbye."

Lyle Lovett, b 1957, singer, songwriter, bandleader, actor; "Cowboy Man."

Loretta Lynn, b 1935?, singer; "Coal Miner's Daughter."

Barbara Mandrell, b 1948, singer; "I Was Country When Country Wasn't Cool."

Kathy Mattea, b 1959, singer, songwriter; "Eighteen Wheels and a Dozen Roses."

Martina McBride, b 1966, singer, songwriter; "Independence Day."

Reba McEntire, b 1955, singer, songwriter, actress; "Whoever's in New England."

Tim McGraw, b 1967, singer; "It's Your Love," "I Like It, I Love It."

Roger Miller, 1936-92, singer, songwriter; "King of the Road."

Ronnie Milsap, b 1944, singer, songwriter; "There's No Gettin' Over Me."

Bill Monroe, 1911-96, singer, songwriter, mandolin player, "father of bluegrass music"; "Mule Skinner Blues."

Anne Murray, b 1945, singer; "You Needed Me."

Willie Nelson, b 1933, singer, songwriter, actor; "On the Road Again."

Mark O'Connor, b 1961, fiddler, country-classical crossover composer.

Buck Owens, 1929-2006, singer, guitarist; "Act Naturally."

Brad Paisley, b 1972, singer, songwriter; "Whiskey Lullaby," "When I Get Where I'm Going."

Dolly Parton, b 1946, singer, songwriter, actress; "Here You Come Again," "9 to 5."

Johnny Paycheck, (Don Lytle), 1938-2003, singer, guitarist; "Take This Job and Shove It."

Minnie Pearl, 1912-96, comedienne, Grand Ole Opry star.

Kellie Pickler, b 1986, singer, songwriter.

Ray Price, b 1926, country singer, guitarist, and songwriter; "Crazy Arms."

Charley Pride, b 1938, singer; 1st African American country star; "Kiss an Angel Good Mornin'."

Eddie Rabbit, 1941-98, singer, songwriter; "I Love a Rainy Night."

Rascal Flatts (Jay DeMarcus, b 1971; Gary LeVox, b 1970; Joe Don Rooney, b 1975); "Life Is a Highway."

Jim Reeves, 1923-64, singer, songwriter; "Four Walls."

Charlie Rich, 1932-95, singer, songwriter called the "Silver Fox"; "The Most Beautiful Girl."

LeAnn Rimes, b 1982, singer; "Blue."

Tex Ritter, 1905-74, singer, songwriter; "Jingle, Jangle, Jingle."

Marty Robbins, 1925-82, singer, songwriter; "A White Sport Coat and a Pink Carnation."

Jimmie Rodgers, 1897-1933, singer, songwriter; "T for Texas."

Kenny Rogers, b 1938, singer, songwriter; "The Gambler."

Roy Rogers (Leonard Slye), 1911-98, singer, actor, "King of the Cowboys," sang with Sons of the Pioneers.

Fred Rose, 1898-1954, songwriter, singer, producer; "Blue Eyes Cryin' in the Rain."

Blake Shelton, b 1976, singer; "Home."

Ricky Skaggs, b 1954, singer, songwriter, bandleader; "Don't Cheat in Our Hometown."

Ralph Stanley, b 1927, singer, banjo player; "Man of Constant Sorrow."

George Strait, b 1952, singer, bandleader; "Ace in the Hole."

Sugarland (Kristian Bush, b 1970; Jennifer Nettles, b 1974); "Stay."

Taylor Swift, b 1989, singer, songwriter; "You Belong With Me."

Lonnie "Mel" Tillis, b 1932, singer, songwriter, bandleader; "I Ain't Never."

Merle Travis, 1917-83, singer, guitarist, songwriter; "Divorce Me C.O.D."

Randy Travis, b 1959, singer, songwriter; "Forever and Ever, Amen."

Ernest Tubb, 1914-84, singer, songwriter, guitarist; "Walking the Floor Over You."

Josh Turner, b 1977, singer; "Why Don't We Just Dance."

Shania Twain, b 1965, singer, songwriter; "You're Still the One."

Conway Twitty, 1933-93, singer, songwriter; "Hello Darlin'."

Carrie Underwood, b 1983, singer, songwriter; *American Idol* winner.

Keith Urban, b 1967, guitarist, singer, songwriter; "It's a Love Thing."

Porter Wagoner, 1927-2007, singer, songwriter, guitarist; "I Will Always Love You."

Kitty Wells (Ellen Deason), 1919-2012, singer, songwriter; "It Wasn't God Who Made Honky-Tonk Angels."

Dottie West, 1932-91, singer, songwriter; "Here Comes My Baby."

Hank Williams Jr., b 1949, singer, songwriter; "Bocephus"; "All My Rowdy Friends (Have Settled Down)."

Hank Williams Sr., 1923-53, singer, songwriter; "Your Cheatin' Heart."

Bob Wills, 1905-75, Western Swing fiddler, singer, bandleader, songwriter; "New San Antonio Rose."

Lee Ann Womack, b 1966, singer, songwriter; "I Hope You Dance."

Tammy Wynette, 1942-98, singer; "Stand By Your Man."

Trisha Yearwood, b 1964, singer, songwriter; "How Do I Live."

Dwight Yoakam, b 1957, singer, songwriter, actor; "Ain't That Lonely Yet."

Zac Brown Band (Coy Bowles, b 1979; Zac Brown, b 1978; Clay Cook, Jimmy De Martini, Chris Fryar, b 1970; John Driskell Hopkins, b 1971); "Chicken Fried."

Dance Figures of the Past

Alvin Ailey, 1931-89, (U.S.) modern dancer, choreographer; melded modern dance and Afro-Caribbean techniques.

Frederick Ashton, 1904-88, (Br.) ballet choreographer; director of Great Britain's Royal Ballet, 1963-70.

Fred Astaire, 1899-1987, (U.S.) dancer, actor; teamed with dancer/actress **Ginger Rogers**, 1911-95, (U.S.) in movie musicals.

George Balanchine, 1904-83, (Russ.-U.S.) ballet choreographer, teacher; most influential exponent of neoclassical style; founded, with Lincoln Kirstein, School of American Ballet and New York City Ballet.

Pina Bausch, 1940-2009, (Ger.) modern dance choreographer influencing the Tanztheater style of dance.

Carlo Blasis, 1795-1878, (It.) ballet dancer, choreographer, writer; his teaching methods are standards of classical dance.

August Bournonville, 1805-79, (Den.) ballet dancer, choreographer, teacher; exuberant, light style.

Fernando Bujones, 1955-2005, (Cuba-U.S.) ballet dancer.

Gisella Caccialanza, 1914-98, (U.S.) ballerina; charter member of Balanchine's American Ballet.

Irene, 1893-1969, (U.S.) and **Vernon Castle**, 1887-1918, (Br.) husband-and-wife ballroom dancers.

Enrico Cecchetti, 1850-1928, (It.) ballet dancer, leading dancer of Russia's Imperial Ballet; his technique was basis for Britain's Imperial Soc. of Teachers of Dancing.

Gower Champion, 1921-80, (U.S.) dancer, choreographer, director; with wife **Marge**, b 1923, (U.S.) choreographed, danced in Broadway musicals and films.

John Cranko, 1927-73, (S. Africa) choreographer; created narrative ballets based on literary works.

Merce Cunningham, 1919-2009, (U.S.) dancer, choreographer of avant-garde dance.

Alexandra Danilova, 1903-97, (Russ.) ballerina; noted teacher at the School of American Ballet.

Agnes de Mille, 1905-93, (U.S.) ballerina, choreographer; known for using American themes, she choreographed the ballet *Rodeo* and the musical *Oklahoma!*

Dame Ninette De Valois, 1898-2001, (Br.) choreographer, founding director of London's Royal Ballet; *The Rake's Progress*.

Sergei Diaghilev, 1872-1929, (Russ.) impresario; founded Les Ballet Russes; saw ballet as art unifying dance, drama, music, and decor.

Isadora Duncan, 1877-1927, (U.S.) expressive dancer who united free movement with serious music; one of the founders of modern dance.

Katherine Dunham, 1910-2006, (U.S.) dancer, choreographer; internationally known for African, Caribbean, and African American dance forms.

Fanny Eissler, 1810-84, (Austria) ballerina of the Romantic era; known for dramatic skill, sensual style.

Michel Fokine, 1880-1942, (Russ.) ballet dancer, choreographer, teacher; rejected strict classicism in favor of dramatically expressive style.

Margot Fonteyn, 1919-91, (Br.) prima ballerina, Royal Ballet of Great Britain; famed performance partner of Rudolf Nureyev.

Bob Fosse, 1927-87, (U.S.) jazz dancer, choreographer, director; Broadway musicals and film.

Serge Golovine, 1924-98, (Fr.) ballet dancer with Grand Ballet du Marquis de Cuevas, choreographer.

Martha Graham, 1894-1991, (U.S.) modern dancer, choreographer; created and codified her own dramatic technique.

Melissa Hayden, 1923-2006, (Can.) ballet dancer.

Martha Hill, 1900-95, (U.S.) educator; leading figure in modern dance; founded American Dance Festival.

Gregory Hines, 1946-2003, (U.S.) tap-dance innovator; master of improvisation.

Doris Humphrey, 1895-1958, (U.S.) modern dancer, choreographer, writer, teacher.

Michael Jackson, 1958-2009, (U.S.) singer and dancer who perfected the "moonwalk."

Robert Joffrey, 1930-88, (U.S.) ballet dancer, choreographer; cofounded with **Gerald Arpino**, 1928-2008, (U.S.) the Joffrey Ballet.

Kurt Jooss, 1901-79, (Ger.) choreographer, teacher; created expressionist works using modern and classical techniques.

Tamara Karsavina, 1885-1978, (Russ.) prima ballerina of Russia's Imperial Ballet and Diaghilev's Ballets Russes; partner of Nijinsky.

Nora Kaye, 1920-87, (U.S.) ballerina with Metropolitan Opera Ballet and Ballet Theater (now American Ballet Theatre).

Gene Kelly, 1912-96, (U.S.) dancer, actor in movie musicals.

Michael Kidd, 1915-2003, (U.S.) dancer, film and theater choreographer.

Lincoln Kirstein, 1907-96 (U.S.) brought ballet as an art form to U.S.; founded, with George Balanchine, School of American Ballet and New York City Ballet.

Serge Lifar, 1905-86, (Russ.-Fr.) prem. danseur, choreographer; director of dance at Paris Opera, 1930-45, 1947-58.

José Limón, 1908-72, (Mex.-U.S.) modern dancer, choreographer, teacher; developed technique based on Humphrey.

Catherine Littlefield, 1908-51, (U.S.) ballerina, choreographer, teacher; pioneer of American ballet.

Kenneth MacMillan, 1929-92, (Br.) dancer, choreographer; directed Royal Ballet of Great Britain, 1970-77.

Dame Alicia Markova, 1910-2004, (Br.) ballerina; helped popularize ballet in U.S. and Britain; known for title role in *Giselle*.

Léonide Massine, 1896-1979, (Russ.-U.S.) ballet dancer, choreographer; known for his "symphonic ballet."

Fayard Nicholas, 1914-2006, (U.S.) tap dancer, choreographer, actor; together with brother **Harold Nicholas**, 1921-2000, (U.S.) formed the "Nicholas Brothers."

Vaslav Nijinsky, 1890-50, (Russ.) prem. danseur, choreographer; leading member of Diaghilev's Ballets Russes; his ballets were revolutionary for their time.

Alwin Nikolais, 1910-93, (U.S.) modern choreographer; created dance theater utilizing mixed media effects.

Jean-George Noverre, 1727-1810, (Fr.) ballet choreographer, teacher, writer; "Shakespeare of the Dance."

Rudolf Nureyev, 1938-93, (Russ.) prem. danseur, choreographer; leading male dancer of his generation; director of dance at Paris Opera, 1983-89.

Ruth Page, 1899-1991, (U.S.) ballerina, choreographer; danced, directed ballet at Chicago Lyric Opera.

Anna Pavlova, 1881-1931, (Russ.) prima ballerina; toured with her own company to world acclaim.

Marius Petipa, 1818-1910, (Fr.) ballet dancer, choreographer; ballet master of the Imperial Ballet; established Russian classicism as leading style of late 19th cent.

Roland Petit, 1924-2011, (Fr.) dancer, choreographer; founder Les Ballets de Paris.

Pearl Primus, 1919-95, (Trinidad-U.S.) modern dancer, choreographer, scholar; combined African, Caribbean, and African American styles.

Jerome Robbins, 1918-98, (U.S.) choreographer, director, dancer; *The King and I, West Side Story, Fiddler on the Roof.*

Bill "Bojangles" Robinson, 1878-1949, (U.S.) famed tap dancer; called "King of Tapology" on stage and screen.

Ruth St. Denis, 1877-1968, (U.S.) influential interpretive dancer, choreographer, teacher.

Ted Shawn, 1891-1972, (U.S.) modern dancer, choreographer; formed dance company and school with Ruth St. Denis; established Jacob's Pillow Dance Festival.

Marie Taglioni, 1804-84, (It.) ballerina, teacher; in title role of *La Sylphide* established image of the ethereal ballerina.

Maria Tallchief, 1925-2013, (U.S.) prima ballerina, 1st of American Indian descent.

Glen Tetley, 1926-2007, (U.S.) dancer, choreographer, ballet director; fused elements of modern dance with ballet.

Antony Tudor, 1908-87, (Br.) choreographer, teacher; exponent of the "psychological ballet."

Galina Ulanova, 1910-98, (Russ.) revered ballerina with Bolshoi Ballet.

Agrippina Vaganova, 1879-1951, (Russ.) ballet teacher, director; codified Soviet ballet technique; called "queen of variations."

Mary Wigman, 1886-1973, (Ger.) modern dancer, choreographer, teacher; influenced European expressionist dance.

Opera Singers of the Past

Frances Alda, 1883?-1952, (N.Z.) soprano.

Pasquale Amato, 1878-1942, (It.) baritone.

Marian Anderson, 1897-1993, (U.S.) contralto.

Charles Anthony, 1929-2012, (U.S.) tenor.

Jussi Björling, 1911-60, (Swed.) tenor.

Lucrezia Bori, 1887-1960, (It.) soprano.

Maria Callas, 1923-77, (U.S.) soprano.

Emma Calvé, 1858-1942, (Fr.) soprano.

Enrico Caruso, 1873-1921, (It.) tenor.

Feodor Chaliapin, 1873-1938, (Russ.)

Lili Chookasian, 1921-2012, (U.S.) contralto.

Boris Christoff, 1914-93, (Bulg.) bass.

Franco Corelli, 1921-2003, (It.) tenor.

Hughes Cuenod, 1902-2010, (Switz.) tenor.

Victoria De Los Angeles, 1923-2005, (Sp.) soprano.

Giuseppe De Luca, 1876-1950, (It.) baritone.

Fernando De Lucia, 1860-1925, (It.) tenor.

Edouard De Reszke, 1853-1917, (Pol.) bass.

Jean De Reszke, 1850-1925, (Pol.) tenor.

Emmy Destinn, 1878-1930, (Czech.) soprano.

Emma Eames, 1865-1952, (U.S.) soprano.

(Carlo Broschi) Farinelli, 1705-82, (It.) castrato.

Geraldine Farrar, 1882-1967, (U.S.) soprano.

Eileen Farrell, 1920-2002, (U.S.) soprano.

Kathleen Ferrier, 1912-53, (Eng.) contralto.

Dietrich Fischer-Dieskau, 1925-2012, (Ger.) baritone.

Kirsten Flagstad, 1895-1962, (Nor.) soprano.
Olive Fremstad, 1871-1951, (Swed.-U.S.) soprano.
Amelita Galli-Curci, 1882-1963, (It.) soprano.
Mary Garden, 1874-1967, (Br.) soprano.
Nicolai Ghiaurov, 1929-2004, (Bulg.) bass.
Beniamino Gigli, 1890-1957, (It.) tenor.
Tito Gobbi, 1913-84, (It.) baritone.
Giulia Grisi, 1811-69, (It.) soprano.
Frieda Hempel, 1885-1955, (Ger.) soprano.
Jerome Hines, 1921-2003, (U.S.) bass.
Hans Hotter, 1909-2003, (Ger.) bass-baritone.
Maria Jeritza, 1887-1982, (Czech.) soprano.
Sena Jurinac, 1921-2011, (Yugo.) soprano.
Alexander Kipnis, 1891-1978, (Russ.-U.S.) bass.
Dorothy Kirsten, 1910-92, (U.S.) soprano.
Alfredo Kraus, 1927-99, (Sp.) tenor.
Luigi Lablache, 1794-1858, (It.) bass.
Lilli Lehmann, 1848-1929, (Ger.) soprano.
Lotte Lehmann, 1888-1976, (Ger.-U.S.) soprano.
Jenny Lind, 1820-87, (Swed.) soprano.
Cornell MacNeil, 1922-2011, (U.S.) baritone.
Maria Malibran, 1808-36, (Sp.) mezzo-soprano.
Giovanni Martinelli, 1885-1969, (It.) tenor.
John McCormack, 1884-1945, (Ire.) tenor.

Nellie Melba, 1861-1931, (Austral.) soprano.
Lauritz Melchior, 1890-1973, (Den.) tenor.
Robert Merrill, 1919-2004, (U.S.) baritone.
Zinka Milanov, 1906-89, (Yugo.) soprano.
Patricia Neway, 1919-2012, (U.S.) soprano.
Birgit Nilsson, 1918-2005, (Swed.) soprano.
Lillian Nordica, 1857-1914, (U.S.) soprano.
Giuditta Pasta, 1797-1865, (It.) soprano.
Adelina Patti, 1843-1919, (It.) soprano.
Luciano Pavarotti, 1935-2007, (It.) tenor.
Peter Pears, 1910-86, (Eng.) tenor.
Jan Peerce, 1904-84, (U.S.) tenor.
Ezio Pinza, 1892-1957, (It.) bass.
Lily Pons, 1898-1976, (Fr.) soprano.
Rosa Ponselle, 1897-1981, (U.S.) soprano.
Hermann Prey, 1929-98, (Ger.) baritone.
Margaret Price, 1941-2011, (U.K.) soprano.
Regina Resnik, 1922-2013, (U.S.) soprano turned mezzo-soprano.
Elisabeth Rethberg, 1894-1976, (Ger.) soprano.
Giovanni Battista Rubini, 1794-1854, (It.) tenor.
Leonie Rysanek, 1926-98, (Austria) soprano.
Dorothy Sarnoff, 1914-2008, (U.S.) soprano.
Bidú Sayão, 1902-99, (Braz.) soprano.
Friedrich Schorr, 1888-1953, (Hung.) bass-baritone.
Elisabeth Schwarzkopf, 1915-2006, (Ger.) soprano.

Marcella Sembrich, 1858-1935, (Pol.) soprano.
Cesare Siepi, 1923-2010, (It.) bass.
Beverly Sills, 1929-2007, (U.S.) soprano.
Elisabeth Söderström, 1927-2009, (Swed.) soprano.
Eleanor Steber, 1914-90, (U.S.) soprano.
Risë Stevens, 1913-2013, (U.S.) mezzo-soprano.
Joan Sutherland, 1926-2010, (Austral.) soprano.
Ferrucio Tagliavini, 1913-95, (It.) tenor.
Renata Tebaldi, 1922-2004 (It.) soprano.
Luisa Tetrazzini, 1871-1940, (It.) soprano.
Lawrence Tibbett, 1896-1960, (U.S.) baritone.
Giorgio Tozzi, 1923-2011, (U.S.) bass-baritone.
Tatiana Troyanos, 1938-93, (U.S.) mezzo-soprano.
Richard Tucker, 1913-75, (U.S.) tenor.
Shirley Verrett, 1931-2010, (U.S.) mezzo-soprano.
Pauline Viardot, 1821-1910, (Fr.) mezzo-soprano.
William Warfield, 1920-2002, (U.S.) bass-baritone.
Leonard Warren, 1911-60, (U.S.) baritone.
Ljuba Welitsch, 1913-96, (Bulg.) soprano.
Camilla Williams, 1919-2012, (U.S.) soprano.
Wolfgang Windgassen, 1914-74, (Ger.) tenor.

Rock and Roll, Rhythm and Blues, and Rap Artists

Titles in quotation marks are singles; others are albums. *Inducted into Rock and Roll Hall of Fame as performer between 1986 and 2013; year is in parentheses.

*ABBA (2010): "Dancing Queen"
Paula Abdul: "Straight Up"
*AC/DC (2003): "Back in Black"
Bryan Adams: "Cuts Like a Knife"
Adele: "Rolling in the Deep"
*Aerosmith (2001): "Sweet Emotion"
Christina Aguilera: "What a Girl Wants"
Alice in Chains: "Heaven Beside You"
*The Allman Brothers Band (1995): "Ramblin' Man"
*The Animals (1994): "House of the Rising Sun"
Paul Anka: "Lonely Boy"
Fiona Apple: "Criminal"
Frankie Avalon: "Venus"
The B-52s: "Love Shack"
Bachman Turner Overdrive: "Takin' Care of Business"
Backstreet Boys: "I Want It That Way"
Bad Company: "Can't Get Enough"
Erykah Badu: "On and On"
*La Vern Baker (1991): "I Cried a Tear"
*Hank Ballard[1] and the Midnighters (1990): "Work With Me, Annie"
*The Band (1994): "The Weight"
Barenaked Ladies: "One Week"
*The Beach Boys (1988): "Good Vibrations"
*Beastie Boys (2012): "(You Gotta) Fight for Your Right (to Party)"
*The Beatles (1988): Sgt. Pepper's Lonely Hearts Club Band
Beck: "Loser"
*Jeff Beck (2009): "Escape"
*The Bee Gees (1997): "Stayin' Alive"
Pat Benatar: "Hit Me With Your Best Shot"
*Chuck Berry (1986): "Johnny B. Goode"
Beyoncé: "Crazy in Love"
The Big Bopper: "Chantilly Lace"
Björk: "Human Behavior"
The Black Crowes: "Hard to Handle"
Black Eyed Peas: Elephunk
*Black Sabbath (2006): "Paranoid"
*Bobby "Blue" Bland (1992): "Turn On Your Love Light"
Mary J. Blige: My Life
Blind Faith: "Can't Find My Way Home"
Blink-182: "All the Small Things"
*Blondie (2006): "Heart of Glass"
Blood, Sweat, and Tears: "Spinning Wheel"
Blues Traveler: "Run-Around"
Gary "U.S." Bonds: "Quarter to Three"
Bon Jovi: "Livin' on a Prayer"
*Booker T. and the M.G.'s (1992): "Green Onions"
Boston: "More Than a Feeling"

*David Bowie (1996): "Space Oddity"
Boyz II Men: "I'll Make Love to You"
Toni Braxton: "Un-Break My Heart"
Chris Brown: "Kiss Kiss"
*James Brown (1986): "Papa's Got a Brand New Bag"
*Ruth Brown (1993): "Lucky Lips"
*Jackson Browne (2004): "Doctor My Eyes"
*Buffalo Springfield (1997): "For What It's Worth"
Jimmy Buffett: "Margaritaville"
*Solomon Burke (2001): "Over and Over (Huggin' and Lovin')"
*The Byrds (1991): "Turn! Turn! Turn!"
Mariah Carey: "Vision of Love"
The Carpenters: "(They Long to Be) Close to You"
The Cars: "Shake It Up"
*Johnny Cash (1992): "I Walk the Line"
*Ray Charles (1986): "Georgia on My Mind"
Cheap Trick: "Surrender"
Chubby Checker: "The Twist"
Chicago: "Saturday in the Park"
*Eric Clapton (2000): "Layla"
Kelly Clarkson: "Since U Been Gone"
*The Clash (2003): "Rock the Casbah"
*Jimmy Cliff (2010): "I Can See Clearly Now"
*The Coasters (1987): "Yakety Yak"
*Eddie Cochran (1987): "Summertime Blues"
Joe Cocker: "With a Little Help From My Friends"
*Leonard Cohen (2008): "Suzanne"
Coldplay: "Clocks"
Collective Soul: "The World I Know"
Phil Collins: "Against All Odds"
*Sam Cooke (1986): "You Send Me"
Coolio: "Gangsta's Paradise"
*Alice Cooper (2011): "School's Out"
*Elvis Costello and the Attractions (2003): "Alison"
Counting Crows: "Mr. Jones"
*Cream (1993): "Sunshine of Your Love"
Creed: "Arms Wide Open"
*Creedence Clearwater Revival (1993): "Proud Mary"
*Crosby, Stills, and Nash (1997): "Suite: Judy Blue Eyes"
Sheryl Crow: "All I Want to Do"
The Crystals: "Da Doo Ron Ron"
The Cure: "Boys Don't Cry"
Daft Punk: "Get Lucky"
Danny and the Juniors: "At the Hop"
*Bobby Darin (1990): "Splish Splash"
Daughtry: "It's Not Over"

*The Dave Clark Five (2008): "Glad All Over"
Dave Matthews Band: "Don't Drink the Water"
*Miles Davis (2006): Bitches Brew
Spencer Davis Group: "Gimme Some Lovin'"
Deep Purple: "Smoke on the Water"
Def Leppard: "Photograph"
*The Dells (2004): "Oh, What a Night"
Depeche Mode: "Strange Love"
Destiny's Child: "Survivor"
*Neil Diamond (2011): "Cracklin' Rosie"
*Bo Diddley (1987): "Who Do You Love?"
*Dion[1] and the Belmonts (1989): "A Teenager in Love"
Celine Dion: "Because You Loved Me"
Dire Straits: "Money for Nothing"
DMX: "What's My Name"
*Fats Domino (1986): "Blueberry Hill"
*Donovan (2012): "Mellow Yellow"
The Doobie Brothers: "What a Fool Believes"
*The Doors (1993): "Light My Fire"
Drake: "Over"
Dr. Dre: "Nothin' But a 'G' Thang"
*The Drifters (1988): "Save the Last Dance for Me"
*Dr. John (2011): "Right Place, Wrong Time"
Duran Duran: "Hungry Like the Wolf"
*Bob Dylan (1988): "Like a Rolling Stone"
*The Eagles (1998): "Hotel California"
*Earth, Wind, and Fire (2000): "Shining Star"
*Duane Eddy (1994): "Rebel-Rouser"
Missy Elliott: "Sock It 2 Me"
Eminem: "The Real Slim Shady"
En Vogue: "Hold On"
The Eurythmics: "Sweet Dreams (Are Made of This)"
Everclear: "Father Of Mine"
*The Everly Brothers (1986): "Wake Up, Little Susie"
50 Cent (Curtis Jackson): Get Rich or Die Tryin'
The Five Satins: "In the Still of the Night"
Roberta Flack: "The First Time Ever I Saw Your Face"
*The Flamingos (2001): "I Only Have Eyes for You"
*Fleetwood Mac (1998): Rumours
The Foo Fighters: "I'll Stick Around"
Foreigner: "Double Vision"
*The Four Seasons (1990): "Sherry"
*The Four Tops (1990): "I Can't Help Myself (Sugar Pie, Honey Bunch)"

*Aretha Franklin (1987): "Respect"
fun.: "We Are Young"
Nelly Furtado: "I'm Like a Bird"
Peter Gabriel: "Shock the Monkey"
*Gamble (Kenny) and Huff (Leon) (2008): "If You Don't Know Me By Now"
*Marvin Gaye (1987): "I Heard It Through the Grapevine"
*Genesis (2010): "No Reply at All"
Goo Goo Dolls: "Iris"
Grand Funk Railroad: "We're an American Band"
*Grandmaster Flash and the Furious Five (2007): "The Message"
*The Grateful Dead (1994): "Uncle John's Band"
*Al Green (1995): "Let's Stay Together"
Green Day: "Boulevard of Broken Dreams"
The Guess Who: "American Woman"
*Guns N' Roses (2012): "Sweet Child o' Mine"
*Buddy Guy (2005): A Man and His Blues
*Bill Haley[1] and His Comets (1987): "Rock Around the Clock"
Hall and Oates: "Kiss on My List"
*George Harrison (2004): "My Sweet Lord"
*Isaac Hayes (2002): "Theme From 'Shaft'"
*Heart (2013): "Barracuda"
*Jimi Hendrix (1992): "Purple Haze"
Lauryn Hill: "Doo-Wop (That Thing)"
*The Hollies (2010): "Long Cool Woman (In a Black Dress)"
*Buddy Holly (1986): "Peggy Sue"
*John Lee Hooker (1991): "Boogie Chillen"
Hootie and the Blowfish: Cracked Rear View
Whitney Houston: "I Will Always Love You"
*The Impressions (1991): "For Your Precious Love"
Indigo Girls: "Closer to Fine"
INXS: "Need You Tonight"
*The Isley Brothers (1992): "It's Your Thing"
Ja Rule: Venni, Vetti, Vecci
*The Jackson Five (1997): "ABC"
Janet Jackson: Rhythm Nation
*Michael Jackson (2001): Thriller
*Etta James (1993): "At Last"
Tommy James and the Shondells: "Crimson and Clover"
Jane's Addiction: "Jane Says"
Jay and the Americans: "This Magic Moment"
Jay-Z: "Can I Live"
*Jefferson Airplane (1996): "White Rabbit"
Jethro Tull: Aqualung
Joan Jett: "I Love Rock 'n' Roll"
Jewel: "You Were Meant For Me"
*Billy Joel (1999): "Piano Man"
*Elton John (1994): "Candle in the Wind"
*Little Willie John (1996): "Sleep"
Norah Jones: Come Away With Me
*Janis Joplin (1995): "Me and Bobby McGee"
Journey: "Don't Stop Believin'"
K.C. and the Sunshine Band: "Get Down Tonight"
R. Kelly: "I Can't Sleep Baby (If I)"
Alicia Keys: "Fallin'"
Kid Rock: "Cowboy"
*B.B. King (1987): "The Thrill Is Gone"
Carole King: Tapestry
*The Kinks (1990): "You Really Got Me"
Kiss: "Rock 'n' Roll All Night"
*Gladys Knight and the Pips (1996): "Midnight Train to Georgia"
Korn: "Blind"
Lenny Kravitz: "Are You Gonna Go My Way?"
Lady Gaga: "Poker Face"
*Led Zeppelin (1995): "Stairway to Heaven"
*Brenda Lee (2002): "I'm Sorry"
John Legend: "Ordinary People"
*John Lennon (1994): "Imagine"
*Jerry Lee Lewis (1986): "Whole Lotta Shakin' Going On"
Lil' Kim: "No Matter What They Say"
Lil Wayne: The Block Is Hot.
Limp Bizkit: "Break Stuff"
Linkin Park: "One Step Closer"
*Little Anthony and the Imperials (2009): "Tears on My Pillow"
*Little Richard (1986): "Tutti Frutti"
*Little Walter (2008): "Juke"
L. L. Cool J: "Mama Said Knock You Out"
Jennifer Lopez: "Love Don't Cost a Thing"

*Darlene Love (2011): "He's a Rebel"
*The Lovin' Spoonful (2000): "Summer in the City"
Ludacris: "Money Maker"
*Frankie Lymon and the Teenagers (1993): "Why Do Fools Fall in Love?"
*Lynyrd Skynyrd (2006): "Free Bird"
*Madonna (2008): "Material Girl"
*The Mamas and the Papas (1998): "Monday, Monday"
Marilyn Manson: "Beautiful People"
*Bob Marley (1994): Exodus
Maroon 5: Songs About Jane
Bruno Mars: "Just the Way You Are"
*Martha and the Vandellas (1995): "Dancin' in the Streets"
The Marvelettes: "Please, Mr. Postman"
Matchbox 20: "Push"
John Mayer: "Daughters"
*Curtis Mayfield (1999): "Superfly"
*Paul McCartney (1999): "Band on the Run"
Don McLean: "American Pie"
*Clyde McPhatter (1987): "A Lover's Question"
Meat Loaf: "Paradise by the Dashboard Light"
*John (Cougar) Mellencamp (2008): "Jack and Diane"
Men at Work: "Who Can It Be Now?"
*Metallica (2009): "Enter Sandman"
George Michael: "Faith"
Nicki Minaj: Pink Friday.
*Joni Mitchell (1997): "Both Sides Now"
Moby: "Bodyrock"
The Monkees: "I'm a Believer"
Moody Blues: "Nights in White Satin"
*The Moonglows (2000): "Blue Velvet"
Alanis Morissette: "Ironic"
*Van Morrison (1993): "Brown-Eyed Girl"
Mötley Crüe: "Live Wire"
Motörhead: "Ace of Spades"
Jason Mraz: "I'm Yours"
Mumford & Sons: "Little Lion Man"
Nelly: Country Grammar
*Ricky Nelson (1987): "Hello, Mary Lou"
Nine Inch Nails: "Closer"
Nirvana: Nevermind
No Doubt: Rock Steady
The Notorious B.I.G.: "Mo Money Mo Problems"
'N Sync: "Bye, Bye, Bye"
Ted Nugent: "Strangehold"
*The O'Jays (2005): "Back Stabbers"
*Roy Orbison (1987): "Oh, Pretty Woman"
Ozzy Osbourne: "Crazy Train"
OutKast: Speakerboxxx/The Love Below
*Parliament/Funkadelic (1997): "One Nation Under a Groove"
Pearl Jam: "Jeremy"
*Carl Perkins (1987): "Blue Suede Shoes"
Katy Perry: "I Kissed a Girl"
Peter, Paul, and Mary: "Leaving on a Jet Plane"
*Tom Petty and the Heartbreakers (2002): "Refugee"
Liz Phair: Exile in Guyville
Phish: "Sample in a Jar"
*Wilson Pickett (1991): "Land of 1,000 Dances"
Pink: Missundaztood!
*Pink Floyd (1996): The Wall
*Gene Pitney (2002): "Only Love Can Break a Heart"
*The Platters (1990): "The Great Pretender"
The Pointer Sisters: "I'm So Excited"
*The Police (2003): "Every Breath You Take"
Iggy Pop: "Lust for Life"
*Elvis Presley (1986): "Love Me Tender"
*The Pretenders (2005): "Back on the Chain Gang"
*Lloyd Price (1998): "Stagger Lee"
*Prince (The Artist) (2004): "Purple Rain"
*Public Enemy (2013): "Fight the Power"
Puff Daddy and the Family: No Way Out
*Queen (2001): "Bohemian Rhapsody"
Radiohead: OK Computer
Rage Against the Machine: Bulls on Parade"
*Bonnie Raitt (2000): "Something to Talk About"
*The Ramones (2002): "I Wanna Be Sedated"
*Red Hot Chili Peppers (2012): "Under the Bridge"
*Otis Redding (1989): "(Sittin' on) The Dock of the Bay"

*Jimmy Reed (1991): "Ain't That Loving You, Baby?"
Lou Reed: "Walk on the Wild Side"
*R.E.M. (2007): "Losing My Religion"
REO Speedwagon: "Can't Fight This Feeling"
Busta Rhymes: "What's It Gonna Be?"
*The Righteous Brothers (2003): "You've Lost That Lovin' Feelin'"
Rihanna: "Rude Boy"
Johnny Rivers: "Poor Side of Town"
*Smokey Robinson[1] and the Miracles (1987): "Shop Around"
*The Rolling Stones (1989): "Satisfaction"
*The Ronettes (2007): "Be My Baby"
Linda Ronstadt: "You're No Good"
Diana Ross: "I'm Coming Out"
*Run-D.M.C. (2009): "Raisin' Hell"
*Rush (2013): "Tom Sawyer"
Sade: "Smooth Operator"
Salt-N-Pepa: "Shoop"
*Sam and Dave (1992): "Soul Man"
*Santana (1998): "Black Magic Woman"
Seal: "Kiss From a Rose"
Neil Sedaka: "Breaking Up Is Hard to Do"
*Bob Seger (2004): "Old Time Rock & Roll"
*Sex Pistols (2006): "Anarchy in the UK"
Shakira: "Whenever, Wherever"
Tupac Shakur: "How Do U Want It"
*Del Shannon (1999): "Runaway"
*The Shirelles (1996): "Soldier Boy"
Carly Simon: "You're So Vain"
*Paul Simon (2001): "50 Ways to Leave Your Lover"
*Simon and Garfunkel (1990): "Bridge Over Troubled Water"
*Percy Sledge (2005): "When a Man Loves a Woman"
*Sly and the Family Stone (1993): "Everyday People"
Smashing Pumpkins: "Today"
*Patti Smith (2007): "Because the Night"
Will Smith: "Gettin' Jiggy With It"
The Smiths: "This Charming Man"
Snoop Lion (née Dogg): "Gin and Juice"
Sonic Youth: "Bull in the Heather"
Soundgarden: "Black Hole Sun"
Britney Spears: "Hit Me Baby One More Time"
Spice Girls: "Wannabe"
*Dusty Springfield (1999): "I Only Want to Be With You"
*Bruce Springsteen (1999): "Born to Run"
*Staple Singers (1999): "I'll Take You There"
*Steely Dan (2001): "Rikki Don't Lose That Number"
Gwen Stefani: "Hollaback Girl"
Steppenwolf: "Born to Be Wild"
*Rod Stewart (1994): "Maggie Mae"
Sting: "If You Love Somebody, Set Them Free"
Stone Temple Pilots: "Plush"
*The Stooges (2010): "I Wanna Be Your Dog"
Styx: "Come Sail Away"
The Sugar Hill Gang: "Rapper's Delight"
*Donna Summer (2013): "Bad Girls"
*The Supremes (1988): "Stop! In the Name of Love"
*Talking Heads (2002): "Once in a Lifetime"
*James Taylor (2001): "You've Got a Friend"
*The Temptations (1989): "My Girl"
Robin Thicke: "Blurred Lines"
Three Dog Night: "Joy to the World"
Justin Timberlake: "SexyBack"
TLC: "Waterfalls"
Traffic (2004): Traffic
*Big Joe Turner (1987): "Shake, Rattle & Roll"
*Ike and Tina Turner (1991): "Proud Mary"
*Tina Turner (1991): "What's Love Got to Do With It?"
The Turtles: "Happy Together"
*U2 (2005): "With or Without You"
Usher: "You Make Me Wanna"
*Ritchie Valens (2001): "La Bamba"
*Van Halen (2007): "Running With the Devil"
Stevie Ray Vaughan: "Crossfire"
*The Velvet Underground (1996): "Sweet Jane"
*The Ventures (2008): "Walk, Don't Run"
*Gene Vincent (1998): "Be-Bop-A-Lula"

*Tom Waits (2011): "Downtown Train"
The Wallflowers: "One Headlight"
Dionne Warwick: "I Say a Little Prayer"
*Muddy Waters (1987): "I Can't Be Satisfied"
Mary Wells: "My Guy"
Kanye West: "Gold Digger"
The White Stripes: "Seven Nation Army"

Whitesnake: "Here I Go Again"
*The Who (1990): Tommy
*Jackie Wilson (1987): "That's Why"
*Bobby Womack (2009): "Lookin' for a Love"
*Stevie Wonder (1989): "You Are the Sunshine of My Life"
Wu-Tang Clan: "Protect Ya Neck"

*The Yardbirds (1992): "For Your Love"
Yes: "Roundabout"
*Neil Young (1995): "Down by the River"
*The Young Rascals/The Rascals (1997): "Good Lovin' "
*Frank Zappa[1]/Mothers of Invention (1995): Hot Rats
*ZZ Top (2004): "Legs"

(1) Only individual performer is in Rock and Roll Hall of Fame.

Entertainment Personalities of the Present

Living actors, musicians, dancers, singers, producers, directors, and radio-TV performers.

Name	Birthplace	Birthdate
Abbado, Claudio	Milan, Italy	6/26/33
Abdul, Paula	San Fernando, CA	6/19/62
Abraham, F. Murray	Pittsburgh, PA	10/24/39
Abrams, J(effrey) J(acob)	New York, NY	6/27/66
Adams, Amy	Vicenza, Italy	8/20/74
Adams, Bryan	Kingston, ON, Canada	11/5/59
Adams, Yolanda	Houston, TX	8/27/61
Adele	London, England, UK	5/5/88
Adjani, Isabelle	Paris, France	6/27/55
Ad-Rock	South Orange, NJ	10/31/66
Affleck, Ben	Berkeley, CA	8/15/72
Affleck, Casey	Falmouth, MA	8/12/75
Aghdashloo, Shohreh	Tehran, Iran	5/11/52
Agron, Dianna	Savannah, GA	4/30/86
Aguilera, Christina	Staten Island, NY.	12/18/80
Aiello, Danny	New York, NY	6/20/33
Aiken, Clay	Raleigh, NC.	11/30/78
Aimee, Anouk	Paris, France	4/27/32
Alba, Jessica	Pomona, CA	4/28/81
Albanese, Licia	Bari, Italy.	7/22/1913
Alberghetti, Anna Maria	Pesaro, Italy	5/15/36
Albert, Marv	Brooklyn, NY.	6/12/41
Alda, Alan	New York, NY	1/28/36
Alexander, Jane	Boston, MA	10/28/39
Alexander, Jason	Newark, NJ	9/23/59
Allen, Debbie	Houston, TX	1/16/50
Allen, Joan	Rochelle, IL	8/20/56
Allen, Karen	Carrollton, IL	10/5/51
Allen, Kris	Jacksonville, AR	6/21/85
Allen, Ted	Columbus, OH.	5/20/65
Allen, Tim	Denver, CO	6/13/53
Allen, Woody	Bronx, NY	12/1/35
Alley, Kirstie	Wichita, KS	1/12/51
Allman, Gregg	Nashville, TN.	12/8/47
Alonso, Maria Conchita	Cienfuegos, Cuba	6/29/57
Alpert, Herb	Los Angeles, CA	3/31/35
Almodóvar, Pedro	Calzada de Calatrava, Spain	9/24/49
Ambrose, Lauren	New Haven, CT	2/20/78
Ames, Ed	Malden, MA	7/9/27
Amos, John	Newark, NJ	12/27/39
Amos, Tori	Newton, NC	8/22/63
Anderson, Gillian	Chicago, IL	8/9/68
Anderson, Harry	Newport, RI	10/14/52
Anderson, Ian	Dunfermline, Scotland, UK	8/10/47
Anderson, Kevin	Gurnee, IL.	1/13/60
Anderson, Loni	St. Paul, MN	8/5/46?
Anderson, Lynn	Grand Forks, ND	9/26/47
Anderson, Melissa Sue	Berkeley, CA	9/26/62
Anderson, Pamela	Ladysmith, BC, Canada	7/1/67
Anderson, Richard	Long Branch, NJ	8/8/26
Anderson, Richard Dean	Minneapolis, MN	1/23/50
Anderson, Wes	Houston, TX	5/1/69
Andersson, Bibi	Stockholm, Sweden	11/11/35
André 3000	Atlanta, GA	5/27/75
Andress, Ursula	Bern, Switzerland	3/19/36
Andrews, Julie	Walton-on-Thames, Surrey, England, UK	10/1/35
Andrews, Naveen	London, England, UK	1/17/69
Aniston, Jennifer	Sherman Oaks, CA	2/11/69
Anka, Paul	Ottawa, ON, Canada	7/30/41
Ann-Margret	Stockholm, Sweden	4/28/41
Ansari, Aziz	Columbia, SC	2/23/83
Anthony, Marc	New York, NY	9/16/68
Apatow, Judd	Syosset, NY.	12/6/67
Apple, Fiona	New York, NY	9/13/77
Applegate, Christina	Los Angeles, CA	11/25/71
Archer, Anne	Los Angeles, CA	8/24/47
Archuleta, David	Miami, FL	12/28/90
Arkin, Adam	Brooklyn, NY.	8/19/56
Arkin, Alan	New York, NY	3/26/34
Armisen, Fred	Hattiesburg, MS.	12/4/66
Arnaz, Desi, Jr.	Hollywood, CA.	1/19/53
Arnaz, Lucie	Hollywood, CA.	7/17/51
Arnett, Will	Toronto, ON, Canada.	5/4/70
Arnold, Tom	Ottumwa, IA.	3/6/59
Arquette, David	Winchester, VA	9/8/71
Arquette, Patricia	Chicago, IL	4/8/68
Arquette, Rosanna	New York, NY	8/10/59
Arroyo, Martina	New York, NY.	2/2/36
Ashanti (Douglas)	Glen Cove, NY.	10/13/80
Ashley, Elizabeth	Ocala, FL.	8/30/39
Asner, Ed	Kansas City, KS.	11/15/29
Assante, Armand	New York, NY.	10/4/49

Name	Birthplace	Birthdate
Astin, John	Baltimore, MD	3/30/30
Astin, Sean	Santa Monica, CA	2/25/71
Atkins, Eileen	London, England, UK	6/16/34
Atkins, Sharif	Pittsburgh, PA	1/29/75
Atkinson, Rowan	Newcastle upon Tyne, England, UK	1/6/55
Attenborough, Richard	Cambridge, England, UK.	8/29/23
Auberjonois, Rene	New York, NY	6/1/40
Austin, Patti	New York, NY	8/10/48
Avalon, Frankie	Philadelphia, PA	9/18/40
Aykroyd, Dan	Ottawa, ON, Canada	7/1/52
Azaria, Hank	Forest Hills, Queens, NY	4/25/64
Aznavour, Charles	Paris, France	5/22/24
Babyface	Indianapolis, IN	4/10/59
Bacall, Lauren	Bronx, NY	9/16/24
Baccarin, Morena	Rio de Janeiro, Brazil	6/2/79
Bacon, Kevin	Philadelphia, PA	7/8/58
Badalucco, Michael	Brooklyn, NY.	12/20/54
Bader, Diedrich	Alexandria, VA.	12/24/66
Badu, Erykah	Dallas, TX	2/26/71
Baez, Joan	Staten Island, NY.	1/9/41
Baio, Scott	Brooklyn, NY.	9/22/60
Baker, Anita	Toledo, OH	1/26/58
Baker, Carroll	Johnstown, PA.	5/28/31
Baker, Diane	Hollywood, CA.	2/25/38
Baker, Joe Don	Groesbeck, TX.	2/12/36
Baker, Kathy	Midland, TX.	6/8/50
Baker, Simon	Launceston, Tasmania, Australia	7/30/69
Bakula, Scott	St. Louis, MO.	10/9/54
Baldwin, Alec	Massapequa, NY.	4/3/58
Baldwin, Daniel	Massapequa, NY.	10/5/60
Baldwin, Stephen	Massapequa, NY.	5/12/66
Baldwin, William	Massapequa, NY.	2/21/63
Bale, Christian	Pembrokeshire, Wales, UK	1/30/74
Ballard, Kaye	Cleveland, OH.	11/20/26
Ballas, Mark	Houston, TX.	5/24/86
Bana, Eric	Melbourne, Australia	8/9/68
Banderas, Antonio	Málaga, Spain.	8/10/60
Banks, Elizabeth	Pittsfield, MA	2/10/74
Banks, Jonathan	Washington, D.C.	1/31/47
Banks, Tyra	Los Angeles, CA	12/4/73
Baranski, Christine	Buffalo, NY	5/2/52
Barbeau, Adrienne	Sacramento, CA	6/11/45
Bardem, Javier	Las Palmas, Canary Islands, Spain.	3/1/69
Bardot, Brigitte	Paris, France.	9/28/34
Barker, Bob	Darrington, WA	12/12/23
Barkin, Ellen	Bronx, NY	4/16/55
Barrie, Barbara	Chicago, IL	5/23/31
Barrino, Fantasia	High Point, NC.	6/30/84
Barrymore, Drew	Los Angeles, CA	2/22/75
Bartoli, Cecilia	Rome, Italy	6/4/66
Barton, Misha	London, England, UK	1/24/86
Baryshnikov, Mikhail	Riga, Latvia	1/28/48
Basinger, Kim	Athens, GA	12/8/53
Bass, Lance	Laurel, MS.	5/4/79
Bassett, Angela	New York, NY.	8/16/58
Bassey, Shirley	Cardiff, Wales, UK	1/8/37
Bateman, Jason	Rye, NY.	1/14/69
Bateman, Justine	Rye, NY.	2/19/66
Bates, Kathy	Memphis, TN.	6/28/48
Batt, Bryan	New Orleans, LA	3/1/63
Battle, Kathleen	Portsmouth, OH.	8/13/48
Baxter, Meredith	South Pasadena, CA	6/21/47
Bean, Orson	Burlington, VT	7/22/28
Bean, Sean	Sheffield, England, UK.	4/17/59
Beatty, Ned	Louisville, KY.	7/6/37
Beatty, Warren	Richmond, VA	3/30/37
Beauvais, Garcelle	St. Marc, Haiti	11/26/66
Beck	Los Angeles, CA	7/8/70
Beck, Jeff	Wallington, Surrey, Eng., UK.	6/24/44
Beckham, Victoria	Hertfordshire, England, UK.	4/17/74
Beckinsale, Kate	London, England, UK	7/26/73
Bedelia, Bonnie	New York, NY	3/25/48
Begley, Ed, Jr.	Los Angeles, CA	9/16/49
Behar, Joy	Brooklyn, NY.	10/7/42
Belafonte, Harry	New York, NY.	3/1/27
Bell, Art	Camp Lejeune, NC	6/17/45
Bell, Catherine	London, England, UK.	8/14/68
Bell, Kristen	Huntington Woods, MI	7/18/80
Bello, Maria	Norristown, PA.	4/18/67
Belmondo, Jean-Paul	Neuilly-sur-Seine, France.	4/9/33

Name	Birthplace	Birthdate
Belushi, Jim	Chicago, IL	6/15/54
Belzer, Richard	Bridgeport, CT.	8/4/44
Benanti, Laura	Kinnelon, NJ	7/15/79
Benatar, Pat	Brooklyn, NY	1/10/53
Benedict, Dirk	Helena, MT	3/1/45
Benigni, Roberto	Misericordia, Italy.	10/27/52
Bening, Annette	Topeka, KS	5/29/58
Benjamin, Richard	New York, NY	5/22/38
Bennett, Alan	Leeds, England, UK.	5/9/34
Bennett, Tony	Astoria, Queens, NY	8/3/26
Benson, George	Pittsburgh, PA	3/22/43
Benson, Robby	Dallas, TX	1/21/56
Berenger, Tom	Chicago, IL	5/31/50
Bergen, Candice	Beverly Hills, CA	5/9/46
Bergen, Polly	Knoxville, TN	7/14/30
Bergeron, Tom	Haverhill, MA	5/6/55
Berman, Shelley	Chicago, IL	2/3/26
Bernard, Crystal	Garland, TX.	9/30/61
Bernhard, Sandra	Flint, MI	6/6/55
Bernsen, Corbin	N. Hollywood, CA.	9/7/54
Berry, Chuck	St. Louis, MO.	10/18/26
Berry, Halle	Cleveland, OH.	8/14/66
Berry, Ken	Moline, IL	11/3/33
Bertinelli, Valerie	Wilmington, DE	4/23/60
Bertolucci, Bernardo	Parma, Italy	3/16/40
Bettany, Paul	London, England, UK	5/27/71
Bialik, Mayim	San Diego, CA.	12/12/75
Bichir, Demián	Mexico City, Mexico	8/1/63
Bieber, Justin	Stratford, ON, Canada	3/1/94
Biel, Jessica	Ely, MN	3/3/82
Big Boi	Savannah, GA	2/1/75
Bigelow, Kathryn	San Carlos, CA	11/27/51
Biggs, Jason	Pompton Plains, NJ	5/12/78
Bikel, Theodore	Vienna, Austria	5/2/24
Bilson, Rachel	Los Angeles, CA	8/25/81
Binoche, Juliette	Paris, France	3/9/64
Birch, Thora	Beverly Hills, CA	3/11/82
Birney, David	Washington, DC	4/23/39
Bisset, Jacqueline	Weybridge, England, UK	9/13/44
Bissett, Josie	Seattle, WA	10/5/70
Björk (Gudmundsdottir)	Reykjavik, Iceland	11/21/65
Black, Clint	Long Branch, NJ	2/4/62
Black, Jack	Santa Monica, CA	4/7/69
Black, Lewis	Washington, DC	8/30/48
Blades, Ruben	Panama City, Panama	7/16/48
Blair, Linda	St. Louis, MO.	1/22/59
Blake, Robert	Nutley, NJ	9/18/33
Blanchett, Cate	Melbourne, Australia	5/14/69
Bledsoe, Tempestt	Chicago, IL	8/1/73
Bleeth, Yasmine	New York, NY	6/14/68
Blethyn, Brenda	Ramsgate, Kent, Eng., UK.	2/20/46
Blige, Mary J.	Bronx, NY	1/11/71
Bloom, Claire	London, England, UK	2/15/31
Bloom, Orlando	Canterbury, England, UK	1/13/77
Blyth, Ann	Mt. Kisco, NY.	8/16/28
Bochco, Steven	New York, NY	12/16/43
Bocelli, Andrea	Lajatico, Italy	9/22/58
Bogdanovich, Peter	Kingston, NY	7/30/39
Bogosian, Eric	Woburn, MA	4/24/53
Bologna, Joseph	Brooklyn, NY	12/30/34?
Bolton, Michael	New Haven, CT.	2/26/53
Bon Jovi, Jon	Sayreville, NJ.	3/2/62
Bonet, Lisa	San Francisco, CA.	11/16/67
Bonham Carter, Helena	London, England, UK	5/26/66
Bonneville, Hugh	London, England, UK	11/10/63
Bono	Dublin, Ireland	5/10/60
Boone, Debby	Hackensack, NJ.	9/22/56
Boone, Pat	Jacksonville, FL.	6/1/34
Boreanaz, David	Buffalo, NY	5/16/69
Bosco, Philip	Jersey City, NJ.	9/26/30
Bostwick, Barry	San Mateo, CA	2/24/45
Bosworth, Kate	Los Angeles, CA	1/2/83
Bottoms, Timothy	Santa Barbara, CA.	8/30/51
Bow Wow	Columbus, OH.	3/9/87
Bowen, Julie	Baltimore, MD	3/3/70
Bowie, David	London, England, UK	1/8/47
Bowles, Peter	London, England, UK	10/16/36
Boxleitner, Bruce	Elgin, IL	5/12/50
Boy George	Bexleyheath, England, UK.	6/14/61
Boyle, Lara Flynn	Davenport, IA	3/24/70
Boyle, Susan	Blackburn, Scotland, UK	4/1/61
Bracco, Lorraine	Brooklyn, NY	10/2/55
Brady, Wayne	Orlando, FL	6/2/72
Braff, Zach	South Orange, NJ	4/6/75
Branagh, Kenneth	Belfast, N. Ireland, UK	12/10/60
Brand, Russell	Grays, Essex, UK	6/4/75
Brandauer, Klaus Maria	Steiermark, Austria	6/22/44
Brandy (Norwood)	McComb, MS.	2/11/79
Bratt, Benjamin	San Francisco, CA	12/16/63
Braugher, Andre	Chicago, IL	7/1/62
Braxton, Toni	Severn, MD	10/7/66
Bremner, Ewen	Edinburgh, Scotland, UK	1/23/72
Brendon, Nicholas	Los Angeles, CA	4/12/71
Brenneman, Amy	Glastonbury, CT.	6/22/64
Brenner, David	Philadelphia, PA	2/4/45?
Bridges, Beau	Los Angeles, CA	12/9/41
Bridges, Jeff	Los Angeles, CA	12/4/49
Brightman, Sarah	Berkhamsted, England, UK	8/14/60
Brimley, Wilford	Salt Lake City, UT	9/27/34
Brinkley, Christie	Monroe, MI	2/2/54
Britton, Connie	Boston, MA	3/6/67
Broadbent, Jim	Lincolnshire, England, UK	5/24/49
Broderick, Matthew	New York, NY	3/21/62
Brody, Adam	San Diego, CA.	12/15/79
Brody, Adrien	New York, NY	4/14/73
Brolin, James	Los Angeles, CA	7/18/40
Brolin, Josh	Los Angeles, CA	2/12/68
Brooks, Albert	Beverly Hills, CA	7/22/47
Brooks, Garth	Tulsa, OK	2/7/62
Brooks, James L.	North Bergen, NJ.	5/9/40
Brooks, Mel	Brooklyn, NY	6/28/26
Brosnan, Pierce	Navan, Co. Meath, Ireland	5/16/53
Brown, Blair	Washington, DC	4/23/46
Brown, Bobby	Roxbury, MA	2/5/69
Brown, Bryan	Panania, Australia	6/23/47
Brown, Chris	Tappahannock, VA.	5/5/89
Brown, Foxy	Brooklyn, NY	9/6/79
Browne, Jackson	Heidelberg, Germany.	10/9/48
Bryson, Peabo	Greenville, SC	4/13/51
Bublé, Michael	Burnaby, BC, Canada	9/9/75
Buckley, Betty	Big Spring, TX	7/3/47
Buffett, Jimmy	Pascagoula, MS	12/25/46
Bujold, Geneviève	Montreal, QC, Canada.	7/1/42
Bullock, Sandra	Arlington, VA	7/26/64
Bumbry, Grace	St. Louis, MO.	1/4/37
Bündchen, Gisele	Horizontina, Brazil	7/20/80
Burghoff, Gary	Bristol, CT.	5/24/43
Burke, Cheryl	San Francisco, CA.	5/3/84
Burke, Delta	Orlando, FL.	7/30/56
Burnett, Carol	San Antonio, TX.	4/26/33
Burns, Edward	Woodside, Queens, NY	1/29/68
Burrell, Ty	Grants Pass, OR.	8/22/67
Burstyn, Ellen	Detroit, MI	12/7/32
Burton, LeVar	Landstuhl, Germany	2/16/57
Burton, Tim	Burbank, CA	8/25/58
Buscemi, Steve	Brooklyn, NY	12/13/57
Busey, Gary	Goose Creek, TX.	6/29/44
Busfield, Timothy	Lansing, MI	6/12/57
Butler, Brett	Montgomery, AL	1/30/58
Butler, Dan	Fort Wayne, IN.	12/2/54
Butler, Gerard	Glasgow, Scot., UK	11/13/69
Butz, Norbert Leo	St. Louis, MO.	1/30/67
Buzzi, Ruth	Westerly, RI	7/24/36
Bynes, Amanda	Thousand Oaks, CA	4/3/86
Byrne, David	Dumbarton, Scotland, UK	5/14/52
Byrne, Gabriel	Dublin, Ireland	5/12/50
Byrne, Rose	Sydney, NSW, Australia	7/24/79
Caan, James	Bronx, NY	3/26/40
Caballe, Montserrat	Barcelona, Spain	4/12/33
Caesar, Sid	Yonkers, NY	9/8/22
Cage, Nicolas	Long Beach, CA	1/7/64
Cain, Dean	Mt. Clemens, MI	7/31/66
Caine, Michael	London, England, UK	3/14/33
Caldwell, Zoe	Hawthorn, Australia	9/14/33
Callies, Sarah Wayne	LaGrange, IL	6/1/77
Callow, Simon	London, England, UK	6/15/49
Cameron, James	Kapuskasing, ON, Canada.	8/16/54
Cameron, Kirk	Panorama City, CA	10/12/70
Campanella, Joseph	New York, NY	11/21/27
Campbell, Bruce	Royal Oak, MI	6/22/58
Campbell, Glen	Delight, AR	4/22/36
Campbell, Naomi	South London, Eng., UK	5/22/70
Campbell, Neve	Guelph, ON, Canada	10/3/73
Campion, Jane	Waikanae, New Zealand	4/30/54
Cannavale, Bobby	Union City, NJ	5/3/71
Cannon, Dyan	Tacoma, WA	1/4/37
Cannon, Nick	San Diego, CA	10/8/80
Capshaw, Kate	Ft. Worth, TX.	11/3/53
Cara, Irene	New York, NY	3/18/59
Cardellini, Linda	Redwood City, CA	6/25/75
Cardinale, Claudia	Tunis, Tunisia	4/15/38
Carell, Steve	Concord, MA.	8/16/62
Carey, Drew	Cleveland, OH.	5/23/58
Carey, Mariah	Huntington, NY	3/27/70
Cariou, Len	St. Boniface, MB, Canada	9/30/39
Carlton, Vanessa	Milford, PA.	8/16/80
Carlyle, Robert	Glasgow, Scotland, UK	4/14/61
Carmen, Eric	Cleveland, OH.	8/11/49
Caron, Leslie	Boulogne, France	7/1/31
Carpenter, John	Carthage, NY	1/16/48
Carpenter, Mary Chapin	Princeton, NJ.	2/21/58
Carr, Vikki	El Paso, TX	7/19/41
Carreras, Jose	Barcelona, Spain.	12/5/46
Carrere, Tia	Honolulu, HI	1/2/67
Carrey, Jim	Newmarket, ON, Canada.	1/17/62
Carroll, Diahann	Bronx, NY	7/17/35
Carroll, Pat	Shreveport, LA	5/5/27
Carter, Jack	Brooklyn, NY	6/24/23
Carter, Jim	Harrogate, Yorkshire, England, UK.	8/19/48
Carter, Lynda	Phoenix, AZ.	7/24/51
Carter, Nick	Jamestown, NY.	1/28/80

Name	Birthplace	Birthdate
Carter, Ron	Ferndale, MI	5/4/37
Cartwright, Nancy	Kettering, OH	10/25/57
Caruso, David	Forest Hills, Queens, NY	1/17/56
Carvey, Dana	Missoula, MT	6/2/55
Case, Sharon	Detroit, MI	2/9/71
Cash, Rosanne	Memphis, TN	5/24/55
Cassidy, David	New York, NY	4/12/50
Castellaneta, Dan	Chicago, IL	10/29/57
Castle-Hughes, Keisha	Donnybrook, Australia	3/24/90
Cates, Phoebe	New York, NY	7/16/63
Cattrall, Kim	Liverpool, England, UK	8/21/56
Cavanagh, Tom	Ottawa, ON, Canada	10/26/63
Cavett, Dick	Gibbon, NE	11/19/36
Caviezel, Jim	Mount Vernon, WA	9/26/68
Cavill, Henry	Jersey, Channel Islands	5/5/83
Cedric the Entertainer	Jefferson City, MO	4/24/64
Cera, Michael	Brampton, ON, Canada	6/7/88
Chalke, Sarah	Ottawa, ON, Canada	8/27/76
Chamberlain, Richard	Beverly Hills, CA	3/31/34
Chambers, Justin	Springfield, OH	7/11/70
Chan, Jackie	Hong Kong	4/7/54
Chandler, Kyle	Buffalo, NY	9/17/65
Channing, Carol	Seattle, WA	1/31/21
Channing, Stockard	New York, NY	2/13/44
Chaplin, Geraldine	Santa Monica, CA	7/31/44
Chapman, Tracy	Cleveland, OH	3/30/64
Chappelle, Dave	Washington, DC	8/24/73
Charles, Josh	Baltimore, MD	9/15/71
Charo	Murcia, Spain	1/15/51?
Chase, Chevy	New York, NY	10/8/43
Chasez, J.C. (Joshua)	Washington, DC	8/8/76
Chastain, Jessica	Sacramento, CA	3/29/77
Cheadle, Don	Kansas City, MO	11/29/64
Checker, Chubby	Spring Gulley, SC	10/3/41
Chenoweth, Kristin	Broken Arrow, OK	7/24/68
Cher	El Centro, CA	5/20/46
Chesney, Kenny	Lutrelle, TN	3/26/68
Chianese, Dominic	Bronx, NY	2/24/31
Chiba, Sonny	Fukuoka, Kyushu, Japan	1/23/39
Chiklis, Michael	Lowell, MA	8/30/63
Chmerkovskiy, Maksim	Odessa, Ukraine	1/17/80
Cho, Margaret	San Francisco, CA	12/5/68
Chong, Thomas	Edmonton, AB, Canada	5/24/38
Chow Yun-Fat	Lamma Island, Hong Kong	5/18/55
Christensen, Hayden	Vancouver, BC, Canada	4/19/81
Christie, Julie	Chukua, Assam, India	4/14/41
Christopher, William	Evanston, IL	10/20/32
Chuck D	Roosevelt, NY	8/1/60
Church, Charlotte	Llandaff, Cardiff, Wales, UK	2/21/86
Church, Thomas Haden	El Paso, TX	6/17/60
Clapp, Gordon	North Conway, NH	9/24/48
Clapton, Eric	Ripley, Surrey, England, UK	3/30/45
Clark, Anthony	Lynchburg, VA	4/4/64
Clark, Petula	Epson, Surrey, England, UK	11/15/32
Clark, Roy	Meherrin, VA	4/15/33
Clarkson, Kelly	Burleson, TX	4/24/82
Clarkson, Patricia	New Orleans, LA	12/29/59
Clay, Andrew Dice	Brooklyn, NY	9/29/57
Cleese, John	Weston-super-Mare, Eng., UK	10/27/39
Clooney, George	Lexington, KY	5/6/61
Close, Glenn	Greenwich, CT	3/19/47
Cocker, Joe	Sheffield, England, UK	5/20/44
Coen, Ethan	St. Louis Park, MN	9/21/57
Coen, Joel	St. Louis Park, MN	11/29/54
Cohen, Leonard	Montreal, QC, Canada	9/21/34
Cohen, Sacha Baron	London, England, UK	10/13/71
Colbert, Stephen	Washington, DC	5/13/64
Cole, Gary	Park Ridge, IL	9/20/56
Cole, Natalie	Los Angeles, CA	2/6/50
Cole, Olivia	Memphis, TN	11/26/42
Coleman, Dabney	Austin, TX	1/3/32
Coleman, Ornette	Fort Worth, TX	3/19/30
Colfer, Chris	Fresno, CA	5/27/90
Collette, Toni	Blacktown, Australia	11/1/72
Collins, Joan	London, England, UK	5/23/33
Collins, Judy	Seattle, WA	5/1/39
Collins, Pauline	Exmouth, England, UK	9/3/40
Collins, Phil	London, England, UK	1/30/51
Collins, Stephen	Des Moines, IA	10/1/47
Colvin, Shawn	Vermillion, SD	1/10/56
Combs, Sean	New York, NY	11/4/69
Connelly, Jennifer	Round Top, NY	12/12/70
Connery, Sean	Edinburgh, Scotland, UK	8/25/30
Connick, Harry, Jr.	New Orleans, LA	9/11/67
Connolly, Kevin	Patchogue, NY	3/5/74
Connors, Mike	Fresno, CA	8/15/25
Conrad, Robert	Chicago, IL	3/1/35
Conroy, Frances	Monroe, GA	11/13/53
Constantine, Michael	Reading, PA	5/22/27
Conti, Tom	Paisley, Scotland, UK	11/22/41
Conway, Tim	Willoughby, OH	12/15/33
Cook, Barbara	Atlanta, GA	10/25/27
Cook, David	Houston, TX	12/20/82
Coolidge, Rita	Nashville, TN	5/1/45
Coolio	Compton, CA	8/1/63
Cooper, Alice	Detroit, MI	2/4/48

Name	Birthplace	Birthdate
Cooper, Bradley	Philadelphia, PA	1/5/75
Cooper, Chris	Kansas City, MO	7/9/51
Copperfield, David	Metuchen, NJ	9/16/56
Coppola, Francis Ford	Detroit, MI	4/7/39
Coppola, Sofia	New York, NY	5/14/71
Corbett, John	Wheeling, WV	5/9/61
Corbin, Barry	Lamesa, TX	10/16/40
Corea, Chick	Chelsea, MA	6/12/41
Corgan, Billy	Elk Grove, IL	3/17/67
Cornell, Chris	Seattle, WA	7/20/64
Corwin, Jeff	Norwell, MA	7/11/67
Cosby, Bill	Philadelphia, PA	7/12/37
Cosgrove, Miranda	Los Angeles, CA	5/14/93
Costas, Bob	Astoria, Queens, NY	3/22/52
Costello, Elvis	London, England, UK	8/25/54
Costner, Kevin	Compton, CA	1/18/55
Cotillard, Marion	Paris, France	9/30/75
Cowell, Simon	London, England, UK	10/7/59
Cox, Brian	Dundee, Scotland, UK	6/1/46
Cox, Courteney	Birmingham, AL	6/15/64
Cox, Ronny	Cloudcroft, NM	7/23/38
Coyote, Peter	New York, NY	10/10/41
Craig, Daniel	Chester, England, UK	3/2/68
Cranston, Bryan	San Fernando Valley, CA	3/7/56
Crawford, Cindy	DeKalb, IL	2/20/66
Crawford, Michael	Salisbury, England, UK	1/19/42
Criss, Darren	San Francisco, CA	2/5/87
Cromwell, James	Los Angeles, CA	1/27/40
Crosby, David	Los Angeles, CA	8/14/41
Cross, Ben	London, England, UK	12/16/47
Cross, Marcia	Marlborough, MA	3/25/62
Crouse, Lindsay	New York, NY	5/12/48
Crow, Sheryl	Kennett, MO	2/11/62
Crowe, Cameron	Palm Springs, CA	7/13/57
Crowe, Russell	Wellington, New Zealand	4/7/64
Crudup, Billy	Manhasset, NY	7/8/48
Cruise, Tom	Syracuse, NY	7/3/62
Cruz, Penelope	Madrid, Spain	4/28/74
Cryer, Jon	New York, NY	4/16/65
Crystal, Billy	Long Beach, NY	3/14/48
Culkin, Kieran	New York, NY	9/30/82
Culkin, Macaulay	New York, NY	8/26/80
Culkin, Rory	New York, NY	7/21/89
Cullum, John	Knoxville, TN	3/2/30
Cumming, Alan	Aberfeldy, Perthshire, Scotland, UK	1/27/65
Cuoco, Kaley	Camarillo, CA	11/30/85
Curry, Tim	Grappenhall, Cheshire, England, UK	4/19/46
Curtin, Jane	Cambridge, MA	9/6/47
Curtis, Jamie Lee	Los Angeles, CA	11/22/58
Cusack, Joan	New York, NY	10/11/62
Cusack, John	Evanston, IL	6/28/66
Cyrus, Billy Ray	Flatwoods, KY	8/25/61
Cyrus, Miley	Nashville, TN	11/23/92
Dafoe, Willem	Appleton, WI	7/22/55
Dahl, Arlene	Minneapolis, MN	8/11/25
Dale, Jim	Rothwell, England, UK	8/15/35
Dalton, Timothy	Colwyn Bay, Wales, UK	3/21/46
Daltrey, Roger	London, England, UK	3/1/44
Daly, Carson	Santa Monica, CA	6/22/73
Daly, Timothy	New York, NY	3/1/56
Daly, Tyne	Madison, WI	2/21/46
Damon, Matt	Cambridge, MA	10/8/70
Damone, Vic	Brooklyn, NY	6/12/28
Dane, Eric	San Francisco, CA	11/9/72
Danes, Claire	New York, NY	4/12/79
D'Angelo	Richmond, VA	2/11/74
D'Angelo, Beverly	Columbus, OH	11/15/54
Daniels, Anthony	Salisbury, England, UK	2/21/46
Daniels, Charlie	Wilmington, NC	10/28/36
Daniels, Jeff	Athens, GA	2/19/55
Daniels, William	Brooklyn, NY	3/31/27
Danner, Blythe	Rosemont, PA	2/3/43
Danson, Ted	San Diego, CA	12/29/47
Danza, Tony	Brooklyn, NY	4/21/51
Darby, Kim	Hollywood, CA	7/8/48
Daughtry, Chris	Roanoke Rapids, NC	12/26/79
David, Larry	Brooklyn, NY	7/2/47
Davidson, John	Pittsburgh, PA	12/13/41
Davis, Ann B.	Schenectady, NY	5/5/26
Davis, Clifton	Chicago, IL	10/4/45
Davis, Geena	Wareham, MA	1/21/56
Davis, Hope	Englewood, NJ	3/23/64
Davis, Judy	Perth, Australia	4/23/55
Davis, Kristin	Boulder, CO	2/24/65
Davis, Mac	Lubbock, TX	1/21/42
Davis, Viola	Saint Matthews, SC	8/11/65
Dawber, Pam	Farmington Hills, MI	10/18/51
Dawson, Rosario	New York, NY	5/9/79
Day, Doris	Cincinnati, OH	4/3/24
Day-Lewis, Daniel	London, England, UK	4/29/57
De Havilland, Olivia	Tokyo, Japan	7/1/16
De Mornay, Rebecca	Santa Rosa, CA	8/29/62
De Niro, Robert	New York, NY	8/17/43
De Rossi, Portia	Melbourne, Victoria, Austral.	1/31/73

Name	Birthplace	Birthdate
Dee, Ruby	Cleveland, OH	10/27/24
DeFranco, Buddy	Camden, NJ	2/17/23
DeGeneres, Ellen	Metairie, LA	1/26/58
DeGraw, Gavin	Middletown, NY	2/4/77
DeHaven, Gloria	Los Angeles, CA	7/23/25
Del Toro, Benicio	Santurce, Puerto Rico	2/19/67
Delaney, Kim	Philadelphia, PA	11/29/61
Delany, Dana	New York, NY	3/13/56
Delon, Alain	Sceaux, France	11/8/35
Demme, Jonathan	Baldwin, NY.	2/22/44
Dempsey, Patrick	Lewiston, ME.	1/13/66
Dench, Judi	York, England, UK	12/9/34
Deneuve, Catherine	Paris, France	10/22/43
Dennehy, Brian	Bridgeport, CT.	7/9/38
DePalma, Brian	Newark, NJ	9/11/40
Depardieu, Gerard	Chateauroux, France	12/27/48
Depp, Johnny	Owensboro, KY	6/9/63
Derek, Bo	Long Beach, CA	11/20/56
Dern, Bruce	Winnetka, IL	6/4/36
Dern, Laura	Santa Monica, CA	2/10/67
Deschanel, Zooey	Los Angeles, CA	1/17/80
Devine, Loretta	Houston, TX	8/21/49
DeVito, Danny	Neptune, NJ	11/17/44
DeWitt, Joyce	Wheeling, WV	4/23/49
Dey, Susan	Pekin, IL	12/10/52
Diamond, Neil	Brooklyn, NY	1/24/41
Diaz, Cameron	San Diego, CA	8/30/72
DiCaprio, Leonardo	Hollywood, CA.	11/11/74
Dick, Andy	Charleston, SC	12/21/65
Dickinson, Angie	Kulm, ND	9/30/31
Diesel, Vin	New York, NY	7/18/67
Diggs, Taye	Essex Co., NJ	1/2/72
Dillahunt, Garret	Castro Valley, CA	11/24/64
Dillman, Bradford	San Francisco, CA	4/14/30
Dillon, Kevin	Mamaroneck, NY.	8/19/65
Dillon, Matt	New Rochelle, NY	2/18/64
Dinklage, Peter	Morristown, NJ	6/11/69
DioGuardi, Kara	Scarsdale, NY	12/9/70
Dion, Celine	Charlemagne, QC, Canada	3/30/68
Djalili, Omid	London, England, UK	9/30/65
Dobrev, Nina	Sofia, Bulgaria	1/9/89
Dobson, Kevin	Jackson Heights, Queens, NY	3/18/43
Dockery, Michelle	Barking, Essex, England, UK	12/15/81
Doherty, Shannen	Memphis, TN	4/12/71
Dolenz, Mickey	Los Angeles, CA	3/8/45
Domingo, Placido	Madrid, Spain	1/21/41
Domino, Fats	New Orleans, LA	2/26/28
Donahue, Phil	Cleveland, OH	12/21/35
D'Onofrio, Vincent	Brooklyn, NY	6/30/59
Donovan (Leitch)	Glasgow, Scotland, UK	5/10/46
Donovan, Tate	New York, NY	9/25/63
Dorn, Michael	Luling, TX	12/9/52
Dotrice, Roy	Guernsey, England, UK	5/26/23
Douglas, Kirk	Amsterdam, NY	12/9/16
Douglas, Michael	New Brunswick, NJ	9/25/44
Dourdan, Gary	Philadelphia, PA	12/11/66
Dovolani, Tony	Pristina, Kosovo	7/17/73
Dow, Tony	Hollywood, CA.	4/13/45
Down, Lesley-Anne	London, England, UK	3/17/54
Downey, Robert, Jr.	New York, NY	4/4/65
Downey, Roma	Derry, N. Ireland, UK	5/6/60
Downs, Hugh	Akron, OH	2/14/21
Drake	Toronto, ON, Canada	10/24/86
Drescher, Fran	Flushing, Queens, NY	9/30/57
Dreyfuss, Richard	Brooklyn, NY	10/29/47
Driver, Adam	San Bernardino, CA.	11/19/83
Driver, Minnie	London, England, UK	1/31/70
Dryer, Fred	Hawthorne, CA	7/6/46
Duchovny, David	New York, NY	8/7/60
Duff, Haylie	Houston, TX	2/19/85
Duff, Hilary	Houston, TX	9/28/87
Duffy (Aimee Anne)	Bangor, Gwynedd, Wales, UK	6/23/84
Duffy, Julia	Minneapolis, MN	6/27/51
Duffy, Patrick	Townsend, MT	3/17/49
Duhamel, Josh	Minot, ND	11/14/72
Dujardin, Jean	Rueil-Malmaison, France	6/19/72
Dukakis, Olympia	Lowell, MA.	6/20/31
Duke, Patty	Elmhurst, Queens, NY	12/14/46
Dullea, Keir	Cleveland, OH	5/30/36
Dunaway, Faye	Bascom, FL.	1/14/41
Duncan, Lindsay	Edinburgh, Scotland, UK	11/7/50
Duncan, Sandy	Henderson, TX	2/20/46
Dunham, Lena	New York, NY	5/13/86
Dunne, Griffin	New York, NY	6/8/55
Dunst, Kirsten	Point Pleasant, NJ	4/30/82
Dussault, Nancy	Pensacola, FL	6/30/36
Dutton, Charles S.	Baltimore, MD	1/30/51
Duvall, Robert	San Diego, CA.	1/5/31
Duvall, Shelley	Houston, TX	7/7/49
Dylan, Bob	Duluth, MN	5/24/41
Dylan, Jakob	New York, NY	12/9/69
Dysart, Richard	Brighton, MA	3/30/29
Dzundza, George	Rosenheim, Germany	7/19/45
Eads, George	Fort Worth, TX.	3/1/67
Easton, Sheena	Bellshill, Scotland, UK	4/27/59
Eastwood, Clint	San Francisco, CA.	5/31/30
Ebersole, Christine	Chicago, IL	2/21/53
Eckhart, Aaron	Cupertino, CA	3/12/68
Eden, Barbara	Tucson, AZ	8/23/31
Edwards, Anthony	Santa Barbara, CA.	7/19/62
Efron, Zac	San Luis Obispo, CA	10/18/87
Ehle, Jennifer	Winston-Salem, NC	12/29/69
Eikenberry, Jill	New Haven, CT.	1/21/47
Eisenberg, Jesse	Bayside, NY	10/5/83
Ekberg, Anita	Malmo, Sweden	9/29/31
Ekland, Britt	Stockholm, Sweden	10/6/42
Electra, Carmen	Cincinnati, OH	4/20/72
Elfman, Jenna	Los Angeles, CA	9/30/71
Elizondo, Hector	New York, NY	12/22/36
Elliott, Bob	Boston, MA	3/26/23
Elliott, Chris	New York, NY	5/31/60
Elliott, Missy	Portsmouth, VA	7/1/71
Elliott, Sam	Sacramento, CA	8/9/44
Elvira	Manhattan, KS.	9/17/51
Emerson, Michael	Cedar Rapids, IA	9/7/54
Eminem	St. Joseph, MO	10/17/72
Enberg, Dick	Mt. Clemens, MI	1/9/35
Englund, Robert	Glendale, CA.	6/6/49
Enya	Gweedore, Ireland	5/17/61
Estefan, Gloria	Havana, Cuba	9/1/57
Estevez, Emilio	New York, NY	5/12/62
Estrada, Erik	New York, NY	3/16/49
Etheridge, Melissa	Leavenworth, KS.	5/29/61
Evans, Chris	Framingham, MA.	6/13/81
Evans, Linda	Hartford, CT	11/18/42
Evans, Robert	New York, NY	6/29/30
Everett, Rupert	Norfolk, England, UK.	5/29/59
Everly, Don	Brownie, KY.	2/1/37
Everly, Phil	Chicago, IL	1/19/39
Evigan, Greg	South Amboy, NJ	10/14/53
Fabares, Shelley	Santa Monica, CA	1/19/44
Fabian	Philadelphia, PA	2/6/43
Fabio (Lanzoni)	Milan, Italy	3/15/59
Fabolous	Brooklyn, NY	11/18/77
Fairchild, Morgan	Dallas, TX	2/3/50
Faison, Donald	New York, NY	6/22/74
Falana, Lola	Philadelphia, PA	9/11/42
Falco, Edie	Brooklyn, NY	7/5/63
Fallon, Jimmy	Brooklyn, NY	9/19/74
Fanning, Dakota	Conyers, GA	2/23/94
Fargo, Donna	Mt. Airy, NC	11/10/49
Farr, Jamie	Toledo, OH	7/1/34
Farrell, Colin	Dublin, Ireland	5/31/76
Farrell, Mike	St. Paul, MN	2/6/39
Farrell, Perry	Bayside, Queens, NY.	3/29/59
Farrell, Suzanne	Cincinnati, OH.	8/16/45?
Farrelly, Bobby	Cumberland, RI	6/17/58
Farrelly, Peter	Phoenixville, PA.	12/17/56
Farrow, Mia	Los Angeles, CA	2/9/45
Fassbender, Michael	Heidelberg, Germany.	4/2/77
Fatone, Joey	Brooklyn, NY.	1/28/77
Feinstein, Michael	Columbus, OH	9/7/56
Feldon, Barbara	Bethel Park, PA	3/12/33
Feldshuh, Tovah	New York, NY	12/27/52
Feliciano, Jose	Lares, Puerto Rico.	9/10/45
Fenn, Sherilyn	Detroit, MI	2/1/65
Fergie	Hacienda Heights, CA	3/27/75
Ferguson, Craig	Glasgow, Scotland, UK	5/17/62
Ferguson, Jesse Tyler	Missoula, MT.	10/22/75
Ferrara, Jerry	Brooklyn, NY.	11/29/79
Ferrell, Conchata	Charleston, WV	3/28/43
Ferrell, Will	Irvine, CA	7/16/67
Ferrera, America	Los Angeles, CA	4/18/84
Feuerstein, Mark	New York, NY	6/8/71
Fey, Tina	Upper Darby, PA	5/18/70
Field, Sally	Pasadena, CA	11/6/46
Fiennes, Joseph	Salisbury, England, UK	5/27/70
Fiennes, Ralph	Suffolk, England, UK	12/22/62
Fierstein, Harvey	Brooklyn, NY	6/6/54
50 Cent	Jamaica, Queens, NY	7/6/76
Fillion, Nathan	Edmonton, AB, Canada	3/27/71
Fincher, David	Denver, CO	8/28/62
Finney, Albert	Salford, England, UK	5/9/36
Fiorentino, Linda	Philadelphia, PA	3/9/60
Firth, Colin	Grayshott, England, UK	9/10/60
Firth, Peter	Bradford, Yorkshire, Eng., UK	10/27/53
Fischer, Jenna	Ft. Wayne, IN.	3/7/74
Fishburne, Laurence	Augusta, GA	7/30/61
Fisher, Carrie	Beverly Hills, CA	10/21/56
Flack, Roberta	Black Mountain, NC	2/10/39
Flanagan, Fionnula	Dublin, Ireland	12/10/41
Flavor Flav	Roosevelt, NY	3/16/59
Fleetwood, Mick	Redruth, Cornwall, Eng., UK.	6/24/42
Fleming, Rhonda	Hollywood, CA.	8/10/23
Fletcher, Louise	Birmingham, AL	7/22/34
Flockhart, Calista	Freeport, IL	11/11/64
Florek, Dann	Flat Rock, MI	5/1/50
Fogerty, John	Berkeley, CA.	5/28/45
Foley, Dave	Etobicoke, ON, Canada	1/4/63
Fonda, Bridget	Los Angeles, CA	1/27/64
Fonda, Jane	New York, NY	12/21/37
Fonda, Peter	New York, NY	2/23/40

Name	Birthplace	Birthdate
Fontaine, Joan	Tokyo, Japan	10/22/17
Ford, Faith	Alexandria, LA	9/14/64
Ford, Harrison	Chicago, IL	7/13/42
Forman, Milos	Caslav, Czechoslovakia	2/18/32
Forte, Will	Alameda Co., CA	6/17/70
Foster, Jodie	Los Angeles, CA	11/19/62
Foster, Sutton	Statesboro, GA	3/18/75
Fox, James	London, England, UK	5/19/39
Fox, Jorja	New York, NY	7/7/68
Fox, Matthew	Abington, PA	7/14/66
Fox, Megan	Rockwood, TN	5/16/86
Fox, Michael J.	Edmonton, AB, Canada	6/9/61
Fox, Vivica A.	South Bend, IN	7/30/64
Foxworth, Robert	Houston, TX	11/1/41
Foxworthy, Jeff	Atlanta, GA	9/6/58
Foxx, Jamie	Terrell, TX	12/13/67
Frampton, Peter	Kent, England, UK	4/22/50
Francis, Connie	Newark, NJ	12/12/38
Franco, James	Palo Alto, CA	4/19/78
Franken, Al	New York, NY	5/21/51
Franklin, Aretha	Memphis, TN	3/25/42
Franz, Dennis	Maywood, IL	10/28/44
Fraser, Brendan	Indianapolis, IN	12/3/68
Freeman, Mona	Baltimore, MD	6/9/26
Freeman, Morgan	Memphis, TN	6/1/37
French, Dawn	Holyhead, Wales, UK.	10/11/57
Fricker, Brenda	Dublin, Ireland	2/17/45
Friedkin, William	Chicago, IL	8/29/39
Fry, Stephen	London, England, UK	8/24/57
Fuentes, Daisy	Havana, Cuba	11/17/66
Fuller, Robert	Troy, NY	7/29/34
Furlong, Edward	Pasadena, CA	8/2/77
Furtado, Nelly	Victoria, BC, Canada	12/2/78
Gabor, Zsa Zsa	Budapest, Hungary	2/6/17
Gabriel, Peter	Surrey, England, UK	2/13/50
Gaines, Boyd	Atlanta, GA	5/11/53
Galecki, Johnny	Bree, Belgium	4/30/75
Galifianakis, Zach	Wilkesboro, NC	10/1/69
Gallagher, Peter	Armonk, NY	8/19/55
Gallo, Vincent	Buffalo, NY	4/11/61
Galway, James	Belfast, N. Ireland, UK	12/8/39
Garagiola, Joe	St. Louis, MO.	2/12/26
Garber, Victor	London, ON, Canada.	3/16/49
Garcia, Andy	Havana, Cuba	4/12/56
Garfield, Andrew	Los Angeles, CA	8/20/83
Garfunkel, Art	Forest Hills, Queens, NY	11/5/41
Garlin, Jeff	Chicago, IL	6/5/62
Garner, James	Norman, OK	4/7/28
Garner, Jennifer	Houston, TX	4/17/72
Garofalo, Janeane	Newton, NJ	9/28/64
Garr, Teri	Lakewood, OH.	12/11/44
Garrett, Brad	Woodland Hills, CA	4/14/60
Garth, Jennie	Urbana, IL	4/3/72
Gatlin, Larry	Seminole, TX.	5/2/48
Gavin, John	Los Angeles, CA	4/8/31
Gayle, Crystal	Paintsville, KY	1/9/51
Gaynor, Mitzi	Chicago, IL	9/4/31
Geary, Anthony	Coalville, UT	5/29/47
Gedda, Nicolai	Stockholm, Sweden	7/11/25
Gellar, Sarah Michelle	New York, NY	4/14/77
Gere, Richard	Philadelphia, PA	8/31/49
Gervais, Ricky	Reading, England, UK	6/25/61
Giannini, Giancarlo	La Spezia, Italy	8/1/42
Gibb, Barry	Isle of Man, England, UK	9/1/46
Gibbons, Leeza	Hartsville, SC	3/26/57
Gibbs, Marla	Chicago, IL	6/14/31
Gibson, Deborah	Brooklyn, NY	8/31/70
Gibson, Mel	Peekskill, NY	1/3/56
Gibson, Thomas	Charleston, SC	7/3/62
Gifford, Frank	Santa Monica, CA	8/16/30
Gifford, Kathie Lee	Neuilly-sur-Seine, France	8/16/53
Gilbert, Melissa	Los Angeles, CA	5/8/64
Gilbert, Sara	Santa Monica, CA	1/29/75
Gilberto, Astrud	Salvador, Brazil	3/30/40
Gill, Vince	Norman, OK	4/12/57
Gillette, Anita	Baltimore, MD	8/16/36
Gilley, Mickey	Natchez, MS	3/9/36
Gilliam, Terry	Minneapolis, MN	11/22/40
Gilmour, David	Cambridge, England, UK	3/6/46
Gilpin, Peri	Waco, TX.	5/27/61
Gilsig, Jessalyn	Montreal, QC, Canada	11/30/71
Ginty, Robert	Brooklyn, NY	11/14/48
Givens, Robin	New York, NY	11/27/64
Glaser, Paul Michael	Cambridge, MA	3/25/43
Gleeson, Brendan	Belfast, N. Ireland, UK	11/29/55?
Glenn, Scott	Pittsburgh, PA	1/26/41
Gless, Sharon	Los Angeles, CA	5/31/43
Glover, Crispin	New York, NY	4/20/64
Glover, Danny	San Francisco, CA	7/22/47
Glover, John	Kingston, NY	8/7/44
Glover, Julian	London, England, UK	3/27/35
Glover, Savion	Newark, NJ	11/19/73
Godard, Jean Luc	Paris, France	12/3/30
Goldberg, Whoopi	New York, NY	11/13/55
Goldblum, Jeff.	Pittsburgh, PA	10/22/52
Goldthwait, Bobcat	Syracuse, NY	5/26/62

Name	Birthplace	Birthdate
Goldwyn, Tony	Los Angeles, CA	5/20/60
Gomez, Selena	Grand Prairie, TX	7/22/92
Gooding, Cuba, Jr.	Bronx, NY	1/2/68
Goodman, John	Affton, MO	6/20/52
Goodman, Len	London, England, UK	4/25/44
Gordon-Levitt, Joseph.	Los Angeles, CA	2/17/81
Gosling, Ryan	London, ON, Canada.	11/12/80
Gosselaar, Mark-Paul	Panorama City, CA	3/1/74
Gossett, Louis, Jr.	Brooklyn, NY	5/27/36
Gould, Elliott	Brooklyn, NY	8/29/38
Grace, Topher	New York, NY	7/12/78
Graham, Heather	Milwaukee, WI	1/29/70
Grammer, Kelsey	St. Thomas, U.S. Virgin Isls.	2/21/55
Grant, Amy	Augusta, GA	11/25/60
Grant, Hugh	London, England, UK	9/9/60
Grant, Lee	New York, NY	10/31/27?
Gray, Linda	Santa Monica, CA	9/12/40
Gray, Macy	Canton, OH	9/6/69
Green, Al	Forrest City, AR	4/13/46
Green, Cee Lo	Atlanta, GA	5/30/74
Green, Seth	Philadelphia, PA	2/8/74
Green, Tom	Pembroke, ON, Canada.	7/30/71
Greene, Shecky	Chicago, IL	4/8/26
Greenfield, Max	Dobbs Ferry, NY	9/4/80
Greenwood, Bruce	Noranda, QC, Canada.	8/12/56
Gregory, Cynthia	Los Angeles, CA	7/8/46
Gregory, Dick	St. Louis, MO.	10/12/32
Grenier, Adrian	Santa Fe, NM	7/10/76
Grey, Jennifer	New York, NY	3/26/60
Grey, Joel	Cleveland, OH.	4/11/32
Grier, David Alan.	Detroit, MI	6/30/55
Grier, Pam	Winston-Salem, NC	5/26/49
Gries, Jon	Glendale, CA	6/17/57
Griffin, Kathy	Oak Park, IL	11/4/61
Griffith, Melanie	New York, NY	8/9/57
Griffiths, Rachel	Melbourne, Australia	12/18/68
Grimes, Tammy.	Lynn, MA.	1/30/34
Grint, Rupert.	Walton-at-Stone, Hertfordshire, Eng., UK	8/24/88
Groban, Josh	Los Angeles, CA	2/27/81
Grodin, Charles	Pittsburgh, PA	4/21/35
Groff, Jonathan	Lancaster, PA	3/26/85
Grohl, David	Warren, OH	1/14/69
Gross, Michael	Chicago, IL	6/21/47
Guest, Christopher	New York, NY	2/5/48
Guillaume, Robert.	St. Louis, MO.	11/30/27
Gumbel, Greg	New Orleans, LA	5/3/46
Gunn, Anna.	Santa Fe, NM	8/11/68
Gunn, Tim.	Washington, DC	7/29/53
Guthrie, Arlo	Brooklyn, NY	7/10/47
Guttenberg, Steve	Brooklyn, NY	8/24/58
Guy, Buddy	Lettsworth, LA	7/30/36
Guy, Jasmine	Boston, MA	3/10/64
Gyllenhaal, Jake	Los Angeles, CA	12/19/80
Gyllenhaal, Maggie	New York, NY	11/16/77
Hackman, Gene	San Bernardino, CA.	1/30/30
Hader, Bill	Tulsa, OK	6/7/78
Hagerty, Julie	Cincinnati, OH.	6/15/55
Haggard, Merle	Bakersfield, CA	4/6/37
Haid, Charles	San Francisco, CA	6/2/43
Hale, Barbara	DeKalb, IL	4/18/22
Hale, Tony	West Point, NY	9/30/70
Hall, Anthony Michael	West Roxbury, MA	4/14/68
Hall, Arsenio	Cleveland, OH	2/12/55
Hall, Daryl	Pottstown, PA.	10/11/46
Hall, Deidre	Milwaukee, WI	10/31/47
Hall, Michael C.	Raleigh, NC.	2/1/71
Hall, Monty	Winnipeg, MB, Canada	8/25/21
Hall, Tom T.	Olive Hill, KY	5/25/36
Halliwell, Geri	Watford, England, UK	8/6/72
Hamill, Mark	Oakland, CA	9/25/51
Hamilton, George	Memphis, TN.	8/12/39
Hamilton, Linda	Salisbury, MD	9/26/56
Hamlin, Harry	Pasadena, CA.	10/30/51
Hamm, Jon	St. Louis, MO.	3/10/71
Hammer, Armie.	Los Angeles, CA	8/28/86
Hammer (M.C.)	Oakland, CA	3/30/63
Hammond, Darrell.	Melbourne, FL	10/8/55
Hancock, Herbie	Chicago, IL	4/12/40
Handler, Chelsea	Livingston, NJ	2/25/75
Hanks, Tom	Concord, CA	7/9/56
Hannah, Daryl	Chicago, IL	12/3/60
Hannigan, Alyson	Washington, DC	3/24/74
Hanson, Curtis	Reno, NV.	3/24/45
Hanson, Isaac.	Tulsa, OK	11/17/80
Hanson, Taylor	Tulsa, OK	3/14/83
Hanson, Zac.	Tulsa, OK	10/22/85
Harden, Marcia Gay	La Jolla, CA.	8/14/59
Harewood, Dorian.	Dayton, OH	8/6/50
Hargitay, Mariska	Los Angeles, CA	1/23/64
Harmon, Angie	Highland Park, TX	8/10/72
Harmon, Mark.	Burbank, CA	9/2/51
Harper, Ben	Claremont, CA.	10/28/69
Harper, Tess	Mammoth Spring, AR	8/15/50
Harper, Valerie	Suffern, NY	8/22/39
Harrelson, Woody	Midland, TX.	7/23/61

Name	Birthplace	Birthdate
Harrington, Pat	New York, NY	8/13/29
Harris, Barbara	Evanston, IL	7/25/35
Harris, Ed	Tenafly, NJ	11/28/50
Harris, Emmylou	Birmingham, AL	4/2/47
Harris, Neil Patrick	Albuquerque, NM	6/15/73
Harris, Rosemary	Ashby, England, UK	9/19/27?
Harris, Steve	Chicago, IL	12/3/65
Harrison, Gregory	Avalon, CA	5/31/50
Harry, Deborah	Miami, FL	7/1/45
Hart, Mary	Madison, SD	11/8/50
Hart, Melissa Joan	Smithtown, NY	4/18/76
Hartley, Mariette	New York, NY	6/21/40
Hartman, David	Pawtucket, RI	5/19/35
Hartman Black, Lisa	Houston, TX	6/1/56
Hartnett, Josh	San Francisco, CA	7/21/78
Harvey, P.J.	Yeovil, Somerset, Eng., UK	10/9/69
Harvey, Steve	Welch, WV.	11/23/56
Hasselbeck, Elisabeth	Cranston, RI	5/28/77
Hasselhoff, David	Baltimore, MD	7/17/52
Hatcher, Teri	Sunnyvale, CA	12/8/64
Hatfield, Juliana	Wiscasset, ME	7/27/67
Hathaway, Anne	Brooklyn, NY	11/12/82
Hauer, Rutger	Breukelen, Netherlands	1/23/44
Hawke, Ethan	Austin, TX	11/6/70
Hawn, Goldie	Washington, DC	11/21/45
Hayek, Salma	Coatzacoalcos, Mexico	9/2/66
Hayes, Sean	Glen Ellyn, IL	6/26/70
Haynes, Roy	Roxbury, MA	3/13/25
Hays, Robert	Bethesda, MD	7/24/47
Head, Anthony	Camden Town, Eng., UK	2/20/54
Heard, John	Washington, DC	3/7/45
Hearn, George	St. Louis, MO.	6/18/34
Heaton, Patricia	Bay Village, OH	3/4/58
Heche, Anne	Aurora, OH	5/25/69
Heder, Jon	Fort Collins, CO.	10/26/77
Hedren, Tippi	New Ulm, MN	1/19/30?
Heigl, Katherine	Washington, DC	11/24/78
Helberg, Simon	Los Angeles, CA	12/9/80
Helfgott, David	Melbourne, Australia	5/19/47
Helgenberger, Marg	Fremont, NE	11/16/58
Helmond, Katherine	Galveston, TX	7/5/28?
Helms, Ed	Atlanta, GA	1/24/74
Hemingway, Mariel	Mill Valley, CA	11/22/61
Hemsworth, Chris	Melbourne, Victoria, Australia	8/11/83
Hemsworth, Liam	Melbourne, Victoria, Australia	1/13/90
Henderson, Florence	Dale, IN	2/14/34
Hendricks, Christina	Knoxville, TN	5/3/75
Henley, Don	Gilmer, TX	7/22/47
Henner, Marilu	Chicago, IL	4/6/52
Hennessy, Jill	Edmonton, AB, Canada	11/25/68
Henry, Buck	New York, NY	12/9/30
Herman, Pee-Wee	Peekskill, NY.	8/27/52
Herrmann, Edward	Washington, DC	7/21/43
Hershey, Barbara	Hollywood, CA.	2/5/48
Hesseman, Howard	Lebanon, OR.	2/27/40
Hetfield, James	Downey, CA.	8/3/63
Hewitt, Jennifer Love	Waco, TX.	2/21/79
Hicks, Catherine	Scottsdale, AZ	8/6/51
Higgins, John Michael	Boston, MA	2/12/63
Hightower, Chelsie	Las Vegas, NV.	7/21/89
Hill, Dulé	Orange, NJ	5/3/75
Hill, Faith	Jackson, MS	9/21/67
Hill, Jonah	Los Angeles, CA	12/20/83
Hill, Lauryn	South Orange, NJ	5/26/75
Hill, Steven	Seattle, WA	2/24/22
Hillerman, John.	Denison, TX.	12/20/32
Hilton, Paris	New York, NY	2/17/81
Hines, Cheryl	Miami Beach, FL	9/21/65
Hirsch, Emile	Palms, CA	3/13/85
Hirsch, Judd	Bronx, NY	3/15/35
Hodgman, John	Cambridge, MA	6/3/71
Hoffman, Dustin	Los Angeles, CA	8/8/37
Hoffman, Philip Seymour	Fairport, NY.	7/23/67
Hogan, Hulk	Augusta, GA	8/11/53
Hogan, Paul	Lightning Ridge, NSW, Australia	10/8/39
Holbrook, Hal	Cleveland, OH	2/17/25
Holder, Geoffrey	Port of Spain, Trinidad	8/1/30
Holliday, Polly	Jasper, AL	7/2/37
Holliman, Earl	Delhi, LA	9/11/28
Holloway, Josh	San Jose, CA.	7/20/69
Holly, Lauren.	Bristol, PA	10/28/63
Holm, Ian	Ilford, England, UK	9/12/31
Holmes, Katie	Toledo, OH	12/18/78
Hooks, Jan	Decatur, GA.	4/23/57
Hopkins, Anthony	Port Talbot, South Wales, UK	12/31/37
Hopkins, Bo	Greenville, SC	2/2/42
Hopkins, Telma	Louisville, KY.	10/28/48
Horne, Marilyn	Bradford, PA	1/16/34
Hornsby, Bruce	Williamsburg, VA	11/23/54
Horsley, Lee	Muleshoe, TX	5/15/55
Hoskins, Bob	Suffolk, England, UK	10/26/42
Hough, Derek	Salt Lake City, UT	5/17/85
Hough, Julianne	Salt Lake City, UT	7/20/88
Hounsou, Djimon	Cotonou, Benin	4/24/64
Howard, Clint	Burbank, CA.	4/20/59
Howard, Ken	El Centro, CA.	3/28/44
Howard, Ron	Duncan, OK.	3/1/54
Howard, Terrence	Chicago, IL	3/11/69
Howell, C. Thomas	Van Nuys, CA	12/7/66
Howes, Sally Ann	St. John's Wood, London, England, UK	7/20/30
Hudgens, Vanessa	Salinas, CA	12/14/88
Hudson, Jennifer	Chicago, IL	9/12/81
Hudson, Kate	Los Angeles, CA	4/19/79
Huffman, Felicity	Bedford, NY.	12/9/62
Hughley, D. L.	Los Angeles, CA	3/6/63
Hulce, Tom	Detroit, MI	12/6/53
Humperdinck, Engelbert	Madras, India.	5/2/36
Humphries, Barry	Melbourne, Australia	2/17/34
Hunt, Bonnie	Chicago, IL	9/22/64
Hunt, Helen.	Culver City, CA	6/15/63
Hunt, Linda	Morristown, NJ	4/2/45
Hunter, Holly	Conyers, GA	3/20/58
Hunter, Tab	New York, NY	7/11/31
Hurley, Elizabeth	Hampshire, England, UK	6/10/65
Hurt, John	Chesterfield, England, UK	1/22/40
Hurt, Mary Beth	Marshalltown, IA	9/26/48
Hurt, William	Washington, DC	3/20/50
Huston, Anjelica	Santa Monica, CA	7/8/51
Hutcherson, Josh	Union, KY	10/12/92
Hutton, Lauren	Charleston, SC	11/17/43
Hutton, Timothy.	Malibu, CA.	8/16/60
Hyman, Earle	Rocky Mount, NC	10/11/26
Ian, Janis	Bronx, NY	4/7/51
Ice Cube	Los Angeles, CA	6/15/69
Ice-T	Newark, NJ	2/16/58
Idle, Eric	S. Shields, England, UK.	3/29/43
Idol, Billy	Middlesex, England, UK	11/30/55
Iglesias, Enrique	Madrid, Spain	5/8/75
Iglesias, Julio	Madrid, Spain	9/23/43
Iler, Robert	New York, NY	3/2/85
Iman	Mogadishu, Somalia	7/25/55
Imbruglia, Natalie	Sydney, Australia	2/4/75
Imperioli, Michael	Mount Vernon, NY	3/26/66
Imus, Don	Riverside, CA.	7/23/40
Ingram, James	Akron, OH	2/16/52
Innes, Laura	Pontiac, MI	8/16/57?
Ireland, Kathy	Glendale, CA.	3/20/63
Irons, Jeremy	Cowes, Isle of Wight, England, UK	9/19/48
Irving, Amy	Palo Alto, CA	9/10/53
Irving, George S.	Springfield, MA	11/1/22
Irwin, Bill	Santa Monica, CA	4/11/50
Ivanek, Zeljko	Ljubljana, Yugoslavia	8/15/57
Ivey, Judith	El Paso, TX	9/4/51
Ivory, James	Berkeley, CA	6/7/28
Izzard, Eddie	Aden, Yemen.	2/7/62
Ja Rule	Hollis, Queens, NY	2/29/76
Jackée (Harry)	Winston-Salem, NC	8/14/56
Jackman, Hugh	Sydney, Australia	10/12/68
Jackson, Anne	Allegheny, PA	9/3/26
Jackson, Cheyenne	Newport, WA	7/12/75
Jackson, Glenda	Birkenhead, England, UK	5/9/36
Jackson, Janet	Gary, IN.	5/16/66
Jackson, Jermaine	Gary, IN.	12/11/54
Jackson, Jonathan	Orlando, FL	5/11/82
Jackson, Joshua	Vancouver, BC, Canada.	6/11/78
Jackson, Kate	Birmingham, AL.	10/29/48
Jackson, La Toya	Gary, IN.	5/29/56
Jackson, Peter	Wellington, New Zealand	10/31/61
Jackson, Samuel L.	Washington, DC	12/21/48
Jacobi, Derek	London, England, UK	10/22/38
Jagger, Mick	Dartford, England, UK	7/26/43
James, Kevin	Mineola, NY	4/26/65
Jamison, Judith	Philadelphia, PA	5/10/43
Janis, Conrad	New York, NY	2/11/28
Janney, Allison	Dayton, OH	11/19/59
Janssen, Famke	Amsterdam, Netherlands	11/5/65
Jardine, Al	Lima, OH.	9/3/42
Jarmusch, Jim	Akron, OH.	1/22/53
Jarreau, Al	Milwaukee, WI	3/12/40
Jarrett, Keith	Allentown, PA	5/8/45
Jay Z	Brooklyn, NY	12/4/69
Jeffreys, Anne	Goldsboro, NC.	1/26/23
Jenner, Kris	San Diego, CA.	11/5/55
Jepsen, Carly Rae	Mission, BC, Can.	11/21/85
Jett, Joan	Philadelphia, PA	9/22/58
Jewel (Kilcher)	Payson, UT	5/23/74
Jewison, Norman	Toronto, ON, Canada.	7/21/26
Jillette, Penn	Greenfield, MA	3/5/55
Jillian, Ann	Cambridge, MA	1/29/50
Joel, Billy	Bronx, NY	5/9/49
Johansson, Scarlett	New York, NY	11/22/84
John, Elton	Pinner, Middlesex, Eng., UK.	3/25/47
Johns, Glynis	Durban, S. Africa.	10/5/23
Johnson, Arte	Benton Harbor, MI	1/20/29
Johnson, Beverly	Buffalo, NY	10/13/52
Johnson, Don	Flatt Creek, MO.	12/15/49
Johnson, Dwayne "The Rock".	Hayward, CA.	5/2/72
Johnston, Bruce	Los Angeles, CA	6/24/42

Name	Birthplace	Birthdate
Johnston, Kristen	Washington, DC	9/20/67
Jolie, Angelina	Los Angeles, CA	6/4/75
Jonas, Joe	Casa Grande, AZ	8/15/89
Jonas, Kevin	Teaneck, NJ	11/5/87
Jonas, Nick	Dallas, TX	9/16/92
Jones, Angus T.	Austin, TX	10/8/93
Jones, Bill T.	Bunnell, FL	2/15/52
Jones, Cherry	Paris, TN	11/21/56
Jones, Dean	Decatur, AL	1/25/31
Jones, Gemma	London, England, UK	12/4/42
Jones, Grace	Spanish Town, Jamaica	5/19/48
Jones, Jack	Hollywood, CA	1/14/38
Jones, James Earl	Arkabutla, MS	1/17/31
Jones, John Paul	Sidcup, Eng., UK	1/3/46
Jones, January	Sioux Falls, SD	1/5/78
Jones, Mick	London, England, UK	6/26/55
Jones, Norah	New York, NY	3/30/79
Jones, Quincy	Chicago, IL	3/14/33
Jones, Shirley	Charleroi, PA	3/31/34
Jones, Star	Badin, NC	3/24/62
Jones, Tom	Pontypridd, Wales, UK.	6/7/40
Jones, Tommy Lee	San Saba, TX	9/15/46
Jonze, Spike	Rockville, MD	10/22/69
Jourdan, Louis	Marseilles, France	6/19/19
Jovovich, Milla	Kiev, Ukraine	12/17/75
Judd, Ashley	Granada Hills, CA	4/19/68
Judd, Naomi	Ashland, KY	1/11/46
Judd, Wynonna	Ashland, KY	5/30/64
Kaczmarek, Jane	Milwaukee, WI	12/21/55
Kanaly, Steve	Burbank, CA	3/14/46
Kane, Carol	Cleveland, OH	6/18/52
Kaplan, Gabe	Brooklyn, NY	3/31/45
Kardashian, Khloe	Los Angeles, CA	6/27/84
Kardashian, Kim	Los Angeles, CA	10/21/80
Kardashian, Kourtney	Los Angeles, CA	4/18/79
Karlen, John	New York, NY	5/28/40
Karn, Richard	Seattle, WA	2/17/56
Kasem, Casey	Detroit, MI	4/27/32
Kattan, Chris	Sherman Oaks, CA	10/19/70
Kavner, Julie	Burbank, CA	9/7/51
Kaye, Judy	Phoenix, AZ.	12/11/48
Kazan, Lainie	New York, NY	5/15/40
Ke$ha	Los Angeles, CA	3/1/87
Keach, Stacy	Savannah, GA	6/2/41
Keaton, Diane	Santa Ana, CA	1/5/46
Keaton, Michael	Coraopolis, PA	9/5/51
Keener, Catherine	Miami, FL	3/23/59
Keillor, Garrison	Anoka, MN	8/7/42
Keitel, Harvey	Brooklyn, NY	5/13/39
Keith, David	Knoxville, TN	5/8/54
Keith, Penelope	Sutton, Surrey, Eng., UK	4/2/40
Kellerman, Sally	Long Beach, CA	6/2/37
Kelly, Minka	Los Angeles, CA	6/24/80
Kelly, R(obert)	Chicago, IL	1/8/67
Kennedy, George	New York, NY	2/18/25
Kennedy, Jamie	Upper Darby, PA	5/25/70
Kennedy, Jayne	Washington, DC	10/27/51
Kenny G	Seattle, WA	6/5/56
Kent, Allegra	Santa Monica, CA	8/11/37
Keoghan, Phil	Christchurch, New Zealand	5/31/67
Kercheval, Ken	Wolcottville, IN.	7/15/35
Kerns, Joanna	San Francisco, CA	2/12/53
Keys, Alicia	New York, NY	1/25/81
Khan, Chaka	Great Lakes, IL	3/23/53
Kid Rock	Romeo, MI.	1/17/71
Kidder, Margot	Yellowknife, NT, Canada	10/17/48
Kidman, Nicole	Honolulu, HI	6/20/67
Kiel, Richard	Detroit, MI	9/13/39
Kilborn, Craig	Kansas City, KS.	8/24/62
Kilmer, Val	Los Angeles, CA	12/31/59
Kim, Daniel Dae	Pusan, S. Korea	8/4/68
Kimmel, Jimmy	Brooklyn, NY	11/13/67
King, B. B.	Itta Bena, MS.	9/16/25
King, Carole	Brooklyn, NY	2/9/42
King, Larry	Brooklyn, NY	11/19/33
King, Perry	Alliance, OH	4/30/48
Kingsley, Ben	Scarborough, England, UK	12/31/43
Kingston, Alex	London, England, UK	3/11/63
Kinnear, Greg	Logansport, IN.	6/17/63
Kinney, Kathy	Stevens Point, WI	11/3/54
Kinski, Nastassja	Berlin, W. Germany	1/24/60
Kirkland, Gelsey	Bethlehem, PA.	12/29/52
Kirkpatrick, Chris	Clarion, PA	10/17/71
Kirshner, Mia.	Toronto, ON, Canada.	1/25/75
Kitsch, Taylor	Kelowna, BC, Canada	4/8/81
Klein, Robert.	Bronx, NY	2/8/42
Kline, Kevin	St. Louis, MO.	10/24/47
Klum, Heidi	Bergish-Gladbach, Germany.	6/1/73
Knight, Gladys	Atlanta, GA	5/28/44
Knight, Shirley	Goessel, KS	7/5/36
Knight, T. R.	Minneapolis, MN	3/26/73
Knight, Wayne	New York, NY	8/7/55
Knightley, Keira	Teddington, England, UK	3/26/85
Knopfler, Mark	Glasgow, Scotland, UK	8/12/49
Knowles, Beyoncé	Houston, TX	9/4/81
Knoxville, Johnny	Knoxville, TN	3/11/71

Name	Birthplace	Birthdate
Konitz, Lee	Chicago, IL	10/13/27
Kopell, Bernie	Brooklyn, NY	6/21/33
Kotto, Yaphet	New York, NY	11/15/37
Krakowski, Jane	Parsippany, NJ.	10/11/68
Krasinski, John	Newton, MA.	10/20/79
Krause, Peter	Alexandria, MN	8/12/65
Kressley, Carson	Allentown, PA	11/11/69
Kretschmann, Thomas	Dessau, E. Germany	9/8/62
Kristofferson, Kris	Brownsville, TX	6/22/36
Kudrow, Lisa	Encino, CA	7/30/63
Kunis, Mila	Kiev, Ukraine	8/14/83
Kuriyama, Chiaki	Tsuchiura, Ibaraki, Japan.	10/10/84
Kurtz, Swoosie	Omaha, NE	9/6/44
Kutcher, Ashton	Cedar Rapids, IA	2/7/78
Kwan, Nancy	Hong Kong	5/19/39
LaBelle, Patti	Philadelphia, PA	5/24/44
LaBeouf, Shia	Los Angeles, CA	6/11/86
Lachey, Nick	Harlan, KY	11/9/73
Ladd, Cheryl	Huron, SD	7/12/51
Ladd, Diane	Meridian, MS.	11/29/32
Lady Gaga	New York, NY	3/28/86
Lagasse, Emeril	Fall River, MA	10/15/59
Lahti, Christine	Birmingham, MI	4/4/50
Laine, Cleo	Southall, England, UK	10/28/27
Lake, Ricki	Hastings-on-Hudson, NY.	9/21/68
Lamas, Lorenzo	Santa Monica, CA	1/20/58
Lambert, Adam	Indianapolis, IN	1/29/82
Lambert, Christopher	Great Neck, NY	3/29/57
Lambert, Miranda	Longview, TX.	11/10/83
Landau, Martin	Brooklyn, NY	6/20/28
Landis, John	Chicago, IL	8/3/50
Lane, Diane	New York, NY	1/22/65
Lane, Nathan	Jersey City, NJ.	2/3/56
lang, k.d.	Consort, AB, Canada.	11/2/61
Lang, Stephen	Jamaica Estates, Queens, NY	7/11/52
Lange, Jessica	Cloquet, MN	4/20/49
Langella, Frank	Bayonne, NJ	1/1/38
Lansbury, Angela	London, England, UK	10/16/25
LaPaglia, Anthony	Adelaide, Australia.	1/31/59
Larroquette, John	New Orleans, LA	11/25/47
LaSalle, Eriq	Hartford, CT	6/23/62
Lauper, Cyndi	Ozone Park, Queens, NY	6/22/53
Laurie, Hugh	Oxford, England, UK	6/11/59
Laurie, Piper	Detroit, MI	1/22/32
Lautner, Taylor	Grand Rapids, MI	2/11/92
Lavigne, Avril	Belleville, ON, Canada.	9/27/84
Lavin, Linda	Portland, ME	10/15/37
Law, Jude	London, England, UK	12/29/72
Lawless, Lucy	Mount Albert, New Zealand.	3/29/68
Lawrence, Carol	Melrose Park, IL	9/5/34
Lawrence, Jennifer	Louisville, KY.	8/15/90
Lawrence, Joey	Montgomery, PA	4/20/76
Lawrence, Martin	Frankfurt, Germany	4/16/65
Lawrence, Steve	Brooklyn, NY	7/8/35
Lawrence, Vicki	Inglewood, CA	3/26/49
Leach, Robin	London, England, UK	8/29/41
Leachman, Cloris	Des Moines, IA	4/30/26
Lear, Norman	New Haven, CT	7/27/22
Learned, Michael	Washington, DC	4/9/39
Leary, Denis	Worcester, MA.	8/18/57
LeBlanc, Matt	Newton, MA.	7/25/67
LeBon, Simon	Bushey, England, UK.	10/27/58
Lee, Ang	Pingtung, Taiwan	10/23/54
Lee, Brenda	Lithonia, GA	12/11/44
Lee, Christopher	London, England, UK	5/27/22
Lee, Jason	Huntington Beach, CA.	4/25/70
Lee, Michele	Los Angeles, CA	6/24/42
Lee, Spike	Atlanta, GA	3/20/57
Leeves, Jane	Ilford, England, UK	4/18/61
Legrand, Michel	Paris, France.	2/24/32
Leguizamo, John	Bogotá, Colombia	7/22/64
Lehmkuhl, Reichen	Cincinnati, OH.	12/26/73
Leibman, Ron	New York, NY	10/11/37
Leigh, Jennifer Jason	Hollywood, CA.	2/5/62
Leighton, Laura	Iowa City, IA	7/24/68
Lennox, Annie	Aberdeen, Scotland, UK	12/25/54
Leno, Jay	New Rochelle, NY.	4/28/50
Leo, Melissa	New York, NY	9/14/60
Leonard, Robert Sean	Westwood, NJ.	2/28/69
Leoni, Tea	New York, NY	2/25/66
Leslie, Joan	Detroit, MI	1/26/25
Leto, Jared	Bossier City, LA	12/26/71
Letterman, David	Indianapolis, IN	4/12/47
Levin, Harvey	Los Angeles, CA	9/2/60
Levine, Adam	Los Angeles, CA	3/18/79
Levine, James	Cincinnati, OH	6/23/43
Levine, Ted	Bellaire, OH.	5/29/57
Levinson, Barry	Baltimore, MD	4/6/42
Levy, Eugene	Hamilton, ON, Canada.	12/17/46
Lewis, Damian	London, Eng., UK	2/11/71
Lewis, Huey	New York, NY	7/5/50
Lewis, Jason	Newport Beach, CA.	6/25/71
Lewis, Jerry	Newark, NJ	3/16/26
Lewis, Jerry Lee	Ferriday, LA.	9/29/35
Lewis, Juliette	Los Angeles, CA	6/21/73
Lewis, Leona	London, England, UK	4/3/85

Name	Birthplace	Birthdate
Lewis, Richard	Brooklyn, NY	6/29/47
Li, Jet	Beijing, China	4/26/63
Light, Judith	Trenton, NJ	2/9/49
Lightfoot, Gordon	Orillia, ON, Canada	11/17/38
Lil' Kim	Brooklyn, NY	7/11/75
Lil' Romeo	New Orleans, LA	8/19/89
Lilly, Evangeline	Fort Saskatchewan, AB, Can.	8/3/79
Lincoln, Andrew	London, England, UK	9/14/73
Linden, Hal	Bronx, NY	3/20/31
Ling, Lisa	Sacramento, CA	8/30/73
Linn-Baker, Mark	St. Louis, MO.	6/17/54
Linney, Laura	New York, NY	2/5/64
Liotta, Ray	Newark, NJ	12/18/54
Lithgow, John	Rochester, NY	10/19/45
Little, Rich	Ottawa, ON, Canada	11/26/38
Little Richard	Macon, GA	12/5/32
Littrell, Brian	Lexington, KY	2/20/75
Liu, Lucy	Jackson Heights, Queens, NY	12/2/68
Lively, Blake	Tarzana, CA	8/25/87
LL Cool J	St. Albans, Queens, NY	1/14/68
Lloyd, Christopher	Stamford, CT.	10/22/38
Lloyd, Emily	North London, Eng., UK	9/29/70
Lloyd Webber, Andrew	London, England, UK	3/22/48
Locke, Sondra	Shelbyville, TN.	5/28/47
Lockhart, June	New York, NY	6/25/25
Locklear, Heather	Westwood, CA.	9/25/61
Loggia, Robert	Staten Island, NY.	1/3/30
Loggins, Kenny	Everett, WA	1/7/48
Lohan, Lindsay	New York, NY	7/2/86
Lollobrigida, Gina	Subiaco, Italy	7/4/27
Lonergan, Kenneth	New York, NY	10/16/62
Long, Nia	Brooklyn, NY	10/30/70
Long, Shelley	Ft. Wayne, IN.	8/23/49
Longoria, Eva	Corpus Christi, TX	3/15/75
Lopez, George	Mission Hills, CA	4/23/61
Lopez, Jennifer	Bronx, NY	7/24/69
Lopez, Mario	San Diego, CA	10/10/73
Loren, Sophia	Rome, Italy	9/20/34
Loring, Gloria	New York, NY	12/10/46
Louis C.K.	Washington, DC	9/12/67
Louis-Dreyfus, Julia	New York, NY	1/13/61
Lovato, Demi	Dallas, TX	8/20/92
Love, Courtney	San Francisco, CA	7/9/64
Love, Mike	Baldwin Hills, CA	3/15/41
Loveless, Patty	Pikeville, KY	1/4/57
Lovett, Lyle	Klein, TX	11/1/57
Lovitz, Jon	Tarzana, CA	7/21/57
Lowe, Rob	Charlottesville, VA	3/17/64
Lucas, George	Modesto, CA	5/14/44
Lucci, Susan	Scarsdale, NY	12/23/46
Luckinbill, Laurence	Ft. Smith, AR	11/21/34
Ludacris	Champaign, IL	9/11/77
Ludwig, Christa	Berlin, Germany	3/16/24
Luhrmann, Baz	Sydney, Australia	9/17/62
LuPone, Patti	Northport, NY	4/21/49
Lynch, David	Missoula, MT.	1/20/46
Lynch, Jane	Dolton, IL.	7/14/60
Lynley, Carol	New York, NY	2/13/42
Lynn, Loretta	Butcher Hollow, KY	4/14/32
Lynn, Vera	London, England, UK	3/20/17
Lynne, Shelby	Quantico, VA	10/22/68
Ma, Yo-Yo	Paris, France	10/7/55
Maazel, Lorin	Neuilly-sur-Seine, France	3/6/30
Macchio, Ralph	Huntington, NY	11/4/61
MacDonald, Kelly	Glasgow, Scotland, UK	2/23/76
MacDowell, Andie	Gaffney, SC	4/21/58
MacFarlane, Seth	Kent, CT	10/26/73
MacGowan, Shane	Tunbridge, Kent, Eng., UK	12/25/57
MacGraw, Ali	Pound Ridge, NY	4/1/39
MacLachlan, Kyle	Yakima, WA.	2/22/59
MacLaine, Shirley	Richmond, VA	4/24/34
MacLeod, Gavin	Mt. Kisco, NY.	2/28/31
MacNee, Patrick	London, England, UK	2/6/22
MacNicol, Peter	Dallas, TX	4/10/54
MacPherson, Elle	Sydney, Australia	3/29/64
Macy, Bill	Revere, MA	5/18/22
Macy, William H.	Miami, FL	3/13/50
Madden, John	Austin, MN.	4/10/36
Madigan, Amy	Chicago, IL	9/11/50
Madonna (Ciccone)	Bay City, MI	8/16/58
Madsen, Michael	Chicago, IL	9/25/59
Maguire, Tobey	Santa Monica, CA	6/27/75
Maher, Bill	New York, NY	1/20/56
Mahoney, John	Blackpool, Lancashire, England, UK	6/20/40
Majors, Lee	Wyandotte, MI	4/23/39
Makarova, Natalia	Leningrad, Russia	11/21/40
Malick, Terrence	Ottawa, IL	11/30/43
Malick, Wendie	Buffalo, NY	12/13/50
Malina, Joshua	New York, NY	1/17/66
Malkovich, John	Christopher, IL	12/9/53
Malone, Dorothy	Chicago, IL	1/30/25
Mamet, David	Chicago, IL	11/30/47
Manchester, Melissa	Bronx, NY	2/15/51
Mandel, Howie	Toronto, ON, Canada	11/29/55
Mandrell, Barbara	Houston, TX	12/25/48
Mangione, Chuck	Rochester, NY	11/29/40
Manheim, Camryn	Caldwell, NJ	3/8/61
Manilow, Barry	Brooklyn, NY	6/17/43
Mann, Aimee	Richmond, VA	8/9/60
Manoff, Dinah	New York, NY	1/25/58
Manson, Marilyn	Canton, OH	1/5/69
Mantegna, Joe	Chicago, IL	11/13/47
Mantello, Joe	Rockford, IL	12/27/62
Mara, Rooney	Bedford, NY.	4/17/85
Marcil, Vanessa	Indio, CA	10/15/69
Margulies, Julianna	Spring Valley, NY	6/8/66
Marie, Constance	Hollywood, CA.	9/9/65
Marin, Cheech	Los Angeles, CA	7/13/46
Marinaro, Ed	New York, NY	3/31/50
Marriner, Neville	Lincoln, England, UK	4/15/24
Mars, Bruno	Honolulu, HI	10/8/85
Marsalis, Branford	Breaux Bridge, LA	8/26/60
Marsalis, Wynton	New Orleans, LA	10/18/61
Marsh, Jean	London, England, UK	7/1/34
Marshall, Garry	Bronx, NY	11/13/34
Marshall, Penny	Bronx, NY	10/15/42
Marshall, Peter	Huntington, WV	3/30/26
Martin, Chris	Devon, England, UK	3/22/77
Martin, Jesse L.	Rocky Mount, VA	1/18/69
Martin, Kellie	Riverside, CA.	10/16/75
Martin, Ricky	San Juan, Puerto Rico	12/24/71
Martin, Steve	Waco, TX.	8/14/45
Martindale, Margo	Jacksonville, TX	7/18/51
Martins, Peter	Copenhagen, Denmark	10/27/46
Mason, Jackie	Sheboygan, WI	6/9/31
Mason, Marsha	St. Louis, MO.	4/3/42
Masterson, Christopher	Long Island, NY	1/22/80
Masterson, Mary Stuart	New York, NY	6/28/66
Mastrantonio, Mary Elizabeth	Lombard, IL.	11/17/58
Masur, Kurt	Brieg, Germany	7/18/27
Masur, Richard	New York, NY	11/20/48
Mathers, Jerry	Sioux City, IA	6/2/48
Matheson, Tim	Glendale, CA.	12/31/47
Mathis, Johnny	Gilmer, TX	9/30/35
Matlin, Marlee	Morton Grove, IL	8/24/65
Matthews, Dave	Johannesburg, S. Africa	1/9/67
May, Elaine	Philadelphia, PA	4/21/32
Mayer, John	Bridgeport, CT	10/16/77
Mays, Jayma	Bristol, TN	7/16/79
Mazar, Debi	Jamaica, Queens, NY	8/13/64
Mazursky, Paul	Brooklyn, NY	4/25/30
McAdams, Rachel	London, ON, Canada.	10/7/76
McArdle, Andrea	Abington, PA	11/5/63
McAvoy, James	Glasgow, Scotland, UK	4/21/79?
McBride, Patricia	Teaneck, NJ	8/23/42
McCallum, David	Glasgow, Scotland, UK	9/19/33
McCarthy, Andrew	Westfield, NJ	11/29/62
McCarthy, Jenny	Chicago, IL	11/1/72
McCarthy, Melissa	Plainfield, IL.	8/26/70
McCartney, Paul	Liverpool, England, UK	6/18/42
McCarver, Tim	Memphis, TN.	10/16/41
McConaughey, Matthew	Uvalde, TX	11/4/69
McCoo, Marilyn	Jersey City, NJ.	9/30/43
McCormack, Eric	Toronto, ON, Canada	4/18/63
McCormack, Mary	Plainsfield, NJ	2/8/69
McCrane, Paul	Philadelphia, PA	1/19/61
McCreery, Scotty	Garner, NC	10/9/93
McDaniel, James	Washington, DC	3/25/58
McDermott, Dylan	Waterbury, CT	10/26/61
McDiarmid, Ian	Carnoustie, Tayside, Scot., UK	4/17/44?
McDonald, Audra	Berlin, Germany	7/3/70
McDonnell, Mary	Wilkes-Barre, PA	4/28/52
McDormand, Frances	Chicago, IL	6/23/57
McDowell, Malcolm	Leeds, England, UK.	6/13/43
McEntire, Reba	McAlester, OK	3/28/55
McFerrin, Bobby	New York, NY	3/11/50
McGillis, Kelly	Newport Beach, CA.	7/9/57
McGovern, Elizabeth	Evanston, IL	7/18/61
McGovern, Maureen	Youngstown, OH	7/27/49
McGraw, Tim	Delhi, LA	5/1/67
McGregor, Ewan	Crieff, Scotland, UK	3/31/71
McHale, Joel	Rome, Italy	11/20/71
McHale, Kevin	Plano, TX.	6/14/88
McKean, Michael	New York, NY	10/17/47
McKechnie, Donna	Pontiac, MI	11/16/42
McKellen, Ian	Burnley, England, UK.	5/25/39
McKenzie, Benjamin	Austin, TX	9/12/78
McKidd, Kevin	Elgin, Scotland, UK	8/9/73
McLachlan, Sarah	Halifax, NS, Canada	1/28/68
McLean, A. J.	West Palm Beach, FL	1/9/78
McNichol, Kristy	Los Angeles, CA	9/11/62
McRaney, Gerald	Collins, MS	8/19/47
McQueen, Steven R.	Los Angeles, CA	7/13/88
McShane, Ian	Blackburn, England, UK.	9/29/42
Meadows, Jayne	Wu Chang, China	9/27/20
Meara, Anne	Brooklyn, NY	9/20/29
Meat Loaf	Dallas, TX	9/27/47
Meester, Leighton	Marco Island, FL	4/9/86
Mehta, Zubin	Bombay, India	4/29/36
Mellencamp, John	Seymour, IN	10/7/51

Name	Birthplace	Birthdate
Meloni, Christopher	Washington, DC	4/2/61
Mendes, Sam	Redding, England, UK	8/1/65
Mendes, Sergio	Niteroi, Brazil	2/11/41
Menzel, Idina	Syosset, NY	5/30/71
Merchant, Natalie	Jamestown, NY	10/26/63
Merkerson, S. Epatha	Saginaw, MI	11/28/52
Merrill, Dina	New York, NY	12/9/25
Messing, Debra	Brooklyn, NY	8/15/68
Metcalf, Laurie	Carbondale, IL	6/16/55
Meyers, Seth	Bedford, NH	12/28/73
Michael, George	London, England, UK	6/25/63
Michaels, Al	Brooklyn, NY	11/12/44
Michaels, Bret	Butler, PA	3/15/63
Michaels, Lorne	Toronto, ON, Canada	11/17/44
Michele, Lea	Bronx, NY	8/29/86
Midler, Bette	Honolulu, HI	12/1/45
Midori (Goto)	Osaka, Japan	10/25/71
Mike D	Brooklyn, NY	11/20/65
Milano, Alyssa	Brooklyn, NY	12/19/72
Miles, Sarah	Ingatestone, England, UK	12/31/41
Miles, Vera	nr. Boise City, OK	8/23/30
Miller, Dennis	Pittsburgh, PA	11/3/53
Miller, Jonny Lee	Kingston Upon Thames, England, UK	11/15/72
Miller, Penelope Ann	Santa Monica, CA	1/13/64
Mills, Donna	Chicago, IL	12/11/43
Mills, Hayley	London, England, UK	4/18/46
Milner, Martin	Detroit, MI	12/28/31
Milnes, Sherrill	Downers Grove, IL	1/10/35
Milsap, Ronnie	Robinsville, NC	1/16/44
Mimieux, Yvette	Hollywood, CA	1/8/42
Minaj, Nicki	St. James, Trinidad and Tobago	12/8/82
Ming-Na (Wen)	Coloane Island, Macao	11/20/63
Minnelli, Liza	Los Angeles, CA	3/12/46
Minogue, Kylie	Melbourne, Australia	5/28/68
Mirren, Helen	London, England, UK	7/26/45
Mitchell, Brian Stokes	Seattle, WA	10/31/57
Mitchell, Elizabeth	Los Angeles, CA	3/27/70
Mitchell, Jerry	Paw Paw, MI	1/15/60
Mitchell, Joni	Fort McLeod, AB, Canada	11/7/43
Moby	New York, NY	9/11/65
Modine, Matthew	Loma Linda, CA	3/22/59
Moffat, Donald	Plymouth, England, UK	12/26/30
Molina, Alfred	London, England, UK	5/24/53
Molinaro, Al	Kenosha, WI	6/24/19
Moll, Richard	Pasadena, CA	1/13/43
Moloney, Janel	Woodland Hills, CA	10/3/69
Monaghan, Dominic	Berlin, Germany	12/8/76
Monica (Arnold)	College Park, GA	10/24/80
Mo'Nique	Woodlawn, MD	12/11/67
Moody, Ron	London, England, UK	1/8/24
Moore, Demi	Roswell, NM	11/11/62
Moore, Julianne	Fort Bragg, NC	12/3/60
Moore, Mandy	Nashua, NH	4/10/84
Moore, Mary Tyler	Brooklyn, NY	12/29/36
Moore, Melba	New York, NY	10/29/45
Moore, Michael	Flint, MI	4/23/54
Moore, Roger	London, England, UK	10/14/27
Moore, Terry	Los Angeles, CA	1/7/29
Morales, Esai	Brooklyn, NY	10/1/62
Moranis, Rick	Toronto, ON, Canada	4/18/53
Moreau, Jeanne	Paris, France	1/23/28
Moreno, Rita	Humacao, Puerto Rico	12/11/31
Morgan, Jeffrey Dean	Seattle, WA	4/22/66
Morgan, Piers	Guildford, Surrey, UK	3/30/65
Morgan, Tracy	Bronx, NY	11/10/68
Moriarty, Michael	Detroit, MI	4/5/41
Morris, Garrett	New Orleans, LA	2/1/37
Morissette, Alanis	Ottawa, ON, Canada	6/1/74
Morrison, Matthew	Fort Ord, CA	10/30/78
Morrison, Van	Belfast, N. Ireland, UK	8/31/45
Morrissey (Steven Patrick)	Manchester, England, UK	5/22/59
Morrow, Rob	New Rochelle, NY	9/21/62
Morse, David	Beverly, MA	10/11/53
Morse, Robert	Newton, MA	5/18/31
Mortensen, Viggo	New York, NY	10/20/58
Mortimer, Emily	London, England, UK	12/1/71
Morton, Joe	New York, NY	10/18/47
Morton, Samantha	Nottingham, England, UK	5/13/77
Moses, William	Los Angeles, CA	11/17/59
Moss, Carrie-Anne	Vancouver, BC, Canada	8/21/67
Moss, Elisabeth	Los Angeles, CA	7/24/82
Moss, Kate	Croydon, Surrey, Eng., UK	1/16/74
Moyer, Stephen	Brentwood, UK	10/11/69
Moynahan, Bridget	Binghamton, NY	4/28/71
Mueller-Stahl, Armin	Tilsit, E. Prussia	12/17/30
Muldaur, Diana	Brooklyn, NY	8/19/38
Mulgrew, Kate	Dubuque, IA	4/29/55
Mull, Martin	Chicago, IL	8/18/43
Mullally, Megan	Los Angeles, CA	11/12/58
Mullan, Peter	Peterhead, Scotland, UK	11/2/59
Mulroney, Dermot	Alexandria, VA	10/31/63
Muniz, Frankie	Wood-Ridge, NJ	12/5/85
Munsel, Patrice	Spokane, WA	5/14/25
Murphy, Ben	Jonesboro, AR	3/6/42
Murphy, Donna	Corona, Queens, NY	3/7/58
Murphy, Eddie	Brooklyn, NY	4/3/61
Murphy, Michael	Los Angeles, CA	5/5/38
Murray, Anne	Springhill, NS, Canada	6/20/45
Murray, Bill	Wilmette, IL	9/21/50
Murray, Don	Hollywood, CA	7/31/29
Musburger, Brent	Portland, OR	5/26/39
Muti, Riccardo	Naples, Italy	7/28/41
Myers, Mike	Scarborough, ON, Canada	5/25/63
Nabors, Jim	Sylacauga, AL	6/12/30
Nagra, Parminder	Leicester, England, UK	10/5/75
Nash, Graham	Blackpool, England, UK	2/2/42
Naughton, James	Middletown, CT	12/6/45
Navarro, Dave	Santa Monica, CA	6/7/67
Nealon, Kevin	St. Louis, MO	11/18/53
Neeson, Liam	Ballymena, N. Ireland, UK	6/7/52
Neff, Lucas	Chicago, IL	11/7/85
Neill, Sam	Ulster, N. Ireland, UK	9/14/47
Nelligan, Kate	London, ON, Canada	3/16/51
Nelly	Austin, TX	11/2/74
Nelson, Craig T.	Spokane, WA	4/4/44
Nelson, Ed	New Orleans, LA	12/21/28
Nelson, Judd	Portland, ME	11/28/59
Nelson, Tracy	Santa Monica, CA	10/25/63
Nelson, Willie	Abbott, TX	4/30/33
Nero, Peter	Brooklyn, NY	5/22/34
Nesmith, Mike	Houston, TX	12/30/42
Neuwirth, Bebe	Newark, NJ	12/31/58
Neville, Aaron	New Orleans, LA	1/24/41
Newhart, Bob	Oak Park, IL	9/5/29
Newman, Randy	New Orleans, LA	11/28/43
Newton, Wayne	Norfolk, VA	4/3/42
Newton-John, Olivia	Cambridge, England, UK	9/26/48
Nicholas, Denise	Detroit, MI	7/12/44
Nichols, Mike	Berlin, Germany	11/6/31
Nicholson, Jack	Neptune, NJ	4/22/37
Nicks, Stevie	Phoenix, AZ	5/26/48
Nighy, Bill	Caterham, Surrey, Eng., UK	12/12/49
Nimoy, Leonard	Boston, MA	3/26/31
Nixon, Cynthia	New York, NY	4/9/66
Nolte, Nick	Omaha, NE	2/8/41
Noone, Peter	Manchester, England, UK	11/5/47
Norman, Jessye	Augusta, GA	9/15/45
Norris, Chuck	Ryan, OK	3/10/40
Northam, Jeremy	Cambridge, England, UK	12/1/61
Norton, Edward	Boston, MA	8/18/69
Noth, Christopher	Madison, WI	11/13/54
Novak, Kim	Chicago, IL	2/13/33
Nuyen, France	Marseilles, France	7/31/39
Oates, John	New York, NY	4/7/49
O'Brian, Hugh	Rochester, NY	4/19/25
O'Brien, Conan	Brookline, MA	4/18/63
O'Brien, Margaret	San Diego, CA	1/15/37
Ocean, Billy	Fyzabad, Trinidad	1/21/50
O'Connor, Sinead	Glenageary, Ireland	12/8/66
O'Donnell, Chris	Winnetka, IL	6/26/70
O'Donnell, Rosie	Commack, NY	3/21/62
O'Grady, Gail	Detroit, MI	1/23/63
Oh, Sandra	Nepean, ON, Canada	7/20/71
O'Hara, Catherine	Toronto, ON, Canada	3/4/54
O'Hara, Maureen	Dublin, Ireland	8/17/20
O'Hare, Denis	Kansas City, MO	1/17/62
Oka, Masi	Tokyo, Japan	12/27/74
Oldman, Gary	South London, Eng., UK	3/21/58
Olin, Ken	Chicago, IL	7/30/54
Olin, Lena	Stockholm, Sweden	3/22/55
Olmos, Edward James	E. Los Angeles, CA	2/24/47
Olsen, Ashley	Sherman Oaks, CA	6/13/86
Olsen, Mary-Kate	Sherman Oaks, CA	6/13/86
Olson, Nancy	Milwaukee, WI	7/14/28
Olyphant, Timothy	Honolulu, HI	5/20/68
O'Malley, Mike	Boston, MA	10/31/66
O'Neal, Ryan	Los Angeles, CA	4/20/41
O'Neal, Tatum	Los Angeles, CA	11/5/63
O'Neill, Ed	Youngstown, OH	4/12/46
Ontkean, Michael	Vancouver, BC, Canada	1/24/46
O'Quinn, Terry	Newbury, MI	7/15/52
Orlando, Tony	New York, NY	4/3/44
Ormond, Julia	Epsom, England, UK	1/4/65
Osbourne, Jack	London, England, UK	11/8/85
Osbourne, Kelly	London, England, UK	10/27/84
Osbourne, Ozzy	Birmingham, England, UK	12/3/48
Osbourne, Sharon	London, England, UK	10/9/52
Osment, Haley Joel	Los Angeles, CA	4/10/88
Osmond, Donny	Ogden, UT	12/9/57
Osmond, Marie	Ogden, UT	10/13/59
O'Toole, Annette	Houston, TX	4/1/51
O'Toole, Peter	Connemara, Ireland	8/2/32
Owen, Clive	Keresley, England, UK	10/3/64
Oz, Frank	Herford, England, UK	5/25/44
Ozawa, Seiji	Shenyang, China	9/1/35
Pacino, Al	New York, NY	4/25/40
Packer, Billy	Wellsville, NY	2/25/40
Page, Ellen	Halifax, NS, Canada	2/21/87
Page, Jimmy	Heston, England, UK	1/9/44
Page, Patti	Claremore, OK	11/8/27

Name	Birthplace	Birthdate
Paget, Debra	Denver, CO	8/19/33
Paige, Janis	Tacoma, WA	9/16/22
Paisley, Brad	Glen Dale, WV	10/28/72
Palin, Michael	Sheffield, England, UK	5/5/43
Palmer, Betsy	East Chicago, IN	11/1/26
Palmer, Geoffrey	London, England, UK	6/4/27
Palminteri, Chazz	Bronx, NY	5/15/51
Paltrow, Gwyneth	Los Angeles, CA	9/27/72
Panettiere, Hayden	Palisades, NY	8/21/89
Panjabi, Archie	Edgware, England, UK	5/31/72
Pantoliano, Joe	Hoboken, NJ	9/12/51
Papas, Irene	Chiliomodi, Greece	9/3/26
Paquin, Anna	Winnipeg, MB, Canada	7/24/82
Parker, Alan	Islington, England, UK	2/14/44
Parker, Eleanor	Cedarville, OH	6/26/22
Parker, Jameson	Baltimore, MD	11/18/47
Parker, Mary-Louise	Fort Jackson, SC	8/2/64
Parker, Sarah Jessica	Nelsonville, OH	3/25/65
Parsons, Estelle	Marblehead, MA	11/20/27
Parsons, Jim	Houston, TX	3/24/73
Parton, Dolly	Sevierville, TN	1/19/46
Pasdar, Adrian	Pittsfield, MA	4/30/65
Patinkin, Mandy	Chicago, IL	11/30/52
Patric, Jason	Queens, NY	6/17/66
Pattinson, Robert	London, England, UK	5/13/86
Patton, Will	Charleston, SC	6/14/54
Paul, Aaron	Emmett, ID	8/27/79
Paul, Adrian	London, England, UK	5/29/59
Paulson, Sarah	Tampa, FL	12/17/75
Paxton, Bill	Fort Worth, TX	5/17/55
Pearce, Guy	Ely, England, UK	10/5/67
Peet, Amanda	New York, NY	1/11/72
Penn, Kal	Montclair, NJ	4/23/77
Penn, Sean	Burbank, CA	8/17/60
Pepper, Barry	Campbell River, BC, Can.	4/4/70
Perez, Rosie	Brooklyn, NY	9/6/64
Perkins, Elizabeth	Queens, NY	11/18/60
Perlman, Itzhak	Tel Aviv, Israel	8/31/45
Perlman, Rhea	Brooklyn, NY	3/31/48
Perlman, Ron	New York, NY	4/13/50
Perrine, Valerie	Galveston, TX	9/3/43
Perry, Katy	Santa Barbara, CA	10/25/84
Perry, Luke	Mansfield, OH	10/11/65
Perry, Matthew	Williamstown, MA	8/19/69
Perry, Tyler	New Orleans, LA	9/13/69
Persoff, Nehemiah	Jerusalem, Israel	8/2/19
Pesci, Joe	Newark, NJ	2/9/43
Peters, Bernadette	Ozone Park, Queens, NY	2/28/48
Peters, Roberta	Bronx, NY	5/4/30
Petersen, Wolfgang	Emden, Germany	3/14/41
Petty, Lori	Chattanooga, TN	3/23/63
Petty, Tom	Gainesville, FL	10/20/50
Pfeiffer, Michelle	Santa Ana, CA	4/29/58
Phair, Liz	New Haven, CT	4/17/67
Philbin, Regis	New York, NY	8/25/31
Phillippe, Ryan	New Castle, DE	9/10/74
Phillips, Lou Diamond	Subic Bay, Philippines	2/17/62
Phillips, Mackenzie	Alexandria, VA	11/10/59
Phillips, Michelle	Long Beach, CA	6/4/44
Phillips, Phillip	Leesburg, GA	9/20/90
Phillips, Sian	Bettws, Wales, UK	5/14/34
Phoenix, Joaquin	San Juan, Puerto Rico	10/28/74
Pierce, David Hyde	Albany, NY	4/3/59
Pinchot, Bronson	New York, NY	5/20/59
Pink	Doylestown, PA	9/8/79
Pinkett Smith, Jada	Baltimore, MD	9/18/71
Pirner, David	Green Bay, WI	4/16/64
Piscopo, Joe	Passaic, NJ	6/17/51
Pitt, Brad	Shawnee, OK	12/18/63
Piven, Jeremy	New York, NY	7/26/65
Plant, Robert	W. Bromwich, England, UK	8/20/48
Plimpton, Martha	New York ,NY	11/16/70
Plowright, Joan	Brigg, England, UK	10/28/29
Plummer, Amanda	New York, NY	3/23/57
Plummer, Christopher	Toronto, ON, Canada	12/13/27
Poehler, Amy	Newton, MA	9/16/71
Poitier, Sidney	Miami, FL	2/20/27
Polanski, Roman	Paris, France	8/18/33
Pompeo, Ellen	Everett, MA	11/10/69
Pop, Iggy	Muskegon, MI	4/21/47
Portman, Natalie	Jerusalem, Israel	6/9/81
Posey, Parker	Baltimore, MD	11/8/68
Post, Markie	Palo Alto, CA	11/4/50
Potente, Franka	Dulmen bei Munster, Germany	7/22/74
Potts, Annie	Nashville, TN	10/28/52
Povich, Maury	Washington, DC	1/17/39
Powell, Jane	Portland, OR	4/1/28
Powers, Stefanie	Hollywood, CA	11/2/42
Prentiss, Paula	San Antonio, TX	3/4/39
Prepon, Laura	Watchung, NJ	3/7/80
Presley, Priscilla	Brooklyn, NY	5/24/45
Pressly, Jaime	Kinston, NC	7/30/77
Previn, Andre	Berlin, Germany	4/6/29
Price, Leontyne	Laurel, MS	2/10/27
Price, Molly	North Plainfield, NJ	12/15/66
Price, Ray	Perryville, TX	1/12/26
Pride, Charley	Sledge, MS	3/18/38
Priestley, Jason	Vancouver, BC, Canada	8/28/69
Prince (The Artist)	Minneapolis, MN	6/7/58
Prince, Faith	Augusta, GA	8/5/57
Principal, Victoria	Fukuoka, Japan	1/3/50
Probst, Jeff	Wichita, KS	11/4/62
Proctor, Emily	Raleigh, NC	10/8/68
Pryce, Jonathan	Holywell, N. Wales, UK	6/1/47
Puck, Wolfgang	St. Veit, Austria	1/8/49
Pulliam, Keshia Knight	Newark, NJ	4/9/79
Pullman, Bill	Hornell, NY	12/17/53
Purcell, Sarah	Richmond, IN	10/8/48
Purefoy, James	Taunton, England, UK	6/3/64
Quaid, Dennis	Houston, TX	4/9/54
Quaid, Randy	Houston, TX	10/1/50
Queen Latifah	Newark, NJ	3/18/70
Quinn, Aidan	Chicago, IL	3/8/59
Quinn, Colin	Brooklyn, NY	6/6/59
Quinn, Martha	Albany, NY.	5/11/59
Quinto, Zachary	Pittsburgh, PA	6/2/77
Rachins, Alan	Cambridge, MA	10/3/42
Radcliffe, Daniel	London, England, UK	7/23/89
Radnor, Josh	Columbus, OH	7/29/74
Rae, Charlotte	Milwaukee, WI	4/22/26
Raffi (Cavoukian)	Cairo, Egypt.	7/8/48
Rainer, Luise	Düsseldorf, Germany	1/12/1910
Raitt, Bonnie	Burbank, CA	11/8/49
Ramey, Samuel	Colby, KS.	3/28/42
Ramirez, Efren	Los Angeles, CA	10/2/73
Ramirez, Sara	Mazatlan, Mexico.	8/31/75
Ramone, Tommy	Budapest, Hungary	1/29/52
Rampling, Charlotte	Sturmer, MA	2/5/46
Rancic, Giuliana	Naples, Italy.	8/17/75
Randolph, Joyce	Detroit, MI	10/21/24
Raphael, Sally Jessy	Easton, PA.	2/25/35
Rashad, Phylicia	Houston, TX	6/19/48
Ratzenberger, John	Bridgeport, CT.	4/6/47
Raver, Kim	New York, NY	3/15/69
Ray, Rachael	Glen Falls, NY	8/25/68
Reddy, Helen	Melbourne, Australia	10/25/41
Redford, Robert	Santa Monica, CA	8/18/36
Redgrave, Vanessa	London, England, UK	1/30/37
Reed, Lou	Brooklyn, NY	3/2/42
Reed, Rex	Ft. Worth, TX	10/2/38
Reese, Della	Detroit, MI	7/6/31
Reeves, Keanu	Beirut, Lebanon	9/2/64
Reeves, Martha	Eufaula, AL	7/18/41
Regalbuto, Joe	New York, NY	8/24/49
Reid, Tara	Wyckoff, NJ	11/8/75
Reid, Tim	Norfolk, VA	12/19/44
Reid, Vernon	London, England, UK	8/22/58
Reilly, John C.	Chicago, IL	5/24/65
Reiner, Carl	Bronx, NY	3/20/22
Reiner, Rob	Bronx, NY	3/6/47
Reinhold, Judge	Wilmington, DE	5/21/57
Roinking, Ann	Seattle, WA	11/10/49
Reiser, Paul	New York, NY	3/30/57
Reitman, Ivan	Komarno, Czechoslovakia	10/26/46
Remini, Leah	Brooklyn, NY	6/15/70
Renner, Jeremy	Modesto, CA	1/7/71
Reynolds, Burt	Waycross, GA	2/11/36
Reynolds, Debbie	El Paso, TX	4/1/32
Reynolds, Ryan	Vancouver, BC, Canada.	10/23/76
Reznor, Trent	Mercer, PA.	5/17/65
Rhames, Ving	New York, NY	5/12/59
Rhymes, Busta	Brooklyn, NY	5/20/72
Rhys Meyers, Jonathan	Dublin, Ireland	7/27/77
Ribisi, Giovanni	Los Angeles, CA	12/17/74
Ricci, Christina	Santa Monica, CA	2/12/80
Richards, Denise	Downers Grove, IL	2/17/71
Richards, Keith	Dartford, Kent, Eng., UK	12/18/43
Richards, Michael	Culver City, CA	7/24/49
Richardson, Kevin	Lexington, KY	10/3/71
Richardson, Miranda	Lancashire, England, UK	3/3/58
Richardson, Patricia	Bethesda, MD	2/23/51
Richie, Lionel	Tuskegee, AL	6/20/49
Richie, Nicole	Berkeley, CA	9/21/81
Richter, Andy	Grand Rapids, MI	10/28/66
Rickles, Don	Jackson Heights, Queens, NY	5/8/26
Rickman, Alan	Hammersmith, Eng., UK	2/21/46
Riegert, Peter	New York, NY	4/11/47
Rigg, Diana	Doncaster, England, UK	7/20/38
Rihanna	St. Michael, Barbados	2/20/88
Riley, Amber	Long Beach, CA	2/15/86
Rimes, LeAnn	Jackson, MS	8/28/82
Ringwald, Molly	Roseville, CA	2/18/68
Ripa, Kelly	Stratford, NJ	10/2/70
Rivera, Chita	Washington, DC	1/23/33
Rivera, Geraldo	New York, NY	7/4/43
Rivers, Joan	Brooklyn, NY	6/8/33
Robbins, Tim	W. Covina, CA	10/16/58
Roberts, Doris	St. Louis, MO.	11/4/25
Roberts, Eric	Biloxi, MS	4/18/56
Roberts, Julia	Smyrna, GA.	10/28/67
Roberts, Tony	New York, NY	10/22/39
Robinson, Smokey	Detroit, MI	2/19/40

Name	Birthplace	Birthdate
Rock, Chris	Andrews, SC	2/7/65
Rodgers, Jimmy	Camas, WA	9/18/33
Rodriguez, Johnny	Sabinal, TX	12/10/51
Rodriguez, Michelle	Bexar County, TX.	7/12/78
Rogan, Joe	Newark, NJ	8/11/67
Rogen, Seth	Vancouver, BC, Canada.	4/15/82
Rogers, Kenny	Houston, TX	8/21/38
Rogers, Mimi.	Coral Gables, FL	1/27/56
Rogers, Wayne	Birmingham, AL	4/7/33
Rohm, Elisabeth	Dusseldorf, Germany...	4/28/73
Rollins, Henry	Washington, DC	2/13/61
Rollins, Sonny	New York, NY	9/7/30
Romano, Ray	Forest Hills, Queens, NY	12/21/57
Romijn, Rebecca	Berkeley, CA	11/6/72
Ronstadt, Linda	Tucson, AZ	7/15/46
Rooney, Mickey	Brooklyn, NY	9/23/20
Root, Stephen	Sarasota, FL	11/17/51
Rose, Axl	Lafayette, IN	2/6/62
Rose Marie	New York, NY	8/15/23
Roseanne	Salt Lake City, UT	11/3/52
Ross, Charlotte	Winnetka, IL	1/21/68
Ross, Diana	Detroit, MI	3/26/44
Ross, Katharine	Hollywood, CA.	1/29/40
Ross, Marion	Albert Lea, MN	10/25/28
Rossdale, Gavin	London, England, UK	10/30/65
Rossellini, Isabella	Rome, Italy	6/18/52
Rossum, Emmy	New York, NY	9/12/86
Roth, David Lee	Bloomington, IN.	10/10/55
Roth, Tim	London, England, UK	5/14/61
Rotten, Johnny	London, England, UK	1/31/56
Rourke, Mickey	Schenectady, NY	9/16/52
Routh, Brandon	Des Moines, IA	10/9/79
Routledge, Patricia	Birkenhead, England, UK	2/17/29
Rowan, Kelly	Ottawa, ON, Canada	10/26/65
Rowlands, Gena	Cambria, WI	6/19/30
Rubinstein, John	Beverly Hills, CA	12/8/46
Rudd, Paul	Passaic, NJ	4/6/1969
Rudner, Rita	Miami, FL	9/17/55?
Rudolph, Maya	Gainesville, FL.	7/27/72
Ruehl, Mercedes	Jackson Heights, Queens, NY	2/28/48
Ruffalo, Mark.	Kenosha, WI	11/22/67
Rupp, Debra Jo	Glendale, CA.	2/24/51
Rush, Barbara	Denver, CO	1/4/27
Rush, Geoffrey	Toowoomba, Australia	7/6/51
Russell, Keri	Fountain Valley, CA	3/23/76
Russell, Kurt	Springfield, MA	3/17/51
Russell, Leon	Lawton, OK	4/2/41
Russell, Mark	Buffalo, NY	8/23/32
Russell, Theresa	San Diego, CA.	3/20/57
Russo, Rene	Burbank, CA	2/17/54
Ruttan, Susan	Oregon City, OR	9/16/50
Ryan, Meg	Fairfield, CT	11/19/61
Ryan, Roz	Detroit, MI	7/7/51
Rydell, Bobby	Philadelphia, PA	4/26/42
Ryder, Winona	Winona, MN	10/29/71
Sabato, Antonio, Jr.	Rome, Italy	2/29/72
Sade (Adu)	Ibadan, Nigeria	1/16/59
Sagal, Katey	Hollywood, CA.	1/19/54
Saget, Bob	Philadelphia, PA	5/17/56
Sagnier, Ludivine	La Celle-St.-Cloud, France...	7/3/79
Sahl, Mort	Montreal, QC, Canada.	5/11/27
Saint, Eva Marie	Newark, NJ	7/4/24
St. James, Susan	Hollywood, CA	8/14/46
St. John, Jill	Los Angeles, CA	8/19/40
St. Patrick, Mathew	Philadelphia, PA	3/17/68
Sajak, Pat	Chicago, IL	10/26/46
Saks, Gene	New York, NY	11/8/21
Saldana, Zoë	Passaic, NJ	6/19/78
Salling, Mark	Dallas, TX	8/17/82
Salonga, Lea	Manila, Philippines	2/22/71
Samberg, Andy	Berkeley, CA	8/18/78
Samms, Emma	London, England, UK	8/28/60
San Giacomo, Laura	Hoboken, NJ	11/14/62
Sandler, Adam	Brooklyn, NY	9/9/66
Sands, Julian	West Yorkshire, Eng., UK.	1/15/58
Santana, Carlos	Autlan, Mexico	7/20/47
Sara, Mia	Brooklyn, NY	6/19/67
Sarandon, Susan	New York, NY	10/4/46
Sartain, Gailard	Tulsa, OK	9/18/46
Savage, Ben	Highland Park, IL.	9/13/80
Savage, Fred	Highland Park, IL.	7/9/76
Sawa, Devon	Vancouver, BC, Canada.	9/7/78
Saxon, John	Brooklyn, NY	8/5/36
Sayles, John	Schenectady, NY	9/28/50
Scacchi, Greta	Milan, Italy	2/18/60
Scaggs, Boz	Canton, OH	6/8/44
Scales, Prunella	Sutton Abinger, Eng., UK	6/22/32
Scalia, Jack	Brooklyn, NY	11/10/51
Schallert, William	Los Angeles, CA	7/6/22
Schell, Maximilian	Vienna, Austria	12/8/30
Schiff, Richard	Bethesda, MD	5/27/55
Schiffer, Claudia	Rheinbach, Germany.	8/25/70
Schneider, John	Mt. Kisco, NY.	4/8/60
Schneider, Rob	San Francisco, CA	10/31/63
Schram, Bitty	New York, NY	7/17/68
Schreiber, Liev	San Francisco, CA.	10/4/67

Name	Birthplace	Birthdate
Schroder, Rick	Staten Island, NY	4/13/70
Schwarzenegger, Arnold..	Thal, Austria	7/30/47
Schwimmer, David	Astoria, Queens, NY	11/2/66
Sciorra, Annabella	Wethersfield, CT	3/24/64
Scolari, Peter	New Rochelle, NY	9/12/54
Scorsese, Martin.	Flushing, Queens, NY	11/17/42
Scott, Lizabeth	Scranton, PA	9/29/22
Scott, Ridley	South Shields, England, UK.	11/30/37
Scott, Seann William	Cottage Grove, MN	10/3/76
Scott Thomas, Kristin	Redruth, England, UK	5/24/60
Scotto, Renata	Savona, Italy	2/24/34
Scully, Vin	Bronx, NY	11/29/27
Seacrest, Ryan	Atlanta, GA	12/24/74
Seagal, Steven	Lansing, MI	4/10/51
Secor, Kyle	Tacoma, WA	5/31/57
Sedaka, Neil	Brooklyn, NY	3/13/39
Sedgwick, Kyra	New York, NY	8/19/65
Seeger, Pete	New York, NY	5/3/19
Segal, George	Great Neck, NY	2/13/34
Segel, Jason	Los Angeles, CA	1/18/80
Seidelman, Susan	Abington, PA	12/11/52
Seinfeld, Jerry	Brooklyn, NY	4/29/54
Seldes, Marian	New York, NY	8/23/28
Sellecca, Connie	Bronx, NY	5/25/55
Selleck, Tom	Detroit, MI	1/29/45
Severinsen, Doc	Arlington, OR.	7/7/27
Sevigny, Chloë	Springfield, MA	11/18/74
Sewell, Rufus	Twickenham, Middlesex, England, UK.	10/29/67
Seyfried, Amanda	Allentown, PA	12/3/85
Seymour, Jane	Hillingdon, England, UK.	2/15/51
Shackelford, Ted	Oklahoma City, OK	6/23/46
Shaffer, Paul	Thunder Bay, ON, Canada..	11/28/49
Shakira (Mebarak Ripoll)	Barranquilla, Colombia	2/2/77
Shalhoub, Tony	Green Bay, WI	10/9/53
Shandling, Garry	Chicago, IL	11/29/49
Shannon, Molly	Shaker Heights, OH.	9/16/64
Sharif, Omar	Alexandria, Egypt	4/10/32
Shatner, William	Montreal, QC, Canada.	3/22/31
Shaughnessy, Charles	London, England, UK	2/9/55
Shaver, Helen	St. Thomas, ON, Canada..	2/24/51
Shawkat, Alia	Riverside, CA.	4/18/89
Shea, John	N. Conway, NH	4/14/49
Shearer, Harry	Los Angeles, CA	12/23/43
Sheedy, Ally	New York, NY	6/13/62
Sheen, Charlie	Los Angeles, CA	9/3/65
Sheen, Martin	Dayton, OH	8/3/40
Sheen, Michael	Newport, Wales, UK	2/5/69
Sheindlin, Judy	Brooklyn, NY	10/21/42
Shelley, Carole	London, England, UK	8/16/39
Shelton, Blake	Ada, OK	6/18/76
Shepard, Sam	Ft. Sheridan, IL	11/5/43
Shepherd, Cybill	Memphis, TN.	2/18/50
Shepherd, Sherri	Chicago, IL	4/22/67
Sheridan, Nicollette	Worthing, England, UK	11/21/63
Shields, Brooke	New York, NY	5/31/65
Shire, Talia	Lake Success, NY	4/25/46
Short, Martin	Hamilton, ON, Canada.	3/26/50
Shortz, Will	Crawfordsville, IN.	8/26/52
Show, Grant	Detroit, MI.	2/27/62
Shue, Andrew	South Orange, NJ	2/20/67
Shue, Elisabeth	Wilmington, DE	10/6/63
Shyamalan, M. Night.	Pondicherry, India	8/6/70
Sidibe, Gabourey	Brooklyn, NY	5/6/83
Sigler, Jamie-Lynn	Jericho, NY	5/15/81
Sikking, James B.	Los Angeles, CA	3/5/34
Silverman, Jonathan	Beverly Hills, CA	8/5/66
Silverman, Sarah	Bedford, NH.	12/1/70
Silverstone, Alicia	San Francisco, CA	10/4/76
Simmons, Gene	Haifa, Israel.	8/25/49
Simmons, Henry	Stamford, CT	7/1/70
Simmons, Richard	New Orleans, LA	7/12/48
Simon, Carly	New York, NY	6/25/45
Simon, Paul	Newark, NJ	10/13/41
Simpson, Ashlee	Waco, TX.	10/3/84
Simpson, Jessica	Abilene, TX	7/10/80
Sinatra, Nancy	Jersey City, NJ.	6/8/40
Sinbad	Benton Harbor, MI	11/10/56
Singleton, John	Los Angeles, CA	1/6/68
Sinise, Gary	Blue Island, IL	3/17/55
Sirico, Tony	Brooklyn, NY	7/29/42
Sisto, Jeremy	Grass Valley, CA	10/6/74
Sizemore, Tom	Detroit, MI	9/29/61
Skerritt, Tom	Detroit, MI	8/25/33
Slater, Christian	New York, NY	8/18/69
Slater, Helen	Massapequa, NY.	12/15/63
Slattery, John	Boston, MA	8/13/62
Sledge, Percy	Leighton, AL	11/25/40
Slezak, Erika	Hollywood, CA.	8/5/46
Slick, Grace	Evanston, IL	10/30/39
Smirnoff, Karina	Kharkiv, Ukraine	1/2/78
Smirnoff, Yakov	Odessa, Ukraine	1/24/51
Smith, Allison	New York, NY	12/9/69
Smith, Jaclyn	Houston, TX	10/26/45
Smith, Jaden	Malibu, CA.	7/8/98
Smith, Keely	Norfolk, VA	3/9/32

Name	Birthplace	Birthdate
Smith, Kevin	Red Bank, NJ	8/2/70
Smith, Maggie	Ilford, England, UK	12/28/34
Smith, Patti	Chicago, IL	12/30/46
Smith, Robert	Blackpool, England, UK	4/21/59
Smith, Will	Philadelphia, PA	9/25/68
Smith, Willow	Los Angeles, CA	10/31/2000
Smits, Jimmy	Brooklyn, NY	7/9/55
Smothers, Dick	Governor's Island, NY	11/20/38
Smothers, Tom	Governor's Island, NY	2/2/37
Smulders, Cobie	Vancouver, BC, Canada	4/3/82
Snipes, Wesley	Orlando, FL	7/31/62
Snooki (Nicole Polizzi)	Santiago, Chile	11/23/87
Snoopzilla (née Snoop Dogg, Snoop Lion)	Long Beach, CA	10/20/71
Soderbergh, Steven	Atlanta, GA	1/14/63
Somerhalder, Ian	Covington, LA	12/8/78
Somers, Suzanne	San Bruno, CA	10/16/46
Sommer, Elke	Berlin, Germany	11/5/40
Sorbo, Kevin	Mound, MN	9/24/58
Sorvino, Mira	Tenafly, NJ	9/28/67
Sorvino, Paul	Brooklyn, NY	4/13/39
Soul, David	Chicago, IL	8/28/43
Spacek, Sissy	Quitman, TX	12/25/49
Spacey, Kevin	South Orange, NJ	7/26/59
Spade, David	Birmingham, MI	7/22/64
Spader, James	Boston, MA	2/7/60
Spalding, Esperanza	Portland, OR	10/18/84
Spano, Joe	San Francisco, CA	7/7/46
Sparks, Jordin	Phoenix, AZ	12/22/89
Spears, Britney	Kentwood, LA	12/2/81
Spears, Jamie-Lynn	McComb, MS	4/4/91
Spector, Phil	Bronx, NY	12/26/40
Spelling, Tori	Los Angeles, CA	5/16/73
Spencer, Octavia	Montgomery, AL	5/25/72
Spielberg, Steven	Cincinnati, OH	12/18/46
Spiner, Brent	Houston, TX	2/2/49
Springer, Jerry	London, England, UK	2/13/44
Springfield, Rick	Sydney, Australia	8/23/49
Springsteen, Bruce	Long Branch, NJ	9/23/49
Spurlock, Morgan	Parksburg, WV	11/7/70
Stahl, Nick	Harlingen, TX	12/5/79
Stallone, Sylvester	New York, NY	7/6/46
Stamos, John	Cypress, CA	8/19/63
Stamp, Terence	Stepney, England, UK	7/22/38
Stanton, Harry Dean	West Irvine, KY	7/14/26
Starr, Ringo	Liverpool, England, UK	7/7/40
Steenburgen, Mary	Newport, AR	2/8/53
Stefani, Gwen	Fullterton, CA	10/3/69
Stein, Ben	Washington, DC	11/25/44
Stephens, James	Mt. Kisco, NY	5/18/51
Stern, Daniel	Bethesda, MD	8/28/57
Stern, Howard	Roosevelt, NY	1/12/54
Sternhagen, Frances	Washington, DC	1/13/30
Stevens, Andrew	Memphis, TN	6/10/55
Stevens, Cat (Yusef Islam)	London, England, UK	7/21/48
Stevens, Connie	Brooklyn, NY	8/8/38
Stevens, Stella	Yazoo City, MS	10/1/36
Stevenson, Parker	Philadelphia, PA	6/4/52
Stewart, French	Albuquerque, NM	2/20/64
Stewart, Jon	New York, NY	11/28/62
Stewart, Kristen	Los Angeles, CA	4/9/90
Stewart, Patrick	Mirfield, England, UK	7/13/40
Stewart, Rod	London, England, UK	1/10/45
Stiers, David Ogden	Peoria, IL	10/31/42
Stiles, Julia	New York, NY	3/28/81
Stiller, Ben	New York, NY	11/30/65
Stiller, Jerry	Brooklyn, NY	6/8/27
Stills, Stephen	Dallas, TX	1/3/45
Sting	Newcastle upon Tyne, England, UK	10/2/51
Stipe, Michael	Decatur, GA	1/4/60
Stockwell, Dean	North Hollywood, CA	3/5/36
Stoltz, Eric	Whittier, CA	9/30/61
Stone, Dee Wallace	Kansas City, KS	12/14/48
Stone, Emma	Scottsdale, AZ	11/6/88
Stone, Oliver	New York, NY	9/15/46
Stone, Sharon	Meadville, PA	3/10/58
Stonestreet, Eric	Kansas City, KS	9/9/71
Stookey, Paul	Baltimore, MD	12/30/37
Storch, Larry	New York, NY	1/8/23
Stowe, Madeleine	Eagle Rock, CA	8/18/58
Strait, George	Pearsall, TX	5/18/52
Strasser, Robin	New York, NY	5/7/45
Stratas, Teresa	Toronto, ON, Canada	5/26/38
Strathairn, David	San Francisco, CA	1/26/49
Strauss, Peter	Croton-on-Hudson, NY	2/20/47
Streep, Meryl	Summit, NJ	6/22/49
Streisand, Barbra	Brooklyn, NY	4/24/42
Stringfield, Sherry	Colorado Springs, CO	6/24/67
Stritch, Elaine	Detroit, MI	2/2/25
Stroman, Susan	Wilmington, DE	10/17/54
Struthers, Sally	Portland, OR	7/28/48
Studdard, Ruben	Frankfurt, Germany	9/12/78
Styles, Harry	Holmes Chapel, Cheshire, Eng., UK	2/1/94
Suchet, David	London, England, UK	5/2/46
Sudeikis, Jason	Fairfax, VA	9/18/75
Sullivan, Erik Per	Worcester, MA	7/12/91
Sullivan, Susan	New York, NY	11/18/42
Sunjata, Daniel	Evanston, IL	12/30/71
Sutherland, Donald	St. John, NB, Canada	7/17/34
Sutherland, Kiefer	London, England, UK	12/21/66
Suvari, Mena	Newport, RI	2/9/79
Swank, Hilary	Lincoln, NE	7/30/74
Swift, Taylor	Wyomissing, PA	12/13/89
Swinton, Tilda	London, England, UK	11/5/60
Swit, Loretta	Passaic, NJ	11/4/37
Sykes, Wanda	Portsmouth, VA	3/7/64
Szmanda, Eric	Milwaukee, WI	7/24/75
T, Mr.	Chicago, IL	5/21/52
Takei, George	Los Angeles, CA	4/20/37
Tamblyn, Amber	Santa Monica, CA	5/14/83
Tamblyn, Russ	Los Angeles, CA	12/30/34
Tambor, Jeffrey	San Francisco, CA	7/8/44
Tarantino, Quentin	Knoxville, TN	3/27/63
Tatum, Channing	Cullman, AL	4/26/80
Tautou, Audrey	Beaumont, France	8/9/76?
Taylor, Buck	Hollywood, CA	5/13/38
Taylor, James	Boston, MA	3/12/48
Taylor, Paul	Englewood, CA	7/29/30
Taylor, Rip	Washington, DC	1/13/34
Taylor, Rod	Sydney, Australia	1/11/30
Taymor, Julie	Newton, MA	12/15/52
Te Kanawa, Kiri	Gisborne, New Zealand	3/6/44
Teller	Philadelphia, PA	2/14/48
Temple Black, Shirley	Santa Monica, CA	4/23/28
Tennant, Victoria	London, England, UK	9/30/50
Tennille, Toni	Montgomery, AL	5/8/40
Tesh, John	Garden City, NY	7/9/52
Tharp, Twyla	Portland, IN	7/1/41
Theron, Charlize	Benoni, South Africa	8/7/75
Thicke, Alan	Kirkland Lake, ON, Canada	3/1/47
Thicke, Robin	Los Angeles, CA	3/10/77
Thiessen, Tiffani	Long Beach, CA	1/23/74
Thomas, Jay	Kermit, TX	7/12/48
Thomas, Jonathan Taylor	Bethlehem, PA	9/8/81
Thomas, Marlo	Deerfield, MI	11/21/37
Thomas, Michael Tilson	Hollywood, CA	12/21/44
Thomas, Philip Michael	Columbus, OH	5/26/49
Thomas, Richard	New York, NY	6/13/51
Thomas, Sean Patrick	Wilmington, DE	12/17/70
Thompson, Emma	London, England, UK	4/15/59
Thompson, Jack	Sydney, Australia	8/31/40
Thompson, Kenan	Atlanta, GA	5/10/78
Thompson, Lea	Rochester, MN	5/31/61
Thorne-Smith, Courtney	San Francisco, CA	11/8/67
Thornton, Billy Bob	Hot Springs, AR	8/4/55
Thurman, Uma	Boston, MA	4/29/70
Tiegs, Cheryl	Breckenridge, MN	9/25/47
Tierney, Maura	Boston, MA	2/3/65
Tillis, Mel	Tampa, FL	8/8/32
Tilly, Jennifer	Harbor City, CA	9/16/58
Tilly, Meg	Long Beach, CA	2/14/60
Timberlake, Justin	Memphis, TN	1/31/81
Tisdale, Ashley	West Deal, NJ	7/2/85
Tomei, Marisa	Brooklyn, NY	12/4/64
Tomlin, Lily	Detroit, MI	9/1/39
Tonioli, Bruno	Ferrara, Italy	11/25/55
Tork, Peter	Washington, DC	2/13/42
Torn, Rip	Temple, TX	2/6/31
Townsend, Robert	Chicago, IL	2/6/57
Townshend, Peter	Chiswick, England, UK	5/19/45
Travanti, Daniel J.	Kenosha, WI	3/7/40
Travis, Nancy	Astoria, Queens, NY	9/21/61
Travis, Randy	Marshville, NC	5/4/59
Travolta, John	Englewood, NJ	2/18/54
Trebek, Alex	Sudbury, ON, Canada	7/22/40
Tripplehorn, Jean	Tulsa, OK	6/10/63
Tritt, Travis	Marietta, GA	2/9/63
Tucci, Stanley	Peekskill, NY	1/11/60
Tucker, Chris	Decatur, GA	8/31/72
Tucker, Michael	Baltimore, MD	2/6/44
Tucker, Tanya	Seminole, TX	10/10/58
Tune, Tommy	Wichita Falls, TX	2/28/39
Turlington, Christy	Walnut Creek, CA	1/2/69
Turner, Janine	Lincoln, NE	12/6/62
Turner, Kathleen	Springfield, MO	6/19/54
Turner, Tina	Nutbush, TN	11/26/39
Turturro, John	Brooklyn, NY	2/28/57
Tveit, Aaron	Middletown, NY	10/21/83
Twain, Shania	Windsor, ON, Canada	8/28/65
Twiggy (Lawson)	London, England, UK	9/19/49
Tyler, Liv	New York, NY	7/1/77
Tyler, Steven	Yonkers, NY	3/26/48
Tyson, Cicely	New York, NY	12/19/33
Uecker, Bob	Milwaukee, WI	1/26/35
Uggams, Leslie	New York, NY	5/25/43
Ullman, Tracey	Slough, England, UK	12/30/59
Ullmann, Liv	Tokyo, Japan	12/16/38
Ulrich, Skeet	Lynchburg, VA	1/20/70
Underwood, Blair	Tacoma, WA	8/25/64

Name	Birthplace	Birthdate
Underwood, Carrie	Muskogee, OK.	3/10/83
Urban, Keith	Whangarei, North Island, New Zealand	10/26/67
Urie, Michael	Dallas, TX	8/8/80
Usher (Raymond IV)	Dallas, TX	10/14/78
Vaccaro, Brenda	Brooklyn, NY	11/18/39
Vale, Jerry	Bronx, NY	7/8/32
Valley, Mark	Ogdensburg, NY	12/24/64
Valli, Frankie	Newark, NJ	5/3/34
Van Ark, Joan	New York, NY	6/16/43
Van Damme, Jean-Claude	Brussels, Belgium	10/18/60
Van Der Beek, James	Cheshire, CT	3/8/77
Van Doren, Mamie	Rowena, SD	2/6/31
Van Dyke, Dick	West Plains, MO	12/13/25
Van Dyke, Jerry	Danville, IL	7/27/31
Van Halen, Eddie	Nijmegen, Netherlands	1/26/55
Van Patten, Dick	Kew Gardens, Queens, NY	12/9/28
Van Peebles, Mario	Mexico City, Mexico	1/15/57
Van Sant, Gus	Louisville, KY	7/24/52
Van Zandt, Steven	Winthrop, MA	11/22/50
VanCamp, Emily	Port Perry, ON, Canada	5/12/86
Vance, Courtney B.	Detroit, MI	3/12/60
Vardalos, Nia	Winnipeg, MB, Canada	9/24/62
Vaughn, Robert	New York, NY	11/22/32
Vaughn, Vince	Minneapolis, MN	3/28/70
Vedder, Eddie	Evanston, IL	12/23/64
Vega, Alexa	Miami, FL	8/27/88
Ventimiglia, Milo	Anaheim, CA	7/8/77
Vereen, Ben	Miami, FL	10/10/46
Vergara, Sofia	Barranquilla, Colombia	7/10/72
Vickers, Jon	Prince Albert, SK, Canada	10/29/26
Vieira, Meredith	Providence, RI	12/30/53
Vigoda, Abe	New York, NY	2/24/21
Villella, Edward	Long Island, NY	10/1/36
Vincent, Jan-Michael	Denver, CO	7/15/44
Vinton, Bobby	Canonsburg, PA	4/16/35
Visnjic, Goran	Sibenik, Yugo. (Croatia)	9/9/72
Vitale, Dick	East Rutherford, NJ	6/9/39
Voight, Jon	Yonkers, NY	12/29/38
Von Stade, Frederica	Somerville, NJ	6/1/45
Von Sydow, Max	Lund, Sweden	4/10/29
Von Trier, Lars	Copenhagen, Denmark	4/30/56
Wagner, Jack	Washington, MO	10/3/59
Wagner, Lindsay	Los Angeles, CA	6/22/49
Wagner, Robert	Detroit, MI	2/10/30
Wahl, Ken	Chicago, IL	10/31/54
Wahlberg, Donnie	Dorchester, MA	8/17/69
Wahlberg, Mark	Dorchester, MA	6/5/71
Wain, Bea	Bronx, NY	4/30/17
Waite, Ralph	White Plains, NY	6/22/28
Waits, Tom	Pomona, CA	12/7/49
Walden, Robert	New York, NY	9/25/43
Walken, Christopher	Astoria, Queens, NY	3/31/43
Walker, Clint	Hartford, IL	5/30/27
Wallace, Marcia	Creston, IA	11/1/42
Wallach, Eli	Brooklyn, NY	12/7/15
Wallis, Quvenzhané	Houma, LA	8/23/08
Walsh, Kate	San Jose, CA.	10/13/67
Walter, Jessica	Brooklyn, NY	1/31/41
Waltz, Christoph	Vienna, Austria	10/4/56
Warburton, Patrick	Paterson, NJ	11/14/64
Ward, Fred	San Diego, CA.	12/30/42
Ward, Sela	Meridian, MS.	7/11/56
Ward, Simon	Kent, London, Eng., UK	10/19/41
Warfield, Marsha	Chicago, IL	3/5/54
Warnor, Malcolm-Jamal	Jersey City, NJ.	8/18/70
Warren, Lesley Ann	New York, NY	8/16/46
Warwick, Dionne	East Orange, NJ	12/12/40
Washington, Denzel	Mt. Vernon, NY	12/28/54
Washington, Isaiah	Houston, TX	8/3/63
Washington, Kerry	Bronx, NY	1/31/77
Wasikowska, Mia	Canberra, Australia	10/14/89
Watanabe, Ken	Koide, Niigata, Japan.	10/21/59
Waters, John	Baltimore, MD	4/22/46
Waters, Roger	Great Bookham, Eng., UK	9/6/43
Waterston, Sam	Cambridge, MA	11/15/40
Watson, Emily	London, England, UK	1/14/67
Watson, Emma	Paris, France	4/15/90
Watts, Naomi	Shoreham, England, UK	9/28/68
Wayans, Damon	New York, NY	9/4/60
Wayans, Keenen Ivory	Brooklyn, NY	6/8/58
Wayans, Marlon	New York, NY	7/23/72
Wayans, Shawn	New York, NY	1/19/71
Weathers, Carl	New Orleans, LA	1/14/48
Weaver, Fritz	Pittsburgh, PA	1/19/26
Weaver, Sigourney	New York, NY	10/8/49
Weiland, Scott	Santa Cruz, CA	10/27/67
Weir, Peter	Sydney, Australia	8/21/44
Weisz, Rachel	London, England, UK	3/7/71
Weitz, Bruce	Norwalk, CT	5/27/43
Welch, Raquel	Chicago, IL	9/5/40
Weld, Tuesday	New York, NY	8/27/43
Weller, Peter	Stevens Point, WI	6/24/47
Welling, Tom	Putnam Valley, NY	4/26/77
Wendt, George	Chicago, IL	10/17/48
Wentz, Pete	Wilmette, IL	6/5/79
West, Adam	Walla Walla, WA	9/19/28
West, Kanye	Atlanta, GA	6/8/77
West, Shane	Baton Rouge, LA	6/10/78
Wettig, Patricia	Cincinnati, OH	12/4/51
Whalley, Joanne	Manchester, England, UK	8/25/64
Wheaton, Wil	Burbank, CA	7/29/72
Whitaker, Forest	Longview, TX.	7/15/61
White, Betty	Oak Park, IL	1/17/22
White, Jack	Detroit, MI	7/9/75
White, Jaleel	Pasadena, CA	11/27/76
White, Vanna	N. Myrtle Beach, SC	2/18/57
Whitford, Bradley	Madison, WI	10/10/59
Wiest, Dianne	Kansas City, MO	3/28/48
Wiig, Kristen	Canandaigua, NY	8/22/73
Wilde, Olivia	New York, NY	3/10/84
Wilder, Gene	Milwaukee, WI	6/11/33
Wilkinson, Tom	Leeds, England, UK.	12/12/48
Williams, Armstrong	Marion, SC	2/5/59
Williams, Barry	Santa Monica, CA	9/30/54
Williams, Billy Dee	New York, NY	4/6/37
Williams, Cindy	Van Nuys, CA	8/22/47
Williams, Hal	Columbus, OH	12/14/38
Williams, Hank, Jr.	Shreveport, LA	5/26/49
Williams, JoBeth	Houston, TX	12/6/48
Williams, Kimberly	Rye, NY.	9/14/71
Williams, Lucinda	Lake Charles, LA	1/26/53
Williams, Michelle	Kalispell, MT	9/9/80
Williams, Montel	Baltimore, MD	7/3/56
Williams, Paul	Omaha, NE	9/19/40
Williams, Robin	Chicago, IL	7/21/51
Williams, Treat	Rowayton, CT	12/1/51
Williams, Vanessa	Millwood, NY	3/18/63
Williamson, Kevin	New Bern, NC	3/14/65
Willis, Bruce	Idar-Oberstein, W. Ger.	3/19/55
Wilson, Brian	Inglewood, CA	6/20/42
Wilson, Cassandra	Jackson, MS	12/4/55
Wilson, Chandra	Houston, TX	8/27/69
Wilson, Demond	Valdosta, GA	10/13/46
Wilson, Elizabeth	Grand Rapids, MI	4/4/21
Wilson, Luke	Dallas, TX	9/21/71
Wilson, Nancy	Chillicothe, OH	2/20/37
Wilson, Owen	Dallas, TX	11/18/68
Wilson, Rainn	Seattle, WA	1/20/66
Winfrey, Oprah	Kosciusko, MS.	1/29/54
Winger, Debra	Cleveland, OH	5/16/55
Winkler, Henry	New York, NY	10/30/45
Winningham, Mare	Phoenix, AZ.	5/16/59
Winokur, Marissa Jaret	New York, NY	2/2/73
Winslet, Kate	Reading, England, UK	10/5/75
Winter, Johnny	Beaumont,TX	2/23/44
Winwood, Steve	Birmingham, England, UK.	5/12/48
Withers, Jane	Atlanta, GA	4/12/26
Witherspoon, Reese	New Orleans, LA	3/22/76
Witt, Alicia	Worcester, MA.	8/21/75
Wolf, Scott	Boston, MA	6/4/68
Wonder, Stevie	Saginaw, MI.	5/13/50
Wong, Faye	Beijing, China	8/8/69
Woo, John	Guangzhou, China	5/1/46
Wood, Elijah	Cedar Rapids, IA	1/28/81
Woodard, Alfre	Tulsa, OK	11/8/52
Woods, James	Vernal, UT.	4/18/47
Woodward, Joanne	Thomasville, GA	2/27/30
Wopat, Tom	Lodi, WI.	9/9/51
Worthington Sam	Godalming, Surrey, Eng., UK	8/2/76
Wright, Jeffrey	Washington, DC	12/7/65
Wright, Max	Detroit, MI	8/2/43
Wright, Robin	Dallas, TX	4/8/66
Wright, Steven	New York, NY	12/6/55
Wyle, Noah	Hollywood, CA.	6/4/71
Wyman, Bill	London, England, UK	10/24/36
Yankovic, Weird Al	Lynwood, CA	10/23/59
Yanni (Chrysomallis)	Kalamata, Greece	11/14/54
Yarrow, Peter	New York, NY	5/31/38
Yearwood, Trisha	Monticello, GA	9/19/64
Yoakam, Dwight	Pikesville, KY.	10/23/56
York, Michael	Fulmer, England, UK	3/27/42
Young, Alan	North Shields, England, UK.	11/19/19
Young, Burt	New York, NY	4/30/40
Young, Neil	Toronto, ON, Canada.	11/12/45
Young, Sean	Louisville, KY	11/20/59
Zane, Billy	Chicago, IL	2/24/66
Zeffirelli, Franco	Florence, Italy	2/12/23
Zellweger, Renée	Katy, TX.	4/25/69
Zemeckis, Robert	Chicago, IL	5/14/52
Zerbe, Anthony	Long Beach, CA	5/20/36
Zeta-Jones, Catherine	Swansea, Wales, UK	9/25/69
Zimbalist, Efrem, Jr.	New York, NY	11/30/18
Zimbalist, Stephanie	New York, NY	10/8/56
Zimmer, Kim	Grand Rapids, MI	2/2/55
Zhang, Ziyi	Beijing, China	2/9/79
Zukerman, Pinchas	Tel Aviv, Israel	7/16/48
Zuniga, Daphne	Berkeley, CA.	10/28/62

Entertainment Personalities of the Past

See also other lists for some deceased entertainers not included here.

Name	Born	Died	Name	Born	Died	Name	Born	Died
Aaliyah (Haughton)	1979	2001	Beery, Noah, Sr.	1884	1946	Brynner, Yul	1915	1985
Abbott, Bud	1895	1974	Beery, Wallace	1885	1949	Buchanan, Edgar	1903	1979
Abbott, George	1887	1995	Begley, Ed	1901	1970	Buchholz, Horst	1933	2003
Acuff, Roy	1903	1992	Bel Geddes, Barbara	1922	2005	Buñuel, Luis	1900	1983
Adams, Don	1923	2005	Bellamy, Ralph	1904	1991	Buono, Victor	1938	1982
Adams, Edie	1927	2008	Belushi, John	1949	1982	Burke, Billie	1885	1970
Adams, Joey	1911	1999	Benaderet, Bea	1906	1968	Burnette, Smiley	1911	1967
Adams, Maude	1872	1953	Bendix, William	1906	1964	Burns, George	1896	1996
Adler, Jacob P.	1855	1926	Bennett, Constance	1904	1965	Burr, Raymond	1917	1993
Adoree, Renee	1898	1933	Bennett, Joan	1910	1990	Burton, Richard	1925	1984
Agar, John	1921	2002	Bennett, Michael	1943	1987	Busch, Mae	1897	1946
Aherne, Brian	1902	1986	Benny, Jack	1894	1974	Bushman, Francis X.	1883	1966
Ailey, Alvin	1931	1989	Berg, Gertrude	1899	1966	Buttons, Red	1919	2006
Akins, Claude	1918	1994	Bergen, Edgar	1903	1978	Byington, Spring	1893	1971
Albert, Eddie	1906	2005	Bergman, Ingmar	1918	2007	Cabot, Bruce	1904	1972
Albertson, Frank	1909	1964	Bergman, Ingrid	1915	1982	Cabot, Sebastian	1918	1977
Albertson, Jack	1907	1981	Berkeley, Busby	1895	1976	Cagney, James	1899	1986
Alda, Robert	1914	1986	Berle, Milton	1908	2002	Caldwell, Sarah	1924	2006
Allen, Fred	1894	1956	Berlin, Irving	1888	1989	Calhern, Louis	1895	1956
Allen, Gracie	1906	1964	Bernardi, Herschel	1923	1986	Calhoun, Rory	1922	1999
Allen, Mel	1913	1996	Bernhardt, Sarah	1844	1923	Callas, Charlie	1927	2011
Allen, Peter	1944	1992	Bernstein, Leonard	1918	1990	Callas, Maria	1923	1977
Allen, Steve	1921	2000	Berry, Jan	1941	2004	Calloway, Cab	1907	1994
Allgood, Sara	1883	1950	Bessell, Ted	1939	1996	Cambridge, Godfrey	1933	1976
Allyson, June	1917	2006	Bickford, Charles	1889	1967	Campbell, Mrs. Patrick	1865	1940
Altman, Robert	1925	2006	Big Bopper, The	1930	1959	Candy, John	1950	1994
Ameche, Don	1908	1993	Billingsley, Barbara	1915	2010	Cantinflas	1911	1993
Ames, Leon	1903	1993	Bing, Rudolf	1902	1997	Cantor, Eddie	1892	1964
Amsterdam, Morey	1908	1996	Bishop, Joey	1918	2007	Capra, Frank	1897	1991
Anderson, G. M. "Bronco Billy"	1882	1971	Bitzer, Billy	1872	1944	Carey, Harry	1878	1947
Anderson, Judith	1897	1992	Bixby, Bill	1934	1993	Carey, Harry, Jr.	1921	2012
Anderson, Marian	1897	1993	Black, Karen	1939	2013	Carey, Macdonald	1913	1994
Andre the Giant	1946	1993	Blackstone, Harry, Jr.	1934	1997	Carle, Frankie	1903	2001
Andrews, Dana	1909	1992	Blackstone, Harry, Sr.	1885	1965	Carlin, George	1937	2008
Andrews, Laverne	1913	1967	Blaine, Vivian	1921	1995	Carlisle Hart, Kitty	1910	2007
Andrews, Maxene	1916	1995	Blake, Amanda	1931	1989	Carney, Art	1918	2003
Andrews, Patty	1918	2013	Blake, Eubie	1883	1983	Carpenter, Karen	1950	1983
Angeli, Pier	1932	1971	Blanc, Mel	1908	1989	Carradine, David	1936	2009
Antonioni, Michelangelo	1912	2007	Blocker, Dan	1928	1972	Carradine, John	1906	1988
Arbuckle, Fatty (Roscoe)	1887	1933	Blondell, Joan	1909	1979	Carrillo, Leo	1880	1961
Archerd, Army	1922	2009	Blondin, Charles	1824	1897	Carroll, Leo G.	1892	1972
Arden, Eve	1908	1990	Blore, Eric	1887	1959	Carroll, Madeleine	1906	1987
Arlen, Richard	1900	1976	Blue, Ben	1901	1975	Carson, Jack	1910	1963
Arliss, George	1868	1946	Blyden, Larry	1925	1975	Carson, Johnny	1925	2005
Armstrong, Louis	1901	1971	Bogarde, Dirk	1921	1999	Carter, Benny	1907	2003
Arnaz, Desi	1917	1986	Bogart, Humphrey	1899	1957	Carter, Dixie	1039	2010
Arness, James	1923	2011	Boland, Mary	1880	1965	Carter, Nell	1948	2003
Arnold, Eddy	1918	2008	Boles, John	1895	1969	Caruso, Enrico	1873	1921
Arnold, Edward	1890	1956	Bolger, Ray	1904	1987	Casals, Pablo	1876	1973
Arquette, Cliff	1905	1974	Bond, Ward	1903	1960	Cash, Johnny	1932	2003
Arthur, Beatrice	1922	2009	Bondi, Beulah	1888	1981	Cash, June Carter	1929	2003
Arthur, Joan	1900	1991	Bono, Sonny	1935	1998	Cass, Peggy	1924	1999
Ashcroft, Peggy	1907	1991	Boone, Richard	1917	1981	Cassavetes, John	1929	1989
Astaire, Fred	1899	1987	Booth, Edwin	1833	1893	Cassidy, Jack	1927	1976
Astor, Mary	1906	1987	Booth, John Wilkes	1838	1865	Castle, Irene	1893	1969
Atkins, Chet	1924	2001	Booth, Junius Brutus	1796	1852	Castle, Vernon	1887	1918
Atwill, Lionel	1885	1946	Booth, Shirley	1898	1992	Chaliapin, Feodor	1873	1938
Auer, Mischa	1905	1967	Borge, Victor	1909	2000	Champion, Gower	1919	1980
Aumont, Jean-Pierre	1911	2001	Borgnine, Ernest	1917	2012	Chandler, Jeff	1918	1961
Austin, Gene	1900	1972	Borzage, Frank	1893	1962	Chaney, Lon	1883	1930
Autry, Gene	1907	1998	Bosley, Tom	1927	2010	Chaney, Lon, Jr.	1905	1973
Axton, Hoyt	1938	1999	Bow, Clara	1905	1965	Chapin, Harry	1942	1981
Ayres, Lew	1908	1996	Bowes, Maj. Edward	1874	1946	Chaplin, Charles	1889	1977
Backus, Jim	1913	1989	Bowman, Lee	1914	1979	Chapman, Graham	1941	1989
Bailey, Pearl	1918	1990	Boxcar Willie	1931	1999	Charisse, Cyd	1921	2008
Bain, Conrad	1923	2013	Boyd, Stephen	1928	1977	Charles, Ray	1930	2004
Bainter, Fay	1892	1968	Boyd, William	1898	1972	Chase, Ilka	1905	1978
Baker, Josephine	1906	1975	Boyer, Charles	1899	1978	Chatterton, Ruth	1893	1961
Balanchine, George	1904	1983	Boyle, Peter	1935	2006	Cherrill, Virginia	1908	1996
Ball, Lucille	1911	1989	Bracken, Eddie	1915	2002	Chevalier, Maurice	1888	1972
Balsam, Martin	1919	1996	Brady, Alice	1892	1939	Child, Julia	1912	2004
Bancroft, Anne	1931	2005	Brando, Marlon	1924	2004	Clair, René	1898	1981
Bankhead, Tallulah	1902	1968	Branigan, Laura	1957	2004	Clark, Dick	1929	2012
Bara, Theda	1885?	1955	Brazzi, Rossano	1916	1994	Clayburgh, Jill	1944	2010
Barnett, Etta Moten	1902	2004	Brennan, Eileen	1932	2013	Clayton, Jan	1917	1983
Barnum, Phineas T.	1810	1891	Brennan, Walter	1894	1974	Clemons, Clarence	1942	2011
Barrett, Syd	1946	2006	Brent, George	1904	1979	Cliburn, Van	1934	2013
Barry, Gene	1919	2009	Brett, Jeremy	1935	1995	Clift, Montgomery	1920	1966
Barrymore, Ethel	1879	1959	Brewer, Teresa	1931	2007	Cline, Patsy	1932	1963
Barrymore, John	1882	1942	Brice, Fanny	1891	1951	Clooney, Rosemary	1928	2002
Barrymore, Lionel	1878	1954	Bridges, Lloyd	1913	1998	Clyde, Andy	1892	1967
Barrymore, Maurice	1848	1905	Broderick, Helen	1891	1959	Cobain, Kurt	1967	1994
Barthelmess, Richard	1895	1963	Bronson, Charles	1921	2003	Cobb, Lee J.	1911	1976
Bartholomew, Freddie	1924	1992	Brooks, Foster	1912	2001	Coburn, Charles	1877	1961
Barty, Billy	1924	2000	Brooks, Louise	1906	1985	Coburn, James	1928	2002
Basehart, Richard	1914	1984	Brown, Clarence	1890	1987	Coca, Imogene	1908	2001
Basie, Count	1904	1984	Brown, James	1933	2006	Coco, James	1930	1987
Bates, Alan	1934	2003	Brown, Joe E.	1892	1973	Cody, Buffalo Bill	1846	1917
Bavier, Frances	1902	1989	Brown, Les	1912	2001	Cody, Iron Eyes	1907	1999
Baxter, Anne	1923	1985	Browne, Roscoe Lee	1925	2007	Cohan, George M.	1878	1942
Baxter, Warner	1889	1951	Brubeck, Dave	1920	2012	Cohen, Myron	1902	1986
Beaumont, Hugh	1909	1982	Bruce, Lenny	1925	1966	Colbert, Claudette	1903	1996
Beavers, Louise	1902	1962	Bruce, Nigel	1895	1953	Cole, Nat "King"	1919	1965
Beery, Noah, Jr.	1913	1994	Bruce, Virginia	1910	1982	Coleman, Gary	1968	2010

Name	Born	Died	Name	Born	Died	Name	Born	Died
Collins, Gary	1938	2012	Denver, Bob.	1935	2005	Ferrer, Jose	1912	1992
Collins, Ray	1890	1965	Denver, John	1943	1997	Ferrer, Mel	1917	2008
Colman, Ronald.	1891	1958	Derek, John.	1926	1998	Fetchit, Stepin	1898	1985
Columbo, Russ	1908	1934	DeSica, Vittorio	1901	1974	Fiedler, Arthur	1894	1979
Comden, Betty.	1917	2006	Devine, Andy	1905	1977	Fiedler, John	1925	2005
Como, Perry	1912	2001	Dewhurst, Colleen	1924	1991	Fields, Gracie	1898	1979
Conniff, Ray	1916	2002	Diamond, Selma	1920	1985	Fields, Totie	1930	1978
Connors, Chuck.	1921	1992	Diddley, Bo	1928	2008	Fields, W. C.	1879	1946
Conrad, William	1920	1994	Dietrich, Marlene	1901	1992	Finch, Peter.	1916	1977
Conried, Hans	1917	1982	Diller, Phyllis	1917	2012	Fine, Larry.	1902	1975
Conte, Richard.	1911	1975	Disney, Walt.	1901	1966	Firkusny, Rudolf	1912	1994
Convy, Bert	1933	1991	Dix, Richard.	1894	1949	Fisher, Eddie	1928	2010
Conway, Tom	1904	1967	Dmytryk, Edward	1908	1999	Fiske, Minnie Maddern	1865	1932
Coogan, Jackie	1914	1984	Donahue, Troy	1936	2001	Fitzgerald, Barry	1888	1961
Cook, Elisha, Jr.	1904	1995	Donat, Robert	1905	1958	Fitzgerald, Ella.	1917	1996
Cooke, Alistair	1908	2004	Donlevy, Brian	1901	1972	Fitzgerald, Geraldine	1913	2005
Cooke, Sam.	1931	1964	Dors, Diana	1931	1984	Flagstad, Kirsten	1895	1962
Cooper, Gary	1901	1961	Dorsey, Jimmy	1904	1957	Fleischer, Richard	1916	2006
Cooper, Gladys	1888	1971	Dorsey, Tommy	1905	1956	Fleming, Art.	1924	1995
Cooper, Jackie.	1922	2011	Douglas, Melvyn	1901	1981	Fleming, Victor.	1889	1949
Cooper, Melville.	1896	1973	Douglas, Paul	1907	1959	Flynn, Errol	1909	1959
Copland, Aaron	1900	1990	Dove, Billie	1900	1998	Flynn, Joe	1925	1974
Corby, Ellen	1913	1999	Downey, Morton, Jr.	1933	2001	Foch, Nina.	1924	2008
Corelli, Franco	1921	2003	Doyle, David	1929	1997	Fogelberg, Dan	1951	2007
Corey, Jeff	1914	2002	Drake, Alfred	1914	1992	Foley, Red	1910	1968
Corio, Ann	1914	1999	Draper, Ruth	1884	1956	Fonda, Henry	1905	1982
Corley, Pat.	1930	2006	Dressler, Marie	1869	1934	Fontaine, Frank	1920	1978
Cornelius, Don.	1936	2012	Drew, Ellen	1915	2003	Fontanne, Lynn	1887	1983
Cornell, Katharine	1893	1974	Drew, Mrs. John.	1820	1897	Fonteyn, Margot	1919	1991
Correll, Charles ("Andy")	1890	1972	Dru, Joanne.	1923	1996	Ford, Glenn.	1916	2006
Costello, Dolores	1905	1979	Duchin, Eddy.	1909	1951	Ford, John.	1895	1973
Costello, Lou	1906	1959	Duff, Howard	1917	1990	Ford, Paul	1901	1976
Cotten, Joseph	1905	1994	Duggan, Andrew	1923	1988	Ford, Tennessee Ernie.	1919	1991
Coward, Noel.	1899	1973	Dumbrille, Douglass	1890	1974	Forrest, Helen	1917	1999
Cox, Wally	1924	1973	Dumont, Margaret	1889	1965	Forsythe, John.	1918	2010
Crabbe, Buster	1908	1983	Duncan, Isadora	1878	1927	Fosse, Bob	1927	1987
Crain, Jeanne	1925	2003	Duncan, Michael Clarke.	1957	2012	Foster, Phil	1914	1985
Crane, Bob	1928	1978	Dunham, Katherine	1910	2006	Foster, Preston	1901	1970
Crawford, Broderick.	1911	1986	Dunn, James	1905	1967	Foxx, Redd	1922	1991
Crawford, Joan	1904	1977	Dunne, Irene	1898	1990	Foy, Eddie	1856	1928
Crenna, Richard.	1926	2003	Dunnock, Mildred.	1901	1991	Franchi, Sergio	1926	1990
Crews, Laura Hope	1880	1942	Durante, Jimmy	1893	1980	Franciosa, Anthony	1928	2006
Crisp, Donald.	1880	1974	Durbin, Deanna	1921	2013	Francis, Anne	1930	2011
Crisp, Quentin	1908	1999	Durning, Charles	1923	2012	Francis, Arlene	1907	2001
Croce, Jim.	1942	1973	Duryea, Dan	1907	1968	Francis, Kay.	1905	1968
Cronyn, Hume	1911	2003	Duse, Eleanora	1858	1924	Franciscus, James	1934	1991
Crosby, Bing	1903	1977	Dvorak, Ann.	1912	1979	Frankenheimer, John	1930	2002
Crothers, Scatman.	1910	1986	Eagels, Jeanne	1894	1929	Franklin, Bonnie.	1944	2013
Cruz, Celia	1925	2003	Ebert, Roger	1942	2013	Frann, Mary.	1943	1998
Cugat, Xavier.	1900	1990	Ebsen, Buddy	1908	2003	Frawley, William	1887	1966
Cukor, George	1899	1983	Eckstine, Billy	1914	1993	Frederick, Pauline	1885	1938
Cullen, Bill.	1920	1990	Eddington, Paul	1927	1995	Freed, Alan	1921	1965
Culp, Robert	1930	2010	Eddy, Nelson	1901	1967	Freeman, Al, Jr.	1934	2012
Cummings, Constance	1910	2005	Edelman, Herb	1933	1996	French, Victor	1934	1989
Cummings, Robert	1908	1990	Edwards, Blake	1922	2010	Friganza, Trixie	1870	1955
Curtis, Ken	1916	1991	Edwards, Cliff	1895	1971	Froman, Jane	1907	1980
Curtis, Tony.	1925	2010	Edwards, Ralph	1913	2005	Frost, David.	1939	2013
Curtiz, Michael	1888	1962	Edwards, Vince	1928	1996	Funicello, Annette	1942	2013
Cushing, Peter.	1913	1994	Egan, Richard	1923	1987	Funt, Allen	1914	1999
Da Silva, Howard.	1909	1986	Eisenstein, Sergei	1898	1948	Furness, Betty.	1916	1994
Dailey, Dan	1915	1978	Elam, Jack.	1916	2003	Gabin, Jean.	1904	1976
Dandridge, Dorothy	1923	1965	Ellington, Duke	1899	1974	Gable, Clark	1901	1960
Dangerfield, Rodney	1921	2004	Elliot, Cass	1941	1974	Gabor, Eva	1920	1995
Daniell, Henry	1894	1963	Elliott, Denholm	1922	1992	Gandolfini, James	1961	2013
Daniels, Bebe	1901	1971	Ellis, Mary.	1897	2003	Garbo, Greta	1905	1990
Darin, Bobby	1936	1973	Elman, Mischa.	1891	1967	Garcia, Jerry	1942	1995
Darnell, Linda	1923	1965	Ephron, Nora	1941	2012	Gardenia, Vincent	1922	1992
Darwell, Jane.	1879	1967	Errol, Leon.	1881	1951	Gardner, Ava	1922	1990
Davenport, Harry	1866	1949	Evans, Dale	1912	2001	Garfield, John	1913	1952
Davies, Marion	1897	1961	Evans, Edith	1888	1976	Garland, Beverly	1926	2008
Davis, Bette	1908	1989	Evans, Maurice	1901	1989	Garland, Judy	1922	1969
Davis, Joan	1907	1961	Everett, Chad.	1936?	2012	Garrett, Betty	1919	2011
Davis, Ossie	1917	2005	Ewell, Tom.	1909	1994	Garson, Greer	1904	1996
Davis, Sammy, Jr.	1925	1990	Fadiman, Clifton.	1904	1999	Gassman, Vittorio	1922	2000
Dawson, Richard	1932	2012	Fairbanks, Douglas	1883	1939	Gaye, Marvin.	1939	1984
Day, Dennis	1917	1988	Fairbanks, Douglas, Jr.	1909	2000	Gaynor, Janet	1906	1984
Day, Laraine	1920	2007	Falk, Peter.	1927	2011	Gazzara, Ben	1930	2012
De Carlo, Yvonne.	1922	2007	Farentino, James	1938	2012	Gebel-Williams, Gunther	1934	2001
De Laurentiis, Dino	1919	2010	Farina, Dennis	1944	2013	Geer, Will.	1902	1978
de Mille, Agnes	1905	1993	Farley, Chris	1964	1997	George, Gladys	1904	1954
De Mille, Cecil B.	1881	1959	Farmer, Frances	1913	1970	Gershwin, George	1898	1937
De Wilde, Brandon.	1942	1972	Farnsworth, Richard	1920	2000	Getty, Estelle.	1923	2008
De Wolfe, Billy	1907	1974	Farnum, Dustin	1874	1929	Ghostley, Alice.	1926	2007
Dean, James	1931	1955	Farnum, William.	1876	1953	Gibb, Andy.	1958	1988
Dean, Jimmy	1928	2010	Farrar, Geraldine	1882	1967	Gibb, Maurice	1949	2003
Dearie, Blossom	1924	2009	Farrell, Charles	1901	1990	Gibb, Robin	1949	2012
De Carlo, Yvonne.	1922	2007	Farrell, Eileen	1920	2002	Gibson, Henry.	1935	2009
Dee, Frances	1907	2004	Fassbinder, Rainer Werner	1946	1982	Gibson, Hoot.	1892	1962
Dee, Sandra	1942	2005	Fawcett, Farrah	1947	2009	Gielgud, John	1904	2000
Defore, Don.	1917	1993	Faye, Alice.	1915	1998	Gilbert, Billy.	1894	1971
Dekker, Albert	1905	1968	Fazenda, Louise	1895	1962	Gilbert, John	1895	1936
Del Rio, Dolores	1905	1983	Feld, Fritz	1900	1993	Gilford, Jack	1907	1990
DeLuise, Dom	1933	2009	Feldman, Marty	1933	1982	Gillespie, Dizzy	1917	1993
Demarest, William	1892	1983	Fell, Norman	1924	1998	Gillette, William	1853	1937
Dennis, Sandy.	1937	1992	Fellini, Federico	1920	1993	Gingold, Hermione	1897	1987
Denny, Reginald	1891	1967	Fenneman, George	1919	1997	Gish, Dorothy	1898	1968

Name	Born	Died	Name	Born	Died	Name	Born	Died
Gish, Lillian	1893	1993	Hayworth, Rita	1918	1987	James, Dennis	1917	1997
Giulini, Carlo Maria	1914	2005	Head, Edith	1897	1981	James, Etta	1938	2012
Gleason, Jackie	1916	1987	Healy, Ted	1896	1937	James, Harry	1916	1983
Gleason, James	1886	1959	Heckart, Eileen	1919	2001	James, Rick	1948	2004
Gluck, Alma	1884	1938	Heflin, Van	1910	1971	Janis, Elsie	1889	1956
Gobel, George	1919	1991	Heifetz, Jascha	1901	1987	Jannings, Emil	1886	1950
Goddard, Paulette	1905?	1990	Held, Anna	1873	1918	Janssen, David	1930	1980
Godfrey, Arthur	1903	1983	Helm, Levon	1940	2012	Jenkins, Allen	1900	1974
Godunov, Alexander	1949	1995	Hemingway, Margaux	1955	1996	Jennings, Waylon	1937	2002
Goldwyn, Samuel	1882	1974	Hemmings, David	1941	2003	Jessel, George	1898	1981
Goodman, Benny	1909	1986	Hemsley, Sherman	1938	2012	Jeter, Michael	1952	2003
Gorcey, Leo	1917	1969	Henderson, Skitch	1918	2005	Johnson, Ben	1918	1996
Gordon, Gale	1906	1995	Hendrix, Jimi	1942	1970	Johnson, Celia	1908	1982
Gordon, Ruth	1896	1985	Henie, Sonja	1912	1969	Johnson, Chic	1892	1962
Gorme, Eydie	1932	2013	Henreid, Paul	1908	1992	Johnson, J.J.	1924	2001
Gorshin, Frank	1934	2005	Henson, Jim	1936	1990	Johnson, Robert	1911	1938
Gosden, Freeman ("Amos")	1899	1982	Hepburn, Audrey	1929	1993	Johnson, Van	1916	2008
Gottschalk, Louis	1829	1869	Hepburn, Katharine	1907	2003	Jolson, Al	1886	1950
Gould, Glenn	1932	1982	Hersholt, Jean	1886	1956	Jones, Brian	1942	1969
Gould, Harold	1923	2010	Heston, Charlton	1923	2008	Jones, Buck	1889	1942
Gould, Morton	1913	1996	Hewett, Christopher	1922	2001	Jonoc, Carolyn	1933	1983
Goulet, Robert	1933	2007	Hickey, William	1928	1997	Jones, Charlie	1930	2008
Grable, Betty	1916	1973	Hickson, Joan	1906	1998	Jones, Davy	1945	2012
Graham, Martha	1894	1991	Hildegarde	1906	2005	Jones, Elvin	1927	2004
Graham, Virginia	1912	1998	Hill, Arthur	1922	2006	Jones, George	1931	2013
Grahame, Gloria	1925	1981	Hill, Benny	1925	1992	Jones, Henry	1912	1999
Granger, Farley	1925	2011	Hill, George Roy	1921	2002	Jones, Jennifer	1919	2009
Granger, Stewart	1913	1993	Hiller, Wendy	1912	2003	Jones, Spike	1911	1965
Grant, Cary	1904	1986	Hines, Gregory	1946	2003	Joplin, Janis	1943	1970
Granville, Bonita	1923	1988	Hines, Jerome	1921	2003	Joplin, Scott	1868	1917
Grapewin, Charley	1869	1956	Hingle, Pat	1924	2009	Jordan, Richard	1937	1993
Graves, Peter	1926	2010	Hirt, Al	1922	1999	Jory, Victor	1902	1982
Gray, Dolores	1924	2002	Hitchcock, Alfred	1899	1980	Joslyn, Allyn	1905	1981
Gray, Spalding	1941	2004	Ho, Don	1930	2007	Julia, Raul	1940	1994
Grayson, Kathryn	1922	2010	Hobson, Valerie	1917	1998	Jump, Gordon	1932	2003
Greco, Jose	1918	2000	Hodiak, John	1914	1955	Jurado, Katy	1924	2002
Green, Adolph	1915	2002	Holden, William	1918	1981	Jurgens, Curt	1915	1982
Greene, Lorne	1915	1987	Holiday, Billie	1915	1959	Kahn, Madeline	1942	1999
Greenstreet, Sydney	1879	1954	Holliday, Judy	1921	1965	Kane, Helen	1904	1966
Greenwood, Charlotte	1890	1978	Holloway, Sterling	1905	1992	Kanin, Garson	1912	1999
Gregory, James	1911	2002	Holly, Buddy	1936	1959	Karloff, Boris	1887	1969
Griffin, Merv	1925	2007	Holm, Celeste	1919	2012	Karns, Roscoe	1893	1970
Griffith, Andy	1926	2012	Holt, Jack	1888	1951	Karras, Alex	1935	2012
Griffith, David Wark	1874	1948	Holt, Tim	1918	1973	Kaufman, Andy	1949	1984
Griffith, Hugh	1912	1980	Homolka, Oscar	1898	1978	Kaye, Danny	1913	1987
Griffiths, Richard	1947	2013	Hooker, John Lee	1917	2001	Kaye, Stubby	1918	1997
Grizzard, George	1928	2007	Hoon, Shannon	1967	1995	Kazan, Elia	1909	2003
Guardino, Harry	1925	1995	Hope, Bob	1903	2003	Kean, Charles	1811	1868
Guinness, Sir Alec	1914	2000	Hopkins, Miriam	1902	1972	Kean, Mrs. Charles	1806	1880
Guthrie, Woody	1912	1967	Hopper, Dennis	1936	2010	Kean, Edmund	1787	1833
Gwenn, Edmund	1875	1959	Hopper, DeWolf	1858	1935	Keaton, Buster	1895	1966
Gwynne, Fred	1926	1993	Hopper, Hedda	1885	1966	Keel, Howard	1919	2004
Hackett, Buddy	1924	2003	Hopper, William	1915	1970	Keeler, Ruby	1910	1993
Hackett, Joan	1934	1983	Horowitz, Vladimir	1904	1989	Keeshan, Bob (Captain		
Hagen, Uta	1919	2004	Horne, Lena	1917	2010	Kangaroo)	1927	2004
Hagman, Larry	1931	2012	Horton, Edward Everett	1886	1970	Keith, Brian	1921	1997
Haines, William	1900	1973	Houdini, Harry	1874	1926	Kellaway, Cecil	1893	1973
Hale, Alan, Jr.	1918	1990	Houseman, John	1902	1988	Kelley, DeForest	1920	1999
Hale, Alan, Sr.	1892	1950	Houston, Whitney	1963	2012	Kelly, Emmett	1898	1979
Haley, Bill	1925	1981	Howard (Horwitz), Curly	1903	1952	Kelly, Gene	1912	1996
Haley, Jack	1899	1979	Howard, Leslie	1890	1943	Kelly, Grace	1929	1982
Hall, Huntz	1919	1999	Howard (Horwitz), Moe	1897	1975	Kelly, Jack	1927	1992
Hall, Jon	1915	1979	Howard (Horwitz), Shemp	1895	1955	Kelly, Patsy	1910	1981
Hamilton, Margaret	1902	1985	Howard, Trevor	1916	1988	Kennedy, Arthur	1914	1990
Hammerstein, Oscar	1847	1919	Hudson, Rock	1925	1985	Kennedy, Edgar	1890	1948
Hammerstein, Oscar, II	1895	1960	Hughes, Bernard	1915	2006	Kerr, Deborah	1921	2007
Hampton, Lionel	1908	2002	Hughes, John	1950	2009	Kibbee, Guy	1886	1956
Hardwicke, Cedric	1893	1964	Hull, Henry	1890	1977	Kilbride, Percy	1888	1964
Hardy, Oliver	1892	1957	Hull, Josephine	1886	1957	Kiley, Richard	1922	1999
Harlow, Jean	1911	1937	Humphrey, Doris	1895	1958	King, Alan	1927	2004
Harris, Julie	1925	2013	Hunter, Jeffrey	1926	1969	King, Henry	1896	1982
Harris, Phil.	1904	1995	Hunter, Kim	1922	2002	Kinski, Klaus	1926	1991
Harris, Richard	1930	2002	Hunter, Ross	1920	1996	Kirby, Bruno	1949	2006
Harrison, George	1943	2001	Hussey, Ruth	1911	2005	Kirby, George	1923	1995
Harrison, Rex	1908	1990	Huston, John	1906	1987	Kirby, Durward	1912	2000
Hart, William S.	1864	1946	Huston, Walter	1884	1950	Kirsten, Dorothy	1910	1992
Hartman, Phil	1948	1998	Hutchence, Michael	1960	1997	Kitt, Eartha	1927	2008
Harvey, Laurence	1928	1973	Hutton, Betty	1921	2007	Klemperer, Werner	1920	2000
Harvey, Paul	1918	2009	Hutton, Jim	1934	1979	Klugman, Jack	1922	2012
Harwell, Ernie	1918	2010	Hyde-White, Wilfrid	1903	1991	Knight, Ted	1923	1986
Hatfield, Bobby	1940	2003	Ingram, Rex	1895	1969	Knotts, Don	1924	2006
Hatfield, Bobby	1940	2003	Ireland, Jill	1936	1990	Korman, Harvey	1927	2008
Havens, Richie	1941	2013	Ireland, John	1915	1992	Kostelanetz, Andre	1901	1980
Havoc, June	1912	2010	Irving, Henry	1838	1905	Kovacs, Ernie	1919	1962
Hawkins, Jack	1910	1973	Ives, Burl	1909	1995	Kramer, Stanley	1913	2001
Hawkins, Screamin' Jay	1929	2000	Irwin, Steve	1962	2006	Kruger, Otto	1885	1974
Hawks, Howard	1896	1977	Iturbi, Jose	1895	1980	Kubrick, Stanley	1928	1999
Hawthorne, Nigel	1929	2001	Jack, Wolfman	1938	1995	Kulp, Nancy	1921	1991
Hayakawa, Sessue	1890	1973	Jackson, Joe	1875	1942	Kurosawa, Akira	1910	1998
Hayden, Sterling	1916	1986	Jackson, Mahalia	1911	1972	Kyser, Kay	1906	1985
Hayes, Gabby	1885	1969	Jackson, Michael	1958	2009	Ladd, Alan	1913	1964
Hayes, Helen	1900	1993	Jackson, Milt	1923	1999	Lahr, Bert	1895	1967
Hayes, Isaac	1942	2008	Jaeckel, Richard	1926	1997	Laine, Frankie	1913	2007
Hayward, Leland	1902	1971	Jaffe, Sam	1891	1984	Lake, Arthur	1905	1987
Hayward, Louis	1909	1985	Jagger, Dean	1903	1991	Lake, Veronica	1919	1973
Hayward, Susan	1917	1975	Jam Master Jay	1965	2002	LaLanne, Jack	1914	2011

Name	Born	Died
Lamarr, Hedy	1913	2000
Lamas, Fernando	1915	1982
Lamour, Dorothy	1914	1996
Lancaster, Burt	1913	1994
Lanchester, Elsa	1902	1986
Landis, Carole	1919	1948
Landis, Jessie Royce	1904	1972
Landon, Michael	1936	1991
Lane, Priscilla	1917	1995
Lang, Fritz	1890	1976
Langdon, Harry	1884	1944
Lange, Hope	1931	2003
Langford, Frances	1914	2005
Langtry, Lillie	1853	1929
Lanza, Mario	1921	1959
LaRue, Lash (Alfred)	1917	1996
Lauder, Harry	1870	1950
Laughton, Charles	1899	1962
Laurel, Stan	1890	1965
Lawford, Peter	1923	1984
Lawrence, Florence	1886	1938
Lawrence, Gertrude	1898	1952
Lean, David	1908	1991
Ledger, Heath	1979	2008
Lee, Anna	1913	2004
Lee, Bernard	1908	1981
Lee, Bruce	1940	1973
Lee, Canada	1907	1952
Lee, Gypsy Rose	1914	1970
Lee, Peggy	1920	2002
LeGallienne, Eva	1899	1991
Lehmann, Lotte	1888	1976
Leigh, Janet	1927	2004
Leigh, Vivien	1913	1967
Leighton, Margaret	1922	1976
Lemmon, Jack	1925	2001
Lennon, John	1940	1980
Lenya, Lotte	1898	1981
Leonard, Eddie	1870	1941
Leonard, Sheldon	1907	1997
Leone, Sergio	1929	1989
LeRoy, Mervyn	1900	1987
Levant, Oscar	1906	1972
Levene, Sam	1905	1980
Levenson, Sam	1911	1980
Lewis, Al	1923	2006
Lewis, Joe E.	1902	1971
Lewis, Shari	1934	1998
Lewis, Ted	1892	1971
Liberace	1919	1987
Lillie, Beatrice	1894	1989
Lincoln, Elmo	1889	1952
Lind, Jenny	1820	1887
Lindfors, Viveca	1920	1995
Lindley, Audra	1918	1997
Linkletter, Art	1912	2010
Linville, Larry	1939	2000
Little, Cleavon	1939	1992
Llewelyn, Desmond	1914	1999
Lloyd, Harold	1893	1971
Lloyd, Marie	1870	1922
Lockhart, Gene	1891	1957
Logan, Ella	1913	1969
Lom, Herbert	1917	2012
Lombard, Carole	1908	1942
Lombardo, Guy	1902	1977
Long, Richard	1927	1974
Lopes, Lisa	1971	2002
Lopez, Vincent	1895	1975
Lord, Jack	1920	1998
Lorne, Marion	1888	1968
Lorre, Peter	1904	1964
Loudon, Dorothy	1933	2003
Lowe, Edmund	1890	1971
Loy, Myrna	1905	1993
Lubitsch, Ernst	1892	1947
Ludden, Allen	1918	1981
Lugosi, Bela	1882	1956
Lukas, Paul	1894	1971
Lumet, Sidney	1924	2011
Lunt, Alfred	1892	1977
Lupino, Ida	1918	1995
Lymon, Frankie	1942	1968
Lynde, Paul	1926	1982
Mac, Bernie	1957	2008
MacArthur, James	1937	2010
MacCorkindale, Simon	1952	2010
MacDonald, Jeanette	1903	1965
Mack, Ted	1904	1976
MacKenzie, Gisele	1927	2003
MacLane, Barton	1902	1969
MacMurray, Fred	1908	1991
MacRae, Gordon	1921	1986
Macready, George	1909	1973
Madison, Guy	1922	1996
Magnani, Anna	1908	1973
Mancini, Henry	1924	1994
Main, Marjorie	1890	1975
Malden, Karl	1912	2009
Malle, Louis	1932	1995
Mamoulian, Rouben	1897	1987
Mankiewicz, Joseph	1909	1993
Mann, Herbie	1930	2003
Mansfield, Jayne	1932	1967
Mantovani, Annunzio	1905	1980
Marais, Jean	1913	1998
March, Fredric	1897	1975
March, Hal	1920	1970
Marchand, Nancy	1928	2000
Markova, Alicia	1910	2004
Marley, Bob	1945	1981
Marshall, E.G.	1910	1998
Marshall, Herbert	1890	1966
Martin, Barney	1923	2005
Martin, Dean	1917	1995
Martin, Dick	1922	2008
Martin, Mary	1913	1990
Martin, Ross	1920	1981
Martin, Tony	1913	2012
Marvin, Lee	1924	1987
Marx, Harpo (Arthur)	1888	1964
Marx, Zeppo (Herbert)	1901	1979
Marx, Groucho (Julius)	1890	1977
Marx, Chico (Leonard)	1887	1961
Marx, Gummo (Milton)	1893	1977
Mason, James	1909	1984
Massey, Raymond	1896	1983
Mastroianni, Marcello	1924	1996
Matthau, Walter	1920	2000
Mature, Victor	1913	1999
Maxwell, Marilyn	1921	1972
Mayer, Louis B.	1885	1957
Mayfield, Curtis	1942	1999
Mayo, Virginia	1920	2005
Mazurki, Mike	1909	1990
MCA (Adam Yauch)	1964	2012
McCambridge, Mercedes	1916	2004
McCarey, Leo	1898	1969
McCarthy, Kevin	1914	2010
McCartney, Linda	1941	1998
McClanahan, Rue	1934	2010
McClure, Doug	1935	1995
McCormack, John	1884	1945
McCrary, Tex	1910	2003
McCrea, Joel	1905	1990
McDaniel, Hattie	1895	1952
McDowall, Roddy	1928	1998
McFarland, Spanky (George)	1928	1993
McGoohan, Patrick	1928	2009
McGuire, Al	1931	2001
McGuire, Dorothy	1916	2001
McHugh, Frank	1898	1981
McIntire, John	1907	1991
McLaglen, Victor	1886	1959
McMahon, Ed	1923	2009
McNeill, Don	1907	1996
McPartland, Marian	1918	2013
McQueen, Butterfly	1911	1995
McQueen, Steve	1930	1980
Meader, Vaughn	1936	2004
Meadows, Audrey	1924	1996
Meek, Donald	1880	1946
Meeker, Ralph	1920	1988
Melba, Nellie	1861	1931
Melchior, Lauritz	1890	1973
Menjou, Adolphe	1890	1963
Menken, Helen	1902	1966
Menuhin, Yehudi	1916	1999
Mercer, Marian	1935	2011
Mercouri, Melina	1925	1994
Mercury, Freddie	1946	1991
Meredith, Burgess	1909	1997
Merman, Ethel	1908	1984
Merrick, David	1911	2000
Merrill, Gary	1915	1990
Milestone, Lewis	1895	1980
Mifune, Toshiro	1920	1997
Milland, Ray	1905	1986
Miller, Ann	1923	2004
Miller, Glenn	1904	1944
Miller, Marilyn	1898	1936
Miller, Mitch	1911	2010
Miller, Roger	1936	1992
Mills, Donald	1915	1999
Mills, Harry	1913	1982
Mills, Herbert	1912	1989
Mills, John	1889	1967
Mills, Sir John	1908	2005
Mineo, Sal	1939	1976
Miner, Jan	1917	2004
Minghella, Anthony	1954	2008
Mingus, Charles	1922	1979
Minnelli, Vincente	1903	1986
Miranda, Carmen	1909	1955
Mitchell, Thomas	1892	1962
Mitchum, Robert	1917	1997
Mix, Tom	1880	1940
Monica, Corbett	1930	1998
Moffo, Anna	1932	2006
Monroe, Marilyn	1926	1962
Monroe, Vaughn	1911	1973
Montalban, Ricardo	1920	2009
Montand, Yves	1921	1991
Monteith, Cory	1982	2013
Montez, Maria	1917	1951
Montgomery, Elizabeth	1933	1995
Montgomery, George	1916	2000
Montgomery, Robert	1904	1981
Moore, Clayton	1914	1999
Moore, Colleen	1900	1988
Moore, Dudley	1935	2002
Moore, Garry	1915	1993
Moore, Grace	1898	1947
Moorehead, Agnes	1906	1974
Moreland, Mantan	1902	1973
Morgan, Dennis	1910	1994
Morgan, Frank	1890	1949
Morgan, Harry	1915	2011
Morgan, Helen	1900	1941
Morgan, Henry	1915	1994
Morita, Pat	1932	2005
Morley, Robert	1908	1992
Morris, Chester	1901	1970
Morris, Greg	1934	1996
Morris, Howard	1919	2005
Morris, Wayne	1914	1959
Morrison, Jim	1943	1971
Morrow, Vic	1929	1982
Morton, Jelly Roll	1885	1941
Mostel, Zero	1915	1977
Mowbray, Alan	1897	1969
Mulhare, Edward	1923	1997
Mulligan, Gerry	1927	1996
Mulligan, Richard	1932	2000
Muni, Paul	1895	1967
Munshin, Jules	1915	1970
Murnau, F. W.	1888	1931
Murphy, Audie	1924	1971
Murphy, Brittany	1977	2009
Murphy, George	1902	1992
Murray, Arthur	1895	1991
Murray, Kathryn	1906	1999
Murray, Mae	1889	1965
Nagel, Conrad	1897	1970
Naish, J. Carroll	1900	1973
Naldi, Nita	1898	1961
Nance, Jack	1943	1996
Natwick, Mildred	1908	1994
Nazimova, Alla	1879	1945
Neal, Patricia	1926	2010
Negri, Pola	1897	1987
Nelson, David	1936	2011
Nelson, Harriet (Hilliard)	1909	1994
Nelson, Ozzie	1906	1975
Nelson, Rick	1940	1985
Nesbit, Evelyn	1884	1967
Nettleton, Lois	1927	2008
Newley, Anthony	1931	1999
Newman, Edwin	1919	2010
Newman, Paul	1925	2008
Nicholas, Fayard	1914	2006
Nicholas, Harold	1924	2000
Nielsen, Leslie	1926	2010
Nijinsky, Vaslav	1890	1950
Nilsson, Anna Q.	1888	1974
Niven, David	1910	1983
Nolan, Lloyd	1902	1985
Normand, Mabel	1894	1930
North, Sheree	1933	2005
Notorious B.I.G.	1972	1997
Novarro, Ramon	1899	1968
Nureyev, Rudolf	1938	1993
Oakie, Jack	1903	1978
Oakley, Annie	1860	1926
Oates, Warren	1928	1982
Oberon, Merle	1911	1979
O'Brien, Edmond	1915	1985
O'Brien, Pat	1899	1983
O'Connell, Arthur	1908	1981
O'Connell, Helen	1921	1993
O'Connor, Carroll	1924	2001
O'Connor, Donald	1925	2003
O'Connor, Una	1880	1959
Odetta (Holmes)	1930	2008
O'Herlihy, Daniel	1919	2005
O'Keefe, Dennis	1908	1968
Oland, Warner	1880	1938
Olcott, Chauncey	1860	1932

Name	Born	Died	Name	Born	Died	Name	Born	Died
Oliver, Edna May	1883	1942	Pyle, Denver	1920	1997	Ruggles, Charles	1886	1970
Olivier, Laurence	1907	1989	Quayle, Anthony	1913	1989	Russell, Harold	1914	2002
Olsen, Merlin	1940	2010	Questel, Mae	1908	1998	Russell, Jane	1921	2011
Olsen, Ole	1892	1963	Quinn, Anthony	1915	2001	Russell, Ken	1927	2011
O'Neal, Ron	1937	2004	Quintero, José	1924	1999	Russell, Lillian	1861	1922
O'Neill, James	1849	1920	Rabb, Ellis	1930	1998	Russell, Nipsey	1923	2005
Ophuls, Max	1902	1957	Rabbit, Eddie	1941	1998	Russell, Rosalind	1911	1976
Orbach, Jerry	1935	2004	Radner, Gilda	1946	1989	Rutherford, Ann	1917	2012
Orbison, Roy	1936	1988	Rafferty, Gerry	1947	2011	Rutherford, Margaret	1892	1972
Ormandy, Eugene	1899	1985	Raft, George	1895	1980	Ryan, Irene	1903	1973
O'Shea, Milo	1926	2013	Rains, Claude	1889	1967	Ryan, Robert	1909	1973
O'Sullivan, Maureen	1911	1998	Raitt, John	1917	2005	Sabu (Dastagir)	1924	1963
Ouspenskaya, Maria	1876	1949	Ralston, Esther	1902	1994	St. Cyr, Lili	1917	1999
Owen, Reginald	1887	1972	Ramone, Dee Dee	1952	2002	St. Denis, Ruth	1877	1968
Owens, Buck	1929	2006	Ramone, Joey	1951	2001	Sakall, S. Z.	1883	1955
Paar, Jack	1918	2004	Ramone, Johnny	1948	2004	Sale (Chic), Charles	1885	1936
Paderewski, Ignace	1860	1941	Rampal, Jean-Pierre	1922	2000	Sales, Soupy	1926	2009
Page, Bettie	1923	2008	Randall, Tony	1920	2004	Sanders, George	1906	1972
Page, Geraldine	1924	1987	Randolph, John	1915	2004	Sanford, Isabel	1917	2004
Page, Patti	1927	2013	Rathbone, Basil	1892	1967	Sargent, Dick	1933	1994
Pakula, Alan	1928	1998	Ratoff, Gregory	1897	1960	Sarrazin, Michael	1940	2011
Palance, Jack	1919	2006	Rawls, Lou	1933	2006	Savalas, Telly	1924	1994
Pallette, Eugene	1889	1954	Ray, Aldo	1926	1991	Scheider, Roy	1935	2008
Palmer, Lilli	1914	1986	Ray, Johnnie	1927	1990	Schell, Maria	1926	2005
Palmer, Robert	1949	2003	Ray, Nicholas	1911	1979	Schenkel, Chris	1923	2005
Pangborn, Franklin	1894	1958	Rayburn, Gene	1917	1999	Schiavelli, Vincent	1948	2005
Parker, Fess	1925	2010	Raye, Martha	1916	1994	Schildkraut, Joseph	1896	1964
Parker, Jean	1915	2005	Raymond, Gene	1908	1998	Schipa, Tito	1888	1965
Parks, Bert	1914	1992	Reagan, Ronald	1911	2004	Schlesinger, John	1926	2003
Parks, Larry	1914	1975	Redding, Otis	1941	1967	Schnabel, Artur	1882	1951
Pasternack, Josef A.	1881	1940	Redgrave, Corin	1939	2010	Schneider, Maria	1952	2011
Pastor, Tony (vaudevillian)	1837	1908	Redgrave, Lynn	1943	2010	Schneider, Romy	1938	1982
Pastor, Tony (bandleader)	1907	1969	Redgrave, Michael	1908	1985	Schwartzkopf, Elizabeth	1915	2006
Patrick, Gail	1911	1980	Reed, Donna	1921	1986	Scofield, Paul	1922	2008
Patti, Adelina	1843	1919	Reed, Jerry	1937	2008	Scott, George C.	1927	1999
Patti, Carlotta	1840	1889	Reed, Oliver	1938	1999	Scott, Gordon	1926	2007
Paul, Les	1915	2009	Reed, Robert	1932	1992	Scott, Hazel	1920	1981
Pavarotti, Luciano	1935	2007	Reeve, Christopher	1952	2004	Scott, Martha	1914	2003
Pavlova, Anna	1885	1931	Reeves, George	1914	1959	Scott, Randolph	1898	1987
Paycheck, Johnny	1938	2003	Reeves, Steve	1926	2000	Scott, Zachary	1914	1965
Payne, John	1912	1989	Reid, Wallace	1891	1923	Scott-Heron, Gil	1949	2011
Pearl, Minnie	1912	1996	Reilly, Charles Nelson	1931	2007	Scott-Siddons, Mrs.	1843	1896
Peck, Gregory	1916	2003	Reinhardt, Max	1873	1943	Seberg, Jean	1938	1979
Peckinpah, Sam	1925	1984	Remick, Lee	1935	1991	Seeley, Blossom	1892	1974
Peerce, Jan	1904	1984	Renaldo, Duncan	1904	1980	Segovia, Andres	1893	1987
Pendergrass, Teddy	1950	2010	Rennie, Michael	1909	1971	Selena (Quintanilla)	1971	1995
Penn, Arthur	1922	2010	Renoir, Jean	1894	1979	Sellers, Peter	1925	1980
Penn, Chris	1965	2006	Rettig, Tommy	1941	1996	Selznick, David O.	1902	1965
Penner, Joe	1905	1941	Reynolds, Marjorie	1921	1997	Sennett, Mack	1880	1960
Peppard, George	1928	1994	Rich, Charlie	1932	1995	Señor Wences	1896	1999
Perkins, Anthony	1932	1992	Richardson, Ian	1934	2007	Serling, Rod	1924	1975
Perkins, Carl	1932	1998	Richardson, Natasha	1963	2009	Shakur, Tupac	1971	1996
Perkins, Marlin	1905	1986	Richardson, Ralph	1902	1983	Shankar, Ravi	1920	2012
Peters, Brock	1927	2005	Riddle, Nelson	1921	1985	Shaw, Artie	1910	2004
Peters, Jean	1926	2000	Riefenstahl, Leni	1902	2003	Shaw, Robert (actor)	1927	1978
Peters, Susan	1921	1952	Ripperton, Minnie	1947	1979	Shaw, Robert (conductor)	1916	1999
Peterson, Oscar	1925	2007	Ritchard, Cyril	1898	1977	Shawn, Ted	1891	1972
Phillips, John	1935	2001	Ritter, John	1948	2003	Shean, Al	1868	1949
Phoenix, River	1970	1993	Ritter, Tex	1905	1974	Shearer, Moira	1926	2006
Piaf, Edith	1915	1963	Ritter, Thelma	1905	1969	Shearer, Norma	1902	1983
Pickens, Slim	1919	1983	Ritz, Al	1901	1965	Shearing, George	1919	2011
Pickett, Wilson	1941	2006	Ritz, Harry	1906	1986	Sheppard, Bob	1910	2010
Pickford, Mary	1893	1979	Ritz, Jimmy	1903	1985	Sheridan, Ann	1915	1967
Picon, Molly	1898	1992	Roach, Hall	1892	1992	Shore, Dinah	1917	1994
Pidgeon, Walter	1897	1984	Roach, Max	1924	2007	Short, Bobby	1924	2005
Pinza, Ezio	1892	1957	Robards, Jason	1922	2000	Shubert, Lee	1875	1953
Pitney, Gene	1941	2006	Robbins, Jerome	1918	1998	Shull, Richard B.	1929	1999
Pitts, Zasu	1898	1963	Robbins, Marty	1925	1982	Siddons, Sarah	1755	1831
Plato, Dana	1964	1999	Roberts, Pernell	1928	2010	Sidney, Sylvia	1910	1999
Pleasence, Donald	1919	1995	Roberts, Rachel	1927	1980	Siegel, Don	1912	1991
Pleshette, Suzanne	1937	2008	Robertson, Cliff	1925	2011	Signoret, Simone	1921	1985
Pollack, Sydney	1934	2008	Robertson, Dale	1923	2013	Sills, Beverly	1929	2007
Pons, Lily	1904	1976	Robeson, Paul	1898	1976	Silver, Ron	1946	2009
Ponselle, Rosa	1897	1981	Robinson, Bill	1878	1949	Silverheels, Jay	1912	1980
Ponti, Carlo	1912	2007	Robinson, Edward G.	1893	1973	Silvers, Phil	1912	1985
Porter, Edwin S.	1870	1941	Robson, Flora	1902	1984	Sim, Alastair	1900	1976
Porter, Eric	1928	1995	Roche, Eugene	1928	2004	Simmons, Jean	1929	2010
Porter, Nyree Dawn	1940	2001	Rochester (Eddie Anderson)	1905	1977	Simone, Nina	1933	2003
Postlethwaite, Pete	1946	2011	Roddenberry, Gene	1921	1991	Sinatra, Frank	1915	1998
Poston, Tom	1921	2007	Rodgers, Jimmie	1897	1933	Sinclair, Madge	1938	1995
Powell, Dick	1904	1963	Rogers, Buddy	1904	1999	Singleton, Penny	1908	2003
Powell, Eleanor	1912	1982	Rogers, Fred	1928	2003	Sirk, Douglas	1900	1987
Powell, William	1892	1984	Rogers, Ginger	1911	1995	Siskel, Gene	1946	1999
Power, Tyrone	1914	1958	Rogers, Roy	1911	1998	Sitka, Emil	1914	1998
Preminger, Otto	1905	1986	Rogers, Will	1879	1935	Sjostrom, Victor	1879	1960
Presley, Elvis	1935	1977	Roland, Gilbert	1905	1994	Skelton, Red	1913	1997
Preston, Billy	1946	2006	Rolle, Esther	1920?	1998	Skinner, Otis	1858	1942
Preston, Robert	1918	1987	Rollins, Howard	1950	1996	Smith, Alexis	1921	1993
Price, Vincent	1911	1993	Roman, Ruth	1924	1999	Smith, Bessie	1894?	1937
Prima, Louis	1911	1978	Romero, Cesar	1907	1994	Smith, Buffalo Bob	1917	1998
Prinze, Freddie	1954	1977	Rose, Billy	1899	1966	Smith, C. Aubrey	1863	1948
Prosky, Robert	1930	2008	Rossellini, Roberto	1906	1977	Smith, Elliott	1969	2003
Provine, Dorothy	1937	2010	Rostropovich, Mstislav	1927	2007	Smith, Jeff	1939	2004
Prowse, Juliet	1936	1996	Rowan, Dan	1922	1987	Smith, Kate	1907	1986
Pryor, Richard	1940	2005	Rubinstein, Artur	1887	1982	Smith, Kent	1907	1985
Puente, Tito	1923	2000	Rubinstein, Zelda	1933	2010	Snodgrass, Carrie	1946	2004
						Snow, Hank	1914	1999

Name	Born	Died	Name	Born	Died	Name	Born	Died
Snyder, Tom	1936	2007	Thompson, Sada	1927	2011	Webb, Clifton	1891	1966
Solti, George	1912	1997	Thorndike, Sybil	1882	1976	Webb, Jack	1920	1982
Sondergaard, Gale	1899	1985	Thulin, Ingrid	1926	2004	Weems, Ted	1901	1963
Sothern, Ann	1909	2001	Tibbett, Lawrence	1896	1960	Weissmuller, Johnny	1904	1984
Sousa, John Philip	1854	1932	Tierney, Gene	1920	1991	Welk, Lawrence	1903	1992
Sparks, Ned	1884	1957	Tiny Tim	1932	1996	Welles, Orson	1915	1985
Spelling, Aaron	1923	2006	Tippett, Sir Michael	1905	1998	Wellman, William	1896	1975
Spencer, John	1946	2005	Todd, Michael	1909	1958	Wells, Kitty	1919	2012
Sperber, Wendy Jo	1958	2005	Todd, Richard	1919	2009	Werner, Oskar	1922	1984
Springfield, Dusty	1939	1999	Tomlinson, David	1917	2000	West, Mae	1893	1980
Stack, Robert	1919	2003	Tone, Franchot	1905	1968	Weston, Jack	1924	1996
Stafford, Jo	1917	2008	Torme, Mel	1925	1999	Whale, James	1889	1957
Stander, Lionel	1908	1994	Toscanini, Arturo	1867	1957	Wheeler, Bert	1895	1968
Stang, Arnold	1918	2009	Tracy, Lee	1898	1968	White, Barry	1944	2003
Stanley, Kim	1925	2001	Tracy, Spencer	1900	1967	White, Jesse	1919	1997
Stanwyck, Barbara	1907	1990	Traubel, Helen	1899	1972	White, Pearl	1889	1938
Stapleton, Jean	1923	2013	Travers, Henry	1874	1965	Whiteman, Paul	1891	1967
Stapleton, Maureen	1925	2006	Travers, Mary	1936	2009	Whiting, Margaret	1924	2011
Steiger, Rod	1925	2002	Treacher, Arthur	1894	1975	Whitmore, James	1921	2009
Sterling, Jan	1921	2004	Tree, Herbert Beerbohm	1853	1917	Whitty, May	1865	1948
Stern, Isaac	1920	2001	Trevor, Claire	1909	2000	Wickes, Mary	1910	1995
Stevens, Craig	1918	2000	Truex, Ernest	1890	1973	Widmark, Richard	1914	2008
Stevens, George	1904	1975	Truffaut, Francois	1932	1984	Wilde, Cornel	1915	1989
Stevens, Inger	1934	1970	Tucker, Forrest	1919	1986	Wilder, Billy	1906	2002
Stevens, Mark	1916	1994	Tucker, Richard	1913	1975	Wilding, Michael	1912	1979
Stevens, Risë	1913	2013	Tucker, Sophie	1884	1966	Williams, Andy	1927	2012
Stevenson, McLean	1929	1996	Turner, Big Joe	1911	1985	Williams, Bert	1874	1922
Stewart, James	1908	1997	Turner, Ike	1931	2008	Williams, Esther	1921	2013
Stickney, Dorothy	1896	1998	Turner, Lana	1920	1995	Williams, Guy	1924	1989
Stokowski, Leopold	1882	1977	Turpin, Ben	1869	1940	Williams, Hank, Sr.	1923	1953
Stone, Fred	1873	1959	Twelvetrees, Helen	1908	1958	Williamson, Nicol	1936	2011
Stone, Lewis	1879	1953	Twitty, Conway	1933	1993	Wills, Bob	1905	1975
Stone, Milburn	1904	1980	Urich, Robert	1946	2002	Wills, Chill	1902	1978
Storm, Gale	1922	2009	Ustinov, Peter	1921	2004	Wilson, Carl	1946	1998
Straight, Beatrice	1918	2001	Valens, Ritchie	1941	1959	Wilson, Dennis	1944	1983
Strasberg, Lee	1901	1982	Valentino, Rudolph	1895	1926	Wilson, Dooley	1894	1953
Strasberg, Susan	1938	1999	Vallee, Rudy	1901	1986	Wilson, Flip	1933	1998
Strode, Woody	1914	1994	Van, Bobby	1928	1980	Wilson, Jackie	1934	1984
Strummer, Joe	1952	2002	Van Cleef, Lee	1925	1989	Wilson, Marie	1917	1972
Stuart, Gloria	1910	2010	Van Fleet, Jo	1922	1996	Windom, William	1923	2012
Stuarti, Enzo	1919	2005	Vance, Vivian	1912	1979	Windsor, Marie	1919	2000
Sturges, Preston	1898	1959	Vandross, Luther	1951	2005	Winehouse, Amy	1983	2011
Sullavan, Margaret	1911	1960	Varney, Jim	1949	2000	Winfield, Paul	1941	2004
Sullivan, Barry	1912	1994	Vaughan, Sarah	1924	1990	Winninger, Charles	1884	1969
Sullivan, Ed	1902	1974	Veidt, Conrad	1893	1943	Winters, Jonathan	1925	2013
Sullivan, Francis L.	1903	1956	Velez, Lupe	1908	1944	Winters, Shelley	1920	2006
Sumac, Yma	1922	2008	Vera-Ellen (Rohe)	1926	1981	Wise, Robert	1914	2005
Summer, Donna	1948	2012	Verdon, Gwen	1925	2000	Wiseman, Joseph	1918	2009
Summerville, Slim	1892	1946	Vernon, Jackie	1925	1987	Wong, Anna May	1907	1961
Sutherland, Joan	1926	2010	Vernon, John	1932	2005	Wood, Natalie	1938	1981
Swanson, Gloria	1899	1983	Verrett, Shirley	1931	2010	Wood, Peggy	1892	1978
Swarthout, Gladys	1904	1969	Vidor, King	1894	1982	Wood, Sam	1884	1949
Swayze, Patrick	1952	2009	Villechaize, Herve	1943	1993	Woodard, Edward	1930	2009
Sweet, Blanche	1896	1986	Vincent, Gene	1935	1971	Wooley, Sheb	1921	2003
Switzer, Carl "Alfalfa"	1927	1959	Vicious, Sid	1957	1979	Woolley, Monty	1888	1963
Talbot, Lyle	1902	1996	Vinson, Helen	1907	1999	Worth, Irene	1916	2002
Tallchief, Maria	1925	2013	Von Stroheim, Erich	1885	1957	Wray, Fay	1907	2004
Talmadge, Constance	1900	1973	Von Zell, Harry	1906	1981	Wright, Teresa	1918	2005
Talmadge, Norma	1893	1957	Walker, Junior	1942	1995	Wyatt, Jane	1910	2006
Tamiroff, Akim	1899	1972	Walker, Nancy	1922	1992	Wyler, William	1902	1981
Tandy, Jessica	1909	1994	Walker, Robert	1918	1951	Wyman, Jane	1914?	2007
Tanguay, Eva	1878	1947	Wallenda, Karl	1905	1978	Wynette, Tammy	1942	1998
Tati, Jacques	1908	1982	Walsh, J. T.	1943	1998	Wynn, Ed.	1886	1966
Taylor, Billy	1921	2010	Walsh, Raoul	1887	1980	Wynn, Keenan	1916	1986
Taylor, Deems	1885	1966	Walston, Ray	1914	2001	Yankovic, Frank	1915	1998
Taylor, Dub	1907	1994	Walter, Bruno	1876	1962	York, Dick	1928	1992
Taylor, Elizabeth	1932	2011	Ward, Helen	1916	1998	York, Susannah	1939	2011
Taylor, Estelle	1899	1958	Warden, Jack	1920	2006	Young, Clara Kimball	1890	1960
Taylor, Laurette	1887	1946	Waring, Fred	1900	1984	Young, Gig	1913	1978
Taylor, Robert	1911	1969	Warner, H. B.	1876	1958	Young, Loretta	1913	2000
Tebaldi, Renata	1922	2004	Warrick, Ruth	1915	2005	Young, Robert	1907	1998
Terry, Ellen	1847	1928	Washington, Dinah	1924	1963	Young, Roland	1887	1953
Thalberg, Irving	1899	1936	Waters, Ethel	1896	1977	Youngman, Henny	1906	1998
Thaw, John	1942	2002	Waters, Muddy	1915	1983	Zanuck, Darryl F.	1902	1979
Thaxter, Phyllis	1919	2012	Waxman, Al	1935	2001	Zappa, Frank	1940	1993
Thigpen, Lynne	1948	2003	Wayne, David	1914	1995	Zevon, Warren	1947	2003
Thomas, Danny	1912	1991	Wayne, John	1907	1979	Ziegfeld, Florenz	1869	1932
Thomas, John Charles	1891	1960	Weaver, Dennis	1924	2006	Zinneman, Fred	1907	1997
						Zukor, Adolph	1873	1976

Original Names of Selected Entertainers

Adele: Adele Laurie Blue Adkins
Ad-Rock: Adam Horovitz
Clay Aiken: Clayton Grissom
Alan Alda: Alphonso D'Abruzzo
Jason Alexander: Jay Greenspan
Woody Allen: Allen Konigsberg
André 3000: Andre Benjamin
Julie Andrews: Julia Wells
Criss Angel: Christopher Sarantakos
Beatrice Arthur: Bernice Frankel
Fred Astaire: Frederick Austerlitz
Babyface: Kenneth Edmonds

Lauren Bacall: Betty Joan Perske
Erykah Badu: Erica Wright
Eric Bana: Eric Banadinovich
Anne Bancroft: Anna Maria Italiano
Theda Bara: Theodosia Goodman
Beck: Bek David Campbell
Pat Benatar: Patricia Andrejewski
Tony Bennett: Anthony Benedetto
Jack Benny: Benjamin Kubelsky
Milton Berle: Mendel Berlinger
Irving Berlin: Israel Baline
Sarah Bernhardt: Henriette-Rosine Bernard

Jello Biafra: Eric Reed Boucher
Big Boi: Antwan Patton
The Big Bopper: Jiles Perry "J.P."
Richardson
Robert Blake: Michael James Vijencio
Gubitosi
Jon Bon Jovi: John Francis Bongiovi
Bono: Paul Hewson
David Bowie: David Robert Jones
Boy George: George Alan O'Dowd
Fanny Brice: Fanny Borach
Charles Bronson: Charles Buchinski

Albert Brooks: Albert Einstein
Mel Brooks: Melvin Kaminsky
Foxy Brown: Inga Marchand
George Burns: Nathan Birnbaum
Ellen Burstyn: Edna Gilhooley
Richard Burton: Richard Jenkins
Red Buttons: Aaron Chwatt
Nicolas Cage: Nicholas Coppola
Michael Caine: Maurice Micklewhite
Maria Callas: Maria Kalogeropoulos
Jackie Chan: Chan Kwong-Sung
Cyd Charisse: Tula Finklea
Ray Charles: Ray Charles Robinson
Charo: Maria Rosario Pilar Martinez Molina Baeza
Chubby Checker: Ernest Evans
Cher: Cherilyn Sarkisian
Chuck D: Carlton Ridenhour
Patsy Cline: Virginia Patterson Hensley
Claudette Colbert: Lily Chauchoin
Coolio: Artis Leon Ivey Jr.
Alice Cooper: Vincent Furnier
David Copperfield: David Kotkin
Howard Cosell: Howard Cohen
Elvis Costello: Declan McManus
Lou Costello: Louis Cristillo
Peter Coyote: Peter Cohon
Quentin Crisp: Denis Pratt
Tom Cruise: Thomas Cruise Mapother IV
Tony Curtis: Bernard Schwartz
Miley Cyrus: Destiny Hope Cyrus
Vic Damone: Vito Farinola
D'Angelo: Michael D'Angelo Archer
Rodney Dangerfield: Jacob Cohen
Bobby Darin: Walden Robert Cassotto
Doris Day: Doris von Kappelhoff
Yvonne De Carlo: Peggy Middleton
Portia de Rossi: Amanda Lee Rogers
Sandra Dee: Alexandra Zuck
John Denver: Henry John Deutschendorf Jr.
Bo Derek: Mary Cathleen Collins
Danny DeVito: Daniel Michaeli
Angie Dickinson: Angeline Brown
Bo Diddley: Elias Bates
Vin Diesel: Mark Vincent
Phyllis Diller: Phyllis Driver
Divine: Harris Glenn Milstead
DMX: Earl Simmons
Troy Donahue: Merle Johnson Jr.
Kirk Douglas: Issur Danielovitch
Drake: Aubrey Drake Graham
Bob Dylan: Robert Zimmerman
Barbara Eden: Barbara Huffman
Elvira: Cassandra Peterson
Eminem: Marshall Mathers
Enya: Eithne Ni Bhraonian
Dale Evans: Frances Smith
Chad Everett: Raymon Cramton
Fabian: Fabian Anthony Forte
Fabolous: John Jackson
Douglas Fairbanks: Douglas Ullman
Morgan Fairchild: Patsy McClenny
Jamie Farr: Jameel Farah
Fergie: Stacy Ferguson
Stepin Fetchit: Lincoln Perry
W. C. Fields: William Claude Dukenfield
50 Cent: Curtis Jackson
Flavor Flav: William Drayton
Joan Fontaine: Joan de Havilland
Jodie Foster: Alicia Christian Foster
Jamie Foxx: Eric Bishop
Redd Foxx: John Sanford
Arlene Francis: Arlene Kazanjian
Connie Francis: Concetta Franconero
Greta Garbo: Greta Gustafsson
Judy Garland: Frances Gumm
James Garner: James Bumgarner
Crystal Gayle: Brenda Gail Webb
George Gershwin: Jacob Gershowitz
Kathie Lee Gifford: Kathie Epstein
Whoopi Goldberg: Caryn Johnson
Eydie Gormé: Edith Garmezano
Cary Grant: Archibald Leach
Lee Grant: Lyova Rosenthal
Robert Guillaume: Robert Williams
Buddy Hackett: Leonard Hacker
Hammer: Stanley Kirk Burrell
Jean Harlow: Harlean Carpenter
Helen Hayes: Helen Brown
Susan Hayward: Edythe Marrener
Rita Hayworth: Margarita Cansino

Pee-Wee Herman: Paul Reubenfeld
Charlton Heston: John Charles Carter
Perez Hilton: Mario Armando Lavandeira Jr.
Hulk Hogan: Terry Gene Bollea
Billie Holiday: Eleanora Fagan
Judy Holliday: Judith Tuvim
Bob Hope: Leslie Townes Hope
Harry Houdini: Erik Weisz
Howlin' Wolf: Chester Burnett
Rock Hudson: Roy Scherer Jr. (later Fitzgerald)
Engelbert Humperdinck: Arnold Dorsey
Kim Hunter: Janet Cole
Ice Cube: O'Shea Jackson
Ice-T: Tracy Morrow
Billy Idol: William Broad
Etta James: Jamesetta Hawkins
Ja Rule: Jeffrey Atkins
Jay-Z: Shawn Carter
Elton John: Reginald Dwight
Al Jolson: Asa Yoelson
Jennifer Jones: Phylis Isley
Tom Jones: Thomas Woodward
Spike Jonze: Adam Spiegel
Wynonna Judd: Christina Ciminella
Boris Karloff: William Henry Pratt
Ke$ha: Kesha Rose Sebert
Diane Keaton: Diane Hall
Michael Keaton: Michael Douglas
Alicia Keys: Alicia Augello Cook
Chaka Khan: Yvette Stevens
Kid Rock: Robert Ritchie
Carole King: Carole Klein
Larry King: Larry Zeiger
Ben Kingsley: Krishna Banji
Ted Knight: Tadewurz Wladziu Konopka
Cheryl Ladd: Cheryl Stoppelmoor
Lady Gaga: Stefani Germanotta
Veronica Lake: Constance Ockleman
Hedy Lamarr: Hedwig Kiesler
Dorothy Lamour: Mary Leta Dorothy Slaton
Michael Landon: Eugene Orowitz
Mario Lanza: Alfredo Cocozza
Queen Latifah: Dana Owens
Stan Laurel: Arthur Jefferson
Steve Lawrence: Sidney Leibowitz
Brenda Lee: Brenda Mae Tarpley
Gypsy Rose Lee: Rose Louise Hovick
Peggy Lee: Norma Egstrom
Janet Leigh: Jeanette Morrison
Vivien Leigh: Vivian Hartley
Huey Lewis: Hugh Cregg
Jerry Lewis: Joseph Levitch
Lil' Kim: Kimberly Denise Jones
Little Richard: Richard Penniman
LL Cool J: James Todd Smith
Carole Lombard: Jane Peters
Sophia Loren: Sophia Scicolone
Peter Lorre: Laszlo Lowenstein
Louis C.K.: Louis Szekely
Myrna Loy: Myrna Williams
Bela Lugosi: Bela Ferenc Blasko
Moms Mabley: Loretta Mary Aiken
Shirley MacLaine: Shirley Beaty
Elle Macpherson: Eleanor Gow
Madonna: Madonna Louise Veronica Ciccone
Lee Majors: Harvey Lee Yeary
Karl Malden: Mladen Sekulovich
Barry Manilow: Barry Alan Pincus
Jayne Mansfield: Vera Jane Palmer
Marilyn Manson: Brian Warner
Bruno Mars: Peter Gene Hernandez
Dean Martin: Dino Crocetti
Ricky Martin: Enrique Jose Martin Morales
MCA: Adam Yauch
Meat Loaf: Marvin Lee Aday
Freddie Mercury: Frederick Bulsara
Ethel Merman: Ethel Zimmermann
George Michael: Georgios Panayiotou
Mike D: Michael Diamond
Helen Mirren: Ilynea Lydia Mironoff
Joni Mitchell: Roberta Joan Anderson
Moby: Richard Melville Hall
Mo'Nique: Monique Imes
Marilyn Monroe: Norma Jean Mortenson (later Baker)
Yves Montand: Ivo Livi
Demi Moore: Demetria Guynes
Rita Moreno: Rosita Alverio
Harry Morgan: Harry Bratsburg

Morrissey: Steven Patrick Morrissey
Mr. T: Lawrence Tureaud
Paul Muni: Mehilem Weisenfreund
Nelly: Cornell Haynes Jr.
Mike Nichols: Michael Igor Peschowsky
Chuck Norris: Carlos Ray Norris
Notorious B.I.G.: Christopher Wallace
Hugh O'Brian: Hugh Krampke
Maureen O'Hara: Maureen FitzSimons
Jack Palance: Vladimir Palanuik
Minnie Pearl: Sarah Ophelia Cannon
Katy Perry: Kathryn Hudson
Bernadette Peters: Bernadette Lazzara
Joaquin Phoenix: Joaquin Bottom
Edith Piaf: Edith Gassion
Slim Pickens: Louis Lindley
Mary Pickford: Gladys Smith
Pink: Alecia Moore
Iggy Pop: James Newell Osterberg
Natalie Portman: Natalie Hershlag
Prince: Prince Rogers Nelson
Dee Dee Ramone: Douglas Colvin
Joey Ramone: Jeffrey Hyman
Johnny Ramone: John Cummings
Tommy Ramone: Tom Erdelyi
Tony Randall: Leonard Rosenberg
Della Reese: Delloreese Patricia Early
Busta Rhymes: Trevor Smith Jr.
Joan Rivers: Joan Sandra Molinsky
Edward G. Robinson: Emmanuel Goldenberg
The Rock: Dwayne Johnson
Ginger Rogers: Virginia McMath
Roy Rogers: Leonard Franklin Slye
Mickey Rooney: Joe Yule Jr.
Johnny Rotten: John Lydon
Lillian Russell: Helen Leonard
Meg Ryan: Margaret Hyra
Winona Ryder: Winona Horowitz
Sade: Helen Folsade Abu
Soupy Sales: Milton Supman
Susan Sarandon: Susan Tomaling
Seal: Seal Henry Olusegun Olumide Adeola Samuel
Jane Seymour: Joyce Frankenberg
Omar Sharif: Michael Shalhoub
Charlie Sheen: Carlos Irwin Estevez
Martin Sheen: Ramon Estevez
Talia Shire: Talia Coppola
Beverly Sills: Belle Silverman
Phil Silvers: Philip Silversmith
Gene Simmons: Chaim Witz
Sinbad: David Adkins
Anna Nicole Smith: Vickie Lynn Hogan
Snoop Lion (née Snoop Dogg): Calvin Broadus
Barbara Stanwyck: Ruby Stevens
Jean Stapleton: Jeanne Murray
Ringo Starr: Richard Starkey
Cat Stevens: Stephen Demetre Georgiou
Connie Stevens: Concetta Ingolia
Jon Stewart: Jonathan Stuart Leibowitz
Sting: Gordon Sumner
Joe Strummer: John Graham Mellor
Donna Summer: La Donna Gaines
Rip Taylor: Charles Elmer Taylor Jr.
Robert Taylor: Spangler Brugh
Danny Thomas: Muzyad Yakhoob (later Amos Jacobs)
Tiny Tim: Herbert Khaury
Rip Torn: Elmore Rual Torn Jr.
Randy Travis: Randy Traywick
Tina Turner: Annie Mae Bullock
Shania Twain: Eilleen Regina Edwards
Twiggy: Lesley Hornby
Conway Twitty: Harold Lloyd Jenkins
Steven Tyler: Stephen Tallarico
Rudolph Valentino: Rudolpho D'Antonguolla
Frankie Valli: Frank Castelluccio
Eddie Vedder: Edward Louis Seversen III
Sid Vicious: John Simon Ritchie
John Wayne: Marion Morrison
Raquel Welch: Raquel Tejada
Gene Wilder: Jerome Silberman
Shelley Winters: Shirley Schrift
Stevie Wonder: Stevland Morris
Jane Wyman: Sarah Jane Mayfield
Loretta Young: Gretchen Michaels Young
Buckwheat Zydeco: Stanley Dural Jr.

ARTS AND MEDIA

Some Notable Movies, Sept. 2012-Aug. 2013

Film (rating)	Stars	Director(s)
2 Guns (R)	Denzel Washington, Mark Wahlberg, Paula Patton	Baltasar Kormákur
42 (PG-13)	Chadwick Boseman, T. R. Knight, Harrison Ford	Brian Helgeland
After Earth (PG-13)	Jaden Smith, Will Smith, David Denman	M. Night Shyamalan
Amour (PG-13)	Jean-Louis Trintignant, Emmanuelle Riva, Isabelle Huppert	Michael Haneke
Argo (R)	Ben Affleck, Bryan Cranston, John Goodman, Alan Arkin	Ben Affleck
Blood Brother (NR)	Documentary	Steve Hoover
Blue Is the Warmest Color	Léa Seydoux, Adèle Exarchopoulos	Abdellatif Kechiche
The Call (R)	Halle Berry, Abigail Breslin, Evie Thompson	Brad Anderson
The Conjuring (R)	Patrick Wilson, Vera Farmiga, Lili Taylor	James Wan
The Croods (PG)	Animated, Nicolas Cage, Ryan Reynolds, Emma Stone	Kirk De Micco, Chris Sanders
Despicable Me 2 (PG)	Animated, Steve Carell, Kristen Wiig, Benjamin Bratt	Pierre Coffin, Chris Renaud
Django Unchained (R)	Jamie Foxx, Christoph Waltz, Leonardo DiCaprio, Kerry Washington	Quentin Tarantino
Elysium (R)	Matt Damon, Jodie Foster	Neill Blomkamp
End of Watch (R)	Jake Gyllenhaal, Michael Peña, Anna Kendrick	David Ayer
Epic (PG)	Animated, Amanda Seyfried, Josh Hutcherson, Beyoncé	Chris Wedge
Escape From Planet Earth (PG)	Animated, Brendan Fraser, Sarah Jessica Parker, Jessica Alba	Cal Brunker
Flight (R)	Denzel Washington, Nadine Velazquez, Don Cheadle	Robert Zemeckis
Frankenweenie (PG)	Animated, Winona Ryder, Catherine O'Hara, Martin Short	Tim Burton
Fruitvale Station (R)	Michael B. Jordan, Melonie Diaz, Octavia Spencer	Ryan Coogler
The Gatekeepers (PG-13)	Documentary	Dror Moreh
G.I. Joe: Retaliation (PG-13)	Dwayne Johnson, Channing Tatum	Jon M. Chu
The Great Gatsby (2013) (PG-13)	Leonardo DiCaprio, Tobey Maguire, Carey Mulligan	Baz Luhrmann
Grown Ups 2 (PG-13)	Adam Sandler, Kevin James, Chris Rock, David Spade	Dennis Dugan
The Hangover Part III (R)	Bradley Cooper, Zach Galifianakis, Ed Helms	Todd Phillips
Hansel and Gretel: Witch Hunters (R)	Jeremy Renner, Gemma Arterton	Tommy Wirkola
The Heat (R)	Sandra Bullock, Melissa McCarthy	Paul Feig
Here Comes the Boom (PG)	Kevin James, Salma Hayek, Henry Winkler	Frank Coraci
The Hobbit: An Unexpected Journey (PG-13)	Martin Freeman, Ian McKellen, Richard Armitage	Peter Jackson
Hotel Transylvania (PG)	Animated, Adam Sandler, Selena Gomez, Andy Samberg	Genndy Tartakovsky
The House I Live In (NR)	Documentary	Eugene Jarecki
How to Survive a Plague (NR)	Documentary	David France
Identity Thief (R)	Jason Bateman, Melissa McCarthy, John Cho	Seth Gordon
The Impossible (PG-13)	Naomi Watts, Ewan McGregor	J.A. Bayona
Iron Man 3 (PG-13)	Robert Downey Jr., Don Cheadle, Gwyneth Paltrow	Shane Black
Jack the Giant Slayer (PG-13)	Stanley Tucci, Ewan McGregor, Nicholas Hoult	Bryan Singer
Jack Reacher (PG-13)	Tom Cruise, Rosamund Pike	Christopher McQuarrie
Lee Daniels' The Butler (PG-13)	Forest Whitaker, Oprah Winfrey, John Cusack	Lee Daniels
Les Miserables (2012) (PG-13)	Hugh Jackman, Russell Crowe, Anne Hathaway	Tom Hooper
Life of Pi (PG)	Suraj Sharma, Irrfan Khan, Adil Hussain	Ang Lee
Lincoln (PG-13)	Daniel Day-Lewis, Sally Field, David Strathairn	Steven Spielberg
The Lone Ranger (PG-13)	Johnny Depp, Armie Hammer	Gore Verbinski
Looper (R)	Joseph Gordon-Levitt, Bruce Willis, Emily Blunt	Rian Johnson
Mama (PG-13)	Jessica Chastain, Nikolaj Coster-Waldau, Megan Charpentier	Andrés Muschietti
Man of Steel (PG-13)	Henry Cavill, Amy Adams, Michael Shannon	Zack Snyder
The Master (R)	Philip Seymour Hoffman, Joaquin Phoenix, Amy Adams	Paul Thomas Anderson
Monsters University (G)	Animated, Billy Crystal, John Goodman, Steve Buscemi	Dan Scanlon
Now You See Me (PG-13)	Jesse Eisenberg, Woody Harrelson, Mark Ruffalo	Louis Leterrier
Oblivion (PG-13)	Tom Cruise, Morgan Freeman	Joseph Kosinski
Olympus Has Fallen (R)	Gerard Butler, Aaron Eckhart, Morgan Freeman	Antoine Fuqua
Oz: The Great and Powerful (PG)	James Franco, Michelle Williams, Mila Kunis	Sam Raimi
Parental Guidance (PG)	Billy Crystal, Bette Midler, Marisa Tomei	Andy Fickman
Pitch Perfect (PG-13)	Anna Kendrick, Brittany Snow, Rebel Wilson	Jason Moore
Red 2 (PG-13)	Bruce Willis, Helen Mirren, John Malkovich	Dean Parisot
Red Dawn (2012) (PG-13)	Chris Hemsworth, Isabel Lucas, Josh Hutcherson	Dan Bradley
Rise of the Guardians (PG)	Animated, Hugh Jackman, Alec Baldwin, Chris Pine, Jude Law, Isla Fisher	Peter Ramsey
Safe Haven (PG-13)	Julianne Hough, Josh Duhamel, Cobie Smulders	Lasse Hallström
The Sessions (R)	John Hawkes, Helen Hunt, William H. Macy	Ben Lewin
Silver Linings Playbook (R)	Bradley Cooper, Jennifer Lawrence, Robert De Niro	David O. Russell
Skyfall (R)	Daniel Craig, Javier Bardem, Judi Dench	Sam Mendes
The Smurfs 2 (PG)	Animated, Neil Patrick Harris, Jayma Mays, Katy Perry	Raja Gosnell
Star Trek Into Darkness (PG-13)	Chris Pine, Zachary Quinto, Zoe Saldana	J.J. Abrams
Taken 2 (PG-13)	Liam Neeson, Famke Janssen, Maggie Grace	Olivier Megaton
This Is 40 (R)	Paul Rudd, Leslie Mann, Maude Apatow	Judd Apatow
This Is the End (R)	James Franco, Jonah Hill, Seth Rogen	Evan Goldberg, Seth Rogen
Turbo (PG)	Animated, Ryan Reynolds, Paul Giamatti, Maya Rudolph	David Soren
The Twilight Saga: Breaking Dawn Part 2 (PG-13)	Kristen Stewart, Robert Pattinson, Taylor Lautner	Bill Condon
Temptation: Confessions of a Marriage Counselor (PG-13)	Jurnee Smollett-Bell, Vanessa Williams, Brandy Norwood	Tyler Perry
We're the Millers (R)	Jason Sudeikis, Jennifer Aniston, Emma Roberts	Rawson Marshall Thurber
White House Down (PG-13)	Channing Tatum, Jamie Foxx, Maggie Gyllenhaal	Roland Emmerich
The Wolverine (PG-13)	Hugh Jackman, Will Yun Lee, Tao Okamoto	James Mangold
World War Z (PG-13)	Brad Pitt, Mireille Enos, Daniella Kertesz	Marc Forster
Wreck-It Ralph (PG-13)	Animated, John C. Reilly, Sarah Silverman, Jane Lynch	Rich Moore
Zero Dark Thirty (R)	Jessica Chastain, Joel Edgerton, Kyle Chandler	Kathryn Bigelow

50 Top-Grossing Movies, 2012
Source: Rentrak Corporation

Rank	Title	Gross (mil)	Rank	Title	Gross (mil)
1.	Marvel's The Avengers	$622.7	26.	Journey 2: The Mysterious Island	$103.9
2.	The Dark Knight Rises	448.1	27.	Rise of the Guardians	94.6
3.	The Hunger Games	408.0	28.	Flight	92.2
4.	Skyfall	291.5	29.	Think Like a Man	91.5
5.	The Twilight Saga: Breaking Dawn Part 2	287.8	30.	Life of Pi	88.2
6.	The Amazing Spider-Man	262.0	31.	Les Miserables	87.5
7.	The Hobbit: An Unexpected Journey	246.3	32.	The Campaign	86.9
8.	Brave	237.3	33.	Django Unchained	86.3
9.	Ted	218.8	34.	The Expendables 2	85.0
10.	Madagascar 3: Europe's Most Wanted	216.4	35.	Wrath of the Titans	83.7
11.	Dr. Seuss' The Lorax	214.0	36.	Dark Shadows	79.7
12.	Men in Black 3	179.0	37.	John Carter	73.1
13.	Wreck-It Ralph	177.3	38.	Act of Valor	70.0
14.	Ice Age: Continental Drift	161.2	39.	Contraband	66.5
15.	Snow White and the Huntsman	155.3	40.	Looper	66.5
16.	Hotel Transylvania	145.5	41.	Tyler Perry's Madea's Witness Protection	65.7
17.	Taken 2	139.1	42.	Battleship	65.4
18.	Lincoln	138.7	43.	Mirror Mirror	64.9
19.	21 Jump Street	138.4	44.	Chronicle	64.6
20.	Prometheus	126.5	45.	Pitch Perfect	64.5
21.	Safe House	126.4	46.	Hope Springs	63.5
22.	The Vow	125.0	47.	Underworld Awakening	62.3
23.	Magic Mike	113.7	48.	The Lucky One	60.5
24.	The Bourne Legacy	113.2	49.	Mission: Impossible—Ghost Protocol	59.7
25.	Argo	109.3	50.	The Dictator	59.7

Note: Box-office grosses in the U.S. and Canada Jan. 6, 2012-Jan. 3, 2013; some films may have had 2011 release dates.

All-Time Top-Grossing American Movies
Source: Rentrak Corporation

Rank	Title (original release)	Gross (mil)	Rank	Title (original release)	Gross (mil)
1.	Avatar (2009)	$760.5	27.	Forrest Gump (1994)	$329.7
2.	The Avengers (2012)	623.4	28.	Despicable Me 2 (2013)	328.0
3.	Titanic (1997)	600.8	29.	Shrek the Third (2007)	322.7
4.	The Dark Knight (2008)	533.3	30.	Transformers (2007)	319.2
5.	Star Wars (1977)	461.0	31.	Iron Man (2008)	318.6
6.	The Dark Knight Rises (2012)	448.1	32.	Harry Potter and the Sorcerer's Stone (2001)	317.6
7.	Shrek 2 (2004)	436.7	33.	Indiana Jones and the Kingdom of the Crystal Skull (2008)	317.1
8.	E.T. the Extra-Terrestrial (1982)	435.0			
9.	Star Wars: Episode I—The Phantom Menace (1999)	431.1	34.	The Lord of the Rings: Fellowship of the Ring (2001)	314.2
10.	Pirates of the Caribbean: Dead Man's Chest (2006)	423.3	35.	The Lion King (1994)	312.9
11.	Toy Story 3 (2010)	415.0	36.	Iron Man 2 (2010)	312.4
12.	The Hunger Games (2012)	408.0	37.	Star Wars: Episode II—Attack of the Clones (2002)	310.7
13.	Iron Man 3 (2013)	407.7	38.	Pirates of the Caribbean: At World's End (2007)	309.4
14.	Spider-Man (2002)	403.7	39.	Star Wars: Episode VI—Return of the Jedi (1983)	309.2
15.	Transformers: Revenge of the Fallen (2009)	402.1	40.	Independence Day (1996)	306.2
16.	Harry Potter and the Deathly Hallows: Part 2 (2011)	381.0	41.	Pirates of the Caribbean: The Curse of the Black Pearl (2003)	305.4
17.	Star Wars: Episode III—Revenge of the Sith (2005)	380.3	42.	Skyfall (2012)	304.4
18.	The Lord of the Rings: Return of the King (2003)	377.0	43.	The Hobbit: An Expected Journey (2012)	303.0
19.	Spider-Man 2 (2004)	373.4	44.	Harry Potter and the Half Blood Prince (2010)	302.0
20.	The Passion of the Christ (2004)	370.3	45.	The Twilight Saga: Eclipse (2010)	300.5
21.	Jurassic Park (1993)	357.1	46.	The Twilight Saga: New Moon (2009)	296.6
22.	Transformers: Dark of the Moon (2011)	352.4	47.	Harry Potter and the Deathly Hallows: Part 1 (2010)	296.0
23.	The Lord of the Rings: Two Towers (2002)	341.7	48.	The Sixth Sense (1999)	293.5
24.	Finding Nemo (2003)	339.7	49.	Up (2009)	293.0
25.	Spider-Man 3 (2007)	336.5	50.	Inception (2010)	292.6
26.	Alice in Wonderland (2010)	334.2			

Note: Box-office grosses in the U.S. and Canada through Aug. 30, 2013, in absolute dollars. Rising ticket prices favor newer films. Revenues from re-releases are included.

100 Best American Movies of All Time
Source: American Film Institute

First unveiled in 1998 based on ballots sent to 1,500 individuals, mostly from the film world, in 1997. Updated in 2007 (the version shown here) to include newly eligible films and reflect shifting cultural perspectives. Criteria for judging included historical significance, cultural impact, critical recognition and awards, and popularity. The year each film was first released is in parentheses.

1. Citizen Kane (1941)	14. Psycho (1960)	27. High Noon (1952)
2. The Godfather (1972)	15. 2001: A Space Odyssey (1968)	28. All About Eve (1950)
3. Casablanca (1942)	16. Sunset Boulevard (1950)	29. Double Indemnity (1944)
4. Raging Bull (1980)	17. The Graduate (1967)	30. Apocalypse Now (1979)
5. Singin' in the Rain (1952)	18. The General (1927)	31. The Maltese Falcon (1941)
6. Gone With the Wind (1939)	19. On the Waterfront (1954)	32. The Godfather Part II (1974)
7. Lawrence of Arabia (1962)	20. It's a Wonderful Life (1946)	33. One Flew Over the Cuckoo's Nest (1975)
8. Schindler's List (1993)	21. Chinatown (1974)	
9. Vertigo (1958)	22. Some Like It Hot (1959)	34. Snow White and the Seven Dwarfs (1937)
10. The Wizard of Oz (1939)	23. The Grapes of Wrath (1940)	
11. City Lights (1931)	24. E.T. the Extra-Terrestrial (1982)	35. Annie Hall (1977)
12. The Searchers (1956)	25. To Kill a Mockingbird (1962)	36. The Bridge on the River Kwai (1957)
13. Star Wars (1977)	26. Mr. Smith Goes to Washington (1939)	37. The Best Years of Our Lives (1946)

38. The Treasure of the Sierra Madre (1948)
39. Dr. Strangelove (1964)
40. The Sound of Music (1965)
41. King Kong (1933)
42. Bonnie and Clyde (1967)
43. Midnight Cowboy (1969)
44. The Philadelphia Story (1940)
45. Shane (1953)
46. It Happened One Night (1934)
47. A Streetcar Named Desire (1951)
48. Rear Window (1954)
49. Intolerance (1916)
50. The Lord of the Rings: The Fellowship of the Ring (2001)
51. West Side Story (1961)
52. Taxi Driver (1976)
53. The Deer Hunter (1978)
54. M*A*S*H (1970)
55. North by Northwest (1959)
56. Jaws (1975)
57. Rocky (1976)
58. The Gold Rush (1925)
59. Nashville (1975)
60. Duck Soup (1933)
61. Sullivan's Travels (1941)
62. American Graffiti (1973)
63. Cabaret (1972)
64. Network (1976)
65. The African Queen (1951)
66. Raiders of the Lost Ark (1981)
67. Who's Afraid of Virginia Woolf? (1966)
68. Unforgiven (1992)
69. Tootsie (1982)
70. A Clockwork Orange (1971)
71. Saving Private Ryan (1998)
72. The Shawshank Redemption (1994)
73. Butch Cassidy and the Sundance Kid (1969)
74. The Silence of the Lambs (1991)
75. In the Heat of the Night (1967)
76. Forrest Gump (1994)
77. All the President's Men (1976)
78. Modern Times (1936)
79. The Wild Bunch (1969)
80. The Apartment (1960)
81. Spartacus (1960)
82. Sunrise (1927)
83. Titanic (1997)
84. Easy Rider (1969)
85. A Night at the Opera (1935)
86. Platoon (1986)
87. 12 Angry Men (1957)
88. Bringing Up Baby (1938)
89. The Sixth Sense (1999)
90. Swing Time (1936)
91. Sophie's Choice (1982)
92. Goodfellas (1990)
93. The French Connection (1971)
94. Pulp Fiction (1994)
95. The Last Picture Show (1971)
96. Do the Right Thing (1989)
97. Blade Runner (1982)
98. Yankee Doodle Dandy (1942)
99. Toy Story (1995)
100. Ben-Hur (1959)

National Film Registry, 2012
Source: National Film Registry, Library of Congress

The National Film Registry adds 25 "culturally, historically, or aesthetically significant" American films annually.

3:10 to Yuma (1957)
Anatomy of a Murder (1959)
The Augustas (1930s-1950s)
Born Yesterday (1950)
Breakfast at Tiffany's (1961)
A Christmas Story (1983)
The Corbett-Fitzsimmons Title Fight (1897)
Dirty Harry (1971)

Hours for Jerome: Parts 1 and 2 (1980-82)
The Kidnappers Foil (1930s-1950s)
Kodachrome Color Motion Picture Tests (1922)
A League of Their Own (1992)
The Matrix (1999)

The Middleton Family at the New York World's Fair (1939)
One Survivor Remembers (1995)
Parable (1964)
Samsara: Death and Rebirth in Cambodia (1990)
Slacker (1991)
Sons of the Desert (1933)

The Spook Who Sat by the Door (1973)
They Call It Pro Football (1966)
The Times of Harvey Milk (1984)
Two-Lane Blacktop (1971)
Uncle Tom's Cabin (1914)
The Wishing Ring; An Idyll of Old England (1914)

Film and Television Production by State, 2010-11
Source: Motion Picture Association of America

State	Number of productions, examples
Alabama*	12, The One Warrior, The Man in the Maze
Alaska*	17, Big Miracle, Deadliest Catch (TV)
Arizona*	31, Under the Bridge, The Coalition
Arkansas*	5, Mud, Then the Night Comes
California*	1,117, The Avengers, Drive, The Big Bang Theory (TV)
Colorado*	15, The Girl With the Dragon Tattoo, Unwrapped (TV)
Connecticut*	32, The Big C (TV), Maury (TV)
Delaware	2, Infamous, Punkin Chunkin (TV)
Florida*	42, Magic Mike, Parker, Burn Notice (TV)
Georgia*	103, Lawless, Flight, The Vampire Diaries (TV)
Hawaii*	16, Rise of the Planet of the Apes, Battleship
Idaho*	1, Leap
Illinois*	53, Man of Steel, Lincoln
Indiana*	6, Transformers: Dark of the Moon, Resurrection
Iowa	2, At Any Price, Scribble
Kansas*	3, The Casserole Club, Earthwork
Kentucky*	9, The Ides of March, Land of Tomorrow
Louisiana*	125, 21 Jump Street, Treme (TV)
Maine*	7, Anatomy of the Tide, Black Rock, American Loggers (TV)
Maryland*	10, Dead Money, The Haunting of Pearson Place, Ace of Cakes (TV)
Massachusetts*	30, R.I.P.D., That's My Boy, Ted, Frontline (TV)
Michigan*	61, The Five-Year Engagement, The Ides of March, Detroit 1-8-7 (TV)
Minnesota*	18, Fun Size, Young Adult, Thin Ice
Mississippi*	8, The Help, The Dynamiter, Mud
Missouri*	10, A Horrible Way to Die, Small Pond, Turbine
Montana*	6, Winter in the Blood, Treasure State, Frontier Force (TV)
Nebraska	3, Vino Veritas, Geocachers, Trunk'd
Nevada	34, My Mother's Curse, Pretty Obsession, Bachelor Pad (TV)
New Hampshire	9, The Resurrection of Victor Jara, The A Plate, Joy and the Apocalypse (TV)
New Jersey*	46, Gimme Shelter, Drama Class, Bad Parents, Brick City (TV)
New Mexico*	42, The Avengers, Gambit, The Last Stand, Breaking Bad (TV)
New York*	470, Extremely Loud and Incredibly Close, The Bourne Legacy, Damages (TV)
North Carolina*	29, The Hunger Games, Piranha 3DD, Homeland (TV), One Tree Hill (TV)
North Dakota	4, The Legend of Hell's Gate: An American Conspiracy, The Aviators (TV)
Ohio*	24, The Avengers, Fun Size, Liberal Arts, One Born Every Minute (TV)
Oklahoma*	10, The Killer Inside Me, A Christmas Snow, Yellow
Oregon*	27, Gone, ParaNorman, Shiver, Grimm (TV)
Pennsylvania*	37, The Dark Knight Rises, Learning to Fly, One Shot
Rhode Island*	9, Moonrise Kingdom, Hall Pass, Body of Proof (TV)
South Carolina*	4, The Bay, Little Red Wagon, Army Wives (TV)
South Dakota	2, The Great Mystery, Full Throttle Saloon (TV)
Tennessee*	18, Country Strong, Water for Elephants, Fall Away
Texas*	86, Abel's Field, The Ghost of Goodnight Lane, Friday Night Lights (TV)
Utah*	16, John Carter, 127 Hours, My Girlfriend's Boyfriend
Vermont	1, Dug Up
Virginia*	12, Lincoln, J. Edgar, To Have and to Hold
Washington*	21, Dancing on the Edge, Desert Cathedral, 21 and Over
Wash., DC*	19, Safe House, J. Edgar, The Chris Matthews Show (TV)
West Virginia*	6, Super 8, Cut, Pilgrim Song, Jamie Oliver's Food Revolution (TV)
Wisconsin*	4, Transformers: Dark of the Moon, House of Purgatory
Wyoming*	5, Django Unchained, Tree Fight, Deeper

* = State has enacted incentives to increase production.

Movie Theaters, 1946-2012

Source: Motion Picture Association of America (MPAA); Rentrak Corporation

Year	Box office (mil)	Admissions (mil)	Admissions per week (mil)	Screens	Avg. ticket price	Films produced	Films released
1946	$1,692.0	4,067.3	78.2	NA	$0.42	NA	400
1950	1,379.0	3,017.5	58.0	NA	0.46	NA	483
1955	1,204.0	2,072.3	39.9	NA	0.58	NA	319
1960	984.4	1,304.5	25.1	NA	0.76	NA	248
1965	1,041.8	1,031.5	19.8	NA	1.01	NA	279
1970	1,429.2	920.6	17.7	NA	1.55	279	306
1975	2,114.8	1,032.8	19.9	15,030	2.05	258	233
1980	2,748.5	1,021.5	19.6	17,590	2.69	214	233
1985	3,749.4	1,056.1	20.3	21,147	3.55	264	470
1990	5,021.8	1,188.6	22.9	23,689	4.23	346	410
1995	5,269.0	1,211.0	23.3	27,805	4.35	631	411
2000	7,468.0	1,383.0	26.6	37,396	5.39	683	475
2001	8,125.0	1,438.0	27.7	36,764	5.66	611	454
2002	9,272.0	1,599.0	30.8	35,280	5.81	546	475
2003	9,165.0	1,521.0	29.3	35,786	6.03	593	455
2004	9,215.0	1,484.0	28.5	36,594	6.21	611	489
2005	8,832.0	1,376.0	26.5	38,852	6.41	920	507
2006	9,138.0	1,395.0	26.8	38,415	6.55	928	594
2007	9,629.0	1,400.0	26.9	38,974	6.88	789	611
2008	9,791.0	1,364.0	26.2	38,834	7.18	773	638
2009	10,543.6	1,415.0	27.2	39,233	7.50	751	558
2010	10,741.0	1,341.0	25.8	39,547	7.89	795	563
2011	10,186.1	1,285.0	24.7	39,641	7.93	818	609
2012	10,774.5	1,358.0	26.0	39,918	7.96	476[1]	677

NA = Not available. (1) Non-MPAA members with est. budget under $1 mil were not tracked in 2012.

Top Film Websites, 2013

Source: comScore Media Metrix, Inc.; ranked by number of visitors.

Rank	Website	Visitors[1]	% change[2]	Rank	Website	Visitors[1]	% change[2]
1.	IMDb.	38,330	9.0%	11.	Cinemablend.com.	2,830	79.3%
2.	Yahoo! Movies	21,947	−11.0	12.	AMC Entertainment Inc.	2,687	13.5
3.	Moviefone	14,639	−5.0	13.	Collider.com	2,262	110.9
4.	Fandango	13,557	0.4	14.	Screenrant.com	2,209	45.9
5.	MSN Movies	12,385	−5.7	15.	Guardian Film	1,789	232.9
6.	Flixster	7,130	−11.1	16.	Tubeplus.me	1,700	48.1
7.	Hollywood.com sites.	4,538	−19.1	17.	Hollywoodreporter.com Movies.	1,682	NA
8.	Megashare.info.	3,953	818.0	18.	Regal Entertainment	1,412	0.8
9.	Disney Movies	3,392	7.8	19.	Cinemark.com	1,401	−11.0
10.	Solarmovie.so.	2,955	NA	20.	Lumovies.com	1,399	NA

NA = Not available. (1) Number of unique visitors, in thousands, who visited website at least once in June 2013. (2) Percent change over June 2012.

Most Popular Movie DVDs, 2012

Source: Rentrak Corporation

Top Rentals, 2012

Rank	Movie	Rank	Movie
1.	Marvel's The Avengers	11.	The Expendables 2
2.	Snow White and the Huntsman	12.	Prometheus
3.	The Amazing Spider-Man	13.	The Hunger Games
4.	That's My Boy	14.	The Watch
5.	Madagascar 3: Europe's Most Wanted	15.	Brave
		16.	Magic Mike
6.	Men in Black 3	17.	Madea's Witness Protection
7.	The Campaign	18.	Abraham Lincoln: Vampire Hunter
8.	Dark Shadows	19.	Lawless
9.	Battleship	20.	Total Recall (2012)
10.	Five-Year Engagement		

Top-Selling DVDs, 2012

Rank	Movie	Rank	Movie
1.	Marvel's The Avengers	11.	Hop
2.	The Hunger Games	12.	Puss in Boots
3.	Brave	13.	Secret of the Wings
4.	The Twilight Saga: Breaking Dawn Part 1	14.	The Amazing Spider-Man
5.	The Dark Knight Rises	15.	Prometheus
6.	Ted	16.	The Muppets
7.	Madagascar 3: Europe's Most Wanted	17.	Real Steel
8.	Sherlock Holmes: A Game of Shadows	18.	The Expendables 2
9.	Dr. Seuss' The Lorax	19.	Snow White and the Huntsman
10.	Alvin and the Chipmunks: Chipwrecked	20.	The Girl With the Dragon Tattoo (2011)

Note: Includes Blu-ray format titles. Top-selling DVDs exclude units sold into the rental channel, online, and in Canada. Top rentals exclude kiosk and online/by-mail channels.

Top-Selling Video Games, 2012

Source: The NPD Group/Retail Tracking Service; ranked by retail units sold

U.S. consumers spent $14.8 bil on video game content in 2012: $7.1 bil on physical software, $5.9 bil on content in digital format, and $1.8 bil on other physical formats (including rental/used content). Spending decreased 21% on physical content, but digital content spending grew 16%.

Rank	Game (console)	Rank	Game (console)
1.	Call of Duty: Black Ops II (360, PS3, PC, Wii U)*	7.	Borderlands 2 (360, PS3, PC)*
2.	Madden NFL 13 (360, PS3, Wii, PSV, Wii U)*	8.	Call of Duty: Modern Warfare 3 (360, PS3, Wii, PC)*
3.	Halo 4 (360)*	9.	Lego Batman 2: DC Super Heroes (Wii, 360, NDS, PS3, 3DS, PSV, PC)
4.	Assassin's Creed III (360, PS3, PC, Wii U)*	10.	FIFA Soccer 13 (360, PS3, Wii, PSV, 3DS, Wii U, PSP)
5.	Just Dance 4 (Wii, 360, Wii U, PS3)		
6.	NBA 2K13 (360, PS3, Wii, PSP, Wii U, PC)*		

* = Includes bundled, collector's, or game-of-the-year editions, except those bundled with hardware. 3DS = Nintendo 3DS; 360 = Microsoft Xbox 360; iOS = Apple mobile operating system devices (iPad, iPhone); NDS = Nintendo DS; PC = personal computer; PSP = PlayStation Portable; PSV = PlayStation Vita; PS3 = PlayStation 3; PS2 = PlayStation 2; Wii/Wii U = Nintendo Wii.

Film and TV Content Ratings

The Motion Picture Association of America (MPAA) began rating movies in 1968. The system was heavily revised in 1984 and again in 1990. The MPAA, National Cable Television Association, and National Association of Broadcasters developed and revised the TV ratings system in 1997, in accordance with the Telecommunications Act of 1996; it was implemented in Oct. 1997.

Film Ratings

G: General Audience. All ages admitted. Does not contain themes, language, nudity, sex, or violence that the MPAA ratings board believes would offend parents whose younger children see the film. Does not necessarily denote a certificate of approval nor children's movie. No nudity, sex scenes, or drug use depicted.

PG: Parental Guidance Suggested. Some material may not be suited for children. The MPAA ratings board recommends that parents determine whether the content of the film is appropriate for their children. The film may contain more mature themes, some profanity, violence, or brief nudity. No drug use depicted.

PG-13: Parents Strongly Cautioned. Some material may be inappropriate for children under 13. The MPAA urges more strongly that parents vet the movie to see if its content is appropriate for their children. Any movie depicting drug use or more than brief nudity is automatically rated at least PG-13. Violence is permitted, though it is generally not both realistic or extreme and persistent violence. The single use of one sexually-derived expletive rates a PG-13; more than one use requires at least an R rating.

R: Restricted. Under 17 requires accompanying parent or adult guardian. Movies given R ratings contain some adult material, defined as adult themes or activity, hard language, intense or persistent violence, sexually-oriented nudity, or drug abuse.

NC-17: No One 17 and Under Admitted. The ratings board considers NC-17 films those that most parents would consider too adult for children under 17. An NC-17 rating does not mean the film is obscene or pornographic. The rating can be based on violence, sex, aberrational behavior, drug abuse, or any other element that most parents would consider too adult for children.

TV Ratings

TV-Y: All Children. Program designed to be acceptable for children of all ages. Its themes and elements are designed for a very young audience.

TV-Y7: Directed to Older Children. Program designed for children ages 7 and older, and more appropriate for those who have the skills to distinguish between make-believe and reality. May include mild fantasy/comedic violence. Programs with more than mild fantasy violence are denoted with FV.

TV-G: General Audience. Program not necessarily designed for children, but most parents would find it suitable for all ages. Little or no violence, no strong language, and little or no sexual dialogue or situations.

TV-PG: Parental Guidance Suggested. Program might contain material that parents would consider inappropriate for children, such as an adult theme or one or more of the following: suggestive dialogue (D), infrequent coarse language (L), some sexual situations (S), or moderate violence (V).

TV-14: Parents Strongly Cautioned. Program contains material that many parents would consider inappropriate for children under 14, such as one or more of the following: intensely suggestive dialogue (D), strong coarse language (L), intense sexual situations (S), or intense violence (V).

TV-MA: Mature Audience Only. Program specifically designed for adults and may be unsuitable for children under 17. Contains one or more of the following: crude indecent language (L), explicit sexual activity (S), or graphic violence (V).

Longest-Running Broadway Shows

Source: The Broadway League, New York, NY

Rank	Title (run)[1]	Performances[2]	Rank	Title (run)[1]	Performances[2]	Rank	Title (run)[1]	Performances[2]
1.	*The Phantom of the Opera (1988-)	10,353	17.	Tobacco Road (1933-41)	3,182	35.	Gemini (1977-81)	1,819
2.	Cats (1982-2000)	7,485	18.	*Jersey Boys (2005-)	3,124	36.	Deathtrap (1978-82)	1,793
3.	*Chicago (revival, 1996-)	6,861	19.	Hello Dolly! (1964-70)	2,844	37.	Harvey (1944-49)	1,775
4.	Les Misérables (1987-2003)	6,880	20.	My Fair Lady (1956-62)	2,717	38.	Dancin' (1978-82)	1,774
5.	*The Lion King (1997-)	6,452	21.	Hairspray (2002-09)	2,642	39.	La Cage aux Folles (1983-87)	1,761
6.	A Chorus Line (1975-90)	6,137	22.	Mary Poppins (2006-13)	2,619	40.	Hair (1968-72)	1,750
7.	Oh! Calcutta! (revival, 1976-89)	5,959	23.	Avenue Q (2003-09)	2,534	41.	The Wiz (1975-79)	1,672
8.	Beauty and the Beast (1994-2007)	5,461	24.	The Producers (2001-07)	2,502	42.	Born Yesterday (1946-49)	1,642
9.	Rent (1996-2008)	5,123	25.	Cabaret (revival, 1998-2004)	2,377	43.	*Rock of Ages (2009-)	1,640
10.	*Mamma Mia! (2001-)	4,811	26.	Annie (1977-83)	2,377	44.	Crazy For You (1992-96)	1,622
11.	Miss Saigon (1991-2001)	4,092	27.	Man of La Mancha (1965-71)	2,328	45.	Ain't Misbehavin' (1978-82)	1,604
12.	*Wicked (2003-)	3,975	28.	Abie's Irish Rose (1922-27)	2,327	46.	The Best Little Whorehouse in Texas (1978-82)	1,584
13.	42nd Street (1980-89)	3,486	29.	Oklahoma! (1943-48)	2,212	47.	Spamalot (2005-09)	1,575
14.	Grease (1972-80)	3,388	30.	Smokey Joe's Cafe (1995-2000)	2,036	48.	Mary, Mary (1961-64)	1,572
15.	Fiddler on the Roof (1964-72)	3,242	31.	Pippin (1972-77)	1,944	49.	Evita (1979-83)	1,567
16.	Life With Father (1939-47)	3,224	32.	South Pacific (1949-54)	1,925	50.	The Voice of the Turtle (1943-48)	1,557
			33.	The Magic Show (1974-78)	1,920			
			34.	Aida (2000-04)	1,852			

* = Still running as of Sept. 1, 2013. (1) Unless noted, listings reflect a play's first run on Broadway. (2) Number of performances through May 26, 2013.

Broadway Season Statistics, 1959-2013

Source: The Broadway League, New York, NY

Season	Gross (mil $)	Attendance (mil)	Playing weeks	New productions	Season	Gross (mil $)	Attendance (mil)	Playing weeks	New productions
1959-1960	$46	7.9	1,156	58	2004-2005	$769	11.5	1,494	39
1964-1965	50	8.2	1,250	67	2005-2006	862	12.0	1,501	39
1969-1970	53	7.1	1,047	62	2006-2007	939	12.3	1,509	35
1974-1975	57	6.6	1,101	54	2007-2008	938	12.3	1,560	36
1979-1980	146	9.6	1,540	61	2008-2009	943	12.2	1,548	43
1984-1985	209	7.3	1,078	33	2009-2010	1,020	11.9	1,464	39
1989-1990	282	8.0	1,070	40	2010-2011	1,080	12.5	1,588	42
1994-1995	406	9.0	1,120	33	2011-2012	1,139	12.3	1,522	41
1999-2000	603	11.4	1,464	37	2012-2013	1,139	11.6	1,430	46

Notable U.S. Museums

This unofficial list of some of the largest museums in the U.S., by budget, was compiled with the assistance of the American Association of Museums, a national association representing the concerns of the museum community. Association members also include zoos, aquariums, arboretums, botanical gardens, and planetariums, but these are not included in *The World Almanac* listings.

Museum	City	State
American Museum of Natural History	New York	NY
Amon Carter Museum of Western Art	Ft. Worth	TX
The Art Institute of Chicago	Chicago	IL
Boston Children's Museum	Boston	MA
Brooklyn Museum of Art	Brooklyn	NY
Busch-Reisinger Museum	Cambridge	MA
California Academy of Sciences	San Francisco	CA
California Science Center	Los Angeles	CA
Carnegie Museums of Pittsburgh	Pittsburgh	PA
Children's Museum of Indianapolis	Indianapolis	IN
Cincinnati Art Museum	Cincinnati	OH
Cincinnati Museum Center	Cincinnati	OH
Cleveland Museum of Art	Cleveland	OH
Colonial Williamsburg	Williamsburg	VA
Corning Museum of Glass	Corning	NY
Crystal Bridges Museum of American Art	Bentonville	AR
Dallas Museum of Art	Dallas	TX
Denver Art Museum	Denver	CO
Denver Museum of Nature and Science	Denver	CO
Detroit Institute of Arts	Detroit	MI
Exploratorium	San Francisco	CA
The Field Museum	Chicago	IL
Fine Arts Museums of San Francisco	San Francisco	CA
Franklin Institute	Philadelphia	PA
The Frick Collection	New York	NY
J. Paul Getty Museum	Los Angeles	CA
Solomon R. Guggenheim Museum of Art	New York	NY
Harvard University Art Museums	Cambridge	MA
Henry F. Dupont Winterthur Museum	Winterthur	DE
Henry Ford Museum/Greenfield Village	Dearborn	MI
High Museum of Art	Atlanta	GA
Houston Museum of Natural Science	Houston	TX
Jamestown-Yorktown Foundation	Williamsburg	VA
Jewish Museum	New York	NY
L.A. County Museum of Art	Los Angeles	CA
Liberty Science Center, Liberty State Park	Jersey City	NJ
Maryland Science Center	Baltimore	MD
Mashantucket Pequot Museum and Research Center	Mashantucket	CT
Metropolitan Museum of Art	New York	NY
Milwaukee Public Museum	Milwaukee	WI
Minneapolis Institute of Arts	Minneapolis	MN
Museum of African American History	Detroit	MI
Museum of the American West	Los Angeles	CA
Museum of Contemporary Art	Los Angeles	CA
Museum of Fine Arts	Boston	MA
Museum of Fine Arts	Houston	TX
Museum of Modern Art	New York	NY
Museum of New Mexico	Santa Fe	NM
Museum of Science	Boston	MA
Museum of Science and Industry	Chicago	IL
Musical Instrument Museum	Phoenix	AZ
Mystic Seaport Museum	Mystic	CT
National Air and Space Museum	Washington	DC
National Baseball Hall of Fame and Museum, Inc.	Cooperstown	NY
National Constitution Center	Philadelphia	PA
National Gallery of Art	Washington	DC
National Museum of American History	Washington	DC
National Museum of the American Indian	Washington	DC
National Museum of Natural History	Washington	DC
Nelson-Atkins Museum of Art	Kansas City	MO
New York Historical Society	New York	NY
New York State Museum	Albany	NY
Peabody Essex Museum	Salem	MA
Philadelphia Museum of Art	Philadelphia	PA
Rock and Roll Hall of Fame and Museum, Inc.	Cleveland	OH
St. Louis Science Center	St. Louis	MO
San Diego Museum of Art	San Diego	CA
San Francisco Museum of Modern Art	San Francisco	CA
Science Museum of Minnesota	St. Paul	MN
Toledo Museum of Art	Toledo	OH
U.S. Holocaust Memorial Museum	Washington	DC
Univ. of Pennsylvania Museum of Archaeology and Anthropology	Philadelphia	PA
Virginia Museum of Fine Arts	Richmond	VA
Wadsworth Atheneum	Hartford	CT
Walker Art Center	Minneapolis	MN
Whitney Museum of American Art	New York	NY

Opera: Most Produced Works, 2012-13

Source: OPERA America

Work, composer	Productions	Work, composer	Productions	Work, composer	Productions
La bohème, Giacomo Puccini	13	Tosca, Giacomo Puccini	9	Le nozze di Figaro [The Marriage of Figaro], Wolfgang Amadeus Mozart	8
Don Giovanni, Wolfgang Amadeus Mozart	11	La traviata, Giuseppe Verdi	9		
		Aida, Giuseppe Verdi	8		
The Magic Flute, Wolfgang Amadeus Mozart	11	Madama Butterfly, Giacomo Puccini	8	Die Fledermaus, Johann Strauss Jr.	7
				Rigoletto, Giuseppe Verdi	7

Note: Scheduled productions of a given work (not individual performances) during the 2012-13 season (generally Oct.-Sept.) by members of OPERA America and Opera.ca.

Best-Selling U.S. Magazines, 2013

Source: Audit Bureau of Circulations (ABC)

General magazines, exclusive of comics; also excludes magazines that failed to file reports to ABC by press time. Based on total average paid and verified circulation during the six months ending June 30, 2013; ranked by paid circulation size.

Publication	Paid circ.	Publication	Paid circ.	Publication	Paid circ.
1. AARP The Magazine	21,931,184	18. AAA Going Places	2,483,456	35. American Rifleman	1,938,564
2. AARP Bulletin	21,701,445	19. AAA Living	2,431,751	36. Money	1,930,480
3. Game Informer Magazine	7,829,179	20. O, The Oprah Magazine	2,417,589	37. Men's Health	1,884,156
4. Better Homes and Gardens	7,624,505	21. Glamour	2,300,854	38. Cooking Light	1,796,440
5. Reader's Digest	5,241,484	22. Parenting	2,245,062	39. In Style	1,775,821
6. Good Housekeeping	4,396,795	23. American Legion Magazine	2,232,287	40. Entertainment Weekly	1,773,561
7. Family Circle	4,014,881	24. Redbook	2,229,809	41. Guideposts	1,766,571
8. National Geographic	4,001,937	25. FamilyFun Magazine	2,130,223	42. Every Day With Rachael Ray	1,733,495
9. People	3,542,185	26. ESPN The Magazine	2,128,345	43. Food Network Magazine	1,713,949
10. Woman's Day	3,394,754	27. Smithsonian	2,121,281	44. Country Living	1,671,727
11. Time	3,301,056	28. Martha Stewart Living	2,088,788	45. Golf Digest	1,668,141
12. Ladies' Home Journal	3,229,809	29. Parents	2,068,756	46. Shape	1,614,641
13. Taste of Home	3,207,340	30. TV Guide Magazine	2,021,689	47. Women's Health	1,574,269
14. Sports Illustrated	3,065,507	31. Real Simple	2,020,064	48. All You	1,560,503
15. Cosmopolitan	3,017,987	32. Seventeen	2,010,619	49. Bon Appetit	1,529,385
16. Prevention	2,884,542	33. Maxim	2,001,935	50. Self	1,520,570
17. Southern Living	2,824,751	34. Us Weekly	1,959,784		

Most Challenged Books, 2012

Source: Office for Intellectual Freedom, American Library Association (ALA)

A challenge is a formal, written complaint filed with a library or school requesting that materials be removed because of content or appropriateness.

Rank	Title, author	Common reasons given for challenge
1.	*Captain Underpants* (series), Dav Pilkey	Offensive language, unsuited for age group
2.	*The Absolutely True Diary of a Part-Time Indian*, Sherman Alexie	Offensive language, racism, sexually explicit, unsuited for age group
3.	*Thirteen Reasons Why*, Jay Asher	Drugs/alcohol/smoking, sexually explicit, suicide, unsuited for age group
4.	*Fifty Shades of Grey*, E. L. James	Offensive language, sexually explicit
5.	*And Tango Makes Three*, Peter Parnell and Justin Richardson	Homosexuality, unsuited for age group
6.	*The Kite Runner*, Khaled Hossein	Homosexuality, offensive language, religious viewpoint, sexually explicit
7.	*Looking for Alaska*, John Green	Offensive language, sexually explicit, unsuited for age group
8.	*Scary Stories* (series), Alvin Schwartz	Unsuited for age group, violence
9.	*The Glass Castle*, Jeanette Walls	Offensive language, sexually explicit
10.	*Beloved*, Toni Morrison	Sexually explicit, religious viewpoint, violence

Some Notable New Books, 2013

Source: Reference and User Services Association, American Library Association (ALA)

Fiction

This Is How You Lose Her, Junot Díaz
Half-Blood Blues, Esi Edugyan
A Hologram for the King, Dave Eggers
The Round House, Louise Erdrich
Canada, Richard Ford
Billy Lynn's Long Halftime Walk, Ben Fountain
The Dog Stars, Peter Heller
The Orphan Master's Son, Adam Johnson
The Unlikely Pilgrimage of Harold Fry, Rachel Joyce
The Headmaster's Wager, Vincent Lam
One Last Thing Before I Go, Jonathan Tropper
Battleborn, Claire Vaye Watkins

Poetry

Inferno, Dante Alighieri, Mary Jo Bang (trans.)
Stag's Leap, Sharon Olds

Nonfiction

Behind the Beautiful Forevers: Life, Death, and Hope in a Mumbai Undercity, Katherine Boo
Quiet: The Power of Introverts in a World That Can't Stop Talking, Susan Cain
Some of My Best Friends Are Black: The Strange Story of Integration in America, Tanner Colby
Turing's Cathedral: The Origins of the Digital Universe, George Dyson
Short Nights of the Shadow Catcher: The Epic Life and Immortal Photographs of Edward Curtis, Timothy Egan
Why Does the World Exist?: An Existential Detective Story, Jim Holt
Engines of Change: A History of the American Dream in Fifteen Cars, Paul Ingrassia
Full Body Burden: Growing up in the Nuclear Shadow of Rocky Flats, Kristen Iversen
Leonardo and the Last Supper, Ross King
Shooting Victoria: Madness, Mayhem, and the Rebirth of the British Monarchy, Paul Thomas Murphy
The Ocean of Life: The Fate of Man and the Sea, Callum Roberts
Why Be Happy When You Could Be Normal?, Jeanette Winterson

Some Notable New Books for Children, 2013

Source: Association for Library Service to Children, American Library Association (ALA)

Younger Readers

And Then It's Spring, Julie Fogliano, Erin E. Stead (illus.)
Bear Has a Story to Tell, Philip C. Stead, Erin E. Stead (illus.)
Black Dog, Levi Pinfold
Charley's First Night, Amy Hest, Helen Oxenbury (illus.)
Creepy Carrots!, Aaron Reynolds, Peter Brown (illus.)
Demolition, Sally Sutton, Brian Lovelock (illus.)
Dogs on Duty, Dorothy Hinshaw Patent
Dreaming Up: A Celebration of Building, Christy Hale
Extra Yarn, Mac Barnett, Jon Klassen (illus.)
Golden Domes and Silver Lanterns: A Muslim Book of Colors, Hena Khan, Mehrdokht Amini (illus.)
Goldilocks and the Three Dinosaurs, Mo Willems
Green, Laura Vaccaro Seeger
Hippopposites, Janik Coat
Infinity and Me, Kate Hosford, Gabi Swiatkowska (illus.)
Just Ducks!, Nicola Davies, Salvatore Rubbino (illus.)
Let's Go for a Drive!, Mo Willems
Machines Go to Work in the City, William Low
Magritte's Marvelous Hat: A Picture Book, D. B. Johnson
Martin de Porres: The Rose in the Desert, Gary D. Schmidt, David Diaz (illus.)
More, I. C. Springman, Brian Lies (illus.)
Nighttime Ninja, Barbara DaCosta, Ed Young (illus.)
Oh, No!, Candace Fleming, Eric Rohmann (illus.)
One Cool Friend, Toni Buzzeo, David Small (illus.)
One Special Day: A Story for Big Brothers and Sisters, Lola M. Schaefer, Jessica Meserve (illus.)
Penny and Her Doll, Kevin Henkes
Pete the Cat and His Four Groovy Buttons, Eric Litwin, James Dean (illus.)
Rabbit and Robot: The Sleepover, Cece Bell
Sleep Like a Tiger, Mary Logue, Pamela Zagarenski (illus.)
This Is Not My Hat, Jon Klassen
This Moose Belongs to Me, Oliver Jeffers
Up, Tall, and High!, Ethan Long
Z Is for Moose, Kelly Bingham, Paul O. Zelinsky (illus.)

Middle Readers

Abraham Lincoln & Frederick Douglass: The Story Behind an American Friendship, Russell Freedman
The Beetle Book, Steve Jenkins
A Black Hole Is Not a Hole, Carolyn Cinami DeCristofano, Michael Carroll (illus.)
Bomb: The Race to Build—and Steal—the World's Most Dangerous Weapon, Steve Sheinkin
Brothers at Bat: The True Story of an Amazing All-Brother Baseball Team, Audrey Vernick, Steven Salerno (illus.)
Chuck Close: Face Book, Chuck Close
Each Kindness, Jacqueline Woodson, E. B. Lewis (illus.)
Electric Ben: The Amazing Life and Times of Benjamin Franklin, Robert Byrd
George Bellows: Painter With a Punch!, Robert Burleigh, George Bellows (illus.)
Helen's Big World: The Life of Helen Keller, Doreen Rappaport, Matt Tavares (illus.)
Iceberg, Right Ahead!: The Tragedy of the Titanic, Stephanie Sammartino McPherson
In a Glass Grimmly, Adam Gidwitz
Island: A Story of the Galápagos, Jason Chin
Liar & Spy, Rebecca Stead

Lulu and the Duck in the Park, Hilary McKay, Priscilla Lamont (illus.)
May B., Caroline Starr Rose
The Mighty Mars Rovers: The Incredible Adventures of Spirit and Opportunity, Elizabeth Rusch
Moonbird: A Year on the Wind With the Great Survivor B95, Phillip M. Hoose
The One and Only Ivan, Katherine Applegate, Patricia Castelao (illus.)
See You at Harry's, Jo Knowles
Splendors and Glooms, Laura Amy Schlitz
Starry River of the Sky, Grace Lin
Three Times Lucky, Sheila Turnage
Titanic: Voices From the Disaster, Deborah Hopkinson
Twelve Kinds of Ice, Ellen Bryan Obed, Barbara McClintock (illus.)
Unspoken: A Story From the Underground Railroad, Henry Cole
Wonder, R. J. Palacio
Zombie Makers: True Stories of Nature's Undead, Rebecca L. Johnson

Older Readers

Aristotle and Dante Discover the Secrets of the Universe, Benjamin Alire Sáenz
Beyond Courage: The Untold Story of Jewish Resistance During the Holocaust, Doreen Rappaport

Drama, Raina Telgemeier
A Game for Swallows: To Die, to Leave, to Return, Zeina Abirached
Invincible Microbe: Tuberculosis and the Never-Ending Search for a Cure, Jim Murphy and Alison Blank
My Family for the War, Anne C. Voorhoeve, Tammi Reichel (trans.)
My Sister Lives on the Mantelpiece, Annabel Pitcher
The Revolution of Evelyn Serrano, Sonia Manzano
Seraphina, Rachel Hartman
Son, Lois Lowry
Son of a Gun, Anne de Graaf
Steve Jobs: The Man Who Thought Different, Karen Blumenthal
Temple Grandin: How the Girl Who Loved Cows Embraced Autism and Changed the World, Sy Montgomery
We've Got a Job: The 1963 Birmingham Children's March, Cynthia Y. Levinson

All Ages

Little Bird, Germano Zullo, Albertine (illus.)
National Geographic Book of Animal Poetry: 200 Poems With Photographs That Squeak, Soar, and Roar!, J. Patrick Lewis (ed.), National Geographic (illus.)
Step Gently Out, Helen Frost, Rick Lieder (illus.)
Water Sings Blue: Ocean Poems, Kate Coombs, Meilo So (illus.)
The Year Comes Round: Haiku Through the Seasons, Sid Farrar, Ilse Plume (illus.)

Best-Selling Books, 2012
Source: Publishers Weekly

Hardcover Fiction

1. *The Casual Vacancy*, J.K. Rowling
2. *The Racketeer*, John Grisham
3. *Gone Girl: A Novel*, Gillian Flynn
4. *Notorious Nineteen*, Janet Evanovich
5. *Merry Christmas, Alex Cross*, James Patterson
6. *Calico Joe*, John Grisham
7. *Winter of the World*, Ken Follett
8. *The Last Man*, Vince Flynn
9. *Threat Vector*, Tom Clancy with Mark Greaney
10. *The Forgotten*, David Baldacci
7. *The Perks of Being a Wallflower*, Stephen Chbosky
8. *Reflected in You*, Sylvia Day
9. *To Heaven and Back: A Doctor's Extraordinary Account of Her Death, Heaven, Angels, and Life Again: A True Story*, Mary C. Neal, M.D.
10. *The Lucky One*, Nicholas Sparks

E-books

1. *Fifty Shades of Grey: Book One*, E. L. James
2. *Fifty Shades Darker: Book Two*, E. L. James
3. *Fifty Shades Freed: Book Three*, E. L. James
4. *Gone Girl: A Novel*, Gillian Flynn
5. *Fifty Shades Trilogy Bundle*, E. L. James
6. *Bared to You*, Sylvia Day
7. *The Racketeer*, John Grisham
8. *Reflected in You*, Sylvia Day
9. *The Lucky One*, Nicholas Sparks
10. *No Easy Day*, Mark Owen

Hardcover Nonfiction

1. *Killing Kennedy: The End of Camelot*, Bill O'Reilly and Martin Dugard
2. *No Easy Day: The Firsthand Accounts of the Mission That Killed Osama Bin Laden*, Mark Owen with Kevin Maurer
3. *Killing Lincoln: The Shocking Assassination That Changed America*, Bill O'Reilly and Martin Dugard
4. *Barefoot Contessa Foolproof: Recipes You Can Trust*, Ina Garten
5. *Cross Roads*, William Paul Young
6. *The Pioneer Woman Cooks: Food From My Frontier*, Ree Drummond
7. *American Sniper*, Chris Kyle
8. *I Declare: 31 Promises to Speak Over Your Life*, Joel Osteen
9. *The Amateur: Barack Obama in the White House*, Edward Klein
10. *Thomas Jefferson: The Art of Power*, Jon Meacham

Children's and Young Adult Hardcover

1. *The Mark of Athena (Heroes of Olympus #3)*, Rick Riordan
2. *The Third Wheel (Diary of a Wimpy Kid #7)*, Jeff Kinney
3. *The Serpent's Shadow (Kane Chronicles #3)*, Rick Riordan
4. *Tales From a Not-So-Graceful Ice Princess (Dork Diaries #4)*, Rachel Renée Russell
5. *Insurgent*, Veronica Roth
6. *Tales From a Not-So-Smart Miss Know-It-All (Dork Diaries #5)*, Rachel Renée Russell
7. *Middle School: Get Me Out of Here!* James Patterson and Chris Tebbetts
8. *Junie B., First Grader: Turkeys We Have Loved and Eaten (and Other Thankful Stuff) (Junie B. Jones #28)*, Barbara Park, Denise Brunkus (illus.)
9. *Hidden*, P.C. Cast and Kristin Cast
10. *"Who Could That Be at This Hour?" (All the Wrong Questions #1)*, Lemony Snicket, Seth (illus.)

Mass Market Fiction

1. *A Game of Thrones*, George R.R. Martin
2. *The Lucky One*, Nicholas Sparks
3. *Chasing Fire*, Nora Roberts
4. *A Clash of Kings*, George R.R. Martin
5. *Safe Haven*, Nicholas Sparks
6. *A Storm of Swords*, George R.R. Martin
7. *The Hobbit*, J.R.R. Tolkien
8. *The Litigators*, John Grisham
9. *A Feast for Crows*, George R.R. Martin
10. *To Kill a Mockingbird*, Harper Lee

Children's and Young Adult Paperback

1. *Divergent (Divergent #1)*, Veronica Roth
2. *Look for the Lorax (Dr. Seuss)*, Tish Rabe, Christopher Moroney and Jan Gerardi (illus.)
3. *One Direction: Dare to Dream*, One Direction
4. *A Fairy-Tale Adventure (Barbie)*, Tish Rabe, Christopher Moroney and Jan Gerardi (illus.)
5. *Pinkalicious: The Princess of Pink Slumber Party*, Victoria Kann
6. *Happy Birthday, Princess! (Disney Princess)*, Jennifer Weinberg, Elisa Marrucchi (illus.)
7. *Game On! (Disney's Wreck-It Ralph)*, Susan Amerikaner
8. *The Hunger Games Tribute Guide*, Emily Seife
9. *Breaking Dawn (Twilight Saga #4)*, Stephenie Meyer
10. *The Lost Hero (Heroes of Olympus #1)*, Rick Riordan

Trade Paperback

1. *Fifty Shades of Grey: Book One*, E. L. James
2. *Fifty Shades Darker: Book Two*, E. L. James
3. *Fifty Shades Freed: Book Three*, E. L. James
4. *Fifty Shades Trilogy Bundle: 3-Volume Boxed Set*, E. L. James
5. *Bared to You*, Sylvia Day
6. *Proof of Heaven: A Neurosurgeon's Journey Into the Afterlife*, Eben Alexander

U.S. Daily Newspapers, 2012
Source: Alliance for Audited Media
(ranked by daily paid circulation for the six months ending Mar. 31, 2013)

Rank	Newspaper	Circulation	Rank	Newspaper	Circulation
1.	New York (NY) *Wall Street Journal*	2,378,827	27.	Portland (OR) *Oregonian*	228,909
2.	New York (NY) *Times*	1,865,318	28.	San Francisco (CA) *Chronicle*	218,987
3.	McLean (VA) *USA Today*	1,674,306	29.	Detroit (MI) *Free Press*	209,652
4.	Los Angeles (CA) *Times*	653,868	30.	St. Paul (MN) *Pioneer Press*	208,280
5.	New York (NY) *Daily News*	516,165	31.	Pittsburgh (PA) *Tribune-Review*	202,175
6.	New York (NY) *Post*	500,521	32.	Sacramento (CA) *Bee*	200,802
7.	Washington (DC) *Post*	474,767	33.	Milwaukee (WI) *Journal Sentinel*	198,469
8.	Chicago (IL) *Sun-Times*	470,548	34.	Tampa (FL) *Tribune*	191,477
9.	Denver (CO) *Post*	416,676	35.	Kansas City (MO) *Star*	189,283
10.	Chicago (IL) *Tribune*	414,930	36.	Fort Worth (TX) *Star-Telegram*	188,593
11.	Dallas (TX) *Morning News*	409,265	37.	Pittsburgh (PA) *Post-Gazette*	180,433
12.	Long Island (NY) *Newsday*	377,744	38.	Baltimore (MD) *Sun*	177,054
13.	Houston (TX) *Chronicle*	360,251	39.	St. Louis (MO) *Post-Dispatch*	167,199
14.	Orange County (CA) *Register*	356,165	40.	Ft. Lauderdale (FL) *South Florida*	
15.	Newark (NJ) *Star-Ledger*	340,778		*Sun-Sentinel*	163,728
16.	St. Petersburg (FL) *Times*	340,260	41.	Orlando (FL) *Sentinel*	161,070
17.	Cleveland (OH) *Plain Dealer*	311,605	42.	Little Rock (AR) *Democrat-Gazette*	158,090
18.	Philadelphia (PA) *Inquirer*	306,831	43.	Los Angeles (CA) *Investor's*	
19.	Minneapolis (MN) *Star Tribune*	301,345		*Business Daily*	157,161
20.	Phoenix (AZ) *Republic*	293,640	44.	Indianapolis (IN) *Star*	156,850
21.	Honolulu (HI) *Star-Advertiser*	268,244	45.	Woodland Park (NJ) *Record/Herald News*	154,823
22.	Las Vegas (NV) *Review-Journal*	252,047	46.	Miami (FL) *Herald*	147,130
23.	San Diego (CA) *Union-Tribune*	250,678	47.	Buffalo (NY) *News*	145,386
24.	Boston (MA) *Globe*	245,572	48.	San Antonio (TX) *Express-News*	139,005
25.	Atlanta (GA) *Journal-Constitution*	231,094	49.	Charlotte (NC) *Observer*	137,829
26.	Seattle (WA) *Times*	229,764	50.	Riverside (CA) *Press-Enterprise*	137,581

Note: Excludes newspapers for which no average M-F circulation number was available, including the San Jose *Mercury News*.

Paid U.S. Newspaper Circulation, 1940-2012
Source: *Editor & Publisher International Data Book*, 2013
(circulation figures in thousands)

Year	Number of daily newspapers			Circulation of daily newspapers			Sunday newspapers	
	Morning	Evening	Total	Morning	Evening	Total	Number	Circulation
1940	380	1,498	1,878	16,114	25,018	41,132	525	32,371
1945	330	1,419	1,749	19,240	29,144	48,384	485	39,860
1950	322	1,450	1,772	21,266	32,563	53,829	549	46,582
1955	316	1,454	1,760	22,183	33,964	56,147	541	46,448
1960	312	1,459	1,763	24,029	34,853	58,882	563	47,699
1965	320	1,444	1,751	24,107	36,251	60,358	562	48,600
1970	334	1,429	1,748	25,934	36,174	62,108	586	49,217
1975	339	1,436	1,756	25,490	35,165	60,655	639	51,096
1980	387	1,388	1,745	29,414	32,787	62,202	736	54,676
1985	482	1,220	1,676	36,362	26,405	62,766	798	58,826
1990	559	1,084	1,611	41,311	21,017	62,328	863	62,635
1995	656	891	1,533	44,310	13,883	58,193	888	61,229
2000	766	727	1,480	46,772	9,000	55,773	917	59,421
2005	817	645	1,452	46,122	7,222	53,345	914	55,270
2006	833	614	1,437	45,441	6,888	52,329	907	53,179
2007	867	565	1,422	44,548	6,194	50,742	902	51,246
2008	872	546	1,408	42,758	5,840	48,598	902	49,115
2009	869	528	1,397	40,796	5,482	46,278	919	46,850
2011	931	451	1,382	40,321	4,100	44,421	900	48,510
2012	985	442	1,427	38,723	4,709	43,432	981	48,821

Newspaper Advertising Revenues, 1950-2012
Source: Research Dept., Newspaper Association of America

Year	National ad revenue (mil $)	Retail ad revenue (mil $)	Classified ad revenue (mil $)	Print advertising total revenue (mil $)	% change[1]	Online advertising total revenue (mil $)	% change	Total advertising revenue (mil $)	% change
1950	$518	$1,175	$377	$2,070	—	—	—	—	—
1955	712	1,755	610	3,077	48.7%	—	—	—	—
1960	778	2,100	803	3,681	19.6	—	—	—	—
1965	783	2,429	1,214	4,426	20.2	—	—	—	—
1970	891	3,292	1,521	5,704	28.9	—	—	—	—
1975	1,109	4,966	2,159	8,234	44.4	—	—	—	—
1980	1,963	8,609	4,222	14,794	79.7	—	—	—	—
1985	3,352	13,443	8,375	25,170	70.1	—	—	—	—
1990	4,122	16,652	11,506	32,280	28.3	—	—	—	—
1995	4,251	18,099	13,742	36,092	11.8	—	—	—	—
2000	7,653	21,409	19,608	48,670	5.1	—	—	—	—
2005	7,910	22,187	17,312	47,408	1.5	$2,027	31.5%	$49,435	2.5%
2006	7,505	22,121	16,986	46,611	−1.7	2,664	31.4	49,275	−0.3
2007	7,005	21,018	14,186	42,209	−9.4	3,166	18.8	45,375	−7.9
2008	5,996	18,769	9,975	34,740	−17.7	3,109	−1.8	37,848	−16.6
2009	4,424	14,218	6,179	24,821	−28.6	2,743	−11.8	27,564	−27.2
2010	4,221	12,926	5,648	22,795	−8.2	3,042	10.9	25,838	−6.3
2011[2]	3,777	11,887	5,028	20,692	−9.2	3,249	6.8	23,941	−7.3
2012[2]	3,335	10,894	4,626	18,931	−8.5	3,370	3.7	22,314	−6.8

(1) Percent change for years 1950-2000 refers to the rate of change over the preceding five-year period; for 2005 and on, they represent the rate of change over the past year. (2) Revenue from niche publications, direct marketing, and non-daily publication advertising ($3,000 in 2011 and $2,900 in 2012) is excluded from total revenue.

Canadian Daily Newspapers, 2012
Source: *Editor & Publisher International Data Book*, 2013
(ranked by circulation as of Sept. 30, 2012)

Newspaper	Circulation	Newspaper	Circulation
1. Toronto (ON) *Globe and Mail*	285,853	6. Vancouver (BC) *Sun*	152,803
2. Toronto (ON) *Star*	252,743	7. Toronto (ON) *Sun*	135,522
3. Montreal (QC) *La Presse*	213,719	8. Vancouver (BC) *Province*	131,329
4. Montreal (QC) *Le Journal de Montréal*	199,686	9. Calgary (AB) *Herald*	117,198
5. Toronto (ON) *National Post*	162,243	10. Halifax (NS) *The Chronicle Herald*	108,639

Top Newspaper Websites, 2013
Source: comScore Media Metrix, Inc.; ranked by number of visitors.

Rank Website	Visitors[1]	% change[2]	Rank Website	Visitors[1]	% change[2]
1. The New York Times Brand	27,157	5.3%	12. Topix	6,676	0.8%
2. T365-Tribune Newspapers	23,679	−1.3	13. NYPost.com	6,104	1.2
3. NYDailyNews.com	16,793	55.2	14. CSMonitor.com	6,012	35.3
4. Mail Online: CA/US	16,665	NA	15. Boston.com	5,491	−9.2
5. Hearst Newspapers	16,444	13.4	16. Sun-Times Media/Chicago		
6. WashingtonPost.com	15,701	−3.4	Region-Wide Network (CRWN)	5,231	59.6
7. The Guardian	12,707	54.6	17. Philly.com Sites	4,131	36.4
8. McClatchy Corporation	11,450	−11.4	18. News World Communications, Inc.	3,795	40.6
9. MediaNews Group	10,976	−21.4	19. Independent.co.uk	3,240	84.8
10. Telegraph Media Group	7,196	59.6	20. The Sun Online	3,223	66.7
11. Lee Enterprises Inc.	7,115	−0.8			

NA = Not available. (1) Number of unique visitors, in thousands, who visited website at least once in June 2013. (2) Percent change over June 2012.

Top News/Information Websites, 2013
Source: comScore Media Metrix, Inc.; ranked by number of visitors.

Rank Website	Visitors[1]	% change[2]	Rank Website	Visitors[1]	% change[2]
1. Yahoo!-ABC News Network	83,460	2.6%	11. T365-Tribune Newspapers	23,679	−1.3%
2. CNN Network	61,280	10.0	12. The Washington Post Company	23,276	4.9
3. HPMG News	60,321	2.3	13. WorldNow Sites	19,126	−4.7
4. About.com	58,526	12.1	14. NYDailyNews.com	16,793	55.2
5. The Weather Channel	54,177	NA	15. Mail Online: CA/US	16,665	NA
6. NBC News Digital	52,291	4.7	16. Hearst Newspapers	16,444	13.4
7. Gannett Sites	48,098	6.2	17. Advance Digital	14,563	−15.0
8. CBS News	32,478	−3.6	18. BBC	13,707	15.5
9. New York Times Digital	30,600	−54.5	19. Examiner.com Sites	13,334	34.4
10. Fox News Digital Network	26,720	1.3	20. Digital First Media	12,762	−26.2

NA = Not available. (1) Number of unique visitors, in thousands, who visited website at least once in June 2013. (2) Percent change over June 2012.

Top-Selling Albums of All-Time
Source: Recording Industry Assn. of America (RIAA)
(As of Aug. 31, 2013. Sales figures represent RIAA multi-platinum certifications; albums ranked by latest sales certification.)

Rank Title, artist	Unit sales (mil)	Rank Title, artist	Unit sales (mil)
1. *Thriller*, Michael Jackson	29.0	16. *Jagged Little Pill*, Alanis Morissette	16.0
Eagles/Their Greatest Hits 1971-1975, Eagles	29.0	*Cracked Rear View*, Hootie & the Blowfish	16.0
3. *Greatest Hits Volume I & Volume II*, Billy Joel	23.0	*Greatest Hits*, Elton John	16.0
Led Zeppelin IV, Led Zeppelin	23.0	*Metallica*, Metallica	16.0
The Wall, Pink Floyd	23.0	*Physical Graffiti*, Led Zeppelin	16.0
6. *Back in Black*, AC/DC	22.0	*Hotel California*, Eagles	16.0
7. *Double Live*, Garth Brooks	21.0	22. *Dark Side of the Moon*, Pink Floyd	15.0
8. *Come on Over*, Shania Twain	20.0	*The Beatles 1962-1966*, The Beatles	15.0
9. *The Beatles*, The Beatles	19.0	*Supernatural*, Santana	15.0
Rumours, Fleetwood Mac	19.0	*Born in the U.S.A.*, Bruce Springsteen	15.0
11. *Appetite for Destruction*, Guns N' Roses	18.0	*Greatest Hits*, Journey	15.0
12. *Boston*, Boston	17.0	*Saturday Night Fever* (soundtrack), Bee Gees	15.0
The Beatles 1967-1970, The Beatles	17.0		
The Bodyguard (soundtrack), Whitney Houston	17.0		
No Fences, Garth Brooks	17.0		

Top-Selling Artists by Digital Sales
Source: Recording Industry Assn. of America (RIAA)
(As of Aug. 31, 2013. Sales figures represent RIAA-confirmed digital units sold.)

Artist	Unit sales (mil)	Artist	Unit sales (mil)	Artist	Unit sales (mil)	Artist	Unit sales (mil)
Taylor Swift	45.0	Lil Wayne	21.0	Drake	13.5	David Guetta	10.5
Rihanna	42.5	Eminem	21.0	Nicki Minaj	13.5	Luke Bryan	10.5
Katy Perry	29.5	Carrie Underwood	21.0	Lady Antebellum	13.0	The Fray	10.5
Lady Gaga	28.5	Jason Aldean	18.5	Kenny Chesney	13.0	Blake Shelton	10.5
Kanye West	25.0	Bruno Mars	18.5	Akon	12.5	Fun.	10.0
Flo Rida	24.5	Beyoncé	18.0	Tim McGraw	12.5	One Republic	10.0
Justin Bieber	24.0	LMFAO	18.0	Train	12.0	Justin Timberlake	10.0
Adele	22.0	Maroon 5	15.0	Jason Derulo	11.0	Miranda Lambert	10.0
The Black Eyed Peas	22.0	Selena Gomez & the Scene	14.0	Linkin Park	11.0	Nelly	10.0
				Toby Keith	10.5	Timbaland	10.0

U.S. Commercial Radio Stations by Format, 2003-13
Source: The Radio Book by Inside Radio © 2013
(ranked by 2013 numbers)

Primary format	2013	2012	2011	2010	2009	2008	2007	2006	2005	2004	2003
1. Country.................	2,042	2,020	1,987	1,997	1,995	2,018	2,027	2,038	2,022	2,047	2,077
2. News/Talk..............	1,453	1,503	1,455	1,437	1,416	1,365	1,368	1,338	1,326	1,287	1,225
3. Spanish.................	835	816	818	806	803	799	786	706	696	665	633
4. Sports..................	740	692	670	665	634	595	564	535	508	472	433
5. Classic Hits............	678	657	657	637	582	524	477	429	271	237	236
6. Adult Contemporary......	605	597	607	634	626	670	665	660	683	696	680
7. Top 40	573	559	523	495	484	472	472	484	503	502	487
8. Oldies..................	566	597	628	637	649	708	709	725	762	811	812
9. Classic Rock............	486	477	477	481	477	474	456	456	461	451	427
10. Hot Adult Contemporary....	428	420	435	417	409	373	373	378	374	420	409
11. Religion (Teaching, Variety)	336	342	332	322	324	299	287	311	319	329	350
12. Rock...................	299	295	301	294	298	287	281	276	269	282	275
13. Adult Standards	227	240	251	265	327	358	369	368	404	458	492
14. Black Gospel	212	214	225	235	242	244	253	267	286	274	268
15. Southern Gospel	172	170	188	197	209	211	204	208	206	204	207
Stations off the air.	237	264	261	253	223	135	92	88	72	81	124
Total operating stations[1] . .	**11,107**	**11,078**	**11,034**	**11,024**	**10,977**	**10,853**	**10,760**	**10,711**	**10,674**	**10,732**	**10,906**

NA = Not available. (1) As of June 2013. Totals include stations that are changing or did not report format, as well as formats not listed here.

Multi-Platinum and Platinum Awards for Recorded Music and Music Videos, 2012-13
Source: Recording Industry Assn. of America (RIAA)

To achieve platinum status, an **album** must reach minimum total sales of 1 mil units in LPs, CDs, and digital with a manufacturer's dollar volume of at least $2 mil based on one-third of the suggested retail list price for each record, CD, or digital copy sold. To achieve multi-platinum status, an album must reach minimum total sales of at least 2 mil units in LPs, CDs, and digital with a manufacturer's dollar volume of at least $4 mil based on one-third of the list price.

Singles must sell 1 mil units to achieve a platinum award and 2 mil to achieve a multi-platinum award. **Digital singles** are certified at the same levels; the digital sales award was first given in 2004. **Music videos** (longform) must sell 100,000 units to qualify for a platinum award and more than 200,000 units for a multi-platinum award.

Awards listed here are for albums, digital singles, and music videos (released Sept. 2011-Aug. 2013) that were certified Sept. 2012-Aug. 2013. Number in parentheses represents millions sold. Alphabetized by artist name.

Albums, Multi-Platinum
Babel, Mumford & Sons (2)
Joyas Prestadas (Pop), Jenni Rivera (2)
Joyas Prestadas (Banda), Jenni Rivera (2)
La Misma Gran Senora, Jenni Rivera (2)
Red, Taylor Swift (2)
The 20/20 Experience, Justin Timberlake (2)

Albums, Platinum
Night Train, Jason Aldean
Independiente, Ricardo Arjona
Stronger, Kelly Clarkson
Here's to the Good Times, Florida Georgia Line
Some Nights, fun.
Hunter Hayes, Hunter Hayes
Night Visions, Imagine Dragons
Magna Carta... Holy Grail, Jay-Z
Tornado, Little Big Town
Overexposed, Maroon 5
Unorthodox Jukebox, Bruno Mars
Take Me Home, One Direction
Truth About Love, Pink
Phase II, Prince Royce
Unapologetic, Rihanna
Ultimate Hits: Rock and Roll Never Forgets, Bob Seger and the Silver Bullet Band
Merry Christmas, Baby, Rod Stewart
El Camino, The Black Keys
The Lumineers, The Lumineers
Trilogy, The Weeknd
Blow Away, Carrie Underwood

Music Videos, Multi-Platinum
Live at the Royal Albert Hall, Adele (10)
Up All Night: The Live Tour, One Direction (5)
Gangnam Style, Psy (5)

Digital Singles, Platinum and Multi-Platinum
"Skyfall," Adele
"Take a Little Ride," Jason Aldean
"Every Storm (Runs out of Rain)," Gary Allan
"F**kin' Problems," ASAP Rocky
"Levels," Avicii
"As Long As You Love Me" (2), "Beauty and a Beat" (2), "Boyfriend" (3), Justin Bieber
"Hard to Love," Lee Brice
"We Run the Night," Havana Brown

"Crash My Party," Luke Bryan
"Cashin' Out," Ca$h Out
"Sweet Nothing," Calvin Harris feat. Florence Welch
"Beautiful," Mariah Carey
"Come Over," Kenny Chesney
"Stronger (What Doesn't Kill You)" (4), Kelly Clarkson
"Get Lucky" (2), Daft Punk
"Started From the Bottom," Drake
"Whistle" (2), Flo Rida
"Shake It Out," Florence and the Machine
"Cruise" (5), "Get Your Shine On," Florida Georgia Line
"Carry On," "Some Nights" (4), fun.
"(Kissed You) Good Night," Gloriana
"Come & Get It" (2), Selena Gomez
"Somebody That I Used to Know" (7), Gotye
"Anything Could Happen," Ellie Goulding
"The Way," Ariana Grande
"Tongue Tied," Grouplove
"The Fighter," Gym Class Heroes feat. Ryan Tedder
"I Want Crazy," Hunter Hayes
"I Love It" (2), Icona Pop
"It's Time," "Radioactive" (2), Imagine Dragons
"Power Trip," J.Cole feat. Miguel
"Call Me Maybe" (9), Carly Rae Jepsen
"Bandz a Make Her Dance," Juicy J feat. Lil Wayne and 2 ChainZ
"Downtown," Lady Antebellum
"Mama's Broken Heart," "Over You," Miranda Lambert
"Here's to Never Growing Up," Avril Lavigne
"Burn It Down," Linkin Park
"Pontoon" (2), Little Big Town
"Want U Back" (2), Cher Lloyd
"Give Your Heart a Break" (2), "Heart Attack" (2), Demi Lovato
"Angel Eyes," Love and Theft
"Cowboys and Angels," Dustin Lynch
"Can't Hold Us," Macklemore and Ryan Lewis feat. Ray Dalton
"Thrift Shop" (5), Macklemore and Ryan Lewis feat. Wanz
"Daylight," "Payphone" (5), Maroon 5
"It Will Rain" (3), "Locked out of Heaven" (3), "When I Was Your Man" (2), Bruno Mars
"Highway Don't Care," Tim McGraw feat. Taylor Swift
"Ready or Not," Bridgit Mendler

"Pound the Alarm," "Starships" (4), Nicki Minaj
"Pop That," French Montana
"I Will Wait" (2), Mumford & Sons
"Madness," Muse
"Everybody Talks" (2), Neon Trees
"Let Me Love You (Until You Learn to Love Yourself)," Ne-Yo
"Thinkin Bout You," Frank Ocean
"Little Talks" (3), Of Monsters and Men
"Troublemaker," Olly Murrs
"Little Things," "Live While We're Young," "One Thing," "What Makes You Beautiful" (4), One Direction
"Good Time" (2), Owl City and Carly Rae Jepsen
"A Thousand Years" (3), Christina Perri
"Gone, Gone, Gone," "Home" (4), Phillip Phillips
"Just Give Me A Reason" (2), Pink feat. Nate Reuss
"Don't Stop the Party," Pitbull
"Feel This Moment," Pitbull feat. Christina Aguilera
"Gangnam Style" (4), Psy
"Birthday Cake," "Diamonds" (2), "Stay," "We Found Love" (7), Rihanna
"Wagon Wheel" (2), Darius Rucker
"Next to Me," Emeli Sande
"The A-Team," Ed Sheeran
"Sure Be Cool If You Did," Blake Shelton
"Young, Wild & Free" (3), Snoop Dogg and Wiz Khalifa
"Don't You Worry Child" (2), Swedish House Mafia
"Begin Again," "Eyes Open," "I Knew You Were Trouble" (4), "Red," "22," "We Are Never Getting Back Together" (4), Taylor Swift
"Better Dig Two," The Band Perry
"Lonely Boy," The Black Keys
"Ho Hey," The Lumineers
"Hall of Fame" (2), The Script feat. will.i.am
"Mirrors" (2), "Suit & Tie" (2), Justin Timberlake
"Drive By" (3), Train
"Faded," Tyga
"Blown Away" (2), Carrie Underwood
"Scream," Usher
"Clique," "Mercy" (2), Kanye West
"Scream & Shout" (3), will.i.am
"Clarity," Zedd

Top-Grossing North American Concert Tours, 1985-2012

Source: Pollstar

Rank Artist (year)	Total gross[1]	Cities/ shows	Rank Artist (year)	Total gross[1]	Cities/ shows
1. The Rolling Stones (2005)	$162.0	38/42	14. Pink Floyd (1994)	$103.5	39/59
2. U2 (2011)	156.0	21/25	15. Paul McCartney (2002)	103.3	43/53
3. U2 (2005)	138.9	43/78	16. The Rolling Stones (1989)	98.0	33/60
4. The Rolling Stones (2006)	138.5	35/39	17. Taylor Swift (2011)	97.7	59/80
5. Madonna (2012)	133.7	31/45	18. Kenny Chesney and Tim McGraw		
6. The Police (2007)	133.2	41/54	(2012)	96.5	22/23
7. U2 (2009)	123.0	16/20	19. Bruce Springsteen & The E Street		
8. The Rolling Stones (1994)	121.2	43/60	Band (2009)	94.5	44/58
9. Bruce Springsteen & The E Street			20. Céline Dion (2008)	94.0	31/47
Band (2003)	115.9	30/47	21. Barbra Streisand (2006)	92.5	16/20
10. U2 (2001)	109.7	56/80	22. Roger Waters (2012)	90.2	38/42
11. Bon Jovi (2010)	108.2	38/51	23. Roger Waters (2010)	89.5	36/56
12. Madonna (2008)	105.3	19/30	24. The Rolling Stones (1997)	89.3	26/33
13. Bruce Springsteen & The E Street			25. Tim McGraw and Faith Hill (2006)	88.8	55/73
Band (2012)	104.7	42/52			

(1) In millions. Not adjusted for inflation.

Sales of Recorded Music and Music Videos, by Units Shipped and Value, 2000-12

Source: Recording Industry Assn. of America

(in millions, net after returns)

	2000	2005	2007	2008	2009	2010	2011	2012	% change, 2011-12
Physical units shipped...	1,079.2	748.7	543.9	385.5	309.2	233.0	222.0	182.9	-17.6%
Dollar value ...	$14,323.7	11,195.0	7,985.8	5,758.5	4,555.9	3,438.7	3,170.9	2,584.3	-18.5
Compact discs (CDs) ...	942.5	705.4	511.1	368.4	292.9	253.0	240.8	210.9	-12.4
Dollar value ...	$13,214.5	10,520.2	7,452.3	5,471.3	4,274.1	3,389.4	3,100.7	2,532.0	-18.3
Cassettes ...	76.0	2.5	0.4	0.1	—	—	—	—	—
Dollar value ...	$626.0	13.1	3.0	0.9	—	—	—	—	—
LP/EP ...	2.2	1.0	1.3	2.9	3.2	4.2	5.5	7.1	28.8
Dollar value ...	$27.7	14.2	22.9	56.7	60.2	88.9	119.4	162.6	36.2
CD singles ...	34.2	2.8	2.6	0.7	0.9	1.0	1.3	1.1	-16.2
Dollar value ...	$142.7	10.9	12.2	3.5	3.1	2.9	3.5	3.2	-7.6
Vinyl singles ...	4.8	2.3	0.6	0.4	0.3	0.3	0.4	0.4	6.6
Dollar value ...	$26.3	13.2	4.0	2.9	2.5	2.3	4.6	4.7	3.3
Music videos[1] ...	18.2	33.8	27.5	12.8	11.8	9.1	7.7	6.2	-19.2
Dollar value ...	$281.0	602.2	484.9	218.9	212.0	177.6	151.0	118.2	-21.7
Digital formats[2] ...	—	383.1	868.4	1,128.6	1,236.8	1,283.4	1,454.7	1,521.4	11.3
Dollar value ...	—	$503.6	1,257.5	1,711.5	2,030.7	2,232.9	2,628.3	2,849.9	17.3
Download albums ...	—	13.6	42.5	63.6	76.4	85.8	103.9	116.7	12.3
Dollar value ...	—	$135.7	424.9	635.3	763.4	872.4	1,070.8	1,204.8	12.5
Download singles ...	—	366.9	809.9	1,042.7	1,138.3	1,177.4	1,332.3	1,392.2	4.5
Dollar value ...	—	$363.3	801.6	1,032.2	1,220.3	1,317.4	1,522.4	1,623.6	6.7
Music videos ...	—	1.9	14.2	20.8	20.4	18.4	16.3	10.5	-35.6
Dollar value ...	—	$3.7	28.2	41.3	40.6	36.6	32.4	20.8	-35.6
Mobile formats[3] ...	—	170.0	362.0	405.1	305.8	188.5	115.4	69.3	-40.0
Dollar value ...	—	$421.6	880.8	977.1	728.8	448.0	276.2	166.9	-39.6
Subscription formats[4] ...	—	1.3	1.8	1.6	1.2	1.5	1.8	3.4	86.3
Dollar value ...	—	$149.2	201.3	221.4	213.1	212.4	359.2	570.8	58.9
Digital performances[5] ...	—	27.4	47.0	100.0	155.5	249.2	292.0	462.0	58.2
Total units[6] ...	1,079.2	1,301.8	1,774.3	1,919.2	1,851.8	1,739.6	1,824.9	1,816.5	-0.5
Total value ...	$14,323.7	12,296.9	10,372.1	8,768.4	7,683.9	6,995.0	7,133.1	7,065.5	-0.9

— = Not available or not applicable. (1) Includes DVD videos. (2) Includes kiosk singles and albums. (3) Includes master ringtones, ringbacks, music videos, full-length downloads, and other mobile music. (4) Weighted annual average. (5) Estimated royalty payments in dollars to artists and copyright holders distributed by SoundExchange. (6) Includes albums and singles; excludes subscriptions and royalties.

Top Cable TV Networks, 2012

Source: SNL Kagan

Rank	Network (year began)	Subscribers (mil)	Rank	Network (year began)	Subscribers (mil)
1.	The Weather Channel (1982)	99.9	11.	USA Network (1980)	99.0
2.	C-SPAN (1979)	99.8	12.	CNN (1980)	98.9
3.	A&E (1984)	99.7		AMC (1984)	98.9
	TBS (1976)	99.7		Cartoon Network (1992)	98.9
	TNT (1988)	99.7	15.	HGTV (1994)	98.7
6.	Lifetime Television (1984)	99.5		HLN (1982)	98.7
7.	Food Network (1993)	99.4	17.	History (1995)	98.6
8.	Disney Channel (1983)	99.3	18.	ESPN (1979)	98.5
9.	Nickelodeon/Nick At Nite (1979)	99.2		TLC (1980)	98.5
10.	Discovery Channel (1985)	99.1		ESPN2 (1993)	98.5

U.S. Television Set Owners, 2013

Source: Nielsen Media Research, July 2013

Of the 114.2 mil U.S. households that owned at least one TV set in 2013:

84.9% had 2 or more TV sets	51.1% had a VCR	90.5% received basic cable
33.6% had 4 or more TV sets	82.5% had a DVD player	47.6% received premium cable

U.S. Households With Cable Television, 1979-2013
Source: Nielsen Media Research

Year[1]	Subscribers[2] (mil)	As % of households with TVs	Year[1]	Subscribers[2] (mil)	As % of households with TVs	Year[1]	Subscribers[2] (mil)	As % of households with TVs
1979	14.9	19.4%	1991	56.1	60.3%	2002	87.8	83.8%
1980	17.7	22.6	1992	56.2	61.1	2003	88.4	82.9
1981	23.2	28.3	1993	57.6	61.9	2004	92.4	85.3
1982	27.4	33.4	1994	59.7	63.4	2005	94.0	85.7
1983	31.8	37.9	1995	62.1	65.1	2006	95.0	86.2
1984	35.8	42.5	1996	63.6	66.3	2007	94.5	83.8
1985	38.7	45.3	1997	65.1	67.2	2008	99.7	88.2
1986	40.9	47.4	1998	65.9	67.2	2009	103.0	89.7
1987	43.3	49.2	1999	76.4	76.9	2010	104.1	90.6
1988	46.3	52.0	2000	78.6	77.9	2011	104.8	90.4
1989	50.2	55.6	2001	81.5	79.8	2012	103.6	90.3
1990	53.9	58.6				2013	103.3	90.5

(1) After 1998, figures include wired-cable households as well as households that receive TV programming via alternate delivery systems (including satellite receivers, SMATV, MMDS). (2) Households that subscribe to basic cable service.

Selected Reality TV Show Winners, 2000-13
Numbers in parentheses represent the season, edition, or cycle of the show. As of Sept. 2013.

The Amazing Race. Debuted Aug. 2001 on CBS. Rob Frisbee & Brennan Swain (1); Chris Luca & Alex Boylan (2); Flo Pesenti & Zach Behr (3); Reichen Lehmkuhl & Chip Arndt (4); Chip & Kim McAllister (5); Freddy Holliday & Kendra Bentley (6); Uchenna & Joyce Agu (7); The Linz Family (8); B. J. Averell & Tyler MacNiven (9); Tyler Denk & James Branaman (10); All-Stars: Eric Sanchez & Danielle Turner (11); TK Erwin & Rachel Morales (12); Nick & Starr Spangler (13); Tammy & Victor Jih (14); Meghan Rickey & Cheyne Whitney (15); Dan & Jordan Pious (16); Natalie Strand & Katherine Chang (17); LaKisha & Jennifer Hoffman (18); Ernie Halvorsen & Cindy Chiang (19); Rachel Brown & Dave Brown Jr. (20); Josh Kilmer-Purcell & Brent Ridge (21); Bates & Anthony Battaglia (22).

American Idol. Debuted July 2002 on Fox. Kelly Clarkson (1); Ruben Studdard (2); Fantasia Barrino (3); Carrie Underwood (4); Taylor Hicks (5); Jordin Sparks (6); David Cook (7); Kris Allen (8); Lee DeWyze (9); Scotty McCreery (10); Phillip Phillips (11); Candice Glover (12).

America's Got Talent. Debuted June 2006 on NBC. Bianca Ryan (1); Terry Fator (2); Neil E. Boyd (3); Kevin Skinner (4); Michael Grimm (5); Landau Eugene Murphy Jr. (6); Olate Dogs (7); Kenichi Ebina (8).

America's Next Top Model. Debuted May 2003 on UPN. Adrianne Curry (1); Yoanna House (2); Eva Pigford (3); Naima Mora (4); Nicole Linkletter (5); Danielle Evans (6); CariDee English (7); Jaslene Gonzalez (8); Saleisha Stowers (9); Whitney Thompson (10); McKey Sullivan (11); Teyona Anderson (12); Nicole Fox (13); Krista White (14); Ann Ward (15); Brittani Kline (16); Lisa D'Amato (17); Sophie Sumner (18); Laura James (19).

The Apprentice. Debuted Jan. 2004 on NBC. Bill Rancic (1); Kelly Perdew (2); Kendra Todd (3); Randal Pinkett (4); Sean Yazbeck (5); Stefani Schaeffer (6); Brandy Kuentzel (7). *Celebrity Apprentice:* Piers Morgan (1); Joan Rivers (2); Bret Michaels (3); John Rich (4); Arsenio Hall (5); Trace Adkins (6).

The Bachelor. Debuted Mar. 2002 on ABC. Alex Michel chose Amanda Marsh (1); Aaron Buerge chose Helene Eksterowicz (2); Andrew Firestone chose Jen Schefft (3); Bob Guiney chose Estella Gardinier (4); Jesse Palmer chose Jessica Bowlin (5); Byron Velvick chose Mary Delgado (6); Charlie O'Connell chose Sarah Brice (7); Travis Stork chose Sarah Stone (8); Lorenzo Borghese chose Jennifer Wilson (9); Andy Baldwin chose Tessa Horst (10); Brad Womack chose no one (11); Matt Grant chose Shayne Lamas (12); Jason Mesnick chose Melissa Rycroft (13); Jake Pavelka chose Vienna Girardi (14); Brad Womack chose Emily Maynard (15); Ben Flajnik chose Courtney Robertson (16); Sean Lowe chose Catherine Giudici (17).

The Bachelorette. Debuted Jan. 2003 on ABC. Trista Rehn chose Ryan Sutter (1); Meredith Phillips chose Ian McKee (2); Jen Schefft chose Jerry Ferris (3); DeAnna Pappas chose Jesse Csincsak (4); Jillian Harris chose Ed Swiderski (5); Ali Fedotowsky chose Roberto Martinez (6); Ashley Hebert chose J. P. Rosenbaum (7); Emily Maynard chose Jef Holm (8); Desiree Hartsock chose Chris Siegfried (9).

The Biggest Loser. Debuted Oct. 2004 on NBC. Ryan Benson (1); Matt Hoover (2); Erik Chopin (3); Bill Germanakos (4); Ali Vincent (5); Michelle Aguilar (6); Helen Phillips (7); Danny Cahill (8); Michael Ventrella (9); Patrick House (10);

Olivia Ward (11); John Rhode (12); Jeremy Britt (13); Danni Allen (14).

Big Brother. Debuted July 2000 on CBS. Eddie McGee (1); Will Kirby (2); Lisa Donahue (3); Jun Song (4); Drew Daniel (5); Maggie Ausburn (6); Mike Malinto (7); Dick Donato (8); Adam Jasinski (9); Dan Gheesling (10); Jordan Lloyd (11); Hayden Moss (12); Rachel Reilly (13); Ian Terry (14); Andy Herren (15).

Dancing With the Stars. Debuted June 2005 on ABC. Kelly Monaco & Alex Mazo (1); Drew Lachey & Cheryl Burke (2); Emmitt Smith & Cheryl Burke (3); Apolo Anton Ohno & Julianne Hough (4); Helio Castroneves & Julianne Hough (5); Kristi Yamaguchi & Mark Ballas (6); Brooke Burke & Derek Hough (7); Shawn Johnson & Mark Ballas (8); Donny Osmond & Kym Johnson (9); Nicole Scherzinger & Derek Hough (10); Jennifer Grey & Derek Hough (11); Hines Ward & Kym Johnson (12); J.R. Martinez & Karina Smirnoff (13); Donald Driver & Peta Murgatroyd (14). All-Stars: Melissa Rycroft & Tony Dovolani.

Food Network Star. Debuted June 2005 on Food Network. Steve McDonagh & Dan Smith (1); Guy Fieri (2); Amy Finley (3); Aaron McCargo Jr. (4); Melissa d'Arabian (5); Aarti Sequeria (6); Jeff Mauro (7); Justin Warner (8); Damaris Phillips (9).

Hell's Kitchen. Debuted Mar. 2005 on FOX. Michael Wray (1); Heather West (2); Rock Harper (3); Christina Machamer (4); Danny Veltri (5); Dave Levey (6); Holli Ugalde (7); Nona Sivley (8); Paul Niedermann (9); Christina Wilson (10); Ja'Nel Witt (11).

Project Runway. Debuted Dec. 2004 on Bravo. Jay McCarroll (1); Chloe Dao (2); Jeffrey Sebelia (3); Christian Siriano (4); Leanne Marshall (5); Irina Shabayeva (6); Seth Aaron Henderson (7); Gretchen Jones (8); Anya Ayoung-Chee (9); Dmitry Sholokhov (10); Michelle Lesniak Franklin (11); Dom Streater (12). All-Stars: Mondo Guerra (1); Anthony Ryan Auld (2).

So You Think You Can Dance. Debuted July 2005 on FOX. Nick Lazzarini (1); Benji Schwimmer (2); Sabra Johnson (3); Joshua Allen (4); Jeanine Mason (5); Russell Ferguson (6); Lauren Froderman (7); Melanie Moore (8); Eliana Girard & Chehon Wespi-Tschopp (9); DuShaunt "Fik-Shun" Stegall & Amy Yakima (10).

Survivor. Debuted May 2000 on CBS. Borneo: Richard Hatch (1); Outback: Tina Wesson (2); Africa: Ethan Zohn (3); Marquesas: Vecepia Towery (4); Thailand: Brian Heidik (5); The Amazon: Jenna Morasca (6); Pearl Islands: Sandra Diaz-Twine (7); All-Stars, Panama: Amber Brkich (8); Vanuatu: Chris Daugherty (9); Palau: Tom Westman (10); Guatemala: Danni Boatwright (11); Panama: Aras Baskauskas (12); Cook Islands: Yul Kwon (13); Fiji: Earl Cole (14); China: Todd Herzog (15); Micronesia: Parvati Shallow (16); Gabon: Robert Crowley (17); Tocantins: James "JT" Thomas (18); Samoa: Natalie White (19); Heroes vs. Villains: Sandra Diaz-Twine (20); Nicaragua: Jud Birza (21); Redemption Island: Rob Mariano (22); South Pacific: Sophie Clarke (23); One World: Kim Spradlin (24); Philippines: Denise Stapley (25); Caramoan—Fans vs. Favorites: John Cochran (26).

Top Chef. Debuted Mar. 2006 on Bravo. Harold Dieterle (1); Ilan Hall (2); Hung Huynh (3); Stephanie Izard (4); Hosea Rosenberg (5); Michael Voltaggio (6); Kevin Sbraga (7); Richard Blais (8); Paul Qui (9); Kristen Kish (10). *Top Chef Masters:* Rick Bayless (1); Marcus Samuelsson (2); Floyd Cardoz (3); Chris Cosentino (4); Douglas Keane (5).

The Voice. Debuted Apr. 2011 on NBC. Javier Colon (1); Jermaine Paul (2); Cassadee Pope (3); Danielle Bradbery (4).

Average U.S. Television Viewing Time, 2012-13
Source: Nielsen Media Research (hours:minutes per week)

Group	Age	Total per week	M-F 7-10 AM	M-F 10 AM-4 PM	M-Sun. 8-11 PM	M-F 11:30 PM-1 AM	Sat. 7 AM-1 PM	Sun. 1-7 PM
Men	18+	34:47	2:02	4:33	8:24	1:44	1:02	1:54
	18-24	21:36	1:00	3:02	4:33	1:20	0:33	1:06
	25-54	32:07	1:46	3:48	7:51	1:45	0:59	1:47
	55+	44:35	2:54	6:25	10:52	1:50	1:18	2:25
Women	18+	39:46	2:37	6:05	9:18	1:55	1:09	1:49
	18-24	25:30	1:19	4:11	5:25	1:27	0:39	1:07
	25-54	36:00	2:22	5:05	8:32	1:53	1:04	1:40
	55+	50:10	3:26	8:09	11:44	2:08	1:25	2:16
Children	2-11	25:19	1:48	4:08	5:10	0:50	1:12	1:18
Teens	12-17	22:14	0:58	2:34	5:13	1:07	0:44	1:10
All viewers		34:28	2:09	4:57	8:03	1:38	1:04	1:43

Note: For viewing period Sept. 24, 2012-Aug. 4, 2013. Includes DVR playback.

Favorite Prime-Time Television Programs, 2012-13
Source: Nielsen Media Research

Data are for regularly scheduled network programs Sept. 24, 2012-Aug. 4, 2013. Ranked by average audience percentages, or ratings, which are estimates of the percentage of all TV-owning households watching a particular program live or on DVR within seven days of broadcast. Audience share percentages are estimates of the percentage of those watching TV at a certain time that are tuned in to a particular program.

Rank	Program, network	Avg. audience	Audience share	Rank	Program, network	Avg. audience	Audience share
1.	NCIS, CBS	11.4%	18%	25.	CSI, CBS	6.9%	12%
2.	The Big Bang Theory, CBS	10.1	17	26.	Survivor: Caramoan, CBS	6.7	11
3.	Dancing With the Stars, ABC	9.9	15	27.	Revolution, NBC	6.6	11
4.	Under the Dome, CBS	9.7	16	28.	Golden Boy, CBS	6.5	11
5.	NCIS: Los Angeles, CBS	9.4	14	29.	Hawaii Five-0, CBS	6.5	11
6.	Dancing With the Stars-Results, ABC	9.2	14	30.	Modern Family, ABC	6.5	10
7.	American Idol-Wednesday, FOX	9.2	14	31.	The Amazing Race 21, CBS	6.5	10
8.	Person of Interest, CBS	9.0	14	32.	The Bachelor, ABC	6.3	9
9.	American Idol-Thursday, FOX	8.9	14	33.	The Mentalist, CBS	6.3	11
10.	The Voice, NBC	8.6	13	34.	The Good Wife, CBS	6.3	10
11.	The Voice-Results, NBC	8.4	13	35.	Once Upon a Time, ABC	6.2	9
12.	Grey's Anatomy, ABC	7.8	12	36.	The Amazing Race 22, CBS	6.0	9
13.	Vegas, CBS	7.7	13	37.	Revenge, ABC	6.0	9
14.	Two and a Half Men, CBS	7.7	12	38.	Scandal, ABC	6.0	10
15.	America's Got Talent-Tuesday, NBC	7.5	12	39.	2 Broke Girls, CBS	6.0	9
16.	America's Got Talent-Wednesday, NBC	7.4	12	40.	Mike & Molly, CBS	5.9	9
17.	60 Minutes, CBS	7.4	12	41.	Bones, FOX	5.9	9
18.	The Following, FOX	7.3	11	42.	X Factor-Wednesday, FOX	5.8	9
19.	Survivor: Philippines, CBS	7.3	11	43.	Body of Proof, ABC	5.8	10
20.	CSI: NY, CBS	7.3	12	44.	X Factor-Thursday, FOX	5.7	9
21.	Criminal Minds, CBS	7.2	11	45.	Unforgettable, CBS	5.7	9
22.	Blue Bloods, CBS	7.2	13	46.	Made in Jersey, CBS	5.4	9
23.	Elementary, CBS	7.1	12	47.	The Bachelorette, ABC	5.3	9
24.	Castle, ABC	7.0	11	48.	60 Minutes Presents, CBS	5.2	9
				49.	Glee, FOX	5.2	8
				50.	Last Resort, ABC	5.1	8

Favorite Syndicated Programs, 2012-13
Source: Nielsen Media Research

Average audience percentages, or ratings, are estimates of the percentage of TV-owning households watching a program live or on DVR within seven days of broadcast, Sept. 24, 2012-Aug. 4, 2013.

Rank	Program	Avg. audience	Rank	Program	Avg. audience
1.	The Big Bang Theory	7.1%	14.	Dr. Phil	3.0%
2.	Judge Judy	7.1	15.	Inside Edition	3.0
3.	Wheel of Fortune	6.8	16.	Wheel of Fortune (weekend)	3.0
4.	Jeopardy	6.2	17.	Law & Order	2.9
5.	The Big Bang Theory (weekend B)	5.4	18.	Law & Order: Criminal Intent	2.7
6.	Two and a Half Men	4.9	19.	How I Met Your Mother	2.6
7.	The Big Bang Theory (weekend A)	4.9	20.	Criminal Minds	2.6
8.	Litton's Weekend Adventure	4.8	21.	Live With Kelly & Michael	2.6
9.	Family Feud	4.7	22.	The Ellen DeGeneres Show	2.5
10.	Law & Order: Special Victims Unit	3.7	23.	House	2.4
11.	Family Guy (weekend)	3.7	24.	Castle	2.4
12.	Family Guy	3.6	25.	CSI: Miami	2.4
13.	Entertainment Tonight	3.6			

Favorite Basic Cable Programs, 2012-13

Source: Nielsen Media Research

Data are for regularly scheduled basic cable programs Sept. 24, 2012-Aug. 4, 2013; excludes children's series, miniseries, movies, and news events. Average audience percentages, or ratings, are estimates of the percentage of TV-owning households watching a program live or on DVR within seven days of broadcast. The highest-rated cable program for the period was Discovery Channel's special *Skywire: Live With Nik Wallenda* with a 4.6% average audience.

Rank	Program, channel	Avg. audience	Rank	Program, channel	Avg. audience
1.	Walking Dead, AMC	1.6%	16.	Mountain Men, History	0.9%
2.	Major Crimes, TNT	1.5	17.	Dallas, TNT	0.9
3.	Rizzoli & Isles, TNT	1.4	18.	Necessary Roughness, USA	0.9
4.	King & Maxwell, TNT	1.4	19.	The Americans, FX	0.9
5.	Talking Dead, AMC	1.3	20.	Pawn Stars, History	0.9
6.	Sons of Anarchy, FX	1.3	21.	Longmire, A&E	0.9
7.	Royal Pains, USA	1.2	22.	Graceland, USA	0.9
8.	White Collar, USA	1.1	23.	The Vikings, A&E	0.9
9.	Army Wives, Lifetime	1.1	24.	The Glades, A&E	0.8
10.	Covert Affairs, USA	1.1	25.	American Pickers, History	0.8
11.	Perception, TNT	1.0	26.	Teen Mom II, MTV	0.8
12.	Duck Dynasty, A&E	1.0	27.	American Horror Story, FX	0.8
13.	Suits, USA	1.0	28.	The Client List, Lifetime	0.8
14.	Psych, USA	1.0	29.	Sister Wives, TLC	0.8
15.	Falling Skies, TNT	1.0	30.	Burn Notice, USA	0.7

Favorite Premium Cable Programs, 2011-13

Source: Nielsen Media Research

Average audience percentages, or ratings, are estimates of the percentage of TV-owning households watching a program live or on DVR within seven days of broadcast, Sept. 24, 2012-Aug. 4, 2013.

Highest-Rated Series

Rank	Program, channel	Avg. audience
1.	Game of Thrones, HBO	3.8%
2.	True Blood, HBO	3.6
3.	Dexter, Showtime	2.2
4.	Boardwalk Empire, HBO	2.0
5.	Homeland, Showtime	2.0
6.	The Newsroom, HBO	1.9
7.	Ray Donovan, Showtime	1.6
8.	Shameless, Showtime	1.5
9.	Real Time With Bill Maher, HBO	1.2
10.	Veep, HBO	1.0
11.	House of Lies, Showtime	0.9
12.	Californication, Showtime	0.8
13.	Nurse Jackie, Showtime	0.8
14.	Girls, HBO	0.7
15.	The Borgias, Showtime	0.6
16.	Magic City, STARZ	0.6
17.	Vice, HBO	0.6

Highest-Rated Movies

Rank	Program, channel	Avg. audience
1.	Ted, HBO	0.6%
2.	Rise of the Guardians, HBO	0.6
3.	The Bourne Legacy, HBO	0.5
4.	The Dark Knight Rises, HBO	0.5
5.	Pitch Perfect, HBO	0.4
6.	Abraham Lincoln: Vampire Hunter, HBO	0.4
7.	Battleship, HBO	0.4
8.	Prometheus, HBO	0.4
9.	Savages, HBO	0.4
10.	Snow White and the Huntsman, HBO	0.4
11.	Behind the Candelabra, HBO	0.4
12.	The Watch, HBO	0.3
13.	American Reunion, HBO	0.3
14.	The Day After Tomorrow, HBO	0.3
15.	Safe House, HBO	0.3

All-Time Most Watched Television Programs

Source: Nielsen Media Research, Jan. 1961-Aug. 2013

Estimates exclude unsponsored or joint network telecasts (e.g., presidential addresses) or programs under 30 minutes long. Ranked by number of TV-owning households tuned in to the program. (Rating is percentage of all TV-owning households tuned in.)

Rank	Program	Telecast date	Network	Rating	Avg. audience (thous.)
1.	Super Bowl XLVI	2/5/2012	NBC	47.0%	53,910
2.	Super Bowl XLV	2/6/2011	FOX	46.1	53,435
3.	Super Bowl XLVII	2/3/2013	CBS	46.7	53,363
4.	Super Bowl XLIV	2/7/2010	CBS	45.2	51,873
5.	Super Bowl XLVII Delay	2/3/2013	CBS	44.5	50,861
6.	M*A*S*H (last episode)	2/28/1983	CBS	60.2	50,150
7.	Super Bowl XLII	2/3/2008	FOX	43.2	48,721
8.	Super Bowl XLIII	2/1/2009	NBC	42.0	48,139
9.	Super Bowl XLI	2/4/2007	CBS	42.7	47,535
10.	Super Bowl XL	2/5/2006	ABC	41.6	45,869
11.	XVII Winter Olympics (Women's figure skating)	2/23/1994	CBS	48.5	45,690
12.	Super Bowl XXXIX	2/6/2005	FOX	41.1	45,080
13.	Super Bowl XXXVIII	2/1/2004	CBS	41.4	44,910
14.	Super Bowl XXX	1/28/1996	NBC	46.0	44,150
15.	Super Bowl XXXII	1/25/1998	NBC	44.5	43,630
16.	Super Bowl XXXIV	1/30/2000	ABC	43.3	43,620
17.	Super Bowl XXXVII	1/26/2003	ABC	40.7	43,430
18.	Super Bowl XXVIII	1/30/1994	NBC	45.5	42,860
19.	Super Bowl XXXVI	2/3/2002	FOX	40.4	42,660
20.	Cheers (last episode)	5/20/1993	NBC	45.5	42,360
21.	Super Bowl XXXI	1/26/1997	FOX	43.3	42,000
22.	Super Bowl XXVII	1/31/1993	NBC	45.1	41,990

Highest-Rated Television Programs by Season, 1950-2013

Source: Nielsen Media Research; regular series programs, Sept.-May season

Rating is percentage of TV-owning households tuned in to the program. Data prior to 1988-89 exclude Alaska and Hawaii.

Season	Program	Rating	TV-owning households (thous.)	Season	Program	Rating	TV-owning households (thous.)
1950-51	Texaco Star Theatre	61.6%	10,320	1981-82	Dallas	28.4%	81,500
1951-52	Godfrey's Talent Scouts	53.8	15,300	1982-83	60 Minutes	25.5	83,300
1952-53	I Love Lucy	67.3	20,400	1983-84	Dallas	25.7	83,800
1953-54	I Love Lucy	58.8	26,000	1984-85	Dynasty	25.0	84,900
1954-55	I Love Lucy	49.3	30,700	1985-86	Cosby Show	33.8	85,900
1955-56	$64,000 Question	47.5	34,900	1986-87	Cosby Show	34.9	87,400
1956-57	I Love Lucy	43.7	38,900	1987-88	Cosby Show	27.8	88,600
1957-58	Gunsmoke	43.1	41,920	1988-89	Roseanne	25.5	90,400
1958-59	Gunsmoke	39.6	43,950	1989-90	Roseanne	23.4	92,100
1959-60	Gunsmoke	40.3	45,750	1990-91	Cheers	21.6	93,100
1960-61	Gunsmoke	37.3	47,200	1991-92	60 Minutes	21.7	92,100
1961-62	Wagon Train	32.1	48,555	1992-93	60 Minutes	21.6	93,100
1962-63	Beverly Hillbillies	36.0	50,300	1993-94	Home Improvement	21.9	94,200
1963-64	Beverly Hillbillies	39.1	51,600	1994-95	Seinfeld	20.5	95,400
1964-65	Bonanza	36.3	52,700	1995-96	E.R.	22.0	95,900
1965-66	Bonanza	31.8	53,850	1996-97	E.R.	21.2	97,000
1966-67	Bonanza	29.1	55,130	1997-98	Seinfeld	22.0	98,000
1967-68	Andy Griffith	27.6	56,670	1998-99	E.R.	17.8	99,400
1968-69	Rowan & Martin's Laugh-In	31.8	58,250	1999-2000	Who Wants to Be a Millionaire	18.6	100,800
1969-70	Rowan & Martin's Laugh-In	26.3	58,500	2000-01	Survivor II	17.4	102,200
1970-71	Marcus Welby, M.D.	29.6	60,100	2001-02	Friends	15.3	105,500
1971-72	All in the Family	34.0	62,100	2002-03	CSI	16.1	106,700
1972-73	All in the Family	33.3	64,800	2003-04	CSI	15.9	108,400
1973-74	All in the Family	31.2	66,200	2004-05	CSI	16.3	106,900
1974-75	All in the Family	30.2	68,500	2005-06	American Idol-Tuesday	17.6	110,200
1975-76	All in the Family	30.1	69,600	2006-07	American Idol-Wednesday	17.3	112,800
1976-77	Happy Days	31.5	71,200	2007-08	American Idol-Tuesday	16.1	113,050
1977-78	Laverne & Shirley	31.6	72,900	2008-09	American Idol-Wednesday	15.1	114,900
1978-79	Laverne & Shirley	30.5	74,500	2009-10	American Idol-Tuesday	13.7	114,900
1979-80	60 Minutes	28.2	76,300	2010-11	American Idol-Wednesday	14.5	115,900
1980-81	Dallas	31.2	79,900	2011-12	Dancing With the Stars	12.0	114,700
				2012-13	NCIS	11.4	114,200

All-Time Highest-Rated Television Programs

Source: Nielsen Media Research, Jan. 1961-Aug. 2013

Estimates exclude unsponsored or joint network telecasts (e.g., presidential addresses) and programs under 30 minutes long. Ranked by rating (percentage of TV-owning households tuned in to the program). Average audience is number of TV-owning households tuned in.

Rank	Program	Telecast date	Network	Rating	Avg. audience (thous.)
1.	M*A*S*H (last episode)	2/28/1983	CBS	60.2%	50,150
2.	Dallas ("Who Shot J.R.?" episode)	11/21/1980	CBS	53.3	41,470
3.	Roots-Pt. 8	1/30/1977	ABC	51.1	36,380
4.	Super Bowl XVI	1/24/1982	CBS	49.1	40,020
5.	Super Bowl XVII	1/30/1983	NBC	48.6	40,480
6.	XVII Winter Olympics (Women's figure skating)	2/23/1994	CBS	48.5	45,690
7.	Super Bowl XX	1/26/1986	NBC	48.3	41,490
8.	Gone With the Wind-Pt. 1	11/7/1976	NBC	47.7	33,960
9.	Gone With the Wind-Pt. 2	11/8/1976	NBC	47.4	33,750
10.	Super Bowl XII	1/15/1978	CBS	47.2	34,410
11.	Super Bowl XIII	1/21/1979	NBC	47.1	35,090
12.	Super Bowl XLVI	2/5/2012	NBC	47.0	53,910
13.	Super Bowl XLVII	2/3/2013	CBS	46.7	53,363
14.	Bob Hope Christmas Show	1/15/1970	NBC	46.6	27,260
15.	Super Bowl XIX	1/20/1985	ABC	46.4	39,390
16.	Super Bowl XVIII	1/22/1984	CBS	46.4	38,880
17.	Super Bowl XIV	1/20/1980	CBS	46.3	35,330
18.	Super Bowl XLV	2/6/2011	FOX	46.1	53,435
19.	Super Bowl XXX	1/28/1996	NBC	46.0	44,150
20.	ABC Theater ("The Day After")	11/20/1983	ABC	46.0	38,550
21.	Roots-Pt. 6	1/28/1977	ABC	45.9	32,680
22.	The Fugitive (last episode)	8/29/1967	ABC	45.9	25,700
23.	Super Bowl XXI	1/25/1987	CBS	45.8	40,030
24.	Roots-Pt. 5	1/27/1977	ABC	45.7	32,540
25.	Super Bowl XXVIII	1/30/1994	NBC	45.5	42,860
26.	Cheers (last episode)	5/20/1993	NBC	45.5	42,360
27.	The Ed Sullivan Show (First live U.S. TV appearance of The Beatles.)	2/9/1964	CBS	45.3	23,240

AWARDS — MEDALS — PRIZES

Alfred B. Nobel Prizes, 1901-2013

Alfred B. Nobel (1833-96) bequeathed $9 mil, the interest on which was to be distributed yearly to those judged to have most benefited humankind in chemistry, literature, promotion of peace, physics, and physiology or medicine. Prizes were first awarded in 1901. The prize in economics, funded by Sweden's central bank, was first awarded in 1969. Each prize is now worth 8 mil Swedish krona (about $1.2 mil). If year is omitted, no award was given. The Royal Swedish Academy selects prize winners for chemistry, economics, and physics; the Nobel Assembly at Karolinska Institutet, physiology or medicine; the Swedish Academy, literature; and the Norwegian Nobel Committee, the peace prize. The 2013 Nobel Prizes were announced Oct. 7-14. Winners sharing a prize are generally listed in alphabetical order, except when the awarding body has given a larger proportion of a shared prize to one or more recipients.

Nobel Prizes, 2013

Chemistry: Martin Karplus, Austria-U.S.; Michael Levitt, S. Afr.-U.S.; and Arieh Warshel, Isr.-U.S. shared the prize for developing computer programs and models that allow researchers to study molecules virtually.

Economics: Americans Eugene F. Fama, Lars Peter Hansen, and Robert J. Shiller "for their empirical analysis of asset prices."

Literature: Canadian Alice Munro, whose work focuses on ordinary lives and relationships in narratives in which time is not always linear, won the prize as the "master of the contemporary short story."

Peace: The Hague-based Organization for the Prohibition of Chemical Weapons (OPCW) "for its extensive efforts to eliminate chemical weapons."

Physics: Belgium's François Englert and the UK's Peter W. Higgs for separately theorizing what became known as the Higgs field, an invisible ocean of energy; its existence was confirmed by the discovery of the fundamental particle, the Higgs boson, in 2012. (Englert worked in collaboration with Robert Brout, deceased.)

Physiology or Medicine: James E. Rothman, U.S.; Randy W. Schekman, U.S.; and Thomas C. Südhof, Ger.-U.S. shared the prize "for their discoveries of machinery regulating vesicle traffic, a major transport system in our cells."

Physics

1901 Wilhelm C. Röntgen, Ger.	1955 Polykarp Kusch, Willis E. Lamb, U.S.	1987 J. Georg Bednorz, Ger.;
1902 Hendrik A. Lorentz,	1956 John Bardeen, Walter H. Brattain,	K. Alex Müller, Switz.
Pieter Zeeman, Neth.	William Shockley, U.S.	1988 Leon M. Lederman, Melvin
1903 Antoine Henri Becquerel, Pierre	1957 Tsung-Dao Lee, Chen Ning Yang,	Schwartz, Jack Steinberger, U.S.
Curie, Fr.; Marie Curie, Pol.-Fr.	U.S.-China	1989 Norman F. Ramsey, U.S.;
1904 Lord Rayleigh (John W. Strutt), UK	1958 Pavel Cherenkov, Il'ja Frank,	Hans G. Dehmelt, Ger.-U.S.;
1905 Philipp E. A. von Lenard, Ger.	Igor Y. Tamm, USSR	Wolfgang Paul, Ger.
1906 Sir Joseph J. Thomson, UK	1959 Owen Chamberlain,	1990 Jerome I. Friedman, Henry W.
1907 Albert A. Michelson, U.S.	Emilio G. Segre, U.S.	Kendall, U.S.; Richard E. Taylor, Can.
1908 Gabriel Lippmann, Fr.	1960 Donald A. Glaser, U.S.	1991 Pierre-Gilles de Gennes, Fr.
1909 Carl F. Braun, Ger.;	1961 Robert Hofstadter, U.S.;	1992 Georges Charpak, Pol.-Fr.
Guglielmo Marconi, Ital.	Rudolf L. Mossbauer, Ger.	1993 Russell A. Hulse,
1910 Johannes D. van der Waals, Neth.	1962 Lev D. Landau, USSR	Joseph H. Taylor, U.S.
1911 Wilhelm Wien, Ger.	1963 Maria Goeppert-Mayer, Eugene P.	1994 Bertram N. Brockhouse, Can.;
1912 Nils G. Dalén, Swed.	Wigner, U.S.; J. Hans D. Jensen, Ger.	Clifford G. Shull, U.S.
1913 Heike Kamerlingh Onnes, Neth.	1964 Nicolay G. Basov,	1995 Martin Perl, Frederick Reines, U.S.
1914 Max von Laue, Ger.	Aleksandr M. Prokhorov, USSR;	1996 David M. Lee, Douglas D. Osheroff,
1915 Sir William H. Bragg,	Charles H. Townes, U.S.	Robert C. Richardson, U.S.
William L. Bragg, UK	1965 Richard P. Feynman,	1997 Steven Chu, William D. Phillips,
1917 Charles G. Barkla, UK	Julian S. Schwinger, U.S.;	U.S.; Claude Cohen-Tannoudji, Fr.
1918 Max K. E. L. Planck, Ger.	Sin-Itiro Tomonaga, Jpn.	1998 Robert B. Laughlin, U.S.;
1919 Johannes Stark, Ger.	1966 Alfred Kastler, Fr.	Horst L. Störmer, Ger.-U.S;
1920 Charles E. Guillaume, Fr.-Switz.	1967 Hans A. Bethe, U.S.	Daniel C. Tsui, China-U.S.
1921 Albert Einstein, Ger.-U.S.	1968 Luis W. Alvarez, U.S.	1999 Gerardus 't Hooft,
1922 Niels Bohr, Den.	1969 Murray Gell-Mann, U.S.	Martinus J. G. Veltman, Neth.
1923 Robert A. Millikan, U.S.	1970 Hannes Alfvén, Swed.;	2000 Jack S. Kilby, U.S.;
1924 Karl M. G. Siegbahn, Swed.	Louis Néel, Fr.	Herbert Kroemer, Ger.-U.S.;
1925 James Franck, Gustav Hertz, Ger.	1971 Dennis Gabor, UK	Zhores I. Alferov, Russ.
1926 Jean B. Perrin, Fr.	1972 John Bardeen, Leon N. Cooper,	2001 Eric A. Cornell, Carl E. Wieman,
1927 Arthur H. Compton, U.S.;	John R. Schrieffer, U.S.	U.S.; Wolfgang Ketterle, Ger.
Charles T. R. Wilson, UK	1973 Brian D. Josephson, UK;	2002 Raymond Davis Jr.,
1928 Owen W. Richardson, UK	Leo Esaki, Jpn.; Ivar Giaever, U.S.	Riccardo Giacconi, U.S.;
1929 Prince Louis-Victor de Broglie, Fr.	1974 Antony Hewish, Sir Martin Ryle, UK	Masatoshi Koshiba, Jpn.
1930 Sir Chandrasekhara V. Raman,	1975 Aage Bohr, Den.;	2003 Alexei A. Abrikosov,
India	Ben Mottelson, U.S.-Den.;	Vitaly L. Ginzburg, Russ.;
1932 Werner Heisenberg, Ger.	Leo James Rainwater, U.S.	Anthony J. Leggett, UK
1933 Paul A. M. Dirac, UK;	1976 Burton Richter,	2004 David J. Gross, H. David Politzer,
Erwin Schrödinger, Austria	Samuel C. C. Ting, U.S.	Frank Wilczek, U.S.
1935 Sir James Chadwick, UK	1977 Philip W. Anderson,	2005 Roy J. Glauber, John L. Hall, U.S.;
1936 Carl D. Anderson, U.S.;	John H. van Vleck, U.S.;	Theodor W. Hänsch, Ger.
Victor F. Hess, Austria	Sir Nevill F. Mott, UK	2006 John C. Mather,
1937 Clinton J. Davisson, U.S.;	1978 Pyotr Kapitsa, USSR;	George F. Smoot, U.S.
Sir George P. Thomson, UK	Arno Penzias, Robert Wilson, U.S.	2007 Albert Fert, Fr.;
1938 Enrico Fermi, Ital.-U.S.	1979 Sheldon L. Glashow,	Peter Grünberg, Ger.
1939 Ernest O. Lawrence, U.S.	Steven Weinberg, U.S.;	2008 Yoichiro Nambu, U.S.;
1943 Otto Stern, U.S.	Abdus Salam, Pakistan	Makoto Kobayashi,
1944 Isidor Isaac Rabi, U.S.	1980 James W. Cronin, Val L. Fitch, U.S.	Toshihide Maskawa, Jpn.
1945 Wolfgang Pauli, U.S.-Austria	1981 Nicolaas Bloembergen,	2009 Charles K. Kao, U.S.-UK;
1946 Percy W. Bridgman, U.S.	Arthur Schawlow, U.S.;	Willard S. Boyle, U.S.-Can.;
1947 Sir Edward V. Appleton, UK	Kai M. Siegbahn, Swed.	George E. Smith, U.S.
1948 Patrick M. S. Blackett, UK	1982 Kenneth G. Wilson, U.S.	2010 Andre Geim, Russ.-Neth.;
1949 Hideki Yukawa, Jpn.	1983 Subramanyan Chandrasekhar,	Konstantin Novoselov, Russ.-UK
1950 Cecil F. Powell, UK	William A. Fowler, U.S.	2011 Saul Perlmutter, Adam G. Riess,
1951 Sir John D. Cockcroft, UK;	1984 Carlo Rubbia, Ital.;	U.S.; Brian P. Schmidt, Austral.-U.S.
Ernest T. S. Walton, Ire.	Simon van der Meer, Neth.	2012 Serge Haroche, Fr.;
1952 Felix Bloch, Edward M. Purcell, U.S.	1985 Klaus von Klitzing, Ger.	David J. Wineland, U.S.
1953 Frits Zernike, Neth.	1986 Ernest Ruska, Gerd Binnig, Ger.;	2013 François Englert, Belg.;
1954 Max Born, UK; Walter Bothe, Ger.	Heinrich Rohrer, Switz.	Peter W. Higgs, UK

Chemistry

1901 Jacobus H. van 't Hoff, Neth.	1953 Hermann Staudinger, Ger.	1989 Sidney Altman,
1902 Emil Fischer, Ger.	1954 Linus C. Pauling, U.S.	Thomas R. Cech, U.S.
1903 Svante A. Arrhenius, Swed.	1955 Vincent du Vigneaud, U.S.	1990 Elias James Corey, U.S.
1904 Sir William Ramsay, UK	1956 Sir Cyril N. Hinshelwood, UK;	1991 Richard R. Ernst, Switz.
1905 Adolf von Baeyer, Ger.	Nikolay N. Semenov, USSR	1992 Rudolph A. Marcus, Can.-U.S.
1906 Henri Moissan, Fr.	1957 Lord (Alexander R.) Todd, UK	1993 Kary B. Mullis, U.S.;
1907 Eduard Buchner, Ger.	1958 Frederick Sanger, UK	Michael Smith, UK-Can.
1908 Ernest Rutherford, UK	1959 Jaroslav Heyrovsky, Czech.	1994 George A. Olah, U.S.
1909 Wilhelm Ostwald, Ger.	1960 Willard F. Libby, U.S.	1995 Paul Crutzen, Neth.;
1910 Otto Wallach, Ger.	1961 Melvin Calvin, U.S.	Mario Molina, Mex.-U.S.;
1911 Marie Curie, Pol.-Fr.	1962 John C. Kendrew, Max F. Perutz, UK	Sherwood Rowland, U.S.
1912 Victor Grignard, Paul Sabatier, Fr.	1963 Giulio Natta, Ital.; Karl Ziegler, Ger.	1996 Robert F. Curl Jr.,
1913 Alfred Werner, Switz.	1964 Dorothy C. Hodgkin, UK	Richard E. Smalley, U.S.;
1914 Theodore W. Richards, U.S.	1965 Robert B. Woodward, U.S.	Sir Harold W. Kroto, UK
1915 Richard M. Willstätter, Ger.	1966 Robert S. Mulliken, U.S.	1997 Paul D. Boyer, U.S.; John E. Walker,
1918 Fritz Haber, Ger.	1967 Manfred Eigen, Ger.; Ronald G. W.	UK; Jens C. Skou, Den.
1920 Walther H. Nernst, Ger.	Norrish, George Porter, UK	1998 Walter Kohn, U.S.;
1921 Frederick Soddy, UK	1968 Lars Onsager, U.S.	John A. Pople, UK
1922 Francis W. Aston, UK	1969 Derek H. R. Barton, UK;	1999 Ahmed H. Zewail, U.S.
1923 Fritz Pregl, Austria	Odd Hassel, Nor.	2000 Alan J. Heeger, U.S.;
1925 Richard A. Zsigmondy, Ger.	1970 Luis F. Leloir, Arg.	Alan G. MacDiarmid, N. Zea.-U.S.;
1926 Theodor Svedberg, Swed.	1971 Gerhard Herzberg, Can.	Hideki Shirakawa, Jpn.
1927 Heinrich O. Wieland, Ger.	1972 Christian B. Anfinsen, Stanford	2001 K. Barry Sharpless,
1928 Adolf O. R. Windaus, Ger.	Moore, William H. Stein, U.S.	William S. Knowles, U.S.;
1929 Sir Arthur Harden, UK;	1973 Ernst Otto Fischer, Ger.;	Ryoji Noyori, Jpn.
Hans von Euler-Chelpin, Swed.	Geoffrey Wilkinson, UK	2002 John B. Fenn, U.S.;
1930 Hans Fischer, Ger.	1974 Paul J. Flory, U.S.	Koichi Tanaka, Jpn.;
1931 Friedrich Bergius, Carl Bosch, Ger.	1975 John Cornforth, Austral.-UK;	Kurt Wüthrich, Switz.
1932 Irving Langmuir, U.S.	Vladimir Prelog, Bosnia-Switz.	2003 Peter Agre,
1934 Harold C. Urey, U.S.	1976 William N. Lipscomb, U.S.	Roderick MacKinnon, U.S.
1935 Frédéric Joliot, Irene Joliot-Curie, Fr.	1977 Ilya Prigogine, Belg.	2004 Aaron Ciechanover, Avram Hershko,
1936 Peter J. W. Debye, Neth.	1978 Peter Mitchell, UK	Isr.; Irwin Rose, U.S.
1937 Walter N. Haworth, UK;	1979 Herbert C. Brown, U.S.;	2005 Yves Chauvin, Fr.; Robert H.
Paul Karrer, Switz.	Georg Wittig, Ger.	Grubbs, Richard R. Schrock, U.S.
1938 Richard Kuhn, Ger.	1980 Paul Berg, Walter Gilbert, U.S.;	2006 Roger D. Kornberg, U.S.
1939 Adolf F. J. Butenandt, Ger.;	Frederick Sanger, UK	2007 Gerhard Ertl, Ger.
Leopold Ruzicka, Switz.	1981 Kenichi Fukui, Jpn.;	2008 Martin Chalfie, Osamu Shimomura,
1943 George de Hevesy, Hung.	Roald Hoffmann, U.S.	Roger Y. Tsien, U.S.
1944 Otto Hahn, Ger.	1982 Aaron Klug, UK-Lith.	2009 Venkatraman Ramakrishnan, UK;
1945 Artturi I. Virtanen, Fin.	1983 Henry Taube, Can.	Thomas A. Steitz, U.S.;
1946 James B. Sumner, John H.	1984 Robert Bruce Merrifield, U.S.	Ada E. Yonath, Isr.
Northrop, Wendell M. Stanley, U.S.	1985 Herbert A. Hauptman,	2010 Richard F. Heck, U.S.; Ei-ichi
1947 Sir Robert Robinson, UK	Jerome Karle, U.S.	Negishi, Jpn -U.S ; Akira Suzuki,
1948 Arne W. K. Tiselius, Swed.	1986 Dudley Herschbach, Yuan T. Lee,	Jpn.
1949 William F. Giauque, U.S.	U.S.; John C. Polanyi, Can.	2011 Dan Shechtman, Isr.
1950 Kurt Alder, Otto P. H. Diels, Ger.	1987 Donald J. Cram,	2012 Brian K. Kobilka,
1951 Edwin M. McMillan,	Charles J. Pedersen, U.S.;	Robert J. Lefkowitz, U.S.
Glenn T. Seaborg, U.S.	Jean-Marie Lehn, Fr.	2013 Martin Karplus, Austria-U.S.;
1952 Archer J. P. Martin,	1988 Johann Deisenhofer, Robert Huber,	Michael Levitt, S. Afr.-U.S.;
Richard L. M. Synge, UK	Hartmut Michel, Ger.	Arieh Warshel, Isr.-U.S.

Physiology or Medicine

1901 Emil A. von Behring, Ger.	1934 George R. Minot, William P. Murphy,	1958 George W. Beadle, Edward L.
1902 Sir Ronald Ross, UK	G. H. Whipple, U.S.	Tatum, Joshua Lederberg, U.S.
1903 Niels R. Finsen, Den.	1935 Hans Spemann, Ger.	1959 Arthur Kornberg,
1904 Ivan P. Pavlov, Russ.	1936 Sir Henry H. Dale, UK;	Severo Ochoa, U.S.
1905 Robert Koch, Ger.	Otto Loewi, U.S.	1960 Sir Frank Macfarlane Burnet,
1906 Camillo Golgi, Ital.;	1937 Albert Szent-Gyorgyi, Hung.-U.S.	Austral.; Peter B. Medawar, UK
Santiago Ramón y Cajal, Spain	1938 Corneille J. F. Heymans, Belg.	1961 Georg von Békésy, U.S.
1907 Charles L. A. Laveran, Fr.	1939 Gerhard Domagk, Ger.	1962 Francis H. C. Crick,
1908 Paul Ehrlich, Ger.;	1943 Henrik C. P. Dam, Den.;	Maurice H. F. Wilkins, UK;
Ilya Mechnikov, Fr.	Edward A. Doisy, U.S.	James D. Watson, U.S.
1909 Emil T. Kocher, Switz.	1944 Joseph Erlanger,	1963 Sir John C. Eccles, Austral.;
1910 Albrecht Kossel, Ger.	Herbert S. Gasser, U.S.	Alan L. Hodgkin,
1911 Allvar Gullstrand, Swed.	1945 Ernst B. Chain, Sir Alexander	Andrew F. Huxley, UK
1912 Alexis Carrel, Fr.	Fleming, Sir Howard W. Florey, UK	1964 Konrad E. Bloch, U.S.;
1913 Charles R. Richet, Fr.	1946 Hermann J. Muller, U.S.	Feodor Lynen, Ger.
1914 Robert Bárány, Austria	1947 Carl F. Cori, Gerty T. Cori, U.S.;	1965 François Jacob, André Lwoff,
1919 Jules Bordet, Belg.	Bernardo A. Houssay, Arg.	Jacques Monod, Fr.
1920 Schack A. S. Krogh, Den.	1948 Paul H. Müller, Switz.	1966 Charles B. Huggins,
1922 Archibald V. Hill, UK;	1949 Walter R. Hess, Switz.;	Peyton Rous, U.S.
Otto F. Meyerhof, Ger.	Antonio Egas Moniz, Port.	1967 Ragnar Granit, Swed.;
1923 Frederick G. Banting, Can.;	1950 Philip S. Hench, Edward C. Kendall,	Haldan Keffer Hartline,
John J. R. Macleod, UK	U.S.; Tadeus Reichstein, Switz.	George Wald, U.S.
1924 Willem Einthoven, Neth.	1951 Max Theiler, U.S.	1968 Robert W. Holley,
1926 Johannes A. G. Fibiger, Den.	1952 Selman A. Waksman, U.S.	H. Gobind Khorana,
1927 Julius Wagner-Jauregg, Austria	1953 Hans A. Krebs, Ger.;	Marshall W. Nirenberg, U.S.
1928 Charles J. H. Nicolle, Fr.	Fritz A. Lipmann, U.S.	1969 Max Delbrück, Alfred D. Hershey,
1929 Christiaan Eijkman, Neth.;	1954 John F. Enders, Frederick C.	Salvador Luria, U.S.
Sir Frederick G. Hopkins, UK	Robbins, Thomas H. Weller, U.S.	1970 Julius Axelrod, U.S.;
1930 Karl Landsteiner, U.S.	1955 Alex H. T. Theorell, Swed.	Sir Bernard Katz, UK;
1931 Otto H. Warburg, Ger.	1956 André F. Cournand,	Ulf von Euler, Swed.
1932 Edgar D. Adrian,	Dickinson W. Richards, U.S.;	1971 Earl W. Sutherland Jr., U.S.
Sir Charles S. Sherrington, UK	Werner Forssmann, Ger.	1972 Gerald M. Edelman, U.S.;
1933 Thomas H. Morgan, U.S.	1957 Daniel Bovet, Ital.	Rodney R. Porter, UK

1973 Konrad Lorenz, Austria;
Nikolaas Tinbergen, UK;
Karl von Frisch, Ger.
1974 Albert Claude, Lux.-U.S.;
Christian de Duve, Belg.;
George Emil Palade, Rom.-U.S.
1975 David Baltimore,
Howard Temin, U.S.;
Renato Dulbecco, Ital.-U.S.
1976 Baruch S. Blumberg,
Daniel Carleton Gajdusek, U.S.
1977 Rosalyn S. Yalow,
Roger C.L. Guillemin,
Andrew V. Schally, U.S.
1978 Werner Arber, Switz.;
Daniel Nathans,
Hamilton O. Smith, U.S.
1979 Allan M. Cormack, U.S.;
Godfrey N. Hounsfield, UK
1980 Baruj Benacerraf, George Snell,
U.S.; Jean Dausset, Fr.
1981 Roger W. Sperry, David H. Hubel,
Torsten N. Wiesel, U.S.
1982 Sune K. Bergström,
Bengt I. Samuelsson, Swed.;
John R. Vane, UK
1983 Barbara McClintock, U.S.
1984 Niels K. Jerne, UK-Den.;
Georges J. F. Köhler, Ger.;
César Milstein, UK-Arg.

1985 Michael S. Brown,
Joseph L. Goldstein, U.S.
1986 Stanley Cohen, U.S.;
Rita Levi-Montalcini, Ital.-U.S.
1987 Susumu Tonegawa, Jpn.
1988 Sir James W. Black, UK;
Gertrude B. Elion,
George H. Hitchings, U.S.
1989 J. Michael Bishop,
Harold E. Varmus, U.S.
1990 Joseph E. Murray,
E. Donnall Thomas, U.S.
1991 Edwin Neher, Bert Sakmann, Ger.
1992 Edmond H. Fisher,
Edwin G. Krebs, U.S.
1993 Richard J. Roberts, UK;
Phillip A. Sharp, U.S.
1994 Alfred G. Gilman,
Martin Rodbell, U.S.
1995 Edward B. Lewis,
Eric F. Wieschaus, U.S.;
Christiane Nüsslein-Volhard, Ger.
1996 Peter C. Doherty, Austral.;
Rolf M. Zinkernagel, Switz.
1997 Stanley B. Prusiner, U.S.
1998 Robert F. Furchgott,
Louis J. Ignarro, Ferid Murad, U.S.
1999 Günter Blobel, U.S.
2000 Arvid Carlsson, Swed.;
Paul Greengard, U.S.;
Eric R. Kandel, Austria-U.S.

2001 Leland H. Hartwell, U.S.;
R. Timothy (Tim) Hunt,
Sir Paul M. Nurse, UK
2002 Sydney Brenner, John E. Sulston,
UK; H. Robert Horvitz, U.S.
2003 Paul C. Lauterbur, U.S.;
Sir Peter Mansfield, UK
2004 Richard Axel, Linda B. Buck, U.S.
2005 Barry J. Marshall,
J. Robin Warren, Austral.
2006 Andrew Z. Fire, Craig C. Mello,
U.S.
2007 Mario R. Capecchi,
Oliver Smithies, U.S.;
Sir Martin J. Evans, UK
2008 Harald zur Hausen, Ger.;
Françoise Barré-Sinoussi,
Luc Montagnier, Fr.
2009 Elizabeth H. Blackburn,
Carol W. Greider,
Jack W. Szostak, U.S.
2010 Robert G. Edwards, UK
2011 Bruce A. Beutler, U.S.;
Jules A. Hoffmann, Fr.;
Ralph M. Steinman, Can.-U.S.
2012 John B. Gurdon, UK;
Shinya Yamanaka, Jpn.-U.S.
2013 James E. Rothman, U.S.;
Randy W. Schekman, U.S.;
Thomas C. Südhof, Ger.-U.S.

Literature

1901 Rene F. A. Sully Prudhomme, Fr.
1902 Theodor Mommsen, Ger.
1903 Bjørnstjerne Bjørnson, Nor.
1904 José Echegaray y Eizaguirre, Spain;
Fréderic Mistral, Fr.
1905 Henryk Sienkiewicz, Pol.
1906 Giosuè Carducci, Ital.
1907 Rudyard Kipling, UK
1908 Rudolf C. Eucken, Ger.
1909 Selma Lagerlöf, Swed.
1910 Paul J. L. Heyse, Ger.
1911 Maurice Maeterlinck, Belg.
1912 Gerhart Hauptmann, Ger.
1913 Rabindranath Tagore, India
1915 Romain Rolland, Fr.
1916 Verner von Heidenstam, Swed.
1917 Karl A. Gjellerup,
Henrik Pontoppidan, Den.
1919 Carl F. G. Spitteler, Switz.
1920 Knut Hamsun, Nor.
1921 Anatole France, Fr.
1922 Jacinto Benavente, Spain
1923 William Butler Yeats, Ire.
1924 Wladyslaw S. Reymont, Pol.
1925 George Bernard Shaw, Ire.-UK
1926 Grazia Deledda, Ital.
1927 Henri Bergson, Fr.
1928 Sigrid Undset, Nor.
1929 Thomas Mann, Ger.
1930 Sinclair Lewis, U.S.
1931 Erik A. Karlfeldt, Swed.
1932 John Galsworthy, UK
1933 Ivan A. Bunin, USSR
1934 Luigi Pirandello, Ital.
1936 Eugene O'Neill, U.S.
1937 Roger Martin du Gard, Fr.
1938 Pearl S. Buck, U.S.

1939 Frans E. Sillanpää, Fin.
1944 Johannes V. Jensen, Den.
1945 Gabriela Mistral, Chile
1946 Hermann Hesse, Ger.-Switz.
1947 André Gide, Fr.
1948 T. S. Eliot, UK
1949 William Faulkner, U.S.
1950 Bertrand Russell, UK
1951 Pär F. Lagerkvist, Swed.
1952 François Mauriac, Fr.
1953 Sir Winston Churchill, UK
1954 Ernest Hemingway, U.S.
1955 Halldór K. Laxness, Ice.
1956 Juan Ramón Jiménez, Spain
1957 Albert Camus, Fr.
1958 Boris L. Pasternak, USSR
(declined)
1959 Salvatore Quasimodo, Ital.
1960 Saint-John Perse, Fr.
1961 Ivo Andric, Yugo.
1962 John Steinbeck, U.S.
1963 Giorgos Seferis, Greece
1964 Jean-Paul Sartre, Fr. (declined)
1965 Mikhail Sholokhov, USSR
1966 Shmuel Yosef Agnon, Isr.;
Nelly Sachs, Swed.
1967 Miguel Angel Asturias, Guat.
1968 Yasunari Kawabata, Jpn.
1969 Samuel Beckett, Ire.
1970 Aleksandr I. Solzhenitsyn, USSR
1971 Pablo Neruda, Chile
1972 Heinrich Böll, Ger.
1973 Patrick White, Austral.
1974 Eyvind Johnson,
Harry Edmund Martinson, Swed.
1975 Eugenio Montale, Ital.
1976 Saul Bellow, U.S.

1977 Vicente Aleixandre, Spain
1978 Isaac Bashevis Singer, U.S.
1979 Odysseus Elytis, Greece
1980 Czeslaw Milosz, Pol.-U.S.
1981 Elias Canetti, Bulg.-UK
1982 Gabriel García Márquez, Colombia
1983 William Golding, UK
1984 Jaroslav Siefert, Czech.
1985 Claude Simon, Fr.
1986 Wole Soyinka, Nigeria
1987 Joseph Brodsky, USSR-U.S.
1988 Naguib Mahfouz, Egypt
1989 Camilo José Cela, Spain
1990 Octavio Paz, Mex.
1991 Nadine Gordimer, S. Afr.
1992 Derek Walcott, St. Lucia
1993 Toni Morrison, U.S.
1994 Kenzaburo Oe, Jpn.
1995 Seamus Heaney, Ire.
1996 Wislawa Szymborska, Pol.
1997 Dario Fo, Ital.
1998 Jose Saramago, Por.
1999 Günter Grass, Ger.
2000 Gao Xingjian, China-Fr.
2001 Sir V. S. Naipaul, UK
2002 Imre Kertész, Hung.
2003 J. M. Coetzee, S. Afr.
2004 Elfriede Jelinek, Austria
2005 Harold Pinter, UK
2006 Orhan Pamuk, Turk.
2007 Doris Lessing, UK
2008 Jean-Marie Gustave Le Clézio, Fr.
2009 Herta Müller, Ger.
2010 Mario Vargas Llosa, Peru
2011 Tomas Tranströmer, Swed.
2012 Mo Yan, China
2013 Alice Munro, Can.

Peace

1901 Jean H. Dunant, Switz.;
Frédéric Passy, Fr.
1902 Élie Ducommun,
Charles A. Gobat, Switz.
1903 Sir William R. Cremer, UK
1904 Institute of International Law
1905 Baroness Bertha von Suttner,
Austria
1906 Theodore Roosevelt, U.S.
1907 Ernesto T. Moneta, Ital.;
Louis Renault, Fr.

1908 Klas P. Arnoldson, Swed.;
Fredrik Bajer, Den.
1909 Auguste M. F. Beernaert, Belg.;
Paul H. B. B. d'Estournelles
de Constant, Fr.
1910 Permanent Intl. Peace Bureau
1911 Tobias M. C. Asser, Neth.;
Alfred H. Fried, Austria
1912 Elihu Root, U.S.
1913 Henri La Fontaine, Belg.
1917 Intl. Committee of the Red Cross
1919 Woodrow Wilson, U.S.

1920 Léon V. A. Bourgeois, Fr.
1921 Karl H. Branting, Swed.;
Christian L. Lange, Nor.
1922 Fridtjof Nansen, Nor.
1925 Sir Austen Chamberlain, UK;
Charles G. Dawes, U.S.
1926 Aristide Briand, Fr.;
Gustav Stresemann, Ger.
1927 Ferdinand E. Buisson, Fr.;
Ludwig Quidde, Ger.
1929 Frank B. Kellogg, U.S.
1930 Nathan Söderblom, Swed.

1931 Jane Addams,	1970 Norman E. Borlaug, U.S.	1994 Yasser Arafat, Pal.; Shimon Peres,
Nicholas Murray Butler, U.S.	1971 Willy Brandt, Ger.	Yitzhak Rabin, Isr.
1933 Sir Norman Angell, UK	1973 Henry Kissinger, U.S.;	1995 Joseph Rotblat, Pol.-UK;
1934 Arthur Henderson, UK	Le Duc Tho, N. Viet. (Tho declined)	Pugwash Conferences
1935 Carl von Ossietzky, Ger.	1974 Seán MacBride, Ire.;	1996 Bishop Carlos Ximenes Belo,
1936 Carlos Saavedra Lamas, Arg.	Eisaku Sato, Jpn.	José Ramos-Horta, Timor-Leste
1937 Lord Robert Cecil, UK	1975 Andrei Sakharov, USSR	1997 Jody Williams, U.S.;
1938 Nansen Intl. Office for Refugees	1976 Mairead Corrigan,	Intl. Campaign to Ban Landmines
1944 Intl. Committee of the Red Cross	Betty Williams, N. Ire.	1998 John Hume, David Trimble, N. Ire.
1945 Cordell Hull, U.S.	1977 Amnesty International	1999 Doctors Without Borders
1946 Emily G. Balch, John R. Mott, U.S.	1978 Anwar al-Sadat, Egypt;	(Médecins Sans Frontières), Fr.
1947 Friends Service Council, UK; Amer.	Menachem Begin, Isr.	2000 Kim Dae Jung, S. Kor.
Friends Service Committee, U.S.	1979 Mother Teresa of Calcutta,	2001 UN; Kofi Annan, Ghana
1949 Lord John Boyd Orr of Brechin, UK	Alb.-India	2002 Jimmy Carter, U.S.
1950 Ralph J. Bunche, U.S.	1980 Adolfo Pérez Esquivel, Arg.	2003 Shirin Ebadi, Iran
1951 Léon Jouhaux, Fr.	1981 Office of UN High Commissioner	2004 Wangari Maathai, Kenya
1952 Albert Schweitzer, Fr.	for Refugees	2005 Mohamed ElBaradei, Egypt;
1953 George C. Marshall, U.S.	1982 Alfonso García Robles, Mex.;	Intl. Atomic Energy Agency, Austria
1954 Office of UN High Commissioner	Alva Myrdal, Swed.	2006 Muhammad Yunus,
for Refugees	1983 Lech Walesa, Pol.	Grameen Bank, Bangl.
1957 Lester B. Pearson, Can.	1984 Bishop Desmond Tutu, S. Afr.	2007 Intergovernmental Panel on Climate
1958 Georges Pire, Belg.	1985 Intl. Physicians for the Prevention	Change, Switz.;
1959 Philip J. Noel-Baker, UK	of Nuclear War, U.S.	Albert Arnold Gore Jr., U.S.
1960 Albert J. Lutuli, S. Afr.	1986 Elie Wiesel, Rom.-U.S.	2008 Martti Ahtisaari, Fin.
1961 Dag Hammarskjöld, Swed.	1987 Oscar Arias Sánchez, Costa Rica	2009 Barack H. Obama, U.S.
1962 Linus C. Pauling, U.S.	1988 UN Peacekeeping Forces	2010 Liu Xiaobo, China
1963 Intl. Committee of the Red Cross,	1989 Dalai Lama (Tenzin Gyatso), Tibet	2011 Leymah Gbowee,
League of Red Cross Societies	1990 Mikhail S. Gorbachev, USSR	Ellen Johnson Sirleaf, Liberia;
1964 Martin Luther King Jr., U.S.	1991 Aung San Suu Kyi, Burma	Tawakkol Karman, Yemen
1965 UN Children's Fund (UNICEF)	1992 Rigoberta Menchú Tum, Guat.	2012 European Union
1968 René Cassin, Fr.	1993 Frederik W. de Klerk,	2013 Organization for the Prohibition of
1969 Intl. Labor Organization	Nelson Mandela, S. Afr.	Chemical Weapons

Nobel Memorial Prize in Economic Sciences

1969 Ragnar Frisch, Nor.;	1987 Robert M. Solow, U.S.	2002 Daniel Kahneman, U.S.-Isr.;
Jan Tinbergen, Neth.	1988 Maurice Allais, Fr.	Vernon L. Smith, U.S.
1970 Paul A. Samuelson, U.S.	1989 Trygve Haavelmo, Nor.	2003 Robert F. Engle, U.S.;
1971 Simon Kuznets, U.S.	1990 Harry M. Markowitz,	Clive W. J. Granger, UK
1972 Kenneth J. Arrow, U.S.;	Merton H. Miller,	2004 Finn E. Kydland, Nor.;
John R. Hicks, UK	William F. Sharpe, U.S.	Edward C. Prescott, U.S.
1973 Wassily Leontief, U.S.	1991 Ronald H. Coase, UK-U.S.	2005 Robert J. Aumann, Isr.-U.S.;
1974 Gunnar Myrdal, Swed.;	1992 Gary S. Becker, U.S.	Thomas C. Schelling, U.S.
Friedrich A. von Hayek, Austria	1993 Robert W. Fogel,	2006 Edmund S. Phelps, U.S.
1975 Leonid Kantorovich, USSR;	Douglass C. North, U.S.	2007 Leonid Hurwicz, Eric S. Maskin,
Tjalling C. Koopmans, Neth.-U.S.	1994 John C. Harsanyi, John F. Nash,	Roger B. Myerson, U.S.
1976 Milton Friedman, U.S.	U.S.; Reinhard Selten, Ger.	2008 Paul Krugman, U.S.
1977 James E. Meade, UK;	1995 Robert E. Lucas Jr., U.S.	2009 Elinor Ostrom,
Bertil Ohlin, Swed.	1996 James A. Mirrlees, UK;	Oliver E. Williamson, U.S.
1978 Herbert A. Simon, U.S.	William Vickrey, Can.-U.S.	2010 Peter A. Diamond, Dale T.
1979 Sir Arthur Lewis, UK;	1997 Robert C. Merton, U.S.;	Mortensen, U.S.; Christopher A.
Theodore W. Schultz, U.S.	Myron S. Scholes, Can.-U.S.	Pissarides, Cyprus-UK
1980 Lawrence R. Klein, U.S.	1998 Amartya Sen, India	2011 Thomas J. Sargent,
1981 James Tobin, U.S.	1999 Robert A. Mundell, Can.	Christopher A. Sims, U.S.
1982 George J. Stigler, U.S.	2000 James J. Heckman,	2012 Alvin E. Roth, Lloyd S. Shapley, U.S.
1983 Gerard Debreu, Fr.-U.S.	Daniel L. McFadden, U.S.	2013 Eugene F. Fama, Lars Peter
1984 Richard Stone, UK	2001 George A. Akerlof, A. Michael	Hansen, Robert J. Shiller, U.S.
1985 Franco Modigliani, Ital.-U.S.	Spence, Joseph E. Stiglitz, U.S.	
1986 James M. Buchanan, U.S.		

Pulitzer Prizes in Journalism, Letters, and Music, 1917-2013

Endowed by Joseph Pulitzer (1847-1911), publisher of the *New York World*, in a bequest to Columbia Univ. and awarded annually, in years shown, for work published the previous year. Prizes are currently $10,000 in each category except Public Service (in Journalism), for which a gold medal is given. The prize board began considering submissions from online-only publications in 2009. For letters and music, prizes in past years are listed; if a year is omitted, no award was given that year.

Pulitzer Prizes in Journalism, 2013

Public Service: *Sun Sentinel* (Ft. Lauderdale, FL) for its investigation of off-duty police officers who speed and endanger civilian lives.

Breaking News Reporting: *Denver Post* staff, for coverage of a mass shooting at an Aurora, CO, movie theater that killed 12 people.

Investigative Reporting: David Barstow and Alejandra Xanic von Bertrab, *NY Times*, for reports on how Walmart used bribery to dominate the market in Mexico.

Explanatory Reporting: *NY Times* staff, for reporting on business practices by Apple and other technology companies that illustrates the darker side of the changing global economy for workers and consumers.

Local Reporting: Brad Schrade, Jeremy Olson, and Glenn Howatt, *Star Tribune* (Minneapolis, MN), for reports on spike in infant deaths at poorly regulated day-care facilities, resulting in legislation.

National Reporting: Lisa Song, Elizabeth McGowan, and David Hasemyer, *InsideClimate News* (Brooklyn, NY), for reports on flawed U.S. pipeline regulation, focusing on ecological dangers of diluted bitumen.

International Reporting: David Barboza, *NY Times*, for exposure of corruption at high levels of the Chinese government.

Feature Writing: John Branch, *NY Times*, for narrative about skiers killed in an avalanche and the science that explains such disasters, enhanced by multimedia elements.

Commentary: Bret Stephens, *Wall Street Journal* (New York, NY), for incisive columns on American foreign policy and domestic politics.

Criticism: Philip Kennicott, *Washington Post*, for eloquent, passionate essays on art and underlying social forces.

Editorial Writing: Tim Nickens and Daniel Ruth, *Tampa Bay Times* (St. Petersburg, FL), for campaign that helped reverse decision to end fluoridation of the water supply in the paper's home county.

Editorial Cartooning: Steve Sack, *Star Tribune* (Minneapolis, MN), for diverse cartoons using an original style to represent his unmistakable point of view.

Breaking News Photography: Rodrigo Abd, Manu Brabo, Narciso Contreras, Khalil Hamra, and Muhammed Muheisen, Associated Press, for coverage of the Syrian civil war under extreme hazard.

Feature Photography: Javier Manzano, Agence France-Presse, for extraordinary picture of two Syrian rebel soldiers guarding their position.

Pulitzer Prizes in Letters, 1917-2013

Fiction

1918 Ernest Poole, *His Family*
1919 Booth Tarkington, *The Magnificent Ambersons*
1921 Edith Wharton, *The Age of Innocence*
1922 Booth Tarkington, *Alice Adams*
1923 Willa Cather, *One of Ours*
1924 Margaret Wilson, *The Able McLaughlins*
1925 Edna Ferber, *So Big*
1926 Sinclair Lewis, *Arrowsmith* (refused)
1927 Louis Bromfield, *Early Autumn*
1928 Thornton Wilder, *Bridge of San Luis Rey*
1929 Julia M. Peterkin, *Scarlet Sister Mary*
1930 Oliver LaFarge, *Laughing Boy*
1931 Margaret Ayer Barnes, *Years of Grace*
1932 Pearl S. Buck, *The Good Earth*
1933 T. S. Stribling, *The Store*
1934 Caroline Miller, *Lamb in His Bosom*
1935 Josephine W. Johnson, *Now in November*
1936 Harold L. Davis, *Honey in the Horn*
1937 Margaret Mitchell, *Gone With the Wind*
1938 John P. Marquand, *The Late George Apley*
1939 Marjorie Kinnan Rawlings, *The Yearling*
1940 John Steinbeck, *The Grapes of Wrath*
1942 Ellen Glasgow, *In This Our Life*
1943 Upton Sinclair, *Dragon's Teeth*
1944 Martin Flavin, *Journey in the Dark*
1945 John Hersey, *A Bell for Adano*
1947 Robert Penn Warren, *All the King's Men*
1948 James A. Michener, *Tales of the South Pacific*
1949 James Gould Cozzens, *Guard of Honor*
1950 A. B. Guthrie Jr., *The Way West*
1951 Conrad Richter, *The Town*
1952 Herman Wouk, *The Caine Mutiny*
1953 Ernest Hemingway, *The Old Man and the Sea*
1955 William Faulkner, *A Fable*
1956 MacKinlay Kantor, *Andersonville*
1958 James Agee, *A Death in the Family*
1959 Robert Lewis Taylor, *The Travels of Jaimie McPheeters*
1960 Allen Drury, *Advise and Consent*
1961 Harper Lee, *To Kill a Mockingbird*
1962 Edwin O'Connor, *The Edge of Sadness*
1963 William Faulkner, *The Reivers*
1965 Shirley Ann Grau, *The Keepers of the House*
1966 Katherine Anne Porter, *Collected Stories*
1967 Bernard Malamud, *The Fixer*
1968 William Styron, *The Confessions of Nat Turner*
1969 N. Scott Momaday, *House Made of Dawn*
1970 Jean Stafford, *Collected Stories*
1972 Wallace Stegner, *Angle of Repose*
1973 Eudora Welty, *The Optimist's Daughter*
1975 Michael Shaara, *The Killer Angels*
1976 Saul Bellow, *Humboldt's Gift*
1978 James Alan McPherson, *Elbow Room*
1979 John Cheever, *The Stories of John Cheever*
1980 Norman Mailer, *The Executioner's Song*
1981 John Kennedy Toole, *A Confederacy of Dunces*
1982 John Updike, *Rabbit Is Rich*
1983 Alice Walker, *The Color Purple*
1984 William Kennedy, *Ironweed*
1985 Alison Lurie, *Foreign Affairs*
1986 Larry McMurtry, *Lonesome Dove*
1987 Peter Taylor, *A Summons to Memphis*
1988 Toni Morrison, *Beloved*
1989 Anne Tyler, *Breathing Lessons*
1990 Oscar Hijuelos, *The Mambo Kings Play Songs of Love*
1991 John Updike, *Rabbit at Rest*
1992 Jane Smiley, *A Thousand Acres*
1993 Robert Olen Butler, *A Good Scent From a Strange Mountain*
1994 E. Annie Proulx, *The Shipping News*
1995 Carol Shields, *The Stone Diaries*
1996 Richard Ford, *Independence Day*
1997 Steven Millhauser, *Martin Dressler: The Tale of an American Dreamer*
1998 Philip Roth, *American Pastoral*
1999 Michael Cunningham, *The Hours*
2000 Jhumpa Lahiri, *Interpreter of Maladies*
2001 Michael Chabon, *The Amazing Adventures of Kavalier & Clay*
2002 Richard Russo, *Empire Falls*
2003 Jeffrey Eugenides, *Middlesex*
2004 Edward P. Jones, *The Known World*
2005 Marilynne Robinson, *Gilead*
2006 Geraldine Brooks, *March*
2007 Cormac McCarthy, *The Road*
2008 Junot Díaz, *The Brief Wondrous Life of Oscar Wao*
2009 Elizabeth Strout, *Olive Kitteridge*
2010 Paul Harding, *Tinkers*
2011 Jennifer Egan, *A Visit From the Goon Squad*
2012 No award
2013 Adam Johnson, *The Orphan Master's Son*

Drama

1918 Jesse Lynch Williams, *Why Marry?*
1920 Eugene O'Neill, *Beyond the Horizon*
1921 Zona Gale, *Miss Lulu Bett*
1922 Eugene O'Neill, *Anna Christie*
1923 Owen Davis, *Icebound*
1924 Hatcher Hughes, *Hell-Bent for Heaven*
1925 Sidney Howard, *They Knew What They Wanted*
1926 George Kelly, *Craig's Wife*
1927 Paul Green, *In Abraham's Bosom*
1928 Eugene O'Neill, *Strange Interlude*
1929 Elmer Rice, *Street Scene*
1930 Marc Connelly, *The Green Pastures*
1931 Susan Glaspell, *Alison's House*
1932 George S. Kaufman, Morrie Ryskind, and Ira Gershwin, *Of Thee I Sing*
1933 Maxwell Anderson, *Both Your Houses*
1934 Sidney Kingsley, *Men in White*
1935 Zoe Akins, *The Old Maid*
1936 Robert E. Sherwood, *Idiot's Delight*
1937 George S. Kaufman and Moss Hart, *You Can't Take It With You*
1938 Thornton Wilder, *Our Town*
1939 Robert E. Sherwood, *Abe Lincoln in Illinois*
1940 William Saroyan, *The Time of Your Life*
1941 Robert E. Sherwood, *There Shall Be No Night*
1943 Thornton Wilder, *The Skin of Our Teeth*
1945 Mary Chase, *Harvey*
1946 Russel Crouse and Howard Lindsay, *State of the Union*
1948 Tennessee Williams, *A Streetcar Named Desire*
1949 Arthur Miller, *Death of a Salesman*
1950 Richard Rodgers, Oscar Hammerstein II, and Joshua Logan, *South Pacific*
1952 Joseph Kramm, *The Shrike*
1953 William Inge, *Picnic*
1954 John Patrick, *Teahouse of the August Moon*
1955 Tennessee Williams, *Cat on a Hot Tin Roof*
1956 Frances Goodrich and Albert Hackett, *The Diary of Anne Frank*
1957 Eugene O'Neill, *Long Day's Journey Into Night*
1958 Ketti Frings, *Look Homeward, Angel*
1959 Archibald MacLeish, *J. B.*
1960 George Abbott, Jerome Weidman, Sheldon Harnick, and Jerry Bock, *Fiorello!*
1961 Tad Mosel, *All the Way Home*
1962 Frank Loesser and Abe Burrows, *How to Succeed in Business Without Really Trying*
1965 Frank D. Gilroy, *The Subject Was Roses*
1967 Edward Albee, *A Delicate Balance*
1969 Howard Sackler, *The Great White Hope*
1970 Charles Gordone, *No Place to Be Somebody*
1971 Paul Zindel, *The Effect of Gamma Rays on Man-in-the-Moon Marigolds*
1973 Jason Miller, *That Championship Season*
1975 Edward Albee, *Seascape*
1976 Michael Bennett, James Kirkwood, Nicholas Dante, Marvin Hamlisch, and Edward Kleban, *A Chorus Line*
1977 Michael Cristofer, *The Shadow Box*
1978 Donald L. Coburn, *The Gin Game*
1979 Sam Shepard, *Buried Child*
1980 Lanford Wilson, *Talley's Folly*
1981 Beth Henley, *Crimes of the Heart*
1982 Charles Fuller, *A Soldier's Play*
1983 Marsha Norman, *'night, Mother*
1984 David Mamet, *Glengarry Glen Ross*
1985 Stephen Sondheim and James Lapine, *Sunday in the Park With George*
1987 August Wilson, *Fences*
1988 Alfred Uhry, *Driving Miss Daisy*
1989 Wendy Wasserstein, *The Heidi Chronicles*
1990 August Wilson, *The Piano Lesson*
1991 Neil Simon, *Lost in Yonkers*
1992 Robert Schenkkan, *The Kentucky Cycle*
1993 Tony Kushner, *Angels in America: Millennium Approaches*
1994 Edward Albee, *Three Tall Women*
1995 Horton Foote, *The Young Man From Atlanta*
1996 Jonathan Larson, *Rent*
1998 Paula Vogel, *How I Learned to Drive*
1999 Margaret Edson, *Wit*
2000 Donald Margulies, *Dinner With Friends*
2001 David Auburn, *Proof*
2002 Suzan-Lori Parks, *Topdog/Underdog*
2003 Nilo Cruz, *Anna in the Tropics*
2004 Doug Wright, *I Am My Own Wife*

2005 John Patrick Shanley, *Doubt, a parable*
2007 David Lindsay-Abaire, *Rabbit Hole*
2008 Tracy Letts, *August: Osage County*
2009 Lynn Nottage, *Ruined*
2010 Tom Kitt and Brian Yorkey, *Next to Normal*
2011 Bruce Norris, *Clybourne Park*
2012 Quiara Alegría Hudes, *Water by the Spoonful*
2013 Ayad Akhtar, *Disgraced*

History (U.S.)

1917 J. J. Jusserand, *With Americans of Past and Present Days*
1918 James Ford Rhodes, *History of the Civil War*
1920 Justin H. Smith, *The War With Mexico*
1921 William Sowden Sims, *The Victory at Sea*
1922 James Truslow Adams, *The Founding of New England*
1923 Charles Warren, *The Supreme Court in United States History*
1924 Charles Howard McIlwain, *The American Revolution: A Constitutional Interpretation*
1925 Frederick L. Paxton, *A History of the American Frontier*
1926 Edward Channing, *A History of the U.S.*
1927 Samuel Flagg Bemis, *Pinckney's Treaty*
1928 V. L. Parrington, *Main Currents in American Thought*
1929 Fred A. Shannon, *The Organization and Administration of the Union Army, 1861-1865*
1930 Claude H. Van Tyne, *The War of Independence*
1931 Bernadotte E. Schmitt, *The Coming of the War, 1914*
1932 Gen. John J. Pershing, *My Experiences in the World War*
1933 Frederick J. Turner, *The Significance of Sections in American History*
1934 Herbert Agar, *The People's Choice*
1935 Charles McLean Andrews, *The Colonial Period of American History*
1936 Andrew C. McLaughlin, *The Constitutional History of the United States*
1937 Van Wyck Brooks, *The Flowering of New England*
1938 Paul Herman Buck, *The Road to Reunion, 1865-1900*
1939 Frank Luther Mott, *A History of American Magazines*
1940 Carl Sandburg, *Abraham Lincoln: The War Years*
1941 Marcus Lee Hansen, *The Atlantic Migration, 1607-1860*
1942 Margaret Leech, *Reveille in Washington*
1943 Esther Forbes, *Paul Revere and the World He Lived In*
1944 Merle Curti, *The Growth of American Thought*
1945 Stephen Bonsal, *Unfinished Business*
1946 Arthur M. Schlesinger Jr., *The Age of Jackson*
1947 James Phinney Baxter III, *Scientists Against Time*
1948 Bernard De Voto, *Across the Wide Missouri*
1949 Roy F. Nichols, *The Disruption of American Democracy*
1950 O. W. Larkin, *Art and Life in America*
1951 R. Carlyle Buley, *The Old Northwest: Pioneer Period 1815-1840*
1952 Oscar Handlin, *The Uprooted*
1953 George Dangerfield, *The Era of Good Feelings*
1954 Bruce Catton, *A Stillness at Appomattox*
1955 Paul Horgan, *Great River: The Rio Grande in North American History*
1956 Richard Hofstadter, *The Age of Reform*
1957 George F. Kennan, *Russia Leaves the War*
1958 Bray Hammond, *Banks and Politics in America—From the Revolution to the Civil War*
1959 Leonard D. White and Jean Schneider, *The Republican Era, 1869-1901*
1960 Margaret Leech, *In the Days of McKinley*
1961 Herbert Feis, *Between War and Peace: The Potsdam Conference*
1962 Lawrence H. Gibson, *The Triumphant Empire: Thunderclouds Gather in the West*
1963 Constance McLaughlin Green, *Washington: Village and Capital, 1800-1878*
1964 Sumner Chilton Powell, *Puritan Village: The Formation of a New England Town*
1965 Irwin Unger, *The Greenback Era*
1966 Perry Miller, *Life of the Mind in America*
1967 William H. Goetzmann, *Exploration and Empire: The Explorer and Scientist in the Winning of the American West*
1968 Bernard Bailyn, *The Ideological Origins of the American Revolution*
1969 Leonard W. Levy, *Origin of the Fifth Amendment*
1970 Dean Acheson, *Present at the Creation: My Years in the State Department*
1971 James McGregor Burns, *Roosevelt: The Soldier of Freedom*
1972 Carl N. Degler, *Neither Black nor White*
1973 Michael Kammen, *People of Paradox: An Inquiry Concerning the Origins of American Civilization*
1974 Daniel J. Boorstin, *The Americans: The Democratic Experience*
1975 Dumas Malone, *Jefferson and His Time*
1976 Paul Horgan, *Lamy of Santa Fe*

1977 David M. Potter, *The Impending Crisis*
1978 Alfred D. Chandler Jr., *The Visible Hand: The Managerial Revolution in American Business*
1979 Don E. Fehrenbacher, *The Dred Scott Case: Its Significance in American Law and Politics*
1980 Leon F. Litwack, *Been in the Storm So Long*
1981 Lawrence A. Cremin, *American Education: The National Experience, 1783-1876*
1982 C. Vann Woodward, ed., *Mary Chesnut's Civil War*
1983 Rhys L. Issac, *The Transformation of Virginia, 1740-1790*
1985 Thomas K. McCraw, *Prophets of Regulation*
1986 Walter A. McDougall, *The Heavens and the Earth*
1987 Bernard Bailyn, *Voyagers to the West*
1988 Robert V. Bruce, *The Launching of Modern American Science, 1846-1876*
1989 Taylor Branch, *Parting the Waters: America in the King Years, 1954-63*; James M. McPherson, *Battle Cry of Freedom: The Civil War Era*
1990 Stanley Karnow, *In Our Image: America's Empire in the Philippines*
1991 Laurel Thatcher Ulrich, *A Midwife's Tale: The Life of Martha Ballard, Based on Her Diary, 1785-1812*
1992 Mark E. Neely Jr., *The Fate of Liberty: Abraham Lincoln and Civil Liberties*
1993 Gordon S. Wood, *The Radicalism of the American Revolution*
1995 Doris Kearns Goodwin, *No Ordinary Time: Franklin and Eleanor Roosevelt: The Home Front in World War II*
1996 Alan Taylor, *William Cooper's Town: Power and Persuasion on the Frontier of the Early American Republic*
1997 Jack N. Rakove, *Original Meanings: Politics and Ideas in the Making of the Constitution*
1998 Edward J. Larson, *Summer for the Gods: The Scopes Trial and America's Continuing Debate Over Science and Religion*
1999 Edwin G. Burrows and Mike Wallace, *Gotham: A History of New York City to 1898*
2000 David M. Kennedy, *Freedom From Fear: The American People in Depression and War, 1929-1945*
2001 Joseph J. Ellis, *Founding Brothers: The Revolutionary Generation*
2002 Louis Menand, *The Metaphysical Club: A Story of Ideas in America*
2003 Rick Atkinson, *An Army at Dawn: The War in North Africa, 1942-1943*
2004 Steven Hahn, *A Nation Under Our Feet: Black Political Struggles in the Rural South From Slavery to the Great Migration*
2005 David Hackett Fischer, *Washington's Crossing*
2006 David M. Oshinsky, *Polio: An American Story*
2007 Gene Roberts and Hank Klibanoff, *The Race Beat: The Press, the Civil Rights Struggle, and the Awakening of a Nation*
2008 Daniel Walker Howe, *What Hath God Wrought: The Transformation of America, 1815-1848*
2009 Annette Gordon-Reed, *The Hemingses of Monticello: An American Family*
2010 Liaquat Ahamed, *Lords of Finance: The Bankers Who Broke the World*
2011 Eric Foner, *The Fiery Trial: Abraham Lincoln and American Slavery*
2012 Manning Marable, *Malcolm X: A Life of Reinvention*
2013 Fredrik Logevall, *Embers of War: The Fall of an Empire and the Making of America's Vietnam*

Biography or Autobiography

1917 Laura E. Richards and Maude Howe Elliott, assisted by Florence Howe Hall, *Julia Ward Howe*
1918 William Cabell Bruce, *Benjamin Franklin, Self-Revealed*
1919 Henry Adams, *The Education of Henry Adams*
1920 Albert J. Beveridge, *The Life of John Marshall*
1921 Edward Bok, *The Americanization of Edward Bok*
1922 Hamlin Garland, *A Daughter of the Middle Border*
1923 Burton J. Hendrick, *The Life and Letters of Walter H. Page*
1924 Michael Pupin, *From Immigrant to Inventor*
1925 M. A. DeWolfe Howe, *Barrett Wendell and His Letters*
1926 Harvey Cushing, *Life of Sir William Osler*
1927 Emory Holloway, *Whitman: An Interpretation in Narrative*
1928 Charles Edward Russell, *The American Orchestra and Theodore Thomas*
1929 Burton J. Hendrick, *The Training of an American: The Earlier Life and Letters of Walter H. Page*
1930 Marquis James, *The Raven (Sam Houston)*
1931 Henry James, *Charles W. Eliot*
1932 Henry F. Pringle, *Theodore Roosevelt*
1933 Allan Nevins, *Grover Cleveland*
1934 Tyler Dennett, *John Hay*
1935 Douglas Southall Freeman, *R. E. Lee*
1936 Ralph Barton Perry, *The Thought and Character of William James*

1937 Allan Nevins, *Hamilton Fish: The Inner History of the Grant Administration*
1938 Odell Shepard, *Pedlar's Progress*; Marquis James, *Andrew Jackson*, 2 vols.
1939 Carl Van Doren, *Benjamin Franklin*
1940 Ray Stannard Baker, *Woodrow Wilson, Life and Letters*
1941 Ola Elizabeth Winslow, *Jonathan Edwards*
1942 Forrest Wilson, *Crusader in Crinoline* (Harriet Beecher Stowe)
1943 Samuel Eliot Morison, *Admiral of the Ocean Sea* (Christopher Columbus)
1944 Carleton Mabee, *The American Leonardo: The Life of Samuel F. B. Morse*
1945 Russell Blaine Nye, *George Bancroft: Brahmin Rebel*
1946 Linny Marsh Wolfe, *Son of the Wilderness* (John Muir)
1947 William Allen White, *Autobiography of William Allen White*
1948 Margaret Clapp, *Forgotten First Citizen: John Bigelow*
1949 Robert E. Sherwood, *Roosevelt and Hopkins*
1950 Samuel Flagg Bemis, *John Quincy Adams and the Foundations of American Foreign Policy*
1951 Margaret Louise Coit, *John C. Calhoun: American Portrait*
1952 Merlo J. Pusey, *Charles Evans Hughes*
1953 David J. Mays, *Edmund Pendleton, 1721-1803*
1954 Charles A. Lindbergh, *The Spirit of St. Louis*
1955 William S. White, *The Taft Story*
1956 Talbot F. Hamlin, *Benjamin Henry Latrobe*
1957 John F. Kennedy, *Profiles in Courage*
1958 Douglas Southall Freeman, *George Washington, Vols. I-VI*
1959 Arthur Walworth, *Woodrow Wilson: American Prophet*
1960 Samuel Eliot Morison, *John Paul Jones*
1961 David Donald, *Charles Sumner and the Coming of the Civil War*
1963 Leon Edel, *Henry James: Vols. 2-3*
1964 Walter Jackson Bate, *John Keats*
1965 Ernest Samuels, *Henry Adams*
1966 Arthur M. Schlesinger Jr., *A Thousand Days* (JFK)
1967 Justin Kaplan, *Mr. Clemens and Mark Twain*
1968 George F. Kennan, *Memoirs (1925-1950)*
1969 B. L. Reid, *The Man From New York: John Quinn and His Friends*
1970 T. Harry Williams, *Huey Long*
1971 Lawrence Thompson, *Robert Frost: The Years of Triumph, 1915-1938*
1972 Joseph P. Lash, *Eleanor and Franklin*
1973 W. A. Swanberg, *Luce and His Empire*
1974 Louis Sheaffer, *O'Neill, Son and Artist*
1975 Robert A. Caro, *The Power Broker: Robert Moses and the Fall of New York*
1976 R. W. B. Lewis, *Edith Wharton: A Biography*
1977 John E. Mack, *A Prince of Our Disorder: The Life of T. E. Lawrence*
1978 Walter Jackson Bate, *Samuel Johnson*
1979 Leonard Baker, *Days of Sorrow and Pain: Leo Baeck and the Berlin Jews*
1980 Edmund Morris, *The Rise of Theodore Roosevelt*
1981 Robert K. Massie, *Peter the Great: His Life and World*
1982 William S. McFeely, *Grant: A Biography*
1983 Russell Baker, *Growing Up*
1984 Louis R. Harlan, *Booker T. Washington*
1985 Kenneth Silverman, *The Life and Times of Cotton Mather*
1986 Elizabeth Frank, *Louise Bogan: A Portrait*
1987 David J. Garrow, *Bearing the Cross: Martin Luther King Jr. and the Southern Christian Leadership Conference*
1988 David Herbert Donald, *Look Homeward: A Life of Thomas Wolfe*
1989 Richard Ellmann, *Oscar Wilde*
1990 Sebastian de Grazia, *Machiavelli in Hell*
1991 Steven Naifeh and Gregory White Smith, *Jackson Pollock: An American Saga*
1992 Lewis B. Puller Jr., *Fortunate Son: The Healing of a Vietnam Vet*
1993 David McCullough, *Truman*
1994 David Levering Lewis, *W.E.B. DuBois: Biography of a Race, 1868-1919*
1995 Joan D. Hedrick, *Harriet Beecher Stowe: A Life*
1996 Jack Miles, *God: A Biography*
1997 Frank McCourt, *Angela's Ashes: A Memoir*
1998 Katharine Graham, *Personal History*
1999 A. Scott Berg, *Lindbergh*
2000 Stacy Schiff, *Véra (Mrs. Vladimir Nabokov)*
2001 David Levering Lewis, *W.E.B. Du Bois: The Fight for Equality and the American Century, 1919-1963*
2002 David McCullough, *John Adams*
2003 Robert Caro, *The Years of Lyndon Johnson: Master of the Senate*
2004 William Taubman, *Khrushchev: The Man and His Era*
2005 Mark Stevens and Annalyn Swan, *de Kooning: An American Master*

2006 Kai Bird and Martin J. Sherwin, *American Prometheus: The Triumph and Tragedy of J. Robert Oppenheimer*
2007 Debby Applegate, *The Most Famous Man in America: The Biography of Henry Ward Beecher*
2008 John Matteson, *Eden's Outcasts: The Story of Louisa May Alcott and Her Father*
2009 Jon Meacham, *American Lion: Andrew Jackson in the White House*
2010 T. J. Stiles, *The First Tycoon: The Epic Life of Cornelius Vanderbilt*
2011 Ron Chernow, *Washington: A Life*
2012 John Lewis Gaddis, *George F. Kennan: An American Life*
2013 Tom Reiss, *The Black Count: Glory, Revolution, Betrayal, and the Real Count of Monte Cristo* (Alex Dumas)

Poetry

1922 Edwin Arlington Robinson, *Collected Poems*
1923 Edna St. Vincent Millay, *The Ballad of the Harp-Weaver; A Few Figs From Thistles*; and other works
1924 Robert Frost, *New Hampshire: A Poem With Notes and Grace Notes*
1925 Edwin Arlington Robinson, *The Man Who Died Twice*
1926 Amy Lowell, *What's O'Clock*
1927 Leonora Speyer, *Fiddler's Farewell*
1928 Edwin Arlington Robinson, *Tristram*
1929 Stephen Vincent Benet, *John Brown's Body*
1930 Conrad Aiken, *Selected Poems*
1931 Robert Frost, *Collected Poems*
1932 George Dillon, *The Flowering Stone*
1933 Archibald MacLeish, *Conquistador*
1934 Robert Hillyer, *Collected Verse*
1935 Audrey Wurdemann, *Bright Ambush*
1936 Robert P. Tristram Coffin, *Strange Holiness*
1937 Robert Frost, *A Further Range*
1938 Marya Zaturenska, *Cold Morning Sky*
1939 John Gould Fletcher, *Selected Poems*
1940 Mark Van Doren, *Collected Poems*
1941 Leonard Bacon, *Sunderland Capture*
1942 William Rose Benet, *The Dust Which Is God*
1943 Robert Frost, *A Witness Tree*
1944 Stephen Vincent Benet, *Western Star*
1945 Karl Shapiro, *V-Letter and Other Poems*
1947 Robert Lowell, *Lord Weary's Castle*
1948 W. H. Auden, *The Age of Anxiety*
1949 Peter Viereck, *Terror and Decorum*
1950 Gwendolyn Brooks, *Annie Allen*
1951 Carl Sandburg, *Complete Poems*
1952 Marianne Moore, *Collected Poems*
1953 Archibald MacLeish, *Collected Poems*
1954 Theodore Roethke, *The Waking*
1955 Wallace Stevens, *Collected Poems*
1956 Elizabeth Bishop, *Poems, North and South*
1957 Richard Wilbur, *Things of This World*
1958 Robert Penn Warren, *Promises: Poems 1954-1956*
1959 Stanley Kunitz, *Selected Poems 1928-1958*
1960 W. D. Snodgrass, *Heart's Needle*
1961 Phyllis McGinley, *Times Three: Selected Verse From Three Decades*
1962 Alan Dugan, *Poems*
1963 William Carlos Williams, *Pictures From Breughel*
1964 Louis Simpson, *At the End of the Open Road*
1965 John Berryman, *77 Dream Songs*
1966 Richard Eberhart, *Selected Poems*
1967 Anne Sexton, *Live or Die*
1968 Anthony Hecht, *The Hard Hours*
1969 George Oppen, *Of Being Numerous*
1970 Richard Howard, *Untitled Subjects*
1971 William S. Merwin, *The Carrier of Ladders*
1972 James Wright, *Collected Poems*
1973 Maxine Winokur Kumin, *Up Country*
1974 Robert Lowell, *The Dolphin*
1975 Gary Snyder, *Turtle Island*
1976 John Ashbery, *Self-Portrait in a Convex Mirror*
1977 James Merrill, *Divine Comedies*
1978 Howard Nemerov, *Collected Poems*
1979 Robert Penn Warren, *Now and Then: Poems 1976-1978*
1980 Donald Justice, *Selected Poems*
1981 James Schuyler, *The Morning of the Poem*
1982 Sylvia Plath, *The Collected Poems*
1983 Galway Kinnell, *Selected Poems*
1984 Mary Oliver, *American Primitive*
1985 Carolyn Kizer, *Yin*
1986 Henry Taylor, *The Flying Change*
1987 Rita Dove, *Thomas and Beulah*
1988 William Meredith, *Partial Accounts*
1989 Richard Wilbur, *New and Collected Poems*
1990 Charles Simic, *The World Doesn't End*
1991 Mona Van Duyn, *Near Changes*
1992 James Tate, *Selected Poems*

1993 Louise Glück, *The Wild Iris*
1994 Yusef Komunyakaa, *Neon Vernacular*
1995 Philip Levine, *The Simple Truth*
1996 Jorie Graham, *The Dream of the Unified Field*
1997 Lisel Mueller, *Alive Together: New and Selected Poems*
1998 Charles Wright, *Black Zodiac*
1999 Mark Strand, *Blizzard of One*
2000 C. K. Williams, *Repair*
2001 Stephen Dunn, *Different Hours*
2002 Carl Dennis, *Practical Gods*
2003 Paul Muldoon, *Moy Sand and Gravel*
2004 Franz Wright, *Walking to Martha's Vineyard*
2005 Ted Kooser, *Delights & Shadows*
2006 Claudia Emerson, *Late Wife*
2007 Natasha Trethewey, *Native Guard*
2008 Robert Hass, *Time and Materials*; Philip Schultz, *Failure*
2009 W. S. Merwin, *The Shadow of Sirius*
2010 Rae Armantrout, *Versed*
2011 Kay Ryan, *The Best of It: New and Selected Poems*
2012 Tracy K. Smith, *Life on Mars*
2013 Sharon Olds, *Stag's Leap*

General Nonfiction

1962 Theodore H. White, *The Making of the President 1960*
1963 Barbara W. Tuchman, *The Guns of August*
1964 Richard Hofstadter, *Anti-Intellectualism in American Life*
1965 Howard Mumford Jones, *O Strange New World*
1966 Edwin Way Teale, *Wandering Through Winter*
1967 David Brion Davis, *The Problem of Slavery in Western Culture*
1968 Will and Ariel Durant, *Rousseau and Revolution*
1969 Norman Mailer, *The Armies of the Night*; Rene Jules Dubos, *So Human an Animal: How We Are Shaped by Surroundings and Events*
1970 Eric H. Erikson, *Gandhi's Truth*
1971 John Toland, *The Rising Sun*
1972 Barbara W. Tuchman, *Stilwell and the American Experience in China, 1911-1945*
1973 Frances FitzGerald, *Fire in the Lake: The Vietnamese and the Americans in Vietnam*; Robert Coles, *Children of Crisis, Vols. II and III*
1974 Ernest Becker, *The Denial of Death*
1975 Annie Dillard, *Pilgrim at Tinker Creek*
1976 Robert N. Butler, *Why Survive? Being Old in America*
1977 William W. Warner, *Beautiful Swimmers*
1978 Carl Sagan, *The Dragons of Eden*
1979 Edward O. Wilson, *On Human Nature*
1980 Douglas R. Hofstadter, *Gödel, Escher, Bach: An Eternal Golden Braid*
1981 Carl E. Schorske, *Fin-de-Siecle Vienna: Politics and Culture*
1982 Tracy Kidder, *The Soul of a New Machine*
1983 Susan Sheehan, *Is There No Place on Earth for Me?*
1984 Paul Starr, *Social Transformation of American Medicine*
1985 Studs Terkel, *The Good War*
1986 Joseph Lelyveld, *Move Your Shadow*; J. Anthony Lukas, *Common Ground*
1987 David K. Shipler, *Arab and Jew*
1988 Richard Rhodes, *The Making of the Atomic Bomb*

1989 Neil Sheehan, *A Bright Shining Lie: John Paul Vann and America in Vietnam*
1990 Dale Maharidge and Michael Williamson, *And Their Children After Them*
1991 Bert Holldobler and Edward O. Wilson, *The Ants*
1992 Daniel Yergin, *The Prize: The Epic Quest for Oil, Money, and Power*
1993 Garry Wills, *Lincoln at Gettysburg*
1994 David Remnick, *Lenin's Tomb: The Last Days of the Soviet Empire*
1995 Jonathan Weiner, *The Beak of the Finch: A Story of Evolution in Our Time*
1996 Tina Rosenberg, *The Haunted Land: Facing Europe's Ghosts After Communism*
1997 Richard Kluger, *Ashes to Ashes: America's Hundred-Year Cigarette War, the Public Health, and the Unabashed Triumph of Philip Morris*
1998 Jared Diamond, *Guns, Germs, and Steel: The Fates of Human Societies*
1999 John McPhee, *Annals of the Former World*
2000 John W. Dower, *Embracing Defeat: Japan in the Wake of World War II*
2001 Herbert P. Bix, *Hirohito and the Making of Modern Japan*
2002 Diane McWhorter, *Carry Me Home: Birmingham, Alabama, the Climactic Battle of the Civil Rights Revolution*
2003 Samantha Power, *A Problem From Hell: America and the Age of Genocide*
2004 Anne Applebaum, *Gulag: A History*
2005 Steve Coll, *Ghost Wars*
2006 Caroline Elkins, *Imperial Reckoning: The Untold Story of Britain's Gulag in Kenya*
2007 Lawrence Wright, *The Looming Tower: Al-Qaeda and the Road to 9/11*
2008 Saul Friedländer, *The Years of Extermination: Nazi Germany and the Jews, 1939-1945*
2009 Douglas A. Blackmon, *Slavery by Another Name: The Re-Enslavement of Black Americans From the Civil War to World War II*
2010 David E. Hoffman, *The Dead Hand: The Untold Story of the Cold War Arms Race and Its Dangerous Legacy*
2011 Siddhartha Mukherjee, *The Emperor of All Maladies: A Biography of Cancer*
2012 Stephen Greenblatt, *The Swerve: How the World Became Modern*
2013 Gilbert King, *Devil in the Grove: Thurgood Marshall, the Groveland Boys, and the Dawn of a New America*

Special Citation in Letters

1944 Richard Rodgers and Oscar Hammerstein II, for *Oklahoma!*
1957 Kenneth Roberts, for his historical novels
1960 *The Armada*, by Garrett Mattingly
1961 *American Heritage Picture History of the Civil War*
1973 *George Washington, Vols. I-IV*, by James Thomas Flexner
1977 Alex Haley, for *Roots*
1978 E. B. White
1984 Theodore Seuss Geisel (Dr. Seuss)
1992 Art Spiegelman, for *Maus*
2006 Edmund S. Morgan
2007 Ray Bradbury

Pulitzer Prizes in Music, 1943-2013

1943 William Schuman, *Secular Cantata No. 2, A Free Song*
1944 Howard Hanson, *Symphony No. 4, Op. 34*
1945 Aaron Copland, *Appalachian Spring*
1946 Leo Sowerby, *The Canticle of the Sun*
1947 Charles E. Ives, *Symphony No. 3*
1948 Walter Piston, *Symphony No. 3*
1949 Virgil Thomson, *Louisiana Story*
1950 Gian-Carlo Menotti, *The Consul*
1951 Douglas Moore, *Giants in the Earth*
1952 Gail Kubik, *Symphony Concertante*
1954 Quincy Porter, *Concerto for Two Pianos and Orchestra*
1955 Gian-Carlo Menotti, *The Saint of Bleecker Street*
1956 Ernest Toch, *Symphony No. 3*
1957 Norman Dello Joio, *Meditations on Ecclesiastes*
1958 Samuel Barber, *Vanessa*
1959 John La Montaine, *Concerto for Piano and Orchestra*
1960 Elliott Carter, *Second String Quartet*
1961 Walter Piston, *Symphony No. 7*
1962 Robert Ward, *The Crucible*
1963 Samuel Barber, *Piano Concerto No. 1*
1966 Leslie Bassett, *Variations for Orchestra*
1967 Leon Kirchner, *Quartet No. 3*
1968 George Crumb, *Echoes of Time and the River*
1969 Karel Husa, *String Quartet No. 3*
1970 Charles W. Wuorinen, *Time's Encomium*
1971 Mario Davidovsky, *Synchronisms No. 6*
1972 Jacob Druckman, *Windows*
1973 Elliott Carter, *String Quartet No. 3*
1974 Donald Martino, *Notturno*

1975 Dominick Argento, *From the Diary of Virginia Woolf*
1976 Ned Rorem, *Air Music*
1977 Richard Wernick, *Visions of Terror and Wonder*
1978 Michael Colgrass, *Deja Vu for Percussion and Orchestra*
1979 Joseph Schwantner, *Aftertones of Infinity*
1980 David Del Tredici, *In Memory of a Summer Day*
1982 Roger Sessions, *Concerto for Orchestra*
1983 Ellen T. Zwilich, *Three Movements for Orchestra*
1984 Bernard Rands, *Canti del Sole*
1985 Stephen Albert, *Symphony, RiverRun*
1986 George Perle, *Wind Quintet IV*
1987 John Harbison, *The Flight Into Egypt*
1988 William Bolcom, *12 New Etudes for Piano*
1989 Roger Reynolds, *Whispers Out of Time*
1990 Mel Powell, *Duplicates: A Concerto for Two Pianos and Orchestra*
1991 Shulamit Ran, *Symphony*
1992 Wayne Peterson, *The Face of the Night, The Heart of the Dark*
1993 Christopher Rouse, *Trombone Concerto*
1994 Gunther Schuller, *Of Reminiscences and Reflections*
1995 Morton Gould, *Stringmusic*
1996 George Walker, *Lilacs for Voice and Orchestra*
1997 Wynton Marsalis, *Blood on the Fields*
1998 Aaron Jay Kernis, *String Quartet No. 2 (musica instrumentalis)*
1999 Melinda Wagner, *Concerto for Flute, Strings, and Percussion*
2000 Lewis Spratlan, *Life is a Dream, Opera in Three Acts: Act II, Concert Version*
2001 John Corigliano, *Symphony No. 2 for String Orchestra*

2002 Henry Brant, *Ice Field*
2003 John Adams, *On the Transmigration of Souls*
2004 Paul Moravec, *Tempest Fantasy*
2005 Steven Stucky, *Second Concerto for Orchestra*
2006 Yehudi Wyner, *Piano Concerto: "Chiavi in Mano"*
2007 Ornette Coleman, *Sound Grammar*
2008 David Lang, *The Little Match Girl Passion*
2009 Steve Reich, *Double Sextet*
2010 Jennifer Higdon, *Violin Concerto*
2011 Zhou Long, *Madame White Snake*
2012 Kevin Puts, *Silent Night: Opera in Two Acts*
2013 Caroline Shaw, *Partita for 8 Voices*

Special Citation in Music
1974 Roger Sessions
1976 Scott Joplin
1982 Milton Babbitt
1985 William Schuman
1998 George Gershwin
1999 Edward Kennedy "Duke" Ellington
2006 Thelonious Monk
2007 John Coltrane
2008 Bob Dylan
2010 Hank Williams

Man Booker Prize for Fiction, 1969-2013

The Booker Prize for fiction, established in 1968, is awarded annually in Oct. for what is judged the best full-length novel written in English by a citizen of the UK, the Commonwealth, or the Irish Republic. In 2002, sponsorship of the award was taken over by Man Group PLC, the name was changed to the Man Booker Prize, and the amount was increased from £20,000 to £50,000 (about $80,000).

Year	Author, book	Year	Author, book
1969	P. H. Newby, *Something to Answer For*	1992	Michael Ondaatje, *The English Patient*; Barry Unsworth, *Sacred Hunger*
1970	Bernice Rubens, *The Elected Member*	1993	Roddy Doyle, *Paddy Clarke Ha Ha Ha*
1971	V. S. Naipaul, *In a Free State*	1994	James Kelman, *How Late It Was, How Late*
1972	John Berger, *G*	1995	Pat Barker, *The Ghost Road*
1973	J. G. Farrell, *The Siege of Krishnapur*	1996	Graham Swift, *Last Orders*
1974	Nadine Gordimer, *The Conservationist*; Stanley Middleton, *Holiday*	1997	Arundhati Roy, *The God of Small Things*
1975	Ruth Prawer Jhabvala, *Heat and Dust*	1998	Ian McEwan, *Amsterdam*
1976	David Storey, *Saville*	1999	J. M. Coetzee, *Disgrace*
1977	Paul Scott, *Staying On*	2000	Margaret Atwood, *The Blind Assassin*
1978	Iris Murdoch, *The Sea, The Sea*	2001	Peter Carey, *True History of the Kelly Gang*
1979	Penelope Fitzgerald, *Offshore*	2002	Yann Martel, *Life of Pi*
1980	William Golding, *Rites of Passage*	2003	DBC Pierre, *Vernon God Little*
1981	Salman Rushdie, *Midnight's Children*[1]	2004	Alan Hollinghurst, *The Line of Beauty*
1982	Thomas Keneally, *Schindler's Ark*	2005	John Banville, *The Sea*
1983	J. M. Coetzee, *Life and Times of Michael K*	2006	Kiran Desai, *The Inheritance of Loss*
1984	Anita Brookner, *Hotel du Lac*	2007	Anne Enright, *The Gathering*
1985	Keri Hulme, *The Bone People*	2008	Aravind Adiga, *The White Tiger*
1986	Kingsley Amis, *The Old Devils*	2009	Hilary Mantel, *Wolf Hall*
1987	Penelope Lively, *Moon Tiger*	2010	Howard Jacobson, *The Finkler Question*
1988	Peter Carey, *Oscar and Lucinda*	2011	Julian Barnes, *The Sense of an Ending*
1989	Kazuo Ishiguro, *The Remains of the Day*	2012	Hilary Mantel, *Bring up the Bodies*
1990	A. S. Byatt, *Possession*	2013	Eleanor Catton, *The Luminaries*
1991	Ben Okri, *The Famished Road*		

(1) Rushdie's *Midnight's Children* also won the Booker of Booker prize in 1993 and the Best of the Booker prize in 2008.

Newbery Medal, 1922-2013

The Newbery Medal is awarded annually by the Association for Library Service to Children, a division of the American Library Association, to the most distinguished contribution to American children's literature published in the previous year.

Year	Book, author	Year	Book, author
1922	*The Story of Mankind*, Hendrik Willem van Loon	1956	*Carry On, Mr. Bowditch*, Jean Lee Latham
1923	*The Voyages of Dr. Dolittle*, Hugh Lofting	1957	*Miracles on Maple Hill*, Virginia Sorensen
1924	*The Dark Frigate*, Charles Boardman Hawes	1958	*Rifles for Watie*, Harold Keith
1925	*Tales From Silver Lands*, Charles Joseph Finger	1959	*The Witch of Blackbird Pond*, Elizabeth George Speare
1926	*Shen of the Sea*, Arthur Bowie Chrisman	1960	*Onion John*, Joseph Krumgold
1927	*Smoky, the Cowhorse*, Will James	1961	*Island of the Blue Dolphins*, Scott O'Dell
1928	*Gay-Neck*, Dhan Gopal Mukerji	1962	*The Bronze Bow*, Elizabeth George Speare
1929	*The Trumpeter of Krakow*, Eric P. Kelly	1963	*A Wrinkle in Time*, Madeleine L'Engle
1930	*Hitty, Her First Hundred Years*, Rachel Field	1964	*It's Like This, Cat*, Emily Cheney Neville
1931	*The Cat Who Went to Heaven*, Elizabeth Coatsworth	1965	*Shadow of a Bull*, Maja Wojciechowska
1932	*Waterless Mountain*, Laura Adams Armer	1966	*I, Juan de Pareja*, Elizabeth Borton de Trevino
1933	*Young Fu of the Upper Yangtze*, Elizabeth Foreman Lewis	1967	*Up a Road Slowly*, Irene Hunt
1934	*Invincible Louisa*, Cornelia Lynde Meigs	1968	*From the Mixed-Up Files of Mrs. Basil E. Frankweiler*, E. L. Konigsburg
1935	*Dobry*, Monica Shannon	1969	*The High King*, Lloyd Alexander
1936	*Caddie Woodlawn*, Carol Ryrie Brink	1970	*Sounder*, William H. Armstrong
1937	*Roller Skates*, Ruth Sawyer	1971	*The Summer of the Swans*, Betsy Byars
1938	*The White Stag*, Kate Seredy	1972	*Mrs. Frisby and the Rats of NIMH*, Robert C. O'Brien
1939	*Thimble Summer*, Elizabeth Enright	1973	*Julie of the Wolves*, Jean George
1940	*Daniel Boone*, James Daugherty	1974	*The Slave Dancer*, Paula Fox
1941	*Call It Courage*, Armstrong Sperry	1975	*M. C. Higgins the Great*, Virginia Hamilton
1942	*The Matchlock Gun*, Walter D. Edmonds	1976	*Grey King*, Susan Cooper
1943	*Adam of the Road*, Elizabeth Janet Gray	1977	*Roll of Thunder, Hear My Cry*, Mildred D. Taylor
1944	*Johnny Tremain*, Esther Forbes	1978	*Bridge to Terabithia*, Katherine Paterson
1945	*Rabbit Hill*, Robert Lawson	1979	*The Westing Game*, Ellen Raskin
1946	*Strawberry Girl*, Lois Lenski	1980	*A Gathering of Days*, Joan Blos
1947	*Miss Hickory*, Carolyn S. Bailey	1981	*Jacob Have I Loved*, Katherine Paterson
1948	*Twenty-One Balloons*, William Pène Du Bois	1982	*A Visit to William Blake's Inn: Poems for Innocent and Experienced Travelers*, Nancy Willard
1949	*King of the Wind*, Marguerite Henry	1983	*Dicey's Song*, Cynthia Voigt
1950	*The Door in the Wall*, Marguerite de Angeli	1984	*Dear Mr. Henshaw*, Beverly Cleary
1951	*Amos Fortune, Free Man*, Elizabeth Yates	1985	*The Hero and the Crown*, Robin McKinley
1952	*Ginger Pye*, Eleanor Estes	1986	*Sarah, Plain and Tall*, Patricia MacLachlan
1953	*Secret of the Andes*, Ann Nolan Clark	1987	*The Whipping Boy*, Sid Fleischman
1954	*...And Now Miguel*, Joseph Krumgold	1988	*Lincoln: A Photobiography*, Russell Freedman
1955	*The Wheel on the School*, Meindert DeJong		

Year	Book, author
1989	*Joyful Noise: Poems for Two Voices*, Paul Fleischman
1990	*Number the Stars*, Lois Lowry
1991	*Maniac Magee*, Jerry Spinelli
1992	*Shiloh*, Phyllis Reynolds Naylor
1993	*Missing May*, Cynthia Rylant
1994	*The Giver*, Lois Lowry
1995	*Walk Two Moons*, Sharon Creech
1996	*The Midwife's Apprentice*, Karen Cushman
1997	*The View From Saturday*, E. L. Konigsburg
1998	*Out of the Dust*, Karen Hesse
1999	*Holes*, Louis Sachar
2000	*Bud, Not Buddy*, Christopher Paul Curtis
2001	*A Year Down Yonder*, Richard Peck

Year	Book, author
2002	*A Single Shard*, Linda Sue Park
2003	*Crispin: The Cross of Lead*, Avi
2004	*The Tale of Despereaux*, Kate DiCamillo
2005	*Kira-Kira*, Cynthia Kadohata
2006	*Criss Cross*, Lynne Rae Perkins
2007	*The Higher Power of Lucky*, Susan Patron
2008	*Good Masters! Sweet Ladies! Voices From a Medieval Village*, Laura Amy Schlitz
2009	*The Graveyard Book*, Neil Gaiman
2010	*When You Reach Me*, Rebecca Stead
2011	*Moon Over Manifest*, Clare Vanderpool
2012	*Dead End in Norvelt*, Jack Gantos
2013	*The One and Only Ivan*, Katherine Applegate

Caldecott Medal, 1938-2013

The Caldecott Medal is awarded annually by the Association for Library Service to Children, a division of the American Library Association, to the illustrator of the most distinguished American picture book for children.

Year	Book, illustrator
1938	*Animals of the Bible*, Dorothy P. Lathrop
1939	*Mei Li*, Thomas Handforth
1940	*Abraham Lincoln*, Ingri and Edgar Parin d'Aulaire
1941	*They Were Strong and Good*, Robert Lawson
1942	*Make Way for Ducklings*, Robert McCloskey
1943	*The Little House*, Virginia Lee Burton
1944	*Many Moons*, Louis Slobodkin
1945	*Prayer for a Child*, Elizabeth Orton Jones
1946	*The Rooster Crows*, Maude and Miska Petersham
1947	*The Little Island*, Leonard Weisgard
1948	*White Snow, Bright Snow*, Roger Duvoisin
1949	*The Big Snow*, Berta and Elmer Hader
1950	*Song of the Swallows*, Leo Politi
1951	*The Egg Tree*, Katherine Milhous
1952	*Finders Keepers*, Nicolas, pseud. (Nicholas Mordvinoff)
1953	*The Biggest Bear*, Lynd Ward
1954	*Madeline's Rescue*, Ludwig Bemelmans
1955	*Cinderella, or the Little Glass Slipper*, Marcia Brown
1956	*Frog Went A-Courtin'*, Feodor Rojankovsky
1957	*A Tree Is Nice*, Marc Simont
1958	*Time of Wonder*, Robert McCloskey
1959	*Chanticleer and the Fox*, Barbara Cooney
1960	*Nine Days to Christmas*, Marie Hall Ets
1961	*Baboushka and the Three Kings*, Nicolas Sidjakov
1962	*Once a Mouse*, Marcia Brown
1963	*The Snowy Day*, Ezra Jack Keats
1964	*Where the Wild Things Are*, Maurice Sendak
1965	*May I Bring a Friend?*, Beni Montressor
1966	*Always Room for One More*, Nonny Hogrogian
1967	*Sam, Bang, and Moonshine*, Evaline Ness
1968	*Drummer Hoff*, Ed Emberley
1969	*The Fool of the World and the Flying Ship*, Uri Shulevitz
1970	*Sylvester and the Magic Pebble*, William Steig
1971	*A Story A Story*, Gail E. Haley
1972	*One Fine Day*, Nonny Hogrogian
1973	*The Funny Little Woman*, Blair Lent
1974	*Duffy and the Devil*, Margot Zemach
1975	*Arrow to the Sun*, Gerald McDermott
1976	*Why Mosquitoes Buzz in People's Ears*, Leo and Diane Dillon

Year	Book, illustrator
1977	*Ashanti to Zulu: African Traditions*, Leo and Diane Dillon
1978	*Noah's Ark*, Peter Spier
1979	*The Girl Who Loved Wild Horses*, Paul Goble
1980	*Ox-Cart Man*, Barbara Cooney
1981	*Fables*, Arnold Lobel
1982	*Jumanji*, Chris Van Allsburg
1983	*Shadow*, Marcia Brown
1984	*The Glorious Flight: Across the Channel With Louis Bleriot*, Alice and Martin Provensen
1985	*Saint George and the Dragon*, Trina Schart Hyman
1986	*The Polar Express*, Chris Van Allsburg
1987	*Hey, Al*, Richard Egielski
1988	*Owl Moon*, John Schoenherr
1989	*Song and Dance Man*, Stephen Grammell
1990	*Lon Po Po: A Red-Riding Hood Story From China*, Ed Young
1991	*Black and White*, David Macaulay
1992	*Tuesday*, David Wiesner
1993	*Mirette on the High Wire*, Emily Arnold McCully
1994	*Grandfather's Journey*, Allen Say
1995	*Smoky Night*, David Diaz
1996	*Officer Buckle and Gloria*, Peggy Rathmann
1997	*Golem*, David Wisniewski
1998	*Rapunzel*, Paul O. Zelinsky
1999	*Snowflake Bentley*, Mary Azarian
2000	*Joseph Had a Little Overcoat*, Simms Taback
2001	*So You Want to be President?*, David Small
2002	*The Three Pigs*, David Wiesner
2003	*My Friend Rabbit*, Eric Rohmann
2004	*The Man Who Walked Between the Towers*, Mordicai Gerstein
2005	*Kitten's First Full Moon*, Kevin Henkes
2006	*The Hello, Goodbye Window*, Chris Raschka
2007	*Flotsam*, David Wiesner
2008	*The Invention of Hugo Cabret*, Brian Selznick
2009	*The House in the Night*, Beth Krommes
2010	*The Lion & the Mouse*, Jerry Pinkney
2011	*A Sick Day for Amos McGee*, Erin E. Stead
2012	*A Ball for Daisy*, Chris Raschka
2013	*This Is Not My Hat*, Jon Klassen

National Book Awards, 1950-2012

The National Book Awards (known as American Book Awards 1980-86) are administered by the National Book Foundation and have been given annually in the years shown, since 1950. The prizes, each valued at $10,000, are awarded to U.S. citizens for works published in the U.S. In some years, multiple awards were given for nonfiction in various categories; in such cases, the history and biography (if any) or biography winner is listed. Selected additional awards in nonfiction are listed in footnotes.

Other National Book Awards, 2012: Poetry: David Ferry, *Bewilderment: New Poems and Translations*. Young People's Literature: William Alexander, *Goblin Secrets*. Distinguished Contribution to American Letters: Elmore Leonard. Literarian Award: Arthur O. Sulzberger Jr.

Fiction

Year	Author, book
1950	Nelson Algren, *The Man With the Golden Arm*
1951	William Faulkner, *The Collected Stories*
1952	James Jones, *From Here to Eternity*
1953	Ralph Ellison, *Invisible Man*
1954	Saul Bellow, *The Adventures of Augie March*
1955	William Faulkner, *A Fable*
1956	John O'Hara, *Ten North Frederick*
1957	Wright Morris, *The Field of Vision*
1958	John Cheever, *The Wapshot Chronicle*
1959	Bernard Malamud, *The Magic Barrel*

Year	Author, book
1960	Philip Roth, *Goodbye, Columbus*
1961	Conrad Richter, *The Waters of Kronos*
1962	Walker Percy, *The Moviegoer*
1963	J. F. Powers, *Morte d'Urban*
1964	John Updike, *The Centaur*
1965	Saul Bellow, *Herzog*
1966	Katherine Anne Porter, *The Collected Stories*
1967	Bernard Malamud, *The Fixer*
1968	Thornton Wilder, *The Eighth Day*
1969	Jerzy Kosinski, *Steps*

Year	Author, book
1970	Joyce Carol Oates, *Them*
1971	Saul Bellow, *Mr. Sammler's Planet*
1972	Flannery O'Connor, *The Complete Stories*
1973	John Barth, *Chimera*
1974	Thomas Pynchon, *Gravity's Rainbow*
1974	Isaac Bashevis Singer, *A Crown of Feathers*
1975	Robert Stone, *Dog Soldiers*
1976	William Gaddis, *JR*
1977	Wallace Stegner, *The Spectator Bird*
1978	Mary Lee Settle, *Blood Ties*
1979	Tim O'Brien, *Going After Cacciato*
1980	William Styron, *Sophie's Choice*
1981	Wright Morris, *Plains Song*
1982	John Updike, *Rabbit Is Rich*
1983	Alice Walker, *The Color Purple*
1984	Ellen Gilchrist, *Victory Over Japan*
1985	Don DeLillo, *White Noise*
1986	E. L. Doctorow, *World's Fair*
1987	Larry Heinemann, *Paco's Story*
1988	Pete Dexter, *Paris Trout*
1989	John Casey, *Spartina*
1990	Charles Johnson, *Middle Passage*

Year	Author, book
1991	Norman Rush, *Mating*
1992	Cormac McCarthy, *All the Pretty Horses*
1993	E. Annie Proulx, *The Shipping News*
1994	William Gaddis, *A Frolic of His Own*
1995	Philip Roth, *Sabbath's Theater*
1996	Andrea Barrett, *Ship Fever and Other Stories*
1997	Charles Frazier, *Cold Mountain*
1998	Alice McDermott, *Charming Billy*
1999	Ha Jin, *Waiting*
2000	Susan Sontag, *In America*
2001	Jonathan Franzen, *The Corrections*
2002	Julia Glass, *Three Junes*
2003	Shirley Hazzard, *The Great Fire*
2004	Lily Tuck, *The News From Paraguay*
2005	William T. Vollmann, *Europe Central*
2006	Richard Powers, *The Echo Maker*
2007	Denis Johnson, *Tree of Smoke*
2008	Peter Matthiessen, *Shadow Country*
2009	Colum McCann, *Let the Great World Spin*
2010	Jaimy Gordon, *Lord of Misrule*
2011	Jesmyn Ward, *Salvage the Bones*
2012	Louise Erdrich, *The Round House*

Nonfiction

Year	Author, book
1950	Ralph L. Rusk, *Ralph Waldo Emerson*
1951	Newton Arvin, *Herman Melville*
1952	Rachel Carson, *The Sea Around Us*
1953	Bernard A. De Voto, *The Course of an Empire*
1954	Bruce Catton, *A Stillness at Appomattox*
1955	Joseph Wood Krutch, *The Measure of Man*
1956	Herbert Kubly, *An American in Italy*
1957	George F. Kennan, *Russia Leaves the War*
1958	Catherine Drinker Bowen, *The Lion and the Throne*
1959	J. Christopher Herold, *Mistress to an Age: A Life of Madame De Stael*
1960	Richard Ellman, *James Joyce*
1961	William L. Shirer, *The Rise and Fall of the Third Reich*
1962	Lewis Mumford, *The City in History: Its Origins, Its Transformations, and Its Prospects*
1963	Leon Edel, *Henry James, Vol. II: The Conquest of London and Vol. III: The Middle Years*
1964	WIlliam H. McNeill, *The Rise of the West: A History of the Human Community*
1965	Louis Fisher, *The Life of Lenin*
1966	Arthur M. Schlesinger Jr., *A Thousand Days: John F. Kennedy in the White House*
1967	Peter Gay, *The Enlightenment, An Interpretation, Vol I: The Rise of Modern Paganism*
1968	George F. Kennan, *Memoirs: 1925-1950*[1]
1969	Winthrop D. Jordan, *White Over Black: American Attitudes Toward the Negro, 1550-1812*[2]
1970	T. Harry Williams, *Huey Long*[3]
1971	James MacGregor Burns, *Roosevelt: The Soldier of Freedom*
1972	Joseph P. Lash, *Eleanor and Franklin: The Story of Their Relationship, Based on Eleanor Roosevelt's Private Papers*
1973	James Thomas Flexner, *George Washington, Vol. IV: Anguish and Farewell, 1793-1799*[4]
1974	John Clive, *Macaulay, The Shaping of the Historian*; Douglas Day, *Malcolm Lowry: A Biography*[5]
1975	Richard B. Sewall, *The Life of Emily Dickinson*[6]
1976	David Brion Davis, *The Problem of Slavery in the Age of Revolution, 1770-1823*
1977	W. A. Swanberg, *Norman Thomas: The Last Idealist*[7]
1978	W. Jackson Bate, *Samuel Johnson*
1979	Arthur M. Schlesinger Jr., *Robert Kennedy and His Times*
1980	Tom Wolfe, *The Right Stuff*
1981	Maxine Hong Kingston, *China Men*
1982	Tracy Kidder, *The Soul of a New Machine*
1983	Fox Butterfield, *China: Alive in the Bitter Sea*

Year	Author, book
1984	Robert V. Remini, *Andrew Jackson and the Course of American Democracy, 1833-1845*
1985	J. Anthony Lukas, *Common Ground: A Turbulent Decade in the Lives of Three American Families*
1986	Barry Lopez, *Arctic Dreams*
1987	Richard Rhodes, *The Making of the Atom Bomb*
1988	Neil Sheehan, *A Bright Shining Lie: John Paul Vann and America in Vietnam*
1989	Thomas L. Friedman, *From Beirut to Jerusalem*
1990	Ron Chernow, *The House of Morgan: An American Banking Dynasty and the Rise of Modern Finance*
1991	Orlando Patterson, *Freedom*
1992	Paul Monette, *Becoming a Man: Half a Life Story*
1993	Gore Vidal, *United States: Essays 1952-1992*
1994	Sherwin B. Nuland, *How We Die: Reflections on Life's Final Chapter*
1995	Tina Rosenberg, *The Haunted Land: Facing Europe's Ghosts After Communism*
1996	James Carroll, *An American Requiem: God, My Father, and the War That Came Between Us*
1997	Joseph J. Ellis, *American Sphinx: The Character of Thomas Jefferson*
1998	Edward Ball, *Slaves in the Family*
1999	John W. Dower, *Embracing Defeat: Japan in the Wake of World War II*
2000	Nathaniel Philbrick, *In the Heart of the Sea: The Tragedy of the Whaleship Essex*
2001	Andrew Solomon, *The Noonday Demon: An Atlas of Depression*
2002	Robert A. Caro, *Master of the Senate: The Years of Lyndon Johnson*
2003	Carlos Eire, *Waiting for Snow in Havana: Confessions of a Cuban Boy*
2004	Kevin Boyle, *Arc of Justice: A Saga of Race, Civil Rights, and Murder in the Jazz Age*
2005	Joan Didion, *The Year of Magical Thinking*
2006	Timothy Egan, *The Worst Hard Time: The Untold Story of Those Who Survived the Great American Dust Bowl*
2007	Tim Weiner, *Legacy of Ashes: The History of the CIA*
2008	Annette Gordon-Reed, *The Hemingses of Monticello: An American Family*
2009	T. J. Stiles, *The First Tycoon: The Epic Life of Cornelius Vanderbilt*
2010	Patti Smith, *Just Kids*
2011	Stephen Greenblatt, *The Swerve: How the World Became Modern*
2012	Katherine Boo, *Behind the Beautiful Forevers: Life, Death, and Hope in a Mumbai Undercity*

(1) Science, Philosophy, & Religion: Jonathan Kozol, *Death at an Early Age*. (2) Arts & Letters: Norman Mailer, *The Armies of the Night: History as a Novel, the Novel as History*. (3) Arts & Letters: Lillian Hellman, *An Unfinished Woman: A Memoir*. (4) Contemp. Affairs: Frances FitzGerald, *Fire in the Lake: The Vietnamese and the Americans in Vietnam*. (5) Arts & Letters: Pauline Kael, *Deeper Into the Movies*. (6) Arts & Letters: Roger Shattuck, *Marcel Proust*; Lewis Thomas, *The Lives of a Cell: Notes of a Biology Watcher*. (7) Contemp. Thought: Bruno Bettelheim, *The Uses of Enchantment: The Meaning and Importance of Fairy Tales*.

Journalism Awards, 2013

National Magazine Awards, by American Society of Magazine Editors and Columbia Journalism School. Magazine of the Year: *New York*. General Excellence: Lifestyle, *Martha Stewart Living*; Literary/Political/Professional, *The Paris Review*; News/Sports/Entertainment, *National Geographic*; Service/Fashion, *Vogue*; Special-Interest, *Outside*. Columns and Commentary: *Slate*. Design: *Time*. Essays and Criticism: *The Atlantic*. Feature Photography: *W.* Feature Writing inc. Profile Writing: *Texas Monthly*. Fiction: *Harper's Magazine*. Leisure Interests: *Wired*. Magazine Section: *New York*. Personal Service: *Los Angeles*. Photography: *National Geographic*. Public Interest: *Texas Monthly*. Reporting: *GQ*. Single-Topic Issue: *Saveur*. **Digital awards:** General Excellence: *Pitchfork*. Website: *The Atlantic*. Tablet Magazine: *National Geographic*. Multimedia: *National Geographic*. Video: *Mother Jones*.

George Foster Peabody Awards, by Univ. of Georgia, awarded to the best in electronic media. Lorne Michaels. "Robin's Journey," "Superstorm Sandy," ABC. *Switched at Birth*, ABC Family. *Sheikh Jarrah [My Neighborhood]*, Al Jazeera. *Putin, Russia & the West*, BBC2. *Doctor Who*, BBC America. "Deception at Duke," "Joy in the Congo," *60 Minutes*, CBS. *Sri Lanka's Killing Fields: War Crimes Unpunished*, Channel 4, UK. *CNN's Coverage Inside Syria & Homs 2012*, CNN. *D.L. Hughley: The Endangered List*, Comedy Central. *Under Fire: Journalists in Combat*, documentary channel hd. *Louie*, FX. "Salat [Bone Dry]," *Reel Time*, GMA News TV. *Game Change*, *Girls*, *The Loving Story*, *Marina Abramovic: The Artist Is Present*, *Real Sports With Bryant Gumbel*, HBO. "Banaz: An Honour Killing," "The Other Side of Jimmy Savile," *Exposure*; Michael Apted's *Up* series; ITV1. *Design Ah!*, NHK Educational Channel, Japan. *Syria 2012*, NPR. "Teen Contender," NPR's All Things Considered. "Summer Pasture," *Independent Lens*; *Why Poverty?*; PBS. *MLK: The Assassination Tapes*, Smithsonian Channel. *Southland*, TNT. *Rapido y Furioso [Fast & Furious]*, Univision. *Investigating the Fire*, KMGH-TV, Denver. *Ford Escape: Exposing a Deadly Defect*, KNXV-TV, Phoenix. *Investigating the IRS*, WTHR-TV, Indianapolis. *Breaking News: Tragedy at Sandy Hook Elementary School*, WVIT-TV, West Hartford, CT. "What Happened at Dos Erres," *This American Life*, WBEZ Radio. *The Leonard Lopate Show*, WNYC. *Inside the National Recording Registry*, WNYC/PRI. *Snow Fall: The Avalanche at Tunnel Creek*, www.nytimes.com. SCOTUSblog, www.scotusblog.com.

Scripps Howard Awards, by Scripps Howard Foundation. Breaking News: *Denver Post*. Business/Economics Reporting: Lou Kilzer, Andrew Conte, Jim Wilhelm, *Pittsburgh Tribune-Review*. Commentary: James Carroll, *Boston Globe*. Community Journalism: Brandon Stahl, *News Tribune* (Duluth, MN). Distinguished Service to the First Amendment: *Wall Street Journal*. Editorial Writing: Tim Nickens, *Tampa Bay Times*. Environmental Reporting: Kenneth R. Weiss, Rick Loomis, *L.A. Times*. Human Interest Storytelling: Michael M. Phillips, *Wall Street Journal*. Investigative Reporting: Spencer S. Hsu, *Washington Post*. Digital Innovation: *NY Times*. Photojournalism: Lisa Krantz, *San Antonio Express-News*. Public Service Reporting: Patricia Callahan, Sam Roe, Michael Hawthorne, *Chicago Tribune*. Radio In-Depth Coverage: Robert Wildeboer, Cate Cahan, WBEZ, Chicago Public Media. TV/Cable In-Depth Local Coverage: KMGH-TV (Denver, CO). TV/Cable In-Depth Natl. and Intl. Coverage: *Need to Know*, PBS; and The Investigative Fund at The Nation Institute.

Miscellaneous Book Awards, 2013

Bollingen Prize in American Poetry, by the Yale Univ. Library, $150,000 (biennial): Charles Wright.

Coretta Scott King Awards, by American Library Assn., for African American authors and illustrators of outstanding books for children and young adults. Author: Andrea Davis Pinkney, *Hand in Hand: Ten Black Men Who Changed America*. Illustrator: Bryan Collier, *I, Too, Am America*.

Costa Book Awards: Book of the Year (formerly Whitbread Award): Hilary Mantel, *Bring up the Bodies*. Short Story: Avril Joy, "Millie and Bird."

Edgar Awards, by the Mystery Writers of America. Novel: *Live by Night*, Dennis Lehane. First Novel: *The Expats*, Chris Pavone. Paperback Original: *The Last Policeman: A Novel*, Ben H. Winters. Fact Crime: *Midnight in Peking: How the Murder of a Young Englishwoman Haunted the Last Days of Old China*, Paul French. Critical/Biographical: *The Scientific Sherlock Holmes: Cracking the Case With Science and Forensics*, James O'Brien. Juvenile: *The Quick Fix*, Jack D. Ferraiolo. Young Adult: *Code Name Verity*, Elizabeth Wein. TV Episode: "A Scandal in Belgravia," *Sherlock*, BBC/Masterpiece. Grand Master: Ken Follett, Margaret Maron. Raven Award: Oline Cogdill.

Golden Kite Awards, by the Society of Children's Book Writers and Illustrators. Fiction: *The Five Lives of Our Cat Zook*, Joanne Rocklin. Nonfiction: *Noah Webster and His Words*, Jeri Chase Ferris. Picture Book Text: *Me and Momma and Big John*, Mara Rockliff. Picture Book Illustration: *Lester's Dreadful Sweaters*, K. G. Campbell.

Hugo Awards, by the World Science Fiction Society (WSFS). Novel: *Redshirts: A Novel With Three Codas*, John Scalzi. Novella: "The Emperor's Soul," Brandon Sanderson. Novelette: "The Girl-Thing Who Went Out for Sushi," Pat Cadigan. Short Story: "Mono no Aware," Ken Liu. Related Work: *Writing Excuses Season Seven*, Brandon Sanderson, Dan Wells, Mary Robinette Kowal, Howard Tayler, Jordan Sanderson. Graphic Story: *Saga, Volume One*, Brian K. Vaughan. Dramatic Presentation, long form: *The Avengers*. Dramatic Presentation, short form: "Blackwater," *Game of Thrones*, HBO.

Lincoln Prize, by Gettysburg College and the Gilder Lehrman Inst. of American History, $50,000: James Oakes, *Freedom National: The Destruction of Slavery in the United States, 1861-1865*.

National Book Critics Circle Awards. Fiction: Ben Fountain, *Billy Lynn's Long Halftime Walk*. Nonfiction: Andrew Solomon, *Far From the Tree: Parents, Children, and the Search for Identity*. Biography: Robert A. Caro, *The Passage of Power: The Years of Lyndon Johnson*. Autobiography: Leanne Shapton, *Swimming Studies*. Criticism: Marina Warner, *Stranger Magic: Charmed States and the Arabian Nights*. Poetry: D. A. Powell, *Useless Landscape, or A Guide for Boys*. Ivan Sandrof Lifetime Achievement Award: Sandra Gilbert and Susan Gubar. Nona Balakian Citation for Excellence in Reviewing: William Deresiewicz.

Nebula Awards, by the Science Fiction and Fantasy Writers of America. Novel: *2312*, Kim Stanley Robinson. Novella: "After the Fall, Before the Fall, During the Fall," Nancy Kress. Novelette: "Close Encounters," Andy Duncan. Short Story: "Immersion," Aliette de Bodard. Ray Bradbury Award: *Beasts of the Southern Wild*, Benh Zeitlin (dir.). Andre Norton Award: *Fair Coin*, E. C. Myers. Damon Knight Grand Master Award: Gene Wolfe. Solstice Award: Carl Sagan and Ginjer Buchanan.

PEN/Faulkner Award, for fiction, $15,000: Benjamin Alire Sáenz, *Everything Begins and Ends at the Kentucky Club*.

Spingarn Medal, 1915-2013

The Spingarn Medal has been awarded annually since 1915 (except in 1938 and 2012) by the National Assn. for the Advancement of Colored People for outstanding achievement by an African American.

1915 Ernest E. Just	1928 Charles W. Chesnutt	1942 A. Philip Randolph	1955 Carl Murphy
1916 Charles Young	1929 Mordecai W. Johnson	1943 William H. Hastie	1956 Jack R. Robinson
1917 Harry T. Burleigh	1930 Henry A. Hunt	1944 Charles Drew	1957 Martin Luther King Jr.
1918 William S. Braithwaite	1931 Richard B. Harrison	1945 Paul Robeson	1958 Daisy Bates and the
1919 Archibald H. Grimké	1932 Robert R. Moton	1946 Thurgood Marshall	Little Rock Nine
1920 W. E. B. Du Bois	1933 Max Yergan	1947 Dr. Percy L. Julian	1959 Duke Ellington
1921 Charles S. Gilpin	1934 William T. B. Williams	1948 Channing H. Tobias	1960 Langston Hughes
1922 Mary B. Talbert	1935 Mary McLeod Bethune	1949 Ralph J. Bunche	1961 Kenneth B. Clark
1923 George W. Carver	1936 John Hope	1950 Charles H. Houston	1962 Robert C. Weaver
1924 Roland Hayes	1937 Walter White	1951 Mabel K. Staupers	1963 Medgar W. Evers
1925 James W. Johnson	1939 Marian Anderson	1952 Harry T. Moore	1964 Roy Wilkins
1926 Carter G. Woodson	1940 Louis T. Wright	1953 Paul R. Williams	1965 Leontyne Price
1927 Anthony Overton	1941 Richard Wright	1954 Theodore K. Lawless	1966 John H. Johnson

1967 Edward W. Brooke	1979 Rosa L. Parks	1991 Gen. Colin L. Powell	2003 Constance Baker Motley
1968 Sammy Davis Jr.	1980 Dr. Rayford W. Logan	1992 Barbara Jordan	2004 Robert L. Carter
1969 Clarence M. Mitchell Jr.	1981 Coleman Young	1993 Dorothy I. Height	2005 Oliver W. Hill
1970 Jacob Lawrence	1982 Dr. Benjamin E. Mays	1994 Maya Angelou	2006 Dr. Benjamin S. Carson
1971 Leon H. Sullivan	1983 Lena Horne	1995 John Hope Franklin	2007 John Conyers Jr.
1972 Gordon Parks	1984 Thomas Bradley	1996 A. Leon Higginbotham	2008 Ruby Dee
1973 Wilson C. Riles	1985 Bill Cosby	1997 Carl T. Rowan	2009 Julian Bond
1974 Damon Keith	1986 Dr. Benjamin L. Hooks	1998 Myrlie Evers-Williams	2010 Cicely Tyson
1975 Henry (Hank) Aaron	1987 Percy E. Sutton	1999 Earl G. Graves Sr.	2011 Frankie Muse Freeman
1976 Alvin Ailey	1988 Frederick D. Patterson	2000 Oprah Winfrey	2012 No award
1977 Alex Haley	1989 Jesse Jackson	2001 Vernon E. Jordan Jr.	2013 Harry Belafonte
1978 Andrew Young	1990 L. Douglas Wilder	2002 John Lewis	

Miscellaneous Awards, 2013

Congressional Gold Medal, by Congress: May 24, 2013: Addie Mae Collins, Denise McNair, Carole Robertson, Cynthia Wesley; July 12, 2013: First Special Service Force, World War II.

Intel Science Talent Search. First place, $100,000: Sara Volz, Colorado Springs, CO; second place, $75,000: Jonah Kallenbach, Ambler, PA; third place, $50,000: Adam Bowman, Brentwood, TN.

John F. Kennedy Center Honors (2012): Buddy Guy, Dustin Hoffman, Led Zeppelin, David Letterman, Natalia Makarova.

Library of the Year Award, by Gale and *Library Journal*, $10,000: Howard County Library System, MD.

MacArthur Fellows, by the John D. and Catherine T. MacArthur Foundation, $500,000 each: Kyle Abraham, Donald Antrim, Phil Baran, C. Kevin Boyce, Jeremy Brenner, Colin Camerer, Jeremy Denk, Angela Duckworth, Craig Fennie, Robin Fleming, Carl Haber, Vijay Iyer, Dina Katabi, Julie Livingston, David Lobell, Tarell McCraney, Susan Murphy, Sheila Nirenberg, Alexei Ratmansky, Ana Maria Rey, Karen Russell, Sara Seager, Margaret Stock, Carrie Mae Weems.

National Humanities Medal, by National Endowment for the Humanities: Edward L. Ayers, William G. Bowen, Jill Ker Conway,

Natalie Zemon Davis, Frank Deford, Joan Didion, Robert D. Putnam, Marilynne Robinson, Kay Ryan, Robert B. Silvers, Anna Deavere Smith, Camilo José Vergara.

National Medal of the Arts, by the National Endowment for the Arts and the White House: Herb Alpert, Lin Arison, Joan Myers Brown, Renée Fleming, Ernest J. Gaines, Ellsworth Kelly, Tony Kushner, George Lucas, Elaine May, Laurie Olin, Allen Toussaint, Washington Performing Arts Society, Washington, DC.

Presidential Medal of Freedom, by the White House: Ernie Banks, Ben Bradlee, Bill Clinton, Daniel Inouye (posthumous), Daniel Kahneman, Richard Lugar, Loretta Lynn, Mario Molina, Sally Ride (posthumous), Bayard Rustin (posthumous), Arturo Sandoval, Dean Smith, Gloria Steinem, Cordy Tindell "C. T." Vivian, Patricia Wald, Oprah Winfrey.

Pritzker Architecture Prize, by the Hyatt Foundation, $100,000: Toyo Ito, Japan.

Teacher of the Year, by Council of Chief State School Officers: Jeffrey Charbonneau, Zillah High School, Zillah, WA.

Templeton Prize, by Templeton Foundation, £1.1 mil (about $1.7 mil): Desmond Tutu.

Miss America Winners, 1921-2014

Year	Winner, hometown	Year	Winner, hometown
1921	Margaret Gorman, Washington, DC	1973	Terry Anne Meeuwsen, DePere, Wisconsin
1922-23	Mary Campbell, Columbus, Ohio	1974	Rebecca Ann King, Denver, Colorado
1924	Ruth Malcolmson, Philadelphia, Pennsylvania	1975	Shirley Cothran, Fort Worth, Texas
1925	Fay Lamphier, Oakland, California	1976	Tawney Elaine Godin, Yonkers, New York
1926	Norma Smallwood, Tulsa, Oklahoma	1977	Dorothy Kathleen Benham, Edina, Minnesota
1927	Lois Delander, Joliet, Illinois	1978	Susan Perkins, Columbus, Ohio
1933	Marion Bergeron, West Haven, Connecticut	1979	Kylene Barker, Galax, Virginia
1935	Henrietta Leaver, Pittsburgh, Pennsylvania	1980	Cheryl Prewitt, Ackerman, Mississippi
1936	Rose Coyle, Philadelphia, Pennsylvania	1981	Susan Powell, Elk City, Oklahoma
1937	Bette Cooper, Bertrand Island, New Jersey	1982	Elizabeth Ward, Russellville, Arkansas
1938	Marilyn Meseke, Marion, Ohio	1983	Debra Maffett, Anaheim, California
1939	Patricia Donnelly, Detroit, Michigan	1984[1]	Suzette Charles, Mays Landing, New Jersey
1940	Frances Marie Burke, Philadelphia, Pennsylvania	1985	Sharlene Wells, Salt Lake City, Utah
1941	Rosemary LaPlanche, Los Angeles, California	1986	Susan Akin, Meridian, Mississippi
1942	Jo-Caroll Dennison, Tyler, Texas	1987	Kellye Cash, Memphis, Tennessee
1943	Jean Bartel, Los Angeles, California	1988	Kaye Lani Rae Rafko, Monroe, Michigan
1944	Venus Ramey, Washington, DC	1989	Gretchen Carlson, Anoka, Minnesota
1945	Bess Myerson, New York City, New York	1990	Debbye Turner, Columbia, Missouri
1946	Marilyn Buferd, Los Angeles, California	1991	Marjorie Vincent, Oak Park, Illinois
1947	Barbara Walker, Memphis, Tennessee	1992	Carolyn Suzanne Sapp, Honolulu, Hawaii
1948	BeBe Shopp, Hopkins, Minnesota	1993	Leanza Cornett, Jacksonville, Florida
1949	Jacque Mercer, Litchfield, Arizona	1994	Kimberly Aiken, Columbia, South Carolina
1951	Yolande Betbeze, Mobile, Alabama	1995	Heather Whitestone, Birmingham, Alabama
1952	Coleen Kay Hutchins, Salt Lake City, Utah	1996	Shawntel Smith, Muldrow, Oklahoma
1953	Neva Jane Langley, Macon, Georgia	1997	Tara Dawn Holland, Overland Park, Kansas
1954	Evelyn Margaret Ay, Ephrata, Pennsylvania	1998	Kate Shindle, Evanston, Illinois
1955	Lee Meriwether, San Francisco, California	1999	Nicole Johnson, Roanoke, Virginia
1956	Sharon Ritchie, Denver, Colorado	2000	Heather Renee French, Maysville, Kentucky
1957	Marian McKnight, Manning, South Carolina	2001	Angela Perez Baraquio, Honolulu, Hawaii
1958	Marilyn Van Derbur, Denver, Colorado	2002	Katie Harman, Gresham, Oregon
1959	Mary Ann Mobley, Brandon, Mississippi	2003	Erika Harold, Urbana, Illinois
1960	Lynda Lee Mead, Natchez, Mississippi	2004	Ericka Dunlap, Orlando, Florida
1961	Nancy Fleming, Montague, Michigan	2005[2]	Deidre Downs, Birmingham, Alabama
1962	Maria Fletcher, Asheville, North Carolina	2006	Jennifer Berry, Tulsa, Oklahoma
1963	Jacquelyn Mayer, Sandusky, Ohio	2007	Lauren Nelson, Lawton, Oklahoma
1964	Donna Axum, El Dorado, Arkansas	2008	Kirsten Haglund, Farmington Hills, Michigan
1965	Vonda Kay Van Dyke, Phoenix, Arizona	2009	Katie Stam, Seymour, Indiana
1966	Deborah Irene Bryant, Overland Park, Kansas	2010	Caressa Cameron, Fredricksburg, Virginia
1967	Jane Anne Jayroe, Laverne, Oklahoma	2011	Teresa Scanlan, Gering, Nebraska
1968	Debra Dene Barnes, Moran, Kansas	2012	Laura Kaeppeler, Kenosha, Wisconsin
1969	Judith Anne Ford, Belvidere, Illinois	2013	Mallory Hytes Hagen, Brooklyn, New York
1970	Pamela Anne Eldred, Birmingham, Michigan	2014	Nina Davuluri, Fayetteville, New York
1971	Phyllis Ann George, Denton, Texas		
1972	Laurie Lea Schaefer, Columbus, Ohio		

(1) Miss New York, Vanessa Williams, resigned July 23, 1984. (2) The Sept. 2005 Miss America Pageant and award were postponed until Jan. 2006, when the pageant was broadcast from Las Vegas, NV, by Country Music Television (CMT).

Entertainment Awards
Tony (Antoinette Perry) Awards, 2013

Play: Vanya and Sonia and Masha and Spike, Christopher Durang
Musical: Kinky Boots
Book of a musical: Matilda the Musical, Dennis Kelly
Original score: Kinky Boots, Cyndi Lauper
Play revival: Who's Afraid of Virginia Woolf?
Musical revival: Pippin
Actor, play: Tracy Letts, Who's Afraid of Virginia Woolf?
Actress, play: Cicely Tyson, The Trip to Bountiful
Actor, musical: Billy Porter, Kinky Boots
Actress, musical: Patina Miller, Pippin
Featured actor, play: Courtney B. Vance, Lucky Guy
Featured actress, play: Judith Light, The Assembled Parties
Featured actor, musical: Gabriel Ebert, Matilda the Musical
Featured actress, musical: Andrea Martin, Pippin
Director, play: Pam MacKinnon, Who's Afraid of Virginia Woolf?

Director, musical: Diane Paulus, Pippin
Choreography: Jerry Mitchell, Kinky Boots
Orchestrations: Stephen Oremus, Kinky Boots
Scenic design, play: John Lee Beatty, The Nance
Scenic design, musical: Rob Howell, Matilda the Musical
Costume design, play: Ann Roth, The Nance
Costume design, musical: William Ivey Long, Rodgers + Hammerstein's Cinderella
Regional theater: Huntington Theatre Company, Boston
Special Tony Award, lifetime achievement: Bernard Gersten, Paul Libin, Ming Cho Lee
Isabelle Stevenson Award: Larry Kramer
Tony Honors for Excellence in the Theatre: Michael R. Bloomberg, Career Transition For Dancers, William Craver, Peter Lawrence, The Lost Colony, Sophia Gennusa, Oona Laurence, Bailey Ryon, and Milly Shapiro

Tony Awards, 1948-2013

Year	Play	Musical
1948	Mister Roberts	No award
1949	Death of a Salesman	Kiss Me Kate
1950	The Cocktail Party	South Pacific
1951	The Rose Tattoo	Guys and Dolls
1952	The Fourposter	The King and I
1953	The Crucible	Wonderful Town
1954	The Teahouse of the August Moon	Kismet
1955	The Desperate Hours	The Pajama Game
1956	The Diary of Anne Frank	Damn Yankees
1957	Long Day's Journey Into Night	My Fair Lady
1958	Sunrise at Campobello	The Music Man
1959	J.B.	Redhead
1960	The Miracle Worker	Fiorello!, The Sound of Music
1961	Becket	Bye, Bye Birdie
1962	A Man for All Seasons	How to Succeed in Business Without Really Trying
1963	Who's Afraid of Virginia Woolf?	A Funny Thing Happened on the Way to the Forum
1964	Luther	Hello, Dolly!
1965	The Subject Was Roses	Fiddler on the Roof
1966	Marat/Sade	Man of La Mancha
1967	The Homecoming	Cabaret
1968	Rosencrantz and Guildenstern Are Dead	Hallelujah, Baby!
1969	The Great White Hope	1776
1970	Borstal Boy	Applause
1971	Sleuth	Company
1972	Sticks and Bones	Two Gentlemen of Verona
1973	That Championship Season	A Little Night Music
1974	The River Niger	Raisin
1975	Equus	The Wiz
1976	Travesties	A Chorus Line
1977	The Shadow Box	Annie
1978	Da	Ain't Misbehavin'
1979	The Elephant Man	Sweeney Todd
1980	Children of a Lesser God	Evita
1981	Amadeus	42nd Street
1982	The Life and Adventures of Nicholas Nickleby	Nine
1983	Torch Song Trilogy	Cats
1984	The Real Thing	La Cage aux Folles
1985	Biloxi Blues	Big River
1986	I'm Not Rappaport	The Mystery of Edwin Drood
1987	Fences	Les Miserables
1988	M. Butterfly	Phantom of the Opera
1989	The Heidi Chronicles	Jerome Robbins' Broadway
1990	The Grapes of Wrath	City of Angels
1991	Lost in Yonkers	The Will Rogers Follies
1992	Dancing at Lughnasa	Crazy for You
1993	Angels in America: Millennium Approaches	Kiss of the Spider Woman
1994	Angels in America: Perestroika	Passion
1995	Love! Valour! Compassion!	Sunset Boulevard
1996	Master Class	Rent
1997	The Last Night of Ballyhoo	Titanic
1998	Art	The Lion King
1999	Side Man	Fosse
2000	Copenhagen	Contact
2001	Proof	The Producers
2002	Edward Albee's The Goat or Who Is Sylvia?	Thoroughly Modern Millie
2003	Take Me Out	Hairspray
2004	I Am My Own Wife	Avenue Q
2005	Doubt	Monty Python's Spamalot
2006	The History Boys	Jersey Boys
2007	The Coast of Utopia	Spring Awakening
2008	August: Osage County	In the Heights
2009	God of Carnage	Billy Elliot, The Musical
2010	Red	Memphis
2011	War Horse	The Book of Mormon
2012	Clybourne Park	Once
2013	Vanya and Sonia and Masha and Spike	Kinky Boots

Selected Daytime Emmy Awards, 2013

Drama: Days of Our Lives, NBC
Game show: The Price is Right, CBS
Animated show, special class: Star Wars: The Clone Wars, Cartoon Network
Culinary show: Best Thing I Ever Made and Trisha's Southern Kitchen, Food Network
Legal/courtroom show: Last Shot With Judge Gunn, synd.
Morning show: CBS Sunday Morning, CBS

Talk show, entertainment: The Ellen DeGeneres Show, synd.
Talk show, informative: The Dr. Oz Show, synd.
Lead actress: Heather Tom, The Bold and the Beautiful, CBS
Lead actor: Doug Davidson, The Young and the Restless, CBS
Game show host: Ben Bailey, Cash Cab, Discovery Channel
Lifestyle/culinary host: Lidia Bastianich, Lidia's Italy, PBS
Talk show host: Ricki Lake, The Ricki Lake Show, synd.

Selected Prime-Time Emmy Awards, 2013

Drama series: Breaking Bad, AMC
Comedy series: Modern Family, ABC
Miniseries or movie: Behind the Candelabra, HBO
Variety series: The Colbert Report, Comedy Central
Lead actor, drama: Jeff Daniels, The Newsroom, HBO
Lead actress, drama: Claire Danes, Homeland, Showtime
Lead actor, comedy: Jim Parsons, The Big Bang Theory, CBS
Lead actress, comedy: Julia Louis-Dreyfus, Veep, HBO
Lead actor, miniseries/movie: Michael Douglas, Behind the Candelabra, HBO
Lead actress, miniseries/movie: Laura Linney, The Big C: Hereafter, Showtime
Sup. actor, drama: Bobby Cannavale, Boardwalk Empire, HBO

Sup. actress, drama: Anna Gunn, Breaking Bad, AMC
Sup. actor, comedy: Tony Hale, Veep, HBO
Sup. actress, comedy: Merritt Wever, Nurse Jackie, Showtime
Sup. actor, miniseries/movie: James Cromwell, American Horror Story: Asylum, FX
Sup. actress, miniseries/movie: Ellen Burstyn, Political Animals, USA
Reality-competition program: The Voice, NBC
Director, drama: David Fincher, House of Cards, Netflix
Director, comedy: Gail Mancuso, Modern Family, ABC
Writing, drama: Henry Bromell, Homeland, Showtime
Writing, comedy: Tina Fey, Tracey Wigfield, 30 Rock, NBC
Writing, variety: The Colbert Report, Comedy Central

Prime-Time Emmy Awards, 1952-2013

The Academy of Television Arts and Sciences presented the first Emmy Awards in 1949. Through the years, award categories have changed, but since 1952, the Academy has given out an outstanding comedy and drama award annually.

Year	Comedy	Drama	Year	Comedy	Drama
1952	Red Skelton Show, NBC	Studio One, CBS	1980	Taxi, ABC	Lou Grant, CBS
1953	I Love Lucy, CBS	Robert Montgomery Presents, NBC	1981	Taxi, ABC	Hill Street Blues, NBC
			1982	Barney Miller, ABC	Hill Street Blues, NBC
1954	I Love Lucy, CBS	The U.S. Steel Hour, ABC	1983	Cheers, NBC	Hill Street Blues, NBC
1955	Make Room for Daddy, ABC	The U.S. Steel Hour, ABC	1984	Cheers, NBC	Hill Street Blues, NBC
1956	Phil Silvers Show, CBS	Producers' Showcase, NBC	1985	The Cosby Show, NBC	Cagney & Lacey, CBS
1957	Phil Silvers Show, CBS	"Requiem for a Heavyweight," CBS[1]	1986	Golden Girls, NBC	Cagney & Lacey, CBS
			1987	Golden Girls, NBC	L.A. Law, NBC
1958	Phil Silvers Show, CBS	Gunsmoke, CBS	1988	The Wonder Years, ABC	thirtysomething, ABC
1959[2]	Jack Benny Show, CBS	(3)	1989	Cheers, NBC	L.A. Law, NBC
1960	Art Carney Special, NBC	Playhouse 90, CBS	1990	Murphy Brown, CBS	L.A. Law, NBC
1961	Jack Benny Show, CBS	Hallmark Hall of Fame: Macbeth, NBC	1991	Cheers, NBC	L.A. Law, NBC
			1992	Murphy Brown, CBS	Northern Exposure, CBS
1962	Bob Newhart Show, CBS	The Defenders, CBS	1993	Seinfeld, NBC	Picket Fences, CBS
1963	Dick Van Dyke Show, CBS	The Defenders, CBS	1994	Frasier, NBC	Picket Fences, CBS
1964	Dick Van Dyke Show, CBS	The Defenders, CBS	1995	Frasier, NBC	NYPD Blue, ABC
1965	Dick Van Dyke Show, CBS	Hallmark Hall of Fame: The Magnificent Yankee, NBC	1996	Frasier, NBC	ER, NBC
			1997	Frasier, NBC	Law & Order, NBC
1966	Dick Van Dyke Show, CBS	The Fugitive, ABC	1998	Frasier, NBC	The Practice, ABC
1967	The Monkees, NBC	Mission: Impossible, CBS	1999	Ally McBeal, FOX	The Practice, ABC
1968	Get Smart, NBC	Mission: Impossible, CBS	2000	Will & Grace, NBC	The West Wing, NBC
1969	Get Smart, NBC	NET Playhouse, NET	2001	Sex and the City, HBO	The West Wing, NBC
1970	My World and Welcome to It, NBC	Marcus Welby, M.D., ABC	2002	Friends, NBC	The West Wing, NBC
1971	All in the Family, CBS	The Bold Ones: The Senator, NBC	2003	Everybody Loves Raymond, CBS	The West Wing, NBC
1972	All in the Family, CBS	Masterpiece Theatre: Elizabeth R, PBS	2004	Arrested Development, FOX	The Sopranos, HBO
			2005	Everybody Loves Raymond, CBS	Lost, ABC
1973	All in the Family, CBS	The Waltons, CBS			
1974	M*A*S*H, CBS	Masterpiece Theatre: Upstairs, Downstairs; PBS	2006	The Office, NBC	24, FOX
			2007	30 Rock, NBC	The Sopranos, HBO
1975	Mary Tyler Moore Show, CBS	Masterpiece Theatre: Upstairs, Downstairs; PBS	2008	30 Rock, NBC	Mad Men, AMC
			2009	30 Rock, NBC	Mad Men, AMC
1976	Mary Tyler Moore Show, CBS	Police Story, NBC	2010	Modern Family, ABC	Mad Men, AMC
1977	Mary Tyler Moore Show, CBS	Masterpiece Theatre: Upstairs, Downstairs; PBS	2011	Modern Family, ABC	Mad Men, AMC
			2012	Modern Family, ABC	Homeland, Showtime
1978	All in the Family, CBS	The Rockford Files, NBC	2013	Modern Family, ABC	Breaking Bad, AMC
1979	Taxi, ABC	Lou Grant, CBS			

(1) Best single program of the year; shown on *Playhouse 90*, which was named best new series. (2) Beginning in 1959, Emmys awarded for work in the season encompassing the previous and current year. (3) *Playhouse 90* (CBS) was best dramatic series of one hour or longer, *Alcoa-Goodyear Theatre* (NBC) of less than one hour.

Golden Globe Awards, 2013

The Hollywood Foreign Press Association (then the Hollywood Foreign Correspondents Association) presented its first awards for achievement in film in 1944; television was considered for the first time in 1955.

Film

Drama: *Argo*
Comedy/musical: *Les Misérables*
Actress, drama: Jessica Chastain, *Zero Dark Thirty*
Actor, drama: Daniel Day-Lewis, *Lincoln*
Actress, comedy/musical: Jennifer Lawrence, *Silver Linings Playbook*
Actor, comedy/musical: Hugh Jackman, *Les Misérables*
Supporting actress: Anne Hathaway, *Les Misérables*
Supporting actor: Christoph Waltz, *Django Unchained*
Director: Ben Affleck, *Argo*
Screenplay: Quentin Tarantino, *Django Unchained*
Animated film: *Brave*
Foreign-language film: *Amour*, Austria
Original score: Mychael Danna, *Life of Pi*
Original song: "Skyfall," *Skyfall*, w/m by Adele and Paul Epworth
Cecil B. DeMille Award: Jodie Foster

Television

Series, drama: *Homeland*, Showtime
Series, comedy/musical: *Girls*, HBO
Actress, drama: Claire Danes, *Homeland*, Showtime
Actor, drama: Damian Lewis, *Homeland*, Showtime
Actress, comedy/musical: Lena Dunham, *Girls*, HBO
Actor, comedy/musical: Don Cheadle, *House of Lies*, Showtime
Miniseries or made-for-TV movie: *Game Change*, HBO
Actress, miniseries/movie: Julianne Moore, *Game Change*, HBO
Actor, miniseries/movie: Kevin Costner, *Hatfields & McCoys*, History
Supporting actress: Maggie Smith, *Downton Abbey*, PBS
Supporting actor: Ed Harris, *Game Change*, HBO

Selected People's Choice Awards, 2013

The first People's Choice Awards were presented in 1975. Sponsored by Procter & Gamble, the nominees and awards were initially selected by a Gallup Poll. Since 2005, winners have been selected by Internet voting.

Film

Actor: Robert Downey Jr.
Actress: Jennifer Lawrence
Action movie: *The Hunger Games*
Comedy movie: *Ted*
Comedic actor: Adam Sandler
Comedic actress: Jennifer Aniston
Drama: *The Perks of Being a Wallflower*
Dramatic actor: Zac Efron
Dramatic actress: Emma Watson
Movie franchise: *The Hunger Games*
Movie superhero: Robert Downey Jr., as Iron Man in *Iron Man*

Music

Album: *Up All Night*, One Direction
Song: "What Makes You Beautiful," One Direction
Male artist: Jason Mraz
Female artist: Katy Perry
Band: Maroon 5

Television

Network comedy: *The Big Bang Theory*
Network drama: *Grey's Anatomy*
Cable comedy: *Awkward*
Cable drama: *Leverage*
New comedy: *The New Normal*
New drama: *Beauty and the Beast*
Premium cable show: *True Blood*
Competition show: *The X Factor*
Crime drama: *Castle*
Sci-fi/fantasy show: *Supernatural*
Comedic actor: Chris Colfer
Comedic actress: Lea Michele
Dramatic actor: Nathan Fillion
Dramatic actress: Ellen Pompeo
Daytime host: Ellen DeGeneres
Late-night host: Jimmy Fallon

Academy Awards (Oscars), 1927-2012

Year	Picture	Actor	Actress	Supporting actor[1]	Supporting actress[1]	Director
1927 -28	Wings	Emil Jannings *The Way of All Flesh*	Janet Gaynor *Seventh Heaven*	NA	NA	Frank Borzage *Seventh Heaven*; Lewis Milestone *Two Arabian Knights*
1928 -29	Broadway Melody	Warner Baxter *In Old Arizona*	Mary Pickford *Coquette*	NA	NA	Frank Lloyd *The Divine Lady*
1929 -30	All Quiet on the Western Front	George Arliss *Disraeli*	Norma Shearer *The Divorcee*	NA	NA	Lewis Milestone *All Quiet on the Western Front*
1930 -31	Cimarron	Lionel Barrymore *Free Soul*	Marie Dressler *Min and Bill*	NA	NA	Norman Taurog *Skippy*
1931 -32	Grand Hotel	Fredric March *Dr. Jekyll and Mr. Hyde*; Wallace Beery *The Champ*	Helen Hayes *The Sin of Madelon Claudet*	NA	NA	Frank Borzage *Bad Girl*
1932 -33	Cavalcade	Charles Laughton *The Private Life of Henry VIII*	Katharine Hepburn *Morning Glory*	NA	NA	Frank Lloyd *Cavalcade*
1934	It Happened One Night	Clark Gable *It Happened One Night*	Claudette Colbert *It Happened One Night*	NA	NA	Frank Capra *It Happened One Night*
1935	Mutiny on the Bounty	Victor McLaglen *The Informer*	Bette Davis *Dangerous*	NA	NA	John Ford *The Informer*
1936	The Great Ziegfeld	Paul Muni *Story of Louis Pasteur*	Luise Rainer *The Great Ziegfeld*	Walter Brennan *Come and Get It*	Gale Sondergaard *Anthony Adverse*	Frank Capra *Mr. Deeds Goes to Town*
1937	Life of Emile Zola	Spencer Tracy *Captains Courageous*	Luise Rainer *The Good Earth*	Joseph Schildkraut *Life of Emile Zola*	Alice Brady *In Old Chicago*	Leo McCarey *The Awful Truth*
1938	You Can't Take It With You	Spencer Tracy *Boys Town*	Bette Davis *Jezebel*	Walter Brennan *Kentucky*	Fay Bainter *Jezebel*	Frank Capra *You Can't Take It With You*
1939	Gone With the Wind	Robert Donat *Goodbye Mr. Chips*	Vivien Leigh *Gone With the Wind*	Thomas Mitchell *Stage Coach*	Hattie McDaniel *Gone With the Wind*	Victor Fleming *Gone With the Wind*
1940	Rebecca	James Stewart *The Philadelphia Story*	Ginger Rogers *Kitty Foyle*	Walter Brennan *The Westerner*	Jane Darwell *The Grapes of Wrath*	John Ford *The Grapes of Wrath*
1941	How Green Was My Valley	Gary Cooper *Sergeant York*	Joan Fontaine *Suspicion*	Donald Crisp *How Green Was My Valley*	Mary Astor *The Great Lie*	John Ford *How Green Was My Valley*
1942	Mrs. Miniver	James Cagney *Yankee Doodle Dandy*	Greer Garson *Mrs. Miniver*	Van Heflin *Johnny Eager*	Teresa Wright *Mrs. Miniver*	William Wyler *Mrs. Miniver*
1943	Casablanca	Paul Lukas *Watch on the Rhine*	Jennifer Jones *The Song of Bernadette*	Charles Coburn *The More the Merrier*	Katina Paxinou *For Whom the Bell Tolls*	Michael Curtiz *Casablanca*
1944	Going My Way	Bing Crosby *Going My Way*	Ingrid Bergman *Gaslight*	Barry Fitzgerald *Going My Way*	Ethel Barrymore *None But the Lonely Heart*	Leo McCarey *Going My Way*
1945	The Lost Weekend	Ray Milland *The Lost Weekend*	Joan Crawford *Mildred Pierce*	James Dunn *A Tree Grows in Brooklyn*	Anne Revere *National Velvet*	Billy Wilder *The Lost Weekend*
1946	The Best Years of Our Lives	Fredric March *The Best Years of Our Lives*	Olivia de Havilland *To Each His Own*	Harold Russell *The Best Years of Our Lives*	Anne Baxter *The Razor's Edge*	William Wyler *The Best Years of Our Lives*
1947	Gentleman's Agreement	Ronald Colman *A Double Life*	Loretta Young *The Farmer's Daughter*	Edmund Gwenn *Miracle on 34th Street*	Celeste Holm *Gentleman's Agreement*	Elia Kazan *Gentleman's Agreement*
1948	Hamlet	Laurence Olivier *Hamlet*	Jane Wyman *Johnny Belinda*	Walter Huston *Treasure of Sierra Madre*	Claire Trevor *Key Largo*	John Huston *Treasure of Sierra Madre*
1949	All the King's Men	Broderick Crawford *All the King's Men*	Olivia de Havilland *The Heiress*	Dean Jagger *Twelve O'Clock High*	Mercedes McCambridge *All the King's Men*	Joseph L. Mankiewicz *Letter to Three Wives*
1950	All About Eve	Jose Ferrer *Cyrano de Bergerac*	Judy Holliday *Born Yesterday*	George Sanders *All About Eve*	Josephine Hull *Harvey*	Joseph L. Mankiewicz *All About Eve*
1951	An American in Paris	Humphrey Bogart *The African Queen*	Vivien Leigh *A Streetcar Named Desire*	Karl Malden *A Streetcar Named Desire*	Kim Hunter *A Streetcar Named Desire*	George Stevens *A Place in the Sun*
1952	The Greatest Show on Earth	Gary Cooper *High Noon*	Shirley Booth *Come Back Little Sheba*	Anthony Quinn *Viva Zapata!*	Gloria Grahame *The Bad and the Beautiful*	John Ford *The Quiet Man*
1953	From Here to Eternity	William Holden *Stalag 17*	Audrey Hepburn *Roman Holiday*	Frank Sinatra *From Here to Eternity*	Donna Reed *From Here to Eternity*	Fred Zinnemann *From Here to Eternity*

Year Picture	Actor	Actress	Supporting actor[1]	Supporting actress[1]	Director
1954 On the Waterfront	Marlon Brando On the Waterfront	Grace Kelly The Country Girl	Edmond O'Brien The Barefoot Contessa	Eva Marie Saint On the Waterfront	Elia Kazan On the Waterfront
1955 Marty	Ernest Borgnine Marty	Anna Magnani The Rose Tattoo	Jack Lemmon Mister Roberts	Jo Van Fleet East of Eden	Delbert Mann Marty
1956 Around the World in 80 Days	Yul Brynner The King and I	Ingrid Bergman Anastasia	Anthony Quinn Lust for Life	Dorothy Malone Written on the Wind	George Stevens Giant
1957 The Bridge on the River Kwai	Alec Guinness The Bridge on the River Kwai	Joanne Woodward The Three Faces of Eve	Red Buttons Sayonara	Miyoshi Umeki Sayonara	David Lean The Bridge on the River Kwai
1958 Gigi	David Niven Separate Tables	Susan Hayward I Want to Live	Burl Ives The Big Country	Wendy Hiller Separate Tables	Vincente Minnelli Gigi
1959 Ben-Hur	Charlton Heston Ben-Hur	Simone Signoret Room at the Top	Hugh Griffith Ben-Hur	Shelley Winters Diary of Anne Frank	William Wyler Ben-Hur
1960 The Apartment	Burt Lancaster Elmer Gantry	Elizabeth Taylor Butterfield 8	Peter Ustinov Spartacus	Shirley Jones Elmer Gantry	Billy Wilder The Apartment
1961 West Side Story	Maximilian Schell Judgment at Nuremberg	Sophia Loren Two Women	George Chakiris West Side Story	Rita Moreno West Side Story	Jerome Robbins, Robert Wise West Side Story
1962 Lawrence of Arabia	Gregory Peck To Kill a Mockingbird	Anne Bancroft The Miracle Worker	Ed Begley Sweet Bird of Youth	Patty Duke The Miracle Worker	David Lean Lawrence of Arabia
1963 Tom Jones	Sidney Poitier Lilies of the Field	Patricia Neal Hud	Melvyn Douglas Hud	Margaret Rutherford The V.I.P.s	Tony Richardson Tom Jones
1964 My Fair Lady	Rex Harrison My Fair Lady	Julie Andrews Mary Poppins	Peter Ustinov Topkapi	Lila Kedrova Zorba the Greek	George Cukor My Fair Lady
1965 The Sound of Music	Lee Marvin Cat Ballou	Julie Christie Darling	Martin Balsam A Thousand Clowns	Shelley Winters A Patch of Blue	Robert Wise The Sound of Music
1966 A Man for All Seasons	Paul Scofield A Man for All Seasons	Elizabeth Taylor Who's Afraid of Virginia Woolf?	Walter Matthau The Fortune Cookie	Sandy Dennis Who's Afraid of Virginia Woolf?	Fred Zinnemann A Man for All Seasons
1967 In the Heat of the Night	Rod Steiger In the Heat of the Night	Katharine Hepburn Guess Who's Coming to Dinner	George Kennedy Cool Hand Luke	Estelle Parsons Bonnie and Clyde	Mike Nichols The Graduate
1968 Oliver!	Cliff Robertson Charly	Katharine Hepburn The Lion in Winter; Barbra Streisand Funny Girl	Jack Albertson The Subject Was Roses	Ruth Gordon Rosemary's Baby	Sir Carol Reed Oliver!
1969 Midnight Cowboy	John Wayne True Grit	Maggie Smith The Prime of Miss Jean Brodie	Gig Young They Shoot Horses Don't They?	Goldie Hawn Cactus Flower	John Schlesinger Midnight Cowboy
1970 Patton	George C. Scott Patton (refused)	Glenda Jackson Women in Love	John Mills Ryan's Daughter	Helen Hayes Airport	Franklin Schaffner Patton
1971 The French Connection	Gene Hackman The French Connection	Jane Fonda Klute	Ben Johnson The Last Picture Show	Cloris Leachman The Last Picture Show	William Friedkin The French Connection
1972 The Godfather	Marlon Brando The Godfather (refused)	Liza Minnelli Cabaret	Joel Grey Cabaret	Eileen Heckart Butterflies Are Free	Bob Fosse Cabaret
1973 The Sting	Jack Lemmon Save the Tiger	Glenda Jackson A Touch of Class	John Houseman The Paper Chase	Tatum O'Neal Paper Moon	George Roy Hill The Sting
1974 The Godfather Part II	Art Carney Harry and Tonto	Ellen Burstyn Alice Doesn't Live Here Anymore	Robert DeNiro The Godfather Part II	Ingrid Bergman Murder on the Orient Express	Francis Ford Coppola The Godfather Part II
1975 One Flew Over the Cuckoo's Nest	Jack Nicholson One Flew Over the Cuckoo's Nest	Louise Fletcher One Flew Over the Cuckoo's Nest	George Burns The Sunshine Boys	Lee Grant Shampoo	Milos Forman One Flew Over the Cuckoo's Nest
1976 Rocky	Peter Finch Network	Faye Dunaway Network	Jason Robards All the President's Men	Beatrice Straight Network	John G. Avildsen Rocky
1977 Annie Hall	Richard Dreyfuss The Goodbye Girl	Diane Keaton Annie Hall	Jason Robards Julia	Vanessa Redgrave Julia	Woody Allen Annie Hall
1978 The Deer Hunter	Jon Voight Coming Home	Jane Fonda Coming Home	Christopher Walken The Deer Hunter	Maggie Smith California Suite	Michael Cimino The Deer Hunter
1979 Kramer vs. Kramer	Dustin Hoffman Kramer vs. Kramer	Sally Field Norma Rae	Melvyn Douglas Being There	Meryl Streep Kramer vs. Kramer	Robert Benton Kramer vs. Kramer
1980 Ordinary People	Robert DeNiro Raging Bull	Sissy Spacek Coal Miner's Daughter	Timothy Hutton Ordinary People	Mary Steenburgen Melvin and Howard	Robert Redford Ordinary People
1981 Chariots of Fire	Henry Fonda On Golden Pond	Katharine Hepburn On Golden Pond	John Gielgud Arthur	Maureen Stapleton Reds	Warren Beatty Reds
1982 Gandhi	Ben Kingsley Gandhi	Meryl Streep Sophie's Choice	Louis Gossett Jr. An Officer and a Gentleman	Jessica Lange Tootsie	Richard Attenborough Gandhi
1983 Terms of Endearment	Robert Duvall Tender Mercies	Shirley MacLaine Terms of Endearment	Jack Nicholson Terms of Endearment	Linda Hunt The Year of Living Dangerously	James L. Brooks Terms of Endearment

Year	Picture	Actor	Actress	Supporting actor[1]	Supporting actress[1]	Director
1984	Amadeus	F. Murray Abraham *Amadeus*	Sally Field *Places in the Heart*	Haing S. Ngor *The Killing Fields*	Peggy Ashcroft *A Passage to India*	Milos Forman *Amadeus*
1985	Out of Africa	William Hurt *Kiss of the Spider Woman*	Geraldine Page *The Trip to Bountiful*	Don Ameche *Cocoon*	Anjelica Huston *Prizzi's Honor*	Sydney Pollack *Out of Africa*
1986	Platoon	Paul Newman *The Color of Money*	Marlee Matlin *Children of a Lesser God*	Michael Caine *Hannah and Her Sisters*	Dianne Wiest *Hannah and Her Sisters*	Oliver Stone *Platoon*
1987	The Last Emperor	Michael Douglas *Wall Street*	Cher *Moonstruck*	Sean Connery *The Untouchables*	Olympia Dukakis *Moonstruck*	Bernardo Bertolucci *The Last Emperor*
1988	Rain Man	Dustin Hoffman *Rain Man*	Jodie Foster *The Accused*	Kevin Kline *A Fish Called Wanda*	Geena Davis *The Accidental Tourist*	Barry Levinson *Rain Man*
1989	Driving Miss Daisy	Daniel Day-Lewis *My Left Foot*	Jessica Tandy *Driving Miss Daisy*	Denzel Washington *Glory*	Brenda Fricker *My Left Foot*	Oliver Stone *Born on the Fourth of July*
1990	Dances With Wolves	Jeremy Irons *Reversal of Fortune*	Kathy Bates *Misery*	Joe Pesci *Goodfellas*	Whoopi Goldberg *Ghost*	Kevin Costner *Dances With Wolves*
1991	The Silence of the Lambs	Anthony Hopkins *The Silence of the Lambs*	Jodie Foster *The Silence of the Lambs*	Jack Palance *City Slickers*	Mercedes Ruehl *The Fisher King*	Jonathan Demme *The Silence of the Lambs*
1992	Unforgiven	Al Pacino *Scent of a Woman*	Emma Thompson *Howards End*	Gene Hackman *Unforgiven*	Marisa Tomei *My Cousin Vinny*	Clint Eastwood *Unforgiven*
1993	Schindler's List	Tom Hanks *Philadelphia*	Holly Hunter *The Piano*	Tommy Lee Jones *The Fugitive*	Anna Paquin *The Piano*	Steven Spielberg *Schindler's List*
1994	Forrest Gump	Tom Hanks *Forrest Gump*	Jessica Lange *Blue Sky*	Martin Landau *Ed Wood*	Dianne Wiest, *Bullets Over Broadway*	Robert Zemeckis *Forrest Gump*
1995	Braveheart	Nicolas Cage *Leaving Las Vegas*	Susan Sarandon *Dead Man Walking*	Kevin Spacey *The Usual Suspects*	Mira Sorvino *Mighty Aphrodite*	Mel Gibson *Braveheart*
1996	The English Patient	Geoffrey Rush *Shine*	Frances McDormand *Fargo*	Cuba Gooding Jr. *Jerry Maguire*	Juliette Binoche *The English Patient*	Anthony Minghella *The English Patient*
1997	Titanic	Jack Nicholson *As Good As It Gets*	Helen Hunt *As Good As It Gets*	Robin Williams *Good Will Hunting*	Kim Basinger *L.A. Confidential*	James Cameron *Titanic*
1998	Shakespeare in Love	Roberto Benigni *Life Is Beautiful*	Gwyneth Paltrow *Shakespeare in Love*	James Coburn *Affliction*	Judi Dench *Shakespeare in Love*	Steven Spielberg *Saving Private Ryan*
1999	American Beauty	Kevin Spacey *American Beauty*	Hilary Swank *Boys Don't Cry*	Michael Caine, *The Cider House Rules*	Angelina Jolie *Girl Interrupted*	Sam Mendes *American Beauty*
2000	Gladiator	Russell Crowe *Gladiator*	Julia Roberts *Erin Brockovich*	Benicio Del Toro *Traffic*	Marcia Gay Harden *Pollock*	Steven Soderbergh *Traffic*
2001	A Beautiful Mind	Denzel Washington *Training Day*	Halle Berry *Monster's Ball*	Jim Broadbent *Iris*	Jennifer Connelly *A Beautiful Mind*	Ron Howard *A Beautiful Mind*
2002	Chicago	Adrien Brody *The Pianist*	Nicole Kidman *The Hours*	Chris Cooper *Adaptation*	Catherine Zeta-Jones, *Chicago*	Roman Polanski *The Pianist*
2003	The Lord of the Rings: The Return of the King	Sean Penn *Mystic River*	Charlize Theron *Monster*	Tim Robbins *Mystic River*	Renée Zellweger *Cold Mountain*	Peter Jackson *The Lord of the Rings: The Return of the King*
2004	Million Dollar Baby	Jamie Foxx *Ray*	Hilary Swank *Million Dollar Baby*	Morgan Freeman *Million Dollar Baby*	Cate Blanchett *The Aviator*	Clint Eastwood *Million Dollar Baby*
2005	Crash	Philip Seymour Hoffman *Capote*	Reese Witherspoon *Walk the Line*	George Clooney *Syriana*	Rachel Weisz *The Constant Gardener*	Ang Lee *Brokeback Mountain*
2006	The Departed	Forest Whitaker *The Last King of Scotland*	Helen Mirren *The Queen*	Alan Arkin *Little Miss Sunshine*	Jennifer Hudson *Dreamgirls*	Martin Scorsese *The Departed*
2007	No Country for Old Men	Daniel Day-Lewis *There Will Be Blood*	Marion Cotillard *La Vie en Rose*	Javier Bardem *No Country for Old Men*	Tilda Swinton *Michael Clayton*	Joel Coen and Ethan Coen, *No Country for Old Men*
2008	Slumdog Millionaire	Sean Penn *Milk*	Kate Winslet *The Reader*	Heath Ledger *The Dark Knight*	Penelope Cruz, *Vicky Cristina Barcelona*	Danny Boyle *Slumdog Millionaire*
2009	The Hurt Locker	Jeff Bridges *Crazy Heart*	Sandra Bullock *The Blind Side*	Christoph Waltz *Inglourious Basterds*	Mo'Nique *Precious*	Kathryn Bigelow *The Hurt Locker*
2010	The King's Speech	Colin Firth *The King's Speech*	Natalie Portman *Black Swan*	Christian Bale *The Fighter*	Melissa Leo *The Fighter*	Tom Hooper *The King's Speech*
2011	The Artist	Jean Dujardin *The Artist*	Meryl Streep *The Iron Lady*	Christopher Plummer, *Beginners*	Octavia Spencer *The Help*	Michel Hazanavicius *The Artist*
2012	Argo	Daniel Day-Lewis *Lincoln*	Jennifer Lawrence *Silver Linings Playbook*	Christoph Waltz *Django Unchained*	Anne Hathaway *Les Misérables*	Ang Lee *Life of Pi*

(1) Award not given until 1936.

Other Academy Award Winners, 2012

Animated film: *Brave*
Cinematography: *Life of Pi*
Costume design: *Anna Karenina*
Documentary: *Searching for Sugar Man*
Film editing: *Argo*
Foreign language film: *Amour*, Austria
Makeup: *Les Misérables*
Original score: *Life of Pi*, Mychael Danna
Original song: "Skyfall," *Skyfall*, Adele Adkins and Paul Epworth

Production design: *Lincoln*
Screenplay, adapted: *Argo*, Chris Terrio
Screenplay, original: *Django Unchained*, Quentin Tarantino
Short films: *Paperman* (animated), *Inocente* (documentary), *Curfew* (live-action)
Sound editing: *Skyfall, Zero Dark Thirty*
Sound mixing: *Les Misérables*
Visual effects: *Life of Pi*

Other Film Awards, 2013
(Awarded in 2013, unless otherwise noted.)

British Academy of Film and Television Awards (BAFTAs)
Awarded in 2013 to films released in the UK in 2012.
Best film: *Argo*
British film: *Skyfall*
Director: Ben Affleck, *Argo*
Original screenplay: Quentin Tarantino, *Django Unchained*
Adapted screenplay: David O. Russell, *Silver Linings Playbook*
Foreign language film: *Amour*, France/Austria
Animated film: *Brave*
Actor: Daniel Day-Lewis, *Lincoln*
Actress: Emmanuelle Riva, *Amour*
Supporting actor: Christoph Waltz, *Django Unchained*
Supporting actress: Anne Hathaway, *Les Misérables*

Canadian Screen Awards
Awarded to Canadian-produced or Canadian-coproduced films.
Motion picture: *Rebelle [War Witch]*
Actor: James Cromwell, *Still Mine*
Actress: Rachel Mwanza, *Rebelle [War Witch]*
Supporting actor: Serge Kanyinda, *Rebelle [War Witch]*
Supporting actress: Seema Biswas, *Midnight's Children*
Documentary: *Stories We Tell*
Director: Kim Nguyen, *Rebelle [War Witch]*

Cannes International Film Festival Awards
Palme d'Or: *La vie d'Adèle — Chapitre 1 & 2 [Blue Is the Warmest Colour]*, France/Belgium/Spain
Grand Prix: *Inside Llewyn Davis*, U.S.
Best Director: Amat Escalante, *Heli*, Mexico/Germany/Netherlands/France
Best Screenplay: Jia Zhangke, *Tian Zhu Ding [A Touch of Sin]*, China/Japan
Best Actress: Bérénice Bejo, *Le passé [The Past]*, France/Italy
Best Actor: Bruce Dern, *Nebraska*, U.S.

Jury Prize: *Soshite Chichi Ni Naru [Like Father, Like Son]*, Japan
Palme d'Or, short film: *Safe*, Byoung-Gon Moon, South Korea

Director's Guild of America Awards
Feature film: Ben Affleck, *Argo*
Documentary: Malik Bendjelloul, *Searching for Sugar Man*

Sundance Film Festival Awards
Grand Jury Prize: *Fruitvale Station* (drama); *Blood Brother* (doc.)
World Cinema Jury Prize: *Jiseul*, South Korea (drama); *A River Changes Course*, Cambodia/U.S. (doc.)
Audience Award: *Fruitvale Station* (drama); *Blood Brother* (doc.)
World Cinema Audience Award: *Metro Manila*, UK/Philippines (drama); *The Square*, Egypt/U.S. (doc.)
Best of Next Audience Award: *This Is Martin Bonner*
Directing: Jill Soloway, *Afternoon Delight* (drama); Zachary Heinzerling, *Cutie and the Boxer* (doc.)
World Cinema Directing Award: Sebastián Silva, *Crystal Fairy*, Chile (drama); Tinatin Gurchiani, *The Machine Which Makes Everything Disappear*, Georgia/Germany (doc.)
Waldo Salt Screenwriting Award: Lake Bell, *In a World...*
World Cinema Screenwriting Award: Barmak Akram, *Wajma (An Afghan Love Story)*, Afghanistan

Toronto International Film Festival
Prize of the International Critics (FIPRESCI Prize) for Discovery: *The Amazing Catfish*
FIPRESCI Prize for Special Presentations: *Ida*
People's Choice Award: *12 Years a Slave*
People's Choice Award (documentary): *The Square*
People's Choice Award (Midnight Madness): *Jigoku de Naze Warui [Why Don't You Play in Hell?]*
Canadian Feature Film: *When Jews Were Funny*
Canadian Short Film: *Noah*
Canadian First Feature Film: *Asphalt Watches*

Academy of Country Music Awards, 2013

Entertainer of the year: Luke Bryan
Male vocalist: Jason Aldean
Female vocalist: Miranda Lambert
Vocal duo: Thompson Square
Vocal group: Little Big Town
New artist: Florida Georgia Line
New male vocalist: Brantley Gilbert
New female vocalist: Jana Kramer

New vocal duo: Florida Georgia Line
Album: *Chief*, Eric Church
Record (single): "Over You," Miranda Lambert
Song: "Over You," Miranda Lambert
Vocal event: "The Only Way I Know," Jason Aldean with Luke Bryan and Eric Church
Video: "Tornado," Little Big Town

Selected Grammy Awards, 2012
Source: National Academy of Recording Arts and Sciences
For albums released Oct. 1, 2011–Sept. 30, 2012, awarded in Feb. 2013.

Record of the year (single): "Somebody That I Used to Know," Gotye feat. Kimbra
Album of the year: *Babel*, Mumford & Sons
Song of the year: "We Are Young," fun. feat. Janelle Monae
New artist: fun.
Pop perf., solo: "Set Fire to the Rain" (live), Adele
Pop perf., duo/group: "Somebody That I Used to Know," Gotye feat. Kimbra
Pop album, instrumental: *Impressions*, Chris Botti
Pop album, traditional: *Kisses on the Bottom*, Paul McCartney
Pop album, vocal: *Stronger*, Kelly Clarkson
Dance recording: "Bangarang," Skrillex feat. Sirah
Dance/electronica album: *Bangarang*, Skrillex
Rock perf.: "Lonely Boy," The Black Keys
Hard rock/metal perf.: "Love Bites (So Do I)," Halestorm
Rock song: "Lonely Boy," The Black Keys
Rock album: *El Camino*, The Black Keys
Alternative album: *Making Mirrors*, Gotye
R&B perf.: "Climax," Usher
R&B perf., traditional: "Love on Top," Beyoncé
R&B song: "Adorn," Miguel Pimentel
R&B album: *Black Radio*, Robert Glasper Experiment
Urban contemporary album: *Channel Orange*, Frank Ocean
Rap perf.: "N****s in Paris," Jay-Z and Kanye West

Rap/sung collaboration: "No Church in the Wild," Jay-Z and Kanye West feat. Frank Ocean and The Dream
Rap song: "N****s in Paris," Jay-Z and Kanye West
Rap album: *Take Care*, Drake
Country perf., solo: "Blown Away," Carrie Underwood
Country perf., duo/group: "Pontoon," Little Big Town
Country song: "Blown Away," Carrie Underwood
Country album: *Uncaged*, Zac Brown Band
Bluegrass album: *Nobody Knows You*, Steep Canyon Rangers
Jazz album, instrumental: *Unity Band*, Pat Metheny Unity Band
Jazz album, vocal: *Radio Music Society*, Esperanza Spalding
New age album: *Echoes of Love*, Omar Akram
Comedy album: *Blow Your Pants Off*, Jimmy Fallon
Spoken-word album: *Society's Child: My Autobiography*, Janis Ian
Soundtrack album, compilation: *Midnight in Paris*, various artists
Soundtrack album, score: *The Girl With the Dragon Tattoo*, Trent Reznor and Atticus Ross
Song, visual media: "Safe & Sound," *The Hunger Games*
Music video, short form: "We Found Love," Rihanna feat. Calvin Harris
Music video, long form: *Big Easy Express*, Mumford & Sons, Edward Sharpe & The Magnetic Zeros, and Old Crow Medicine Show

Grammy Awards, 1958-2012

Record of the Year (single)	Year	Album of the Year
Domenico Modugno, "Nel Blu Dipinto Di Blu (Volare)"	1958	Henry Mancini, *The Music From Peter Gunn*
Bobby Darin, "Mack the Knife"	1959	Frank Sinatra, *Come Dance With Me*
Percy Faith, "Theme From a Summer Place"	1960	Bob Newhart, *Button Down Mind*
Henry Mancini, "Moon River"	1961	Judy Garland, *Judy at Carnegie Hall*
Tony Bennett, "I Left My Heart in San Francisco"	1962	Vaughn Meader, *The First Family*
Henry Mancini, "The Days of Wine and Roses"	1963	Barbra Streisand, *The Barbra Streisand Album*
Stan Getz and Astrud Gilberto, "The Girl From Ipanema"	1964	Stan Getz and João Gilberto, *Getz/Gilberto*
Herb Alpert, "A Taste of Honey"	1965	Frank Sinatra, *September of My Years*
Frank Sinatra, "Strangers in the Night"	1966	Frank Sinatra, *A Man and His Music*
5th Dimension, "Up, Up and Away"	1967	The Beatles, *Sgt. Pepper's Lonely Hearts Club Band*
Simon and Garfunkel, "Mrs. Robinson"	1968	Glen Campbell, *By the Time I Get to Phoenix*
5th Dimension, "Aquarius/Let the Sunshine In"	1969	Blood, Sweat & Tears, *Blood, Sweat & Tears*
Simon and Garfunkel, "Bridge Over Troubled Water"	1970	Simon and Garfunkel, *Bridge Over Troubled Water*
Carole King, "It's Too Late"	1971	Carole King, *Tapestry*
Roberta Flack, "The First Time Ever I Saw Your Face"	1972	George Harrison and Friends, *The Concert for Bangla Desh*
Roberta Flack, "Killing Me Softly With His Song"	1973	Stevie Wonder, *Innervisions*
Olivia Newton-John, "I Honestly Love You"	1974	Stevie Wonder, *Fulfillingness' First Finale*
Captain & Tennille, "Love Will Keep Us Together"	1975	Paul Simon, *Still Crazy After All These Years*
George Benson, "This Masquerade"	1976	Stevie Wonder, *Songs in the Key of Life*
Eagles, "Hotel California"	1977	Fleetwood Mac, *Rumours*
Billy Joel, "Just the Way You Are"	1978	Bee Gees, *Saturday Night Fever*
The Doobie Brothers, "What a Fool Believes"	1979	Billy Joel, *52nd Street*
Christopher Cross, "Sailing"	1980	Christopher Cross, *Christopher Cross*
Kim Carnes, "Bette Davis Eyes"	1981	John Lennon and Yoko Ono, *Double Fantasy*
Toto, "Rosanna"	1982	Toto, *Toto IV*
Michael Jackson, "Beat It"	1983	Michael Jackson, *Thriller*
Tina Turner, "What's Love Got to Do With It"	1984	Lionel Richie, *Can't Slow Down*
USA for Africa, "We Are the World"	1985	Phil Collins, *No Jacket Required*
Steve Winwood, "Higher Love"	1986	Paul Simon, *Graceland*
Paul Simon, "Graceland"	1987	U2, *The Joshua Tree*
Bobby McFerrin, "Don't Worry, Be Happy"	1988	George Michael, *Faith*
Bette Midler, "Wind Beneath My Wings"	1989	Bonnie Raitt, *Nick of Time*
Phil Collins, "Another Day in Paradise"	1990	Quincy Jones, *Back on the Block*
Natalie Cole, with Nat "King" Cole, "Unforgettable"	1991	Natalie Cole, with Nat "King" Cole, *Unforgettable*
Eric Clapton, "Tears in Heaven"	1992	Eric Clapton, *Unplugged*
Whitney Houston, "I Will Always Love You"	1993	Whitney Houston, *The Bodyguard*
Sheryl Crow, "All I Wanna Do"	1994	Tony Bennett, *MTV Unplugged*
Seal, "Kiss From a Rose"	1995	Alanis Morissette, *Jagged Little Pill*
Eric Clapton, "Change the World"	1996	Celine Dion, *Falling Into You*
Shawn Colvin, "Sunny Came Home"	1997	Bob Dylan, *Time Out of Mind*
Celine Dion, "My Heart Will Go On"	1998	Lauryn Hill, *The Miseducation of Lauryn Hill*
Santana feat. Rob Thomas, "Smooth"	1999	Santana, *Supernatural*
U2, "Beautiful Day"	2000	Steely Dan, *Two Against Nature*
U2, "Walk On"	2001	Various artists, *O Brother, Where Art Thou?*
Norah Jones, "Don't Know Why"	2002	Norah Jones, *Come Away With Me*
Coldplay, "Clocks"	2003	OutKast, *Speakerboxxx/The Love Below*
Ray Charles and Norah Jones, "Here We Go Again"	2004	Ray Charles and various artists, *Genius Loves Company*
Green Day, "Boulevard of Broken Dreams"	2005	U2, *How to Dismantle an Atomic Bomb*
Dixie Chicks, "Not Ready to Make Nice"	2006	Dixie Chicks, *Taking the Long Way*
Amy Winehouse, "Rehab"	2007	Herbie Hancock, *River: The Joni Letters*
Robert Plant and Alison Krauss, "Please Read the Letter"	2008	Robert Plant and Alison Krauss, *Raising Sand*
Kings of Leon, "Use Somebody"	2009	Taylor Swift, *Fearless*
Lady Antebellum, "Need You Now"	2010	Arcade Fire, *The Suburbs*
Adele, "Rolling in the Deep"	2011	Adele, *21*
Gotye, "Somebody That I Used to Know"	2012	Mumford & Sons, *Babel*

MTV Video Music Awards, 2013

Video of the year: "Mirrors," Justin Timberlake
Artist to watch: "What About Love," Austin Mahone
Female video: "I Knew You Were Trouble," Taylor Swift
Male video: "Locked out of Heaven," Bruno Mars
Song of the summer: "Best Song Ever," One Direction
Video with a social message: "Same Love," Macklemore and Ryan Lewis feat. Mary Lambert
Hip-hop video: "Can't Hold Us," Macklemore and Ryan Lewis feat. Ray Dalton
Pop video: "Come and Get It," Selena Gomez

Rock video: "Up in the Air," 30 Seconds to Mars
Collaboration: "Just Give Me a Reason," Pink feat. Nate Ruess
Art direction: "Q.U.E.E.N.," Janelle Monae feat. Erykah Badu
Choreography: "Treasure," Bruno Mars
Cinematography: "Can't Hold Us," Macklemore and Ryan Lewis feat. Ray Dalton
Direction: "Suit & Tie," Justin Timberlake feat. Jay-Z
Editing: "Mirrors," Justin Timberlake
Visual effects: "Safe and Sound," Capital Cities

Science and Technology News, 2013

The following were some of the more newsworthy developments in science and technology in the past year.

Earliest Primate Found

In the June 6, 2013, issue of *Nature*, scientists described a nearly complete fossil skeleton of a tiny, previously unknown primate: a creature that lived 55 mil years ago, in the early Eocene epoch. The slender-limbed animal, just 2.8 in. long, ranks as the earliest known animal that can be classified as a primate. Primates include humans and other such mammals as apes, monkeys, tarsiers, lemurs, and galagos.

A Chinese farmer discovered the fossil in 2002, near Jingzhou. Analysis of the fragile specimen, which had been encased in rock, took years of careful work. Using powerful X-ray equipment, the scientists made a detailed three-dimensional digital reconstruction of the skeleton. The creature had grasping feet, long back limbs, and a lengthy tail. It probably spent its life in trees. Its hip, pelvis, knee, and elbow looked somewhat similar to those of a tarsier. But its foot featured a distinctive heel bone and toes that were more like the feet of anthropoids (monkeys, apes, and humans). The scientists dubbed it *Archicebus achilles*, from the Greek meaning "first [or beginning] monkey Achilles." (Achilles was a legendary ancient Greek hero whose heel was said to be his only vulnerable spot.) The unusual mix of features led researchers to suggest that the animal represented a point not long after tarsiers and anthropoids began to follow separate evolutionary paths.

Life Deep Below

Even as speculation raged about the possibility of life on or below the surface of Mars and other solar system bodies, scientists in 2013 continued to uncover evidence on Earth of extremophiles—organisms that flourish in extreme conditions inhospitable to most known life-forms.

A study in the Mar. 15 issue of *Science* hinted that a vast ecosystem may exist in the "dark biosphere," the little-studied region below the ocean floor. Researchers found microbes in rock gathered 1,150-1,900 ft beneath the Pacific Ocean floor on the eastern side of the Juan de Fuca Ridge, off the northwestern U.S. coast. The organisms derive their energy from chemical reactions, or chemosynthesis.

A study reported online on Mar. 17 in *Nature Geoscience* analyzed sediment from the Mariana Trench, in the central west Pacific Ocean, the deepest point on Earth's surface. Researchers found high rates of oxygen consumption in the sediment, indicating the presence of an unexpectedly active community of microbes.

Another study analyzed sediment taken from six sites around the globe, at depths between 6 ft and 158 ft under the seafloor. It revealed evidence at least 70 varieties of living fungi. The scientists also found evidence of living algae, though they could not understand how it could have survived without sunlight. The research was published online on Feb. 13 in *PLoS One*.

Success and Setback in the Hunt for Planets

By Sept. 2013, the number of known exoplanets—planets outside our solar system—had grown to more than 900. More than 3,000 potential planets spotted by NASA's space observatory Kepler (launched in 2009) awaited confirmation by astronomers. A study in the July 10 issue of *Astrophysical Journal Letters* estimated that, in our galaxy, red dwarf stars alone may have as many as 60 bil planets orbiting them in their habitable zones. In Sept., Japanese astronomers reported that the atmosphere of a large planet orbiting the star Gliese 1214, just 40 light-years from Earth, was probably rich in water.

Jan. 2013 had brought news of the possible discovery by Kepler of the most Earth-like exoplanet yet. Just a bit larger than Earth, it seemed to lie in the habitable zone of its star, Kepler-69, which is of the same type as the Sun. Further study suggested that the planet may be more like the torridly hot Venus than Earth.

Kepler's primary mission was completed Nov. 2012, though the data it collected are still being analyzed. A planned four-year follow-up mission abruptly ended when a second of Kepler's four gyroscope-like reaction wheels

failed in May 2013. NASA put out a call in Aug. for new mission proposals needing only two reaction wheels.

Universe Older, More Puzzling

The most accurate map yet of the early universe was released by scientists on Mar. 21, 2013. It showed, with unprecedented detail and resolution, tiny variations in the so-called cosmic microwave background radiation—an afterglow from the Big Bang. Based on the first 15.5 months of observations by the European Space Agency's Planck space telescope (launched in 2009), the map refined astronomers' notions of the universe's age and makeup. It dovetailed with the general outlines of astronomers' standard model of the cosmos, but it also contained puzzling features.

The cosmic background is a relic dating from some 370,000-380,000 years after the Big Bang. The variations detected in it indicate slight temperature differences and are believed to stem from random fluctuations that occurred right after the Big Bang. The universe, as depicted by the Planck data, is not quite as uniform as many researchers expected. It seems slightly lopsided, and there is an unexplained large cool spot. According to the Planck results, the universe is 13.8 bil years old—100 mil years older than previously believed. It also appears to be expanding more slowly, and to have a higher proportion of matter and dark matter to dark energy than had been thought.

Storing Data in DNA

Current methods of storing large quantities of digital data for long periods have their limits. For example, magnetic tape degrades with time. Hard drives also wear out, and they consume substantial amounts of electricity. Nature uses DNA to carry the complex genetic information of living creatures. This long, sturdy molecule can hold a wealth of information; the contents of 45 1-terabyte hard drives could fit into DNA the size of a speck of dust.

In the Sept. 28, 2012, issue of *Science*, researchers reported success in encoding a 54,000-word book in DNA. A project described in the Feb. 7, 2013, issue of *Nature* dealt with a slightly larger collection of data (about 739 kilobytes' worth) and reduced the chances of error in the archival process. It assembled a variety of media: a photograph, the sonnets of William Shakespeare, the historic 1953 paper by Francis Crick and James Watson on DNA's "double helix" structure, and an audio clip from Martin Luther King Jr.'s "I Have a Dream" speech. These items were converted into code carried by DNA, and the DNA was then "read"—the original files were recreated from it—with virtually 100% accuracy. Researchers predicted that, based on current rates of technological progress, the approach could become cost-effective within a decade.

New Wonder Material

Graphene is an odd material. Like graphite, commonly found in pencils, it is made of carbon atoms. But it consists of a single layer just one atom thick, with the carbon atoms linked together in a hexagonally patterned crystal. Two British scientists won the 2010 Nobel Prize in physics for their research on this remarkable substance, which, among other attributes, conducts electricity better than silicon. Recent years have seen an explosion of research on ways to produce and use graphene.

Among the numerous graphene-related developments in 2013, a study reported in the May 31 issue of *Science* found a way of making sheets of graphene that are sufficiently large for many potential applications and that retain nearly all of the strength exhibited by graphene grains, shown by previous research to be the strongest material ever measured.

On Aug. 30 another group of researchers reported in the online journal *Nature Communications* success in using strands of DNA as a template for "growing" tiny ribbons of graphene, which they then used to make primitive transistors. If the method can be refined and adapted for mass production, it may supply a way of producing graphene transistors that are smaller, faster, and use less power than silicon-based transistors.

Science Glossary

This glossary covers some concepts that come up frequently in the news, in biology, chemistry, geology, and physics.

Biology

Amino acid: one of about 20 similar small molecules that are the building blocks of proteins.

Antibiotic: a substance produced by or derived from a bacterium, fungus, or other organism that battles infections and diseases caused by microorganisms, especially bacteria; it works by killing the microorganism or halting its growth.

Archaea: a group of single-celled microorganisms; they are prokaryotes, like bacteria, but they share some similarities with eukaryotes.

Autoimmunity: a condition in which an individual's immune system reacts against his or her own tissues; leads to diseases such as lupus, some forms of diabetes, inflammatory bowel disease, and rheumatoid arthritis.

Bacterium (plural, bacteria): one of a large, varied class of microscopic and simple, single-celled organisms; bacteria live almost everywhere—some forms cause disease, while others are useful in digestion and other natural processes.

Biodiversity: richness of variety of life-forms—both plant and animal—in a given environment.

Cell: the smallest unit of life capable of living independently, or with other cells; usually bounded by a membrane. May include a nucleus and other specialized parts.

Cholesterol: a fatty substance in animal tissues. It is produced by the liver in humans; is found in foods such as butter, eggs, and meat; and is an essential body constituent.

Chromosome: one of the rod-like structures in cell nuclei that carry genetic material (DNA).

Cloning: the process of copying a particular piece of DNA to allow it to be sequenced, studied, or used in some other way; can also refer to producing a genetic copy of an organism.

DNA (deoxyribonucleic acid): the double-stranded chemical substance that carries genetic information, which determines the form and functioning of all living things.

Ecosystem: an interdependent community of living organisms and their climatic and geographical habitat.

Enzyme: a protein that promotes a particular chemical reaction in the body.

Estrogen: one of a group of hormones that promote development of female secondary sex characteristics and the growth and health of the female reproductive system; males also produce small amounts of estrogen.

Eukaryote: any of the group of single- or multi-celled organisms whose cells have distinct nuclei.

Evolution: the process of gradual change that may occur as a species adapts to its environment; natural selection is the process by which evolution occurs.

Gene: a portion of a DNA molecule that provides the blueprint for the assembly of a protein.

Gene pool: the collection and total diversity of genes in an interbreeding population.

Gene therapy: a treatment in which scientists try to implant functioning genes into a person's cells so the genes can produce proteins that the person lacks or that help the person fight disease.

Genetic sequencing: the process of finding the order of subunits in a gene or the order of all an organism's genes.

Genome: the complete set of an organism's genetic material.

Hormone: a substance secreted in one part of an organism that regulates the functioning of other tissues or organs.

Meiosis: the process of cell division that results in gametes (sperm or egg cells), all of which contain half the number of chromosomes as their precursor.

Metabolism: the sum total of the body's chemical processes providing energy for vital functions and enabling new material to be synthesized.

Mitosis: the process by which a cell divides its nucleus and other cell materials into two duplicate daughter cells with the same DNA.

Neuron or nerve cell: any of the cells in the nervous system that send electrical and chemical messages to other cells.

Nucleus (plural, nuclei): the center of an atom; or the portion of a eukaryotic cell that contains genetic material and regulates growth and metabolism.

Organism: a living entity, capable of growth, metabolism, and usually reproduction.

Phenotype: the observable properties and characteristics of an organism arising at least in part from its genetic makeup.

Pheromone: a chemical secreted by an animal or plant to influence the behavior of other members of its species.

Placebo effect: a phenomenon in which patients show improvements even though they have taken a medically inactive substance, called a placebo.

Prokaryote: a single-celled organism that does not have a distinct nucleus, such as a bacterium or archaeon.

Protein: a complex molecule made up of one or more chains of amino acids; essential to the structure and function of all cells.

RNA (ribonucleic acid): a complex molecule similar to the genetic material DNA but usually single-stranded; several forms of RNA translate the genetic code of DNA and use that code to assemble proteins for structural and biological functions in the body. RNA also serves as the genetic material of some viruses.

Species: a population of organisms that breed with each other in nature and produce fertile offspring; other definitions of species exist to accommodate the diversity of life on Earth.

Stem cell: a cell that can give rise to other types of cells; for instance, bone marrow stem cells may divide and produce different types of blood cells.

Steroid: a type of chemical substance with a certain molecular structure. Some steroids are hormones that can suppress immune response or influence stress reaction, blood pressure, or sexual development.

Testosterone: a steroid hormone that stimulates the development and maintenance of male sexual characteristics and the production of sperm; women also produce small amounts of testosterone.

Virus: a microscopic, often disease-causing, "organism" made of genetic material surrounded by a protein shell; can only reproduce inside a living cell.

Chemistry

Acid: a class of compound that contrasts with bases. Acids taste sour, turn litmus red/pink, and often produce hydrogen gas in contact with some metals. Acids donate protons (hydrogen atoms minus the electron) in chemical reactions.

Base: a substance that yields hydroxyl ions (OH-) when dissolved in water; any of a class of compounds whose aqueous solutions taste bitter, feel slippery, turn litmus blue, and react with acids to form salts; also known as **alkaline**.

Carbon fiber: an extremely strong, thin fiber made by pyrolyzing (decomposing by heat) synthetic fibers, such as rayon, until charred; used to make high-strength composites.

Chlorofluorocarbon (CFC): one of a group of industrial chemicals that contain chlorine, fluorine, and carbon and have been found to damage Earth's ozone layer.

Element: a substance that cannot be chemically decomposed into simpler substances; the atoms of an element all have the same number of protons and electrons.

Isotope: an atom of a chemical element with the same number of protons in its nucleus as other atoms of that element, but with a different number of neutrons.

Molecule: the basic unit of a chemical compound, composed of two or more atoms bound together.

Noble gases or inert gases: a group of gases including helium, neon, argon, krypton, xenon, and radon that are not reactive except in rare and limited instances.

Osmosis: the transfer of a fluid across a semipermeable membrane, usually from an area of higher concentration to one of lower concentration.

Phase: any of the possible states of matter—solid, liquid, gas, or plasma—that change according to temperature and pressure.

Polymer: a huge molecule containing hundreds or thousands of smaller molecules arranged in repeating units.

Salt: a neutral compound produced by the reaction of an acid and a base.

Geology

Fault, tectonic: a crack or break in Earth's crust, often due to the slippage of tectonic plates past or over one another; usually geologically unstable.

Igneous: a type of rock formed by solidification from a molten state, especially from molten magma.

Magma: hot liquid rock material under Earth's crust, from which igneous rock is formed by cooling.

Metamorphic: in geology, the name given to rocks or minerals that have recrystallized under the influence of heat and pressure since their original formation.

Pangaea: a single supercontinent that scientists believe began to break apart at least 200 mil years ago to form the current continents.

Plate tectonics: theory that Earth's lithosphere—the uppermost layer that includes the crust—is made up of many separate rigid plates of rock that float on top of hot semi-liquid rock.

Sedimentary: a type of rock formed by the buildup of material at the bottoms of bodies of water.

Physics

Absolute zero: the theoretical temperature at which all motion within a molecule stops, corresponding to $-273.15°C$ ($-459.67°F$).

Antimatter: matter that consists of antiparticles, such as antiprotons, that have an opposite charge from normal particles; when matter meets antimatter, both are destroyed, and their combined mass is converted to energy. Antimatter is created in certain radioactive decay processes but appears to be present in only small amounts in the universe.

Atom: the basic unit of a chemical element.

Atomic mass: the total mass of an atom of a given element; atoms of the same element with different atomic masses (different numbers of neutrons, not protons) are called **isotopes**.

Atomic number: the number of protons in an atom of a given element of the periodic table; the characteristic that sets atoms of different elements apart.

Axion: a hypothetical subatomic particle with low mass and energy that is thought to exist because of the properties of the strong nuclear force.

Bose-Einstein condensate (BEC): a "super-atom" comprising thousands of atoms super-cooled to within a few hundred millionths of a degree of absolute zero and thus condensed into the lowest energy state. Atoms bound in the BEC behave synchronously, giving the BEC wavelike properties.

Boson: force-carrying particles including photons, gluons, and the W and Z particles; one of the two primary categories of particles in the Standard Model, the other being fermions.

Dark energy: a mysterious, undefined energy leading to a repulsive force pervading all of space-time; proposed by cosmologists as counteracting gravity and accelerating the expansion of the universe; predicted to make up 73% of the universe's composition.

Dark matter: hypothetical, invisible matter that some scientists believe makes up 83% of the matter in the universe (excluding dark energy). Its existence was proposed to account for otherwise inexplicable gravitational forces observed in space.

Doppler effect: a change in the frequency of sound, light, or radio waves caused by the motion of the source emitting the waves or the motion of the person or instrument perceiving the waves.

Electron: negatively charged particle that is the least massive electrically charged fundamental particle; the most common charged lepton in the Standard Model.

Energy: capacity to perform work. Energy can take various forms, such as potential energy, kinetic energy, and chemical energy.

Entropy: a measure of disorder in a system.

Fermion: any one of a number of matter particles including electrons, protons, neutrons, and quarks; one of the two primary categories of particles in the Standard Model, the other being bosons.

Field: the effects of forces (gravitational, electric, etc.) are visualized and described mathematically by physicists in terms of fields, which show the strength and direction of a force at a given position.

Fission: a nuclear reaction that occurs when the nuclei of large, unstable atoms break apart, releasing large amounts of energy.

Fluorescence: luminescence that is caused by the absorption of radiation at one wavelength followed by an almost immediate re-radiation, usually at a different wavelength, that stops almost immediately when the radiation stops.

Force: in classical physics, something that causes acceleration in a body; can be thought of as a push or pull.

Fusion: a nuclear reaction occurring when atomic nuclei collide at high temperatures and combine to form one heavier atomic nucleus, releasing enormous energy in the process.

Gravity: an attractive force between any two objects or particles, proportional to the mass (or energy) of the objects; strength of the force decreases with greater distance; the only fundamental force still unaccounted for by the Standard Model.

Half-life: the time it takes for half of a given amount of a radioactive element to decay.

Hertz (Hz): a measure of frequency, or how many times a given event occurs per second; applied to sound waves, electrical current, and microchip clock speeds.

Laser: light consisting of a cascade of photons all having the same wavelength; stands for Light Amplification by Stimulated Emission of Radiation.

Light-emitting diode (LED): a semiconductor that emits light when an electrical current is passed through it. The color of the light depends on the material used in making the diode.

Neutrino: a tiny fundamental particle with no electrical charge and very small mass that moves very quickly through the universe; comes in three varieties, or flavors, called electron, muon, and tau.

Neutron: a neutral particle found in the nuclei of atoms.

Particle accelerator: a large machine with a circular or long, straight tunnel in which atoms smash into each other at high speeds. Physicists use these machines to study subatomic particles.

Phosphorescence: luminescence that is caused by the absorption of radiation at one wavelength followed by a delayed re-radiation, usually at a different wavelength, that continues for at least a hundredth of a second after the radiation stops.

Photon: the elementary unit, or quantum, of light or electromagnetic radiation. It has no mass or electrical charge and is one of the fundamental force-carrying particles, or bosons, described by the Standard Model.

Plasma: a high-energy state of matter different from solid, liquid, or gas in which atomic nuclei and the electrons orbiting them separate from each other.

Proton: a positively charged subatomic particle found in the nuclei of atoms.

Quantum: a natural unit of some physically measurable property, such as energy or electrical charge.

Quark: a fermion and a fundamental matter particle that makes up neutrons and protons, forming atomic nuclei; there are six different varieties, or flavors, of quarks grouped in pairs: up and down, charm and strange, top and bottom.

Radiation: energy emitted as rays or particles. Radiation includes heat, light, ultraviolet rays, gamma rays, X-rays, cosmic rays, alpha particles, and beta particles.

Relativity, general theory of: a theory of space-time proposed by Albert Einstein in 1915; it links gravity to the curvature of space-time.

Relativity, special theory of: Einstein's theory of space and time: all laws of physics are valid in all uniformly moving frames of reference, and the speed of light in a vacuum is always the same, so long as the source and the observer are moving without (not accelerating).

Standard Model: prevailing theory of the interaction of subatomic particles. Matter particles are fermions: either leptons or quarks; force-carrying particles are bosons, such as gluons, W or Z bosons, and photons; successfully explains three of the four elementary forces acting on particles (strong, weak, electromagnetic) but thus far has not incorporated gravity.

String theory: a theory that seeks to unify quantum mechanics and general relativity, positing that the basic constituents of matter can best be understood not as point objects but as tiny oscillating "strings."

Subatomic particle: one of the small particles, such as electrons, neutrons, and protons, which make up an atom.

Superconductivity: the property of certain materials, usually metals and chemically complex ceramics, to conduct electricity without resistance, generally at very cold temperatures.

Thermodynamics: the branch of physics that describes how energy, heat, and temperature flow in physical systems.

Ultraviolet radiation: a form of light, invisible to the human eye, that has a shorter wavelength and greater energy than visible light but has a longer wavelength and less energy than X-rays.

Virtual particle: subatomic particles that rapidly pop into and out of existence and can exert real forces; usually occur in particle-antiparticle pairs and are rapidly annihilated.

Mohs Scale of Hardness

Hardness is the ability of a solid substance to resist abrasion or deformation on its surface. Soft minerals scratch more easily than hard ones. For example, a diamond will scratch graphite because the graphite is softer. In 1812, German mineralogist Frederich Mohs (1773-1839) created the arbitrary scale shown below to measure relative hardness using 10 minerals that were readily available at that time. The numbers in the Mohs scale are arranged in order of increasing hardness. An item's hardness is obtained by determining which mineral in the Mohs scale can scratch it.

Mohs Scale		Selected items and their relative hardness		
1 . . . . . . Talc	6 . . . . . Orthoclase feldspar	2.5 . . . . . Fingernail	5.5 . . . . . Knife blade	
2 . . . . . . Gypsum	7 . . . . . Quartz	2.5-3 . . . . . Gold, silver	6-7 . . . . . Glass	
3 . . . . . . Calcite	8 . . . . . Topaz	3 . . . . Copper penny	6.5 . . . . . Iron pyrite	
4 . . . . . . Fluorite	9 . . . . . Corundum	4-4.5 . . . . . Platinum	7+ . . . . . . Hardened steel file	
5 . . . . . . Apatite	10 . . . . . . Diamond	4-5 . . . . . Iron		

Chemical Elements, Atomic Numbers, Year Discovered

See Periodic Table of the Elements on the following page for atomic weights.

Element	Symbol	Atomic number	Year discov.	Element	Symbol	Atomic number	Year discov.	Element	Symbol	Atomic number	Year discov.
Actinium	Ac	89	1899	Gold	Au	79	BCE	Protactinium	Pa	91	1917
Aluminum	Al	13	1825	Hafnium	Hf	72	1923	Radium	Ra	88	1898
Americium	Am	95	1944	Hassium	Hs	108	1984	Radon	Rn	86	1900
Antimony	Sb	51	1450	Helium	He	2	1868	Rhenium	Re	75	1925
Argon	Ar	18	1894	Holmium	Ho	67	1878	Rhodium	Rh	45	1803
Arsenic	As	33	13th cent.	Hydrogen	H	1	1766	Roentgenium	Rg	111	1995
Astatine	At	85	1940	Indium	In	49	1863	Rubidium	Rb	37	1861
Barium	Ba	56	1808	Iodine	I	53	1811	Ruthenium	Ru	44	1845
Berkelium	Bk	97	1949	Iridium	Ir	77	1804	Rutherfordium	Rf	104	1969
Beryllium	Be	4	1798	Iron	Fe	26	BCE	Samarium	Sm	62	1879
Bismuth	Bi	83	15th cent.	Krypton	Kr	36	1898	Scandium	Sc	21	1879
Bohrium	Bh	107	1981	Lanthanum	La	57	1839	Seaborgium	Sg	106	1974
Boron	B	5	1808	Lawrencium	Lr	103	1961	Selenium	Se	34	1817
Bromine	Br	35	1826	Lead	Pb	82	BCE	Silicon	Si	14	1823
Cadmium	Cd	48	1817	Lithium	Li	3	1817	Silver	Ag	47	BCE
Calcium	Ca	20	1808	Livermorium	Lv	116	2000	Sodium	Na	11	1807
Californium	Cf	98	1950	Lutetium	Lu	71	1907	Strontium	Sr	38	1790
Carbon	C	6	BCE	Magnesium	Mg	12	1829	Sulfur	S	16	BCE
Cerium	Ce	58	1803	Manganese	Mn	25	1774	Tantalum	Ta	73	1802
Cesium	Cs	55	1860	Meitnerium	Mt	109	1982	Technetium	Tc	43	1937
Chlorine	Cl	17	1774	Mendelevium	Md	101	1955	Tellurium	Te	52	1782
Chromium	Cr	24	1797	Mercury	Hg	80	BCE	Terbium	Tb	65	1843
Cobalt	Co	27	1735	Molybdenum	Mo	42	1782	Thallium	Tl	81	1861
Copernicium	Cn	112	1996	Neodymium	Nd	60	1885	Thorium	Th	90	1828
Copper	Cu	29	BCE	Neon	Ne	10	1898	Thulium	Tm	69	1879
Curium	Cm	96	1944	Neptunium	Np	93	1940	Tin	Sn	50	BCE
Darmstadtium	Ds	110	1995	Nickel	Ni	28	1751	Titanium	Ti	22	1791
Dubnium (Hahnium)[1]	Db (Ha)	105	1970	Niobium[2]	Nb	41	1801	Tungsten (Wolfram)	W	74	1783
				Nitrogen	N	7	1772				
Dysprosium	Dy	66	1886	Nobelium	No	102	1958	*Ununoctium	Uuo	118	2006
Einsteinium	Es	99	1952	Osmium	Os	76	1804	*Ununpentium	Uup	115	2004
Erbium	Er	68	1843	Oxygen	O	8	1774	*Ununseptium	Uus	117	2010
Europium	Eu	63	1901	Palladium	Pd	46	1803	*Ununtrium	Uut	113	2004
Fermium	Fm	100	1953	Phosphorus	P	15	1669	Uranium	U	92	1789
Flerovium	Fl	114	1999	Platinum	Pt	78	1735	Vanadium	V	23	1830
Fluorine	F	9	1771	Plutonium	Pu	94	1941	Xenon	Xe	54	1898
Francium	Fr	87	1939	Polonium	Po	84	1898	Ytterbium	Yb	70	1878
Gadolinium	Gd	64	1886	Potassium	K	19	1807	Yttrium	Y	39	1794
Gallium	Ga	31	1875	Praseodymium	Pr	59	1885	Zinc	Zn	30	BCE
Germanium	Ge	32	1886	Promethium	Pm	61	1945	Zirconium	Zr	40	1789

Note: 118 elements are listed here; only 114 have been independently confirmed. (*) Indicates element whose existence has been reported or hypothesized, but not yet confirmed. Between 2004 and 2010, observation of isotopes of elements 113, 115, 117, and 118 were reported in refereed journals. These reports all await confirmation and are shown in italics in the periodic table. (1) The name Dubnium (Db) has been approved by IUPAC for element 105, but the name Hahnium (Ha) was used in most of the scientific literature before 1998 and is still sometimes used in the U.S. (2) Formerly Columbium.

Periodic Table of the Elements

Source: Los Alamos National Laboratory Chemistry Division; International Union of Pure and Applied Chemistry (IUPAC)

Legend (key):
- atomic number — 14
- name — Silicon
- atomic weight† — 28.09
- symbol — Si

Categories shown: alkali metals · alkaline earth metals · transitional metals · other metals · nonmetals · noble gases · Lanthanide series · Actinide series

Period	1	2	3	4	5	6	7	8	9	10	11	12	13	14	15	16	17	18
1	H 1 (1.007–1.009)																	He 2 (4.003)
2	Li 3 (6.938–6.997)	Be 4 (9.012)											B 5 (10.80–10.83)	C 6 (12.00–12.02)	N 7 (14.00–14.01)	O 8 (15.99–16.00)	F 9 (19.00)	Ne 10 (20.18)
3	Na 11 (22.99)	Mg 12 (24.30–24.31)											Al 13 (26.98)	Si 14 (28.08–28.09)	P 15 (30.97)	S 16 (32.05–32.08)	Cl 17 (35.44–35.46)	Ar 18 (39.95)
4	K 19 (39.10)	Ca 20 (40.08)	Sc 21 (44.96)	Ti 22 (47.87)	V 23 (50.94)	Cr 24 (52.00)	Mn 25 (54.94)	Fe 26 (55.85)	Co 27 (58.93)	Ni 28 (58.69)	Cu 29 (63.55)	Zn 30 (65.38)	Ga 31 (69.72)	Ge 32 (72.63)	As 33 (74.92)	Se 34 (78.96)	Br 35 (79.90–79.91)	Kr 36 (83.80)
5	Rb 37 (85.47)	Sr 38 (87.62)	Y 39 (88.91)	Zr 40 (91.22)	Nb 41 (92.91)	Mo 42 (95.96)	Tc 43 ([98])	Ru 44 (101.1)	Rh 45 (102.9)	Pd 46 (106.4)	Ag 47 (107.9)	Cd 48 (112.4)	In 49 (114.8)	Sn 50 (118.7)	Sb 51 (121.8)	Te 52 (127.6)	I 53 (126.9)	Xe 54 (131.3)
6	Cs 55 (132.9)	Ba 56 (137.3)	La 57–71 (Lanthanoids)	Hf 72 (178.5)	Ta 73 (180.9)	W 74 (183.8)	Re 75 (186.2)	Os 76 (190.2)	Ir 77 (192.2)	Pt 78 (195.1)	Au 79 (197.0)	Hg 80 (200.6)	Tl 81 (204.3–204.4)	Pb 82 (207.2)	Bi 83 (209.0)	Po 84 ([209])	At 85 ([210])	Rn 86 ([222])
7	Fr 87 ([223])	Ra 88 ([226])	Ac 89–103 (Actinoids)	Rf 104 ([265])	Db 105 ([268])	Sg 106 ([271])	Bh 107 ([270])	Hs 108 ([277])	Mt 109 ([276])	Ds 110 ([281])	Rg 111 ([280])	Cn 112 ([285])	113 ([284])	Fl 114 ([289])	115 ([288])	Lv 116 ([293])	117 ([294])	118

Lanthanide series

La 57 (138.9)	Ce 58 (140.1)	Pr 59 (140.9)	Nd 60 (144.2)	Pm 61 ([145])	Sm 62 (150.4)	Eu 63 (152.0)	Gd 64 (157.3)	Tb 65 (158.9)	Dy 66 (162.5)	Ho 67 (164.9)	Er 68 (167.3)	Tm 69 (168.9)	Yb 70 (173.1)	Lu 71 (175.0)
Lanthanum	Cerium	Praseodymium	Neodymium	Promethium	Samarium	Europium	Gadolinium	Terbium	Dysprosium	Holmium	Erbium	Thulium	Ytterbium	Lutetium

Actinide series

Ac 89 ([227])	Th 90 (232.0)	Pa 91 (231.0)	U 92 (238.0)	Np 93 ([237])	Pu 94 ([244])	Am 95 ([243])	Cm 96 ([247])	Bk 97 ([247])	Cf 98 ([251])	Es 99 ([252])	Fm 100 ([257])	Md 101 ([258])	No 102 ([259])	Lr 103 ([262])
Actinium	Thorium	Protactinium	Uranium	Neptunium	Plutonium	Americium	Curium	Berkelium	Californium	Einsteinium	Fermium	Mendelevium	Nobelium	Lawrencium

*Element has no stable nuclides. The value enclosed in brackets, e.g., [209], indicates the mass number of the longest-lived isotope of the element. However, three such elements (Th, Pa, and U) do have a characteristic terrestrial isotopic composition, and for these an atomic weight is tabulated. (†) For elements whose atomic weight varies, a range is shown.

Basic Laws of Physics

Newton's Laws of Motion

1. An object in motion moves at a constant velocity in a straight line unless acted upon by a force. Likewise, an object at rest will stay at rest. These two properties are known as inertia.

2. The acceleration of an object is proportional to the force acting on it and inversely proportional to the mass of an object.

Force (F) equals mass (m) times acceleration (a):

$$F = ma$$

3. For every action, there is an equal and opposite reaction. For example, if a force of one ton pushes down on an object, the object pushes up with an equal force. As per the second law, the amount of movement (acceleration) produced in the object will depend on the object's mass.

Law of Gravity

In common usage, gravity refers to the gravitational force between planets and objects on or near them. But in scientific parlance, gravitation represents one of four basic forces controlling the interactions of matter. The others are the strong and weak nuclear forces and electromagnetic force. The gravitational force (F) between objects is proportional to the product of their masses (m_1 and m_2) and inversely proportional to the square of the distance (d) between them. G represents the gravitational constant in Newton's law of gravity, a fixed ratio of approximately 6.67384×10^{-11} newton m^2/kg^2.

The basic law of gravity is:

$$F = G \frac{m_1 m_2}{d^2}$$

Near Earth's surface, Earth's gravitational force pulls objects downward at a constant acceleration of 9.8 m/s^2 (g). This allows calculation of the vertical velocity (v) of an object with an initial vertical velocity of v_0 in free fall at a given point in time (t) and calculation of the distance (d) of an object from Earth at any given time with a given initial velocity (v_0) and a known initial height (a) via the following equations:

$$v = v_0 - gt$$

$$d = -\tfrac{1}{2}g(t^2) + v_0 t + a$$

Assuming that height is measured in feet and speeds in feet per second, the maximum height (H) reached by an object with a positive initial velocity is expressed as:

$$H = a + \frac{v_0^2}{64}$$

For motion not near Earth's surface, more complicated equations are required. Also, if the object's upward velocity is very great, the object may escape Earth's gravity. Even near Earth's surface, there are slight complications. Gravity is lessened by the centrifugal force of the Earth's rotation. At the poles, where centrifugal force is absent, acceleration due to gravity is greater.

Gravity is weaker on a mountaintop than at sea level because the mountaintop is farther from Earth's center.

Conservation Laws

In physics, laws of conservation state that in a closed system, where neither mass nor energy is added or subtracted, certain measurable quantities remain constant.

Conservation of Mass: Mass is neither created nor destroyed within a closed system except when converted to energy.

Conservation of Momentum: All moving objects have momentum, and in a closed system, total momentum is always conserved. Linear momentum is the product of the mass of an object and its velocity. In the following equation, M and V represent the initial total mass and velocity of objects within a closed system. After a collision between those objects, the mass and velocity of individual objects may change (for example, one object breaks into smaller pieces, each traveling at a different velocity), but the product of the total mass and velocity in the system after the collision (mv) will remain the same.

$$MV = mv$$

Any object moving in a circle has another kind of momentum—angular momentum. This is because circular motion requires acceleration toward the center of the circle. The amount of acceleration depends on the speed of the object and the square of the radius of the circle. (Angular momentum is the product of this speed, the mass of the object, and the square of the radius.)

Conservation of Energy: The total amount of energy in a closed system will not change except when converted to mass.

Conservation of Mass-Energy: Although mass and energy can be converted into one another, the total amount of mass and energy together must be conserved. This is reflected in Einstein's famous equation, where m is mass, E is energy, and c is the speed of light in a vacuum (which is constant):

$$E = mc^2$$

Relativistic mass can describe how mass increases with velocity. The following equation—where m is the mass of a moving object, m_0 is the object's mass when not moving, v is the object's velocity in relation to a stationary observer, and c is the speed of light—shows the relationship:

$$m = \frac{m_0}{\sqrt{1 - \dfrac{v^2}{c^2}}}$$

The theory that no object can travel faster than the speed of light is based in this equation. As an object approaches c, so much energy is converted to mass that it no longer accelerates.

Laws of Thermodynamics

1. Heat is a form of energy. Within a closed system energy must be conserved except in nuclear reactions or other extreme conditions. It is neither created nor destroyed.

2. Within a self-sustaining system, heat can never go from an area of low temperature to an area of high temperature, for this would require added energy. Without added energy, disorder, or entropy, can only increase.

3. Absolute zero cannot be attained by any procedure in a finite number of steps. Although it can be approached asymptotically, it can never be reached.

Laws of Current Electricity

Electric current generally represents the flow of electrons through a conductor. The rate at which electrons flow can be measured in amperes, defined as the number of electrons (measured in a unit called the coulomb, equal to about 6.24 quintillion or 6.24×10^{18} electrons) moving past a particular point every second. One ampere is equal to 1 coulomb of charge passing each second. Like water, electrons tend to move from areas of high pressure to low pressure. The difference between these two pressures, known as potential difference, is measured in volts.

Certain substances, such as copper and carbon, allow electric currents to pass more readily than others—that is, they have greater conductivity. Resistance to conductivity is measured in ohms.

Ohm's Law: Electric current is directly proportional to the potential difference and inversely proportional to the total resistance of the circuit. I is electric current (measured in amperes), V is the potential difference (measured in volts), and R is resistance (measured in ohms):

$$I = \frac{V}{R}$$

Law of Electric Power: Electric power (P), measured in watts, represents the rate at which electricity is converted into some other form of energy (such as light, in the case of a lightbulb). For a direct-current circuit, P is the product of current and potential difference:

$$P = IV$$

Two Basic Laws of Quantum Physics

1. Heisenberg's uncertainty principle: Certain pairs of observable quantities like energy and time or position and momentum cannot be measured with complete accuracy simultaneously. Also known as the indeterminacy principle.

2. Pauli's exclusion principle: Two electrons in an atom cannot simultaneously occupy the same quantum or energy state. This has since been shown to be true for many subatomic particles.

Breaking the Sound Barrier; Speed of Sound

The prefix **Mach** is used to describe supersonic speed. It was named for Ernst Mach (1838-1916), a Czech-born Austrian physicist. Mach may be defined as the ratio of the velocity of an object to the velocity of sound in a particular medium. A plane moving at the speed of sound moves at Mach 1. At twice the speed of sound, it moves at Mach 2.

When a plane passes the sound barrier—that is, flies faster than the speed at which sound travels—people in the area, though not the people on the plane, hear what seem to be thunderclaps. These sounds are sometimes called sonic booms.

Sound is produced by vibrations of an object. It is transmitted by the alternating increase and decrease in pressure that radiates outward from a source through a material medium of molecules, like waves spreading out on a pond after a rock has been tossed in.

The **frequency of sound** is determined by the number of times the vibrating waves undulate per second. It is measured in cycles per second. The slower the cycle of waves, the lower the frequency. As the frequency increases, the sound becomes higher in pitch. The human ear is sensitive to frequencies between 20 and 20,000 vibrations per second, although this range varies among individuals.

Intensity, or loudness, is the strength of the pressure of these radiating waves and is measured in decibels.

The **speed of sound** varies depending on temperature and altitude. It moves faster in water than in air, for example. At sea level and a temperature of 59°F (15°C), the speed of sound is approximately 761 mph, or 1,100 ft per sec.

Light; Colors of the Spectrum

Light, a form of electromagnetic radiation similar to radiant heat, radio waves, and X-rays, is emitted from a source in straight lines and spreads in area as it travels. For emission from a point source, light per unit area diminishes in proportion to the square of the distance.

The English mathematician and physicist Isaac Newton (1642-1727) described light as an **emission of particles**; the Dutch astronomer, mathematician, and physicist Christiaan Huygens (1629-95) and others developed the theory that light travels in a **wave motion**. It is now believed that these two theories are essentially complementary. The development of quantum theory has led to results where light acts like a series of particles in some experiments and like a wave in others.

The first relatively accurate measurement of the **speed of light** was made by French physicist Armand Hippolyte Louis Fizeau (1819-96). Today the speed of light is known precisely as 299,792.458 km per sec (or 186,282.397 mi/sec) in a vacuum. In water the speed of light is about 25% less, and in glass, 33% less.

Color sensations are produced through the excitation of the retina of the eye by light vibrating at different frequencies. The different colors of the visible spectrum may be seen by viewing light refracted by passage through a prism, which separates light into its component wavelengths.

Customarily, the basic colors are taken to be the six monochromatic (single) colors that occupy relatively large areas of the spectrum: red, orange, yellow, green, blue, and violet. So-called primary colors can be combined to produce the sensation of other colors. However, scientists disagree about how many and what primary colors to recognize. The color sensation of **black** is due to complete lack of stimulation of the retina, that of **white** to complete stimulation.

Infrared and ultraviolet rays, which are below the red (long) end and above the violet (short) end of the visible spectrum, respectively, are invisible to the naked eye. Heat is the principal effect of infrared rays, and chemical action that of ultraviolet rays.

Discoveries and Innovations: Biology, Chemistry, Medicine, Physics

Discovery	Date	Discoverer(s)	Nationality
Acetylene gas	1862	Berthelot	French
ACTH	1927	Evans, Long	U.S.
Adrenaline	1901	Takamine	Japanese
Aluminum, electrolytic process	1886	Hall	U.S.
Aluminum, isolated	1825	Oersted	Danish
Anesthesia, ether	1842	Long	U.S.
Anesthesia, local	1885	Koller	Austrian
Anesthesia, spinal	1898	Bier	German
Aniline dye	1856	Perkin	English
Anti-rabies	1885	Pasteur	French
Antiseptic surgery	1867	Lister	English
Antitoxin, diphtheria	1891	Von Behring	German
Argyrol	1897	Bayer	German
Arsphenamine	1910	Ehrlich	German
Aspirin	1853	Gerhardt	French
Atabrine	1932	Mietzsch, et al.	German
Atomic numbers	1913	Moseley	English
Atomic theory	1803	Dalton	English
Atomic time clock	1948	Lyons	U.S.
Atom-smashing theory	1919	Rutherford	English
Bacitracin	1943	Johnson, Meleneyl	U.S.
Bacteria, description	1676	Leeuwenhoek	Dutch
Bleaching powder	1798	Tennant	English
Blood, circulation	1628	Harvey	English
Bordeaux mixture	1885	Millardet	French
Bromine from the sea	1826	Balard	French
Calcium carbide	1888	Wilson	U.S.
Calculus	1670	Newton	English
Camphor synthetic	1896	Haller	French
Canning (food)	1804	Appert	French
Carbon oxides	1925	Fisher	German
Chemotherapy	1909	Ehrlich	German
Chloamphenicol	1947	Burkholder	U.S.
Chlorine	1774	Scheele	Swedish
Chloroform	1831	Guthrie, S.	U.S.
Chlortetracycline	1948	Duggen	U.S.
Classification of plants and animals	1735	Linnaeus	Swedish
Cloning, DNA	1973	Boyer, Cohen	U.S.
Cloning, mammal	1996	Wilmut, et al.	Scottish
Cocaine	1860	Niermann	German
Combustion explained	1777	Lavoisier	French

Discovery	Date	Discoverer(s)	Nationality
Conditioned reflex	1914	Pavlov	Russian
Cortisone	1936	Kendall	U.S.
Cortisone, synthesis	1946	Sarett	U.S.
Cosmic rays	1910	Gockel	Swiss
Cyanamide	1905	Frank, Caro.	German
Cyclotron	1930	Lawrence	U.S.
DDT (not applied as insecticide until 1939)	1874	Zeidler	German
Denisovan humans (DNA analysis)	2010	Krause, et al.	Germany
		Pääbo	Swedish
Deuterium	1932	Urey, Brickwedde, Murphy	U.S.
DNA (structure)	1953	Crick, Wilkins	English
		Watson	U.S.
Electric resistance, law of	1827	Ohm	German
Electric waves	1888	Hertz	German
Electrolysis	1852	Faraday	English
Electromagnetism	1819	Oersted	Danish
Electron	1897	Thomson, J.	English
Electron diffraction	1936	Thomson	English
		Davisson, G.	U.S.
Electroshock treatment	1938	Cerletti, Bini	Italian
Erythromycin	1952	McGuire	U.S.
Evolution, natural selection	1858	Darwin	English
Falling bodies, law of	1590	Galileo	Italian
Gases, law of combining volumes	1808	Gay-Lussac	French
Geometry, analytic	1619	Descartes	French
Gold, cyanide process for extraction	1887	MacArthur, Forest.	British
Gravitation, law	1687	Newton	English
HIV (human immuno-deficiency virus)	1984	Montagnier	French
		Gallo	U.S.
Holograph	1948	Gabor	British
Homo floresiensis ("hobbit" human)	2003	Morwood, et al.	New Zeal.
Human heart transplant	1967	Barnard	S. African
Indigo, synthesis of	1880	Baeyer	German
Induction, electric	1830	Henry	U.S.
Insulin	1922	Banting, Best.	Canadian
		Macleod	Scottish
Intelligence testing	1905	Binet, Simon	French

Discovery	Date	Discoverer(s)	Nationality
In vitro fertilization	1978	Steptoe, Edwards	English
Isotopes, theory	1912	Soddy	English
Laser	1957	Gould	U.S.
Light, velocity	1675	Roemer	Danish
Light, wave theory	1690	Huygens	Dutch
Lithography	1796	Senefelder	Bohemian
Logarithms	1614	Napier	Scottish
LSD-25	1943	Hoffman	Swiss
Mendelian laws	1866	Mendel	Austrian
Mercator projection (map)	1568	Mercator (Kremer)	Flemish
Methanol	1661	Boyle	Irish
Milk condensation	1853	Borden	U.S.
Molecular hypothesis	1811	Avogadro	Italian
Motion, laws of	1687	Newton	English
Neomycin	1949	Waksman, Lechevalier	U.S.
Neutrino	1956	Reines, Cowan	U.S.
Neutron	1932	Chadwick	English
Nitric acid	1648	Glauber	German
Nitric oxide	1772	Priestley	English
Nitroglycerin	1846	Sobrero	Italian
Oil cracking process	1891	Dewar	U.S.
Oxygen	1774	Priestley	English
Oxytetracycline	1950	Finlay, et al.	U.S.
Ozone	1840	Schonbein	German
Paper, sulfite process	1867	Tilghman	U.S.
Paper, wood pulp, sulfate process	1884	Dahl	German
Penicillin	1928	Fleming	Scottish
Penicillin, practical use	1941	Florey, Chain	English
Periodic law and table of elements	1869	Mendeleyev	Russian
Physostigmine synthesis	1935	Julian	U.S.
Pill, birth-control	1954	Pincus, Rock	U.S.
Planetary motion, laws	1609	Kepler	German
Plutonium fission	1940	Kennedy, Wahl, Seaborg, Segre	U.S.
Polymyxin	1947	Ainsworth	English
Positron	1932	Anderson	U.S.
Proton	1919	Rutherford	N. Zeal.
Psychoanalysis	1900	Freud	Austrian
Pulsars	1967	Bell	English
Quantum theory	1900	Planck	German
Quasars	1963	Matthews, Sandage	U.S.
Quinine synthetic	1946	Woodward, Doering	U.S.
Radioactivity	1896	Becquerel	French
Radiocarbon dating	1947	Libby	U.S.
Radium	1898	Curie, Pierre	French
		Curie, Marie	Pol.-Fr.
Relativity theory	1905	Einstein	German
Reserpine	1949	Jal Vaikl	Indian
Schick test	1913	Schick	U.S.
Silicon	1823	Berzelius	Swedish
Smallpox eradication	1979	World Health Org.	UN
Streptomycin	1944	Waksman, et al.	U.S.
Sulfanilamide	1935	Bovet, Trefouel	French
Sulfanilamide theory	1908	Gelmo	German
Sulfapyridine	1938	Ewins, Phelps	English
Sulfathiazole	1939	Fosbinder, Walter	U.S.
Sulfuric acid	1831	Phillips	English
Sulfuric acid, lead	1746	Roebuck	English
Superconductivity	1911	Onnes	Dutch
Superconductivity theory	1957	Bardeen, Cooper, Schreiffer	U.S.
Superconductors, high-temp.	1986	Bednorz, Muller	Ger., Swiss
Syphilis test	1906	Wassermann	German
Transplant, heart	1967	Barnard	S. African
Tuberculin	1890	Koch	German
Uranium fission, atomic reactor	1942	Fermi, Szilard	U.S.
Uranium fission theory	1939	Hahn, Meitner, Strassmann	German
		Bohr	Danish
		Fermi	Italian
		Einstein, Pegram, Wheeler	U.S.
Vaccine, measles	1963	Enders	U.S.
Vaccine, measles-mumps-rubella	1971	Hilleman	U.S.
Vaccine, meningitis (first conjugate)	1987	Gordon, et al., Connaught Labs	U.S.
Vaccine, polio	1954	Salk	U.S.
Vaccine, polio, oral	1960	Sabin	U.S.
Vaccine, rabies	1885	Pasteur	French
Vaccine, smallpox	1796	Jenner	English
Vaccine, typhus	1909	Nicolle	French
Vaccine, varicella	1974	Takahashi	Japanese
Van Allen belts, radiation	1958	Van Allen	U.S.
Vitamin A	1913	McCollum, Davis	U.S.
Vitamin B	1916	McCollum	U.S.
Vitamin C	1928	Szent-Gyorgyi, King	Hungarian, U.S.
Vitamin D	1922	McCollum	U.S.
Vitamin K	1935	Dam, Doisy	U.S.
Xerography	1938	Carlson	U.S.
X-ray	1895	Roentgen	German

Inventions

Invention	Date	Inventor(s)	Nationality
Adding machine	1642	Pascal	French
Adding machine	1885	Burroughs	U.S.
Aerosol spray	1926	Rotheim	Norwegian
Air brake	1868	Westinghouse	U.S.
Air conditioning	1902	Carrier	U.S.
Air pump	1654	Guericke	German
Airbag	1952	Hetrick	U.S.
Airplane, automatic pilot	1912	Sperry	U.S.
Airplane, experimental	1896	Langley	U.S.
Airplane, hydro	1911	Curtiss	U.S.
Airplane jet engine	1939	Ohain	German
Airplane with motor	1903	Wright Bros.	U.S.
Airship	1852	Giffard	French
Aqua-Lung	1943	Cousteau, Gagnan	French
Arc welder	1919	Thomson	U.S.
Aspartame	1965	Schlatter	U.S.
Autogyro	1920	de la Cierva	Spanish
Automobile, differential gear	1885	Benz	German
Automobile, electric	1892	Morrison	U.S.
Automobile, exp'mtl	1864	Marcus	Austrian
Automobile, gasoline	1889	Daimler	German
Automobile, gasoline	1892	Duryea	U.S.
Automobile magneto.	1897	Bosch	German
Automobile muffler	1904	Pope	U.S.
Automobile self-starter	1911	Kettering	U.S.
Bakelite	1907	Baekeland	Belg., U.S.
Balloon	1783	Montgolfier	French
Barometer	1643	Torricelli	Italian
Bicycle, modern	1885	Starley	English
Bifocal lens	1780	Franklin	U.S.
Bottle machine	1895	Owens	U.S.
Braille printing	1829	Braille	French
Brassiere, modern	1913	Jacob	U.S
Bubble gum	1928	Diemer	U.S.
Burner, gas	1855	Bunsen	German
Calculating machine	1833	Babbage	English
Calculator, electronic pocket	1972	Merryman, Van Tassel	U.S.
Camera, digital	1977	Lloyd, Sasson	U.S.
Camera, Kodak	1888	Eastman, Walker	U.S.
Camera, Polaroid Land	1948	Land	U.S.
Can, pop-top	1959	Fraze	U.S.
Car coupler	1873	Janney	U.S.
Carburetor, gasoline	1893	Maybach	German
Carding machine	1797	Whittemore	U.S.
Carpet sweeper	1876	Bissell	U.S.
Cash register	1879	Ritty	U.S.
Cassette, audio	1963	Philips Co.	Dutch
Cassette, videotape	1969	Sony	Japanese
CAT, or CT, scan	1973	Hounsfield	English
Cathode-ray tube	1897	Braun	German
Cellophane	1908	Brandenberger	Swiss
Celluloid	1870	Hyatt	U.S.
Cement, Portland	1824	Aspdin	English
Chronometer	1735	Harrison	English
Circuit breaker	1925	Hilliard	U.S.
Circuit, integrated	1959	Kilby, Noyce, Texas Instr.	U.S.
Clock, pendulum	1657	Huygens	Dutch
Coaxial cable system	1929	Affel, Espensched.	U.S.
Coca-Cola	1885	Pemberton	U.S.
Coffeemaker, automatic drip	1963	Bunn Corp.	U.S.
Compressed air rock drill	1871	Ingersoll	U.S.
Comptometer	1887	Felt	U.S.
Computer, automatic sequence	1944	Aiken, et al.	U.S.
Computer, electronic	1942	Atanasoff, Berry	U.S.
Computer, laptop	1987	Sinclair	English
Computer, mini	1960	Digital Corp.	U.S.
Condenser microphone (telephone)	1916	Wente	U.S.
Contact lens, corneal	1948	Tuohy	U.S.
Contraceptive, oral	1954	Pincus, Rock	U.S.
Corn, hybrid	1917	Jones	U.S.
Cotton gin	1793	Whitney	U.S.
Cream separator	1878	DeLaval	Swedish

Invention	Date	Inventor(s)	Nationality
Cultivator, disc	1878	Mallon	U.S.
Cyclotron	1931	Lawrence	U.S.
Cystoscope	1878	Nitze	German
Diapers, disposable	1950	Donovan	U.S.
Diesel engine	1895	Diesel	German
Disc, compact	1972	RCA	U.S.
Disc player, compact	1979	Sony, Philips Co.	Japanese, Dutch
Dishwasher	1893	Cochrane	U.S.
Disk, floppy	1970	IBM	U.S.
Disk, video	1972	Philips Co.	Dutch
Dynamite	1866	Nobel	Swedish
Dynamo, contin. current	1871	Gramme	Belgian
Electric battery	1800	Volta	Italian
Electric fan	1882	Wheeler	U.S.
Electrocardiograph	1903	Einthoven	Dutch
Electroencephalograph	1929	Berger	German
Electromagnet	1824	Sturgeon	English
Electron microscope	1931	Ruska, Knoll	German
Electron spectrometer	1944	Deutsch, Elliott, Evans	U.S.
Electron tube multigrid	1913	Langmuir	U.S.
Electronic paper (e-ink)	1974	Sheridon	U.S.
Electroplating	1805	Brugnatelli	Italian
Electrostatic generator	1929	Van de Graaff	U.S.
Elevator brake	1852	Otis	U.S.
Elevator, push button	1922	Larson	U.S.
Engine, automatic transmission	1910	Fottinger	German
Engine, coal-gas 4-cycle	1876	Otto	German
Engine, compression ignition	1883	Daimler	German
Engine, electric ignition	1883	Benz	German
Engine, gas, compound	1926	Eickemeyer	U.S.
Engine, gasoline	1872	Brayton, Geo.	U.S.
Engine, gasoline	1889	Daimler	German
Engine, jet	1930	Whittle	English
Engine, steam, piston	1705	Newcomen	English
Engine, steam, piston	1769	Watt	Scottish
Engraving, half-tone	1852	Talbot	English
Ferris wheel	1893	Ferris	U.S.
Fiberglass	1938	Owens-Corning	U.S.
Fiber optic wire	1970	Keck, Maurer Schulz	U.S.
Fiber optics	1955	Kapany	English
Filament, tungsten	1913	Coolidge	U.S.
Flanged rail	1831	Stevens	U.S.
Flatiron, electric	1882	Seely	U.S.
Food, frozen	1923	Birdseye	U.S.
Freon	1930	Midgley, et al.	U.S.
Furnace (for steel)	1858	Siemens	German
Galvanometer	1820	Sweigger	German
Garbage bag, polyethylene	1950	Wasylyk	Canadian
Gas discharge tube	1922	Hull	U.S.
Gas lighting	1792	Murdoch	Scottish
Gas mantle	1885	Welsbach	Austrian
Gasoline, cracked	1913	Burton	U.S.
Gasoline, high octane	1930	Ipatieff	Russian
Gasoline (lead ethyl)	1922	Midgley	U.S.
Geiger counter	1913	Geiger	German
Geodesic dome	1948	Fuller	U.S.
Glass, laminated safety	1909	Benedictus	French
Glider	1853	Cayley	English
Google search software	1996	Brin, Page	U.S.
Gun, breechloader	1811	Thornton	U.S.
Gun, Browning	1897	Browning	U.S.
Gun, magazine	1875	Hotchkiss	U.S.
Gun, silencer	1908	Maxim, H. P.	U.S.
Guncotton	1847	Schoenbein	German
Gyrocompass	1911	Sperry	U.S.
Gyroscope	1852	Foucault	French
Hard drive, computer	1955	Johnson	U.S.
Harvester-thresher	1818	Lane	U.S.
Heart, artificial	1982	Jarvik	U.S.
Helicopter	1939	Sikorsky	U.S.
Hovercraft	1955	Cockerell	English
Hydrometer	1768	Baume	French
Ice resurfacing machine	1949	Zamboni	U.S.
Iron lung	1928	Drinker, Shaw	U.S.
Jet Ski	1973	Jacobsen	U.S.
Kaleidoscope	1817	Brewster	Scottish
Kevlar	1965	Kwolek, Blades	U.S.
Kidney dialysis machine	1941	Kolff	Dutch
Kinetoscope	1889	Edison	U.S.
Lamp, arc	1847	Staite	English
Lamp, fluorescent	1938	General Electric, Westinghouse	U.S.
Lamp, incandescent	1879	Edison	U.S.
Lamp, incand., gas	1913	Langmuir	U.S.
Lamp, klieg	1911	Kliegl, A. and J.	U.S.
Lamp, mercury vapor	1912	Hewitt	U.S.
Lamp, miner's safety	1816	Davy	English
Lamp, neon	1909	Claude	French
Lathe, turret	1845	Fitch	U.S.
Launderette	1934	Cantrell	U.S.
Lens, achromatic	1758	Dollond	English
Lens, fused bifocal	1908	Borsch	U.S.
Leyden jar (condenser)	1745	von Kleist	German
Lightning rod	1752	Franklin	U.S.
Linoleum	1860	Walton	English
Linotype	1884	Mergenthaler	U.S.
Linux	1991	Torvalds	Finnish
Liquid Paper	c.1951	Graham	U.S.
Lock, cylinder	1851	Yale	U.S.
Locomotive, electric	1851	Vail	U.S.
Locomotive, exp'mtl	1802	Trevithick	English
Locomotive, exp'mtl	1812	Fenton, et al.	English
Locomotive, exp'mtl	1814	Stephenson	English
Locomotive, 1st U.S.	1830	Cooper, P.	U.S.
Locomotive, practical	1829	Stephenson	English
Loom, power	1785	Cartwright	English
Loudspeaker, dynamic	1924	Rice, Kellogg	U.S.
Machine gun	1862	Gatling	U.S.
Machine gun, improved	1872	Hotchkiss	U.S.
Machine gun (Maxim)	1883	Maxim, H. S.	U.S.-Eng.
Magnet, electro	1828	Henry	U.S.
Magnetic Resonance Imaging (MRI)	1971	Damadian	U.S.
Maser	1953	Townes	U.S.
Mason jar	1858	Mason, J.	U.S.
Match, friction	1827	Walker, J.	English
Mercerized textiles	1843	Mercer, J.	English
Meter, induction	1888	Shallenberger	U.S.
Metronome	1816	Malezel	German
Microcomputer	1973	Truong, et al.	French
Micrometer	1636	Gascoigne	English
Microphone	1877	Berliner	U.S.
Microprocessor	1971	Intel Corp.	U.S.
Microscope, compound	1590	Janssen	Dutch
Microscope, electronic	1931	Knoll, Ruska	German
Microscope, field ion	1951	Mueller	German
Microwave oven	1947	Spencer	U.S.
Monitor, warship	1861	Ericsson	U.S.
Monotype	1887	Lanston	U.S.
Motor, AC	1892	Tesla	U.S.
Motor, DC	1837	Davenport	U.S.
Motor, induction	1887	Tesla	U.S.
Motorcycle	1885	Daimler	German
Mouse, computer	1968	Engelbart	U.S.
Movie machine	1894	Jenkins	U.S.
Movie, panoramic	1952	Waller	U.S.
Movie, talking	1927	Warner Bros.	U.S.
Mower, lawn	1831	Budding, Ferrabee	English
Mowing machine	1822	Bailey	U.S.
Neoprene	1930	Carothers	U.S.
Nylon	1937	DuPont lab	U.S.
Oil cracking furnace	1891	Gavrilov	Russian
Oil filled power cable	1921	Emanueli	Italian
Oleomargarine	1869	Mege-Mouries	French
Ophthalmoscope	1851	Helmholtz	German
Pacemaker	1952	Zoll	U.S.
Pacemaker, implantable cardiac	1958	Greatbatch	U.S.
Paper	105	Ts'ai	Chinese
Paper clip	1900	Waaler	Norwegian
Paper machine	1809	Dickinson	U.S.
Parachute	1785	Blanchard	French
Pen, ballpoint	1888	Loud	U.S.
Pen, fountain	1884	Waterman	U.S.
Pen, steel	1780	Harrison	English
Pendulum	1583	Galileo	Italian
Percussion cap	1807	Forsythe	Scottish
Phonograph	1877	Edison	U.S.
Photo, color	1892	Ives	U.S.
Photo film, celluloid	1893	Reichenbach	U.S.
Photo film, transparent	1884	Eastman, Goodwin	U.S.
Photocopier	1938	Carlson	U.S.
Photoelectric cell	1895	Elster	German
Photographic paper	1835	Talbot	English
Photography	1816	Niepce	French
Photography	1835	Talbot	English
Photography	1835	Daguerre	French

Invention	Date	Inventor(s)	Nationality
Photophone	1880	Bell	U.S.-Scot.
Phototelegraphy	1925	Bell Labs	U.S.
Piano	1709	Cristofori	Italian
Piano, player	1863	Fourneaux	French
Pin, safety	1849	Hunt	U.S.
Pistol (revolver)	1836	Colt	U.S.
Plow, cast iron	1785	Ransome	English
Plow, disc	1896	Hardy	U.S.
Pneumatic hammer	1890	King	U.S.
Post-it note	1980	Fry, Silver	U.S.
Potato chip	1853	Crum	U.S.
Powder, smokeless	1884	Vieille	French
Printing press, rotary	1845	Hoe	U.S.
Printing press, web	1865	Bullock	U.S.
Propeller, screw	1804	Stevens	U.S.
Propeller, screw	1837	Ericsson	Swedish
Punch card accounting	1889	Hollerith	U.S.
Radar	1940	Watson-Watt	Scottish
Radio amplifier	1906	De Forest	U.S.
Radio beacon	1928	Donovan	U.S.
Radio crystal oscillator	1918	Nicolson	U.S.
Radio FM, 2-path	1933	Armstrong	U.S.
Radio, magnetic detector	1902	Marconi	Italian
Radio receiver, cascade tuning	1913	Alexanderson	U.S.
Radio receiver, heterodyne	1913	Fessenden	Canadian
Radio, signals	1895	Marconi	Italian
Radio transmitter triode modulation	1914	Alexanderson	U.S.
Radio tube diode	1904	Fleming	English
Radio tube oscillator	1915	De Forest	U.S.
Radio tube triode	1906	De Forest	U.S.
Rayon (acetate)	1895	Cross	English
Rayon (cuprammonium)	1890	Despeissis	French
Rayon (nitrocellulose)	1884	Chardonnet	French
Razor, electric	1917	Schick	U.S.
Razor, safety	1895	Gillette	U.S.
Reaper	1834	McCormick	U.S.
Record, cylinder	1887	Bell, Tainter	U.S.
Record, disc	1887	Berliner	U.S.
Record, long playing	1947	Goldmark	U.S.
Record, wax cylinder	1888	Edison	U.S.
Refrigerator car	1868	David	U.S.
Remote control	1898	Tesla	U.S.
Resin, synthetic	1931	Hill	English
Richter scale	1935	Richter	U.S.
Rifle, repeating	1860	Henry	U.S.
Rocket, liquid fuel	1926	Goddard	U.S.
Rollerblades	1980	Olson	U.S.
Rubber, vulcanized	1839	Goodyear	U.S.
Saccharin	1879	Remsen, Fahlberg	U.S.
Saw, circular	1777	Miller	English
Scotch tape	1930	Drew	U.S.
Seat belt	1959	Volvo	Swedish
Segway human transporter	2001	Kamen	U.S.
Seismograph	1880	Milne, Ewing, Gray	Eng.-Scot.
Sewing machine	1846	Howe	U.S.
Shoe-lasting machine	1883	Matzeliger	U.S.
Shoe-sewing machine	1860	McKay	U.S.
Shrapnel shell	1784	Shrapnel	English
Shuttle, flying	1733	Kay	English
Skates, in-line	1759	Merlin	Belgian
Sleeping-car	1865	Pullman	U.S.
Slide rule	1620	Oughtred	English
Slinky	1943	James	U.S.
Smoke detector	1969	Smith, House	U.S.
Soap, hardwater	1928	Bertsch	German
Spectroscope	1859	Kirchoff, Bunsen	German
Spectroscope (mass)	1918	Dempster	U.S.
Spinning jenny	c.1764	Hargreaves	English
Spinning mule	1779	Crompton	English
Steam car	1770	Cugnot	French
Steam turbine	1884	Parsons	English
Steamboat, exp'mtl	1778	Jouffroy	French
Steamboat, exp'mtl	1785	Fitch	U.S.
Steamboat, exp'mtl	1787	Rumsey	U.S.
Steamboat, exp'mtl	1803	Fulton	U.S.
Steamboat, exp'mtl	1804	Stevens	U.S.
Steamboat, practical	1802	Symington	Scottish
Steamboat, practical	1807	Fulton	U.S.
Steel (converter)	1856	Bessemer	English
Steel alloy	1891	Harvey	U.S.
Steel alloy, high-speed	1901	Taylor, White	U.S.
Steel, manganese	1884	Hadfield	English
Steel, stainless	1916	Brearley	English
Stereoscope	1838	Wheatstone	English
Stethoscope	1819	Laennec	French
Stethoscope, binaural	1840	Cammann	U.S.
Stock ticker	1870	Edison	U.S.
Storage battery, rechargeable	1859	Plante	French
Stove, electric	1896	Hadaway	U.S.
Submarine	1891	Holland	U.S.
Submarine, even keel	1894	Lake	U.S.
Submarine, torpedo	1776	Bushnell	U.S.
Synthesizer	1964	Moog	U.S.
Tank, military	1914	Swinton	English
Tape recorder, magnetic	1899	Poulsen	Danish
Teflon	1938	Du Pont	U.S.
Telegraph, magnetic	1837	Morse	U.S.
Telegraph, quadruplex	1864	Edison	U.S.
Telegraph, railroad	1887	Woods	U.S.
Telegraph, wireless high frequency	1895	Marconi	Italian
Telephone[1]	1871	Meucci	U.S.-Italian
Telephone[1]	1876	Bell	U.S.-Scot.
Telephone amplifier	1912	De Forest	U.S.
Telephone answering machine (1st practical)	1954	Hashimoto	Japanese
Telephone, automatic	1891	Strowger	U.S.
Telephone, cellular	1947	Bell Labs	U.S.
Telephone, cordless[2]	1950	Gross	U.S.
Telephone, radio	1900	Poulsen / Fessenden	Danish / Canadian
Telephone, radio	1906	De Forest	U.S.
Telephone, radio, long dist.	1915	AT&T	U.S.
Telephone, recording	1898	Poulsen	Danish
Telescope	1608	Lippershey	Dutch
Telescope	1609	Galileo	Italian
Telescope, astronomical	1611	Kepler	German
Telescope, reflecting	1668	Newton	English
Teletype	1928	Morkrum, Kleinschmidt	U.S.
Television, color	1928	Baird	Scottish
Television, electronic	1927	Farnsworth	U.S.
Television, iconoscope	1923	Zworykin	U.S.
Television, mech. scanner	1923	Baird	Scottish
Tesla Coil	1891	Tesla	U.S.
Thermometer	1593	Galileo	Italian
Thermometer	1730	Reaumur	French
Thermometer, mercury	1714	Fahrenheit	German
3D printing (stereolithography)	1984	Hull	U.S.
Time recorder	1890	Bundy	U.S.
Tire, double-tube	1845	Thomson	Scottish
Tire, pneumatic	1888	Dunlop	Scottish
Toaster, automatic	1918	Strite	U.S.
Toilet, flush	1589	Harington	English
Torpedo, marine	1804	Fulton	U.S.
Tractor, crawler	1904	Holt	U.S.
Transformer, AC	1885	Stanley	U.S.
Transistor	1947	Shockley, Brattain, Bardeen	U.S.
Trolley car, electric	1884-87	Van DePoele, Sprague	U.S.
Tungsten, ductile	1912	Coolidge	U.S.
Tupperware®	1945	Tupper	U.S.
Turbine, gas	1849	Bourdin	French
Turbine, hydraulic	1849	Francis	U.S.
Turbine, steam	1884	Parsons	English
Type, movable	1447	Gutenberg	German
Typewriter	1867	Sholes, Soule, Glidden	U.S.
Universal Serial Bus (USB)	1994	Bhatt et al.	U.S.
Vacuum cleaner, electric	1907	Spangler	U.S.
Vacuum evaporating pan	1846	Rillieux	U.S.
Velcro	1948	de Mestral	Swiss
Video game ("Pong")	1972	Bushnell	U.S.

Invention	Date	Inventor(s)	Nationality
Video home system (VHS)	1975	Matsushita, JVC	Japanese
Vinyl	1926	Semon	U.S.
Washer, electric	1901	Fisher	U.S.
Welding, atomic hydrogen	1924	Langmuir, Palmer	U.S.
Welding, electric	1877	Thomson	U.S.
Wheelchair, multiterrain	1986	Twitchell	U.S.
Wheelchair, stair-climbing	1962	Blanco	U.S.
Wiki software	1995	Cunningham	U.S.
Wind tunnel	1912	Eiffel	French
Windshield wiper	1903	Anderson	U.S.
Wire, barbed	1874	Glidden	U.S.
World Wide Web	1989	Berners-Lee	English
Wrench, double-acting	1913	Owen	U.S.
X-ray tube	1913	Coolidge	U.S.
Zeppelin	1900	Zeppelin	German
Zipper, early model	1893	Judson	U.S.
Zipper, improved	1913	Sundback	Canadian

(1) While Alexander Graham Bell has traditionally been credited with invention of the telephone, which he patented, Antonio Meucci developed a working model before Bell. (2) Al Gross held a number of important early patents in the field of wireless communication; other people were also involved in the development of practical cordless telephones.

U.S. Patent-Receiving Corporations, 2012

Source: U.S. Patent and Trademark Office, U.S. Dept. of Commerce

(ranked by number of "utility patents," or patents for inventions, granted)

Rank	Company	No. of patents	Rank	Company	No. of patents
1.	International Business Machines Corp.	6,457	11.	Seiko Epson Corp.	1,454
2.	Samsung Electronics Co., Ltd.	5,043	12.	Hitachi, Ltd	1,428
3.	Canon Kabushiki Kaisha	3,173	13.	Ricoh Co., Ltd.	1,407
4.	Sony Corp.	3,017	14.	Hewlett-Packard Development Co., L.P.	1,393
5.	Panasonic Corp.	2,748	15.	GM Global Technology Operations, Inc.	1,374
6.	Microsoft Corp.	2,610	16.	Qualcomm, Inc.	1,292
7.	Toshiba Corp.	2,415	17.	Intel Corp.	1,287
8.	General Electric Co.	1,650	18.	Toyota Jidosha K.K.	1,173
9.	LG Electronics Inc.	1,617	19.	Broadcom Corp.	1,157
10.	Fujitsu Limited	1,527	20.	Google, Inc.	1,151

Note: Reflects patent ownership at time of patent granting. Changes may occur after patent is granted. Where more than one assignee exists, patents are attributed to first-named assignee.

U.S. Patents by Country, 2012

Source: U.S. Patent and Trademark Office, U.S. Dept. of Commerce

Rank	Country	Patents	% change, 2011-12	% share of total issued	Rank	Country	Patents	% change, 2011-12	% share of total issued
1.	Japan	50,677	9.8%	20.0%	7.	UK	5,213	21.4%	2.1%
2.	Germany	13,835	16.1	5.5	8.	China	4,637	46.1	1.8
3.	South Korea	13,233	7.9	5.2	9.	Israel	2,474	24.9	1.0
4.	Taiwan	10,646	21.2	4.2	10.	Italy	2,120	12.5	0.8
5.	Canada	5,775	15.2	2.3		United States	121,026	11.4	47.8
6.	France	5,386	18.8	2.1		All countries	253,155	12.8	100.0

Note: Country of origin is determined by residence of first-named inventor in patent.

U.S. Patents by Category, 1992-2012

Source: U.S. Patent and Trademark Office, U.S. Dept. of Commerce

(ranked by number of patents issued in 2012)

Rank	Category	Pre-1992	1992	2001	2011	2012	% change 1992-2012
1.	Multiplex communications	3,764	425	1,942	7,718	8,403	1,877.2%
2.	Telecommunications	3,075	327	1,820	5,578	7,615	2,228.7
3.	Active solid-state devices (e.g., transistors, solid-state diodes)	6,821	1,119	2,979	7,028	6,885	515.3
4.	Drug, bio-affecting and body treating compositions (class 514)	26,334	2,390	4,101	4,601	5,365	124.5
5.	Electrical computers and digital processing systems: multicomputer data transferring	358	83	1,155	4,871	5,310	6,297.6
6.	Semiconductor device manufacturing: process	6,276	893	5,672	5,909	5,176	479.6
7.	Image analysis	2,435	439	1,416	3,742	5,145	1,072.0
8.	Data processing: database and file management or data structures	332	84	935	4,244	4,977	5,825.0
9.	Computer graphics processing and selective visual display systems	3,478	419	1,876	3,523	4,855	1,058.7
10.	Data processing: financial, business practice, management, or cost/price determination	822	89	485	4,064	4,854	5,353.9
11.	Pulse or digital communications	3,401	476	1,357	3,073	4,369	817.9
12.	Television	7,982	822	1,016	2,780	4,330	426.8
13.	Drug, bio-affecting and body treating compositions (class 424)	8,901	1,206	3,198	2,895	3,845	218.8
14.	Chemistry: molecular biology and microbiology	8,301	1,250	3,933	3,740	3,708	196.6
15.	Data processing: vehicles, navigation, and relative location	2,421	288	1,250	2,138	3,212	1,015.3
16.	Surgery (class 600)	6,848	828	1,768	2,293	2,940	255.1
17.	Surgery (class 606)	3,775	613	1,434	2,214	2,895	372.3
18.	Communications: electrical	7,789	620	1,431	2,282	2,751	343.7
19.	Stock material or miscellaneous articles	18,811	1,952	2,955	2,755	2,684	37.5
20.	Static information storage and retrieval	4,502	368	1,981	2,765	2,667	624.7

Geologic Time Scale

Our understanding of Earth's ancient history is largely a result of geoscientists' study of climate, rock strata, ice samples, mineral deposits, and fossils from around the world; clues to the planet's origin have also been found through the study of extraterrestrial bodies. Geologists divide Earth's history into the following units (MYA = million years ago):

PRECAMBRIAN TIME (4,600-541 MYA)

HADEAN EON (4,600-4,000 MYA) Earth has no continents, oceans, or life; surface conditions are defined by intense volcanic activity and widespread meteorite impact. Oldest known minerals and rocks, many of meteoric origin, date to this era.

ARCHEAN EON (4,000-2,500 MYA) Earth's surface cools and water vapor in atmosphere condenses to form early oceans, which define small protocontinents; the first single-celled organisms, bacteria and archaea, appear in these oceans.

PROTEROZOIC EON (2,500-541 MYA) Protocontinents merge into larger landmasses as Earth's crust continues to shift. Atmospheric oxygen levels increase, and first known multicellular life appears. Later, soft-bodied marine animals emerge.

PHANEROZOIC EON (541 MYA-present)

Paleozoic Era (541-251 MYA)

Cambrian Period (541-485 MYA) The supercontinent known as Gondwana, or Gondwanaland, dominates the Southern Hemisphere. Seas experience an explosion of invertebrate animal life, including thousands of species of trilobites; the first known vertebrates appear. There is no life on land.

Ordovician Period (485-443 MYA) Gondwanaland extends from South Pole to tropic regions; Northern Hemisphere is mostly open ocean. Average global temperatures are warmer than in the current era. First primitive land plants, early ancestors of starfish and mollusks, and first armored, jawless fishes appear. The period ends in extinction of a majority of species, possibly a result of a global drop in sea level due to glaciation.

Silurian Period (443-419 MYA) South Pole remains covered by supercontinent, but precursors of present-day N America, Europe, and Asia coalesce around the equator and middle latitudes. Appearance of first known vascular land plants, first freshwater fish, first jawed fish, first coral reefs, and first air-breathing animals (certain eurypterids, a scorpion-like creature).

Devonian Period (419-359 MYA) Collisions between Gondwanaland and ancestral landmasses of N America and Eurasia produce mountains visible today as northern Appalachians. Newly-formed ozone layer offers protection from sun's rays, allowing first air-breathing spiders and mites to appear on dry land. Fish with fins and scales and first amphibians emerge.

Carboniferous Period (359-299 MYA) Precursors of modern N America and Northern Europe lie in tropical latitudes north of the equator; warm and humid conditions there facilitate spread of lush forests and peat swamps that later form most of the world's coal and limestone. Later period sees emergence of first true conifers, Lepidodendrales ("scale trees") as tall as 100 ft, and first true reptiles.

Permian Period (299-252 MYA) All major landmasses collide to form the supercontinent Pangaea, surrounded by the world ocean Panthalassa. Gradual warming through much of the Permian allows for initial flourishing of species—including dinosaur precursors (up to 10 ft in length) and marine species in shallow inland seas. The period ended with a mass extinction of as much as 95% of all marine species and most land species.

Mesozoic Era (252-66 MYA)

Triassic Period (252-201 MYA) Pangaea separates into supercontinents of Laurasia and Gondwana; subtropical conditions extend as far north as present-day Wyoming and New England. Emergence of icthyosaurs and plesiosaurs (large marine reptiles), several species of dinosaurs (up to 15 ft long), first true mammals, and first insects to undergo metamorphosis from larva to pupa to adult.

Jurassic Period (201-145 MYA) N American continent drifts westward, opening Gulf of Mexico; rift forms between S America and Africa. Warm, moist climate contributes to flourishing of coral reefs and temperate and subtropical forests. Appearance of first angiosperms (flowering plants), pterosaurs (winged reptiles), the earliest known birds, and huge dinosaurs such as the carnivorous *Allosaurus* and herbivorous *Apatosaurus*.

Cretaceous Period (145-66 MYA) African continental plate drifts north, creating roots of European Alps; gap between S America and Africa broadens; western movement of N America drives formation of Sierra Nevada and Rocky Mountains, turning the western interior of continent into a vast swamp. Later, sea levels rise and cover about one-third of Earth's present land area. The global climate is warm and mild. The period ends in a mass extinction of plant and animal species (including dinosaurs), likely caused by the impact of one or more asteroids or comet fragments.

Cenozoic Era (66 MYA-present)

Paleogene Period (66-23 MYA)

• Paleocene Epoch (66-56 MYA) Australia begins to separate from Antarctica; N America and Greenland begin to spread apart. Mammalian life predominates, including early marsupials, insectivores, creodonts (carnivorous relatives of cats and dogs), and primitive hoofed mammals.

• Eocene Epoch (56-33.9 MYA) Australia drifts farther from Antarctica; the Indian subcontinent becomes welded to Asia, and tectonic forces drive the upheaval of the Alpine-Himalayan system. Climate in N America and Europe is subtropical and moist, with temperate forests as far north as Greenland and Siberia. Ancestors of modern horses, elephants, rhinoceroses, camels, bats, primates, and squirrel-like rodents emerge; earliest known marine mammals appear in later Eocene.

• Oligocene Epoch (33.9-23 MYA) San Andreas fault develops between N American and Pacific plates. Mammalian species continue to diversify, producing modern horse and multiple rodent, camel, and rhinoceros-like species, as well as first known species of great ape. Long-term cooling trend begins that would later cause Pleistocene ice ages.

Neogene Period (23 MYA-2.6 MYA)

• Miocene Epoch (23-5.3 MYA) Crustal plate collisions continue to drive uplift of Alps, Himalayas, and Cordilleran Ranges in Americas; eroded sediment is deposited in shallow marine basins, forming reservoirs for oil fields of California, Romania, and Caspian Sea. Ocean currents prevent Antarctica from receiving warmer waters, fostering growth of Antarctic ice sheet. Northern forests become grassy prairies. Large apes related to the orangutan live in Asia and southern Europe. Oldest hominid fossils from Africa date to this epoch.

• Pliocene Epoch (5.3-2.6 MYA) Alps continue to rise in Europe, and subduction of the Pacific tectonic plate elevates the Sierra Nevada and volcanic Cascade Range. Climate becomes cooler and drier, driving formation of permanent Arctic ice cap. Rapid primate evolution produces *Australopithecus*, earliest direct ancestor of *Homo sapiens*.

Quarternary Period (2.6 MYA-present)

• Pleistocene Epoch (2.6 MYA-11,700 years ago) Glacier ice covers as much as 25% or more of Earth's land surface, carving numerous present-day features including the Great Lakes; increased rainfall in lower latitudes allows plant and animal life to flourish in northern and eastern Africa. Late Pleistocene brings worldwide extinction of many large mammals, including the mastodon, saber-toothed tiger, and ground sloth. Evidence of Neanderthals and Denisovans dates from the latter part of the Pleistocene.

• Holocene Epoch (11,700 years ago to present-day) Melting ice caused sea levels to rise 100 ft or more in early Holocene, covering large areas of land and extending continental shelf of N America. Humans proliferate, and civilization begins.

Biological Classification

Source: *Funk & Wagnalls New Encyclopedia*

In biology, classification is the identification, naming, and grouping of organisms into a formal system. The two fields that are most directly concerned with classification are taxonomy and systematics. Although they overlap, taxonomy is more concerned with nomenclature (naming) and with constructing hierarchical systems, and systematics with uncovering evolutionary relationships. Two kingdoms of living forms, Plantae and Animalia, have been recognized since Aristotle established the first taxonomy in the 4th century BCE. Plants and animals are examples of eukaryotes; their cells have nuclei bound by membranes. Two other kingdoms of eukaryotes that have been identified are Protista (one-celled organisms) and Fungi. The single-celled bacteria and archaea lack such nuclei. They are referred to as prokaryotes (or procaryotes) and are commonly placed in separate kingdoms. The seven basic categories of classification (from most general to most specific) are kingdom, phylum (or division), class, order, family, genus, and species. (In addition, many scientists group all eukaryotes together in a single "domain." The bacteria and archaea are also often treated as separate domains.) Below are two examples of classification:

ZOOLOGICAL HIERARCHY

Kingdom	Phylum	Class	Order	Family	Genus	Species name	Common name
Animalia	Chordata	Mammalia	Primates	Hominidae	*Homo*	*Homo sapiens*	Human

BOTANICAL HIERARCHY

Kingdom	Division*	Class	Order	Family	Genus	Species name	Common name
Plantae	Magnoliophyta	Magnoliopsida	Magnoliales	Magnoliaceae	*Magnolia*	*M. virginiana*	Sweet bay

*In botany, the division is generally used in place of the phylum.

Gestation, Longevity, and Incubation of Selected Animals

Information reviewed by Ronald M. Nowak, author of *Walker's Mammals of the World* (6th ed., Johns Hopkins University Press, 1999). Average longevity figures supplied by Ronald T. Reuther. These apply to animals in captivity; the potential life span of animals is rarely attained in nature. Figures on gestation and incubation are averages based on estimates.

Animal	Gestation (days)	Average longevity (yrs.)	Maximum longevity (yrs.-mos.)	Animal	Gestation (days)	Average longevity (yrs.)	Maximum longevity (yrs.-mos.)
Ass	365	12	47	Leopard	98	12	23
Baboon	187	20	45	Lion	100	15	30
Bear (black)	219	18	36-10	Monkey (rhesus)	166	15	37
Bear (grizzly)	225	25	50	Moose	240	12	27
Bear (polar)	240	20	45	Mouse (domestic white)	19	3	6
Beaver	105	5	50	Mouse (meadow)	21	3	4
Bison	285	15	40	Opossum (American)	13	1	5
Camel	406	12	50	Pig (domestic)	112	10	27
Cat (domestic)	63	12	38	Puma	90	12	20
Chimpanzee	230	20	60	Rabbit (domestic)	31	5	18-10
Chipmunk	31	6	10	Rhinoceros (black)	450	15	45-10
Cow	284	15	30	Rhinoceros (white)	480	20	50
Deer (white-tailed)	201	8	20	Sea lion (California)	350	12	34
Dog (domestic)	61	12	21	Sheep (domestic)	154	12	23
Elephant (African)	660	35	70	Squirrel (gray)	44	10	23-6
Elephant (Asian)	645	40	77	Tiger	105	16	26-3
Elk	250	15	26-8	Wolf (maned)	63	5	15-8
Fox (red)	52	7	14	Zebra (Grant's)	365	15	50
Giraffe	457	10	36-2				

Animal	Incubation time (days)
Goat (domestic)	151	8	18
Gorilla	258	20	54

Animal	Gestation (days)	Average longevity (yrs.)	Maximum longevity (yrs.-mos.)
Guinea pig	68	4	8
Hippopotamus	238	41	61
Horse	330	20	50
Kangaroo (gray)	36	7	24

Animal	Incubation time (days)
Chicken	21
Duck	30
Goose	30
Pigeon	18
Turkey	26

Major Venomous Animals

Snakes

Asian pit viper—2 ft to 5 ft long; throughout Asia; reactions and mortality vary, but most bites cause tissue damage; mortality generally low.

Australian brown snake—4 ft to 7 ft long; very slow onset of cardiac or respiratory distress; moderate mortality, but because death can be sudden and unexpected, it is the most dangerous of the Australian snakes; antivenom.

Barba amarilla or fer-de-lance—up to 7 ft long; from tropical Mexico to Brazil; severe tissue damage common; moderate mortality; antivenom.

Black mamba—up to 14 ft long; southern and central Africa; rapid onset of dizziness, difficulty breathing, erratic heartbeat; mortality high, nears 100% without antivenom.

Boomslang—less than 6 ft long; African savannahs; rapid onset of nausea and dizziness, often followed by slight recovery and then sudden death from internal hemorrhaging; bites rare, mortality high; antivenom.

Bushmaster—up to 12 ft long; tropical forests of Central and S America; few bites occur, but mortality high.

Common, or Asian, cobra—4 ft to 8 ft long; throughout southern Asia; considerable tissue damage, sometimes paralysis; mortality probably not over 10%; antivenom.

Copperhead—less than 4 ft long; from New England to Texas; pain and swelling; very seldom fatal; antivenom seldom needed.

Coral snake—2 ft to 5 ft long; in Americas south of Canada; bite may be painless; slow onset of paralysis, impaired breathing; mortalities rare but high without antivenom and mechanical respiration.

Cottonmouth water moccasin—up to 5 ft long; wetlands of southern U.S. from Virginia to Texas; rapid onset of severe pain, swelling, tissue destruction can be extensive; mortality low; antivenom.

Death adder—less than 3 ft long; Australia; rapid onset of faintness, cardiac and respiratory distress; at least 50% mortality without antivenom.

Desert horned viper—up to 2 ft long; dry areas of Africa and western Asia; swelling and tissue damage; low mortality; antivenom.

European viper—1 ft to 3 ft long; throughout Europe; bleeding and tissue damage; mortality low; antivenom.

Gaboon viper—more than 6 ft long; S of the Sahara; massive tissue damage, internal bleeding; few recorded bites.

King cobra—up to 16 ft long; throughout southern Asia; rapid swelling, dizziness, loss of consciousness, difficulty breathing, erratic heartbeat; mortality varies with amount of venom involved, but most bites involve nonfatal amounts; antivenom.

Krait—up to 5 ft long; SE Asia; rapid onset of sleepiness, numbness; up to 50% mortality even with use of antivenom.

Puff adder—up to 5 ft long, fat; S of the Sahara, throughout the Middle East; rapid large swelling, great pain, dizziness; moderate mortality, often from internal bleeding; antivenom.

Rattlesnakes—2 ft to 6 ft long; throughout Western Hemisphere; rapid onset of severe pain, swelling; mortality low, but amputation of affected digits is sometimes necessary; antivenom. Mojave rattler may produce temporary paralysis.

Ringhals, or spitting, cobra—5 ft to 7 ft long; southern Africa; squirts venom through holes in front of fangs as a defense; venom severely irritating and can cause blindness.

Russell's viper or tic-polonga—more than 5 ft long; throughout Asia; internal bleeding; bite reports common; moderate mortality rate; antivenom.

Saw-scaled, or carpet, viper—up to 2 ft long; dry areas from India to Africa; severe bleeding, fever; high mortality, causes more human fatalities than any other snake; antivenom.

Sea snakes—3 ft to 10 ft long; throughout Pacific, Indian Oceans except NE Pacific; almost painless bite; variety of muscle pain, paralysis; mortality low, many bites not envenomed; some antivenoms.

Sharp-nosed pit viper or one hundred pace snake—up to 5 ft long; S Vietnam, Taiwan, and China; the most toxic of Asian pit vipers; very rapid onset of swelling and tissue damage, internal bleeding; moderate mortality; antivenom.

Taipan—up to 11 ft long; Australia and New Guinea; rapid paralysis with severe breathing difficulty; mortality nears 100% without antivenom.

Tiger snake—2 ft to 6 ft long; southern Australia; pain, numbness, mental disturbances with rapid paralysis; may be deadliest of all land snakes, but antivenom is quite effective.

Yellow, or cape, cobra—7 ft long; southern Africa; most toxic venom of any cobra; rapid onset of swelling, breathing and cardiac difficulties; mortality is high without treatment; antivenom.

Note: Not all bites by venomous snakes are actually envenomed. Any animal bite, however, carries the danger of tetanus, and anyone suffering a venomous snake bite should seek medical attention. Antivenoms do not cure; they are only an aid in the treatment of bites. Mortality rates above are for envenomed bites; low mortality, c. 2% or less; moderate, 2%-5%; high, 5%-15%.

Lizards

Gila monster—up to 24 in. long, with heavy body and tail; high desert in SW U.S. and N Mexico; immediate severe pain and transient low blood pressure; no recent mortality.

Mexican beaded lizard—similar to Gila monster; W coast of Mexico; reaction and mortality similar to Gila monster.

Insects

Ants, bees, hornets, wasps—global distribution; usual reaction is piercing pain in area of sting, though many people suffer allergic reactions (swelling, rashes); not directly fatal, except in cases of massive multiple stings, and a few may die within minutes from severe sensitivity to the venom (anaphylactic shock).

Spiders, scorpions

Black widow—small, round-bodied with red hourglass marking; the widow and its relatives are found in tropical and temperate zones; severe musculoskeletal pain, weakness, breathing difficulty, convulsions, which may be more serious in small children; low mortality; antivenom. The **redback** spider of Australia has the hourglass marking on its back, rather than on its front, but is otherwise identical to the black widow.

Brown recluse, or fiddleback, spider—small, oblong body; throughout U.S.; pain with later ulceration, which may last months, at place of bite; fever, nausea, and stomach cramps in severe cases; very low mortality.

Funnel web spider—several varieties, often large; Australia; slow onset of breathing, circulation difficulties; low mortality; antivenom.

Scorpions—crablike body with stinger in tail, various sizes; many varieties throughout tropical and subtropical areas; severe pain spreading from the wound, numbness, severe agitation, cramps, and even respiratory failure; low mortality, usually in children; antivenoms.

Tarantula—large, hairy spider; around the world; the American tarantula, and probably all other tarantulas, are harmless to humans, though their bite may cause some pain and swelling.

Sea life

Cone-shell—mollusk in small shell; S Pacific and Indian Oceans; shoots barbs into victims; paralysis; low mortality.

Octopus—global distribution, usually in warm waters; rapid onset of paralysis with breathing difficulty; all varieties produce venom, but only a few can cause death.

Portuguese man-of-war—jellyfish-like, with tentacles up to 100 ft long; in most warm water areas; immediate severe pain; not directly fatal, though shock may cause death in rare cases.

Sea wasp—jellyfish, with tentacles up to 30 ft long; S Pacific; very rapid onset of circulatory problems; high mortality because of speed of toxic reaction; antivenom.

Stingray—several varieties of differing sizes; tropical and temperate seas and some freshwater; severe pain, rapid onset of nausea, vomiting, breathing difficulties; wound area may ulcerate, gangrene may occur; seldom fatal.

Stonefish—brownish fish that lies motionless on bottom of shallow waters; throughout S Pacific and Indian Oceans; extraordinary pain, rapid paralysis; low mortality; antivenom, warm water relieves pain.

Speeds of Selected Animals

Source: *Natural History* magazine. © American Museum of Natural History

Animal	Speed (mph)	Animal	Speed (mph)	Animal	Speed (mph)
Cheetah	70	Mongolian wild ass	40	Human	27.89
Pronghorn antelope	61	Greyhound	39.35	Elephant	25
Wildebeest	50	Whippet	35.50	Black mamba snake	20
Lion	50	Rabbit (domestic)	35	Six-lined race runner (lizard)	18
Thomson's gazelle	50	Mule deer	35	Wild turkey	15
Quarterhorse	47.5	Jackal	35	Squirrel	12
Elk	45	Reindeer	32	Pig (domestic)	11
Cape hunting dog	45	Giraffe	32	Chicken	9
Coyote	43	White-tailed deer	30	Spider (*Tegenaria atrica*)	1.17
Gray fox	42	Warthog	30	Giant tortoise	0.17
Hyena	40	Grizzly bear	30	Three-toed sloth	0.15
Zebra	40	Cat (domestic)	30	Garden snail	0.03

Note: Most of these measurements are for maximum speeds over approximate quarter-mile distances. Exceptions are the lion and elephant, whose speeds were clocked in the act of charging; the whippet, which was timed over a 200-yd course; the cheetah, timed over a 100-yd distance; a human, timed over a 15-yd segment of a 100-yd run; and the black mamba, six-lined race runner, spider, giant tortoise, three-toed sloth, and garden snail, which were measured over various small distances.

Top American Kennel Club Breed Registrations, 2002-12

Source: American Kennel Club (AKC)

Breed	Rank				Breed	Rank			
	2012	2011	2007	2002		2012	2011	2007	2002
Labrador Retrievers	1	1	1	1	French Bulldogs	14	18	34	58
German Shepherd Dogs	2	2	3	3	German Shorthaired Pointers	15	15	18	22
Golden Retrievers	3	4	4	2	Siberian Huskies	16	16	24	21
Beagles	4	3	5	4	Great Danes	17	19	23	28
Bulldogs	5	6	10	18	Chihuahuas	18	14	12	9
Yorkshire Terriers	6	5	2	6	Pomeranians	19	17	13	12
Boxers	7	7	6	7	Cavalier King Charles				
Poodles	8	8	8	8	Spaniels	20	21	25	40
Rottweilers	9	10	15	13	Shetland Sheepdogs	21	20	20	16
Dachshunds	10	9	7	5	Australian Shepherds	22	24	33	35
Shih Tzu	11	11	9	10	Boston Terriers	23	22	16	17
Doberman Pinschers	12	13	21	23	Pembroke Welsh Corgis	24	25	22	25
Miniature Schnauzers	13	12	11	11	Maltese	25	23	19	20

Dog Breeds by Type

Source: American Kennel Club (AKC)

The AKC currently recognizes more than 175 breeds and uses the following seven groups to classify breeds, according to functions and other distinctive traits.

Herding Group: Australian Cattle Dog, Australian Shepherd, Bearded Collie, Beauceron, Belgian Malinois, Belgian Sheepdog, Belgian Tervuren, Border Collie, Bouvier des Flandres, Briard, Canaan Dog, Cardigan Welsh Corgi, Collie, Entlebucher Mountain Dog, Finnish Lapphund, German Shepherd Dog, Icelandic Sheepdog, Norwegian Buhund, Old English Sheepdog, Pembroke Welsh Corgi, Polish Lowland Sheepdog, Puli, Pyrenean Shepherd, Shetland Sheepdog, Swedish Vallhund.

Hound Group: Afghan Hound, American English Coonhound, American Foxhound, Basenji, Basset Hound, Beagle, Black and Tan Coonhound, Bloodhound, Bluetick Coonhound, Borzoi, Dachshund, English Foxhound, Greyhound, Harrier, Ibizan Hound, Irish Wolfhound, Norwegian Elkhound, Otterhound, Petit Basset Griffon Vendéen, Pharaoh Hound, Plott, Redbone Coonhound, Rhodesian Ridgeback, Saluki, Scottish Deerhound, Treeing Walker Coonhound, Whippet.

Non-Sporting Group: American Eskimo Dog, Bichon Frise, Boston Terrier, Bulldog, Chinese Shar-Pei, Chow Chow, Dalmatian, Finnish Spitz, French Bulldog, Keeshond, Lhasa Apso, Löwchen, Norwegian Lundehund, Poodle (standard and miniature), Schipperke, Shiba Inu, Tibetan Spaniel, Tibetan Terrier, Xoloitzcuintli.

Sporting Group: American Water Spaniel, Boykin Spaniel, Brittany, Chesapeake Bay Retriever, Clumber Spaniel, Cocker Spaniel, Curly-Coated Retriever, English Cocker Spaniel, English Setter, English Springer Spaniel, Field Spaniel, Flat-Coated Retriever, German Shorthaired Pointer, German Wirehaired Pointer, Golden Retriever, Gordon Setter, Irish Red and White Setter, Irish Setter, Irish Water Spaniel, Labrador Retriever, Nova Scotia Duck Tolling Retriever, Pointer, Spinone Italiano, Sussex Spaniel, Vizsla, Weimaraner, Welsh Springer Spaniel, Wirehaired Pointing Griffon.

Terrier Group: Airedale Terrier, American Staffordshire Terrier, Australian Terrier, Bedlington Terrier, Border Terrier, Bull Terrier, Cairn Terrier, Cesky Terrier, Dandie Dinmont Terrier, Glen of Imaal Terrier, Irish Terrier, Kerry Blue Terrier, Lakeland Terrier, Manchester Terrier, Miniature Bull Terrier, Miniature Schnauzer, Norfolk Terrier, Norwich Terrier, Parson Russell Terrier, Rat Terrier, Russell Terrier, Scottish Terrier, Sealyham Terrier, Skye Terrier, Smooth Fox Terrier, Soft Coated Wheaten Terrier, Staffordshire Bull Terrier, Welsh Terrier, West Highland White Terrier, Wire Fox Terrier.

Toy Group: Affenpinscher, Brussels Griffon, Cavalier King Charles Spaniel, Chihuahua, Chinese Crested, English Toy Spaniel, Havanese, Italian Greyhound, Japanese Chin, Maltese, Manchester Terrier (toy), Miniature Pinscher, Papillon, Pekingese, Pomeranian, Poodle (toy), Pug, Shih Tzu, Silky Terrier, Toy Fox Terrier, Yorkshire Terrier.

Working Group: Akita, Alaskan Malamute, Anatolian Shepherd Dog, Bernese Mountain Dog, Black Russian Terrier, Boxer, Bullmastiff, Cane Corso, Chinook, Doberman Pinscher, Dogue de Bordeaux, German Pinscher, Giant Schnauzer, Great Dane, Great Pyrenees, Greater Swiss Mountain Dog, Komondor, Kuvasz, Leonberger, Mastiff, Neapolitan Mastiff, Newfoundland, Portuguese Water Dog, Rottweiler, Saint Bernard, Samoyed, Siberian Husky, Standard Schnauzer, Tibetan Mastiff.

Registrations for Pedigreed Cats, 2012

Source: The Cat Fanciers' Association
(ranked by total registrations)

Rank	Breed	Rank	Breed	Rank	Breed	Rank	Breed	Rank	Breed
1.	Persian	7.	American	12.	Cornish Rex	17.	Burmese	22.	Japanese
2.	Exotic		Shorthair	13.	Norwegian	18.	Siberian		Bobtail
3.	Maine Coon	8.	British Shorthair		Forest Cat	19.	Russian Blue	23.	Selkirk Rex
4.	Ragdoll	9.	Siamese	14.	Scottish Fold	20.	Ocicat	24.	Turkish Angora
5.	Abyssinian	10.	Devon Rex	15.	Birman	21.	Egyptian Mau	25.	Singapura
6.	Sphynx	11.	Oriental	16.	Tonkinese				

Trees of the U.S.

Source: American Forests

More than 870 native and naturalized species of trees grow in the U.S. The trunk of the world's largest known living tree, the General Sherman giant sequoia in California, weighs almost 1,400 tons—about as much as 15 adult blue whales. To determine the country's largest trees, American Forests uses a point system whereby trunk circumference, or girth (in inches) + height (in feet) + ¼ average crown spread (in feet) = total points. As of Apr. 29, 2013.

10 Largest National Champion Trees

Tree type	Girth at 4.5 ft (in.)	Height (ft)	Crown spread (ft)	Total points	Location
Giant sequoia (Gen. Sherman tree)	1,020	274	107	1,321	Sequoia National Park, CA
Coast redwood	950	321	75	1,290	Jedediah Smith Redwoods State Park, CA
Coast redwood	895	307	83	1,223	Jedediah Smith Redwoods State Park, CA
Coast redwood	844	349	89	1,216	Redwood National Park, CA
Coast redwood	867	299	101	1,191	Prairie Creek Redwoods State Park, CA
Western red cedar	761	159	45	931	Olympic National Park, WA
Sitka spruce	668	191	96	883	Olympic National Park, WA
Coast Douglas-fir	505	281	71	804	Olympic National Forest, WA
Port-Orford-cedar	522	242	35	773	Coos, OR
Common baldcypress	647	96	74	762	Cat Island, LA

ENVIRONMENT

U.S. Greenhouse Gas Emissions From Human Activities, 1990-2011

Source: U.S. Environmental Protection Agency

Gas and major source(s)	1990	2005	2007	2008	2009	2010	2011	% change, 1990-2011
Carbon dioxide (CO$_2$)	5,108.8	6,109.3	6,128.6	5,944.8	5,517.9	5,736.4	5,612.9	9.9%
Fossil fuel combustion	4,748.5	5,748.7	5,767.7	5,590.6	5,222.4	5,408.1	5,277.2	11.1
Methane (CH$_4$)	639.9	593.6	618.6	618.8	603.8	592.7	587.2	-8.2
Landfills	147.8	112.5	111.6	113.6	113.3	106.8	103.0	-30.3
Enteric fermentation[1]	132.7	137.0	141.8	141.4	140.6	139.3	137.4	3.5
Natural gas systems	161.2	159.0	168.4	163.4	150.7	143.6	144.7	-10.2
Coal mining	84.1	56.9	57.9	67.1	70.3	72.4	63.2	-24.9
Nitrous oxide (N$_2$O)	344.3	356.1	376.1	349.7	338.7	343.9	356.9	3.7
Agricultural soil management	227.9	237.5	252.3	245.4	242.8	244.5	247.2	8.5
Hydrofluorocarbons, etc.	90.1	136.2	140.0	135.5	126.2	137.3	145.4	61.4
Total U.S. emissions	6,183.3	7,195.3	7,263.2	7,048.8	6,586.6	6,810.3	6,702.3	8.4
Net U.S. emissions[2]	5,388.7	6,197.4	6,334.0	6,146.2	5,704.0	5,921.5	5,797.3	7.6

Note: Emissions given in terms of equivalent emissions of carbon dioxide (CO$_2$), using units of teragrams of carbon dioxide equivalents (Tg CO$_2$ eq.). (1) Digestive process of ruminant animals, such as cattle and sheep, producing methane as a by-product. (2) Total emissions minus carbon dioxide absorbed by forests or other means.

U.S. Greenhouse Gas Emissions, 2011

Source: U.S. Environmental Protection Agency

World Carbon Dioxide Emissions From the Use of Fossil Fuels, 2011

Source: U.S. Energy Information Administration

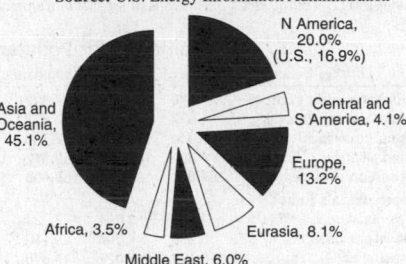

HFCs, PFCs, and sulfur hexafluoride, 2.2%
Methane, 8.8%
Nitrous oxide, 5.3%
Carbon dioxide, 83.7%

N America, 20.0% (U.S., 16.9%)
Asia and Oceania, 45.1%
Central and S America, 4.1%
Europe, 13.2%
Eurasia, 8.1%
Africa, 3.5%
Middle East, 6.0%

HFC = hydrofluorocarbon; PFC = perfluorocarbon. **Note:** Emissions sources are independently rounded; percentages may not add up to 100.

Top 20 Nations Producing Carbon Dioxide Emissions, 1980-2011

Source: U.S. Dept. of Energy

(in million metric tons of carbon dioxide emitted from the consumption of energy; ranked by 2011 totals)

Country	1980	1990	1995	2000	2005	2010	2011	% change, 1980-2011	% change, 1990-2011
China	1,448.5	2,177.7	2,722.7	3,271.8	5,463.7	7,997.0	8,715.3	502%	300%
United States	4,775.8	5,040.4	5,319.1	5,863.3	5,999.2	5,636.7	5,490.6	15	9
Russia[1]	3,081.9	3,820.9	1,603.1	1,498.8	1,587.5	1,642.3	1,788.1	NA	NA
India	291.2	578.6	870.2	991.0	1,181.4	1,601.2	1,725.8	493	198
Japan	947.0	1,047.0	1,116.2	1,201.4	1,241.3	1,179.8	1,180.6	25	13
Germany[2]	759.3	698.1	890.8	854.7	847.4	793.3	748.5	NA	NA
Iran	116.8	202.1	262.3	321.5	451.1	564.6	624.9	435	209
Korea, South	131.7	242.1	381.4	438.7	493.8	581.1	611.0	364	152
Canada	457.4	470.6	508.7	573.3	623.8	546.7	552.6	21	17
Saudi Arabia	176.9	208.0	235.3	290.5	401.9	468.7	513.5	190	147
United Kingdom	613.6	601.8	560.1	560.3	583.1	528.9	496.8	-19	-17
Brazil	185.7	237.3	289.1	344.4	370.8	451.0	475.4	156	100
Mexico	240.3	302.2	321.4	382.9	397.8	432.2	462.3	92	53
South Africa	235.0	298.0	347.5	386.0	432.4	473.2	461.6	96	55
Indonesia	85.8	156.0	214.8	266.2	330.8	414.5	426.8	397	174
Italy	371.5	415.4	431.4	447.7	471.9	416.8	400.9	8	-3
Australia	198.8	267.6	289.1	356.3	412.6	423.7	392.3	97	47
France	488.9	367.7	372.5	401.7	414.0	388.7	374.3	-23	2
Spain	195.0	224.1	243.4	315.6	379.4	312.4	318.6	63	42
Poland	428.9	333.8	308.2	292.6	287.6	304.7	307.9	-28	-8
World total[3]	18,433.2	21,523.2	22,009.8	24,149.9	28,261.8	31,502.4	32,578.6	77	51

NA = Not applicable. (1) Numbers for 1980-90 are for the former Soviet Union. (2) Numbers for 1980-90 are for former West Germany. (3) Includes nations not listed.

Atmospheric Concentration of Carbon Dioxide, 1744-2012

Source: Carbon Dioxide Information Analysis Center, U.S. Dept. of Energy

Year[1]	CO_2 in ppm	Year[1]	CO_2 in ppm	Year[1]	CO_2 in ppm	Year[1]	CO_2 in ppm	Year[1]	CO_2 in ppm
1744	277	1878	290	1960	317	2005	380	2009	387
1791	280	1903	295	1970	326	2006	382	2010	390
1816	284	1915	301	1980	339	2007	384	2011	392
1843	287	1927	306	1990	354	2008	386	2012	394
1869	289	1943	308	2000	369				

ppm = Parts per million. (1) Measurements for the years 1744-1943 were derived from a 200-m ice core sample drilled near Siple Station in Antarctica in 1983-84. Measurements from 1960-2012 were taken directly from the atmosphere at Mauna Loa Observatory in Hawaii.

Emissions of Principal Air Pollutants in the U.S., 1970-2012

Source: Office of Air Quality Planning and Standards, U.S. Environmental Protection Agency; in est. million tons

Pollutant	1970	1975	1980	1985	1990	1995	2000	2005	2010	2012
Carbon monoxide	204.0	188.4	185.4	176.8	154.2	126.8	114.5	92.4	76.2	64.7
Nitrogen oxides[1]	26.9	26.4	27.1	25.8	25.5	25.0	22.6	19.0	14.7	11.4
Particulate matter[2]										
PM10	13.0	7.6	7.0	41.3	27.8	25.8	23.0	14.4	18.2	18.1
PM2.5	NA	NA	NA	NA	7.6	6.9	6.5	2.5	3.3	3.2
Sulfur dioxide	31.2	28.0	25.9	23.3	23.1	18.6	16.3	14.8	7.6	5.5
Volatile org. compounds[1]	34.7	30.8	31.1	27.4	24.1	22.0	17.5	18.3	17.0	15.7
Ammonia	NA	NA	NA	NA	4.3	4.7	4.9	4.1	4.3	4.3
Total[3]	309.8	281.2	276.5	294.6	266.6	229.8	189.3	165.5	141.3	122.9

NA = Not available. (1) Ozone, a major air pollutant and the primary constituent of smog, is not emitted directly to the air but is formed by sunlight acting on emissions of nitrogen oxides and volatile organic compounds. (2) PM10 = particulates 10 microns or smaller in diameter. PM2.5 = particulates 2.5 microns or smaller in diameter. (3) Totals are rounded, as are components of totals.

Sources of Air Pollutants in the U.S., 1970-2012

Source: Office of Air Quality Planning and Standards, U.S. Environmental Protection Agency; in thousand tons

Carbon monoxide sources	1970	1975	1980	1985	1990	1995	2000	2005	2010	2012
Fuel combustion, elec. util.	237	276	322	291	363	372	484	642	722	722
Industrial processes[1]	10,610	8,304	7,700	5,894	5,572	5,631	3,628	3,068	2,606	2,606
Transportation[2]	174,602	167,884	160,512	153,216	131,702	107,755	92,239	68,606	47,826	36,282
Total carbon dioxide[3]	204,042	188,398	185,408	176,845	154,188	126,778	114,467	92,415	76,221	64,678
Nitrogen oxide sources										
Fuel combustion, elec. util.	4,900	5,694	7,024	6,127	6,663	6,384	5,330	3,791	2,106	1,679
Industrial processes[1]	5,100	4,546	4,110	4,009	3,831	3,909	3,518	2,764	2,361	2,361
Transportation[2]	15,276	15,029	14,846	14,508	13,373	12,989	12,560	11,325	9,295	6,403
Total nitrogen oxide[3]	26,882	26,378	27,080	25,757	25,527	24,955	22,598	19,046	14,717	11,397
Sulfur dioxide sources										
Fuel combustion, elec. util.	17,398	18,268	17,469	16,272	15,909	12,080	11,396	10,404	5,147	3,218
Industrial processes[1]	11,661	7,993	6,725	5,597	5,402	4,945	3,516	2,709	1,817	1,817
Transportation[2]	551	635	717	809	874	741	697	977	165	27
Total sulfur dioxide[3]	31,218	28,044	25,926	23,307	23,077	18,619	16,347	14,826	7,578	5,512

(1) Industrial fuel combustion, chemical and allied manufacturing, metals processing, and petroleum and other industrial sectors. (2) Highway and off-highway vehicles. (3) Numbers may not add up to totals because not all categories are listed.

Changes in Global Land and Ocean Temperature, 1880-2012

Source: National Climatic Data Center, Natl. Oceanic and Atmospheric Admin., U.S. Dept. of Commerce

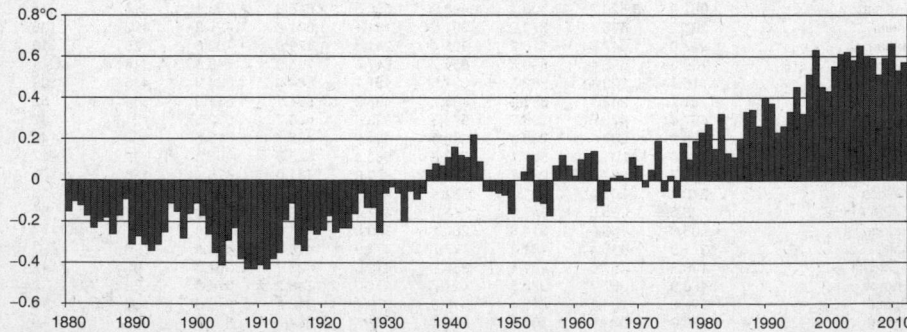

Note: Temperature anomalies measure the departure from a reference value or long-term average. The Natl. Climatic Data Center uses a 20th-cent. average (for the period 1901-2000) of 13.9°C (57.0°F) as its baseline. The graph shows the amount in degrees Celsius that the annual land and ocean temperature was above or below this average.

Air Pollution in Selected World Cities

Source: *World Development Indicators 2013*, The World Bank

Particulate matter in the following table refers to smoke, soot, dust, and liquid droplets from combustion that are in the air—specifically, to particulates less than 10 microns in diameter (PM10) capable of reaching deep into the respiratory tract. The level of particulates, an important indicator of air quality, is significantly affected by the state of technology and pollution controls. Particulate pollution causes an estimated 500,000 premature deaths each year. **Sulfur dioxide** is a pollutant formed when fossil fuels containing sulfur are burned. **Nitrogen dioxide** is a poisonous, pungent gas formed when nitric oxide combines with hydrocarbons and sunlight, producing a photochemical reaction. Nitrogen oxides are emitted by bacteria, nitrogenous fertilizers, aerobic decomposition of organic matter, biomass combustion, and, especially, burning fuel for vehicles and industrial activities. Emissions of sulfur dioxide and nitrogen oxides lead to **acid rain**.

Data in the table represent the annual average of outdoor particulates, in micrograms per cubic meter (mpcm), that a resident of a city is exposed to. They are based on reports from urban monitoring sites. The figures give a general indication of air quality, but results should be interpreted with caution. World Health Organization standards for acceptable air quality are annual mean concentrations of 20 mpcm for particulate matter less than 10 microns in diameter and 40 mpcm for nitrogen dioxide and daily mean concentrations of 20 mpcm for sulfur dioxide.

City, country	Particulate matter[1]	Sulfur dioxide[2]	Nitrogen dioxide[2]	City, country	Particulate matter[1]	Sulfur dioxide[2]	Nitrogen dioxide[2]
Accra, Ghana	22	NA	NA	Montréal, QC, Canada	14	10	42
Amsterdam, Netherlands	30	10	58	Moscow, Russia	15	109	NA
Athens, Greece	29	34	64	Mumbai, India	45	33	39
Bangkok, Thailand	60	11	23	Nairobi, Kenya	32	NA	NA
Barcelona, Spain	25	11	43	New York, NY, U.S.	17	26	79
Beijing, China	72	90	122	Oslo, Norway	20	8	43
Berlin, Germany	18	18	26	Paris, France	9	14	57
Cairo, Egypt	99	69	NA	Prague, Czech Republic	16	14	33
Cape Town, South Africa	11	21	72	Quito, Ecuador	23	22	NA
Caracas, Venezuela	15	33	57	Rio de Janeiro, Brazil	23	129	NA
Chicago, IL, U.S.	20	14	57	Rome, Italy	22	NA	NA
Delhi, India	108	24	41	São Paulo, Brazil	27	43	83
Jakarta, Indonesia	62	NA	NA	Seoul, South Korea	33	44	60
Kolkata, India	92	49	34	Shanghai, China	59	53	73
London, England, UK	16	25	77	Sofia, Bulgaria	44	39	122
Los Angeles, CA, U.S.	28	9	74	Tokyo, Japan	31	18	68
Manila, Philippines	23	33	NA	Toronto, ON, Canada	17	17	43
Mexico City, Mexico	40	74	130	Warsaw, Poland	37	16	32
Milan, Italy	23	31	248				

NA = Not available. (1) Urban-population weighted PM10 data as of 2010. (2) As of 2001.

Air Quality of Selected U.S. Urban Areas, 2000-12

Source: Office of Air Quality Planning and Standards, U.S. Environmental Protection Agency

Data indicate the number of days metropolitan statistical areas or corresponding core based statistical areas failed to meet acceptable air-quality standards.

Urban area	2000	2005	2007	2008	2009	2010	2011	2012
Atlanta-Sandy Springs-Marietta, GA	26	5	15	4	0	2	0	3
Bakersfield, CA	62	33	29	40	23	14	10	17
Baltimore-Towson, MD	7	6	5	4	1	6	5	2
Baton Rouge, LA	19	9	5	0	0	3	1	0
Boston-Cambridge-Quincy, MA-NH	1	3	2	0	0	0	0	1
Chicago-Naperville-Joliet, IL-IN-WI	1	6	2	0	1	0	1	10
Cincinnati-Middletown, OH-KY-IN	3	5	4	0	0	0	3	4
Cleveland-Elyria-Mentor, OH	2	6	2	0	0	1	0	5
Dallas-Fort Worth-Arlington, TX	17	16	3	1	3	0	6	4
Denver-Aurora, CO	0	0	2	0	0	0	1	3
Detroit-Warren-Livonia, MI	1	7	4	1	0	0	0	3
Fresno, CA	69	19	19	17	10	11	22	16
Houston-Sugar Land-Baytown, TX	30	19	5	3	6	1	7	4
Indianapolis-Carmel, IN	6	1	0	0	0	1	0	2
Kansas City, MO-KS	6	4	2	0	0	0	2	4
Las Vegas-Paradise, NV	1	3	2	0	0	0	0	2
Los Angeles-Long Beach-Santa Ana, CA	36	29	18	31	18	4	11	10
Memphis, TN-MS-AR	6	4	2	1	0	0	0	1
Miami-Fort Lauderdale-Pompano Beach, FL	0	1	0	0	0	0	1	0
Minneapolis-St. Paul-Bloomington, MN-WI	1	2	0	0	0	0	0	1
Nashville-Davidson–Murfreesboro–Franklin, TN	5	1	2	0	0	0	0	1
New Orleans-Metairie-Kenner, LA	5	0	1	0	16	26	7
New York-Northern New Jersey-Long Island, NY-NJ-PA	7	12	7	2	0	1	3	0
Philadelphia-Camden-Wilmington, PA-NJ-DE-MD	9	9	7	4	0	3	3	2
Phoenix-Mesa-Scottsdale, AZ	2	1	92	84	17	3	45	16
Pittsburgh, PA	7	13	8	2	3	10	3	4
Riverside-San Bernardino-Ontario, CA	65	50	52	57	47	31	35	34
Sacramento–Arden-Arcade–Roseville, CA	22	22	4	19	8	4	3	6
Salt Lake City, UT	9	2	9	1	4	5	1	0
San Francisco-Oakland-Fremont, CA	1	0	0	1	0	1	0	0
Seattle-Tacoma-Bellevue, WA	1	0	2	0	1	0	0	1
Tucson, AZ	0	0	0	0	1	0	0	0
Washington-Arlington-Alexandria, DC-VA-MD-WV	5	4	3	3	0	0	3	3
Winston-Salem, NC	4	0	2	0	1	0	0	0

Toxics Release Inventory in the U.S., 2010-11

Source: U.S. Environmental Protection Agency

Releases of toxic chemicals into the environment, by manner of release and industry sector; pollutant transfers by destination of transfer. Numbers may not add up to totals because of rounding.

	2010	2011		2010	2011
Pollutant releases	mil lbs	mil lbs	**Top industries, total releases**	%	%
Air releases...............	860	799	Metal mining......................	41%	45%
Surface water discharges	226	213	Electric utilities	18	15
Underground injection	229	195	Chemicals........................	13	12
On-site land releases...............	2,205	2,121	Primary metals	10	10
Off-site releases..................	410	412	Paper	5	4
Total on- and off-site releases	3,929	4,083	All others........................	14	14
Pollutant transfers	mil lbs	mil lbs	**Top carcinogens, air/water/land**		
To recycling......................	1,889	2,267	**releases**	mil lbs	mil lbs
To energy recovery	429	354	Lead compounds	555	764
To treatment	250	288	Arsenic compounds...............	222	341
To publicly owned treatment works.....	231	239	Chromium compounds	54	38
Other transfers....................	<1	<1	Styrene	25	26
Off-site to disposal.................	444	444	Nickel compounds.................	32	23
Total	**3,244**	**3,592**	Formaldehyde....................	19	19

Note: This information does not indicate whether or to what degree the public has been exposed to toxic chemicals.

States With Most Toxics Releases, 2011

Source: U.S. Environmental Protection Agency

State	Pounds	State	Pounds	State	Pounds	State	Pounds
Alaska.......	1,048,767,437	Utah	196,603,470	Louisiana	130,209,437	Arizona......	97,702,283
Nevada	529,280,580	Indiana	149,399,233	Illinois	105,411,076		
Texas	209,158,006	Ohio	148,611,221	Pennsylvania	100,872,163	**U.S. total**	**4,082,694,962**

Note: Total includes states not shown, DC, Puerto Rico, American Samoa, Guam, Northern Marianas, and U.S. Virgin Islands.

Hazardous Waste Sites in the U.S., 2013

Source: *National Priorities List*, U.S. Environmental Protection Agency; as of May 2013

State/territory	Proposed Gen.	Proposed Fed.	Final Gen.	Final Fed.	Total	State/territory	Proposed Gen.	Proposed Fed.	Final Gen.	Final Fed.	Total
Alabama..........	1	0	11	3	15	Nebraska	0	0	12	1	13
Alaska...........	0	0	1	5	6	Nevada...........	0	0	1	0	1
Arizona..........	0	0	7	2	9	New Hampshire	2	0	19	1	22
Arkansas.........	0	0	9	0	9	New Jersey	1	0	107	6	114
California	1	0	74	24	99	New Mexico	1	0	13	1	15
Colorado..........	2	0	15	3	20	New York..........	1	0	83	4	88
Connecticut.......	1	0	13	1	15	North Carolina	2	0	35	2	39
Delaware.........	1	0	12	1	14	North Dakota	0	0	0	0	0
District of Columbia	0	0	0	1	1	Ohio	4	2	34	3	43
Florida	1	0	49	6	56	Oklahoma.........	2	0	7	1	10
Georgia...........	1	0	14	2	17	Oregon...........	1	0	12	2	15
Guam	0	0	1	1	2	Pennsylvania......	2	0	90	6	98
Hawaii...........	0	0	1	2	3	Puerto Rico........	0	0	15	1	16
Idaho............	3	0	4	2	9	Rhode Island	0	0	10	2	12
Illinois	3	1	40	4	48	South Carolina	0	0	25	2	27
Indiana	3	0	34	0	37	South Dakota	0	0	1	1	2
Iowa	1	0	10	1	12	Tennessee	0	0	13	3	16
Kansas	1	0	11	1	13	Texas	1	0	46	4	51
Kentucky..........	0	0	13	1	14	Utah	3	0	11	5	19
Louisiana	3	0	8	1	12	Vermont	0	0	11	0	11
Maine	0	0	10	3	13	Virgin Islands	0	0	1	0	1
Maryland..........	1	0	10	10	21	Virginia	0	0	20	11	31
Massachusetts	1	0	26	6	33	Washington........	1	0	36	13	50
Michigan..........	1	1	65	0	67	West Virginia.......	0	0	7	2	9
Minnesota........	0	0	23	2	25	Wisconsin..........	1	0	38	0	39
Mississippi	1	0	8	0	9	Wyoming..........	0	0	1	1	2
Missouri	0	0	30	3	33	**Total**.............	**50**	**4**	**1,163**	**157**	**1,374**
Montana	2	0	16	0	18						

Note: Fed. = Hazardous waste produced by federal agency; Gen. = Non-fed. sites. Sites that have been proposed for federal Superfund financing are listed under Proposed; sites that have qualified for Superfund financing are under Final.

Renewable Water Resources, 2011

Source: Food and Agriculture Organization, United Nations

Globally, water supplies are abundant, but they are unevenly distributed among and within countries. In some areas, water withdrawals are so high, relative to supply, that surface water supplies are shrinking, and groundwater reserves are being depleted faster than they can be replenished by precipitation. The U.S. (including Alaska and Hawaii) has 9,001 cubic meters per capita and 2,818 cubic kilometers of internal renewable water resources total.

These numbers, and those in the tables below, were published by the Food and Agriculture Organization. The tables, which take into account countries for which data are available, draw upon studies done over a number of years and use 2011 population data. Numbers represent each country's internal resources.

Countries With Greatest Internal Water Resources

Country	Cubic m per capita	Total cubic km
Iceland	524,691	170.0
Guyana	318,783	241.0
Suriname	166,352	88.0
Papua New Guinea	114,200	801.0
Gabon	106,910	164.0
Bhutan	105,691	78.0
Canada	82,969	2,850.0
Solomon Islands	80,978	44.7
Norway	77,563	382.0
New Zealand	74,066	327.0

Countries With Lowest Internal Water Resources

Country	Cubic m per capita	Total cubic km
Kuwait	0	0
Bahrain	3.021	0.004
United Arab Emirates	19.01	0.15
Egypt	21.81	1.8
Qatar	29.95	0.056
Bahamas, The	57.64	0.02
Yemen	84.68	2.1
Saudi Arabia	85.46	2.4
Maldives	93.75	0.03
Israel	99.18	0.75

Top 50 Countries by Forest Area, 1990-2011

Source: Food and Agriculture Organization, United Nations
(in square kilometers; ranked by 2011 area)

Country	Forest area, 1990	Forest area, 2011	% change, 1990-2011	% of land area covered by forest in 2011	Country	Forest area, 1990	Forest area, 2011	% change, 1990-2011	% of land area covered by forest in 2011
Russia	8,089,500	8,091,500	0.0%	49.4%	Congo Rep.	227,260	223,990	−1.4%	65.6%
Brazil	5,748,390	5,173,276	−10.0	61.2	Finland	218,890	221,570	1.2	72.9
Canada	3,101,340	3,101,340	0.0	34.1	Gabon	220,000	220,000	0.0	85.4
United States	2,963,350	3,044,048	2.7	33.3	Malaysia	223,760	203,692	−9.0	62.0
China	1,571,410	2,096,239	33.4	22.5	Cameroon	243,160	196,960	−19.0	41.7
Congo, Dem. Rep.	1,603,630	1,538,236	−4.1	67.9	Thailand	195,490	189,868	−2.9	37.2
Australia	1,545,000	1,483,760	−4.0	19.3	Spain	138,180	183,493	32.8	36.8
Indonesia	1,185,450	937,470	−20.9	51.7	Paraguay	211,570	174,034	−17.7	43.8
India	639,390	685,790	7.3	23.1	Chile	152,630	162,686	6.6	21.9
Peru	701,560	678,420	−3.3	53.0	France	145,370	160,020	10.1	29.2
Mexico	702,910	646,468	−8.0	33.3	Laos	173,140	156,728	−9.5	67.9
Colombia	625,190	603,980	−3.4	54.4	Zimbabwe	221,640	152,970	−31.0	39.5
Angola	609,760	583,552	−4.3	46.8	Guyana	152,050	152,050	0.0	77.2
Bolivia	627,950	568,884	−9.4	52.5	South Sudan	NA	148,196	NA	NA
Sudan	NA	550,752	NA	NA	Suriname	147,760	147,544	−0.1	94.6
Zambia	528,000	493,014	−6.6	66.3	Vietnam	93,630	139,410	48.9	45.0
Venezuela	520,260	459,874	−11.6	52.1	Madagascar	136,920	124,960	−8.7	21.5
Mozambique	433,780	388,106	−10.5	49.4	Mali	140,720	124,110	−11.8	10.2
Tanzania	414,950	330,246	−20.4	37.3	Ethiopia	151,140	121,552	−19.6	12.2
Myanmar	392,180	314,634	−19.8	48.2	Turkey	96,800	114,528	18.3	14.9
Argentina	347,930	291,602	−16.2	10.7	Chad	131,100	114,458	−12.7	9.1
Papua New Guinea	315,230	285,838	−9.3	63.1	Botswana	137,180	112,326	−18.1	19.8
Sweden	272,810	282,030	3.4	68.7	Germany	107,410	110,760	3.1	31.8
Japan	249,500	249,878	0.2	68.6	Iran	110,750	110,750	0.0	6.8
Central African Rep.	232,030	225,750	−2.7	36.2	Mongolia	125,360	108,160	−13.7	7.0
					World	40,330,620	40,274,668	−0.1	31.5

NA = Not available.

Selected Endangered Animal Species

Source: Fish and Wildlife Service, U.S. Dept. of the Interior

Common name	Scientific name	Range
Albatross, Amsterdam	Diomedia amsterdamensis	Amsterdam Island, Indian Ocean
Antelope, giant sable	Hippotragus niger variani	Angola
Armadillo, giant	Priodontes maximus	Venezuela, Guyana to Argentina
Babirusa	Babyrousa babyrussa	Indonesia
Bandicoot, desert	Perameles eremiana	Australia
Bat, gray	Myotis grisescens	Central, southeastern U.S.
Bear, Mexican grizzly	Ursus arctos	Mexico
Bobcat, Mexican	Lynx rufus escuinapae	Central Mexico
Caiman, black	Melanosuchus niger	Amazon Basin
Camel, Bactrian	Camelus bactrianus	Mongolia, China
Caribou, woodland	Rangifer tarandus caribou	Canada, northern U.S.

Common name	Scientific name	Range
Cheetah	Acinonyx jubatus	Africa to India
Chimpanzee, pygmy	Pan paniscus	Dem. Rep. of the Congo
Condor, California	Gymnogyps californianus	U.S. (AZ, CA, OR), Mexico (Baja California)
Crane, whooping	Grus americana	Canada, Mexico, U.S. (Rocky Mts. to Carolinas)
Crocodile, American	Crocodylus acutus	U.S. (FL), Mexico, Caribbean Sea, Central and South America
Deer, Columbian white-tailed	Odocoileus virginianus leucurus	U.S. (OR, WA)
Dolphin, Chinese river	Lipotes vexillifer	China
Dugong	Dugong dugon	East Africa to southern Japan, Palau
Elephant, Asian	Elephas maximus	South-central and southeastern Asia
Fox, northern swift	Vulpes velox hebes	U.S. (northern Great Plains), Canada
Frog, mountain yellow-legged	Rana muscosa	U.S. (CA, NV)
Gorilla	Gorilla gorilla	Central and West Africa
Hartebeest, Tora	Alcelaphus buselaphus tora	Egypt, Ethiopia, Sudan
Hawk, Hawaiian	Buteo solitarius	U.S. (HI)
Hyena, brown	Parahyaena brunnea	Southern Africa
Impala, black-faced	Aepyceros melampus petersi	Angola, Namibia
Kangaroo, Tasmanian forester	Macropus giganteus tasmaniensis	Australia (Tasmania)
Leopard	Panthera pardus	Africa, Asia
Lion, Asiatic	Panthera leo persica	Turkey to India
Manatee, West Indian	Trichechus manatus	Southeastern U.S., Caribbean Sea, Mexico
Monkey, spider	Ateles geoffroyi frontatus	Costa Rica, Nicaragua
Ocelot	Leopardus pardalis	U.S. (AZ, TX) to Central and S America
Orangutan	Pongo pygmaeus	Borneo, Sumatra
Ostrich, West African	Struthio camelus spatzi	Western Sahara
Otter, marine	Lontra felina	Peru south to Straits of Magellan
Panda, giant	Ailuropoda melanoleuca	China
Panther, Florida	Puma concolor coryi	U.S. (LA, AR to SC, FL)
Parakeet, golden	Aratinga guarouba	Brazil
Parrot, imperial	Amazona imperialis	West Indies (Dominica)
Penguin, Galapagos	Spheniscus mendiculus	Ecuador (Galapagos Islands)
Puma, eastern	Puma concolor couguar	Eastern N America (presumed extinct in wild)
Python, Indian	Python molurus molurus	Sri Lanka, India
Rat-kangaroo, brush-tailed	Bettongia penicillata	Australia
Rhinoceros, black	Diceros bicornis	Sub-Saharan Africa
Rhinoceros, northern white	Ceratotherium simum cottoni	Dem. Rep. of the Congo, Sudan, Uganda, Central African Rep.
Salamander, Chinese giant	Andrias davidianus	Western China
Sea-lion, Steller	Eumetopias jubatus	U.S. (AK, CA, OR, WA), Russia, Canada, N Pacific Ocean
Squirrel, Carolina northern flying	Glaucomys sabrinus coloratus	U.S. (NC, TN)
Tiger	Panthera tigris	Asia
Tortoise, Galapagos	Geochelone nigra	Ecuador (Galapagos Islands)
Whale, gray	Eschrichtius robustus	N Pacific Ocean, Bering Sea
Whale, humpback	Megaptera novaeangliae	All major oceans
Wolf, red	Canis rufus	Southeastern U.S.
Woodpecker, ivory-billed	Campephilus principalis	South-central and southeastern U.S., Cuba
Yak, wild	Bos mutus	China (Tibet), India
Zebra, mountain	Equus zebra zebra	South Africa

Status of Endangered and Threatened Species, 2013

Source: Fish and Wildlife Service, U.S. Dept. of the Interior; as of June 2013

Group	Endangered U.S.	Endangered Foreign	Threatened U.S.	Threatened Foreign	Total species[1]	U.S. species with recovery plans
Mammals	69	256	16	20	361	62
Birds	78	208	15	16	317	86
Reptiles	14	69	22	19	124	35
Amphibians	16	8	10	1	35	17
Fishes	83	11	70	1	165	102
Clams	72	2	12	0	86	70
Snails	30	1	13	0	44	29
Insects	57	4	10	0	71	40
Arachnids	12	0	0	0	12	12
Crustaceans	19	0	3	0	22	18
Corals	0	0	2	0	2	0
Animal subtotal	**450**	**559**	**173**	**57**	**1,239**	**471**
Flowering plants	670	1	148	0	819	640
Conifers and cycads	2	0	1	2	5	3
Ferns and allies	28	0	2	0	30	26
Lichens	2	0	0	0	2	2
Plant subtotal	**702**	**1**	**151**	**2**	**856**	**671**
Grand total	**1,152**	**560**	**324**	**59**	**2,095**	**1,142**

(1) Some species are counted more than once in the above table, primarily because these animals have distinct population segments (each with its own individual listing status). The dual status species, all tallied as endangered, are (U.S.) California tiger salamander, chinook salmon, chum salmon, coho salmon, green sea turtle, piping plover, roseate tern, sockeye salmon, steelhead, Steller sea-lion, loggerhead sea turtle; (foreign) argali, chimpanzee, dugong, leopard, saltwater crocodile, loggerhead sea turtle.

METEOROLOGY

National Weather Service Watches and Warnings

Source: National Weather Service, National Oceanic and Atmospheric Admin. (NOAA), U.S. Dept. of Commerce; *Glossary of Meteorology*, American Meteorological Society

The National Weather Service issues watches, warnings, and advisories for specific geographic areas to alert people to the possibility or imminent arrival of severe weather or of flooding. Often the weather hazard is a convective storm (a storm involving upward and downward movement of heat and moisture). A severe thunderstorm or tornado watch is issued when a severe convective storm, covering a relatively small geographic area or moving in a narrow path, is sufficiently intense to threaten life and property. Excessive localized convective rains are not classified as severe storms but are often the product of severe local storms. Such rainfall may result in phenomena, such as flash floods, that threaten life and property. Lightning occurs with all thunderstorms and, along with flash floods, is a leading cause of storm deaths and injuries.

Cyclone: Atmospheric circulation of winds rotating counterclockwise in the Northern Hemisphere and clockwise in the Southern Hemisphere. Tornadoes, hurricanes, and the lows shown on weather maps are all examples of cyclones. Cyclones are usually accompanied by precipitation or stormy weather.

Severe thunderstorm: Thunderstorm (any local atmospheric disturbance) that produces a tornado, winds of at least 50 knots (58 mph), and/or hail at least 1 in. in diameter. A severe thunderstorm watch indicates conditions are favorable for the development of a severe thunderstorm within 4 to 8 hours. A severe thunderstorm warning indicates a severe thunderstorm has been sighted by radar or reported by a spotter.

Tornado: Violently rotating column of air that extends from the base of a thunderstorm to the ground. On a local scale, it is the most destructive of all atmospheric phenomena. Tornado paths range from a few feet to more than 100 mi long (average 5 mi) and from a few feet to more than 1 mi in diameter (avg. 220 yds). The average forward speed is 30 mph, and wind speeds can reach to more than 200 mph. A rotating column of air over water, whether or not linked to a thunderstorm, is called a **waterspout**.

Tropical storm: Cyclone that develops over tropical or subtropical waters with 1-min. sustained surface winds between 34 and 63 knots (39-73 mph). A tropical storm watch is issued when tropical storm conditions pose a threat to specified coastal areas within 48 hours. A tropical storm warning is issued when such conditions are expected in a specified coastal area within 36 hours.

Hurricane: Tropical cyclone having 1-min. sustained surface winds of 64 knots (74 mph) or more. (In the northwest Pacific Ocean, west of the International Date Line, such storms are known as **typhoons**.) The hurricane-force winds form a circle or oval, sometimes as wide as 300 mi in diameter. In the lower latitudes, hurricanes usually move W or NW at 10-15 mph. When the center approaches 25° to 30° N, the direction of motion often changes to the NE, with increased forward speed. In the Atlantic, hurricane season is June 1-Nov. 30.

Hurricane season is May 15-Nov. 30 in the eastern Pacific. A hurricane warning is issued when a hurricane is forecast for an area within 36 hours.

Winter storm and **blizzard:** A winter storm watch is issued when there is a potential for heavy snow or significant ice accumulations, usually at least 24-36 hours in advance. A winter storm warning is issued when a winter storm is producing or is forecast to produce heavy snow or significant ice accumulations. A blizzard warning is issued for winter storm conditions where winds speeds of 35 mph or more, there is sufficient falling and/or blowing snow to frequently reduce visibility to less than ¼ mi, and the conditions are expected to prevail for at least 3 hours.

River flooding: Occurs when rains, sometimes coupled with melting snow, quickly fill river basins with an excess of water. Torrential rains from decaying hurricanes or tropical systems are also a major cause. **Coastal flooding:** Tropical storm and hurricane winds or intense offshore low-pressure systems can drive ocean water inland. Coastal floods can also be produced by sea waves called **tsunamis**, produced by earthquakes or underwater volcanic eruptions or landslides. **Flash flooding:** Usually due to copious amounts of rain falling in a short time. Ice can also cause flash flooding. When ice accumulates at natural or artificial obstructions, it can stop the flow of water. The resulting buildup of water can lead to flooding upstream. If the jam suddenly gives way, a flash flood can occur downstream. Flash flooding typically occurs within 6 hours of the causative event.

Flash floods account for the majority of flood deaths in the U.S. and are the leading cause of deaths associated with thunderstorms. Urbanization significantly increases runoff because less rain is absorbed by the terrain, making flash flooding in urban areas extremely dangerous. Streets can become swift-moving rivers, and basements can fill with water.

A (flash) flood watch indicates flooding or flash flooding is possible within a designated area. A (flash) flood warning indicates flooding is in progress, imminent, or highly likely.

National Weather Service Marine Warnings and Advisories

Primary sources of dissemination are commercial radio, TV, U.S. Coast Guard radio stations, and NOAA VHF radio broadcasts. The NOAA Weather Radio All Hazards (NWR) network broadcasts on seven frequencies between 162.40 and 162.55 MHz. These broadcasts can usually be received within about 40 mi of the transmission site using a special radio receiver. The following are examples of the warnings and advisories that may be addressed to mariners.

Small craft advisory: Alerts mariners to sustained weather and/or sea conditions, present or forecast, potentially hazardous to small boats, including winds 20-33 knots (23-38 mph) and/or dangerous wave conditions. The advisory is also issued when sea or lake ice exists that could be hazardous to small boats. Criteria vary depending on region and type of marine environment.

Special marine warning: Indicates potentially hazardous weather conditions not covered by existing marine warnings.

The conditions are usually of short duration (2 hours or less) and involve wind speeds of 34 knots (39 mph) or more, and/or hail at least ¾ in. in diameter or waterspouts.

Gale warning: Indicates winds of 34-47 knots (39-54 mph) not directly associated with a tropical storm are forecast for the area.

Storm warning: Indicates winds 48-63 knots (55-73 mph) not directly associated with a tropical storm are forecast for the area.

Hurricane and Tornado Classifications

Source: National Weather Service, NOAA, U.S. Dept. of Commerce

The Saffir-Simpson Hurricane Wind Scale rates a hurricane's intensity from 1 to 5. The scale, updated in 2012, provides examples of the type of damage and impacts associated with winds of the indicated intensity. The Fujita (or F) Scale was created by T. Theodore Fujita in 1971 to classify tornadoes. The Enhanced Fujita Scale, an update to the original, was implemented in the U.S. in 2007. It uses 3-sec. gusts estimated at the point of damage based on a judgment of eight levels of damage to 28 indicators.

Saffir-Simpson Wind Scale (Hurricanes)			Enhanced Fujita Scale (Tornadoes)	
Category	Wind speed[1]	Summary of damage	Rank	3-sec. gust
1	74-95 mph	Very dangerous winds will produce some damage.	EF-0	65-85 mph
2	96-110 mph	Extremely dangerous winds will cause extensive damage.	EF-1	86-110 mph
3	111-129 mph	Devastating damage will occur.	EF-2	111-135 mph
4	130-156 mph	Catastrophic damage will occur.	EF-3	136-165 mph
5	Over 156 mph	Catastrophic damage will occur.	EF-4	166-200 mph
(1) 1-min. sustained winds.			EF-5	Over 200 mph

Monthly Normal Mean Temperatures, Precipitation in U.S. Cities

Source: National Climatic Data Center, NESDIS, NOAA, U.S. Dept. of Commerce

Normals are averages covering a 30-year period. The temperature and precipitation normals given here are based on records for 1981-2010. Temperatures listed below represent means of the normal daily maximum and normal daily minimum temperatures for each month. For stations that did not have continuous records from the same site for the entire 30 years, the means have been adjusted to the record at the present site. (*) = city station. Other figures are for airport stations. T = Temperature in Fahrenheit; P = Precipitation in inches.

	Jan.		Feb.		Mar.		Apr.		May		June		July		Aug.		Sept.		Oct.		Nov.		Dec.	
Station	T	P	T	P	T	P	T	P	T	P	T	P	T	P	T	P	T	P	T	P	T	P	T	P
Albany, NY	23	2.6	26	2.2	35	3.2	48	3.2	58	3.6	67	3.8	72	4.1	70	3.5	62	3.3	50	3.7	40	3.3	29	2.9
Albuquerque, NM	36	0.4	41	0.5	48	0.5	56	0.6	66	0.5	75	0.7	78	1.5	76	1.6	69	1.1	58	1.0	45	0.6	36	0.5
Anchorage, AK	17	0.7	20	0.7	27	0.6	37	0.5	48	0.7	55	1.0	59	1.8	57	3.3	49	3.0	35	2.0	22	1.2	19	1.1
Asheville, NC	37	3.7	40	3.8	47	3.8	55	3.3	63	3.7	71	4.7	74	4.3	73	4.4	66	3.8	56	2.9	47	3.7	39	3.6
Atlanta, GA	43	4.2	47	4.7	54	4.8	62	3.4	70	3.7	77	4.0	80	5.3	79	3.9	74	4.5	63	3.4	54	4.1	45	3.9
Atlantic City, NJ	33	3.2	35	2.9	42	4.2	52	3.6	61	3.4	71	3.1	76	3.7	74	4.1	67	3.2	56	3.4	47	3.3	37	3.7
Baltimore, MD	33	3.1	36	2.9	44	3.9	54	3.2	54	4.0	72	3.5	77	4.1	75	3.3	68	4.0	56	3.3	47	3.3	37	3.4
Barrow, AK	–13	0.1	–14	0.1	–13	0.1	2	0.2	21	0.2	36	0.3	41	1.0	39	1.1	32	0.1	17	0.4	–2	0.2	–8	0.1
Birmingham, AL	44	4.8	48	4.5	55	5.2	63	4.4	71	5.0	78	4.4	81	4.8	81	3.9	75	3.9	64	3.4	54	4.9	46	4.5
Bismarck, ND	13	0.4	18	0.5	30	0.9	44	1.3	56	2.4	65	3.2	71	2.9	70	2.3	59	1.6	45	1.3	29	0.7	16	0.5
Boise, ID	31	1.2	37	1.0	45	1.4	51	1.2	59	1.4	68	0.7	76	0.3	75	0.2	65	0.6	53	0.8	40	1.4	31	1.6
Boston, MA	29	3.4	32	3.3	38	4.3	48	3.7	58	3.5	68	3.7	73	3.4	72	3.4	65	3.4	54	3.9	45	4.0	35	3.8
Buffalo, NY	25	3.2	26	2.5	34	2.9	46	3.0	57	3.5	66	3.7	71	3.2	70	3.3	62	3.9	51	3.5	41	4.0	30	3.9
Burlington, VT	19	2.1	22	1.8	31	2.2	45	2.8	56	3.5	66	3.7	71	4.2	69	3.9	61	3.6	48	3.6	38	3.1	26	2.4
Caribou, ME	10	2.7	14	2.2	25	2.5	39	2.7	52	3.3	61	3.5	66	4.1	64	3.8	55	3.3	43	3.5	32	3.6	18	3.3
Charleston, SC	48	3.7	52	3.0	58	3.7	65	2.9	73	3.0	79	5.7	82	6.5	81	7.2	76	6.1	67	3.8	59	2.4	51	3.1
Charleston, WV	34	3.0	38	3.2	46	3.9	56	3.2	64	4.8	72	4.3	75	4.9	74	3.7	67	3.3	57	2.7	47	3.7	37	3.3
Chicago, IL	24	1.7	28	1.8	38	2.5	49	3.4	59	3.7	69	3.5	74	3.7	72	4.9	65	3.2	53	3.2	40	3.2	28	2.3
Cleveland, OH	28	2.7	31	2.3	38	2.9	50	3.5	60	3.7	69	3.4	74	3.5	72	3.5	65	3.8	54	3.1	44	3.6	32	3.1
Columbus, OH	30	2.7	33	2.3	42	3.0	53	3.4	63	4.2	72	4.0	75	4.8	74	3.3	67	2.8	55	2.6	44	3.2	34	3.0
Dallas-Ft. Worth, TX	46	2.1	50	2.7	58	3.5	66	3.1	74	4.9	81	3.8	85	2.2	86	1.9	78	2.6	68	4.2	57	2.7	47	2.6
Denver, CO	31	0.4	33	0.3	40	0.9	47	1.7	57	2.2	67	2.0	74	3.0	73	1.6	63	1.0	51	1.0	38	0.6	30	0.3
Des Moines, IA	23	1.0	27	1.3	39	2.3	52	3.9	62	4.7	72	4.9	76	4.5	74	4.1	66	3.1	53	2.6	39	2.2	26	1.4
Detroit, MI	26	2.0	28	2.0	37	2.3	49	2.9	60	3.4	69	3.5	74	3.4	72	3.0	64	3.3	52	2.5	42	2.8	30	2.4
Dodge City, KS	32	0.6	36	0.7	44	1.6	54	1.8	64	2.9	74	3.2	80	3.1	78	2.8	69	1.7	57	1.7	43	0.8	33	0.8
Duluth, MN	10	1.0	15	0.8	26	1.5	40	2.4	51	3.2	60	4.2	66	3.9	64	3.7	56	4.1	43	2.9	29	2.1	15	1.2
Fairbanks, AK	–8	0.6	–1	0.4	11	0.3	33	0.3	49	0.6	60	1.4	63	2.2	56	1.9	45	1.1	24	0.8	3	0.7	–4	0.6
Fresno, CA	47	2.2	52	2.0	57	2.0	62	1.0	70	0.4	77	0.2	83	0.0	82	0.0	76	0.2	66	0.6	54	1.1	47	1.8
Galveston, TX*	53	3.7	55	3.0	61	2.9	68	2.2	76	3.0	82	4.8	84	3.9	84	3.4	80	5.4	73	4.2	64	3.4	56	3.4
Grand Rapids, MI	24	2.1	27	1.8	36	2.4	48	3.4	59	4.0	68	3.8	73	3.8	71	3.6	63	4.3	51	3.3	40	3.5	29	2.5
Helena, MT	23	0.4	28	0.3	36	0.6	45	1.0	54	1.9	62	2.1	70	1.2	68	1.2	58	1.1	46	0.7	33	0.5	22	0.4
Honolulu, HI	73	2.3	73	2.0	75	2.0	76	0.6	78	0.6	80	0.3	81	0.5	82	0.6	82	0.7	80	1.8	78	2.4	75	3.2
Houston, TX	53	3.4	56	3.2	63	3.4	70	3.3	77	5.1	82	5.9	84	3.8	85	3.8	80	4.1	72	5.7	62	4.3	54	3.7
Huron, SD	17	0.5	22	0.6	33	1.5	47	2.3	58	3.1	68	3.9	74	2.9	72	2.4	62	2.5	48	1.8	33	0.9	19	0.5
Indianapolis, IN	28	2.7	32	2.3	42	3.6	53	3.8	63	5.1	72	4.3	75	4.6	74	3.1	67	3.1	55	3.1	44	3.7	32	3.2
Jackson, MS	46	5.0	50	4.8	57	5.0	64	5.0	72	4.4	79	4.1	82	4.8	81	4.2	76	3.0	65	3.9	56	4.8	48	5.2
Jacksonville, FL	53	3.3	56	3.2	62	4.0	67	2.6	74	2.5	80	6.5	82	6.6	82	6.8	78	8.2	70	3.9	62	2.1	55	2.8
Juneau, AK	28	5.4	30	4.1	34	3.8	41	2.9	49	3.4	55	3.2	57	4.6	56	5.7	50	8.6	42	8.6	33	6.0	30	5.8
Kansas City, MO	29	1.1	34	1.5	44	2.4	55	3.7	65	5.2	74	5.2	78	4.5	77	3.9	68	4.6	56	3.2	44	2.2	32	1.5
Knoxville, TN	38	4.3	42	4.3	50	4.3	59	4.0	67	4.5	75	3.8	78	5.1	78	3.3	71	3.2	60	2.5	50	4.0	41	4.5
Lander, WY	22	0.4	25	0.6	36	1.2	44	1.9	53	2.2	63	1.3	71	0.8	70	0.6	59	1.1	46	1.3	31	0.9	21	0.6
Lexington, KY	33	3.2	37	3.2	46	4.1	55	3.6	64	5.3	73	4.4	76	4.7	75	3.3	68	2.9	57	3.1	46	3.5	36	3.9
Little Rock, AR	41	3.6	45	3.7	53	4.7	62	5.1	71	4.9	79	3.7	83	3.3	83	2.6	75	3.2	64	4.9	53	5.3	43	5.0
Los Angeles, CA*	58	3.1	59	3.8	61	2.4	63	0.9	66	0.3	69	0.1	73	0.0	74	0.0	73	0.2	69	0.7	62	1.0	58	2.3
Louisville, KY	35	3.2	39	3.2	48	4.2	58	4.0	67	5.3	76	3.8	79	4.2	78	3.3	71	3.1	60	3.2	49	3.6	38	3.8
Marquette, MI*	19	1.8	21	1.3	29	2.0	40	2.5	51	2.5	60	2.7	67	2.8	67	2.6	59	3.2	47	3.1	35	2.6	24	2.0
Memphis, TN	41	4.0	46	4.4	54	5.2	63	5.5	72	5.3	80	3.6	83	4.6	82	2.9	75	3.1	64	4.0	53	5.5	44	5.7
Miami, FL	68	1.6	70	2.3	73	3.0	76	3.1	80	5.3	83	9.7	84	6.5	84	8.9	83	9.9	80	6.3	75	3.3	71	2.0
Milwaukee, WI	22	1.8	26	1.7	35	2.3	46	3.6	56	3.4	66	3.9	72	3.7	71	4.0	63	3.2	51	2.7	39	2.7	27	2.0
Minneapolis, MN	16	0.9	21	0.8	33	1.9	48	2.7	59	3.4	69	4.2	74	4.0	71	4.3	62	3.1	49	2.4	34	1.8	20	1.2
Mobile, AL	50	5.7	54	5.1	60	6.1	66	4.8	74	5.1	80	6.1	82	7.2	82	7.0	78	5.1	68	3.7	60	5.1	52	5.1
Moline, IL	23	1.5	27	1.6	39	2.9	51	3.6	62	4.3	72	4.5	75	4.3	74	4.5	65	3.1	53	3.0	40	2.6	27	2.2
Nashua, NH	24	3.7	27	3.2	35	4.3	46	4.0	57	2.9	66	4.3	71	3.7	70	4.5	62	3.4	50	4.7	40	4.1	30	3.7
Nashville, TN	38	3.8	42	3.9	50	4.1	59	4.0	68	5.5	76	4.1	79	3.6	79	3.2	72	3.4	60	3.0	50	4.3	40	4.2
New Orleans, LA	53	5.2	57	5.3	63	4.6	69	4.6	77	4.6	82	8.1	83	5.9	83	6.0	80	5.1	71	3.6	63	4.5	56	5.3
New York, NY*	33	3.7	35	3.1	43	4.4	53	4.5	62	4.2	71	4.4	77	4.6	75	4.4	68	4.3	57	4.4	48	4.0	38	4.0
Newark, NJ	32	3.5	35	2.9	42	4.2	53	4.2	63	4.1	72	4.0	77	4.8	76	3.7	68	3.8	57	3.6	47	3.7	37	3.8
Norfolk, VA	40	3.4	43	3.1	49	3.7	58	3.4	67	3.4	75	4.3	80	5.1	78	5.5	72	4.8	62	3.4	53	3.2	44	3.3
Oklahoma City, OK	39	1.4	44	1.6	52	3.1	61	3.1	70	4.7	78	4.9	83	2.9	82	3.3	74	4.1	63	3.7	51	2.0	41	1.9
Omaha, NE	24	0.7	28	0.9	40	2.0	52	3.0	62	4.8	72	4.2	77	3.8	75	3.8	66	2.7	53	2.2	39	1.6	26	1.0
Philadelphia, PA	33	3.0	36	2.7	44	3.8	54	3.6	64	3.7	73	3.4	78	4.4	77	3.5	69	3.8	58	3.2	48	3.0	38	3.6
Phoenix, AZ	56	0.9	60	0.9	65	1.0	73	0.3	82	0.1	91	0.0	95	1.1	94	1.0	88	0.6	77	0.6	64	0.7	55	0.9
Pittsburgh, PA	29	2.7	32	2.7	40	3.1	52	3.2	61	4.2	69	4.0	73	3.8	72	3.5	65	3.4	53	2.5	43	3.4	33	2.9
Portland, ME	22	3.4	26	3.3	34	4.2	44	4.3	54	4.0	63	3.8	69	3.6	68	3.1	60	3.7	49	4.9	39	4.9	29	4.0
Portland, OR	41	4.9	44	3.7	48	3.7	52	2.7	58	2.5	64	1.7	69	0.7	70	0.7	65	1.5	55	3.0	47	5.6	40	5.5
Providence, RI	29	3.9	32	3.3	39	5.0	49	4.4	59	3.6	68	3.6	74	3.3	72	3.6	65	3.9	54	3.9	45	4.5	34	4.2
Raleigh, NC	41	3.5	45	3.2	52	4.1	60	2.9	68	3.3	76	3.5	80	4.7	79	4.3	72	4.4	61	3.3	52	3.1	44	3.1
Rapid City, SD	25	0.3	27	0.4	35	0.9	45	1.8	55	3.2	65	2.5	73	1.9	72	1.6	61	1.3	48	1.4	35	0.5	25	0.4
Reno, NV	36	1.0	40	1.0	46	0.8	51	0.5	60	0.5	68	0.5	75	0.2	73	0.2	65	0.4	54	0.5	43	0.8	35	1.0
Richmond, VA	38	3.0	41	2.8	49	4.0	58	3.3	66	3.8	75	3.9	79	4.5	78	4.7	71	4.1	60	3.0	50	3.2	41	3.3
St. Louis, MO	32	2.4	36	2.2	46	3.3	57	3.7	67	4.7	76	4.3	80	4.1	79	3.0	70	3.1	59	3.3	47	3.9	35	2.8
Salt Lake City, UT	30	1.3	34	1.3	44	1.8	51	2.0	60	2.0	70	1.0	79	0.6	77	0.7	66	1.2	53	1.5	40	1.5	30	1.4
San Antonio, TX	52	1.8	56	1.8	62	2.3	69	2.1	77	4.0	82	4.1	85	2.7	85	2.1	80	3.0	71	4.1	61	2.3	53	1.9
San Diego, CA	57	2.0	58	2.3	59	1.8	62	0.8	64	0.1	66	0.1	70	0.0	72	0.0	71	0.2	67	0.6	61	1.0	57	1.5
San Francisco, CA	50	4.2	53	4.1	55	3.0	57	1.3	60	0.5	62	0.1	64	0.0	65	0.0	65	0.2	62	1.0	56	2.4	51	4.0
San Juan, PR	78	3.8	78	2.4	79	2.0	80	4.7	82	5.9	83	4.4	83	5.1	84	5.5	84	5.8	83	5.6	81	6.4	79	5.0
Santa Fe, NM	32	0.6	36	0.5	43	0.8	50	0.7	60	0.9	69	1.1	73	1.8	71	2.6	64	1.6	53	1.4	40	0.7	31	0.8
Savannah, GA	50	3.7	53	2.8	59	3.7	66	3.1	73	3.0	80	6.0	83	5.6	82	6.6	77	4.6	68	3.7	59	2.4	52	3.0
Seattle, WA	42	5.6	43	3.5	47	3.7	50	2.7	56	1.9	61	1.6	66	0.7	66	0.9	61	1.5	53	3.5	45	6.6	41	5.4
Spokane, WA	30	1.8	33	1.3	40	1.6	47	1.3	55	1.6	62	1.3	70	0.6	69	0.6	60	0.7	48	1.2	36	2.3	27	2.3
Springfield, MO	33	2.5	37	2.5	46	3.6	56	4.3	65	5.1	73	4.9	78	3.7	78	3.6	69	4.6	58	3.6	46	4.2	35	3.0
Tampa, FL	61	2.2	63	2.8	67	3.0	72	2.0	78	2.1	82	6.7	83	7.1	83	7.8	82	6.3	76	2.3	69	1.6	63	2.5
Washington, DC	36	2.8	39	2.6	47	3.5	57	3.1	66	4.0	75	3.8	80	3.7	78	2.9	71	3.7	60	3.4	50	3.2	40	3.1
Wilmington, DE	32	3.0	35	2.7	43	3.9	53	3.5	63	4.0	72	3.9	77	4.6	75	3.2	68	4.3	56	3.4	47	3.1	37	3.5
Windsor Locks, CT	26	3.2	30	2.9	38	3.6	49	3.7	60	4.4	69	4.4	74	4.2	72	3.9	64	3.9	52	4.4	42	3.9	32	3.4

Normal High and Low Temperatures, Precipitation in U.S. Cities

Source: National Climatic Data Center, NESDIS, NOAA, U.S. Dept. of Commerce

The normal temperatures and precipitation data given here are based on records for the period 1981-2010. The extreme temperatures are based on records from the time of each station's installation. (*) = City station. Other figures are for airport stations.

| | | NORMAL TEMPERATURE (°F) | | | | EXTREME | | AVG. ANNUAL |
| | | January | | July | | TEMPERATURE (°F) | | PRECIPITATION |
State	Station	Max.	Min.	Max.	Min.	Highest	Lowest	(in.)
Alabama	Mobile	61	40	91	73	105	3	66.15
Alaska	Anchorage	23	11	65	52	85	−34	16.58
Alaska	Barrow	−7	−20	47	35	79	−56	4.53
Alaska	Juneau	33	24	64	50	90	−22	62.27
Arizona	Phoenix	67	46	106	78	122	17	8.03
Arkansas	North Little Rock	50	33	92	73	111	−6	50.03
California	Los Angeles	65	49	74	64	110	23	12.82
California	San Francisco	56	44	72	55	106	20	20.65
Colorado	Denver	44	17	89	59	105	−19	14.92
Connecticut	Windsor Locks	35	18	85	63	102	−26	45.85
Delaware	Wilmington	40	25	86	68	103	11	43.08
District of Columbia	Washington–Reagan	43	29	88	71	105	−5	39.74
Florida	Jacksonville	65	41	92	73	105	7	52.39
Florida	Miami	76	60	91	77	98	30	61.90
Georgia	Atlanta	52	34	89	71	105	−8	49.71
Georgia	Savannah	60	39	92	73	105	3	47.96
Hawaii	Honolulu	80	66	88	75	95	53	17.10
Idaho	Boise	38	25	91	60	111	−25	11.73
Illinois	Chicago	31	17	84	64	104	−27	36.89
Indiana	Indianapolis	36	21	85	66	104	−27	42.44
Iowa	Des Moines	31	14	86	67	108	−26	36.01
Kansas	Dodge City	44	20	93	66	110	−21	21.60
Kentucky	Lexington	41	25	86	66	103	−21	45.17
Kentucky	Louisville	43	27	89	70	106	−22	44.91
Louisiana	New Orleans	62	45	91	75	102	11	62.66
Maine	Caribou	20	1	76	55	96	−41	38.49
Maine	Portland	31	13	79	59	103	−39	47.25
Maryland	Baltimore	41	24	87	67	105	−7	41.88
Massachusetts	Boston	36	22	81	65	102	−12	43.77
Michigan	Detroit	32	19	83	64	104	−21	33.47
Michigan	Grand Rapids	31	18	83	62	100	−22	38.27
Michigan	Sault Ste. Marie	23	8	76	54	98	−36	32.95
Minnesota	Duluth	19	2	76	55	97	−39	30.96
Minnesota	Minneapolis	24	8	83	64	105	−34	30.61
Mississippi	Jackson	56	35	92	72	107	2	54.14
Missouri	Kansas City	38	20	88	68	109	−23	38.86
Missouri	St. Louis	40	24	89	71	107	−18	40.96
Montana	Helena	33	13	86	54	105	−42	11.22
Nebraska	Omaha	33	14	87	66	114	−23	30.62
Nevada	Reno	46	25	92	58	108	−16	7.40
New Hampshire	Concord	31	10	82	58	102	−37	40.61
New Jersey	Atlantic City	42	25	86	67	106	−11	41.75
New Mexico	Albuquerque	47	26	90	66	107	−17	9.45
New York	Albany	31	15	82	61	100	−28	39.35
New York	Buffalo	31	19	80	62	99	−20	40.48
New York	New York–Central Park*	38	27	84	69	106	−15	49.94
North Carolina	Raleigh	51	31	90	70	105	−9	43.34
North Dakota	Bismarck	23	2	85	57	112	−44	17.85
Ohio	Cleveland	34	22	83	64	104	−20	39.14
Ohio	Columbus	37	23	85	66	102	−22	39.31
Oklahoma	Oklahoma City	50	29	94	72	110	−8	36.52
Oregon	Portland	47	36	81	58	107	−3	36.03
Pennsylvania	Philadelphia	40	26	87	69	104	−7	41.53
Pennsylvania	Pittsburgh	36	21	83	63	103	−22	38.19
Puerto Rico	San Juan	83	72	89	78	98	60	56.35
Rhode Island	Providence	37	21	83	64	104	−13	47.18
South Carolina	Charleston	59	38	91	73	105	6	51.03
South Dakota	Huron	27	7	86	61	112	−41	22.90
South Dakota	Rapid City	37	13	87	58	111	−31	16.29
Tennessee	Memphis	50	33	92	74	108	−13	53.68
Tennessee	Nashville	47	28	89	68	107	−17	47.25
Texas	Dallas-Fort Worth	56	36	96	75	113	−1	36.14
Texas	Houston	63	43	94	75	109	7	49.77
Utah	Salt Lake City	37	22	93	65	107	−30	16.10
Vermont	Burlington	27	10	81	60	101	−30	36.82
Virginia	Norfolk	48	33	87	72	105	−3	46.53
Virginia	Richmond	47	28	90	69	105	−12	43.60
Washington	Seattle-Tacoma	47	37	76	56	103	0	37.49
Washington	Spokane	34	25	83	56	108	−25	16.56
West Virginia	Charleston	43	26	85	66	104	−16	44.03
Wisconsin	Milwaukee	29	16	80	64	103	−26	34.76
Wyoming	Lander	33	10	87	56	101	−37	12.66

Mean annual snowfall (in.): Based on climate normals 1981-2010: Albany, NY, 59.1; Anchorage, AK, 74.5; Boston, MA, 43.8; Burlington, VT, 81.2; Lander, WY, 91.4; Sault Ste. Marie, MI, 123.4.

World's wettest spot: Mawsynram, India, may be the rainiest place in the world. It has a recorded average annual rainfall of 467.4 in.

Temperature extremes: The world's highest temperature ever recorded under standard conditions was 134°F in Death Valley, CA, on July 10, 1913. The world record low of −128.5°F was recorded at the Soviet station of Vostok in Antarctica on July 21, 1983. The record low in the U.S. was −80°F at Prospect Creek, AK, Jan. 23, 1971.

Annual Climatological Data for U.S. Cities, 2012

Source: National Climatic Data Center, NESDIS, NOAA, U.S. Dept. of Commerce

Station	TEMPERATURE (°F)					PRECIPITATION[1]			Snowfall[2]			FASTEST[3] WIND		NO. OF DAYS	
	Elev. (ft)	Highest	Date	Lowest	Date	Total (in.)	Greatest in 24 hr. (in.)	Date	Total snowfall (in.)	Greatest in 24 hr. (in.)	Date	MPH	Date	Prec. 0.01 in. or more	Snow, sleet 1 in. or more
Albany, NY	281	98	7/17	0	1/22+	36.99	3.27	9/18-19	30.6	4.9	12/27	37	3/8	134	8
Albuquerque, NM	5,308	101	6/30	13	12/29	5.46	0.81	3/11	6.2	1.9	3/11	55	4/26	42	3
Anchorage, AK	222	75	6/22	-15	1/28	21.48	1.74	10/5-6	92.5	9.1	2/3	109	1/30	117	24
Asheville, NC	2,174	98	7/1	13	1/4	44.66	3.94	9/17-18	T	T	12/30+	39	12/29	136	0
Atlanta, GA	974	106	6/30	19	2/12	37.03	2.18	1/20-21	T	T	12/29	40	6/13	103	0
Atlantic City, NJ	117	101	7/18	10	1/16	48.59	5.05	10/28-29	6.8	2.5	11/7	54	6/30	113	3
Baltimore, MD	196	104	7/18+	13	1/4	37.42	5.70	10/29-30	3.2	1.0	12/26	47	6/29	119	1
Barrow, AK	38	67	7/23	-45	1/30+	6.27	0.42	9/22-23	60.8	1.9	10/17	36	12/23	124	20
Birmingham, AL	630	104	7/1	20	2/12	49.36	4.31	7/31	T	T	12/26	37	12/20	109	0
Bismarck, ND	1,654	104	7/19	-18	12/24	14.91	1.50	8/11	31.8	9.1	11/10	47	6/15	103	11
Boise, ID	2,861	103	7/12+	13	12/31+	11.45	4.80	1/18	10.7	4.8	1/18	41	6/4	97	2
Boston, MA	180	97	7/17	6	1/15	36.73	2.48	4/22-23	12.1	2.9	1/21	46	10/29	122	4
Buffalo, NY	717	96	8/4	2	1/15	32.79	1.85	10/29-30	54.9	10.1	12/26	45	3/3	146	12
Burlington, VT	348	97	6/21	-11	1/16	35.94	3.06	9/4-5	60.2	13.1	12/27	51	7/4	161	14
Caribou, ME	626	89	8/26+	-23	1/22	38.61	1.84	6/22	112.1	11.0	2/25	33	7/15	157	29
Charleston, SC	48	98	7/27+	20	1/4	43.97	3.45	6/11-12	0.0	0.0	—	38	7/31	107	0
Chicago, IL	658	103	7/6+	5	1/20+	26.91	1.65	7/18-19	19.0	5.4	1/20	43	7/26	109	4
Cleveland, OH	805	98	1/17+	6	1/20	44.62	2.51	10/29-30	46.3	5.0	12/26	47	10/30	153	18
Columbus, OH	812	101	7/7+	8	1/20+	37.27	2.04	3/18	27.4	5.9	12/29	53	6/29	130	10
Dallas-Ft. Worth, TX	562	108	8/9	22	12/26	31.26	4.27	1/24-25	0.8	0.4	12/25	48	7/20	56	0
Denver, CO	5,382	105	7/26+	-6	1/11	10.11	1.63	9/25-26	38.5	12.5	2/3	52	6/2	52	13
Des Moines, IA	971	106	7/25	1	1/18	26.29	3.66	4/14-15	30.7	6.8	12/20	46	8/8	92	7
Detroit, MI	631	102	7/17+	4	1/20	27.11	1.76	7/5	30.7	5.8	12/26	45	6/18	126	12
Duluth, MN	1,429	92	7/16	-18	1/19	33.20	6.99	6/19-20	61.8	9.7	2/1	41	2/29	126	15
Fairbanks, AK	464	86	6/23	-51	1/29	10.62	0.83	8/26-27	61.7	9.5	12/12	26	8/27	112	20
Fresno, CA	375	111	8/11	28	1/17	9.97	1.52	3/16-17	0.0	0.0	—	33	6/4	42	0
Grand Rapids, MI	788	104	7/6	3	2/11	33.85	2.27	8/9-10	53.5	6.2	2/10	40	4/16	128	16
Helena, MT	3,867	98	7/25+	-9	1/18	9.77	1.09	11/8-9	51.3	10.0	1/18	47	2/22	78	12
Honolulu, HI	18	89	10/11+	60	2/9+	8.58	3.91	3/5-6	—	—	—	30	12/16	51	—
Houston, TX	107	105	7/26	30	12/30	42.32	3.10	8/18-19	T	T	6/12	41	6/12	91	0
Huron, SD	1,284	104	7/16	-10	12/25+	19.66	2.06	6/19-20	39.6	8.1	2/23	52	8/3	91	11
Indianapolis, IN	797	105	7/7+	11	1/20	38.00	2.95	9/7-8	22.3	7.5	12/26	48	3/17	111	6
Jackson, MS	296	100	7/4	22	12/30	69.52	4.00	3/21-22	—	—	—	39	12/20	99	—
Jacksonville, FL	34	96	7/26	21	2/13+	53.41	7.37	6/25-26	—	—	—	39	5/27	107	—
Kansas City, MO	1,008	106	7/25+	5	2/12+	22.28	1.60	9/3-4	7.5	2.5	12/20	49	8/8	85	3
Knoxville, TN	982	105	7/1	16	2/12	53.64	5.82	9/17-18	T	T	12/31+	49	8/9	130	0
Lander, WY	5,560	99	7/1	-10	12/31	6.60	0.93	5/18-19	50.5	4.9	2/2	50	3/26	52	18
Lexington, KY	984	105	7/7	13	2/12	42.62	2.81	7/12-13	11.0	5.0	3/5	44	7/1	118	2
Los Angeles, CA	326	98	9/15	41	12/31	8.89	1.42	12/24	—	—	—	41	3/18	39	—
Louisville, KY	484	106	7/7	17	2/12	44.68	3.17	5/29	9.7	2.8	3/5	43	7/19	122	3
Marquette, MI	1,415	91	7/5+	-12	12/20	36.11	2.21	10/25	196.4	10.0	11/23	—	—	169	45
Memphis, TN	286	103	7/5	21	12/30	36.90	2.24	5/22-23	0.9	0.9	12/26	44	7/7	110	0
Miami, FL	29	94	6/14	43	1/4	86.94	9.81	5/22-23	—	—	—	38	8/26	148	—
Milwaukee, WI	680	103	7/5	-1	1/20	29.29	2.53	5/6-7	35.3	6.1	1/12	37	11/11	104	10
Minneapolis, MN	874	102	7/6	-11	1/19	29.59	3.39	5/23-24	27.8	10.5	12/9	45	8/3	109	7
Mobile, AL	212	97	7/3	25	1/14+	69.10	7.24	6/8-9	0.0	0.0	—	39	8/28	116	0
Moline, IL	607	104	7/7	-4	1/14	27.23	1.80	12/19-20	20.8	4.9	12/20	55	4/14	92	5
Nashville, TN	574	109	6/29	18	2/13+	45.82	2.48	7/19-20	0.4	0.2	2/19	43	8/16	124	0
New Orleans, LA	7	98	6/26	32	1/14	68.26	7.98	8/28-29	—	—	—	53	8/28	112	—
New York, NY	161	100	7/18	13	1/4	38.51	2.67	4/22-23	9.6	4.3	11/7	38	10/29	134	2
Newark, NJ	28	104	7/18	12	1/4	36.35	2.78	4/22-23	12.1	5.7	11/7	43	10/29	128	3
Norfolk, VA	69	102	7/8	22	2/13	48.35	4.55	10/28-29	0.5	0.3	11/7	43	10/28	122	0
North Little Rock, AR	565	107	7/30	21	2/12+	44.33	5.14	3/20-21	10.6	10.3	12/25-26	23	12/25	90	2
Oklahoma City, OK	1,284	113	8/3	13	12/26	29.47	3.03	3/19-20	3.2	0.9	2/13+	53	5/20	66	0
Philadelphia, PA	62	101	7/7	14	1/4	35.94	3.12	9/4	4.1	2.3	1/21	44	10/29	111	1
Phoenix, AZ	1,106	116	8/23	37	12/29	4.28	0.80	8/23	—	—	—	44	5/9	27	—
Pittsburgh, PA	1,175	98	7/7	3	1/20	41.74	2.15	9/29-30	48.6	5.2	2/11	39	1/1	145	17
Portland, ME	72	93	6/20	-4	1/16	54.47	5.31	6/2-3	62.9	13.0	3/1	43	10/29	141	12
Portland, OR	223	102	8/4	26	1/13	50.44	2.14	11/18-19	—	—	—	38	12/17	170	—
Providence, RI	53	96	7/18	9	1/16	41.19	3.17	4/22-23	26.1	7.6	12/29	41	10/29	131	7
Raleigh-Durham, NC	430	105	7/8	19	1/4	40.79	2.31	9/2-3	0.9	0.9	2/19	36	2/24	121	0
Rapid City, SD	3,153	109	6/26	-8	2/11	11.41	1.49	4/14-15	16.7	2.4	12/24	56	10/18	74	5
Reno, NV	4,407	103	8/9	8	1/17	5.77	0.92	1/20-21	16.2	3.4	2/27	52	1/19	41	6
Richmond, VA	167	104	7/7	17	1/4	36.55	2.10	10/29-30	4.5	3.9	2/19	48	8/2	125	1
St. Louis, MO	710	108	7/25	13	1/14	32.30	2.29	4/13-14	6.4	1.8	2/13	47	2/29	105	3
Salt Lake City, UT	4,224	103	8/8	12	12/31	12.66	1.11	11/9-10	47.8	8.5	11/10	43	2/25	74	16
San Antonio, TX	821	106	6/26	27	12/21	39.40	4.01	5/14-15	T	T	5/11	41	8/10	73	0
San Diego, CA	81	101	9/15	41	12/31	6.64	1.56	12/13	—	—	—	32	3/25	40	—
San Francisco, CA	89	93	10/2	34	1/17	0.46	2.01	11/29-30	—	—	—	45	5/24	64	—
San Juan, PR	10	95	6/22+	69	2/20	3.24	3.40	3/24-25	0.0	0.0	—	30	8/23	208	—
Sault Ste. Marie, MI	727	91	8/4	-9	3/5	0.73	1.81	6/18	119.0	10.3	12/20	35	11/23	159	36
Savannah, GA	143	100	7/26	21	2/13	40.21	3.22	3/3-4	T	T	5/15	43	7/1	99	0
Scottsbluff, NE	3,949	106	6/26+	-9	1/17	6.99	1.09	6/6-7	23.9	3.7	11/10	49	1/22	63	9
Seattle, WA	434	94	8/16	26	1/15	48.26	2.26	11/18-19	11.1	6.8	1/18	39	1/24	177	2
Spokane, WA	2,384	98	7/8	6	2/28	21.32	1.22	3/14-15	51.8	6.0	1/19	48	12/17	132	19
Springfield, MO	1,280	106	8/4	10	2/12+	30.94	2.32	10/13-14	3.7	1.7	2/13	48	6/11	86	2
Tampa, FL	40	96	5/25+	34	2/12	55.99	8.57	6/24-25	T	T	7/21	37	6/25	103	0
Washington, DC	3	105	7/7	17	1/4	32.45	4.10	10/29-30	2.2	0.6	1/21+	49	6/29	122	0
Wilmington, DE	77	101	7/18+	13	1/4	36.29	3.88	10/29-30	5.2	2.4	1/21	46	10/30	117	2
Windsor Locks, CT	165	100	7/18	4	1/16	38.44	2.68	4/22-23	30.2	6.8	12/29	43	7/18	131	9

(+) = Indicates value for extreme also occurred on an earlier date(s). (T) = Trace amount. — = Data not available or unreported. (1) Where one date is shown, it is the starting date of the storm. (2) Comprises all forms of frozen precipitation, including hail and sleet. (3) Sustained for at least 2 min., not peak gust.

Record Temperatures by State

Source: National Climatic Data Center, NESDIS, NOAA, U.S. Dept. of Commerce
(as of May 22, 2013)

State	°F	Latest date	Station	Approx. elevation (ft)	°F	Latest date	Station	Approx. elevation (ft)
		LOWEST TEMPERATURE				HIGHEST TEMPERATURE		
Alabama	-27	Jan. 30, 1966	New Market	732	112	Sept. 6, 1925	Centerville	220
Alaska	-80	Jan. 23, 1971	Prospect Creek Camp	955	100	June 27, 1915	Fort Yukon	445
Arizona	-40	Jan. 7, 1971	Hawley Lake	8,180	128	June 29, 1994	Lake Havasu City	505
Arkansas	-29	Feb. 13, 1905	Gravette	1,260	120	Aug. 10, 1936	Ozark	390
California	-45	Jan. 20, 1937	Boca	5,575	134	July 10, 1913	Greenland Ranch	-194
Colorado	-61	Feb. 1, 1985	Maybell	5,944	114	July 11, 1954[1]	Sedgwick	3,584
Connecticut	-32	Jan. 22, 1961[1]	Coventry	480	106	July 15, 1995[1]	Danbury	405
Delaware	-17	Jan. 17, 1893	Millsboro	20	110	July 21, 1930	Millsboro	20
Florida	-2	Feb. 13, 1899	Tallahassee	192	109	June 29, 1931	Monticello	98
Georgia	-17	Jan. 27, 1940	CCC Fire Camp F-16	1,000	112	Aug. 20, 1983[1]	Greenville	960
Hawaii	12	May 17, 1979	Mauna Kea Observ.	13,773	100	Apr. 27, 1931	Pahala	840
Idaho	-60	Jan. 18, 1943	Island Park	6,290	118	July 28, 1934	Orofino	1,320
Illinois	-36	Jan. 5, 1999	Congerville	635	117	July 14, 1954	East St. Louis	410
Indiana	-36	Jan. 19, 1994	New Whiteland	785	116	July 14, 1936	Collegeville	650
Iowa	-47	Feb. 3, 1996[1]	Elkader	788	118	July 20, 1934	Keokuk	651
Kansas	-40	Feb. 13, 1905	Lebanon	1,874	121	July 24, 1936[1]	Alton	1,591
Kentucky	-37	Jan. 19, 1994	Shelbyville	730	114	July 28, 1930	Greensburg	590
Louisiana	-16	Feb. 13, 1899	Minden	200	114	Aug. 10, 1936	Plain Dealing	290
Maine	-50	Jan. 16, 2009	Big Black River	885	105	July 10, 1911[1]	North Bridgton	449
Maryland	-40	Jan. 13, 1912	Oakland	2,420	109	July 10, 1936[1]	Cumberland	899
							Frederick	380
Massachusetts	-35	Jan. 12, 1981[1]	Chester	640	107	Aug. 2, 1975	Chester	640
							New Bedford	70
Michigan	-51	Feb. 9, 1934	Vanderbilt	905	112	July 13, 1936	Mio	960
							Stanwood	830
Minnesota	-60	Feb. 2, 1996	Tower	1,485	115	July 29, 1917	Beardsley	1,089
Mississippi	-19	Jan. 30, 1966	Corinth	420	115	July 29, 1930	Holly Springs	502
Missouri	-40	Feb. 13, 1905	Warsaw	705	118	July 14, 1954	Warsaw	705
							Union	540
Montana	-70	Jan. 20, 1954	Rogers Pass	5,545	117	July 5, 1937[1]	Medicine Lake	1,942
Nebraska	-47	Dec. 22, 1909[1]	Oshkosh	3,390	118	July 24, 1936[1]	Minden	2,160
Nevada	-50	Jan. 8, 1937	San Jacinto	5,203	125	June 29, 1994	Laughlin	605
New Hampshire	-50	Jan. 22, 1885	Mt. Washington	6,267	106	July 4, 1911	Nashua	140
New Jersey	-34	Jan. 5, 1904	River Vale	70	110	July 10, 1936	Runyon	20
New Mexico	-50	Feb. 1, 1951	Gavilan	7,425	122	June 27, 1994	Waste Isolat. Pilot Plant	3,411
New York	-52	Feb. 18, 1979	Old Forge	1,748	108	July 22, 1926	Troy	35
North Carolina	-34	Jan. 21, 1985	Mt. Mitchell	6,240	110	Aug. 21, 1983	Fayetteville	186
North Dakota	-60	Feb. 15, 1936	Parshall	1,952	121	July 6, 1936	Steele	1,885
Ohio	-39	Feb. 10, 1899	Milligan	875	113	July 21, 1934	Gallipolis	669
Oklahoma	-31	Feb. 10, 2011	Nowata	NA	120	Aug. 12, 1936	Altus Irig. Res. Station	1,380
Oregon	-54	Feb. 10, 1933[1]	Seneca	4,660	119	Aug. 10, 1898[1]	Pendleton	1,040
Pennsylvania	-42	Jan. 5, 1904	Smethport	1,469	111	July 10, 1936[1]	Phoenixville	105
Rhode Island	-28	Jan. 11, 1942	Wood River Junction	49	104	Aug. 2, 1975	Providence	60
South Carolina	-19	Jan. 21, 1985	Caesars Head	3,200	113	June 29, 2012	Columbia	242
South Dakota	-58	Feb. 17, 1936	McIntosh	2,175	120	July 15, 2006[1]	Fort Pierre	1,590
Tennessee	-32	Dec. 30, 1917	Mountain City	2,503	113	Aug. 9, 1930[1]	Perryville	371
Texas	-23	Feb. 8, 1933	Seminole	3,336	120	June 28, 1994[1]	Monahans	2,547
Utah	-50	Jan. 5, 1913	East Portal	7,615	117	July 5, 1985	Saint George	2,770
Vermont	-50	Dec. 30, 1933	Bloomfield	1,040	107	July 7, 1912	Vernon	226
Virginia	-30	Jan. 21, 1985	Mountain Lake Bio. Station	3,870	110	July 15, 1954[1]	Balcony Falls	732
Washington	-48	Dec. 30, 1968	Mazama / Winthrop	2,106 / 1,749	118	Aug. 5, 1961[1]	Ice Harbor Dam	368
West Virginia	-37	Dec. 30, 1917	Lewisburg	2,251	112	July 10, 1936[1]	Martinsburg	534
Wisconsin	-55	Feb. 4, 1996[1]	Couderay	1,300	114	July 13, 1936	Wisconsin Dells	835
Wyoming	-66	Feb. 9, 1933	Riverside Ranger Sta.	6,500	115	July 15, 1988[1]	Diversion Dam	5,575

NA = Not available. (1) Also on earlier dates at the same or other places.

Tropical Cyclone Names in 2014

Source: National Weather Service, NOAA, U.S. Dept. of Commerce

Atlantic: Arthur, Bertha, Cristobal, Dolly, Edouard, Fay, Gonzalo, Hanna, Isaias, Josephine, Kyle, Laura, Marco, Nana, Omar, Paulette, Rene, Sally, Teddy, Vicky, Wilfred. If there are more than 21 named Atlantic storms in one season, remaining storms take names from the Greek alphabet, starting with Alpha. (This has so far only been necessary in 2005.)

Eastern North Pacific: Amanda, Boris, Cristina, Douglas, Elida, Fausto, Genevieve, Hernan, Iselle, Julio, Karina, Lowell, Marie, Norbert, Odile, Polo, Rachel, Simon, Trudy, Vance, Winnie, Xavier, Yolanda, Zeke.

World Temperature and Precipitation

Source: World Meteorological Organization

Average daily maximum and minimum temperatures and annual precipitation based on records for the period 1961-90. Records of extreme temperatures include all available years of data for a given location and are usually for a longer period. Surface elevations are supplied by the WMO and may differ from figures in other sections of *The World Almanac*.

Station	Surface elevation (ft)	Temperature (°F) AVERAGE DAILY January Max.	January Min.	July Max.	July Min.	EXTREME Max.	EXTREME Min.	Avg. annual precipitation (in.)
Algiers, Algeria	82	61.7	42.6	87.1	65.3	NA	NA	27.0
Athens, Greece	49	56.1	44.6	88.9	73.0	NA	NA	14.6
Auckland, New Zealand	20	74.8	61.2	58.5	46.4	NA	NA	49.4
Bangkok, Thailand	66	89.6	69.8	90.9	77.0	104	51	59.0
Beijing, China	177	34.9	15.1	87.4	70.9	105	-17	22.7
Berlin, Germany	190	35.2	26.8	73.6	55.2	107	-4	23.3
Bogotá, Colombia	8,357	67.3	41.7	64.6	45.5	75	21	32.4
Bucharest, Romania	298	34.7	22.1	83.8	60.1	105	-18	23.4
Budapest, Hungary	456	34.2	24.8	79.7	59.7	103	-10	20.3
Buenos Aires, Argentina	82	85.8	67.3	59.7	45.7	104	22	45.2
Cairo, Egypt	243	65.8	48.2	93.9	71.1	118	34	1.0
Cape Town, South Africa	138	79.0	60.3	63.3	44.6	105	28	20.5
Caracas, Venezuela	2,739	79.9	60.8	81.3	66.0	96	45	36.1
Casablanca, Morocco	203	62.8	47.1	77.7	66.7	NA	NA	16.8
Copenhagen, Denmark	16	35.6	28.4	68.9	55.0	NA	NA	NA
Damascus, Syria	2,004	54.3	32.9	97.2	61.9	NA	NA	5.6
Dubai, United Arab Emirates[1]	16	75.2	56.7	105.1	84.0	117	45	3.7
Dublin, Ireland	279	45.7	36.5	66.0	52.5	86	8	28.8
Geneva, Switzerland	1,364	38.3	27.9	76.3	53.2	101	-3	35.6
Havana, Cuba	164	78.4	65.5	88.3	74.8	NA	NA	46.9
Hong Kong, China	203	65.5	56.5	88.7	79.9	97	32	87.2
Istanbul, Turkey	108	47.8	37.2	82.8	65.3	105	7	27.4
Jerusalem, Israel	2,483	53.4	39.4	83.8	63.0	107	26	23.2
Karachi, Pakistan	69	78.4	50.7	91.6	81.3	117	34	8.6
Lagos, Nigeria	125	90.0	72.3	82.8	72.1	NA	NA	59.3
Lima, Peru	43	79.0	66.9	66.4	59.4	NA	NA	0.2
London, England	203	44.1	32.7	71.1	52.3	99	2	29.7
Manila, Philippines	79	85.8	74.8	89.1	76.8	NA	NA	49.6
Mexico City, Mexico	7,570	70.3	43.7	73.8	53.2	NA	NA	33.4
Montreal, Canada	118	21.6	5.2	79.2	59.7	100	-36	37.0
Mumbai (Bombay), India	36	85.3	66.7	86.2	77.5	110	46	85.4
Nairobi, Kenya	5,897	77.9	50.9	71.6	48.6	NA	NA	41.9
New Delhi, India[2]	709	69.8	45.7	94.5	80.2	113	34	31.3
Paris, France	213	42.8	33.6	75.2	55.2	105	-1	25.6
Prague, Czech Republic	1,197	32.7	22.5	73.9	53.2	98	-16	20.7
Reykjavik, Iceland	200	35.4	26.6	55.9	46.9	76	-3	31.5
Riyadh, Saudi Arabia	2,034	68.4	46.8	109.0	81.3	120	28	NA
Rome, Italy	79	53.8	35.4	88.2	62.1	NA	NA	33.0
San Salvador, El Salvador	2,037	86.5	61.3	86.2	66.4	105	45	68.3
São Paulo, Brazil	2,598	81.1	65.7	71.2	53.1	NA	NA	57.4
Seoul, South Korea	285	33.4	19.2	83.3	70.9	NA	NA	NA
Shanghai, China	23	45.9	32.9	88.9	76.6	104	10	43.8
Singapore	52	85.8	73.6	87.4	75.6	NA	NA	84.6
Stockholm, Sweden	171	30.7	23.0	71.4	56.1	97	-26	21.2
Sydney, Australia	10	79.5	65.5	62.4	43.9	114	32	46.4
Tehran, Iran	3,906	45.0	30.0	98.2	75.2	109	-5	9.1
Tokyo, Japan	118	49.1	34.2	83.8	72.1	NA	NA	55.4
Toronto, Canada	567	27.5	12.0	80.2	57.6	105	-26	30.8

NA = Not available. (1) Records are for 1974-91. (2) Records are for 1971-90.

Speed of Winds in the U.S.

Source: National Climatic Data Center, NESDIS, NOAA, U.S. Dept. of Commerce

Based on available records through 2012. Average and maximum speeds are annual. Max. speeds are highest 1-min. average.

Station	Avg. mph	Max. mph	Station	Avg. mph	Max. mph	Station	Avg. mph	Max. mph
Albuquerque, NM	8.9	55	Helena, MT[2]	7.7	73	Oklahoma City, OK	12.2	74
Anchorage, AK[1,2]	7.1	75	Honolulu, HI	11.2	46	Omaha, NE	10.5	70
Atlanta, GA	9.1	60	Houston, TX	7.6	51	Philadelphia, PA[2]	9.5	73
Baltimore, MD[2]	8.6	80	Indianapolis, IN	9.6	60	Phoenix, AZ	6.2	54
Birmingham, AL[2]	7.1	65	Jackson, MS	6.8	55	Pittsburgh, PA	8.9	58
Bismarck, ND	10.2	64	Jacksonville, FL	7.8	57	Portland, ME	8.7	57
Boise, ID[2]	8.7	61	Little Rock, AR[2]	7.7	65	Portland, OR[2]	7.9	68
Boston, MA	12.3	54	Los Angeles, CA[2]	4.8	49	Providence, RI	10.3	90
Buffalo, NY[2]	11.8	91	Louisville, KY	8.3	56	Richmond, VA	7.7	51
Burlington, VT	8.9	51	Miami, FL	9.2	86	St. Louis, MO	9.6	53
Charleston, SC	8.6	52	Milwaukee, WI	11.5	54	Salt Lake City, UT[2]	8.8	71
Chicago, IL	10.3	58	Minn.-St. Paul, MN	10.5	51	San Francisco, CA[2]	8.7	47
Cleveland, OH	10.5	53	Mobile, AL	7.6	66	San Juan, PR	8.3	79
Dallas-Ft. Worth, TX	10.7	73	Mount Washington, NH[1,2]	35.1	231	Seattle, WA[2]	8.8	66
Denver, CO	8.7	54	Nashville, TN	7.9	58	Sioux Falls, SD	11.0	70
Des Moines, IA[2]	10.7	76	New Orleans, LA	8.2	69	Washington, DC	9.4	49
Detroit, MI	10.1	61	New York, NY	9.1	40	Wichita, KS	12.2	70
Hartford, CT	8.4	46	Newark, NJ	10.2	82	Wilmington, DE	9.0	58

(1) Max. speed based on short gusts. (2) Max. speed calculated from minimum time during which 1 mi of wind passed the station.

Wind Chill Temperature

Source: National Weather Service, NOAA, U.S. Dept. of Commerce

Temperature and wind combine to cause heat loss from body surfaces. For example, a temperature of 5°F, plus a 10-mph wind, causes body heat loss equal to that which would occur in –10°F with no wind. In other words, a 10-mph wind makes 5°F feel like –10°F. Wind speeds greater than 45 mph have little additional chilling effect. Direct sunlight can increase the wind chill temperature 10° to 15°F. When the wind chill temperature falls within the shaded area, frostbite can occur in 30 min. or less.

	Calm	\multicolumn{18}{c}{Air temperature (°F)}																
		40	35	30	25	20	15	10	5	0	–5	–10	–15	–20	–25	–30	–35	–40	–45
		\multicolumn{18}{c}{Wind chill temperature (°F)}																
Wind speed (mph)	5	36	31	25	19	13	7	1	–5	–11	–16	–22	–28	–34	–40	–46	–52	–57	–63
	10	34	27	21	15	9	3	–4	–10	–16	–22	–28	–35	–41	–47	–53	–59	–66	–72
	15	32	25	19	13	6	0	–7	–13	–19	–26	–32	–39	–45	–51	–58	–64	–71	–77
	20	30	24	17	11	4	–2	–9	–15	–22	–29	–35	–42	–48	–55	–61	–68	–74	–81
	25	29	23	16	9	3	–4	–11	–17	–24	–31	–37	–44	–51	–58	–64	–71	–78	–84
	30	28	22	15	8	1	–5	–12	–19	–26	–33	–39	–46	–53	–60	–67	–73	–80	–87
	35	28	21	14	7	0	–7	–14	–21	–27	–34	–41	–48	–55	–62	–69	–76	–82	–89
	40	27	20	13	6	–1	–8	–15	–22	–29	–36	–43	–50	–57	–64	–71	–78	–84	–91
	45	26	19	12	5	–2	–9	–16	–23	–30	–37	–44	–51	–58	–65	–72	–79	–86	–93

Heat Index

Source: National Weather Service, NOAA, U.S. Dept. of Commerce

The heat index, or apparent temperature, is a measure of how hot it feels when the relative humidity is factored in with the actual air temperature. For example, when air temperature is 100°F, and relative humidity is 50%, it feels as if it's 118°F with no humidity. Full sunlight can make one feel even hotter. On the chart, the shaded area above 103°–105°F apparent temperature corresponds to a level that may cause increasingly severe heat disorders with continued exposure and/or physical activity.

	\multicolumn{16}{c}{Temperature (°F)}															
	80	82	84	86	88	90	92	94	96	98	100	102	104	106	108	110
	\multicolumn{16}{c}{Apparent temperature (°F)}															
Relative humidity (%) 40	80	81	83	85	88	91	94	97	101	105	109	114	119	124	130	136
45	80	82	84	87	89	93	96	100	104	109	114	119	124	130	137	
50	81	83	85	88	91	95	99	103	108	113	118	124	131	137		
55	81	84	86	89	93	97	101	106	112	117	124	130	137			
60	82	84	88	91	95	100	105	110	116	123	129	137				
65	82	85	89	93	98	103	108	114	121	128	136					
70	83	86	90	95	100	105	112	119	126	134						
75	84	88	92	97	103	109	116	124	132							
80	84	89	94	100	106	113	121	129								
85	85	90	96	102	110	117	126	135								
90	86	91	98	105	113	122	131									
95	86	93	100	108	117	127										
100	87	95	103	112	121	132										

☐ Caution ▨ Extreme caution ▨ Danger ▨ Extreme danger

Ultraviolet (UV) Index Forecast

Source: National Weather Service, NOAA, U.S. Dept. of Commerce; U.S. Environmental Protection Agency; U.S. Food and Drug Administration, U.S. Dept. of Health and Human Services

The National Weather Service (NWS) and the Environmental Protection Agency (EPA) developed and began offering a UV index in 1994 in response to increasing incidences of skin cancer, cataracts, and other effects from exposure to the sun's harmful rays. In 2004, they adapted their index to the Global Solar UV Index sponsored by the World Health Organization. The UV index is now a regular element of NWS atmospheric forecasts.

The UV index, ranging from 0 to 11+, is an indication of the expected intensity of UV radiation reaching the Earth's surface during the solar noon hour (time of day when the sun appears to have reached its highest point in the sky; it depends on location and the time of year). The lower the UV index value, the less the radiation. The UV index forecast is produced daily for 58 cities by the NWS Climate Prediction Center and uses the following scale.

UV index	Exposure	Minimum precautions
0-2	Low	Sunscreen with an SPF of at least 15
3-5	Moderate	Sunscreen, covering up
6-7	High	Sunscreen, hat, UV-blocking sunglasses, avoid sun 10 AM-4 PM
8-10	Very high	Same as above
11+	Extreme	Same as above

The index value is valid for a radius of about 30 miles around a listed city and is based on several factors:

Ozone. Ozone, a form of oxygen, the molecules of which consist of three atoms rather than two, absorbs UV radiation. The more ozone, the less the radiation at the surface.

Sun height. The higher the sun is in the sky, the higher the UV radiation level.

Cloudiness. UV radiation levels are highest under cloudless skies. Even with cloud cover, UV radiation levels can be high due to the scattering of UV radiation by water molecules and fine particles in the atmosphere.

Reflectivity. Reflective surfaces intensify UV exposure. White sand reflects about 15% of UV radiation that reaches it; sea foam, 25%; snow, as much as 80%; water, up to 100% depending on reflection angle.

Elevation. At higher elevations, UV radiation travels a shorter distance to reach Earth's surface so there is less atmosphere to absorb the rays. For every 1,000 m (3,281 ft) one travels above sea level, UV levels increase by 10%-12%. Snow and lack of pollutants intensify UV exposure at higher altitudes.

Latitude. The closer a location is to the equator, the higher the UV radiation level.

SPF (sun protection factor) number. The UV index is not linked in any way to the SPF number on sunscreens. The Centers for Disease Control and Prevention recommends using a sunscreen with at least SPF 15. Under a Food and Drug Administration rule that took effect in 2012, sunscreens that protect against cancer and early skin aging as well as sunburn are labeled "broad spectrum."

Further information. For precautions to take after learning the UV index value, call the EPA's Stratospheric Ozone Hotline (800-296-1996). For questions on scientific aspects, visit the NWS Climate Prediction Center online at www.cpc.ncep.noaa.gov.

Lightning

Source: National Weather Service, NOAA, U.S. Dept. of Commerce

Lightning is a powerful electric discharge, or spark, that can occur in the atmosphere when an imbalance of positive and negative charges develops. It can travel within a cloud, between clouds, between a cloud and clear sky, or between a cloud and the ground. Lightning generally accompanies rainstorms but it can also be seen with snowstorms, volcano eruption clouds, and violent forest fires. In a common form of cloud-to-ground lightning, a negatively charged area in a thunderstorm sends charges down toward positively charged objects. Lightning can travel miles away from the area of a storm.

The transfer of charges in lightning generates a huge amount of heat, sending the temperature in the channel to 50,000°F or more and causing the air within it to expand rapidly. The sound of that expansion is thunder. Sound travels more slowly than light, so lightning is usually observed before thunder is heard.

An estimated 25 mil cloud-to-ground lightning bolts happen in the U.S. each year. They killed an annual average of 52 people in 1983-2012. This is a small number compared to U.S. deaths from fire (about 3,000 a year) and motor vehicle crashes (more than 30,000 annually in recent years), but it is still significant. In comparison, tornadoes caused an average of 74 deaths a year and hurricanes an average of 47 over the same 30-year time period. According to preliminary figures from the National Weather Service, 28 people were struck and killed by lightning in 2012; 139 more were injured.

Most lightning deaths and injuries occur in summer when people are outdoors. If outdoors, one should run to a safe building or vehicle when thunder is first heard, lightning is seen, or dark threatening clouds are observed developing overhead. Even while indoors, one is advised to stay away from windows and doors and to avoid contact with anything conducting electricity, including corded phones, computers and other electrical equipment, and tubs, showers, and other plumbing. One should stay inside until 30 min. after the last occurrence of lightning or thunder.

More information about lightning can be found online at www.lightningsafety.noaa.gov.

Global Temperature Extremes and Precipitation Records

Source: World Weather/Climate Extremes Archive, World Meteorological Organization (WMO) Commission for Climatology

(records in each category ranked from most to least extreme)

Highest Temperature Extremes

Continent	Highest temp. (°F)	Place	Elevation (ft)	Date
North America	134	Death Valley, CA, U.S. (Furnace Creek Ranch)	-179	July 10, 1913
Africa	131[1]	Kebili, Tunisia	125	July 7, 1931
Asia	129.2	Tirat Tsvi, Israel	-722	June 21, 1942
Australia	123	Oodnadatta, South Australia	367	Jan. 2, 1960
South America	120	Rivadavia, Argentina	2,192	Dec. 11, 1905
Europe	118.4	Athens, Greece (and Elefsina, Greece)	774	July 10, 1977
Oceania	108	Tuguegarao, Philippines	676	Apr. 29, 1912
Antarctica	59	Vanda Station (New Zealand), Wright Valley	49	May 1, 1974

(1) Previous record of 136.4°F set on Sept. 13, 1922, in El Azizia, Libya, was invalidated in Sept. 2012 after the WMO determined that an error had been made in recording the temperature.

Lowest Temperature Extremes

Continent	Lowest temp. (°F)	Place	Elevation (ft)	Date
Antarctica	-128.6	Vostok Station (Russia)	11,220	July 21, 1983
Asia	-90	Verkhoyansk, Russia	350	Feb. 5 and 7, 1892
	-90	Oimekon, Russia	2,625	Feb. 6, 1933
North America	-81.4	Snag, Yukon, Canada	2,120	Feb. 3, 1947
Europe	-72.6	Ust'-Shchugor, Russia	279	Dec. 31, 1978
South America	-27	Sarmiento, Argentina	879	June 1, 1907
Africa	-11	Ifrane, Morocco	5,364	Feb. 11, 1935
Australia	-9.4	Charlotte Pass, New South Wales	5,758	June 29, 1994

Highest Measured Average Annual Precipitation Extremes

Continent	Highest avg. (in.)[1]	Place	Elevation (ft)	Years in averaging period
Asia	467.4	Mawsynram, India	4,695	38
Oceania	460	Mt. Waialeale, Kauai, HI, U.S.	5,148	30
Africa	405	Debundscha, Cameroon	30	32
South America	354	Quibdo, Colombia	230	29
Australia	316.3	Bellenden Ker, Queensland	5,102	34
North America	276	Henderson Lake, British Columbia, Canada	12	15
Europe	183	Crkvica, Bosnia-Herzegovina	4,298	22
Antarctica	>31.5[2]	Along coast of E and W and over the Antarctic Peninsula		3[3]

(1) Official greatest average annual precipitation. The frequently cited record of 523.6 in. in Lloro, Colombia (14 mi SE and at a higher elevation than Quibdo) is an estimate. (2) Water equivalent. (3) July 1996-June 1999.

Lowest Measured Average Annual Precipitation Extremes

Continent	Lowest avg. (in.)	Place	Elevation (ft)	Years in averaging period
South America	0.03	Arica, Chile	213	59
Antarctica	0.08	Amundsen-Scott South Pole Station (U.S.)	9,301	10
Africa	<0.1	Wadi Halfa, Sudan	590	39
North America	1.2	Batagues, Mexico	69	14
Asia	1.8	Aden, Yemen	63	50
Australia	4.05	Troudaninna, South Australia	46	42
Europe	6.4	Astrakhan, Russia	66	25
Oceania	7.41	Mauna Kea Observatory, HI, U.S.	13,780	11[1]

(1) 1972-82.

OCEANOGRAPHY

Tides and Their Causes

Source: National Ocean Service, NOAA, U.S. Dept. of Commerce

The tides are natural phenomena involving the movement of waves in the Earth's large fluid bodies as a result of the gravitational attraction of the sun and moon. These two variable influences combined produce the complex recurrent cycle of the tides. Tides may occur in both oceans and seas; to a limited extent in large lakes in the atmosphere; and, to a very minute degree, in the Earth itself. The length of time between succeeding tides can vary.

The tide-generating force represents the difference between (1) the centrifugal force produced by Earth's revolution around the common center-of-gravity of the Earth-moon system and (2) the gravitational attraction of the moon acting upon the Earth's overlying waters. The moon is about 390 times closer to Earth than is the sun. So despite its smaller mass, the moon's tide-raising force is two and a half times greater.

The tide-generating forces of the moon and sun acting tangentially to the Earth's surface tend to cause a maximum accumulation of waters at two diametrically opposite points on the Earth's surface and to withdraw compensating amounts of water from all points 90° removed from these tidal bulges. As the Earth rotates beneath the maxima and minima of these tide-generating forces, a sequence of two high tides, separated by two low tides, is produced each lunar day (24 hr. and 50 min., the time it takes for a specific site on the Earth to rotate from an exact point under the moon to the same point under the moon) in what is called a semidiurnal tide. Each ocean basin reacts differently to tidal forces.

Twice each month, when the sun, moon, and Earth are directly aligned—the moon between the Earth and sun (at new moon) or on the opposite side of Earth from the sun (at full moon)—the sun and moon exert gravitational forces in a mutual or additive fashion. The highest high tides and lowest low tides, called spring tides, are produced at these times. At two positions 90° in between, the moon and sun's gravitational forces—imposed at right angles—counteract each other to the greatest extent, and the range between high and low tides is reduced, resulting in neap tides.

The inclination of the moon's monthly orbit and of the sun to the equator during Earth's yearly passage through its orbit produce a difference in the height of succeeding high and low tides, known as the diurnal inequality. In most cases, this produces a so-called mixed tide. In extreme cases, these phenomena may result in a diurnal tide, with only one high tide and one low tide each day. There are other monthly and yearly variations in the tides because of the elliptical shape of the orbits.

The range of tides in the open ocean is generally less than in the coastal regions, where the incoming tide can be augmented by the continental shelves, as well as by bays and estuaries. The largest tidal ranges in the world occur in the Bay of Fundy and in Ungava Bay, Canada, where the range of tide reaches 53.5 ft. In New Orleans, the periodic rise and fall of the diurnal tide is affected by the seasonal stages of the Mississippi River, being about 10 in. at low stage and 0 at high.

In every case, actual high or low tide can vary considerably from the average as a result of weather conditions such as strong winds, abrupt barometric pressure changes, or prolonged periods of extreme high or low pressure.

Mean Ranges of Tide

Place	Ft	In.	Place	Ft	In.	Place	Ft	In.
Baltimore, MD.	1	2	Key West, FL	1	3	Provincetown, MA	9	3
Biloxi, MS	1	6	Los Angeles, CA.	3	8	St. Petersburg, FL	1	6
Boston, MA.	9	6	Miami Beach, FL	2	5	San Diego, CA	4	1
Charleston, SC	5	3	New London, CT	2	6	San Francisco, CA	4	1
Eastport, ME.	18	4	New York, NY.	4	6	San Juan, PR.	1	1
Ft. Pulaski, GA	6	10	Newport, RI	3	5	Sandy Hook, NJ	4	8
Galveston, TX.	1	0	Philadelphia, PA.	6	1	Seattle, WA	7	7
Honolulu, HI	1	3	Portland, ME.	9	1	Washington, DC.	2	8

Note: Mean range is the difference in height between mean high water and mean low water.

El Niño and La Niña

Source: National Weather Service, NOAA, U.S. Dept. of Commerce

El Niño is a climatically significant disruption of the ocean-atmosphere system characterized by large-scale weakening of trade winds and warming of surface layer waters in the central and eastern equatorial Pacific. The term El Niño, Spanish for "the little boy" or "the Christ Child," was originally used by fishing crews to refer to a warm ocean current that appeared around Christmas off the west coast of Ecuador and Peru lasting several months. The term has come to be reserved for exceptionally strong, warm currents that bring heavy rains.

El Niño events generally occur at irregular intervals of two to seven years, at an average of once every three to four years. They typically last 12 to 18 months. The intensity of El Niño events varies depending on the area encompassed by the abnormally warm ocean temperatures. Some are strong, such as in 1982-83 and 1997-98. Others are considerably weaker, such as the 2009-10 event. The eastward extent of warmer than normal water varies from episode to episode.

El Niño influences weather around the globe, and its impacts are most clearly seen in the winter. During El Niño years, winter temperatures in the continental U.S. tend to be warmer than normal in the northern states and on the West Coast and cooler than normal in the Southeast. Conditions tend to be wetter than normal over central and southern California, the Southwest and across much of the South, and drier than normal over the northern portions of the Rocky Mountains and in the Ohio Valley. Globally, El Niño brings wetter than normal conditions to Peru and Chile and dry conditions to Australia and Indonesia. It should be noted that El Niño is only one of a number of factors influencing seasonal variations of climate.

La Niña ("the little girl") is characterized by colder than normal sea surface temperatures in the equatorial Pacific. La Niña typically brings wetter, cooler conditions to the Pacific Northwest and drier, warmer conditions to much of the southern U.S. El Niño and La Niña are opposite phases of the El Niño-Southern Oscillation (ENSO) cycle, which involves a shift in tropical sea-level pressure between the Eastern and Western Hemispheres.

The National Oceanographic and Atmospheric Administration and other agencies monitor these events using satellites, weather balloons, and buoys in the Pacific Ocean. Numerical computer models of the ocean and atmosphere use these data to predict the onset and evolution of El Niño and La Niña.

DISASTERS

Some Notable Aircraft Disasters Since 1937

Source: National Transportation Safety Board; World Almanac research. As of Sept. 2013.

Particularly notable disasters are in bold. Asterisk (*) indicates number of deaths includes people on the ground.

Date	Aircraft	Site of accident	Deaths
1937, May 6	**German zeppelin Hindenburg**	**Burned at mooring, Lakehurst, NJ**	**36***
1944, Aug. 23	U.S. Air Force B-24 Liberator bomber	Hit school, Freckleton, England	61*
1945, July 28	U.S. Army B-25	Hit Empire State Building after getting lost in fog, New York, NY	14*
1952, Dec. 20	U.S. Air Force C-124	Crashed at Moses Lake, WA	87
1953, Mar. 3	**Canadian Pacific DH-106 Comet**	**Crashed on takeoff from Karachi, Pakistan; world's first fatal commercial passenger jet crash**	**11**
1953, June 18	U.S. Air Force C-124	Crashed, burned near Tokyo, Japan	129
1955, Oct. 6	United Airlines DC-4	Crashed in Medicine Bow Peak, WY	66
1955, Nov. 1	United Airlines DC-6	Bomb on board exploded near Longmont, CO	44¹
1956, June 20	Venezuelan Super Constellation	Crashed into Atlantic off Asbury Park, NJ	74
1956, June 30	TWA Super Const., United DC-7	Collided over Grand Canyon, AZ	128
1960, Dec. 16	United DC-8, TWA Super Const.	Collided over New York, NY, killing all 128 on planes, 6 on ground.	134*
1962, Mar. 16	Flying Tiger Super Constellation	Vanished in W Pacific en route to Philippines from Guam	107
1962, June 3	Air France Boeing 707	Crashed on takeoff from Paris, France	130
1962, June 22	Air France Boeing 707	Crashed in storm, Guadeloupe, French W Indies	113
1963, Feb. 1	Lebanese Middle East Airlines Vickers Viscount 754, Turkish Mil. Douglas C-47	Collided over Ankara, Turkey, killing all 17 on planes, 87 on ground	104*
1963, Nov. 29	Trans-Canada Air Lines DC-8	Crashed after takeoff from Montreal, QC, Canada.	118
1965, May 20	Pakistani Boeing 720	Crashed at airport in Cairo, Egypt	121
1966, Jan. 24	Air India Boeing 707	Crashed on Mont Blanc, France-Italy	117
1966, Feb. 4	All-Nippon Boeing 727	Plunged into Tokyo Bay, Japan	133
1966, Mar. 5	BOAC Boeing 707	Crashed into Mt. Fuji, Japan, after encountering severe turbulence	124
1966, Dec. 24	U.S. military-chartered CL-44	Crashed into village in S Vietnam	129*
1967, Apr. 20	Globe Air Bristol Britannia	Crashed on approach to airport, Nicosia, Cyprus.	126
1967, July 19	Piedmont Boeing 727, Cessna 310	Collided over Hendersonville, NC	82
1968, Apr. 20	S. African Airways Boeing 707	Crashed on takeoff from Windhoek, Namibia	122
1968, May 3	Braniff International Electra	Crashed in storm near Dawson, TX	85
1968, May 12	U.S. Air Force Lockheed C-130B	Hit by enemy mortar while evacuating Kham Duc Camp, S Vietnam	155
1969, Mar. 16	Venezuelan DC-9	Crashed after takeoff from Maracaibo, Venezuela	155²
1970, July 3	British-chartered DH-106 Comet	Crashed near Barcelona, Spain	112
1970, July 5	Air Canada DC-8	Crashed near Toronto Intl. Airport, ON, Canada	108
1970, Nov. 14	Southern Airways DC-9	Crashed into mountains near Huntington, WV	75³
1971, July 30	All-Nippon Boeing 727, Japan Air Force F-86 fighter	Collided over Morioka, Japan.	162⁴
1971, Sept. 4	Alaska Airlines Boeing 727	Crashed into mountain near Juneau, AK	111
1972, May 18	Aeroflot Antonov 10A	Wings separated from fuselage; crashed on approach to Kharkov, U.S.S.R.	122
1972, June 18	British European Airways Trident-1C	Crashed near A30 motorway after takeoff from London.	118
1972, Aug. 14	East German Ilyushin 62	Crashed on takeoff from East Berlin.	156
1972, Aug. 31	Aeroflot Ilyushin 18V	Crashed in field near Magnitogorsk, U.S.S.R.	101
1972, Oct. 1	Aeroflot Ilyushin 18V	Crashed into Black Sea, U.S.S.R.	109
1972, Oct. 13	Aeroflot Ilyushin 62	Crashed near Moscow, U.S.S.R.	174
1972, Dec. 3	Spanish-chartered Convair CV-990	Crashed on takeoff from Canary Islands, Spain.	155
1972, Dec. 29	Eastern Airlines Lockheed Tristar	Crashed on approach to Miami Intl. Airport, FL	99
1973, Jan. 22	Nigerian-chartered Boeing 707	Burst into flames upon landing at Kano Airport, Nigeria.	176
1973, Feb. 21	**Libyan Arab Boeing 727**	**Flew off course, shot down by Israeli fighter planes over Sinai Desert**	**108**
1973, Apr. 10	Invicta Airways Vickers Vanguard	Crashed during snowstorm on approach to Basel, Switzerland	108
1973, June 3	Soviet Supersonic Tu-144	Crashed near Goussainville, France	14⁵
1973, July 11	Varig Airlines (Brazil) Boeing 707	Crashed on approach to Orly Airport, Paris, France	123
1973, July 31	Delta Airlines DC-9	Crashed while attempting landing in fog, Logan Airport, Boston, MA	89
1973, Sept. 30	Aeroflot Tupolev 104B	Crashed after takeoff from Sverdlovsk, U.S.S.R.	108
1973, Oct. 13	Aeroflot Tupolev 104B	Crashed on approach to Moscow, U.S.S.R.	122
1973, Dec. 22	Royal Air Maroc SE 210 Caravelle VIN	Flew into side of a mountain near Tangier, Morocco	106
1974, Mar. 3	Turkish DC-10	Crashed in Ermenonville, near Paris, France.	346
1974, Apr. 22	Pan American Boeing 707	Crashed in Bali, Indonesia	107
1974, Apr. 27	Aeroflot Ilyushin 18V	Crashed after takeoff from Leningrad, U.S.S.R.	109
1974, Dec. 1	TWA Boeing 727	Crashed on approach in storm, Upperville, VA	92
1974, Dec. 4	Dutch-chartered DC-8	Crashed in storm near Colombo, Sri Lanka	191
1975, Apr. 4	U.S. Air Force Galaxy C-5A	First mission of Operation Babylift, bringing Vietnamese orphans to U.S., crashed on takeoff near Saigon.	155
1975, Apr. 4	Air Force Galaxy C-5A	Crashed on takeoff nr. Saigon, S Vietnam; carried orphans	172
1975, June 24	Eastern Airlines 727	Crashed in storm, JFK Airport, New York, NY	113
1975, Aug. 3	Alia Royal Jordanian Boeing 707	Hit mountainside in heavy fog near Agadir, Morocco.	188
1975, Aug. 20	Czechoslovakian Air Ilyushin 62	Crashed on approach to Damascus, Syria.	126
1976, Mar. 6	Aeroflot Ilyushin 18E	Crashed between Moscow, U.S.S.R., and Yerevan, Armenia	111
1976, Sept. 10	British Airways Trident; Yugoslavian DC-9	Collided near Zagreb, Yugoslavia	176
1976, Sept. 19	Turkish Boeing 727	Hit mountain in S Turkey	154
1976, Oct. 13	Lloyd Aero Boliviano Boeing 707	Crashed into soccer field after takeoff from Santa Cruz, Bolivia	91⁶
1977, Mar. 27	**KLM 747, Pan American 747**	**Collided on runway, Tenerife, Canary Islands, Spain; world's worst airline disaster**	**583**
1977, Nov. 19	TAP Portugal Boeing 727	Crashed in Madeira, Portugal.	131
1977, Dec. 4	Malaysian Airlines Boeing 737	Hijacked and forced to fly to Singapore, crashed near Johor Strait	100
1978, Jan. 1	Air India 747	Crashed into sea after takeoff from Bombay, India	213
1978, Sept. 25	Pacific SW Air Boeing 727, Cessna 172	Collided over San Diego, CA	144*
1978, Nov. 15	Indonesian-chartered DC-8	Crashed on approach to airport, Colombo, Sri Lanka	183
1979, May 25	**American Airlines DC-10**	**Crashed after takeoff from O'Hare Airport, Chicago, IL; highest death toll in U.S. aviation history**	**275***
1979, Aug. 11	Aeroflot/Moldova Tu-134, Aeroflot Tu-134	Collided over Ukraine	178
1979, Nov. 26	Pakistani Boeing 707	Crashed near Jidda, Saudi Arabia	156

Date	Aircraft	Site of accident	Deaths
1979, Nov. 28	Air New Zealand DC-10	Crashed into mountain after takeoff from Antarctica	257
1980, Mar. 14	PLL LOT Ilyushin 62	Crashed making emergency landing, Warsaw, Poland	87[7]
1980, Apr. 25	Dan-Air Services Boeing 727	Crashed into mountain, Tenerife, Canary Islands, Spain	146
1980, July 8	Aeroflot Tupolev 154B	Crashed after takeoff from Alma-Ata, U.S.S.R.	166
1980, Aug. 19	Saudi Arabian Tristar	Burned after emergency landing in Riyadh, Saudi Arabia	301
1981, Dec. 1	Inex Adria DC-9	Crashed into mountain on island of Corsica, France	180
1982, Jan. 13	Air Florida Boeing 737	Crashed into Potomac R. after takeoff from Washington, DC	78
1982, June 8	VASP (Brazil) Boeing 727	Crashed into mountain near Fortaleza, Brazil	137
1982, June 28	Aeroflot Yokovlev 42	Crashed near Mozyr, U.S.S.R.	132
1982, July 9	Pan Am Boeing 727	Crashed after takeoff from Kenner, LA, near New Orleans	153*
1983, July 11	Ecuadorean Boeing 737	Inexperienced pilot crashed into hill near Cuenca, Ecuador	119
1983, Sept. 1	**S. Korean Boeing 747**	**Shot down after violating Soviet airspace near Sakhalin; plane apparently misidentified**	**269**
1983, Sept. 23	Gulf Air Boeing 737	Bomb exploded in cargo hold over Mina Jebel Ali, U.A.E.	112
1983, Nov. 27	Avianca Boeing 747	Crashed near Barajas Airport, Madrid, Spain.	181
1984, Oct. 11	Aeroflot/East Siberia Tu-154	Crashed into vehicles on runway while landing in poor weather, Omsk, Russia.	178*
1985, Feb. 19	Spanish Boeing 727	Crashed into Mt. Oiz, Spain	148
1985, June 23	Air India Boeing 747	Crashed into Atlantic off Ireland after bomb detonated on board.	329
1985, July 10	Aeroflot Tupolev 154B	Crashed after takeoff from Uzbekistan, U.S.S.R.	200
1985, Aug. 2	Delta Air Lines L-1011	Crashed at Dallas-Ft. Worth Airport, TX.	135
1985, Aug. 12	**Japan Air Lines Boeing 747**	**Crashed into Mt. Ogura, Japan; world's worst single-plane disaster**	**520**
1985, Dec. 12	Arrow Air DC-8	Crashed after takeoff from Gander, NL, Canada	256[8]
1986, Mar. 31	Mexican Boeing 727	Crashed NW of Mexico City	167
1986, Aug. 31	Aeromexico DC-9, Piper PA-28	Collided over Cerritos, CA	82*
1987, May 9	Polish IL-62M	Crashed after takeoff from Warsaw, Poland.	183
1987, Aug. 16	Northwest Airlines MD-82	Crashed after takeoff from Romulus, MI.	156
1987, Nov. 28	S. African Boeing 747	Crashed into Indian Ocean near Mauritius.	159
1987, Nov. 29	Korean Air Boeing 707	Bomb planted by 2 N. Korean agents exploded while plane over Andaman Sea off Burma.	115
1988, Mar. 17	Colombian Boeing 707	Crashed into mountainside near Venezuela border	143
1988, July 3	**Iran Air Airbus A300**	**Misidentified as hostile aircraft, shot down by U.S. Navy warship Vincennes over Persian Gulf.**	**290**
1988, Oct. 19	Indian Airlines Boeing 737	Exploded after striking trees near runway, Ahmedabad, India	131
1988, Dec. 21	**Pan Am Boeing 747**	**Libyan agent planted bomb on board; exploded over Lockerbie, Scotland**	**270[9]**
1989, Feb. 8	U.S.-chartered Boeing 707	Crashed into mountain on Azores Isls., off Portugal	144
1989, June 7	Suriname DC-8	Crashed near Paramaribo Airport, Suriname	176
1989, July 19	United Airlines DC-10	Crashed on landing in Sioux City, IA	111
1989, Sept. 3	Cubana Aviacion Ilyushin 62M	Crashed on takeoff from Havana, Cuba.	171*
1989, Sept. 19	**UTA DC-10**	**Bomb exploded on board flight from Chad to France while over desert in Niger**	**170**
1989, Oct. 21	Honduran Boeing 727	Crashed into mountain near Tegucigalpa, Honduras.	131
1989, Nov. 27	Avianca Boeing 727	Bomb exploded on flight from Bogotá, Colombia.	107
1990, Jan. 25	Avianca Boeing 707	Crashed on landing at JFK Airport, New York, NY.	73
1990, Oct. 2	Xiamen Airlines Boeing 737	Hijacked after takeoff from Xiamen; collided with China Southern Airlines 757 on runway, Guangzhou, China	128
1991, May 26	Lauda-Air Boeing 767-300	Exploded over rural Thailand	223
1991, July 11	Nigerian DC-8	Crashed on landing at Jidda, Saudi Arabia	261
1991, Oct. 5	U.S. Air Force Lockheed C-130 Hercules	Crashed after takeoff from Jakarta, Indonesia	135*
1992, July 31	Thai Airbus A300-310	Crashed into mountain N of Kathmandu, Nepal.	113
1992, Sept. 26	Nigerian Air Force Lockheed C-130 Hercules	Transport full of military officers crashed near Lagos, Nigeria	158
1992, Sept. 28	Pakistan Intl. Air Airbus A300	Crashed into hillside near Kathmandu, Nepal	167
1992, Oct. 4	**El Al Boeing 747-200F**	**Crashed into 2 apartment bldgs., Amsterdam, Netherlands**	**120***
1992, Nov. 24	China Southern Airlines Boeing 737	Crashed on approach to Giulin, China	141
1992, Dec. 22	Libyan Arab Air Boeing 727	Collided with MiG-23 on approach to Tripoli, Libya	159
1993, Feb. 8	Iran Air Tu-154, Iranian Air Force jet	Collided after military jet took off from Tehran, Iran	131
1993, May 19	SAM Colombia Boeing 727	Crashed into mountain near Medellin, Colombia	132
1993, Nov. 20	Macedonian Yakovlev 42D	Crashed into mountain near Skopje, Macedonia	116
1994, Jan. 3	Aeroflot Tu-154	Crashed and exploded after takeoff from Irkutsk, Russia.	125*
1994, Apr. 26	China Airlines Airbus A300	Crashed on approach to Nagoya Airport, Japan	264
1994, June 6	China Northwest Airlines Tu-154	Crashed near Xian, China	160
1994, Sept. 8	USAir Boeing 737-300	Crashed near Pittsburgh Intl. Airport, Aliquippa, PA.	132
1994, Oct. 31	American Eagle ATR-72-210	Crashed in field near Roselawn, IN	68
1995, Dec. 18	Zairean Lockheed L-188C Electra	Overloaded charter crashed in Lunda Norte, Angola	141
1995, Dec. 20	American Airlines Boeing 757	Crashed into mountain N of Cali, Colombia	159
1996, Jan. 8	African Air Antonov-32 cargo plane	Crashed into a market in Kinshasa, Zaire; all deaths on ground	237*
1996, Feb. 6	Dominican Boeing 757	Crashed into Atlantic off Dominican Republic	189
1996, Feb. 29	Peruvian Boeing 737	Crashed into hillside near Arequipa, Peru	123
1996, Apr. 3	U.S. Air Force Boeing T-43A	Crashed into mountain near Dubrovnik, Croatia	35[10]
1996, May 11	ValuJet DC-9	Crashed into Florida Everglades after takeoff	110
1996, July 17	Trans World Airlines Boeing 747	Exploded and crashed into Atlantic off Long Island, NY.	230
1996, Aug. 29	Vnukovo Airlines Tu-154	Crashed into mountain on Arctic island of Spitsbergen	141
1996, Nov. 7	Nigerian Boeing 727	Crashed into lagoon SE of Lagos, Nigeria	144
1996, Nov. 12	**Saudi Arabian Boeing 747, Kazakh Ilyushin 76 cargo plane**	**Collided near New Delhi, India; world's worst midair collision**	**349**
1996, Nov. 23	Ethiopian Airlines Boeing 767	Hijacked, then crashed into Indian Ocean off the Comoros	127
1997, Aug. 6	Korean Air Boeing 747-300	Crashed into jungle on Guam on approach to airport.	228
1997, Sept. 26	Indonesian Airbus A300	Crashed near airport, Medan, Indonesia	234
1998, Feb. 16	China Airlines Airbus A300	Crashed on approach to airport in Taipei, Taiwan	203*
1998, Sept. 2	Swissair MD-11	Crashed into Atlantic off Nova Scotia, Canada	229

Date	Aircraft	Site of accident	Deaths
1999, Oct. 31	EgyptAir Boeing 767	Crashed off Nantucket, MA; result of deliberate actions by copilot, motives unknown	217
2000, Jan. 30	Kenya Airways Airbus A310	Crashed into Atlantic after takeoff from Abidjan, Ivory Coast	169
2000, Jan. 31	Alaska Airlines MD-83	Crashed into Pacific off coast of Southern CA	88
2000, Apr. 19	Air Philippines Boeing 737-200	Crashed on approach to airport, Davao, Philippines	131
2000, July 25	**Air France Concorde**	**Crashed into hotel after takeoff from Paris; world's first Concorde crash**	**113***
2000, Aug. 23	Gulf Air Airbus A320	Crashed into Persian Gulf on approach to airport in Bahrain	143
2001, July 3	Vladivostokavia Tu-154	Crashed on approach to airport, Irkutsk, Russia	145
2001, Sept. 11	**2 Boeing 767s, 2 Boeing 757s**	**September 11 terrorist attacks**	**265[11]**
2001, Oct. 8	Cessna 525A Citation, Scandinavian Airlines System (SAS) MD-87	Collided in heavy fog on takeoff from Milan, Italy	118*
2001, Nov. 12	**American Airlines Airbus A300**	**Crashed after takeoff from JFK Airport, New York, NY**	**265***
2002, Feb. 12	Iran Air Tours Tu-154	Crashed in Khorramabad, Iran	119
2002, Apr. 15	Air China Boeing 767	Crashed into mountainside in rain and fog on approach to airport, Pusan, S. Korea	129
2002, May 4	EAS Airlines BAC 1-11	Crashed shortly after takeoff from Kano, Nigeria	149
2002, May 7	China Northern Airlines MD-82	Plunged into sea, apparently after a passenger started fire in cabin, NE China	112
2002, May 25	China Airlines Boeing 747	Broke apart in midair, plunged into Taiwan Strait en route to Hong Kong airport	225
2002, July 27	**Ukraine Air Force Sukhoi Su-27**	**Crashed while performing, Lviv, Ukraine; world's worst air-show crash**	**77[12]**
2002, Aug. 19	Russian Mi-26 transport helicopter	Hit by Chechen missile near Grozny, Chechnya	127
2003, Jan. 8	Turkish Airlines British Aerospace RJ-100	Crashed on approach to airport in Diyarbakir, Turkey	75
2003, Feb. 19	Iranian Revolutionary Guard Ilyushin 76	Crashed into mountain near Kerman, Iran; passengers were Revolutionary Guard members	275
2003, May 26	Ukrain.-Medit. Airlines Yak-42	Crashed into mountain in fog approaching Trabzon, Turkey; passengers incl. Spanish peacekeepers returning from Afghan.	75
2003, July 8	Sudan Airways Boeing 737-200	Mechanical problems reported shortly after takeoff; crashed upon return to Port Sudan Airport	115
2003, Dec. 25	Union Transp. Africains Boeing 727	Overloading caused crash on takeoff from Cotonou, Benin	141
2004, Jan. 3	Flash Airlines Boeing 737-300	Crashed into Red Sea after takeoff from Sharm el-Sheik, Egypt	148
2004, Aug. 24	Volga-Aviaexpress Tu-134, Sibir Airlines Tu-154	2 planes that took off from Moscow crashed within minutes of each other; brought down by Chechen suicide bombers	90
2005, Aug. 14	Helios Airways Boeing 737-300	Crashed after air pressure failure on board, near Athens, Greece	121
2005, Aug. 16	West Caribbean Airways MD-82	Crashed after engine failure, near Machiques, Venezuela	160
2005, Sept. 5	Mandala Airlines Boeing 737-200	Crashed shortly after takeoff from Medan, Sumatra, Indonesia	145*
2005, Oct. 22	Bellview Airlines Boeing 737-200	Crashed during heavy electrical storm near Lagos, Nigeria	117
2005, Dec. 6	Islamic Rep. of Iran Air Force Lockheed C-130	Crashed into apartment building after reportedly attempting emergency landing back at airport, Tehran, Iran	116*
2005, Dec. 10	Sosoliso Airlines DC-9-30	Crashed during storm on approach to Port Harcourt, Nigeria	107
2006, May 3	Armavia Airbus A320	Crashed into Black Sea on approach to airport, Sochi, Russia	113
2006, July 9	S7 Airlines Airbus A310	Skidded off runway, crashed into concrete barrier after landing, Irkutsk, Russia	125
2006, Aug. 22	Pulkovo Aviation Tu-154	Crashed after encountering storm, near Donetsk, Ukraine	170
2006, Sept. 29	Gol Airlines Boeing 737	Crashed into Amazon jungle after midair collision with Embraer Legacy jet, Brazil	154
2007, May 5	Kenya Airways Boeing 737-800	Crashed shortly after takeoff from Douala, Cameroon	114
2007, July 17	TAM Airlines Airbus 320	Crashed into cargo depot, gas station after skidding off airport runway, São Paulo, Brazil	199*
2008, Aug. 20	Spanair Boeing-MD-82	Swerved off runway, caught fire on takeoff attempt, Madrid, Spain	154
2009, Feb. 12	Colgan Air Bombardier Dash 8 Q400	Crashed into house near airport, Buffalo, NY	50*
2009, June 1	**Air France Airbus A330**	**Plunged into Atlantic Ocean en route from Rio de Janeiro, Brazil, to Paris, France**	**228**
2009, June 29	Yemenia Airbus A310-300	Fell into Indian Ocean on approach to Moroni, Comoros	152
2009, July 15	Caspian Airlines Tupolev 154	Crashed after takeoff from Tehran, Iran	168
2010, Apr. 10	Polish Air Force Tupolev 154M	Crashed on approach to Smolensk Air Base, killing Polish Pres. Lech Kaczynski, his wife, and several members of parliament	96
2010, May 12	Afriqiyah Airways Airbus A330-200	Crashed short of runway in Tripoli, Libya	103
2010, May 22	Air India Express Boeing 737-800	Overran runway on landing at Mangalore, India	158
2010, July 28	Airblue Airbus 321-231	Crashed into Margalla Hills near Islamabad, Pakistan	152
2012, Apr. 20	Bhoja Airlines Boeing 737-236	Crashed on approach to airport in Islamabad, Pakistan	127
2012, June 3	Dana Air MD-83	Crashed into residential area of Lagos, Nigeria	163*

(1) Bomb was planted by Jack G. Graham in insurance plot to kill his mother, Daisie E. King, a passenger. (2) 84 on plane, 71 on ground killed. (3) Incl. 43 Marshall Univ. (WV) football players and coaches. (4) Fighter pilot parachuted to safety. (5) First supersonic plane crash; killed 8 on ground. (6) Crew of 3, 88 on ground killed. (7) Incl. 22 members of U.S. amateur boxing team. (8) Incl. 248 members of U.S. 101st Airborne Division. (9) Incl. 11 on ground. (10) Incl. U.S. Sec. of Commerce Ron Brown. (11) 4 planes were hijacked and crashed, with all on board killed (265, incl. 19 hijackers). American Airlines Flight 11, a Boeing 767-200, with 81 passengers, 11 crew, crashed into Tower 1 of World Trade Center (WTC); United Airlines Flight 175, a Boeing 767-200, with 56 passengers, 9 crew, crashed into Tower 2 of WTC; American Airlines Flight 77, a Boeing 757-200, with 58 passengers, 6 crew, crashed into Pentagon outside Washington, DC; United Airlines Flight 93, a Boeing 757-200, with 37 passengers, 7 crew, crashed near Shanksville, PA. The official death toll of 2,977 includes all those who perished on the ground at the Pentagon and the WTC, as well as those who died as many as 10 years later from pulmonary sarcoidosis, a lung disease caused by exposure to toxic dust created by the disaster. (12) The two pilots ejected to safety. All spectator deaths.

Crash Landing

Date: July 6, 2013. **Aircraft:** Boeing 777. **Location:** San Francisco Intl. Airport. **Fatalities:** 3.

Asiana Airlines Flight 214 from Seoul, South Korea, crashed while attempting to land at San Francisco Intl. Airport. The aircraft's landing gear hit a sea wall before the runway and broke off, and a ruptured oil tank caused the fuselage to burst into flames after the crash. Three people were killed, and more than 180 of the 307 people onboard were injured. It was the first commercial airline crash in the U.S. in more than four years. Less than 24 hours later, an air taxi crashed in Soldotna, Alaska, killing the pilot and all nine passengers.

Some Notable Shipwrecks Since 1854

Figures are estimated deaths. Does not include most wartime disasters.

Date—vessel(s)	Incident	Deaths
1854, Mar. 1—City of Glasgow	British steamer left Liverpool for Philadelphia, never heard from again	480
1854, Sept. 27—Arctic and Vesta	U.S. Collins Line steamer sunk in collision with French steamer nr. Cape Race, Canada	285-351
1856, Jan. 23—Pacific	U.S. Collins Line steamer went missing in N Atlantic	186-286
1857, Sept. 12—Central America	U.S. mail steamship sank off Florida coast with $1.5 mil in gold	427
1858, Sept. 23—Austria	German steamer destroyed by fire in N Atlantic	471
1863, Apr. 27—Anglo-Saxon	British steamer wrecked at Cape Race, Canada	238
1865, Apr. 27—Sultana	Mississippi R. steamer carrying 2,300 released Civil War prisoners exploded nr. Memphis, TN. Worst maritime disaster in U.S. history	1,700+
1869, Feb. 20—Radetzky	Austrian steam frigate exploded in Adriatic Sea	345
1869, Oct. 27—Stonewall	U.S. steamer burned, Mississippi R. below Cairo, IL	200
1872, Nov. 7—Mary Celeste	U.S. half-brig sailing from New York to Genoa, Italy, found abandoned	Unknown
1873, Jan. 22—Northfleet	British steamer rammed by Spanish steamer Murillo off Dungeness, England	300
1873, Apr. 1—Atlantic	British White Star steamer off Halifax, Nova Scotia, Canada	585
1873, Nov. 23—Ville du Havre and Loch Earn	French steamer sank after collision with British sailing ship	226
1874, Nov. 17—Cospatrick	Burned off Auckland, New Zealand	468
1875, May 7—Schiller	German steamer off Scilly Isles, UK	312
1875, Nov. 4—Pacific	U.S. steamer sank after collision off Cape Flattery, WA	236
1878, Mar. 24—Eurydice	British frigate sank off Isle of Wight, England	398
1878, Sept. 3—Princess Alice	British steamer sank after collision with Bywell Castle in Thames R.	700
1878, Dec. 12—Byzantin and Rinaldo	French and British steamers collided in Dardanelles, off Turkey	210
1883, Jan. 19—Cimbria and Sultan	German steamer sank in collision with British steamer in North Sea	389
1887, Nov. 15—Wah Yeung	Chinese steamer burned in Canton R., Hong Kong	400
1890, Feb. 17—Duburg	British steamer wrecked, China Sea	400
1890, Sept. 19—Ertogrul	Turkish frigate off Japan	540
1891, Mar. 17—Utopia and Anson	British steamer sank in collision with British ironclad off Gibraltar	562
1893, June 22—Victoria	British battleship sank after collision with warship Camperdown, off Syrian coast	358
1895, Jan. 30—Elbe and Craithie	German steamer sank in collision with British steamer in North Sea	332
1895, Mar. 11—Reina Regenta	Spanish cruiser foundered nr. Gibraltar	400
1898, Feb. 15—USS Maine	Explosion caused battleship to sink in Havana Harbor, Cuba	260
1898, July 4—La Bourgogne and Cromartyshire	French steamer sank in collision with British sailing ship off Nova Scotia, Canada	549
1904, May 15—Yoshino	Japanese cruiser sank after collision with cruiser Kasuga in fog off Liao-Tung Peninsula, China	329
1904, June 15—General Slocum	Excursion steamer burned off N. Brother Isl., New York, NY	1,021
1904, June 28—Norge	Danish steamer wrecked on Rockall Isl., Scotland	620
1906, Aug. 4—Sirio	Italian steamer wrecked off Cape Palos, Spain	350
1907, Feb. 11—Larchmont	U.S. steamer sank after collision with U.S. schooner Harry Knowlton nr. Block Island, RI	131
1908, Mar. 23—Mutsu Maru	Japanese steamer sank in collision with another steamer nr. Hakodate, Japan	300
1909, Aug. 1—Waratah	British steamer vanished en route from Sydney to London	300
1911, Sept. 25—Liberté	French battleship exploded at Toulon	285
1912, Apr. 14-15—Titanic	British White Star steamer hit iceberg in N Atlantic	1,503
1912, Sept. 28—Kichemaru	Japanese steamer sank off Japan coast	1,000
1914, May 29—Empress of Ireland	Canadian Pacific steamer collided with Norwegian coal transporter Storstad in St. Lawrence R., Canada	1,014
1914, Nov. 26—Bulwark	British battleship exploded in Sheerness Harbor, England	788
1915, May 7—Lusitania	British Cunard Line steamer torpedoed and sunk by German submarine off Ireland	1,198
1915, July 24—Eastland	Steamer capsized, Chicago R., IL	844
1916, Feb. 26—Provence	French cruiser sank in Mediterranean; then-worst disaster in maritime history	3,100
1916, Mar. 5—Principe de Asturias	Spanish steamer wrecked nr. Santos, Brazil	558
1917, Dec. 6—Mont Blanc and Imo	French ammunition ship and Belgian steamer collided in Halifax Harbor, Canada	1,600
1918, Apr. 25—Kiang-Kwan	Chinese steamer sank after collision with Chinese gunboat Chutai off Hankow, China	500
1918, July 12—Kawachi	Japanese battleship blew up in Tokayama Bay	500
1918, Oct. 25—Princess Sophia	Canadian-Pacific steamer sank off Vanderbilt Reef, Alaska	398
1919, Jan. 17—Chaonia	French steamer lost in Straits of Messina, Italy	460
1919, Sept. 9—Valbanera	Spanish steamer lost off FL coast	500
1920, Jan. 11—Afrique	French liner sank nr. La Rochelle, France	553
1921, Mar. 18—Hong Kong	Chinese steamer wrecked, S China Sea	1,000
1922, Aug. 26—Niitaka	Japanese cruiser sank in storm off Kamchatka, USSR	300
1927, Sept. 20—Gentoku Maru	Japanese steamer capsized in Tsingtao Bay, China	278
1927, Oct. 25—Principessa Mafalda	Italian steamer blew up, sank off Porto Seguro, Brazil	314
1934, Sept. 8—Morro Castle	U.S. steamer en route from Havana to New York, burned off Asbury Park, NJ	134
1940, June 17—Lancastria	Nazi forces sank Cunard liner evacuating British troops from France	2,500-6,000
1940, July 24—Meknes	French liner torpedoed by Nazis in English Channel	350
1942, Feb. 18—USS Truxtun and USS Pollux	Destroyer and cargo ship ran aground, sank off Newfoundland, Canada	204
1942, Oct. 2—Curacao and Queen Mary	British cruiser sank off Ireland after collision with liner carrying U.S. troops	338
1944, Dec. 17-18—Spence, Monaghan, Hull	3 U.S. destroyers sank during typhoon, Philippine Sea	790
1945, Jan. 30—Wilhelm Gustloff	Liner with German refugees, soldiers sunk by Soviet submarine in Baltic	5,000-9,000
1945, Apr. 16—Goya	Cargo ship carrying German refugees, soldiers sunk by Soviet submarine in Baltic	6,000-7,000
1945, May 3—Cap Arcona and Thielbeck	German liners carrying concentration camp inmates sunk by British warplanes in Lubeck Bay, Germany	7,000-8,000

Date—vessel(s)	Incident	Deaths
1947, Jan. 19—Himera	Greek steamer hit mine off Athens, Greece	392
1947, Apr. 16—Grandcamp	Ammonium nitrate explosion aboard French freighter caused fires throughout port, Texas City, TX	576+
1948, Dec. 3—Kiangya	Chinese refugee ship wrecked in explosion S of Shanghai	1,100+
1954, Sept. 26—Toya Maru	Japanese ferry sank, Tsugaru Strait, Japan	1,172
1956, July 26—Andrea Doria and Stockholm	Italian liner and Swedish liner collided off Nantucket Isl., MA	51
1957, July 14—Eshghabad	Soviet fishing boat ran aground in Caspian Sea	270
1961, Apr. 8—Dara	British liner exploded in Persian Gulf	236
1961, July 8—Save	Portuguese ship ran aground off Mozambique	259
1965, Nov. 13—Yarmouth Castle	Cruise ship burned and sank off Nassau, Bahamas	89
1970, Dec. 15—Namyong-Ho	S. Korean ferry sank in Korea Strait	308
1975, Nov. 10—Edmund Fitzgerald	U.S. cargo ship sank during storm on Lake Superior	29
1980, Apr. 22—Don Juan	Sank off Mindoro Isl., Philippines, after colliding with barge	1,000+
1981, Jan. 27—Tamponas II	Indonesian car ferry caught fire and sank in Java Sea	580
1983, May 25—10th of Ramadan	Nile steamer caught fire and sank in Lake Nasser, Egypt	357
1986, May 25—Shamia	Ferry capsized in storm, Meghna R., Bangladesh	500+
1986, Sept. 1—Admiral Nakhimov and Pyotr Vasev	Soviet cruise ship collided with Soviet freighter in Black Sea	425
1987, Dec. 20—Doña Paz and Victor	Philippine ferry and oil tanker collided in Tablas Strait, Philippines	4,341
1988, Aug. 6	Indian ferry capsized on Ganges R.	400+
1988, Oct. 24—Doña Marilyn	Philippine ferry sank by typhoon near Leyte Isl.	350+
1991, Dec. 14—Salem Express	Ferry rammed coral reef nr. Safaga, Egypt	462
1993, Feb. 17—Neptune	Ferry capsized off Port-au-Prince, Haiti	500+
1993, Oct. 10—Seohae	S. Korean ferry capsized in Yellow Sea during storm	292
1994, Sept. 28—Estonia	Ferry sank in Baltic Sea off Finland	850+
1996, May 21—Bukoba	Overcrowded Tanzanian ferry sank in Lake Victoria	500+
1997, Sept. 8—Pride of la Gonâve	Haitian ferry sank off Montrouis, Haiti	200+
1999, Feb. 6—Harta Rimba	Cargo ship sank off Indonesia	280+
1999, May 1—Miss Majestic	"Duck" boat on tour sank, Lake Hamilton, AR	13
1999, Nov. 24—Dashun	Passenger ferry capsized nr. Yantai, China.	280
2000, June 29—Cahaya Bahari	Overloaded ferry carrying refugees from religious strife capsized in storm off Sulawesi Isl., Indonesia	500+
2001, Oct. 19	Fishing boat overloaded with refugees, mainly from Middle East, sank off Indonesia	350+
2002, May 4—Salahuddin-2	Overloaded Bangladesh ferry sank in Meghna R.	300+
2002, Sept. 26—Joola	Overloaded Senegalese ferry capsized in ocean off The Gambia	1,863
2003, July 8—MV-Nasrin 1	Overcrowded ferry sank nr. Chandpur in Bangladesh R.	400
2003, Oct. 15—Andrew J. Barberi	NYC ferry crashed into dock on approach to Staten Island	11
2006, Feb. 3—Al-Salam Boccaccio 98	Ferry caught fire, sank in Red Sea off Egypt	1,000+
2006, Dec. 30—Senopati Nusantara	High waves capsized ferry en route to Java, Indonesia	400+
2007, Nov. 23—Explorer	Canadian cruise ship hit Antarctic iceberg; first commercial passenger ship to sink in region	0
2008, June 23—Princess of the Stars	Philippine ferry capsized during Typhoon Fengshen nr. Manila	800
2011, Sept. 10—MV Spice Islander	Overloaded ferry sank off coast of Tanzania.	240+
2012, Jan 17—Costa Concordia	Cruise ship ran aground off Italian coast; captain abandoned ship before passengers	32

Some Notable Railroad Disasters Since 1925

Date	Location	Deaths	Date	Location	Deaths
1925, June 16	Hackettstown, NJ	50	1981, June 6	Bihar, India	800+
1933, Dec. 23	Lagny-Pomponne, France	230	1982, Jan. 27	El Asnam, Algeria	130
1938, June 19	Saugus, MT	47	1982, July 11	Tepic, Mexico	120
1939, Dec. 22	Near Magdeburg, Germany	132	1983, Feb. 19	Empalme, Mexico	100
1939, Dec. 22	Near Friedrichshafen, Germany	99	1985, Jan. 14	Awash, Ethiopia	392
1940, July 31	Cuyahoga Falls, OH	43	1987, July 2	Kasumbalesha Shaba, Zaire	125
1943, Sept. 6	Frankford Junction, Philadelphia, PA	79	1987, Aug. 6	U.S.S.R.	106
1943, Dec. 16	Between Rennert and Buie, NC	72	1988, June 4	Arzamas, U.S.S.R.	100
1944, Jan. 16	León Province, Spain	500	1988, June 27	Gare de Lyon train station, Paris	57
1944, Mar. 2	Salerno, Italy	521	1988, July 8	Kerala, India	108
1944, Aug. 4	Near Stockton, GA	47	1989, Jan. 15	Maizdi Khan, Bangladesh	110+
1944, Dec. 31	Bagley, UT	50	1989, June 4	Ufa, U.S.S.R.	645
1946, Mar. 20	Aracaju, Mexico	185	1989, Aug. 11	Sinaloa, Mexico	112
1946, Apr. 25	Naperville, IL	45	1990, Jan. 4	Sindh Province, Pakistan	210+
1949, Oct. 22	Near Dwor, Poland	200+	1991, Sept. 5	Near Pointe Noir, Congo	110
1950, Nov. 22	Richmond Hill, NY	79	1993, Jan. 30	Train fell into river, rural Kenya	140+
1951, Feb. 6	Woodbridge, NJ	84	1993, Sept. 22	Big Bayou Conot, AL	47
1952, Mar. 4	Near Rio de Janeiro, Brazil	119	1994, Dec. 30	Near Namkham, Myanmar	102
1952, July 9	Rzepin, Poland	160	1994, Sept. 22	Tolunda, Angola	300
1952, Oct. 8	Harrow, England	112	1995, Aug. 20	Firozabad, India	358
1953, Dec. 24	Tangiwai, New Zealand	151	1995, Dec. 21	Near Badrasheen, Egypt	75
1953, Dec. 24	Sakvice, Czechoslovakia	103	1997, Mar. 3	Punjab Province, Pakistan	125
1955, Apr. 3	Guadalajara, Mexico	300	1997, May 4	Kisangani, Zaire	100+
1957, Sept. 1	Kendal, Jamaica	178	1997, Sept. 14	Madhya Pradesh state, India	77
1957, Sept. 29	Montgomery, W Pakistan	250	1998, Feb. 19	Yaounde, Cameroon	100+
1957, Dec. 4	London, England	90	1998, June 3	Eschede, Germany	102
1958, May 8	Rio de Janeiro, Brazil	128	1998, Nov. 26	Khanna, India	200+
1958, Sept. 15	Elizabethport, NJ	48	1999, Aug. 2	Gauhati, India	285+
1962, May 3	Tokyo, Japan	163	2000, Nov. 11	Kaprun, Austria	155
1963, Nov. 9	Yokohama, Japan	120+	2002, Feb. 20	S of Cairo, Egypt	373
1970, Feb. 1	Buenos Aires, Argentina	236	2002, May 25	Muamba, Mozambique	196+
1972, June 16	Vierzy, France	107	2002, June 24	Igandu, Tanzania	281+
1972, Oct. 6	Saltillo, Mexico	208	2002, Sept. 10	Bihar, India	118
1972, Oct. 30	Chicago, IL	45	2004, Feb. 18	Neyshabur, NE Iran	300+
1974, Aug. 30	Zagreb, Yugoslavia	153	2004, Apr. 22	Ryongchon, N. Korea	161

Date	Location	Deaths	Date	Location	Deaths
2005, Apr. 25	Near Amagasaki, Japan	107+	2010, May 28	W Bengal, India	148
2005, July 13	Ghotki, Pakistan	133	2011, July 23	Wenzhou, China	40
2005, Oct. 29	Near Veligonda, India	114+	2013, July 6	Lac-Megantic, Quebec, Canada	47
2007, Aug. 2	Near Benaleka, Dem. Rep. of Congo	70+	2013, July 24	Near Santiago de Compostela, Spain	79
2008, Sept. 12	Los Angeles, CA	25			

Principal U.S. Mine Disasters Since 1900

Source: Bureau of Mines, U.S. Dept. of the Interior; Mine Safety and Health Admin., U.S. Dept. of Labor; World Almanac research
All are bituminous coal mines unless otherwise noted.

Date	Location	Deaths	Date	Location	Deaths	Date	Location	Deaths
1900, May 1	Scofield, UT	200	1913, Oct. 22	Dawson, NM	263	1940, Mar. 16	St. Clairesville, OH	72
1902, May 19	Coal Creek, TN	184	1914, Apr. 28	Eccles, WV	181	1942, Mar. 26	Allentown, PA[4]	31
1902, July 10	Johnstown, PA	112	1915, Mar. 2	Layland, WV	115	1943, Feb. 27	Washoe, MT	74
1903, June 30	Hanna, WY	169	1917, Apr. 27	Hastings, CO	121	1947, Mar. 25	Centralia, IL	111
1904, Jan. 25	Cheswick, PA	179	1917, June 8	Butte, MT[1]	163	1951, Dec. 21	West Frankfort, IL.	119
1905, Feb. 20	Virginia City, AL	112	1919, June 5	Wilkes-Barre, PA[2]	92	1968, Mar. 6	Belle Isle, LA[5]	21
1907, Jan. 29	Stuart, WV	84	1922, Nov. 6	Spangler, PA	79	1968, Nov. 20	Farmington, WV	78
1907, Dec. 6	Monongah, WV	362	1922, Nov. 22	Dolomite, AL	90	1970, Dec. 30	Hyden, KY	38
1907, Dec. 19	Jacobs Creek, PA.	239	1923, Feb. 8	Dawson, NM	120	1972, May 2	Kellogg, ID[6]	91
1908, Nov. 28	Marianna, PA	154	1923, Aug. 14	Kemmerer, WY	99	1976, Mar. 9	Oven Fork, KY	15
1909, Nov. 13	Cherry, IL	259	1924, Mar. 8	Castle Gate, UT	172	1981, Apr. 15	Redstone, CO.	15
1910, Jan. 31	Primero, CO	75	1924, Apr. 28	Benwood, WV	119	1981, Dec. 8	Whitwell, TN	13
1910, May 5	Palos, AL	84	1926, Jan. 13	Wilburton, OK	91	1984, Dec. 19	Orangeville, UT.	27
1910, Nov. 8	Delagua, CO	79	1926, Nov. 3	Ishpeming, MI[3]	51	1989, Sept. 13	Wheatcroft, KY	10
1911, Apr. 8	Littleton, AL	128	1927, Apr. 30	Everettville, WV	97	2001, Sept. 23	Brookwood, AL	13
1911, Dec. 9	Briceville, TN	84	1928, May 19	Mather, PA	195	2006, Jan. 2	Buckhannon, WV	12
1912, Mar. 26	Jed, WV	81	1930, Nov. 5	Millfield, OH	82	2010, Apr. 5	Montcoal, WV	29
1913, Apr. 23	Finleyville, PA	98	1940, Jan. 10	Bartley, WV.	91			

Note: The world's worst mine disaster killed 1,549 workers in Manchuria, China, Apr. 25, 1942. (1) Copper mine. (2) Anthracite mine. (3) Iron mine. (4) Limestone mine. (5) Salt mine. (6) Silver mine.

Some Notable U.S. Tornadoes Since 1925

Date	Location	Deaths	Date	Location	Deaths
1925, Mar. 18	MO, IL, IN.	747	1973, May 26-27	South, Midwest.	47
1927, Apr. 12	Rocksprings, TX.	74	1974, Apr. 3-4	AL; GA; KY; Xenia, OH; other states	315
1927, May 9	AR; Poplar Bluff, MO	92	1977, Apr. 4	AL, MS, GA	22
1927, Sept. 29	St. Louis, MO	90	1979, Apr. 10	TX, OK.	60
1930, May 6	Hill, Navarro, Ellis Cos., TX	41	1984, Mar. 28	NC, SC	57
1932, Mar. 21	Alabama	268	1985, May 31	NY; PA; OH; Ontario, Can.	75
1936, Apr. 5-6	Tupelo, MS; Gainesville, GA	454	1987, May 22	Saragosa, TX.	30
1938, Sept. 29	Charleston, SC.	32	1989, Nov. 15	Huntsville, AL.	18
1942, Mar. 16	Central to NE Mississippi	75	1990, Aug. 28	Northern IL.	25
1942, Apr. 27	Rogers and Mayes Cos., OK.	52	1991, Apr. 26	KS, OK	23
1944, June 23	OH, PA, WV, MD	150	1992, Nov. 21-23	South, Midwest.	26
1945, Apr. 12	OK, AR.	102	1994, Mar. 27-28	AL, TN, GA, NC, SC.	52
1947, Apr. 9	TX; Woodward, OK; KS.	181	1995, May 6-7	S Oklahoma, N Texas.	23
1948, Mar. 19	Bunker Hill and Gillespie, IL.	33	1997, Mar. 1	Central AR.	26
1949, Jan. 3	LA, AR.	58	1997, May 27	Jarrell, TX.	27
1952, Mar. 21-22	AR, MO, TN.	208	1998, Feb. 22-23	Central FL.	42
1953, May 11	Waco, TX.	114	1998, Apr. 8	AL, GA, MS.	39
1953, June 8	Flint-Beecher, MI; OH	142	1999, May 3	OK, KS.	54
1953, June 9	Worcester and vicinity, MA	90	2000, Feb. 14	SW Georgia.	22+
1953, Dec. 5	Vicksburg, MS	38	2002, Nov. 10-11	AL, MS, TN, IN, OH, PA.	36
1955, May 25	Udall, KS; MO; Blackwell, OK; TX.	115	2003, May 4-11	TN, MO, KS, IL, OK, WV, AL.	48
1957, May 20	KS, MO.	48	2005, Nov. 6	KY, IN	22
1958, June, 4	NW Wisconsin	30	2007, Mar. 1	AL, GA, MO, Midwest	20
1959, Feb. 10	St. Louis, MO	21	2008, Feb. 25	"Super Tuesday"—TN, AR, KY,	
1960, May 5-6	Southeastern OK, AR	30		AL, MO	57
1962, Mar. 31	Milton, FL	17	2008, May 10	MS, OK, GA.	23
1965, Apr. 11	IA, IN, IL, OH, MI, WI.	271	2011, Apr. 14-16	Southeast, Midwest U.S., OK to VA.	38
1966, Mar. 3	Jackson, MS; AL	57	2011, Apr. 25-28	305 funnels from TX to NY	321
1967, Apr. 21	IL, MO, IA, MI.	33	2011, May 22	Joplin, MO.	161
1968, May 15	Midwest	71	2012, Mar. 2-3	IL, IN, KY, OH, AL	42
1969, Jan. 23	Mississippi	32	2013, May 20	Moore, OK.	24
1970, May 11	Lubbock, TX.	23	2013, May 31	El Reno, OK.	21
1971, Feb. 21	Mississippi Delta: MS, LA, AR, TN.	110			

The Widest Tornado in History

Date: May 31, 2013. **Location:** El Reno, OK.
Fatalities: 21. **Damages:** $30 mil (est.).

Most tornadoes range in width between a half-mile and three-quarters of a mile. The May 31 twister that blew through El Reno, OK, was a record-breaking 2.6 mi wide (about as wide as the island of Manhattan) and cut a 16.2-mi path. That made it exponentially more powerful than a typical tornado. Luckily, the tornado did not hit any major population centers, limiting both casualties and damages. Eight people—including three storm-chasers—were directly killed by the tornado; the remaining 13 were killed by flash floods caused by the accompanying very large hail and heavy rains.

Some Notable Hurricanes, Typhoons, Blizzards, Other Storms

C. = cyclone; H. = hurricane; TS. = tropical storm; T. = typhoon[1].

Date	Location	Deaths	Date	Location	Deaths
1881, Aug. 24-29	H., GA, SC	700	1990, May 6-11	C. (mult.), SE India	450
1888, Mar. 11-14	Blizzard, Eastern U.S.	400	1991, Apr. 30	C., Bangladesh	139,000
1893, Aug. 15-Sept. 2	H., GA, SC	1,000+	1991, Nov. 5	TS. Thelma, flash floods, central Philippines	7,000+
1893, Oct. 1	H., LA	1,100+	1992, Aug. 24-26	H. Andrew, Southern FL, LA.	65
1900, Sept. 8	H., Galveston, TX	8,000+	1993, Mar. 12-14	Blizzard, Eastern U.S.	270+
1906, Sept. 18	T., Hong Kong	10,000+	1993, June	Monsoon, Bangladesh	2,000
1906, Sept. 19-24	H., LA, MS	350	1994, Nov. 8-18	TS. Gordon, Caribbean, FL	830
1909, Sept. 20	H., LA	350+	1995, Oct. 2-4	H. Opal, S Mexico, FL, AL	59
1915, Aug. 16	H., Galveston, TX	275	1995, Nov. 2-3	T. Angela, Philippines	600+
1915, Sept. 29	H., LA	275	1996, Jan. 7-8	Blizzard, NE U.S.	100
1919, Sept. 6-14	H., Carib., FL Keys, Gulf, TX	600+[2]	1996, Aug. 22	Blizzard, Himalayas, N India.	239
1922, July 27	T. Swatow, China	100,000	1996, Aug. 29-Sept. 6	H. Fran, Carib., NC, VA, WV	30
1926, Sept. 11-22	H., FL, AL, MS	370+	1996, Sept. 9	T. Sally, S China.	114
1926, Oct. 20	H., Cuba	600	1996, Nov. 6	C., Andhra Pradesh, India	1,000+
1928, Sept. 6-20	H., southern FL.	2,500+	1996, Dec. 25	TS. Greg, Eastern Malaysia	100+
1930, Sept. 3	H., Dominican Republic	2,000	1997, May 19	C., Bangladesh	108
1935, Aug. 29-Sept. 10	H., "Labor Day Hurricane," Caribbean, SE U.S.	400+	1997, Aug. 18-21	T. Winnie, Taiwan, E China	140+
1937, Sept. 2	T., "The Great Typhoon," Hong Kong	10,000+	1997, Oct. 8-10	H. Pauline, SW Mexico.	230
1938, Sept. 21	H., "Long Isl. Express," NY, New England	682	1998, June 9	C., Gujarat, India	1,320
1940, Nov. 11-12	"Armistice Day Blizzard," NE, Midwest U.S.	154	1998, Aug.	Monsoon, Bangladesh	326
1942, Oct.	T., W. Sundarbans, Bangladesh	61,000	1998, Sept. 21-23	H. Georges, Carib., FL, U.S. Gulf	600+
1942, Oct. 15-16	H., Bengal, India	40,000	1998, Oct. 27-29	H. Mitch, Honduras, Nicaragua, Guatemala, El Salvador	14,600
1947, Dec. 26	Blizzard, NYC, N Atl. states	55	1999, Sept. 4-17	H. Floyd, Bahamas, E seaboard U.S.	56
1952, Oct. 22	T., Philippines	440	1999, Oct. 29	C., E India.	9,392
1954, Aug. 30	H. Carol, northeastern U.S.	68	1999, Dec. 26-29	Gales, France, Switz., Germany	120
1954, Oct. 5-18	H. Hazel, E Canada, U.S., Haiti	347	2000, Dec. 27	Winter storm, TX, OK, AR	40+
1955, Aug. 7-21	H. Diane, Eastern U.S.	400	2001, July 30	T. Toraji, Taiwan.	200
1955, Sept. 19	H. Hilda, Mexico	200	2001, Nov. 6-12	T. Lingling, S Philip., Vietnam.	220+
1956, Feb. 1-29	Blizzard, W Europe	1,000	2002, Aug.-Sept.	T. Rusa, N. and S. Korea	115+
1957, June 25-30	H. Audrey, TX to AL	390	2003, Feb. 16-17	Blizzard, E seaboard U.S.	59
1958, Feb. 15-16	Blizzard, NE U.S.	171	2003, Sept. 7-19	H. Isabel, NC, VA, E seaboard..	40+
1959, Sept. 17-19	T. Sarah, Japan, S. Korea	2,000	2003, Sept. 12	T. Maemi, S. Korea.	130
1959, Sept. 26-27	T. Vera, Honshu, Japan	4,466	2004, Mar. 7-19	C. Gafilo, Madagascar	198
1960, Sept. 4-12	H. Donna, Caribbean, E U.S..	148	2004, May 19	C., Myanmar.	220
1961, Oct. 31	H. Hattie, Brit. Honduras.	400	2004, Aug. 12-15	T. Rananim, Eastern China	164
1962, Sept. 1	T. Wanda, Hong Kong	130-200	2004, Aug. 13-14	H. Charley, FL, SC	36
1963, May 28-29	Windstorm, Bangladesh	22,000	2004, Sept. 5-6	H. Frances, Bahamas, FL.	35
1963, Oct. 4-8	H. Flora, Caribbean	6,000	2004, Sept. 7-16	H. Ivan, Barbados, Grenada, U.S. Gulf Coast.	115
1964, June 30	T. Winnie, N Philippines	107	2004, Sept. 16-26	H. Jeanne, Dom. Rep., Haiti, FL	1,500+
1964, Sept. 5	T. Ruby, Hong Kong, China	735	2005, July 7-11	H. Dennis, Jamaica, Haiti, Cuba, FL.	50
1965, May 11-12	Windstorm, Bangladesh	17,000	2005, Aug. 25-29	H. Katrina, LA, MS, FL, AL, GA	1,833+[3]
1965, June 1-2	Windstorm, Bangladesh	30,000	2005, Aug. 31-Sept. 1	T. Talim, Taiwan, E China	129+
1965, Sept. 7-12	H. Betsy, FL, MS, LA	74	2005, Sept. 21-24	H. Rita, TX, LA	62[4]
1965, Dec. 15	Windstorm, Bangladesh	10,000	2005, Sept. 21-28	T. Damrey, SE Asia; Philippines; Hainan, China.	145
1966, June 4-10	H. Alma, Honduras, SE U.S.	51	2005, Oct. 4	H. Stan, Central Amer., Mex.	1,000+[5]
1966, Sept. 24-30	H. Inez, Carib., FL, Mexico	293	2006, Jul. 14	TS. Bilis, SE China	612
1967, July 9	T. Billie, SW Japan	347	2006, Aug. 10	T. Saomai, SE China	295
1967, Sept. 5-23	H. Beulah, Carib., Mex., TX	54	2006, Nov. 30	T. Durian, Philippines	450-1,000+
1967, Dec. 12-20	Blizzard, SW U.S.	51	2007, June 6-7	C. Gonu, Oman, Iran	54[6]
1969, Aug. 17-18	H. Camille, MS, LA	256	2007, Nov. 15	C. Sidr, Southern Bangladesh	3,363
1970, Sept. 15	T. Georgia, Philippines	300	2008, May 2-3	C. Nargis, Southern Myanmar	138,366
1970, Oct. 14	T. Sening, Philippines	583	2008, June 20-25	T. Fengshen, Philippines, China	233
1970, Oct. 15	T. Titang, Philippines	526	2008, Aug. 26-Sept. 1	H. Gustav, Haiti, Dom. Rep., U.S.	138
1970, Nov. 12	C., Bay of Bengal, Bangladesh	300,000	2008, Sept. 1-4	TS. Hanna, Haiti	529
1971, Aug. 1	T. Rose, Hong Kong	130	2008, Sept. 7-13	H. Ike, Haiti; Cuba; Galveston, TX	164
1972, June 19-29	H. Agnes, FL to NY.	118	2009, May 23-26	C. Alia, India, Bangladesh	260
1972, Dec. 3	T. Theresa, Philippines	169	2009, Aug. 7-9	T. Morakot, mudslides, Taiwan	700+
1973, June-Aug.	Monsoon rains, India	1,217	2009, Sept. 23-30	T. Ketsana, Philippines, Vietnam, Cambodia, Laos	498+
1974, July 11	T. Gilda, Japan, S. Korea	108	2009, Oct. 3-10	T. Parma, Philippines	375
1974, Sept. 19-20	H. Fifi, Honduras.	2,000	2009, Oct. 30-Nov. 3	T. Mirinae, Philippines, Vietnam	159+
1975, Sept. 13-27	H. Eloise, Caribbean, NE U.S.	71	2009, Dec. 11-22	Snowstorms, central Europe	90+
1976, May 20	T. Olga, floods, Philippines	215	2010, Apr. 13	C., India, Bangladesh	137
1976, Sept. 25-Oct. 2	H. Liza, Western Mexico	630	2010, May 29	TS. Agatha, Guatemala, El Salvador, Honduras	184
1978, Oct. 27	T. Rita, Philippines	400	2010, July 13-17	T. Conson, Luzon Isl., Philippines	105+
1979, Aug. 30-Sept. 7	H. David, Caribbean, E U.S.	1,100	2011, Dec. 16	TS. Washi, Philippines	1,257
1980, Aug. 4-11	H. Allen, Caribbean, TX	272	2012, Jan. 24-Feb. 14	Blizzard/cold snap, E Europe	650+
1981, Nov. 25	T. Irma, Luzon Isl., Philippines	176	2012, Oct. 22-31	H. Sandy, Cuba, Haiti, Jamaica, Eastern U.S.	245[7]
1983, June	Monsoon, India	900	2012, Dec. 4	T. Bopha Philippines	1,146
1984, Sept. 2	T. Ike, S Philippines	1,363			
1985, May 25	C., Bangladesh	15,000			
1985, Oct. 26-Nov. 6	H. Juan, SE U.S.	97			
1987, Nov. 25	H. Nina, Philippines	650			
1988, Sept. 10-17	H. Gilbert, Carib., Gulf of Mex.	260			
1989, Sept. 16-22	H. Hugo, Caribbean, SE U.S..	86			

(1) What hurricanes are called W of Intl. Date Line and N of equator. (2) Incl. about 500 lost on ships at sea. (3) Official toll as of Aug. 2006 was 1,577 in LA, 238 in MS, 14 in FL, and 2 each in AL and GA. (4) Incl. 55 indirect deaths, among them 20 people, mostly elderly evacuees from a nursing home, whose bus exploded and caught fire outside Dallas. (5) Incl. deaths from floods and landslides generated by heavy rainstorms. (6) First documented super cyclone in Arabian Sea. (7) Includes 87 indirect deaths in the U.S.

Frankenstorm

Date: Oct. 29, 2012. **Location:** Eastern U.S. **U.S. fatalities:** 159. **Damages:** $65 bil.

What would happen if a late-season tropical cyclone met up with an early-season snowstorm? Residents of the East Coast found out in Oct. 2012 when Sandy, the last hurricane of the 2012 season, merged with the first nor'easter of winter. The resulting Superstorm Sandy ceased to carry hurricane-strength winds after making landfall, but it was as destructive as a Category 5. Sandy's torrential rains caused flooding and record-high storm surges in densely populated coastal areas of New York and New Jersey. The New York Stock Exchange closed for two days and 8 mil homes lost power, many for a week or longer. Further inland, the storm turned into a blizzard, dropping more than a foot of snow on six states from North Carolina to Pennsylvania.

Some Notable Floods, Tidal Waves

Source: EM-DAT: The OFDA/CRED Intl. Disaster Database, Université catholique de Louvain, Brussels, Belgium, www.emdat.be; World Almanac research

Date	Location	Deaths	Date	Location	Deaths
1703	Awa, Japan	100,000+	1981, Apr.	N China	550
1889, May 31	Johnstown, PA	2,200+	1981, July	Sichuan, Hubei Prov.,	
1903, June 15	Heppner, OR	325		China	1,300
1911	Chang Jiang R., China	100,000	1982, Jan. 23	Near Lima, Peru	600
1913, Mar. 25-27	OH, IN	732	1982, May 12	Guangdong, China	430
1915, Aug. 17	Galveston, TX	275	1982, Sept. 17-21	El Salvador, Guatemala	1,300+
1927, Jan.-July	Mississippi Valley	246+	1984, Aug.-Sept.	South Korea	200+
1927, Nov. 1	Mostagenem, Algeria	3,000	1987, July 22	Bangladesh	2,055
1928, Mar. 13	Dam collapse, Saugus,		1987, Aug.-Sept.	N Bangladesh	1,000+
	CA	450	1988, June-Sept.	Bangladesh	2,379
1928, Sept. 16	Lake Okeechobee, FL	1,770+	1988, Sept.	N India	1,000+
1931, Aug.	Huang He R., China	3,700,000	1989, July 14	China	2,000
1933	Shandong, China	18,000	1994, May-Oct.	Assam, India	2,001
1937, Jan. 22	OH, MS valleys	250	1995, July	NE China	1,200
1939, July	Hunan province, China	500,000	1995, Sept. 1-20	India	1,479
1946, Apr. 1	HI, AK	159	1996, June-July	Guizho, Hebei, China	2,775
1947, Sept. 20	Honshu Isl., Japan	2,000	1997, Oct.-Nov.	Somalia	2,311
1949, July	China	57,000	1998, July-Aug.	Hunan, Sichuan, China	3,656
1949, Oct.	Guatemala	40,000	1998, July-Sept.	Bangladesh	1,441
1950	Pakistan	2,900	1998, July 17	Papua New Guinea	3,000
1951, Aug. 28	Manchuria	4,800	1998, Aug.	India	1,811
1953, Jan. 31	Storm surge, Zuiderzee,		1999, Oct.-Dec.	Central Vietnam	700+
	Netherlands	2,000	1999, Dec. 15-20	NW Venezuela	30,000
1953, June 23	Japan	2,566	2000, Feb.-Mar.	Mozambique	700
1954, Aug. 17	Farahzad, Iran	2,000	2000, Sept. 19-30	India, Bangladesh	1,000+
1954, Aug.	China	30,000	2001, Aug. 1-6	Taiwan	100+
1955, Oct. 7-12	India, Pakistan	1,700	2001, Nov. 9-10	N Algeria	711+
1959-1961	China	2,000,000	2002, Apr.-Aug.	China	800+
1959, Nov. 1	W Mexico	2,000	2002, July-Aug.	India, Nepal, Bangladesh	1,100+
1959, Dec. 2	Frejus, France	412	2004, May 23-Jun. 1	Dom. Republic, Haiti	2,665
1960, Oct. 10	Bangladesh	6,000	2004, June-Sept.	Bangladesh, India,	
1960, Oct. 31	Bangladesh	4,000		Myanmar, Nepal	2,000+
1961, July	N India	2,000	2004, June-Sept.	China	500
1962, Sept. 27	Barcelona, Spain	445	2004, Nov.-Dec.	Philippines	1,060+
1963, Oct. 9	Dam collapse, Vaiont, Italy	1,800	2004, Dec. 26	12 Indian Ocean nations	227,898
1967, Jan. 18-24	E Brazil	894	2005, July 26-Aug. 5	W Maharashtra state,	
1967, Mar. 19	Rio de Janeiro, Brazil	436		India	1,200
1967, Nov. 26	Lisbon, Portugal	464	2006, Feb. 17	Leyte Isl., Philippines	1,000
1968, July	Rajasthan, Gujarat states,		2006, July 17	S of Java, Indonesia	530+
	India	4,892	2007, July-Sept.	India	1,103
1968, Oct. 7	NE India	780	2007, July 21-Aug. 3	Bangladesh	1,110
1969, Jan. 18-26	Southern CA	100	2008, June-July	India	1,063
1969, Aug. 20-22	Western VA	189	2009, July-Sept.	India	992
1969, Oct. 1-8	Tunisia	500	2010, May-Aug.	China	1,691
1970, July 22	Himalayas, India	500	2010, June 13-24	Cenxi, China	377+
1972, Feb. 26	Buffalo Creek, WV	118	2010, July-Aug.	Pakistan	1,985
1972, June 9	Rapid City, SD	238	2010, Aug. 1-4	Zhouqu county, China	1,500+
1972, Aug. 7	Luzon Isl., Philippines	454	2011, Jan. 11-12	SE Brazil	900
1972, Aug. 19-31	Pakistan	1,500	2011, Mar. 11	NE Japan	20,896
1974, Mar. 29	Tubaro, Brazil	1,000	2011, Apr.-May	Northern Colombia	425+
1974, July	Bangladesh	28,700	2011, July-Dec.	Thailand	708+
1974, Aug. 12	Monty-Long, Bangladesh	2,500	2011, July-Dec.	Philippines, Cambodia,	
1976, July 31	Big Thompson Canyon, CO	140		Myanmar	2,000+
1978, July	N, NE India	3,800	2012, July-Oct.	Nigeria	363
1979, July 17	Lomblem Isl., Indonesia	539	2012, Aug.-Oct.	Pakistan	480
1979, Aug. 11	Morvi, India	15,000	2012-Sept-Oct.	Nigeria	431
1980, June	Sichuan, China	6,200	2013, June	Uttarakhand, India	5,700+

Extra-Dangerous Flooding

Date: Jan. 25, 2013. **Location:** Limpopo Province, South Africa.

When driving rains pushed the Limpopo River over its banks, the owners of the Rakwena Crocodile Farm feared for the survival of their animals and opened a floodgate that released 15,000 crocodiles into a river that borders Botswana and Zimbabwe. The lightly populated province is home to dozens of game reserves and crocodile farms, but the Limpopo River, one of South Africa's longest, had been largely crocodile-free before the flooding, which killed at least 10 people in the province. Crocodile farmers, local residents, police, and the Natl. Society for the Prevention of Cruelty to Animals quickly recaptured thousands of crocodiles within the first three days.

Some Major Earthquakes

Source: Global Volcanism Network, Smithsonian Institution; U.S. Geological Survey, U.S. Dept. of the Interior; World Almanac research
Magnitude of earthquakes (mag.) is a relative measurement of an earthquake's energy.

Date	Location	Deaths	Mag.	Date	Location	Deaths	Mag.
526, May 20	Antioch, Syria	250,000	NA	1949, July 10	Khait, Tajikistan	12,000	7.5
856	Corinth, Greece	45,000	NA	1949, Aug. 5	Pelileo, Ecuador	5,050	6.8
856, Dec. 22	Damghan, Iran	200,000	NA	1950, Aug. 15	Assam, India	1,526	8.6
893, Mar. 23	Ardabil, Iran	150,000	NA	1954, Sept. 9	Orleansville, Algeria	1,250	6.8
1057	Chihli, China	25,000	NA	1956, June 10-17	N Afghanistan	2,000	7.7
1138, Aug. 9	Aleppo, Syria	230,000	NA	1957, July 2	N Iran	1,200	7.1
1169, Feb. 11	Nr. Mt. Etna, Sicily	15,000	NA[1]	1960, Feb. 29	Agadir, Morocco	12,000	5.7
1268	Silicia, Asia Minor	60,000	NA	1960, May 21-30	S Chile	1,655	9.5[5]
1290, Sept. 27	Chihli, China	100,000	NA	1962, Sept. 1	NW Iran	12,255	7.1
1293, May 20	Kamakura, Japan	30,000	NA	1964, Mar. 27	Prince Wm. Sound, AK	131	9.2[6]
1531, Jan. 26	Lisbon, Portugal	30,000	NA	1966, Aug. 19	E Turkey	2,529	6.8
1556, Jan. 24	Shaanxi, China	830,000	NA	1968, Aug. 31	NE Iran	12,000	7.3
1667, Nov.	Shemakha, Caucasia			1969, July 25	Guangdong, China	3,000	5.9
	(now Azerbaijan)	80,000	NA	1970, Jan. 5	Yunnan Prov., China	10,000	7.5
1693, Jan. 11	Catania, Italy	60,000	NA	1970, May 31	Chimbote, Peru	70,000	7.9
1737, Oct. 11	India, Calcutta	300,000	NA	1971, Feb. 9	San Fernando Valley, CA	65	6.6
1755, June 7	N Persia (current-day Iran)	40,000	NA	1972, Apr. 10	S Iran	5,054	7.1
1755, Nov. 1	Lisbon, Portugal	60,000	8.75[2]	1972, Dec. 23	Managua, Nicaragua	5,000	6.2
1783, Feb. 4	Calabria, Italy	30,000	NA	1974, May 10	China	20,000	6.8
1797, Feb. 4	Quito, Ecuador	41,000	NA	1974, Dec. 28	N Pakistan	5,300	6.2
1822, Sept. 5	Asia Minor, Aleppo	22,000	NA	1975, Feb. 4	Haicheng, China	2,000	7.0
1828, Dec. 28	Echigo, Japan	30,000	NA	1975, Sept. 6	E Turkey	2,300	6.7
1868, Aug. 13-15	Peru, Ecuador	40,000	NA	1976, Feb. 4	Guatemala	23,000	7.5
1875, May 16	Venezuela, Colombia	16,000	NA	1976, May 6	NE Italy	1,000	6.5
1886, Aug. 31	Charleston, SC	60	6.6	1976, June 25	Irian Jaya, New Guinea	422	7.1
1896, June 15	Sanriku, Japan (tsunami)	27,120	8.5	1976, July 28	Tangshan, China	242,769	7.5
1902, Apr. 19	Quezaltenango and San			1976, Aug. 16	Mindanao, Philippines	8,000	7.9
	Marcos, Guatemala	2,000	7.5	1976, Nov. 24	NW Iran-Turkey border	5,000	7.3
1902, Dec. 16	Uzbekistan, Russia	4,700	6.4	1977, Mar. 4	Romania	1,500	7.2
1903, Apr. 28	Malazgirt, Turkey	3,500	7.0	1978, Sept. 16	NE Iran	15,000	7.8
1905, Apr. 4	Kangra, India	19,000	7.5	1980, Oct. 10	NW Algeria	5,000	7.7
1906, Jan. 31	Off coast of Esmeraldas,			1980, Nov. 23	S Italy	2,735	6.5
	Ecuador	1,000	8.8	1981, June 11	S Iran	3,000	6.9
1906, Mar. 16	Chia-i, Taiwan	1,250	6.8	1981, July 28	S Iran	1,500	7.3
1906, Apr. 18-19	San Francisco, CA	3,000+	7.7[3]	1982, Dec. 13	W Arabian Peninsula	2,800	6.0
1906, Aug. 17	Valparaiso, Chile	3,882	8.6	1983, Oct. 30	E Turkey	1,342	6.9
1907, Oct. 21	Central Asia	12,000	8.1	1985, Sept. 19	Michoacan, Mexico	9,500	8.0
1908, Dec. 28	Messina, Italy	72,000	7.2	1986, Oct. 10	El Salvador	1,000+	5.5
1909, Jan. 23	Silakhor, Iran	5,000-		1987, Mar. 6	Colombia-Ecuador	1,000	7.0
		6,000	7.3	1988, Aug. 20	India-Nepal border	1,000	6.8
1912, Aug. 9	Murefte, Turkey	2,800	7.4	1988, Dec. 7	Spitak, Armenia	25,000	6.8
1914, Oct. 3	Burdur, Turkey	4,000	7.0	1989, Oct. 17	San Francisco Bay area, CA	63	6.9
1915, Jan. 13	Avezzano, Italy	32,610	7.0	1990, June 20	W Iran	40,000+	7.4
1917, July 30	Yunnan, China	1,800	7.5	1990, July 16	Luzon, Philippines	1,621	7.7
1920, Dec. 16	Gansu, China	200,000	7.8[4]	1991, Feb. 1	Pakistan-Afgh. border	1,200	6.8
1923, Mar. 24	Sichuan, China	3,500	7.3	1991, Oct. 19	N India	2,000	7.0
1923, Mar. 25	Torbat-e Heydariyeh, Iran	2,200	5.7	1992, Dec. 12	Flores Isl., Indonesia	2,500	7.5
1923, Sept. 1	Yokohama, Japan	142,800	7.9	1993, Sept. 30	Maharashtra, S India	9,748	6.2
1925, Mar. 16	Yunnan, China	5,800	7.0	1994, Jan. 17	Northridge, CA	61	6.8
1927, Mar. 7	Tango, Japan	3,020	7.6	1994, June 6	Cauca, SW Colombia	1,000	6.8
1927, May 22	Gansu, China	40,900	7.6	1995, Jan. 16	Kobe, Japan	5,502	6.9
1929, May 1	Koppeh Dagh, Iran	3,800	7.2	1995, May 27	Sakhalin Isl., Russia	1,989	7.5
1930, May 6	Salmas, Iran	2,500	7.2	1997, Feb. 28	NW Iran	1,000+	6.1
1930, July 23	Irpinia, Italy	1,404	6.5	1997, May 10	N Iran	1,567	7.3
1931, Mar. 31	Managua, Nicaragua	2,500	6.0	1998, Feb. 4, 8	Hindu Kush, Afghanistan	2,323	5.9
1931, Apr. 27	Armenia-Azerbaijan border	2,800	5.7	1998, May 30	Afghanistan-Tajikistan	4,000+	6.6
1931, Aug. 10	Xinjiang, China	10,000	8.0		border		
1933, Mar. 2	Sanriku, Japan (tsunami)	2,990	8.4	1998, July 17	Papua New Guinea	2,183	7.0
1933, Mar. 10	Long Beach, CA	115	6.2	1999, Jan. 25	Armenia, Colombia	1,185+	6.1
1933, Aug. 25	Sichuan, China	9,300	7.5	1999, Aug. 17	Izmit, W Turkey	17,118+	7.6
1934, Jan. 15	Bihar, India-Nepal	10,700	8.1	1999, Sept. 20	Taichung, Taiwan	2,400	7.6
1935, Apr. 21	Miao-li, Taiwan	3,270	7.1	2001, Jan. 26	Gujarat, India	20,085	7.6
1935, May 30	Quetta, Pakistan	30,000	7.6	2002, Mar. 25-26	Hindu Kush, Afghanistan	1,000+	6.1
1939, Jan. 25	Chillan, Chile	28,000	7.8	2003, May 21	N Algeria	2,266	6.8
1939, Dec. 26	Erzincan, Turkey	32,700	7.8	2003, Dec. 26	Bam, SE Iran	31,000	6.6
1943, Sept. 10	Tottori, Japan	1,190	7.4	2004, Dec. 26	Sumatra-Andaman Isls.,		
1943, Nov. 26	Ladik, Turkey	4,000	7.6		Indonesia	227,898	9.1[7]
1944, Jan. 15	San Juan, Argentina	8,000	7.4	2005, Mar. 28	N Sumatra, Indonesia	1,313	8.6
1944, Feb. 1	Gerede, Turkey	2,790	7.4	2005, Oct. 8	Kashmir, Pakistan, India	86,000	7.6
1945, Jan. 12	Mikawa, Japan	1,961	7.1	2006, May 26	Java, Indonesia	5,749	6.3
1945, Nov. 27	Makran Coast, Pakistan	4,000	8.0	2008, May 12	E Sichuan Prov., China	87,857	7.9
1946, May 31	Ustukran, Turkey	1,300	5.9	2009, Sept. 30	Sumatra, Indonesia	1,117	7.5
1946, Nov. 10	Ancash, Peru	1,400	7.3	2010, Jan. 12	Haiti	316,000	7.0
1946, Dec. 20	Honshu, Japan	1,362	8.1	2010, Feb. 27	Chile	800	8.8
1948, June 28	Fukui, Japan	3,769	7.3	2010, Apr. 13	S Qinghai, China	2,698+	6.9
1948, Oct. 5	Ashgabat, Turkmenistan	110,000	7.3	2011, Mar. 11	NE Japan	20,896	9.0[8]

NA = Not available. (1) Once thought to have been a volcanic eruption; evidence indicates a destructive earthquake and tsunami occurred on this date. (2) This earthquake caused the most deadly tsunami to date in the Atlantic Ocean. (3) Incl. deaths from resulting fires; revised estimates of magnitude range from 7.7 to 7.9. (4) Commonly referred to as the Gansu quake; actually located within the Ningxia autonomous region. (5) The largest recorded earthquake; caused a deadly tsunami that spread across the Pacific Ocean as far as Japan. (6) The "Good Friday" earthquake sent a tsunami that hit British Columbia, Canada, and the U.S. Pacific coast. (7) This undersea earthquake triggered devastating tsunamis that hit 12 Indian Ocean nations. (8) The most powerful earthquake in Japan's history set off a tsunami that inundated much of the coast and caused a partial meltdown of the Fukushima nuclear power plant.

Some Notable Fires Since 1918

See also Some Notable Explosions Since 1920.

Date	Location	Deaths
1918, Oct. 12	Cloquet-Moose Lake, MN.	453
1922, Oct. 4-5	Wind-blown fire, Haileybury, ON,	
	Canada	43
1929, May 10	Forest fire, Xochilapa, Mexico	60
1930, Apr. 21	Penitentiary, Columbus, OH.	320
1931, July 24	Home for aged, Pittsburgh, PA.	48
1934, Dec. 11	Hotel Kerns, Lansing, MI	34
1938, May 16	Terminal Hotel, Atlanta, GA	35
1940, Apr. 23	Nightclub, Natchez, MS	198
1942, Nov. 28	Cocoanut Grove Nightclub,	
	Boston, MA.	492
1942, Dec. 12	Hostel, St. John's, NL, Canada	100
1943, Sept. 7	Gulf Hotel, Houston, TX	55
1944, July 6	Ringling Circus, Hartford, CT	168
1946, June 5	LaSalle Hotel, Chicago, IL	61
1946, Dec. 7	Winecoff Hotel, Atlanta, GA	119
1946, Dec. 12	Ice plant, tenement, New York, NY . . .	37
1949, Apr. 5	Hospital, Effingham, IL	77
1949, Aug.	Forest fire, Landes, France	80
1950, Jan. 7	Mercy Hospital, Davenport, IA	41
1953, Mar. 29	Nursing home, Largo, FL	35
1953, Apr. 16	Metalworking plant, Chicago, IL	35
1957, Feb. 17	Home for aged, Warrenton, MO	72
1958, Mar. 19	Loft building, New York, NY	24
1958, Dec. 1	Parochial school, Chicago, IL.	95
1958, Dec. 16	Store, Bogotá, Colombia	83
1960, Mar. 12	Chemical plant, Pusan, Korea	68
1960, July 14	Mental hospital, Guatemala City.	225
1960, Nov. 13	Movie theater, Amude, Syria	152
1960, Dec. 19	USS Constellation, Brooklyn, NY	49
1961, Jan. 6	Thomas Hotel, San Francisco, CA	20
1961, Dec. 17	Circus, Niteroi, Brazil	323
1963, May 4	Theater, Diourbel, Senegal.	64
1963, Nov. 18	Surfside Hotel, Atlantic City, NJ	25
1963, Nov. 23	Rest home, Fitchville, OH.	63
1963, Dec. 29	Roosevelt Hotel, Jacksonville, FL.	22
1964, Dec. 18	Nursing home, Fountaintown, IN	20
1965, Aug. 11-16	Watts riot fires, Los Angeles, CA . . .	30+
1966, Dec. 7	Barracks, Erzurum, Turkey.	68
1967, Feb. 7	Restaurant, Montgomery, AL	25
1967, Feb. 7	Scrub fire, Hobart, Tasmania,	
	Australia	62
1967, May 22	Dept. store, Brussels, Belgium	322
1967, July 16	State prison, Jay, FL.	37
1967, July 29	USS Forrestal, off N Vietnam	134
1968, May 11	Wedding hall, Vijayawada, India.	58
1969, Dec. 2	Nursing home, Notre Dame,	
	QC, Can	54
1970, Jan. 9	Nursing home, Marietta, OH.	27
1970, Nov. 1	Dance hall, Grenoble, France.	145
1970, Dec. 20	Hotel, Tucson, AZ.	28
1971, Dec., 25	Hotel, Seoul, S. Korea	162
1972, May 13	Nightclub, Osaka, Japan	116
1972, July 5	Hospital, Sherborne, England.	30
1973, June 24	Bar, New Orleans, LA.	32
1973, Aug. 3	Amusement park, Isle of Man, Eng. . . .	51
1973, Nov. 29	Dept. store, Kumamoto, Japan.	107
1973, Dec. 2	Theater, Seoul, S. Korea	50
1974, Feb. 1	Bank building, São Paulo, Brazil	189
1974, June 30	Discotheque, Port Chester, NY	24
1974, Nov. 3	Hotel, disco, Seoul, S. Korea	88
1975, Dec. 12	Tent city, Mina, Saudi Arabia	138
1976, Oct. 24	Social club, Bronx, NY	25
1977, Feb. 25	Rossiya Hotel, Moscow, Russia	45
1977, May 28	Nightclub, Southgate, KY	164
1977, June 9	Nightclub, Abidjan, Ivory Coast	41
1977, June 26	Jail, Columbia, TN	42
1977, Nov. 14	Hotel, Manila, Philippines	47
1978, Aug. 19	Movie theater, Abadan, Iran.	425+
1979, July 14	Hotel, Saragossa, Spain.	80
1979, Dec. 31	Social club, Chapais, QC, Can.	42
1980, May 20	Nursing home, Kingston, Jamaica	157
1980, Nov. 21	MGM Grand Hotel, Las Vegas, NV . . .	84
1980, Dec. 4	Stouffer Inn, Harrison, NY	26
1981, Jan. 9	Boarding home, Keansburg, NJ	30
1981, Feb. 14	Discotheque, Dublin, Ireland	44
1982, Nov. 8	County jail, Biloxi, MS.	29
1983, Feb. 13	Movie theater, Turin, Italy.	64

Date	Location	Deaths
1983, Feb. 16	"Ash Wednesday" bushfires,	
	S Australia.	75
1983, Dec. 17	Discotheque, Madrid, Spain	83
1984, May 11	Great Adventure Amusement Park,	
	Jackson Twp., NJ	8
1985, Apr. 21	Movie theaters, Tabaco, Philippines. . .	44
1985, Apr. 26	Hospital, Buenos Aires, Argentina . . .	79
1985, May 11	Soccer stadium, Bradford, England . . .	53
1985, May 13	MOVE headquarters, row houses,	
	Philadelphia, PA.	11
1986, Dec. 31	Dupont Plaza Hotel, Puerto Rico	96
1987, May 6-		
June 2	Forest fire, Mohe, China.	191
1987, Nov. 17	Subway, London, England	30
1988, Mar. 20	About 2,000 buildings, Lashio, Myan.	134
1990, Mar. 25	Social club, Bronx, NY	87
1991, Mar. 3	Munitions dump, Addis Ababa, Ethiopia	260+
1991, Aug-Oct.	Wildfires, Sumatra, Borneo, Indonesia	57
1991, Sept. 3	Processing plant, Hamlet, NC	25
1991, Oct. 20-21	Wildfire, Oakland, Berkeley, CA	24
1992, Mar.	Forest fire, Terai, Nepal	56
1993, Apr. 19	Cult compound, Waco, TX	72
1994, May 10	Toy factory, Bangkok, Thailand	213
1994, July 4-10	Glenwood Springs, CO.	14
1994, Nov. 2	Burning fuel flood, Durunka, Egypt. . .	500
1994, Dec. 10	Theater, Karamay, China	300
1995, Oct. 28	Subway train, Baku, Azerbaijan	300
1995, Dec. 23	School, Mandi Dabwali, India	500+
1996, Mar. 19	Nightclub, Quezon City, Philippines . . .	150+
1996, Mar. 28	Shopping mall, Bogor, Indonesia	78
1996, Nov. 20	Building, Hong Kong.	39
1997, Feb. 23	Worship site, Baripada, India	164
1997, Apr. 15	Encampment, Mina, Saudi Arabia . . .	343
1997, June 7	Temple, Thanjavur, India	60+
1997, June 13	Movie theater, New Delhi, India	60
1997, July 11	Hotel, Pattaya, Thailand	90
1997, Sept.-Nov.	Drought-fueled fire, Sumatra, Indonesia	240
1997, Sept. 29	Children's home, nr. Colina, Chile . . .	30
1998, Apr.-June	Wildfire, Oaxaca, Mexico	50
1998, Dec. 3	Orphanage, Manila, Philippines	28
1999, Mar. 24	Mt. Blanc Tunnel, France, Italy.	40
1999, Oct. 30	Karaoke salon, Inchon, S. Korea	55+
2000, Mar. 17	Church, Kanungu, Uganda	530
2000, Nov. 11	Cable car, Kaprun, Austria	155
2000, Dec. 25	Shopping center, Luoyang, China	309
2001, Mar. 6	School, central China	41
2001, Mar. 26	School, Machakos, Kenya	64
2001, Aug. 18	Hotel, Quezon City, Philippines	73
2001, Sept. 1	Nightclub, Tokyo, Japan.	44
2001, Dec. 29	Fireworks accident, Lima, Peru	291
2003, Feb. 18	Subway train, Taegu, S. Korea.	198
2003, Feb. 20	Pyrotechnics in nightclub, Warwick, RI	100
2003, Sept. 15	Prison, Riyadh, Saudi Arabia	94
2003, Nov. 24	Students' hostel, Moscow, Russia	36
2004, May 17	Prison, San Pedro Sula, Honduras . . .	104
2004, July 16	Pvt. school, Kumbakonam, India	80+
2004, Aug. 1	Market, Asunción, Paraguay	400+
2004, Dec. 30	Club, Buenos Aires, Argentina	194
2005, Feb. 14	Mosque, Tehran, Iran	59
2005, Mar. 7	Prison, Higuey, Dom. Republic.	159
2005, Apr. 15	Hotel, Paris, France	22
2005, Sept. 5	Theater, Beni Suef, Egypt	32
2006, Dec. 9	Drug treatment center, Moscow, Russ.	45
2007, Mar. 20	Nursing home Kamyshevatskaya,	
	Russia.	62
2007, Aug. 24-		
Sept. 2	Wildfires (arson), Greece	67
2008, Apr. 26	Factory fire, Casablanca, Morocco. . .	55
2008, Sept.	Wildfires, Mozambique, S. Africa,	
	Swaziland.	89
2009, Jan. 1	Nightclub fire, Bangkok, Thailand. . . .	67
2009, Jan.-Feb.	Wildfires (arson), Victoria, Australia. . .	173
2010, July	Bushfires, Nizhny Novgorod, Russia. .	53
2010, Dec. 2-5	Grassland fire, Israel	44
2012, Feb. 14	Prison fire, Comayagua, Honduras . . .	360+
2013, Jan. 27	Pyrotechnics in nightclub,	
	Santa Maria, Brazil.	241
2013, June 30	Wildfire, Prescott, AZ	19

Some Notable Explosions Since 1920

See also Principal U.S. Mine Disasters Since 1900. Some bombings related to political conflicts and terrorism are not included.

Date	Location	Deaths
1920, Sept. 16	Wall Street, New York, NY	30
1921, Sept. 21	Chem. storage facility, Oppau, Ger.	561
1924, Jan. 3	Food plant, Pekin, IL.	42
1927, May 18	School bombing, Bath, MI	45
1928, Apr. 13	Dance hall, West Plains, MO	40
1937, Mar. 18	School, New London, TX	311
1940, Sept. 12	Hercules Powder factory, Kenvil, NJ . . .	55
1942, June 5	Ordnance plant, Elwood, IL	49
1944, Apr. 14	Harbor, Bombay, India	700
1944, July 17	Munitions ships, depot, Port Chicago, CA	322
1944, Oct. 20	Liquid natural gas tanks, Cleveland, OH	130
1947, Apr. 16	Freighter, chemical co. plant, Texas City, TX.	576
1948, July 28	Farben works, Ludwigshafen, Ger.	184
1950, May 19	Munitions barges, S. Amboy, NJ	30
1954, May 26	USS *Bennington*, off RI	103
1956, Aug. 7	Dynamite trucks, Cali, Colombia	1,100
1958, Apr. 18	Sunken munitions ship, Okinawa, Japan	40
1959, Apr. 10	WWII bomb, Philippines	38
1959, June 28	Rail tank cars, Meldrim, GA	25
1959, Nov. 2	Explosives, Jamuri Bazar, India	46
1959, Dec. 13	2 apt. bldgs., Dortmund, Ger.	26
1960, Mar. 4	Belgian munitions ship, Havana, Cuba. .	100
1962, Oct. 3	New York Telephone Co. office, New York, NY	23
1963, Jan. 2	Packing plant, Terre Haute, IN	17
1963, Mar. 9	Dynamite plant, S. Africa	45
1963, Aug. 13	Explosives dump, Gauhaiti, India	32
1963, Oct. 31	State Fair Coliseum, Indianapolis, IN . . .	73
1964, July 23	Harbor munitions, Bone, Algeria.	100
1965, Aug. 9	Missile silo, Searcy, AR	53
1965, Oct. 21	Bridge, Tila Bund, Pakistan	80
1965, Nov. 24	Armory, Keokuk, IA.	20
1967, Dec. 25	Apartment bldg., Moscow, USSR.	20
1968, Apr. 6	Sports store, Richmond, IN	43
1969, Mar. 31	Coal mine, nr. Barroteran, Mexico	180
1970, Apr. 8	Subway construction, Osaka, Japan . . .	73
1971, June 24	Tunnel, Sylmar, CA	17
1973, Feb., 10	Liquid gas tank, Staten Island, NY	40
1975, Dec. 27	Coal mine, Chasnala, India	431
1976, Apr. 13	Munitions works, Lapua, Finland	40
1977, Nov. 11	Freight train, Iri, S. Korea.	57
1977, Dec. 22	Grain elevator, Westwego, LA	35
1978, July 11	Propylene tank truck, Tarragona, Spain	150
1980, Oct. 23	School, Ortuella, Spain.	64
1982, Apr. 25	Antiques exhibition, Todi, Italy	33
1982, Nov. 2	Salang Tunnel, Afghanistan	1,000+
1984, Feb. 25	Oil pipeline, Cubatao, Brazil	508
1984, June 21	Naval supply depot, Severomorsk, USSR	200+
1984, Nov. 19	Gas storage area, NE Mexico City	334
1984, Dec. 3	Chemical plant, Bhopal, India.	3,849
1984, Dec. 5	Coal mine, Taipei, Taiwan	94
1985, June 25	Fireworks factory, Hallett, OK.	21
1988, Apr. 10	Army ammunitions dump nr. Rawalpindi and Islamabad, Pakistan	100
1988, July 6	Oil rig, North Sea off NE Scotland	167
1989, June 3	Gas pipeline, between Ufa, Asha, USSR	650+
1992, Mar. 3	Coal mine, Kozlu, Turkey	270+
1992, Apr. 22	Gas leak in sewers, Guadalajara, Mexico.	200+
1992, May 9	Coal mine, Plymouth, Nova Scotia, Can.	26
1993, Feb. 26	World Trade Center, New York, NY	6
1994, July 18	Jewish comm. center, Buenos Aires, Arg.	100
1995, Apr. 19	Fed. office building, Oklahoma City, OK	168
1995, Apr. 29	Subway construction, S. Korea	110
1996, Jan. 31	Bank, Colombo, Sri Lanka	53
1996, Mar. 3-4	Jerusalem and Tel Aviv, Israel	33
1996, June 25	U.S. military housing complex, nr. Dhahran, Saudi Arabia	19
1996, July 24	Train, Colombo, Sri Lanka	86
1996, Nov. 16	Military apt., Dagestan region, Russia . .	68
1996, Nov. 21	Propane gas leak in bldg., San Juan, Puerto Rico.	33
1996, Nov. 27	Coal mine, Shanxi Prov., China	91+
1996, Dec. 30	Train, Assam, India.	59+

Date	Location	Deaths
1997, Dec. 2	Coal mine, Novokuznetsk, Siberia	68
1998, Feb. 14	2 oil tankers, Yaounde, Cameroon	120
1998, Feb. 14	17 bombs, Coimbatore, India	50
1998, Apr. 4	Coal mine, Donetsk, Ukraine	63
1998, Aug. 7	Bomb, U.S. emb., Nairobi, Kenya.	213
1998, Aug. 7	Bomb, U.S. emb., Dar-es-Salaam, Tanz.	11
1998, Sept. 8	2 buses, São Paulo, Brazil	59
1998, Oct. 17	Oil pipeline, Jesse, Nigeria.	700+
1999, May 16	Fuel truck, Punjab Prov., Pakistan	75
1999, Sept. 10	Apartment building, Moscow, Russia . . .	94
1999, Sept. 13	Apartment building, Moscow, Russia . . .	118
1999, Sept. 16	Apartment building, Moscow, Russia . . .	18
1999, Sept. 26	Fireworks factory, Celaya, Mexico	56
2000, Feb. 25	Bombs on 2 buses, Ozamis, Philippines	41
2000, Mar. 11	Coal mine, Krasnodon, Ukraine	80
2000, Apr. 16	Airport hangar, Dem. Rep. of Congo . . .	100+
2000, July 16	Oil pipeline, Warri, Nigeria	30
2000, Sept. 9	Truck explosion, Urumqi, China	60
2000, Oct. 12	U.S. destroyer, Yemen.	17
2001, Mar. 6	School, Wanzai Co., China.	41
2001, Apr. 21	Coal mine, Shaanxi, China.	51
2001, June 1	Dance club, Tel Aviv, Israel	21
2001, July 17	Coal mine, Guanxi, China.	76+
2001, Aug. 19	Coal mine, Donetsk region, Ukraine. . . .	52
2001, Sept. 21	Chem. plant, Toulouse, France	29
2002, Jan. 21	Volcanic lava caused gas station blast, Goma, Dem. Rep. of Congo.	50+
2002, Jan. 27	Munitions dump, Lagos, Nigeria.	1,000+
2002, May 9	Land mine at parade, Kaspiisk, Russia.	34+
2002, June 14	Car bomb outside U.S. consulate, Karachi, Pakistan	12
2002, June 18	Bomb on bus, Jerusalem, Israel.	20
2002, July 5	Bomb in market, Larba, Algeria	35+
2002, Aug. 9	Explosion, Jalalabad, Afghanistan	25+
2002, Sept. 5	Car bomb, Kabul, Afghanistan	30
2002, Oct. 12	Nightclub bombings, Bali, Indonesia . . .	202
2003, Aug. 25	Bombs in 2 taxis, Mumbai, India.	52
2003, Dec. 5	Bomb on train, Yessentuki, Russia.	45
2003, Dec. 23	Gas well explosion, Chongqing, China. .	233
2004, Jan. 19	Natural gas facility, Skikda, Algeria	27
2004, Feb. 6	Bomb on subway car, Moscow, Russia	39
2004, Mar. 11	Bombs on commuter trains, Madrid, Spain	191
2005, Feb. 14	Coal mine, NE China	214
2005, Mar. 23	Oil refinery, Texas City, TX.	15
2005, May 2	Arms cache, Baghlan Prov., Afghan. . . .	34+
2005, July 7	Bombs in mass transit, London, Eng. . .	56
2005, Oct. 1	Bombings of restaurants, Bali, Indonesia	26
2005, Nov. 27	Coal mine, NE China	161+
2006, May 12	Oil pipeline, nr. Lagos, Nigeria	200
2006, July 1	Bombings of trains, station, Mumbai, India	207
2007, Mar. 19	Coal mine, Siberia, Russia.	108
2007, Mar. 22	Natl. weapons depot, Maputo, Mozambique.	117
2007, June 9	Oil pipeline, Pyongan Prov., N. Korea . .	110
2007, Nov. 18	Methane gas buildup in coal mine, E Ukraine	90
2008, May 15	Pipeline explosion in Lagos, Nigeria. . . .	100+
2008, Sept. 20	Truck bomb outside hotel, Islamabad, Pakistan.	40+
2009, Feb. 22	Coal mine, N China	74
2010, Apr. 5	Coal mine, Montcoal, WV	29
2010, May 8-9	Coal mine, Siberia, Russia	91
2010, June 17	Coal mine, Amaga, Colombia.	73
2010, Nov. 19	Coal mine, Ataru, New Zealand	29
2011, Mar. 28	Munitions factory, Abyan, Yemen.	150+
2011, July 13	Bombs in three locations in Mumbai, India	27
2012, Mar. 4	Arms depot, Brazzaville, Congo Rep. . . .	250+
2013, Apr. 17	Fire at fertilizer plant, West, TX.	14
2013, June 3	Poultry plant, Mishzai, China	119+
2013, June 30	Fuel tanker, Kampala, Uganda	30+
2013, July 6	Derailed oil train, Lac-Megantic, QC, Canada	47
2013, Aug. 1	Weapons cache, Homs, Syria	40

Notable Nuclear Accidents

Oct. 7, 1957: Fire in the Windscale plutonium production reactor N of Liverpool, England, released radioactive material; later blamed for 39 cancer deaths.

Jan. 3, 1961: Reactor explosion at a federal installation near Idaho Falls, ID, killed 3 workers. Radiation contained.

Oct. 5, 1966: Sodium cooling system malfunction caused a partial core meltdown at the Enrico Fermi demonstration breeder reactor, near Detroit, MI. Radiation contained.

Jan. 21, 1969: Coolant malfunction from an experimental underground reactor at Lucens Vad, Switzerland, released radiation into a cavern, which was then sealed.

Mar. 22, 1975: Fire at the Brown's Ferry reactor in Decatur, AL, caused dangerous lowering of cooling water levels.

Mar. 28, 1979: Worst commercial nuclear accident in the U.S. occurred as equipment failures and human mistakes led to a loss of coolant and a partial core meltdown at the Three Mile Island reactor in Middletown, PA.

Feb. 11, 1981: Eight workers were contaminated when 100,000 gallons of radioactive coolant fluid leaked into the containment building of TVA's Sequoyah 1 plant near Chattanooga, TN.

Apr. 25, 1981: Some 100 workers were exposed to radiation during repairs of a nuclear plant at Tsuruga, Japan.

Jan. 6, 1986: Cylinder of nuclear material burst after being improperly heated at a Kerr-McGee plant at Gore, OK. One worker died; 100 were hospitalized.

Apr. 26, 1986: Fires and explosions resulting from an unauthorized experiment at the Chernobyl nuclear power plant near Kiev, USSR (now in Ukraine), left at least 31 dead in the immediate aftermath and spread radioactive material over much of Europe. An estimated 135,000 people were evacuated from the region, some of which was uninhabitable for years. As a result of the radiation released, tens of thousands of excess cancer deaths (as well as increased birth defects) were expected.

Mar. 11, 2011: A 9.0-magnitude earthquake caused a devastating tsunami that inundated the Fukushima Daiichi nuclear power plant on Japan's NE coast. Three of the plant's reactors suffered partial meltdowns, and more than 12,000 tons of radioactive water was released into the sea. More than two years later, the plant's owners reported that 300 tons of radioactive water was still leaking into the ocean every day.

Record Oil Spills

The exact number of barrels in a ton varies with the type of oil, but a good approximation is 7 barrels per ton. Each barrel contains 42 gallons.

Name, location	Date	Cause	Tons
BP *Deepwater Horizon* rig, Gulf of Mexico, U.S.	Apr. 20-July 15, 2010	Explosion	700,000[1]
Ixtoc I oil well, S Gulf of Mexico	June 3, 1979	Blowout	600,000
Nowruz oil field, Persian Gulf	Feb. 1983	Blowout	600,000 (est.)
Atlantic Empress and *Aegean Captain*, off Trinidad and Tobago	July 19, 1979	Collision	300,000
ABT Summer, off Angola	May 28, 1991	Explosion	260,000
Castillo de Bellver, off Cape Town, South Africa	Aug. 6, 1983	Fire	250,000
Amoco Cadiz, near Portsall, France	Mar. 16, 1978	Grounding	223,000
Torrey Canyon, off Land's End, England	Mar. 18, 1967	Grounding	119,000
Sea Star, Gulf of Oman	Dec. 19, 1972	Collision	115,000
Urquiola, La Coruna, Spain	May 12, 1976	Grounding	100,000

(1) The Dept. of Energy estimated the spill at 4.9 mil barrels, or more than 200 mil gallons.

Other Notable Oil Spills

Name, location	Date	Cause	Gallons
Persian Gulf	Began Jan. 21, 1991	Intentional spillage by Iraq	130,000,000[1]
Braer, off Shetland Islands, UK	Jan. 5, 1993	Grounding	26,000,000
Prestige, off N Spain	Nov. 13-19, 2002	Ship broke in half	22,600,000
Aegean Sea, off N Spain	Dec. 3, 1992	Grounding	21,500,000
Sea Empress, off SW Wales, UK	Feb. 15, 1996	Grounding	18,000,000
Newtown Creek, Greenpoint, Brooklyn, NY	Oct. 5, 1950-present.	Industrial explosion[2]	17,000,000
World Glory, off South Africa	June 13, 1968	Hull failure.	13,524,000
Exxon Valdez, Prince William Sound, AK.	Mar. 24, 1989	Grounding	10,080,000
Ashland Oil facility, Floreffe, PA; Monongahela R.	Jan. 2, 1988	Storage tank collapse.	3,850,000

(1) Est. by Saudi Arabia. Some estimates as low as 25 mil gal. (2) Preceded by leaks in 1940s-50s.

Notable Droughts

Source: EM-DAT: The OFDA/CRED Intl. Disaster Database, Université catholique de Louvain, Brussels, Belgium, www.emdat.be; World Almanac research

Date	Location	Est. deaths	Date	Location	Est. deaths
1900	Bengal, India	1,250,000	1981-85	Chad	3,000
1900	Cape Verde Islands	11,000	1982	East Timor, Indonesia	280
1910-14	Zinder dept., Niger	85,000	1983	Swaziland	500
1920	China	500,000	1983-84	Eritrea, Ethiopia	300,000
1920	Cape Verde Islands	24,000	1983-85	N Sudan	150,000
1921	S Ukraine, Volga, U.S.S.R.	1,200,000	1984	Indonesia	230
1928	Shensi, Honan, Kansu, China	3,000,000	1987	Somalia	600
1940-44	Cape Verde Islands	20,000	1987	Eritrea, Ethiopia	367
1942	Calcutta, Bengal, India	1,500,000	1987	NW India	300
1943	Bangladesh	1,900,000	1988	Central China	1,400
1946	Cape Verde Islands	30,000	1988-92	S Madagascar	200
1965	Ethiopia	2,000	1989	S Rwanda	237
1965-67	India	1,500,000	1991	Jiangxi, Hunan Provinces, China	2,000
1966	Lombok, Indonesia	8,000	1997	Irian Jaya, Indonesia	672
1967-69	SE Australia	600	1999-2003	Pakistan	143
1973-78	Ethiopia	100,000	2002	Malawi	500
1974-76	Somalia	19,000	2005-06	Burundi	120
1981-85	Mozambique	100,000	2006	SW China	134

Some Notable Miscellaneous Disasters Since 1950

Date	Event	Location	Details	Est. deaths
1952, Dec.	Pollution	London, England	Heavy smog blanketed city; impeded breathing	4,000
1980, summer	Heat wave	United States	June through Sept.	1,265
1984, Dec. 3	Industrial accident	Bhopal, India	Toxic gas leaked from a Union Carbide factory	16,000
1986, Aug. 21	Gas	Nr. Lake Nyos, Cameroon	Volcanic lake released cloud of carbon dioxide gas.	1,700
1990, July 2	Stampede	Mecca, Saudi Arabia	Pilgrims panicked in tunnel leading to the holy city	1,426
2003, summer	Heat wave	Europe	Abnormally high temperatures from Russia to Britain; France suffered most, with 14,800 dead	35,000
2013, Apr. 24	Building collapse	Savar, Bangladesh	Garment factory found to have substandard foundation collapsed.	1,100+

AEROSPACE

Notable Human Spaceflight Missions

Source: National Aeronautics and Space Administration (NASA); Congressional Research Service; World Almanac research

The spaceflights listed are a selection of notable U.S. missions by NASA, unless otherwise noted, plus non-U.S. missions (shown with an asterisk). The non-U.S missions were sponsored by the USSR—later, the Commonwealth of Independent States (CIS) and, from 1997, Russia—or by China. Launch dates are Eastern standard time. **EVA** = extravehicular activity. **ASTP** = Apollo-Soyuz Test Project. **STS** = Space Transportation System, NASA's name for the overall shuttle program.

For shuttle flights, mission name is in parentheses following name of orbiter. Duration of flight is listed in hours:minutes for 1961-Apr. 1970; days (d.), hours (hr.), and minutes (min.) for June 1970-Apr. 1981; days only thereafter. Number of total flights taken by each crew member is given in parentheses when flight listed is not the person's first.

4/12/1961: *Vostok 1*; 1:48; Yuri A. Gagarin. **1st human orbital flight.**

5/5/1961: *Mercury-Redstone 3*; 0:15; Alan B. Shepard Jr. **1st American in space.**

7/21/1961: *Mercury-Redstone 4*; 0:15; Virgil I. Grissom. Flight successful but spacecraft sank shortly after splashdown; Grissom rescued.

8/6/1961: **Vostok 2*; 25:18; Gherman S. Titov. 1st spaceflight of more than 24 hours.

2/20/1962: *Mercury-Atlas 6*; 4:55; John H. Glenn Jr. **1st American in orbit.**

5/24/1962: *Mercury-Atlas 7*; 4:56; M. Scott Carpenter. Manual retrofire error caused 250-mi landing overshoot.

8/11/1962: **Vostok 3*; 94:22; Andrian G. Nikolayev. *Vostok 3* and *4* made 1st group flight.

8/12/1962: **Vostok 4*; 70:57; Pavel R. Popovich. On 1st orbit, it came within 3 mi of *Vostok 3*.

10/3/1962: *Mercury-Atlas 8*; 9:13; Walter M. Schirra Jr. Landed 5 mi from target; six orbits.

5/15/1963: *Mercury-Atlas 9*; 34:19; L. Gordon Cooper. 1st U.S. evaluation of effects of one day in space on a person; 22 orbits.

6/14/1963: **Vostok 5*; 119:06; Valery F. Bykovsky. *Vostok 5* and *6* made 2nd group flight.

6/16/1963: **Vostok 6*; 70:50; Valentina V. Tereshkova. **1st woman in space**; passed within 3 mi of *Vostok 5*.

10/12/1964: **Voskhod 1*; 24:17; Vladimir M. Komarov, Konstantin P. Feoktistov, Boris B. Yegorov. 1st three-person orbital flight; 1st without space suits.

3/18/1965: **Voskhod 2*; 26:02; Pavel I. Belyayev, Aleksei A. Leonov. Leonov made **1st spacewalk** (10 min.).

3/23/1965: *Gemini-Titan 3*; 4:53; Virgil I. Grissom (2), John W. Young. 1st piloted spacecraft to change its orbital path.

6/3/1965: *Gemini-Titan 4*; 97:56; James A. McDivitt, Edward H. White II. White was **1st American to "walk in space"** (36 min.).

8/21/1965: *Gemini-Titan 5*; 190:55; L. Gordon Cooper (2), Charles Conrad Jr. Longest-duration human flight to date.

12/4/1965: *Gemini-Titan 7*; 330:35; Frank Borman, James A. Lovell Jr. Longest-duration *Gemini* flight.

12/15/1965: *Gemini-Titan 6A*; 25:51; Walter M. Schirra Jr. (2), Thomas P. Stafford. Completed 1st U.S. space rendezvous, with *Gemini 7*.

3/16/1966: *Gemini-Titan 8*; 10:41; Neil A. Armstrong, David R. Scott. **1st docking of one space vehicle with another**; mission aborted, control malfunction; 1st Pacific landing.

6/3/1966: *Gemini-Titan 9A*; 72:21; Thomas P. Stafford (2), Eugene A. Cernan. Performed simulation of lunar module rendezvous.

7/18/1966: *Gemini-Titan 10*; 70:47; John W. Young (2), Michael Collins. 1st use of Agena target vehicle's propulsion systems; 1st orbital docking.

9/12/1966: *Gemini-Titan 11*; 71:17; Charles Conrad Jr. (2), Richard F. Gordon Jr. 1st tethered flight; highest Earth-orbit altitude (850 mi).

11/11/1966: *Gemini-Titan 12*; 94:34; James A. Lovell Jr., Edwin E. "Buzz" Aldrin Jr. Final *Gemini* mission; 5-hr. EVA.

4/23/1967: **Soyuz 1*; 26:40; Vladimir M. Komarov (2). Crashed on reentry, killing Komarov; **1st space fatality.**

10/11/1968: *Apollo-Saturn 7*; 260:09; Walter M. Schirra Jr. (3), Donn F. Eisele, R. Walter Cunningham. **1st piloted flight of Apollo** spacecraft command-service module only; live TV footage of crew.

12/21/1968: *Apollo-Saturn 8*; 147:00; Frank Borman (2), James A. Lovell Jr. (3), William A. Anders. **1st lunar orbit** and piloted lunar return reentry (command-service module only); views of lunar surface televised to Earth.

1/14/1969: **Soyuz 4*; 71:21; Vladimir A. Shatalov. Docked with *Soyuz 5.*

1/15/1969: **Soyuz 5*; 72:54; Boris V. Volyanov, Aleksei S. Yeliseyev, Yevgeny V. Khrunov. Docked with *Soyuz 4*; Yeliseyev and Khrunov transferred to *Soyuz 4* via a spacewalk.

3/3/1969: *Apollo-Saturn 9*; 241:00; James A. McDivitt (2), David R. Scott (2), Russell L. Schweickart. 1st piloted flight of lunar module.

5/18/1969: *Apollo-Saturn 10*; 192:03; Thomas P. Stafford (3), John W. Young (3), Eugene A. Cernan (2). 1st lunar module orbit of Moon, 50,000 ft from Moon's surface.

7/16/1969: *Apollo-Saturn 11*; 195:18; Neil A. Armstrong (2), Michael Collins (2), Edwin E. "Buzz" Aldrin Jr. (2). **1st Moon landing** made by Armstrong and Aldrin (7/20); collected 48.5 lbs of soil, rock samples; lunar stay time 21:36.

10/11/1969: **Soyuz 6*; 118:43; Georgi S. Shonin, Valery N. Kubasov. 1st welding of metals in space.

10/12/1969: **Soyuz 7*; 118:40; Anatoly V. Flipchenko, Vladislav N. Volkov, Viktor V. Gorbatko. Space lab construction test made; *Soyuz 6, 7,* and *8*: 1st time three spacecraft, seven crew members orbited the Earth at once.

10/13/1969: **Soyuz 8*; 118:51; Vladimir A. Shatalov (2), Aleksei S. Yeliseyev (2). Part of space lab construction team.

11/14/1969: *Apollo-Saturn 12*; 244:36; Charles Conrad Jr. (3), Richard F. Gordon Jr. (2), Alan L. Bean. Conrad and Bean made **2nd Moon landing** (11/18); collected 74.7 lbs of samples; lunar stay time 31:31.

4/11/1970: *Apollo-Saturn 13*; 142:54; James A. Lovell Jr. (4), Fred W. Haise Jr., John L. Swigert Jr. Aborted after service module oxygen tank ruptured; crew returned in lunar module.

6/1/1970: **Soyuz 9*; 17 d., 16 hr., 59 min.; Andrian G. Nikolayev (2), Vitaly I. Sevastyanov. Longest human spaceflight to date.

1/31/1971: *Apollo-Saturn 14*; 9 d., 2 min.; Alan B. Shepard Jr. (2), Stuart A. Roosa, Edgar D. Mitchell. Shepard and Mitchell made **3rd Moon landing** (2/3); collected 96 lbs of lunar samples; lunar stay 33:31.

4/19/1971: **Salyut 1*; launched without crew. **1st space station.**

4/22/1971: **Soyuz 10*; 1 d., 23 hr., 46 min.; Vladimir A. Shatalov (3), Aleksei S. Yeliseyev (3), Nikolay N. Rukavishnikov. **1st successful docking with a space station**; failed to enter space station.

6/6/1971: **Soyuz 11*; 23 d., 28 hr., 22 min.; Georgi T. Dobrovolskiy, Vladislav N. Volkov (2), Viktor I. Patsayev. Docked and entered *Salyut 1* space station; **crew died** during reentry from loss of pressurization.

7/26/1971: *Apollo-Saturn 15*; 12 d., 17 hr., 12 min.; David R. Scott (3), James B. Irwin, Alfred M. Worden. Scott and Irwin made **4th Moon landing** (7/30). 1st lunar rover use; 1st deep spacewalk; 170 lbs of samples; 66:55 stay.

4/16/1972: *Apollo-Saturn 16*; 11 d., 1 hr., 51 min.; John W. Young (4), Charles M. Duke Jr., Thomas K. Mattingly II. Young and Duke made **5th Moon landing** (4/20); collected 213 lbs of lunar samples; lunar stay 71:02.

12/7/1972: *Apollo-Saturn 17*; 12 d., 13 hr., 52 min.; Eugene A. Cernan (3), Ronald E. Evans, Harrison H. Schmitt. Cernan and Schmitt made 6th and **last lunar landing** (12/11); collected 243 lbs of samples; record lunar stay over 75 hr.

5/14/1973: *Skylab 1*; launched without crew. **1st U.S. space station**; fell out of orbit 7/11/1979.

5/25/1973: *Skylab 2*; 28 d., 49 min.; Charles Conrad Jr. (4), Joseph P. Kerwin, Paul J. Weitz. 1st U.S.-piloted orbiting space station; crew repaired damage caused in boost.

7/28/1973: *Skylab 3*; 59 d., 11 hr., 1 min.; Alan L. Bean (2), Owen K. Garriott, Jack R. Lousma. Crew systems and operational tests; scientific activities; three EVAs, 13:44.

11/16/1973: *Skylab 4*; 84 d., 1 hr., 16 min.; Gerald P. Carr, Edward G. Gibson, William R. Pogue. Final *Skylab* mission.

7/15/1975: **Soyuz 19 (ASTP)*; 6 d., 11 hr., 31 min.; Aleksei A. Leonov (2), Valery N. Kubasov (2). U.S.-USSR joint flight; crews linked up in space (7/17), conducted experiments, shared meals, held a joint news conference.

7/15/1975: *Apollo (ASTP)*; 9 d., 7 hr., 28 min.; Vance D. Brand, Thomas P. Stafford (4), Donald K. Slayton. Joint flight with *Soyuz 19*.

12/10/1977: **Soyuz 26*; 96 d., 10 hr.; Yuri V. Romanenko, Georgiy M. Grechko (2). 1st multiple docking at a space station (*Soyuz 26* and *27* docked at *Salyut 6*).

1/10/1978: **Soyuz 27*; 5 d., 22 hr., 59 min.; Vladimir A. Dzhanibekov. See *Soyuz 26*.

3/2/1978: **Soyuz 28*; 7 d., 22 hr., 16 min.; Aleksei A. Gubarev (2), Vladimir Remek. 1st international crew launch; Remek was 1st Czech in space.

4/12/1981: *Columbia (STS-1)*; 2 d., 6 hr., 21 min.; John W. Young (5), Robert L. Crippen. **1st reusable space shuttle** to fly into Earth's orbit.

11/12/1981: *Columbia (STS-2)*; 3 days; Joe H. Engle, Richard H. Truly. 1st scientific payload; 1st reuse of space shuttle.

11/11/1982: *Columbia (STS-5)*; 6 days; Vance D. Brand (2), Robert F. Overmyer, Joseph P. Allen, William B. Lenoir. 1st four-person crew.

6/18/1983: *Challenger (STS-7)*; 7 days; Robert L. Crippen (2), Frederick H. Hauck, John M. Fabian, Sally K. Ride, Norman E. Thagard. Ride was **1st U.S. woman in space**; 1st 5-person crew.

6/27/1983: **Soyuz T-9*; 150 days; Vladimir A. Lyakhov (2), Aleksandr Pavlovich. Docked at *Salyut 7*. 1st construction in space.

8/30/1983: *Challenger (STS-8)*; 7 days; Richard H. Truly (2), Daniel C. Brandenstein, Dale A. Gardner, Guion S. Bluford Jr., William E. Thornton. Bluford was **1st African American in space**; 1st night launch.

11/28/1983: *Columbia (STS-9)*; 11 days; John W. Young (6), Brewster H. Shaw Jr., Owen K. Garriott (2), Robert A.R. Parker, Byron K. Lichtenberg, Ulf Merbold. 1st six-person crew; 1st Spacelab mission.

2/3/1984: *Challenger (41-B)*; 8 days; Vance Brand (3), Robert L. Gibson, Ronald E. McNair, Bruce McCandless II, Robert L. Stewart. 1st untethered EVA.

2/8/1984: **Soyuz T-10B*; 63 days; Leonid Kizim, Vladimir Solovyov, Oleg Atkov. Docked with *Salyut 7*; crew set space duration record of 237 days.

4/3/1984: **Soyuz T-11*; 182 days; Yury Malyshev (2), Gennady Strekalov (3), Rakesh Sharma. Docked with *Salyut 7*; Sharma was 1st Indian in space.

4/6/1984: *Challenger (41-C)*; 7 days; Robert L. Crippen (3), Francis R. Scobee, George D. Nelson, Terry J. Hart, James D. van Hoften. 1st in-orbit satellite repair.

7/17/1984: **Soyuz T-12*; 12 days; Vladimir A. Dzhanibekov (4), Svetlana Y. Savitskaya (2), Igor P. Volk. Docked at *Salyut 7*; Savitskaya was 1st woman to perform EVA.

8/30/1984: *Discovery (41-D)*; 7 days; Henry W. Hartsfield Jr. (2), Michael L. Coats, Richard M. Mullane, Steven A. Hawley, Judith A. Resnik, Charles D. Walker. 1st flight of non-astronaut (payload specialist Walker).

10/5/1984: *Challenger (41-G)*; 9 days; Robert L. Crippen (4), Jon A. McBride, Kathryn D. Sullivan, Sally K. Ride (2), David C. Leestma, Marc Garneau, Paul D. Scully-Power. 1st seven-person crew.

11/8/1984: *Discovery (51-A)*; 8 days; Frederick H. Hauck (2), David M. Walker, Anna L. Fisher, Dale A. Gardner (2), Joseph P. Allen (2). 1st satellite retrieval/repair.

4/12/1985: *Discovery (51-D)*; 7 days; Karol J. Bobko, Donald E. Williams, Charles D. Walker (2), M. Rhea Seddon, Jeffrey A. Hoffman, S. David Griggs, E. Jake Garn. Garn (R, UT) was **1st U.S. senator in space**.

6/17/1985: *Discovery (51-G)*; 8 days; Daniel C. Brandenstein (2), John O. Creighton, Shannon W. Lucid, John M. Fabian (2), Steven R. Nagel, Prince Sultan Salman al-Saud, Patrick Baudry. Launched three satellites; Salman al-Saud was 1st Arab in space; Baudry was 1st French person on U.S. mission.

10/3/1985: *Atlantis (51-J)*; 5 days; Karol J. Bobko (3), Ronald J. Grabe, David C. Hilmers, Robert L. Stewart (2), William A. Pailes. 1st *Atlantis* flight.

10/30/1985: *Challenger (61-A)*; 8 days; Henry W. Hartsfield Jr. (3), Steven R. Nagel (2), James F. Buchli (2), Guion S. Bluford (2), Bonnie J. Dunbar, Wubbo J. Ockels, Richard Furrer, Ernst Messerschmid. 1st eight-person crew; 1st German Spacelab mission.

1/12/1986: *Columbia (61-C)*; 7 days; Robert L. Gibson (2), Charles F. Bolden Jr., Franklin R. Chang-Diaz, Steven A. Hawley (2), George D. Nelson (2), Robert J. Cenker, Bill Nelson. Nelson (D, FL) was **1st U.S. representative in space**.

1/28/1986: *Challenger (51-L)*; 73 seconds; Francis R. Scobee (2), Michael J. Smith, Judith A. Resnik (2), Ellison S. Onizuka (2), Ronald E. McNair, Gregory B. Jarvis, Christa McAuliffe. **Exploded 73 seconds after liftoff; all aboard were killed**, including McAuliffe, a New Hampshire schoolteacher who won a national competition to become 1st private citizen in space.

2/20/1986: **Mir[1]*; launched without crew. **Space station** with six docking ports launched.

3/13/1986: **Soyuz T-15*; 125 days; Leonid Kizim (3), Vladimir Solovyov (2). Ferry between stations; docked at *Mir*.

2/5/1987: **Soyuz TM-2*; 327 days; Yuri V. Romanenko (3), Aleksandr I. Laveikin. Romanenko set endurance record, since broken.

7/22/1987: **Soyuz TM-3*; 161 days; Aleksandr Viktorenko, Aleksandr Pavlovich Aleksandrov (2), Mohammed Faris. Docked with *Mir*; Faris was 1st Syrian in space.

9/29/1988: **Discovery (STS 26)*; 4 days; Frederick H. Hauck (3), Richard O. Covey (2), George D. Nelson (3), John M. Lounge (2), David C. Hilmers (2). **1st shuttle flight since *Challenger* explosion** 1/28/1986.

5/4/1989: *Atlantis (STS-30)*; 4 days; David M. Walker (2), Ronald J. Grabe (2), Norman E. Thagard (3), Mary L. Cleave (2), Mark C. Lee. Launched Venus orbiter *Magellan*.

10/18/1989: *Atlantis (STS-34)*; 5 days; Donald E. Williams (2), Michael J. McCulley, Shannon W. Lucid (2), Franklin R. Chang Díaz (2), Ellen S. Baker. Launched Jupiter probe and orbiter *Galileo*.

4/24/1990: *Discovery (STS-31)*; 6 days; Loren J. Shriver (2), Charles F. Bolden Jr. (2), Steven A. Hawley (3), Bruce McCandless (2), Kathryn D. Sullivan (2). **Launched Hubble Space Telescope**.

10/6/1990: *Discovery (STS-41)*; 5 days; Richard N. Richards (2), Robert D. Cabana, Bruce E. Melnick, William M. Shepherd (2), Thomas D. Akers. Launched *Ulysses* spacecraft to investigate interstellar space and the Sun.

5/18/1991: **Soyuz TM-12*; 145 days; Anatoly Artsebarsky, Sergei Krikalev (2) (to *Mir*), Helen Sharman. Docked with *Mir*; Sharman was 1st Briton in space.

3/17/1992: **Soyuz TM-14*; 146 days; Aleksandr Viktorenko (3) (to *Mir*), Alexandr Kaleri (to *Mir*), Klaus-Dietrich Flade, Aleksandr Volkov (3) (from *Mir*), Sergei Krikalev (2) (from *Mir*). 1st human CIS space mission; docked with *Mir* 3/19; Krikalev was in space 313 days.

5/7/1992: *Endeavour (STS-49)*; 9 days; Daniel C. Brandenstein (4), Kevin P. Chilton, Pierre J. Thuot (2), Kathryn Thornton (2), Richard J. Hieb (2), Thomas D. Akers (2), Bruce E. Melnick (2). 1st 3-person EVA; satellite recovery and redeployment.

9/12/1992: *Endeavour (STS-47)*; 8 days; Robert L. Gibson (4), Curtis L. Brown Jr., Mark C. Lee (2), N. Jan Davis, Jay Apt (2), Mae Carol Jemison, Mamoru Mohri. Jemison was **1st black woman in space**; Lee and Davis were **1st married couple to travel together in space**; 1st Japanese Spacelab.

6/21/1993: *Endeavour (STS-57)*; 10 days; Ronald J. Grabe (4), Brian J. Duffy (2), G. David Low (3), Nancy J. Sherlock, Janice E. Voss, Peter J. K. Wisoff. Carried Spacelab commercial payload module.

12/2/1993: *Endeavour (STS-61)*; 11 days; Richard O. Covey (3), Kenneth D. Bowersox (2), F. Story Musgrave (5), Kathryn Thornton (3), Claude Nicollier (2), Jeffrey A. Hoffman (4), Thomas D. Akers (3). Hubble Space Telescope repaired; Akers set new U.S. EVA duration record (29 hr., 40 min.).

2/3/1994: *Discovery (STS-60)*; 9 days; Charles F. Bolden Jr. (3), Kenneth S. Reightler Jr. (2), N. Jan Davis (2), Franklin R. Chang Díaz (3), Ronald M. Sega, Sergei Krikalev (3). Krikalev was 1st Russian on U.S. shuttle.

7/1/1994: **Soyuz TM-19*; 126 days; Yuri I. Malenchenko, Talgat A. Musabayev, Ulf Merbold (2) (from *Mir*). Docked with *Mir*.

9/9/1994: *Discovery (STS-64)*; 11 days; Richard N. Richards (4), L. Blaine Hammond Jr. (2), Jerry M. Linenger, Susan J. Helms (2), Carl J. Meade (3), Mark C. Lee (3). Performed atmospheric research; 1st untethered EVA in more than 10 years.

2/3/1995: *Discovery (STS-63)*; 9 days; James D. Wetherbee (3), Eileen M. Collins, Bernard A. Harris (2), C. Michael Foale (3), Janice E. Voss (2), Vladimir Titov (4). *Discovery* and Russian space station rendezvous.

3/2/1995: *Endeavour (STS-67)*; 17 days; Stephen S. Oswald (3), William G. Gregory, Tamara E. Jernigan (3), John M. Grunsfeld, Wendy B. Lawrence, Ronald Parise (2), Samuel T. Durrance (2). Shuttle data made available on the Internet.

3/14/1995: **Soyuz TM-21*; 112 days; Norman E. Thagard (5), Vladimir Dezhurov, Gennady Strekalov (3). Docked with *Mir* 3/16. Thagard was 1st American onboard Russian spacecraft; Valery Polyakov returned to Earth, 3/22/1995, after record stay in space (439 days).

6/27/1995: *Atlantis (STS-71)*; 10 days; Robert L. Gibson (5), Charles J. Precourt (2), Ellen S. Baker (3), Bonnie J. Dunbar (4), Gregory J. Harbaugh (3), Anatoly Solovyev (4) (to *Mir*), Nikolai M. Budarin (to *Mir*), Norman E. Thagard (5) (from *Mir*), Gennady Strekalov (from *Mir*), Vladimir Dezhurov (from *Mir*). **1st shuttle-*Mir* docking**; exchanged crew members with *Mir*.

11/12/1995: *Atlantis (STS-74)*; 9 days; Kenneth D. Cameron (3), James D. Halsell Jr. (2), Jerry L. Ross (5), William S. McArthur Jr. (2), Chris A. Hadfield. 2nd shuttle-*Mir* docking (11/15-11/18); erected a 15-ft permanent docking tunnel to *Mir* for future use by U.S. orbiters.

2/22/1996: *Columbia (STS-75)*; 16 days; Andrew M. Allen (3), Scott J. Horowitz, Franklin R. Chang Díaz (5), Umberto Guidoni, Jeffrey A. Hoffman (5), Maurizio Cheli, Claude Nicollier (3). Lost an Italian satellite when its tether was severed; microgravity experiments performed; singe marks found on two O-rings.

3/22/1996: *Atlantis (STS-76)*; 10 days; Kevin P. Chilton (2), Richard A. Searfoss (2), Shannon W. Lucid (5) (to *Mir*), Linda M. Godwin (3), Michael R. Clifford (3), Ronald M. Sega (2). 3rd shuttle-*Mir* docking (5 days); two-person EVA.

9/16/1996: *Atlantis (STS-79)*; 11 days; William F. Readdy (3), Terry W. Wilcutt (2), Thomas D. Akers (4), John E. Blaha (5) (to *Mir*), Jay Apt (4), Carl E. Walz (3), Shannon W. Lucid (5) (from *Mir*). Docked with *Mir* 9/18; exchanged crew members; Lucid set **U.S. and women's duration in space record** (188 days).

11/19/1996: *Columbia (STS-80)*; 18 days; Kenneth D. Cockrell (3), Kent V. Rominger (2), Tamara E. Jernigan (4), Thomas D. Jones (3), F. Story Musgrave (6). Longest-duration shuttle flight; Musgrave, 61, oldest thus far to fly in space; two science satellites deployed, retrieved.

1/12/1997: *Atlantis (STS-81)*; 11 days; Michael A. Baker (4), Brent W. Jett (2), John M. Grunsfeld (2), Marsha S. Ivins (4), Peter J. K. Wisoff (3), Jerry M. Linenger (2) (to *Mir*), John E. Blaha (5) (from *Mir*). Docked with *Mir* 1/14-1/19; Blaha spent 128 days in space.

2/11/1997: *Discovery (STS-82)*; 10 days; Kenneth D. Bowersox (4), Scott J. Horowitz (2), Mark C. Lee (4), Steven A. Hawley (4), Gregory J. Harbaugh (4), Steven L. Smith (2), Joseph R. Tanner (2). Increased capabilities of Hubble Space Telescope; five EVAs conducted to service it.

5/15/1997: *Atlantis (STS-84)*; 10 days; Charles J. Precourt (3), Eileen M. Collins (2), C. Michael Foale (4) (to *Mir*), Carlos I. Noriega, Edward T. Lu, Jean-François Clervoy (2), Elena Kondakova, Jerry M. Linenger (2) (from *Mir*). Docked with *Mir* 5/16-5/21. Foale's stay on *Mir* marked by major collision with cargo ship 6/25/1997.

8/5/1997: **Soyuz TM-26*; 198 days; Anatoly Solovyev (5), Pavel Vinogradov. Docked with *Mir* 8/7; repaired damaged space station.

8/7/1997: *Discovery (STS-85)*; 12 days; Curtis L. Brown Jr. (4), Kent V. Rominger (3), N. Jan Davis (3), Robert L. Curbeam Jr., Stephen K. Robinson, Bjarni V. Tryggvason. Deployed and retrieved satellite designed to study Earth's middle atmosphere; demonstrated robotic arm.

9/25/1997: *Atlantis (STS-86)*; 11 days; James D. Wetherbee (4), Michael J. Bloomfield, Vladimir Titov (4), Scott E. Parazynski (2), Jean-Loup J. Chrétien (3), Wendy B. Lawrence (2), David A. Wolf (2) (to *Mir*), C. Michael Foale (4) (from *Mir*). Docked with *Mir* 9/27-10/3; delivered new computer to *Mir*.

4/17/1998: *Columbia (STS-90)*; 16 days; Richard A. Searfoss (3), Scott D. Altman, Richard M. Linnehan (2), Dave R. Williams, Kathryn P. Hire, Jay C. Buckey, James A. Pawelczyk. Studied effects of microgravity on the nervous systems of the crew and more than 2,000 live animals; 1st surgery in space on animals meant to survive.

6/2/1998: *Discovery (STS-91)*; 10 days; Charles J. Precourt (4), Dominic L. Gorie, Wendy B. Lawrence (3), Franklin R. Chang Díaz (6), Janet L. Kavandi, Valery Y. Ryumin (4), Andrew S.W. Thomas (2) (from *Mir*). Final docking mission with *Mir*; Thomas from *Mir*, 141 days in space.

10/29/1998: *Discovery (STS-95)*; 10 days; Curtis L. Brown Jr. (5), Steven W. Lindsey (2), Scott E. Parazynski (3), Stephen K. Robinson (2), Pedro Duque, Chiaki Mukai (2), John H. Glenn Jr. (2). The 77-year-old Glenn, one of the original *Mercury* astronauts, and at that point a senator (D, OH), became **oldest person to fly in space**; Duque was 1st Spaniard in space; experiments to study aging performed on Glenn.

12/4/1998: *Endeavour (STS-88)*; 12 days; Robert D. Cabana (4), Frederick W. Sturckow, Nancy J. Currie (3), Jerry L. Ross (6), James H. Newman (3), Sergei K. Krikalev (4). **1st assembly of International Space Station (ISS)**; attached U.S.-built *Unity* connecting module to Russian-built *Zarya* control module; 1st crew to enter ISS.

7/23/1999: *Columbia (STS-93)*; 5 days; Eileen M. Collins (3), Jeffrey S. Ashby, Steven A. Hawley (5), Catherine G. Coleman (2), Michel Tognini (2). Collins was **1st woman space shuttle commander**; deployed Chandra X-ray Observatory telescope.

2/11/2000: *Endeavour (STS-99)*; 12 days; Kevin R. Kregel (4), Dominic L. Gorie (2), Janet L. Kavandi (2), Janice E. Voss (5), Mamoru Mohri (2), Gerhard P.J. Thiele. Used radar to make most complete topographic map of Earth's surface ever produced.

9/8/2000: *Atlantis (STS-106)*; 12 days; Terry W. Wilcutt (4), Scott D. Altman (2), Edward T. Lu (2), Richard A. Mastracchio, Daniel C. Burbank (2), Yuri I. Malenchenko (2), Boris V. Morukov.

Prepared ISS for 1st permanent crew; one EVA by all seven crew members.

10/31/2000: *Soyuz TM-31*; William M. Shepherd (4), Yuri Gidzenko (2), Sergei Krikalev (5). Established **1st permanent manning of ISS** with three-person crew for a 4-month stay.

3/8/2001: *Discovery (STS-102)*; 13 days; James D. Wetherbee (5), James M. Kelly, Andrew S.W. Thomas (2), Paul Richards, Susan J. Helms (4) (to ISS), James S. Voss (5) (to ISS), Yuri V. Usachev (4) (to ISS), William M. Shepherd (4) (from ISS), Sergei K. Krikalev (5) (from ISS), Yuri P. Gidzenko (2) (from ISS). Transported 2nd permanent crew to ISS and returned 1st crew to Earth; two EVAs.

7/12/2001: *Atlantis (STS-104)*; 13 days; Steven W. Lindsey (3), Charles O. Hobaugh, Michael L. Gernhardt (4), Janet L. Kavandi (3), James F. Reilly II (2). Installed the Joint Airlock, with nitrogen and oxygen tanks to permit future spacewalks from the ISS; three EVAs.

3/1/2002: *Columbia (STS-109)*; 11 days; Scott D. Altman (3), Duane G. Carey, John M. Grunsfeld (4), Nancy J. Currie (4), Richard M. Linnehan (3), James H. Newman (4), Michael J. Massimino. Installed powerful new camera and upgraded other equipment on Hubble Space Telescope; five EVAs.

4/8/2002: *Atlantis (STS-110)*; 11 days; Michael J. Bloomfield (3), Stephen N. Frick, Jerry L. Ross (7), Steven L. Smith (4) Ellen Ochoa (4), Lee M.E. Morin, Rex J. Walheim. Installed S0 Truss, backbone for expansion of ISS; Ross set records with 7th spaceflight, 9th spacewalk.

10/30/2002: *Soyuz TMA-1*[2]; Sergei Zalyotin (2), Frank De Winne (2), Yuri Lonchakov (2). 1st launch of *Soyuz TMA* (crew returned 11/10/2002 on *Soyuz TM-34* already docked at ISS).

1/16/2003: *Columbia (STS 107)*; 16 days; Rick D. Husband (2), William C. McCool, Michael P. Anderson (2), David M. Brown, Kalpana Chawla (2), Laurel B. Clark, Ilan Ramon. **Entire crew lost when** *Columbia* **burned** during reentry, 2/1; Ramon was 1st Israeli astronaut.

10/15/2003: *Shenzhou 5*; 21 hr.; Yang Liwei. **1st Chinese manned spacecraft.**

6/21/2004: SpaceShipOne; 90 min.; Mike Melvill. **1st privately funded manned spaceflight**[3].

7/26/2005: *Discovery (STS-114)*; 14 days; Eileen M. Collins (4), James M. Kelly (2), Charles J. Camarda, Wendy B. Lawrence (4), Soichi Noguchi, Stephen K. Robinson (3), Andrew S.W. Thomas (3). **1st space shuttle flight since** *Columbia* **disaster;** tested new safety modifications to craft.

7/4/2006: *Discovery (STS-121)*; 13 days; Steven W. Lindsey (4), Mark E. Kelly, Michael E. Fossum, Piers J. Sellers (2), Lisa M. Nowak, Thomas Reiter (to ISS), Stephanie D. Wilson. 1st shuttle to launch on Independence Day; conducted more safety tests to craft; brought supplies to and performed maintenance on ISS.

4/7/2007: *Soyuz TMA-10*[2]; Oleg Kotov (to ISS), Sheikh Muszaphar Shukor (to ISS), Charles Simonyi (U.S.) Fyodor Yurchikhin (to ISS). Kotov and Yurchikhin joined ISS expedition 15; Simonyi became **5th space tourist** (returned on *TMA-9*); Shukor was 1st Malaysian in space (arrived on *TMA-11*).

6/8/2007: *Atlantis (STS-117)*; 14 days; Frederick W. Sturckow (3), Lee J. Archambault, Patrick G. Forrester (2), John "Danny" Olivas, James F. Reilly (3), Steven R. Swanson, Clayton C. Anderson (to ISS), Sunita L. Williams (from ISS). Delivered truss segments and solar arrays to ISS; Williams set record for longest spaceflight by a woman.

8/8/2007: *Endeavour (STS-118)*; 13 days; Scott J. Kelly (2), Charles O. Hobaugh (2), Alvin B. Drew, Barbara R. Morgan, Tracy Caldwell Dyson, Rick A. Mastracchio (2), Dave R. Williams (2). Brought **Teacher in Space** project participant Morgan to ISS; attached new truss segment; repaired faulty gyroscope.

10/10/2007: *Soyuz TMA-11*[2]; Yuri I. Malenchenko (3), Sheikh Muszaphar Shukor (to ISS), Peggy A. Whitson (2) (from ISS), Yi So-yeon (from ISS). Delivered and installed components of ISS; malfunctioned on return to Earth, landing short of its touchdown area but causing no fatalities.

10/23/2007: *Discovery (STS-120)*; 16 days; Pamela A. Melroy (3), George D. Zamka, Scott E. Parazynski (5), Douglas H. Wheelock, Stephanie D. Wilson (2), Paolo Nespoli, Daniel M. Tani (2) (to ISS), Clayton C. Anderson (from ISS). Installed living space (Harmony Node 2) on ISS.

2/7/2008: *Atlantis (STS-122)*; 13 days; Stephen N. Frick (2), Stanley G. Love, Leland D. Melvin, Alan G. Poindexter, Hans Schlegel (2), Léopold Eyharts (to ISS), Daniel M. Tani (from ISS), Rex J. Walheim (2). Installed European Space Agency's Columbus laboratory on the ISS; minor damage to a thermal plate caused concern about the shuttle's safety during reentry, but *Atlantis* landed safely.

3/11/2008: *Endeavour (STS-123)*; 16 days; Dominic L. Gorie (4), Gregory H. Johnson, Richard M. Linnehan (4), Robert L. Behnken, Michael J. Foreman, Takao Doi (2), Garrett Reisman (to ISS), Léopold Eyharts (from ISS). Delivered and installed components of the Japanese Kibo science laboratory.

4/8/2008: *Soyuz TMA-12*[2]; Oleg Kononenko, Sergei Volkov, Yi So-yeon (to ISS), Richard Garriott (from ISS). Yi became 1st S. Korean in space.

5/31/2008: *Discovery (STS-124)*; 14 days; Mark E. Kelly (3), Kenneth T. Ham, Karen L. Nyberg, Ronald J. Garan Jr., Michael E. Fossum (2), Akihiko Hoshide, Gregory E. Chamitoff (to ISS), Garrett E. Reisman (from ISS). Delivered and installed pressurized and experimental modules of Kibo.

9/25/2008: *Shenzhou 7*; 68 hr.; Jing Haipeng, Liu Boming, Zhai Zhigang. Zhai completed 1st Chinese spacewalk.

10/12/2008: *Soyuz TMA-13*[2]; Richard Garriott (to ISS), Yuri V. Lonchakov (3), Michael Fincke. Garriott became 6th space tourist.

3/15/2009: *Discovery (STS-119)*; 13 days; Lee J. Archambault (2), Dominic A. Antonelli, Joseph M. Acaba, John L. Phillips, Steven R. Swanson (2), Richard R. Arnold, Koichi Wakata (to ISS), Sandra H. Magnus (from ISS). Delivered final solar panels and last U.S.-made truss segment.

5/11/2009: *Atlantis (STS-125)*; 13 days; Scott D. Altman (4), Gregory C. Johnson, Andrew J. Feustel, Michael T. Good, John M. Grunsfeld (5), Michael J. Massimino (2), K. Megan McArthur. Final Hubble Space Telescope servicing mission.

11/16/2009: *Atlantis (STS-129)*; 11 days; Charles O. Hobaugh (3), Barry E. Wilmore, Leland D. Melvin (2), Michael J. Foreman (2), Randolph J. Bresnik, Robert L. Satcher Jr., Nicole P. Stott (from ISS). Final Space Shuttle crew rotation flight.

6/15/2010: *Soyuz TMA-19*[2]; Fyodor Yurchikhin (3), Shannon Walker, Douglas H. Wheelock (2). 100th mission since launching of the International Space Station.

7/8/2011: *Atlantis (STS-135)*; 13 days; Christopher Ferguson (3), Doug Hurley (2), Sandy H. Magnus (3), Rex J. Walheim (3). Final Space Shuttle mission.

Note: Four Soviet cosmonauts have died during spaceflight: Vladimir Komarov was killed on *Soyuz 1* (1967) when parachute lines tangled during descent; the three-person *Soyuz 11* crew (1971) was asphyxiated. Six Americans and an Israeli astronaut died aboard the *Columbia*; seven Americans died in the *Challenger* explosion; and three astronauts—Virgil I. Grissom, Edward H. White, and Roger B. Chaffee—died in the Jan. 27, 1967, *Apollo 1* fire on the ground at Cape Canaveral, FL. (1) Space stations, such as the *Salyuts* and *Mir*, were used to house crews starting in 1971. (2) *Soyuz* crew often return from the ISS on spacecraft that launched and were docked at the station before their arrival. (3) Date of first successful flight; later, *SpaceShipOne* flew at least 100 km (62 mi) into space, 9/29/2004, piloted by Mike Melvill, and 10/4/2004, piloted by Brian Binnie, winning the $10 mil Ansari Prize for first private venture to accomplish this feat twice within two weeks.

U.S. Manned Space Program

Source: National Aeronautics and Space Administration (NASA)

After 50 years of sending men and women into space, the United States ended its manned space program with the safe landing of the *Atlantis* space shuttle on July 21, 2011, at Florida's Kennedy Space Center. In the short term, all U.S. astronauts will have to rent space on Russian rockets. In Oct. 2012, Hawthorne, CA-based SpaceX became the first private company to resupply cargo to the International Space Station. Under a $1.6-bil deal with NASA, SpaceX will send a total of 12 such flights to the space station, with the hope of eventually carrying passengers into space.

The surviving space shuttles are now on display at museums around the country. *Discovery* was placed at the Smithsonian National Air and Space Museum's Udvar-Hazy Center at Washington-Dulles Intl. Airport in Virginia. It replaced *Enterprise*, which performed test runs but never went into space. *Enterprise* was moved to New York City's Intrepid Air, Sea, and Space Museum. *Endeavour* took up residence at the California Science Center in Los Angeles. *Atlantis* remained on permanent display at the Kennedy Space Center.

International Space Station

Source: National Aeronautics and Space Administration (NASA)

The International Space Station (ISS) is considered the largest cooperative scientific project in history. Construction began in 1998 and was completed in 2011. It has been inhabited by more than 200 international crew members since 2000.

15 cooperating nations: Belgium, Canada, Denmark, France, Germany, Italy, Japan, Netherlands, Norway, Russia, Spain, Sweden, Switzerland, United Kingdom, and the U.S.

About the ISS

- It has a mass of 924,739 lbs and is about as long as a football field at 357.5 feet.
- It is entirely powered by an acre of solar panels.
- Its internal volume is roughly equivalent to that of a five-bedroom house or a 747 jumbo jet.
- It requires three people to keep it running but has room for up to 10 people to live aboard.
- Astronauts typically spend 4-6 months aboard the Space Station.

ISS Research

- Studying the effects of long-term exposure to reduced gravity on plants, crystals, plant and animal cells, and pathogens
- Studying the effects on humans of long-term exposure to reduced gravity
- Recording large-scale long-term changes in Earth's environment by observing the planet from orbit
- Testing recycling technologies for human life support

Summary of Worldwide Successful Launches, 1957-2013

Source: National Aeronautics and Space Administration (NASA); Space Launch Report

Country	1957-59	1960-69	1970-79	1980-89	1990-99	2000-09	2010-13[1]	Total
Russia[2]	6	399	1,028	1,132	542	246	106	3,459
U.S.	18	614	247	191	300	206	55	1,631
China	—	—	8	16	33	52	57	166
ESA[3]	—	2	5	14	55	63	23	162
Japan	—	—	18	26	23	18	9	94
India	—	—	1	9	11	13	8	42
France	—	4	14	5	16	0	0	39
UK	—	1	6	4	7	0	0	18
Germany	—	—	3	7	6	0	0	16
Canada	—	—	4	5	4	0	0	13
Israel	—	—	—	—	—	3	1	4
Iran	—	—	—	—	—	1	2	3
S. Korea	—	—	—	—	—	1	1	2
N. Korea	—	—	—	—	—	—	1	1
Total[4]	24	1,020	1,334	1,409	997	603	263	5,650

— = Not applicable. (1) As of Aug. 8, 2013. (2) Data for 1957-91 apply to the Soviet Union, for 1992-96 to the Commonwealth of Independent States, after 1996 to Russia. (3) European Space Agency. Member states are Austria, Belgium, Denmark, Finland, France, Germany, Greece, Ireland, Italy, Luxemburg, the Netherlands, Norway, Portugal, Spain, Sweden, Switzerland, and the United Kingdom. Canada, Hungary, and the Czech Republic also participate in some projects under cooperation agreements. (4) Includes launches sponsored by countries not shown.

Notable Lunar and Planetary Science Missions

Source: National Aeronautics and Space Administration (NASA)

Spacecraft	Launch date[1]	Mission	Remarks
Mariner 2	Aug. 27, 1962	Venus	Passed within 22,000 mi of Venus 12/14/1962; confirmed high surface temperature on planet; contact lost 1/3/1963 at 54 mil mi.
Ranger 7	July 28, 1964	Moon	Yielded over 4,000 photos of lunar surface.
Mariner 4	Nov. 28, 1964	Mars	1st probe to fly by Mars; passed behind planet 7/14/1965.
Ranger 8	Feb. 17, 1965	Moon	Yielded over 7,000 photos of lunar surface.
Venera 3	Nov. 16, 1965	Venus	Soviet probe; 1st artificial probe to impact on the surface of another planet, 3/1/1966; probe failed to send back data.
Surveyor 3	Apr. 17, 1967	Moon	Scooped and tested lunar soil.
Mariner 5	June 14, 1967	Venus	In solar orbit; closest Venus flyby 10/19/1967; allowed scientists to obtain accurate readings on the composition of the Venusian atmosphere.
Mariner 6	Feb. 24, 1969	Mars	Came within 2,000 mi of Mars 7/31/1969; collected data, photos.
Mariner 7	Mar. 27, 1969	Mars	Came within 2,000 mi of Mars 8/5/1969.
Venera 7	Aug. 17, 1970	Venus	Soviet probe; 1st probe to land safely on the surface of another planet.
Mariner 9	May 30, 1971	Mars	1st craft to orbit Mars 11/13/1971; sent back over 7,000 photos.
Pioneer 10	Mar. 2, 1972	Jupiter	Passed Jupiter 12/4/1973; took readings on Jupiter's composition and found that the planet is composed mostly of hydrogen. Exited the planetary system 6/13/1983; transmission ended 3/31/1997 at 6.39 bil mi.
Pioneer 11	Apr. 5, 1973	Jupiter, Saturn	Passed Jupiter 12/3/1974, Saturn 9/1/1979; discovered an additional ring and 2 moons around Saturn. Transmission ended 9/30/1995.
Mariner 10	Nov. 3, 1973	Venus, Mercury	Passed Venus 2/5/1974, arrived at Mercury 3/29/1974. 1st time gravity of 1 planet (Venus) used to whip spacecraft toward another (Mercury); 1st probe to visit 2 planets; took cloud and wind pattern readings in Venusian atmosphere.

Spacecraft	Launch date[1]	Mission	Remarks
Viking 1	Aug. 20, 1975	Mars	Landed on Mars 7/20/1976; 1st probe to land safely on Mars; performed chemical analysis of soil; functioned 6 years.
Viking 2	Sept. 9, 1975	Mars	Sister probe of *Viking 1*; landed on Mars 9/3/1976; functioned 3 years.
Voyager 2	Aug. 20, 1977	Jupiter, Saturn, Uranus, Neptune	Encountered Jupiter 7/9/1979, Saturn 8/25/1981, Uranus 1/24/1986, Neptune 8/25/1989. Confirmed existence of rings around Neptune; observed Neptune's "great dark spot," which has since dissipated. Entered boundary of solar system 10/2007; as of 9/2013, it was 9.5 bil mi (15.3 bil km) from Sun and still returning data to Earth.
Voyager 1	Sept. 5, 1977	Jupiter, Saturn	Encountered Jupiter 3/5/1979; provided evidence of rings around Jupiter; passed near Saturn 11/12/1980; passed *Pioneer 10* to become most distant human-made object 2/17/1998; as of 9/2013, it had reached a distance of 11.6 bil mi (18.7 bil km) from Sun and was still returning data to Earth.
Pioneer Venus 1	May 20, 1978	Venus	Entered Venus orbit 12/4/1978; studied atmosphere, magnetic field, weather, and surface; fuel ran out, and probe was destroyed in atmospheric entry, 8/1992.
Pioneer Venus 2 (multiprobe)	Aug. 8, 1978	Venus	Consisted of a "bus" carrying 1 large and 3 small atmospheric probes. All 4 probes entered the Venus atmosphere 12/9/1978, followed by the bus; took readings of atmosphere; probes impacted surface.
Magellan	May 4, 1989	Venus	Landed on Venus 8/10/1990; monitored geological activity; mapped more than 99% of planet surface, observed more than 1,600 volcanoes and volcanic features, enabling creation of a 3-D map; showed that about 85% of the surface is covered by volcanic flows; ceased operating 10/11/1994.
Galileo	Oct. 18, 1989	Jupiter	Used Earth's gravity to propel itself towards Jupiter; encountered Venus 2/1990, Jupiter 12/7/1995; encountered moons. Released probe into Jovian atmosphere; intentionally flown into Jupiter 9/21/2003 to prevent accidental contamination of Jupiter's moon Europa.
Mars Global Surveyor	Nov. 7, 1996	Mars	Began orbiting Mars 9/11/1997; began mapping entire surface 3/9/1999; discovered a weak magnetic field on planet; observed Martian moon Phobos; found evidence of liquid water in past 6/22/2000.
Mars Pathfinder	Dec. 4, 1996	Mars	Landed on Mars 7/4/1997; rover *Sojourner* made measurements of climate and soil composition, sending thousands of surface images; ceased operating 9/27/1997.
Cassini-Huygens	Oct. 15, 1997	Saturn	Began orbiting Saturn 6/30/2004; 4-year mission to study planet's atmosphere, rings, and moons; spotted evidence of a subterranean ocean and 300-mi-wide hot spot region on moon Titan; detected an atmosphere on moon Enceladus. *Huygens* probe landed on Titan 1/14/2005; found a muddy surface, possible deposits of water ice, channels carved by liquid methane springs.
Lunar Prospector	Jan. 6, 1998	Moon	Began orbiting Moon 1/11/1998; mapped abundance of 11 elements on Moon's surface; discovered evidence of water ice at both lunar poles; crashed into crater near Moon's south pole 7/31/1999 to end mission.
Deep Space 1	Oct. 24, 1998	Comet Borrelly	Flew within 1,500 mi of comet; sent back photos showing 6-mi-long nucleus.
Stardust	Feb. 7, 1999	Comet Wild-2	Reached comet 1/2/2004; gathered dust samples, returned to Earth 1/15/2006.
2001 Mars Odyssey	Apr. 7, 2001	Mars	Reached Mars 10/24/2001; detected evidence of water ice near south pole; primary mission to study climate and geologic history completed 8/2004; began extended mission, aiming to identify minerals on Mars.
Genesis	Aug. 8, 2001	Sun	Orbited Sun, collected particles from solar wind; capsule containing specimens crashed to Earth 9/8/2004; some samples survived.
Mars Express/ Beagle 2 lander	June 3, 2003	Mars	1st European Space Agency probe to another planet; arrived at Mars 12/2003; performed remote sensing including photography in search of subsurface water; *Beagle 2* lander was deployed 12/19/2003, but contact was lost soon after.
Mars Exploration Rovers	June 7 and July 10, 2003	Mars	Rovers *Spirit* and *Opportunity* landed on Mars 1/2004, found further evidence that water existed on surface; *Spirit* took 1st photo of a Martian meteor; survived severe dust storms in 2007. *Opportunity* explored massive Victoria Crater 9/2007-8/2008; sighted larger Endeavour Crater 3/2009.
MESSENGER	Mar. 2, 2004	Mercury	Began returning images of Mercury during initial flyby 1/14/2008; entered orbit 3/17/2011; delivered 100,000th image 5/3/2012.
Deep Impact	Jan. 12, 2005	Comet Tempel 1	Reached comet 7/4/2005; deployed an impact probe that slammed into comet 7/4/2005 with a force roughly equivalent to 5 tons of TNT.
Mars Reconnaissance Orbiter	Aug. 12, 2005	Mars	Reached Mars 3/10/2006 and began taking detailed images of Martian surface; in 3/2008, found salt deposits suggesting ancient water supplies; in 6/2008, found largest known crater in solar system.
New Horizons (Pluto)	Jan. 19, 2006	Pluto, Charon	Flew by Jupiter 7/2007. Due to reach Pluto and Charon in 7/2015; may examine other Kuiper Belt Objects.
Phoenix Mars Lander	Aug. 4, 2007	Mars	Landed on Mars 5/25/2008; examined northern polar region; monitored weather and analyzed minerals; evidence of water ice verified 7/31/2008; lost contact 11/2/2008.
Dawn	Sept. 27, 2007	Asteroid Belt (bet. Jupiter and Mars)	Will compare the evolution of dwarf planet Ceres with Vesta, an asteroid, in an effort to shed light on formation of the solar system. Departed Vesta 8/2012; expected to arrive at Ceres 2/2015.
Lunar CRater Observation and Sensing Satellite (LCROSS)	June 18, 2009	Moon	Impact into Cabeus crater detected presence of water ice in Moon's surface on 10/9/2009; subsequent analysis found methane, ammonia, hydrogen gas, and large amounts of sodium and mercury.
Mars Science Laboratory Curiosity Rover (Mars Rover)	Nov. 26, 2011	Mars	Landed on Mars 8/6/2012 and began assessing whether Mars is or ever was able to support microbial life and other factors in the planet's potential for habitability.

(1) In Coordinated Universal Time.

Notable U.S. Space Missions in 2013

Source: National Aeronautics and Space Administration (NASA)

Scheduled launch	Mission	Purpose
Sept. 6, 2013	Lunar Atmosphere and Dust Environment Explorer (LADEE)	Orbit the moon for 100 days to study the fragile lunar atmosphere before it is further disturbed by human activity.
Nov. 18, 2013	Mars Atmosphere and Volatile Evolution (MAVEN)	Explore the red planet's upper atmosphere to determine how the loss of volatile organic compounds like carbon dioxide and nitrogen dioxide have affected the Martian climate over time.

General Aviation and Air Taxi Active Aircraft, 2010

Source: Federal Aviation Administration; aircraft not associated with major airlines or the military

Aircraft	Total active	Personal	Busi- ness	Cor- porate	Instruc- tional	Aerial apps.	Aerial obser- vation	Other work	Sight- seeing	Air medical	Other	On-demand operations
Fixed wing.....	176,272	117,015	20,476	9,680	12,685	2,709	3,614	618	311	121	3,203	5,545
Piston........	155,419	114,059	17,572	1,300	12,508	1,439	3,017	427	308	73	2,129	2,421
Turboprop.....	9,369	1,771	1,716	1,980	124	1,266	582	178	3	29	195	1,402
Turbojet	11,484	1,185	1,189	6,400	53	3	15	13	0	19	879	1,723
Rotorcraft.....	10,102	1,520	486	565	1,324	519	2,124	73	181	89	216	2,421
Piston........	3,588	1,193	314	16	1,215	195	327	15	117	4	57	87
Turbine........	6,514	327	173	550	109	325	1,798	58	65	85	159	2,334
Other aircraft....	5,684	4,534	73	0	329	0	3	78	550	0	77	39
Gliders........	1,899	1,621	0	0	211	0	3	0	30	0	34	0
Lighter-than-air..	3,785	2,914	73	0	118	0	0	78	520	0	43	39
Experimental....	24,784	22,047	575	160	445	85	164	30	415	22	731	106
Amateur.......	21,270	19,604	411	3	388	0	111	5	400	0	349	0
Exhibition......	2,029	1,716	40	0	32	4	7	9	12	0	207	0
Other	1,485	726	125	157	25	80	46	16	2	22	175	106
Light sport.....	6,528	5,738	55	0	621	0	24	7	0	0	83	0
Total aircraft	223,370	150,854	21,666	10,405	15,404	3,313	5,929	806	1,457	232	4,311	8,112

Note: Columns may not add up to totals due to rounding. Personal—Flying for personal reasons; Business—Individual or group use for business transportation without a paid, professional crew; Corporate—Individual or group business transportation with a paid, professional crew (includes fractional ownership); Instructional—Flying under the supervision of a flight instructor; Aerial applications—Includes agriculture, forestry, public health, fire fighting, and other applications; Aerial observation—Includes aerial mapping/photography, patrol, search and rescue, hunting, traffic advisory, ranching, surveillance, oil and mineral exploration, etc.; Other work—Construction work, parachuting, aerial advertising, towing gliders, etc.; Sightseeing—Commercial sightseeing; Air medical—Air ambulance services, rescue, human organ transportation, emergency medical services; Other—Positioning flights, proficiency flights, training, ferrying, sales demos; On-demand operations—On-demand air taxi, air tours, commuter, and air medical services.

Estimated Active Airmen Certificates Held, 2012

Source: Federal Aviation Administration, U.S. Dept. of Transportation

Category	Certificates	Category	Certificates	Category	Certificates
Pilot total..............	610,576	Airline Transport.....	145,590	Parachute Rigger	8,474
Student	119,946	Rotorcraft (helicopters)		Ground Instructor	73,599
Recreational (only)	218	(only)	15,126	Dispatcher............	21,862
Sport (only)..........	4,493	Glider (only)	20,802	Flight Navigator.......	141
Airplane[1]		Nonpilot total	701,291	Flight Attendant.......	172,357
Private	188,001	Mechanic............	337,775	Flight Engineer	46,639
Commercial........	116,400	Repairmen	40,444		

Note: The term airmen includes men and women certified as pilots, mechanics, or other aviation technicians. (1) Includes pilots with an airplane-only certificate as well as those with an airplane and a helicopter and/or glider certificate.

Aircraft Operating Statistics

Source: Airbus S.A.S.; The Boeing Company; Embraer S.A.

Manufacturer and model	Max. # of seats	Typical # of seats	Fuel capacity (gal)	Typical cruising speed (mph)[1]	Max. range (naut. mi)	Max. thrust (thous. lbs)	Manufacturer and model	Max. # of seats	Typical # of seats	Fuel capacity (gal)	Typical cruising speed (mph)[1]	Max. range (naut. mi)	Max. thrust (thous. lbs)
Airbus							**Boeing**						
A318	132	107	6,400	630	3,200	24.0	727-200*....	189	148	9,806	605	2,500	17.4
A319	156	124	6,400	630	3,700	27.0	737-600	132	110	6,875	602	3,225	22.7
A320	180	150	6,400	630	3,300	27.0	737-700	149	126	6,875	602	3,440	26.3
A321	220	185	6,350	630	6,200	33.0	737-700C ...	140	126	6,875	599	3,285	27.3
A330-200...	380	253	36,750	660	7,250	72.0	737-800	189	162	6,875	602	3,115	27.3
A330-300...	440	295	26,765	660	5,850	72.0	737-900	215	180	7,837	599	3,265	27.3
A340-300...	440	295	37,150	660	7,400	34.0	747-100	452	366	48,445	645	6,100	50.1
A340-500...	375	313	56,870	660	9,000	56.0	747-200/300	452	366	52,410	645	7,900	54.8
A340-600...	475	380	51,750	660	7,900	60.0	747-400	524	416	57,285	653	7,260	63.3
A380	853	525	84,600	684	8,300	70.0	747-8	467	467	64,055	653	8,000	66.5
Embraer							757-200*....	228	200	11,489	614	3,900	43.5
190	114	98	NA	630	2,400	20.0	757-300*....	280	243	11,466	614	3,395	43.5
195	122	108	NA	630	2,200	20.0	767-200ER ..	255	181	23,980	614	6,385	63.3
McDonnell- Douglas							767-300ER ..	350	218	23,980	614	5,990	63.3
DC-10 series*	380	250	36,650	600	6,220	24.0	767-400ER ..	375	245	23,980	614	5,625	63.5
MD-11*	410	285	NA	NA	7,360	NA	777-200	440	305	31,000	645	5,420	77.0
MD-80 series*	172	155	5,840	584	2,504	21.0	777-200ER ..	440	301	45,220	645	7,725	93.7
MD-90 series*	172	153	7,620	584	3,205	28.0	777-200LR ..	NA	301	47,890	645	9,395	115.3
							777-300	550	368	45,220	645	6,005	98.0
							777-300ER ..	NA	365	47,890	645	7,390	115.3
							787-8 Dreamliner	250	210	NA	652	8,200	NA
							787-9 Dreamliner	290	250	NA	652	8,500	NA

* = Aircraft no longer in production. NA = Not available. Note: Figures are for most commonly flown passenger models. When models within a series vary, maximums are shown. McDonnell-Douglas merged with Boeing in 1997. (1) Figures shown are converted from Mach speed (speed of sound), which varies depending on altitude and temperature. For comparison purposes, this table uses 768 mph as equivalent to Mach 1.

Milestones in Aviation History

Source: National Aeronautics and Space Administration (NASA); National Air and Space Museum; Air Transport Association of America; National Museum of the U.S. Air Force (USAF); U.S. National Park Service

1903, Dec. 17: Brothers Wilbur and Orville Wright (U.S.) made the first human-carrying, powered flight near Kitty Hawk, NC. Each brother made two flights; the longest, about 852 ft, lasted 59 seconds.

1908, May 14: Charles Furnas (U.S.), worker for Wright brothers, became first American airplane passenger.

1911, Feb.: The Burgess Company and Curtiss, Inc. receive authorization to build Wright planes, becoming the first licensed airplane manufacturer in the U.S.

1911, Sept. 23: First transportation of mail by airplane officially approved by the U.S. Postal Service.

1914, Jan. 1: First scheduled passenger airline service began. A seaplane that landed on water operated between St. Petersburg and Tampa, FL.

1918, Mar. 6: The Curtiss-Sperry "Flying Bomb" (U.S.) made its first successful flight. The first radio-controlled plane led to the development of both autopilot systems and cruise missiles.

1918, May 14: First scheduled airmail service began, between New York and Washington, DC, with intermediate stop in Philadelphia. In 1921, scheduled transcontinental airmail service began between New York City and San Francisco.

1919, June 14-15: Capt. John Alcock (UK) and Lt. Arthur W. Brown (U.S.) completed the first nonstop flight across the Atlantic Ocean. They traveled from Newfoundland, Canada, to Ireland in 16 hours and 12 minutes.

1923, Aug.: Rotating beacons enabled the first night flights in the U.S.

1924, Apr. 6-Sept. 28: Two U.S. Army planes landed in Seattle, completing the first circumnavigation of the globe. They completed the 26,000-mi journey in 371 hours of flying time.

1926, May 12-13: Roald Amundsen (Norway), Umberto Nobile (Italy), Lincoln Ellsworth (U.S.), and Oscar Wisting (Norway) made the first flight over the North Pole, in a dirigible that flew between Spitsbergen, Norway, and Teller, AK. Two weeks earlier, Adm. Richard E. Byrd and Floyd Bennett (both U.S.) claimed to have made the first flight over the Pole (May 9, 1926) in a Fokker F-VII. But when Byrd's diary was released to the public in 1996, some historians began to question whether his plane had reached the Pole.

1927, May 20-21: Charles Lindbergh (U.S.) completed the first solo transatlantic flight in the *Spirit of St. Louis.* "Lucky Lindy" traveled 3,610 mi from New York to Paris in 33 hours, 29 minutes, and 30 seconds.

1929, Aug. 8-29: Hugo Eckener (Germany) piloted the *Graf Zeppelin* around the world in record time: 20,373 mi in 21 days, 5 hours, and 31 minutes.

1929, Nov. 29: Adm. Richard E. Byrd (U.S.) and Bernt Balchen (Norway) became the first to fly to the South Pole and back, in 18 hours and 41 minutes.

1930, May 15: Ellen Church (U.S.) became first flight attendant.

1931, June 23-July 1: Wiley Post and Harold Gatty (both U.S.) broke the speed record for around-the-world flight. They traveled 15,474 mi in 8 days, 15 hours, and 51 minutes in the monoplane *Winnie Mae.*

1931, Oct. 3-5: Clyde Pangborn and Hugh Herndon (both U.S.) completed the first nonstop transpacific flight. They traveled 4,558 mi from Misawa, Japan, to East Wenatchee, WA, in 41 hours and 34 minutes.

1932, May 20-21: Amelia Earhart (U.S.) completed first solo transoceanic flight by a woman. She completed the 2,026-mi journey from Newfoundland, Canada, to Ireland in 14 hours and 56 minutes.

1933, July 15-22: Wiley Post (U.S.) completed the first solo circumnavigation of the globe. His 15,596-mi trip took 7 days, 18 hours, and 49 minutes.

1936, June 25: American Airlines began scheduled passenger service of the first Douglas DC-3 aircraft. The DC-3 was the first aircraft with a kitchen onboard and hence offered the first in-flight hot meal service.

1937, May 6: German *Hindenburg* zeppelin exploded and burst into flames in Lakehurst, NJ, killing 35 of the 97 people aboard (and one on the ground). The airship had made 34 transatlantic flights in 1936.

1938, July 10-13: Howard Hughes (U.S.) and four assistants established a new speed record for circumnavigating the globe: 14,824 mi in 3 days, 9 hours, 17 minutes.

1939, Aug. 27: The German-made Heinkel He 178 made the first successful flight powered by a jet engine.

1947, June 17-30: Pan American Airways began the first scheduled around-the-world passenger flights, from New York or San Francisco.

1947, Oct. 14: Chuck Yeager (U.S.) broke the sound barrier, reaching Mach 1 speed in a Bell X-1 rocket-powered aircraft.

1947, Nov. 2: Howard Hughes (U.S.) piloted the *Spruce Goose* on its maiden and only flight. The largest airplane ever built, it could carry 750 troops or two Sherman tanks.

1949, Mar. 2: James Gallagher (U.S.) piloted the first round-the-world flight to be refueled in midair. The *Lucky Lady* USAF B-50 covered 23,452 mi in 94 hours and 1 minute and was refueled four times.

1950, Sept. 22: Col. David Schilling (USAF) made the first nonstop transatlantic jet flight, covering 3,300 mi in 10 hours and 1 minute.

1952, Aug. 26: The UK bomber Canberra made the first round-trip transatlantic crossing on the same day, from Northern Ireland to Newfoundland, Canada, and back in 7 hours and 59 minutes.

1953, May 18: Jacqueline Cochran (U.S.) became the first woman to fly faster than the speed of sound.

1956, Mar. 10: Britain's Fairey FD-2 aircraft set a world speed record of 1,132 mph.

1956, Nov. 11: Convair B-58 (USAF), the first supersonic bomber, was introduced.

1957, Jan. 15-18: Three USAF B-52 Stratofortresses made the first nonstop global flight by jet planes. They were refueled in flight by KC-97 aerial tankers.

1958, Oct. 24: A Mirage III-A achieved Mach 2 (twice the speed of sound) in level flight, the first European plane to reach that speed.

1962, Nov. 29: Britain and France signed an agreement to jointly develop the Concorde, a supersonic plane that could fly twice as fast as most U.S. jets.

1969, June 5: The Soviet Tupolev Tu-144 became the first passenger airliner to reach Mach 2.

1970, May 26: The Tupolev Tu-144 reached a top speed of about 1,335 mph at 53,475 ft.

1976, Aug. 23: The Concorde began the first scheduled supersonic commercial service.

1977, Aug. 23: The *Gossamer Condor,* built by aeronautical engineer Paul MacCready (U.S.), successfully demonstrated human-powered flight through pedalling, completing a figure-8 course of 1.15 mi.

1979, June 12: The human-powered *Gossamer Albatross,* developed by MacCready, crossed the English Channel in 2 hours and 49 minutes.

1981, July 7: The MacCready-developed *Solar Challenger* became the first solar-powered airplane to cross the English Channel.

1995, Aug. 15-16: The Concorde set a new around-the-world speed record of 31 hours, 27 minutes, and 49 seconds.

1999, Mar. 1-21: Bertrand Piccard (Switz.) and Brian Jones (UK) completed the first around-the-world flight in a hot-air balloon. Their 29,055-mi journey began in Chateau-d'Oex, Switzerland, and ended 19 days, 21 hours, and 55 minutes later in the Egyptian desert.

2001, Aug. 13: Solar-powered, propeller-driven plane *Helios* (NASA) reached 96,863 ft, breaking altitude record for non-rocket-powered aircraft.

2002, June 19-July 4: Steve Fossett (U.S.) completed the first nonstop solo circumnavigation of globe in a balloon.

2003, Nov. 26: The Concorde flew its final flight.

2005, Mar. 1-3: Steve Fossett (U.S.) achieved the first nonstop solo circumnavigation in an airplane without refueling.

2005, Apr. 27: The Airbus A380, the biggest-ever commercial jet, made its maiden voyage. It was 240 ft long, had a wingspan of 262 ft, and could seat a maximum of 840 passengers. Its first commercial flight was Oct. 25, 2007.

2006, Feb. 8-11: Steve Fossett (U.S.) flew the longest nonstop, non-refueled solo flight (25,766 mi).

2009, Dec. 15: Boeing's 787 Dreamliner, the company's most fuel-efficient plane and the first to be constructed primarily from composite materials, made its maiden voyage, two years after it was originally scheduled.

2011, Feb. 4: Northrop Grumman and the U.S. Navy reported the first successful flight for the X-47B, an unmanned fighter jet that can operate safely from an aircraft carrier.

2013, July 6: *Solar Impulse* became the first solar-powered airplane to fly across the U.S. without fuel. Flying during the day as well as at night, the aircraft traveled from San Francisco to New York with stops in Phoenix, Dallas, St. Louis, and Washington, DC, in 62 days.

ASTRONOMY

Edited by Michael J. Kaufman, Dept. of Physics and Astronomy, San Jose State University.

Celestial Events Summary, 2014

There are four eclipses in 2014: two total lunar eclipses, one annular solar eclipse, and one partial solar eclipse. Both lunar eclipses will be visible across wide areas of the U.S., with the entire Apr. lunar eclipse visible throughout the U.S. The annular solar eclipse in Apr. will only be visible in a small, uninhabited region of the Antarctic, but a partially eclipsed Sun will be seen across wide swaths of the Indian Ocean and Australia. The Oct. partial solar eclipse will be visible in Alaska, western Canada, and the western and midwestern United States.

The most likely viewing successes for meteor showers will be the Quadrantids in Jan., the Lyrids in Apr., the Orionids in Oct., the Leonids in Nov. and the Geminids in Dec. Astronomers have predicted that debris from the comet 209P/LINEAR will result in a strong meteor shower on May 24. One of the typically strong meteor showers—the Perseids in Aug.—will peak when the Moon is just past full, so viewing conditions will not be ideal. At the start of the year, Jupiter is in the East at sunset and up much of the night. Venus is low in the West at sunset at the start of the year, but soon becomes a pre-dawn object, which it remains through mid-Oct. when it returns to the evening sky. Mars rises in the pre-dawn hours through Mar., but becomes predominantly an evening object from Apr. onward. Saturn is high in the East before sunrise through Apr., moves to the evening sky in May, then returns to the morning sky in late Nov. The best opportunities for seeing Mercury in the morning sky occur in mid-Mar., mid-July, and late Oct.; the planet will be visible in the evening sky in early Feb., late May, and late Sept.

The crescent Moon, with its subdued light, regularly makes pretty pairings with the two brightest planets, Venus and Jupiter. Waxing crescent pairings are visible in the early evening soon after sunset, while waning crescent pairings are visible in the early morning before sunrise. The waning crescent Moon pairs with Venus in each of the months from Jan. through Aug. The waxing crescent Moon pairs with Jupiter in the evening in Apr., May, and June and the waning crescent pairs with Jupiter from Aug.-Nov. The waning crescent Moon joins Mercury and Venus in the early morning sky July 25. The waxing crescent Moon joins Mars and Saturn on the nights of June 6-7, Aug. 3-4, and Aug. 31.

Astronomical Positions and Constants

Two celestial bodies are in **conjunction** when they are due north and south of each other, either in **right ascension** (with respect to the north celestial pole) or in **celestial longitude** (with respect to the north ecliptic pole). Celestial bodies in conjunction will rise and set at nearly the same time. For the inner planets—Mercury and Venus—**inferior conjunction** occurs when either planet passes between Earth and the Sun, while **superior conjunction** occurs when either Mercury or Venus is on the far side of the Sun. Celestial bodies are in **opposition** when their right ascensions differ by exactly 12 hours, or when their celestial longitudes differ by 180°. In this case one of the two objects in opposition will rise while the other is setting. **Quadrature** refers to the arrangement where the coordinates of two bodies differ by exactly 90°. These terms may refer to the relative positions of any two bodies as seen from Earth, but one of the bodies is so frequently the Sun that mention of the Sun is omitted in that case.

When objects are in conjunction, the alignment is not perfect, and one is usually passing above or below the other. The geocentric angular separation between the Sun and an object is termed **elongation**. Elongation is limited only for Mercury and Venus; the greatest elongation for each of these bodies is approximately the time for longest observation. **Perihelion** is the point in an object's orbit when it is nearest the Sun, and **aphelion** is the point farthest from the Sun. **Perigee** is the point in an orbit that is nearest Earth, and **apogee** the point that is farthest from Earth. An **occultation** of a planet or a star is an eclipse of it by some other body, usually the Moon. A **transit** of the Sun occurs when Mercury or Venus passes directly between Earth and the Sun, appearing to cross the Sun's disk.

The following were adopted as part of the International Astronomical Union System of Astronomical Constants (1976): **Speed of light**, 299,792.458 km per sec., or about 186,282 statute mi per sec.; **solar parallax**, 8".794148; **astronomical unit** (AU, mean distance between the Earth and Sun), 149,597,870 km, or 92,955,807 mi; **constant of nutation**, 9".2025; and **constant of aberration**, 20".49552.

Celestial Events Highlights, 2014

(In Coordinated Universal Time, or UTC, the standard time of the prime meridian.)

January

Mercury is visible low in the SW after sunset by the middle of the month.
Venus is visible low in the SW after sunset early in the month and low in the SE before sunrise late in the month.
Mars rises around midnight and is high overhead at sunrise.
Jupiter is in the E at sunset and sets in the early morning.
Saturn rises in the middle of the night and is high in the SE at sunrise.
Uranus and **Neptune** are in the SW after sunset and set several hours later.

Jan. 1: Mercury, Venus, and Sun in Sagittarius, Mars in Virgo, Jupiter in Gemini, Saturn in Libra all year, Uranus in Pisces all year, Neptune in Aquarius all year. New Moon, Mercury 6.62° S of Moon, Moon at perigee
Jan. 2: Venus 2.02° S of Moon
Jan. 3: Quadrantid meteor shower
Jan. 4: Earth at perihelion
Jan. 5: Neptune 5.40° S of Moon, Jupiter at opposition
Jan. 7: Venus 6.44° N of Mercury, Uranus 3.05° S of Moon

Jan. 8: First Quarter Moon
Jan. 11: Venus in inferior conjunction 5.19° North
Jan. 12: Aldebaran 2.55° S of Moon, Mercury enters Capricorn
Jan. 15: Jupiter 4.90° N of Moon
Jan. 16: Full Moon, Moon at apogee, Pollux 11.81° N of Moon
Jan. 19: Regulus 5.19° N of Moon, Sun enters Capricorn
Jan. 23: Mars 3.66° N of Moon, Spica 1.34° S of Moon
Jan. 24: Last Quarter Moon, Venus enters Scutum
Jan. 25: Saturn 0.57° N of Moon
Jan. 26: Antares 7.62° S of Moon
Jan. 28: Spica 4.90° S of Mars, Mercury enters Aquarius
Jan. 29: Venus 2.25° N of Moon
Jan. 30: New Moon, Moon at perigee
Jan. 31: Mercury at greatest elongation 18.4° E, Venus enters Sagittarius

February

Mercury is visible low in the SW after sunset early in the month, and low in the SE before sunrise late in the month.
Venus is visible in the SE before sunrise all month.

Mars rises late in the evening and is high in the SW at sunrise.
Jupiter is high in the E at sunset and sets in the middle of the night.
Saturn rises after midnight and is high in the SW at sunrise.
Uranus sets several hours after the Sun.
Neptune begins the month setting just after the Sun and is lost in the Sun's glare by the end of the month.

Feb. 1: Mercury 4.11° S of Moon, Neptune 5.18° S of Moon
Feb. 3: Uranus 2.69° S of Moon
Feb. 6: First Quarter Moon
Feb. 8: Aldebaran 2.32° S of Moon
Feb. 11: Jupiter 4.97° N of Moon
Feb. 12: Moon at apogee, Pollux 11.88° N of Moon
Feb. 14: Mercury enters Capricorn
Feb. 15: Full Moon, Regulus 5.10° N of Moon, Mercury in inferior conjunction
Feb. 16: Sun enters Aquarius
Feb. 19: Spica 1.59° S of Moon
Feb. 20: Mars 3.12° N of Moon
Feb. 21: Saturn 0.31° N of Moon
Feb. 22: Last Quarter Moon
Feb. 23: Antares 7.87° S of Moon, Neptune 0.67° S of Sun, Mercury enters Aquarius

March

Mercury is low in the SE before sunrise all month.
Venus is visible in the SE before sunrise all month.
Mars rises mid-evening and is low in the SW at sunrise.
Jupiter is high overhead at sunset and sets after midnight.
Saturn rises before midnight and is high in the SW at sunrise.
Uranus is low in the SW at sunset at the start of the month and lost in the Sun's glare by late in the month.
Neptune is visible low in the SE before sunrise.

Mar. 1: New Moon, Neptune 5.08° S of Moon
Mar. 3: Uranus 2.39° S of Moon
Mar. 5: Mercury enters Capricorn, Venus enters Capricorn
Mar. 7: Aldebaran 2.09° S of Moon
Mar. 8: First Quarter Moon
Mar. 10: Jupiter 5.17° N of Moon
Mar. 11: Moon at apogee, Pollux 12.04° N of Moon
Mar. 12: Sun enters Pisces
Mar. 14: Regulus 5.14° N of Moon, Mercury at greatest elongation 27.6° W
Mar. 15: Mercury enters Aquarius
Mar. 16: Full Moon
Mar. 18: Spica 1.71° S of Moon
Mar. 19: Mars 3.22° N of Moon
Mar. 20: Equinox
Mar. 21: Saturn 0.25° N of Moon, Antares 8.05° S of Moon, Mercury 1.25° S of Neptune, Venus at greatest elongation 46.6° W
Mar. 22: Venus enters Aquarius
Mar. 24: Last Quarter Moon
Mar. 26: Venus enters Capricorn
Mar. 27: Venus 3.59° S of Moon, Moon at perigee
Mar. 28: Neptune 5.08° S of Moon
Mar. 29: Mercury 6.24° S of Moon
Mar. 30: New Moon
Mar. 31: Uranus 2.20° S of Moon, Spica 5.11° S of Mars

April

Mercury is visible low in the SE before sunrise early in the month, but lost in the Sun's glare by late in the month.
Venus is low in the E before sunrise all month.
Mars rises after sunset and is up all night.
Jupiter is high overhead at sunset and sets after midnight.
Saturn rises mid-evening and is visible the rest of the night.
Uranus and **Neptune** are low in the SE at sunrise by the end of the month.

Apr. 2: Uranus 0.65° S of Sun
Apr. 3: Venus enters Aquarius
Apr. 4: Aldebaran 1.96° S of Moon
Apr. 5: Mercury enters Pisces
Apr. 6: Jupiter 5.37° N of Moon
Apr. 7: First Quarter Moon
Apr. 8: Moon at apogee, Pollux 12.15° N of Moon, Mars at opposition
Apr. 11: Regulus 5.21° N of Moon, Mercury enters Cetus
Apr. 12: Neptune 0.69° S of Venus
Apr. 13: Mercury enters Pisces
Apr. 14: Uranus 1.39° N of Mercury, Mars 3.49° N of Moon
Apr. 15: Full Moon, Spica 1.72° S of Moon, Total Lunar eclipse
Apr. 17: Saturn 0.38° N of Moon
Apr. 18: Antares 8.09° S of Moon, Sun enters Aries
Apr. 21: Pluto 2.46° S of Moon
Apr. 22: Last Quarter Moon
Apr. 23: Moon at perigee, Mercury enters Aries
Apr. 24: Neptune 5.08° S of Moon
Apr. 25: Venus 4.36° S of Moon, Lyrid meteor shower
Apr. 26: Mercury in superior conjunction 0.37° S
Apr. 27: Uranus 2.07° S of Moon
Apr. 28: Venus enters Pisces
Apr. 29: New Moon, Mercury 1.60° N of Moon, Annular Solar Eclipse

May

Mercury is visible low in the W after sunset by mid-month.
Venus is low in the E before sunrise all month.
Mars is high in the SE at sunset and sets a few hours before sunrise.
Jupiter is high in the W at sunset and sets around midnight.
Saturn is in the SE at sunset and up most of the night.
Uranus and **Neptune** rise a few hours before the Sun.

May 1: Aldebaran 1.97° S of Moon
May 4: Jupiter 5.49° N of Moon, Mercury enters Taurus
May 5: Pollux 12.13° N of Moon
May 6: Moon at apogee
May 7: First Quarter Moon
May 8: Regulus 5.18° N of Moon, Venus enters Cetus
May 10: Saturn at opposition
May 11: Mars 2.97° N of Moon
May 12: Spica 1.73° S of Moon, Venus enters Pisces
May 13: Aldebaran 7.75° S of Mercury
May 14: Full Moon, Saturn 0.57° N of Moon, Sun enters Taurus
May 15: Uranus 1.27° N of Venus, Antares 8.06° S of Moon
May 18: Pluto 2.40° S of Moon, Moon at perigee
May 21: Last Quarter Moon
May 22: Neptune 4.98° S of Moon
May 24: Uranus 1.89° S of Moon, predicted meteor shower due to Comet 209P/LINEAR
May 25: Venus 2.26° S of Moon, Mercury at greatest elongation 22.7° E
May 28: New Moon
May 29: Aldebaran 2.00° S of Moon, Mercury enters Gemini
May 30: Mercury 5.88° N of Moon

June

Mercury is visible low in the W after sunset early in the month and low in the E before sunrise at the very end of the month.
Venus is low in the E before sunrise all month.
Mars is high in the S at sunset and sets after midnight.
Jupiter is in the W at sunset and sets late evening.
Saturn is in the SE at sunset and sets in the early morning hours.
Uranus and **Neptune** rise in the middle of the night and are high overhead at sunrise.

June 1: Jupiter 5.50° N of Moon, Pollux 12.02° N of Moon, Venus enters Aries
June 3: Moon at apogee

June 4: Regulus 5.03° N of Moon
June 5: First Quarter Moon
June 8: Mars 1.62° N of Moon, Spica 1.84° S of Moon
June 10: Saturn 0.63° N of Moon
June 12: Antares 8.06° S of Moon, Mercury enters Orion
June 13: Full Moon
June 14: Pluto 2.31° S of Moon
June 15: Moon at perigee
June 17: Venus enters Taurus
June 18: Neptune 4.80° S of Moon
June 19: Last Quarter Moon, Mercury in inferior conjunction 3.79° S
June 21: Uranus 1.65° S of Moon, Pollux 6.44° N of Jupiter, Solstice, Mercury enters Taurus, Sun enters Gemini
June 24: Venus 1.28° N of Moon
June 25: Aldebaran 1.97° S of Moon
June 26: Mercury 0.27° S of Moon
June 27: New Moon
June 29: Pollux 11.90° N of Moon, Jupiter 5.48° N of Moon
June 30: Moon at apogee

July

Mercury is visible low in the NE before sunrise all month.
Venus is visible low in the NE before sunrise all month.
Mars is high in the SW at sunset and sets around midnight.
Jupiter is lost in the Sun's glare most of the month.
Saturn is high in the SE at sunset and sets after midnight.
Uranus and **Neptune** rise in the middle of the night and are high overhead at sunrise.

July 2: Regulus 4.81° N of Moon, Aldebaran 4.15° S of Venus
July 4: Earth at aphelion
July 5: First Quarter Moon
July 6: Mars 0.21° S of Moon, Spica 2.06° S of Moon, Jupiter enters Cancer
July 8: Saturn 0.44° N of Moon
July 9: Antares 8.16° S of Moon
July 10: Mercury enters Orion
July 11: Pluto 2.32° S of Moon
July 12: Full Moon, Spica 1.43° S of Mars, Mercury at greatest elongation 20.9° W
July 13: Moon at perigee
July 15: Neptune 4.61° S of Moon
July 16: Mercury enters Gemini, Venus enters Orion
July 18: Uranus 1.37° S of Moon, Venus enters Gemini
July 19: Last Quarter Moon
July 20: Sun enters Cancer
July 22: Aldebaran 1.82° S of Moon
July 24: Venus 4.42° N of Moon, Jupiter 0.40° N of Sun
July 25: Mercury 5.11° N of Moon
July 26: New Moon, Pollux 11.87° N of Moon, Jupiter 5.46° N of Moon
July 28: Moon at apogee
July 29: Pollux 6.05° N of Mercury, Regulus 4.65° N of Moon
July 30: Mercury enters Cancer

August

Mercury is visible low in W after sunset late in the month.
Venus is visible low in the E before sunrise all month.
Mars is in the SW at sunset and sets late in the evening.
Jupiter is visible in the E before sunrise by late in the month.
Saturn is high in the SW at sunset and sets around midnight.
Uranus and **Neptune** rise in the late evening and in the W at sunrise.

Aug. 2: Spica 2.33° S of Moon, Jupiter 0.96° S of Mercury
Aug. 3: Mars 2.22° S of Moon
Aug. 4: First Quarter Moon, Saturn 0.07° N of Moon
Aug. 6: Antares 8.37° S of Moon
Aug. 7: Pollux 6.58° N of Venus

Aug. 8: Mercury in superior conjunction 1.74° North
Aug. 9: Mercury enters Leo, Mars enters Libra
Aug. 10: Full Moon, Moon at perigee, Venus enters Cancer
Aug. 11: Sun enters Leo
Aug. 12: Neptune 4.52° S of Moon
Aug. 13: Perseid meteor shower
Aug. 14: Uranus 1.16° S of Moon
Aug. 15: Regulus 1.27° S of Mercury
Aug. 17: Last Quarter Moon
Aug. 18: Jupiter 0.20° S of Venus, Aldebaran 1.61° S of Moon
Aug. 22: Pollux 11.96° N of Moon
Aug. 23: Jupiter 5.45° N of Moon
Aug. 24: Moon at apogee, Venus 5.69° N of Moon
Aug. 25: New Moon, Regulus 4.60° N of Moon
Aug. 26: Venus enters Leo
Aug. 27: Mercury 3.36° N of Moon, Saturn 3.56° N of Mars
Aug. 29: Spica 2.53° S of Moon, Neptune at opposition, Mercury enters Virgo
Aug. 31: Saturn 0.36° S of Moon

September

Mercury is low in the W after sunset all month.
Venus is visible low in the E before sunrise all month.
Mars is low in the SW at sunset and sets a few hours later.
Jupiter rises several hours before sunrise and is high in the E at sunrise.
Saturn is in the SW at sunset and sets several hours later.
Uranus and **Neptune** rise around sunset and set near sunrise.

Sept. 1: Mars 4.13° S of Moon
Sept. 2: First Quarter Moon, Antares 8.57° S of Moon
Sept. 4: Pluto 2.68° S of Moon
Sept. 5: Regulus 0.78° S of Venus
Sept. 8: Neptune 4.56° S of Moon, Moon at perigee
Sept. 9: Full Moon
Sept. 11: Uranus 1.11° S of Moon
Sept. 12: Mars enters Scorpius
Sept. 15: Aldebaran 1.43° S of Moon
Sept. 16: Last Quarter Moon
Sept. 17: Sun enters Virgo
Sept. 18: Pollux 12.09° N of Moon
Sept. 20: Moon at apogee, Jupiter 5.44° N of Moon
Sept. 21: Spica 0.62° N of Mercury, Regulus 4.65° N of Moon, Mercury at greatest elongation 26.4° E
Sept. 23: Venus 4.02° N of Moon, Equinox
Sept. 24: New Moon, Venus enters Virgo, Mars enters Ophiuchus
Sept. 26: Spica 2.60° S of Moon, Mercury 4.24° S of Moon
Sept. 27: Antares 3.12° S of Mars
Sept. 28: Saturn 0.73° S of Moon
Sept. 29: Antares 8.69° S of Moon, Mars 5.65° S of Moon

October

Mercury is low in the SW after sunset early in the month and low in the SE before sunrise at the end of the month.
Venus is close to the Sun and difficult to observe all month.
Mars is in the SW at sunset and sets early evening.
Jupiter rises in the middle of the night and is high in the W at sunrise.
Saturn is visible low in the SW after sunset and sets soon afterwards.
Uranus and **Neptune** are high in the SE at sunset and set in the early morning.

Oct. 5: Neptune 4.64° S of Moon
Oct. 6: Moon at perigee
Oct. 7: Uranus at opposition
Oct. 8: Full Moon, Uranus 1.19° S of Moon, Total Lunar Eclipse
Oct. 12: Aldebaran 1.37° S of Moon
Oct. 13: Jupiter enters Leo

Oct. 15: Last Quarter Moon
Oct. 16: Pollux 12.14° N of Moon, Spica 0.48° S of Mercury, Mercury in inferior conjunction
Oct. 17: Venus 2.73° N of Mercury
Oct. 18: Moon at apogee, Spica 3.50° S of Venus, Jupiter 5.38° N of Moon
Oct. 19: Regulus 4.68° N of Moon
Oct. 20: Mars enters Sagittarius
Oct. 21: Orionid meteor shower
Oct. 22: Mercury 0.72° N of Moon
Oct. 23: New Moon, Spica 2.59° S of Moon, Venus 0.07° N of Moon, Partial Solar Eclipse
Oct. 25: Saturn 1.01° S of Moon, Venus in superior conjunction
Oct. 26: Antares 8.68° S of Moon
Oct. 28: Mars 6.53° S of Moon
Oct. 29: Pluto 2.92° S of Moon, Venus enters Libra
Oct. 31: First Quarter Moon, Sun enters Libra

November

Mercury is low in the SE before sunrise early in the month.
Venus is visible in the SW after sunset late in the month.
Mars is low in the S at sunset and sets a few hours later.
Jupiter rises around midnight and is high overhead at sunrise.
Saturn is visible low in the SE before sunrise late in the month.
Uranus and **Neptune** are high overhead at sunset and set after midnight.

Nov. 1: Mercury at greatest elongation 18.7° W
Nov. 2: Neptune 4.64° S of Moon
Nov. 3: Spica 4.57° S of Mercury, Moon at perigee
Nov. 4: Uranus 1.28° S of Moon
Nov. 6: Full Moon
Nov. 8: Aldebaran 1.41° S of Moon
Nov. 10: Pluto 3.76° N of Mars
Nov. 12: Pollux 12.06° N of Moon
Nov. 13: Saturn 1.60° N of Venus, Mercury enters Libra
Nov. 14: Last Quarter Moon, Jupiter 5.25° N of Moon
Nov. 15: Moon at apogee, Regulus 4.58° N of Moon
Nov. 17: Leonid meteor shower
Nov. 18: Saturn 1.91° N of Sun
Nov. 19: Spica 2.63° S of Moon, Venus enters Scorpius
Nov. 21: Mercury 1.92° S of Moon

Nov. 22: New Moon, Saturn 1.26° S of Moon, Venus 3.94° S of Moon, Venus enters Ophiuchus
Nov. 23: Antares 8.62° S of Moon
Nov. 24: Antares 4.56° S of Venus, Sun enters Scorpius
Nov. 25: Pluto 2.89° S of Moon
Nov. 26: Saturn 1.71° N of Mercury, Mars 6.61° S of Moon
Nov. 27: Moon at perigee
Nov. 28: Mercury enters Scorpius
Nov. 29: First Quarter Moon, Neptune 4.47° S of Moon
Nov. 30: Sun enters Ophiuchus

December

Mercury is low in the SW after sunset late in the month.
Venus is in the SW after sunset all month.
Mars is low in the S at sunset and sets a few hours later.
Jupiter rises late in the evening and is high in the W at sunrise.
Saturn is visible in the SE before sunrise all month.
Uranus and **Neptune** are overhead at sunset and in the late evening.

Dec. 2: Uranus 1.22° S of Moon, Mercury enters Ophiuchus
Dec. 3: Mars enters Capricorn
Dec. 4: Antares 4.01° S of Mercury
Dec. 6: Full Moon, Aldebaran 1.45° S of Moon
Dec. 7: Venus enters Sagittarius
Dec. 8: Mercury in superior conjunction 1.05° S
Dec. 9: Pollux 11.89° N of Moon
Dec. 12: Moon at apogee, Jupiter 5.10° N of Moon, Regulus 4.36° N of Moon
Dec. 14: Last Quarter Moon, Mercury enters Sagittarius, Gemenid meteor shower
Dec. 17: Spica 2.80° S of Moon
Dec. 18: Sun enters Sagittarius
Dec. 19: Saturn 1.54° S of Moon
Dec. 20: Antares 8.65° S of Moon
Dec. 21: Solstice
Dec. 22: New Moon, Mercury 7.06° S of Moon
Dec. 23: Venus 6.19° S of Moon
Dec. 24: Moon at perigee
Dec. 25: Mars 5.73° S of Moon
Dec. 26: Neptune 4.19° S of Moon
Dec. 28: First Quarter Moon
Dec. 29: Uranus 0.97° S of Moon

Meteorites and Meteor Showers

When a chunk of material, ice or rock, plunges into Earth's atmosphere and burns up in a fiery display, the event is a **meteor**. While the chunk of material is still in space, it is a **meteoroid**. If a portion of the material survives passage through the atmosphere and reaches the ground, the remnant on the ground is a **meteorite**.

Meteorites found on Earth are classified into types, depending on their composition: **irons**, those composed chiefly of iron, a small percentage of nickel, and traces of other metals such as cobalt; **stones**, stony meteors consisting of silicates; and **stony irons**, containing varying proportions of both iron and stone.

Serious study of meteorites as non-earth objects began in the 20th century. Scientists use sophisticated chemical analysis, X-rays, and mass spectrography in determining their origin and composition. Although most meteorites are now believed to be fragments of asteroids or comets, geochemical studies have shown that a few Antarctic stones came from the Moon or from Mars, presumably ejected by the explosive impact of asteroids.

The **largest known meteorite**, estimated to weigh about 55 metric tons, is situated at Hoba West near Grootfontein, Namibia. The Manicouagan impact crater in Quebec, Canada, with an estimated diameter of 60 mi, is one of the largest crater structures still visible on the surface of the Earth. Although not obvious to the eye, larger impact craters identified include the Vredefort crater in South Africa at 185 mi across and the Sudbury crater in Ontario, Canada,

estimated at 125 mi across. The Bedout impact site off the NW coast of Australia gained attention in 2004 when scientists identified further evidence in support of the idea that it may be linked to the Permian extinction event 250 mil years ago.

Meteor showers vary in strength, but usually the three most visible meteor showers of the year are the **Perseids**, around Aug. 13, the **Orionids**, around Oct. 21, and the **Geminids**, around Dec. 14. These showers feature meteors at the rate of about 60 per hour. Best observing conditions occur in the absence of moonlight, usually when the Moon's phase is between waning crescent and waxing quarter. Bright Moons can adversely affect viewing of some of the best showers of the year.

For most meteor showers the cometary debris is relatively uniformly scattered along the comet's orbit. However, in the case of the **Leonid** meteor shower, which occurs every year around Nov. 17-18, the cometary debris, from Comet Temple-Tuttle, seems to be bunched up in one stretch. Hence, most years when Earth crosses the orbit of this comet, the meteor shower produced is relatively weak. However, about every 33 years, Earth encounters the bunched-up debris. Sometimes the expected shower is a disappointment; as in 1899 and 1933; at other times, the dense debris provides a spectacular show, as in 1833 and 1866. The Leonids stormed again more recently, producing rates of 1,000-3,000 meteors per hour in 2001.

Rising and Setting of Planets, 2014

(In Coordinated Universal Time, the standard time of the prime meridian. 0 in the *h* column designates 12 AM.)

Venus, 2014

Date	20° N Latitude Rise	20° N Latitude Set	30° N Latitude Rise	30° N Latitude Set	40° N Latitude Rise	40° N Latitude Set	50° N Latitude Rise	50° N Latitude Set	60° N Latitude Rise	60° N Latitude Set
	h m	h m	h m	h m	h m	h m	h m	h m	h m	h m
Jan. 1	7 34	18 42	7 50	18 26	8 10	18 07	8 37	17 39	9 22	16 55
11	6 29	17 41	6 43	17 26	7 01	17 08	7 26	16 44	8 05	16 05
21	5 25	16 40	5 39	16 26	5 56	16 09	6 19	15 46	6 56	15 09
31	4 36	15 52	4 50	15 38	5 06	15 21	5 30	14 58	6 07	14 21
Feb. 10	4 04	15 19	4 18	15 05	4 36	14 48	4 59	14 24	5 38	13 46
20	3 46	15 00	4 00	14 46	4 18	14 28	4 42	14 03	5 22	13 24
Mar. 1	3 36	14 51	3 50	14 36	4 08	14 18	4 32	13 54	5 12	13 15
12	3 31	14 48	3 44	14 34	4 01	14 17	4 25	13 54	5 02	13 17
22	3 28	14 50	3 40	14 38	3 56	14 22	4 17	14 01	4 50	13 29
Apr. 1	3 26	14 55	3 36	14 45	3 49	14 32	4 07	14 15	4 34	13 48
11	3 24	15 02	3 32	14 54	3 42	14 44	3 54	14 32	4 14	14 12
21	3 22	15 09	3 26	15 05	3 32	14 59	3 40	14 51	3 52	14 40
May 1	3 19	15 18	3 20	15 17	3 22	15 15	3 24	15 13	3 28	15 10
11	3 16	15 27	3 14	15 29	3 11	15 32	3 08	15 36	3 02	15 42
21	3 13	15 37	3 08	15 43	3 01	15 50	2 51	16 00	2 36	16 15
31	3 12	15 48	3 02	15 57	2 51	16 09	2 35	16 25	2 10	16 51
June 10	3 12	16 00	2 59	16 13	2 43	16 29	2 21	16 51	1 46	17 27
20	3 14	16 13	2 58	16 29	2 39	16 49	2 11	17 17	1 25	18 04
30	3 20	16 27	3 01	16 46	2 38	17 09	2 05	17 43	1 08	18 40
July 10	3 28	16 41	3 07	17 02	2 42	17 28	2 05	18 05	1 00	19 11
20	3 39	16 55	3 18	17 17	2 51	17 44	2 12	18 22	1 02	19 32
30	3 52	17 08	3 31	17 29	3 05	17 55	2 27	18 33	1 19	19 41
Aug. 9	4 08	17 18	3 48	17 38	3 23	18 02	2 48	18 37	1 47	19 37
19	4 23	17 26	4 06	17 43	3 45	18 04	3 14	18 34	2 23	19 24
29	4 39	17 30	4 25	17 44	4 07	18 01	3 43	18 25	3 04	19 04
Sept. 8	4 54	17 33	4 43	17 43	4 31	17 55	4 13	18 12	3 45	18 40
18	5 08	17 33	5 02	17 39	4 54	17 47	4 43	17 57	4 27	18 13
28	5 22	17 33	5 20	17 34	5 17	17 37	5 13	17 40	5 08	17 45
Oct. 8	5 35	17 32	5 37	17 29	5 40	17 26	5 44	17 22	5 49	17 17
18	5 49	17 31	5 56	17 24	6 04	17 16	6 14	17 05	6 31	16 49
28	6 04	17 32	6 15	17 21	6 28	17 08	6 46	16 50	7 13	16 22
Nov. 7	6 20	17 35	6 34	17 21	6 52	17 02	7 17	16 38	7 57	15 57
17	6 37	17 41	6 55	17 23	7 17	17 01	7 48	16 30	8 40	15 38
27	6 55	17 51	7 15	17 30	7 41	17 04	8 17	16 28	9 20	15 25
Dec. 7	7 12	18 03	7 34	17 42	8 02	17 14	8 41	16 34	9 51	15 24
17	7 28	18 19	7 50	17 57	8 18	17 29	8 58	16 49	10 09	15 38
27	7 41	18 36	8 02	18 15	8 28	17 49	9 06	17 12	10 11	16 07

Mars, 2014

Date	20° N Latitude Rise	20° N Latitude Set	30° N Latitude Rise	30° N Latitude Set	40° N Latitude Rise	40° N Latitude Set	50° N Latitude Rise	50° N Latitude Set	60° N Latitude Rise	60° N Latitude Set
	h m	h m	h m	h m	h m	h m	h m	h m	h m	h m
Jan. 1	0 05	12 01	0 07	11 59	00 10	11 57	0 13	11 54	0 17	11 49
11	23 42	11 35	23 45	11 32	23 49	11 28	23 55	11 23	0 05	11 14
21	23 18	11 08	23 23	11 04	23 28	10 58	23 36	10 51	23 47	10 40
31	22 52	10 39	22 58	10 34	23 05	10 27	23 13	10 19	23 27	10 05
Feb. 10	22 23	10 08	22 30	10 02	22 37	9 55	22 47	9 45	23 02	9 30
20	21 51	9 34	21 57	9 28	22 05	9 20	22 16	9 09	22 32	8 53
Mar. 1	21 13	8 57	21 20	8 50	21 28	8 42	21 39	8 31	21 55	8 15
12	20 31	8 15	20 37	8 09	20 45	8 01	20 55	7 51	21 11	7 35
22	19 43	7 29	19 48	7 24	19 55	7 17	20 05	7 07	20 19	6 53
Apr. 1	18 50	6 40	18 55	6 35	19 01	6 29	19 08	6 21	19 20	6 09
11	17 55	5 48	17 58	5 44	18 03	5 39	18 09	5 33	18 19	5 24
21	17 00	4 56	17 03	4 53	17 06	4 49	17 11	4 45	17 18	4 38
May 1	16 08	4 06	16 10	4 04	16 13	4 01	16 17	3 57	16 22	3 52
11	15 21	3 20	15 23	3 18	15 25	3 15	15 29	3 12	15 34	3 07
21	14 40	2 38	14 42	2 36	14 45	2 33	14 48	2 29	14 53	2 24
31	14 04	2 00	14 06	1 57	14 10	1 54	14 14	1 49	14 21	1 43
June 10	13 32	1 25	13 36	1 22	13 41	1 17	13 46	1 11	13 55	1 02
20	13 05	0 54	13 10	0 49	13 16	0 43	13 24	0 35	13 36	0 24
30	12 41	0 25	12 47	0 19	12 55	0 11	13 05	0 01	13 21	23 42
July 10	12 20	23 56	12 28	23 48	12 37	23 38	12 50	23 25	13 10	23 05
20	12 01	23 31	12 10	23 22	12 22	23 10	12 38	22 54	13 02	22 29
30	11 44	23 09	11 55	22 57	12 09	22 43	12 28	22 24	12 58	21 55
Aug. 9	11 29	22 48	11 42	22 35	11 59	22 18	12 21	21 56	12 56	21 21
19	11 16	22 29	11 31	22 14	11 50	21 55	12 15	21 29	12 57	20 48
29	11 04	22 11	11 21	21 54	11 42	21 33	12 11	21 04	12 59	20 16
Sept. 8	10 54	21 56	11 13	21 37	11 36	21 14	12 08	20 41	13 02	19 47
18	10 45	21 42	11 05	21 21	11 30	20 56	12 06	20 21	13 07	19 20
28	10 37	21 29	10 58	21 08	11 25	20 41	12 03	20 03	13 10	18 56
Oct. 8	10 30	21 19	10 52	20 57	11 20	20 29	12 00	19 49	13 13	18 36
18	10 23	21 10	10 46	20 47	11 15	20 19	11 56	19 37	13 12	18 22
28	10 16	21 03	10 39	20 40	11 08	20 11	11 50	19 30	13 06	18 13
Nov. 7	10 09	20 57	10 32	20 35	11 00	20 06	11 41	19 25	12 55	18 11
17	10 01	20 52	10 23	20 30	10 50	20 03	11 29	19 24	12 39	18 14
27	9 53	20 48	10 13	20 27	10 39	20 02	11 15	19 25	12 18	18 22
Dec. 7	9 43	20 44	10 02	20 25	10 25	20 01	10 58	19 29	11 54	18 33
17	9 32	20 39	9 49	20 23	10 10	20 02	10 39	19 33	11 27	18 45
27	9 20	20 35	9 35	20 21	9 53	20 03	10 18	19 38	10 58	18 58

Jupiter, 2014

Date		20° N Latitude Rise h m	20° N Latitude Set h m	30° N Latitude Rise h m	30° N Latitude Set h m	40° N Latitude Rise h m	40° N Latitude Set h m	50° N Latitude Rise h m	50° N Latitude Set h m	60° N Latitude Rise h m	60° N Latitude Set h m
Jan.	1	17 47	7 04	17 26	7 25	16 59	7 51	16 21	8 29	15 13	9 38
	11	17 01	6 19	16 40	6 40	16 13	7 07	15 35	7 46	14 26	8 55
	21	16 16	5 35	15 55	5 56	15 28	6 23	14 49	7 02	13 39	8 12
	31	15 32	4 51	15 10	5 12	14 43	5 39	14 04	6 18	12 53	7 29
Feb.	10	14 49	4 07	14 27	4 29	14 00	4 56	13 20	5 36	12 09	6 47
	20	14 07	3 26	13 45	3 47	13 17	4 15	12 38	4 54	11 26	6 06
Mar.	1	13 26	2 45	13 04	3 07	12 37	3 34	11 57	4 14	10 45	5 26
	12	12 47	2 06	12 25	2 28	11 57	2 55	11 18	3 35	10 06	4 47
	22	12 09	1 28	11 47	1 50	11 20	2 17	10 40	2 57	9 28	4 09
Apr.	1	11 33	0 51	11 11	1 13	10 43	1 41	10 04	2 20	8 52	3 32
	11	10 57	0 16	10 36	0 38	10 08	1 05	9 29	1 44	8 18	2 56
	21	10 23	23 38	10 02	0 03 0 00	9 35	0 30	8 56	1 09	7 45	2 20
May	1	9 50	23 05	9 29	23 26	9 02	23 53	8 23	0 35	7 13	1 45
	11	9 18	22 32	8 57	22 53	8 30	23 20	7 52	0 01 23 58	6 43	1 10
	21	8 47	22 00	8 26	22 21	7 59	22 47	7 21	23 25	6 14	0 36
	31	8 16	21 28	7 55	21 49	7 29	22 15	6 52	22 52	5 46	0 01 23 58
June	10	7 46	20 57	7 25	21 17	7 00	21 43	6 23	22 19	5 18	23 24
	20	7 16	20 25	6 56	20 45	6 30	21 11	5 55	21 46	4 52	22 49
	30	6 46	19 55	6 26	20 14	6 02	20 39	5 27	21 14	4 26	22 15
July	10	6 17	19 24	5 57	19 43	5 33	20 07	4 59	20 41	4 00	21 40
	20	5 47	18 53	5 29	19 11	5 05	19 35	4 32	20 08	3 35	21 05
	30	5 18	18 22	5 00	18 40	4 37	19 03	4 05	19 35	3 10	20 30
Aug.	9	4 49	17 51	4 31	18 08	4 09	18 31	3 37	19 02	2 45	19 54
	19	4 19	17 19	4 02	17 37	3 40	17 58	3 10	18 28	2 19	19 19
	29	3 49	16 48	3 33	17 04	3 12	17 25	2 43	17 54	1 54	18 43
Sept.	8	3 19	16 16	3 03	16 32	2 43	16 52	2 15	17 20	1 28	18 07
	18	2 49	15 44	2 33	15 59	2 13	16 19	1 46	16 46	1 02	17 30
	28	2 17	15 11	2 02	15 26	1 44	15 45	1 17	16 11	0 34	16 54
Oct.	8	1 46	14 38	1 31	14 52	1 13	15 10	0 47	15 36	0 06	16 17
	18	1 13	14 03	0 59	14 18	0 41	14 35	0 17	15 00	23 34	15 40
	28	0 40	13 29	0 26	13 43	0 08	14 00	23 41	14 24	23 03	15 02
Nov.	7	0 05	12 53	23 48	13 07	23 31	13 24	23 08	13 47	22 30	14 25
	17	23 26	12 17	23 12	12 30	22 56	12 47	22 33	13 09	21 56	13 47
	27	22 49	11 39	22 35	11 52	22 19	12 09	21 56	12 32	21 20	13 08
Dec.	7	22 10	11 01	21 57	11 14	21 41	11 30	21 18	11 53	20 41	12 29
	17	21 30	10 21	21 17	10 34	21 01	10 51	20 38	11 14	20 01	11 50
	27	20 49	9 40	20 36	9 54	20 19	10 10	19 56	10 34	19 18	11 11

Saturn, 2014

Date		20° N Latitude Rise h m	20° N Latitude Set h m	30° N Latitude Rise h m	30° N Latitude Set h m	40° N Latitude Rise h m	40° N Latitude Set h m	50° N Latitude Rise h m	50° N Latitude Set h m	60° N Latitude Rise h m	60° N Latitude Set h m
Jan.	1	2 52	14 09	3 06	13 55	3 23	13 38	3 46	13 15	4 23	12 38
	11	2 17	13 32	2 31	13 19	2 48	13 02	3 11	12 38	3 48	12 01
	21	1 41	12 56	1 55	12 42	2 12	12 25	2 36	12 01	3 13	11 23
	31	1 04	12 19	1 18	12 04	1 35	11 47	1 59	11 23	2 37	10 45
Feb.	10	0 26	11 41	0 41	11 27	0 58	11 09	1 22	10 45	2 01	10 07
	20	23 44	11 03	0 03 23 59	10 48	0 20	10 31	0 44	10 07	1 23	9 28
Mar.	1	23 05	10 24	23 20	10 10	23 37	9 52	0 05	9 28	0 44	8 50
	12	22 26	9 44	22 40	9 30	22 57	9 13	23 21	8 49	0 04 0 00	8 10
	22	21 45	9 04	21 59	8 50	22 17	8 33	22 40	8 09	23 18	7 31
Apr.	1	21 04	8 23	21 18	8 09	21 35	7 52	21 59	7 29	22 37	6 51
	11	20 23	7 42	20 36	7 28	20 53	7 11	21 16	6 48	21 54	6 11
	21	19 40	7 01	19 54	6 47	20 11	6 30	20 34	6 07	21 10	5 31
May	1	18 58	6 19	19 11	6 05	19 28	5 49	19 51	5 26	20 27	4 50
	11	18 15	5 37	18 29	5 24	18 45	5 07	19 07	4 45	19 43	4 09
	21	17 33	4 55	17 46	4 42	18 02	4 26	18 24	4 04	18 59	3 29
	31	16 50	4 13	17 03	4 00	17 19	3 44	17 41	3 22	18 15	2 48
June	10	16 08	3 31	16 21	3 19	16 37	3 03	16 58	2 41	17 32	2 07
	20	15 27	2 50	15 39	2 37	15 55	2 22	16 16	2 01	16 50	1 27
	30	14 46	2 09	14 58	1 57	15 14	1 41	15 35	1 20	16 09	0 46
July	10	14 05	1 29	14 18	1 16	14 33	1 01	14 55	0 40	15 28	0 06
	20	13 26	0 49	13 38	0 37	13 54	0 21	14 15	23 56	14 48	23 22
	30	12 47	0 10	12 59	23 53	13 15	23 38	13 36	23 17	14 10	22 43
Aug.	9	12 08	23 28	12 21	23 15	12 37	22 59	12 58	22 38	13 32	22 04
	19	11 31	22 50	11 44	22 37	12 00	22 21	12 21	21 59	12 56	21 25
	29	10 54	22 12	11 07	21 59	11 23	21 43	11 45	21 21	12 20	20 46
Sept.	8	10 18	21 35	10 31	21 22	10 47	21 05	11 10	20 43	11 45	20 07
	18	9 42	20 58	9 55	20 45	10 12	20 28	10 35	20 05	11 11	19 29
	28	9 06	20 22	9 20	20 09	9 37	19 52	10 00	19 28	10 38	18 51
Oct.	8	8 32	19 47	8 46	19 32	9 03	19 15	9 27	18 51	10 05	18 13
	18	7 57	19 11	8 11	18 57	8 29	18 39	8 53	18 15	9 32	17 36
	28	7 23	18 36	7 37	18 21	7 55	18 03	8 20	17 38	9 00	16 58
Nov.	7	6 48	18 01	7 03	17 46	7 22	17 27	7 47	17 02	8 28	16 21
	17	6 14	17 26	6 30	17 10	6 48	16 52	7 14	16 26	7 56	15 44
	27	5 40	16 51	5 56	16 35	6 15	16 16	6 41	15 50	7 24	15 07
Dec.	7	5 06	16 16	5 22	16 00	5 41	15 41	6 08	15 14	6 52	14 30
	17	4 32	15 41	4 48	15 25	5 08	15 05	5 35	14 38	6 19	13 53
	27	3 57	15 05	4 14	14 49	4 34	14 29	5 01	14 02	5 46	13 16

Morning and Evening "Stars," 2014

(In Coordinated Universal Time, the standard time of the prime meridian)

	Morning	Evening		Morning	Evening
Jan.	Venus from Jan. 12 Mars Jupiter to Jan. 5 Saturn	Mercury Venus to Jan. 11 Jupiter from Jan. 6 Uranus Neptune	July	Mercury Venus Jupiter from July 25 Uranus Neptune	Mars Jupiter to July 24 Saturn
Feb.	Mercury from Feb. 16 Venus Mars Saturn Neptune from Feb. 24	Mercury to Feb. 15 Jupiter Uranus Neptune to Feb.23	Aug.	Mercury to Aug. 8 Venus Jupiter Uranus Neptune to Aug. 29	Mercury from Aug. 9 Mars Saturn Neptune from Aug. 30
Mar.	Mercury Venus Mars Saturn Neptune	Jupiter Uranus	Sept.	Venus Jupiter Uranus	Mercury Mars Saturn Neptune
Apr.	Mercury to Apr. 26 Venus Mars to Apr. 8 Saturn Uranus from Apr. 3 Neptune	Mercury from Apr. 27 Mars from Apr. 9 Jupiter Uranus to Apr. 2	Oct.	Mercury from Oct. 17 Venus to Oct. 25 Jupiter Uranus to Oct. 7	Mercury to Oct. 16 Venus from Oct. 26 Mars Saturn Uranus from Oct. 8 Neptune
May	Venus Saturn to May 10 Uranus Neptune	Mercury Mars Jupiter Saturn from May 11	Nov.	Mercury Jupiter Saturn from Nov. 19	Venus Mars Saturn to Nov. 18 Uranus Neptune
June	Mercury from June 20 Venus Uranus Neptune	Mercury to June 19 Mars Jupiter Saturn	Dec.	Mecury to Dec. 8 Jupiter Saturn	Mercury from Dec. 9 Venus Mars Uranus Neptune

Greenwich Sidereal Time for 0h UTC, 2014

UTC = Coordinated Universal Time. Add 12 hours to obtain right ascension of mean sun.

Date	d	h	m	Date	d	h	m	Date	d	h	m	Date	d	h	m
Jan.	1	6	42.3	Apr.	1	12	37.1	July	10	19	11.4	Oct.	8	1	6.2
	11	7	21.7		11	13	16.5		20	19	50.8		18	1	45.6
	21	8	1.1		21	13	56.0		30	20	30.2		28	2	25.1
	31	8	40.6	May	1	14	35.4	Aug.	9	21	9.6	Nov.	7	3	4.5
Feb.	10	9	20.0		11	15	14.8		19	21	49.1		17	3	43.9
	20	9	59.4		21	15	54.2		29	22	28.5		27	4	23.3
Mar.	1	10	38.8		31	16	33.7	Sept.	8	23	7.9	Dec.	7	5	2.8
	12	11	18.3	June	10	17	13.1		18	23	47.3		17	5	42.2
	22	11	57.7		20	17	52.5		28	0	26.8		27	6	21.6
					30	18	31.9								

Largest Telescopes

Astronomers indicate the size of telescopes not by length or magnification but by the diameter of the primary light-gathering component of the system, such as the lens or mirror. This measurement is a direct indication of the telescope's light-gathering power. The larger the diameter, the fainter the objects that can be detected. In principle, larger telescopes have better resolving power (ability to discern small details) than smaller telescopes. However, the Earth's atmosphere limits the resolution of what can be seen from ground-based telescopes. That is why the Hubble Space Telescope, which orbits the Earth outside of its atmosphere, can achieve higher resolution with its 2.4-m (7.9-ft) mirror than much larger telescopes on Earth. Adaptive optics systems, which help compensate for the blurring effects of the Earth's atmosphere, allow ground-based telescopes to achieve similar levels of detail as space-based telescopes. Telescopes to detect ultraviolet, X-ray, and gamma radiation must be placed in space or high-altitude balloons because the Earth's atmosphere absorbs most of these types of radiation; as a result, telescopes to detect such radiation are generally much smaller than optical, infrared, and radio telescopes.

Refracting (lens) telescopes are currently not made with lens diameters of more than 40 in. Because **reflecting telescopes** can be made less expensively and with more precision than refracting telescopes, all modern large optical telescopes are made with mirrors. **Radio telescopes** view at wavelengths not visible to optical telescopes or to the human eye. Radio telescopes are larger than optical telescopes because larger diameters are required at longer wavelengths to obtain equivalent resolution. Arrays of telescopes are used to achieve even better resolution through a technique called interferometry. Originally developed for radio telescopes, the technique is now also used with optical and infrared telescopes.

Largest refracting (lens) optical telescope: Yerkes Observatory, 1 m (40 in.), at Williams Bay, WI

Largest reflecting (mirror) optical/infrared telescope: Gran Telescopio Canarias, 10.4 m (34 ft), on La Palma, Canary Islands (segmented mirror)

Largest infrared interferometer: Four 8.2-m (27-ft) telescopes of the Very Large Telescope Interferometer (VLTI) with a 200-m (656-ft) baseline on Cerro Paranal in Chile

Largest fully steerable radio dish: Robert Byrd Green Bank Telescope (GBT), 100 m × 110 m (328 ft × 360 ft), in Green Bank, WV

Largest single radio dish: Arecibo Observatory, 305 m (1,000 ft), in Puerto Rico

Largest radio interferometer: Ten 25-m (82-ft) diameter telescopes of the Very Long Baseline Array (VLBA), dispersed from Hawaii to the Virgin Islands with a resolution equal to a radio dish of 8,600 km (5,000 mi), making it the highest resolution telescope in the solar system

Largest airborne telescope: Stratospheric Observatory for Infrared Astronomy (SOFIA), 2.5-m (8.2-ft) infrared telescope aboard a NASA 747

Constellations

Culturally, constellations are imagined patterns among the stars that, in some cases, have been recognized through millennia. Knowledge of constellations was once necessary in order to function as an astronomer. For today's astronomers, constellations are simply areas of the sky in which objects await observation and interpretation.

Because Western culture has dominated much of modern scientific discourse, constellations and celestial traditions of other cultures are not well known outside their regions of origin. Even the patterns with which we are most familiar today have undergone considerable change over the centuries.

Today, **88 constellations** are officially recognized. Although many have ancient origins, some are modern, devised out of unclaimed stars by astronomers a few centuries ago. Unclaimed stars were those too faint or inconveniently placed to be included in the more prominent constellations. Stars in a constellation are not necessarily near each other; they are just located in the same direction on the celestial sphere.

When Western astronomers began to travel to South Africa in the 16th and 17th centuries, they found an unfamiliar sky that showed numerous brilliant stars. Thus, constellations in the Southern Hemisphere are named after technological marvels of the time, as well as some arguably traditional forms, such as Musca, the fly.

Many of the commonly recognized constellations have their origins in ancient Asia Minor. These were adopted by the Greeks and Romans, who translated their names and stories into their own languages, modifying some details in the process. After the decline of those cultures, most such knowledge entered oral tradition or remained hidden in monastic libraries. In the 8th century, Muslims began to spread through the Mediterranean world. Wherever possible, everything was translated into Arabic to be taught in the universities the Muslims established throughout their new-found world.

In the 13th century, Alfonso X of Castile, an avid student of astronomy, had Ptolemy's astronomical treatise *Almagest* translated into Latin. It thus became widely available to European scholars. In the process, the constellation names were translated, but the star names were retained in their Arabic forms. Thus the names of many stars—Altair, Alnitak, and Mirfak, among others—have Arabic roots, although linguistic adaptation and the inaccuracies of transliteration have wrought changes.

Until the 1920s, astronomers used curved boundaries for the constellation areas. As these were rather arbitrary, the International Astronomical Union adopted new constellation boundaries that run due N-S and E-W. These boundaries divide the sky into the 88 constellations, much as the contiguous U.S. is made up of the lower 48 states.

Common names of stars often referred to parts of the traditional figures they represented: Deneb, the tail of the swan, and Betelgeuse, the armpit of the giant. Astronomers may avoid traditional names by labeling stars with Greek letters, generally to denote order of brightness. Thus, the "alpha star" would typically be the brightest star in a constellation. The "of" implies possession, so the genitive (possessive) form of the constellation name is used as in Alpha Orionis, the first star of Orion (Betelgeuse). Astronomers usually use a three-letter abbreviation for the constellation name, as indicated below.

Asterisms are widely recognized patterns of stars. The so-called Big Dipper is a small part of the constellation Ursa Major, the big bear; the Sickle is the traditional head and mane of Leo, the lion; the three stars of the Summer Triangle are each in a different constellation, with Vega in Lyra the lyre, Deneb in Cygnus the swan, and Altair in Aquila the eagle. The northeast star of the Great Square of Pegasus is Alpha Andromedae.

Name	Genitive case	Abbr.	Meaning
Andromeda	Andromedae	And	Chained Maiden
Antlia	Antliae	Ant	Air Pump
Apus	Apodis	Aps	Bird of Paradise
Aquarius	Aquarii	Aqr	Water Bearer
Aquila	Aquilae	Aql	Eagle
Ara	Arae	Ara	Altar
Aries	Arietis	Ari	Ram
Auriga	Aurigae	Aur	Charioteer
Boötes	Boötis	Boo	Herdsmen
Caelum	Caeli	Cae	Chisel
Camelopardalis	Camelopardalis	Cam	Giraffe
Cancer	Cancri	Cnc	Crab
Canes Venatici	Canum Venaticorum	CVn	Hunting Dogs
Canis Major	Canis Majoris	CMa	Greater Dog
Canis Minor	Canis Minoris	CMi	Littler Dog
Capricornus	Capricorni	Cap	Sea-Goat
Carina	Carinae	Car	Keel
Cassiopeia	Cassiopeiae	Cas	Queen
Centaurus	Centauri	Cen	Centaur
Cepheus	Cephei	Cep	King
Cetus	Ceti	Cet	Whale
Chamaeleon	Chamaeleontis	Cha	Chameleon
Circinus	Circini	Cir	Compasses (art)
Columba	Columbae	Col	Dove
Coma Berenices	Comae Berenices	Com	Berenice's Hair
Corona Australis	Coronae Australis	CrA	Southern Crown
Corona Borealis	Coronae Borealis	CrB	Northern Crown
Corvus	Corvi	Crv	Crow
Crater	Crateris	Crt	Cup
Crux	Crucis	Cru	Cross (southern)
Cygnus	Cygni	Cyg	Swan
Delphinus	Delphini	Del	Dolphin
Dorado	Doradus	Dor	Goldfish
Draco	Draconis	Dra	Dragon
Equuleus	Equulei	Equ	Little Horse
Eridanus	Eridani	Eri	River
Fornax	Fornacis	For	Furnace
Gemini	Geminorum	Gem	Twins
Grus	Gruis	Gru	Crane (bird)
Hercules	Herculis	Her	Hercules
Horologium	Horologii	Hor	Clock
Hydra	Hydrae	Hya	Water Snake (female)
Hydrus	Hydri	Hyi	Water Snake (male)
Indus	Indi	Ind	Indian
Lacerta	Lacertae	Lac	Lizard
Leo	Leonis	Leo	Lion
Leo Minor	Leonis Minoris	LMi	Littler Lion
Lepus	Leporis	Lep	Hare
Libra	Librae	Lib	Balance
Lupus	Lupi	Lup	Wolf
Lynx	Lyncis	Lyn	Lynx
Lyra	Lyrae	Lyr	Lyre
Mensa	Mensae	Men	Table Mountain
Microscopium	Microscopii	Mic	Microscope
Monoceros	Monocerotis	Mon	Unicorn
Musca	Muscae	Mus	Fly
Norma	Normae	Nor	Square (rule)
Octans	Octantis	Oct	Octant
Ophiuchus	Ophiuchi	Oph	Serpent Bearer
Orion	Orionis	Ori	Hunter
Pavo	Pavonis	Pav	Peacock
Pegasus	Pegasi	Peg	Flying Horse
Perseus	Persei	Per	Hero
Phoenix	Phoenicis	Phe	Phoenix
Pictor	Pictoris	Pic	Painter
Pisces	Piscium	Psc	Fishes
Piscis Austrinus	Piscis Austrini	PsA	Southern Fish
Puppis	Puppis	Pup	Stern (deck)
Pyxis	Pyxidis	Pyx	Compass (sea)
Reticulum	Reticuli	Ret	Reticle
Sagitta	Sagittae	Sge	Arrow
Sagittarius	Sagittarii	Sgr	Archer
Scorpius	Scorpii	Sco	Scorpion
Sculptor	Sculptoris	Scl	Sculptor
Scutum	Scuti	Sct	Shield
Serpens	Serpentis	Ser	Serpent
Sextans	Sextantis	Sex	Sextant
Taurus	Tauri	Tau	Bull
Telescopium	Telescopii	Tel	Telescope
Triangulum	Trianguli	Tri	Triangle
Triangulum Australe	Trianguli Australis	TrA	Southern Triangle
Tucana	Tucanae	Tuc	Toucan
Ursa Major	Ursae Majoris	UMa	Greater Bear
Ursa Minor	Ursae Minoris	UMi	Littler Bear
Vela	Velorum	Vel	Sail
Virgo	Virginis	Vir	Maiden
Volans	Volantis	Vol	Flying Fish
Vulpecula	Vulpeculae	Vul	Fox

Eclipses, 2014

(In Coordinated Universal Time, or UTC, the standard time of the prime meridian.)

There will be four eclipses in 2014: two total lunar eclipses, one annular solar eclipse, and one partial solar eclipse. Both lunar eclipses will be visible across wide areas of the United States, with the entire lunar eclipse in Apr. visible throughout the U.S. The annular phase of the solar eclipse in Apr. will only be visible in a small, uninhabited region of the Antarctic, but a partially eclipsed Sun will be visible across wide swaths of the Indian Ocean and Australia. The Oct. partial solar eclipse will be visible in Alaska, western Canada, and the western and midwestern United States.

During an annular eclipse of the Sun, the Moon's angular diameter is not large enough to block the entire disk of the Sun, and the Sun appears as a bright ring about the dark disk of the Moon. During a partial solar eclipse, the Moon blocks some of the Sun's disk. The tables below give the times, in UTC, when the Moon or Sun reaches certain phases of eclipse. In the case of the lunar eclipses, the times are relevant for any observer who can see the Moon. In the case of solar eclipses, the tabulated times refer to when the given event begins or ends from specific points along the eclipse path; as the Moon's shadow sweeps quickly across the Earth, the observed duration and degree of eclipse depends precisely on the observer's location.

I. Total Eclipse of the Moon: Apr. 15

This eclipse is an excellent viewing opportunity for the Americas. The entire total phase of this eclipse, when the Moon is completely within the Earth's shadow, will be visible everywhere in the U.S., Canada, Mexico, and South America.

Event	Date	h	m
Penumbral eclipse begins	Apr. 15	4	53.7
Partial eclipse begins	15	5	58.3
Total eclipse begins	15	7	6.8
Greatest eclipse	15	7	46.8
Total eclipse ends	15	8	24.5
Partial eclipse ends	15	9	33
Penumbral eclipse ends	15	10	37.5

II. Annular Eclipse of the Sun: Apr. 29

This event will be visible as a partial eclipse across a wide area of the southern Indian Ocean and across most of Australia. It will be seen as an annular eclipse only in a small, uninhabited region of the Antarctic continent.

Event	Date	h	m
Penumbral eclipse begins	Apr. 29	3	52.6
Annular eclipse begins	29	5	57.8
Greatest eclipse	29	6	3.4
Annular eclipse ends	29	6	9.3
Penumbral eclipse ends	29	8	14.5

III. Total Eclipse of the Moon: Oct. 8

Although not positioned quite as well for the U.S. as the Apr. 15 eclipse, viewers in the western half of the country will be able to see the entire eclipse. Observers in much of Asia will also be able to see much of the eclipse.

Event	Date	h	m
Penumbral eclipse begins	Oct. 8	8	15.6
Partial eclipse begins	8	9	14.8
Total eclipse begins	8	10	25.2
Greatest eclipse	8	10	55.7
Total eclipse ends	8	11	24
Partial eclipse ends	8	12	34.3
Penumbral eclipse ends	8	13	33.7

IV. Partial Eclipse of the Sun: Oct. 23

The partially eclipsed Sun will be visible over a wide area extending from the north Pacific Ocean, through Alaska, western Canada, the western and midwestern U.S., and most of Mexico. More northern observers will see a greater fraction of the Sun blocked by the Moon.

Event	Date	h	m
Partial eclipse begins	Oct. 23	19	37.5
Greatest eclipse	23	21	44.5
Penumbral eclipse ends	23	23	51.6

Total Solar Eclipses, 2014-35

Total solar eclipses actually take place nearly as often as total lunar eclipses. Total lunar eclipses are visible over at least half of the Earth, while total solar eclipses can be seen only along a very narrow path up to a few hundred miles wide and a few thousand miles long. Observing a total solar eclipse is thus a rarity for most people.

Solar eclipses can be dangerous to observe. This is not because the Sun emits more potent rays, but because the Sun is always dangerous to observe directly, and people are particularly likely to stare at it during a solar eclipse.

Date	Duration[1] m	s	Width (mi)	Path of totality
2015, Mar. 20	2	47	304	N Atlantic Ocean, Arctic Ocean
2016, Mar. 9	4	10	96	Indonesia, Pacific Ocean
2017, Aug. 21	2	40	71	Pacific Ocean, U.S., Atlantic Ocean
2019, July 2	4	33	125	S Pacific Ocean, S America
2020, Dec. 14	2	10	56	S Pacific Ocean, S America, S Atlantic Ocean
2021, Dec. 04	1	54	260	Antarctica
2024, Apr. 08	4	27	123	Mexico, midwestern U.S., E Canada
2026, Aug. 12	2	18	183	Greenland, Iceland, Spain
2027, Aug. 02	6	24	160	Spain, N Africa, Arabian peninsula
2028, July 22	5	10	140	Indian Ocean, Australia, New Zealand
2030, Nov. 25	3	45	105	Namibia, Botswana, South Africa, Indian Ocean, E Australia
2033, Mar. 30	2	37	485	Alaska, E Russia, Arctic
2034, Mar. 20	4	9	100	Central and NE Africa, Arabian Peninsula, Central and E Asia
2035, Sept. 2	2	54	72	China, Korea, Japan, Pacific Ocean

(1) Length of time at optimal viewing area.

Total Solar Eclipses in the U.S. in the 21st Century

During the 21st century there will be eight total solar eclipses visible somewhere in the continental U.S. The first comes after a long gap. The last total solar eclipse was on Feb. 26, 1979, in the northwestern U.S.

Date	Path of totality	Date	Path of totality
Aug. 21, 2017	Oregon to South Carolina	Mar. 30, 2052	Florida to Georgia
Apr. 8, 2024	Mexico to Texas and N through Maine	May 11, 2078	Louisiana to North Carolina
Aug. 23, 2044	Montana to North Dakota	May 1, 2079	New Jersey to the lower edge of New England
Aug. 12, 2045	Northern California to Florida	Sept. 14, 2099	North Dakota to Virginia

Beginnings of the Universe

One of the dominating astronomical discoveries of the 20th century was that the galaxies of the universe all seem to be moving away from Earth. Doppler redshifts were observed for the spiral nebulae around 1920 even though they were not yet known to be galaxies. By the early 1930s, Edwin Hubble and M. L. Humason had established that the more distant a galaxy, the faster it was receding. It turned out that they are moving away not just from the Earth but from one another—that is, the **universe is expanding**. Scientists conclude that the universe must once, very long ago, have been extremely compact and dense, until an explosion or a similar event caused the matter to spread out. The explosion that gave birth to the universe is called the **Big Bang**.

On the subatomic level, according to this theory, there were vast changes of energy and matter and the way physical laws operated during the first few minutes. After those early minutes the percentages of the basic matter of the universe—hydrogen, helium, and lithium—were set. Everything was so compact and so hot that radiation dominated the early universe and there were no stable, un-ionized atoms. The universe was opaque, in the sense that any energy emitted was quickly absorbed and then re-emitted by free electrons. As the universe expanded, density and temperature continued to drop. A few hundred thousand years after the Big Bang, the temperature dropped far enough that electrons and nuclei could combine to form stable atoms as the universe became transparent. Once that occurred, the radiation that had been trapped was free to escape.

In the 1940s, George Gamov and others predicted that astronomers should be able to see remnants of this escaped radiation. They were starting to search for this background radiation when physicists Arno Penzias and Robert Wilson, using a radio telescope, inadvertently beat them to the punch (the two were later awarded a Nobel Prize).

In 2003, NASA's Wilkinson Microwave Anisotropy Probe made measurements of the temperature of this **cosmic microwave background radiation** to within millionths of a degree. From these measurements, scientists were able to deduce that our universe is 13.7 bil years old and that first-generation stars began to form a mere 200 mil years after the Big Bang.

A related mystery is evidence suggesting hidden matter and hidden energy that cannot be directly observed. This **dark matter** may be composed of gas; large numbers of cool, small objects; or even subatomic particles. The presence of dark matter is indicated by the rotation curves of galaxies and the dynamics of clusters of galaxies. Evidence for **dark energy** is derived from studies of distant Type Ia supernovae in far galaxies indicating that the expansion of the universe is accelerating rather than slowing. The visible matter we see seems to constitute only about 4% of the total mass of the universe while the rest of the mass of the universe is in the form of dark matter (23%) and dark energy (73%). Dark energy is a mysterious force that seems to work on the very fabric of the universe, spreading it apart.

Galaxies

The 20th century might be called the century of the galaxy. By the start of the century, more than 10,000 **nebulae**—cloud-like luminous objects in the sky—had been discovered. Some were correctly identified as star clusters and others as clouds of gas and dust. Those nebulae which were spiral or elliptical in shape were found in regions of the sky far from the glowing band that is our own Milky Way galaxy. Immanuel Kant had written in 1775 that some of these fuzzy objects might be **"island universes"** apart from our own. But the idea remained speculative until 1923-24, when Edwin Hubble discovered the existence of variable stars in some of these nebulae. This provided conclusive evidence that these systems were outside our own island universe, the Milky Way galaxy.

Galaxies range in size from small dwarf elliptical ones, with perhaps 1 mil stars, to spiral galaxies containing 300 bil stars, to giant elliptical galaxies that may be home to more than 10 tril stars. The diameters of galaxies range from 3,000 light-years in dwarf elliptical galaxies to over 500,000 light-years in giant elliptical galaxies. It is estimated that the Milky Way galaxy is about 100,000 light-years in diameter with about 400 bil stars.

Galaxies also congregate into **clusters**. The smallest are poor clusters of only a few dozen galaxies, while the largest rich clusters may contain thousands of galaxies. The Milky Way is part of a poor cluster of about three dozen galaxies called the **Local Group**. The largest member of the Local Group is the Andromeda Galaxy, a spiral galaxy visible to the unaided eye in the constellation of Andromeda on a very dark night away from lights. The Milky Way is the second largest galaxy in this group; most other galaxies in our Local Group are small.

The Solar System

The major planets of the solar system, in order of mean distance from the Sun, are **Mercury**, **Venus**, **Earth**, **Mars**, **Jupiter**, **Saturn**, **Uranus**, and **Neptune**. The dwarf planets in order of average distance from the Sun are **Ceres** (located between Mars and Jupiter), **Pluto**, **Haumea**, **Makemake**, and **Eris**. All planets orbit counterclockwise around the Sun as viewed from above the Earth's North Pole.

Because **Mercury** and **Venus** are nearer to the Sun than is Earth, their motions about the Sun appear from Earth as wide swings first to one side of the Sun then to the other, though both planets move around the Sun in almost circular orbits. When their passage takes them between Earth and the Sun or beyond the Sun in relation to Earth, they cannot be seen. The planets that lie farther from the Sun than does Earth may be seen for longer periods. They are invisible only when so located in the sky that they rise and set at about the same time as the Sun and are thus overwhelmed by the Sun's light.

The giant planets emit their own energy. On occasion, radio emissions from Jupiter exceed even those emitted by the Sun in intensity.

Mercury and Venus, because they are between Earth and the Sun, show phases much as the Moon does. The planets farther from the Sun are always seen as full, although Mars does occasionally present a slightly gibbous phase, like the Moon when it is not quite full.

The planets appear to move rapidly among the stars because they are relatively closer to Earth. The stars are also in motion, some at tremendous speeds, but they are so far away that their motion does not change their apparent positions in the heavens enough to be perceived. The nearest star is over 9,000 times farther away than Neptune. The count for identified **moons** in the solar system orbiting planets and dwarf planets stood at 180 as of July 2013. Several dwarf planet candidates are also known to have moons.

Planet Superlatives			
Largest, most massive planet	Jupiter	Smallest, least massive planet	Mercury
Fastest orbiting planet	Mercury	Slowest orbiting planet	Neptune
Fastest sidereal rotation	Jupiter	Slowest sidereal rotation	Venus
Longest (synodic) day	Mercury	Shortest (synodic) day	Jupiter
Rotational pole closest to ecliptic	Uranus	Hottest planet	Venus
Most moons	Jupiter	No moons	Mercury, Venus
Planet with largest moon	Jupiter	Planet with moon with most eccentric orbit	Neptune
Greatest average density	Earth	Lowest average density	Saturn
Tallest mountain	Mars	Deepest oceans	Jupiter
Strongest magnetic fields	Jupiter	Greatest amount of liquid, surface water	Earth
Most circular orbit	Venus		

Selected Characteristics of the Sun and Planets

Sun and planets	Radius— at unit distance[1] "	Radius— at mean least distance[2] "	in mi mean radius	Volume[3]	Mass[3]	Density[3]	Sidereal period d	h	m	s	Gravity at surface[3]	Reflecting power[4]	Daytime surface temp. (°F)
Sun	959.50	976.0	432,500	1,304,000	333,000	0.26	25	9	7		28.00	—	9,941
Mercury	3.36	6.5	1,516	0.0562	0.0553	0.98	58	15	36		0.38	0.11	845
Venus	8.34	33.0	3,760	0.857	0.815	0.95	243		30R		0.91	0.65	867
Earth	8.78	—	3,959	1.000	1.000	1.00		23	56	4.2	1.00	0.37	59
Moon	2.40	986.2	1,079	0.0203	0.0123	0.61	27	7	43	40	0.16	0.12	260
Mars	4.67	12.8	2,106	0.151	0.107	0.71		24	37	22	0.38	0.15	-24
Jupiter	96.40	24.5	43,441	1,321	317.8	0.24		9	55	30	2.53	0.52	-162
Saturn	80.29	10.05	36,184	764	95.16	0.12		10	39	20	1.06	0.47	-218
Uranus	34.97	2.05	15,759	63.1	14.54	0.23		17	14	20R	0.90	0.51	-323
Neptune	33.95	1.2	15,301	57.7	17.15	0.30		16	6	40	1.14	0.41	-330

R = Retrograde rotation. (1) Angular radius, in seconds of arc, if object were seen at a distance of 1 astronomical unit. (2) Angular radius, in seconds of arc, when object is closest to Earth. (3) Earth = 1. (4) A value of 1 would indicate a perfect reflector.

Planets: Motion, Distance, and Brightness

Planet	Mean daily motion[1]	Orbital velocity (mi per sec.[2])	Sidereal revolution days[3]	Synodic revolution days[4]	Distance from Sun (mil of mi) Max.	Min.	Distance from Earth (mil of mi) Max.	Min.	Light at[5] perihelion	aphelion
Mercury	14,732	29.75	87.97	115.9	43.4	28.6	137.9	48	10.56	4.59
Venus	5,768	21.76	224.7	583.9	67.7	66.8	162.2	23.7	1.94	1.89
Earth	3,548	18.50	365.256	—	94.5	91.4	—	—	1.03	0.97
Mars	1,887	15.00	686.98	779.9	154.9	128.4	249.4	33.9	0.52	0.36
Jupiter	299	8.12	4,332.6	398.9	507.4	460.1	602	366	0.041	0.034
Saturn	120	6.02	10,759.2	378.1	941.1	840.4	1,031	743	0.012	0.0098
Uranus	42	4.23	30,685.4	369.7	1,866.4	1,703.4	1,962	1,605	0.0030	0.0025
Neptune	22	3.37	60,189.0	367.5	2,824.5	2,761.7	2,913	2,676	0.0011	0.0011

(1) Average angular motion measured in seconds of arc per day. (2) Speed of revolution around Sun. (3) Number of Earth days to orbit Sun with respect to background stars. (4) Number of Earth days to get back to the same position in its orbit around Sun, relative to Earth. (5) Solar illumination measured in units of mean illumination at Earth.

Planets of the Solar System

The International Astronomical Union (IAU) on Aug. 24, 2006, at their General Assembly in Prague, Czech Republic, agreed on a new definition for planet, and in the process effectively removed Pluto's planet status. The ruling came after years of debate as to whether Pluto, discovered in 1930, should still be considered the ninth planet in our solar system because of its size, orbit, and other characteristics. New discoveries of other Pluto-like objects in the solar system, such as the 2003 discovery of Eris, a **Kuiper Belt object** (KBO) bigger than Pluto, also contributed to the debate.

Under the IAU's new definition, Mercury, Venus, Earth, Mars, Jupiter, Saturn, Uranus, and Neptune are regarded as "classical" planets. A **planet** is now defined as a celestial body that (a) is in orbit around the Sun, (b) has sufficient mass for its self-gravity to overcome rigid body forces so that it assumes a hydrostatic equilibrium (nearly round) shape, and (c) has cleared the neighborhood around its orbit.

Pluto, Eris, Ceres, Makemake, and Haumea are regarded as dwarf planets, with the status of Pluto's largest moon, Charon, still to be determined. A **dwarf planet** is a celestial body that (a) is in orbit around the Sun, (b) has sufficient mass for its self-gravity to overcome rigid body forces so that it assumes a hydrostatic equilibrium (nearly round) shape, (c) has not cleared the neighborhood around its orbit, and (d) is not a satellite.

The IAU also created a new category, **small solar system bodies**, for all other objects orbiting the Sun, including comets, asteroids, KBOs, and other small objects. It has not yet established a process by which other solar system objects will be classified.

Note: AU = astronomical unit (92.96 mil mi, mean distance of Earth from the Sun); d = 1 Earth synodic (solar) day (24 hours); **synodic day** = rotation period of a planet measured with respect to the Sun (the "true" day, i.e., the time from midday to midday, or from sunrise to sunrise); **sidereal day** = rotation period of a planet with respect to the stars.

Mercury

```
Distance from the Sun
  Perihelion .............................28.6 mil mi
  Semi-major axis (mean distance) .. 36 mil mi (0.387 AU)
  Aphelion...............................43.4 mil mi
Period of revolution around Sun.............87.97 d
Orbital eccentricity........................0.2056
Orbital inclination.........................7.00°
Synodic day (midday to midday) ............175.94 d
Sidereal day...............................58.65 d
Rotational inclination.....................0.01°
Mass (Earth = 1)...........................0.0553
Mean radius................................1,516 mi
Mean density (Earth = 1)...................0.984
Natural satellites.........................0
Average surface temperature................333°F
```

Mercury, named for the Roman gods' messenger, is the closest planet to the Sun and the smallest in the solar system. Mercury is too much in line with the Sun to be observed against a dark sky; therefore it is always seen during morning or evening twilight. In 2008, the MESSENGER spacecraft made the first flybys of Mercury since the 1970s. Messenger went into orbit about Mercury in Mar. 2011 for a reconnaissance mission; the original one-year science program was extended in 2012. The goals of the mission include mapping, imaging, and measuring the surface composition of Mercury, as well as probing the planet's interior structure and interactions with the Sun.

Among the early discoveries are that at least part of Mercury's metallic core is liquid, that there may be water ice in shadowed craters near the poles, and that the planet's magnetic field is offset from the planet's center.

Orbit and rotation. Mercury moves with great speed around the Sun, averaging about 30 mi per second to complete its orbit, which takes about 88 Earth days. Mercury takes nearly 59 days to rotate on its axis. Because its orbital period is only about 50% longer than its sidereal rotation, the time from one sunrise to the next on Mercury is about 176 days—twice as long as a Mercurial year. Oddly, Mercury has a magnetic field, albeit a very weak one. It has been held that both a fluid core and rapid rotation—neither of which Mercury was believed to have—are necessary for the generation of a planetary magnetic field. Mercury may demonstrate the contrary.

Atmosphere. Mercury's atmosphere is almost nonexistent. What very little it has is composed of 42% oxygen, 29% sodium, 22% hydrogen, 6% helium, 0.5% potassium, and 0.5% other particles. Because of Mercury's lack of atmosphere, the surface during the day may reach a temperature of about 845°F, while the temperature at night may fall as low as -300°F. Earth-based observation has provided evidence of water ice near the poles.

Surface and composition. Mercury's surface is rocky and cratered similar to that of the Earth's moon. The most imposing feature on Mercury, the Caloris Basin, is a huge impact crater

more than 800 mi in diameter. Mercury has a huge iron core that takes up about 75% of the planet's radius; it has a higher percentage of iron than any other planet in the solar system.

Venus

Distance from the Sun	
Perihelion	66.8 mil mi
Semi-major axis (mean distance)	67.2 mil mi (0.723 AU)
Aphelion	67.7 mil mi
Period of revolution around Sun	224.7 d
Orbital eccentricity	0.0067
Orbital inclination	3.39°
Synodic day (midday to midday)	116.75 d (retrograde)
Sidereal day	243.02 d (retrograde)
Rotational inclination	177.4°
Mass (Earth = 1)	0.815
Mean radius	3,760 mi
Mean density (Earth = 1)	0.951
Natural satellites	0
Average surface temperature	867°F

Venus, named for the Roman goddess of love, is the second planet out from the Sun. Because Venus is almost the same size as Earth, it is believed that the two planets were formed at the same time by the same general process and from the same mixture of chemical elements. Venus can easily be seen from Earth with the naked eye; it is the third-brightest object in the sky, exceeded only by the Sun and the Moon.

Orbit and rotation. It takes Venus 225 Earth days to complete its orbit around the Sun. Its synodic revolution—the amount of time it takes for Venus to return to the same position relative to Earth and the Sun, which is a result of the combination of its own motion with that of Earth—is 584 days. Because of this, every 19 months Venus is closer to Earth than any other planet. The rotation period of Venus appears to be 243 days clockwise. In other words, its rotation is contrary to the rotation of the other planets and contrary to its own motion around the Sun. This rate and sense of rotation makes for a solar day (sunrise to sunrise) on Venus of 116.8 Earth days. Night lasts 58 days, and day lasts 58 days. Venus has no detectible magnetic field.

Atmosphere. The Venusian atmosphere is very thick and toxic. It is composed primarily of 96.5% carbon dioxide, 3.5% nitrogen, and trace concentrations of sulfur dioxide, argon, water, carbon monoxide, helium, and neon. In addition, it exerts an atmospheric pressure at the surface more than 90 times Earth's normal sea-level pressure. The planet is covered with a dense, white, cloudy atmosphere that conceals whatever is below it. These clouds are believed to contain sulfuric acid, meaning that it rains sulfuric acid on Venus. Due to the thickness of the atmosphere and resulting extreme greenhouse effect, the temperature is essentially the same day and night; the planet has an average surface temperature of about 867°F, making it the hottest planet in the solar system. Winds of about 200 mph in the clouds may account for the transfer of heat into the night side despite the low rotation speed of the planet. However, at the surface, the winds are very slow.

Surface and composition. Radar-produced maps of the planet show large craters, continent-sized highlands, and extensive dry lowlands. No tectonic activity has been found similar to Earth's moving tectonic plates, but a system of global rift zones and numerous broad, low, dome-like structures, called coronae, may have been produced by the upwelling and subsidence of magma from the mantle. Volcanic surface features, such as vast lava plains, fields of small lava domes, and large shield volcanoes, are common. About 1,600 volcanoes and volcanic features appear on the Venusian surface; more than 85% of the surface is covered by volcanic flows. Theia Mons, a huge shield volcano, has a diameter of over 600 mi and a height of over 3.5 mi. (The largest Hawaiian volcano is only about 125 mi in diameter, but rises nearly 5.5 mi from the ocean floor.) Aside from volcanoes, there are highly deformed mountain belts across Venus along with a few meteor-impact craters more than 20 mi wide. Erosion is a very slow process on Venus due to the lack of water. There are indications of some wind movement of dust and sand. The few impact craters on Venus suggest that the surface is generally geologically young—less than 800 mil years old. Despite the fact that probes have landed on Venus, there are very few pictures because the probes couldn't survive the high temperature and atmospheric pressure.

Mars

Distance from the Sun	
Perihelion	128.4 mil mi
Semi-major axis (mean distance)	141.6 mil mi (1.524 AU)
Aphelion	154.9 mil mi
Period of revolution around Sun	686.98 d (1.88 y)
Orbital eccentricity	0.0935
Orbital inclination	1.85°
Synodic day (midday to midday)	24h 39m 35s
Sidereal day	24h 37m 22s
Rotational inclination	25.19°
Mass (Earth = 1)	0.107
Mean radius	2,106 mi
Mean density (Earth = 1)	0.713
Natural satellites	2
Average surface temperature	−81°F

Named for the Roman god of war, the Red Planet has some features much like Earth. Mars has climate, seasons, volcanoes, and possibly once had liquid water flowing across its surface. Mars can easily be seen with the naked eye on most clear nights, which is why it was one of the first planets to be studied by ancient astronomers. Later, when telescopes came into use, many observers claimed that canals made by Martians existed on the planet's surface, which led to speculation as to whether there was intelligent life there. Unmanned probes have since put all those theories to rest; the canals turned out to be topographic patterns and dust storms.

Mars is currently being explored by a number of robotic craft, both on the surface and in orbit. The *Curiosity*/Mars Science Laboratory, an SUV-sized robot, landed on the surface in Aug. 2012. Its mission was to understand the history of the Martian geology and climate, search for the presence of organic matter, and to assess the planet's past suitability for life.

Orbit and rotation. Although Mars's orbital path is nearly circular, it is somewhat more eccentric than that of most other planets. Mars is more than 26 mil mi farther from the Sun at its most distant point compared to its closest approach. Its orbit and speed in relation to Earth's bring it fairly close to Earth about every two years. Every 15-17 years the close approaches are especially favorable for observation.

Mars rotates in 24 hours and 37 minutes, almost the same period of time as Earth. Mars's mean distance from the Sun is 142 mil mi. Because Mars's axis of rotation is inclined by about 25° from the vertical to the plane of its solar orbit about the Sun, the planet has seasons.

Unlike Earth's global magnetic field, the Martian magnetic field is small, weak, and localized and may be the remnant of a stronger field from the planet's past.

Atmosphere. The Martian atmosphere is composed primarily of 95.32% carbon dioxide, 2.7% nitrogen, 1.6% argon, 0.13% oxygen, 0.08% carbon monoxide, and in very minor quantities, water, hydrogen oxide, and neon. The atmosphere on Mars is very thin. It has an atmospheric pressure between 1% and 2% of Earth's (if Earth's atmosphere were that thin, we would not have enough oxygen to breathe). Because the Martian atmosphere is so thin and because of the planet's weak magnetic field, its surface is bombarded by cosmic radiation about 100 times as intense as on Earth.

Martian weather systems consist mainly of huge dust storms. On the poles, white caps (believed to be both water ice and carbon dioxide ice) grow in winter and shrink in summer. It is mainly the carbon dioxide that comes and goes with the seasons. The water ice is apparently in many layers with dust between them, indicating climatic cycles.

Surface and composition. Mars is an alien world with rust-red sand and pink skies. In the planet's beginning stages when it was much hotter, Mars's surface melted to a sufficient extent to separate into dense and lighter layers. Mars later cooled enough to allow liquid water to possibly flow across its surface. Today, Mars is very dry.

Natural satellites. Mars has two satellites called Phobos and Deimos, each discovered in 1877 by Asaph Hall. (Phobos measures about 11 by 17 mi and Deimos about 7 by 9 mi.) Deimos, the outer satellite, revolves around the planet at about 31 hours. Phobos, the inner satellite, whips around Mars in a little more than 7 hours, making three trips each Martian day. Since it orbits Mars faster than the planet rotates, Phobos rises in the west and sets in the east, opposite to what other bodies appear to do in the Martian sky. Both moons are irregularly shaped and pitted with numerous craters. Their origins are not known; however, some astronomers consider them to be asteroid-like objects that were captured by Mars very early in its history.

Jupiter

Distance from the Sun	
Perihelion	460.1 mil mi
Semi-major axis (mean distance)	483.8 mil mi (5.204 AU)
Aphelion	507.4 mil mi
Period of revolution around Sun	11.862 y
Orbital eccentricity	0.0489
Orbital inclination	1.304°
Synodic day (midday to midday)	9h 55m 33s
Sidereal day	9h 55m 30s
Rotational inclination	3.13°
Mass (Earth = 1)	317.8
Mean radius	43,441 mi
Mean density (Earth = 1)	0.24
Natural satellites	67
Average temperature*	−162°F

*i.e., temperature where atmospheric pressure equals 1 Earth atmosphere.

Jupiter, named for the Roman ruler of the gods, is the largest planet in the solar system (11 times the diameter of Earth). Its mass is more than twice the mass of all the other planets, moons, and asteroids put together. Visible to the naked eye and known to the ancients, it was a focus of the Italian scientist Galileo Galilei, who viewed the planet and its four largest moons through a homemade telescope.

Orbit and rotation. Jupiter is at an average distance of 484 mil mi from the Sun and takes almost 12 Earth years to make a complete revolution. The largest of the planets, Jupiter has an equatorial diameter of 88,846 mi; its polar diameter is more than 5,700 mi shorter. This noticeable oblateness is a result of the liquidity of the planet and its extremely rapid rotation rate—a Jupiter day is less than 10 Earth hours long. For a planet this size, this rotational speed is amazing. A point on Jupiter's equator moves at a speed of 22,000 mph, as compared with 1,000 mph for a point on Earth's equator. Jupiter's magnetic field is by far the strongest of any planet. Electrical activity caused by this field is so strong that it discharges billions of watts into Earth's magnetic field daily.

Atmosphere. Jupiter's atmosphere is primarily composed of 90% molecular hydrogen and 10% helium. Minor constituents include methane, ammonia, hydrogen deuteride, ethane, and water. Jupiter has a turbulent atmosphere characterized by thick clouds, high winds, and huge lightning storms many times larger than those on Earth. The atmospheric temperature varies, but the temperature at the tops of clouds may be about −280°F. The Great Red Spot seen prominently on Jupiter is a huge hurricane-like storm that is three times the diameter of Earth. In 2006, the Hubble Space Telescope detected the appearance of a second, smaller red spot.

Surface and composition. Gas giant planets like Jupiter, Saturn, and Neptune do not have a surface like Earth or any of the other rocky planets. The gases become denser with depth, until they may turn into a slush or slurry. Jupiter has a liquid hydrogen ocean more than 35,000 mi deep. It likely has a rocky core about the size of Earth, but 13 times more massive. There is no sharp interface between the gaseous atmosphere and the hydrogen ocean that accounts for most of Jupiter's volume. At lower depths, under enormous pressure, the liquid hydrogen takes on the properties of a metal. It is likely that this liquid metallic hydrogen is the source for both Jupiter's persistent radio noise and for its improbably strong magnetic field.

Natural satellites. Jupiter has 66 known satellites. Four of the moons (in order of distance from Jupiter), Io, Europa, Ganymede, and Callisto—all discovered by Galileo in 1610—are large and bright and are close in diameter to Earth's moon and Mercury. Because they move so rapidly around Jupiter, their change in position from night to night can be seen from Earth using binoculars.

Io is one of the most intriguing moons because it is the most volcanically active body in the solar system. A gaseous, doughnut-shaped ring, or torus, enveloping Io's orbit around Jupiter may have been formed by material ejected from Io's active volcanoes. (This is not to be confused with Jupiter's rings.) These volcanoes, hotter than Earth's volcanoes, erupt mainly molten sulfur.

Europa may have a 30-mi-deep salty, liquid ocean beneath its icy crust, perhaps a small metallic core, and a very tenuous atmosphere. Ganymede is the biggest moon in the solar system. With a diameter of 3,120 mi, it is bigger than both Mercury and Pluto. Ganymede also has its own magnetic field produced by a molten core perhaps of iron sulfide. Callisto has the oldest, most heavily cratered surface in the solar system, a very thin atmosphere of carbon dioxide, and possibly a subsurface liquid ocean.

The other satellites are much smaller, with four closer to Jupiter than Io, five between Ganymede and Callisto, and the rest farther out. Most of Jupiter's moons revolve around Jupiter clockwise as seen from the north, contrary to the motions of most satellites in the solar system and to the direction of revolution of planets around the Sun. These moons may be captured asteroids.

Rings. Jupiter has a set of rings that cannot be seen from Earth without powerful telescopes. They are composed of small dust grains possibly blasted off the four innermost moons by meteoroid impacts.

Saturn

Distance from the Sun	
Perihelion	840.44 mil mi
Semi-major axis (mean distance)	890.8 mil mi (9.582 AU)
Aphelion	941.07 mil mi
Period of revolution around Sun	29.458 y
Orbital eccentricity	0.0565
Orbital inclination	2.485°
Synodic day (midday to midday)	10h 39m 23s
Sidereal day	10h 39m 22s
Rotational inclination	26.73°
Mass (Earth = 1)	95.159
Mean radius	36,184 mi
Mean density (Earth = 1)	0.125
Natural satellites	62
Average temperature*	−218°F

*i.e., temperature where atmospheric pressure equals 1 Earth atmosphere.

Saturn, named for the Roman ruler of the Titans, is the sixth planet from the Sun and most distant of the planets visible to the unaided eye. Saturn is second in size to Jupiter, but its mass is much smaller. Saturn is the only planet less dense than water, meaning that Saturn would float if there were a pool of water gigantic enough to hold it.

Orbit and rotation. Saturn's diameter is almost 74,900 mi at the equator, while its polar diameter is more than 7,300 mi shorter. Like Jupiter, its noticeable oblateness is a result of the liquidity of the planet and its extremely rapid rate of rotation; a day is little more than 10 Earth hours long.

Atmosphere. Saturn's atmosphere is composed primarily of 96.3% hydrogen, 3.3% helium, and traces of methane, ammonia, hydrogen deuteride, ethane, and water. Saturn's atmosphere is much like that of Jupiter, except that the temperature at the top of its cloud layer is at least 50°F colder.

Surface and composition. Saturn's atmosphere resembles Jupiter's; it likely has a small dense center surrounded by a deep ocean of hydrogen.

Natural satellites. Saturn has 62 known natural satellites, most of which were not discovered until space probes reached the planet. Saturn's moon Mimas has an impact crater 81 mi across (the moon itself is only 249 mi across). Enceladus has an atmosphere and shows evidence of geysers that spit water ice and vapor. Two tiny moons orbit within the rings, plowing through and making gaps in their orbits. Pan, the innermost satellite, creates the Encke Gap of Saturn's A-ring. 2005 S1 creates the Keeler Gap. The most intriguing Saturnian moon is Titan. The second-biggest moon in the solar system, Titan is bigger than Mercury. Its atmosphere is similar to Earth's atmosphere of long ago; it is made up of approximately 95% nitrogen with traces of methane. Titan's atmosphere extends about 360 mi into space whereas Earth's atmosphere extends about 37 mi. Photographs from its surface show a muddy terrain, with possible deposits of water ice, channels carved by liquid methane springs, and an interesting boundary between

light and dark material on the surface. In 2006, scientists found sand dunes on Titan's surface. The "sand" is believed to be tiny water ice crystals or organic compounds. Surface phenomena such as sand dunes are signs of erosion and wind. Unlike winds on Earth or Mars, Titan's winds are not the result of uneven solar heating on the moon's surface but rather Saturn's gravitational pull (similar to how the Moon acts on the Earth's oceans).

Rings. Saturn's ring system is the planet's most recognizable feature. It begins about 4,000 mi above the visible disk of Saturn lying above its equator and extends about 260,000 mi into space. The diameter of the ring system visible from Earth is about 170,000 mi; the rings are estimated to be about 700 ft thick. The rings are composed of rock and ice and range in size from tiny particles to large chunks of material the size of a bus. There are several divisions in the rings. The 2,920-mi Cassini division, the gap between the A and B rings, is the largest division.

Uranus

Distance from the Sun	
Perihelion	1,703.4 mil mi
Semi-major axis (mean distance)	1,784.8 mil mi (19.201 AU)
Aphelion	1,866.4 mil mi
Period of revolution around Sun	84.01 y
Orbital eccentricity	0.0457
Orbital inclination	0.772°
Synodic day (midday to midday)	17h 14m 23s (retrograde)
Sidereal day	17h 14m 24s (retrograde)
Rotational inclination	97.77°
Mass (Earth = 1)	14.536
Mean radius	15,759 mi
Mean density (Earth = 1)	0.23
Natural satellites	27
Average temperature*	−323°F
*i.e., temperature where atmospheric pressure equals 1 Earth atmosphere.	

Uranus, discovered by Sir William Herschel in 1781, was the first planet discovered using a telescope. It was named for the father of the Titans in Roman mythology.

Orbit and rotation. Uranus has a diameter of over 31,000 mi and spins once in approximately 17.23 hours, according to flyby magnetic data. One of the most fascinating features of Uranus is how far over it is tipped. Its north pole lies 98° from its orbital plane. Thus, its seasons are extreme. Over its 84-year orbit, when the Sun rises at the north pole, it shines there for about 42 Earth years; then it sets, and the north pole is in darkness for 42 Earth years. In addition to its rotational tilt, Uranus's magnetic field axis is tipped 58.6° from its rotational axis and is displaced about 30% of its radius away from the planet's center.

Atmosphere. The atmosphere is composed primarily of 82.5% hydrogen, 15.2% helium, and 2.3% methane, with small amounts of hydrogen deuteride, ammonia ice, water ice, ammonia hydrosulfide, and methane ice.

Surface and composition. Uranus has no solid surface, and likely no rocky core but rather a mixture of rocks and assorted ices with about 15% hydrogen and some helium.

Natural satellites. Uranus has 27 known moons, which have orbits lying in the plane of the planet's equator. Five moons are relatively large, while 22 are very small and were only discovered with the *Voyager 2* mission or in later observations. Miranda has grooved markings, reminiscent of Jupiter's Ganymede, but often arranged in a chevron pattern. Rifts and channels on Ariel provide evidence of liquid flowing over its surface in the past. Umbriel is extremely dark, prompting some observers to regard its surface as among the oldest in the system. Titania has rifts and fractures, but not the evidence of flow found on Ariel. Oberon's main feature is its surface saturated with craters, unrelieved by other formations.

Rings. In the equatorial plane there is also a complex of 11 rings, 9 of which were discovered in 1978 by observers watching Uranus pass before a star.

Neptune

Distance from the Sun	
Perihelion	2,761.7 mil mi
Semi-major axis (mean distance)	2,793.1 mil mi (30.047 AU)
Aphelion	2,824.5 mil mi
Period of revolution around Sun	164.79 y
Orbital eccentricity	0.0113
Orbital inclination	1.769°
Synodic day (midday to midday)	16h 6m 37s
Sidereal day	16h 6m 36s
Rotational inclination	28.32°
Mass (Earth = 1)	17.147
Mean radius	15,301 mi
Mean density (Earth = 1)	0.297
Natural satellites	14
Average temperature*	−330°F
*i.e., temperature where atmospheric pressure equals 1 Earth atmosphere.	

Named for the Roman god of the sea, Neptune was the first planet discovered through mathematical calculations and not observation. Its approximate orbit and position were first calculated independently by British astronomer John Couch Adams and French astronomer Urbain Le Verrier in 1845. In 1846, German astronomer Johann Galle first observed Neptune through a telescope.

Orbit and rotation. Neptune orbits the Sun in 164.8 years in a nearly circular orbit. Its magnetic field is considerably asymmetric to the planet's structure, similar to, but not so extreme as, Uranus's magnetic field. Neptune's magnetic field axis is tipped 46.9° from its rotational axis and is displaced more than 55% of its radius away from the planet's center.

Atmosphere. The Neptunian atmosphere is composed primarily of 80% hydrogen, 19% helium, 1.5% methane, and small amounts of hydrogen deuteride, ethane, ammonia ice, water ice, ammonia hydrosulfide, and methane ice. Neptune's atmosphere is quite blue, with quickly changing white clouds often suspended high above an apparent surface. A Great Dark Spot was discovered in 1989 when *Voyager 2* visited the planet, reminiscent of Jupiter's Great Red Spot. Observations with the Hubble Space Telescope have shown that the Great Dark Spot originally seen by *Voyager* has apparently dissipated, but a new dark spot has since appeared. Lightning and auroras have been found on other giant planets, but only the aurora phenomenon has been seen on Neptune. As with the other giant planets, Neptune emits more energy than it receives from the Sun. The excess has been found to be 2.7 times the solar contribution.

Surface and composition. As with the other giant planets, Neptune may have no solid surface or exact diameter. However, a mean value of 30,600 mi may be assigned to a diameter between atmosphere levels where the pressure is about the same as sea level on Earth.

Natural satellites. Largest of Neptune's 14 satellites is Triton. It is the only large moon in a retrograde orbit, which suggests that it was captured rather than having been there from the beginning. Triton's large size, sufficient to raise significant tides on the planet, may one day, billions of years from now, bring Triton close enough to Neptune for Triton to be torn apart. Triton has a tenuous atmosphere of nitrogen with a trace of hydrocarbons and evidence of active geysers injecting material into it. Triton is the coldest object yet measured in the solar system with a surface temperature of −391°F. Only about half of Triton has been observed, but its terrain shows cratering and a strange regional feature described as resembling the skin of a cantaloupe. Nereid has the highest orbital eccentricity (0.75) of any moon. Its long looping orbit suggests that it was also captured. In 2003, two more moons, which orbit farther from their parent planet than any other moons in the solar system, were discovered. In July 2013, Hubble Space Telescope observations confirmed the existence of the 14th natural satellite of Neptune. At less than 20 km diameter, it is the smallest of Neptune's known moons. The *Voyager 2* probe in 1989 confirmed the existence of six rings around Neptune composed of very fine particles. There may be some clumps in the rings' structure. It is not known whether Neptune's satellites influence the formation or maintenance of the rings.

Dwarf Planets

Ceres

Distance from the Sun	
Perihelion	237 mil mi (2.55 AU)
Semi-major axis (mean distance)	257 mil mi (2.77 AU)
Period of revolution around Sun	4.6 y
Orbital eccentricity	0.0789
Orbital inclination	10.58°
Sidereal day	9.075 h
Mass (Earth = 1)	0.00016
Mean radius	300 mi

Ceres was the first asteroid ever discovered, on Jan. 1, 1801, by the Italian astronomer Guiseppe Piazzi. In the 1800s, it was considered a planet, but as more asteroids were discovered, it lost that designation. In Aug. 2006, it was designated a dwarf planet by the International Astronomical Union.

No probe has ever visited Ceres. NASA's Dawn space probe, launched in Sept. 2007, may become the first. The probe's mission is to Vesta and Ceres, the solar system's two largest asteroids. When Dawn arrives at Ceres in Feb. 2015, months before the New Horizons probe arrives at Pluto, it will be the first mission to study a dwarf planet.

Orbit and rotation. Ceres orbits the Sun in the asteroid belt region between Mars and Jupiter.

Surface and composition. Ceres is in a class of stony meteorites known as carbonaceous chondrites. These are considered to be the oldest materials in the solar system, with a composition reflecting that of the primitive solar nebula. Extremely dark in color, probably because of their hydrocarbon content, they show evidence of having absorbed water of hydration. Thus, unlike the Earth and the Moon, they have never either melted or been reheated since they first formed.

Pluto

Distance from the Sun	
Perihelion	2,756.9 mil mi
Semi-major axis (mean distance)	3,647.2 mil mi
	(39.482 AU)
Aphelion	4,583.2 mil mi
Period of revolution around Sun	247.68 y
Orbital eccentricity	0.2488
Orbital inclination	17.16°
Synodic day (midday to midday)	6d 9h 17m (retrograde)
Sidereal day	6d 9h 18m (retrograde)
Rotational inclination	122.53°
Mass (Earth = 1)	0.0021
Mean radius	742.5 mi
Mean density (Earth = 1)	0.317
Natural satellites	5
Average surface temperature	−369°F

Pluto, named for the Roman god of the underworld, is the second-largest known Kuiper Belt object (KBO) in the solar system. It was first discovered in 1930 by American astronomer Clyde Tombaugh and classified as a planet until 2006, when the International Astronomical Union (IAU) changed its designation to dwarf planet. The New Horizons spacecraft was launched on a voyage to Pluto and beyond in 2006; the spacecraft will make its closest approach to Pluto in July 2015. In 2008, Pluto was designated by the IAU as the prototype for a class of objects called **plutoids**, bodies that (a) have an average distance from the Sun greater than Neptune's; (b) are large enough that gravity determines their shape; and (c) have not cleared their orbit of other objects. Haumea, Makemake, and Eris are also plutoids. At least 10 other plutoid candidates have been identified through mid-2012.

Orbit and rotation. Pluto's orbit and rotation are highly irregular. Although on average it stays about 3.6 bil mi from the Sun, it may get as close as 2.76 bil mi. And for about 20 years of its orbit, it is closer to the Sun than Neptune. Currently, it is beyond Neptune's orbit.

Atmosphere and surface. Because no probes have visited Pluto, it is difficult for astronomers to accurately take readings of the dwarf planet's atmospheric composition. It is believed that an atmosphere of methane, nitrogen, and carbon monoxide exists when the dwarf planet is closer to the Sun. When Pluto is farther away from the Sun, the atmosphere freezes and becomes part of the surface. Large regions of Pluto are dark, others light; Pluto has spots and perhaps polar caps. There is also evidence of temperature fluctuations on the dwarf planet that may indicate primitive weather. Its core may be rocky with a mantle of water ice surrounding it.

Natural satellites. Pluto has five natural satellites. Charon, the biggest, has a diameter of 737 mi—about half of Pluto's diameter of 1,485 mi. No other planet in the solar system has a moon so close to its size. Discovered in 1978, Charon orbits Pluto at a distance of 12,200 mi and takes 6.39 days to move around the dwarf planet. In this same length of time, Pluto and Charon both rotate once on their axes, meaning that a person standing on Pluto would always see the same face of Charon in the same part of the sky, every day and night. The Pluto-Charon system thus appears to rotate as virtually a rigid body. Both worlds are roughly spherical and have comparable densities. Because of these similarities and their peculiar relationship, there is debate as to whether Charon should one day be designated a dwarf planet.

Two other moons, discovered in 2005 and 2006, were officially named Nix and Hydra. Two moons, discovered in 2011 and 2012, were officially named Kerberos and Styx by the IAU in 2013.

Haumea

Distance from the Sun	
Semi-major axis (mean distance)	43.335 AU
Period of revolution around Sun	285 y
Orbital eccentricity	0.189
Orbital inclination	28.19°
Mass (Earth = 1)	0.0007
Mean radius	420 mi
Natural satellites	2

Haumea was discovered in 2004 and was accepted as a dwarf planet by the IAU in 2008.
Orbit and rotation. Haumea has a moderately eccentric orbit and takes about 285 years to go around the Sun.
Surface and composition. Spectra of Haumea indicate the presence of almost pure crystalline water ice. The surface reflects about 60% of the sunlight that reaches it. Haumea has a very oblong shape, twice as long as it is wide.
Natural satellites. Haumea has two natural satellites.

Makemake

Distance from the Sun	
Semi-major axis (mean distance)	45.791 AU
Period of revolution around Sun	310 y
Orbital eccentricity	0.159
Orbital inclination	28.96°
Mass (Earth = 1)	0.0007
Mean radius	450 mi

Makemake was discovered in 2005 and was accepted as a dwarf planet by the IAU in 2008.
Orbit and rotation. Makemake has a moderately eccentric orbit and takes about 310 years to go around the Sun.
Surface and composition. Spectra of Makemake indicate the presence of frozen methane, as well as several organic compounds. The surface is highly reflective and appears similar to that of Pluto.

Eris

Distance from the Sun	
Semi-major axis (mean distance)	67.6681 AU
Period of revolution around Sun	560 y
Orbital eccentricity	0.44177
Orbital inclination	44.177°
Mass (Earth = 1)	0.0027
Mean radius	925 mi
Natural satellites	1

Eris is the largest dwarf planet. Discovered in 2003 by astronomers at the California Institute of Technology, it is the most distant object ever seen in orbit around the Sun.
Orbit and rotation. Eris has a highly elliptical orbit and takes about 560 years to go around the Sun—more than twice the time it takes Pluto. Its inclination is steep, tilted at 44° to the planetary plane. It also has an extremely eccentric orbit. It will be at its closest to the Sun, actually coming inside part of Pluto's orbit, in about 280 years.
Surface and composition. Eris, with a surface covered in frozen methane, may be similar to Pluto and the Neptunian moon Triton. Observations made by the Hubble Space Telescope show that Eris's surface is almost white and uniform, reflecting 86% of the light that hits it. This makes it the most reflective body in the solar system. The dwarf planet's interior is likely a mixture of rock and ice.
Natural satellites. Eris has one moon, Dysnomia.

Small Solar System Bodies: Asteroids, Comets, Kuiper Belt, and the Oort Cloud

Asteroids

Besides planets and moons, many smaller objects orbit the Sun. In 2006, the International Astronomical Union (IAU) officially designated these objects "small solar system bodies." **Asteroids** or minor planets are found mainly in a belt between the orbits of Mars and Jupiter. Within this belt there may be millions of asteroids of varying sizes. Most asteroids are very small. Ceres, which can be classified both as an asteroid and a dwarf planet, is 588 mi in diameter, about one-quarter the diameter of our Moon.

Some of these objects, or asteroids, are gravitationally locked with Jupiter and the Sun so that they have roughly the same orbit as Jupiter but are either 60° ahead or behind the planet. These are the **Trojan asteroids**. Many of the smaller moons of the solar system, especially those in retrograde orbits, may be captured asteroids. Asteroids whose orbits either cross or come close to the Earth's orbit are labeled **Near Earth asteroids** or NEAs. A handful of asteroids have actually been imaged by the Arecibo and Goldstone radio telescopes and by the NEAR Shoemaker space probe. The *Galileo* spacecraft imaged the asteroids Gaspra and Ida (including its moon Dactyl) on its way to Jupiter.

Comets

Comets are small icy bodies that orbit the Sun. When one approaches the Sun, the energy from the Sun boils off material from the comet's icy nucleus, producing an enlarged head (or **coma**), and in many cases an extended tail. Because of that, comets are brighter when near the Sun. For large comets, the head may be 100,000 mi across and the tail more than a million mi long, though both are mainly empty space.

Comets have been known since ancient times. British astronomer Edmund Halley (1656-1742) ultimately realized that a group of historical reports were just repeated visits of the same object. Comets are the only astronomical objects named after their discoverers. In 1986, the European spacecraft *Giotto* took the first close-up images of a comet's nucleus, specifically of Comet Halley, showing it had a peanut-shaped nucleus whose longest dimension was about 10 mi.

In 1995, U.S. observers Alan Hale (1958-) and Thomas Bopp (1949-) independently discovered a comet that was then beyond the orbit of Jupiter. It is one of the brightest comets of all time. It also holds the record for length of naked-eye visibility—19 months—and is the most photographed comet in history. In July 2009, an amateur astronomer discovered a large impact scar in the upper atmosphere of Jupiter, likely the result of another cometary impact.

Kuiper Belt

The **Kuiper Belt** is a doughnut-shaped region that extends to about 50 AU (astronomical units) from the Sun and is thought to be the source of short-period comets such as Comets Halley or Swift-Tuttle. It is filled with icy bodies that are in solar orbit. The more than 1,000 objects found in this region in recent years are called Kuiper Belt objects (KBOs). It is estimated that there are more than 70,000 objects 60 mi in diameter or larger within the Kuiper Belt. Dwarf planets Pluto and Eris are considered KBO. There are at least six KBOs larger than 300 mi in diameter.

Oort Cloud

The Oort Cloud is a vast spherical shell hypothesized to exist around the Sun. Dutch astronomer Jan Oort (1900-92) proposed its existence as the origin for long-period comets that enter the inner part of the solar system where the planets orbit. Current technology is not sufficient to detect any members of the Oort Cloud other than observed comets whose orbits may reach out as far as 50,000 AU. Recent examples of such long-period comets are Comets Hale-Bopp and Hyakutake.

The Sun

Distance from Earth, mean	92.96 mil mi (1 AU)
Sidereal day	25.38 d
Mass (Earth=1)	332,900
Mean radius	432,200 mi
Mean density (Earth=1)	0.255
Average surface temperature	9,941°F

The Sun is the Earth's primary source of light and heat and its closest star. The biggest object in the solar system, the Sun is 332,900 times more massive than Earth and contains 99.86% of the mass of the entire solar system. On the whole, the Sun is made up of about 92.1% hydrogen and 7.8% helium, with trace amounts of other elements. It has a mass and luminosity greater than that of 90% of the stars in the Milky Way galaxy. Although most of the stars that can be easily seen on a clear night are bigger and brighter than the Sun, its proximity to Earth makes it appear tremendously large and bright. The Sun is 400,000 times as bright as the full moon, and it gives Earth 6 mil times as much light as do all the other stars put together. Because of the great distance between the Sun and Earth, it takes about 499 seconds, or slightly more than 8 minutes, for light from the Sun to reach Earth.

Composition. The Sun has six regions. The first three from the inside out are the core, the radiative zone, and the convective zone. Together they form the interior. The others, which comprise the visible surface, are the photosphere, the chromosphere, and the outermost region, the corona.

The Sun's core is where its heat and energy are produced. Through a series of nuclear fusion reactions, hydrogen nuclei are converted to helium nuclei. Temperatures in the core are theorized to be 28 mil °F. From the core, photons transport the energy outward through the radiative zone. It can take photons several million years to pass through this area. In the convective zone, gases move energy outward at a faster rate. Like a boiling pot, bubbles of gas bring energy to the surface.

The photosphere is the visible surface of the Sun, that is, the light that we see as sunlight. When sunlight is analyzed with a spectroscope, it is found to consist of a continuous spectrum composed of all the colors of the rainbow, crossed by many dark lines. The dark "absorption lines" are produced by gaseous materials in the outer layers of the Sun. More than 60 of the natural terrestrial elements have been identified in the Sun, all in gaseous form because of the Sun's intense heat.

Just above the photosphere is the chromosphere, which is visible to the naked eye only in total solar eclipses, during which it appears to be a pinkish-violet layer with occasional great prominences projecting above its general level. With proper instruments, the chromosphere can be seen or photographed whenever the Sun is visible. Above the chromosphere is the corona, also visible to the naked eye only at times of total eclipse or with instruments that permit the brighter portions of the corona to be seen. The light of the corona surges millions of miles from the Sun; its atoms are all in a state of extreme attenuation and high ionization that indicates temperatures nearly 2 mil °F.

Sunspots. These dark, irregularly shaped regions may reach diameters of thousands of miles. There is an intimate connection between sunspots and the corona. At times of low sunspot activity, the fine streamers of the corona are longer above the Sun's equator than over the polar regions of the Sun; during periods of high sunspot activity, the corona extends fairly evenly outward from all regions of the Sun but to a much greater distance in space. The average life of a sunspot group is two months, but some have lasted for more than a year. Sunspots reach a low point, on average, every 11.3 years, with a peak of activity occurring irregularly between two successive periods of minimal activity. Currently, the number of sunspots is declining. Solar minimum occurred late in 2006.

Solar wind and magnetic field. Magnetic arches, called prominences, may extend tens of thousands of miles into the corona and may release enormous amounts of energy heating the corona. Coronal mass ejections are enormous releases of solar energy. Coronal holes are regions where the corona appears dark in X-rays, and are associated with open magnetic field lines, where the magnetic field lines project out into space instead of back toward the Sun. It is in these regions where the high-speed solar wind originates.

The solar wind carries the Sun's magnetic field, which extends beyond the planets. This is called the interplanetary magnetic field (IMF). Far past Pluto and the Kuiper Belt, the solar wind and the IMF lose their influence. The boundary between them and interstellar space is called the heliopause.

Searching for Extrasolar Planets

During the last 10 years of the 20th century, astronomers began to detect the presence of planets orbiting stars other than the Sun. Except in a few possible instances, they have not seen those objects, but merely inferred their existence by their effect on their parent star. The Sun is a typical star in many respects. With over 200 bil stars in the Milky Way, it seems plausible that many other stars might have planets.

As of summer 2013, astronomers had found more than 900 planets orbiting some 700 stars. Of those, more than 400 were at least as massive as Jupiter, which is about 318 times more massive than the Earth. Planets with masses less than Jupiter are now regularly discovered; at the time of this writing, the minimum confirmed mass for an extrasolar planet was slightly smaller than the mass of Earth.

Astronomers use the Doppler effect to detect radial velocity changes in the motion of an individual star. They are more likely to find high-mass planets in close and eccentric orbits around a star because that situation produces larger and more noticeable changes.

In addition to the radial velocity method, astronomers use optical gravitational lensing to detect extrasolar planets. With that technique, Southern Hemisphere astronomers found the most distant planet yet detected, about halfway to the center of our own Milky Way galaxy. Astronomers have also found planets by looking for the periodic dimming of starlight as an orbiting planet passes in front of its host star. About 16 planets have been discovered this way.

In 2005, astronomers obtained the first direct photograph of an extrasolar planet. The unnamed planet orbits a star called GQ Lupi, which is like our Sun but younger. The planet is about 100 AU (astronomical units) away from its star, and it is estimated to be about twice as massive as Jupiter.

In 2006, astronomers discovered what they call a "super Earth" orbiting a red dwarf star 9,000 light-years away. The planet appears to have about 13 times the mass of Earth and may be composed of rock and ice. Although the planet is similar in structure to Earth, it is believed to orbit too far from its star for there to be any liquid on its surface. In 2007, astronomers for the first time detected water in the atmosphere of an extrasolar planet.

In Apr. 2009, NASA launched Kepler, the first telescope sensitive enough to detect Earth-sized planets around other stars. Kepler's first released data, in summer 2010, included indications that small planets are more common than large planets, with suggestions of planets with diameters as small as twice the diameter of Earth. More recently released data show that Earth-sized planets are common. Some of the planets are known to orbit within their host star's habitable zone, meaning that the conditions are such that liquid water could exist on the planetary surface. Kepler has identified nearly 3,000 candidate planets, of which 150 have thus far been confirmed as planets as of Aug. 2013. In 2012, the 3.5-year-long Kepler project was approved for an extended mission, though in Aug. 2013, NASA ended attempts to restore Kepler to full working order. NASA approved the Transiting Exoplanet Survey Satellite (TESS) mission in Apr. 2013. The mission, scheduled for launch in 2017, would conduct an all-sky survey of extrasolar planets.

Earth: Size, Computation of Time, Seasons

Distance from the Sun	
Perihelion	91.4 mil mi
Semi-major axis (mean distance)	93 mil mi (1.0000 AU)
Aphelion	94.5 mil mi
Period of revolution	365.256 d
Orbital eccentricity	0.0167
Orbital inclination	0°
Synodic day (midday to midday)	24h 0m 0s
Sidereal day (rotation period)	23h 56m 4.2s
Rotational inclination	23.45°
Mass (Earth = 1)	1
Mean radius	3,958.8 mi
Mean density (Earth = 1)	1
Natural satellites	1
Average surface temperature	59°F

Earth is the fifth-largest planet and the third from the Sun. Its mass is 5.9736×10^{24} kg. Earth's equatorial diameter is 7,926 mi while its polar diameter is only 7,900 mi.

Size and dimensions. Earth is considered a solid mass, yet it has a large, liquid iron, **magnetic core** with a radius of about 2,160 mi. Surprisingly, it has a solid **inner core** that may be a large iron crystal, with a radius of 760 mi. Around the core is a thick shell, or **mantle**, of dense rock. This mantle is composed of materials rich in iron and magnesium. It is somewhat plastic-like, and under slow steady pressure, it can flow like a liquid. The mantle, in turn, is covered by a thin **crust** forming the solid granite and basalt base of the continents and ocean basins. Over broad areas of Earth's surface, the crust has a thin cover of sedimentary rock such as sandstone, shale, and limestone formed by weathering and by deposits of sands, clays, and plant and animal remains.

The temperature inside the Earth increases about 1°F with every 100 to 200 ft in depth, in the upper 100 km of Earth. It reaches nearly 8,000°F-9,000°F at the center. The heat is believed to come from radioactivity in rocks, pressures within Earth, and the original heat of formation.

Atmosphere. Earth's atmosphere is a blanket composed of 78% nitrogen, 21% oxygen, and 1% argon. Present in minute quantities are carbon dioxide, hydrogen, neon, helium, krypton, and xenon. Water vapor displaces other gases and varies from nearly zero to about 4% by volume. The atmosphere rests on Earth's surface with a weight equivalent to a layer of water 34 ft deep. For about 300,000 ft upward, the gases remain in the proportions stated. Gravity holds the gases to Earth. The weight of the air compresses it at the bottom so that the greatest density is at Earth's surface. Pressure and density decrease as height increases.

The lowest layer of the atmosphere extending up from the Earth's surface about 7.5 mi is the **troposphere**, which contains 90% of the air. This is also where most weather phenomena occur. The temperature drops with increasing height through this layer. The **stratosphere** extends about 23 mi above the troposphere; the temperature generally increases with height in this layer. The stratosphere contains **ozone**, which prevents ultraviolet rays from reaching Earth's surface. Since there is very little convection in the stratosphere, jets regularly cruise in the lower parts to provide a smoother ride for passengers.

Above the stratosphere is the **mesosphere**, where the temperature again decreases with height for another 19 mi. Extending above the mesosphere to the outer fringes of the atmosphere is the **thermosphere**, a region where temperature once more increases with height to a value measured in thousands of degrees Fahrenheit. The lower portion of this region, extending from 50 to about 400 mi in altitude, is characterized by high ion density and is thus called the **ionosphere**. Most meteors are in the lower thermosphere or the mesosphere at the time they are observed.

Longitude and latitude. Position on the globe is measured by meridians and parallels. Meridians, which are imaginary lines drawn around Earth through the poles, determine **longitude**. The meridian running through Greenwich, England, is the **prime meridian** of longitude; all others are either E or W. Parallels, which are imaginary circles parallel with the equator, determine **latitude**. The length of a degree of longitude varies as the cosine of the latitude. At the equator a degree of longitude is 69.171 statute mi; this is gradually reduced toward the poles. Value of a longitude degree at the poles is zero.

Latitude is reckoned by the number of degrees N or S of the **equator**, an imaginary circle on Earth's surface everywhere equidistant between the two poles. According to the International Astronomical Union, the length of a degree of latitude is 68.708 statute mi at the equator and varies slightly N and S because of the oblate form of the globe. At the poles, it is 69.403 statute mi.

Definitions of time. Earth rotates on its axis and follows an elliptical orbit around the Sun. The rotation makes the Sun appear to move across the sky from E to W. This rotation determines day and night, and the complete rotation, in relation to the Sun, is called the **apparent or true solar day**. A sundial thus measures **apparent solar time**. This length of time varies, but an average determines a mean solar day of 24 hours.

The mean solar day and **mean solar time** are in universal use for civil purposes. Mean solar time may be obtained from apparent solar time by correcting observations of the Sun for the **equation of time**. Mean solar time may be up to 16 minutes different from apparent solar time.

Sidereal time is the measure of time defined by the diurnal motion of the vernal equinox and is determined from observation of the meridian transits of stars. One complete rotation of Earth relative to the equinox is called the **sidereal day**. The **mean sidereal day** is 23 hours, 56 minutes, 4.2 seconds of mean solar time.

The interval required for Earth to make one absolute revolution around the Sun is a **sidereal year**; it consisted of 365 days, 6 hours, 9 minutes, and 9.5 seconds of mean solar time (approximately 24 hours per day) in 1900 and has been increasing at the rate of 0.0001 second annually.

The **tropical year**, upon which our calendar is based, is the interval between two consecutive returns of the Sun to the vernal equinox. The tropical year consisted of 365 days, 5 hours, 48 minutes, and 46 seconds in 1900. It has been decreasing at the rate of 0.53 second per century. The **calendar year** begins at 12 o'clock midnight precisely, local clock time, on the night of Dec. 31-Jan. 1. The day and the calendar month also begin at midnight by the clock.

On Jan. 1, 1972, the Bureau International des Poids et Mesures in Paris introduced **International Atomic Time** (TAI) as the most precisely determined time scale for astronomical usage. The fundamental unit of TAI in the international system of units is the second, defined as the duration of 9,192,631,770 periods of the radiation corresponding to the transition between two hyperfine levels of the ground state of the cesium-133 atom. **Coordinated Universal Time** (UTC), which serves as the basis for civil timekeeping and is the standard time of the prime meridian, is officially defined by a formula which relates UTC to mean sidereal time in Greenwich, England. (UTC has replaced GMT as the basis for standard time for the world.)

Zones and seasons. The five zones of Earth's surface are the Torrid, lying between the Tropics of Cancer and Capricorn; the N Temperate, between Cancer and the Arctic Circle; the S Temperate, between Capricorn and the Antarctic Circle; and the two Frigid Zones, between the Polar Circles and the Poles.

The inclination, or tilt, of Earth's axis, 23°45′ away from a perpendicular to Earth's orbit of the Sun, determines the seasons. These are commonly marked in the N Temperate Zone, where spring begins at the vernal equinox, summer at the summer solstice, autumn at the autumnal equinox, and winter at the winter solstice. In the S Temperate Zone, the seasons are reversed. Spring begins at the autumnal equinox, summer at the winter solstice and so on.

The points at which the Sun crosses the equator are the **equinoxes**, when day and night are most nearly equal. The points at which the Sun is at a maximum distance from the equator are the **solstices**. Days and nights are then most unequal. However, at the equator, day and night are equal throughout the year.

In June, the North Pole is tilted 23°27′ toward the Sun, and the days in the Northern Hemisphere are longer than the nights, while the days in the Southern Hemisphere are shorter than the nights. In Dec., the North Pole is tilted 23°27′ away from the Sun, and the situation is reversed.

The Seasons in 2014. In 2014, the four seasons begin in the Northern Hemisphere as shown. (Add 1 hour to Eastern Standard Time for Atlantic Time; subtract 1 hour for Central, 2 for Mountain, 3 for Pacific, 4 for Alaska, 5 for Hawaii-Aleutian. Also shown is Coordinated Universal Time.)

Season	Date	UTC	EST/EDT
Vernal Equinox (spring)	Mar. 20	16:57	12:57 EDT
Northern Solstice (summer)	June 21	10:51	06:51 EDT
Autumnal Equinox (fall)	Sept. 23	02:29	22:29 EDT (Sept. 22)
Southern Solstice (winter)	Dec. 21	23:03	18:03 EST

Poles. The geographic (rotation) poles, or points where Earth's axis of rotation cuts the surface, are not absolutely fixed in the body of Earth. The pole of rotation describes an irregular curve about its mean position.

Two periods have been detected in this motion: (1) an annual period due to seasonal changes in barometric pressure, to load of ice and snow on the surface, and to other seasonal phenomena; (2) a period of about 14 months due to the shape and constitution of Earth. In addition, there are small but as yet unpredictable irregularities. The whole motion is so small that the actual pole at any time remains within a circle of 30 or 40 ft in radius centered at the mean position of the pole.

The pole of rotation for the time being is of course the pole having a latitude of 90° and an indeterminate longitude.

Magnetic poles. Although Earth's magnetic field resembles that of an ordinary bar magnet, this magnetic field is probably produced by electric currents in the liquid currents of the Earth's outer core. The **north magnetic pole** of Earth is that region where the magnetic force is downward, and the **south magnetic pole** is that region where the magnetic force is upward. A compass placed at the magnetic poles experiences no directive force in azimuth (i.e., direction).

There are slow changes in the distribution of Earth's magnetic field. This slow temporal change is referred to as the secular change of the main magnetic field, and the magnetic poles shift due to this. The location of the N magnetic pole was first measured in 1831 at Cape Adelaide on the W coast of Boothia Peninsula in Canada's Northwest Territories (about latitude 70° N and longitude 96° W). Since then it has moved over 500 mi. It is now estimated to be at 82.7° N and 114.4° W, NW of Ellef Ringnes Island in northern Canada. Measurement for several decades by Canadian scientists indicates the motion of the pole has accelerated, now averaging about 25 mi per year.

The direction of the horizontal components of the magnetic field at any point is known as magnetic N at that point, and the angle by which it deviates E or W of true N is known as the magnetic declination.

A compass without error points in the direction of magnetic north. (In general, this is not the direction of the true rotational north pole.) If you follow the direction indicated by the N end of the compass, you will go along an irregular curve that eventually reaches the north magnetic pole (though not usually by a great-circle route). However, the action of the compass should not be thought of as due to any influence of the distant pole, but simply as an indication of the distribution of Earth's magnetism at the place of observation.

Rotation. The speed of Earth's rotation about its axis is slightly variable. The variations may be classified as:

(A) **Secular.** Tidal friction acts as a brake on the rotation and causes a slow secular increase in the length of the day, about 1 millisecond per century.

(B) **Irregular.** The speed of rotation may increase for a number of years (about 5 to 10) and then start decreasing. The maximum difference from the mean in the length of the day during a century is about 5 milliseconds. The accumulated difference in time has amounted to approximately 44 seconds since 1900. The cause is probably motion in the interior of Earth.

(C) **Periodic.** Seasonal variations exist with periods of 1 year and 6 months. The cumulative effect is such that each year, Earth is late about 30 milliseconds near June 1 and is ahead about 30 milliseconds near Oct. 1. The maximum seasonal variation in the length of the day is about 0.5 millisecond. It is believed that the principal cause of the annual variation is the seasonal change in the wind patterns of the Northern and Southern Hemispheres. The semiannual variation is due chiefly to tidal action of the Sun, which distorts the shape of Earth slightly.

The Moon

Distance from Earth	
Perigee	225,744 mi
Semi-major axis (mean distance)	238,855 mi
Apogee	251,966 mi
Period of revolution	27.322 d
Orbital eccentricity	0.0549
Orbital inclination	5.145°
Synodic orbital period (period of phases)	29.53 d
Sidereal day (rotation period)	27.322 d
Rotational inclination	6.68°
Mass (Earth = 1)	0.0123
Mean radius	1,079 mi
Mean density (Earth = 1)	0.607
Average surface temperature	–100°F

The Moon is the second-brightest object in the sky (the Sun is the first). Earth's only natural satellite, the Moon is the force behind the rising and falling of tides, and it helps to regulate the Earth's orbit around the Sun. Many probes have been sent to the Moon, and between 1969 and 1972, 12 U.S. astronauts walked on its surface. The Moon is the subject of renewed international interest. In 2007, Japan and China orbited satellites around the Moon, India orbited a spacecraft in fall 2008, and the U.S. sent an orbiter and impactor in 2009. It is expected that several nations, including the U.S. and China, will send humans back to the Moon in the next 15 years. In Sept. 2009, American scientists announced the discovery of a thin layer of water ice near the lunar poles. The LCROSS impactor mission impacted the lunar south polar region in Oct. 2009. The plume of material thrown up in the impact included water plus a variety of other chemical species, indicating that the lunar regolith harbors a rich and active chemistry.

Orbit and rotation. The Moon completes a circuit around Earth in a period that averages 27 days, 7 hours, 43.2 minutes. This is the Moon's sidereal period. Because of the motion of the Moon in common with Earth around the Sun, the mean duration of the lunar month—the period from one new moon to the next new moon—is 29 days, 12 hours, 44.05 minutes. This is the Moon's synodic period.

The mean distance of the Moon from Earth is 238,855 mi, but its orbit about Earth is elliptical, and thus the actual distance varies considerably. The maximum distance from Earth that the Moon may reach is 251,966 mi and the least distance is 225,744 mi.

The Moon rotates on its axis in a period of time that is exactly equal to its sidereal revolution about Earth—27.322 days. Thus the backside, or farside, of the Moon always faces away from Earth. But this does not mean that the backside is always dark. The farside of the Moon gets just as much direct sunlight as the nearside; at new moon phase, the farside of the Moon is fully lit but not visible from Earth.

The Moon's revolution about Earth is irregular because of its elliptical orbit. The Moon's rotation, however, is regular, and this, together with the irregular revolution, produces what is called libration in longitude, which permits an observer on Earth to see first farther around the eastern side and then farther around the western side of the Moon. The Moon's variation north or south of the ecliptic permits one to see farther over first one pole of the Moon and then the other; this is called libration in latitude. These two libration effects permit observers on Earth to see a total of about 60% of the Moon's surface over a period of time.

Atmosphere and surface. The Moon, like the planet Mercury, has no real atmosphere to speak of. What little exists is variable and tenuous. With its long day and night, the daytime temperature can reach 260°F. The coldest nighttime temperature is –280°F. This day-to-night contrast is exceeded only by that on Mercury.

The lunar surface has not changed much since humans began observing it. The side visible from Earth has large craters and vast dark areas called *maria* that were once lava. The farside has almost no maria but is pockmarked with craters.

Recent findings show that up to 300 mil metric tons of water ice may exist in craters at the lunar poles. In its interior, the Moon may have a small core, which supports the idea that most of the Moon's mass was ripped away from the early Earth when a Mars-size object collided with Earth. The hidden side of the Moon was first photographed in 1959 by the Soviet space probe *Lunik III*.

Harvest moon and hunter's moon. The harvest moon, the full Moon nearest the autumnal equinox, ushers in a period of several successive days when the Moon rises soon after sunset. This phenomenon gives farmers in temperate latitudes extra hours of light in which to harvest their crops before the onset of cold weather. The 2014 harvest moon falls on Sept. 9. Harvest moon in the Southern Hemisphere temperate latitudes falls on Mar. 16.

The next full moon after harvest moon is called the hunter's moon; it is accompanied by a similar but less marked phenomenon. In 2014, the hunter's moon occurs on Oct. 8 in the Northern Hemisphere and on Apr. 15 in the Southern Hemisphere.

Moon's Perigee and Apogee, 2014

Perigee is the point in the Moon's orbit where it is closest to the Earth. Apogee is the point where it is farthest.

(In Coordinated Universal Time, or UTC, the standard time of the prime meridian.)

Perigee

Month	Day	Hour	Month	Day	Hour
Jan.	1	21	July	13	8
Jan.	30	10	Aug.	10	18
Feb.	27	20	Sept.	8	3
Mar.	27	19	Oct.	6	10
Apr.	23	0	Nov.	3	0
May	18	12	Nov.	27	23
June	15	4	Dec.	24	17

Apogee

Month	Day	Hour	Month	Day	Hour
Jan.	16	2	July	28	3
Feb.	12	5	Aug.	24	6
Mar.	11	20	Sept.	20	14
Apr.	8	15	Oct.	18	6
May	6	10	Nov.	15	2
June	3	4	Dec.	12	23
June	30	19			

Moon Phases, 2014

(In Coordinated Universal Time, or UTC, the standard time of the prime meridian.)

New Moon

Month	d	h	m
Jan.	1	11	14
Jan.	30	21	39
Mar.	1	8	0
Mar.	30	18	45
Apr.	29	6	14
May	28	18	40
June	27	8	8
July	26	22	42
Aug.	25	14	13
Sept.	24	6	14
Oct.	23	21	57
Nov.	22	12	32
Dec.	22	1	36

Waxing Quarter

Month	d	h	m
Jan.	8	3	39
Feb.	6	19	22
Mar.	8	13	27
Apr.	7	8	31
May	7	3	15
June	5	20	39
July	5	11	59
Aug.	4	0	50
Sept.	2	11	11
Oct.	1	19	33
Oct.	31	2	48
Nov.	29	10	6
Dec.	28	18	31

Full Moon

Month	d	h	m
Jan.	16	4	52
Feb.	14	23	53
Mar.	16	17	8
Apr.	15	7	42
May	14	19	16
June	13	4	11
July	12	11	25
Aug.	10	18	9
Sept.	9	1	38
Oct.	8	10	51
Nov.	6	22	23
Dec.	6	12	27

Waning Quarter

Month	d	h	m
Jan.	24	5	19
Feb.	22	17	15
Mar.	24	1	46
Apr.	22	7	52
May	21	12	59
June	19	18	39
July	19	2	8
Aug.	17	12	26
Sept.	16	2	5
Oct.	15	19	12
Nov.	14	15	16
Dec.	14	12	51

CALENDAR

Western Calendars

The **Julian calendar**, under which all Western nations measured time until 1582 CE, was authorized by Julius Caesar in 46 BCE. It called for a year of 365¼ days, starting in Jan., with every fourth year being a **leap year** of 366 days. St. Bede, an Anglo-Saxon monk also known as the Venerable Bede, announced in 730 CE that the Julian year was 11 min., 14 sec. too long, a cumulative error of about a day every 128 years, but nothing was done about this for centuries.

By 1582 the accumulated error was estimated at 10 days. In that year, Pope Gregory XIII decreed that the day following Oct. 4, 1582, should be called Oct. 15, thus dropping 10 days and initiating the **Gregorian calendar**.

The Gregorian calendar perpetuated a chronological system devised by the monk Dionysius Exiguus (fl. 6th cent.). His chronology started with the first year following the birth of Jesus Christ, which he inaccurately took to be year 753 in the Roman calendar. Leap years were continued but, to prevent further displacements, centesimal years (years ending in 00) were made common years, not leap years, unless divisible by 400. Under this plan, 1600 and 2000 were leap years; 1700, 1800, and 1900 were not.

The Gregorian calendar was adopted at once by France, Italy, Spain, Portugal, and Luxembourg. Within two years, most German Catholic states, Belgium, and parts of Switzerland and the Netherlands were brought under the new calendar, and Hungary followed in 1587. The rest of the Netherlands, along with Denmark and the German Protestant states, made the change in 1699-1700.

The British government adopted the Gregorian calendar and imposed it on all its possessions, including the American colonies, in 1752, decreeing that the day following Sept. 2, 1752, should be called Sept. 14, a loss of 11 days. All dates preceding were marked OS, for Old Style. In addition, New Year's Day was moved to Jan. 1 from Mar. 25 (under the old reckoning, for example, Mar. 24, 1700, was followed by Mar. 25, 1701). Thus George Washington's birth date, which was Feb. 11, 1731, OS, became Feb. 22, 1732, NS (New Style). In 1753, Sweden also went Gregorian.

In 1793, the French revolutionary government adopted a calendar of 12 months of 30 days each with 5 extra days in Sept. of each common year and 6 extra days every fourth year. Napoleon reinstated the Gregorian calendar in 1806.

The Gregorian system later spread to non-European regions, replacing traditional calendars at least for official purposes. Japan in 1873, Egypt in 1875, China in 1912, and Turkey in 1925 made the change, usually in conjunction with political upheaval. In China, the republican government began reckoning years from its 1911 founding. After 1949, the People's Republic adopted the Common, or Christian Era, year count, even for the traditional lunar calendar, which it retained. In 1918, the Soviet Union decreed that the day after Jan. 31, 1918, OS, would be Feb. 14, 1918, NS. Greece changed over in 1923. For the first time in history, all major nations had one calendar. The Russian Orthodox church and some other Christian sects retained the Julian calendar.

To convert from the Julian to the Gregorian calendar, add 10 days to dates Oct. 5, 1582, through Feb. 28, 1700; after that date, add 11 days through Feb. 28, 1800; 12 days through Feb. 28, 1900; and 13 days through Feb. 28, 2100.

A **century** consists of 100 consecutive years. The 1st century CE may be said to have run from the years 1 through 100. The 20th century by this reckoning consisted of the years 1901 through 2000 and ended Dec. 31, 2000, as did the 2nd millennium CE. The 21st century thus technically began on Jan. 1, 2001.

For a **perpetual calendar**, see pages 350-51.

Gregorian Calendar

Choose the desired year from the table below or from the perpetual calendar (for years 1803 to 2080). The number after each year designates which calendar to use for that year, as shown in the perpetual calendar. (The Gregorian calendar was inaugurated Oct. 15, 1582. From that date through Dec. 31, 1582, use calendar 6.)

1583-1802

1583 7	1603 4	1623 1	1643 5	1663 6	1683 6	1703 2	1723 6	1743 3	1763 7	1783 4
1584 8	1604 12	1624 9	1644 13	1664 10	1684 14	1704 10	1724 14	1744 11	1764 8	1784 12
1585 3	1605 7	1625 4	1645 1	1665 5	1685 2	1705 5	1725 2	1745 6	1765 3	1785 7
1586 4	1606 1	1626 5	1646 2	1666 6	1686 3	1706 6	1726 3	1746 7	1766 4	1786 1
1587 5	1607 2	1627 6	1647 3	1667 7	1687 4	1707 7	1727 4	1747 1	1767 5	1787 2
1588 13	1608 10	1628 14	1648 11	1668 8	1688 12	1708 8	1728 12	1748 9	1768 13	1788 10
1589 1	1609 5	1629 2	1649 6	1669 3	1689 7	1709 3	1729 7	1749 4	1769 1	1789 5
1590 2	1610 6	1630 3	1650 7	1670 4	1690 1	1710 4	1730 1	1750 5	1770 2	1790 6
1591 3	1611 7	1631 4	1651 1	1671 5	1691 2	1711 5	1731 2	1751 6	1771 3	1791 7
1592 11	1612 8	1632 12	1652 9	1672 13	1692 10	1712 13	1732 10	1752 14	1772 11	1792 8
1593 6	1613 3	1633 7	1653 4	1673 1	1693 5	1713 1	1733 5	1753 2	1773 6	1793 3
1594 7	1614 4	1634 1	1654 5	1674 2	1694 6	1714 2	1734 6	1754 3	1774 7	1794 4
1595 1	1615 5	1635 2	1655 6	1675 3	1695 7	1715 3	1735 7	1755 4	1775 1	1795 5
1596 9	1616 13	1636 10	1656 11	1676 11	1696 8	1716 11	1736 8	1756 12	1776 9	1796 13
1597 4	1617 1	1637 5	1657 2	1677 6	1697 3	1717 6	1737 3	1757 7	1777 4	1797 1
1598 5	1618 2	1638 6	1658 3	1678 7	1698 4	1718 7	1738 4	1758 1	1778 5	1798 2
1599 6	1619 3	1639 7	1659 4	1679 1	1699 5	1719 1	1739 5	1759 2	1779 6	1799 3
1600 14	1620 11	1640 8	1660 12	1680 9	1700 6	1720 9	1740 13	1760 10	1780 14	1800 4
1601 2	1621 6	1641 3	1661 7	1681 4	1701 7	1721 4	1741 1	1761 5	1781 2	1801 5
1602 3	1622 7	1642 4	1662 1	1682 5	1702 1	1722 5	1742 2	1762 6	1782 3	1802 6

The Julian Period

How many days have you lived? To determine this, multiply your age by 365, add the number of days since your last birthday, and account for all leap years. Chances are your calculations will go wrong somewhere. Astronomers, however, find it convenient to express dates and time intervals in days rather than in years, months, and days. This is done by placing events within the Julian period.

The Julian period was devised in 1582 by the French classical scholar Joseph Scaliger (1540-1609), who named it after his father, Julius Caesar Scaliger, not after the Julian calendar as might be supposed.

Scaliger began with a zero hour, or starting time, of noon on Jan. 1, 4713 BCE (on the Julian calendar). This was the most recent time that three major chronological cycles began on the same day: (1) the 28-year solar cycle, after which dates in the Julian calendar (e.g., Feb. 11) return to the same days of the week (e.g., Monday); (2) the 19-year lunar cycle, after which the phases of the moon return to the same dates of the year; and (3) the 15-year indiction cycle, used in ancient Rome to regulate taxes.

It will take 7,980 years to complete the period, the product of the numbers 28, 19, and 15.

Noon (Universal Time) of Jan. 1, 2014, will be Julian date (JD) 2,456,659; that many days will have passed since the start of the Julian period. The JD at noon of any date in 2014 may be found by adding to that number the day of the year for that date and subtracting one. The day of the year can be obtained from the left half of the "How Far Apart Are Two Dates?" chart on the next page.

Julian Calendar

To find which of the 14 calendars of the Perpetual Calendar (pages 350-51) applies to any year under the Julian system, find the century for the desired year in the three leftmost columns below. Locate the desired year from among the four top rows. Then read down. The number at the intersection of that row and column is the calendar designation for that year. For some years and countries, the Julian new year did not start Jan. 1; to find the correct Perpetual Calendar for Britain and its possessions, you can generally add one year for dates from Jan. 1 to Mar. 24. For example, to look up Feb. 2, 1705, Old Style, use the year 1706.

Year (last 2 digits of desired year)

Century	00	01 / 29 / 57 / 85	02 / 30 / 58 / 86	03 / 31 / 59 / 87	04 / 32 / 60 / 88	05 / 33 / 61 / 89	06 / 34 / 62 / 90	07 / 35 / 63 / 91	08 / 36 / 64 / 92	09 / 37 / 65 / 93	10 / 38 / 66 / 94	11 / 39 / 67 / 95	12 / 40 / 68 / 96	13 / 41 / 69 / 97	14 / 42 / 70 / 98	15 / 43 / 71 / 99	16 / 44 / 72	17 / 45 / 73	18 / 46 / 74	19 / 47 / 75	20 / 48 / 76	21 / 49 / 77	22 / 50 / 78	23 / 51 / 79	24 / 52 / 80	25 / 53 / 81	26 / 54 / 82	27 / 55 / 83	28 / 56 / 84
0 700 1400	12	7	1	2	10	5	6	7	8	3	4	5	13	1	2	3	11	6	7	1	9	4	5	6	14	2	3	4	12
100 800 1500	11	6	7	1	9	4	5	6	14	2	3	4	12	7	1	2	10	5	6	7	8	3	4	5	13	1	2	3	11
200 900 1600	10	5	6	7	8	3	4	5	13	1	2	3	11	6	7	1	9	4	5	6	14	2	3	4	12	7	1	2	10
300 1000 1700	9	4	5	6	14	2	3	4	12	7	1	2	10	5	6	7	8	3	4	5	13	1	2	3	11	6	7	1	9
400 1100 1800	8	3	4	5	13	1	2	3	11	6	7	1	9	4	5	6	14	2	3	4	12	7	1	2	10	5	6	7	8
500 1200 1900	14	2	3	4	12	7	1	2	10	5	6	7	8	3	4	5	13	1	2	3	11	6	7	1	9	4	5	6	14
600 1300 2000	13	1	2	3	11	6	7	1	9	4	5	6	14	2	3	4	12	7	1	2	10	5	6	7	8	3	4	5	13

How Far Apart Are Two Dates?

This table covers a range of two years. To use, find the numbers listed in the tables for each date and subtract the smaller number from the larger. For example, to find the number of days between Mar. 15, 2013, and Sept. 22, 2014, subtract 74 from 630; the result is 556. For leap years, such as 2012, where Feb. 29 intervenes, one day must be added to the result; thus Feb. 4, 2012, and Mar. 13, 2013, were 403 days apart.

First year

Date	Jan.	Feb.	Mar.	Apr.	May	June	July	Aug.	Sept.	Oct.	Nov.	Dec.
1	1	32	60	91	121	152	182	213	244	274	305	335
2	2	33	61	92	122	153	183	214	245	275	306	336
3	3	34	62	93	123	154	184	215	246	276	307	337
4	4	35	63	94	124	155	185	216	247	277	308	338
5	5	36	64	95	125	156	186	217	248	278	309	339
6	6	37	65	96	126	157	187	218	249	279	310	340
7	7	38	66	97	127	158	188	219	250	280	311	341
8	8	39	67	98	128	159	189	220	251	281	312	342
9	9	40	68	99	129	160	190	221	252	282	313	343
10	10	41	69	100	130	161	191	222	253	283	314	344
11	11	42	70	101	131	162	192	223	254	284	315	345
12	12	43	71	102	132	163	193	224	255	285	316	346
13	13	44	72	103	133	164	194	225	256	286	317	347
14	14	45	73	104	134	165	195	226	257	287	318	348
15	15	46	74	105	135	166	196	227	258	288	319	349
16	16	47	75	106	136	167	197	228	259	289	320	350
17	17	48	76	107	137	168	198	229	260	290	321	351
18	18	49	77	108	138	169	199	230	261	291	322	352
19	19	50	78	109	139	170	200	231	262	292	323	353
20	20	51	79	110	140	171	201	232	263	293	324	354
21	21	52	80	111	141	172	202	233	264	294	325	355
22	22	53	81	112	142	173	203	234	265	295	326	356
23	23	54	82	113	143	174	204	235	266	296	327	357
24	24	55	83	114	144	175	205	236	267	297	328	358
25	25	56	84	115	145	176	206	237	268	298	329	359
26	26	57	85	116	146	177	207	238	269	299	330	360
27	27	58	86	117	147	178	208	239	270	300	331	361
28	28	59	87	118	148	179	209	240	271	301	332	362
29	29	—	88	119	149	180	210	241	272	302	333	363
30	30	—	89	120	150	181	211	242	273	303	334	364
31	31	—	90	—	151	—	212	243	—	304	—	365

Second year

Date	Jan.	Feb.	Mar.	Apr.	May	June	July	Aug.	Sept.	Oct.	Nov.	Dec.
1	366	397	425	456	486	517	547	578	609	639	670	700
2	367	398	426	457	487	518	548	579	610	640	671	701
3	368	399	427	458	488	519	549	580	611	641	672	702
4	369	400	428	459	489	520	550	581	612	642	673	703
5	370	401	429	460	490	521	551	582	613	643	674	704
6	371	402	430	461	491	522	552	583	614	644	675	705
7	372	403	431	462	492	523	553	584	615	645	676	706
8	373	404	432	463	493	524	554	585	616	646	677	707
9	374	405	433	464	494	525	555	586	617	647	678	708
10	375	406	434	465	495	526	556	587	618	648	679	709
11	376	407	435	466	496	527	557	588	619	649	680	710
12	377	408	436	467	497	528	558	589	620	650	681	711
13	378	409	437	468	498	529	559	590	621	651	682	712
14	379	410	438	469	499	530	560	591	622	652	683	713
15	380	411	439	470	500	531	561	592	623	653	684	714
16	381	412	440	471	501	532	562	593	624	654	685	715
17	382	413	441	472	502	533	563	594	625	655	686	716
18	383	414	442	473	503	534	564	595	626	656	687	717
19	384	415	443	474	504	535	565	596	627	657	688	718
20	385	416	444	475	505	536	566	597	628	658	689	719
21	386	417	445	476	506	537	567	598	629	659	690	720
22	387	418	446	477	507	538	568	599	630	660	691	721
23	388	419	447	478	508	539	569	600	631	661	692	722
24	389	420	448	479	509	540	570	601	632	662	693	723
25	390	421	449	480	510	541	571	602	633	663	694	724
26	391	422	450	481	511	542	572	603	634	664	695	725
27	392	423	451	482	512	543	573	604	635	665	696	726
28	393	424	452	483	513	544	574	605	636	666	697	727
29	394	—	453	484	514	545	575	606	637	667	698	728
30	395	—	454	485	515	546	576	607	638	668	699	729
31	396	—	455	—	516	—	577	608	—	669	—	730

Signs of the Zodiac

The zodiac is the apparent yearly path of the sun among the stars as viewed from Earth and was divided by the ancients into 12 equal sections or signs, each named for the constellation situated within its limits in ancient times. Astrologers claim that the temperament and destiny of each individual depend on the zodiac sign under which the person was born and the relationships between the planets at that time and throughout the person's life.

Below are the 12 traditional signs and the traditional range of dates pertaining to each:

♈ **Aries** (Ram), March 21-April 19

♎ **Libra** (Scales), September 23-October 23

♉ **Taurus** (Bull), April 20-May 20

♏ **Scorpio** (Scorpion), October 24-November 21

♊ **Gemini** (Twins), May 21-June 21

♐ **Sagittarius** (Archer), November 22-December 21

♋ **Cancer** (Crab), June 22-July 22

♑ **Capricorn** (Goat), December 22-January 19

♌ **Leo** (Lion), July 23-August 22

♒ **Aquarius** (Water Bearer), January 20-February 18

♍ **Virgo** (Virgin), August 23-September 22

♓ **Pisces** (Fishes), February 19-March 20

Calendar for the Year 2014

January

S	M	T	W	T	F	S
			1	2	3	4
5	6	7	8	9	10	11
12	13	14	15	16	17	18
19	20	21	22	23	24	25
26	27	28	29	30	31	

February

S	M	T	W	T	F	S
						1
2	3	4	5	6	7	8
9	10	11	12	13	14	15
16	17	18	19	20	21	22
23	24	25	26	27	28	

March

S	M	T	W	T	F	S
						1
2	3	4	5	6	7	8
9	10	11	12	13	14	15
16	17	18	19	20	21	22
23	24	25	26	27	28	29
30	31					

April

S	M	T	W	T	F	S
		1	2	3	4	5
6	7	8	9	10	11	12
13	14	15	16	17	18	19
20	21	22	23	24	25	26
27	28	29	30			

May

S	M	T	W	T	F	S
				1	2	3
4	5	6	7	8	9	10
11	12	13	14	15	16	17
18	19	20	21	22	23	24
25	26	27	28	29	30	31

June

S	M	T	W	T	F	S
1	2	3	4	5	6	7
8	9	10	11	12	13	14
15	16	17	18	19	20	21
22	23	24	25	26	27	28
29	30					

July

S	M	T	W	T	F	S
		1	2	3	4	5
6	7	8	9	10	11	12
13	14	15	16	17	18	19
20	21	22	23	24	25	26
27	28	29	30	31		

August

S	M	T	W	T	F	S
					1	2
3	4	5	6	7	8	9
10	11	12	13	14	15	16
17	18	19	20	21	22	23
24	25	26	27	28	29	30
31						

September

S	M	T	W	T	F	S
	1	2	3	4	5	6
7	8	9	10	11	12	13
14	15	16	17	18	19	20
21	22	23	24	25	26	27
28	29	30				

October

S	M	T	W	T	F	S
			1	2	3	4
5	6	7	8	9	10	11
12	13	14	15	16	17	18
19	20	21	22	23	24	25
26	27	28	29	30	31	

November

S	M	T	W	T	F	S
						1
2	3	4	5	6	7	8
9	10	11	12	13	14	15
16	17	18	19	20	21	22
23	24	25	26	27	28	29
30						

December

S	M	T	W	T	F	S
	1	2	3	4	5	6
7	8	9	10	11	12	13
14	15	16	17	18	19	20
21	22	23	24	25	26	27
28	29	30	31			

Federal Holidays and Other Notable Dates, 2014

Some dates may be subject to change.

The dates in **bold** on the calendar above and shown below in *italics* are U.S. federal holidays, designated by the president or Congress and applicable to federal employees and in the District of Columbia. Most U.S. states also observe these holidays, and many states observe others; practices vary by state. In most states the secretary of state's office can provide details.

January

1 *New Year's Day*; Rose Bowl; Fiesta Bowl
2 Sugar Bowl
3 Orange Bowl
6 BCS Football Championship Game (Pasadena, CA)
13-26 Australian Open tennis tournament
20 *Martin Luther King Jr. Day*
26 Australia Day; NFL Pro Bowl (Honolulu, HI)
27 Australia Day (observed)

February

2 Groundhog Day; Super Bowl XLVIII (East Rutherford, NJ)
10-11 Westminster Dog Show
12 Lincoln's Birthday
14 Valentine's Day
16 NBA All-Star Game (New Orleans, LA)
17 *Washington's Birthday* (observed); President's Day, or Washington-Lincoln Day (3rd Mon. in Feb.)
23 Daytona 500
28-Mar. 5 Carnival, Brazil

March

1 Iditarod Trail Sled Dog Race begins
2 Academy Awards
4 Mardi Gras
5 Ash Wednesday
9 Daylight-saving time begins in U.S.
16 Purim (Feast of Lots) begins previous night
17 St. Patrick's Day
20 First day of spring (Northern Hemisphere)
21 Benito Juárez's Birthday, Mexico

April

1 April Fools' Day
5, 7 NCAA Men's Basketball Final Four (Arlington, TX)
6, 8 NCAA Women's Basketball Final Four (Nashville, TN)
7-13 Masters golf tournament
15 Passover, 1st full day; Tax Day (IRS filing deadline)
18 Good Friday
20 Easter; Easter (Orthodox)
21 Patriot's Day; Boston Marathon (3rd Mon. in Apr.)
22 Earth Day
24 Take Our Daughters and Sons to Work Day
25 Arbor Day

May

1 May Day (International Workers' Day)
3 Kentucky Derby
5 Cinco de Mayo (Battle of Puebla Day), Mexico
6 Buddha's Birthday, Korea, Hong Kong
11 Mother's Day
17 Armed Forces Day; Preakness Stakes
19 Victoria Day, Canada
25-June 8 French Open tennis tournament
26 *Memorial Day*, or Decoration Day (last Mon. in May)

June

2 Dragon Boat Festival, China
7 Belmont Stakes
12-15 U.S. Open golf tournament (Pinehurst, NC)
14 Flag Day
15 Father's Day
19-22 U.S. Women's Open golf tournament (Pinehurst, NC)
21 First day of summer (Northern Hemisphere)
23-July 6 Wimbledon tennis tournament
28 Ramadan (Islamic month of fasting), 1st full day

July

1 Canada Day, Canada
4 *Independence Day*
6-14 Running of the Bulls (Pamplona, Spain)
14 Bastille Day, France
17-20 British Open golf tournament

August

4-10 PGA Championship (Louisville, KY)

September

1 *Labor Day*, U.S., Canada, (1st Mon. in Sept.)
7 Grandparents' Day, U.S.
16 Independence Day, Mexico
17 Constitution Day and Citizenship Day, U.S.
22 First day of autumn (Northern Hemisphere)
25 Rosh Hashanah (New Year), 1st full day

October

3 German Unity Day, Germany
6 U.S. Supreme Court session begins
4 Yom Kippur (Day of Atonement) begins previous night
12 Día de la Raza, Spain, Mexico
13 *Columbus Day* (2nd Mon. in Oct.); Thanksgiving Day, Canada
25 Islamic New Year (Muharram 1) begins previous night
31 Halloween

November

1 All Saints' Day
2 New York City Marathon; daylight-saving time ends in U.S.
4 Election Day (1st Tues. after 1st Mon. in Nov.)
5 Guy Fawkes Day, UK
9 Remembrance Sunday, UK
11 *Veterans Day*; Remembrance Day, Canada
27 *Thanksgiving Day* (4th Thurs. in Nov.)

December

10 Nobel Prizes awarded (winners announced in Oct.)
12 Día de la Virgen de Guadalupe, Mexico
17-24 Hannukah (Festival of Lights) begins previous night
21 First day of winter (Northern Hemisphere)
25 *Christmas Day*
26 Boxing Day, Australia, Canada, New Zealand, UK
26-Jan. 1 Kwanzaa

Perpetual Calendar

The number shown for each year indicates which Gregorian calendar to use. For 1583–1802, see "Gregorian Calendar" on page 347. For 1803–20, use numbers for 1983–2000, respectively. The years in the calendar labels are the last and next occurrences of each calendar.

Year	No.		Year	No.		Year	No.		Year	No.		Year	No.		Year	No.		Year	No.		Year	No.		Year	No.
1821	2		1847	6		1873	4		1899	1		1925	5		1951	2		1977	7		2003	4		2029	2		2055	5
1822	3		1848	14		1874	5		1900	2		1926	6		1952	10		1978	1		2004	12		2030	3		2056	6
1823	4		1849	7		1875	6		1901	3		1927	7		1953	5		1979	2		2005	7		2031	4		2057	7
1824	12		1850	3		1876	14		1902	4		1928	8		1954	6		1980	10		2006	1		2032	12		2058	1
1825	7		1851	4		1877	2		1903	5		1929	3		1955	7		1981	5		2007	2		2033	7		2059	2
1826	1		1852	12		1878	3		1904	13		1930	4		1956	8		1982	6		2008	10		2034	1		2060	10
1827	2		1853	7		1879	4		1905	1		1931	5		1957	3		1983	7		2009	5		2035	2		2061	5
1828	10		1854	1		1880	12		1906	2		1932	13		1958	4		1984	8		2010	6		2036	10		2062	6
1829	5		1855	2		1881	7		1907	3		1933	1		1959	5		1985	3		2011	7		2037	5		2063	7
1830	6		1856	10		1882	1		1908	11		1934	2		1960	13		1986	4		2012	8		2038	6		2064	8
1831	7		1857	5		1883	2		1909	6		1935	3		1961	1		1987	5		2013	3		2039	7		2065	3
1832	8		1858	6		1884	10		1910	7		1936	11		1962	2		1988	13		2014	4		2040	8		2066	4
1833	3		1859	7		1885	5		1911	1		1937	6		1963	3		1989	1		2015	5		2041	3		2067	5
1834	4		1860	8		1886	6		1912	9		1938	7		1964	11		1990	2		2016	13		2042	4		2068	13
1835	5		1861	3		1887	7		1913	4		1939	1		1965	6		1991	3		2017	1		2043	5		2069	1
1836	13		1862	4		1888	8		1914	5		1940	9		1966	7		1992	11		2018	2		2044	13		2070	2
1837	1		1863	5		1889	3		1915	6		1941	4		1967	1		1993	6		2019	3		2045	1		2071	3
1838	2		1864	13		1890	4		1916	14		1942	5		1968	9		1994	7		2020	11		2046	2		2072	11
1839	3		1865	1		1891	5		1917	2		1943	6		1969	4		1995	1		2021	6		2047	3		2073	6
1840	11		1866	2		1892	13		1918	3		1944	14		1970	5		1996	9		2022	7		2048	11		2074	7
1841	6		1867	3		1893	1		1919	4		1945	2		1971	6		1997	4		2023	1		2049	6		2075	1
1842	7		1868	11		1894	2		1920	12		1946	3		1972	14		1998	5		2024	9		2050	7		2076	9
1843	1		1869	6		1895	3		1921	7		1947	4		1973	2		1999	6		2025	4		2051	1		2077	4
1844	9		1870	7		1896	11		1922	1		1948	12		1974	3		2000	14		2026	5		2052	9		2078	5
1845	4		1871	1		1897	6		1923	2		1949	7		1975	4		2001	2		2027	6		2053	4		2079	6
1846	5		1872	9		1898	7		1924	10		1950	3		1976	12		2002	3		2028	14		2054	5		2080	14

1 — 2006/2017

2 — 2007/2018

3 — 2013/2019

4 — 2003/2014

5 — 2009/2015

6 — 2010/2021

Each numbered calendar shows twelve months (January through December) with columns labeled S M T W T F S.

7 — 2011/2022

JANUARY · FEBRUARY · MARCH · APRIL · MAY · JUNE · JULY · AUGUST · SEPTEMBER · OCTOBER · NOVEMBER · DECEMBER

8 — 2012/2040

JANUARY · FEBRUARY · MARCH · APRIL · MAY · JUNE · JULY · AUGUST · SEPTEMBER · OCTOBER · NOVEMBER · DECEMBER

9 — 1996/2024

JANUARY · FEBRUARY · MARCH · APRIL · MAY · JUNE · JULY · AUGUST · SEPTEMBER · OCTOBER · NOVEMBER · DECEMBER

10 — 2008/2036

JANUARY · FEBRUARY · MARCH · APRIL · MAY · JUNE · JULY · AUGUST · SEPTEMBER · OCTOBER · NOVEMBER · DECEMBER

11 — 1992/2020

JANUARY · FEBRUARY · MARCH · APRIL · MAY · JUNE · JULY · AUGUST · SEPTEMBER · OCTOBER · NOVEMBER · DECEMBER

12 — 2004/2032

JANUARY · FEBRUARY · MARCH · APRIL · MAY · JUNE · JULY · AUGUST · SEPTEMBER · OCTOBER · NOVEMBER · DECEMBER

13 — 1988/2016

JANUARY · FEBRUARY · MARCH · APRIL · MAY · JUNE · JULY · AUGUST · SEPTEMBER · OCTOBER · NOVEMBER · DECEMBER

14 — 2000/2028

JANUARY · FEBRUARY · MARCH · APRIL · MAY · JUNE · JULY · AUGUST · SEPTEMBER · OCTOBER · NOVEMBER · DECEMBER

Chinese Calendar and Asian Festivals

The Chinese calendar, like the Jewish and Islamic calendars (see the Religion chapter), is a lunar calendar. It is divided into 12 months of 29 or 30 days (compensating for the lunar month's mean duration of 29 days, 12 hr., 44.05 min.). This calendar is synchronized with the solar year by the addition of extra months at fixed intervals.

The Chinese calendar runs on a 60-year cycle. The cycles 1876-1935 and 1936-95, along with the first 24 years of the current cycle, are shown below grouped by their association with 1 of 12 animals in the Chinese zodiac. This cycle began in 1996 and will last until 2055. Jan. 31, 2014, marks the beginning of the year 4712 in the Chinese calendar and is designated the Year of the Horse. (Note: The first 3-7 weeks of each Western year belong to the previous Chinese year.)

Both the Western (Gregorian) and traditional lunar calendars are used publicly in China and in North and South Korea, and two New Year's celebrations are held. In Taiwan, overseas Chinese communities, and Vietnam, the lunar calendar is used only to set the dates for traditional festivals, with the Gregorian system in general use.

The 4-day Chinese New Year; the 3-day Vietnamese New Year festival, Tet; and the 3-to-4-day Korean festival, Suhl, begin at the second new moon after the winter solstice. The new moon in East Asia, which is west of the International Date Line, may be a day later than the new moon in the U.S. The festivals may start, therefore, anywhere between Jan. 21 and Feb. 19 of the Gregorian calendar.

Rat	Ox	Tiger	Hare (Rabbit)	Dragon	Snake	Horse	Sheep (Goat)	Monkey	Rooster	Dog	Pig (Boar)
1876	1877	1878	1879	1880	1881	1882	1883	1884	1885	1886	1887
1888	1889	1890	1891	1892	1893	1894	1895	1896	1897	1898	1899
1900	1901	1902	1903	1904	1905	1906	1907	1908	1909	1910	1911
1912	1913	1914	1915	1916	1917	1918	1919	1920	1921	1922	1923
1924	1925	1926	1927	1928	1929	1930	1931	1932	1933	1934	1935
1936	1937	1938	1939	1940	1941	1942	1943	1944	1945	1946	1947
1948	1949	1950	1951	1952	1953	1954	1955	1956	1957	1958	1959
1960	1961	1962	1963	1964	1965	1966	1967	1968	1969	1970	1971
1972	1973	1974	1975	1976	1977	1978	1979	1980	1981	1982	1983
1984	1985	1986	1987	1988	1989	1990	1991	1992	1993	1994	1995
1996	1997	1998	1999	2000	2001	2002	2003	2004	2005	2006	2007
2008	2009	2010	2011	2012	2013	2014	2015	2016	2017	2018	2019

Other Calendars: Year and New Year's Day, 2014

Era	Year	Begins in 2014	Era	Year	Begins in 2014
Byzantine	7523	Sept. 14	Islamic/Muslim (Hijra)	1436	Oct. 25[1]
Chinese (Year of the Horse)	4712	Jan. 31	Japanese (starts at 0 with new emperor)	26	Jan. 1
Diocletian	1731	Sept. 11	Jewish	5775	Sept. 25[1]
Grecian (Seleucidae)	2326	Sept. 14 or Oct. 14	Nabonassar (Babylonian)	2763	Apr. 23
Indian (Saka)	1936	Mar. 22	Roman (Ab Urbe Condita)	2767	Jan. 14

(1) Year begins the previous night.

Chronological Cycles, 2014

Dominical Letter	E	Roman Indiction	7	Solar Cycle	7
Golden Number (Lunar Cycle)	1	Epact	29	Julian Period (year of)	6727

Special Months

There are many thousands of special months, days, and weeks because of anniversaries, official proclamations, and promotional events, both trivial and serious. Here are a few of the special months:

January: Jump Out of Bed Month, National Mentoring Month, National Poverty in America Awareness Month

February: Black History Month, American Heart Month, Library Lovers Month, Youth Leadership Month, Return Shopping Carts to the Supermarket Month

March: Irish-American Heritage Month, Women's History Month, American Red Cross Month, National Frozen Food Month, National Talk With Your Teen About Sex Month, National Colorectal Cancer Awareness Month

April: National Child Abuse Prevention Month, National Humor Month, Stress Awareness Month, Grange Month

May: Clean Air Month, Get Caught Reading Month, National Barbecue Month, Asian Pacific American Heritage Month, National Inventors Month, National Mental Health Month

June: National Candy Month; Lesbian, Gay, Bisexual, and Transgender Pride Month; Potty Training Awareness Month; National Safety Month

July: Cell Phone Courtesy Month, National HIV Awareness Month, National Hot Dog Month, Women's Motorcycle Month

August: National Black Business Month, Happiness Happens Month, National Immunization Awareness Month, National Toddler Month

September: Library Card Sign-Up Month, National Hispanic Heritage Month (Sept. 15-Oct. 15), National Biscuit Month

October: National Domestic Violence Awareness Month, National Breast Cancer Awareness Month, Diversity Awareness Month, National Popcorn Poppin' Month

November: National American Indian Heritage Month, National Adoption Month, American Diabetes Month, National Peanut Butter Lovers' Month

December: Universal Human Rights Month, National Impaired Driving Prevention Month, National Tie Month

Wedding Anniversary Gifts

The traditional names for wedding anniversaries go back many years in social usage and have been used to suggest types of appropriate anniversary gifts. Traditional products for gifts are listed here in capital letters, with allowable revisions in parentheses, followed by common modern gifts in each category.

1st	PAPER, clocks	9th	POTTERY (CHINA), leather goods	25th	SILVER, sterling silver
2nd	COTTON, china	10th	TIN, ALUMINUM, diamond	30th	PEARL, diamond
3rd	LEATHER, crystal, glass	11th	STEEL, fashion jewelry	35th	CORAL (JADE), jade
4th	LINEN (SILK), appliances	12th	SILK, pearls, colored gems	40th	RUBY, ruby
5th	WOOD, silverware	13th	LACE, textiles, furs	45th	SAPPHIRE, sapphire
6th	IRON, wood objects	14th	IVORY, gold jewelry	50th	GOLD, gold
7th	WOOL (COPPER), desk sets	15th	CRYSTAL, watches	55th	EMERALD, emerald
8th	BRONZE, linens, lace	20th	CHINA, platinum	60th	DIAMOND, diamond

Birthstones

Source: Jewelry Industry Council

Birth month	Ancient birthstone	Modern birthstone	Birth month	Ancient birthstone	Modern birthstone
January	Garnet	Garnet	July	Onyx	Ruby
February	Amethyst	Amethyst	August	Carnelian	Sardonyx or Peridot
March	Jasper	Bloodstone or Aquamarine	September	Chrysolite	Sapphire
April	Sapphire	Diamond	October	Aquamarine	Opal or Tourmaline
May	Agate	Emerald	November	Topaz	Topaz
June	Emerald	Pearl, Moonstone, or Alexandrite	December	Ruby	Turquoise or Zircon

Standard Time and Daylight Saving Time

Source: National Institute of Standards and Technology, U.S. Dept. of Commerce

See also Time Zone map, page 462.

Standard Time

Standard Time is reckoned from the prime meridian of longitude in Greenwich, England. The world is divided into 24 zones, each 15 deg of arc, or one hour in time apart. The Greenwich meridian (0 deg) extends through the center of the initial zone. Zones to the east are numbered from 1 to 12, with the prefix "minus" indicating the number of hours to be subtracted to obtain Greenwich Time. Each zone extends 7.5 deg on either side of its central meridian.

Westward zones are similarly numbered, but prefixed "plus," showing the number of hours that must be added to get Greenwich Time. Although these zones apply generally to ocean areas, the standard time maintained in many countries does not coincide with zone time.

The U.S. and possessions are divided into nine standard time zones. All places in each zone use, instead of their own local time, the time counted from the transit of the "mean sun" across the standard time meridian that passes near the middle of that zone. These time zones are designated as Atlantic, Eastern, Central, Mountain, Pacific, Alaska, Hawaii-Aleutian, Samoa, and Chamorro (Guam and Northern Mariana Isls.); the time in these zones is reckoned from the 60th, 75th, 90th, 105th, 120th, 135th, 150th, and 165th meridians west of Greenwich and the 150th meridian east of Greenwich. The time zone line wanders to conform to local geography. The time in the various zones in the U.S. and U.S. territories west of Greenwich is earlier than Greenwich Time by 4, 5, 6, 7, 8, 9, 10, and 11 hours, respectively. However, Chamorro crosses the International Date Line and is 10 hours later than Greenwich Time.

24-Hour Time

With the 24-hour system, the day begins at midnight, and times are designated 00:00 through 23:59. Twenty-four-hour time is widely used in scientific work throughout the world. In the U.S., it is also used in operations of the armed forces. In Europe, it is frequently used by the transportation networks in preference to the 12-hour AM and PM system.

International Date Line

The Date Line, approximately coinciding with the 180th meridian, separates the calendar dates. The date must be advanced one day when crossing in a westerly direction and set back one day when crossing in an easterly direction. The Date Line frequently deviates from the 180th meridian because of decisions made by individual nations affected. The line is deflected eastward through the Bering Strait and westward of the Aleutians to prevent separating these areas by date. The line is deflected eastward of the Tonga and New Zealand Islands in the South Pacific. In 1995, Kiribati announced that all of its islands east of the Date Line would observe the same date as islands to the west, though most maps and atlases do not depict this as a deviation in the Date Line. The line is established by international custom; there is no international authority prescribing its exact course.

Daylight-Saving Time

Daylight-saving time is achieved by advancing the clock one hour. Since 2007, daylight-saving time has begun at 2 AM on the 2nd Sunday in Mar. and has ended at 2 AM on the first Sunday in Nov. **In 2014, daylight-saving time begins at 2 AM on Mar. 9 and ends at 2 AM on Nov. 2.** Prior to 2007, daylight-saving time traditionally ran from the first Sunday in Apr. to the last Sunday in Oct.

Daylight-saving time was first observed in the U.S. during World War I, and then again during World War II. In the intervening years, some states and communities observed daylight-saving time, using whatever beginning and ending dates they chose. In 1966, Congress passed the Uniform Time Act, which provided that any state or territory choosing to observe daylight-saving time must begin and end on the federal dates. Any state could, by law, exempt itself; a 1972 amendment to the act authorized states in more than one time zone to exempt the entire state or one time zone only. Currently, most of Arizona, Hawaii, Puerto Rico, the U.S. Virgin Islands, Guam, and American Samoa do not observe daylight-saving time. On Apr. 2, 2006, all of Indiana observed daylight-saving time for the first time. (The state is divided between two time zones.)

Congress and the secretary of transportation both have authority to change time zone boundaries, which they have done on a number of occasions since 1966. In addition, efforts to conserve energy have prompted various changes in the times that daylight-saving time is observed.

Daylight-Saving Time: International Usage

Adjusting clock time so as to gain daylight on summer evenings is common throughout the world.

Canada, which extends over 6 time zones, generally observes daylight-saving time during the same period as the U.S. Most provincial governments observe the 4-week extension to daylight-saving time that went into effect in 2007. Most of Saskatchewan remains on standard time year-round. Communities elsewhere in Canada also may exempt themselves from daylight-saving time. Except for the state of Sonora, which shares a border with Arizona, most of Mexico observes daylight-saving time.

Member nations of the European Union (EU) observe a "summer-time period," a version of daylight-saving time, from the last Sunday of Mar. until the last Sunday in Oct.

Russia, which extends geographically over 11 time zones and uses 9, historically has maintained its standard time one hour ahead of its zone designation. Additionally, Russian observation of daylight-saving time ended in 2011. Though an hour of time was added in Mar. 2011, clocks were not set back an hour in the fall, meaning that standard time in most of Russia is effectively 2 hours ahead of the zone designation.

China, which extends across 5 time zones, has decreed that the entire country be placed on Greenwich time plus 8 hours. Daylight-saving time is not observed. Japan, which lies within one time zone, also does not modify its legal time during the summer months.

Many countries in the Southern Hemisphere maintain daylight-saving time generally from Oct. to Mar. However, most countries near the equator do not deviate from standard time.

Standard Time Differences: World Cities

The time indicated in the table is fixed by law and is called the legal time or, more generally, standard time. Use of daylight-saving time varies widely. An asterisk (*) indicates morning of the following day. At 12:00 noon, Eastern Standard Time, the standard time (in 24-hour time) in selected cities is as shown.

City	Hr	Min	City	Hr	Min	City	Hr	Min
Addis Ababa	20	00	Hong Kong	1	00*	Paris	18	00
Amsterdam	18	00	Islamabad	22	00	Prague	18	00
Ankara	19	00	Istanbul	19	00	Quito	12	00
Athens	19	00	Jakarta	0	00*	Rio de Janeiro	14	00
Auckland	5	00*	Jerusalem	19	00	Riyadh	20	00
Baghdad	20	00	Johannesburg	19	00	Rome	18	00
Bangkok	0	00*	Kabul	21	50	St. Petersburg	20	00
Beijing	1	00*	Karachi	22	00	Santiago	13	00
Belfast	17	00	Kathmandu	22	45	São Paulo	14	00
Belgrade	18	00	Kiev	19	00	Sarajevo	18	00
Berlin	18	00	Kolkata (Calcutta)	22	30	Seoul	2	00*
Bogotá	12	00	Lagos	18	00	Shanghai	1	00*
Brussels	18	00	Lima	12	00	Singapore	1	00*
Bucharest	19	00	Lisbon	17	00	Stockholm	18	00
Budapest	18	00	London	17	00	Sydney	3	00*
Buenos Aires	14	00	Madrid	18	00	Taipei	1	00*
Cairo	19	00	Manila	1	00*	Tashkent	22	00
Cape Town	19	00	Mecca	20	00	Tehran	20	30
Caracas	13	00	Melbourne	3	00*	Tel Aviv	19	00
Casablanca	17	00	Montevideo	14	00	Tokyo	2	00*
Copenhagen	18	00	Moscow	20	00	Vienna	18	00
Dhaka	23	00	Mumbai (Bombay)	22	30	Vladivostok	3	00*
Dublin	17	00	Munich	18	00	Warsaw	18	00
Edinburgh	17	00	Nagasaki	2	00*	Wellington	5	00*
Geneva	18	00	Nairobi	20	00	Yangon (Rangoon)	23	30
Helsinki	19	00	New Delhi	22	30	Yokohama	2	00*
Ho Chi Minh City	0	00*	Oslo	18	00	Zurich	18	00

Standard Time Differences: North American Cities

At 12:00 noon, Eastern Standard Time, the standard time in selected North American cities is as shown.

City	Hr	Min		City	Hr	Min		City	Hr	Min	
Akron, OH	12	00	Noon	Fort Wayne, IN[1]	12	00	Noon	Ottawa, ON	12	00	Noon
Albuquerque, NM	10	00	AM	Frankfort, KY	12	00	Noon	*Panama City, Panama	12	00	Noon
Anchorage, AK	8	00	AM	Havana, Cuba	12	00	Noon	Peoria, IL	11	00	AM
Atlanta, GA	12	00	Noon	Helena, MT	10	00	AM	*Phoenix, AZ	10	00	AM
Austin, TX	11	00	AM	*Honolulu, HI	7	00	AM	Pierre, SD	11	00	AM
Baltimore, MD	12	00	Noon	Houston, TX	11	00	AM	Pittsburgh, PA	12	00	Noon
Birmingham, AL	11	00	AM	Indianapolis, IN[1]	12	00	Noon	*Regina, SK	11	00	AM
Bismarck, ND	11	00	AM	Jackson, MS	11	00	AM	Reno, NV	9	00	AM
Boise, ID	10	00	AM	Jacksonville, FL	12	00	Noon	Richmond, VA	12	00	Noon
Boston, MA	12	00	Noon	Juneau, AK	8	00	AM	Rochester, NY	12	00	Noon
Buffalo, NY	12	00	Noon	Kansas City, MO	11	00	AM	Sacramento, CA	9	00	AM
Butte, MT	10	00	AM	*Kingston, Jamaica	12	00	Noon	St. John's, NL	1	30	PM
Calgary, AB	10	00	AM	Knoxville, TN	12	00	Noon	St. Louis, MO	11	00	AM
Charleston, SC	12	00	Noon	Las Vegas, NV	9	00	AM	St. Paul, MN	11	00	AM
Charleston, WV	12	00	Noon	Lexington, KY	12	00	Noon	Salt Lake City, UT	10	00	AM
Charlotte, NC	12	00	Noon	Lincoln, NE	11	00	AM	San Antonio, TX	11	00	AM
Charlottetown, PE	1	00	PM	Little Rock, AR	11	00	AM	San Diego, CA	9	00	AM
Chattanooga, TN	12	00	Noon	Los Angeles, CA	9	00	AM	San Francisco, CA	9	00	AM
Cheyenne, WY	10	00	AM	Louisville, KY	12	00	Noon	San Jose, CA	9	00	AM
Chicago, IL	11	00	AM	Madison, WI	11	00	AM	*San Juan, PR	1	00	PM
Cincinnati, OH	12	00	Noon	Mexico City, Mexico	11	00	AM	Santa Fe, NM	10	00	AM
Cleveland, OH	12	00	Noon	Memphis, TN	11	00	AM	Savannah, GA	12	00	Noon
Colorado Spr., CO	10	00	AM	Miami, FL	12	00	Noon	Seattle, WA	9	00	AM
Columbus, OH	12	00	Noon	Milwaukee, WI	11	00	AM	Shreveport, LA	11	00	AM
Dallas, TX	11	00	AM	Minneapolis, MN	11	00	AM	Sioux Falls, SD	11	00	AM
*Dawson, YT	9	00	AM	Mobile, AL	11	00	AM	Spokane, WA	9	00	AM
Dayton, OH	12	00	Noon	Montréal, QC	12	00	Noon	Tampa, FL	12	00	Noon
Denver, CO	10	00	AM	Nashville, TN	11	00	AM	Toledo, OH	12	00	Noon
Des Moines, IA	11	00	AM	Nassau, The Bahamas	12	00	Noon	Topeka, KS	11	00	AM
Detroit, MI	12	00	Noon	New Haven, CT	12	00	Noon	Toronto, ON	12	00	Noon
Duluth, MN	11	00	AM	New Orleans, LA	11	00	AM	*Tucson, AZ	10	00	AM
Edmonton, AB	10	00	AM	New York, NY	12	00	Noon	Tulsa, OK	11	00	AM
El Paso, TX	10	00	AM	Nome, AK	8	00	AM	Vancouver, BC	9	00	AM
Erie, PA	12	00	Noon	Norfolk, VA	12	00	Noon	Washington, DC	12	00	Noon
Evansville, IN[1]	11	00	AM	Oklahoma City, OK	11	00	AM	Wichita, KS	11	00	AM
Fairbanks, AK	8	00	AM	Omaha, NE	11	00	AM	Wilmington, DE	12	00	Noon
Flint, MI	12	00	Noon	Orlando, FL	12	00	Noon	Winnipeg, MB	11	00	AM

Note: This same table can be used for daylight-saving time when it is in effect, but allowance must be made for cities that do not observe it; they are marked with an asterisk (*). Daylight-saving time is one hour later than standard time. (1) While most of Indiana is in the Eastern Time Zone, 12 counties in the southwestern and northwestern parts of the state observe Central Time.

WEIGHTS AND MEASURES

Source: National Institute of Standards and Technology (NIST), U.S. Dept. of Commerce

International System of Units (SI)

Two systems of weights and measures coexist in the U.S. today: the **U.S. Customary System** and the **International System of Units** (SI, for Système International). The SI is a more complete, coherent version of the **metric system**. Throughout U.S. history, the Customary System—parts of which were inherited but are now different from the British Imperial System—has been generally used. Federal and state legislation gave it, through implication, standing as the primary weights and measures system. The metric system, however, is the only system that Congress has ever specifically sanctioned, dating back to an 1866 law. Along with 17 other nations, the U.S. signed the International Metric Convention (a.k.a. the Treaty of the Meter) May 20, 1875, establishing several intergovernmental organizations to oversee and refine the SI. The U.S. is represented at these organizations by the Natl. Institute of Standards and Technology (NIST).

Since that time, use of the metric system in the U.S. has slowly increased, particularly in the scientific community, the pharmaceutical industry, and the manufacturing sector—the last motivated by the predominant use of the metric system in international commerce.

On Dec. 23, 1975, Pres. Gerald R. Ford signed the Metric Conversion Act of 1975. It defined the "metric system of measurement" as the SI, as established in 1960 by the General Conference on Weights and Measures and interpreted in the U.S. by the secretary of commerce, who delegated that authority to the director of the NIST. The Trade and Competitiveness Act of 1988 declared the metric system the preferred system of weights and measures for U.S. trade and commerce, but explicitly permitted "the continued use of traditional systems of weights and measures in nonbusiness activities." The Code of Federal Regulations made the use of metric units mandatory for federal agencies in 1991. However, the metric system has still not become the system of choice for most Americans' daily use.

The following are the seven base SI units: **length**—meter; **mass**—kilogram; **time**—second; **electric current**—ampere; **thermodynamic temperature**—kelvin; **amount of substance**—mole; and **luminous intensity**—candela.

Frequently Used Conversions

Boldface indicates exact values. For greater accuracy, use the "multiply by" number in parentheses. For weights, avoirdupois (avdp) weight is the system applied to all goods except medicines, precious metals, and precious stones.

U.S. Customary to Metric

	If you have:	Multiply by:		To get:
Length	inches	25.4		millimeters
	inches	2.54		centimeters
	inches	0.0254		meters
	feet	0.3	(0.3048)	meters
	yards	0.9	(0.9144)	meters
	miles[1]	1.6	(1.609344)	kilometers
Area	sq inches	6.5	(6.4516)	sq cm
	sq feet	0.09	(0.09290304)	sq meters
	sq yards	0.84	(0.83612736)	sq meters
	acres	0.4	(0.4046873)	hectares
	sq miles[1]	2.6	(2.58998811)	sq kilometers
Weight	ounces (avdp)	28	(28.34952)	grams
	pounds (avdp)	454	(453.59237)	grams
	pounds (avdp)	0.45	(0.45359237)	kilograms
	short tons[2]	0.91	(0.90718474)	metric tons
	long tons[3]	1	(1.016047)	metric tons
Liquid	ounces	0.03	(0.02957353)	liters
	cups	0.24	(0.23658824)	liters
	pints	0.47	(0.473176473)	liters
	quarts	0.95	(0.946352946)	liters
	gallons	3.79	(3.785412)	liters

Metric to U.S. Customary

	If you have:	Multiply by:		To get:
Length	millimeters	0.04	(0.03937)	inches
	centimeters	0.4	(0.3937)	inches
	meters	39	(39.37)	inches
	meters	3.3	(3.280840)	feet
	meters	1.1	(1.093613)	yards
	kilometers	0.6	(0.621371)	miles[1]
Area	sq cm	0.16	(0.15500)	sq inches
	sq meters	10.8	(10.76391)	sq feet
	sq meters	1.2	(1.195990)	sq yards
	hectares	2.5	(2.471044)	acres
	sq kilometers	0.39	(0.386102)	sq miles[1]
Weight	grams	0.035	(0.03527396)	ounces (avdp)
	grams	0.002	(0.00220462)	pounds (avdp)
	kilograms	2.2	(2.204623)	pounds (avdp)
	metric tons	1.1	(1.102311)	short tons[2]
	metric tons	0.98	(0.9842065)	long tons[3]
Liquid	liters	33.8	(33.81402)	ounces
	liters	4.2	(4.226752)	cups
	liters	2.1	(2.113376)	pints
	liters	1.1	(1.056688)	quarts
	liters	0.26	(0.264172)	gallons

(1) Survey mile. (2) A short ton is 2,000 pounds. (3) A long ton is 2,240 pounds.

Temperature Conversions

The left-hand column below gives a temperature according to the **Celsius** scale, and the right-hand gives the same temperature according to the **Fahrenheit** scale. The lowest number on each scale is equivalent to absolute zero, the theoretical temperature at which all molecular motion would stop.

For temperatures not shown: To convert Fahrenheit to Celsius, subtract 32 degrees and divide by 1.8; to convert Celsius to Fahrenheit, multiply by 1.8 and add 32 degrees.

Celsius	Fahrenheit	Celsius	Fahrenheit	Celsius	Fahrenheit	Celsius	Fahrenheit	Celsius	Fahrenheit
−273.15	−459.67	−45.6	−50	−1.1	30	30	86	65.6	150
−250	−418	**−40**	**−40**	**0**	**32**	32.2	90	70	158
−200	−328	−34.4	−30	4.4	40	35	95	80	176
−184.4	−300	−30	−22	10	50	**37**	**98.6**	90	194
−156.7	−250	−28.9	−20	15.6	60	37.8	100	93.3	200
−150	−238	−23.3	−10	**20**	**68**	40	104	**100**	**212**
−128.9	−200	−20	−4	21.1	70	43.3	110	121.1	250
−101.1	−150	−17.8	0	23.9	75	48.9	120	148.9	300
−100	−148	−12.2	10	25	77	50	122	150	302
−73.3	−100	−10	14	26.7	80	54.4	130	200	392
−50	−58	−6.7	20	29.4	85	60	140	300	572

Note: Although the term *centigrade* is still frequently used, the International Committee on Weights and Measures and the National Institute of Standards and Technology have recommended since 1948 that this scale be called *Celsius*.

Boiling and Freezing Points

Water boils at 212°F (100°C) at sea level. For every 550 feet above sea level, the boiling point of water is lower by about 1°F. Methyl alcohol boils at 148.5°F. Average human oral temperature is 98.6°F. **Water freezes** at 32°F (0°C).

Mathematical Formulas

The value of π (the Greek letter pi) is approximately 3.14159265 (equal to the ratio of the circumference of a circle to its diameter). The equivalence is typically rounded further to 3.1416 or 3.14.

Calculating Circumference
Circle: Multiply the diameter by π.

Calculating Area
Circle: Multiply the square of the radius (equal to ½ the diameter) by π.

Rectangle: Multiply the length of the base by the height.

Sphere (surface): Multiply the square of the radius by π and multiply by 4.

Square: Square the length of one side.

Trapezoid: Add the 2 parallel sides, multiply by the height, and divide by 2.

Triangle: Multiply the base by the height and divide by 2.

Calculating Volume
Cone: Multiply the square of the radius of the base by π, multiply by the height, and divide by 3.

Cube: Cube the length of one edge.

Cylinder: Multiply the square of the radius of the base by π and multiply by the height.

Pyramid: Multiply the area of the base by the height and divide by 3.

Rectangular prism: Multiply the length by the width by the height.

Sphere: Multiply the cube of the radius by π, multiply by 4, and divide by 3.

Playing Cards and Dice Chances

5-Card Poker Hands

Hand	Number possible	Odds against
Royal flush	4	649,739 to 1
Other straight flush	36	72,192 to 1
Four of a kind	624	4,164 to 1
Full house	3,744	693 to 1
Flush	5,108	508 to 1
Straight	10,200	254 to 1
Three of a kind	54,912	46 to 1
Two pairs	123,552	20 to 1
One pair	1,098,240	4 to 3 (1.37 to 1)
Nothing	1,302,540	1 to 1
Total	**2,598,960**	

Bridge

The odds—against suit distribution in a hand of 4-4-3-2 are about 4 to 1; against 5-4-2-2 about 8 to 1; against 6-4-2-1 about 20 to 1; against 7-4-1-1 about 254 to 1; against 8-4-1-0 about 2,211 to 1; and against 13-0-0-0 about 158,753,389,899 to 1.

Dice
(probabilities on 2 dice)

Total	Odds against (single toss)	Total	Odds against (single toss)
2	35 to 1	8	31 to 5
3	17 to 1	9	8 to 1
4	11 to 1	10	11 to 1
5	8 to 1	11	17 to 1
6	31 to 5	12	35 to 1
7	5 to 1		

Large Numbers

No. of zeros	U.S.	British[1], French, German	No. of zeros	U.S.	British[1], French, German
6	million	million	42	tredecillion	septillion
9	billion	milliard	45	quattuordecillion	1,000 septillion
12	trillion	billion	48	quindecillion	octillion
15	quadrillion	1,000 billion	51	sexdecillion	1,000 octillion
18	quintillion	trillion	54	septendecillion	nonillion
21	sextillion	1,000 trillion	57	octodecillion	1,000 nonillion
24	septillion	quadrillion	60	novemdecillion	decillion
27	octillion	1,000 quadrillion	63	vigintillion	1,000 decillion
30	nonillion	quintillion	100	googol	googol
33	decillion	1,000 quintillion	303	centillion	NA
36	undecillion	sextillion	600	NA	centillion
39	duodecillion	1,000 sextillion	googol	googolplex	googolplex

(1) In recent years, it has become more common in Britain to use U.S. terminology for large numbers.

Prime Numbers to 1,009

A prime number is any positive integer greater than 1 that is divisible only by two positive integers—1 and itself.

	2	3	5	7	11	13	17	19	23
29	31	37	41	43	47	53	59	61	67
71	73	79	83	89	97	101	103	107	109
113	127	131	137	139	149	151	157	163	167
173	179	181	191	193	197	199	211	223	227
229	233	239	241	251	257	263	269	271	277
281	283	293	307	311	313	317	331	337	347
349	353	359	367	373	379	383	389	397	401
409	419	421	431	433	439	443	449	457	461
463	467	479	487	491	499	503	509	521	523
541	547	557	563	569	571	577	587	593	599
601	607	613	617	619	631	641	643	647	653
659	661	673	677	683	691	701	709	719	727
733	739	743	751	757	761	769	773	787	797
809	811	821	823	827	829	839	853	857	859
863	877	881	883	887	907	911	919	929	937
941	947	953	967	971	977	983	991	997	1,009

Common Fractions Converted to Decimals

8ths	16ths	32nds	64ths	
			1	= 0.015625
		1	2	= 0.03125
			3	= 0.046875
	1	2	4	= 0.0625
			5	= 0.078125
		3	6	= 0.09375
			7	= 0.109375
1	2	4	8	= 0.125
			9	= 0.140625
		5	10	= 0.15625
			11	= 0.171875
	3	6	12	= 0.1875
			13	= 0.203125
		7	14	= 0.21875
			15	= 0.234375
2	4	8	16	= 0.25

8ths	16ths	32nds	64ths	
			17	= 0.265625
		9	18	= 0.28125
			19	= 0.296875
	5	10	20	= 0.3125
			21	= 0.328125
		11	22	= 0.34375
			23	= 0.359375
3	6	12	24	= 0.375
			25	= 0.390625
		13	26	= 0.40625
			27	= 0.421875
	7	14	28	= 0.4375
			29	= 0.453125
		15	30	= 0.46875
			31	= 0.484375
4	8	16	32	= 0.5

8ths	16ths	32nds	64ths	
			33	= 0.515625
		17	34	= 0.53125
			35	= 0.546875
	9	18	36	= 0.5625
			37	= 0.578125
		19	38	= 0.59375
			39	= 0.609375
5	10	20	40	= 0.625
			41	= 0.640625
		21	42	= 0.65625
			43	= 0.671875
	11	22	44	= 0.6875
			45	= 0.703125
		23	46	= 0.71875
			47	= 0.734375
6	12	24	48	= 0.75

8ths	16ths	32nds	64ths	
			49	= 0.765625
		25	50	= 0.78125
			51	= 0.796875
	13	26	52	= 0.8125
			53	= 0.828125
		27	54	= 0.84375
			55	= 0.859375
7	14	28	56	= 0.875
			57	= 0.890625
		29	58	= 0.90625
			59	= 0.921875
	15	30	60	= 0.9375
			61	= 0.953125
		31	62	= 0.96875
			63	= 0.984375
8	16	32	64	= 1.0

Roman Numerals

I — 1	IV — 4	VII — 7	X — 10	XX — 20
II — 2	V — 5	VIII — 8	XI — 11	XXX — 30
III — 3	VI — 6	IX — 9	XIX — 19	XL — 40

L — 50	C — 100	D — 500
LX — 60	CC — 200	CM — 900
XC — 90	CD — 400	M — 1,000

Note: The numerals V, X, L, C, D, or M shown with a horizontal line on top denote 1,000 times the original value.

Ancient Measures

Biblical

Cubit	=	21.8 inches
Omer	=	0.45 peck
	=	3.964 liters
Ephah	=	10 omers
Shekel	=	0.497 ounce
	=	14.1 grams

Greek

Cubit	=	18.3 inches
Stadion	=	607.2 or 622 feet
Obolos	=	715.38 milligrams
Drachma	=	4.2923 grams
Mina	=	0.9463 pound
Talent	=	60 mina

Roman

Cubit	=	17.5 inches
Stadium	=	202 yards
As, libra, pondus	=	325.971 grams
	=	0.71864 pound

Metric System Prefixes

The following prefixes, in combination with the basic unit names, provide the multiples and submultiples in the metric system. For example, the unit name *meter*, with the prefix *kilo* added, produces *kilometer*, meaning "1,000 meters."

Prefix	Symbol	Multiples	Equivalent	Prefix	Symbol	Multiples	Equivalent
yotta	Y	10^{24}	septillionfold	deci	d	10^{-1}	tenth part
zetta	Z	10^{21}	sextillionfold	centi	c	10^{-2}	hundredth part
exa	E	10^{18}	quintillionfold	milli	m	10^{-3}	thousandth part
peta	P	10^{15}	quadrillionfold	micro	μ	10^{-6}	millionth part
tera	T	10^{12}	trillionfold	nano	n	10^{-9}	billionth part
giga	G	10^{9}	billionfold	pico	p	10^{-12}	trillionth part
mega	M	10^{6}	millionfold	femto	f	10^{-15}	quadrillionth part
kilo	k	10^{3}	thousandfold	atto	a	10^{-18}	quintillionth part
hecto	h	10^{2}	hundredfold	zepto	z	10^{-21}	sextillionth part
deka	da	10	tenfold	yocto	y	10^{-24}	septillionth part

Weight and Measurement Equivalents

In this table, there is a distinction between the international foot and the survey foot. The international foot, defined in 1959 as exactly equal to 0.3048 meter, is shorter than the survey foot by exactly 2 parts in 1 million. This means that an international mile is about ⅛ inch shorter than the survey mile. The survey foot is still used in the publication of some geodetic surveys within the U.S. In this table, the survey foot is indicated with capital letters, as FEET.

When the name of a unit is enclosed in brackets, e.g., [1 hand], either (1) the unit is not in general current use in the U.S. or (2) the unit is believed to be based on custom and usage rather than on formal definition.

Equivalents involving decimals are, in most instances, rounded to the third decimal place; exact equivalents are so designated.

Lengths

1 angstrom (Å)	= 0.1 nanometer (exactly)
	= 0.0001 micrometer (exactly)
	= 0.0000001 millimeter (exactly)
	= 0.000000004 inch
1 cable's length	= 120 fathoms (exactly)
	= 720 FEET (exactly)
	= 219 meters
1 centimeter (cm)	= 0.3937 inch
1 chain (ch) (engineer's)	= 30.48 meters (exactly)
	= 100 feet
1 chain (Gunter's or surveyor's)	= 66 FEET (exactly)
	= 20.1168 meters
1 decimeter (dm)	= 3.937 inches
1 degree (geographical)	= 364,566.929 feet
	= 69.047 miles (avg.)
	= 111.123 kilometers (avg.)
of latitude	= 68.708 miles at equator
	= 69.403 miles at poles
of longitude	= 69.171 miles at equator

1 dekameter (dam)	= 32.808 feet
1 fathom (fath)	= 6 FEET (exactly)
	= 1.8288 meters
1 foot (ft)	= 12 inches (exactly)
	= 0.3048 meters (exactly)
	= 0.015 chains (surveyor's)
1 furlong (fur)	= 660 FEET (exactly)
	= ⅛ survey mile (exactly)
	= 201.168 meters
[1 hand (height measure for horses, from ground to top of their shoulders)]	= 4 inches
1 inch (in.)	= 2.54 centimeters (exactly)
1 kilometer (km)	= 0.621371 mile
	= 3,280.8 feet
1 league (land)	= 3 survey miles (exactly)
	= 4.828 kilometers
1 link (engineer's)	= 1 foot
	= 0.305 meter
1 link (Gunter's or surveyor's)	= 7.92 inches (exactly)
	= 0.201 meter

1 meter (m). . . . . = 39.37 inches
= 1.09361 yards
1 micrometer (μm) . . . . = 0.001 millimeter (exactly)
= 0.00003937 inch
1 mil . . . . = 0.001 inch (exactly)
= 0.0254 millimeter (exactly)
1 mile (mi) (statute or land). . . . = 5,280 FEET (exactly)
= 1.609344 kilometers (exactly)
1 international nautical mile
(nmi). . . . . = 1.852 kilometers (exactly)
= 1.151 miles
= 6,076.1 feet
1 millimeter (mm) . . . . = 0.03937 inch
1 nanometer (nm). . . . . = 0.001 micrometer (exactly)
= 0.00000003937 inch
1 pica (typography). . . . . = 12 points
1 point (pt) (typography) . . . . . . = 0.013837 inch (exactly)
= 0.351 millimeter
1 rod (rd), pole, or perch. . . . . . = 16½ FEET (exactly)
= 5.029 meters
1 yard (yd) . . . . = 3 feet (exactly)
= 0.9144 meter (exactly)

Areas or Surfaces

1 acre (A) . . . . = 43,560 square FEET (exactly)
= 4,840 square yards
= 0.405 hectare
1 are (a) . . . . = 119.599 square yards
= 0.025 acre
1 bolt (cloth measure):
length . . . . = 100 yards
width. . . . . = 45 or 60 inches
1 hectare (ha) . . . . = 2.471 acres
[1 square (building)] . . . . = 100 square feet
1 square centimeter (cm²) . . . . = 0.155 square inch
1 square decimeter (dm²). . . . . = 15.500 square inches
1 square foot (ft²) . . . . = 929.030 square centimeters
1 square inch (in.²) . . . . = 6.4516 square centimeters
(exactly)
1 square kilometer (km²) . . . . . = 247.104 acres
= 0.386102 square mile
1 square meter (m²) . . . . = 1.196 square yards
= 10.764 square feet
1 square mile (mi²) . . . . = 640 acres (exactly)
= 258.999 hectares
1 square millimeter (mm²) . . . . = 0.002 square inch
1 square rod (rd²), square
pole, or square perch . . . . . . = 25.293 square meters
1 square yard (yd²) . . . . = 0.836127 square meter

Capacities or Volumes

1 barrel (bbl), liquid . . . . = 31 to 42 gallons*
*There are a variety of "barrels" established by law or usage. For
example, federal taxes on fermented liquors are based on a
barrel of 31 gallons. Many state laws fix the "barrel for liquids" as
31½ gallons; one state fixes a 36-gallon barrel for cistern
measurement. Federal law recognizes a 40-gallon barrel for
"proof spirits." By custom, 42 gallons constitute a barrel of
crude oil or petroleum products for statistical purposes, and this
equivalent is recognized "for liquids" by some states.

1 barrel (bbl), standard for
fruits, vegetables, and other
dry commodities except dry
cranberries . . . . = 7,056 cubic inches
= 105 dry quarts
= 3.281 bushels, struck measure
1 barrel, standard, cranberry . . = 86⁴⁵⁄₆₄ dry quarts
= 2.709 bushels, struck measure
= 5,826 cubic inches
1 board foot (lumber measure) = a foot-square board 1 inch
thick
1 bushel (U.S.) (struck
measure) . . . . = 2,150.42 cu in. (exactly)
= 35.239 liters
[1 bushel, heaped (U.S.)] . . . . = 2,747.715 cubic inches
= 1.278 bushels,
struck measure**
**Frequently recognized as 1¼ bushels, struck measure.
[1 bushel (bu) (British Imperial)
(struck measure)] . . . . = 1.032 U.S. bushels,
struck measure
= 2,219.36 cubic inches
1 cord (cd) (firewood) . . . . = 128 cubic feet (exactly)

1 cubic centimeter (cm³) . . . . . = 0.061 cubic inch
1 cubic decimeter (dm³). . . . . . = 61.024 cubic inches
1 cubic inch (in³) . . . . = 0.554 fluid ounce
= 4.433 fluid drams
= 16.387 cubic centimeters
1 cubic foot (ft³) . . . . = 7.481 gallons
= 28.317 cubic decimeters
1 cubic meter (m³) . . . . = 1.308 cubic yards
1 cubic yard (yd³). . . . . = 0.765 cubic meter
1 cup, measuring . . . . = 8 fluid ounces (exactly)
= ½ liquid pint (exactly)
1 dekaliter (daL). . . . . = 2.642 gallons
= 1.135 pecks
[1 dram, fluid (fl dr) (British)] = 0.961 U.S. fluid dram
= 0.217 cubic inch
= 3.552 milliliters
1 gallon (gal) (U.S.) . . . . = 4 quarts, liquid (exactly)
= 231 cubic inches (exactly)
= 3.785 liters
= 0.833 British gallon
= 128 U.S. fluid ounces (exactly)
[1 gallon (British Imperial)]. . . . = 277.42 cubic inches
= 1.201 U.S. gallons
= 4.546 liters
= 160 British fluid ounces
(exactly)
1 gill (gi) . . . . = 7.219 cubic inches
= 4 fluid ounces (exactly)
= 0.118 liter
1 hectoliter (hL) . . . . = 26.418 gallons
= 2.838 bushels
1 liter (L) (1 cubic decimeter
exactly). . . . . = 1.057 liquid quarts
= 0.908 dry quart
= 61.024 cubic inches
1 milliliter (mL) (1 cu cm
exactly). . . . . = 0.271 fluid dram
= 16.231 minims
= 0.061 cubic inch
1 ounce, liquid (U.S.) . . . . = 1.805 cubic inches
= 29.574 milliliters
= 1.041 British fluid ounces
[1 ounce, fluid (fl oz) (British)] = 0.961 U.S. fluid ounce
= 1.734 cubic inches
= 28.412 milliliters
1 peck (pk) . . . . = 8.810 liters
1 pint (pt), dry. . . . . = 33.600 cubic inches
= 0.551 liter
1 pint, liquid . . . . = 28.875 cubic inches (exactly)
= 0.473 liter
1 quart (qt), dry (U.S.) . . . . = 67.201 cubic inches
= 1.101 liters
= 0.969 British quart
1 quart, liquid (U.S.). . . . . = 2 pints, liquid (exactly)
= 4 cups (exactly)
= 57.75 cubic inches (exactly)
= 0.946 liter
= 0.833 British quart
[1 quart (British)] . . . . = 69.354 cubic inches
= 1.032 U.S. dry quarts
= 1.201 U.S. liquid quarts
1 tablespoon (T., Tbs, tbsp.) . . = 3 teaspoons (exactly)
= 4 fluid drams
= ½ fluid ounce (exactly)
1 teaspoon (t., tsp.) . . . . = ⅓ tablespoon (exactly)
= 1⅓ fluid drams***

***The equivalent "1 teaspoon = 1⅓ fluid drams" has been found
to correspond more closely with the actual capacities of
teaspoons in use than the equivalent "1 teaspoon = 1 fluid dram"
given by many dictionaries.

Weights or Masses

1 assay ton* (AT) . . . . = 29.167 grams
*Used in assaying. The assay ton bears the same relation to the
milligram that a ton of 2,000 pounds avoirdupois bears to the
ounce troy; hence, the weight in milligrams of precious metal
obtained from one assay ton of ore gives directly the number of
troy ounces to the net ton.

1 carat (c). . . . . = 200 milligrams (exactly)
= 3.086 grains
1 dram avoirdupois (dr avdp). . = 27¹¹⁄₃₂ (= 27.344) grains
= 1.772 grams
1 gamma (γ) . . . . = 1 microgram (exactly)
1 grain (gr) . . . . = 64.79891 milligrams (exactly)

1 gram (g) . . . . = 15.432 grains
       = 0.035 ounce, avoirdupois

1 hundredweight, gross or
  long** (gross cwt) . . . . = 112 pounds (exactly)
       = 50.802 kilograms

**The gross, or long, ton and hundredweight are used commercially in the U.S. to only a limited extent, usually in restricted industrial fields. These units are the same as the British ton and hundredweight.

1 hundredweight, gross or
  short (cwt or net cwt) . . . . . = 100 pounds (exactly)
       = 45.359 kilograms

1 kilogram (kg) . . . . = 2.20462 pounds

1 microgram (µg) . . . . = 0.000001 gram (exactly)

1 milligram (mg) . . . . = 0.015 grain

1 ounce, avoirdupois (oz avdp) = 437.5 grains (exactly)
       = 0.911 troy ounce
       = 28.3495 grams

1 ounce, troy (oz t) . . . . = 480 grains (exactly)
       = 1.097 avoirdupois ounces
       = 31.103 grams

1 pennyweight (dwt) . . . . = 1.555 grams

1 pound, avoirdupois (lb avdp) = 7,000 grains (exactly)
       = 1.215 troy pounds
       = 453.59237 grams (exactly)

1 pound, troy (lb t) . . . . = 5,760 grains (exactly)
       = 0.823 pound, avoirdupois
       = 373.242 grams

1 stone (st) . . . . = 14 pounds avdp (exactly)
       = 6.350 kilograms

1 ton, gross or long . . . . = 2,240 pounds (exactly)
       = 1.12 net tons (exactly)
       = 1.016 metric tons

1 ton, metric (t) . . . . = 2,204.623 pounds
       = 0.984 gross ton
       = 1.102 net tons

1 ton, net or short (sh ton) . . . . = 2,000 pounds (exactly)
       = 0.893 gross ton
       = 0.907 metric ton

Electrical Units

The **watt** (W) is the unit of power (electrical, mechanical, thermal). Electrical power is given by the product of the voltage and the current.

Energy is sold by the **joule** (J), but in common practice the billing of electrical energy is expressed in terms of the **kilowatt-hour** (kWh), which is 3,600,000 joules, or 3.6 megajoules.

The **horsepower** (hp) is a nonmetric unit sometimes used in mechanics. It is equal to 746 watts.

The **ohm** (Ω) is the unit of electrical resistance and represents the physical property of a conductor that offers a resistance to the flow of electricity, permitting just 1 ampere to flow at 1 volt of pressure.

Measures of Force and Pressure

Dyne (dyn) = force necessary to accelerate a 1-gram mass 1 centimeter per second squared = 0.000072 poundal

Poundal (pdl) = force necessary to accelerate a 1-pound mass 1 foot per second squared = 13,825.5 dynes = 0.138255 newton

Newton (N) = force needed to accelerate a 1-kilogram mass 1 meter per second squared = 100,000 dynes (exactly)

Pascal (pressure) (Pa) = 1 newton per square meter = 0.020885 pound per square foot

Atmosphere (air pressure at sea level) (atm) = 2,116.217 pounds per square foot = 14.6959 pounds per square inch = 1.0332 kilograms per square centimeter = 101,325 newtons per square meter

Measures of Alcohol

Pony . . . . = 1.0 fluid ounce

Shot . . . . = varies, usu. 1.0-1.5 fluid ounces

Jigger . . . . = 1.5 fluid ounces

Pint (pt) . . . . = 16 fluid ounces
       = 0.625 fifth

Fifth. . . . . = 25.6 fluid ounces
       = 1.6 pints
       = 0.8 quart
       = 0.757 liter

Quart (qt) . . . . = 32 fluid ounces
       = 1.25 fifths

Wine bottle
  (standard) . . . . = 0.75 liter
       = 25.4 fluid ounces

Magnum . . . . = 1.5 liters

For champagne and brandy:
Jeroboam . . . . = 2 magnums
       = 3 liters
       = 101 fluid ounces

For champagne:
Rehoboam . . . . = 3 magnums
Methuselah . . . . = 4 magnums
Salmanazar . . . . = 6 magnums
Balthazar . . . . = 8 magnums
Nebuchadnezzar . . . = 10 magnums

Miscellaneous Measures

Caliber (cal)—the diameter of a gun bore. In the U.S., caliber is traditionally expressed in hundredths of inches, e.g., .22. In Britain, caliber is often expressed in thousandths of inches, e.g., .270. Now it is commonly expressed in millimeters, e.g., the 5.56 mm M16 rifle. The caliber of heavier weapons has long been expressed in millimeters, e.g., the 155 mm howitzer. Naval guns' caliber refers to the barrel length as a multiple of the bore diameter. A 5-inch, 50-caliber naval gun has a 5-inch bore and a barrel length of 250 inches.

Decibel (dB)—a measure of the relative intensity of sound. The threshold of hearing is given as 0 decibels. A 20-decibel sound is 10 times more intense than a 10-decibel sound; 30 decibels is 100 times more intense. (A 10-decibel increase corresponds generally to the perception of a sound being twice as loud.) One decibel is the smallest difference between sounds detectable by the human ear. A 125-decibel sound is painful.

   10 decibels . . . breathing
   20 . . . . rustling leaves
   30 . . . . whisper
   40 . . . . refrigerator humming
   50 . . . . quiet conversation
   60 . . . . conversation, laughter
   70 . . . . vacuum cleaner
   80 . . . . city traffic
   90 . . . . subway, lawn mower
  100 . . . . chainsaw

Em—a printer's measure designating the square width of any given type size. For example, an em of 10-point type is 10 points. An en is half an em.

Gauge (ga)—the diameter of a shotgun bore. Gauge numbers originally referred to the number of lead balls—of equal diameter as the gun barrel—required to make a pound. Thus, a 16-gauge shotgun's bore was smaller than a 12-gauge shotgun's. Today, an international agreement assigns millimeter measures to each gauge.

Gauge	Bore diameter (mm)	Gauge	Bore diameter (mm)
6	23.34	14	17.60
10	19.67	16	16.81
12	18.52	20	15.90

Horsepower (hp)—the power needed to lift 550 pounds 1 foot in 1 second or to lift 33,000 pounds 1 foot in 1 minute. Equivalent to 746 watts or 2,546 British thermal units per hour.

Karat or carat (k or c)—a measure of fineness for gold equal to $\frac{1}{24}$ part of pure gold in an alloy. Thus 24-karat gold is pure; 18-karat gold is $\frac{18}{24}$ alloy. The carat is also used as a unit of weight for precious stones; it is equal to 200 milligrams or 3.086 grains.

Knot (kn or kt)—a measure of the speed of ships. A knot equals 1 nautical mile per hour.

Quire (qr)—25 sheets of paper of the same size and quality.

Ream (rm)—500 sheets of paper of the same size and quality.

Computer Milestones

1623: German mathematician Wilhelm Schickard developed the first mechanical calculator, capable of adding, subtracting, multiplying, and dividing.

1642: French mathematician Blaise Pascal built the first of more than four dozen copies of an adding and subtracting machine that he invented.

1801: French inventor Joseph Marie Jacquard demonstrated a new control system for looms. He "programmed" the loom, communicating desired weaving operations to the machine via patterns of holes in paper cards.

1833-71: British mathematician and scientist Charles Babbage used the Jacquard punch-card system in his design for a sophisticated, programmable "Analytical Engine" that foreshadowed basic features of today's computers. Babbage's concept was beyond the capabilities of the technology of his time, and the machine remained unfinished at his death in 1871.

1889: American engineer Herman Hollerith patented an electromechanical punch-card tabulating system that facilitated the handling of large amounts of statistical data and quickly found use in censuses in the U.S. and other countries.

1911: Hollerith's Tabulating Machine Company merged with two other enterprises to form the Computing-Tabulating-Recording Company, which was renamed the International Business Machines Corporation (IBM) in 1924.

1941: German engineer Konrad Züse completed the Z3, the first fully functional digital computer to be controlled by a program; the Z3 was not electronic—it was based on electrical switches called relays.

1942: Iowa State Coll. physicist John Vincent Atanasoff and his assistant Clifford Berry completed a working model of the first fully electronic computer using vacuum tubes, which could operate much more quickly than relays; the rudimentary machine was not programmable.

1943: IBM and Harvard professor Howard Aiken completed the first large-scale automatic digital computer, the Mark I, a relay-based machine 55 ft long and 8 ft high. British scientists built the Colossus, an electronic computer for breaking German codes during World War II.

1946: ENIAC (Electronic Numerical Integrator and Computer), a 30-ton room-sized electronic computer with more than 18,000 vacuum tubes, was completed by physicist John Mauchly and engineer J. Presper Eckert at the Univ. of Pennsylvania for the U.S. Army. ENIAC could be programmed to do different tasks, but cables had to be plugged in and switches had to be set by hand.

1951: Eckert and Mauchly's UNIVAC (Universal Automatic Computer) became the first commercially available computer in the U.S. The first customer was the Census Bureau. CBS-TV used a UNIVAC in 1952 to predict election results.

1967: Computer pioneer Doug Engelbart applied for a patent on the mouse.

1969-71: The powerful Unix operating system was developed at Bell Laboratories; later versions became widely used on large computers and formed the basis for the Macintosh OS X operating system.

1971: Intel released the 4004, the first commercial microprocessor (an entire computer processing unit on a chip).

1973: The Alto computer, developed at Xerox's Palo Alto Research Center, became operational, implementing many features of modern commercial personal computers, including a graphical user interface (GUI) featuring windows, icons, and pointers that could be manipulated by a mouse.

1975: The first widely marketed personal computer (PC), the MITS Altair 8800, was introduced in kit form, with no keyboard, video display, or printer, for under $400. Microsoft was founded by Bill Gates and Paul Allen.

1976: The first word-processing program for personal computers, Electric Pencil, was written. Apple Computer Company was founded by Steven Jobs and Stephen Wozniak.

1977: Apple introduced the Apple II; capable of displaying text and graphics in color, the machine enjoyed phenomenal success.

1981: IBM unveiled its Personal Computer (IBM 5150), which used an operating system from Microsoft known as MS-DOS (Disk Operating System).

1984: Apple introduced the first Macintosh. The easy-to-use Macintosh came with a proprietary operating system and was the first popular computer to have a GUI and a mouse.

1990: Microsoft released Windows 3.0, the first workable version of its own GUI.

1991: The Unix-like Linux operating system was invented by Helsinki Univ. student Linus Torvalds and made available for free.

1996: The Palm Pilot, the first widely successful handheld computer and personal information manager, arrived.

1997: The IBM computer Deep Blue beat world chess champion Garry Kasparov in a 6-game match, 2-1, with 3 draws.

2000: Microsoft was found guilty of antitrust violations by a federal district judge. Microsoft settled in 2001 by accepting certain restrictions on its competitive practices.

2001: Apple introduced the Unix-based operating system OS X for the Macintosh.

2002: The total number of personal computers, including desktop and laptop machines of all types, shipped by manufacturers since 1975 reached 1 bil.

2006: Apple began using Intel microprocessors instead of the IBM PowerPC in its Macintosh computers.

2007: Apple introduced the iPhone, a touchscreen-equipped smartphone. Amazon released the Kindle, a proprietary hardware/software system for displaying books electronically.

2008: Google released the Linux-based Android operating system for mobile devices.

2010: Apple released the iPad tablet computer and sold more than 3 mil devices in the first 80 days.

2012: Microsoft released its Windows 8 operating system, featuring enhanced support for touchscreens and an interface with a grid of tiles displaying actively updated content and apps. By late in the year more than 1 bil smartphones of all types were in use worldwide.

Nations With the Most Personal Computers in Use, 2012

Source: Computer Industry Almanac at www.c-i-a.com for year-end 2012

Rank	Nations	PCs in use (mil)	% of world total	Rank	Nations	PCs in use (mil)	% of world total
1.	U.S.	326.0	18.60%	10.	Italy	47.6	2.71%
2.	China	229.9	13.12	11.	South Korea	42.9	2.45
3.	Japan	102.1	5.83	12.	Canada	32.5	1.86
4.	Germany	74.6	4.25	13.	Mexico	30.7	1.75
5.	India	68.9	3.93	14.	Spain	26.8	1.53
6.	Russia	60.4	3.45	15.	Australia	20.3	1.16
7.	United Kingdom	57.0	3.25	**Top 15 countries**		**1,229**	**70.12**
8.	France	56.5	3.22	**World**		**1,753**	**100.00**
9.	Brazil	53.0	3.02				

World's Fastest Supercomputers, 2013

Source: Top500.org, as of midyear 2013

Rank	Name	Location	Manufacturer/ vendor	Processors (cores)	Top speed[1]
1.	Tianhe-2 (Milky Way-2)	National University of Defense Technology (NUDT), China	NUDT	3,120,000	33.86
2.	Titan	Oak Ridge National Laboratory, TN, U.S.	Cray	560,640	17.59
3.	Sequoia	Lawrence Livermore National Laboratory, CA, U.S.	IBM	1,572,864	17.17
4.	K Computer	RIKEN Advanced Institute for Computational Science, Japan	Fujitsu	705,024	10.51
5.	Mira	Argonne National Laboratory, IL, U.S.	IBM	786,432	8.59
6.	Stampede	Texas Advanced Computing Center/Univ. of Texas, TX, U.S.	Dell	462,462	5.17
7.	JUQUEEN	Forschungszentrum Juelich, Germany	IBM	458,752	5.01
8.	Vulcan	Lawrence Livermore National Laboratory, CA, U.S.	IBM	393,216	4.29
9.	SuperMUC	Leibniz Rechenzentrum, Germany	IBM	147,456	2.90
10.	Tianhe-1A (Milky Way-1A)	National Supercomputing Center, China	NUDT	186,368	2.57

Note: The 10 fastest supercomputers, and almost all of the 500 fastest supercomputers, use a version of the Linux operating system. (1) Top speed, in petaflops, achieved as measured according to the Linpack Benchmark. 1 petaflop = 1 quadrillion floating-point operations per sec.

U.S. Sales of Selected Hardware, 2010-13

Source: Consumer Electronics Association

(factory sales to dealers in thousands of units and millions of dollars)

Hardware	2010		2012		2013	
	Units	Sales	Units	Sales	Units	Sales
Desktop computers[1]	10,739	$7,390	10,527	$6,997	10,359	$6,876
Tablets	NA	NA	60,102	23,139	87,084	27,312
Mobile PCs[2]	NA	NA	25,095	16,331	26,025	17,181
Smartphones	54,136	17,594	111,037	33,228	126,582	37,880
Electronic gaming hardware[3]	NA	5,809	NA	2,752	NA	2,702
Digital video recorders (DVRs)	16,891	2,618	16,669	2,745	13,545	2,249
Digital cameras	36,545	6,778	23,702	6,470	15,395	4,563
Digital camcorders	7,246	1,150	2,663	237	1,670	137
Portable media/MP3 players[4]	39,686	7,030	26,472	3,929	20,402	2,959

NA = Not available. (1) Includes all-in-one computers. (2) Includes notebooks, netbooks, ultrabooks. (3) Does not include systems or software for direct use with personal computer. (4) Includes flash media and hard-drive based portable MP3 players.

U.S. Sales and Household Penetration of Selected Products, 1985-2012

Source: Consumer Electronics Association

Product	1985		1990		1995		2000		2005		2012	
	Sales (mil)	% of all house-holds	Sales (mil)	% of all house-holds	Sales (mil)	% of all house-holds	Sales (mil)	% of all house-holds	Sales (mil)	% of all house-holds	Sales (mil)	% of all house-holds
Cordless telephones	$280	11%	$842	28%	$1,141	55%	$1,307	80%	$943	88%	$701	NA
Pagers	NA	NA	118	1	300	11	750	23	525	11	7	NA
Modems/fax modems	10	0	191	2.7	770	16	1,564	55	1,525	70	1,372	70%
Telephone answering devices	325	7	827	35	1,077	57	984	75	1,279	76	577	63
Cellular phones[1]	116	0.1	1,098	5	2,574	29	8,995	60	14,265	NA	39,473	91

NA = Not available. (1) For 2005 and 2012, also includes other wireless communication devices such as PDAs and smartphones. Smartphones were 27% of sales in 2005 and 85% of sales in 2012.

About the Internet

The Internet is not owned or funded by any one institution, organization, or government. It has no CEO and is not a commercial service. Its development is guided by the Internet Society (ISOC), which is composed of volunteers. The ISOC appoints the Internet Architecture Board (IAB), which oversees issues of standards and network resources, among others.

Major Historical Highlights

1969: ARPANET, an experimental four-computer network, was established by the Advanced Research Projects Agency (ARPA) of the U.S. Defense Dept. Two years later, ARPANET linked about 23 computers ("hosts") at 15 sites, including MIT and Harvard.

1978: The first spam, or junk email, was sent over ARPANET.

1983: The set of communications rules (protocol) known as TCP/IP became the main networking protocol of ARPANET. Its adoption was tantamount to the birth of the Internet. The military portion of ARPANET was moved onto MILNET.

1986: The U.S. National Science Foundation (NSF) launched NSFNET, the first large-scale network using Internet technology.

1988: Internet Relay Chat (IRC) was developed by Finnish student Jarkko Oikarinen, enabling people to communicate via the Internet in "real time."

1988: A "worm" crafted by Cornell Univ. computer science graduate student Robert Morris Jr. infected thousands of computers, shutting many down and causing millions of dollars of damage—the first known case of large-scale damage caused by a computer virus spread via the Internet.

1989: The World—the first commercial Internet service provider supplying dial-up access—debuted.

1989-90: Tim Berners-Lee invented the World Wide Web. Created as an environment in which scientists at the European Center for Nuclear Research in Switzerland could share information, it gradually evolved into a medium with text, graphics, audio, animation, and video.

1990: ARPANET was disbanded.

1991: NSFNET was opened to commercial traffic. Berners-Lee introduced the first browser, or software for accessing the web.

1993: The National Center for Supercomputing Applications released versions of Mosaic, the first web browser able to present both text and images in a single page.

1994: Netscape Communications released the Netscape Navigator browser.

1995: Microsoft released its Internet Explorer browser. It initially failed to make a dent in Netscape's dominance of the browser market but surpassed it by 1999.

1996: A group of universities launched Internet2, an advanced, high-performance network for the research community and a test bed for development of new capabilities that might find use in the commercial Internet.

1998: Under a contract with the U.S. Dept. of Commerce, the nonprofit Internet Corporation for Assigned Numbers and Names (ICANN) took over the management of assigning domain names and Internet Protocol (IP) addresses.

1999: Release of the free Napster file-sharing service enabled users to easily exchange files containing music or other content without regard to copyright restrictions.

2003: Niue, a self-governing Pacific island associated with New Zealand, became the first country to offer free nationwide wireless access to the Internet, using Wi-Fi technology.

2004: The Mozilla Foundation released the first official version of the open-source browser Mozilla Firefox.

2008: Google introduced its Chrome browser. By 2012, Chrome ranked as the most widely used browser in the world, according to StatCounter.com.

2011: ICANN decided to allow generic top-level domains to be almost any word in any alphabet.

Safety and Security on the Internet

Common sense dictates some basic security rules:

- Pick passwords that are difficult to guess, preferably consisting of both letters and numbers and other symbols, if permitted. Avoid using the same password for multiple websites.

- Do not give out your phone number, address, credit card number, or other personal information unless needed for a transaction at a site you trust.

- If you feel someone is being threatening or dangerous, inform your Internet service provider.

- Use protective "firewall," antivirus, and antispyware software to guard your system against attacks by hackers.

- Be careful about opening email and file attachments from unknown correspondents.

- To avoid falling victim to the scam known as **phishing**—which uses a forged email message, purportedly from a respectable organization, to elicit personal data—do not click on hyperlinks in emails from companies with which you do business. Phishing emails typically contain a link leading to a fabricated website resembling the site of the ostensible sender. If you want to visit a company's website, open your browser and manually enter the site's address.

- Users of so-called **peer-to-peer** (P2P) file-sharing networks or protocols should open up only part of their computer system to sharing, not the entire hard drive.

- When manufacturers provide **patches** to solve security flaws or other problems with operating systems, web browsers, or other software, it is usually advisable to install these fixes. If a fix is not available for a serious security problem, you may want to consider switching to an alternative program.

Internet Addresses

The fundamental part of an address on the Internet is called the domain. The final part of a domain name, known as the **top-level domain (TLD)**, is its most basic part. For example, .com is the top-level domain of *The World Almanac*'s web address (www.worldalmanac.com).

So-called generic top-level domains (gTLDs), consisting of three or more letters, include the following:

Domain	What it is (usually)
.aero	an organization in the air-transport industry
.asia	an entity or individual associated with the Pan-Asia and Asia-Pacific region
.biz	a business
.cat	a site associated with Catalan language and culture
.com	generally a commercial organization, business, or company
.coop	a nonprofit business cooperative, such as a rural electric co-op
.edu	an educational institution
.gov	a nonmilitary governmental entity in the U.S.
.info	an informational site for an individual or organization
.int	an international organization
.jobs	information about employment
.mil	a U.S. military organization
.mobi	a site providing content for mobile devices
.museum	a museum
.name	an individual
.net	suggested for a network administration but actually used by a wide variety of sites
.org	suggested for a nonprofit organization but actually used by a wide variety of sites
.post	postal services
.pro	a professional, such as an accountant, lawyer, or physician
.tel	contact data for a group or individual
.travel	information about travel
.xxx	adult entertainment community

Domain names with two letters are generally for countries or regions. The **top-level domain** .us, for instance, is available to persons, organizations, and entities in the U.S. More examples: .ca (Canada), .eu (European Union), .jp (Japan), .ru (Russia), .uk (United Kingdom).

Nations With Highest Percentage of Population Using the Internet, 2000-12
Source: © International Telecommunication Union; ranked by 2012 figures

Rank	Nation	2000	2005	2006	2007	2008	2009	2010	2011	2012
1.	Iceland	44.47%	87.00%	89.51%	90.60%	91.00%	93.00%	93.39%	95.02%	96.00%
2.	Norway	52.00	81.99	82.55	86.93	90.57	92.08	93.39	93.97	95.00
3.	Sweden	45.69	84.83	87.76	82.01	90.00	91.00	90.00	94.00	94.00
4.	Denmark	39.17	82.74	86.65	85.03	85.02	86.84	88.72	90.00	93.00
	Netherlands	43.98	81.00	83.70	85.82	87.42	89.63	90.72	92.30	93.00
6.	Luxembourg	22.89	70.00	72.51	78.92	82.23	87.31	90.62	90.89	92.00
7.	Finland	37.25	74.48	79.66	80.78	83.67	82.49	86.89	89.37	91.00
8.	New Zealand	47.38	62.72	69.00	69.76	72.03	79.70	83.00	86.00	89.51
9.	Liechtenstein	36.52	63.37	64.21	65.08	70.00	75.00	80.00	85.00	89.41
10.	Qatar	4.86	24.73	28.97	37.00	44.30	53.10	81.60	86.20	88.10
11.	Bahrain	6.15	21.30	28.24	32.91	51.95	53.00	55.00	77.00	88.00
12.	United Kingdom	26.82	70.00	68.82	75.09	78.39	83.56	85.00	86.84	87.02
13.	Monaco	42.18	55.46	61.48	64.38	67.25	70.10	75.00	80.30	87.00
14.	Canada	51.30	71.66	72.40	73.20	76.70	80.30	80.30	83.00	86.77
15.	Andorra	10.54	37.61	48.94	70.87	70.04	78.53	81.00	81.00	86.43
16.	Switzerland	47.10	70.10	75.70	77.20	79.20	81.30	83.90	85.20	85.20
17.	United Arab Emirates	23.63	40.00	52.00	61.00	63.00	64.00	68.00	78.00	85.00
18.	South Korea	44.70	73.50	78.10	78.80	81.00	81.60	83.70	83.80	84.10
19.	Germany	30.22	68.71	72.16	75.16	78.00	79.00	82.00	83.00	84.00
20.	Antigua and Barbuda	6.48	34.72	62.64	70.06	75.03	74.20	80.00	82.00	83.79

Note: As of 2012, 81.03% of Americans were Internet users.

Nations With the Most Internet Users, 2012

Source: Computer Industry Almanac at www.c-i-a.com for year-end 2012

Rank	Nation	Internet users (mil)	% of worldwide users	Rank	Nation	Internet users (mil)	% of worldwide users
1.	China	489.5	19.91%	10.	France	50.9	2.07%
2.	U.S.	271.4	11.04	11.	Italy	46.1	1.88
3.	India	190.3	7.74	12.	South Korea	41.3	1.68
4.	Japan	108.1	4.40	13.	Mexico	36.0	1.46
5.	Brazil	80.7	3.28	14.	Spain	31.1	1.26
6.	Germany	67.6	2.75	15.	Turkey	30.9	1.26
7.	Russia	61.7	2.51				
8.	Indonesia	55.9	2.27		Top 15 total	1,613	65.62
9.	United Kingdom	51.6	2.10		World total	2,458	100.00

Most-Visited World Websites, 2013

Source: comScore Media Metrix

Some websites represent an aggregation of commonly owned domain names; popular domains within a group added in parentheses by World Almanac editors.

Rank	Website	Visitors[1]	Rank	Website	Visitors[1]
1.	Google sites (YouTube, Blogger)	1,194,404	11.	Apple Inc. (iTunes)	300,297
2.	Microsoft sites (Bing, Xbox Live)	891,369	12.	Ask Network	283,949
3.	Facebook	835,176	13.	Glam Media (Glam, Brash)	283,805
4.	Yahoo! sites (Yahoo! Voices, Flickr)	711,502	14.	CBS Interactive (CNET, ZDNet)	281,473
5.	Wikimedia Foundation sites (Wikipedia)	499,578	15.	Youku Inc.	267,873
6.	Amazon sites (Zappos, Audible, IMDb)	383,802	16.	Vevo	248,616
7.	Baidu.com Inc.	356,664	17.	BitTorrent Network	244,552
8.	Tencent Inc. (QQ)	338,853	18.	SINA Corp.	241,203
9.	Alibaba.com Corp.	314,272	19.	eBay (PayPal, Half.com, Stubhub)	240,614
10.	Sohu.com Inc.	312,305	20.	Tudou sites	217,058

(1) Number of persons age 15 or older, in thousands, who visited a website from any location at least once in June 2013.

Top Web Browsers Worldwide, 2009-13

Source: StatCounter Global Stats, gs.statcounter.com

Browser	% of browser market				
	2009	2010	2011	2012	2013
Chrome	3.01%	9.88%	22.14%	33.81%	43.12%
Internet Explorer	60.11	52.68	42.45	32.04	24.53
Firefox	30.50	30.69	27.95	23.73	20.09
Safari	3.02	4.09	5.17	7.12	8.59
Opera	2.64	1.91	1.66	1.72	1.10

Note: Percent of World Wide Web users accessing the Web via a particular browser, for July of year shown.

Top Operating Systems Worldwide, 2009-13

Source: StatCounter Global Stats, gs.statcounter.com

Operating system	% of OS market				
	2009	2010	2011	2012	2013
Windows 7	0.98%	17.85%	36.06%	51.14%	52.48%
Windows XP	69.95	56.31	43.89	29.10	20.45
Mac OSX	4.12	5.53	6.23	6.92	7.35
Windows 8	—	—	—	0.20	6.61
Windows Vista	22.71	18.46	11.56	8.12	5.24
Apple iOS	—	0.14	0.83	2.64	4.35
Android	—	—	0.07	0.40	1.56
Linux	0.76	0.77	0.76	0.83	1.29

— = Not available. Note: Percent of World Wide Web users accessing Web with a particular operating system (OS), for July of year shown. Includes mobile devices' operating systems.

U.S. Broadband and Dial-Up Adoption, 2000-13

Source: Pew Internet & American Life Project, Aug. 2013

(% of American adults who access the Internet via broadband or dial-up)

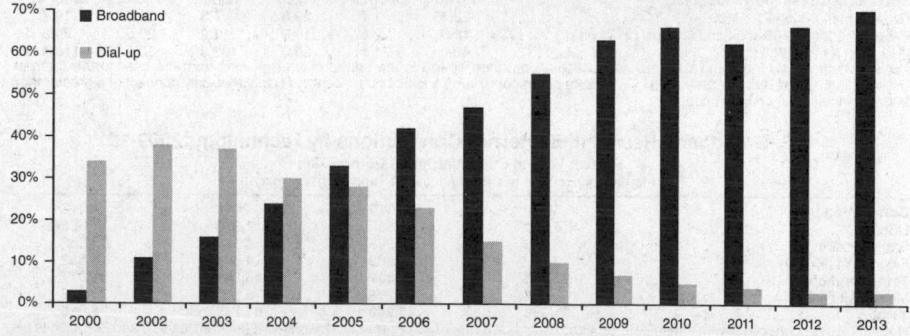

Note: Based on annual survey of adults (persons age 18 and older), which takes place Mar.-June of each year.

U.S. Broadband Internet Access by Selected Characteristics, 2012-13

Source: Pew Internet & American Life Project, Aug. 2013

	% broadband 2012	2013		% broadband 2012	2013		% broadband 2012	2013
All adults	66%	70%	Race/ethnicity			Annual household income		
Gender			White.............	70%	74%	Less than $30,000 ..	46%	54%
Male	66	71	Black.............	54	64	$30,000-$49,999 ...	68	70
Female	66	69	Hispanic	51	53	$50,000-$74,999 ...	85	84
Age			**Education**			$75,000 or more....	87	88
18-29	75	80	No high school diploma	34	37	**Geography**		
30-49	76	78	High school graduate	55	57	Urban.............	67	70
50-64	62	69	Some college	74	78	Suburban	70	73
65+..............	39	43	College graduate....	87	89	Rural.............	53	62

Note: Survey of persons age 18 and older who had broadband Internet access at home. Respondents were contacted Mar. 15-Apr. 3, 2012, and Apr. 17-May 19, 2013. Interviews were conducted in English and Spanish by landline and cell phone.

Most-Visited U.S. Websites, 2013

Source: comScore Media Metrix; comScore qSearch

Some websites represent an aggregation of commonly owned domain names; popular domains within a group as of June 2013 added in parentheses by World Almanac editors.

All U.S. Sites

Rank	Website	Visitors[1]
1.	Google sites (YouTube, Blogger)	192,590
2.	Yahoo! sites (Flickr, Rivals.com)............	188,727
3.	Microsoft sites (Bing, Xbox Live)...........	174,998
4.	Facebook (Instagram)...................	144,659
5.	AOL, Inc. (Moviefone, Patch, Huffington Post)	113,352
6.	Amazon sites (Zappos, Audible, IMDb)......	98,332
7.	Glam Media (Glam, Brash)..............	91,090
8.	Wikimedia Foundation sites (Wikipedia)......	81,439
9.	CBS Interactive (CNET, GameSpot)........	76,185
10.	Apple Inc. (iTunes)....................	75,040

Blog Sites

Rank	Website	Visitors[1]
1.	Blogger........................	58,902
2.	Federated Media Publishing	33,450
3.	Wordpress.com....................	28,316
4.	Gawker Media (Gizmodo, Lifehacker).......	21,149
5.	Technorati Media	18,117

Email

Rank	Website	Visitors[1]
1.	Yahoo! Mail......................	83,249
2.	Google Gmail......................	75,312
3.	Outlook.........................	30,771
4.	AOL Email	19,358
5.	Xfinity.com WebMail	7,294

Social Networking Sites

Rank	Website	Visitors[1]
1.	Facebook	144,659
2.	LinkedIn	50,615
3.	Twitter	39,085
4.	Tumblr..........................	35,863
5.	Pinterest	27,927

Search and Navigation

Rank	Website	Searches (mil)	% of searches
1.	Google sites	12,823	66.7%
2.	Microsoft sites (Bing)	3,434	17.9
3.	Yahoo! sites	2,197	11.4
4.	Ask Network	524	2.7
5.	AOL, Inc.	253	1.3

Video Sites

Rank	Website	Visitors[1]
1.	Google sites (YouTube).................	158,337
2.	Facebook	61,646
3.	AOL, Inc.	51,014
4.	Vevo	49,293
5.	Microsoft sites (Xbox Live)	46,801
6.	NDN (News Distribution Network)	46,605
7.	Yahoo! sites	41,391
8.	Viacom Digital (BET, Comedy Central, MTV)..	40,457
9.	Amazon sites (IMDb)	33,784
10.	Turner Digital (CNN, SI, Golf, NCAA, PGA) ...	27,587

(1) Number of persons age 2 and older in any U.S. location, in thousands, who visited the website at least once in June 2013.

Internet Connections in the U.S. by Speed, 2010-12

Source: Federal Communications Commission

(Internet connections in millions, as of June of given year)

	2010 Fixed	Mobile	2011 Fixed	Mobile	2012 Fixed	Mobile
Speeds, upstream/downstream						
Greater than 6 Mbps/1.5 Mbps......................	23.4	1.7	29.6	4.3	36.8	18.7
Between 3 Mbps/768 kbps and 6 Mbps/1.5 Mbps	18.0	2.5	19.0	11.9	20.5	24.3
Less than 3 Mbps/768 kbps[1]........................	40.4	71.1	38.0	103.3	32.7	110.4

Note: Includes residential and business connections. Upstream speed is the speed of transmission from the user to the Internet. Downstream speed is the reverse. Mbps = megabits per second; kbps = kilobits per second. (1) Includes only connections greater than 200 kbps in at least one direction.

U.S. Broadband Residential Internet Connections by Technology, 2009-12

Source: Federal Communications Commission

(Internet connections in thousands, as of June of given year)

Connection type	2009	2010	2011	2012
DSL.............................	4,897	5,559	7,913	11,583
Cable modem......................	23,025	29,398	32,321	36,583
Fiber optic (FTTP)	3,177	3,982	4,894	5,632
Total nonmobile[1].................	**31,161**	**39,037**	**45,263**	**53,077**
Mobile wireless.....................	196	3,206	6,520	25,539
Total[1,2].........................	**31,356**	**42,243**	**51,783**	**78,616**

Note: Includes connections with transmission speeds of at least 3 megabits per second downstream (Internet to user) and 768 kilobits per second upstream (user to Internet). (1) Includes categories not listed individually. (2) Numbers may not add up to totals due to rounding.

Internet Use in the U.S., 2000-12

Source: The 2013 Digital Future Report, USC Annenberg School Center for the Digital Future

	2000	2001	2002	2003	2005	2006	2007	2008	2009	2010	2012
% of Americans accessing Internet ...	67%	72%	71%	76%	79%	78%	79%	80%	82%	82%	86%
% of households with broadband connection....................	10	13	22	36	48	51	76	79	82	84	83
% of Internet users who make purchases online..............	45	51	40	43	46	51	67	65	65	68	78
Weekly time online[1]	9.4	9.8	11.1	12.5	13.3	14.0	15.3	17.3	19.0	18.3	20.4
Weekly time online, at home[1]........	3.3	5.9	6.8	6.9	7.8	8.9	10.0	10.1	10.6	12.3	14.1
Weekly time online, at work[2]	NA	4.6	5.5	4.9	5.6	7.8	7.4	8.3	9.0	9.2	9.2

NA = Not available. (1) Average number of active-use hours per week among Internet users. (2) Average number of hours per week among Internet users who access the Internet at work.

U.S. Internet Use by Race and Ethnicity, 2000-11

Source: Current Population Survey, U.S. Census Bureau, U.S. Dept. of Commerce

Year	White, non-Hispanic Households (thous.)	% with Internet use	Black Households (thous.)	% with Internet use	Asian Households (thous.)	% with Internet use	Hispanic[1] Households (thous.)	% with Internet use
2000	78,719	46.1%	13,171	23.6%	3,457	56.2%	9,565	23.6%
2001	80,734	55.2	13,304	31.1	4,081	67.5	10,476	32.2
2003	81,857	59.9	13,746	36.0	4,009	66.7	12,023	36.0
2007	83,294	66.9	14,730	45.3	4,576	75.2	13,619	43.4
2009	83,810	73.3	15,254	54.5	4,625	80.5	13,799	52.8
2010	83,613	74.9	15,357	58.1	4,744	82.6	14,142	59.1
2011	83,148	76.2	15,369	56.9	4,795	82.7	14,222	58.3

Note: Numbers by race/ethnicity of householder. (1) Hispanic persons may be of any race.

U.S. Internet Use by Educational Attainment, 2000-11

Source: Current Population Survey, U.S. Census Bureau, U.S. Dept. of Commerce

Year	Less than high school Households (thous.)	% with Internet use	High school degree[1] Households (thous.)	% with Internet use	Some college Households (thous.)	% with Internet use	Bachelor's degree or more Households (thous.)	% with Internet use
2000	17,402	11.7%	32,278	29.9%	27,883	49.0%	27,684	66.0%
2001	17,463	18.0	33,469	39.7	29,410	57.7	28,765	75.2
2003	16,972	20.2	34,377	43.1	30,320	62.6	31,457	78.3
2007	13,978	24.0	33,099	49.5	30,434	68.9	33,302	84.0
2009	13,711	32.2	32,990	57.5	31,050	74.7	34,910	88.5
2010	13,257	35.5	33,008	60.4	31,549	77.2	35,156	89.2
2011	13,183	36.9	33,060	61.2	31,586	77.3	35,301	89.9

Note: Numbers by educational attainment of householders 25 years and older. (1) Includes householders with GEDs.

Popular U.S. Online Purchases, 2002-12

Source: The 2013 Digital Future Report, USC Annenberg School Center for the Digital Future

(percent of Internet users who buy item(s) online)

Item	2002	2006	2008	2010	2012	Item	2002	2006	2008	2010	2012
Books	29%	34%	60%	63%	66%	Videos/DVDs	6%	13%	48%	47%	42%
Clothes	39	42	61	59	66	Computers/peripherals	10	11	43	44	40
Travel	16	17	57	57	66	Software/games	12	11	43	44	37
Gifts	10	12	61	63	60	CDs................	15	17	42	41	35
Electronic goods/ appliances.........	14	11	47	50	51	Products for hobbies....	5	2	40	41	34

Frequency of Selected Internet Activities in the U.S., 2012

Source: The 2013 Digital Future Report, USC Annenberg School Center for the Digital Future

(as % of all Internet users age 12 and older)

Online activity	Several times a day	Daily	Weekly	Monthly	Less than monthly	Never
Check email	55%	32%	8%	2%	1%	2%
Browse (surf)	29	30	19	7	7	9
Look for news..............................	15	33	18	8	13	13
Instant message	9	11	11	6	17	46
Find or check a fact	8	21	32	16	14	9
Play games.................................	8	14	14	7	16	42
Listen/download music......................	7	10	16	16	17	34
Watch/download videos.....................	6	10	19	10	18	37
Listen to online radio.......................	6	8	14	8	18	48
Look up a definition	5	10	28	21	23	15
Online banking	3	17	38	16	4	22

Informative and Useful Websites

Name	URL	Description
Daily Data		
Federal Register	www.federalregister.gov	Online magazine approach to the government's daily journal. Browse by topic, date, or agency.
Flowing Data	flowingdata.com	Online data visualizations and statistics.
ResourceShelf	www.resourceshelf.com	Running list of newly published databases, reports, and other research aids.
Today's Front Pages	www.newseum.org/todaysfrontpages/	Today's front page from more than 800 newspapers worldwide.
Education and Exhibits		
American Memory	memory.loc.gov	More than 9 mil items from the Library of Congress, including audio, maps, movies, photos, prints, and sheet music.
Europeana	europeana.eu	Network of European cultural organizations linking to more than 20 mil digital items.
Internet Archive	www.archive.org	Digital library of free cultural artifacts and Internet sites.
MIT OpenCourseWare	ocw.mit.edu	Free and open educational course material from the Massachusetts Institute of Technology.
New York Public Library Digital Gallery	digitalgallery.nypl.org	More than 800,000 images digitized from primary sources and printed rarities in the library's collections.
Our Documents	www.ourdocuments.gov	Digitized images and text of 100 milestone documents from America's history.
World Digital Library	www.wdl.org	Collection of significant primary documents from countries around the world.
Statistics		
DATA.gov	www.data.gov	Open access to raw U.S. government data files.
FedStats	www.fedstats.gov	Statistics by topic or program from more than 100 federal agencies.
United Nations Statistics Division	unstats.un.org	International data sets and country profiles with demographics and stats on society, industry, and the environment.
U.S. Economy at a Glance	stats.bls.gov/eag/	Quick reference tables on employment and wages from the U.S. Bureau of Labor Statistics.
Online Tools		
Kayak	www.kayak.com	One-stop search of multiple travel-booking sites for the lowest fares and price trends.
LibraryThing	www.librarything.com	Track the books you've read, receive suggestions for new books, and compare lists with other readers.
Wolfram Alpha	www.wolframalpha.com	Ready reference through computation of databases maintained by Wolfram Research.
Open Congress	www.opencongress.org	Easily follow Congress and find news about specific members, bills, committees, and issues. Receive updates by RSS feed.
Downloadable Tools		
Google Earth	earth.google.com	Free downloadable interactive world atlas and mapping software.
Stellarium	www.stellarium.org	Free downloadable planetarium that visualizes astronomical phenomena in real time from any point on Earth.

Note: Websites are subject to change. The World Almanac cannot take responsibility for contents.

Worldwide Telecommunications: Market Data, 1990-2013

Source: © International Telecommunication Union

	1990		2000		2005		2010		2012[1]		2013[1]	
	No. (mil)	Per 100 pop.	No. (mil)	Per 100 pop.	No. (mil)	Per 100 pop.	No. (mil)	Per 100 pop.	No. (mil)	Per 100 pop.	No. (mil)	Per 100 pop.
Fixed telephone lines	520	NA	975	15.9	1,243	19.1	1,228	17.8	1,186	16.9	1,171	16.5
Mobile cellular subscriptions	11	NA	739	12.0	2,205	33.9	5,320	77.2	6,411	91.2	6,835	96.2
Internet users	NA	NA	394	6.4	1,024	15.8	2,023	29.5	2,497	35.7	2,749	38.8
Wired broadband subscriptions ...	NA	NA	NA	NA	220	3	527	8	638	9	696	10
Active mobile broadband subscriptions................	NA	NA	NA	NA	NA	NA	778	11.3	1,556	22.1	2,096	29.5

NA = Not available. (1) Estimated.

World Cell Phone Use by Nation, 2012

Source: © International Telecommunication Union, estimated; ranked by countries with most subscriptions

Rank	Country	Subscriptions (thous.)	Per 100 pop.	Rank	Country	Subscriptions (thous.)	Per 100 pop.
1.	China	1,100,000	81.26	14.	Italy...............	97,226	159.48
2.	India	864,720	68.72	15.	Bangladesh.........	97,180	63.76
3.	United States	310,000	98.17	16.	Egypt	96,799	115.29
4.	Indonesia	281,964	115.20	17.	Thailand	84,075	120.29
5.	Russia.............	261,886	183.52	18.	United Kingdom	82,109	130.75
6.	Brazil..............	248,324	125.19	19.	South Africa	68,394	134.80
7.	Japan	138,363	109.43	20.	Turkey.............	67,681	90.84
8.	Vietnam	134,066	149.41	21.	France.............	62,280	98.14
9.	Pakistan	120,151	66.77	22.	Ukraine	59,344	132.05
10.	Nigeria	112,778	67.68	23.	Argentina	58,599	142.51
11.	Germany...........	107,658	131.30	24.	Iran	58,158	76.92
12.	Philippines	103,000	106.77	25.	South Korea	53,624	110.36
13.	Mexico	100,786	86.77		**World**	**6,411,000**	**91.20**

U.S. Wireless Industry, 1985-2012

Source: CTIA Semi-Annual Industry Survey, used with permission of CTIA. As of Dec. of year shown.

Year	Est. total subscribers	Total service revenues (thous.)	Cell phone antennas	Avg. monthly revenue per subscriber unit	Avg. local call length (min.)
1985	340,213	$482,428	913	NA	NA
1987	1,230,855	1,151,519	2,305	NA	2.33
1989	3,508,944	3,340,595	4,169	NA	2.48
1991	7,557,148	5,708,522	7,847	NA	2.38
1993	16,009,461	10,892,175	12,824	$76.98	2.41
1995	33,785,661	19,081,239	22,663	59.47	2.15
1996	44,042,992	23,634,971	30,045	54.66	2.32
1997	55,312,293	27,485,633	51,600	48.62	2.31
1998	69,209,321	33,133,175	65,887	47.93	2.39
1999	86,047,003	40,018,489	81,698	45.82	2.38
2000	109,478,031	52,466,020	104,288	48.21	2.56
2001	128,374,512	65,316,235	127,540	50.41	2.74
2002	140,766,842	76,508,187	139,338	51.97	2.73
2003	158,721,981	87,624,093	162,986	52.18	3.07
2004	182,140,362	102,121,210	175,725	52.75	3.05
2005	207,896,198	113,538,221	183,689	49.92	3.00
2006	233,040,781	125,456,825	195,613	49.34	3.03
2007	255,395,599	138,869,304	213,299	49.41	NA
2008	270,333,881	148,084,170	242,130	49.04	2.27
2009	285,646,191	152,551,854	247,081	47.74	1.81
2010	296,285,629	159,929,648	253,086	47.36	1.79
2011	315,963,848	169,767,314	283,385	46.11	1.78
2012	326,475,248	185,013,936	301,779	48.73	1.80

NA = Not available.

U.S. Use of Selected Cell Phone Functions, 2007-12

Source: The 2013 Digital Future Report, USC Annenberg School Center for the Digital Future
(as % of cell phone users age 12 and older)

Function	2007	2008	2009	2010	2012
Text message	31%	45%	54%	62%	82%
Take pictures	33	47	52	60	79
Access the Internet	8	13	18	23	59
Play games	17	22	20	23	43

U.S. Use of Selected Cell Phone Functions, 2012

Source: The 2013 Digital Future Report, USC Annenberg School Center for the Digital Future
(% of cell phone users age 12 and older who used function)

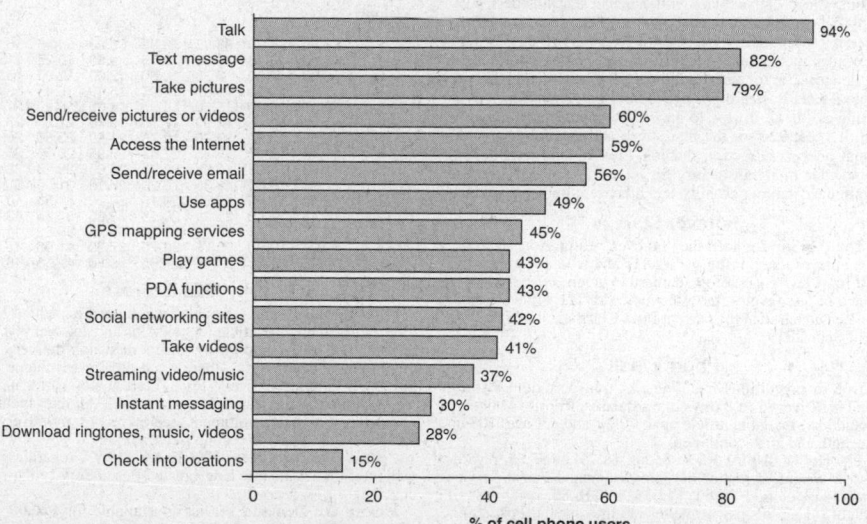

Function	%
Talk	94%
Text message	82%
Take pictures	79%
Send/receive pictures or videos	60%
Access the Internet	59%
Send/receive email	56%
Use apps	49%
GPS mapping services	45%
Play games	43%
PDA functions	43%
Social networking sites	42%
Take videos	41%
Streaming video/music	37%
Instant messaging	30%
Download ringtones, music, videos	28%
Check into locations	15%

% of cell phone users

POSTAL INFORMATION

Basic U.S. Postal Service

The Postal Reorganization Act, creating a government-owned postal service under the executive branch and replacing the old Post Office Department, was signed into law by Pres. Richard Nixon, Aug. 12, 1970. The service officially came into being on July 1, 1971. The U.S. Postal Service is governed by an 11-person board of governors. Nine of the members are appointed by the president, with Senate approval. These nine choose a postmaster general. The board and the postmaster general choose the 11th member, who serves as deputy postmaster general.

Congress passed the Postal Accountability and Enhancement Act, which overhauled postal service operations for the first time since 1971, on Dec. 8, 2006. New operating provisions included the ability to adjust rates annually, negotiate for contracts, and invest profits in internal improvements. (The Postal Service last received a public service subsidy, i.e., taxpayer dollars, in 1982.)

Historical Postage Rates, 1851-2013

Postage cost for a prepaid, one-ounce letter (the first-class standard after July 1, 1885).

Effective date	Rate	2013 dollars	Effective date	Rate	2013 dollars	Effective date	Rate	2013 dollars
July 1, 1851	$0.06[1]	$1.78	May 16, 1971	$0.08	$0.46	Jan. 10, 1999	$0.33	$0.46
July 1, 1863	0.06	1.08	Mar. 2, 1974	0.10	0.50	Jan. 7, 2001	0.34	0.45
Oct. 1, 1883	0.04	1.89	Dec. 31, 1975	0.13	0.58	June 30, 2002	0.37	0.48
July 1, 1885	0.02	0.47	May 29, 1978	0.15	0.55	Jan. 8, 2006	0.39	0.46
Nov. 2, 1917	0.03[2]	0.59	Mar. 22, 1981	0.18	0.48	May 14, 2007	0.41	0.47
July 1, 1919	0.02[2]	0.28	Nov. 1, 1981	0.20	0.53	May 12, 2008	0.42	0.46
July 6, 1932	0.03	0.47	Feb. 17, 1985	0.22	0.48	May 11, 2009	0.44	0.48
Aug. 1, 1958	0.04	0.32	Apr. 3, 1988	0.25	0.50	June 24, 2012	0.45	0.46
Jan. 7, 1963	0.05	0.38	Feb. 3, 1991	0.29	0.50	Jan. 27, 2013	0.46	0.46
Jan. 7, 1968	0.06	0.41	Jan. 1, 1995	0.32	0.49			

(1) For domestic letters traveling under 3,000 miles. (2) The price increased one cent during World War I; Congress restored its prewar rate in 1919.

Status of the U.S. Postal Service, 2001-12

Source: *Postal Facts 2013*, U.S. Postal Service

	2001	2005	2006	2007	2008	2009	2010	2011	2012	% change, 2001-12
Total mail items (bil)	207.5	211.7	213.1	212.2	202.7	177.0	171.0	168.0	160.0	−22.9%
First-class mail items (bil)	103.7	98.1	97.7	95.9	91.7	83.8	78.2	73.5	68.7	−33.8
Stamped mail items (bil)	53.6	45.9	44.4	42.3	35.4	31.6	28.9	25.8	23.2	−56.7
Advertising mail items (bil)	89.9	100.9	102.5	103.5	99.1	82.7	82.5	84.7	79.5	−11.6
Annual revenue (bil)	$65.8	$69.9	$72.7	$74.7	$74.9	$68.0	$67.1	$65.7	$65.2	−0.9
Total retail revenue (bil)	$14.8	$17.3	$17.8	$18.5	$18.7	$17.7	$17.5	$16.9	$17.5	18.2
Total customer visits (bil)	1.4	1.3	1.3	1.2	1.2	1.1	1.1	0.9	1.0	−28.6
Delivery points (mil)	137.7	144.3	146.2	148.0	149.2	150.0	150.7	151.5	152.7	10.5
Total delivery routes	242,600	243,000	244,700	246,500	244,800	232,900	230,600	228,160	227,000	−6.4
Total retail offices	38,123	37,142	36,826	36,451	36,723	36,496	36,222	35,756	35,369	−7.2
Career employees	775,903	704,716	696,138	684,762	663,238	623,128	583,908	551,570	522,144	−32.7

U.S. Domestic Mail Rates

Source: *Price List (Notice 123)*, U.S. Postal Service. Effective July 28, 2013. Rates are for domestic retail customers unless otherwise noted. Domestic rates apply to the U.S., its territories and possessions, and APOs and FPOs.

First-Class Mail

First-Class Mail includes written matter such as letters, postcards, bills, account statements, and any matter sealed or closed against inspection. In most cases, **delivery is in 3 days or less.**

Written matter sealed against inspection costs **46¢** for the first ounce, 20¢ for each additional ounce or fraction thereof, up to 3.5 oz. Postcard postage is **33¢**. Large envelopes measuring up to 12 in. by 15 in. (or standard envelopes over 3.5 oz.) cost **92¢** for the first ounce and 20¢ for each additional ounce or fraction thereof. Presort- and automation-compatible mail can qualify for lower rates if certain piece minimums, mailing permits, and other requirements are met.

Forever Stamps

The USPS introduced the "Forever" stamp Apr. 12, 2007. The Forever stamp initially cost 41¢ and will always be valid as First-Class postage on standard envelopes weighing one ounce or less, even after rates increase. The Forever stamp can be purchased at the current First-Class standard rate (46¢ as of Sept. 2013).

Priority Mail

Due to expeditious handling and transportation, Priority Mail is **delivered in 2 days** in most cases. Priority Mail may include any mailable article up to 70 lbs and not over 108 in. in length and girth combined.

Priority Mail Flat Rate: $5.60, $5.75, or $5.95, regardless of weight, if matter fits into designated Postal Service flat-rate envelopes. **$5.80, $12.35, or $16.85**, regardless of weight (under 70 lbs), if matter fits into special Postal Service flat-rate boxes.

Priority Mail Rates

Weight not over	Zone						
	1-2	3	4	5	6	7	8
1 lb	$5.60	$5.70	$5.85	$6.00	$6.20	$6.45	$6.95
2	5.80	6.15	6.85	8.75	9.50	10.25	11.25
3	6.60	7.60	8.75	10.60	12.00	12.90	15.25
4	7.45	8.90	10.05	14.05	15.40	16.45	18.35
5	8.85	10.20	11.50	15.95	17.55	18.90	21.20
6	9.75	11.25	12.90	17.75	19.70	21.20	23.95
7	10.35	12.20	13.90	19.75	21.80	23.85	26.90
8	11.10	13.30	15.55	21.45	23.95	26.30	30.15
9	11.85	14.35	16.85	23.25	26.05	28.45	33.55
10	12.65	15.40	18.35	25.20	28.15	31.30	36.50
11	13.50	16.45	19.80	27.15	30.20	34.55	40.10
12	14.45	17.65	21.20	29.15	32.85	37.35	43.05
13	15.35	18.75	22.40	30.80	35.25	38.85	44.60
14	16.25	19.90	23.65	32.75	37.20	41.05	46.80
15	16.95	21.00	25.05	34.65	38.80	41.95	48.15

Priority Mail Express

Priority Mail Express provides guaranteed expedited service for any mailable article (up to 70 lbs and not over 108 in. in combined length and girth). Offers **next-day delivery** by noon to most destinations; there is a $12.50 extra charge for Sunday or holiday delivery. Prices start at $14.10 for items weighing up to 8 oz., dependent on distance. All rates include insurance up to $100, shipment receipt, record of delivery at the destination post office, and free tracking.

Priority Mail Express Flat Rate: $19.95, regardless of weight, if matter fits into a designated Postal Service flat-rate envelope.

Pickup On Demand service is available for **$20.00** per stop, regardless of the number of pieces or service used.

Standard Post

Standard Post applies to packages not sent as Priority Mail, Priority Mail Express, Media Mail, or Library Mail. (Parcel Select, a separate service, is used for medium-to-large volumes of packages.) Standard Post is a ground service for nonurgent shipping and oversized packages; delivery depends on distance and takes 2-8 days.

Any package matter may be mailed at Standard Post rates provided it does not exceed 70 lbs or 130 in. in combined length and girth. Packages under 20 lbs that are over 84 in. and up to 108 in. in combined length and girth use the 20-lb "balloon" price. Packages exceeding 108 in. use the oversized price. Fractions of a pound are counted as a full pound.

Standard Post Rates

Weight not over	Zone						
	1-2	3	4	5	6	7	8
1 lb	$5.60	$5.70	$5.85	$5.95	$6.15	$6.35	$6.85
2	5.80	6.15	6.85	7.53	8.16	8.92	9.79
3	6.60	7.60	8.75	8.91	10.01	10.81	12.77
4	7.45	8.90	10.05	10.40	10.75	12.07	13.58
5	8.85	10.20	11.50	11.64	11.76	12.66	14.20
6	9.75	11.25	12.90	13.12	13.20	14.20	16.05
7	10.35	12.20	13.90	14.39	14.61	15.98	18.02
8	11.10	13.30	15.55	15.66	16.05	17.62	20.20
9	11.85	14.35	16.85	16.97	17.45	19.06	22.48
10	12.65	15.40	18.35	18.45	18.86	20.97	24.46
11	13.50	16.45	19.80	19.94	20.23	23.15	26.87
12	14.45	17.65	21.20	21.31	22.01	25.02	28.84
13	15.35	18.75	22.40	22.49	23.62	26.03	29.88
14	16.25	19.90	23.75	23.91	24.92	27.50	31.36
15	16.95	21.00	25.05	25.29	26.00	28.11	32.26
Balloon	17.39	22.01	26.18	27.15	27.96	30.21	34.58
Oversized	62.42	65.30	66.60	68.57	91.83	97.79	108.23

Standard Mail

Standard Mail is limited to items less than 16 oz. such as solicitations, newsletters, advertising materials, books, cassettes, and other merchandise. It may not be used for personal correspondence. A minimum volume of 200 pieces or 50 lbs of such items is necessary, and specific bulk mail preparation and sortation requirements apply.

The minimum rate per piece for mail 3.3 oz. or less is $0.408 for basic nonmachinable letters. Contact a post office for discounts for automation, presorted, carrier route, and destination entry, among others. Separate rates are available for some nonprofit organizations.

Any mailer who uses standard mail is required to pay an annual fee of $200, good for 365 days. Additional standards apply to mailings of nonidentical-weight pieces.

Library Mail

Applies to books, printed music, bound academic theses, periodicals, sound recordings, museum materials, and other library materials mailed between schools, colleges, universities, public libraries, museums, veterans' and fraternal organizations, and nonprofit religious, educational, scientific, and labor organizations or associations (or to or from such organizations). Advertising restrictions apply. Packages may not exceed 108 in. in combined length and girth. Contact a post office for further information.

Rates are calculated by weight only. Single-piece rates: $2.40, up to 1 lb; 43¢ for each additional pound or fraction thereof up to 7 lbs; additional pounds thereafter, 41¢.

Periodicals

Periodicals include newspapers and magazines.

For the general public, the applicable retail postage is paid for periodicals.

For publishers, rates vary according to the following:
(1) whether item is sent to same county,
(2) percentage of editorial and advertising matter,
(3) whether the publisher is a nonprofit or produces educational material for use in classrooms,
(4) weight,
(5) distance,
(6) level of presort, and
(7) automation compatibility.

Media Mail

Applies to books of at least 8 printed pages; 16-mm or narrower-width films; printed music; printed test materials; sound recordings, playscripts, and manuscripts for books; printed educational charts; loose-leaf pages and binders consisting of medical information; and computer-readable media. Advertising restrictions apply. Packages may not exceed 108 in. in combined length and girth. Contact a post office for further information.

Rates are calculated by weight only. Single-piece rates: $2.53, up to 1 lb; 45¢ for each additional pound or fraction thereof up to 7 lbs; additional pounds thereafter, 43¢.

Bound Printed Matter

Applies to advertising, promotional, directory, or editorial material that is bound by permanent fastening and consists of sheets of which at least 90% are imprinted by any process other than handwriting or typewriting. Does not include stationery (or pads of blank forms) or personal correspondence. Packages may not exceed 108 in. in combined length and girth.

Bound Printed Matter Rates
(zone rate for nonpresorted commercial parcels)

Weight not over	Zone						
	1-2	3	4	5	6	7	8
1.0 lb	$2.48	$2.54	$2.60	$2.69	$2.81	$2.87	$3.08
1.5	2.48	2.54	2.60	2.69	2.81	2.87	3.08
2.0	2.59	2.67	2.75	2.87	3.03	3.11	3.39
2.5	2.71	2.81	2.91	3.06	3.26	3.36	3.71
3.0	2.82	2.94	3.06	3.24	3.48	3.60	4.02
3.5	2.94	3.08	3.22	3.43	3.71	3.85	4.34
4.0	3.05	3.21	3.37	3.61	3.93	4.09	4.65
4.5	3.17	3.35	3.53	3.80	4.16	4.34	4.97
5.0	3.28	3.48	3.68	3.98	4.38	4.58	5.28
6.0	3.51	3.75	3.99	4.35	4.83	5.07	5.91
7.0	3.74	4.02	4.30	4.72	5.28	5.56	6.54
8.0	3.97	4.29	4.61	5.09	5.73	6.05	7.17
9.0	4.20	4.56	4.92	5.46	6.18	6.54	7.80
10.0	4.43	4.83	5.23	5.83	6.63	7.03	8.43
11.0	4.66	5.10	5.54	6.20	7.08	7.52	9.06
12.0	4.89	5.37	5.85	6.57	7.53	8.01	9.69
13.0	5.12	5.64	6.16	6.94	7.98	8.50	10.32
14.0	5.35	5.91	6.47	7.31	8.43	8.99	10.95
15.0	5.58	6.18	6.78	7.68	8.88	9.48	11.58

Domestic Mail Special Services

Delivery Confirmation

Applies to First-Class Mail parcels, Priority Mail, and Package Services. Available for purchase at the time of mailing only. Provides mailer with the date and time an article was delivered or date and time of any unsuccessful delivery attempts. Electronic confirmation is available for bar-coded matter.

Confirmation is accessible to retail purchasers on the Internet (www.usps.com) or toll-free by phone at (800) 222-1811. First-Class Mail parcels fees: retail, 90¢; electronic, free. Priority Mail fees: free. Standard Mail fee: electronic, 20¢.

Change of Address

The USPS will forward mail to another address provided a Change of Address (COA) form has been filed, either in

person (free), on www.usps.com ($1 fee), or by phone at (800) ASK-USPS ($1). The COA form, which can be picked up at any post office or printed off the Internet, can also be dropped in any mailbox for free filing.

Special Handling

Provides preferential handling, but not preferential delivery, to the extent practicable in dispatch and transportation. Available for First-Class Mail, Priority Mail, and Package Services for the following surcharge: up to 10 lb, $9.00; over 10 lb, $11.95. Pieces must be marked "Special Handling."

Registered Mail

Provides sender with mailing receipt, and a delivery record is maintained. Only matter prepaid with postage at First-Class Mail or Priority Mail rates may be registered. Stamps or meter stamps must be attached. The face of the article must be at least 5 in. long, 3.5 in. high.

Declared value	Fee
$0.00	$11.20
$0.01 to $100.00	12.05
$100.01 to $500.00	13.95
$500.01 to $1,000.00	15.40
$1,000.01 to $2,000.00	16.85
$2,000.01 to $3,000.00	18.30
$3,000.01 to $4,000.00	19.75
$4,000.01 to $5,000.00	21.20
$5,000.01 to $6,000.00	22.65
$6,000.01 to $7,000.00	24.10
$7,000.01 to $8,000.00	25.55
$8,000.01 to $9,000.00	27.00
$9,000.01 to $10,000.00	28.45
$10,000.01 to $11,000.00	29.90
Each additional $1,000 or fraction thereof	1.45

Note: The mailer is required to declare the value of mail presented for registration. Fee for articles with declared value of $0.01 up to $25,000 includes insurance.

Collect on Delivery (C.O.D.)

Fee: $5.35 for up to $50; increases incrementally. Items must be sent as bona fide orders or be in conformity with agreements between senders and addressees. Maximum amount collectible is $1,000. For details, consult a post office.

Certified Mail

Available for any matter having no intrinsic value on which First-Class Mail or Priority Mail postage is paid. A receipt is furnished at the time of mailing, and evidence of delivery is obtained. Basic fee is $3.10 in addition to regular postage. Return receipt and restricted delivery available upon payment of additional fees. No indemnity.

Insured Mail

Applicable to Standard Mail, First-Class Mail, or Priority Mail packages. Matter for sale addressed to prospective purchasers who have not ordered it or authorized its sending cannot be insured. **Note:** For Priority Mail Express, insurance is included up to $100; additional insurance can be purchased for significantly lower fees than those shown here.

Declared value	Fee[1]
$0.01 to $50.00	$1.95
$50.01 to $100.00	2.45
$100.01 to $200.00	3.05
$200.01 to $300.00	5.10
$300.01 to $400.00	6.25
$400.01 to $500.00	7.40
$500.01 to $600.00	8.55
Each additional $100 or fraction thereof	1.15

(1) In addition to postage. (Maximum liability is $5,000.) See a post office for details on bulk discounts.

International Mail Special Services

Customs Clearance and Delivery: $5.50 to most countries.

Insurance: Available to many countries for loss of or damage to items paid at parcel post rate. Consult a post office for indemnity limits for individual countries.

International postcards (single): $1.10 to all countries.

Registration: Available for letter-post items only to most countries. Fee: $12.95.

Return Receipt: Shows to whom and when item is delivered. Fee: $3.50 (must be purchased at time of mailing).

First-Class Mail International: Letter-post items weighing under 1 oz. can be sent for $1.10 to all countries.

International Business Reply: Provides foreign addressees with a prepaid means of responding to communications initiated by a U.S. sender. Fee: $1.25 per card; $1.75 per envelope.

International Postal Money Order: $4.50 per money order.

Priority Mail International Insurance Rates

Limit of indemnity not over	Fee
$50	$2.45
$100	3.60
$200	4.75
$300	5.90
$400	7.05
$500	8.20
$600	9.35
$700	10.50
Each additional $100 or fraction thereof	1.15

Note: Maximum insurance $5,000 ($2,499 in Canada). Varies by country.

U.S. Postal Abbreviations

The abbreviations below are approved by the U.S. Postal Service for use in addresses.

Alabama	AL	Illinois	IL	Missouri	MO	Pennsylvania	PA
Alaska	AK	Indiana	IN	Montana	MT	Puerto Rico	PR
American Samoa	AS	Iowa	IA	Nebraska	NE	Rhode Island	RI
Arizona	AZ	Kansas	KS	Nevada	NV	South Carolina	SC
Arkansas	AR	Kentucky	KY	New Hampshire	NH	South Dakota	SD
California	CA	Louisiana	LA	New Jersey	NJ	Tennessee	TN
Colorado	CO	Maine	ME	New Mexico	NM	Texas	TX
Connecticut	CT	Marshall Islands[1]	MH	New York	NY	Utah	UT
Delaware	DE	Maryland	MD	North Carolina	NC	Vermont	VT
District of Columbia	DC	Massachusetts	MA	North Dakota	ND	Virgin Islands	VI
Florida	FL	Michigan	MI	Northern Mariana Isls.	MP	Virginia	VA
Georgia	GA	Micronesia, Federated		Ohio	OH	Washington	WA
Guam	GU	States of.	FM	Oklahoma	OK	West Virginia	WV
Hawaii	HI	Minnesota	MN	Oregon	OR	Wisconsin	WI
Idaho	ID	Mississippi	MS	Palau[1]	PW	Wyoming	WY

(1) Although an independent nation, this country is subject to domestic rates and fees.

Canadian Province and Territory Postal Abbreviations

Source: Canada Post

Alberta	AB	Newfoundland and		Nunavut	NU	Quebec	QC
British Columbia	BC	Labrador	NL	Ontario	ON	Saskatchewan	SK
Manitoba	MB	Northwest Territories	NT	Prince Edward Island	PE	Yukon	YT
New Brunswick	NB	Nova Scotia	NS				

SOCIAL SECURITY AND WELFARE
Social Security Coverage
Source: Social Security Administration; World Almanac research; provisions shown are as under current law, Sept. 2013

Social Security Benefits

Social Security's **Old-Age, Survivors, and Disability Insurance (OASDI)** program benefits are based on a worker's **primary insurance amount (PIA)**, which is related by law to the average indexed monthly earnings (AIME) on which Social Security contributions have been paid. The full PIA is payable to a worker who retires at full retirement age (FRA), which is 65-67 depending on birth year, and to an entitled disabled worker at any age. Spouses and children of retired or disabled workers and survivors of deceased workers receive set proportions of the PIA subject to a family maximum amount.

The PIA is calculated by applying varying percentages to succeeding parts of the AIME. The formula is adjusted annually to reflect changes in average annual wages.

Increases in Social Security benefits are initiated for Dec. of each year, assuming the Consumer Price Index (CPI) for the third calendar quarter of the year increased relative to the base quarter, which is the third calendar quarter of the year in which an increase last took effect. The size of the benefit increase is determined by the percentage rise of the CPI between the quarters measured.

The **average monthly benefit** payable to all retired workers amounted to $1,262 in Dec. 2012. The average benefit for disabled workers in that month was $1,130.

Maximum Monthly Retired-Worker Benefits Payable for Individuals who Retired at Age 65[1]

Year attaining age 65	Maximum benefit— Payable at retirement	Payable effective Dec. 2012
1990	$975	$1,792
1995	1,199	1,857
1998	1,342	1,929
1999	1,373	1,947
2000	1,435	1,986
2001	1,538	2,057
2002	1,660	2,164
2003	1,721	2,213
2004	1,784	2,247
2005	1,874	2,298
2006	1,961	2,310
2007	1,998	2,278
2008	2,030	2,263
2009	2,172	2,288
2010	2,191	2,309
2011	2,249	2,370
2012	2,310	2,349
2013	2,414	2,414

(1) Assumes retirement at beginning of year.

Amount of Work Required

To qualify for benefits, the worker generally must have worked a certain length of time in covered employment. Just how long depends on when the worker reaches age 62 or, if earlier, when he or she dies or becomes disabled. A person born after 1929 who dies, becomes disabled, or reaches 62 after 1991 must generally have had at least 10 years of work credit to qualify for benefits.

Contribution and Benefit Base

Calendar year	OASDI[1]	Calendar year	OASDI[1]	Calendar year	OASDI[1]
1994	$60,600	2001	$80,400	2008	$102,000
1995	61,200	2002	84,900	2009	106,800
1996	62,700	2003	87,000	2010	106,800
1997	65,400	2004	87,900	2011	106,800
1998	68,400	2005	90,000	2012	110,100
1999	72,600	2006	94,200	2013	113,700
2000	76,200	2007	97,500		

(1) Old-Age, Survivors, and Disability Insurance.

A person is **fully insured** when he or she has one quarter of coverage for every year after age 21 is reached (or 1950, if later) up to but not including the year the worker reaches 62, dies, or becomes disabled. In 2013, a person earns one quarter of coverage for each $1,160 of annual earnings in covered employment, up to four quarters per year.

To receive **disability benefits**, the worker, in addition to being fully insured, must generally have credit for 20 quarters of coverage out of the 40 calendar quarters before he or she became disabled. A disabled blind worker need meet only the fully insured requirement. Persons disabled before age 31 can qualify with a briefer period of coverage. Certain survivor benefits are payable if the deceased worker had 6 quarters of coverage in the 13 quarters preceding death.

Tax Rate Schedule
(percentage of covered earnings)

Year	Total (for employees and employers, each)	OASDI[1]	HI[2]
1979-80	6.13%	5.08%	1.05%
1981	6.65	5.35	1.30
1982-83	6.70	5.40	1.30
1984	7.00	5.70	1.30
1985	7.05	5.70	1.35
1986-87	7.15	5.70	1.45
1988-89	7.51	6.06	1.45
1990 and after[3]	7.65	6.20	1.45

Year	(for self-employed)		
1979-80	8.10%	7.05%	1.05%
1981	9.30	8.00	1.30
1982-83	9.35	8.05	1.30
1984	14.00	11.40	2.60
1985	14.10	11.40	2.70
1986-87	14.30	11.40	2.90
1988-89	15.02	12.12	2.90
1990 and after[3]	15.30	12.40	2.90

(1) Old-Age, Survivors, and Disability Ins. (2) Hospital Ins. (Medicare). (3) Public Law 111-147 exempted most employers from paying the employer share of OASDI payroll tax on wages paid Mar. 19-Dec. 31, 2010, to certain qualified individuals hired after Feb. 3, 2010. PL 111-312 reduced the OASDI payroll tax rate for 2011 by 2 percentage points for employees and for self-employed workers. PL 112-96 extended the 2011 rate reduction through 2012. The laws require that the general fund of the Treasury reimburses the OASI and DI Trust Funds for these temporary reductions.

What Aged Workers Receive

A person may receive monthly old-age benefits when he or she has enough work in covered employment and has reached retirement age—age 62 for reduced benefits or the age below for full benefits.

Full Retirement Age (FRA) by Birth Year

Year of birth	FRA	Year of birth	FRA
1937 or earlier	65	1955	66 and 2 mos.
1938	65 and 2 mos.	1956	66 and 4 mos.
1939	65 and 4 mos.	1957	66 and 6 mos.
1940	65 and 6 mos.	1958	66 and 8 mos.
1941	65 and 8 mos.	1959	66 and 10 mos.
1942	65 and 10 mos.	1960 or	
1943-54	66	later	67

Note: If born on Jan. 1, refer to the previous birth year.

In 2000, the retirement earnings test was eliminated beginning with the month when the beneficiary reaches **full retirement age (FRA)**. A person at or above FRA no longer receives reduced benefits because of earnings. However, a person's benefits are reduced $1 for every $3 of earnings above the limit allowed by law ($40,080 for 2013) if he or she retires in the same calendar year but months prior to FRA. For retirees who have not yet attained FRA, the reduction is $1 for every $2 of earnings over the exempt amount ($15,120 for 2013).

For workers who reached age 65 between 1982 and 1989, Social Security benefits are raised by 3% for each year in which the worker did not receive benefits between FRA and 70 (72 before 1984), whether because of earnings from work, because the worker did not apply for benefits, or because the worker declined benefits after entitlement. The **delayed retirement credit** is 1% per year for workers who reached age 65 before 1982. The delayed retirement credit rose to 8% per year for 2008 and years after. The rate for workers who reached age 65 in 1998-99 is 5.5%; 2000-01, 6.0%; 2002-03, 6.5%; 2004-05, 7.0%. For 2006-07, it is 7.5%.

For workers retiring early, benefits are permanently reduced 5/9 of 1% for each month before the FRA, up to 36 months. If the number of months exceeds 36, then the benefit is further reduced 5/12 of 1% per month.

For example, when FRA reaches 67, for workers who retire at exactly age 62, there are a total of 60 months of reduction. The reduction for the first 36 months is 5/9 of 36%, or 20%. The reduction for the remaining 24 months is 5/12 of 24%, or 10%. Thus, when the FRA reaches 67, the amount of reduction at age 62 will be 30%. The nearer to FRA a person is when he or she begins collecting a benefit, the larger the monthly benefit will be.

Benefits for Worker's Spouse

The spouse of a worker who is getting Social Security retirement or disability payments may become entitled to an insurance benefit of **one-half of the worker's PIA** if claiming benefits at full retirement age. Reduced spouse's benefits are available at age 62 and are permanently reduced $^{25}/_{36}$ of 1% for each month before FRA, up to 36 months. If the number of months exceeds 36, then the benefit is further reduced $^5/_{12}$ of 1% per month. Benefits are also payable to the aged divorced spouse of an insured worker if he or she was married to the worker for at least 10 years. To qualify for divorced spouse benefits, the insured worker does not have to be receiving benefits if the divorce occurred at least two years earlier. Benefits received as a spouse are reduced by the amount of one's PIA.

Benefits for Children of Workers

If a retired or disabled worker has a child under age 18, the child will usually get a benefit equal to **one-half of the worker's unreduced benefit**. So will the worker's spouse, regardless of age, if he or she is caring for an entitled child of the worker, and the child is under 16 or became disabled before age 22. However, total benefits paid on a worker's earnings record are subject to a family maximum. Total monthly benefits paid to the family of a worker who retired in 2013 at age 66 and always had the maximum earnings creditable under Social Security cannot exceed $4,464.

Entitled children generally stop receiving benefits at age 18, though they can continue receiving benefits until age 19 if they attend elementary or secondary school full-time. A child disabled before age 22 may get a benefit as long as the disability meets the definition in the law.

Benefits may also be paid to a grandchild or step-grandchild of a worker or of his or her spouse, in special circumstances.

OASDI Beneficiaries

Beneficiaries	May 2005	May 2010	May 2012	May 2013
Total (in thous.)[1]	48,068	53,349	56,158	57,457
Age 65 and over, total. .	33,811	36,914	38,905	40,150
Retired workers.	27,413	30,734	32,714	33,999
Disabled workers . . .	112	339	453	452
Survivors/				
dependents	6,286	5,841	5,738	5,699
Under age 65, total . . .	14,257	16,435	17,253	17,307
Retired workers.	2,809	3,314	3,407	3,296
Disabled workers . . .	6,239	7,628	8,254	8,426
Survivors/				
dependents	5,209	5,492	5,592	5,584
Total monthly benefits (in mil)	**$42,074**	**$56,966**	**$63,243**	**$66,492**

OASDI = Old-Age, Survivors, and Disability Ins. (1) Numbers may not add up to totals due to rounding or incomplete enumeration.

What Disabled Workers Receive

A worker who becomes unable to work may be eligible for a monthly disability benefit. Benefits continue until it is determined that the individual is no longer disabled. When a disabled-worker beneficiary reaches FRA (66 years for workers born 1943-54), the disability benefit becomes a retired-worker benefit.

Benefits—like those for dependents of retired-worker beneficiaries generally—may be paid to dependents of disabled beneficiaries. However, the maximum family benefit in disability cases is generally lower than in retirement cases.

Survivor Benefits

If an insured worker should die, one or more types of benefits may be payable to survivors, again subject to a maximum family benefit described above.

1. If claiming benefits at FRA, the **surviving spouse** will receive a benefit equal to 100% of the deceased worker's benefit. Benefits claimed before FRA are reduced, with a maximum reduction of 28.5% at age 60. However, if the deceased worker claimed benefits before FRA, the surviving spouse's benefits are limited to the reduced amount the worker would be getting if alive, but not less than 82.5% of the worker's PIA. Remarriage after the worker's death ends the surviving spouse's benefit rights. However, if the widow(er) marries, and the marriage later ends, he or she regains benefit rights.

(A marriage after age 60, age 50 if disabled, is deemed not to have occurred for benefit purposes.) Survivor benefits may also be paid to a divorced spouse if the marriage lasted for at least 10 years.

Disabled widows and widowers may under certain circumstances qualify for benefits after attaining age 50 at the rate of 71.5% of the deceased worker's PIA. The widow or widower must have become totally disabled before or within seven years after the spouse's death or the last month in which he or she received mother's or father's insurance benefits.

2. There is a benefit for each **child under age 18**. The monthly benefit for a child of a deceased worker is $^3/_4$ of the PIA, subject to the family maximum. A child who became disabled before age 22 may also qualify for benefits. Also, a child can receive benefits until age 19 if he or she is in full-time attendance at an elementary or secondary school.

3. There is a **mother's or father's benefit** for the widow(er) if children of the worker who are under age 16 are in his or her care. The benefit is 75% of the PIA (subject to the family maximum), and it continues until the youngest child reaches age 16, at which time payments stop even if the child's benefit continues. Benefits may continue if the widow(er) has a disabled child beneficiary age 16 or over in his or her care.

4. Dependent parents may be eligible for benefits if they have been receiving at least half their support from the worker before his or her death, have reached age 62, and (except in certain circumstances) have not remarried since the worker's death. Each parent gets 75% of the worker's PIA; if only one parent survives, the benefit is 82% (could be reduced for the family maximum).

5. A lump sum cash payment of **$255** is made if the worker was living with a spouse or has a child who is eligible for immediate monthly survivor benefits.

Self-Employed Workers

A self-employed person who has **net earnings of $400 or more** in a year must report such earnings for Social Security tax and credit purposes. Income from real estate, savings, dividends, loans, pensions, or insurance policies are not included unless it is part of a person's business.

A self-employed person receives one quarter of coverage for each $1,160 for 2013, up to a maximum of four quarters per year.

The nonfarm self-employed have the option of reporting their earnings as $^2/_3$ of their gross income from self-employment. This option can be used only if actual net earnings from self-employment income are less than $1,600 and less than $^2/_3$ of their gross income. The option may be used only five times. Also, the self-employed person must have actual net earnings of $400 or more in two of the three taxable years immediately preceding the year in which he or she uses the option.

When a person has both taxable wages and earnings from self-employment, wages are credited for Social Security purposes first; only as much self-employment income as brings total earnings up to the current taxable maximum becomes subject to the self-employment tax.

Farm Owners and Workers

Self-employed farmers whose gross annual earnings from farming are from **$600 to $2,400** may report $^2/_3$ of their gross earnings instead of net earnings for Social Security purposes. (Farmers whose gross annual earnings are under $600 cannot use the optional method.) Farmers whose gross income is over $2,400 and whose net earnings are less than $1,600 can report $1,600. Cash or crop shares received from a tenant or share farmer count if the owner participated materially in production or management. The self-employed farmer pays contributions at the same rate as other self-employed persons.

Agricultural employees. A worker's earnings from farm work count toward benefits if (1) the employer pays the worker $150 or more in cash during the year or (2) the employer spends $2,500 or more in the year for agricultural labor. Under these rules, a person gets credit for one calendar quarter for each $1,160 in cash pay in 2013.

Foreign farm workers admitted to the U.S. on a temporary basis are not covered.

Household Workers

If an employer pays a household worker (e.g., maid, cook, laundry worker, nurse, babysitter, chauffeur, gardener) who is age 18 or older **$1,800 or more** in wages in 2013, the wages are covered under Social Security. This includes transportation costs paid for in cash. The job need not be regular or full-time.

The employee should get a Social Security card at the Social Security office and show it to the employer. The employer deducts the amount of the employee's Social Security tax from the worker's pay, adds an identical amount as the employer's Social Security tax, and sends the total amount to the federal government.

Medicare Coverage

The Medicare health insurance program provides acute-care coverage for Social Security and Railroad Retirement beneficiaries age 65 and over; workers and spouses age 65 and over with sufficient Medicare-only coverage in federal, state, or local government employment; certain persons entitled to receive Social Security or Railroad Retirement disability benefits; certain disabled persons with Medicare-only coverage through government employment; certain persons with end-stage kidney disease; and certain persons in the vicinity of Libby, MT, with asbestos-related conditions. What follows is a basic description that may not cover all circumstances.

The **basic Medicare plan**, available nationwide, is a fee-for-service arrangement where the beneficiary may use any provider accepting Medicare. Some services are not covered, and there are some out-of-pocket costs.

Hospital insurance (Part A). The basic hospital insurance program pays covered services for hospital and post-hospital care, including:

* All necessary inpatient hospital care for the first 60 days of each benefit period, except for a deductible ($1,184 in 2013). For days 61-90, Medicare pays for services over and above the coinsurance ($296 per day in 2013). After 90 days, the beneficiary has 60 lifetime reserve days for which Medicare helps pay. The coinsurance amount for reserve days was $592 in 2013.
* Up to 100 days of care in a skilled-nursing facility in each benefit period. Hospital insurance pays for all covered services for the first 20 days; for days 21-100, the beneficiary pays coinsurance ($148 per day in 2013).
* Part-time home health care provided by nurses or other health workers.
* Limited coverage of hospice care for terminally ill.

There is a premium for this insurance in certain—but not most—cases.

Medical insurance (Part B). Eligible elderly and disabled persons can receive benefits under this supplementary program only if they sign up and agree to a monthly premium. As of 2007, the monthly premium is tied to annual income. Individuals with an income of $85,000 or less and couples with an income of $170,000 or less pay $104.90 per person if they sign up upon becoming eligible in 2013. Part B covers certain medical services and supplies, including:

* Physicians' and surgeons' services, as well as some services furnished by other medical professionals.
* Services in an emergency room, outpatient clinic, or ambulatory surgical center.
* Home health care not covered under Part A.
* Laboratory tests, X-rays, and other diagnostic radiology services.
* Certain preventative care services and screening tests.
* Most physical and occupational therapy and speech pathology services.
* Comprehensive outpatient rehabilitation facility services and mental health care in a partial hospitalization psychiatric program, if inpatient care would otherwise be required.
* Radiation therapy, renal (kidney) dialysis and transplants, heart, lung, heart-lung, liver, pancreas, bone marrow, and intestinal transplants.
* Approved durable medical equipment for home use.
* Drugs that are not usually self-administered. Certain services for diabetes.
* Ambulance services when other transportation methods are contraindicated.
* Rural health clinic and health center services, including some telemedicine.

Part B services are generally subject to a deductible ($147 in 2013), coinsurance (generally 20% of the remaining allowed charges with certain exceptions), a deductible for blood, and amounts above the allowed charge if a doctor or supplier does not accept the Medicare-approved rate as payment in full. For outpatient mental health services, coinsurance is being phased from 50% to 20% of allowed charges over the period 2010-14. For outpatient hospital services, coinsurance varies by service, usually falling between 20% and 50% of allowed charges. There are no deductibles or coinsurance for certain services, such as clinical lab tests, home health agency services (except some durable medical equipment, which is subject to 20% coinsurance), and some preventative care services. Payments for certain physical, speech, and occupational therapy services are subject to certain limits. Dental care, hearing aids, and routine eye care are generally not covered under the basic plan.

To get medical insurance (Part B), persons approaching age 65 may enroll during the seven-month initial enrollment period, which includes the month of their 65th birthday as well as the three months before and after. If new enrollees desire coverage to begin in the month they reach age 65, they must enroll in the three months before their birthday. Persons who enroll after their initial enrollment period may be subject to late-enrollment premiums.

The monthly premium is deducted from the cash benefit for persons receiving Social Security, Railroad Retirement, or Civil Service Retirement benefits. Income from the medical premiums and the federal matching payments are put in a Supplementary Medical Insurance Trust Fund, from which benefits and administrative expenses are paid.

Medicare Advantage (Part C) (formerly Medicare+Choice). Persons eligible for Medicare may have the option of getting services through a Medicare-certified local coordinated care plan, such as a health maintenance organization (HMO), local preferred provider organization (PPO), provider-sponsored organization (PSO), or other local Medicare-certified **managed care** plan, or through a regional preferred provider organization (RPPO). Any such plan must provide at least the same benefits as Parts A and B, except for hospice services. They may provide added benefits (such as vision or hearing coverage) or reduce cost sharing or premiums. Enrollees may be required to use the plan's network of participating providers or pay higher out-of-pocket costs to go outside the network. Also available as options in some areas are Medicare-approved private fee-for-service plans and, for certain beneficiaries, special needs plans.

Prescription Drug Coverage (Part D). Effective Jan. 1, 2006, a Medicare prescription drug plan provides insurance coverage for prescription drugs. Medicare recipients pay a monthly premium (averaging about $30 in 2013, depending on the provider) and a portion of drug costs. Enrollment is scheduled to take place Oct. 15-Dec. 7 and is optional. Coverage varies depending on the drug plan selected.

Further details are available on the Internet at www.medicare.gov or by calling 1-800-MEDICARE (1-800-633-4227).

Medicare card. Persons qualifying for hospital insurance under Social Security receive a health insurance card. The card indicates whether the individual has taken out medical insurance protection. It is to be shown to the hospital, skilled-nursing facility, home health agency, doctor, or whoever provides the covered services.

Payments are generally made only in the 50 states, Puerto Rico, U.S. Virgin Isls., Guam, American Samoa, and N. Mariana Isls.

Social Security Financing

Social Security is paid for by a tax on certain earnings (for 2013, on earnings up to $113,700) for **Old-Age, Survivors, and Disability Insurance (OASDI)** and on all earnings (no upper limit) for hospital insurance with the **Medicare** program; the taxable earnings base for OASDI is adjusted annually to reflect changes in average wages. The employed worker and his or her employer share Social Security taxes equally.

Employers remit amounts withheld from employee wages for Social Security and income taxes to the Internal Revenue Service; employer Social Security taxes are also payable at the same time. (Self-employed workers pay Social Security taxes when filing their regular income tax forms.) The Social Security taxes (along with revenues arising from partial taxation of the Social Security benefits of certain high-income people) are transferred to the Social Security Trust Funds; they can be used only to pay benefits, the cost of rehabilitation services, and administrative expenses. By law, money not immediately needed for those purposes is invested in obligations of the federal government, which must pay interest on the money borrowed and must repay the principal when the obligations are redeemed or mature.

On Jan. 1, 1974, the **Supplemental Security Income (SSI)** program, established by the Social Security Amendments of 1972, replaced federal grants to states for aid to the needy aged, blind, and disabled in the 50 states and the District of Columbia. The program provides for federal payments, based on uniform national standards and eligibility requirements, and for state supplementary payments, which vary by state. The Social Security Administration administers the federal payments—financed by general funds of the Treasury—as well as the state supplement for those states that choose to have it federally administered. States may supplement the federal payment of all recipients and must supplement it for persons otherwise adversely affected by the transition from the former public assistance programs. In May 2013, the number of persons receiving federally administered SSI payments was 8,311,121; the payments totaled about $4.6 bil.

The **maximum monthly federal SSI payment** for individuals without an eligible spouse and with no other countable income, living in their own household, was $710 in 2013. For couples where both members were eligible, the maximum payment was $1,066.

For further information, contact the Social Security Administration toll-free at 1-800-772-1213 or visit its website at www.socialsecurity.gov.

Examples of Monthly Social Security Benefits Available, 2013

Benefit or beneficiary	For low earnings[1]	For med. earnings[1]	For max. earnings[1,2]
Primary insurance amount (worker retiring at 66 years, 0 months) ..	$965.60	$1,590.40	$2,533.50
Maximum family benefit (worker retiring at 66 years, 0 months).....	1,448.50	2,904.90	4,434.60
Maximum family disability benefit (worker disabled at 55; in 2013) ..	1,391.40	2,434.80	3,879.40
Disabled worker (worker disabled at 55):			
Worker alone...	982.60	1,623.20	2,586.30
Worker, spouse, and 1 child	1,391.40	2,434.80	3,879.30
Retired worker claiming benefits at age 62:			
Worker alone[3]	730.70	1,203.20	1,912.50
Worker with spouse claiming benefits at—			
FRA or over..	1,217.80	2,005.30	3,187.50
Age 62[3]	1,071.60	1,764.60	2,805.00
Widow or widower claiming benefits at—			
Age 66 or over[4]..	965.60	1,590.40	2,533.50
Age 60[4]	694.20	1,143.40	1,821.50
Disabled widow or widower claiming benefits at age 50-59[5]	690.40	1,137.10	1,811.40
1 surviving child[4]	724.20	1,192.80	1,900.10
Widow or widower at FRA or over and 1 child[4]..................	1,448.50	2,783.20	4,433.60
Widowed mother or father and 1 child[4].......................	1,448.40	2,385.60	3,800.20
Widowed mother or father and 2 children[4]	1,448.40	2,904.90	4,434.60

FRA = Full retirement age. **Note:** Effective Jan. 2013. (1) Career average earnings: an average of lifetime earnings indexed to the year prior to entitlement (2012 in this case). (2) Assumes work beginning at age 22. (3) Assumes maximum reduction. (4) Assumes worker lived and worked until FRA without receiving reduced benefits. (5) Effective Jan. 1984, disabled widow(er) claiming a benefit at age 50-59 receives a benefit equal to 71.5% of the primary insurance amount.

Social Security Recipients by Age, Sex, Race, and Hispanic Origin, 2012
Source: Social Security Administration

Characteristic/benefit	Total[2]	White	Black	American Indian, Alaska Native	Asian	Hispanic
Social Security beneficiaries (thous.)[1]	**46,931**	**40,422**	**4,846**	**695**	**1,388**	**3,314**
Sex						
Male......................................	20,830	18,119	1,962	307	607	1,511
Female	26,101	22,303	2,885	388	782	1,803
Age						
15-54 years...............................	5,257	4,064	969	205	158	557
55-64 years...............................	6,505	5,332	912	124	191	555
65-74 years...............................	18,886	16,417	1,752	232	613	1,292
75 years or older...........................	16,283	14,610	1,214	133	426	910
Supplemental Security Income recipients (thous.)[1] ..	**6,118**	**4,036**	**1,614**	**235**	**357**	**989**
Sex						
Male......................................	2,571	1,704	695	86	129	417
Female	3,547	2,332	920	149	228	571
Age						
15-54 years...............................	3,413	2,268	972	157	105	535
55-64 years...............................	1,408	947	379	51	49	199
65-74 years...............................	691	431	159	12	98	135
75 years or older...........................	606	390	104	14	105	120
Average annual benefit in 2011 (dollars)						
Social Security	$13,327	$13,514	$12,092	$11,693	$12,435	$11,155
Supplemental Security Income	7,371	7,467	7,190	7,106	7,024	7,190

Note: Race categories include people who reported being of that race, alone or in combination with another race. Persons of Hispanic origin may be of any race. (1) Persons 15 or older receiving Social Security benefits or Supplemental Security Income in Mar. 2012. (2) The sum of the individual categories may not add up to totals because of rounding and because the totals include persons who reported being of more than one race.

OASDI Recipients and Monthly Payments, 1940-2012

Source: Social Security Administration

Year	Total recipients	Monthly benefits Total (thous.)	Avg.[1]	Avg. (2012 dollars)[2]	Year	Total recipients	Monthly benefits Total (thous.)	Avg.[1]	Avg. (2012 dollars)[2]
1940	222,488	$4,070	$18.29	$293.29	1995	43,387,259	$28,148,078	$648.76	$979.52
1945	1,288,107	23,801	18.48	230.97	2000	45,414,794	34,848,920	767.35	1,027.31
1950	3,477,243	126,857	36.48	340.97	2005	48,434,445	44,351,772	915.71	1,084.17
1955	7,960,616	411,613	51.71	433.85	2006	49,122,831	46,938,176	955.53	1,095.96
1960	14,844,589	936,321	63.07	479.35	2007	49,864,982	49,218,232	987.03	1,101.22
1965	20,866,767	1,516,802	72.69	518.35	2008	50,898,396	53,666,202	1,054.38	1,130.20
1970	26,228,629	2,628,326	100.21	580.62	2009	52,522,819	55,905,731	1,064.41	1,148.69
1975	32,085,372	5,727,903	178.52	745.66	2010	54,032,097	58,048,364	1,074.33	1,135.90
1980	35,618,840	10,694,022	300.23	818.62	2011	55,404,480	62,213,382	1,122.89	1,146.48
1985	37,058,353	15,901,643	429.10	907.48	2012	56,758,185	65,430,104	1,122.89	1,152.79
1990	39,832,125	21,686,763	544.45	954.00					

OASDI = Old-Age, Survivors, and Disability Insurance. **Note:** Disability insurance payments began in 1957. (1) Avg. monthly benefit does not necessarily reflect individual payments to OASDI recipients. (2) Adjusted for inflation.

Social Security Trust Funds

Source: Social Security Administration

Old-Age and Survivors Insurance Trust Fund, 1940-2012

(in millions)

Fiscal year[1]	Total	INCOME Net payroll tax contribs.	Income from taxing benefits	General fund reimburse-ments[2]	Net interest[3]	Total	DISBURSEMENTS Benefit pymts.[4]	Admin. expenses	Transfers to Railroad Retirement program	Net increase in fund[5]	Year-end balance
1940	$592	$550	—	—	$42	$28	$16	$12	—	$564	$1,745
1950	2,367	2,106	—	$4	257	784	727	57	—	1,583	12,893
1960	10,360	9,843	—	—	517	11,073	10,270	202	$600	−713	20,829
1970	31,746	29,955	—	442	1,350	27,321	26,268	474	579	4,425	32,616
1980	100,051	97,608	—	557	1,886	103,228	100,626	1,160	1,442	−3,177	24,566
1990	278,607	260,069	$2,924	1,471	14,143	223,481	218,948	1,564	2,969	55,126	203,445
1995	326,067	289,525	5,114	11	31,417	294,456	288,607	1,797	4,052	31,611	447,946
2000	484,228	418,219	12,476	1	53,532	353,396	347,868	1,990	3,538	130,832	893,003
2005	599,992	502,998	15,332	—	81,662	436,919	430,439	2,900	3,579	163,073	1,615,623
2006	632,157	530,006	15,176	−350	87,324	455,560	449,191	2,911	3,458	176,597	1,792,220
2007	603,376	553,414	16,661	—	93,300	488,553	481,828	3,151	3,575	174,822	1,967,042
2008	692,873	573,750	16,396	—	102,727	509,864	502,973	3,259	3,632	183,009	2,150,052
2009	697,326	571,228	18,967	—	107,131	551,542	544,484	3,369	3,690	145,784	2,295,835
2010	682,448	552,037	21,068	737	108,606	579,907	572,515	3,462	3,930	102,541	2,398,377
2011	692,510	495,031	21,174	68,886	107,419	599,232	591,477	3,645	4,110	93,278	2,491,654
2012	728,981	500,661	27,150	95,927	105,243	634,700	627,208	3,352	4,139	94,281	2,585,936

Note: Numbers may not add up to totals due to rounding. (1) Fiscal years 1977 and later consist of the 12 months ending on Sept. 30 of each year. Fiscal years prior to 1977 consisted of the 12 months ending on June 30 of each year. (2) Includes reimbursements from the general fund of the Treasury to the OASI Trust Fund for certain legislated measures since 1957. (3) Includes net profits or losses on marketable investments. Beginning in 1967, the trust fund paid administrative expenses on an estimated basis, with a final adjustment including interest made in the following fiscal year. Net interest includes these interest adjustments. Beginning in Oct. 1973, figures include relatively small gifts to the fund. (4) Beginning in 1967, includes payments for vocational rehabilitation services furnished to disabled persons receiving benefits because of their disabilities; beginning in 1983, includes reimbursements paid from the general fund to the trust fund for unnegotiated benefit checks. (5) Net change in assets during fiscal year, including amounts borrowed or repaid by other funds.

Disability Insurance Trust Fund, 1960-2012

(in millions)

Fiscal year[1]	Total	INCOME Net payroll tax contribs.	Income from taxing benefits	General fund reimburse-ments[2]	Net interest[3]	Total	DISBURSEMENTS Benefit pymts.[4]	Admin. expenses	Transfers to Railroad Retirement program	Net increase in fund[5]	Year-end balance
1960	$1,034	$987	—	—	$47	$533	$528	$32	−$27	$501	$2,167
1970	4,380	4,141	—	$16	223	2,954	2,795	149	10	1,426	5,104
1980	17,376	16,805	—	118	453	15,320	14,998	334	−12	2,056	7,680
1990	28,215	27,154	$158	138	766	25,124	24,327	717	80	3,091	11,455
1995	70,209	67,986	335	—	1,888	41,374	40,234	1,072	68	28,835	35,206
2000	77,023	70,001	756	—	6,266	56,008	54,244	1,608	159	21,014	113,752
2005	96,765	85,418	1,164	—	10,183	86,360	83,721	2,301	338	10,405	193,298
2006	101,571	90,001	1,174	—	10,396	92,932	90,064	2,480	388	8,640	201,938
2007	108,396	93,973	1,351	—	13,072	96,758	93,955	2,357	445	11,638	213,577
2008	109,816	97,432	1,373	8	11,003	107,153	104,222	2,513	418	2,663	216,239
2009	109,681	97,008	1,841	—	10,832	118,144	115,073	2,623	448	−8,462	207,777
2010	105,513	93,739	1,745	125	9,904	126,344	122,935	2,947	462	−20,831	186,946
2011	106,225	84,031	1,878	11,745	8,571	131,449	127,990	3,034	465	−25,264	161,682
2012	108,845	85,072	383	16,234	7,156	138,546	135,114	2,920	512	−29,701	131,981

Note: Numbers may not add up to totals due to rounding. (1) Fiscal years 1977 and later consist of the 12 months ending on Sept. 30 of each year. Fiscal years prior to 1977 consisted of the 12 months ending on June 30 of each year. (2) Includes reimbursements from the general fund of the Treasury to the DI Trust Fund for certain legislated measures since 1957. (3) Includes net profits or losses on marketable investments. Beginning in 1967, the trust fund paid administrative expenses on an estimated basis, with a final adjustment including interest made in the following fiscal year. Net interest includes these interest adjustments. The 1970 report describes the accounting for administrative expenses for years prior to 1967. Beginning in July 1974, figures include relatively small gifts to the fund. (4) Beginning in 1967, includes payments for vocational rehabilitation services furnished to persons receiving benefits because of a disability; beginning in 1983, includes reimbursements paid from the general fund to the trust fund for unnegotiated benefit checks. (5) Net change in assets during fiscal year, including amounts borrowed or repaid by other funds.

Supplementary Medical Insurance Trust Fund (Medicare SMI), 1975-2012

Source: Centers for Medicare & Medicaid Services, Dept. of Health and Human Services

(in millions)

Fiscal year[1]	INCOME					DISBURSEMENTS			Net change	Year-end balance[9]
	Total	Premium from participants[2]	Govt. contribs.[3]	Transfers from states[4]	Interest and other income[5,6]	Total	Benefit pymts.[6,7,8]	Admin. expenses		
1975	$4,322	$1,887	$2,330	—	$106	$4,170	$3,765	$404	$152	$1,424
1980	10,275	2,928	6,932	—	416	10,737	10,144	593	-462	4,532
1990	46,138[10]	11,494[10]	33,210	—	1,434[10]	43,022[10]	41,498	1,524[10]	3,115[10]	14,527[10]
1995	58,169	19,244	36,988	—	1,937	65,213	63,491	1,722	-7,044	13,874
2000	89,239	20,515	65,561	—	3,164	88,992	87,212[11]	1,780	247	45,896
2005	152,505	35,939	115,200	—	1,366	152,735	149,820[12]	2,914	-230	16,885
2006	211,951	44,241[13]	162,601	$3,630	1,478	195,557	192,083[12,13]	3,474	16,394	33,279
2007	237,890	49,666[13]	179,181	6,977	2,065	232,022	228,596[12,13]	3,426	5,867	39,146
2008	244,872	54,158[13]	180,434	7,042	3,238	224,869	221,445[13,14]	3,423	20,003	59,149
2009	262,573	57,709[13]	194,267	7,504	3,093	260,257	256,938[13]	3,318	2,317	61,466
2010	282,734	61,364[13]	213,709	4,493	3,168	272,224	268,710[13]	3,514	10,510	71,976
2011	301,523	64,502[13]	225,178	6,536	5,307	300,672	296,842[13]	3,830	851	72,827
2012	290,850	66,053[13]	210,508	8,324	5,965	291,893	287,763[13]	4,130	-1,043	71,783

Note: Numbers may not add up to totals because of rounding. (1) Fiscal year 1975 consists of the 12 months ending on June 30, 1975; fiscal years 1980 and later consist of the 12 months ending on Sept. 30 of each year. (2) For Part D, premiums include both amounts withheld from Social Security benefit checks (and certain other federal benefit payments) and amounts paid directly to Part D plans (estimated). (3) For Part B, includes matching payments from the general fund, plus certain interest-adjustment items. For Part D, includes all federal govt. transfers. (4) As of 2006, Medicaid is no longer the primary payer for full-benefit dual eligibles; states pay 90% of estimated costs. (5) Other income includes recoveries of amounts reimbursed from the trust fund that are not trust fund obligations and other miscellaneous income. In 2008, includes an adjustment of $812 mil for interest inadvertently unearned as a result of HI hospice costs misallocated to, and paid from, the Part B account of the SMI trust fund May 2005-Sept. 2007. (6) Values after 2005 include additional premiums for Medicare Advantage (MA) plans that are deducted from beneficiaries' Social Security checks, transferred to Hospital Insurance (HI) and SMI trust funds, and then transferred to the plans. (7) Includes costs of Peer Review Organizations in 1983-2001 and costs of Quality Review Organizations beginning in 2002. (8) For Part D, includes payments to plans, subsidies to employer-sponsored retiree drug plans, payments to states for low-income eligibility determinations, and Part D drug premiums (the amount collected from beneficiaries and transferred to plans and an estimated amount for premiums paid directly by enrollees to plans). Includes amounts for transitional assistance benefits in 2004-06. (9) The financial status of SMI depends on the trust fund's assets and liabilities. (10) Includes the impact of the Medicare Catastrophic Coverage Act of 1988. (11) Benefit payments less monies transferred from the HI trust fund for home health agency costs. (12) Certain HI hospice costs were misallocated to, and paid from, the Part B account of the SMI trust fund. See also footnote 14. (13) Includes an estimated $1.804 bil (2006), $2.295 bil (2007), $2.970 bil (2008), $3.699 bil (2009), $4.221 bil (2010), $4.843 bil (2011), and $5.209 bil (2012) for premiums paid directly to Part D plans. (14) Benefit payments were $229.9 bil; amount shown does not include $8.5 bil transferred from the general fund of the Treasury for HI hospice costs that were misallocated to, and paid from, the Part B account of the SMI trust fund from May 2005 to Sept. 2007. (The HI trust fund, in turn, transferred $8.5 bil to the general fund.)

Hospital Insurance Trust Fund (Medicare HI), 1975-2012

Source: Centers for Medicare & Medicaid Services, Dept. of Health and Human Services

(in millions)

Fiscal year[1]	INCOME								DISBURSEMENTS			Net change	Year-end balance
	Total	Payroll taxes	Taxation of benefits	Transfers from Railroad Retirement acct.	Reimb. for uninsured persons	Premiums from voluntary enrollees	Pymts. for military wage credits	Interest and other income[2,3]	Total	Benefit pymts.[3,4]	Admin. expenses[5]		
1975	$12,568	$11,291	—	$132	$481	$6	$48	$609	$10,612	$10,353	$259	$1,956	$9,870
1980	25,415	23,244	—	244	697	17	141	1,072	24,288	23,790	497	1,127	14,490
1990	79,563	70,655	—	367	413	113	107	7,908	66,687	65,912	774	12,876	95,631
1995	114,847	98,053	$3,913	396	462	998	61	10,963	114,883	113,583	1,300	-36	129,520
2000	159,681	137,738	8,787	465	470	1,392	2	10,827	130,284	127,934[6]	2,350	29,397	168,084
2005	196,921	168,954	8,765	445	286	2,303	0	16,168	184,142	181,292[7]	2,850	12,779	277,723
2006	210,309	180,392	10,319	471	408	2,632	0	16,086	184,901	181,815[7]	3,086	25,408	303,130
2007	219,207	187,992	10,593	483	468	2,761	0	16,910	202,827	200,191[7]	2,636	16,380	319,510
2008	229,729	197,195	11,733	526	506	2,913	0	16,856	230,240	227,008[8]	3,231	-511	319,000
2009	228,915	194,102	12,376	524	614	2,817	968[9]	17,514	238,001	234,659	3,343	-9,086	309,914
2010	218,004	183,603	13,760	535	-142	3,314	0	16,933	248,978	245,650	3,328	-30,975	278,939
2011	226,486	192,063	15,143	477	275	3,273	0	15,255	259,628	255,717	3,911	-33,142	245,797
2012	241,760	204,752	18,643	511	262	3,400	0	14,162	258,155	254,459	3,696	-16,425	229,372

Note: Numbers may not add up to totals because of rounding. (1) Fiscal year 1975 consists of the 12 months ending on June 30, 1975; fiscal years 1980 and later consist of the 12 months ending on Sept. 30 of each year. (2) Other income includes recoveries of amounts reimbursed from the trust fund that are not trust fund obligations, receipts from the fraud and abuse control program, and other small amounts of miscellaneous income. In 2008, includes an adjustment of -$853 mil for interest inadvertently earned as a result of HI hospice costs that were misallocated to, and paid from, the Part B account of the Supplementary Advantage Medical Insurance (SMI) trust fund from May 2005 to Sept. 2007. (3) Values after 2005 include additional premiums for Medicare Advantage (MA) plans that are deducted from beneficiaries' Social Security checks, transferred to the HI and SMI trust funds, and then transferred to the plans. (4) Includes costs of Peer Review Organizations from 1983 through 2001 (beginning with implementation of the Prospective Payment System on Oct. 1, 1983), and costs of Quality Improvement Organizations beginning in 2002. (5) Includes costs of experiments and demonstration projects. Beginning in 1997, includes fraud and abuse control expenses. (6) Includes monies transferred to the SMI trust fund for home health agency costs. (7) Certain HI hospice costs were misallocated to, and paid from, the Part B account of the SMI trust fund. (8) Benefit payments were $218.5 bil. Amount shown includes transfer of $8.484 bil to the general fund of the Treasury for HI hospice costs that were misallocated to, and paid from, the Part B account of the SMI trust fund from May 2005 to Sept. 2007. (The general fund, in turn, transferred $8.484 bil to the Part B account.) (9) Includes the lump-sum general revenue adjustment of -$968 mil.

Temporary Assistance for Needy Families (TANF), 2010

Source: Office of Family Assistance, Admin. for Children and Families, U.S. Dept. of Health and Human Services

State/territory	Total federal and state TANF expenditures, 2010[1]	2010 average monthly expenditure per— Family	Recipient	2010 average monthly number of— Families	Recipients	Children
Alabama	$191,087	$750.39	$310.84	21,221	51,228	38,019
Alaska	61,678	1,555.17	558.80	3,305	9,198	6,374
Arizona	350,059	898.33	426.72	32,473	68,362	51,473
Arkansas	232,779	2,269.60	999.14	8,547	19,415	14,019
California	7,238,867	1,047.02	414.03	576,151	1,456,979	1,129,407
Colorado	323,266	2,338.24	901.42	11,521	29,885	22,294
Connecticut	500,225	2,414.02	1,219.05	17,268	34,195	24,332
Delaware	74,570	1,204.53	553.31	5,159	11,231	8,800
Dist. of Columbia	251,234	2,394.07	1,058.29	8,745	19,783	14,266
Florida	900,886	1,288.44	701.91	58,267	106,956	85,739
Georgia	563,258	2,281.88	1,244.55	20,570	37,715	34,106
Guam	NA	NA	NA	1,257	3,757	2,957
Hawaii	377,776	3,490.17	1,247.08	9,020	25,244	17,076
Idaho	34,772	1,673.96	1,094.27	1,731	2,648	2,461
Illinois	1,254,679	4,712.30	2,220.26	22,188	47,092	39,656
Indiana	343,572	790.61	314.73	36,214	90,969	67,255
Iowa	193,662	900.33	354.19	17,925	45,564	30,953
Kansas	206,622	1,180.32	461.48	14,588	37,311	25,167
Kentucky	280,819	774.66	386.73	30,209	60,511	47,170
Louisiana	263,506	2,072.96	953.82	10,593	23,022	19,802
Maine	141,372	1,068.96	457.09	11,021	25,774	17,140
Maryland	563,872	1,915.82	809.57	24,527	58,042	43,031
Massachusetts	1,021,678	1,727.01	903.53	49,299	94,230	63,465
Michigan	1,703,006	2,079.89	803.99	68,233	176,517	127,731
Minnesota	475,283	1,727.15	797.43	22,932	49,668	37,465
Mississippi	105,666	728.21	346.55	12,092	25,409	18,685
Missouri	404,574	943.64	496.00	35,728	67,973	41,389
Montana	47,291	1,050.08	410.60	3,753	9,598	6,690
Nebraska	98,456	1,042.00	431.73	7,874	19,004	15,057
Nevada	108,254	878.48	339.75	10,269	26,552	19,518
New Hampshire	86,261	1,351.72	652.48	5,318	11,017	8,058
New Jersey	1,445,745	3,600.47	1,478.21	33,462	81,503	57,883
New Mexico	237,088	997.99	378.01	19,797	52,266	37,081
New York	5,346,657	3,974.92	1,638.55	121,242	271,920	206,191
North Carolina	563,445	1,918.75	975.07	24,471	48,154	40,239
North Dakota	36,885	1,510.46	592.59	2,035	5,187	3,883
Ohio	1,331,348	1,076.84	470.50	103,029	235,803	170,131
Oklahoma	178,999	1,584.34	599.64	9,415	24,876	20,781
Oregon	391,635	1,204.56	471.38	27,094	69,235	48,349
Pennsylvania	964,229	1,548.72	645.47	51,883	124,487	93,533
Puerto Rico	NA	NA	NA	13,003	34,874	23,531
Rhode Island	148,626	1,664.05	708.96	7,443	17,470	11,989
South Carolina	179,919	811.28	318.88	18,481	47,019	32,518
South Dakota	30,853	795.75	381.18	3,231	6,745	5,703
Tennessee	338,332	459.62	182.78	61,343	154,254	111,049
Texas	908,117	1,480.98	653.15	51,099	115,864	99,874
Utah	131,859	1,654.11	753.50	6,643	14,583	10,702
Vermont	78,080	2,249.10	1,028.07	2,893	6,329	4,480
Virgin Islands	NA	NA	NA	519	1,499	1,062
Virginia	298,535	716.14	319.16	34,739	77,947	56,110
Washington	1,494,308	1,898.75	783.50	65,583	158,936	110,002
West Virginia	198,862	1,701.95	797.68	9,737	20,775	15,714
Wisconsin	523,552	2,011.96	877.27	21,685	49,733	38,943
Wyoming	29,373	7,485.41	3,647.88	327	671	547
Totals by year						
2010 totals	33,255,476	1,500.30	634.89	1,847,152	4,364,979	3,280,150
2009 totals	30,577,765	1,475.65	630.53	1,726,799	4,041,292	3,084,413
2008 totals	28,129,745	1,438.71	620.06	1,629,344	3,780,543	2,911,078
2007 totals	26,921,973	1,321.70	566.92	1,697,432	3,957,330	3,047,043
2006 totals	25,593,809	1,191.88	510.33	1,789,460	4,179,295	3,207,216
2005 totals	25,580,110	1,120.87	474.21	1,901,810	4,495,175	3,428,885
2004 totals	25,821,230	1,094.51	455.63	1,965,960	4,722,588	3,581,448
2003 totals	26,339,994	1,092.22	447.88	2,009,666	4,900,889	3,693,056
2002 totals	25,414,383	1,039.00	417.89	2,038,373	5,067,963	3,791,560
2001 totals	25,667,381	1,024.57	400.86	2,087,646	5,335,891	3,968,499
2000 totals	24,780,711	926.32	353.72	2,229,315	5,838,043	4,303,943
1999 totals	23,114,572	267.99	267.99	2,673,610	7,187,658	NA
1998 totals	22,036,420	208.91	208.91	3,199,700	8,790,149	NA
1997 totals	19,010,190	144.87	144.87	3,936,610	10,935,125	NA

NA = Not available. **Note:** Under 1996 legislation, the Aid to Families with Dependent Children (AFDC) program was converted to this state block-grant program. Covers period from previous Oct. to Sept. of fiscal years shown. (1) In thousands.

Adults Receiving TANF Funds by Employment Status, 2010

Source: Office of Family Assistance, Admin. for Children and Families, U.S. Dept. of Health and Human Services

State/terr.	Adults	Employed	State/terr.	Adults	Employed	State/terr.	Adults	Employed	State/terr.	Adults	Employed
AL	13,209	31.2%	IL	7,436	15.7%	NE	3,947	46.4%	SC	14,501	22.3%
AK	2,824	29.6	IN	23,714	24.5	NV	7,034	41.1	SD	1,042	17.9
AZ	16,889	14.5	IA	14,611	36.8	NH	2,959	24.3	TN	42,905	28.6
AR	5,396	25.8	KS	12,144	31.7	NJ	23,620	10.4	TX	15,990	30.6
CA	327,572	25.1	KY	13,341	22.7	NM	15,185	21.3	UT	3,881	14.9
CO	7,591	23.9	LA	3,220	23.9	NY	65,729	27.4	VT	1,849	20.3
CT	9,863	25.5	ME	8,634	18.2	NC	7,915	17.0	Virgin Isls.	437	3.7
DE	2,431	26.4	MD	15,011	12.9	ND	1,304	41.4	VA	21,837	25.3
DC	5,517	16.9	MA	30,765	8.8	OH	65,672	16.2	WA	48,934	13.2
FL	21,217	10.5	MI	48,786	22.0	OK	4,095	8.3	WV	5,061	14.9
GA	3,609	11.0	MN	12,203	31.1	OR	20,886	6.4	WI	10,790	18.9
Guam	800	3.3	MS	6,724	19.0	PA	30,954	36.8	WY	124	8.9
HA	8,168	39.3	MO	26,584	14.5	Puerto Rico	11,343	2.6	U.S.	1,084,828	22.3
ID	187	9.9	MT	2,908	30.8	RI	5,481	18.0			

NA = Not available. TANF = Temporary Assistance for Needy Families state block-grant program. **Note:** For fiscal year 2010; covers period from Oct. 2009 to Sept. 2010.

TAXES

Federal Personal Income Tax Return Facts, 2013

Source: George W. Smith III, CPA, Managing Partner, George W. Smith & Company, P.C.

Deadlines. The deadline for filing a 2013 U.S. individual income tax return (1040, 1040A, or 1040EZ) is Apr. 15, 2014.

Extensions. Individuals who cannot file their 2013 individual income tax return by the due date may apply for a six-month extension to Oct. 15, 2014. To qualify for an extension, Form 4868 must be filed no later than Apr. 15, 2014. Approximately 9 mil extensions were filed in 2013.

E-Filing. On June 10, 2011, the IRS announced that 1 bil individual tax returns had been processed since the electronic filing program began as a pilot program in 1986. For the tax period ending May 10, 2013, 113.9 mil returns were e-filed and received by the IRS.

Penalties. The IRS can levy two potential penalties after the filing due date when there is a balance owed. One penalty is for failing to file a timely tax return; the other is for failure to pay the tax when due. In addition, interest can be charged on any unpaid tax balance.

Refunds. For the tax period ending May 10, 2013, the average taxpayer refund was $2,651.

Statute of Limitations. Taxpayers who have not yet filed their 2010 federal tax return have until Apr. 15, 2014, to file and claim their refund. After that date any refunds for 2010 income tax or withholding tax, including the refundable earned income tax credit, will be lost.

Individual Federal Income Tax Rates and Brackets, 2013

Tax rate	Single	Married filing jointly or qualifying widow(er)	Married filing separately	Head of household
10%	$1 to $8,925	$1 to $17,850	$1 to $8,925	$1 to $12,750
15%	$8,926 to $36,250	$17,851 to $72,500	$8,926 to $36,250	$12,751 to $48,600
25%	$36,251 to $87,850	$72,501 to $146,400	$36,251 to $73,200	$48,601 to $125,450
28%	$87,851 to $183,250	$146,401 to $223,050	$73,201 to $111,525	$125,451 to $203,150
33%	$183,251 to $398,350	$223,051 to $398,350	$111,526 to $199,175	$203,151 to $398,350
35%	$398,351 to $400,000	$398,351 to $450,000	$199,176 to $225,000	$398,351 to $425,000
39.6%	More than $400,000	More than $450,000	More than $225,000	More than $425,000

Standard Deduction, 2013

The standard deduction is a flat dollar amount that is subtracted from the adjusted gross income of taxpayers who do not itemize deductions.

Single	$6,100
Married filing jointly or qualifying widow(er)	$12,200
Married filing separately	$6,100
Head of household	$8,950

Dependents. An individual reported as a dependent on another person's 2013 income tax return generally may claim on his or her own tax return the greater of $1,000 (up from $950) or $350 plus earned income (up from $300) not to exceed the regular standard deduction.

Additional Standard Deduction, 2013

Taxpayers in 2013 who do not itemize, are 65 or older, and/or blind may claim an additional standard deduction.

Single or head of household, 65 or older OR blind	$1,500
Single or head of household, 65 or older AND blind	$3,000
Married filing jointly or qualifying widow(er), 65 or older OR blind (per person)	$1,200
Married filing jointly or qualifying widow(er), 65 or older AND blind (per person)	$2,400
Married filing separately, 65 or older OR blind	$1,200
Married filing separately, 65 or older AND blind	$2,400

IRS Rulings on Deductions and Other Tax Matters

Auto Damage. Damage to a person's car may be a deductible casualty loss unless it was caused by the person's willful conduct, such as drunken driving.

Charitable Giving. Charitable donations of real estate and securities that result in long-term capital gains are deductible at fair market value. Donations also include tangible personal property such as furniture, books, jewelry, paintings, and cars.

Combat Pay. For enlisted personnel or warrant officers serving in a combat zone for any part of a month, all pay received for military service that month is not taxable. For officers, tax-free income is capped at the highest enlisted pay level plus any hostile-fire or imminent-danger pay.

Community Property. In community property states (Arizona, California, Idaho, Louisiana, Nevada, New Mexico, Texas, Washington, Wisconsin), each spouse or registered domestic partner is (usually) considered to own half the community property.

Counseling. Parent(s) of a child with psychological problems may deduct as a medical expense that part of a private school fee directly related to psychological aid given to the child.

Day Camp. The cost of day camps for children may qualify for the child care credit. The child must be under the age of 13, and the expenses must be incurred so the parent(s) can work.

Dependent Children. Dependent children can open IRAs and Roth IRAs as long as they have earned income from a job up to a maximum of $5,500. This is $500 more than 2012.

Estate Taxes. In general, after the death of an individual, federal estate tax returns only need to be filed for 2013 when a decedent's gross estate, plus adjusted taxable gifts and specific exemptions, is more than $5.25 mil.

First Jobs. Graduates may not deduct expenses for seeking their first job. First job expenses include auto rental, plane travel, lodging costs, and meals.

Frivolous Claims. Taxpayers may have to pay a penalty if they file an erroneous claim for refund or credit. The penalty for filing a frivolous individual income tax return is $5,000.

Garage Sales. Revenues received from a garage sale usually do not result in taxable income. In most cases, the items that were sold cost more than the revenue received. These losses are considered personal and, therefore, not deductible.

Investment Expenses. Investors may take a miscellaneous deduction on Schedule A, Form 1040, for financial newspapers, reports, and other expenses incurred in managing their investment portfolio. However, investors cannot deduct expenses for attending a convention, seminar, or similar meeting.

Mileage, Business. Beginning Jan. 1, 2013, the standard mileage rate for the use of a car, van, pickup, or panel truck is 56.5 cents per mile for business-miles driven. The business portion of parking fees and tolls may be deducted in addition to the mileage.

Mileage, Personal. The IRS mileage allowance deduction for moving and medical expenses is 24 cents per mile. The rate for volunteer work or charitable activities is 14 cents per mile. Charitable rates are set by Congress, not the IRS.

Parking Expenses. Reimbursement for parking expenses provided to an employee who commutes caps out at $245 per month.

Penalties. Penalties and fines paid to a governmental agency or department are not deductible. This includes parking and speeding tickets as well as penalties for late filing of a tax return.

Refunds. Not all taxpayers expecting a refund will necessarily receive one. If an individual owes taxes to the federal government, has failed to pay child support, or has unpaid

education loans, the IRS can take the individual's refund to satisfy the debt.

Sale of Residence. Married couples filing jointly who have lived in their principal residence for at least two years out of the last five can exclude up to $500,000 of the gain on its sale. Single taxpayers can exclude up to $250,000.

Smoking. Taxpayers can deduct the cost of two types of aids for quitting cigarette smoking as a medical expense: (1) participation in a smoking-cessation program or (2) prescription drugs to alleviate the effects of nicotine withdrawal. Over-the-counter products such as nicotine patches and chewing gum are nondeductible.

Full-Time Students. For 2013, a taxpayer may not claim a dependency exemption for an individual who qualifies as a full-time student and is over age 23 at the end of the year, unless the student's gross income is less than $3,900.

Student Loans. For the tax year beginning in 2013, the income phase-out range for the $2,500 maximum deduction for interest paid on qualified education loans is $60,000-$75,000 income for single taxpayers and $125,000-$155,000 for married taxpayers filing jointly.

Weight Loss. The IRS allows a medical deduction for costs of certain weight-loss programs. Participation must be for treatment of a physician-diagnosed disease, including obesity. No deduction is allowed for diets that are not prescribed by a physician or for special diet foods.

Working Abroad. Many Americans who live and work abroad are eligible to exclude a certain amount of their pay from U.S. income taxes. The amount of earned income excludable for 2013 is $97,600.

Savings Plans

401(k) Plan. The maximum amount that an individual can contribute to a 401(k) plan for 2013 is $17,500, a $500 increase over 2012. Individuals born before 1964 can put away an additional $5,500, for a total of $23,000.

IRAs. The 2013 limits for IRAs and Roth IRAs increased to $5,500, $500 more than for 2012. Anyone who was born before 1964 can put in an extra $1,000. Funds may be deposited into a traditional IRA for 2013 up to Apr. 15, 2014. Contributions after Apr. 15 will automatically be considered funds deposited for 2014.

Roth IRA. Contributions paid into a Roth IRA are not tax deductible. Distributions of funds including investment earnings held in the account for five years or longer and distributed after age 59½ are both free of income tax and the 10% early-withdrawal penalty. Withdrawals from the account in less than five years can be subject to tax and a 10% withdrawal penalty regardless of age. There are income limitations on contributions.

Distributions. There is a 10% penalty for IRA distributions before age 59½. Distributions paid to a beneficiary due to disability/death of the owner are not subject to this penalty, nor are payments used for certain unreimbursed medical expenses, higher-education expenses, or first-time homebuyer acquisition costs (up to $10,000). The owner of a traditional IRA (or a SIMPLE plan, pension, or profit-sharing plan account) must begin receiving distributions by Apr. 1 of the calendar year following the year in which he or she reaches age 70½. Any employee who works beyond 70½ and is not a 5% or more owner of the business can continue to defer profit-sharing and pension plan distributions.

Common Income Tax Errors

Periodically, the IRS issues a list of the most commonly made income tax errors. The most common were:
1. Incorrect or missing Social Security numbers.
2. Incorrect tax entered based on taxable income and filing status.
3. Computation errors in figuring the taxable income, withholding and estimated tax payments, Earned Income Credit, standard deduction for those age 65 or over or blindness, taxable amount of Social Security benefits, and child and dependent care credit. Also, missing or incorrect identification numbers for child care providers.
4. Withholding and estimated tax payments entered on the wrong line.
5. Math errors, both addition and subtraction.

2013 Itemized Deductions

If the total amount of itemized deductions is more than the standard deduction, taxpayers generally should itemize their deductions in Schedule A, Form 1040. The following examples are just a few of the many deductions that may be itemized. Some are subject to income limitations.

Business Expenses. Deductible miscellaneous expenses include unreimbursed employee business expenses such as travel, automobile, telephone, and gifts. However, only 50% of the cost of customer meals and entertainment is deductible.

Charitable Contributions. Individuals may not deduct the value of volunteer work they personally perform for charities.

Gambling. Lottery, slots, poker, craps, bingo, or other gambling expenses are deductible if the taxpayer itemizes on Schedule A. However, expenses are limited to gambling winnings reported on page one of Form 1040. If there are no winnings on page one, the taxpayer cannot deduct expenses on Schedule A.

Interest. Mortgage interest paid on a primary residence or a second home is deductible. However, there are limitations on mortgages in excess of $1 mil. Interest on home equity loans also is deductible, but only covering the first $100,000 of equity debt. Personal credit card interest is not deductible.

Lamaze Classes. A mother-to-be may deduct as a medical expense the cost of classes taken for Lamaze breathing and relaxation techniques, stages of labor, and delivery procedures.

Long-Term Care Insurance. Based on various annual limits, long-term care insurance premiums are deductible as medical expenses. For 2013, taxpayers age 71 and older can claim as much as $4,550 per person; ages 61-70, up to $3,640; ages 51-60, up to $1,360; ages 41-50, up to $680; and ages 40 and younger, limited to $360.

Medical Expenses. Cosmetic surgery for a congenital abnormality including personal injury from an accident, trauma, or for a disfiguring disease may qualify as a medical deduction.

Medical Traveling. Taxpayers may deduct part of the travel expense, including auto expenses and airfare, to seek health care.

Moving Expenses. Taxpayers who change jobs or are transferred usually can deduct part of their moving expenses, including travel and the cost of moving household goods, but not the cost of meals.

Personal Losses. Casualty and theft losses are deductible subject to a $100 reduction and further reduced 10% for each occurrence. Separate rules apply for federally declared disasters. Unreimbursed automobile accident damage may be a deductible casualty loss.

Taxes. State and local income taxes including real estate taxes are deductible. An auto license fee based on weight, model, year, or horsepower is not deductible. A tax based on the car's value qualifies as a personal property tax deduction.

Tax Credits

A tax deduction reduces a taxpayer's taxable income whereas tax credits reduce, dollar-for-dollar, the amount of tax owed.

Adoption Credit. The adoption credit for qualified expenses is $12,970 in 2013. The credit limit is per person, not per year; is adjusted annually for inflation; and is nonrefundable. The exclusion phases out for taxpayers whose income is between $194,580 and $234,580, when the credit is completely phased out.

American Opportunity Tax Credit. This credit provides a $2,500 credit to cover each of four years of college. Up to 40% of the credit is refundable, which means that a taxpayer may be able to receive up to $1,000 even if he or she owes no taxes. The credit begins to phase out for higher-income individuals.

Child and Dependent Care Credit. This credit is for expenses for the care of taxpayers' qualifying children under age 13, or for a disabled spouse or dependent, while the taxpayer works or looks for work.

Child Tax Credit. The maximum child tax credit is $1,000 for each qualifying child.

Earned Income Credit. Lower-income workers who maintain a household may be eligible for an Earned Income Credit (EIC). This credit is based on total earned income such as

wages, commissions, and tips. Military personnel can include tax-free combat pay in income to compute the credit. There are phase-out rules.

Energy Credits. There are many energy-related credits—from the purchase of an alternative fuel vehicle and the installation of solar/fuel cell property in a residence, to the production of biodiesel or ethanol.

Alternative Minimum Tax

The Alternative Minimum Tax (AMT) was established in 1969 to prevent individuals with very high incomes from using special tax breaks to pay little or no tax. Because of changes in the tax law, this tax affects more and more middle-income taxpayers every year.

The AMT exemption for a single taxpayer is $51,900, $80,800 for married filing jointly.

Instructions included with tax forms 1040 and 1040A help individuals determine if they are subject to the AMT. Tax Form 6251 is used to figure how much additional tax, if any, is owed.

Estate and Gift Taxes

Estate Tax. The Tax Relief Reconciliation Act of 2001 increased the estate tax exclusion from $675,000 in 2001 to $3.5 mil through 2009. The maximum tax rate in 2001, based on the value of an estate, was 55%. The rate was decreased over the years to a maximum 45% in 2009. The estate tax was set to expire in 2010. The Tax Relief Act of 2010 reinstated the estate tax with a 35% flat rate and increased the exemptions to $5 mil in 2011, $5.12 mil in 2012, and $5.25 mil in 2013. The estate tax rate increased to 40% in 2013.

Gifting. U.S. citizens, residents, and nonresident aliens have an annual gift tax exclusion of up to $14,000 per individual (increased from $13,000 in 2012) to as many individuals as he or she chooses. For married couples the exclusion is twice that amount, $28,000, even if only one spouse does all the gifting. The annual $14,000 gift tax does not include gifts to most charities or for tuition that donors pay directly to schools or medical expenses paid on behalf of donees.

International Property. All property owned worldwide by American citizens is subject to U.S. estate tax rules and regulations.

Resident Aliens. Aliens residing in the U.S. are subject to the same rules as American citizens.

Taxable Social Security Benefits

Earnings Limitations. For 2013, Social Security recipients who have not reached the full retirement age of 66 will lose $1 of their benefits for every $2 of earned income over $15,120. Recipients who reached full retirement age in 2013 will not lose any benefits if they earned $40,080 or less. Recipients will have to pay back some benefits if their income exceeded that amount.

Taxable Benefits. Up to 50% of Social Security benefits may be taxable if the person's total income is more than $25,000 but less than $34,000 for a single individual, head of household, qualifying widow(er), or a married person who is filing separately if spouses lived apart all year; or more than $32,000 but less than $44,000 for married individuals filing jointly. For higher incomes, 85% of Social Security benefits may become taxable.

Tax-Free. If the only income received during the year was Social Security, these benefits are not taxable, and the recipient probably does not have to file a tax return.

Retention of Income Tax Records

How long should a taxpayer keep copies of his or her tax returns and supporting records? The answer is a combination of judgment and the statutes of limitations. Because federal tax returns generally can be audited for up to three years after filing, or six years if the IRS suspects underreported income, it's wise to keep copies of an income tax return and records at least seven years after filing a return.

Tax Audits

Odds of an Audit. The IRS audit rate for individual returns filed in 2012 was 1.03%. The odds of an audit increase with higher taxpayer income. For taxpayers with incomes of $200,000 or higher, the audit rate is 3.39%. For taxpayers with gross income of $1 mil or more, the rate is 12.5%. If income is lower than $200,000, the audit rate drops to one in 100. Most taxpayers have no reason to be concerned about being audited.

Decision to Audit. The audit selection process is not random. It is based on a set of formulas that are designed to spot questionable returns. If the IRS concludes that the taxpayer owes more tax and he or she disagrees with the findings, the taxpayer can meet with a supervisor.

If the taxpayer still does not agree, he or she can appeal to a separate Appeals Office, or take it to the U.S. Tax Court, Federal District Court, or the U.S. Court of Federal Claims.

Tax Court. The U.S. Tax Court is a federal court where taxpayers can dispute tax deficiencies as determined by the Commissioner of Internal Revenue before payment of the disputed amounts. The Tax Court is composed of presidentially appointed members. Many taxpayers choose the Tax Court because they are not required to pay the contested tax up front.

Appeals. For more information about audits, call the IRS at (800) TAX-FORM (829-3676) for its free Publication 556, *Examination of Returns, Appeal Rights, and Claims for Refund* or visit www.irs.gov.

IRS Contact Information

Website: www.irs.gov
Fax: (703) 368-9694
Tax questions: (800) 829-1040
Forms/publications: (800) TAX-FORM (829-3676)
Spanish forms/publications: The IRS provides instructions in Spanish at participating libraries. Taxpayers can also view and download tax forms and publications in Spanish directly from www.irs.gov/Spanish/. For more information, call (800) TAX-FORM and ask for IRS Publication 1SP, *Derechos del Contribuyente.*

Hearing impaired: The IRS telephone service for hearing impaired persons is available for taxpayers with access to TDD equipment. The number is (800) 829-4059.

Report wrongdoing: Confidentially report misconduct, waste, fraud, or abuse by an IRS employee to the Treasury Inspector General for Tax Administration at (800) 366-4484.

Additional services: Request Publication 910, *IRS Guide to Free Tax Services.* This guide contains a list of free tax publications and other information including tax education and assistance programs

Working With a Tax Preparer

The following are some suggestions when using a tax preparer:

- **Choose** wisely. Regulations in effect in 2013 require all paid tax return preparers including attorneys, certified public accountants, and IRS-enrolled agents to have a Preparer Tax Identification Number. Check the preparer's qualifications and history. Ask about service fees in advance.
- **Review** last year's tax return. Make note of any changes since then such as marriage, divorce, number of dependents, retirement, job changes, additional income, or new deductions.
- **Organize** your records with income items first, followed by itemized deductions (medical, taxes, interest, and charitable and other miscellaneous deductions), followed by gains, losses, rentals, or other items.
- **Time** spent with your preparer may affect your bill. If you provide disorganized records and deductions, there may be

an additional cost to have your tax preparer organize your information.

- **Prepare** a list of questions in advance. Ask about any invoices or bills that you are not sure apply.
- **Alert** your preparer if you're waiting to receive additional information. He or she can begin preparing your tax return and include the missing data later to finalize your return. Amending a return after it is completed may incur additional fees.
- **Review** your tax return before signing it. Ask questions about any item you don't understand. Even though your preparer is required to sign the return, you are responsible for its contents.

U.S. Total Tax Collections by Type, 1960-2012

Source: *Internal Revenue Service Data Book, 2012*, Internal Revenue Service, U.S. Dept. of the Treasury
(as percent of total gross collection or total income taxes)

Fiscal year	Total gross collection in current dollars (bil)[1]	Income taxes Total	Business[2]	Individual[3]	Estate and trust[3]	Employment taxes[4]	Estate taxes	Gift taxes	Excise taxes[5]
1960	$92	73.1%	24.2%	49.0%	—	12.2%	1.6%	0.20%	12.9%
1965	114	69.7	22.8	46.9	—	14.9	2.1	0.25	12.9
1970	196	70.9	17.9	53.0	—	19.1	1.7	0.22	8.1
1975	294	68.8	15.6	53.2	—	23.9	1.5	0.13	5.7
1980	519	69.3	13.9	55.4	—	24.7	1.2	0.04	4.7
1985	743	63.8	10.4	53.4	—	30.3	0.8	0.04	5.0
1990	1,056	61.6	10.4	51.1	—	34.8	0.9	0.20	2.6
1995	1,376	61.8	12.7	49.1	—	33.8	1.0	0.13	3.3
2000	2,097	65.5	11.2	54.2	—	30.5	1.2	0.20	2.6
2005	2,269	62.3	13.5	48.8	—	34.0	1.0	0.09	2.5
2010	2,345	62.0	11.9	49.6	0.5%	35.1	0.7	0.12	2.0
2011	2,415	65.8	10.1	55.1	0.6	31.8	0.1	0.27	2.0
2012	2,524	66.1	11.1	54.3	0.7	31.1	0.5	0.08	2.2

Note: Numbers may not add up to totals because of rounding. (1) Credits to taxpayer accounts excluded beginning with fiscal year 2009. (2) Includes taxes on corporation income and unrelated business income from tax-exempt organizations. (3) Income tax reported for estates and trusts is included in individual income tax in FY1960-2007. From FY2008 on, estate and trust income tax is reported separately. (4) Includes taxes for Old-Age, Survivors, Disability, and Hospital Insurance; federal unemployment insurance; and Railroad Retirement. (5) Excludes excise taxes collected by the U.S. Customs and Border Protection and the Alcohol and Tobacco Tax and Trade Bureau. The IRS collected taxes on alcohol and tobacco until FY1988 and taxes on firearms until FY1991.

Taxes Collected by State Governments, 2012

Source: Annual Survey of State Government Tax Collections, U.S. Census Bureau, U.S. Dept. of Commerce
(as percent of total taxes collected or total sales and gross receipts)

State	Total taxes collected in dollars (mil)[1]	Property taxes	Sales and gross receipts taxes Total	General	Selective[2]	License taxes[3]	Individual income taxes	Corporation net income taxes	Other taxes[4]
Alabama	$9,053	3.6%	51.1%	25.1%	26.0%	5.7%	33.3%	4.6%	1.7%
Alaska	7,049	3.1	3.5	—	3.5	1.9	—	9.4	82.1
Arizona	12,973	5.8	62.2	47.9	14.3	2.9	23.8	5.0	0.3
Arkansas	8,288	12.2	48.1	33.9	14.2	4.3	29.0	4.9	1.6
California	112,372	1.9	34.4	25.4	9.0	7.7	49.0	7.1	<0.1
Colorado	10,251	—	39.9	22.5	17.4	6.0	47.6	4.8	1.7
Connecticut	15,420	—	43.3	24.4	18.9	2.9	47.8	4.1	2.0
Delaware	3,360	—	14.6	—	14.6	36.6	39.0	7.8	1.9
Florida	32,997	<0.1	82.6	58.8	23.8	6.7	—	6.1	4.6
Georgia	16,577	0.4	43.8	32.0	11.8	3.1	40.1	3.6	0.1
Hawaii	5,516	—	64.9	48.9	16.0	4.7	27.9	1.5	1.0
Idaho	3,374	—	49.3	36.3	13.0	8.9	36.0	5.6	0.2
Illinois	36,438	0.2	39.2	22.0	17.2	7.1	43.1	9.6	0.8
Indiana	15,705	<0.1	58.4	42.2	16.2	4.0	30.3	6.1	1.1
Iowa	7,832	—	45.1	30.9	14.2	9.6	38.7	5.4	1.2
Kansas	7,418	1.0	49.7	38.1	11.6	4.3	39.0	4.3	1.8
Kentucky	10,473	5.1	48.1	29.1	18.9	4.1	33.5	5.5	3.7
Louisiana	8,994	0.6	54.4	31.3	23.0	4.5	27.5	3.2	9.9
Maine	3,777	1.0	46.3	28.2	18.1	6.7	38.2	6.1	1.7
Maryland	17,064	4.4	42.0	23.9	18.1	4.4	41.7	5.2	2.2
Massachusetts	22,806	<0.1	32.1	22.3	9.8	3.9	52.3	8.8	2.8
Michigan	23,969	7.5	54.7	39.9	14.8	5.9	28.5	2.5	0.8
Minnesota	20,561	3.9	44.4	24.0	20.4	5.8	38.9	5.2	1.8
Mississippi	6,953	0.3	63.2	44.2	19.0	7.4	21.6	5.7	1.7
Missouri	10,801	0.3	44.1	28.7	15.4	5.2	47.5	2.8	0.1
Montana	2,459	10.5	22.1	—	22.1	12.8	36.6	5.4	12.6
Nebraska	4,358	<0.1	47.9	33.4	14.4	4.2	42.2	5.4	0.4
Nevada	6,775	3.5	77.2	50.7	26.5	8.6	—	—	10.7
New Hampshire	2,206	17.3	39.7	—	39.7	12.0	3.7	23.6	3.8
New Jersey	27,456	<0.1	43.7	29.5	14.2	5.2	40.5	7.0	3.5
New Mexico	5,088	1.2	52.1	39.1	13.0	3.5	22.6	5.5	15.1
New York	71,546	—	32.0	16.6	15.3	2.7	54.2	6.4	4.8
North Carolina	22,713	—	42.0	24.5	17.5	6.5	45.7	5.4	0.4
North Dakota	5,620	<0.1	28.4	20.0	8.4	3.3	7.7	3.8	56.7
Ohio	25,924	—	50.6	31.9	18.7	13.8	34.8	0.5	0.3
Oklahoma	8,826	—	42.2	27.4	14.8	11.6	31.4	5.1	9.8
Oregon	8,700	0.2	16.1	—	16.1	10.4	67.0	5.0	1.4
Pennsylvania	32,950	0.1	52.1	27.8	24.2	8.0	30.7	5.6	3.6
Rhode Island	2,805	0.1	52.6	29.9	22.6	3.8	37.9	4.4	1.3
South Carolina	8,036	0.1	52.2	36.4	15.8	5.6	38.5	3.1	0.4
South Dakota	1,521	—	78.7	55.1	23.6	16.5	—	3.9	0.9
Tennessee	11,982	—	74.8	54.3	20.4	10.7	1.5	10.2	2.8
Texas	48,597	—	77.0	50.4	26.6	15.5	—	—	7.5
Utah	5,810	—	46.9	32.0	14.9	4.4	42.5	4.5	1.8
Vermont	2,757	34.4	35.1	12.4	22.7	3.7	21.7	3.5	1.6
Virginia	18,138	0.2	32.3	19.2	13.0	4.3	56.3	4.6	2.3
Washington	17,625	10.8	80.4	60.2	20.2	5.6	—	—	3.2
West Virginia	5,356	0.1	49.1	23.8	25.2	2.6	32.8	3.6	11.8
Wisconsin	14,748	1.1	43.4	26.3	17.1	6.7	42.5	6.0	0.4
Wyoming	2,551	12.4	43.9	39.0	4.9	5.5	—	—	38.2
U.S. total	**794,570**	**1.6**	**47.2**	**30.5**	**16.6**	**6.8**	**35.3**	**5.3**	**3.9**

— = Tax not collected by state. **Note:** For fiscal year 2012, July 1, 2011-June 30, 2012, for all states except Alabama and Michigan (ends Sept. 30), New York (Mar. 31), and Texas (Aug. 31). (1) Includes taxes not shown separately. (2) Includes taxes on sale of alcoholic beverages, insurance premiums, motor fuel, public utilities, and tobacco products. (3) Includes taxes on licenses for motor vehicles and corporations among others. (4) Includes death and gift taxes and severance taxes (on extraction of natural resources).

State Government Personal Income Tax Rates, 2013

Source: Reproduced with permission from *CCH State Tax Guide*, published and copyrighted by CCH Inc., a Wolters Kluwer business Alaska, Florida, Nevada, South Dakota, Texas, Washington, and Wyoming did not have state income taxes and are thus not listed. Tax rates apply in stages—for example, a single person in Arizona making $60,000 in taxable income would pay 2.59% on the first $10,000 of income, 2.88% on the next $15,000, and so on. For further details, see notes at end of table.

Alabama

Single, Head of household, or Married filing separately

$0 to $500	2%
$501 to $3,000	4%
$3,001 and over	5%

Married filing jointly

$0 to $1,000	2%
$1,001 to $6,000	4%
$6,001 and over	5%

Arizona[1]

Single or Married filing separately

$0 to $10,000	2.59%
$10,001 to $25,000	2.88%
$25,001 to $50,000	3.36%
$50,001 to $150,000	4.24%
$150,001 and over	4.54%

Married filing jointly or Head of household

$0 to $20,000	2.59%
$20,001 to $50,000	2.88%
$50,001 to $100,000	3.36%
$100,001 to $300,000	4.24%
$300,001 and over	4.54%

Arkansas[2,3]

Single, Head of household, Married filing jointly, or Married filing separately

$0 to $4,099	1%
$4,100 to $8,199	2.5%
$8,200 to $12,199	3.5%
$12,200 to $20,399	4.5%
$20,400 to $33,999	6%
$34,000 and over	7%

California[1,2]

Single, Married filing separately, or Registered domestic partner filing separately

$0 to $7,582	1%
$7,583 to $17,976	2%
$17,977 to $28,371	4%
$28,372 to $39,384	6%
$39,385 to $49,774	8%
$49,775 to $254,250	9.3%
$254,251 to $305,100	10.3%
$305,101 to $508,500	11.3%
$508,501 and over	12.3%

Head of household

$0 to $15,174	1%
$15,175 to $35,952	2%
$35,953 to $46,346	4%
$46,347 to $57,359	6%
$57,360 to $67,751	8%
$67,752 to $345,780	9.3%
$345,781 to $414,936	10.3%
$414,937 to $691,560	11.3%
$691,561 and over	12.3%

Married filing jointly, Registered domestic partner filing jointly, or Qualifying widow(er)

$0 to $15,164	1%
$15,165 to $35,952	2%
$35,953 to $56,742	4%
$56,743 to $78,768	6%
$78,769 to $99,548	8%
$99,549 to $508,500	9.3%
$508,501 to $610,200	10.3%
$610,201 to $1,017,000	11.3%
$1,017,001 and over	12.3%

Colorado

4.63% of federal taxable income

Connecticut

Single or Married filing separately

$0 to $10,000	3%
$10,001 to $50,000	5%
$50,001 to $100,000	5.5%
$100,001 to $200,000	6%
$200,001 to $250,000	6.5%
$250,001 and over	6.7%

Head of household

$0 to $16,000	3%
$16,001 to $80,000	5%
$80,001 to $160,000	5.5%
$160,001 to $320,000	6%
$320,001 to $400,000	6.5%
$400,001 and over	6.7%

Married filing jointly or Qualifying widow(er)

$0 to $20,000	3%
$20,001 to $100,000	5%
$100,001 to $200,000	5.5%
$200,001 to $400,000	6%
$400,001 to $500,000	6.5%
$500,001 and over	6.7%

Delaware

Single, Head of household, Married filing jointly, or Married filing separately

$0 to $2,000	0%
$2,001 to $5,000	2.2%
$5,001 to $10,000	3.9%
$10,001 to $20,000	4.8%
$20,001 to $25,000	5.2%
$25,001 to $60,000	5.55%
$60,001 and over	6.75%

District of Columbia

$0 to $10,000	4%
$10,001 to $40,000	6%
$40,001 to $350,000	8.5%
$350,001 and over	8.95%

Georgia

Single

$0 to $750	1%
$751 to $2,250	2%
$2,251 to $3,750	3%
$3,751 to $5,250	4%
$5,251 to $7,000	5%
$7,001 and over	6%

Head of household, Married filing jointly, or Qualifying widow(er)

$0 to $1,000	1%
$1,001 to $3,000	2%
$3,001 to $5,000	3%
$5,001 to $7,000	4%
$7,001 to $10,000	5%
$10,001 and over	6%

Married filing separately

$0 to $500	1%
$501 to $1,500	2%
$1,501 to $2,500	3%
$2,501 to $3,500	4%
$3,501 to $5,000	5%
$5,001 and over	6%

Hawaii

Single or Married filing separately

$0 to $2,400	1.4%
$2,401 to $4,800	3.2%
$4,801 to $9,600	5.5%
$9,601 to $14,400	6.4%
$14,401 to $19,200	6.8%
$19,201 to $24,000	7.2%
$24,001 to $36,000	7.6%
$36,001 to $48,000	7.9%
$48,001 to $150,000	8.25%
$150,001 to $175,000	9%
$175,001 to $200,000	10%
$200,001 and over	11%

Head of household

$0 to $3,600	1.4%
$3,601 to $7,200	3.2%
$7,201 to $14,400	5.5%
$14,401 to $21,600	6.4%
$21,601 to $28,800	6.8%
$28,801 to $36,000	7.2%
$36,001 to $54,000	7.6%
$54,001 to $72,000	7.9%
$72,001 to $225,000	8.25%
$225,001 to $262,500	9%
$262,501 to $300,000	10%
$300,001 and over	11%

Idaho[1,2]

Single or Married filing separately

$0 to $1,408	1.6%
$1,409 to $2,817	3.6%
$2,818 to $4,226	4.1%
$4,227 to $5,635	5.1%
$5,636 to $7,044	6.1%
$7,045 to $10,567	7.1%
$10,568 and over	7.4%

Head of household, Married filing jointly, or Surviving spouse

$0 to $2,817	1.6%
$2,818 to $5,635	3.6%
$5,636 to $8,453	4.1%
$8,454 to $11,271	5.1%
$11,272 to $14,089	6.1%
$14,090 to $21,135	7.1%
$21,136 and over	7.4%

Illinois

5% of federal AGI with modifications

Indiana

3.4% of AGI

Iowa[2]

$0 to $1,494	0.36%
$1,495 to $2,988	0.72%
$2,989 to $5,977	2.43%
$5,977 to $13,446	4.5%
$13,447 to $22,410	6.12%
$22,411 to $29,880	6.48%
$29,881 to $44,820	6.8%
$44,821 to $67,230	7.92%
$67,231 and over	8.98%

Kansas

Single, Head of household, or Married filing separately

$0 to $15,000	3%
$15,001 and over	4.9%

Married filing jointly

$0 to $30,000	3%
$30,001 and over	4.9%

Kentucky

Single, Head of household, Married filing jointly, or Married filing separately

$0 to $3,000	2%
$3,001 to $4,000	3%
$4,001 to $5,000	4%
$5,001 to $8,000	5%
$8,001 to $75,000	5.8%
$75,001 and over	6%

Louisiana[1]

Single, Head of household, or Married filing separately

$0 to $12,500	2%
$12,501 to $50,000	4%
$50,001 and over	6%

Married filing jointly

$0 to $25,000	2%
$25,001 to $100,000	4%
$100,001 and over	6%

Maine[2]

Single or Married filing separately

$0 to $5,199	0%
$5,200 to $20,899	6.5%
$20,900 and over	7.950%

Head of household

$0 to $7,849	0%
$7,850 to $31,349	6.5%
$31,350 and over	7.95%

Married filing jointly or Qualifying widow(er)

$0 to $10,449	0%
$10,450 to $41,849	6.5%
$41,850 and over	7.95%

Maryland

Single, Married filing separately, or Dependent taxpayers

$0 to $1,000	2%
$1,001 to $2,000	3%
$2,001 to $3,000	4%
$3,001 to $100,000	4.75%
$100,001 to $125,000	5%
$125,001 to $150,000	5.25%
$150,001 to $250,000	5.5%
$250,001 and over	5.75%

Head of household, Married filing jointly, or Qualifying widow(er)

$0 to $1,000	2%
$1,001 to $2,000	3%
$2,001 to $3,000	4%
$3,001 to $150,000	4.75%
$150,001 to $175,000	5%
$175,001 to $225,000	5.25%
$225,001 to $300,000	5.5%
$300,001 and over	5.75%

Massachusetts

Part A income (short-term capital gains)	12.0%
Part A income (interest and dividends)	5.25%
Part B income	5.25%
Part C income	5.25%

Michigan

4.25% of taxable income

Minnesota[2]

Single

$0 to $24,270	5.35%
$24,271 to $79,730	7.05%
$79,731 to $150,000	7.85%
$150,001 and over	9.85%

Head of household

$0 to $29,880	5.35%
$29,881 to $120,070	7.05%
$120,071 to $200,000	7.85%
$200,001 and over	9.85%

Married filing jointly

$0 to $35,480	5.35%
$35,481 to $140,960	7.05%
$140,961 to $250,000	7.85%
$250,001 and over	9.85%

Married filing separately

$0 to $17,740	5.35%
$17,741 to $70,480	7.05%
$70,481 to $125,000	7.85%
$125,001 and over	9.85%

Mississippi

$0 to $5,000	3%
$5,001 to $10,000	4%
$10,001 and over	5%

Missouri

$0 to $1,000	1.5%
$1,001 to $2,000	2%
$2,001 to $3,000	2.5%
$3,001 to $4,000	3%
$4,001 to $5,000	3.5%
$5,001 to $6,000	4%
$6,001 to $7,000	4.5%
$7,001 to $8,000	5%
$8,001 to $9,000	5.5%
$9,001 and over	6%

Montana[2]

$0 to $2,800	1%
$2,801 to $4,900	2%
$4,901 to $7,400	3%

$7,401 to $10,100. . . . . 4%
$10,101 to $13,000 . . . . . . 5%
$13,001 to $16,700. . . . . . . 6%
$16,701 and over 6.9%

Nebraska

Single
$0 to $2,400 . . . . 2.46%
$2,401 to $17,500. . . . . . . 3.51%
$17,501 to $27,000. . . . . 5.01%
$27,001 and over 6.84%
Head of household
$0 to $4,500 . . . . 2.46%
$4,501 to $28,000. . . . . . . 3.51%
$28,001 to $40,000. . . . . 5.01%
$40,001 and over 6.84%
Married filing jointly or Surviving spouse
$0 to $4,800 . . . . 2.46%
$4,801 to $35,000. . . . . . . 3.51%
$35,001 to $54,000. . . . . 5.01%
$54,001 and over 6.84%
Married filing separately
$0 to $2,400 . . . . 2.46%
$2,401 to $17,500. . . . . . . 3.51%
$17,501 to $27,000. . . . . 5.01%
$27,001 and over 6.84%

New Hampshire

5% on interest and dividends only

New Jersey

Single or Married/civil-union partner filing separately
$0 to $20,000 . . . . 1.4%
$20,001 to $35,000. . . . . 1.75%
$35,001 to $40,000. . . . . . 3.5%
$40,001 to $75,000. . . . 5.525%
$75,001 to $500,000. . . . 6.37%
$500,001 and over 8.97%
Head of household, Married/civil-union couple filing jointly, or Qualifying widow(er)/Surviving civil-union partner
$0 to $20,000 . . . . 1.4%
$20,001 to $50,000. . . . . 1.75%
$50,001 to $70,000. . . . . 2.45%
$70,001 to $80,000. . . . . . 3.5%
$80,001 to $150,000. . . 5.525%
$150,001 to $500,000. . . 6.37%
$500,001 and over 8.97%

New Mexico[1]

Single
$0 to $5,500 . . . . 1.7%
$5,501 to $11,000. . . . . . . 3.2%
$11,001 to $16,000. . . . . . 4.7%
$16,001 and over 4.9%
Head of household
$0 to $8,000 . . . . 1.7%
$8,001 to $16,000. . . . . . . 3.2%
$16,001 to $24,000. . . . . . 4.7%
$24,001 and over 4.9%
Married filing jointly or Qualifying widow(er)
$0 to $8,000 . . . . 1.7%
$8,001 to $16,000. . . . . . . 3.2%
$16,001 to $24,000. . . . . . 4.7%
$24,001 and over 4.9%
Married filing separately
$0 to $4,000 . . . . 1.7%
$4,001 to $8,000. . . . . 3.2%
$8,001 to $12,000. . . . . . . 4.7%
$12,001 and over 4.9%

New York

Single or Married filing separately
$0 to $8,200 . . . . 4%
$8,201 to $11,300. . . . . . . 4.5%
$11,301 to $13,350. . . . 5.25%
$13,351 to $20,550. . . . . 5.9%
$20,551 to $77,150. . . . 6.45%
$77,151 to $205,850. . . 6.65%
$205,851 to $1,029,250 6.85%
$1,029,251 and over. . . 8.82%
Head of household
$0 to $12,350 . . . . 4%
$12,351 to $16,950. . . . . . 4.5%
$16,951 to $20,050. . . . 5.25%
$20,051 to $30,850. . . . . 5.9%
$30,851 to $102,900. . . 6.45%
$102,901 to $257,300. . 6.65%
$257,301 to $1,543,900 6.85%
$1,543,901 and over. . . 8.82%
Married filing jointly or Qualifying widow(er)
$0 to $16,450 . . . . 4%
$16,451 to $22,600. . . . . 4.5%
$22,601 to $26,750. . . . 5.25%
$26,751 to $41,150. . . . . 5.9%
$41,151 to $154,350. . . 6.45%
$154,351 to $308,750. . 6.65%
$308,751 to $2,058,550 6.85%
$2,058,551 and over. . . 8.82%

North Carolina

Single
$0 to $12,750 . . . . 6%
$12,751 to $60,000. . . . . . . 7%
$60,001 and over 7.75%
Head of household
$0 to $17,000 . . . . 6%
$17,001 to $80,000. . . . . . . 7%
$80,001 and over 7.75%
Married filing jointly or Qualifying widow(er)
$0 to $21,250 . . . . 6%
$21,251 to $100,000. . . . . . 7%
$100,001 and over 7.75%
Married filing separately
$0 to $10,625 . . . . 6%
$10,626 to $50,000. . . . . . . 7%
$50,001 and over 7.75%

North Dakota[2]

Single
$0 to $36,250 . . . . 1.22%
$36,251 to $87,850. . . . 2.27%
$87,851 to $183,250. . . 2.52%
$183,251 to $398,350. . 2.93%
$398,351 and over 3.22%
Head of household
$0 to $48,600 . . . . 1.22%
$48,601 to $125,450. . . 2.27%
$125,451 to $203,150. . 2.52%
$203,151 to $398,350. . 2.93%
$398,351 and over 3.22%
Married filing jointly or Surviving spouse
$0 to $60,650 . . . . 1.22%
$60,651 to $146,400. . . 2.27%
$146,401 to $223,050. . 2.52%
$223,051 to $398,350. . 2.93%
$398,351 and over 3.22%
Married filing separately
$0 to $30,325 . . . . 1.22%
$30,326 to $73,200. . . . 2.27%
$73,201 to $111,525. . . 2.52%
$111,526 to $199,175. . 2.93%
$199,176 and over 3.22%

Ohio

$0 to $5,200 . . . . 0.537%
$5,201 to $10,400. . . . . 1.074%
$10,401 to $15,650 . . . . 2.148%
$15,651 to $20,900. . . . 2.686%
$20,901 to $41,700. . . . 3.222%
$41,701 to $83,350. . . . 3.760%
$83,351 to $104,250. . . 4.296%
$104,251 to $208,500. . 4.988%
$208,501 and over 5.421%

Oklahoma

Single or Married filing separately
$0 to $1,000 . . . . 0.5%
$1,001 to $2,500. . . . . 1%
$2,501 to $3,750. . . . . 2%
$3,751 to $4,900. . . . . 3%
$4,901 to $7,200 . . . . 4%
$7,201 to $8,700 . . . . 5%
$8,701 and over 5.25%
Head of household, Married filing jointly, or Qualifying widow(er)
$0 to $2,000 . . . . 0.5%
$2,001 to $5,000. . . . . 1%
$5,001 to $7,500. . . . . 2%
$7,501 to $9,800. . . . . 3%
$9,801 to $12,200. . . . . 4%
$12,201 to $15,000. . . . . . . 5%
$15,001 and over 5.25%

Oregon[2]

Single or Married filing separately
$0 to $3,250 . . . . 5%
$3,251 to $8,150. . . . . 7%
$8,151 to $125,000. . . . . . . 9%
$125,001 and over 9.9%
Married filing jointly, Head of household, or Qualifying widow(er)
$0 to $6,500 . . . . 5%
$6,501 to $16,300. . . . . 7%
$16,301 to $250,000. . . . . . 9%
$250,001 and over 9.9%

Pennsylvania

3.07% of taxable compensation, net profits, net gains from the sale of property, rent, royalties, patents or copyrights, income from estates or trusts, dividends, interest, and winnings

Rhode Island[2]

Single, Head of household, Married filing jointly, Qualifying widow(er), or Married filing separately
$0 to $58,600 . . . . 3.75%
$58,601 to $133,250. . . . 4.75%
$133,251 and over 5.99%

South Carolina[2]

$0 to $2,850 . . . . 0%
$2,851 to $5,700. . . . . 3%
$5,701 to $8,550. . . . . 4%
$8,551 to $11,400. . . . . 5%
$11,401 to $14,250. . . . . . . 6%
$14,251 and over 7%

Tennessee

6% on interest and dividend income

Utah

5% on state taxable income

Vermont[2]

Single
$0 to $36,250 . . . . 3.55%
$36,251 to $87,850. . . . . . 6.8%
$87,851 to $183,250. . . . . 7.8%
$183,251 to $398,350. . . . 8.8%
$398,351 and over 8.95%
Head of household
$0 to $48,600 . . . . 3.55%
$48,601 to $125,450. . . . . 6.8%
$125,451 to $203,150. . . . 7.8%
$203,151 to $398,350. . . . 8.8%
$398,351 and over 8.95%
Married or Civil union filing jointly
$0 to $60,550 . . . . 3.55%
$60,551 to $146,400. . . . . 6.8%
$146,401 to $223,050. . . . 7.8%
$223,051 to $398,350. . . . 8.8%
$398,351 and over 8.95%
Married or Civil union filing separately
$0 to $30,275 . . . . 3.55%
$30,276 to $73,200. . . . . . 6.8%
$73,201 to $111,525. . . . . 7.8%
$111,526 to $199,175. . . . 8.8%
$199,176 and over 8.95%

Virginia

Single, Head of household, Married filing jointly, or Married filing separately
$0 to $3,000 . . . . 2%
$3,001 to $5,000. . . . . 3%
$5,001 to $17,000. . . . . 5%
$17,001 and over 5.75%

West Virginia

Single, Head of household, Married filing jointly, or Widower with dependent child
$0 to $10,000 . . . . 3%
$10,001 to $25,000. . . . . . . 4%
$25,001 to $40,000. . . . . . 4.5%
$40,001 to $60,000. . . . . . . 6%
$60,001 and over 6.5%
Married filing separately
$0 to $5,000 . . . . 3%
$5,001 to $12,500. . . . . 4%
$12,501 to $20,000. . . . . . 4.5%
$20,001 to $30,000. . . . . . . 6%
$30,001 and over 6.5%

Wisconsin[1,2]

Single or Head of household
$0 to $10,750. . . . . 4.4%
$10,751 to $21,490 . . . . 5.84%
$21,491 to $236,600 . . . 6.27%
$236,601 and over. 7.65%
Married filing jointly
$0 to $14,330. . . . . 4.4%
$14,331 to $28,650 . . . . 5.84%
$28,651 to $315,460 . . . 6.27%
$315,461 and over. 7.65%
Married filing separately
$0 to $7,160. . . . . 4.4%
$7,161 to $14,330 . . . . . 5.84%
$14,331 to $157,730 . . . 6.27%
$157,731 and over. 7.65%

AMT = Alternative minimum tax; AGI = Adjusted gross income. (1) Community property state in which, in general, one-half of the community income is taxable to each spouse. (2) Brackets indexed for inflation annually. (3) 2013 adjusted brackets were not available. Bracketed rates listed are for 2012. **Arkansas:** Married filing separately combined-status couples calculate taxes separately and add the results. **California:** An additional 1% tax is imposed on taxable income in excess of $1 mil. **Colorado:** Individual taxpayers are subject to an AMT equal to the amount by which 3.47% of their Colorado alternative minimum taxable income exceeds their Colorado normal tax. **Connecticut:** Resident estates and trusts are subject to 6.7% rate on all income. **Indiana:** Counties may impose an AGI tax on residents or on nonresidents, or a county option income tax. **Iowa:** An AMT of 6.7% of alternative minimum income is imposed if the minimum tax exceeds the taxpayer's regular income tax liability. **Massachusetts:** Part A income represents either interest and dividends or short-term capital gains. Part B income represents wages, salaries, tips, pensions, state bank interest, partnership income, business income, rents, alimony, winnings, and certain other items of income. Part C income represents gains from the sale of capital assets held for more than one year. **Minnesota:** A 6.75% AMT is imposed. **Montana:** Minimum tax, $1. **Nebraska:** There is an additional tax on taxpayers with federal AGI of more than a certain amount, which is $300,000 ($150,000 for married filing separately) in 2013. **New Mexico:** Qualified nonresident taxpayers may pay alternative tax of 0.75% of gross receipts from sales in New Mexico. **New York:** A supplemental tax is imposed to recapture the tax table benefit. **Vermont:** The tax amount is increased by 24% for certain items.

EDUCATION

U.S. Public Schools: Students, Staff, Spending, 1899-2011

Source: National Center for Education Statistics, U.S. Dept. of Education

	1899-1900	1919-20	1939-40	1959-60	1969-70	1979-80	1989-90	1999-2000	2010-11[1]
Population (thous.)									
Total U.S. population[2]	75,995	104,514	131,028	177,830	201,385	225,055	246,819	279,040	309,330
Population 5-17 years of age	21,573	27,571	30,151	43,881	52,386	48,043	44,947	52,811	53,931
Percentage 5-17 years of age	28.4%	26.4%	23.0%	24.7%	26.0%	21.3%	18.2%	18.9%	17.4%
Enrollment (thous.)									
Elementary and secondary[3]	15,503	21,578	25,434	36,087	45,550	41,651	40,543	46,857	49,484
Pre-kindergarten and grades 1-8	14,984	19,378	18,833	27,602	32,513	28,034	29,152	33,486	34,625
Grades 9-12	519	2,200	6,601	8,485	13,037	13,616	11,390	13,371	14,860
Percentage pop. ages 5-17 enrolled	71.9%	78.3%	84.4%	82.2%	87.0%	86.7%	90.2%	88.7%	91.8%
Percentage high school of all enrolled	3.3%	10.2%	26.0%	23.5%	28.6%	32.7%	28.1%	28.5%	30.0%
High school graduates	62	231	1,143	1,627	2,589	2,748	2,320	2,554	3,104
Instructional staff (thous.)									
Total instructional staff	*	678	912	1,457	2,286	2,406	2,986	3,819	4,151
Teachers, librarians, and other nonsupervisory instructional staff	423	657	875	1,393	2,195	2,300	2,860	3,682	3,986
Revenue and expenditures (mil)									
Total revenue	$220	$970	$2,261	$14,747	$40,267	$96,881	$208,548	$372,944	$597,486
Total expenditures	215	1,036	2,344	15,613	40,683	95,962	212,770	381,838	607,236
Current expenditures[4,5]	180	861	1,942	12,329	34,218	86,984	188,229	323,889	525,498
Capital outlay	35	154	258	2,662	4,659	6,506	17,781	43,357	55,651
Interest on school debt	*	18	131	490	1,171	1,874	3,776	9,135	17,679
Others	*	3	13	133	636	598	2,983	5,457	8,408
Salaries and pupil cost									
Avg. annual salary of instruct. staff[6]	$325	$871	$1,441	$4,995	$8,626	$15,970	$31,367	$41,807	$55,623
Expenditure per capita total pop.	2.83	9.91	17.89	88	202	426	862	1,368	1,963
Current expenditure per pupil ADA[5,7]	16.67	53.32	88.09	375	816	2,272	4,980	7,394	10,652

* = Data not collected. **Note:** Because of rounding, details may not add up to totals. Prior to 1959-60, data do not include Alaska and Hawaii. (1) Revenues and expenditures are fiscal year 2010 (2009-10 school year) provisional data. (2) Data for 1899-1900 are based on total population from the decennial census. From 1919-20 to 1959-60, total population includes armed forces overseas, as of July 1 preceding the school year. Data for later years are for resident population excluding armed forces overseas. (3) Data for 1899-1960 are school year enrollment; data for later years are fall enrollment. (4) In 1899-1900, includes interest on school debt. (5) Because of changes in the definition of "current expenditures," data for 1959-60 and later years are not entirely comparable with prior years. (6) Data prior to 1959-60 include supervisors, principals, teachers, and nonsupervisory instructional staff. (7) ADA = average daily attendance.

U.S. Public High School Graduation Rates, 2009-10

Source: National Center for Education Statistics, U.S. Dept. of Education

State	Rate	Rank	State	Rate	Rank	State	Rate	Rank	State	Rate	Rank
Alabama	71.8%	43	Illinois	81.9%	16	Montana	81.9%	17	Rhode Island	76.4%	33
Alaska	75.5	38	Indiana	77.2	30	Nebraska	83.8	11	South Carolina	68.2	47
Arizona	74.7	42	Iowa	87.9	5	Nevada	57.8	51	South Dakota	81.8	18
Arkansas	75.0	41	Kansas	84.5	8	New Hampshire	86.3	7	Tennessee	80.4	21
California	78.2	29	Kentucky	79.9	23	New Jersey	87.2	6	Texas	78.9	25
Colorado	79.8	24	Louisiana	68.8	46	New Mexico	67.3	48	Utah	78.6	26
Connecticut	75.1	40	Maine	82.8	13	New York	76.0	35	Vermont	91.4	1
Delaware	75.5	37	Maryland	82.2	15	North Carolina	76.9	32	Virginia	81.2	20
Dist. of Columbia	59.9	50	Massachusetts	82.6	14	North Dakota	88.4	4	Washington	77.2	31
Florida	70.8	44	Michigan	75.9	36	Ohio	81.4	19	West Virginia	78.3	28
Georgia	69.9	45	Minnesota	88.2	4	Oklahoma	78.5	27	Wisconsin	91.1	2
Hawaii	75.4	39	Mississippi	63.8	49	Oregon	76.3	34	Wyoming	80.3	22
Idaho	84.0	10	Missouri	83.7	12	Pennsylvania	84.1	9	**Total U.S.**	**78.2**	

Note: The averaged freshman graduation rate provides an estimate of the percentage of students who receive a regular diploma within four years of entering ninth grade. The rate uses aggregate student enrollment data to estimate the size of an incoming freshman class and aggregate counts of the number of diplomas awarded four years later.

High School Dropouts by Sex, Race, and Ethnicity, 1960-2011

Source: Current Population Survey, U.S. Census Bureau, U.S. Dept. of Commerce

(data for Oct. of year shown unless otherwise noted)

Year[1]	Total dropout rate				Male dropout rate				Female dropout rate			
	All races[2]	White	Black	Hispanic	All races[2]	White	Black	Hispanic	All races[2]	White	Black	Hispanic
1960[3]	27.2%	NA	NA	NA	27.8%	NA	NA	NA	26.7%	NA	NA	NA
1970[4]	15.0	13.2%	27.9%	NA	14.2	12.2%	29.4%	NA	15.7	14.1%	26.6%	NA
1980	14.1	11.4	19.1	35.2%	15.1	12.3	20.8	37.2%	13.1	10.5	17.7	33.2%
1985	12.6	10.4	15.2	27.6	13.4	11.1	16.1	29.9	11.8	9.8	14.3	25.2
1990	12.1	9.0	13.2	32.4	12.3	9.3	11.9	34.3	11.8	8.7	14.4	30.3
1995	12.0	8.6	12.1	30.0	12.2	9.0	11.1	30.0	11.7	8.2	12.9	30.0
2000	10.9	6.9	13.1	27.8	12.0	7.0	15.3	31.8	9.9	6.9	11.1	23.5
2001	10.7	7.3	10.9	27.0	12.2	7.9	13.0	31.6	9.3	6.7	9.0	22.1
2002	10.5	6.5	11.3	25.7	11.8	6.7	12.8	29.6	9.2	6.3	9.9	21.2
2003[5]	9.9	6.3	10.9	23.5	11.3	7.1	12.5	26.7	8.4	5.6	9.5	20.1
2004[5]	10.3	6.8	11.8	23.8	11.6	7.1	13.5	28.5	9.0	6.4	10.2	18.5
2005[5]	9.4	6.0	10.4	22.4	10.8	6.6	12.0	26.4	8.0	5.3	9.0	18.1
2006[5]	9.3	5.8	10.7	22.1	10.3	6.4	9.7	25.7	8.3	5.3	11.7	18.1
2007[5]	8.7	5.3	8.4	21.4	9.8	6.0	8.0	24.7	7.7	4.5	8.8	18.0
2008[5]	8.0	4.8	9.9	18.3	8.5	5.4	11.7	19.9	7.5	4.2	11.1	16.7
2009[5]	8.1	5.2	9.3	17.6	9.1	6.3	10.6	19.0	7.0	4.1	8.1	16.1
2010[5]	7.4	5.1	8.0	15.1	8.5	5.9	9.5	17.3	6.3	4.2	6.7	12.8
2011[5]	7.1	5.0	7.3	13.6	7.7	5.4	8.3	14.6	6.5	4.6	6.4	12.4

NA = Not available. **Note:** Table shows "status" dropouts, defined as 16- to 24-year-olds who are not enrolled in school and who have not completed a high school program, regardless of when they left school. People who have received GED credentials are not shown. Excludes persons in prisons or in the military, and other persons not living in households. Race categories exclude persons of Hispanic ethnicity unless otherwise noted. (1) Because of changes in data collection procedures, data for years prior to 1992 may not be comparable to later years. (2) Includes other racial/ethnic categories not separately shown. (3) Based on the Apr. 1960 decennial census. (4) White and black data include persons of Hispanic ethnicity. (5) White and black data exclude persons identifying themselves as being of two or more races.

Overview of U.S. Public Schools, 2011-12

Source: National Center for Education Statistics, U.S. Dept. of Education; National Education Association (NEA)

State	Local school districts	Elementary schools[1,2]	Secondary schools[2,3]	Classroom teachers	Total enrollment	Pupils per teacher	Teacher's avg. pay	Expend. per pupil
Alabama	132	945	420	45,519	736,339	16.2	$48,003	$8,597
Alaska	54	197	83	8,220	127,699*	15.5*	62,425	17,032*
Arizona	627*	1,346	737	59,715*	1,072,826*	18.0*	48,691*	6,683*
Arkansas	256	716	386	31,083	468,190	15.1	46,314	9,440
California	1,042*	6,789	2,531	242,308	6,204,065*	25.6*	68,531	9,053*
Colorado	178	1,282	397	47,927	854,234	17.8	49,049	10,001
Connecticut	199	826	278	41,528	554,398	13.3	69,465	15,790*
Delaware	37*	152	38	8,936*	129,917*	14.5*	58,800*	14,396*
Dist. of Columbia	41*	165	40	6,080*	77,076*	12.7*	68,720*	13,952*
Florida	67*	2,714	673	168,502	2,661,945	15.8	46,479	8,436
Georgia	196	1,802	457	110,788	1,684,430	15.2	52,938	9,586*
Hawaii	1	209	52	11,292	177,734	15.7	54,070	11,906
Idaho	137*	444	234	15,897*	289,486*	18.2*	48,551*	8,323*
Illinois	865*	3,189	1,006	128,166	2,087,628	16.3	57,636	12,455*
Indiana	355	1,385	437	62,463	1,040,313	16.7	50,516	10,820
Iowa	351	986	403	34,200	496,009	14.5	50,240	9,435
Kansas	286	956	384	34,074	482,796	14.2	46,718	9,518
Kentucky	174*	991	445	41,183	659,089*	16.0*	49,730	9,847*
Louisiana	126	986	304	49,712*	703,390	14.1*	50,179*	9,998
Maine	229*	469	151	15,507	185,033	11.9	47,338	10,396
Maryland	24	1,123	260	58,351	854,086	14.6	63,634	14,616*
Massachusetts	400	1,412	370	69,242	952,370	13.8	71,721	14,938
Michigan	855	2,460	1,065	84,092	1,543,573	18.4	61,560	13,313*
Minnesota	519	1,258	854	52,899*	839,738	15.9*	54,959*	11,398*
Mississippi	152	624	319	33,479*	490,037*	14.6*	41,646*	9,060*
Missouri	524*	1,572	651	68,652*	905,755*	13.2*	46,406*	9,760*
Montana	417*	479	348	10,645*	139,650*	13.1*	48,546*	10,309*
Nebraska	249	722	342	28,137	300,996	10.7	48,154	9,402
Nevada	17*	474	137	25,762*	470,068*	18.2*	54,559*	8,247*
New Hampshire	161*	375	105	15,619*	190,931*	12.2*	54,177*	14,587*
New Jersey	591	1,935	538	113,250	1,361,813	12.0	67,078	18,485*
New Mexico	89	602	239	21,352	333,643	15.6	45,622	10,203
New York	695*	3,325	1,101	206,000	2,617,556*	12.7*	73,398	18,616*
North Carolina	115	1,883	529	93,964	1,430,007	15.2	45,947	8,492
North Dakota	179	298	183	7,848*	95,858	12.2*	46,058	8,757
Ohio	1,016	2,547	1,023	108,399	1,875,491*	17.3*	56,715	9,842*
Oklahoma	522	1,235	547	41,377	665,841	16.1	44,391	8,285*
Oregon	196	915	309	27,800	560,950	20.2	57,348	10,897
Pennsylvania	499*	2,290	832	120,544	1,750,104*	14.5*	61,934	13,904*
Rhode Island	49*	233	74	11,029*	137,175*	12.4*	62,186*	16,683*
South Carolina	87	901	275	47,310	721,398	15.2	47,428	8,776
South Dakota	152	431	256	9,075	124,739	13.7	38,804	9,218*
Tennessee	135	1,308	350	64,702	959,322	14.8	47,082	8,577
Texas	1,227	5,894	2,151	324,243	4,978,120	15.4	48,373	8,498
Utah	41*	628	315	27,245*	597,397*	21.9*	48,159*	6,849*
Vermont	286*	235	69	8,964*	84,008*	9.4*	51,306*	18,571*
Virginia	132	1,508	402	103,908*	1,260,334*	12.1*	48,703*	11,192*
Washington	295	1,514	622	53,020	1,045,987	19.7	52,232	10,000*
West Virginia	55*	567	135	19,860	282,091	14.2	45,320*	11,777*
Wisconsin	424	1,552	587	56,180	871,105	15.5	53,792	12,172*
Wyoming	48	237	100	7,220	88,994	12.3	57,222	16,666
Total U.S.	15,504*	67,086	24,544	3,083,266*	49,221,735*	16.0*	55,418*	10,834*

* = NEA estimate. (1) Includes primary and middle schools (schools with no grade higher than 8th). (2) 2010-11 estimates. (3) Includes schools with no grade lower than 7th.

Programs for the Disabled, 1995-2012

Source: Office of Special Education and Rehabilitative Services, U.S. Dept. of Education

Number of children and young adults 3-21 years old served annually in federally funded educational programs for the disabled. (in thousands)

Type of disability	1995 -96	2000 -01	2002 -03	2003 -04	2004 -05	2005 -06	2006 -07	2007 -08	2008 -09	2009 -10	2010 -11	2011 -12
Learning disabilities	2,578	2,868	2,848	2,831	2,798	2,735	2,665	2,577	2,537	2,498	2,423	2,364
Speech impairments	1,022	1,409	1,412	1,441	1,463	1,468	1,475	1,458	1,451	1,449	1,429	1,413
Intellectual disabilities[1]	571	624	602	593	578	556	534	500	488	473	457	443
Emotional disturbance	437	481	485	489	489	477	464	442	421	409	391	375
Multiple disabilities	93	133	138	140	140	141	142	138	132	132	131	133
Hearing impairments	67	78	78	79	79	79	80	79	79	79	79	79
Orthopedic impairments	63	83	83	77	73	71	69	67	70	66	79	79
Other health impairments[2] . .	133	303	403	464	521	570	611	641	666	698	724	755
Visual impairments	25	29	29	28	29	29	29	29	29	29	29	29
Autism	28	94	137	163	191	223	258	296	338	380	419	458
Deaf-blindness	1	1	2	2	2	2	2	2	2	2	2	2
Traumatic brain injury	9	16	22	23	24	24	25	25	26	25	26	26
Developmental delay	—	178	283	305	332	339	333	358	354	368	381	393
All disabilities	5,572	6,296	6,523	6,634	6,719	6,713	6,686	6,613	6,593	6,608	6,553	6,531

— = Not available or not reliable data. **Note:** Counts based on reports from states and District of Columbia. Details may not add up to totals because of rounding and/or incomplete enumeration. (1) Referred to in some prior years as "mental retardation." (2) Includes limited strength, vitality, or alertness due to chronic or acute health problems such as a heart condition, tuberculosis, rheumatic fever, nephritis, asthma, sickle cell anemia, hemophilia, epilepsy, lead poisoning, leukemia, or diabetes.

Revenues for Public Elementary and Secondary Schools by State, 2009-10

Source: National Center for Education Statistics, U.S. Dept. of Education; amounts in thousands

State/territory	Total	Federal Amount	% of tot. rev.	State Amount	% of tot. rev.	Local and intermediate Amount	% of tot. rev.
Alabama	$7,239,691	$1,168,016	16.1%	$3,800,153	52.5%	$2,271,522	31.4%
Alaska	2,338,215[1]	369,729	15.8	1,461,906	62.5	506,580[1]	21.7
American Samoa	75,691	64,364	85.0	11,051[3]	14.6[3]	277	0.4
Arizona	10,069,959	1,893,298	18.8	3,896,117	38.7	4,280,545	42.5
Arkansas	5,160,401	819,459	15.9	2,686,231	52.1	1,654,711	32.1
California	64,130,242	8,855,246	13.8	34,743,249	54.2	20,531,747	32.0
Colorado	8,852,609	730,363	8.3	3,860,026	43.6	4,262,220	48.1
Connecticut	9,895,487	854,645	8.6	3,463,790	35.0	5,577,052	56.4
Delaware	1,784,101	218,204	12.2	1,046,317	58.6	519,580	29.1
District of Columbia[2]	1,720,917	156,202	9.1	0	0.0	1,564,715	90.9
Florida	26,056,857	4,200,101	16.1	8,216,579	31.5	13,640,177	52.3
Georgia	17,835,791	2,645,785	14.8	6,764,686	37.9	8,425,320	47.2
Guam	252,926	50,166	19.8	0	0.0	202,760	80.2
Hawaii[2]	2,564,855	382,399	14.9	2,093,299	81.6	89,157	3.5
Idaho	2,222,539	462,867	20.8	1,284,139	57.8	475,533	21.4
Illinois	28,263,059	3,508,917	12.4	8,021,217	28.4	16,732,925	59.2
Indiana	13,641,695	1,513,137	11.1	6,441,408	47.2	5,687,150	41.7
Iowa	5,541,140	743,561	13.4	2,217,893	40.0	2,579,686	46.6
Kansas	5,487,071	641,619	11.7	2,893,517	52.7	1,951,936	35.6
Kentucky	6,873,286	1,139,931	16.6	3,582,406	52.1	2,150,950	31.3
Louisiana	8,215,973[1]	1,572,272	19.1	3,533,026	43.0	3,110,675[1]	37.9
Maine	2,639,779	315,277	11.9	1,079,330	40.9	1,245,173	47.2
Maryland	13,352,511	1,039,305	7.8	5,544,364	41.5	6,768,842	50.7
Massachusetts	15,570,234	1,175,524	7.5	6,476,420	41.6	7,918,291	50.9
Michigan	19,401,180	2,575,799	13.3	10,516,655	54.2	6,308,726	32.5
Minnesota	10,639,251	1,326,127	12.5	6,309,625	59.3	3,003,499	28.2
Mississippi	4,443,683	945,971	21.3	2,109,083	47.5	1,388,629	31.2
Missouri	10,157,112	1,515,939	14.9	2,971,265	29.3	5,669,907	55.8
Montana	1,616,262	259,304	16.0	753,976	46.6	602,983	37.3
Nebraska	3,693,930[1]	469,503[1]	12.7	1,220,466	33.0	2,003,961	54.3
Nevada	4,310,014	367,140	8.5	1,406,630	32.6	2,536,244	58.8
New Hampshire	2,810,018	351,279	12.5	902,020	32.1	1,556,719	55.4
New Jersey	25,856,286[1]	2,422,449[1]	9.4	9,412,795	36.4	14,021,042	54.2
New Mexico	3,760,801	789,309	21.0	2,384,730	63.4	586,762	15.6
New York	57,146,375	5,122,664	9.0	23,438,008	41.0	28,585,703	50.0
North Carolina	13,056,767	1,991,491	15.3	7,602,930	58.2	3,462,346	26.5
North Dakota	1,256,048	277,989	22.1	552,862	44.0	425,197	33.9
Northern Mariana Islands	72,628	41,148	56.7	31,220[3]	43.0[3]	260	0.4
Ohio	22,729,890	2,452,032	10.8	10,017,540	44.1	10,260,318	45.1
Oklahoma	5,699,758	978,847	17.2	2,726,116	47.8	1,994,795	35.0
Oregon	6,211,294	820,955	13.2	2,945,986	47.4	2,444,352	39.4
Pennsylvania	26,408,846	2,887,079	10.9	9,456,502	35.8	14,065,265	53.3
Puerto Rico	4,345,726	1,617,604	37.2	2,725,019[3]	62.7[3]	3,103	0.1
Rhode Island	2,262,193	259,486	11.5	790,260	34.9	1,212,447	53.6
South Carolina	7,837,314	1,092,174	13.9	3,431,142	43.8	3,313,999	42.3
South Dakota	1,300,147	253,761	19.5	404,402	31.1	641,985	49.4
Tennessee	8,528,047	1,158,247	13.6	3,842,346	45.1	3,527,454	41.4
Texas	50,045,607	7,787,692	15.6	19,714,162	39.4	22,543,753	45.0
Utah	4,464,562	560,352	12.6	2,283,683	51.2	1,620,527	36.3
Vermont	1,638,396	174,139	10.6	1,337,034	81.6	127,223	7.8
Virgin Islands (U.S.)	266,086	89,574	34	0	0	176,513	66
Virginia	14,692,849[1]	1,527,093	10.4	5,485,997	37.3	7,679,759[1]	52.3
Washington	11,817,488	1,401,295	11.9	6,931,627	58.7	3,484,566	29.5
West Virginia	3,432,220	536,424	15.6	1,899,967	55.4	995,830	29.0
Wisconsin	11,104,749	1,163,103	10.5	4,975,033	44.8	4,966,614	44.7
Wyoming	1,708,365	124,360	7.3	880,853	51.6	703,152	41.2

NA = Not applicable. **Note:** Included as revenue receipts are all appropriations from general funds of federal, state, county, and local governments; receipts from taxes levied for school purposes; income from permanent school funds and endowments; and income from leases of school lands and miscellaneous sources (interest on bank deposits, tuition, gifts, school lunch charges, etc.). (1) Value affected by redistribution of reported values to correct for missing data items and/or to distribute state direct support expenditures. (2) Both DC and Hawaii have only one school district each; therefore, neither is comparable to other states. Local revenues in Hawaii consist almost entirely of student fees and charges for services, such as food services, summer school, and student activities. (3) Reported state revenue data are revenues received from the central government of the jurisdiction.

Students Reporting School Bullying and Cyberbullying, 2011

Source: National Center for Education Statistics, U.S. Dept. of Education

(percentage of students ages 12-18)

	Total	Male	Female		Total	Male	Female
Bullied students	27.8%	24.5%	31.4%	Cyberbullied students	9.0%	6.9%	11.2%
Made fun of, called names, or insulted	17.6	16.2	19.1	Hurtful information on Internet	3.6	1.7	5.7
Subject of rumors	18.3	13.2	23.8	Private information purposefully shared on Internet	1.1	0.7	1.5
Threatened with harm	5.0	5.0	5.1	Subject of harassing instant messages	2.7	1.5	4.0
Tried to make do things they did not want to do	3.3	3.6	3.0	Subject of harassing text messages	4.4	2.4	6.5
Excluded from activities on purpose	5.6	4.8	6.4	Subject of harassing emails	1.9	1.1	2.7
Property destroyed on purpose	2.8	3.3	2.3	Subject of harassing while gaming	1.5	2.7	0.2
Pushed, shoved, tripped, or spit on	7.9	8.9	6.8	Excluded online	1.2	1.0	1.4
				Total bullied or cyberbullied	**29.7**	**26.7**	**32.9**

Note: Includes bullying taking place in the school building, on school property, on a school bus, or going to and from school and cyberbullying anywhere during the school year.

Fighting, Bullying, and Safety Concerns of High School Students, 2011

Source: *Youth Risk Behavior Surveillance–United States, 2011*, Centers for Disease Control and Prevention

	In a physical fight on school property[1]			Bullied on school property[2]			Electronically bullied[2,3]			Did not go to school because of safety concerns[4]		
	Female	Male	Total	Female	Male	Total	Female	Male	Total	Female	Male	Total
Race/ethnicity[5]												
White......	5.6%	13.8%	9.9%	25.2%	20.7%	22.9%	25.9%	11.8%	18.6%	4.8%	4.0%	4.4%
Black......	13.1	19.6	16.4	12.2	11.1	11.7	11.0	6.9	8.9	5.3	8.0	6.7
Hispanic ...	9.0	19.4	14.4	19.3	16.0	17.6	18.0	9.5	13.6	9.6	8.5	9.1
Grade												
9	10.4	21.7	16.2	27.1	21.5	24.2	22.6	8.9	15.5	6.3	5.4	5.8
10	8.0	17.0	12.8	24.6	20.4	22.4	24.2	12.6	18.1	7.1	6.4	6.8
11	6.0	12.3	9.2	17.5	16.7	17.1	19.8	12.4	16.0	5.1	5.3	5.2
12	6.1	11.5	8.8	17.2	13.4	15.2	21.5	8.8	15.0	5.1	5.9	5.5
Total......	7.8	16.0	12.0	22.0	18.2	20.1	22.1	10.8	16.2	6.0	5.8	5.9

(1) One or more times during the 12 months before the survey. (2) During the 12 months before the survey. (3) Including being bullied through email, chat rooms, instant messaging, websites, or texting. (4) On at least one day during the 30 days before the survey. (5) Race categories include non-Hispanics only. Hispanics may be of any race.

Trends in International Mathematics and Science Study (TIMSS), 1995-2011

Source: National Center for Education Statistics, U.S. Dept. of Education

The TIMSS is an international assessment test that was administered to 4th and 8th graders in 1995, 1999 (5th graders only), 2003, 2007, and 2011 to measure the degree to which students have learned concepts of mathematics and science. Listed below are the average scaled scores for each country. Scores are reported on a scale of 0 to 1,000, with the scale average set at 500. Student achievement is considered "high" with a score of at least 550; a score of at least 475 is considered "intermediate."

	4th grade						**8th grade**			
	Mathematics		Science				Mathematics		Science	
	2011	% change, 1995-2011	2011	% change, 1995-2011			2011	% change, 1995-2011	2011	% change, 1995-2011
Australia	516	−5%	516	−8%		Australia	505	−5%	519	−5%
Austria	508	−9	532	−6		England	507	0	533	−3
Czech Republic	511	−10	536	−4		Hong Kong	586	0	535	2
England	542	6	529	−4		Hungary	505	−6	522	−6
Hong Kong	602	3	535	0		Iran...........	415	−3	474	1
Hungary	515	−6	534	0		Israel..........	516	−1	516	−2
Iran...........	431	0	453	9		Japan.........	570	−6	558	−2
Japan.........	585	−2	559	−3		Korea, South...	613	1	560	−1
Ireland........	527	−4	(1)	NA		Lithuania......	502	5	514	8
Kuwait.........	342	−15	347	−13		Norway	475	−6	494	−6
Netherlands ...	540	−6	531	−5		Romania.......	458	−5	465	−4
New Zealand ...	486	−3	497	6		Russia........	539	1	542	1
Norway........	495	−1	494	−7		Singapore	611	−5	590	−3
Portugal	532	12	522	9		Slovenia	505	−7	543	−3
Singapore	606	−3	583	7		Sweden........	484	−7	509	−5
Slovenia	513	−7	(1)	NA		Thailand	427	−18	(1)	NA
Thailand	458	−7	472	0		**United States**...	509	1.8	525	−2
United States...	541	−1	544	−4						

NA = Not applicable. (1) Did not participate.

Mathematics, Reading, and Science Achievement of U.S. Students, 1998-2011

Source: National Assessment of Educational Progress, National Center for Education Statistics, U.S. Dept. of Education

Percent of public school students who scored at or above basic levels in national tests. Basic level denotes a partial mastery of prerequisite knowledge and skills fundamental for proficient work at each grade.

	4th grade				**8th grade**							**4th grade**				**8th grade**					
	Math		Reading		Math		Reading		Science				Math		Reading		Math		Reading		Science	
State	2000	2011	1998	2011	2000	2011	1998	2011	2000	2011	State	2000	2011	1998	2011	2000	2011	1998	2011	2000	2011
AL	55	75	56	68	52	60	67	69	53	54	MT	72	87	72	73	80	83	83	85	79	80
AK	NA	78	NA	55	NA	74	NA	68	NA	68	NE	65	82	NA	70	74	75	NA	80	52	72
AZ	57	77	51	58	62	68	72	71	55	57	NV	60	79	51	59	58	67	70	69	NA	58
AR	55	80	54	63	52	70	68	71	53	62	NH	93	75	77	NA	82	NA	84	NA	79	
CA	50	74	48	57	52	61	63	66	38	52	NJ	NA	89	NA	77	NA	82	NA	84	NA	69
CO	NA	84	69	70	NA	80	77	81	NA	74	NM	50	75	51	53	50	64	71	68	48	58
CT	76	81	76	73	72	75	81	83	64	69	NY	66	79	62	68	68	70	76	76	NA	62
DE	NA	84	53	72	NA	74	64	76	NA	63	NC	73	89	58	68	70	75	74	74	54	61
DC	24	59	27	44	23	48	44	51	NA	24	ND	73	89	NA	74	77	84	NA	83	72	82
FL	NA	83	53	71	NA	68	67	72	NA	62	OH	73	86	NA	72	75	79	NA	80	72	73
GA	57	80	54	66	55	69	68	75	52	63	OK	67	83	66	63	64	71	80	73	60	63
HI	55	80	45	59	52	68	59	68	40	55	OR	65	77	58	62	71	71	78	76	68	71
ID	68	83	NA	68	71	78	NA	81	71	75	PA	NA	87	NA	73	NA	73	NA	77	NA	66
IL	63	79	NA	66	68	73	NA	77	59	60	RI	65	84	64	71	64	74	76	76	58	63
IN	77	86	NA	77	76	77	NA	78	66	68	SC	59	79	53	61	55	70	66	72	48	61
IA	75	86	67	68	NA	77	NA	77	NA	73	SD	NA	86	NA	68	NA	81	NA	82	NA	79
KS	76	90	70	71	77	79	81	79	NA	70	TN	59	76	57	61	53	64	71	70	55	64
KY	59	85	62	72	63	71	74	79	60	71	TX	76	85	59	65	68	81	74	75	52	67
LA	57	73	44	56	48	63	63	65	44	56	UT	69	85	62	68	68	73	77	79	67	77
ME	73	87	72	69	76	79	83	80	72	78	VT	73	88	NA	73	75	70	NA	83	71	80
MD	60	87	58	75	65	75	70	80	57	64	VA	71	87	62	72	67	78	78	78	61	73
MA	77	92	70	83	76	85	79	84	70	76	WA	NA	84	64	66	NA	76	76	77	NA	72
MI	71	78	62	65	70	71	NA	77	68	72	WV	65	78	60	61	62	65	75	68	57	64
MN	76	88	69	70	80	83	78	81	72	76	WI	NA	86	72	77	NA	79	78	79	NA	75
MS	45	72	47	55	41	58	62	65	41	47	WY	71	87	64	72	70	80	76	82	69	77
MO	71	83	61	67	67	73	75	79	66	72	U.S.	64	81	58	66	65	73	71	75	57	65

NA = Not administered.

Enrollment in U.S. Public and Private Schools, 1899-2022

Source: National Center for Education Statistics, U.S. Dept. of Education

Of all students enrolled at private schools in 2009-10, 77% attended religious schools, and 23% attended nonsectarian schools.

School year[1]	Public school[2]	Private school[2]	% private[3]	School year[1]	Public school[2]	Private school[2]	% private[3]
1899-1900	15,503	1,352	8.0%	1979-80	41,651	5,000[4]	10.7%
1909-10	17,814	1,558	8.0	1989-90	40,543	5,599	12.1
1919-20	21,578	1,699	7.3	1999-2000	46,857	6,018	11.4
1929-30	25,678	2,651	9.4	2008-09	49,266	5,707	10.4
1939-40	25,434	2,611	9.3	2009-10	49,373	5,488	10.0
1949-50	25,111	3,380	11.9	2010-11	49,484	5,391	9.8
1959-60	35,182	5,675	13.9	2020-21[4]	52,688	5,287	9.1
1969-70	45,550	5,500[4]	10.8	2021-22[4]	53,113	5,331	9.1

Note: "Private" includes all nonpublic schools. (1) Fall enrollment. (2) In thousands. Data from fall 1980 onward covers an expanded universe of private schools; comparisons with earlier years should be avoided. (3) Percent of U.S. students enrolled in private schools. (4) Projected.

Characteristics of Public Charter Schools and Students, 1999-2011

Source: National Center for Education Statistics, U.S. Dept. of Education

	1999-2000	2001-02	2003-04	2005-06	2007-08	2009-10	2010-11
Number of charter school students	339,678	571,029	789,479	1,012,906	1,276,731	1,611,332	1,787,091
			percentage of charter school students who were—				
Sex							
Male	51.1%	50.8%	50.4%	49.9%	49.5%	49.5%	49.5%
Female	48.9	49.2	49.6	50.1	50.5	50.5	50.5
Race/ethnicity							
White	42.5	42.6	41.8	40.5	38.8	37.3	36.2
Black	33.5	32.5	31.9	32.1	31.8	30.3	28.9
Hispanic	19.6	20.1	21.5	22.4	24.5	26.1	27.3
Asian/Pacific Islander	2.8	3.1	3.2	3.6	3.8	3.8	3.7
American Indian/Alaska Native	1.5	1.7	1.5	1.4	1.2	1.1	0.9
Other[1]	NA	NA	NA	NA	NA	1.4	2.9
Number of charter schools	1,524	2,348	2,977	3,780	4,388	4,952	5,274
			percentage of charter school that were—				
School level							
Elementary	55.7%	51.7%	52.1%	52.9%	54.1%	54.3%	54.3%
Secondary	24.9	24.6	26.4	28.1	27.5	26.7	25.9
Combined	18.9	23.0	21.4	18.8	18.4	18.8	19.5
Enrollment size							
Under 300	77.0	73.5	70.9	69.5	65.5	61.3	59.0
300-499	12.0	13.7	15.6	16.6	19.4	21.0	22.3
500-999	8.7	10.0	10.3	10.9	12.0	14.0	14.8
1,000 or more	2.4	2.8	3.2	3.0	3.1	3.7	3.9
Locale							
City	NA	NA	52.5	53.4	54.6	54.8	55.5
Suburban	NA	NA	22.2	21.9	21.8	21.1	21.3
Town	NA	NA	9.6	8.8	8.5	8.0	7.6
Rural	NA	NA	15.8	15.8	15.2	16.1	15.6

NA = Not available. **Note:** Race categories exclude persons of Hispanic ethnicity, who may be of any race. (1) Includes data for states reporting students of two or more races.

Homeschooled Students, 2011-12

Source: National Center for Education Statistics, U.S. Dept. of Education

A total of 1,770,000 U.S. students in grades K-12 were homeschooled in 2011-12, up from 1.5 mil in 2007 and 850,000 in 1999. In a 2012 U.S. Dept. of Education survey of parents who homeschool their children, the reasons they gave as most important in their decision to homeschool included concern over the school environment, including such factors as safety, drugs, or negative peer pressure (25%); dissatisfaction with academic instruction in schools (19%); desire to provide religious instruction (16%); desire to provide moral instruction (5%); desire to provide a nontraditional approach to education (5%); and the child having a physical or mental health problem (5%). In all, 91% cited concern over school environment as one of their reasons, 77% cited moral instruction, 74% cited dissatisfaction with academic instruction, and 64% cited religious instruction.

Characteristic	No. of students (thous.)	% distrib.	Home-schooling rate[1]	Characteristic	No. of students (thous.)	% distrib.	Home-schooling rate[1]
Total	1,770	NA	3.4%	**Grade equivalent**			
Household locale				Kindergarten-2nd grade	415	23%	3.1%
City	489	28%	3.2	3rd-5th grade	416	23	3.4
Suburban	601	34	3.1	6th-8th grade	425	24	3.5
Town	132	7	2.7	9th-12th grade	514	29	3.7
Rural	548	31	4.5				
Race/ethnicity[2]				**Parents' education**			
White	1,201	68	4.5	Less than high school	203	11	3.4
Black	139	8	1.9	High school	355	20	3.4
Hispanic	267	15	2.3	Vocational/technical			
Asian or Pacific Islander	73	4	2.6	or some college	525	30	3.4
Other race(s)	90	5	3.2	Bachelor's degree	436	25	3.7
Poverty status				Graduate/professional			
Poor	348	20	3.5	school	252	14	3.3
Nonpoor	1,422	80	3.4				

Note: Numbers may not add up to totals because of rounding. Homeschooled students are school-age children in a grade equivalent to K-12 who receive instruction at home all or most of the time. Excludes students who were enrolled in public or private school more than 25 hours per week and students who were homeschooled because of temporary illness only. (1) Percentage of the total group or subgroup within the general homeschooled population. (2) Race categories include non-Hispanic population only.

School Progress Under NCLB Mandates, 2006-11

Source: Center on Education Policy

(percentage of schools not making adequate yearly progress [AYP])

State	2006	2011	State	2006	2011	State	2006	2011	State	2006	2011
Alabama*	11%	27%	Illinois	18%	67%	Montana	10%	28%	Rhode Island*	32%	19%
Alaska*	38	54	Indiana*	51	49	Nebraska	18	27	South Carolina*	62	76
Arizona*	33	42	Iowa	16	26	Nevada*	47	53	South Dakota*	19	17
Arkansas*	39	35	Kansas*	14	16	New Hampshire*	40	71	Tennessee*	17	49
California	34	66	Kentucky*	34	57	New Jersey*	29	53	Texas	19	28
Colorado*	25	58	Louisiana*	9	22	New Mexico*	54	86	Utah*	12	24
Connecticut*	34	47	Maine*	21	63	New York*	29	47	Vermont	24	72
Dist. of Columbia*	85	87	Maryland*	23	45	North Carolina*	56	72	Virginia*	23	61
Delaware*	18	22	Massachusetts*	41	82	North Dakota	9	53	Washington*	16	62
Florida*	71	91	Michigan*	14	15	Ohio*	39	40	West Virginia*	14	48
Georgia*	21	27	Minnesota*	31	55	Oklahoma*	11	30	Wisconsin*	4	11
Hawaii*	65	59	Mississippi*	16	48	Oregon*	32	46	Wyoming	15	7
Idaho*	27	38	Missouri*	29	75	Pennsylvania*	18	25	U.S.	29	48

* = State approved for a waiver under the U.S. Dept. of Education's Elementary and Secondary Education Act (ESEA) flexibility plan, as of Aug. 12, 2013. Waivered states were not required to conform to AYP targets but had developed their own alternative accountability measures. **Note:** Under the No Child Left Behind Act (NCLB), public schools and districts were required to show AYP by meeting targets set by their state for the percentages of students scoring proficient on state tests and other performance indicators. If a school failed to make AYP for two consecutive years or more, it would be considered "in need of improvement" and would have to submit to interventions intended to improve achievement mandated by NCLB.

Top 50 Libraries in U.S. by Volumes Held, 2010

Source: ALA Library Fact Sheet Number 22, American Library Association (ALA)

Rank	Institution	Volumes held	Rank	Institution	Volumes held
1.	Library of Congress	34,528,818	26.	Univ. of Pennsylvania	6,438,305
2.	Boston Public Library[1]	19,090,261	27.	Duke Univ.	6,174,814
3.	Harvard Univ.	16,832,952	28.	Ohio State Univ.	6,161,657
4.	New York Public Library[1]	16,342,365	29.	Univ. of Pittsburgh	6,148,036
5.	Univ. of Illinois–Urbana-Champaign	13,158,748	30.	Univ. of Arizona	5,998,148
6.	Yale Univ.	12,787,962	31.	Chicago Public Library	5,790,289
7.	Univ. of California–Berkeley	11,545,418	32.	Univ. of Oklahoma	5,662,666
8.	Columbia Univ.	11,189,036	33.	Michigan State Univ.	5,609,761
9.	Univ. of Michigan	10,778,736	34.	Univ. of Virginia	5,607,915
10.	Univ. of Texas–Austin	9,990,941	35.	San Diego Public Library	5,535,415
11.	Univ. of Chicago	9,837,021	36.	Univ. of Iowa	5,490,825
12.	Univ. of California–Los Angeles	9,151,964	37.	Pennsylvania State Univ.	5,441,121
13.	Public Library of Cincinnati and Hamilton County (OH)	8,819,759	38.	New York Univ.	5,382,424
14.	Indiana Univ.	8,677,974	39.	Northwestern Univ.	5,047,970
15.	Stanford Univ.	8,500,000	40.	Free Library of Philadelphia	5,043,943
16.	Univ. of Wisconsin–Madison	8,421,198	41.	Dallas Public Library	4,972,494
17.	Cornell Univ.	8,173,778	42.	Hennepin County Library (MN)	4,961,514
18.	Princeton Univ.	7,226,744	43.	Univ. of Georgia	4,810,192
19.	Univ. of Washington	7,203,156	44.	Rutgers Univ.	4,722,407
20.	Univ. of Minnesota	7,111,311	45.	Univ. of Colorado	4,681,261
21.	Detroit Public Library	7,070,433	46.	Texas A&M Univ.	4,577,498
22.	Univ. of North Carolina–Chapel Hill	7,012,787	47.	Arizona State Univ.	4,497,114
23.	County of Los Angeles Public Library	6,795,552	48.	Univ. of Florida	4,414,450
24.	Queens Borough Public Library (NY)	6,544,609	49.	Univ. of Cincinnati	4,379,445
25.	Los Angeles Public Library	6,459,552	50.	North Carolina State Univ.	4,332,899

Note: For academic libraries, a volume is a single physical unit of any printed, typewritten, handwritten, mimeographed, or processed work, distinguished from other units by a separate binding, encasement, portfolio, or other clear distinction, which has been cataloged, classified, and made ready for use, and which is typically the unit used to charge circulation transactions. For public libraries, holdings are the number of cataloged items plus paperbacks and videocassettes even if uncataloged. (1) Includes both public library and research library collection numbers.

Number of Public Libraries and Operating Income by State, 2010

Source: Public Libraries Survey, Institute of Museum and Library Services

State	No.[1]	Income[2] (thous.)	State	No.[1]	Income[2] (thous.)	State	No.[1]	Income[2] (thous.)	State	No.[1]	Income[2] (thous.)
AL	212	$96,305	IL	622	$768,867	MT	80	$23,577	RI	48	$46,959
AK	75	32,959	IN	238	323,997	NE	216	50,740	SC	42	119,901
AZ	89	186,204	IA	531	107,616	NV	22	101,509	SD	102	21,942
AR	55	66,069	KS	311	111,469	NH	221	52,257	TN	186	104,405
CA	181	1,289,759	KY	117	161,879	NJ	284	487,394	TX	549	448,673
CO	114	267,817	LA	68	212,687	NM	81	44,326	UT	72	90,604
CT	183	176,707	ME	215	39,726	NY	756	1,080,620	VT	159	20,045
DE	21	26,834	MD	24	262,198	NC	77	206,845	VA	91	270,772
DC	1	41,005	MA	360	256,863	ND	73	14,888	WA	61	351,372
FL	80	573,009	MI	384	428,033	OH	251	690,226	WV	97	35,850
GA	61	200,457	MN	138	202,880	OK	116	103,290	WI	381	220,891
HI	1	30,922	MS	50	48,091	OR	126	183,536	WY	23	30,917
ID	102	45,789	MO	147	218,974	PA	457	322,005	**Total U.S.**	**8,951**	**11,300,660**

(1) Includes central libraries only. (2) Some totals may be underestimated because of nonresponse.

Population With Upper Secondary Education in Selected Countries, 2011

Source: Organization for Economic Cooperation and Development

Percentage of the population ages 25-64 that have received at least an upper secondary (senior high school) education.

Country	%	Country	%	Country	%	Country	%	Country	%
Czech Republic	92%	Germany	86%	Norway	82%	Ireland	73%	Greece	67%
Slovakia	91	Switzerland	86	Korea	81	Chile	72	Italy	56
Canada	89	Finland	84	Denmark	77	France	72	Spain	54
Estonia	89	Slovenia	84	Luxembourg	77	Netherlands	72	Mexico	36
Poland	89	Israel	83	United Kingdom	77	Belgium	71	Portugal	35
United States	89	Austria	82	Australia	74	Iceland	71	Turkey	32
Sweden	87	Hungary	82	New Zealand	74				

Financial Aid to U.S. Undergraduate Students, 2000-11

Source: National Center for Education Statistics, U.S. Dept. of Education

Control and level of institution/ year	Number enrolled	Number receiving financial aid	Percent receiving aid	Percent of enrolled students in student aid programs				Average award[1]			
				Federal grants	State/ local grants	Institu- tional grants	Student loans[2]	Federal grants	State/ local grants	Institu- tional grants	Student loans[2]
All institutions											
2000-01	1,976,600	1,390,527	70.3%	31.6%	31.2%	31.1%	40.1%	$3,232	$2,650	$6,160	$4,892
2010-11	2,654,501	2,184,367	82.3	47.8	30.9	35.7	50.1	4,894	2,927	8,631	6,812
Public											
2000-01	1,333,236	872,109	65.4	30.0	33.5	22.7	30.7	3,129	2,218	2,956	3,964
2010-11	1,802,565	1,421,056	78.8	46.0	35.9	27.2	40.2	4,907	2,759	4,279	5,951
4-year											
2000-01	804,793	573,430	71.3	26.6	36.5	29.6	40.7	3,339	2,688	3,400	4,174
2010-11	1,039,170	858,433	82.6	38.9	38.3	39.6	51.5	5,134	3,576	4,765	6,310
2-year											
2000-01	528,443	298,679	56.5	35.2	28.8	12.1	15.3	2,888	1,312	1,305	3,114
2010-11	763,395	562,623	73.7	55.6	32.7	10.3	24.8	4,691	1,460	1,730	4,940
Private nonprofit											
2000-01	439,369	363,044	82.6	28.4	31.8	68.1	57.7	3,741	3,896	9,576	5,224
2010-11	518,433	463,163	89.3	36.4	27.7	78.2	64.3	5,214	3,648	14,735	7,516
4-year											
2000-01	419,499	347,638	82.9	27.4	32.2	70.1	58.1	3,809	3,901	9,693	5,198
2010-11	504,874	450,906	89.3	35.4	27.7	79.6	64.3	5,248	3,671	14,826	7,529
2-year											
2000-01	19,870	15,406	77.5	49.2	23.9	25.7	49.5	2,949	3,759	2,817	5,861
2010-11	13,559	12,257	90.4	73.5	27.4	28.4	65.2	4,601	2,775	5,289	7,045
Private for-profit											
2000-01	203,995	155,374	76.2	49.3	15.2	6.2	63.5	3,005	3,241	2,001	7,171
2010-11	333,503	300,148	90.0	75.2	8.9	15.3	82.0	4,610	3,108	1,936	8,237
4-year											
2000-01	81,075	51,739	63.8	36.1	11.9	8.3	57.7	2,983	3,754	2,100	7,471
2010-11	113,482	102,643	90.4	73.5	11.3	23.6	82.8	4,875	3,036	2,872	8,733
2-year											
2000-01	122,920	103,635	84.3	58.0	17.3	4.8	67.3	3,014	3,007	1,888	7,001
2010-11	220,021	197,505	89.8	76.1	7.6	11.0	81.5	4,478	3,164	902	7,978

Note: Data for full-time, first-time, degree-seeking undergraduate students. (1) Average amounts for students participating in indicated programs, in constant 2011-12 dollars. (2) Includes only loans made directly to students. Does not include Parent Loans for Undergraduate Students (PLUS) and other loans made directly to parents.

Undergraduate Students Taking Distance Education Courses, 2003-08

Source: National Center for Education Statistics, U.S. Dept. of Education; percentages are as of all undergraduate students

Selected characteristic	2003-04				2007-08			
	Taking any distance education courses		Taking entire program through distance education		Taking any distance education courses		Taking entire program through distance education	
	Number (thous.)	Percent	Number (thous.)	Percent	Number (thous.)	Percent	Number (thous.)	Percent
Total	2,961	15.5%	973	5.1%	4,277	20.4%	769	3.7%
Sex								
Male	1,099	13.6	365	4.5	1,679	18.6	297	3.3
Female	1,862	17.0	609	5.5	2,598	21.8	472	4.0
Age								
15-23 years	1,283	11.7	353	3.2	1,891	15.1	169	1.4
24-29 years	592	18.4	213	6.6	938	25.9	192	5.3
30 years or older	1,086	22.4	408	8.4	1,448	30.1	408	8.5
Attendance status								
Exclusively full-time	1,179	12.7	360	3.9	1,648	16.5	299	3.0
Exclusively part-time	1,251	18.7	470	7.0	1,839	24.8	373	5.0
Mixed full-time and part-time	531	17.3	143	4.7	791	22.3	97	2.7
Work status								
No job	533	12.4	158	3.7	708	16.1	121	2.8
Regular job only	2,282	17.2	768	5.8	3,259	22.3	607	4.2
Work-study/assistantship only	60	8.8	18	2.6	112	12.9	13	1.5
Both regular job and work-study/assistantship	86	11.1	29	3.7	198	18.7	27	2.5
Housing status								
On-campus	194	7.2	48	1.8	263	8.9	13	0.5
Off-campus	1,851	17.7	634	6.1	2,709	24.0	606	5.4
With parents or relatives	604	13.2	171	3.7	854	17.1	83	1.7
Attended more than one institution	312	23.4	120	9.1	452	27.1	66	4.0

	2003-04				2007-08			
	Taking any distance education courses		Taking entire program through distance education		Taking any distance education courses		Taking entire program through distance education	
Selected characteristic Dependency status	Number (thous.)	Percent	Number (thous.)	Percent	Number (thous.)	Percent	Number (thous.)	Percent
Dependent	1,064	11.1%	291	3.0%	1,589	14.3%	108	1.0%
Independent, no dependents, not married	454	15.6	152	5.2	788	24.0	155	4.7
Independent, no dependents, married	269	19.6	101	7.4	356	28.7	83	6.6
Independent, with dependents, not married	522	20.5	180	7.1	712	25.5	197	7.0
Independent, with dependents, married	653	25.1	251	9.6	833	33.0	227	9.0

Note: Distance education courses include live, interactive audio- or video-conferencing; prerecorded instructional videos; webcasts; CD-ROMs or DVDs; or computer-based systems accessed over the Internet. Does not include correspondence courses. Estimates pertain to all postsecondary students who enrolled at any time during the school year at an institution participating in Title IV programs. Includes students attending more than one institution.

Charges at U.S. Institutions of Higher Education, 1969-2012

Source: National Center for Education Statistics, U.S. Dept. of Education

Figures for 1969-70 are average charges for full-time resident degree-credit students; figures for later years are average charges per full-time equivalent student. Room and board are based on full-time students. These figures are enrollment-weighted according to the number of full-time equivalent undergraduates and thus may vary from averages given elsewhere.

Public (in-state)	Tuition and fees			Board rates			Dormitory charges		
	All institutions	2-yr	4-yr	All institutions	2-yr	4-yr	All institutions	2-yr	4-yr
1969-70	$323	$178	NA	$511	$465	NA	$369	$308	NA
1979-80	583	355	$738	867	893	$865	715	574	$725
1989-90	1,356	756	1,780	1,635	1,581	1,638	1,513	962	1,557
1999-2000	2,504	1,348	3,349	2,364	1,834	2,406	2,440	1,549	2,519
2001-02	2,700	1,380	3,735	2,598	2,036	2,645	2,723	1,722	2,816
2002-03	2,903	1,483	4,046	2,669	2,164	2,712	2,930	1,954	3,029
2003-04	3,319	1,702	4,587	2,822	2,221	2,876	3,106	2,089	3,212
2004-05	3,629	1,849	5,027	2,931	2,353	2,981	3,304	2,174	3,418
2005-06	3,874	1,935	5,351	3,035	2,306	3,093	3,545	2,251	3,664
2006-07	4,102	2,018	5,666	3,191	2,390	3,253	3,757	2,407	3,878
2007-08	4,291	2,061	5,943	3,331	2,409	3,404	3,952	2,506	4,082
2008-09	4,512	2,136	6,312	3,554	2,769	3,619	4,190	2,664	4,331
2009-10	4,751	2,285	6,695	3,653	2,574	3,754	4,399	2,845	4,565
2010-11	5,076	2,439	7,136	3,848	2,685	3,958	4,640	2,960	4,824
2011-12	5,500	2,647	7,701	3,947	2,829	4,052	4,844	3,085	5,036
Private									
1969-70	$1,533	$1,034	NA	$561	$546	NA	$436	$413	NA
1979-80	3,130	2,062	$3,225	955	923	$957	827	766	$831
1989-90	8,147	5,196	8,396	1,948	1,811	1,953	1,923	1,663	1,935
1999-2000	14,100	8,225	14,616	2,877	2,753	2,879	3,236	3,067	3,242
2001-02	15,742	10,076	16,211	3,104	2,633	3,109	3,567	3,116	3,576
2002-03	16,383	10,651	16,826	3,206	3,870	3,197	3,752	3,232	3,764
2003-04	17,315	11,545	17,763	3,364	4,432	3,354	3,945	3,581	3,952
2004-05	18,154	12,122	18,604	3,485	3,700	3,483	4,178	4,475	4,173
2005-06	18,862	12,450	19,292	3,645	4,781	3,637	4,400	4,173	4,404
2006-07	20,048	12,708	20,517	3,785	3,429	3,788	4,606	4,147	4,613
2007-08	20,972	13,126	21,427	3,992	4,074	3,991	4,804	4,484	4,808
2008-09	21,570	13,562	22,036	4,209	4,627	4,206	5,025	4,537	5,032
2009-10	21,444	14,876	21,908	4,331	4,390	4,331	5,249	5,217	5,249
2010-11	22,186	14,467	22,771	4,434	4,475	4,433	5,406	4,928	5,413
2011-12	22,817	13,879	23,479	4,591	4,456	4,591	5,639	5,111	5,646

NA = Not available.

Top 20 Colleges and Universities in Endowment Assets, 2012

Source: 2012 NACUBO-Commonfund Study of Endowments, National Association of College and University Business Officers (NACUBO)

Rank	College/university	Endowment assets[1]	% change, 2011-12	Rank	College/university	Endowment assets[1]	% change, 2011-12
1.	Harvard University	$30,435,375	−4.1%	11.	University of Pennsylvania	$6,754,658	2.6%
2.	Yale University	19,345,000	−0.1	12.	University of Chicago	6,570,875	−0.1
3.	University of Texas System . . .	18,263,850	6.5	13.	University of Notre Dame	6,329,866	1.1
4.	Stanford University	17,035,804	3.2	14.	University of California	5,962,906	−6.0
5.	Princeton University	16,954,128	−0.9	15.	Duke University	5,555,196	−3.3
6.	Massachusetts Institute of Technology	10,149,564	4.5	16.	Emory University	5,461,158	1.1
7.	University of Michigan	7,691,052	−1.8	17.	Washington University in St. Louis	5,225,992	−1.0
8.	Columbia University	7,654,152	−1.7	18.	Cornell University	4,946,954	−2.2
9.	Texas A&M University System & Foundations	7,638,555	9.1	19.	University of Virginia	4,788,852	0.6
10.	Northwestern University	7,118,595	−0.9	20.	Rice University	4,418,595	−0.7

Note: Market value of endowment assets, excluding pledges and working capital, in the fiscal year. (1) In thousands.

U.S. Higher Education Trends: Bachelor's Degrees Conferred, 1899-2022
Source: National Center for Education Statistics, U.S. Dept. of Education
(*) figures are projected.

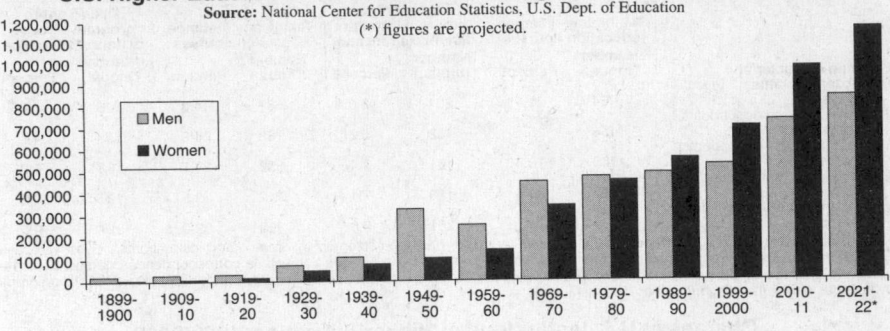

Financial Aid for College and Other Postsecondary Education
As of Aug. 2013. Reviewed by National Assoc. of Student Financial Aid Administrators.

The cost of postsecondary education in the U.S. continues to increase, but financial aid—in the form of **grants** (no repayment needed), **loans**, and/or **work-study** programs—is widely available to help families meet these expenses. Most federal aid is limited to families that demonstrate financial need as determined by standard formulas and is designed to help students attend the college of their choice regardless of their ability to pay. Financial aid personnel at each school can provide information about all aid programs (federal, state, institutional, and private) available to students, how to apply, and deadlines.

All applicants for federal aid must file a Free Application for Federal Student Aid (**FAFSA**), generally as soon as possible after Jan. 1 for the academic year starting the following Sept. Figures provided should match federal income tax forms filed for the previous year. Applicants may also import certain information from their tax forms if they filed their taxes online. Many other sources of aid—state governments, employers and unions, civic organizations, and the institutions themselves—also use the FAFSA to determine eligibility for aid. There are also federal programs that pay for postsecondary education in return for service: AmeriCorps (1-800-942-2677), Reserve Officers' Training Corps (1-800-USA-ROTC), the G.I. Bill (1-888-GIBILL-1), and the National Health Service Corps (1-800-221-9393). A student must reapply for aid annually.

A **federal formula**, based on information provided in the FAFSA, takes into account such factors as family income in the preceding calendar year, parental and student assets (excluding the parents' home, farm, or small business), length of time to parents' retirement, and unusual expenses (such as very high medical expenses). Outside scholarships are also taken into account in determining eligibility for federal, institutional, and state financial aid programs.

The formula determines a family's **expected family contribution** (EFC), which is divided among the number of family members—excluding parents—in college. The EFC is subtracted from the total cost of attending college for each person. The difference determines financial need and the maximum federal aid for which the family may be eligible. (Some institutions use a separate formula for need-based institutional aid.) Some schools guarantee to meet the full financial need of each admitted student; most do their best to cover a student's financial need using various forms of financial aid but may not be able to because of a lack of funds.

The **aid package** offered by each school may include one or more of the following resources: Federal Pell Grants, for those who demonstrate sufficient financial need; Federal Supplemental Educational Opportunity Grants, for those who still have need after receiving Pell Grants; grants from the school; Federal Work-Study or other work programs; low-interest Perkins loans; and federal Direct Subsidized and Unsubsidized loans (also called Stafford loans). Parents of undergraduates and students in graduate or professional school may apply for a federal PLUS loan. Unsubsidized Stafford loans and PLUS loans are available regardless of financial need, but students and parents must still complete the FAFSA to get these loans.

Loans have varying interest rates and other requirements. Repayment of Perkins and Stafford loans does not begin until after graduation; deferments, income-based repayment plans, and loan forgiveness are available on federal loans for students who meet certain requirements. For PLUS loans, parents and graduate-level students must pass a credit check and may need to begin repayment of both principal and interest while the student is still in school.

Terms may vary, but federal student loans must be repaid, even if financial circumstances change, education is incomplete or not as expected, or post-graduation income is less than expected. The loan servicer or lender is required to provide a loan repayment schedule that states the first payment due date, the number and frequency of payments, and the amount due. Some loans have a grace period, a set period of time (in most cases six months) after graduation before repayment begins. Some loan servicers have a number of repayment plan options—including graduated repayments, extended repayment, income-based repayment—or offer loan consolidation.

Certain federal income **tax credits and refunds** are also available to families who meet requirements; see the chapter on taxes.

Rules for financial aid are complex and changeable. *Funding Your Education: The Guide to Federal Student Aid*, a comprehensive resource on financial aid from the U.S. Dept. of Education, is available online in English and Spanish at studentaid.ed.gov/resources/.

Further information and FAFSA forms are available from schools or from the Federal Student Aid Information Center: 1-800-4-FED-AID, Mon.-Fri., 8 AM-10 PM EST; www.fafsa.ed.gov.

Average Salaries of U.S. College Professors, 2012-13

Source: American Association of University Professors

Teaching level		Men Public institution	Men Private/ independent institution	Men Religiously affiliated institution	Women Public institution	Women Private/ independent institution	Women Religiously affiliated institution
Doctoral level	Professor	$126,469	$170,244	$142,502	$113,456	$156,632	$129,741
	Associate	86,825	106,812	96,654	80,500	99,623	90,794
	Assistant	76,219	94,514	83,409	69,936	85,573	75,548
Master's level	Professor	90,392	106,952	96,370	86,263	98,860	89,231
	Associate	72,693	79,893	74,795	69,696	76,073	71,155
	Assistant	62,345	67,658	62,597	59,873	64,722	60,610
Baccalaureate level	Professor	87,894	106,021	79,614	83,750	101,238	76,624
	Associate	71,479	77,866	63,970	68,268	75,983	62,398
	Assistant	59,611	63,518	54,020	57,496	62,088	53,801
2-year	Professor	75,260	NA	NA	74,394	NA	NA
	Associate	61,771	NA	NA	60,111	NA	NA
	Assistant	53,027	NA	NA	52,531	NA	NA

NA = Not available. **Note:** Salaries are for full-time faculty members only.

Average ACT Scores and Characteristics of College-Bound Students, 1990-2013

Source: ACT, Inc. (formerly American College Testing)

(for class graduating in spring of year shown)

SCORES[1]	Unit	1990	1995	2000	2005	2007	2008	2009	2010	2011	2012	2013
Composite score	Points	20.6	20.8	21.0	20.9	21.2	21.1	21.1	21.0	21.1	21.1	20.9
Male	Points	21.0	21.0	21.2	21.1	21.2	21.2	21.3	21.2	21.2	21.2	20.9
Female	Points	20.3	20.7	20.9	20.9	21.0	21.0	20.9	20.9	21.0	21.0	20.9
English score	Points	20.5	20.2	20.5	20.4	20.7	20.6	20.6	20.5	20.6	20.5	20.2
Male	Points	20.1	19.8	20.0	20.0	20.2	20.1	20.2	20.1	20.2	20.0	19.8
Female	Points	20.9	20.6	20.9	20.8	21.0	21.0	20.9	20.8	20.9	20.9	20.6
Math score	Points	19.9	20.2	20.7	20.7	21.0	21.0	21.0	21.0	21.1	21.1	20.9
Male	Points	20.7	20.9	21.4	21.3	21.6	21.6	21.6	21.6	21.6	21.7	21.4
Female	Points	19.3	19.7	20.2	20.2	20.4	20.4	20.4	20.5	20.6	20.6	20.5
PARTICIPANTS												
Total number	(Thous.)	817	945	1,065	1,186	1,301	1,422	1,480	1,569	1,623	1,666	1,799
Male	Percent	46%	44%	43%	44%	42%	44%	45%	45%	46%	46%	46%
White	Percent	79	80	72	66	60	63	64	62	60	59	58
Black	Percent	9	9	10	12	12	13	13	14	14	13	13
Hispanic[2]	Percent	4	5	5	7	7	8	9	10	12	14	14
Composite score												
27 or above	Percent	12	13	14	14	15	9[3]	12	16	17	17	13
18 or below	Percent	35	34	32	34	32	33	34	35	34	34	36

(1) Minimum score, 1; maximum score, 36. Test scores and characteristics of college-bound students are based on the performance of all ACT-tested students who graduated in the spring of a given school year and took the ACT assessment during junior or senior year of high school. (2) Persons of Hispanic origin may be of any race. (3) Composite score of 28 or above.

Average ACT Composite Scores by State, 2013

Source: ACT, Inc. (formerly American College Testing)

State	Avg. comp. score	% grads taking ACT	State	Avg. comp. score	% grads taking ACT	State	Avg. comp. score	% grads taking ACT
Alabama	20.4	78%	Louisiana	19.5	100%	Ohio	21.8	72%
Alaska	21.1	37	Maine	23.5	8	Oklahoma	20.8	75
Arizona	19.6	50	Maryland	22.3	21	Oregon	21.5	34
Arkansas	20.2	90	Massachusetts	24.1	22	Pennsylvania	22.7	18
California	22.2	26	Michigan	19.9	100	Rhode Island	22.7	14
Colorado	20.4	100	Minnesota	23.0	74	South Carolina	20.4	51
Connecticut	24.0	27	Mississippi	18.9	95	South Dakota	21.9	78
Delaware	22.9	15	Missouri	21.6	74	Tennessee	19.5	100
Dist. of Columbia	20.4	38	Montana	21.3	72	Texas	20.9	37
Florida	19.6	74	Nebraska	21.5	84	Utah	20.7	100
Georgia	20.7	51	Nevada	21.3	32	Vermont	23.0	26
Hawaii	20.1	40	New Hampshire	23.8	19	Virginia	22.6	26
Idaho	22.1	49	New Jersey	23.0	23	Washington	22.8	21
Illinois	20.6	100	New Mexico	19.9	70	West Virginia	20.6	63
Indiana	21.7	38	New York	23.4	26	Wisconsin	22.1	71
Iowa	22.1	66	North Carolina	18.7	100	Wyoming	19.8	100
Kansas	21.8	75	North Dakota	20.5	98	U.S. average	20.9	54
Kentucky	19.6	100						

Mean SAT Scores of College-Bound Seniors, 1975-2013

Source: The College Board

(recentered scale; for school year ending in year shown)

	1975	1980	1985	1990	1995	2000	2004	2005	2006	2007	2008	2009	2010	2011	2012	2013
Critical reading score[1]	512	502	509	500	504	505	508	508	503	501	500	499	500	497	496	496
Male	515	506	514	505	505	507	512	513	505	503	502	502	502	500	498	499
Female	509	498	503	496	502	504	504	505	502	500	499	497	498	495	493	494
Math score	498	492	500	501	506	514	518	520	518	514	514	514	515	514	514	514
Male	518	515	522	521	525	533	537	538	536	532	532	533	533	531	532	531
Female	479	473	480	483	490	498	501	504	502	499	499	498	499	500	499	499
Writing score	NA	NA	NA	NA	NA	NA	NA	NA	497	493	493	492	491	489	488	488
Male	NA	NA	NA	NA	NA	NA	NA	NA	491	487	486	485	485	482	481	482
Female	NA	NA	NA	NA	NA	NA	NA	NA	499	499	499	499	498	497	496	493

NA = Not applicable. **Note:** In 1995, the College Board recentered the scoring scale for the SAT by reestablishing the original mean score of 500 on the 200-800 scale. Earlier scores have been adjusted to account for this recentering. The writing test was first given in Mar. 2005; only the scores of the first graduating class to take the revised test are given. (1) Pre-2006 scores are for the Verbal section.

Mean SAT Scores by State, 1990-2013

Source: The College Board

(for school year ending in year shown; V = Verbal, M = Math, CR = Critical reading, W = Writing)

State	1990		2000		2010			2012			2013			% grads taking SAT[1]
	V	M	V	M	CR	M	W	CR	M	W	CR	M	W	
Alabama	545	534	559	555	556	550	544	538	531	527	544	534	530	8%
Alaska	514	501	519	515	518	515	491	512	507	485	508	505	482	54
Arizona	521	520	521	523	519	525	500	517	525	499	521	528	502	27
Arkansas	545	532	563	554	566	566	552	565	566	549	572	570	555	4
California	494	508	497	518	501	516	500	495	512	496	498	512	495	55
Colorado	533	534	534	537	568	572	555	575	581	562	578	581	562	17
Connecticut	506	496	508	509	509	514	513	506	512	510	508	512	512	88
Delaware	510	496	502	496	493	495	481	456	462	444	451	457	443	100
District of Columbia	483	467	494	486	474	464	466	466	460	456	473	466	461	83
Florida	495	493	498	500	496	498	479	492	492	476	492	490	475	66
Georgia	478	473	488	486	488	490	475	488	489	475	490	487	475	81
Hawaii	480	505	488	519	483	505	470	478	500	467	481	504	468	66
Idaho	542	524	540	541	543	541	517	547	541	525	454	459	451	20
Illinois	542	547	568	586	585	600	577	596	615	587	600	617	590	5
Indiana	486	486	498	501	494	505	477	493	501	476	493	500	477	69
Iowa	584	588	589	600	603	613	582	603	606	580	592	601	570	3
Kansas	566	563	574	580	590	595	567	584	594	561	589	595	568	6
Kentucky	548	541	548	550	575	576	563	579	575	566	585	584	572	6
Louisiana	551	537	562	558	555	550	547	542	536	529	556	553	546	9
Maine	501	490	504	500	468	467	454	470	472	452	462	467	451	93
Maryland	506	502	507	509	501	506	488	497	502	488	497	500	486	74
Massachusetts	503	498	511	513	512	526	509	513	530	508	515	529	509	89
Michigan	529	534	557	569	585	605	576	586	603	574	590	610	582	4
Minnesota	552	558	581	594	594	607	580	592	606	573	595	608	577	7
Mississippi	552	538	562	549	566	548	552	561	544	551	568	547	558	4
Missouri	548	541	572	577	593	595	580	589	592	575	596	595	582	5
Montana	540	542	543	546	538	538	517	536	536	511	539	540	516	28
Nebraska	559	562	560	571	585	593	568	576	585	562	584	583	567	5
Nevada	511	511	510	517	496	501	473	491	493	466	492	494	468	49
New Hampshire	518	510	520	519	520	524	510	521	525	510	524	528	515	75
New Jersey	495	498	498	513	495	514	497	495	517	499	499	522	500	78
New Mexico	554	546	549	543	553	549	534	550	546	529	550	545	531	13
New York	489	496	494	506	484	499	478	483	500	475	485	501	477	90
North Carolina	478	470	492	496	497	511	477	491	506	472	495	506	478	68
North Dakota	579	578	588	609	580	594	559	588	610	568	609	609	581	3
Ohio	526	522	533	539	538	548	522	543	552	525	548	556	531	19
Oklahoma	553	542	563	560	569	568	547	568	566	546	571	569	549	5
Oregon	515	509	527	527	523	524	499	521	523	498	520	520	499	57
Pennsylvania	497	490	498	497	492	501	480	491	501	480	494	504	482	74
Rhode Island	498	488	505	500	494	495	488	490	491	485	491	490	487	69
South Carolina	475	467	484	482	484	495	468	481	488	462	484	487	465	73
South Dakota	580	570	587	588	592	603	571	589	610	570	592	601	567	3
Tennessee	558	544	563	553	576	571	565	576	570	566	574	569	566	10
Texas	490	489	493	500	484	505	473	474	499	461	477	499	461	62
Utah	566	555	570	569	568	559	547	568	566	548	569	566	549	6
Vermont	507	493	513	508	519	521	506	519	523	505	516	519	505	69
Virginia	501	496	509	500	512	512	497	510	512	495	516	514	498	72
Washington	513	511	526	528	524	532	508	519	530	503	515	523	499	58
West Virginia	520	514	526	511	515	507	500	516	502	497	514	501	498	17
Wisconsin	552	559	584	597	595	604	579	594	605	577	591	604	576	4
Wyoming	534	538	545	545	570	567	546	567	579	549	581	588	558	5
National average	500	501	505	514	501	516	492	496	514	488	496	514	488	

Note: In 1995, the College Board recentered the scoring scale for the SAT by reestablishing the original mean score of 500 on the 200-800 scale. In 2005, the SAT was changed. The Verbal portion became Critical reading, and a writing test was added. The 2006 graduating class was the first to take the new test. (1) Based on number of high school graduates in 2012, as projected by the Western Interstate Commission for Higher Education, and number of students in the class of 2012 who took the SAT.

Four-Year Colleges and Universities

Source: Peterson's College Database © 2013 Peterson's Nelnet, LLC. All rights reserved.

Note: These listings **include only accredited degree-granting institutions** in the U.S. and U.S. territories with a total enrollment of 1,000 or more. Only four-year colleges and universities (which award a bachelor's degree as their highest undergraduate degree) are included. Data reported **only for institutions that provided updated information** on Peterson's Annual Survey of Undergraduate Institutions for the 2011-12 academic year.

All institutions are coeducational except those where the ZIP code is followed directly by a number in parentheses. (1) = men only, (2) = primarily men, (3) = women only, (4) = primarily women.

The **Tuition & fees** column shows the annual tuition and required fees for full-time students or, where indicated, the tuition and standard fees per unit for part-time students. Where tuition varies according to residence, the figure is given for the most local resident and is coded as follows: (A) = area residents; (S) = state residents; all other figures apply to all students regardless of residence. Where annual expenses are expressed as a lump sum (including full-time tuition, mandatory fees, and room and board), the figure is entered under Tuition & fees and coded (C) = comprehensive fee. **Room & board** is the average cost for one academic year.

Control: 1 = independent (nonprofit), 2 = independent-religious, 3 = independent (profit-making), 4 = federal, 5 = state, 6 = commonwealth (Puerto Rico), 7 = territory (U.S. territories), 8 = county, 9 = district, 10 = city, 11 = state and local, 12 = state-related, 13 = private (unspecified). **Degree** means the highest degree offered: B = bachelor's, M = master's, D = doctorate.

Enrollment is the total number of matriculated undergraduate and (if applicable) graduate students.

Faculty is the total number of faculty members teaching undergraduate courses and (if available) graduate courses.

Grad. rate is the percentage of full-time, first-time bachelor's (or equivalent) degree-seeking undergraduate students who obtain their degrees within six years.

NA indicates category is inapplicable, or data is not available from a consistent source.

Name, address	Year founded	Tuition & fees	Room & board	Control, degree	Enrollment	Faculty	Grad. rate
Abilene Christian Univ., Abilene, TX 79699-9100	1906	$28,350	$8,800	2-D	4,367	346	59.0%
Abraham Baldwin Agr. Coll., Tifton, GA 31793	1933	$3,848(S)	$7,117	5-B	3,327	162	NA
Academy of Art Univ., San Francisco, CA 94105-3410	1929	$23,840	$13,400	3-M	18,115	1,468	35.0
Adams State Univ., Alamosa, CO 81102	1921	$6,448(S)	$7,900	5-M	3,283	177	24.0
Adelphi Univ., Garden City, NY 11530-0701	1896	$29,320	$11,900	1-D	7,859	999	66.0
Adrian Coll., Adrian, MI 49221-2575	1859	$29,156	$8,796	2-M	1,678	176	50.0
Adventist Univ. of Health Sci., Orlando, FL 32803	1913	$10,030	$3,500	1-M	2,671	252	NA
Alabama Agr. and Mech. Univ., Huntsville, AL 35811	1875	$8,160(S)	$6,980	5-D	5,814	290	100.0
Alabama State Univ., Montgomery, AL 36101-0271	1867	$6,312(S)	$5,366	5-D	5,816	430	27.0
Albany Coll. of Pharm. and Health Sci., Albany, NY 12208	1881	$27,630	$9,760	1-D	1,701	142	68.0
Albany State Univ., Albany, GA 31705-2717	1903	$5,912(S)	$7,388	5-M	4,663	270	40.0
Albertus Magnus Coll., New Haven, CT 06511-1189	1925	$28,358	$11,754	2-M	2,010	76	62.0
Albion Coll., Albion, MI 49224-1831	1835	$34,194	$9,690	2-B	1,382	151	72.0
Albright Coll., Reading, PA 19612-5234	1856	$36,660	$10,000	2-M	1,690	173	53.0
Alcorn State Univ., Alcorn State, MS 39096-7500	1871	$5,724(S)	$7,999	5-M	3,950	214	32.0
Alfred Univ., Alfred, NY 14802-1205	1836	$28,774	$11,498	1-D	2,362	190	64.0
Allegheny Coll., Meadville, PA 16335	1815	$39,100	$9,920	1-B	2,140	200	78.0
Alliant Intl. Univ., San Diego, CA 92131-1799	1952	$16,930	$7,340	1-D	3,554	670	NA
Alma Coll., Alma, MI 48801-1599	1006	$31,060	$8,900	2-B	1,464	174	66.0
Alvernia Univ., Reading, PA 19607-1799	1958	$29,060	$10,190	2-D	2,891	292	51.0
Alverno Coll., Milwaukee, WI 53234-3922	1887	$22,126	$7,050	2-M	2,522	269	39.0
Amberton Univ., Garland, TX 75041-5595	1971	$5,640	NA	2-M	1,461	40	NA
Amer. InterContinental Univ. Online, Hoffman Estates, IL 60192	1970	NA	NA	3-M	22,424	396	NA
Amer. Intl. Coll., Springfield, MA 01109-3189	1885	$29,158	$11,710	1-D	3,401	323	34.0
Amer. Public Univ. System, Charles Town, WV 25414	1991	$6,400	NA	3-M	58,115	NA	NA
Amer. Univ. of Puerto Rico, Bayamón, PR 00960-2037	1963	$5,347	NA	1-M	2,468	162	NA
American Univ., Washington, DC 20016-8001	1893	$39,499	$13,920	2-D	12,904	1,327	77.0
Amherst Coll., Amherst, MA 01002-5000	1821	$44,610	$11,650	1-B	1,817	253	95.0
Andorson Univ., Anderson, IN 46012-3495	1917	$26,200	$9,110	2-D	2,516	274	57.0
Anderson Univ., Anderson, SC 29621-4035	1911	$22,790	$8,348	2-D	2,922	302	49.0
Andrews Univ., Berrien Springs, MI 49104	1874	$24,478	$7,528	2-D	3,551	292	59.0
Angelo State Univ., San Angelo, TX 76909	1928	$7,493(S)	$8,026	5-D	6,886	356	31.0
Anna Maria Coll., Paxton, MA 01612	1946	$30,456	$11,450	2-M	1,456	200	46.0
Antioch Univ. Seattle, Seattle, WA 98121-1814	1975	$19,335	NA	1-D	1,080	NA	NA
Appalachian State Univ., Boone, NC 28608	1899	$5,859(S)	$7,060	5-D	17,589	1,256	67.0
Aquinas Coll., Grand Rapids, MI 49506-1799	1886	$25,250	$7,810	2-M	2,327	251	NA
Arcadia Univ., Glenside, PA 19038-3295	1853	$35,620	$12,150	2-D	4,027	487	65.0
Arizona State Univ., Tempe, AZ 85287	1885	$9,724(S)	$9,094	5-D	73,378	2,762	57.0
Arkansas State Univ., State University, AR 72467	1909	$7,180(S)	$7,150	5-D	13,877	660	39.0
Arkansas Tech. Univ., Russellville, AR 72801	1909	$6,798(S)	$5,846	5-M	10,950	519	42.0
Armstrong Atlantic State Univ., Savannah, GA 31419-1997	1935	$5,844(S)	$9,770	5-D	7,439	424	31.0
Art Ctr. Coll. of Design, Pasadena, CA 91103	1930	$35,552	NA	1-M	1,869	431	70.0
Asbury Univ., Wilmore, KY 40390-1198	1890	$26,076	$5,962	2-M	1,765	187	76.0
Ashford Univ., Clinton, IA 52733-2967	1918	NA	NA	3-M	10,568	748	NA
Ashland Univ., Ashland, OH 44805-3702	1878	$28,858	$9,502	2-D	6,491	591	59.0
Ashworth Coll., Norcross, GA 30092	1987	$1,846	NA	3-M	57,650	NA	NA
Assumption Coll., Worcester, MA 01609-1296	1904	$33,805	$10,590	2-M	2,588	228	75.0
Athens State Univ., Athens, AL 35611	1822	$5,340(S)	NA	5-B	3,415	218	NA
Atlantic Univ. Coll., Guaynabo, PR 00970	1983	NA	NA	1-M	1,236	NA	NA
Auburn Univ., Auburn University, AL 36849	1856	$9,446(S)	$10,606	5-D	25,134	1,368	68.0
Auburn Univ. at Montgomery, Montgomery, AL 36124-4023	1967	$8,150(S)	$3,270	5-D	4,989	333	33.0
Augsburg Coll., Minneapolis, MN 55454-1351	1869	$30,418	$8,072	2-M	3,841	400	61.0
Augustana Coll., Rock Island, IL 61201-2296	1860	$34,614	$8,784	2-B	2,551	286	78.0
Augustana Coll., Sioux Falls, SD 57197	1860	$27,780	$6,626	2-M	1,839	206	66.0
Aurora Univ., Aurora, IL 60506-4892	1893	$20,720	$9,542	1-D	4,702	382	52.0
Austin Coll., Sherman, TX 75090-4400	1849	$33,830	$10,715	2-M	1,260	123	77.0
Austin Peay State Univ., Clarksville, TN 37044	1927	$6,648(S)	$7,380	5-M	10,597	615	37.0
Avila Univ., Kansas City, MO 64145-1698	1916	$24,850	$6,800	2-M	1,818	209	40.0
Azusa Pacific Univ., Azusa, CA 91702-7000	1899	$31,076	$4,242	2-D	10,184	1,020	63.0
Babson Coll., Babson Park, MA 02457-0310	1919	$43,520	$14,142	1-M	3,250	261	90.0
Baker Coll. of Allen Park, Allen Park, MI 48101 (4)	2003	$7,740	NA	1-B	3,954	88	NA
Baker Coll. of Auburn Hills, Auburn Hills, MI 48326-1586	1911	$7,740	NA	1-B	3,803	155	NA
Baker Coll. of Cadillac, Cadillac, MI 49601	1986	$7,740	NA	1-B	1,639	105	NA
Baker Coll. of Clinton Township, Clinton Township, MI 48035-4701	1990	$7,920	NA	1-B	5,138	208	NA
Baker Coll. of Flint, Flint, MI 48507-5508	1911	$7,740	$3,000	1-B	6,329	315	NA
Baker Coll. of Jackson, Jackson, MI 49202	1994	$7,740	NA	1-B	2,730	85	NA
Baker Coll. of Muskegon, Muskegon, MI 49442-3497	1888	$7,740	NA	1-B	4,994	177	NA
Baker Coll. of Owosso, Owosso, MI 48867-4400	1984	$7,740	$3,000	1-B	3,078	144	NA
Baker Coll. of Port Huron, Port Huron, MI 48060-2597	1990	$7,920	NA	1-B	1,177	126	NA
Baldwin Wallace Univ., Berea, OH 44017-2088	1845	$27,060	$7,520	2-M	4,173	424	68.0

Name, address	Year founded	Tuition & fees	Room & board	Control, degree	Enroll- ment	Faculty	Grad. rate
Ball State Univ., Muncie, IN 47306-1099	1918	$8,980(S)	$8,870	5-D	21,053	1,140	55.0%
Baptist Bible Coll. of Pennsylvania, Clarks Summit, PA 18411-1297.	1932	$19,710	$7,180	2-D	1,001	47	36.0
Baptist Coll. of Health Sci., Memphis, TN 38104 (4)	1994	$11,870	$2,200	2-B	1,043	107	60.0
Bard Coll., Annandale-on-Hudson, NY 12504	1860	$46,370	$13,502	1-D	2,322	265	79.0
Barnard Coll., New York, NY 10027-6598 (3)	1889	$43,502	$13,810	1-B	2,445	335	88.0
Barry Univ., Miami Shores, FL 33161-6695	1940	$28,160	$11,988	2-D	9,070	838	41.0
Barton Coll., Wilson, NC 27893-7000.	1902	$24,180	$7,940	2-M	1,106	111	47.0
Baruch Coll. of the City Univ. of New York, New York, NY 10010-5585	1919	$5,430(S)	$11,590	11-M	17,373	1,070	63.0
Bastyr Univ., Kenmore, WA 98028-4966	1978	$21,990	$7,050	1-D	1,028	160	NA
Bates Coll., Lewiston, ME 04240-6028	1855	$44,300	$12,935	1-B	1,753	195	88.0
Bayamón Central Univ., Bayamón, PR 00960-1725	1970	$8,200	NA	2-M	1,202	153	NA
Baylor Univ., Waco, TX 76798	1845	$36,137	$10,748	2-D	15,364	1,238	75.0
Bay Path Coll., Longmeadow, MA 01106-2292	1897	$28,532	$11,440	1-M	2,370	230	50.0
Becker Coll., Worcester, MA 01609	1784	$30,340	$11,050	1-B	1,826	193	29.0
Belhaven Univ., Jackson, MS 39202-1789.	1883	$19,200	$6,890	2-M	3,519	335	48.0
Bellarmine Univ., Louisville, KY 40205-0671	1950	$33,180	$9,770	2-D	3,602	376	66.0
Bellevue Univ., Bellevue, NE 68005-3098	1965	$7,700	NA	1-D	10,304	411	37.0
Belmont Abbey Coll., Belmont, NC 28012-1802	1876	$27,622	$10,403	2-B	1,706	157	43.0
Belmont Univ., Nashville, TN 37212-3757	1951	$26,130	$12,420	2-D	6,665	735	67.0
Beloit Coll., Beloit, WI 53511-5596.	1846	$41,250	$7,256	1-B	1,359	137	78.0
Bemidji State Univ., Bemidji, MN 56601-2699	1919	$8,106(S)	$6,970	5-M	5,017	260	46.0
Benedict Coll., Columbia, SC 29204	1870	$18,286	$8,104	2-B	2,641	NA	NA
Benedictine Coll., Atchison, KS 66002-1499	1859	$23,175	$8,190	2-M	2,149	158	56.0
Benedictine Univ., Lisle, IL 60532-0900	1887	$25,850	$8,380	2-D	6,516	702	49.0
Bentley Univ., Waltham, MA 02452-4705.	1917	$39,628	$12,960	1-D	5,565	448	89.0
Berea Coll., Berea, KY 40404	1855	$910	$5,792	1-B	1,658	171	67.0
Berkeley Coll., Woodland Park, NJ 07424-3353	1931	$21,750	$6,900	3-B	3,709	NA	NA
Berkeley Coll.–New York City campus, New York, NY 10017-4604	1936	$21,750	NA	3-B	4,430	NA	NA
Berklee Coll. of Mus., Boston, MA 02215-3693.	1945	$36,490	$16,950	1-M	4,521	569	52.0
Berry Coll., Mount Berry, GA 30149-0159	1902	$27,650	$9,679	2-M	2,166	207	61.0
Bethel Coll., Mishawaka, IN 46545-5591	1947	$24,970	$7,460	2-M	1,963	221	62.0
Bethel Univ., McKenzie, TN 38201	1842	$14,520	$8,364	2-M	4,295	291	34.0
Bethel Univ., St. Paul, MN 55112-6999	1871	$30,840	$8,900	2-D	5,326	306	71.0
Beth Medrash Govoha, Lakewood, NJ 08701-2797 (1)	1943	NA	NA	2-M	5,639	NA	NA
Bethune-Cookman Univ., Daytona Beach, FL 32114-3099	1904	$14,410	$8,548	2-M	3,543	248	43.0
Binghamton Univ., State Univ. of New York, Binghamton, NY 13902-6000.	1946	$7,645(S)	$12,446	5-D	15,308	866	79.0
Biola Univ., La Mirada, CA 90639-0001.	1908	$31,004	$7,912	2-D	6,302	515	65.0
Birmingham-Southern Coll., Birmingham, AL 35254	1856	$30,700	$10,700	2-B	1,231	114	65.0
Black Hills State Univ., Spearfish, SD 57799	1883	$7,320(S)	$5,641	5-M	4,412	NA	28.0
Bloomfield Coll., Bloomfield, NJ 07003-9981	1868	$25,050	$10,700	2-M	2,045	226	37.0
Bloomsburg Univ. of Pennsylvania, Bloomsburg, PA 17815-1301.	1839	$8,343(S)	$7,498	5-D	9,950	519	64.0
Bluefield State Coll., Bluefield, WV 24701-2198	1895	$217/cr. hr.(A)	NA	5-B	1,935	140	26.0
Bluffton Univ., Bluffton, OH 45817	1899	$27,426	$9,010	2-M	1,198	107	56.0
Bob Jones Univ., Greenville, SC 29614	1927	$13,430	$5,790	2-D	3,469	260	64.0
Boise State Univ., Boise, ID 83725-0399	1932	$5,884(S)	$7,174	5-D	22,674	1,272	30.0
Boricua Coll., New York, NY 10032-1560	1974	$10,000	NA	1-M	1,058	133	NA
Boston Coll., Chestnut Hill, MA 02467-3800	1863	$43,878	$12,608	2-D	13,783	1,363	92.0
Boston Univ., Boston, MA 02215	1839	$42,994	$13,190	1-D	32,603	2,630	84.0
Bowdoin Coll., Brunswick, ME 04011	1794	$44,118	$12,010	1-B	1,839	228	95.0
Bowie State Univ., Bowie, MD 20715-9465	1865	$6,639(S)	$9,597	5-D	5,421	408	40.0
Bowling Green State Univ., Bowling Green, OH 43403	1910	$10,513(S)	$8,064	5-D	17,286	1,067	58.0
Bradley Univ., Peoria, IL 61625-0002.	1897	$29,664	$9,050	1-D	5,451	579	75.0
Brandeis Univ., Waltham, MA 02454-9110	1948	$44,294	$12,256	1-D	5,808	511	90.0
Briarcliffe Coll., Bethpage, NY 11714	1966	NA	NA	3-B	1,779	NA	NA
Briar Cliff Univ., Sioux City, IA 51104-0100	1930	$25,642	$7,542	2-M	1,185	106	45.0
Bridgewater Coll., Bridgewater, VA 22812-1599	1880	$29,090	$10,790	2-B	1,760	138	57.0
Bridgewater State Univ., Bridgewater, MA 02325-0001.	1840	$8,052(S)	$10,700	5-M	11,417	775	54.0
Brigham Young Univ., Provo, UT 84602-1001.	1875	$4,710	$7,200	2-D	34,409	1,739	77.0
Brigham Young Univ.–Hawaii, Laie, HI 96762-1294	1955	$4,630	$5,048	2-B	2,555	228	52.0
Brigham Young Univ.–Idaho, Rexburg, ID 83460	1888	NA	NA	2-B	14,944	NA	NA
Brookline Coll., Phoenix, AZ 85021	1979	$13,750	NA	3-B	1,072	43	NA
Brooklyn Coll. of the City Univ. of New York, Brooklyn, NY 11210-2889	1930	$5,884(S)	NA	11-D	17,094	1,401	43.0
Brooks Institute, Santa Barbara, CA 93101	1945	NA	NA	3-M	1,240	NA	NA
Brown Univ., Providence, RI 02912	1764	$43,758	$11,258	1-D	8,885	977	95.0
Bryan Coll., Dayton, TN 37321	1930	$18,740	$5,454	2-M	1,304	66	55.0
Bryant & Stratton Coll.–Wauwatosa campus, Wauwatosa, WI 53226	1854	$15,695	NA	3-B	1,264	NA	NA
Bryant Univ., Smithfield, RI 02917	1863	$37,234	$13,664	1-M	3,418	308	80.0
Bryn Mawr Coll., Bryn Mawr, PA 19010-2899	1885	$42,246	$13,340	1-D	1,774	201	82.0
Bucknell Univ., Lewisburg, PA 17837.	1846	$46,902	$11,258	1-M	3,618	386	90.0
Buffalo State Coll., State Univ. of New York, Buffalo, NY 14222-1095	1867	$6,694(S)	$11,192	5-M	11,214	842	48.0
Butler Univ., Indianapolis, IN 46208-3485	1855	$33,138	$11,110	1-D	4,771	480	73.0
Cabrini Coll., Radnor, PA 19087-3698.	1957	$29,000	NA	2-M	2,801	293	48.0
Cairn Univ., Langhorne, PA 19047-2990	1913	$22,455	$4,625	2-M	1,200	115	NA
Caldwell Coll., Caldwell, NJ 07006-6195	1939	$29,000	$11,000	2-D	2,213	227	51.0
California Baptist Univ., Riverside, CA 92504-3206.	1950	$26,900	$8,990	2-M	6,031	531	58.0
California Coll., San Diego, CA 92111	1978	NA	NA	3-B	1,299	NA	NA
California Coll. of the Arts, San Francisco, CA 94107	1907	$40,334	$8,000	1-M	1,932	466	44.0
California Institute of Integral Studies, San Francisco, CA 94103	1968	NA	NA	1-D	1,166	NA	NA
California Institute of Tech., Pasadena, CA 91125-0001	1891	$41,538	$12,507	1-D	2,243	341	92.0
California Institute of the Arts, Valencia, CA 91355-2340	1961	$38,260	$9,626	1-D	1,454	314	60.0
California Lutheran Univ., Thousand Oaks, CA 91360-2787	1959	$34,360	$11,510	2-D	4,103	373	NA
California Polytechnic State Univ., San Luis Obispo, San Luis Obispo, CA 93407	1901	$8,523(S)	$10,679	5-M	18,679	1,259	73.0
California State Polytechnic Univ., Pomona, Pomona, CA 91768-2557	1938	$6,623(S)	$11,615	5-D	22,156	1,077	51.0
California State Univ., Bakersfield, Bakersfield, CA 93311	1970	$6,709(S)	$8,787	5-M	8,002	NA	41.0
California State Univ., Channel Islands, Camarillo, CA 93012	2002	$6,316(S)	$10,200	5-D	3,599	294	NA
California State Univ., Chico, Chico, CA 95929-0722	1887	$8,906(S)	$11,208	5-M	16,470	862	59.0
California State Univ., Dominguez Hills, Carson, CA 90747-0001.	1960	$6,095(S)	$10,733	5-M	13,933	743	28.0
California State Univ., East Bay, Hayward, CA 94542-3000	1957	$6,309(S)	$11,321	5-D	13,851	709	41.0
California State Univ., Fresno, Fresno, CA 93740-8027	1911	NA	$10,192	5-D	22,565	1,186	48.0
California State Univ., Fullerton, Fullerton, CA 92834-9480.	1957	$6,182(S)	$12,096	5-D	37,677	1,680	50.0
California State Univ., Long Beach, Long Beach, CA 90840	1949	$6,240(S)	$11,300	5-D	36,279	1,908	57.0
California State Univ., Los Angeles, Los Angeles, CA 90032-8530.	1947	$6,335(S)	$9,728	5-D	21,755	1,117	37.0
California State Univ., Monterey Bay, Seaside, CA 93955-8001	1994	$5,963(S)	$9,498	5-M	5,609	383	37.0
California State Univ., Northridge, Northridge, CA 91330	1958	$6,520(S)	$12,404	5-M	36,164	1,857	48.0
California State Univ., Sacramento, Sacramento, CA 95819	1947	$6,620(S)	$11,724	5-D	28,016	1,400	42.0
California State Univ., San Bernardino, San Bernardino, CA 92407-2397.	1965	$12,021(S)	$9,972	5-D	18,234	730	46.0

Name, address	Year founded	Tuition & fees	Room & board	Control, degree	Enroll-ment	Faculty	Grad. rate
California State Univ., San Marcos, San Marcos, CA 92096-0001	1990	$7,298(S)	NA	5-M	10,363	609	47.0%
California State Univ., Stanislaus, Turlock, CA 95382	1957	$6,584(S)	$9,056	5-D	8,882	446	49.0
California Univ. of Pennsylvania, California, PA 15419-1394.	1852	$9,016(S)	$10,172	5-M	8,608	404	54.0
Calumet Coll. of St. Joseph, Whiting, IN 46394-2195	1951	$15,620	NA	2-M	1,030	130	NA
Calvin Coll., Grand Rapids, MI 49546-4388	1876	$28,250	$9,335	2-M	4,008	394	77.0
Cambridge Coll., Cambridge, MA 02138-5304.	1971	$13,280	NA	1-D	3,757	453	NA
Cameron Univ., Lawton, OK 73505-6377.	1908	$4,770(S)	$3,884	5-M	6,112	319	17.0
Campbellsville Univ., Campbellsville, KY 42718-2799	1906	$22,196	$8,200	2-M	3,664	311	42.0
Campbell Univ., Buies Creek, NC 27506	1887	$23,720	$8,300	2-D	4,743	305	51.7
Canisius Coll., Buffalo, NY 14208-1098	1870	$32,030	$11,820	2-M	4,908	519	68.0
Capella Univ., Minneapolis, MN 55402	1993	NA	NA	3-D	36,375	NA	NA
Capital Univ., Columbus, OH 43209-2394	1830	$31,364	$8,460	2-D	3,584	450	59.0
Cardinal Stritch Univ., Milwaukee, WI 53217-3985	1937	$24,330	$7,030	2-D	4,641	431	NA
Caribbean Univ., Bayamón, PR 00960-0493	1969	$4,465	$9,000	1-M	5,846	424	NA
Carleton Coll., Northfield, MN 55057-4001.	1866	$44,445	$11,553	1-B	2,055	243	94.0
Carlos Albizu Univ., Miami campus, Miami, FL 33172-2209.	1980	$12,048	NA	1-D	1,046	48	39.0
Carlow Univ., Pittsburgh, PA 15213-3165 (4).	1929	$24,438	$9,630	2-D	2,967	280	57.0
Carnegie Mellon Univ., Pittsburgh, PA 15213-3891.	1900	$47,642	$11,990	1-D	12,569	NA	87.0
Carroll Coll., Helena, MT 59625-0002	1909	$26,554	$8,062	2-B	1,464	170	62.0
Carroll Univ., Waukesha, WI 53186-5593	1846	$25,248	$7,736	2-D	3,385	330	57.0
Carson-Newman Univ., Jefferson City, TN 37760	1851	$22,652	$6,406	2-M	1,967	206	55.0
Carthage Coll., Kenosha, WI 53140.	1847	$33,000	$9,000	2-M	2,778	NA	54.0
Case Western Reserve Univ., Cleveland, OH 44106.	1826	$40,490	$12,436	1-D	10,026	932	78.0
Castleton State Coll., Castleton, VT 05735	1787	$10,286(S)	$9,138	5-M	2,156	234	41.0
Catawba Coll., Salisbury, NC 28144-2488.	1851	$26,820	$9,410	2-M	1,293	129	51.0
The Catholic Univ. of America, Washington, DC 20064.	1887	$36,820	$14,274	2-D	6,838	814	67.0
Cazenovia Coll., Cazenovia, NY 13035-1084.	1824	$28,022	$11,398	1-B	1,092	129	44.0
Cedar Crest Coll., Allentown, PA 18104-6196 (4)	1867	$31,196	$9,990	2-M	1,567	156	61.0
Cedarville Univ., Cedarville, OH 45314-0601.	1887	$25,496	$5,540	2-D	3,380	311	72.0
Centenary Univ., Hackettstown, NJ 07840-2100.	1867	$28,500	$10,116	2-M	2,644	222	50.0
Central Coll., Pella, IA 50219	1853	$30,700	$9,980	2-B	1,486	120	69.0
Central Connecticut State Univ., New Britain, CT 06050-4010	1849	$8,321(S)	$10,056	5-D	12,521	968	47.0
Central Methodist Univ., Fayette, MO 65248-1198	1854	$20,590	NA	2-M	1,173	123	50.0
Central Michigan Univ., Mount Pleasant, MI 48859	1892	$10,950(S)	$8,368	5-D	27,626	1,113	58.0
Central Penn Coll., Summerdale, PA 17093-0309	1881	$16,167	$6,960	3-B	1,342	133	44.0
Central State Univ., Wilberforce, OH 45384.	1887	$5,870(S)	$8,782	5-M	2,152	243	27.0
Central Washington Univ., Ellensburg, WA 98926	1891	$8,946(S)	$9,240	5-M	11,320	589	6.0
Centre Coll., Danville, KY 40422-1394.	1819	$36,000	$9,100	2-B	1,344	142	87.0
Chadron State Coll., Chadron, NE 69337	1911	$5,330(S)	$5,311	5-M	2,649	NA	NA
Chamberlain Coll. of Nursing, Addison, IL 60101-6106	2005	$16,960	NA	3-M	11,120	353	NA
Chaminade Univ. of Honolulu, Honolulu, HI 96816-1578.	1955	$19,330	$11,290	2-M	2,144	NA	36.0
Champlain Coll., Burlington, VT 05402-0670	1878	$31,350	$13,500	1-M	3,233	350	66.0
Chapman Univ., Orange, CA 92866.	1861	$43,573	$12,204	2-D	7,566	781	72.0
Charleston Southern Univ., Charleston, SC 29423-8087.	1964	$22,090	$8,650	2-M	3,130	298	38.0
Charter Oak State Coll., New Britain, CT 06053-2142.	1973	$7,692(S)	NA	5-B	1,644	153	NA
Chatham Univ., Pittsburgh, PA 15232-2826.	1809	$32,454	$9,086	1-D	2,178	323	59.0
Chestnut Hill Coll., Philadelphia, PA 19118-2693	1924	$31,170	$9,875	2-D	2,301	354	47.0
Cheyney Univ. of Pennsylvania, Cheyney, PA 19319	1837	$9,036(S)	$11,552	5-M	1,284	107	22.0
Chicago State Univ., Chicago, IL 60628.	1867	$9,254(S)	$8,221	5-D	6,107	291	21.0
Chowan Univ., Murfreesboro, NC 27855	1848	$22,160	$7,870	2-M	1,316	105	24.0
Christian Brothers Univ., Memphis, TN 38104-5581	1871	$27,284	$6,140	2-M	1,598	153	60.0
Christopher Newport Univ., Newport News, VA 23606-2998.	1960	$10,572(S)	$9,728	5-M	5,186	392	67.0
The Citadel, The Military Coll. of South Carolina, Charleston, SC 29409 (2)	1842	$11,772(S)	$6,115	5-M	3,499	266	70.0
City Coll. of the City Univ. of New York, New York, NY 10031-9198	1847	$5,131(S)	NA	11-D	16,161	1,922	41.0
City Univ. of Seattle, Bellevue, WA 98005	1973	$15,600	NA	1-D	2,065	332	28.0
Claflin Univ., Orangeburg, SC 29115	1869	$14,424	$8,040	2-M	1,946	153	44.0
Claremont McKenna Coll., Claremont, CA 91711	1946	$44,085	$13,980	1-M	1,295	162	92.0
Clarion Univ. of Pennsylvania, Clarion, PA 16214	1867	$9,141(S)	$7,186	5-M	6,520	387	50.0
Clark Atlanta Univ., Atlanta, GA 30314	1865	$19,830	$8,956	2-D	3,419	320	39.0
Clark Univ., Worcester, MA 01610-1477	1887	$39,550	$7,470	1-D	3,503	291	80.0
Clarke Univ., Dubuque, IA 52001-3198	1843	$28,000	$8,400	2-D	1,191	160	63.0
Clarkson Univ., Potsdam, NY 13699	1896	$40,610	$12,998	1-D	3,604	273	72.0
Clayton State Univ., Morrow, GA 30260-0285	1969	$5,916(S)	$8,862	5-M	7,140	367	28.0
Clemson Univ., Clemson, SC 29634	1889	$13,076(S)	$7,552	5-D	20,768	1,157	82.0
Cleveland State Univ., Cleveland, OH 44115.	1964	$9,314(S)	$11,848	5-D	17,525	1,041	30.0
Coastal Carolina Univ., Conway, SC 29528-6054	1954	$9,760(S)	$7,700	5-M	9,335	645	47.0
Coe Coll., Cedar Rapids, IA 52402-5092	1851	$35,730	$7,700	2-M	1,367	169	70.0
Coker Coll., Hartsville, SC 29550.	1908	$24,576	$7,610	1-M	1,163	103	56.0
Colby Coll., Waterville, ME 04901-8840.	1813	$55,700(C)	NA	1-B	1,863	216	90.0
Colegio Univ.ersitario de San Juan, San Juan, PR 00918.	1971	NA	NA	10-B	1,785	NA	NA
Colgate Univ., Hamilton, NY 13346-1386.	1819	$44,640	$11,075	1-M	2,865	349	90.0
The Coll. at Brockport, State Univ. of New York, Brockport, NY 14420-2997	1867	$7,210(S)	$11,528	5-M	8,271	604	NA
Coll. for Creative Studies, Detroit, MI 48202-4034.	1926	$35,710	$8,050	1-M	1,441	252	57.0
Coll. of Charleston, Charleston, SC 29424-0001	1770	$9,918(S)	$10,461	5-M	11,723	957	69.0
Coll. of Coastal Georgia, Brunswick, GA 31520.	1961	$3,927(S)	$8,126	5-B	3,156	186	NA
The Coll. of Idaho, Caldwell, ID 83605.	1891	$23,000	$8,646	1-M	1,059	113	64.0
Coll. of Mount St. Joseph, Cincinnati, OH 45233-1670	1920	$25,800	$8,080	2-D	2,294	233	60.0
Coll. of Mount St. Vincent, Riverdale, NY 10471-1093.	1911	$30,290	$12,060	1-M	1,925	232	57.0
The Coll. of New Jersey, Ewing, NJ 08628	1855	$14,378(S)	$10,998	5-M	7,270	754	87.0
The Coll. of New Rochelle, New Rochelle, NY 10805-2308 (4)	1904	$31,260	$11,690	1-M	1,670	NA	35.0
Coll. of St. Benedict, Saint Joseph, MN 56374 (3)	1887	$36,218	$9,271	2-B	2,070	189	81.0
Coll. of St. Elizabeth, Morristown, NJ 07960-6989 (4)	1899	$29,907	$12,254	2-D	1,687	289	58.0
Coll. of St. Mary, Omaha, NE 68106 (3).	1923	$25,310	$6,800	2-D	1,037	158	36.0
The Coll. of St. Rose, Albany, NY 12203-1419	1920	$27,684	$11,250	1-M	4,698	426	65.0
The Coll. of St. Scholastica, Duluth, MN 55811-4199	1912	$31,612	$8,348	2-D	4,144	383	65.0
Coll. of Staten Island of the City Univ. of New York, Staten Island, NY 10314-6600	1955	$5,858(S)	NA	11-D	14,321	1,219	47.0
Coll. of the Holy Cross, Worcester, MA 01610-2395	1843	$44,272	$11,960	2-B	2,926	316	93.0
Coll. of the Ozarks, Point Lookout, MO 65726	1906	$430	$5,900	2-B	1,379	129	64.0
The Coll. of William & Mary, Williamsburg, VA 23187-8795.	1693	$13,570(S)	$9,072	5-D	8,258	NA	91.0
The Coll. of Wooster, Wooster, OH 44691-2363	1866	$39,810	$9,590	2-B	2,080	213	77.0
Colorado Christian Univ., Lakewood, CO 80226	1914	$22,960	$9,840	2-M	2,511	NA	NA
The Colorado Coll., Colorado Springs, CO 80903-3294	1874	$41,942	$9,728	1-M	2,026	198	90.0
Colorado Mesa Univ., Grand Junction, CO 81501-3122	1925	$6,870(S)	$9,103	5-D	9,482	607	29.0
Colorado Mountain Coll., Glenwood Springs, CO 81601	1965	$1,860(A)	$8,164	9-B	2,465	NA	NA
Colorado Mountain Coll., Alpine campus, Steamboat Springs, CO 80487	1965	$1,860(A)	$8,164	9-B	1,550	NA	NA
Colorado Mountain Coll., Timberline campus, Leadville, CO 80461	1965	$1,860(A)	$8,164	9-B	1,209	NA	NA

Name, address	Year founded	Tuition & fees	Room & board	Control/degree	Enrollment	Faculty	Grad. rate
Colorado Sch. of Mines, Golden, CO 80401-1887	1874	$14,454(S)	$8,838	5-D	5,632	368	67.0%
Colorado State Univ., Fort Collins, CO 80523-0015	1870	$8,648(S)	$10,278	5-D	30,647	966	64.0
Colorado State Univ.–Pueblo, Pueblo, CO 81001-4901	1933	$7,327(S)	$8,600	5-M	5,049	418	32.0
Colorado Tech. Univ. Colorado Springs, Colorado Springs, CO 80907-3896	1965	$13,275	NA	3-D	2,359	343	NA
Colorado Tech. Univ. Online, Colorado Springs, CO 80907	NA	NA	NA	3-M	25,797	613	NA
Columbia Centro Universitario, Caguas, PR 00726	1966	$9,435	NA	3-M	1,744	127	24.0
Columbia Coll., Columbia, MO 65216-0002	1851	$19,386	NA	2-M	1,193	118	43.0
Columbia Coll., Columbia, SC 29203-5998	1854	$27,250	$6,978	2-D	1,263	134	49.0
Columbia Coll. Chicago, Chicago, IL 60605-1996	1890	$21,750	$11,920	1-M	10,783	1,675	NA
Columbia Southern Univ., Orange Beach, AL 36561	1993	$4,895	NA	3-D	22,658	285	35.0
Columbia Univ., New York, NY 10027	1754	$47,346	$11,496	1-D	6,068	1,965	98.0
Columbia Univ., Sch. of General Studies, New York, NY 10027-6939	1754	$45,699	$10,233	1-B	1,632	NA	NA
Columbus Coll. of Art and Design, Columbus, OH 43215-1758	1879	$28,524	$7,490	1-M	1,400	193	55.0
Columbus State Univ., Columbus, GA 31907-5645	1958	$6,592(S)	$8,542	5-D	8,239	511	34.0
Concordia Coll., Moorhead, MN 56562	1891	$32,814	$7,160	2-M	2,631	252	68.0
Concord Univ., Athens, WV 24712-1000	1872	$5,716(S)	$7,386	5-M	2,888	216	37.3
Concordia Univ. Chicago, River Forest, IL 60305-1499	1864	$27,788	$8,664	2-D	5,454	507	49.0
Concordia Univ., Irvine, CA 92612-3299	1972	$29,630	$9,050	2-M	3,519	319	52.0
Concordia Univ., Nebraska, Seward, NE 68434-1599	1894	$24,750	$6,700	2-M	2,091	161	64.0
Concordia Univ., Portland, OR 97211-6099	1905	$25,392	$7,040	2-M	3,111	259	45.0
Concordia Univ., St. Paul, St. Paul, MN 55104-5494	1893	$19,700	$7,750	2-M	3,013	325	46.0
Concordia Univ. Texas, Austin, TX 78726	1926	$23,600	$8,460	2-M	2,584	278	35.0
Concordia Univ. Wisconsin, Mequon, WI 53097-2402	1881	$23,970	$9,050	2-D	7,751	382	59.0
Connecticut Coll., New London, CT 06320-4196	1911	$46,085	$12,695	1-M	1,933	249	NA
Converse Coll., Spartanburg, SC 29302-0006	1889	$28,276	$8,854	1-M	1,221	83	54.0
Coppin State Univ., Baltimore, MD 21216-3698	1900	$5,732(S)	$8,018	5-M	3,800	312	15.0
Corban Univ., Salem, OR 97301-9392	1935	$26,430	$8,145	2-D	1,160	107	55.0
Cornell Coll., Mount Vernon, IA 52314-1098	1853	$34,705	$7,900	2-B	1,180	116	70.0
Cornell Univ., Ithaca, NY 14853-0001	1865	$43,413	$13,678	1-D	21,131	1,827	93.0
Cornerstone Univ., Grand Rapids, MI 49525-5897	1941	$24,168	$7,910	2-M	2,747	114	43.0
Covenant Coll., Lookout Mountain, GA 30750	1955	$28,270	$8,040	2-M	1,135	101	61.0
Creighton Univ., Omaha, NE 68178-0001	1878	$33,330	$9,446	2-D	7,736	764	74.0
Crown Coll., St. Bonifacius, MN 55375-9001	1916	$22,430	$7,480	2-M	1,269	160	50.0
The Culinary Institute of America, Hyde Park, NY 12538-1499	1946	$27,130	$8,580	1-B	2,827	192	NA
Cumberland Univ., Lebanon, TN 37087	1842	$20,200	$7,800	1-M	1,375	122	31.0
Curry Coll., Milton, MA 02186-9984	1879	$33,465	$12,760	1-M	3,040	292	43.0
Daemen Coll., Amherst, NY 14226-3592	1947	$23,130	$10,700	1-D	3,005	291	44.0
Dakota State Univ., Madison, SD 57042-1799	1881	$7,950(S)	$5,235	5-D	3,110	119	42.0
Dallas Baptist Univ., Dallas, TX 75211-9299	1965	$21,110	$6,498	2-D	5,622	568	56.0
Dalton State Coll., Dalton, GA 30720	1963	$3,162(S)	$6,320	5-B	5,047	215	15.0
Dartmouth Coll., Hanover, NH 03755	1769	$45,212	$12,954	1-D	6,277	702	96.0
Davenport Univ., Grand Rapids, MI 49512	1866	$13,022	$8,434	1-M	11,304	982	NA
Davidson Coll., Davidson, NC 28035	1837	$42,849	$11,834	2-B	1,790	176	93.0
Defiance Coll., Defiance, OH 43512-1610	1850	$27,360	$8,850	2-M	1,021	107	51.0
Delaware State Univ., Dover, DE 19901-2277	1891	$6,481(S)	$9,386	5-D	4,178	357	35.0
Delaware Valley Coll., Doylestown, PA 18901-2697	1896	$31,746	$11,262	1-M	2,253	195	55.0
Delta State Univ., Cleveland, MS 38733-0001	1924	$5,724(S)	$7,100	5-D	4,763	257	32.0
Denison Univ., Granville, OH 43023	1831	$42,280	$10,360	1-B	2,336	223	83.0
DePaul Univ., Chicago, IL 60604-2287	1898	$32,295	$11,717	2-D	24,966	1,987	68.0
DePauw Univ., Greencastle, IN 46135	1837	$38,750	$10,200	2-B	2,336	267	78.0
DeSales Univ., Center Valley, PA 18034-9568	1964	$30,150	$10,970	2-D	3,255	308	67.0
DeVry Coll. of New York, New York, NY 10016-5267	1998	$16,156	NA	3-M	1,953	68	NA
DeVry Univ., Phoenix, AZ 85021-2995	1967	$16,156	NA	3-M	1,318	157	NA
DeVry Univ., Fremont, CA 94555	1998	$15,374	NA	3-M	1,553	231	39.0
DeVry Univ., Long Beach, CA 90806	1984	$15,374	NA	3-M	1,172	101	32.0
DeVry Univ., Pomona, CA 91768-2642	1983	$16,156	NA	3-M	2,637	98	NA
DeVry Univ., Orlando, FL 32839	2000	$16,156	NA	3-M	1,594	98	NA
DeVry Univ., Decatur, GA 30030-2556	1969	$16,156	NA	3-M	2,554	152	NA
DeVry Univ., Addison, IL 60101-6106	1982	$15,374	NA	3-B	1,508	154	36.0
DeVry Univ., Chicago, IL 60618-5994	1931	$16,156	NA	3-M	1,776	130	NA
DeVry Univ., Naperville, IL 60563-2361	NA	NA	NA	3-M	8,828	2,248	NA
DeVry Univ., Tinley Park, IL 60477	2000	$15,374	NA	3-M	1,471	79	39.0
DeVry Univ., North Brunswick, NJ 08902-3362	1969	$16,156	NA	3-M	1,414	159	NA
DeVry Univ., Columbus, OH 43209-2705	1952	$16,156	NA	3-M	2,476	107	NA
DeVry Univ., Houston, TX 77041	NA	$16,156	NA	3-M	1,332	165	NA
DeVry Univ., Irving, TX 75063-2439	1969	$16,156	NA	3-M	1,220	102	NA
DeVry Univ. Online, Addison, IL 60101-6106	2000	$16,156	NA	3-M	24,623	2,809	NA
Dickinson Coll., Carlisle, PA 17013-2896	1773	$44,551	$11,178	1-B	2,386	253	85.0
Dickinson State Univ., Dickinson, ND 58601-4896	1918	$5,717(S)	$4,950	5-B	2,668	233	38.0
DigiPen Institute of Tech., Redmond, WA 98052	1988	$26,560	$10,441	3-M	1,041	95	NA
Dillard Univ., New Orleans, LA 70122-3097	1869	$14,850	$8,686	2-B	1,307	NA	31.0
Dixie State Coll. of Utah, St. George, UT 84770-3876	1911	$4,709(S)	$4,348	5-B	9,044	NA	32.0
Doane Coll., Crete, NE 68333-2430	1872	$25,080	$7,140	2-M	1,149	123	64.0
Dominican Coll., Orangeburg, NY 10962-1210	1952	$23,970	$11,980	1-D	2,051	237	34.0
Dominican Univ., River Forest, IL 60305-1099	1901	$28,690	$8,818	2-D	3,589	404	66.0
Dominican Univ. of California, San Rafael, CA 94901-2298	1890	$39,050	$13,940	2-M	2,278	371	56.0
Dordt Coll., Sioux Center, IA 51250-1697	1955	$25,520	$7,230	2-M	1,400	102	65.0
Dowling Coll., Oakdale, NY 11769-1999	1955	$27,124	$10,590	1-D	4,416	431	36.0
Drake Univ., Des Moines, IA 50311-4516	1881	$30,880	$8,700	1-D	5,270	450	74.0
Drew Univ., Madison, NJ 07940-1493	1867	$44,068	$11,944	2-D	2,447	300	69.0
Drexel Univ., Philadelphia, PA 19104-2875	1891	$37,505	$14,415	1-D	25,500	2,014	65.0
Drury Univ., Springfield, MO 65802	1873	$22,415	$8,200	1-M	2,060	169	65.0
Duke Univ., Durham, NC 27708-0586	1838	$42,033	$11,640	2-D	14,350	1,155	95.0
Duquesne Univ., Pittsburgh, PA 15282-0001	1878	$30,034	$10,198	2-D	9,956	987	74.0
D'Youville Coll., Buffalo, NY 14201-1084	1908	$22,240	$10,250	1-D	2,971	322	63.0
Earlham Coll., Richmond, IN 47374-4095	1847	$41,450	$8,260	2-M	1,211	120	73.0
East Carolina Univ., Greenville, NC 27858-4353	1907	$5,869(S)	$8,300	5-D	26,947	1,491	58.0
East Central Univ., Ada, OK 74820-6899	1909	$4,957(S)	$4,824	5-M	4,819	277	33.0
East Stroudsburg Univ. of Pennsylvania, East Stroudsburg, PA 18301-2999	1893	$8,315(S)	$9,176	5-M	7,353	319	59.0
East Tennessee State Univ., Johnson City, TN 37614	1911	$6,271(S)	$6,000	5-D	15,133	845	41.0
East Texas Baptist Univ., Marshall, TX 75670-1498	1912	$21,530	$6,145	2-M	1,290	118	32.0
Eastern Connecticut State Univ., Willimantic, CT 06226-2295	1889	$9,376(S)	$11,168	5-M	5,440	478	53.0
Eastern Illinois Univ., Charleston, IL 61920-3099	1895	$10,930(S)	$9,174	5-M	10,417	720	60.0
Eastern Kentucky Univ., Richmond, KY 40475-3102	1906	$7,320(S)	$7,316	5-D	16,062	1,114	38.0
Eastern Mennonite Univ., Harrisonburg, VA 22802-2462	1917	$29,080	$9,690	2-M	1,519	205	59.0
Eastern Michigan Univ., Ypsilanti, MI 48197	1849	$9,026(S)	$8,286	5-D	23,502	1,226	37.0
Eastern Nazarene Coll., Quincy, MA 02170	1918	$26,884	$8,300	2-M	1,036	122	52.0

Name, address	Year founded	Tuition & fees	Room & board	Control, degree	Enrollment	Faculty	Grad. rate
Eastern New Mexico Univ., Portales, NM 88130	1934	$5,776(S)	$6,090	5-M	5,814	378	29.0%
Eastern Oregon Univ., La Grande, OR 97850-2899	1929	$7,046(S)	$8,100	5-M	4,298	128	32.0
Eastern Univ., St. Davids, PA 19087-3696	1952	$28,040	$9,614	2-D	4,263	568	59.0
Eastern Washington Univ., Cheney, WA 99004-2431	1882	$7,976(S)	$8,412	5-D	12,587	649	47.0
Eckerd Coll., St. Petersburg, FL 33711	1958	$37,362	$10,144	2-B	1,893	164	60.0
ECPI Coll. of Tech., Virginia Beach, VA 23462	1966	NA	NA	3-B	13,717	1,371	NA
Edgewood Coll., Madison, WI 53711-1997 (4)	1927	$23,740	$8,476	2-D	3,064	319	53.0
Edinboro Univ. of Pennsylvania, Edinboro, PA 16444	1857	$8,578(S)	$7,362	5-M	7,462	410	45.0
EDP Univ. of Puerto Rico, Hato Rey, PR 00918	1968	$6,240	NA	3-M	1,198	93	25.0
Elizabeth City State Univ., Elizabeth City, NC 27909-7806	1891	$4,428(S)	$7,213	5-M	2,878	218	43.0
Elizabethtown Coll., Elizabethtown, PA 17022-2298	1899	$38,200	$9,400	2-B	1,911	212	74.0
Elmhurst Coll., Elmhurst, IL 60126-3296	1871	$32,945	$9,112	2-M	3,298	392	74.0
Elmira Coll., Elmira, NY 14901	1855	$38,150	$11,800	1-M	1,533	192	57.0
Elms Coll., Chicopee, MA 01013-2839 (4)	1928	$28,128	$10,202	2-M	1,260	NA	NA
Elon Univ., Elon, NC 27244-2010	1889	$28,980	$9,480	2-D	6,029	535	83.0
Embry-Riddle Aeron Univ.–Daytona, Daytona Beach, FL 32114-3900	1926	$31,334	$9,550	1-D	5,120	392	58.0
Embry-Riddle Aeron Univ.–Prescott, Prescott, AZ 86301-3720	1978	$31,034	$9,550	1-M	1,724	136	55.0
Embry-Riddle Aeron Univ.–Worldwide, Daytona Beach, FL 32114-3900	1970	$7,032	NA	1-D	16,482	2,711	NA
Emerson Coll., Boston, MA 02116-4624	1880	$35,730	$14,516	1-D	4,513	444	82.0
Emmanuel Coll., Boston, MA 02115	1919	$33,650	$12,990	2-M	2,488	242	58.0
Emory Univ., Atlanta, GA 30322-1100	1836	$44,008	$12,360	2-D	14,236	1,452	90.0
Emporia State Univ., Emporia, KS 66801-5087	1863	$5,272(S)	$6,629	5-D	5,867	296	42.0
Endicott Coll., Beverly, MA 01915-2096	1939	$28,166	$13,200	1-D	4,625	386	72.0
Eugene Lang Coll.–The New School for Liberal Arts, New York, NY 10011-8601	1978	$38,570	$17,300	1-B	1,457	149	52.0
Evangel Univ., Springfield, MO 65802	1955	$19,050	$6,640	2-M	2,079	154	52.0
Everest Univ., Pompano Beach, FL 33062	1940	NA	NA	3-M	1,633	NA	NA
Everest Univ., Tampa, FL 33614-5899	1890	$15,336	NA	3-M	3,430	61	NA
Everest Univ., Tampa, FL 33619	1890	$16,452	NA	3-M	12,695	61	NA
Everglades Univ., Boca Raton, FL 33431	1989	NA	NA	1-M	1,039	NA	NA
The Evergreen State Coll., Olympia, WA 98505	1967	$8,395(S)	$9,240	5-M	4,509	240	54.0
Excelsior Coll., Albany, NY 12203-5159	1970	$390/cr. hr.	NA	1-M	37,194	NA	NA
Fairfield Univ., Fairfield, CT 06824-5195	1942	$41,690	$12,550	2-D	4,999	587	81.0
Fairleigh Dickinson Univ., Coll. at Florham, Madison, NJ 07940-1099	1942	$36,352	$11,972	1-D	3,067	378	58.0
Fairleigh Dickinson Univ., Metropolitan campus, Teaneck, NJ 07666-1914	1942	$33,792	$12,406	1-D	9,130	753	47.0
Fairmont State Univ., Fairmont, WV 26554	1865	$5,804(S)	$7,686	5-M	4,451	326	31.0
Farmingdale State Coll., Farmingdale, NY 11735	1912	$7,125(S)	$11,860	5-B	7,889	592	45.0
Fashion Institute of Tech., New York, NY 10001-5992 (4)	1944	$6,358(S)	$12,598	11-M	10,052	977	NA
Faulkner Univ., Montgomery, AL 36109-3398	1942	$17,380	$6,650	2-D	3,327	349	32.0
Fayetteville State Univ., Fayetteville, NC 28301-4298	1867	$5,671(S)	$6,142	5-D	6,060	334	31.0
Felician Coll., Lodi, NJ 07644-2117	1942	$29,990	$11,650	2-D	2,109	241	36.0
Ferris State Univ., Big Rapids, MI 49307	1884	$10,710(S)	$8,744	5-D	14,533	969	56.0
Ferrum Coll., Ferrum, VA 24088	1913	$27,425	$9,130	2-B	1,510	125	31.0
Fisher Coll., Boston, MA 02116-1500	1903	$26,775	$13,924	1-B	1,751	155	40.0
Fitchburg State Univ., Fitchburg, MA 01420-2697	1894	$8,710(S)	$8,602	5-M	6,889	274	47.0
Flagler Coll., St. Augustine, FL 32085-1027	1968	$15,340	$8,350	1-B	2,847	228	65.0
Florida Agr. & Mech. Univ., Tallahassee, FL 32307-3200	1887	$5,187(S)	$8,754	5-D	12,057	724	40.0
Florida Atlantic Univ., Boca Raton, FL 33431-0991	1961	$5,986(S)	$11,353	5-D	30,038	1,226	42.0
Florida Gulf Coast Univ., Fort Myers, FL 33965-6565	1991	$4,855(S)	$9,424	5-D	13,471	630	45.0
Florida Institute of Tech., Melbourne, FL 32901-6975	1958	$36,020	$12,270	1-D	5,384	467	55.0
Florida Intl. Univ., Miami, FL 33199	1965	$6,417(S)	$11,330	5-D	46,261	2,052	43.0
Florida Memorial Univ., Miami-Dade, FL 33054	1879	NA	NA	2-M	1,750	173	33.0
Florida Natl Univ., Hialeah, FL 33012	1982	$13,230	NA	3-M	2,506	150	NA
Florida Southern Coll., Lakeland, FL 33801-5698	1885	$27,200	$9,100	2-M	2,238	229	55.0
Florida State Univ., Tallahassee, FL 32306	1851	$6,402(S)	$9,626	5-D	40,695	1,624	75.0
Fontbonne Univ., St. Louis, MO 63105-3098	1917	$22,054	$8,600	2-M	2,293	276	43.0
Fordham Univ., New York, NY 10458	1841	$41,732	$15,370	2-D	15,170	1,510	78.0
Fort Hays State Univ., Hays, KS 67601-4099	1902	$135/cr. hr.(S)	$6,625	5-M	12,802	479	NA
Fort Lewis Coll., Durango, CO 81301-3999	1911	$6,923(S)	$8,590	5-B	3,891	205	38.0
Fort Valley State Univ., Fort Valley, GA 31030	1895	$6,030(S)	$7,418	5-D	3,571	202	39.0
Framingham State Univ., Framingham, MA 01701-9101	1839	$8,080(S)	$9,540	5-M	6,506	313	52.0
Franciscan Univ. of Steubenville, Steubenville, OH 43952-1763	1946	$22,180	$7,400	2-M	2,823	223	70.0
Francis Marion Univ., Florence, SC 29502-0547	1970	$9,066(S)	$6,820	5-M	4,093	270	42.0
Franklin & Marshall Coll., Lancaster, PA 17604-3003	1787	$44,360	$11,750	1-B	2,365	288	83.0
Franklin Coll., Franklin, IN 46131	1834	$26,895	$7,950	2-B	1,053	103	59.0
Franklin Pierce Univ., Rindge, NH 03461-0060	1962	$29,950	$11,260	1-D	2,267	315	50.0
Franklin Univ., Columbus, OH 43215-5399	1902	$12,450	NA	1-M	6,885	843	11.0
Freed-Hardeman Univ., Henderson, TN 38340-2399	1869	$20,468	$7,296	2-D	1,904	149	54.0
Fresno Pacific Univ., Fresno, CA 93702-4709	1944	$25,525	$7,288	2-M	3,759	353	59.0
Friends Univ., Wichita, KS 67213	1898	$22,500	$6,600	2-M	2,502	206	33.0
Frostburg State Univ., Frostburg, MD 21532-1099	1898	$7,728(S)	$7,990	5-D	5,421	378	45.0
Full Sail Univ., Winter Park, FL 32792-7437 (2)	1979	NA	NA	3-M	8,921	702	NA
Furman Univ., Greenville, SC 29613	1826	$41,532	$10,509	1-M	2,915	268	83.0
Gallaudet Univ., Washington, DC 20002-3625	1864	$12,806	$10,790	1-D	1,546	185	41.0
Gannon Univ., Erie, PA 16541-0001	1925	$27,546	$10,940	2-D	4,008	363	66.0
Gardner-Webb Univ., Boiling Springs, NC 28017	1905	$24,640	$7,940	2-D	4,854	258	37.0
Geneva Coll., Beaver Falls, PA 15010-3599	1848	$25,220	$9,250	2-M	1,646	202	59.0
George Fox Univ., Newberg, OR 97132-2697	1891	$30,230	$9,360	2-D	3,484	377	64.0
George Mason Univ., Fairfax, VA 22030	1957	$9,620(S)	$9,250	5-D	32,961	2,379	66.0
The George Washington Univ., Washington, DC 20052	1821	$47,335	$11,378	1-D	25,653	NA	80.0
Georgetown Coll., Georgetown, KY 40324-1696	1829	$30,770	$7,920	2-M	1,543	148	60.0
Georgetown Univ., Washington, DC 20057	1789	$43,070	$13,312	2-D	17,357	1,757	94.0
Georgia Coll. & State Univ., Milledgeville, GA 31061	1889	$8,618(S)	$9,268	5-D	6,444	446	57.0
Georgia Gwinnett Coll., Lawrenceville, GA 60043	2006	$5,082(S)	$12,350	5-B	9,397	562	NA
Georgia Institute of Tech., Atlanta, GA 30332-0001	1885	$10,098(S)	$9,236	5-D	21,557	1,251	79.0
Georgian Court Univ., Lakewood, NJ 08701-2697 (4)	1908	$26,740	$12,860	2-M	2,555	272	51.0
Georgia Southern Univ., Statesboro, GA 30460	1906	$6,724(S)	$9,290	5-D	20,574	884	50.0
Georgia Southwestern State Univ., Americus, GA 31709-4693	1906	$5,780(S)	$7,378	5-M	2,973	169	29.0
Georgia State Univ., Atlanta, GA 30302-3083	1913	$9,664(S)	$11,546	5-D	32,092	1,658	51.0
Gettysburg Coll., Gettysburg, PA 17325-1483	1832	$44,210	$10,560	2-B	2,597	312	84.0
Glenville State Coll., Glenville, WV 26351-1200	1872	$5,860(S)	$8,400	5-B	1,857	112	30.0
Global Univ., Springfield, MO 65804	1948	$3,870	NA	2-D	4,551	633	NA
Globe Univ.–Woodbury, Woodbury, MN 55125	1885	$16,848	NA	3-D	1,542	159	NA
Golden Gate Univ., San Francisco, CA 94105-2968	1901	NA	NA	1-D	3,528	489	NA
Goldey-Beacom Coll., Wilmington, DE 19808-1999	1886	$22,140	$5,353	1-M	1,352	56	49.0
Gonzaga Univ., Spokane, WA 99258	1887	$33,652	$8,730	2-D	7,781	784	81.0
Gordon Coll., Wenham, MA 01984-1899	1889	$33,230	$9,430	2-M	1,909	177	74.0

Name, address	Year founded	Tuition & fees	Room & board	Control, degree	Enroll-ment	Faculty	Grad. rate
Goucher Coll., Baltimore, MD 21204-2794.	1885	$39,084	$11,168	1-M	2,254	218	66.0%
Governors State Univ., University Park, IL 60484	1969	$9,116(S)	NA	5-D	5,609	413	NA
Grace Coll., Winona Lake, IN 46590-1294.	1948	$23,290	$7,454	2-D	1,616	85	55.0
Graceland Univ., Lamoni, IA 50140	1895	$23,530	$7,890	2-D	2,318	97	50.0
Grambling State Univ., Grambling, LA 71245	1901	$5,240(S)	$9,674	5-D	5,277	239	31.0
Grand Canyon Univ., Phoenix, AZ 85017-1097	1949	$19,000	$8,100	2-D	NA	NA	NA
Grand Valley State Univ., Allendale, MI 49401-9403.	1960	$10,078(S)	$7,920	5-D	24,654	1,678	63.0
Grand View Univ., Des Moines, IA 50316-1599.	1896	$22,708	$7,264	2-M	2,232	269	49.0
Granite State Coll., Concord, NH 03301	1972	$6,840(S)	NA	11-M	2,018	189	59.0
Grantham Univ., Kansas City, MO 64153	1951	$6,480	NA	3-M	9,463	10	NA
Greensboro Coll., Greensboro, NC 27401-1875	1838	$25,000	$9,100	2-M	1,264	96	43.0
Greenville Coll., Greenville, IL 62246-0159	1892	$22,920	$7,576	2-M	1,463	185	52.0
Grinnell Coll., Grinnell, IA 50112-1690.	1846	$41,004	$9,614	1-B	1,674	211	90.0
Grove City Coll., Grove City, PA 16127-2104	1876	$14,880	$8,108	2-B	2,506	228	82.0
Guilford Coll., Greensboro, NC 27410-4173	1837	$32,470	$8,800	2-B	2,462	190	57.0
Gustavus Adolphus Coll., St. Peter, MN 56082-1498	1862	$37,606	$8,880	2-B	2,524	230	83.0
Gwynedd-Mercy Coll., Gwynedd Valley, PA 19437-0901	1948	$28,340	$9,850	2-M	2,710	272	52.0
Hamilton Coll., Clinton, NY 13323-1296.	1812	$44,350	$11,270	1-B	1,884	223	91.0
Hamline Univ., St. Paul, MN 55104-1284.	1854	$33,752	$8,700	2-D	4,683	448	63.0
Hampden-Sydney Coll., Hampden-Sydney, VA 23943 (1).	1776	$35,570	$11,166	2-B	1,080	106	68.0
Hampshire Coll., Amherst, MA 01002	1965	$46,625	$12,030	1-B	1,461	145	64.0
Hampton Univ., Hampton, VA 23668	1868	$20,724	$9,230	1-D	4,754	330	65.0
Hannibal-LaGrange Univ., Hannibal, MO 63401-1999.	1858	$17,800	$6,570	2-M	1,128	146	50.0
Hanover Coll., Hanover, IN 47243-0108	1827	$30,268	$9,230	2-B	1,123	101	65.0
Harding Univ., Searcy, AR 72149-0001	1924	$15,240	$6,192	2-D	6,672	585	61.0
Hardin-Simmons Univ., Abilene, TX 79698-0001.	1891	$23,460	$6,792	2-D	2,301	206	47.0
Harrison Coll., Indianapolis, IN 46204	1902	NA	NA	3-B	4,547	345	29.0
Harris-Stowe State Univ., St. Louis, MO 63103-2136	1857	NA	NA	5-B	1,484	203	8.0
Hartwick Coll., Oneonta, NY 13820-4020.	1797	$38,930	$10,485	1-B	1,558	183	55.0
Harvard Univ., Cambridge, MA 02138	1636	$40,866	$13,630	1-D	10,573	1,113	97.0
Hastings Coll., Hastings, NE 68901-7696	1882	$23,734	$6,780	2-M	1,138	123	62.3
Haverford Coll., Haverford, PA 19041-1392.	1833	$43,702	$13,290	1-B	1,205	138	94.0
Hawai'i Pacific Univ., Honolulu, HI 96813	1965	$19,980	$13,230	1-M	7,463	696	40.0
Heidelberg Univ., Tiffin, OH 44883-2462	1850	$24,582	$8,974	2-M	1,317	150	57.0
Henderson State Univ., Arkadelphia, AR 71999-0001.	1890	$6,984(S)	$5,332	5-M	3,771	259	33.0
Hendrix Coll., Conway, AR 72032-3080.	1876	$37,816	$10,620	2-M	1,388	142	72.0
Heritage Univ., Toppenish, WA 98948-9599	1982	$15,480	NA	1-M	1,115	NA	NA
High Point Univ., High Point, NC 27262-3598	1924	$39,800(C)	NA	2-D	4,263	338	60.0
Hilbert Coll., Hamburg, NY 14075-1597.	1957	$20,500	$8,650	1-M	1,075	122	50.0
Hillsdale Coll., Hillsdale, MI 49242-1298	1844	$22,890	$9,000	1-D	1,447	163	77.0
Hiram Coll., Hiram, OH 44234-0067.	1850	$28,950	$9,460	1-M	1,324	139	63.0
Hobart and William Smith Colls. Geneva, NY 14456-3397	1822	$44,438	$11,261	1-M	2,300	231	76.0
Hodges Univ., Naples, FL 34119	1990	$12,260	NA	1-M	2,255	157	NA
Hofstra Univ., Hempstead, NY 11549	1935	$35,950	$12,370	1-D	11,023	1,135	61.0
Holy Family Univ., Philadelphia, PA 19114	1954	$25,590	$12,350	2-D	3,094	375	61.0
Holy Names Univ., Oakland, CA 94619-1699 (4).	1868	$30,390	$10,260	2-M	1,353	209	41.0
Hood Coll., Frederick, MD 21701-8575	1893	$32,300	$10,910	1-M	2,422	262	60.0
Hope Coll., Holland, MI 49422-9000	1866	$28,720	$8,810	2-B	3,343	329	77.0
Hope Intl. Univ., Fullerton, CA 92831-3138	1928	$26,050	$8,600	2-M	1,652	208	39.0
Houghton Coll., Houghton, NY 14744	1883	$27,728	$8,012	2-M	1,165	125	67.0
Houston Baptist Univ., Houston, TX 77074-3298.	1960	$27,930	$6,500	2-M	2,589	225	44.0
Howard Payne Univ., Brownwood, TX 76801-2715.	1889	$23,200	$6,800	2-M	1,130	120	43.0
Howard Univ., Washington, DC 20059-0002.	1867	$22,883	$9,342	1-D	10,288	1,520	65.0
Humboldt State Univ., Arcata, CA 95521-8299	1913	$7,130(S)	$11,440	5-M	8,116	538	42.0
Hunter Coll. of the City Univ. of New York, New York, NY 10021-5085.	1870	$5,829(S)	$5,500	11-D	23,007	1,908	45.0
Huntingdon Coll., Montgomery, AL 36106-2148	1854	$22,500	$8,250	2-B	1,118	120	46.0
Huntington Univ., Huntington, IN 46750-1299	1897	$24,040	$8,180	2-M	1,189	109	60.0
Husson Univ., Bangor, ME 04401-2999.	1898	$15,130	$8,256	1-D	3,077	320	41.0
Idaho State Univ., Pocatello, ID 83209.	1901	$6,070(S)	$5,838	5-D	14,209	787	27.0
Illinois Institute of Tech., Chicago, IL 60616-3793	1890	$38,512	NA	1-D	7,684	742	68.0
Illinois State Univ., Normal, IL 61790-2200	1857	$12,726(S)	$9,364	5-D	20,706	1,212	71.0
Illinois Wesleyan Univ., Bloomington, IL 61702-2900	1850	$37,954	$8,838	1-B	2,013	226	82.0
Immaculata Univ., Immaculata, PA 19345 (4)	1920	$29,000	$11,740	2-D	4,117	426	53.0
Indian River State Coll., Fort Pierce, FL 34981-5596.	1960	NA	NA	5-B	17,806	874	NA
Indiana State Univ., Terre Haute, IN 47809	1865	$8,098(S)	$8,262	5-D	12,114	689	39.0
Indiana Tech., Fort Wayne, IN 46803-1297.	1930	$24,860	$9,380	1-D	4,912	306	NA
Indiana Univ. Bloomington, Bloomington, IN 47405-7000	1820	$10,033(S)	$8,853	5-D	42,133	2,284	75.0
Indiana Univ. East, Richmond, IN 47374-1289	1971	$6,496(S)	NA	5-M	4,186	271	24.0
Indiana Univ. Kokomo, Kokomo, IN 46904-9003	1945	$6,542(S)	NA	5-M	3,719	194	22.0
Indiana Univ. Northwest, Gary, IN 46408-1197	1959	$6,627(S)	NA	5-M	6,184	424	22.0
Indiana Univ. of Pennsylvania, Indiana, PA 15705-1087	1875	$8,672(S)	$10,466	5-D	15,379	708	52.0
Indiana Univ.–Purdue Univ. Fort Wayne, Fort Wayne, IN 46805-1499	1917	$6,876(S)	$7,210	5-M	13,771	860	26.0
Indiana Univ.–Purdue Univ. Indianapolis, Indianapolis, IN 46202-2896.	1969	$8,605(S)	$7,944	5-D	30,451	3,256	38.0
Indiana Univ. South Bend, South Bend, IN 46634-7111	1922	$6,728(S)	$6,838	5-M	8,490	535	23.0
Indiana Univ. Southeast, New Albany, IN 47150-6405	1941	$6,575(S)	$6,570	5-M	6,904	498	27.0
Indiana Wesleyan Univ., Marion, IN 46953-4974.	1920	$23,628	$7,560	2-D	3,094	300	71.0
Inter Amer. Univ. of Puerto Rico, Aguadilla campus, Aguadilla, PR 00605 .	1957	$5,614	NA	1-M	4,626	264	21.0
Inter Amer. Univ. of Puerto Rico, Arecibo campus, Arecibo, PR 00614-4050 .	1957	NA	NA	1-M	4,878	298	NA
Inter Amer. Univ. of Puerto Rico, Barranquitas campus, Barranquitas, PR 00794 .	1957	NA	NA	1-M	2,418	135	NA
Inter Amer. Univ. of Puerto Rico, Bayamón campus, Bayamón, PR 00957.	1912	$5,620	NA	1-M	4,915	329	24.0
Inter Amer. Univ. of Puerto Rico, Fajardo campus, Fajardo, PR 00738-7003 .	1965	$4,338	NA	1-M	2,199	120	NA
Inter Amer. Univ. of Puerto Rico, Guayama campus, Guayama, PR 00785 .	1958	$4,562	NA	1-M	2,358	203	26.0
Inter Amer. Univ. of Puerto Rico, Metropolitan campus, San Juan, PR 00919-1293.	1960	NA	NA	1-D	10,093	599	25.0
Inter Amer. Univ. of Puerto Rico, Ponce campus, Mercedita, PR 00715-1602 .	1962	$4,080	NA	1-M	5,983	294	28.0
Inter Amer. Univ. of Puerto Rico, San Germán campus, San Germán, PR 00683-5008.	1912	$5,620	$2,700	1-D	5,355	316	36.0
Intl. Academy of Design & Tech., Chicago, IL 60602-9736	1977	NA	NA	3-B	1,832	113	15.0
Iona Coll., New Rochelle, NY 10801-1890.	1940	$32,770	$13,175	2-M	4,241	353	65.0
Iowa State Univ. of Sci. & Tech., Ames, IA 50011	1858	$7,726(S)	$7,721	5-D	30,748	1,745	71.0
Ithaca Coll., Ithaca, NY 14850	1892	$37,000	$13,400	1-D	6,760	701	74.0
Jackson State Univ., Jackson, MS 39217	1877	$5,988(S)	$6,996	5-D	8,783	525	36.4
Jacksonville State Univ., Jacksonville, AL 36265-1602	1883	$7,950(S)	$6,300	5-D	9,161	497	29.0
Jacksonville Univ., Jacksonville, FL 32211	1934	$29,900	$10,030	1-D	3,936	335	37.0
James Madison Univ., Harrisonburg, VA 22807.	1908	$9,176(S)	$8,873	5-D	19,722	1,400	81.0
Jefferson Coll. of Health Sci., Roanoke, VA 24031-3186.	1982	NA	NA	1-M	1,032	128	69.0

Name, address	Year founded	Tuition & fees	Room & board	Control, degree	Enroll-ment	Faculty	Grad. rate
John Brown Univ., Siloam Springs, AR 72761-2121	1919	$22,734	$8,262	2-M	2,215	156	68.0%
John Carroll Univ., University Heights, OH 44118-4581	1886	$34,480	$10,040	2-M	3,583	366	75.0
John F. Kennedy Univ., Pleasant Hill, CA 94523-4817 (4)	1964	$15,120	NA	1-D	1,580	237	NA
John Hancock Univ., Chicago, IL 60606-7204	NA	NA	NA	3-M	1,950	NA	NA
John Jay Coll. of Criminal Justice of the City Univ. of New York, New York, NY 10019-1093	1964	$5,760(S)	NA	11-M	14,996	NA	43.0
The Johns Hopkins Univ., Baltimore, MD 21218-2699	1876	$45,970	$13,832	1-D	7,221	609	94.0
Johnson & Wales Univ., Denver, CO 80220	1993	$25,107	$10,314	1-B	1,532	87	53.0
Johnson & Wales Univ., North Miami, FL 33181	1992	$25,107	$9,261	1-B	2,098	90	51.0
Johnson & Wales Univ., Providence, RI 02903-3703	1914	$25,107	$10,314	1-D	10,974	519	56.0
Johnson & Wales Univ.–Charlotte campus, Charlotte, NC 28202	2004	$25,107	$10,314	1-B	2,587	110	62.0
Johnson C. Smith Univ., Charlotte, NC 28216-5398	1867	$18,236	$7,100	1-B	1,669	159	42.0
Johnson State Coll., Johnson, VT 05656	1828	$10,543(S)	$9,138	5-M	1,882	137	35.0
Jones Intl. Univ., Centennial, CO 80112	1995	$12,720	NA	3-D	3,196	111	NA
Judson Univ., Elgin, IL 60123-1498	1963	$27,530	$8,990	2-M	1,128	218	50.0
The Juilliard School, New York, NY 10023-6588	1905	$33,630	$12,770	1-D	1,009	307	93.0
Juniata Coll., Huntingdon, PA 16652-2119	1876	$37,170	$10,200	2-M	1,565	143	75.0
Kalamazoo Coll., Kalamazoo, MI 49006-3295	1833	$37,710	$8,274	2-B	1,379	114	80.0
Kansas State Univ., Manhattan, KS 66506	1863	$8,047(S)	$7,450	5-D	24,378	1,203	59.0
Kean Univ., Union, NJ 07083	1855	$10,601(S)	$13,934	5-D	15,391	1,481	50.0
Keene State Coll., Keene, NH 03435	1909	$12,776(S)	$8,762	5-M	5,060	464	62.0
Kendall Coll., Chicago, IL 60201-2899	1934	$22,920	$9,900	3-B	2,545	209	37.0
Kennesaw State Univ., Kennesaw, GA 30144-5591	1963	$6,486(S)	$7,966	5-D	24,604	1,356	41.0
Kent State Univ., Kent, OH 44242-0001	1910	$9,672(S)	$9,176	5-D	28,172	1,688	52.0
Kent State Univ. at Geauga, Burton, OH 44021-9500	1964	$5,472(S)	NA	5-B	2,535	125	23.0
Kent State Univ. at Stark, Canton, OH 44720-7599	1967	$5,472(S)	NA	5-M	4,864	255	26.0
Kentucky State Univ., Frankfort, KY 40601	1886	$6,858(S)	$6,580	12-M	2,524	162	14.0
Kenyon Coll., Gambier, OH 43022-9623	1824	$45,640	$11,170	1-B	1,667	201	90.0
Kettering Univ., Flint, MI 48504 (2)	1919	$33,946	$6,660	1-M	2,079	154	58.0
Keuka Coll., Keuka Park, NY 14478-0098	1890	$26,320	$10,280	2-M	2,083	153	51.0
Keystone Coll., La Plume, PA 18440	1868	$21,200	$9,800	1-B	1,683	244	42.0
King Coll., Bristol, TN 37620-2699	1867	$24,960	$8,180	2-M	2,342	212	50.0
King's Coll., Wilkes-Barre, PA 18711-0801	1946	$29,174	$11,020	2-M	2,494	237	68.0
Knox Coll., Galesburg, IL 61401	1837	$38,952	$8,400	1-B	1,430	140	79.0
Kutztown Univ. of Pennsylvania, Kutztown, PA 19530-0730	1866	$8,596(S)	$8,890	5-M	9,804	464	54.0
Lafayette Coll., Easton, PA 18042-1798	1826	$43,970	$13,080	2-B	2,488	258	88.0
Lake Erie Coll., Painesville, OH 44077-3389	1856	$27,368	$8,336	1-M	1,199	114	48.0
Lake Forest Coll., Lake Forest, IL 60045	1857	$38,300	$9,050	1-M	1,516	161	68.0
Lakeland Coll., Sheboygan, WI 53082-0359	1862	$21,242	$7,340	2-M	3,749	71	42.0
Lake Superior State Univ., Sault Sainte Marie, MI 49783	1946	$9,715(S)	$8,481	5-M	2,530	184	35.0
Lamar Univ., Beaumont, TX 77710	1923	$9,011(S)	$7,966	5-D	14,288	645	30.0
Lander Univ., Greenwood, SC 29649-2099	1872	$9,504(S)	$6,740	5-M	3,049	249	40.0
Lane Coll., Jackson, TN 38301-4598	1882	$8,560	$6,040	2-B	1,512	91	38.0
Langston Univ., Langston, OK 73050	1897	$4,285(S)	$8,690	5-M	2,338	205	NA
La Roche Coll., Pittsburgh, PA 15237-5898	1963	$24,058	$9,732	2-M	1,465	194	47.0
La Salle Univ., Philadelphia, PA 19141-1199	1863	$36,650	$12,210	2-D	6,580	457	68.0
Lasell Coll., Newton, MA 02466-2709	1851	$29,000	$12,300	1-M	1,980	229	47.0
La Sierra Univ., Riverside, CA 92515	1922	$28,314	$7,300	2-D	2,393	212	45.0
Lawrence Tech. Univ., Southfield, MI 48075-1058	1932	$27,870	$8,987	1-D	4,154	398	42.0
Lawrence Univ., Appleton, WI 54911	1847	$40,023	$8,247	1-B	1,525	196	73.0
Lebanon Valley Coll., Annville, PA 17003-1400	1866	$34,470	$9,180	2-M	1,984	219	72.0
Lee Univ., Cleveland, TN 37320-3450	1918	$13,750	$6,762	2-M	4,954	388	49.0
Lehigh Univ., Bethlehem, PA 18015-3094	1865	$42,220	$11,230	1-D	7,080	691	88.0
Lehman Coll. of the City Univ. of New York, Bronx, NY 10468-1589	1931	$5,808(S)	$8,085	11-M	11,862	912	34.0
Le Moyne Coll., Syracuse, NY 13214	1946	$30,460	$11,740	2-M	3,339	326	69.0
Lenoir-Rhyne Univ., Hickory, NC 28601	1891	$27,718	$9,796	2-M	1,860	178	47.0
Lesley Univ., Cambridge, MA 02138-2790	1909	$32,250	$14,000	1-D	5,528	270	46.0
LeTourneau Univ., Longview, TX 75607-7001	1946	$24,540	$8,940	2-M	2,843	232	50.0
Lewis & Clark Coll., Portland, OR 97219-7899	1867	$41,928	$10,636	1-D	3,703	417	76.0
Lewis-Clark State Coll., Lewiston, ID 83501-2698	1893	$5,562(S)	NA	5-B	4,525	260	26.0
Lewis Univ., Romeoville, IL 60446	1932	$26,780	$9,530	2-D	6,539	662	59.0
Liberty Univ., Lynchburg, VA 24502	1971	$20,892	$7,976	2-D	12,645	620	52.0
Life Univ., Marietta, GA 30060-2903	1974	$11,978	$12,854	1-D	2,655	181	18.0
LIM Coll., New York, NY 10022-5268 (4)	1939	$23,645	$15,850	3-M	1,552	202	52.0
Lincoln Christian Univ., Lincoln, IL 62656-2167	1944	$15,060	$7,080	2-D	1,071	118	48.0
Lincoln Memorial Univ., Harrogate, TN 37752-1901	1897	$19,460	$6,740	1-D	4,338	275	45.0
Lincoln Univ., Jefferson City, MO 65102	1866	$6,624(S)	$4,750	5-M	3,205	214	24.0
Lincoln Univ., Lincoln University, PA 19352	1854	$7,018(S)	$8,554	12-M	2,101	146	37.0
Lindenwood Univ., St. Charles, MO 63301-1695	1827	$14,600	$7,580	2-D	11,903	920	41.0
Lindsey Wilson Coll., Columbia, KY 42728	1903	$22,070	$8,400	2-M	2,677	256	32.0
Linfield Coll., McMinnville, OR 97128-6894	1849	$34,328	$9,500	2-B	1,663	196	68.0
Lipscomb Univ., Nashville, TN 37204-3951	1891	$24,754	$9,224	2-D	4,254	490	56.0
Lock Haven Univ. of Pennsylvania, Lock Haven, PA 17745-2390	1870	$8,564(S)	$8,016	5-M	5,328	245	49.0
Logan Univ.–Coll. of Chiropractic, Chesterfield, MO 63006-1065	1935	$5,220	NA	1-D	1,015	102	NA
Loma Linda Univ., Loma Linda, CA 92350	1905	NA	NA	2-D	4,270	840	NA
Long Island Univ.–Brooklyn campus, Brooklyn, NY 11201-8423	1926	$34,120	$12,064	1-D	8,567	863	22.0
Long Island Univ.–C. W. Post campus, Brookville, NY 11548-1300	1954	$34,070	$12,534	1-D	11,012	798	42.0
Longwood Univ., Farmville, VA 23909	1839	$10,890(S)	$8,448	5-M	4,834	288	61.0
Loras Coll., Dubuque, IA 52004-0178	1839	$28,165	$7,650	2-M	1,555	141	58.0
Louisiana Coll., Pineville, LA 71359-0001	1906	$13,780	$4,448	2-M	1,557	115	46.0
Louisiana State Univ. and Agr. & Mech. Coll., Baton Rouge, LA 70803	1860	$6,989(S)	$10,218	5-D	30,225	1,399	67.0
Louisiana State Univ. at Alexandria, Alexandria, LA 71302-9121	1960	NA	NA	5-B	2,430	139	NA
Louisiana State Univ. Health Sci. Ctr., New Orleans, LA 70112-2223	1931	$4,491(S)	$3,708	5-D	2,644	893	NA
Louisiana State Univ. in Shreveport, Shreveport, LA 71115-2399	1965	$4,942(S)	NA	5-M	4,535	188	30.0
Louisiana Tech. Univ., Ruston, LA 71272	1894	$5,955(S)	$5,289	5-D	11,304	406	48.0
Lourdes Univ., Sylvania, OH 43560-2898	1958	$17,455	NA	2-M	2,460	280	28.0
Loyola Marymount Univ., Los Angeles, CA 90045-2659	1911	$38,900	$14,395	2-D	9,492	1,115	75.0
Loyola Univ. Chicago, Chicago, IL 60660	1870	$35,503	$12,900	2-D	15,720	1,463	70.0
Loyola Univ. Maryland, Baltimore, MD 21210-2699	1852	$42,430	$12,120	2-D	5,978	556	84.0
Loyola Univ. New Orleans, New Orleans, LA 70118-6195	1912	$36,610	$12,185	2-D	4,933	492	58.0
Lubbock Christian Univ., Lubbock, TX 79407-2099	1957	$17,760	$6,674	2-M	2,135	187	43.0
Luther Coll., Decorah, IA 52101	1861	$37,480	$6,850	2-B	2,473	255	77.0
Luther Rice Univ., Lithonia, GA 30038-2454	1962	$5,352	NA	2-M	1,650	NA	NA
Lycoming Coll., Williamsport, PA 17701-5192	1812	$32,756	$9,420	2-B	1,365	119	70.0
Lynchburg Coll., Lynchburg, VA 24501-3199	1903	$32,005	$8,680	2-D	2,756	297	57.0
Lyndon State Coll., Lyndonville, VT 05851-0919	1911	$9,864(S)	$8,786	5-M	1,436	160	39.0
Lynn Univ., Boca Raton, FL 33431-5598	1962	$33,400	$10,900	1-D	2,097	181	40.0

Name, address	Year founded	Tuition & fees	Room & board	Control, degree	Enroll-ment	Faculty	Grad. rate
Macalester Coll., St. Paul, MN 55105-1899	1874	$45,388	$10,068	2-B	2,070	237	90.0%
Madonna Univ., Livonia, MI 48150-1173	1947	$15,300	$7,694	2-D	4,429	415	35.0
Maharishi Univ. of Mgmt., Fairfield, IA 52557	1971	$26,430	$7,400	1-D	1,132	94	50.0
Maine Maritime Academy, Castine, ME 04420 (2)	1941	$11,525(S)	$9,548	5-M	1,013	90	NA
Malone Univ., Canton, OH 44709	1892	$25,678	$8,656	2-M	2,373	223	63.0
Manchester Univ., North Manchester, IN 46962-1225	1889	$27,920	$9,250	2-D	1,345	102	51.0
Manhattan Coll., Riverdale, NY 10471	1853	$35,725	$13,080	2-M	3,800	408	75.0
Manhattanville Coll., Purchase, NY 10577-2132	1841	$35,370	$14,340	1-D	3,019	352	57.0
Mansfield Univ. of Pennsylvania, Mansfield, PA 16933	1857	$8,926(S)	$8,592	5-M	3,131	188	47.0
Marian Univ., Indianapolis, IN 46222-1997	1851	$28,400	$8,658	2-D	2,580	269	59.0
Marian Univ., Fond du Lac, WI 54935-4699	1936	$23,440	$6,140	2-D	2,306	257	60.0
Marietta Coll., Marietta, OH 45750-4000	1835	$30,940	$9,560	1-M	1,622	173	63.0
Marist Coll., Poughkeepsie, NY 12601-1387	1929	$30,000	$12,600	1-M	6,377	558	80.0
Marquette Univ., Milwaukee, WI 53201-1881	1881	$34,640	$10,730	2-D	11,749	1,161	80.0
Marshall Univ., Huntington, WV 25755	1837	$5,930(S)	$8,988	5-D	13,708	768	45.0
Mars Hill Coll., Mars Hill, NC 28754	1856	$25,636	$9,188	2-M	1,370	184	38.0
Martin Univ., Indianapolis, IN 46218-3867	1977	NA	NA	1-M	1,236	43	13.0
Mary Baldwin Coll., Staunton, VA 24401-3610 (4)	1842	$28,720	$8,400	1-M	1,804	128	47.0
Marygrove Coll., Detroit, MI 48221-2599 (4)	1905	$17,840	$7,600	2-M	2,953	64	34.0
Maryland Institute Coll. of Art, Baltimore, MD 21217	1826	$39,340	$10,880	1-M	2,168	363	70.0
Marylhurst Univ., Marylhurst, OR 97036-0261 (4)	1893	$18,405	NA	2-M	1,722	263	NA
Marymount Coll., Palos Verdes, California, Rancho Palos Verdes, CA 90275-6299	1932	$28,867	$12,075	2-B	1,001	105	NA
Marymount Manhattan Coll., New York, NY 10021-4597	1936	$25,688	$14,430	1-B	1,908	293	40.0
Marymount Univ., Arlington, VA 22207-4299	1950	$26,430	$11,550	2-D	3,702	370	48.0
Maryville Coll., Maryville, TN 37804-5907	1819	$31,132	$9,890	2-B	1,093	106	48.0
Maryville Univ. of St. Louis, St. Louis, MO 63141-7299	1872	$23,746	$9,242	1-D	4,203	433	70.0
Marywood Univ., Scranton, PA 18509-1598	1915	$30,440	$13,566	2-D	3,479	398	63.0
Massachusetts Coll. of Art and Design, Boston, MA 02115-5882	1873	$10,400(S)	$12,150	5-M	2,326	277	68.0
Massachusetts Coll. of Liberal Arts, North Adams, MA 01247-4100	1894	$8,525(S)	$9,102	5-M	1,799	174	47.0
Massachusetts Coll. of Pharm. and Health Sci., Boston, MA 02115-5896	1823	$27,440	$13,448	1-D	6,010	259	63.0
Massachusetts Institute of Tech., Cambridge, MA 02139-4307	1861	$42,050	$12,188	1-D	11,189	1,447	93.0
Massachusetts Maritime Academy, Buzzards Bay, MA 02532-1803 (2)	1891	$6,867(S)	$9,700	5-M	1,415	137	61.0
The Master's Coll., Santa Clarita, CA 91321-1200	1927	$29,480	$9,360	2-D	1,534	191	65.0
Mayville State Univ., Mayville, ND 58257-1299	1889	$6,193(S)	$4,854	5-B	1,020	81	36.0
McDaniel Coll., Westminster, MD 21157-4390	1867	$36,960	$8,640	1-M	3,284	380	74.0
McKendree Univ., Lebanon, IL 62254-1299	1828	$26,050	$8,690	2-D	3,308	313	53.0
McMurry Univ., Abilene, TX 79697	1923	$23,305	$7,460	2-M	1,368	126	37.0
McNeese State Univ., Lake Charles, LA 70609	1939	$5,120(S)	$7,468	5-M	8,588	428	37.0
Medaille Coll., Buffalo, NY 14214-2695	1875	$22,678	$10,760	1-D	2,634	281	NA
Medgar Evers Coll. of the City Univ. of New York, Brooklyn, NY 11225-2298	1969	$5,800(S)	NA	11-B	6,540	536	4.0
Med. Univ. of South Carolina, Charleston, SC 29425	1824	$15,438(S)	NA	5-D	2,679	223	NA
Mercer Univ., Macon, GA 31207-0003	1833	$32,466	$10,697	2-D	6,288	685	64.0
Mercy Coll., Dobbs Ferry, NY 10522-1189	1951	$17,556	$12,184	1-D	11,454	893	34.0
Mercy Coll. of Ohio, Toledo, OH 43604 (4)	1993	NA	NA	2-B	1,205	166	50.0
Mercyhurst Univ., Erie, PA 16546	1926	$29,037	$10,104	2-M	3,122	249	66.0
Meredith Coll., Raleigh, NC 27607-5298	1891	$29,106	$8,348	1-M	1,980	207	59.0
Merrimack Coll., North Andover, MA 01845-5800	1947	$33,920	$11,690	2-M	2,657	315	64.0
Messiah Coll., Mechanicsburg, PA 17055	1909	$30,470	$9,070	2-M	3,017	312	76.0
Methodist Univ., Fayetteville, NC 28311-1498	1956	$25,625	$9,521	2-M	2,416	213	44.0
Metropolitan Coll. of New York, New York, NY 10013 (4)	1964	NA	NA	1-M	1,084	183	40.0
Metropolitan State Univ., St. Paul, MN 55106-5000	1971	$6,642(S)	NA	5-D	8,474	NA	NA
Metropolitan State Univ. of Denver, Denver, CO 80217-3362	1963	$4,834(S)	NA	5-M	23,381	1,494	25.0
Miami Univ., Oxford, OH 45056	1809	$13,595(S)	$10,596	12-D	17,683	1,114	80.0
Miami Univ. Hamilton, Hamilton, OH 45011-3399	1968	NA	NA	5-M	4,194	224	NA
Michigan State Univ., East Lansing, MI 48824	1855	$13,800(S)	$8,476	5-D	48,906	2,789	77.0
Michigan Tech. Univ., Houghton, MI 49931	1885	$13,353(S)	$8,865	5-D	7,034	469	65.0
MidAmerica Nazarene Univ., Olathe, KS 66062-1899	1966	$22,730	$7,440	2-M	1,978	80	50.0
Mid-Continent Univ., Mayfield, KY 42066-9007	1949	$13,350	$6,800	2-M	2,264	199	NA
Middlebury Coll., Middlebury, VT 05753-6002	1800	$43,731	$11,839	1-D	2,516	337	94.0
Middle Georgia State Coll., Cochran, GA 31014-1599	1884	NA	NA	5-B	3,614	170	NA
Middle Tennessee State Univ., Murfreesboro, TN 37132	1911	$7,210(S)	$7,532	5-D	25,394	NA	NA
Midland Univ., Midland, NE 79705-6399	1969	$2,160(A)	$4,650	11-D	5,530	271	NA
Midway Coll., Midway, KY 40347-1120 (4)	1847	$19,800	$7,640	2-D	1,600	118	38.0
Midwestern State Univ., Wichita Falls, TX 76308	1922	$7,238(S)	$6,350	5-M	5,916	342	41.0
Miles Coll., Fairfield, AL 35064	1905	$10,490	$5,306	2-B	1,738	147	NA
Millersville Univ. of Pennsylvania, Millersville, PA 17551-0302	1855	$8,600(S)	$9,234	5-M	8,368	442	65.0
Milligan Coll., Milligan College, TN 37682	1866	$26,760	$5,850	2-M	1,208	134	65.0
Millikin Univ., Decatur, IL 62522-2084	1901	$28,644	$8,970	2-M	2,347	305	55.0
Mills Coll., Oakland, CA 94613-1000	1852	$41,494	$12,625	1-D	1,533	211	63.0
Milwaukee Sch. of Engineering, Milwaukee, WI 53202-3109 (2)	1903	$34,470	$8,271	1-M	2,564	231	56.0
Minnesota Sch. of Business–Blaine, Blaine, MN 55449 (4)	1877	$16,848	NA	3-B	1,012	132	NA
Minnesota State Univ. Mankato, Mankato, MN 56001	1868	$8,396(S)	$7,053	5-D	15,195	762	55.0
Minnesota State Univ. Moorhead, Moorhead, MN 56563-0002	1885	$7,834(S)	$6,984	5-D	6,904	469	45.0
Minot State Univ., Minot, ND 58707-0002	1913	$5,921(S)	$4,994	5-M	3,560	276	34.0
Misericordia Univ., Dallas, PA 18612-1098	1924	$27,230	$11,190	2-D	3,012	323	68.0
Mississippi Coll., Clinton, MS 39058	1826	$14,868	$7,150	2-D	5,070	461	62.0
Mississippi State Univ., Mississippi State, MS 39762	1878	$6,264(S)	$8,486	5-D	20,365	1,005	60.0
Mississippi Univ. for Women, Columbus, MS 39701-9998 (4)	1884	$5,316(S)	$5,991	5-M	2,650	214	39.0
Mississippi Valley State Univ., Itta Bena, MS 38941-1400	1946	$5,778(S)	$6,510	5-M	2,479	165	22.0
Missouri Baptist Univ., St. Louis, MO 63141-8660	1964	$20,654	$8,230	2-M	5,212	309	28.0
Missouri Southern State Univ., Joplin, MO 64801-1595	1937	$5,090(S)	$5,976	5-M	5,591	306	NA
Missouri State Univ., Springfield, MO 65897	1905	$6,792(S)	$6,844	5-D	20,629	1,056	55.0
Missouri Univ. of Sci. & Tech., Rolla, MO 65409 (2)	1870	$9,350(S)	$8,900	5-D	7,647	493	65.0
Missouri Valley Coll., Marshall, MO 65340-3197	1889	$17,780	$6,700	2-B	1,639	90	23.0
Missouri Western State Univ., St. Joseph, MO 64507-2294	1915	$6,386(S)	$6,918	5-M	6,056	393	30.0
Molloy Coll., Rockville Centre, NY 11571-5002	1955	$24,420	$12,080	1-D	4,482	674	62.0
Monmouth Coll., Monmouth, IL 61462-1998	1853	$31,500	$7,600	2-B	1,247	118	58.0
Monmouth Univ., West Long Branch, NJ 07764-1898	1933	$29,710	$10,802	1-D	6,472	597	66.0
Monroe Coll., Bronx, NY 10468-5407	1933	NA	NA	3-M	5,068	251	66.0
Monroe Coll., New Rochelle, NY 10801	1983	NA	NA	3-M	2,222	93	75.0
Montana State Univ., Bozeman, MT 59717	1893	$6,749(S)	$8,070	5-D	14,660	917	49.0
Montana State Univ. Billings, Billings, MT 59101-0298	1927	$5,711(S)	$6,320	5-M	5,081	343	33.0
Montana State Univ.–Northern, Havre, MT 59501-7751	1929	$5,070(S)	$6,275	5-M	1,273	96	30.0
Montana Tech. of The Univ. of Montana, Butte, MT 59701-8997	1895	$6,693(S)	$7,626	5-M	2,816	213	48.0
Montclair State Univ., Montclair, NJ 07043-1624	1908	$11,058(S)	$13,443	5-D	18,382	1,589	63.0
Moody Bible Institute, Chicago, IL 60610-3284	1886	NA	NA	2-M	3,349	211	NA

Name, address	Year founded	Tuition & fees	Room & board	Control, degree	Enrollment	Faculty	Grad. rate
Moravian Coll., Bethlehem, PA 18018-6650	1742	$34,484	$10,146	2-M	1,909	167	74.0%
Morehead State Univ., Morehead, KY 40351	1922	$276/cr. hr.(A)	NA	5-D	11,172	479	NA
Morehouse Coll., Atlanta, GA 30314 (1)	1867	$24,744	$12,672	1-B	2,377	223	55.0
Morgan State Univ., Baltimore, MD 21251	1867	$6,928(S)	$8,750	5-D	7,005	558	100.0
Morningside Coll., Sioux City, IA 51106	1894	$25,000	$7,620	2-M	2,224	180	59.0
Morrisville State Coll., Morrisville, NY 13408-0901	1908	$7,792(S)	$10,720	5-B	3,095	252	31.0
Mount Aloysius Coll., Cresson, PA 16630-1999	1939	$18,750	$8,120	2-M	1,768	184	33.0
Mount Carmel Coll. of Nursing, Columbus, OH 43222 (4)	1903	$11,365	$5,000	1-M	1,056	107	72.0
Mount Holyoke Coll., South Hadley, MA 01075 (3)	1837	$41,456	$12,140	1-M	2,344	268	81.0
Mount Ida Coll., Newton, MA 02459-3310	1899	$26,929	$12,500	1-M	1,481	189	38.0
Mount Marty Coll., Yankton, SD 57078-3724	1936	$22,130	$6,390	2-M	1,178	61	51.0
Mount Mary Coll., Milwaukee, WI 53222-4597	1913	$25,098	$7,738	2-D	1,640	206	35.0
Mount Mercy Univ., Cedar Rapids, IA 52402-4797	1928	$26,310	$8,075	2-M	1,810	152	54.0
Mount Olive Coll., Mount Olive, NC 28365	1951	$16,300	$6,500	2-B	3,855	183	44.0
Mount St. Mary Coll., Newburgh, NY 12550-3494	1960	$26,250	$13,290	1-M	2,581	279	56.0
Mount St. Mary's Coll., Los Angeles, CA 90049-1599 (4)	1925	$33,852	$10,530	2-D	3,146	347	61.0
Mount St. Mary's Univ., Emmitsburg, MD 21727-7799	1808	$32,954	$11,018	2-M	2,350	193	67.0
Mount Vernon Nazarene Univ., Mount Vernon, OH 43050-9500	1964	$23,690	$6,980	2-M	2,267	235	55.0
Muhlenberg Coll., Allentown, PA 18104-5586	1848	$41,510	$11,140	2-B	2,422	262	87.0
Murray State Univ., Murray, KY 42071	1922	$6,840(S)	$7,638	5-D	10,832	611	52.0
Musicians Institute, Hollywood, CA 90028	1976	$30,420	NA	3-B	1,337	204	NA
Muskingum Univ., New Concord, OH 43762	1837	$21,610	$8,540	2-M	2,099	NA	NA
Naropa Univ., Boulder, CO 80302-6697	1974	$28,790	$8,980	1-M	1,019	164	27.0
National Louis Univ., Chicago, IL 60603	1886	$18,975	NA	1-D	5,737	521	20.0
National Univ., La Jolla, CA 92037-1011	1971	$14,670	NA	1-D	17,898	2,756	23.0
National Univ., Bayamón, PR 00960	1983	NA	NA	13-B	2,703	NA	NA
Nazareth Coll. of Rochester, Rochester, NY 14618-3790	1924	$27,222	$11,144	1-D	2,910	461	73.0
Nebraska Wesleyan Univ., Lincoln, NE 68504-2796	1887	$27,240	$7,550	2-M	2,071	156	65.0
Neumann Univ., Aston, PA 19014-1298	1965	$24,232	$11,070	2-D	3,100	308	51.0
Nevada State Coll. at Henderson, Henderson, NV 89015	2002	NA	NA	5-B	2,988	94	17.0
Newberry Coll., Newberry, SC 29108-2197	1856	$23,800	$9,000	2-B	1,042	121	40.0
Newbury Coll., Brookline, MA 02445	1962	$28,950	$12,900	1-B	1,003	107	42.0
New England Coll., Henniker, NH 03242-3293	1946	$31,744	$12,434	1-D	2,016	180	42.0
New England Institute of Tech., East Greenwich, RI 02818	1940	$21,995	NA	1-M	2,764	294	NA
New Jersey City Univ., Jersey City, NJ 07305-1597	1927	$245/cr. hr.(S)	NA	5-M	8,493	752	34.0
New Jersey Institute of Tech., Newark, NJ 07102	1881	$14,740(S)	$11,750	5-D	9,944	691	55.0
Newman Univ., Wichita, KS 67213-2097	1933	$22,298	$6,390	2-M	3,108	233	46.0
New Mexico Highlands Univ., Las Vegas, NM 87701	1893	$3,504(S)	$5,920	5-M	3,738	331	16.0
New Mexico Institute of Mining and Tech., Socorro, NM 87801	1889	$5,496(S)	$6,304	5-D	2,105	162	49.0
New Mexico State Univ., Las Cruces, NM 88003-8001	1888	$6,040(S)	$7,182	5-D	17,651	833	44.0
New Orleans Baptist Theol. Sem., New Orleans, LA 70126-4858 (2)	1917	NA	NA	2-D	2,036	NA	NA
The New School for Public Engagement, New York, NY 10011-8603	1919	$24,630	$14,910	1-M	2,224	385	NA
New York City Coll. of Tech. of the City Univ. of New York, Brooklyn, NY 11201-2983	1946	$5,769(S)	NA	11-B	16,207	1,350	23.0
New York Institute of Tech., Old Westbury, NY 11568-8000	1955	$28,940	$11,650	1-D	7,883	1,248	46.0
New York Univ., New York, NY 10012-1019	1831	$43,204	$16,133	1-D	44,516	6,574	85.0
Niagara Univ., Niagara University, NY 14109	1856	$27,230	$11,300	2-D	4,045	333	67.0
Nicholls State Univ., Thibodaux, LA 70310	1948	$5,679(S)	$8,560	5-M	6,606	298	39.0
Nichols Coll., Dudley, MA 01571-5000	1815	$31,740	$10,700	1-M	1,547	80	38.0
Norfolk State Univ., Norfolk, VA 23504	1935	$6,860(S)	$8,130	5-D	8,343	417	32.0
North Carolina Agr. & Tech. State Univ., Greensboro, NC 27411	1891	$5,058(S)	$7,349	5-D	10,881	674	43.0
North Carolina Central Univ., Durham, NC 27707-3129	1910	$3,244(S)	$9,923	5-D	8,604	598	43.0
North Carolina State Univ., Raleigh, NC 27695	1887	$7,788(S)	$8,414	5-D	34,340	1,821	72.0
North Carolina Wesleyan Coll., Rocky Mount, NC 27804-8677	1956	$26,981	$8,679	2-B	1,522	213	24.0
North Central Coll., Naperville, IL 60566-7063	1861	$31,071	$8,883	2-M	3,042	256	68.0
North Central Univ., Minneapolis, MN 55404-1322	1930	$19,066	$5,886	2-B	1,125	102	37.0
North Dakota State Univ., Fargo, ND 58108	1890	$7,233(S)	$6,910	5-D	14,443	833	52.0
North Greenville Univ., Tigerville, SC 29688-1892	1892	$13,936	$8,164	2-D	2,428	183	54.0
North Park Univ., Chicago, IL 60625-4895	1891	$22,090	$8,040	2-D	2,181	NA	NA
Northcentral Univ., Prescott Valley, AZ 86314	1996	$9,760	NA	3-D	9,252	481	NA
Northeastern Illinois Univ., Chicago, IL 60625-4699	1961	$9,926(S)	NA	5-M	11,149	669	21.0
Northeastern State Univ., Tahlequah, OK 74464-2399	1846	$4,857(S)	$5,914	5-D	9,361	513	26.0
Northeastern Univ., Boston, MA 02115-5096	1898	$39,736	$13,620	1-D	24,540	1,536	79.0
Northern Arizona Univ., Flagstaff, AZ 86011	1899	$9,271(S)	$8,784	5-D	26,002	1,539	49.0
Northern Illinois Univ., De Kalb, IL 60115-2854	1895	$13,061(S)	$10,648	5-D	21,869	1,148	52.0
Northern Kentucky Univ., Highland Heights, KY 41099	1968	$8,064(S)	$7,430	5-D	15,634	1,060	37.0
Northern Michigan Univ., Marquette, MI 49855-5301	1899	$8,710(S)	$8,404	5-M	9,098	NA	47.0
Northern State Univ., Aberdeen, SD 57401-7198	1901	$7,269(S)	$6,147	5-M	3,449	101	46.0
Northwest Missouri State Univ., Maryville, MO 64468-6001	1905	$7,720(S)	$8,614	5-M	6,831	300	49.0
Northwest Nazarene Univ., Nampa, ID 83686-5897	1913	$26,550	$6,400	2-D	2,232	107	55.0
Northwest Univ., Kirkland, WA 98033	1934	$23,470	$6,884	2-D	1,612	206	48.0
Northwestern Coll., Orange City, IA 51041-1996	1882	$26,764	$8,084	2-B	1,241	126	63.0
Northwestern Coll., St. Paul, MN 55113-1598	1902	$26,960	$8,210	2-M	3,267	159	68.0
Northwestern Oklahoma State Univ., Alva, OK 73717-2799	1897	$5,198(S)	$3,780	5-M	2,295	182	26.0
Northwestern State Univ. of Louisiana, Natchitoches, LA 71497	1884	$5,480(S)	$7,826	5-M	9,447	498	40.0
Northwestern Univ., Evanston, IL 60208	1851	$43,779	$13,329	1-D	18,431	1,153	93.0
Northwood Univ., Michigan campus, Midland, MI 48640-2398	1959	$20,996	$8,770	1-M	1,787	130	54.0
Norwich Univ., Northfield, VT 05663 (2)	1819	$31,782	$10,976	1-M	3,452	327	54.0
Notre Dame Coll., South Euclid, OH 44121-4293	1922	$24,652	$8,054	2-M	1,393	118	NA
Notre Dame de Namur Univ., Belmont, CA 94002-1908	1851	$31,206	$12,152	2-D	2,001	226	47.0
Notre Dame of Maryland Univ., Baltimore, MD 21210-2476 (4)	1873	$30,850	$10,150	2-D	2,731	121	60.0
Nova Southeastern Univ., Fort Lauderdale, FL 33314-7796	1964	$24,500	$9,516	1-D	26,808	1,725	43.0
Nyack Coll., Nyack, NY 10960-3698	1882	$23,250	$8,650	2-D	3,318	315	46.0
Oakland City Univ., Oakland City, IN 47660-1099	1885	$18,600	$8,100	2-D	2,519	202	65.0
Oakland Univ., Rochester, MI 48309-4401	1957	$11,183(S)	$8,208	5-D	19,740	NA	47.0
Oakwood Univ., Huntsville, AL 35896	1896	$15,414	$8,536	2-M	1,824	171	46.0
Oberlin Coll., Oberlin, OH 44074	1833	$43,210	$11,550	1-M	2,974	285	86.0
Occidental Coll., Los Angeles, CA 90041-3314	1887	$46,270	$12,940	1-M	2,178	265	84.0
Oglala Lakota Coll., Kyle, SD 57752-0490	1970	NA	NA	11-M	1,000	NA	NA
Oglethorpe Univ., Atlanta, GA 30319	1835	$31,280	$11,300	1-M	1,079	116	56.0
Ohio Dominican Univ., Columbus, OH 43219-2099	1911	$26,790	$9,090	2-M	3,052	170	44.0
Ohio Northern Univ., Ada, OH 45810-1599	1871	$36,720	$10,520	2-D	3,557	305	67.0
The Ohio State Univ., Columbus, OH 43210	1870	$10,037(S)	$10,370	5-D	56,387	4,974	82.0
The Ohio State Univ. at Lima, Lima, OH 45804	1960	$7,140(S)	NA	5-M	1,134	89	38.0
The Ohio State Univ. at Marion, Marion, OH 43302-5695	1958	$7,140(S)	NA	5-M	1,273	103	44.0
The Ohio State Univ.–Mansfield campus, Mansfield, OH 44906-1599	1958	$7,140(S)	$6,020	5-M	1,265	92	40.0
The Ohio State Univ.–Newark campus, Newark, OH 43055-1797	1957	$6,903(S)	$7,185	5-M	2,390	151	37.0

Name, address	Year founded	Tuition & fees	Room & board	Control, degree	Enroll- ment	Faculty	Grad. rate
Ohio Univ., Athens, OH 45701-2979	1804	$10,282(S)	$10,010	5-D	27,402	1,229	64.0%
Ohio Univ.–Chillicothe, Chillicothe, OH 45601	1946	$4,956(S)	NA	5-M	2,200	NA	NA
Ohio Univ.–Lancaster, Lancaster, OH 43130-1097	1968	NA	NA	5-M	1,728	NA	NA
Ohio Univ.–Southern campus, Ironton, OH 45638-2214	1956	NA	NA	5-M	1,836	NA	NA
Ohio Univ.–Zanesville, Zanesville, OH 43701-2695	1946	$5,104(S)	NA	5-B	1,972	130	NA
Ohio Wesleyan Univ., Delaware, OH 43015	1842	$39,150	$10,310	2-B	1,821	219	68.0
Oklahoma Baptist Univ., Shawnee, OK 74804	1910	$20,856	$6,200	2-M	1,979	192	51.0
Oklahoma Christian Univ., Oklahoma City, OK 73136-1100	1950	$18,800	$6,175	2-M	2,271	194	48.0
Oklahoma City Univ., Oklahoma City, OK 73106-1402	1904	$28,190	$9,170	2-D	NA	342	NA
Oklahoma Panhandle State Univ., Goodwell, OK 73939-0430	1909	NA	NA	5-B	1,387	91	38.0
Oklahoma State Univ., Stillwater, OK 74078	1890	$7,442(S)	$6,868	5-D	25,544	1,344	62.0
Oklahoma Wesleyan Univ., Bartlesville, OK 74006-6299	1909	$21,140	$7,240	2-M	1,178	168	45.0
Old Dominion Univ., Norfolk, VA 23529	1930	$8,450(S)	$9,066	5-D	24,670	1,294	49.0
Olivet Coll., Olivet, MI 49076-9701	1844	$21,118	$7,000	2-M	1,206	90	43.0
Olivet Nazarene Univ., Bourbonnais, IL 60914	1907	$28,090	$7,900	2-M	4,636	NA	NA
Oral Roberts Univ., Tulsa, OK 74171	1963	$22,438	$9,296	2-D	3,335	273	NA
Oregon Health & Sci. Univ., Portland, OR 97239-3098	1974	NA	NA	12-D	2,849	111	NA
Oregon Institute of Tech., Klamath Falls, OR 97601-8801	1947	NA	NA	5-M	3,911	257	45.0
Oregon State Univ., Corvallis, OR 97331	1868	$8,138(S)	$10,563	5-D	26,393	1,345	60.0
Otis Coll. of Art and Design, Los Angeles, CA 90045-9785	1918	$35,354	NA	1-M	1,165	544	53.0
Otterbein Univ., Westerville, OH 43081	1847	$30,658	$8,684	2-D	2,997	337	62.0
Ouachita Baptist Univ., Arkadelphia, AR 71998-0001	1886	$22,340	$6,640	2-B	1,532	155	63.0
Our Lady of Holy Cross Coll., New Orleans, LA 70131-7399	1916	$9,170	NA	2-M	1,298	NA	NA
Our Lady of the Lake Coll., Baton Rouge, LA 70808 (4)	1990	NA	NA	2-M	1,748	183	67.0
Our Lady of the Lake Univ. of San Antonio, San Antonio, TX 78207-4689	1895	$22,756	$7,326	2-D	2,751	249	32.0
Pace Univ., New York, NY 10038	1906	$36,564	$12,590	1-D	12,772	1,324	56.0
Pacific Lutheran Univ., Tacoma, WA 98447	1890	$34,740	$10,100	2-M	3,473	254	69.0
Pacific Oaks Coll., Pasadena, CA 91103 (4)	1945	NA	NA	1-M	1,028	125	NA
Pacific Union Coll., Angwin, CA 94508-9707	1882	$26,850	$7,485	2-M	1,564	139	40.0
Pacific Univ., Forest Grove, OR 97116-1797	1849	$35,260	$9,992	1-D	3,416	NA	63.0
Palm Beach Atlantic Univ., West Palm Beach, FL 33416-4708	1968	$25,532	$8,350	2-D	3,579	332	50.0
Palm Beach State Coll., Lake Worth, FL 33461-4796	1933	$2,314(S)	NA	5-B	29,974	1,473	NA
Palmer Coll. of Chiropractic, Davenport, IA 52803-5287	1897	NA	NA	1-D	2,310	15	NA
Park Univ., Parkville, MO 64152-3795	1875	$9,900	$7,151	1-M	2,458	174	41.0
Parsons The New School for Design, New York, NY 10011-8878	1896	$40,140	$15,100	1-M	4,916	1,046	73.0
Patten Univ., Oakland, CA 94601-2699	1944	NA	NA	2-M	1,050	125	37.0
Peirce Coll., Philadelphia, PA 19102-4699 (4)	1865	$16,500	NA	1-B	2,261	149	56.0
Penn State Abington, Abington, PA 19001	1950	$13,356(S)	NA	12-B	3,516	226	47.0
Penn State Altoona, Altoona, PA 16601-3760	1939	$13,900(S)	$9,690	12-B	3,863	292	67.0
Penn State Berks, Reading, PA 19610-6009	1924	$13,900(S)	$10,560	12-B	2,747	217	54.0
Penn State Erie, The Behrend Coll., Erie, PA 16563-0001	1948	$13,900(S)	$9,690	12-M	4,149	299	67.0
Penn State Harrisburg, Middletown, PA 17057-4898	1966	$13,900(S)	$11,000	12-D	4,376	341	61.0
Penn State Univ. Park, University Park, PA 16802-1503	1855	$16,444(S)	$9,690	12-D	45,783	2,910	86.0
Pennsylvania Coll. of Tech., Williamsport, PA 17701-5778	1965	$14,370(S)	$10,500	12-B	5,671	477	NA
Pepperdine Univ., Malibu, CA 90263	1937	$42,772	$12,600	2-D	7,319	707	80.0
Peru State Coll., Peru, NE 68421	1867	$4,200(S)	$5,970	5-M	2,358	109	NA
Pfeiffer Univ., Misenheimer, NC 28109-0960	1885	$21,650	$8,720	2-M	2,019	150	59.0
Philadelphia Univ., Philadelphia, PA 19144	1884	$31,874	$10,178	1-D	3,540	488	61.0
Piedmont Coll., Demorest, GA 30535-0010	1897	$20,730	$8,530	2-D	2,464	245	52.0
Pittsburg State Univ., Pittsburg, KS 66762	1903	$5,494(S)	$6,758	5-M	7,107	411	48.0
Pitzer Coll., Claremont, CA 91711-6101	1963	$43,402	$13,864	1-B	1,084	121	87.0
Plymouth State Univ., Plymouth, NH 03264-1595	1871	$12,560(S)	$9,440	5-D	5,431	418	55.0
Point Loma Nazarene Univ., San Diego, CA 92106-2899	1902	$29,510	$9,550	2-M	3,192	362	75.0
Point Park Univ., Pittsburgh, PA 15222-1984	1960	$25,190	$8,000	1-M	3,827	442	50.0
Point Univ., East Point, GA 30344-1999	1937	$16,226	$5,980	2-B	1,483	129	35.0
Polk State Coll., Winter Haven, FL 33881-4299	1964	$3,307(S)	NA	5-B	11,862	623	NA
Polytechnic Institute of New York Univ., Brooklyn, NY 11201-2990	1854	$37,882	$10,080	1-D	4,652	396	62.0
Polytechnic Univ. of Puerto Rico, Hato Rey, PR 00919 (2)	1966	$7,548	NA	1-M	4,743	248	22.0
Pomona Coll., Claremont, CA 91711	1887	$41,438	$13,526	1-B	1,607	241	96.0
Pontifical Catholic Univ. of Puerto Rico, Ponce, PR 00717-0777	1948	NA	NA	2-D	7,682	385	39.0
Portland State Univ., Portland, OR 97207-0751	1946	$7,653(S)	$11,019	5-D	28,731	1,734	40.0
Prairie View A&M Univ., Prairie View, TX 77446-0519	1878	$7,738(S)	$7,467	5-D	8,336	461	34.0
Pratt Institute, Brooklyn, NY 11205-3899	1887	$41,092	$10,506	1-M	4,722	1,005	62.0
Presbyterian Coll., Clinton, SC 29325	1880	$32,680	$8,750	2-D	1,403	126	68.0
Prescott Coll., Prescott, AZ 86301	1966	$28,019	$5,900	1-D	1,065	149	45.0
Princeton Univ., Princeton, NJ 08544-1019	1746	$40,715	$13,080	1-D	8,010	1,098	96.1
Providence Coll., Providence, RI 02918	1917	$42,206	$12,440	2-M	4,336	395	87.0
Purchase Coll., State Univ. of New York, Purchase, NY 10577-1400	1967	$7,230(S)	$11,566	5-M	4,267	403	63.0
Purdue Univ., West Lafayette, IN 47907	1869	$10,466(S)	$9,990	5-D	39,256	2,314	68.0
Purdue Univ. Calumet, Hammond, IN 46323-2094	1951	$6,991(S)	$7,717	5-M	10,054	606	28.0
Purdue Univ. North Central, Westville, IN 46391-9542	1967	$7,045(S)	NA	5-M	6,048	277	18.0
Queens Coll. of the City Univ. of New York, Flushing, NY 11367-1597	1937	$5,730(S)	NA	11-M	20,100	1,508	52.0
Queens Univ. of Charlotte, Charlotte, NC 28274-0002	1857	$27,576	$9,412	2-M	2,386	254	59.0
Quincy Univ., Quincy, IL 62301-2699	1860	$25,834	$9,880	2-M	1,632	165	56.0
Quinnipiac Univ., Hamden, CT 06518-1940	1929	$39,330	$14,250	1-D	8,614	942	75.0
Radford Univ., Radford, VA 24142	1910	$8,590(S)	$7,881	5-D	9,573	663	60.0
Ramapo Coll. of New Jersey, Mahwah, NJ 07430-1680	1969	$13,144(S)	$11,370	5-M	5,817	503	73.4
Randolph-Macon Coll., Ashland, VA 23005-5505	1830	$33,525	$10,400	2-B	1,312	148	56.0
Reed Coll., Portland, OR 97202-8199	1908	$44,460	$11,460	1-M	1,455	139	73.0
Regent Univ., Virginia Beach, VA 23464-9800	1977	$15,960	$8,430	2-D	5,863	569	NA
Regis Coll., Weston, MA 02493	1927	$33,060	$12,800	2-D	1,991	177	53.0
Regis Univ., Denver, CO 80221-1099	1877	$32,424	$9,380	2-D	10,683	1,181	62.0
Reinhardt Univ., Waleska, GA 30183-2981	1883	$18,290	$6,958	2-M	1,154	157	39.0
Rensselaer Polytechnic Institute, Troy, NY 12180-3590	1824	$44,475	$12,450	1-D	6,999	500	84.0
Rhode Island Coll., Providence, RI 02908-1991	1854	$7,598(S)	$9,534	5-D	8,869	743	43.0
Rhode Island Sch. of Design, Providence, RI 02903-2784	1877	$41,332	$11,980	1-M	2,386	530	87.0
Rhodes Coll., Memphis, TN 38112-1690	1848	$38,092	$9,504	1-M	1,927	207	81.0
Rice Univ., Houston, TX 77251-1892	1912	$38,942	$13,000	1-D	6,484	771	92.0
The Richard Stockton Coll. of New Jersey, Galloway, NJ 08205-9441	1969	$12,322(S)	$10,796	5-D	8,400	626	64.0
Rider Univ., Lawrenceville, NJ 08648-3001	1865	$33,420	$12,340	1-M	5,485	626	67.0
Ringling Coll. of Art and Design, Sarasota, FL 34234-5895	1931	$35,300	$12,230	1-B	1,364	152	65.0
Rivier Univ., Nashua, NH 03060	1933	$26,755	$10,118	2-D	2,316	200	50.0
Roanoke Coll., Salem, VA 24153-3794	1842	$36,472	$11,524	2-B	2,060	212	65.0
Robert Morris Univ., Moon Township, PA 15108-1189	1921	$24,064	$11,360	1-D	5,181	469	54.0
Robert Morris Univ. Illinois, Chicago, IL 60605	1913	$22,800	$11,754	1-M	3,802	261	74.0
Roberts Wesleyan Coll., Rochester, NY 14624-1997	1866	$27,464	$9,630	2-M	1,752	259	59.0
Rochester Institute of Tech., Rochester, NY 14623-5603	1829	$34,424	$11,740	1-D	16,362	1,475	62.0

Name, address	Year founded	Tuition & fees	Room & board	Control, degree	Enrollment	Faculty	Grad. rate
Rockford Coll., Rockford, IL 61108-2393	1847	$26,310	$7,320	1-M	1,238	162	39.0%
Rockhurst Univ., Kansas City, MO 64110-2561	1910	$29,840	$8,060	2-D	2,808	253	67.0
Rocky Mountain Coll., Billings, MT 59102-1796	1878	$23,718	$7,430	2-M	1,087	127	48.0
Rogers State Univ., Claremore, OK 74017-3252	1909	$5,047(S)	$6,425	5-B	4,646	281	23.0
Roger Williams Univ., Bristol, RI 02809	1956	$31,668	$14,120	1-D	5,274	511	61.0
Rollins Coll., Winter Park, FL 32789-4499	1885	$39,900	$12,470	1-M	2,459	216	72.0
Roosevelt Univ., Chicago, IL 60605	1945	$25,950	$12,100	1-D	6,343	722	44.0
Rose-Hulman Institute of Tech., Terre Haute, IN 47803-3999 (2)	1874	$39,078	$10,935	1-M	2,214	181	82.0
Rowan Univ., Glassboro, NJ 08028-1701	1923	$12,380(S)	$10,972	5-D	12,133	1,125	70.0
Rush Univ., Chicago, IL 60612-3832	1969	NA	NA	1-D	1,566	796	NA
Rutgers, The State Univ. of New Jersey, Camden, Camden, NJ 08102-1401	1927	$12,923(S)	$11,206	5-D	6,343	537	64.0
Rutgers, The State Univ. of New Jersey, Newark, Newark, NJ 07102	1892	$12,590(S)	$12,285	5-D	12,011	819	60.0
Rutgers, The State Univ. of New Jersey, New Brunswick, Piscataway, NJ 08854-8097	1766	$13,073(S)	$11,412	5-D	40,434	2,890	79.0
Sacred Heart Univ., Fairfield, CT 06825-1000	1963	$34,030	$13,230	2-D	6,347	634	68.0
Saginaw Valley State Univ., University Center, MI 48710	1963	$8,120(S)	$8,190	5-M	10,552	767	39.0
St. Ambrose Univ., Davenport, IA 52803-2898	1882	$26,740	$9,016	2-D	3,671	425	63.0
St. Anselm Coll., Manchester, NH 03102-1310	1889	$35,634	$12,690	2-B	1,954	217	74.0
St. Augustine Coll., Chicago, IL 60640-3501	1980	NA	NA	1-B	1,430	154	NA
St. Augustine's Coll., Raleigh, NC 27610-2298	1867	$17,160	$7,562	2-B	1,506	151	NA
St. Bonaventure Univ., St. Bonaventure, NY 14778-2284	1858	$28,727	$10,704	2-M	2,329	220	64.0
St. Catherine Univ., St. Paul, MN 55105	1905	$32,690	$8,568	2-D	5,075	330	59.0
St. Cloud State Univ., St. Cloud, MN 56301-4498	1869	$7,439(S)	$6,994	5-D	17,231	872	48.0
St. Edward's Univ., Austin, TX 78704	1885	$33,720	$10,954	2-M	5,095	532	69.0
St. Francis Coll., Brooklyn Heights, NY 11201-4398	1884	$19,200	$13,000	2-M	2,903	281	51.0
St. Francis Univ., Loretto, PA 15940-0600	1847	$29,992	$10,346	2-D	2,451	203	65.0
St. John Fisher Coll., Rochester, NY 14618-3597	1948	$28,430	$10,940	2-D	4,008	415	75.0
St. John's Univ., Collegeville, MN 56321 (1)	1857	$35,486	$8,639	2-M	1,983	167	77.0
St. John's Univ., Queens, NY 11439	1870	$35,520	$15,270	2-D	21,087	1,467	59.0
St. Joseph's Coll., Rensselaer, IN 47978	1889	$27,350	$8,250	2-M	1,084	119	50.0
St. Joseph's Coll., Long Island campus, Patchogue, NY 11772-2399	1916	$20,125	NA	1-M	4,113	453	69.0
St. Joseph's Coll., New York, Brooklyn, NY 11205-3688	1916	$20,115	NA	1-M	1,519	189	62.0
St. Joseph's Coll. of Maine, Standish, ME 04084	1912	$29,000	$11,400	2-M	3,355	126	50.0
St. Joseph's Univ., Philadelphia, PA 19131-1395	1851	$37,830	$12,800	2-D	8,805	786	79.0
St. Lawrence Univ., Canton, NY 13617-1455	1856	$44,390	$11,435	1-M	2,488	201	80.0
St. Leo Univ., Saint Leo, FL 33574-6665	1889	$19,610	$5,000	2-M	5,383	190	45.0
St. Louis Coll. of Pharm., St. Louis, MO 63110-1088	1864	$26,125	$9,280	1-D	1,299	134	65.0
St. Louis Univ., St. Louis, MO 63103-2097	1818	$35,266	$9,612	2-D	13,981	1,340	70.0
St. Martin's Univ., Lacey, WA 98503	1895	$29,834	$9,660	2-M	1,823	218	54.0
St. Mary's Coll., Notre Dame, IN 46556 (3)	1844	$33,280	$10,140	2-B	1,469	196	78.0
St. Mary's Coll. of California, Moraga, CA 94556	1863	$39,890	$13,660	2-D	4,228	458	58.0
St. Mary's Coll. of Maryland, St. Mary's City, MD 20686-3001	1840	$14,773(S)	$11,305	5-M	1,933	225	81.0
St. Mary's Univ., San Antonio, TX 78228-8507	1852	$24,520	$8,870	2-D	3,988	393	53.0
St. Mary's Univ. of Minnesota, Winona, MN 55987-1399	1912	$29,315	$7,700	2-D	5,574	555	62.0
St. Michael's Coll., Colchester, VT 05439	1904	$39,015	$9,725	2-M	2,410	217	82.0
St. Norbert Coll., De Pere, WI 54115-2099	1898	$30,675	$7,813	2-M	2,287	201	75.0
St. Olaf Coll., Northfield, MN 55057-1098	1874	$39,560	$9,090	2-B	3,176	340	87.0
St. Petersburg Coll., St. Petersburg, FL 33733-3489	1927	$3,088(S)	NA	11-B	31,793	1,731	28.0
St. Peter's Univ., Jersey City, NJ 07306-5997	1872	$32,230	$13,458	2-D	3,045	279	53.0
St. Thomas Aquinas Coll., Sparkill, NY 10976	1952	$26,840	$11,300	1-M	1,957	143	49.0
St. Thomas Univ., Miami Gardens, FL 33054-6459	1961	$25,110	$7,140	2-D	2,472	238	38.0
St. Vincent Coll., Latrobe, PA 15650-2690	1846	$29,144	$9,594	2-M	1,766	NA	73.0
St. Xavier Univ., Chicago, IL 60655-3105	1847	$28,110	$9,490	2-M	4,709	431	52.0
Salem State Univ., Salem, MA 01970-5353	1854	$8,050(S)	$8,292	5-M	9,456	783	45.0
Salisbury Univ., Salisbury, MD 21801-6837	1925	$7,700(S)	$9,120	5-D	8,657	661	67.0
Salve Regina Univ., Newport, RI 02840-4192	1934	$33,950	$11,900	2-D	2,615	236	73.0
Samford Univ., Birmingham, AL 35229	1841	$25,150	$8,250	2-D	4,758	487	71.0
Sam Houston State Univ., Huntsville, TX 77341	1879	$8,120(S)	$8,092	5-D	18,461	797	49.0
Samuel Merritt Univ., Oakland, CA 94609-3108 (4)	1909	$39,456	NA	1-D	1,530	271	NA
San Diego State Univ., San Diego, CA 92182	1897	$6,766(S)	$13,812	5-D	31,597	1,370	67.0
San Diego State Univ.–Imperial Valley campus, Calexico, CA 92231	1959	NA	NA	5-M	1,003	NA	NA
San Francisco State Univ., San Francisco, CA 94132-1722	1899	$6,440(S)	$11,576	5-D	30,500	1,712	46.0
San Jose State Univ., San Jose, CA 95192-0001	1857	$7,303(S)	$11,733	5-M	30,448	1,656	47.0
Santa Clara Univ., Santa Clara, CA 95053	1851	$40,572	$12,276	2-D	8,519	839	86.0
Santa Fe Coll., Gainesville, FL 32606	1966	$2,456(S)	NA	11-B	15,745	829	NA
Sarah Lawrence Coll., Bronxville, NY 10708-5999	1926	$46,924	$9,324	1-M	1,744	311	70.0
Savannah Coll. of Art and Design, Savannah, GA 31402-3146	1978	$32,405	$12,990	1-M	11,415	657	65.0
Savannah State Univ., Savannah, GA 31404	1890	$6,031(S)	$6,604	5-M	4,080	200	35.0
School of the Art Institute of Chicago, Chicago, IL 60603-3103	1866	$39,020	$13,810	1-M	3,308	744	60.0
School of Visual Arts, New York, NY 10010-3994	1947	$31,030	$16,200	3-M	4,214	929	69.0
Schreiner Univ., Kerrville, TX 78028-5697	1923	$21,540	$10,062	2-M	1,126	119	34.0
Seattle Pacific Univ., Seattle, WA 98119-1997	1891	$32,067	$9,492	2-D	4,095	348	72.0
Seattle Univ., Seattle, WA 98122-1090	1891	$34,800	$10,296	2-D	7,484	739	77.0
Seton Hall Univ., South Orange, NJ 07079-2697	1856	$34,750	$12,952	2-D	9,616	879	63.0
Seton Hill Univ., Greensburg, PA 15601	1883	$29,450	$9,944	2-M	2,091	196	57.0
Sewanee: The Univ. of the South, Sewanee, TN 37383-1000	1857	$35,756	$10,214	2-D	1,554	181	78.0
Shawnee State Univ., Portsmouth, OH 45662-4344	1986	$6,988(S)	$9,012	5-M	4,652	328	20.0
Shaw Univ., Raleigh, NC 27601-2399	1865	$13,228	$7,560	2-M	2,183	187	26.0
Shenandoah Univ., Winchester, VA 22601-5195	1875	$27,850	$9,240	2-D	4,176	404	47.0
Shepherd Univ., Shepherdstown, WV 25443	1871	$5,834(S)	$8,424	5-M	4,326	367	43.0
Shippensburg Univ. of Pennsylvania, Shippensburg, PA 17257-2299	1871	$9,154(S)	$7,910	5-M	7,724	397	57.0
Shorter Univ., Rome, GA 30165	1873	$17,870	$8,600	2-M	1,696	186	43.0
Siena Coll., Loudonville, NY 12211-1462	1937	$31,368	$12,495	2-M	3,289	354	73.0
Siena Heights Univ., Adrian, MI 49221-1796	1919	$21,570	$8,710	2-M	2,629	NA	43.0
Silicon Valley Univ., San Jose, CA 95131	1997	NA	NA	3-M	1,090	31	NA
Simmons Coll., Boston, MA 02115	1899	$35,370	$13,400	1-D	4,830	623	67.0
Simpson Coll., Indianola, IA 50125-1297	1860	$30,999	$7,963	2-M	1,897	202	67.0
Simpson Univ., Redding, CA 96003-8606	1921	$23,300	$7,500	2-M	1,297	154	41.0
Skidmore Coll., Saratoga Springs, NY 12866	1903	$44,020	$11,744	1-M	2,689	335	88.0
Slippery Rock Univ. of Pennsylvania, Slippery Rock, PA 16057-1383	1889	$8,747(S)	$9,364	5-D	8,559	407	62.0
Smith Coll., Northampton, MA 01063	1871	$41,460	$13,860	1-D	3,212	299	85.0
Sojourner-Douglass Coll., Baltimore, MD 21205-1814 (4)	1980	$8,850	NA	1-M	1,268	240	22.0
Sonoma State Univ., Rohnert Park, CA 94928-3609	1960	$7,396(S)	$11,241	5-M	9,021	514	59.0
South Carolina State Univ., Orangeburg, SC 29117-0001	1896	$9,258(S)	$9,286	5-D	4,326	279	36.0
South Dakota Sch. of Mines & Tech., Rapid City, SD 57701-3995	1885	$8,820(S)	$5,700	5-D	2,311	153	46.0
South Dakota State Univ., Brookings, SD 57007	1881	$7,404(S)	$5,586	5-D	12,583	693	56.0
Southeastern Baptist Theol. Sem., Wake Forest, NC 27588-1889	1950	$6,358	$1,935	2-M	2,332	85	NA

Name, address	Year founded	Tuition & fees	Room & board	Control, degree	Enrollment	Faculty	Grad. rate
Southeastern Louisiana Univ., Hammond, LA 70402.	1925	$5,427(S)	$6,510	5-D	15,602	610	33.0%
Southeastern Oklahoma State Univ., Durant, OK 74701-0609	1909	$5,060(S)	$4,970	5-M	4,120	262	30.0
Southeastern Univ., Lakeland, FL 33801-6099	1935	$18,596	$8,606	2-M	2,703	169	42.0
Southeast Missouri State Univ., Cape Girardeau, MO 63701-4799.	1873	$6,750(S)	$8,110	5-M	11,729	598	46.0
Southern Adventist Univ., Collegedale, TN 37315-0370	1892	$19,124	$5,584	2-M	3,053	269	48.0
Southern Arkansas Univ.–Magnolia, Magnolia, AR 71753.	1909	$7,346(S)	$4,974	5-M	3,383	174	34.0
Southern Baptist Theol. Sem., Louisville, KY 40280-0004.	1858	NA	NA	2-D	3,190	NA	NA
Southern Connecticut State Univ., New Haven, CT 06515-1355.	1893	$8,570(S)	$10,641	5-D	11,117	1,055	44.0
Southern Illinois Univ. Carbondale, Carbondale, IL 62901-4701	1869	$11,528(S)	$9,126	5-D	18,847	996	50.0
Southern Illinois Univ. Edwardsville, Edwardsville, IL 62026-0001	1957	$9,251(S)	$8,281	5-D	14,055	920	52.0
Southern Methodist Univ., Dallas, TX 75275	1911	$43,800	$13,955	2-D	10,893	1,155	79.0
Southern Nazarene Univ., Bethany, OK 73008	1899	$21,174	$7,600	2-M	2,184	189	41.0
Southern New Hampshire Univ., Manchester, NH 03106-1045.	1932	$28,884	$11,620	1-D	17,534	1,167	61.0
Southern Oregon Univ., Ashland, OR 97520	1926	$7,521(S)	$9,918	5-M	6,307	334	32.0
Southern Polytechnic State Univ., Marietta, GA 30060-2896.	1948	$6,678(S)	$7,280	5-M	6,202	309	37.0
Southern Univ. and Agr. & Mech. Coll., Baton Rouge, LA 70813	1880	$5,126(S)	$5,614	5-D	7,699	546	30.0
Southern Univ. at New Orleans, New Orleans, LA 70126-1009 (4)	1959	$3,906(S)	$7,680	5-M	3,141	102	5.2
Southern Utah Univ., Cedar City, UT 84720-2498.	1897	$5,576(S)	$2,878	5-M	8,297	420	36.0
Southern Wesleyan Univ., Central, SC 29630-1020	1906	$20,550	$7,550	2-M	1,883	193	39.0
Southwest Baptist Univ., Bolivar, MO 65613-2597.	1878	$19,150	$6,350	2-D	3,864	304	54.0
Southwest Florida Coll., Fort Myers, FL 33907	1940	NA	NA	1-B	1,263	NA	NA
Southwest Minnesota State Univ., Marshall, MN 56258	1963	$7,743(S)	$6,944	5-M	6,588	180	39.0
Southwestern Assemblies of God Univ., Waxahachie, TX 75165-5735.	1927	$16,630	$6,784	2-M	2,064	142	39.0
Southwestern Coll., Winfield, KS 67156-2499	1885	$23,886	$6,636	2-M	1,637	119	51.0
Southwestern Oklahoma State Univ., Weatherford, OK 73096-3098	1901	$4,755(S)	$4,240	5-D	5,340	234	30.0
Southwestern Univ., Georgetown, TX 78626	1840	$35,240	$11,010	2-B	1,394	165	75.0
Spalding Univ., Louisville, KY 40203-2188.	1814	$20,550	$8,400	2-D	2,432	169	42.0
Spelman Coll., Atlanta, GA 30314-4399 (3)	1881	$23,794	$11,541	1-B	2,145	247	72.0
Spring Arbor Univ., Spring Arbor, MI 49283-9799	1873	$22,538	$7,900	2-M	4,125	143	52.0
Springfield Coll., Springfield, MA 01109-3797	1885	$31,690	$10,630	1-D	5,000	342	NA
Spring Hill Coll., Mobile, AL 36608-1791	1830	$29,450	$11,296	2-M	1,328	134	62.0
Stanford Univ., Stanford, CA 94305-9991	1891	$42,690	$13,166	1-D	18,217	1,508	95.0
State Coll. of Florida Manatee-Sarasota, Bradenton, FL 34206-7046	1957	$2,460(S)	NA	5-B	10,765	445	NA
State Univ. of New York at Albany, Albany, NY 12222-0001.	1844	$7,563(S)	$11,276	5-D	17,316	1,198	63.0
State Univ. of New York at Buffalo, Buffalo, NY 14260	1846	$7,989(S)	$11,310	5-D	28,952	1,719	70.0
State Univ. of New York at Fredonia, Fredonia, NY 14063-1136.	1826	$7,058(S)	$11,100	5-M	5,523	482	64.0
State Univ. of New York at New Paltz, New Paltz, NY 12561	1828	$6,458(S)	$9,950	5-M	7,767	634	73.0
State Univ. of New York at Oswego, Oswego, NY 13126	1861	$6,841(S)	$12,510	5-M	7,921	576	58.0
State Univ. of New York at Plattsburgh, Plattsburgh, NY 12901-2681	1889	$6,808(S)	$10,582	5-M	6,167	519	60.0
State Univ. of New York Coll. at Cortland, Cortland, NY 13045	1868	$6,942(S)	$11,430	5-M	7,098	641	67.1
State Univ. of New York Coll. at Geneseo, Geneseo, NY 14454-1401	1871	$7,095(S)	$10,960	5-M	5,557	359	79.0
State Univ. of New York Coll. at Old Westbury, Old Westbury, NY 11568-0210.	1965	$6,624(S)	$9,700	5-M	4,422	311	35.0
State Univ. of New York Coll. at Oneonta, Oneonta, NY 13820-4015	1889	$6,887(S)	$10,540	5-M	6,023	483	67.0
State Univ. of New York Coll. at Potsdam, Potsdam, NY 13676	1816	$6,842(S)	$10,180	5-M	4,224	362	51.0
State Univ. of New York Coll. of Agr. and Tech. at Cobleskill, Cobleskill, NY 12043	1916	$8,262(S)	$10,866	5-B	2,519	150	48.0
State Univ. of New York Coll. of Environmental Sci. and Forestry, Syracuse, NY 13210-2779.	1911	$6,593(S)	$14,400	5-D	2,401	183	67.0
State Univ. of New York Coll. of Tech. at Canton, Canton, NY 13617.	1906	$6,970(S)	$10,952	5-M	3,780	220	46.0
State Univ. of New York Coll. of Tech. at Delhi, Delhi, NY 13753	1913	$7,090(S)	$10,346	5-B	3,151	227	57.0
State Univ. of New York Downstate Med. Ctr., Brooklyn, NY 11203-2098	1858	$5,789(S)	$12,134	5-D	1,694	981	NA
State Univ. of New York Empire State Coll., Saratoga Springs, NY 12866-4391.	1971	$5,915(S)	NA	5-M	12,091	1,400	NA
State Univ. of New York Institute of Tech., Utica, NY 13504-3050	1966	$6,764(S)	$10,290	5-M	2,377	180	NA
State Univ. of New York Maritime Coll., Throggs Neck, NY 10465-4198 (2).	1874	$6,782(S)	$10,444	5-M	1,761	149	47.0
State Univ. of New York Upstate Med. Univ., Syracuse, NY 13210-2334	1950	$5,880(S)	$10,710	5-D	1,787	54	NA
Stephen F. Austin State Univ., Nacogdoches, TX 75962.	1923	$7,928(S)	$8,476	5-D	12,999	673	43.0
Stetson Univ., DeLand, FL 32723.	1883	$36,644	$10,688	1-D	3,961	381	64.0
Stevens Institute of Tech., Hoboken, NJ 07030.	1870	$41,942	$13,800	1-D	5,541	406	79.0
Stevenson Univ., Stevenson, MD 21153	1952	$25,310	$11,894	1-M	4,418	502	64.0
Stillman Coll., Tuscaloosa, AL 35403-9990	1876	$15,665	$7,056	2-B	1,072	61	34.0
Stonehill Coll., Easton, MA 02357	1948	$36,160	$13,810	2-B	2,599	278	80.0
Stony Brook Univ., State Univ. of New York, Stony Brook, NY 11794.	1957	$7,560(S)	$10,934	5-D	24,149	1,467	69.0
Suffolk Univ., Boston, MA 02108-2770.	1906	$30,792	$14,730	1-D	9,044	863	56.0
Sullivan Univ., Louisville, KY 40205.	1864	NA	NA	3-D	5,478	340	NA
Sul Ross State Univ., Alpine, TX 79832.	1920	$6,000(S)	$6,810	5-M	1,782	175	23.0
Susquehanna Univ., Selinsgrove, PA 17870	1858	$37,280	$10,000	2-B	2,215	254	74.0
Swarthmore Coll., Swarthmore, PA 19081-1397	1864	$43,080	$12,670	1-B	1,552	205	92.0
Syracuse Univ., Syracuse, NY 13244	1870	$39,004	$13,692	1-D	21,029	1,563	82.0
Tarleton State Univ., Stephenville, TX 76402.	1899	$6,939(S)	$7,336	5-D	10,279	601	40.0
Taylor Univ., Upland, IN 46989-1001	1846	$28,088	$7,757	2-M	2,358	253	77.0
Temple Univ., Philadelphia, PA 19122-6096	1884	$13,596(S)	$10,276	12-D	36,744	2,888	68.0
Tennessee State Univ., Nashville, TN 37209-1561	1912	$6,088(S)	$5,910	5-M	8,775	603	35.0
Tennessee Tech. Univ., Cookeville, TN 38505	1915	$6,724(S)	$7,642	5-D	11,538	640	48.0
Tennessee Wesleyan Coll., Athens, TN 37303	1857	$19,700	$6,480	2-M	1,116	106	44.0
Texas A&M Intl. Univ., Laredo, TX 78041-1900.	1969	$6,838(S)	$6,275	5-D	7,213	306	39.0
Texas A&M Univ., College Station, TX 77843	1876	$8,506(S)	$8,400	5-D	50,227	2,451	80.0
Texas A&M Univ. at Galveston, Galveston, TX 77553-1675	1962	$7,464(S)	$7,100	5-M	1,774	170	53.0
Texas A&M Univ.–Commerce, Commerce, TX 75429-3011	1889	$8,376(S)	$3,627	5-D	11,187	610	37.0
Texas A&M Univ.–Corpus Christi, Corpus Christi, TX 78412-5503	1947	$6,968(S)	$9,528	5-D	10,162	547	36.0
Texas A&M Univ.–Kingsville, Kingsville, TX 78363	1925	$6,940(S)	$7,484	5-D	7,234	399	34.0
Texas A&M Univ.–Texarkana, Texarkana, TX 75505-5518.	1971	$5,167(S)	NA	5-M	1,653	NA	NA
Texas Christian Univ., Fort Worth, TX 76129-0002	1873	$36,590	NA	2-D	9,727	886	75.0
Texas Lutheran Univ., Seguin, TX 78155-5999	1891	$24,990	$7,340	2-M	1,318	129	46.0
Texas Southern Univ., Houston, TX 77004-4584.	1947	$7,646(S)	$10,566	5-D	9,646	602	12.0
Texas State Univ.–San Marcos, San Marcos, TX 78666	1899	$8,772(S)	$7,070	5-D	34,225	1,590	54.0
Texas Tech. Univ., Lubbock, TX 79409	1923	$8,942(S)	$8,275	5-D	32,327	1,348	61.0
Texas Wesleyan Univ., Fort Worth, TX 76105-1536	1890	$20,840	$7,470	2-D	3,204	274	36.0
Texas Woman's Univ., Denton, TX 76201 (4)	1901	$6,703(S)	$6,930	5-D	15,168	886	47.0
Thiel Coll., Greenville, PA 16125-2181	1866	$25,988	$10,120	2-B	1,109	105	39.0
Thomas Edison State Coll., Trenton, NJ 08608-1176.	1972	$5,508(S)	NA	5-M	20,606	NA	NA
Thomas Jefferson Univ., Philadelphia, PA 19107	1824	NA	NA	1-D	3,326	NA	NA
Thomas More Coll., Crestview Hills, KY 41017-3495.	1921	$27,220	$7,500	2-M	1,761	159	51.0
Thomas Univ., Thomasville, GA 31792-7499.	1950	$13,320	$3,550	1-M	1,124	53	NA
Tiffin Univ., Tiffin, OH 44883-2161.	1888	$20,700	$9,573	1-M	6,920	506	37.0
Touro Coll., New York, NY 10010	1971	$15,370	$10,400	1-D	17,544	NA	NA

Name, address	Year founded	Tuition & fees	Room & board	Control, degree	Enrollment	Faculty	Grad. rate
Towson Univ., Towson, MD 21252-0001	1866	$8,132(S)	$10,338	5-D	21,960	1,643	66.0%
Transylvania Univ., Lexington, KY 40508-1797	1780	$29,865	$8,750	2-B	1,074	108	74.0
Trevecca Nazarene Univ., Nashville, TN 37210-2877	1901	$21,290	$7,488	2-D	2,472	223	54.0
Trine Univ., Angola, IN 46703-1764	1884	$28,850	$9,500	1-M	1,948	137	45.0
Trinity Christian Coll., Palos Heights, IL 60463-0929	1959	$23,513	$8,442	2-M	1,369	157	56.0
Trinity Coll., Hartford, CT 06106-3100	1823	$45,730	$11,800	1-M	2,387	250	83.0
Trinity Intl. Univ., Deerfield, IL 60015-1284	1897	NA		2-D	2,671	82	52.0
Trinity Univ., San Antonio, TX 78212-7200	1869	$33,688	$10,496	2-M	2,525	309	80.0
Trinity Washington Univ., Washington, DC 20017-1094	1897	$20,775	$9,210	2-M	1,630	NA	NA
Troy Univ., Troy, AL 36082	1887	$9,070(S)	$7,071	5-D	22,554	1,284	35.0
Truman State Univ., Kirksville, MO 63501-4221	1867	$7,216(S)	$7,504	5-M	6,237	373	74.0
Tufts Univ., Medford, MA 02155	1852	$46,598	$12,182	1-D	10,837	1,045	92.0
Tulane Univ., New Orleans, LA 70118-5669	1834	$45,240	$11,547	1-D	13,486	1,179	75.0
Tusculum Coll., Greeneville, TN 37743-9997	1794	$22,250	$8,500	2-M	2,199	224	28.0
Tuskegee Univ., Tuskegee, AL 36088	1881	$18,900	$8,450	1-D	3,152	297	NA
Union Coll., Barbourville, KY 40906-1499	1879	$20,800	$6,650	2-M	1,194	110	34.0
Union Coll., Schenectady, NY 12308-2311	1795	$46,785	$11,463	1-B	2,241	236	83.0
Union Institute & Univ., Cincinnati, OH 45206-1925	1969	$11,592	NA	1-D	1,650	353	NA
Union Univ., Jackson, TN 38305-3697	1823	$25,650	$8,430	2-D	3,996	248	67.0
United States Air Force Academy, USAF Academy, CO 80840-5025 (2)	1954	$0(C)	NA	4-B	4,120	523	80.0
United States Coast Guard Academy, New London, CT 06320-8100	1876	$0(C)	NA	4-B	1,045	143	NA
United States Merchant Marine Academy, Kings Point, NY 11024-1699	1943	$0(C)	NA	4-M	1,012	NA	74.0
United States Military Academy, West Point, NY 10996	1802	$0(C)	NA	4-B	4,592	617	83.0
United States Naval Academy, Annapolis, MD 21402-5000 (2)	1845	$0(C)	NA	4-B	4,536	528	87.0
United Talmudical Sem, Brooklyn, NY 11211 (1)	1949	NA	NA	2-M	1,500	NA	NA
Universidad Adventista de las Antillas, Mayagüez, PR 00681-0118	1957	$5,550	$2,900	2-M	1,322	95	30.0
Universidad del Este, Carolina, PR 00984	1949	NA	NA	1-M	13,317	NA	NA
Universidad del Turabo, Gurabo, PR 00778-3030	1972	$19,512	$8,600	1-D	17,040	1,317	16.0
Universidad Metropolitana, San Juan, PR 00928-1150	1980	NA	NA	1-M	12,622	903	24.0
Univ. of Advancing Tech., Tempe, AZ 85283-1042 (2)	1983	$19,500	$11,060	3-M	1,073	60	NA
The Univ. of Akron, Akron, OH 44325	1870	$9,863(S)	$9,878	5-D	26,580	1,706	38.0
The Univ. of Alabama, Tuscaloosa, AL 35487	1831	$9,200(S)	$8,650	5-D	33,503	1,663	67.0
The Univ. of Alabama at Birmingham, Birmingham, AL 35294	1969	$8,400(S)	$5,400	5-D	17,999	943	45.0
The Univ. of Alabama in Huntsville, Huntsville, AL 35899	1950	$8,794(S)	$8,070	5-D	7,629	486	45.0
Univ. of Alaska Anchorage, Anchorage, AK 99508	1954	$4,950(S)	$9,780	5-D	18,107	1,390	26.0
Univ. of Alaska Fairbanks, Fairbanks, AK 99775-7520	1917	$5,580(S)	$7,200	5-D	9,314	1,060	33.0
Univ. of Alaska Southeast, Juneau, AK 99801	1972	$5,477(S)	$7,100	5-M	3,458	229	31.0
The Univ. of Arizona, Tucson, AZ 85721	1885	$10,035(S)	$9,714	5-D	40,223	NA	61.0
Univ. of Arkansas, Fayetteville, AR 72701-1201	1871	$7,553(S)	$8,672	5-D	23,199	1,087	59.0
Univ. of Arkansas at Little Rock, Little Rock, AR 72204-1099	1927	$6,854(S)	$8,989	5-D	12,872	804	20.0
Univ. of Arkansas at Monticello, Monticello, AR 71656	1909	$5,700(S)	$4,880	5-M	3,920	240	24.0
Univ. of Arkansas at Pine Bluff, Pine Bluff, AR 71601-2799	1873	$3,975(S)	$6,148	5-M	3,428	234	24.0
Univ. of Arkansas for Med. Sci., Little Rock, AR 72205-7199	1879	$6,856(S)	$5,900	5-D	2,809	1,271	NA
Univ. of Arkansas–Fort Smith, Fort Smith, AR 72913-3649	1928	$5,436(S)	$7,828	11-B	7,352	449	25.0
Univ. of Atlanta, Atlanta, GA 30360	1991	NA	NA	1-D	1,410	209	NA
Univ. of Baltimore, Baltimore, MD 21201-5779	1925	NA	NA	5-D	6,501	404	NA
Univ. of Bridgeport, Bridgeport, CT 06604	1927	$28,140	$12,050	1-D	4,877	470	32.0
Univ. of California, Berkeley, Berkeley, CA 94720-1500	1868	$12,874(S)	$15,000	5-D	35,899	NA	91.0
Univ. of California, Davis, Davis, CA 95616	1905	NA	NA	5-D	32,354	1,620	82.0
Univ. of California, Irvine, Irvine, CA 92697	1965	$14,226(S)	$11,735	5-D	27,479	1,906	86.0
Univ. of California, Los Angeles, Los Angeles, CA 90095	1919	$12,692(S)	$12,675	5-D	41,341	2,553	91.0
Univ. of California, Merced, Merced, CA 95343	2005	NA	$14,272	5-D	5,760	306	58.0
Univ. of California, Riverside, Riverside, CA 92521-0102	1954	$12,960(S)	$13,200	5-D	21,005	902	69.0
Univ. of California, San Diego, La Jolla, CA 92093	1959	$13,234(S)	$11,924	5-D	26,723	1,444	84.0
Univ. of California, Santa Barbara, Santa Barbara, CA 93106-2014	1909	$15,036(S)	$13,275	5-D	21,927	1,050	80.0
Univ. of California, Santa Cruz, Santa Cruz, CA 95064	1965	$13,417(S)	$14,856	5-D	17,404	804	74.0
Univ. of Central Arkansas, Conway, AR 72035-0001	1907	$7,332(S)	$5,270	5-D	11,107	726	40.0
Univ. of Central Florida, Orlando, FL 32816	1963	$6,247(S)	$9,357	5-D	59,767	1,842	65.0
Univ. of Central Missouri, Warrensburg, MO 64093	1871	$7,785(S)	$7,094	5-M	11,637	NA	50.0
Univ. of Central Oklahoma, Edmond, OK 73034-5209	1890	$5,091(S)	$6,708	5-M	17,211	1,024	32.0
Univ. of Charleston, Charleston, WV 25304-1099	1888	$25,700	$9,000	1-D	1,427	126	41.0
Univ. of Chicago, Chicago, IL 60637-1513	1891	$44,574	$13,137	1-D	12,508	1,723	92.0
Univ. of Cincinnati, Cincinnati, OH 45221	1819	$10,784(S)	$10,170	5-D	33,347	1,195	62.0
Univ. of Colorado Boulder, Boulder, CO 80309	1876	$9,482(S)	$11,730	5-D	31,725	1,899	65.0
Univ. of Colorado Colorado Springs, Colorado Springs, CO 80933-7150	1965	$8,339(S)	$8,300	5-D	10,257	712	46.0
Univ. of Colorado Denver, Denver, CO 80217-3364	1912	$7,494(S)	$10,410	5-D	22,396	3,417	45.0
Univ. of Connecticut, Storrs, CT 06269	1881	$12,022(S)	$11,722	5-D	25,483	1,421	82.0
Univ. of Dallas, Irving, TX 75062-4736	1955	$31,070	$9,890	2-D	2,725	235	73.0
Univ. of Dayton, Dayton, OH 45469-1300	1850	$33,400	$10,350	2-D	11,159	935	78.0
Univ. of Delaware, Newark, DE 19716	1743	$11,682(S)	$10,758	12-D	21,081	1,484	80.0
Univ. of Denver, Denver, CO 80208	1864	$40,707	$11,080	1-D	11,656	1,349	76.0
Univ. of Detroit Mercy, Detroit, MI 48221	1877	$34,530	$9,470	2-D	5,725	NA	NA
Univ. of Dubuque, Dubuque, IA 52001-5099	1852	$24,530	$7,880	2-D	2,003	166	41.0
Univ. of Evansville, Evansville, IN 47722	1854	$30,556	$10,010	2-D	2,757	238	68.0
The Univ. of Findlay, Findlay, OH 45840-3653	1882	$29,798	$9,258	2-D	4,955	293	51.0
Univ. of Florida, Gainesville, FL 32611	1853	$6,143(S)	$9,370	5-D	49,913	3,701	85.1
Univ. of Georgia, Athens, GA 30602	1785	$9,842(S)	$8,970	5-D	34,519	2,205	83.0
Univ. of Great Falls, Great Falls, MT 59405	1932	$20,960	$6,800	2-M	1,058	116	29.0
Univ. of Guam, Mangilao, GU 96923	1952	$5,098(S)	$4,800	7-M	3,702	258	27.0
Univ. of Hartford, West Hartford, CT 06117-1599	1877	$33,358	$12,248	1-D	6,894	846	52.0
Univ. of Hawaii at Hilo, Hilo, HI 96720-4091	1970	$6,496(S)	NA	5-D	4,157	300	38.0
Univ. of Hawaii at Manoa, Honolulu, HI 96822	1907	$9,884(S)	$10,029	5-D	20,426	1,265	55.0
Univ. of Hawaii–West Oahu, Pearl City, HI 96782-3366	1976	$5,592(S)	NA	5-B	1,997	101	NA
Univ. of Houston, Houston, TX 77204	1927	$9,888(S)	NA	5-D	40,747	1,966	46.0
Univ. of Houston–Clear Lake, Houston, TX 77058-1098	1971	$6,580(S)	$8,354	5-D	8,155	484	NA
Univ. of Houston–Downtown, Houston, TX 77002	1974	$5,997(S)	NA	5-M	13,916	673	12.0
Univ. of Houston–Victoria, Victoria, TX 77901-4450	1973	$6,117(S)	$7,042	5-M	4,335	212	NA
Univ. of Idaho, Moscow, ID 83844-2282	1889	$6,212(S)	$7,682	5-D	12,420	687	56.0
Univ. of Illinois at Chicago, Chicago, IL 60607-7128	1946	$13,354(S)	$10,882	5-D	27,875	1,672	58.0
Univ. of Illinois at Springfield, Springfield, IL 62703-5407	1969	$11,132(S)	$10,350	5-D	5,048	374	47.0
Univ. of Illinois at Urbana-Champaign, Champaign, IL 61820	1867	$15,338(S)	$10,636	5-D	44,520	1,854	82.0
Univ. of Indianapolis, Indianapolis, IN 46227-3697	1902	$23,830	$9,090	2-D	5,417	493	52.0
The Univ. of Iowa, Iowa City, IA 52242-1316	1847	$8,061(S)	$9,420	5-D	30,119	1,635	70.0
The Univ. of Kansas, Lawrence, KS 66045	1866	$9,678(S)	$7,258	5-D	27,135	1,722	64.0

Name, address	Year founded	Tuition & fees	Room & board	Control, degree	Enrollment	Faculty	Grad. rate
Univ. of Kentucky, Lexington, KY 40506-0032	1865	$9,676(S)	$10,192	5-D	28,034	1,683	60.0%
Univ. of La Verne, La Verne, CA 91750-4443	1891	$35,000	$11,910	1-D	4,973	665	57.0
Univ. of Louisiana at Lafayette, Lafayette, LA 70504	1898	$5,374(S)	$8,102	5-D	16,687	754	44.0
Univ. of Louisiana at Monroe, Monroe, LA 71209-0001	1931	$5,443(S)	$6,486	5-D	8,545	407	24.0
Univ. of Louisville, Louisville, KY 40292-0001	1798	$9,466(S)	$7,570	5-D	21,242	2,299	52.0
Univ. of Maine, Orono, ME 04469	1865	$10,588(S)	$8,644	5-D	11,168	789	60.0
Univ. of Maine at Augusta, Augusta, ME 04330-9410	1965	$7,448(S)	NA	5-B	4,974	290	20.0
Univ. of Maine at Farmington, Farmington, ME 04938-1990	1863	$9,137(S)	$8,454	5-B	2,180	171	57.0
Univ. of Maine at Fort Kent, Fort Kent, ME 04743-1292	1878	$7,575(S)	$7,400	5-B	1,169	74	50.0
Univ. of Maine at Presque Isle, Presque Isle, ME 04769-2888	1903	$7,435(S)	$7,422	5-B	1,453	103	30.0
Univ. of Mary, Bismarck, ND 58504-9652	1959	$13,600	$6,290	2-D	3,135	257	52.0
Univ. of Mary Hardin-Baylor, Belton, TX 76513	1845	$24,150	$6,620	2-D	3,287	286	46.0
Univ. of Maryland Baltimore Cty, Baltimore, MD 21250	1963	$9,764(S)	$10,142	5-D	13,637	776	57.0
Univ. of Maryland College Park, College Park, MD 20742	1856	$8,909(S)	$9,893	5-D	37,197	2,375	82.0
Univ. of Maryland Eastern Shore, Princess Anne, MD 21853-1299	1886	$6,998(S)	$8,374	5-D	4,454	345	32.0
Univ. of Maryland Univ. Coll., Adelphi, MD 20783	1947	$6,384(S)	NA	5-D	42,268	2,712	NA
Univ. of Mary Washington, Fredericksburg, VA 22401-5358	1908	$9,246(S)	$10,238	5-M	5,093	386	76.0
Univ. of Massachusetts Amherst, Amherst, MA 01003	1863	$13,415(S)	$10,767	5-D	28,236	1,361	70.0
Univ. of Massachusetts Boston, Boston, MA 02125-3393	1964	$11,966(S)	NA	5-D	15,874	1,193	38.0
Univ. of Massachusetts Dartmouth, North Dartmouth, MA 02747-2300	1895	$11,681(S)	NA	5-D	9,210	660	50.0
Univ. of Massachusetts Lowell, Lowell, MA 01854-2881	1894	$11,852(S)	$10,282	5-D	15,431	NA	50.0
Univ. of Med. and Dentistry of New Jersey, Newark, NJ 07107-1709	1970	$7,658(S)	NA	5-D	1,454	448	NA
Univ. of Memphis, Memphis, TN 38152	1912	$8,234(S)	$6,860	5-D	22,139	1,517	41.0
Univ. of Miami, Coral Gables, FL 33124	1925	$42,852	$12,314	1-D	16,172	1,452	81.0
Univ. of Michigan, Ann Arbor, MI 48109	1817	$13,819(S)	$9,752	5-D	42,716	3,139	90.0
Univ. of Michigan–Dearborn, Dearborn, MI 48128-1491	1959	$10,482(S)	NA	5-D	8,789	571	52.0
Univ. of Michigan–Flint, Flint, MI 48502-1950	1956	$9,514(S)	$7,506	5-D	8,289	549	36.0
Univ. of Minnesota, Crookston, Crookston, MN 56716-5001	1966	$11,455(S)	$7,018	5-B	2,764	90	47.0
Univ. of Minnesota, Duluth, Duluth, MN 55812-2496	1947	$12,748(S)	$6,732	5-D	11,491	596	60.0
Univ. of Minnesota, Morris, Morris, MN 56267-2134	1959	$12,550(S)	$7,324	5-B	1,607	153	66.0
Univ. of Minnesota, Twin Cities campus, Minneapolis, MN 55455-0213	1851	$13,459(S)	$8,000	5-D	51,853	2,837	73.0
Univ. of Mississippi, University, MS 38677	1844	$6,282(S)	$9,200	5-D	18,774	875	58.0
Univ. of Mississippi Med. Ctr., Jackson, MS 39216-4505	1955	NA	NA	5-D	2,092	836	NA
Univ. of Missouri, Columbia, MO 65211	1839	$9,257(S)	$8,944	5-D	34,748	1,489	69.0
Univ. of Missouri–Kansas City, Kansas City, MO 64110-2499	1929	$9,220(S)	$11,428	5-D	16,019	1,187	47.5
Univ. of Missouri–St. Louis, St. Louis, MO 63121	1963	$9,474(S)	$8,830	5-D	16,719	1,005	47.0
Univ. of Mobile, Mobile, AL 36613	1961	$17,680	$8,650	2-M	1,719	178	46.0
The Univ. of Montana, Missoula, MT 59812-0002	1893	$6,216(S)	$7,262	5-D	14,207	800	42.0
The Univ. of Montana Western, Dillon, MT 59725-3598	1893	$4,719(S)	$6,180	5-B	1,483	108	40.0
Univ. of Montevallo, Montevallo, AL 35115	1896	$9,280(S)	$5,522	5-M	3,085	223	43.0
Univ. of Mount Union, Alliance, OH 44601-3993	1846	$26,650	$8,480	2-M	2,253	236	65.0
Univ. of Nebraska at Kearney, Kearney, NE 68849-0001	1903	$6,506(S)	$8,038	5-M	7,199	406	56.0
Univ. of Nebraska at Omaha, Omaha, NE 68182	1908	$6,550(S)	$8,090	5-D	14,786	984	45.0
Univ. of Nebraska–Lincoln, Lincoln, NE 68588	1869	$7,897(S)	$9,122	5-D	24,207	1,089	65.0
Univ. of Nebraska Med. Ctr., Omaha, NE 68198	1869	$8,424(S)	NA	5-D	3,625	1,232	NA
Univ. of Nevada, Las Vegas, Las Vegas, NV 89154	1957	$6,585(S)	$10,524	5-D	27,402	NA	42.0
Univ. of Nevada, Reno, Reno, NV 89557	1874	$6,365(S)	$9,518	5-D	18,227	566	54.0
Univ. of New England, Biddeford, ME 04005-9526	1831	$31,870	$12,500	1-D	5,666	437	61.0
Univ. of New Hampshire, Durham, NH 03824	1866	$16,422(S)	$9,764	5-D	15,301	987	77.0
Univ. of New Haven, West Haven, CT 06516-1916	1920	$32,750	$13,700	1-D	6,351	572	56.0
Univ. of New Mexico, Albuquerque, NM 87131-2039	1889	$6,661(S)	NA	5-D	NA	1,548	NA
Univ. of New Orleans, New Orleans, LA 70148	1958	$5,922(S)	$8,310	5-D	10,071	519	34.0
Univ. of North Alabama, Florence, AL 35632-0001	1830	$8,148(S)	$5,678	5-M	7,016	331	32.0
Univ. of North Carolina at Asheville, Asheville, NC 28804-3299	1927	$5,866(S)	$7,584	5-M	3,751	270	55.0
The Univ. of North Carolina at Chapel Hill, Chapel Hill, NC 27599	1789	$7,690(S)	$9,734	5-D	29,278	1,936	89.5
The Univ. of North Carolina at Charlotte, Charlotte, NC 28223-0001	1946	$5,873(S)	$8,130	5-D	26,232	1,412	53.0
The Univ. of North Carolina at Greensboro, Greensboro, NC 27412-5001	1891	$6,229(S)	$8,948	5-D	18,172	1,006	54.0
The Univ. of North Carolina at Pembroke, Pembroke, NC 28372-1510	1887	$4,857(S)	$7,010	5-M	6,269	402	34.0
The Univ. of North Carolina Wilmington, Wilmington, NC 28403-3297	1947	$5,800(S)	$8,016	5-D	13,733	1,027	68.0
Univ. of North Dakota, Grand Forks, ND 58202	1883	$7,254(S)	$6,332	5-D	14,697	703	51.0
Univ. of Northern Colorado, Greeley, CO 80639	1890	$6,514(S)	$10,040	5-D	12,497	737	46.0
Univ. of Northern Iowa, Cedar Falls, IA 50614	1876	$7,635(S)	$7,597	5-D	12,273	788	66.0
Univ. of North Florida, Jacksonville, FL 32224	1965	$6,235(S)	$8,190	5-D	16,201	827	50.0
Univ. of North Georgia, Dahlonega, GA 30597	1873	$6,570(S)	$8,430	5-D	6,413	353	53.0
Univ. of North Texas, Denton, TX 76203	1890	$9,078(S)	$7,150	5-D	35,836	1,489	48.0
Univ. of Northwestern Ohio, Lima, OH 45805-1498	1920	NA	NA	1-B	3,848	127	NA
Univ. of Notre Dame, Notre Dame, IN 46556	1842	$42,971	$11,934	2-D	12,126	1,221	97.0
Univ. of Oklahoma, Norman, OK 73019-0390	1890	$7,341(S)	$8,382	5-D	27,507	1,403	68.0
Univ. of Oklahoma Health Sci. Ctr., Oklahoma City, OK 73190	1890	$6,052(S)	NA	5-D	3,583	448	NA
Univ. of Oregon, Eugene, OR 97403	1872	$9,310(S)	$10,580	5-D	24,518	1,505	68.0
Univ. of Pennsylvania, Philadelphia, PA 19104	1740	$43,738	$12,368	1-D	21,339	2,250	96.0
Univ. of Phoenix–Online campus, Phoenix, AZ 85034-7209	1989	NA	NA	3-D	292,797	11,477	NA
Univ. of Pikeville, Pikeville, KY 41501	1889	$17,050	$6,700	2-D	2,031	109	27.0
Univ. of Pittsburgh, Pittsburgh, PA 15260	1787	$16,590(S)	$9,870	12-D	28,769	2,206	79.0
Univ. of Pittsburgh at Bradford, Bradford, PA 16701-2812	1963	$12,810(S)	$7,960	12-B	1,518	155	49.0
Univ. of Pittsburgh at Greensburg, Greensburg, PA 15601-5860	1963	$12,890(S)	$8,730	12-B	1,733	133	48.0
Univ. of Pittsburgh at Johnstown, Johnstown, PA 15904-2990	1927	$12,892(S)	$8,230	12-B	2,957	NA	60.0
Univ. of Portland, Portland, OR 97203-5798	1901	$35,260	$7,290	2-D	3,981	335	74.0
Univ. of Puerto Rico, Aguadilla Univ. Coll., Aguadilla, PR 00604	1972	NA	NA	6-B	3,076	NA	NA
Univ. of Puerto Rico at Arecibo, Arecibo, PR 00613	1967	NA	NA	6-B	4,352	NA	NA
Univ. of Puerto Rico at Bayamón, Bayamón, PR 00959	1971	$2,212(S)	NA	6-B	5,051	261	32.0
Univ. of Puerto Rico at Carolina, Carolina, PR 00984-4800	1974	NA	NA	6-B	4,321	NA	NA
Univ. of Puerto Rico at Humacao, Humacao, PR 00791	1962	$3,012(S)	$8,280	6-B	3,774	257	45.0
Univ. of Puerto Rico at Ponce, Ponce, PR 00732-7186	1970	$2,819(S)	$8,280	6-B	3,089	193	38.0
Univ. of Puerto Rico at Utuado, Utuado, PR 00641-2500	1979	NA	NA	6-B	1,623	107	NA
Univ. of Puerto Rico, Cayey Univ. Coll., Cayey, PR 00736	1967	NA	NA	6-B	3,830	164	41.0
Univ. of Puerto Rico, Mayagüez campus, Mayagüez, PR 00681-9000	1911	$2,746(S)	$8,280	6-D	13,852	NA	NA
Univ. of Puerto Rico, Med. Sci. campus, San Juan, PR 00936-5067 (4)	1950	NA	NA	6-D	2,381	NA	NA
Univ. of Puerto Rico, Río Piedras, San Juan, PR 00931-3300	1903	NA	NA	6-D	18,966	1,084	47.0
Univ. of Puget Sound, Tacoma, WA 98416	1888	$41,868	$10,780	1-D	2,857	281	77.0
Univ. of Redlands, Redlands, CA 92373-0999	1907	$39,338	$11,924	1-D	4,956	492	72.0
Univ. of Rhode Island, Kingston, RI 02881	1892	$12,450(S)	NA	5-D	16,451	1,169	63.0
Univ. of Richmond, University of Richmond, VA 23173	1830	$45,320	$10,270	1-D	3,626	427	83.0
Univ. of Rio Grande, Rio Grande, OH 45674	1876	$19,520	$8,220	1-M	2,278	182	42.0
Univ. of Rochester, Rochester, NY 14627	1850	$43,666	$12,618	1-D	10,510	762	85.0

Name, address	Year founded	Tuition & fees	Room & board	Control, degree	Enroll- ment	Faculty	Grad. rate
Univ. of St. Francis, Joliet, IL 60435-6169	1920	$26,824	$8,268	2-D	2,345	254	56.0%
Univ. of St. Francis, Fort Wayne, IN 46808-3994	1890	$24,560	$8,170	2-M	2,464	249	NA
Univ. of St. Joseph, West Hartford, CT 06117-2700	1932	$31,826	$13,598	2-D	2,525	309	58.0
Univ. of St. Mary, Leavenworth, KS 66048-5082	1923	$21,980	$7,250	2-D	1,044	148	37.0
Univ. of St. Thomas, St. Paul, MN 55105-1096	1885	$33,787	$8,778	2-D	10,316	NA	74.0
Univ. of St. Thomas, Houston, TX 77006-4696	1947	$26,890	$7,900	2-D	3,711	335	48.0
Univ. of San Diego, San Diego, CA 92110-2492	1949	$41,392	$11,910	2-D	8,105	875	76.0
Univ. of San Francisco, San Francisco, CA 94117-1080	1855	$40,294	$12,990	2-D	10,017	1,043	67.0
The Univ. of Scranton, Scranton, PA 18510	1888	$37,456	$12,804	2-D	5,898	522	84.0
Univ. of Sioux Falls, Sioux Falls, SD 57105-1699	1883	$22,850	$6,570	2-M	1,564	140	49.2
Univ. of South Alabama, Mobile, AL 36688-0002	1963	$7,950(S)	$7,150	5-D	14,636	858	37.0
Univ. of South Carolina, Columbia, SC 29208	1801	$10,488(S)	$8,459	5-D	31,288	2,051	72.0
Univ. of South Carolina Aiken, Aiken, SC 29801-6309	1961	$9,024(S)	$6,780	5-M	3,210	237	43.0
Univ. of South Carolina Beaufort, Bluffton, SC 29909	1959	$8,558(S)	$6,910	5-B	1,874	141	20.0
Univ. of South Carolina Upstate, Spartanburg, SC 29303-4999	1967	$9,892(S)	$7,250	5-M	5,561	406	38.0
The Univ. of South Dakota, Vermillion, SD 57069-2390	1862	$7,704(S)	$6,648	5-D	10,284	579	52.0
Univ. of South Florida, Tampa, FL 33620-9951	1956	$6,334(S)	$8,960	5-D	40,111	1,188	56.0
Univ. of South Florida–St. Petersburg campus, St. Petersburg, FL 33701	1965	$5,199(S)	$7,570	5-M	4,391	255	29.0
Univ. of South Florida–Sarasota-Manatee, Sarasota, FL 34243	1956	$5,529(S)	NA	5-M	1,943	121	NA
Univ. of Southern California, Los Angeles, CA 90089	1880	$44,463	$12,440	1-D	39,958	3,264	90.0
Univ. of Southern Indiana, Evansville, IN 47712-3590	1965	$6,325(S)	$7,502	5-D	10,467	681	36.0
Univ. of Southern Maine, Portland, ME 04104-9300	1878	$8,920(S)	$9,130	5-D	9,382	680	31.0
Univ. of Southern Mississippi, Hattiesburg, MS 39406-0001	1910	$6,336(S)	$6,907	5-D	16,468	903	50.0
The Univ. of Tampa, Tampa, FL 33606-1490	1931	$25,222	$9,116	1-M	6,912	564	57.0
The Univ. of Tennessee, Knoxville, TN 37996	1794	$9,092(S)	$8,752	5-D	29,833	2,008	66.0
The Univ. of Tennessee at Chattanooga, Chattanooga, TN 37403-2598	1886	$7,212(S)	$8,300	5-D	11,660	751	38.0
The Univ. of Tennessee at Martin, Martin, TN 38238-1000	1900	$7,049(S)	$5,593	5-M	7,751	563	49.0
The Univ. of Texas at Arlington, Arlington, TX 76019	1895	$8,878(S)	$7,708	5-D	33,237	1,399	42.0
The Univ. of Texas at Austin, Austin, TX 78712-1111	1883	$9,792(S)	$10,946	5-D	52,186	3,034	79.0
The Univ. of Texas at Brownsville, Brownsville, TX 78520-4991	1973	$5,116(S)	$6,602	5-D	13,713	642	17.0
The Univ. of Texas at Dallas, Richardson, TX 75080	1969	$11,592(S)	$9,050	5-D	19,727	940	64.0
The Univ. of Texas at El Paso, El Paso, TX 79968-0001	1913	$6,869(S)	$4,725	5-D	22,749	1,215	36.0
The Univ. of Texas at San Antonio, San Antonio, TX 78249-0617	1969	$8,419(S)	$9,693	5-D	30,474	NA	28.0
The Univ. of Texas at Tyler, Tyler, TX 75799-0001	1971	$7,222(S)	$8,979	5-D	6,858	449	41.0
The Univ. of Texas Health Sci. Ctr. at Houston, Houston, TX 77225-0036	1972	NA	NA	5-D	4,489	NA	NA
The Univ. of Texas Health Sci. Ctr. at San Antonio, San Antonio, TX 78229-3900	1976	NA	NA	5-D	3,093	NA	NA
The Univ. of Texas Med. Branch, Galveston, TX 77555	1891	NA	NA	5-D	2,430	NA	NA
The Univ. of Texas of the Permian Basin, Odessa, TX 79762-0001	1969	$6,458(S)	$7,616	5-M	4,021	186	34.0
The Univ. of Texas–Pan Amer., Edinburg, TX 78539	1927	$5,164(S)	$5,656	5-D	19,302	775	39.0
The Univ. of the Arts, Philadelphia, PA 19102-4944	1870	$34,840	$12,700	1-M	2,126	505	62.0
Univ. of the Cumberlands, Williamsburg, KY 40769-1372	1889	$19,640	$7,500	2-D	4,297	194	45.0
Univ. of the District of Columbia, Washington, DC 20008-1175	1976	$7,255(S)	$6,600	9-M	5,110	NA	16.0
Univ. of the Incarnate Word, San Antonio, TX 78209-6397	1881	$23,690	$10,094	2-D	8,442	533	47.0
Univ. of the Pacific, Stockton, CA 95211-0197	1851	$38,320	$12,038	1-D	6,652	812	63.0
Univ. of the Sacred Heart, San Juan, PR 00914-0383	1935	NA	NA	2-M	5,666	367	35.3
Univ. of the Sci., Philadelphia, PA 19104-4495	1821	$32,148	$12,564	1-D	2,770	323	74.0
The Univ. of Toledo, Toledo, OH 43606-3390	1872	$9,275(S)	$9,738	5-D	21,501	1,249	45.0
Univ. of Tulsa, Tulsa, OK 74104-3189	1894	$34,350	$10,476	1-D	4,326	404	66.0
Univ. of Utah, Salt Lake City, UT 84112-1107	1850	$7,138(S)	$7,155	5-D	32,388	2,116	59.0
Univ. of Vermont, Burlington, VT 05405	1791	$15,254(S)	$10,094	5-D	13,097	755	72.0
Univ. of the Virgin Islands, Saint Thomas, VI 00802-9990	1962	$4,594(S)	$9,900	7-M	2,423	254	31.0
Univ. of Virginia, Charlottesville, VA 22903	1819	$12,458(S)	$9,717	5-D	23,907	1,307	93.0
The Univ. of Virginia's Coll. at Wise, Wise, VA 24293	1954	$8,509(S)	$9,440	5-B	2,420	196	42.0
Univ. of Washington, Seattle, WA 98195	1861	$11,305(S)	NA	5-D	42,428	3,602	80.0
Univ. of Washington, Bothell, WA 98011-8246	1990	$10,241(S)	$8,340	5-M	4,159	219	64.0
Univ. of Washington, Tacoma, Tacoma, WA 98402-3100	1990	$11,902(S)	NA	5-D	3,912	232	NA
The Univ. of West Alabama, Livingston, AL 35470	1835	$7,320(S)	$5,920	5-M	4,943	268	28.0
Univ. of West Florida, Pensacola, FL 32514-5750	1963	$7,022(S)	$9,210	5-D	12,651	603	48.0
Univ. of West Georgia, Carrollton, GA 30118	1933	$6,710(S)	$7,482	5-D	11,769	644	36.0
Univ. of Wisconsin–Eau Claire, Eau Claire, WI 54702-4004	1916	$8,691(S)	$6,300	5-D	11,046	583	66.0
Univ. of Wisconsin–Green Bay, Green Bay, WI 54311-7001	1968	$7,648(S)	$7,076	5-M	6,790	335	51.0
Univ. of Wisconsin–La Crosse, La Crosse, WI 54601-3742	1909	$8,754(S)	$6,000	5-D	10,227	572	71.0
Univ. of Wisconsin–Madison, Madison, WI 53706-1380	1848	$10,385(S)	$8,080	5-D	42,820	2,925	83.0
Univ. of Wisconsin–Milwaukee, Milwaukee, WI 53201-0413	1956	$9,187(S)	$7,945	5-D	29,114	1,626	40.0
Univ. of Wisconsin–Oshkosh, Oshkosh, WI 54901	1871	$7,067(S)	$6,852	5-M	12,669	608	52.0
Univ. of Wisconsin–Parkside, Kenosha, WI 53141-2000	1968	$7,287(S)	$7,082	5-M	4,769	259	30.0
Univ. of Wisconsin–Platteville, Platteville, WI 53818-3099	1866	$7,463(S)	$6,464	5-M	8,442	417	51.0
Univ. of Wisconsin–River Falls, River Falls, WI 54022	1874	$7,700(S)	$6,902	5-M	6,455	365	51.0
Univ. of Wisconsin–Stevens Point, Stevens Point, WI 54481-3897	1894	$7,505(S)	$6,538	5-D	9,677	481	59.0
Univ. of Wisconsin–Stout, Menomonie, WI 54751	1891	$8,944(S)	$6,054	5-M	9,247	472	52.5
Univ. of Wisconsin–Superior, Superior, WI 54880-4500	1893	$7,904(S)	$5,992	5-M	2,700	219	35.0
Univ. of Wisconsin–Whitewater, Whitewater, WI 53190-1790	1868	$7,528(S)	$5,736	5-M	11,629	529	56.0
Univ. of Wyoming, Laramie, WY 82070	1886	$4,278(S)	$9,084	5-D	12,903	837	53.0
Upper Iowa Univ., Fayette, IA 52142-1857	1857	$24,400	$7,510	1-M	5,178	586	41.0
Urbana Univ., Urbana, OH 43078-2091	1850	$21,566	$8,100	1-M	1,551	120	NA
Ursinus Coll., Collegeville, PA 19426-1000	1869	$41,820	$10,300	1-B	1,742	194	83.0
Ursuline Coll., Pepper Pike, OH 44124-4398 (4)	1871	$26,760	$8,900	2-D	1,496	202	53.0
Utah State Univ., Logan, UT 84322	1888	$6,183(S)	$5,620	5-D	28,786	1,074	50.0
Utah Valley Univ., Orem, UT 84058-5999	1941	$4,786(S)	NA	5-M	31,562	1,717	17.0
Utica Coll., Utica, NY 13502-4892	1946	$29,996	$11,650	1-D	3,839	378	47.0
Valdosta State Univ., Valdosta, GA 31698	1906	$5,792(S)	$7,070	5-D	12,515	644	41.0
Valencia Coll., Orlando, FL 32802-3028	1967	$2,377(S)	NA	5-B	42,915	1,602	NA
Valley City State Univ., Valley City, ND 58072	1890	$6,324(S)	$5,480	5-M	1,362	109	41.0
Valley Forge Christian Coll., Phoenixville, PA 19460	1938	NA	NA	1-M	1,204	77	39.0
Valparaiso Univ., Valparaiso, IN 46383	1859	$32,250	$9,164	2-D	4,078	380	74.0
Vanderbilt Univ., Nashville, TN 37240-1001	1873	$42,118	$13,818	1-D	12,710	1,148	92.0
Vanguard Univ. of Southern California, Costa Mesa, CA 92626-9601	1920	$28,500	$8,700	2-M	2,197	203	55.0
Vassar Coll., Poughkeepsie, NY 12604	1861	$46,270	$10,800	1-M	2,406	320	91.0
Vaughn Coll. of Aeronautics and Tech., Flushing, NY 11369 (2).	1932	$20,450	$11,880	1-M	1,812	216	57.0
Vermont Tech. Coll., Randolph Center, VT 05061-0500	1866	$12,544(S)	$8,786	5-B	1,645	194	NA
Villanova Univ., Villanova, PA 19085-1699	1842	$42,740	$11,370	2-D	10,661	951	91.0
Virginia Coll. in Birmingham, Birmingham, AL 35209	1989	NA	NA	3-M	3,826	NA	NA
Virginia Commonwealth Univ., Richmond, VA 23284-9005	1838	$9,885(S)	$8,748	5-D	31,752	3,253	53.0
Virginia Military Institute, Lexington, VA 24450 (2)	1839	$13,835(S)	$7,733	5-B	1,569	180	73.0

Name, address	Year founded	Tuition & fees	Room & board	Control, degree	Enrollment	Faculty	Grad. rate
Virginia State Univ., Petersburg, VA 23806-0001	1882	$7,420(S)	$9,680	5-D	6,208	426	40.0%
Virginia Tech., Blacksburg, VA 24061	1872	$9,187(S)	$7,406	5-D	31,087	1,579	83.0
Virginia Union Univ., Richmond, VA 23220-1170	1865	$14,630	$7,672	2-D	1,710	114	31.0
Virginia Wesleyan Coll., Norfolk, VA 23502-5599	1961	$32,182	$8,508	2-B	1,431	119	48.0
Viterbo Univ., La Crosse, WI 54601-4797	1890	$22,670	$7,400	2-M	2,830	415	52.0
Wagner Coll., Staten Island, NY 10301-4495	1883	$39,220	$11,660	1-M	2,208	275	66.0
Wake Forest Univ., Winston-Salem, NC 27109	1834	$44,742	$12,000	1-D	7,432	690	88.0
Walden Univ., Minneapolis, MN 55401	1970	$13,335	NA	3-D	50,208	2,705	NA
Waldorf Coll., Forest City, IA 50436-1713	1903	$20,316	$6,856	2-B	1,105	41	31.0
Walla Walla Univ., College Place, WA 99324-1198	1892	$25,377	$5,970	2-M	1,940	202	53.0
Walsh Coll. of Accountancy and Business Admin., Troy, MI 48007-7006	1922	NA	NA	1-M	3,106	178	NA
Walsh Univ., North Canton, OH 44720-3396	1958	$24,690	$8,940	2-D	2,864	254	60.0
Warner Pacific Coll., Portland, OR 97215-4099	1937	$18,290	$7,260	2-M	1,333	116	53.0
Wartburg Coll., Waverly, IA 50677-0903	1852	$34,250	$4,150	2-B	1,747	160	65.0
Washburn Univ., Topeka, KS 66621	1865	$5,486(S)	$6,216	10-D	7,204	555	37.0
Washington Adventist Univ., Takoma Park, MD 20912	1904	$20,220	$7,600	2-M	1,493	134	26.0
Washington & Jefferson Coll., Washington, PA 15301	1781	$38,310	$9,960	1-B	1,429	151	74.0
Washington & Lee Univ., Lexington, VA 24450-0303	1749	$43,362	$9,450	1-D	2,302	311	90.0
Washington Coll., Chestertown, MD 21620-1197	1782	$39,944	$8,824	1-M	1,607	172	69.0
Washington State Univ., Pullman, WA 99164	1890	$12,300(S)	$10,524	5-D	27,679	1,701	67.0
Washington Univ. in St. Louis, St. Louis, MO 63130-4899	1853	$44,841	$13,977	1-D	13,952	1,102	94.0
Wayland Baptist Univ., Plainview, TX 79072-6998	1908	$14,630	$4,157	2-M	1,824	153	36.0
Waynesburg Univ., Waynesburg, PA 15370-1222	1849	$19,810	$8,250	2-D	2,270	278	60.0
Wayne State Coll., Wayne, NE 68787	1910	$5,520(S)	$5,960	5-M	3,555	216	51.0
Wayne State Univ., Detroit, MI 48202	1868	$325/cr. hr.(S)	$8,504	5-D	28,938	1,873	28.0
Weber State Univ., Ogden, UT 84408-1001	1889	$4,761(S)	$5,200	5-M	26,532	976	43.0
Webster Univ., St. Louis, MO 63119-3194	1915	$23,010	$9,950	1-D	5,119	641	61.0
Wellesley Coll., Wellesley, MA 02481 (3)	1870	$43,554	$13,488	1-B	2,481	346	92.0
Wentworth Institute of Tech., Boston, MA 02115-5998	1904	$27,950	$12,526	1-M	4,155	310	64.0
Wesleyan Univ., Middletown, CT 06459	1831	$45,628	$12,574	1-D	3,262	389	91.0
Wesley Coll., Dover, DE 19901-3875	1873	$22,392	$10,438	2-M	1,770	170	33.0
West Chester Univ. of Pennsylvania, West Chester, PA 19383	1871	$8,620(S)	$6,786	5-M	15,411	890	69.0
West Coast Univ., North Hollywood, CA 91606	1909	NA	NA	3-B	1,792	NA	NA
West Liberty Univ., West Liberty, WV 26074	1837	$5,805(S)	$8,200	5-M	2,804	240	41.0
West Texas A&M Univ., Canyon, TX 79016-0001	1909	$6,790(S)	$5,000	5-D	7,909	384	43.0
West Virginia State Univ., Institute, WV 25112-1000	1891	$5,442(S)	$6,698	5-M	2,644	179	21.0
West Virginia Univ., Morgantown, WV 26506	1867	$6,090(S)	$8,782	5-D	29,707	1,360	56.0
West Virginia Univ. Institute of Tech., Montgomery, WV 25136	1895	$5,558(S)	$8,414	5-B	1,107	99	30.0
West Virginia Wesleyan Coll., Buckhannon, WV 26201	1890	$26,794	$7,740	2-M	1,394	156	58.0
Western Carolina Univ., Cullowhee, NC 28723	1889	$6,479(S)	$7,477	5-D	9,608	657	48.0
Western Connecticut State Univ., Danbury, CT 06810-6885	1903	$8,893(S)	$10,907	5-D	6,176	588	43.0
Western Governors Univ., Salt Lake City, UT 84107	1998	NA	NA	1-M	9,022	NA	NA
Western Illinois Univ., Macomb, IL 61455-1390	1899	$9,955(S)	$8,820	5-D	12,205	737	54.0
Western Intl. Univ., Phoenix, AZ 85021-2718	1978	$12,900	NA	3-M	2,993	369	NA
Western Kentucky Univ., Bowling Green, KY 42101	1906	$8,472(S)	$7,320	5-D	21,110	1,131	50.0
Western Michigan Univ., Kalamazoo, MI 49008	1903	$9,982(S)	$8,414	5-D	24,598	1,456	56.0
Western New England Univ., Springfield, MA 01119	1919	$31,912	$12,144	1-D	3,729	337	61.0
Western New Mexico Univ., Silver City, NM 88062-0680	1893	$4,054(S)	$5,660	5-M	2,697	259	NA
Western Oregon Univ., Monmouth, OR 97361-1394	1856	$8,529(S)	NA	5-M	6,187	406	46.0
Western State Colorado Univ., Gunnison, CO 81231	1901	$7,343(S)	$8,792	5-M	2,301	163	38.0
Western Washington Univ., Bellingham, WA 98225-5996	1893	$8,805(S)	$9,372	5-M	14,833	783	73.0
Westfield State Univ., Westfield, MA 01086	1838	$8,297(S)	$9,233	5-M	6,079	469	60.0
Westminster Coll., Fulton, MO 65251-1299	1851	$20,850	$8,450	2-B	1,084	97	70.0
Westminster Coll., New Wilmington, PA 16172-0001	1852	$31,410	$9,570	2-M	1,608	163	74.0
Westminster Coll., Salt Lake City, UT 84105-3697	1875	$28,210	$7,890	1-M	3,301	410	57.0
Westmont Coll., Santa Barbara, CA 93108-1099	1937	$35,650	$11,340	2-B	1,378	151	77.0
Westwood Coll.–Anaheim, Anaheim, CA 92806	NA	NA	NA	3-B	1,206	82	NA
Westwood Coll.–Inland Empire, Upland, CA 91786	NA	NA	NA	3-B	1,140	94	NA
Westwood Coll.–Online campus, Broomfield, CO 80021	NA	NA	NA	3-M	7,584	281	NA
Wheaton Coll., Wheaton, IL 60187-5593	1860	$30,120	$8,560	2-D	3,034	283	90.0
Wheaton Coll., Norton, MA 02766	1834	$45,074	$11,500	1-B	1,616	171	82.0
Wheeling Jesuit Univ., Wheeling, WV 26003-6295	1954	$25,640	$5,000	2-M	1,563	156	58.0
Wheelock Coll., Boston, MA 02215-4176 (4)	1888	$30,955	$12,800	1-M	1,308	167	58.0
Whitman Coll., Walla Walla, WA 99362-2083	1859	$42,106	$10,560	1-B	1,539	205	88.0
Whittier Coll., Whittier, CA 90608-0634	1887	$40,096	$11,494	1-D	2,448	169	67.0
Whitworth Univ., Spokane, WA 99251-0001	1890	$34,346	$9,364	2-M	2,568	331	76.0
Wichita State Univ., Wichita, KS 67260	1895	$6,442(S)	$6,460	5-D	14,893	814	41.0
Widener Univ., Chester, PA 19013-5792	1821	$36,382	$12,248	1-D	6,238	656	55.0
Wilkes Univ., Wilkes-Barre, PA 18766-0002	1933	$29,326	$12,034	1-D	5,030	407	61.0
Willamette Univ., Salem, OR 97301-3931	1842	$40,874	$9,820	2-D	2,933	320	77.0
William Carey Univ., Hattiesburg, MS 39401-5499	1906	$10,350	$3,900	2-M	3,248	NA	NA
William Jewell Coll., Liberty, MO 64068-1843	1849	$31,100	$8,020	1-B	1,052	141	69.0
William Paterson Univ. of New Jersey, Wayne, NJ 07470-8420	1855	$11,694(S)	$10,540	5-D	11,423	1,060	48.0
William Penn Univ., Oskaloosa, IA 52577-1799	1873	$23,210	$5,472	2-M	1,865	50	26.0
William Woods Univ., Fulton, MO 65251-1098	1870	$19,200	$7,900	2-M	2,020	357	50.0
Williams Coll., Williamstown, MA 01267	1793	$43,190	$11,370	1-M	2,106	334	96.0
Wilmington Coll., Wilmington, OH 45177	1870	$26,840	$8,870	2-M	1,458	119	52.0
Wilmington Univ., New Castle, DE 19720-6491	1967	$7,586	NA	1-D	11,795	1,116	34.0
Wingate Univ., Wingate, NC 28174-0159	1896	$25,040	$9,950	2-D	2,648	266	45.0
Winona State Univ., Winona, MN 55987	1858	$8,930(S)	$7,800	5-D	8,890	556	54.0
Winston-Salem State Univ., Winston-Salem, NC 27110-0003	1892	$4,584(S)	NA	5-M	6,427	336	37.0
Winthrop Univ., Rock Hill, SC 29733	1886	$13,026(S)	$7,464	5-M	6,170	525	53.0
Wittenberg Univ., Springfield, OH 45501-0720	1845	$38,030	$9,736	2-M	1,894	194	65.0
Wofford Coll., Spartanburg, SC 29303-3663	1854	$35,515	$10,280	2-B	1,588	153	84.0
Woodbury Univ., Burbank, CA 91504-1099	1884	$31,444	$9,952	1-M	1,771	315	59.0
Worcester Polytechnic Institute, Worcester, MA 01609-2280	1865	$42,778	$13,082	1-D	5,957	460	85.0
Worcester State Univ., Worcester, MA 01602-2597	1874	$8,157(S)	$10,500	5-M	6,221	422	51.0
Wright State Univ., Dayton, OH 45435	1964	$8,354(S)	$8,629	5-D	16,780	647	40.0
Xavier Univ., Cincinnati, OH 45207	1831	$33,000	$10,740	2-D	6,650	677	78.0
Xavier Univ. of Louisiana, New Orleans, LA 70125-1098	1925	$18,700	$7,600	2-D	3,178	261	47.0
Yale Univ., New Haven, CT 06520	1701	$44,000	$13,500	1-D	11,906	1,666	96.0
Yeshiva Univ., New York, NY 10033-3201	1886	$37,600	$11,150	1-D	6,753	1,477	89.0
York Coll. of Pennsylvania, York, PA 17405-7199	1787	$17,010	$9,580	1-D	5,439	550	59.0
York Coll. of the City Univ. of New York, Jamaica, NY 11451-0001	1967	$6,096(S)	NA	11-M	8,389	553	17.0
Young Harris Coll., Young Harris, GA 30582	1886	$25,280	$9,660	2-B	1,034	105	NA
Youngstown State Univ., Youngstown, OH 44555-0001	1908	$7,712(S)	$8,150	5-D	13,799	1,054	33.0

DIRECTORY

Associations and Organizations

Source: World Almanac research

Selected list, generally by category and first distinctive key word in each title. Listed by acronym when that is the official name. Year established is in parentheses. Entries for religious organizations include addresses and leadership information for 2013.

Academic and Educational

Academies, Natl. (1863): (202) 334-2000; www.nationalacademies.org

African American Life and History, Assn. for the Study of (1915): (202) 238-5910; www.asalh.org

Alpha Delta Kappa (1947): (816) 363-5525; www.alphadeltakappa.org

AMIDEAST (America-Mideast Educational and Training Services, Inc.) (1951): (202) 776-9600; www.amideast.org

Anthropological Assn., American (1902): (703) 528-1902; www.aaanet.org

Archaeological Institute of America (1879): (617) 353-9361; www.archaeological.org

Arts, Americans for the (1960): (202) 371-2830; www.artsusa.org

Arts and Sciences, American Academy of (1780): (617) 576-5000; www.amacad.org

Beta Gamma Sigma Honor Society (1913): (314) 432-5650; www.betagammasigma.org

Beta Sigma Phi Intl. (1931): (816) 444-6800; www.betasigmaphi.org

Biological Sciences, American Institute of (1947): (703) 674-2500; www.aibs.org

College Board (1900): (212) 713-8000; www.collegeboard.org

Colleges and Universities, Assn. of American (1915): (202) 387-3760; www.aacu.org

Community Colleges, American Assn. of (1920): (202) 728-0200; www.aacc.nche.edu

Consumer Interests, American Council on (1953): (727) 493-2131; www.consumerinterests.org

Delta Kappa Gamma Society Intl. (1929): (512) 478-5748; www.dkg.org

Education, American Council on (1918): (202) 939-9300; www.acenet.edu

Education, Council for Advancement and Support of (1974): (202) 328-2273; www.case.org

Education of Young Children, Natl. Assn. for the (1926): (202) 232-8777; www.naeyc.org

Educators for World Peace, Intl. Assn. of (1973): (256) 534-5501; www.iaewp.org

English-Speaking Union of the U.S. (1920): (212) 818-1200; www.esuus.org

Entomological Society of America (1889): (301) 731-4535; www.entsoc.org

Family Relations, Natl. Council on (1938): (888) 781-9331; www.ncfr.org

Foreign Study, American Institute for (1964): (866) 906-2437; www.aifs.com

Freedom of Information Center, Natl. (1958): (573) 882-3075; www.nfoic.org/foi-center

French Institute/Alliance Française (1971): (212) 355-6100; www.fiaf.org

Genealogical Society, Natl. (1903): (703) 525-0050; www.ngsgenealogy.org

Genetic Assn., American (1914): (541) 867-0334; www.theaga.org

Geological Society of America (1888): (303) 357-1000; www.geosociety.org

Hemispheric Affairs, Council on (1975): (202) 223-4975; www.coha.org

Industrial and Applied Mathematics, Society for (1952): (215) 382-9800; www.siam.org

Intl. Education, Institute of (1919): (212) 883-8200; www.iie.org

Intl. Educational Exchange, Council on (1947): (207) 553-4000; www.ciee.org

Intl. Law, American Society of (1906): (202) 939-6000; www.asil.org

Irish American Cultural Inst. (1962): (973) 605-1991; www.iaci-usa.org

Law Libraries, American Assn. of (1906): (312) 939-4764; www.aallnet.org

Learned Societies, American Council of (1919): (212) 697-1505; www.acls.org

Libraries Assn., Special (1909): (703) 647-4900; www.sla.org

Linguistic Society of America (1924): (202) 835-1714; www.lsadc.com

Mathematical Society, American (1888): (401) 455-4000; www.ams.org

Mensa, Ltd., American (1960): (817) 607-0060; www.us.mensa.org

Meteorological Society, American (1919): (617) 227-2425; www.ametsoc.org

Metric Assn., Inc., U.S. (1916): (310) 832-3763; www.metric.org

Microbiology, American Society for (1899): (202) 737-3600; www.asm.org

Modern Language Assn. of America (1883): (646) 576-5000; www.mla.org

Museums, American Assn. of (1906): (202) 289-1818; www.aam-us.org

Music Education, Natl. Assn. for (formerly Music Educators Natl. Conference) (1907): (703) 860-4000; musiced.nafme.org

Musicological Society, American (1934): (207) 798-4243; www.ams-net.org

Negro College Fund, United (1944): (800) 331-2244; www.uncf.org

Oriental Society, American (1842): (734) 647-4760; www.umich.edu/~aos/

ORT America (1922): (212) 505-7700; www.ortamerica.org

PEN American Center (1922): (212) 334-1660; www.pen.org

Phi Beta Kappa Society (1776): (202) 265-3808; www.pbk.org

Phi Theta Kappa Honor Society (1918): (800) 946-9995; www.ptk.org

Philological Assn., American (1869): (215) 898-4975; www.apaclassics.org

Philosophical Assn., American (1900): (302) 831-1112; www.apaonline.org

Physics, American Inst. of (1931): (301) 209-3100; www.aip.org

Physiological Society, American (1887): (301) 634-7118; www.the-aps.org

Poetry Society of America (1910): (212) 254-9628; www.poetrysociety.org

Poets, Academy of American (1934): (212) 274-0343; www.poets.org

Political Science, Academy of (1880): (212) 870-2500; www.psqonline.org

Radio and Television Society Foundation, Intl. (1939): (212) 867-6650; www.irts.org

Reading Assn., Intl. (1956): (302) 731-1600; www.reading.org

Religion, American Academy of (1909): (404) 727-3049; www.aarweb.org

Science, American Assn. for the Advancement of (1848): (202) 326-6400; www.aaas.org

Science Fiction Society, World (1939): www.wsfs.org

Sciences, Natl. Academy of (1863): (202) 334-2000; www.nasonline.org

Sigma Beta Delta (1994): (314) 516-4723; www.sigmabetadelta.org

Sociological Assn., American (1905): (202) 383-9005; www.asanet.org

Tau Beta Pi Assn. (1885): (865) 546-4578; www.tbp.org

Teach For America (1990): (212) 279-2080; www.teachforamerica.org

Theological Schools in the U.S. and Canada, Assn. of (1918): (412) 788-6505; www.ats.edu

Theosophical Society in America (1875): (630) 668-1571; www.theosophical.org

Universities, Assn. of American (1900): (202) 408-7500; www.aau.edu

World Learning (1932): (802) 257-7751; www.worldlearning.org

Animal Welfare and Environment

Animal Welfare Institute (1951): (202) 337-2332; www.awionline.org

Animals, American Society for the Prevention of Cruelty to (ASPCA) (1866): (212) 876-7700; www.aspca.org

Animals, People for the Ethical Treatment of (PETA) (1980): (757) 622-7382; www.peta.org

Appalachian Trail Conservancy (1925): (304) 535-6331; www.appalachiantrail.org

Audubon Society, Natl. (1905): (212) 979-3000; www.audubon.org

Cat Fanciers' Assn., Inc., The (1906): (330) 680-4070; www.cfa.org

Conservation Intl. (1987): (703) 341-2400; www.conservation.org

Defenders of Wildlife (1947): (800) 385-9712; www.defenders.org

Ducks Unlimited (1937): (901) 758-3825; www.ducks.org

Forest History Society (1946): (919) 682-9319; www.foresthistory.org

Foresters, Society of American (1900): (301) 897-8720; www.safnet.org

Friends of the Earth (1969): (202) 783-7400; www.foe.org

Garden Club of America (1913): (212) 753-8287; www.gcamerica.org

Garden Clubs, Inc., Natl. (1929): (314) 776-7574; www.gardenclub.org

Geographic Society, Natl. (1888): (813) 979-6845; www.nationalgeographic.com

Green Mountain Club (1910): (802) 244-7037; www.greenmountainclub.org

Greenpeace (1971): (202) 462-1177; www.greenpeaceusa.org

Hiking Society, American (1976): (301) 565-6704; www.americanhiking.org

Horse Council, American (1969): (202) 296-4031; www.horsecouncil.org

Humane Society of the U.S., The (1954): (202) 452-1100; www.humanesociety.org

Natural Resources Defense Council (1970): (212) 727-2700; www.nrdc.org

Nature Conservancy, The (1951): (703) 841-5300; www.nature.org

Ocean Conservancy (1972): (202) 429-5609; www.oceanconservancy.org

Ornithologists' Union, American (1883): (505) 326-1579; www.aou.org

Recreation and Park Assn., Natl. (1965): (800) 626-6772; www.nrpa.org

Recycling Coalition, Inc., Natl. (1978): (202) 618-2107; www.nrcrecycles.org

Rose Society, American (1892): (318) 938-5402; www.ars.org

Save the Redwoods League (1918): (415) 362-2352; www.savetheredwoods.org

Sierra Club (1892): (415) 977-5500; www.sierraclub.org

Water Environment Federation (1928): (800) 666-0206; www.wef.org

Wildflower Center, Lady Bird Johnson (1982): (512) 232-0100; www.wildflower.org

Wildlife Federation, Natl. (1936): (800) 822-9919; www.nwf.org

World Wildlife Fund (1961): (202) 293-4800; www.worldwildlife.org

Children and Social Services

Big Brothers Big Sisters of America (1904): (215) 567-7000; www.bbbs.org

Boy Scouts of America (1910): (972) 580-2000; www.scouting.org

Boys & Girls Clubs of America (1906): (404) 487-5700; www.bgca.org

Camp Fire USA (formerly Camp Fire Boys & Girls) (1910): (816) 285-2010; www.campfireusa.org

Child Welfare League of America (1920): (202) 688-4200; www.cwla.org

Children's Aid Society (1913): (205) 251-7148; www.childrensaid.org

Children's Book Council, The (1945): (212) 966-1990; www.cbcbooks.org

Feeding America (formerly America's Second Harvest) (1976): (800) 771-2303; feedingamerica.org

4-H Council, Natl. (1914): (301) 961-2800; www.4-h.org

Future Business Leaders of America-Phi Beta Lambda, Inc. (1942): (800) 325-2946; www.fbla-pbl.org

Future Farmers of America Org., Natl. (1928): (317) 802-6060; www.ffa.org

Gifted Children, Natl. Assn. for (1954): (202) 785-4268; www.nagc.org
Girl Scouts of the USA (1912): (212) 852-8000; www.girlscouts.org
Honor Society, Natl. (1921): (703) 860-0200; www.nhs.us
Junior Achievement, Inc. (1919): (719) 540-8000; www.ja.org
Junior Auxiliaries, Inc., Natl. Assn. of (1941): (662) 332-3000; www.najanet.org
Junior Chamber, U.S. (1914): (636) 681-1857; www.usjaycees.org
Junior Honor Society, Natl. (1929): (703) 860-0200; www.njhs.us
Missing and Exploited Children, Natl. Center for (1984): (703) 224-2150; www.missingkids.com
Pilot Intl. (1921): (478) 477-1208; www.pilotinternational.org
Student Councils, Natl. Assn. of (1931): (703) 860-0200; www.nasc.us

Fraternal

Eagles, Fraternal Order of (1898): (614) 883-2200; www.foe.com
Eastern Star, General Grand Chapter, Order of the (1876): (202) 667-4737; www.easternstar.org
Elks of the USA, Benevolent and Protective Order of (1868): (773) 755-4700; www.elks.org
Freemasonry, Scottish Rite of, Supreme Council, 33°, Northern Masonic Jurisdiction (1813): (781) 862-4410; www.scottishritenmj.org
Freemasonry, Supreme Council, 33°, Scottish Rite of, Southern Jurisdiction (1802): (202) 232-3579; www.srmason-sj.org
Kiwanis Intl. (1915): (317) 875-8755; www.kiwanis.org
Knights of Columbus (1882): (203) 752-4000; www.kofc.org
Knights of Pythias, Order of (1864): (781) 341-2422; www.pythias.org
Lions Clubs Intl. (1917): (630) 571-5466; www.lionsclubs.org
Men, Natl. Coalition for (1977): (888) 223-1280; www.ncfm.org
Moose Intl., Inc. (1888): (630) 859-2000; www.mooseintl.org
Odd Fellows, Independent Order of (1819): (336) 725-5955; www.ioof.org
Rotary Intl. (1905): (847) 866-3000; www.rotary.org
Shriners Intl. (1872): (813) 281-0300; www.shrinersinternational.org
Sons of Italy in America, Order (1905): (202) 547-2900; www.osia.org
Sons of Norway (1895): (612) 827-3611; www.sofn.com
Woodmen of America, Modern (1883): (800) 447-9811; www.modern-woodmen.org

Historical

Civil War Trust (1987): (202) 367-1861; www.civilwar.org
Colonial Dames XVII Century, Natl. Soc. (1915): (202) 293-1700; www.colonialdames17c.org
Daughters of the American Revolution (1890): (202) 628-1776; www.dar.org
Daughters of the Confederacy, United (1894): (804) 355-1636; www.hqudc.org
Historic Preservation, Natl. Trust for (1949): (202) 588-6000; www.preservationnation.org
Historical Assn., American (1884): (202) 544-2422; www.historians.org
Lewis and Clark Trail Heritage Foundation (1969): (406) 454-1234; lewisandclark.org
Mayflower Descendants, General Soc. of (1897): (508) 746-3188; www.themayflowersociety.com
Pilgrims, Natl. Soc. Sons and Daughters of the (1908): www.nssdp.com
Railway Historical Society, Natl. (1935): (215) 557-6606; www.nrhs.com
Sons of the American Revolution, Natl. Soc. (1889): (502) 589-1776; www.sar.org
Sons of Confederate Veterans (1896): (800) 380-1896; www.scv.org
State and Local History, American Assn. for (1940): (615) 320-3203; www.aaslh.org

Supreme Court Historical Society (1974): (202) 543-0400; www.supremecourthistory.org
Theodore Roosevelt Assn. (1920): (516) 921-6319; www.theodoreroosevelt.org
Thoreau Society (1941): (978) 369-5310; www.thoreausociety.org
Titanic Historical Society, Inc. (1963): (413) 543-4770; www.titanichistoricalsociety.org
Victorian Society in America (1966): (215) 636-9872; www.victoriansociety.org

Industrial and Trade

Aerospace Industries Assn. (1919): (703) 358-1000; www.aia-aerospace.org
Better Business Bureaus, Council of (1912): (703) 276-0100; www.bbb.org
Chamber of Commerce of the U.S.A. (1912): (202) 659-6000; www.uschamber.com
Chemistry Council, American (1872): (202) 249-7000; www.americanchemistry.com
Construction Specifications Institute (1948): (800) 689-2900; www.csinet.org
CropLife America (1933): (202) 296-1585; www.croplifeamerica.org
Electrical Manufacturers Assn., Natl. (1926): (703) 841-3200; www.nema.org
Fire Protection Assn., Natl. (NFPA) (1896): (617) 770-3000; www.nfpa.org
Fisheries Soc., American (1870): (301) 897-8616; www.fisheries.org
Foreign Trade Council, Inc., Natl. (1914): (202) 887-0278; www.nftc.org
Funeral Consumers Alliance (1963): (802) 865-8300; www.funerals.org
Hotel & Lodging Assn., American (1910): (202) 289-3100; www.ahla.com
Insurance Assn., American (1866): (202) 828-7100; www.aiadc.org
Magazine Media, Assn. of (1919): (212) 872-3700; www.magazine.org
Manufacturers, Natl. Assn. of (1895): (202) 637-3000; www.nam.org
Newspaper Assn. of America (1992): (571) 366-1000; www.naa.org
Nuclear Society, American (1954): (708) 352-6611; www.ans.org
Orchestras, League of American (1942): (212) 262-5161; www.symphony.org
Petroleum Institute, American (1919): (202) 682-8000; www.api.org
Printing Industries of America, Inc. (1887): (412) 741-6860; www.printing.org
Publishers, Assn. of American (1970): (202) 347-3375; www.publishers.org
Retail Federation, Natl. (1908): (202) 783-7971; www.nrf.com
Safety Council, Natl. (1913): (630) 285-1121; www.nsc.org
Shipbuilders Council of America (1920): (202) 772-5577; www.shipbuilders.org
Small Business Assn., Natl. (1937): (800) 345-6728; www.nsba.biz
Software & Information Industry Assn. (1999): (202) 289-7442; www.siia.net
Tall Buildings and Urban Habitat, Council on (1969): (312) 567-3307; www.ctbuh.org
Toy Industry Assn., Inc. (1916): (212) 675-1141; www.toyassociation.org
Water Works Assn., American (1881): (303) 794-7711; www.awwa.org
Zoos & Aquariums, Assn. of (1924): (301) 562-0777; www.aza.org

Lifestyle and Travel

AAA (American Automobile Assn.) (1902): (407) 444-7000; www.aaa.com
AARP (formerly American Assn. of Retired Persons) (1958): (888) 687-2277; www.aarp.org
AFS Intercultural Programs USA (1947): (800) 237-4636; www.afsusa.org
Aircraft Owners and Pilots Assn. (1939): (800) 872-2672; www.aopa.org
Appalachian Mountain Club (1876): (617) 523-0636; www.outdoors.org
Boat Owners Assn. of the U.S. (1966): (703) 461-4666; www.boatus.com
Camp Assn., American (1910): (765) 342-8456; www.acacamps.org
Consumer Federation of America (1968): (202) 387-6121; www.consumerfed.org

Consumers Union (1936): (914) 378-2000; www.consumersunion.org
Green America (formerly Co-op America) (1982): (800) 584-7336; www.greenamerica.org
Helicopter Society Intl., American (1943): (703) 684-6777; www.vtol.org
Hostelling Intl. USA (1934): (240) 650-2100; www.hiusa.org
Jewish Community Centers Assn. of North America (1917): (212) 532-4949; www.jcca.org
Motorcyclist Assn., American (1924): (800) 262-5646; www.americanmotorcyclist.com
Parents Without Partners, Inc. (1957): (800) 637-7974; www.parentswithoutpartners.org
Planetary Society (1980): (626) 793-5100; www.planetary.org
SCRABBLE® Players Assn., N. American (2009): www.scrabbleplayers.org
Sports Car Club of America (1944): (785) 357-7222; www.scca.org
Toastmasters Intl. (1924): (949) 858-8255; www.toastmasters.org
YMCA (Young Men's Christian Assn.) of the USA (1851): (800) 872-9622; www.ymca.net
YWCA (Young Women's Christian Assn.) USA (1858): (202) 467-0801; www.ywca.org

Military and Veterans'

Air Force Assn. (1946): (703) 247-5800; www.afa.org
American Legion (1919): (317) 630-1200; www.legion.org
American Legion Auxiliary (1919): (317) 569-4500; www.alaforveterans.org
AMVETS (American Veterans) (1944): (877) 726-8387; www.amvets.org
Army, Assn. of the United States (1950): (703) 841-4300; www.ausa.org
Blinded Veterans Assn. (1958): (202) 371-8880; www.bva.org
Civil Air Patrol (1941): (877) 227-9142; www.gocivilairpatrol.com
Coast Guard Combat Veterans Assn. (1985): (610) 539-1000; www.coastguardcombatvets.com
Disabled American Veterans (1920): (859) 441-7300; www.dav.org
82nd Airborne Division Assn., Inc. (1944): (910) 223-1182; www.82ndassociation.org
Ex-Prisoners of War, American (1942): (817) 649-2979; www.axpow.org
Fleet Reserve Assn. (1924): (703) 683-1400; www.fra.org
Iraq and Afghanistan Veterans of America (2004): (212) 982-9699; www.iava.org
Jewish War Veterans of the U.S.A. (1896): (202) 265-6280; www.jwv.org
Legion of Valor Museum (1991): (559) 498-0510; www.fresnovetmuseum.com
Marine Corps League (1937): (703) 207-9588; www.mcleague.org
Military Officers Assn. of America (1929): (703) 549-2311; www.moaa.org
Military Order of the World Wars (1919): (703) 683-4911; www.militaryorder.net
National Guard Assn. of the U.S. (1878): (202) 789-0031; www.ngaus.org
Naval Institute, U.S. (1873): (410) 268-6110; www.usni.org
Navy League of the United States (1902): (703) 528-1775; www.navyleague.org
Ninety-Nines, Inc. (Intl. Org. of Women Pilots) (1929): (405) 685-7969; www.ninety-nines.org
Non-Commissioned Officers Assn. (1960): (800) 662-2620; www.ncoausa.org
Paralyzed Veterans of America (1946): (800) 424-8200; www.pva.org
POW/MIA Families, Natl. League of (1970): (703) 465-7432; www.pow-miafamilies.org
Purple Heart, Military Order of the (1932): (703) 354-2140; www.purpleheart.org
Reserve Officers Assn. of the U.S. (1922): (202) 479-2200; www.roa.org
Sons of the American Legion (1932): (317) 630-1200; www.legion.org/sons
Tin Can Sailors (Natl. Assn. of Destroyer Veterans) (1976): (508) 677-0515; www.destroyers.org
Uniformed Services, Natl. Assn. for (1968): (800) 842-3451; www.naus.org

USO, Inc. (United Service Org.) (1941): (888) 484-3876; www.uso.org

USS Los Angeles CA-135 Assn. (1977): www.uss-la-ca135.org/2la-assoc.htm

USS Missouri Memorial Assn., Inc. (1998): (808) 455-1600; www.ussmissouri.org

Veterans of Foreign Wars (1899): (816) 756-3390; www.vfw.org

Veterans of Foreign Wars, Ladies Auxiliary to the (1914): (816) 561-8655; www.ladiesauxvfw.org

Vietnam Veterans of America (1978): (301) 585-4000; www.vva.org

Women's Army Corps Veterans' Assn. (1946): (256) 820-6824; www.armywomen.org

Political

Abortion Federation, National (1977): (202) 667-5881; www.prochoice.org

Action Network, American (2010): (202) 559-6420; americanactionnetwork.org

Advancement and Support of Education, Council for (1974): (202) 328-2273; www.case.org

American Indians, Natl. Congress of (1944): (202) 466-7767; www.ncai.org

American-Islamic Relations, Council on (1994): (202) 488-8787; www.cair.com

Brady Campaign to Prevent Gun Violence (1974): (202) 898-0792; www.brady campaign.org

Center for Responsive Politics (1983): (202) 857-0044; www.opensecrets.org

Cities, Natl. League of (1924): (202) 626-3100; www.nlc.org

Civil Liberties Union, American (ACLU) (1920): (212) 549-2500; www.aclu.org

Coffee Party USA (2010): (301) 259-1869; www.coffeepartyusa.com

Common Cause (1970): (202) 833-1200; www.commoncause.org

Concerned Women for America (1979): (202) 488-7000; www.cwfa.org

Congress of Racial Equality (CORE) (1942): (212) 598-4000; www.core-online.org

Conservation Voters, League of (1969): (202) 785-8683; www.lcv.org

Crime and Delinquency, Natl. Council on (1907): (800) 306-6223; www.nccdglobal.org

Crossroads GPS (Grassroots Political Strategies) (2010): (202) 706-7051; www.crossroadsgps.org

Democratic Natl. Committee (1848): (202) 863-8000; www.democrats.org

Feminists for Life of America (1972): (703) 836-3354; www.feministsforlife.org

Future Fund, Amer. (2007): (515) 661-4233; www.americanfuturefund.com

Gay & Lesbian Alliance Against Defamation (GLAAD) (1985): (212) 629-3322; www.glaad.org

Gay and Lesbian Task Force, Natl. (1973): (202) 393-5177; www.thetaskforce.org

Governors Assn., Natl. (1908): (202) 624-5300; www.nga.org

Grange of the Order of Patrons of Husbandry, Natl. (1867): (202) 628-3507; www.nationalgrange.org

Gray Panthers (1970): (202) 737-6637; www.graypanthers.org

Greens/Green Party USA (1984): (202) 319-7191; www.gp.org

Homeless, Natl. Coalition for the (1984): (202) 462-4822; www.nationalhomeless.org

Human Rights Campaign (1980): (202) 628-4160; www.hrc.org

Immigration Equality (1994): (202) 347-0002; immigrationequality.org

Immigration Reform, Federation for American (FAIR) (1979): 202-328-7004; www.fairus.org

Japanese American Citizens League (1929): (415) 921-5225; www.jacl.org

Jewish Committee, American (1906): (212) 751-4000; www.ajc.org

John Birch Society (1958): (920) 749-3780; www.jbs.org

Libertarian Party (1971): (202) 333-0008; www.lp.org

Marriage, Natl. Org. for (2007): (888) 894-3604; www.nationformarriage.org

Marry, Freedom to (2003): 212.851.8418; www.freedomtomarry.org

Mayors, U.S. Conference of (1932): (202) 293-7330; www.usmayors.org

NAACP (Natl. Assn. for the Advancement of Colored People) (1909): (410) 580-5777; www.naacp.org

National Tea Party Federation (2010): www.thenationalteapartyfederation.com

NRA (National Rifle Assn.) (1871): (800) 672-3888; www.nra.org

Parliamentarians, Natl. Assn. of (1930): (816) 833-3892; www.parliamentarians.org

Patriot Majority (2005): www.patriotmajority.org

Progress, Center for American (2003): (202) 682-1611; www.americanprogress.org

Reform Party Natl. Committee (1995): (972) 275-9297; www.reformparty.org

Republican Natl. Committee (1856): (202) 863-8500; www.rnc.org

Southern Christian Leadership Conference (1957): (404) 522-1420; sclcnational.org

Southern Poverty Law Center (1971): (334) 956-8200; www.splcenter.org

State Governments, Council of (1933): (859) 244-8000; www.csg.org

Tax Foundation (1937): (202) 464-6200; www.taxfoundation.org

Tax Reform, Americans for (1985): (202) 785-0266; www.atr.org

Taxpayers Union, Natl. (1969): (703) 683-5700; www.ntu.org

Tea Party Patriots (2009): www.teaparty patriots.org

Term Limits, U.S. (1992): (703) 383-0907; www.termlimits.org

Urban League, Natl. (1910): (212) 558-5300; www.nul.org

Women, Natl. Organization for (NOW) (1966): (202) 628-8669; www.now.org

Women and Families, Natl. Partnership for (1971): (202) 986-2600; www.national partnership.org

Women Voters of the U.S., League of (1920): (202) 429-1965; www.lwv.org

Women's Christian Temperance Union (1874): (847) 864-1397; www.wctu.org

Zionist Organization of America (1897): (212) 481-1500; www.zoa.org

Religious

African Methodist Episcopal Church (1787): 500 8th Ave. S., Nashville, TN 37203; (615) 254-0911; www.ame-church.com; Gen. Sec., Dr. Jefferey Cooper

African Methodist Episcopal Zion Church (1796): 3225 West Sugar Creek Rd., Charlotte, NC 28269; (704) 599-4630; www.amez.org; Senior Bishop, George E. Battle Jr.

American Baptist Churches USA (1907): P.O. Box 851, Valley Forge, PA 19482; (610) 768-2000; www.abc-usa.org; Gen. Sec., A. Roy Medley

Antiochian Orthodox Christian Archdiocese of North America (1895): P.O. Box 5238, Englewood, NJ 07631; (201) 871-1355; www.antiochian.org; Primate, Archbishop, Metropolitan Philip Saliba

Armenian Apostolic Church of America: *Eastern Prelacy* (1958): 138 E. 39th St., New York, NY 10016; (212) 689-7810; www.armenianprelacy.org; Prelate, Archbishop Oshagan Choloyan; *Western Prelacy (1973)*: 6252 Honolulu Ave., La Crescenta, CA 91214; (818) 248-7737; www.westernprelacy.org; Prelate, Archbishop Moushegh Mardirossian

Assemblies of God USA (1914): 1445 N. Boonville Ave., Springfield, MO 65802; (417) 862-2781; www.ag.org; Gen. Supt., George O. Wood

Atheists, American (1963): P.O. Box 158, Cranford, NJ 07016; (908) 276-7300; www.atheists.org; Pres., David P. Silverman

Bahá'ís of the U.S., National Spiritual Assembly of the (1909): 1233 Central St., Evanston, IL 60201; (847) 733-3400; www.bahai.us; Sec., Kenneth E. Bowers

Baptist Bible Fellowship Intl. (1950): 720 E. Kearney St., Springfield, MO 65803; (417) 862-5001; www.bbfi.org; Pres., Linzy Slayden

Baptist Convention, Southern (1845): 901 Commerce St., Nashville, TN 37203; (615) 244-2355; www.sbc.net; Pres. Frank S. Page

Baptist Convention, USA, Inc., National (1886): 1700 Baptist World Center Dr., Nashville, TN 37207; (615) 228-6292; www.nationalbaptist.com; Pres., Dr. Julius R. Scruggs

Baptist Convention of America, Inc., Intl., National (1880): 777 S.R.L. Thornton Freeway, Ste. 210, Dallas, TX 75203; (214) 942-3311; www.nbcainc.com; Pres., Rev. Stephen J. Thurston

Baptist Conventional of America, National Missionary (1880): 6925 Wofford Dr., Dallas, TX 75227; (877) 886-6222; www.nmbca.com; Pres., Dr. Nehemiah Davis

Bible Society, American (1816): 1865 Broadway, New York, NY 10023; (212) 408-1200; www.americanbible.org; Pres. and CEO, S. Douglas Birdsall

Biblical Literature, Society of (1880): 825 Houston Mill Rd., Atlanta, GA 30329; (404) 727-3100; www.sbl-site.org

B'nai B'rith Intl. (1843): 2020 K St. NW, 7th Fl., Washington, DC 20006; (202) 857-6600; www.bnaibrith.org

Brethren in Christ Church (c. 1778): 431 Grantham Rd., Mechanicsburg, PA 17055; (717) 697-2634; www.bic-church.org; Moderator, Dr. Alan Robinson

Buddhist Churches of America (1899): 1710 Octavia St., San Francisco, CA 94109; (415) 776-5600; www.buddhist churchesofamerica.com; Pres., Ron Murakami

Catholic Bishops, U.S. Conference of (2001): 3211 4th St. NE, Washington, DC 20017; (202) 541-3000; www.usccb.org; Gen. Sec., Msgr. Ronny E. Jenkins

Christian Church (Disciples of Christ) (1832): Disciples Center, 130 E. Washington St., Indianapolis, IN 46204; (317) 635-3100; www.disciples.org; Gen. Min. and Pres., Rev. Dr. Sharon E. Watkins

Christian Methodist Episcopal Church (1870): 4466 Elvis Presley Blvd., Memphis, TN 38116; (901) 345-0580; www.c-m-e.org; Senior Bishop, Thomas L. Hoyt, Jr.

Church of the Brethren (1708): General Offices, 1451 Dundee Ave., Elgin, IL 60120; (847) 742-5100; www.brethren.org; Gen. Sec., Stanley J. Noffsinger

Church of Christ (1830): P.O. Box 472, Independence, MO 64051; (816) 833-3995; www.churchofchrist-tl.org; Council of Apostles, Sec., Duane L. Ely

Church of God (Anderson, IN) (1881): Box 2420, Anderson, IN 46018; (765) 642-0256; www.chog.org; Gen. Dir., Dr Ronald V. Duncan

Church of God (Cleveland, TN) (1886): 2490 Keith St. NW, Cleveland, TN 37320; (423) 472-3361; www.churchofgod.org; Gen. Overseer, Dr. Mark Williams

Church of God in Christ (1897): Mason Temple, 930 Mason St., Memphis, TN 38126; (901) 947-9300; www.cogic.org; Presiding Bishop, Bishop Charles E. Blake Sr.

Church of Jesus Christ (1862): 525 6th St., Monongahela, PA 15063; (412) 771-1686; www.thechurchofjesuschrist.org; Pres., Paul A. Palmieri

Church of Jesus Christ of Latter-day Saints, The (Mormons) (1830): 50 W. North Temple St., Salt Lake City, UT 84150; (801) 240-2640; www.lds.org; Pres., Thomas S. Monson

Church of the Nazarene (1908): Global Ministry Center, 17001 Prairie Star Pkwy., Lenexa, KS 66220; (913) 577-0500; www.nazarene.org; Gen. Sec., David P. Wilson

Community of Christ (reorganized Church of Jesus Christ of Latter-Day Saints) (1830): Intl. Headquarters, 1001 W. Walnut, Independence, MO 64050; (816) 833-1000; www.cofchrist.org; Pres., Stephen M. Veazey

Community Churches, International Council of (1950): 21116 Washington Pkwy., Frankfort, IL 60423; (815) 464-5690; www.icccusa.com; Interim Exec. Dir., Don Ashmall

Conservative Judaism, United Synagogue of (1913): 820 Second Ave., New York, NY 10017; (212) 533-7800; www.uscj.org; Pres., Richard Skolnik

Converge Worldwide (formerly Baptist General Conference) (1852): 2002 S. Arlington Heights Rd., Arlington Heights, IL 60005; (800) 323-4215; www.convergeworldwide.org; Pres. and CEO, Jerry Sheveland

Cumberland Presbyterian Church (1810): 8207 Traditional Pl., Cordova, TN 38016; (901) 276-4572; www.cumberland.org; Moderator, Forest Prosser

Episcopal Church (1789): 815 Second Ave., New York, NY 10017; (212) 716-6000; www.episcopalchurch.org; Presiding Bishop and Primate, Most Rev. Katharine Jefferts Schori

Evangelical Lutheran Church in America (1988): 8765 W. Higgins Rd., Chicago, IL 60631; (773) 380-2700; www.elca.org; Presiding Bishop, Rev. Mark S. Hanson

First Church of Christ, Scientist, The (1879): 210 Massachusetts Ave., Boston, MA 02115; (617) 450-2000; www.christianscience.com; Pres., Bosede Bakarey

Free Methodist Church USA (1860): 770 N. High School Rd., Indianapolis, IN 46214; (317) 244-3660; www.fmcusa.org; Larry Roberts

Freedom From Religion Foundation (1978): PO Box 750, Madison, WI 53701; (608) 256-8900; www.ffrf.org

Friends General Conference (1900): 1216 Arch St., #2B, Philadelphia, PA 19107; (215) 561-1700; www.fgcquaker.org; Gen. Sec., Barry Crossno

Gideons Intl. (1899): P.O. Box 140800, Nashville, TN 37214; (615) 564-5000; www.gideons.org

Greek Orthodox Archdiocese of America (1922): 8 E. 79th St., New York, NY 10075; (212) 570-3500; www.goarch.org; Primate, Archbishop Demetrios

Hadassah, the Women's Zionist Organization of America, Inc. (1912): 50 W. 58th St., New York, NY 10019; (888) 303-3640; www.hadassah.org; Exec. Dir., Janice Weinman

Interfaith Alliance (1994): 1212 New York Ave. NW, Ste. 1250, Washington, DC 20005; (202) 238-3300; www.interfaithalliance.org; Pres., Rev. Dr. C. Welton Gaddy

Islamic Society of North America: 6555 S. County Rd. 750 East, Plainfield, IN 46168; (317) 839-8157; www.isna.net; Pres., Mohamed Hagmagid

Jehovah's Witnesses (1931): 25 Columbia Heights, Brooklyn, NY 11201; (718) 560-5000; www.jw.org

Jewish Congress, American (1918): 115 E. 57th St., Ste. 11, New York, NY 10022; (212) 879-4500; www.ajcongress.org; Pres., Richard S. Gordon

Jewish Reconstructionist Federation (1955): Beit Devora, 101 Greenwood Ave., Ste. 430, Jenkintown, PA 19046; (215) 885-5601; www.jrf.org; Pres., Jack Rosen

Jewish Women, Natl. Council of (1893): 475 Riverside Dr., Ste. 1901, New York, NY 10115; (212) 645-4048; www.ncjw.org; Pres., Linda Slucker

Lutheran Church—Missouri Synod (1847): 1333 S. Kirkwood Rd., St. Louis, MO 63122; (800) 248-1930; www.lcms.org; Pres., Rev. Dr. Matthew C. Harrison

Mennonite Church USA (2001): 718 N. Main St., Newton, KS 67114; (316) 283-5100; www.mennoniteusa.org; Exec. Dir., Ervin Stutzman

Moravian Church in North America (1735): www.moravian.org; *Northern Prov.*: 1021 Center St., P.O. Box 1245, Bethlehem, PA 18016; (610) 867-7566; Pres., Betsy Miller; *Southern Prov.*: 459 S. Church St., Winston-Salem, NC 27101; (336) 725-5811; Pres., Rt. Rev. David Guthrie

North American Shia Ithnasheri Muslim Communities, Org. of (1986): P.O. Box 29691, Minneapolis, MN 55429; (905) 763-7512; www.nasimco.info; Pres., Gulamabbas Najafi

Orthodox Union (1898): 11 Broadway, New York, NY 10004; (212) 563-4000; www.ou.org; Exec. Vice Pres., Rabbi Steven Weil

Pentecostal Assemblies of the World, Inc. (1906): 3939 N. Meadows Dr., Indianapolis, IN 46205; (317) 547-9541;

www.pawinc.org; Presiding Bishop, Charles H. Ellis, III

Presbyterian Church (U.S.A.) (1983): 100 Witherspoon St., Louisville, KY 40202; (800) 728-7228; www.pcusa.org; Exec. Dir., Linda Valentine

Progressive National Baptist Convention, Inc. (1961): 601 50th St. NE, Washington, DC 20019; (202) 396-0558; www.pnbc.org; Pres., Dr. Carroll A. Baltimore Sr.

Rabbis, Central Conference of American (1889): 355 Lexington Ave., New York, NY 10017; (212) 972-3636; www.ccarnet.org; Pres., Richard Block

Reform Judaism, Union for (1873): 633 3rd Ave., New York, NY 10017; (212) 650-4000; www.urj.org; Pres., Rabbi Rick Jacobs

Secular Humanism, Council for (1980): P.O. Box 664, Amherst, NY 14226; (716) 636-7571; www.secularhumanism.org; Pres. and CEO, Ronald A. Lindsay

Separation of Church and State, Americans United for (1947): 1301 K St. NW, Ste. 850E, Washington, DC 20005; (202) 466-3234; www.au.org; Exec. Dir., Rev. Barry W. Lynn

Seventh-day Adventist Church (1863): 12501 Old Columbia Pike, Silver Spring, MD 20904; (301) 680-6000; www.adventist.org; Pres., Ted N. C. Wilson

Unitarian Universalist Assn. of Congregations (1961): 25 Beacon St., Boston, MA 02108; (617) 742-2100; www.uua.org; Pres., Rev. Peter Morales

United Church of Christ (1957): 700 Prospect Ave., Cleveland, OH 44115; (216) 736-2100; www.ucc.org; Pres., Rev. Geoffrey A. Black

United Methodist Church (1968): 100 Maryland Ave. NE, Washington, DC 20002; (202) 488-5600; www.umc.org

United Pentecostal Church Intl. (1945): 8855 Dunn Rd., Hazelwood, MO 63042; (314) 837-7300; www.upci.org; Gen. Supt., David K. Bernard

Wesleyan Church (1843): 13300 Olio Rd., Fishers, IN 46037; (317) 774-7900; www.wesleyan.org; Gen. Supt., Dr. Jo Anne Lyon

Businesses and Corporations

Source: World Almanac research

Listed below are major corporations offering products and services to U.S. consumers, as of June 2013. Alphabetization is by first key word or founder last name. Listings generally include examples of products offered.

Company name (NYSE/Nasdaq symbol, if traded on those markets): Address; Telephone number; Website; Top executive; Business, products, or services.

A&P: see Great Atlantic & Pacific Tea Co., Inc.

Abbott Laboratories (ABT): 100 Abbott Park Rd., Abbott Park, IL 60064; (847) 937-6100; www.abbott.com; Miles D. White; develops, mfr. pharmaceutical, nutritional, diagnostic prods. Spun off indep. pharm. co. Abvie, 1/1/2013.

ABC: see Disney Co.

adidas Group: Adi-Dassler-Strasse 1, D-91074 Herzogenaurach, Germany; +49 9132-84-0; www.adidas-group.com; Herbert Hainer; apparel and accessories mfr. (Reebok, Rockport, Taylor Golf).

Advance Publications, Inc.: 950 W. Fingerboard Rd., Staten Island, NY, 10305; (718) 981-1234; www.advance.net; Steven Newhouse; communications, newspaper and magazine publisher (*Parade*; Condé Nast subsids.: *New Yorker*, *Vanity Fair*, *Vogue*).

Aetna, Inc. (AET): 151 Farmington Ave., Hartford, CT 06156; (860) 273-0123; www.aetna.com; Mark T. Bertolini; health care, employee benefits.

Aflac, Inc. (AFL): 1932 Wynnton Rd., Columbus, GA 31999; (706) 323-3431; www.aflac.com; Daniel P. Amos; supplemental health and life insurance.

Alaska Air Group, Inc. (ALK): 19300 International Blvd., Seattle, WA 98188; (206) 392-5040; www.alaskaair.com; William S. Ayer; airline carriers (Alaska Airlines, Horizon Air).

Alcatel-Lucent (ALU): 3 av. Octave Gréard, Paris 75007, France; +33 (1) 4076-1010;

www.alcatel-lucent.com; Michel Combes; telecom. equip., broadband networks.

Alcoa, Inc. (AA): 201 Isabella St., Pittsburgh, PA 15212; (412) 553-4545; www.alcoa.com; Klaus Kleinfeld; prod., mfr. of aluminum, aluminum prods. (aerospace, automotive, industrial materials and components).

Allegheny Technologies Inc. (ATI): 1000 Six PPG Pl., Pittsburgh, PA 15222; (412) 394-2800; www.atimetals.com; Richard J. Harshman; specialty metals mfr. (titanium, alloys).

Allstate Corp. (ALL): 2775 Sanders Rd., Northbrook, IL 60062; (847) 402-5000; www.allstate.com; Thomas J. Wilson; personal property and casualty insurance; financial services.

Altria Group, Inc. (MO): 6601 W. Broad St., Richmond, VA 23230; (804) 484-8897; www.altria.com; Martin J. Barrington; largest U.S. tobacco company (Marlboro, Merit, Parliament, Virginia Slims).

Amazon.com, Inc. (AMZN): 440 Terry Ave. N., Seattle, WA 98109; (206) 266-1000; www.amazon.com; Jeffrey P. Bezos; online retailer of books, music, other consumer and household prods. Announced acquisition of automation and robotic co. Kiva Systems, 5/19/2012.

American Electric Power Co., Inc. (AEP): 1 Riverside Plz., Columbus, OH 43215; (614) 716-1000; www.aep.com; Nick Adams; public utilities.

American Express Co. (AXP): World Financial Ctr., 200 Vesey St., NY, NY 10285;

(212) 640-2000; www.americanexpress.com; Kenneth I. Chenault; charge and credit cards, travel-related services.

American Greetings Corp. (AM): 1 American Rd., Cleveland, OH 44144; (216) 252-7300; www.americangreetings.com; Morry Weiss; greeting cards, stationery, party goods, gift items.

American Intl. Group, Inc. (AIG): 180 Maiden Ln., NY, NY 10038; (212) 770-7000; www.aigcorporate.com; Robert H. Benmosche; insurance, financial services. AIG received $182 bil in govt. bailouts, 2008.

American Standard Brands (AS America, Inc.): 1 Centennial Plz., Piscataway, NJ 08855; (800) 442-1902; www.americanstandard-us.com; Jay D. Gould; kitchen and bath prods. Japan's Lixil Corp. announced plans to acquire, 6/28/2013.

AmerisourceBergen (ABC): 1300 Morris Dr., Chesterbrook, PA 19087; (610) 727-7000; www.amerisourcebergen.com; Steven H. Collis; distrib. of generic and brand-name pharmaceuticals.

AMR Corp. (AMR): 4333 Amon Carter Blvd., Ft. Worth, TX 76155; (817) 963-1234; www.aa.com; Thomas W. Horton; one of the world's largest air carriers (American Airlines, American Eagle). Filed for Chap. 11 reorganization, 11/29/2011.

Anheuser-Busch InBev (BUD): Brouwerijplein 1, 3000 Leuven, Belgium; +32 (16) 276111; www.ab-inbev.com; Carlos Brito; world's largest brewer (Budweiser, Bud Light, Michelob, Busch), soft drinks.

Acquired Grupo Modelo SAB de CV, 6/29/12.

Apple Inc. (AAPL): 1 Infinite Loop, Cupertino, CA 95014; (408) 996-1010; www.apple.com; Tim Cook; mfr. of computers (Mac), digital media devices (iPod, iPhone, iPad) and distrib. (iTunes store).

ARAMARK Corp.: 1101 Market St., Philadelphia, PA 19107; (215) 238-3000; www.aramark.com; Eric J. Foss; food/support services to institutions and facilities, uniforms and career apparel.

ArcelorMittal USA, Inc.: 1 South Dearborn, Chicago, IL 60603; (312) 899-3440; www.arcelormittal.com; Michael G. Rippey; U.S. subsidiary of Arcelor Mittal, world's largest steel co., based in Luxembourg.

Archer Daniels Midland Co. (ADM): 4666 Faries Pkwy., Decatur, IL 62526; (217) 424-5200; www.adm.com; Patricia A. Woertz; agricultural commodities and prods.

Armstrong World Industries, Inc. (AWI): 2500 Columbia Ave., P.O. Box 3001, Lancaster, PA 17604; (717) 397-0611; www.armstrong.com; Matthew J. Espe; mfr. of flooring, ceiling prods., cabinets.

ArvinMeritor, Inc.: see Meritor, Inc.

Ashland Inc. (ASH): 50 E. RiverCenter Blvd., P.O. Box 391, Covington, KY 41012; (859) 815-3333; www.ashland.com; James J. O'Brien; petroleum producer and refiner (Valvoline, plastics), chemicals, road construction.

AT&T Inc. (T): 208 S. Akard St., Dallas, TX 75202; (210) 821-4105; www.att.com; Randall L. Stephenson; telecommunications, global information management.

AutoNation, Inc. (AN): 200 SW 1st Ave., Ste. 1600, Ft. Lauderdale, FL 33301; (954) 769-6000; www.autonation.com; Mike Jackson; largest U.S. auto retailer; new and used vehicles; auto parts, maintenance, and repair; auto finance and insurance.

Avon Products, Inc. (AVP): 777 Third Ave., NY, NY 10017; (212) 282-7000; www.avon.com; Sheri E. McCoy; cosmetics, fragrances, skin and personal care items; fashion.

Bank of America Corp. (BAC): 100 N. Tryon St., Charlotte, NC 28255; (704) 386-5681; www.bankofamerica.com; Brian T. Moynihan; banking and nonbanking financial services.

Barnes & Noble, Inc. (BKS): 122 Fifth Ave., NY, NY 10011; (212) 633-3300; www.barnesandnobleinc.com; Leonard S. Riggio; leading U.S. bookseller (retail and college), publisher (Sterling Pub. Co.).

Bausch + Lomb Inc.: One Bausch & Lomb Pl., Rochester, NY 14604; (585) 338-6000; www.bausch.com; Brent L. Saunders; vision care prods., pharmaceuticals, surgical equip. Acquired by Valeant Pharmaceuticals, 5/28/2013.

Baxter International Inc. (BAX): 1 Baxter Pkwy., Deerfield, IL 60015; (224) 948-2000; www.baxter.com; Robert L. Parkinson Jr.; mfr. of health care prods.

Beam Inc. (BEAM): 510 Lake Cook Rd., Deerfield, IL 60015; (847) 948-8888; www.beamglobal.com; Matt Shattock; spirits (Jim Beam, Maker's Mark, Courvoisier, Sauza). Spun off from Fortune Brands, Inc., 10/3/2011.

Bear Stearns Cos. Inc.: see JPMorgan Chase & Co.

Becton, Dickinson & Co. (BDX): 1 Becton Dr., Franklin Lakes, NJ 07417; (201) 847-6800; www.bd.com; Vincent A. Forlenza; medical, laboratory, diagnostic prods.

Berkshire Hathaway Inc. (BRK.A): 3555 Farnam St., Ste. 1440, Omaha, NE 68131; (402) 346-1400; www.berkshirehathaway.com; Warren E. Buffett; insurance (GEICO), building materials (Benjamin Moore & Co., Shaw), apparel (Fruit of the Loom), food (Dairy Queen). Merged Burlington Northern Santa Fe Corp. rail transportation co. into Berkshire subsidiary, 2/12/2010.

Bertelsmann AG: Carl-Bertelsmann-Str. 270, 33311 Gütersloh, Germany; +49-5241-80-6613; www.bertelsmann.de; Thomas Rabe; intl. media corp., world's largest trade book publisher (Random House: Knopf, Doubleday). Formed Penguin Random House with Pearson, 7/1/2013

Best Buy Co., Inc. (BBY): 7601 Penn Ave. S., Richfield, MN 55423; (612) 291-1000; www.bestbuy.com; Hubert Joly; retailer of software, appliances, cellular phones, largest U.S. retailer of consumer electronics.

Blackstone Group LP, The (BX): 345 Park Ave., NY, NY 10154; (212) 583-5000; www.blackstone.com; Stephen A. Schwarzman; asset mgmt., financial services.

Blockbuster LLC: 9601 S. Meridian Blvd., Englewood, CO 80112; (303) 723-1000; www.blockbuster.com; Michael Kelly; in-home movie and video game rental, purchases. Filed for bankruptcy 9/23/2010; acquired by DISH Network, 4/26/2011.

Boeing Co. (BA): 100 N. Riverside, Chicago, IL 60606; (312) 544-2000; www.boeing.com; W. James McNerney Jr.; world's leading aerospace co., largest mfr. of commercial jet and military aircraft; one of the largest U.S. defense contractors.

Brink's Co., The (BCO): 1801 Bayberry Ct., P.O. Box 18100, Richmond, VA 23226; (469) 549-6000; www.brinkscompany.com; Thomas C. Schievelbein; security (armored transport, money processing, trans. of valuables).

Bristol-Myers Squibb Co. (BMY): 345 Park Ave., NY, NY 10154; (212) 546-4000; www.bms.com; Lamberto Andreotti; development, mfr., and sale of pharmaceuticals (Plavix, Abilify, Atripla). Acquired ZymoGenetics, Inc., 10/12/2010.

Brown-Forman Corp. (BFB): 850 Dixie Hwy., Louisville, KY 40210; (502) 585-1100; www.brown-forman.com; Paul C. Varga; distilled spirits (Jack Daniel's, Southern Comfort, Finlandia), wine and champagne (Sonoma-Cutrer, Korbel).

Brown Shoe Co., Inc. (BWS): 8300 Maryland Ave., St. Louis, MO 63105; (314) 854-4000; www.brownshoe.com; Diane M. Sullivan; shoe mfr (Buster Brown, Naturalizer, Dr. Scholl's, AVIA) and retailer (Famous Footwear, shoes.com). Acquired American Sporting Goods Corp., 2/17/2011.

Brunswick Corp. (BC): 1 N. Field Ct., Lake Forest, IL 60045; (847) 735-4700; www.brunswick.com; Dustan E. McCoy; leisure and recreation prods., incl. marine engines and boats; billiards, bowling, and fitness equipment; bowling centers.

Burger King Holdings, Inc. (BKW): 5505 Blue Lagoon Dr., Miami, FL 33126; (305) 378-3000; www.bk.com; Daniel Schwartz; world's 2nd-largest fast food hamburger restaurant chain. Acquired by 3G Capital 10/19/2010.

Cablevision Systems Corp. (CVC): 1111 Stewart Ave., Bethpage, NY 11714; (516) 803-2300; www.cablevision.com; James L. Dolan; cable and Internet services provider (Optimum); local media and programming; movie theaters (Clearview). Spun off Madison Square Garden, 2/9/2010; spun off AMC Networks, 6/30/2011. Sold Optimum West to Charter, 7/1/2013.

Caesars Entertainment Corp. (CZR): One Caesars Palace Dr., Las Vegas, NV 89109; (702) 407-6000; www.caesars.com; Gary W. Loveman; world's largest provider of branded casino entertainment (Caesars, Harrah's, Horseshoe, World Series of Poker). Changed name from Harrah's Entertainment, Inc., 11/23/2010.

Campbell Soup Co. (CPB): One Campbell Pl., Camden, NJ 08103; (856) 342-4800; www.campbellsoupcompany.com; Denise Morrison; world's largest soup mfr.; sauces (Pace, Prego), V8 juice, Pepperidge Farm prods.

Cardinal Health, Inc. (CAH): 7000 Cardinal Pl., Dublin, OH 43017; (614) 757-5000; www.cardinalhealth.com; George S. Barrett; pharmaceutical and medical equip. dist. co.

Caterpillar Inc. (CAT): 100 NE Adams St., Peoria, IL 61629; (309) 675-1000; www.caterpillar.com; Douglas R. Oberhelman; world's largest mfr. of construction and mining equip. Announced agreement to acquire Berg Propulsion, 7/1/2013.

CBS Corp. (CBS): 51 W. 52nd St., NY, NY 10019; (212) 975-4321; www.cbscorporation.com; Leslie Moonves; TV networks (CBS, Showtime); TV distribution; radio stations; book publishing (Simon & Schuster); advertising.

CenturyLink, Inc. (CTL): 100 CenturyLink Dr., Monroe, LA 71203; (318) 388-9000; www.centurylink.com; Glen F. Post III; 3rd-largest telecommunications provider in the U.S. Acquired Qwest Communications, 4/1/2011; acquired Savvis, 7/15/2011; acquired AppFog, Inc., 6/14/2013.

Chevron Corp. (CVX): 6001 Bollinger Canyon Rd., San Ramon, CA 94583; (925) 842-1000; www.chevron.com; John S. Watson; one of the world's largest integrated-energy co. Acquired Atlas Energy, 2/18/2011.

Chiquita Brands International, Inc. (CQB): 550 S. Caldwell St., Charlotte, NC 28202; (980) 636-5000; www.chiquita.com; Edward F. Lonergan; bananas and other fruits and vegetables.

CHS, Inc. (CHSCP): 550 Cenex Dr., Inver Grove Heights, MN 55077; (655) 355-2000; www.chsinc.com; Carl Casale; grain marketing, oil refining, and pipeline operations.

Church & Dwight Co., Inc. (CHD): Princeton South Corporate Center, 500 Charles Ewing Blvd., Ewing, NJ 08628; (800) 524-1328; www.churchdwight.com; James R. Craigie; top world producer of sodium bicarbonate (ARM & HAMMER baking soda); household (OxiClean) and personal care prods. (Arrid, Trojan, First Response). Acquired Avid Health, Inc., 10/1/2012.

Cigna Corp. (CI): 900 Cottage Grove Rd., Bloomfield, CT 06002; (860) 226-6000; www.cigna.com; David M. Cordani; health-care, life, and accident insurance provider.

Cintas Corp. (CTAS): 6800 Cintas Blvd., Cincinnati, OH 45262; (513) 459-1200; www.cintas.com; Scott D. Farmer; largest uniform supplier in U.S.

Circuit City Stores, Inc.: see Systemax Inc.

Cisco Systems, Inc. (CSCO): 170 W. Tasman Dr., San Jose, CA 95134; (408) 526-4000; www.cisco.com; John T. Chambers; networking and communication prods.

Citigroup, Inc. (C): 399 Park Ave., NY, NY 10022; (212) 559-1000; www.citigroup.com; Michael L. Corbat; diversified financial services.

Clear Channel Communications, Inc.: 200 E. Basse Rd., San Antonio, TX 78209; (210) 822-2828; www.clearchannel.com; Bob Pittman; largest radio station owner in U.S. (850+ stations); outdoor advertising (billboards, mass transit ads).

Clorox Co. (CLX): 1221 Broadway, Oakland, CA 94612; (510) 271-7000; www.clorox.com; Donald R. Knauss; retail consumer prods. (Clorox, Formula 409, Pine-Sol, S.O.S., Tilex; Scoop Away, Fresh Step cat litters; Kingsford charcoal; Hidden Valley dressing; Glad plastic bags; Brita water systems; Burt's Bees personal care prods.).

Coca-Cola Co. (KO): 1 Coca-Cola Plz., Atlanta, GA 30313; (404) 676-2121; www.coca-cola.com; Muhtar Kent; world's largest beverage co. (Coca-Cola, Sprite, DAS-ANI water), world's largest dist. of juice prods. (Minute Maid).

Colgate-Palmolive Co. (CL): 300 Park Ave., NY, NY 10022; (212) 310-2000; www.colgate.com; Ian M. Cook; soap (Irish Spring), detergent (Palmolive), household cleansers (Ajax), toothpaste (Colgate, Tom's of Maine), pet food (Hill's Science Diet).

Comcast Corp. (CMCSA): 1701 JFK Blvd., Philadelphia, PA 19103; (215) 286-1700; www.comcast.com; Brian L. Roberts; largest U.S. cable company; broadband cable, Internet, and voice services. Some programming (E!, Golf Channel); controlling stake in NBCUniversal (NBC, Bravo, USA, Telemundo).

Computer Sciences Corp. (CSC): 3170 Fairview Park Dr., Falls Church, VA 22042; (703) 876-1000; www.csc.com; Mike Lawrie; technology services.

ConAgra Foods, Inc. (CAG): 1 ConAgra Dr., Omaha, NE 68102; (402) 240-4000; www.conagrafoods.com; Gary M. Rodkin; food processor (Chef Boyardee, Healthy Choice frozen dinners, Egg Beaters, Reddi-wip); food service supplier. Acquired Ralcorp Holdings, 1/29/2013.

ConocoPhillips Co. (COP): 600 N. Dairy Ashford, P.O. Box 2197, Houston, TX 77079; (281) 293-1000; www.conoco phillips.com; Ryan M. Lance; oil and gas exploration and prod. company. Spun off refining and marketing segment of co. 5/1/2012, as new independent co., Phillips 66.

Consolidated Edison, Inc. (ED): 4 Irving Pl., NY, NY 10003; (212) 460-4600; www.conedison.com; Kevin Burke; electric, natural gas utilities.

Continental Airlines, Inc.: see United Continental Holdings, Inc.

Corning Inc. (GLW): 1 Riverfront Plz., Corning, NY 14831; (607) 974-9000; www.corning.com; Wendell P. Weeks; mfr. of telecommunications, specialty equipment, fiber optics.

Costco Wholesale Corp. (COST): 999 Lake Dr., Issaquah, WA 98027; (425) 313-8100; www.costco.com; W. Craig Jelinek; largest U.S. chain of wholesale warehouse stores.

Countrywide Financial: see Bank of America Corp.

Crane Co. (CR): 100 First Stamford Pl., Stamford, CT 06902; (203) 363-7300; www.craneco.com; Eric C. Fast; mfr. of fluid control devices, vending machines, aircraft components.

A. T. Cross Co. (ATX): 1 Albion Rd., Lincoln, RI 02865; (401) 333-1200; www.cross.com; David G. Whalen; writing instruments, timepieces, personal accessories.

Crown Holdings, Inc. (CCK): 1 Crown Way, Philadelphia, PA 19154; (215) 698-5100; www.crowncork.com; John W. Conway; leading producer of packaging prods.

CSX Corp. (CSX): 500 Water St., 15th Fl., Jacksonville, FL 32202; (904) 359-3200; www.csx.com; Michael J. Ward; rail freight transport.

CVS Caremark Corp. (CVS): 1 CVS Dr., Woonsocket, RI 02895; (401) 765-1500; www.cvs.com; Larry J. Merlo. Nation's largest drugstore chain.

Dana Holding Corp. (DAN): 3939 Technology Dr., Maumee, OH 43537; (419) 887-3000; www.dana.com; Roger J. Wood; truck and auto parts, supplies.

Darden Restaurants, Inc. (DRI): 1000 Darden Center Dr., Orlando, FL 32837; (407) 245-4000; www.darden.com; Clarence Otis Jr.; casual-dining restaurants (Red Lobster, Olive Garden).

Dean Foods Co. (DF): 2711 N. Haskell Ave., Ste. 3400, Dallas, TX 75204; (214) 303-3400; www.deanfoods.com; Greg A. Tanner; milk and specialty dairy prods. (LAND O LAKES, Horizon Organic, Silk soy milk, International Delight coffee creamers). Spun off WhiteWave Foods Co., 5/23/2013.

Deere & Co. (DE): One John Deere Pl., Moline, IL 61265; (309) 765-8000; www.deere.com; Samuel R. Allen; one of the world's largest mfrs. of farm equip.; mfr. industrial equip., lawn and garden tractors.

Dell Inc. (DELL): 1 Dell Way, Round Rock, TX 78682; (512) 338-4400; www.dell.com; Michael S. Dell; laptop and desktop computers, network accessories, peripherals, tablets, smartphones.

Delta Air Lines, Inc. (DAL): 1030 Delta Blvd., Atlanta, GA 30320; (404) 715-2600; www.delta.com; Richard H. Anderson; air transportation.

Dial Corp. 19001 N. Scottsdale Rd., Scottsdale, AZ 85255; (480) 754-3425; www.henkelna.com; Jeffrey C. Piccolomini; consumer prods. (Dial soap, Purex detergent, Right Guard antiperspirant, Renuzit air fresheners); U.S. subsidiary of Germany's Henkel company.

Diebold, Inc. (DBD): 5995 Mayfair Rd., North Canton, OH 44720; (330) 490-4000; www.diebold.com; Andy W. Mattes; mfr. ATMs, security systems and prods.

Dillard's, Inc. (DDS): 1600 Cantrell Rd., Little Rock, AR 72201; (501) 376-5200; www.dillards.com; William Dillard II; dept. store chain.

Walt Disney Co., The (DIS): 500 S. Buena Vista St., Burbank, CA 91521; (818) 560-1000; disney.go.com; Robert A. Iger; one of the world's largest media conglomerates; motion pictures (Touchstone, Pixar); TV (ABC, ESPN) and radio; publishing; theme parks (Walt Disney World, Disneyland) and resorts.

Doctor's Associates Inc.: 325 Bic Dr., Milford, CT 06461; (203) 877-4281; www.subway.com; Frederick A. DeLuca; restaurants (Subway).

Dole Food Co., Inc. (DOLE): One Dole Dr., Westlake Village, CA 91362; (818) 879-6600; www.dole.com; C. Michael Carter; food prods., fresh fruits, and vegetables.

R. R. Donnelley & Sons Co. (RRD): 111 S. Wacker Dr., Chicago, IL 60606; (312) 326-8000; www.rrdonnelley.com; Thomas J. Quinlan III; commercial printing; photos/graphics, translation; printer of *The World Almanac*.

Dow Chemical Co. (DOW): 2030 Dow Ctr., Midland, MI 48674; (989) 636-1000; www.dow.com; Andrew N. Liveris; chemicals, plastics (world's 2nd-largest chemical co.).

Dow Jones & Co., Inc.: see News Corp.

Dr Pepper Snapple Group, Inc. (DPS): 5301 Legacy Dr., Plano, TX 75024; (972) 673-7000; www.drpeppersnapplegroup.com; Larry D. Young; bottler and distributor of nonalcoholic beverages (Dr Pepper, Hawaiian Punch, 7UP, Snapple, Mott's).

Duke Energy Corp. (DUK): 550 S. Tryon St., Charlotte, NC 28202; (704) 594-6200; www.duke-energy.com; James E. Rogers; utilities, fiber optic networks.

Dun & Bradstreet Corp. (DNB): 103 JFK Pkwy., Short Hills, NJ 07078; (973) 921-5500; www.dnb.com; Sara Mathew; business information, research.

Dupont (E. I. du Pont de Nemours & Co.) (DD): 1007 Market St., Wilmington, DE 19898; (302) 774-1000; www.dupont.com; Ellen J. Kullman; 3rd-largest U.S. chemical co.; petroleum, consumer prods.

Eastman Kodak Co.: 343 State St., Rochester, NY 14650; (585) 724-4000; www.kodak.com; Antonio M. Perez; photo printers, high-speed commercial inkjet presses, workflow software and packaging. Filed for Chap. 11 reorganization, 1/19/2012.

Eaton Corp. (ETN): Eaton Ctr., 1111 Superior Ave., Cleveland, OH 44114; (216) 523-5000; www.eaton.com; Sandy Cutler; mfr. vehicle components, controls. Acquired Cooper Industries PLC, 11/30/2012.

eBay Inc. (EBAY): 2065 Hamilton Ave., San Jose, CA 95125; (408) 376-7400; www.ebay.com; John Donahoe; e-commerce (PayPal, StubHub.com).

Edison Intl. (EIX): 2244 Walnut Grove Ave., Rosemead, CA 91770; (626) 302-2222; www.edison.com; Theodore F. Craver Jr.; electric utilities.

Electronic Arts Inc. (EA): 209 Redwood Shores Pkwy., Redwood City, CA 94065; (650) 628-1500; www.ea.com; Lawrence F. Probst III; leading U.S. video game publisher (Madden NFL, Battlefield, The Sims).

Electronic Data Systems: see Hewlett-Packard Co.

Eli Lilly and Co. (LLY): Lilly Corporate Center, Indianapolis, IN 46285; (317) 276-2000; www.lilly.com; John C. Lechleiter; pharmaceutical research, development, and manufacturing (Prozac, Strattera, Cialis).

EMC Corp. (EMC): 176 South St., Hopkinton, MA 01748; (508) 435-1000; www.emc.com; Joseph M. Tucci; data storage/protection.

Emerson Electric Co. (EMR): 8000 W. Florissant Ave., St. Louis, MO 63136; (314) 553-2000; www.emerson.com; David N. Farr; electrical, electronics prods. and systems.

Energizer Holdings, Inc. (ENR): 533 Maryville Univ. Dr., St. Louis, MO 63141; (314) 985-2000; www.energizer.com; Ward M. Klein; batteries, flashlights, personal care prods.

Enterprise Products Partners L.P. (EPD): 1100 Louisiana St., Houston, TX 77002; (731) 381-6500; www.enterpriseproducts.com; Michael A. Creel; oil processing/transport and waterborne freight.

Estée Lauder Cos. Inc. (EL): 767 Fifth Ave., NY, NY 10153; (212) 572-4200; www.elcompanies.com; Fabrizio Freda; cosmetics (Clinique, Bobbi Brown), fragrance, skin care prods.

Exelon Corp. (EXC): 10 S. Dearborn St., 48th Fl., Chicago, IL 60680; (800) 483-3220; www.exeloncorp.com; Christopher M. Crane; electricity generation/distribution; natural gas. Merged with Constellation Energy, 3/12/2012.

Express Scripts Holding Co. (ESRX): 1 Express Way, St. Louis, MO 63121; 314-996-0900; www.express-scripts.com; George Paz; largest U.S. pharmacy benefits management co. Acquired Medco Health Solutions Inc., 4/2/2012.

ExxonMobil Corp. (XOM): 5959 Las Colinas Blvd., Irving, TX 75039; (972) 444-1000; www.exxonmobil.com; Rex W. Tillerson; world's largest integrated oil co.

Facebook, Inc. (FB): 1601 Willow Rd., Menlo Park, CA 94025; (650) 308-7300; www.facebook.com; Mark Zuckerberg; social networking. Acquired Instagram, 9/6/2012.

Federal Home Loan Mortgage Corp. (Freddie Mac): 8200 Jones Branch Dr., McLean, VA 22102; (703) 903-2000; www.freddiemac.com; Donald H. Layton; residential mortgage provider. Taken over by U.S. government, 9/7/2008.

Federal National Mortgage Assn. (Fannie Mae): 3900 Wisconsin Ave. NW, Washington, DC 20016; (202) 752-7000; www.fanniemae.com; Timothy J. Mayopoulos; largest U.S. provider of residential mortgage funds. Taken over by U.S. government, 9/7/2008.

FedEx Corp. (FDX): 942 S. Shady Grove Rd., Memphis, TN 38120; (901) 818-7500; www.fedex.com; Frederick W. Smith; world's largest express delivery service.

Fifth & Pacific Cos., Inc. (FNP): 1441 Broadway, NY, NY 10018; (212) 354-4900; fifthandpacific.com; William L. McComb; women's apparel (kate spade, Juicy Couture, Lucky Brand Jeans). Sold Liz Claiborne brand to J.C. Penney Co. Inc., 11/2/2011; changed name from Liz Claiborne, Inc., 5/15/2012.

First Data Corp.: 5565 Glenridge Connector NE, Ste. 2000, Atlanta, GA 30342; (404) 890-2000; www.firstdata.com; Frank Bisignano; financial transaction processing.

FirstEnergy Corp. (FE): 76 S. Main St., Akron, OH 44308; (800) 736-3402; www.firstenergycorp.com; Anthony J. Alexander; public electricity supplier.

Fluor Corp. (FLR): 6700 Las Colinas Blvd., Irving, TX 75039; (469) 398-7000; www.fluor.com; David T. Seaton; international engineering and construction co.

Foot Locker, Inc. (FL): 112 W. 34th St., NY, NY 10120; (212) 720-3700; www.foot locker-inc.com; Ken C. Hicks; retail athletic stores (Footaction, Foot Locker, Champs Sports). Acquired Runners Point Group, 7/10/2013.

Ford Motor Co. (F): 1 American Rd., Dearborn, MI 48126; (313) 322-3000; www.ford.com; William C. Ford Jr.; auto mfr.; motor vehicle sales (Ford, Lincoln); one of the largest U.S. auto finance co. (Ford Motor Credit).

Fortune Brands Home and Security, Inc. (FBHS): 520 Lake Cook Rd., Deerfield, IL 60015; (847) 484-4400; www.fbhs.com; Christopher Klein; cabinetry, plumbing (Moen), windows and doors, security and storage (Master Lock). Spun off from Fortune Brands, Inc., 10/3/2011.

Fox: see News Corp.

Gannett Co., Inc. (GCI): 7950 Jones Branch Dr., McLean, VA 22107; (703) 854-6000; www.gannett.com; Gracia Martore; largest U.S. newspaper publisher (*USA Today*); network and cable TV; employment web site (CareerBuilder).

Gap Inc. (GPS): 2 Folsom St., San Francisco, CA 94105; (650) 952-4400; www.gapinc.com; Glenn K. Murphy; casual apparel retailer (Gap, Banana Republic, Old Navy).

General Dynamics Corp. (GD): 2941 Fairview Park Dr., Ste. 100, Falls Church, VA 22042; (703) 876-3000; www.generaldynamics.com; Phebe N. Novakovic; defense contractor: aerospace, combat systems, marine systems, computing devices.

General Electric Co. (GE): 3135 Easton Tpke., Fairfield, CT 06828; (203) 373-2211; www.ge.com; Jeffrey Immelt; electrical, electronic equip., financial services, radio and TV broadcasting, aircraft engines, power generation, appliances.

General Mills, Inc. (GIS): One General Mills Blvd., Minneapolis, MN 55426; (763) 764-7600; www.generalmills.com; Kendall J. Powell; food mfr. (Betty Crocker, Bisquick, Cheerios, Chex, Green Giant, Häagen-Dazs, Pillsbury, Progresso, Total, Wheaties, Yoplait).

General Motors Co. (GM): 300 Renaissance Ctr., Detroit, MI 48265; (313) 556-5000; www.gm.com; Daniel F. Akerson; world's largest auto mfr. (Chevrolet, Cadillac, Buick, GMC); auto financing (GM Financial); vehicle security (OnStar). General Motors Corp. filed for Chap. 11 reorganization, 6/1/2009; sold its profitable components to a new, smaller company called General Motors Co., 7/10/2009.

Genuine Parts Co. (GPC): 2999 Circle 75 Pkwy., Atlanta, GA 30339; (770) 953-1700; www.genpt.com; Thomas C. Gallagher; distrb. of auto (NAPA), industrial replacement parts.

Goldman Sachs Group, Inc. (GS): 200 West St., 29th Fl., NY, NY 10282; (212) 902-1000; www.goldmansachs.com; Lloyd C. Blankfein; investment banking, asset mgmt., securities services.

Goodyear Tire & Rubber Co. (GT): 200 Innovation Way, Akron, OH 44316; (330) 796-2121; www.goodyear.com; Richard J. Kramer; tires and other auto prods.

Google, Inc. (GOOG): 1600 Amphitheatre Pkwy., Mountain View, CA 94043; (650) 253-0000; www.google.com; Larry Page; Internet-related prods. and services (leading search engine, ad sales; YouTube.

W. R. Grace & Co. (GRA): 7500 Grace Dr., Columbia, MD 21044; (410) 531-4000; www.grace.com; Fred E. Festa; chemicals, construction prods.

Great Atlantic & Pacific Tea Co., Inc.: 2 Paragon Dr., Montvale, NJ 07645; (201) 573-9700; www.aptea.com; Samuel Martin; supermarkets (A&P, The Food Emporium, Super Fresh, Waldbaum's, Pathmark) Emerged from Chap. 11 reorganization, 3/13/2012.

Halliburton Co. (HAL): 3000 N. Sam Houston Pkwy. E., Houston, TX 77032; (281) 871-4000; www.halliburton.com; David J. Lesar; oil field mgmt., energy services.

Hanesbrands Inc. (HBI): 1000 E. Hanes Mill Rd., Winston-Salem, NC 27105; (336) 519-8080; www.hanesbrands.com; Richard A. Noll; apparel mfr. (Hanes, L'eggs, Champion, Just My Size, Playtex, Wonderbra).

Harley-Davidson, Inc. (HOG): 3700 W. Juneau Ave., Milwaukee, WI 53208; (414) 342-4680; www.harley-davidson.com; Keith E. Wandell; mfr. motorcycles, parts, and accessories.

Hartford Financial Services Group, Inc. (HIG): One Hartford Plz., Hartford, CT 06155; (860) 547-5000; www.thehartford.com; Liam E. McGee; insurance, financial services.

Hasbro, Inc. (HAS): 1027 Newport Ave., Pawtucket, RI 02862; (401) 431-8697; www.hasbro.com; Brian Goldner; toy and game mfr. (Milton Bradley, Playskool, G.I. Joe, Parker Bros., Nerf, Play-Doh).

HCA Holdings, Inc. (HCA): 1 Park Plz., Nashville, TN 37203; (615) 344-9551; www.hcahealthcare.com; Richard M. Bracken; owns and operates hospitals; other diagnostic, surgical, health treatment centers.

H. J. Heinz Co.: 1 PPG Pl., Ste. 3100, Pittsburgh, PA 15222; (412) 456-5700; www.heinz.com; Bernardo Hees; food mfr. (Orelda, 57 Varieties ketchup, Weight Watchers foods). Acquired by Berkshire Hathaway and 3G Capital, 6/7/2013.

Hershey Co., The (HSY): 100 Crystal A Dr., Hershey, PA 17033; (717) 534-4200; www.thehersheycompany.com; John P. Bilbrey; largest North American producer of chocolate prods. (Reese's, Kit Kat, Mounds, Almond Joy, Jolly Rancher, Twizzlers, Milk Duds, Good & Plenty, York). Agreed to acquire Canadian confectionary Brookside Foods, 12/8/2011.

Hertz Global Holdings, Inc. (HTZ): 225 Brae Blvd., Park Ridge, NJ 07656; (201) 307-2000; www.hertz.com; Mark P. Frissora; car rentals.

Hess Corp. (HES): 1185 Ave. of the Americas, 40th Fl., NY, NY 10036; (212) 997-8500; www.hess.com; John B. Hess; integrated oil and gas co.

Hewlett-Packard Co. (HPQ): 3000 Hanover St., Palo Alto, CA 94304; (650) 857-1501; www.hp.com; Margaret C. Whitman; computers, electronic prods. and systems.

Hillenbrand, Inc. (HI): One Batesville Blvd., Batesville, IN 47006; (812) 934-7000; www.hillenbrandinc.com; Kenneth A. Camp; holder of Batesville Caskets, coffin mfr. Acquired Coperion Capital GmbH, 12/3/2012.

Hill-Rom Holdings, Inc. (HRC): 1069 State Rte. 46 E., Batesville, IN 47006; (812) 934-7777; www.hill-rom.com; John J. Greisch; mfr. hospital beds, other hospital equip.

Hillshire Brands Co. (HSH): 400 S. Jefferson St., Chicago, IL 60607; (312) 614-6000; www.hillshirebrands.com; Sean Connolly; split from Sara Lee, 6/28/2012.

Hilton Worldwide: 7930 Jones Branch Dr., Ste. 1100, McLean, VA 22102; (703) 883-1000; www.hiltonworldwide.com; Christopher J. Nassotta; hotels and resorts (Doubletree, Embassy, Hampton).

Home Depot, Inc. (HD): 2455 Paces Ferry Rd. NW, Atlanta, GA 30339; (770) 433-8211; www.homedepot.com; Francis S. Blake; world's largest home improvement retailer; 5th-largest retailer in the world; home improvement warehouse stores.

Honeywell Intl. Inc. (HON): 101 Columbia Rd., Morristown, NJ 07962; (973) 455-2000; www.honeywell.com; David Cote; industrial and home control systems, aerospace guidance systems.

Hormel Foods Corp. (HRL): 1 Hormel Pl., Austin, MN 55912; (507) 437-5611; www.hormelfoods.com; Jeffrey M. Ettinger; meat processor; pork, turkey, and beef prods. (SPAM, Dinty Moore, Jennie-O).

Hostess Brands: 1 E Armour Blvd., Kansas City, MO 64111; (816) 701-4600; www.hostessbrands.com; Dean Metropoulos; baked goods wholesaler, distributor (Hostess, Dolly Madison). Filed for Chap. 11 reorganization, 1/11/2012. Wonder Bread and Nature's Pride brands acquired by Flowers Food, 2/28/2013. Acquired and reorganized by Apollo Global Management and C. Dean Metropoulos & Co., 3/12/2013. Drake's and Nature's brands acquired by McKee Foods, 3/14/2013.

Houghton Mifflin Harcourt: 222 Berkeley St., Boston, MA 02116; (617) 351-5000; www.hmhco.com; Linda K. Zecher; publisher of textbooks and other educational prods. (Holt McDougal Clarion), trade and reference books. Emerged from Chap. 11 reorganization, 6/22/2012.

H&R Block, Inc. (HRB): 1 H&R Block Way, Kansas City, MO 64105; (816) 854-3000; www.hrblock.com; William C. Cobb; tax return preparation; business and consulting services.

Humana Inc. (HUM): 500 W. Main St., Louisville, KY 40202; (502) 580-1000; www.humana.com; Bruce D. Broussard; managed health care service provider, related specialty prods.

IAC/InterActiveCorp (IACI): 555 W. 18th St., NY, NY 10011; (212) 314-7300; www.iac.com; Barry Diller; Internet

conglomerate (Ask.com, Match.com, Citysearch, Urbanspoon, Vimeo).

Illinois Tool Works Inc. (ITW): 3600 W. Lake Ave., Glenview, IL 60026; (847) 724-7500; www.itw.com; E. Scott Santi; consumer, industrial tools; food equip. (Hobart), packaging (Zip-Pak).

Ingersoll-Rand plc (IR): 170/175 Lakeview Dr., Airside Business Park, Swords, Dublin, Ireland; 353-1-870-7400; company.ingersollrand.com; Michael W. Lamach; locks and security systems (Schlage, Kryptonite); refrigeration equip. (Thermo King, Hussmann); industrial equip.; air conditioning systems (Trane). Announced plans to spin off security prods. business as Allegion, 6/17/2013.

Ingram Micro Inc. (IM): 1600 E. St. Andrew Pl., Santa Ana, CA 92705; (714) 566-1000; www.ingrammicro.com; Alain Moné; IT equipment wholesaler and distributor in over 160 countries.

Intel Corp. (INTC): 2200 Mission College Blvd., Santa Clara, CA 95054; (408) 765-8080; www.intel.com; Andy D. Bryant; mfr. semiconductors, microprocessors (Core, Centrino).

International Business Machines Corp. (IBM): One New Orchard Rd., Armonk, NY 10504; (914) 499-1900; www.ibm.com; Virginia M. Rometty; world's largest supplier of advanced information processing technology equip., services.

International Paper Co. (IP): 6400 Poplar Ave., Memphis, TN 38197; (901) 419-7000; www.internationalpaper.com; John V. Faraci Jr.; world's largest paper/forest prods. co.

International Textile Group, Inc.: 804 Green Valley, Greensboro, NC 27408; (336) 379-6220; www.itg-global.com; Joseph L. Gorga; apparel and home textiles/fabrics.

INTL FCStone Inc. (INTL): 708 Third Ave., 15th Fl., NY, NY 10017; (212) 485-3500; www.intlfcstone.com; Sean O'Connor; securities and commodities advising. Announced IPO, 7/15/2013.

J.C. Penney Co., Inc. (JCP): 6501 Legacy Dr., Plano, TX 75024; (972) 431-1000; www.jcpenney.net; Mike Ullman; dept. store retailer, general merchandise catalog sales.

J. Crew Group, Inc.: 770 Broadway, NY, NY 10003; (212) 209-2500; www.jcrew.com; Millard S. Drexler; retail and mail order apparel and accessories. Acquired by TPG Capital and Leonard Green & Partners, 3/7/2011.

JetBlue Airways Corp. (JBLU): 27-01 Queens Plz. N., Long Island City, NY 11101; (718) 286-7900; www.jetblue.com; David Barger; air transportation.

Jo-Ann Stores, Inc.: 5555 Darrow Rd., Hudson, OH 44236; (330) 656-2600; www.joann.com; Travis Smith; nation's largest specialty fabric and craft stores. Acquired by Leonard Green & Partners, 3/18/2011.

Johnson Controls, Inc. (JCI): 5757 N. Green Bay Ave., Milwaukee, WI 53209; (414) 524-1200; www.johnsoncontrols.com; Stephen A. Roell; equipment and controls for heating, ventilating, AC, refrigeration, and building security; auto interiors, batteries.

Johnson & Johnson (JNJ): 1 Johnson & Johnson Plz., New Brunswick, NJ 08933; (732) 524-0400; www.jnj.com; Alex Gorsky; health care prods. (Band-Aid, Neosporin), pharmaceuticals (Tylenol, Motrin, Sudafed), toiletries (Neutrogena, Aveeno).

S. C. Johnson & Son, Inc.: 1525 Howe St., Racine, WI 53403; (262) 260-2000; www.scjohnson.com; H. Fisk Johnson; cleaning and other household prods. (Johnson's Wax, Windex, Pledge, Fantastik, Raid, OFF!, Shout, Glade, Scrubbing Bubbles, Ziploc bags).

Jones Group, Inc. (JNY): 1411 Broadway, NY, NY 10018; (212) 642-3860; www.jny.com; Wesley R. Card; apparel (Jones New York, Gloria Vanderbilt), shoes (Nine West, Anne Klein); retail and outlet stores.

JPMorgan Chase & Co. (JPM): 270 Park Ave., NY, NY 10017; (212) 270-6000; www.jpmorganchase.com; James Dimon; financial services.

KBR, Inc. (KBR): 601 Jefferson St., Ste. 3400, Houston, TX 77002; (713) 753-2000; www.kbr.com; William P. Utt; engineering; construction mgmt. services.

Kellogg Co. (K): One Kellogg Sq., Battle Creek, MI 49016; (269) 961-2000; www. kelloggcompany.com; John A. Bryant; world's largest mfr. of ready-to-eat cereals, other food prods. (Frosted Flakes, Rice Krispies, Froot Loops, Pop-Tarts, Nutri-Grain, Keebler, Eggo, Pringles). Acquired Pringles from Procter & Gamble, 6/1/2012.

Kelly Services, Inc. (KELYA): 999 W. Big Beaver Rd., Troy, MI 48084; (248) 362-4444; www.kellyservices.com; Carl T. Camden; temporary staffing services.

Kimberly-Clark Corp. (KMB): 351 Phelps Dr., Irving, TX 75038; (972) 281-1200; www.kimberly-clark.com; Thomas J. Falk; personal care prods. (Kleenex, Scott, Cottonelle, Huggies, Kotex).

Kinder Morgan, Inc. (KMI): 1001 Louisiana St., Ste. 1000, Houston, TX 77002; (713) 369-9000; www.kindermorgan.com; Richard D. Kinder; energy trans. and storage. Acquired El Paso Corp., 5/24/2012.

Kmart Corp.: see Sears Holdings Corp.

Koch Industries, Inc.: P.O. Box 2256, Wichita, KS 67201; (316) 828-5500; www. kochind.com; Charles G. Koch; forest prod. mfr.; oil refineries/pipeline; chemicals; pollution-control equipment; ranching.

Kraft Foods Group Inc.: Three Lakes Dr., Northfield, IL 60093; (847) 646-2000; www.kraftfoodsgroup.com; W. Anthony Vernon; global packaged food co. (Maxwell House, Oscar Mayer, Planters, Velveeta, Capri Sun, Jell-O, Lunchables). Kraft Foods split into two public cos., Mondelēz International and Kraft Foods Group Inc., 10/1/2012.

Kroger Co. (KR): 1014 Vine St., Cincinnati, OH 45202; (513) 762-4000; www. thekrogerco.com; David B. Dillon; one of the largest U.S. grocery retailers, convenience stores, mail jewelry stores.

La-Z-Boy Inc. (LZB): 1284 N. Telegraph Rd., Monroe, MI 48162; (734) 242-1444; www.la-z-boy.com; Kurt L. Darrow; reclining chairs, other furniture.

Leggett & Platt, Inc. (LEG): No. 1 Leggett Rd., Carthage, MO 64836; (417) 358-8131; www.leggett.com; David S. Haffner; furniture and its components, industrial materials, automotive suspension, control and power train cable systems.

Levi Strauss & Co.: 1155 Battery St., San Francisco, CA 94111; (415) 501-6000; www.levistrauss.com; Charles Bergh; blue jeans, casual sportswear (Dockers).

Lexmark Intl., Inc. (LXK): 740 W. New Circle Rd., Lexington, KY 40550; (859) 232-2000; www.lexmark.com; Paul Rooke; computer printers and peripherals.

Liberty Mutual Holding Co. Inc.: 175 Berkeley St., Boston, MA 02116; (617) 357-9500; www.libertymutual.com; David H. Long; insurance prods. and services.

Limited Brands, Inc. (LTD): 3 Limited Pkwy., Columbus, OH 43216; (614) 415-7000; www.limitedbrands.com; Leslie H. Wexner; apparel stores (La Senza, Victoria's Secret, PINK, Henri Bendel), home decor (White Barn Candle Co.), personal care (Bath & Body Works).

Liz Claiborne, Inc.: See J.C. Penney Co., Inc.

L.L. Bean, Inc.: 15 Casco St., Freeport, ME 04033; (207) 552-2000; www.llbean.com; Christopher J. McCormick; catalog and retail outdoor apparel, footwear, gear.

Lockheed Martin Corp. (LMT): 6801 Rockledge Dr., Bethesda, MD 20817; (301) 897-6000; www.lockheedmartin.com; Marillyn A. Hewlson; leading U.S. defense contractor; commercial and military aircraft, electronics, missiles, information tech., and communications.

Loews Corp. (L): 667 Madison Ave., NY, NY 10065; (212) 521-2000; www.loews.com; James S. Tisch; hotels, insurance (CNA Financial), offshore drilling (Diamond).

Longs Drug Stores: see CVS Caremark Corp.

Lorillard, Inc. (LO): 714 Green Valley Rd., Greensboro, NC 27408; (336) 335-7000; www.lorillard.com; Murray S. Kessler; 3rd-largest U.S. cigarette mfr. (Newport, Kent).

Lowe's Cos., Inc. (LOW): 1000 Lowe's Blvd., Mooresville, NC 28117; (704) 758-1000; www.lowes.com; Robert A. Niblock; building material and home improvement superstores.

Macy's, Inc. (M): 7 W. 7th St., Cincinnati, OH 45202; (513) 579-7000; www. macysinc.com; Terry J. Lundgren; dept. stores (Macy's, Bloomingdale's).

ManpowerGroup (MAN): 100 Manpower Pl., Milwaukee, WI 53212; (414) 961-1000; www.manpowergroup.com; Jeffrey A. Joerres; employment services.

Marathon Oil Corp. (MRO): 5555 San Felipe Rd., Houston, TX 77056; (713) 629-6600; www.marathonoil.com; Clarence P. Cazalot Jr.; integrated oil co. Spun off Marathon Petroleum Corp., 7/1/2011.

Marriott International, Inc. (MAR): 10400 Fernwood Rd., Bethesda, MD 20817; (301) 380-3000; www.marriott.com; Arne M. Sorenson; hotels (Renaissance, Courtyard, Fairfield Inn, Ritz-Carlton).

Mars, Inc.: 6885 Elm St., McLean, VA 22101; (703) 821-4900; www.mars.com; Paul S. Michaels; one of the largest food mfrs. in the world, including chocolate (M&M's, Snickers, Dove), food (Uncle Ben's), pet food (Pedigree, Whiskas).

Masco Corp. (MAS): 21001 Van Born Rd., Taylor, MI 48180; (313) 274-7400; www. masco.com; Timothy Wadhams; mfr. kitchen, bathroom prods. (Delta, Peerless faucets; Merillat cabinets); paints (Behr).

Massachusetts Mutual Life Insurance Co. (MassMutual Financial Group): 1295 State St., Springfield, MA 01111; (413) 744-1000; www.massmutual.com; Roger W. Crandall; financial planning and investment, life insurance.

Mattel, Inc. (MAT): 333 Continental Blvd., El Segundo, CA 90245; (310) 252-2000; www.mattel.com; Bryan Stockton; world's largest toymaker (Barbie, Fisher-Price, Hot Wheels, Matchbox, American Girls).

McClatchy Co. (MNI): 2100 Q St., Sacramento, CA 95816; (916) 321-1855; www. mcclatchy.com; Patrick J. Talamantes; 3rd-largest U.S. newspaper publisher.

McDonald's Corp. (MCD): 2111 McDonald's Dr., Oak Brook, IL 60523; (630) 623-3000; www.mcdonalds.com; Don Thompson; world's largest fast food co.

McGraw-Hill Cos., Inc. (MHP): 1221 Ave. of the Americas, NY, NY 10020; (212) 512-2000; www.mcgraw-hill.com; Harold McGraw III; book, textbook publishing; information and financial services (Standard & Poor's). Sold broadcasting group to E.W. Scripps Co., 12/30/2011.

McKesson Corp. (MCK): 1 Post St., San Francisco, CA 94104; (415) 983-8300; www.mckesson.com; John H. Hammergren; distributor of drugs and toiletries; provides mgmt. software and services.

MeadWestvaco Corp. (MWV): 501 S. 5th St., Richmond, VA 23219; (804) 444-1000; www.meadwestvaco.com; John A. Luke Jr.; packaging, shipping containers, chemicals. Spun off consumer and office prods., 5/1/2012.

Medco Health Solutions, Inc.: see Express Scripts Holding Co.

Medtronic, Inc. (MDT): 710 Medtronic Pkwy., Minneapolis, MN 55432; (763) 514-4000; www.medtronic.com; Omar Ishrak; mfr. of implantable biomedical devices.

Merck & Co., Inc. (MRK): 1 Merck Dr., Whitehouse Station, NJ 08889; (908) 423-1000; www.merck.com; Kenneth C. Frazier; pharmaceuticals (Gardasil, Propecia, Singulair, Vytorin, Zocor); consumer health prods. (Claritin, Coppertone, Dr. Scholl's, MiraLAX).

Meredith Corp. (MDP): 1716 Locust St., Des Moines, IA 50309; (515) 284-3000; www.meredith.com; Stephen M. Lacy; magazine publishing (*Better Homes and Gardens, Ladies' Home Journal, Parents, Family Circle, Every Day With Rachael Ray, FamilyFun*), book publishing, broadcasting, online media (allrecipes.com).

Meritor, Inc. (MTOR): 2135 W. Maple Rd., Troy, MI 48084; (248) 435-1000; www. meritor.com; Ivor J. Evans; commercial vehicles systems and components. ArvinMeritor completed divestiture of its light vehicle business, 1/2011; and changed name to Meritor, 3/30/2011.

Merrill Lynch & Co., Inc.: see Bank of America Corp.

MetLife, Inc. (MET): 200 Park Ave., NY, NY 10166; (212) 578-2211; www.metlife.com; Steven A. Kandarian; insurance, financial services. Acquired American Life Insurance Co. (Alico) from American International Group, Inc. (AIG), 11/1/2010.

MGM Resorts Intl. (MGM): 3600 Las Vegas Blvd. S., Las Vegas, NV 89109; (702) 693-7120; www.mgmresorts.com; James J. Murren; hotel-casino operator (Mirage, New York-New York, Luxor, Bellagio, Circus Circus, Monte Carlo).

Microsoft Corp. (MSFT): One Microsoft Way, Redmond, WA 98052; (425) 882-8080; www.microsoft.com; William H. Gates III; world's largest consumer software maker (Windows, Word, Excel); video game consoles (Xbox). Acquired enterprise social network co. Yammer, 6/25/2012.

Miller Brewing Co.: see SABMiller plc.

Molson Coors Brewing Co. (TAP): 1225 17th St., Ste. 3200, Denver, CO 80202; (303) 927-2337; www.molsoncoors.com; Peter Swinburn; brewer (Coors, Killian's, Molson, Heineken, Miller).

Mondelēz International, Inc. (MDLZ): 3 Pkwy N., Northfield, IL 60093; (847) 646-2000; www.mondelezinternational.com; Irene B. Rosenfeld; global snack food co., including Nabisco (Oreo), Cadbury, Tang, Trident. Spun off from Kraft Foods, 10/1/2012.

Morgan Stanley (MS): 1585 Broadway, NY, NY 10036; (212) 761-4000; www.morgan stanley.com; James P. Gorman; diversified financial services.

Motorola Solutions, Inc. (MSI): 1303 E. Algonquin Rd., Schaumburg, IL 60196; (847) 576-5000; www.motorolasolutions. com; Greg Brown; electronic equipment and components; communication devices. Spun off from Motorola, Inc., 1/4/2011.

Murphy Oil Corp. (MUR): 200 Peach St., El Dorado, AR 71730; (870) 862-6411; www. murphyoilcorp.com; Steven A. Cossé; oil and gas exploration and production.

National Semiconductor Corp.: see Texas Instruments, Inc.

Nationwide Mutual Insurance Co.: One Nationwide Plz., Columbus, OH 43215; (614) 249-7111; www.nationwide.com; Stephen S. Rasmussen; property/casualty, life insurance; financial services.

Navistar Intl. Corp. (NAV): 2701 Navistar Dr., Lisle, IL 60532; (331) 332-5000; www. navistar.com; Troy Clarke; mfr. heavy-duty trucks, parts, school buses.

NBC Universal: 30 Rockefeller Plaza, NY, NY 10112; (212) 664-4444; www.nbcuni. com; Stephen B. Burke; news/entertainment producer and developer; TV and CATV stations (NBC, Bravo, USA, Telemundo); film production. Owned by Comcast and General Electric.

NCR Corp. (NCR): 3097 Satellite Blvd., Duluth, GA 30096; (937) 445-5000; www. ncr.com; William R. Nuti; mfr. ATMs, retail technology, hardware and software; computer services and supplies.

Nestlé USA, Inc.: 800 N. Brand Blvd., Glendale, CA 91203; (818) 549-6000; www. nestleusa.com; Brad Alford; candy (Baby Ruth, Raisinets), beverages (Nestea, Juicy Juice), food (Buitoni, Coffee-Mate), frozen foods (Stouffer's, Häagen-Dazs, Lean Cuisine), pet foods (Purina, Alpo, Friskies). Subsidiary of Nestlé SA in Switzerland, world's largest food co.

Netflix, Inc. (NFLX): 100 Winchester Cir., Los Gatos, CA 95032; (408) 540-3700; www.netflix.com; Reed Hastings; online DVD rentals; streaming video.

New York Life Insurance Co.: 51 Madison Ave., NY, NY 10010; (212) 576-7000; www. newyorklife.com; Theodore A. Mathas; life insurance, annuities, mutual funds.

New York Times Co. (NYT): 620 8th Ave., NY, NY 10018; (212) 556-1234; www.nytco.com; Arthur O. Sulzberger Jr.; newspapers. Announced plans to sell *Boston Globe,* 8/3/2013.

Newell Rubbermaid Inc. (NWL): 3 Glenlake Pkwy., Atlanta, GA 30328; (770) 418-7000; www.newellrubbermaid.com; Michael B. Polk; housewares (Rubbermaid, Levolor, Calphalon); hair accessories (Goody); writing utensils (Parker, Sharpie, Paper Mate); hardware and tools (Irwin, Amerock); juvenile prods. (Graco).

News Corp. (NWS): 1211 Ave. of the Americas, NY, NY 10036; (212) 852-7000; www.newscorp.com; K. Rupert Murdoch; global newspaper, magazine, book publishing (HarperCollins; Wall Street Journal;) TV and CATV stations (FOX, Fox News Channel, FX); film production; websites (hulu.com). Sold RottenTomatoes.com to Flixter, 1/4/2010; sold MySpace.com to Specific Media Inc., 6/29/2011. Announced plans to split into 2 cos., publishing and entertainment, 6/28/2012.

NIKE, Inc. (NKE): 1 Bowerman Dr., Beaverton, OR 97005; (503) 671-6453; nikeinc.com; Mark G. Parker; world's largest mfr. athletic footwear and apparel.

Nordstrom, Inc. (JWN): 1617 6th Ave., Seattle, WA 98101; (206) 628-2111; www.nordstrom.com; Blake W. Nordstrom; upscale dept. store chain.

Norfolk Southern Corp. (NSC): Three Commercial Pl., Norfolk, VA 23510; (757) 629-2600; www.nscorp.com; Charles W. Moorman; railway operator; freight carrier.

Northrop Grumman Corp. (NOC): 2980 Fairview Park Dr., Falls Church, VA 22042; (703) 280-2900; www.northropgrumman.com; Wes Bush; defense contractor: aircraft, electronics, data systems, information systems, missiles. Spun off shipbuilding sector, 3/31/2011.

Northwest Airlines Corp.: see Delta Air Lines, Inc.

Northwestern Mutual Life Insurance Co.: 720 E. Wisconsin Ave., Milwaukee, WI 53202; (414) 271-1444; www.northwesternmutual.com; John E. Schlifske; life insurance, investment products and services, annuities.

Occidental Petroleum Corp. (OXY): 10889 Wilshire Blvd., Los Angeles, CA 90024; (310) 208-8800; www.oxy.com; Stephen I. Chazen; oil, natural gas, chemicals, plastics.

Office Depot, Inc. (ODP): 6600 N. Military Trl., Boca Raton, FL 33496; (561) 438-4800; www.officedepot.com; Neil R. Austrian; office supply retail stores.

Omnicom Group Inc. (OMC): 437 Madison Ave., NY, NY 10022; (212) 415-3600; www.omnicomgroup.com; John D. Wren; advertising, marketing, interactive/digital media.

Oracle Corp. (ORCL): 500 Oracle Pkwy., Redwood City, CA 94065; (650) 506-7000; www.oracle.com; Lawrence J. Ellison; database and file management software. Acquired Sun Microsystems, 1/27/2010.

Owens Corning (OC): 1 Owens Corning Pkwy., Toledo, OH 43659; (419) 248-8000; www.owenscorning.com; Michael H. Thaman; world leader in insulation, advanced glass, composite materials.

Owens-Illinois, Inc. (OI): 1 Michael Owens Way, Perrysburg, OH 43551; (567) 336-5000; Albert P. L. Stroucken; www.o-i.com; mfr. glass containers.

Payless Holdings, Inc. (formerly Collective Brands, Inc.) (PSS): 3231 SE 6th Ave., Topeka, KS 66607; (785) 233-5171; www.collectivebrands.com; W. Paul Jones; shoe mfr./retailer, Collective Brands, Inc. acquired by Blum Capital and Golden Gate Capital and renamed Payless Holdings. Collective Brands' Performance Group (Sperry Top-Sider, Stride Rite, Saucony, Keds) acquired by Wolverine Worldwide, 10/9/2012.

PepsiCo, Inc. (PEP): 700 Anderson Hill Rd., Purchase, NY 10577; (914) 253-2000; www.pepsico.com; Indra K. Nooyi; soft drinks and other beverages (Pepsi-Cola, Mountain Dew, Gatorade, Tropicana), snacks and cereals (Fritos, Lay's, Ruffles, Quaker). Acquired Pepsi Bottling Group and Pepsi Americas, 3/1/2010, making it largest food and beverage co. in North America.

Pfizer, Inc. (PFE): 235 E. 42nd St., NY, NY 10017; (212) 733-2323; www.pfizer.com; Ian Read; biopharmaceuticals (Celebrex, Lipitor, Viagra, Zoloft); human and animal health care prods.

PG&E Corp. (PCG): One Market, Spear Tower, Ste. 2400, San Francisco, CA 94105; (415) 973-1000; www.pgecorp.com; Anthony F. Earley Jr.; operates Pacific Gas and Electric public utility.

Philip Morris Intl. Inc. (PM): 120 Park Ave., NY, NY 10017; (917) 663-2000; www.pmi.com; André Calantzopoulos; mfr. and distributor of tobacco.

Phillips 66 Co. (PSX): P.O. Box 4428, Houston, TX 77210; (281) 293-6600; www.phillips66.com; Greg C. Garland; oil, gas co. Formed when refining and marketing segment of ConocoPhillips was spun off, 5/1/2012.

Pitney Bowes Inc. (PBI): 1 Elmcroft Rd., Stamford, CT 06926; (203) 356-5000; www.pb.com; Marc B. Lautenbach; postage meters and mailing equip.

Plains All American Pipeline, L.P. (PAA): 333 Clay St., Ste. 1600, Houston, TX 77002; (713) 646-4100; www.paalp.com; Greg L. Armstrong; oil and natural gas transportation, storage.

Post Holdings, Inc. (POST): 2503 S. Hanley Rd., St. Louis, MO 63144; (314) 644-7600; www.postfoods.com; William Stiritz; ready-to-eat cereals. Spun off from Ralcorp Holdings, 2/6/2012.

PPG Industries, Inc. (PPG): 1 PPG Pl., Pittsburgh, PA 15272; (412) 434-3131; www.ppg.com; Charles E. Bunch; glass prods., silicas, fiberglass, chemicals, sealants; world's leading supplier of automobile/industrial coatings. Spun off chemical commodities co. Axiall to Georgia Gulf Corp., 6/28/2013.

Procter & Gamble Co. (PG): 1 Procter & Gamble Plz., Cincinnati, OH 45202; (513) 983-1100; www.pg.com; Alan G. Lafley; soaps and detergents (Ivory, Cheer, Tide, Mr. Clean); toiletries (Crest, Scope, Head & Shoulders, Old Spice); pharmaceuticals (Pepto-Bismol, Vicks cough medicines); paper prods. (Charmin toilet tissues, Bounty towels, Tampax tampons; disposable diapers (Pampers, Luvs); CoverGirl and Max Factor cosmetics, Clairol hair care; Gillette razors; sold Pringles to Kellogg, 6/1/2012.

Prudential Financial, Inc. (PRU): 751 Broad St., Newark, NJ 07102; (973) 802-6000; www.prudential.com; John R. Strangfeld Jr.; insurance, financial services.

Publix Super Markets Inc.: 3300 Publix Corporate Pkwy., Lakeland, FL 33811; (863) 688-1188; www.publix.com; William Crenshaw; supermarket chain.

PVH Corp. (PVH): 200 Madison Ave., NY, NY 10016; (212) 381-3500; www.pvh.com; Emanuel Chirico; mfr. of apparel, including licensed brands (Calvin Klein, IZOD, Geoffrey Beene, Kenneth Cole, Tommy Hilfiger, Sean John).

Quest Diagnostics Inc. (DGX): 3 Giralda Farms, Madison, NJ 07940; (800) 222-0446; www.questdiagnostics.com; Stephen H. Rusckowski; leading clinical laboratory.

RadioShack Corp. (RSH): 300 RadioShack Cir., Fort Worth, TX 76102; (817) 415-3011; www.radioshack.com; Joseph C. Magnacca; consumer electronics retailer.

Ralcorp Holdings, Inc.: see ConAgra Foods, Inc.

Ralph Lauren Corp. (RL): 650 Madison Ave., NY, NY 10022; (212) 318-7000; www.ralphlauren.com; Ralph Lauren; men's and women's apparel, home furnishings, fragrances.

Raytheon Co. (RTN): 870 Winter St., Waltham, MA 02451; (781) 522-3000; www.raytheon.com; William Swanson; defense, communications systems.

Reader's Digest Assn., Inc.: 750 Third Ave., NY, NY 10017; (914) 238-1000; www.rda.com; Robert E. Guth; magazine publisher; marketer of books, music, video prods.

Emerged from Chap. 11 reorganization, 2/22/2010; filed for Chap. 11 reorganization, 2/17/2013.

Republic Services, Inc. (RSG): 18500 N. Allied Way, Phoenix, AZ 85054; (480) 627-2700; www.republicservices.com; Donald W. Slager; waste management co.

Revlon, Inc. (REV): 237 Park Ave., NY, NY 10017; (212) 527-4000; www.revlon.com; Alan T. Ennis; cosmetics, skin care.

Reynolds American Inc. (RAI): 401 N. Main St., Winston-Salem, NC 27101; (336) 741-2000; www.reynoldsamerican.com; Daniel M. Delen; 2nd-largest U.S. producer of cigarettes (Winston, Camel, Pall Mall, Kool, Doral).

Rite Aid Corp. (RAD): 30 Hunter Ln., Camp Hill, PA 17011; (717) 761-2633; www.riteaid.com; John T. Standley; 3rd-largest U.S. drugstore chain.

Rock-Tenn Co. (RKT): 504 Thrasher St., Norcross, GA 30071; (770) 448-2193; www.rocktenn.com; James A. Rubright; corrugated and consumer packaging. Acquired Smurfit-Stone Container Corp., 5/27/2011.

Rockwell Automation, Inc. (ROK): 1201 S. 2nd St., Milwaukee, WI 53204; (414) 382-2000; www.rockwellautomation.com; Keith D. Nosbusch; industrial automation co.

Rohm and Haas Co.: see Dow Chemical Co.

Ryder System, Inc. (R): 11690 NW 105th St., Miami, FL 33178; (305) 500-3726; www.ryder.com; Robert E. Sanchez; truck-leasing service.

SABMiller plc: 1 Stanhope Gate, London, W1K 1AF, United Kingdom; + 44 1483 264000; www.sabmiller.com; Alan Clark; brewing company (Miller, Peroni, Grolsch). Acquired Foster's Group Ltd., 12/16/2011.

Safeway Inc. (SWY): 5918 Stoneridge Mall Rd., Pleasanton, CA 94588; (925) 467-3000; www.safeway.com; Robert Edwards; supermarkets.

Sara Lee Corp.: see Hillshire Brands Co.

Schering-Plough Corp.: see Merck & Co., Inc.

Sears Holdings Corp. (SHLD): 3333 Beverly Rd., Hoffman Estates, IL 60179; (847) 286-2500; www.searsholdings.com; Edward S. Lampert; U.S. retailer.

Shell Oil Co.: 910 Louisiana St., Houston, TX 77002; (713) 241-6161; www.shell.us; Peter Voser; integrated oil co.; subsidiary of Royal Dutch Shell, world's 2nd-largest oil co.

Sherwin-Williams Co. (SHW): 101 W. Prospect Ave., Cleveland, OH 44115; (216) 566-2000; www.sherwin-williams.com; Christopher M. Connor; paint and varnish producer (Dutch Boy, Krylon, Minwax).

Smithfield Foods, Inc. (SFD): 200 Commerce St., Smithfield, VA 23430; (757) 365-3000; www.smithfieldfoods.com; C. Larry Pope; world's largest producer and processor of pork.

J. M. Smucker Co. (SJM): One Strawberry Ln., Orrville, OH 44667; (330) 682-3000; www.smuckers.com; Timothy P. Smucker; leading producer of fruit spreads, peanut butter (Jif), oils (Crisco), coffee (Folgers).

Smurfit-Stone Container Corp.: see Rock-Tenn Co.

Sony Corp. of America: 550 Madison Ave., NY, NY 10022; (212) 833-6800; www.sony.com; Michael Lynton; U.S. subsidiary of Japan-based Sony Corp.; electronics, movies, music.

Southwest Airlines Co. (LUV): 2702 Love Field Dr., Dallas, TX 75235; (214) 792-4000; www.southwest.com; Gary C. Kelly; air transportation. Acquired AirTran Holdings, Inc., 5/2/2011.

Sprint Nextel Corp. (S): 6200 Sprint Pkwy., Overland Park, KS 66251; (703) 433-4000; www.sprint.com; Dan Hesse; wireless and long-distance telecommunications. Sold 72 percent of co. shares to SoftBank Corp, 7/5/2013.

Stanley Black & Decker, Inc. (SWK): 1000 Stanley Dr., New Britain, CT 06053; (860) 225-5111; www.stanleyblackanddecker.com; John F. Lundgren; one of the top U.S. mfrs. of hand and power tools (DeWalt, Bostitch), household prods. (Kwikset, Baldwin). The Stanley Works and Black & Decker merged, 3/12/2010.

Staples, Inc. (SPLS): 500 Staples Dr., Framingham, MA 01702; (508) 253-5000; www.staples.com; Ronald L. Sargent; largest U.S. office-supply retailer.

Starbucks Corp. (SBUX): 2401 Utah Ave. S., Seattle, WA 98134; (206) 447-1575; www.starbucks.com; Howard D. Schultz; coffee producer; world's leading specialty coffee retailer.

Starwood Hotels & Resorts Worldwide, Inc. (HOT): 1 StarPoint, Stamford, CT 06902; (203) 964-6000; www.starwood hotels.com; Frits van Paasschen; hotel and resort co. (Westin, Sheraton, W Hotels).

State Farm Mutual Automobile Ins. Co.: 1 State Farm Plz., Bloomington, IL 61710; (309) 766-2311; www.statefarm.com; Edward B. Rust Jr.; largest U.S. provider of auto/homeowners insurance.

Sun Microsystems, Inc.: see Oracle Corp.

Sunoco, Inc. (SUN): 1735 Market St., Ste. LL, Philadelphia, PA 19103; (215) 977-3000; www.sunocoinc.com; Brian P. MacDonald; energy resources co., gasoline retailer.

SUPERVALU Inc. (SVU): East View Innovation Ctr., 7075 Flying Cloud Dr., Eden Prairie, MN 55344; (952) 828-4000; www. supervalu.com; Sam Duncan; food retailer, wholesale distrib. (Acme, Albertsons, Shoppers).

SYSCO Corp. (SYY): 1390 Enclave Pkwy., Houston, TX 77077; (281) 584-1390; www. sysco.com; William J. DeLaney; world's largest food-service distributor.

Systemax Inc. (SYX): 11 Harbor Park Dr., Port Washington, NY 11050; (516) 608-7000; www.systemax.com; Richard Leeds; computers, electronics, industrial prod. retailer.

Target Corp. (TGT): 1000 Nicollet Mall, Minneapolis, MN 55403; (612) 304-6073; www.target.com; Gregg W. Steinhafel; 2nd-largest U.S. discount retailer.

Tenneco Inc. (TEN): 500 N. Field Dr., Lake Forest, IL 60045; (847) 482-5000; www. tenneco.com; Gregg M. Sherrill; automotive parts (Monroe, Walker).

Texas Instruments Inc. (TXN): 12500 TI Blvd., Dallas, TX 75266; (972) 995-2011; www.ti.com; Richard K. Templeton; processors, semiconductors, software, handheld calculators. Acquired Natl. Semiconductor Corp., 9/23/2011.

Textron Inc. (TXT): 40 Westminster St., Providence, RI 02903; (401) 421-2800; www.textron.com; Scott C. Donnelly; aircraft (Cessna, Bell), industrial, automotive prods.; financial services.

3M Co. (MMM): 3M Center, St. Paul, MN 55144; (651) 733-1110; www.3m.com; Inge G. Thulin; abrasives, adhesives, electrical, health care, cleaning (Scotch-Brite, O-Cel-O sponges, Scotchgard), printing, consumer prods. (Scotch Tape, Post-it).

TIAA-CREF: 730 Third Ave., NY, NY 10017; (212) 490-9000; www.tiaa-cref.org; Roger W. Ferguson Jr.; financial services provider.

Time Warner Inc. (TWX): One Time Warner Ctr., NY, NY 10019; (212) 484-8000; www. timewarner.com; Jeffrey L. Bewkes; magazine publishing (*Time, Sports Illustrated, Fortune, Money, People,* DC Comics), TV and CATV (Cartoon Network, HBO, CNN, TBS, TNT), motion pictures (Warner Bros.), recordings. AOL and Time Warner completed the largest corporate merger in history in 2001; Time Warner spun off AOL, 12/9/2009. Announced plans to spin off magazine holdings as Time Inc., 3/6/2013.

TJX Cos., Inc. (TJX): 770 Cochituate Rd., Framingham, MA 01701; (508) 390-1000; www.tjx.com; Carol Meyrowitz; world's largest off-price apparel retailer (T.J. Maxx, Marshalls); home furnishing retailer (HomeGoods).

Toro Co. (TTC): 8111 Lyndale Ave. S, Bloomington, MN 55420; (952) 888-8801; www.thetorocompany.com; Michael J. Hoffman; lawn and turf maintenance prods. (Lawn-Boy), snow removal equip.; irrigation systems.

Toys "R" Us, Inc.: 1 Geoffrey Way, Wayne, NJ 07470; (973) 617-3500; www.toysrus.com; Antonio Urcelay; children's specialty retailer.

Tribune Co.: 435 N. Michigan Ave., Chicago, IL 60611; (312) 222-9100; www.tribune. com; Peter Liguori; newspapers (*Los Angeles Times, Chicago Tribune*), broadcasting (incl. WGN and 23 other television and radio stations). Emerged from Chap. 11 reorganization, 12/31/2012.

Trinity Industries, Inc. (TRN): 2525 Stemmons Fwy., Dallas, TX 75207; (214) 631-4420; www.trin.net; Timothy R. Wallace; mfr. metal prods., rail and freight equip.

Tyco Intl. Ltd. (TYC): 9 Roszel Rd., Princeton, NJ 08540; (609) 720-4200; www. tyco.com; George R. Oliver; security and engineered prods. Spun off ADT Corp. and Pentair Ltd., 9/28/2012. Announced plans to acquire Exacq Technologies, 6/19/2013.

Tyson Foods, Inc. (TSN): 2200 W. Don Tyson Pkwy., Springdale, AR 72762; (479) 290-4000 www.tysonfoods.com; Donnie Smith; fresh and processed poultry; beef and pork prods.

UBS Financial Services Inc.: 1285 Ave. of the Americas, NY, NY 10019; (212) 713-2000; www.ubs.com; Sergio P. Ermotti; financial services; subsidiary of Switzerland's UBS AG.

Unilever USA (UN/UL): 800 Sylvan Ave., Englewood Cliffs, NJ 07632; (201) 894-4000; www.unilever.com; Paul Polman; food (Hellmann's mayonnaise, Knorr soups, Wish-Bone salad dressing, Lipton, Skippy peanut butter, Slim-Fast), hygiene prods. (Dove, Q-tips, Vaseline). Subsidiary of Unilever NV (Neth.) and Unilever plc (UK). Acquired Alberto Culver, 5/10/2011.

Union Pacific Corp. (UNP): 1400 Douglas St., Omaha, NE, 68179; (402) 544-5000; www.up.com; James R. Young; one of the largest railroad freight cos. in U.S.

Unisys Corp. (UIS): 801 Lakeview Dr., Ste. 100, Blue Bell, PA 19422; (215) 986-4011; www.unisys.com; J. Edward Coleman; designs, manuf. computer information systems; IT consulting.

United Continental Holdings, Inc. (UAL): 77 W. Wacker Dr., Chicago IL 60601; (312) 997-8000; www.unitedcontinentalholdings. com; Jeffery A. Smisek; air transportation (United Airlines, Continental Airlines); formed by merger of United Airlines and Continental Airlines, 10/1/2010.

United Parcel Service, Inc. (UPS): 55 Glenlake Pkwy. NE, Atlanta, GA 30328; (404) 828-6000; www.ups.com; D. Scott Davis; world's largest package delivery co.

United States Steel Corp. (X): 600 Grant St., Pittsburgh, PA 15219; (412) 433-1121; www.ussteel.com; John P. Surma Jr.; steel, tin prods., resource mgmt.

United Technologies Corp. (UTX): One Financial Plz., Hartford, CT 06103; (860) 728-7000; www.utc.com; Louis R. Chênevert; aerospace, industrial prods. and services (Carrier, Otis, Pratt & Whitney, Sikorsky).

UnitedHealth Group Inc. (UNH): UHG Center, 9900 Bren Rd. E., Minnetonka, MN 55343; (952) 936-1300; www.unitedhealth group.com; Stephen J. Hemsley; health insurer.

US Airways Group, Inc. (LCC): 111 W. Rio Salado Pkwy., Tempe, AZ 85281; (480) 693-0800; www.usairways.com; William Douglas Parker; air transportation. Shareholders approved merger with American Airlines, 7/15/2013.

Valero Energy Corp. (VLO): One Valero Way, San Antonio, TX 78249; (210) 345-2000; www.valero.com; Bill Klesse; fuel mfg. and marketing. Spun off CST Brands, 5/1/2013.

Verizon Communications Inc. (VZ): 140 West St., NY, NY 10007; (212) 395-1000; www.verizon.com; Lowell C. McAdam; broadband, wireless, wireline services provider.

VF Corp. (VFC): 105 Corporate Center Blvd., Greensboro, NC 27408; (336) 424-6000; www.vfc.com; Eric C. Wiseman; apparel (Lee, Wrangler, North Face, Timberland). Acquired Timberland 9/13/2011.

Viacom Inc. (VIA): 1515 Broadway, NY, NY 10036; (212) 258-6000; www.viacom.com; Philippe P. Dauman; media networks (BET, Comedy Central, MTV, VH1, Nickelodeon); movies (Paramount).

Visteon Corp. (VC): One Village Center Dr., Van Buren Twp., MI 48111; (734) 710-5000; www.visteon.com; Timothy D. Leuliette; automotive parts mfr. Emerged from Chap. 11 reorganization, 10/1/2010.

Walgreen Co. (Walgreens) (WAG): 200 Wilmot Rd., Deerfield, IL 60015; (847) 940-2500; www.walgreens.com; Gregory D. Wasson; retail drugstores. Formed joint venture co. with global pharm. group Alliance Boots, 10/1/2012.

Wal-Mart Stores, Inc. (WMT): 702 SW 8th St., Bentonville, AR 72716; (479) 273-4000; www.walmartstores.com; Michael T. Duke; world's largest retailer; discount stores, membership warehouse clubs (Sam's Club).

Washington Post Co. (WPO): 1150 15th St. NW, Washington, DC 20071; (202) 334-6000; www.washpostco.com; Donald E. Graham; media (newspapers, Slate. com, TV) and education (Kaplan). Sold *Newsweek,* 9/30/2010. Announced sale of *Washington Post* newspaper, 8/5/2013.

Waste Management, Inc. (WM): 1001 Fannin St., Ste. 4000, Houston, TX 77002; (713) 512-6200; www.wm.com; David P. Steiner; North America's largest waste co., recycler.

WellPoint, Inc. (WLP): 120 Monument Cir., Indianapolis, IN 46204; (317) 488-6000; www.wellpoint.com; Joseph R. Swedish; U.S. health benefits co.; HMOs and PPOs, an independent licensee of the Blue Cross Blue Shield Assn.

Wells Fargo & Co. (WFC): 420 Montgomery St., San Francisco, CA 94163; (866) 249-3302; www.wellsfargo.com; John G. Stumpf; financial services.

Wendy's Co. (WEN): 1 Dave Thomas Blvd., Dublin, OH 43017; (614) 764-3100; www. aboutwendys.com; Emil J. Brolick; one of the largest fast food restaurant companies in the U.S. Sold Arby's Restaurant Group, Inc., 7/4/2011.

Western Union Co. (WU): 12500 E. Belford Ave., Englewood, CO 80112; (720) 332-1000; www.westernunion.com; Hikmet Ersek; money transfers, payment services.

Weyerhaeuser Co. (WY): 33663 Weyerhaeuser Way S., Federal Way, WA 98001; (253) 924-2345; www. weyerhaeuser.com; Daniel S. Fulton; produces, distributes wood prods.; real estate development.

Whirlpool Corp. (WHR): 2000 N. M-63, Benton Harbor, MI 49022; (269) 923-5000; www.whirlpoolcorp.com; Jeff M. Fettig; mfr. of major home appliances (KitchenAid, Amana, Maytag).

Whole Foods Market, Inc. (WFM): 550 Bowie St., Austin, TX 78703; (512) 477-4455; www.wholefoodsmarket.com; John P. Mackey/Walter Robb; largest U.S. retailer of natural and organic foods.

Winn-Dixie Stores, Inc.: 5050 Edgewood Ct., Jacksonville, FL 32254; (904) 783-5000; www.winndixie.com; R. Randall Onstead; one of the largest food retailers in U.S. Acquired by BI-LO Holding, 3/12/2012.

Winnebago Industries, Inc. (WGO): 605 W. Crystal Lake Rd., Forest City, IA 50436; (641) 585-3535; www.winnebagoind.com; Randy J. Potts; mfr. of motor homes, or recreational vehicles (RVs).

Wm. Wrigley Jr. Co. see Mars, Inc.

World Fuel Services Corp. (INT): 9800 NW 41st St., Ste. 400, Miami, FL 33178; www. wfscorp.com; Paul H. Stebbins; marketer and financer of fuel to large-scale aviation and marine-related firms.

Xerox Corp. (XRX): 45 Glover Ave., P.O. Box 4505, Norwalk, CT 06856; (203) 968-3000; www.xerox.com; Ursula M. Burns; printers, multifunction devices, document publishing technology and support.

Yahoo! Inc. (YHOO): 701 First Ave., Sunnyvale, CA 94089; (408) 349-3300; www. yahoo.com; Marissa Mayer; Internet media company.

Yum! Brands, Inc. (YUM): 1441 Gardiner Ln., Louisville, KY 40213; (502) 874-8300; www.yum.com; David C. Novak; fast food restaurants (Pizza Hut, KFC, Taco Bell). Sold Long John Silver's, 12/5/2011; sold A&W, 12/19/2011.

Labor Unions and Professional Organizations

Source: Bureau of Labor Statistics, U.S. Dept. of Labor; AFL-CIO; World Almanac research

= Member of Change to Win Federation, formed in 2005 by unions disaffiliated from AFL-CIO. * = Independent union or one not otherwise affiliated with Change to Win or AFL-CIO. All other groups listed here are affiliated with AFL-CIO as of 2013. Year established is in parenthesis.

Labor Unions

Air Line Pilots Assn. (ALPA) (1931): nearly 50,000+ members, 33 U.S. and Canadian airlines; (703) 689-2270; www.alpa.org

American Federation of Labor and Congress of Industrial Organizations (AFL-CIO) (1955): federation of 57 unions, 11.5 mil+ members; (202) 637-5000; www.aflcio.org

Automobile, Aerospace & Agricultural Implement Workers of America, International Union, United (UAW) (1935): 382,500 members, 750 locals; (313) 926-5000; www.uaw.org

Bakery, Confectionery, Tobacco Workers, and Grain Millers International Union (BCTGM) (1886): 80,000+ members; (301) 933-8600; www.bctgm.org

Bricklayers and Allied Craftworkers, International Union of (BAC) (1865): 100,000 members, 50 locals; (202) 783-3788; www.bacweb.org

***Carpenters and Joiners of America, United Brotherhood of** (UBC) (1881): 500,000 members, 600+ locals; (202) 546-6206; www.carpenters.org

#Change to Win Federation (2005): 4 unions, ex-affiliates of AFL-CIO, 4.2 mil+ members; (202) 721-0660; www.changetowin.org

Communications Workers of America (CWA) (1938): 467,000+ members, 1,200 locals; (202) 434-1100; www.cwa-union.org

***Education Assn., National** (NEA) (1857): 3 mil+ members, 14,000+ affiliates; (202) 833-4000; www.nea.org

Electrical Workers, International Brotherhood of (IBEW) (1891): 660,000+ members, 900+ locals; (202) 833-7000; www.ibew.org

Engineers, International Union of Operating (IUOE) (1896): 380,000+ members, 123 locals; (202) 429-9100; www.iuoe.org

#Farm Workers of America, United (UFW) (1962): 15,000+ members; (661) 823-6151; www.ufw.org

***Federal Employees, National Federation of** (NFFE; affiliated with IAMAW) (1917): 110,000 members, nearly 200 locals; (202) 216-4420; www.nffe.org

Fire Fighters, International Assn. of (IAFF) (1918): nearly 294,000 members, 3,200+ locals; (202) 737-8484; www.iaff.org

Flight Attendants, Assn. of (AFA-CWA) (1945): nearly 39,000 members, 20 airlines; merged with Communications Workers of America in 2004; (202) 434-1300; www.afanet.org

#Food and Commercial Workers International Union (UFCW) (1979): 1.3 mil members, 400+ locals; (202) 223-3111; www.ufcw.org

Glass, Molders, Pottery, Plastics and Allied Workers Intl. Union (GMP) (1842): 28,000 members, 250+ locals; (610) 565-5051; www.gmpiu.org

Government Employees, American Federation of (AFGE) (1932): nearly 300,000 members; 1,100 locals; (202) 737-8700; www.afge.org

#Graphic Communications Conference (GCC/IBT) (1983): 73,000 members; merged with Teamsters in 2005; (202) 462-1400; www.gciu.org

Iron Workers, Intl. Assn. of Bridge, Structural, Ornamental, and Reinforcing (1896): 120,000 members, 200+ locals; (202) 383-4800; www.ironworkers.org

Laborers' International Union of North America (LiUNA) (1903): 571,000 members, 500+ locals; (202) 737-8320; www.liuna.org

Letter Carriers, National Assn. of (NALC) (1889): nearly 270,000 members, 2,500 locals; (202) 393-4695; www.nalc.org

#Locomotive Engineers and Trainmen, Brotherhood of (BLET) (1863): 54,800+ members; (216) 241-2630; www.ble-t.org

Longshoremen's Assn., Intl. (ILA) (1892): 43,500 members, approx. 200 locals; (212) 425-1200; www.ilaunion.org

Machinists and Aerospace Workers, International Assn. of (IAM) (1888): 577,000 members; affiliated with TCU in 2005; (301) 967-4500; www.goiam.org

#Maintenance of Way Employes, Division of the Intl. Brotherhood of Teamsters; Brotherhood of (BMWED) (1887): 35,700 members, 710 locals; merged with Teamsters in 2004; (248) 662-2660; www.bmwed.org (Note: In honor of tradition, the union maintains the variant spelling of "employes" in its logo.)

Mine Workers of America, United (UMWA) (1890): nearly 74,600 members, 600 locals; (703) 291-2400; www.umwa.org

Musicians of the United States and Canada, American Federation of (AFM) (1896): 80,000 members, 240+ locals; (212) 869-1330; www.afm.org

Newspaper Guild—Communications Workers of America, The (TNG) (CWA) (1933): 34,000+ members, 90 locals; (202) 434-7177; www.newsguild.org

***Nurses Assn., American** (ANA) (1911): 146,000 members, 54 constituent state and territorial assns.; (301) 628-5000; www.nursingworld.org

Office and Professional Employees Intl. Union (OPEIU) (1945): 87,000 members, 200 locals; (800) 346-7348; www.opeiu.org

Painters and Allied Trades, International Union of (IUPAT) (1887): 160,000+ members, 425 locals; (410) 564-5900; www.iupat.org

Plumbing and Pipe Fitting Industry of the U.S. and Canada, United Assn. of Journeymen and Apprentices of the (UA) (1889): 340,000 members, 300+ locals; (410) 269-2000; www.ua.org

***Police, Fraternal Order of** (1915): 325,000+ members, 2,100+ affiliates; (615) 399-0900; www.grandlodgefop.org

Police Assns., International Union of (IUPA) (1979): 80,000 members; (941) 487-2560; www.iupa.org

Postal Workers Union, American (APWU) (1971): 246,000+ members, 1,000+ locals; (202) 842-4200; www.apwu.org

Roofers, Waterproofers and Allied Workers, United Union of (1906): 22,000 members; (202) 463-7663; www.unionroofers.com

***Rural Letter Carriers' Assn., National** (1903): 100,000+ members; 50 state org; (703) 684-5545; www.nrlca.org

***Security, Police, Fire Professionals of America, Intl. Union,** (SPFPA) (1948): 24,500+ members, 200 locals; (586) 772-7250; www.spfpa.org

#Service Employees International Union (SEIU) (1921): 1.9 mil members, 150+ locals; (202) 730-7000; www.seiu.org

Sheet Metal Workers' International Assn. (SMWIA) (1888): 134,000 members, 185 locals; (202) 783-5880; www.smwia.org

State, County, and Municipal Employees, American Federation of (AFSCME) (1932): 1.4 mil members, 3,400 locals; (202) 429-1000; www.afscme.org

Steel, Paper and Forestry, Rubber, Manufacturing, Energy, Allied Industrial and Service Workers International Union, United (USW) (2005): 614,000 members, 1,800+ locals; formed from merger of the various United Steelworkers of America (USWA) (1936) and Paper, Allied-Industrial, Chemical and Energy Workers (PACE) (1999); (412) 562-2400; www.usw.org

Teachers, American Federation of (AFT) (1916): 848,000 members, 3,000+ locals; (202) 879-4400; www.aft.org

#Teamsters, International Brotherhood of (IBT) (1903): 1.3 mil. members, 440 locals; (202) 624-6800; www.teamster.org

Theatrical Stage Employees, Moving Picture Technicians, Artists and Allied Crafts of the U.S., Its Territories, and Canada, Intl. Alliance of (IATSE) (1893): 114,542 members, 555+ locals; (212) 730-1770; www.iatse-intl.org

Transit Union, Amalgamated (ATU) (1892): 190,000+ members, 270 locals; (202) 537-1645; www.atu.org

Transport Workers Union of America (TWU) (1934): nearly 116,000 members, 114 locals; (212) 719-3900; www.twu.org

Transportation Communications Intl. Union (TCU) (1899): affiliated with IAM in 2005; see Machinists and Aerospace Workers.

Transportation Union, United (UTU) (1969): 70,600+ members, 500+ locals; (216) 228-9400; www.utu.org

***Treasury Employees Union, National** (NTEU) (1938): 82,500+ members, 270+ chapters; (202) 572-5500; www.nteu.org

UNITE HERE (UNITE, 1900; HERE, 1891; merged 2004): 251,000+ members; (212) 265-7000; www.unitehere.org

#Workers United (affiliated with SEIU) (2009): 83,796 members

***Writers Guild of America, West** (1933): 12,000+ members; (323) 951-4000; www.wga.org

Professional Organizations and Societies

Accountants, American Institute of Certified Public (1887): nearly 386,000 members; (888) 777-7077; www.aicpa.org

ACMP—The Chamber Music Network (1947): over 6,000 members; (212) 645-7424; www.acmp.net

Actuaries, Soc. of (1949): 22,000 members; (847) 706-3500; www.soa.org

Administrative Professionals, Intl. Assn. of (1942): 22,000 members; (816) 891-6600; www.iaap-hq.org

Aerospace Medical Assn. (1929): 2,600+ members; (703) 739-2240; www.asma.org

Agricultural and Biological Engineers, American Soc. of (1907): 8,000 members; (269) 429-0300; www.asabe.org

AIGA (formerly American Institute of Graphic Arts) (1914): 23,000+ members; (212) 807-1990; www.aiga.org

Air & Waste Management Assn. (1907): 5,000+ members; (412) 232-3444; www.awma.org

AMSUS—The Society of the Federal Health Professionals (1891): nearly 8,000 members; (301) 897-8800; www.amsus.org

APICS—The Assn. for Operations Management (1957): 43,000+ members; (773) 867-1777; www.apics.org

Architects, American Institute of (1857): nearly 80,000 members; (202) 626-7300; www.aia.org

ASIS Intl. (formerly Amer. Soc. for Industrial Security) (1955): 38,000+ members; (703) 519-6200; www.asisonline.org

Astrologers, Inc., American Federation of (1938): 4,000 members; (480) 838-1751; www.astrologers.com

Astronautical Society, American (1954): 1,400 members; (703) 866-0020; www.astronautical.org

Astronomical Society, American (1899): 7,000 members; (202) 328-2010 www.aas.org

Authors Guild, The (1912): 9,000+ members; (212) 563-5904; www.authorsguild.org

Bankers of America, Independent Community (1930): nearly 5,000 members; (202) 659-8111; www.icba.org

Bar Assn., American (1878): nearly 400,000 members; (312) 988-5000; www.abanet.org

Bar Assn., Federal (1920): 15,000+ members; (571) 481-9100; www.fedbar.org

Biochemistry and Molecular Biology, American Society for (1906): 12,000+ members; (240) 283-6600; www.asbmb.org

Broadcasters, Natl. Assn. of (1923): 8,300 members; (202) 429-5300; www.nab.org

Business Women's Assn., American (1949): 40,000 members; (800) 228-0007; www.abwa.org

Cartoonists Society, Natl. (1946): 500+ members; (407) 647-8839; www.reuben.org

Ceramic Society, American (1898): 9,500+ members; (240) 646-7054; www.ceramics.org

Chemical Society, American (1876): 164,000+ members; (202) 872-4600; www.chemistry.org

Chiefs of Police, Intl. Assn. of (1893): 20,000+ members; (703) 836-6767; www.theiacp.org

Chiropractic Assn., American (1963): 15,000 members; (703) 276-8800; www.acatoday.org

Civil Engineers, American Soc. of (1852): 140,000+ members; (703) 295-6300; www.asce.org

College Admission Counseling, Natl. Assn. for (1937): nearly 13,000 members; (703) 836-2222; www.nacacnet.org

Commercial Law League of America (1895): 3,000+ members; (312) 240-1400; www.clla.org

Communication Assn., Natl. (1914): 8,000+ members; (202) 464-4622; www.natcom.org

Composers, Authors & Publishers, American Soc. of (ASCAP) (1914): 460,000+ members; (212) 621-6000; www.ascap.com

Computing Machinery, Assn. for (1947): 100,000+ members; (212) 626-0500; www.acm.org

Computing Professionals, Institute for Certification of (1973): nearly 55,000 members; (847) 299-4227; www.iccp.org

Construction Inspectors, Assn. of (1974): 1,000 members; (760) 327-5284; www.aci-assoc.org

Counseling Assn., American (1952): 50,000+ members; (800) 347-6647; www.counseling.org

Country Music Assn. (1958): 13,000+ members; (615) 244-2840; www.cmaworld.com

Customs Brokers and Forwarders Assn. of America, Inc., Natl. (1897): nearly 940 cos.; (202) 466-0222; www.ncbfaa.org

Dental Assn., American (1859): 157,000+ members; (312) 440-2500; www.ada.org

Directors Guild of America (1936): 15,000+ members; (310) 289-2000; www.dga.org

Electrical and Electronics Engineers, Institute of (1963): 425,000 members; (732) 981-0060; www.ieee.org

Electronics Technicians, Intl. Soc. of Certified (1980): 50,000+ members; (817) 921-9101; www.iscet.org

Energy Engineers, Assn. of (1977): 16,000+ members; (770) 447-5083; www.aeecenter.org

Engineers, Natl. Society of Professional (1934): 35,000 members; (703) 684-2800; www.nspe.org

Environmental Assessment Association (1972): 3,500 members; (760) 327-5284; www.eaa-assoc.org

Environmental Health Assn., Natl. (1937): 4,500+ members; (303) 756-9090; www.neha.org

Family Physicians, American Academy of (1947): 110,600+; (913) 906-6000; www.aafp.org

Farm Bureau Federation, American (1919): 6.2 mil+ members; (202) 406-3600; www.fb.org

Farmers Union, Natl. (1902): 250,000 families; (202) 554-1600; www.nfu.org

Financial Professionals, Assn. for (1979): 16,000+ members; (301) 907-2862; www.AFPonline.org

Financial Service Professionals, Soc. of (1928): 15,000 members; (610) 526-2500; www.financialpro.org

Fire Chiefs, Intl. Assn. of (1873): 10,000+ members; (703) 273-0911; www.iafc.org

Fire Protection Engineers, Soc. of (1950): 4,500+ members; (301) 718-2910; www.sfpe.org

Food Technologists, Institute of (1939): 22,000 members; (312) 782-8424; www.ift.org

Forensic Sciences, American Academy of (1948): 6,260 members; (719) 636-1100; www.aafs.org

Funeral Directors Assn., Natl. (1882): 19,000 members; (262) 789-1880; www.nfda.org

General Contractors of America, Associated (1918): nearly 30,000 cos.; (703) 548-3118; www.agc.org

Geographers, Assn. of American (1904): 10,000 members; (202) 234-1450; www.aag.org

Ground Water Assn., Natl. (1948): 12,000+ members; (614) 898-7791; www.ngwa.org

Heating, Refrigerating and Air-Conditioning Engineers, Inc., American Soc. of (1894): 54,000+ members; (404) 636-8400; www.ashrae.org

Home Builders, Natl. Assn. of (1942): 140,000+ members; (202) 266-8200; www.nahb.org

Human Resource Management, Soc. for (SHRM) (1948): 250,000+ members; (703) 548-3440; www.shrm.org

Illustrators, Society of (1901): 1,000 members; (212) 838-2560; www.societyillustrators.org

Industrial Designers Society of America (1965): 3,200+ members; (703) 707-6000; www.idsa.org

Intelligence Officers, Assn. of Former (1975): 24 chap., 5,000+ members; (703) 790-0320; www.afio.com

Interior Designers, American Soc. of (1975): 30,000+ members; (202) 546-3480; www.asid.org

Investigative Pathology, American Soc. for (1900): 1,718 members; (301) 634-7130; www.asip.org

Jail Assn., American (1981): 4,000+ members; (301) 790-3930; www.aja.org

Journalists, Society of Professional (1909): 9,000 members; (317) 927-8000; www.spj.org

Journalists and Authors, American Soc. of (1948): 1,300+ members; (212) 997-0947; www.asja.org

Judicature Society, American (1913): 6,000 members; (515) 271-2281; www.ajs.org

Landscape Architects, American Society of (1899): 15,000+ members; (202) 898-2444; www.asla.org

Legal Administrators, Assn. of (1971): 10,000+ members; (847) 267-1252; www.alanet.org

Library Assn., American (1876): 61,000+ members; (800) 545-2433; www.ala.org

Lifesaving Assn., U.S. (1964): 11,000 members; (866) 367-8752; www.usla.org

Logistics, Intl. Society of (SOLE) (1966): 3,000+ members; (301) 459-8446; www.sole.org

Magicians, Intl. Brotherhood of (1922): 13,000 members; (636) 724-2400; www.magician.org

Management Accountants, Inst. of (1919): 65,000+ members; (201) 573-9000; www.imanet.org

Management Assn., American (1923): 4,100 cos., 38,000 ind.; (212) 903-7976; www.amanet.org

Marketing Assn., American (1937): 30,000+ members; (312) 542-9000; www.marketingpower.com

Master Brewers Assn. of the Americas (1887): 2,700+ members; (651) 454-7250; www.mbaa.com

Material and Process Engineering, Soc. for the Advancement of (1944): 4,500 members; (626) 331-0616; www.sampe.org

Mechanical Engineers, American Soc. of (1880): 130,000+ members; (973) 882-1170; www.asme.org

Medical Assn., American (1847): 250,000 members; (800) 621-8335; www.ama-assn.org

Medical Library Assn. (1898): 4,000+ members; (312) 419-9094; www.mlanet.org

Motion Picture Arts & Sciences, Academy of (1927): 6,000+ members; (310) 247-3000; www.oscars.org

Motion Picture and Television Engineers, Soc. of (1916): 5,000+ members; (914) 761-1100; www.smpte.org

Mystery Writers of America (1945): 3,000+ members; (212) 888-8171; www.mysterywriters.org

NALS...the association for legal professionals (formerly the Natl. Assn. of Legal Secretaries) (1929): 6,000 members; (918) 582-5188; www.nals.org

Notaries, American Society of (1965): approx. 20,000 members; (850) 671-5164; www.notaries.org

Nursing, Natl. League for (1893): 33,000 members, 1,200 institutions; (212) 812-0300; www.nln.org

Operations Management, Assn. for (APICS) (1957): nearly 40,000 members; (773) 867-1777; www.apics.org

Optometric Assn., American (1898): 36,000 members; (800) 365-2219; www.aoa.org

Organists, American Guild of (1896): 20,000 members; (212) 870-2310; www.agohq.org

Pen Women, Natl. League of American (1897): 2,600+ members; (202) 785-1997; www.nlapw.org

Pharmacists Assn., American (1852): 60,000+ members; (202) 628-4410; www.pharmacist.com

Physical Therapy Assn., American (1921): 85,000+ members; (703) 684-2782; www.apta.org

Plastics Engineers, Society of (1942): nearly 20,000 members; (203) 775-0471; www.4spe.org

Police Assn.—United States Section, Intl. (1962): 10,000 members; (855) 241-9998; www.ipa-usa.org

Population Assn. of America (1930): 3,300 members; (301) 565-6710; www.populationassociation.org

Postmasters of the U.S., Natl. Assn. of (1898): 42,000+ members, 95 clubs; (703) 683-9027; www.napus.org

Press Club, National (1908): 3,500+ members; (202) 662-7500; www.press.org

Professional Ball Players of America, Assn. of (1924): 11,000 members; (714) 528-2012; www.apbpa.org

Professional Beauty Assn. (1904): 12,000+ members; (480) 281-0424; www.probeauty.org

Psychiatric Assn., American (1844): 33,000+ members; (703) 907-7300; www.psychiatry.org

Psychological Assn., American (1892): 134,000+ members; (202) 336-5500; www.apa.org

Public Administration, American Soc. for (1939): 9,000 members; (202) 393-7878; www.aspanet.org

Public Health Assn., American (1872): 25,000+ members; (202) 777-2742; www.apha.org

Public Relations Soc. of America (1947): 21,000+ members; (212) 460-1400; www.prsa.org

Range Management, Society for (1948): 4,000+ members; (303) 986-3309; www.rangelands.org

Real Estate Appraisers, Natl. Assn. of (1966): 5,500 members; (760) 327-5284; www.narea-assoc.org

Rehabilitation Assn., Natl. (1923): 5,500+ members; (703) 836-0850; www.nationalrehab.org

Road & Transportation Builders Assn., American (1902): 5,000+ members; (202) 289-4434; www.artba.org

Safety Engineers, American Soc. of (1911): 34,000+ members; (847) 699-2929; www.asse.org

School Administrators, American Assn. of (1865): 13,000+ members; (703) 528-0700; www.aasa.org

Science Teachers Assn., Natl. (1944): 60,000 members; (703) 243-7100; www.nsta.org

Science Writers, Natl. Assn. of (1955): 2,200 members; (510) 647-9500; www.nasw.org

Screen Actors Guild—American Federation of Television and Radio Artists (2012): 165,000+ members; (855) SAG-AGTRA; www.sagaftra.org

Songwriters Guild of America (1931): 5,000+ members; (615) 742-9945; www.songwritersguild.com

Sportscasters Assn., American (1980): 500+ members; (212) 227- 8080; www.americansportscastersonline.com

Surgeons, American College of (1913): 78,000 members; (312) 202-5000; www.facs.org

Tax Administrators, Federation of (1937): (202) 624-5890; www.taxadmin.org

Teachers of English, Natl. Council of (1911): 35,000+ members; (217) 328-3870; www.ncte.org

Teachers of English to Speakers of Other Languages, Inc. (1966): nearly 12,150 members; (703) 836-0774; www.tesol.org

Teachers of French, American Assn. of (1927): nearly 10,000 members; (618) 453-5731; www.frenchteachers.org

Teachers of German, American Assn. of (1926): 5,000 members; (856) 795-5553; www.aatg.org

Teachers of Mathematics, Natl. Council of (1920): 80,000 members; (703) 620-9840; www.nctm.org

Teachers of Spanish and Portuguese, American Assn. of (1917): 11,000+ members; (248) 960-2180; www.aatsp.org

Television Arts and Sciences, Natl. Academy of (1955): (212) 586-8424; www.emmyonline.org

Theological Library Assn., American (1946): nearly 1,000 members; (312) 454-5100; www.atla.com

Transportation Engineers, Inst. of (1930): nearly 17,000 members; (202) 785-0060; www.ite.org

Travel Agents, American Soc. of (1931): 12,000 members; (703) 739-2782; www.asta.org

Underwriters Soc., Chartered Property Casualty (1944): 22,000+ members; (800) 932-2728; www.cpcusociety.org

University Women, American Assn. of (1881): 100,000+ members; (202) 785-7700; www.aauw.org

Veterinary Medical Assn., American (1863): 84,000+ members; (800) 248-2862; www.avma.org

Women in Communications, The Assn. for (1909): 3,000+ members; (703) 370-7436; www.womcom.org

Women Engineers, Society of (1950): 17,000 members; (877) 793-4636; societyofwomenengineers.swe.org

Women in Media, Alliance for (1951): nearly 10,000 members; (703) 506-3290; www.allwomeninmedia.org

Professional Sports Organizations

Source: World Almanac research

Major League Baseball

Office of the Commissioner, 245 Park Ave., 31st Fl., New York, NY 10167; www.mlb.com

American League

Baltimore Orioles (1953): 333 W. Camden St., Baltimore, MD 21201; (410) 685-9800; www.orioles.com

Boston Red Sox (1901): 4 Yawkey Way, Boston, MA 02215; (617) 267-9440; www.redsox.com

Chicago White Sox (1900, as Chicago White Stockings): 333 W. 35th St., Chicago, IL 60616; (312) 674-1000; www.whitesox.com

Cleveland Indians (1901, as Cleveland Blues): 2401 Ontario St., Cleveland, OH 44115; (216) 420-4200; www.indians.com

Detroit Tigers (1901): 2100 Woodward Ave., Detroit, MI 48201; (313) 471-2000; www.tigers.com

Houston Astros (1962, as Houston Colt .45s): 501 Crawford St., Houston, TX 77002; (713) 259-8000; www.astros.com. (The Astros were a National League team, 1962-2012; the franchise joined the AL West beginning with the 2013 season.)

Kansas City Royals (1969): One Royal Way, Kansas City, MO 64129; (816) 921-8000; www.royals.com

Los Angeles Angels of Anaheim (1961): 2000 Gene Autry Way, Anaheim, CA 92806; (714) 940-2000; www.angelsbaseball.com

Minnesota Twins (1960): 1 Twins Way, Minneapolis, MN 55403; (612) 659-3400; www.twinsbaseball.com

New York Yankees (1903): One E. 161st St., Bronx, NY 10451; (718) 293-4300; www.yankees.com

Oakland Athletics (1901, as Philadelphia Athletics): 7000 Coliseum Way, Oakland, CA 94621; (510) 638-4900; oakland.athletics.mlb.com

Seattle Mariners (1977): P.O. Box 4100, Seattle, WA 98194; (206) 346-4000; www.mariners.com

Tampa Bay Rays (1995, as Tampa Bay Devil Rays): One Tropicana Dr., St. Petersburg, FL 33705; (727) 825-3137; www.raysbaseball.com

Texas Rangers (1960, as Washington Senators): 1000 Ballpark Way, Arlington, TX 76011; (817) 273-5222; www.texasrangers.com

Toronto Blue Jays (1976): One Blue Jays Way, Ste. 3200, Toronto, ON M5V 1J1, Canada; (416) 341-1000; www.bluejays.com

National League

Arizona Diamondbacks (1998): 401 E. Jefferson St., Phoenix, AZ 85004; (602) 462-6500; www.dbacks.com

Atlanta Braves (1876, as Boston Red Stockings): 755 Hank Aaron Dr., Atlanta, GA 30315; (404) 522-7630; www.braves.com

Chicago Cubs (1876, as Chicago White Stockings): 1060 W. Addison, Chicago, IL 60613; (773) 404-2827; www.cubs.com

Cincinnati Reds (1869, as Cincinnati Red Stockings): 100 Main St., Cincinnati, OH 45202; (513) 765-7000; www.reds.com

Colorado Rockies (1991): 2001 Blake St., Denver, CO 80205; (303) 292-0200; www.coloradorockies.com

Houston Astros see American League.

Los Angeles Dodgers (1890): 1000 Elysian Park Ave., Los Angeles, CA 90012; (323) 224-1500; www.dodgers.com

Miami Marlins (1991, as Florida Marlins): 501 Marlins Way, Miami, FL 33125; (305) 480-1300; www.marlins.com

Milwaukee Brewers (1970): One Brewers Way, Milwaukee, WI 53214; (414) 902-4400; www.brewers.com

New York Mets (1961): Citi Field, Flushing, NY 11368; (718) 507-6387; www.mets.com

Philadelphia Phillies (1883): One Citizens Bank Way, Philadelphia, PA 19148; (215) 463-6000; www.phillies.com

Pittsburgh Pirates (1887, as Pittsburgh Alleghenies): 115 Federal St., Pittsburgh, PA 15212; (412) 323-5000; www.pirates.com

St. Louis Cardinals (1892, as St. Louis Browns): 700 Clark St., St. Louis, MO 63102; (314) 345-9600; www.cardinals.com

San Diego Padres (1969): 100 Park Blvd., San Diego, CA 92101; (619) 795-5000; www.padres.com

San Francisco Giants (1883, as New York Gothams): 24 Willie Mays Plz., San Francisco, CA 94107; (415) 972-2000; www.sfgiants.com

Washington Nationals (1969, as Montréal Expos): 1500 South Capitol St., SE, Washington, DC 20003; (202) 675-6287; www.nationals.com

National Basketball Association

League Office, 645 Fifth Ave., New York, NY 10022; www.nba.com

Atlanta Hawks (1949, as Tri-Cities Blackhawks): 101 Marietta St. NW, Ste. 1900, Atlanta, GA 30303; (866) 715-1500; www.nba.com/hawks/

Boston Celtics (1946): 226 Causeway St., 4th Fl., Boston, MA 02114; (866) 423-5849; www.nba.com/celtics/

Brooklyn Nets (1967, as New Jersey Americans): 15 MetroTech Ctr., 11th Fl., Brooklyn, NY 11201; (718) 933-3000; www.nba.com/nets/

Charlotte Bobcats (2004): 333 E. Trade St., Charlotte, NC 28202; (704) 688-8600; www.nba.com/bobcats/

Chicago Bulls (1966): 1901 W. Madison St., Chicago, IL 60612; (312) 455-4000; www.nba.com/bulls/

Cleveland Cavaliers (1970): One Center Ct., Cleveland, OH 44115; (216) 420-2000; www.nba.com/cavaliers/

Dallas Mavericks (1980): 2909 Taylor St., Dallas, TX 75226; (214) 747-6287; www.nba.com/mavericks/

Denver Nuggets (1967, as Denver Rockets): 1000 Chopper Cir., Denver, CO 80204; (303) 405-1100; www.nba.com/nuggets/

Detroit Pistons (1957): Six Championship Dr., Auburn Hills, MI 48326; (248) 377-0100; www.nba.com/pistons/

Golden State Warriors (1946, as Philadelphia Warriors): 1011 Broadway, Oakland, CA 94605; (510) 986-2200; www.nba.com/warriors/

Houston Rockets (1967, as San Diego Rockets): 1510 Polk St., Houston, TX 77002; (713) 627-3865; www.nba.com/rockets/

Indiana Pacers (1967): 125 S. Pennsylvania St., Indianapolis, IN 46204; (317) 917-2500; www.nba.com/pacers/

Los Angeles Clippers (1970, as Buffalo Braves): 1111 S. Figueroa St., Ste. 1100, Los Angeles, CA 90015; (213) 742-7500; www.nba.com/clippers/

Los Angeles Lakers (1947, as Minneapolis Lakers): 555 N. Nash St., El Segundo, CA 90245; (310) 426-6000; www.nba.com/lakers/

Memphis Grizzlies (1995, as Vancouver Grizzlies): 191 Beale St., Memphis, TN 38103; (901) 888-4667; www.nba.com/grizzlies/

Miami Heat (1988): 601 Biscayne Blvd., Miami, FL 33132; (786) 777-1000; www.nba.com/heat/

Milwaukee Bucks (1968): 1001 N. 4th St., Milwaukee, WI 53203; (414) 227-0500; www.nba.com/bucks/

Minnesota Timberwolves (1989): 600 1st Ave. North, Minneapolis, MN 55403; (612) 673-1600; www.nba.com/timberwolves/

New Orleans Hornets (1988, as Charlotte Hornets): 1250 Poydras St., 19th Fl., New Orleans, LA 70113; (504) 593-4700; www.nba.com/hornets/

New York Knickerbockers (1946): Two Pennsylvania Plz., New York, NY 10121; (212) 465-6471; www.nba.com/knicks/

Oklahoma City Thunder (1967, as Seattle SuperSonics): 2 Leadership Square, 211 N. Robinson Ave., Ste. 300; Oklahoma City, OK 73102; (405) 208-4800; www.nba.com/thunder/

Orlando Magic (1989): 8701 Maitland Summit Blvd., Orlando, FL 32810; (407) 916-2400; www.nba.com/magic/

Philadelphia 76ers (1937, as Syracuse Nationals): 3601 S. Broad St., Philadelphia, PA 19148; (215) 339-7676; www.nba.com/sixers/

Phoenix Suns (1968): 201 E. Jefferson St., Phoenix, AZ 85004; (602) 379-7900; www.nba.com/suns/

Portland Trail Blazers (1970): One Center Ct., Ste. 200, Portland, OR 97227; (503) 234-9291; www.nba.com/blazers/

Sacramento Kings (1945, as Rochester Royals): One Sports Pkwy., Sacramento, CA 95834; (916) 928-0000; www.nba.com/kings/

San Antonio Spurs (1967, as Dallas Chaparrals): One AT&T Center, San Antonio, TX 78219; (210) 444-5000; www.nba.com/spurs/

Toronto Raptors (1995): 40 Bay St., Toronto, ON M5J 2X2, Canada; (416) 366-3865; www.nba.com/raptors/

Utah Jazz (1974, as New Orleans Jazz): 301 W. South Temple, Salt Lake City, UT 84101; (801) 325-2500; www.nba.com/jazz/

Washington Wizards (1961, as Chicago Packers): 601 F St. NW, Washington, DC 20004; (202) 661-5000; www.nba.com/wizards/

National Hockey League

NHL Headquarters, 1185 Ave. of the Americas, 15th Fl., New York, NY 10036; www.nhl.com

Anaheim Ducks (1993): 2695 E. Katella Ave., Anaheim, CA 92806; (877) 945-3946; ducks.nhl.com

Boston Bruins (1924): 100 Legends Way, Boston, MA 02114; (617) 624-1900; bruins.nhl.com

Buffalo Sabres (1970): One Seymour H. Knox III Plz., Buffalo, NY 14203; (716) 855-4100; sabres.nhl.com

Calgary Flames (1980): P.O. Box 1540, Station M, Calgary, AB T2P 3B9, Canada; (403) 777-2177; flames.nhl.com

Carolina Hurricanes (1972, as New England Whalers): 1400 Edwards Mill Rd., Raleigh, NC 27607; (919) 467-7825; hurricanes.nhl.com

Chicago Blackhawks (1926): 1901 W. Madison St., Chicago, IL 60612; (312) 455-7000; blackhawks.nhl.com

Colorado Avalanche (1972, as Quebec Nordiques): 1000 Chopper Cir., Denver, CO 80204; (303) 405-1100; avalanche.nhl.com

Columbus Blue Jackets (2000): 200 W. Nationwide Blvd., Suite Level, Columbus, OH 43215; (614) 246-4625; bluejackets.nhl.com

Dallas Stars (1967, as Minnesota North Stars): 2601 Ave. of the Stars, Frisco, TX 75034; (214) 387-5500; stars.nhl.com

Detroit Red Wings (1926, as Detroit Cougars): 600 Civic Center Dr., Detroit, MI 48226; (313) 471-6606; redwings.nhl.com

Edmonton Oilers (1972, as Alberta Oilers): 11230 - 110 St., Edmonton, AB T5G 3H7, Canada; (780) 414-4000; oilers.nhl.com

Florida Panthers (1993): One Panther Pkwy., Sunrise, FL 33323; (954) 835-7000; panthers.nhl.com

Los Angeles Kings (1967): 1111 S. Figueroa St., Ste. 3100, Los Angeles, CA 90015; (213) 742-7100; kings.nhl.com

Minnesota Wild (2000): 317 Washington St., St. Paul, MN 55102; (651) 602-6000; wild.nhl.com

Montréal Canadiens (1917): 1909, avenue des Canadiens-de-Montréal, Montréal, QC H3C 5L2, Canada; (514) 932-2582; canadiens.nhl.com

Nashville Predators (1998): 501 Broadway, Nashville, TN 37203; (615) 770-2355; predators.nhl.com

New Jersey Devils (1974, as Kansas City Scouts): Prudential Center, 165 Mulberry St., Newark, NJ 07102; (973) 757-6100; devils.nhl.com

New York Islanders (1972): 1255 Hempstead Tpke., Uniondale, NY 11553; (516) 501-6700; islanders.nhl.com

New York Rangers (1926): Two Pennsylvania Plz., New York, NY 10121; (212) 465-6000; rangers.nhl.com

Ottawa Senators (1992): 1000 Palladium Dr., Ottawa, ON K2V 1A5, Canada; (613) 599-0250; senators.nhl.com

Philadelphia Flyers (1967): 3601 S. Broad St., Philadelphia, PA 19148; (215) 336-3600; flyers.nhl.com

Phoenix Coyotes (1979, as Winnipeg Jets): 6751 N. Sunset Blvd. #200, Glendale, AZ 85305; (623) 772-3200; coyotes.nhl.com

Pittsburgh Penguins (1967): 1001 5th Ave., Pittsburgh, PA 15219; (412) 642-1800; penguins.nhl.com

St. Louis Blues (1967): 1401 Clark Ave. at Brett Hull Way, St. Louis, MO 63103; (314) 622-2500; blues.nhl.com

San Jose Sharks (1991): 525 W. Santa Clara St., San Jose, CA 95113; (408) 287-7070; sharks.nhl.com

Tampa Bay Lightning (1992): 401 Channelside Dr., Tampa, FL 33602; (813) 301-6500; lightning.nhl.com

Toronto Maple Leafs (1919, as Toronto St. Pats): 40 Bay St., Ste. 400, Toronto, ON M5J 2X2, Canada; (416) 703-5323; mapleleafs.nhl.com

Vancouver Canucks (1946): 800 Griffiths Way, Vancouver, BC V6B 6G1, Canada; (604) 899-7400; canucks.nhl.com

Washington Capitals (1974): 627 N. Glebe Rd., Ste. 850, Arlington, VA 22203; (202) 266-2200; capitals.nhl.com

Winnipeg Jets (1999, as Atlanta Thrashers): 345 Graham Ave., Winnipeg, MB R3C 5S6, Canada; (204) 987-7825; jets.nhl.com

National Football League

League Office, 345 Park Ave., New York, NY 10154 www.nfl.com

Arizona Cardinals (1898, as Morgan Athletic Club): P.O. Box 888, Phoenix, AZ 85001; (602) 379-0101; www.azcardinals.com

Atlanta Falcons (1965): 4400 Falcon Pkwy., Flowery Branch, GA 30542; (770) 965-3115; www.atlantafalcons.com

Baltimore Ravens (1996): 1101 Russell St., Baltimore, MD 21230; (410) 261-7283; www.baltimoreravens.com

Buffalo Bills (1960): One Bills Dr., Orchard Park, NY 14127; (716) 648-1800; www.buffalobills.com

Carolina Panthers (1993): 800 S. Mint St., Charlotte, NC 28202; (704) 358-7000; www.panthers.com

Chicago Bears (1920, as Decatur Staleys): 1000 Football Dr., Lake Forest, IL 60045; (847) 615-2327; www.chicagobears.com

Cincinnati Bengals (1968): One Paul Brown Stadium, Cincinnati, OH 45202; (513) 621-3550; www.bengals.com

Cleveland Browns (1946): 76 Lou Groza Blvd., Berea, OH 44017; (440) 824-3434; www.clevelandbrowns.com

Dallas Cowboys (1960): One Legends Way, Arlington, TX 76011; (817) 892-5000; www.dallascowboys.com

Denver Broncos (1960): 13655 Broncos Pkwy., Englewood, CO 80112; (303) 649-9000; www.denverbroncos.com

Detroit Lions (1934): 222 Republic Dr., Allen Park, MI 48101; (313) 262-2000; www.detroitlions.com

Green Bay Packers (1919): 1265 Lombardi Ave., Green Bay, WI 54304; (920) 569-7500; www.packers.com

Houston Texans (2002): Two Reliant Park, Houston, TX 77054; (832) 667-2002; www.houstontexans.com

Indianapolis Colts (1946, as Baltimore Colts): 7001 W. 56th St., Indianapolis, IN 46254; (317) 297-2658; www.colts.com

Jacksonville Jaguars (1995): One Ever-Bank Field Dr., Jacksonville, FL 32202; (904) 633-2000; www.jaguars.com

Kansas City Chiefs (1960, as Dallas Texans): One Arrowhead Dr., Kansas City, MO 64129; (816) 920-9300; www.kcchiefs.com

Miami Dolphins (1966): 347 Don Shula Dr., Miami Gardens, FL 33056; (305) 943-8000; www.miamidolphins.com

Minnesota Vikings (1961): 9520 Viking Dr., Eden Prairie, MN 55344; (952) 828-6500; www.vikings.com

New England Patriots (1960): One Patriot Pl., Foxboro, MA 02035; (508) 543-8200; www.patriots.com

New Orleans Saints (1967): 5800 Airline Dr., Metairie, LA 70003; (504) 733-0255; www.neworleanssaints.com

New York Giants (1925): MetLife Stadium, E. Rutherford, NJ 07073; (201) 935-8111; www.giants.com

New York Jets (1960, as New York Titans): One Jets Dr., Florham Park, NJ 07932; (800) 469-5387; www.newyorkjets.com

Oakland Raiders (1960): 1220 Harbor Bay Pkwy., Alameda, CA 94502; (510) 864-5000; www.raiders.com

Philadelphia Eagles (1933): One NovaCare Way, Philadelphia, PA 19145; (215) 463-2500; www.philadelphiaeagles.com

Pittsburgh Steelers (1933): 3400 S. Water. St., Pittsburgh, PA 15203; (412) 432-7800; www.steelers.com

St. Louis Rams (1937, as Cleveland Rams): One Rams Way, St. Louis, MO 63045; (314) 982-7267; www.stlouisrams.com

San Diego Chargers (1960, as Los Angeles Chargers): P.O. Box 609609, San Diego, CA 92160; (858) 874-4500; www.chargers.com

San Francisco 49ers (1950): 4949 Centennial Blvd., Santa Clara, CA 95054; (408) 562-4949; www.49ers.com

Seattle Seahawks (1976): 12 Seahawks Way, Renton, WA 98056; (888) 635-4295; www.seahawks.com

Tampa Bay Buccaneers (1976): One Buccaneer Pl., Tampa, FL 33607; (813) 870-2700; www.buccaneers.com

Tennessee Titans (1960, as Houston Oilers): 460 Great Circle Rd., Nashville, TN 37228; (615) 565-4000; www.titansonline.com

Washington Redskins (1937): 21300 Redskin Park Dr., Ashburn, VA 20147; (703) 726-7000; www.redskins.com

Health Organizations

Source: World Almanac research

Entries are roughly alphabetized by the basic condition addressed or organization name. Year established is in parentheses. In addition to these selected sites, there is a vast array of medical information on the Internet. It is important, however, to be certain that the source of information is reliable and accurate. Always check with a physician before embarking on any new health-related undertaking.

Al-Anon Family Groups (1951): (757) 563-1600; www.al-anon.alateen.org

Alcohol and Drug Information, SAMHSA National Clearinghouse: (877) SAMHSA-7 (726-4727); store.samhsa.gov

Alcoholics Anonymous (1935): (212) 870-3400; www.aa.org

Alcoholism and Drug Dependence, Inc., National Council on (1944): (212) 269-7797; www.ncadd.org

Aging, National Institute on (1974): (301) 496-1752; www.nia.nih.gov

Aging's Eldercare Locator, Administration on (1991): (800) 677-1116; www.eldercare.gov

AIDSInfo (800) HIV-0440 (448-0440); www.aidsinfo.nih.gov

AIDS Society, Canadian (1988): (613) 230-3580; www.cdnaids.ca

Allergy, Asthma, and Immunology, American Academy of (1943): (414) 272-6071; www.aaaai.org

ALS Assn. [Lou Gehrig's disease] (1985): (202) 407-8580; www.alsa.org

Alzheimer's Assn. (1979): (312) 335-8700; www.alz.org

Alzheimer Society of Canada (1978): (416) 488-8772; www.alzheimer.ca

Anorexia Nervosa and Associated Disorders, National Assn. of (1976): (630) 577-1333; www.anad.org

Arc of the United States, The [intellectual and developmental disabilities] (1950): (800) 433-5255; www.thearc.org

Arthritis Foundation (1948): (800) 283-7800; www.arthritis.org

Arthritis and Musculoskeletal and Skin Diseases, National Institute of (1986): (877) 226-4267; www.niams.nih.gov

Asthma and Allergy Foundation of America (1953): (800) 727-8462; www.aafa.org

Autism Society (1965): (800) 328-8476; www.autism-society.org

Blind, American Council of the (1961): (202) 467-5081; www.acb.org

Blind, Inc., Guide Dog Foundation for the (1946): (800) 548-4337; www.guidedog.org

Blind, National Federation of the (1940): (410) 659-9314; www.nfb.org

Blind and Physically Handicapped, National Library Service for the (1931): (202) 707-5100; TDD (202) 707-0744; www.loc.gov/nls/

Blindness Foundation Fighting (1971): (800) 683-5555; www.blindness.org

Blindness America, Prevent (1908): (800) 331-2020; www.preventblindness.org

Brain Tumor Society, National (2008): (800) 770-8287; www.braintumor.org

Breast Cancer Diagnosis, After (ABCD) (1999): (414) 977-1780; www.abcdbreastcancersupport.org

Cancer Institute's Cancer Information Service, National (1975): (800) 422-6237; www.cancer.gov/aboutnci/cis/

Cancer Society, American (1913): (800) 227-2345; www.cancer.org

Cancer Society, Canadian (1938): (416) 961-7223; www.cancer.ca

Centers for Disease Control and Prevention (CDC) (1946): (800) 232-4636; www.cdc.gov

Cerebral Palsy, United (1949): (202) 776-0406; www.ucp.org

CFIDS Assn. of America [chronic fatigue syndrome] (1987): (704) 365-2343; www.cfids.org

Child Abuse and Family Violence, National Council on (1984): (202) 429-6695; www.nccafv.org

Childhelp National Child Abuse Hotline (1959): (800) 4-A-CHILD (422-4453); www.childhelp.org

Children, National Center for Missing and Exploited (1984): (703) 224-2150; www.missingkids.com

Children's Tumor Foundation (1978): (212) 344-6633; www.ctf.org

Chronic Pain Assn., American (1980): (800) 533-3231; www.theacpa.org

Continence, National Assn. for (1982): (843) 377-0900; www.nafc.org

Continence, Simon Foundation for (1983): (800) 237-4666; www.simonfoundation.org

Cooley's Anemia Foundation [thalassemia major] (1954): (800) 522-7222; www.thalassemia.org

Crohn's and Colitis Foundation of America (1967): (800) 932-2423; www.ccfa.org

Crohn's and Colitis Foundation of Canada (1974): (416) 920-5035; www.ccfc.ca

Cystic Fibrosis Foundation (1955): (800) 344-4823 or (301) 951-4422; www.cff.org

Deaf, Natl. Assn. of the (1880): (301) 587-1788, TTY (301) 587-1789; www.nad.org

Depression and Bipolar Support Alliance (1985): (800) 826-3632; www.dbsalliance.org

Diabetes Assn., American (1940): (800) 342-2383; www.diabetes.org

Diabetes Assn., Canadian (1953): (416) 363-3373; www.diabetes.ca

Dial-A-Hearing Screening Test: (800) 222-EARS (222-3277)

Domestic Violence Hotline, National (1996): (800) 799-7233; TTY (800) 787-3224; www.thehotline.org

Down Syndrome Congress, Natl. (1973): (800) 232-6372; www.ndsccenter.org

Down Syndrome Society, National (1979): (800) 221-4602; www.ndss.org

Dyslexia Assn., International (1949): (410) 296-0232; www.interdys.org

Easter Seals [disabilities, special needs] (1919): (800) 221-6827; www.easterseals.com

Endometriosis Assn. (1980): (414) 355-2200; www.endometriosisassn.org

Epilepsy Foundation (1967): (800) 332-1000; www.epilepsyfoundation.org

Fat Acceptance, Natl. Assn. to Advance (1969): (916) 558-6880; www.naafa.org

First Candle [sudden infant death syndrome] (1987): (800) 221-7437; www.sidsalliance.org

FoodSafety.gov—Gateway to Federal Food Safety Information: Food (except for meat, poultry, eggs): (888) 723-3366 (FDA Center for Food Safety and Applied Nutrition); Meat, poultry, eggs: (888) 674-6854 (USDA Meat and Poultry Hotline); Illness or food poisoning: (800) 232-4636 (CDC)

Gamblers Anonymous (1957): (626) 960-3500; www.gamblersanonymous.org

Geriatrics Society, American (1942): (212) 308-1414; www.americangeriatrics.org

Hard of Hearing Assn., Canadian (1982): (613) 526-1584, TTY (613) 526-2692; www.chha.ca

Headache Foundation, National (1970): (888) 643-5552; www.headaches.org

HealthyWomen (1988): (877) 986-9472; www.healthywomen.org

Hearing Society, Intl. (1951): (734) 522-7200; www.ihsinfo.org

Heart Assn., American (1924): (800) 242-8721; www.heart.org

Hearts, Inc., Mended (1951): (214) 206-9259; www.mendedhearts.org

Hospice Education Institute (1985): (800) 331-1620; www.hospiceworld.org

Hospice International, Children's (1983): (800) 242-4453; www.chionline.org

Hospital Assn., American (1899): (312) 422-3000; www.aha.org

Huntington's Disease Society of America (1967): (800) 345-4372; www.hdsa.org

JDRF (formerly Juvenile Diabetes Research Foundation) (1970): (800) 533-2873; www.jdrf.org

Kidney Foundation, National (1950): (212) 889-2210; www.kidney.org

Kidney Foundation of Canada (1964): (514) 369-4806; www.kidney.ca

Kidney Fund, American (1971): (800) 638-8299; www.kidneyfund.org

Kidney and Urologic Diseases Information Clearinghouse, National: (800) 891-5390; www.kidney.niddk.nih.gov

La Leche League Intl. [breastfeeding] (1957): (800) 525-3243; www.llli.org

Leukemia and Lymphoma Society (1949): (800) 955-4572; www.lls.org

Liver Foundation, American (1976): (212) 668-1000; www.liverfoundation.org

Living Bank [organ donation] (1968): (800) 528-2971; www.livingbank.org

Lung Assn., American (1904): (800) 548-8252; www.lungusa.org

Lung Line (1983): (800) 222-5864; www.nationaljewish.org/about/contact/lung-line/

Lupus Foundation of America, Inc. (1977): (202) 349-1155; www.lupus.org

March of Dimes [babies' health] (1938): (914) 997-4488; www.marchofdimes.com

Marfan Foundation, Natl. (1981): (800) 8-MARFAN (862-7326); www.marfan.org

Mayo Clinic (1889): (507) 284-2511; www.mayoclinic.com

Mental Health, National Institute of (1946): (301) 443-4513, TTY (301) 443-8431; www.nimh.nih.gov

Mental Health America (1909): (800) 969-6642; www.nmha.org

Mental Illness, Natl. Alliance on (1979): (703) 524-7600; www.nami.org

Multiple Sclerosis Society, National (1946): (800) 344-4867; www.nationalmssociety.org

Multiple Sclerosis Society of Canada (1948): (416) 922-6065; www.mssociety.ca

Muscular Dystrophy Assn. (1950): (800) 572-1717; www.mdausa.org

Myeloma Foundation, Intl. (1990): (800) 452-2873; www.myeloma.org

Narcotics Anonymous (1953): (818) 773-9999; www.na.org

National Health Council (1920): (202) 785-3910; www.nationalhealthcouncil.org

National Health Information Center (1979): (240) 453-8282; www.health.gov/NHIC/

National Institutes of Health (NIH) (1887): (301) 496-4000; www.nih.gov

Neurological Disorders and Stroke, Natl. Institute of (1950): (800) 352- 9424; www.ninds.nih.gov

Organ Sharing, United Network for (1984): (804) 782-4800; www.unos.org

Osteoporosis Foundation, National (1984): (800) 231-4222; www.nof.org

Overeaters Anonymous (1960): (505) 891-2664; www.oa.org

Parkinson Foundation, National (1957): (800) 327-4545; www.parkinson.org

Parkinson's Disease Foundation (1957): (212) 923-4700; www.pdf.org

Parkinson Society Canada (1965): (416) 227-9700; www.parkinson.ca

Pediatrics, American Academy of (1930): (847) 434-4000; www.aap.org

Phoenix House [substance abuse] (1967): (800) DRUG-HELP (378-4435); www.phoenixhouse.org

Planned Parenthood Federation of America, Inc. (1916): (212) 541-7800; www.plannedparenthood.org

Plastic Surgeons, American Society of (1931): (847) 228-9900; www.plasticsurgery.org

Post-Polio Health International (1960): (314) 534-0475; www.post-polio.org

Psoriasis Foundation, Natl. (1966): (800) 723-9166; www.psoriasis.org

Rare Disorders, Natl. Organization for (1983): (203) 744-0100; www.rarediseases.org

Rehabilitation Information Center, National (1977): (800) 346-2742; TTY (301) 459-5984; www.naric.com

Reye's Syndrome Foundation, Natl. (1974): (800) 233-7393; www.reyessyndrome.org

Runaway Switchboard, National (1971): (773) 880-9860; www.1800runaway.org

Scleroderma Foundation (1989): (800) 722-HOPE (722-4673); www.scleroderma.org

Sexual Health Assn., American (1914): (919) 361-8400; www.ashastd.org

Sickle Cell Disease Assn. of America (1971): (800) 421-8453; www.sicklecelldisease.org

Sjögren's Syndrome Foundation (1983): (800) 475-6473; www.sjogrens.org

Speech-Language-Hearing Assn., American (1925): (800) 638-8255, TTY (301) 296-5650; www.asha.org

Spinal Cord Injury Assn., National (1948): (718) 803-3782; www.spinalcord.org

Stroke Assn., National (1984): (800) 787-6537; www.stroke.org

Stuttering Assn., Natl. (1977): (212) 944-4050; www.nsastutter.org

Stuttering Foundation of America (1947): (800) 992-9392; www.stutteringhelp.org

Sudden Infant Death Syndrome Institute, American (1983): (239) 431-5425; www.sids.org

Suicide Prevention Lifeline, National (2004): (800) 273-TALK (273-8255); www.suicidepreventionlifeline.org

Therapy Dogs Intl. (1976): (973) 252-9800; www.tdi-dog.org

Tourette Syndrome Assn. (1972): (718) 224-2999; tsa-usa.org

Tuberous Sclerosis Alliance (1974): (301) 562-9890; www.tsalliance.org

Urological Assn., American (1902): (866) 746-4282; www.auanet.org

Visual Impairments, Natl. Assn. for Parents of Children with (1980): www.napvi.org

Women's Health Network, National (1975): (202) 682-2640; www.nwhn.org

UNITED STATES FACTS

Superlative U.S. Statistics

Source: U.S. Geological Survey, U.S. Dept. of the Interior; U.S. Census Bureau, U.S. Dept. of Commerce; World Almanac research

Superlative Statistics for the 50 States

Total area for 50 states and Washington, DC		3,796,742 sq mi
Land area for 50 states and Washington, DC		3,531,905 sq mi
Water area for 50 states and Washington, DC		264,837 sq mi
Largest state	Alaska	665,384 sq mi
Smallest state	Rhode Island	1,545 sq mi
Largest county (excluding Alaska)	San Bernardino County, CA	20,105 sq mi
Smallest county	Arlington County, VA[1]	26 sq mi
Largest incorporated city (by area, pop. 1,000+)	Sitka, AK	4,811 sq mi
Northernmost city	Barrow, AK	71°17′ N
Northernmost point	Point Barrow, AK	71°23′ N
Southernmost city	Hilo, HI	19°44′ N
Southernmost settlement	Naalehu, HI	19°03′ N
Southernmost point	Ka Lae (South Cape), island of Hawaii	18°55′ N (155°41′ W)
Easternmost city	Eastport, ME	66°59′05′′ W
Easternmost settlement[2]	Attu Station, AK	173°11′ E
Easternmost point[2]	Pochnoi Point, Semisopochnoi Island, AK	179°52′ E
Westernmost city	Adak Station, AK	173°11′ E
Westernmost settlement	Adak Station, AK	173°11′ E
Westernmost point	Amatignak Island, AK	179°09′ W
Highest settlement	Tordal Estates, CO	10,653 ft
Lowest settlement	Bombay Beach, CA	−223 ft
Highest point on Atlantic coast	Cadillac Mountain, Mount Desert Island, ME	1,530 ft
Oldest national park	Yellowstone National Park (1872), WY-MT-ID	2,219,791 acres
Largest national park	Wrangell-St. Elias, AK	8,323,147 acres
Highest waterfall	Yosemite Falls—total in three sections	2,425 ft
	(Upper Yosemite Fall, 1,430 ft; Cascades, 675 ft; Lower Yosemite Fall, 320 ft)	
Longest river system	Mississippi-Missouri-Red Rock	3,710 mi
Highest mountain	Mount McKinley (Denali), AK	20,237 ft
Lowest point	Death Valley, CA	−282 ft
Deepest lake	Crater Lake, OR	1,958 ft
Rainiest spot	Mount Waialeale, Kauai, HI	annual avg. rainfall 423 in.
Largest gorge	Grand Canyon, Colorado River, AZ	277 mi long, 600 ft to 18 mi wide, 1 mi deep
Deepest gorge	Hells Canyon, Snake River, OR-ID	7,900 ft
Largest dam	New Cornelia Tailings, Ten Mile Wash, AZ[3]	274,026,000 cu yds material used
Tallest building	Willis Tower (formerly Sears Tower), Chicago, IL	1,451 ft
Largest building	Boeing Manufacturing Plant, Everett, WA	472,000,000 cu ft; covers 98 acres
Largest office building	Pentagon, Arlington, VA	77,015,000 cu ft; covers 29 acres
Tallest supported structure	KVLY-TV Tower, Blanchard, ND	2,063 ft
Tallest freestanding tower	Stratosphere Tower, Las Vegas, NV	1,149 ft
Longest bridge span	Verrazano-Narrows Bridge, New York, NY	4,260 ft
Highest bridge	Royal Gorge Bridge, Cañon City, CO	1,053 ft above water
Deepest well	Bertha Rogers gas well (inactive), Washita County, OK	31,441 ft

Superlative Statistics for the 48 Contiguous States

Total area for 48 states and Washington, DC		3,129,611 sq mi
Land area for 48 states and Washington, DC		2,958,868 sq mi
Water area for 48 states and Washington, DC		170,743 sq mi
Largest state	Texas	268,596 sq mi
Northernmost city	Bellingham, WA	48°46′ N
Northernmost settlement	Angle Inlet, MN	49°21′ N
Northernmost point	Northwest Angle, MN	49°23′ N
Southernmost city	Key West, FL	24°32′ N
Southernmost mainland city	Florida City, FL	25°27′ N
Southernmost point	Ballast Key, FL	24°31′ N
Easternmost settlement	Lubec, ME	66°58′49′′ W
Easternmost point	West Quoddy Head, ME	66°57′ W
Westernmost town	La Push, WA	124°38′ W
Westernmost point	Bodelteh Islands, WA	124°46′ W
Highest mountain	Mount Whitney, CA	14,500 ft

(1) Smallest county by land area is Kalawao County, Hawaii, at 12 sq mi; its total area (including water) is 53 sq mi. Superlative shown is for smallest total area. (2) Alaska's Aleutian Islands extend into the Eastern Hemisphere (across 180° longitude) and thus technically contain the easternmost point and settlement in the U.S. (3) Privately owned industrial dam composed of tailings, remnants of a mining process.

Highest and Lowest Altitudes in U.S. States and Territories

Source: U.S. Geological Survey, U.S. Dept. of the Interior
(negative sign indicates below sea level)

State/territory	Highest point Name	County	Elev. (ft)	Lowest point Name	County	Elev. (ft)
Alabama	Cheaha Mountain	Cleburne	2,407	Gulf of Mexico		Sea level
Alaska	Mount McKinley/Denali	Denali	20,237	Pacific Ocean		Sea level
American Samoa	Lata Mountain	Tau Island	3,160	Pacific Ocean		Sea level
Arizona	Humphreys Peak	Coconino	12,637	Colorado R.	Yuma	70
Arkansas	Magazine Mountain	Logan	2,753	Ouachita R.	Ashley-Union	55
California	Mount Whitney	Inyo-Tulare	14,500	Death Valley	Inyo	−282
Colorado	Mount Elbert	Lake	14,440	Arikaree R.	Yuma	3,315
Connecticut	S. slope of Mt. Frissell	Litchfield	2,380	Long Island Sound		Sea level
Delaware	Ebright Azimuth	New Castle	448	Atlantic Ocean		Sea level
Dist. of Columbia	Tenleytown	NW quadrant	410	Potomac R.		1
Florida	Britton Hill	Walton	345	Atlantic Ocean		Sea level
Georgia	Brasstown Bald	Towns-Union	4,784	Atlantic Ocean		Sea level
Guam	Mount Lamlam	Agat District	1,332	Pacific Ocean		Sea level
Hawaii	Pu'u Wekiu, Mauna Kea	Hawaii	13,796	Pacific Ocean		Sea level
Idaho	Borah Peak	Custer	12,661	Snake R.	Nez Perce	710
Illinois	Charles Mound	Jo Daviess	1,235	Mississippi R.	Alexander	279
Indiana	Hoosier Hill	Wayne	1,257	Ohio R.	Posey	320
Iowa	Hawkeye Point	Osceola	1,670	Mississippi R.	Lee	480
Kansas	Mount Sunflower	Wallace	4,039	Verdigris R.	Montgomery	679
Kentucky	Black Mountain	Harlan	4,145	Mississippi R.	Fulton	257
Louisiana	Driskill Mountain	Bienville	535	New Orleans	Orleans	−8
Maine	Mount Katahdin	Piscataquis	5,268	Atlantic Ocean		Sea level
Maryland	Hoye Crest	Garrett	3,360	Atlantic Ocean		Sea level
Massachusetts	Mount Greylock	Berkshire	3,491	Atlantic Ocean		Sea level
Michigan	Mount Arvon	Baraga	1,979	Lake Erie		571
Minnesota	Eagle Mountain	Cook	2,301	Lake Superior		601
Mississippi	Woodall Mountain	Tishomingo	806	Gulf of Mexico		Sea level
Missouri	Taum Sauk Mountain	Iron	1,772	St. Francis R.	Dunklin	230
Montana	Granite Peak	Park	12,804	Kootenai R.	Lincoln	1,800
Nebraska	Panorama Point	Kimball	5,424	Missouri R.	Richardson	840
Nevada	Boundary Peak	Esmeralda	13,146	Colorado R.	Clark	479
New Hampshire	Mount Washington	Coos	6,288	Atlantic Ocean		Sea level
New Jersey	High Point	Sussex	1,803	Atlantic Ocean		Sea level
New Mexico	Wheeler Peak	Taos	13,166	Red Bluff Reservoir	Eddy	2,842
New York	Mount Marcy	Essex	5,344	Atlantic Ocean		Sea level
North Carolina	Mount Mitchell	Yancey	6,684	Atlantic Ocean		Sea level
North Dakota	White Butte	Slope	3,506	Red R. of the North	Pembina	750
Ohio	Campbell Hill	Logan	1,550	Ohio R.	Hamilton	455
Oklahoma	Black Mesa	Cimarron	4,973	Little R.	McCurtain	289
Oregon	Mount Hood	Clackamas-Hood R.	11,240	Pacific Ocean		Sea level
Pennsylvania	Mount Davis	Somerset	3,213	Delaware R.	Delaware	Sea level
Puerto Rico	Cerro de Punta	Ponce District	4,390	Atlantic Ocean		Sea level
Rhode Island	Jerimoth Hill	Providence	812	Atlantic Ocean		Sea level
South Carolina	Sassafras Mountain	Pickens	3,560	Atlantic Ocean		Sea level
South Dakota	Harney Peak	Pennington	7,242	Big Stone Lake	Roberts	966
Tennessee	Clingmans Dome	Sevier	6,643	Mississippi R.	Shelby	178
Texas	Guadalupe Peak	Culberson	8,749	Gulf of Mexico		Sea level
Utah	Kings Peak	Duchesne	13,534	Beaver Dam Wash	Washington	2,000
Vermont	Mount Mansfield	Chittenden	4,393	Lake Champlain		95
Virginia	Mount Rogers	Grayson-Smyth	5,729	Atlantic Ocean		Sea level
Virgin Islands	Crown Mountain	St. Thomas Island	1,556	Atlantic Ocean		Sea level
Washington	Mount Rainier	Pierce	14,416	Pacific Ocean		Sea level
West Virginia	Spruce Knob	Pendleton	4,863	Potomac R.	Jefferson	240
Wisconsin	Timms Hill	Price	1,951	Lake Michigan		579
Wyoming	Gannett Peak	Fremont	13,810	Belle Fourche R.	Crook	3,099

U.S. Coastline by State

Source: National Oceanic and Atmospheric Administration, U.S. Dept. of Commerce
(in statute miles; only states with coastline or shoreline are shown)

	Coastline[1]	Shoreline[2]		Coastline[1]	Shoreline[2]
Atlantic Coast	2,069	28,673	Gulf Coast	1,631	17,141
Connecticut	0	618	Alabama	53	607
Delaware	28	381	Florida	770	5,095
Florida	580	3,331	Louisiana	397	7,721
Georgia	100	2,344	Mississippi	44	359
Maine	228	3,478	Texas	367	3,359
Maryland	31	3,190			
Massachusetts	192	1,519	Pacific Coast	7,623	40,298
New Hampshire	13	131	Alaska	5,580	31,383
New Jersey	130	1,792	California	840	3,427
New York	127	1,850	Hawaii	750	1,052
North Carolina	301	3,375	Oregon	296	1,410
Pennsylvania	0	89	Washington	157	3,026
Rhode Island	40	384			
South Carolina	187	2,876	Arctic Coast	1,060	2,521
Virginia	112	3,315	United States	12,383	88,633

(1) Length of general outline of seacoast. Measurements were made in 1948 with a unit measure of 30 minutes of latitude on charts as near the scale of 1:1,200,000 as possible. Includes coastlines of large sounds and bays. (2) Shoreline of outer coast, offshore islands, sounds, bays, rivers, and creeks to the head of tidewater or to a point where tidal waters narrow to a width of 100 ft. Figures obtained in 1939-40 with a recording instrument on the largest-scale charts and maps then available.

States: Capitals, Key Dates, Geographic Data

Source: *Statistical Abstract of the United States,* U.S. Census Bureau, U.S. Dept. of Commerce

The 13 colonies that declared independence from Great Britain and fought the War of Independence (American Revolution) became the 13 original states. They were, in the order in which they ratified the Constitution: Delaware, Pennsylvania, New Jersey, Georgia, Connecticut, Massachusetts, Maryland, South Carolina, New Hampshire, Virginia, New York, North Carolina, and Rhode Island.

State	Settled[1]	Capital	Entered Union Date	Order	Extent (mi) Length (approx. mean)	Width	Area (sq mi) Land	Water	Total	Rank by tot. area
AL	1702	Montgomery	Dec. 14, 1819	22	330	190	50,645	1,775	52,420	30
AK	1784	Juneau	Jan. 3, 1959	49	1,480[2]	810	570,641	94,743	665,384	1
AZ	1776	Phoenix	Feb. 14, 1912	48	400	310	113,594	396	113,990	6
AR	1686	Little Rock	June 15, 1836	25	260	240	52,035	1,143	53,179	29
CA	1769	Sacramento	Sept. 9, 1850	31	770	250	155,779	7,916	163,695	3
CO	1858	Denver	Aug. 1, 1876	38	380	280	103,642	452	104,094	8
CT	1634	Hartford	Jan. 9, 1788	5	110	70	4,842	701	5,543	48
DE	1638	Dover	Dec. 7, 1787	1	96	30	1,949	540	2,489	49
DC	NA	NA	NA	NA	NA	NA	61	7	68	51
FL	1565	Tallahassee	Mar. 3, 1845	27	447	361	53,625	12,133	65,758	22
GA	1733	Atlanta	Jan. 2, 1788	4	300	230	57,513	1,912	59,425	24
HI	1820	Honolulu	Aug. 21, 1959	50	NA	NA	6,423	4,509	10,932	43
ID	1842	Boise	July 3, 1890	43	570	300	82,643	926	83,569	14
IL	1720	Springfield	Dec. 3, 1818	21	390	210	55,519	2,395	57,914	25
IN	1733	Indianapolis	Dec. 11, 1816	19	270	140	35,826	593	36,420	38
IA	1788	Des Moines	Dec. 28, 1846	29	310	200	55,857	416	56,273	26
KS	1727	Topeka	Jan. 29, 1861	34	400	210	81,759	520	82,278	15
KY	1774	Frankfort	June 1, 1792	15	380	140	39,486	921	40,408	37
LA	1699	Baton Rouge	Apr. 30, 1812	18	380	130	43,204	9,174	52,378	31
ME	1624	Augusta	Mar. 15, 1820	23	320	190	30,843	4,537	35,380	39
MD	1634	Annapolis	Apr. 28, 1788	7	250	90	9,707	2,699	12,406	42
MA	1620	Boston	Feb. 6, 1788	6	190	50	7,800	2,754	10,554	44
MI	1668	Lansing	Jan. 26, 1837	26	490	240	56,539	40,175	96,714	11
MN	1805	St. Paul	May 11, 1858	32	400	250	79,627	7,309	86,936	12
MS	1699	Jackson	Dec. 10, 1817	20	340	170	46,923	1,509	48,432	32
MO	1735	Jefferson City	Aug. 10, 1821	24	300	240	68,742	965	69,707	21
MT	1809	Helena	Nov. 8, 1889	41	630	280	145,546	1,494	147,040	4
NE	1823	Lincoln	Mar. 1, 1867	37	430	210	76,824	524	77,348	16
NV	1849	Carson City	Oct. 31, 1864	36	490	320	109,781	791	110,572	7
NH	1623	Concord	June 21, 1788	9	190	70	8,953	397	9,349	46
NJ	1660	Trenton	Dec. 18, 1787	3	150	70	7,354	1,368	8,723	47
NM	1610	Santa Fe	Jan. 6, 1912	47	370	343	121,298	292	121,590	5
NY	1614	Albany	July 26, 1788	11	330	283	47,126	7,429	54,555	27
NC	1660	Raleigh	Nov. 21, 1789	12	500	150	48,618	5,201	53,819	28
ND	1812	Bismarck	Nov. 2, 1889	39	340	211	69,001	1,698	70,698	19
OH	1788	Columbus	Mar. 1, 1803	17	220	220	40,861	3,965	44,826	34
OK	1889	Oklahoma City	Nov. 16, 1907	46	400	220	68,595	1,304	69,899	20
OR	1811	Salem	Feb. 14, 1859	33	360	261	95,988	2,391	98,379	9
PA	1682	Harrisburg	Dec. 12, 1787	2	283	160	44,743	1,312	46,054	33
RI	1636	Providence	May 29, 1790	13	40	30	1,034	511	1,545	50
SC	1670	Columbia	May 23, 1788	8	260	200	30,061	1,960	32,020	40
SD	1859	Pierre	Nov. 2, 1889	40	380	210	75,811	1,305	77,116	17
TN	1769	Nashville	June 1, 1796	16	440	120	41,235	909	42,144	36
TX	1682	Austin	Dec. 29, 1845	28	790	660	261,232	7,365	268,596	2
UT	1847	Salt Lake City	Jan. 4, 1896	45	350	270	82,170	2,727	84,897	13
VT	1724	Montpelier	Mar. 4, 1791	14	160	80	9,217	400	9,616	45
VA	1607	Richmond	June 25, 1788	10	430	200	39,490	3,285	42,775	35
WA	1811	Olympia	Nov. 11, 1889	42	360	240	66,456	4,842	71,298	18
WV	1727	Charleston	June 20, 1863	35	240	130	24,038	192	24,230	41
WI	1766	Madison	May 29, 1848	30	310	260	54,158	11,339	65,496	23
WY	1834	Cheyenne	July 10, 1890	44	360	280	97,093	720	97,813	10

NA = Not applicable. **Note:** Land and water areas may not add up to totals because of rounding. (1) First permanent settlement by Europeans. (2) Does not include Aleutian Islands or Alexander Archipelago.

Continental Divide of the U.S.

The Continental Divide of the U.S., also known as the Great Divide, is located at the watershed created by the mountain ranges, or tablelands, of the Rocky Mountains. This watershed separates the waters that ultimately drain into the Atlantic Ocean and its marginal seas from those waters that drain into the Pacific Ocean. The majority of water flowing E in the U.S. drains into the Gulf of Mexico and then the Atlantic. The majority of water flowing W drains through the Columbia River or Colorado River, which flows into the Gulf of California before reaching the Pacific.

The location and route of the Continental Divide across the U.S. can be described as follows:

Beginning at the U.S.-Mexico border, near longitude 108°45′ W, the Divide, in a northerly direction, follows New Mexico along the western edge of the Rio Grande drainage basin, entering Colorado near longitude 106°41′ W. From there by an irregular route N across Colorado along the western summits of the Rio Grande and Arkansas, South Platte,

and North Platte river basins, and across Rocky Mountain National Park, entering Wyoming near longitude 106°52′ W.

From there in a northwesterly direction, the western rims of the North Platte, Big Horn, and Yellowstone river basins, crossing the SW portion of Yellowstone National Park. From there in a westerly and then northerly direction forming the boundary between Idaho and Montana, to a point on the boundary near longitude 114°00′ W. From there northeasterly and northwesterly through Montana and Glacier National Park, entering Canada near longitude 114°04′ W.

Depending on how a "divide" is defined, the U.S. can also be characterized as having a Northern (or Laurentian) Divide, Eastern Divide, and St. Lawrence Seaway Divide. Some of the waters at the Northern Divide drain into Hudson Bay and the Arctic Ocean. The Appalachian Mountains mark the Eastern Divide, with waters joining the Atlantic or Gulf of Mexico. The waters at the St. Lawrence Seaway Divide, near Chicago, flow into the Gulf of St. Lawrence or Gulf of Mexico.

Chronological List of Territories, With State Admissions to Union

Source: U.S. National Archives and Records Administration

Territory	Date of act creating territory	When act took effect	Date of admission as state	Years as terr.
Northwest Territory[1]	July 13, 1787	No fixed date	Mar. 1, 1803[2]	16
Territory southwest of Ohio River	May 26, 1790	No fixed date	June 1, 1796[3]	6
Mississippi	Apr. 7, 1798	When president acted	Dec. 10, 1817	19
Indiana	May 7, 1800	July 4, 1800	Dec. 11, 1816	16
Orleans	Mar. 26, 1804	Oct. 1, 1804	Apr. 30, 1812[4]	7
Michigan	Jan. 11, 1805	June 30, 1805	Jan. 26, 1837	31
Louisiana-Missouri[5]	Mar. 3, 1805	July 4, 1805	Aug. 10, 1821	16
Illinois	Feb. 3, 1809	Mar. 1, 1809	Dec. 3, 1818	9
Alabama	Mar. 3, 1817	When MS became a state	Dec. 14, 1819	2
Arkansas	Mar. 2, 1819	July 4, 1819	June 15, 1836	17
Florida	Mar. 30, 1822	No fixed date	Mar. 3, 1845	23
Wisconsin	Apr. 20, 1836	July 3, 1836	May 29, 1848	12
Iowa	June 12, 1838	July 3, 1838	Dec. 28, 1846	8
Oregon	Aug. 14, 1848	Date of act	Feb. 14, 1859	10
Minnesota	Mar. 3, 1849	Date of act	May 11, 1858	9
New Mexico	Sept. 9, 1850	On president's proclamation	Jan. 6, 1912	61
Utah	Sept. 9, 1850	Date of act	Jan. 4, 1896	46
Washington	Mar. 2, 1853	Date of act	Nov. 11, 1889	36
Nebraska	May 30, 1854	Date of act	Mar. 1, 1867	12
Kansas	May 30, 1854	Date of act	Jan. 29, 1861	6
Colorado	Feb. 28, 1861	Date of act	Aug. 1, 1876	15
Nevada	Mar. 2, 1861	Date of act	Oct. 31, 1864	3
Dakota	Mar. 2, 1861	Date of act	Nov. 2, 1889	28
Arizona	Feb. 24, 1863	Date of act	Feb. 14, 1912	49
Idaho	Mar. 3, 1863	Date of act	July 3, 1890	27
Montana	May 26, 1864	Date of act	Nov. 8, 1889	25
Wyoming	July 25, 1868	When officers were qualified	July 10, 1890	22
Alaska	May 17, 1884[6]	No fixed date	Jan. 3, 1959	75
Oklahoma	May 2, 1890	Date of act	Nov. 16, 1907	17
Hawaii	Apr. 30, 1900	June 14, 1900	Aug. 21, 1959	59

(1) Included what is now Ohio, Indiana, Illinois, Michigan, Wisconsin, and E Minnesota. (2) Date of admission for Ohio, the first state created out of NW territory. (3) Admitted as the state of Tennessee. (4) Admitted as the state of Louisiana. (5) The act renaming Louisiana Territory as Missouri Territory (June 4, 1812) became effective Dec. 7, 1812. (6) Act constituted Alaska as a district, though it was often referred to and administered as a territory. The Territory of Alaska was formally organized by an act of Aug. 24, 1912.

U.S. Geographic Centers

Source: U.S. Geological Survey, U.S. Dept. of the Interior

There is no generally accepted definition of a geographic center and no uniform method for determining it. Geographic center is defined here as the center of gravity of the surface of an area, or that point on which an area would balance if it were a plane of uniform thickness.

No government agency has officially established any points marking the geographic center of the U.S., the conterminous U.S. (48 states), or the North American continent. Private citizens erected a monument in Lebanon, KS, marking it as the geographic center of the conterminous U.S.; a cairn in Rugby, ND, asserts that location as the center of the North American continent.

The geographic centers in the following list are approximate. They are indicated by county then city unless otherwise noted.

U.S., including Alaska and Hawaii: W of Castle Rock, Butte County, South Dakota; 44°58′ N, 103°46′ W
Conterminous U.S. (48 states): near Lebanon, Smith County, Kansas; 39°50′ N, 98°35′ W
North American continent: 6 mi W of Balta, Pierce County, North Dakota; 48°10′ N, 100°10′ W
Alabama: Chilton, 12 mi SW of Clanton
Alaska: approx. 60 mi NW of Mt. McKinley (Denali); 63°50′ N, 152° W
Arizona: Yavapai, 55 mi E-SE of Prescott
Arkansas: Pulaski, 12 mi NW of Little Rock
California: Madera, 38 mi E of Madera
Colorado: Park, 30 mi NW of Pikes Peak
Connecticut: Hartford, at East Berlin
Delaware: Kent, 11 mi S of Dover
District of Columbia: near 4th and L Sts. NW
Florida: Hernando, 12 mi N-NW of Brooksville
Georgia: Twiggs, 18 mi SE of Macon
Hawaii: off Maui; 20°15′ N, 156°20′ W
Idaho: Custer, SW of Challis
Illinois: Logan, 28 mi NE of Springfield
Indiana: Boone, 14 mi N-NW of Indianapolis
Iowa: Story, 5 mi NE of Ames
Kansas: Barton, 15 mi NE of Great Bend
Kentucky: Marion, 3 mi N-NW of Lebanon
Louisiana: Avoyelles, 3 mi SE of Marksville
Maine: Piscataquis, 18 mi N of Dover
Maryland: Prince George's, 4.5 mi NW of Davidsonville
Massachusetts: Worcester, N part of city of Worcester

Michigan: Wexford, 5 mi N-NW of Cadillac
Minnesota: Crow Wing, 10 mi SW of Brainerd
Mississippi: Leake, 9 mi W-NW of Carthage
Missouri: Miller, 20 mi SW of Jefferson City
Montana: Fergus, 11 mi W of Lewistown
Nebraska: Custer, 10 mi NW of Broken Bow
Nevada: Lander, 26 mi SE of Austin
New Hampshire: Belknap, 3 mi E of Ashland
New Jersey: Mercer, 5 mi SE of Trenton
New Mexico: Torrance, 12 mi S-SW of Willard
New York: Madison, 12 mi S of Oneida and 26 mi SW of Utica
North Carolina: Chatham, 10 mi NW of Sanford
North Dakota: Sheridan, 5 mi SW of McClusky
Ohio: Delaware, 25 mi N-NE of Columbus
Oklahoma: Oklahoma, 8 mi N of Oklahoma City
Oregon: Crook, 25 mi S-SE of Prineville
Pennsylvania: Centre, 2.5 mi SW of Bellefonte
Rhode Island: Kent, 1 mi S-SW of Crompton
South Carolina: Richland, 13 mi SE of Columbia
South Dakota: Hughes, 8 mi NE of Pierre
Tennessee: Rutherford, 5 mi NE of Murfreesboro
Texas: McCulloch, 15 mi NE of Brady
Utah: Sanpete, 3 mi N of Manti
Vermont: Washington, 3 mi E of Roxbury
Virginia: Buckingham, 5 mi SW of Buckingham
Washington: Chelan, 10 mi W-SW of Wenatchee
West Virginia: Braxton, 4 mi E of Sutton
Wisconsin: Wood, 9 mi SE of Marshfield
Wyoming: Fremont, 58 mi E-NE of Lander

Lengths of U.S. Boundaries

The length of the N boundary of the conterminous U.S.—the U.S.-Canadian border excluding Alaska—is 3,987 mi according to the U.S. Geological Survey. The length of the Alaskan-Canadian border is 1,538 mi. The U.S.-Mexican border, from the Gulf of Mexico to the Pacific Ocean, is about 1,933 mi per a 1963 boundary agreement.

Origins of the Names of U.S. States

Source: State officials; Smithsonian Institution; Topographic Division, U.S. Geological Survey, U.S. Dept. of the Interior

Alabama: Choctaw word for a Chickasaw tribe. First noted in accounts of Hernando de Soto expedition.

Alaska: Russian version of Aleutian (Eskimo) word *alakshak* for "peninsula," "great lands," or "land that is not an island."

Arizona: Spanish version of Pima Indian word for "little spring place" or Aztec *arizuma*, meaning "silver-bearing."

Arkansas: Algonquin name for Quapaw Indians, meaning "south wind."

California: Bestowed by Spanish conquistadors (possibly Hernán Cortés). It was the name of an imaginary island in the 1510 Spanish novel *Las Sergas de Esplandián*, by Garci Rodríguez de Montalvo. The Spanish first visited *Baja* (Lower) *California* in 1533. The present-day U.S. state was called *Alta* (Upper) *California*.

Colorado: From Spanish for "red," first applied to Colorado River.

Connecticut: From Mohican and other Algonquin words meaning "long river place."

Delaware: Named for Lord De La Warr, early governor of Virginia; first applied to river, then to Indian tribe (Lenni-Lenape).

District of Columbia: For Christopher Columbus, 1791.

Florida: Named by Juan Ponce de León *Pascua Florida*, "Flowery Easter," on Easter Sunday, 1513.

Georgia: Named by colonial administrator James Oglethorpe for King George II of England in 1732.

Hawaii: Possibly derived from *Hawaiki* or *Owhyhee*, Polynesian word for "homeland."

Idaho: Said to be a coined name with the invented meaning "gem of the mountains"; suggested for the Pikes Peak mining territory (Colorado), then applied to the new mining territory of the Pacific Northwest. Another theory suggests *Idaho* may be Kiowa Apache term for the Comanche.

Illinois: French for *Illini* or "land of *Illini*," Algonquin word meaning "men" or "warriors."

Indiana: Means "land of the Indians."

Iowa: Indian word variously translated as "here I rest" or "beautiful land." Named for the Iowa River, which was named for the Iowa Indians.

Kansas: Sioux word for "south wind people."

Kentucky: Indian word variously translated as "dark and bloody ground," "meadowland," and "land of tomorrow."

Louisiana: Part of territory called Louisiana by René-Robert Cavelier Sieur de La Salle for French King Louis XIV.

Maine: From Maine, ancient French province. Also descriptive, referring to the mainland as distinct from coastal islands.

Maryland: For Queen Henrietta Maria, wife of Charles I of England.

Massachusetts: From Indian tribe whose name meant "at or about the Great Hill" in Blue Hills region south of Boston.

Michigan: From Chippewa *mici gama*, meaning "great water," after lake of the same name.

Minnesota: From Dakota Sioux word meaning "cloudy water" or "sky-tinted water" of the Minnesota River.

Mississippi: Probably Chippewa *mici zibi*, meaning "great river" or "gathering-in of all the waters." Also Algonquin word *messipi*.

Missouri: Algonquin Indian term meaning "river of the big canoes."

Montana: Latin or Spanish for "mountainous."

Nebraska: From Omaha or Otos Indian word meaning "broad water" or "flat river," describing the Platte River.

Nevada: Spanish, meaning "snow-clad."

New Hampshire: Named by Capt. John Mason of Plymouth Council, in 1629, for his home county in England.

New Jersey: The Duke of York, in 1664, gave a patent to Lord John Berkeley and Sir George Carteret for *Nova Caesaria*, or New Jersey, after England's Isle of Jersey.

New Mexico: Spaniards in Mexico applied term to land north and west of Rio Grande in the 16th century.

New York: For James, Duke of York and Albany, who received patent for New Netherland from his brother Charles II and sent an expedition to capture it, 1664.

North Carolina: In 1619, Charles I gave patent to Sir Robert Heath for Province of Carolana, from *Carolus*, Latin name for Charles. Charles II granted a new patent to Earl of Clarendon and others. Divided into North and South Carolina, 1710.

North Dakota: Sioux word *Dakota*, meaning "friend" or "ally."

Ohio: Iroquois word for "fine or good river."

Oklahoma: Choctaw word meaning "red man," proposed by Rev. Allen Wright, Choctaw-speaking Indian.

Oregon: Origin unknown. One theory is that the name derives from *wauregan*, meaning "beautiful," term used by Indians in New England.

Pennsylvania: William Penn, Quaker who was made full proprietor of area by King Charles II in 1681, suggested "Sylvania," or "woodland," for his tract. The king's government owed 16,000 pounds to Penn's father, Adm. William Penn, and the land was granted as partial settlement. Charles II added "Penn" to "Sylvania," against the modest proprietor's desires, in honor of the admiral.

Puerto Rico: Spanish for "rich port."

Rhode Island: Origin unknown. One theory notes that Giovanni de Verrazano recorded observing an island about the size of the Greek island of Rhodes in 1524. Another theory is that Dutch explorer Adriaen Block named the state *Roode Eylandt* for its red clay.

South Carolina: See North Carolina.

South Dakota: See North Dakota.

Tennessee: *Tanasi* was the name of Cherokee villages on the Little Tennessee River. From 1784 to 1788, this was the State of Franklin, or Frankland.

Texas: Variant of word used by Caddo and other Indians meaning "friends" or "allies" and applied to them by the Spanish in eastern Texas. Also written *Texias*, *Tejas*, *Teysas*.

Utah: From a Navajo word meaning "upper," or "higher up," as applied to Shoshone tribe called Ute. Proposed name *Deseret*, "land of honeybees," from Book of Mormon, was rejected by Congress.

Vermont: From French words *vert* (green) and *mont* (mountain). The Green Mountains were said to have been named by Samuel de Champlain. When the state was formed in 1777, Dr. Thomas Young suggested combining *vert* and *mont*.

Virginia: Named by Sir Walter Raleigh, who outfitted an expedition in 1584, in honor of England's Queen Elizabeth, the Virgin Queen.

Washington: Named after George Washington. When the bill creating the Territory of Columbia was introduced in the 32nd Congress, its name was changed to Washington because of the existence of the District of Columbia.

West Virginia: So named when western counties of Virginia refused to secede from Virginia in 1863.

Wisconsin: Indian name, spelled *Ouisconsin* or *Mesconsing* by early chroniclers, believed to mean "grassy place" in Chippewa. Congress made it *Wisconsin*.

Wyoming: From Algonquin words for "large prairie place," "at the big plains," or "on the great plain."

Territorial Sea of the U.S.

According to a Dec. 27, 1988, proclamation by Pres. Ronald Reagan, "The territorial sea of the United States henceforth extends to 12 nautical miles from the baselines of the United States determined in accordance with international law. In accordance with international law, as reflected in the applicable provisions of the 1982 United Nations Convention on the Law of the Sea, within the territorial sea of the United States, the ships of all countries enjoy the right of innocent passage and the ships and aircraft of all countries enjoy the right of transit passage through international straits."

Major Accessions of Territory by the U.S.

Source: U.S. Dept. of the Interior; U.S. Census Bureau, U.S. Dept. of Commerce

Not including territories such as the Panama Canal Zone and the Philippines, which are no longer under U.S. jurisdiction. Area figures are for total area and may differ from figures given elsewhere in *The World Almanac*.

Accession	Date	Area (sq mi)	Accession	Date	Area (sq mi)	Accession	Date	Area (sq mi)
Territory in 1790[1]	NA	888,685	Mexican Cession	1848	529,017	Guam[3]	1899	212
Louisiana Purchase	1803	827,192	Gadsden Purchase	1853	29,640	American Samoa[4]	1900	76
Treaty of Florida	1819	72,003	Alaska	1867	586,412	U.S. Virgin Islands	1917	133
Texas	1845	390,143	Hawaii	1898	6,450	Northern Marianas[5]	1986	179
Oregon Territory	1846	285,680	Puerto Rico[2]	1899	3,435			

NA = Not applicable. (1) Includes that part of a drainage basin of Red River of the North, south of 49th parallel, sometimes considered part of Louisiana Purchase. (2) Ceded by Spain in 1898, ratified in 1899, and became the Commonwealth of Puerto Rico by Act of Congress on July 25, 1952. (3) Acquired in 1898; ratified 1899. (4) Acquired in 1899; ratified 1900. (5) Part of the UN Trust Territory of the Pacific Islands, which U.S. began administering in 1947; became U.S. commonwealth Nov. 3, 1986.

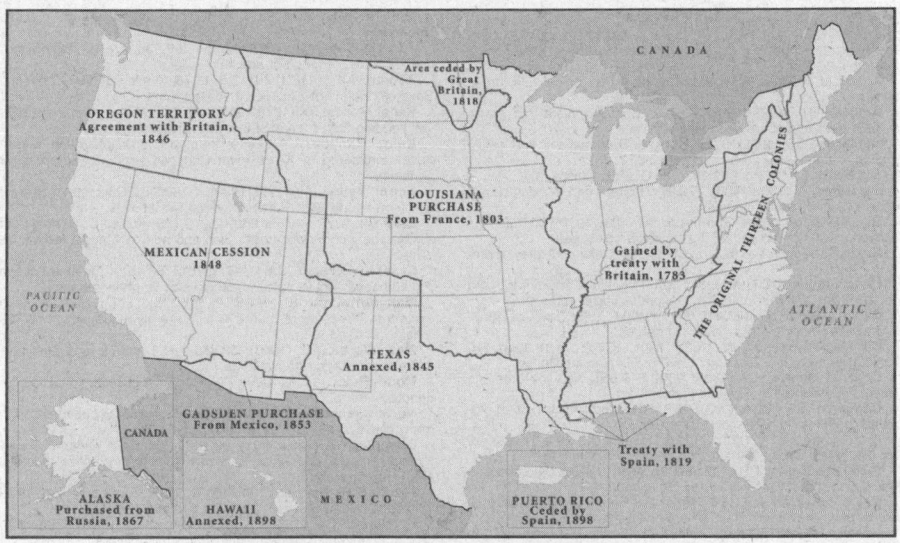

U.S. Forest Service Special Designated Areas

Source: U.S. Forest Service, U.S. Dept. of Agriculture; as of Sept. 30, 2012

These areas within the National Forest System have been specially designated by presidential proclamation or act of Congress. Size of an area does not include acreage within National Forest boundaries that is not federally owned or administered by the Forest Service.

NM = Natl. Monument; NRA = Natl. Recreation Area; NS(A) = Natl. Scenic (Area); NVM = Natl. Volcanic Monument; SRA = Scenic Recreation Area

Area	Location	Estab.	Acreage	Area	Location	Estab.	Acreage
Admiralty Island NM	AK	1980	974,278	Mount Baker NRA	WA	1984	8,473
Allegheny NRA	PA	1984	24,145	Mount Hood NRA	OR	2009	34,474
Arapaho NRA	CO	1978	32,521	Mount Pleasant NSA	VA	1994	7,580
Bear Creek NSA	VA	2009	5,128	Mount Rogers NRA	VA	1966	118,509
Beech Creek NSA	OK	1988	6,200	Mount St. Helens NVM	WA	1989	112,605
Cascade Head NS Research Area	OR	1974	6,637	Newberry NVM	OR	1990	54,822
Chimney Rock NM	CO	2012	4,726	Opal Creek SRA	OR	1996	12,645
Columbia River Gorge NSA	OR-WA	1986	72,974	Oregon Dunes NRA	OR	1972	27,232
Coosa Bald NSA	GA	1991	7,100	Pine Ridge NRA	NE	1986	6,600
Ed Jenkins NRA	GA	1991	23,166	Rattlesnake NRA	MT	1980	59,119
Flaming Gorge NRA	UT-WY	1968	189,825	Robert T. Stafford White Rocks NRA	VT	1984	36,152
Giant Sequoia NM	CA	2000	327,769	Santa Rosa and			
Grand Island NRA	MI	1990	12,974	San Jacinto Mountains NM	CA	2000	64,400
Hells Canyon NRA	OR-ID	1975	537,770	Sawtooth NRA	ID	1972	729,428
Indian Nations NS and Wildlife Area	OK	1988	39,171	Seng Mountain NSA	VA	2009	5,192
Jemez NRA	NM	1993	44,670	Smith River NRA	CA	1990	305,169
Jewel Cave NM	SD	1908	1,120	Spring Mountains NRA	NV	1993	314,367
Land Between the Lakes NRA	KY-TN	1998	170,310	Spruce Knob-Seneca Rocks NRA	WV	1965	57,232
Misty Fiords NM	AK	1980	2,293,842	Whiskeytown-Shasta-Trinity NRA	CA	1965	176,367
Mono Basin NSA	CA	1984	128,303	Winding Stair Mountain NRA	OK	1988	25,890
Moosalamoo NRA	VT	2006	15,170				

Most-Visited Sites in the National Park System, 2012

Source: National Park Service (NPS), U.S. Dept. of the Interior
Attendance at 367 of 398 NPS sites totaled 282,765,682 recreation visits in 2012. (Not all units report public use statistics.)

Rank	Site (location)	Recreation visits
1.	Blue Ridge Parkway (NC-VA)	15,205,059
2.	Golden Gate Natl. Recreation Area (CA)	14,540,338
3.	Great Smoky Mountains Natl. Park (NC-TN)	9,685,829
4.	George Washington Memorial Parkway (VA-MD-DC)	7,425,577
5.	Lake Mead Natl. Recreation Area (AZ-NV)	6,285,439
6.	Lincoln Memorial (DC)	6,191,361
7.	Natchez Trace Parkway (MS-AL-TN)	5,560,668
8.	Gateway Natl. Recreation Area (NJ-NY)	5,043,863
9.	Gulf Islands National Seashore (FL-MS)	4,973,462
10.	Delaware Water Gap Natl. Recreation Area (NJ-PA)	4,970,802
11.	Chesapeake & Ohio Canal Natl. Historical Park (DC-MD-WV)	4,712,377
12.	Cape Cod National Seashore (MA)	4,441,290
13.	Vietnam Veterans Memorial (DC)	4,424,407
14.	Grand Canyon National Park (AZ)	4,421,352
15.	World War II Memorial (DC)	4,161,685
16.	San Francisco Maritime Natl. Historical Park (CA)	4,129,983
17.	Yosemite National Park (CA)	3,853,404
18.	Martin Luther King Jr. Memorial (DC)	3,738,336
19.	Independence National Historical Park (PA)	3,594,549
20.	Yellowstone National Park (ID-MT-WY)	3,447,729

National Parks and Other Areas Administered by National Park Service

As of Dec. 31, 2012, the National Park Service (NPS) administered about 84,422,725 acres of federal and non-federal land across 398 sites. Date when area was authorized or established by Congress or by presidential proclamation is given in parentheses; any date that follows indicates when a site received its current designation or was transferred to the NPS. Figure after the date is gross area acres as of Dec. 31, 2012. Refer to the National Trails System for National Park Service trails.

National Parks

Acadia, ME (1916/1929): 47,458. Incl. Mount Desert Isl., half of Isle au Haut, Schoodic Peninsula on mainland. Highest elevation on Eastern seaboard.

American Samoa, AS (1988): 9,000. Paleotropical rain forest, coral reef.

Arches, UT (1929/1971): 76,679. Contains giant red sandstone arches and other products of erosion.

Badlands, SD (1929/1978): 242,756. Reformations and native prairie; animal fossils 23-37 mil years old.

Big Bend, TX (1935): 801,163. Rio Grande, Chisos Mts.

Biscayne, FL (1968/1980): 172,971. Aquatic park encompassing chain of islands south of Miami.

Black Canyon of the Gunnison, CO (1933/1999): 30,750. Has canyon 2,900 ft deep and 40 ft wide at narrowest part.

Bryce Canyon, UT (1923/1928): 35,835. Colorful display of erosion effects.

Canyonlands, UT (1964): 337,598. At junction of Colorado and Green Rivers; extensive evidence of prehistoric peoples.

Capitol Reef, UT (1937/1971): 241,904. 70-mi uplift of sandstone cliffs dissected by high-walled gorges.

Carlsbad Caverns, NM (1923/1930): 46,766. More than 110 limestone caves, incl. Carlsbad Cavern; Chihuahuan Desert.

Channel Islands, CA (1938/1980): 249,561. Sea lion breeding place, nesting seabirds, unique plants.

Congaree, SC (1976/2003): 26,546. Largest intact tract of old-growth bottomland hardwood forest in U.S.

Crater Lake, OR (1902): 183,224. Deepest U.S. lake, in crater of Mt. Mazama, volcano that erupted about 7,700 years ago.

Cuyahoga Valley, OH (1974/2000): 32,831. Along Ohio and Erie Canal system between Akron and Cleveland.

Death Valley, CA-NV (1933/1994): 3,373,063. Large desert. Incl. lowest point in Western Hemisphere and Scotty's Castle.

Denali, AK (1917/1980): 4,740,911. Formerly known as Mt. McKinley; highest mountain in U.S.

Dry Tortugas, FL (1935/1992): 64,701. Ft. Jefferson and seven coral reef and sand islands near Key West.

Everglades, FL (1934): 1,508,976. Largest remaining subtropical wilderness in continental U.S.

Gates of the Arctic, AK (1978/1984): 7,523,897. Vast wilderness in north central region. Limited federal facilities.

Glacier, MT (1910): 1,013,322. Rocky Mt. scenery, numerous glaciers and glacial lakes. Part of Waterton-Glacier Intl. Peace Park established by U.S. and Canada in 1932.

Glacier Bay, AK (1925/1986): 3,223,383. Tidewater glaciers that move down mountainsides and break up into sea.

Grand Canyon, AZ (1893/1919): 1,217,191. Carved by Colorado River.

Grand Teton, WY (1929): 310,044. Most impressive part of Teton Mts.; winter feeding ground of largest American elk herd.

Great Basin, NV (1922/1986): 77,180. Incl. Wheeler Peak, Lexington Arch, Lehman Caves.

Great Sand Dunes, CO (1932/2000): 44,246. North America's tallest dunes.

Great Smoky Mountains, NC-TN (1926/1934): 522,427. Largest Eastern U.S. mountain range; magnificent forests.

Guadalupe Mountains, TX (1966): 86,367. Extensive Permian limestone fossil reef; tremendous earth fault.

Haleakalā, HI (1916/1960): 33,265. Dormant volcano on island of Maui with large craters.

Hawai'i Volcanoes, HI (1916/1961): 323,431. Contains Kilauea and Mauna Loa, active volcanoes.

Hot Springs, AR (1832/1921): 5,549. Waters from park's 47 hot springs used for bathing and drinking.

Isle Royale, MI (1931): 571,790. Largest island in Lake Superior.

Joshua Tree, CA (1936/1994): 790,636. Desert region incl. Joshua trees, other plant and animal life.

Katmai, AK (1918/1980): 3,674,378. "Valley of Ten Thousand Smokes," scene of 1912 volcanic eruption.

Kenai Fjords, AK (1978/1980): 669,984. Marine mammals, birdlife; Harding Icefield, one of four major icecaps in U.S.

Kings Canyon, CA (1890/1940): 461,901. Mountain wilderness, dominated by Kings River Canyons and High Sierra; giant sequoias.

Kobuk Valley, AK (1978/1980): 1,750,716. Contains geological and recreational sites. Limited federal facilities.

Lake Clark, AK (1978/1980): 2,619,713. Across Cook Inlet from Anchorage; scenic wilderness, fish and wildlife. Limited federal facilities.

Lassen Volcanic, CA (1907/1916): 106,452. Contains Lassen Peak, recently active volcano; other volcanic phenomena.

Mammoth Cave, KY (1926/1941): 52,830. Longest known cave system in world (more than 390 mi currently surveyed); river 300 ft below surface.

Mesa Verde, CO (1906): 52,485. Most notable and best preserved prehistoric cliff dwellings in U.S.

Mount Rainier, WA (1899): 236,381. Most glaciated peak in contiguous U.S.

North Cascades, WA (1968): 504,781. Mountainous region with many glaciers, lakes.

Olympic, WA (1909/1938): 922,650. Mountain wilderness containing remnant of Pacific Northwest rain forest, active glaciers, shoreline, rare elk.

Petrified Forest, AZ (1906/1962): 221,415. Extensive petrified wood and Indian artifacts. Contains part of Painted Desert.

Redwood, CA (1968): 139,044. 40 mi of Pacific coastline, groves of ancient redwoods and world's tallest trees.

Rocky Mountain, CO (1915): 265,761. On Continental Divide; incl. peaks over 14,000 ft.

Saguaro, AZ (1933/1994): 91,442. Part of Sonoran Desert; incl. giant saguaro cacti, unique to region.

Sequoia, CA (1890): 404,063. Giant sequoia groves; world's largest tree (by volume). Mt. Whitney, highest mountain in conterminous U.S.

Shenandoah, VA (1926): 199,100. Portion of Blue Ridge Mts.; overlooks Shenandoah Valley; Skyline Drive.

Theodore Roosevelt, ND (1947/1978): 70,447. Contains part of Roosevelt's ranch and scenic badlands.

Virgin Islands, VI (1956): 14,951. Covers 75% of St. John Isl. and Hassel Isl.; beaches, Carib Indian petroglyphs, evidence of colonial Danes.

Voyageurs, MN (1971): 218,200. Abundant lakes, forests, wildlife.

Wind Cave, SD (1903): 33,847. Limestone caverns in Black Hills; extensive wildlife incl. bison herd.

Wrangell-St. Elias, AK (1978/1980): 8,323,147. Largest area in park system; most peaks over 16,000 ft. No federal facilities.

Yellowstone, ID-MT-WY (1872): 2,219,791. World's first national park. World's greatest geyser area with about 10,000 geysers, hot springs; falls and canyons of Yellowstone River; grizzly bear, moose, bison.

Yosemite, CA (1890): 761,268. Yosemite Valley, country's highest waterfall, grove of sequoias, mountains.

Zion, UT (1909/1919): 146,597. Unusual shapes, landscapes resulting from erosion and faulting; evidence of past volcanic activity; contains 2,394-ft monolith "Great White Throne."

National Historical Parks

Abraham Lincoln Birthplace, Hodgenville, KY (1916/1959): 345. Memorial building, sinking spring.

Adams, Quincy, MA (1946/1998): 24. Home of Pres. John Adams, John Quincy Adams, and descendants.

Appomattox Court House, VA (1930/1954): 1,774. Where Confederate Gen. Lee surrendered to Gen. Grant, signaling Civil War's end.

Boston, MA (1974): 44. Incl. Faneuil Hall, Old North Church, Bunker Hill, Paul Revere House.

Cane River Creole, LA (1994): 206. Preserves Creole culture as it developed along the Cane River.

Cedar Creek & Belle Grove, VA (2002): 3,712. Civil War battle site and an antebellum plantation in Shenandoah Valley.

Chaco Culture, NM (1907/1980): 33,960. Ruins of pueblos built by prehistoric peoples incl. Pueblo, Hopi, and Navajo.

Chesapeake & Ohio Canal, MD-DC-WV (1938/1971): 19,612. 184-mi historic canal; DC to Cumberland, MD.

Colonial, VA (1930/1936): 8,677. Incl. most of Jamestown Isl., site of first successful English colony; Yorktown, site of Cornwallis's surrender to George Washington; Colonial Parkway.

Cumberland Gap, KY-TN-VA (1940): 24,547. Mountain pass of Wilderness Road, which carried first great migration of pioneers into America's interior.

Dayton Aviation Heritage, OH (1992): 111. Commemorates area's involvement in aviation.

George Rogers Clark, Vincennes, IN (1966): 26. Commemorates American defeat of British in West during Revolution.

Harpers Ferry, MD-VA-WV (1944/1963): 3,670. At confluence of Shenandoah and Potomac Rivers, the site of John Brown's 1859 raid on the Army arsenal.

Hopewell Culture, OH (1923/1992): 1,765. Remains of ceremonial mounds built in the Ohio River Valley, 200 BCE-500 CE.

Independence, Philadelphia, PA (1948): 45. Several properties associated with American Revolution and founding of U.S., incl. Independence Hall, Liberty Bell Center.

Jean Lafitte (and Preserve), LA (1907/1978): 23,664. Incl. Chalmette, site of 1815 Battle of New Orleans; French Quarter.

Kalaupapa, HI (1980): 10,779. Molokai's former leper colony.

Kaloko-Honokohau, HI (1978): 1,163. Preserves native culture of Hawaii.

Keweenaw, MI (1992): 1,869. Site of first significant copper mine in U.S.

Klondike Gold Rush, AK-WA (1976): 12,996. Preserves Chilkoot Trail used in 1898 Gold Rush. Museum in Seattle.

Lewis and Clark, OR-WA (1958/2004): 3,410. Lewis and Clark encampment, 1805-06. Incorporates former Fort Clatsop Natl. Mem. Park and OR-WA state parks.

Lowell, MA (1978): 141. Textile mills, canal, 19th cent. structures; park shows planned city of Industrial Revolution.

Lyndon B. Johnson, TX (1969/1980): 1,570. President's birthplace, boyhood home, ranch.

Marsh-Billings-Rockefeller, VT (1992): 643. Boyhood home of conservationist George Perkins Marsh.

Minute Man, MA (1959): 1,027. Where Minute Men battled British, Apr. 19, 1775. Also contains Nathaniel Hawthorne's home.

Morristown, NJ (1933): 1,711. Site of important military encampments during the American Revolution; Washington's headquarters, 1779-80.

Natchez, MS (1988): 108. Mansions, townhouses, and villas related to history of Natchez.

New Bedford Whaling, MA (1996): 34. Preserves structures and relics associated with the city's 19th-cent. whaling industry.

New Orleans Jazz, LA (1994): 5. Preserves, educates, and interprets jazz as it has evolved in New Orleans.

Nez Perce, ID-MT-OR-WA (1965): 4,565. Illustrates history and culture of Nez Perce, or Nimiipuu, homeland (38 separate sites).

Palo Alto Battlefield, TX (1978): 3,442. Scene of first battle of the Mexican War.

Paterson Great Falls, NJ (2011): 36. Falls helped make city one of U.S.'s earliest industrial centers.

Pecos, NM (1965/1990): 6,703. Ruins of ancient Pueblo of Pecos, archaeological sites, and two associated Spanish colonial missions from 17th and 18th centuries.

Pu'uhonua o Hōnaunau, HI (1955/1978): 420. Until 1819, a sanctuary for Hawaiians vanquished in battle and for those guilty of crimes or breaking taboos.

Rosie the Riveter/WWII Home Front, Richmond, CA (2000): 145. Site of shipyard that employed thousands of women during WWII; commemorates women who worked in wartime industries.

Salt River Bay (and Ecological Preserve), St. Croix, VI (1992): 986. Only known site where, in 1493, members of a Columbus party landed on what is now U.S. territory.

San Antonio Missions, TX (1978): 824. Four Spanish missions, 18th-cent. irrigation system.

San Francisco Maritime, CA (1988): 50. Artifacts, photographs, and historic vessels related to development of the Pacific Coast.

San Juan Island, WA (1966): 2,146. Commemorates peaceful relations between U.S., Canada, and Great Britain since the 1872 boundary disputes.

Saratoga, NY (1938): 3,394. Scene of a major 1777 battle that became a turning point in the American Revolution.

Sitka, AK (1910/1972): 112. Scene of last major resistance of Tlingit to the Russians, 1804.

Thomas Edison, West Orange, NJ (1955/1962): 21. Inventor's home and laboratory.

Tumacacori, AZ (1908/1990): 360. Historic Spanish mission building near site first visited by Father Kino in 1691.

Valley Forge, PA (1976): 3,468. Continental Army campsite in 1777-78 winter.

War in the Pacific, GU (1978): 2,037. Seven distinct units illustrating the Pacific theater of WWII. Limited federal facilities.

Women's Rights, NY (1980): 7. Seneca Falls site where Lucretia Mott, Elizabeth Cady Stanton organized movement in 1848.

National Battlefields/Parks/Sites

Antietam, MD (1890/1978): 3,230. Battle here ended first Confederate invasion of North, Sept. 17, 1862.

Big Hole, MT (1910/1963): 1,011. Site of major battle with Nez Perce Indians, Aug. 9-10, 1877.

Brices Cross Roads, Baldwyn, MS (1929): 1. Site of Confederate victory, June 10, 1864.

Cowpens, SC (1929/1972): 842. American Revolution battlefield, Jan. 17, 1781.

Fort Donelson, TN-KY (1928/1985): 1,025. Site of first major Union victory, Feb. 14-16, 1862.

Fort Necessity, PA (1931/1961): 903. Site of first battle of French and Indian War, July 3, 1754.

Kennesaw Mountain, GA (1917/1935): 2,853. Site of major battle of Atlanta campaign in Civil War.

Manassas, VA (1940): 5,073. Scene of two Civil War battles.

Monocacy, MD (1934/1976): 1,647. Civil War battle in defense of Washington, DC, fought here, July 9, 1864.

Moores Creek, Currie, NC (1926/1980): 88. Commemorates Feb. 27, 1776, battle between Patriots and Loyalists.

Petersburg, VA (1926/1962): 2,740. Scene of Union campaigns, 1864-65.

Richmond, VA (1936): 6,956. Site of battles defending Confederate capital.

River Raisin, Monroe, MI (2010): 42. Site of major battles of War of 1812.

Stones River, TN (1927/1960): 709. Scene of battle that began federal offensive to trisect Confederacy, Dec. 31, 1862-Jan. 2, 1863.

Tupelo, MS (1929/1961): 1. Site of crucial battle over Union Gen. Sherman's supply line, July 14-15, 1865.

Wilson's Creek, MO (1960/1970): 2,369. Scene of Civil War battle for control of Missouri, Aug. 10, 1861.

National Military Parks

Chickamauga and Chattanooga, GA-TN (1890): 9,036. Where Gen. Sherman and Union armies gained control of TN, 1863.

Fredericksburg and Spotsylvania, VA (1927/1933): 8,382. Sites of several major Civil War battles and campaigns.

Gettysburg, PA (1895/1933): 5,989. Site of decisive Confederate defeat in North, July 1863, and of Gettysburg Address.

Guilford Courthouse, NC (1917/1933): 250. American Revolution battle site.

Horseshoe Bend, AL (1956): 2,040. On Tallapoosa River, where Gen. Andrew Jackson broke power of Upper Creek Indian Confederacy on Mar. 27, 1814.

Kings Mountain, SC (1931/1933): 3,945. Site of American Revolution battle, fought on Oct. 7, 1780.

Pea Ridge, AR (1956): 4,300. Civil War battle, Mar. 7-8, 1862.

Shiloh, TN-MS (1894/1933): 5,976. Major Civil War battle site; incl. Indian burial mounds.

Vicksburg, MS-LA (1899/1933): 1,802. Union victory gave North control of Mississippi and split Confederate forces.

National Memorials

Arkansas Post, AR (1960): 758. First permanent French settlement in lower Mississippi River valley.

Arlington House, The Robert E. Lee Memorial, VA (1925/1972): 28. Lee's home overlooking the Potomac River.

Chamizal, El Paso, TX (1966/1974): 55. Commemorates 1963 settlement of 99-year border dispute with Mexico.

Coronado, AZ (1941/1952): 4,830. Commemorates first European exploration of the Southwest.

De Soto, Bradenton, FL (1948): 30. Commemorates 16th-cent. Spanish explorations.

Federal Hall, New York, NY (1939/1955): 0.45. First seat of U.S. government under the Constitution.

Flight 93, Shanksville, PA (2002): 2,321. Commemorates passengers and crew of Flight 93, who died thwarting an attack on Sept. 11, 2001. First features of memorial completed and dedicated in 2011.

Fort Caroline, Jacksonville, FL (1950): 138. On St. Johns River, site of first attempt by France, in 16th cent., at permanent North American settlement.

Franklin Delano Roosevelt Memorial, DC (1982): 8. Statues of Pres. Roosevelt and Eleanor Roosevelt; waterfalls and plaza.

General Grant, New York, NY (1958): 0.76. Tomb of Ulysses Grant and wife; largest mausoleum in U.S.

Hamilton Grange, New York, NY (1962): 1. Home of Alexander Hamilton.

Jefferson National Expansion, St. Louis, MO (1935): 193. Commemorates 19th cent. westward expansion; incl. Gateway Arch.

Johnstown Flood, PA (1964): 178. Commemorates 1889 flood.

Korean War Veterans Memorial, DC (1986): 2. Honors those who served in the Korean War.

Lincoln Boyhood, Lincoln City, IN (1962): 200. Site of Abraham Lincoln's boyhood home and grave site of his mother.

Lincoln Memorial, DC (1911/1933): 7. Marble statue of 16th president.

Lyndon Baines Johnson Memorial Grove on the Potomac, DC (1973): 17. Overlooks Potomac River; vista of the Capitol.

Martin Luther King Jr., DC (1996): 3. Granite statue of Dr. King close to where he delivered "I Have a Dream" speech.

Mount Rushmore, SD (1925): 1,278. World-famous sculpture of presidents Washington, Jefferson, Lincoln, T. Roosevelt.

Perry's Victory and International Peace Memorial, Put-in-Bay, OH (1936/1972): 25. World's most massive Doric column promotes pursuit of peace through arbitration and disarmament.

Port Chicago Naval Magazine, Danville, CA (2009): 5. Where 1944 munitions ship explosion killed 320 men.

Roger Williams, Providence, RI (1965): 5. Memorial to founder of Rhode Island.

Thaddeus Kosciuszko, Philadelphia, PA (1972): 0.02. Memorial to Polish hero of American Revolution.

Theodore Roosevelt Island, DC (1932/1933): 89. Statue of Roosevelt in wooded island sanctuary.

Thomas Jefferson Memorial, DC (1934): 18. Statue of Jefferson in an inscribed circular, colonnaded structure.

Vietnam Veterans Memorial, DC (1980): 2. Black granite wall with names of those missing or killed in action in Vietnam War.

Washington Monument, DC (1848/1933): 106. Obelisk honoring the first U.S. president.

World War II Memorial, DC (1994/2004): 8. Oval plaza with central pool commemorating those who fought and died.

Wright Brothers, Kill Devil Hills, NC (1927/1953): 428. Site of first powered flight.

National Historic Sites

Allegheny Portage Railroad, PA (1964): 1,284. Linked Pennsylvania Canal system and the West.

Andersonville, GA (1970): 515. Noted Civil War POW camp.

Andrew Johnson, Greeneville, TN (1935/1963): 17. Two homes and the tailor shop of 17th U.S. president.

Bent's Old Fort, CO (1960): 799. Replica of fort on Sante Fe Trail.

Boston African-American, MA (1980): 0.59. Pre-Civil War black-owned structures.

Brown v. Board of Education, Topeka, KS (1992): 2. Commemorates landmark 1954 U.S. Supreme Court decision, which ended legal segregation in schools.

Carl Sandburg Home, Flat Rock, NC (1968): 264. Home of Pulitzer Prize-winning poet and biographer.

Carter G. Woodson Home, DC (1976/2006): 0.15. Home of "Father of Black History."

Charles Pinckney, Mt. Pleasant, SC (1988): 28. Farm of a principal author and signer of the Constitution.

Christiansted, St. Croix, VI (1952/1961): 27. Commemorates Danish colony.

Clara Barton, Glen Echo, MD (1974): 9. Home of American Red Cross founder.

Edgar Allan Poe, Philadelphia, PA (1978/1980): 0.52. Writer's home.

Eisenhower, Gettysburg, PA (1967): 690. Home of 34th president.

Eleanor Roosevelt, Hyde Park, NY (1977): 181. Former first lady's personal retreat.

Eugene O'Neill, Danville, CA (1976): 13. Home where playwright wrote his final plays, incl. *The Iceman Cometh.*

First Ladies, Canton, OH (2000): 0.46. Home of first lady Ida Sexton McKinley. Library now devoted to America's first ladies.

Ford's Theatre, DC (1866/1970): 0.30. Incl. theater where Lincoln was assassinated, house where he died, and Lincoln Museum.

Fort Bowie, AZ (1964): 999. Focal point of operations against Geronimo and Apaches.

Fort Davis, TX (1961): 523. Frontier outpost in West Texas; established to guard the San Antonio-El Paso Road.

Fort Laramie, WY (1938/1960): 833. Military post on Oregon Trail.

Fort Larned, KS (1964/1966): 718. Military post on Santa Fe Trail.

Fort Point, CA (1970): 29. West Coast fortification; protected San Francisco during and after Civil War.

Fort Raleigh, NC (1941): 513. First attempted English settlement in North America.

Fort Scott, KS (1965/1978): 17. Commemorates U.S. frontier. Focal point of black troop activity, training during Civil War.

Fort Smith, AR-OK (1961): 75. One of the earliest U.S. posts in Missouri Territory, active 1817-90.

Fort Union Trading Post, MT-ND (1966): 440. Principal fur-trading post on upper Missouri, 1829-67.

Fort Vancouver, WA-OR (1948/1961): 207. Headquarters for Hudson's Bay Company.

Frederick Douglass, DC (1962/1988): 9. Home of black abolitionist, writer, orator.

Frederick Law Olmsted, Brookline, MA (1979): 7. Home of city planner, famous for designing Central Park in NYC.

Friendship Hill, PA (1978): 675. Home of Albert Gallatin, Jefferson's and Madison's secretary of treasury.

Golden Spike, UT (1957): 2,735. Commemorates completion of first transcontinental railroad in 1869.

Grant-Kohrs Ranch, MT (1972): 1,618. Ranch house owned by John Grant, 19th-cent. range-cattle industry pioneer.

Hampton, Towson, MD (1948): 62. 18th-cent. Georgian mansion, which in 1790 was largest house in U.S.

Harry S. Truman, MO (1983): 10. House of 33rd president from 1919 on and farm where he worked as young man.

Herbert Hoover, West Branch, IA (1965): 187. Birthplace and boyhood home of 31st president.

Home of Franklin D. Roosevelt, Hyde Park, NY (1944): 836. FDR's birthplace, home, and "summer White House."

Hopewell Furnace, PA (1938/1985): 848. 19th-cent. iron-making village.

Hubbell Trading Post, AZ (1965): 160. Oldest continuously operating trading post in SW; founded in 1878 on Navajo Nation.

James A. Garfield, Mentor, OH (1980): 8. Home of 20th president; site of his front-porch campaign.

Jimmy Carter, Plains, GA (1987): 72. Birthplace and home of 39th president.

John Fitzgerald Kennedy, Brookline, MA (1967): 0.09. Birthplace and childhood home of 35th president.

John Muir, Martinez, CA (1964): 344. Home of Sierra Club cofounder and "Father of the National Park Service."

Knife River Indian Villages, ND (1974): 1,749. Remnants of villages last occupied by Hidatsa and Mandan Indians.

Lincoln Home, Springfield, IL (1971): 12. Lincoln's residence when he was elected 16th president, 1860.

Little Rock Central High School, AR (1998): 27. Commemorates 1957 desegregation during which federal troops were called in to protect nine black students.

Longfellow House–Washington's Headquarters, Cambridge, MA (1972): 2. Poet's home, 1837-82; Washington's headquarters during Boston siege, 1775-76.

Maggie L. Walker, Richmond, VA (1978): 1. Home of black leader and first female bank president, daughter of former slave.

Manzanar, Lone Pine, CA (1992): 814. Manzanar War Relocation Ctr., a WWII Japanese-American internment camp.

Martin Luther King Jr., Atlanta, GA (1980): 39. Birthplace, grave, church of the civil rights leader.

Martin Van Buren, Kinderhook, NY (1974): 285. Lindenwald, home of 8th president.

Mary McLeod Bethune Council House, DC (1982/1991): 0.07. Commemorates Bethune's leadership in the black women's movement.

Minidoka, ID (2008): 218. WWII Japanese internment center.

Minuteman Missile, SD (1999): 15. Missile launch facilities dating back to Cold War era.

Nicodemus, KS (1996): 5. Only remaining Western town established by African Americans during Reconstruction.

Ninety Six, SC (1976): 1,022. Colonial trading village and site of Gen. Nathanael Greene's siege on Loyalist-held fort in 1781.

Pennsylvania Avenue, DC (1965): 19. Incl. area between Capitol and White House, encompassing U.S. Navy Memorial, Freedom Plaza, Old Post Office Pavilion, and other sites.

President William Jefferson Clinton Birthplace Home, Hope, AR (2010): 1. Birthplace and early home of 42nd president.

Pu'ukoholā Heiau, Kawaihae, HI (1972): 86. Ruins of temple built by King Kamehameha, first king of united Hawaiian islands.

Sagamore Hill, Oyster Bay, NY (1962): 83. Home of Pres. Theodore Roosevelt from 1885 until his death in 1919.

Saint-Gaudens, Cornish, NH (1964): 191. Home, studio, and gardens of American sculptor Augustus Saint-Gaudens.

Saint Paul's Church, New York, NY (1943): 6. Site associated with John Peter Zenger's "freedom of press" trial.

Salem Maritime, MA (1938): 9. Major fishing and whaling port famous for 1692 witchcraft trials.

Sand Creek Massacre, CO (2000): 12,583. Site where more than 160 Cheyenne and Arapaho Indians were killed by U.S. soldiers in 1864.

San Juan, PR (1949): 75. 16th-cent. Spanish fortifications.

Saugus Iron Works, MA (1974): 9. Reconstructed 17th-cent. colonial ironworks.

Springfield Armory, MA (1974): 55. Small-arms manufacturing center for nearly 200 years.

Steamtown, Scranton, PA (1986): 62. Rail yard, roadhouse, repair shops of former Delaware, Lackawanna & Western Railroad.

Theodore Roosevelt Birthplace, New York, NY (1962): 0.11. Reconstructed brownstone where 26th president was born.

Theodore Roosevelt Inaugural, Buffalo, NY (1966): 1. Wilcox House, where 26th president took oath of office, 1901.

Thomas Stone, Port Tobacco, MD (1978): 328. Home of signer of Declaration of Independence.

Tuskegee Airmen, AL (1998): 90. Airfield where pilots of all-black WWII air corps unit received flight training.

Tuskegee Institute, AL (1974): 58. College founded by Booker T. Washington in 1881 for blacks.

Ulysses S. Grant, St. Louis, MO (1989): 10. Home of Grant during pre-Civil War years.

Vanderbilt Mansion, Hyde Park, NY (1940): 212. Mansion of 19th-cent. financier.

Washita Battlefield, OK (1996): 315. Scene of Nov. 27, 1868, battle between Plains tribes and U.S. army.

Weir Farm, Wilton, CT (1990): 74. Home and studio of American impressionist painter J. Alden Weir.

Whitman Mission, Walla Walla, WA (1936/1963): 139. Site of Protestant missionaries to Cayuse Indians beginning in 1830s.

William Howard Taft, Cincinnati, OH (1969): 4. Birthplace and early home of 27th president.

Name	Location	Year[1]	Acreage
National Lakeshores			
Apostle Islands	WI	1970	69,372
Indiana Dunes	IN	1966	15,314
Pictured Rocks	MI	1966	73,236
Sleeping Bear Dunes	MI	1970	71,210
National Monuments			
African Burial Ground	NY	2006	0.35
Agate Fossil Beds	NE	1965	3,058
Alibates Flint Quarries	TX	1965	1,371
Aniakchak[2]	AK	1978	137,176
Aztec Ruins	NM	1923	318
Bandelier	NM	1916	33,677
Booker T. Washington	VA	1956	239
Buck Island Reef	VI	1961	19,015
Cabrillo	CA	1913	160
Canyon de Chelly	AZ	1931	83,840
Cape Krusenstern	AK	1978	649,125
Capulin Volcano	NM	1916	793
Casa Grande Ruins	AZ	1889	473
Castillo de San Marcos	FL	1924	19
Castle Clinton	NY	1946	1
Cedar Breaks	UT	1933	6,155
César E. Chávez	CA	2012	NA
Chiricahua	AZ	1924	11,985
Colorado	CO	1911	20,536
Craters of the Moon	ID	1924	53,571
Devils Postpile	CA	1911	798
Devils Tower	WY	1906	1,347
Dinosaur	CO-UT	1915	210,283
Effigy Mounds	IA	1949	2,526
El Malpais	NM	1987	114,314
El Morro	NM	1906	1,279
Florissant Fossil Beds	CO	1969	5,998
Fort Frederica	GA	1936	284
Fort Matanzas	FL	1924	300
Fort McHenry (and Historic Shrine)	MD	1925	43
Fort Monroe	VA	2011	325
Fort Pulaski	GA	1924	5,623
Fort Stanwix	NY	1935	16
Fort Sumter	SC	1948	235
Fort Union	NM	1954	721
Fossil Butte	WY	1972	8,198
George Washington Birthplace	VA	1930	662
George Washington Carver	MO	1943	210
Gila Cliff Dwellings	NM	1907	533
Governors Island	NY	2001	23
Grand Portage	MN	1951	710
Hagerman Fossil Beds	ID	1988	4,351
Hohokam Pima[3]	AZ	1972	1,690
Homestead NM of America	NE	1936	211
Hovenweep	CO-UT	1923	785
Jewel Cave	SD	1908	1,274
John Day Fossil Beds	OR	1974	14,062
Lava Beds	CA	1925	46,692
Little Bighorn Battlefield	MT	1879	765
Montezuma Castle	AZ	1906	859
Muir Woods	CA	1908	554
Natural Bridges	UT	1908	7,636
Navajo	AZ	1909	360
Ocmulgee	GA	1934	702
Oregon Caves	OR	1909	488
Organ Pipe Cactus	AZ	1937	330,689
Petroglyph	NM	1990	7,209
Pinnacles	CA	1908	26,606
Pipe Spring	AZ	1923	40
Pipestone	MN	1937	282
Poverty Point[2]	LA	1988	911
Rainbow Bridge	UT	1910	160
Russell Cave	AL	1961	310
Salinas Pueblo Missions	NM	1909	1,071
Scotts Bluff	NE	1919	3,005
Statue of Liberty	NJ-NY	1924	61
Sunset Crater Volcano	AZ	1930	3,040
Timpanogos Cave	UT	1922	250
Tonto	AZ	1907	1,120
Tuzigoot	AZ	1939	812
Virgin Islands Coral Reef	VI	2001	12,708
Walnut Canyon	AZ	1915	3,529
White Sands	NM	1933	143,733
World War II Valor in the Pacific	HI-CA	2008	59
Wupatki	AZ	1924	35,422
Yucca House[2]	CO	1919	34
National Parkways			
Blue Ridge	NC-VA	1933	95,948
George Washington Memorial	MD-DC-VA	1930	7,022
John D. Rockefeller Jr. Mem.	WY	1972	23,777
Natchez Trace	MS-TN-AL	1938	52,302
National Preserves			
Aniakchak[2]	AK	1980	464,118
Bering Land Bridge	AK	1980	2,697,391
Big Cypress	FL	1974	720,564
Big Thicket	TX	1974	107,006
Craters of the Moon	ID	2002	410,733

Name	Location	Year[1]	Acreage
Denali	AK	1917	1,334,118
Gates of the Arctic	AK	1978	948,608
Glacier Bay	AK	1925	58,406
Great Sand Dunes	CO	2000	41,686
Katmai	AK	1918	418,699
Lake Clark	AK	1978	1,410,294
Little River Canyon	AL	1992	15,288
Mojave	CA	1994	1,538,415
Noatak	AK	1978	6,587,071
Tallgrass Prairie	KS	1996	10,894
Timucuan Ecological and Historic	FL	1988	46,301
Wrangell-St. Elias	AK	1978	4,852,653
Yukon-Charley Rivers	AK	1978	2,526,512
National Recreation Areas			
Amistad	TX	1965	58,500
Bighorn Canyon	MT-WY	1966	120,296
Boston Harbor Islands	MA	1996	1,482
Chattahoochee River	GA	1978	9,792
Chickasaw	OK	1902	9,899
Curecanti	CO	1965	43,095
Delaware Water Gap	NJ-PA	1965	66,741
Gateway	NJ-NY	1972	26,607
Gauley River	WV	1988	11,560
Glen Canyon	AZ-UT	1958	1,254,117
Golden Gate	CA	1972	80,033
Lake Chelan	WA	1968	61,949
Lake Mead	AZ-NV	1936	1,495,806
Lake Meredith	TX	1965	44,978
Lake Roosevelt[4]	WA	1946	100,390
Ross Lake	WA	1968	117,575
Santa Monica Mountains	CA	1978	156,670
Whiskeytown-Shasta-Trinity[5]	CA	1965	42,503
National Reserves			
City of Rocks	ID	1988	14,407
Ebey's Landing Historical	WA	1978	19,333
National Rivers			
Big South Fork (and Rec. Area)	KY-TN	1976	125,310
Buffalo	AR	1972	94,293
Mississippi (and Rec. Area)	MN	1988	53,775
New River Gorge	WV	1978	72,186
Ozark Scenic Riverways	MO	1964	80,785
National Seashores			
Assateague Island[6]	MD-VA	1965	41,320
Canaveral	FL	1975	57,662
Cape Cod	MA	1961	43,607
Cape Hatteras	NC	1937	30,351
Cape Lookout	NC	1966	28,243
Cumberland Island	GA	1972	36,347
Fire Island	NY	1964	19,580
Gulf Islands	FL-MS	1971	137,989
Padre Island	TX	1962	130,434
Point Reyes	CA	1962	71,055
International Historic Site			
Saint Croix Island	ME	1949	6.5
Other Designations			
Catoctin Mountain Park	MD	1954	5,891
Constitution Gardens	DC	1974	39
Fort Washington Park	MD	1930	341
Greenbelt Park	MD	1950	1,175
National Capital Parks	DC-MD	1933	6,841
National Mall	DC	1933	156
Piscataway Park	MD	1961	4,626
Prince William Forest Park	VA	1948	16,084
Rock Creek Park	DC	1890	1,755
White House	DC	1933	18
Wolf Trap Park for Performing Arts	VA	1966	130

National Wild and Scenic Rivers

Rivers in this system are designated by Congress or the Secretary of the Interior. As of Sept. 2012, the system included 12,602 miles of 203 rivers in 39 states and Puerto Rico. Not all of the rivers that the NPS administers are official units of the park system. Only official NPS units are listed here.

Name	Location	Year[1]	Acreage
Alagnak Wild[2]	AK	1980	30,665
Bluestone Scenic	WV	1978	4,310
Delaware Scenic	NJ-PA-NY	1978	1,973
Great Egg Harbor Scenic and Rec.	NJ	1992	43,311
Missouri Recreational	NE-SD	1991	34,099
Niobrara Scenic	NE	1991	29,101
Obed	TN	1976	5,073
Rio Grande	TX	1978	9,600
Saint Croix Scenic Riverway	MN-WI	1968	67,470
Upper Delaware Scenic and Rec.	NY-PA	1978	75,000

Affiliated Areas

Affiliated areas are administered in connection with the NPS but are not owned by that agency.

Name	Location	Year[1]	Acreage
Aleutian World War II Natl. Historic Site (NHS)	AK	1996	81
American Memorial Park	MP	1978	133
Benjamin Franklin Natl. Memorial	PA	1972	NA

Name	Location	Year[1]	Acreage	Name	Location	Year[1]	Acreage
Chicago Portage NHS	IL	1952	NA	Jamestown NHS	VA	1940	23
Chimney Rock NHS	NE	1956	83	Kate Mullany NHS	NY	2004	0.06
Fallen Timbers Battlefield and Fort Miamis NHS	OH	1999	185	Lower East Side Tenement NHS	NY	1998	NA
Father Marquette Natl. Memorial	MI	1975	52	New Jersey Coastal Heritage Trail Route	NJ	1988	NA
Gloria Dei (Old Swedes') Church NHS	PA	1942	4	Oklahoma City Natl. Memorial	OK	2004	3
Green Springs Natl. Historic Landmark District	VA	1974	14,004	Pinelands Natl. Reserve	NJ	1978	1,100,000
Historic Camden Revolutionary War Site	SC	1982	107	Red Hill Patrick Henry Natl. Memorial	VA	1986	117
Ice Age Natl. Scientific Reserve	WI	1964	32,500	Roosevelt Campobello Intl. Park	NB	1964	2,861
International Peace Garden	ND-MB	1949	2,339	Sewall-Belmont House NHS	DC	1974	0.35
Iñupiat Heritage Center	AK	1999	NA	Thomas Cole NHS	NY	1999	3
				Touro Synagogue NHS	RI	1946	0.23

NA = Not available. (1) Year current designation received. (2) No federal facilities. (3) Not open to the public. (4) Formerly Coulee Dam NRA. (5) Shasta and Trinity units are administered by the Forest Service. Figure given is NPS acreage only. (6) Figure given includes acreage administered by Fish and Wildlife Service.

National Trails System

Source: National Park Service (NPS) and Bureau of Land Management (BLM), U.S. Dept. of the Interior; U.S. Forest Service, U.S. Dept. of Agriculture

The National Trails System Act of 1968 authorized the creation of national trails. National scenic trails and national historic trails are established by Congress; they are administered by the NPS, Forest Service, or BLM. Not all of the trails that the NPS administers are official units of the park system. Official NPS units are indicated by an asterisk.

Name	Location	Year[1]	Length (mi)[2]	Name	Location	Year[1]	Length (mi)[2]
National Scenic Trails				El Camino Real de los Tejas	TX, LA	2004	2,580
*Appalachian	ME to GA	1968	2,184	El Camino Real de Tierra Adentro	NM, TX	2000	404
Arizona	AZ	2009	819	Iditarod	AK	1978	2,300
Continental Divide	MT, ID, WY, CO, NM	1978	3,100	Juan Bautista de Anza	AZ, CA	1990	1,200
				Lewis and Clark	IL to Pacific	1978	3,700
Florida	FL	1983	1,300	Mormon Pioneer	IL to UT	1978	1,200
Ice Age	WI	1980	1,200	Nez Perce (Nee-Me-Poo)	OR to MT	1986	1,182
*Natchez Trace	MS-AL-TN	1983	150	Old Spanish	NM to CA	2002	2,700
New England	MA, CT	2009	215	Oregon	MO to OR	1978	2,170
North Country	NY to ND	1980	4,600	Overmountain Victory	NC, SC, TN, VA	1980	330
Pacific Crest	CA, OR, WA	1968	2,650	Pony Express	MO to CA	1992	2,005
Pacific Northwest	MT, ID, WA	2009	1,206	Santa Fe	MO, KS, OK, CO, NM	1987	1,203
*Potomac Heritage	VA to PA	1983	836	Selma to Montgomery	AL	1996	54
National Historic Trails[3]				Star-Spangled Banner	VA, DC, MD	2008	560
Ala Kahakai	HI	2000	175	Trail of Tears	GA, AL, TN to OK	1987	5,045
California	MO, NE to CA, OR	1992	2,000	Washington-Rochambeau Revolutionary Route	MA to VA	2009	680
Captain John Smith Chesapeake	VA, DC, MD, DE	2006	3,000				

(1) Year designation was received. (2) Authorized length; some trails are not yet complete. (3) Trails may include both overland and water routes.

National Heritage Areas

Source: National Park Service (NPS), U.S. Dept. of the Interior; Alliance of National Heritage Areas

National Heritage Areas (NHAs) are designated by Congress for their national importance. NHAs are not units of the National Park system, though the NPS advises and provides limited financial assistance.

Name	Location	Year[1]	Size (sq mi)	Name	Location	Year[1]	Size (sq mi)
Abraham Lincoln	IL	2008	25,975	Mississippi Delta	MS	2009	10,976
Arabia Mountain	GA	2006	64	Mississippi Gulf Coast	MS	2004	4,289
Atchafalaya	LA	2006	10,400	Mississippi Hills	MS	2009	(5)
Augusta Canal	GA	1996	NA	Mormon Pioneer	UT	2006	16,070
Baltimore	MD	2009	18	MotorCities	MI	1998	10,000
Blue Ridge	NC	2003	11,000	Muscle Shoals	AL	2009	3,913
Cache La Poudre River[2]	CO	1996	45	National Aviation Heritage Area	OH	2004	(6)
Cane River	LA	1994	181	National Coal Heritage Area	WV	1996	5,300
Champlain Valley National Heritage Partnership	NY, VT	2006	(3)	Niagara Falls	NY	2008	NA
				Northern Plains	ND	2009	800
Crossroads of the American Revolutions	NJ	2006	2,155	Northern Rio Grande	NM	2006	10,000
				Ohio & Erie Canalway[2]	OH	1996	110
Delaware & Lehigh National Heritage Corridor (NHC)[2]	PA	1988	165	Oil Region	PA	2004	708
Erie Canalway NHC[2]	NY	2000	524	Path of Progress National Heritage Tour Route[2]	PA	1988	500
Essex	MA	1996	500	Quinebaug and Shetucket Rivers Valley NHC	CT, MA	1994	1,086
Freedom's Frontier	KS, MO	2006	31,000	Rivers of Steel	PA	1996	5,000+
Freedom's Way	MA, NH	2009	(4)	Sangre de Cristo	CO	2009	3,000+
Great Basin Natl. Heritage Route	NV, UT	2006	15,704	Schuylkill River Valley	PA	2000	1,750
Gullah Geechee Cultural Heritage Corridor	NC, SC, GA, FL	2006	12,818	Shenandoah Valley Battlefields National Historic District	VA	1996	3,939
Hudson River Valley[2]	NY	1996	154	Silos and Smokestacks	IA	1996	20,000+
Illinois & Michigan Canal NHC	IL	1984	862	South Carolina NHC[2]	SC	1996	240
John H. Chafee Blackstone River Valley NHC	MA, RI	1986	550	South Park	CO	2009	1,800
Journey Through Hallowed Ground[2]	PA, MD, WV, VA	2008	180	Tennessee Civil War[7]	TN	1996	42,144
				Upper Housatonic Valley	MA, CT	2006	964
Kenai Mountains-Turnagain Arm	AK	2009	NA	Wheeling	WV	2000	12
Lackawanna River Heritage Trail[2]	PA	2000	70	Yuma Crossing	AZ	2000	NA

NA = Not available. (1) Year designation was received. (2) Figure given is length of area. (3) Covers 11 counties in both states. (4) 45 cities and towns. (5) Parts of 30 counties. (6) 8 counties. (7) Spans entire state of Tennessee.

UNITED STATES HISTORY

This chapter includes the following sections:

Chronology of Events

1492 Christopher Columbus and crew sighted land Oct. 12 in what is now the Bahamas.

1513 Juan Ponce de León explored Florida coast.

1524 Giovanni da Verrazano led French expedition along coast from Carolina north to Nova Scotia; entered New York Harbor.

1526 San Miguel de Guadalupe, **first European settlement** in what became U.S. territory, was established in the summer off South Carolina coast; abandoned in Oct.

1539 Hernando de Soto landed in Florida May 28; crossed Mississippi River, 1541.

1540 Francisco Vásquez de Coronado explored Southwest north of Rio Grande. **Hernando de Alarcón** reached Colorado River; **García López de Cárdenas** reached Grand Canyon. Others explored California coast.

1562 First French colony in what became U.S. territory founded on Parris Island off South Carolina coast; abandoned, 1564.

1565 St. Augustine, FL, oldest continuously occupied European settlement in U.S., founded Sept. 8 by Pedro Menéndez de Avilés. Spain ceded settlement to U.S. in 1821.

1579 Sir Francis Drake entered San Francisco Bay and claimed region for Britain.

1585 First English colony in America, sponsored by Sir Walter Raleigh, founded on **Roanoke Island**, off North Carolina coast; colony failed.

1587 Second colony attempted on Roanoke Island. Virginia Dare of colony became **first English infant born** in the New World. Settlers of second colony found to have vanished, 1590.

1607 Capt. **John Smith** and 105 cavaliers in three ships landed on Virginia coast and started Jamestown, **first permanent English settlement** in New World.

1609 Henry Hudson, English explorer of Northwest Passage, employed by Dutch, sailed into New York Harbor in Sept. and up Hudson to Albany. **Samuel de Champlain** explored Lake Champlain, to the north. Spaniards settled **Santa Fe, NM**.

1619 House of Burgesses, **first representative assembly** in New World, elected July 30 at Jamestown, VA. **First black laborers**—indentured servants—in English North American colonies, brought by Dutch to Jamestown in Aug. Chattel slavery legally recognized, 1650.

1620 Pilgrims, Puritan separatists, left Plymouth, England, Sept. 16 on *Mayflower*; reached Cape Cod Nov. 19; 103 passengers landed at Plymouth, Dec. 26. **Mayflower Compact**, signed Nov. 11, was agreement to form a self-government. Half of colony died during harsh winter.

1624 Dutch settled in Albany and along Hudson River, establishing the colony of **New Netherland** in May.

1626 Peter Minuit bought **Manhattan** for Dutch West India Co. from Manahatta Indians during summer for goods valued at $24; named island **New Amsterdam**.

1630 Settlement of **Boston** established by Massachusetts colonists led by John Winthrop; Winthrop began *The History of New England*. **William Bradford**, a governor of Plymouth Colony, began his chronicle *History of Plymouth Plantation (1620-1647)*, first published in entirety in 1856.

1634 Maryland founded as Catholic colony under charter to Lord Baltimore. Act of Toleration passed 1649 provided for religious tolerance.

1635 Boston Latin School, **oldest public school** in continuous existence in U.S., founded Apr. 23.

1636 Roger Williams founded **Providence, RI**, in June, as a democratically ruled colony with separation of church and state. Charter granted, 1644. **Harvard College** founded; oldest institution of higher learning in U.S.

1640 First book printed in America, the so-called *Bay Psalm Book*.

1647 Liberal constitution drafted in Rhode Island. First law in America providing for **free compulsory basic education** enacted in Massachusetts.

1660 British Parliament passed first **Navigation Act** Dec. 1, regulating colonial commerce to suit English needs.

1661 Missionary John Eliot's translation of the New Testament into Algonquian became the **first Bible printed** in North America.

1664 British troops Sept. 8 seized New Netherland from Dutch. Charles II granted New Netherland and city of New Amsterdam to brother, Duke of York; both renamed **New York**. Dutch recaptured colony 1673 but ceded it to Britain Nov. 10, 1674.

1670 Charles Town, SC, founded by English colonists in Apr.

1673 Regular mail service on horseback instituted Jan. 1 between New York and Boston. **Jacques Marquette** and **Louis Jolliet** reached the upper Mississippi and traveled down it.

1674 Future **Salem witch trial** judge Samuel Sewall began renowned diary covering events through 1729.

1676 Bloody **Indian war** in New England ended Aug. 12. King Philip, Wampanoag chief, and Narragansett Indians killed. **Nathaniel Bacon** led planters against autocratic British Gov. Sir William Berkeley, burned Jamestown, VA, Sept. 19. Rebellion collapsed when Bacon died; 23 followers executed.

1678 A book of poetry by **Anne Bradstreet** (first published in Britain) revised and expanded for posthumous publication in Massachusetts. Considered first female poet in American colonies.

1679 Fire destroyed 150 houses in Boston. City imported **first fire engines** from England.

1681 John Bunyan's *The Pilgrim's Progress* published in America; became best seller.

1682 René-Robert Cavelier, Sieur de La Salle, claimed lower Mississippi River country for France and called it Louisiana Apr. 9. Had French outposts built in Illinois and Texas, 1684. Killed during mutiny, 1687. Spanish colonists became the **first Europeans to settle Texas**, at site of present-day El Paso.

1683 William Penn signed treaty with Delaware Indians Apr. 23 and made payment for **Pennsylvania** lands. The **first German colonists** in America settled near Philadelphia.

1689 New York's English colonial governor, **Sir Edmund Andros**, resigned after armed uprising in Boston on Apr. 18.

1690 First colonial newspaper, *Publick Occurrences*, published by Benjamin Harris but promptly shut down for lack of official permission. Harris also published *New England Primer* for use as elementary school textbook. Large-scale **whaling** operations began in Nantucket, MA.

1626: Peter Minuit buys the island of Manhattan from Native Americans for goods valued at $24 (according to a 19th-cent. estimate).

1692 Hysteria over **witchcraft** began in Salem Village (now Danvers), MA; 19 women and 1 man were executed by special court.

1697 *The Essays* of **Sir Francis Bacon**, first published in England in 1597, was published in America; it became a best seller.

1699 Former privateer Capt. **William Kidd** arrested and sent to England; hanged for piracy, 1701. French settlements made in Mississippi, Louisiana.

1702 Legislation enacted making **Church of England** the established church in Maryland.

1704 Indians attacked **Deerfield**, MA, Feb. 28-29; killed 40, carried off 100. *Boston News Letter*, **first regular newspaper**, started by postmaster John Campbell.

1710 British-colonial troops captured French fort, Port Royal, Nova Scotia, in **Queen Anne's War**, 1702-13. France yielded Nova Scotia by treaty, 1713.

1712 Slaves revolted in New York Apr. 6; 21 were executed. Second uprising, 1741; 13 slaves hanged, 13 burned, 71 deported.

1716 **First theater** in colonies opened in Williamsburg, VA.

1726 **Great Awakening**, general revival of evangelical religion, began in colonies.

1731 America's **first circulating library** founded in Philadelphia by Benjamin Franklin.

1732 Benjamin Franklin published the **first *Poor Richard's Almanack***; published annually until 1757. Georgia, last of 13 colonies, chartered.

1733 **Influenza epidemic** swept through New York City and Philadelphia.

1735 Editor **John Peter Zenger** was acquitted of libel Aug. 5 in New York after criticizing the British governor's conduct in office.

1739 A series of **slave uprisings** put down in South Carolina.

1741 Famous sermon "Sinners in the Hands of an Angry God," delivered July 8 at Enfield, MA, by Jonathan Edwards, one of the most important preachers in the **Great Awakening** religious revival. Danish navigator **Vitus Bering**, commanding Russian expedition, reached Alaska.

1744 **King George's War** pitted British and colonials versus French. Colonials captured Louisbourg, Cape Breton Isl., Nova Scotia, June 17, 1745. Returned to France 1748 by Treaty of Aix-la-Chapelle.

1752 According to legend, **Benjamin Franklin**, flying kite in thunderstorm, proved lightning is electricity, June 15; invented lightning rod. **Liberty Bell**, cast in England, was delivered to Pennsylvania.

1752: According to legend, Benjamin Franklin's kite experiment proves that lightning is electricity.

1754 **French and Indian War** began with Ft. Necessity campaign in Pennsylvania. Skirmish May 28, battle at fort July 3-4. British moved Acadian French from Nova Scotia to Louisiana Oct. 8, 1755. British captured Québec Sept. 18, 1759, in battles in which French Gen. Joseph de Montcalm and British Gen. James Wolfe were killed. Peace pact signed Feb. 10, 1763. French lost Canada and Midwest. Delegates from seven colonies to New York for **Albany Congress**, July 19, approved plan of union by Benjamin Franklin; plan rejected by the colonies.

1757 **First streetlights** appeared in Philadelphia.

1764 **Sugar Act**, Apr. 5, placed duties on lumber, foodstuffs in colonies. First law passed by Parliament to specifically raise revenue from colonies, alleviate French and Indian War debts. British enforced this act, unlike with **Molasses Act** of 1733.

1765 **Stamp Act**, enacted by Parliament Mar. 22, required revenue stamps to help fund royal troops. Nine colonies, at Stamp Act Congress in New York Oct. 7-25, adopted Declaration of Rights. Stamp Act repealed Mar. 17, 1766. **Quartering Act**, requiring colonists to house British troops, went into effect Mar. 24.

1767 **Townshend Acts** levied taxes on glass, lead, paper, paint, and tea. In 1770 all duties except on tea were repealed.

1770 British troops fired Mar. 5 into Boston mob, killed five including **Crispus Attucks**, a black man, reportedly leader of group; later called **Boston Massacre**.

1773 East India Co. tea ships turned back at Boston, New York, and Philadelphia in May. Cargo ship burned at Annapolis, Oct. 14; cargo thrown overboard at **Boston Tea Party**, Dec. 16, to protest the tea tax. **First museum** in the colonies was officially established in Charleston, SC; later named the Charleston Museum.

1774 **"Intolerable Acts"** of Parliament curtailed Massachusetts self-rule; barred use of Boston Harbor until dumped tea was paid for. **First Continental Congress** held in Philadelphia Sept. 5-Oct. 26; called for civil disobedience against British. Rhode Island **abolished slavery**.

1775 **Patrick Henry** addressed Virginia convention, Mar. 23, said, "Give me liberty or give me death!" **Paul Revere**, **William Dawes**, and Dr. **Samuel Prescott**, Apr. 18, rode to alert patriots that British were on their way to Concord, MA, to destroy arms. At **Lexington**, MA, Apr. 19, Minutemen lost eight. On return from **Concord**, British suffered 273 casualties. Col. Ethan Allen (joined by Col. Benedict Arnold) captured **Ft. Ticonderoga** in New York, May 10, also Crown Point. Colonials headed for **Bunker Hill** and fortified nearby Breed's Hill, Charlestown, MA. Repulsed British under Gen. William Howe twice before retreating, June 17. Continental Congress June 15 named **George Washington** commander in chief; established a postal system, July 26. Benjamin Franklin became the **first postmaster general**.

1776 **Thomas Paine**'s *Common Sense*, famous pro-independence pamphlet, published Jan. 10; quickly sold some 100,000 copies. France and Spain agreed May 2 to provide arms to U.S. In Continental Congress June 7, Richard Henry Lee (VA) moved "that these united colonies are, and of right ought to be, free and independent states." Resolution adopted July 2. **Declaration of Independence** approved July 4, signed Aug. 2. Col. William Moultrie's batteries at **Charleston, SC**, repulsed British sea attack June 28. Washington lost **Battle of Long Island** Aug. 27; evacuated New York. **Nathan Hale** executed as spy by British Sept. 22. Brig. Gen. Arnold's Lake Champlain fleet was defeated in **Battle of Valcour Island** Oct. 11, but British returned to Canada. Howe failed to destroy Washington's army at White Plains, NY, Oct. 28. Hessians captured Ft. Washington, Manhattan, and 3,000 men, Nov. 16; captured Ft. Lee, NJ, Nov. 20. Washington, in Pennsylvania, recrossed **Delaware River** Dec. 25-26, defeated Hessians at **Battle of Trenton**, NJ, Dec. 26.

1777 Washington defeated Lord Charles Cornwallis at **Princeton**, NJ, Jan. 3. Continental Congress, June 14, authorized an **American flag**, the Stars and Stripes. Maj. Gen. John Burgoyne's force of 8,000 from Canada captured **Ft. Ticonderoga**, NY, July 6. Americans beat back Burgoyne at Bemis Heights, Oct. 7, cut off British escape route. Burgoyne surrendered 5,000 men at Saratoga, NY, Oct. 17. **Articles of Confederation** adopted by Continental Congress, Nov. 15; took effect Mar. 1, 1781.

1776: George Washington's army crosses the Delaware River to defeat Hessian forces in the Battle of Trenton.

1778 **France signed treaty** of aid with U.S. Feb. 6; sent fleet. British evacuated Philadelphia, June 18.

1779 **George Rogers Clark** took Ft. Vincennes in what is now Indiana in Feb. **John Paul Jones** on the *Bonhomme Richard* defeated *Serapis* in British North Sea waters, Sept. 23.

1780 Charleston, SC, fell to the British May 12, but Loyalists were defeated in battle of **Kings Mountain**, NC, Oct. 7 in what Thomas Jefferson called "the turn of the tide of success." **Benedict Arnold** found to be a traitor Sept. 23. Arnold escaped, made brigadier general in British army.

1781 Bank of North America, **first commercial bank**, incorporated May 26. Cornwallis retired to **Yorktown, VA.** Adm. Francois Joseph de Grasse landed 3,000 French and stopped British fleet in **Hampton Roads**, VA. Washington and Jean Baptiste de Rochambeau joined forces, arrived near Williamsburg, Sept. 26. Siege of Cornwallis began, Oct. 6; **Cornwallis surrendered** Oct. 19.

1782 New British cabinet agreed in Mar. to **recognize U.S. independence**. Preliminary agreement signed in Paris, Nov. 30. Use of **scarlet letter A**, sewn on clothing or branded on skin of adulterers, discontinued in New England.

1783 Massachusetts Supreme Court decision in final Quock Walker trial **declared slavery illegal**. Newspapers typically published weekly; **first regular daily newspaper**, *Pennsylvania Evening Post*, went on sale in Philadelphia, May 30. Britain, U.S. signed **Paris peace treaty**, Sept. 3, recognizing American independence; Congress ratified it Jan. 14, 1784. Washington ordered army disbanded Nov. 3, bade farewell to his officers at Fraunces Tavern, New York City, Dec. 4.

1784 Thomas Jefferson's proposal to **ban slavery in new territories** after 1802 was narrowly defeated, Mar. 1.

1785 Regular **stagecoach routes** established between Albany, New York City, and Philadelphia.

1786 Delegates from five states at Annapolis, MD, Sept. 11-14 asked Congress to call a **constitutional convention**.

1787 Shays's Rebellion of debt-ridden farmers in Massachusetts failed, Jan. 25. **Constitutional convention** opened in Philadelphia, May 25, with Washington presiding. Constitution accepted by delegates, Sept. 17. Delaware was first state to ratify it, Dec. 7; Pennsylvania and New Jersey followed. **Northwest Ordinance** adopted July 13 by Continental Congress for Northwest Territory, north of Ohio River, west of New York; made rules for statehood and guaranteed freedom of religion, support for schools, no slavery. *Federalist Papers* first appeared in *NY Independent Journal*.

1788 A large fire in **New Orleans**, then a Spanish territory, destroyed much of the city, Mar. 21. **Constitution adopted** June 21 after being ratified by the requisite ninth state (New Hampshire); also ratified by Georgia, Connecticut, Massachusetts, Maryland, South Carolina, Virginia, and New York throughout the year. **First U.S. senators elected** Sept. 30, from Pennsylvania.

1789 **George Washington** chosen president by all electors voting (73 eligible, 69 voting, 4 absent); **John Adams**, vice president, got 34 votes. **First Congress** met at Federal Hall, New York City, and declared Constitution in effect, Mar. 4; Washington inaugurated there Apr. 30; **first inaugural ball** held May 7. U.S. **State Dept.** established by Congress July 27. (Thomas Jefferson installed as first secretary of state Feb. 1790.) **War Dept.** created Aug. 7, with Henry Knox as secretary; **Treasury Dept.** created Sept. 2, with Alexander Hamilton to be secretary. **Supreme Court** created by Federal Judiciary Act, Sept. 24; **John Jay** confirmed by Congress as first Supreme Court chief justice, Sept. 26.

1790 **First Supreme Court session** held Feb. 2 in New York City. Congress, Mar. 1, authorized decennial **U.S. census**. Collection of data took 18 months. **Naturalization Act** (two-year residency) passed Mar. 26. John Carroll consecrated as **first American Catholic bishop**, Aug. 15. Congress met in **Philadelphia**, new temporary capital, Dec. 6.

1791 **Bill of Rights**, submitted to states, Sept. 25, 1789, went into effect Dec. 15. First Bank of the United States, **first bank chartered by federal government**, established in Philadelphia.

1792 Coinage Act established **U.S. Mint** in Philadelphia, Apr. 2. Gen. **"Mad" Anthony Wayne** made commander in Ohio-Indiana area, trained American Legion, established string of forts. Routed Indians at Fallen Timbers on Maumee River, Aug. 20, 1794; checked British at Fort Miami, OH, same year. **White House** cornerstone laid Oct. 13.

1793 **Washington** inaugurated for second term, Mar. 4, having received 132 electoral votes; **John Adams** again became vice president, having received second highest total, 77. Washington declared **U.S. neutrality**, Apr. 22, in war between Britain and France. Eli Whitney invented **cotton gin**, reviving Southern slavery.

1794 Whiskey Rebellion, western Pennsylvania farmers protesting liquor tax of 1791, suppressed by federal militia in Sept. **Jay's Treaty**, controversial treaty with Britain negotiated by John Jay, signed Nov. 19, ratified June 24, 1795. This treaty intended to settle long-standing differences between U.S. and Britain.

1795 U.S. bought peace from **Algerian pirates** by paying $1 mil ransom for 115 seamen Sept. 5, followed by annual tributes. Gen. Wayne signed **Treaty of Greenville** with Indians, opening Northwest Territory to settlers. Univ. of North Carolina became **first operating state university**.

1796 **Washington's farewell address** as president delivered Sept. 17. Warned against permanent alliances with foreign powers, big public debt, large military establishment, and devices of "small, artful, enterprising minority."

1797 **John Adams** inaugurated as second president Mar. 4, having received 71 electoral votes; **Thomas Jefferson** became vice president, having received 68. U.S. frigate *United States* launched at Philadelphia, July 10; *Constellation* at Baltimore, Sept. 7; *Constitution* (Old Ironsides) at Boston, Sept. 20.

1798 **Alien and Sedition Acts** passed by Federalists June-July; intended to silence political opposition. **War with France threatened** over French raids on U.S. shipping and rejection of U.S. diplomats. Navy (45 ships) and 365 privateers captured 84 French ships. USS *Constellation* took French warship *Insurgente*, 1799. Napoleon stopped French raids after becoming first consul.

1800 Federal government moved to **Washington, DC**.

1801 **John Marshall** named Supreme Court chief justice, Jan. 20. **Thomas Jefferson**, who had received same number of electoral votes as Aaron Burr in 1800 election, won out over Burr in House vote Feb. 17; Burr named vice president. **Tripoli declared war** June 10 against U.S., which refused added tribute to commerce-raiding Arab corsairs. Land and naval campaigns forced Tripoli to negotiate peace, June 4, 1805. **Oldest U.S. art institution**, Pennsylvania Academy of Fine Arts, founded in Philadelphia.

1802 Congress established U.S. Military Academy at **West Point**, NY.

1803 Supreme Court, in *Marbury v. Madison*, overturned U.S. law for first time, Feb. 24. Napoleon sold all of Louisiana, stretching to Canadian border, to U.S. for $11.25 mil in bonds, plus $3.75 mil indemnities to American citizens with

1808: Laws outlawing slave importation go into effect, but an estimated 250,000 slaves are illegally imported, 1808-60.

claims against France. U.S. took title Dec. 20. **Louisiana Purchase** doubled U.S. area.

1804 **Meriwether Lewis** and **William Clark** expedition ordered by Pres. Thomas Jefferson to explore what is now Northwest U.S. Started from St. Louis May 14; ended Sept. 23, 1806, back in St. Louis. Vice Pres. **Aaron Burr** shot Alexander Hamilton in duel July 11 in Weehawken, NJ; Hamilton died next day.

1805 U.S. Marines aided by Arab mercenaries, Apr. 27, captured Tripolitan port of Derna. Major victory in war against **Barbary pirates**; inspiration for "to the shores of Tripoli" in Marines Corps hymn.

1807 Robert Fulton made **first practical steamboat trip**; left New York City Aug. 17 and reached Albany, 150 mi away, in 32 hr. **Embargo Act** banned all trade with foreign countries, forbidding ships to set sail for foreign ports Dec. 22.

1808 Slave importation outlawed. Some 250,000 slaves were illegally imported 1808-60.

1810 Third U.S. **Census** found population of 7,239,814. The slave population was put at 1,191,364 and the population of all other non-white free persons at 186,446.

1811 Indiana Territory governor William Henry Harrison defeated Indians led by Tenskwatawa, called the Prophet, in **Battle of Tippecanoe**, Nov. 7. Construction began on **Cumberland Road** in Cumberland, MD; road became important route to West. About 400 **slaves revolted** in Louisiana, killing the son of a plantation owner and marching on New Orleans. The insurrection was suppressed; some 75 slaves killed.

1812 **War of 1812** had three main causes: Britain seized U.S. ships trading with France; Britain had seized 4,000 naturalized U.S. sailors by 1810; Britain armed Indians, who raided Western border. U.S. stopped trade with Europe 1807 and 1809. Trade with Britain only was stopped 1810. Unaware that Britain had raised blockade against France two days before, **Congress declared war** June 18. British took **Detroit** Aug. 16.

1813 Oliver H. Perry defeated British fleet at **Battle of Lake Erie**, Sept. 10. U.S. won **Battle of the Thames**, Ontario, Oct. 5, but failed in Canadian invasion attempts. York (Toronto) and Buffalo, NY, were burned.

1814 Troops under Andrew Jackson defeated Creek Indians led by Chief Weatherford at Battle of Horseshoe Bend in Alabama, Mar. 29, ending **Creek Indian War**, begun a year earlier. British landed in Maryland in Aug., defeated U.S. force Aug. 24, **burned Capitol and White House**. Maryland militia stopped British advance, Sept. 12. British bombardment of Ft. McHenry, Baltimore, for 25 hr., Sept. 13-14, failed, inspiring **Francis Scott Key** to write the words to **"The Star-Spangled Banner."** U.S. won naval **Battle of Lake Champlain** Sept. 11. Peace treaty with Great Britain signed at Ghent, Belgium, Dec. 24.

1815 Some 5,300 British, unaware of peace treaty, attacked U.S. entrenchments near **New Orleans**, Jan. 8. British had more than 2,000 casualties; Americans lost 71. U.S. flotilla finally ended attacks by **pirates** from Ottoman states of Algiers, Tunis, Tripoli.

1816 **Second Bank of the U.S.** chartered Apr. 10. The **American Colonization Society**, which sought to address slavery issue by transporting freed blacks to Africa, formed in Washington, DC, Dec. 1816-Jan. 1817.

1817 Thomas Hopkins Gallaudet established the **first free public school for the deaf** in Hartford, CT.

1818 Connecticut expanded **suffrage** among white male voters. Massachusetts followed suit in 1820, and New York in 1821, reducing or eliminating property qualifications.

1819 Spain ceded **Florida** to U.S. Feb. 22. American steamship *Savannah* made first part-steam-powered, part-sail-powered **crossing of Atlantic**, traveling from Savannah, GA, to Liverpool, England, in 29 days. **Washington Irving**'s *Sketch Book* became best seller.

1820 **First organized immigration of blacks to Africa** from U.S. began with 86 free blacks sailing to Sierra Leone in Feb. Henry Clay's **Missouri Compromise** bill passed by Congress, Mar. 3. Slavery was allowed in Missouri but not west of the Mississippi River, north of 36° 30′ (the southern line of Missouri). Compromise repealed 1854.

1821 Emma Willard founded Troy Female Seminary, **first U.S. women's college**. Stephen Austin established **first American community in Texas**, San Felipe de Austin. **James Fenimore Cooper**'s *The Spy*, novel set during American Revolution, published and became a best seller.

1822 Tension between sports and academics surfaced when Yale College Pres. Timothy Dwight banned a **primitive form of football**, setting fines for violators.

1823 **Monroe Doctrine**, opposing European intervention in the Americas, enunciated by Pres. James Monroe Dec. 2. The **Hudson River School**, painters who focused on the beauties of nature, began to receive public attention.

1824 Pawtucket, RI, **weavers strike**, first such action by women workers. **Slavery abolished** in state of Illinois Aug. 2.

1825 After a deadlocked election, **John Quincy Adams** was elected president by the House, Feb. 9. **Erie Canal** opened; first boat left Buffalo, NY, Oct. 26, reached New York City Nov. 4. John Stevens, of Hoboken, NJ, built and operated **first experimental steam locomotive** in U.S.

1826 Thomas Jefferson and John Adams both died July 4. James Fenimore Cooper's *The Last of the Mohicans* published.

1827 Massachusetts became first state to pass a law providing for tax-supported **public high schools**.

1828 Baltimore & Ohio, the **first U.S. passenger railroad**, began operations July 4. South Carolina Dec. 19 declared right of **state nullification of federal laws**, opposing the "Tariff of Abominations." **Noah Webster** published his *American Dictionary of the English Language*.

1829 **Andrew Jackson** inaugurated as president, Mar. 4.

1830 Famous **debate** Jan. 27 between Sen. **Daniel Webster** (MA) and Robert Hayne (SC), on state right to nullify federal law. **Mormon church** organized by Joseph Smith in Fayette, NY, Apr. 6. Pres. Jackson, May 28, signed **Indian Removal Act**, granting president authority to negotiate treaties whereby Indians living east of Mississippi R. give up lands in exchange for lands in West.

1831 William Lloyd Garrison began abolitionist newspaper *The Liberator* Jan. 1. **Nat Turner**, black slave in Virginia, led local slave rebellion, starting Aug. 21; 57 whites killed. Troops called in, 100 slaves killed. Turner captured, tried, and hanged Nov. 11.

1832 **Black Hawk War** in Illinois and Wisconsin Apr.-Sept. pushed Sauk and Fox Indians west across Mississippi.

1833 **American Anti-Slavery Society** founded in Philadelphia, Dec. 4. **Oberlin College** became first to adopt coeducation in U.S.

1835 **Liberty Bell cracked** July 8 while tolling death of Chief Justice John Marshall. **Seminole Indians** in Florida under Osceola began attacks Nov. 1, protesting forced removal. The unpopular war ended Aug. 14, 1842; most of the Indians sent to Oklahoma. **Texas** proclaimed right to secede from Mexico; **Sam Houston** put in command of Texas army, Nov. 2-4. **Gold** discovered on Cherokee land in Georgia. Indians forced to cede lands, Dec. 20, and to cross Mississippi.

1836 Texans besieged at **Alamo** in San Antonio by Mexicans under Antonio López de Santa Anna, Feb. 23-Mar. 6; entire garrison killed. Texas independence had been declared, Mar. 2. At San Jacinto Apr. 21, Sam Houston and Texans defeated Mexicans. Ralph Waldo Emerson published his first work, *Nature*, espousing his philosophy of **transcendentalism**. Marcus Whitman, H. H. Spaulding, and wives reached

1838: Cherokee Indians are marched from their homes in southeast U.S. to present-day Oklahoma on the "Trail of Tears."

Fort Walla Walla on Columbia River, OR, **first white women to cross the Continental Divide**, in the Rocky Mountains.

1838 Cherokee Indians forced to walk **"Trail of Tears"** from southeast U.S. to area in present-day Oklahoma. At least 4,000—nearly one-fifth of Cherokee population—are estimated to have died.

1841 **First emigrant wagon train bound for California**, 47 people, left Independence, MO, May 1, reached California Nov. 4. Edgar Allan Poe published one of the **first American detective stories**, *The Murders in the Rue Morgue*.

1842 **Webster-Ashburton Treaty** signed Aug. 9, fixing U.S.-Canada border in Maine and Minnesota. **First use of anesthetic** (sulfuric ether gas) in an operation performed by Georgia doctor Crawford Long.

1843 More than 1,000 settlers left Independence, MO, for Oregon May 22, arriving in Oct. via **Oregon Trail.**

1844 **First message over first telegraph line** sent May 24 by inventor Samuel F. B. Morse from Washington to Baltimore: "What hath God wrought?"

1845 Congress **overrode a presidential veto for the first time**, Mar. 3, after Pres. John Tyler vetoed a tariff bill. Congress of **Texas** voted for annexation by U.S., July 4; Texas admitted to Union, Dec. 29. **Edgar Allan Poe**'s poem "The Raven" published.

1846 **Mexican War** began after Pres. James K. Polk ordered Gen. Zachary Taylor to seize disputed Texan land settled by Mexicans. After border clash, U.S. declared war May 13; Mexico declared war May 23. About 12,000 U.S. troops took Vera Cruz Mar. 27, 1847, and Mexico City Sept. 14, 1847. Treaty signed Feb. 2, 1848, ended war, and Mexico ceded claims to Texas, California, and other territory. Bear flag of **Republic of California** raised by American settlers at Sonoma, June 14. Treaty with Britain June 15 set **Oregon territory** boundary at 49th parallel (extension of existing line). Expansionists had used slogan "54° 40´ or fight." The term **"manifest destiny,"** coined by journalist in 1845, also came into play. **Mormons**, after violent clashes with settlers over polygamy, left Nauvoo, IL, for West under Brigham Young. They settled July 1847 at Salt Lake City, UT. Elias Howe invented **sewing machine.**

1847 **First adhesive U.S. postage stamps**—Benjamin Franklin 5¢, Washington 10¢—sold July 1. **Henry Wadsworth Longfellow**'s *Evangeline* published.

1848 **Gold discovered** Jan. 24 in California; 80,000 prospectors emigrated in 1849. Lucretia Mott and Elizabeth Cady Stanton led Seneca Falls, NY, **Women's Rights Convention** July 19-20.

1850 Sen. Henry Clay's **Compromise of 1850** admitted California as 31st state Sept. 9, with slavery forbidden; made Utah and New Mexico territories; made **Fugitive Slave Law** harsher; and ended District of Columbia slave trade. **Nathaniel Hawthorne**'s *The Scarlet Letter* published.

1851 **Herman Melville**'s *Moby-Dick* published.

1852 **Harriet Beecher Stowe**'s *Uncle Tom's Cabin* published.

1853 Japan receives Comm. Matthew C. Perry, July 14. He negotiated treaty to **open Japan** to U.S. ships. New York City hosted **first World's Fair** in the U.S., beginning July 14. **Stephen Foster** published "My Old Kentucky Home."

1854 **Republican Party** formed at Ripon, WI, Feb. 28. Opposed Kansas-Nebraska Act, which left issue of slavery to

vote of settlers. Act became law May 30. Treaty ratified with Mexico Apr. 25, providing for **Gadsden Purchase** of a strip of land. **Henry David Thoreau**'s *Walden* published.

1855 **First railroad train crossed Mississippi River** on river's first bridge, between Rock Island, IL, and Davenport, IA, Apr. 21. **Walt Whitman**'s *Leaves of Grass* published.

1856 Proslavery group sacked **Lawrence, KS**, May 21; abolitionist John Brown led antislavery contingent against Missourians at Osawatomie, KS, Aug. 30. Antislavery Republican Party's **first presidential nominee**, John C. Frémont, defeated by James Buchanan. Abraham Lincoln made 50 speeches for Frémont. **First U.S. kindergarten** opened in Watertown, WI.

1857 In **Dred Scott** case, which involved determination of constitutionality of already-repealed Missouri Compromise, Supreme Court decided Mar. 6 that slaves did not become free in a free state, and blacks were not and could not be citizens. **Currier & Ives**, firm of American lithographers, issued their first print.

1858 **First Atlantic cable** completed, by Cyrus W. Field Aug. 5. **Lincoln-Douglas debates** in Illinois, Aug. 21-Oct. 15.

1859 Edwin L. Drake drilled the **first commercially productive oil well** near Titusville, PA, Aug. 27. Abolitionist John Brown, with 21 men, seized U.S. armory at **Harpers Ferry**, WV, Oct. 16. U.S. Marines captured raiders, killing several. Brown was hanged for treason Dec. 2.

1860 Shoeworkers in Lynn, MA, went on strike Feb. 22. Within a week, strike spread to include 20,000 shoeworkers throughout New England in country's **largest strike to date**. **First Pony Express** between Sacramento, CA, and St. Joseph, MO, started Apr. 3. Republican **Abraham Lincoln** elected president Nov. 6 in four-way race.

1861 Seven southern states set up **Confederate States of America** Feb. 8, with **Jefferson Davis** as president. **Civil War** began as Confederates fired on **Ft. Sumter** in Charleston, SC, Apr. 12; they captured it Apr. 14. Pres. Lincoln called for 75,000 volunteers Apr. 15. Lincoln blockaded Southern ports Apr. 19, cutting off vital exports and aid. By May, 11 states had seceded. Confederates repelled Union forces at first **Battle of Bull Run**, July 21. **First transcontinental telegraph line** put in operation.

1862 Union forces were victorious in Western campaigns, took New Orleans May 1. Battles in East were largely inconclusive despite heavy casualties. The **Battle of Antietam**, in western Maryland Sept. 17, was bloodiest one-day battle of war; each side lost more than 2,000 men. **Homestead Act**, which granted free farms to settlers, approved May 20. **Land Grant Act**, which provided for public land sale to benefit agricultural education, approved July 7. It eventually led to establishment of state university systems.

1863 Pres. Lincoln issued **Emancipation Proclamation** Jan. 1, freeing "all slaves in areas still in rebellion." Union forces won major victory at Gettysburg, PA, July 1-3. Confederate forces under siege surrendered **Vicksburg, MS**, to Union forces under Gen. Ulysses S. Grant, July 4; control of Mississippi River in Union hands. About 1,000 were killed or

1848: Gold is discovered in California, encouraging thousands to move west.

1863: Pres. Abraham Lincoln's Gettysburg Address commemorates the sacrifice of thousands in fewer than 300 words.

wounded in **draft riots** in New York City; some blacks were hanged by mobs July 13-16. Pres. Lincoln gave his **Gettysburg Address** Nov. 19. Lincoln declared **Thanksgiving** a national holiday.

1864 Gen. **William Tecumseh Sherman** marched through Georgia, taking Atlanta Sept. 1 and Savannah Dec. 22. **Sand Creek massacre** of Cheyenne and Arapaho Indians Nov. 29. Soldiers drove Indians out of village; about 150 killed.

1865 Gen. **Robert E. Lee surrendered** 27,800 Confederate troops to Gen. Grant at Appomattox Court House in VA, Apr. 9. J. E. Johnston surrendered 31,200 to Sherman at Durham Station, NC, Apr. 18. Last rebel troops surrendered May 26. Pres. Lincoln shot Apr. 14 by **John Wilkes Booth** in Ford's Theater, Washington, DC; died the following morning. Vice Pres. **Andrew Johnson** was sworn in as president. Booth was hunted down and fatally wounded, perhaps by his own hand, Apr. 26. Four co-conspirators were hanged July 7. **13th Amendment**, abolishing slavery, ratified Dec. 6.

1866 Congress took control of Southern **Reconstruction**, backed freedmen's rights in legislation vetoed by Pres. Johnson; veto overridden by Congress, Apr. 9. **Ku Klux Klan** formed secretly in South to terrorize blacks who voted. Disbanded 1869-71.

1867 Alaska sold to U.S. by Russia for $7.2 mil Mar. 30, through efforts of Sec. of State William H. Seward. Fraternal society the **Grange** was organized Dec. 4 to protect farmer interests. **Horatio Alger**'s *Ragged Dick* published.

1868 Pres. Johnson dismissed Sec. of War Edwin M. Stanton without Senate approval. **Johnson impeached** by the House Feb. 24 for violation of Tenure of Office Act, though charges were actually made in response to his opposition to congressional Reconstruction. He was acquitted by the Senate Mar.-May. **14th Amendment**, providing for citizenship of all persons born or naturalized in U.S. and subject to the jurisdiction thereof, ratified July 9. **Louisa May Alcott**'s *Little Women* published. *The World Almanac*, a publication of the *New York World* newspaper, appeared for first time.

1869 Transcontinental railroad completed; golden spike driven at Promontory Summit, UT, May 10, marking junction of Central Pacific and Union Pacific lines. Attempt to "corner" gold led to financial **"Black Friday"** in New York Sept. 24. **Woman suffrage law** passed in Wyoming Territory Dec. 10. **Knights of Labor** labor union formed in Philadelphia. By 1886, it had 700,000 members nationally.

1870 15th Amendment, making race no bar to voting rights, ratified Feb. 8. **First U.S. boardwalk** completed, in Atlantic City, NJ. **U.S. Weather Bureau** founded.

1871 Great Chicago fire destroyed city Oct. 8-11. **National Rifle Association (NRA)** founded.

1872 Amnesty Act May 22 restored civil rights to citizens of the South, except for 500 Confederate leaders. Congress

established Yellowstone, **first national park**. James McNeill Whistler painted famous portrait known informally as **"Whistler's Mother."**

1873 First U.S. postal card issued May 1. **Jesse James** and his gang robbed their first passenger train July 21. Banks failed, panic began in Sept. **Depression** lasted five years. **"Boss" William Tweed** of New York City was convicted Nov. 19 of stealing public funds; he died in jail in 1878. New York's Bellevue Hospital started **first nursing school**.

1874 Women's Christian Temperance Union established in Cleveland. **First public zoo** in U.S. established in Philadelphia.

1875 Congress passed **Civil Rights Act** Mar. 1, giving equal rights to blacks in public accommodations and jury duty. Supreme Court invalidated act in 1883. First **Kentucky Derby** held May 17. First **Jim Crow segregation law** enacted, in Tennessee.

1876 Alexander Graham Bell patented the telephone Mar. 7. Col. **George A. Custer** and 264 soldiers of the 7th Cavalry were killed June 25 in "last stand," **Battle of the Little Bighorn**, MT, in Sioux Indian War. Democrat **Samuel J. Tilden** received majority of popular votes for president over Republican **Rutherford B. Hayes**, Nov. 7, but 22 electoral votes were in dispute. Congress agreed to certify Hayes as winner in Feb. 1877 after Republicans agreed to end federal Reconstruction of South.

1877 Molly Maguires—Irish terrorist society in mining areas of Scranton, PA—was broken up by hanging, June 21, of 11 leaders for murders of mine officials and police. Pres. Rutherford B. Hayes sent federal troops to control violent national **railroad strike**, which began in July.

1878 First commercial telephone exchange opened, New Haven, CT, Jan. 28. **Thomas A. Edison** founded Edison Electric Light Co. on Oct. 15.

1879 F. W. Woolworth opened his first five-and-ten store, in Utica, NY, Feb. 22. French actress **Sarah Bernhardt** made her U.S. debut Nov. 8 at New York City's Booth Theater. Economist and social philosopher **Henry George** published *Progress & Poverty*, advocating single tax on land.

1881 Clara Barton founded **American Red Cross** May 21. Pres. **James A. Garfield** shot in Washington, DC, July 2; died Sept. 19. Famous gun battle between the Earp brothers and outlaw rustlers Oct. 26 near the **OK Corral**, Tombstone, AZ. **Booker T. Washington** founded Tuskegee Institute for blacks. **Helen Hunt Jackson**'s *A Century of Dishonor*, about mistreatment of Indians, published.

1882 Chinese Exclusion Act, barring immigration of Chinese laborers for 10 years, later made permanent, passed by Congress May 6; prohibited naturalization of Chinese resident aliens.

1883 Civil Service Act, or **Pendleton Act**, passed Jan. 16, created foundations of American civil service system. The **Brooklyn Bridge** opened May 24 as world's longest suspension bridge. Transcontinental **Northern Pacific Railroad** was completed Sept. 8. **Buffalo Bill Cody**'s Wild West Show began its 30-year touring run.

1884 First long-distance telephone call completed, Mar. 27, between Boston and New York. Switchback Railway—**first U.S. roller coaster** built as amusement park ride—opened at Coney Island in New York City. **Mark Twain**'s *The Adventures of Huckleberry Finn* published.

1885 Washington Monument dedicated Feb. 21.

1886 Haymarket riot and bombing, May 4, followed labor battles for 8-hr. work day in Chicago; seven police and four workers died. Eight anarchists found guilty Aug. 20; four hanged Nov. 11. **Coca-Cola** first sold, May 8, at Jacob's Pharmacy in Atlanta. Apache Indian **Geronimo** surrendered Sept. 4, ending last major Indian war. **Statue of Liberty** dedicated Oct. 28. **American Federation of Labor** (AFL) formed Dec. 8 by 25 craft unions.

1887 Interstate Commerce Act enacted Feb. 4, created Interstate Commerce Commission.

1888 Great blizzard struck Eastern U.S. Mar. 11-14, causing about 400 deaths. Ernest Thayer's poem **"Casey at the Bat"** recited for first time in public at New York City theater in May.

1889 U.S. opened 2-mil. acre **Oklahoma District** to settlement Apr. 22, initiating land run; "sooner" settlers illegally entered the territory before that date to stake favorable claims. More than 2,200 lives lost in **Johnstown flood** (PA) May 31. **Electric lights** installed at White House.

1889: A dam failure causes a massive flood in Johnstown, PA, that kills more than 2,200.

1890 **Sherman Antitrust Act** passed July 2, began federal effort to curb monopolies. Massacre at **Wounded Knee,** SD, Dec. 29, the last major conflict between Indians and U.S. troops; about 200 Indian men, women, and children and 29 soldiers were killed. **Jacob Riis's** *How the Other Half Lives,* about city slums, published, instigating reform legislation in New York City. **Emily Dickinson's** poems published, four years after her death.

1891 **Forest Reserve Act,** Mar. 3, let president close public forest land to settlement for establishment of national parks. **Carnegie Hall,** in New York City, opened May 5.

1892 **Ellis Island,** in New York Bay, opened Jan. 1 to receive immigrants; closed 1954. **Homestead strike** (PA) at Carnegie steel mills; 7 guards and 11 strikers and spectators shot to death July 6. James J. Corbett defeated John L. Sullivan Sept. 7 to become **first world heavyweight champion** under Marquess of Queensbury rules.

1893 **Columbian Exposition** world's fair held May-Oct. in Chicago. Financial panic led to four-year **depression. Mormon Temple** dedicated in Salt Lake City, UT.

1894 Thomas A. Edison's **kinetoscope,** for motion pictures (invented 1887), given first public showing Apr. 14. **Jacob S. Coxey** led army of unemployed from the Midwest, reaching Washington, DC, Apr. 30. Coxey arrested May 1 for trespassing on Capitol grounds; his army disbanded. **Pullman strike** began May 11 at railroad car plant in Chicago. Milton Hershey started **Hershey Chocolate Company.**

1895 **"America, the Beautiful"** appeared for first time, in church publication, July 4. **Stephen Crane's** *The Red Badge of Courage* published.

1896 Supreme Court, in *Plessy v. Ferguson,* May 18, approved racial segregation under the **"separate but equal"** doctrine. **William Jennings Bryan** delivered **"Cross of Gold"** speech July 9; won Democratic Party nomination. **John Philip Sousa** composed "Stars and Stripes Forever" on Dec. 25.

1897 **Olney-Pauncefote Treaty** with Britain, Jan. 11, gave wide scope to arbitration in settling disputes; never ratified by U.S. John J. McDermott won **first Boston Marathon** Apr. 19. First Klondike gold arrived in San Francisco July 14, helping set off **Klondike gold rush. First subway service** in country opens to public in Boston, Sept. 1.

1898 U.S. battleship *Maine* blown up Feb. 15 in Havana, Cuba; 260 killed. U.S. blockaded Cuba Apr. 22 in aid of independence forces. U.S. declared **war on Spain** Apr. 24; destroyed Spanish fleet in Philippines May 1; took Guam June 20. U.S. took **Puerto Rico** July 25-Aug. 12. Spain agreed Dec. 10 to cede Philippines, Puerto Rico, and Guam, and approved independence for Cuba. Annexation of **Hawaii** signed by Pres. William McKinley, July 7.

1899 Filipino insurgents, unable to get recognition of independence from U.S., started guerrilla war Feb. 4. Their leader, Emilio Aguinaldo, captured May 23, 1901. **Philippine insurrection** ended 1902. Killed were 20,000 Filipino troops and some 200,000 civilians, mostly from disease and starvation. Pres. McKinley signed treaty officially ending **Spanish-American War,** Feb. 10. U.S. declared **Open Door Policy**

Sept. 6, to make China an open international market. Philosopher **John Dewey's** *School and Society,* advocating progressive education ("learn by doing"), published. Pianist Scott Joplin's "Maple Leaf Rag" published, popularizing **ragtime music.**

1900 **International Ladies' Garment Workers Union** founded in New York City June 3. Fought sweatshop working conditions. **Carry Nation,** Kansas temperance leader, began raiding saloons with a hatchet. U.S. helped suppress **Boxer Rebellion** in Beijing, China. Eastman Kodak Co. introduced the **Brownie camera,** popularizing picture-taking.

1901 Texas had first significant oil strike at **Spindletop** well near Beaumont, Jan. 10. U.S. withdrew troops from **Cuba** May 20, and Cuba became independent. Pres. **McKinley** shot Sept. 6 in Buffalo, NY, by anarchist Leon Czolgosz; died Sept. 14. Vice Pres. **Theodore Roosevelt** sworn in as youngest-ever president, at age 42 years, 11 months. **Booker T. Washington's** *Up From Slavery* published.

1902 Permanent **Bureau of the Census** established Mar. 6. **Helen Keller** autobiography appeared in serial form.

1903 Treaty between U.S. and Colombia to have U.S. dig **Panama Canal** signed Jan. 22, but rejected by Colombia's Congress; Panama declared independence from Colombia with U.S. support Nov. 3; recognized by Pres. Roosevelt Nov. 6. U.S., Panama signed canal treaty Nov. 18. Wisconsin set first **direct primary voting system,** May 23. **Henry Ford** founded Ford Motor Co., June 16. Boston defeated Pittsburgh, 5 games to 3, Oct. 13 in **first modern World Series. First successful flight** in heavier-than-air mechanically propelled airplane by **Orville Wright** Dec. 17 near Kitty Hawk, NC, 120 ft in 12 secs. Later flight same day by **Wilbur Wright,** 852 ft in 59 secs. Improved plane patented, 1906. **Iroquois Theater fire** in Chicago killed about 600 out of 1,900 in audience, Dec. 30. Pioneering film *Great Train Robbery* produced.

1904 St. Louis hosted **first Olympics in U.S.,** July 1-Nov. 23. First section of New York subway system opened, Oct. 27. **Ida Tarbell** published muckraking *The History of the Standard Oil Company.* **Henry James's** last major novel, *The Golden Bowl,* published.

1905 **Industrial Workers of the World,** which advocated Marxian theory of class struggle between workers and capitalists, founded in Chicago, June 27. **Rotary,** oldest service club organization in U.S., founded in Chicago.

1906 **San Francisco earthquake** and fire, Apr. 18-19, caused more than 3,000 deaths and $400 mil in damages. **Upton Sinclair's** *The Jungle,* which exposed working conditions in meat-packing industry, published. Helped spur passage of the **Pure Food and Drug Act** and **Meat Inspection Act** June 30.

1907 Financial panic and **depression** started Mar. 13. Pres. Roosevelt sent **"Great White Fleet"** of 16 U.S. battleships around the world in show of power.

1908 Springfield, IL, torn by **anti-black rioting,** Aug. 14-15. Henry Ford introduced **Model T** car, priced at $850, Oct. 1.

1909 Adm. Robert E. Peary claimed to have reached **North Pole** Apr. 6 on sixth attempt, accompanied by black explorer

1903: Orville and Wilbur Wright achieve the first sustained, controlled flight in a powered airplane at Kitty Hawk, NC.

Matthew Henson and four Inuit; may have fallen short. National Conference on the Negro convened May 30, leading to founding of **National Association for the Advancement of Colored People** (NAACP).

1910 **Boy Scouts** of America founded Feb. 8. Former Pres. Roosevelt called for **"new nationalism"** in famous speech in Kansas, Aug. 10.

1911 Building with New York City's **Triangle Shirtwaist Co.** factory caught fire Mar. 25; 146 died. Supreme Court ruled May 15 that **Standard Oil Co.** must be dissolved because it unreasonably restrained trade. **First transcontinental airplane flight** (with numerous stops) by C. P. Rodgers, from New York to Pasadena, CA, Sept. 17-Nov. 5; time in air 82 hr., 4 min.

1912 American Girl Guides founded Mar. 12; name changed in 1913 to **Girl Scouts**. U.S. Marines, Aug. 14, sent to **Nicaragua**, which was in default of loans to U.S. and Europe.

1913 **16th Amendment**, authorizing federal income tax, ratified Feb. 3. The **Armory Show** in New York City brought modern art to U.S. for first time, Feb. 17. **17th Amendment**, providing for direct popular election of U.S. senators, ratified Apr. 8. **Federal Reserve System** authorized Dec. 23, in major reform of U.S. banking and finance.

1914 **Ford Motor Co.** raised basic wage rates from $2.40 for 9-hr. day to $5 for 8-hr. day, Jan. 5, increasing stability in labor force. When U.S. sailors were arrested in Tampico, Mexico, Apr. 9, Atlantic fleet was sent to **Veracruz**, occupied city. Pres. Woodrow Wilson proclaimed **U.S. neutrality** in the European war, Aug. 4. The **Panama Canal** officially opened Aug. 15. The **Clayton Antitrust Act** passed Oct. 15, strengthening federal antimonopoly powers.

1915 **First transcontinental telephone call**, New York to San Francisco, completed Jan. 25 by Alexander Graham Bell and Thomas A. Watson. British ship *Lusitania* sunk May 7 by German submarine; 1,198 passengers died, including 128 Americans. (In notice in morning newspapers the day *Lusitania* set sail, Germany had warned Americans against taking passage on British vessels.) As result of U.S. campaign, Germany issued apology and promise of payments, Oct. 5. U.S. troops landed in **Haiti**, July 28. Haiti became virtual U.S. protectorate under Sept. 16 treaty. Pres. Wilson asked for a military fund increase, Dec. 7. D. W. Griffith's film *The Birth of a Nation* released. William J. Simmons partly inspired by film to revive **Ku Klux Klan**, which peaks in 1920s.

1916 Gen. **John J. Pershing** entered Mexico in Mar. to pursue **Francisco (Pancho) Villa**, who had raided U.S. border areas. Forces withdrew Feb. 5, 1917. **Rural Credits Acts** passed July 17, followed by **Warehouse Act** Aug. 11; both provided financial aid to farmers. Bomb exploded during **San Francisco Preparedness Day parade** July 22, killed 10. Thomas J. Mooney, labor organizer, and Warren K. Billings, shoeworker, convicted 1917; both later pardoned. U.S. bought **Virgin Islands** from Denmark Aug. 4. U.S. established military government in the **Dominican Republic** Nov. 29. Jeannette Rankin (R, MT) elected to House of Representatives, **first female member of Congress**.

1917 Germany, suffering from British blockade, declared almost unrestricted **submarine warfare** Jan. 31. U.S. cut diplomatic ties with Germany Feb. 3 and formally **declared war** Apr. 6. Jones Act, passed Mar. 2, made **Puerto Rico** a U.S. territory, its inhabitants U.S. citizens. **Conscription law** passed May 18. First U.S. troops arrived in Europe June 26.

1918 Pres. Wilson set out his **14 Points** as basis for peace, Jan. 8. More than 1 mil American troops were in Europe by July. Allied counteroffensive launched at Château-Thierry July 18. War ended with signing of **armistice** Nov. 11. **Influenza epidemic** killed an estimated 20 mil worldwide, 548,000 in U.S.

1919 **18th Amendment**, providing for prohibition of manufacture, sale, or transportation of alcoholic beverages, ratified Jan. 16, to take effect on Jan. 16, 1920. **First transatlantic flight**, by U.S. Navy seaplane, left Rockaway, NY, May 8; stopped at Newfoundland, Azores, Lisbon May 27. **Boston police strike** Sept. 9, earliest strike conducted by government employees. About 250 **foreign-born radicals** deported Dec. 21 to Soviet Union.

1920 In national **Red Scare**, some 2,700 Communists, anarchists, and other radicals were arrested Jan.-May. **League of**

1920: The ratification of the 19th Amendment gives all women the right to vote.

Women Voters founded Feb. 14. Senate refused Mar. 19 to ratify **League of Nations Covenant**. Nicola Sacco and **Bartolomeo Vanzetti** accused of killing two men in Massachusetts payroll holdup Apr. 15; found guilty 1921. A seven-year campaign for their release failed; both executed Aug. 23, 1927. Verdict repudiated 1977 by proclamation of Massachusetts Gov. Michael Dukakis. **19th Amendment** ratified Aug. 18, giving women the vote. **First regular licensed radio broadcasting** began Aug. 20. **Wall St. bombing** in New York City killed 30, injured 100, did $2 mil damage, Sept. 16. **Sinclair Lewis**'s *Main Street* published.

1921 Congress sharply curbed immigration, set **national quota system** May 19. Joint congressional resolution declaring **peace with Germany, Austria, and Hungary** signed July 2 by Pres. Warren G. Harding; treaties were signed in Aug. In so-called **Black Sox scandal**, eight Chicago White Sox players were banned from baseball Aug. 4 for conspiring with gamblers to throw the 1919 World Series. Limitation of Armaments Conference met in Washington, DC, Nov. 12-Feb. 6, 1922. Major powers agreed to curtail naval construction, outlaw poison gas, restrict submarine attacks on merchant vessels, and respect China's integrity.

1922 During nationwide coal strike, union miners killed some 21 strikebreakers at Herrin, IL, June 21-22, in incident referred to as the **Herrin Massacre**. T. S. Eliot's *The Waste Land* published in London.

1923 **First sound-on-film motion picture**, *Phonofilm*, shown at Rivoli Theater, New York City, beginning in Apr. Pres. Calvin Coolidge addressed Congress, Dec. 6; **first radio broadcast of president's annual speech**.

1924 Law approved by Congress June 15 made all **Native Americans U.S. citizens**. Nellie Tayloe Ross elected governor of Wyoming, and **Miriam (Ma) Ferguson** elected governor of Texas Nov. 9. Ross inaugurated as nation's **first female governor** Jan. 5, 1925. Ferguson installed Jan. 20, 1925. George Gershwin wrote "Rhapsody in Blue."

1925 John T. Scopes found guilty of having taught **evolution** in Dayton, TN, high school, fined $100 and costs, July 24. **F. Scott Fitzgerald**'s *The Great Gatsby* published.

1926 Dr. Robert H. Goddard, Mar. 16, demonstrated **first liquid-fuel rocket**. Congress established **Army Air Corps** July 2. **Air Commerce Act** passed Nov. 2, established government agencies for development of airports, radio navigation, and other services. **Ernest Hemingway**'s *The Sun Also Rises* published.

1927 Capt. **Charles A. Lindbergh** left Roosevelt Field, NY, May 20 alone in *Spirit of St. Louis* on first New York-Paris nonstop flight. Reached Le Bourget airfield May 21, 3,610 mi in 33½ hr. *The Jazz Singer*, **first feature-length film** in which **spoken dialogue was part of narrative action**, released Oct. 6. The musical *Show Boat* opened in New York City Dec. 27.

1928 **Amelia Earhart** became first woman to fly across the Atlantic, June 17. **Herbert Hoover** elected president Nov. 6, defeating New York Gov. Alfred E. Smith, a Catholic.

1929 Gangsters killed seven rivals in Chicago **St. Valentine's Day massacre** Feb. 14, which won Al Capone control of Chicago's underworld. Stock market crash Oct. 29 marked end of past prosperity as stock prices plummeted. Stock losses for 1929-31 estimated at $50 bil; beginning of **Great Depression**. Albert B. Fall, former interior sec., was convicted of accepting $10,000 bribe in leasing of the **Elk Hills (Teapot Dome)** naval oil reserve; sentenced Nov. 1 to a year in prison and fined. **William Faulkner**'s *The Sound and the Fury* published.

1930 London **Naval Reduction Treaty** signed by U.S., Britain, Italy, France, and Japan Apr. 22; in effect Jan. 1, 1931; expired Dec. 31, 1936. **Hawley-Smoot Tariff** signed; rate hikes slash world trade. **Sinclair Lewis** became first American to win a Nobel Prize in literature. **Dashiell Hammett**'s *The Maltese Falcon* published.

1931 Empire State Building opened in New York City May 1, displacing NYC's Chrysler Building as world's tallest. **Al Capone** convicted of tax evasion Oct. 17. **Pearl Buck**'s *The Good Earth* published. **Charlie Chaplin** film *City Lights* released.

1932 Reconstruction Finance Corp. established Jan. 22 to stimulate banking and business. Unemployment at 12 mil. Twenty-month-old **Charles Lindbergh Jr.** kidnapped Mar. 1; found dead May 12. Bruno Hauptmann found guilty Feb. 1935; executed Apr. 3, 1936. Unemployed World War I veterans demanding Congress pay promised bonus early launched **Bonus March** on Washington, DC, May 29. **Franklin D. Roosevelt** elected president for first time in Democratic landslide, Nov. 8. Chicago Bears won **first NFL title game** Dec. 18, defeating the Portsmouth (OH) Spartans, 9-0.

1933 Pres. Roosevelt named **Frances Perkins** U.S. sec. of labor; **first woman in U.S. cabinet**. Pres. Roosevelt ordered **all U.S. banks closed** Mar. 6. In a "100 days" special session, Mar. 9-June 16, Congress passed **New Deal**, including measures to regulate banks, distribute funds to the jobless, create jobs, raise agricultural prices, and set wage and production standards for industry. **Gold standard** dropped by U.S. in favor of "modified gold bullion standard"; announced by Pres. Roosevelt Apr. 19, ratified by Congress June 5. **Tennessee Valley Authority (TVA)** created by act of Congress, May 18. **Prohibition** ended in the U.S. as 36th state ratified **21st Amendment** Dec. 5. Pres. Roosevelt foreswore armed intervention in **Western Hemisphere** nations, Dec. 26.

1934 Pres. Roosevelt signed law creating **Securities and Exchange Commission**, June 6. U.S. troops pulled out of **Haiti**, Aug. 6.

1935 Works Progress Administration (WPA) instituted May 6. Rural Electrification Administration created May 11. National Industrial Recovery Act struck down by Supreme Court May 27. **Boulder Dam** (later renamed **Hoover Dam**) completed, May 29. **Social Security Act** passed by Congress Aug. 8-9. Comedian **Will Rogers** and aviator Wiley Post killed Aug. 15 in Alaska plane crash. **Huey Long**, Louisiana senator and national political leader, shot Sept. 8; died Sept. 10. George Gershwin's jazz opera *Porgy and Bess* opened Oct. 10 in New York. **Committee for Industrial Organization** (later Congress of Industrial Organizations) formed to expand industrial unionism Nov. 9.

1936 Jesse Owens won four gold medals at the Berlin Olympics in Aug. **Baseball Hall of Fame** founded in Cooperstown, NY. **Margaret Mitchell**'s *Gone With the Wind* published.

1937 Airship *Hindenburg* caught fire May 6 as it was landing in Lakehurst, NJ; 36 killed. **Golden Gate Bridge** opened May 27. **Joe Louis** knocked out James J. Braddock to become world heavyweight champ June 22. Aviator **Amelia Earhart** and copilot Fred Noonan disappeared July 2 near Howland Isl., in the Pacific. Pres. Roosevelt proposed judicial reforms that would allow him to appoint additional Supreme Court justices; his **"court-packing"** plan defeated. **Auto, steel labor unions** won first big contracts.

1938 National minimum wage enacted June 25. Orson Welles's radio dramatization of H. G. Wells's *War of the Worlds*, Oct. 30, caused Martian invasion scare. **Seabiscuit** beat War Admiral in match race of the century, at Pimlico track, MD, Nov. 1. Artist Anna Mary Robertson, **"Grandma Moses,"** discovered. **Thornton Wilder**'s *Our Town* produced on Broadway.

1936: Jesse Owens wins four gold medals at the Olympic Games in Berlin, Germany, but is not acknowledged by German Chancellor Adolf Hitler nor officially by the U.S. government.

1939 Opera singer **Marian Anderson** performed for integrated crowd of 75,000 at Lincoln Memorial Apr. 9 after Daughters of the American Revolution refused to let Anderson sing in DC's Constitution Hall. **New York World's Fair**—theme: "The World of Tomorrow"—opened Apr. 30, closed Oct. 31. Reopened for second season May 11-Oct. 27, 1940. **Lou Gehrig**, seriously ill, said farewell to fans at Yankee Stadium, July 4. Albert Einstein alerted Pres. Roosevelt to **A-bomb possibilities** in Aug. 2 letter. **U.S. declared its neutrality** in European war Sept. 5. Pres. Roosevelt proclaimed limited **national emergency** Sept. 8, unlimited emergency May 27, 1941. Both ended by Pres. Harry Truman, Apr. 28, 1952.

Pocket Books, **first paperback publisher** in U.S., established. **John Steinbeck**'s *The Grapes of Wrath* published. *The Wizard of Oz* and *Gone With the Wind* released, the latter to become highest-grossing film of all time (inflation-adjusted).

1940 U.S. OK'd sale of **surplus war material** to Britain June 3; announced transfer of 50 overaged destroyers Sept. 3. **First peacetime military draft** in U.S. history approved, Sept. 14. **Forty-hour work week** went into effect, Oct. 24. Pres. **Roosevelt** elected Nov. 5 to third presidential term. **Richard Wright**'s *Native Son* published.

1941 Four Freedoms—freedom of speech and religion, freedom from want and fear—termed essential by Pres. Roosevelt in speech to Congress Jan. 6. **Lend-Lease Act** signed Mar. 11 provided $7 bil in military credits for Britain. Lend-lease for USSR approved in Nov. Pres. Roosevelt signed executive order June 25 barring federal government and war contractors from **racial discrimination**. Order also established Fair Employment Practice Committee. The **Atlantic Charter**, 8-point declaration of principles, issued by Pres. Roosevelt and British Prime Min. Winston Churchill, Aug. 14. Japan attacked **Pearl Harbor**, Hawaii, 7:55 AM Hawaiian time, Dec. 7; 19 ships sunk or damaged, 2,300 dead. Pres. Roosevelt called it "a date which will live in infamy." U.S. declared war on Japan Dec. 8. Germany and Italy declared war on U.S. Dec. 11. U.S. responded with declaration of war later on same

day. Japanese invaded **Philippines**, Dec. 22; Wake Island fell, Dec. 23. *Citizen Kane*, directed by Orson Welles, released.
1942 Pres. Roosevelt issued executive order Feb. 19 authorizing relocation of Japanese-Americans. Federal government began forcibly moving 110,000 Japanese-Americans from West Coast to **detention camps**; exclusion lasted three years. Japanese troops took **Bataan** peninsula Apr. 8 and **Corregidor** May 6. **Battle of Midway** June 4-7 was Japan's first major defeat. Marines landed on **Guadalcanal** Aug. 7; last Japanese not expelled until Feb. 9, 1943. U.S., Britain invaded **North Africa** Nov. 8. **First nuclear chain reaction** (fission of uranium isotope U-235) produced at Univ. of Chicago under physicists Arthur Compton, Enrico Fermi, others, Dec. 2. The movie *Casablanca*, starring Humphrey Bogart and Ingrid Bergman, released.
1943 *Oklahoma!* opened Mar. 31 on Broadway. Pres. Roosevelt signed June 10 pay-as-you-go income tax bill. Starting July 1, wage and salary earners were subject to **paycheck withholding tax**. **Detroit race riot** June 21 left 34 dead, 700 injured. Six killed in riot in New York City's **Harlem** section Aug. 2. U.S., Britain invaded **Sicily** July 9, Italian **mainland** Sept. 3. Marines in Nov. recaptured the **Gilbert Islands**, captured by Japan in 1941 and 1942.
1944 U.S., Allied forces invaded Europe at Normandy, France, on **"D Day,"** June 6, in greatest amphibious landing in history. **GI Bill of Rights**, providing benefits to veterans, signed by Pres. Roosevelt June 22. Representatives of the U.S. and other major powers met at **Dumbarton Oaks**, Washington, DC, Aug. 21-Oct. 7, to work out formation of postwar world organization that would become the **United Nations**. U.S. forces landed on **Leyte**, Philippines, Oct. 20. Pres. **Roosevelt** elected to fourth term as president Nov. 7. **Battle of the Bulge**, failed Nazi counteroffensive, waged Dec. 16 to Jan. 28, 1945.
1945 Yalta Conference met in the Crimea, USSR, Feb. 4-11. Pres. Roosevelt, Prime Min. Churchill, and Soviet leader Joseph Stalin agreed that their countries, plus France, would occupy Germany and that the Soviet Union would enter war against Japan. Marines landed on **Iwo Jima** Feb. 19, won control Mar. 16 after heavy casualties. U.S. forces invaded **Okinawa** Apr. 1, captured it June 21. Pres. **Roosevelt** died in Warm Springs, GA, Apr. 12; Vice Pres. **Harry S. Truman** became president. Germany surrendered May 7; May 8 proclaimed **V-E Day**. **First atomic bomb**, produced at Los Alamos, NM, exploded at Alamogordo, NM, July 16. Bomb dropped on **Hiroshima**, Japan, Aug. 6, killing about 75,000; bomb dropped on **Nagasaki**, Japan, Aug. 9, killing about 40,000. Japan agreed to surrender Aug. 14; formally surrendered Sept. 2. At **Potsdam Conference**, July 17-Aug. 2, leaders of U.S., USSR, and Britain agreed on disarmament of Germany, occupation zones, war crimes trials. **Empire State Building** struck accidentally by Army B-25 bomber, July 28, killing 14. U.S. forces entered **Korea** south of 38th parallel to displace Japanese Sept. 8. Gen. **Douglas MacArthur** took over supervision of Japan Sept. 9.
1946 Steel strike by 750,000 started Jan. 21, settled in four weeks. Strike by 400,000 **mine workers** began Apr. 1

1944: More than 160,000 Allied troops storm a heavily fortified stretch of French coastline on D-Day (June 6).

(settled May 29); other industries (including rail, maritime) followed. Former Prime Min. Winston Churchill employed the phrase **"Iron Curtain"** in Mar. 5 speech at Westminster College in Fulton, MO. Atomic bomb tested off **Bikini Atoll** in Pacific, July 1. In all, U.S. conducted 23 nuclear tests between 1946 and 1958. **Philippines** given independence by U.S. July 4. Mother Frances Xavier Cabrini **first American to be canonized**, July 7. Dr. Benjamin Spock's *Baby and Child Care* published as **baby boom** began.
1947 Pres. Truman asked Congress for financial and military aid for Greece and Turkey to help combat Communist subversion, Mar. 12; **Truman Doctrine** approved May 15. UN Security Council voted Apr. 2 to place under U.S. trusteeship the **Pacific islands** formerly mandated to Japan. **Jackie Robinson** joined Brooklyn Dodgers Apr. 11, breaking color barrier in major league baseball. The **Marshall Plan** for U.S. aid to European countries proposed by Sec. of State George C. Marshall June 5. Congress authorized some $12 bil in next four years. **Taft-Hartley Labor Act** restricting labor union power vetoed by Pres. Truman June 20; Congress overrode veto. Air Force Capt. **Chuck Yeager** broke sound barrier, Oct. 14, in X-1 rocket plane.
1948 Organization of American States (OAS) founded Apr. 30 by 21 countries. USSR halted all surface traffic into **West Berlin** June 24; in response, U.S. and British troops launched an **airlift**. Soviet blockade halted May 12, 1949; airlift ended Sept. 30. Pres. **Truman** elected Nov. 2, defeating NY Gov. Thomas E. Dewey in historic upset. **Alger Hiss** indicted Dec. 15 for perjury, after denying he had passed secret documents to Whittaker Chambers to go to a Communist spy ring; convicted Jan. 21, 1950. **Kinsey Report** on sexuality in the human male published.
1949 North Atlantic Treaty Organization (**NATO**) established Aug. 24 by U.S., Canada, and 10 Western European nations, agreeing that an armed attack against one would be considered an attack against all. Eleven leaders of U.S. **Communist Party** convicted Oct. 14 of advocating violent overthrow of U.S. government; sentenced to prison. Supreme Court upheld convictions, 1951. Pres. Truman, Oct. 26, signed legislation raising **federal minimum wage** from 40¢ an hour to 75¢. **Arthur Miller's** *Death of a Salesman* opened on Broadway.
1950 Masked bandits robbed **Brink's, Inc.**, Boston express office, Jan. 17, of $2.8 mil. Case solved 1956; eight sentenced to life. Pres. Truman authorized production of **H-bomb** Jan. 31. Special Senate committee to investigate organized crime established May 3, chaired by Sen. **Estes Kefauver** (D, TN).
  North Korean forces **invaded South Korea** June 25. UN asked for troops to restore peace. Pres. Truman ordered Air Force and Navy to Korea June 27. Truman approved ground forces, air strikes against North Korea June 30. U.S. sent 35 military advisers to **South Vietnam** June 27 and agreed to aid anti-Communist government. U.S. forces landed at **Inchon**, South Korea, Sept. 15. UN forces took Pyongyang Oct. 20, reached China border Nov. 20. China sent troops across border Nov. 26. U.S. banned shipments Dec. 8 to **Communist China** and to Asiatic ports trading with it.
  Army **seized all railroads** Aug. 27 on Truman's order to prevent general strike; returned to owners in 1952. Two members of **Puerto Rican nationalist movement** tried to kill Pres. Truman Nov. 1.
  Peanuts comic strip appeared in newspapers. Variety show *Your Show of Shows* debuted on TV. David Riesman's *The Lonely Crowd* published.
1951 22nd Amendment, limiting presidential term of office, ratified Feb. 27. **Julius Rosenberg**; his wife, **Ethel Rosenberg**; and **Morton Sobell** found guilty Mar. 29 of conspiracy to commit wartime espionage. Rosenbergs received death penalty. Sobell sentenced to 30 years; released 1969.
  Pres. Truman removed Gen. **Douglas MacArthur** from Korea command Apr. 11 for unauthorized policy statements. **Korea cease-fire** talks began in July; lasted two years. Fighting ended July 27, 1953.
  Transcontinental TV began Sept. 4 with Pres. Truman's address at Japanese Peace Treaty Conference in San Francisco. **Japanese peace treaty** signed in San Francisco Sept. 8 by U.S., Japan, and 47 other nations. **J. D. Salinger's** *Catcher in the Rye* published. *I Love Lucy* sitcom premiered on TV.
1952 Pres. Truman ordered seizure of nation's **steel mills** Apr. 8 to avert strike. Ruled illegal by Supreme Court June 2.

1951: Julius and Ethel Rosenberg are sentenced to death for spying for the Soviet Union amidst heightening Cold War suspicions.

Peace contract between West Germany, U.S., Great Britain, and France signed May 26. Last racial and ethnic barriers to naturalization removed, June 26-27, with passage of **Immigration and Naturalization Act** of 1952. **Puerto Rico** proclaimed commonwealth July 25, after referendum Mar. 3. Richard Nixon, as vice-pres. candidate, gave **"Checkers" speech**, so called because of sentimental reference to his dog Checkers, Sept. 23. **First hydrogen device explosion** Nov. 1 in Pacific. **Ralph Ellison**'s *Invisible Man* published.

1953 Federal jury in New York convicted 13 **Communist** leaders on conspiracy charges, Jan. 20. **Julius and Ethel Rosenberg** executed in electric chair, June 19, for relaying nuclear secrets to Soviet Union. **Korean War armistice** signed July 27. California Gov. **Earl Warren** sworn in Oct. 5 as 14th chief justice of U.S. Supreme Court.

1954 *Nautilus*, **first atomic-powered submarine**, launched at Groton, CT, Jan. 21. Five members of Congress were wounded in the House Mar. 1 by four **Puerto Rican independence supporters** who fired at random from a spectators' gallery.

At televised hearings, Apr. 22-June 17, before a Senate subcommittee, Army officials accused Sen. **Joseph McCarthy** (R, WI) of seeking preferential treatment for a draftee, and McCarthy accused Army of hindering probe of Communist infiltration. McCarthy was cleared in the hearings, but the Senate later voted to condemn him, 67-22, for abuse of the Senate during hearings and debates.

Supreme Court ruled unanimously May 17 that racial segregation in public schools was unconstitutional, in *Brown v. Board of Education* of *Topeka*. **Ernest Hemingway** won Nobel Prize in literature for *The Old Man and the Sea*.

1955 U.S. agreed Feb. 12 to help train **South Vietnamese army.** Supreme Court ordered "all deliberate speed" in **integration** of public schools, May 31. A summit meeting of leaders of **Big 4**—U.S., Britain, France, and USSR—took place July 18-23 in Geneva, Switzerland.

Rosa Parks refused Dec. 1 to give her seat to white man on bus in Montgomery, AL. Her arrest, detention, and conviction sparked boycott of bus system, organized by Rev. **Martin Luther King Jr.**, by Montgomery's black community, Dec. 5. Bus segregation ordinance declared unconstitutional by federal court in 1956. Boycott ended Dec. 23 of that year.

America's two largest labor organizations merged Dec. 5, creating **AFL-CIO.** Russian-born U.S. citizen **Vladimir Nabokov**'s *Lolita* published.

1956 Massive resistance to Supreme Court **desegregation rulings** was called for Mar. 12 by 101 Southern congressmen. U.S. Supreme Court, Apr. 23, unanimously ruled against **racial segregation** on intrastate buses.

Federal-Aid Highway Act signed June 29, creating **interstate highway system. First transatlantic telephone cable** activated Sept. 25. On Oct. 8, in Game 5, Yankee right-hander Don Larsen pitched **only perfect World Series game. Eugene O'Neill**'s *Long Day's Journey Into Night* opened Nov. 7 on Broadway.

1957 Congress approved **Civil Rights Act of 1957**, Apr. 29, first such bill since Reconstruction to protect voting rights. Pres. Eisenhower signed act into law Sept. 9; provided for creation of Civil Rights Commission. The U.S. surgeon general July 12 said studies showed "direct link" between cigarette smoking and lung cancer.

Arkansas Gov. Orval Faubus (D) called National Guardsmen Sept. 4 to bar nine black students from entering all-white high school in Little Rock. Faubus complied Sept. 21 with federal court order to remove Guardsmen, but local authorities ordered black students to withdraw. Pres. Eisenhower sent troops Sept. 24 to enforce court order.

Jack Kerouac's *On the Road* published.

1958 Army launched **first U.S. Earth-orbiting satellite,** *Explorer I*, Jan. 31 from Cape Canaveral, FL; discovered Van Allen radiation belt. U.S. Marines sent to Lebanon to protect elected government from threatened overthrow July-Oct. Nuclear sub *Nautilus* made **first undersea crossing of North Pole** Aug. 5. Presidential aide **Sherman Adams** resigned Sept. 22 over scandal involving alleged improper gifts. **First domestic jet airline passenger service** in U.S. opened by National Airlines Dec. 10 between New York and Miami.

1959 Alaska admitted as 49th state, Jan. 3; Hawaii admitted as 50th, Aug. 21. St. Lawrence Seaway opened to traffic, Apr. 25.

Vice Pres. Richard Nixon, on tour of USSR, held **"kitchen debate,"** July 24, with Soviet Prem. Nikita Khrushchev at U.S. exhibit in Moscow. Prem. Khrushchev paid unprecedented visit to U.S. Sept. 15-27; made transcontinental tour.

Pres. Eisenhower issued injunction Oct. 12, upheld and made effective by Supreme Court Nov. 7, ending record **116-day steel strike.** In **quiz show scandal,** Columbia Univ. Prof. Charles Van Doren admitted to U.S. House subcommittee Nov. 2 that he had been coached before appearances on NBC-TV's *21* in 1956; he had won $129,000. William Wyler's *Ben-Hur* released; the movie won a record 11 Academy Awards the following year.

1960 Sit-ins began Feb. 1 when four black college students in Greensboro, NC, refused to move from a Woolworth lunch counter after being denied service. By Sept. 1961, more than 70,000 students, whites and blacks, had participated in sit-ins. Pres. Eisenhower signed **Civil Rights Act** May 6.

A U.S. **U-2 reconnaissance plane** was shot down in the Soviet Union May 1; pilot Gary Powers captured. The incident led to cancellation of a Paris summit conference. A **birth control pill** approved as safe for first time by Food and Drug Administration May 9. Vice Pres. **Richard Nixon** and Sen. **John F. Kennedy** faced each other Sept. 26 in first in series of televised debates. Kennedy defeated Nixon to win presidency, Nov. 8. U.S. announced Dec. 15 its backing of rightist group in **Laos,** which took power the next day.

Alfred Hitchcock film *Psycho* released.

1961 U.S. severed diplomatic and consular relations with Cuba Jan. 3, after disputes over nationalizations of U.S. firms, U.S. military presence at Guantánamo base. U.S.-directed invasion of Cuba's **Bay of Pigs** Apr. 17 by Cuban exiles unsuccessfully attempted to overthrow the regime of Prem. Fidel Castro.

Peace Corps created by executive order, Mar. 1. **23rd Amendment,** giving DC citizens the right to vote in presidential elections, ratified Mar. 29. Comm. Alan B. Shepard Jr. rocketed from Cape Canaveral, FL, in a Mercury capsule May 5, in **first U.S.-crewed suborbital space flight.**

"Freedom Rides" from Washington, DC, across Deep South were launched May 20 to protest segregation in interstate transportation.

Joseph Heller's *Catch-22* published.

1962 Pres. Kennedy said Feb. 14 that U.S. military advisers in **Vietnam** would fire if fired upon. Lt. Col. John H. Glenn Jr. became **first American in orbit** Feb. 20 when he circled the Earth three times in the Mercury capsule *Friendship 7.*

In *Baker v. Carr*, Mar. 26, Supreme Court ruled that constitutional challenges to unequal distribution of voters among legislative districts could be resolved by federal courts. James

Meredith became first black student at Univ. of Mississippi Oct. 1 after 3,000 troops put down riots.

A Soviet **offensive missile buildup** in Cuba was revealed Oct. 22 by Pres. Kennedy, who ordered naval and air quarantine on shipment of offensive military equipment to the island. He and Soviet Prem. Khrushchev agreed Oct. 28 on formula to end crisis. Kennedy announced Nov. 2 that missile bases in Cuba were being dismantled. **Rachel Carson**'s *Silent Spring* launched environmentalist movement.

1963 In *Gideon v. Wainwright*, Mar. 18, Supreme Court ruled that all criminal defendants must have counsel.

March for civil rights began May 2 in Birmingham, AL; led to desegregation accord, which in turn sparked rioting and violence. Univ. of Alabama **desegregated** after Gov. George Wallace stepped aside when confronted by federally deployed National Guard troops June 11. Civil rights leader **Medgar Evers** assassinated June 12. On Aug. 28, 200,000 joined in **March on Washington** in support of black demands for equal rights led by **Rev. Martin Luther King Jr.**; highlight was King's **"I Have a Dream" speech.**

Supreme Court ruled June 17 that laws requiring **recitation of Lord's Prayer or Bible verses** in public schools were unconstitutional. Pres. Kennedy, on Europe trip, addressed huge crowd in **West Berlin**, June 23. **Limited nuclear test-ban treaty** agreed upon July 25 by the U.S., the Soviet Union, and Britain. Four black girls killed in bombing of **16th St. Baptist Church** in Birmingham, AL, Sept. 15.

South Vietnam Pres. **Ngo Dinh Diem** assassinated Nov. 2; U.S. had earlier withdrawn support. Pres. **Kennedy** shot and fatally wounded Nov. 22 as he rode in motorcade through downtown Dallas, TX. Vice Pres. **Lyndon B. Johnson** sworn in as president. **Lee Harvey Oswald** arrested and charged with murder but was himself shot and fatally wounded Nov. 24. Nightclub owner **Jack Ruby** convicted of Oswald's murder; Ruby died in 1967 while awaiting retrial following reversal of his conviction. **Betty Friedan**'s feminist work *The Feminine Mystique* published.

1964 **Panama** suspended relations with U.S. Jan. 9 after riots. U.S. offered Dec. 18 to negotiate new canal treaty. **The Beatles** appeared Feb. 9 on *The Ed Sullivan Show.* Supreme Court ruled Feb. 17 that **congressional districts** as near as practicable be equal in population. U.S. reported May 27 it was sending military planes to **Laos.**

1964: Martin Luther King Jr. becomes, at age 35, the youngest-ever Nobel Peace Prize laureate for his leadership in the civil rights movement.

Three **civil rights workers** reported missing in Mississippi June 22; bodies found Aug. 4. Eighteen white men tried. On Oct. 20, 1967, an all-white federal jury convicted seven of conspiracy in the slayings. Omnibus **civil rights bill** signed by Pres. Johnson July 2, banning discrimination in voting, jobs, public accommodations.

Congress Aug. 7 passed **Tonkin Gulf Resolution**, authorizing presidential action in Vietnam, after North Vietnamese boats reportedly attacked U.S. destroyers Aug. 2. Congress approved **War on Poverty** bill Aug. 11, providing for a domestic Peace Corps (VISTA), **Job Corps**, and antipoverty funding. The **Warren Commission** released a report Sept. 27 concluding that Lee Harvey Oswald was solely responsible for the Kennedy assassination. Pres. **Johnson** elected to full term, Nov. 3, defeating Sen. **Barry Goldwater** (R, AZ) in landslide. **Verrazano-Narrows Bridge** opened in New York City, Nov. 21, with world's then-longest suspension span.

1965 In State of the Union address Jan. 4, Pres. Johnson outlined plans for **"Great Society,"** program of civil rights, antipoverty, and health-care legislation. Johnson in Feb. ordered continuous bombing of **North Vietnam** below 20th parallel.

Malcolm X assassinated Feb. 21 at New York City rally. March from **Selma to Montgomery**, AL, Mar. 21-25, by Rev. Martin Luther King Jr. to demand federal protection of blacks' voting rights. Some 14,000 U.S. troops sent to **Dominican Republic** during civil war Apr. 28. All troops withdrawn by next year. Bill establishing **Medicare**, government health insurance program for elderly, signed by Pres. Johnson July 30.

New **Voting Rights Act**, which banned literacy tests and other voter qualification tests, signed Aug. 6. Arrest of black motorist by white police officers precipitated **Watts riot** in predominantly-black Los Angeles neighborhood Aug. 11-16. Riots resulted in 34 deaths and $200 mil in property damage. National **immigration quota system** abolished Oct. 3. **Electric power failure** blacked out most of northeastern U.S., parts of two Canadian provinces the night of Nov. 9-10.

1966 U.S. forces began firing into **Cambodia** May 1. Bombing of Hanoi area of North Vietnam by U.S. planes began June 29. By Dec. 31, 385,300 U.S. troops were stationed in South Vietnam, plus 60,000 offshore and 33,000 in Thailand.

Supreme Court ruled June 13, in *Miranda v. Arizona*, that suspects must be read their rights before police questioning. **Medicare** began July 1. In **Univ. of Texas shooting** rampage, 25-year-old student Charles Whitman killed 15 and wounded 31 from tower observation deck on Austin campus, Aug. 1; shot dead by police.

Dept. of Transportation created, Oct. 15. Edward Brooke (R, MA) elected Nov. 8 as first black U.S. senator in 85 years. Robert C. Weaver named secretary of newly created Dept. of Housing and Urban Development, becoming **first black cabinet member.**

1967 Green Bay Packers beat Kansas City Chiefs, 35-10, in **first Super Bowl**, Jan. 15, in Los Angeles. Three astronauts died Jan. 27 in *Apollo 1* fire on ground at Cape Canaveral, FL. **25th Amendment**, providing for presidential succession, ratified Feb. 10. Pres. Johnson and Soviet Prem. **Aleksei Kosygin** met June 23 and 25 at Glassboro State College in New Jersey; agreed not to let any crisis push them into war.

Riots erupted among residents of predominantly black **Newark**, NJ, July 12-17; 26 killed, 1,500 injured, more than 1,000 arrested. In **Detroit**, MI, July 23-30, 43 died, 2,000 injured; 5,000 left homeless by rioting, looting, and burning in city's black neighborhoods. **Thurgood Marshall** sworn in Oct. 2 as first black U.S. Supreme Court justice. **Antiwar march** on Washington, DC, Oct. 21-22, drew 50,000 participants. Carl B. Stokes (D, Cleveland) and Richard G. Hatcher (D, Gary, IN) elected **first black mayors** of major U.S. cities Nov. 7.

1968 In **"Tet offensive,"** Communist troops attacked several provincial capitals and other major cities, including Saigon, Jan. 30, but suffered heavy casualties. Pres. Johnson **curbed bombing** of North Vietnam Mar. 31. Peace talks began in Paris May 10. All bombing of North halted Oct. 31.

Rev. **Martin Luther King Jr.** assassinated Apr. 4 in Memphis, TN. **James Earl Ray**, an escaped convict, pleaded guilty to slaying, was sentenced to 99 years. Students at **Columbia Univ.**, Apr. 23-24, seized school buildings in protest against school's involvement in military research, among other issues.

Sen. **Robert F. Kennedy** (D, NY) shot June 5 in Los Angeles after celebrating presidential primary victories, died June 6. **Sirhan Sirhan** convicted of murder, 1969; death sentence commuted to life in prison, 1972.

Vice Pres. Hubert Humphrey nominated for president at **Democratic National Convention** in Chicago, marked by clash between police and antiwar protestors, Aug. 26-29. Republican nominee **Richard Nixon** won presidency, defeating Humphrey in close race Nov. 5.

Apollo 8 orbited moon in five-day mission, Dec. 21-27. North Korea released 82-man crew of the USS *Pueblo* Dec. 22, 11 months after seizing the ship in Sea of Japan; one crew member had been killed in battle.

1969 Expanded four-party **Vietnam peace talks** began Jan. 18. U.S. force peaked at 543,400 in Apr.; withdrawal started July 8. Pres. Nixon set Vietnamization policy Nov. 3. Earl Warren retired upon swearing in **Warren Burger**, June 23, as Supreme Court chief justice. In incident that marked birth of **gay rights** movement, police clashed with patrons of gay bar, the **Stonewall Inn**, in New York City June 27.

U.S. astronaut **Neil Armstrong**, commander of the *Apollo 11* mission, became the **first person to set foot on the moon**, July 20, followed by astronaut **Edwin "Buzz" Aldrin**. Astronaut **Michael Collins** remained aboard command module.

Woodstock rock music festival near Bethel, NY, drew 300,000-500,000 people, Aug. 15-18. **Anti-Vietnam War demonstrations** held in cities across the U.S., marking Vietnam Moratorium day, Oct. 15; on Nov. 15, some 250,000 marched in Washington, DC. Massacre of hundreds of civilians by U.S. troops at **My Lai**, South Vietnam, in 1968 reported Nov. 16. **Kurt Vonnegut**'s *Slaughterhouse Five* published. *Sesame Street* launched on public TV.

1970 A federal jury Feb. 18 found the **"Chicago 7"** antiwar activists not guilty of conspiring to incite riots during 1968 Democratic National Convention. However, five were convicted of crossing state lines with intent to incite riots.

Three astronauts safely returned to Earth Apr. 17 after oxygen tank on *Apollo 13* ruptured. Lunar landing had been cancelled. Millions of Americans participated in antipollution demonstrations Apr. 22 to mark **first Earth Day**.

U.S. and South Vietnamese forces crossed **Cambodian** borders Apr. 30 to get at enemy bases. Four students killed May 4 at **Kent State Univ.** in Ohio by National Guardsmen during war protest. In protest at **Jackson State Univ.** in Mississippi, two killed when police fired on protesters.

First female U.S. generals appointed June 11. **Postal reform** measure signed Aug. 12 created an independent U.S. Postal Service. Pres. Nixon, Dec. 31, signed **clean air bill** calling for development of cleaner auto engine and national air quality standards for 10 major pollutants. Garry Trudeau's *Doonesbury* comic strip launched in 30 papers.

1971 **Charles Manson** and three of his cult followers found guilty Jan. 25 of first-degree murder in 1969 slaying of actress Sharon Tate and six others. A court-martial jury Mar. 29 convicted Lt. **William Calley** in murder of 22 South Vietnamese at **My Lai** on Mar. 16, 1968. He was sentenced to life in prison Mar. 31, later reduced to 20 years.

Pres. Nixon, Apr. 14, relaxed 20-year **trade embargo with China**. *New York Times* began publishing June 13 classified **Pentagon Papers**, secret Pentagon study on U.S. involvement in Vietnam leaked by Daniel Ellsberg, military analyst consulting for government. Supreme Court June 30 upheld, 6-3, right to publish the documents. **26th Amendment**, lowering the minimum voting age to 18, ratified June 30. Pres. Nixon, Aug. 15, instituted 90-day **wage and price freeze**.

U.S. bombers initiated massive five-day strike Dec. 26 in North Vietnam in retaliation for alleged violations of agreements reached prior to 1968 bombing halt.

1972 Pres. Nixon arrived in **Beijing** Feb. 21 for eight-day visit to China, in "journey for peace." Joint communiqué released Feb. 27 called for increased Sino-U.S. contacts. Senate, Mar. 22, approved **Equal Rights Amendment** banning discrimination on basis of sex; sent measure to states for ratification.

North Vietnamese forces launched biggest attacks in four years across the demilitarized zone Mar. 30. The U.S. responded Apr. 15 with **resumption of bombing** of Hanoi and Haiphong. Pres. Nixon announced May 8 the mining of North Vietnam ports.

Gov. **George C. Wallace** (D, AL), campaigning for president at Laurel, MD, shopping center May 15, shot and seriously wounded. **Arthur Bremer** convicted Aug. 4, sentenced to 63 years for shooting Wallace and three others. In **first visit of U.S. president to Moscow**, Pres. Nixon arrived May 22 for summit talks with Kremlin leaders that culminated in landmark strategic arms pact (**SALT I**). Five men arrested June 17 for breaking into Democratic National Committee offices in **Watergate** office complex in Washington, DC. Supreme Court in *Furman v. Georgia* June 29 ruled **capital punishment** as currently practiced was unconstitutional. **Mark Spitz** won seven gold medals in world record times at the Munich Olympics in Aug.-Sept.

Last U.S. combat troops left Vietnam Aug. 11. Pres. **Nixon** reelected Nov. 7 in landslide, carrying 49 states to defeat Sen. George McGovern (D, SD). Three astronauts, part of *Apollo 17*, made 6th and last lunar landing on Dec. 11. Full-scale **bombing of North Vietnam** resumed after Paris peace negotiations reached impasse Dec. 18.

The Godfather, directed by Francis Ford Coppola, is released.

1973 In *Roe v. Wade*, Supreme Court ruled, 7-2, Jan. 22, fetus not a person with constitutional rights and that right to privacy protected woman's decision to have abortion; states may not ban abortions during first three months of pregnancy but may regulate, not ban, abortions during second trimester.

Four-party **Vietnam peace pacts** signed in Paris Jan. 27. **End of military draft** announced on same day. Last U.S. troops left Vietnam Mar. 29. North Vietnam released some 590 U.S. prisoners by Apr. 1. Pres. Nixon announced, Apr. 30, resignation of top Nixon aides H. R. Haldeman and John Ehrlichman and firing of White House Counsel **John Dean** as a consequence of the widening **Watergate** scandal. Dean told Senate hearings June 25 that Nixon, his aides, and Justice Dept. had conspired to cover up Watergate facts. The U.S. officially ceased bombing in **Cambodia** at midnight Aug. 14 in accord with June congressional action.

Vice Pres. **Spiro Agnew**, Oct. 10, resigned and pleaded no contest to charge of tax evasion while Maryland governor. **Gerald R. Ford**, Oct. 12, became **first appointed vice president** under 25th Amendment; sworn in Dec. 6. The "**Saturday Night Massacre**" occurred Oct. 20, when Pres. Nixon ordered Atty. Gen. Elliot Richardson to fire Watergate special prosecutor **Archibald Cox**, who had sought handover of Nixon's subpoenaed **White House tapes**. Richardson refused to comply and resigned; Dep. Atty. Gen. William Ruckelshaus refused and was fired. Solicitor Gen. Robert Bork, as acting atty. gen., then fired Cox. Nixon administration named **Leon Jaworski**, Nov. 1, to succeed Cox.

Skylab, **first U.S. space station**, launched May 14. **Secretariat** became first Triple Crown winner since *Citation* in 1948 by winning Belmont Stakes June 9 in record time. **Billie Jean King** defeated Bobby Riggs in three straight sets in tennis's nationally televised "Battle of the Sexes," Sept. 20. Total **ban on oil exports** to U.S. imposed by Arab oil-producing nations Oct. 19-21 after outbreak of an Arab-Israeli war; lifted Mar. 1974. Congress overrode Nov. 7 Pres. Nixon's veto of **war powers bill** curbing curbed president's power to commit forces to hostilities abroad without congressional approval.

1974 On Apr. 8, **Hank Aaron** of the Atlanta Braves hit his 715th career home run to break Babe Ruth's record.

House Judiciary Committee opened **impeachment** hearings May 9 against Pres. Nixon. John Ehrlichman and three **White House "plumbers"** found guilty July 12 of conspiring to violate the civil rights of the psychiatrist of **Pentagon Papers** leaker Daniel Ellsberg by breaking into psychiatrist's office. Supreme Court ruled, 8-0, July 24 that Pres. Nixon had to turn over 64 **audio tapes of White House conversations**. House Judiciary Committee, in televised hearings July 24-30, recommended **articles of impeachment** against Pres. Nixon, involving conspiracy to obstruct justice in Watergate cover-up, abuses of power, and defiance of committee subpoenas.

Pres. **Nixon** announced his **resignation**, Aug. 8, and stepped down the next day. His support in Congress had begun to collapse Aug. 5 after release of tapes appearing to implicate him in Watergate cover-up. Vice Pres. **Ford** sworn in Aug. 9 as 38th U.S. president. Pres. Ford, Aug. 20, nominated

1974: Pres. Richard Nixon resigns from office and departs the White House.

Nelson Rockefeller to be vice president; Rockefeller sworn in Dec. 10. Citing need to move on, Pres. Ford, Sept. 8, issued **pardon to Nixon** for any federal crimes he committed while president.

New York Times published article Dec. 22 on CIA engagement in illegal domestic surveillance. Reports of other apparently illegal CIA activities, recorded in **"family jewels"** file kept by the CIA, leaked out over the years.

1975 Former Atty. Gen. John Mitchell and ex-presidential advisers H. R. Haldeman and John Ehrlichman found guilty Jan. 1 of **Watergate cover-up** charges. Mitchell released 1979, last of 25 jailed over scandal to leave prison.

U.S. launched **evacuation from Saigon** of Americans and some South Vietnamese Apr. 29 as Communist forces completed takeover of South Vietnam; **South Vietnamese** government officially surrendered Apr. 30. U.S. merchant ship *Mayaguez* and its crew of 39 seized by Cambodian forces in Gulf of Siam May 12. In rescue operation, U.S. Marines attacked Tang Island, planes bombed air base; Cambodia surrendered ship and crew. Congress voted $405 mil for **South Vietnam refugees** May 16; 140,000 flown to U.S.

Publishing heiress **Patricia (Patty) Hearst**, kidnapped Feb. 5, 1974, by Symbionese Liberation Army (SLA), captured in San Francisco Sept. 18 with other militants. She was convicted Mar. 20, 1976, of bank robbery.

1976 In **right-to-die** case, New Jersey Supreme Court, Mar. 31, allowed comatose Karen Ann Quinlan to be removed from respirator; she survived until 1985. U.S. Supreme Court reinstated **death penalty**, July 2, subject to conditions.

U.S. celebrated **200th anniversary of independence** July 4 with festivals, parades, and New York City's Operation Sail, gathering of tall ships from around the world. **"Legionnaire's disease"** killed 29 people who attended American Legion convention July 21-24 in Philadelphia.

Viking I made successful landing on Mars, July 20. Two U.S. officers on routine mission near DMZ slain by **North Korean soldiers** Aug. 18; North Korea stated "regret."

1977 Convicted murderer Gary Gilmore executed by Utah firing squad Jan. 17; **first use of capital punishment** in U.S. since 1967. Pres. Jimmy Carter Jan. 21 pardoned most Vietnam War **draft evaders.**

Natural gas shortage caused by severe winter weather led Congress Feb. 2 to approve emergency gas bill temporarily authorizing reallocation from surplus areas. Pres. Carter signed act Aug. 4 creating new cabinet-level **Energy Dept.** FBI Dec. 7 released 40,000 pages of previously secret files relating to **Kennedy assassination.**

George Lucas's first *Star Wars* film released.

1978 Senate voted Apr. 18 to turn over **Panama Canal** to Panama on Dec. 31, 1999; Mar. 16 vote had given approval to treaty guaranteeing area's neutrality after the year 2000. Californians, June 6, approved **Proposition 13**, state constitutional amendment slashing property taxes.

Supreme Court, June 28, ruled that while race could be a factor in admission to institutions of higher education, **numerical quotas** could not be used.

Egyptian Pres. **Anwar al-Sadat** and Israeli Prem. **Menachem Begin** reached accord on "framework for peace," Sept. 17, after Pres. Carter-mediated talks at **Camp David**. New York's Chemical Bank Dec. 20 initiated industry-wide move to raise **lending rate** to near-record 11.75%.

1979 Partial meltdown released radioactive material Mar. 28 at nuclear reactor on **Three Mile Island** near Middletown, PA. American Airlines DC-10 **jetliner crashed** May 25 after takeoff from Chicago, killing 275 people.

In speech July 15, Pres. Carter spoke of national "crisis of confidence" and outlined proposed 10-year $140 bil program to reduce **dependence on foreign oil.** Militant followers of **Ayatollah Khomeini** took hostage some 90 people, including 66 Americans, Nov. 4 at **American embassy in Tehran**, Iran. Khomeini demanded return of ailing former Shah Muhammad Reza Pahlavi to stand trial.

1980 Pres. Carter announced, Jan. 4, economic sanctions against USSR in retaliation for Soviet invasion of Afghanistan. At Carter's request, U.S. Olympic Committee voted, Apr. 12, against U.S. participation in **Moscow Summer Olympics**. At **Winter Olympics** in Lake Placid, NY, U.S. hockey team defeated Russian team Feb. 22 en route to gold medal in "miracle on ice."

Eight Americans killed, Apr. 24, in ill-fated attempt to rescue hostages held by Iranian militants. **Mt. St. Helens**, in Washington state, erupted May 18. The blast, with others May 25 and June 12, left 57 dead. In sweeping victory, Nov. 4, **Ronald Reagan** (R) was elected 40th president, defeating incumbent Pres. Carter. Republicans gained control of Senate. Former Beatle **John Lennon** was shot and killed by Mark David Chapman, Dec. 8, in New York City.

1981 Minutes after Reagan's inauguration Jan. 20, 52 **American hostages in Iran** were freed after being held for 444 days. Pres. **Reagan** was shot and seriously wounded, Mar. 30, in Washington, DC; also seriously wounded were a Secret Service agent, a policeman, and Press Sec. **James Brady.** **John W. Hinckley Jr.** arrested, found not guilty by reason of insanity in 1982, and committed to mental institution.

World's **first reusable spacecraft**, space shuttle *Columbia*, sent into space, Apr. 12. U.S. Centers for Disease Control, June 5, reported first cases of what became known as **AIDS.**

Air controllers went on **strike** Aug. 3; most were fired by Pres. Reagan after defying back-to-work order. Reagan signed into law Aug. 13 **tax-cut legislation**, expected to save taxpayers $750 bil over five years, largest tax cut to date. The Senate confirmed, Sept. 21, appointment of **Sandra Day O'Connor** as **first female Supreme Court justice.**

1982 The 13-year-old Justice Dept. lawsuit against **AT&T** was settled Jan. 8. AT&T agreed to give up 22 Bell System companies and was allowed to expand. **Equal Rights Amendment**, sent to states in 1972, defeated when deadline for ratification passed June 30 with support from only 35 of the 38 states needed. The economy showed signs of recovery from a **recession** that began in mid-1981, as Dow Jones Industrial Average hit 1,016.93 Oct. 13, its highest level in 18 months.

NFL strike ended Nov. 16 after 57 days when players and team owners settled with $1.6 bil pact. Singer **Michael Jackson**'s album *Thriller*, released Nov. 30, became monumental best-seller. Retired dentist Dr. Barney B. Clark became **first permanent artificial heart recipient**, Dec. 2; he died Mar. 23, 1983. The House, Dec. 16, cited EPA administrator Anne Gorsuch for contempt after she refused to release records relating to enforcement of **Superfund** law.

1983 Pres. Reagan, Jan. 3, declared Times Beach, MO, a federal disaster area because of toxic **dioxin** in soil, prompting evacuation of residents and town's closure. Harold Washington (D) elected Apr. 12 as **first black mayor of Chicago**. On Apr. 20, Pres. Reagan signed compromise bipartisan bill designed to save **Social Security** from bankruptcy.

Sally Ride became **first American woman to travel in space**, June 18, when space shuttle *Challenger* launched from

1984: The Democratic presidential ticket of former Vice Pres. Walter Mondale and Rep. Geraldine Ferraro (NY) makes history with the first female major-party nominee, but Pres. Ronald Reagan scores a landslide victory.

Cape Canaveral, FL. On Sept. 1, **South Korean passenger jet** in Soviet air space and apparently misidentified was shot down; 269 people, including 61 Americans, killed.

On Oct. 23, 241 U.S. Marines and sailors were killed when TNT-laden **suicide truck bomb** blew up Marine barracks at Beirut International Airport in **Lebanon**. U.S. troops, with small force from six Caribbean nations, invaded **Grenada** Oct. 25; deposed Marxist regime.

1984 Seven regional companies took over **local telephone service** from AT&T, Jan. 1. On space shuttle *Challenger*'s fourth trip, launched Feb. 3, two astronauts became **first humans to fly free of a spacecraft**. On May 7, Vietnam War veterans reached out-of-court settlement with chemical companies in class-action suit over the herbicide **Agent Orange**.

Former Vice Pres. **Walter Mondale** won Democratic presidential nomination, June 6. He chose Rep. **Geraldine Ferraro** (D, NY) as vice presidential candidate, first woman to be nominated for position by major political party. Pres. Reagan signed bill July 17 cutting federal transportation aid to states that keep their **drinking age** under 21. Pres. **Reagan** reelected Nov. 6 in Republican landslide, carrying 49 states for record 525 electoral votes. **Bernhard Goetz** shot and wounded four allegedly menacing teenage boys on NYC subway train, Dec. 22; later acquitted of major charges but was successfully sued.

1985 Visiting Germany, Pres. Reagan, May 5, laid wreath at Bergen-Belsen Nazi concentration camp site and also at military cemetery at **Bitburg**, where some Nazis were buried. Philadelphia police bombed a rowhouse occupied by **MOVE radical group**, May 13; 11 killed, and fire damaged two blocks of houses. On June 14, **terrorists seized TWA jet** after takeoff from Athens, Greece, with 153 passengers and crew. Thirty-nine Americans held hostage for 17 days; one U.S. service member killed.

Reversing an Apr. 23 decision to market "new" Coke, the **Coca-Cola Co.** said, July 10, it would resume marketing soda made under its original "Classic" formula. **Live Aid** rock concert broadcast around the world July 13, raised $70 mil for famine relief in Ethiopia.

On Oct. 7, four **Palestinian hijackers** seized Italian cruise ship *Achille Lauro* in the Mediterranean for two days. One American, Leon Klinghoffer, killed. For first time in six years U.S. and Soviet leaders met at **summit in Geneva**, Nov. 19-20. **General Electric** agreed Dec. 11 to buy RCA Corp.

1986 The U.S. officially observed **Martin Luther King Jr. Day** for first time Jan. 20. Space shuttle *Challenger* exploded 73 seconds after liftoff, Jan. 28, killing six astronauts and Teacher in Space Project participant Christa McAuliffe. In four-day extravaganza in July, the U.S. celebrated 100th birthday of the **Statue of Liberty**.

The Senate confirmed, Sept. 17, Reagan's nomination of **William Rehnquist** as chief justice and **Antonin Scalia** as associate justice of Supreme Court. Congress completed action Oct. 2 overriding a veto to place economic sanctions on **South Africa**.

Lebanese newspaper first broke news of **Iran-Contra scandal** Nov. 3, involving secret U.S. sale of arms to Iran and diversion of some of the proceeds to support the Contras, a right-wing, anti-Communist insurgent movement in Nicaragua.

Financier **Ivan Boesky** agreed Nov. 14 to pay $100 mil in fines and illicit profits for **insider trading**. Robert Penn Warren named America's **first poet laureate**.

1987 Pres. Reagan produced nation's **first trillion-dollar budget**, Jan. 5. FDA approved, Mar. 20, AZT—first drug shown to be effective in fight against **AIDS**. Nearly 1.4 mil **illegal aliens** met May 4 deadline for applying for amnesty under immigration measure passed in 1986.

Joint public hearings by Senate and House committees investigating **Iran-Contra affair** opened May 5. Lt. Col. **Oliver North**, former National Security Council staff member, said he had believed all his activities were authorized by his superiors. Hearings ended Aug. 3. Pres. Reagan, Aug. 12, denied knowing of diversion of funds to Contras.

An **Iraqi missile** killed 37 sailors on the USS *Stark* in the Persian Gulf, May 17. Iraq called it an accident. The 200th anniversary of **U.S. Constitution** signing was observed, Sept. 17, in Philadelphia and around the U.S. **Stock market crashed**, Oct. 19, with the Dow Jones plummeting a then-record 508 points to 1,738, ending bull market that began mid-1982. Pres. Reagan and Soviet leader Mikhail Gorbachev Dec. 8, signed **pact to dismantle** all 1,752 U.S. and 859 Soviet missiles with 300- to 3,400-mi range.

1988 *Phantom of the Opera*, longest running Broadway play ever, opened Jan. 26. In report issued May 16, Surgeon Gen. C. Everett Koop declared **cigarettes addictive**. Congress approved, in June, expansion of **Medicare** benefits to protect against "catastrophic" medical costs; act was repealed in Nov. 1989.

A missile, fired from U.S. Navy warship *Vincennes* in the Persian Gulf, mistakenly struck a commercial **Iranian airliner**, July 3, killing all 290 aboard. **George H. W. Bush** (R) elected 41st U.S. president, Nov. 8, decisively defeating Massachusetts Gov. **Michael Dukakis** (D). **Pan Am Flight 103** exploded and crashed, due to terrorist bomb, into town of Lockerbie, Scotland, Dec. 21, killing all 259 people aboard and 11 on the ground. **Drexel Burnham Lambert** agreed, Dec. 21, to plead guilty to insider trading and other violations, and pay penalties of $650 mil. U.S. suffered widespread **drought** conditions, the worst in over 50 years.

1989 Major oil spill occurred when *Exxon Valdez* struck Bligh Reef in Alaska's Prince William Sound, Mar. 24. Oliver North convicted, May 4, on charges related to **Iran-Contra scandal**. Conviction thrown out on appeal in 1991 because of his immunized testimony. TV comedy series *Seinfeld* premiered July 5 on NBC.

A measure to rescue **savings and loan industry** signed into law, Aug. 9, by Pres. Bush, launching largest federal rescue to date. Army Gen. **Colin Powell** became **first black chairman of Joint Chiefs of Staff** after being nominated Aug. 10 by Pres. Bush.

Baseball legend **Pete Rose** banned from game for life Aug. 24 for involvement with gamblers. **Hurricane Hugo** swept through the Carolinas Sept. 22, causing at least 86 deaths and $7 bil damage. Just before a World Series

1989: The *Exxon Valdez* oil spill causes environmental devastation in Alaska's Prince William Sound.

game, Oct. 17, an **earthquake** struck the San Francisco Bay area, causing 63 deaths.

L. Douglas Wilder (D) declared governor of Virginia Nov. 27, **first elected black governor** in U.S. history. U.S. troops invaded Panama, Dec. 20, overthrowing the government of **Manuel Noriega**. Noriega, wanted by U.S. authorities on drug charges, surrendered Jan. 3, 1990.

1990 Junk bond financier **Michael Milken** pleaded guilty to fraud-related charges, Apr. 14; agreed to pay $500 mil in restitution and sentenced Nov. 21 to 10 years in prison. Pres. Bush signed **Americans With Disabilities Act** barring discrimination against, and requiring accommodations for, the disabled, July 26. **Operation Desert Shield** forces left for Saudi Arabia Aug. 7 to defend that country following invasion of **Kuwait** by Iraq, Aug. 2. David Souter confirmed Sept. 27 to serve on Supreme Court, replacing retiring Justice **William Brennan**. Pres. Bush Nov. 15 signed new **Clean Air Act**, focused on urban pollution, cancer-causing emissions from industrial sources.

1991 The U.S. and its allies defeated Iraq in **Persian Gulf War** and liberated Kuwait, which Iraq had invaded. On Jan. 17, the allies launched devastating air attacks, followed by rapid ground war starting Feb. 24. Pres. Bush ordered cease-fire Feb. 27.

An 8-month **recession** showed signs of having ended in Mar. The **Dow Jones** Industrial Average closed above 3,000 for first time, Apr. 17. Justice **Thurgood Marshall** announced, June 17, plans to retire. Senate, voting 52-48 on Oct. 15, confirmed nomination of **Clarence Thomas** to replace Marshall, after contentious hearings marked by allegations that Thomas had sexually harassed former aide Anita Hill. House Speaker Tom Foley announced Oct. 3 closure of **House Bank** by end of year after revelations that House members had written numerous bad checks.

1992 Retail giant **R.H. Macy & Co.** filed for bankruptcy, Jan. 27. Major U.S. carrier Trans World Airlines (**TWA**) filed for bankruptcy, Jan. 31. **Riots** swept South Central Los Angeles Apr. 29 after jury acquitted four white police officers on all but one count in 1991 videotaped beating of black motorist **Rodney King**. Death toll in L.A. violence was put at 53. **27th Amendment**, regarding congressional pay raises, ratified May 7.

Hurricane Andrew ravaged South Florida and Louisiana Aug. 24-26, causing 65 deaths. White supremacist and fugitive Randall Weaver surrendered Aug. 31 after 11-day **FBI siege** at his **Ruby Ridge**, ID, cabin, during which his wife, son, and a deputy sheriff were killed.

Bill Clinton (D) elected 42nd president, Nov. 3, defeating Pres. Bush (R) and independent Ross Perot. A UN-sanctioned military force, led by U.S. troops, arrived in **Somalia** Dec. 9. Presidents of U.S., Canada, and Mexico Dec. 17 signed **North American Free Trade Agreement** (NAFTA), which took effect Jan. 1, 1994.

1993 A bomb exploded in a parking garage beneath the **World Trade Center** in New York City, Feb. 26, killing six. Four men found guilty, Mar. 4, 1994. Four federal agents killed, Feb. 28, during unsuccessful raid on **Branch Davidian** compound near **Waco**, TX. A 51-day siege by agents ended Apr. 19 when the compound burned down, leaving more than 70 cult members dead. Eleven cult members acquitted Feb. 26, 1994, of deaths of federal agents.

Janet Reno became **first female attorney general** Mar. 12. Federal jury, Apr. 17, found two Los Angeles police officers guilty and two not guilty of violating civil rights of motorist **Rodney King** in 1991 videotaped beating.

Defense Sec. Les Aspin, Apr. 28, removed restrictions on aerial **combat roles for women** in the armed forces. In a May 14 plebiscite, voters in **Puerto Rico** supported continuing commonwealth status with U.S. **"Motor-voter" bill** signed by Pres. Clinton, May 20, easing voting procedures. **"Great Flood of 1993"** inundated parts of nine Midwestern states in summer, leaving about 50 dead and $15 bil in damages.

Pres. Clinton, July 2, approved recommendations that 33 major U.S. military bases be closed. On July 19 he announced **"don't ask, don't tell, don't pursue"** policy for homosexuals in the military. **Ruth Bader Ginsburg** sworn in, Aug. 10, as 107th Supreme Court justice, replacing retiring Justice **Byron White**. Pres. Clinton, Aug. 10, signed measure designed to **cut federal budget deficits** by $496 bil over five years, through

spending cuts and new taxes. **Brady Bill**, a major gun-control measure, signed into law by Pres. Clinton Nov. 30.

1994 A predawn **earthquake** in the Los Angeles area, Jan. 17, claimed 61 lives. Pres. Clinton Feb. 3 lifted 19-year ban on U.S. trade with **Vietnam**. Byron De La Beckwith convicted Feb. 5 of 1963 murder of civil rights leader **Medgar Evers**. Longtime CIA officer **Aldrich Ames** and his wife charged, Feb. 21, with spying for Russians. Under plea bargain, he received life in prison, while she drew 63 months.

U.S. troops, Mar. 25, officially ended peacekeeping and humanitarian aid mission in **Somalia**, begun in 1992. Congressional committees, late July, began **Whitewater hearings**. Kenneth Starr named Aug. 5 as independent counsel to probe Whitewater affair. Major league **baseball players** went on strike following Aug. 11 games. World Series canceled; strike ended Apr. 25, 1995. Senate Majority Leader George Mitchell (D, ME), Sept. 26, dropped efforts to pass Pres. Clinton's **health-care reform** package.

Republicans gained control of both House and Senate in Nov. 8 elections after many years of Democratic control. House speaker **Tom Foley** (MA) was among the defeated Democrats.

1995 104th Congress opened Jan. 4. **Newt Gingrich** (R, GA) elected House speaker. A bill to end Congress's exemption from federal labor laws, first in series of measures in Republicans' **"Contract With America,"** cleared Congress Jan. 17; signed into law Jan. 23. Pres. Clinton, Jan. 31, authorized $20 bil loan to **Mexico** to help it avert financial collapse. Last UN peacekeeping troops withdrew from **Somalia** Feb. 28-Mar. 3, with aid of U.S. Marines. In **Haiti**, peacekeeping responsibilities were transferred from U.S. to UN forces Mar. 31, with U.S. providing 2,400 soldiers.

Truck **bomb exploded outside Oklahoma City federal office** building Apr. 19, killing 168 in deadliest terrorist attack up to then on U.S. soil; Timothy McVeigh arrested as key suspect, Apr. 21. U.S. space shuttle *Atlantis* made first in series of dockings with Russian space station *Mir*, June 29-July 4. The U.S. announced July 11 it was reestablishing diplomatic **relations with Vietnam**.

1995: The Murrah Federal Building in Oklahoma City is targeted in the deadliest act of domestic terrorism in U.S. history.

Ten Muslim militants convicted, Oct. 1, in failed **plot to blow up UN Headquarters**, other buildings and assassinate political leaders. Former football star **O. J. Simpson** found not guilty Oct. 3 of June 1994 murders of former wife, Nicole Brown Simpson, and a friend of hers. Hundreds of thousands of black men participated in **Million Man March** and rally in Washington, DC, Oct. 16, organized by Rev. Louis Farrakhan.

Five Americans among seven killed, Nov. 13, in **bombing** of U.S. military post in **Riyadh, Saudi Arabia**. Budget impasse between Congress and Pres. Clinton led to partial **government shutdown** beginning Nov. 14; operations resumed Nov. 20 under continuing resolutions. After talks outside Dayton, OH, warring parties in **Bosnia and Herzegovina** reached agreement Nov. 21 to end their conflict; treaty signed Dec. 14, after which U.S. peacekeeping troops arrived. A 1973 federal law imposing **55-mph speed limit** repealed Nov. 28.

1996 Senate, Jan. 26, approved, 87-4, Second Strategic Arms Reduction Treaty (**START II**). Congress, Mar. 27-28, approved **line item veto**; struck down by Supreme Court, June 1998.

James and Susan McDougal convicted May 28 of fraud and conspiracy in **Whitewater** case; Arkansas Gov. Jim Guy Tucker (D) convicted on similar charges. The antitax **Freemen** surrendered to federal authorities June 13 after 81-day standoff near Jordan, MT; four were convicted, July 1998, of conspiring to defraud banks.

Bomb exploded at **Khobar Towers** military complex near Dhahran, Saudi Arabia, June 25, killing 19 American service personnel. Homemade pipe bomb exploded July 27 in **Atlanta**, GA, park during **Summer Olympics**; one person killed. Extremist Eric Robert Rudolph, arrested in May 2003, pleaded guilty to this and other bombings.

Major **welfare reform bill** signed into law, Aug. 22. U.S. signed **Comprehensive Test Ban Treaty**, Sept. 24, which banned all nuclear weapons tests and explosions; Senate failed to ratify treaty. Pres. **Clinton reelected**, Nov. 5.

1997 Madeleine Albright sworn in as sec. of state Jan. 23, becoming first female State Dept. head. Former CIA official Harold Nicholson pleaded guilty, Mar. 3, to **spying for Russia**. Thirty-nine members of **Heaven's Gate** religious cult found dead in Rancho Santa Fe, CA, house Mar. 26, in apparent mass suicide.

Timothy McVeigh convicted of conspiracy and murder, June 2, in 1995 **Oklahoma City** bombing; executed June 2001. Terry Nichols convicted Dec. 23 on related charges. Two Islamic militants convicted, Nov. 12, of key roles in 1993 bombing of **World Trade Center**. The film *Titanic*, released Dec. 14, went on to win 11 Oscars and gross over $600 mil.

1998 Media outlets reported Jan. 21 on evidence of sexual relationship between Pres. Clinton and former White House intern **Monica Lewinsky**. Clinton initially denied affair, but in grand jury testimony and address to the nation, Aug. 17, acknowledged relationship that was "not appropriate." On Sept. 9, independent counsel **Kenneth Starr** sent findings to House of Representatives; Judiciary Committee, Oct. 5, voted 21-16 to recommend full inquiry. House, Dec. 19, approved two articles of **impeachment** charging Pres. Clinton with grand jury perjury and obstruction of justice in cover-up.

"**Unabomber**" Theodore Kaczynski, arrested in Montana in 1993, pleaded guilty Jan. 22 to California and New Jersey bombings that killed three people; sentenced in May to four life terms plus 30 years. Texas, Feb. 3, executed its first female convict in 135 years.

Bombs at U.S. embassies in Nairobi, Kenya, and Dar-es-Salaam, Tanzania, killed at least 257, Aug. 7; U.S. launched retaliatory strikes, Aug. 20, against targets in Afghanistan and Sudan. On Sept. 30, Pres. Clinton announced federal **budget surplus** of $70 bil for fiscal 1998, first since 1969.

Pres. Clinton, Nov. 13, settled suit by agreeing to pay $850,000 to **Paula Jones**, who alleged he had made an unwanted sexual advance in 1991. Country's four largest **tobacco companies**, in settlement Nov. 23, agreed to pay states and territories $206 bil over 25 years to cover public health costs.

1999 *The Sopranos* TV drama debuted on HBO, Jan. 10. Pres. **Clinton** was acquitted, Feb. 12, at end of Senate impeachment trial. Perjury article failed with 45 votes; obstruction of justice article drew 50-50 vote, with two-thirds vote needed for conviction.

Dr. **Jack Kevorkian** convicted of second-degree murder Mar. 26 in death of terminally ill man. One man pleaded guilty Apr. 5, another convicted Nov. 4, in 1998 kidnapping and beating death of **Matthew Shepard**, an openly gay student at the Univ. of Wyoming.

Eric Harris, 18, and Dylan Klebold, 17, killed 12 fellow students and a teacher Apr. 20 at **Columbine High School** in Littleton, CO, then fatally shot themselves. One NYC police officer pleaded guilty to six charges, May 25, another convicted of assault, June 8, in 1997 police-station torture of **Abner Louima**, Haitian immigrant. **John F. Kennedy Jr.** killed in crash of private plane July 16.

2000 Across U.S., midnight celebrations marked changeover to year 2000 on Jan. 1; feared **Y2K** computer glitch caused only minor problems. Vermont Gov. Howard Dean (D) signed legislation Apr. 26 allowing same-sex couples in **civil unions** to gain legal rights. Scientists from U.S. and Britain announced jointly, June 26, that they had determined structure of the **human genome**.

Six-year-old **Elián González** was returned to father in Cuba June 28, seven months after rescue from boat wreck in which his mother and other refugees drowned. **Tiger Woods** became youngest player, at age 24, to win all four of golf's majors, with record score in British Open, July 23.

Food and Drug Administration announced, Sept. 28, approval of **RU-486**, a pill that induces abortions. Seventeen U.S. sailors died Oct. 12 in terrorist bombing of **USS Cole**, which was refueling in Aden, Yemen.

On election night, Nov. 7, the winner of **Florida's electoral votes** remained uncertain, leaving national result in doubt. Florida Supreme Court, Dec. 8, ordered manual recount of certain ballots; on Dec. 12, U.S. Supreme Court reversed that decision, and Vice Pres. **Al Gore** (D), next day, conceded to Texas Gov. **George W. Bush** (R).

2001 AOL-Time Warner merger completed Jan. 11. FBI agent **Robert Hanssen** arrested Feb. 20, charged with spying for Soviet Union and Russia over 20-year period; under plea bargain, sentenced in 2002 to life in prison. **U.S. Navy spy plane** collided with Chinese fighter plane over South China Sea Apr. 1, killing fighter pilot; 24 U.S. crew members detained in Hainan until U.S. apology, Apr. 12.

Sen. **James Jeffords** (R, VT) announced May 24 he was leaving his party, giving Democrats control of Senate. Pres. Bush signed, June 7, $1.35-tril tax-cut package. Bush announced Aug. 9 he would allow federal funding of limited research on existing **stem-cell** lines derived from human embryos.

On morning of **Sept. 11**, two hijacked commercial airliners struck **World Trade Center twin towers** in New York City in **worst-ever terrorist attack** on American soil. A third hijacked plane destroyed a portion of the **Pentagon**; a fourth crashed in a field near Shanksville, PA. Some 3,000 people were killed, including about 2,750 at World Trade Center. Five people died and 14 became ill from exposure to **anthrax** through U.S. postal system, Oct. 4-Nov. 21.

U.S. and Britain, Oct. 7, launched air-strike campaign against Afghan-based terrorist organization **al-Qaeda** and Afghanistan's ruling **Taliban** militia. Pres. Bush created **Office of**

2001: The attacks of Sept. 11, 2001, kill more than 2,750 people in New York, including 343 firefighters.

Homeland Security, Oct. 8, and signed federal **antiterrorism bill**, Oct. 26. **Taliban** surrendered Kabul, Nov. 13, and fled from Kandahar, their stronghold, Dec. 7. Taliban member and U.S. citizen **John Walker Lindh** captured Dec. 2 in Afghanistan; under plea bargain, sentenced in Oct. 2002 to 20 years. U.S. government, Dec. 11, indicted al-Qaeda member **Zacarias Moussaoui** as Sept. 11 co-conspirator; he pleaded guilty, sentenced in May 2006 to life in prison. Operation in Afghanistan's **Tora Bora** cave complex, Dec. 12-17, failed to capture al-Qaeda leader **Osama bin Laden**.

Leading energy-trading company **Enron** filed for bankruptcy, Dec. 2. Pres. Bush announced, Dec. 13, U.S. withdrawal from **1972 Antiballistic Missile Treaty**.

2002 Taliban and al-Qaeda fighters captured in Afghanistan flown to U.S. naval base at **Guantánamo Bay** in Cuba, starting Jan. 11. House committee, Jan. 14, released parts of whistle-blowing letter from Enron employee to CEO **Kenneth Lay**. Lay resigned Jan. 23; Congress, Jan. 24, began hearings into **Enron bankruptcy**.

In State of the Union address, Jan. 29, Pres. Bush called Iran, Iraq, and North Korea part of **"axis of evil."** By Mar. 6, 1,200 U.S. troops were involved in **Operation Anaconda** against al-Qaeda and Taliban forces in Afghanistan.

Independent prosecutor's report, Mar. 20, found insufficient evidence that Pres. Clinton or Hillary Clinton committed any crime in connection with **Whitewater**. Pres. Bush, Mar. 27, signed into law McCain-Feingold **campaign-finance reform bill** banning unregulated, unrestricted "soft money" donations; part of bill struck down by Supreme Court, June 2007.

Ceremonial last girder removed May 30 from **World Trade Center** site, signaling end of massive clean-up and recovery operation. FBI agent Coleen Rowley testified before congressional committee June 6 that Washington FBI agents had stymied investigative efforts in Minneapolis prior to Sept. 11. **WorldCom** filed for bankruptcy, July 21.

Richard Reid pleaded guilty Oct. 4 to all charges stemming from incident aboard plane in Dec. 2001, when he tried to ignite explosives in his shoes; sentenced Jan. 2003 to life in prison. On Oct. 10-11 the House, 296-133, and Senate, 77-23, gave Bush backing to use military force against **Iraq**. Bush administration revealed Oct. 16 that **North Korea** had acknowledged developing nuclear arms. Bush signed measure, Nov. 25, creating **Dept. of Homeland Security**.

U.S. Roman Catholic bishops, Nov. 13, approved revised, Vatican-vetted policies dealing with priests who **sexually abuse minors**. Cardinal **Bernard Law**, Dec. 13, resigned as archbishop of Boston; he had been accused of covering up sexual abuse by priests. **Trent Lott** (R, MS) bowed out as new Senate majority leader Dec. 20 after remarks apparently supporting segregation.

2003 On Jan. 10-11, Illinois Gov. George Ryan (R) pardoned or **commuted death sentences** of all 171 Illinois death row convicts.

Space shuttle *Columbia* broke apart Feb. 1 during descent toward planned landing; all seven crew members killed. Report issued Aug. 26 blamed damage sustained during liftoff; also cited "broken safety culture" at NASA. Senate, Mar. 6, approved the **Strategic Offensive Reductions Treaty (Moscow Treaty)** for reducing nuclear stockpiles signed in 2002 by U.S. and Russian leaders.

U.S.-led military offensive aimed at ousting **Saddam Hussein** got underway Mar. 19, when 40 Tomahawk cruise missiles hit targets in Baghdad. U.S. forces Mar. 21 seized oil fields near Basra. By Apr. 9, U.S. forces reported control over much of Baghdad. Pres. Bush, speaking from aircraft carrier May 1, declared **end of major combat operations in Iraq**; insurgents continued to mount attacks.

Pres. Bush signed bill May 28 providing $330 bil in **tax cuts** over several years. Under settlement in private antitrust suit brought by Netscape (unit of AOL), **Microsoft** agreed May 29 to pay $750 mil. A power failure caused **blackouts** affecting some 50 mil people in Ohio, Michigan, and the Northeast, as well as eastern Canada, on Aug. 14.

The Roman Catholic archdiocese of Boston agreed to pay up to $85 mil in **sex abuse settlement** announced Sept. 9. Californians, Oct. 7, voted to recall Gov. Gray Davis (D) and replace him with actor-turned-politician **Arnold Schwarzenegger** (R). Rev. V. Gene Robinson consecrated Nov. 2 as Episcopal Church's **first openly gay bishop**.

Senate, Nov. 3, approved $87.5 bil for **U.S. military forces in Iraq** and help rebuilding the country. Virginia jury, Nov. 17, found **John Muhammad** guilty in 2002 Washington, DC, area **sniper attacks** that killed 10; sentenced to death. Another Virginia jury found accomplice **Lee Malvo** guilty of murder in the attacks, Dec. 18; sentenced to life in prison without parole. Massachusetts court decided 4-3, Nov. 18, that **gay couples had right to marry**.

Pres. Bush signed bill Dec. 8 to overhaul **Medicare**, adding prescription drug benefit and expanding role of private insurance companies. **Saddam Hussein captured** by U.S. forces Dec. 13, in underground hideout southeast of Tikrit.

2004 On Feb. 12, San Francisco began issuing marriage licenses to same-sex couples; process blocked Mar. 11 by state supreme court. *The Lord of the Rings: The Return of the King* won 11 Oscars, Feb. 29.

Photos showing abuse of **Abu Ghraib prison inmates** in Iraq by American soldiers emerged Apr. 3. **National World War II Memorial** in Washington, DC, opened Apr. 29.

U.S.-led coalition transferred power to **interim Iraqi government**, June 28. **9/11 Commission Report**, released July 22, called for restructuring U.S. intelligence operations. In Boston, July 28-29, Democrats nominated Sen. **John Kerry** (MA) for president and Sen. **John Edwards** (NC) for vice president.

Four hurricanes hit Florida and surrounding states, Aug. 13-Sept. 25; blamed for over 50 deaths and $20 bil in damage in U.S. **Boston Red Sox** won World Series Oct. 27, for first time since 1918.

Pres. **Bush reelected** Nov. 2. U.S. forces took control of the Iraqi city of **Fallujah** from insurgents, Nov. 14. Pres. Bush signed intelligence reform bill Dec. 17, creating a **director of national intelligence**.

2005 Two U.S. soldiers found guilty, Jan. 14, in **Abu Ghraib prisoner abuses** in Iraq and sentenced to prison terms.

Condoleezza Rice became first black woman sec. of state, Jan. 26. **Alberto Gonzales** became first Hispanic U.S. atty. gen., Feb. 3. **Terri Schiavo**, in a persistent vegetative state since 1990, died Mar. 31, 13 days after feeding tube was removed.

Vanity Fair article revealed May 31 that former FBI official W. Mark Felt was **"Deep Throat"**—key source for *Washington Post* reporters Bob Woodward and Carl Bernstein probing 1972 **Watergate break-in**.

Hurricane Katrina hit Gulf coast, Aug. 29, causing devastation in Louisiana, Mississippi, and Alabama. Breach in a levee on Lake Pontchartrain, Aug. 30, flooded **New Orleans**. Relief efforts widely criticized as insufficient.

Chief Justice **William H. Rehnquist** died Sept. 3. Bush Sept. 5 nominated as successor **John G. Roberts Jr.**; on Sept. 29 he was confirmed by Senate, 78-22, and sworn in as 17th chief justice. White House counsel **Harriet Miers**, nominated Oct. 3 to Supreme Court, withdrew Oct. 27. In her place, Bush, Oct. 31, nominated **Samuel A. Alito Jr.**; confirmed Jan. 31, 2006.

House Majority Leader **Tom DeLay** (R, TX) indicted in Texas Sept. 28 on money laundering charges; stepped down from leadership, and later convicted.

2005: Hurricane Katrina and subsequent failure of levees cause unprecedented destruction in New Orleans and along the Gulf Coast.

New York Times, Dec. 16, reported that Pres. Bush in 2002 had secretly authorized National Security Agency to **eavesdrop without court warrant** on people in U.S. suspected of terrorist activities. Senate, Dec. 21, passed $453 bil defense appropriations bill with **anti-torture amendment**.

2006 Former top Republican lobbyist **Jack Abramoff** pleaded guilty Jan. 3 to bribery and other charges; in plea agreement, promised to cooperate with investigation into his dealings with members of Congress. Former Enron CEO **Jeffrey Skilling** and **Kenneth Lay**, Enron's founder and Skilling's successor as CEO, convicted May 25 on charges related to **Enron**'s collapse.

U.S. Supreme Court ruled June 29 that Pres. Bush's system for trying terrorism detainees at **Guantánamo** Bay was unauthorized under federal law and Geneva Conventions. Bush, July 19, issued his **first veto**, rejecting bill to end federal funding constraints on human embryonic **stem cell research**.

British authorities announced Aug. 10 they had foiled terrorist plot to use **liquid explosives** on flights between Britain and U.S.; new security restrictions introduced. In speech Sept. 6 Bush confirmed existence of **secret overseas prisons** for terrorism suspects run by CIA.

Pres. Bush signed bill Oct. 26 authorizing construction of 700-mi fence along **U.S.-Mexico border**; broader immigration bill failed in Congress.

Democrats won control of House and Senate in **midterm congressional elections** Nov. 7. Pres. Bush announced Nov. 8 that Defense Sec. **Donald Rumsfeld**, a focus of criticism over Iraq war, had resigned.

2007 Rep. Nancy Pelosi (D, CA) chosen Jan. 4 as **first woman Speaker of the House**. Pres. Bush announced Jan. 10 he was sending more than 20,000 additional troops to Iraq, in troop "surge" backed by Lt. Gen. **David Petraeus**, new top U.S. commander in Iraq.

Reports of substandard conditions at **Walter Reed Army Medical Center** in Washington, DC, resulted in dismissals of military officials, Mar. 1-2. I. Lewis "Scooter" Libby, former chief of staff for Vice Pres. Cheney, found guilty Mar. 6 of perjury and obstructing justice in the investigation into a leak exposing undercover CIA agent Valerie Plame Wilson; Bush commuted his prison sentence.

A senior at **Virginia Tech** killed 27 students and five faculty members on Apr. 16 before killing himself. On Apr. 18, Supreme Court upheld, 5-4, a 2003 federal law that banned so-called **partial birth abortions**.

U.S. Senate and House May 24 approved Iraq and Afghanistan **war-funding bill** without timetable for withdrawal of U.S. troops from Iraq; Congress also raised **minimum wage** from $5.15 to $7.25 per hour over two years.

Dow Jones closed over 14,000 July 19, just 59 trading days after passing 13,000. Pres. Bush issued an executive order July 20 requiring that **imprisoned terror suspects** receive "the basic necessities of life" and barring cruel, inhuman, or degrading treatment. *Harry Potter and the Deathly Hallows*, final novel in J. K. Rowling's series, released July 21, earning record U.S. sales.

A **Minneapolis highway bridge** collapsed Aug. 1, causing the deaths of 13 people. Congress, Aug. 4, cleared measure allowing **National Security Agency** to monitor communications without court warrants if believed related to terrorism. Barry Bonds tied Hank Aaron's all-time career **home-run record** at 755 on Aug. 4 in San Diego; hit No. 756 on Aug. 7.

Karl Rove, Bush's chief political strategist, announced Aug. 13 that he was resigning. **José Padilla** convicted of conspiracy in terrorism case, Aug. 16; sentenced to 17 years, 4 months. Atty. Gen. **Alberto Gonzales**, blamed for alleged firing of U.S. attorneys, announced resignation Aug. 27.

Congress voted, Nov. 6 and 8, to **overturn veto** by Pres. Bush for first time on a $23 bil water projects bill. Report by former U.S. Sen. George J. Mitchell, released Dec. 13, presented evidence of **performance-enhancing drug use** by 86 Major League Baseball players.

On Dec. 6 Pres. Bush announced accord among mortgage lenders to freeze interest rates for some and provide refinancing options. Under law signed Dec. 17, New Jersey became the first state to **repeal the death penalty** since Supreme Court reinstated it in 1976. An energy bill mandating an increase in automobile **fuel-economy standards** to 35 mi per gallon by 2030 signed by Pres. Bush Dec. 19.

2007: Pres. George W. Bush sends a "surge" of additional U.S. troops to Iraq.

2008 Sen. **John McCain** (AZ) won New Hampshire primary, Jan. 8; clinched 2008 Republican presidential nomination by early Mar. Among Democrats, Sen. **Barack Obama** (IL) moved ahead of closest rival Sen. **Hillary Clinton** (NY) to clinch nomination in early June.

The Federal Reserve cut key interest rates, Jan. 22 and 30, to aid U.S. economy; $168 bil **economic stimulus** package, signed Feb. 13 by Pres. Bush, provided tax rebates.

In Mar. 18 speech, Sen. Obama discussed America's racial divide and condemned inflammatory rhetoric used by Rev. **Jeremiah Wright**, his former pastor.

Justice Dept., Apr. 1, declassified 2003 legal brief that sanctioned use of extreme methods in questioning detainees linked to al-Qaeda. U.S. Supreme Court ruled June 12 that foreign prisoners at **Guantánamo** Bay could challenge detention by filing writs of **habeas corpus**.

Oil prices spiked above $140 per barrel in June; national average price for gallon of regular gas topped $4.

Sec. of State Condoleezza Rice signed agreements in Czech Republic, July 8, and Poland, Aug. 20, to place components of a U.S. **missile defense system** there (agreements rescinded by Obama administration, Sept. 17, 2009). Measure signed July 10 by Pres. Bush expanded government power to spy on suspected terrorists. U.S., Sept. 1, gave Iraqi forces security responsibilities in Anbar province, formerly center of a Sunni insurgency. U.S. air strike in **Afghanistan** village of Azizabad, Aug. 22, killed up to 90 civilians, according to Afghan sources.

Meeting Aug. 25-28 in Denver, CO, Democrats nominated Sen. **Barack Obama** (IL) for president and Sen. **Joe Biden** (DE) for vice president. Meeting Sept. 3 in St. Paul, MN, Republicans nominated Sen. **John McCain** (AZ) for president and Alaska Gov. **Sarah Palin** for vice president.

With financial system in crisis, federal government Sept. 7 took control of mortgage finance companies **Fannie Mae** and **Freddie Mac**. On Wall Street a week later, investment titan **Merrill Lynch** agreed to sell itself to Bank of America for $50 bil, and **Lehman Brothers** declared bankruptcy, after finding no buyer. The Fed Sept. 16 took control of insurance giant **AIG**, giving it a credit line that expanded to $144 bil by Oct. 31.

On Sept. 20, a Treasury Dept. plan was introduced to purchase up to $700 bil of **"toxic" mortgage-backed securities** to restore confidence. Legislation to implement Troubled Assets Relief Program (**TARP**) failed in the House, Sept. 29, sending Dow Jones down 778 points. Revised **bailout plan** passed Senate Oct. 1, 74-25, and House Oct. 3, 263-171; gave Treasury immediate access to half of $700 bil in TARP funds, with broad discretion in their use. On Oct. 21 Fed pledged $540 bil as a backup to protect money market funds.

Barack Obama elected, Nov. 4, as **first African-American president** in U.S. history, earning 53% of popular vote and 365 of 538 electoral votes. Democrats also increased majorities in House and Senate. California voters approved Proposition 8, banning same-sex marriages in the state.

Dow Jones fell 427 points, or 5.1%, Nov. 19, going below 8,000. U.S. officials Nov. 23 announced plan to provide $20 bil in cash and up to $306 bil more as backup to protect ailing **Citigroup** from potential mortgage losses; Dow Jones rose 397 points. Pres.-elect Obama Nov. 24 named

Timothy Geithner to be treasury sec.; he was confirmed Jan. 26, 2009. Dow Jones dropped 680 points Dec. 1 after reports that manufacturing had hit 26-year low and that U.S economy fell into **recession** in Dec. 2007.

Pres.-elect Obama named former rival **Hillary Clinton**, Dec. 1, to be sec. of state (confirmed Jan. 2009). Illinois Gov. **Rod Blagojevich** (D) arrested Dec. 9, accused of seeking to sell Senate seat being vacated by Obama. Convicted in a state senate trial, he was removed from office, Jan. 2009. **Bernard Madoff** arrested Dec. 11 on charges he had defrauded investment clients in massive **Ponzi scheme**; sentenced to 150 years in jail in guilty plea, June 2009. Fed, Dec. 16, cut benchmark interest rate to near zero. On Dec. 19, Pres. Bush announced that $17 bil in **TARP funds** would be used to help keep **General Motors** and **Chrysler** afloat.

2009 Treasury Dept., Jan. 15, gained access to remaining $350 bil in TARP funds; provided funds to prop up **Bank of America.**

Barack Obama inaugurated Jan. 20 as 44th U.S. president. He issued executive orders Jan. 22 restricting CIA interrogation practices and calling for closing of U.S. military prison at **Guantánamo Bay**, Cuba, within a year (closing blocked by Congress). Treasury Sec. Geithner, Feb. 10, outlined $2 tril program to stabilize banking and ease credit markets with "stress tests" that led to greater capital requirements for some banks. Pres. Obama signed **economic stimulus** bill Feb. 17, providing for $212 bil in tax cuts and $575 bil in new spending; introduced $275 bil program Feb. 18 to help protect homeowners from **foreclosure** and ease terms for refinancing.

Pres. Obama announced, Feb. 17, that U.S. would send 17,000 more troops to **Afghanistan** and said, Feb. 27, that most U.S. troops would be out of Iraq by Aug. 2010. California legislators, ending 15-week deadlock, closed $42 bil budget gap, Feb. 19; revised plan passed July 24.

Treasury Sec. Geithner, Mar. 23, introduced Public-Private Investment Program (PPIP), offering incentives to encourage purchases of **"toxic assets."**

Iowa's Supreme Court Apr. 3 struck down state law barring **same-sex marriage**, while laws allowing it were enacted in three other states, Apr.-June.

Justice Dept. Apr. 16 released memos offering legal rationale for CIA interrogation methods that included **waterboarding**. On Aug. 24, Atty. Gen. Eric Holder appointed special prosecutor to investigate **possible detainee abuse**.

Obama administration Apr. 13 eased restrictions on family travel and remittances to **Cuba**. After outbreak of influenza A (H1N1), or **swine flu**, in Mexico and then in U.S., U.S. officials declared public health emergency Apr. 26.

Chrysler LLC filed for bankruptcy protection Apr. 30; auto workers' union retirement health-care fund given 55% stake in reorganized company. Pres. Obama, May 19, tightened **fuel efficiency** standards for vehicles. **General Motors** filed for bankruptcy June 1, under plan providing new federal funds. On June 9, 10 financial firms got permission from U.S. Treasury to return some $68 bil in **TARP funds**.

George Tiller, Kansas doctor who performed **late-term abortions**, murdered May 31; anti-abortion activist was convicted Jan. 2010 and sentenced Mar. 2010 to life in prison.

Speaking June 4 in Egypt, Pres. Obama called for "new beginning" in relations with **Muslim world**. U.S. military completed **withdrawal from Iraq's cities** and towns June 30; some 130,000 U.S. troops remained at bases.

Pres. Obama, June 22, signed measure to regulate content and marketing of tobacco products. Pop superstar **Michael Jackson**, 50, died June 25; death attributed to intoxication from a powerful anesthetic. Jackson's physician convicted of manslaughter in 2011. Obama and Russian Pres. Dmitri Medvedev, in Russia July 6, agreed on reducing **nuclear arsenals** and allowing U.S. flights to Afghanistan through Russian airspace.

Judge **Sonia Sotomayor** confirmed Aug. 6 for Supreme Court vacancy left by retirement of David Souter; sworn in Aug. 8, she became first Hispanic to join the court.

Short-term federal **"cash for clunkers"** program, for trading in old gas-guzzling vehicles, began July 24; ultimately funded at $3 bil.

Airport shuttle driver Najibullah Zazi charged, Sept. 24, with plot to produce bombs for **terror attacks** in the New York City subway system; he later pleaded guilty.

Government reported Oct. 29 that real GDP grew at 3.5% annual rate in July-Sept., signaling **recession** ended. However, **unemployment** in Oct. passed 10%. Pres. Obama Nov. 6 signed measure extending unemployment benefits and $8,000 tax credit for first-time homebuyers.

Pres. Obama announced Oct. 30 end to U.S. travel and immigration restrictions on people infected with AIDS virus. On Nov. 5, 12 soldiers and a civilian were killed in mass shooting at **Ft. Hood**, TX; Army psychiatrist Maj. Nidal Malik Hasan, shot and captured by police SWAT team, was charged in the shootings.

Pres. Obama Dec. 1 announced a **surge** of 30,000 additional troops to **Afghanistan** so as to peak at 100,000, with drawdown to begin within 18 months. Accepting **Nobel Peace Prize**, Dec. 10 in Oslo, Norway, Obama defended U.S.-led military action in Afghanistan as a "just war."

Pres. Obama brokered **greenhouse-gas accord**, Dec. 18 in Copenhagen, establishing nonbinding reduction goals.

Detroit-bound airline passengers, Dec. 25, thwarted attempt by Nigerian man to ignite **explosives hidden in his underwear**. On Dec. 30, a Jordanian CIA informant acting as a double agent set off **bomb at CIA meeting** site near Afghan-Pakistan border, killing himself and eight others.

2010 In special election Jan. 19 in Massachusetts, state Sen. **Scott Brown** (R) won U.S. Senate seat long held by Sen. Edward Kennedy (D); result cost Democrats filibuster-proof majority. U.S. Supreme Court Jan. 21 held that corporations and unions had right to spend unlimited funds on advertising to influence election outcomes.

Pres. Obama Feb. 18 created bipartisan National Commission on Fiscal Responsibility and Reform, headed by former Clinton chief of staff Erskine **Bowles** (D) and former Sen. Alan **Simpson** (R, WY).

U.S. and other coalition troops launched offensive in **Helmand Province**, Afghanistan, Feb. 13, targeting Taliban.

Pres. Obama, Mar. 18, signed $18 bil **job-stimulus** measure providing tax cuts and other employer incentives.

Long effort by Democrats to enact **health care reform** legislation succeeded on Mar. 21 when the House voted, 219-212, with no Republican support, to approve bill as passed by Senate in Dec. 2009. The wide-ranging, controversial measure, signed by Pres. Obama on Mar. 23, aimed in part at extending **health insurance** to an estimated 32 mil uninsured.

Meeting Apr. 8 in Prague, Pres. Obama and Russian Pres. Dmitri Medvedev signed New Strategic Arms Reduction Treaty, or **New START** (ratified by Senate Dec. 2010; in force Feb. 2011). On Apr. 15, Pres. Obama outlined plans for **NASA** to send manned missions to an asteroid by 2025 and to Mars by the mid-2030s; defended decision to terminate Bush administration program to return astronauts to the moon by 2020.

On Apr. 20, a gas explosion and fire engulfed *Deepwater Horizon* drilling platform off Louisiana, killing 11 people on board and damaging the ecology and state economy. Oil flow was stopped July 15.

Arizona Gov. Jan Brewer (R), Apr. 23, signed controversial **immigration measure** which, among other things, authorized police to arrest anyone reasonably suspected of being an illegal immigrant. (Key provisions struck down by U.S. Supreme Court, June 2012.) New York City police May 1 dismantled **car bomb in Times Square**; suspect pleaded guilty to terrorism charges.

Pres. Obama May 10 nominated **Elena Kagan** to the U.S. Supreme Court to replace retiring Justice John Paul Stevens; confirmed by Senate, Aug. 5.

Pres. Obama June 23 named Gen. **David Petraeus** as commander of troops in Afghanistan, replacing Gen. Stanley McChrystal, forced to resign after publication of disparaging comments about Obama administration. Ten **Russian agents** were arrested June 27 on spy charges; later exchanged for four Americans held by Russia as alleged spies.

Investment giant **Goldman Sachs** agreed July 15 to pay $550 mil to settle case brought by the SEC, alleging it had duped investors. Pres. Obama signed major **financial reform measure**, July 21.

More than 75,000 Afghanistan documents, many of them classified, were published July 25 on website run by **WikiLeaks** and in some news outlets. U.S. had filed charges, July 6, against Pfc. Bradley Manning, arrested May 26 in connection with earlier WikiLeaks releases.

New York City's landmark commission Aug. 3 cleared way for construction of an **Islamic cultural center** near site of former World Trade Center, generating controversy. Plans by a tiny Pentecostal church in Gainesville, FL, to **burn Korans** on Sept. 11 sparked denunciations in U.S. and riots abroad before being called off.

Last U.S. combat unit left Iraq Aug. 19 and Pres. Obama, Aug. 31, declared **U.S. combat mission in Iraq ended**; however, 50,000 troops remained in noncombat units.

Congress passed measures to **aid small businesses** with loans and tax breaks; signed into law Sept. 27. **TARP program** reached two-year mark Oct. 3, the day its authority to make new commitments expired. Treasury Dept. estimated net cost at $51 bil or less, though this figure was disputed. Taxpayers continued to pay for federal bailout of **Fannie Mae** and **Freddie Mac**.

WikiLeaks released documents covering Iraq conflict Oct. 22. Authorities in UK and UAE Oct. 29 confiscated packages with bombs concealed in printer cartridges, bound for Chicago area.

In Nov. 2 elections **Republicans gained control** of the U.S. House and picked up six more seats in the Senate. The Fed Nov. 3 announced plan to buy $600 bil worth of Treasury securities over eight months as means of stimulating the sluggish economy. On Dec. 2, U.S. House voted, 333-79, to censure veteran Rep. **Charles Rangel** (D, NY) for ethics violations.

Pres. Obama, Dec. 17, signed $858 bil compromise measure that extended **Bush-era tax cuts** for two years, including tax cuts for the wealthy, while also extending **unemployment** insurance benefits and reducing the Social Security payroll tax rate for one year. **"Don't ask, don't tell"** policy for gays in the military was repealed, Dec. 22.

2011 The 112th Congress convened Jan. 5; **John Boehner** (R, OH) elected House Speaker. Gunman in Tucson, AZ, Jan. 8, killed six people and injured 13 others, including Rep. **Gabrielle Giffords** (D, AZ), making a public appearance.

Atty. Gen. Eric Holder disclosed Feb. 23 that the Obama administration would no longer defend in court the 1996 **Defense of Marriage Act** (DOMA), which allowed federal government and states to deny recognition to same-sex marriages legal in some states.

A measure to limit **collective bargaining** by most public sector employees, championed by Wisconsin Gov. **Scott Walker** (R), passed state legislature Mar. 9-10 despite large demonstrations by opponents and a walkout by Senate Democrats.

With federal government shutdown looming, congressional leaders reached agreement Apr. 9 on **omnibus appropriations bill**. Pres. Obama outlined plan, Apr. 13, to cut $4 tril from projected deficits over 12 years by cutting spending and raising taxes on the wealthy. Two days later, House approved budget resolution based on plan by Rep. Paul Ryan (R, WI). **Ryan plan** would reduce deficits by $4.4 tril over 10 years while cutting spending and taxes; would replace Medicaid with block grants to states and transform Medicare into subsidized private insurance for new recipients. House plan defeated in Senate, May 25.

Former baseball slugger **Barry Bonds** was convicted Apr. 13 of obstructing justice in 2003 for evasive answers to a grand jury investigating use of banned **performance-enhancing drugs**. Pres. Obama Apr. 27 denounced rumors by so-called birthers and released copies of his "long-form" **birth certificate**.

On May 2, in Abbottabad, Pakistan, a CIA-led squadron of U.S. Navy SEALs breached hideout of al-Qaeda leader **Osama bin Laden**, responsible for Sept. 11, 2001, attacks on U.S., and killed him; he was buried at sea the same day.

Early candidates for the 2012 GOP presidential nomination met May 5 for first televised **campaign debate**.

The single **deadliest U.S. tornado** in more than a half-century hit Joplin, MO, May 22, claiming an estimated 161 lives.

House rejected measure to raise federal **debt ceiling** from $14.3 tril to $16.7 tril without compensating deficit reductions May 31; talks between Obama and House Speaker Boehner on possible "grand bargain" collapsed July 22. Budget control act shaped by Vice Pres. Biden and Senate minority leader Mitch McConnell (R, KY) passed by bipartisan votes in

Congress, Aug. 1-2. It called for rise in the debt ceiling and some $900 bil in spending cuts, with an additional $1.5 tril in cuts to be worked out by supercommittee. Standard & Poor's, Aug. 5, downgraded nation's **credit rating**.

U.S. stepped up **drone attacks** against jihadists in Yemen after Pres. Ali Abdullah Saleh and others were wounded June 3 in a rocket attack. Former Sen. and vice-pres. nominee **John Edwards** (D, NC) indicted June 3 on charges related to use of campaign funds to conceal affair; found not guilty on one count, mistrial on others, May 2012.

Obama administration June 22 announced timetable for drawing down troops in **Afghanistan**, with all combat troops to be out by the end of 2014.

After a deadlocked jury failed to reach a verdict on most counts in Aug. 2010, former Gov. **Rod Blagojevich** (D, IL) was convicted in a retrial on 17 felony corruption charges June 27 and sentenced Dec. 7 to 14 years in prison. **Bank of America**, June 29, agreed to pay $8.5 bil to cover investor losses on mortgage-backed securities issued by its Countrywide Financial unit.

Leon Panetta was confirmed by Senate, replacing Robert Gates as sec. of defense July 1. Gen. **David Petraeus**, commander of troops in Afghanistan, succeeded Panetta as CIA director.

Minnesota Gov. Mark Dayton (D) signed two-year, $36 bil budget bills July 20, ending a 20-day state **government shutdown** caused by budget deadlock. After 30 years and 135 missions, NASA's **space shuttle** program ended with landing of the *Atlantis*, July 21, at Florida's Kennedy Space Center.

Taliban insurgents in **Afghanistan** shot down U.S. transport helicopter Aug. 6, killing 38 people, including 17 Navy SEAL commandos.

Atty. Gen. Eric Holder announced Aug. 30 the departure of two senior Justice Dept. officials who had overseen **Operation Fast and Furious**, a failed sting operation that had arranged for sale of guns to be smuggled to drug traffickers in Mexico. Pres. Obama, Sept. 8, proposed $447 bil economic **stimulus plan**, to be paid for by limiting tax breaks and raising taxes on high incomes. **Solyndra**, a solar panel manufacturer touted by the Obama administration, filed for bankruptcy Sept. 6 after having received $535 mil in federal loan guarantees.

A diffuse left-wing movement that began Sept. 17 as **Occupy Wall Street** in New York City expanded to demonstrations in hundreds of cities in the U.S. and overseas. **Anwar al-Awlaki**, a U.S. citizen and Muslim cleric linked to terrorist attacks in U.S., was killed Sept. 30 in U.S. drone attack in Yemen.

Formalities Dec. 12-15 marked the end of the U.S. military mission in Iraq. Last U.S. troop convoy crossed into Kuwait, Dec. 18. Since U.S.-led invasion in Mar. 2003, nearly 4,500 U.S. service members had been killed and another 32,000 wounded.

Averting new government shutdown, Congress Dec. 16-17 passed $915 bil omnibus measure to fund agencies through 2012 fiscal year. Congress Dec. 23 also approved two-month extension of a **payroll tax** break, extended benefits for long-term **unemployed**, and continued Medicare reimbursement rates for physicians. A $662 bil military spending

2011: As administration officials monitored the operation from Washington, U.S. forces kill Osama bin Laden, mastermind of the Sept. 11, 2001, terrorist attacks.

bill approved by Congress Dec. 14-15 was signed Dec. 31 by Obama, with signing statement saying the administration would not authorize indefinite military detention of U.S citizens without trial.

2012 Former Massachusetts Gov. **Mitt Romney**, front-runner for Republican presidential nomination, won New Hampshire primary, Jan. 10. But conservative challengers emerged: former House Speaker **Newt Gingrich** (GA) won South Carolina primary Jan. 21 and former Sen. **Rick Santorum** (PA) swept two caucuses and a primary Feb. 7.

Pres. Obama Jan. 18 denied Canadian company a permit to construct proposed 1,700-mi **Keystone XL oil pipeline**. In State of the Union address Jan. 24 he called for a millionaires' tax (the **"Buffett Rule"**) and more government action to attract manufacturing jobs.

Pres. Obama Feb. 10 announced a compromise health insurance mandate, requiring insurers to separately provide free contraception coverage so that religiously affiliated employers would not have to directly provide policies with such coverage. Congress voted Feb. 17 to extend a 2% **payroll tax cut** through 2012; the bill also extended unemployment benefits and halted a 27% cut in Medicare reimbursement rates.

Defense Sec. Leon Panetta announced Feb. 1 that the U.S. combat mission in **Afghanistan** would end as early as mid-2013. Of 90,000 U.S. troops there, 22,000 were scheduled to withdraw in 2012, with the rest to leave by end of 2014.

Oil-and-gas giant BP and lawyers for victims of the 2010 *Deepwater Horizon* explosion in Gulf of Mexico announced settlement in class-action suit Mar. 2; BP agreed to cover medical expenses for related illnesses and accept court administration of a $20-bil escrow fund.

Mitt Romney won six of 10 primary contests on **"Super Tuesday,"** Mar. 6, and many thereafter; a May 29 victory in Texas clinched his Republican presidential nomination.

A dozen **Secret Service** agents were implicated in a prostitution scandal while in Colombia preparing for Pres. Obama's Apr. 13 arrival for a summit; most were fired or resigned. Obama became first sitting president to endorse **same-sex marriage** in May 9 TV interview. Social networking giant **Facebook**'s initial public offering raised $16 bil May 18 but the stock lost value in following days.

Wisconsin Gov. **Scott Walker** (R) comfortably survived a June 5 recall election that Democrats and unions had sought over Walker's support of legislation limiting collective bargaining rights of public-sector employees. Pres. Obama June 15 announced an executive action ending deportation of qualified **undocumented immigrants** under age 30.

Key provisions of **"Obamacare"** health insurance law were upheld June 28 by U.S. Supreme Court, including the individual mandate, penalizing those who decline to buy health insurance. Chief Justice John G. Roberts Jr. provided the swing vote, construing the penalty as a permissible tax.

The House June 28 found Atty. Gen. **Eric Holder** in contempt of Congress for rebuffing a subpoena for Justice Dept. documents related to failed gun-trafficking sting **Operation Fast and Furious**. An inspector general's report on the operation, Sept. 19, cited "misguided strategies, tactics, errors in judgment, and management failures" by Justice Dept. officials.

2012: Hurricane Sandy devastates coastal areas of mid-Atlantic and Northeast states, causing more than 200 deaths and $65 bil in estimated property damages.

Jerry Sandusky, former assistant football coach at Penn State Univ., was convicted June 22 in sexual abuse of 10 boys; an investigation later concluded that head coach Joe Paterno had covered up Sandusky's actions. NCAA July 23 fined the university $60 mil, stripped it of 14 years of victories, and banned team from postseason participation for four years.

A man shot at patrons in a crowded movie theater, July 20, in **Aurora**, CO, killing 12 people; suspect James Holmes, arrested outside theater, was charged July 30. A gunman opened fire Aug. 5 at a **Sikh temple** in Oak Creek, WI, leaving six dead; he killed himself after being wounded in shootout with police.

The NASA rover *Curiosity* guided itself to a safe landing on Mars Aug. 6. Cyclist **Lance Armstrong** announced Aug. 23 that he would stop fighting doping charges; he was subsequently banned from cycling and stripped of his seven Tour de France wins.

U.S. District Court jury in San Jose, CA, ruled Aug. 24 that Samsung Electronics had infringed on **Apple** patents. Samsung was ordered to pay Apple $1.05 bil in damages.

Mitt Romney, Aug. 11, chose Rep. **Paul Ryan** (WI), chairman of the House Budget Committee, as running mate. Both were nominated at the Republican National Convention, Aug. 27-30, in Tampa, FL. Meeting Sept. 4-6 in Charlotte, NC, the Democratic National Convention nominated the **Obama-Biden** ticket. Leftist magazine *Mother Jones* Sept. 17 posted a damaging video of Romney, covertly recorded at a May 2012 fundraising dinner, in which he appeared to write off 47% of Americans as believing they are victims entitled to government handouts.

Chicago public-school teachers went on strike Sept. 10; returned to work Sept. 19 after agreement on pay raises and role of standardized tests in evaluating teachers. **Federal Reserve** announced Sept. 13 it would begin buying mortgage-backed securities at a rate of $40 bil per month, continuing until job market significantly improved, unless inflation spiraled.

Protests broke out Sept. 11 outside U.S. embassy in Cairo fueled by a widely publicized **anti-Islamic film** produced by a small group of Americans. On the night of Sept. 11-12, U.S. facility in **Benghazi**, Libya, was attacked by Islamic terrorists, who killed ambassador J. Christopher Stevens and three other Americans. Report released Dec. 18 blamed State Dept. management for "grossly inadequate" security.

Obama and Romney met for three **debates**: Oct. 3 at the Univ. of Denver in Denver, CO; Oct. 16 at Hofstra Univ. in Hempstead, NY; and Oct. 22 at Lynn Univ. in Boca Raton, FL. The vice-presidential nominees met in one debate, Oct. 11, at Centre Coll. in Danville, KY.

Hurricane **Sandy** made landfall in the Northeast U.S. as a tropical storm Oct. 29, causing devastation especially in coastal areas of New Jersey and New York; the storm caused more than 200 deaths and damages were estimated at $65 bil.

Obama and Biden were reelected, Nov. 6, with 51% of the popular vote, taking 332 electoral votes. Democrats gained two Senate seats, for a majority of 53, with two more won by independents who caucus with Democrats. Republicans held onto the House majority with 233 seats. Voters in Maine, Maryland, and Washington state, Nov. 6, approved measures to legalize **same-sex marriage**, becoming the first states to do so by popular vote. Ballot measures legalizing recreational use of **marijuana** won in Colorado and Washington state but lost in Oregon.

Retired Army Gen. **David Petraeus** resigned as CIA director Nov. 9 after FBI cybercrime investigation accidentally uncovered involvement in an extramarital affair. **BP pleaded guilty** Nov. 15 to criminal charges in relation to 2010 oil rig explosion in the Gulf of Mexico; agreed to pay record $4.5 bil in criminal and civil fines and penalties.

On Dec. 14, an armed man entered **Sandy Hook** Elementary School in Newtown, CT, and shot to death 20 children, the school principal, and five others. The shooter, 20-year-old Adam Lanza, fatally shot himself as police arrived.

With **"fiscal cliff"** of automatic budget cuts and expiring tax breaks looming as of Jan. 1, 2013, Vice Pres. Biden and Senate Minority Leader Mitch McConnell (R, KY) negotiated compromise Dec. 30-31, to make **Bush-era tax cuts** permanent only to certain ceilings while deferring automatic budget and spending cuts to Mar. 1, 2013.

Dow Jones Industrial Average closed Dec. 31 at 13,104, up 7.26% for 2013—its fourth straight year of increase.

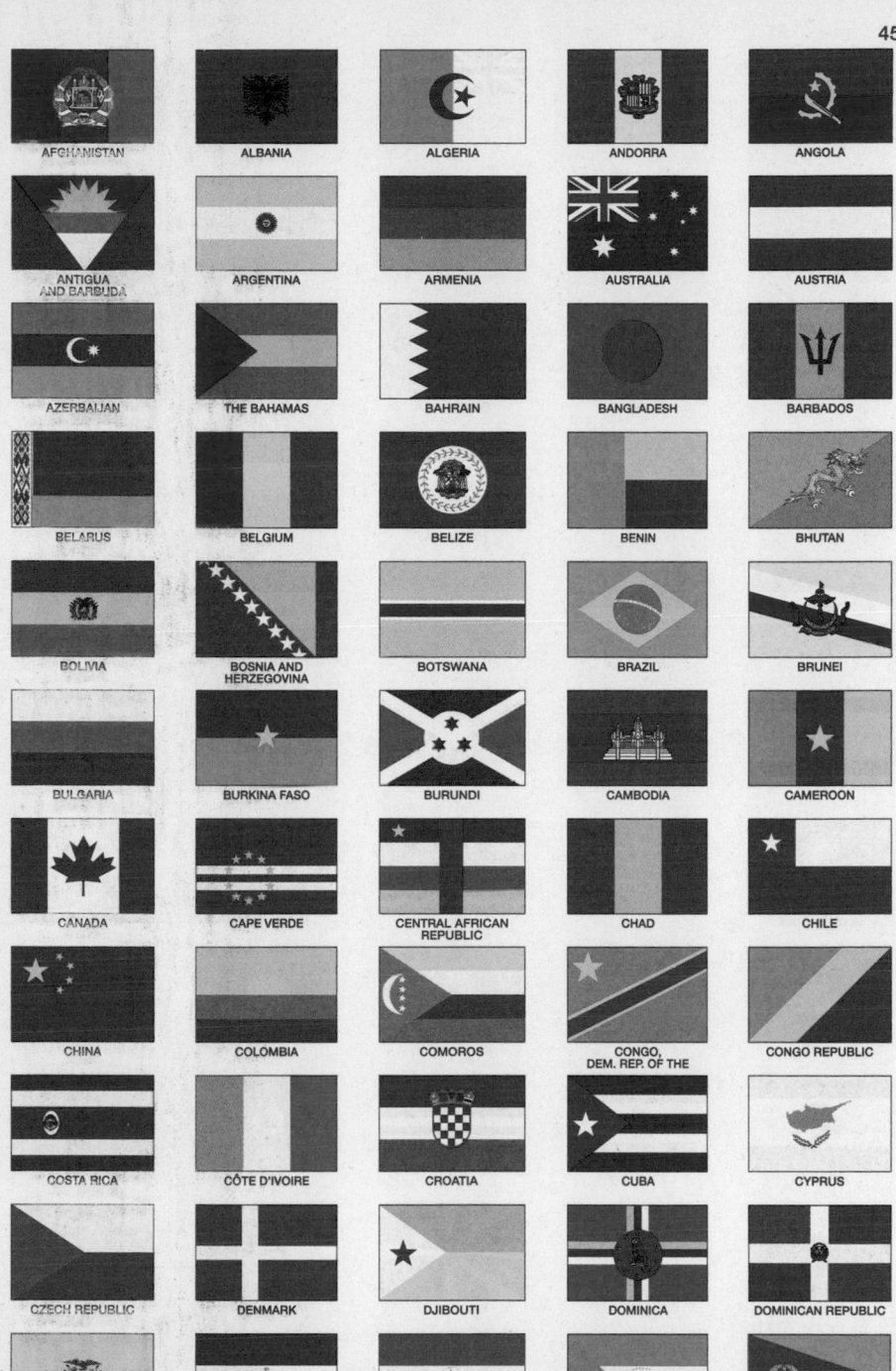

AFGHANISTAN	ALBANIA	ALGERIA	ANDORRA	ANGOLA
ANTIGUA AND BARBUDA	ARGENTINA	ARMENIA	AUSTRALIA	AUSTRIA
AZERBAIJAN	THE BAHAMAS	BAHRAIN	BANGLADESH	BARBADOS
BELARUS	BELGIUM	BELIZE	BENIN	BHUTAN
BOLIVIA	BOSNIA AND HERZEGOVINA	BOTSWANA	BRAZIL	BRUNEI
BULGARIA	BURKINA FASO	BURUNDI	CAMBODIA	CAMEROON
CANADA	CAPE VERDE	CENTRAL AFRICAN REPUBLIC	CHAD	CHILE
CHINA	COLOMBIA	COMOROS	CONGO, DEM. REP. OF THE	CONGO REPUBLIC
COSTA RICA	CÔTE D'IVOIRE	CROATIA	CUBA	CYPRUS
CZECH REPUBLIC	DENMARK	DJIBOUTI	DOMINICA	DOMINICAN REPUBLIC
ECUADOR	EGYPT	EL SALVADOR	EQUATORIAL GUINEA	ERITREA

Note: Flag proportions have been standardized to fit page.

460

ESTONIA	ETHIOPIA	FIJI	FINLAND	FRANCE
GABON	THE GAMBIA	GEORGIA	GERMANY	GHANA
GREECE	GRENADA	GUATEMALA	GUINEA	GUINEA-BISSAU
GUYANA	HAITI	HONDURAS	HUNGARY	ICELAND
INDIA	INDONESIA	IRAN	IRAQ	IRELAND
ISRAEL	ITALY	JAMAICA	JAPAN	JORDAN
KAZAKHSTAN	KENYA	KIRIBATI	NORTH KOREA	SOUTH KOREA
KOSOVO	KUWAIT	KYRGYZSTAN	LAOS	LATVIA
LEBANON	LESOTHO	LIBERIA	LIBYA	LIECHTENSTEIN
LITHUANIA	LUXEMBOURG	MACEDONIA	MADAGASCAR	MALAWI
MALAYSIA	MALDIVES	MALI	MALTA	MARSHALL ISLANDS

Note: Flag proportions have been standardized to fit page.

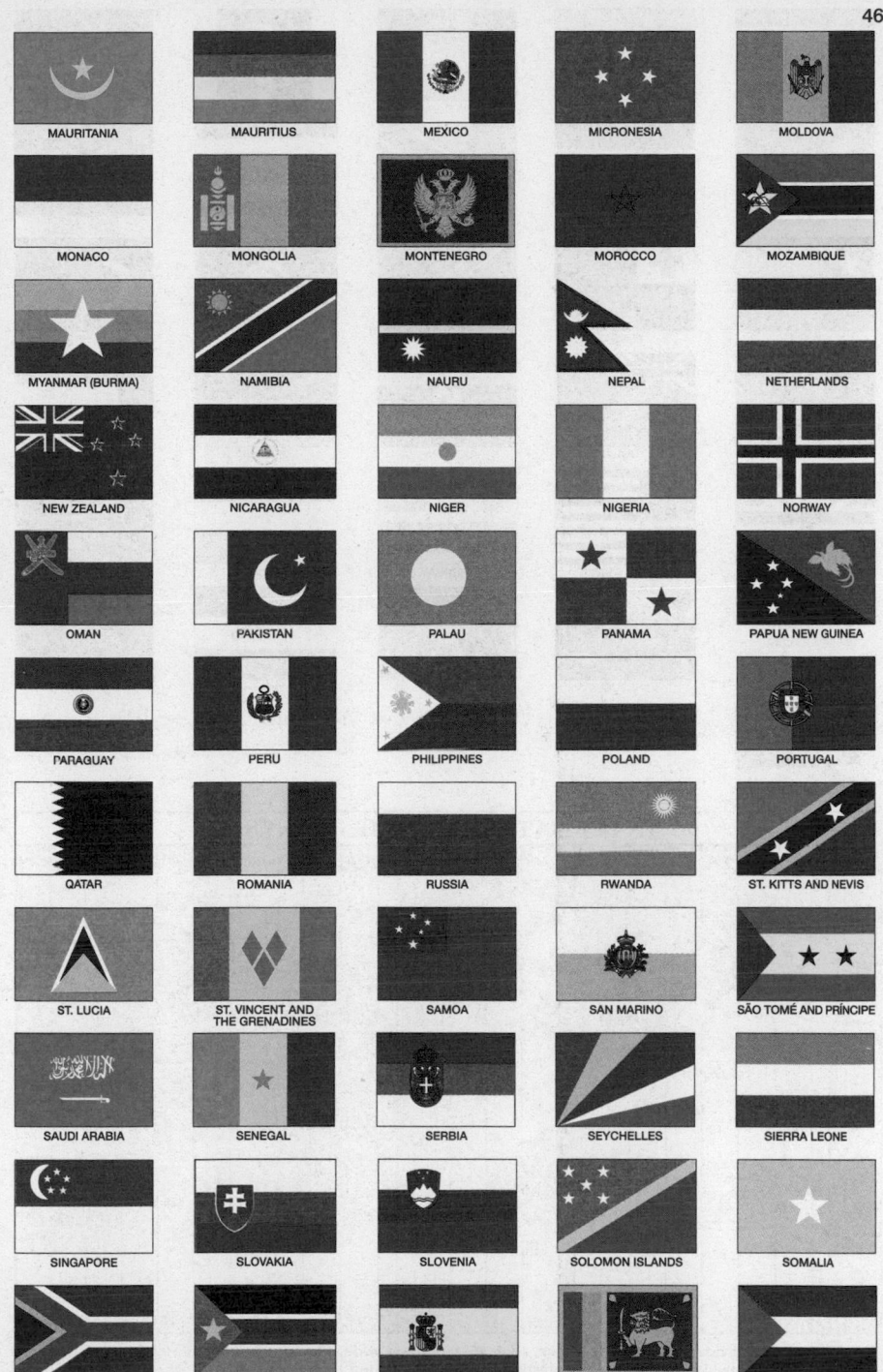

MAURITANIA   MAURITIUS   MEXICO   MICRONESIA   MOLDOVA

MONACO   MONGOLIA   MONTENEGRO   MOROCCO   MOZAMBIQUE

MYANMAR (BURMA)   NAMIBIA   NAURU   NEPAL   NETHERLANDS

NEW ZEALAND   NICARAGUA   NIGER   NIGERIA   NORWAY

OMAN   PAKISTAN   PALAU   PANAMA   PAPUA NEW GUINEA

PARAGUAY   PERU   PHILIPPINES   POLAND   PORTUGAL

QATAR   ROMANIA   RUSSIA   RWANDA   ST. KITTS AND NEVIS

ST. LUCIA   ST. VINCENT AND THE GRENADINES   SAMOA   SAN MARINO   SÃO TOMÉ AND PRÍNCIPE

SAUDI ARABIA   SENEGAL   SERBIA   SEYCHELLES   SIERRA LEONE

SINGAPORE   SLOVAKIA   SLOVENIA   SOLOMON ISLANDS   SOMALIA

SOUTH AFRICA   SOUTH SUDAN   SPAIN   SRI LANKA   SUDAN

Note: Flag proportions have been standardized to fit page.

SURINAME

SWAZILAND

SWEDEN

SWITZERLAND

SYRIA

TAIWAN

TAJIKISTAN

TANZANIA

THAILAND

TIMOR-LESTE (EAST TIMOR)

TOGO

TONGA

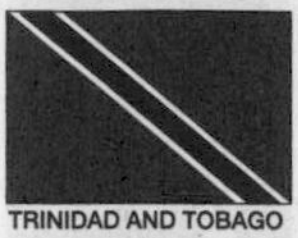

TRINIDAD AND TOBAGO

TUNISIA

TURKEY

TURKMENISTAN

TUVALU

UGANDA

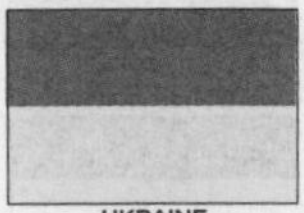

UKRAINE

UNITED ARAB EMIRATES

UNITED KINGDOM

UNITED STATES

URUGUAY

UZBEKISTAN

VANUATU

VATICAN CITY

VENEZUELA

VIETNAM

YEMEN

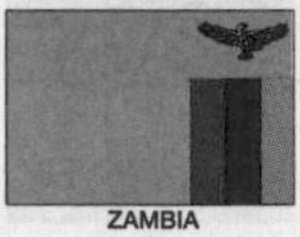

ZAMBIA

ZIMBABWE

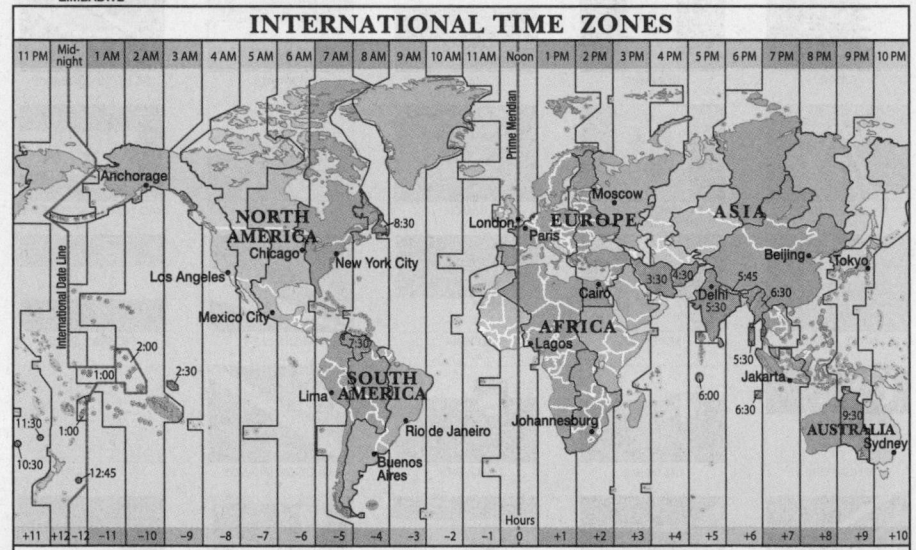

INTERNATIONAL TIME ZONES

The world is divided into 24 time zones, each 15° longitude wide. The longitudinal meridian passing through Greenwich, England, is the starting point, and is called the *prime meridian*. The 12th zone is divided by the 180th meridian (International Date Line). When the line is crossed going west, the date is advanced one day; when crossed going east, the date becomes a day earlier.

UNITED STATES

ATLANTIC OCEAN

PACIFIC OCEAN

Gulf of Mexico

CANADA

MEXICO

CUBA

THE BAHAMAS

Tropic of Cancer

States and regions: Maine, N.H., Vt., Mass., R.I., Conn., New York, Pennsylvania, New Jersey, Del., Md., D.C., Virginia, W. Va., North Carolina, South Carolina, Georgia, Florida, Alabama, Mississippi, Louisiana, Tennessee, Kentucky, Ohio, Indiana, Illinois, Michigan, Wisconsin, Minnesota, Iowa, Missouri, Arkansas, Oklahoma, Kansas, Nebraska, South Dakota, North Dakota, Montana, Wyoming, Colorado, New Mexico, Texas, Arizona, Utah, Nevada, Idaho, Washington, Oregon, California, Hawai'i

ROCKY MOUNTAINS · APPALACHIAN MOUNTAINS · GREAT PLAINS · COLORADO PLATEAU · GREAT BASIN · SIERRA NEVADA · CASCADE RANGE · COAST RANGES · BLACK HILLS · EDWARDS PLATEAU · MOJAVE · GRAND CANYON

Lake Superior · Lake Michigan · Lake Huron · Lake Ontario · Lake Erie · Lake of the Woods

Chesapeake Bay · Cape Cod · Cape Hatteras · Cape Canaveral · Cape Sable · Cape Flattery · Cape Mendocino · Key West · Strait of Florida

Mt. Washington 1917 m (6,289 ft)
Mt. Mitchell 2037 m (6,683 ft)
Mt. Rainier 4392 m (14,410 ft)
Mt. Whitney 4418 m (14,491 ft)
Mt. Elbert 4399 m (14,433 ft)
Wheeler Pk. 4011 m (13,161 ft)
Death Valley −86 m (−282 ft) Lowest point in the U.S.
Mt. McKinley 6194 m (20,320 ft) Highest point in the U.S.

Scale bars (main map):
0 — 250 — 500 — 750 Miles
0 — 250 — 500 — 750 Kilometers

ALASKA....See page 464
0 — 100 — 200 Miles
0 — 150 — 300 Kilometers

HAWAI'I inset: Ni'ihau, Kaua'i, O'ahu, Moloka'i, Lāna'i, Kaho'olawe, Maui, Hawai'i
Honolulu, Hilo, Kailua-Kona, Kahului
Mauna Kea 4205 m (13,796 ft)
Mauna Loa 4169 m (13,680 ft)
0 — 100 Miles
0 — 150 Kilometers

EUROPE

NORWAY
⊙Oslo

GREAT BRITAIN

60°

0°

10°

20°

30°

40°

-40°

ICELAND

Reykjavík•

Denmark Strait

Arctic Circle

Tasiilaq•

70°

Greenland
Sea

Labrador
Sea

Newfoundland and
Labrador

St. Anthony•

Newfoundland

Corner Brook•

St. John's•

St. Pierre and
Miquelon Is. (Fr.)

Sydney•
Cape Breton I.

GREENLAND
(KALAALLIT NUNAAT)
(Den.)

Ittoqqortoormiit
(Scoresbysund)•

Nuuk•

Hebron•

Happy Valley-
Goose Bay•

Labrador City•

P.E.I.

New
Bruns

80°

Nord•

Cape
Morris Jesup

Qaanaaq
(Thule)•

Grise Fiord•

Baffin
Bay

Davis Strait

Pangnirtung•

Iqaluit•

Schefferville•

Sept-
Îles•

Anticosti I.

Chibougamau•

Chicoutimi•

Quebec

CANADIAN

SHIELD

Svalbard
(Nor.)

Cape Columbia

Albert•

Ellesmere
I.

Dewon I.

Pond Inlet•

UNGAVA
PENINSULA

Puvirnituq•

Belcher
Is.•

James
Bay

Moosonee•

North Pole

Queen
Elizabeth
Islands

Melville I.

Resolute•

Arctic Bay•

Baffin Island

Repulse Bay•

Southampton
I.

Hudson
Bay

Ontario

+ North Pole

ARCTIC OCEAN

Banks
I.

Victoria
I.

Cambridge
Bay•

Nunavut

Rankin Inlet•

Arviat•

Churchill•

Lake Winnipeg

CANADA

Sachs
Harbour•

Kugluktuk•

CANADA

Thompson•

Manitoba

Flin Flon•

80°

Beaufort
Sea

Great
Bear Lake

Yellowknife•

Great Slave
Lake

Fort
Smith•

Uranium
City•

Lake Athabasca

La Loche•

Saskatchewan

Prince
Albert•

Saskatoon•

Regina•

Point
Barrow

Inuvik•

Fort McPherson•

Déline•

Mackenzie

Fort
Simpson•

Hay
River•

La Ronge•

Chukchi
Sea

Point
Hope

Barrow•

BROOKS RANGE

Fort Yukon•

Dawson•

YUKON
PLATEAU

Whitehorse•

Watson
Lake•

Carmacks•

Yukon

Northwest
Territories

British
Columbia

Peace
River•

Fort
McMurray•

Grande
Prairie•

Alberta

Edmonton•

Peace

Athabasca

GREAT

Calgary•

ROCKY

ASIA

RUSSIA

Bering Strait

Arctic Circle

Kotzebue•

SEWARD
PENINSULA

Nome•

Fairbanks•

Alaska

ALASKA RANGE

Anchorage•

Skagway•

Juneau•

Dawson
Creek•

Prince
George•

Williams
Lake•

Mt. Waddington
3994 m
(13,104 ft)

Jasper•

ROCKY

RANGE

Bering
Sea

60°

Bethel•

Mt. Katmai
2047 m
(6,716 ft)

Kenai•

Valdez•

Seward•

Highest point
in North America
Mt. McKinley
6168 m (20,237 ft)

ALASKA

Kodiak•
Kodiak I.

Mt. Logan
5959 m
(19,551 ft)

Gulf of
Alaska

Sitka•

Ketchikan•

Alexander
Archipelago

Prince Rupert•

Kitimat•

Queen
Charlotte Is.

Port Hardy•

Vancouver
I.

Vancouver•

Victoria•

Seattle•

Tacoma•

COAST MOUNTAINS

70°

60°

180°

170°

160°

150°

140°

130°

50°

160°

NORTH AMERICA AND THE CARIBBEAN

10°

0°

10°

20°

ATLANTIC

OCEAN

Natal
João Pessoa
Recife
Maceió
Aracaju
Salvador
Alagoinhas
Ilhéus
Itabuna
Vitória

Fortaleza
Mossoró
Juazeiro do Norte
Campina Grande
Petrolina
Juazeiro
Feira de Santana
Jequié
Vitória da Conquista
Teófilo Otoni
Governador Valadares

Paraíba
São Luís
Teresina
Caxias
Floriano
Montes Claros
Juiz de Fora
Volta Redonda
Niterói
Rio de Janeiro

Belém

Macapá

Marajó Island

Kourou
Cayenne
French Guiana (Fr.)

Santarém

Imperatriz

Araguaína

Marabá

Altamira

Itaituba

Manaus

BRAZIL

Pico da Bandeira 2890 m (9,482 ft)
Belo Horizonte
Ribeirão Preto
Campinas
Jundiaí
São Paulo
Sorocaba
Santos

BRAZILIAN HIGHLANDS

Brasília
Goiânia
Uberlândia
Anápolis
São José do Rio Preto
Bauru
Londrina
Presidente Prudente

MATO GROSSO PLATEAU

Cuiabá

Rondonópolis

Campo Grande

Corumbá

Dourados

Concepción

Maturín
El Tigre

Ciudad Guayana
Ciudad Bolívar

Georgetown
New Amsterdam
Paramaribo

GUYANA
SURINAME
GUIANA HIGHLANDS

Boa Vista

Pico da Neblina 2994 m (9,823 ft)

VENEZUELA
San Fernando de Apure
Puerto Ayacucho

Orinoco

Barcelona
Caracas
Valencia
Maracay
Maracaibo
Cabimas
Valera
Mérida
San Cristóbal
Barquisimeto

Aruba (Neth.)
Bonaire (Neth.)
Curaçao (Neth.)
Margarita I.

TRINIDAD AND TOBAGO
Port-of-Spain

Caribbean Sea

Pico Cristóbal Colón 5775 m (18,947 ft)
Santa Marta
Barranquilla
Cartagena
Sincelejo
Montería
Barrancabermeja
Cúcuta
Bucaramanga
Tunja
Medellín
Manizales
Pereira
Armenia
Ibagué
Bogotá
Villavicencio

COLOMBIA
LLANOS
Nevada del Huila 5364 m (17,598 ft)
Cali
Palmira
Neiva
Florencia
Popayán
Pasto

AMAZON BASIN
SELVAS

Boa Vista

Negro

Amazon

Branco
Río Madeira

Leticia
Benjamin Constant
Crazeiro do Sul

Iquitos

Porto Velho

Ji-Paraná

Guajará-Mirim

Riberalta
Cobija

Puerto Maldonado

Trinidad
Santa Cruz
Camiri

BOLIVIA
Cochabamba
La Paz
Sucre
Oruro
Potosí
Tarija

San Salvador de Jujuy

PARAGUAY
CHACO

ALTIPLANO

ANDES

ATACAMA DESERT

Arica
Iquique
Antofagasta

Juliaca
Puno

Cuzco

LA MONTAÑA
PERU
Pucallpa
Huánuco
Cerro de Pasco
Lima
Callao
Ica
Ayacucho
Abancay
Arequipa
Tacna

Yurimaguas

Cajamarca
Nev. Huascarán 6768 m (22,205 ft)
Chimbote
Nev. Yerupajá 6634 m (21,765 ft)

Trujillo
Chiclayo
Piura
Sullana
Talara
Tumbes

Aguja Point

ECUADOR
Quito
Ambato
Riobamba
Cuenca
Loja
Machala
Portoviejo
Guayaquil

Cotopaxi 5911 m (19,393 ft)
Chimborazo 6310 m (20,702 ft)

Esmeraldas
Tumaco
Buenaventura

ANDES

Galápagos Islands (Ecuador)

Equator

CENTRAL AMERICA
HONDURAS
Tegucigalpa
EL SALVADOR
San Salvador
NICARAGUA
Managua
COSTA RICA
San José
PANAMA
Panama City

PACIFIC OCEAN

40°

50°

60°

70°

80°

90°

0°

20°

10°

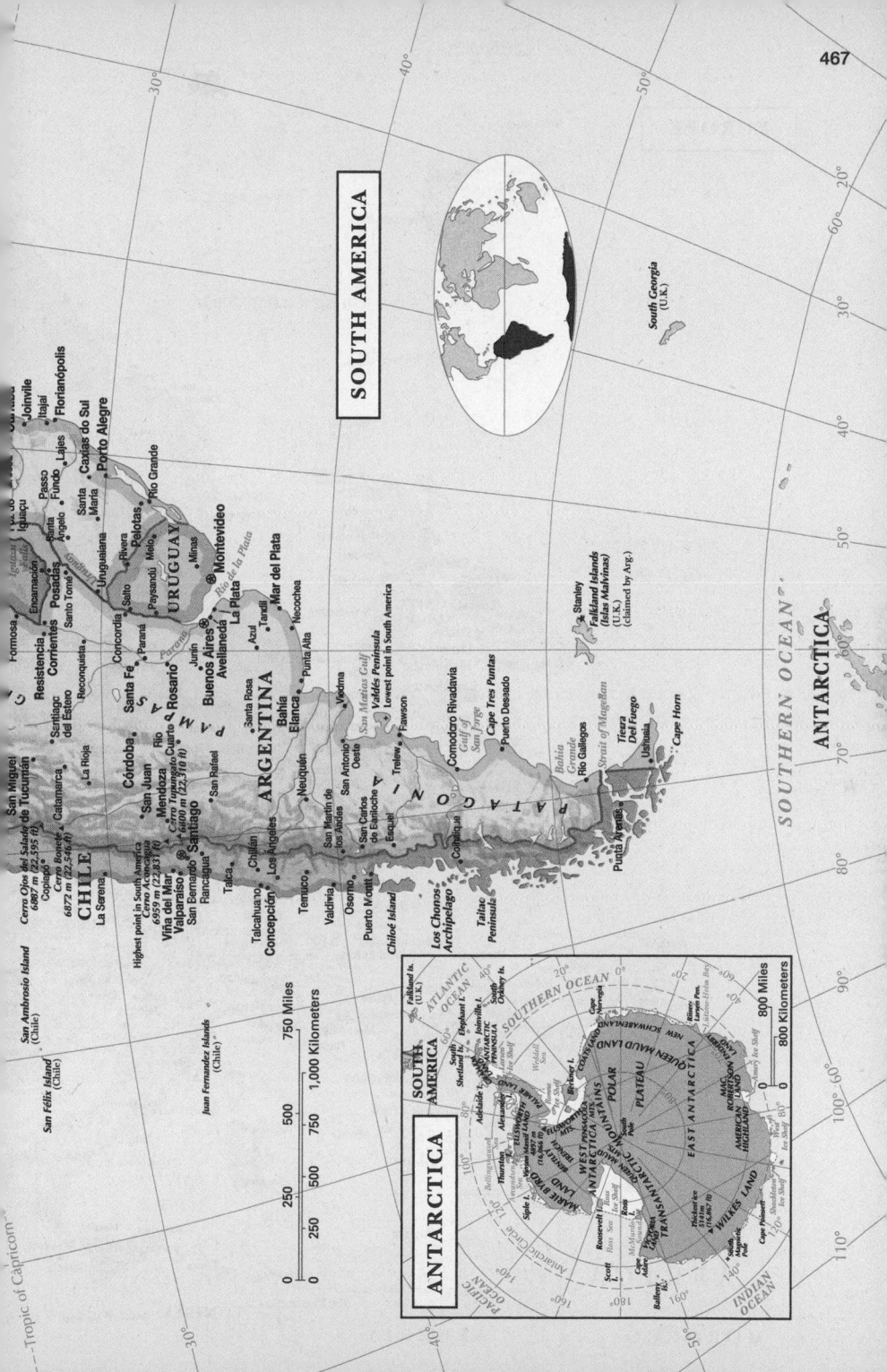

EUROPE

GREENLAND
(KALAALLIT NUNAAT)
(Denmark)

Ísafjörður

ICELAND

Keflavík
Reykjavík
Akureyri

Arctic Circle

Seydhisfjördhur

Norwegian Sea

Namsos

Torshavn
Faroe
Islands
(Den.)

Trondheim

Molde
Ålesund

Bergen

Östersund

Sundsvall

Borlänge

*ATLANTIC
OCEAN*

Shetland
Islands
(U.K.)

Orkney
Islands

Thurso

Inverness

Haugesund
Stavanger

NORWAY SWEDEN

Oslo
Drammen
Skien
Karlstad

Uppsala
Örebro

Stockholm
Norrköping
Linköping

Hebrides

Scotland Aberdeen

Dundee

Kristiansand

Göteborg
Ålborg
Halmstad
Jönköping

Växjö
Öland

*North
Sea*

Jutland
Århus

Helsingborg
Malmö

Bornholm
(Den.)

Glasgow
Ayr
Edinburgh

Esbjerg
Copenhagen
Odense

Londonderry
Northern
Ireland
Belfast

Newcastle

DENMARK

Galway
UNITED
KINGDOM
Dublin
IRELAND
Limerick

Liverpool
Leeds
Kingston upon Hull

Kiel
Lübeck
Rostock

Szczecin
Bydgoszcz

Cork
Waterford
Manchester
Sheffield

Hamburg
NORTHERN

POLAN

Birmingham
Wales Swansea
Coventry
Norwich

Groningen
Bremen

Oder

Poznań

Cardiff
Bristol
England
London Amsterdam
NETHERLANDS

Hannover
Bielefeld
Berlin

Wrocła

Plymouth
Land's End

The Hague Rotterdam
Antwerp
Essen

Madgeburg
Magdeburg

GERMANY
Leipzig
Dresden

Liberec
CZECH REP.
Walbrz

Channel Is.
(U.K.)

Portsmouth
Dover
Brussels
Lille
BELGIUM
Cologne
Liège Bonn

Kassel
Erfurt
Chemnitz

Plzen
Prague

Ostrav

Brno

Brest

Le Havre
Caen
Rouen

LUXEMBOURG
Luxembourg
Wiesbaden
Frankfurt

Rennes
Paris
Le Mans
Orleans

Nancy
Strasbourg
Saarbrucken
Mannheim

Nürnberg

Regensburg
Linz

Bratisla

Nantes
Tours

Dijon

Basel
Stuttgart
Augsburg

Munich

Vienna

HU

Limoges
FRANCE
Clermont-Ferrand
Lyon
Zürich
Bern
SWITZERLAND
Geneva
LIECHTENSTEIN
Salzburg
Innsbruck
AUSTRIA
Klagenfurt

Graz

Györ

Bay
of
Biscay

Bordeaux
Saint-Etienne
Grenoble
Mt. Blanc
4807 m (15,771 ft)
Matterhorn
4478 m (14,692 ft)
Bergamo
Udine
SLOVENIA
Trieste
Ljubljana
Zagreb
CROATIA

A Coruña
Vigo

Gijón
Santander
Bilbao

Toulouse
Montpellier

Avignon
Torino
Milan
Verona
Genoa
Parma

Venice

Bologna

Rijeka
BOS.
HER.

Porto
Braga
Leon
Vitoria-Gasteiz
Pamplona
PYRENEES
Marseille
Toulon
Nice
MONACO
Pisa
Florence
Perugia
SAN
MARINO
Ancona

Luc
Sarajev

Coimbra
Valladolid
IBERIAN
Salamanca
Pico de Aneto
3404 m
(11,169 ft)
ANDORRA

Split.

Dubrovnik

PORTUGAL
Lisbon
Setubal
Badajoz
Madrid
SPAIN
Toledo
Zaragoza

Barcelona
Tarragona

Corsica
(Fr.)
Ajaccio
Elba

VATICAN CITY
Rome
ITALY

Foggia

Adriatic
Sea

Valencia
Castellon de la Plana

Naples
Bari

Cape
St. Vincent
Seville
PENINSULA
Cordoba
Alicante
Murcia
Majorca
Palma de
Mallorca
Balearic
(Sp.)
Minorca

Sardinia
(It.)

Vesuvius
1277 m (4,190 ft)
Salerno
Taranto

Cádiz
Málaga
Granada
Cartagena
Almería

Cagliari

Tyrrhenian
Sea

Ionia
Sea

Strait of
Gibraltar
GIBRALTAR
(U.K.)

Rabat
Algiers

Palermo
Messina
Etna
3369 m (11,053 ft)
Reggio di
Calabria
Sicily
(It.)
Catania

AFRICA

250

500 Miles

Tunis

MOROCCO

250   500   750 Kilometers

ALGERIA

TUNISIA

MALTA Valletta

Mediterranean Sea

Barents Sea

ASIA

Novaya Zemlya

North Cape
Hammerfest
Vardø
Tromsø
Alta
Murmansk
Ivalo
Apatity
KOLA PENINSULA
Kiruna
LAPLAND
Rovaniemi
Belomorsk
White Sea
Nar'yan-Mar
Pechora
Ukhta
URAL
Luleå
Skellefteå
Oulu
FINLAND
Lake Onega
Petrozavodsk
Arkhangel'sk
Dvina
Syktyvkar
Berezniki
RUSSIA
MOUNTAINS
Pori
Vaasa
Jyväskylä
Kuopio
Lahti
Tampere
Turku
Kotka
Helsinki
Åland Is. (Fin.)
Gulf of Bothnia
Lake Ladoga
St. Petersburg
Cherepovets
Vologda
Kostroma
Rybinsk
Yaroslavl'
Yoshkar Ola
Nizhniy Novgorod
Cheboksary
Kazan'
Kirov
Izhevsk
Perm'
Naberezhnye Chelny
Ufa
Sterlitamak
Tallinn
ESTONIA
Tartu
Pskov
Velikiy Novgorod
Ivanovo
Ul'yanovsk
Saransk
Tol'yatti
Samara
Orsk
Orenburg
Gotland (Swe.)
Riga
LATVIA
Liepaja
Daugavpils
Vitsyebsk
Tver'
Vladimir
Moscow
Ryazan'
Penza
Saratov
EUROPEAN
PLAIN
Volga
KAZAKHSTAN
Klaipeda
LITHUANIA
Kaunas
Vilnius
Kaliningrad (RUSSIA)
Minsk
Smolensk
Kaluga
Tula
Tambov
Mahilyow
Orsha
Hrodna
Babruysk
Bryansk
Lipetsk
Homyel'
Bialystok
Warsaw
Brest
Pinsk
BELARUS
Voronezh
Łódź
Radom
Lublin
Chernihiv
Sumy
Kursk
Belgorod
Volgograd
Astrakhan'
Caspian
Sea
Kielce
Katowice
Kraków
Zhytomyr
Kyiv (Kiev)
Cherkasy
Kharkiv
Poltava
Luhans'k
Horlivka
Donets'k
Rostov-na-Donu
Don
L'viv
UKRAINE
Vinnytsia
Dnieper
Dnipropetrovs'k
Zaporizhzhia
CARPATHIAN MOUNTAINS
Košice
Chernivtsi
MOLDOVA
Iasi
Chisinău
Kryvyy Rih
Mykolaiv
Mariupol'
Stavropol'
Nal'chik
Groznyy
Makhachkala
Slovenska
Miskolc
Budapest
Debrecen
Oradea
Cluj-Napoca
Odesa
Sea of Azov
Krasnodar
Mt. Elbrus 5633 m (18,481 ft) Highest point in Europe
Vladikavkaz
CAUCASUS MTS.
Kecskemét
Szeged
Timişoara
ROMANIA
Galaţi
Braşov
Ploieşti
CRIMEA PENINSULA
Simferopol
Sevastopol
GEORGIA
Tbilisi
Baku
Novi Sad
Belgrade
Bucharest
Craiova
Constanţa
ARMENIA
Yerevan
AZERBAIJAN
SERBIA
Danube
Ruse
Pleven
Varna
Black Sea
AZER.
Niš
Priština
KOSOVO
Burgas
BULGARIA
Stara Zagora
Sofia
Plovdiv
Skopje
BALKAN
MACEDONIA
Podgorica
Shkodër
PENINSULA
Kavala
İstanbul
Durrës
Tirana
Thessaloniki
ALBANIA
Vlorë
Olympus 2917 m (9,570 ft)
Larisa
Ioannina
Volos
Aegean Sea
Dardanelles
Ankara
TURKEY
IRAN
ASIA
Corfu
GREECE
Patras
Athens
Corinth
Peloponnese
Kalamata
Sparta
Cyclades
Sea of Crete
Hania
Crete (Gr.)
Iraklion
Rhodes (Gr.)
CYPRUS
Nicosia
LEBANON
Beirut
SYRIA
Damascus
Baghdad
IRAQ

470

ATLANTIC OCEAN

ARCTIC OCEAN

10°

PORT.

SPAIN

⊕ Madrid

IRELAND

Paris ⊕

FRANCE

BEL.

UNITED KINGDOM

⊕ London

NETH.

DEN.

⊕ Copenhagen

NORWAY

⊕ Oslo

SWEDEN

⊕ Stockholm

GERMANY

⊕ Berlin

SWITZ.

Baltic Sea

FINLAND

⊕ Helsinki

EST.

Severnaya Zemlya

Kara Sea

Dickson

ITALY

⊕ Rome

AUS.

CZECH REP.

POLAND

⊕ Warsaw

SLOV.

HUNG.

LITH.

LAT.

BELARUS

Noril'sk

CE

SLOV.

CRO.

BOS. & HERZ.

MONT.

SERB.

ALB.

KOS.

MAC.

ROMANIA

MOL.

⊕ Bucharest

UKRAINE

EUROPE

⊕ Moscow

Vorkuta

Salekhard

Novyy Urengoy

Tu

RUSSIA

SIB.

BUL.

GREECE

⊕ Athens

Izmir

Bursa

Ankara

TURKEY

Samsun

Black Sea

Kyiv (Kiev) ⊕

Serov

Nizhniy Tagil

Yekaterinburg

Surgut

Nizhnevartovsk

WEST SIBERIAN PLAIN

PL

Mediterranean Sea

LIBYA

CYPRUS

Nicosia

Latakia

Beirut

LEBANON

Adana

Aleppo

SYRIA

Diyarbakir

Erzurum

Trabzon

Mt. Ararat 5137 m (16,854 ft)

GEORGIA

⊕ Tbilisi

Ganca

Basht

ARMENIA

Yerevan

AZERBAIJAN

Tabriz

Baku

Caspian Sea

Aktau

Oral

Atyrau'

Chelyabinsk

Kurgan

Tyumen

Tobol'sk

Tara

Omsk

Magnitogorsk

Petropavlovsk

KAZAKHSTAN

Astana

Qaraghandy (Karaganda)

Kolpashevo

Tomsk

Lesosibirsk

Achinsk

Novosibirsk

Barnaul

Kemerovo

Novokuznetsk

Krasnoya

SAYAN MT

URAL MOUNTAINS

CAUCASUS MTS.

Cairo

Tel Aviv-Yafo

Jerusalem

ISRAEL

JORDAN

Amman

Damascus

Mosul

Arbil

Kirkuk

Lake Urmia

Mashhad

Tehran

AFRICA

EGYPT

Al 'Aqabah

Tabuk

IRAQ

Baghdad

Al Hillah

ZAGROS

Kermanshah

Qom

Esfahan

IRAN

Yazd

Mt. Damavand 5610 m (18,406 ft)

DASHT-E KAVIR

DASHT-E LUT

KARA KUM DESERT

Urganch

Ashgabat

Nukus

TURKMENISTAN

Turkmenbashy

Aral Sea

Zhezkazgan

Qyzylorda

Balqash

KAZAKH UPLAND

Taldykorgan

Lake Balkhash

Taraz

Bishkek

Almaty

Semey (Semipalatinsk)

Ökemen (Ust'-Kamenogorsk)

Ayagoz

Dund-

ALTAI MTS.

KYZYL KUM DESERT

Bukhara

UZBEKISTAN

Tashkent

Dushanbe

TAJIKISTAN

Kashi

KYRGYZSTAN

Yining

Jenghis Chotasu 7439 m (24,406 ft)

TIEN SHAN

Ürümqi

Turpan Depression

Amu Darya

Syr Darya

Mt. Everest 8850 m (29,035 ft)

SUDAN

Khartoum

Asmara

ERITREA

Jeddah

Mecca

At Taif

Riyadh

Manama

BAHRAIN

Doha

QATAR

SAUDI ARABIA

Buraydah

Hail

Kuwait City

KUWAIT

Al Basrah

Shiraz

Kerman

Zahedan

AFGHANISTAN

Kabul

Peshawar

Herat

Farah

Kandahar

HINDU KUSH

Islamabad

Rawalpindi

Srinagar

PAMIRS

K2 8611 m (28,250 ft)

Shache

Lenin Peak 7134 m (23,406 ft)

Ismail Semani Pk. 7495 m (24,590 ft)

Highest point in Asia

TAKLIMAKAN DESERT

Tarim

KUNLUN MTS.

PLATEAU OF TIBET

Red Sea

Birjand

Zabol

Helmand

Quetta

Faisalabad

Lahore

Multan

Chandigarh

Delhi

New Delhi

HIMALAYA

Brahmaputra

Lha

Abha

Abu Dhabi

UNITED ARAB EMIRATES

Muscat

Ras al Hadd

Sur

OMAN

Bandar-e Abbas

Gulf of Oman

Turbat

Sukkur

THAR DESERT

Hyderabad

Karachi

Jodhpur

Jaipur

Agra

Lucknow

Kanpur

Allahabad

Varanasi

Patna

NEPAL

Kathmandu

BHUTAN

Thimphu

Persian Gulf

AN NAFUD

Jeddah

Sanaa

Aden

Al Mukalla

YEMEN

RU' AL KHALI

Salalah

Ahmadabad

DECCAN PLATEAU

Nagpur

Mumbai (Bombay)

Pune

Solapur

WESTERN GHATS

Raipur

Asansol

Kolkata (Calcutta)

Khulna

BANGLADESH

Dhaka

Chittagong

Akyab

INDIA

Imphal

Cuttack

MYANMAR (BURMA)

Pathe

Addis Ababa

ETHIOPIA

DJI.

SOMALIA

Socotra (Yemen)

Arabian Sea

Gulf of Aden

Panaji

Hyderabad

Vijayawada

Visakhapatnam

Bay of Bengal

Andaman Is. (India)

Bengaluru (Bangalore)

Laccadive Is. (India)

Mysuru (Mysore)

Coimbatore

Kochi

Thiruvananthapuram

Cape Comorin

Madurai

Chennai (Madras)

EASTERN GHATS

Hubballi (Hubli)

Colombo

Sri Jayewardenepura Kotte

Galle

SRI LANKA

Trincomalee

Nicobar Is. (India)

⊕ Male

MALDIVES

Equator

INDIAN OCEAN

Inset map:

TURKEY

Antalya

Mersin

Adana

Şanlıurfa

CYPRUS

Nicosia

Limassol

Antakya

Latakia

Al Hasakah

Ar Raqqah

Mosul

Mediterranean Sea

LEBANON

Beirut

Aleppo

Hamah

Hims

Bayji

SYRIA

Tadmur

Abu Kamal

ISRAEL

Halfa

Tel Aviv-Yafo

Port Said

Jerusalem

Amman

Jericho

WEST BANK

GAZA STRIP

The West Bank currently occupied by Israel. Permanent status to be determined.

Ar Ramadi

IRAQ

SYRIAN DESERT

JORDAN

Ma'an

Tanta

Cairo

Suez

Giza

Canal

EGYPT

SINAI

Gulf of Suez

Elat

Al 'Aqabah

Tabuk

SAUDI ARABIA

AN NAFUD

0   250 Miles

0   250 Kilometers

ATLANTIC OCEAN

INDIAN OCEAN

AFRICA

SOMALIA — Mogadishu, Marka, Kismaayo, Marsabit

KENYA — Nairobi, Nakuru, Eldoret, Kisumu, Machakos, Meru, Mt. Kenya 5199 m (17,057 ft)

Mt. Kilimanjaro 5895 m (19,344 ft) Highest point in Africa

UGANDA — Kampala, Jinja

RWANDA — Kigali

BURUNDI — Bujumbura

TANZANIA — Dodoma, Dar es Salaam, Arusha, Tabora, Mwanza, Morogoro, Iringa, Mbeya, Songea, Mtwara, Tanga, Zanzibar, Pemba I., Mombasa

SERENGETI PLAIN, Mt. Meru 4565 m (14,977 ft), Lake Victoria, RIFT VALLEY, HIGHLANDS

COMOROS — Moroni, Mayotte (Fr.)

MADAGASCAR — Antananarivo, Antsiranana, Mahajanga, Toamasina, Fianarantsoa, Antsirabe, Toliara, Tolanaro

Mozambique Channel

DEMOCRATIC REPUBLIC OF THE CONGO — Kinshasa, Kisangani, Mbandaka, Goma, Bukavu, Kindu, Kalemie, Kabalo, Kalima, Kananga, Mbuji-Mayi, Ilebo, Tshikapa, Kikwit, Bandundu, Kolwezi, Likasi, Lubumbashi, Kabinda, Mwene-Ditu, Buta, Bumba, Beni

CONGO BASIN, KATANGA PLATEAU, Kasai, Congo

REPUBLIC OF THE CONGO — Brazzaville, Pointe-Noire, Loubomo

GABON — Libreville, Port-Gentil, Lambaréné, Franceville

EQUATORIAL GUINEA — Bioko

SÃO TOMÉ AND PRÍNCIPE — São Tomé, Príncipe, Annobon (Eq. Guinea)

Gulf of Guinea

ANGOLA — Luanda, Huambo, Lobito, Benguela, Lubango, Namibe, Malanje, Menongue, Luena, Cabinda (Angola), Mbanza-Ngungu, Matadi, Soyo

ZAMBIA — Lusaka, Ndola, Kitwe, Chingola, Kabwe, Livingstone, Lake Kariba, Kafue

MALAWI — Lilongwe, Blantyre, Lake Nyasa (Lake Malawi)

MOZAMBIQUE — Beira, Quelimane, Nampula, Nacala, Chimoio, Tete, Inhambane, Xai-Xai, Maputo

ZIMBABWE — Harare, Bulawayo, Gweru, Mutare, Gwanda, Masvingo, Francistown

BOTSWANA — Gaborone, Francistown, Serowe, Mahalapye

KALAHARI DESERT

NAMIBIA — Windhoek, Walvis Bay, Tsumeb, Grootfontein, Keetmanshoop, Lüderitz, Swakopmund

NAMIB DESERT, Ruacana Falls, Cunene, Okavango, Orange

SOUTH AFRICA — Pretoria (Tshwane), Johannesburg, Klerksdorp, Vereeniging, Welkom, Kimberley, Bloemfontein, Upington, Springbok, Cape Town, Cape of Good Hope, Cape Agulhas, Worcester, Middelburg, East London, Port Elizabeth, Umtata, Pietermaritzburg, Durban, Newcastle, Bisho

LESOTHO — Maseru

SWAZILAND — Mbabane, Lobamba

Tropic of Capricorn

Equator

Ascension (U.K.)

SEYCHELLES

SCALE: 0 250 500 750 Miles; 0 250 500 750 1,000 Kilometers

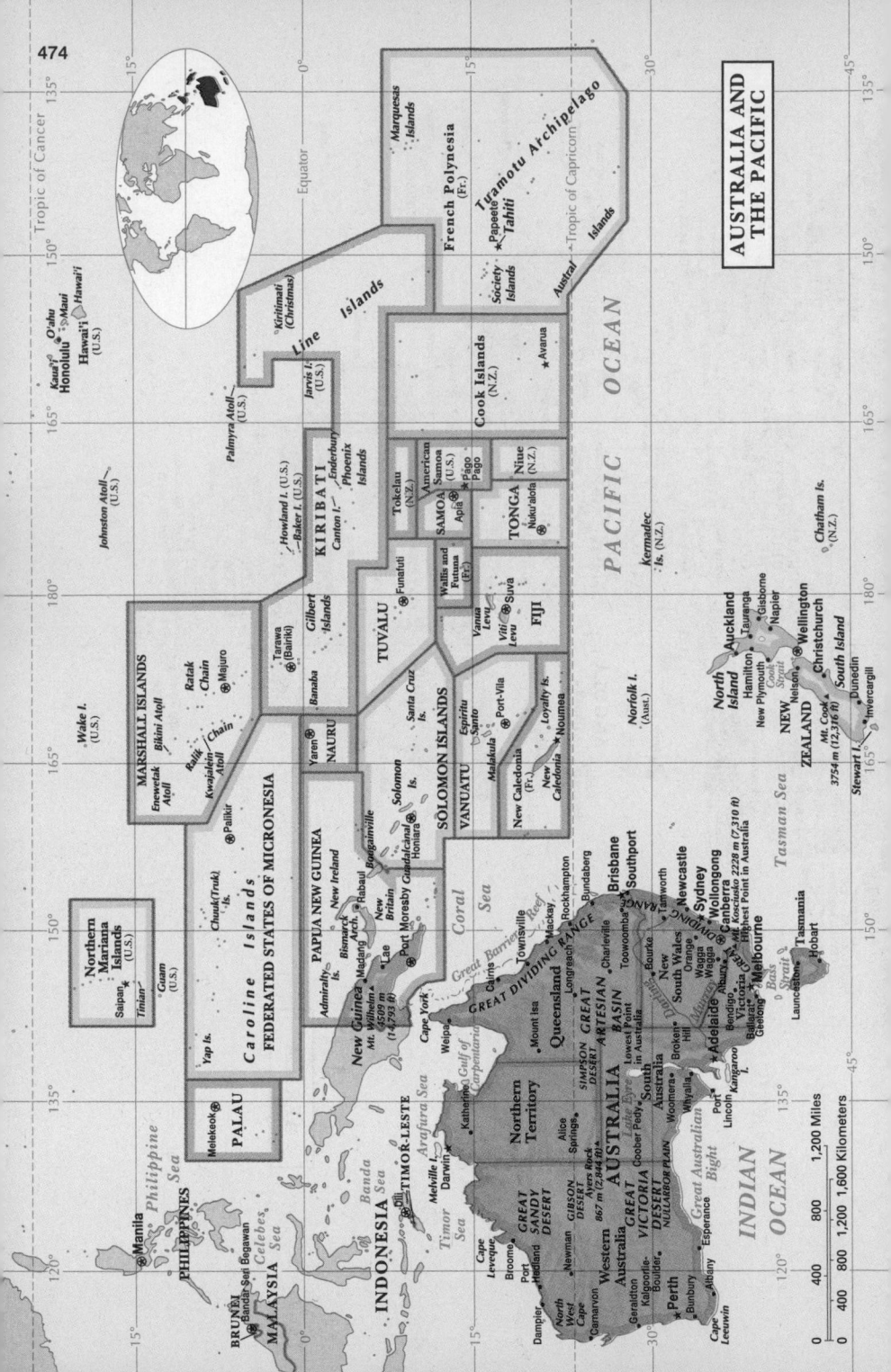

AUSTRALIA AND THE PACIFIC

PACIFIC OCEAN

INDIAN OCEAN

Tropic of Cancer

Equator

Tropic of Capricorn

Coral Sea

Tasman Sea

Philippine Sea

Banda Sea

Timor Sea

Arafura Sea

Celebes Sea

Countries and regions:

PHILIPPINES
MALAYSIA
BRUNEI
INDONESIA
TIMOR-LESTE
PALAU
Northern Mariana Islands (U.S.)
Guam (U.S.)
FEDERATED STATES OF MICRONESIA
Caroline Islands
PAPUA NEW GUINEA
MARSHALL ISLANDS
NAURU
SOLOMON ISLANDS
TUVALU
KIRIBATI
Gilbert Islands
Line Islands
VANUATU
New Caledonia (Fr.)
FIJI
TONGA
SAMOA
American Samoa (U.S.)
Niue (N.Z.)
Cook Islands (N.Z.)
French Polynesia (Fr.)
Tuamotu Archipelago
AUSTRALIA
NEW ZEALAND

Cities and places:

Manila
Bandar Seri Begawan
Dili
Melekeok
Saipan
Tinian
Palikir
Yap Is.
Chuuk (Truk) Is.
Madang
Lae
Port Moresby
Rabaul
Bougainville
Honiara
Guadalcanal I.
Santa Cruz Is.
Yaren
Majuro
Ratak Chain
Ralik Chain
Kwajalein Atoll
Bikini Atoll
Enewetak Atoll
Wake I. (U.S.)
Tarawa (Bairiki)
Banaba
Funafuti
Wallis and Futuna (Fr.)
Suva
Viti Levu
Vanua Levu
Nuku'alofa
Apia
Pago Pago
Kermadec Is. (N.Z.)
Norfolk I. (Aust.)
Port-Vila
Espiritu Santo
Malakula
Loyalty Is.
Nouméa
Canton I.
Baker I. (U.S.)
Howland I. (U.S.)
Enderbury
Phoenix Islands
Tokelau (N.Z.)
Palmyra Atoll (U.S.)
Jarvis I. (U.S.)
Kiritimati (Christmas)
Johnston Atoll (U.S.)
Kaua'i
O'ahu
Honolulu
Maui
Hawai'i (U.S.)
Avarua
Society Islands
Tahiti
Papeete
Austral Islands
Marquesas Islands
Chatham Is. (N.Z.)

Australia:

Darwin
Melville I.
Katherine
Gulf of Carpentaria
Cape York
Weipa
Cairns
Townsville
Great Barrier Reef
Mount Isa
Mackay
Longreach
Rockhampton
Bundaberg
Charleville
Maryborough
Brisbane
Southport
Toowoomba
Bourke
Tamworth
Newcastle
Orange
Wollongong
Wagga Wagga
Sydney
Albury
Canberra
Broken Hill
Whyalla
Port Lincoln
Adelaide
Geelong
Ballarat
Bendigo
Melbourne
Launceston
Hobart
Tasmania
Bass Strait
Kangaroo I.
Woomera
Coober Pedy
Alice Springs
Ayers Rock (Uluru)
Lake Eyre Lowest Point in Australia
Simpson Desert
Great Artesian Basin
Great Dividing Range
Mt. Kosciusko 2228 m (7,310 ft) Highest Point in Australia
Great Sandy Desert
Gibson Desert
Great Victoria Desert
Nullarbor Plain
Great Australian Bight
Newman
Port Hedland
Broome
Cape Leveque
Dampier
North West Cape
Carnarvon
Geraldton
Kalgoorlie-Boulder
Esperance
Perth
Bunbury
Albany
Cape Leeuwin
Western Australia
Northern Territory
Queensland
South Australia
New South Wales
Victoria
Murray
Darling

Papua New Guinea:

New Guinea
Mt. Wilhelm 4509 m (14,793 ft)
Admiralty Is.
Bismarck Arch.
New Ireland
New Britain

New Zealand:

North Island
Auckland
Tauranga
Hamilton
Gisborne
New Plymouth
Napier
Nelson
Wellington
Cook Strait
South Island
Christchurch
Mt. Cook 3754 m (12,316 ft)
Dunedin
Invercargill
Stewart I.

Solomon Is.

Scale:
0   400   800   1,200 Miles
0   400   800   1,200   1,600 Kilometers

Patrick Henry's Speech to the Virginia Convention

The following is an excerpt from Patrick Henry's speech to the Virginia Convention, which met at St. John's Church in Richmond, on Mar. 23, 1775, to react to British oppression.

Gentlemen may cry, peace, peace—but there is no peace. The war is actually begun! The next gale that sweeps from the north will bring to our ears the clash of resounding arms! Our brethren are already in the field! Why stand we here idle? What is it that gentlemen wish? What would they have? Is life so dear, or peace so sweet, as to be purchased at the price of chains and slavery? Forbid it, Almighty God! I know not what course others may take; but as for me, give me liberty, or give me death!

Adoption of the Declaration of Independence

On June 7, 1776, Richard Henry Lee, who had issued the first call for a congress of the colonies, introduced in the Continental Congress at Philadelphia a resolution declaring "that these United Colonies are, and of right ought to be, free and independent states, that they are absolved from all allegiance to the British Crown, and that all political connection between them and the state of Great Britain is, and ought to be, totally dissolved."

The resolution, seconded by John Adams on behalf of the Massachusetts delegation, came up again June 11 when a committee of five chaired by Thomas Jefferson (VA) was appointed to express the purpose of the resolution in a declaration of independence. The other four were John Adams, Benjamin Franklin (PA), Robert R. Livingston (NY), and Roger Sherman (CT).

Drafting the Declaration was assigned to Jefferson, who worked on a portable desk of his own construction in a room at Market and 7th St. The committee reported the result on June 28, 1776. The members of the Congress suggested a number of changes, which Jefferson called "deplorable." They did not approve Jefferson's arraignment of the British people and King George III for encouraging and fostering the slave trade, which Jefferson called "an execrable commerce." They eliminated 630 words and added 146, leaving 1,322 words in the final draft. In its final form, capitalization was erratic. Jefferson had written that men were endowed with "inalienable" rights; in the final copy it came out as "unalienable" and has been thus ever since.

The Lee-Adams resolution of independence was adopted by 12 yeas on July 2—the actual date of the act of independence. The Declaration, which explains the act, was adopted July 4.

After the Declaration was adopted, July 4, 1776, it was turned over to printer John Dunlap to be printed on broadsides. The original copy was lost and one of his broadsides was attached to a page in the journal of the Congress. It was read aloud July 8 in Philadelphia, PA; Easton, PA; and Trenton, NJ. On July 9, it was read by order of Gen. George Washington to the troops assembled on the Common in New York City (now City Hall Park).

The Continental Congress of July 19, 1776, adopted the following resolution:

"Resolved, That the Declaration passed on the 4th, be fairly engrossed on parchment with the title and stile of 'The Unanimous Declaration of the thirteen United States of America' and that the same, when engrossed, be signed by every member of Congress." (Engrossing meant clearly writing out an official document.)

Not all delegates who signed the engrossed Declaration had been present on July 4. Among them were Robert Morris (PA), William Williams (CT), and Samuel Chase (MD), who signed on Aug. 2. Oliver Wolcott (CT), George Wythe (VA), Richard Henry Lee (VA), and Elbridge Gerry (MA) signed in Aug. and Sept.; Matthew Thornton (NH) joined the Congress Nov. 4 and signed later. Thomas McKean (DE) rejoined Washington's army before signing and said later that he signed in 1781.

Charles Carroll of Carrollton was appointed a delegate by Maryland on July 4, 1776, presented his credentials July 18, and signed the engrossed Declaration on Aug. 2. Born Sept. 19, 1737, he was 95 years old and the last surviving signer when he died Nov. 14, 1832.

Two Pennsylvania delegates who did not support the Declaration July 4, 1776, were replaced. The four New York delegates did not have authority from their state to vote on July 4. On July 9, the New York state convention authorized its delegates to approve the Declaration, and the Congress was so notified on July 15, 1776. The four signed the Declaration on Aug. 2.

Declaration of Independence

The Declaration of Independence was adopted by the Continental Congress in Philadelphia on July 4, 1776. John Hancock was president of the Congress, and Charles Thomson was secretary. A copy of the Declaration, engrossed (i.e., written in a clear hand) on parchment, was signed by members of Congress on and after Aug. 2, 1776. On Jan. 18, 1777, Congress ordered that "an authenticated copy, with the names of the members of Congress subscribing the same, be sent to each of the United States, and that they be desired to have the same put on record." Authenticated copies were printed in broadside form in Baltimore, where the Continental Congress was then in session. The following text is that of the original printed by John Dunlap in Philadelphia for the Continental Congress. The original is on display at the National Archives in Washington, DC.

In CONGRESS, July 4, 1776.
A DECLARATION
By the REPRESENTATIVES of the
UNITED STATES OF AMERICA,
In GENERAL CONGRESS assembled.

When in the Course of human Events, it becomes necessary for one People to dissolve the Political Bands which have connected them with another, and to assume among the Powers of the Earth, the separate and equal Station to which the Laws of Nature and of Nature's God entitle them, a decent Respect to the Opinions of Mankind requires that they should declare the causes which impel them to the Separation.

We hold these Truths to be self-evident, that all Men are created equal, that they are endowed by their Creator with certain unalienable Rights, that among these are Life, Liberty, and the Pursuit of Happiness—That to secure these Rights, Governments are instituted among Men, deriving their just Powers from the Consent of the Governed, that whenever any Form of Government becomes destructive of these Ends, it is the Right of the People to alter or to abolish it, and to institute new Government, laying its Foundation on such Principles, and organizing its Powers in such Form, as to them shall seem most likely to effect their Safety and Happiness. Prudence, indeed, will dictate that Governments long established should not be changed for light and transient Causes; and accordingly all Experience hath shewn, that Mankind are more disposed to suffer, while Evils are sufferable, than to right themselves by abolishing the Forms to which they are accustomed. But when a long Train of Abuses and Usurpations, pursuing invariably the same Object, evinces a Design to reduce them under absolute Despotism, it is their Right, it is their Duty, to throw off such Government, and to provide new Guards for their future Security. Such has been the patient Sufferance of these Colonies; and such is now the Necessity which constrains them to alter their former Systems of Government. The History of the present King of Great Britain is a History of repeated Injuries and Usurpations, all having in direct Object the Establishment of an absolute Tyranny over these States. To prove this, let Facts be submitted to a candid World.

He has refused his Assent to Laws, the most wholesome and necessary for the public Good.

He has forbidden his Governors to pass Laws of immediate and pressing Importance, unless suspended in their Operation till his Assent should be obtained; and when so suspended, he has utterly neglected to attend to them.

He has refused to pass other Laws for the Accommodation of large Districts of People, unless those People would relinquish the Right of Representation in the Legislature, a Right inestimable to them, and formidable to Tyrants only.

He has called together Legislative Bodies at Places unusual, uncomfortable, and distant from the Depository of their Public Records, for the sole Purpose of fatiguing them into Compliance with his Measures.

He has dissolved Representative Houses repeatedly, for opposing with manly Firmness his Invasions on the Rights of the People.

He has refused for a long Time, after such Dissolutions, to cause others to be elected; whereby the Legislative Powers, incapable of Annihilation, have returned to the People at large for their exercise; the State remaining in the mean time exposed to all the Dangers of Invasion from without, and Convulsions within.

He has endeavoured to prevent the Population of these States; for that Purpose obstructing the Laws for Naturalization of Foreigners; refusing to pass others to encourage their Migrations hither, and raising the Conditions of new Appropriations of Lands.

He has obstructed the Administration of Justice, by refusing his Assent to Laws for establishing Judiciary Powers.

He has made Judges dependent on his Will alone, for the Tenure of their Offices, and the Amount and payment of their Salaries.

He has erected a Multitude of new Offices, and sent hither Swarms of Officers to harrass our People, and eat out their Substance.

He has kept among us, in Times of Peace, Standing Armies, without the consent of our Legislatures.

He has affected to render the Military independent of, and superior to the Civil Power.

He has combined with others to subject us to a Jurisdiction foreign to our Constitution, and unacknowledged by our Laws; giving his Assent to their Acts of pretended Legislation:

For Quartering large bodies of armed troops among us:

For protecting them, by a mock Trial, from Punishment for any Murders which they should commit on the Inhabitants of these States:

For cutting off our Trade with all Parts of the World:

For imposing Taxes on us without our Consent:

For depriving us, in many Cases, of the Benefits of Trial by Jury:

For transporting us beyond Seas to be tried for pretended Offences:

For abolishing the free System of English Laws in a neighbouring Province, establishing therein an arbitrary Government, and enlarging its Boundaries, so as to render it at once an Example and fit Instrument for introducing the same absolute Rule into these Colonies:

For taking away our Charters, abolishing our most valuable Laws, and altering fundamentally the Forms of our Governments:

For suspending our own Legislatures, and declaring themselves invested with Power to legislate for us in all Cases whatsoever.

He has abdicated Government here, by declaring us out of his Protection and waging War against us.

He has plundered our Seas, ravaged our Coasts, burnt our towns, and destroyed the Lives of our People.

He is, at this Time, transporting large Armies of foreign Mercenaries to complete the works of Death, Desolation, and Tyranny, already begun with circumstances of Cruelty

and Perfidy, scarcely paralleled in the most barbarous Ages, and totally unworthy the Head of a civilized Nation.

He has constrained our fellow Citizens taken Captive on the high Seas to bear Arms against their Country, to become the Executioners of their Friends and Brethren, or to fall themselves by their Hands.

He has excited domestic Insurrections amongst us, and has endeavoured to bring on the Inhabitants of our Frontiers, the merciless Indian Savages, whose known Rule of Warfare, is an undistinguished Destruction, of all Ages, Sexes and Conditions.

In every stage of these Oppressions we have Petitioned for Redress in the most humble Terms: Our repeated Petitions have been answered only by repeated Injury. A Prince, whose Character is thus marked by every act which may define a Tyrant, is unfit to be the Ruler of a free People.

Nor have we been wanting in Attentions to our British Brethren. We have warned them from Time to Time of Attempts by their Legislature to extend an unwarrantable Jurisdiction over us. We have reminded them of the Circumstances of our Emigration and Settlement here. We have appealed to their native Justice and Magnanimity, and we have conjured them by the Ties of our common Kindred to disavow these Usurpations, which, would inevitably interrupt our Connections and Correspondence. They too have been deaf to the Voice of Justice and of Consanguinity. We must, therefore, acquiesce in the Necessity, which denounces our Separation, and hold them, as we hold the rest of Mankind, Enemies in War, in Peace, Friends.

We, therefore, the Representatives of the UNITED STATES OF AMERICA, in General Congress, Assembled, appealing to the Supreme Judge of the World for the Rectitude of our Intentions, do, in the Name, and by Authority of the good People of these Colonies, solemnly Publish and Declare, That these United Colonies are, and of Right ought to be, Free and Independent States; that they are absolved from all Allegiance to the British Crown, and that all political Connection between them and the State of Great Britain, is and ought to be totally dissolved; and that as Free and Independent States, they have full Power to levy War, conclude Peace, contract Alliances, establish Commerce, and to do all other Acts and Things which Independent States may of right do. And for the support of this declaration, with a firm Reliance on the Protection of Divine Providence, we mutually pledge to each other our lives, our Fortunes, and our sacred Honor.

JOHN HANCOCK, President.

Attest.

CHARLES THOMSON, Secretary.

Signers of the Declaration of Independence

Delegate (state)	Occupation	Birthplace	Born	Died
Adams, John (MA)	Lawyer	Braintree (Quincy), MA	Oct. 30, 1735	July 4, 1826
Adams, Samuel (MA)	Political leader	Boston, MA	Sept. 27, 1722	Oct. 2, 1803
Bartlett, Josiah (NH)	Physician, judge	Amesbury, MA	Nov. 21, 1729	May 19, 1795
Braxton, Carter (VA)	Farmer	Newington Plantation, VA	Sept. 10, 1736	Oct. 10, 1797
Carroll, Charles, of Carrollton (MD)	Merchant	Annapolis, MD	Sept. 19, 1737	Nov. 14, 1832
Chase, Samuel (MD)	Judge	Princess Anne, MD	Apr. 17, 1741	June 19, 1811
Clark, Abraham (NJ)	Surveyor	Elizabethtown, NJ	Feb. 15, 1726	Sept. 15, 1794
Clymer, George (PA)	Merchant	Philadelphia, PA	Mar. 16, 1739	Jan. 23, 1813
Ellery, William (RI)	Lawyer	Newport, RI	Dec. 22, 1727	Feb. 15, 1820
Floyd, William (NY)	Soldier	Brookhaven, NY	Dec. 17, 1734	Aug. 4, 1821
Franklin, Benjamin (PA)	Printer, publisher	Boston, MA	Jan. 17, 1706	Apr. 17, 1790
Gerry, Elbridge (MA)	Merchant	Marblehead, MA	July 17, 1744	Nov. 23, 1814
Gwinnett, Button (GA)	Merchant	Gloucester, England	c. 1735	May 19, 1777
Hall, Lyman (GA)	Physician	Wallingford, CT	Apr. 12, 1724	Oct. 19, 1790
Hancock, John (MA)	Merchant	Braintree (Quincy), MA	Jan. 12, 1737	Oct. 8, 1793
Harrison, Benjamin (VA)	Farmer	Charles City County, VA	Apr. 5, 1726	Apr. 24, 1791
Hart, John (NJ)	Farmer	Stonington, CT	c. 1711	May 11, 1779
Hewes, Joseph (NC)	Merchant	Kingston, NJ	Jan. 23, 1730	Nov. 10, 1779
Heyward, Thomas, Jr. (SC)	Lawyer, farmer	St. Luke's Parish, SC	July 28, 1746	Mar. 6, 1809
Hooper, William (NC)	Lawyer	Boston, MA	June 17, 1742	Oct. 14, 1790
Hopkins, Stephen (RI)	Judge, educator	Providence, RI	Mar. 7, 1707	July 13, 1785
Hopkinson, Francis (NJ)	Judge, author	Philadelphia, PA	Oct. 2, 1737	May 9, 1791
Huntington, Samuel (CT)	Judge	Windham, CT	July 3, 1731	Jan. 5, 1796
Jefferson, Thomas (VA)	Lawyer	Shadwell, VA	Apr. 13, 1743	July 4, 1826
Lee, Francis Lightfoot (VA)	Farmer	Westmoreland County, VA	Oct. 14, 1734	Jan. 11, 1797
Lee, Richard Henry (VA)	Farmer	Westmoreland County, VA	Jan. 20, 1732	June 19, 1794
Lewis, Francis (NY)	Merchant	Llandaff, Wales	Mar. 21, 1713	Dec. 31, 1802
Livingston, Philip (NY)	Merchant	Albany, NY	Jan. 15, 1716	June 12, 1778
Lynch, Thomas, Jr. (SC)	Farmer	Winyah, SC	Aug. 5, 1749	(at sea) 1779
McKean, Thomas (DE)	Lawyer	New London, PA	Mar. 19, 1734	June 24, 1817
Middleton, Arthur (SC)	Farmer	Charleston, SC	June 26, 1742	Jan. 1, 1787
Morris, Lewis (NY)	Farmer	Morrisania (Bronx County), NY	Apr. 8, 1726	Jan. 22, 1798
Morris, Robert (PA)	Merchant	Liverpool, England	Jan. 31, 1734	May 8, 1806
Morton, John (PA)	Judge	Ridley, PA	c. 1724	Apr. 1777
Nelson, Thomas, Jr. (VA)	Farmer	Yorktown, VA	Dec. 26, 1738	Jan. 4, 1789
Paca, William (MD)	Judge	Abingdon, MD	Oct. 31, 1740	Oct. 23, 1799
Paine, Robert Treat (MA)	Judge	Boston, MA	Mar. 11, 1731	May 12, 1814
Penn, John (NC)	Lawyer	Caroline County, VA	May 17, 1741	Sept. 14, 1788
Read, George (DE)	Judge	Cecil County, MD	Sept. 18, 1733	Sept. 21, 1798
Rodney, Caesar (DE)	Judge	Dover, DE	Oct. 7, 1728	June 29, 1784
Ross, George (PA)	Judge	New Castle, DE	May 10, 1730	July 14, 1779
Rush, Benjamin (PA)	Physician	Byberry (Philadelphia), PA	Jan. 4, 1746	Apr. 19, 1813
Rutledge, Edward (SC)	Lawyer	Charleston, SC	Nov. 23, 1749	Jan. 23, 1800
Sherman, Roger (CT)	Lawyer	Newton, MA	Apr. 19, 1721	July 23, 1793
Smith, James (PA)	Lawyer	Northern Ireland	c. 1719	July 11, 1806
Stockton, Richard (NJ)	Lawyer	Princeton, NJ	Oct. 1, 1730	Feb. 28, 1781
Stone, Thomas (MD)	Lawyer	Charles County, MD	c. 1743	Oct. 5, 1787
Taylor, George (PA)	Ironmaster	Ireland	c. 1716	Feb. 23, 1781
Thornton, Matthew (NH)	Physician	Ireland	c. 1714	June 24, 1803
Walton, George (GA)	Judge	Cumberland County, VA	c. 1741	Feb. 2, 1804
Whipple, William (NH)	Merchant, judge	Kittery, ME	Jan. 14, 1730	Nov. 28, 1785
Williams, William (CT)	Merchant	Lebanon, CT	Apr. 8, 1731	Aug. 2, 1811
Wilson, James (PA)	Judge	Carskerdo, Scotland	Sept. 14, 1742	Aug. 21, 1798
Witherspoon, John (NJ)	Clergyman, educator	Gifford, Scotland	Feb. 5, 1723	Nov. 15, 1794
Wolcott, Oliver (CT)	Judge	Windsor, CT	Nov. 20, 1726	Dec. 1, 1797
Wythe, George (VA)	Lawyer	Elizabeth City County, VA	c. 1726	June 8, 1806

Origin of the Constitution

The War of Independence was conducted by delegates from the original 13 states, who composed the Congress of the United States of America, known as the Continental Congress. In 1777 the Congress submitted to the legislatures of the states the Articles of Confederation and Perpetual Union, which were ratified by New Hampshire, Massachusetts, Rhode Island, Connecticut, New York, New Jersey, Pennsylvania, Delaware, Virginia, North Carolina, South Carolina, Georgia, and finally, in 1781, Maryland.

The first article read: "The stile of this confederacy shall be the United States of America." This did not signify a sovereign nation, because the states delegated only those powers they could not handle individually, such as to wage war, make treaties, and contract debts for general expenses (e.g., paying the army). Taxes for payment of such debts were levied by the individual states. The president signed himself "President of the United States in Congress assembled," but here the United States were considered in the plural, a cooperating group.

When the war was over, it became evident that a stronger federal union was needed. The Congress left the initiative to the legislatures. Virginia in Jan. 1786 appointed commissioners to meet with representatives of other states; delegates from Virginia, Delaware, New York, New Jersey, and Pennsylvania met at Annapolis. Alexander Hamilton prepared their call asking delegates from all states to meet in Philadelphia in May 1787 "to render the Constitution of the federal government adequate to the exigencies of the union." Congress endorsed the plan on Feb. 21, 1787. Delegates were appointed by all states except Rhode Island.

The convention was called for May 14, 1787, but a quorum was not present until May 25. George Washington was chosen president (presiding officer). The states certified 65 delegates, but 10 did not attend. The work was done by 55, not all of whom were present at all sessions. Of the 55 attending delegates, 39 signed Sept. 17, 1787, some with reservations, and 16 failed to sign. Some historians have said 74 delegates (nine more than the 65 actually certified) were named, and 19 failed to attend. These additional persons refused the appointment, were never delegates, and were never counted as absentees. Washington sent the Constitution to Congress, and that body, Sept. 28, 1787, ordered it sent to the legislatures, "in order to be submitted to a convention of delegates chosen in each state by the people thereof."

The Constitution was ratified by votes of state conventions as follows: Delaware, Dec. 7, 1787, unanimous; Pennsylvania, Dec. 12, 1787, 46 to 23; New Jersey, Dec. 18, 1787, unanimous; Georgia, Jan. 2, 1788, unanimous; Connecticut, Jan. 9, 1788, 128 to 40; Massachusetts, Feb. 6, 1788, 187 to 168; Maryland, Apr. 28, 1788, 63 to 11; South Carolina, May 23, 1788, 149 to 73; New Hampshire, June 21, 1788, 57 to 46; Virginia, June 25, 1788, 89 to 79; New York, July 26, 1788, 30 to 27. Nine states were needed to establish the operation of the Constitution "between the states so ratifying the same," and New Hampshire was the ninth state. The government did not declare the Constitution in effect until the first Wednesday in Mar. 1789, which was Mar. 4. After that, North Carolina ratified it on Nov. 21, 1789, 194 to 77; and Rhode Island, May 29, 1790, 34 to 32. Vermont in convention ratified it on Jan. 10, 1791, and by act of Congress approved on Feb. 18, 1791, was admitted into the Union as the 14th state, Mar. 4, 1791.

Constitution of the United States

The text of the Constitution given here (except for Amendment XXVII) is from the pocket-size edition of the Constitution published by the U.S. Government Printing Office as a result of a congressional resolution to print the Constitution in its original form as amended through July 5, 1971. *Text in brackets* indicates that an item has been superseded or amended, or provides background information. **Boldface text** preceding an article, section, or amendment is a brief summary, added by *The World Almanac*.

The Original 7 Articles

PREAMBLE

We, the People of the United States, in Order to form a more perfect Union, establish Justice, insure domestic Tranquility, provide for the common defence, promote the general Welfare, and secure the Blessings of Liberty to ourselves and our Posterity, do ordain and establish this Constitution for the United States of America.

ARTICLE I.

Section 1—Legislative powers; in whom vested.

All legislative Powers herein granted shall be vested in a Congress of the United States, which shall consist of a Senate and House of Representatives.

Section 2—House of Representatives, how and by whom chosen. Qualifications of a Representative. Representatives and direct taxes, how apportioned. Enumeration. Vacancies to be filled. Power of choosing officers, and of impeachment.

The House of Representatives shall be composed of Members chosen every second Year by the People of the several States, and the Electors in each State shall have the Qualifications requisite for Electors of the most numerous Branch of the State Legislature.

No Person shall be a Representative who shall not have attained to the Age of twenty five Years, and been seven Years a Citizen of the United States, and who shall not, when elected, be an Inhabitant of that State in which he shall be chosen.

[Representatives and direct taxes shall be apportioned among the several States which may be included within this Union, according to their respective Numbers, which shall be determined by adding to the whole Number of free Persons, including those bound to Service for a Term of Years, and excluding Indians not taxed, three-fifths of all other persons.] [The previous sentence was superseded by Amendment XIV, section 2.] The actual Enumeration shall be made within three Years after the first Meeting of the Congress of the United States, and within every subsequent Term of ten Years, in such Manner as they shall by Law direct. The Number of Representatives shall not exceed one for every thirty Thousand, but each State shall have at Least one Representative; and until such enumeration shall be made, the State of New Hampshire shall be entitled to chuse three, Massachusetts eight, Rhode-Island and Providence Plantations one, Connecticut five, New-York six, New Jersey four, Pennsylvania eight, Delaware one, Maryland six, Virginia ten, North Carolina five, South Carolina five, and Georgia three.

When vacancies happen in the Representation from any State, the Executive Authority thereof shall issue Writs of Election to fill such Vacancies.

The House of Representatives shall chuse their Speaker and other Officers; and shall have the sole Power of Impeachment.

Section 3—Senators, how and by whom chosen. How classified. Qualifications of a Senator. President of the Senate, his right to vote. President pro tem., and other officers of the Senate, how chosen. Power to try impeachments. When President is tried, Chief Justice to preside. Sentence.

The Senate of the United States shall be composed of two Senators from each State, *[chosen by the Legislature thereof] [The preceding five words were superseded by Amendment XVII.]* for six Years; and each Senator shall have one Vote.

Immediately after they shall be assembled in Consequence of the first Election, they shall be divided as equally as may be into three Classes. The Seats of the Senators of the first Class shall be vacated at the Expiration of the second Year, of the second Class at the Expiration of the fourth Year, and of the third Class at the Expiration of the Sixth year, so that one-third may be chosen every second Year; *[and if Vacancies happen by Resignation, or otherwise, during the Recess of the Legislature of any State, the Executive thereof may make temporary Appointments until the next Meeting of the Legislature, which shall then fill such Vacancies.] [The words in brackets were superseded by Amendment XVII.]*

No Person shall be a Senator who shall not have attained to the Age of thirty Years, and been nine Years a Citizen of the United States, and who shall not, when elected, be an Inhabitant of that State for which he shall be chosen.

The Vice President of the United States shall be President of the Senate, but shall have no Vote, unless they be equally divided.

The Senate shall chuse their other Officers, and also a President pro tempore, in the absence of the Vice President, or when he shall exercise the Office of President of the United States.

The Senate shall have the sole Power to try all Impeachments. When sitting for that Purpose, they shall be on Oath or Affirmation. When the President of the United States is tried, the Chief Justice shall preside: And no Person shall be convicted without the Concurrence of two thirds of the Members present.

Judgment in Cases of Impeachment shall not extend further than to removal from Office, and disqualification to hold and enjoy any Office of honor, Trust or Profit under the United States: but the Party convicted shall nevertheless be liable and subject to Indictment, Trial, Judgment and Punishment, according to Law.

Section 4—Times, etc., of holding elections, how prescribed. One session each year.

The Times, Places and Manner of holding Elections for Senators and Representatives, shall be prescribed in each State by the Legislature thereof; but the Congress may at any time by Law make or alter such Regulations, except as to the Place of Chusing Senators.

The Congress shall assemble at least once in every Year, and such Meeting shall be *[on the first Monday in December,] [The words in brackets were superseded by Amendment XX, section 2.]* unless they shall by Law appoint a different Day.

Section 5—Membership, quorum, adjournments, rules. Power to punish or expel. Journal. Time of adjournments, how limited, etc.

Each House shall be the Judge of the Elections, Returns and Qualifications of its own Members, and a Majority of each shall constitute a Quorum to do Business; but a smaller number may adjourn from day to day, and may be authorized to compel the Attendance of absent Members, in such manner, and under such Penalties as each House may provide.

Each House may determine the Rules of its Proceedings, punish its members for disorderly Behavior, and, with the Concurrence of two thirds, expel a Member.

Each House shall keep a Journal of its Proceedings, and from time to time publish the same, excepting such Parts as may in their Judgment require Secrecy; and the Yeas and Nays of the Members of either House on any question shall, at the Desire of one fifth of those Present, be entered on the Journal.

Neither House, during the Session of Congress, shall, without the Consent of the other, adjourn for more than three days, nor to any other Place than that in which the two Houses shall be sitting.

Section 6—Compensation, privileges, disqualifications in certain cases.

The Senators and Representatives shall receive a Compensation for their Services, to be ascertained by Law, and paid out of the Treasury of the United States. They shall in all Cases, except Treason, Felony and Breach of the Peace, be privileged from Arrest during their Attendance at the Session of their respective Houses, and in going to and returning from the same; and for any Speech or Debate in either House, they shall not be questioned in any other Place.

No Senator or Representative shall, during the Time for which he was elected, be appointed to any civil Office under the Authority of the United States, which shall have been created, or the Emoluments whereof shall have been encreased during such time; and no Person holding any Office under the United States, shall be a Member of either House during his Continuance in Office.

Section 7—House to originate all revenue bills. Veto. Bill may be passed by two-thirds of each House, notwithstanding, etc. Bill, not returned in ten days, to become a law. Provisions as to orders, concurrent resolutions, etc.

All bills for raising Revenue shall originate in the House of Representatives; but the Senate may propose or concur with Amendments as on other Bills.

Every Bill which shall have passed the House of Representatives and the Senate, shall, before it become a Law, be presented to the President of the United States; If he approve he shall sign it, but if not he shall return it, with his Objections to that House in which it shall have originated, who shall enter the Objections at large on their Journal, and proceed to reconsider it. If after such Reconsideration two thirds of that House shall agree to pass the Bill, it shall be sent, together with the Objections, to the other House, by which it shall likewise be reconsidered, and if approved by two thirds of that House, it shall become a Law. But in all such Cases the Votes of both Houses shall be determined by Yeas and Nays, and the Names of the Persons voting for and against the Bill shall be entered on the Journal of each House respectively. If any Bill shall not be returned by the President within ten Days (Sundays excepted) after it shall have been presented to him, the Same shall be a Law, in like Manner as if he had signed it, unless the Congress by their Adjournment prevent its Return, in which Case it shall not be a Law.

Every order, Resolution, or Vote to which the Concurrence of the Senate and House of Representatives may be necessary (except on a question of Adjournment) shall be presented to the President of the United States; and before the Same shall take Effect, shall be approved by him, or being disapproved by him, shall be repassed by two thirds of the Senate and House of Representatives, according to the Rules and Limitations prescribed in the Case of a Bill.

Section 8—Powers of Congress.

The Congress shall have Power To lay and collect Taxes, Duties, Imposts and Excises, to pay the Debts and provide for the common Defence and general Welfare of the United States; but all Duties, Imposts and Excises shall be uniform throughout the United States;

To borrow money on the credit of the United States;

To regulate Commerce with foreign Nations, and among the several States, and with the Indian Tribes;

To establish an uniform Rule of Naturalization, and uniform Laws on the subject of Bankruptcies throughout the United States;

To coin Money, regulate the Value thereof, and of foreign Coin, and fix the Standard of Weights and Measures;

To provide for the Punishment of counterfeiting the Securities and current Coin of the United States;

To establish Post Offices and post Roads;

To promote the Progress of Science and useful Arts, by securing for limited Times to Authors and Inventors the exclusive Right to their respective Writings and Discoveries;

To constitute Tribunals inferior to the supreme Court;

To define and punish Piracies and Felonies committed on the high Seas, and Offenses against the Law of Nations;

To declare War, grant Letters of Marque and Reprisal, and make Rules concerning Captures on Land and Water;

To raise and support Armies, but no Appropriation of Money to that Use shall be for a longer Term than two Years;

To provide and maintain a Navy;

To make Rules for the Government and Regulation of the land and naval Forces;

To provide for calling forth the Militia to execute the Laws of the Union, suppress Insurrections and repel Invasions;

To provide for organizing, arming, and disciplining the Militia, and for governing such Part of them as may be employed in the Service of the United States, reserving to the States respectively, the Appointment of the Officers, and the Authority of training the Militia according to the discipline prescribed by Congress;

To exercise exclusive Legislation in all Cases whatsoever, over such District (not exceeding ten Miles square) as may, by Cession of particular States, and the acceptance of Congress, become the Seat of the Government of the United States, and to exercise like Authority over all Places purchased by the Consent of the Legislature of the State in which the Same shall be, for the Erection of Forts, Magazines, Arsenals, dock-Yards, and other needful Buildings;—And

To make all Laws which shall be necessary and proper for carrying into Execution the foregoing Powers, and all other Powers vested by this Constitution in the Government of the United States, or in any Department or Officer thereof.

Section 9—Provision as to migration or importation of certain persons. Habeas corpus, bills of attainder, etc. Taxes, how apportioned. No export duty. No commercial preference. Money, how drawn from Treasury, etc. No titular nobility. Officers not to receive presents, etc.

The Migration or Importation of such Persons as any of the States now existing shall think proper to admit, shall not be prohibited by the Congress prior to the Year one thousand eight hundred and eight, but a tax or duty may be imposed on such Importation, not exceeding ten dollars for each Person.

The privilege of the Writ of Habeas Corpus shall not be suspended, unless when in Cases of Rebellion or Invasion the public Safety may require it.

No Bill of Attainder or ex post facto Law shall be passed.

[No capitation, or other direct, Tax shall be laid, unless in Proportion to the Census or Enumeration herein before directed to be taken.] [Words in brackets modified by Amendment XVI.]

No Tax or Duty shall be laid on Articles exported from any State.

No Preference shall be given by any Regulation of Commerce or Revenue to the Ports of one State over those of another: nor shall Vessels bound to, or from, one State, be obliged to enter, clear, or pay Duties in another.

No Money shall be drawn from the Treasury, but in Consequence of Appropriations made by Law; and a regular Statement and Account of the Receipts and Expenditures of all public Money shall be published from time to time.

No Title of Nobility shall be granted by the United States: and no Person holding any Office of Profit or Trust under them, shall, without the Consent of the Congress, accept of any present, Emolument, Office, or Title, of any kind whatever, from any King, Prince, or foreign State.

Section 10—States prohibited from the exercise of certain powers.

No State shall enter into any Treaty, Alliance, or Confederation; grant Letters of Marque and Reprisal; coin Money; emit Bills of Credit; make any Thing but gold and silver Coin a Tender in Payment of Debts; pass any Bill of Attainder, ex post facto Law, or Law impairing the Obligation of Contracts, or grant any Title of Nobility.

No State shall, without the Consent of the Congress, lay any Imposts or Duties on Imports or Exports, except what may be absolutely necessary for executing its inspection Laws: and the net Produce of all Duties and Imposts, laid by any State on Imports or Exports, shall be for the Use of the Treasury of the United States; and all such Laws shall be subject to the Revision and Control of the Congress.

No State shall, without the Consent of Congress, lay any duty of Tonnage, keep Troops, or Ships of War in time of Peace, enter into any Agreement or Compact with another State, or with a foreign Power, or engage in War, unless actually invaded, or in such imminent Danger as will not admit of delay.

ARTICLE II.

Section 1—President: his term of office. Electors of President; number and how appointed. Electors to vote on same day. Qualification of President. On whom his duties devolve in case of his removal, death, etc. President's compensation. His oath of office.

The executive Power shall be vested in a President of the United States of America. He shall hold his Office during the Term of four Years, and, together with the Vice President, chosen for the same Term, be elected, as follows.

Each State shall appoint, in such Manner as the Legislature thereof may direct, a Number of Electors, equal to the whole Number of Senators and Representatives to which the State may be entitled in the Congress: but no Senator or Representative, or Person holding an Office of Trust or Profit under the United States, shall be appointed an Elector.

[The Electors shall meet in their respective States, and vote by Ballot for two persons, of whom one at least shall not be an Inhabitant of the same State with themselves. And they shall make a List of all the Persons voted for, and of the Number of Votes for each; which List they shall sign and certify, and transmit sealed to the Seat of the Government of the United States, directed to the President of the Senate. The President of the Senate shall, in the Presence of the Senate and House of Representatives, open all the Certificates, and the Votes shall then be counted. The Person having the greatest Number of Votes shall be the President, if such Number be a Majority of the whole Number of Electors appointed; and if there be more than one who have such Majority, and have an equal Number of Votes, then the House of Representatives shall immediately chuse by Ballot one of them for President; and if no Person have a Majority, then from the five highest on the List the said House shall in like Manner chuse the President. But in chusing the President,

the Votes shall be taken by States, the Representation from each State having one Vote; a quorum for this Purpose shall consist of a Member or Members from two thirds of the States, and a Majority of all the States shall be necessary to a Choice. In every Case, after the Choice of the President, the Person having the greatest Number of Votes of the Electors shall be the Vice President. But if there should remain two or more who have equal Votes, the Senate shall chuse from them by Ballot the Vice-President.] [This clause was superseded by Amendment XII.]

The Congress may determine the Time of chusing the Electors, and the Day on which they shall give their Votes; which Day shall be the same throughout the United States.

No person except a natural born Citizen, or a Citizen of the United States, at the time of the Adoption of this Constitution, shall be eligible to the Office of President; neither shall any Person be eligible to that Office who shall not have attained to the Age of thirty-five Years, and been fourteen Years a Resident within the United States. [For qualification of the Vice President, see Amendment XII.]

[In Case of the Removal of the President from Office, or of his Death, Resignation, or Inability to discharge the Powers and Duties of the said Office, the same shall devolve on the Vice President, and the Congress may by Law, provide for the Case of Removal, Death, Resignation or Inability, both of the President and Vice President, declaring what Officer shall then act as President, and such Officer shall act accordingly, until the Disability be removed, or a President shall be elected.] [This clause was superseded by Amendment XXV.]

The President shall, at stated Times, receive for his Services, a Compensation, which shall neither be encreased nor diminished during the Period for which he shall have been elected, and he shall not receive within that Period any other Emolument from the United States, or any of them.

Before he enter on the Execution of his Office, he shall take the following Oath or Affirmation:–"I do solemnly swear (or affirm) that I will faithfully execute the Office of President of the United States, and will to the best of my Ability, preserve, protect and defend the Constitution of the United States."

Section 2—President to be Commander-in-Chief. He may require opinions of cabinet officers, etc., may pardon. Treaty-making power. Nomination of certain officers. When President may fill vacancies.

The President shall be Commander in Chief of the Army and Navy of the United States, and of the Militia of the several States, when called into the actual Service of the United States; he may require the Opinion in writing, of the principal Officer in each of the executive Departments, upon any subject relating to the Duties of their respective Offices, and he shall have Power to Grant Reprieves and Pardons for Offenses against the United States, except in Cases of Impeachment.

He shall have Power, by and with the Advice and Consent of the Senate, to make Treaties, provided two-thirds of the Senators present concur; and he shall nominate, and by and with the Advice and Consent of the Senate, shall appoint Ambassadors, other public Ministers and Consuls, Judges of the supreme Court, and all other Officers of the United States, whose Appointments are not herein otherwise provided for, and which shall be established by Law: but the Congress may by Law vest the Appointment of such inferior Officers, as they think proper, in the President alone, in the Courts of Law, or in the Heads of Departments.

The President shall have Power to fill up all Vacancies that may happen during the Recess of the Senate, by granting Commissions which shall expire at the End of their next Session.

Section 3—President shall communicate to Congress. He may convene and adjourn Congress, in case of disagreement, etc. Shall receive ambassadors, execute laws, and commission officers.

He shall from time to time give to the Congress Information of the State of the Union, and recommend to their Consideration such Measures as he shall judge necessary and expedient; he may, on extraordinary Occasions, convene both Houses, or either of them, and in Case of Disagreement between them, with Respect to the Time of Adjournment, he may adjourn them to such Time as he shall think proper; he shall receive Ambassadors and other public Ministers; he shall take Care that the Laws be faithfully executed, and shall Commission all the Officers of the United States.

Section 4—All civil offices forfeited for certain crimes.

The President, Vice President and all civil Officers of the United States, shall be removed from Office on Impeachment for, and Conviction of, Treason, Bribery, or other high Crimes and Misdemeanors.

ARTICLE III.

Section 1—Judicial powers, tenure. Compensation.

The judicial Power of the United States, shall be vested in one supreme Court, and in such inferior Courts as the Congress may from time to time ordain and establish. The Judges, both of the supreme and inferior Courts, shall hold their Offices during good Behaviour, and shall, at stated Times, receive for their Services, a Compensation, which shall not be diminished during their Continuance in Office.

Section 2—Judicial power; to what cases it extends. Original jurisdiction of Supreme Court; appellate jurisdiction. Trial by jury, etc. Trial, where.

The judicial Power shall extend to all Cases, in Law and Equity, arising under this Constitution, the Laws of the United States, and Treaties made, or which shall be made, under their Authority;–to all Cases affecting Ambassadors, other public Ministers and Consuls;–to all Cases of admiralty and maritime Jurisdiction;–to Controversies to which the United States shall be a Party;–to Controversies between two or more States; [–between a State and Citizens of another State;–] between Citizens of different States; –between Citizens of the same State claiming Lands under Grants of different States, [and between a State, or the Citizens thereof, and foreign States, Citizens or Subjects.] [This section is modified by Amendment XI.]

In all Cases affecting Ambassadors, other public Ministers and Consuls, and those in which a State shall be Party, the supreme Court shall have original Jurisdiction. In all the other Cases before mentioned, the supreme Court shall have appellate Jurisdiction, both as to Law and Fact, with such Exceptions, and under such Regulations as the Congress shall make.

The trial of all Crimes, except in Cases of Impeachment, shall be by Jury; and such Trial shall be held in the State where the said Crimes shall have been committed; but when not committed within any State, the Trial shall be at such Place or Places as the Congress may by Law have directed.

Section 3—Treason Defined. Proof of. Punishment of.

Treason against the United States, shall consist only in levying War against them, or in adhering to their Enemies, giving them Aid and Comfort. No Person shall be convicted of Treason unless on the Testimony of two Witnesses to the same overt Act, or on Confession in open Court.

The Congress shall have Power to declare the Punishment of Treason, but no Attainder of Treason shall work Corruption of Blood, or Forfeiture except during the Life of the Person attainted.

ARTICLE IV.

Section 1—Each State to give credit to the public acts, etc., of every other State.

Full Faith and Credit shall be given in each State to the public Acts, Records, and judicial Proceedings of every other State. And the Congress may by general Laws prescribe the Manner in which such Acts, Records and Proceedings shall be proved, and the Effect thereof.

Section 2—Privileges of citizens of each State. Fugitives from justice to be delivered up. Persons held to service having escaped, to be delivered up.

The Citizens of each State shall be entitled to all Privileges and Immunities of Citizens in the several States.

A Person charged in any State with Treason, Felony, or other Crime, who shall flee from Justice, and be found in another State, shall on demand of the executive Authority of the State from which he fled, be delivered up, to be removed to the State having Jurisdiction of the Crime.

[No Person held to Service or Labour in one State, under the Laws thereof, escaping into another, shall, in Consequence of any Law or Regulation therein, be discharged from such Service or Labour, but shall be delivered up on Claim of the Party to whom such Service or Labour may be due.] [This clause was superseded by Amendment XIII.]

Section 3—Admission of new States. Power of Congress over territory and other property.

New States may be admitted by the Congress into this Union; but no new State shall be formed or erected within the Jurisdiction of any other State; nor any State be formed by the Junction of two or more States, or parts of States, without the Consent of the Legislatures of the States concerned as well as of the Congress.

The Congress shall have Power to dispose of and make all needful Rules and Regulations respecting the Territory or other Property belonging to the United States; and nothing in this Constitution shall be so construed as to Prejudice any Claims of the United States, or of any particular State.

Section 4—Republican form of government guaranteed. Each State to be protected.

The United States shall guarantee to every State in this Union a Republican Form of Government, and shall protect each of them against Invasion; and on Application of the Legislature, or of the Executive (when the Legislature cannot be convened) against domestic Violence.

ARTICLE V.

Constitution: how amended; proviso.

The Congress, whenever two-thirds of both Houses shall deem it necessary, shall propose Amendments to this Constitution, or, on the Application of the Legislatures of two-thirds of the several States, shall call a Convention for proposing Amendments, which, in either Case, shall be valid to all Intents and Purposes, as part of this Constitution, when ratified by the Legislatures of three-fourths of the several States, or by Conventions in three-fourths thereof, as the one or the other Mode of Ratification may be proposed by the Congress: Provided that no Amendment which may be made prior to the Year One thousand eight hundred and eight shall in any Manner affect the first and fourth Clauses in the Ninth Section of the first Article; and that no State, without its Consent, shall be deprived of its equal Suffrage in the Senate.

ARTICLE VI.

Certain debts, etc., declared valid. Supremacy of Constitution, treaties, and laws of the United States. Oath to support Constitution, by whom taken. No religious test.

All Debts contracted and Engagements entered into, before the Adoption of this Constitution, shall be as valid against the United States under this Constitution, as under the Confederation.

This Constitution, and the Laws of the United States which shall be made in Pursuance thereof; and all Treaties made, or which shall be made, under the Authority of the United States, shall be the supreme Law of the Land; and the Judges in every State shall be bound thereby, any Thing in the Constitution or Laws of any State to the Contrary notwithstanding.

The Senators and Representatives before mentioned, and the Members of the several State Legislatures, and all executive and judicial Officers, both of the United States and of the several States, shall be bound by Oath or Affirmation, to support this Constitution; but no religious Test shall ever be required as a Qualification to any Office or public Trust under the United States.

ARTICLE VII.

What ratification shall establish Constitution.

The Ratification of the Conventions of nine States shall be sufficient for the Establishment of this Constitution between the States so ratifying the Same.

Done in Convention by the Unanimous Consent of the States present the Seventeenth Day of September in the Year of our Lord one thousand seven hundred and Eighty seven and of the Independence of the United States of America the Twelfth.

In Witness whereof We have hereunto subscribed our Names.

G°. Washington, Presidt and deputy from Virginia

New Hampshire—John Langdon, Nicholas Gilman

Massachusetts—Nathaniel Gorham, Rufus King

Connecticut—Wm. Saml. Johnson, Roger Sherman

New York—Alexander Hamilton

New Jersey—Wil: Livingston, David Brearley, Wm. Paterson, Jona: Dayton

Pennsylvania—B Franklin, Thomas Mifflin, Robt. Morris, Geo. Clymer, Thos. FitzSimons, Jared Ingersoll, James Wilson, Gouv Morris

Delaware—Geo: Read, Gunning Bedford jun, John Dickinson, Richard Bassett, Jaco: Broom

Maryland—James McHenry, Dan of St Thos. Jenifer, Danl Carroll

Virginia—John Blair, James Madison Jr.

North Carolina—Wm. Blount, Rich'd Dobbs Spaight, Hu Williamson

South Carolina—J. Rutledge, Charles Cotesworth Pinckney, Charles Pinckney, Pierce Butler

Georgia—William Few, Abr Baldwin

Attest: William Jackson, Secretary.

The Bill of Rights
In force Dec. 15, 1791

[Congress, at its first session in New York, NY, submitted to the states 12 amendments Sept. 25, 1789, to clarify certain individual and state rights not named in the Constitution. They are generally called the Bill of Rights.]

[Influential in framing these amendments was the Declaration of Rights of Virginia, written by George Mason (1725-92) in 1776. Mason, a Virginia delegate to the Constitutional Convention, did not sign the Constitution and opposed its ratification on the ground that it did not sufficiently oppose slavery or safeguard individual rights.]

[In the preamble to the resolution offering the proposed amendments, Congress said: "The conventions of a number of the States having at the time of their adopting the Constitution, expressed a desire, in order to prevent misconstruction or abuse of its powers, that further declaratory and restrictive clauses should be added, and as extending the ground of public confidence in the government will best insure the beneficent ends of its institution, be it resolved," etc.]

[Ten of these amendments, now commonly known as one to 10 inclusive, but originally three to 12 inclusive, were ratified by the states as follows: New Jersey, Nov. 20, 1789; Maryland, Dec. 19, 1789; North Carolina, Dec. 22, 1789; South Carolina, Jan. 19, 1790; New Hampshire, Jan. 25, 1790; Delaware, Jan. 28, 1790; New York, Feb. 27, 1790; Pennsylvania, Mar. 10, 1790; Rhode Island, June 7, 1790; Vermont, Nov. 3, 1791; Virginia, Dec. 15, 1791; Massachusetts, Mar. 2, 1939; Georgia, Mar. 18, 1939; Connecticut, Apr. 19, 1939. These original 10 ratified amendments follow as Amendments I to X inclusive.]

[Of the two original proposed amendments that were not ratified promptly by the necessary number of states, the first related to apportionment of Representatives; the second, relating to compensation of members of Congress, was ratified in 1992 and became Amendment XXVII.]

AMENDMENT I.

Religious establishment prohibited. Freedom of speech, of press, right to assemble and to petition.

Congress shall make no law respecting an establishment of religion, or prohibiting the free exercise thereof; or abridging the freedom of speech, or of the press; or the right of the people peaceably to assemble, and to petition the Government for a redress of grievances.

AMENDMENT II.

Right to keep and bear arms.

A well regulated Militia, being necessary to the security of a free State, the right of the people to keep and bear Arms, shall not be infringed.

AMENDMENT III.

Conditions for quarters for soldiers.

No Soldier shall, in time of peace be quartered in any house, without the consent of the Owner, nor in time of war, but in a manner to be prescribed by law.

AMENDMENT IV.

Protection from unreasonable search and seizure.

The right of the people to be secure in their persons, houses, papers, and effects, against unreasonable searches and seizures, shall not be violated, and no Warrants shall issue, but upon probable cause, supported by Oath or affirmation, and particularly describing the place to be searched, and the persons or things to be seized.

AMENDMENT V.

Provisions concerning prosecution and due process of law. Double jeopardy restriction. Private property not to be taken without compensation.

No person shall be held to answer for a capital, or otherwise infamous crime, unless on a presentment or indictment of a Grand Jury, except in cases arising in the land or naval forces, or in the Militia, when in actual service in time of War or public danger; nor shall any person be subject for the same offence to be twice put in jeopardy of life or limb; nor shall be compelled in any criminal case to be a witness against himself, nor be deprived of life, liberty, or property, without due process of law; nor shall private property be taken for public use, without just compensation.

AMENDMENT VI.

Right to speedy trial, witnesses, etc.

In all criminal prosecutions, the accused shall enjoy the right to a speedy and public trial, by an impartial jury of the State and district wherein the crime shall have been committed, which district shall have been previously ascertained by law, and to be informed of the nature and cause of the accusation; to be confronted with the witnesses against him; to have compulsory process for obtaining witnesses in his favor, and to have the Assistance of Counsel for his defence.

AMENDMENT VII.

Right of trial by jury.

In suits at common law, where the value in controversy shall exceed twenty dollars, the right of trial by jury shall be preserved, and no fact tried by a jury, shall be otherwise reexamined in any Court of the United States, than according to the rules of the common law.

AMENDMENT VIII.

Excessive bail or fines; cruel and unusual punishment.

Excessive bail shall not be required, nor excessive fines imposed, nor cruel and unusual punishments inflicted.

AMENDMENT IX.

Rule of construction of Constitution.

The enumeration in the Constitution, of certain rights, shall not be construed to deny or disparage others retained by the people.

AMENDMENT X.

Rights of States under Constitution.

The powers not delegated to the United States by the Constitution, nor prohibited by it to the States, are reserved to the States respectively, or to the people.

Amendments Since the Bill of Rights

AMENDMENT XI.

Judicial powers construed.

The Judicial power of the United States shall not be construed to extend to any suit in law or equity, commenced or prosecuted against one of the United States by Citizens of another State, or by Citizens or Subjects of any Foreign State.

[This amendment was proposed to the Legislatures of the several States by the Third Congress on Mar. 4, 1794, and was declared to have been ratified in a message from the President to Congress, dated Jan. 8, 1798.]

[It was on Jan. 5, 1798, that Secretary of State Pickering received from 12 of the States authenticated ratifications, and informed President John Adams of that fact.]

[As a result of later research in the Department of State, it is now established that Amendment XI became part of the Constitution on Feb. 7, 1795, for on that date it had been ratified by 12 States as follows.]

[1. New York, Mar. 27, 1794. 2. Rhode Island, Mar. 31, 1794. 3. Connecticut, May 8, 1794. 4. New Hampshire, June 16, 1794. 5. Massachusetts, June 26, 1794. 6. Vermont, between Oct. 9, 1794, and Nov. 9, 1794. 7. Virginia, Nov. 18, 1794. 8. Georgia, Nov. 29, 1794. 9. Kentucky, Dec. 7, 1794. 10. Maryland, Dec. 26, 1794. 11. Delaware, Jan. 23, 1795. 12. North Carolina, Feb. 7, 1795]

[On June 1, 1796, more than a year after Amendment XI had become a part of the Constitution—but before anyone was officially aware of this—Tennessee had been admitted as a State; but not until Oct. 16, 1797, was a certified copy of the resolution of Congress proposing the amendment sent to the Governor of Tennessee, John Sevier, by Secretary of State Pickering, whose office was then at Trenton, New Jersey, because of the epidemic of yellow fever at Philadelphia; it seems, however, that the Legislature of Tennessee took no action on Amendment XI, owing doubtless to the fact that public announcement of its adoption was made soon thereafter.]

[Besides the necessary 12 States, one other, South Carolina, ratified Amendment XI, but this action was not taken until Dec. 4, 1797; the two remaining States, New Jersey and Pennsylvania, failed to ratify.]

AMENDMENT XII.

Manner of choosing President and Vice-President.

[Proposed by Congress Dec. 9, 1803; ratified June 15, 1804.]

The Electors shall meet in their respective states and vote by ballot for President and Vice-President, one of whom, at least, shall not be an inhabitant of the same state with themselves; they shall name in their ballots the person voted for as President, and in distinct ballots the person voted for as Vice-President, and they shall make distinct lists of all persons voted for as President, and of all persons voted for as Vice-President, and of the number of votes for each, which lists they shall sign and certify, and transmit sealed to the seat of the government of the United States, directed to the President of the Senate;—the President of the Senate shall, in presence of the Senate and House of Representatives, open all the certificates and the votes shall then be counted;—The person having the greatest number of votes for President, shall be the President, if such number be a majority of the whole number of Electors appointed; and if no person have such majority, then from the persons having the highest numbers not exceeding three on the list of those voted for as President, the House of Representatives shall choose immediately, by ballot, the President. But in choosing the President, the votes shall be taken by states, the representation from each state having one vote; a quorum for this purpose shall consist of a member or members from two-thirds of the states, and a majority of all the states shall be necessary to a choice. *[And if the House of Representatives shall not choose a President whenever the right of choice shall devolve upon them, before the fourth day of March next following, then the Vice-President shall act as President, as in the case of the death or other constitutional disability of the President.] [The words in brackets were superseded by Amendment XX, section 3.]* The person having the greatest number of votes as Vice-President, shall be the Vice-President, if such number be a majority of the whole number of Electors appointed, and if no person have a majority, then from the two highest numbers on the list, the Senate shall choose the Vice-President; a quorum for the purpose shall consist of two-thirds of the whole number of Senators, and a majority of the whole number shall be necessary to a choice. But no person constitutionally ineligible to the office of President shall be eligible to that of Vice-President of the United States.

THE RECONSTRUCTION AMENDMENTS

[Amendments XIII, XIV, and XV are commonly known as the Reconstruction Amendments, inasmuch as they followed the Civil War, and were drafted by Republicans who were bent on imposing their own policy of reconstruction on the South. Postbellum legislatures there—Mississippi, South Carolina, Georgia, for example—had set up laws which, it was charged, were contrived to perpetuate Negro slavery under other names.]

AMENDMENT XIII.

Slavery abolished.

[Proposed by Congress Jan. 31, 1865; ratified Dec. 6, 1865. The amendment, when first proposed by a resolution in Congress, was passed by the Senate, 38 to 6, on Apr. 8, 1864, but was defeated in the House, 95 to 66 on June 15, 1864. On reconsideration by the House, on Jan. 31, 1865, the resolution passed, 119 to 56. It was approved by President Lincoln on Feb. 1, 1865, although the Supreme Court had decided in 1798 that the President has nothing to do with the proposing of amendments to the Constitution, or their adoption.]

1. Neither slavery nor involuntary servitude, except as a punishment for crime whereof the party shall have been duly convicted, shall exist within the United States, or any place subject to their jurisdiction.

2. Congress shall have power to enforce this article by appropriate legislation.

AMENDMENT XIV.

Citizenship rights not to be abridged.

[The following amendment was proposed to the Legislatures of the several states by the 39th Congress, June 13, 1866, ratified July 9, 1868, and declared to have been ratified in a proclamation by the Secretary of State, July 28, 1868.]

[The 14th Amendment was adopted only by virtue of ratification subsequent to earlier rejections. Newly constituted legislatures in both North Carolina and South Carolina (respectively July 4 and 9, 1868), ratified the proposed amendment, although earlier legislatures had rejected the proposal. The Secretary of State issued a proclamation, which, though doubtful as to the effect of attempted withdrawals by Ohio and New Jersey, entertained no doubt as to the validity of the ratification by North and South Carolina. The following day (July 21, 1868), Congress passed a resolution which declared the 14th Amendment to be a part of the Constitution and directed the Secretary of State so to promulgate it. The Secretary waited, however, until the newly constituted Legislature of Georgia had ratified the amendment, subsequent to an earlier rejection, before the promulgation of the ratification of the new amendment.]

1. All persons born or naturalized in the United States, and subject to the jurisdiction thereof, are citizens of the United States and of the State wherein they reside. No State shall make or enforce any law which shall abridge the privileges or immunities of citizens of the United States; nor shall any State deprive any person of life, liberty, or property, without due process of law; nor deny to any person within its jurisdiction the equal protection of the laws.

2. Representatives shall be apportioned among the several States according to their respective numbers, counting the whole number of persons in each State, excluding Indians not taxed. But when the right to vote at any election for the choice of electors for President and Vice-President of the United States, Representatives in Congress, the Executive and Judicial officers of a State, or the members of the Legislature thereof, is denied to any of the male inhabitants of such State, being *[twenty-one] [The words in brackets were changed by Amendment XXVI.]* years of age, and citizens of the United States, or in any way abridged, except

for participation in rebellion, or other crime, the basis of representation therein shall be reduced in the proportion which the number of such male citizens shall bear to the whole number of male citizens twenty-one years of age in such State.

3. No person shall be a Senator or Representative in Congress, or elector of President and Vice-President, or hold any office, civil or military, under the United States, or under any State, who, having previously taken an oath, as a member of Congress, or as an officer of the United States, or as a member of any State legislature, or as an executive or judicial officer of any State, to support the Constitution of the United States, shall have engaged in insurrection or rebellion against the same, or given aid or comfort to the enemies thereof. But Congress may by a vote of two-thirds of each House, remove such disability.

4. The validity of the public debt of the United States, authorized by law, including debts incurred for payment of pensions and bounties for services in suppressing insurrection or rebellion, shall not be questioned. But neither the United States nor any State shall assume or pay any debt or obligation incurred in aid of insurrection or rebellion against the United States, or any claim for the loss or emancipation of any slave; but all such debts, obligations and claims shall be held illegal and void.

5. The Congress shall have power to enforce, by appropriate legislation, the provisions of this article.

AMENDMENT XV.

Race no bar to voting rights.

[The following amendment was proposed to the legislatures of the several States by the 40th Congress, Feb. 26, 1869, and ratified Feb. 3, 1870.]

1. The right of citizens of the United States to vote shall not be denied or abridged by the United States or by any State on account of race, color, or previous condition of servitude–

2. The Congress shall have power to enforce this article by appropriate legislation.

AMENDMENT XVI.

Income taxes authorized.

[Proposed by Congress July 12, 1909; ratified Feb. 3, 1913.]

The Congress shall have power to lay and collect taxes on incomes, from whatever source derived, without apportionment among the several States, and without regard to any census or enumeration.

AMENDMENT XVII.

United States Senators to be elected by direct popular vote.

[Proposed by Congress May 13, 1912; ratified Apr. 8, 1913.]

The Senate of the United States shall be composed of two Senators from each State, elected by the people thereof, for six years; and each Senator shall have one vote. The electors in each State shall have the qualifications requisite for electors of the most numerous branch of the State legislatures.

When vacancies happen in the representation of any State in the Senate, the executive authority of such State shall issue writs of election to fill such vacancies: *Provided,* That the legislature of any State may empower the executive thereof to make temporary appointments until the people fill the vacancies by election as the legislature may direct.

This amendment shall not be so construed as to affect the election or term of any Senator chosen before it becomes valid as part of the Constitution.

AMENDMENT XVIII.

Liquor prohibition amendment.

[Proposed by Congress Dec. 18, 1917; ratified Jan. 16, 1919. Repealed by Amendment XXI, effective Dec. 5, 1933.]

1. After one year from the ratification of this article the manufacture, sale, or transportation of intoxicating liquors within, the importation thereof into, or the exportation thereof from the United States and all territory subject to the jurisdiction thereof for beverage purposes is hereby prohibited.

2. The Congress and the several States shall have concurrent power to enforce this article by appropriate legislation.

3. This article shall be inoperative unless it shall have been ratified as an amendment to the Constitution by the legislatures of the several States as provided in the Constitution, within seven years from the date of the submission hereof to the States by the Congress.

[The total vote in the Senates of the various States was 1,310 for, 237 against—84.6% dry. In the lower houses of the States the vote was 3,782 for, 1,035 against—78.5% dry.

[The amendment ultimately was adopted by all the States except Rhode Island.]

AMENDMENT XIX.

Giving nationwide suffrage to women.

[Proposed by Congress June 4, 1919; ratified Aug. 18, 1920.]

The right of citizens of the United States to vote shall not be denied or abridged by the United States or by any State on account of sex.

Congress shall have power to enforce this Article by appropriate legislation.

AMENDMENT XX.

Terms of President and Vice President to begin on Jan. 20; those of Senators, Representatives, Jan. 3.

[Proposed by Congress Mar. 2, 1932; ratified Jan. 23, 1933.]

1. The terms of the President and Vice President shall end at noon on the 20th day of January, and the terms of Senators and Representatives at noon on the 3d day of January, of the years in which such terms would have ended if this article had not been ratified; and the terms of their successors shall then begin.

2. The Congress shall assemble at least once in every year, and such meeting shall begin at noon on the 3d day of January, unless they shall by law appoint a different day.

3. If, at the time fixed for the beginning of the term of the President, the President elect shall have died, the Vice President elect shall become President. If a President shall not have been chosen before the time fixed for the beginning of his term, or if the President elect shall have failed to qualify, then the Vice President elect shall act as President until a President shall have qualified; and the Congress may by law provide for the case wherein neither a President elect nor a Vice President elect shall have qualified, declaring who shall then act as President, or the manner in which one who is to act shall be selected, and such person shall act accordingly until a President or Vice President shall have qualified.

4. The Congress may by law provide for the case of the death of any of the persons from whom the House of Representatives may choose a President whenever the right of choice shall have devolved upon them, and for the case of the death of any of the persons from whom the Senate may choose a Vice President whenever the right of choice shall have devolved upon them.

5. Sections 1 and 2 shall take effect on the 15th day of October following the ratification of this article. *[Oct. 1933]*

6. This article shall be inoperative unless it shall have been ratified as an amendment to the Constitution by the legislatures of three-fourths of the several States within seven years from the date of its submission.

AMENDMENT XXI.

Repeal of Amendment XVIII.

[Proposed by Congress Feb. 20, 1933; ratified Dec. 5, 1933.]

1. The eighteenth article of amendment to the Constitution of the United States is hereby repealed.

2. The transportation or importation into any State, Territory, or possession of the United States for delivery or use therein of intoxicating liquors, in violation of the laws thereof, is hereby prohibited.

3. This article shall be inoperative unless it shall have been ratified as an amendment to the Constitution by conventions in the several States, as provided in the Constitution, within seven years from the date of the submission hereof to the States by the Congress.

AMENDMENT XXII.

Limiting Presidential terms of office.

[Proposed by Congress Mar. 24, 1947; ratified Feb. 27, 1951.]

1. No person shall be elected to the office of the President more than twice, and no person who has held the office of President, or acted as President, for more than two years of a term to which some other person was elected President shall be elected to the office of the President more than once. But this Article shall not apply to any person holding the office of President when this Article was proposed by the Congress, and shall not prevent any person who may be holding the office of President, or acting as President, during the term within which this Article becomes operative from holding the office of President or acting as President during the remainder of such term.

2. This article shall be inoperative unless it shall have been ratified as an amendment to the Constitution by the legislatures of three-fourths of the several States within seven years from the date of its submission to the States by the Congress.

AMENDMENT XXIII.

Presidential vote for District of Columbia.

[Proposed by Congress June 16, 1960; ratified Mar. 29, 1961.]

1. The District constituting the seat of Government of the United States shall appoint in such manner as the Congress may direct:

A number of electors of President and Vice President equal to the whole number of Senators and Representatives in Congress to which the District would be entitled if it were a State, but in no event more than the least populous State; they shall be in addition to those appointed by the States, but they shall be considered, for the purposes of the election of President and Vice President, to be electors appointed by a State; and they shall meet in the District and perform such duties as provided by the twelfth article of amendment.

2. The Congress shall have power to enforce this article by appropriate legislation.

AMENDMENT XXIV.

Barring poll tax in federal elections.

[Proposed by Congress Sept. 14, 1962; ratified Jan. 23, 1964.]

1. The right of citizens of the United States to vote in any primary or other election for President or Vice President, for electors for President or Vice President, or for Senator or Representative in Congress, shall not be denied or abridged by the United States or any State by reason of failure to pay any poll tax or other tax.

2. The Congress shall have power to enforce this article by appropriate legislation.

AMENDMENT XXV.

Presidential disability and succession.

[Proposed by Congress July 6, 1965; ratified Feb. 10, 1967.]

1. In case of the removal of the President from office or of his death or resignation, the Vice President shall become President.

2. Whenever there is a vacancy in the office of the Vice President, the President shall nominate a Vice President who shall take office upon confirmation by a majority vote of both houses of Congress.

3. Whenever the President transmits to the President pro tempore of the Senate and the Speaker of the House of Representatives his written declaration that he is unable to discharge the powers and duties of his office, and until he transmits to them a written declaration to the contrary, such powers and duties shall be discharged by the Vice President as Acting President.

4. Whenever the Vice President and a majority of either the principal officers of the executive departments or of such other body as Congress may by law provide, transmit to the President pro tempore of the Senate and the Speaker of the House of Representatives their written declaration that the President is unable to discharge the powers and duties of his office, the Vice President shall immediately assume the powers and duties of the office as Acting President.

Thereafter, when the President transmits to the President pro tempore of the Senate and the Speaker of the House of Representatives his written declaration that no inability exists, he shall resume the powers and duties of his office unless the Vice President and a majority of either the principal officers of the executive department or of such other body as Congress may by law provide, transmit within four days to the President pro tempore of the Senate and the Speaker of the House of Representatives their written declaration that the President is unable to discharge the powers and duties of his office. Thereupon Congress shall decide the issue, assembling within forty-eight hours for that purpose if not in session. If the Congress, within twenty-one days after receipt of the latter written declaration, or, if Congress is not in session, within twenty-one days after Congress is required to assemble, determines by two-thirds vote of both Houses that the President is unable to discharge the powers and duties of his office, the Vice President shall continue to discharge the same as Acting President; otherwise, the President shall resume the powers and duties of his office.

AMENDMENT XXVI.

Lowering voting age to 18 years.

[Proposed by Congress Mar. 23, 1971; ratified July 1, 1971.]

1. The right of citizens of the United States, who are eighteen years of age or older, to vote shall not be denied or abridged by the United States or by any State on account of age.

2. The Congress shall have the power to enforce this article by appropriate legislation.

AMENDMENT XXVII.

Congressional pay.

[Proposed by Congress Sept. 25, 1789; ratified May 7, 1992.]

No law, varying the compensation for the services of the Senators and Representatives, shall take effect, until an election of Representatives shall have intervened.

How a Bill Becomes a Law

A senator or representative introduces a bill in Congress by sending it to the clerk of the Senate or the House, who assigns it a number and title. This procedure is termed the first reading. The clerk then refers the bill to the appropriate committee of the Senate or House.

If the committee does not wish to consider the bill, it will table it. Otherwise, the committee holds hearings to listen to opinions and facts offered by members and other interested parties. The committee then debates the bill and may offer amendments. A vote is taken, and if favorable, the bill is sent back to the clerk of the Senate or House.

The clerk reads the bill to the house—the second reading. Members may then debate the bill and suggest amendments.

After debate and any amendments, the bill is given a third reading, simply of the title, and put to a voice or roll-call vote.

If the bill has passed, it goes to the other house, where it may be defeated or passed, with or without amendments. If defeated, the bill dies. If passed with amendments, a conference committee made up of members of both houses works out the differences between the two bills and arrives at a compromise.

After passage of the final version by both houses, the bill is sent to the president. If the president signs it, the bill becomes a law. The president may instead veto the bill by refusing to sign it and sending it back to the house where it originated, with reasons for the veto.

The president's objections are then read and debated, and a roll-call vote is taken. If the bill receives less than a two-thirds majority, it is defeated. If it receives at least two-thirds, it is sent to the other house. If that house also passes it by at least a two-thirds majority, the president's veto is overridden, and the bill becomes a law.

If the president neither signs nor vetoes the bill within 10 days—not including Sundays—it automatically becomes a law even without the president's signature. However, if Congress has adjourned within those 10 days, the bill is automatically killed; this indirect rejection is termed a pocket veto.

Note: Under the Line Item Veto Act, effective Jan. 1, 1997, the president was authorized, under certain circumstances, to veto a bill in part. The legislation was found unconstitutional by the Supreme Court, June 25, 1998.

Confederate States and Secession

The American Civil War (1861-65) grew out of sectional disputes over the continued existence of slavery in the South. Southern legislators contended that the states retained many rights, including the right to own slaves and the right to secede.

The war was not fought by state against state but by one federal regime against another. A Confederate government in Richmond assumed control over the economic, political, and military life of the seceding states, under protest from Georgia and South Carolina.

South Carolina voted unanimously in convention to secede from the Union, repealing its 1788 ratification of the U.S. Constitution on Dec. 20, 1860, to take effect on Dec. 24. Other states seceded in 1861. Their votes in conventions were: Mississippi, Jan. 9, 84-15; Florida, Jan. 10, 62-7; Alabama, Jan. 11, 61-39; Georgia, Jan. 19, 208-89; Louisiana, Jan. 26, 113-17; Texas, Feb. 1, 166-7, ratified by popular vote (34,794 to 11,325) Feb. 23; Virginia, Apr. 17, 88-55, ratified by popular vote (128,884 to 32,134) May 23; Arkansas, May 6,

69-1; Tennessee, May 7, ratified by popular vote (104,019 to 47,238) June 8; North Carolina, unanimous, May 20.

Missouri Unionists stopped secession in conventions Feb. 28 and Mar. 9, 1861. The legislature condemned secession Mar. 7. Under the protection of Confederate troops, secessionist members of the legislature adopted a resolution of secession at Neosho, Oct. 31. The Confederate Congress seated the secessionists' representatives.

Kentucky did not secede, and its government remained Unionist. In a part of the state occupied by Confederate troops, Kentuckians approved secession, and the Confederate Congress admitted their representatives.

The Maryland legislature voted against secession Apr. 27, 1861, 53-13. Delaware did not secede. Western Virginia held conventions at Wheeling, named a pro-Union governor on June 11, 1861, and was admitted to the Union as West Virginia on June 20, 1863. Its constitution provided for gradual abolition of slavery.

Confederate Government

Forty-two delegates from South Carolina, Georgia, Alabama, Mississippi, Louisiana, and Florida met in convention at Montgomery, AL, on Feb. 4, 1861. They adopted a provisional constitution of the Confederate States of America and elected Jefferson Davis (MS) as provisional president and Alexander H. Stephens (GA) as provisional vice president.

A permanent constitution was adopted Mar. 11. It banned African slave trade, but it did not bar interstate commerce in

slaves. On July 20 the Congress moved to Richmond, VA. Davis was elected president in Nov. 1861 and was inaugurated Feb. 22, 1862.

The Congress adopted a flag, consisting of a red field with a white stripe, and a blue jack with a circle of white stars. Later the more popular flag was the red field with blue diagonal crossbars that held 13 white stars, for the 11 states in the Confederacy plus Kentucky and Missouri.

The Gettysburg Address

Delivered by Pres. Abraham Lincoln at Gettysburg, PA, on Nov. 19, 1863. Five handwritten copies of the Gettysburg Address as made by Lincoln are known to exist. The text differs slightly between copies. The text of the Bliss version, considered the standard, is reproduced here.

Four score and seven years ago our fathers brought forth on this continent, a new nation, conceived in Liberty, and dedicated to the proposition that all men are created equal.

Now we are engaged in a great civil war, testing whether that nation, or any nation so conceived and so dedicated, can long endure. We are met on a great battle-field of that war. We have come to dedicate a portion of that field, as a final resting place for those who here gave their lives that that nation might live. It is altogether fitting and proper that we should do this.

But, in a larger sense, we can not dedicate—we can not consecrate—we can not hallow—this ground. The brave men, living and dead, who struggled here, have consecrated

it, far above our poor power to add or detract. The world will little note, nor long remember what we say here, but it can never forget what they did here.

It is for us the living, rather, to be dedicated here to the unfinished work which they who fought here have thus far so nobly advanced. It is rather for us to be here dedicated to the great task remaining before us—that from these honored dead we take increased devotion to that cause for which they gave the last full measure of devotion—that we here highly resolve that these dead shall not have died in vain—that this nation, under God, shall have a new birth of freedom—and that government of the people, by the people, for the people, shall not perish from the earth.

Presidential Oath of Office

The Constitution (Article II) directs that the president-elect shall take the following oath or affirmation to be inaugurated as president: "I do solemnly swear [affirm] that I will faithfully execute the office of President of the United States, and will, to the best of my ability, preserve, protect, and defend the Constitution of the United States."

Custom decrees the addition of the words "So help me God" at the end of the oath when taken by the president-elect, with the left hand on the Bible for the duration of the oath, and the right hand slightly raised.

Presidential Succession

If, by reason of death, resignation, removal from office, inability, or failure to qualify, there is neither a president nor vice president to discharge the powers and duties of the office of president, then the speaker of the House of Representatives shall upon his resignation as speaker and as representative, act as president. The same rule shall apply in the case of the death, resignation, removal from office, or inability of an individual acting as president.

If, at the time when a speaker is to begin the discharge of the powers and duties of the office of president, there is no speaker, or the speaker fails to qualify as acting president, then the president pro tempore of the Senate, upon his resignation as president pro tempore and as senator, shall act as president.

An individual acting as president shall continue to act until the expiration of the then current presidential term, except that (1) if his discharge of the powers and duties of the office is founded in whole or in part in the failure of both the president-elect and the vice president-elect to qualify, then

he shall act only until a president or vice president qualifies, and (2) if his discharge of the powers and duties of the office is founded in whole or in part on the inability of the president or vice president, then he shall act only until the removal of the disability of one of such individuals.

If, by reason of death, resignation, removal from office, or failure to qualify, there is no president pro tempore to act as president, then the officer of the United States who is highest on the following list, and who is not under any disability to discharge the powers and duties of president shall act as president: the secretaries of state, treasury, defense, attorney general, secretaries of interior, agriculture, commerce, labor, health and human services, housing and urban development, transportation, energy, education, veterans affairs, homeland security.

Legislation approved July 18, 1947; amended Sept. 9, 1965, Oct. 15, 1966, Aug. 4, 1977, Sept. 27, 1979, and Mar. 9, 2006. See also Constitutional Amendment XXV.

Origin of the United States National Motto

In God We Trust, designated as the U.S. National Motto by Congress in 1956, originated during the Civil War as an inscription for U.S. coins, although it was used by Francis Scott Key in a slightly different form when he wrote "The Star-Spangled Banner" in 1814. On Nov. 13, 1861, when Union morale had been shaken by battlefield defeats, the Rev. M. R. Watkinson, of Ridleyville, PA, wrote to Sec. of the Treasury Salmon P. Chase. "From my heart I have felt our national shame in disowning God as not the least of our present national disasters," the minister wrote,

suggesting "recognition of the Almighty God in some form on our coins." Sec. Chase ordered designs prepared with the inscription *In God We Trust* and backed coinage legislation that authorized use of this slogan. The motto first appeared on some U.S. coins in 1864, and it appeared sporadically on coins until 1938, after which all U.S. coins bear the inscription. A joint resolution passed by the 84th Congress and signed by Pres. Dwight D. Eisenhower July 30, 1956, declared *In God We Trust* the national motto of the United States.

The Great Seal of the U.S.

On July 4, 1776, the Continental Congress appointed a committee consisting of Benjamin Franklin, John Adams, and Thomas Jefferson "to bring in a device for a seal of the United States of America." The designs submitted by this and a subsequent committee were

considered unacceptable. After many delays, a third committee, appointed early in 1782, presented a design prepared by lawyer William Barton. Charles Thomson, the secretary of Congress, suggested certain changes, and Congress finally approved the design on June 20, 1782. The obverse side of the seal shows an American bald eagle. In its mouth is a ribbon bearing the motto *E Pluribus Unum* (out of many, one). In the eagle's talons are 13 arrows of war and an olive branch of peace. The reverse side shows an unfinished pyramid with an eye (Eye of Providence) above it.

The Flag of the U.S.—The Stars and Stripes

The 50-star flag of the United States was raised for the first time officially at 12:01 AM on July 4, 1960, at Ft. McHenry National Monument in Baltimore, MD. The 50th star had been added for Hawaii; a year earlier the 49th, for Alaska. Before that, no star had been added since 1912, when New Mexico and Arizona were admitted to the Union.

The true history of the Stars and Stripes has become so cluttered by myth and tradition that the facts are difficult, and in some cases impossible, to establish. For example, it is not certain who designed the Stars and Stripes, who made the first such flag, or even whether it ever flew during any battle of the American Revolution.

All agree, however, that the Stars and Stripes originated as the result of a resolution offered by the Marine Committee of the Second Continental Congress at Philadelphia and adopted on June 14, 1777. It read:

"Resolved: that the flag of the United States be thirteen stripes, alternate red and white; that the union be thirteen stars, white in a blue field, representing a new constellation."

Congress gave no hint as to the designer of the flag, no instructions as to the arrangement of the stars, and no information on its appropriate uses. Historians have been unable to find the original flag details.

The resolution establishing the flag was not even published until Sept. 2, 1777. Despite repeated requests, Washington did not get the flags until 1783, after the American Revolution was over. And there is no certainty that they were the Stars and Stripes.

Early Flags

Many historians consider the first flag of the U.S. to have been the Grand Union (sometimes called Great Union) flag, although the Continental Congress never officially adopted it. This flag was a modification of the British Meteor flag, which had the red cross of St. George and the white cross of St. Andrew combined in the blue canton. For the Grand Union flag, six horizontal stripes were imposed on the red field, dividing it into 13 alternating red and white stripes. On

Jan. 1, 1776, when the Continental Army came into formal existence, this flag was unfurled on Prospect Hill, Somerville, MA. Washington wrote that "we hoisted the Union Flag in compliment to the United Colonies."

One of several flags about which controversy has raged for years is at Easton, PA. Containing the devices of the national flag in reversed order, this flag has been in the public library at Easton for more than 150 years. Some contend that this flag was actually the first Stars and Stripes, first displayed on July 8, 1776. This flag has 13 red and white stripes in the canton, 13 white stars centered in a blue field.

A flag was hastily improvised from garments by the defenders of Ft. Schuyler at Rome, NY, Aug. 3-22, 1777. Historians believe it was the Grand Union Flag.

The Sons of Liberty had a flag of nine red and white stripes, to signify nine colonies, when they met in New York in 1765 to oppose the Stamp Tax. By 1775, the flag had grown to 13 red and white stripes, with a rattlesnake on it.

At Concord, Apr. 19, 1775, the minutemen from Bedford, MA, are said to have carried a flag having a silver arm with sword on a red field. At Cambridge, MA, the Sons of Liberty used a plain red flag with a green pine tree on it.

In June 1775, Washington went from Philadelphia to Boston to take command of the army, escorted to New York by the Philadelphia Light Horse Troop. It carried a yellow flag that had an elaborate coat of arms—the shield charged with 13 knots, the motto "For These We Strive"—and a canton of 13 blue and silver stripes.

In Feb. 1776, Col. Christopher Gadsden, a member of the Continental Congress, gave the South Carolina Provincial Congress a flag "such as is to be used by the commander-in-chief of the American Navy." It had a yellow field, with a rattlesnake about to strike and the words "Don't Tread on Me."

At the Battle of Bennington, Aug. 16, 1777, patriots used a flag of 7 white and 6 red stripes with a blue canton extending down 9 stripes and showing an arch of 11 white stars over the figure 76 and a star in each of the upper corners. The stars are seven-pointed. This flag is preserved in the historical museum in Bennington, VT.

At the Battle of Cowpens, Jan. 17, 1781, the 3rd Maryland Regiment is said to have carried a flag of 13 red and white stripes, with a blue canton containing 12 stars in a circle around one star.

Who Designed the Flag? No one knows for certain. Francis Hopkinson, designer of a naval flag, declared he had designed the flag and in 1781 asked Congress to reimburse him for his services. Congress did not do so. Dumas Malone of Columbia Univ. wrote, "This talented man . . . designed the American flag."

Who Called the Flag "Old Glory"? The flag is said to have been named Old Glory by William Driver, a sea captain of Salem, MA. One legend has it that when he raised the flag on his brig, the *Charles Doggett*, in 1824, he said: "I name thee Old Glory." But his daughter, who presented the flag to the Smithsonian Institution, said he named it at his 21st birthday celebration on Mar. 17, 1824, when his mother presented the homemade flag to him.

The Betsy Ross Legend. The widely publicized legend that Betsy Ross made the first Stars and Stripes in June 1776, at the request of a committee composed of George Washington, Robert Morris, and George Ross, an uncle, was first made public in 1870, by a grandson of Ross. Historians have been unable to find a historical record of such a meeting or committee.

Adding New Stars

The flag of 1777 was used until 1795. Then, on the admission of Vermont and Kentucky to the Union, Congress passed and Pres. Washington signed an act that after May 1, 1795, the flag should have 15 stripes, alternating red and white, and 15 white stars on a blue field.

When new states were admitted, it became evident that the flag would become burdened with stripes. Congress thereupon ordered that after July 4, 1818, the flag should have 13 stripes, symbolizing the 13 original states; that the union have 20 stars, and that whenever a new state was admitted a new star should be added on the July 4 following admission.

No law designates the permanent arrangement of the stars. However, since 1912, when a new state has been admitted, the new design has been announced by executive order. No star is specifically identified with any state.

Code of Etiquette for Display and Use of the U.S. Flag

Reviewed by National Flag Foundation

Although the Stars and Stripes originated in 1777, it was not until 146 years later that there was a serious attempt to establish a uniform code of etiquette for the U.S. flag. On Feb. 15, 1923, the War Department issued a circular on the rules of flag usage. These rules were adopted almost in their entirety June 14, 1923, by a conference of 68 patriotic organizations in Washington, DC. A joint resolution of Congress June 22, 1942, amended by Public Law 94-344, July 7, 1976, codified "existing rules and customs pertaining to the display and use of the flag." Military branches have their own codes of etiquette regarding the flag; this guide is for civilian purposes.

When to Display the Flag. The flag should be displayed on all days, especially on legal holidays and other special occasions, on official buildings when in use, in or near polling places on election days, and in or near schools when in session. Citizens may fly the flag at any time. It is customary to display it only from sunrise to sunset on buildings and on stationary flagstaffs in the open. It may be displayed at night, however, on special occasions, preferably lighted. The flag

now flies over the White House both day and night. It flies over the Senate wing of the Capitol when the Senate is in session and over the House wing when that body is in session. It flies day and night over the east and west fronts of the Capitol, without floodlights at night but receiving illumination from the Capitol Dome. It flies 24 hours a day at several other places, including the Ft. McHenry National Monument in Baltimore, where it inspired Francis Scott Key to write "The Star Spangled Banner." The flag also flies 24 hours a day, properly illuminated, at U.S. Customs ports of entry.

Flying the Flag at Half-Staff. Flying the flag at half-staff, that is, halfway up the staff, is a signal of mourning. The flag should be hoisted to the top of the staff for an instant before being lowered to half-staff. It should be hoisted to the peak again before being lowered for the day.

As provided by presidential proclamation, the flag should fly at half-staff for 30 days from the day of death of a president or former president; for 10 days from the day of death of a vice president, chief justice or retired chief justice of the U.S., or speaker of the House of Representatives; from day

of death until burial of an associate justice of the Supreme Court, cabinet member, former vice president, Senate president pro tempore, or majority or minority Senate or House leader; for a U.S. senator, representative, territorial delegate, or the resident commissioner of Puerto Rico, on day of death and the following day within the metropolitan area of the District of Columbia and from day of death until burial within the decedent's state, congressional district, territory or commonwealth; and for the death of the governor of a state, territory, or possession of the U.S., from day of death until burial.

On Memorial Day, the flag should fly at half-staff until noon and then be raised to the peak. The flag should also fly at half-staff on Korean War Veterans Armistice Day (July 27), National Pearl Harbor Remembrance Day (Dec. 7), and Peace Officers Memorial Day (May 15).

How to Fly the Flag. The flag should be hoisted briskly and lowered ceremoniously and should never be allowed to touch the ground or the floor. When the flag is hung over a sidewalk from a rope extending from a building to a pole, the union (the blue field with white stars) should be away from the building. When the flag is hung over the center of a street the union should be to the north in an east-west street and to the east in a north-south street. No other flag may be flown above or, if on the same level, to the right of the U.S. flag, except that at the United Nations Headquarters, the UN flag may be placed above flags of all member nations and other national flags may be flown with equal prominence or honor with the flag of the U.S.

When two flags are placed against a wall with crossed staffs, the U.S. flag should be at right—its own right, and its staff should be in front of the staff of the other flag; when a number of flags are grouped and displayed from staffs, it should be at the center and highest point of the group.

Church and Platform Use. In an auditorium, the flag may be displayed flat, above and behind the speaker. When displayed from a staff in a church or in a public auditorium, the flag should hold the position of superior prominence, in advance of the audience, and in the position of honor at the speaker's right as she or he faces the audience. Any other flag so displayed should be placed on the left of the speaker or to the right of the audience.

When the flag is displayed horizontally or vertically against a wall, the stars should be uppermost and at the observer's left.

When used to cover a casket, the flag should be placed so that the union is at the head and over the left shoulder. It should not be lowered into the grave nor touch the ground.

How to Dispose of Worn Flags. When the flag is in such condition that it is no longer a fitting emblem for display, it should be destroyed in a dignified way, preferably by burning.

When to Salute the Flag. All persons present should face the flag, stand at attention, and salute on the following occasions: (1) when the flag is passing in a parade or in a review, (2) during the ceremony of hoisting or lowering, (3) when the national anthem is played, and (4) during the Pledge of Allegiance. Those present in uniform should render the military salute. Those not in uniform should place the right hand over the heart. A man wearing a hat should remove it with his right hand and hold it to his left shoulder during the salute.

Prohibited Uses of the Flag. The flag should not be dipped to any person or thing. (An exception—customarily, ships salute by dipping their colors.) It should never be displayed with the union down save as a distress signal. It should never be carried flat or horizontally, but always aloft and free.

It should not be displayed on a float, an automobile, or a boat except from a staff. It should never be used as a covering for a ceiling, nor have placed on it any word, design, or drawing. It should never be used as a receptacle for carrying anything. It should not be used to cover a statue or a monument.

The flag should never be used for advertising purposes, nor be embroidered on such articles as cushions or handkerchiefs, printed or otherwise impressed on boxes or anything that is designed for temporary use and discard; or used as a costume or athletic uniform. Advertising signs should not be fastened to its staff or halyard.

The flag should never be used as drapery of any sort, never festooned, drawn back, nor up, in folds, but always allowed to fall free. Bunting of blue, white, and red, always arranged with the blue above and the white in the middle, should be used for covering a speaker's desk, draping the front of a platform, and for decoration in general.

An act of Congress approved on Feb. 8, 1917, provided certain penalties for the desecration, mutilation, or improper use of the flag within the District of Columbia. A 1968 federal law provided penalties of as much as a year's imprisonment or a $1,000 fine or both for publicly burning or otherwise desecrating any U.S. flag. In addition, many states have laws against flag desecration. In 1989, the Supreme Court ruled that no laws could prohibit political protesters from burning the flag. The decision had the effect of declaring unconstitutional the flag desecration laws of 48 states, as well as a similar federal statute, in cases of peaceful political expression.

The Supreme Court, in June 1990, declared that a new federal law making it a crime to burn or deface the American flag violated the free-speech guarantee of the First Amendment. The 5-4 Court decision led to renewed calls in Congress for a constitutional amendment to make it possible to prosecute flag burners. In 2005, the House passed a flag desecration amendment with the requisite two-thirds majority, but the measure failed by one vote to achieve two-thirds majority in the Senate in 2006.

Pledge of Allegiance to the Flag

I pledge allegiance to the flag of the United States of America and to the republic for which it stands, one nation under God, indivisible, with liberty and justice for all.

This, the current official version of the Pledge of Allegiance, developed from the original pledge, which was first published in the Sept. 8, 1892, issue of *Youth's Companion,* a weekly magazine. The original pledge contained the phrase "my flag," which was changed more than 30 years later to "flag of the United States of America." A 1954 act of Congress added the words "under God." (In 2002, the 9th Circuit U.S. Court of Appeals ruled that recitation of the pledge in public schools could not include that phrase. In 2004, however, the U.S. Supreme Court voted to decline to decide the case on a technicality. The lower court's decision was thus overturned.)

The authorship of the pledge was in dispute for many years. *Youth's Companion* stated in 1917 that the original draft was written by James B. Upham, an executive of the magazine who died in 1910. A leaflet circulated by the magazine later named Upham as the originator of the draft "afterwards condensed and perfected by him and his associates of the Companion force."

Francis Bellamy, a former member of *Youth's Companion* editorial staff, publicly claimed authorship of the pledge in 1923. In 1939, the United States Flag Association, acting on the advice of a committee named to study the controversy, upheld the claim of Bellamy, who had died eight years earlier. In 1957 the Library of Congress issued a report attributing the authorship to Bellamy.

History of the National Anthem

"The Star-Spangled Banner" was ordered played by the military and naval services by Pres. Woodrow Wilson in 1916. It was designated the national anthem by Act of Congress, Mar. 3, 1931. The words were written by Francis Scott Key, of Georgetown, MD, during the bombardment of Ft. McHenry in Baltimore MD, Sept. 13-14, 1814. Key was a lawyer, a graduate of St. John's College, Annapolis, MD, and a volunteer in a light artillery company. When a friend, Dr. Beanes, a Maryland physician, was taken aboard Adm. Cockburn's British squadron for interfering with ground troops, Key and J. S. Skinner, carrying a note from Pres. Madison, went to the fleet under a flag of truce on a cartel ship to ask Beanes's release. Cockburn consented, but as the fleet was about to sail up the Patapsco to bombard Ft. McHenry, he detained them, first on HMS *Surprise* and then on a supply ship.

Key witnessed the bombardment from his own vessel. It began at 7 AM, Sept. 13, 1814, and lasted 25 hours. The British fired more than 1,500 shells, each weighing as much as 220 lbs. They were unable to approach closely because the U.S. had sunk 22 vessels. Only four Americans were killed and 24 wounded. A British bomb-ship was disabled.

During the event, Key wrote a stanza on the back of an envelope. The next day at Indian Queen Inn in Baltimore, he wrote out the poem and gave it to his brother-in-law, Judge J. H. Nicholson. Nicholson suggested use of the tune, "Anacreon in Heaven" (attributed to a British composer named John Stafford Smith), and had the poem printed on broadsides, of which two survive. On Sept. 20 it appeared in the *Baltimore American*. Later Key made three copies; one is in the Library of Congress, and one in the Pennsylvania Historical Society. The copy Key wrote on Sept. 14 remained in the Nicholson family for 93 years. In 1907, it was sold to Henry Walters of Baltimore. In 1934, it was bought by Walters Art Gallery in Baltimore for $26,400. In 1953, it was sold to the Maryland Historical Society for the same price.

The flag that Key saw during the bombardment is preserved in the Smithsonian Institution, Washington, DC. It measures 30 by 42 ft and has 15 alternating red and white stripes and 15 stars, for the original 13 states plus Kentucky and Vermont. It was made by Mary Pickersgill. The Star-Spangled Banner Flag House, a museum, occupies her premises, which were restored in 1953.

The Star-Spangled Banner

Note: The second and third verses are commonly omitted.

I

Oh, say can you see by the dawn's early light
What so proudly we hailed at the twilight's last gleaming?
Whose broad stripes and bright stars thru the perilous fight,
O'er the ramparts we watched were so gallantly streaming?
And the rocket's red glare, the bombs bursting in air,
Gave proof through the night that our flag was still there.
Oh, say does that star-spangled banner yet wave
O'er the land of the free and the home of the brave?

II

On the shore, dimly seen through the mists of the deep,
Where the foe's haughty host in dread silence reposes,
What is that which the breeze, o'er the towering steep,
As it fitfully blows, half conceals, half discloses?
Now it catches the gleam of the morning's first beam,
In full glory reflected now shines in the stream.
'Tis the star-spangled banner! Oh long may it wave
O'er the land of the free and the home of the brave!

III

And where is that band who so vauntingly swore
That the havoc of war and the battle's confusion,
A home and a country should leave us no more!
Their blood has washed out their foul footsteps' pollution.
No refuge could save the hireling and slave
From the terror of flight, or the gloom of the grave:
And the star-spangled banner in triumph doth wave
O'er the land of the free and the home of the brave!

IV

Oh! thus be it ever, when freemen shall stand
Between their loved home and the war's desolation!
Blest with victory and peace, may the heav'n rescued land
Praise the Power that hath made and preserved us a nation.
Then conquer we must, when our cause it is just,
And this be our motto: "In God is our trust."
And the star-spangled banner in triumph shall wave
O'er the land of the free and the home of the brave!

History of the Liberty Bell

The Liberty Bell is housed in the Liberty Bell Center, located in Philadelphia's Independence National Historical Park.

The original bell was ordered by Isaac Norris, Assembly Speaker and Chairman of the State House Superintendents, from Thomas Lester of Whitechapel Foundry in London. It reached Philadelphia at the end of Aug. 1752. It bore an inscription from Leviticus 25:10: "Proclaim LIBERTY throughout all the land unto all the inhabitants thereof."

The bell was cracked by a stroke of its clapper in Sept. 1752 while it hung on a truss in the State House yard for testing. Pass & Stow, Philadelphia founders, recast the bell, adding 1½ ounces of copper to a pound of the original Whitechapel metal to reduce its high tone and brittleness. That proved to be too much copper, injuring its tone, so Pass & Stow recast it once more.

In June 1753, the bell was hung in the old wooden steeple of the State House. It rang out in defiance of British tax and trade restrictions while the Continental Congress was in session in the State House. It proclaimed the Boston Tea Party as well as the first public reading of the Declaration of Independence, on July 8, 1776.

On Sept. 18, 1777, when the British Army was about to occupy Philadelphia, the Liberty Bell was moved in a baggage train to Allentown, PA, where it was hidden until June 27, 1778. The bell was moved back to Philadelphia after the British left the city.

In 1781, the wooden steeple became insecure and had to be taken down. The bell was lowered into the brick section of the tower, where it remained until 1828. Between 1828 and 1844, the old State House bell continued to ring on special occasions. According to tradition, it cracked in 1835 as it tolled the death of U.S. Supreme Court Chief Justice John Marshall. It rang for the last time on Feb. 23, 1846, in honor of George Washington's birthday. In 1852 it was placed on exhibition in the Declaration Chamber of Independence Hall.

In 1876, when thousands of Americans visited Philadelphia for the Centennial Exposition, the bell was placed in its old wooden support in the tower hallway. In 1877, it was hung from the ceiling of the tower by a chain of 13 links. In 1896, it was placed within a glass case to prevent souvenir hunters and vandals from taking some of the metal. In 1915, the case was removed so that the public might touch the bell. To mark the opening of the Bicentennial Year, the bell was moved just after midnight on Jan. 1, 1976, to a new glass and steel pavilion behind Independence Hall for easier viewing. On Oct. 9, 2003, the bell was transferred to its present location, where exhibits and displays explain the history of the bell.

Measurements of the bell: circumference around the lip, 12 ft ½ in.; circumference around the crown, 6 ft 11¼ in.; lip to the crown, 3 ft; height over the crown, 2 ft 3 in.; thickness at lip, 3 in.; thickness at crown, 1¼ in.; weight, 2,080 lbs; length of clapper, 3 ft 2 in.

Statue of Liberty National Monument

Since 1886, the Statue of Liberty, formally known as "Liberty Enlightening the World," has stood as a symbol of freedom in New York harbor. It also commemorates French-American friendship because it was given by the people of France to the people of the U.S. It was designed by French sculptor Frédéric Auguste Bartholdi (1834-1904).

On Washington's Birthday, Feb. 22, 1877, Congress approved the use of a site on Bedloe's Island suggested by Bartholdi. This island of 12 acres had been owned in the 17th cent. by a Walloon colonist named Isaac Bedloe. On Aug. 3, 1956, Pres. Dwight Eisenhower approved a measure changing the name to Liberty Island.

The statue was finished on May 21, 1884, and presented to the U.S. minister to France, Levi Parsons Morton, July 4, 1884, by Ferdinand de Lesseps, head of the Franco-American Union, promoter of the Panama Canal, and builder of the Suez Canal.

On Aug. 5, 1884, the cornerstone for the pedestal was laid on the foundations of Fort Wood, erected by the government in 1811. The American Committee for the Statue of Liberty had raised an inadequate $125,000, and *New York World* newspaper owner Joseph Pulitzer appealed Mar. 16, 1885, for general donations. By Aug. 11, 1885, he had raised $100,000. The statue itself arrived dismantled, in 214 packing cases, from Rouen, France, in June 1885. The last rivet of the statue was driven on Oct. 28, 1886, when Pres. Grover Cleveland dedicated the monument.

The Statue of Liberty National Monument was designated as such in 1924. It is administered by the National Park Service. A $2.5-mil building housing the American Museum of Immigration was opened by Pres. Richard Nixon on Sept. 26, 1972, at the base of the statue. It houses a permanent exhibition tracing the history of American immigration.

Four years of restoration work funded and led by the Statue of Liberty-Ellis Island Foundation were completed before the statue's 1986 centennial. The $87-mil project included the replacement of the 1,600 wrought iron bands that hold the statue's copper skin to its frame, replacement of the torch, and installation of an elevator. A four-day "Liberty Weekend" extravaganza of concerts, tall ships, ethnic festivals, and fireworks, July 3-6, 1986, celebrated the 100th anniversary. U.S. Supreme Court Chief Justice Warren E. Burger swore in 5,000 new citizens on Ellis Island, while 20,000 others across the country were sworn in through a satellite telecast. Other ceremonies followed on Oct. 28, 1986, the statue's exact 100th birthday.

After the Sept. 11, 2001, terrorist attacks, Liberty Island was closed to visitors. On Dec. 20, 2001, the secretary of the interior reopened the island after installing airport-type screening facilities at passenger embarkation areas at Battery Park in Manhattan and Liberty State Park in New Jersey.

To open the statue, the federal government needed to increase security throughout the park. In addition to federally funded security upgrades, significant safety improvements were made to meet building codes. Access to the statue was restored on Aug. 3, 2004.

Following the 125th anniversary celebration Oct. 28, 2011, the statue was closed. A $30-mil renovation brought the statue up to contemporary safety standards and allowed for increased visitor access. The island remained open to visitors, and views of the statue were largely unobstructed, but visitors could not go inside. The statue interior reopened Oct. 28, 2012, but damages caused by Hurricane Sandy the next week forced all of Liberty Island to close again.

The island and the statue officially reopened for visitors July 4, 2013. Advance reservations are required to visit the statue interior and to access the crown. Reservations are available by visiting www.statuecruises.com or by calling 1-877-LADY-TIX. Visitors to the statue's interior must follow a number of guidelines including ones on height requirements and locker rentals, for which there is a $2 fee. (Inside the statue, visitors may carry only a camera, a ferry ticket with crown reservation, and necessary medication.) For more information, visit www.nps.gov/stli/ and www.statueof liberty.org.

Statue Statistics

The statue weighs 450,000 lbs, or 225 tons. The copper sheeting weighs 200,000 lbs. There are 377 steps from the main lobby to the crown platform. There are 146 steps from the top of the pedestal (the statue's feet) to the crown platform.

	Ft	In.
Height from base to torch tip	151	1
Foundation of pedestal to torch tip	305	1
Heel to top of head	111	1
Hand, length	16	5
Index finger, length	8	0
Fingernail size		13x10
Head from chin to cranium	17	3
Head thickness, ear to ear	10	0
Nose, length	4	6
Right arm, length	42	0
Right arm, max. thickness	12	0
Waist, thickness	35	0
Mouth, width	3	0
Tablet, length	23	7
Tablet, width	13	7

Ellis Island

Ellis Island was the gateway to America for over 12 mil immigrants between 1892 and 1924. In the late 18th cent., Samuel Ellis, a New York City merchant, purchased the island and gave it his name. From Ellis, it passed to New York state, and the U.S. government bought it in 1808. On Jan. 1, 1892, the government opened the first federal immigration center in the U.S. there. The 27.5-acre site eventually supported more than 35 buildings, including the Main Building with its Great Hall, in which as many as 5,000 people a day were processed.

Closed as an immigration station in 1954, Ellis Island was proclaimed part of the Statue of Liberty National Monument in 1965 by Pres. Lyndon B. Johnson. After a six-year, $170 mil restoration project funded by the Statue of Liberty-Ellis Island Foundation, Ellis Island was reopened as a museum in 1990. Artifacts, historic photographs and documents, oral histories, and ethnic music depicting 400 years of American immigration are housed in the museum. The museum also includes The American Immigrant Wall of Honor (www.wallofhonor.org), which is inscribed with more than 700,000 names that have been placed in tribute. Registrations are still being accepted for inclusion in the memorial.

The American Family Immigration History Center® opened in Apr. 2001. It contains an electronic database of ship passenger arrival information through the Port of New York and Ellis Island from 1892 to 1924. Data on over 25 mil individuals are available, as well as an interactive database which features a Living Family Archive, multimedia presentations on various immigration groups and patterns, reproductions of original ships' passenger manifests, and pictures of over 800 immigrant ships (www.ellis island.org).

In 1998, the U.S. Supreme Court ruled that nearly 90% of the island (the 24.2 acres that are landfill) lies in New Jersey, while the original 3.3 acres, on which the museum is located, are in New York.

Damages caused by storm surges of Hurricane Sandy in late Oct. 2012 forced Ellis Island to close for repairs. As of Sept. 2013, the island was still closed indefinitely.

U.S. SUPREME COURT

Justices of the U.S. Supreme Court

The Supreme Court comprises the chief justice of the U.S. and eight associate justices, all appointed for life by the president with advice and consent of the U.S. Senate. Names of chief justices are in **boldface**. Terms of service begin with the year each justice took the judicial oath. Service years are the number of complete years served by a justice. Current salaries: chief justice, $223,500; associate justice, $213,900. The U.S. Supreme Court Building is at 1 First St. NE, Washington, DC 20543. The Court website is www.supremecourt.gov.

Current membership. Chief justice: John G. Roberts Jr.; associate justices in seniority order: Antonin Scalia, Anthony M. Kennedy, Clarence Thomas, Ruth Bader Ginsburg, Stephen G. Breyer, Samuel A. Alito Jr., Sonia Sotomayor, Elena Kagan.

Name, appointed from	Term	Yrs.	Born	Died
John Jay, NY	1789-1795	5	1745	1829
John Rutledge, SC[1]	1790-1791	1	1739	1800
William Cushing, MA	1790-1810*	20	1732	1810
James Wilson, PA	1789-1798	8	1742	1798
John Blair, VA	1790-1795*	5	1732	1800
James Iredell, NC	1790-1799	9	1751	1799
Thomas Johnson, MD	1792-1793	<1	1732	1819
William Paterson, NJ	1793-1806	13	1745	1806
John Rutledge, SC[2,3]	1795	<1	1739	1800
Samuel Chase, MD	1796-1811	15	1741	1811
Oliver Ellsworth, CT	1796-1800	4	1745	1807
Bushrod Washington, VA	1799-1829*	30	1762	1829
Alfred Moore, NC	1800-1804	3	1755	1810
John Marshall, VA	1801-1835	34	1755	1835
William Johnson, SC	1804-1834	30	1771	1834
Henry B. Livingston, NY	1807-1823	16	1757	1823
Thomas Todd, KY	1807-1826	18	1765	1826
Gabriel Duvall, MD	1811-1835	23	1752	1844
Joseph Story, MA	1812-1845*	33	1779	1845
Smith Thompson, NY	1823-1843	20	1768	1843
Robert Trimble, KY	1826-1828	2	1777	1828
John McLean, OH	1830-1861*	31	1785	1861
Henry Baldwin, PA	1830-1844	14	1780	1844
James M. Wayne, GA	1835-1867	32	1790	1867
Roger B. Taney, MD	1836-1864	28	1777	1864
Philip P. Barbour, VA	1836-1841	4	1783	1841
John Catron, TN	1837-1865	28	1786	1865
John McKinley, AL	1838-1852*	14	1780	1852
Peter V. Daniel, VA	1842-1860*	18	1784	1860
Samuel Nelson, NY	1845-1872	27	1792	1873
Levi Woodbury, NH	1845-1851	5	1789	1851
Robert C. Grier, PA	1846-1870	23	1794	1870
Benjamin R. Curtis, MA	1851-1857	5	1809	1874
John A. Campbell, AL	1853-1861*	8	1811	1889
Nathan Clifford, ME	1858-1881	23	1803	1881
Noah H. Swayne, OH	1862-1881	18	1804	1884
Samuel F. Miller, IA	1862-1890	28	1816	1890
David Davis, IL	1862-1877	14	1815	1886
Stephen J. Field, CA	1863-1897	33	1816	1899
Salmon P. Chase, OH	1864-1873	8	1808	1873
William Strong, PA	1870-1880	10	1808	1895
Joseph P. Bradley, NJ	1870-1892	21	1813	1892
Ward Hunt, NY	1873-1882	9	1810	1886
Morrison R. Waite, OH	1874-1888	14	1816	1888
John M. Harlan, KY	1877-1911	33	1833	1911
William B. Woods, GA	1881-1887	6	1824	1887
Stanley Matthews, OH	1881-1889	7	1824	1889
Horace Gray, MA	1882-1902	20	1828	1902
Samuel Blatchford, NY	1882-1893	11	1820	1893
Lucius Q.C. Lamar, MS.	1888-1893	5	1825	1893
Melville W. Fuller, IL	1888-1910	21	1833	1910
David J. Brewer, KS	1890-1910	20	1837	1910
Henry B. Brown, MI	1891-1906	15	1836	1913
George Shiras Jr., PA	1892-1903	10	1832	1924
Howell E. Jackson, TN	1893-1895	2	1832	1895
Edward D. White, LA[1]	1894-1910	16	1845	1921
Rufus W. Peckham, NY	1896-1909	13	1838	1909
Joseph McKenna, CA	1898-1925	26	1843	1926
Oliver W. Holmes, MA	1902-1932	29	1841	1935
William R. Day, OH	1903-1922	19	1849	1923
William H. Moody, MA	1906-1910	3	1853	1917
Horace H. Lurton, TN	1910-1914	4	1844	1914
Charles E. Hughes, NY[1]	1910-1916	5	1862	1948
Willis Van Devanter, WY	1911-1937	26	1859	1941
Joseph R. Lamar, GA	1911-1916	5	1857	1916
Edward D. White, LA[2]	1910-1921	10	1845	1921
Mahlon Pitney, NJ	1912-1922	10	1858	1924
James C. McReynolds, TN	1914-1941	26	1862	1946
Louis D. Brandeis, MA	1916-1939	22	1856	1941
John H. Clarke, OH	1916-1922	5	1857	1945
William H. Taft, CT	1921-1930	8	1857	1930
George Sutherland, UT	1922-1938	15	1862	1942
Pierce Butler, MN	1923-1939	16	1866	1939
Edward T. Sanford, TN	1923-1930	7	1865	1930
Harlan F. Stone, NY[1]	1925-1941	16	1872	1946
Charles E. Hughes, NY[2]	1930-1941	11	1862	1948
Owen J. Roberts, PA	1930-1945	15	1875	1955
Benjamin N. Cardozo, NY	1932-1938	6	1870	1938
Hugo L. Black, AL	1937-1971	34	1886	1971
Stanley F. Reed, KY	1938-1957	19	1884	1980
Felix Frankfurter, MA	1939-1962	23	1882	1965
William O. Douglas, CT	1939-1975	36[4]	1898	1980
Frank Murphy, MI	1940-1949	9	1890	1949
Harlan F. Stone, NY[2]	1941-1946	4	1872	1946
James F. Byrnes, SC	1941-1942	1	1879	1972
Robert H. Jackson, NY	1941-1954	13	1892	1954
Wiley B. Rutledge, IA	1943-1949	6	1894	1949
Harold H. Burton, OH	1945-1958	13	1888	1964
Fred M. Vinson, KY	1946-1953	7	1890	1953
Tom C. Clark, TX	1949-1967	17	1899	1977
Sherman Minton, IN	1949-1956	7	1890	1965
Earl Warren, CA	1953-1969	15	1891	1974
John Marshall Harlan, NY	1955-1971	16	1899	1971
William J. Brennan Jr., NJ	1956-1990	33	1906	1997
Charles E. Whittaker, MO	1957-1962	5	1901	1973
Potter Stewart, OH	1958-1981	22	1915	1985
Byron R. White, CO	1962-1993	31	1917	2002
Arthur J. Goldberg, IL	1962-1965	2	1908	1990
Abe Fortas, TN	1965-1969	3	1910	1982
Thurgood Marshall, NY	1967-1991	24	1908	1993
Warren E. Burger, VA	1969-1986	17	1907	1995
Harry A. Blackmun, MN	1970-1994	24	1908	1999
Lewis F. Powell Jr., VA	1972-1987	15	1907	1998
William H. Rehnquist, AZ[1]	1972-1986	14	1924	2005
John Paul Stevens, IL	1975-2010	34	1920	
Sandra Day O'Connor, AZ	1981-2006	24	1930	
William H. Rehnquist, VA[2]	1986-2005	18	1924	2005
Antonin Scalia, VA	1986-		1936	
Anthony M. Kennedy, CA	1988-		1936	
David H. Souter, NH	1990-2009	18	1939	
Clarence Thomas, GA	1991-		1948	
Ruth Bader Ginsburg, NY	1993-		1933	
Stephen G. Breyer, MA	1994-		1938	
John G. Roberts Jr., MD	2005-		1955	
Samuel A. Alito Jr., NJ	2006-		1950	
Sonia Sotomayor, NY	2009-		1954	
Elena Kagan, MA	2010-		1960	

*Because of inadequate government record keeping, date of oath is estimated. (1) Later, chief justice, as listed. (2) Formerly associate justice. (3) Named acting chief justice; confirmation rejected by the Senate. (4) Longest term of service.

Supreme Court History and Notable Firsts

The U.S. Supreme Court first convened Feb. 1, 1790, in New York, NY. Acting on the authority of Congress as outlined in the Judiciary Act of 1789, the Court consisted of Chief Justice John Jay and five associate justices who held sessions for a few weeks in Feb. and Aug. The justices also served twice a year in each of the nation's then-13 judicial districts, a requirement known as "riding circuit."

The Court's first major legal decision, *Chisholm v. Georgia* (1793), ruled that federal courts held jurisdiction over disputes between individual states and citizens of other states. (The 11th Amendment, which the states ratified in 1795, removed that jurisdiction.)

Since it was established, 112 justices have served on the Court for an average of 16 years. Of 160 nominations to the Court (including Chief Justice nominations), just 12 have been rejected by the Senate, most recently Robert Bork in 1987. (George W. Bush nominee Harriet Miers's nomination was withdrawn in 2005, before the Senate considered it.) Justices may be removed from the Court by impeachment. In 1805, the House of Representatives impeached Samuel Chase; he was later acquitted by the Senate. No other justice has ever been impeached.

The Court over time has expanded its impact on the nation's affairs. Since 1803 it has declared unconstitutional 169 acts of Congress and more than 1,070 state and territorial laws and municipal statutes. Operating on an est. $88-mil budget, the Court receives approximately 10,000 petitions annually and hears oral arguments in about 100 cases per term. The Court begins its term the first Monday in October and recesses in late June or early July.

First fully vested justice: James Wilson took the Constitutional Oath of the Court Oct. 5, 1789
First Jewish justice: Louis D. Brandeis (1916-39)
First and only person to serve as both U.S. president and chief justice: William Howard Taft (president, 1909-13; chief justice, 1921-30)

First justice to take an oath at the White House: Frank Murphy, Jan. 18, 1940
First African-American justice: Thurgood Marshall (1967-91)
First woman justice: Sandra Day O'Connor (1981-2006)
First Hispanic justice: Sonia Sotomayor (2009-)

U.S. Supreme Court Decisions by Issue and Leadership Era, 1946-2013

Source: The Supreme Court Database, supremecourtdatabase.org

Decisions through the end of the 2012-13 term. Figures are the number of cases decided in each issue category (number of 5-4 decisions in parentheses).

Issue	Vinson (1946-53)	Warren (1953-69)	Burger (1969-86)	Rehnquist (1986-2005)	Roberts (2005-)
Attorneys[1]	2 (0)	12 (1)	37 (5)	31 (7)	13 (2)
Civil rights	74 (7)	316 (27)	555 (78)	323 (69)	110 (22)
Criminal procedure	123 (29)	462 (70)	626 (109)	509 (136)	194 (50)
Due process	47 (6)	40 (5)	144 (18)	86 (23)	14 (4)
Economic activity	225 (37)	493 (48)	451 (52)	346 (40)	126 (14)
Federal taxation	49 (2)	118 (5)	75 (7)	56 (3)	8 (2)
Federalism	30 (1)	94 (3)	108 (6)	123 (26)	38 (9)
First amendment	44 (8)	206 (44)	236 (56)	140 (36)	30 (9)
Interstate relations	12 (2)	14 (0)	40 (0)	23 (1)	5 (1)
Judicial power	134 (18)	300 (20)	365 (33)	286 (28)	86 (20)
Miscellaneous[2]	1 (0)	13 (0)	13 (0)	22 (0)	1 (0)
Privacy	4 (0)	2 (0)	48 (9)	42 (6)	13 (1)
Private action[3]	0 (0)	0 (0)	0 (0)	0 (0)	1 (1)
Unions	41 (4)	131 (8)	109 (24)	54 (11)	12 (3)
Total	**786 (114)**	**2,201 (231)**	**2,807 (397)**	**2,041 (386)**	**651 (138)**

Note: Decision types include orally argued judgments, per curiams, and opinions; per curiams without oral arguments; equally divided votes; and decrees. (1) Includes cases on commercial fees, attorneys' fees, admission to state or federal bar, attorney discipline and disbarment. (2) Includes cases that could not be classified. (3) Includes cases on commercial transactions, civil procedures, contracts, evidence, personal and real property, torts, and wills and trusts.

Selected Landmark Decisions of the U.S. Supreme Court, 1803-2012

1803: *Marbury v. Madison.* The Court ruled that Congress exceeded its power in the Judiciary Act of 1789. The Court thus established its power to review acts of Congress and to declare invalid those it found to be in conflict with the Constitution.

1819: *Trustees of Dartmouth College v. Woodward.* The Court ruled that a state could not arbitrarily alter the terms of a college's contract. The Court later used a similar principle to limit the states' ability to interfere with business contracts.

1819: *McCulloch v. Maryland.* The Court ruled that Congress had the authority to charter a national bank, under the Constitution's granting of power to enact all laws "necessary and proper" to responsibilities of government.

1824: *Gibbons v. Ogden.* The Court ruled that New York state had overstepped its authority in granting a monopoly to two steamboat operators. According to the ruling, Congress's power to regulate interstate commerce included transportation.

1857: *Dred Scott v. Sandford.* The Court declared unconstitutional the already-repealed Missouri Compromise of 1820 because it deprived a person of property—a slave—without due process of law. The Court also ruled that slaves were not citizens of any state nor of the U.S. The latter part of the decision was overturned by ratification of the 14th Amendment in 1868.

1880: *Strauder v. West Virginia.* The Court struck down a state law mandating that jurors must be white, ruling it a violation of the right to equal protection under the 14th Amendment.

1896: *Plessy v. Ferguson.* The Court ruled that a state law requiring federal railroad trains to provide separate but equal facilities for black and white passengers neither infringed upon federal authority to regulate interstate commerce nor violated the 13th and 14th Amendments. The "separate but equal" doctrine remained effective until the 1954 *Brown v. Board of Education* decision.

1904: *Northern Securities Co. v. U.S.* The Court ruled that a holding company formed solely to eliminate competition between two railroad lines was a combination in restraint of trade, violating the 1890 federal Sherman Antitrust Act.

1908: *Muller v. Oregon.* The Court upheld a state law limiting the working hours of women. (Louis D. Brandeis, counsel for the state, cited evidence from social workers, physicians, and factory inspectors that the number of hours women worked affected their health and morals.)

1911: *Standard Oil Co. of New Jersey v. U.S.* The Court ruled that the Standard Oil Trust must be dissolved because of its unreasonable restraint of trade.

1919: *Schenck v. U.S.* The Court sustained the Espionage Act of 1917, maintaining that freedom of speech and press could be constrained if "the words used ... create a clear and present danger."

1925: *Gitlow v. New York.* The Court ruled that the 1st Amendment prohibition against government abridgment of the freedom of speech applied to the states as well as to the

federal government. The decision was the first of a number of rulings holding that the 14th Amendment extended the guarantees of the Bill of Rights to state action.

1935: *Schechter Poultry Corp. v. U.S.* The Court ruled that Congress exceeded its authority to delegate legislative powers and to regulate interstate commerce when it enacted the National Industrial Recovery Act (1933), which afforded the U.S. president too much discretionary power.

1944: *Korematsu v. U.S.* The Court upheld the constitutionality of an order barring U.S. citizens of Japanese ancestry from much of the West Coast, forcing them into internment camps, ruling that the need to prevent espionage outweighed the petitioner's civil rights. The ruling, never officially overturned, followed *Hirabayashi v. U.S.* (1943), in which the Court upheld the imposition of curfews on minority populations perceived to be a potential wartime threat.

1951: *Dennis v. U.S.* The Court upheld convictions under the Smith Act of 1940 for invoking Communist theory advocating the forcible overthrow of the government. In *Yates v. U.S.* (1957), the Court moderated this ruling by allowing such advocacy in the abstract, if not connected to action to achieve the goal.

1952: *Youngstown Sheet & Tube Co. v. Sawyer.* The Court ruled that the president had exceeded his wartime power in ordering the seizure of private steel mills during a nationwide steelworkers' strike. The Court held that neither the Constitution nor his role as commander-in-chief gave the president the authority to interfere in labor issues.

1954: *Brown v. Board of Education of Topeka.* The Court ruled that separate public schools for black and white students were inherently unequal, so state-sanctioned segregation in public schools violated the equal protection guarantee of the 14th Amendment. And in *Bolling v. Sharpe* the same year, the Court ruled that the congressionally mandated segregated public school system in the District of Columbia violated the 5th Amendment's due process guarantee of personal liberty. The Brown ruling also led to abolition of state-sponsored segregation in other public facilities.

1957: *Roth v. U.S.; Alberts v. California.* The Court ruled obscene material was not protected by 1st Amendment guarantees of freedom of speech and press, defining as obscene something "utterly without redeeming social value" in the average person's view. This definition was modified in later decisions, and the "average person" standard was replaced by the "local community" standard in *Miller v. California* (1973).

1958: *Cooper v. Aaron.* The Court held that Arkansas could not nullify *Brown v. Board of Education* by arguing mandatory school desegregation was unconstitutional. The opinion of the Court affirmed its reading of the Constitution as the "supreme law of the land."

1961: *Mapp v. Ohio.* The Court ruled that evidence obtained in violation of the 4th Amendment guarantee against unreasonable search and seizure must be excluded from use in state as well as federal trials.

1962: *Baker v. Carr.* The Court held that constitutional challenges to the unequal distribution of voters among legislative districts could be resolved by federal courts.

1962: *Engel v. Vitale.* The Court held that government bodies could not encourage the recitation of a state-composed prayer in public schools, even if nondenominational, because that would be an unconstitutional attempt to establish religion.

1963: *Gideon v. Wainwright.* The Court ruled that defendants in state cases must have access to an attorney even if they could not afford one.

1964: *New York Times Co. v. Sullivan.* The Court ruled that the 1st Amendment protected the press from libel suits for defamatory reports about public officials unless an injured party could prove that a defamatory report was made out of malice or "reckless disregard" for the truth.

1964: *Heart of Atlanta Motel v. U.S.* The Court upheld the constitutionality of Title II of the 1964 Civil Rights Act banning racial discrimination in motels/hotels engaged in interstate commerce (by accommodating travelers from other states). The Court in *Katzenbach v. McClung* (1964) held that Title II also applied to restaurants and businesses that purchased a substantial percentage of food or goods from other states.

1965: *Griswold v. Connecticut.* The Court ruled that a state unconstitutionally interfered with personal privacy in the marriage relationship when it prohibited everyone, including married couples, from using contraceptives.

1966: *Miranda v. Arizona.* The Court ruled that, under the guarantee of due process, suspects in custody, before being questioned, must be informed that they have the right to remain silent, that anything they say may be used against them, and that they have the right to counsel.

1968: *Terry v. Ohio.* The Court ruled that a "stop and frisk" performed without a warrant or probable cause was not a violation of 4th Amendment rights, provided that the law enforcement officer had a reasonable suspicion that the subject was armed and dangerous, or had committed or was about to commit a crime.

1973: *Roe v. Wade; Doe v. Bolton.* The Court ruled that the fetus was not a "person" with constitutional rights and that a right to privacy inherent in the 14th Amendment's due process guarantee of personal liberty protected a woman's decision to have an abortion. During the first trimester of pregnancy, the Court maintained, the decision should be left entirely to a woman and her physician. Some regulation of abortion procedures was allowed in the second trimester and some restriction of abortion in the third.

1974: *U.S. v. Nixon.* The Court ruled that neither the separation of powers nor the need to preserve the confidentiality of presidential communications could alone justify an absolute executive privilege of immunity from judicial demands for evidence to be used in a criminal trial.

1976: *Gregg v. Georgia; Proffitt v. Florida; Jurek v. Texas.* The Court held that death, as a punishment for persons convicted of first-degree murder, was not in and of itself cruel and unusual punishment in violation of the 8th Amendment. But the Court ruled that the sentencing judge and jury must consider the character of the offender and the circumstances of the particular crime.

1978: *Regents of the Univ. of Calif. v. Bakke.* The Court ruled that an admissions program for a state medical school, under which a set number of places were reserved for minorities, violated the 1964 Civil Rights Act, which forbids the exclusion of anyone from a federally funded program based on race. However, the Court ruled that race could be considered as one of a complex of factors.

1985: *New Jersey v. T.L.O.* The Court ruled that officials who carry out searches on school grounds do not violate students' 4th Amendment rights because students' privacy rights can be outweighed by schools' need to maintain learning environments. The ruling put in place less stringent standards of required "reasonableness" for such searches.

1986: *Bowers v. Hardwick.* The Court refused to extend any right of privacy to homosexual activity, upholding a Georgia antisodomy law that in effect made such activity a crime. However, the law was struck down by the state supreme court in 1998, and in *Lawrence v. Texas* (2003), the U.S. Supreme Court struck down all state antisodomy laws as violations of liberty prohibited in the 14th Amendment's due process clause. In *Romer v. Evans* (1996), the Court struck down a Colorado constitutional provision that barred homosexuals from recognition as a protected class, ruling that it violated the 14th Amendment's Equal Protection clause.

1989: *Texas v. Johnson.* The Court held the actions of a political activist who burned an American flag outside of the 1984 Republican National Convention were expressive and therefore protected by the 1st Amendment. The ruling invalidated laws in 48 states prohibiting flag desecration.

1990: *Cruzan v. Missouri.* The Court ruled that a person had the right to refuse life-sustaining medical treatment. However, the Court ruled a state could require evidence that a comatose patient would not have wanted to live before withholding treatment. In two 1997 rulings, *Washington v. Glucksberg* and *Vacco v. Quill*, the Court ruled that states could ban doctor-assisted suicide.

1995: *U.S. Term Limits, Inc. v. Thornton.* The Court ruled that neither states nor Congress could limit terms of members of Congress because the Constitution reserves to the people the right to choose federal lawmakers.

1995: *Adarand Constructors, Inc. v. Peña*. The Court held that federal programs that classify people by race, unless "narrowly tailored" to accomplish a "compelling governmental interest," may violate the right to equal protection.

1997: *Clinton v. Jones*. Rejecting an appeal by Pres. Clinton in a sexual harassment suit, the Court ruled that a sitting president did not have temporary immunity from a lawsuit for actions outside the realm of official duties.

1997: *City of Boerne v. Flores*. The Court overturned a 1993 law banning enforcement of laws that "substantially burden" religious practice unless there is a "compelling need" to do so. The Court held that the act was an unwarranted intrusion by Congress on states' prerogatives and an infringement of the judiciary's role.

1997: *Reno v. ACLU*. Citing the right to free expression, the Court overturned a provision making it a crime to display or distribute "indecent" or "patently offensive" material on the Internet. The Court ruled, however, in *NEA v. Finley* (1998) that "general standards of decency" may be used as a criterion in federal arts funding.

1998: *Clinton v. City of New York*. The Court struck down the Line-Item Veto Act (1996), holding that it unconstitutionally gave the president "the unilateral power to change the text of duly enacted statutes."

1998: *Faragher v. City of Boca Raton; Burlington Industries, Inc. v. Ellerth*. The Court issued new guidelines for workplace sexual harassment suits, holding employers responsible for misconduct by supervisory employees. And in *Oncale v. Sundowner Offshore Services, Inc.*, the Court ruled that the law against discrimination based on sex applies regardless of whether the harasser and harassed are the same sex.

1999: *Dept. of Commerce v. U.S. House of Representatives*. Upholding a challenge to plans for the 2000 census, the Court prohibited statistical sampling, favored by Democrats, in apportioning seats in the U.S. House. The Court maintained that an actual head count was required.

1999: *Alden v. Maine; Florida Prepaid v. College Savings Bank; College Savings Bank v. Florida Prepaid*. In a series of rulings, the Court applied the principle of sovereign immunity to shield states in large part from being sued under federal law.

2000: *Boy Scouts of America v. Dale*. The Court ruled that the Boy Scouts could dismiss a troop leader after learning he was gay, holding that the right to freedom of association outweighed a New Jersey antidiscrimination statute.

2000: *Bush v. Gore*. The Court ruled that manual recounts of presidential ballots in the Nov. 2000 election could not proceed because inconsistent evaluation standards in different counties violated the equal protection clause. In effect, the ruling meant existing official results leaving George W. Bush as narrow winner of the election would prevail.

2001: *Good News Club v. Milford Central School*. The justices found that religious and secular organizations were entitled to equal access to public elementary school grounds for after-school meetings.

2002: *Federal Maritime Commission v. South Carolina State Ports Authority*. The Court ruled that the 11th Amendment gave states immunity from private lawsuits involving federal agencies.

2002: *Atkins v. Virginia*. The Court ruled that the execution of mentally retarded felons violated the 8th Amendment ban on cruel and unusual punishment. The Court ruled in *Roper v. Simmons* (2005) that executions of convicts who committed their crimes before age 18 were also prohibited on the same grounds.

2002: *Zelman v. Simmons-Harris*. The Court ruled that publicly funded tuition vouchers could be used at religious schools without violating the separation of church and state.

2003: *Grotter v. Bollinger; Gratz v. Bollinger*. The Court upheld affirmative action in admission policies at the Univ. of Michigan Law School. However, in a second decision, the Court ruled against a strict point system based on racial and ethnic backgrounds, as used in the university's undergraduate admissions process.

2004: *Tennessee v. Lane*. The Court ruled that disabled individuals could sue states under the Americans With Disabilities Act (1990) for failing to provide adequate access to state courthouses, despite states' usual immunity from private lawsuits in federal court under the 11th Amendment, which the Court ruled on in *Federal Maritime Commission v. South Carolina State Ports Authority* (2002).

2004: *Locke v. Davey*. The justices decided that a scholarship program provided by the state of Washington did not violate the right to free exercise of religion in denying aid to students preparing for the clergy.

2004: *Ashcroft v. ACLU*. The Court struck down federal legislation passed in 1998 to restrict online access to pornography by minors, on the basis that the law violated the 1st Amendment right of free speech.

2005: *Kelo v. City of New London*. The Court ruled that local governments could force property owners to sell their land in order to facilitate private development projects deemed to be economically beneficial to the community.

2006: *Garcetti v. Ceballos*. The Court ruled that the 1st Amendment guarantee of free speech did not protect statements made by public employees in the course of their official duties.

2006: *Hamdan v. Rumsfeld*. The Court ruled that Pres. George W. Bush's system for trying terrorism detainees at the U.S. military base in Guantánamo Bay, Cuba, was unauthorized under federal law and the international Geneva Conventions. The Court furthermore ruled in *Boumediene v. Bush* (2008) that habeas corpus applied and that detainees had a right to challenge their detention in federal court.

2007: *Gonzales v. Carhart; Gonzales v. Planned Parenthood Federation of America*. The Court upheld a 2003 federal law prohibiting the abortion procedure known as intact dilation and extraction, or "partial-birth" abortion.

2007: *Parents Involved in Community Schools v. Seattle School District No. 1; Meredith v. Jefferson County Board of Education*. The Court ruled that two school districts could not, to encourage diversity, use "racial classifications in making school assignments."

2008: *Crawford v. Marion County Election Board*. The Court upheld the constitutionality of an Indiana law requiring voters to present valid government photo identification.

2008: *District of Columbia v. Heller*. The Court over-turned DC's handgun ban, ruling that the 2nd Amendment protected an individual's right to own guns for personal use.

2010: *Citizens United v. Federal Election Commission*. The Court ruled that a federal law barring corporations from using general funds to finance campaign advertisements was unconstitutional. The decision cast doubt on many laws restricting political spending by corporations and unions.

2011: *Snyder v. Phelps*. The justices found that an antigay church whose members protested at the funeral of a Marine could not be held liable for intrusion or the emotional distress of the father of the deceased; their protests were protected by the 1st Amendment.

2012: *U.S. v. Jones*. The Court ruled that attaching a GPS tracking device to a suspect's car and monitoring its movements requires a search warrant, as the 4th Amendment prohibition against unreasonable search and seizure applies.

2012: *Miller v. Alabama*. The Court ruled that mandatory life sentences without the possibility of parole violate juvenile offenders' 8th Amendment right to freedom from cruel and unusual punishment. The decision extended *Graham v. Florida*, a 2010 case in which the Court held that juveniles may not receive life sentences for crimes that do not result in homicides.

2012: *Natl. Federation of Independent Business v. Sebelius*. The Court ruled Congress acted within its powers of taxation in enacting the individual-mandate provision of the Patient Protection and Affordable Care Act, which required Americans without government- or employer-provided health insurance to purchase it or pay a fine. The Court ruled unconstitutional the provision of the act's Medicaid expansion that threatened noncompliant states with loss of funding.

See also Year in Review: Notable Supreme Court Decisions, 2012-13.

PRESIDENTS OF THE UNITED STATES

U.S. Presidents

	Name	Politics	Born	Birthplace	Inaug.	Age at inaug.	Died	Age at death
1.	George Washington	Fed.	1732, Feb. 22	VA	1789	57	1799, Dec. 14	67
2.	John Adams	Fed.	1735, Oct. 30	MA	1797	61	1826, July 4	90
3.	Thomas Jefferson	Dem.-Rep.	1743, Apr. 13	VA	1801	57	1826, July 4	83
4.	James Madison	Dem.-Rep.	1751, Mar. 16	VA	1809	57	1836, June 28	85
5.	James Monroe	Dem.-Rep.	1758, Apr. 28	VA	1817	58	1831, July 4	73
6.	John Quincy Adams	Dem.-Rep.	1767, July 11	MA	1825	57	1848, Feb. 23	80
7.	Andrew Jackson	Dem.	1767, Mar. 15	SC	1829	61	1845, June 8	78
8.	Martin Van Buren	Dem.	1782, Dec. 5	NY	1837	54	1862, July 24	79
9.	William Henry Harrison	Whig	1773, Feb. 9	VA	1841	68	1841, Apr. 4	68
10.	John Tyler	Whig	1790, Mar. 29	VA	1841	51	1862, Jan. 18	71
11.	James Knox Polk	Dem.	1795, Nov. 2	NC	1845	49	1849, June 15	53
12.	Zachary Taylor	Whig	1784, Nov. 24	VA	1849	64	1850, July 9	65
13.	Millard Fillmore	Whig	1800, Jan. 7	NY	1850	50	1874, Mar. 8	74
14.	Franklin Pierce	Dem.	1804, Nov. 23	NH	1853	48	1869, Oct. 8	64
15.	James Buchanan	Dem.	1791, Apr. 23	PA	1857	65	1868, June 1	77
16.	Abraham Lincoln	Rep.	1809, Feb. 12	KY	1861	52	1865, Apr. 15	56
17.	Andrew Johnson	(1)	1808, Dec. 29	NC	1865	56	1875, July 31	66
18.	Ulysses S. Grant	Rep.	1822, Apr. 27	OH	1869	46	1885, July 23	63
19.	Rutherford Birchard Hayes	Rep.	1822, Oct. 4	OH	1877	54	1893, Jan. 17	70
20.	James Abram Garfield	Rep.	1831, Nov. 19	OH	1881	49	1881, Sept. 19	49
21.	Chester Alan Arthur	Rep.	1829, Oct. 5	VT	1881	51	1886, Nov. 18	57
22.	Grover Cleveland	Dem.	1837, Mar. 18	NJ	1885	47	1908, June 24	71
23.	Benjamin Harrison	Rep.	1833, Aug. 20	OH	1889	55	1901, Mar. 13	67
24.	Grover Cleveland	Dem.	1837, Mar. 18	NJ	1893	55	1908, June 24	71
25.	William McKinley	Rep.	1843, Jan. 29	OH	1897	54	1901, Sept. 14	58
26.	Theodore Roosevelt	Rep.	1858, Oct. 27	NY	1901	42	1919, Jan. 6	60
27.	William Howard Taft	Rep.	1857, Sept. 15	OH	1909	51	1930, Mar. 8	72
28.	(Thomas) Woodrow Wilson	Dem.	1856, Dec. 28	VA	1913	56	1924, Feb. 3	67
29.	Warren Gamaliel Harding	Rep.	1865, Nov. 2	OH	1921	55	1923, Aug. 2	57
30.	(John) Calvin Coolidge	Rep.	1872, July 4	VT	1923	51	1933, Jan. 5	60
31.	Herbert Clark Hoover	Rep.	1874, Aug. 10	IA	1929	54	1964, Oct. 20	90
32.	Franklin Delano Roosevelt	Dem.	1882, Jan. 30	NY	1933	51	1945, Apr. 12	63
33.	Harry S. Truman	Dem.	1884, May 8	MO	1945	60	1972, Dec. 26	88
34.	Dwight David Eisenhower	Rep.	1890, Oct. 14	TX	1953	62	1969, Mar. 28	78
35.	John Fitzgerald Kennedy	Dem.	1917, May 29	MA	1961	43	1963, Nov. 22	46
36.	Lyndon Baines Johnson	Dem.	1908, Aug. 27	TX	1963	55	1973, Jan. 22	64
37.	Richard Milhous Nixon[2]	Rep.	1913, Jan. 9	CA	1969	56	1994, Apr. 22	81
38.	Gerald Rudolph Ford	Rep.	1913, July 14	NE	1974	61	2006, Dec. 26	93
39.	James Earl (Jimmy) Carter	Dem.	1924, Oct. 1	GA	1977	52		
40.	Ronald Wilson Reagan	Rep.	1911, Feb. 6	IL	1981	69	2004, June 5	93
41.	George Herbert Walker Bush	Rep.	1924, June 12	MA	1989	64		
42.	Wm. Jefferson (Bill) Clinton	Dem.	1946, Aug. 19	AR	1993	46		
43.	George Walker Bush	Rep.	1946, July 6	CT	2001	54		
44.	Barack Hussein Obama	Dem.	1961, Aug. 4	HI	2009	47		

(1) Andrew Johnson, a Democrat, had been nominated vice president by Republicans and elected with Lincoln on National Union ticket. (2) Resigned Aug. 9, 1974.

U.S. Presidents, Vice Presidents, Congresses

President	Service	Vice President	Congresses
1. George Washington	Apr. 30, 1789-Mar. 3, 1797	1. John Adams	1, 2, 3, 4
2. John Adams	Mar. 4, 1797-Mar. 3, 1801	2. Thomas Jefferson	5, 6
3. Thomas Jefferson	Mar. 4, 1801-Mar. 3, 1805	3. Aaron Burr	7, 8
	Mar. 4, 1805-Mar. 3, 1809	4. George Clinton	9, 10
4. James Madison	Mar. 4, 1809-Mar. 3, 1813	George Clinton[1]	11, 12
	Mar. 4, 1813-Mar. 3, 1817	5. Elbridge Gerry[2]	13, 14
5. James Monroe	Mar. 4, 1817-Mar. 3, 1825	6. Daniel D. Tompkins	15, 16, 17, 18
6. John Quincy Adams	Mar. 4, 1825-Mar. 3, 1829	7. John C. Calhoun	19, 20
7. Andrew Jackson	Mar. 4, 1829-Mar. 3, 1833	John C. Calhoun[3]	21, 22
	Mar. 4, 1833-Mar. 3, 1837	8. Martin Van Buren	23, 24
8. Martin Van Buren	Mar. 4, 1837-Mar. 3, 1841	9. Richard M. Johnson	25, 26
9. William Henry Harrison[4]	Mar. 4, 1841-Apr. 4, 1841	10. John Tyler	27
10. John Tyler	Apr. 6, 1841-Mar. 3, 1845	(None)	27, 28
11. James K. Polk	Mar. 4, 1845-Mar. 3, 1849	11. George M. Dallas	29, 30
12. Zachary Taylor[4]	Mar. 5, 1849-July 9, 1850	12. Millard Fillmore	31
13. Millard Fillmore	July 10, 1850-Mar. 3, 1853	(None)	31, 32
14. Franklin Pierce	Mar. 4, 1853-Mar. 3, 1857	13. William R. King[5]	33, 34
15. James Buchanan	Mar. 4, 1857-Mar. 3, 1861	14. John C. Breckinridge	35, 36
16. Abraham Lincoln	Mar. 4, 1861-Mar. 3, 1865	15. Hannibal Hamlin	37, 38
(4)	Mar. 4, 1865-Apr. 15, 1865	16. Andrew Johnson	39
17. Andrew Johnson	Apr. 15, 1865-Mar. 3, 1869	(None)	39, 40
18. Ulysses S. Grant	Mar. 4, 1869-Mar. 3, 1873	17. Schuyler Colfax	41, 42
	Mar. 4, 1873-Mar. 3, 1877	18. Henry Wilson[6]	43, 44
19. Rutherford B. Hayes	Mar. 4, 1877-Mar. 3, 1881	19. William A. Wheeler	45, 46
20. James A. Garfield[4]	Mar. 4, 1881-Sept. 19, 1881	20. Chester A. Arthur	47
21. Chester A. Arthur	Sept. 20, 1881-Mar. 3, 1885	(None)	47, 48
22. Grover Cleveland[7]	Mar. 4, 1885-Mar. 3, 1889	21. Thomas A. Hendricks[8]	49, 50
23. Benjamin Harrison	Mar. 4, 1889-Mar. 3, 1893	22. Levi P. Morton	51, 52
24. Grover Cleveland[7]	Mar. 4, 1893-Mar. 3, 1897	23. Adlai E. Stevenson	53, 54
25. William McKinley	Mar. 4, 1897-Mar. 3, 1901	24. Garret A. Hobart[9]	55, 56
(4)	Mar. 4, 1901-Sept. 14, 1901	25. Theodore Roosevelt	57
26. Theodore Roosevelt	Sept. 14, 1901-Mar. 3, 1905	(None)	57, 58
	Mar. 4, 1905-Mar. 3, 1909	26. Charles W. Fairbanks	59, 60
27. William H. Taft	Mar. 4, 1909-Mar. 3, 1913	27. James S. Sherman[10]	61, 62

President	Service	Vice President	Congresses
28. Woodrow Wilson	Mar. 4, 1913-Mar. 3, 1921	28. Thomas R. Marshall	63, 64, 65, 66
29. Warren G. Harding[4]	Mar. 4, 1921-Aug. 2, 1923	29. Calvin Coolidge	67
30. Calvin Coolidge	Aug. 3, 1923-Mar. 3, 1925	(None)	68
	Mar. 4, 1925-Mar. 3, 1929	30. Charles G. Dawes	69, 70
31. Herbert C. Hoover	Mar. 4, 1929-Mar. 3, 1933	31. Charles Curtis	71, 72
32. Franklin D. Roosevelt[11]	Mar. 4, 1933-Jan. 20, 1941	32. John N. Garner	73, 74, 75, 76, 77
	Jan. 20, 1941-Jan. 20, 1945	33. Henry A. Wallace	77, 78, 79
(4)	Jan. 20, 1945-Apr. 12, 1945	34. Harry S. Truman	79
33. Harry S. Truman	Apr. 12, 1945-Jan. 20, 1949	(None)	79, 80, 81
	Jan. 20, 1949-Jan. 20, 1953	35. Alben W. Barkley	81, 82, 83
34. Dwight D. Eisenhower	Jan. 20, 1953-Jan. 20, 1961	36. Richard M. Nixon	83, 84, 85, 86, 87
35. John F. Kennedy[4]	Jan. 20, 1961-Nov. 22, 1963	37. Lyndon B. Johnson	87, 88
36. Lyndon B. Johnson	Nov. 22, 1963-Jan. 20, 1965	(None)	88, 89
	Jan. 20, 1965-Jan. 20, 1969	38. Hubert H. Humphrey	89, 90, 91
37. Richard M. Nixon	Jan. 20, 1969-Jan. 20, 1973	39. Spiro T. Agnew[12]	91, 92, 93
(13)	Jan. 20, 1973-Aug. 9, 1974	40. Gerald R. Ford[14]	93
38. Gerald R. Ford[15]	Aug. 9, 1974-Jan. 20, 1977	41. Nelson A. Rockefeller[16]	93, 94, 95
39. Jimmy Carter	Jan. 20, 1977-Jan. 20, 1981	42. Walter F. Mondale	95, 96, 97
40. Ronald W. Reagan	Jan. 20, 1981-Jan. 20, 1989	43. George H. W. Bush	97, 98, 99, 100, 101
41. George H. W. Bush	Jan. 20, 1989-Jan. 20, 1993	44. Dan Quayle	101, 102, 103
42. Bill Clinton	Jan. 20, 1993-Jan. 20, 2001	45. Al Gore	103, 104, 105, 106, 107
43. George W. Bush	Jan. 20, 2001-Jan. 20, 2009	46. Dick Cheney	107, 108, 109, 110, 111
44. Barack H. Obama	Jan. 20, 2009-	47. Joe Biden	111, 112, 113

(1) Died Apr. 20, 1812. (2) Died Nov. 23, 1814. (3) Resigned Dec. 28, 1832, to become U.S. senator. (4) Died in office. (5) Died Apr. 18, 1853. (6) Died Nov. 22, 1875. (7) Terms not consecutive. (8) Died Nov. 25, 1885. (9) Died Nov. 21, 1899. (10) Died Oct. 30, 1912. (11) First president to be inaugurated under 20th Amendment, Jan. 20, 1937. (12) Resigned Oct. 10, 1973, after pleading no contest to a charge of tax evasion. (13) Resigned Aug. 9, 1974. (14) First nonelected vice president, chosen under 25th Amendment procedure. (15) First president never elected president or vice president. (16) Second nonelected vice president, chosen under 25th Amendment. Confirmed Dec. 19, 1974.

Vice Presidents of the U.S.

The numerals given vice presidents do not coincide with those given presidents, because some presidents (Tyler, Fillmore, A. Johnson, Arthur) had none, and some had more than one.

Name	Birthplace	Year	Home	Inaug.	Politics	Place of death	Year	Age at death
1. John Adams	Quincy, MA	1735	MA	1789	Fed.	Quincy, MA	1826	90
2. Thomas Jefferson	Shadwell, VA	1743	VA	1797	Dem.-Rep.	Monticello, VA	1826	83
3. Aaron Burr	Newark, NJ	1756	NY	1801	Dem.-Rep.	Staten Island, NY	1836	80
4. George Clinton	Little Britain, NY	1739	NY	1805	Dem.-Rep.	Washington, DC	1812	73
5. Elbridge Gerry	Marblehead, MA	1744	MA	1813	Dem.-Rep.	Washington, DC	1814	70
6. Daniel D. Tompkins	Scarsdale, NY	1774	NY	1817	Dem.-Rep.	Staten Island, NY	1825	51
7. John C. Calhoun[1]	Abbeville, SC	1782	SC	1825	Dem.-Rep.	Washington, DC	1850	68
8. Martin Van Buren	Kinderhook, NY	1782	NY	1833	Dem.	Kinderhook, NY	1862	79
9. Richard M. Johnson[2]	Louisville, KY	1780	KY	1837	Dem.	Frankfort, KY	1850	70
10. John Tyler	Greenway, VA	1790	VA	1841	Whig	Richmond, VA	1862	71
11. George M. Dallas	Philadelphia, PA	1792	PA	1845	Dem.	Philadelphia, PA	1864	72
12. Millard Fillmore	Cayuga Co., NY	1800	NY	1849	Whig	Buffalo, NY	1874	74
13. William R. King	Sampson Co., NC	1786	AL	1853	Dem.	Cahaba, AL	1853	67
14. John C. Breckinridge	Lexington, KY	1821	KY	1857	Dem.	Lexington, KY	1875	54
15. Hannibal Hamlin	Paris, ME	1809	ME	1861	Rep.	Bangor, ME	1891	81
16. Andrew Johnson	Raleigh, NC	1808	TN	1865	(3)	Carter Co., TN	1875	66
17. Schuyler Colfax	New York, NY	1823	IN	1869	Rep.	Mankato, MN	1885	62
18. Henry Wilson	Farmington, NH	1812	MA	1873	Rep.	Washington, DC	1875	63
19. William A. Wheeler	Malone, NY	1819	NY	1877	Rep.	Malone, NY	1887	68
20. Chester A. Arthur	Fairfield, VT	1829	NY	1881	Rep.	New York, NY	1886	57
21. Thomas A. Hendricks	Zanesville, OH	1819	IN	1885	Dem.	Indianapolis, IN	1885	66
22. Levi P. Morton	Shoreham, VT	1824	NY	1889	Rep.	Rhinebeck, NY	1920	96
23. Adlai E. Stevenson[4]	Christian Co., KY	1835	IL	1893	Dem.	Chicago, IL	1914	78
24. Garret A. Hobart	Long Branch, NJ	1844	NJ	1897	Rep.	Paterson, NJ	1899	55
25. Theodore Roosevelt	New York, NY	1858	NY	1901	Rep.	Oyster Bay, NY	1919	60
26. Charles W. Fairbanks	Unionville Centre, OH	1852	IN	1905	Rep.	Indianapolis, IN	1918	66
27. James S. Sherman	Utica, NY	1855	NY	1909	Rep.	Utica, NY	1912	57
28. Thomas R. Marshall	N. Manchester, IN	1854	IN	1913	Dem.	Washington, DC	1925	71
29. Calvin Coolidge	Plymouth Notch, VT	1872	MA	1921	Rep.	Northampton, MA	1933	60
30. Charles G. Dawes	Marietta, OH	1865	IL	1925	Rep.	Evanston, IL	1951	85
31. Charles Curtis	Topeka, KS	1860	KS	1929	Rep.	Washington, DC	1936	76
32. John Nance Garner	Red River Co., TX	1868	TX	1933	Dem.	Uvalde, TX	1967	98
33. Henry A. Wallace	Adair County, IA	1888	IA	1941	Dem.	Danbury, CT	1965	77
34. Harry S. Truman	Lamar, MO	1884	MO	1945	Dem.	Kansas City, MO	1972	88
35. Alben W. Barkley	Graves County, KY	1877	KY	1949	Dem.	Lexington, VA	1956	78
36. Richard M. Nixon	Yorba Linda, CA	1913	CA	1953	Rep.	New York, NY	1994	81
37. Lyndon B. Johnson	Stonewall, TX	1908	TX	1961	Dem.	San Antonio, TX	1973	64
38. Hubert H. Humphrey	Wallace, SD	1911	MN	1965	Dem.	Waverly, MN	1978	66
39. Spiro T. Agnew[5]	Baltimore, MD	1918	MD	1969	Rep.	Berlin, MD	1996	77
40. Gerald R. Ford[6]	Omaha, NE	1913	MI	1973	Rep.	Rancho Mirage, CA	2006	93
41. Nelson A. Rockefeller[7]	Bar Harbor, ME	1908	NY	1974	Rep.	New York, NY	1979	70
42. Walter F. Mondale	Ceylon, MN	1928	MN	1977	Dem.			
43. George H. W. Bush	Milton, MA	1924	TX	1981	Rep.			
44. James Danforth (Dan) Quayle Jr.	Indianapolis, IN	1947	IN	1989	Rep.			
45. Albert A. Gore	Washington, DC	1948	TN	1993	Dem.			
46. Richard B. Cheney	Lincoln, NE	1941	WY	2001	Rep.			
47. Joseph R. Biden Jr.	Scranton, PA	1942	DE	2009	Dem.			

(1) Resigned Dec. 28, 1832, having been elected to the Senate to fill a vacancy. (2) Richard M. Johnson was the only vice president to be chosen by the Senate because of a tied vote in the Electoral College. (3) Democrat Andrew Johnson was nominated vice president by Republicans and elected with Lincoln on the National Union Ticket. (4) Grandfather of Democratic candidate for president in 1952 and 1956. (5) Resigned Oct. 10, 1973, after pleading no contest to a charge of tax evasion. (6) First nonelected vice president, chosen under 25th Amendment procedure. (7) Second nonelected vice president, chosen under 25th Amendment.

Biographies of the Presidents

George Washington (1789-97), first president, Federalist, was born on Feb. 22, 1732, in Wakefield on Pope's Creek, Westmoreland Co., VA, the son of Augustine and Mary Ball Washington. He spent his early childhood on a farm near Fredericksburg. His father died when Washington was 11. He studied mathematics and surveying, and at 16, he went to live with his elder half brother, Lawrence, who built and named Mount Vernon in Virginia. Washington surveyed the lands of Thomas Fairfax in the Shenandoah Valley. He accompanied Lawrence to Barbados, West Indies, where he contracted smallpox and was deeply scarred. Lawrence died in 1752, and Washington inherited his property. He valued land, and when he died, he owned 70,000 acres in Virginia and 40,000 acres in what is now West Virginia.

Washington's military service began in 1753, when Lt. Gov. Robert Dinwiddie of Virginia sent him on missions deep into Ohio country. He clashed with the French and had to surrender Fort Necessity on July 3, 1754. He was an aide to the British general Edward Braddock and was at his side when the army was ambushed and defeated (July 9, 1755) on a march to Fort Duquesne. He helped take Fort Duquesne from the French in 1758.

After Washington's marriage to Martha Dandridge Custis, a widow, in 1759, he managed his family estate at Mount Vernon. Although not at first for independence, he opposed the repressive measures of the British crown and took charge of the Virginia troops before war broke out. He was made commander of the newly created Continental Army by the Continental Congress on June 15, 1775.

The American victory was due largely to Washington's leadership. He was resourceful, a disciplinarian, and the one dependable force for unity. Washington favored a federal government. He became chairman of the Constitutional Convention of 1787 and helped get the Constitution ratified. Unanimously elected president by the Electoral College he was inaugurated Apr. 30, 1789, on the balcony of New York's Federal Hall. He was reelected in 1792. Washington made an effort to avoid partisan politics as president.

Refusing to consider a third term, Washington retired to Mount Vernon in Mar. 1797. A ride in snow and rain around his estate led to what present-day doctors believe to have been an attack of acute epiglottitis. Doctors were unsuccessful in treating the inflammation in his throat, and Washington died Dec. 14, 1799.

John Adams (1797-1801), second president, Federalist, was born on Oct. 30, 1735, in Braintree (now Quincy), MA, the son of John and Susanna Boylston Adams. He was a great-grandson of Henry Adams, who came from England in 1636. He graduated from Harvard in 1755, then taught school and studied law. He married Abigail Smith in 1764. In 1765 he argued against taxation without representation before the royal governor. In 1770, he successfully defended in court the British soldiers who fired on civilians in the Boston Massacre. He was a delegate to the Continental Congress and a signer of the Declaration of Independence. In 1778, Congress sent Adams and John Jay to join Benjamin Franklin as diplomatic representatives in Europe. Because he ran second to Washington in Electoral College balloting in Feb. 1789, Adams became the nation's first vice president, a post he characterized as highly insignificant; he was reelected in 1792.

In 1796 Adams was chosen president by the electors. His administration was marked by growing conflict with fellow Federalist Alexander Hamilton and with others in his own cabinet who supported Hamilton's strongly anti-French position. Adams avoided full-scale war with France but became unpopular, especially after securing passage of the Alien and Sedition Acts in 1798. His foreign policy contributed significantly to the election of Thomas Jefferson in 1800.

Adams lived for a quarter century after he left office, during which time he wrote extensively. He died July 4, 1826, on the same day as his rival Thomas Jefferson (the 50th anniversary of the Declaration of Independence).

Thomas Jefferson (1801-09), third president, Democratic-Republican, was born on Apr. 13, 1743, in Shadwell in Goochland (now Albemarle) Co., VA, the son of Peter and Jane Randolph Jefferson. His father died when Jefferson was 14, leaving him 2,750 acres and his slaves. Jefferson attended (1760-62) the College of William and Mary, read Greek and Latin classics, and played the violin. In 1769 he was elected to the Virginia House of Burgesses. In 1770 he began building his home, Monticello, and in 1772 he married Martha Wayles Skelton, a wealthy widow. Jefferson helped establish the Virginia Committee of Correspondence. As a member of the Second Continental Congress he drafted the Declaration of Independence. He also was a member of the Virginia House of Delegates (1776-79) and was elected governor of Virginia in 1779. Reelected in 1780, he resigned the next year after British troops invaded Virginia. During his term he wrote the statute on religious freedom. After his wife's death in 1782, Jefferson again became a delegate to the Congress, and in 1784 he drafted the report that was the basis for the Ordinances of 1784, 1785, and 1787. He was minister to France from 1785 to 1789, when George Washington appointed him secretary of state.

Jefferson's strong faith in the consent of the governed conflicted with the emphasis on executive control, favored by Sec. of the Treasury Alexander Hamilton, and Jefferson resigned on Dec. 31, 1793. In the 1796 election Jefferson was the Democratic-Republican candidate for president; John Adams won the election, and Jefferson became vice president. In 1800, Jefferson and Aaron Burr received equal Electoral College votes; the House of Representatives elected Jefferson president. Jefferson was a strong advocate of westward expansion; major events of his first term were the Louisiana Purchase (1803) and the Lewis and Clark expedition. An important development during his second term was passage of the Embargo Act, barring U.S. ships from setting sail to foreign ports. Jefferson established the Univ. of Virginia and designed its buildings. He died July 4, 1826, on the same day as John Adams (the 50th anniversary of the Declaration of Independence).

Analysis of contemporary accounts, plantation records, and DNA taken from descendants of Jefferson and of Sally Hemings, one of his slaves, has caused many historians to conclude Jefferson fathered one or more of her six children.

James Madison (1809-17), fourth president, Democratic-Republican, was born on Mar. 16, 1751, in Port Conway, King George Co., VA, the son of James and Eleanor Rose Conway Madison. Madison graduated from the College of New Jersey in 1771. He served in the Virginia Constitutional Convention (1776), and, in 1780, became a delegate to the Second Continental Congress. He was chief recorder at the Constitutional Convention in 1787 and supported ratification in the *Federalist Papers*, written with Alexander Hamilton and John Jay. In 1789, Madison was elected to the House of Representatives, where he helped frame the Bill of Rights and fought against passage of the Alien and Sedition Acts. In the 1790s, he helped found the Democratic-Republican Party, which ultimately became the Democratic Party. He became Jefferson's secretary of state in 1801.

Madison was elected president in 1808. His first term was marked by tensions with Great Britain, and his conduct of foreign policy was criticized by the Federalists and by his own party. Nevertheless, he was reelected in 1812, the year war was declared on Great Britain. The war that many considered a second American revolution ended with a treaty that did not settle any of the issues. Madison's most important action after the war was demilitarizing the U.S.-Canadian border.

In 1817, Madison retired to his estate, Montpelier, where he served as an elder statesman. He edited his famous papers on the Constitutional Convention and helped found the Univ. of Virginia, of which he became rector in 1826. He died June 28, 1836.

James Monroe (1817-25), fifth president, Democratic-Republican, was born on Apr. 28, 1758, in Westmoreland Co., VA, the son of Spence and Elizabeth Jones Monroe. He entered the College of William and Mary in 1774 but left to serve in the Third Virginia Regiment during the American Revolution. After the war, he studied law with Thomas Jefferson. In 1782 he was elected to the Virginia House of Delegates, and he served (1783-86) as a delegate to the Continental Congress. He opposed ratification of the Constitution because it lacked a bill of rights. Monroe was elected to the U.S. Senate in 1790. In 1794, Pres. Washington appointed Monroe minister to France. He served twice as governor of Virginia (1799-1802, 1811). Pres. Jefferson also sent him to France as minister (1803), and from 1803 to 1807, he served as minister to Great Britain.

In 1816 Monroe was elected president; he was reelected in 1820 with all but one Electoral College vote. His administration became known as the Era of Good Feeling. He obtained Florida from Spain, settled boundary disputes with Britain over Canada, and eliminated border forts. He supported the antislavery position that led to the Missouri Compromise. His most significant contribution was the Monroe Doctrine, which opposed European intervention in the Western Hemisphere and became a cornerstone of U.S. foreign policy.

Although Monroe retired to Oak Hill, VA, financial problems forced him to sell his property and move to New York City. He died there on July 4, 1831.

John Quincy Adams (1825-29), sixth president, independent Federalist, later Democratic-Republican, was born on July 11, 1767, in Braintree (now Quincy), MA, the son of John and Abigail Adams. His father was the second president. He studied abroad and at Harvard College, from which he graduated in 1787. In 1803, he was elected to the U.S. Senate. President Monroe chose him as his secretary of state in 1817. In this capacity he negotiated the cession of Florida from Spain, supported exclusion of slavery in the Missouri Compromise, and helped formulate the Monroe Doctrine.

After no candidate won an Electoral College majority in 1824, the presidential election was thrown into the House of Representatives; Adams won with support from rival Henry Clay, whom he named secretary of state, fueling accusations of a "corrupt bargain." His expansion of executive powers was strongly opposed, and in the 1828 election he lost to Andrew Jackson. In 1831 he entered the House of Representatives and served 17 years with distinction. He opposed slavery, the annexation of Texas, and the Mexican War. He helped establish the Smithsonian Institution.

Adams suffered a stroke in the House and died in the Speaker's Room on Feb. 23, 1848.

Andrew Jackson (1829-37), seventh president, Democratic-Republican, later a Democrat, was born on Mar. 15, 1767, in the Waxhaw district, on the border of North and South Carolina, the son of Andrew and Elizabeth Hutchinson Jackson. At the age of 13, he joined the militia to fight in the American Revolution and was captured. Orphaned at age 14, Jackson was brought up by a well-to-do uncle. By age 20, he was practicing law, and he later served as prosecuting attorney in Nashville, TN. In 1796 he helped draft the constitution of Tennessee, and for a year he occupied its one seat in the House of Representatives. The next year he served in the U.S. Senate.

In the War of 1812, Jackson crushed the Creek Indians at Horseshoe Bend, AL (1814), and, with a greatly outnumbered army consisting chiefly of backwoods militia members and volunteers, defeated Gen. Edward Pakenham's British troops at the Battle of New Orleans (1815). Nicknamed "Old Hickory" for his toughness, he emerged a national hero.

In 1818 Jackson briefly invaded Spanish Florida to quell Seminoles and outlaws who harassed frontier settlements. He ran for president against John Quincy Adams in 1824, but, although he won the most popular and electoral votes, he did not have a majority. The House of Representatives decided the election and chose Adams. In the 1828 election, however, Jackson defeated Adams, carrying the West and the South.

As president, Jackson introduced what became known as the spoils system—rewarding party members with government posts. A self-professed champion of the common man, he also viewed the Second Bank of the U.S. as a bastion of privilege and made it a major issue in the election of 1832, the first where candidates were chosen at national conventions rather than in congressional caucuses. Defeating Henry Clay, Jackson increasingly diverted funds from the national bank into so-called pet banks run by members of his own party. When South Carolina refused to collect imports under a federal tariff, which it declared null and void, Jackson won passage of legislation confirming his right to use military force to obtain compliance; eventually the tariff rate was reduced and the nullifiers backed down. After leaving office in 1837, he retired to the Hermitage, his estate outside Nashville, where he died on June 8, 1845.

Martin Van Buren (1837-41), eighth president, Democrat, was born on Dec. 5, 1782, in Kinderhook, NY, the son of Abraham and Maria Hoes Van Buren. After attending local schools, he studied law and became a lawyer at the age of 20. A consummate politician, Van Buren began his career in the New York state senate and then served as state attorney general (1816-19). He was elected to the U.S. Senate in 1821. He helped swing Eastern support to Andrew Jackson in the 1828 election and then served as Jackson's secretary of state from 1829 to 1831. In 1832 he was elected vice president. Known as the "Little Magician," Van Buren was extremely influential in Jackson's administration.

In 1836, Van Buren defeated William Henry Harrison for president and took office as the financial panic of 1837 initiated a nationwide depression. Although he instituted the independent treasury system, his refusal to spend land revenues led to his defeat by William Henry Harrison in 1840. In 1844 he lost the Democratic nomination to James K. Polk. In 1848 he again ran for president on the Free Soil ticket but lost. He died in Kinderhook on July 24, 1862.

William Henry Harrison (1841), ninth president, Whig, who served only 31 days, was born on Feb. 9, 1773, in Berkeley, Charles City Co., VA, the son of Benjamin Harrison—a signer of the Declaration of Independence—and of Elizabeth Bassett Harrison. He attended Hampden-Sydney College. Harrison served as secretary of the Northwest Territory in 1798 and was its delegate to the House of Representatives in 1799. He was the first governor of Indiana Territory and served as superintendent of Indian affairs. With 900 men he put down a Shawnee uprising at Tippecanoe, IN, on Nov. 7, 1811. A generation later, in 1840, he waged a rousing presidential campaign, using the slogan "Tippecanoe and Tyler Too." The Tyler of the slogan was his running mate, John Tyler.

Although born to one of the wealthiest, most prestigious, and most influential families in Virginia, Harrison was elected president with the slogan, "Log Cabin and Hard Cider." He caught pneumonia during his inauguration and died Apr. 4, 1841, after only one month in office.

John Tyler (1841-45), 10th president, independent Whig, was born on Mar. 29, 1790, in Greenway, Charles City Co., VA, the son of John and Mary Armistead Tyler. His father was governor of Virginia (1808-11). Tyler graduated from the College of William and Mary in 1807 and in 1811 was elected to the Virginia legislature. In 1816 he was chosen for the U.S. House of Representatives. He served in the Virginia legislature again from 1823 to 1825, when he was elected governor of Virginia. After a stint in the U.S. Senate (1827-36), he was elected vice president (1840).

When William Henry Harrison died only a month after taking office, Tyler succeeded him. Because he was the first person to occupy the presidency without having been elected to that office, he was referred to as "His Accidency." He gained passage of the Preemption Act of 1841, which gave squatters on government land the right to buy 160 acres at the minimum auction price. His last act as president was to sign a resolution annexing Texas. Tyler accepted renomination in 1844 from some Democrats but withdrew in favor of the official party candidate, James K. Polk. A strong advocate of states' rights, he served briefly in the Confederate House of Representatives before he died in Richmond, VA, on Jan. 18, 1862.

James Knox Polk (1845-49), 11th president, Democrat, was born on Nov. 2, 1795, in Mecklenburg Co., NC, the son of Samuel and Jane Knox Polk. He graduated from the Univ. of North Carolina in 1818 and served in the Tennessee state legislature from 1823 to 1825. He served in the U.S. House of Representatives from 1825 to 1839, the last four years as Speaker. He was governor of Tennessee from 1839 to 1841. In 1844, after the Democratic National Convention became deadlocked, it nominated Polk, who became the first "dark horse" candidate for president. He was nominated primarily because he favored annexation of Texas.

As president, Polk reestablished the independent treasury system originated by Van Buren. He was so intent on acquiring California from Mexico that he sent troops to the Mexican border and, when Mexicans attacked, declared that a state of war existed. The Mexican War ended with the annexation of California and much of the Southwest as part of America's "manifest destiny." Polk compromised on the Oregon boundary ("54-40 or fight!") by accepting the 49th parallel and yielding Vancouver Island to the British. Polk died in Nashville, TN, on June 15, 1849, a few months after leaving office.

Zachary Taylor (1849-50), 12th president, Whig, who served only 16 months, was born on Nov. 24, 1784, in Orange Co., VA, the son of Richard and Sarah Strother Taylor. He grew up on his father's plantation near Louisville, KY, where he was educated by private tutors. In 1808 Taylor joined the regular army and was commissioned first lieutenant. He fought in the War of 1812, the Black Hawk War (1832), and the second Seminole War (beginning in 1837). He was called "Old Rough and Ready." In 1846 Pres. Polk sent him with an army to the Rio Grande. When the Mexicans attacked him, Polk declared war. Outnumbered four to one, Taylor defeated Antonio López de Santa Anna at Buena Vista (1847).

A national hero, Taylor received the Whig nomination in 1848 and was elected president, even though he had never bothered to vote. He resumed the spoils system and, though a slaveholder, worked to admit California as a free state. He fell ill, likely from a case of acute gastroenteritis, and died in office on July 9, 1850.

Millard Fillmore (1850-53), 13th president, Whig, was born on Jan. 7, 1800, in Cayuga Co., NY, the son of Nathaniel and Phoebe Millard Fillmore. Although he had little schooling, he became a law clerk at the age of 22 and a year later was admitted to the bar. He was elected to the New York state assembly in 1828 and served until 1831. From 1833 until 1835 and again from 1837 to 1843, he represented his district in the U.S. House of Representatives. He opposed the entrance of Texas as a slave state and voted for a protective tariff. In 1844 he was defeated for governor of New York.

In 1848, he was elected vice president, and he succeeded as president after Taylor's death. Fillmore favored the Compromise of 1850 and signed the Fugitive Slave Law. His policies pleased neither expansionists nor slaveholders, and he was not renominated in 1852. In 1856 he was nominated by the American (Know-Nothing) Party, but despite the support of the Whigs, he was defeated by James Buchanan. He died in Buffalo, NY, on Mar. 8, 1874.

Franklin Pierce (1853-57), 14th president, Democrat, was born on Nov. 23, 1804, in Hillsboro, NH, the son of Benjamin Pierce, Revolutionary War general and governor of New Hampshire, and Anna Kendrick. He graduated from Bowdoin College in 1824 and was admitted to the bar in 1827. He was elected to the New Hampshire state legislature in 1829 and was chosen Speaker in 1831. He went to the U.S. House in 1833 and was elected a U.S. senator in 1837. He enlisted in the Mexican War and became brigadier general under Gen. Winfield Scott.

In 1852 Pierce was nominated as the Democratic presidential candidate on the 49th ballot. He decisively defeated Gen. Scott, his Whig opponent, in the election. Although he was against slavery, Pierce was influenced by proslavery Southerners. He supported the controversial Kansas-Nebraska Act, which left the question of slavery in the new territories of Kansas and Nebraska to popular vote. Pierce signed a reciprocity treaty with Canada and approved the Gadsden Purchase of a border area on a proposed railroad route, from Mexico. Denied renomination, he spent most of his remaining years in Concord, NH, where he died on Oct. 8, 1869.

James Buchanan (1857-61), 15th president, Federalist, later Democrat, was born on Apr. 23, 1791, near Mercersburg, PA, the son of James and Elizabeth Speer Buchanan. He graduated from Dickinson College in 1809 and was admitted to the bar in 1812. He fought in the War of 1812 as a volunteer. He was twice elected to the Pennsylvania general assembly, and in 1821 he entered the U.S. House of Representatives. After briefly serving (1832-33) as minister to Russia, he was elected U.S. senator from Pennsylvania. As Polk's secretary of state (1845-49), he ended the Oregon dispute with Britain and supported the Mexican War and annexation of Texas. As minister to Great Britain, he signed the Ostend Manifesto (1854), declaring a U.S. right to take Cuba by force should efforts to purchase it fail.

Nominated by Democrats, Buchanan was elected president in 1856. On slavery he favored popular sovereignty and choice by state constitutions but did not consistently uphold this position. He denied the right of states to secede but opposed coercion and attempted to keep peace by not provoking secessionists. Buchanan left office having failed to deal decisively with the situation. He died at Wheatland, his estate, near Lancaster, PA, on June 1, 1868.

Abraham Lincoln (1861-65), 16th president, Whig, then Republican, was born on Feb. 12, 1809, in a log cabin on a farm in Hardin (now Larue) Co., KY, the son of Thomas and Nancy Hanks Lincoln. The Lincolns moved to Spencer Co., IN, near Gentryville, when Lincoln was 7. After Lincoln's mother died, his father married Mrs. Sarah Bush Johnston in 1819. In 1830 the family moved to Macon Co., IL.

Defeated in 1832 in a race for the state legislature, Lincoln was elected on the Whig ticket two years later and served in the lower house from 1834 to 1842. In 1837 Lincoln was admitted to the bar and became partner in a Springfield, IL, law office. In 1846, he was elected to Congress, where he attracted attention during a single term for his opposition to the Mexican War and his position on slavery. In 1856 he campaigned for the newly founded Republican Party, and in 1858 he became its senatorial candidate against Stephen A. Douglas. Although he lost the election, Lincoln gained national recognition from his debates with Douglas.

In 1860, Lincoln was nominated for president by the Republican Party on a platform of restricting slavery. He ran against Douglas, a northern Democrat; John C. Breckinridge, a Southern proslavery Democrat; and John Bell, of the Constitutional Union Party. In response to Lincoln's victory, South Carolina seceded from the Union on Dec. 20, 1860, soon followed by six other Southern states.

The Civil War erupted when Fort Sumter, which Lincoln decided to resupply, was attacked by Confederate forces on Apr. 12, 1861. Lincoln called successfully for recruits from the North, and four more Southern states seceded. Hundreds of thousands of Union and Confederate soldiers were killed or wounded in four years of battle that followed. On Sept. 22, 1862, five days after the Battle of Antietam, Lincoln announced that slaves in territory then in rebellion would be free Jan. 1, 1863, under his Emancipation Proclamation. His speeches, including his Gettysburg and inaugural addresses, are remembered for their eloquence.

Lincoln was reelected, in 1864, over Gen. George B. McClellan, a Democrat. Confederate Gen. Robert E. Lee surrendered on Apr. 9, 1865. On Apr. 14, Lincoln was shot by actor John Wilkes Booth in Ford's Theater, in Washington, DC. He died the next day.

Andrew Johnson (1865-69), 17th president, Democrat, was born on Dec. 29, 1808, in Raleigh, NC, the son of Jacob and Mary McDonough Johnson. He was apprenticed to a tailor as a youth but ran away after two years and eventually settled in Greeneville, TN, where he was elected councilman and later mayor. In 1835 he was sent to the state general assembly. In 1843 he was elected to the U.S. House of Representatives, where he served for 10 years. Johnson was also governor of Tennessee from 1853 to 1857, when he was elected to the U.S. Senate. Although Johnson had held slaves, he opposed secession and tried to prevent Tennessee from seceding. In Mar. 1862, Lincoln appointed him military governor of occupied Tennessee.

In 1864, in order to balance Lincoln's ticket with a Southern Democrat, the Republicans nominated Johnson for vice president. He was elected vice president with Lincoln and then succeeded to the presidency upon Lincoln's death. Soon afterward, in a controversy with Congress over the president's power over the South, he proclaimed an amnesty to all Confederates, except certain leaders, if they would ratify the 13th Amendment abolishing slavery. States doing so added anti-Negro provisions that enraged Congress, which restored military control over the South. When Johnson removed Sec. of War Edwin M. Stanton without notifying the Senate, the House impeached him in Feb. 1868. Charging him with thereby having violated the Tenure of Office Act, the House was actually responding to his opposition to harsh congressional Reconstruction, expressed in repeated vetoes. He was acquitted in the Senate by one-vote margins on each of two counts.

Johnson was denied renomination but remained politically active. He was reelected to the Senate in 1874. Johnson died July 31, 1875, at Carter Station, TN.

Ulysses S. Grant (1869-77), 18th president, Republican, was born on Apr. 27, 1822, in Point Pleasant, OH, the son of Jesse R. and Hannah Simpson Grant. The next year the family moved to Georgetown, OH. Grant was named Hiram Ulysses. Upon entering West Point in 1839, he found his name had been put down as Ulysses S. Grant, with his middle name first and his mother's maiden name as his middle name. He eventually adopted it as his true name but maintained the "S" did not stand for anything. Grant graduated in 1843. During the Mexican War, Grant served under both Gen. Zachary Taylor and Gen. Winfield Scott. In 1854, he resigned his commission because of loneliness and drinking problems, and in the following years he engaged in generally unsuccessful farming and business ventures. With the start of the Civil War, he was named colonel and then brigadier general of the Illinois Volunteers. He took Forts Henry and Donelson and fought at Shiloh. His brilliant campaign against Vicksburg and his victory at Chattanooga made him so prominent that Lincoln placed him in command of all Union armies. Grant accepted Confederate Gen. Robert E. Lee's surrender at Appomattox Court House on Apr. 9, 1865.

Grant was nominated for president by the Republicans in 1868 and elected over Democrat Horatio Seymour. The 15th Amendment, the amnesty bill, and peaceful settlement of disputes with Great Britain were events of his administration. The Liberal Republicans and Democrats opposed him with Horace Greeley in the 1872 election, but Grant was reelected. His second administration was marked by scandals, including the Crédit Mobilier affair, the Whiskey Ring, in which high-ranked officials conspired to defraud the government of taxes, and the impeachment of his secretary of war. An attempt by the Stalwarts (Old Guard Republicans) to nominate him in 1880 failed. Left penniless by the 1884 collapse of an investment firm in which he was a partner, he wrote his well-regarded memoirs to provide income for his family while he was suffering from cancer. He died at Mt. McGregor, NY, on July 23, 1885.

Rutherford Birchard Hayes (1877-81), 19th president, Republican, was born on Oct. 4, 1822, in Delaware, OH, the son of Rutherford and Sophia Birchard Hayes. He was reared by his uncle, Sardis Birchard. Hayes graduated from Kenyon College in 1842 and from Harvard Law School in 1845. He practiced law in Lower Sandusky (now Fremont), OH, and was city solicitor of Cincinnati from 1858 to 1861. During the Civil War, he was major of the 23rd Ohio Volunteers. He was wounded several times, and by the end of the war he had risen to the rank of brevet major general. While serving (1865-67) in the U.S. House of Representatives, Hayes supported Reconstruction and Johnson's impeachment. He was twice elected governor of Ohio (1867, 1869). After losing a race for the U.S. House in 1872, he was reelected governor of Ohio in 1875.

In 1876, Hayes was nominated for president and believed he had lost the election to Democrat Samuel J. Tilden. But a few Southern states submitted two sets of electoral votes, and the result was in dispute. An electoral commission, consisting of 8 Republicans and 7 Democrats, awarded all disputed votes to Hayes, allowing him to become president by one electoral vote. Hayes, keeping a promise to Southerners, withdrew troops from areas still occupied in the South, ending the era of Reconstruction. He proposed civil service reforms, alienating those favoring the spoils system, and advocated repeal of the Tenure of Office Act restricting presidential power to dismiss officials. He supported sound money and specie payments.

Hayes died in Fremont, OH, on Jan. 17, 1893.

James Abram Garfield (1881), 20th president, Republican, was born on Nov. 19, 1831, in Orange, Cuyahoga Co., OH, the son of Abram and Eliza Ballou Garfield. His father died in 1833, and he was reared in poverty by his mother. He worked as a canal bargeman, a farmer, and a carpenter. He attended Western Reserve Eclectic Institute and graduated from Williams College in 1856. He returned to Western Reserve to teach and in 1857, at age 25, he became the school's president. In 1859 he was elected to the Ohio legislature. Antislavery and antisecession, he volunteered for military service in the Civil War, becoming colonel of the 42nd Ohio Infantry and brigadier in 1862. He fought at Shiloh, TN, was chief of staff for Gen. William Starke Rosecrans, and was made major general for gallantry at Chickamauga, GA. He entered Congress as a radical Republican in 1863, calling for execution or exile of Confederate leaders, but he moderated his views after the Civil War. On the electoral commission in 1877 he voted for Hayes against Tilden on strict party lines.

Garfield was a senator-elect in 1880 when he became the Republican nominee for president. He was chosen as a compromise over Gen. Grant, James G. Blaine, and John Sherman, and won election despite some bitterness among Grant's supporters. For much of his brief tenure as president, Garfield was concerned with a fight between New York Sen. Roscoe Conkling, who opposed two major appointments made by Garfield. On July 2, 1881, Garfield was shot and seriously wounded by a mentally disturbed office seeker, Charles J. Guiteau, while entering a railroad station in Washington, DC. He died on Sept. 19, 1881, in Elberon, NJ.

Chester Alan Arthur (1881-85), 21st president, Republican, was born on Oct. 5, 1829, in Fairfield, VT, to William and Malvina Stone Arthur. He graduated from Union College in 1848, taught school in Vermont, then studied law and practiced in New York City. In 1853, he argued in a fugitive slave case that slaves transported through New York State were thereby freed. In 1871, he was appointed collector of the Port of New York. Pres. Hayes, an opponent of the spoils system, forced him to resign in 1878. This made the New York machine enemies of Hayes. Arthur and the Stalwarts (Old Guard Republicans) tried to nominate Grant for a third term as president in 1880. When Garfield was nominated, Arthur was nominated for vice president in the interests of harmony.

Upon Garfield's assassination, Arthur became president. Despite his past connections, he signed major civil service reform legislation. Arthur tried to dissuade Congress from enacting the high protective tariff of 1883. He was defeated for renomination in 1884 by James G. Blaine. He died in New York City on Nov. 18, 1886.

Grover Cleveland (1885-89; 1893-97) *(According to a State Dept. ruling, Grover Cleveland should be counted as both the 22nd and the 24th president because his two terms were not consecutive),* Democrat, was born Stephen Grover Cleveland on Mar. 18, 1837, in Caldwell, NJ, the son of Richard F. and Ann Neal Cleveland. When he was a small boy, his family moved to New York. Prevented by his father's death from attending college, he studied by himself and was admitted to the bar in Buffalo, NY, in 1859. In succession he became assistant district attorney (1863), sheriff (1871), mayor (1881), and governor of New York (1882). He was an independent, honest administrator who hated corruption. Cleveland was nominated for president over Tammany Hall opposition in 1884 and defeated Republican James G. Blaine.

As president, he enlarged the civil service and vetoed many pension raids on the Treasury. In the 1888 election he was defeated by Benjamin Harrison, although his popular vote was larger. Reelected over Harrison in 1892, he faced a money crisis brought about by a lowered gold reserve, circulation of paper, and exorbitant silver purchases under the Sherman Silver Purchase Act. He obtained a repeal of the Sherman Act but was unable to secure effective tariff reform. A severe economic depression and labor troubles racked his administration, but he refused to interfere in business matters and rejected Jacob Coxey's demand for unemployment relief. In 1894, he broke the Pullman strike. Cleveland was not renominated in 1896. He died in Princeton, NJ, on June 24, 1908.

Benjamin Harrison (1889-93), 23rd president, Republican, was born on Aug. 20, 1833, in North Bend, OH, the son of John Scott and Elizabeth Irwin Harrison. His great-grandfather, Benjamin Harrison, was a signer of the Declaration of Independence; his grandfather, William Henry Harrison, was the ninth president; his father was a member of Congress. He attended school on his father's farm and graduated from Miami Univ. in Oxford, OH, in 1852. He was admitted to the bar in 1854 and practiced in Indianapolis, IN. During the Civil War, he rose to the rank of brevet brigadier general and fought at Kennesaw Mountain, Peachtree Creek, Nashville, and in the Atlanta campaign. He lost the 1876 gubernatorial election in Indiana but succeeded in becoming a U.S. senator in 1881.

In 1888 he defeated Cleveland for president despite receiving fewer popular votes. As president, he expanded the pension list and signed the McKinley high tariff bill, the Sherman Antitrust Act, and the Sherman Silver Purchase Act. During his administration, six states were admitted to the Union. He was defeated for reelection in 1892. He died in Indianapolis, IN, on Mar. 13, 1901.

William McKinley (1897-1901), 25th president, Republican, was born on Jan. 29, 1843, in Niles, OH, the son of William and Nancy Allison McKinley. McKinley briefly attended Allegheny College. When the Civil War broke out in 1861, he enlisted and served for the duration. He rose to captain and in 1865 was made brevet major. After studying law in Albany, NY, he opened a law office in Canton, OH (1867). He served twice in the U.S. House (1877-83; 1885-91) and led the fight there for the McKinley Tariff, passed in 1890; he was not reelected to the House as a result. He served two terms (1892-96) as governor of Ohio.

In 1896 he was elected president as a proponent of a protective tariff and sound money (gold standard) over William Jennings Bryan, the Democrat and a proponent of free silver. McKinley was reluctant to intervene in Cuba, but the loss of the battleship *Maine* at Havana crystallized opinion. He demanded Spain's withdrawal from Cuba; Spain made some concessions,

but Congress announced a state of war as of Apr. 21, 1898. He was reelected in the 1900 campaign, defeating Bryan's anti-imperialist arguments with the promise of a "full dinner pail." He was known for a conservative stance on business issues. On Sept. 6, 1901, at the Pan-American Exposition, in Buffalo, NY, he was shot by Leon Czolgosz, an anarchist. He died Sept. 14.

Theodore Roosevelt (1901-09), 26th president, Republican, was born on Oct. 27, 1858, in New York City, the son of Theodore and Martha Bulloch Roosevelt. He was a 5th cousin of Franklin D. Roosevelt and an uncle of Eleanor Roosevelt. Roosevelt graduated from Harvard Univ. in 1880. He attended Columbia Law School briefly but abandoned law to enter politics. He was elected to the New York State Assembly in 1881 and served until 1884. He spent the next two years ranching and hunting in the Dakota Territory. In 1886, he ran unsuccessfully for mayor of New York City. He was civil service commissioner in Washington, DC, from 1889 to 1895. From 1895 to 1897, he served as New York City's police commissioner. He was assistant secretary of the Navy under McKinley. The Spanish-American War made him nationally known. He organized the First U.S. Volunteer Cavalry (Rough Riders) and, as lieutenant colonel, led the charge up Kettle Hill in San Juan. Elected New York governor in 1898, he fought the spoils system and achieved taxation of corporation franchises.

Nominated for vice president in 1900, Roosevelt became the nation's youngest president when McKinley was assassinated. He was reelected in 1904. As president he fought corruption of politics by big business, dissolved the Northern Securities Co. and others for violating antitrust laws, intervened in the 1902 coal strike on behalf of the public, obtained the Elkins Law (1903) forbidding rebates to favored corporations, and helped pass the Hepburn Railway Rate Act of 1906 (extending jurisdiction of the Interstate Commerce Commission). He helped obtain passage of the Pure Food and Drug Act (1906) and of employers' liability laws. Roosevelt vigorously organized conservation efforts. He mediated the peace between Japan and Russia in 1905, for which he won the Nobel Peace Prize. He abetted the 1903 revolution in Panama that led to U.S. acquisition of territory for the Panama Canal.

In 1908 Roosevelt obtained the nomination of William H. Taft, who was elected. Feeling that Taft had abandoned his policies, he unsuccessfully sought the nomination in 1912. He then ran on the Progressive "Bull Moose" ticket against Taft and Woodrow Wilson, splitting the Republicans and ensuring Wilson's election. During the campaign he was shot by a mentally deranged man but was not seriously wounded. In 1916, after unsuccessfully seeking the presidential nomination, he supported the Republican candidate, Charles E. Hughes. He strongly promoted U.S. intervention in World War I.

Roosevelt was a voracious reader and wrote some 40 books, including *The Winning of the West*. He died Jan. 6, 1919, at Sagamore Hill, his home in Oyster Bay, NY.

William Howard Taft (1909-13), 27th president, Republican, and 10th chief justice of the U.S., was born on Sept. 15, 1857, in Cincinnati, OH, the son of Alphonso and Louisa Maria Torrey Taft. His father was secretary of war and attorney general in Grant's cabinet and minister to Austria and Russia under Arthur. Taft graduated from Yale in 1878 and from Cincinnati Law School in 1880. After working as a law reporter for Cincinnati newspapers, he served as assistant prosecuting attorney (1881-82), assistant county solicitor (1885), superior court judge (1887), U.S. solicitor-general (1890), and federal circuit judge (1892). In 1900 he became head of the U.S. Philippines Commission and was the first civil governor of the Philippines (1901-04). In 1904 he served as secretary of war, and in 1906 he was sent to Cuba to help avert a threatened revolution.

Taft was groomed for the presidency by Theodore Roosevelt and elected over William Jennings Bryan in 1908. Taft vigorously continued Roosevelt's trust-busting, instituted the Dept. of Labor, and drafted amendments calling for direct election of senators and an income tax. However, his tariff and

conservation policies angered progressives. Although renominated in 1912, he was opposed by Roosevelt, who ran on the Progressive Party ticket; the result was Wilson's election.

Taft, with some reservations, supported the League of Nations. After leaving office, he was professor of constitutional law at Yale (1913-21) and chief justice of the U.S. (1921-30). Taft was the only person in U.S. history to have been both president and chief justice. He died in Washington, DC, on Mar. 8, 1930.

(Thomas) Woodrow Wilson (1913-21), 28th president, Democrat, was born on Dec. 28, 1856, in Staunton, VA, the son of Joseph Ruggles and Janet (Jessie) Woodrow Wilson. He grew up in Georgia and South Carolina. He attended Davidson College in North Carolina before graduating from Princeton Univ. in 1879. He studied law at the Univ. of Virginia and political science at Johns Hopkins Univ., where he received his PhD in 1886. He taught at Bryn Mawr (1885-88) and at Wesleyan (1888-90) before joining the faculty at Princeton. He was president of Princeton from 1902 until 1910, when he was elected governor of New Jersey. In 1912 he was nominated for president with the aid of William Jennings Bryan, who sought to block James "Champ" Clark and Tammany Hall. Wilson won because the Republican vote for Taft was split by the Progressives.

As president, Wilson protected American interests in revolutionary Mexico and fought for American rights on the high seas. He oversaw the creation of the Federal Reserve system, cut the tariff, and developed a reputation as a reformer. His sharp warnings to Germany led to the resignation of his secretary of state, Bryan, a pacifist. In 1916 he was reelected by a slim margin with the slogan, "He kept us out of war," although his attempts to mediate in the war failed. After several American ships were sunk by the Germans, he secured a declaration of war against Germany on Apr. 6, 1917.

Wilson outlined his peace program on Jan. 8, 1918, in the Fourteen Points, a state paper that enunciated a doctrine of self-determination for the settlement of territorial disputes. The Germans accepted his terms and an armistice on Nov. 11, 1918. Wilson went to Paris to help negotiate the peace treaty, the crux of which he considered the League of Nations. The Senate demanded reservations that would not make the U.S. subordinate to the votes of other nations in case of war. Wilson refused and toured the country to get support. After he suffered a severe stroke in Oct. 1919, his wife, Edith Wilson, concealed the extent of his infirmity, controlled access to him, and in effect largely acted in his place.

Wilson was awarded the 1919 Nobel Peace Prize, but the treaty embodying the League of Nations was ultimately rejected by the Senate in 1920. He left the White House in Mar. 1921. He died in Washington, DC, on Feb. 3, 1924.

Warren Gamaliel Harding (1921-23), 29th president, Republican, was born on Nov. 2, 1865, near Corsica (now Blooming Grove), OH, the son of George Tryon and Phoebe Elizabeth Dickerson Harding. He attended Ohio Central College, studied law, and became editor and publisher of a county newspaper. He entered the political arena as state senator (1901-04) and then served as lieutenant governor (1904-06). In 1910 he ran unsuccessfully for governor of Ohio; in 1914 he was elected to the U.S. Senate. In the Senate he voted for antistrike legislation, women's suffrage, and the Volstead Prohibition Enforcement Act over Pres. Wilson's veto. He opposed the League of Nations.

In 1920 he was nominated for president and defeated James M. Cox in the election. The Republicans capitalized on war weariness and fear that Wilson's League of Nations would curtail U.S. sovereignty. Harding stressed a return to "normalcy" and worked for tariff revision and the repeal of excess profits law and high income taxes. In what became known as the Teapot Dome scandal, his secretary of the interior, Albert B. Fall, resigned and was later convicted of accepting bribes in the leasing of government-owned oil reserves to private companies.

As rumors began to circulate about the corruption in his administration, Harding fell ill after a trip to Alaska, and he died suddenly in San Francisco on Aug. 2, 1923.

(John) Calvin Coolidge (1923-29), 30th president, Republican, was born on July 4, 1872, in Plymouth Notch, VT, the son of John Calvin and Victoria J. Moor Coolidge. Coolidge graduated from Amherst College in 1895. He entered Republican state politics and served as mayor of Northampton, MA, as state senator, as lieutenant governor, and, in 1919, as governor. In Sept. 1919, Coolidge attained national prominence by calling out the state guard in the Boston police strike. He declared, "There is no right to strike against the public safety by anybody, anywhere, anytime." This brought his name before the Republican convention of 1920, where he was nominated for vice president.

Coolidge succeeded to the presidency on Harding's death. As president, he opposed the League of Nations and the soldiers' bonus bill, which was passed over his veto. In 1924 he was elected to the presidency by a huge majority. He substantially reduced the national debt. He twice vetoed legislation to aid financially hard-pressed farmers.

With Republicans eager to renominate him, Coolidge simply announced on Aug. 2, 1927, "I do not choose to run for president in 1928." He died in Northampton, MA, on Jan. 5, 1933.

Herbert Clark Hoover (1929-33), 31st president, Republican, was born on Aug. 10, 1874, in West Branch, IA, the son of Jesse Clark and Hulda Randall Minthorn Hoover. Hoover grew up in Indian Territory (now Oklahoma) and Oregon and graduated from Stanford Univ. with a degree in geology in 1895. He worked briefly with the U.S. Geological Survey and then managed mines in Australia, Asia, Europe, and Africa. While chief engineer of imperial mines in China, he directed food relief for victims of the Boxer Rebellion. He gained a reputation not only as an engineer but as a humanitarian as he directed the American Relief Committee, London (1914-15) and the U.S. Commission for Relief in Belgium (1915-19). He was U.S. Food Administrator (1917-19), American Relief Administrator (1918-23), and in charge of Russian Relief (1918-23). He served as secretary of commerce under both Harding and Coolidge. Some historians believe that he was the most effective secretary of commerce ever to hold that office.

In 1928 Hoover was elected president over Alfred E. Smith. In 1929 the stock market crashed, and the economy collapsed. During the Great Depression, Hoover inaugurated some government assistance programs, but he was opposed to administration of aid through a federal bureaucracy. As the effects of the depression continued, he was defeated in the 1932 election by Franklin D. Roosevelt. Hoover remained active after leaving office. President Truman named him coordinator of the European Food Program (1946) and chairman of the Commission on Organization of the Executive Branch (1947-49); he was later appointed by President Eisenhower to serve in the same role (1953-55).

Hoover died in New York City on Oct. 20, 1964.

Franklin Delano Roosevelt (1933-45), 32nd president, Democrat, was born on Jan. 30, 1882, in Hyde Park, NY, the son of James and Sara Delano Roosevelt. He graduated from Harvard Univ. in 1903. He attended Columbia University Law School without taking a degree and was admitted to the New York State bar in 1907. His political career began when he was elected to the New York State senate in 1910. In 1913 Pres. Wilson appointed him assistant secretary of the navy, a post he held during World War I.

In 1920 Roosevelt ran for vice president with James Cox and was defeated. From 1921 to 1928 he worked in his New York law office and was also vice president of a bank. In Aug. 1921, he was stricken with poliomyelitis, which left his legs paralyzed. As a result of therapy he was able to stand, or walk a few steps, with the aid of leg braces.

Roosevelt served two terms as governor of New York (1929-33). In 1932, Democratic convention delegate W. G. McAdoo, pledged to nominee John N. Garner, threw his votes to Roosevelt, who was nominated for president. The Depression and the promise to repeal Prohibition ensured his election. Asked for emergency powers, proclaimed the New Deal, and put into effect a vast number of administrative changes. Foremost was

the use of public funds for relief and public works, resulting in deficit financing. He greatly expanded the federal government's regulation of business and by an excess profits tax and progressive income taxes produced a redistribution of earnings on an unprecedented scale. He also promoted legislation establishing the Social Security system. He was the last president inaugurated on Mar. 4 (1933) and the first inaugurated on Jan. 20 (1937).

Roosevelt was the first president to use radio for "fireside chats." When the Supreme Court nullified some New Deal laws, he sought power to "pack" the Court with additional justices, but Congress refused to give him the authority. He was the first president to break the "no third term" tradition (1940) and was elected to a fourth term in 1944, despite failing health.

Roosevelt was openly hostile to fascist governments before World War II and launched a lend-lease program on behalf of the Allies. With British Prime Min. Winston Churchill he wrote a declaration of principles to be followed after Nazi defeat (the Atlantic Charter of Aug. 14, 1941) and urged the Four Freedoms (freedom of speech, of worship, from want, from fear) Jan. 6, 1941. After Japan attacked Pearl Harbor on Dec. 7, 1941, the U.S. entered the war. Roosevelt guided the nation through the war and conferred with allied heads of state but did not live to see the end of the war. He died of a cerebral hemorrhage in Warm Springs, GA, on Apr. 12, 1945.

Harry S. Truman (1945-53), 33rd president, Democrat, was born on May 8, 1884, in Lamar, MO, the son of John Anderson and Martha Ellen Young Truman. A family disagreement over whether his middle name should be Shipp or Solomon, after his two grandfathers, resulted in his using only the middle initial S. After graduating from high school (1901) in Independence, MO, he worked in the mailroom of the *Kansas City Star*, as a railroad timekeeper, and as a clerk in Kansas City banks until about 1905. He ran his family's farm from 1906 to 1917, then served in France during World War I. After the war he opened a haberdashery, was a judge on the Jackson Co. Court (1922-24), and attended Kansas City School of Law (1923-25).

Truman was elected to the U.S. Senate in 1934 and reelected in 1940. In 1944, with Roosevelt's backing, he was nominated for vice president and elected. On Roosevelt's death in 1945, Truman became president. In 1948, in a famous upset victory, he defeated Republican Thomas E. Dewey to win a new term.

Truman authorized the first uses of the atomic bomb (Hiroshima and Nagasaki, Aug. 6 and 9, 1945), bringing World War II to a rapid end. He was responsible for what came to be called the Truman Doctrine to aid nations such as Greece and Turkey, threatened by Communist takeover, and his strong commitment to NATO and to the Marshall Plan helped bring the two about. In 1948-49, he broke a Soviet blockade of West Berlin with a massive airlift. When Communist North Korea invaded South Korea (June 1950), he won UN approval for a "police action" and, without prior congressional consent, sent in forces under Gen. Douglas MacArthur. When MacArthur opposed his policy of limited objectives, Truman removed him.

He died in Kansas City, MO, on Dec. 26, 1972.

Dwight David Eisenhower (1953-61), 34th president, Republican, was born on Oct. 14, 1890, in Denison, TX, the son of David Jacob and Ida Elizabeth Stover Eisenhower, as David Dwight Eisenhower. He grew up on a small farm in Abilene, KS, and graduated from West Point in 1915. He was on the staff of Gen. Douglas MacArthur in the Philippines from 1935 to 1939. In 1942, he was made commander of Allied forces landing in North Africa; the next year he was made full general. He became supreme Allied commander in Europe that same year and led the Normandy invasion (June 6, 1944). He was subsequently given the rank of general of the Army.

On May 7, 1945, Eisenhower received the surrender of Germany at Rheims, France. He returned to the U.S. to serve as chief of staff (1945-48). His memoir, *Crusade in Europe* (1948), was a best-seller. In 1948 he became president of Columbia Univ.; in 1950 he became commander of NATO forces.

Eisenhower was nominated for president by the Republicans in 1952. He defeated Illinois Gov. Adlai E. Stevenson in the 1952 election and defeated Stevenson in 1956 to win reelection. Eisenhower called himself a moderate, favored the "free market system" versus government price and wage controls, kept government out of labor disputes, reorganized the defense establishment, and promoted missile programs. He continued foreign aid, helped negotiate a cease fire truce in the Korean War, endorsed Taiwan and SE Asia defense treaties, backed the UN in condemning the Anglo-French raid on Egypt, and advocated the "open skies" policy of mutual inspection with the USSR. He sent U.S. troops into Little Rock, AR, in Sept. 1957, to enforce school integration.

Eisenhower died on Mar. 28, 1969, in Washington, DC.

John Fitzgerald Kennedy (1961-63), 35th president, Democrat, was born on May 29, 1917, in Brookline, MA, the son of Joseph P. and Rose Fitzgerald Kennedy. He graduated from Harvard Univ. in 1940. While serving in the Navy (1941-45), he commanded a PT (patrol torpedo) boat in the Solomons and won the Navy and Marine Corps Medal. In 1956, while recovering from spinal surgery, he wrote *Profiles in Courage*, which won a Pulitzer Prize in 1957. He served in the House of Representatives from 1947 to 1953 and was elected to the Senate in 1952 and 1958. In 1960, he won the Democratic nomination for president and narrowly defeated Republican Vice Pres. Richard M. Nixon. Kennedy was the youngest president ever elected to the office and the first Catholic.

Despite the image of youth and vigor he conveyed to the public, Kennedy suffered from serious medical problems, including Addison's disease and severe chronic back pain that required him to wear a back brace. The public was not aware of the extent of these problems, or of his frequent sexual liaisons.

In Apr. 1961, the new Kennedy administration suffered a severe setback when an invasion force of anti-Castro Cubans, trained and directed by the CIA, failed to establish a beachhead at the Bay of Pigs in Cuba. But he weathered a major foreign crisis with his successful demand on Oct. 22, 1962, that the Soviet Union dismantle its missile bases in Cuba. Kennedy also dodged Soviet attempts to force the Allies out of Berlin. He established the Peace Corps, spurred space exploration, and won passage of other "New Frontier" legislation. But Congress balked at initiatives such as medical coverage for the aged and aid to education. After some delay he introduced major civil rights legislation, but death intervened before it could be passed.

On Nov. 22, 1963, Kennedy was assassinated while riding in a motorcade in Dallas, TX. A commission chaired by Chief Justice Earl Warren concluded in Sept. 1964 that the sole assassin had been Lee Harvey Oswald, a former U.S. Marine and an ardent Marxist. Oswald was captured a short time after the assassination and charged, but two days later, he was shot dead by nightclub owner Jack Ruby while being moved to a county jail.

Lyndon Baines Johnson (1963-69), 36th president, Democrat, was born on Aug. 27, 1908, near Stonewall, TX, the son of Sam Ealy and Rebekah Baines Johnson. He graduated from Southwest Texas State Teachers College in 1930 and attended Georgetown University Law School. He taught public speaking in Houston (1930-31) and then served as secretary to Rep. R. M. Kleberg (1931-35). In 1937 Johnson won an election to fill the vacancy caused by the death of a U.S. representative. In 1938 he was elected to the first of five full terms. During 1941 and 1942 he also served in the Navy in the Pacific, earning a Silver Star for bravery. He was elected U.S. senator in 1948 and reelected in 1954. He was Democratic leader of the Senate in 1953. Johnson had strong support for the Democratic presidential nomination at the 1960 convention and was elected vice president on the ticket led by the successful Democratic nominee, John F. Kennedy.

Johnson became president when Kennedy was assassinated. He was elected to a full term in 1964. Johnson's domestic program was of considerable importance. He won passage of major civil rights, anti-poverty, aid to education, and health-care (Medicare, Medicaid) legislation—the "Great Society" program. However, his escalation of the war in Vietnam came to overshadow the achievements of his administration. In the face

of increasing division in the nation and in his own party over his handling of the war, Johnson declined to seek another term.

Johnson died on Jan. 22, 1973, in San Antonio, TX.

Richard Milhous Nixon (1969-74), 37th president, Republican, was born on Jan. 9, 1913, in Yorba Linda, CA, the son of Francis Anthony and Hannah Milhous Nixon. He graduated from Whittier College in 1934 and from Duke University Law School in 1937. After practicing law in Whittier, CA, and serving briefly in the Office of Price Administration in 1942, he entered the Navy and served in the South Pacific. Nixon was elected to the House of Representatives in 1946 and 1948. He achieved prominence as the House Un-American Activities Committee member who forced the showdown leading to the Alger Hiss perjury conviction. In 1950 he was elected to the Senate.

Nixon was elected vice president in the Eisenhower landslides of 1952 and 1956. He won the Republican nomination for president in 1960 but was narrowly defeated by John F. Kennedy. He ran unsuccessfully for governor of California in 1962. In 1968 he again won the GOP presidential nomination, then defeated Hubert Humphrey for the presidency.

As president, Nixon appointed four Supreme Court justices, including the chief justice, moving the court to the right. As a "new federalist," he sought to shift greater responsibility to state and local governments. At the same time, he championed important federal initiatives, including creation of the Office of Management and Budget and the Environmental Protection Agency. The economy suffered periods of high unemployment and inflation, and he imposed wage and price controls in 1971.

In foreign affairs, Nixon dramatically altered relations with China, which he visited in 1972—the first U.S. president to do so. With adviser Henry Kissinger, he pursued détente with the Soviet Union, signing major arms limitation and other treaties and increasing trade. He began a gradual withdrawal from Vietnam, but U.S. troops remained there through his first term. He ordered an incursion into Cambodia (1970) and the bombing of Hanoi and mining of Haiphong Harbor (1972). Reelected by a large majority in Nov. 1972, he secured a Vietnam cease-fire in Jan. 1973.

Nixon's second term was cut short by scandal, after disclosures relating to a June 1972 burglary of Democratic Party headquarters in the Watergate office complex in DC. The courts and Congress sought tapes of Nixon's office conversations; Nixon claimed executive privilege, but the Supreme Court ruled against him. In July 1974, the House Judiciary Committee recommended adoption of three impeachment articles charging him with obstruction of justice, abuse of power, and contempt of Congress. On Aug. 5, he released transcripts of conversations that linked him to cover-up activities. He resigned on Aug. 9, becoming the first president ever to do so.

In later years, Nixon emerged as an elder statesman. He died Apr. 22, 1994, in New York City.

Gerald Rudolph Ford (1974-77), 38th president, Republican, was born on July 14, 1913, in Omaha, NE, the son of Leslie and Dorothy Gardner King, and was named Leslie Lynch King Jr. When he was two, his parents divorced, and he and his mother moved to Grand Rapids, MI. There she married Gerald R. Ford, who formally adopted him and gave him his name. Ford graduated from the Univ. of Michigan in 1935 and from Yale Law School in 1941. He began practicing law in Grand Rapids, but in 1942, he joined the Navy and served in the Pacific, leaving the service in 1946 as a lieutenant commander. He entered the House of Representatives in 1949 and spent 25 years in the House, eight of them as Republican leader.

On Oct. 12, 1973, after Vice Pres. Spiro T. Agnew resigned, Pres. Nixon nominated Ford to replace him. It was the first use of the procedures set out in the 25th Amendment. When Nixon resigned, Aug. 9, 1974, because of the Watergate scandal, Ford became president; he was the only president who was never elected either to the presidency or to the vice presidency.

Ford was widely credited with having contributed to rebuilding morale after the Nixon presidency. But he was also criticized by many when he pardoned Nixon for any federal crimes he might have committed as president. Ford vetoed 48 bills in his first 21 months in office, mostly in the interest of fighting high inflation; he was less successful in curbing high unemployment. In foreign policy, Ford continued to pursue détente.

Ford was narrowly defeated in the 1976 election. He died Dec. 26, 2006, at home in Rancho Mirage, CA.

James Earl (Jimmy) Carter (1977-81), 39th president, Democrat, was the first president from the Deep South since before the Civil War. He was born on Oct. 1, 1924, in Plains, GA, the son of James and Lillian Gordy Carter. Carter graduated from the U.S. Naval Academy in 1946 and in 1952 entered the Navy's nuclear submarine program as an aide to Capt. (later Adm.) Hyman Rickover. He studied nuclear physics at Union College. Carter's father died in 1953, and he left the Navy to take over the family peanut farming businesses. He served in the Georgia state senate (1963-67) and as governor of Georgia (1971-75). In 1976, Carter won the Democratic nomination and defeated Pres. Gerald R. Ford.

On his first full day in office, Carter pardoned all Vietnam draft evaders. He played a major role in the negotiations leading to the 1979 peace treaty between Israel and Egypt, and he won passage of new treaties with Panama providing for U.S. control of the Panama Canal to end in 2000. Carter was widely criticized, however, for the poor state of the economy and was viewed by some as weak in his handling of foreign policy. In Nov. 1979, Iranian student militants attacked the U.S. embassy in Tehran and held members of the embassy staff hostage. Efforts to obtain release of the hostages were a major preoccupation during the rest of his term. He reacted to the Soviet invasion of Afghanistan by imposing a grain embargo and boycotting the Moscow Olympic Games.

Carter was defeated by Ronald Reagan in the 1980 election. The 52 American hostages in Iran were finally released on inauguration day, 1981, just after Reagan officially became president. After leaving office, Carter played an active role in diplomatic and humanitarian efforts around the world, especially through the Carter Center, which he founded with his wife in 1982. He was awarded the Nobel Peace Prize in 2002.

Ronald Wilson Reagan (1981-89), 40th president, Republican, was born on Feb. 6, 1911, in Tampico, IL, the son of John Edward and Nellie Wilson Reagan. Reagan graduated from Eureka College in 1932, after which he worked as a sports announcer in Des Moines, IA. He began a successful career as a movie actor in 1937. During World War II Reagan served in the Army Air Force, making training films. He was president of the Screen Actors Guild in 1947-52 and in 1959-60. Reagan was elected governor of California in 1966 and reelected in 1970.

In 1980, Reagan gained the Republican presidential nomination and won a landslide victory over Jimmy Carter. He was easily reelected in 1984. Reagan forged a bipartisan coalition in Congress, which led to enactment of his program of large-scale tax cuts, cutbacks in many government programs, and a major defense buildup. He signed a Social Security reform bill designed to provide for the long-term solvency of the system. In 1986, he signed into law a major tax-reform bill. He was shot and seriously wounded in 1981 by John Hinckley, who was tried and found not guilty by reason of insanity.

In 1982, the U.S. joined France and Italy in maintaining a peacekeeping force in Beirut, Lebanon, and the next year Reagan sent a task force to invade Grenada after two Marxist coups on the island. Reagan's opposition to international terrorism led to the U.S. bombing of Libyan military installations in 1986. He strongly supported El Salvador, the Nicaraguan contras, and other anticommunist governments and forces throughout the world. He also held four summit meetings with Soviet leader Mikhail Gorbachev and signed a treaty in 1987 eliminating short- and medium-range missiles from Europe.

In 1986, it was revealed that the U.S. had sold weapons through Israeli brokers to Iran in exchange for the release of U.S. hostages being held in Lebanon and that subsequently some of the money had been illegally diverted to the Nicaraguan contras. The scandal led to the resignation of leading White House aides, but no proof of Reagan's involvement was discovered. As Reagan left office in Jan. 1989, the nation was experiencing its sixth consecutive year of economic prosperity, and had piled up large budget deficits.

In 1994, Reagan revealed that he was suffering from Alzheimer's disease. He died on June 5, 2004, in Los Angeles, CA, from complications of the disease.

George Herbert Walker Bush (1989-93), 41st president, Republican, was born on June 12, 1924, in Milton, MA, the son of Prescott and Dorothy Walker Bush. He served as a U.S. Navy pilot in World War II. After graduating from Yale Univ. in 1948, he settled in Texas, where, in 1953, he helped found an oil company. After losing a bid for a U.S. Senate seat in 1964, he was elected to the House of Representatives in 1966 and 1968. He lost a second U.S. Senate race in 1970. Subsequently he served as U.S. ambassador to the United Nations (1971-73), headed the U.S. Liaison Office in Beijing (1974-75), and was director of the CIA (1976-77). Following an unsuccessful bid for the 1980 Republican presidential nomination, Bush became Ronald Reagan's running mate, and served as vice president from 1981 to 1989.

In 1988, Bush gained the GOP presidential nomination and defeated Gov. Michael Dukakis (D, MA) to win the presidency. Bush took office faced with U.S. budget and trade deficits, and insolvent U.S. savings and loan institutions. He faced a severe budget deficit annually, struggled with military cutbacks, and vetoed abortion-rights legislation. In 1990 he agreed to a budget deficit-reduction plan that included tax hikes, despite a campaign promise to the contrary, angering many conservatives.

Bush supported Soviet reforms, Eastern Europe democratization, and good relations with Beijing. In Dec. 1989, he sent troops to Panama; they overthrew the government and captured military dictator Gen. Manuel Noriega. Bush reacted to Iraq's Aug. 1990 invasion of Kuwait by sending U.S. forces to the Persian Gulf area and assembling a UN-backed coalition, including NATO and Arab League members. After a month-long air war, in Feb. 1991, Allied forces retook Kuwait in a four-day ground assault. The quick victory, with extremely light casualties on the U.S. side, gave Bush at that time one of the highest presidential approval ratings in history. His popularity plummeted by the end of 1991, however, as the economy slipped into recession. He was defeated by Bill Clinton in the 1992 election.

Bush saw his son George W. inaugurated as the 43rd president in 2001. In 2005 the elder Bush teamed with former Pres. Clinton to raise money for natural disaster victims.

William Jefferson (Bill) Clinton (1993-2001), 42nd president, Democrat, was born Aug. 19, 1946, in Hope, AR, son of William Blythe and Virginia Cassidy Blythe, and was named William Jefferson Blythe IV. Blythe died in an auto accident before his son was born. His widow married Roger Clinton, whose last name Bill Clinton then took. Clinton earned his undergraduate degree from Georgetown Univ. in 1968. While attending Oxford Univ. as a Rhodes scholar, he legally avoided the draft and possible service in Vietnam, according to some critics by misleading his draft board. Clinton worked on George McGovern's 1972 presidential campaign and earned a degree from Yale Law School in 1973. He taught at the Univ. of Arkansas law school until 1976, when he was elected state attorney general. In 1978 he was elected governor, becoming the nation's youngest at the time. Though defeated for reelection in 1980, he was returned to office several times thereafter. He married law school classmate Hillary Rodham in 1975.

Clinton won most of the 1992 presidential primaries, moving his party toward the center as he tried to broaden his appeal; as the Democratic nominee he defeated Pres. George H. W. Bush and independent candidate H. Ross Perot in the Nov. election. In 1993, Clinton won passage of a measure to reduce the federal budget deficit and won congressional approval of the North American Free Trade Agreement. However, his administration's plan for major health care reform legislation died in Congress. After 1994 midterm elections, Clinton faced Republican majorities in both houses of Congress. He followed a centrist course at home, sent troops to Bosnia to help implement a peace settlement, and cultivated relations with Russia and China.

Though accused of improprieties in his involvement in the Whitewater Development Corp., an Arkansas land-development venture, Clinton won reelection with 49% of the vote in 1996. Independent prosecutor Kenneth Starr did not find wrongdoing related to Whitewater, but did report evidence of an affair between Clinton and White House intern Monica Lewinsky. In 1998, Clinton became only the second U.S. president to be impeached by the House of Representatives. He was charged with perjury and obstruction of justice in an attempted cover-up of the affair but was acquitted by the Senate.

In 1999 the United States joined other NATO nations in an aerial bombing campaign that induced Serbia to withdraw troops from Kosovo, where they had been terrorizing ethnic Albanians. On Clinton's last full day in office, the Whitewater investigation ended in a deal; Clinton admitted having given false testimony and agreed to penalties. Clinton remained active in politics, supporting candidates he favored, including his wife, who became a U.S. senator (D, NY), ran unsuccessfully for the 2008 Democratic presidential nomination, then served as Pres. Obama's secretary of state. He took a leadership role in various humanitarian programs and founded an institute to promote practical solutions to global problems.

George Walker Bush (2001-09), 43rd president, Republican, was born on July 6, 1946, in New Haven, CT. He was the oldest of six children born to the 41st president, George Herbert Walker Bush, and the former Barbara Pierce. He became the first son of a former president to occupy the White House since John Quincy Adams took office in 1825.

Bush grew up in Midland and Houston, TX. He attended Andover Prep in Massachusetts and then Yale Univ., graduating in 1968. Eligible for the draft, he fulfilled his military service requirement with the Texas Air National Guard. After earning a master's degree from Harvard Business School, he returned to Midland in 1975 and went into the oil business. Two years later he married Laura Welch, a librarian; they had twin daughters, Barbara and Jenna, in 1981. After aiding his father's winning 1988 presidential campaign, he became managing partner of the Texas Rangers baseball team. He was elected governor of Texas in 1994 and reelected in 1998.

In 2000, Bush won the Republican presidential nomination and, with running mate Dick Cheney, defeated the Democratic ticket led by Vice Pres. Al Gore, in one of the closest-ever U.S. presidential elections. The result was not settled until a mid-Dec. ruling by the U.S. Supreme Court left Florida's crucial electoral votes in Bush's column.

In May 2001, Bush won passage of a tax cut package projected at $1.35 tril over 10 years. After the Sept. 11, 2001, terrorist attacks on the U.S., he rallied support for a "war against terrorism." By Dec. 2001, the U.S. military, aided by forces from other nations, had deposed Afghanistan's Taliban regime, which was sheltering al-Qaeda terrorists. In Mar. 2003, the U.S., aided mainly by UK forces, launched an air and ground war against Iraq and deposed its autocratic leader, Saddam Hussein. No evidence was found that his regime had developed weapons of mass destruction, the key rationale for the war. A sovereign government was formed in June 2004, but insurgent violence and U.S. troop casualties continued.

Bush was reelected in Nov. 2004 with 51% of the popular vote, but his push for Social Security and immigration reforms in his second term failed in Congress, and his administration drew criticism for its response to Hurricane Katrina in Aug.-Sept. 2005. The Senate confirmed Bush's nominations of a new chief justice and associate justice of the Supreme Court. In 2006, Bush exercised his first veto to maintain restrictions on federal funding for stem cell research.

After Democrats won majorities in House and Senate 2006 midterm elections, Bush accepted the resignation of Defense Sec. Donald Rumsfeld, a target of widespread criticism over the Iraq war. Two months later, he announced a "surge" in U.S. troop strength in Iraq. A sharp drop in casualties ensued, aided also by a shift in alliances, and in late 2008 the administration reached an agreement with Iraq allowing U.S. troops to remain there through but not beyond 2011. But the Taliban was gaining strength in Afghanistan and Pakistan, and the Bush administration was damaged by revelations of prisoner abuse and memos that had given legal sanction to extreme interrogation methods.

The U.S. economy fell into recession in Dec. 2007; Bush and congressional leaders responded with a $168-bil stimulus plan. Problems in home finance and credit markets triggered a deep economic crisis in Sept. and the Treasury Dept. announced a bailout of mortgage finance firms Fannie Mae and Freddie Mac. Lehman Bros. filed for bankruptcy, and the Federal Reserve

rescued insurance giant AIG with a line of credit reaching $144 bil. A Bush administration-backed plan to buy up to $700 bil in devalued mortgage-related assets cleared Congress Oct. 3, after a severe stock market plunge bolstered support. The economic crisis added to Bush's unpopularity and contributed to the Nov. 2008 defeat of GOP presidential candidate Sen. John McCain (AZ).

In early 2010 Bush and former Pres. Clinton established a nonprofit organization to raise funds for earthquake relief in Haiti. In Nov. 2010, Bush published a memoir entitled *Decision Points*. The George W. Bush Presidential Center, including his presidential library, opened in Dallas, TX, in 2013.

 **Barack Hussein Obama (2009-)**, 44th president, Democrat, was born Aug. 4, 1961, in Honolulu, HI. His father, Barack Obama Sr., was a black Kenyan, and his mother, Stanley Ann Dunham, a white American born in Kansas. After his parents divorced, his mother married an Indonesian man and Obama lived in Indonesia. He later moved to Hawaii to live with his maternal grandparents and attend high school. He earned his bachelor's degree from Columbia Univ. (1983). After working as a community organizer in Chicago, he earned a law degree from Harvard Univ. (1991), where he was president of the law review. He practiced civil rights law in Chicago and taught at the Univ. of Chicago Law School. In 1992, he married attorney Michelle Robinson (1964-). They have two daughters, Malia (1998-) and Natasha (Sasha) (2001-).

Obama won election to the Illinois state senate in 1996 and was twice reelected. He lost the Democratic nomination for a U.S. House seat in 2000, but was nominated to a U.S. Senate seat in a Mar. 2004 primary. Already somewhat known for his 1995 memoir, *Dreams From My Father*, he gained national attention with his keynote address at the Democratic National Convention in July and was easily elected in Nov. 2004. His second book, *The Audacity of Hope* (2006), was an immediate best-seller.

Stressing his opposition to the Iraq war and aim to bring change to Washington, he ran for the 2008 Democratic presidential nomination, and eventually pulled ahead of expected front-runner Sen. Hillary Clinton (NY) in the primaries. With running mate Sen. Joe Biden (DE), he won 53% of the popular vote to defeat Sen. John McCain (R, AZ) and his running mate, Alaska Gov. Sarah Palin, and become the nation's first African-American president. Sen. Clinton served as secretary of state in Obama's first term.

Obama sounded a cooperative and conciliatory note in foreign relations; on that basis he was awarded the 2009 Nobel Peace Prize. Over the next few years, he gradually ended U.S. military involvement in Iraq. He began winding down U.S. military involvement in Afghanistan, after authorizing a temporary troop surge there. But in Mar. 2011, in reaction to massacres of civilians in a Libyan civil war, he authorized U.S. military action, with a multi-state coalition, against the regime of Muammar al-Qaddafi, leading to his overthrow by rebel forces. He also ordered an operation in which al-Qaeda terrorist leader Osama bin Laden was killed by U.S. Navy SEALs in Pakistan May 2011.

In an effort to revive the economy, the administration won passage, in Feb. 2009, of a $787-bil stimulus package; the U.S. technically pulled out of recession in third quarter 2009, but economic growth fell short of expectations and unemployment remained high. Obama's approval rating, which was close to 70% early in his presidency, drifted downward. Democrats lost their filibuster-proof Senate majority after a Jan. 2010 special election in Massachusetts, but still held majorities in both chambers of Congress. Congress passed Obama's top priority in Mar. 2010: a controversial health care reform bill aimed in part at extending coverage to uninsured Americans. (Doggedly opposed by Republicans in Congress, "Obamacare" was being rolled out gradually, with its impact unclear; it survived a major obstacle when most components of the legislation were upheld by the Supreme Court in June 2012.) In July 2010 the administration won passage of a major financial reform bill. The president also won confirmation, in 2009 and 2010, of Sonia Sotomayor and Elena Kagan to the Supreme Court.

In Nov. 2010 elections Democrats lost their majority in the House; many of the new Republicans were allied with the small-government Tea Party movement. During the ensuing lame-duck session, Obama reached a compromise with Republicans on an $858-bil spending plan that kept the G.W. Bush-era tax cuts for all income levels for two years but extended unemployment benefits and temporarily reduced payroll taxes. Obama also won

passage of a measure to repeal the "don't ask, don't tell" policy for gays in the military.

The bipartisan Simpson-Bowles commission, formed by the president to recommend deficit reduction measures, released a detailed $4-tril plan, calling for entitlement and other spending cuts along with tax reforms. Obama outlined a smaller plan with higher taxes on the wealthy and no entitlement cuts. With the federal government set to run out of funds in Aug. 2011, Republicans insisted that the debt ceiling should not be raised without compensating cost savings. A last-minute compromise was passed by Congress and signed by Obama; it called for cuts to be determined by a bipartisan congressional committee. When the committee deadlocked, automatic cuts in domestic programs and defense were slated to take effect at the start of 2013.

As 2012 elections approached, Obama became the first sitting president to publicly support same-sex marriage. He also issued an executive order allowing many undocumented immigrants under 30 to remain and work in the U.S. for a time. Obama and Biden were reelected in Nov. 2012 with 51% of the vote, defeating a ticket headed by former Gov. Mitt Romney (R, MA). Control of the House and Senate was unchanged. A compromise reached in Congress averted a year-end fiscal cliff by making expiring Bush-era tax cuts permanent for individuals earning under $400,000 a year, while postponing automatic spending cuts. Obama and congressional leaders failed to reach agreement on the follow-up deal to this so-called sequester, which took effect Mar. 1, 2013, triggering $85 bil in automatic cuts.

Obama remained moderately popular in the first eight months of 2013, with his job approval in polls dropping from about 50% to around 45% as of late-Aug. 2013. But relations with Congress were acrimonious and the administration had to contend with a series of scandals, many of which it sought to dismiss as overblown. The Sept. 11, 2012, attack on the U.S. Consulate in Benghazi, Libya, in which the U.S. ambassador and three other Americans were killed, raised questions about U.S. security procedures, and critics charged that the administration tried to mischaracterize or conceal the circumstances surrounding the attack. Revelations in May 2013 that the Internal Revenue Service targeted Tea Party organizations for greater scrutiny caused widespread concern, but no link to the White House was found.

In June 2013, leaked information about the wide scope of surveillance programs by the Natl. Security Agency (NSA) generated controversy. Obama defended the program while announcing intentions to address limited reforms. The administration's continued use of unmanned drones to attack militants in Pakistan and Yemen also brought steady criticism, but the Boston Marathon bombing in Apr. 2013 and intelligence that led to the temporary closing of U.S. embassies in the Mideast in Aug. 2013 underlined the continuing threat of terrorism.

The second-term Obama administration faced challenges in defining and asserting U.S. interests abroad. In Egypt, after the elected government was overthrown in July 2013 in a military-supported revolt, the administration had limited leverage to promote transition to broad-based democratic rule. In Syria, after concluding that the regime had used chemical weapons against civilians in late Aug., during its long and bloody civil war, Obama at first called for a punitive military strike, for which he then sought congressional backing. But with support flagging, he agreed with Russia in mid-Sept. on a plan to seek removal of the weapons. Reaction to Obama's handling of the Syrian situation varied, but the agreement appeared to mark an improvement in U.S. relations with Russia, which had been strained by sharp differences in policy and by Russia's having granted temporary asylum to fugitive NSA leaker Edward Snowden.

Obama continued efforts to promote immigration reform and gun control, with the latter issue sparked by the Dec. 2012 mass shooting in a Newtown, CT, elementary school, but he faced strong resistance in Congress. The Supreme Court gave the administration a big victory in June 2013 when it overturned key parts of the federal Defense of Marriage Act. After a neighborhood watch volunteer was acquitted in July 2013 in the shooting death of an unarmed black teenager, Obama avoided criticizing the jury verdict, but took the occasion to focus attention on race relations and the fears and concerns of young black males.

With more conflict looming over government funding and raising of the debt ceiling, Obama frequently spoke in 2013 in support of more government spending to boost the still struggling economy and aid the middle class, with the help of tax reform and higher taxes on the wealthy. Republicans in Congress countered that economic growth was being crippled by deficit spending, over-regulation, and Obamacare, and would be threatened by higher taxes.

Presidential Facts

Oldest president: Ronald Reagan, who was 77 when he left office

Youngest president: Theodore Roosevelt, who was 42 when sworn in after McKinley's death

Youngest person elected president: John F. Kennedy, who was 43 when elected in 1960

Tallest president: Abraham Lincoln, who was 6 feet, 4 inches

Shortest president: James Madison, who was 5 feet, 4 inches

Heaviest president: William Howard Taft, who was 332 pounds in 1911

First president to live in the White House: John Adams, who moved there in 1800

First president inaugurated in Washington, DC: Thomas Jefferson, in 1801

First president whose parents were immigrants: Andrew Jackson; his parents immigrated from Ireland in 1765

First president born a U.S. citizen: Martin Van Buren, in Kinderhook, NY, 1782

First president born outside the original colonies: Abraham Lincoln, in Kentucky, 1809

First president born west of the Mississippi: Herbert Hoover, in West Branch, IA, 1874

Most common presidential home state: Virginia, with 8 presidents

First president born in a hospital: Jimmy Carter, in Plains, GA, 1924

First president to be photographed while in office: James K. Polk, in 1849

First president to have a telephone in the White House: Rutherford B. Hayes, in 1879

First president to address the nation on radio: Warren G. Harding, in 1922

First president to appear on TV: Franklin D. Roosevelt, at opening ceremonies for the 1939 World's Fair

First president to give a live, televised news conference: John F. Kennedy, in 1961

First president to hold an Internet chat: Bill Clinton, in 1999

Presidents who lost the popular vote while winning election: John Quincy Adams, in 1824 (elected by the House after general election failed to produce a majority); Rutherford B. Hayes, in 1876; Benjamin Harrison, in 1888; George W. Bush, in 2000. (Popular vote totals before 1824 are unknown.)

Only presidents chosen by the House of Representatives: Thomas Jefferson (1st term) and John Quincy Adams

Only president never elected either president or vice president: Gerald Ford; named vice president when Spiro Agnew resigned (1973), became president when Nixon resigned (1974)

Only left-handed presidents: James Garfield, Herbert Hoover, Harry Truman, Gerald Ford, Ronald Reagan, George H. W. Bush, Bill Clinton, and Barack Obama

Only Catholic president: John F. Kennedy; the most common religious affiliations have been Episcopalian (11) and Presbyterian (7)

Only bachelor presidents: James Buchanan, who never married, and Grover Cleveland, who married Frances Folsom in the White House in 1886

Only divorced president: Ronald Reagan; divorced from Jane Wyman in 1948, married Nancy Davis in 1952

Presidents who died on July 4: John Adams and Thomas Jefferson (both 1826) and James Monroe (1831)

Only president buried in Washington, DC: Woodrow Wilson, interred at Washington National Cathedral

Presidential Libraries

Presidential libraries are coordinated by the National Archives and Records Administration (www.archives.gov/presidential-libraries/). Materials for presidents before Herbert Hoover are held by private institutions. Under the Presidential Records Act, presidential records are not available to the public for the first five years following the end of an administration. The George W. Bush Library and Museum opened to the public in May 2013 but its records weren't subject to FOIA requests until Jan. 20, 2014.

Herbert Hoover Library and Museum
210 Parkside Dr.
West Branch, IA 52358
Phone: (319) 643-5301
Email: hoover.library@nara.gov
Website: hoover.archives.gov

Franklin D. Roosevelt Library and Museum
4079 Albany Post Rd.
Hyde Park, NY 12538-1990
Phone: (800) FDR-VISIT
Email: roosevelt.library@nara.gov
Website: www.fdrlibrary.marist.edu

Harry S. Truman Library and Museum
500 West U.S. Hwy. 24
Independence, MO 64050-2481
Phone: (800) 833-1225
Email: truman.library@nara.gov
Website: www.trumanlibrary.org

Dwight D. Eisenhower Library
200 SE 4th St.
Abilene, KS 67410-2900
Phone: (877) RING-IKE
Email: eisenhower.library@nara.gov
Website: eisenhower.archives.gov

John F. Kennedy Library and Museum
Columbia Pt.
Boston, MA 02125-3312
Phone: (866) JFK-1960

Email: kennedy.library@nara.gov
Website: www.jfklibrary.org

Lyndon Baines Johnson Library and Museum
2313 Red River St.
Austin, TX 78705-5737
Phone: (512) 721-0200
Email: johnson.library@nara.gov
Website: www.lbjlib.utexas.edu

Richard Nixon Library and Museum
18001 Yorba Linda Blvd.
Yorba Linda, CA 92886-3903
Phone: (714) 983-9120
Email: nixon@nara.gov
Website: www.nixonarchives.gov
MD Office: Natl. Archives at College Park
8601 Adelphi Rd.
College Park, MD 20740-6001
Phone: (301) 837-3290

Gerald R. Ford Library and Museum
Library: 1000 Beal Ave.
Ann Arbor, MI 48109-2109
Phone: (734) 205-0555
Museum: 303 Pearl St. NW
Grand Rapids, MI 49504-5353
Phone: (616) 254-0400
Email: ford.library@nara.gov
Website: www.fordlibrarymuseum.gov

Jimmy Carter Library and Museum
441 Freedom Pkwy.

Atlanta, GA 30307-1498
Phone: (404) 865-7100
Email: carter.library@nara.gov
Website: www.jimmycarterlibrary.gov

Ronald Reagan Library and Museum
40 Presidential Dr.
Simi Valley, CA 93065-0600
Phone: (800) 410-8354
Email: reagan.library@nara.gov
Website: www.reagan.utexas.edu

George Bush Library and Museum
1000 George Bush Dr. West
College Station, TX 77845
Phone: (979) 691-4000
Email: library.bush@nara.gov
Website: bushlibrary.tamu.edu

William J. Clinton Library and Museum
1200 President Clinton Ave.
Little Rock, AR 72201
Phone: (501) 374-4242
Email: clinton.library@nara.gov
Website: www.clintonlibrary.gov

George W. Bush Library and Museum
1725 Lakepointe Dr.
Lewisville, TX 75057
Phone: (972) 353-0545
Email: gwbush.library@nara.gov
Website: www.georgewbushlibrary.smu.edu

Presidential Impeachment in U.S. History

The U.S. Constitution provides for impeachment and removal from office of federal officials on grounds of "Treason, Bribery, or other high Crimes and Misdemeanors" (Article II, Sect. 4). Impeachment is the bringing of charges by the House of Representatives. It is followed by a Senate trial; a two-thirds majority vote of Senators present is needed for conviction and removal from office.

In 1868, **Andrew Johnson** became the first president impeached by the House, for his removal of Sec. of War Edwin M. Stanton without first notifying the Senate. He was tried but not convicted. In 1974, impeachment articles against Pres. **Richard Nixon**, in connection with the Watergate scandal, were adopted by the House Judiciary Committee. He resigned Aug. 9, and the House accepted the committee report without taking further action. In 1998, Pres. **Bill Clinton** was impeached by the House in connection with covering up a sexual relationship with former White House intern Monica Lewinsky. He was tried in the Senate in 1999 and acquitted.

Wives and Children of the Presidents

Name (born-died; married)	State	Sons/ daughters	Name (born-died; married)	State	Sons/ daughters
Martha Dandridge Custis Washington (1731-1802; 1759)	VA	None	Mary Scott Lord Dimmick Harrison (1858-1948; 1896)	PA	0/1
Abigail Smith Adams (1744-1818; 1764)	MA	3/2	Ida Saxton McKinley (1847-1907; 1871)	OH	0/2
Martha Wayles Skelton Jefferson (1748-82; 1772)	VA	1/5	Alice Hathaway Lee Roosevelt (1861-84; 1880)	MA	0/1
Dolley Payne Todd Madison (1768-1849; 1794)	NC	None	Edith Kermit Carow Roosevelt (1861-1948; 1886)	CT	4/1
Elizabeth Kortright Monroe (1768-1830; 1786)	NY	1/2	Helen Herron Taft (1861-1943; 1886)	OH	2/1
Louisa Catherine Johnson Adams (1775-1852; 1797)	MD[1]	3/1	Ellen Louise Axson Wilson (1860-1914; 1885)	GA	0/3
Rachel Donelson Robards Jackson (1767-1828; 1791)	VA	1/0[2]	Edith Bolling Galt Wilson (1872-1961; 1915)	VA	None
Hannah Hoes Van Buren (1783-1819; 1807)	NY	4/0	Florence Kling De Wolfe Harding (1860-1924; 1891)	OH	None
Anna Tuthill Symmes Harrison (1775-1864; 1795)	NJ	6/4	Grace Anna Goodhue Coolidge (1879-1957; 1905)	VT	2/0
Letitia Christian Tyler (1790-1842; 1813)	VA	3/5	Lou Henry Hoover (1875-1944; 1899)	IA	2/0
Julia Gardiner Tyler (1820-89; 1844)	NY	5/2	Anna Eleanor Roosevelt (1884-1962; 1905)	NY	5/1
Sarah Childress Polk (1803-91; 1824)	TN	None	Elizabeth Virginia (Bess) Wallace Truman (1885-1982; 1919)	MO	0/1
Margaret (Peggy) Mackall Smith Taylor (1788-1852; 1810)	MD	1/5	Mamie Geneva Doud Eisenhower (1896-1979; 1916)	IA	2/0
Abigail Powers Fillmore (1798-1853; 1826)	NY	1/1	Jacqueline Lee Bouvier Kennedy (1929-94; 1953)	NY	2/1
Caroline Carmichael McIntosh Fillmore (1813-81; 1858)	NJ	None	Claudia (Lady Bird) Alta Taylor Johnson (1912-2007; 1934)	TX	0/2
Jane Means Appleton Pierce (1806-63; 1834)	NH	3/0	Thelma Catherine Patricia Ryan Nixon (1912-93; 1940)	NV	0/2
Mary Todd Lincoln (1818-82; 1842)	KY	4/0	Elizabeth (Betty) Bloomer Warren Ford (1918-2011; 1948)	IL	3/1
Eliza McCardle Johnson (1810-76; 1827)	TN	3/2	Eleanor Rosalynn Smith Carter (1927- ; 1946)	GA	3/1
Julia Boggs Dent Grant (1826-1902; 1848)	MO	3/1	Anne Frances (Nancy) Robbins Davis Reagan (1921- ; 1952)	NY	1/1[3]
Lucy Ware Webb Hayes (1831-89; 1852)	OH	7/1	Barbara Pierce Bush (1925- ; 1945)	NY	4/2
Lucretia Rudolph Garfield (1832-1918; 1858)	OH	5/2	Hillary Diane Rodham Clinton (1947- ; 1975)	IL	0/1
Ellen Lewis Herndon Arthur (1837-80; 1859)	VA	2/1	Laura Lane Welch Bush (1946- ; 1977)	TX	0/2
Frances Folsom Cleveland (1864-1947; 1886)	NY	2/3	Michelle LaVaughn Robinson Obama (1964- ; 1992)	IL	0/2
Caroline Lavinia Scott Harrison (1832-92; 1853)	OH	1/1			

Note: Pres. Buchanan was unmarried. (1) Born in London, father a MD citizen. (2) Adopted son. (3) Pres. Reagan's first wife, whom he later divorced, was Jane Wyman. They had a daughter who died in infancy, a daughter who lived past infancy, and an adopted son.

First Lady Michelle Obama

Michelle Robinson Obama was born in Chicago, IL, Jan. 17, 1964. She graduated from Princeton Univ., 1985, earned a law degree from Harvard Univ., 1988, and joined Chicago law firm Sidley & Austin. She served as assistant commissioner of planning and development for Chicago, then as founding executive director of the Chicago chapter of Public Allies, an AmeriCorps program. She began working for the Univ. of Chicago in 1996, first as associate dean of student services, then as the Univ. of Chicago Medical Center's vice president of community and external affairs. Michelle and Barack Obama were married in 1992; in 1998, their daughter Malia was born, followed by Natasha (Sasha) in 2001.

As First Lady, Michelle Obama has focused on supporting military families, helping women balance career and family, encouraging national service, and promoting the arts and arts education. She has also launched a major campaign to deal with the problem of childhood obesity in the U.S.

Burial Places of the Presidents

President	Burial place	President	Burial place	President	Burial place
Washington	Mt. Vernon, VA	Pierce	Concord, NH	Wilson	Wash. Natl. Cathedral, DC
J. Adams	Quincy, MA	Buchanan	Lancaster, PA	Harding	Marion, OH
Jefferson	Charlottesville, VA	Lincoln	Springfield, IL	Coolidge	Plymouth Notch, VT
Madison	Montpelier Station, VA	A. Johnson	Greeneville, TN	Hoover	West Branch, IA
Monroe	Richmond, VA	Grant	New York, NY	F. Roosevelt	Hyde Park, NY
J. Q. Adams	Quincy, MA	Hayes	Fremont, OH	Truman	Independence, MO
Jackson	Nashville, TN	Garfield	Cleveland, OH	Eisenhower	Abilene, KS
Van Buren	Kinderhook, NY	Arthur	Albany, NY	Kennedy	Arlington Natl. Cem., VA
W. H. Harrison	North Bend, OH	Cleveland	Princeton, NJ	L. B. Johnson	Stonewall, TX
Tyler	Richmond, VA	B. Harrison	Indianapolis, IN	Nixon	Yorba Linda, CA
Polk	Nashville, TN	McKinley	Canton, OH	Ford	Grand Rapids, MI
Taylor	Louisville, KY	T. Roosevelt	Oyster Bay, NY	Reagan	Simi Valley, CA
Fillmore	Buffalo, NY	Taft	Arlington Natl. Cem., VA		

PRESIDENTIAL ELECTIONS

Electoral and Popular Vote, 2008 and 2012

Source: Federal Election Commission

State	2012 Electoral vote Obama	Romney	2012 Popular vote Obama	Romney	Johnson	2008 Electoral vote Obama	McCain	2008 Popular vote Obama	McCain	Nader	State
AL	0	9	795,696	1,255,925	12,328	0	9	813,479	1,266,546	6,788	AL
AK	0	3	122,640	164,676	7,392	0	3	123,594	193,841	3,783	AK
AZ	0	11	1,025,232	1,233,654	32,100	0	10	1,034,707	1,230,111	11,301	AZ
AR	0	6	394,409	647,744	16,276	0	6	422,310	638,017	12,882	AR
CA	55	0	7,854,285	4,839,958	143,221	55	0	8,274,473	5,011,781	108,381	CA
CO	9	0	1,323,102	1,185,243	35,545	9	0	1,288,633	1,073,629	13,352	CO
CT	7	0	905,083	634,892	12,580	7	0	997,772	629,428	19,162	CT
DE	3	0	242,584	165,484	3,882	3	0	255,459	152,374	2,401	DE
DC	3	0	267,070	21,381	2,083	3	0	245,800	17,367	958	DC
FL	29	0	4,237,756	4,163,447	44,726	27	0	4,282,074	4,045,624	28,124	FL
GA	0	16	1,773,827	2,078,688	45,324	0	15	1,844,123	2,048,759	1,158	GA
HI	4	0	306,658	121,015	3,840	4	0	325,871	120,566	3,825	HI
ID	0	4	212,787	420,911	9,453	0	4	236,440	403,012	7,175	ID
IL	20	0	3,019,512	2,135,216	56,229	21	0	3,419,348	2,031,179	30,948	IL
IN	0	11	1,152,887	1,420,543	50,111	11	0	1,374,039	1,345,648	909	IN
IA	6	0	822,544	730,617	12,926	7	0	828,940	682,379	8,014	IA
KS	0	6	440,726	692,634	20,456	0	6	514,765	699,655	10,527	KS
KY	0	8	679,370	1,087,190	17,063	0	8	751,985	1,048,462	15,378	KY
LA	0	8	809,141	1,152,262	18,157	0	9	782,989	1,148,275	6,997	LA
ME	4	0	401,306	292,276	9,352	4	0	421,923	295,273	10,636	ME
MD	10	0	1,677,844	971,869	30,195	10	0	1,629,467	959,862	14,713	MD
MA	11	0	1,921,290	1,188,314	30,920	12	0	1,904,097	1,108,854	28,841	MA
MI	16	0	2,564,569	2,115,256	7,774	17	0	2,872,579	2,048,639	33,085	MI
MN	10	0	1,546,167	1,320,225	35,098	10	0	1,573,354	1,275,409	30,152	MN
MS	0	6	562,949	710,746	6,676	0	6	554,662	724,597	4,011	MS
MO	0	10	1,223,796	1,482,440	43,151	0	11	1,441,911	1,445,814	17,813	MO
MT	0	3	201,839	267,928	14,165	0	3	231,667	242,763	3,686	MT
NE[1]	0	5	302,081	475,064	11,109	1	4	333,319	452,979	5,406	NE[1]
NV	6	0	531,373	463,567	10,968	5	0	533,736	412,827	6,150	NV
NH	4	0	369,561	329,918	8,212	4	0	384,826	316,534	3,503	NH
NJ	14	0	2,125,101	1,477,568	21,045	15	0	2,215,422	1,613,207	21,298	NJ
NM	5	0	415,335	335,788	27,788	5	0	472,422	346,832	5,327	NM
NY	29	0	4,337,622	2,228,060	47,256	31	0	4,804,945	2,752,771	41,249	NY
NC	0	15	2,178,391	2,270,395	44,515	15	0	2,142,651	2,128,474	1,448	NC
ND	0	3	124,827	108,163	5,231	0	3	141,278	168,601	4,189	ND
OH	18	0	2,827,710	2,661,433	49,493	20	0	2,940,044	2,677,820	42,337	OH
OK	0	7	443,547	891,325	—	0	7	502,496	960,165	—	OK
OR	7	0	970,488	754,175	24,089	7	0	1,037,291	738,475	18,614	OR
PA	20	0	2,990,274	2,680,434	49,991	21	0	3,276,363	2,655,885	42,977	PA
RI	4	0	279,677	157,204	4,388	4	0	296,571	165,391	4,829	RI
SC	0	9	865,941	1,071,645	16,321	0	8	862,449	1,034,896	5,053	SC
SD	0	3	145,039	210,610	5,795	0	3	170,924	203,054	4,267	SD
TN	0	11	960,709	1,462,330	18,623	0	11	1,087,437	1,479,178	11,560	TN
TX	0	38	3,308,124	4,569,843	88,580	0	34	3,528,633	4,479,328	5,751	TX
UT	0	6	251,813	740,600	12,572	0	5	327,670	596,030	8,416	UT
VT	3	0	199,239	92,698	3,487	3	0	219,262	98,974	3,339	VT
VA	13	0	1,971,820	1,822,522	31,216	13	0	1,959,532	1,725,005	11,483	VA
WA	12	0	1,755,396	1,290,670	42,202	11	0	1,750,848	1,229,216	29,489	WA
WV	0	5	238,269	417,655	6,302	0	5	303,857	397,466	7,219	WV
WI	10	0	1,620,985	1,410,966	20,439	10	0	1,677,211	1,262,393	17,605	WI
WY	0	3	69,286	170,962	5,326	0	3	82,868	164,958	2,525	WY
Total	332	206	65,915,796	60,933,500	1,275,971	365	173	69,498,516	59,948,323	739,034	Total

— = Not listed on state's ballot. (1) Nebraska is one of two states (the other is Maine) that allows electoral votes to be split between candidates.

Presidential Popular Vote, 2012

Candidate (party)	Vote total	Percent of vote
Barack Obama (Democrat)	65,915,796	51.06%
Mitt Romney (Republican)	60,933,500	47.20
Gary Johnson (Libertarian)	1,275,971	0.99
Jill Stein (Green)	469,628	0.36
Virgil Goode (Constitution/U.S. Taxpayers)	122,388	0.09
Roseanne Barr (Peace and Freedom)	67,326	0.05
Ross C. "Rocky" Anderson (Justice/Natural Law)	43,018	0.03
Tom Hoefling (American Independent, America's Party)	40,628	0.03
Randall Terry (Independent/no party affiliation)	13,105	0.01
Richard Duncan (Independent)	12,557	0.01
Peta Lindsay (Socialism and Liberation)	7,791	0.01
Chuck Baldwin (Reform)	5,017	<0.01
Will Christensen (Constitution)	4,453	<0.01
Stewart Alexander (Socialist)	4,405	<0.01
James Harris (Socialist Workers)	4,117	<0.01
Thomas Robert Stevens (Objectivist)	4,091	<0.01%
Jim Carlson (Grassroots)	3,149	<0.01
Jill Reed (Unaffiliated)	2,875	<0.01
Merlin Miller (American Third Position)	2,701	<0.01
Sheila "Samm" Tittle (We the People)	2,572	<0.01
Gloria La Riva (Socialism and Liberation)	1,608	<0.01
Jerry White (Socialist Equality)	1,279	<0.01
Dean Morstad (Constitutional Govt.)	1,094	<0.01
Jerry Litzel (Nominated by petition)	1,027	<0.01
Barbara Dale Washer (Reform)	1,016	<0.01
Jeff Boss (NSA Did 911)	1,007	<0.01
Andre Barnett (Reform)	956	<0.01
Jack Fellure (Prohibition)	518	<0.01
Write-in votes (other/miscellaneous)	136,040	0.11
None of these candidates (Nevada)	5,770	<0.01
Total	129,085,403	

Voting age population, Nov. 2012 235,248,000
Percentage casting vote for president 54.87%

Note: Party designations vary from one state to another; party label listed may not necessarily represent a political party organization. Vote totals for the candidates listed above include any write-in votes they received.

The Electoral College

The president and the vice president are the only elective federal officials not chosen by direct vote of the people. They are elected by the members of the Electoral College, an institution provided for in the U.S. Constitution.

On presidential election day, the first Tuesday after the first Monday in Nov. of every fourth year, each state chooses as many electors as it has senators and representatives in Congress. In 1964, for the first time, as provided by the 23rd Amendment to the Constitution, the District of Columbia voted for three electors. Thus, with 100 senators and 435 representatives, there are 538 members of the Electoral College, with a majority of 270 electoral votes needed to elect the president and vice president.

Although political parties were not part of the original plan created by the Founding Fathers, today political parties customarily nominate their lists of electors at their respective state conventions. Some states print names of the candidates for president and vice president at the top of the Nov. ballot; others list only the electors' names. In either case, the electors of the party receiving the highest vote are elected. Two states, Maine and Nebraska, allow for proportional allocation.

The electors meet on the first Monday after the second Wednesday in Dec. in their respective state capitals or in some other place prescribed by state legislatures. By long-established custom, they vote for their party nominees, although this is not required by federal law; some states do require it.

The Constitution requires electors to cast a ballot for at least one person who is not an inhabitant of that elector's home state. This ensures that presidential and vice presidential candidates from the same party will not be from the same state. (In 2000, Republican vice presidential nominee Dick Cheney changed his voter registration to Wyoming, where he grew up and which he'd once represented in Congress, from George W. Bush's home state of Texas.) Also, an elector cannot be a member of Congress or hold federal office.

Certified and sealed lists of the votes of the electors in each state are sent to the president of the U.S. Senate, who then opens them in the presence of the members of the Senate and House of Representatives in a joint session held in early Jan., and the electoral votes of all the states are then officially counted.

If no candidate for president has a majority, the House of Representatives chooses a president from the top three candidates, with all representatives from each state combining to cast one vote for that state. The House decided the outcome of the 1800 and 1824 presidential elections. If no candidate for vice president has a majority, the Senate chooses from the top two, with the senators voting as individuals. The Senate chose the vice president following the 1836 election.

Under the electoral college system, a candidate who fails to be the top vote getter in the popular vote still may win a majority of electoral votes. This happened in the elections of 1876, 1888, and 2000.

Electoral Votes for President, 2012

Electoral votes based on the 2010 Census were in force beginning with the 2012 elections.

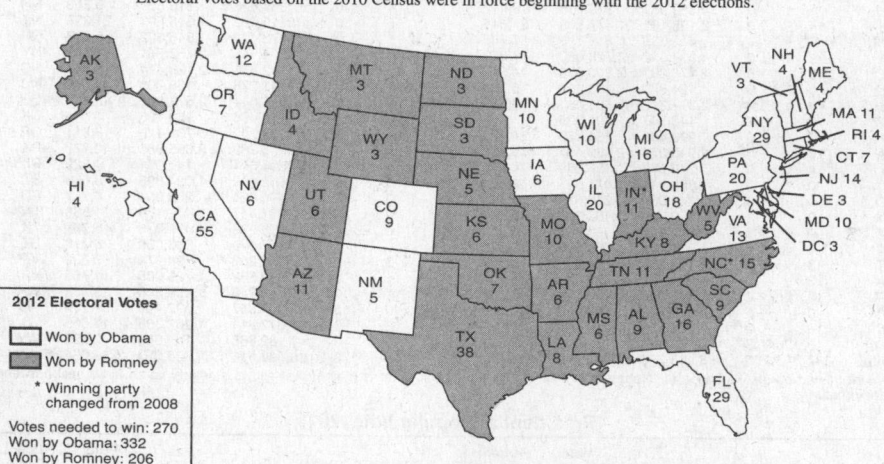

2012 Electoral Votes
- ☐ Won by Obama
- ▨ Won by Romney
- * Winning party changed from 2008

Votes needed to win: 270
Won by Obama: 332
Won by Romney: 206

Voter Turnout in Presidential Elections, 1932-2012

Source: Federal Election Commission; Center for the Study of the American Electorate, American Univ.; *Congressional Quarterly*

Year	Candidates	Voter participation (% of voting-age population)	Year	Candidates	Voter participation (% of voting-age population)
1932	F. D. Roosevelt-Hoover	52.4%	1976	Carter-Ford	53.5%
1936	F. D. Roosevelt-Landon	56.0	1980	Reagan-Carter	54.0
1940	F. D. Roosevelt-Willkie	58.9	1984	Reagan-Mondale	53.1
1944	F. D. Roosevelt-Dewey	56.0	1988	G. H. W. Bush-Dukakis	50.2
1948	Truman-Dewey	51.1	1992	Clinton-G. H. W. Bush-Perot	55.9
1952	Eisenhower-Stevenson	61.6	1996	Clinton-Dole-Perot	49.0
1956	Eisenhower-Stevenson	59.3	2000	G. W. Bush-Gore	51.3
1960	Kennedy-Nixon	62.8	2004	G. W. Bush-Kerry	60.7
1964	L. B. Johnson-Goldwater	61.9	2008	Obama-McCain	58.2
1968	Nixon-Humphrey	60.9	2012	Obama-Romney	54.9
1972	Nixon-McGovern	55.2[1]			

(1) The drop in voter participation followed the expansion of eligibility with the enfranchisement of 18- to 20-year-olds.

Major-Party Nominees for President and Vice President, 1856-2012

Asterisk (*) denotes winning ticket.

Democratic			Republican		
Year	President	Vice President	Year	President	Vice President
1856	James Buchanan*	John Breckinridge	1856	John Frémont	William Dayton
1860	Stephen A. Douglas[1]	Herschel V. Johnson	1860	Abraham Lincoln*	Hannibal Hamlin
1864	George McClellan	G. H. Pendleton	1864	Abraham Lincoln*	Andrew Johnson
1868	Horatio Seymour	Francis Blair	1868	Ulysses S. Grant*	Schuyler Colfax
1872	Horace Greeley	B. Gratz Brown	1872	Ulysses S. Grant*	Henry Wilson
1876	Samuel J. Tilden	Thomas Hendricks	1876	Rutherford B. Hayes*	William Wheeler
1880	Winfield Hancock	William English	1880	James A. Garfield*	Chester A. Arthur
1884	Grover Cleveland*	Thomas Hendricks	1884	James G. Blaine	John Logan
1888	Grover Cleveland	A. G. Thurman	1888	Benjamin Harrison*	Levi Morton
1892	Grover Cleveland*	Adlai Stevenson	1892	Benjamin Harrison	Whitelaw Reid
1896	William J. Bryan	Arthur Sewall	1896	William McKinley*	Garret Hobart
1900	William J. Bryan	Adlai Stevenson	1900	William McKinley*	Theodore Roosevelt
1904	Alton Parker	Henry Davis	1904	Theodore Roosevelt*	Charles Fairbanks
1908	William J. Bryan	John Kern	1908	William H. Taft*	James Sherman
1912	Woodrow Wilson*	Thomas Marshall	1912	William H. Taft	James Sherman[2]
1916	Woodrow Wilson*	Thomas Marshall	1916	Charles E. Hughes	Charles Fairbanks
1920	James M. Cox	Franklin D. Roosevelt	1920	Warren G. Harding*	Calvin Coolidge
1924	John W. Davis	Charles W. Bryan	1924	Calvin Coolidge*	Charles G. Dawes
1928	Alfred E. Smith	Joseph T. Robinson	1928	Herbert Hoover*	Charles Curtis
1932	Franklin D. Roosevelt*	John N. Garner	1932	Herbert Hoover	Charles Curtis
1936	Franklin D. Roosevelt*	John N. Garner	1936	Alfred M. Landon	Frank Knox
1940	Franklin D. Roosevelt*	Henry A. Wallace	1940	Wendell L. Willkie	Charles McNary
1944	Franklin D. Roosevelt*	Harry S. Truman	1944	Thomas E. Dewey	John W. Bricker
1948	Harry S. Truman*	Alben W. Barkley	1948	Thomas E. Dewey	Earl Warren
1952	Adlai E. Stevenson	John J. Sparkman	1952	Dwight D. Eisenhower*	Richard M. Nixon
1956	Adlai E. Stevenson	Estes Kefauver	1956	Dwight D. Eisenhower*	Richard M. Nixon
1960	John F. Kennedy*	Lyndon B. Johnson	1960	Richard M. Nixon	Henry Cabot Lodge
1964	Lyndon B. Johnson*	Hubert H. Humphrey	1964	Barry M. Goldwater	William E. Miller
1968	Hubert H. Humphrey	Edmund S. Muskie	1968	Richard M. Nixon*	Spiro T. Agnew
1972	George S. McGovern	R. Sargent Shriver Jr.[3]	1972	Richard M. Nixon*	Spiro T. Agnew
1976	Jimmy Carter*	Walter F. Mondale	1976	Gerald R. Ford	Bob Dole
1980	Jimmy Carter	Walter F. Mondale	1980	Ronald Reagan*	George H. W. Bush
1984	Walter F. Mondale	Geraldine Ferraro	1984	Ronald Reagan*	George H. W. Bush
1988	Michael S. Dukakis	Lloyd Bentsen	1988	George H. W. Bush*	Dan Quayle
1992	Bill Clinton*	Al Gore	1992	George H. W. Bush	Dan Quayle
1996	Bill Clinton*	Al Gore	1996	Bob Dole	Jack Kemp
2000	Al Gore	Joseph Lieberman	2000	George W. Bush*	Richard Cheney
2004	John Kerry	John Edwards	2004	George W. Bush*	Richard Cheney
2008	Barack Obama*	Joseph Biden	2008	John McCain	Sarah Palin
2012	Barack Obama*	Joseph Biden	2012	Mitt Romney	Paul Ryan

(1) Douglas and Johnson were nominated at the Baltimore convention. An earlier convention in Charleston, SC, failed to reach a consensus and resulted in a split in the party. The Southern faction of the Democrats nominated John Breckinridge for president and Joseph Lane for vice president. (2) Died Oct. 30; replaced on ballot by Nicholas Butler. (3) Chosen by Democratic National Committee after Thomas Eagleton withdrew because of controversy over past treatments for depression.

Third-Party and Independent Presidential Candidates

In most elections since 1860, fewer than one vote in 20 has been cast for a third-party candidate. Still, independent and third-party candidates often bring attention to prominent issues and can affect the outcome between major-party candidates.

Major vote getters among third-party and independent candidates include James B. Weaver (People's Party), 1892; former Pres. Theodore Roosevelt (Progressive Party), 1912; Robert M. La Follette (Progressive Party), 1924; George C. Wallace (American Independent Party), 1968; and H. Ross Perot, as an independent in 1992 and with the Reform Party in 1996. In these six elections, non-major-party candidates combined polled at least 10% of the vote.

Roosevelt outpolled the Republican candidate, William Howard Taft, in 1912, capturing 28% of the popular vote and 88 electoral votes. In 1948, Strom Thurmond (States' Rights [Dixiecrat]) won 39 electoral votes from five Southern states; however, third-party candidates received only 5.75% of the popular vote. George Wallace's popularity in the same region in 1968 allowed him to get 46 electoral votes and 13.5% of the popular vote.

In 1992, Ross Perot captured 19% of the popular vote. However, he did not win a single electoral vote. In 1996, Perot won 8% of the popular vote; all third-party candidates combined won just over 10%. In 2000, Ralph Nader (Green, independent) won about 3% of the vote.

Notable Third-Party and Independent Campaigns by Year

Party	Presidential nominee	Year	Issues	Strength in
Anti-Masonic	William Wirt	1832	Against secret societies and oaths	PA, VT
Liberty	James G. Birney	1844	Anti-slavery	North
Free Soil	Martin Van Buren	1848	Anti-slavery	NY, OH
American (Know-Nothing)	Millard Fillmore	1856	Anti-immigrant	Northeast, South
Greenback	Peter Cooper	1876	For "cheap money," labor rights	National
Greenback	James B. Weaver	1880	For "cheap money," labor rights	National
Prohibition	John P. St. John	1884	Anti-liquor	National
People's (Populist)	James B. Weaver	1892	For "cheap money," end of national banks	South, West
Socialist	Eugene V. Debs	1900-12; 1920	For public ownership	National
Progressive (Bull Moose)	Theodore Roosevelt	1912	Against high tariffs	Midwest, West
Progressive	Robert M. La Follette	1924	For farmer and labor rights	Midwest, West
Socialist	Norman Thomas	1928-48	For liberal reforms	National
Union	William Lemke	1936	Anti-New Deal	National
States' Rights (Dixiecrat)	Strom Thurmond	1948	For states' rights	South
Progressive	Henry A. Wallace	1948	Anti-Cold War	NY, CA
American Independent	George C. Wallace	1968	For states' rights	South
American	John G. Schmitz	1972	For "law and order"	West, OH, LA
None (independent)	John B. Anderson	1980	A third choice	National
None (independent)	H. Ross Perot	1992	Federal budget deficit	National
Reform	H. Ross Perot	1996	Deficit, campaign finance	National
Green, independent	Ralph Nader	2000-08	Corporate power, domestic priorities	National
Libertarian	Gary Johnson	2012	Public debt, civil liberties	National

Popular and Electoral Vote for President, 1789-2012

(D) Democrat; (DR) Democratic Republican; (F) Federalist; (LB) Libertarian; (LR) Liberal Republican; (NR) National Republican; (P) People's; (PR) Progressive; (R) Republican; (W) Whig; * = See notes below table.

Year	President elected	Popular	Elec.	Major losing candidate(s)	Popular	Elec.
1789	George Washington	Unknown	69	No major opposition	—	—
1792	George Washington	Unknown	132	No major opposition	—	—
1796	John Adams (F)	Unknown	71	Thomas Jefferson (DR)	Unknown	68
1800*	Thomas Jefferson (DR)	Unknown	73	Aaron Burr (DR)	Unknown	73
1804	Thomas Jefferson (DR)	Unknown	162	Charles Pinckney (F)	Unknown	14
1808	James Madison (DR)	Unknown	122	Charles Pinckney (F)	Unknown	47
1812	James Madison (DR)	Unknown	128	DeWitt Clinton (F)	Unknown	89
1816	James Monroe (DR)	Unknown	183	Rufus King (F)	Unknown	34
1820	James Monroe (DR)	Unknown	231	John Quincy Adams (DR)	Unknown	1
1824*	John Quincy Adams (DR)	113,122	84	Andrew Jackson (DR)	151,271	99
				Henry Clay (DR)	46,587	37
				William H. Crawford (DR)	44,282	41
1828	Andrew Jackson (D)	642,553	178	John Quincy Adams (NR)	500,897	83
1832	Andrew Jackson (D)	701,780	219	Henry Clay (NR)	484,205	49
1836	Martin Van Buren (D)	764,176	170	William H. Harrison (W)	550,816	73
1840	William H. Harrison (W)	1,275,390	234	Martin Van Buren (D)	1,128,854	60
1844	James K. Polk (D)	1,339,494	170	Henry Clay (W)	1,300,004	105
1848	Zachary Taylor (W)	1,361,393	163	Lewis Cass (D)	1,223,460	127
				Martin Van Buren (Free Soil)	291,501	—
1852	Franklin Pierce (D)	1,607,510	254	Winfield Scott (W)	1,386,942	42
1856	James Buchanan (D)	1,836,072	174	John C. Fremont (R)	1,342,345	114
				Millard Fillmore (W-American)	873,053	8
1860	Abraham Lincoln (R)	1,865,908	180	Stephen A. Douglas (D)	848,019	12
				John C. Breckinridge (D)	845,763	72
				John Bell (Constitutional Union)	589,581	39
1864	Abraham Lincoln (R)	2,218,388	212	George McClellan (D)	1,812,807	21
1868	Ulysses S. Grant (R)	3,013,650	214	Horatio Seymour (D)	2,708,744	80
1872*	Ulysses S. Grant (R)	3,598,235	286	Horace Greeley (D-LR)	2,834,671	—
1876*	Rutherford B. Hayes (R)	4,034,311	185	Samuel J. Tilden (D)	4,288,546	184
1880	James A. Garfield (R)	4,446,158	214	Winfield S. Hancock (D)	4,444,260	155
1884	Grover Cleveland (D)	4,874,621	219	James G. Blaine (R)	4,848,936	182
1888	Benjamin Harrison (R)	5,443,892	233	Grover Cleveland (D)	5,534,488	168
1892	Grover Cleveland (D)	5,551,883	277	Benjamin Harrison (R)	5,179,244	145
				James Weaver (P)	1,027,329	22
1896	William McKinley (R)	7,108,480	271	William J. Bryan (D-P)	6,511,495	176
1900	William McKinley (R)	7,218,039	292	William J. Bryan (D)	6,358,345	155
1904	Theodore Roosevelt (R)	7,626,593	336	Alton B. Parker (D)	5,082,898	140
1908	William H. Taft (R)	7,676,258	321	William J. Bryan (D)	6,406,801	162
1912	Woodrow Wilson (D)	6,293,152	435	Theodore Roosevelt (PR)	4,119,207	88
				William H. Taft (R)	3,483,922	8
1916	Woodrow Wilson (D)	9,126,300	277	Charles E. Hughes (R)	8,546,789	254
1920	Warren G. Harding (R)	16,153,115	404	James M. Cox (D)	9,133,092	127
1924	Calvin Coolidge (R)	15,719,921	382	John W. Davis (D)	8,386,704	136
				Robert M. La Follette (PR)	4,822,856	13
1928	Herbert Hoover (R)	21,437,277	444	Alfred E. Smith (D)	15,007,698	87
1932	Franklin D. Roosevelt (D)	22,829,501	472	Herbert Hoover (R)	15,760,684	59
1936	Franklin D. Roosevelt (D)	27,757,333	523	Alfred Landon (R)	16,684,231	8
1940	Franklin D. Roosevelt (D)	27,313,041	449	Wendell Willkie (R)	22,348,480	82
1944	Franklin D. Roosevelt (D)	25,612,610	432	Thomas E. Dewey (D)	22,117,617	99
1948	Harry S. Truman (D)	24,179,345	303	Thomas E. Dewey (D)	21,991,291	189
				Strom Thurmond (States' Rights)	1,169,021	39
				Henry A. Wallace (PR)	1,157,172	—
1952	Dwight D. Eisenhower (R)	33,936,234	442	Adlai E. Stevenson (D)	27,314,992	89
1956*	Dwight D. Eisenhower (R)	35,590,472	457	Adlai E. Stevenson (D)	26,022,752	73
1960*	John F. Kennedy (D)	34,226,731	303	Richard M. Nixon (R)	34,108,157	219
1964	Lyndon B. Johnson (D)	43,129,566	486	Barry M. Goldwater (R)	27,178,188	52
1968	Richard M. Nixon (R)	31,785,480	301	Hubert H. Humphrey (D)	31,275,166	191
				George C. Wallace (Amer. Indep.)	9,906,473	46
1972*	Richard M. Nixon (R)	47,169,911	520	George S. McGovern (D)	29,170,383	17
1976*	Jimmy Carter (D)	40,830,763	297	Gerald R. Ford (R)	39,147,793	240
1980	Ronald Reagan (R)	43,904,153	489	Jimmy Carter (D)	35,483,883	49
				John B. Anderson (independent)	5,719,437	—
1984	Ronald Reagan (R)	54,455,075	525	Walter F. Mondale (D)	37,577,185	13
1988*	George H. W. Bush (R)	48,886,097	426	Michael S. Dukakis (D)	41,809,074	111
1992	Bill Clinton (D)	44,908,254	370	George H. W. Bush (R)	39,102,343	168
				H. Ross Perot (independent)	19,741,065	—
1996	Bill Clinton (D)	45,590,703	379	Bob Dole (R)	37,816,307	159
				H. Ross Perot (Reform)	7,866,284	—
2000*	George W. Bush (R)	50,459,211	271	Al Gore (D)	51,003,894	266
				Ralph Nader (Green)	2,834,410	—
2004*	George W. Bush (R)	62,040,610	286	John Kerry (D)	59,028,444	251
2008	Barack H. Obama (D)	69,498,516	365	John McCain (R)	59,948,283	173
2012	Barack H. Obama (D)	65,915,796	332	Mitt Romney (R)	60,933,500	206

*1800—Elected by House of Representatives because of tied electoral vote. 1824—Elected by House of Representatives because no candidate polled a majority. By 1824, the Democratic Republicans had become a loose coalition of competing political groups. By 1828, the supporters of Jackson were known as Democrats, and the John Q. Adams and Henry Clay supporters as National Republicans. 1872—Greeley died Nov. 29, 1872. His electoral votes were split among four individuals. 1876—FL, LA, OR, and SC election returns were disputed. Congress in joint session (Mar. 2, 1877) declared Hayes and Wheeler elected president and vice president. 1956—Democrats elected 74 electors, but one from AL refused to vote for Stevenson. 1960—Sen. Harry F. Byrd (D, VA) received 15 electoral votes. 1972—John Hospers of CA received a vote from an elector of VA. 1976—Ronald Reagan of CA received a vote from an elector of WA. 1988—Sen. Lloyd Bentsen (D, TX) received a vote from an elector of WV. 2000—One Gore elector from Washington, DC, abstained. Nader was listed as "independent" on the ballot in some states; he was not on the ballot in all states. 2004—One MN elector voted for VP candidate John Edwards for both president and vice president.

Presidential Election Results by State, 1960-2012
Source: Federal Election Commission; local secretaries of state; state elections offices.

Alabama

County	2012 Obama (D)	Romney (R)	2008 Obama (D)	McCain (R)
Autauga	6,363	17,379	6,093	17,403
Baldwin	18,424	66,016	19,386	61,271
Barbour	5,912	5,550	5,697	5,866
Bibb	2,202	6,132	2,299	6,262
Blount	2,970	20,757	3,522	20,389
Bullock	4,061	1,251	4,011	1,391
Butler	4,374	5,087	4,188	5,485
Calhoun	15,511	30,278	16,334	32,348
Chambers	6,871	7,626	6,799	8,067
Cherokee	2,132	7,506	2,306	7,298
Chilton	3,397	13,932	3,674	13,960
Choctaw	3,786	4,152	3,636	4,223
Clarke	6,334	7,470	5,914	7,466
Clay	1,777	4,817	1,760	4,984
Cleburne	971	5,272	1,168	5,216
Coffee	4,925	14,666	5,079	14,919
Colbert	9,166	13,936	9,703	14,739
Conecuh	3,555	3,439	3,429	3,470
Coosa	2,191	3,049	2,273	3,248
Covington	3,158	12,153	3,240	12,444
Crenshaw	2,050	4,331	1,938	4,319
Cullman	5,052	28,999	5,864	28,896
Dale	5,286	13,108	5,270	13,886
Dallas	14,612	6,288	13,986	6,798
De Kalb	5,239	18,331	5,658	17,957
Elmore	8,954	26,253	8,301	25,777
Escambia	5,489	9,287	5,188	9,375
Etowah	12,803	29,130	13,497	30,595
Fayette	1,817	6,054	1,994	5,883
Franklin	3,171	7,567	3,469	8,048
Geneva	2,039	9,175	2,134	9,417
Greene	4,521	804	4,408	876
Hale	5,411	3,210	4,982	3,200
Henry	3,083	5,628	3,018	5,585
Houston	12,367	29,270	12,225	29,254
Jackson	5,822	14,400	6,374	14,083
Jefferson	159,876	141,683	166,121	149,921
Lamar	1,646	5,457	1,614	5,419
Lauderdale	12,511	23,911	13,329	24,068
Lawrence	5,069	8,874	5,164	9,277
Lee	21,381	32,194	21,498	32,230
Limestone	9,829	25,295	9,536	23,598
Lowndes	5,747	1,756	5,449	1,809
Macon	9,045	1,331	9,450	1,396
Madison	62,015	90,884	64,117	86,965
Marengo	6,167	5,336	5,926	5,516
Marion	2,249	9,697	2,600	9,536
Marshall	6,299	25,867	7,038	25,727
Mobile	78,760	94,893	82,181	98,049
Monroe	4,914	5,741	5,025	6,175
Montgomery	63,085	38,332	62,166	42,031
Morgan	13,439	35,391	13,895	36,014
Perry	4,568	1,506	4,457	1,679
Pickens	4,455	5,124	4,594	5,434
Pike	6,035	7,963	5,879	8,004
Randolph	3,078	7,224	3,064	7,175
Russell	10,500	8,278	10,085	8,705
St. Clair	5,801	29,031	6,091	27,649
Shelby	20,051	71,436	20,625	69,060
Sumter	5,421	1,586	5,264	1,731
Talladega	13,905	19,246	13,779	20,112
Tallapoosa	6,319	12,396	6,063	13,116
Tuscaloosa	32,048	45,748	32,796	45,405
Walker	6,557	21,651	7,420	20,722
Washington	2,976	5,761	3,067	5,654
Wilcox	4,868	1,679	4,612	1,868
Winston	1,286	8,312	1,757	8,103
Totals	**795,696**	**1,255,925**	**813,479**	**1,266,546**

Alabama Vote Since 1960

2012: Romney, R., 1,255,925; Obama, D., 795,696; Johnson, Ind., 12,328; Stein, Ind., 3,397; Goode, Ind., 2,981.
2008: McCain, R., 1,266,546; Obama, D., 813,479; Nader, Ind., 6,788; Barr, Ind., 4,991; Baldwin, Ind., 4,310.
2004: Bush, R., 1,176,394; Kerry, D., 693,933; Nader, Ind., 6,701; Badnarik, Ind., 3,529; Peroutka, Ind., 1,994.
2000: Bush, R., 941,173; Gore, D., 692,611; Nader, Ind., 18,323; Buchanan, Ind., 6,351; Browne, LB., 5,893; Phillips, Ind., 775; Hagelin, Ind., 447.

1996: Dole, R., 769,044; Clinton, D., 662,165; Perot, RF., 92,149; Browne, LB., 5,290; Phillips, Ind., 2,365; Hagelin, Natural Law, 1,697; Harris, Ind., 516.
1992: Bush, R., 804,283; Clinton, D., 690,080; Perot, Ind., 183,109; Marrou, LB., 5,737; Fulani, New Alliance, 2,161.
1988: Bush, R., 815,576; Dukakis, D., 549,506; Paul, LB., 8,460; Fulani, Ind., 3,311.
1984: Reagan, R., 872,849; Mondale, D., 551,899; Bergland, LB., 9,504.
1980: Reagan, R., 654,192; Carter, D., 636,730; Anderson, Ind., 16,481; Rarick, Amer. Ind., 15,010; Clark, LB., 13,318; Bubar, Statesman, 1,743; Hall, Comm., 1,629; DeBerry, Soc. Workers, 1,303; McReynolds, Soc., 1,006; Commoner, Citizens, 517.
1976: Carter, D., 659,170; Ford, R., 504,070; Maddox, Amer. Ind., 9,198; Bubar, Prohib., 6,669; Hall, Comm., 1,954; MacBride, LB., 1,481.
1972: Nixon, R., 728,701; McGovern, D., 219,108 plus 37,815 Natl. Dem. Party of AL; Schmitz, Conservative, 11,918; Munn, Prohib., 8,551.
1968: Wallace, 3rd party, 691,425; Humphrey, D., 196,579; Nixon, R., 146,923; Munn, Prohib., 4,022.
1964: Goldwater, R., 479,085; D. (electors unpledged), 209,848; scattered, 105.
1960: Kennedy, D., 324,050; Nixon, R., 237,981; Faubus, States' Rights, 4,367; Decker, Prohib., 2,106; King, Afro-Americans, 1,485; scattered, 236.

Alaska

	2012 Obama (D)	Romney (R)	2008 Obama (D)	McCain (R)
Totals	122,640	164,676	123,594	193,841

Alaska Vote Since 1960

2012: Romney, R., 164,676; Obama, D., 122,640; Johnson, LB., 7,392; Stein, Green, 2,917.
2008: McCain, R., 193,841; Obama, D., 123,594; Nader, Ind., 3,783; Baldwin, AK Ind., 1,660; Barr, LB., 1,589.
2004: Bush, R., 190,889; Kerry, D., 111,025; Nader, Populist, 5,069; Peroutka, AK Ind., 2,092; Badnarik, LB., 1,675; Cobb, Green, 1,058.
2000: Bush, R., 167,398; Gore, D., 79,004; Nader, Green, 28,747; Buchanan, RF., 5,192; Browne, LB., 2,636; Hagelin, Natural Law, 919; Phillips, Const., 596.
1996: Dole, R., 122,746; Clinton, D., 80,380; Perot, RF., 26,333; Nader, Green, 7,597; Browne, LB., 2,276; Phillips, U.S. Taxpayers, 925; Hagelin, Natural Law, 729.
1992: Bush, R., 102,000; Clinton, D., 78,294; Perot, Ind., 73,481; Gritz, Populist/America First, 1,379; Marrou, LB., 1,378.
1988: Bush, R., 119,251; Dukakis, D., 72,584; Paul, LB., 5,484; Fulani, New Alliance, 1,024.
1984: Reagan, R., 138,377; Mondale, D., 62,007; Bergland, LB., 6,378.
1980: Reagan, R., 86,112; Carter, D., 41,842; Clark, LB., 18,479; Anderson, Ind., 11,155; write-in, 857.
1976: Ford, R., 71,555; Carter, D., 44,058; MacBride, LB., 6,785.
1972: Nixon, R., 55,349; McGovern, D., 32,967; Schmitz, Amer., 6,903.
1968: Nixon, R., 37,600; Humphrey, D., 35,411; Wallace, 3rd party, 10,024.
1964: Johnson, D., 44,329; Goldwater, R., 22,930.
1960: Nixon, R., 30,953; Kennedy, D., 29,809.

Arizona

County	2012 Obama (D)	Romney (R)	2008 Obama (D)	McCain (R)
Apache	17,147	8,250	15,390	8,551
Cochise	18,546	29,497	18,943	29,026
Coconino	29,257	21,220	31,433	22,186
Gila	7,697	13,455	7,884	14,095
Graham	3,609	8,076	3,487	8,376
Greenlee	1,310	1,592	1,165	1,712
La Paz	1,880	3,714	1,929	3,509
Maricopa	602,288	749,885	602,166	746,448
Mohave	19,533	49,168	22,092	44,333
Navajo	16,945	19,884	15,579	19,761
Pima	201,251	174,779	206,254	182,406
Pinal	44,306	62,079	44,254	59,421
Santa Cruz	9,486	4,235	8,683	4,518
Yavapai	33,918	64,468	36,889	61,192
Yuma	18,059	23,352	18,559	24,577
Totals	**1,025,232**	**1,233,654**	**1,034,707**	**1,230,111**

Arizona Vote Since 1960

2012: Romney, R., 1,233,654; Obama, D., 1,025,232; Johnson, LB., 32,100; Stein, Green, 7,816.
2008: McCain, R., 1,230,111; Obama, D., 1,034,707; Barr, LB., 12,555; Nader, New Prog., 11,301; McKinney, Green, 3,406.
2004: Bush, R., 1,104,294; Kerry, D., 893,524; Badnarik, LB., 11,856.
2000: Bush, R., 781,652; Gore, D., 685,341; Nader, Green, 45,645; Buchanan, RF., 12,373; Smith, LB., 5,775; Hagelin, Natural Law, 1,120.
1996: Clinton, D., 653,288; Dole, R., 622,073; Perot, RF., 112,072; Browne, LB., 14,358.
1992: Bush, R., 572,086; Clinton, D., 543,050; Perot, Ind., 353,741; Gritz, Populist/America First, 8,141; Marrou, LB., 6,759; Hagelin, Natural Law, 2,267.
1988: Bush, R., 702,541; Dukakis, D., 454,029; Paul, LB., 13,351; Fulani, New Alliance, 1,662.
1984: Reagan, R., 681,416; Mondale, D., 333,854; Bergland, LB., 10,585.
1980: Reagan, R., 529,688; Carter, D., 246,843; Anderson, Ind., 76,952; Clark, LB., 18,784; De Berry, Soc. Workers, 1,100; Commoner, Citizens, 551; Hall, Comm., 25; Griswold, Workers World, 2.
1976: Ford, R., 418,642; Carter, D., 295,602; McCarthy, Ind., 19,229; MacBride, LB., 7,647; Camejo, Soc. Workers, 928; Anderson, Amer., 564; Maddox, Amer. Ind., 85.
1972: Nixon, R., 402,812; McGovern, D., 198,540; Jenness, Soc. Workers, 30,945; Schmitz, Amer. Ind., 21,208.
1968: Nixon, R., 266,721; Humphrey, D., 170,514; Wallace, 3rd party, 46,573; McCarthy, New Party, 2,751; Cleaver, Peace/Freedom, 217; Halstead, Soc. Workers, 85; Blomen, Soc. Labor, 75.
1964: Goldwater, R., 242,535; Johnson, D., 237,753; Hass, Soc. Labor, 482.
1960: Nixon, R., 221,241; Kennedy, D., 176,781; Hass, Soc. Labor, 469.

Arkansas

County	2012 Obama (D)	Romney (R)	2008 Obama (D)	McCain (R)
Arkansas	2,455	3,897	2,619	4,185
Ashley	2,859	4,867	2,976	5,406
Baxter	5,172	13,688	6,539	12,852
Benton	22,636	54,646	23,331	51,174
Boone	3,772	11,159	4,435	10,575
Bradley	1,449	2,134	1,680	2,262
Calhoun	660	1,458	691	1,462
Carroll	3,696	6,125	4,172	6,083
Chicot	2,649	1,670	3,043	2,119
Clark	3,811	4,343	4,267	4,608
Clay	1,738	3,225	2,244	3,032
Cleburne	2,620	8,693	2,951	7,962
Cleveland	845	2,313	911	2,451
Columbia	3,557	5,790	3,554	5,861
Conway	3,005	4,514	3,149	4,691
Craighead	10,527	20,350	11,294	18,881
Crawford	4,881	15,145	5,238	14,688
Crittenden	9,487	6,998	10,330	7,650
Cross	2,279	4,269	2,580	4,393
Dallas	1,337	1,665	1,471	1,757
Desha	2,443	1,896	2,569	1,999
Drew	2,630	3,887	2,598	3,860
Faulkner	13,621	26,722	14,955	25,362
Franklin	1,726	4,631	1,869	4,411
Fulton	1,452	2,949	1,819	2,702
Garland	13,804	26,014	15,899	26,825
Grant	1,468	4,829	1,562	5,023
Greene	4,000	9,071	4,541	8,578
Hempstead	2,468	4,284	2,869	4,273
Hot Spring	3,830	7,097	4,288	7,209
Howard	1,471	2,892	1,746	2,957
Independence	3,281	8,728	3,688	8,255
Izard	1,524	3,575	1,792	3,193
Jackson	2,095	3,072	2,207	3,118
Jefferson	17,470	9,520	18,465	10,655
Johnson	2,799	5,064	3,034	4,922
Lafayette	1,173	1,713	1,133	1,685
Lawrence	1,788	3,536	2,138	3,357
Lee	2,107	1,280	2,263	1,454
Lincoln	1,425	2,199	1,710	2,513
Little River	1,552	3,385	1,753	3,247
Logan	2,009	5,079	2,286	5,350
Lonoke	5,625	17,880	5,968	17,242
Madison	2,099	4,263	2,144	3,972
Marion	2,037	4,774	2,384	4,524
Miller	4,518	10,622	4,869	9,913
Mississippi	6,467	6,603	6,667	6,976
Monroe	1,583	1,585	1,615	1,754
Montgomery	920	2,369	1,092	2,365
Nevada	1,314	1,996	1,474	2,062
Newton	993	2,508	1,182	2,588
Ouachita	4,633	5,521	4,346	5,427
Perry	1,187	2,581	1,352	2,743
Phillips	5,202	2,598	5,695	3,097
Pike	851	2,847	1,089	2,727
Poinsett	2,390	4,974	2,742	4,903
Polk	1,556	5,955	1,957	5,473
Pope	5,126	14,763	6,002	15,568
Prairie	880	2,153	1,048	2,223
Pulaski	87,248	68,984	88,854	70,212
Randolph	2,046	3,701	2,469	3,615
St. Francis	4,910	3,368	5,486	3,917
Saline	12,869	32,963	12,695	30,981
Scott	897	2,631	1,053	2,791
Searcy	814	2,699	961	2,726
Sebastian	13,092	29,169	13,673	28,637
Sevier	1,042	3,136	1,291	3,125
Sharp	2,092	4,921	2,436	4,535
Stone	1,356	3,776	1,598	3,534
Union	6,196	10,689	6,190	10,677
Van Buren	1,832	4,365	2,151	4,276
Washington	28,236	39,688	29,021	37,963
White	5,765	20,011	6,732	19,467
Woodruff	1,340	1,227	1,412	1,206
Yell	1,722	4,042	2,003	3,808
Totals	**394,409**	**647,744**	**422,310**	**638,017**

Arkansas Vote Since 1960

2012: Romney, R., 647,744; Obama, D., 394,409; Johnson, LB., 16,276; Stein, Green, 9,305; Lindsay, Socialism/Liberation, 1,734.
2008: McCain, R., 638,017; Obama, D., 422,310; Nader, Ind., 12,882; Barr, LB., 4,776; Baldwin, Const., 4,023; McKinney, Green, 3,470; La Riva, Socialism/Liberation, 1,139.
2004: Bush, R., 572,898; Kerry, D., 469,953; Nader, Populist, 6,171; Badnarik, LB., 2,352; Peroutka, Const., 2,083; Cobb, Green, 1,488.
2000: Bush, R., 472,940; Gore, D., 422,768; Nader, Green, 13,421; Buchanan, RF., 7,358; Browne, LB., 2,781; Phillips, Const., 1,415; Hagelin, Natural Law, 1,098.
1996: Clinton, D., 475,171; Dole, R., 325,416; Perot, RF., 69,884; Nader, Ind., 3,649; Browne, Ind., 3,076; Phillips, Ind., 2,065; Forbes, Ind., 932; Collins, Ind., 823; Masters, Ind., 749; Moorehead, Ind., 747; Hagelin, Ind., 729; Hollis, Ind., 538; Dodge, Ind., 483.
1992: Clinton, D., 505,823; Bush, R., 337,324; Perot, Ind., 99,132; Phillips, U.S. Taxpayers, 1,437; Marrou, LB., 1,261; Fulani, New Alliance, 1,022.
1988: Bush, R., 466,578; Dukakis, D., 349,237; Duke, Populist, 5,146; Paul, LB., 3,297.
1984: Reagan, R., 534,774; Mondale, D., 338,646; Bergland, LB., 2,220.
1980: Reagan, R., 403,164; Carter, D., 398,041; Anderson, Ind., 22,468; Clark, LB., 8,970; Commoner, Citizens, 2,345; Bubar, Statesman, 1,350; Hall, Comm., 1,244.
1976: Carter, D., 498,604; Ford, R., 267,903; McCarthy, Ind., 639; Anderson, Amer. Ind., 389.
1972: Nixon, R., 445,751; McGovern, D., 198,899; Schmitz, Amer. Ind., 3,016.
1968: Wallace, 3rd party, 235,627; Nixon, R., 189,062; Humphrey, D., 184,901.
1964: Johnson, D., 314,197; Goldwater, R., 243,264; Kasper, Natl. States' Rights, 2,965.
1960: Kennedy, D., 215,049; Nixon, R., 184,508; Faubus, Natl. States' Rights, 28,952.

California

County	2012 Obama (D)	Romney (R)	2008 Obama (D)	McCain (R)
Alameda	469,684	108,182	489,106	119,555
Alpine	389	236	422	252
Amador	6,830	10,281	7,813	10,561
Butte	42,669	44,479	49,013	46,706
Calaveras	8,670	12,365	9,813	12,835
Colusa	2,314	3,601	2,569	3,733
Contra Costa	290,824	136,517	306,983	136,436
Del Norte	3,791	4,614	4,323	4,967
El Dorado	35,166	50,973	40,529	50,314
Fresno	129,129	124,490	136,706	131,015
Glenn	3,301	5,632	3,734	5,910
Humboldt	34,457	18,825	39,692	21,713
Imperial	25,136	12,777	24,162	14,008
Inyo	3,422	4,340	3,743	4,523
Kern	89,495	126,618	93,457	134,793
Kings	12,979	17,671	14,747	19,710
Lake	13,163	9,200	14,854	9,935
Lassen	3,053	7,296	3,586	7,483
Los Angeles	2,216,903	885,333	2,295,853	956,425

County	2012 Obama (D)	Romney (R)	2008 Obama (D)	McCain (R)
Madera	16,018	22,852	17,952	23,583
Marin	99,896	30,880	109,320	28,384
Mariposa	3,498	5,140	4,100	5,298
Mendocino	23,193	9,658	27,843	10,721
Merced	33,005	27,581	34,031	28,704
Modoc	1,111	2,777	1,313	2,981
Mono	2,733	2,285	3,093	2,354
Monterey	82,920	37,390	88,453	38,797
Napa	35,870	19,526	38,849	19,484
Nevada	24,663	24,986	28,617	25,663
Orange	512,440	582,332	549,558	579,064
Placer	66,818	99,921	75,112	94,647
Plumas	4,026	5,721	4,715	6,035
Riverside	329,063	318,127	325,017	310,041
Sacramento	300,503	202,514	316,506	213,583
San Benito	11,276	7,343	11,917	7,425
San Bernardino	305,109	262,358	315,720	277,408
San Diego	626,957	536,726	666,581	541,032
San Francisco	301,723	47,076	322,220	52,292
San Joaquin	114,121	86,071	113,974	91,607
San Luis Obispo	61,258	59,967	68,176	61,055
San Mateo	206,085	72,756	222,826	75,057
Santa Barbara	94,129	64,606	105,614	65,585
Santa Clara	450,818	174,843	462,241	190,039
Santa Cruz	90,805	24,047	98,745	25,244
Shasta	25,819	48,067	28,867	49,588
Sierra	653	1,056	743	1,158
Siskiyou	8,046	11,077	9,292	11,520
Solano	96,783	52,092	102,095	56,035
Sonoma	153,942	54,784	168,888	55,127
Stanislaus	77,724	73,459	80,279	77,497
Sutter	12,192	18,122	13,412	18,911
Tehama	7,934	14,235	8,945	14,843
Trinity	2,674	2,716	3,233	2,940
Tulare	41,752	56,956	43,634	59,765
Tuolumne	9,998	13,880	11,532	14,988
Ventura	170,930	147,958	187,601	145,853
Yolo	48,715	23,368	53,488	24,592
Yuba	4,711	11,275	8,866	12,007
Totals	**7,854,285**	**4,839,958**	**8,274,473**	**5,011,781**

California Vote Since 1960

2012: Obama, D., 7,854,285; Romney, R., 4,839,958; Johnson, LB., 143,221; Stein, Green, 85,638; Barr, Peace/Freedom, 53,824; Hoefling, Amer. Ind., 38,372.

2008: Obama, D., 8,274,473; McCain, R., 5,011,781; Nader, Peace/Freedom, 108,381; Barr, LB., 67,582; Alan Keyes, Amer. Ind., 40,673; McKinney, Green, 38,774.

2004: Kerry, D., 6,745,485; Bush, R., 5,509,826; Badnarik, LB., 50,165; Cobb, Green, 40,771; Peltier, Peace/Freedom, 27,607; Peroutka, Amer. Ind., 26,645.

2000: Gore, D., 5,861,203; Bush, R., 4,567,429; Nader, Green, 418,707; Browne, LB., 45,520; Buchanan, RF., 44,987; Phillips, Amer. Ind., 17,042; Hagelin, Natural Law, 10,934.

1996: Clinton, D., 5,119,835; Dole, R., 3,828,380; Perot, RF., 697,847; Nader, Green, 237,016; Browne, LB., 73,600; Feinland, Peace/Freedom, 25,332; Phillips, Amer. Ind., 21,202; Hagelin, Natural Law, 15,403.

1992: Clinton, D., 5,121,325; Bush, R., 3,630,575; Perot, Ind., 2,296,006; Marrou, LB., 48,139; Daniels, Ind., 18,597; Phillips, U.S. Taxpayers, 12,711.

1988: Bush, R., 5,054,917; Dukakis, D., 4,702,233; Paul, LB., 70,105; Fulani, Ind., 31,181.

1984: Reagan, R., 5,305,410; Mondale, D., 3,815,947; Bergland, LB., 48,400.

1980: Reagan, R., 4,524,858; Carter, D., 3,083,661; Anderson, Ind., 739,833; Clark, LB., 148,434; Commoner, Ind., 61,063; Smith, Peace/Freedom, 18,116; Rarick, Amer. Ind., 9,856.

1976: Ford, R., 3,882,244; Carter, D., 3,742,284; McCarthy, write-in, 58,412; MacBride, LB., 56,388; Maddox, Amer. Ind., 51,098; Wright, People's, 41,731; Camejo, Soc. Workers, 17,259; Hall, Comm., 12,766; write-in, 4,935.

1972: Nixon, R., 4,602,096; McGovern, D., 3,475,847; Schmitz, Amer. Ind., 232,554; Spock, Peace/Freedom, 55,167; Hospers, LB., 980; Jenness, Soc. Workers, 574; Hall, Comm., 373; Fisher, Soc. Labor, 197; Munn, Prohib., 53; Green, Universal, 21.

1968: Nixon, R., 3,467,664; Humphrey, D., 3,244,318; Wallace, 3rd party, 487,270; Peace/Freedom, 27,707; McCarthy, Alternative, 20,721; Gregory, write-in, 3,230; Blomen, Soc. Labor, 341; Mitchell, Comm., 260; Munn, Prohib., 59; Soeters, Defense, 17.

1964: Johnson, D., 4,171,877; Goldwater, R., 2,879,108; Hass, Soc. Labor, 489; DeBerry, Soc. Workers, 378; Munn, Prohib., 305; Hensley, Universal, 19.

1960: Nixon, R., 3,259,722; Kennedy, D., 3,224,099; Decker, Prohib., 21,706; Hass, Soc. Labor, 1,051.

Colorado

County	2012 Obama (D)	Romney (R)	2008 Obama (D)	McCain (R)
Adams	100,649	70,972	93,443	63,976
Alamosa	3,811	2,705	3,521	2,635
Arapahoe	153,905	125,588	148,218	113,866
Archuleta	2,679	3,872	2,836	3,638
Baca	467	1,559	536	1,572
Bent	815	1,075	799	1,077
Boulder	125,091	49,981	124,159	44,904
Broomfield	16,966	15,008	16,168	12,757
Chaffee	5,086	5,070	4,861	4,873
Cheyenne	172	889	198	890
Clear Creek	3,119	2,430	3,332	2,300
Conejos	2,213	1,835	2,154	1,653
Costilla	1,340	446	1,245	415
Crowley	535	924	552	976
Custer	868	1,788	912	1,672
Delta	4,622	10,915	5,084	10,067
Denver	222,018	73,111	204,882	62,567
Dolores	334	859	369	818
Douglas	61,094	104,397	61,960	88,108
Eagle	12,792	9,411	13,187	8,179
El Paso	111,819	170,952	108,899	160,318
Elbert	3,603	10,266	3,819	9,108
Fremont	6,704	13,174	6,844	12,668
Garfield	11,305	12,535	11,357	11,359
Gilpin	1,892	1,346	1,954	1,253
Grand	3,684	4,253	4,037	4,128
Gunnison	5,044	3,341	5,556	3,131
Hinsdale	229	353	240	344
Huerfano	1,953	1,646	1,989	1,580
Jackson	216	600	277	624
Jefferson	159,296	144,197	158,153	131,627
Kiowa	118	677	178	650
Kit Carson	838	2,785	912	2,455
La Plata	15,489	12,794	16,057	11,503
Lake	1,839	1,098	1,859	1,078
Larimer	92,747	82,376	89,822	73,641
Las Animas	3,445	3,263	3,562	3,086
Lincoln	552	1,687	546	1,717
Logan	2,712	6,179	2,846	6,002
Mesa	23,846	47,472	24,008	44,578
Mineral	291	344	270	334
Moffat	1,330	4,695	1,582	4,135
Montezuma	4,542	7,401	4,661	6,961
Montrose	6,138	13,552	6,495	12,199
Morgan	3,912	6,602	3,813	6,272
Otero	3,647	4,382	3,546	4,393
Ouray	1,646	1,481	1,636	1,367
Park	3,862	5,236	4,250	4,896
Phillips	588	1,637	622	1,612
Pitkin	6,849	3,024	7,349	2,484
Prowers	1,519	3,230	1,487	3,043
Pueblo	42,551	31,894	41,097	30,257
Rio Blanco	568	2,724	655	2,437
Rio Grande	2,478	2,918	2,448	2,930
Routt	7,547	5,469	8,270	4,725
Saguache	1,865	964	1,730	953
San Juan	266	212	264	218
San Miguel	2,992	1,154	3,349	933
Sedgwick	419	881	468	857
Summit	9,347	5,571	9,802	4,883
Teller	4,333	8,702	4,513	8,146
Washington	468	2,076	529	1,949
Weld	49,050	63,775	47,292	56,526
Yuma	987	3,490	1,117	3,286
Totals	**1,323,102**	**1,185,243**	**1,288,633**	**1,073,629**

Colorado Vote Since 1960

2012: Obama, D., 1,323,102; Romney, R., 1,185,243; Johnson, LB., 35,545; Stein, Green, 7,508; Goode, Const., 6,234; Barr, Peace/Freedom, 5,059; Reed, unaff., 2,589; Anderson, Justice, 1,260; Tittle, We the People, 792; Hoefling, Amer. Ind., 679; La Riva, Socialism/Liberation, 317; Alexander, Soc. USA, 308; Miller, A3P, 266; Stevens, Objectivist, 235; Harris, Soc. Workers, 192; White, Soc. Equality, 189.

2008: Obama, D., 1,288,633; McCain, R., 1,073,629; Nader, Unaff., 13,352; Barr, LB., 10,898; Baldwin, Const., 6,233; Alan Keyes, Amer. Ind., 3,051; McKinney, Green, 2,822; McEnulty, unaff., 829; Jay, Boston Tea, 598; Allen, HeartQuake'08, 348; Stevens, Objectivist, 336; Moore, Soc. USA, 226; La Riva, Socialism/Liberation, 158; Harris, Soc. Workers, 154; Lyttle, U.S. Pacifist, 110; Amondson, Prohib., 85.

2004: Bush, R., 1,101,255; Kerry, D., 1,001,732; Nader, RF., 12,718; Badnarik, LB., 7,664; Peroutka, Amer. Const., 2,562; Cobb, Green, 1,591; Andress, Ind., 804; Amondson, Concerns of People, 378; Van Auken, Soc. Equal., 329; Harris, Soc. Workers, 241; Brown, Soc., 216; Dodge, Prohib., 140.

2000: Bush, R., 883,748; Gore, D., 738,227; Nader, Green, 91,434; Browne, LB., 12,799; Buchanan, RF., 10,465; Hagelin,

RF., 2,240; Phillips, Amer. Const., 1,319; McReynolds, Soc., 712; Harris, Soc. Workers, 216; Dodge, Prohib., 208.

1996: Dole, R., 691,848; Clinton, D., 671,152; Perot, RF., 99,629; Nader, Green, 25,070; Browne, LB., 12,392; Phillips, Amer. Const., 2,813; Collins, Ind., 2,809; Hagelin, Natural Law, 2,547; Hollis, Soc., 669; Moorehead, Workers World, 599; Templin, Amer., 557; Dodge, Prohib., 375; Harris, Soc. Workers, 244.

1992: Clinton, D., 629,681; Bush, R., 562,850; Perot, Ind., 366,010; Marrou, LB., 8,669; Fulani, New Alliance, 1,608.

1988: Bush, R., 728,177; Dukakis, D., 621,453; Paul, LB., 15,482; Dodge, Prohib., 4,604.

1984: Reagan, R., 821,817; Mondale, D., 454,975; Bergland, LB., 11,257.

1980: Reagan, R., 652,264; Carter, D., 367,973; Anderson, Ind., 130,633; Clark, LB., 25,744; Commoner, Citizens, 5,614; Bubar, Statesman, 1,180; Pulley, Soc., 520; Hall, Comm., 487.

1976: Ford, R., 584,367; Carter, D., 460,353; McCarthy, Ind., 26,107; MacBride, LB., 5,330; Bubar, Prohib., 2,882.

1972: Nixon, R., 597,189; McGovern, D., 329,980; Schmitz, Amer., 17,269; Fisher, Soc. Labor, 4,361; Spock, People's, 2,403; Hospers, LB., 1,111; Jenness, Soc. Workers, 555; Munn, Prohib., 467; Hall, Comm., 432.

1968: Nixon, R., 409,345; Humphrey, D., 335,174; Wallace, 3rd party, 60,813; Blomen, Soc. Labor, 3,016; Gregory, New Party, 1,393; Munn, Prohib., 275; Halstead, Soc. Workers, 235.

1964: Johnson, D., 476,024; Goldwater, R., 296,767; DeBerry, Soc. Workers, 2,537; Munn, Prohib., 1,356; Hass, Soc. Labor, 302.

1960: Nixon, R., 402,242; Kennedy, D., 330,629; Hass, Soc. Labor, 2,803; Dobbs, Soc. Workers, 572.

Connecticut

	2012		2008	
City	Obama (D)	Romney (R)	Obama (D)	McCain (R)
Bridgeport	32,135	5,168	33,976	6,507
Bristol	14,146	10,004	15,966	10,203
Danbury	15,290	10,590	16,028	10,732
East Hartford	14,149	4,556	14,811	5,195
Fairfield	15,283	14,357	17,236	13,071
Greenwich	13,079	16,456	16,233	13,937
Hamden	19,181	7,482	19,960	8,531
Hartford	31,735	2,138	31,741	2,686
Manchester	15,565	7,961	17,782	8,457
Meriden	14,886	6,880	15,913	7,363
Middletown	13,834	6,105	15,143	5,907
Milford	13,668	11,462	14,873	11,772
New Britain	16,052	4,783	16,742	5,442
New Haven	39,865	4,430	39,112	5,098
Norwalk	22,369	12,773	24,489	12,651
Shelton	8,362	10,327	9,655	10,428
Southington	10,727	10,452	12,066	9,845
Stamford	29,623	17,473	31,733	17,510
Stratford	13,483	9,324	14,626	10,199
Wallingford	11,560	9,259	12,833	9,372
Waterbury	20,931	11,043	22,599	12,821
West Hartford	21,069	10,511	23,576	10,021
West Haven	14,286	5,789	14,186	7,005
Other	483,805	425,569	546,493	414,675
Totals	**905,083**	**634,892**	**997,772**	**629,428**

Connecticut Vote Since 1960

2012: Obama, D., 905,083; Romney, R., 634,892; Johnson, LB., 12,580; Anderson, Ind., 5,487.

2008: Obama, D., 997,772; McCain, R., 629,428; Nader, Ind., 19,162.

2004: Kerry, D., 857,488; Bush, R., 693,826; Nader, petitioning cand., 12,969; Cobb, Green, 9,564; Badnarik, LB., 3,367; Peroutka, Concerned Citizens, 1,543.

2000: Gore, D., 816,015; Bush, R., 561,094; Nader, Green, 64,452; Phillips, Concerned Citizens, 9,695; Buchanan, RF., 4,731; Browne, LB., 3,484.

1996: Clinton, D., 735,740; Dole, R., 483,109; Perot, RF., 139,523; Nader, Green, 24,321; Browne, LB., 5,788; Phillips, Concerned Citizens, 2,425; Hagelin, Natural Law, 1,703.

1992: Clinton, D., 682,318; Bush, R., 578,313; Perot, Ind., 348,771; Marrou, LB., 5,391; Fulani, New Alliance, 1,363.

1988: Bush, R., 750,241; Dukakis, D., 676,584; Paul, LB., 14,071; Fulani, New Alliance, 2,491.

1984: Reagan, R., 890,877; Mondale, D., 569,597.

1980: Reagan, R., 677,210; Carter, D., 541,732; Anderson, Ind., 171,807; Clark, LB., 8,570; Commoner, Citizens, 6,130; scattered, 836.

1976: Ford, R., 719,261; Carter, D., 647,895; Maddox, George Wallace Party, 7,101; LaRouche, U.S. Labor, 1,789.

1972: Nixon, R., 810,763; McGovern, D., 555,498; Schmitz, Amer., 17,239; scattered, 777.

1968: Humphrey, D., 621,561; Nixon, R., 556,721; Wallace, 3rd party, 76,650; scattered, 1,300.

1964: Johnson, D., 826,269; Goldwater, R., 390,996; scattered, 1,313.

1960: Kennedy, D., 657,055; Nixon, R., 565,813.

Delaware

	2012		2008	
County	Obama (D)	Romney (R)	Obama (D)	McCain (R)
Kent	35,527	32,135	36,392	29,827
New Castle	167,082	81,230	178,768	74,608
Sussex	39,975	52,119	40,299	47,939
Totals	**242,584**	**165,484**	**255,459**	**152,374**

Delaware Vote Since 1960

2012: Obama, D., 242,584; Romney, R., 165,484; Johnson, LB., 3,882; Stein, Green, 1,940.

2008: Obama, D., 255,459; McCain, R., 152,374; Nader, Ind. (DE), 2,401; Barr, LB., 1,109; Baldwin, Const., 626; McKinney, Green, 385; Calero, Soc. Workers, 58.

2004: Kerry, D., 200,152; Bush, R., 171,660; Nader, Ind., 2,153; Badnarik, LB., 586; Peroutka, Const., 289; Cobb, Green, 250; Brown, Natural Law, 100.

2000: Gore, D., 180,068; Bush, R., 137,288; Nader, Green, 8,307; Buchanan, RF., 777; Browne, LB., 774; Phillips, Const., 208; Hagelin, Natural Law, 107.

1996: Clinton, D., 140,355; Dole, R., 99,062; Perot, RF., 28,719; Browne, LB., 2,052; Phillips, U.S. Taxpayers, 348; Hagelin, Natural Law, 274.

1992: Clinton, D., 126,054; Bush, R., 102,313; Perot, Ind., 59,213; Fulani, New Alliance, 1,105.

1988: Bush, R., 139,639; Dukakis, D., 108,647; Paul, LB., 1,162; Fulani, New Alliance, 443.

1984: Reagan, R., 152,190; Mondale, D., 101,656; Bergland, LB., 268.

1980: Reagan, R., 111,252; Carter, D., 105,754; Anderson, Ind., 16,288; Clark, LB., 1,974; Greaves, Amer., 400.

1976: Carter, D., 122,596; Ford, R., 109,831; McCarthy, nonpartisan, 2,437; Anderson, Amer., 645; LaRouche, U.S. Labor, 136; Bubar, Prohib., 103; Levin, Soc. Labor, 86.

1972: Nixon, R., 140,357; McGovern, D., 92,283; Schmitz, Amer., 2,638; Munn, Prohib., 238.

1968: Nixon, R., 96,714; Humphrey, D., 89,194; Wallace, 3rd party, 28,459.

1964: Johnson, D., 122,704; Goldwater, R., 78,078; Munn, Prohib., 425; Hass, Soc. Labor, 113.

1960: Kennedy, D., 99,590; Nixon, R., 96,373; Faubus, States' Rights, 354; Decker, Prohib., 284; Hass, Soc. Labor, 82.

District of Columbia

	2012		2008	
	Obama (D)	Romney (R)	Obama (D)	McCain (R)
Totals	267,070	21,381	245,800	17,367

District of Columbia Vote Since 1964

2012: Obama, D., 267,070; Romney, R., 21,381; Stein, DC Statehood Green, 2,458; Johnson, LB., 2,083.

2008: Obama, D., 245,800; McCain, R., 17,367; Nader, Ind., 958; McKinney, Green, 590.

2004: Kerry, D., 202,970; Bush, R., 21,256; Nader, Ind., 1,485; Cobb, DC Statehood Green, 737; Badnarik, LB., 502; Harris, Soc. Workers, 130.

2000: Gore, D., 171,923; Bush, R., 18,073; Nader, Green, 10,576; Browne, LB., 669; Harris, Soc. Workers, 114.

1996: Clinton, D., 158,220; Dole, R., 17,339; Nader, Green, 4,780; Perot, RF., 3,611; Browne, LB., 588; Hagelin, Natural Law, 283; Harris, Soc. Workers, 257.

1992: Clinton, D., 192,619; Bush, R., 20,698; Perot, Ind., 9,681; Fulani, New Alliance, 1,459; Daniels, Ind., 1,186.

1988: Dukakis, D., 159,407; Bush, R., 27,590; Fulani, New Alliance, 2,901; Paul, LB., 554.

1984: Mondale, D., 180,408; Reagan, R., 29,009; Bergland, LB., 279.

1980: Carter, D., 130,231; Reagan, R., 23,313; Anderson, Ind., 16,131; Commoner, Citizens, 1,826; Clark, LB., 1,104; Hall, Comm., 369; DeBerry, Soc. Workers, 173; Griswold, Workers World, 52; write-in, 690.

1976: Carter, D., 137,818; Ford, R., 27,873; Camejo, Soc. Workers, 545; MacBride, LB., 274; Hall, Comm., 219; LaRouche, U.S. Labor, 157.

1972: McGovern, D., 127,627; Nixon, R., 35,226; Reed, Soc. Workers, 316; Hall, Comm., 252.

1968: Humphrey, D., 139, 566; Nixon, R., 31,012.

1964: Johnson, D., 169,796; Goldwater, R., 28,801.

Florida

	2012		2008	
County	Obama (D)	Romney (R)	Obama (D)	McCain (R)
Alachua	69,699	48,797	75,565	48,513
Baker	2,311	8,975	2,327	8,672
Bay	22,051	56,876	23,653	56,683
Bradford	3,325	8,219	3,430	8,136
Brevard	122,993	159,300	127,620	157,589
Broward	508,312	244,101	492,640	237,729
Calhoun	1,664	4,366	1,821	4,345

County	2012 Obama (D)	Romney (R)	2008 Obama (D)	McCain (R)
Charlotte	35,906	47,996	39,031	45,205
Citrus	28,460	44,662	31,460	43,706
Clay	25,759	70,022	26,697	67,203
Collier	51,698	96,520	54,450	86,379
Columbia	8,462	18,429	9,171	18,670
De Soto	4,174	5,587	4,383	5,632
Dixie	1,798	5,052	1,925	5,194
Duval	196,737	211,615	202,618	210,537
Escambia	58,185	88,711	61,572	91,411
Flagler	23,207	26,969	24,726	23,951
Franklin	1,845	3,570	2,134	3,818
Gadsden	15,770	6,630	15,582	6,811
Gilchrist	1,885	5,917	1,996	5,656
Glades	1,603	2,344	1,381	1,938
Gulf	2,014	4,995	2,149	4,980
Hamilton	2,228	3,138	2,364	3,179
Hardee	2,463	4,696	2,568	4,763
Hendry	4,751	5,355	4,998	5,780
Hernando	37,830	44,938	41,886	45,021
Highlands	16,148	25,915	18,135	26,221
Hillsborough	286,467	250,186	272,963	236,355
Holmes	1,264	6,919	1,446	7,033
Indian River	27,492	43,450	29,710	40,176
Jackson	7,342	13,418	7,671	13,717
Jefferson	3,945	3,808	4,088	3,797
Lafayette	687	2,668	642	2,679
Lake	61,799	87,643	62,948	82,802
Lee	110,157	154,163	119,701	147,608
Leon	90,881	55,805	91,747	55,705
Levy	6,119	12,054	6,711	11,754
Liberty	942	2,301	895	2,339
Madison	4,176	4,474	4,270	4,544
Manatee	66,503	85,627	70,034	80,721
Marion	66,831	93,043	70,839	89,628
Martin	30,107	48,183	33,508	44,143
Miami-Dade	541,440	332,981	499,831	360,551
Monroe	19,404	19,234	20,907	18,933
Nassau	10,251	29,929	10,618	27,403
Okaloosa	23,421	70,168	25,872	68,789
Okeechobee	4,856	7,328	5,108	7,561
Orange	273,665	188,589	273,009	186,632
Osceola	67,239	40,592	59,962	40,086
Palm Beach	349,651	247,398	361,271	226,037
Pasco	98,263	112,427	102,417	110,104
Pinellas	239,104	213,250	248,299	210,066
Polk	114,622	131,577	113,865	128,878
Putnam	11,667	19,326	13,236	19,637
St. Johns	35,190	78,513	35,791	69,222
St. Lucie	65,869	56,202	67,125	52,512
Santa Rosa	17,768	58,186	19,470	55,972
Sarasota	95,119	110,504	102,686	102,897
Seminole	96,445	109,943	99,335	105,070
Sumter	19,524	40,646	17,655	30,866
Suwannee	4,751	12,672	4,916	12,534
Taylor	2,764	6,249	2,803	6,457
Union	1,039	3,980	1,300	3,940
Volusia	114,748	117,490	127,795	113,938
Wakulla	5,175	9,290	5,311	8,877
Walton	6,671	21,490	7,174	19,561
Washington	2,820	8,038	2,863	8,178
Totals	**4,237,756**	**4,163,447**	**4,282,074**	**4,045,624**

Florida Vote Since 1960

2012: Obama, D., 4,237,756; Romney, R., 4,163,447; Johnson, LB., 44,726; Stein, Green, 8,947; Barr, Peace/Freedom, 8,154; Stevens, Objectivist, 3,856; Goode, Const., 2,607; Anderson, Justice, 1,754; Hoefling, Amer. Ind., 946; Barnett, RF., 820; Alexander, Soc., 799; Lindsay, Socialism/Liberation, 322.

2008: Obama, D., 4,282,074; McCain, R., 4,045,624; Nader, Ecology (FL), 28,124; Barr, LB., 17,218; Baldwin, Const., 7,915; McKinney, Green, 2,887; Keyes, Amer. Ind., 2,550; La Riva, Socialism/Liberation, 1,516; Jay, Boston Tea, 795; Harris, Soc. Workers, 533; Stevens, Objectivist, 419; Moore, Soc. USA, 405; Amondson, Prohib., 293.

2004: Bush, R., 3,964,522; Kerry, D., 3,583,544; Nader, RF., 32,971; Badnarik, LB., 11,996; Peroutka, Const., 6,626; Cobb, Green, 3,917; Brown, Soc., 3,502; Harris, Soc. Workers, 2,732.

2000: Bush, R., 2,912,790; Gore, D., 2,912,253; Nader, Green, 97,488; Buchanan, RF., 17,484; Browne, LB., 16,415; Hagelin, Natural Law, 2,281; Moorehead, Workers World, 1,804; Phillips, Const., 1,371; McReynolds, Soc., 622; Harris, Soc. Workers, 562.

1996: Clinton, D., 2,545,968; Dole, R., 2,243,324; Perot, RF., 483,776; Browne, LB., 23,312.

1992: Bush, R., 2,171,781; Clinton, D., 2,071,651; Perot, Ind., 1,052,481; Marrou, LB., 15,068.

1988: Bush, R., 2,616,597; Dukakis, D., 1,655,851; Paul, LB., 19,796, Fulani, New Alliance, 6,655.

1984: Reagan, R., 2,728,775; Mondale, D., 1,448,344.

1980: Reagan, R., 2,046,951; Carter, D., 1,419,475; Anderson, Ind., 189,692; Clark, LB., 30,524; write-in, 285.

1976: Carter, D., 1,636,000; Ford, R., 1,469,531; McCarthy, Ind., 23,643; Anderson, Amer., 21,325.

1972: Nixon, R., 1,857,759; McGovern, D., 718,117; scattered, 7,407.

1968: Nixon, R., 886,804; Humphrey, D., 676,794; Wallace, 3rd party, 624,207.

1964: Johnson, D., 948,540; Goldwater, R., 905,941.

1960: Nixon, R., 795,476; Kennedy, D., 748,700.

Georgia

County	2012 Obama (D)	Romney (R)	2008 Obama (D)	McCain (R)
Appling	1,758	5,233	1,846	5,085
Atkinson	930	1,938	938	1,941
Bacon	791	3,093	817	3,089
Baker	794	785	846	828
Baldwin	8,483	7,589	8,587	7,823
Banks	780	5,354	1,027	5,120
Barrow	6,028	18,725	6,657	17,625
Bartow	8,396	26,876	9,662	25,976
Ben Hill	2,512	3,396	2,590	3,417
Berrien	1,273	4,843	1,471	4,901
Bibb	38,585	25,623	38,987	27,037
Bleckley	1,269	3,587	1,380	3,657
Brantley	939	4,964	1,119	5,080
Brooks	3,138	3,554	2,669	3,507
Bryan	3,707	9,560	3,636	9,112
Bulloch	9,593	14,174	9,586	14,174
Burke	5,405	4,301	5,233	4,344
Butts	2,968	6,306	3,065	5,947
Calhoun	1,298	883	1,342	862
Camden	6,377	11,343	6,482	10,502
Candler	1,157	2,344	1,209	2,286
Carroll	12,688	28,280	14,334	28,661
Catoosa	5,365	17,858	6,025	18,218
Charlton	1,197	2,527	1,197	2,466
Chatham	60,246	47,204	62,755	46,829
Chattahoochee	729	735	830	811
Chattooga	2,232	5,452	2,596	5,572
Cherokee	19,841	76,514	22,350	70,279
Clarke	25,431	13,815	29,591	15,333
Clay	862	537	879	558
Clayton	81,479	14,164	82,527	16,506
Clinch	852	1,598	989	1,678
Cobb	133,124	171,722	141,216	170,957
Coffee	5,057	9,248	4,811	8,872
Colquitt	3,973	9,243	4,139	9,185
Columbia	16,451	41,765	15,703	39,322
Cook	2,042	3,935	2,075	3,782
Coweta	15,168	39,653	15,521	37,571
Crawford	1,706	3,368	1,832	3,358
Crisp	3,167	4,182	3,085	4,424
Dade	1,411	4,471	1,612	4,703
Dawson	1,241	8,847	1,632	8,242
Decatur	4,591	5,824	4,424	5,890
DeKalb	238,224	64,392	254,594	65,581
Dodge	2,442	5,214	2,595	5,543
Dooly	2,285	1,985	2,138	1,991
Dougherty	26,295	11,449	26,135	12,547
Douglas	28,441	26,241	27,825	26,812
Early	2,765	2,557	2,603	2,711
Echols	173	917	201	981
Effingham	4,947	15,596	4,936	15,230
Elbert	3,181	4,859	3,366	4,868
Emanuel	2,927	5,100	3,068	5,110
Evans	1,268	2,268	1,374	2,462
Fannin	2,028	7,857	2,611	7,807
Fayette	19,736	38,075	20,313	38,501
Floyd	9,640	22,733	10,691	23,132
Forsyth	14,571	65,908	15,406	59,166
Franklin	1,499	6,114	1,914	6,069
Fulton	255,470	137,124	272,000	130,136
Gilmer	1,958	8,926	2,614	8,408
Glascock	176	1,135	210	1,202
Glynn	11,950	20,893	12,676	20,479
Gordon	3,440	13,197	4,268	13,113
Grady	3,419	5,924	3,539	5,775
Greene	3,201	5,071	3,339	4,532
Gwinnett	132,509	159,855	129,025	158,746
Habersham	2,301	12,166	2,900	11,766
Hall	12,999	47,481	14,457	44,962
Hancock	3,308	769	3,535	795
Haralson	1,789	8,446	2,248	8,658
Harris	4,145	11,197	4,184	10,648
Hart	2,870	6,517	3,365	6,537
Heard	948	3,160	1,042	3,133
Henry	43,761	46,774	40,567	47,157
Houston	22,702	34,662	22,094	33,392
Irwin	1,141	2,538	1,197	2,605
Jackson	4,238	19,135	4,950	17,776
Jasper	1,845	4,136	1,935	3,916

County	2012 Obama (D)	Romney (R)	2008 Obama (D)	McCain (R)
Jeff Davis	1,275	3,996	1,356	3,867
Jefferson	4,261	2,999	4,149	3,061
Jenkins	1,488	1,887	1,482	1,936
Johnson	1,305	2,440	1,198	2,426
Jones	4,274	7,744	4,572	7,782
Lamar	2,602	4,899	2,752	4,873
Lanier	1,114	1,820	1,062	1,787
Laurens	7,513	11,950	7,769	12,052
Lee	3,196	10,314	3,100	9,925
Liberty	10,457	5,565	10,474	5,828
Lincoln	1,586	2,807	1,650	2,731
Long	1,442	2,306	1,288	2,119
Lowndes	17,470	21,327	17,597	21,269
Lumpkin	2,055	8,647	2,586	8,326
Macon	3,211	1,545	3,251	1,712
Madison	2,494	8,443	2,965	8,226
Marion	1,412	1,733	1,381	1,772
McDuffie	4,044	5,475	3,989	5,400
McIntosh	2,864	3,409	2,905	3,282
Meriwether	4,331	4,856	4,465	4,982
Miller	852	1,905	818	1,899
Mitchell	4,081	4,155	3,872	4,201
Monroe	3,785	8,361	4,106	7,933
Montgomery	1,135	2,662	1,045	2,521
Morgan	2,753	6,186	3,091	5,987
Murray	2,542	8,443	3,026	8,180
Muscogee	42,573	27,510	44,158	29,568
Newton	21,851	20,982	20,827	20,337
Oconee	4,421	13,098	4,825	12,120
Oglethorpe	1,914	4,251	2,232	4,144
Paulding	15,825	40,846	17,229	39,192
Peach	6,148	5,287	5,927	5,173
Pickens	1,975	10,547	2,595	10,004
Pierce	1,124	5,667	1,253	5,500
Pike	1,356	6,668	1,575	6,547
Polk	3,615	9,811	4,052	9,850
Pulaski	1,219	2,444	1,377	2,553
Putnam	2,926	6,215	3,102	5,966
Quitman	612	510	597	509
Rabun	1,559	5,754	2,001	5,487
Randolph	1,770	1,271	1,833	1,370
Richmond	52,560	25,845	52,100	26,842
Rockdale	22,023	15,716	20,526	16,921
Schley	448	1,286	479	1,252
Screven	2,774	3,287	3,024	3,423
Seminole	1,478	2,245	1,660	2,315
Spalding	9,898	14,911	10,141	14,885
Stephens	2,131	7,221	2,705	7,689
Stewart	1,323	745	1,305	783
Sumter	6,375	5,378	6,454	5,717
Talbot	2,265	1,202	2,369	1,301
Taliaferro	636	323	643	339
Tattnall	1,897	4,706	1,932	4,730
Taylor	1,572	1,948	1,536	2,021
Telfair	1,805	2,480	1,862	2,486
Terrell	2,544	1,834	2,501	1,890
Thomas	7,653	11,156	7,720	10,642
Tift	4,660	9,185	4,749	9,431
Toombs	2,746	6,524	2,964	6,658
Towns	1,273	4,876	1,391	4,292
Treutlen	1,074	1,652	1,112	1,826
Troup	10,547	15,179	10,455	15,391
Turner	1,510	2,028	1,427	2,096
Twiggs	2,270	1,907	2,402	2,087
Union	2,139	8,773	2,486	8,013
Upson	3,959	7,230	4,061	7,291
Walker	5,274	16,247	6,095	17,110
Walton	8,148	29,036	8,469	27,253
Ware	3,900	7,941	4,034	8,311
Warren	1,529	990	1,554	1,087
Washington	4,714	4,035	4,607	4,216
Wayne	2,596	7,557	2,858	7,601
Webster	582	601	515	588
Wheeler	772	1,366	794	1,408
White	1,671	8,651	2,174	8,467
Whitfield	7,210	19,305	8,167	19,230
Wilcox	1,060	2,053	978	2,159
Wilkes	2,087	2,635	2,315	2,705
Wilkinson	2,181	2,246	2,298	2,349
Worth	2,487	5,869	2,542	5,780
Totals	1,773,827	2,078,688	1,844,123	2,048,759

Georgia Vote Since 1960

2012: Romney, R., 2,078,688; Obama, D., 1,773,827; Johnson, LB., 45,324.
2008: McCain, R., 2,048,759; Obama, D., 1,844,123; Barr, LB., 28,731.
2004: Bush, R., 1,914,254; Kerry, D., 1,366,149; Badnarik, LB., 18,387.

2000: Bush, R., 1,419,720; Gore, D., 1,116,230; Browne, LB., 36,332; Buchanan, Ind., 10,926.
1996: Dole, R., 1,080,843; Clinton, D., 1,053,849; Perot, RF., 146,337; Browne, LB., 17,870.
1992: Clinton, D., 1,008,966; Bush, R., 995,252; Perot, Ind., 309,657; Marrou, LB., 7,110.
1988: Bush, R., 1,081,331; Dukakis, D., 714,792; Paul, LB., 8,435; Fulani, New Alliance, 5,099.
1984: Reagan, R., 1,068,722; Mondale, D., 706,628.
1980: Carter, D., 890,955; Reagan, R., 654,168; Anderson, Ind., 36,055; Clark, LB., 15,627.
1976: Carter, D., 979,409; Ford, R., 483,743; write-in, 4,306.
1972: Nixon, R., 881,496; McGovern, D., 289,529; Schmitz, Amer., 812; scattered, 2,935.
1968: Wallace, 3rd party, 535,550; Nixon, R., 380,111; Humphrey, D., 334,440; write-in, 162.
1964: Goldwater, R., 616,600; Johnson, D., 522,557.
1960: Kennedy, D., 458,638; Nixon, R., 274,472; write-in, 239.

Hawaii

County	2012 Obama (D)	Romney (R)	2008 Obama (D)	McCain (R)
Hawaii	47,224	14,753	50,819	14,866
Honolulu	204,349	88,461	214,909	88,301
Kauai	18,641	6,121	20,416	6,245
Maui	36,052	11,602	39,727	11,154
Overseas	392	78	NA	NA
Totals	306,658	121,015	325,871	120,566

Hawaii Vote Since 1960

2012: Obama, D., 306,658; Romney, R., 121,015; Johnson, LB., 3,840; Stein, Green, 3,184.
2008: Obama, D., 325,871; McCain, R., 120,566; Nader, Ind. (HI), 3,825; Barr, LB., 1,314; Baldwin, Const., 1,013; McKinney, Green, 979.
2004: Kerry, D., 231,708; Bush, R., 194,191; Cobb, Green, 1,737; Badnarik, LB., 1,377.
2000: Gore, D., 205,286; Bush, R., 137,845; Nader, Green, 21,623; Browne, LB., 1,477; Buchanan, RF., 1,071; Phillips, Const., 343; Hagelin, Natural Law, 306.
1996: Clinton, D., 205,012; Dole, R., 113,943; Perot, RF., 27,358; Nader, Green, 10,386; Browne, LB., 2,493; Hagelin, Natural Law, 570; Phillips, Taxpayers, 358.
1992: Clinton, D., 179,310; Bush, R., 136,822; Perot, Ind., 53,003; Gritz, Populist/America First, 1,452; Marrou, LB., 1,119.
1988: Dukakis, D., 192,364; Bush, R., 158,625; Paul, LB., 1,999; Fulani, New Alliance, 1,003.
1984: Reagan, R., 184,934; Mondale, D., 147,098; Bergland, LB., 2,167.
1980: Carter, D., 135,879; Reagan, R., 130,112; Anderson, Ind., 32,021; Clark, LB., 3,269; Commoner, Citizens, 1,548; Hall, Comm., 458.
1976: Carter, D., 147,375; Ford, R., 140,003; MacBride, LB., 3,923.
1972: Nixon, R., 168,865; McGovern, D., 101,409.
1968: Humphrey, D., 141,324; Nixon, R., 91,425; Wallace, 3rd party, 3,469.
1964: Johnson, D., 163,249; Goldwater, R., 44,022.
1960: Kennedy, D., 92,410; Nixon, R., 92,295.

Idaho

County	2012 Obama (D)	Romney (R)	2008 Obama (D)	McCain (R)
Ada	77,137	97,554	82,236	93,328
Adams	577	1,413	728	1,517
Bannock	13,214	21,010	14,792	19,356
Bear Lake	302	2,489	502	2,377
Benewah	1,164	2,596	1,407	2,646
Bingham	3,822	13,440	4,424	12,230
Blaine	5,992	3,939	6,947	3,439
Boise	1,053	2,284	1,240	2,433
Bonner	6,500	11,367	7,840	11,145
Bonneville	9,903	32,276	11,417	29,334
Boundary	1,225	3,138	1,484	3,078
Butte	258	1,001	318	1,056
Camas	159	402	187	422
Canyon	19,866	44,369	20,147	42,752
Caribou	386	2,608	553	2,656
Cassia	1,098	7,154	1,332	6,309
Clark	66	235	64	305
Clearwater	1,032	2,541	1,211	2,569
Custer	530	1,744	611	1,694
Elmore	2,513	5,227	2,591	5,665
Franklin	325	5,195	600	4,246
Fremont	810	4,907	1,065	4,700
Gem	1,957	5,311	2,166	5,585
Gooding	1,287	3,696	1,489	3,765
Idaho	1,708	5,921	2,017	5,895
Jefferson	1,303	9,895	1,641	8,540
Jerome	1,699	4,804	1,794	4,897

County	2012 Obama (D)	Romney (R)	2008 Obama (D)	McCain (R)
Kootenai	18,851	39,381	22,120	38,387
Latah	8,306	7,589	9,195	7,988
Lemhi	960	3,029	1,061	2,938
Lewis	396	1,173	479	1,275
Lincoln	469	1,141	545	1,232
Madison	832	13,445	1,627	11,131
Minidoka	1,390	5,442	1,630	5,087
Nez Perce	6,451	9,967	7,123	10,357
Oneida	217	1,838	381	1,724
Owyhee	833	2,794	944	3,024
Payette	2,271	6,004	2,415	5,988
Power	982	1,870	1,027	1,754
Shoshone	2,277	2,699	2,521	2,953
Teton	1,926	2,458	2,302	2,263
Twin Falls	7,541	19,773	8,621	19,032
Valley	2,095	2,664	2,405	2,772
Washington	1,104	3,128	1,241	3,168
Totals	212,787	420,911	236,440	403,012

Idaho Vote Since 1960

2012: Romney, R., 420,911; Obama, D., 212,787; Johnson, LB., 9,453; Stein, Ind., 4,402; Anderson, Ind., 2,499; Goode, Const., 2,222.
2008: McCain, R., 403,012; Obama, D., 236,440; Nader, Ind., 7,175; Baldwin, Const., 4,747; Barr, LB., 3,658.
2004: Bush, R., 409,235; Kerry, D., 181,098; Badnarik, LB., 3,844; Peroutka, Const., 3,084.
2000: Bush, R., 336,937; Gore, D., 138,637; Buchanan, RF., 7,615; Browne, LB., 3,488; Phillips, Const., 1,469; Hagelin, Natural Law, 1,177.
1996: Dole, R., 256,595; Clinton, D., 165,443; Perot, RF., 62,518; Browne, LB., 3,325; Phillips, U.S. Taxpayers, 2,230; Hagelin, Natural Law, 1,600.
1992: Bush, R., 202,645; Clinton, D., 137,013; Perot, Ind., 130,395; Gritz, Populist/America First, 10,281; Marrou, LB., 1,167.
1988: Bush, R., 253,881; Dukakis, D., 147,272; Paul, LB., 5,313; Fulani, Ind., 2,502.
1984: Reagan, R., 297,523; Mondale, D., 108,510; Bergland, LB., 2,823.
1980: Reagan, R., 290,699; Carter, D., 110,192; Anderson, Ind., 27,058; Clark, LB., 8,425; Rarick, Amer., 1,057.
1976: Ford, R., 204,151; Carter, D., 126,549; Maddox, Amer., 5,935; MacBride, LB., 3,558; LaRouche, U.S. Labor, 739.
1972: Nixon, R., 199,384; McGovern, D., 80,826; Schmitz, Amer., 28,869; Spock, People's, 903.
1968: Nixon, R., 165,369; Humphrey, D., 89,273; Wallace, 3rd party, 36,541.
1964: Johnson, D., 148,920; Goldwater, R., 143,557.
1960: Nixon, R., 161,597; Kennedy, D., 138,853.

Illinois

County	2012 Obama (D)	Romney (R)	2008 Obama (D)	McCain (R)
Adams	9,648	20,416	11,794	18,711
Alexander	1,965	1,487	2,189	1,692
Bond	3,020	4,095	3,843	3,947
Boone	9,883	11,096	11,333	10,403
Brown	787	1,513	986	1,544
Bureau	8,134	8,164	8,889	7,911
Calhoun	1,080	1,440	1,423	1,221
Carroll	3,665	3,555	3,965	3,596
Cass	2,053	2,707	2,690	2,617
Champaign	40,831	35,312	48,597	33,871
Christian	5,494	8,885	6,918	7,872
Clark	2,591	5,144	3,742	4,409
Clay	1,584	4,190	2,425	3,926
Clinton	5,596	10,524	7,657	9,357
Coles	9,262	11,631	11,716	10,978
Cook	1,488,537	495,542	1,629,024	487,736
Crawford	2,858	5,585	3,883	5,070
Cumberland	1,641	3,509	2,055	3,156
DeKalb	21,207	18,934	25,784	18,266
DeWitt	2,601	4,579	3,308	4,348
Douglas	2,430	5,334	3,228	5,005
DuPage	199,460	195,046	228,698	183,626
Edgar	2,565	5,132	3,743	4,398
Edwards	754	2,405	1,140	2,137
Effingham	3,861	12,501	5,262	11,323
Fayette	2,853	5,951	3,967	5,499
Ford	1,656	4,229	2,227	4,079
Franklin	7,254	10,267	8,880	9,404
Fulton	8,328	6,632	9,732	6,251
Gallatin	1,029	1,492	1,587	1,212
Greene	2,023	3,451	2,619	3,053
Grundy	9,451	11,343	11,063	10,687
Hamilton	1,269	2,566	1,796	2,353
Hancock	3,650	5,271	4,141	5,161
Hardin	742	1,535	892	1,330
Henderson	1,978	1,541	2,215	1,541
Henry	12,332	11,583	13,181	11,263
Iroquois	3,413	9,120	4,643	8,695
Jackson	13,319	9,864	15,248	9,687
Jasper	1,436	3,514	2,063	2,964
Jefferson	6,089	9,811	7,462	9,302
Jersey	3,667	6,039	5,042	5,329
Jo Daviess	5,667	5,534	6,403	5,170
Johnson	1,572	3,963	1,871	3,912
Kane	90,332	88,335	106,756	83,963
Kankakee	21,595	23,136	24,750	22,527
Kendall	22,471	24,047	24,742	21,380
Knox	13,451	9,408	14,191	9,419
Lake	153,757	129,764	177,242	118,545
LaSalle	23,073	23,256	27,443	21,872
Lawrence	2,011	3,857	3,016	3,403
Lee	6,937	8,059	7,765	8,258
Livingston	5,020	9,753	6,189	9,191
Logan	3,978	7,844	5,250	7,429
Macon	22,780	25,309	25,487	24,948
Macoupin	9,464	10,946	12,090	9,891
Madison	58,922	60,608	68,979	57,177
Marion	6,225	9,248	8,345	8,691
Marshall	2,455	3,290	3,081	3,145
Mason	2,867	3,265	3,542	3,141
Massac	2,092	4,278	2,693	4,371
McDonough	5,967	6,147	6,783	6,055
McHenry	59,797	71,598	72,288	64,845
McLean	31,883	39,947	37,689	36,767
Menard	2,100	3,948	2,706	3,672
Mercer	4,507	3,876	4,887	3,833
Monroe	6,215	10,888	7,953	9,881
Montgomery	5,058	6,776	6,491	6,150
Morgan	5,806	7,972	7,467	7,591
Moultrie	2,144	3,784	2,668	3,471
Ogle	9,514	13,422	11,253	13,144
Peoria	40,209	36,774	45,906	34,579
Perry	3,819	5,507	4,701	5,086
Piatt	3,090	5,413	3,859	4,991
Pike	2,278	4,860	3,024	4,457
Pope	650	1,512	845	1,343
Pulaski	1,389	1,564	1,638	1,593
Putnam	1,559	1,502	1,900	1,378
Randolph	5,759	8,290	7,395	7,538
Richland	2,362	4,756	3,181	4,329
Rock Island	39,157	24,934	42,210	26,364
St. Clair	67,285	50,125	76,160	47,958
Saline	3,701	6,806	5,083	6,099
Sangamon	42,107	50,225	51,300	46,945
Schuyler	1,727	2,069	1,900	1,833
Scott	910	1,587	1,090	1,455
Shelby	3,342	6,843	4,245	6,396
Stark	1,095	1,528	1,357	1,513
Stephenson	10,165	10,512	11,349	9,909
Tazewell	24,438	35,335	29,384	33,247
Union	3,137	4,957	3,918	5,003
Vermilion	12,878	16,892	16,246	16,054
Wabash	1,590	3,478	2,462	3,254
Warren	4,044	3,618	4,286	3,637
Washington	2,450	4,792	3,342	4,473
Wayne	1,514	5,988	2,547	5,390
White	2,188	4,731	3,315	3,987
Whiteside	14,833	10,448	15,607	10,883
Will	144,229	128,969	160,406	122,597
Williamson	10,647	17,909	12,914	17,387
Winnebago	61,732	55,138	70,034	53,886
Woodford	5,572	12,961	6,999	12,191
Totals	3,019,512	2,135,216	3,419,348	2,031,179

Illinois Vote Since 1960

2012: Obama, D., 3,019,512; Romney, R., 2,135,216; Johnson, LB., 56,229; Stein, Green, 30,222.
2008: Obama, D., 3,419,348; McCain, R., 2,031,179; Nader, Ind., 30,948; Barr, LB., 19,642; McKinney, Green, 11,838; Baldwin, Const., 8,256; Polachek, New Party, 1,149.
2004: Kerry, D., 2,891,550; Bush, R., 2,345,946; Badnarik, LB., 32,442.
2000: Gore, D., 2,589,026; Bush, R., 2,019,421; Nader, Green, 103,759; Buchanan, Ind., 16,106; Browne, LB., 11,623; Hagelin, RF., 2,127.
1996: Clinton, D., 2,341,744; Dole, R., 1,587,021; Perot, RF., 346,408; Browne, LB., 22,548; Phillips, U.S. Taxpayers, 7,606; Hagelin, Natural Law, 4,606.
1992: Clinton, D., 2,453,350; Bush, R., 1,734,096; Perot, Ind., 840,515; Marrou, LB., 9,218; Fulani, New Alliance, 5,267; Gritz, Populist/America First, 3,577; Hagelin, Natural Law, 2,751; Warren, Soc. Workers, 1,361.
1988: Bush, R., 2,310,939; Dukakis, D., 2,215,940; Paul, LB., 14,944; Fulani, Solidarity, 10,276.

1984: Reagan, R., 2,707,103; Mondale, D., 2,086,499; Bergland, LB., 10,086.
1980: Reagan, R., 2,358,049; Carter, D., 1,981,413; Anderson, Ind., 346,754; Clark, LB., 38,939; Commoner, Citizens, 10,692; Hall, Comm., 9,711; Griswold, Workers World, 2,257; DeBerry, Soc. Workers, 1,302; write-in, 604.
1976: Ford, R., 2,364,269; Carter, D., 2,271,295; McCarthy, Ind., 55,939; Hall, Comm., 9,250; MacBride, LB., 8,057; Camejo, Soc. Workers, 3,615; Levin, Soc. Labor, 2,422; LaRouche, U.S. Labor, 2,018; write-in, 1,968.
1972: Nixon, R. 2,788,179; McGovern, D., 1,913,472; Fisher, Soc. Labor, 12,344; Hall, Comm., 4,541; Schmitz, Amer., 2,471; others, 2,229.
1968: Nixon, R., 2,174,774; Humphrey, D., 2,039,814; Wallace, 3rd party, 390,958; Blomen, Soc. Labor, 13,878; write-in, 325.
1964: Johnson, D., 2,796,833; Goldwater, R., 1,905,946; write-in, 62.
1960: Kennedy, D., 2,377,846; Nixon, R., 2,368,988; Hass, Soc. Labor, 10,560; write-in, 15.

Indiana

County	2012		2008	
	Obama (D)	Romney (R)	Obama (D)	McCain (R)
Adams	3,806	8,937	4,928	8,404
Allen	60,036	84,613	71,263	77,793
Bartholomew	10,625	18,083	13,567	17,067
Benton	1,159	2,329	1,563	2,183
Blackford	1,927	2,711	2,677	2,690
Boone	8,328	18,808	9,752	16,622
Brown	3,060	4,332	3,854	4,060
Carroll	2,635	4,999	3,736	4,858
Cass	5,371	8,443	7,011	8,346
Clark	20,807	25,450	21,953	25,326
Clay	3,460	7,096	4,954	6,267
Clinton	3,308	6,338	5,307	6,919
Crawford	2,041	2,421	2,286	2,393
Daviess	2,437	7,638	3,370	7,098
Dearborn	6,528	15,394	7,123	14,886
Decatur	2,941	7,119	3,892	6,449
DeKalb	5,419	10,587	7,175	9,780
Delaware	22,654	21,251	28,384	20,916
Dubois	6,522	11,654	8,748	9,526
Elkhart	24,399	42,378	31,398	39,396
Fayette	3,555	5,045	4,389	4,917
Floyd	14,812	19,878	16,263	19,957
Fountain	2,237	4,664	3,094	4,158
Franklin	2,909	7,424	3,404	7,018
Fulton	2,621	5,317	3,702	5,147
Gibson	4,928	9,487	6,455	8,449
Grant	9,589	15,151	11,293	14,734
Greene	4,350	8,457	5,709	7,691
Hamilton	43,796	90,747	49,704	78,401
Hancock	9,319	22,796	11,874	22,008
Harrison	6,607	10,640	7,288	10,551
Hendricks	21,112	44,312	24,548	39,728
Henry	7,613	10,838	10,059	10,896
Howard	15,135	20,327	17,871	20,248
Huntington	4,596	10,862	5,843	10,291
Jackson	5,838	10,419	7,354	9,726
Jasper	4,672	7,955	5,044	7,669
Jay	3,063	4,645	3,748	4,401
Jefferson	5,728	7,096	6,255	7,053
Jennings	3,821	6,120	5,312	6,261
Johnson	17,260	39,513	21,553	36,487
Knox	5,228	9,612	7,569	8,639
Kosciusko	6,862	22,558	9,236	20,488
LaGrange	2,898	6,231	3,663	5,702
Lake	130,897	68,431	139,301	67,742
LaPorte	24,107	18,615	28,258	17,918
Lawrence	5,779	11,622	7,208	11,018
Madison	24,407	26,769	30,152	26,403
Marion	216,336	136,509	241,987	134,313
Marshall	6,137	11,260	7,889	10,406
Martin	1,351	3,262	1,706	3,122
Miami	4,222	8,174	5,564	8,312
Monroe	33,436	22,481	41,450	21,118
Montgomery	4,271	9,824	6,013	9,060
Morgan	7,969	19,591	10,330	18,129
Newton	2,212	3,291	2,625	3,301
Noble	5,229	10,680	7,064	9,673
Ohio	994	1,759	1,158	1,713
Orange	2,939	4,617	3,390	4,536
Owen	2,823	5,062	3,570	4,415
Parke	2,110	4,234	2,924	3,909
Perry	4,316	3,403	5,141	3,202
Pike	2,125	3,627	2,700	3,221
Porter	37,252	34,406	39,178	33,857
Posey	4,533	7,430	5,828	6,804
Pulaski	1,899	3,366	2,466	3,388
Putnam	4,507	9,005	6,334	8,086

County	2012		2008	
	Obama (D)	Romney (R)	Obama (D)	McCain (R)
Randolph	3,769	6,218	4,839	5,788
Ripley	3,241	7,484	4,187	7,794
Rush	2,221	4,633	3,229	4,271
St. Joseph	56,460	52,578	68,710	48,510
Scott	3,998	4,539	4,271	4,445
Shelby	5,359	10,978	6,987	10,333
Spencer	4,026	5,515	5,039	5,001
Starke	3,809	4,738	4,778	4,473
Steuben	4,853	8,547	6,284	7,674
Sullivan	3,191	4,902	4,284	4,343
Switzerland	1,437	1,872	1,638	1,940
Tippecanoe	26,711	28,757	37,781	29,822
Tipton	2,432	4,773	3,250	4,452
Union	1,018	2,022	1,224	2,061
Vanderburgh	31,725	39,389	39,423	37,512
Vermillion	2,979	3,426	4,003	3,010
Vigo	19,712	19,369	25,040	18,121
Wabash	3,973	8,644	5,456	8,238
Warren	1,324	2,377	1,755	2,166
Warrick	8,793	15,351	12,329	16,013
Washington	3,909	6,533	4,562	6,519
Wayne	10,591	14,321	13,459	14,558
Wells	3,436	9,256	4,403	8,504
White	3,637	5,970	4,839	5,731
Whitley	4,420	10,258	5,862	9,124
Totals	**1,152,887**	**1,420,543**	**1,374,039**	**1,345,648**

Indiana Vote Since 1960

2012: Romney, R., 1,420,543; Obama, D., 1,152,887; Johnson, LB., 50,111.
2008: Obama, D., 1,374,039; McCain, R., 1,345,648; Barr, LB., 29,257.
2004: Bush, R., 1,479,438; Kerry, D., 969,011; Badnarik, LB., 18,058.
2000: Bush, R., 1,245,836; Gore, D., 901,980; Buchanan, Ind., 16,959; Browne, LB., 15,530.
1996: Dole, R., 1,006,693; Clinton, D., 887,424; Perot, RF., 224,299; Browne, LB., 15,632.
1992: Bush, R., 989,375; Clinton, D., 848,420; Perot, Ind., 455,934; Marrou, LB., 7,936; Fulani, New Alliance, 2,583.
1988: Bush, R., 1,297,763; Dukakis, D., 860,643; Fulani, New Alliance, 10,215.
1984: Reagan, R., 1,377,230; Mondale, D., 841,481; Bergland, LB., 6,741.
1980: Reagan, R., 1,255,656; Carter, D., 844,197; Anderson, Ind.,111,639; Clark, LB., 19,627; Commoner, Citizens, 4,852; Greaves, Amer., 4,750; Hall, Comm., 702; DeBerry, Soc., 610.
1976: Ford, R., 1,185,958; Carter, D., 1,014,714; Anderson, Amer., 14,048; Camejo, Soc. Workers, 5,695; LaRouche, U.S. Labor, 1,947.
1972: Nixon, R., 1,405,154; McGovern, D., 708,568; Reed, Soc. Workers, 5,575; Spock, Peace/Freedom, 4,544; Fisher, Soc. Labor, 1,688.
1968: Nixon, R., 1,067,885; Humphrey, D., 806,659; Wallace, 3rd party, 243,108; Munn, Prohib., 4,616; Halstead, Soc. Workers, 1,293; Gregory, write-in, 36.
1964: Johnson, D., 1,170,848; Goldwater, R., 911,118; Munn, Prohib., 8,266; Hass, Soc. Labor, 1,374.
1960: Nixon, R., 1,175,120; Kennedy, D., 952,358; Decker, Prohib., 6,746; Hass, Soc. Labor, 1,136.

Iowa

County	2012		2008	
	Obama (D)	Romney (R)	Obama (D)	McCain (R)
Adair	1,790	2,114	1,924	2,060
Adams	1,028	1,108	1,118	1,046
Allamakee	3,553	3,264	3,971	2,965
Appanoose	2,951	3,161	2,970	3,086
Audubon	1,611	1,802	1,739	1,634
Benton	6,862	6,940	7,058	6,447
Black Hawk	39,821	26,235	39,184	24,662
Boone	7,512	6,556	7,356	6,293
Bremer	6,763	6,405	6,940	5,741
Buchanan	5,911	4,450	6,050	4,139
Buena Vista	3,700	4,554	4,075	4,223
Butler	3,329	4,106	3,364	3,700
Calhoun	2,238	2,891	2,341	2,741
Carroll	4,947	5,601	5,302	4,922
Cass	2,858	4,217	3,211	4,006
Cedar	4,972	4,529	5,221	4,289
Cerro Gordo	13,316	10,128	14,405	9,375
Cherokee	2,634	3,662	2,890	3,372
Chickasaw	3,554	2,836	3,923	2,557
Clarke	2,189	2,124	2,218	2,118
Clay	3,385	4,951	3,925	4,355
Clayton	4,806	4,164	5,195	3,651
Clinton	15,141	9,432	15,018	9,324

County	2012 Obama (D)	Romney (R)	2008 Obama (D)	McCain (R)
Crawford	3,066	3,595	3,715	3,345
Dallas	16,576	20,988	15,149	16,954
Davis	1,520	2,138	1,680	2,029
Decatur	1,791	1,947	1,986	2,020
Delaware	4,616	4,636	4,649	4,113
Des Moines	11,888	8,136	12,462	7,721
Dickinson	4,095	5,912	4,625	5,162
Dubuque	28,768	21,280	28,611	18,651
Emmet	2,099	2,507	2,570	2,373
Fayette	5,732	4,492	5,908	4,205
Floyd	4,680	3,472	4,822	3,051
Franklin	2,266	2,823	2,575	2,501
Fremont	1,637	1,972	1,848	1,989
Greene	2,375	2,380	2,371	2,349
Grundy	2,635	4,215	2,790	3,945
Guthrie	2,569	3,171	2,625	3,074
Hamilton	3,782	3,991	4,018	3,913
Hancock	2,521	3,317	2,805	3,016
Hardin	4,075	4,670	4,393	4,315
Harrison	3,136	4,065	3,555	3,909
Henry	4,460	5,035	4,349	4,822
Howard	2,768	1,795	2,941	1,722
Humboldt	1,972	3,099	2,160	2,895
Ida	1,321	2,286	1,454	2,036
Iowa	4,144	4,569	4,202	4,188
Jackson	5,907	4,177	6,102	3,673
Jasper	10,257	8,877	10,250	8,794
Jefferson	4,798	3,436	5,070	3,324
Johnson	50,666	23,698	51,027	20,732
Jones	5,534	4,721	5,446	4,405
Keokuk	2,303	2,843	2,518	2,712
Kossuth	3,850	4,937	4,625	4,329
Lee	10,714	7,785	9,821	7,062
Linn	68,581	47,622	68,037	43,626
Louisa	2,452	2,420	2,523	2,314
Lucas	1,987	2,254	2,029	2,330
Lyon	1,423	4,978	1,675	4,471
Madison	3,630	4,638	3,733	4,579
Mahaska	4,213	6,448	4,464	6,271
Marion	7,507	9,828	7,421	9,256
Marshall	10,257	8,472	10,023	8,278
Mills	2,848	4,216	2,976	4,183
Mitchell	2,031	2,643	3,179	2,469
Monona	2,101	2,557	2,295	2,411
Monroe	1,731	2,026	1,798	2,000
Montgomery	1,922	3,001	2,326	2,887
Muscatine	11,323	8,168	10,920	7,929
O'Brien	1,969	5,266	2,338	4,894
Osceola	912	2,230	1,037	2,027
Page	2,613	4,348	2,900	4,351
Palo Alto	2,139	2,660	2,428	2,294
Plymouth	4,164	8,597	4,629	7,765
Pocahontas	1,523	2,396	1,800	2,138
Polk	128,465	96,096	120,984	89,668
Pottawattamie	19,644	21,860	20,436	21,237
Poweshiek	5,357	4,424	5,519	4,340
Ringgold	1,186	1,368	1,236	1,401
Sac	2,122	3,094	2,256	2,705
Scott	50,652	38,251	48,927	36,365
Shelby	2,469	3,911	2,863	3,488
Sioux	2,700	14,407	3,030	13,490
Story	26,192	19,668	26,548	18,995
Tama	4,768	4,098	4,899	3,820
Taylor	1,262	1,683	1,347	1,607
Union	3,043	2,813	3,000	2,781
Van Buren	1,402	2,064	1,546	1,986
Wapello	8,663	6,789	8,820	6,663
Warren	12,551	13,052	12,299	12,144
Washington	5,115	5,562	5,170	5,247
Wayne	1,251	1,583	1,357	1,565
Webster	9,537	8,469	9,917	8,337
Winnebago	2,903	2,906	3,254	2,730
Winneshiek	6,256	4,622	6,829	4,273
Woodbury	22,302	21,841	21,983	22,219
Worth	2,350	1,744	2,567	1,612
Wright	2,836	3,349	3,102	3,198
Totals	**822,544**	**730,617**	**828,940**	**682,379**

Iowa Vote Since 1960

2012: Obama, D., 822,544; Romney, R., 730,617; Johnson, LB., 12,926; Stein, Green, 3,769; Goode, Const., 3,038; Litzel, Ind., 1,027; Harris, Soc. Workers, 445; La Riva, Socialism/Liberation, 372.
2008: Obama, D., 828,940; McCain, R., 682,379; Nader, Peace/Freedom, 8,014; Barr, LB., 4,590; Baldwin, Const., 4,445; McKinney, Green, 1,423; Harris, Soc. Workers, 292; Moore, Soc. USA, 182; La Riva, Socialism/Liberation, 121.
2004: Bush, R., 751,957; Kerry, D., 741,898; Nader, petitioning cand., 5,973; Badnarik, LB., 2,992; Peroutka, Const., 1,304;

Cobb, Green, 1,141; Harris, Soc. Workers, 373; Van Auken, petitioning cand., 176.
2000: Gore, D., 638,517; Bush, R., 634,373; Nader, Green, 29,374; Buchanan, RF., 5,731; Browne, LB., 3,209; Hagelin, Ind., 2,281; Phillips, Const., 613; Harris, Soc. Workers, 190; McReynolds, Soc., 107.
1996: Clinton, D., 620,258; Dole, R., 492,644; Perot, RF., 105,159; Nader, Green, 6,550; Hagelin, Natural Law, 3,349; Browne, LB., 2,315; Phillips, Taxpayers, 2,229; Harris, Soc. Workers, 331.
1992: Clinton, D., 586,353; Bush, R., 504,891; Perot, Ind., 253,468; Hagelin, Natural Law, 3,079; Gritz, Populist/America First, 1,177; Marrou, LB., 1,076.
1988: Dukakis, D., 670,557; Bush, R., 545,355; LaRouche, Ind., 3,526; Paul, LB., 2,494.
1984: Reagan, R., 703,088; Mondale, D., 605,620; Bergland, LB., 1,844.
1980: Reagan, R., 676,026; Carter, D., 508,672; Anderson, Ind., 115,633; Clark, LB., 13,123; Commoner, Citizens, 2,273; McReynolds, Soc., 534; Hall, Comm., 298; DeBerry, Soc. Workers, 244; Greaves, Amer., 189; Bubar, Statesman, 150; scattered, 519.
1976: Ford, R., 632,863; Carter, D., 619,931; McCarthy, Ind., 20,051; Anderson, Amer., 3,040; MacBride, LB., 1,452.
1972: Nixon, R., 706,207; McGovern, D., 496,206; Schmitz, Amer., 22,056; Jenness, Soc. Workers, 488; Hall, Comm., 272; Green, Universal, 199; Fisher, Soc. Labor, 195; scattered, 321.
1968: Nixon, R., 619,106; Humphrey, D., 476,699; Wallace, 3rd party, 66,422; Halstead, Soc. Workers, 3,377; Cleaver, Peace/Freedom, 1,332; Munn, Prohib., 362; Blomen, Soc. Labor, 241.
1964: Johnson, D., 733,030; Goldwater, R., 449,148; Munn, Prohib., 1,902; Hass, Soc. Labor, 182; DeBerry, Soc. Workers, 159.
1960: Nixon, R., 722,381; Kennedy, D., 550,565; Hass, Soc. Labor, 230; write-in, 634.

Kansas

County	2012 Obama (D)	Romney (R)	2008 Obama (D)	McCain (R)
Allen	1,869	3,316	2,189	3,552
Anderson	944	2,276	1,175	2,362
Atchison	2,567	3,917	3,241	3,791
Barber	482	1,772	598	1,833
Barton	2,297	7,874	3,027	7,802
Bourbon	1,996	4,102	2,394	4,240
Brown	1,076	2,829	1,317	2,985
Butler	7,282	18,157	9,159	18,155
Chase	358	875	383	976
Chautauqua	280	1,304	401	1,418
Cherokee	2,930	5,456	3,594	5,886
Cheyenne	233	1,159	323	1,148
Clark	174	805	245	897
Clay	834	2,788	1,009	2,998
Cloud	974	2,954	1,233	3,121
Coffey	898	2,903	1,121	3,054
Comanche	143	767	194	765
Cowley	4,319	8,081	5,012	8,492
Crawford	6,826	7,708	7,957	7,735
Decatur	266	1,218	343	1,189
Dickinson	2,020	5,832	2,422	6,081
Doniphan	902	2,414	1,115	2,372
Douglas	29,267	17,401	34,398	17,929
Edwards	298	1,059	333	995
Elk	281	1,049	363	1,042
Ellis	3,057	8,399	4,010	8,207
Ellsworth	702	1,930	851	2,021
Finney	2,682	6,219	3,275	6,926
Ford	2,600	5,602	2,991	5,730
Franklin	3,694	6,984	4,433	7,079
Geary	3,332	4,372	3,491	4,492
Gove	176	1,168	261	1,136
Graham	256	1,056	325	1,060
Grant	456	1,811	635	1,995
Gray	324	1,603	436	1,643
Greeley	113	543	151	591
Greenwood	478	1,590	622	1,619
Hamilton	163	693	233	844
Harper	506	1,759	736	1,999
Harvey	5,373	8,588	6,318	9,006
Haskell	215	1,159	278	1,277
Hodgeman	179	868	211	865
Jackson	1,901	3,527	2,308	3,811
Jefferson	2,977	4,827	3,542	5,220
Jewell	229	1,235	313	1,231
Johnson	110,526	158,401	127,091	152,627
Kearny	268	1,097	309	1,159
Kingman	733	2,397	963	2,603
Kiowa	163	976	200	912
Labette	3,117	4,742	3,839	5,001
Lane	172	739	193	814

County	2012 Obama (D)	Romney (R)	2008 Obama (D)	McCain (R)
Leavenworth	11,357	17,059	13,255	16,791
Lincoln	289	1,165	347	1,204
Linn	1,170	3,177	1,425	3,086
Logan	197	1,126	225	1,187
Lyon	5,111	6,470	5,924	6,698
Marion	1,385	3,889	1,801	4,159
Marshall	1,469	3,195	1,784	3,157
McPherson	3,449	8,545	4,218	8,937
Meade	258	1,428	357	1,540
Miami	4,712	9,858	5,742	9,382
Mitchell	584	2,327	701	2,440
Montgomery	3,501	8,630	4,338	9,309
Morris	718	1,773	907	1,875
Morton	189	1,072	229	1,153
Nemaha	1,000	3,930	1,432	3,817
Neosho	2,050	4,272	2,563	4,473
Ness	218	1,209	289	1,207
Norton	398	1,878	497	1,878
Osage	2,268	4,427	2,534	4,820
Osborne	324	1,479	403	1,490
Ottawa	558	2,295	704	2,323
Pawnee	718	1,836	882	1,946
Phillips	382	2,135	525	2,105
Pottawatomie	2,335	6,804	2,599	6,929
Pratt	980	2,771	1,294	2,822
Rawlins	190	1,223	273	1,247
Reno	8,085	15,718	9,916	16,112
Republic	477	2,134	640	1,978
Rice	911	2,676	1,163	2,780
Riley	8,977	11,507	10,495	12,111
Rooks	361	2,038	468	2,068
Rush	367	1,166	504	1,225
Russell	593	2,553	736	2,509
Saline	7,040	13,840	8,186	14,165
Scott	277	1,728	321	1,823
Sedgwick	71,977	106,506	82,337	106,849
Seward	1,490	3,617	1,493	3,791
Shawnee	36,975	37,782	41,235	41,476
Sheridan	168	1,154	254	1,108
Sherman	577	1,976	688	1,959
Smith	358	1,624	446	1,719
Stafford	404	1,385	542	1,495
Stanton	143	605	188	628
Stevens	252	1,749	283	1,815
Sumner	2,658	6,260	3,353	6,737
Thomas	598	2,788	787	2,837
Trego	291	1,261	420	1,225
Wabaunsee	918	2,256	1,036	2,395
Wallace	68	719	96	690
Washington	524	2,316	659	2,248
Wichita	157	821	163	840
Wilson	1,636	5,650	1,170	2,850
Woodson	380	1,035	512	1,055
Wyandotte	34,302	15,496	39,865	16,506
Totals	**440,726**	**692,634**	**514,765**	**699,655**

Kansas Vote Since 1960

2012: Romney, R., 692,634; Obama, D., 440,726; Johnson, LB., 20,456; Baldwin, RF., 5,017.

2008: McCain, R., 699,655; Obama, D., 514,765; Nader, Ind., 10,527; Barr, LB., 6,706; Baldwin, RF., 4,148.

2004: Bush, R., 736,456; Kerry, D., 434,993; Nader, RF., 9,348; Badnarik, LB., 4,013; Peroutka, Ind., 2,899.

2000: Bush, R., 622,332; Gore, D., 399,276; Nader, Ind., 36,086; Buchanan, RF., 7,370; Browne, LB., 4,525; Hagelin, Ind., 1,373; Phillips, Const., 1,254.

1996: Dole, R., 583,245; Clinton, D., 387,659; Perot, RF., 92,639; Browne, LB., 4,557; Phillips, Ind., 3,519; Hagelin, Ind., 1,655.

1992: Bush, R., 449,951; Clinton, D., 390,434; Perot, Ind., 312,358; Marrou, LB., 4,314.

1988: Bush, R., 554,049; Dukakis, D., 422,636; Paul, Ind., 12,553; Fulani, Ind., 3,806.

1984: Reagan, R., 674,646; Mondale, D., 332,471; Bergland, LB., 3,585.

1980: Reagan, R., 566,812; Carter, D., 326,150; Anderson, Ind., 68,231; Clark, LB., 14,470; Shelton, Amer., 1,555; Hall, Comm., 967; Bubar, Statesman, 821; Rarick, Conservative, 789.

1976: Ford, R., 502,752; Carter, D., 430,421; McCarthy, Ind., 13,185; Anderson, Amer., 4,724; MacBride, LB., 3,242; Maddox, Conservative, 2,118; Bubar, Prohib., 1,403.

1972: Nixon, R., 619,812; McGovern, D., 270,287; Schmitz, Conservative, 21,808; Munn, Prohib., 4,188.

1968: Nixon, R., 478,674; Humphrey, D., 302,996; Wallace, 3rd party, 88,921; Munn, Prohib., 2,192.

1964: Johnson, D., 464,028; Goldwater, R., 386,579; Munn, Prohib., 5,393; Hass, Soc. Labor, 1,901.

1960: Nixon, R., 561,474; Kennedy, D., 363,213; Decker, Prohib., 4,138.

Kentucky

County	2012 Obama (D)	Romney (R)	2008 Obama (D)	McCain (R)
Adair	1,660	5,841	1,668	5,512
Allen	1,808	5,184	2,024	5,258
Anderson	3,315	6,822	3,462	6,885
Ballard	1,189	2,647	1,427	2,537
Barren	5,400	10,922	5,434	11,133
Bath	1,770	2,275	2,210	2,234
Bell	2,224	7,127	2,782	6,681
Boone	15,629	35,922	16,292	33,812
Bourbon	3,075	4,692	3,385	4,820
Boyd	7,776	10,884	8,886	11,430
Boyle	4,471	7,703	4,769	7,701
Bracken	1,147	2,029	1,241	2,066
Breathitt	1,562	3,318	2,205	2,671
Breckinridge	2,825	5,025	3,110	5,281
Bullitt	9,971	21,306	10,177	20,102
Butler	1,293	3,716	1,555	3,696
Caldwell	1,852	3,904	2,212	3,866
Calloway	5,317	9,440	6,165	8,991
Campbell	15,080	24,240	15,622	24,046
Carlisle	750	1,835	879	1,699
Carroll	1,629	1,999	1,716	2,032
Carter	3,383	5,279	4,316	5,252
Casey	1,086	4,904	1,219	4,679
Christian	8,252	13,475	8,880	13,699
Clark	5,228	9,931	5,749	9,664
Clay	1,111	6,176	1,552	5,710
Clinton	752	3,569	761	3,366
Crittenden	960	2,839	1,254	2,604
Cumberland	599	2,216	697	2,056
Daviess	16,208	25,092	19,282	23,692
Edmonson	1,374	3,232	1,652	3,562
Elliott	1,186	1,126	1,535	902
Estill	1,356	3,749	1,555	3,685
Fayette	62,080	60,795	66,042	59,884
Fleming	1,911	3,780	2,279	3,432
Floyd	4,733	9,784	7,530	7,741
Franklin	11,535	11,345	11,767	11,911
Fulton	1,022	1,425	1,238	1,530
Gallatin	1,238	1,758	1,278	1,840
Garrard	1,661	5,310	2,012	5,118
Grant	2,810	5,664	3,112	5,510
Graves	4,547	10,699	5,843	10,056
Grayson	2,744	6,404	3,154	6,605
Green	1,165	3,634	1,204	3,785
Greenup	6,027	8,855	6,621	8,849
Hancock	1,833	2,212	2,135	1,928
Hardin	15,214	23,357	15,650	23,896
Harlan	1,830	8,652	2,586	7,165
Harrison	2,471	4,556	2,916	4,520
Hart	2,283	4,257	2,290	4,397
Henderson	8,091	10,296	10,049	9,523
Henry	2,530	3,940	2,725	4,081
Hickman	686	1,431	812	1,406
Hopkins	5,789	13,681	7,104	11,916
Jackson	612	4,365	743	4,407
Jefferson	186,181	148,423	196,435	153,957
Jessamine	6,001	14,233	6,236	13,711
Johnson	1,723	7,095	2,407	5,948
Kenton	24,920	41,389	26,480	40,714
Knott	1,420	4,130	2,612	3,070
Knox	2,484	8,467	3,074	8,150
LaRue	1,733	3,911	1,913	4,153
Laurel	3,905	18,151	4,618	17,660
Lawrence	1,520	3,995	2,036	3,503
Lee	595	1,977	752	1,978
Leslie	433	4,439	766	3,574
Letcher	1,702	6,811	2,623	5,367
Lewis	1,342	3,326	1,510	3,213
Lincoln	2,582	6,416	2,752	6,273
Livingston	1,346	3,089	1,622	2,890
Logan	3,469	6,899	3,811	6,925
Lyon	1,373	2,412	1,577	2,220
Madison	11,512	21,128	12,392	19,694
Magoffin	1,433	3,391	2,105	2,434
Marion	3,418	3,800	3,596	3,842
Marshall	5,022	10,402	5,683	9,512
Martin	574	3,180	808	2,824
Mason	2,592	4,197	2,891	4,102
McCracken	10,062	19,979	11,285	19,043
McCreary	1,069	4,564	1,258	4,078
McLean	1,432	2,705	1,963	2,386
Meade	4,122	6,606	4,343	6,691
Menifee	1,048	1,484	1,276	1,155
Mercer	2,966	6,820	3,159	6,781
Metcalfe	1,425	2,676	1,350	2,734
Monroe	936	3,762	1,067	3,537
Montgomery	3,701	6,398	4,234	5,947
Morgan	1,369	3,021	1,879	2,396

County	2012 Obama (D)	Romney (R)	2008 Obama (D)	McCain (R)
Muhlenberg	4,771	7,762	6,221	6,447
Nelson	7,611	10,673	7,654	10,139
Nicholas	948	1,583	1,272	1,634
Ohio	2,987	6,470	4,059	5,687
Oldham	9,240	20,179	10,000	18,997
Owen	1,501	2,971	1,694	2,969
Owsley	283	1,279	381	1,279
Pendleton	1,859	3,556	2,027	3,676
Perry	2,047	8,040	3,444	6,762
Pike	5,646	17,590	9,525	12,655
Powell	1,620	2,766	2,065	2,837
Pulaski	4,976	20,714	5,590	19,862
Robertson	340	579	451	533
Rockcastle	1,097	5,028	1,410	4,757
Rowan	3,438	4,035	4,074	3,907
Russell	1,445	6,346	1,569	5,779
Scott	7,532	12,679	7,712	11,782
Shelby	6,634	11,790	6,871	11,451
Simpson	2,650	4,355	2,775	4,437
Spencer	2,549	5,726	2,519	5,378
Taylor	3,285	7,551	3,165	7,568
Todd	1,403	3,247	1,543	3,336
Trigg	2,115	4,520	2,246	4,189
Trimble	1,355	2,133	1,484	2,239
Union	1,942	3,955	2,804	3,120
Warren	16,805	26,384	17,669	25,993
Washington	1,669	3,495	1,890	3,305
Wayne	1,855	5,289	2,201	4,868
Webster	1,765	3,607	2,390	3,037
Whitley	2,683	10,232	3,484	10,015
Wolfe	976	1,542	1,493	1,408
Woodford	4,883	7,219	5,027	7,130
Totals	**679,370**	**1,087,190**	**751,985**	**1,048,462**

Kentucky Vote Since 1960

2012: Romney, R., 1,087,190; Obama, D., 679,370; Johnson, LB., 17,063; Terry, Ind., 6,872; Stein, Green, 6,337.
2008: McCain, R., 1,048,462; Obama, D., 751,985; Nader, Ind., 15,378; Barr, LB., 5,989; Baldwin, Const., 4,694.
2004: Bush, R., 1,069,439; Kerry, D., 712,733; Nader, Ind., 8,856; Badnarik, LB., 2,619; Peroutka, Const., 2,213.
2000: Bush, R., 872,520; Gore, D., 638,923; Nader, Green, 23,118; Buchanan, RF., 4,152; Browne, LB., 2,885; Hagelin, Natural Law, 1,513; Phillips, Const., 915.
1996: Clinton, D., 636,614; Dole, R., 623,283; Perot, RF., 120,396; Browne, LB., 4,009; Phillips, U.S. Taxpayers, 2,204; Hagelin, Natural Law, 1,493.
1992: Clinton, D., 665,104; Bush, R., 617,178; Perot, Ind., 203,944; Marrou, LB., 4,513.
1988: Bush, R., 734,281; Dukakis, D., 580,368; Duke, Populist, 4,494; Paul, LB., 2,118.
1984: Reagan, R., 815,345; Mondale, D., 536,756.
1980: Reagan, R., 635,274; Carter, D., 616,417; Anderson, Ind., 31,127; Clark, LB., 5,531; McCormack, Respect for Life, 4,233; Commoner, Citizens, 1,304; Pulley, Soc., 393; Hall, Comm., 348.
1976: Carter, D., 615,717; Ford, R., 531,852; Anderson, Amer., 8,308; McCarthy, Ind., 6,837; Maddox, Amer. Ind., 2,328; MacBride, LB., 814.
1972: Nixon, R., 676,446; McGovern, D., 371,159; Schmitz, Amer., 17,627; Spock, People's, 1,118; Jenness, Soc. Workers, 685; Hall, Comm., 464.
1968: Nixon, R., 462,411; Humphrey, D., 397,547; Wallace, 3rd party, 193,098; Halstead, Soc. Workers, 2,843.
1964: Johnson, D., 669,659; Goldwater, R., 372,977; Kasper, Natl. States' Rights, 3,469.
1960: Nixon, R., 602,607; Kennedy, D., 521,855.

Louisiana

Parish	2012 Obama (D)	Romney (R)	2008 Obama (D)	McCain (R)
Acadia	6,560	19,931	7,028	19,229
Allen	2,617	6,495	2,891	6,333
Ascension	16,349	33,856	14,625	31,239
Assumption	4,754	6,083	4,756	5,981
Avoyelles	6,077	10,670	6,327	10,236
Beauregard	2,828	11,112	3,071	10,718
Bienville	3,490	3,641	3,589	3,776
Bossier	12,956	34,988	12,703	32,713
Caddo	58,042	52,459	55,536	52,228
Calcasieu	28,359	51,850	30,244	50,449
Caldwell	1,016	3,640	1,118	3,696
Cameron	408	3,260	613	3,089
Catahoula	1,408	2,744	1,659	3,486
Claiborne	3,014	3,649	3,025	3,750
Concordia	3,833	5,450	3,766	5,668
DeSoto	5,553	7,353	5,242	6,883
East Baton Rouge	102,656	92,292	99,652	95,390

Parish	2012 Obama (D)	Romney (R)	2008 Obama (D)	McCain (R)
East Carroll	2,478	1,508	2,267	1,254
East Feliciana	4,648	5,397	4,383	5,432
Evangeline	5,330	10,181	5,853	9,793
Franklin	2,921	6,294	2,961	6,278
Grant	1,422	7,082	1,474	6,907
Iberia	12,132	20,892	12,492	20,127
Iberville	9,548	7,271	9,023	7,185
Jackson	2,305	5,132	2,456	5,190
Jefferson	70,384	102,536	65,096	113,191
Jefferson Davis	3,484	10,014	3,923	9,278
Lafayette	31,768	64,992	32,145	62,055
Lafourche	9,623	28,592	9,662	27,089
LaSalle	764	5,726	860	5,602
Lincoln	7,956	10,739	8,292	10,680
Livingston	7,451	45,513	6,681	43,269
Madison	3,154	2,000	3,100	2,152
Morehouse	5,888	6,591	5,792	7,258
Natchitoches	7,942	9,077	7,801	9,054
Orleans	126,722	28,003	117,102	28,130
Ouachita	26,645	40,948	24,813	41,741
Plaquemines	3,599	6,471	3,380	6,894
Pointe Coupee	5,436	6,548	5,516	6,702
Rapides	20,045	37,193	20,127	36,611
Red River	2,253	2,483	2,080	2,484
Richland	3,387	5,846	3,311	5,751
Sabine	2,194	7,738	2,245	7,226
St. Bernard	5,059	8,501	3,491	9,643
St. Charles	8,896	15,937	8,522	16,457
St. Helena	3,780	2,529	3,567	2,522
St. James	7,059	5,209	6,994	5,432
St. John the Baptist	13,179	7,620	12,424	8,912
St. Landry	19,668	21,475	20,268	21,650
St. Martin	9,422	15,653	9,419	14,443
St. Mary	9,450	13,885	9,345	13,183
St. Tammany	25,728	84,723	24,596	83,078
Tangipahoa	17,722	31,590	16,438	31,434
Tensas	1,564	1,230	1,646	1,367
Terrebonne	12,074	29,503	11,581	28,210
Union	3,075	7,561	3,103	7,619
Vermilion	5,720	18,910	6,266	18,069
Vernon	3,173	12,150	3,534	11,946
Washington	6,466	11,798	6,122	12,215
Webster	6,802	11,400	6,610	11,417
West Baton Rouge	5,692	6,922	5,043	6,654
West Carroll	853	3,628	878	4,045
West Feliciana	3,014	3,257	2,415	3,150
Winn	1,919	4,541	2,047	4,632
Totals	**809,141**	**1,152,262**	**782,989**	**1,148,275**

Louisiana Vote Since 1960

2012: Romney, R., 1,152,262; Obama, D., 809,141; Johnson, LB., 18,157; Stein, Green, 6,978; Goode, Const., 2,508; Tittle, We the People, 1,767; Anderson, Justice, 1,368; Lindsay, Socialism/Liberation, 622; Fellure, Prohib., 518; Harris, Soc. Workers, 389; White, Soc. Equality, 355.
2008: McCain, R., 1,148,275; Obama, D., 782,989; Paul, LA Taxpayers, 9,368; McKinney, Green, 9,187; Nader, Ind., 6,997; Baldwin, Const., 2,581; Harris, Soc. Workers, 735; La Riva, Socialism/Liberation, 354; Amondson, Prohib., 275.
2004: Bush, R., 1,102,169; Kerry, D., 820,299; Nader, Better Life, 7,032; Peroutka, Const., 5,203; Badnarik, LB., 2,781; Brown, Protect Working Families, 1,795; Amondson, Prohib., 1,566; Cobb, Green, 1,276; Harris, Soc. Workers, 985.
2000: Bush, R., 927,871; Gore, D., 792,344; Nader, Green, 20,473; Buchanan, RF., 14,356; Phillips, Const., 5,483; Browne, LB., 2,951; Harris, Soc. Workers, 1,103; Hagelin, Natural Law, 1,075.
1996: Clinton, D., 927,837; Dole, R., 712,586; Perot, RF., 123,293; Browne, LB., 7,499; Nader, Liberty, Ecology, Community, 4,719; Phillips, U.S. Taxpayers, 3,366; Hagelin, Natural Law, 2,981; Moorehead, Workers World, 1,678.
1992: Clinton, D., 815,971; Bush, R., 733,386; Perot, Ind., 211,478; Gritz, Populist/America First, 18,545; Marrou, LB., 3,155; Daniels, Ind., 1,663; Phillips, U.S. Taxpayers, 1,552; Fulani, New Alliance, 1,434; LaRouche, Ind., 1,136.
1988: Bush, R., 883,702; Dukakis, D., 717,460; Duke, Populist, 18,612; Paul, LB., 4,115.
1984: Reagan, R., 1,037,299; Mondale, D., 651,586; Bergland, LB., 1,876.
1980: Reagan, R., 792,853; Carter, D., 708,453; Anderson, Ind., 26,345; Rarick, Amer. Ind., 10,333; Clark, LB., 8,240; Commoner, Citizens, 1,584; DeBerry, Soc. Workers, 783.
1976: Carter, D., 661,365; Ford, R., 587,446; Maddox, Amer., 10,058; Hall, Comm., 7,417; McCarthy, Ind., 6,588; MacBride, LB., 3,325.
1972: Nixon, R., 686,852; McGovern, D., 298,142; Schmitz, Amer., 52,099; Jenness, Soc. Workers, 14,398.

1968: Wallace, 3rd party, 530,300; Humphrey, D., 309,615; Nixon, R., 257,535.
1964: Goldwater, R., 509,225; Johnson, D., 387,068.
1960: Kennedy, D., 407,339; Nixon, R., 230,890; States' Rights (unpledged), 169,572.

Maine

City	2012 Obama (D)	Romney (R)	2008 Obama (D)	McCain (R)
Auburn	6,503	4,462	6,866	4,686
Augusta	5,220	3,351	5,556	3,662
Bangor	8,781	5,788	9,406	6,258
Biddeford	6,618	3,047	6,840	2,903
Brunswick	7,900	3,670	7,845	3,692
Falmouth	4,150	3,319	4,189	2,861
Gorham	5,123	3,742	5,196	3,600
Kennebunk	3,927	2,784	4,237	2,685
Lewiston	9,624	5,796	10,629	5,961
Portland	27,739	7,488	28,317	7,844
Saco	6,179	3,569	6,457	3,374
Sanford	5,588	3,701	5,953	3,607
Scarborough	6,351	5,187	6,750	4,866
S. Portland	9,958	4,104	9,942	4,017
Waterville	4,693	2,107	5,080	2,109
Westbrook	5,528	3,053	5,590	3,030
Windham	4,704	4,107	5,086	4,000
York	4,888	3,594	5,107	3,314
Other	267,832	219,407	278,713	220,686
Totals	**401,306**	**292,276**	**421,923**	**295,273**

Maine Vote Since 1960

2012: Obama, D., 401,306; Romney, R., 292,276; Johnson, LB., 9,352; Stein, Green, 8,119.
2008: Obama, D., 421,923; McCain, R., 295,273; Nader, Ind., 10,636; McKinney, Green, 2,900.
2004: Kerry, D., 396,842; Bush, R., 330,201; Nader, Better Life, 8,069; Cobb, Green, 2,936; Badnarik, LB., 1,965; Peroutka, Const., 735.
2000: Gore, D., 319,951; Bush, R., 286,616; Nader, Green, 37,127; Buchanan, RF., 4,443; Browne, LB., 3,074; Phillips, Const., 579.
1996: Clinton, D., 312,788; Dole, R., 186,378; Perot, RF., 85,970; Nader, Green, 15,279; Browne, LB., 2,996; Phillips, Taxpayers, 1,517; Hagelin, Natural Law, 825.
1992: Clinton, D., 263,420; Perot, Ind., 206,820; Bush, R., 206,504; Marrou, LB., 1,681.
1988: Bush, R., 307,131; Dukakis, D., 243,569; Paul, LB., 2,700; Fulani, New Alliance, 1,405.
1984: Reagan, R., 336,500; Mondale, D., 214,515.
1980: Reagan, R., 238,522; Carter, D., 220,974; Anderson, Ind., 53,327; Clark, LB., 5,119; Commoner, Citizens, 4,394; Hall, Comm., 591; write-in, 84.
1976: Ford, R., 236,320; Carter, D., 232,279; McCarthy, Ind., 10,874; Bubar, Prohib., 3,495.
1972: Nixon, R., 256,458; McGovern, D., 160,584; scattered, 229.
1968: Humphrey, D., 217,312; Nixon, R., 169,254; Wallace, 3rd party, 6,370.
1964: Johnson, D., 262,264; Goldwater, R., 118,701.
1960: Nixon, R., 240,608; Kennedy, D., 181,159.

Maryland

County	2012 Obama (D)	Romney (R)	2008 Obama (D)	McCain (R)
Allegany	9,805	19,230	10,693	18,405
Anne Arundel	126,635	126,832	125,015	129,682
Baltimore	220,322	154,908	214,151	158,714
Calvert	20,529	23,952	20,299	23,095
Caroline	4,970	8,098	4,971	8,015
Carroll	27,939	56,761	28,060	54,503
Cecil	16,557	24,806	17,665	23,855
Charles	48,774	25,178	43,635	25,732
Dorchester	7,257	7,976	6,912	8,168
Frederick	55,146	58,798	54,013	55,170
Garrett	3,124	9,743	3,736	8,903
Harford	49,729	72,911	48,552	71,751
Howard	91,393	57,758	87,120	55,393
Kent	4,842	4,870	4,953	4,905
Montgomery	323,400	123,353	314,444	118,608
Prince George's	347,938	35,734	332,396	38,833
Queen Anne's	8,556	15,823	8,575	15,087
St. Mary's	19,711	26,797	19,023	24,705
Somerset	5,240	5,042	4,779	5,037
Talbot	8,808	11,339	9,035	10,995
Washington	25,042	36,074	26,245	34,169
Wicomico	19,635	21,764	19,436	21,849
Worcester	11,014	15,951	11,374	15,607
City				
Baltimore	221,478	28,171	214,385	28,681
Totals	**1,677,844**	**971,869**	**1,629,467**	**959,862**

Maryland Vote Since 1960

2012: Obama, D., 1,677,844; Romney, R., 971,869; Johnson, LB., 30,195; Stein, Green, 17,110.
2008: Obama, D., 1,629,467; McCain, R., 959,862; Nader, MD Ind., 14,713; Barr, LB., 9,842; McKinney, Green, 4,747; Baldwin, RF., 3,760.
2004: Kerry, D., 1,334,493; Bush, R., 1,024,703; Nader, Populist, 11,854; Badnarik, LB., 6,094; Cobb, Green, 3,632; Peroutka, Const., 3,421.
2000: Gore, D., 1,144,008; Bush, R., 813,827; Nader, Green, 53,768; Browne, LB., 5,310; Buchanan, RF., 4,248; Phillips, Const., 918.
1996: Clinton, D., 966,207; Dole, R., 681,530; Perot, RF., 115,812; Browne, LB., 8,765; Phillips, Taxpayers, 3,402; Hagelin, Natural Law, 2,517.
1992: Clinton, D., 988,571; Bush, R., 707,094; Perot, Ind., 281,414; Marrou, LB., 4,715; Fulani, New Alliance, 2,786.
1988: Bush, R., 876,167; Dukakis, D., 826,304; Paul, LB., 6,748; Fulani, New Alliance, 5,115.
1984: Reagan, R., 879,918; Mondale, D., 787,935; Bergland, LB., 5,721.
1980: Carter, D., 726,161; Reagan, R., 680,606; Anderson, Ind., 119,537; Clark, LB., 14,192.
1976: Carter, D., 759,612; Ford, R., 672,661.
1972: Nixon, R., 829,305; McGovern, D., 505,781; Schmitz, Amer., 18,726.
1968: Humphrey, D., 538,310; Nixon, R., 517,995; Wallace, 3rd party, 178,734.
1964: Johnson, D., 730,912; Goldwater, R., 385,495; write-in, 50.
1960: Kennedy, D., 565,800; Nixon, R., 489,538.

Massachusetts

City	2012 Obama (D)	Romney (R)	2008 Obama (D)	McCain (R)
Arlington	18,850	6,694	18,365	6,407
Barnstable	12,947	12,355	13,559	11,084
Beverly	12,158	8,328	12,247	7,780
Boston	200,190	48,985	185,976	45,548
Brockton	25,262	8,710	23,299	9,646
Brookline	22,277	5,880	22,484	4,842
Cambridge	43,515	5,476	40,876	4,697
Chicopee	14,302	8,241	14,172	8,268
Fall River	21,878	7,390	22,591	7,933
Framingham	18,499	8,978	17,839	8,464
Haverhill	15,592	11,894	15,552	10,814
Lowell	22,771	10,643	20,646	10,393
Lynn	23,124	8,512	20,276	8,719
Malden	15,010	5,730	13,865	6,075
Medford	18,874	8,359	17,598	8,655
Methuen	11,092	10,198	11,263	9,303
New Bedford	25,253	7,550	24,881	8,201
Newton	32,099	12,154	33,360	10,283
Peabody	15,027	11,622	14,818	10,800
Pittsfield	15,648	4,057	15,665	4,404
Plymouth	15,233	14,347	15,180	13,139
Quincy	24,849	14,850	22,810	15,546
Somerville	28,853	4,885	26,665	5,215
Springfield	43,869	10,515	39,516	11,331
Taunton	13,769	8,925	13,243	8,677
Waltham	15,906	8,856	15,276	8,383
Weymouth	15,166	12,362	14,727	12,358
Worcester	42,210	17,949	41,352	18,474
Other	1,137,067	883,869	1,155,996	813,415
Totals	**1,921,290**	**1,188,314**	**1,904,097**	**1,108,854**

Massachusetts Vote Since 1960

2012: Obama, D., 1,921,290; Romney, R., 1,188,314; Johnson, LB., 30,920; Stein, Green, 20,691.
2008: Obama, D., 1,904,097; McCain, R., 1,108,854; Nader, Ind., 28,841; Barr, LB., 13,189; McKinney, Green, 6,550; Baldwin, RF., 4,971.
2004: Kerry, D., 1,803,800; Bush, R., 1,071,109; Badnarik, LB., 15,022; Cobb, Green, 10,623.
2000: Gore, D., 1,616,487; Bush, R., 878,502; Nader, Green, 173,564; Browne, LB., 16,366; Buchanan, RF., 11,149; Hagelin, Natural Law, 2,884.
1996: Clinton, D., 1,571,509; Dole, R., 718,058; Perot, RF., 227,206; Browne, LB., 20,424; Hagelin, Natural Law, 5,183; Moorehead, Workers World, 3,276.
1992: Clinton, D., 1,318,639; Bush, R., 805,039; Perot, Ind., 630,731; Marrou, LB., 9,021; Fulani, New Alliance, 3,172; Phillips, U.S. Taxpayers, 2,218; Hagelin, Natural Law, 1,812; LaRouche, Ind., 1,027.
1988: Dukakis, D., 1,401,415; Bush, R., 1,194,635; Paul, LB., 24,251; Fulani, New Alliance, 9,561.
1984: Reagan, R., 1,310,936; Mondale, D., 1,239,606.
1980: Reagan, R., 1,057,631; Carter, D., 1,053,802; Anderson, Ind., 382,539; Clark, LB., 22,038; DeBerry, Soc. Workers, 3,735; Commoner, Citizens, 2,056; McReynolds, Soc., 62; Bubar, Statesman, 34; Griswold, Workers World, 19; scattered, 2,382.

1976: Carter, D., 1,429,475; Ford, R., 1,030,276; McCarthy, Ind., 65,637; Camejo, Soc. Workers, 8,138; Anderson, Amer., 7,555; LaRouche, U.S. Labor, 4,922; MacBride, LB., 135.
1972: McGovern, D., 1,332,540; Nixon, R., 1,112,078; Jenness, Soc. Workers, 10,600; Schmitz, Amer., 2,877; Fisher, Soc. Labor, 129; Spock, People's, 101; Hall, Comm., 46; Hospers, LB., 43; scattered, 342.
1968: Humphrey, D., 1,469,218; Nixon, R., 766,844; Wallace, 3rd party, 87,088; Blomen, Soc. Labor, 6,180; Munn, Prohib., 2,369; scattered, 53; blank, 25,394.
1964: Johnson, D., 1,786,422; Goldwater, R., 549,727; Hass, Soc. Labor, 4,755; Munn, Prohib., 3,735; scattered, 159; blank, 48,104.
1960: Kennedy, D., 1,487,174; Nixon, R., 976,750; Hass, Soc. Labor, 3,892; Decker, Prohib., 1,633; others, 31; blank and void, 26,024.

Michigan

County	2012 Obama (D)	Romney (R)	2008 Obama (D)	McCain (R)
Alcona	2,472	3,571	2,896	3,404
Alger	2,212	2,330	2,472	2,188
Allegan	20,806	31,123	24,165	30,061
Alpena	6,549	7,298	7,705	7,125
Antrim	5,107	7,917	6,079	7,506
Arenac	3,669	4,057	4,155	3,807
Baraga	1,574	1,866	1,725	1,846
Barry	11,491	16,655	13,449	16,431
Bay	27,877	24,911	32,589	23,795
Benzie	4,685	5,075	5,451	4,687
Berrien	33,465	38,209	40,381	36,130
Branch	6,913	10,035	8,413	9,534
Calhoun	29,267	28,333	34,561	28,553
Cass	9,591	12,659	12,083	11,114
Charlevoix	5,939	8,000	6,817	7,306
Cheboygan	5,831	7,286	6,720	6,920
Chippewa	7,100	8,278	8,184	8,267
Clare	6,338	6,988	7,496	6,793
Clinton	18,191	20,650	20,005	19,726
Crawford	2,994	3,744	3,441	3,561
Delta	8,330	9,534	9,974	8,763
Dickinson	4,952	7,688	5,995	7,049
Eaton	27,913	26,197	30,742	25,900
Emmet	7,225	10,253	8,515	9,314
Genesee	128,978	71,808	143,927	72,451
Gladwin	5,760	6,661	6,590	6,391
Gogebic	4,058	3,444	4,757	3,330
Grand Traverse	20,875	26,534	23,258	24,716
Gratiot	7,610	8,241	9,105	8,322
Hillsdale	7,106	11,727	8,765	11,221
Houghton	6,801	8,196	7,476	8,101
Huron	6,518	8,806	8,367	8,434
Ingham	80,847	45,306	93,994	46,483
Ionia	11,018	14,315	12,565	14,156
Iosco	6,242	6,909	7,309	6,583
Iron	2,687	3,224	3,080	2,947
Isabella	13,038	10,800	10,679	11,220
Jackson	32,301	36,298	37,480	35,692
Kalamazoo	69,051	52,662	77,051	51,554
Kalkaska	3,272	4,901	3,780	4,527
Kent	133,408	155,925	149,909	148,336
Keweenaw	582	774	610	756
Lake	2,752	2,487	2,919	2,269
Lapeer	18,796	23,734	21,457	22,831
Leelanau	6,576	7,483	7,355	6,938
Lenawee	21,776	22,351	24,640	22,225
Livingston	37,216	60,083	42,349	55,592
Luce	991	1,580	1,191	1,490
Mackinac	2,652	3,397	3,027	3,268
Macomb	208,016	191,913	223,784	187,663
Manistee	6,473	5,737	7,235	5,510
Marquette	18,115	13,606	19,635	12,906
Mason	6,856	7,580	7,817	7,147
Mecosta	7,515	9,176	9,101	9,238
Menominee	5,242	5,564	5,981	4,855
Midland	17,450	23,919	20,701	22,263
Missaukee	2,274	4,665	2,898	4,469
Monroe	36,310	35,593	39,180	35,858
Montcalm	11,430	13,621	13,208	13,291
Montmorency	2,049	2,928	2,403	2,841
Muskegon	44,436	30,884	53,821	29,145
Newaygo	8,728	12,457	10,790	11,862
Oakland	349,002	296,514	372,566	276,956
Oceana	5,063	6,239	6,405	5,860
Ogemaw	4,791	5,437	5,391	5,133
Ontonagon	1,586	1,906	1,966	1,823
Osceola	3,981	6,141	4,855	5,973
Oscoda	1,657	2,308	1,887	2,320
Otsego	4,681	7,011	5,634	6,752
Ottawa	42,737	88,166	50,828	83,330

County	2012 Obama (D)	Romney (R)	2008 Obama (D)	McCain (R)
Presque Isle	3,192	3,794	3,722	3,606
Roscommon	6,198	6,701	7,082	6,727
Saginaw	54,381	42,720	60,276	42,225
St. Clair	33,983	39,271	40,677	38,536
St. Joseph	10,112	12,978	12,322	12,886
Sanilac	7,212	10,963	9,047	10,679
Schoolcraft	1,865	2,142	2,184	2,058
Shiawassee	17,197	15,962	19,397	16,268
Tuscola	11,425	14,240	13,503	13,740
Van Buren	16,290	16,141	18,588	15,534
Washtenaw	120,890	56,412	130,578	53,946
Wayne	595,846	213,814	660,085	219,582
Wexford	6,184	8,450	7,379	8,044
Totals	**2,564,569**	**2,115,256**	**2,872,579**	**2,048,639**

Michigan Vote Since 1960

2012: Obama, D., 2,564,569; Romney, R., 2,115,256; Stein, Green, 21,897; Goode, U.S. Taxpayers, 16,119; Johnson, Ind., 7,774, Anderson, Natural Law, 5,147;
2008: Obama, D., 2,872,579; McCain, R., 2,048,639; Nader, Natural Law, 33,085; Barr, LB., 23,716; Baldwin, U.S. Taxpayers, 14,685; McKinney, Green, 8,892.
2004: Kerry, D., 2,479,183; Bush, R., 2,313,746; Nader, Ind., 24,035; Badnarik, LB., 10,552; Cobb, Green, 5,325; Peroutka, U.S. Taxpayers, 4,980; Brown, Natural Law, 1,431.
2000: Gore, D., 2,170,418; Bush, R., 1,953,139; Nader, Green, 84,165; Browne, LB., 16,711; Phillips, U.S. Taxpayers, 3,791; Hagelin, Natural Law, 2,426.
1996: Clinton, D., 1,989,653; Dole, R., 1,481,212; Perot, RF., 336,670; Browne, LB., 27,670; Hagelin, Natural Law, 4,254; Moorehead, Workers World, 3,153; White, Soc. Equality, 1,554.
1992: Clinton, D., 1,871,182; Bush, R., 1,554,940; Perot, Ind., 824,813; Marrou, LB., 10,175; Phillips, U.S. Taxpayers, 8,263; Hagelin, Natural Law, 2,954.
1988: Bush, R., 1,965,486; Dukakis, D., 1,675,783; Paul, LB., 18,336; Fulani, Ind., 2,513.
1984: Reagan, R., 2,251,571; Mondale, D., 1,529,638; Bergland, LB., 10,055.
1980: Reagan, R., 1,915,225; Carter, D., 1,661,532; Anderson, Ind., 275,223; Clark, LB., 41,597; Commoner, Citizens, 11,930; Hall, Comm., 3,262; Griswold, Workers World, 30; Greaves, Amer., 21; Bubar, Statesman, 9.
1976: Ford, R., 1,893,742; Carter, D., 1,696,714; McCarthy, Ind., 47,905; MacBride, LB., 5,406; Wright, People's, 3,504; Camejo, Soc. Workers, 1,804; LaRouche, U.S. Labor, 1,366; Levin, Soc. Labor, 1,148; scattered, 2,160.
1972: Nixon, R., 1,961,721; McGovern, D., 1,459,435; Schmitz, Amer., 63,321; Fisher, Soc. Labor, 2,437; Jenness, Soc. Workers, 1,603; Hall, Comm., 1,210.
1968: Humphrey, D., 1,593,082; Nixon, R., 1,370,665; Wallace, 3rd party, 331,968; Halstead, Soc. Workers, 4,099; Blomen, Soc. Labor, 1,762; Cleaver, New Politics, 4,585; Munn, Prohib., 60; scattered, 29.
1964: Johnson, D., 2,136,615; Goldwater, R., 1,060,152; DeBerry, Soc. Workers, 3,817; Hass, Soc. Labor, 1,704; Prohib. (no candidate listed), 699; scattered, 145.
1960: Kennedy, D., 1,687,269; Nixon, R., 1,620,428; Dobbs, Soc. Workers, 4,347; Decker, Prohib., 2,029; Daly, Tax Cut, 1,767; Hass, Soc. Labor, 1,718; Ind. Amer. (unpledged), 539.

Minnesota

County	2012 Obama (D)	Romney (R)	2008 Obama (D)	McCain (R)
Aitkin	4,412	4,533	4,595	4,589
Anoka	88,614	93,430	86,976	91,357
Becker	6,829	9,204	7,687	8,851
Beltrami	11,818	9,637	12,019	9,762
Benton	8,173	10,849	8,454	10,338
Big Stone	1,345	1,385	1,552	1,362
Blue Earth	18,164	14,916	19,325	14,782
Brown	5,630	7,938	5,809	7,456
Carlton	11,389	6,586	11,501	6,549
Carver	20,745	31,155	20,654	28,156
Cass	6,858	8,957	7,276	8,660
Chippewa	3,083	2,967	3,280	2,907
Chisago	12,524	16,227	12,783	15,789
Clay	15,208	12,920	16,666	11,978
Clearwater	1,753	2,359	1,877	2,291
Cook	1,993	1,221	2,019	1,240
Cottonwood	2,433	3,316	2,759	3,157
Crow Wing	14,760	19,415	15,859	18,567
Dakota	116,255	109,516	116,778	104,364
Dodge	4,487	5,522	4,463	5,468
Douglas	8,653	11,884	9,256	11,241
Faribault	3,407	4,104	3,736	4,196
Fillmore	5,713	4,913	5,921	4,993
Freeborn	9,326	6,969	9,915	6,955

County	2012 Obama (D)	Romney (R)	2008 Obama (D)	McCain (R)
Goodhue	12,212	12,986	12,420	12,775
Grant	1,647	1,748	1,850	1,646
Hennepin	423,982	240,073	420,958	231,054
Houston	5,281	4,951	5,906	4,743
Hubbard	4,676	6,622	4,872	6,558
Isanti	8,024	11,675	8,248	11,324
Itasca	12,852	10,501	13,460	10,309
Jackson	2,268	3,044	2,618	2,858
Kanabec	3,593	4,328	3,743	4,479
Kandiyohi	9,805	11,240	10,125	11,319
Kittson	1,241	1,095	1,492	1,016
Koochiching	3,451	2,841	3,649	2,962
Lac Qui Parle	1,974	1,938	2,160	1,912
Lake	4,043	2,610	4,174	2,636
Lake of the Woods	859	1,306	971	1,278
Le Sueur	6,753	7,715	6,994	7,636
Lincoln	1,429	1,595	1,517	1,491
Lyon	5,465	6,594	6,110	6,315
Mahnomen	1,276	871	1,436	843
Marshall	1,998	2,569	2,311	2,285
Martin	4,054	6,657	4,413	6,053
McLeod	6,968	11,069	7,505	10,993
Meeker	4,969	6,913	5,380	6,737
Mille Lacs	5,829	6,951	6,072	7,049
Morrison	6,153	10,159	6,547	9,735
Mower	11,129	6,938	11,605	7,075
Murray	2,160	2,504	2,345	2,320
Nicollet	9,652	8,214	9,887	7,968
Nobles	3,793	4,581	4,244	4,368
Norman	1,730	1,384	2,129	1,204
Olmsted	39,338	36,832	38,711	36,202
Otter Tail	12,165	18,860	13,856	18,077
Pennington	3,024	3,305	3,394	3,248
Pine	6,750	6,845	7,084	6,862
Pipestone	1,725	2,826	2,023	2,652
Polk	6,773	7,615	7,850	7,148
Pope	2,981	3,142	3,317	3,069
Ramsey	184,938	86,800	182,974	88,942
Red Lake	928	978	1,120	983
Redwood	3,008	4,570	3,250	4,308
Renville	3,394	4,149	3,904	3,956
Rice	17,054	14,384	17,381	13,723
Rock	1,946	2,810	2,079	2,775
Roseau	2,772	4,409	3,097	4,438
St. Louis	73,378	39,131	77,351	38,742
Scott	29,712	40,323	29,208	36,724
Sherburne	17,597	27,848	17,957	26,140
Sibley	2,916	4,693	2,998	4,492
Stearns	33,551	43,015	35,690	41,194
Steele	8,706	9,903	9,016	10,068
Stevens	2,742	2,766	2,781	2,710
Swift	2,751	2,248	2,907	2,184
Todd	4,819	6,719	5,277	6,637
Traverse	943	861	1,043	933
Wabasha	5,415	6,049	5,646	5,935
Wadena	2,492	4,143	2,882	4,128
Waseca	4,370	5,116	4,401	5,211
Washington	70,203	69,137	70,277	64,334
Watonwan	2,494	2,517	2,562	2,526
Wilkin	1,258	1,884	1,550	1,786
Winona	14,980	11,480	16,308	10,975
Wright	25,741	40,466	26,343	37,779
Yellow Medicine	2,465	2,806	2,816	2,579
Totals	1,546,167	1,320,225	1,573,354	1,275,409

Minnesota Vote Since 1960

2012: Obama, D., 1,546,167; Romney, R., 1,320,225; Johnson, LB., 35,098; Stein, Green, 13,023; Goode, Const., 3,722; Carlson, Grassroots, 3,149; Anderson, Justice, 1,996; Morstad, Constitutional, 1,092; Harris, Soc. Workers, 1,051; Lindsay, Socialism/Liberation, 397.

2008: Obama, D., 1,573,354; McCain, R., 1,275,409; Nader, Ind., 30,152; Barr, LB., 9,174; Baldwin, Const., 6,787; McKinney, Green, 5,174; Calero, Soc. Workers, 790.

2004: Kerry, D., 1,445,014; Bush, R., 1,346,695; Nader, Better Life, 18,683; Badnarik, LB., 4,639; Cobb, Green, 4,408; Peroutka, Const., 3,074; Harens, other, 2,387; Van Auken, Soc. Equal., 539; Calero, Soc. Workers, 416.

2000: Gore, D., 1,168,266; Bush, R., 1,109,659; Nader, Green, 126,696; Buchanan, RF. MN, 22,166; Browne, LB., 5,282; Phillips, Const., 3,272; Hagelin, RF., 2,294; Harris, Soc. Workers, 1,022.

1996: Clinton, D., 1,120,438; Dole, R., 766,476; Perot, RF., 257,704; Nader, Green, 24,908; Browne, LB., 8,271; Peron, Grass Roots, 4,898; Phillips, U.S. Taxpayers, 3,416; Hagelin, Natural Law, 1,808; Birrenbach, Ind. Grass Roots, 787; Harris, Soc. Workers, 684; White, Soc. Equality, 347.

1992: Clinton, D., 1,020,997; Bush, R., 747,841; Perot, Ind., 562,506; Marrou, LB., 3,373; Gritz, Populist/America First, 3,363; Hagelin, Natural Law, 1,406.

1988: Dukakis, D., 1,109,471; Bush, R., 962,337; McCarthy, Minn. Prog., 5,403; Paul, LB., 5,109.

1984: Mondale, D., 1,036,364; Reagan, R., 1,032,603; Bergland, LB., 2,996.

1980: Carter, D., 954,173; Reagan, R., 873,268; Anderson, Ind., 174,997; Clark, LB., 31,593; Commoner, Citizens, 8,406; Hall, Comm., 1,117; DeBerry, Soc. Workers, 711; Griswold, Workers World, 698; McReynolds, Soc., 536; write-in, 281.

1976: Carter, D., 1,070,440; Ford, R., 819,395; McCarthy, Ind., 35,490; Anderson, Amer., 13,592; Camejo, Soc. Workers, 4,149; MacBride, LB., 3,529; Hall, Comm., 1,092.

1972: Nixon, R., 898,269; McGovern, D., 802,346; Schmitz, Amer., 31,407; Fisher, Soc. Labor, 4,261; Spock, People's, 2,805; Jenness, Soc. Workers, 940; Hall, Comm., 662; scattered, 962.

1968: Humphrey, D., 857,738; Nixon, R., 658,643; Wallace, 3rd party, 68,931; Cleaver, Peace/Freedom, 935; Halstead, Soc. Workers, 808; McCarthy, write-in, 585; Mitchell, Comm., 415; Blomen, Industrial Govt., 285; scattered, 2,613.

1964: Johnson, D., 991,117; Goldwater, R., 559,624; Hass, Industrial Govt., 2,544; DeBerry, Soc. Workers, 1,177.

1960: Kennedy, D., 779,933; Nixon, R., 757,915; Dobbs, Soc. Workers, 3,077; Hass, Industrial Govt. 962.

Mississippi

County	2012 Obama (D)	Romney (R)	2008 Obama (D)	McCain (R)
Adams	9,061	6,293	9,021	6,566
Alcorn	3,511	11,111	4,130	10,805
Amite	3,242	4,414	3,348	4,245
Attala	3,927	5,126	3,849	5,273
Benton	2,051	2,041	2,227	2,329
Bolivar	10,582	4,701	10,334	4,891
Calhoun	2,586	4,412	2,522	4,467
Carroll	2,007	3,960	2,037	3,902
Chickasaw	4,378	3,994	4,588	4,395
Choctaw	1,428	2,812	1,459	2,624
Claiborne	4,838	625	4,682	748
Clarke	3,111	5,049	3,121	5,229
Clay	6,712	4,291	6,558	4,466
Coahoma	7,792	2,712	7,597	2,917
Copiah	7,749	6,282	7,710	6,701
Covington	3,878	5,405	3,852	5,523
DeSoto	21,575	43,559	19,627	44,222
Forrest	13,272	16,574	11,622	15,296
Franklin	1,726	2,735	1,733	2,909
George	1,359	8,376	1,532	7,700
Greene	1,325	4,531	1,366	4,361
Grenada	5,288	5,986	5,029	6,234
Hancock	3,917	12,964	3,768	13,020
Harrison	23,119	39,470	22,673	38,757
Hinds	76,112	29,664	75,401	32,949
Holmes	7,812	1,435	7,765	1,714
Humphreys	3,903	1,293	3,634	1,462
Issaquena	479	302	579	364
Itawamba	1,706	7,393	2,084	7,663
Jackson	17,299	35,747	17,781	35,993
Jasper	5,097	4,193	5,025	4,135
Jefferson	3,951	468	3,883	551
Jefferson Davis	4,267	2,507	4,454	2,871
Jones	9,211	20,687	8,846	20,157
Kemper	3,239	1,789	3,256	1,935
Lafayette	8,091	11,075	7,997	10,278
Lamar	5,494	19,101	5,159	18,497
Lauderdale	13,814	18,700	13,332	19,582
Lawrence	2,468	4,192	2,587	4,369
Leake	4,079	4,863	4,151	5,148
Lee	12,563	22,415	12,021	22,694
Leflore	9,119	3,587	8,914	4,105
Lincoln	5,471	10,839	5,505	10,781
Lowndes	13,388	13,518	13,209	13,994
Madison	20,722	28,507	19,831	27,203
Marion	4,393	8,237	4,422	8,513
Marshall	9,650	6,473	9,685	6,683
Monroe	7,056	9,723	7,169	10,184
Montgomery	2,675	2,947	2,609	3,071
Neshoba	3,089	7,837	3,114	8,209
Newton	3,319	6,394	3,218	6,579
Noxubee	4,920	1,325	5,030	1,525
Oktibbeha	9,095	8,761	9,326	9,320
Panola	9,079	7,629	8,690	7,620
Pearl River	4,366	17,549	4,320	17,881
Perry	1,527	4,137	1,533	4,067
Pike	9,650	8,181	9,276	8,651

County	2012 Obama (D)	2012 Romney (R)	2008 Obama (D)	2008 McCain (R)
Pontotoc	2,804	9,448	2,982	9,727
Prentiss	2,817	7,075	3,020	7,703
Quitman	2,837	1,116	2,803	1,334
Rankin	14,988	48,444	14,372	48,140
Scott	5,031	6,089	5,025	6,584
Sharkey	1,782	737	1,907	873
Simpson	4,723	7,424	4,817	7,641
Smith	1,979	6,049	1,968	6,265
Stone	2,003	5,420	1,996	5,149
Sunflower	8,199	2,929	7,838	3,245
Tallahatchie	3,959	2,499	4,105	2,786
Tate	4,933	7,332	5,003	7,678
Tippah	2,317	6,717	2,623	6,937
Tishomingo	1,643	6,133	1,962	6,249
Tunica	3,475	883	3,279	1,017
Union	2,742	8,498	2,985	9,072
Walthall	3,422	4,051	3,456	4,253
Warren	10,786	10,457	10,489	11,152
Washington	13,981	5,651	13,148	6,347
Wayne	4,148	6,111	3,890	6,070
Webster	1,190	3,992	1,349	4,072
Wilkinson	3,412	1,415	3,534	1,560
Winston	4,607	5,168	4,653	5,497
Yalobusha	3,030	3,276	3,151	3,628
Yazoo	6,603	4,941	6,116	5,290
Totals	**562,949**	**710,746**	**554,662**	**724,597**

Mississippi Vote Since 1960

2012: Romney, R., 710,746; Obama, D., 562,949; Johnson, LB., 6,676; Goode, Const., 2,609; Stein, Green, 1,588; Washer, RF., 1,016.

2008: McCain, R., 724,597; Obama, D., 554,662; Nader, Ind., 4,011; Baldwin, Const., 2,551; Barr, LB., 2,529; McKinney, Green, 1,034; Weill, RF., 481.

2004: Bush, R., 684,981; Kerry, D., 458,094; Nader, RF., 3,177; Badnarik, LB., 1,793; Peroutka, Const., 1,759; Harris, Ind., 1,268; Cobb, Green, 1,073.

2000: Bush, R., 572,844; Gore, D., 404,614; Nader, Ind., 8,122; Phillips, Const., 3,267; Buchanan, RF., 2,265; Browne, LB., 2,009; Harris, Ind., 613; Hagelin, Natural Law, 450.

1996: Dole, R., 439,838; Clinton, D., 394,022; Perot, RF., 52,222; Browne, LB., 2,809; Phillips, U.S. Taxpayers, 2,314; Hagelin, Natural Law, 1,447; Collins, Ind., 1,205.

1992: Bush, R., 487,793; Clinton, D., 400,258; Perot, Ind., 85,626; Fulani, New Alliance, 2,625; Marrou, LB., 2,154; Phillips, U.S. Taxpayers, 1,652; Hagelin, Natural Law, 1,140.

1988: Bush, R., 557,890; Dukakis, D., 363,921; Duke, Ind., 4,232; Paul, LB., 3,329.

1984: Reagan, R., 582,377; Mondale, D., 352,192; Bergland, LB., 2,336.

1980: Reagan, R., 441,089; Carter, D., 429,281; Anderson, Ind., 12,036; Clark, LB., 5,465; Griswold, Workers World, 2,402; Pulley, Soc. Workers, 2,347.

1976: Carter, D., 381,309; Ford, R., 366,846; Anderson, Amer., 6,678; McCarthy, Ind., 4,074; Maddox, Ind., 4,049; Camejo, Soc. Workers, 2,805; MacBride, LB., 2,609.

1972: Nixon, R., 505,125; McGovern, D., 126,782; Schmitz, Amer., 11,598; Jenness, Soc. Workers, 2,458.

1968: Wallace, 3rd party, 415,349; Humphrey, D., 150,644; Nixon, R., 88,516.

1964: Goldwater, R., 356,528; Johnson, D., 52,618.

1960: D. (electors unpledged), 116,248; Kennedy, D., 108,362; Nixon, R., 73,561. *Mississippi's victorious slate of 8 unpledged Democratic electors cast their votes for Sen. Harry F. Byrd (D, VA).

Missouri

County	2012 Obama (D)	2012 Romney (R)	2008 Obama (D)	2008 McCain (R)
Adair	4,219	5,651	5,735	5,891
Andrew	2,649	5,457	3,345	5,279
Atchison	756	1,902	1,000	1,936
Audrain	3,539	6,186	4,434	6,167
Barry	3,667	9,832	4,630	9,758
Barton	1,230	4,418	1,455	4,414
Bates	2,557	5,020	3,271	4,833
Benton	2,925	6,069	3,629	5,759
Bollinger	1,213	4,095	1,690	3,972
Boone	39,847	37,404	47,062	36,849
Buchanan	15,594	18,660	19,164	19,110
Butler	4,363	12,248	5,316	11,805
Caldwell	1,312	2,721	1,814	2,654
Callaway	6,071	11,745	7,580	11,389
Camden	6,458	15,092	7,773	14,074
Cape Girardeau	9,728	25,370	12,208	24,768
Carroll	1,154	3,072	1,535	2,955

County	2012 Obama (D)	2012 Romney (R)	2008 Obama (D)	2008 McCain (R)
Carter	754	1,978	984	1,840
Cass	17,044	30,912	19,844	29,695
Cedar	1,537	4,376	2,060	4,194
Chariton	1,339	2,402	1,799	2,339
Christian	9,813	27,473	11,883	25,382
Clark	1,398	1,730	1,572	1,782
Clay	47,310	56,191	53,761	54,516
Clinton	3,688	5,931	4,545	5,709
Cole	12,005	24,490	13,959	24,385
Cooper	2,474	4,887	2,996	4,902
Crawford	2,951	6,434	3,911	6,007
Dade	939	2,895	1,184	2,864
Dallas	2,122	4,992	2,656	4,895
Daviess	1,125	2,290	1,400	2,263
DeKalb	1,194	3,056	1,692	2,889
Dent	1,585	4,883	2,056	4,655
Douglas	1,710	4,649	2,140	4,405
Dunklin	3,636	6,850	4,540	7,044
Franklin	16,347	29,396	21,256	27,355
Gasconade	2,099	4,895	2,899	4,763
Gentry	937	1,988	1,235	1,964
Greene	46,219	76,900	56,181	77,683
Grundy	1,212	3,030	1,580	3,006
Harrison	984	2,624	1,287	2,512
Henry	3,606	6,229	4,869	6,095
Hickory	1,733	2,835	2,171	2,850
Holt	551	1,725	802	1,794
Howard	1,723	3,017	2,036	2,708
Howell	4,395	11,544	5,736	10,982
Iron	1,669	2,252	2,213	2,090
Jackson	78,283	93,199	90,722	92,833
Jasper	12,809	31,349	15,730	31,667
Jefferson	41,564	53,978	53,467	50,804
Johnson	7,667	12,763	9,480	12,183
Knox	698	1,205	759	1,212
Laclede	4,093	10,934	5,218	10,875
Lafayette	5,655	9,803	6,902	9,442
Lawrence	4,017	11,421	5,097	11,263
Lewis	1,508	2,677	1,837	2,594
Lincoln	7,734	14,332	10,234	12,924
Linn	2,041	3,344	2,638	3,140
Livingston	1,906	4,006	2,435	3,993
Macon	2,309	4,701	2,784	4,586
Madison	1,588	3,227	2,042	2,897
Maries	1,299	3,165	1,599	2,853
Marion	4,031	7,923	4,703	7,705
McDonald	1,920	5,694	2,454	5,499
Mercer	353	1,255	519	1,169
Miller	2,651	8,099	3,553	7,797
Mississippi	1,858	2,997	2,247	3,034
Moniteau	1,608	4,704	2,084	4,467
Monroe	1,398	2,564	1,703	2,533
Montgomery	1,740	3,490	2,347	3,428
Morgan	2,773	5,733	3,565	5,451
New Madrid	2,814	4,284	3,370	4,593
Newton	6,425	18,181	7,450	17,637
Nodaway	3,172	5,593	4,493	5,568
Oregon	1,419	2,886	1,811	2,652
Osage	1,473	5,329	1,907	5,062
Ozark	1,261	3,080	1,661	2,918
Pemiscot	2,671	3,598	3,029	3,954
Perry	2,184	5,669	3,005	5,527
Pettis	5,904	10,842	6,932	11,018
Phelps	5,798	11,895	7,394	11,706
Pike	2,582	4,577	3,487	4,268
Platte	19,175	25,618	21,459	24,460
Polk	3,580	9,252	4,553	8,956
Pulaski	4,199	9,092	5,249	9,552
Putnam	587	1,673	695	1,591
Ralls	1,736	3,231	2,041	2,987
Randolph	3,031	6,667	3,984	6,457
Ray	4,275	5,815	5,241	5,593
Reynolds	1,157	1,931	1,418	1,782
Ripley	1,396	3,743	1,795	3,407
St. Charles	71,838	110,784	84,183	102,550
St. Clair	1,460	3,019	1,886	2,981
St. Francois	8,829	13,248	11,540	12,660
St. Louis Co.	297,097	224,742	333,123	221,705
Ste. Genevieve	3,813	4,055	4,979	3,732
Saline	3,790	5,104	4,712	4,962
Schuyler	697	1,174	775	1,139
Scotland	643	1,246	793	1,249
Scott	5,122	11,623	6,258	11,563
Shannon	1,302	2,262	1,637	2,075
Shelby	966	2,188	1,114	2,166
Stoddard	3,153	9,496	3,899	9,172

County	2012 Obama (D)	Romney (R)	2008 Obama (D)	McCain (R)
Stone	3,923	11,787	5,029	11,147
Sullivan	908	1,610	1,173	1,607
Taney	5,479	15,746	6,683	14,736
Texas	2,871	7,618	3,410	7,215
Vernon	2,580	5,758	3,381	5,334
Warren	5,219	9,150	6,705	8,675
Washington	3,417	5,071	4,711	4,706
Wayne	1,813	3,790	2,243	3,784
Webster	4,409	10,708	5,685	10,431
Worth	341	664	427	707
Wright	1,953	5,830	2,557	5,784
City				
Kansas City	105,670	29,509	120,102	31,854
St. Louis	118,780	22,943	132,925	24,662
Totals	1,223,796	1,482,440	1,441,911	1,445,814

Missouri Vote Since 1960

2012: Romney, R., 1,482,440; Obama, D., 1,223,796; Johnson, LB., 43,151; Goode, Const., 7,936.
2008: McCain, R., 1,445,814; Obama, D., 1,441,911; Nader, Ind., 17,813; Barr, LB., 11,386; Baldwin, Const., 8,201.
2004: Bush, R., 1,455,713; Kerry, D., 1,259,171; Badnarik, LB., 9,831; Peroutka, Const., 5,355.
2000: Bush, R., 1,189,924; Gore, D., 1,111,138; Nader, Green, 38,515; Buchanan, RF., 9,818; Browne, LB., 7,436; Phillips, Const., 1,957; Hagelin, Natural Law, 1,104.
1996: Clinton, D., 1,025,935; Dole, R., 890,016; Perot, RF., 217,188; Phillips, U.S. Taxpayers, 11,521; Browne, LB., 10,522; Hagelin, Natural Law, 2,287.
1992: Clinton, D., 1,053,873; Bush, R., 811,159; Perot, Ind., 518,741; Marrou, LB., 7,497.
1988: Bush, R., 1,084,953; Dukakis, D., 1,001,619; Fulani, New Alliance, 6,656; Paul, write-in, 434.
1984: Reagan, R., 1,274,188; Mondale, D., 848,583.
1980: Reagan, R., 1,074,181; Carter, D., 931,182; Anderson, Ind., 77,920; Clark, LB., 14,422; DeBerry, Soc. Workers, 1,515; Commoner, Citizens, 573; write-in, 34.
1976: Carter, D., 999,163; Ford, R., 928,808; McCarthy, Ind., 24,329.
1972: Nixon, R., 1,154,058; McGovern, D., 698,531.
1968: Nixon, R., 811,932; Humphrey, D., 791,444; Wallace, 3rd party, 206,126.
1964: Johnson, D., 1,164,344; Goldwater, R., 653,535.
1960: Kennedy, D., 972,201; Nixon, R., 962,221.

Montana

County	2012 Obama (D)	Romney (R)	2008 Obama (D)	McCain (R)
Beaverhead	1,371	3,289	1,617	3,008
Big Horn	2,882	1,667	3,516	1,628
Blaine	1,616	1,178	1,702	1,139
Broadwater	764	2,152	857	1,875
Carbon	2,146	3,533	2,443	3,108
Carter	96	678	111	573
Cascade	15,232	18,345	17,664	16,857
Chouteau	978	1,758	1,122	1,634
Custer	1,833	3,373	2,267	3,047
Daniels	237	740	343	694
Dawson	1,219	3,029	1,593	2,639
Deer Lodge	2,860	1,448	3,402	1,502
Fallon	237	1,128	318	1,064
Fergus	1,640	4,257	1,933	4,108
Flathead	13,892	28,309	16,138	25,559
Gallatin	21,961	24,358	24,205	22,578
Garfield	66	622	110	598
Glacier	2,924	1,415	3,423	1,451
Golden Valley	110	351	124	343
Granite	533	1,107	601	1,013
Hill	3,403	3,164	3,596	2,787
Jefferson	2,272	4,055	2,582	3,538
Judith Basin	337	854	397	801
Lake	5,805	7,135	6,766	6,498
Lewis and Clark	15,620	16,803	17,114	14,966
Liberty	257	702	367	594
Lincoln	2,552	6,057	3,025	5,704
Madison	1,289	3,130	1,607	2,822
McCone	223	745	321	726
Meagher	269	670	298	624
Mineral	700	1,216	845	1,053
Missoula	32,824	22,652	36,531	20,743
Musselshell	492	1,833	636	1,581
Park	3,783	4,709	4,173	4,376
Petroleum	49	240	68	227
Phillips	471	1,688	638	1,423
Pondera	975	1,673	1,223	1,588
Powder River	170	833	208	802

County	2012 Obama (D)	Romney (R)	2008 Obama (D)	McCain (R)
Powell	888	1,806	1,021	1,683
Prairie	167	520	211	503
Ravalli	7,285	14,307	8,400	13,002
Richland	1,002	3,510	1,203	3,184
Roosevelt	2,086	1,514	2,564	1,473
Rosebud	1,422	2,004	1,919	1,768
Sanders	1,720	3,980	1,970	3,563
Sheridan	665	1,207	953	987
Silver Bow	10,857	5,430	11,676	4,818
Stillwater	1,248	3,337	1,512	2,991
Sweet Grass	475	1,594	541	1,494
Teton	1,082	2,113	1,294	1,874
Toole	582	1,440	737	1,317
Treasure	114	319	156	314
Valley	1,385	2,337	1,645	2,121
Wheatland	272	693	289	657
Wibaux	98	421	146	379
Yellowstone	26,403	40,500	32,038	36,483
Totals	201,839	267,928	231,667	242,763

Montana Vote Since 1960

2012: Romney, R., 267,928; Obama, D., 201,839; Johnson, LB., 14,165.
2008: McCain, R., 242,763; Obama, D., 231,667; Paul, Const., 10,638; Nader, Ind., 3,686; Barr, LB., 1,355.
2004: Bush, R., 266,063; Kerry, D., 173,710; Nader, Ind., 6,168; Peroutka, Const., 1,764; Badnarik, LB., 1,733; Cobb, Green, 996.
2000: Bush, R., 240,178; Gore, D., 137,126; Nader, Green, 24,437; Buchanan, RF., 5,697; Browne, LB., 1,718; Phillips, Const., 1,155; Hagelin, Natural Law, 675.
1996: Dole, R., 179,652; Clinton, D., 167,922; Perot, RF., 55,229; Browne, LB., 2,526; Hagelin, Natural Law, 1,754.
1992: Clinton, D., 154,507; Bush, R., 144,207; Perot, Ind., 107,225; Gritz, Populist/America First, 3,658.
1988: Bush, R., 190,412; Dukakis, D., 168,936; Paul, LB., 5,047; Fulani, New Alliance, 1,279.
1984: Reagan, R., 232,450; Mondale, D., 146,742; Bergland, LB., 5,185.
1980: Reagan, R., 206,814; Carter, D., 118,032; Anderson, Ind., 29,281; Clark, LB., 9,825.
1976: Ford, R., 173,703; Carter, D., 149,259; Anderson, Amer., 5,772.
1972: Nixon, R., 183,976; McGovern, D., 120,197; Schmitz, Amer., 13,430.
1968: Nixon, R., 138,835; Humphrey, D., 114,117; Wallace, 3rd party, 20,015; Munn, Prohib., 510; Caton, New RF., 470; Halstead, Soc. Workers, 457.
1964: Johnson, D., 164,246; Goldwater, R., 113,032; Kasper, Natl. States' Rights, 519; Munn, Prohib., 499; DeBerry, Soc. Workers, 332.
1960: Nixon, R., 141,841; Kennedy, D., 134,891; Decker, Prohib., 456; Dobbs, Soc. Workers, 391.

Nebraska

County	2012 Obama (D)	Romney (R)	2008 Obama (D)	McCain (R)
Adams	4,062	8,316	4,685	8,252
Antelope	571	2,596	757	2,383
Arthur	30	227	39	217
Banner	55	346	62	348
Blaine	29	268	43	266
Boone	615	2,138	742	2,042
Box Butte	1,692	2,869	1,886	2,932
Boyd	188	873	250	839
Brown	224	1,302	311	1,208
Buffalo	5,365	13,570	5,867	13,097
Burt	1,291	2,029	1,413	1,907
Butler	1,045	2,738	1,190	2,557
Cass	4,367	7,556	4,753	7,120
Cedar	958	3,278	1,190	2,912
Chase	254	1,584	341	1,477
Cherry	436	2,557	599	2,360
Cheyenne	1,084	3,449	1,173	3,572
Clay	667	2,232	780	2,177
Colfax	969	2,051	1,125	2,018
Cuming	1,031	2,876	1,274	2,732
Custer	1,083	4,296	1,192	4,301
Dakota	2,922	3,094	2,994	3,292
Dawes	1,132	2,478	1,285	2,376
Dawson	2,199	5,460	2,399	5,460
Deuel	215	763	243	732
Dixon	870	1,745	940	1,785
Dodge	5,673	8,995	6,689	8,557
Douglas	106,456	113,220	116,810	106,291
Dundy	176	792	218	783
Fillmore	807	2,007	962	1,913
Franklin	384	1,112	442	1,079
Frontier	271	1,007	349	1,034

County	2012 Obama (D)	Romney (R)	2008 Obama (D)	McCain (R)
Furnas	423	1,782	556	1,725
Gage	3,903	5,513	4,473	5,435
Garden	242	829	283	844
Garfield	149	769	212	800
Gosper	230	734	260	776
Grant	30	322	41	318
Greeley	340	820	458	715
Hall	7,161	12,646	7,855	12,977
Hamilton	1,146	3,600	1,332	3,389
Harlan	354	1,395	402	1,329
Hayes	51	476	85	461
Hitchcock	274	1,178	346	1,001
Holt	882	3,922	1,089	3,746
Hooker	59	330	75	355
Howard	914	1,890	1,083	1,847
Jefferson	1,195	2,166	1,520	2,103
Johnson	790	1,225	914	1,142
Kearney	773	2,349	876	2,224
Keith	928	3,044	974	2,942
Keya Paha	80	393	115	409
Kimball	395	1,235	439	1,346
Knox	1,059	2,885	1,255	2,728
Lancaster	62,015	62,434	65,734	59,398
Lincoln	4,450	10,728	5,046	10,817
Logan	68	356	81	327
Loup	62	290	86	302
Madison	3,485	10,062	4,142	9,655
McPherson	41	237	45	240
Merrick	925	2,490	986	2,375
Morrill	455	1,681	557	1,725
Nance	481	1,106	549	1,116
Nemaha	1,128	2,012	1,240	2,134
Nuckolls	568	1,574	657	1,498
Otoe	2,561	4,258	2,915	4,033
Pawnee	400	899	483	859
Perkins	238	1,135	310	1,092
Phelps	880	3,400	1,050	3,360
Pierce	637	2,707	783	2,385
Platte	3,148	10,061	3,796	9,373
Polk	528	1,890	668	1,822
Red Willow	952	3,891	1,216	3,735
Richardson	1,191	2,443	1,513	2,342
Rock	103	672	139	640
Saline	2,289	2,557	2,674	2,434
Sarpy	26,671	43,213	28,010	38,816
Saunders	3,307	6,770	3,767	6,188
Scotts Bluff	4,327	9,648	4,745	9,708
Seward	2,386	5,003	2,703	4,647
Sheridan	390	2,021	454	1,941
Sherman	552	927	585	950
Sioux	101	624	117	603
Stanton	614	1,949	664	1,781
Thayer	728	1,874	860	1,749
Thomas	42	360	51	331
Thurston	1,247	939	1,120	972
Valley	498	1,657	706	1,657
Washington	3,132	6,899	3,711	6,425
Wayne	1,074	2,493	1,249	2,503
Webster	442	1,258	552	1,233
Wheeler	93	345	96	334
York	1,373	4,874	1,607	4,848
Totals	302,081	475,064	333,319	452,979

Nebraska Vote Since 1960

2012: Romney, R., 475,064; Obama, D., 302,081; Johnson, LB., 11,109; Terry, petitioning cand., 2,408.
2008: McCain, R., 452,979; Obama, D., 333,319; Nader, petitioning cand., 5,406; Baldwin, Nebraska, 2,972; Barr, LB., 2,740; McKinney, Green, 1,028.
2004: Bush, R., 512,814; Kerry, D., 254,328; Nader, petitioning cand., 5,698; Badnarik, LB., 2,041; Peroutka, Nebraska, 1,314; Cobb, Green, 978; Calero, petitioning cand., 82.
2000: Bush, R., 433,862; Gore, D., 231,780; Nader, Green, 24,540; Buchanan, Ind., 3,646; Browne, LB., 2,245; Hagelin, Natural Law, 478; Phillips, Ind., 468.
1996: Dole, R., 363,467; Clinton, D., 236,761; Perot, RF., 71,278; Browne, LB., 2,792; Phillips, Ind., 1,928; Hagelin, Natural Law, 1,189.
1992: Bush, R., 343,678; Clinton, D., 216,864; Perot, Ind., 174,104; Marrou, LB., 1,340.
1988: Bush, R., 397,956; Dukakis, D., 259,235; Paul, LB., 2,534; Fulani, New Alliance, 1,740.
1984: Reagan, R., 459,135; Mondale, D., 187,475; Bergland, LB., 2,075.
1980: Reagan, R., 419,214; Carter, D., 166,424; Anderson, Ind., 44,854; Clark, LB., 9,041.
1976: Ford, R., 359,219; Carter, D., 233,287; McCarthy, Ind., 9,383; Maddox, Amer. Ind., 3,378; MacBride, LB., 1,476.
1972: Nixon, R., 406,298; McGovern, D., 169,991; scattered, 817.

1968: Nixon, R., 321,163; Humphrey, D., 170,784; Wallace, 3rd party, 44,904.
1964: Johnson, D., 307,307; Goldwater, R., 276,847.
1960: Nixon, R., 380,553; Kennedy, D., 232,542.

Nevada

County	2012 Obama (D)	Romney (R)	2008 Obama (D)	McCain (R)
Churchill	2,961	7,061	3,494	6,832
Clark	389,936	289,053	380,765	257,078
Douglas	9,297	16,276	10,672	14,648
Elko	3,511	12,014	4,541	10,969
Esmeralda	92	317	104	303
Eureka	107	663	144	564
Humboldt	1,737	3,810	1,909	3,586
Lander	534	1,580	577	1,466
Lincoln	400	1,691	518	1,498
Lyon	7,380	13,520	8,405	12,154
Mineral	863	1,080	1,082	1,131
Nye	6,320	10,566	7,226	9,537
Pershing	632	1,167	673	1,075
Storey	920	1,321	1,102	1,247
Washoe	95,409	88,453	99,671	76,880
White Pine	983	2,601	1,230	2,440
City				
Carson City	10,291	12,394	11,623	11,419
Totals	531,373	463,567	533,736	412,827

Nevada Vote Since 1960

2012: Obama, D., 531,373; Romney, R., 463,567; Johnson, LB., 10,968; None of These Candidates, 5,770; Goode, Ind. Amer., 3,240.
2008: Obama, D., 533,736; McCain, R., 412,827; None of These Candidates, 6,267; Nader, Ind., 6,150; Barr, LB., 4,263; Baldwin, Const., 3,194; McKinney, Green, 1,411.
2004: Bush, R., 418,690; Kerry, D., 397,190; Nader, Ind., 4,838; None of These Candidates, 3,688; Badnarik, LB., 3,176; Peroutka, Ind. Amer., 1,152; Cobb, Green, 853.
2000: Bush, R., 301,575; Gore, D., 279,978; Nader, Green, 15,008; Buchanan, Citizens First, 4,747; None of These Candidates, 3,315; Browne, LB., 3,311; Phillips, Ind. Amer., 621; Hagelin, Natural Law, 415.
1996: Clinton, D., 203,974; Dole, R., 199,244; Perot, RF., 43,986; None of These Candidates, 5,608; Nader, Green, 4,730; Browne, LB., 4,460; Phillips, Ind. Amer., 1,732; Hagelin, Natural Law, 545.
1992: Clinton, D., 189,148; Bush, R., 175,828; Perot, Ind., 132,580; Gritz, Populist/America First, 2,892; Marrou, LB., 1,835.
1988: Bush, R., 206,040; Dukakis, D., 132,738; Paul, LB., 3,520; Fulani, New Alliance, 835.
1984: Reagan, R., 188,770; Mondale, D., 91,655; Bergland, LB., 2,292.
1980: Reagan, R., 155,017; Carter, D., 66,666; Anderson, Ind., 17,651; Clark, LB., 4,358.
1976: Ford, R., 101,273; Carter, D., 92,479; MacBride, LB., 1,519; Maddox, Amer. Ind., 1,497; scattered, 5,108.
1972: Nixon, R., 115,750; McGovern, D., 66,016.
1968: Nixon, R., 73,188; Humphrey, D., 60,598; Wallace, 3rd party, 20,432.
1964: Johnson, D., 79,339; Goldwater, R., 56,094.
1960: Kennedy, D., 54,880; Nixon, R., 52,387.

New Hampshire

County	2012 Obama (D)	Romney (R)	2008 Obama (D)	McCain (R)
Belknap	15,890	17,571	16,796	16,402
Carroll	13,977	14,207	15,221	13,387
Cheshire	25,380	15,156	26,971	15,205
Coos	9,095	6,342	9,532	6,558
Grafton	29,826	18,208	31,446	17,687
Hillsborough	102,303	99,991	104,820	97,178
Merrimack	44,756	34,524	45,078	34,010
Rockingham	80,142	87,921	83,723	81,917
Strafford	36,026	26,729	37,990	25,021
Sullivan	12,166	9,269	13,249	9,169
Totals	369,561	329,918	384,826	316,534

New Hampshire Vote Since 1960

2012: Obama, D., 369,561; Romney, R., 329,918; Johnson, LB., 8,212; Goode, Const., 708.
2008: Obama, D., 384,826; McCain, R., 316,534; Nader, Ind., 3,503; Barr, LB., 2,217; Phillies, LB., 531.
2004: Kerry, D., 340,511; Bush, R., 331,237; Nader, Ind., 4,479.
2000: Bush, R., 273,559; Gore, D., 266,348; Nader, Green, 22,198; Browne, LB., 2,757; Buchanan, Independence, 2,615; Phillips, Const., 328.

1996: Clinton, D., 246,166; Dole, R., 196,486; Perot, RF., 48,387; Browne, LB., 4,214; Phillips, Taxpayers, 1,344.
1992: Clinton, D., 209,040; Bush, R., 202,484; Perot, Ind., 121,337; Marrou, LB., 3,548.
1988: Bush, R., 281,537; Dukakis, D., 163,696; Paul, LB., 4,502; Fulani, New Alliance, 790.
1984: Reagan, R., 267,051; Mondale, D., 120,377; Bergland, LB., 735.
1980: Reagan, R., 221,705; Carter, D., 108,864; Anderson, Ind., 49,693; Clark, LB., 2,067; Commoner, Citizens, 1,325; Hall, Comm., 129; Griswold, Workers World, 76; DeBerry, Soc. Workers, 72; scattered, 68.
1976: Ford, R., 185,935; Carter, D., 147,645; McCarthy, Ind., 4,095; MacBride, LB., 936; Reagan, write-in, 388; LaRouche, U.S. Labor, 186; Camejo, Soc. Workers, 161; Levin, Soc. Labor, 66; scattered, 215.
1972: Nixon, R., 213,724; McGovern, D., 116,435; Schmitz, Amer., 3,386; Jenness, Soc. Workers, 368; scattered, 142.
1968: Nixon, R., 154,903; Humphrey, D., 130,589; Wallace, 3rd party, 11,173; New Party, 421; Halstead, Soc. Workers, 104.
1964: Johnson, D., 182,065; Goldwater, R., 104,029.
1960: Nixon, R., 157,989; Kennedy, D., 137,772.

New Jersey

County	2012		2008	
	Obama (D)	Romney (R)	Obama (D)	McCain (R)
Atlantic	65,640	46,522	67,830	49,902
Bergen	212,754	169,070	225,367	186,118
Burlington	126,377	87,401	131,219	89,626
Camden	153,682	69,476	159,259	73,819
Cape May	21,657	25,781	22,893	27,288
Cumberland	34,055	20,658	34,919	22,360
Essex	236,618	64,406	240,306	74,063
Gloucester	74,013	59,456	77,267	60,315
Hudson	153,108	42,369	154,140	55,360
Hunterdon	26,876	38,687	29,776	39,092
Mercer	104,377	47,355	107,926	50,223
Middlesex	190,555	107,310	193,812	123,695
Monmouth	133,145	147,513	148,737	160,433
Morris	100,146	124,947	112,275	132,331
Ocean	102,300	146,474	110,189	160,677
Passaic	115,926	64,523	113,257	72,552
Salem	14,719	14,334	16,044	14,816
Somerset	74,592	66,603	79,321	70,085
Sussex	26,104	40,625	28,840	44,184
Union	139,752	68,314	141,417	78,768
Warren	18,745	25,744	20,628	27,500
Totals	**2,125,101**	**1,477,568**	**2,215,422**	**1,613,207**

New Jersey Vote Since 1960

2012: Obama, D., 2,125,101; Romney, R., 1,477,568; Johnson, LB., 21,045; Stein, Green, 9,888; Goode, Const., 2,064; Anderson, Justice, 1,724; Boss, Ind., 1,007; Harris, Soc. Workers, 710; Miller, A3P, 664; Lindsay, Socialism/Liberation, 521.
2008: Obama, D., 2,215,422; McCain, R., 1,613,207; Nader, Ind., 21,298; Barr, Ind., 8,441; Baldwin, Ind., 3,956; McKinney, Ind., 3,636; Moore, Ind., 699; Boss, Ind., 639; Calero, Ind., 523; La Riva, Ind., 416.
2004: Kerry, D., 1,911,430; Bush, R., 1,670,003; Nader, Ind., 19,418; Badnarik, Ind., 4,514; Peroutka, Ind., 2,750; Cobb, Ind., 1,807; Brown, Ind., 664; Van Auken, Ind., 575; Calero, Ind., 530.
2000: Gore, D., 1,788,850; Bush, R., 1,284,173; Nader, Ind., 94,554; Buchanan, Ind., 6,989; Browne, Ind., 6,312; Hagelin, Ind., 2,215; McReynolds, Ind., 1,880; Phillips, Ind., 1,409; Harris, Ind., 844.
1996: Clinton, D., 1,652,361; Dole, R., 1,103,099; Perot, RF., 262,134; Nader, Green, 32,465; Browne, LB., 14,763; Hagelin, Natural Law, 3,887; Phillips, U.S. Taxpayers, 3,440; Harris, Soc. Workers, 1,837; Moorehead, Workers World, 1,337; White, Soc. Equality, 537.
1992: Clinton, D., 1,436,206; Bush, R., 1,356,865; Perot, Ind., 521,829; Marrou, LB., 6,822; Fulani, New Alliance, 3,513; Phillips, U.S. Taxpayers, 2,670; LaRouche, Ind., 2,095; Warren, Soc. Workers, 2,011; Daniels, Ind., 1,996; Gritz, Populist/America First, 1,867; Hagelin, Natural Law, 1,353.
1988: Bush, R., 1,740,604; Dukakis, D., 1,317,541; Lewin, Peace/Freedom, 9,953; Paul, LB., 8,421.
1984: Reagan, R., 1,933,630; Mondale, D., 1,261,323; Bergland, LB., 6,416.
1980: Reagan, R., 1,546,557; Carter, D., 1,147,364; Anderson, Ind., 234,632; Clark, LB., 20,652; Commoner, Citizens, 8,203; McCormack, Right to Life, 3,927; Lynen, Middle Class, 3,694; Hall, Comm., 2,555; Pulley, Soc. Workers, 2,198; McReynolds, Soc., 1,973; Gahres, Down With Lawyers, 1,718; Griswold, Workers World, 1,288; Wendelken, Ind., 923.
1976: Ford, R., 1,509,688; Carter, D., 1,444,653; McCarthy, Ind., 32,717; MacBride, LB., 9,449; Maddox, Amer., 7,716; Levin,

Soc. Labor, 3,686; Hall, Comm., 1,662; LaRouche, U.S. Labor, 1,650; Camejo, Soc. Workers, 1,184; Wright, People's, 1,044; Bubar, Prohib., 554; Zeidler, Soc., 469.
1972: Nixon, R., 1,845,502; McGovern, D., 1,102,211; Schmitz, Amer., 34,378; Spock, People's, 5,355; Fisher, Soc. Labor, 4,544; Jenness, Soc. Workers, 2,233; Mahalchik, Amer. First, 1,743; Hall, Comm., 1,263.
1968: Nixon, R., 1,325,467; Humphrey, D., 1,264,206; Wallace, 3rd party, 262,187; Halstead, Soc. Workers, 8,667; Gregory, Peace/Freedom, 8,084; Blomen, Soc. Labor, 6,784.
1964: Johnson, D., 1,867,671; Goldwater, R., 963,843; DeBerry, Soc. Workers, 8,181; Hass, Soc. Labor, 7,075.
1960: Kennedy, D., 1,385,415; Nixon, R., 1,363,324; Dobbs, Soc. Workers, 11,402; Lee, Conservative, 8,708; Hass, Soc. Labor, 4,262.

New Mexico

County	2012		2008	
	Obama (D)	Romney (R)	Obama (D)	McCain (R)
Bernalillo	150,739	106,408	171,556	110,521
Catron	560	1,494	664	1,398
Chaves	6,604	13,088	8,197	13,651
Cibola	4,961	2,998	5,827	3,131
Colfax	2,828	2,699	3,490	2,805
Curry	4,022	9,251	4,670	9,599
De Baca	287	586	359	676
Doña Ana	37,139	27,322	40,282	28,068
Eddy	6,142	12,583	7,351	12,500
Grant	7,090	5,358	8,142	5,406
Guadalupe	1,488	557	1,557	620
Harding	260	327	260	358
Hidalgo	995	899	993	936
Lea	4,080	12,548	5,108	13,347
Lincoln	2,942	5,961	3,535	6,001
Los Alamos	5,191	4,796	5,824	5,064
Luna	3,583	3,670	4,311	3,870
McKinley	15,841	5,546	16,572	6,382
Mora	1,955	595	2,168	569
Otero	6,829	12,451	8,610	12,806
Quay	1,383	2,202	1,547	2,367
Rio Arriba	11,465	3,397	12,703	4,086
Roosevelt	1,727	4,043	2,303	4,311
San Juan	15,855	28,849	18,028	27,869
San Miguel	8,850	2,303	10,320	2,478
Sandoval	27,236	24,387	32,669	25,193
Santa Fe	50,872	15,500	55,567	15,807
Sierra	1,964	2,928	2,352	3,017
Socorro	4,058	2,722	4,696	3,032
Taos	11,978	2,730	13,816	2,866
Torrance	2,428	3,529	3,087	3,735
Union	472	1,236	492	1,227
Valencia	13,511	12,825	15,366	13,136
Totals	**415,335**	**335,788**	**472,422**	**346,832**

New Mexico Vote Since 1960

2012: Obama, D., 415,335; Romney, R., 335,788; Johnson, LB., 27,788; Stein, Green, 2,691; Anderson, Ind., 1,174; Goode, Const., 982.
2008: Obama, D., 472,422; McCain, R., 346,832; Nader, Ind., 5,327; Barr, LB., 2,428; Baldwin, Const., 1,597; McKinney, Green, 1,552.
2004: Bush, R., 376,930; Kerry, D., 370,942; Nader, Ind., 4,053; Badnarik, LB., 2,382; Cobb, Green, 1,226; Peroutka, Const., 771.
2000: Gore, D., 286,783; Bush, R., 286,417; Nader, Green, 21,251; Browne, LB., 2,058; Buchanan, RF., 1,392; Hagelin, Natural Law, 361; Phillips, Const., 343.
1996: Clinton, D., 273,495; Dole, R., 232,751; Perot, RF., 32,257; Nader, Green, 13,218; Browne, LB., 2,996; Phillips, Taxpayers, 713; Hagelin, Natural Law, 644.
1992: Clinton, D., 261,617; Bush, R., 212,824; Perot, Ind., 91,895; Marrou, LB., 1,615.
1988: Bush, R., 270,341; Dukakis, D., 244,497; Paul, LB., 3,268; Fulani, New Alliance, 2,237.
1984: Reagan, R., 307,101; Mondale, D., 201,769; Bergland, LB., 4,459.
1980: Reagan, R., 250,779; Carter, D., 167,826; Anderson, Ind., 29,459; Clark, LB., 4,365; Commoner, Citizens, 2,202; Bubar, Statesman, 1,281; Pulley, Soc. Workers, 325.
1976: Ford, R., 211,419; Carter, D., 201,148; Camejo, Soc. Workers, 2,462; MacBride, LB., 1,110; Zeidler, Soc., 240; Bubar, Prohib., 211.
1972: Nixon, R., 235,606; McGovern, D., 141,084; Schmitz, Amer., 8,767; Jenness, Soc. Workers, 474.
1968: Nixon, R., 169,692; Humphrey, D., 130,081; Wallace, 3rd party, 25,737; Chavez, 1,519; Halstead, Soc. Workers, 252.
1964: Johnson, D., 194,017; Goldwater, R., 131,838; Hass, Soc. Labor, 1,217; Munn, Prohib., 543.
1960: Kennedy, D., 156,027; Nixon, R., 153,733; Decker, Prohib., 777; Hass, Soc. Labor, 570.

New York

County	2012 Obama (D)	Romney (R)	2008 Obama (D)	McCain (R)
Albany	83,979	40,210	93,937	50,586
Allegany	5,866	9,377	7,016	11,013
Bronx[1]	334,642	26,682	338,261	41,683
Broome	39,971	34,708	47,204	40,077
Cattaraugus	12,040	14,655	14,307	17,770
Cayuga	16,105	11,646	18,128	15,243
Chautauqua	22,463	24,266	29,129	28,579
Chemung	16,205	16,138	18,888	19,364
Chenango	8,642	8,922	10,100	10,337
Clinton	18,072	9,892	20,216	12,579
Columbia	15,241	10,600	17,556	13,337
Cortland	9,965	7,859	11,861	9,678
Delaware	7,881	9,086	9,462	10,524
Dutchess	62,063	48,264	71,060	59,628
Erie	227,325	149,683	256,299	178,815
Essex	9,368	6,076	10,390	7,913
Franklin	9,532	5,231	10,571	6,676
Fulton	8,331	9,830	9,695	11,709
Genesee	9,092	12,814	10,762	15,705
Greene	8,485	9,811	9,850	12,059
Hamilton	1,092	1,771	1,225	2,141
Herkimer	10,826	12,166	12,094	14,619
Jefferson	16,231	16,435	18,166	20,220
Kings (Brooklyn)[1]	585,491	113,752	603,525	151,872
Lewis	4,530	5,129	4,986	5,969
Livingston	11,100	12,641	13,655	16,030
Madison	13,231	12,011	14,692	14,434
Monroe	185,916	114,434	207,371	144,262
Montgomery	8,106	8,046	9,080	10,711
Nassau	294,661	237,862	342,185	288,776
New York (Manhattan)[1]	488,632	85,245	572,126	89,906
Niagara	41,837	38,158	47,303	46,348
Oneida	39,031	40,532	43,506	49,256
Onondaga	117,470	69,357	129,317	84,972
Ontario	22,065	20,919	25,103	25,171
Orange	70,742	58,003	78,326	72,042
Orleans	5,505	7,585	6,614	9,708
Oswego	22,178	17,610	24,777	23,571
Otsego	11,530	10,451	13,570	12,026
Putnam	18,539	20,925	21,613	25,145
Queens[1]	461,545	108,821	480,692	155,221
Rensselaer	35,373	24,903	39,753	32,840
Richmond (Staten Island)[1]	75,565	66,919	79,311	86,062
Rockland	63,908	51,976	69,543	61,752
St. Lawrence	20,488	13,543	23,706	16,956
Saratoga	50,998	44,915	56,645	52,855
Schenectady	35,330	22,952	38,611	29,758
Schoharie	5,119	6,497	6,009	8,071
Schuyler	3,444	3,798	3,933	4,542
Seneca	6,715	5,244	7,422	7,038
Steuben	15,015	20,163	17,148	24,203
Suffolk	292,238	246,044	346,549	307,021
Sullivan	14,612	11,347	16,850	13,900
Tioga	8,544	11,160	10,172	12,536
Tompkins	24,872	10,191	29,826	11,927
Ulster	44,480	26,123	54,320	33,300
Warren	14,276	12,925	16,281	15,429
Washington	10,993	9,793	12,741	12,533
Wayne	15,732	17,248	18,184	22,239
Westchester	234,778	131,139	261,810	147,824
Wyoming	5,357	9,248	6,379	10,998
Yates	4,259	4,269	4,890	5,269
Totals	**4,337,622**	**2,228,060**	**4,804,945**	**2,752,771**

(1) Borough of New York City.

New York Vote Since 1960

2012: Obama, D., 4,337,662; Romney, R., 2,228,060; Johnson, LB., 47,256; Stein, Green, 39,982; Goode, Const., 6,274; Lindsay, Socialism/Liberation, 2,050.
2008: Obama, D., 4,804,945; McCain, R., 2,752,771; Nader, Populist, 41,249; Barr, LB., 19,596; McKinney, Green, 12,801; Calero, Soc. Workers, 3,615; La Riva, Socialism/Liberation, 1,639.
2004: Kerry, D., 4,314,280; Bush, R., 2,962,567; Nader, Ind., 99,873; Badnarik, LB., 11,607; Calero, Soc. Workers, 2,405.
2000: Gore, D., 4,112,965; Bush, R., 2,405,570; Nader, Green, 244,360; Buchanan, RF., 31,554; Hagelin, Independence, 24,369; Browne, LB., 7,664; Harris, Soc. Workers, 1,790; Phillips, Const., 1,503.
1996: Clinton, D., 3,756,177; Dole, R., 1,933,492; Perot, RF., 503,458; Nader, Green, 75,956; Phillips, Right to Life, 23,580; Browne, LB., 12,220; Hagelin, Natural Law, 5,011; Moorehead, Workers World, 3,473; Harris, Soc. Workers, 2,762.
1992: Clinton, D., 3,444,450; Bush, R., 2,346,649; Perot, Ind., 1,090,721; Warren, Soc. Workers, 15,472; Marrou, LB., 13,451; Fulani, New Alliance, 11,318; Hagelin, Natural Law, 4,420.
1988: Dukakis, D., 3,347,882; Bush, R., 3,081,871; Marra, Right to Life, 20,497; Fulani, New Alliance, 15,845.
1984: Reagan, R., 3,664,763; Mondale, D., 3,119,609; Bergland, LB., 11,949.
1980: Reagan, R., 2,893,831; Carter, D., 2,728,372; Anderson, Liberal, 467,801; Clark, LB., 52,648; McCormack, Right to Life, 24,159; Commoner, Citizens, 23,186; Hall, Comm., 7,414; DeBerry, Soc. Workers, 2,068; Griswold, Workers World, 1,416; scattered, 1,064.
1976: Carter, D., 3,389,558; Ford, R., 3,100,791; MacBride, LB., 12,197; Hall, Comm., 10,270; Camejo, Soc. Workers, 6,996; LaRouche, U.S. Labor, 5,413; blank, void, and scattered, 143,037.
1972: Nixon, R., 3,824,642; McGovern, D., 2,767,956 and Liberal, 183,128 (total, 2,951,084); Reed, Soc. Workers, 7,797; Fisher, Soc. Labor, 4,530; Hall, Comm., 5,641; blank, void, and scattered, 161,641.
1968: Humphrey, D., 3,378,470; Nixon, R., 3,007,932; Wallace, 3rd party, 358,864; Gregory, Peace/Freedom, 24,517; Halstead, Soc. Workers, 11,851; Blomen, Soc. Labor, 8,432; blank, void, and scattered, 171,624.
1964: Johnson, D., 4,913,156; Goldwater, R., 2,243,559; Hass, Soc. Labor, 6,085; DeBerry, Soc. Workers, 3,215; scattered, 188; blank and void, 151,383.
1960: Kennedy, D., 3,423,909 and Liberal, 406,176 (total, 3,830,085); Nixon, R., 3,446,419; Dobbs, Soc. Workers, 14,319; scattered, 256; blank and void, 88,896.

North Carolina

County	2012 Obama (D)	Romney (R)	2008 Obama (D)	McCain (R)
Alamance	28,875	38,170	28,918	34,859
Alexander	4,611	12,253	5,167	11,790
Alleghany	1,583	3,390	2,021	3,124
Anson	7,019	4,166	6,456	4,207
Ashe	4,116	8,242	4,872	7,916
Avery	1,882	5,766	2,178	5,681
Beaufort	9,435	13,977	9,454	13,460
Bertie	6,695	3,387	6,365	3,376
Bladen	8,062	7,748	7,853	7,532
Brunswick	22,038	34,743	21,331	30,753
Buncombe	70,625	54,701	69,716	52,494
Burke	13,701	22,267	14,901	22,102
Cabarrus	32,849	49,557	31,546	45,924
Caldwell	10,898	23,229	12,081	22,526
Camden	1,508	3,109	1,597	3,140
Cartaret	10,301	24,775	11,130	23,131
Caswell	5,348	5,594	5,545	5,208
Catawba	24,069	44,538	25,656	42,993
Chatham	18,361	16,665	17,862	14,668
Cherokee	3,378	9,278	3,785	8,643
Chowan	3,556	3,891	3,688	3,773
Clay	1,579	3,973	1,734	3,707
Cleveland	17,062	25,793	17,363	26,078
Columbus	11,050	12,941	11,076	12,994
Craven	18,763	26,928	19,352	24,901
Cumberland	75,792	50,666	74,693	52,151
Currituck	3,562	7,496	3,737	7,234
Dare	7,393	10,248	8,074	9,745
Davidson	20,624	49,383	22,433	45,419
Davie	5,735	14,687	6,178	13,981
Duplin	9,033	11,416	8,958	10,834
Durham	111,224	33,769	103,456	32,353
Edgecombe	18,310	8,546	17,403	8,445
Forsyth	92,323	79,768	91,085	73,674
Franklin	13,436	14,603	13,085	13,273
Gaston	33,171	56,138	31,384	52,507
Gates	2,786	2,564	2,830	2,547
Graham	1,119	2,750	1,265	2,824
Granville	13,598	12,405	13,074	11,447
Greene	3,778	4,411	3,796	4,272
Guilford	146,365	104,789	142,101	97,718
Halifax	17,176	8,763	16,047	8,961
Harnett	17,331	25,565	16,785	23,579
Haywood	11,833	15,633	12,730	14,910
Henderson	18,642	32,994	20,082	30,930
Hertford	7,843	3,007	7,513	3,089
Hoke	10,076	6,819	9,227	6,293
Hyde	1,163	1,193	1,241	1,212
Iredell	26,076	49,299	27,318	45,148
Jackson	8,095	8,254	8,766	7,854
Johnston	27,290	48,427	26,795	43,622
Jones	2,352	2,837	2,378	2,817
Lee	10,801	13,158	10,784	12,775
Lenoir	13,948	13,980	13,378	13,401
Lincoln	11,024	25,267	11,713	23,631

County	2012 Obama (D)	Romney (R)	2008 Obama (D)	McCain (R)
Macon	5,712	10,835	6,620	10,317
Madison	4,484	5,404	5,026	5,192
Martin	6,583	5,995	6,539	5,957
McDowell	6,031	11,775	6,571	11,534
Mecklenburg	272,262	171,668	253,958	153,848
Mitchell	1,838	5,806	2,238	5,499
Montgomery	4,706	6,404	4,926	6,155
Moore	16,505	29,495	17,624	27,314
Nash	24,313	23,842	23,099	23,728
New Hanover	48,668	53,385	49,145	50,544
Northampton	7,232	3,483	6,903	3,671
Onslow	18,490	32,243	19,499	30,278
Orange	53,901	21,539	53,806	20,266
Pamlico	2,647	4,051	2,838	3,823
Pasquotank	10,282	7,633	10,272	7,778
Pender	9,632	14,617	9,907	13,618
Perquimans	2,759	3,822	2,772	3,678
Person	8,418	10,496	8,446	10,030
Pitt	41,843	36,214	40,501	33,927
Polk	4,013	6,236	4,396	5,990
Randolph	14,773	45,160	16,414	40,998
Richmond	9,904	9,332	9,713	9,424
Robeson	24,988	17,510	23,058	17,433
Rockingham	16,351	25,227	17,255	23,899
Rowan	22,650	38,775	23,391	37,451
Rutherford	9,374	18,954	9,641	18,769
Sampson	11,566	14,422	11,836	14,038
Scotland	8,215	5,831	8,151	6,005
Stanly	8,431	19,904	8,878	19,329
Stokes	6,018	15,237	6,875	14,488
Surry	9,112	19,923	10,475	18,730
Swain	2,618	2,976	2,806	2,900
Transylvania	6,826	9,634	7,275	9,401
Tyrrell	837	930	933	960
Union	32,473	61,107	31,189	54,123
Vance	13,323	7,429	13,166	7,606
Wake	267,262	211,596	250,891	187,001
Warren	-6,978	3,140	7,086	3,063
Washington	3,833	2,622	3,748	2,670
Watauga	13,002	13,861	14,558	13,344
Wayne	23,314	27,641	22,671	26,952
Wilkes	8,148	20,515	8,934	20,288
Wilson	20,875	17,954	19,652	17,375
Yadkin	3,957	12,578	4,527	12,409
Yancey	3,981	5,278	4,486	5,045
Totals	**2,178,391**	**2,270,395**	**2,142,651**	**2,128,474**

North Carolina Vote Since 1960

2012: Romney, R., 2,270,395; Obama, D., 2,178,391; Johnson, LB., 44,515.

2008: Obama, D., 2,142,651; McCain, R., 2,128,474; Barr, LB., 25,722.

2004: Bush, R., 1,961,166; Kerry, D., 1,525,849; Badnarik, LB., 11,731.

2000: Bush, R., 1,631,163; Gore, D., 1,257,692; Browne, LB., 13,891; Buchanan, RF., 8,874.

1996: Dole, R., 1,225,938; Clinton, D., 1,107,849; Perot, RF., 168,059; Browne, LB., 8,740; Hagelin, Natural Law, 2,771.

1992: Bush, R., 1,134,661; Clinton, D., 1,114,042; Perot, Ind., 357,864; Marrou, LB., 5,171.

1988: Bush, R., 1,237,258; Dukakis, D., 890,167; Fulani, New Alliance, 5,682; Paul, write-in, 1,263.

1984: Reagan, R., 1,346,481; Mondale, D., 824,287; Bergland, LB., 3,794.

1980: Reagan, R., 915,018; Carter, D., 875,635; Anderson, Ind., 52,800; Clark, LB., 9,677; Commoner, Citizens, 2,287; DeBerry, Soc. Workers, 416.

1976: Carter, D., 927,365; Ford, R., 741,960; Anderson, Amer., 5,607; MacBride, LB., 2,219; LaRouche, U.S. Labor, 755.

1972: Nixon, R., 1,054,889; McGovern, D., 438,705; Schmitz, Amer., 25,018.

1968: Nixon, R., 627,192; Wallace, 3rd party, 496,188; Humphrey, D., 464,113.

1964: Johnson, D., 800,139; Goldwater, R., 624,844.

1960: Kennedy, D., 713,136; Nixon, R., 655,420.

North Dakota

County	2012 Obama (D)	Romney (R)	2008 Obama (D)	McCain (R)
Adams	328	918	435	788
Barnes	2,394	2,964	2,741	2,826
Benson	1,235	868	1,569	773
Billings	89	472	114	375
Bottineau	1,183	2,280	1,387	2,059
Bowman	414	1,280	478	1,107
Burke	230	769	286	640
Burleigh	14,122	27,951	15,600	25,443

County	2012 Obama (D)	Romney (R)	2008 Obama (D)	McCain (R)
Cass	34,712	36,855	37,622	32,566
Cavalier	818	1,195	930	1,128
Dickey	853	1,610	1,044	1,525
Divide	385	733	464	630
Dunn	508	1,506	527	1,080
Eddy	486	634	583	548
Emmons	383	1,435	546	1,230
Foster	607	1,030	687	914
Golden Valley	162	742	210	642
Grand Forks	14,032	15,060	16,104	14,520
Grant	334	1,025	280	587
Griggs	536	771	598	682
Hettinger	313	1,000	406	893
Kidder	393	870	422	752
LaMoure	740	1,377	868	1,310
Logan	232	810	299	726
McHenry	943	1,678	981	1,374
McIntosh	459	1,035	579	916
McKenzie	927	2,458	933	1,740
McLean	1,670	3,141	1,867	2,767
Mercer	1,166	3,152	1,476	2,789
Morton	4,469	8,680	5,079	7,869
Mountrail	1,403	1,962	1,477	1,406
Nelson	767	865	907	800
Oliver	281	693	332	682
Pembina	1,253	1,899	1,494	1,722
Pierce	660	1,465	792	1,301
Ramsey	2,164	2,665	2,314	2,361
Ransom	1,343	1,009	1,371	998
Renville	398	851	505	799
Richland	3,198	4,229	3,513	3,900
Rolette	3,353	1,092	3,403	1,045
Sargent	1,075	879	1,115	778
Sheridan	163	642	229	555
Sioux	900	225	1,145	215
Slope	83	341	106	297
Stark	2,812	8,521	3,802	7,024
Steele	518	498	614	404
Stutsman	3,585	5,685	4,056	5,499
Towner	516	623	621	536
Traill	1,811	1,996	2,136	1,845
Walsh	1,985	2,656	2,325	2,415
Ward	8,441	16,230	10,144	15,061
Wells	673	1,654	841	1,468
Williams	2,322	7,184	2,921	6,291
Totals	**124,827**	**188,163**	**141,278**	**168,601**

North Dakota Vote Since 1960

2012: Romney, R., 188,163; Obama, D., 124,827; Johnson, LB., 5,231; Stein, Green, 1,361; Goode, Const., 1,185.

2008: McCain, R., 168,601; Obama, D., 141,278; Nader, Ind., 4,189; Barr, LB., 1,354; Baldwin, Const., 1,199.

2004: Bush, R., 196,651; Kerry, D., 111,052; Nader, Ind., 3,756; Badnarik, LB., 851; Peroutka, Const., 514.

2000: Bush, R., 174,852; Gore, D., 95,284; Nader, Ind., 9,486; Buchanan, RF., 7,288; Browne, Ind., 660; Phillips, Const., 373; Hagelin, Ind., 313.

1996: Dole, R., 125,050; Clinton, D., 106,905; Perot, RF., 32,515; Browne, LB., 847; Phillips, Ind., 745; Hagelin, Natural Law, 349.

1992: Bush, R., 136,244; Clinton, D., 99,168; Perot, Ind., 71,084.

1988: Bush, R., 166,559; Dukakis, D., 127,739; Paul, LB., 1,315; LaRouche, Natl. Econ. Recovery, 905.

1984: Reagan, R., 200,336; Mondale, D., 104,429; Bergland, LB., 703.

1980: Reagan, R., 193,695; Carter, D., 79,189; Anderson, Ind., 23,640; Clark, LB., 3,743; Commoner, LB., 429; McLain, Natl. People's League, 296; Greaves, Amer., 235; Hall, Comm., 93; DeBerry, Soc. Workers, 89; McReynolds, Soc., 82; Bubar, Statesman, 54.

1976: Ford, R., 153,470; Carter, D., 136,078; Anderson, Amer., 3,698; McCarthy, Ind., 2,952; Maddox, Amer. Ind., 269; MacBride, LB., 256; scattered, 371.

1972: Nixon, R., 174,109; McGovern, D., 100,384; Schmitz, Amer., 5,646; Jenness, Soc. Workers, 288; Hall, Comm., 87.

1968: Nixon, R., 138,669; Humphrey, D., 94,769; Wallace, 3rd party, 14,244; Halstead, Soc. Workers, 128; Munn, Prohib., 38; Troxell, Ind., 34.

1964: Johnson, D., 149,784; Goldwater, R., 108,207; DeBerry, Soc. Workers, 224; Munn, Prohib., 174.

1960: Nixon, R., 154,310; Kennedy, D., 123,963; Dobbs, Soc. Workers, 158.

Ohio

County	2012 Obama (D)	Romney (R)	2008 Obama (D)	McCain (R)
Adams	3,976	6,865	4,170	6,914
Allen	17,914	29,502	19,521	29,941
Ashland	8,281	15,519	9,300	15,158

County	2012 Obama (D)	Romney (R)	2008 Obama (D)	McCain (R)
Ashtabula	23,803	18,298	25,027	18,949
Athens	18,307	8,543	20,722	9,742
Auglaize	5,831	17,169	6,727	16,395
Belmont	14,156	16,758	16,302	15,422
Brown	7,107	11,916	7,503	12,192
Butler	62,388	105,176	66,030	105,340
Carroll	5,543	7,315	6,423	7,097
Champaign	7,044	11,045	7,385	11,141
Clark	31,298	31,816	31,958	33,634
Clermont	30,458	64,208	31,611	62,559
Clinton	5,791	12,009	6,558	12,410
Columbiana	19,821	25,251	21,882	25,585
Coshocton	6,940	8,390	7,689	8,675
Crawford	7,507	11,852	8,288	12,316
Cuyahoga	447,273	190,660	458,204	199,864
Darke	6,826	18,108	7,964	17,290
Defiance	7,732	10,176	8,399	10,407
Delaware	37,292	60,194	36,653	54,778
Erie	21,793	16,952	23,148	17,432
Fairfield	29,890	41,034	29,250	41,580
Fayette	4,249	6,620	4,401	7,102
Franklin	346,373	215,597	334,684	218,478
Fulton	9,073	11,738	9,900	11,689
Gallia	4,557	7,750	4,777	8,247
Geauga	19,659	30,589	21,250	29,096
Greene	32,256	49,819	33,540	48,936
Guernsey	7,450	8,993	7,625	9,197
Hamilton	219,927	193,326	224,644	195,107
Hancock	12,564	22,443	13,870	22,420
Hardin	4,619	7,489	5,013	7,749
Harrison	2,950	4,019	3,683	3,872
Henry	5,658	8,257	6,320	8,239
Highland	6,054	11,413	6,857	11,908
Hocking	6,157	6,285	6,231	6,326
Holmes	2,608	8,702	3,141	7,720
Huron	11,006	13,060	12,076	12,884
Jackson	5,166	7,904	5,397	8,219
Jefferson	15,385	17,034	17,635	17,559
Knox	10,470	17,266	11,014	16,640
Lake	57,680	58,744	60,155	59,142
Lawrence	10,744	14,651	11,262	15,415
Licking	34,201	45,503	33,896	46,886
Logan	7,062	13,663	7,936	13,848
Lorain	81,464	59,405	85,276	59,068
Lucas	136,616	69,940	142,852	73,706
Madison	6,845	10,342	6,532	10,603
Mahoning	77,059	42,641	79,173	45,319
Marion	12,504	14,265	12,870	15,454
Medina	38,785	50,418	40,924	48,189
Meigs	4,027	5,895	4,094	6,015
Mercer	4,745	16,561	5,853	15,100
Miami	16,383	34,606	18,372	33,417
Monroe	3,035	3,548	3,705	3,066
Montgomery	137,139	124,841	145,997	128,679
Morgan	2,814	3,179	2,966	3,440
Morrow	5,933	9,865	6,177	10,067
Muskingum	17,002	19,264	17,730	20,549
Noble	2,131	3,563	2,474	3,450
Ottawa	11,503	10,538	12,049	10,618
Paulding	3,538	5,354	4,165	5,317
Perry	7,033	7,627	7,261	7,721
Pickaway	9,684	14,037	9,077	14,228
Pike	5,684	5,685	6,033	6,162
Portage	39,453	35,242	41,856	34,822
Preble	6,211	13,535	6,999	13,562
Putnam	4,318	13,721	5,281	13,072
Richland	22,687	33,867	25,727	34,034
Ross	14,569	15,008	14,455	16,759
Sandusky	14,541	13,755	15,601	14,190
Scioto	15,077	15,492	14,926	16,994
Seneca	11,353	13,243	13,087	13,823
Shelby	6,343	17,142	7,317	15,924
Stark	89,432	88,581	96,990	86,743
Summit	153,041	111,001	155,105	110,499
Trumbull	61,672	38,279	64,145	40,164
Tuscarawas	18,407	22,242	21,498	20,454
Union	8,805	16,289	8,761	15,744
Van Wert	4,029	9,585	5,178	9,168
Vinton	2,436	2,856	2,463	3,021
Warren	32,909	76,564	33,398	71,691
Washington	11,651	17,284	12,368	17,019
Wayne	19,808	30,251	21,712	29,342
Williams	7,266	10,047	8,174	9,880
Wood	32,802	29,704	34,285	29,648
Wyandot	4,137	6,180	4,461	6,270
Totals	**2,827,710**	**2,661,433**	**2,940,044**	**2,677,820**

Ohio Vote Since 1960

2012: Obama, D., 2,827,710; Romney, R., 2,661,433; Johnson, LB., 49,493; Stein, Green, 18,574; Duncan, Ind., 12,502; Goode, Const., 8,151; Alexander, Soc., 2,944.

2008: Obama, D., 2,940,044; McCain, R., 2,677,820; Nader, Ind., 42,337; Barr, LB., 19,917; Baldwin, Const., 12,565; McKinney, Green, 8,518; Duncan, Ind., 3,905; Moore, Soc., 2,735.

2004: Bush, R., 2,859,768; Kerry, D., 2,741,167; Badnarik, nonpartisan, 14,676; Peroutka, nonpartisan, 939.

2000: Bush, R., 2,351,209; Gore, D., 2,186,190; Nader, Ind., 117,857; Buchanan, Ind., 26,724; Browne, LB., 13,475; Hagelin, Natural Law, 6,169; Phillips, Ind., 3,823.

1996: Clinton, D., 2,148,222; Dole, R., 1,859,883; Perot, RF., 483,207; Browne, Ind., 12,851; Moorehead, Ind., 10,813; Hagelin, Natural Law, 9,120; Phillips, Ind., 7,361.

1992: Clinton, D., 1,984,942; Bush, R., 1,894,310; Perot, Ind., 1,036,426; Marrou, LB., 7,252; Fulani, New Alliance, 6,413; Gritz, Populist/America First, 4,699; Hagelin, Natural Law, 3,437; LaRouche, Ind., 2,446.

1988: Bush, R., 2,416,549; Dukakis, D., 1,939,629; Fulani, Ind., 12,017; Paul, Ind., 11,926.

1984: Reagan, R., 2,678,559; Mondale, D., 1,825,440; Bergland, LB., 5,886.

1980: Reagan, R., 2,206,545; Carter, D., 1,752,414; Anderson, Ind., 254,472; Clark, LB., 49,033; Commoner, Citizens, 8,564; Hall, Comm., 4,729; Congress, Ind., 4,029; Griswold, Workers World, 3,790; Bubar, Statesman, 27.

1976: Carter, D., 2,011,621; Ford, R., 2,000,505; McCarthy, Ind., 58,258; Maddox, Amer. Ind., 15,529; MacBride, LB., 8,961; Hall, Comm., 7,817; Camejo, Soc. Workers, 4,717; LaRouche, U.S. Labor, 4,335; scattered, 130.

1972: Nixon, R., 2,441,827; McGovern, D., 1,558,889; Schmitz, Amer., 80,067; Fisher, Soc. Labor, 7,107; Hall, Comm., 6,437; Wallace, Ind., 460.

1968: Nixon, R., 1,791,014; Humphrey, D., 1,700,586; Wallace, 3rd party, 467,495; Gregory, 372; Blomen, Soc. Labor, 120; Halstead, Soc. Workers, 69; Mitchell, Comm., 23; Munn, Prohib., 19.

1964: Johnson, D., 2,498,331; Goldwater, R., 1,470,865.

1960: Nixon, R., 2,217,611; Kennedy, D., 1,944,248.

Oklahoma

County	2012 Obama (D)	Romney (R)	2008 Obama (D)	McCain (R)
Adair	2,127	4,381	2,052	4,638
Alfalfa	322	1,761	411	2,023
Atoka	1,243	3,538	1,370	3,511
Beaver	244	2,062	265	2,199
Beckham	1,417	5,508	1,625	5,772
Blaine	992	2,824	1,011	3,101
Bryan	3,681	9,520	4,426	9,307
Caddo	3,164	5,607	3,404	6,413
Canadian	10,537	35,625	11,426	36,428
Carter	4,908	12,214	5,603	13,241
Cherokee	6,144	8,162	7,194	9,186
Choctaw	1,494	3,572	1,860	3,730
Cimarron	115	1,082	152	1,119
Cleveland	34,771	59,116	39,681	64,749
Coal	649	1,710	600	1,672
Comanche	12,521	17,664	14,120	20,127
Cotton	657	1,796	690	1,793
Craig	1,747	3,559	2,073	3,858
Creek	7,128	18,986	8,318	20,187
Custer	2,359	7,446	2,660	7,842
Delaware	4,196	10,080	5,085	10,277
Dewey	301	1,792	346	1,857
Ellis	226	1,575	282	1,627
Garfield	4,733	15,177	5,545	17,067
Garvin	2,559	6,925	3,028	7,710
Grady	4,786	14,833	5,520	15,195
Grant	393	1,675	514	1,836
Greer	488	1,344	566	1,548
Harmon	264	659	333	757
Harper	173	1,261	221	1,342
Haskell	1,175	3,069	1,474	3,207
Hughes	1,370	2,838	1,709	3,134
Jackson	1,954	5,965	2,264	6,719
Jefferson	605	1,634	805	1,652
Johnston	1,137	2,649	1,249	2,708
Kay	4,627	11,499	5,463	13,230
Kingfisher	898	4,870	1,009	5,372
Kiowa	1,106	2,316	1,226	2,537
Latimer	1,170	2,628	1,313	2,860
Le Flore	4,662	11,177	5,136	11,605
Lincoln	3,273	9,553	3,504	10,470
Logan	4,724	12,314	5,717	12,556
Love	1,034	2,436	1,257	2,589
Major	446	2,700	515	2,956
Marshall	1,396	3,744	1,643	3,730
Mayes	4,823	9,637	5,749	10,234
McClain	3,194	11,112	3,551	11,193

County	2012 Obama (D)	Romney (R)	2008 Obama (D)	McCain (R)
McCurtain	2,440	7,635	2,794	7,745
McIntosh	2,779	4,509	3,320	4,903
Murray	1,540	3,606	1,592	3,746
Muskogee	9,952	13,404	11,294	15,289
Noble	1,143	3,488	1,174	3,881
Nowata	1,244	2,832	1,411	3,031
Okfuskee	1,256	2,335	1,480	2,643
Oklahoma	106,982	149,728	116,182	163,172
Okmulgee	5,432	7,731	6,191	8,727
Osage	6,704	11,242	7,498	12,160
Ottawa	3,509	6,466	4,268	6,905
Pawnee	1,813	4,232	2,063	4,533
Payne	9,198	16,481	10,601	18,435
Pittsburg	4,831	10,841	5,457	11,752
Pontotoc	3,947	8,945	4,512	9,750
Pottawatomie	7,188	16,250	7,910	17,753
Pushmataha	1,043	3,087	1,265	3,208
Roger Mills	272	1,402	287	1,502
Rogers	9,148	27,553	10,772	27,743
Seminole	2,600	4,856	2,977	5,600
Sequoyah	4,193	9,578	4,454	9,466
Stephens	3,939	12,908	4,538	14,394
Texas	862	4,930	923	5,336
Tillman	906	1,815	1,042	2,195
Tulsa	82,744	145,062	96,133	158,363
Wagoner	7,791	20,900	8,810	21,441
Washington	5,532	15,668	6,308	16,457
Washita	822	3,494	1,052	3,724
Woods	671	2,727	873	3,043
Woodward	1,133	5,945	1,350	6,404
Totals	443,547	891,325	502,496	960,165

Oklahoma Vote Since 1960

2012: Romney, R., 891,325; Obama, D., 443,547.
2008: McCain, R., 960,165; Obama, D., 502,496.
2004: Bush, R., 959,792; Kerry, D., 503,966.
2000: Bush, R., 744,337; Gore, D., 474,276; Buchanan, RF., 9,014; Browne, LB., 6,602.
1996: Dole, R., 582,315; Clinton, D., 488,105; Perot, RF., 130,788; Browne, LB., 5,505.
1992: Bush, R., 592,929; Clinton, D., 473,066; Perot, Ind., 319,878; Marrou, LB., 4,486.
1988: Bush, R., 678,367; Dukakis, D., 483,423; Paul, LB., 6,261; Fulani, New Alliance, 2,985.
1984: Reagan, R., 861,530; Mondale, D., 385,080; Bergland, LB., 9,066.
1980: Reagan, R., 695,570; Carter, D., 402,026; Anderson, Ind., 38,284; Clark, LB., 13,828.
1976: Ford, R., 545,708; Carter, D., 532,442; McCarthy, Ind., 14,101.
1972: Nixon, R., 759,025; McGovern, D., 247,147; Schmitz, Amer., 23,728.
1968: Nixon, R., 449,697; Humphrey, D., 301,658; Wallace, 3rd party, 191,731.
1964: Johnson, D., 519,834; Goldwater, R., 412,665.
1960: Nixon, R., 533,039; Kennedy, D., 370,111.

Oregon

County	2012 Obama (D)	Romney (R)	2008 Obama (D)	McCain (R)
Baker	2,369	5,702	2,805	5,650
Benton	27,776	14,991	29,901	15,264
Clackamas	95,493	88,592	103,476	83,595
Clatsop	9,861	7,249	10,701	7,192
Columbia	12,004	10,772	13,390	10,413
Coos	12,845	14,673	14,401	15,354
Crook	3,104	6,790	3,632	6,371
Curry	4,625	6,598	5,230	6,646
Deschutes	36,961	42,463	38,819	39,064
Douglas	17,145	30,776	20,298	30,919
Gilliam	371	639	430	648
Grant	853	2,926	1,006	2,785
Harney	832	2,607	950	2,595
Hood River	6,058	3,429	6,302	3,265
Jackson	44,468	49,020	49,090	49,043
Jefferson	3,301	4,642	3,682	4,402
Josephine	14,953	23,673	17,412	22,973
Klamath	8,302	18,898	9,370	19,113
Lake	770	2,808	957	2,638
Lane	102,652	62,509	114,037	63,835
Lincoln	13,401	8,686	14,258	8,791
Linn	20,378	28,944	22,163	28,071
Malheur	2,759	6,851	2,949	7,157
Marion	56,376	60,190	61,816	59,059
Morrow	1,202	2,532	1,410	2,509
Multnomah	274,887	75,302	279,696	75,171
Polk	16,292	17,819	17,536	17,714
Sherman	319	678	385	634

County	2012 Obama (D)	Romney (R)	2008 Obama (D)	McCain (R)
Tillamook	6,293	5,684	7,072	5,757
Umatilla	8,584	15,499	9,484	15,254
Union	3,973	7,636	4,613	7,581
Wallowa	1,253	2,804	1,492	2,836
Wasco	5,211	5,229	5,906	5,103
Washington	135,291	93,974	141,544	89,185
Wheeler	266	545	281	498
Yamhill	19,260	22,045	20,797	21,390
Totals	970,488	754,175	1,037,291	738,475

Oregon Vote Since 1960

2012: Obama, D., 970,488; Romney, R., 754,175; Johnson, LB., 24,089; Stein, Pacific Green, 19,427; Christensen, Const., 4,432; Anderson, OR Prog., 3,384.
2008: Obama, D., 1,037,291; McCain, R., 738,475; Nader, Peace Party of OR, 18,614; Baldwin, Const., 7,693; Barr, LB., 7,635; McKinney, Pacific Green, 4,543.
2004: Kerry, D., 943,163; Bush, R., 866,831; Badnarik, LB., 7,260; Cobb, Pacific Green, 5,315; Peroutka, Const., 5,257.
2000: Gore, D., 720,342; Bush, R., 713,577; Nader, Green, 77,357; Browne, LB., 7,447; Buchanan, Ind., 7,063; Hagelin, RF., 2,574; Phillips, Const., 2,189.
1996: Clinton, D., 649,641; Dole, R., 538,152; Perot, RF., 121,221; Nader, Pacific, 49,415; Browne, LB., 8,903; Phillips, Taxpayers, 3,379; Hagelin, Natural Law, 2,798; Hollis, Soc., 1,922.
1992: Clinton, D., 621,314; Bush, R., 475,757; Perot, Ind., 354,091; Marrou, LB., 4,277; Fulani, New Alliance, 3,030.
1988: Dukakis, D., 616,206; Bush, R., 560,126; Paul, LB., 14,811; Fulani, Ind., 6,487.
1984: Reagan, R., 658,700; Mondale, D., 536,479.
1980: Reagan, R., 571,044; Carter, D., 456,890; Anderson, Ind., 112,389; Clark, LB., 25,838; Commoner, Citizens, 13,642; scattered, 1,713.
1976: Ford, R., 492,120; Carter, D., 490,407; McCarthy, Ind., 40,207; write-in, 7,142.
1972: Nixon, R., 486,686; McGovern, D., 392,760; Schmitz, Amer., 46,211; write-in, 2,289.
1968: Nixon, R., 408,433; Humphrey, D., 358,866; Wallace, 3rd party, 49,683; write-ins: McCarthy, 1,496; N. Rockefeller, 69; others, 1,075.
1964: Johnson, D., 501,017; Goldwater, R., 282,779; write-in, 2,509.
1960: Nixon, R., 408,060; Kennedy, D., 367,402.

Pennsylvania

County	2012 Obama (D)	Romney (R)	2008 Obama (D)	McCain (R)
Adams	15,091	26,767	17,633	26,349
Allegheny	352,687	262,039	373,153	272,347
Armstrong	9,045	20,142	11,138	18,542
Beaver	37,055	42,344	40,499	42,895
Bedford	4,788	16,702	6,059	16,124
Berks	83,011	54,702	97,047	80,513
Blair	16,276	33,319	19,813	32,708
Bradford	8,624	14,410	10,306	15,057
Bucks	160,521	156,579	179,031	150,248
Butler	28,550	59,761	32,260	57,074
Cambria	24,249	35,163	32,451	31,995
Cameron	724	1,359	879	1,323
Carbon	11,580	13,504	13,464	12,957
Centre	34,176	34,001	41,950	32,992
Chester	124,311	124,840	137,833	114,421
Clarion	5,056	10,828	6,756	10,737
Clearfield	11,121	20,347	14,555	18,662
Clinton	5,734	7,303	7,097	7,504
Columbia	10,937	14,236	13,230	14,477
Crawford	13,883	20,901	16,780	20,750
Cumberland	44,367	64,809	48,306	63,739
Dauphin	64,965	57,450	69,975	58,238
Delaware	171,792	110,853	178,870	115,273
Elk	5,463	7,579	7,290	6,676
Erie	68,036	49,025	75,775	50,351
Fayette	21,971	26,018	25,866	26,081
Forest	896	1,383	1,038	1,366
Franklin	18,995	43,260	21,169	41,906
Fulton	1,310	4,814	1,576	4,642
Greene	5,852	8,428	7,829	7,889
Huntingdon	5,409	11,979	6,621	11,745
Indiana	14,473	21,257	17,065	19,727
Jefferson	4,787	13,048	6,447	12,057
Juniata	2,547	6,862	3,068	6,484
Lackawanna	61,838	35,085	67,520	39,488
Lancaster	88,481	130,669	99,586	126,568
Lawrence	17,513	21,047	19,711	21,851
Lebanon	19,900	35,872	23,310	34,314
Lehigh	78,283	66,874	87,089	63,382
Luzerne	64,307	58,325	72,492	61,127

County	2012 Obama (D)	Romney (R)	2008 Obama (D)	McCain (R)
Lycoming	15,203	30,658	18,381	30,280
McKean	5,297	9,545	6,465	9,224
Mercer	24,232	25,925	26,411	26,565
Mifflin	4,273	11,939	5,375	10,929
Monroe	35,221	26,867	39,453	28,293
Montgomery	233,356	174,381	253,393	165,552
Montour	3,053	4,652	3,364	4,574
Northampton	67,606	61,446	75,255	58,551
Northumberland	13,072	19,518	14,329	19,018
Perry	5,685	13,120	6,396	13,058
Philadelphia	588,806	96,467	595,980	117,221
Pike	10,210	12,786	11,493	12,518
Potter	1,897	5,231	2,300	5,109
Schuylkill	24,546	32,278	28,300	33,767
Snyder	4,687	10,073	5,382	9,900
Somerset	9,436	23,984	12,878	21,686
Sullivan	1,034	1,868	1,233	1,841
Susquehanna	6,935	10,800	8,381	10,633
Tioga	5,357	11,342	6,390	11,326
Union	6,109	9,896	7,333	9,859
Venango	7,945	13,815	9,238	13,718
Warren	6,995	10,010	8,537	9,685
Washington	40,345	53,230	46,122	50,752
Wayne	8,396	12,896	9,892	12,702
Westmoreland	63,722	103,932	72,721	102,294
Wyoming	5,061	6,587	5,985	6,983
York	73,191	113,304	82,829	109,268
Totals	2,990,274	2,680,434	3,276,363	2,655,885

Pennsylvania Vote Since 1960

2012: Obama, D., 2,990,274; Romney, R., 2,680,434; Johnson, LB., 49,991; Stein, Green, 21,341.
2008: Obama, D., 3,276,363; McCain, R., 2,655,885; Nader, Ind., 42,977; Barr, LB., 19,912.
2004: Kerry, D., 2,938,095; Bush, R., 2,793,847; Badnarik, LB., 21,185; Cobb, Green, 6,319; Peroutka, Const., 6,318.
2000: Gore, D., 2,485,967; Bush, R., 2,281,127; Nader, Green, 103,392; Buchanan, RF., 16,023; Phillips, Const., 14,428; Browno, LB., 11,248.
1996: Clinton, D., 2,215,819; Dole, R., 1,801,169; Perot, RF., 430,984; Browne, LB., 28,000; Phillips, Const., 19,552; Hagelin, Natural Law, 5,783.
1992: Clinton, D., 2,239,164; Bush, R., 1,791,841; Perot, Ind., 902,667; Marrou, LB., 21,477; Fulani, New Alliance, 4,661.
1988: Bush, R., 2,300,087; Dukakis, D., 2,194,944; McCarthy, Consumer, 19,158; Paul, LB., 12,051.
1984: Reagan, R., 2,584,323; Mondale, D., 2,228,131; Bergland, LB., 6,982.
1980: Reagan, R., 2,261,872; Carter, D., 1,937,540; Anderson, Ind., 292,921; Clark, LB., 33,263; DeBerry, Soc. Workers, 20,291; Commoner, Consumer, 10,430; Hall, Comm., 5,184.
1976: Carter, D., 2,328,677; Ford, R., 2,205,604; McCarthy, Ind., 50,584; Maddox, Const., 25,344; Camejo, Soc. Workers, 3,009; LaRouche, U.S. Labor, 2,744; Hall, Comm., 1,891; others, 2,934.
1972: Nixon, R., 2,714,521; McGovern, D., 1,796,951; Schmitz, Amer., 70,593; Jenness, Soc. Workers, 4,639; Hall, Comm., 2,686; others, 2,715.
1968: Humphrey, D., 2,259,405; Nixon, R., 2,090,017; Wallace, 3rd party, 378,582; Gregory, Peace/Freedom, 7,821; Blomen, Soc. Labor, 4,977; Halstead, Soc. Workers, 4,862; others, 2,264.
1964: Johnson, D., 3,130,954; Goldwater, R., 1,673,657; DeBerry, Soc. Workers, 10,456; Hass, Soc. Labor, 5,092; scattered, 2,531.
1960: Kennedy, D., 2,556,282; Nixon, R., 2,439,956; Hass, Soc. Labor, 7,185; Dobbs, Soc. Workers, 2,678; scattered, 440.

Rhode Island

City	2012 Obama (D)	Romney (R)	2008 Obama (D)	McCain (R)
Bristol	6,359	3,707	6,833	3,834
Coventry	9,122	6,969	9,622	7,367
Cranston	21,388	13,008	22,520	13,981
Cumberland	9,291	7,106	9,707	6,941
East Providence	14,095	5,752	15,380	6,216
Johnston	7,503	5,417	7,763	6,066
Lincoln	6,028	4,866	6,264	4,831
Newport	6,174	2,959	6,989	3,215
North Kingstown	7,847	6,451	8,562	6,285
North Providence	9,613	5,404	9,954	5,933
Pawtucket	18,155	5,228	18,486	6,098

City	2012 Obama (D)	Romney (R)	2008 Obama (D)	McCain (R)
Providence	43,617	7,282	46,276	8,548
Smithfield	5,293	4,681	5,464	4,660
South Kingstown	8,611	4,720	9,336	4,689
Warwick	24,448	15,027	25,802	16,541
West Warwick	6,956	4,332	7,475	4,735
Westerly	6,071	4,382	6,490	4,710
Woonsocket	7,985	4,114	8,678	4,398
Other	60,853	45,746	64,970	46,343
Totals	279,677	157,204	296,571	165,391

Rhode Island Vote Since 1960

2012: Obama, D., 279,677; Romney, R., 157,204; Johnson, LB., 4,388; Stein, Green, 2,421; Goode, Const., 430; Anderson, Justice, 416; Lindsay, Socialism/Liberation, 132.
2008: Obama, D., 296,571; McCain, R., 165,391; Nader, Ind., 4,829; Barr, LB., 1,382; McKinney, Green, 797; Baldwin, Const., 675; La Riva, Socialism/Liberation, 122.
2004: Kerry, D., 259,765; Bush, R., 169,046; Nader, RF., 4,651; Cobb, Green, 1,333; Badnarik, LB., 907; Peroutka, Const., 339; Parker, Workers World, 253.
2000: Gore, D., 249,508; Bush, R., 130,555; Nader, Ind., 25,052; Buchanan, RF., 2,273; Browne, Ind., 742; Hagelin, Ind., 271; Moorehead, Ind., 199; Phillips, Ind., 97; McReynolds, Ind., 52; Harris, Ind., 34.
1996: Clinton, D., 233,050; Dole, R., 104,683; Perot, RF., 43,723; Nader, Green, 6,040; Browne, LB., 1,109; Phillips, U.S. Taxpayers, 1,021; Hagelin, Natural Law, 435; Moorehead, Workers World, 186.
1992: Clinton, D., 213,299; Bush, R., 131,601; Perot, Ind., 105,045; Fulani, New Alliance, 1,878.
1988: Dukakis, D., 225,123; Bush, R., 177,761; Paul, LB., 825; Fulani, New Alliance, 280.
1984: Reagan, R., 212,080; Mondale, D., 197,106; Bergland, LB., 277.
1980: Carter, D., 198,342; Reagan, R., 154,793; Anderson, Ind., 59,819; Clark, LB., 2,458; Hall, Comm., 218; McReynolds, Soc., 170; DeBerry, Soc. Workers, 90; Griswold, Workers World, 77.
1976: Carter, D., 227,636; Ford, R., 181,249; MacBride, LB., 715; Camejo, Soc. Workers, 462; Hall, Comm., 334; Levin, Soc. Labor, 188.
1972: Nixon, R., 220,383; McGovern, D., 194,645; Jenness, Soc. Workers, 729.
1968: Humphrey, D., 246,518; Nixon, R., 122,359; Wallace, 3rd party, 15,678; Halstead, Soc. Workers, 383.
1964: Johnson, D., 315,463; Goldwater, R., 74,615.
1960: Kennedy, D., 258,032; Nixon, R., 147,502.

South Carolina

County	2012 Obama (D)	Romney (R)	2008 Obama (D)	McCain (R)
Abbeville	4,543	4,578	4,593	6,264
Aiken	25,322	44,042	26,101	42,849
Allendale	3,297	838	3,029	947
Anderson	22,405	48,709	24,132	48,690
Bamberg	4,624	2,194	4,426	2,309
Barnwell	5,188	4,659	4,931	4,769
Beaufort	29,848	42,687	30,396	37,821
Berkeley	28,542	38,475	27,755	36,205
Calhoun	4,045	3,707	3,970	3,695
Charleston	81,487	77,629	82,698	69,822
Cherokee	7,231	13,314	7,215	13,305
Chester	7,891	6,367	7,478	6,318
Chesterfield	7,958	8,490	7,842	8,325
Clarendon	9,091	7,071	8,673	6,758
Colleton	8,475	8,443	8,616	8,525
Darlington	15,457	14,434	14,505	14,544
Dillon	7,523	5,427	7,408	5,874
Dorchester	23,445	32,531	21,806	29,929
Edgefield	4,967	6,512	5,075	6,334
Fairfield	7,777	3,999	7,591	3,912
Florence	28,614	28,961	28,012	29,861
Georgetown	14,163	16,526	14,199	15,790
Greenville	68,070	121,685	70,886	116,363
Greenwood	11,972	16,348	12,348	16,995
Hampton	5,834	3,312	5,816	3,439
Horry	38,885	72,127	38,879	64,609
Jasper	5,757	4,169	5,389	3,365
Kershaw	11,259	16,324	11,226	16,466
Lancaster	13,419	19,333	12,139	16,441
Laurens	10,318	14,746	10,578	15,334
Lee	5,977	2,832	5,960	3,074
Lexington	34,148	76,662	33,303	74,960
Marion	9,688	5,164	9,608	5,416
Marlboro	6,100	3,676	6,794	3,996
McCormick	2,653	2,467	2,755	2,437

County	2012 Obama (D)	Romney (R)	2008 Obama (D)	McCain (R)
Newberry	6,913	9,260	6,708	9,616
Oconee	8,550	21,611	9,481	21,164
Orangeburg	30,720	12,022	27,263	12,115
Pickens	11,156	33,474	11,691	32,552
Richland	103,989	53,105	105,656	57,941
Saluda	3,328	5,135	3,323	5,191
Spartanburg	41,461	66,969	41,632	65,042
Sumter	27,589	19,274	25,431	18,581
Union	5,796	6,584	5,935	7,449
Williamsburg	11,335	4,824	11,279	5,004
York	39,131	59,546	37,918	54,500
Totals	865,941	1,071,645	862,449	1,034,896

South Carolina Vote Since 1960

2012: Romney, R., 1,071,645; Obama, D., 865,941; Johnson, LB., 16,321; Stein, Green, 5,446; Goode, Const., 4,765.
2008: McCain, R., 1,034,896; Obama, D., 862,449; Barr, LB., 7,283; Baldwin, Const., 6,827; Nader, petitioning cand., 5,053; McKinney, Green, 4,461.
2004: Bush, R., 937,974; Kerry, D., 661,699; Nader, Ind., 5,520; Peroutka, Const., 5,317; Badnarik, LB., 3,608; Brown, United Citizens, 2,124; Cobb, Green, 1,488.
2000: Bush, R., 786,892; Gore, D., 566,039; Nader, United Citizens, 20,279; Browne, LB., 4,898; Buchanan, RF., 3,309; Phillips, Const., 1,682; Hagelin, Natural Law. 943.
1996: Dole, R., 573,458; Clinton, D., 506,283; Perot, RF./Patriot, 64,386; Browne, LB., 4,271; Phillips, U.S. Taxpayers, 2,043; Hagelin, Natural Law, 1,248.
1992: Bush, R., 577,507; Clinton, D., 479,514; Perot, Ind., 138,872; Marrou, LB., 2,719; Phillips, U.S. Taxpayers, 2,680; Fulani, New Alliance, 1,235.
1988: Bush, R., 606,443; Dukakis, D., 370,554; Paul, LB., 4,935; Fulani, United Citizens, 4,077.
1984: Reagan, R., 615,539; Mondale, D., 344,459; Bergland, LB., 4,359.
1980: Reagan, R., 439,277; Carter, D., 428,220; Anderson, Ind., 13,868; Clark, LB., 4,807; Rarick, Amer. Ind., 2,086.
1976: Carter, D., 450,807; Ford, R., 346,149; Anderson, Amer., 2,996; Maddox, Amer. Ind., 1,950; write-in, 681.
1972: Nixon, R., 477,044; McGovern, D., 184,559, and United Citizens, 2,265 (total, 186,824); Schmitz, Amer., 10,075; write-in, 17.
1968: Nixon, R., 254,062; Wallace, 3rd party, 215,430; Humphrey, D., 197,486.
1964: Goldwater, R., 309,048; Johnson, D., 215,700; write-ins: Wallace, 5; Nixon, 1; Powell, 1; Thurmond, 1.
1960: Kennedy, D., 198,129; Nixon, R., 188,558; write-in, 1.

South Dakota

County	2012 Obama (D)	Romney (R)	2008 Obama (D)	McCain (R)
Aurora	556	804	655	794
Beadle	2,881	4,230	3,493	4,054
Bennett	548	626	557	614
Bon Homme	1,167	1,830	1,367	1,712
Brookings	5,827	6,220	7,207	6,431
Brown	7,250	8,321	9,041	8,067
Brule	824	1,499	965	1,407
Buffalo	472	166	454	156
Butte	1,002	3,073	1,306	2,821
Campbell	153	616	243	591
Charles Mix	1,483	2,230	1,807	2,109
Clark	713	1,067	830	1,065
Clay	2,955	2,147	3,808	2,296
Codington	4,588	6,696	5,595	6,374
Corson	648	515	837	535
Custer	1,335	3,062	1,475	2,909
Davison	3,042	4,757	3,554	4,731
Day	1,497	1,320	1,785	1,372
Deuel	941	1,175	1,054	1,088
Dewey	1,207	663	1,328	659
Douglas	332	1,334	424	1,293
Edmunds	622	1,264	819	1,213
Fall River	1,140	2,258	1,338	2,348
Faulk	331	765	426	739
Grant	1,493	2,034	1,786	1,951
Gregory	599	1,507	771	1,423
Haakon	138	940	187	939
Hamlin	921	1,803	1,043	1,661
Hand	575	1,242	718	1,247
Hanson	760	1,627	961	1,426
Harding	82	638	135	575
Hughes	2,786	5,219	3,037	5,298
Hutchinson	923	2,451	1,242	2,285
Hyde	189	531	226	547
Jackson	426	661	435	668
Jerauld	452	538	542	546
Jones	108	490	147	463

County	2012 Obama (D)	Romney (R)	2008 Obama (D)	McCain (R)
Kingsbury	1,092	1,451	1,277	1,435
Lake	2,724	3,419	3,033	2,993
Lawrence	3,973	7,025	4,932	6,787
Lincoln	7,982	13,611	8,642	11,803
Lyman	605	933	710	894
Marshall	1,061	889	1,261	900
McCook	905	1,655	1,219	1,646
McPherson	272	921	441	915
Meade	2,928	7,566	3,751	7,515
Mellette	375	381	373	445
Miner	479	636	605	577
Minnehaha	34,674	40,342	39,838	39,251
Moody	1,429	1,535	1,663	1,508
Pennington	15,125	28,232	17,802	27,603
Perkins	319	1,205	499	1,102
Potter	339	1,029	482	937
Roberts	2,302	1,883	2,672	1,781
Sanborn	389	688	500	669
Shannon	2,937	188	2,971	331
Spink	1,300	1,670	1,550	1,660
Stanley	435	1,063	510	1,017
Sully	186	613	233	581
Todd	1,976	498	2,208	571
Tripp	737	1,905	914	1,859
Turner	1,411	2,715	1,681	2,538
Union	2,782	4,698	3,244	4,310
Walworth	671	1,731	923	1,668
Yankton	4,226	5,495	4,838	5,039
Ziebach	439	314	554	312
Totals	145,039	210,610	170,924	203,054

South Dakota Vote Since 1960

2012: Romney, R., 210,610; Obama, D., 145,039; Johnson, LB., 5,795; Goode, Const., 2,371.
2008: McCain, R., 203,054; Obama, D., 170,924; Nader, Ind., 4,267; Baldwin, Const., 1,895; Barr, Ind., 1,835.
2004: Bush, R., 232,584; Kerry, D., 149,244; Nader, Ind., 4,320; Peroutka, Const., 1,103; Badnarik, LB., 964.
2000: Bush, R., 190,700; Gore, D., 118,804; Buchanan, RF., 3,322; Phillips, Ind., 1,781; Browne, LB., 1,662.
1996: Dole, R., 150,543; Clinton, D., 139,333; Perot, RF., 31,250; Browne, LB., 1,472; Phillips, Taxpayers, 912; Hagelin, Natural Law, 316.
1992: Bush, R., 136,718; Clinton, D., 124,888; Perot, Ind., 73,295.
1988: Bush, R., 165,415; Dukakis, D., 145,560; Paul, LB., 1,060; Fulani, New Alliance, 730.
1984: Reagan, R., 200,267; Mondale, D., 116,113.
1980: Reagan, R., 198,343; Carter, D., 103,855; Anderson, Ind., 21,431; Clark, LB., 3,824; Pulley, Soc. Workers, 250.
1976: Ford, R., 151,505; Carter, D., 147,068; MacBride, LB., 1,619; Hall, Comm., 318; Camejo, Soc. Workers, 168.
1972: Nixon, R., 166,476; McGovern, D., 139,945; Jenness, Soc. Workers, 994.
1968: Nixon, R., 149,841; Humphrey, D., 118,023; Wallace, 3rd party, 13,400.
1964: Johnson, D., 163,010; Goldwater, R., 130,108.
1960: Nixon, R., 178,417; Kennedy, D., 128,070.

Tennessee

County	2012 Obama (D)	Romney (R)	2008 Obama (D)	McCain (R)
Anderson	10,122	18,968	11,396	19,675
Bedford	4,211	10,034	5,027	10,217
Benton	2,258	3,850	2,645	3,696
Bledsoe	1,267	3,022	1,517	3,166
Blount	12,934	35,441	15,253	35,571
Bradley	8,037	27,422	9,357	28,333
Campbell	3,328	8,604	3,867	8,535
Cannon	1,564	3,309	2,011	3,322
Carroll	3,475	7,225	3,980	7,455
Carter	4,789	15,503	5,587	15,852
Cheatham	4,659	10,268	5,498	10,702
Chester	1,624	4,684	1,797	4,587
Claiborne	2,433	7,617	3,078	7,175
Clay	1,037	1,747	1,248	1,676
Cocke	2,804	8,459	3,340	8,945
Coffee	5,870	13,023	7,132	13,250
Crockett	1,669	3,783	1,967	3,994
Cumberland	6,261	18,653	7,889	17,436
Davidson	143,120	97,622	158,423	102,915
Decatur	1,303	2,874	1,566	3,101
DeKalb	2,174	4,143	2,832	4,085
Dickson	6,233	11,296	7,506	11,677
Dyer	3,757	9,921	4,411	9,859
Fayette	6,688	12,689	6,892	12,173
Fentress	1,561	5,243	1,831	4,789

County	2012 Obama (D)	Romney (R)	2008 Obama (D)	McCain (R)
Franklin	5,603	10,262	6,613	10,539
Gibson	6,564	12,883	7,406	13,516
Giles	3,760	6,915	4,614	6,902
Grainger	1,668	5,470	2,066	5,297
Greene	6,225	17,245	7,110	17,151
Grundy	1,643	2,516	1,971	2,563
Hamblen	5,234	14,522	6,807	15,508
Hamilton	58,836	79,933	64,246	81,702
Hancock	475	1,527	604	1,588
Hardeman	5,482	4,865	5,919	5,225
Hardin	2,467	7,886	2,794	7,077
Hawkins	5,088	14,382	5,930	14,756
Haywood	4,569	2,960	4,893	3,165
Henderson	2,517	7,421	3,021	7,669
Henry	4,339	8,193	5,153	8,182
Hickman	2,698	4,758	3,563	4,784
Houston	1,400	1,579	1,678	1,608
Humphreys	2,905	3,833	3,600	3,818
Jackson	1,739	2,383	2,224	2,185
Jefferson	4,232	13,038	5,178	13,092
Johnson	1,483	4,611	1,837	4,621
Knox	59,399	109,707	70,215	113,015
Lake	884	1,163	1,024	1,175
Lauderdale	4,011	4,616	4,322	4,933
Lawrence	4,237	10,770	5,161	10,566
Lewis	1,447	3,117	1,804	2,951
Lincoln	3,290	9,803	3,695	9,231
Loudon	5,058	16,707	6,058	15,815
Macon	1,552	5,260	2,060	5,145
Madison	18,367	21,993	20,209	23,290
Marion	3,953	6,272	4,506	6,746
Marshall	3,725	6,832	4,320	6,755
Maury	11,825	20,708	13,058	20,288
McMinn	4,609	12,967	5,541	12,989
McNairy	2,645	7,015	3,131	7,135
Meigs	1,163	2,734	1,372	2,797
Monroe	4,372	11,731	5,053	11,484
Montgomery	24,499	30,245	25,716	30,175
Moore	705	2,053	881	2,010
Morgan	1,725	4,669	1,969	4,717
Obion	3,321	8,814	4,308	8,873
Overton	2,805	4,775	3,419	4,497
Perry	992	1,578	1,329	1,596
Pickett	712	1,712	854	1,786
Polk	1,856	4,108	2,124	4,267
Putnam	7,802	17,254	9,739	17,101
Rhea	2,628	7,802	2,907	8,042
Roane	6,018	14,724	7,224	15,658
Robertson	8,290	17,643	9,318	17,903
Rutherford	36,414	60,846	40,460	59,892
Scott	1,452	5,117	1,720	4,931
Sequatchie	1,489	3,541	1,717	3,610
Sevier	7,418	25,984	8,604	24,922
Shelby	232,443	135,649	256,297	145,458
Smith	2,470	4,495	2,992	4,563
Stewart	2,069	2,963	2,470	2,956
Sullivan	15,321	43,562	18,354	44,808
Sumner	18,579	46,003	21,487	44,949
Tipton	7,133	16,672	7,931	17,165
Trousdale	1,240	1,612	1,475	1,688
Unicoi	1,913	5,032	2,107	5,011
Union	1,478	4,282	1,829	4,467
Van Buren	875	1,386	849	1,294
Warren	4,752	8,010	5,515	8,562
Washington	14,325	32,808	15,941	32,341
Wayne	1,163	4,253	1,355	4,076
Weakley	3,548	8,605	4,596	8,855
White	2,795	6,197	3,372	6,103
Williamson	25,142	69,850	27,886	64,858
Wilson	14,695	36,109	15,886	34,595
Totals	**960,709**	**1,462,330**	**1,087,437**	**1,479,178**

Tennessee Vote Since 1960

2012: Romney, R., 1,462,330; Obama, D., 960,709; Johnson, Ind., 18,623; Stein, Green, 6,515; Goode, Const., 6,022; Anderson, Ind., 2,639, Miller, Ind., 1,739.

2008: McCain, R., 1,479,178; Obama, D., 1,087,437; Nader, Ind., 11,560; Barr, Ind., 8,547; Baldwin, Ind., 8,191; McKinney, Ind., 2,499; Moore, Ind., 1,326; Jay, Ind., 1,011.

2004: Bush, R., 1,384,375; Kerry, D., 1,036,477; Nader, Ind., 8,992; Badnarik, Ind., 4,866; Peroutka, Ind., 2,570.

2000: Bush, R., 1,061,949; Gore, D., 981,720; Nader, Green, 19,781; Browne, LB., 4,284; Buchanan, RF., 4,250; Brown, Ind., 1,606; Phillips, Ind., 1,015; Hagelin, RF., 613; Venson, Ind., 535.

1996: Clinton, D., 909,146; Dole, R., 863,530; Perot, RF., 105,918; Nader, Ind., 6,427; Browne, Ind., 5,020; Phillips, Ind., 1,818; Collins, Ind., 688; Hagelin, Ind., 636; Michael, Ind., 408; Dodge, Ind., 324.

1992: Clinton, D., 933,521; Bush, R., 841,300; Perot, Ind., 199,968; Marrou, LB., 1,847.

1988: Bush, R., 947,233; Dukakis, D., 679,794; Paul, Ind., 2,041; Duke, Ind., 1,807.

1984: Reagan, R., 990,212; Mondale, D., 711,714; Bergland, LB., 3,072.

1980: Reagan, R., 787,761; Carter, D., 783,051; Anderson, Ind., 35,991; Clark, LB., 7,116; Commoner, Citizens, 1,112; Bubar, Statesman, 521; McReynolds, Soc., 519; Hall, Comm., 503; DeBerry, Soc. Workers, 490; Griswold, Workers World, 400; write-in, 152.

1976: Carter, D., 825,879; Ford, R., 633,969; Anderson, Amer., 5,769; McCarthy, Ind., 5,004; Maddox, Amer. Ind., 2,303; MacBride, LB., 1,375; Hall, Comm., 547; LaRouche, U.S. Labor, 512; Bubar, Prohib., 442; Miller, Ind., 316; write-in, 230.

1972: Nixon, R., 813,147; McGovern, D., 357,293; Schmitz, Amer., 30,373; write-in, 369.

1968: Nixon, R., 472,592; Wallace, 3rd party, 424,792; Humphrey, D., 351,233.

1964: Johnson, D., 635,047; Goldwater, R., 508,965; write-in, 34.

1960: Nixon, R., 556,577; Kennedy, D., 481,453; Faubus, States' Rights, 11,304; Decker, Prohib., 2,458.

Texas

County	2012 Obama (D)	Romney (R)	2008 Obama (D)	McCain (R)
Anderson	3,813	12,262	4,630	11,884
Andrews	795	3,639	790	3,816
Angelina	7,834	20,303	9,379	19,569
Aransas	2,704	6,830	3,006	6,693
Archer	525	3,600	740	3,595
Armstrong	98	828	128	856
Atascosa	5,133	7,461	4,415	5,462
Austin	2,252	9,265	2,821	8,786
Bailey	466	1,339	682	1,618
Bandera	1,864	7,426	2,250	6,935
Bastrop	9,864	14,033	11,687	13,817
Baylor	267	1,297	366	1,262
Bee	3,452	4,356	3,645	4,471
Bell	35,512	49,574	40,413	49,242
Bexar	264,856	241,617	275,527	246,275
Blanco	1,220	3,638	1,467	3,418
Borden	32	324	40	316
Bosque	1,367	5,885	1,797	5,762
Bowie	10,106	24,869	10,815	24,162
Brazoria	34,421	70,862	36,480	67,515
Brazos	17,477	37,209	20,502	37,465
Brewster	1,765	1,976	1,970	1,855
Briscoe	117	578	205	617
Brooks	1,886	507	1,747	556
Brown	1,904	11,895	2,822	12,052
Burleson	1,705	4,671	2,053	4,547
Burnet	3,674	12,843	4,608	12,059
Caldwell	4,791	6,021	5,403	6,107
Calhoun	2,410	4,144	2,729	4,106
Callahan	751	4,378	1,063	4,589
Cameron	49,975	26,099	48,480	26,671
Camp	1,428	2,881	1,734	2,798
Carson	292	2,451	406	2,548
Cass	2,924	8,763	3,490	8,279
Castro	630	1,470	719	1,562
Chambers	2,790	11,787	3,188	9,988
Cherokee	3,875	12,094	4,610	11,695
Childress	320	1,665	497	1,782
Clay	740	4,266	1,085	4,213
Cochran	256	649	284	758
Coke	179	1,218	299	1,252
Coleman	442	3,012	643	3,011
Collin	101,415	196,888	109,047	184,897
Collingsworth	177	962	234	943
Colorado	2,029	6,026	2,508	5,795
Comal	11,450	39,318	12,384	35,233
Comanche	890	3,944	1,334	3,813
Concho	194	793	257	807
Cooke	2,246	11,951	3,051	11,871
Coryell	5,158	11,220	6,619	11,550
Cottle	180	555	187	509
Crane	275	985	319	1,119
Crockett	480	957	512	1,026
Crosby	639	1,132	684	1,221
Culberson	568	295	492	257
Dallam	253	1,248	302	1,269
Dallas	405,571	295,813	422,989	310,000
Dawson	1,019	2,591	1,152	2,906
Deaf Smith	1,239	3,042	1,247	3,466
Delta	454	1,524	589	1,580
Denton	80,978	157,579	91,160	149,935
DeWitt	1,467	5,122	1,716	4,888
Dickens	216	793	234	730
Dimmit	2,141	762	2,692	874

County	2012 Obama (D)	Romney (R)	2008 Obama (D)	McCain (R)
Donley	226	1,287	291	1,374
Duval	3,331	980	3,298	1,076
Eastland	970	5,444	1,271	5,165
Ector	8,118	24,010	9,123	26,199
Edwards	232	642	346	673
El Paso	112,952	57,150	122,021	61,783
Ellis	13,881	39,574	15,333	38,078
Erath	1,965	10,329	3,128	10,768
Falls	2,033	3,356	2,225	3,328
Fannin	2,486	8,161	3,464	8,092
Fayette	2,315	8,106	3,014	7,582
Fisher	512	1,094	687	1,083
Floyd	551	1,523	730	1,784
Foard	140	348	198	327
Fort Bend	101,144	116,126	98,368	103,206
Franklin	751	3,446	1,036	3,392
Freestone	1,850	5,646	2,034	5,205
Frio	2,376	1,559	2,405	1,644
Gaines	535	3,484	650	3,385
Galveston	39,511	69,059	41,805	62,258
Garza	279	1,263	375	1,356
Gillespie	2,055	10,306	2,576	9,563
Glasscock	44	526	52	502
Goliad	1,127	2,294	1,329	2,298
Gonzales	1,777	4,216	2,167	4,076
Gray	886	6,443	1,153	6,924
Grayson	10,670	30,936	13,900	31,136
Gregg	12,398	28,742	13,166	29,203
Grimes	2,339	6,141	2,704	5,562
Guadalupe	15,744	33,117	16,156	30,869
Hale	2,243	6,490	2,708	7,171
Hall	265	832	324	930
Hamilton	591	2,918	863	2,876
Hansford	159	1,788	240	1,847
Hardeman	302	1,176	373	1,199
Hardin	3,359	17,746	3,939	16,603
Harris	587,044	586,073	590,982	571,883
Harrison	8,456	17,512	8,887	17,103
Hartley	184	1,708	250	1,711
Haskell	553	1,424	699	1,388
Hays	25,537	31,661	28,431	29,638
Hemphill	192	1,298	216	1,345
Henderson	6,106	21,231	7,913	20,857
Hidalgo	97,969	39,865	90,261	39,668
Hill	2,752	9,132	3,811	9,264
Hockley	1,486	5,546	1,797	5,795
Hood	3,843	18,409	5,087	17,299
Hopkins	2,777	9,836	3,530	9,299
Houston	2,265	5,880	2,656	5,872
Howard	2,110	6,453	2,545	7,029
Hudspeth	379	471	430	458
Hunt	6,671	21,011	8,594	20,573
Hutchinson	1,045	6,804	1,322	7,361
Irion	112	668	164	644
Jack	303	2,580	470	2,528
Jackson	1,070	3,906	1,301	3,723
Jasper	3,423	9,957	3,658	9,022
Jeff Davis	440	719	468	749
Jefferson	44,668	43,242	44,888	42,905
Jim Hogg	1,301	356	1,336	472
Jim Wells	6,492	4,598	6,706	4,841
Johnson	10,496	37,661	12,912	36,685
Jones	1,226	4,262	1,528	4,203
Karnes	1,325	2,825	1,760	2,736
Kaufman	9,472	24,846	11,161	23,735
Kendall	3,043	14,508	3,599	12,971
Kenedy	82	84	108	94
Kent	66	335	99	342
Kerr	4,338	17,274	5,570	16,752
Kimble	217	1,667	342	1,487
King	5	139	8	151
Kinney	522	880	633	907
Kleberg	4,754	4,058	5,256	4,540
Knox	332	1,160	367	986
La Salle	965	669	1,052	714
Lamar	4,181	12,826	5,243	12,952
Lamb	998	3,058	1,156	3,344
Lampasas	1,479	5,621	1,903	5,651
Lavaca	1,428	6,796	1,869	6,293
Lee	1,632	4,507	2,000	4,312
Leon	1,062	5,814	1,418	5,566
Liberty	5,202	17,323	5,991	15,448
Limestone	2,208	5,288	2,516	5,079
Lipscomb	119	1,044	155	1,093
Live Oak	919	3,154	1,048	3,095
Llano	1,822	7,610	2,250	7,281
Loving	9	54	12	67
Lubbock	26,271	63,469	30,486	66,304
Lynn	506	1,439	627	1,473
Madison	967	3,028	1,146	2,891
Marion	1,495	2,733	1,644	2,567
Martin	248	1,368	314	1,389
Mason	380	1,565	546	1,544
Matagorda	3,980	8,040	4,440	7,835
Maverick	8,303	2,171	8,554	2,316
McCulloch	537	2,419	728	2,263
McLennan	25,694	47,903	29,998	49,044
McMullen	67	431	132	400
Medina	4,784	11,079	5,147	10,480
Menard	171	665	295	712
Midland	8,286	35,689	9,691	36,155
Milam	2,636	5,481	3,044	5,217
Mills	279	1,882	398	1,753
Mitchell	538	1,756	586	1,815
Montague	1,116	6,549	1,597	6,245
Montgomery	32,920	137,969	36,703	119,884
Moore	964	3,968	1,123	4,282
Morris	1,858	3,232	2,055	3,158
Motley	55	538	67	522
Nacogdoches	6,465	13,925	8,393	14,828
Navarro	4,350	10,847	5,400	10,810
Newton	1,677	4,112	1,751	3,446
Nolan	1,216	3,282	1,521	3,485
Nueces	45,771	48,966	47,912	52,391
Ochiltree	253	2,719	243	2,851
Oldham	71	790	102	813
Orange	6,800	23,366	7,646	21,509
Palo Pinto	1,811	7,393	2,499	7,264
Panola	2,211	7,950	2,586	7,582
Parker	7,853	39,243	10,502	36,974
Parmer	529	2,011	719	2,969
Pecos	1,591	2,512	1,476	2,480
Polk	4,859	14,071	6,230	13,731
Potter	7,126	18,918	8,939	20,761
Presidio	1,282	504	1,252	489
Rains	761	3,279	1,048	3,146
Randall	7,574	41,447	9,468	41,948
Reagan	158	676	197	795
Real	277	1,236	375	1,238
Red River	1,482	3,549	1,539	3,461
Reeves	1,655	1,188	1,606	1,445
Refugio	998	1,663	1,382	1,855
Roberts	33	468	41	477
Robertson	2,798	4,419	2,675	3,980
Rockwall	8,120	27,113	8,492	23,300
Runnels	519	3,104	720	3,118
Rusk	4,451	13,924	4,983	13,646
Sabine	807	3,727	1,077	3,749
San Augustine	1,193	2,469	1,328	2,342
San Jacinto	2,410	7,107	2,721	6,151
San Patricio	7,856	12,005	8,854	12,404
San Saba	323	1,905	487	1,941
Schleicher	221	787	324	970
Scurry	838	4,124	1,088	4,414
Shackelford	131	1,218	208	1,284
Shelby	2,322	6,879	2,548	6,630
Sherman	121	908	127	884
Smith	21,456	57,331	23,726	55,187
Somervell	613	2,871	799	2,677
Starr	10,260	1,547	8,274	1,492
Stephens	475	2,892	626	2,869
Sterling	31	459	97	520
Stonewall	160	507	206	524
Sutton	369	1,110	381	1,189
Swisher	579	1,655	813	1,683
Tarrant	253,071	348,920	274,880	348,420
Taylor	9,750	32,904	12,690	34,317
Terrell	184	358	186	323
Terry	1,059	2,602	1,379	2,879
Throckmorton	109	700	166	671
Titus	2,648	6,084	3,145	6,028
Tom Green	9,294	26,878	11,158	27,362
Travis	232,788	140,152	254,017	136,981
Trinity	1,614	4,537	1,925	4,095
Tyler	1,668	5,910	2,166	5,644
Upshur	2,971	12,015	3,790	11,222
Upton	333	953	288	898
Uvalde	3,825	4,529	4,126	4,590
Val Verde	6,285	5,635	6,982	5,752
Van Zandt	3,084	15,794	4,505	15,734
Victoria	8,802	19,692	9,832	19,878
Walker	6,252	12,140	7,334	11,623
Waller	6,514	9,244	7,153	8,265
Ward	841	2,366	899	2,667
Washington	3,381	10,857	4,034	10,176
Webb	37,597	11,078	33,452	13,119
Wharton	4,235	9,750	4,937	9,431
Wheeler	232	1,878	314	1,918
Wichita	10,525	29,812	13,868	31,731
Wilbarger	971	2,956	1,196	3,283

County	2012 Obama (D)	Romney (R)	2008 Obama (D)	McCain (R)
Willacy	3,600	1,416	3,409	1,456
Williamson	61,875	97,006	67,691	88,323
Wilson	4,821	12,218	5,362	10,904
Winkler	398	1,311	477	1,529
Wise	3,221	17,207	4,471	15,973
Wood	3,056	14,351	4,010	13,658
Yoakum	409	1,698	450	1,989
Young	992	6,225	1,303	5,942
Zapata	2,527	997	1,939	919
Zavala	3,042	574	3,263	596
Totals	3,308,124	4,569,843	3,528,633	4,479,328

Texas Vote Since 1960

2012: Romney, R., 4,569,843; Obama, D., 3,308,124; Johnson, LB., 88,580; Stein, Green, 24,657.
2008: McCain, R., 4,479,328; Obama, D., 3,528,633 Barr, LB., 56,116.
2004: Bush, R., 4,526,917; Kerry, D., 2,832,704; Badnarik, LB., 38,787.
2000: Bush, R., 3,799,639; Gore, D., 2,433,746; Nader, Green, 137,994; Browne, LB., 23,160; Buchanan, Ind., 12,394.
1996: Dole, R., 2,736,167; Clinton, D., 2,459,683; Perot, RF., 378,537; Browne, LB., 20,256; Phillips, U.S. Taxpayers, 7,472; Hagelin, Natural Law, 4,422.
1992: Bush, R., 2,496,071; Clinton, D., 2,281,815; Perot, Ind., 1,354,781; Marrou, LB., 19,699.
1988: Bush, R., 3,036,829; Dukakis, D., 2,352,748; Paul, LB., 30,355; Fulani, New Alliance, 7,208.
1984: Reagan, R., 3,433,428; Mondale, D., 1,949,276.
1980: Reagan, R., 2,510,705; Carter, D., 1,881,147; Anderson, Ind., 111,613; Clark, LB., 37,643; write-in, 528.
1976: Carter, D., 2,082,319; Ford, R., 1,953,300; McCarthy, Ind., 20,118; Anderson, Amer., 11,442; Camejo, Soc. Workers, 1,723; write-in, 2,982.
1972: Nixon, R., 2,298,896; McGovern, D., 1,154,289; Jenness, Soc. Workers, 8,664; Schmitz, Amer., 6,039; others, 3,393.
1968: Humphrey, D., 1,266,804; Nixon, R., 1,227,844; Wallace, 3rd party, 584,269; write-in, 489.
1964: Johnson, D., 1,663,185; Goldwater, R., 958,566; Lightburn, Const., 5,060.
1960: Kennedy, D., 1,167,932; Nixon, R., 1,121,699; Sullivan, Const., 18,169; Decker, Prohib., 3,870; write-in, 15.

Utah

County	2012 Obama (D)	Romney (R)	2008 Obama (D)	McCain (R)
Beaver	346	2,174	542	1,902
Box Elder	1,984	17,101	3,311	15,228
Cache	6,244	35,039	10,294	29,127
Carbon	2,275	5,090	3,468	4,091
Daggett	94	406	131	297
Davis	21,889	96,861	30,477	77,341
Duchesne	581	5,698	911	4,689
Emery	569	3,777	973	3,358
Garfield	308	1,832	405	1,710
Grand	1,727	1,996	2,067	1,871
Iron	2,148	14,200	3,258	12,518
Juab	451	3,448	741	2,683
Kane	744	2,522	856	2,212
Millard	431	4,478	758	3,653
Morgan	403	4,114	689	3,311
Piute	74	697	141	635
Rich	83	915	154	831
Salt Lake	146,147	223,811	176,988	176,692
San Juan	2,139	3,074	2,406	2,638
Sanpete	980	8,406	1,631	6,664
Sevier	738	7,207	1,359	6,394
Summit	8,072	8,884	9,532	6,956
Tooele	4,524	14,268	5,830	10,998
Uintah	997	10,421	1,462	8,441
Utah	17,281	156,950	29,567	122,224
Wasatch	2,191	7,220	2,892	5,430
Washington	8,337	44,698	10,826	37,311
Wayne	215	1,089	335	940
Weber	19,841	54,224	25,666	45,885
Totals	251,813	740,600	327,670	596,030

Utah Vote Since 1960

2012: Romney, R., 740,600; Obama, D., 251,813; Johnson, LB., 12,572; Anderson, Justice, 5,335; Stein, Green, 3,817; Goode, Const., 2,871; La Riva, unaff., 393.
2008: McCain, R., 596,030; Obama, D., 327,670; Baldwin, Const., 12,012; Nader, unaff., 8,416; Barr, LB., 6,966; McKinney, unaff., 982; La Riva, unaff., 262.
2004: Bush, R., 663,742; Kerry, D., 241,199; Nader, Ind., 11,305; Peroutka, Const., 6,841; Badnarik, LB., 3,375; Jay, Pers. Choice, 946; Harris, Soc. Workers, 393.

2000: Bush, R., 515,096; Gore, D., 203,053; Nader, Green, 35,850; Buchanan, RF., 9,319; Browne, LB., 3,616; Phillips, Ind. Amer., 2,709; Hagelin, Natural Law, 763; Harris, Soc. Workers, 186; Youngkeit, Ind., 161.
1996: Dole, R., 361,911; Clinton, D., 221,633; Perot, RF., 66,461; Nader, Green, 4,615; Browne, LB., 4,129; Phillips, Taxpayers, 2,601; Templin, Ind. Amer., 1,290; Crane, Ind., 1,101; Hagelin, Natural Law, 1,085; Moorehead, Workers World, 298; Harris, Soc. Workers, 235; Dodge, Prohib., 111.
1992: Bush, R., 322,632; Perot, Ind., 203,400; Clinton, D., 183,429; Gritz, Populist/America First, 28,602; Marrou, LB., 1,900; Hagelin, Natural Law, 1,319; LaRouche, Ind., 1,089.
1988: Bush, R., 428,442; Dukakis, D., 207,352; Paul, LB., 7,473; Dennis, Amer., 2,158.
1984: Reagan, R., 469,105; Mondale, D., 155,369; Bergland, LB., 2,447.
1980: Reagan, R., 439,687; Carter, D., 124,266; Anderson, Ind., 30,284; Clark, LB., 7,226; Commoner, Citizens, 1,009; Greaves, Amer., 965; Rarick, Amer. Ind., 522; Hall, Comm., 139; DeBerry, Soc. Workers, 124.
1976: Ford, R., 337,908; Carter, D., 182,110; Anderson, Amer., 13,304; McCarthy, Ind., 3,907; MacBride, LB., 2,438; Maddox, Amer. Ind., 1,162; Camejo, Soc. Workers, 268; Hall, Comm., 121.
1972: Nixon, R., 323,643; McGovern, D., 126,284; Schmitz, Amer., 28,549.
1968: Nixon, R., 238,728; Humphrey, D., 156,665; Wallace, 3rd party, 26,906; Peace/Freedom, 180; Halstead, Soc. Workers, 89.
1964: Johnson, D., 219,628; Goldwater, R., 181,785.
1960: Nixon, R., 205,361; Kennedy, D., 169,248; Dobbs, Soc. Workers, 100.

Vermont

County	2012 Obama (D)	Romney (R)	2008 Obama (D)	McCain (R)
Addison	12,257	5,203	13,202	5,667
Bennington	11,514	5,687	12,524	6,133
Caledonia	8,192	5,088	8,900	5,472
Chittenden	53,626	21,571	59,611	22,237
Essex	1,539	1,164	1,733	1,284
Franklin	12,057	7,405	13,179	7,853
Grand Isle	2,531	1,471	2,694	1,490
Lamoille	8,371	3,342	8,914	3,515
Orange	9,076	4,588	9,799	5,047
Orleans	7,117	4,306	7,998	4,482
Rutland	17,088	10,835	19,355	11,584
Washington	20,351	8,093	22,324	9,129
Windham	16,026	5,347	17,585	5,997
Windsor	19,494	8,598	21,444	9,084
Totals	199,239	92,698	219,262	98,974

Vermont Vote Since 1960

2012: Obama, D., 199,239; Romney, LB., 92,698; Johnson, LB., 3,487; Anderson, Justice, 1,128; Lindsay, Socialism/Liberation, 695.
2008: Obama, D., 219,262; McCain, R., 98,974; Nader, Ind., 3,339; Barr, LB., 1,067; Baldwin, Const., 500; Calero, Soc. Workers, 150; La Riva, Socialism/Liberation, 149; Moore, Liberty Union, 141.
2004: Kerry, D., 184,067; Bush, R., 121,180; Nader, Ind., 4,494; Badnarik, LB., 1,102; Parker, Liberty Union, 265; Calero, Soc. Workers, 244.
2000: Gore, D., 149,022; Bush, R., 119,775; Nader, Green, 20,374; Buchanan, RF., 2,192; Lane, Grass Roots, 1,044; Browne, LB., 784; Hagelin, Natural Law, 219; McReynolds, Liberty Union, 161; Phillips, Const., 153; Harris, Soc. Workers, 70.
1996: Clinton, D., 137,894; Dole, R., 80,352; Perot, RF., 31,024; Nader, Green, 5,585; Browne, LB., 1,183; Hagelin, Natural Law, 498; Peron, Grass Roots, 480; Phillips, Taxpayers, 382; Hollis, Liberty Union, 292; Harris, Soc. Workers, 199.
1992: Clinton, D., 133,590; Bush, R., 88,122; Perot, Ind., 65,985.
1988: Bush, R., 124,331; Dukakis, D., 115,775; Paul, LB., 1,000; LaRouche, Ind., 275.
1984: Reagan, R., 135,865; Mondale, D., 95,730; Bergland, LB., 1,002.
1980: Reagan, R., 94,598; Carter, D., 81,891; Anderson, Ind., 31,760; Commoner, Citizens, 2,316; Clark, LB., 1,900; McReynolds, Liberty Union, 136; Hall, Comm., 118; DeBerry, Soc. Workers, 75; scattered, 413.
1976: Ford, R., 100,387; Carter, D., 77,798 and Ind. Vermonters, 991 (total, 79,789); McCarthy, Ind., 4,001; Camejo, Soc. Workers, 430; LaRouche, U.S. Labor, 196; scattered, 99.
1972: Nixon, R., 117,149; McGovern, D., 68,174; Spock, Liberty Union, 1,010; Jenness, Soc. Workers, 296; scattered, 318.
1968: Nixon, R., 85,142; Humphrey, D., 70,255; Wallace, 3rd party, 5,104; Gregory, New Party, 579; Halstead, Soc. Workers, 295.
1964: Johnson, D., 107,674; Goldwater, R., 54,868.
1960: Nixon, R., 98,131; Kennedy, D., 69,186.

Virginia

County	2012 Obama (D)	Romney (R)	2008 Obama (D)	McCain (R)
Accomack	7,655	8,213	7,607	7,833
Albemarle	29,757	23,297	29,792	20,576
Alleghany	3,403	3,595	3,553	3,715
Amelia	2,490	4,331	2,488	3,970
Amherst	5,900	8,876	6,094	8,470
Appomattox	2,453	5,340	2,641	4,903
Arlington	81,269	34,474	78,994	29,876
Augusta	9,451	23,624	9,825	23,120
Bath	894	1,274	1,043	1,349
Bedford	10,209	26,679	11,017	24,420
Bland	735	2,144	864	2,031
Botetourt	5,452	12,479	5,693	11,471
Brunswick	4,994	2,968	4,973	2,877
Buchanan	3,094	6,436	4,063	4,541
Buckingham	3,750	3,569	3,489	3,428
Campbell	7,595	17,695	8,091	17,444
Caroline	7,276	6,151	7,163	5,617
Carroll	3,685	8,736	4,109	8,187
Charles City	2,772	1,396	2,838	1,288
Charlotte	2,503	3,311	2,705	3,372
Chesterfield	77,694	90,934	74,310	86,413
Clarke	3,239	4,296	3,457	3,840
Craig	830	1,757	877	1,695
Culpeper	8,285	11,580	8,802	10,711
Cumberland	2,422	2,538	2,255	2,418
Dickenson	2,473	4,274	3,278	3,324
Dinwiddie	6,550	6,875	6,246	6,526
Essex	3,016	2,602	2,934	2,379
Fairfax	315,273	206,773	310,359	200,994
Fauquier	13,965	21,034	14,616	19,227
Floyd	2,732	4,673	2,937	4,441
Fluvanna	5,893	6,678	6,185	6,420
Franklin	9,090	16,718	9,618	15,414
Frederick	12,690	22,858	12,961	20,149
Giles	2,730	4,660	3,192	4,462
Gloucester	6,764	12,137	6,916	12,089
Goochland	4,676	8,448	4,813	7,643
Grayson	2,068	4,801	2,480	4,540
Greene	3,290	5,569	3,174	4,980
Greensville	3,135	1,766	3,122	1,729
Halifax	7,766	8,694	8,126	8,600
Hanover	18,294	39,940	18,447	37,344
Henrico	89,594	70,449	86,323	67,381
Henry	10,317	13,984	11,118	13,758
Highland	459	924	590	930
Isle of Wight	8,761	11,802	8,573	11,258
James City	17,879	22,843	17,352	20,912
King and Queen	1,745	1,865	1,918	1,763
King George	4,477	6,604	4,473	5,888
King William	3,344	5,466	3,344	4,966
Lancaster	3,149	3,753	3,235	3,647
Lee	2,583	6,847	3,219	5,825
Loudoun	82,479	75,292	74,845	63,336
Louisa	6,953	9,215	6,978	8,182
Lunenburg	2,684	2,969	2,703	2,900
Madison	2,639	3,869	2,862	3,758
Mathews	1,807	3,488	1,934	3,456
Mecklenburg	6,921	7,973	7,127	7,817
Middlesex	2,370	3,619	2,391	3,545
Montgomery	19,903	20,006	21,031	19,028
Nelson	4,171	3,947	4,391	3,647
New Kent	3,555	7,246	3,493	6,385
Northampton	3,741	2,676	3,800	2,713
Northumberland	3,191	4,310	3,312	4,041
Nottoway	3,344	3,409	3,413	3,499
Orange	6,870	9,244	7,107	8,506
Page	3,724	6,344	4,235	6,041
Patrick	2,417	5,622	2,879	5,491
Pittsylvania	10,858	19,263	11,445	18,730
Powhatan	4,088	11,200	4,237	10,088
Prince Edward	5,132	3,952	5,101	4,174
Prince George	6,991	8,879	7,130	8,752
Prince William	103,331	74,458	93,435	67,621
Pulaski	5,292	8,920	5,918	8,857
Rappahannock	1,980	2,311	2,105	2,227
Richmond	1,574	2,160	1,618	2,092
Roanoke	18,711	31,624	19,812	30,571
Rockbridge	4,088	5,898	4,347	5,732
Rockingham	10,065	24,186	10,453	22,468
Russell	3,718	8,180	4,932	6,389
Scott	2,395	7,439	2,725	6,980
Shenandoah	6,469	12,538	6,912	12,005
Smyth	4,171	8,379	4,239	7,817
Southampton	4,437	4,733	4,402	4,583
Spotsylvania	25,165	31,844	24,897	28,610
Stafford	27,182	32,480	25,716	29,221
Surry	2,576	1,671	2,626	1,663
Sussex	3,358	2,021	3,301	2,026
Tazewell	3,661	13,843	5,596	11,201
Warren	6,452	9,869	6,997	8,879
Washington	7,076	18,141	8,063	16,077
Westmoreland	4,295	3,731	4,577	3,719
Wise	3,760	11,076	4,995	8,914
Wythe	3,783	8,324	4,107	8,207
York	13,183	20,204	13,700	19,833
City				
Alexandria	52,199	20,249	50,473	19,181
Bedford	1,225	1,527	1,208	1,497
Bristol	2,492	4,780	2,665	4,579
Buena Vista	919	1,564	1,108	1,282
Charlottesville	16,510	4,844	15,705	4,078
Chesapeake	55,052	53,900	53,994	52,625
Colonial Heights	2,544	5,941	2,562	6,161
Covington	1,319	975	1,304	1,020
Danville	12,218	7,763	12,352	8,361
Emporia	1,793	886	1,702	897
Fairfax	6,651	4,775	6,575	4,691
Falls Church	5,015	2,147	4,695	1,970
Franklin	2,833	1,496	2,819	1,576
Fredericksburg	7,131	4,060	6,155	3,413
Galax	900	1,332	1,052	1,317
Hampton	46,966	18,640	46,917	20,476
Harrisonburg	8,654	6,565	8,444	6,048
Hopewell	5,179	3,739	5,285	4,149
Lexington	1,486	1,146	1,543	914
Lynchburg	15,948	19,806	16,269	17,638
Manassas	8,478	6,463	7,518	5,975
Manassas Park	2,879	1,699	2,463	1,634
Martinsville	3,855	2,312	4,139	2,311
Newport News	51,100	27,230	51,972	28,667
Norfolk	62,687	23,147	62,819	24,814
Norton	566	895	743	744
Petersburg	14,283	1,527	13,774	1,583
Poquoson	1,679	5,312	1,748	5,229
Portsmouth	32,501	12,858	32,327	13,984
Radford	2,732	2,520	2,930	2,418
Richmond	75,921	20,050	73,623	18,649
Roanoke	24,134	14,991	24,934	15,394
Salem	4,760	7,299	5,164	7,088
Staunton	5,728	5,272	5,569	5,330
Suffolk	24,267	17,820	22,446	17,165
Virginia Beach	94,299	99,291	98,885	100,319
Waynesboro	3,840	4,790	3,906	4,815
Williamsburg	4,903	2,682	4,328	2,353
Winchester	5,094	4,946	5,268	4,725
Totals	**1,971,820**	**1,822,522**	**1,959,532**	**1,725,005**

Virginia Vote Since 1960

2012: Obama, D., 1,971,820; Romney, R., 1,822,522; Johnson, LB., 31,216; Goode, Const., 13,058; Stein, Green, 8,627.

2008: Obama, D., 1,959,532; McCain, R., 1,725,005; Nader, Ind., 11,483; Barr, LB., 11,067; Baldwin, Ind. Green, 7,474; McKinney, Green, 2,344.

2004: Bush, R., 1,716,959; Kerry, D., 1,454,742; Badnarik, LB., 11,032; Peroutka, Const., 10,161.

2000: Bush, R., 1,437,490; Gore, D., 1,217,290; Nader, Green, 59,398; Browne, LB., 15,198; Buchanan, RF., 5,455; Phillips, Const., 1,809.

1996: Dole, R., 1,138,350; Clinton, D., 1,091,060; Perot, RF., 159,861; Phillips, Taxpayers, 13,687; Browne, LB., 9,174; Hagelin, Natural Law, 4,510.

1992: Bush, R., 1,150,517; Clinton, D., 1,038,650; Perot, Ind., 348,639; LaRouche, Ind., 11,937; Marrou, LB., 5,730; Fulani, New Alliance, 3,192.

1988: Bush, R., 1,309,162; Dukakis, D., 859,799; Fulani, Ind., 14,312; Paul, LB., 8,336.

1984: Reagan, R., 1,337,078; Mondale, D., 796,250.

1980: Reagan, R., 989,609; Carter, D., 752,174; Anderson, Ind., 95,418; Commoner, Citizens, 14,024; Clark, LB., 12,821; DeBerry, Soc. Workers, 1,986.

1976: Ford, R., 836,554; Carter, D., 813,896; Camejo, Soc. Workers, 17,802; Anderson, Amer., 16,686; LaRouche, U.S. Labor, 7,508; MacBride, LB., 4,648.

1972: Nixon, R., 988,493; McGovern, D., 438,887; Schmitz, Amer., 19,721; Fisher, Soc. Labor, 9,918.

1968: Nixon, R., 590,319; Humphrey, D., 442,387; Wallace, 3rd party, 320,272; Blomen, Soc. Labor, 4,671; Gregory, Peace/Freedom, 1,680; Munn, Prohib., 601. *10,561 votes for Wallace were omitted in the count.

1964: Johnson, D., 558,038; Goldwater, R., 481,334; Hass, Soc. Labor, 2,895.

1960: Nixon, R., 404,521; Kennedy, D., 362,327; Coiner, Conservative, 4,204; Hass, Soc. Labor, 397.

Washington

County	2012 Obama (D)	Romney (R)	2008 Obama (D)	McCain (R)
Adams	1,540	3,171	1,552	3,222
Asotin	4,003	5,654	4,139	5,451
Benton	28,145	49,461	26,288	45,345
Chelan	13,112	18,402	13,781	17,605
Clallam	18,580	18,437	19,470	18,199
Clark	93,382	92,951	95,356	84,212
Columbia	645	1,568	686	1,499
Cowlitz	22,726	20,746	24,597	19,554
Douglas	5,166	9,425	5,848	9,098
Ferry	1,294	1,995	1,467	1,916
Franklin	8,398	13,748	7,361	12,037
Garfield	336	913	385	968
Grant	8,950	17,852	9,601	17,153
Gray's Harbor	15,960	11,914	16,354	12,104
Island	21,478	19,605	22,058	19,426
Jefferson	12,739	6,405	13,252	6,330
King	668,004	275,700	648,230	259,716
Kitsap	67,277	52,846	68,624	53,297
Kittitas	7,949	9,782	8,030	9,471
Klickitat	4,598	5,316	4,965	4,944
Lewis	12,664	20,452	13,624	20,278
Lincoln	1,673	4,063	2,032	3,803
Mason	14,764	12,761	15,050	12,600
Okanogan	7,108	9,221	7,613	8,798
Pacific	5,711	4,499	6,094	4,555
Pend Oreille	2,508	3,952	2,562	3,717
Pierce	186,430	148,467	181,824	141,673
San Juan	7,125	3,111	7,374	2,958
Skagit	28,688	25,071	30,053	24,687
Skamania	2,628	2,687	2,817	2,524
Snohomish	188,516	133,016	187,294	126,722
Spokane	102,295	115,285	105,786	108,314
Stevens	7,762	13,691	8,499	13,132
Thurston	74,037	49,287	75,882	48,366
Wahkiakum	1,094	1,119	1,121	1,105
Walla Walla	9,768	14,648	10,081	14,182
Whatcom	57,089	42,703	58,236	40,205
Whitman	8,037	8,507	9,070	8,104
Yakima	33,217	42,239	33,792	41,946
Totals	**1,755,396**	**1,290,670**	**1,750,848**	**1,229,216**

Washington Vote Since 1960

2012: Obama, D., 1,755,396; Romney, R., 1,290,670; Johnson, LB., 42,202; Stein, Green, 20,928; Goode, Const., 8,851; Anderson, Justice, 4,946; Lindsay, Socialism/Liberation, 1,318; Harris, Soc. Workers, 1,205.
2008: Obama, D., 1,750,848; McCain, R., 1,229,216; Nader, Ind., 29,489; Barr, LB., 12,728; Baldwin, Const., 9,432; McKinney, Green, 3,819; La Riva, Socialism/Liberation, 705; Harris, Soc. Workers, 641.
2004: Kerry, D., 1,510,201; Bush, R., 1,304,894; Nader, Ind., 23,283; Badnarik, LB., 11,955; Peroutka, Const., 3,922; Cobb, Green, 2,974; Parker, Workers World, 1,077; Harris, Soc. Workers, 547; Van Auken, Soc. Equality, 231.
2000: Gore, D., 1,247,652; Bush, R., 1,108,864; Nader, Green, 103,002; Browne, LB., 13,135; Buchanan, Freedom, 7,171; Hagelin, Natural Law, 2,927; Phillips, Const., 1,989; Moorehead, Workers World, 1,729; McReynolds, Soc., 660; Harris, Soc. Workers, 304.
1996: Clinton, D., 1,123,323; Dole, R., 840,712; Perot, RF., 201,003; Nader, Ind., 60,322; Browne, LB., 12,522; Hagelin, Natural Law, 6,076; Phillips, U.S. Taxpayers, 4,578; Collins, Ind., 2,374; Moorehead, Workers World, 2,189; Harris, Soc. Workers, 738.
1992: Clinton, D., 993,037; Bush, R., 731,234; Perot, Ind., 541,780; Marrou, LB., 7,533; Gritz, Populist/America First, 4,854; Hagelin, Natural Law, 2,456; Phillips, U.S. Taxpayers, 2,354; Fulani, New Alliance, 1,776; Daniels, Ind., 1,171.
1988: Dukakis, D., 933,516; Bush, R., 903,835; Paul, LB., 17,240; LaRouche, Ind., 4,412.
1984: Reagan, R., 1,051,670; Mondale, D., 798,352; Bergland, LB., 8,844.
1980: Reagan, R., 865,244; Carter, D., 650,193; Anderson, Ind., 185,073; Clark, LB., 29,213; Commoner, Citizens, 9,403; DeBerry, Soc. Workers, 1,137; McReynolds, Soc., 956; Hall, Comm., 834; Griswold, Workers World, 341.
1976: Ford, R., 777,732; Carter, D., 717,323; McCarthy, Ind., 36,986; Maddox, Amer. Ind., 8,585; Anderson, Amer., 5,046; MacBride, LB., 5,042; Wright, People's, 1,124; Camejo, Soc. Workers, 905; LaRouche, U.S. Labor, 903; Hall, Comm., 817; Levin, Soc. Labor, 713; Zeidler, Soc., 358.
1972: Nixon, R., 837,135; McGovern, D., 568,334; Schmitz, Amer., 58,906; Spock, Ind., 2,644; Hospers, LB., 1,537; Fisher, Soc. Labor, 1,102; Jenness, Soc. Workers, 623; Hall, Comm., 566.
1968: Humphrey, D., 616,037; Nixon, R., 588,510; Wallace, 3rd party, 96,990; Cleaver, Peace/Freedom, 1,609; Blomen, Soc. Labor, 488; Mitchell, Free Ballot, 377; Halstead, Soc. Workers, 270.

1964: Johnson, D., 779,699; Goldwater, R., 470,366; Hass, Soc. Labor, 7,772; DeBerry, Freedom Soc., 537.
1960: Nixon, R., 629,273; Kennedy, D., 599,298; Hass, Soc. Labor, 10,895; Curtis, Const., 1,401; Dobbs, Soc. Workers, 705.

West Virginia

County	2012 Obama (D)	Romney (R)	2008 Obama (D)	McCain (R)
Barbour	1,768	3,824	2,419	3,685
Berkeley	14,275	22,156	15,994	20,841
Boone	2,790	5,467	4,529	3,632
Braxton	1,998	2,725	2,704	2,629
Brooke	4,005	5,060	4,717	4,961
Cabell	13,568	17,985	15,292	18,793
Calhoun	818	1,319	993	1,366
Clay	931	1,971	1,421	1,755
Doddridge	575	2,130	735	2,218
Fayette	5,419	8,350	7,242	7,658
Gilmer	840	1,595	1,004	1,445
Grant	718	3,783	997	3,166
Greenbrier	4,710	7,930	5,881	7,567
Hampshire	2,299	5,523	2,983	5,222
Hancock	4,627	7,226	5,504	7,518
Hardy	1,482	3,536	1,901	3,376
Harrison	9,732	15,876	13,582	17,824
Jackson	3,854	7,408	4,861	7,148
Jefferson	10,398	11,258	11,687	10,600
Kanawha	32,480	41,364	40,594	40,952
Lewis	1,736	4,375	2,109	4,335
Lincoln	2,227	4,383	3,029	3,637
Logan	3,469	8,222	5,873	7,326
Marion	8,959	12,054	11,618	11,501
Marshall	4,484	8,135	5,996	7,759
Mason	3,778	5,741	4,484	5,853
McDowell	2,109	3,959	3,430	2,882
Mercer	5,432	15,450	7,450	13,246
Mineral	2,885	7,833	3,750	7,616
Mingo	2,428	6,191	3,582	4,587
Monongalia	13,826	16,831	17,060	15,775
Monroe	1,455	3,616	2,014	3,397
Morgan	2,363	4,513	2,721	4,428
Nicholas	2,664	5,898	4,357	4,804
Ohio	6,786	10,768	8,593	10,694
Pendleton	1,074	2,095	1,310	2,035
Pleasants	955	1,825	1,142	1,772
Pocahontas	1,303	2,182	1,548	2,011
Preston	2,931	7,889	4,205	7,325
Putnam	7,256	16,032	9,334	15,162
Raleigh	7,739	20,614	10,237	17,548
Randolph	3,342	6,160	4,539	6,060
Ritchie	768	2,921	998	2,781
Roane	1,939	2,982	2,511	2,943
Summers	1,621	2,981	2,290	2,891
Taylor	1,941	3,840	2,462	3,605
Tucker	880	2,176	1,288	2,123
Tyler	890	2,314	1,241	2,415
Upshur	2,158	5,939	2,925	5,911
Wayne	4,931	8,688	6,137	8,947
Webster	947	1,710	1,552	1,386
Wetzel	2,217	3,473	2,942	3,342
Wirt	676	1,427	782	1,496
Wood	11,230	22,183	12,573	22,896
Wyoming	1,583	5,769	2,735	4,621
Totals	**238,269**	**417,655**	**303,857**	**397,466**

West Virginia Vote Since 1960

2012: Romney, R., 417,655; Obama, D., 238,269; Johnson, LB., 6,302; Stein, Mountain, 4,406; Terry, NPA, 3,806.
2008: McCain, R., 397,466; Obama, D., 303,857; Nader, unaff., 7,219; Baldwin, Const., 2,465; McKinney, Mountain, 2,355.
2004: Bush, R., 423,778; Kerry, D., 326,541; Nader, Ind., 4,063; Badnarik, LB., 1,405.
2000: Bush, R., 336,475; Gore, D., 295,497; Nader, Green, 10,680; Buchanan, RF., 3,169; Browne, LB., 1,912; Hagelin, Natural Law, 367.
1996: Clinton, D., 327,812; Dole, R., 233,946; Perot, RF., 71,639; Browne, LB., 3,062.
1992: Clinton, D., 331,001; Bush, R., 241,974; Perot, Ind., 108,829; Marrou, LB., 1,873.
1988: Dukakis, D., 341,016; Bush, R., 310,065; Fulani, New Alliance, 2,230.
1984: Reagan, R., 405,483; Mondale, D., 328,125.
1980: Carter, D., 367,462; Reagan, R., 334,206; Anderson, Ind., 31,691; Clark, LB., 4,356.
1976: Carter, D., 435,864; Ford, R., 314,726.
1972: Nixon, R., 484,964; McGovern, D., 277,435.
1968: Humphrey, D., 374,091; Nixon, R., 307,555; Wallace, 3rd party, 72,560.
1964: Johnson, D., 538,087; Goldwater, R., 253,953.
1960: Kennedy, D., 441,786; Nixon, R., 395,995.

Wisconsin

County	2012 Obama (D)	2012 Romney (R)	2008 Obama (D)	2008 McCain (R)
Adams	5,542	4,644	5,806	3,974
Ashland	5,399	2,820	5,818	2,634
Barron	10,890	11,443	12,078	10,457
Bayfield	6,033	3,603	5,972	3,365
Brown	62,526	64,836	67,269	55,854
Buffalo	3,570	3,364	3,949	2,923
Burnett	3,986	4,550	4,337	4,200
Calumet	11,489	14,539	13,295	12,722
Chippewa	15,237	15,322	16,239	13,492
Clark	6,172	7,412	7,454	6,383
Columbia	17,175	13,026	16,661	12,193
Crawford	4,629	3,067	4,987	2,830
Dane	216,071	83,644	205,984	73,065
Dodge	18,762	25,211	19,183	23,015
Door	9,357	8,121	10,142	7,112
Douglas	14,863	7,705	15,830	7,835
Dunn	11,316	10,224	13,002	9,566
Eau Claire	30,666	23,256	33,146	20,959
Florence	953	1,645	1,134	1,512
Fond du Lac	22,379	30,355	23,463	28,164
Forest	2,425	2,172	2,673	1,963
Grant	13,594	10,255	14,875	9,068
Green	11,206	7,857	11,502	6,730
Green Lake	3,793	5,782	4,000	5,393
Iowa	8,105	4,287	7,987	3,829
Iron	1,784	1,790	1,914	1,464
Jackson	5,298	3,900	5,572	3,552
Jefferson	20,158	23,517	21,448	21,096
Juneau	6,242	5,411	6,186	5,148
Kenosha	44,867	34,977	45,836	31,609
Kewaunee	5,153	5,747	5,902	4,711
La Crosse	36,693	25,751	38,524	23,701
Lafayette	4,536	3,314	4,732	2,984
Langlade	4,573	5,816	5,182	5,081
Lincoln	7,563	7,455	8,424	6,519
Manitowoc	20,403	21,604	22,428	19,234
Marathon	32,363	36,617	36,367	30,345
Marinette	9,882	10,619	11,195	9,726
Marquette	4,014	3,992	4,068	3,654
Menominee	1,191	179	1,257	185
Milwaukee	332,438	154,924	319,819	149,445
Monroe	9,515	9,675	10,198	8,666
Oconto	8,865	10,741	9,927	8,755
Oneida	10,452	10,917	11,907	9,630
Outagamie	45,659	47,372	50,294	39,677
Ozaukee	19,159	36,077	20,579	32,172
Pepin	1,876	1,794	2,102	1,616
Pierce	10,235	10,397	11,803	9,812
Polk	10,073	12,094	10,876	11,282
Portage	22,075	16,615	24,817	13,810
Price	3,887	3,884	4,559	3,461
Racine	53,008	49,347	53,408	45,954
Richland	4,969	3,573	5,041	3,298
Rock	49,219	30,517	50,529	27,364
Rusk	3,397	3,676	3,855	3,253
St. Croix	19,910	25,503	21,177	22,837
Sauk	18,736	12,838	18,617	11,562
Sawyer	4,486	4,442	4,765	4,199
Shawano	9,000	11,022	10,259	9,538
Sheboygan	27,918	34,072	30,395	30,801
Taylor	3,763	5,601	4,563	4,586
Trempealeau	7,605	5,707	8,321	4,808
Vernon	8,044	5,942	8,463	5,367
Vilas	5,951	7,749	6,491	7,055
Walworth	22,552	29,006	24,177	25,485
Washburn	4,447	4,699	4,693	4,303
Washington	23,166	54,765	25,719	47,729
Waukesha	78,779	162,798	85,339	145,152
Waupaca	11,578	14,002	12,952	12,232
Waushara	5,335	6,562	5,868	5,770
Winnebago	45,449	42,122	48,167	37,946
Wood	18,581	19,704	21,710	16,581
Totals	**1,620,985**	**1,407,966**	**1,677,211**	**1,262,393**

Wisconsin Vote Since 1960

2012: Obama, D., 1,620,985; Romney, R., 1,407,966; Johnson, LB., 20,439; Stein, Green, 7,665; White, Soc. Equality, 553; La Riva, Socialism/Liberation, 526.

2008: Obama, D., 1,677,211; McCain, R., 1,262,393; Nader, Ind., 17,605; Barr, LB., 8,858; Baldwin, Ind., 5,072; McKinney, Green, 4,216; Wamboldt, Ind., 764; Moore, Ind., 540; La Riva, Ind., 237.

2004: Kerry, D., 1,489,504; Bush, R., 1,478,120; Nader, Ind., 16,390; Badnarik, LB., 6,464; Cobb, Green, 2,661; Brown, Ind., 471; Harris, Ind., 411.

2000: Gore, D., 1,242,987; Bush, R., 1,237,279; Nader, Green, 94,070; Buchanan, RF., 11,446; Browne, LB., 6,640; Phillips, Const., 2,042; Moorehead, Workers World, 1,063; Hagelin, RF., 878; Harris, Soc. Workers, 306.

1996: Clinton, D., 1,071,971; Dole, R., 845,029; Perot, RF., 227,339; Nader, Green, 28,723; Phillips, U.S. Taxpayers, 8,811; Browne, LB., 7,929; Hagelin, Natural Law, 1,379; Moorehead, Workers World, 1,333; Hollis, Soc., 848; Harris, Soc. Workers, 483.

1992: Clinton, D., 1,041,066; Bush, R., 930,855; Perot, Ind., 544,479; Marrou, LB., 2,877; Gritz, Populist/America First, 2,311; Daniels, Ind., 1,883; Phillips, U.S. Taxpayers, 1,772; Hagelin, Natural Law, 1,070.

1988: Dukakis, D., 1,126,794; Bush, R., 1,047,499; Paul, LB., 5,157; Duke, Populist, 3,056.

1984: Reagan, R., 1,198,584; Mondale, D., 995,740; Bergland, LB., 4,883.

1980: Reagan, R., 1,088,845; Carter, D., 981,584; Anderson, Ind., 160,657; Clark, LB., 29,135; Commoner, Citizens, 7,767; Rarick, Const., 1,519; McReynolds, Soc., 808; Hall, Comm., 772; Griswold, Workers World, 414; DeBerry, Soc. Workers, 383; scattered, 1,337.

1976: Carter, D., 1,040,232; Ford, R., 1,004,987; McCarthy, Ind., 34,943; Maddox, Amer. Ind., 8,552; Zeidler, Soc., 4,298; MacBride, LB., 3,814; Camejo, Soc. Workers, 1,691; Wright, People's, 943; Hall, Comm., 749; LaRouche, U.S. Labor, 738; Levin, Soc. Labor, 389; scattered, 2,839.

1972: Nixon, R., 989,430; McGovern, D., 810,174; Schmitz, Amer., 47,525; Spock, Ind., 2,701; Fisher, Soc. Labor, 998; Hall, Comm., 663; Reed, Ind., 506; scattered, 893.

1968: Nixon, R., 809,997; Humphrey, D., 748,804; Wallace, 3rd party, 127,835; Blomen, Soc. Labor, 1,338; Halstead, Soc. Workers, 1,222; scattered, 2,342.

1964: Johnson, D., 1,050,424; Goldwater, R., 638,495; DeBerry, Soc. Workers, 1,692; Hass, Soc. Labor, 1,204.

1960: Nixon, R., 895,175; Kennedy, D., 830,805; Dobbs, Soc. Workers, 1,792; Hass, Soc. Labor, 1,310.

Wyoming

County	2012 Obama (D)	2012 Romney (R)	2008 Obama (D)	2008 McCain (R)
Albany	7,458	7,866	8,644	7,936
Big Horn	868	4,285	1,108	4,045
Campbell	2,163	14,953	2,990	13,011
Carbon	2,110	4,148	2,336	4,331
Converse	1,089	5,043	1,380	4,922
Crook	426	3,109	612	2,967
Fremont	5,333	11,075	6,016	11,083
Goshen	1,458	4,178	1,832	3,942
Hot Springs	523	1,895	619	1,834
Johnson	749	3,363	908	3,334
Laramie	14,295	23,904	16,072	24,549
Lincoln	1,287	7,144	1,823	6,485
Natrona	8,961	22,132	10,475	21,906
Niobrara	200	1,022	244	1,017
Park	2,927	11,234	3,757	10,839
Platte	1,223	3,136	1,407	3,002
Sheridan	3,618	10,267	4,458	10,177
Sublette	767	3,472	936	3,316
Sweetwater	4,774	11,428	5,762	10,360
Teton	6,213	4,858	7,472	4,565
Uinta	1,628	6,615	2,317	5,763
Washakie	794	3,014	1,042	2,956
Weston	422	2,821	658	2,618
Totals	**69,286**	**170,962**	**82,868**	**164,958**

Wyoming Vote Since 1960

2012: Romney, R., 170,962; Obama, D., 69,286; Johnson, LB., 5,326; Goode, Const., 1,452.

2008: McCain, R., 164,958; Obama, D., 82,868; Nader, Ind., 2,525; Barr, LB., 1,594; Baldwin, Ind., 1,192.

2004: Bush, R., 167,629; Kerry, D., 70,776; Nader, Ind., 2,741; Badnarik, LB., 1,171; Peroutka, Ind., 631.

2000: Bush, R., 147,947; Gore, D., 60,481; Buchanan, RF., 2,724; Browne, LB., 1,443; Phillips, Ind., 720; Hagelin, Natural Law, 411.

1996: Dole, R., 105,388; Clinton, D., 77,934; Perot, RF., 25,928; Browne, LB., 1,739; Hagelin, Natural Law, 582.

1992: Bush, R., 79,347; Clinton, D., 68,160; Perot, Ind., 51,263.

1988: Bush, R., 106,867; Dukakis, D., 67,113; Paul, LB., 2,026; Fulani, New Alliance, 545.

1984: Reagan, R., 133,241; Mondale, D., 53,370; Bergland, LB., 2,357.

1980: Reagan, R., 110,700; Carter, D., 49,427; Anderson, Ind., 12,072; Clark, LB., 4,514.

1976: Ford, R., 92,717; Carter, D., 62,239; McCarthy, Ind., 624; Reagan, Ind., 307; Anderson, Amer., 290; MacBride, LB., 89; Brown, Ind., 47; Maddox, Amer. Ind., 30.

1972: Nixon, R., 100,464; McGovern, D., 44,358; Schmitz, Amer., 748.

1968: Nixon, R., 70,927; Humphrey, D., 45,173; Wallace, 3rd party, 11,105.

1964: Johnson, D., 80,718; Goldwater, R., 61,998.

1960: Nixon, R., 77,451; Kennedy, D., 63,331.

UNITED STATES GOVERNMENT

EXECUTIVE BRANCH	LEGISLATIVE BRANCH	JUDICIAL BRANCH
President	CONGRESS	Supreme Court of the United States
Vice President	Senate/House of Representatives	Courts of Appeals
Executive Office of the President	Architect of the Capitol	District Courts
Council of Economic Advisers	U.S. Botanic Garden	Territorial Courts
Council on Environmental Quality	Government Accountability Office	Court of International Trade
Executive Residence	Government Printing Office	Bankruptcy Courts
National Security Council	Library of Congress	Court of Federal Claims
Office of Administration	Congressional Budget Office	Tax Court
Office of Management and Budget	Medicare Payment Advisory Commission	Court of Appeals for the Armed Forces
Office of National Drug Control Policy	Stennis Center for Public Service	Court of Appeals for Veterans Claims
Office of Science and Technology Policy		Administrative Office of the Courts
Office of the U.S. Trade Representative		Federal Judicial Center
Office of the Vice President		Sentencing Commission
White House Office*		Judicial Panel on Multidistrict Litigation

*Includes Domestic Policy Council, National Security Advisor, National Economic Council, Office of Cabinet Affairs, Office of the Chief of Staff, Office of Communications, Office of Digital Strategy, Office of the First Lady, Office of Legislative Affairs, Office of Management and Administration, Oval Office Operations, Office of Presidential Personnel, Office of Public Engagement and Intergovernmental Affairs, Office of Scheduling and Advance, Office of the Staff Secretary, and Office of the White House Counsel.

The Obama Administration

As of Aug. 2013; mailing addresses are for Washington, DC, except where otherwise noted.
Terms of office of the president and vice president: Jan. 20, 2013, to Jan. 20, 2017.

President: By law, Pres. Barack H. Obama received an annual salary of $400,000 (taxable) and an annual expense allowance of $50,000 (nontaxable) for costs resulting from official duties. This does not include amounts available for expenditures within the Executive Office of the President, including $3,850,000 for necessary expenses for the White House, up to $100,000 a year for travel expenses, and up to $19,000 for official entertainment.
Website: www.whitehouse.gov/administration/president-obama
Vice President: By law, Vice Pres. Joseph R. Biden received an annual salary of $230,700 (taxable) and an annual expense allowance of $20,000 for costs resulting from official duties, plus $90,000 for official entertainment expenses (nontaxable).
Website: www.whitehouse.gov/administration/vice-president-biden

Cabinet Department Heads

(Salary: $199,700 per year)

Secretary of State: John Kerry
Secretary of the Treasury: Jack Lew
Secretary of Defense: Chuck Hagel
Attorney General (Dept. of Justice): Eric H. Holder Jr.
Secretary of the Interior: Sally Jewell
Secretary of Agriculture: Thomas J. Vilsack
Secretary of Commerce: Penny Pritzker
Secretary of Labor: Thomas E. Perez
Secretary of Health and Human Services: Kathleen Sebelius
Secretary of Housing and Urban Development: Shaun L.S. Donovan
Secretary of Transportation: Anthony Foxx
Secretary of Energy: Ernest Moniz
Secretary of Education: Arne Duncan
Secretary of Veterans Affairs: Eric K. Shinseki
Secretary of Homeland Security: Vacant

Executive Agencies

Council of Economic Advisers: Jason Furman, chair; www.whitehouse.gov/administration/eop/cea/
Council on Environ. Quality: Nancy Sutley, chair; www.whitehouse.gov/administration/eop/ceq/
Office of Administration: Beth Jones, dir.; www.whitehouse.gov/administration/eop/oa/
Office of Management and Budget: Sylvia Burwell, dir.; www.whitehouse.gov/omb/
Office of Natl. Drug Control Policy: R. Gil Kerlikowske, dir.; www.whitehouse.gov/ondcp/
Office of Science and Technology Policy: John Holdren, dir.; www.whitehouse.gov/administration/eop/ostp/
Office of the U.S. Trade Representative: Amb. Michael Froman; www.ustr.gov

White House Staff

1600 Pennsylvania Ave. NW, 20500; www.whitehouse.gov

Counselor to the President: Peter M. Rouse
Physician to the President: Ronny Jackson
Director, National Intelligence: James R. Clapper
Assistants to the President:
  Chief of Staff: Denis McDonough
  Deputy Chief of Staff for Operations: Alyssa Mastromonaco
  Deputy Chief of Staff for Planning: Mark B. Childress
  Deputy Chief of Staff for Policy: Robert L. Nabors II
  Cabinet Secretary: Danielle C. Gray
  Counsel to the President: Kathryn H. Ruemmler
  White House Press Secretary: Jay Carney
  National Security Advisor: Susan Rice
  Deputy National Security Advisor: Antony J. Blinken
  Director of Communications: Jennifer M. Palmieri
  Director of the Domestic Policy Council: Cecilia Muñoz
  Economic Policy and Director of the National Economic Council: Gene B. Sperling
  Homeland Security and Counterterrorism: Lisa O. Monaco
  Director of Legislative Affairs: Miguel E. Rodriguez
  Director of Speechwriting: Cody S. Keenan
  Director of Scheduling and Advance: Danielle M. Crutchfield
  Management and Administration: Katy A. Kale
  Deputy Senior Advisor for Communications and Strategy: David M. Simas
Senior Advisors: Valerie B. Jarrett, Dan Pfeiffer
Chief of Staff to the Vice President: Bruce Reed
White House Social Secretary: Jeremy M. Bernard
Chief of Staff to the First Lady: Christina M. Tchen
Press Secretary to the First Lady: Hannah M. August

Cabinet-Level Departments

Department of State

2201 C St. NW, 20520; www.state.gov

Conducts U.S. foreign policy. The Foreign Service protects American citizens and interests through embassies in some 180 countries and supports U.S. foreign trade. Promotes democracy, international security, human rights—including issues related to AIDS, human trafficking, war crimes, and migration—and arms and narcotics control. Represents the nation in international organizations. Issues passports to U.S. citizens and visas to foreigners. **Budget** (includes State Dept. and other international programs): $47.0 bil (2012); $55.5 bil (est. 2013); $56.4 bil (est. 2014).

- Intl. Boundary and Water Commission (4171 North Mesa, Ste. C-100, El Paso, TX 79902); www.ibwc.gov
- Intl. Information Programs (2201 C St. NW, SA-5, Rm. 5B17, 20520); www.state.gov/r/iip/
- Intl. Narcotics and Law Enforcement Affairs (2201 C St. NW, Rm. 7333 HST, 20520); www.state.gov/j/inl/
- Intl. Organization Affairs (2201 C St. NW, Rm. 6323, 20520); www.state.gov/p/io/
- Population, Refugees, and Migration (2201 C St. NW, HST, Rm. 6825, 20520); www.state.gov/j/prm/
- U.S. Global AIDS Coordinator (2201 C St. NW, SA-29, Ste. 200, 20520); www.state.gov/s/gac/

Department of the Treasury

1500 Pennsylvania Ave. NW, 20220; www.treasury.gov

Responsible for the fiscal affairs of the U.S. Serves as the government's financial agent; collects, borrows, and disburses funds for the federal government. Monitors the nation's financial infrastructure and economic development; recommends domestic and international financial, monetary, economic, trade, and tax policies. Manufactures currency and coins. Carries out monetary and tax law enforcement activities, sanctions, embargoes, and fights illicit finance—counterfeiting, money laundering, narcotics trafficking, terrorist financing. **Budget** (not including interest on the public debt): $105.5 bil (2012); $70.1 bil (est. 2013); $89.7 bil (est. 2014).

- Alcohol and Tobacco Tax and Trade Bureau (1310 G St. NW, Box 12, 20005); www.ttb.gov
- Bureau of Engraving and Printing (14th and C Sts. SW, 20228); www.moneyfactory.gov
- Bureau of the Public Debt (200 3rd St., Parkersburg, WV 26106); www.publicdebt.treas.gov
- Financial Crimes Enforcement Network (P.O. Box 39, Vienna, VA 22183); www.fincen.gov
- Financial Management Service (401 14th St. SW, 20227); www.fms.treas.gov
- Internal Revenue Service (1111 Constitution Ave. NW, 20224); www.irs.gov
- U.S. Mint (801 9th St. NW, 20220); www.usmint.gov

Department of Defense

1400 Defense Pentagon, 20301; www.defense.gov

Directs and controls the armed forces and assists the president in protecting the nation's security. Military departments of the Army, Navy, and Air Force are each separately organized under its own secretary but all function under the command of the Secretary of Defense. They conduct military operations as unified commands. The chairman of the Joint Chiefs of Staff is the principal military adviser to the President. Undersecretaries supervise acquisition, technology, and logistics; intelligence; personnel and readiness; and policy. **Budget:** $650.9 bil (2012); $633.3 bil (est. 2013); $597.6 bil (est. 2014).

- Def. Advanced Research Projects Agency (675 N. Randolph St., Arlington, VA 22203); www.darpa.mil
- Def. Intelligence Agency (200 MacDill Blvd., 20340); www.dia.mil
- Def. Security Cooperation Agency (2800 Defense Pentagon, 20301); www.dsca.osd.mil
- Missile Def. Agency (5700 18th St., Bldg. 245, Fort Belvoir, VA 22060-5573); www.mda.mil
- Natl. Geospatial-Intelligence Agency (7500 GEOINT Dr., Springfield, VA 22150); www.nga.mil
- Natl. Security Agency/Central Security Service (9800 Savage Road, Ft. Meade, MD 20755); www.nsa.gov

Department of Justice

950 Pennsylvania Ave. NW, 20530; www.justice.gov

Provides for the enforcement of federal laws and investigation of violations; furnishes legal counsel in cases involving the federal government and interprets laws relating to the activities of other federal departments; supervises federal penal institutions. The Attorney General and Office of Legal Counsel render legal advice, upon request, to the president and department heads. The Solicitor General conducts all suits brought before the U.S. Supreme Court in which the federal government is concerned. The Civil Division represents the U.S. government in many civil or criminal matters. The 94 U.S. Attorneys are the principal litigators in the U.S. and its territories. Divisions for suits regarding antitrust laws, civil rights, civil and criminal statutes, natural resources and the environment, national security, and taxes. **Budget:** $31.2 bil (2012); $35.3 bil (est. 2013); $34.5 bil (est. 2014).

- Bureau of Alcohol, Tobacco, Firearms, and Explosives (99 New York Ave. NE, Rm. 5S 144, 20226); www.atf.gov
- Bureau of Prisons (320 First St. NW, 20534); www.bop.gov
- Drug Enforcement Admin. (8701 Morrissette Dr., Springfield, VA 22152); www.dea.gov
- Executive Office for Immigration Review (5107 Leesburg Pike, Falls Church, VA 22041); www.justice.gov/eoir/
- Federal Bureau of Investigation (935 Pennsylvania Ave. NW, 20535); www.fbi.gov
- INTERPOL Washington (U.S. Natl. Central Bureau) (20530); www.justice.gov/interpol-washington/
- U.S. Marshals Service (2604 Jefferson Davis Hwy., Alexandria, VA 22301-1025); www.usmarshals.gov
- U.S. Parole Commission (90 K St. NE, 3rd Fl., 20530); www.justice.gov/uspc/

Department of the Interior

1849 C St. NW, 20240; www.doi.gov

Custodian of natural resources. Has the responsibility of protecting and conserving the country's land, water, minerals, fish, and wildlife; of promoting the wise use of all these natural resources; of maintaining national parks and recreation areas; and of preserving historic places. It also provides for the welfare of American Indian reservation communities and of inhabitants of island territories under U.S. administration. **Budget:** $12.9 bil (2012); $10.4 bil (est. 2013); $13.5 bil (est. 2014).

- Bureau of Indian Affairs (1849 C Street NW, 20240); www.bia.gov
- Bureau of Land Management (1849 C St. NW, 20240); www.blm.gov
- Bureau of Ocean Energy Management (1849 C St. NW, 20240); www.boem.gov
- Bureau of Reclamation (1849 C St. NW, 20240); www.usbr.gov
- Bureau of Safety and Environmental Enforcement (1849 C St. NW, 20240); www.bsee.gov
- National Park Service (1849 C St. NW, 20240); www.nps.gov
- Office of Surface Mining Reclamation and Enforcement (1951 Constitution Ave. NW, 20240); www.osmre.gov
- U.S. Fish and Wildlife Service (1849 C St. NW, 20240); www.fws.gov
- U.S. Geological Survey (12201 Sunrise Valley Dr., Reston, VA 20192); www.usgs.gov

Department of Agriculture

1400 Independence Ave. SW, 20250; www.usda.gov

Provides leadership on food, agriculture, and natural resources; supports scientific research and education for agriculture, nutrition, and food safety. Develops nutrition assistance programs, promotes healthy eating, supplies food stamps, grades and inspects the commercial supply of food. Responsible for the health of the land through sustainable management and conservation, manages public lands in national forests and grasslands; safeguards against invasive pests and diseases; ensures the health and care of animals and plants. Oversees assistance and conservation programs for farmers and ranchers and programs to improve the rural economy and quality of life. Facilitates domestic and international marketing of U.S. agricultural products. **Budget:** $139.7 bil (2012); $156.0 bil (est. 2013); $143.6 bil (est. 2014).

- Agricultural Research Service (1400 Independence Ave. SW, 20250); www.ars.usda.gov
- Economic Research Service (1400 Independence Ave. SW, Mail Stop 1800, 20250); www.ers.usda.gov
- Food and Nutrition Service (3101 Park Center Dr., Alexandria, VA 22302); www.fns.usda.gov
- Food Safety and Inspection Service (1400 Independence Ave. SW, 20250); www.fsis.usda.gov
- Foreign Agricultural Service (1400 Independence Ave. SW, 20250); www.fas.usda.gov
- Forest Service (Mailstop: 1111, 1400 Independence Ave. SW, 20250); www.fs.fed.us
- Natl. Agricultural Statistics Service (1400 Independence Ave. SW, 20250); www.nass.usda.gov
- Natural Resources Conservation Service (1400 Independence Ave. SW, 20250); www.nrcs.usda.gov

Department of Commerce

1401 Constitution Ave. NW, 20230; www.commerce.gov

Fosters, serves, and promotes the nation's economic development and technological advancement; supports the comprehension and use of the environment and its oceanic life; assists states, communities, and individuals with economic progress; promotes trade abroad and ensures an effective export control and treaty compliance system. Issues trademarks and patents, maintains measurement standards, and manages the federal telecommunications spectrum. Collects, analyzes, and distributes statistics regarding the nation and the economy through the Bureaus of the Census and of Economic Analysis. The NOAA explores, monitors, and conserves oceans and coasts, tracks weather and other environmental data. **Budget:** $10.3 bil (2012); $9.9 bil (est. 2013); $9.5 bil (est. 2014).

- Bureau of the Census (4600 Silver Hill Rd., 20233); www.census.gov
- Bureau of Economic Analysis (1441 L St. NW, 20230); www.bea.gov
- Minority Business Development Agency (1401 Constitution Ave. NW, 20230); www.mbda.gov
- Natl. Institute of Standards and Technology (100 Bureau Dr., Stop 1070, Gaithersburg, MD 20899); www.nist.gov
- Natl. Oceanic and Atmospheric Admin. (1401 Constitution Ave. NW, Rm. 5128, 20230); www.noaa.gov
- Natl. Technical Information Service (5301 Shawnee Rd., Alexandria, VA 22312); www.ntis.gov
- Natl. Telecommunications and Information Admin. (1401 Constitution Ave. NW, 20230); www.ntia.doc.gov

Department of Labor

200 Constitution Ave. NW, 20210; www.dol.gov

Administers federal labor laws to foster, promote, and develop the welfare of job seekers, wage earners, and retirees of the U.S.; to improve working conditions; and to advance opportunities for profitable employment. Administers standards for wages and overtime pay, safety and health conditions, workers' compensation. Tracks changes in employment, prices, and other national economic measurements. Regulates pension and welfare benefit plans, the hiring and employment of migrant and seasonal workers, and requirements pertaining to the mining, construction, and transportation industries. Monitors labor unions and their funds. **Budget:** $104.6 bil (2012); $95.2 bil (est. 2013); $86.8 bil (est. 2014).

- Bureau of Labor Statistics (2 Massachusetts Ave. NE, 20212); www.bls.gov
- Employment and Training Admin. (200 Constitution Ave. NW, 20210); www.doleta.gov
- Mine Safety and Health Admin. (1100 Wilson Blvd., 21st Fl., Arlington, VA 22209); www.msha.gov
- Occupational Safety and Health Admin. (200 Constitution Ave. NW, 20210); www.osha.gov
- Office of Federal Contract Compliance Programs (200 Constitution Ave. NW, 20210); www.dol.gov/ofccp/
- Office of Labor-Management Standards (200 Constitution Ave. NW, 20210); www.dol.gov/olms/
- Office of Workers' Compensation Programs (200 Constitution Ave. NW, 20210); www.dol.gov/owcp/
- Wage and Hour Div. (200 Constitution Ave. NW, 20210); www.dol.gov/whd/

Department of Health and Human Services

200 Independence Ave. SW, 20201; www.hhs.gov

Administers a wide range of programs in the fields of health care and social services that affect nearly all Americans. Medicare and Medicaid provide health care insurance for one in four Americans. The HRSA improves health care services for people who are uninsured, isolated, or medically vulnerable; also oversees organ, tissue, and blood cell donations. The FDA assures the safety of food, drugs, cosmetics, biological products, and medical devices. The CDC monitors and safeguards against disease outbreaks. The NIH supports research projects nationwide and 27 health institutes and centers. The Surgeon General is the nation's chief health educator and leads the U.S. Public Health Service Commissioned Corps. **Budget:** $848.1 bil (2012); $907.7 bil (est. 2013); $967.2 bil (est. 2014).

- Agency for Healthcare Research and Quality (540 Gaither Rd., Rockville, MD 20850); www.ahrq.gov
- Centers for Disease Control and Prevention (1600 Clifton Rd., Atlanta, GA 30333); www.cdc.gov
- Centers for Medicare and Medicaid Services (7500 Security Blvd., Baltimore, MD 21244); www.cms.gov
- Food and Drug Admin. (10903 New Hampshire Ave., Silver Spring, MD 20993); www.fda.gov
- Health Resources and Services Admin. (5600 Fishers Ln., Rockville, MD 20857); www.hrsa.gov
- Natl. Institutes of Health (9000 Rockville Pike, Bethesda, MD 20892); www.nih.gov
- Office of the Surgeon General (Tower Bldg., Plaza Level 1, Rm. 100, 1101 Wootton Pkwy., Rockville, MD 20852); www.surgeongeneral.gov

Department of Housing and Urban Development

451 7th St. SW, 20410; www.hud.gov

Responsible for housing needs and the improvement and development of urban areas. Supports affordable housing, provides grants for community development and redevelopment. Enforces fair and safe housing standards. Provides funds to assist homeless individuals and families with emergency and transitional shelters. The FHA provides mortgage insurance on loans made by approved lenders. **Budget:** $49.6 bil (2012); $60.5 bil (est. 2013); $49.3 bil (est. 2014).

- Fannie Mae (Federal Natl. Mortgage Association) (3900 Wisconsin Ave. NW, 20016); www.fanniemae.com
- Federal Housing Admin. (451 7th St. SW, 20410); www.fha.gov
- Freddie Mac (Federal Home Loan Mortgage Corporation) (8200 Jones Branch Dr., McLean, VA 22102); www.freddiemac.com
- Ginnie Mae (Government Natl. Mortgage Association) (451 7th St. SW, Rm. B-133, 20410); www.ginniemae.gov

Note: Fannie Mae and Freddie Mac are government-sponsored enterprises (GSEs).

Department of Transportation

1200 New Jersey Ave. SE, 20590; www.dot.gov

Promotes and develops rapid, safe, efficient, and convenient transportation in the U.S.; monitors and administers assistance to transportation industries; negotiates and implements international transportation agreements. Manages airspace, commercial space transportation, and the movement of hazardous materials. Resolves railroad rate and service disputes and reviews proposed railroad mergers. Analyzes and shares research and statistics to develop and improve transportation through RITA. Develops and enforces regulations on the nation's pipeline transportation system. The Maritime Administration maintains a fleet of cargo ships in reserve for war or national emergencies and commissions officers of the merchant marines. Operates the U.S. portion of the St. Lawrence Seaway between Montreal and Lake Erie. **Budget:** $75.1 bil (2012); $80.1 bil (est. 2013); $88.2 bil (est. 2014).

- Federal Aviation Admin. (800 Independence Ave. SW, 20591); www.faa.gov
- Federal Highway Admin. (1200 New Jersey Ave. SE, 20590); www.fhwa.dot.gov
- Federal Transit Admin. (East Bldg., 1200 New Jersey Ave. SE, 20590); www.fta.dot.gov
- Federal Railroad Admin. (1200 New Jersey Ave. SE, 20590); www.fra.dot.gov
- Maritime Admin. (1200 New Jersey Ave. SE, 20590); www.marad.dot.gov
- Natl. Highway Traffic Safety Admin. (West Bldg., 1200 New Jersey Ave. SE, 20590); www.nhtsa.gov
- Research and Innovative Technology Admin. (1200 New Jersey Ave. SE, 20590); www.rita.dot.gov

Department of Energy

1000 Independence Ave. SW, 20585; energy.gov

Secures the nation's energy and promotes scientific and technological innovation. Oversees the national energy supply and electric grid. Investigates and promotes clean and reliable energy. Manages and cleans up nuclear and other radioactive material, including nuclear weapons. The OSTI supports much of America's scientific research through program offices, education initiatives, national laboratories, and technology centers. Four power administrations sell hydroelectric power across the West and Southeast. **Budget:** $32.5 bil (2012); $28.9 bil (est. 2013); $31.3 bil (est. 2014).

- Energy Information Admin. (1000 Independence Ave. SW, 20585); www.eia.gov
- Federal Energy Regulatory Commission (independent regulatory agency) (888 1st St. NE, 20426); www.ferc.gov
- Natl. Nuclear Security Admin. (1000 Independence Ave. SW, 20585); www.nnsa.energy.gov
- Office of Scientific and Technical Information (P.O. Box 62, Oak Ridge, TN 37831); www.osti.gov

Department of Education

400 Maryland Ave. SW, 20202; www.ed.gov

Works with state agencies and local systems to ensure equal access to all levels of education and seeks to improve the quality of that education through federal support, research programs, and information sharing. Oversees a variety of financial aid distributed through competition, need-based requests, or a set formula. Sets policy goals and initiatives like No Child Left Behind. Conducts research and gathers educational information to disseminate to educators and the general public. **Budget:** $57.2 bil (2012); $48.1 bil (est. 2013); $75.4 bil (est. 2014).

Department of Veterans Affairs

810 Vermont Ave. NW, 20420; www.va.gov

Supports veterans and their families with nationwide programs for health care, financial assistance, and burial benefits. Compensates for disabilities incurred during wartime. Provides pensions for veterans with low incomes, education assistance, loan guaranty, and life insurance. Manages America's largest medical education and health professions training program which includes hospitals, clinics, nursing homes, veterans centers, rehabilitation treatment, readjustment counseling, and home-care programs. Also funds medical research pertaining to veterans issues. Manages 131 national cemeteries; provides headstones and markers. **Budget:** $124.1 bil (2012); $139.2 bil (est. 2013); $147.7 bil (est. 2014).

Department of Homeland Security

20528 (requires no street address); www.dhs.gov

Provides a unified core for the vast national network of organizations and institutions involved in efforts to secure the U.S., its borders, infrastructure, and major events. Provides funding, intelligence, and training for law enforcement and disaster relief.

Leads and coordinates response teams to natural and man-made emergencies. Directs security for borders, customs, and transportation. Identifies threats, administers the National Terrorism Advisory System. **Budget:** $47.4 bil (2012); $60.8 bil (est. 2013); $53.4 bil (est. 2014).

- Fed. Emergency Management Agency (500 C St. SW, 20472); www.fema.gov
- Immigration and Customs Enforcement (500 12th St. SW, 20536); www.ice.gov
- Transportation Security Admin. (601 S. 12th St., Arlington, VA 20598); www.tsa.gov

- U.S. Citizenship and Immigration Services (20 Massachusetts Ave. NW, 20529); www.uscis.gov
- U.S. Coast Guard (2100 2nd St. SW, 20593); www.uscg.mil
- U.S. Customs and Border Protection (1300 Pennsylvania Ave. NW, 20229); www.cbp.gov
- U.S. Fire Admin. (16825 S. Seton Ave., Emmitsburg, MD 21727); www.usfa.dhs.gov
- U.S. Secret Service (245 Murray Dr., Bldg. 410, 20223); www.secretservice.gov

Other Notable U.S. Government Agencies

Source: *The U.S. Government Manual*; National Archives and Records Administration; World Almanac research

All addresses are Washington, DC, unless otherwise noted; as of Aug. 2013.

Administrative Conference of the U.S.: Paul R. Verkuil, chair (1120 20th St. NW, Ste. 706S, 20036); www.acus.gov

African Development Foundation: Shari Berenbach, pres. and CEO (1400 I St. NW, Ste. 1000, 20005); www.adf.gov

AMTRAK (Natl. Railroad Passenger Corporation): Joseph H. Boardman, pres. and CEO (60 Mass. Ave. NE, 20002); www.amtrak.com

Broadcasting Board of Governors: chair vacant (330 Independence Ave. SW, 20237); www.bbg.gov

Central Intelligence Agency: John O. Brennan, dir. (20505); www.cia.gov

Commodity Futures Trading Commission: Gary Gensler, chair (3 Lafayette Ctr., 1155 21st St. NW, 20581); www.cftc.gov

Consumer Financial Protection Bureau: Rich Cordray, dir. (P.O. Box 4503, Iowa City, IA 52244); www.consumerfinance.gov

Consumer Product Safety Commission: Inez Tenenbaum, chair (4330 East-West Hwy., Bethesda, MD 20814); www.cpsc.gov

Corporation for Natl. and Community Service: Wendy Spencer, CEO (1201 New York Ave. NW, 20525); www.nationalservice.gov

Court Services and Offender Supervision Agency for the District of Columbia: Nancy M. Ware, dir. (633 Indiana Ave. NW, 20004); www.csosa.gov

Defense Nuclear Facilities Safety Board: Peter S. Winokur, chair (625 Indiana Ave. NW, Ste. 700, 20004); www.dnfsb.gov

Election Assistance Commission: chair vacant (1201 New York Ave. NW, Ste. 300, 20005); www.eac.gov

Environmental Protection Agency: Gina McCarthy, administrator (Cabinet rank) (1200 Pennsylvania Ave. NW, 20460); www.epa.gov

Equal Employment Opportunity Commission: Jacqueline A. Berrien, chair (131 M St. NE, 20507); www.eeoc.gov

Export-Import Bank of the U.S.: Fred P. Hochberg, pres. and chair (811 Vermont Ave. NW, 20571); www.exim.gov

Farm Credit Admin.: Jill Long Thompson, chair and CEO (1501 Farm Credit Dr., McLean, VA 22102); www.fca.gov

Federal Communications Commission: Mignon Clyburn, act. chair (445 12th St. SW, 20554); www.fcc.gov

Federal Deposit Insurance Corporation: Martin J. Gruenberg, chair (550 17th St. NW, 20429); www.fdic.gov

Federal Election Commission: Ellen L. Weintraub, chair (999 E St. NW, 20463); www.fec.gov

Federal Housing Finance Agency: Edward DeMarco, act. dir. (400 7th St. SW, 20024); www.fhfa.gov

Federal Labor Relations Authority: Ernest DuBester, chair (1400 K St. NW, 20424); www.flra.gov

Federal Maritime Commission: Mario Cordero, chair (800 N. Capitol St. NW, 20573); www.fmc.gov

Federal Mediation and Conciliation Service: George H. Cohen, dir. (2100 K St. NW, 20427); www.fmcs.gov

Federal Mine Safety and Health Review Commission: Mary Lucille Jordan, chair (1331 Pennsylvania Ave. NW, Ste. 520N, 20004); www.fmshrc.gov

Federal Reserve System: Ben S. Bernanke, chair (20th St. and Constitution Ave. NW, 20551); www.federalreserve.gov

Federal Retirement Thrift Investment Board: Michael D. Kennedy, chair (77 K St. NE, 20002); www.frtib.gov

Federal Trade Commission: Edith Ramirez, chair (600 Pennsylvania Ave. NW, 20580); www.ftc.gov

General Services Admin.: Daniel M. Tangherlini, administrator (One Constitution Sq., 1275 1st St. NE, 20417); www.gsa.gov

Institute of Museum and Library Services: Susan Hildreth, dir. (1800 M St. NW, 9th Fl., 20036); www.imls.gov

Inter-American Foundation: Robert N. Kaplan, pres. (1331 Pennsylvania Ave. NW, Ste. 1200N, 20004); www.iaf.gov

Merit Systems Protection Board: Susan Tsui Grundmann, chair (1615 M St. NW, 20419); www.mspb.gov

Natl. Aeronautics and Space Admin.: Charles F. Bolden Jr., administrator (Suite 5K39, 20546); www.nasa.gov

Natl. Archives and Records Admin.: David S. Ferriero, archivist (8601 Adelphi Rd., College Park, MD 20740); www.archives.gov

Natl. Capital Planning Commission: L. Preston Bryant Jr., chair (401 9th St. NW, N. Lobby, Ste. 500, 20004); www.ncpc.gov

Natl. Council on Disability: Jeff Rosen, chair (1331 F St. NW, Ste. 850, 20004); www.ncd.gov

Natl. Credit Union Admin.: Debbie Matz, chair (1775 Duke St., Alexandria, VA 22314); www.ncua.gov

Natl. Endowment for the Arts: chair vacant (1100 Pennsylvania Ave. NW, 20506); www.arts.gov

Natl. Endowment for the Humanities: Carole M. Watson, act. chair (1100 Pennsylvania Ave. NW, 20506); www.neh.gov

Natl. Indian Gaming Commission: Tracie Stevens, chair (1441 L St. NW, Ste. 9100, 20005); www.nigc.gov

Natl. Labor Relations Board: Mark G. Pearce, chair (1099 14th St. NW, 20570); www.nlrb.gov

Natl. Mediation Board: Linda Puchala, chair (1301 K St. NW, Ste. 250 East, 20005); www.nmb.gov

Natl. Science Foundation: Cora Marrett, act. dir. (4201 Wilson Blvd., Arlington, VA 22230); www.nsf.gov

Natl. Transportation Safety Board: Deborah A.P. Hersman, chair (490 L'Enfant Plaza SW, 20594); www.ntsb.gov

Nuclear Regulatory Commission: Allison M. Macfarlane, chair (20555); www.nrc.gov

Nuclear Waste Technical Review Board: Rodney C. Ewing, chair (2300 Clarendon Blvd., Ste. 1300, Arlington, VA 22201); www.nwtrb.gov

Occupational Safety and Health Review Commission: Thomasina V. Rogers, chair (1120 20th St. NW, 9th Fl., 20036); www.oshrc.gov

Office of the Dir. of Natl. Intelligence: James R. Clapper, dir. (20511); www.dni.gov

Office of Government Ethics: Walter M. Shaub Jr., dir. (1201 New York Ave. NW, Ste. 500, 20005); www.oge.gov

Office of Personnel Management: Elaine Kaplan, act. dir. (1900 E St. NW, 20415); www.opm.gov

Office of Special Counsel: Carolyn Lerner, spec. counsel (1730 M St. NW, Ste. 218, 20036); www.osc.gov

Overseas Private Investment Corporation: Elizabeth L. Littlefield, pres. and CEO (1100 New York Ave. NW, 20527); www.opic.gov

Peace Corps: Carrie Hessler-Radelet, act. dir. (1111 20th St. NW, 20526); www.peacecorps.gov

Pension Benefit Guaranty Corporation: Josh Gotbaum, dir. (1200 K St. NW, 20005); www.pbgc.gov

Postal Regulatory Commission: Ruth Y. Goldway, chair (901 New York Ave. NW, Ste. 200, 20268); www.prc.gov

Railroad Retirement Board: Michael S. Schwartz, chair (844 N. Rush St., Chicago, IL 60611); www.rrb.gov

Securities and Exchange Commission: Mary Jo White, chair (100 F St. NE, 20549); www.sec.gov

Selective Service System: Lawrence G. Romo, dir. (Natl. Headquarters, Arlington, VA 22209); www.sss.gov

Small Business Admin.: Karen G. Mills, admin. (Cabinet rank) (409 3rd St. SW, 20416); www.sba.gov

Social Security Admin.: Carolyn W. Colvin, act. comm. (6401 Security Blvd., Baltimore, MD 21235); www.ssa.gov

Tennessee Valley Authority: Bill Johnson, CEO and pres. (400 W. Summit Hill Dr., Knoxville, TN 37902); www.tva.gov

U.S. Agency for Intl. Development: Rajiv Shah, admin. (Ronald Reagan Building, 1300 Pennsylvania Ave. NW, 20523); www.usaid.gov

U.S. Commission on Civil Rights: Martin R. Castro, chair (624 9th St. NW, 20425); www.usccr.gov

U.S. Intl. Trade Commission: Irving A. Williamson, chair (500 E St. SW, 20436); www.usitc.gov

U.S. Postal Service: Patrick R. Donahoe, postmaster general and CEO (475 L'Enfant Plaza SW, 20260); www.usps.com

U.S. Trade and Development Agency: Leocadia I. Zak, dir. (1000 Wilson Blvd., Ste. 1600, Arlington, VA 22209); www.ustda.gov

CABINETS OF THE U.S.

The U.S. Cabinet and Its Role

The heads of major executive departments of the federal government constitute the Cabinet. This institution, not provided for in the U.S. Constitution, developed as an advisory body out of the desire of presidents to consult on policy matters. Aside from its advisory role, the Cabinet as a body has no formal function and wields no executive authority. Individual members exercise authority as heads of their departments, reporting to the president. The Cabinet meets at times set by the president.

In addition to the heads of federal departments as listed below, the Cabinet commonly includes other officials designated by the president as being of Cabinet rank.

The officials so designated by Pres. Barack Obama include Vice Pres. Joseph R. Biden, White House Chief of Staff Denis McDonough, Environmental Protection Agency Administrator Gina McCarthy, Office of Management and Budget Director Sylvia Burwell, U.S. Trade Representative Ambassador Michael Froman, U.S. Ambassador to the United Nations Samantha Power, Council of Economic Advisers Chair Jason Furman, and Small Business Administration Administrator Karen G. Mills.

Members of Pres. Obama's Cabinet listed in this chapter are as of Aug. 2013.

Secretaries of State

The Department of Foreign Affairs was created by act of Congress on July 27, 1789, and the name changed to Department of State on Sept. 15, 1789.

President	Secretary	Home	Sworn in
Washington.....	Thomas Jefferson........	VA	1789
	Edmund J. Randolph.....	VA	1794
	Timothy Pickering........	PA	1795
Adams, J......	Timothy Pickering........	PA	1797
	John Marshall............	VA	1800
Jefferson......	James Madison..........	VA	1801
Madison......	Robert Smith............	MD	1809
	James Monroe..........	VA	1811
Monroe......	John Quincy Adams......	MA	1817
Adams, J. Q...	Henry Clay.............	KY	1825
Jackson......	Martin Van Buren........	NY	1829
	Edward Livingston.......	LA	1831
	Louis McLane...........	DE	1833
	John Forsyth...........	GA	1834
Van Buren.....	John Forsyth...........	GA	1837
Harrison, W. H.	Daniel Webster..........	MA	1841
Tyler.........	Daniel Webster..........	MA	1841
	Abel P. Upshur..........	VA	1843
	John C. Calhoun........	SC	1844
Polk.........	John C. Calhoun........	SC	1845
	James Buchanan........	PA	1845
Taylor........	James Buchanan........	PA	1849
	John M. Clayton........	DE	1849
Fillmore......	John M. Clayton........	DE	1850
	Daniel Webster.........	MA	1850
	Edward Everett.........	MA	1852
Pierce........	William L. Marcy........	NY	1853
Buchanan.....	William L. Marcy........	NY	1857
	Lewis Cass............	MI	1857
	Jeremiah S. Black.......	PA	1860
Lincoln.......	Jeremiah S. Black.......	PA	1861
	William H. Seward......	NY	1861
Johnson, A....	William H. Seward......	NY	1865
Grant.........	Elihu B. Washburne.....	IL	1869
	Hamilton Fish..........	NY	1869
Hayes........	Hamilton Fish..........	NY	1877
	William M. Evarts.......	NY	1877
Garfield......	William M. Evarts.......	NY	1881
	James G. Blaine........	ME	1881
Arthur........	James G. Blaine........	ME	1881
	F. T. Frelinghuysen......	NJ	1881
Cleveland.....	F. T. Frelinghuysen......	NJ	1885
	Thomas F. Bayard......	DE	1885
Harrison, B.	Thomas F. Bayard.......	DE	1889
	James G. Blaine........	ME	1889
	John W. Foster.........	IN	1892
Cleveland.....	Walter Q. Gresham.....	IN	1893
	Richard Olney..........	MA	1895
McKinley......	Richard Olney..........	MA	1897
	John Sherman.........	OH	1897
	William R. Day.........	OH	1898
	John M. Hay...........	DC	1898
Roosevelt, T. ...	John M. Hay...........	DC	1901
	Elihu Root............	NY	1905
	Robert Bacon..........	NY	1909
Taft..........	Robert Bacon..........	NY	1909
	Philander C. Knox......	PA	1909
Wilson........	Philander C. Knox......	PA	1913
	William J. Bryan........	NE	1913
	Robert Lansing.........	NY	1915
	Bainbridge Colby........	NY	1920

President	Secretary	Home	Sworn in
Harding......	Charles E. Hughes.......	NY	1921
Coolidge.....	Charles E. Hughes.......	NY	1923
	Frank B. Kellogg.........	MN	1925
Hoover	Frank B. Kellogg.........	MN	1929
	Henry L. Stimson........	NY	1929
Roosevelt, F. D.	Cordell Hull.............	TN	1933
	Edward R. Stettinius Jr. . . .	VA	1944
Truman.......	Edward R. Stettinius Jr. . . .	VA	1945
	James F. Byrnes........	SC	1945
	George C. Marshall	PA	1947
	Dean G. Acheson........	CT	1949
Eisenhower...	John Foster Dulles.......	NY	1953
	Christian A. Herter	MA	1959
Kennedy.....	D. Dean Rusk..........	NY	1961
Johnson, L. B. . .	D. Dean Rusk..........	NY	1963
Nixon	William P. Rogers.......	NY	1969
	Henry A. Kissinger	DC	1973
Ford	Henry A. Kissinger	DC	1974
Carter	Cyrus R. Vance	NY	1977
	Edmund S. Muskie......	ME	1980
Reagan.......	Alexander M. Haig Jr......	CT	1981
	George P. Shultz	CA	1982
Bush, G. H. W.	James A. Baker III	TX	1989
	Lawrence S. Eagleburger. .	MI	1992
Clinton	Warren M. Christopher....	CA	1993
	Madeleine K. Albright.....	DC	1997
Bush, G. W. ..	Colin L. Powell	NY	2001
	Condoleezza Rice	AL	2005
Obama	Hillary Rodham Clinton...	NY	2009
	John Kerry	MA	2013

Secretaries of the Treasury

The Treasury Department was organized by act of Congress on Sept. 2, 1789.

President	Secretary	Home	Sworn in
Washington....	Alexander Hamilton	NY	1789
	Oliver Wolcott Jr.	CT	1795
Adams, J.....	Oliver Wolcott Jr.	CT	1797
	Samuel Dexter	MA	1801
Jefferson......	Samuel Dexter	MA	1801
	Albert Gallatin...........	PA	1801
Madison	Albert Gallatin...........	PA	1809
	George W. Campbell......	TN	1814
	Alexander J. Dallas.......	PA	1814
	William H. Crawford	GA	1816
Monroe	William H. Crawford	GA	1817
Adams, J. Q...	Richard Rush...........	PA	1825
Jackson	Samuel D. Ingham	PA	1829
	Louis McLane...........	DE	1831
	William J. Duane........	PA	1833
	Roger B. Taney.........	MD	1833
	Levi Woodbury	NH	1834
Van Buren.....	Levi Woodbury	NH	1837
Harrison, W. H.	Thomas Ewing	OH	1841
Tyler	Thomas Ewing	OH	1841
	Walter Forward..........	PA	1841
	John C. Spencer........	NY	1843
	George M. Bibb.........	KY	1844
Polk..........	Robert J. Walker........	MS	1845
Taylor........	William M. Meredith	PA	1849
Fillmore.......	Thomas Corwin..........	OH	1850
Pierce	James Guthrie	KY	1853
Buchanan	Howell Cobb...........	GA	1857
	Phillip F. Thomas	MD	1860
	John A. Dix............	NY	1861

President	Secretary	Home	Sworn in
Lincoln	Salmon P. Chase	OH	1861
	William P. Fessenden	ME	1864
	Hugh McCulloch	IN	1865
Johnson, A.	Hugh McCulloch	IN	1865
Grant	George S. Boutwell	MA	1869
	William A. Richardson	MA	1873
	Benjamin H. Bristow	KY	1874
	Lot M. Morrill	ME	1876
Hayes	John Sherman	OH	1877
Garfield	William Windom	MN	1881
Arthur	Charles J. Folger	NY	1881
	Walter Q. Gresham	IN	1884
	Hugh McCulloch	IN	1884
Cleveland	Daniel Manning	NY	1885
	Charles S. Fairchild	NY	1887
Harrison, B.	William Windom	MN	1889
	Charles Foster	OH	1891
Cleveland	John G. Carlisle	KY	1893
McKinley	Lyman J. Gage	IL	1897
Roosevelt, T.	Lyman J. Gage	IL	1901
	Leslie M. Shaw	IA	1902
	George B. Cortelyou	NY	1907
Taft	Franklin MacVeagh	IL	1909
Wilson	William G. McAdoo	NY	1913
	Carter Glass	VA	1918
	David F. Houston	MO	1920
Harding	Andrew W. Mellon	PA	1921
Coolidge	Andrew W. Mellon	PA	1923
Hoover	Andrew W. Mellon	PA	1929
	Ogden L. Mills	NY	1932
Roosevelt, F. D.	William H. Woodin	NY	1933
	Henry Morgenthau Jr.	NY	1934
Truman	Fred M. Vinson	KY	1945
	John W. Snyder	MO	1946
Eisenhower	George M. Humphrey	OH	1953
	Robert B. Anderson	CT	1957
Kennedy	C. Douglas Dillon	NJ	1961
Johnson, L. B.	C. Douglas Dillon	NJ	1963
	Henry H. Fowler	VA	1965
	Joseph W. Barr	IN	1968
Nixon	David M. Kennedy	IL	1969
	John B. Connally	TX	1971
	George P. Shultz	IL	1972
	William E. Simon	NJ	1974
Ford	William E. Simon	NJ	1974
Carter	W. Michael Blumenthal	MI	1977
	G. William Miller	RI	1979
Reagan	Donald T. Regan	NY	1981
	James A. Baker III	TX	1985
	Nicholas F. Brady	NJ	1988
Bush, G. H. W.	Nicholas F. Brady	NJ	1989
Clinton	Lloyd M. Bentsen	TX	1993
	Robert E. Rubin	NY	1995
	Lawrence H. Summers	CT	1999
Bush, G. W.	Paul H. O'Neill	MO	2001
	John W. Snow	OH	2003
	Henry M. Paulson Jr.	FL	2006
Obama	Timothy F. Geithner	NY	2009
	Jack Lew	NY	2013

Secretaries of Defense

The Department of Defense, originally designated the National Military Establishment, was created on Sept. 18, 1947. It is headed by the secretary of defense, who is a member of the president's Cabinet. The departments of the Army, of the Navy, and of the Air Force function within the Defense Department. A 1949 amendment withdrew Cabinet-level status from the secretaries of those departments.

President	Secretary	Home	Sworn in
Truman	James V. Forrestal	NY	1947
	Louis A. Johnson	WV	1949
	George C. Marshall	PA	1950
	Robert A. Lovett	NY	1951
Eisenhower	Charles E. Wilson	MI	1953
	Neil H. McElroy	OH	1957
	Thomas S. Gates Jr.	PA	1959
Kennedy	Robert S. McNamara	MI	1961
Johnson, L. B.	Robert S. McNamara	MI	1963
	Clark M. Clifford	MD	1968
Nixon	Melvin R. Laird	WI	1969
	Elliot L. Richardson	MA	1973
	James R. Schlesinger	VA	1973

President	Secretary	Home	Sworn in
Ford	James R. Schlesinger	VA	1974
	Donald H. Rumsfeld	IL	1975
Carter	Harold Brown	CA	1977
Reagan	Caspar W. Weinberger	CA	1981
	Frank C. Carlucci	PA	1987
Bush, G. H. W.	Richard B. Cheney	WY	1989
Clinton	Les Aspin	WI	1993
	William J. Perry	CA	1994
	William S. Cohen	ME	1997
Bush, G. W.	Donald H. Rumsfeld	IL	2001
	Robert M. Gates	TX	2006
Obama	Robert M. Gates	TX	2009
	Leon E. Panetta	CA	2011
	Chuck Hagel	NE	2013

Secretaries of War

The War Department (which included jurisdiction over the Navy until 1798) was created by act of Congress on Aug. 7, 1789.

President	Secretary	Home	Sworn in
Washington	Henry Knox	MA	1789
	Timothy Pickering	PA	1795
	James McHenry	MD	1796
Adams, J.	James McHenry	MD	1797
	Samuel Dexter	MA	1800
Jefferson	Henry Dearborn	MA	1801
Madison	William Eustis	MA	1809
	John Armstrong	NY	1813
	James Monroe	VA	1814
	William H. Crawford	GA	1815
Monroe	John C. Calhoun	SC	1817
Adams, J. Q.	James Barbour	VA	1825
	Peter B. Porter	NY	1828
Jackson	John H. Eaton	TN	1829
	Lewis Cass	MI	1831
	Benjamin F. Butler	NY	1837
Van Buren	Joel R. Poinsett	SC	1837
Harrison, W. H.	John Bell	TN	1841
Tyler	John Bell	TN	1841
	John C. Spencer	NY	1841
	James M. Porter	PA	1843
	William Wilkins	PA	1844
Polk	William L. Marcy	NY	1845
Taylor	George W. Crawford	GA	1849
Fillmore	Charles M. Conrad	LA	1850
Pierce	Jefferson Davis	MS	1853
Buchanan	John B. Floyd	VA	1857
	Joseph Holt	KY	1861
Lincoln	Simon Cameron	PA	1861
	Edwin M. Stanton	PA	1862
Johnson, A.	Edwin M. Stanton	PA	1865
	John M. Schofield	IL	1868
Grant	John A. Rawlins	IL	1869
	William T. Sherman	OH	1869
	William W. Belknap	IA	1869
	Alphonso Taft	OH	1876
	James D. Cameron	PA	1876
Hayes	George W. McCrary	IA	1877
	Alexander Ramsey	MN	1879
Garfield	Robert T. Lincoln	IL	1881
Arthur	Robert T. Lincoln	IL	1881
Cleveland	William C. Endicott	MA	1885
Harrison, B.	Redfield Proctor	VT	1889
	Stephen B. Elkins	WV	1891
Cleveland	Daniel S. Lamont	NY	1893
McKinley	Russell A. Alger	MI	1897
	Elihu Root	NY	1899
Roosevelt, T.	Elihu Root	NY	1901
	William H. Taft	OH	1904
	Luke E. Wright	TN	1908
Taft	Jacob M. Dickinson	TN	1909
	Henry L. Stimson	NY	1911
Wilson	Lindley M. Garrison	NJ	1913
	Newton D. Baker	OH	1916
Harding	John W. Weeks	MA	1921
Coolidge	John W. Weeks	MA	1923
	Dwight F. Davis	MO	1925
Hoover	James W. Good	IL	1929
	Patrick J. Hurley	OK	1929
Roosevelt, F. D.	George H. Dern	UT	1933
	Harry H. Woodring	KS	1937
	Henry L. Stimson	NY	1940
Truman	Robert P. Patterson	NY	1945
	Kenneth C. Royall[1]	NC	1947

(1) Last member of Cabinet with this title. The War Department became the Department of the Army with the creation of the Defense Department in 1947, though the Army secretary maintained Cabinet-level status until 1949.

Secretaries of the Navy

The Navy Department was created by act of Congress on Apr. 30, 1798. The Marine Corps is part of this department.

President	Secretary	Home	Sworn in
Adams, J.	Benjamin Stoddert	MD	1798
Jefferson	Benjamin Stoddert	MD	1801
	Robert Smith	MD	1801
Madison	Paul Hamilton	SC	1809
	William Jones	PA	1813
	Benjamin W. Crowninshield	MA	1814
Monroe	Benjamin W. Crowninshield	MA	1817
	Smith Thompson	NY	1818
	Samuel L. Southard	NJ	1823
Adams, J. Q.	Samuel L. Southard	NJ	1825
Jackson	John Branch	NC	1829
	Levi Woodbury	NH	1831
	Mahlon Dickerson	NJ	1834
Van Buren	Mahlon Dickerson	NJ	1837
	James K. Paulding	NY	1838
Harrison, W. H.	George E. Badger	NC	1841
Tyler	George E. Badger	NC	1841
	Abel P. Upshur	VA	1841
	David Henshaw	MA	1843
	Thomas W. Gilmer	VA	1844
	John Y. Mason	VA	1844
Polk	George Bancroft	MA	1845
	John Y. Mason	VA	1846
Taylor	William B. Preston	VA	1849
Fillmore	William A. Graham	NC	1850
	John P. Kennedy	MD	1852
Pierce	James C. Dobbin	NC	1853
Buchanan	Isaac Toucey	CT	1857
Lincoln	Gideon Welles	CT	1861
Johnson, A.	Gideon Welles	CT	1865
Grant	Adolph E. Borie	PA	1869
	George M. Robeson	NJ	1869
Hayes	Richard W. Thompson	IN	1877
	Nathan Goff Jr.	WV	1001
Garfield	William H. Hunt	LA	1881
Arthur	William E. Chandler	NH	1882
Cleveland	William C. Whitney	NY	1885
Harrison, B.	Benjamin F. Tracy	NY	1889
Cleveland	Hilary A. Herbert	AL	1893
McKinley	John D. Long	MA	1897
Roosevelt, T.	John D. Long	MA	1901
	William H. Moody	MA	1902
	Paul Morton	IL	1904
	Charles J. Bonaparte	MD	1905
	Victor H. Metcalf	CA	1906
	Truman H. Newberry	MI	1908
Taft	George von L. Meyer	MA	1909
Wilson	Josephus Daniels	NC	1913
Harding	Edwin Denby	MI	1921
Coolidge	Edwin Denby	MI	1923
	Curtis D. Wilbur	CA	1924
Hoover	Charles Francis Adams	MA	1929
Roosevelt, F. D.	Claude A. Swanson	VA	1933
	Charles Edison	NJ	1940
	Frank Knox	IL	1940
	James V. Forrestal	NY	1944
Truman	James V. Forrestal[1]	NY	1945

(1) Last member of Cabinet with this title. The Navy Department became a branch of the Department of Defense when the latter was created in 1947, though the Navy secretary maintained Cabinet-level status until 1949.

Attorneys General

The Office of Attorney General was established by act of Congress on Sept. 24, 1789. It officially reached Cabinet rank in Mar. 1792, when the first attorney general, Edmund Randolph, attended his initial Cabinet meeting. The Department of Justice, headed by the attorney general, was created June 22, 1870.

President	Attorney General	Home	Sworn in
Washington	Edmund J. Randolph	VA	1789
	William Bradford	PA	1794
	Charles Lee	VA	1795
Adams, J.	Charles Lee	VA	1797
Jefferson	Levi Lincoln	MA	1801
	John Breckenridge	KY	1805
	Caesar A. Rodney	DE	1807
Madison	Caesar A. Rodney	DE	1807
	William Pinkney	MD	1811
	Richard Rush	PA	1814
Monroe	Richard Rush	PA	1817
	William Wirt	VA	1817
Adams, J. Q.	William Wirt	VA	1825
Jackson	John M. Berrien	GA	1829
	Roger B. Taney	MD	1831
	Benjamin F. Butler	NY	1833
Van Buren	Benjamin F. Butler	NY	1837
	Felix Grundy	TN	1838
	Henry D. Gilpin	PA	1840
Harrison, W. H.	John J. Crittenden	KY	1841
Tyler	John J. Crittenden	KY	1841
	Hugh S. Legaré	SC	1841
	John Nelson	MD	1843
Polk	John Y. Mason	VA	1845
	Nathan Clifford	ME	1846
	Isaac Toucey	CT	1848
Taylor	Reverdy Johnson	MD	1849
Fillmore	John J. Crittenden	KY	1850
Pierce	Caleb Cushing	MA	1853
Buchanan	Jeremiah S. Black	PA	1857
	Edwin M. Stanton	PA	1860
Lincoln	Edward Bates	MO	1861
	James Speed	KY	1864
Johnson, A.	James Speed	KY	1865
	Henry Stanbery	OH	1866
	William M. Evarts	NY	1868
Grant	Ebenezer R. Hoar	MA	1869
	Amos T. Akerman	GA	1870
	George H. Williams	OR	1871
	Edwards Pierrepont	NY	1875
	Alphonso Taft	OH	1876
Hayes	Charles Devens	MA	1877
Garfield	I. Wayne MacVeagh	PA	1881
Arthur	Benjamin H. Brewster	PA	1882
Cleveland	Augustus H. Garland	AR	1885
Harrison, B.	William H. H. Miller	IN	1889
Cleveland	Richard Olney	MA	1893
	Judson Harmon	OH	1895
McKinley	Joseph McKenna	CA	1897
	John W. Griggs	NJ	1898
	Philander C. Knox	PA	1901
Roosevelt, T.	Philander C. Knox	PA	1901
	William H. Moody	MA	1904
	Charles J. Bonaparte	MD	1906
Taft	George W. Wickersham	NY	1909
Wilson	James C. McReynolds	TN	1913
	Thomas W. Gregory	TX	1914
	A. Mitchell Palmer	PA	1919
Harding	Harry M. Daugherty	OH	1921
Coolidge	Harry M. Daugherty	OH	1923
	Harlan F. Stone	NY	1924
	John G. Sargent	VT	1925
Hoover	William D. Mitchell	MN	1929
Roosevelt, F. D.	Homer S. Cummings	CT	1933
	Frank Murphy	MI	1939
	Robert H. Jackson	NY	1940
	Francis Biddle	PA	1941
Truman	Thomas C. Clark	TX	1945
	J. Howard McGrath	RI	1949
	James P. McGranery	PA	1952
Eisenhower	Herbert Brownell Jr.	NY	1953
	William P. Rogers	MD	1957
Kennedy	Robert F. Kennedy	MA	1961
Johnson, L. B.	Robert F. Kennedy	MA	1963
	Nicholas Katzenbach	IL	1964
	W. Ramsey Clark	TX	1967
Nixon	John N. Mitchell	NY	1969
	Richard G. Kleindienst	AZ	1972
	Elliot L. Richardson	MA	1973
	William B. Saxbe	OH	1974
Ford	William B. Saxbe	OH	1974
	Edward H. Levi	IL	1975

President	Attorney General	Home	Sworn in
Carter	Griffin B. Bell	GA	1977
	Benjamin R. Civiletti	MD	1979
Reagan	William French Smith	CA	1981
	Edwin Meese III	CA	1985
	Richard L. Thornburgh	PA	1988
Bush, G. H. W.	Richard L. Thornburgh	PA	1989
	William P. Barr	NY	1991
Clinton	Janet Reno	FL	1993
Bush, G. W.	John Ashcroft	MO	2001
	Alberto R. Gonzales	TX	2005
	Michael B. Mukasey	NY	2007
Obama	Eric H. Holder Jr.	DC	2009

Secretaries of the Interior

The Department of the Interior was created by act of Congress on Mar. 3, 1849.

President	Secretary	Home	Sworn in
Taylor	Thomas Ewing	OH	1849
Fillmore	Thomas M. T. McKennan	PA	1850
	Alex H. H. Stuart	VA	1850
Pierce	Robert McClelland	MI	1853
Buchanan	Jacob Thompson	MS	1857
Lincoln	Caleb B. Smith	IN	1861
	John P. Usher	IN	1863
Johnson, A.	John P. Usher	IN	1865
	James Harlan	IA	1865
	Orville H. Browning	IL	1866
Grant	Jacob D. Cox	OH	1869
	Columbus Delano	OH	1870
	Zachariah Chandler	MI	1875
Hayes	Carl Schurz	MO	1877
Garfield	Samuel J. Kirkwood	IA	1881
Arthur	Henry M. Teller	CO	1882
Cleveland	Lucius Q. C. Lamar	MS	1885
	William F. Vilas	WI	1888
Harrison, B.	John W. Noble	MO	1889
Cleveland	M. Hoke Smith	GA	1893
	David R. Francis	MO	1896
McKinley	Cornelius N. Bliss	NY	1897
	Ethan A. Hitchcock	MO	1898
Roosevelt, T.	Ethan A. Hitchcock	MO	1901
	James R. Garfield	OH	1907
Taft	Richard A. Ballinger	WA	1909
	Walter L. Fisher	IL	1911
Wilson	Franklin K. Lane	CA	1913
	John B. Payne	IL	1920
Harding	Albert B. Fall	NM	1921
	Hubert Work	CO	1923
Coolidge	Hubert Work	CO	1923
	Roy O. West	IL	1929
Hoover	Ray Lyman Wilbur	CA	1929
Roosevelt, F. D.	Harold L. Ickes	IL	1933
Truman	Harold L. Ickes	IL	1945
	Julius A. Krug	WI	1946
	Oscar L. Chapman	CO	1949
Eisenhower	Douglas McKay	OR	1953
	Fred A. Seaton	NE	1956
Kennedy	Stewart L. Udall	AZ	1961
Johnson, L. B.	Stewart L. Udall	AZ	1963
Nixon	Walter J. Hickel	AK	1969
	Rogers C. B. Morton	MD	1971
Ford	Rogers C. B. Morton	MD	1971
	Stanley K. Hathaway	WY	1975
	Thomas S. Kleppe	ND	1975
Carter	Cecil D. Andrus	ID	1977
Reagan	James G. Watt	CO	1981
	William P. Clark	CA	1983
	Donald P. Hodel	OR	1985
Bush, G. H. W.	Manuel Lujan	NM	1989
Clinton	Bruce Babbitt	AZ	1993
Bush, G. W.	Gale Norton	CO	2001
	Dirk Kempthorne	ID	2006
Obama	Kenneth L. Salazar	CO	2009
	Sally Jewell	WA	2013

Secretaries of Agriculture

The Department of Agriculture was created by act of Congress on May 15, 1862. On Feb. 8, 1889, its commissioner was renamed secretary of agriculture and became a member of the Cabinet.

President	Secretary	Home	Sworn in
Cleveland	Norman J. Colman	MO	1889
Harrison, B.	Jeremiah M. Rusk	WI	1889
Cleveland	J. Sterling Morton	NE	1893
McKinley	James Wilson	IA	1897
Roosevelt, T.	James Wilson	IA	1901
Taft	James Wilson	IA	1909
Wilson	David F. Houston	MO	1913
	Edwin T. Meredith	IA	1920
Harding	Henry C. Wallace	IA	1921
Coolidge	Henry C. Wallace	IA	1923
	Howard M. Gore	WV	1924
	William M. Jardine	KS	1925
Hoover	Arthur M. Hyde	MO	1929
Roosevelt, F. D.	Henry A. Wallace	IA	1933
	Claude R. Wickard	IN	1940
Truman	Clinton P. Anderson	NM	1945
Truman	Charles F. Brannan	CO	1948
Eisenhower	Ezra Taft Benson	UT	1953
Kennedy	Orville L. Freeman	MN	1961
Johnson, L. B.	Orville L. Freeman	MN	1963
Nixon	Clifford M. Hardin	IN	1969
	Earl L. Butz	IN	1971
Ford	Earl L. Butz	IN	1974
	John A. Knebel	VA	1976
Carter	Bob Bergland	MN	1977
Reagan	John R. Block	IL	1981
	Richard E. Lyng	CA	1986
Bush, G. H. W.	Clayton K. Yeutter	NE	1989
	Edward Madigan	IL	1991
Clinton	Mike Espy	MS	1993
	Dan Glickman	KS	1995
Bush, G. W.	Ann M. Veneman	CA	2001
	Mike Johanns	NE	2005
	Ed Schafer	ND	2008
Obama	Thomas J. Vilsack	IA	2009

Secretaries of Commerce and Labor

The Department of Commerce and Labor, created by Congress on Feb. 14, 1903, was divided by Congress Mar. 4, 1913, into two departments. The secretary of each was made a Cabinet member.

President	Secretary	Home	Sworn in
Roosevelt, T.	George B. Cortelyou	NY	1903
	Victor H. Metcalf	CA	1904
	Oscar S. Straus	NY	1906
Taft	Charles Nagel	MO	1909

Secretaries of Labor

President	Secretary	Home	Sworn in
Wilson	William B. Wilson	PA	1913
Harding	James J. Davis	PA	1921
Coolidge	James J. Davis	PA	1923
Hoover	James J. Davis	PA	1929
	William N. Doak	VA	1930
Roosevelt, F. D.	Frances Perkins	NY	1933
Truman	L. B. Schwellenbach	WA	1945
	Maurice J. Tobin	MA	1949
Eisenhower	Martin P. Durkin	IL	1953
	James P. Mitchell	NJ	1953
Kennedy	Arthur J. Goldberg	IL	1961
	W. Willard Wirtz	IL	1962
Johnson, L. B.	W. Willard Wirtz	IL	1963
Nixon	George P. Shultz	IL	1969
	James D. Hodgson	CA	1970
	Peter J. Brennan	NY	1973
Ford	Peter J. Brennan	NY	1974
	John T. Dunlop	CA	1975
	W. J. Usery Jr.	GA	1976
Carter	F. Ray Marshall	TX	1977
Reagan	Raymond J. Donovan	NJ	1981
	William E. Brock	TN	1985
	Ann D. McLaughlin	DC	1987
Bush, G. H. W.	Elizabeth H. Dole	NC	1989
	Lynn Martin	IL	1991
Clinton	Robert B. Reich	MA	1993
	Alexis M. Herman	AL	1997
Bush, G. W.	Elaine L. Chao	KY	2001
Obama	Hilda L. Solis	CA	2009
	Thomas E. Perez	MD	2013

Secretaries of Commerce

President	Secretary	Home	Sworn in
Wilson	William C. Redfield	NY	1913
	Joshua W. Alexander	MO	1919
Harding	Herbert C. Hoover	CA	1921
Coolidge	Herbert C. Hoover	CA	1923
	William F. Whiting	MA	1928
Hoover	Robert P. Lamont	IL	1929
	Roy D. Chapin	MI	1932
Roosevelt, F. D.	Daniel C. Roper	SC	1933
	Harry L. Hopkins	NY	1939
	Jesse H. Jones	TX	1940
	Henry A. Wallace	IA	1945
Truman	Henry A. Wallace	IA	1945
	W. Averell Harriman	NY	1947
	Charles W. Sawyer	OH	1948
Eisenhower	Sinclair Weeks	MA	1953
	Lewis L. Strauss	NY	1958
	Frederick H. Mueller	MI	1959
Kennedy	Luther H. Hodges	NC	1961
Johnson, L. B.	Luther H. Hodges	NC	1963
	John T. Connor	NJ	1965
	Alex B. Trowbridge	NJ	1967
	Cyrus R. Smith	NY	1968
Nixon	Maurice H. Stans	MN	1969
	Peter G. Peterson	IL	1972
	Frederick B. Dent	SC	1973
Ford	Frederick B. Dent	SC	1974
	Rogers C. B. Morton	MD	1975
	Elliot L. Richardson	MA	1975
Carter	Juanita M. Kreps	NC	1977
	Philip M. Klutznick	IL	1979
Reagan	Malcolm Baldrige	CT	1981
	C. William Verity Jr.	OH	1987
Bush, G. H. W.	Robert A. Mosbacher	TX	1989
	Barbara H. Franklin	PA	1992
Clinton	Ronald H. Brown	DC	1993
	Mickey Kantor	CA	1996
	William M. Daley	IL	1997
	Norman Y. Mineta	CA	2000
Bush, G. W.	Donald L. Evans	TX	2001
	Carlos M. Gutierrez	MI	2005
Obama	Gary F. Locke	WA	2009
	John Bryson	CA	2011
	Penny Pritzker	IL	2013

Secretaries of Housing and Urban Development

The Department of Housing and Urban Development was created by act of Congress on Sept. 9, 1965.

President	Secretary	Home	Sworn in
Johnson, L. B.	Robert C. Weaver	WA	1966
	Robert C. Wood	MA	1969
Nixon	George W. Romney	MI	1969
	James T. Lynn	OH	1973
Ford	James T. Lynn	OH	1974
	Carla Anderson Hills	CA	1975
Carter	Patricia Roberts Harris	DC	1977
	Moon Landrieu	LA	1979
Reagan	Samuel R. Pierce Jr.	NY	1981
Bush, G. H. W.	Jack F. Kemp	NY	1989
Clinton	Henry G. Cisneros	TX	1993
	Andrew M. Cuomo	NY	1997
Bush, G. W.	Mel Martinez	FL	2001
	Alphonso Jackson	TX	2004
	Steve Preston	VA	2008
Obama	Shaun L. S. Donovan	NY	2009

Secretaries of Transportation

The Department of Transportation was created by act of Congress on Oct. 15, 1966.

President	Secretary	Home	Sworn in
Johnson, L. B.	Alan S. Boyd	FL	1966
Nixon	John A. Volpe	MA	1969
	Claude S. Brinegar	CA	1973
Ford	Claude S. Brinegar	CA	1974
	William T. Coleman Jr.	PA	1975
Carter	Brock Adams	WA	1977
	Neil E. Goldschmidt	OR	1979
Reagan	Andrew L. Lewis Jr.	PA	1981
	Elizabeth H. Dole	NC	1983
	James H. Burnley	NC	1987
Bush, G. H. W.	Samuel K. Skinner	IL	1989
	Andrew H. Card Jr.	MA	1992
Clinton	Federico F. Peña	CO	1993
	Rodney E. Slater	AR	1997
Bush, G. W.	Norman Y. Mineta	CA	2001
	Mary E. Peters	AZ	2006
Obama	Raymond L. LaHood	IL	2009
	Anthony Foxx	NC	2013

Secretaries of Energy

The Department of Energy was created by federal law on Aug. 4, 1977.

President	Secretary	Home	Sworn in
Carter	James R. Schlesinger	VA	1977
	Charles W. Duncan Jr.	WY	1979
Reagan	James B. Edwards	SC	1981
	Donald P. Hodel	OR	1982
	John S. Herrington	CA	1985
Bush, G. H. W.	James D. Watkins	CA	1989
Clinton	Hazel R. O'Leary	MN	1993
	Federico F. Peña	CO	1997
	Bill Richardson	NM	1998
Bush, G. W.	Spencer Abraham	MI	2001
	Samuel W. Bodman	MA	2005
Obama	Steven Chu	CA	2009
	Ernest Moniz	MA	2013

Secretaries of Health, Education, and Welfare

The Department of Health, Education, and Welfare was created by Congress on Apr. 11, 1953. On Sept. 27, 1979, Congress approved creation of a separate Department of Education. The existing department was renamed the Department of Health and Human Services.

President	Secretary	Home	Sworn in
Eisenhower	Oveta Culp Hobby	TX	1953
	Marion B. Folsom	NY	1955
	Arthur S. Flemming	OH	1958
Kennedy	Abraham A. Ribicoff	CT	1961
	Anthony J. Celebrezze	OH	1962
Johnson, L. B.	Anthony J. Celebrezze	OH	1963
	John W. Gardner	NY	1965
	Wilbur J. Cohen	MI	1968
Nixon	Robert H. Finch	CA	1969
	Elliot L. Richardson	MA	1970
	Caspar W. Weinberger	CA	1973
Ford	Caspar W. Weinberger	CA	1974
	Forrest D. Mathews	AL	1975
Carter	Joseph A. Califano Jr.	DC	1977
	Patricia Roberts Harris	DC	1979

Secretaries of Health and Human Services

President	Secretary	Home	Sworn in
Carter	Patricia Roberts Harris	DC	1979
Reagan	Richard S. Schweiker	PA	1981
	Margaret M. Heckler	MA	1983
Reagan	Otis R. Bowen	IN	1985
Bush, G. H. W.	Louis W. Sullivan	GA	1989
Clinton	Donna E. Shalala	WI	1993
Bush, G. W.	Tommy Thompson	WI	2001
	Michael O. Leavitt	UT	2005
Obama	Kathleen Sebelius	KS	2009

Secretaries of Education

President	Secretary	Home	Sworn in
Carter	Shirley Hufstedler	CA	1979
Reagan	Terrel H. Bell	UT	1981
	William J. Bennett	NY	1985
	Lauro F. Cavazos	TX	1988
Bush, G. H. W.	Lauro F. Cavazos	TX	1989
	Lamar Alexander	TN	1991
Clinton	Richard W. Riley	SC	1993
Bush, G. W.	Roderick R. Paige	TX	2001
	Margaret Spellings	TX	2005
Obama	Arne Duncan	IL	2009

Secretaries of Veterans Affairs

Pres. Ronald Reagan signed a bill in 1988 granting Cabinet-level status to the Veterans Administration. The agency became the Department of Veterans Affairs on Mar. 15, 1989.

President	Secretary	Home	Sworn in
Bush, G. H. W.	Edward J. Derwinski	IL	1989
Clinton	Jesse Brown	IL	1993
	Togo D. West Jr.	NC	1998
Bush, G. W.	Anthony J. Principi	CA	2001
	R. James Nicholson	CO	2005
	James B. Peake	MO	2007
Obama	Eric K. Shinseki	VA	2009

Secretaries of Homeland Security

The Department of Homeland Security was created by act of Congress on Nov. 25, 2002.

President	Secretary	Home	Sworn in
Bush, G. W.	Thomas Ridge	PA	2003
	Michael Chertoff	DC	2005
Obama	Janet A. Napolitano	AZ	2009

CONGRESS

Floor Leaders in the U.S. Senate, 1920-2013

Majority leaders				Minority leaders			
Name	Party	State	Tenure	Name	Party	State	Tenure
Charles Curtis[1]	Rep.	KS	1925-1929	Oscar W. Underwood[2]	Dem.	AL	1920-1923
James E. Watson	Rep.	IN	1929-1933	Joseph T. Robinson	Dem.	AR	1923-1933
Joseph T. Robinson	Dem.	AR	1933-1937	Charles L. McNary	Rep.	OR	1933-1944
Alben W. Barkley	Dem.	KY	1937-1947	Wallace H. White	Rep.	ME	1944-1947
Wallace H. White	Rep.	ME	1947-1949	Alben W. Barkley	Dem.	KY	1947-1949
Scott W. Lucas	Dem.	IL	1949-1951	Kenneth S. Wherry	Rep.	NE	1949-1951
Ernest W. McFarland	Dem.	AZ	1951-1953	Henry Styles Bridges	Rep.	NH	1952-1953
Robert A. Taft	Rep.	OH	1953	Lyndon B. Johnson	Dem.	TX	1953-1955
William F. Knowland	Rep.	CA	1953-1955	William F. Knowland	Rep.	CA	1955-1959
Lyndon B. Johnson	Dem.	TX	1955-1961	Everett M. Dirksen	Rep.	IL	1959-1969
Mike Mansfield	Dem.	MT	1961-1977	Hugh D. Scott	Rep.	PA	1969-1977
Robert C. Byrd	Dem.	WV	1977-1981	Howard H. Baker Jr.	Rep.	TN	1977-1981
Howard H. Baker Jr.	Rep.	TN	1981-1985	Robert C. Byrd	Dem.	WV	1981-1987
Robert J. Dole	Rep.	KS	1985-1987	Robert J. Dole	Rep.	KS	1987-1995
Robert C. Byrd	Dem.	WV	1987-1989	Thomas A. Daschle	Dem.	SD	1995-2001[3]
George J. Mitchell	Dem.	ME	1989-1995	Trent Lott	Rep.	MS	2001-2002[3,4]
Robert J. Dole	Rep.	KS	1995-1996	Thomas A. Daschle	Dem.	SD	2003-2005
Trent Lott	Rep.	MS	1996-2001[3]	Harry M. Reid	Dem.	NV	2005-2007
Thomas A. Daschle	Dem.	SD	2001-2003[3]	Mitch McConnell	Rep.	KY	2007-
William Frist	Rep.	TN	2003-2007[4]				
Harry M. Reid	Dem.	NV	2007-				

Note: The offices of party (majority and minority) leaders in the Senate did not evolve until the 20th century. (1) First Republican to be formally designated floor leader. Henry Cabot Lodge (MA) served as unofficial party leader prior to Curtis's election. (2) First Democrat to be designated floor leader. (3) Democrats held the majority Jan. 3, 2001, until Dick Cheney (R) was installed as vice pres., Jan. 20. Republicans subsequently lost the majority when Jim Jeffords (VT) switched from Republican to Independent, June 6, 2001. (4) Trent Lott resigned from Republican leadership Dec. 20, 2002. William Frist was elected Republican leader Dec. 23, 2002, and began service Jan. 7, 2003, as majority leader.

Speakers of the U.S. House of Representatives, 1789-2013

Name	Party	State	Tenure	Name	Party	State	Tenure
Frederick A. C. Muhlenberg	Federalist	PA	1789-1791	Michael C. Kerr	Dem.	IN	1875-1876
Jonathan Trumbull	Federalist	CT	1791-1793	Samuel J. Randall	Dem.	PA	1876-1881
Frederick A. C. Muhlenberg	Federalist	PA	1793-1795	J. Warren Keifer	Rep.	OH	1881-1883
Jonathan Dayton	Federalist	NJ	1795-1799	John G. Carlisle	Dem.	KY	1883-1889
Theodore Sedgwick	Federalist	MA	1799-1801	Thomas B. Reed	Rep.	ME	1889-1891
Nathaniel Macon	Dem.-Rep.	NC	1801-1807	Charles F. Crisp	Dem.	GA	1891-1895
Joseph B. Varnum	Dem.-Rep.	MA	1807-1811	Thomas B. Reed	Rep.	ME	1895-1899
Henry Clay	Dem.-Rep.	KY	1811-1814	David B. Henderson	Rep.	IA	1899-1903
Langdon Cheves	Dem.-Rep.	SC	1814-1815	Joseph G. Cannon	Rep.	IL	1903-1911
Henry Clay	Dem.-Rep.	KY	1815-1820	Champ Clark	Dem.	MO	1911-1919
John W. Taylor	Dem.-Rep.	NY	1820-1821	Frederick H. Gillett	Rep.	MA	1919-1925
Philip P. Barbour	Dem.-Rep.	VA	1821-1823	Nicholas Longworth	Rep.	OH	1925-1931
Henry Clay	Dem.-Rep.	KY	1823-1825	John N. Garner	Dem.	TX	1931-1933
John W. Taylor	Dem.	NY	1825-1827	Henry T. Rainey	Dem.	IL	1933-1934
Andrew Stevenson	Dem.	VA	1827-1834	Joseph W. Byrns	Dem.	TN	1935-1936
John Bell	Dem.	TN	1834-1835	William B. Bankhead	Dem.	AL	1936-1940
James K. Polk	Dem.	TN	1835-1839	Sam Rayburn	Dem.	TX	1940-1947
Robert M. T. Hunter	Dem.	VA	1839-1841	Joseph W. Martin Jr.	Rep.	MA	1947-1949
John White	Whig	KY	1841-1843	Sam Rayburn	Dem.	TX	1949-1953
John W. Jones	Dem.	VA	1843-1845	Joseph W. Martin Jr.	Rep.	MA	1953-1955
John W. Davis	Dem.	IN	1845-1847	Sam Rayburn	Dem.	TX	1955-1961
Robert C. Winthrop	Whig	MA	1847-1849	John W. McCormack	Dem.	MA	1962-1971
Howell Cobb	Dem.	GA	1849-1851	Carl B. Albert	Dem.	OK	1971-1977
Linn Boyd	Dem.	KY	1851-1855	Thomas P. O'Neill Jr.	Dem.	MA	1977-1987
Nathaniel P. Banks	American	MA	1856-1857	James C. Wright Jr.	Dem.	TX	1987-1989
James L. Orr	Dem.	SC	1857-1859	Thomas S. Foley	Dem.	WA	1989-1995
William Pennington	Rep.	NJ	1860-1861	Newt Gingrich	Rep.	GA	1995-1999
Galusha A. Grow	Rep.	PA	1861-1863	J. Dennis Hastert	Rep.	IL	1999-2007
Schuyler Colfax	Rep.	IN	1863-1869	Nancy Pelosi	Dem.	CA	2007-2011
Theodore M. Pomeroy	Rep.	NY	1869	John Boehner	Rep.	OH	2011-
James G. Blaine	Rep.	ME	1869-1875				

Political Divisions of Congress, 1901-2012

Source: Office of the Clerk, U.S. House of Representatives; Congressional Research Service, Library of Congress

All figures reflect post-election party breakdown except where noted; **boldface** denotes party in majority immediately after election.

		SENATE					HOUSE OF REPRESENTATIVES				
Congress	Years	Total members	Dem.	Rep.	Other parties	Vacant	Total members	Dem.	Rep.	Other parties	Vacant
57th	1901-1903	90	32	**56**	2		357	151	**200**	6	
58th	1903-1905	90	33	**57**			386	176	**207**	3	
59th	1905-1907	90	32	**58**			386	135	**251**		
60th	1907-1909	92	31	**61**			391	167	**223**	1	
61st	1909-1911	92	32	**60**			391	172	**219**		
62nd	1911-1913	96	44	**52**			394	**230**	162	2	
63rd	1913-1915	96	**51**	44	1		435	**291**	134	10	
64th	1915-1917	96	**56**	40			435	**230**	196	9	
65th	1917-1919	96	**54**	42			435	214[1]	**215**	6	
66th	1919-1921	96	47	**49**			435	192	**240**	2	1
67th	1921-1923	96	37	**59**			435	131	**302**	2	
68th	1923-1925	96	42	**53**	1		435	207	**225**	3	
69th	1925-1927	96	41	**54**	1		435	183	**247**	5	

Congress	Years	SENATE Total members	Dem.	Rep.	Other parties	Vacant	HOUSE OF REPRESENTATIVES Total members	Dem.	Rep.	Other parties	Vacant
70th	1927-1929	96	46	48	1	1	435	194	238	3	
71st	1929-1931	96	39	56	1		435	164	270	1	
72nd	1931-1933	96	47	48	1		435	216[2]	218	1	
73rd	1933-1935	96	59	36	1		435	313	117	5	
74th	1935-1937	96	69	25	2		435	322	103	10	
75th	1937-1939	96	76	16	4		435	334	88	13	
76th	1939-1941	96	69	23	4		435	262	169	4	
77th	1941-1943	96	66	28	2		435	267	162	6	
78th	1943-1945	96	57	38	1		435	222	209	4	
79th	1945-1947	96	57	38	1		435	242	191	2	
80th	1947-1949	96	45	51			435	188	246	1	
81st	1949-1951	96	54	42			435	263	171	1	
82nd	1951-1953	96	49	47			435	235	199	1	
83rd	1953-1955	96	47	48	1		435	213	221	1	
84th	1955-1957	96	48	47	1		435	232	203		
85th	1957-1959	96	49	47			435	234	201		
86th	1959-1961	100	65	35			437[3,4]	283	153	1	
87th	1961-1963	100	64	36			437	263	174		
88th	1963-1965	100	66	34			435	259	176		
89th	1965-1967	100	68	32			435	295	140		
90th	1967-1969	100	64	36			435	247	187		1
91st	1969-1971	100	57	43			435	243	192		
92nd	1971-1973	100	54	44	2		435	255	180		
93rd	1973-1975	100	56	42	2		435	242	192	1	
94th	1975-1977	100	60	38	2		435	291	144		
95th	1977-1979	100	61	38	1		435	292	143		
96th	1979-1981	100	58	41	1		435	277	158		
97th	1981-1983	100	46	53	1		435	242	192	1	
98th	1983-1985	100	46	54			435	269	166		
99th	1985-1987	100	47	53			435	253	182		
100th	1987-1989	100	55	45			435	258	177		
101st	1989-1991	100	55	45			435	260	175		
102nd	1991-1993	100	56	44			435	267	167	1	
103rd	1993-1995	100	57	43			435	258	176	1	
104th	1995-1997	100	48	52			435	204	230	1	
105th	1997-1999	100	45	55			435	206	228	1	
106th	1999-2001	100	45	55			435	211	223	1	
107th	2001-2003	100	50	50[5]			435	212	221	2	
108th	2003-2005	100	48	51	1		435	204	229	1	1
109th	2005-2007	100	44	55	1		435	202	232	1	
110th	2007-2009	100	49	49	2[6]		435	233	202		
111th	2009-2011	100	57	41	2[6]		435	257	178		
112th	2011-2013	100	51	47	2[6]		435	193	242		
113th	2013-	100	53	45	2[6]		435	201	234		

(1) Democrats organized the House with help of other parties. (2) Democrats organized the House because of Republican deaths. (3) Proclamation declaring Alaska a state issued Jan. 3, 1959. (4) Proclamation declaring Hawaii a state issued Aug. 21, 1959. (5) While the Senate was split 50-50, control was held by whichever party had an incumbent vice president. Republican Sen. Jim Jeffords (VT) changed his party designation to Independent on June 6, 2001, switching control of the Senate to Democrats. (6) Both Independent senators chose to caucus with the Democrats.

Congressional Bills Vetoed, 1789-2013

Source: Virtual Reference Desk, U.S. Senate

President	Regular vetoes	Pocket vetoes	Total vetoes	Vetoes overridden	President	Regular vetoes	Pocket vetoes	Total vetoes	Vetoes overridden
Washington	2	—	2	—	B. Harrison	19	25	44	1
J. Adams	—	—	—	—	Cleveland[2]	42	128	170	5
Jefferson	—	—	—	—	McKinley	6	36	42	—
Madison	5	2	7	—	T. Roosevelt	42	40	82	1
Monroe	1	—	1	—	Taft	30	9	39	1
J. Q. Adams	—	—	—	—	Wilson	33	11	44	6
Jackson	5	7	12	—	Harding	5	1	6	—
Van Buren	—	1	1	—	Coolidge	20	30	50	4
W. H. Harrison	—	—	—	—	Hoover	21	16	37	3
Tyler	6	4	10	1	F. D. Roosevelt	372	263	635	9
Polk	2	1	3	—	Truman	180	70	250	12
Taylor	—	—	—	—	Eisenhower	73	108	181	2
Fillmore	—	—	—	—	Kennedy	12	9	21	—
Pierce	9	—	9	5	L. Johnson	16	14	30	—
Buchanan	4	3	7	—	Nixon	26	17	43	7
Lincoln	2	5	7	—	Ford	48	18	66	12
A. Johnson	21	8	29	15	Carter	13	18	31	2
Grant	45	48	93	4	Reagan	39	39	78	9
Hayes	12	1	13	1	G. H. W. Bush[3]	29	15	44	1
Garfield	—	—	—	—	Clinton[4]	36	1	37	2
Arthur	4	8	12	1	G. W. Bush	12	—	12	4
Cleveland[1]	304	110	414	2	Obama	2	—	2	—
					Total[3,4]	1,498	1,066	2,564	110

— = 0. (1) First term only. (2) Second term only. (3) Excluded from the figures are two bills that Pres. Bush claimed to be vetoed but Congress considered enacted into law because the president failed to return them to Congress during a recess period. (4) Does not include line-item vetoes, which were ruled unconstitutional by the U.S. Supreme Court on June 25, 1998.

Members of the 113th Congress: Senate

Source: *Statistics of the Presidential and Congressional Election* (corrected to Feb. 28, 2013), Clerk of the House of Representatives
53 Democrats, 45 Republicans, 2 independents (who were both expected to caucus with Democrats). Boldface denotes the 2012 election winner. * = Incumbent. Third-party or independent candidates receiving fewer than 10,000 votes are not necessarily listed. Terms are for 6 years and end Jan. 3 of the year preceding the senator's name in the following table. Annual salary, $174,000; President Pro Tempore, Majority Leader, and Minority Leader, $193,400. To be eligible to serve in the Senate, one must be at least 30 years old, a U.S. citizen for at least 9 years, and a resident of the state from which chosen.

D = Democrat; R = Republican; CP = Constitution Party; DFL = Dem.-Farmer-Labor; I = Independent; IP = Independence Party; LB = Libertarian; NPA = No party affiliation; RF = Reform; Unaff. = Unaffiliated.

Term ends	Senator/candidate (party); service from[1]	2012 election results
Alabama		
2015	Jeff Sessions (R); 1/7/1997	
2017	Richard Shelby (R); 1/6/1987	
Alaska		
2015	Mark Begich (D); 1/6/2009	
2017	Lisa Murkowski (R); 12/20/2002	
Arizona		
2017	John McCain (R); 1/6/1987	
2019	**Jeff Flake (R)**	1,104,457
	Richard Carmona (D)	1,036,542
	Marc Victor (LB)	102,109
Arkansas		
2015	Mark Pryor (D); 1/7/2003	
2017	John Boozman (R); 1/5/2011	
California		
2017	Barbara Boxer (D); 1993	
2019	**Dianne Feinstein* (D); 11/10/1992**	7,864,624
	Elizabeth Emken (R)	4,713,887
Colorado		
2015	Mark Udall (D); 1/6/2009	
2017	Michael F. Bennet (D); 1/22/2009	
Connecticut		
2017	Richard Blumenthal (D); 1/5/2011	
2019	**Christopher S. Murphy (D)**	828,761
	Linda E. McMahon (R)	651,089
	Paul Passarelli (LB)	25,045
Delaware		
2015	Christopher Coons (D); 11/15/2010	
2019	**Thomas R. Carper* (D); 2001**	265,415
	Kevin Wade (R)	115,700
	Alexander Pires (Ind. Party of DE)	15,300
Florida		
2017	Marco Rubio (R); 1/5/2011	
2019	**Bill Nelson* (D); 2001**	4,523,451
	Connie Mack (R)	3,458,267
	Bill Gaylor (NPA)	126,079
	Chris Borgia (NPA)	82,089
Georgia		
2015	Saxby Chambliss (R); 1/7/2003	
2017	Johnny Isakson (R); 2005	
Hawaii		
2017	Daniel K. Inouye (D); 1963	
2019	**Mazie K. Hirono (D)**	269,489
	Linda Lingle (R)	160,994
Idaho		
2015	Jim Risch (R); 1/6/2009	
2017	Mike Crapo (R); 1/6/1999	
Illinois		
2015	Richard J. Durbin (D); 1/7/1997	
2017	Mark Kirk (R); 11/29/2010	
Indiana		
2017	Dan Coats (R); 1/5/2011	
2019	**Joe Donnelly (D)**	1,281,181
	Richard E. Mourdock (R)	1,133,621
	Andrew "Andy" Horning (LB)	145,282
Iowa		
2015	Tom Harkin (D); 1985	
2017	Chuck Grassley (R); 1981	
Kansas		
2015	Pat Roberts (R); 1/7/1997	
2017	Jerry Moran (R); 1/5/2011	
Kentucky		
2015	Mitch McConnell (R); 1985	
2017	Rand Paul (R); 1/5/2011	

Term ends	Senator/candidate (party); service from[1]	2012 election results
Louisiana		
2015	Mary L. Landrieu (D); 1/7/1997	
2017	David Vitter (R); 2005	
Maine		
2015	Susan M. Collins (R); 1/7/1997	
2019	**Angus King (I)**	370,580
	Charles E. Summers Jr. (R)	215,399
	Cynthia Ann Dill (D)	92,900
	Stephen M. Woods (I)	10,289
Maryland		
2017	Barbara Ann Mikulski (D); 1/6/1987	
2019	**Benjamin L. Cardin* (D); 2007**	1,474,028
	Daniel John Bongino (R)	693,291
	S. Rob Sobhani (Unaff.)	430,934
	Dean Ahmad (LB)	32,252
Massachusetts		
2015	Edward J. Markey (D); 7/16/2013[2]	
2019	**Elizabeth A. Warren (D)**	1,696,346
	Scott P. Brown* (R)	1,458,048
Michigan		
2015	Carl Levin (D); 1979	
2019	**Debbie Stabenow* (D); 2001**	2,735,826
	Pete Hoekstra (R)	1,767,386
	Scotty Boman (LB)	84,480
	Harley Mikkelson (Green)	27,890
	Richard A. Matkin (U.S. Taxpayers)	26,038
	John Litle (Natural Law)	11,229
Minnesota		
2015	Al Franken (DFL); 7/7/2009	
2019	**Amy Klobuchar* (DFL); 2007**	1,854,595
	Kurt Bills (R)	867,974
	Stephen Williams (IP)	73,539
	Tim Davis (Grassroots)	30,531
	Michael Cavlan (MN Open Progressives)	13,986
Mississippi		
2015	Thad Cochran (R); 12/27/1978	
2019	**Roger F. Wicker* (R); 12/31/2007**	709,626
	Albert N. Gore Jr. (D)	503,467
	Thomas Cramer (CP)	15,281
	Shawn O'Hara (RF)	13,194
Missouri		
2017	Roy Blunt (R); 1/5/2011	
2019	**Claire McCaskill* (D); 2007**	1,494,125
	W. Todd Akin (R)	1,066,159
	Jonathan Dine (LB)	165,468
Montana		
2015	Max Baucus (D); 12/15/1978	
2019	**Jon Tester* (D); 2007**	236,123
	Denny Rehberg (R)	218,051
	Dan Cox (LB)	31,892
Nebraska		
2015	Mike Johanns (R); 1/6/2009	
2019	**Deb Fischer (R)**	455,593
	Bob Kerrey (D)	332,979
Nevada		
2017	Harry Reid (D); 1/6/1987	
2019	**Dean Heller* (R); 5/9/2011**	457,656
	Shelley Berkley (D)	446,080
	David Lory VanDerBeek (Independent American)	48,792
	None of these candidates	45,277
New Hampshire		
2015	Jeanne Shaheen (D); 1/6/2009	
2017	Kelly Ayotte (R); 1/5/2011	

Term ends	Senator/candidate (party); service from[1]	2012 election results
New Jersey		
2015	Vacant[3]	
2019	**Robert Menendez* (D); 1/18/2006**	1,987,680
	Joe Kyrillos (R)	1,329,534
	Kenneth R. Kaplan (LB)	16,803
	Ken Wolski (Green)	15,801
New Mexico		
2015	Tom Udall (D); 1/6/2009	
2019	**Martin Heinrich (D)**	395,717
	Heather A. Wilson (R)	351,260
	Jon R. Barrie (Independent American)	28,199
New York		
2017	Charles E. Schumer (D); 1/6/1999	
2019	**Kirsten E. Gillibrand* (D); 1/27/2009**	4,808,878
	Wendy Long (R)	1,755,466
	Colia Clark (Green)	42,442
	Chris Edes (LB)	31,894
	John Mangelli (Common Sense)	21,985
North Carolina		
2015	Kay Hagan (D); 1/6/2009	
2017	Richard Burr (R); 2005	
North Dakota		
2017	John Hoeven (R); 1/5/2011	
2019	**Heidi Heitkamp (Dem.-NPL)**	161,337
	Rick Berg (R)	158,401
Ohio		
2017	Rob Portman (R); 1/5/2011	
2019	**Sherrod Brown* (D); 2007**	2,762,690
	Josh Mandel (R)	2,435,712
	Scott A. Rupert (I)	250,616
Oklahoma		
2015	James M. Inhofe (R); 11/21/1994	
2017	Tom Coburn (R); 2005	
Oregon		
2015	Jeff Merkley (D); 1/6/2009	
2017	Ron Wyden (D); 2/6/1996	
Pennsylvania		
2017	Pat Toomey (H); 1/5/2011	
2019	**Bob Casey Jr.* (D); 2007**	3,021,364
	Tom Smith (R)	2,509,132
	Rayburn Douglas Smith (LB)	96,926
Rhode Island		
2015	John F. Reed (D); 1/7/1997	
2019	**Sheldon Whitehouse* (D); 2007**	271,034
	Benjamin Barrett Hinckley III (R)	146,222
South Carolina		
2015	Lindsey Graham (R); 1/7/2003	
2017	Jim DeMint (R); 2005	

Term ends	Senator/candidate (party); service from[1]	2012 election results
South Dakota		
2015	Tim Johnson (D); 1/7/1997	
2017	John Thune (R); 2005	
Tennessee		
2015	Lamar Alexander (R); 1/7/2003	
2019	**Bob Corker* (R); 2007**	1,506,443
	Mark E. Clayton (D)	705,882
	Martin Pleasant (Green)	38,472
	Shaun E. Crowell (I)	20,936
	Kermit Steck (CP)	18,620
Texas		
2015	John Cornyn (R); 12/2/2002	
2019	**Ted Cruz (R)**	4,440,137
	Paul Sadler (D)	3,194,927
	John Jay Myers (LB)	162,354
	David B. Collins (Green)	67,404
Utah		
2017	Mike Lee (R); 1/5/2011	
2019	**Orrin G. Hatch* (R); 1977**	657,608
	Scott Howell (D)	301,873
	Shaun Lynn McCausland (CP)	31,905
Vermont		
2017	Patrick Leahy (D); 1975	
2019	**Bernard Sanders* (I); 2007**	207,848
	John MacGovern (R)	72,898
Virginia		
2015	Mark Warner (D); 1/6/2009	
2019	**Timothy M. Kaine (D)**	2,010,067
	George F. Allen (R)	1,785,542
Washington		
2017	Patty Murray (D); 1993	
2019	**Maria Cantwell* (D); 2001**	1,855,493
	Michael Baumgartner (R)	1,213,924
West Virginia		
2015	John D. "Jay" Rockefeller IV (D); 1/15/1985	
2019	**Joe Manchin III* (D); 11/15/2010**	399,898
	John R. Raese (R)	240,787
	Bob Henry Raber (Mountain)	19,517
Wisconsin		
2017	Ron Johnson (R); 1/5/2011	
2019	**Tammy Baldwin (D)**	1,547,104
	Tommy G. Thompson (R)	1,380,126
	Joseph Kexel (LB)	62,240
	Nimrod Y. U. Allen III (I)	16,455
Wyoming		
2015	Michael B. Enzi (R); 1/7/1997	
2019	**John Barrasso* (R); 6/22/2007**	185,250
	Tim Chesnut (D)	53,019

(1) Jan. 3, unless otherwise noted. (2) Sen. John F. Kerry resigned effective Feb. 1, 2013, to serve as secretary of state to Pres. Obama; Markey was elected in a special election June 25, 2013. (3) Sen. Frank Lautenberg (D) died in office June 3, 2013; a special election was scheduled to be held Oct. 16, 2013, to fill his seat.

Members of the 113th Congress: House of Representatives

Source: *Statistics of the Presidential and Congressional Election* (corrected to Feb. 28, 2013), Clerk of the House of Representatives

234 Republicans, 201 Democrats. Boldface denotes the 2012 election winner. * = Incumbent. ** = Incumbent running in a different district. Third-party or independent candidates receiving fewer than 10,000 votes are not necessarily listed.

Terms are for two years ending Jan. 3, 2015. Annual salary, $174,000; Majority Leader and Minority Leader, $196,400; Speaker of the House, $223,500. To be eligible for House membership, a person must be at least 25 years of age, a U.S. citizen for at least seven years, and a resident of the state from which chosen.

D = Democrat; R = Republican; Amer. Const. = American Constitution; Amer. Ind. = American Independent Party; CP = Constitution Party; DFL = Dem.-Farmer-Labor; I = Independent; IP = Independence Party; LB = Libertarian; NPA = No party affiliation; NPD = No party designation; Prog. = Progressive; Unaff. = Unaffiliated.

Dist.	Representative/candidate (party)	2012 election results
Alabama		
1	Vacant[1]	NA
2	**Martha Roby* (R)**	180,591
	Therese Ford (D)	103,092
3	**Mike Rogers* (R)**	175,306
	John Andrew Harris (D)	98,141
4	**Robert B. Aderholt* (R)**	199,071
	Daniel H. Boman (D)	69,706
5	**Mo Brooks* (R)**	189,185
	Charlie L. Holley (D)	101,772
6	**Spencer Bachus* (R)**	219,262
	Penny H. Bailey (D)	88,267
7	**Terri A. Sewell* (D)**	232,520
	Don Chamberlain (R)	73,835

Dist.	Representative/candidate (party)	2012 election results
Alaska		
	Don Young* (R)	185,296
	Sharon M. Cissna (D)	82,927
	Jim C. McDermott (LB)	15,028
Arizona		
1	**Ann Kirkpatrick (D)**	122,774
	Jonathan Paton (R)	113,594
	Kim Allen (LB)	15,227
2	**Ron Barber** (D)**	147,338
	Martha McSally (R)	144,884
3	**Raúl M. Grijalva** (D)**	98,468
	Gabriela Saucedo Mercer (R)	62,663
4	**Paul A. Gosar** (R)**	162,907
	Johnnie Robinson (D)	69,154

Dist.	Representative/candidate (party)	2012 election results
5	Matt Salmon (R)	183,470
	Spencer Morgan (D)	89,589
6	David Schweikert** (R)	179,706
	Matt Jette (D)	97,666
	Jack Anderson (LB)	10,167
7	Ed Pastor** (D)	104,489
	Joe Cobb (LB)	23,338
8	Trent Franks** (R)	172,809
	Gene Scharer (D)	95,635
9	Kyrsten Sinema (D)	121,881
	Vernon B. Parker (R)	111,630
	Powell Gammill (LB)	16,620
Arkansas		
1	Rick Crawford* (R)	138,800
	Scott Ellington (D)	96,601
2	Tim Griffin* (R)	158,175
	Herb Rule (D)	113,156
3	Steve Womack* (R)	186,467
	Rebekah J. Kennedy (Green)	39,318
	David Pangrac (LB)	19,875
4	Tom Cotton (R)	154,149
	Gene Jeffress (D)	95,013
California		
1	Doug La Malfa (R)	168,827
	Jim Reed (D)	125,386
2	Jared Huffman (D)	226,216
	Daniel W. Roberts (R)	91,310
3	John Garamendi** (D)	126,882
	Kim Vann (R)	107,086
4	Tom McClintock* (R)	197,803
	Jack Uppal (D)	125,885
5	Mike Thompson** (D)	202,872
	Randy Loftin (R)	69,545
6	Doris O. Matsui** (D)	160,667
	Joseph McCray Sr. (R)	53,406
7	Ami Bera (D)	141,241
	Dan Lungren** (R)	132,050
8	Paul Cook (R)	103,093
	Gregg Imus (R)	76,551
9	Jerry McNerney** (D)	118,373
	Ricky Gill (R)	94,704
10	Jeff Denham** (R)	110,265
	Jose Hernandez (D)	98,934
11	George Miller** (D)	200,743
	Virginia Fuller (R)	87,136
12	Nancy Pelosi** (D)	253,709
	John Dennis (R)	44,478
13	Barbara Lee** (D)	250,436
	Marilyn M. Singleton (NPD)	38,146
14	Jackie Speier** (D)	203,828
	Deborah "Debbie" Bacigalupi (R)	54,455
15	Eric Swalwell (D)	120,388
	Fortney "Pete" Stark** (D)	110,646
16	Jim Costa** (D)	84,649
	Brian Daniel Whelan (R)	62,801
17	Mike Honda** (D)	159,392
	Evelyn Li (R)	57,336
18	Anna G. Eshoo** (D)	212,831
	Dave Chapman (R)	89,103
19	Zoe Lofgren** (D)	162,300
	Robert Murray (R)	59,313
20	Sam Farr** (D)	172,996
	Jeff Taylor (R)	60,566
21	David G. Valadao (R)	67,164
	John Hernandez (D)	49,119
22	Devin Nunes** (R)	132,386
	Otto Lee (D)	81,555
23	Kevin McCarthy** (R)	158,161
	Terry Phillips (NPD)	57,842
24	Lois Capps** (D)	156,749
	Abel Maldonado (R)	127,746
25	Howard P. "Buck" McKeon* (R)	129,593
	Lee C. Rogers (D)	106,982
26	Julia Brownley (D)	139,072
	Tony Strickland (R)	124,863
27	Judy Chu** (D)	154,191
	Jack Orswell (R)	86,817
28	Adam B. Schiff** (D)	188,703
	Phil Jennerjahn (R)	58,008
29	Tony Cardenas (D)	111,287
	David R. Hernandez (NPD)	38,994
30	Brad Sherman* (D)	149,456
	Howard L. Berman** (D)	98,395
31	Gary G. Miller** (R)	88,964
	Bob Dutton (R)	72,255
32	Grace F. Napolitano** (D)	124,903
	David L. Miller (R)	65,208
33	Henry A. Waxman** (D)	171,860
	Bill Bloomfield (NPD)	146,660
34	Xavier Becerra** (D)	120,367
	Stephen C. Smith (R)	20,223
35	Gloria Negrete McLeod (D)	79,698
	Joe Baca** (D)	62,982
36	Raul Ruiz (D)	110,189
	Mary Bono Mack** (R)	97,953
37	Karen Bass** (D)	207,039
	Morgan Osborne (R)	32,541
38	Linda T. Sánchez** (D)	145,280
	Benjamin Campos (R)	69,807
39	Ed Royce** (R)	145,607
	Jay Chen (D)	106,360
40	Lucille Roybal-Allard** (D)	73,940
	David Sanchez (R)	51,163
41	Mark Takano (D)	103,578
	John Tavaglione (R)	72,074
42	Ken Calvert** (R)	130,245
	Michael Williamson (D)	84,702
43	Maxine Waters** (D)	143,123
	Bob Flores (D)	57,771
44	Janice Hahn** (D)	99,909
	Laura Richardson** (D)	65,989
45	John Campbell** (R)	171,417
	Sukhee Kang (D)	121,814
46	Loretta Sanchez** (D)	95,694
	Jerry Hayden (R)	54,121
47	Alan Lowenthal (D)	130,093
	Gary DeLong (R)	99,919
48	Dana Rohrabacher** (R)	177,144
	Ron Varasteh (D)	113,358
49	Darrell E. Issa* (R)	159,725
	Jerry Tetalman (D)	114,893
50	Duncan D. Hunter** (R)	174,838
	David B. Secor (D)	83,455
51	Juan Vargas (D)	113,934
	Michael Crimmins (R)	45,464
52	Scott Peters (D)	151,451
	Brian P. Bilbray** (R)	144,459
53	Susan A. Davis* (D)	164,825
	Nick Popaditch (R)	103,482
Colorado		
1	Diana DeGette* (D)	237,579
	Danny Stroud (R)	93,217
	Frank Atwood (LB)	12,585
2	Jared Polis* (D)	234,758
	Kevin Lundberg (R)	162,639
	Randy Luallin (LB)	13,770
	Susan P. Hall (Green)	10,413
3	Scott R. Tipton* (R)	185,291
	Sal Pace (D)	142,619
	Tisha T. Casida (Unaff.)	11,125
4	Cory Gardner* (R)	200,006
	Brandon Shaffer (D)	125,800
	Josh Gilliland (LB)	10,682
5	Doug Lamborn* (R)	199,639
	Dave Anderson (Unaff.)	53,318
	Jim Pirtle (LB)	22,778
	Misha Luzov (Green)	18,284
	Kenneth R. Harvell (Amer. Const.)	13,212
6	Mike Coffman* (R)	163,938
	Joe Miklosi (D)	156,937
	Kathy Polhemus (Unaff.)	13,442
7	Ed Perlmutter* (D)	182,460
	Joe Coors (R)	139,066
	Douglas "Dayhorse" Campbell (Amer. Const.)	10,296
Connecticut		
1	John B. Larson* (D)	206,973
	John Henry Decker (R)	82,321
2	Joe Courtney* (D)	204,708
	Paul M. Formica (R)	88,103
3	Rosa L. DeLauro* (D)	217,573
	Wayne Winsley (R)	73,726
4	Jim Himes* (D)	175,929
	Steve Obsitnik (R)	117,503
5	Elizabeth Esty (D)	146,098
	Andrew Roraback (R)	128,927
Delaware		
	John C. Carney Jr.* (D)	249,933
	Thomas H. Kovach (R)	129,757

Dist.	Representative/candidate (party)	2012 election results
Florida		
1	**Jeff Miller* (R)**	**238,440**
	Jim Bryan (D)	92,961
	Calen Fretts (LB)	11,176
2	**Steve Southerland II* (R)**	**175,856**
	Al Lawson (D)	157,634
3	**Ted Yoho (R)**	**204,331**
	J. R. Gaillot (D)	102,468
4	**Ander Crenshaw* (R)**	**239,988**
	Jim Klauder (NPA)	75,236
5	**Corrine Brown** (D)**	**190,472**
	LeAnne Kolb (R)	70,700
6	**Ron DeSantis (R)**	**195,962**
	Heather Beaven (D)	146,489
7	**John L. Mica* (R)**	**185,518**
	Jason H. Kendall (D)	130,479
8	**Bill Posey** (R)**	**205,432**
	Shannon Roberts (D)	130,870
	Richard H. Gillmor (NPA)	12,607
9	**Alan Grayson (D)**	**164,891**
	Todd Long (R)	98,856
10	**Daniel Webster** (R)**	**164,649**
	Val B. Demings (D)	153,574
11	**Richard B. Nugent** (R)**	**218,360**
	H. David Werder (D)	120,303
12	**Gus M. Bilirakis** (R)**	**209,604**
	Jonathan Michael Snow (D)	108,770
13	**C. W. Bill Young** (R)**	**189,605**
	Jessica Ehrlich (D)	139,742
14	**Kathy Castor** (D)**	**197,121**
	Evelio "EJ" Otero (R)	83,480
15	**Dennis A. Ross** (R)**	**Unopposed**
16	**Vern Buchanan** (R)**	**187,147**
	Keith Fitzgerald (D)	161,929
17	**Tom Rooney** (R)**	**165,488**
	William Bronson (D)	116,766
18	**Patrick Murphy (D)**	**166,257**
	Allen B. West** (R)	164,353
19	**Trey Radel (R)**	**189,833**
	Jim Roach (D)	109,746
20	**Alcee L. Hastings** (D)**	**214,727**
	Randall Terry (NPA)	29,553
21	**Ted Deutch** (D)**	**221,263**
	Michael "Mike" Trout (NPA)	37,776
	Cesar Henao (NPA)	25,361
22	**Lois Frankel (D)**	**171,021**
	Adam Hasner (R)	142,050
23	**Debbie Wasserman Schultz** (D)**	**174,205**
	Karon Harrington (R)	98,096
24	**Frederica S. Wilson** (D)**	**Unopposed**
25	**Mario Diaz-Balart** (R)**	**151,466**
	Stanley Blumenthal (NPA)	31,664
	VoteForEddie.com (NPA)	17,099
26	**Joe Garcia (D)**	**135,694**
	David Rivera** (R)	108,820
27	**Ileana Ros-Lehtinen** (R)**	**138,488**
	Manny Yevancey (D)	85,020
Georgia		
1	**Jack Kingston* (R)**	**157,191**
	Lesli Rae Messinger (D)	92,399
2	**Sanford D. Bishop Jr.* (D)**	**162,751**
	John House (R)	92,410
3	**Lynn A. Westmoreland* (R)**	**Unopposed**
4	**Henry "Hank" Johnson* (D)**	**208,861**
	J. Chris Vaughn (R)	75,041
5	**John Lewis* (D)**	**234,330**
	Howard Stopeck (R)	43,335
6	**Tom Price* (R)**	**189,669**
	Jeff Kazanow (D)	104,365
7	**Rob Woodall* (R)**	**156,689**
	Steve Reilly (D)	95,377
8	**Austin Scott* (R)**	**Unopposed**
9	**Doug Collins (R)**	**192,101**
	Jody Cooley (D)	60,052
10	**Paul C. Broun* (R)**	**Unopposed**
11	**Phil Gingrey* (R)**	**196,968**
	Patrick Thompson (D)	90,353
12	**John Barrow* (D)**	**139,148**
	Lee Anderson (R)	119,973
13	**David Scott* (D)**	**201,988**
	Shalid Malik (R)	79,550
14	**Tom Graves** (R)**	**159,947**
	Daniel "Danny" Grant (D)	59,245
Hawaii		
1	**Colleen W. Hanabusa* (D)**	**116,505**
	Charles K. Djou (R)	96,824

Dist.	Representative/candidate (party)	2012 election results
2	**Tulsi Gabbard (D)**	**168,503**
	Kawika Crowley (R)	40,707
Idaho		
1	**Raul R. Labrador* (R)**	**199,402**
	Jimmy Farris (D)	97,450
	Rob Oates (LB)	12,265
2	**Mike Simpson* (R)**	**207,412**
	Nicole LeFavour (D)	110,847
Illinois		
1	**Bobby L. Rush* (D)**	**236,854**
	Donald E. Peloquin (R)	83,989
2	**Robin L. Kelly (D)**	**58,834**[2]
	Paul McKinley (R)	18,387
3	**Daniel Lipinski* (D)**	**168,738**
	Richard L. Grabowski (R)	77,653
4	**Luis V. Gutierrez* (D)**	**133,226**
	Hector Concepcion (R)	27,279
5	**Mike Quigley* (D)**	**177,729**
	Dan Schmitt (R)	77,289
	Nancy Wade (Green)	15,359
6	**Peter J. Roskam* (R)**	**193,138**
	Leslie Coolidge (D)	132,991
7	**Danny K. Davis* (D)**	**242,439**
	Rita Zak (R)	31,466
	John H. Monaghan (I)	12,523
8	**Tammy Duckworth (D)**	**123,206**
	Joe Walsh* (R)	101,860
9	**Janice D. Schakowsky* (D)**	**194,869**
	Timothy C. Wolfe (R)	98,924
10	**Brad Schneider (D)**	**133,890**
	Robert J. Dold* (R)	130,564
11	**Bill Foster (D)**	**148,928**
	Judy Biggert** (R)	105,348
12	**William L. Enyart (D)**	**157,000**
	Jason Plummer (R)	129,902
	Paula Bradshaw (Green)	17,045
13	**Rodney Davis (R)**	**137,034**
	David M. Gill (D)	136,032
	John Hartman (I)	21,319
14	**Randy Hultgren* (R)**	**177,603**
	Dennis Anderson (D)	124,351
15	**John Shimkus** (R)**	**205,775**
	Angela Michael (D)	94,162
16	**Adam Kinzinger** (R)**	**181,789**
	Wanda Rohl (D)	112,301
17	**Cheri Bustos (D)**	**153,519**
	Bobby Schilling* (R)	134,623
18	**Aaron Schock* (R)**	**244,467**
	Steve Waterworth (D)	85,164
Indiana		
1	**Peter J. Visclosky* (D)**	**187,743**
	Joel Phelps (R)	91,291
2	**Jackie Walorski (R)**	**134,033**
	Brendan Mullen (D)	130,113
3	**Marlin A. Stutzman* (R)**	**187,872**
	Kevin R. Boyd (D)	92,363
4	**Todd Rokita* (R)**	**168,688**
	Tara E. Nelson (D)	93,015
	Benjamin Gehlhausen (LB)	10,565
5	**Susan Brooks (R)**	**194,570**
	Scott Reske (D)	125,347
	Chard Reid (LB)	13,442
6	**Luke Messer (R)**	**162,613**
	Bradley T. Bookout (D)	96,678
	Rex Bell (LB)	15,962
7	**André Carson* (D)**	**162,122**
	Carlos A. May (R)	95,828
8	**Larry Bucshon* (R)**	**151,533**
	Dave Crooks (D)	122,325
	Bart Gadau (LB)	10,134
9	**Todd C. Young* (R)**	**165,332**
	Shelli Yoder (D)	132,848
Iowa		
1	**Bruce L. Braley* (D)**	**222,422**
	Ben Lange (R)	162,465
2	**David Loebsack* (D)**	**211,863**
	John Archer (R)	161,977
3	**Tom Latham** (R)**	**202,000**
	Leonard Boswell* (D)	168,632
4	**Steve King** (R)**	**200,063**
	Christie Vilsack (D)	169,470
Kansas		
1	**Tim Huelskamp* (R)**	**Unopposed**
2	**Lynn Jenkins* (R)**	**167,463**
	Tobias Schlingensiepen (D)	113,735
	Dennis Hawver (LB)	12,520

Dist.	Representative/candidate (party)	2012 election results
3	Kevin Yoder* (R)	201,087
	Joel Balam (LB)	92,675
4	Mike Pompeo* (R)	161,094
	Robert Leon Tillman (D)	81,770
	Thomas Jefferson (LB)	16,058
Kentucky		
1	Ed Whitfield* (R)	199,956
	Charles Kendall Hatchett (D)	87,199
2	Brett Guthrie* (R)	181,508
	David Lynn Williams (D)	89,541
3	John A. Yarmuth* (D)	206,385
	Brooks Wicker (R)	111,452
4	Thomas Massie (R)	186,036
	William R. "Bill" Adkins (D)	104,734
5	Harold "Hal" Rogers* (R)	195,408
	Kenneth S. Stepp (D)	55,447
6	Garland "Andy" Barr (R)	153,222
	Ben Chandler* (D)	141,438
Louisiana		
1	Steve Scalise* (R)	193,496
	M. V. "Vinny" Mendoza (D)	61,703
	Gary King (R)	24,844
2	Cedric L. Richmond* (D)	158,501
	Gary Landrieu (D)	71,916
	Dwayne Bailey (R)	38,801
	Josue Larose (D)	11,345
3	Charles W. Boustany Jr.** (R)	139,123
	Jeff Landry* (R)	93,527
	Ron Richard (D)	67,070
4	John Fleming* (R)	187,894
	Randall Lord (LB)	61,637
5	Rodney Alexander* (R)	202,536
	Ron Ceasar (NPA)	37,486
	Clay Steven Grant (LB)	20,194
6	Bill Cassidy* (R)	243,553
	Rufus Holt Craig Jr. (LB)	32,185
	Richard Torregano (NPA)	30,975
Maine		
1	Chellie Pingree* (D)	236,363
	Jonathan T. E. Courtney (R)	128,440
2	Mike Michaud* (D)	191,456
	Kevin L. Raye (R)	137,542
Maryland		
1	Andy Harris* (R)	214,204
	Wendy Rosen (D)	92,812
	John LaFerla (write-in, D)	14,858
	Muir Wayne Boda (LB)	12,857
2	C. A. Dutch Ruppersberger* (D)	194,088
	Nancy C. Jacobs (R)	92,071
3	John P. Sarbanes* (D)	213,747
	Eric Delano Knowles (R)	94,549
	Paul W. Drgos Jr. (LB)	11,028
4	Donna F. Edwards* (D)	240,385
	Faith M. Loudon (R)	64,560
5	Steny H. Hoyer* (D)	238,618
	Tony O'Donnell (R)	95,271
6	John Delaney (D)	181,921
	Roscoe G. Bartlett* (R)	117,313
7	Elijah E. Cummings* (D)	247,770
	Frank C. Mirabile (R)	67,405
8	Chris Van Hollen* (D)	217,531
	Ken Timmerman (R)	113,033
Massachusetts		
1	Richard E. Neal** (D)	Unopposed
2	James P. McGovern** (D)	Unopposed
3	Niki Tsongas** (D)	212,119
	Jonathan A. Golnik (R)	109,372
4	Joseph P. Kennedy III (D)	221,303
	Sean Bielat (R)	129,936
	David A. Rosa (I)	10,741
5	Edward J. Markey** (D)	257,490
	Tom Tierney (R)	82,944
6	John F. Tierney* (D)	180,942
	Richard R. Tisei (R)	176,612
	Daniel Fishman (LB)	16,739
7	Michael E. Capuano** (D)	210,794
	Karla Romero (I)	41,199
8	Stephen F. Lynch** (D)	263,999
	Joe Selvaggi (R)	82,242
9	Bill Keating** (D)	212,754
	Christopher Sheldon (R)	116,531
	Daniel S. Botelho (I)	32,655

Dist.	Representative/candidate (party)	2012 election results
Michigan		
1	Dan Benishek* (R)	167,060
	Gary McDowell (D)	165,179
	Emily Salvette (LB)	10,630
2	Bill Huizenga* (R)	194,653
	Willie German Jr. (D)	108,973
3	Justin Amash* (R)	171,675
	Steve Pestka (D)	144,108
	Bill Gelineau (LB)	10,498
4	Dave Camp* (R)	197,386
	Debra Freidell Wirth (D)	104,996
5	Daniel T. Kildee (D)	214,531
	Jim Slezak (R)	103,931
6	Fred Upton* (R)	174,955
	Mike O'Brien (D)	136,563
7	Tim Walberg* (R)	169,668
	Kurt Richard Haskell (D)	136,849
8	Mike Rogers* (R)	202,217
	Lance Enderle (D)	128,657
9	Sander M. Levin** (D)	208,846
	Don Volaric (R)	114,760
10	Candice S. Miller* (R)	226,075
	Chuck Stadler (D)	97,734
11	Kerry Bentivolio (R)	181,788
	Syed Taj (D)	158,879
12	John D. Dingell** (D)	216,884
	Cynthia Kallgren (R)	92,472
13	John Conyers Jr.** (D)	235,336
	Harry T. Sawicki (R)	38,769
14	Gary C. Peters** (D)	270,450
	John Hauler (R)	51,395
Minnesota		
1	Tim Walz* (DFL)	193,211
	Allen Quist (R)	142,164
2	John Kline* (R)	193,587
	Mike Obermueller (DFL)	164,338
3	Erik Paulsen* (R)	222,335
	Brian Barnes (DFL)	159,937
4	Betty McCollum* (DFL)	216,685
	Tony Hernandez (R)	109,659
	Steve Carlson (IP)	21,135
5	Keith Ellison* (DFL)	262,102
	Chris Fields (R)	88,753
6	Michele Bachmann* (R)	179,240
	Jim Graves (DFL)	174,944
7	Collin C. Peterson* (DFL)	197,791
	Lee Byberg (R)	114,151
	Adam Steele (IP)	15,298
8	Richard Nolan (DFL)	191,976
	Chip Cravaack* (R)	160,520
Mississippi		
1	Alan Nunnelee* (R)	186,760
	Brad Morris (D)	114,076
2	Bennie G. Thompson* (D)	214,978
	Bill Marcy (R)	99,160
3	Gregg Harper* (R)	234,717
	John "Luke" Pannell (Reform)	58,605
4	Steven M. Palazzo* (R)	182,998
	Matt Moore (D)	82,344
	Ron Williams (LB)	17,982
Missouri		
1	Wm. Lacy Clay* (D)	267,927
	Robyn Hamlin (R)	60,832
	Robb E. Cunningham (LB)	11,824
2	Ann Wagner (R)	236,971
	Glenn Koenen (D)	146,272
3	Blaine Luetkemeyer** (R)	214,843
	Eric C. Mayer (D)	111,189
	Steven Wilson (LB)	12,353
4	Vicky Hartzler* (R)	192,237
	Teresa Hensley (D)	113,120
	Thomas Holbrook (LB)	10,407
5	Emanuel Cleaver* (D)	200,290
	Jacob Turk (R)	122,149
6	Sam Graves* (R)	216,906
	Kyle Yarber (D)	108,503
7	Billy Long* (R)	203,565
	Jim Evans (D)	98,498
	Kevin Craig (LB)	16,668
8	Jason T. Smith (R)	42,141[3]
	Steve Hodges (D)	17,207

Dist.	Representative/candidate (party)	2012 election results
Montana		
	Steve Daines (R)	**255,468**
	Kim Gillan (D)	204,939
	David Kaiser (LB)	19,333
Nebraska		
1	**Jeff Fortenberry* (R)**	**174,889**
	Korey L. Reiman (D)	81,206
2	**Lee Terry* (R)**	**133,964**
	John W. Ewing Jr. (D)	129,767
3	**Adrian Smith* (R)**	**187,423**
	Mark Sullivan (D)	65,266
Nevada		
1	**Dina Titus (D)**	**113,967**
	Chris Edwards (R)	56,521
2	**Mark E. Amodei* (R)**	**162,213**
	Samuel Koepnick (D)	102,019
	Michael L. Haines (I)	11,166
3	**Joe Heck* (R)**	**137,244**
	John Oceguera (D)	116,823
	Jim Murphy (I)	12,856
4	**Steven A. Horsford (D)**	**120,501**
	Danny Tarkanian (R)	101,261
New Hampshire		
1	**Carol Shea-Porter (D)**	**171,650**
	Frank C. Guinta* (R)	158,659
	Brendan Kelly (LB)	14,521
2	**Ann McLane Kuster (D)**	**169,275**
	Charles Bass* (R)	152,977
	Hardy Macia (LB)	14,936
New Jersey		
1	**Robert E. Andrews* (D)**	**210,470**
	Gregory W. Horton (R)	92,459
2	**Frank A. LoBiondo* (R)**	**166,677**
	Cassandra Shober (D)	116,462
3	**Jon Runyan* (R)**	**174,253**
	Shelley Adler (D)	145,506
4	**Christopher H. Smith* (R)**	**195,145**
	Brian P. Froelich (D)	107,991
5	**Scott Garrett* (R)**	**167,501**
	Adam Gussen (D)	130,100
6	**Frank Pallone Jr.* (D)**	**151,782**
	Anna Little (Π)	84,360
7	**Leonard Lance* (R)**	**175,662**
	Upendra J. Chivukula (D)	123,057
8	**Albio Sires** (D)**	**130,853**
	Maria Karczewski (R)	31,763
9	**Bill Pascrell Jr.** (D)**	**162,822**
	Shmuley Boteach (R)	55,091
10	**Donald M. Payne Jr.* (D)**	**201,435**
	Brian C. Kelemen (R)	24,271
11	**Rodney P. Frelinghuysen* (R)**	**182,237**
	John Arvanites (D)	123,897
12	**Rush D. Holt* (D)**	**189,926**
	Eric A. Beck (R)	80,906
New Mexico		
1	**Michelle Lujan Grisham (D)**	**162,924**
	Janice E. Arnold-Jones (R)	112,473
2	**Steve Pearce* (R)**	**133,180**
	Evelyn Madrid Erhard (D)	92,162
3	**Ben Ray Luján* (D)**	**167,103**
	Jefferson L. Byrd (R)	97,616
New York		
1	**Timothy H. Bishop* (D)**	**145,198**
	Randy Altschuler (R)	131,650
2	**Peter T. King** (R)**	**141,950**
	Vivianne C. Falcone (D)	99,955
3	**Steve Israel** (D)**	**157,602**
	Stephen A. Labate (R)	113,021
4	**Carolyn McCarthy* (D)**	**163,955**
	Francis X. Becker Jr. (R)	85,693
	Frank Scaturro (Conservative)	15,603
5	**Gregory W. Meeks** (D)**	**167,835**
	Allan W. Jennings Jr. (R)	17,875
6	**Grace Meng (D)**	**111,499**
	Daniel J. Halloran (R)	50,845
7	**Nydia M. Velázquez** (D)**	**141,322**
	James Murray (Conservative)	7,811
8	**Hakeem S. Jeffries (D)**	**184,038**
	Alan S. Bellone (R)	17,650
9	**Yvette D. Clarke** (D)**	**186,141**
	Daniel J. Cavanagh (R)	24,164
10	**Jerrold Nadler** (D)**	**165,000**
	Michael W. Chan (R)	39,311
11	**Michael G. Grimm** (R)**	**103,118**
	Mark S. Murphy (D)	92,428

Dist.	Representative/candidate (party)	2012 election results
12	**Carolyn B. Maloney** (D)**	**193,455**
	Christopher R. Wight (R)	46,692
13	**Charles B. Rangel** (D)**	**174,789**
	Craig Schley (D)	12,132
14	**Joseph Crowley** (D)**	**120,761**
	William F. Gibbons Jr. (R)	21,755
15	**José E. Serrano** (D)**	**152,661**
	Frank L. Della Valle (R)	4,427
16	**Eliot L. Engel** (D)**	**179,561**
	Joseph McLaughlin (R)	53,935
17	**Nita M. Lowey** (D)**	**171,417**
	Joe E. Carvin (R)	91,899
18	**Sean Patrick Maloney (D)**	**143,845**
	Nan A. S. Hayworth** (R)	133,049
19	**Christopher P. Gibson** (R)**	**149,736**
	Julian Schreibman (D)	133,567
20	**Paul Tonko** (D)**	**203,400**
	Robert J. Dieterich (R)	93,778
21	**William "Bill" Owens** (D)**	**126,631**
	Matthew A. Doheny (R)	121,646
22	**Richard L. Hanna** (R)**	**157,941**
	Dan Lamb (D)	102,080
23	**Thomas Reed** (R)**	**137,669**
	Nate Shinagawa (D)	127,535
24	**Daniel B. Maffei (D)**	**143,044**
	Ann Marie Buerkle** (R)	127,054
	Ursula Rozum (Green)	22,670
25	**Louise McIntosh Slaughter** (D)**	**179,810**
	Maggie Brooks (R)	133,389
26	**Brian Higgins** (D)**	**212,588**
	Michael H. Madigan (R)	71,666
27	**Chris Collins (R)**	**161,220**
	Kathleen C. Hochul** (D)	156,219
North Carolina		
1	**G. K. Butterfield* (D)**	**254,644**
	Pete DiLauro (R)	77,288
2	**Renee L. Ellmers* (R)**	**174,066**
	Steve Wilkins (D)	128,973
3	**Walter B. Jones* (R)**	**195,571**
	Erik Anderson (D)	114,314
4	**David E. Price* (D)**	**259,534**
	Tim D'Annunzio (R)	88,951
5	**Virginia Foxx* (R)**	**200,945**
	Elisabeth Motsinger (D)	148,252
6	**Howard Coble* (R)**	**222,116**
	Tony Foriest (D)	142,467
7	**Mike McIntyre* (D)**	**168,695**
	David Rouzer (R)	168,041
8	**Richard Hudson (R)**	**160,695**
	Larry Kissell* (D)	137,139
9	**Robert Pittenger (R)**	**194,537**
	Jennifer Roberts (D)	171,503
10	**Patrick T. McHenry* (R)**	**190,826**
	Patsy Keever (D)	144,023
11	**Mark Meadows (R)**	**190,319**
	Hayden Rogers (D)	141,107
12	**Mel Watt* (D)**	**247,591**
	Jack Brosch (R)	63,317
13	**George Holding (R)**	**210,495**
	Charles Malone (D)	160,115
North Dakota		
	Kevin Cramer (R)	**173,585**
	Pam Gulleson (Dem.-NPL)	131,870
	Eric Olson (LB)	10,261
Ohio		
1	**Steve Chabot* (R)**	**201,907**
	Jeff Sinnard (D)	131,490
2	**Brad Wenstrup (R)**	**194,296**
	William R. Smith (D)	137,077
3	**Joyce Beatty (D)**	**201,897**
	Chris Long (R)	77,901
4	**Jim Jordan* (R)**	**182,643**
	Jim Slone (D)	114,214
	Chris Kalla (LB)	16,141
5	**Robert "Bob" Latta* (R)**	**201,514**
	Angela Zimmann (D)	137,806
	Eric Eberly (LB)	12,558
6	**Bill Johnson* (R)**	**164,536**
	Charlie Wilson (D)	144,444
7	**Bob Gibbs** (R)**	**178,104**
	Joyce R. Healy-Abrams (D)	137,708
8	**John Boehner** (R)**	**Unopposed**
9	**Marcy Kaptur* (D)**	**217,771**
	Samuel J. Wurzelbacher (R)	68,668
	Sean Stipe (LB)	11,725

Dist.	Representative/candidate (party)	2012 election results
10	**Mike Turner** (R)**	**208,201**
	Sharen Swartz Neuhardt (D)	131,097
11	**Marcia Fudge* (D)**	**Unopposed**
12	**Pat Tiberi* (R)**	**233,869**
	Jim Reese (D)	134,605
13	**Tim Ryan** (D)**	**235,492**
	Marisha G. Agana (R)	88,120
14	**David P. Joyce (R)**	**183,657**
	Dale Virgil Blanchard (D)	131,637
	Elaine Mastromatteo (Green)	13,038
	David Macko (LB)	11,536
15	**Steve Stivers* (R)**	**205,274**
	Pat Lang (D)	128,188
16	**Jim Renacci* (R)**	**185,165**
	Betty Sutton** (D)	170,600
Oklahoma		
1	**Jim Bridenstine (R)**	**181,084**
	John Olson (D)	91,421
	Craig Allen (I)	12,807
2	**Markwayne Mullin (R)**	**143,701**
	Rob Wallace (D)	96,081
	Michael G. Fulks (I)	10,830
3	**Frank D. Lucas* (R)**	**201,744**
	Timothy Ray Murray (D)	53,472
	William M. Sanders (I)	12,787
4	**Tom Cole* (R)**	**176,740**
	Donna Marie Bebo (D)	71,846
	RJ Harris (I)	11,745
5	**James Lankford* (R)**	**153,603**
	Tom Guild (D)	97,504
Oregon		
1	**Suzanne Bonamici* (D)**	**197,845**
	Delinda Morgan (R)	109,699
	Steven Reynolds (Prog./LB/Pacific Green)	15,009
2	**Greg Walden* (R)**	**228,043**
	Joyce B. Segers (D)	96,741
3	**Earl Blumenauer* (D)**	**264,979**
	Ronald Green (R)	70,325
	Woodrow Broadnax (Pacific Green/Prog.)	13,159
4	**Peter A. DeFazio* (D)**	**212,866**
	Art Robinson (R)	140,549
5	**Kurt Schrader* (D)**	**177,229**
	Fred Thompson (R)	139,223
Pennsylvania		
1	**Robert A. Brady* (D)**	**235,394**
	John Featherman (R)	41,708
2	**Chaka Fattah* (D)**	**318,176**
	Robert Allen Mansfield Jr. (R)	33,381
3	**Mike Kelly* (R)**	**165,826**
	Missa Eaton (D)	123,933
	Steven Porter (I)	12,755
4	**Scott Perry (R)**	**181,603**
	Harry Perkinson (D)	104,643
	Wayne W. Wolff (I)	11,524
5	**Glenn Thompson* (R)**	**177,740**
	Charles Dumas (D)	104,725
6	**Jim Gerlach* (R)**	**191,725**
	Manan M. Trivedi (D)	143,803
7	**Patrick Meehan* (R)**	**209,942**
	George Badey (D)	143,509
8	**Michael G. Fitzpatrick* (R)**	**199,379**
	Kathy Boockvar (D)	152,859
9	**Bill Shuster* (R)**	**169,177**
	Karen Ramsburg (D)	105,128
10	**Tom Marino* (R)**	**179,563**
	Philip Scollo (D)	94,227
11	**Lou Barletta* (R)**	**166,967**
	Gene Stilp (D)	118,231
12	**Keith J. Rothfus (R)**	**175,352**
	Mark S. Critz* (D)	163,589
13	**Allyson Y. Schwartz* (D)**	**209,901**
	Joseph James Rooney (R)	93,918
14	**Mike Doyle* (D)**	**251,932**
	Hans Lessmann (R)	75,702
15	**Charles W. Dent* (R)**	**168,960**
	Rick Daugherty (D)	128,764
16	**Joseph R. Pitts* (R)**	**156,192**
	Aryanna C. Strader (D)	111,185
	John A. Murphy (I)	12,250
17	**Matthew A. Cartwright (D)**	**161,393**
	Laureen A. Cummings (R)	106,284
18	**Tim Murphy* (R)**	**216,727**
	Larry Maggi (D)	122,146

Dist.	Representative/candidate (party)	2012 election results
Rhode Island		
1	**David N. Cicilline* (D)**	**108,612**
	Brendan P. Doherty (R)	83,737
	David S. Vogel (I)	12,504
2	**Jim Langevin* (D)**	**124,067**
	Michael G. Riley (R)	78,189
	Abel G. Collins (I)	20,212
South Carolina		
1	**Mark Sanford (R)**	**77,600[4]**
	Elizabeth Colbert Busch	64,961
2	**Joe Wilson* (R)**	**Unopposed**
3	**Jeff Duncan* (R)**	**169,512**
	Brian "Ryan B." Doyle (D)	84,735
4	**Trey Gowdy* (R)**	**173,201**
	Deb Morrow (D)	89,964
5	**Mick Mulvaney* (R)**	**154,324**
	Joyce Knott (D)	123,443
6	**James E. Clyburn* (D)**	**218,717**
	Nammu Y. Muhammad (Green)	12,920
7	**Tom Rice (R)**	**153,068**
	Gloria Bromell Tinubu (D)	122,389
South Dakota		
	Kristi L. Noem* (R)	**207,640**
	Matt Varilek (D)	153,789
Tennessee		
1	**Phil Roe* (R)**	**182,252**
	Alan Woodruff (D)	47,663
2	**John J. Duncan Jr.* (R)**	**196,894**
	Troy Christopher Goodale (D)	54,522
3	**Chuck Fleischmann* (R)**	**157,830**
	Mary M. Headrick (D)	91,094
4	**Scott DesJarlais* (R)**	**128,568**
	Eric Stewart (D)	102,022
5	**Jim Cooper* (D)**	**171,621**
	Brad Staats (R)	86,240
6	**Diane Black* (R)**	**184,383**
	Scott Beasley (I)	34,766
	Pat Riley (Green)	21,633
7	**Marsha Blackburn* (R)**	**182,730**
	Credo Amouzouvik (D)	61,679
8	**Stephen Lee Fincher* (R)**	**190,923**
	Timothy D. Dixon (D)	79,490
9	**Steve Cohen* (D)**	**188,422**
	George S. Flinn Jr. (R)	59,742
Texas		
1	**Louie Gohmert* (R)**	**178,322**
	Shirley J. McKellar (D)	67,222
2	**Ted Poe* (R)**	**159,664**
	Jim Dougherty (D)	80,512
3	**Sam Johnson* (R)**	**Unopposed**
4	**Ralph M. Hall* (R)**	**182,679**
	VaLinda Hathcox (D)	60,214
5	**Jeb Hensarling* (R)**	**134,091**
	Linda S. Mrosko (D)	69,178
6	**Joe Barton* (R)**	**145,019**
	Kenneth Sanders (D)	98,053
7	**John Abney Culberson* (R)**	**142,793**
	James Cargas (D)	85,553
8	**Kevin Brady* (R)**	**194,043**
	Neil Burns (D)	51,051
9	**Al Green* (D)**	**144,075**
	Steve Mueller (R)	36,139
10	**Michael T. McCaul* (R)**	**159,783**
	Tawana W. Cadien (D)	95,710
11	**Mike Conaway* (R)**	**177,742**
	Jim Riley (D)	41,970
12	**Kay Granger* (R)**	**175,649**
	Dave Robinson (D)	66,080
13	**Mac Thornberry* (R)**	**187,775**
	John Robert Deek (LB)	12,701
14	**Randy Weber (R)**	**131,460**
	Nick Lampson (D)	109,697
15	**Rubén Hinojosa* (D)**	**89,296**
	Dale A. Brueggemann (R)	54,056
16	**Beto O'Rourke (D)**	**101,403**
	Barbara Carrasco (R)	51,043
17	**Bill Flores* (R)**	**143,284**
	Ben Easton (LB)	35,978
18	**Sheila Jackson Lee* (D)**	**146,223**
	Sean Seibert (I)	44,015
19	**Randy Neugebauer* (R)**	**163,239**
	Richard "Chip" Peterson (LB)	28,824

Dist.	Representative/candidate (party)	2012 election results
20	Joaquin Castro (D)	119,032
	David Rosa (R)	62,376
21	Lamar Smith* (R)	187,015
	Candace E. Duval (D)	109,326
	John-Henry Liberty (LB)	12,524
22	Pete Olson* (R)	160,668
	Kesha Rogers (D)	80,203
23	Pete P. Gallego (D)	96,676
	Francisco "Quico" Canseco* (R)	87,547
24	Kenny Marchant* (R)	148,586
	Tim Rusk (D)	87,645
25	Roger Williams (R)	154,245
	Elaine M. Henderson (D)	98,827
	Betsy Dewey (LB)	10,860
26	Michael C. Burgess* (R)	176,642
	David Sanchez (D)	74,237
27	Blake Farenthold* (R)	120,684
	Rose Meza Harrison (D)	83,395
28	Henry Cuellar* (D)	112,456
	William R. Hayward (R)	49,309
29	Gene Green* (D)	86,053
	Jamey Stanczak (LB)	4,996
30	Eddie Bernice Johnson* (D)	171,059
	Travis Washington Jr. (R)	41,222
31	John R. Carter* (R)	145,348
	Stephen M. Wyman (D)	82,977
32	Pete Sessions* (R)	146,653
	Katherine Savers McGovern (D)	99,288
33	Marc Veasey (D)	85,114
	Chuck Bradley (R)	30,252
34	Filemon Vela (D)	89,606
	Jessica Puente Bradshaw (R)	52,448
35	Lloyd Doggett** (D)	105,626
	Susan Narvaiz (R)	52,894
36	Steve Stockman (R)	165,405
	Max Martin (D)	62,143

Utah

Dist.	Representative/candidate (party)	2012 election results
1	Rob Bishop* (R)	175,487
	Donna M. McAleer (D)	60,611
2	Chris Stewart (R)	154,523
	Jay Seegmiller (D)	83,176
3	Jason Chaffetz* (R)	198,828
	Soren D. Simonsen (D)	60,719
4	Jim Matheson** (D)	119,803
	Mia B. Love (R)	119,035

Vermont

Dist.	Representative/candidate (party)	2012 election results
	Peter Welch* (D)	208,600
	Mark Donka (R)	67,543

Virginia

Dist.	Representative/candidate (party)	2012 election results
1	Robert J. Wittman* (R)	200,845
	Adam M. Cook (D)	147,036
2	E. Scott Rigell* (R)	166,231
	Paul O. Hirschbiel Jr. (D)	142,548
3	Bobby Scott* (D)	259,199
	Dean J. Longo (R)	58,931
4	J. Randy Forbes* (R)	199,292
	Ella P. Ward (D)	150,190
5	Robert Hurt* (R)	193,009
	John Wade Douglass (D)	149,214

Dist.	Representative/candidate (party)	2012 election results
6	Bob Goodlatte* (R)	211,278
	Andy B. Schmookler (D)	111,949
7	Eric Cantor* (R)	222,983
	E. Wayne Powell (D)	158,012
8	James P. "Jim" Moran Jr.* (D)	226,847
	J. Patrick Murray (R)	107,370
9	H. Morgan Griffith* (R)	184,882
	Anthony J. Flaccavento (D)	116,400
10	Frank R. Wolf* (R)	214,038
	Kristin A. Cabral (D)	142,024
11	Gerry Connolly* (D)	202,606
	Chris S. Perkins (R)	117,902

Washington

Dist.	Representative/candidate (party)	2012 election results
1	Suzan DelBene (D)	177,025
	John Koster (R)	151,187
2	Rick Larsen* (D)	184,826
	Dan Matthews (R)	117,465
3	Jaime Herrera Beutler* (R)	177,446
	Jon T. Haugen (D)	116,438
4	Doc Hastings* (R)	154,749
	Mary Baechler (D)	78,940
5	Cathy McMorris Rodgers* (R)	191,066
	Rich Cowan (D)	117,512
6	Derek Kilmer (D)	186,661
	Bill Driscoll (R)	129,725
7	Jim McDermott* (D)	298,368
	Ron Bemis (R)	76,212
8	Dave Reichert* (R)	180,204
	Karen Porterfield (D)	121,886
9	Adam Smith* (D)	192,034
	Jim Postma (R)	76,105
10	Denny Heck (D)	163,036
	Richard "Dick" Muri (R)	115,381

West Virginia

Dist.	Representative/candidate (party)	2012 election results
1	David B. McKinley* (R)	133,809
	Sue Thorn (D)	80,342
2	Shelley Moore Capito* (R)	158,206
	Howard Swint (D)	68,560
3	Nick J. Rahall II* (D)	108,199
	Rick Snuffer (R)	92,238

Wisconsin

Dist.	Representative/candidate (party)	2012 election results
1	Paul Ryan* (R)	200,423
	Rob Zerban (D)	158,414
2	Mark Pocan (D)	265,422
	Chad Lee (R)	124,683
3	Ron Kind* (D)	217,712
	Ray Boland (R)	121,713
4	Gwen Moore* (D)	235,257
	Dan Sebring (R)	80,787
5	F. James Sensenbrenner Jr.* (R)	250,335
	Dave Heaster (D)	118,478
6	Tom Petri* (R)	223,460
	Joe Kallas (D)	135,921
7	Sean P. Duffy* (R)	201,720
	Pat Kreitlow (D)	157,524
8	Reid J. Ribble* (R)	198,874
	Jamie Wall (D)	156,287

Wyoming

Dist.	Representative/candidate (party)	2012 election results
	Cynthia M. Lummis* (R)	166,452
	Chris Henrichsen (D)	57,573

(1) Jo Bonner (R) resigned Aug. 2, 2013. (2) Jesse L. Jackson (D) resigned Nov. 21, 2012; Kelly was elected in special election Apr. 9, 2013, and sworn in Apr. 11. (3) Jo Ann Emerson (R) resigned Jan. 22, 2013; Smith was elected in special election June 4, 2013, and sworn in June 5. (4) Tim Scott (R) resigned Jan. 2, 2013; Sanford was elected in special election May 7, 2013, and sworn in May 15.

Nonvoting Members of Congress

Representative/candidate (party)	2012 election results	Representative/candidate (party)	2012 election results
American Samoa		**Puerto Rico—Resident Commissioner[1]**	
Eni F.H. Faleomavaega* (D)	7,221	Pedro R. Pierluisi* (New Prog. Party/D)	905,066
Aumua Amata (Conservative)	4,420	Roberto Cox Alomar (Popular Dem. Party)	881,181
Rosie F. Tago Lancaster (I)	697	Juan Manuel "Juanchin" Mercado Nieves (Puerto Rican IP)	38,941
District of Columbia		Félix Córdova Iturregui (Working People's Party)	13,120
Eleanor Holmes Norton* (D)	246,664	María de Lourdes Guzmán (Sovereign Union)	11,764
Bruce Majors (LB)	16,524	**Virgin Islands**	
Natale Lino Stracuzzi (DC Statehood Green)	13,243	Donna M. Christensen* (D)	11,512
Guam		Warren B. Mosler (NPA)	3,276
Madeleine Z. Bordallo* (D)	19,765	Holland Redfield (R)	2,131
Frank Flores Blas Jr. (R)	12,995	Norma Pickard-Samuel (NPA)	1,927
Northern Mariana Islands			
Gregorio Kilili Camacho Sablan* (D)	9,829		
Ignacia Tudela Demapan (R)	2,503		

(1) The resident commissioner of Puerto Rico is the only member of the House of Representatives who serves a four-year term.

STATES AND OTHER AREAS OF THE U.S.

Sources: Population: Decennial Censuses and Population Estimates Program, U.S. Census Bureau, U.S. Dept. of Commerce; population as of July 1, 2012, unless otherwise noted. Pop. density is for land area only. **Racial distribution** categories are abbreviated here; their full forms are white, black or African American, Asian, American Indian and Alaska Native, Native Hawaiian and Other Pacific Islander, two or more races. Categories may not add up to 100% due to rounding. **Hispanic** or Latino persons may be of any race. **Area:** Geography Division, U.S. Census Bureau, U.S. Dept. of Commerce. **Acres forested:** U.S. Forest Service, U.S. Dept. of Agriculture; source year may vary. **Chief airports:** Federal Aviation Admin., U.S. Dept. of Transportation. Chief airports had 500,000+ boardings in 2012. All **Economy** data as of 2012 unless otherwise noted. **Chief manuf. goods:** Manufacturing and Construction Division, U.S. Census Bureau, U.S. Dept. of Commerce. **Chief crops** and **Livestock:** Agriculture Dept., Natl. Agricultural Statistics Service, U.S. Dept. of Agriculture. Cattle/calves and sheep/lambs as of Jan. 2013; hogs/pigs as of June 2013. Many states do not disclose broiler or hog/pig data. **Nonfuel minerals:** Office of Mineral Information, U.S. Dept. of Interior; preliminary data. Some states exclude small amounts to avoid disclosing proprietary data. **Commercial fishing:** Natl. Marine Fisheries Service, U.S. Dept. of Commerce. **Gross state product** and **Per cap. pers. income:** Bureau of Economic Analysis, U.S. Dept. of Commerce; income data are preliminary. **Sales tax:** Federation of Tax Administrators; as of Jan. 1, 2013. **Employment distrib.** and **Unemployment:** Bureau of Labor Statistics, U.S. Dept. of Labor; distribution is for non-farm jobs as of May 2013. **New private housing:** Manufacturing and Construction Division, U.S. Census Bureau, U.S. Dept. of Commerce. **Broadband Internet:** Industry Analysis and Tech. Division, Fed. Communications Commission. Broadband connections have minimum speeds of at least 768 kilobytes per second (Kbps) downstream and 200 Kbps upstream; figure given is broadband as a percentage of total Internet connections. **Commercial banks** and **Savings institutions:** Federal Deposit Insurance Corp., as of June 30, 2012; FDIC-insured institutions only. **Lottery:** North American Assn. of State and Provincial Lotteries. Data may be unaudited and in some cases were gathered by third party. Some states report round sums; others report exact figures. **Federal employees:** Office of Personnel Mgmt., U.S. Dept. of Labor; as of Mar. 2013. **Energy:** Energy Information Admin., U.S. Dept. of Energy; average per capita monthly electricity consumption and cost for residential customers in 2011. Other information from sources in individual states. NA = Not available.

Famous persons lists may include non-natives associated with the state as well as persons born there. **Websites** are subject to change and are not endorsed by *The World Almanac*.

Alabama (AL)
Heart of Dixie, Camellia State

People. Population: 4,822,023; rank: 23. **Pop. change** (2010-12): 0.9%. **Pop. density:** 95.2 per sq mi. **Racial distribution:** 70.0% white; 26.5% black; 1.2% Asian; 0.7% Amer. Ind.; 0.1% Hawaiian/Pacific Islander; two or more races, 4.1%. **Hispanic pop.:** 4.1%.

Geography. Total area: 52,420 sq mi; rank: 30. **Land area:** 50,645 sq mi; rank: 28. **Acres forested:** 22.9 mil. **Location:** East South Central state extending N-S from Tennessee to the Gulf of Mexico; E of the Mississippi R. **Climate:** long, hot summers; mild winters; generally abundant rain. **Topography:** coastal plains, including Prairie Black Belt, give way to hills, broken terrain; highest elevation, 2,407 ft. **Capital:** Montgomery. **Chief airports:** Birmingham, Huntsville.

Economy. Chief industries: chemicals, electronics, apparel, primary metals, lumber and wood products, food processing, fabricated metals, automotive tires, oil and gas exploration. **Chief manuf. goods:** poultry processing, paper & paperboard, iron & steel, petroleum, automotive tires, aerospace, aluminum, auto body & parts. **Chief crops:** cotton, greenhouse & nursery, hay, peanuts, corn, soybeans. **Livestock:** 15.49 mil chickens (excl. broilers), 1.18 bil broilers, 1.22 mil cattle/calves. **Nonfuel minerals:** $1 bil; cement (portland), stone (crushed), lime, sand and gravel (construction), cement (masonry). **Commercial fishing:** $46.3 mil. **Chief port:** Mobile. **Gross state product:** $183.5 bil. **Sales tax:** 4.0%. **Employment distrib.:** 19.8% govt.; 19.2% trade/trans./util.; 13% mfg.; 11.6% ed./health; 11.6% prof./bus. serv.; 9.7% leisure/hosp.; 4.9% finance; 4.8% constr./mining/log.; 1.1% info.; 4.2% other serv. **Unemployment:** 7.3%. **Per cap. pers. income:** $35,625. **New private housing:** 13,506 units/$2 bil. **Broadband Internet:** 77.2%. **Commercial banks:** 161; deposits: $83.8 bil. **Savings institutions:** 11; deposits: $1 bil.

Federal govt. Fed. civ. employees: 40,871; **avg. salary:** $77,810. **Notable fed. facilities:** Redstone Arsenal; Ft. Rucker; Marshall Space Flight Ctr.; Anniston Army Depot; Maxwell-Gunter AFB; Army Corps of Engineers, Mobile District.

Energy. Electricity use/cost: 1,284 kWh, $142.41.

State data. Motto: Audemus Jura Nostra Defendere (We dare defend our rights). **Flower:** Camellia. **Bird:** Yellowhammer (yellowhammer is local nickname). **Tree:** Southern longleaf pine. **Song:** "Alabama." **Entered union:** Dec. 14, 1819; rank: 22nd. **State fair** at Pelham, mid to late-Aug.

History. Alabama was inhabited by the Creek, Cherokee, Chickasaw, Alabama, and Choctaw peoples when Spanish explorers arrived in the early 1500s. The French made the first permanent settlement at Ft. Louis, 1702, and founded Mobile, 1711. France later gave up the entire region to England under the Treaty of Paris, 1763. Spanish forces took control of the Mobile Bay area, 1780, and it remained under Spanish control until seized by U.S. troops, 1813. Most of present-day Alabama was held by the Creeks until Gen. Andrew Jackson broke their power, 1814. When Alabama became a state, 1819, black slaves made up about one-third of the population.

The Indian Removal Act of 1830 forced most remaining Creeks west. The state seceded, 1861, and the Confederate states were organized Feb. 4, at Montgomery, the first capital. The state was readmitted, 1868. Birmingham, founded 1871, became a center for iron- and steelmaking. The Montgomery bus boycott, 1955, sparked by Rosa Parks, helped launch the civil rights movement. Other confrontations occurred at Birmingham, 1963, and Selma, 1965. The leading political figure from the 1960s through the '80s, 4-term gov. George Wallace, started as a segregationist but later won with black support. Growth in the auto industry boosted the state economy as the 21st cent. began. A string of tornadoes in western Alabama in Apr. 2011 killed at least 248. Jefferson County, which includes the city of Birmingham, filed for the then-most expensive municipal bankruptcy in history in Nov. 2011 due to more than $3.1 bil in sewer-system debt.

Tourist attractions. First White House of the Confederacy, Civil Rights Memorial, Alabama Shakespeare Festival, in Montgomery; Ivy Green (Helen Keller birthplace), Tuscumbia; Barber Vintage Motorsports Museum, Civil Rights Institute, Vulcan Park and Museum (world's largest cast iron statue), in Birmingham; G. W. Carver Interpretive Museum, Tuskegee; W. C. Handy Home, Museum, and Library, Frank Lloyd Wright's Rosenbaum House, in Florence; U.S. Space & Rocket Ctr., Huntsville; Moundville Archaeological Park; USS *Alabama* Memorial Park, Mobile; Gulf State Park, Gulf Shores.

Famous Alabamians. Hank Aaron, Tallulah Bankhead, Charles Barkley, Hugo L. Black, Paul "Bear" Bryant, George Washington Carver, Nat King Cole, Courteney Cox, William Christopher "W. C." Handy, Polly Holliday, Bo Jackson, Helen Keller, Coretta Scott King, Harper Lee, Joe Louis, Willie Mays, Jim Nabors, Jesse Owens, Terrell Owens, Rosa Parks, Condoleezza Rice, Lionel Richie, Octavia Spencer, Channing Tatum, George C. Wallace, Booker T. Washington, Hank Williams.

Tourist information. Alabama Tourism Department, 401 Adams Ave., Ste. 126, P.O. Box 4927, Montgomery, AL 36103; 1-800-ALABAMA, (334) 242-4169; www.alabama.travel

Website. www.alabama.gov

Alaska (AK)
The Last Frontier (unofficial)

People. Population: 731,449; rank: 47. **Pop. change** (2010-12): 3.0%. **Pop. density:** 1.3 per sq mi. **Racial distribution:** 67.5% white; 3.7% black; 5.7% Asian; 14.8% Amer. Ind.; 1.2% Hawaiian/Pacific Islander; two or more races, 7.1%. **Hispanic pop.:** 6.1%.

Geography. Total area: 665,384 sq mi; rank: 1. **Land area:** 570,641 sq mi; rank: 1. **Acres forested:** 15.2 mil. **Location:** NW corner of North America, bordered on E by Canada. **Climate:** SE, SW, and central regions, moist and mild; far N extremely dry. Extended summer days, winter nights throughout. **Topography:** includes Pacific and Arctic mountain systems, central plateau, and Arctic slope. Mt. McKinley, 20,237 ft, is the highest point in N. America. **Capital:** Juneau. **Chief airport:** Anchorage.

Economy. Chief industries: petroleum, tourism, fishing, mining, forestry, transportation, aerospace. **Chief manuf. goods:** petroleum, seafood. **Chief crops:** greenhouse products, barley, oats, hay, potatoes, carrots. **Livestock:** 12,000 cattle/calves. **Nonfuel minerals:** $3.5 bil; gold, zinc, silver, lead, sand and gravel (construction). **Commercial fishing:** $1.7 bil. **Chief ports:** Anchorage, Dutch Harbor, Kodiak, Juneau, Sitka, Valdez. **Gross state product:** $51.9 bil. **Sales tax:** none. **Employment distrib.:** 24.9% govt.; 19.8% trade/trans./util.; 2.7% mfg.; 14.2% ed./health; 8.6% prof./bus. serv.; 10% leisure/hosp.; 4% finance; 10.5% constr./mining/log.; 1.8% info.; 3.5% other serv. **Unemployment:** 7.0%. **Per cap. pers. income:** $46,778. **New private housing:** 994 units/$234.3 mil. **Broadband Internet:** 90.6%. **Commercial banks:** 6; deposits $9.7 bil. **Savings institutions:** 2; deposits: $406 mil.

Federal govt. Fed. civ. employees: 12,301; **avg. salary:** $74,921. **Notable fed. facilities:** Joint Base Elmendorf-Richardson; Ft. Wainwright; Eilson AFB; Ft. Greely.

Energy. Electricity use/cost: 649 kWh, $114.42.

State data. Motto: North to the future. **Flower:** Forget-me-not. **Bird:** Willow ptarmigan. **Tree:** Sitka spruce. **Song:** "Alaska's Flag." **Entered union:** Jan. 3, 1959; rank: 49th. **State fair** at Palmer, late Aug.-early Sept.

History. Early inhabitants included the Tlingit-Haida and Athabascan peoples. Ancestors of the Aleut and Inuit (Eskimo) probably arrived from Siberia between 10,000 and 6,000 years ago. Vitus Bering, a Dane sailing for Russia, was the first European to land in Alaska, 1741. Russians, pursuing the fur trade, established a permanent settlement on Kodiak Island, 1784. Sec. of State William H. Seward bought Alaska from Russia for $7.2 mil in 1867, a deal some called "Seward's Folly." Discovery of gold in the Klondike region of Canada's Yukon Territory, 1896, triggered an Alaskan gold rush. Alaska became a territory, 1912, and a state, 1959. A huge oil find at Prudhoe Bay, 1968, led to construction of the Trans-Alaska Pipeline, 1974-77. The *Exxon Valdez* supertanker ran aground, 1989, spilling about 11 mil gallons of crude oil; the cleanup cost more than $2.2 bil. Repeated attempts by Congress members to allow oil and gas drilling in the Arctic National Wildlife Refuge have failed.

Tourist attractions. Portage Glacier, in Chugach Natl. Forest; Mendenhall Glacier, in Tongass Natl. Forest; Totem Heritage Ctr., Ketchikan; Glacier Bay Natl. Park and Preserve; Mt. McKinley (or Denali, N. America's highest peak), in Denali Natl. Park and Preserve; Mt. Roberts Tramway, Juneau; Alaska Maritime Natl. Wildlife Refuge; St. Michael's Cathedral, Alaska Raptor Ctr., in Sitka; White Pass & Yukon Route railroad, Skagway; Katmai Natl. Park and Preserve; Univ. of Alaska Museum of the North, Fairbanks.

Famous Alaskans. Tom Bodett, Susan Butcher, Ernest Gruening, Jewel (Kilcher), Tony Knowles, Sydney Laurence, Sarah Palin, Libby Riddles, Curt Schilling, Jefferson "Soapy" Smith.

Tourist information. Alaska Travel Industry Association, 2600 Cordova St., Ste. 201, Anchorage, AK 99503; 1-800-327-9372; www.travelalaska.com
Website. www.alaska.gov

Arizona (AZ)
Grand Canyon State

People. Population: 6,553,255; rank: 15. **Pop. change** (2010-12): 2.5%. **Pop. density:** 57.7 per sq mi. **Racial distribution:** 84.3% white; 4.5% black; 3.1% Asian; 5.3% Amer. Ind.; 0.3% Hawaiian/Pacific Islander; two or more races, 2.5%. **Hispanic pop.:** 30.2%.

Geography. Total area: 113,990 sq mi; rank: 6. **Land area:** 113,594 sq mi; rank: 6. **Acres forested:** 18.6 mil. **Location:** southwestern U.S. **Climate:** clear and dry in southern regions and northern plateau; high central areas have heavy winter snows. **Topography:** Colorado Plateau in the N, containing the Grand Canyon; Mexican Highlands run diagonally NW to SE; Sonoran Desert in the SW. **Capital:** Phoenix. **Chief airports:** Mesa, Phoenix, Tucson.

Economy. Chief industries: manufacturing, construction, tourism, mining, agriculture. **Chief manuf. goods:** aerospace, semiconductors, navigational instruments, cement, plastics, structural metals, dairy, printing, furniture. **Chief crops:** cotton, grapes, apples, lettuce, hay, potatoes, sorghum, barley, corn, wheat. **Livestock:** 900,000 cattle/calves,

140,000 sheep/lambs. **Nonfuel minerals:** $8.1 bil; copper, molybdenum concentrates, sand and gravel (construction), cement (portland), silver. **Gross state product:** $266.9 bil. **Sales tax:** 6.6%. **Employment distrib.:** 16.6% govt.; 19.1% trade/trans./util.; 6.2% mfg.; 14.8% ed./health; 14.3% prof./bus. serv.; 11.2% leisure/hosp.; 7.3% finance; 5.6% constr./mining/log.; 1.6% info.; 3.4% other serv. **Unemployment:** 8.3%. **Per cap. pers. income:** $35,979. **New private housing:** 21,726 units/$4.5 bil. **Broadband Internet:** 75.8%. **Commercial banks:** 66; deposits $82.7 bil. **Savings institutions:** 8; deposits: $4.1 bil. **Lottery:** total sales: $646.7 mil; profit: $164.7 mil.

Federal govt. Fed. civ. employees: 41,754; **avg. salary:** $66,151. **Notable fed. facilities:** Luke AFB, Davis-Monthan AFB; Ft. Huachuca; Yuma Proving Ground.

Energy. Electricity use/cost: 1,070 kWh, $118.62.

State data. Motto: Ditat Deus (God enriches). **Flower:** Blossom of the saguaro cactus. **Bird:** Cactus wren. **Tree:** Paloverde. **Song:** "Arizona." **Entered union:** Feb. 14, 1912; rank: 48th. **State fair** at Phoenix, Oct.-early Nov.

History. Paleo-Indians hunted large game in the area at least 12,000 years ago. Anasazi, Mogollon, and Hohokam civilizations lived there c. 300 BCE-1300 CE; Navajo and Apache came c. 15th cent. Marcos de Niza, a Franciscan, and Estevanico, a black former slave, explored, 1539; Spanish explorer Francisco Vásquez de Coronado visited, 1540. Eusebio Francisco Kino, a Jesuit missionary, taught Indians 1692-1711, and left missions. Tubac, a Spanish fort, became the first European settlement, 1752. Spain ceded Arizona to Mexico, 1821. The U.S. took over, 1848, after the Mexican War. The area below the Gila R. came from Mexico in the Gadsden Purchase, 1853. Arizona became a territory, 1863. Apache wars ended with Geronimo's surrender, 1886. Arizona became a state, 1912, and grew rapidly after 1960 with a fourfold rise in population over the next four decades. Barry Goldwater was a leading conservative voice in the U.S. Senate (1953-65, 1969-87). The border with Mexico is a major gateway for illegal immigration to the U.S. In 2012, the U.S. Supreme Court struck down most provisions of a 2010 state immigration law that allowed police to make warrantless arrests of those reasonably suspected of having immigrated illegally, but left a provision requiring police to check the immigration status of those stopped or arrested for any other reason.

Tourist attractions. Grand Canyon; Painted Desert, in Grand Canyon and Petrified Forest Natl. Parks; Glen Canyon Natl. Recreation Area; Canyon de Chelly Natl. Monument; Meteor Crater, near Winslow; London Bridge, Lake Havasu City; Biosphere 2, Oracle; Navajo Natl. Monument; Tombstone historic mining town; Tempe Town Lake.

Famous Arizonans. Bruce Babbitt, Cochise, Alice Cooper, Geronimo, Gabrielle Giffords, Barry Goldwater, Zane Grey, Carl Hayden, George W. P. Hunt, Helen Hull Jacobs, Bil Keane, Percival Lowell, John McCain, John J. Rhodes, Linda Ronstadt, Emma Stone, Morris K. Udall, Stewart L. Udall, Frank Lloyd Wright.

Tourist information. Arizona Office of Tourism, 1110 W. Washington St., Ste. 155, Phoenix, AZ 85007; 1-866-275-5816; www.arizonaguide.com
Website. www.az.gov

Arkansas (AR)
Natural State, Razorback State

People. Population: 2,949,131; rank: 32. **Pop. change** (2010-12): 1.1%. **Pop. density:** 56.7 per sq mi. **Racial distribution:** 80.0% white; 15.6% black; 1.4% Asian; 0.9% Amer. Ind.; 0.3% Hawaiian/Pacific Islander; two or more races, 1.8%. **Hispanic pop.:** 6.8%.

Geography. Total area: 55,179 sq mi; rank: 29. **Land area:** 52,035 sq mi; rank: 27. **Acres forested:** 18.9 mil. **Location:** West South Central state. **Climate:** long, hot summers, mild winters; generally abundant rainfall. **Topography:** eastern delta and prairie, southern lowland forests, and the northwestern highlands, which include the Ozark Plateaus. **Capital:** Little Rock. **Chief airports:** Bentonville, Little Rock.

Economy. Chief industries: manufacturing, agriculture, tourism, forestry. **Chief manuf. goods:** poultry processing, motor vehicles & parts, iron & steel, paper & paperboard, plastics, preserved fruits & vegetables, aerospace, rubber. **Chief crops:** rice, soybeans, cotton, hay, wheat, corn, sorghum, tomatoes, peaches, watermelons, pecans, blueberries,

grapes. **Livestock:** 20.23 mil chickens (excl. broilers), 977.1 mil broilers, 1.6 mil cattle/calves. **Nonfuel minerals:** $800 mil; bromine, stone (crushed), sand and gravel (industrial), cement (portland), sand and gravel (construction). **Chief port:** Helena. **Gross state product:** $109.6 bil. **Sales tax:** 6.0%. **Employment distrib.:** 18.4% govt.; 21.2% trade/trans./util.; 13% mfg.; 14.6% ed./health; 10.4% prof./bus. serv.; 8.8% leisure/hosp.; 4.1% finance; 4.8% constr./mining/log.; 1.2% info.; 3.5% other serv. **Unemployment:** 7.3%. **Per cap. pers. income:** $34,723. **New private housing:** 8,231 units/$1.1 bil. **Broadband Internet:** 82.6%. **Commercial banks:** 138; deposits: $52.5 bil. **Savings institutions:** 6; deposits: $903 mil. **Lottery:** total sales: $473.1 mil; profit: $97.5 mil.

Federal govt. Fed. civ. employees: 14,348; **avg. salary:** $63,966. **Notable fed. facilities:** Little Rock AFB; Pine Bluff Arsenal; Natl. Ctr. for Toxicological Research, Jefferson.

Energy. Electricity use/cost: 1,179 kWh, $106.27.

State data. Motto: Regnat Populus (The people rule). **Flower:** Apple blossom. **Bird:** Mockingbird. **Tree:** Pine. **Song:** "Arkansas." **Entered union:** June 15, 1836; rank: 25th. **State fair** at Little Rock, mid-Oct.

History. Quapaw, Caddo, Osage, Cherokee, and Choctaw peoples lived in the area at the time of European contact. The first European explorers were Hernando de Soto, 1541; Jacques Marquette and Louis Jolliet, 1673; and René-Robert Cavelier, sieur de La Salle, 1682. French fur trader Henri de Tonty founded the first settlement, 1686, at Arkansas Post. In 1762, the area was ceded by France to Spain, then given back, 1800, and was part of the Louisiana Purchase, 1803. It was made a territory, 1819, and entered the Union as a slave state, 1836. Arkansas seceded in 1861, after the Civil War began; it was readmitted, 1868. Pres. Eisenhower sent federal troops, 1957, to keep Gov. Orval Faubus from blocking racial integration at Central High School in Little Rock. Wal-Mart, now the world's leading retailer, opened its first store in Rogers, 1962. Elected five times as governor, Bill Clinton later served two terms as president (1993-2001). His presidential library opened, 2004, in Little Rock.

Tourist attractions. Eureka Springs; Ozark Folk Ctr. State Park, Mountain View; Blanchard Springs Caverns, in Ozark Natl. Forest; Crater of Diamonds State Park, Murfreesboro; Toltec Mounds Archeological State Park, Scott; Buffalo Natl. River; Hot Springs Natl. Park; Pea Ridge Natl. Military Park; William J. Clinton Presidential Library and Museum, Little Rock Central High School Natl. Historic Site, in Little Rock; Crystal Bridges Museum of American Art, Bentonville.

Famous Arkansans. Daisy Bates, Dee Brown, Paul "Bear" Bryant, Glen Campbell, Hattie Wyatt Caraway, Johnny Cash, Wesley Clark, Bill Clinton, Jay Hanna "Dizzy" Dean, Orval Faubus, James William Fulbright, Al Green, John Grisham, Levon Helm, John H. Johnson, Douglas MacArthur, John Little McClellan, James S. McDonnell, Scottie Pippen, Dick Powell, Brooks Robinson, Winthrop Rockefeller, Mary Steenburgen, Edward Durell Stone, Billy Bob Thornton, Sam Walton, Archibald Yell.

Tourist information. Arkansas Dept. of Parks & Tourism, 1 Capitol Mall, Little Rock, AR 72201; 1-800-NATURAL; www.arkansas.com
Website. www.arkansas.gov

California (CA)
Golden State

People. Population: 38,041,430; rank: 1. **Pop. change** (2010-12): 2.1%. **Pop. density:** 244.2 per sq mi. **Racial distribution:** 73.7% white; 6.6% black; 13.9% Asian; 1.7% Amer. Ind.; 0.5% Hawaiian/Pacific Islander; two or more races, 3.6%. **Hispanic pop.:** 38.2%.

Geography. Total area: 163,695 sq mi; rank: 3. **Land area:** 155,779 sq mi; rank: 3. **Acres forested:** 32.6 mil. **Location:** western coast of U.S. **Climate:** moderate temperatures and rainfall along the coast; extremes in the interior. **Topography:** long mountainous coastline; central valley; Sierra Nevada on the E; desert basins in southern interior; rugged mountains in N. **Capital:** Sacramento. **Chief airports:** Burbank, Fresno, Long Beach, Los Angeles, Oakland, Ontario, Palm Springs, Sacramento, San Diego, San Francisco, San Jose, Santa Ana.

Economy. Chief industries: agriculture, tourism, apparel, electronics, telecommunications, entertainment. **Chief manuf. goods:** petroleum, aerospace, precision instruments, semiconductors, telecom. & broadcasting equip.,

pharmaceutical, wineries, plastics, medical equip., preserved fruits & vegetables, printing, dairy, cut & sew apparel, motor vehicles. **Chief crops:** grapes, nursery products, almonds, lettuce, hay, strawberries, floriculture, tomatoes, cotton, oranges, pistachios, walnuts, broccoli, carrots, rice, peaches, lemons. **Livestock:** 24.51 mil chickens (excl. broilers), 5.3 mil cattle/calves, 570,000 sheep/lambs. **Nonfuel minerals:** $3.6 bil; sand and gravel (construction), boron minerals, cement (portland), gold, stone (crushed). **Commercial fishing:** $231.7 mil. **Chief ports:** Long Beach, Los Angeles, San Diego, Port Hueneme, Richmond, Oakland, San Francisco, Stockton. **Gross state product:** $2.0 tril. **Sales tax:** 7.5%. **Employment distrib.:** 16.5% govt.; 18.6% trade/trans./util.; 8.5% mfg.; 13.1% ed./health; 15.7% prof./bus. serv.; 11.4% leisure/hosp.; 5.4% finance; 4.4% constr./mining/log.; 2.9% info.; 3.5% other serv. **Unemployment:** 10.5%. **Per cap. pers. income:** $44,980. **New private housing:** 58,549 units/$12.7 bil. **Broadband Internet:** 77.9%. **Commercial banks:** 269; deposits: $922.2 bil. **Savings institutions:** 25; deposits: $30.8 bil. **Lottery:** total sales: $4.4 bil; profit: $1.3 bil.

Federal govt. Fed. civ. employees: 168,041; **avg. salary:** $77,353. **Notable fed. facilities:** USMC Camp Pendleton; Naval Base Coronado; Marine Corps Air Ground Combat Ctr., 29 Palms; Marine Corps Air Station Miramar; Travis AFB; Naval Research Lab., Monterey; Lawrence Livermore Natl. Lab; Lawrence Berkeley Natl. Lab; NASA Jet Propulsion Lab; Edwards AFB (NASA Dryden Flight Research Ctr., AF Flight Test Ctr.); San Francisco Mint.

Energy. Electricity use/cost: 567 kWh, $83.70.

State data. Motto: Eureka (I have found it). **Flower:** Golden poppy. **Bird:** California valley quail. **Tree:** California redwood. **Song:** "I Love You, California." **Entered union:** Sept. 9, 1850; rank: 31st. **State fair** at Sacramento, mid to late-July.

History. Early inhabitants included more than 100 different Native American tribes with multiple dialects. The first European explorers were Juan Rodríguez Cabrillo, 1542, and Sir Francis Drake, 1579. The first settlement was the Spanish Alta California mission at San Diego, 1769, first in a string founded by Franciscan Father Junípero Serra. California became a province of independent Mexico, 1821. U.S. traders and settlers arrived in the 19th cent. and staged the Bear Flag revolt, 1846, in protest against Mexican rule; later that year U.S. forces occupied California. At the end of the Mexican War, Mexico ceded the territory to the U.S., 1848; that same year gold was discovered, and the famed gold rush began. California became a state, 1850. An economic downturn in the 1870s spurred riots against Chinese immigrants, who had come as laborers in the boom years. An earthquake and related fires devastated San Francisco, 1906. During World War II, Japanese Americans, many of them U.S. citizens, were held in detention camps, 1942-45. Ronald Reagan, a former movie actor, became state governor (1967-75) and U.S. president (1981-89). A budget crisis, 2003, resulted in the recall of Gov. Gray Davis and the election of another actor, Arnold Schwarzenegger. Led by Hollywood in entertainment and Silicon Valley in high-tech, the state's economy dwarfs that of most nations. Still, billion-dollar budget deficits have been a perennial problem. The U.S. Supreme Court in June 2013 effectively upheld the right of same-sex couples to marry in the state.

Tourist attractions. *Queen Mary*, Aquarium of the Pacific, in Long Beach; Palomar Observatory, Palomar Mountain; Disneyland Resort, Anaheim; Getty Center, Universal Studios Hollywood, Griffith Observatory, in Los Angeles; Tournament of Roses and Rose Bowl, Pasadena; The California Museum, California State Railroad Museum, in Sacramento; San Diego Zoo, USS *Midway* Museum, in San Diego; Yosemite Valley; Lassen Volcanic, Sequoia, and Kings Canyon Natl. Parks; Mojave and Sonoran Deserts; Death Valley; Golden Gate Park, Alcatraz Island, in San Francisco; Napa Valley wine region; Monterey Bay Aquarium, Monterey Peninsula; Ancient Bristlecone Pine Forest (oldest known living trees on Earth), in Inyo Natl. Forest; Redwood Natl. and State Parks; Muir Woods Natl. Monument, Mill Valley.

Famous Californians. Tom Brady, Edmund G. (Pat) Brown, Jerry Brown, Luther Burbank, Julia Child, Ted Danson, Cameron Diaz, Leonardo DiCaprio, Joe DiMaggio, Landon Donovan, Clint Eastwood, Dianne Feinstein, John C. Fremont, Tom Hanks, Bret Harte, William Randolph Hearst, Helen Hunt, Steve Jobs, Jimmie Johnson, Angelina Jolie, Jack Kemp, Jason Kidd, Lisa Leslie, Monica Lewinsky, Jack London,

George Lucas, Phil Mickelson, Marilyn Monroe, John Muir, Richard M. Nixon, Gwyneth Paltrow, George S. Patton Jr., Gregory Peck, Nancy Pelosi, Ronald Reagan, Sally K. Ride, William Saroyan, Arnold Schwarzenegger, Father Junípero Serra, O. J. Simpson, Kevin Spacey, Leland Stanford, Gwen Stefani, John Steinbeck, Shirley Temple, Earl Warren, Serena Williams, Ted Williams, Venus Williams, Tiger Woods.

Tourist information. California Tourism, P.O. Box 1499, Sacramento, CA 95812-1499; 1-877-225-4367; www.visit california.com

Website. www.ca.gov

Colorado (CO)
Centennial State

People. Population: 5,187,582; rank: 22. **Pop. change** (2010-12): 3.1%. **Pop. density:** 50.1 per sq mi. **Racial distribution:** 88.1% white; 4.3% black; 3% Asian; 1.6% Amer. Ind.; 0.2% Hawaiian/Pacific Islander; two or more races, 2.8%. **Hispanic pop.:** 21.0%.

Geography. Total area: 104,094 sq mi; rank: 8. **Land area:** 103,642 sq mi; rank: 8. **Acres forested:** 22.9 mil. **Location:** W central U.S. **Climate:** low relative humidity, abundant sunshine, wide daily/seasonal temperature ranges; alpine conditions in the high mountains. **Topography:** eastern dry high plains; hilly to mountainous central plateau; western Rocky Mts. of high ranges with broad valleys, deep, narrow canyons. **Capital:** Denver. **Chief airports:** Colorado Springs, Denver.

Economy. Chief industries: manufacturing, construction, government, tourism, agriculture, aerospace, electronics equipment. **Chief manuf. goods:** animal slaughtering, beer, petroleum, pharmaceuticals, aerospace, medical equip., precision instruments, printing, semiconductors. **Chief crops:** hay, corn, potatoes, wheat, onions, dry edible beans, sunflowers, sugar beets, barley, proso millet, cabbage, peaches, lettuce, apples, cantaloupes. **Livestock:** 5.13 mil chickens (excl. broilers), 2.6 mil cattle/calves, 435,000 sheep/lambs, 145,000 hogs/pigs. **Nonfuel minerals:** $1.9 bil; molybdenum concentrates, gold, cement (portland), sand and gravel (construction), stone (crushed). **Gross state product:** $274.0 bil. **Sales tax:** 2.9%. **Employment distrib.:** 17.4% govt.; 17.5% trade/trans./util.; 5.6% mfg.; 12.3% ed./health; 15.7% prof./ bus. serv.; 11.9% leisure/hosp.; 6.1% finance; 6.4% constr./ mining/log.; 2.9% info.; 4.1% other serv. **Unemployment:** 8.0%. **Per cap. pers. income:** $45,135. **New private housing:** 23,301 units/$4.4 bil. **Broadband Internet:** 79.4%. **Commercial banks:** 142; deposits: $97 bil. **Savings institutions:** 14; deposits: $2./ bil. **Lottery:** total sales: $545.3 mll; profit: $123.2 mil.

Federal govt. Fed. civ. employees: 40,037; **avg. salary:** $76,304. **Notable fed. facilities:** U.S. Air Force Academy; Peterson AFB; Denver Mint; Ft. Carson; Natl. Renewable Energy Laboratory; Transportation Tech. Ctr.; NORAD and USNORTHCOM Alt. Command Ctr., Cheyenne Mtn. Complex; Denver Federal Ctr.; Natl. Ctr. for Atmospheric Research; Natl. Inst. of Standards & Tech., Boulder; Natl. Wildlife Research Ctr.; NOAA Earth Systems Research Environmental Lab.

Energy. Electricity use/cost: 711 kWh, $80.12.

State data. Motto: Nil Sine Numine (Nothing without Providence). **Flower:** Rocky Mountain columbine. **Bird:** Lark bunting. **Tree:** Colorado blue spruce. **Songs:** "Where the Columbines Grow"; "Rocky Mountain High." **Entered union:** Aug. 1, 1876; rank 38th. **State fair** at Pueblo, mid-Aug.-early Sept.

History. Paleo-Indians hunted big game in the area at least 11,000 years ago. Anasazi cliff dwellers flourished around Mesa Verde until about 1300 CE; other Native Americans were the Ute, Pueblo, Cheyenne, and Arapaho. The region was claimed by Spain, but passed to France, 1800. The U.S. acquired eastern Colorado in the Louisiana Purchase, 1803. Lt. Zebulon M. Pike explored the area, 1806, sighting the peak that bears his name. After the Mexican War, 1846-48, U.S. immigrants settled in the east, former Mexicans in the south. Gold was discovered in 1858, causing a population boom. Congress created Colorado Territory, 1861. Conflict between newcomers and displaced Native Americans led to the Sand Creek Massacre, 1864, in which U.S. soldiers and settlers killed some 150 Cheyenne and Arapaho. U.S. Army troops forced the removal to reservations (mostly in present-day Oklahoma) of most Native Americans in the state, 1867. The 1870s brought statehood, 1876, and rich silver finds that turned Leadville into a boomtown. Federal military and civilian

employment in Colorado surged in the 1940s and '50s; since then, tourism and high-tech industries have fueled the economy. The state's Hispanic population grew from 5.8% in 1980 to 20.7% in 2010.

Tourist attractions. Denver Museum of Nature & Science, Denver Botanic Gardens, Denver Zoo; Red Rocks Park and Amphitheatre, Morrison; Natl. Ctr. for Atmospheric Research, Boulder; Rocky Mountain, Black Canyon of the Gunnison, and Mesa Verde (Anasazi cliff dwellings) Natl. Parks; Aspen, Breckenridge, Steamboat, and Vail ski resorts; Garden of the Gods, Colorado Springs; Great Sand Dunes Natl. Park and Preserve; Dinosaur and Colorado Natl. Monuments; Pikes Peak and Mount Evans; Grand Mesa Natl. Forest; historic mining towns of Central City, Silverton, Cripple Creek; Bent's Old Fort Natl. Historic Site, near La Junta; Georgetown Loop Historic Mining and Railroad Park; Durango & Silverton Narrow Gauge Railroad Museum, Durango; Cumbres and Toltec Scenic Railroad, Antonito; gambling in Black Hawk, Central City, Cripple Creek and on tribal land in Ignacio and Towaoc.

Famous Coloradans. Tim Allen, Chauncey Billups, Frederick Bonfils, Molly Brown, William N. Byers, M. Scott Carpenter, Lon Chaney, Jack Dempsey, Mamie Eisenhower, Douglas Fairbanks, Barney Ford, Roy Halladay, Chief Ouray, Trey Parker, "Baby Doe" Tabor, Lowell Thomas, Byron R. White, Paul Whiteman.

Tourist information. Colorado Tourism Office, 1625 Broadway, Ste. 1700, Denver, CO 80202; 1-800-COLORADO; www.colorado.com

Website. www.colorado.gov

Connecticut (CT)
Constitution State, Nutmeg State

People. Population: 3,590,347; rank: 29. **Pop. change** (2010-12): 0.5%. **Pop. density:** 741.4 per sq mi. **Racial distribution:** 82.0% white; 11.2% black; 4.2% Asian; 0.5% Amer. Ind.; 0.1% Hawaiian/Pacific Islander; two or more races, 2.1%. **Hispanic pop.:** 14.2%.

Geography. Total area: 5,543 sq mi; rank: 48. **Land area:** 4,842 sq mi; rank: 48. **Acres forested:** 1.7 mil. **Location:** New England state in NE corner of U.S. **Climate:** moderate; winters avg. slightly below freezing; warm, humid summers. **Topography:** western upland, the Berkshires, in the NW, highest elevations; narrow central lowland N-S; hilly eastern upland drained by rivers. **Capital:** Hartford. **Chief airport:** Windsor Locks.

Economy. Chief industries: manufacturing, retail trade, government, services, finances, insurance, real estate. **Chief manuf. goods:** aerospace, chemicals, fabricated metals, precision instruments, toiletries, medical equip., printing, plastics. **Chief crops:** nursery stock, Christmas trees, mushrooms, sweet corn, apples, tobacco, hay. **Livestock:** 2.97 mil chickens (excl. broilers), 48,000 cattle/calves. **Nonfuel minerals:** $173 mil; stone (crushed), sand and gravel (construction), clays (common), stone (dimension), gemstones (natural). **Commercial fishing:** $20.6 mil. **Chief ports:** New Haven, Bridgeport, New London. **Gross state product:** $229.3 bil. **Sales tax:** 6.35%. **Employment distrib.:** 14.5% govt.; 17.9% trade/trans./util.; 9.7% mfg.; 19.5% ed./health; 12.5% prof./bus. serv.; 9.1% leisure/hosp.; 7.8% finance; 3.3% constr./mining/log.; 1.9% info.; 3.7% other serv. **Unemployment:** 8.4%. **Per cap. pers. income:** $58,908. **New private housing:** 4,669 units/$1 bil. **Broadband Internet:** 77.8%. **Commercial banks:** 37; deposits: $71.5 bil. **Savings institutions:** 34; deposits: $31.1 bil. **Lottery:** total sales: $1.1 bil; profit: $310.0 mil.

Federal govt. Fed. civ. employees: 8,753; **avg. salary:** $78,717. **Notable fed. facilities:** U.S. Coast Guard Academy; Navy Sub Base New London.

Energy. Electricity use/cost: 740 kWh, $134.07.

State data. Motto: Qui Transtulit Sustinet (He who transplanted still sustains). **Flower:** Mountain laurel. **Bird:** American robin. **Tree:** White oak. **Song:** "Yankee Doodle." **Fifth** of the 13 original states to ratify the Constitution, Jan. 9, 1788. **State fair:** no official state fair; district and local fairs, largest at Durham, late Sept.

History. At the time of European contact, inhabitants of the area were Algonquian peoples, including the Mohegan and Pequot. Dutch explorer Adriaen Block was the first European visitor, 1614. By 1634, settlers from Plymouth Bay had started colonies along the Connecticut R.; in 1637 they defeated the

Pequots. The Colony of Connecticut was chartered by England, 1662, adding New Haven, 1665. A Patriot stronghold in the American Revolution, the state actively supported the antislavery movement and the Union cause in the Civil War. The state economy prospered in the 20th cent. from insurance- and defense-related industries. *Nautilus*, the first nuclear-powered submarine, was launched at Groton, 1954. Connecticut Sen. Joseph Lieberman was the Democratic nominee for vice president in 2000. American Indian casinos, starting with Foxwoods in 1992, were an economic boon to the state, but tourism revenues declined sharply with the recession that began in late 2007. Twenty children and six staff members were killed in a mass shooting at Sandy Hook Elementary School in Newtown, CT, Dec. 14, 2012.

Tourist attractions. Mark Twain House and Museum, Hartford; Yale Univ. Art Gallery, Peabody Museum of Natural History, in New Haven; Mystic Seaport, Mystic Aquarium; Barnum Museum, Bridgeport; Gillette Castle State Park, East Haddam; USS *Nautilus* (1st nuclear-powered submarine) at Submarine Force Library and Museum, Groton; Mashantucket Pequot Museum and Research Ctr.; Foxwoods Resort Casino, Ledyard; Mohegan Sun, Uncasville; Lake Compounce (est. 1846; oldest continuously operating amusement park in U.S.), Bristol; Philip Johnson Glass House, New Canaan.

Famous "Nutmeggers." Ethan Allen, P. T. Barnum, Michael Bolton, Glenn Close, Samuel Colt, Ann Coulter, Jonathan Edwards, Nathan Hale, Katharine Hepburn, Isaac Hull, Norman Lear, Seth MacFarlane, John Mayer, Robert Mitchum, J. P. Morgan, Ralph Nader, Israel Putnam, Wallace Stevens, Harriet Beecher Stowe, Mark Twain, Noah Webster, Eli Whitney.

Tourist information. Connecticut Commission on Culture and Tourism, One Constitution Plz., 2nd Fl., Hartford, CT 06103; 1-888-CTVISIT, (860) 256-2800; www.ctvisit.com

Website. www.ct.gov

Delaware (DE)
First State, Diamond State

People. Population: 917,092; rank: 45. **Pop. change** (2010-12): 2.1%. **Pop. density:** 470.6 per sq mi. **Racial distribution:** 71.4% white; 22.0% black; 3.5% Asian; 0.7% Amer. Ind.; 0.1% Hawaiian/Pacific Islander; two or more races, 2.4%. **Hispanic pop.:** 8.6%.

Geography. Total area: 2,489 sq mi; rank: 49. **Land area:** 1,949 sq mi; rank: 50. **Acres forested:** 0.3 mil. **Location:** Delmarva Peninsula on the Atlantic coastal plain. **Climate:** moderate. **Topography:** Piedmont Plateau to the N, sloping to a near sea-level plain. **Capital:** Dover.

Economy. Chief industries: chemicals, agriculture, finance, poultry, shellfish, tourism, auto assembly, food processing, transportation equipment. **Chief manuf. goods:** pharmaceuticals, poultry processing, soap & cleaning compounds, precision instruments, basic chemicals, plastics. **Chief crops:** soybeans, corn, greenhouse & nursery, wheat, potatoes, barley, hay, watermelons, lima beans, green peas, pumpkins, mushrooms, cabbage. **Livestock:** 212 mil broilers, 18,000 cattle/calves. **Nonfuel minerals:** $13.4 mil; magnesium compounds, sand and gravel (construction), stone (crushed), gemstones (natural). **Commercial fishing:** $7.9 mil. **Chief port:** Wilmington. **Gross state product:** $66.0 bil. **Sales tax:** none. **Employment distrib.:** 15.2% govt.; 17.7% trade/trans./util.; 6% mfg.; 16.4% ed./health; 13.8% prof./bus. serv.; 10.6% leisure/hosp.; 10% finance; 4.3% constr./mining/log.; 1.3% info.; 4.7% other serv. **Unemployment:** 7.1%. **Per cap. pers. income:** $41,940. **New private housing:** 4,091 units/$485.6 mil. **Broadband Internet:** 76.2%. **Commercial banks:** 35; deposits: $273.2 bil. **Savings institutions:** 6; deposits $90.5 bil. **Lottery:** total sales: $686.8 mil; profit: $271.3 mil.

Federal govt. Fed. civ. employees: 3,325; **avg. salary:** $69,153. **Notable fed. facilities:** Dover AFB; Bombay Hook National Wildlife Refuge.

Energy. Electricity use/cost: 970 kWh, $132.83.

State data. Motto: Liberty and independence. **Flower:** Peach blossom. **Bird:** Blue hen chicken. **Tree:** American holly. **Song:** "Our Delaware." **First** of original 13 states to ratify the Constitution, Dec. 7, 1787. **State fair** at Harrington, mid to late-July.

History. The Lenni Lenape (Delaware) people lived in the region at the time of European contact. Henry Hudson

located the Delaware R., 1609, and in 1610, English explorer Samuel Argall entered Delaware Bay, naming the area after Virginia's governor, Lord De La Warr. Dutch, Swedish, and Finnish settlers were followed by the British, who took control in 1664. After 1682, Delaware became part of Pennsylvania, and in 1704 it was granted its own assembly. It adopted a constitution as the state of Delaware, 1776, and was first to ratify the federal Constitution, 1787. Although it remained in the Union during the Civil War, Delaware retained slavery until the 13th Amendment abolished it in 1865. The DuPont company, founded as a gunpowder mill in 1802, became an industrial giant in the 20th cent. making nylon, Teflon, and other synthetics. Pro-business laws drew many out-of-state firms to incorporate in Delaware. In 2000, Ruth Ann Minner was elected Delaware's first woman governor.

Tourist attractions. Fort Christina (site of founding of colony of New Sweden), Holy Trinity (Old Swedes) Church (erected 1698, oldest church in U.S. still standing as built and in use), Hagley Museum and Library, Nemours Mansion and Gardens, in Wilmington; Winterthur Museum, Garden, and Library, near Wilmington; New Castle Historic District; John Dickinson "Penman of the Revolution" Plantation, First State Heritage Park, Dover Intl. Speedway, in Dover; Rehoboth Beach.

Famous Delawareans. Thomas F. Bayard, Joseph Biden, Henry Seidel Canby, E. I. du Pont, John P. Marquand, Howard Pyle, Caesar Rodney, Susan Stroman.

Tourist information. Delaware Tourism Office, 99 Kings Hwy., Dover, DE 19901; 1-866-2VISITDE; www.visitdelaware.com

Website. www.delaware.gov

Florida (FL)
Sunshine State

People. Population: 19,317,568; rank: 4. **Pop. change** (2010-12): 2.7%. **Pop. density:** 360.2 per sq mi. **Racial distribution:** 78.3% white; 16.6% black; 2.7% Asian; 0.5% Amer. Ind.; 0.1% Hawaiian/Pacific Islander; two or more races, 1.9%. **Hispanic pop.:** 23.2%.

Geography. Total area: 65,758 sq mi; rank: 22. **Land area:** 53,625 sq mi; rank: 26. **Acres forested:** 17.5 mil. **Location:** peninsula jutting southward 500 mi between the Atlantic and Gulf of Mexico. **Climate:** subtropical N of Bradenton-Lake Okeechobee-Vero Beach line; tropical S of line. **Topography:** land is flat or rolling; highest point is 345 ft in the NW. **Capital:** Tallahassee. **Chief airports:** Fort Lauderdale, Fort Myers, Jacksonville, Miami, Orlando, Pensacola, Sanford, Sarasota, Tampa, West Palm Beach.

Economy. Chief industries: tourism, agriculture, manufacturing, construction, services, international trade. **Chief manuf. goods:** navigational instruments, medical equip., cement, broadcasting equip., beverages, phosphatic fertilizer, preserved fruits & vegetables, structural metal, printing. **Chief crops:** greenhouse & nursery, oranges, sugarcane, tomatoes, green peppers, grapefruit, strawberries, snap beans, sweet corn, potatoes, cucumbers, tangerines. **Livestock:** 10.46 mil chickens (excl. broilers), 59.5 mil broilers, 1.66 mil cattle/calves. **Nonfuel minerals:** $3.6 bil; phosphate rock, stone (crushed), cement (portland), sand and gravel (construction), zirconium concentrates. **Commercial fishing:** $199.4 mil. **Chief ports:** Pensacola, Tampa, Port Manatee, Miami, Port Everglades, Jacksonville, Canaveral. **Gross state product:** $777.2 bil. **Sales tax:** 6.0%. **Employment distrib.:** 14.4% govt.; 20.8% trade/trans./util.; 4.2% mfg.; 15% ed./health; 14.5% prof./bus. serv.; 13.8% leisure/hosp.; 6.6% finance; 4.7% constr./mining/log.; 1.8% info.; 4.2% other serv. **Unemployment:** 8.6%. **Per cap. pers. income:** $40,344. **New private housing:** 64,810 units/$13.2 bil. **Broadband Internet:** 80.8%. **Commercial banks:** 259; deposits: $397.8 bil. **Savings institutions:** 33; deposits $26.1 bil. **Lottery:** total sales: $4.4 bil; profit: $1.3 bil.

Federal govt. Fed. civ. employees: 90,427; **avg. salary:** $71,363. **Notable fed. facilities:** John F. Kennedy Space Ctr.; Eglin AFB; MacDill AFB; Hurlburt Field; Pensacola NAS; Jacksonville NAS; Mayport Naval Sta.

Energy. Electricity use/cost: 1,131 kWh, $130.10.

State data. Motto: In God we trust. **Flower:** Orange blossom. **Bird:** Mockingbird. **Tree:** Sabal palmetto palm. **Song:** "Old Folks at Home." **Entered union:** Mar. 3, 1845; rank: 27th. **State fair** at Tampa, early to mid-Feb.

History. Florida has been inhabited for at least 12,000 years. Timucua, Apalachee, and Calusa peoples were living in the region when the earliest Europeans came; later the Seminole migrated from Georgia to Florida, becoming dominant there in the early 18th cent. The first European to see Florida was Ponce de León, 1513. France established a colony, Ft. Caroline, on the St. Johns R., 1564. Spain settled St. Augustine, 1565, and Spanish troops massacred most of the French. Britain's Sir Francis Drake burned St. Augustine, 1586. In 1763, Spain ceded Florida to Great Britain, which held the area 20 years before returning it to Spain. Florida was ceded to the U.S. in the Adams-Onís Treaty, 1819. The Seminole War, 1835-42, resulted in removal of most Native Americans to Indian Territory. Florida joined the Union in 1845, seceded in 1861, and was readmitted in 1868. In the late 19th cent., hotel and railroad builder Henry M. Flagler laid the foundations of the tourism industry. The state experienced phenomenal population growth in the 20th cent., especially after 1950. The first U.S. astronaut was launched into space from Cape Canaveral, 1961. Walt Disney World opened near Orlando, 1971. Hurricane Andrew slammed Florida, 1992, causing at least $25 bil in property damage. A dispute over Florida's presidential vote in 2000 was decided by the U.S. Supreme Court decision and resulted in George W. Bush's electoral college victory. Four hurricanes hit the state in 2004, causing more than $40 bil in damages.

Tourist attractions. Miami Beach; Castillo de San Marcos Natl. Monument, St. Augustine Lighthouse & Museum, Lightner Museum, in St. Augustine (oldest permanent European settlement in U.S.); Walt Disney World Resort, SeaWorld Orlando, Universal Studios, Discovery Cove, in Orlando; Kennedy Space Ctr., U.S. Astronaut Hall of Fame; Everglades Natl. Park; Ringling Museum of Art, Ringling Circus Museum, in Sarasota; Cypress Gardens at Legoland Florida, Winter Haven; Busch Gardens, Big Cat Rescue, in Tampa; Florida Caverns State Park, Marianna; Key West.

Famous Floridians. Edna Buchanan, Jeb Bush, Marjory Stoneman Douglas, Henry Morrison Flagler, Carl Hiaasen, Perez Hilton, Zora Neale Hurston, James Weldon Johnson, Deacon Jones, MacKinlay Kantor, Osceola, Claude Pepper, Tom Petty, Henry B. Plant, A. Philip Randolph, Marjorie Kinnan Rawlings, Janet Reno, Marco Rubio, Deion Sanders, Emmitt Smith, Joseph W. Stilwell, Amar'e Stoudemire, Charles P. Summerall.

Tourist information. Visit Florida, 2540 W. Executive Center Cir., Ste. 200, Tallahassee, FL 32301; 1-888-7FLA-USA; www.visitflorida.com

Website. www.myflorida.com

Georgia (GA)
Empire State of the South, Peach State

People. Population: 9,919,945; rank: 8. **Pop. change** (2010-12): 2.4%. **Pop. density:** 172.5 per sq mi. **Racial distribution:** 62.8% white; 31.2% black; 3.5% Asian; 0.5% Amer. Ind.; 0.1% Hawaiian/Pacific Islander; two or more races, 1.8%. **Hispanic pop.:** 9.2%.

Geography. Total area: 59,425 sq mi; rank: 24. **Land area:** 57,513 sq mi; rank: 21. **Acres forested:** 24.8 mil. **Location:** South Atlantic state. **Climate:** maritime tropical air masses dominate in summer; polar air masses in winter; E central area drier. **Topography:** most southerly of the Blue Ridge Mts. cover NE and N central; central Piedmont extends to the fall line of rivers; coastal plain levels to the coast flatlands. **Capital:** Atlanta. **Chief airports:** Atlanta, Savannah.

Economy. Chief industries: services, manufacturing, retail trade. **Chief manuf. goods:** carpet & rugs, animal slaughtering & processing, motor vehicles & parts, plastics, aircrafts, paper, chemicals, food. **Chief crops:** cotton, greenhouse & nursery, peanuts, pecans, corn, tomatoes, cucumbers, onions, watermelons, tobacco, squash, blueberries, hay, cabbage, soybeans, peaches, snap beans, wheat. **Livestock:** 25.94 mil chickens (excl. broilers), 1.36 bil broilers, 1.02 mil cattle/calves. **Nonfuel minerals:** $1.4 bil; clays (kaolin), stone (crushed), clays (fuller's earth), cement (portland), sand and gravel (construction). **Commercial fishing:** $16.3 mil. **Chief ports:** Savannah, Brunswick. **Gross state product:** $433.6 bil. **Sales tax:** 4.0%. **Employment distrib.:** 16.8% govt.; 20.9% trade/trans./util.; 8.7% mfg.; 12.6% ed./health; 14.7% prof./bus. serv.; 10.4% leisure/hosp.; 5.7% finance; 3.8% constr./mining/log.; 2.6% info.; 3.8% other serv.

Unemployment: 9.0%. **Per cap. pers. income:** $36,869. **New private housing:** 24,350 units/$3.9 bil. **Broadband Internet:** 76.2%. **Commercial banks:** 258; deposits: $181.5 bil. **Savings institutions:** 20; deposits: $4.7 bil. **Lottery:** total sales: $3.8 bil; profit: $901.3 mil.

Federal govt. Fed. civ. employees: 78,522; **avg. salary:** $71,853. **Notable fed. facilities:** Ft. Benning; Ft. Stewart; Fed. Law Enforcement Training Ctr., Robins AFB; Ft. Gordon; Navy Sub Base Kings Bay; Moody AFB; Centers for Disease Control; Marine Corps Logistics Base.

Energy. Electricity use/cost: 1,186 kWh, $131.15.

State data. Motto: Wisdom, justice, and moderation. **Flower:** Cherokee rose. **Bird:** Brown thrasher. **Tree:** Live oak. **Song:** "Georgia on My Mind." **Fourth** of the 13 original states to ratify the Constitution, Jan. 2, 1788. **State fair** at Macon, early May; at Atlanta, late Oct.-early Nov.

History. Creek and Cherokee peoples were living in the region when Spaniards founded Santa Catalina mission, 1566, on Saint Catherines Island. Gen. James Oglethorpe established a colony at Savannah, 1733, for the poor and religiously persecuted. Oglethorpe defeated a Spanish army from Florida at Bloody Marsh, 1742. Georgia was a battleground in the American Revolution, with the British finally evacuating Savannah in 1782. When Georgia entered the Union, 1788, its plantation economy relied on slaves for rice and cotton growing. The Cherokee were removed to Indian Territory, 1838-39, and thousands died on the long march, known as the Trail of Tears. By 1860 the number of slaves exceeded 462,000 (44% of the total population). Georgia seceded from the Union, 1861, and was invaded by Union forces, 1864, under Gen. William T. Sherman, who took Atlanta, Sept. 2, and proceeded on his famous "march to the sea," ending in Dec., in Savannah. Georgia was readmitted, 1870. Born 1929 in Atlanta, Martin Luther King Jr. made the city his base during the civil rights struggles of the 1960s. Atlanta became the leading city of the "New South," world headquarters of Coca-Cola and CNN, host of the 1996 Summer Olympic Games. Hispanics are a rapidly growing economic and political force in the state.

Tourist attractions. Georgia State Capitol, Stone Mountain, Centennial Olympic Park, Six Flags Over Georgia, Martin Luther King Jr. Natl. Historic Site, Jimmy Carter Library and Museum, Atlanta Botanical Garden, Georgia Aquarium (world's largest), in Atlanta; Kennesaw Mountain Natl. Battlefield Park; Chickamauga and Chattanooga Natl. Military Park; Chattahoochee-Oconee Natl. Forest; Dahlonega, site of earliest U.S. gold rush; Brasstown Bald (highest mtn. in state); Franklin D. Roosevelt's Little White House Historic Site, Warm Springs; Callaway Gardens, Pine Mountain; Andersonville Natl. Historic Site (Confederate military prison); Okefenokee Natl. Wildlife Refuge; Jekyll, St. Simons, and Cumberland barrier islands; Savannah Historic District.

Famous Georgians. Kim Basinger, Griffin Bell, James Brown, Erskine Caldwell, Jimmy Carter, Ray Charles, Ty Cobb, James Dickey, Walt Frazier, John C. Fremont, Newt Gingrich, Nancy Grace, Joel Chandler Harris, "Doc" Holliday, Larry Holmes, Holly Hunter, Alan Jackson, Martin Luther King Jr., Gladys Knight, Sidney Lanier, Little Richard, Juliette Gordon Low, Margaret Mitchell, Jessye Norman, Sam Nunn, Flannery O'Connor, Otis Redding, Burt Reynolds, Julia Roberts, Jackie Robinson, Ryan Seacrest, Clarence Thomas, Travis Tritt, Ted Turner, Carl Vinson, Alice Walker, Herschel Walker, Joanne Woodward, Trisha Yearwood, Andrew Young.

Tourist information. Dept. of Economic Development, 75 Fifth St., NW, Ste. 1200, Atlanta, GA 30308; 1-800-VISITGA; www.exploregeorgia.org

Website. www.georgia.gov

Hawai'i (HI)
Aloha State

People. Population: 1,392,313; rank: 40. **Pop. change** (2010-12): 2.4%. **Pop. density:** 216.8 per sq mi. **Racial distribution:** 26.1% white; 2.1% black; 38.3% Asian; 0.4% Amer. Ind.; 10.1% Hawaiian/Pacific Islander; two or more races, 23%. **Hispanic pop.:** 9.5%.

Geography. Total area: 10,932 sq mi; rank: 43. **Land area:** 6,423 sq mi; rank: 47. **Acres forested:** 1.7 mil **Location:** Islands lie in the North Pacific, 2,397 mi SW of San Francisco. **Climate:** subtropical, with wide variations in rainfall; Mt. Waialeale, on Kaua'i, wettest spot in U.S. (annual rainfall 450 in.). **Topography:** islands are tops of a chain of sub-

merged volcanic mountains; Mauna Loa, Kilauea are active volcanoes. **Capital:** Honolulu. **Chief airports:** Hilo, Honolulu, Kahului, Kailua Kona, Lihue.

Economy. Chief industries: tourism, defense, sugar, pineapples. **Chief manuf. goods:** concrete, printing, baked goods, sugar, preserved fruits & vegetables, apparel. **Chief crops:** flowers & nursery, pineapples, seed crops, sugarcane, macadamia nuts, coffee, algae, papayas, tomatoes, bananas, basil, ginger. **Livestock:** 132,000 cattle/calves. **Nonfuel minerals:** $107 mil; stone (crushed), sand and gravel (construction), gemstones (natural). **Commercial fishing:** $112.3 mil. **Chief ports:** Honolulu, Hilo, Barbers Point, Kahului. **Gross state product:** $72.4 bil. **Sales tax:** 4.0%. **Employment distrib.:** 20.9% govt.; 18.7% trade/trans./util.; 2.1% mfg.; 12.7% ed./health; 12.4% prof./bus. serv.; 17.8% leisure/hosp.; 4.5% finance; 5.1% constr./mining/log.; 1.4% info.; 4.5% other serv. **Unemployment:** 5.8%. **Per cap. pers. income:** $44,024. **New private housing:** 2,993 units/$757 mil. **Broadband Internet:** 85.8%. **Commercial banks:** 8; deposits: $27.4 bil. **Savings institutions:** 5; deposits: $5.7 bil.

Federal govt. Fed. civ. employees: 25,021; **avg. salary:** $70,922. **Notable fed. facilities:** Joint Base Pearl Harbor-Hickam; Schofield Barracks; Marine Corps Base Hawaii Kaneohe Bay; Tripler Army Med. Ctr.; Ft. Shafter; Wheeler Army Airfield; Prince Kuhio Federal Bldg.

Energy. Electricity use/cost: 585 kWh, $202.72.

State data. Motto: Ua mau ke ea o ka aina i ka pono (The life of the land is perpetuated in righteousness). **Flower:** Yellow hibiscus. **Bird:** Hawaiian goose. **Tree:** Kukui (candlenut). **Song:** "Hawai'i Pono'i" (Hawai'i's Own). **Entered union:** Aug. 21, 1959; rank: 50th. **State fair** at Honolulu, late May-June.

History. Polynesians from islands 2,000 mi to the S settled the Hawaiian Islands, probably 300-600 CE. The first European visitor was British captain James Cook, 1778. King Kamehameha I united the islands by 1810. Christian missionaries arrived, 1819, bringing Western culture. Under the reign, 1825-54, of King Kamehameha III, a constitution, legislature, and public school system were instituted. Sugar production began, 1835, and it became the dominant industry. Queen Liliuokalani was deposed, 1893, and a republic was established, 1894, headed by Sanford B. Dole. Annexation by the U.S. came in 1898. The Japanese attack on Pearl Harbor, Dec. 7, 1941, brought the U.S. into World War II. Hawai'i attained statehood, 1959. Hurricane Iniki pounded Kaua'i, 1992, causing about $1 bil in damage. In 2006, Pres. George W. Bush designated the Northwestern Hawaiian Islands Natl. Monument, a marine area of 140,000 sq mi.

Tourist attractions. Oahu Isl.: Natl. Memorial Cemetery of the Pacific, Waikiki Beach, Diamond Head, in Honolulu; USS Arizona Memorial, Pearl Harbor; Polynesian Cultural Ctr., Laie; Hanauma Bay; Nu'uanu Pali. Kaua'i Isl.: Waimea Canyon. Maui Isl.: Haleakala Natl. Park. Hawai'i Isl.: Hawaii Volcanoes Natl. Park, Wailoa and Wailuku River State Parks.

Famous Islanders. Bernice Pauahi Bishop, Tia Carrere, Alexander Cartwright, St. Damien de Veuster, Don Ho, Daniel K. Inouye, Duke Kahanamoku, King Kamehameha, Nicole Kidman, Brook Mahealani Lee, Jason Scott Lee, Queen Liliuokalani, Bruno Mars, Bette Midler, Barack Obama, Ellison S. Onizuka, Michelle Wie.

Tourist information. Hawaii Visitors and Conventions Bureau, 2270 Kalakaua Ave., Ste. 801, Honolulu, HI 96815; 1-800-GOHAWAII; www.gohawaii.com

Website. www.ehawaii.gov

Idaho (ID)
Gem State

People. Population: 1,595,728; rank: 39. **Pop. change** (2010-12): 1.8%. **Pop. density:** 19.3 per sq mi. **Racial distribution:** 93.8% white; 0.8% black; 1.4% Asian; 1.7% Amer. Ind.; 0.2% Hawaiian/Pacific Islander; two or more races, 2.2%. **Hispanic pop.:** 11.6%.

Geography. Total area: 83,569 sq mi; rank: 14. **Land area:** 82,643 sq mi; rank: 11. **Acres forested:** 21.5 mil. **Location:** northwestern Mountain state bordering on British Columbia. **Climate:** tempered by Pacific westerly winds; drier, colder, continental climate in SE; altitude an important factor. **Topography:** Snake R. plains in the S; central region of mountains, canyons, gorges (Hells Canyon, 7,900 ft, deepest in N. America); subalpine northern region. **Capital:** Boise. **Chief airport:** Boise.

Economy. Chief industries: manufacturing, agriculture, tourism, lumber, mining, electronics. **Chief manuf. goods:** computers & electronics, preserved fruits & vegetables, cheese, lumber. **Chief crops:** potatoes, wheat, hay, sugar beets, barley, greenhouse & nursery, onions, dry beans, corn, mint, apples, hops, peaches, lentils, peas, cherries, plums & prunes, oats. **Livestock:** 2.37 mil cattle/calves, 235,000 sheep/lambs. **Nonfuel minerals:** $728 mil; molybdenum concentrates, phosphate rock, sand and gravel (construction), silver, stone (crushed). **Chief port:** Lewiston. **Gross state product:** $58.2 bil. **Sales tax:** 6.0%. **Employment distrib.:** 18.9% govt.; 20.2% trade/trans./util.; 9.1% mfg.; 14.3% ed./health; 12.4% prof./bus. serv.; 9.8% leisure/hosp.; 5% finance; 5.5% constr./mining/log.; 1.5% info.; 3.4% other serv. **Unemployment:** 7.1%. **Per cap. pers. income:** $33,749. **New private housing:** 6,265 units/$1.1 bil. **Broadband Internet:** 71.4%. **Commercial banks:** 33; deposits: $18.5 bil. **Savings institutions:** 2; deposits: $1 bil. **Lottery:** total sales: $175.8 mil; profit: $41.5 mil.

Federal govt. Fed. civ. employees: 8,824; **avg. salary:** $64,970. **Notable fed. facilities:** Idaho Natl. Lab; Mountain Home AFB.

Energy. Electricity use/cost: 1,048 kWh, $82.50.

State data. Motto: Esto Perpetua (It is perpetual). **Flower:** Syringa. **Bird:** Mountain bluebird. **Tree:** White pine. **Song:** "Here We Have Idaho." **Entered union:** July 3, 1890; rank: 43rd. **State fair** at Boise, mid to late-Aug.; at Blackfoot, early Sept.

History. Paleo-Indian hunters roamed the land over 13,000 years ago; later inhabitants included Shoshone, Northern Paiute, Bannock, and Nez Percé peoples. Meriwether Lewis and William Clark Expedition took place, 1804-06. Next came fur traders, 1809-34, and missionaries, 1830s-50s. Mormons made their first permanent settlement at Franklin, 1860. Idaho's gold rush began the same year and brought thousands of permanent settlers. A series of Indian wars followed, including a remarkable campaign by Chief Joseph and the Nez Percé that ended with his surrender in Montana, 1877. Idaho became a territory, 1863, and a state, 1890. In the 20th cent., it emerged as a leader in potato, lumber, and silver output. The Sun Valley ski resort opened in 1936, boosting tourism. Startup of Lewiston's river port, 1975, opened Idaho to oceangoing trade. Fueled by high-tech job growth, the state's population jumped 21.2% in 2000-10.

Tourist attractions. Hells Canyon (deepest river gorge in N. America); World Ctr. for Birds of Prey, Boise Art Museum, in Boise; Craters of the Moon Natl. Monument and Preserve; Sun Valley; Shoshone Falls, near Twin Falls; Lava Hot Springs; Lake Coeur d'Alene; Sawtooth Natl. Recreation Area; Frank Church-River of No Return Wilderness Area; Nez Perce Natl. Historical Park.

Famous Idahoans. William Borah, Frank Church, Lou Dobbs, Fred Dubois, W. Mark Felt, Chief Joseph, Harmon Killebrew, Ezra Pound, Marilynne Robinson, Sacagawea, Picabo Street, Lana Turner.

Tourist information. Idaho Division of Tourism Development, 700 W. State St., P.O. Box 83720, Boise, ID 83720; 1-800-VISITID; www.visitid.org

Website. www.state.id.us

Illinois (IL)
Prairie State

People. Population: 12,875,255; rank: 5. **Pop. change** (2010-12): 0.3%. **Pop. density:** 231.9 per sq mi. **Racial distribution:** 77.9% white; 14.8% black; 5.0% Asian; 0.6% Amer. Ind.; 0.1% Hawaiian/Pacific Islander; two or more races, 1.7%. **Hispanic pop.:** 16.3%.

Geography. Total area: 57,914 sq mi; rank: 25. **Land area:** 55,519 sq mi; rank: 24. **Acres forested:** 4.9 mil. **Location:** East North Central state; western, southern, and eastern boundaries formed by Mississippi, Ohio, and Wabash Rivers, respectively. **Climate:** temperate; typically cold, snowy winters, hot summers. **Topography:** prairie and fertile plains throughout; open hills in the southern region. **Capital:** Springfield. **Chief airports:** Chicago (2).

Economy. Chief industries: services, manufacturing, travel, wholesale and retail trade, finance, insurance, real estate, construction, health care, agriculture. **Chief manuf. goods:** food, petroleum, plastics, chemicals, agricultural machinery, pharmaceuticals, motor vehicles, printing. **Chief**

crops: corn, soybeans, hay, wheat, greenhouse & nursery, apples, peaches, sorghum. **Livestock:** 4.65 mil chickens (excl. broilers), 1.12 mil cattle/calves, 53,000 sheep/lambs, 500,000 hogs/pigs. **Nonfuel minerals:** $1.2 bil; stone (crushed), sand and gravel (industrial), cement (portland), sand and gravel (construction), tripoli. **Chief port:** Chicago. **Gross state product:** $695.2 bil. **Sales tax:** 6.25%. **Employment distrib.:** 14.4% govt.; 19.9% trade/trans./util.; 10% mfg.; 15.2% ed./health; 15.2% prof./bus. serv.; 9.5% leisure/hosp.; 6.4% finance; 3.4% constr./mining/log.; 1.7% info.; 4.4% other serv. **Unemployment:** 8.9%. **Per cap. pers. income:** $44,815. **New private housing:** 13,797 units/$2.6 bil. **Broadband Internet:** 83.5%. **Commercial banks:** 538; deposits: $369.8 bil. **Savings institutions:** 85; deposits: $22.1 bil. **Lottery:** total sales: $2.7 bil; profit: $708.5 mil.

Federal govt. Fed. civ. employees: 48,745; **avg. salary:** $77,244. **Notable fed. facilities:** Great Lakes Naval Station; Fermi Natl. Accelerator Lab; Argonne Natl. Lab; Scott AFB; Rock Island Arsenal.

Energy. Electricity use/cost: 770 kWh, $90.80.

State data. Motto: State sovereignty, national union. **Flower:** Native violet. **Bird:** Cardinal. **Tree:** White oak. **Song:** "Illinois." **Entered union:** Dec. 3, 1818; rank: 21st. **State fair** at Springfield, mid-Aug.; at DuQuoin, late Aug.-Sept.

History. The region has been inhabited for at least 10,000 years; seminomadic Algonquian peoples, including the Peoria, Illinois, Kaskaskia, and Tamaroa, lived there at the time of European contact. Fur traders were the first Europeans in Illinois, followed shortly by Louis Jolliet and Jacques Marquette, 1673, and René-Robert Cavelier, sieur de La Salle, 1680, who built a fort near present-day Peoria. French priests established the first permanent settlements at Cahokia, near present-day St. Louis, 1699, and Kaskaskia, 1703. France ceded the area to Britain, 1763, and in 1778, American Gen. George Rogers Clark took Kaskaskia from the British without a shot. Illinois became a separate territory, 1809, and a state, 1818. Defeat of Native American tribes in the Black Hawk War, 1832, and canal, rail, and road construction brought rapid change. Mormon settlers at Nauvoo, 1839, met with hostility, and a Carthage mob killed Mormon leader Joseph Smith and his brother, 1844. The Great Chicago Fire, 1871, destroyed the city's downtown. Illinois became a center for the labor movement, leading to bitter conflicts such as the Haymarket riot, 1886, and Pullman strike, 1894. Social reformer Jane Addams founded Hull House, 1889, to aid immigrants and the poor. During 1900-70, as manufacturing expanded, many African Americans arrived from the southern U.S. Chicago police violently suppressed antiwar protests at the 1968 Democratic National Convention. Dennis Hastert was the longest serving Republican Speaker of the House, 1999-2007. Barack Obama, elected in 2004, was only the fifth African American to serve in the U.S. Senate; he became the 44th U.S. president in 2009. Political corruption and criminality have plagued the state for decades; since 1960, five former governors have been charged with criminal offenses.

Tourist attractions. Art Institute of Chicago, Field Museum of Natural History, Shedd Aquarium, Millennium Park, Navy Pier, in Chicago; Illinois State Museum, Abraham Lincoln Presidential Library and Museum, in Springfield; Cahokia Mounds State Historic Site, Collinsville; Starved Rock State Park; Crab Orchard Natl. Wildlife Refuge; Forts Kaskaskia, de Chartres, Massac; Shawnee Natl. Forest; Dickson Mounds Museum, Lewistown.

Famous Illinoisans. Jane Addams, Saul Bellow, John Belushi, Jack Benny, Ray Bradbury, Gwendolyn Brooks, St. Frances Xavier Cabrini, Al Capone, Hillary Rodham Clinton, Clarence Darrow, John Deere, Stephen A. Douglas, Katherine Dunham, Wyatt Earp, Roger Ebert, James T. Farrell, Marshall Field, Harrison Ford, Betty Friedan, Benny Goodman, Ulysses S. Grant, Dennis Hastert, Hugh Hefner, Ernest Hemingway, Charlton Heston, Jennifer Hudson, Henry J. Hyde, Abraham Lincoln, Vachel Lindsay, David Mamet, Edgar Lee Masters, Oscar Mayer, Cyrus McCormick, Eliot Ness, Bob Newhart, Michelle Obama, Ronald Reagan, Shonda Rhimes, Donald Rumsfeld, Carl Sandburg, Shel Silverstein, Adlai E. Stevenson, James Watson, Frank Lloyd Wright, Philip K. Wrigley.

Tourist information. Illinois Bureau of Tourism, 100 W. Randolph St., Ste. 3-400, Chicago, IL 60601; 1-800-2CONNECT; www.enjoyillinois.com

Website. www.illinois.gov

Indiana (IN)
Hoosier State

People. Population: 6,537,334; rank: 16. **Pop. change** (2010-12): 0.8%. **Pop. density:** 182.5 per sq mi. **Racial distribution:** 86.6% white; 9.4% black; 1.8% Asian; 0.4% Amer. Ind.; 0.1% Hawaiian/Pacific Islander; two or more races, 1.8%. **Hispanic pop.:** 6.3%.

Geography. Total area: 36,420 sq mi; rank: 38. **Land area:** 35,826 sq mi; rank: 38. **Acres forested:** 4.9 mil. **Location:** East North Central state; Lake Michigan on N border. **Climate:** 4 distinct seasons with temperate climate. **Topography:** hilly southern region; fertile rolling plains of central region; flat, heavily glaciated N; dunes along Lake Michigan shore. **Capital:** Indianapolis. **Chief airport:** Indianapolis.

Economy. Chief industries: manufacturing, services, agriculture, government, wholesale and retail trade, transportation and public utilities. **Chief manuf. goods:** motor vehicles & parts, iron & steel mills, pharmaceuticals, petroleum, plastics, medical equip., printing. **Chief crops:** corn, soybeans, greenhouse & nursery, wheat, hay, tomatoes, watermelons, apples. **Livestock:** 34.28 mil chickens (excl. broilers), 810,000 cattle/calves, 55,000 sheep/lambs, 270,000 hogs/pigs. **Nonfuel minerals:** $838 mil; stone (crushed), cement (portland), lime, sand and gravel (construction), cement (masonry). **Chief ports:** Burns Harbor-Portage, Mt. Vernon, Jeffersonville. **Gross state product:** $298.6 bil. **Sales tax:** 7.0%. **Employment distrib.:** 14.7% govt.; 19.5% trade/trans./util.; 16.5% mfg.; 14.9% ed./health; 10.4% prof./bus. serv.; 10.3% leisure/hosp.; 4.5% finance; 4.4% constr./mining/log.; 1.2% info.; 3.7% other serv. **Unemployment:** 8.4%. **Per cap. pers. income:** $36,902. **New private housing:** 13,781 units/$2.3 bil. **Broadband Internet:** 78.5%. **Commercial banks:** 140; deposits: $95.1 bil. **Savings institutions:** 40; deposits: $7 bil. **Lottery:** total sales: $855.6 mil; profit: $210.8 mil.

Federal govt. Fed. civ. employees: 24,660; **avg. salary:** $67,478. **Notable fed. facilities:** Nav. Surface Warfare Ctr., Crane Div.; Grissom Air Reserve Base.

Energy. Electricity use/cost: 1,030 kWh, $103.54.

State data. Motto: Crossroads of America. **Flower:** Peony. **Bird:** Cardinal. **Tree:** Tulip poplar. **Song:** "On the Banks of the Wabash, Far Away." **Entered union:** Dec. 11, 1816; rank: 19th. **State fair** at Indianapolis, early to mid-Aug.

History. When the Europeans arrived, Miami, Potawatomi, Kickapoo, Piankashaw, Wea, and Shawnee peoples inhabited the region. René-Robert Cavelier, sieur de La Salle visited the present South Bend area, 1679 and 1681. The first French fort was built near present-day Lafayette, 1717. A French trading post was established, 1731-32, at Vincennes. France ceded the area to Britain, 1763. During the American Revolution, American Gen. George Rogers Clark captured Vincennes, 1778, and defeated British forces, 1779. Indiana became a territory, 1800, and a state, 1816. The Miami were beaten, 1794, at Fallen Timbers, and Gen. William H. Harrison defeated Tecumseh's Indian confederation, 1811, at Tippecanoe. Manufacturing grew rapidly after the Civil War. U.S. Steel founded Gary, 1906. An automotive test track was the site of the first Indianapolis 500 race, 1911. The auto industry remains key to the state economy; in 2008, Honda opened a $550-mil plant near Greensburg. Heavy rain in June 2008 flooded southwest and central Indiana.

Tourist attractions. Lincoln Boyhood Natl. Memorial, Lincoln City; George Rogers Clark Natl. Historical Park, Vincennes; Tippecanoe Battlefield Museum and Park, Battle Ground; Benjamin Harrison Presidential Site, Indianapolis Motor Speedway and Hall of Fame Museum, Indianapolis Museum of Art, in Indianapolis; Indiana Dunes Natl. Lakeshore, Chesterton; College Football Hall of Fame, Studebaker Natl. Museum, in South Bend; Hoosier Natl. Forest.

Famous "Hoosiers." Larry Bird, Ambrose Burnside, Meg Cabot, Hoagy Carmichael, Jim Davis, James Dean, Eugene V. Debs, John Dillinger, Theodore Dreiser, Paul Dresser, Jeff Gordon, Benjamin Harrison, Gil Hodges, Michael Jackson, David Letterman, Carole Lombard, Marjorie Main, John Mellencamp, Jane Pauley, Cole Porter, Gene Stratton Porter, Ernie Pyle, Dan Quayle, James Whitcomb Riley, Oscar Robertson, Red Skelton, Tony Stewart, Booth Tarkington, Kurt Vonnegut, Lew Wallace, Ryan White, Wendell L. Willkie, Wilbur Wright.

Tourist information. Indiana Office of Tourism Development, 1 North Capital, Ste. 600, Indianapolis, IN 46204; 1-800-677-9800; www.visitindiana.com
Website. www.in.gov

Iowa (IA)
Hawkeye State

People. Population: 3,074,186; rank: 30. **Pop. change** (2010-12): 0.9%. **Pop. density:** 55.0 per sq mi. **Racial distribution:** 92.8% white; 3.2% black; 2.0% Asian; 0.5% Amer. Ind.; 0.1% Hawaiian/Pacific Islander; two or more races, 1.6%. **Hispanic pop.:** 5.3%.
Geography. Total area: 56,273 sq mi; rank: 26. **Land area:** 55,857 sq mi; rank: 23. **Acres forested:** 3.0 mil. **Location:** West North Central state bordered by Mississippi R. on the E, Missouri R. on the W. **Climate:** humid, continental. **Topography:** watershed from NW to SE; soil especially rich and land level in the N central counties. **Capital:** Des Moines. **Chief airport:** Des Moines.
Economy. Chief industries: agriculture, communications, construction, finance, insurance, trade, services, manufacturing. **Chief manuf. goods:** machinery, vegetable oils, animal slaughtering & processing, laundry equip., plastics, motor vehicles & parts. **Chief crops:** corn, soybeans, hay, greenhouse & nursery, oats. **Livestock:** 64.85 mil chickens (excl. broilers), 3.85 mil cattle/calves, 175,000 sheep/lambs, 1.03 mil hogs/pigs. **Nonfuel minerals:** $731 mil; stone (crushed), cement (portland), sand and gravel (construction), sand and gravel (industrial), lime. **Gross state product:** $152.4 bil. **Sales tax:** 6.0%. **Employment distrib.:** 16.9% govt.; 20.1% trade/trans./util.; 14% mfg.; 14.6% ed./health; 8.6% prof./bus. serv.; 9.1% leisure/hosp.; 6.8% finance; 4.6% constr./mining/log.; 1.7% info.; 3.7% other serv. **Unemployment:** 5.2%. **Per cap. pers. income:** $42,126. **New private housing:** 9,501 units/$1.6 bil. **Broadband Internet:** 76%. **Commercial banks:** 350; deposits: $69.5 bil. **Savings institutions:** 12; deposits: $3.3 bil. **Lottery:** total sales: $310.9 mil; profit: $78.7 mil.
Federal govt. Fed. civ. employees: 9,077; **avg. salary:** $64,982. **Notable fed. facilities:** Ames Lab; Natl. Animal Disease Ctr.
Energy. Electricity use/cost: 898 kWh, $93.94.
State data. Motto: Our liberties we prize, and our rights we will maintain. **Flower:** Wild rose. **Bird:** Eastern goldfinch. **Tree:** Oak. **Song:** "The Song of Iowa." **Entered union:** Dec. 28, 1846; rank: 29th. **State fair** at Des Moines, mid-Aug.
History. Early inhabitants were Mound Builders who dwelt on Iowa's fertile plains. Later, Iowa and Yankton Sioux lived in the area. The first Europeans, Jacques Marquette and Louis Jolliet, gave France its claim to the area, 1673. In 1762, France ceded the region to Spain, but Napoleon took it back, 1800. It became part of the U.S. through the Louisiana Purchase, 1803. Native American Sauk and Fox tribes moved into the area but relinquished their land in defeat, after the 1832 uprising led by Sauk chieftain Black Hawk. Iowa became a territory in 1838, and entered as a free state, 1846, strongly supporting the Union. Fertile land lured farmers from eastern states, 1850-1900 and the population rose rapidly. Growth slowed in the 20th cent., as farming became mechanized. Surging demand for ethanol fuel from Iowa corn contributed more than $2.6 bil to the state economy in 2005. Severe flooding in eastern Iowa in June 2008 caused billions of dollars in damages and forced the evacuation of thousands of residents.
Tourist attractions. Des Moines Art Ctr., Iowa State Fairgrounds, Iowa State Capitol, in Des Moines; Natl. Czech & Slovak Museum & Library, Cedar Rapids; Herbert Hoover Natl. Historic Site, Presidential Library and Museum, in West Branch; Effigy Mounds Natl. Monument, Marquette; Amana Colonies; Figge Art Museum, Davenport; Living History Farms, Urbandale; Adventureland, Altoona; Boone & Scenic Valley Railroad and Museum; riverboat cruises and casino gambling, Mississippi and Missouri Rivers; Iowa Great Lakes, Okoboji; American Gothic House, Eldon; *Field of Dreams* movie site, Dyersville; Natl. Mississippi River Museum & Aquarium, Dubuque.
Famous Iowans. Tom Arnold, Johnny Carson, William F. "Buffalo Bill" Cody, Mamie Dowd Eisenhower, Michael Emerson, Bob Feller, George Gallup, Susan Glaspell, James Norman Hall, Herbert Hoover, Shawn Johnson, Ashton Kutcher, Ann Landers, Cloris Leachman, Glenn Miller, Lillian Russell, Billy Sunday, James A. Van Allen, Abigail Van Buren, Carl Van

Vechten, Henry Wallace, Kurt Warner, John Wayne, Meredith Willson, Elijah Wood, Grant Wood.
Tourist information. Iowa Tourism Office, Iowa Dept. of Economic Development, 200 E. Grand Ave., Des Moines, IA 50309; 1-888-472-6035; www.traveliowa.com
Website. www.iowa.gov

Kansas (KS)
Sunflower State

People. Population: 2,885,905; rank: 33. **Pop. change** (2010-12): 1.1%. **Pop. density:** 35.3 per sq mi. **Racial distribution:** 87.2% white; 6.2% black; 2.6% Asian; 1.2% Amer. Ind.; 0.1% Hawaiian/Pacific Islander; two or more races, 2.7%. **Hispanic pop.:** 11.0%.
Geography. Total area: 82,278 sq mi; rank: 15. **Land area:** 81,759 sq mi; rank: 13. **Acres forested:** 2.5 mil. **Location:** West North Central state, with Missouri R. on E. **Climate:** temperate but continental, with great extremes between summer and winter. **Topography:** hilly Osage Plains in the E; central region level prairie and hills; high plains in the W. **Capital:** Topeka. **Chief airport:** Wichita.
Economy. Chief industries: manufacturing, finance, insurance, real estate, services. **Chief manuf. goods:** animal slaughtering, aerospace, petroleum, plastics, machinery, navigational instruments, printing. **Chief crops:** wheat, corn, soybeans, hay, sorghum, sunflowers, cotton, potatoes. **Livestock:** 5.85 mil cattle/calves, 65,000 sheep/lambs, 170,000 hogs/pigs. **Nonfuel minerals:** $1.2 bil; helium (Grade-A), stone (crushed), salt, cement (portland), helium (crude). **Chief port:** Kansas City. **Gross state product:** $139.0 bil. **Sales tax:** 6.3%. **Employment distrib.:** 19.1% govt.; 18.6% trade/trans./util.; 12% mfg.; 13.6% ed./health; 11.7% prof./bus. serv.; 9% leisure/hosp.; 5.5% finance; 4.7% constr./mining/log.; 2.1% info.; 3.8% other serv. **Unemployment:** 5.7%. **Per cap. pers. income:** $41,835. **New private housing:** 6,252 units/$1.1 bil. **Broadband Internet:** 80.8%. **Commercial banks:** 334; deposits: $56 bil. **Savings institutions:** 14; deposits: $6.9 bil. **Lottery:** total sales: $246.1 mil; profit: $72.0 mil.
Federal govt. Fed. civ. employees: 17,418; **avg. salary:** $66,235. **Notable fed. facilities:** Ft. Riley; Leavenworth Fed. Pen.; McConnell AFB; Colmery-O'Neal VA Medical Ctr; Dwight D. Eisenhower VA Medical Ctr.
Energy. Electricity use/cost: 983 kWh, $104.70.
State data. Motto: Ad Astra per Aspera (To the stars through difficulties). **Flower:** Native sunflower. **Bird:** Western meadowlark. **Tree:** Cottonwood. **Song:** "Home on the Range." **Entered union:** Jan. 29, 1861; rank: 34th. **State fair** at Hutchinson, begins Fri. after Labor Day.
History. Wichita, Pawnee, Kansa, and Osage peoples lived in the area when Francisco de Coronado explored it in 1541. These Native Americans—hunters who also farmed—were joined on the Plains by the nomadic Cheyenne, Arapaho, Comanche, and Kiowa about 1800. France claimed the region, 1682, ceded its claim to Spain, 1762, then regained control, 1800, before selling it to the U.S. in the Louisiana Purchase, 1803. After 1830, thousands of Native Americans were removed from more eastern states to Kansas. Organized as a territory, 1854, the area witnessed violent clashes between pro- and antislavery settlers and became known as "Bleeding Kansas." It entered the Union as a free state, 1861. After the Civil War, rail construction and huge cattle drives from Texas turned Abilene and Dodge City into cowboy capitals. Russian Mennonite immigrants brought a new strain of winter wheat, 1874, transforming Kansas agriculture. Carry Nation launched her anti-saloon crusade in the 1890s. Part of the Dust Bowl, the state experienced drought and depression in the 1930s. Topeka was the focus of the famous *Brown v. Board of Education* decision, 1954, that led to desegregation of U.S. public schools. Bob Dole represented Kansas in the U.S. Senate (1969-96) but failed in several efforts to win higher office.
Tourist attractions. Eisenhower Presidential Library and Museum, Abilene; Natl. Agricultural Ctr. and Hall of Fame, Bonner Springs; Boot Hill Museum, Dodge City; Old Cowtown Museum, Wichita; Ft. Scott and Ft. Larned Natl. Historic Sites; Kansas Cosmosphere and Space Ctr., Hutchinson; U.S. Cavalry Museum, Ft. Riley; Tallgrass Prairie Natl. Preserve, Strong City; Kansas Speedway, Kansas City.
Famous Kansans. Kirstie Alley, Roscoe "Fatty" Arbuckle, Ed Asner, John Brown, Walter P. Chrysler, Glenn Cunningham, John Steuart Curry, Robert Joseph "Bob" Dole, Amelia

Earhart, Dwight D. Eisenhower, Melissa Etheridge, Ron Evans, Georgia Neese Clark Gray, Maurice Greene, James Butler "Wild Bill" Hickok, Cyrus K. Holliday, Dennis Hopper, William Inge, Don Johnson, Walter Johnson, Nancy Landon Kassebaum, Buster Keaton, Emmett Kelly, Alfred M. "Alf" Landon, Hattie McDaniel, Oscar Micheaux, Carry Nation, Charlie Parker, Gordon Parks, Jim Ryun, Barry Sanders, Vivian Vance, William Allen White, Jess Willard.

Tourist information. Kansas Dept. of Commerce, Travel and Tourism Div., 1000 SW Jackson St., Ste. 100, Topeka, KS 66612; (785) 296-2009; www.travelks.com

Website. www.kansas.gov

Kentucky (KY)
Bluegrass State

People. Population: 4,380,415; rank: 26. **Pop. change** (2010-12): 0.9%. **Pop. density:** 110.9 per sq mi. **Racial distribution:** 88.6% white; 8.1% black; 1.3% Asian; 0.3% Amer. Ind.; 0.1% Hawaiian/Pacific Islander; two or more races, 1.6%. **Hispanic pop.:** 3.2%.

Geography. Total area: 40,408 sq mi; rank: 37. **Land area:** 39,486 sq mi; rank: 37. **Acres forested:** 12.5 mil. **Location:** East South Central state, bordered on N by Illinois, Indiana, Ohio; on E by West Virginia and Virginia; on S by Tennessee; on W by Missouri. **Climate:** moderate, with plentiful rainfall. **Topography:** mountainous in E; rounded hills of the Knobs region in the N; Bluegrass region in heart of state; wooded rocky hillsides of the Pennyroyal Plateau; Western Coal Field; the fertile Jackson Purchase region in the SW. **Capital:** Frankfort. **Chief airports:** Greater Cincinnati, Lexington, Louisville.

Economy. Chief industries: manufacturing, services, finance, insurance and real estate, retail trade, public utilities. **Chief manuf. goods:** motor vehicles & parts, aluminum, basic chemicals, plastics, iron & steel, rubber, printing. **Chief crops:** hay, corn, soybeans, tobacco, wheat. **Livestock:** 6.21 mil chickens (excl. broilers), 309.5 mil broilers, 2.24 mil cattle/calves, 43,000 sheep/lambs. **Nonfuel minerals:** $786 mil; stone (crushed), lime, cement (portland), sand and gravel (construction), clays (common). **Chief ports:** Louisville, Hickman-Fulton County. **Gross state product:** $173.5 bil. **Sales tax:** 6.0%. **Employment distrib.:** 18.4% govt.; 20.4% trade/trans./util.; 12.3% mfg.; 14% ed./health; 10.6% prof./bus. serv.; 10% leisure/hosp.; 4.8% finance; 4.5% constr./mining/log.; 1.4% info.; 3.7% other serv. **Unemployment:** 8.2%. **Per cap. pers. income:** $35,041. **New private housing:** 9,725 units/$1.2 bil. **Broadband Internet:** 85.2%. **Commercial banks:** 200; deposits: $68.7 bil. **Savings institutions:** 21; deposits: $2.2 bil. **Lottery:** total sales: $823.6 mil; profit: $216.4 mil.

Federal govt. Fed. civ. employees: 26,140; **avg. salary:** $61,154. **Notable fed. facilities:** U.S. Bullion Depository, Ft. Knox; Ft. Campbell; Fed. Medical Ctr., Lexington; Army Corps of Engineers, Louisville District.

Energy. Electricity use/cost: 1,175 kWh, $108.16.

State data. Motto: United we stand, divided we fall. **Flower:** Goldenrod. **Bird:** Cardinal. **Tree:** Tulip poplar. **Song:** "My Old Kentucky Home." **Entered union:** June 1, 1792; rank: 15th. **State fair** at Louisville, mid-Aug.

History. Paleo-Indians first arrived about 14,000 years ago. Much later, Shawnee, Wyandot, Delaware, and Cherokee peoples also used the area mostly for hunting. Explored by Thomas Walker and Christopher Gist, 1750-51, Kentucky was the first area W of the Alleghenies settled by American pioneers. The first permanent settlement was Harrodsburg, 1774. Daniel Boone blazed the Wilderness Trail through the Cumberland Gap and founded Ft. Boonesborough, 1775. Clashes with Native Americans were frequent, 1774-94. Virginia dropped its claims to the region, and Kentucky became a state, 1792. Tobacco growing, horse breeding, coal mining, and bourbon whiskey making were major industries in the 19th cent. A slave state, Kentucky tried to stay neutral in the Civil War, but then opted for the Union; many Kentuckians sided with the Confederacy. The U.S. gold depository at Ft. Knox opened, 1937. Prior to the 2008 economic downturn, auto manufacturing had grown in recent decades. An ice storm in southwestern Kentucky in Jan. 2009 killed 14 and caused severe power outages.

Tourist attractions. Churchill Downs (Kentucky Derby), Louisville Slugger Museum and Factory, in Louisville; Land Between the Lakes Natl. Recreation Area (Kentucky and Barkley Lakes); Mammoth Cave Natl. Park (world's longest known cave system); Abraham Lincoln Birthplace Natl. Historical Park, Hodgenville; My Old Kentucky Home State Park, Bardstown; Cumberland Gap Natl. Historical Park, Middlesboro; Kentucky Horse Park, Lexington; Shaker Village of Pleasant Hill, Harrodsburg; Natl. Corvette Museum, Bowling Green.

Famous Kentuckians. Muhammad Ali, Alben W. Barkley, Ned Beatty, Louis D. Brandeis, John C. Breckinridge, Kit Carson, Albert B. "Happy" Chandler, Henry Clay, George Clooney, Rosemary Clooney, Jefferson Davis, D. W. Griffith, "Casey" Jones, Jennifer Lawrence, Abraham Lincoln, Mary Todd Lincoln, Thomas Hunt Morgan, Carry Nation, Colonel Harland Sanders, Diane Sawyer, Jesse Stuart, Zachary Taylor, Hunter S. Thompson, Robert Penn Warren, Whitney M. Young Jr.

Tourist information. Kentucky Dept. of Travel, Capital Plaza Tower, 22nd Fl., 500 Mero St., Frankfort, KY 40601; 1-800-225-8747; www.kentuckytourism.com

Website. www.kentucky.gov

Louisiana (LA)
Pelican State

People. Population: 4,601,893; rank: 25. **Pop. change** (2010-12): 1.5%. **Pop. density:** 106.5 per sq mi. **Racial distribution:** 63.7% white; 32.4% black; 1.7% Asian; 0.7% Amer. Ind.; 0.1% Hawaiian/Pacific Islander; two or more races, 1.4%. **Hispanic pop.:** 4.5%.

Geography. Total area: 52,378 sq mi; rank: 31. **Land area:** 43,204 sq mi; rank: 33. **Acres forested:** 14.9 mil. **Location:** West South Central state on the Gulf Coast. **Climate:** subtropical, affected by continental weather patterns. **Topography:** lowlands of marshes and Mississippi R. floodplain; Red R. Valley lowlands; upland hills in the Florida Parishes; avg. elevation, 100 ft. **Capital:** Baton Rouge. **Chief airport:** Metairie.

Economy. Chief industries: wholesale and retail trade, tourism, manufacturing, construction, transportation, communication, public utilities, finance, insurance, real estate, mining. **Chief manuf. goods:** petroleum, chemicals, plastics material & resin, pesticides & fertilizers, cleaning prods., paper & paperboard, ships, structural metals. **Chief crops:** sugarcane, cotton, rice, soybeans, corn, sweet potatoes. **Livestock:** 2.68 mil chickens (excl. broilers), 780,00 cattle/calves. **Nonfuel minerals:** $492 mil; salt, sand and gravel (construction), stone (crushed), sand and gravel (industrial), lime. **Commercial fishing:** $331.2 mil. **Chief ports:** New Orleans, Baton Rouge, Lake Charles, Port of S. Louisiana (La Place), Shreveport, Plaquemine, St. Bernard, Alexandria. **Gross state product:** $243.3 bil. **Sales tax:** 4.0%. **Employment distrib.:** 17.8% govt.; 19.7% trade/trans./util.; 7.3% mfg.; 14.6% ed./health; 10.5% prof./bus. serv.; 11% leisure/hosp.; 4.8% finance; 9.8% constr./mining/log.; 1.4% info.; 3.2% other serv. **Unemployment:** 6.4%. **Per cap. pers. income:** $39,413. **New private housing:** 13,018 units/$2.2 bil. **Broadband Internet:** 84.2%. **Commercial banks:** 135; deposits: $84.3 bil. **Savings institutions:** 23; deposits: $4.5 bil. **Lottery:** total sales: $429.6 mil; profit: $156.9 mil.

Federal govt. Fed. civ. employees: 21,063; **avg. salary:** $67,105. **Notable federal facilities:** Ft. Polk (Joint Readiness Training Ctr.); Barksdale AFB; Strategic Petroleum Reserve, Michoud Assembly Facility, USDA Southern Regional Research Ctr., New Orleans NAS JRB.

Energy. Electricity use/cost: 1,348 kWh, $120.84.

State data. Motto: Union, justice, and confidence. **Flower:** Magnolia. **Bird:** Eastern brown pelican. **Tree:** Cypress. **Song:** "Give Me Louisiana." **Entered union:** Apr. 30, 1812; rank: 18th. **State fair** at Shreveport, late Oct.-early Nov.

History. Caddo, Tunica, Choctaw, Chitimacha, and Chawash peoples lived in the region at the time of European contact. Spanish explorers in the early 16th cent. reached the mouth of the Mississippi. René-Robert Cavelier, sieur de La Salle, 1682, claimed the region for France. Early French and Spanish settlers were the ancestors of Louisiana Creoles. Cajuns descended from the Acadians, French settlers expelled by the British from Nova Scotia, Canada, in 1755. France ceded the Louisiana region to Spain, 1762, took it back, 1800, and sold it to the U.S., 1803, in the Louisiana Purchase. Admitted as a state in 1812, Louisiana witnessed the Battle of New Orleans, 1815. Cotton and sugar plantations relied on

black slaves, who made up 47% of the population in 1860, on the eve of the Civil War. Louisiana seceded, 1861, and was readmitted, 1868. Jazz was born in New Orleans in the early 20th cent. As governor (1928-32), Huey Long pushed populist programs. Many tropical storms and floods have battered Louisiana, including Hurricane Katrina and subsequent flooding, 2005, which devastated New Orleans. The offshore oil and gas industry developed after World War II. An oil rig explosion of the state's Gulf coast spilled millions of barrels of oil into the gulf, damaging coastal wetlands and many of the state's marine-dependent industries in 2010.

Tourist attractions. Mardi Gras, French Quarter, Bourbon Street, in New Orleans; Jean Lafitte Natl. Historical Park and Preserve; Longfellow-Evangeline State Historic Site, St. Martinville; Kent Plantation House, Alexandria; Oak Alley Plantation, Vacherie; Hodges Gardens State Park, Florien; USS *Kidd* Veterans Memorial, Baton Rouge.

Famous Louisianans. Louis Armstrong, Pierre Beauregard, Judah P. Benjamin, Braxton Bragg, Kate Chopin, Harry Connick Jr., Ellen DeGeneres, Fats Domino, George "Buddy" Guy, Lillian Hellman, Grace King, Jerry Lee Lewis, Bob Livingston, Huey Long, Eli Manning, Peyton Manning, Wynton Marsalis, Tim McGraw, Leonidas K. Polk, Anne Rice, Bill Russell, Henry Miller Shreve, Britney Spears, Madam C. J. Walker (Sarah Breedlove), Edward Douglass White Jr.

Tourist information. Louisiana Office of Tourism, P.O. Box 94291, Baton Rouge, LA 70804-9291; 1-800-677-4082; www.louisianatravel.com

Website. www.louisiana.gov

Maine (ME)
Pine Tree State

People. Population: 1,329,192; rank: 41. **Pop. change** (2010-12): 0.1%. **Pop. density:** 43.1 per sq mi. **Racial distribution:** 95.3% white; 1.3% black; 1.1% Asian; 0.7% Amer. Ind.; <0.05% Hawaiian/Pacific Islander; two or more races, 1.5%. **Hispanic pop.:** 1.4%.

Geography. Total area: 35,380 sq mi; rank: 39. **Land area:** 30,843 sq mi; rank: 39. **Acres forested:** 17.6 mil. **Location:** New England state at northeastern tip of U.S. **Climate:** southern interior and coastal influenced by air masses from the S and W; northern clime harsher, avg. over 100 in. snow in winter. **Topography:** Appalachian Mts. extend through state; western borders have rugged terrain; long sand beaches on southern coast; northern coast mainly rocky promontories, peninsulas, fjords. **Capital:** Augusta. **Chief airport:** Portland.

Economy. Chief industries: manufacturing, agriculture, fishing, services, trade, government, finance, insurance, real estate, construction. **Chief manuf. goods:** paper, ships & boats, cardboard, frozen/canned fruits & vegetables, plastics, baked goods. **Chief crops:** potatoes, greenhouse & nursery, wild blueberries, apples, hay, maple syrup. **Livestock:** 3.54 mil chickens (excl. broilers), 85,000 cattle/calves. **Nonfuel minerals:** $133 mil; sand and gravel (construction), cement (portland), stone (crushed), stone (dimension), cement (masonry). **Commercial fishing:** $448.5 mil. **Chief ports:** Searsport, Portland, Eastport. **Gross state product:** $53.7 bil. **Sales tax:** 5.0%. **Employment distrib.:** 17.2% govt.; 19.3% trade/trans./util.; 8.4% mfg.; 20% ed./health; 9.8% prof./bus. serv.; 10.5% leisure/hosp.; 5.2% finance; 4.8% constr./mining/log.; 1.3% info.; 3.3% other serv. **Unemployment:** 7.3%. **Per cap. pers. income:** $39,481. **New private housing:** 3,001 units/$499.4 mil. **Broadband Internet:** 80.4%. **Commercial banks:** 12; deposits: $23.6 bil. **Savings institutions:** 21; deposits: $10 bil. **Lottery:** total sales: $228.3 mil; profit: $54.3 mil.

Federal govt. Fed. civ. employees: 10,861; **avg. salary:** $66,234. **Notable fed. facilities:** Portsmouth Naval Shipyard.

Energy. Electricity use/cost: 521 kWh, $80.09.

State data. Motto: Dirigo (I direct). **Flower:** White pine cone and tassel. **Bird:** Black-capped chickadee. **Tree:** Eastern white pine. **Song:** "State of Maine Song." **Entered union:** Mar. 15, 1820; rank: 23rd. **State fair** at Bangor, late July-early Aug.; at Skowhegan, mid-Aug.

History. Paleo-Indians arrived about 11,500 years ago. Maine was inhabited by Algonquian peoples including the Abnaki, Penobscot, and Passamaquoddy at the time of European contact. French settled, 1604, at the St. Croix R., English, c. 1607, on the Kennebec; both settlements failed. A royal charter, 1691, made Maine part of Massachusetts. Maine broke off, 1819, and became a separate state, 1820.

Drawing on vast forest resources, the pulp and paper industry developed after the Civil War. Bath Iron Works began building U.S. Navy vessels and other ships in the 1890s. Mail-order and retail giant L.L. Bean was founded, 1912. Women have fared well in state politics: Margaret Chase Smith became the first woman to serve in both houses of Congress (House, 1940-49; Senate, 1949-73), and Olympia Snowe and Susan Collins represented Maine in the Senate since the mid-1990s (Snowe retired in Jan. 2013).

Tourist attractions. Acadia Natl. Park, Bar Harbor, on Mt. Desert Island; Old Orchard Beach; Old Port historic waterfront, Victoria Mansion, Portland; Portland Head Light, Cape Elizabeth; Maine Maritime Museum, Bath; Baxter State Park; L.L. Bean flagship store and outlet shopping, Freeport.

Famous "Down Easters." Leon Leonwood (L. L.) Bean, James G. Blaine, Patrick Dempsey, Hannibal Hamlin, Sarah Orne Jewett, Stephen King, Henry Wadsworth Longfellow, Sir Hiram and Hudson Maxim, Edna St. Vincent Millay, George J. Mitchell, Edmund Muskie, Judd Nelson, Edwin Arlington Robinson, Joan Benoit Samuelson, Liv Tyler, Kate Douglas Wiggin, Ben Ames Williams.

Tourist information. Maine Office of Tourism, 59 State House Station, Augusta, ME 04333; 1-888-624-6345; www.visitmaine.com

Website. www.maine.gov

Maryland (MD)
Old Line State, Free State

People. Population: 5,884,563; rank: 19. **Pop. change** (2010-12): 1.9%. **Pop. density:** 606.2 per sq mi. **Racial distribution:** 60.8% white; 30% black; 6.0% Asian; 0.5% Amer. Ind.; 0.1% Hawaiian/Pacific Islander; two or more races, 2.5%. **Hispanic pop.:** 8.7%.

Geography. Total area: 12,406 sq mi; rank: 42. **Land area:** 9,707 sq mi; rank: 42. **Acres forested:** 2.5 mil. **Location:** South Atlantic state stretching from the ocean to the Allegheny Mts. **Climate:** continental in the W; humid subtropical in the E. **Topography:** coastal plain on Eastern Shore separated by Chesapeake Bay from coastal plain, Piedmont Plateau, and the Blue Ridge. **Capital:** Annapolis. **Chief airport:** Glen Burnie.

Economy. Chief industries: manufacturing, biotechnology and information technology, services, tourism. **Chief manuf. goods:** navigational instruments, pharmaceutical & medicine, broadcasting equip., plastics, printing, milk & ice cream. **Chief crops:** greenhouse & nursery, corn, soybeans, wheat, hay, tomatoes, watermelons, barley, potatoes, apples. **Livestock:** 3.22 mil chickens (excl. broilers), 304 mil broilers, 192,000 cattle/calves. **Nonfuel minerals:** $289 mil; cement (portland), stone (crushed), sand and gravel (construction), cement (masonry), stone (dimension). **Commercial fishing:** $77.9 mil. **Chief port:** Baltimore. **Gross state product:** $317.7 bil. **Sales tax:** 6.0%. **Employment distrib.:** 19.7% govt.; 17.3% trade/trans./util.; 4.1% mfg.; 16.2% ed./health; 16.2% prof./bus. serv.; 9.7% leisure/hosp.; 5.5% finance; 5.7% constr./mining/log.; 1.5% info.; 4.2% other serv. **Unemployment:** 6.8%. **Per cap. pers. income:** $51,971. **New private housing:** 15,217 units/$2.4 bil. **Broadband Internet:** 77.5%. **Commercial banks:** 85; deposits: $114.3 bil. **Savings institutions:** 38; deposits: $6.5 bil. **Lottery:** total sales: $2.0 bil; profit: $683.1 mil.

Federal govt. Fed. civ. employees: 135,052; **avg. salary:** $96,282. **Notable fed. facilities:** U.S. Naval Academy; Beltsville Agriculture Res. Ctr.; Ft. Meade; Aberdeen Proving Ground; Andrews AFB; Naval Air Sys. Command; Goddard Space Flight Ctr.; Natl. Inst. of Health; Natl. Inst. of Standards & Technology; Food & Drug Admin.; Bureau of the Census; Natl. Naval Med. Ctr., Bethesda; Natl. Marine Fisheries Serv.; Natl. Oceanic and Atmospheric Admin.

Energy. Electricity use/cost: 1,030 kWh, $137.17.

State data. Motto: Fatti Maschii, Parole Femine (Manly deeds, womanly words). **Flower:** Black-eyed Susan. **Bird:** Baltimore oriole. **Tree:** White oak. **Song:** "Maryland, My Maryland." **Seventh** of the original 13 states to ratify the U.S. Constitution, Apr. 28, 1788. **State fair** at Timonium, late Aug.-early Sept.

History. Europeans encountered Algonquian-speaking Nanticoke and Piscataway and Iroquois-speaking Susquehannock when they first visited the area. Italian navigator Verrazano reached the Chesapeake region in the early

16th cent. English Capt. John Smith explored and mapped the area, 1608. William Claiborne set up a trading post on Kent Island in Chesapeake Bay, 1631. King Charles I granted land to Cecilius Calvert, Lord Baltimore, 1632; Calvert's brother Leonard, with about 200 settlers, founded St. Marys, 1634. During the Revolutionary War, Baltimore (1776-77) and Annapolis (1783-84) served as temporary capitals of the U.S. In the War of 1812, when a British fleet tried to take Ft. McHenry, Marylander Francis Scott Key wrote "The Star-Spangled Banner," 1814. Born into slavery at Tuckahoe in 1818, Frederick Douglass became a leading abolitionist. Although a slaveholding state, Maryland stayed in the Union during the Civil War and was the site of the battle of Antietam, 1862. Gov. Spiro Agnew elected U.S. vice pres. 1968, 1972; pleaded no contest to tax evasion and resigned 1973. Israeli and Egyptian leaders reached a historic peace accord at the Camp David presidential retreat, 1978. A major effort is under way to clean up pollution in the Chesapeake Bay watershed.

Tourist attractions. Ocean City; Ft. McHenry—the defense of which inspired Francis Scott Key to write "The Star-Spangled Banner," Pimlico Race Course (Preakness Stakes), Edgar Allan Poe House and Museum, Oriole Park at Camden Yards, Natl. Aquarium, Inner Harbor, in Baltimore; Antietam Natl. Battlefield, Sharpsburg; South Mountain State Battlefield, Middletown; U.S. Naval Academy, Maryland State House (oldest in continuous legislative use in U.S.), in Annapolis; Natl. Cryptologic Museum, Ft. Meade.

Famous Marylanders. John Astin, Benjamin Banneker, Tom Clancy, Frederick Douglass, Matthew Henson, Francis Scott Key, H. L. Mencken, Kweisi Mfume, Ogden Nash, Charles Willson Peale, Michael Phelps, William Pinkney, Edgar Allan Poe, Cal Ripken Jr., Babe Ruth, Upton Sinclair, Roger B. Taney, Harriet Tubman, John Waters, Montel Williams.

Tourist information. Maryland Office of Tourism Development, 401 E. Pratt St., 14th Fl., Baltimore, MD 21202; 1-866-639-3526; www.visitmaryland.org

Website. www.maryland.gov

Massachusetts (MA)
Bay State, Old Colony

People. Population: 6,646,144; rank: 14. **Pop. change** (2010-12): 1.5%. **Pop. density:** 852.1 per sq mi. **Racial distribution:** 83.7% white; 7.9% black; 5.8% Asian; 0.5% Amer. Ind.; 0.1% Hawaiian/Pacific Islander; two or more races, 2.0%. **Hispanic pop.:** 10.1%.

Geography. Total area: 10,554 sq mi; rank: 44. **Land area:** 7,800 sq mi; rank: 45. **Acres forested:** 3.0 mil. **Location:** New England state along Atlantic seaboard. **Climate:** temperate, with colder, drier clime in western region. **Topography:** jagged indented coast from Rhode Island around Cape Cod; flat land yields to stony upland pastures near central region and gentle hilly country in W; except in W, land is rocky, sandy, and not fertile. **Capital:** Boston. **Chief airport:** Boston.

Economy. Chief industries: services, trade, manufacturing. **Chief manuf. goods:** electronics & instruments, pharmaceuticals, telecom. & broadcasting equip., plastics, medical equip., printing. **Chief crops:** greenhouse & nursery, cranberries, tomatoes, sweet corn, apples, hay, tobacco. **Livestock:** 142,000 chickens (excl. broilers), 39,000 cattle/calves. **Nonfuel minerals:** $209 mil; stone (crushed), sand and gravel (construction), stone (dimension), lime, clays (common). **Commercial fishing:** $618.2 mil. **Chief ports:** Boston, Fall River. **Gross state product:** $403.8 bil. **Sales tax:** 6.25%. **Employment distrib.:** 13.5% govt.; 16.6% trade/trans./util.; 7.5% mfg.; 21.1% ed./health; 15.2% prof./bus. serv.; 10% leisure/hosp.; 6.1% finance; 3.6% constr./mining/log.; 2.7% info.; 3.7% other serv. **Unemployment:** 6.7%. **Per cap. pers. income:** $54,687. **New private housing:** 11,111 units/$2.4 bil. **Broadband Internet:** 76.8%. **Commercial banks:** 63; deposits: $208.5 bil. **Savings institutions:** 122; deposits: $63 bil. **Lottery:** total sales: $4.7 bil; profit: $833.9 mil.

Federal govt. Fed. civ. employees: 28,804; **avg. salary:** $78,534. **Notable fed. facilities:** Thomas P. O'Neill Jr. Fed. Bldg.; J.W. McCormack Bldg.; JFK Fed. Bldg.; Hanscom AFB; Army Natick Soldier Systems Ctr.

Energy. Electricity use/cost: 633 kWh, $92.92.

State data. Motto: Ense Petit Placidam Sub Libertate Quietem (By the sword we seek peace, but peace only under liberty). **Flower:** Mayflower. **Bird:** Black-capped chickadee. **Tree:** American elm. **Song:** "All Hail to Massachusetts." **Sixth**

of the original 13 states to ratify Constitution, Feb. 6, 1788. **State fair** at West Springfield, mid to late-Sept.

History. Early inhabitants were Algonquian peoples: Nauset, Wampanoag, Massachuset, Pennacook, Nipmuc, and Pocumtuc. Pilgrims settled in Plymouth, 1620, giving thanks for their survival with the first Thanksgiving Day, 1621. About 20,000 new settlers arrived, 1630-40. Colonist-Native American relations deteriorated, leading to King Philip's War, 1675-76, which the colonists won. Witch trials at Salem, 1692, led to the execution of 20 people. Demonstrations against British restrictions set off the Boston Massacre, 1770, and the Boston Tea Party, 1773. The first bloodshed of American Revolution was at Lexington, 1775. After statehood, Massachusetts prospered from shipbuilding, seafaring, and the making of textiles, shoes, and metal goods, while artists, writers, and social reformers flourished. The controversial Sacco-Vanzetti case, 1920-27, ended with the execution of two Italian immigrants on murder and robbery charges. After World War II, old industries declined, knowledge-intensive enterprises thrived, and the Kennedys became a dominant political family. The state's highest court ruled, 2003, that same-sex couples could legally marry. Two bombs exploded Apr. 15, 2013, near the finish line of the Boston Marathon, killing three and injuring more than 250.

Tourist attractions. Provincetown art colony; Cape Cod; Plymouth Rock, Plimoth Plantation, Mayflower II, in Plymouth; Freedom Trail, Museum of Fine Arts, New England Aquarium, Faneuil Hall, Boston Harbor Isls. Natl. Recreation Area, Boston Public Garden, in Boston; Tanglewood, Hancock Shaker Village, Berkshire Scenic Railway Museum, Norman Rockwell Museum, in the Berkshires region; Peabody Essex Museum, House of the Seven Gables, in Salem; Old Sturbridge Village; Historic Deerfield; Walden Pond, Louisa May Alcott's Orchard House, in Concord; Naismith Memorial Basketball Hall of Fame, Springfield.

Famous "Bay Staters." John Adams, John Quincy Adams, Samuel Adams, Louisa May Alcott, Horatio Alger, Susan B. Anthony, Crispus Attucks, Clara Barton, Michael Bloomberg, George H. W. Bush, Steve Carell, John Cheever, E. E. Cummings, Bette Davis, Emily Dickinson, Charles Eliot, Ralph Waldo Emerson, William Lloyd Garrison, Edward Everett Hale, John Hancock, Nathaniel Hawthorne, Oliver Wendell Holmes Jr., Winslow Homer, Elias Howe, John F. Kennedy, Jack Kerouac, John Kerry, Emeril Lagasse, Jack Lemmon, James Russell Lowell, Cotton Mather, Maria Mitchell, Samuel F. B. Morse, Conan O'Brien, Paul Revere, Norman Rockwell, Dr. Seuss (Theodor Seuss Geisel), Henry David Thoreau, Barbara Walters, James Abbott McNeil Whistler, John Greenleaf Whittier.

Tourist information. Massachusetts Office of Travel & Tourism, 10 Park Plz., Ste. 4510, Boston, MA 02116; 1-800-227-MASS; www.massvacation.com

Website. www.mass.gov

Michigan (MI)
Great Lakes State, Wolverine State

People. Population: 9,883,360; rank: 9. **Pop. change** (2010-12): <0.05%. **Pop. density:** 174.8 per sq mi. **Racial distribution:** 80.1% white; 14.3% black; 2.6% Asian; 0.7% Amer. Ind.; <0.05% Hawaiian/Pacific Islander; two or more races, 2.2%. **Hispanic pop.:** 4.6%.

Geography. Total area: 96,714 sq mi; rank: 11. **Land area:** 56,539 sq mi; rank: 22. **Acres forested:** 20.3 mil. **Location:** East North Central state bordering on 4 of the 5 Great Lakes, divided into an Upper and Lower Peninsula by the Straits of Mackinac, which link Lakes Michigan and Huron. **Climate:** well-defined seasons tempered by the Great Lakes. **Topography:** low rolling hills give way to northern tableland of hilly belts in Lower Peninsula; Upper Peninsula is level in the E with swampy areas; western region is higher and more rugged. **Capital:** Lansing. **Chief airports:** Detroit, Grand Rapids.

Economy. Chief industries: manufacturing, services, tourism, agriculture, forestry/lumber. **Chief manuf. goods:** motor vehicles & parts, plastics, metalworking machinery, non-wood office furniture, fabricated metals. **Chief crops:** greenhouse & nursery, soybeans, corn, wheat, sugar beets, apples, blueberries, potatoes, dry beans, cherries, hay, cucumbers, tomatoes, grapes. **Livestock:** 15.15 mil chickens (excl. broilers), 1.12 mil cattle/calves, 82,000 sheep/lambs, 110,000 hogs/pigs. **Nonfuel minerals:** $2.2 bil; iron ore (usable shipped),

cement (portland), sand and gravel (construction), salt, stone (crushed). **Commercial fishing:** $9.3 mil. **Chief ports:** Detroit, Escanaba, Calcite, Port Inland, Muskegon, Port Huron. **Gross state product:** $400.5 bil. **Sales tax:** 6.0%. **Employment distrib.:** 14.9% govt.; 18% trade/trans./util.; 13.5% mfg.; 15.6% ed./health; 14.5% prof./bus. serv.; 10% leisure/hosp.; 4.8% finance; 3.4% constr./mining/log.; 1.3% info.; 4.1% other serv. **Unemployment:** 9.1%. **Per cap. pers. income:** $37,497. **New private housing:** 11,692 units/$2.3 bil. **Broadband Internet:** 75.2%. **Commercial banks:** 142; deposits: $154.5 bil. **Savings institutions:** 18; deposits: $12.2 bil. **Lottery:** total sales: $2.4 bil; profit: $770.0 mil.

Federal govt. Fed. civ. employees: 30,166; **avg. salary:** $76,456. **Notable fed. facilities:** Detroit Arsenal (Army TACOM Life Cycle Mgmt.); DLA Logistics Info. Service; Selfridge Air Natl. Guard Base; Hart-Dole-Inouye Fed. Ctr.

Energy. Electricity use/cost: 683 kWh, $90.63.

State data. Motto: Si Quaeris Peninsulam Amoenam, Circumspice (If you seek a pleasant peninsula, look about you). **Flower:** Apple blossom. **Bird:** Robin. **Tree:** White pine. **Song:** "Michigan, My Michigan." **Entered union:** Jan. 26, 1837; rank: 26th. **State fair** at Novi, late Aug.-early Sept.

History. Hunting and fishing peoples lived in the region as early as 11,000 years ago. Ojibwa, Ottawa, Miami, Potawatomi, and Huron inhabited the area at the time of European contact. French fur traders and missionaries arrived in the 17th cent. and established a settlement at Sault Ste. Marie, 1668. British took over, 1763, and crushed a Native American uprising led by Ottawa chieftain Pontiac. Treaty of Paris ceded the area to U.S., 1783, but British remained until 1796. Michigan was organized as a territory, 1805. The British seized Ft. Mackinac and Detroit, 1812, but the U.S. regained control, 1814. The opening of the Erie Canal, 1825, and new land laws and Native American cessions led the way for a flood of settlers. Strongly antislavery, Michigan became a state, 1837, and supplied 90,000 soldiers to the Union army in the Civil War. In the 20th cent., automobile manufacturing was the backbone of the economy. Henry Ford launched the Model T car, 1908; the United Auto Workers union was founded, 1935. Motown music flourished in Detroit in the 1960s, but riots in 1967 dealt the city a heavy blow. As the auto industry faltered, Michigan lost more than 20% of its automotive-related jobs between 2002 and 2007. In 2009, the federal government loaned billions of dollars to GM and Chrysler to keep them solvent. Citing massive budget shortfalls, Detroit city officials filed for bankruptcy in July 2013.

Tourist attractions. Henry Ford Museum and Greenfield Village, Dearborn; Frederik Meijer Gardens and Sculpture Park, Grand Rapids; Tahquamenon Falls (of Longfellow's poem *Song of Hiawatha*); De Zwaan windmill, Tulip Time Festival, in Holland; Soo Locks (bet. Lakes Superior and Huron), Sault Ste. Marie; Air Zoo, Portage; Mackinac Island; Belle Isle Park, Detroit Institute of Arts, Charles H. Wright Museum of African-American History, Motown Historical Museum, in Detroit.

Famous Michiganders. Ralph Bunche, Paul de Kruif, Thomas Edison, Eminem (Marshall Mathers), Edna Ferber, Gerald R. Ford, Henry Ford, Aretha Franklin, Edgar Guest, Lee Iacocca, Magic Johnson, Casey Kasem, Will Kellogg, Ring Lardner, Elmore Leonard, Charles Lindbergh, Joe Louis, Madonna, Malcolm X, Terry McMillan, Michael Moore, Larry Page, Pontiac, Gilda Radner, Mitt Romney, Diana Ross, Tom Selleck, Sinbad (David Adkins), John Smoltz, Lily Tomlin, Serena Williams.

Tourist information. Michigan Economic Development Corp., 300 N. Washington Sq., Lansing, MI 48913; 1-888-784-7328; www.michigan.org

Website. www.michigan.gov

Minnesota (MN)

North Star State, Gopher State

People. Population: 5,379,139; rank: 21. **Pop. change** (2010-12): 1.4%. **Pop. density:** 67.6 per sq mi. **Racial distribution:** 86.5% white; 5.5% black; 4.4% Asian; 1.3% Amer. Ind.; 0.1% Hawaiian/Pacific Islander; two or more races, 2.2%. **Hispanic pop.:** 4.9%.

Geography. Total area: 86,936 sq mi; rank: 12. **Land area:** 79,627 sq mi; rank: 14. **Acres forested:** 17.4 mil. **Location:** West North Central state bounded on the E by Wisconsin and Lake Superior, on the N by Canada, on the W by the Dakotas, and on the S by Iowa. **Climate:** northern part of state lies in

the moist Great Lakes storm belt; the western border lies at the edge of the semiarid Great Plains. **Topography:** central hill and lake region covering approx. half the state; to the NE, rocky ridges and deep lakes; to the NW, flat plain; to the S, rolling plains and deep river valleys. **Capital:** St. Paul. **Chief airport:** Minneapolis.

Economy. Chief industries: agribusiness, forest products, mining, manufacturing, tourism. **Chief manuf. goods:** petroleum & asphalt, computers & electronics, milk & cheese, printing, animal slaughtering, paper & prod., medical equip. **Chief crops:** corn, soybeans, hay, sugar beets, wheat, potatoes, greenhouse & nursery, dry edible beans, green peas, sunflowers. **Livestock:** 13.11 mil chickens (excl. broilers), 45.5 mil broilers, 2.39 mil cattle/calves, 135,000 sheep/lambs, 580,000 hogs/pigs. **Nonfuel minerals:** $4.5 bil; iron ore (usable shipped), sand and gravel (industrial), sand and gravel (construction), stone (crushed), stone (dimension). **Commercial fishing:** $0.3 mil. **Chief ports:** Two Harbors, Silver Bay, Duluth, St. Paul. **Gross state product:** $294.7 bil. **Sales tax:** 6.875%. **Employment distrib.:** 15.2% govt.; 18.3% trade/trans./util.; 10.9% mfg.; 17.6% ed./health; 12.4% prof./bus. serv.; 9.3% leisure/hosp.; 6.4% finance; 3.8% constr./mining/log.; 2% info.; 4.2% other serv. **Unemployment:** 5.6%. **Per cap. pers. income:** $46,227. **New private housing:** 16,095 units/$3 bil. **Broadband Internet:** 79.1%. **Commercial banks:** 399; deposits: $191.9 bil. **Savings institutions:** 29; deposits: $9 bil. **Lottery:** total sales: $520.0 mil; profit: $123.7 mil.

Federal govt. Fed. civ. employees: 18,256; **avg. salary:** $71,961. **Notable fed. facilities:** Bishop Henry Whipple Fed. Bldg.; Minneapolis-St Paul Air Reserve Station.

Energy. Electricity use/cost: 813 kWh, $89.14.

State data. Motto: L'Etoile du Nord (The star of the north). **Flower:** Pink and white lady's-slipper. **Bird:** Common loon. **Tree:** Red pine. **Song:** "Hail! Minnesota." **Entered union:** May 11, 1858; rank: 32nd. **State fair** at St. Paul, late Aug.-early Sept.

History. Inhabited for at least 10,000 years, the region was home to Dakota Sioux when Europeans arrived. French fur traders Pierre Esprit Radisson and Médard Chouart, sieur des Groseilliers, explored in the mid-17th cent. In 1679, Daniel Greysolon, sieur Duluth, claimed the entire region for France. Ojibwa arrived in the 18th cent. and warred with the Sioux for over 100 years. Britain took the area east of the Mississippi, 1763. The U.S. took over that portion after the American Revolution and gained the western area, 1803, in the Louisiana Purchase. The U.S. built Ft. St. Anthony (now Ft. Snelling), 1819, and bought Native American lands, 1837, spurring an influx of settlers from the east. Minnesota became a territory, 1849, and a state, 1858. Sioux staged a bloody uprising, the Battle of Wood Lake, 1862, and were driven from the state. Railroad construction after the Civil War spurred the growth of the grain, timber, and iron mining industries. Opening of the St. Lawrence Seaway, 1959, aided the port of Duluth. Elected as a reformer, former wrestler Jesse Ventura served as governor, 1999-2003. Two-term Sen. Paul Wellstone, one of a long line of liberal Minnesota Democrats, died when his campaign plane crashed, 2002. The I-35W Mississippi River Bridge in Minneapolis collapsed, 2007, killing 13.

Tourist attractions. Minneapolis Institute of Arts, Walker Art Center, Minneapolis Sculpture Garden, Minnehaha Falls (in Longfellow's poem *Song of Hiawatha*), Guthrie Theater, in Minneapolis; Mall of America, Bloomington; Ordway Ctr. for the Performing Arts, Science Museum of Minnesota, in St. Paul; Voyageurs Natl. Park; Mayo Clinic, Rochester; North Shore (Lake Superior); Lake Minnetonka; Boundary Waters Canoe Area Wilderness; Superior Natl. Forest; Aerial Lift Bridge, Duluth.

Famous Minnesotans. Andrews Sisters, Warren E. Burger, Ethan and Joel Coen, Bob Dylan, F. Scott Fitzgerald, Al Franken, Judy Garland, Cass Gilbert, Hubert H. Humphrey, Garrison Keillor, Sister Elizabeth Kenny, Jessica Lange, Sinclair Lewis, Paul Manship, E. G. Marshall, William J. and Charles H. Mayo, Eugene McCarthy, Walter F. Mondale, Prince (Prince Rogers Nelson), Charles M. Schulz, Ann Sothern, Harold Stassen, Thorstein Veblen, Jesse Ventura, Lindsey Vonn, Paul Wellstone.

Tourist information. Explore Minnesota Tourism, Metro Square, 121 7th Pl. E., Ste. 100, St. Paul, MN 55101; 1-888-TOURISM; www.exploreminnesota.com

Website. www.minnesota.gov

Mississippi (MS)

Magnolia State

People. Population: 2,984,926; rank: 31. **Pop. change** (2010-12): 0.6%. **Pop. density:** 63.6 per sq mi. **Racial distribution:** 59.9% white; 37.4% black; 0.9% Asian; 0.6% Amer. Ind.; 0.1% Hawaiian/Pacific Islander; two or more races, 1.1%. **Hispanic pop.:** 2.9%.

Geography. Total area: 48,432 sq mi; rank: 32. **Land area:** 46,923 sq mi; rank: 31. **Acres forested:** 19.5 mil. **Location:** East South Central state bordered on the W by the Mississippi R., on the S by the Gulf of Mexico. **Climate:** semitropical, with abundant rainfall and long growing season. **Topography:** low, fertile delta between the Yazoo and Mississippi Rivers; loess bluffs stretch around delta border; sandy gulf coastal terraces followed by piney woods and prairie; rugged, high sandy hills in extreme NE followed by Prairie Black Belt, Pontotoc Ridge, and flatwoods into the N central highlands. **Capital:** Jackson. **Chief airport:** Jackson.

Economy. Chief industries: warehousing & distribution, services, manufacturing, government, wholesale and retail trade. **Chief manuf. goods:** petroleum, upholstered furniture, poultry processing, motor vehicle parts, plastics, ships & boats, chemicals. **Chief crops:** cotton, soybeans, rice, hay, corn, sweet potatoes. **Livestock:** 9.44 mil chickens (excl. broilers), 751.3 mil broilers, 910,000 cattle/calves. **Nonfuel minerals:** $196 mil; sand and gravel (construction), stone (crushed), clays (fuller's earth), clays (ball), clays (bentonite). **Commercial fishing:** $49.3 mil. **Chief ports:** Pascagoula, Vicksburg, Gulfport, Biloxi, Greenville. **Gross state product:** $101.5 bil. **Sales tax:** 7.0%. **Employment distrib.:** 22.2% govt.; 19.3% trade/trans./util.; 12% mfg.; 11.9% ed./health; 9.3% prof./bus. serv.; 11.4% leisure/hosp.; 4% finance; 5.5% constr./mining/log.; 1.1% info.; 3.3% other serv. **Unemployment:** 9.2%. **Per cap. pers. income:** $33,073. **New private housing:** 6,039 units/$836.5 mil. **Broadband Internet:** 65.3%. **Commercial banks:** 99; deposits: $46.0 bil. **Savings institutions:** 5; deposits $457 mil.

Federal govt. Fed. civ. employees: 18,863; **avg. salary:** $66,026. **Notable fed. facilities:** Keesler AFB; Meridian NAS, Columbus AFB; NASA Stennis Space Ctr.; Army Corps of Eng. Waterways Experiment Sta.; Naval Constr. Battalion Ctr., Gulfport.

Energy. Electricity use/cost: 1,287 kWh, $130.90.

State data. Motto: Virtute et Armis (By valor and arms). **Flower:** Magnolia. **Tree:** Mockingbird. **Tree:** Magnolia. **Song:** "Go, Mississippi!" **Entered union:** Dec. 10, 1817; rank: 20th. **State fair** at Jackson, begins first Wed. in Oct.

History. Choctaw, Chickasaw, and Natchez peoples were living in the region at the time of European contact. The Spaniard Hernando de Soto explored the area, 1540-41. René-Robert Cavelier, sieur de La Salle traced the Mississippi R. from Illinois to its mouth and claimed the entire Mississippi Valley for France, 1682. The first settlement was the French Ft. Maurepas, 1699, on Biloxi Bay. The region was ceded to Britain, 1763, and claimed by Spain, 1779-98, then became a U.S. territory, 1798, and a state, 1817. Slavery spread along with cotton plantations, and slaves made up 55% of the population, 1860. Mississippi seceded, 1861. In the Civil War, Union forces captured Vicksburg, 1863, and caused extensive damage elsewhere. Mississippi reentered the Union, 1870. For the next 100 years, resistance to desegregation and violence against blacks made the state a battleground for the African American civil rights movement. Hurricanes Camille, 1969, and Katrina, 2005, caused substantial damage to the Gulf Coast. Since the early 1990s, casino gambling has boosted the economy, but the state's poverty rate remained the highest in the nation in 2010.

Tourist attractions. Vicksburg Natl. Military Park and Cemetery; Natchez Trace Parkway; antebellum home tours in Natchez and other cities; Tupelo Natl. Battlefield, Elvis Presley Birthplace, in Tupelo; Smith Robertson Museum and Cultural Ctr., Mynelle Gardens, Eudora Welty House, in Jackson; Mardi Gras parades on Gulf Coast; Beauvoir (Jefferson Davis Home and Presidential Library), Biloxi; Gulf Islands Natl. Seashore; Delta Blues Museum, Clarksdale.

Famous Mississippians. Margaret Walker Alexander, Dana Andrews, Jimmy Buffett, Bo Diddley, Medgar Evers, William Faulkner, Brett Favre, Shelby Foote, Morgan Freeman, John Grisham, Fannie Lou Hamer, Jim Henson, Faith Hill, John Lee Hooker, Robert Johnson, James Earl Jones, B. B. King, L. Q. C. Lamar, Trent Lott, Gerald McRaney, Willie Morris, Walter Payton, Elvis Presley, Leontyne Price, Charley Pride, LeAnn Rimes, Robin Roberts, Muddy Waters, Eudora Welty, Tennessee Williams, Oprah Winfrey, Johnny Winter, Richard Wright, Tammy Wynette.

Tourist information. Mississippi Division of Tourism, P.O. Box 849, Jackson, MS 39205; 1-866-SEE-MISS; www.visitmississippi.org

Website. www.ms.gov

Missouri (MO)

Show Me State

People. Population: 6,021,988; rank: 18. **Pop. change** (2010-12): 0.6%. **Pop. density:** 87.6 per sq mi. **Racial distribution:** 83.9% white; 11.7% black; 1.8% Asian; 0.5% Amer. Ind.; 0.1% Hawaiian/Pacific Islander; two or more races, 2.0%. **Hispanic pop.:** 3.7%.

Geography. Total area: 69,707 sq mi; rank: 21. **Land area:** 68,742 sq mi; rank: 18. **Acres forested:** 15.5 mil. **Location:** West North Central state near the geographic center of the conterminous U.S.; bordered on the E by Mississippi R., on the NW by Missouri R. **Climate:** continental, susceptible to cold Canadian air; moist, warm gulf air; and drier SW air. **Topography:** rolling hills, open, fertile plains, and well-watered prairie N of the Missouri R.; S of the river, land is rough and hilly with deep, narrow valleys; alluvial plain in the SE; low elevation in the W. **Capital:** Jefferson City. **Chief airports:** Kansas City, St. Louis.

Economy. Chief industries: agriculture, manufacturing, aerospace, tourism. **Chief manuf. goods:** motor vehicles & parts, aerospace, pharmaceuticals, plastics, soap, animal slaughtering & processing, printing. **Chief crops:** soybeans, corn, hay, cotton & cottonseed, wheat, rice, sorghum. **Livestock:** 11.17 mil chickens (excl. broilers), 271.6 mil broilers, 3.65 mil cattle/calves, 75,000 sheep/lambs, 350,000 hogs/pigs. **Nonfuel minerals:** $2.6 bil; stone (crushed), cement (portland), lead, lime, sand and gravel (industrial). **Gross state product:** $258.8 bil. **Sales tax:** 4.225%. **Employment distrib.:** 16.5% govt.; 19.2% trade/trans./util.; 9.2% mfg.; 15.4% ed./health; 12.5% prof./bus. serv.; 10.8% leisure/hosp.; 6.1% finance; 4.2% constr./mining/log.; 2.1% info.; 4.2% other serv. **Unemployment:** 6.9%. **Per cap. pers. income:** $39,049. **New private housing:** 12,297 units/$1.9 bil. **Broadband Internet:** 86.6%. **Commercial banks:** 345; deposits: $121.6 bil. **Savings institutions:** 32; deposits $20.2 bil. **Lottery:** total sales: $1.1 bil; profit: $280.0 mil.

Federal govt. Fed. civ. employees: 38,794; **avg. salary:** $63,388. **Notable fed. facilities:** Federal Reserve banks; Ft. Leonard Wood; Jefferson Barracks Natl. Cem.; Natl. Personnel Records Ctr.; Whiteman AFB.

Energy. Electricity use/cost: 1,112 kWh, $108.39.

State data. Motto: Salus Populi Suprema Lex Esto (Let the welfare of the people be the supreme law). **Flower:** Hawthorn. **Bird:** Bluebird. **Tree:** Dogwood. **Song:** "Missouri Waltz." **Entered union:** Aug. 10, 1821; rank: 24th. **State fair** at Sedalia, mid-Aug.; at Bethany, late Aug.-early Sept.

History. In the 17th cent., when French explorers arrived, Algonquian Sauk, Fox, and Illinois and Siouan Osage, Missouri, Iowa, and Kansa peoples were living in the region; few remained by the 1830s. French hunters and lead miners made the first settlement c. 1735, at Ste. Genevieve. The territory was ceded to Spain by the French, 1762, then returned to France, 1800, and acquired by the U.S. in the Louisiana Purchase, 1803. Powerful earthquakes rocked New Madrid, 1811-12. Missouri became a territory, 1812, and entered the Union as a slave state, 1821. St. Louis became the gateway for pioneers heading West. Though Missouri stayed with the Union, pro- and antislavery forces battled there during the Civil War. In the late 19th cent. railroad building and the cattle trade made Kansas City a boomtown. The most notable Missourian of the 20th cent., Harry S. Truman, was U.S. president, 1945-53. The state, a political bellwether, voted for the winner in every presidential election from 1960 to 2004. In May 2011, a tornado in Joplin, MO, killed about 162.

Tourist attractions. Silver Dollar City, Branson; Mark Twain Boyhood Home and Museum, Hannibal; Pony Express Natl. Museum, St. Joseph; Harry S. Truman Library and Museum, Independence; Gateway Arch (part of Jefferson Natl. Expansion Memorial), Ulysses S. Grant Natl. Historic Site, St. Louis Zoo, in St. Louis; Worlds of Fun amusement park, Kansas

City; Lake of the Ozarks; Ozark Natl. Scenic Riverways; Natl. Churchill Museum, Fulton; State Capitol, Jefferson City; Wilson's Creek Natl. Battlefield; George Washington Carver Natl. Monument, Diamond; Bass Pro Shops Outdoor World, Springfield.

Famous Missourians. Maya Angelou, Robert Altman, John Ashcroft, Burt Bacharach, Josephine Baker, Scott Bakula, Thomas Hart Benton, Yogi Berra, Chuck Berry, George Caleb Bingham, Daniel Boone, Omar Bradley, William S. Burroughs, Kate Capshaw, Dale Carnegie, George Washington Carver, Bob Costas, Walter Cronkite, Sheryl Crow, Walt Disney, T. S. Eliot, Richard "Dick" Gephardt, John Goodman, Betty Grable, Jon Hamm, Edwin Hubble, Jesse James, Rush Limbaugh, Marianne Moore, Reinhold Niebuhr, J. C. Penney, John J. Pershing, Brad Pitt, Joseph Pulitzer, Ginger Rogers, Bess Truman, Harry S. Truman, Kathleen Turner, Tina Turner, Mark Twain, Dick Van Dyke, Tennessee Williams, Lanford Wilson, Shelley Winters, Jane Wyman.

Tourist information. Missouri Division of Tourism, P.O. Box 1055, Jefferson City, MO 65102; 1-800-519-2100; www.visitmo.com

Website. www.mo.gov

Montana (MT)
Treasure State

People. Population: 1,005,141; rank: 44. **Pop. change** (2010-12): 1.6%. **Pop. density:** 6.9 per sq mi. **Racial distribution:** 89.7% white; 0.6% black; 0.7% Asian; 6.5% Amer. Ind.; 0.1% Hawaiian/Pacific Islander; two or more races, 2.5%. **Hispanic pop.:** 3.1%.

Geography. Total area: 147,040 sq mi; rank: 4. **Land area:** 145,546 sq mi; rank: 4. **Acres forested:** 25.6 mil. **Location:** Mountain state bounded on the E by the Dakotas, on the S by Wyoming, on the SSW by Idaho, on the N by Canada. **Climate:** colder, continental climate with low humidity. **Topography:** Rocky Mts. in western third of state; eastern two-thirds gently rolling northern Great Plains. **Capital:** Helena.

Economy. Chief industries: agriculture, timber, mining, tourism, oil and gas. **Chief manuf. goods:** sawmills, softwood veneer & plywood, petroleum. **Chief crops:** wheat, barley, hay, sugar beets, potatoes, dry beans, flaxseed, cherries, corn, oats. **Livestock:** 550,000 chickens (excl. broilers), 2.6 mil cattle/calves, 235,000 sheep/lambs. **Nonfuel minerals:** $1.4 bil; copper, palladium metal, molybdenum concentrates, platinum metal, gold. **Gross state product:** $40.4 bil. **Sales tax:** none. **Employment distrib.:** 20.3% govt.; 19.9% trade/trans./util.; 3.9% mfg.; 15.4% ed./health; 9.6% prof./bus. serv.; 13.4% leisure/hosp.; 4.8% finance; 7.1% constr./mining/log.; 1.6% info.; 3.9% other serv. **Unemployment:** 6.0%. **Per cap. pers. income:** $37,370. **New private housing:** 2,736 units/$449.8 mil. **Broadband Internet:** 52.3%. **Commercial banks:** 69; deposits: $18.6 bil. **Savings institutions:** 3; deposits: $301 mil. **Lottery:** total sales: $52.6 mil; profit: $13.1 mil.

Federal govt. Fed. civ. employees: 10,116; **avg. salary:** $63,634. **Notable fed. facilities:** Malmstrom AFB and missile silos; Ft. Peck, Hungry Horse, Libby, Yellowtail, and other dams.

Energy. Electricity use/cost: 871 kWh, $84.97.

State data. Motto: Oro y Plata (Gold and silver). **Flower:** Bitterroot. **Bird:** Western meadowlark. **Tree:** Ponderosa pine. **Song:** "Montana." **Entered union:** Nov. 8, 1889; rank: 41st. **State fair** at Great Falls, late July-early Aug.

History. Paleo-Indian hunters reached the area over 12,000 years ago. Cheyenne, Blackfoot, Crow, Assiniboin, Salish (Flatheads), Kootenai, and Kalispel peoples lived in the region before Europeans arrived. French explorers visited the region, 1742. The U.S. acquired the area partly through the Louisiana Purchase, 1803, partly through the Lewis and Clark Expedition, 1804-06. Fur traders and missionaries established posts in the early 19th cent. Gold was discovered on Grasshopper Creek, 1862, and Montana Territory was established, 1864. Indian uprisings reached their peak with the defeat of Gen. George Custer at the Battle of Little Bighorn, 1876. Chief Joseph and the Nez Percé tribe surrendered here, 1877, after a long trek across the state. Mining activity and the coming of the Northern Pacific Railway, 1883, brought population growth. Montana became a state, 1889. Copper wealth from the Butte pits resulted in the turn of the century "War of Copper Kings" as feuding factions contended

for "the richest hill on earth." During the first half of the 20th cent., the Anaconda Copper firm wielded enormous political influence. Jeannette Rankin, a suffragist and pacifist, was the first woman elected to Congress, 1916. Mike Mansfield served 34 years in Congress and was Senate Democratic leader, 1961-77. An 18-year hunt for notorious "Unabomber" Theodore Kaczynski ended with his arrest, 1996, at his cabin near Lincoln.

Tourist attractions. Glacier and Yellowstone Natl. Parks; Museum of the Rockies, Bozeman; Museum of the Plains Indian, Blackfeet Reservation, in Browning; Custer Natl. Cemetery at Little Bighorn Battlefield Natl. Monument; Lewis and Clark Caverns State Park, Whitehall; Lewis and Clark Natl. Historic Trail Interpretive Ctr., Great Falls.

Famous Montanans. Dana Carvey, Gary Cooper, Marcus Daly, Chet Huntley, Phil Jackson, Will James, Myrna Loy, David Lynch, Mike Mansfield, Brent Musburger, Jeannette Rankin, Charles M. Russell, Lester Thurow.

Tourist information. Travel Montana, Dept. of Commerce, 301 S. Park Ave., P.O. Box 200533, Helena, MT 59601; 1-800-VISITMT; www.visitmt.com

Website. www.mt.gov

Nebraska (NE)
Cornhusker State

People. Population: 1,855,525; rank: 37. **Pop. change** (2010-12): 1.6%. **Pop. density:** 24.2 per sq mi. **Racial distribution:** 89.9% white; 4.8% black; 2.0% Asian; 1.3% Amer. Ind.; 0.1% Hawaiian/Pacific Islander; two or more races, 1.9%. **Hispanic pop.:** 9.7%.

Geography. Total area: 77,348 sq mi; rank: 16. **Land area:** 76,824 sq mi; rank: 15. **Acres forested:** 1.6 mil. **Location:** West North Central state with the Missouri R. for a border on NE and E. **Climate:** continental semiarid. **Topography:** till plains of the central lowland in the eastern third rises to the Great Plains and hill country of the N central and NW. **Capital:** Lincoln. **Chief airport:** Omaha.

Economy. Chief industries: agriculture, manufacturing. **Chief manuf. goods:** animal slaughtering, grain & oilseed, farm machinery, medical equip., motor vehicle parts, printing, structural metals. **Chief crops:** corn, sorghum, soybeans, hay, wheat, dry beans, oats, potatoes, sugar beets. **Livestock:** 11.33 mil chickens (excl. broilers), 6.3 mil cattle/calves, 80,000 sheep/lambs, 400,000 hogs/pigs. **Nonfuel minerals:** $335 mil; sand and gravel (construction), cement (portland), stone (crushed), sand and gravel (industrial), lime. **Gross state product:** $99.6 bil. **Sales tax:** 5.5%. **Employment distrib.:** 17.7% govt.; 20.5% trade/trans./util.; 9.9% mfg.; 14.6% ed./health; 11% prof./bus. serv.; 8.9% leisure/hosp.; 7.4% finance; 4.5% constr./mining/log.; 1.7% info.; 3.8% other serv. **Unemployment:** 3.9%. **Per cap. pers. income:** $43,143. **New private housing:** 6,116 units/$918.3 mil. **Broadband Internet:** 66.4%. **Commercial banks:** 217; deposits: $47.4 bil. **Savings institutions:** 12; deposits: $4.2 bil. **Lottery:** total sales: $150.6 mil; profit: $36.1 mil.

Federal govt. Fed. civ. employees: 10,059; **avg. salary:** $67,634. **Notable fed. facilities:** Offutt AFB.

Energy. Electricity use/cost: 1,029 kWh, $95.92.

State data. Motto: Equality before the law. **Flower:** Goldenrod. **Bird:** Western meadowlark. **Tree:** Cottonwood. **Song:** "Beautiful Nebraska." **Entered union:** Mar. 1, 1867; rank: 37th. **State fair** at Grand Island, late Aug.-early Sept.

History. When Europeans arrived, Pawnee, Ponca, Omaha, and Oto peoples lived in the region. Spanish and French explorers and fur traders visited the area prior to its acquisition in the Louisiana Purchase, 1803. Meriwether Lewis and William Clark passed through, 1804-06. The first permanent settlement was Bellevue, near Omaha, 1823. The 1834 Indian Intercourse Act declared Nebraska Indian country and excluded white settlement, but conflicts with settlers eventually forced Native Americans to move to reservations. Nebraska became a territory, 1854, and a state, 1867. Many Civil War veterans settled under free land terms of the 1862 Homestead Act; as agriculture grew, struggles followed between homesteaders and ranchers. Since the mid-1930s, Nebraska has been the only state with a unicameral legislature. A leader in agribusiness, Nebraska has also become a major telemarketing center. The "Oracle of Omaha," investor Warren Buffett, one of the world's

wealthiest men, announced in 2006 he would give most of his $44 bil fortune to charity.

Tourist attractions. Univ. of Nebraska State Museum at Morrill Hall, Nebraska State Capitol, in Lincoln; Stuhr Museum of the Prairie Pioneer, Grand Island; Boys Town; Omaha's Henry Doorly Zoo and Aquarium, Joslyn Art Museum, The Durham Museum, in Omaha; Ashfall Fossil Beds State Hist. Park, near Royal; Strategic Air and Space Museum, Ashland; Arbor Lodge State Historical Park, Nebraska City; Buffalo Bill Ranch State Historical Park, North Platte; Pioneer Village, Minden; Oregon Trail landmarks, incl. at Scotts Bluff Natl. Monument and Chimney Rock Natl. Historic Site; Great Platte River Road Archway, Museum of Nebraska Art, in Kearney.

Famous Nebraskans. Grover Cleveland Alexander, Fred Astaire, Marlon Brando, Charles W. Bryan, William Jennings Bryan, Warren Buffett, Johnny Carson, Willa Cather, Dick Cavett, Dick Cheney, Loren Eiseley, Father Edward J. Flanagan, Henry Fonda, Bob Gibson, Rollin Kirby, Harold Lloyd, Malcolm X, J. Sterling Morton, John G. Neihardt, Nick Nolte, George W. Norris, Tom Osborne, Roscoe Pound, Red Cloud, Mari Sandoz, Robert Taylor, Darryl F. Zanuck.

Tourist information. Nebraska Division of Travel and Tourism, 301 Centennial Mall S., Lincoln, NE 68508; 1-888-444-1867; www.visitnebraska.com

Website. www.nebraska.gov

Nevada (NV)
Sagebrush State, Battle Born State, Silver State

People. Population: 2,758,931; rank: 35. **Pop. change** (2010-12): 2.2%. **Pop. density:** 25.1 per sq mi. **Racial distribution:** 77.1% white; 8.9% black; 7.9% Asian; 1.6% Amer. Ind.; 0.7% Hawaiian/Pacific Islander; two or more races, 3.8%. **Hispanic pop.:** 27.3%.

Geography. Total area: 110,572 sq mi; rank: 7. **Land area:** 109,781 sq mi; rank: 7. **Acres forested:** 11.2 mil. **Location:** Mountain state bordered on N by Oregon and Idaho, on E by Utah, on SE by Arizona, and on SW and W by California. **Climate:** semiarid and arid. **Topography:** rugged N-S mountain ranges; highest elevation, Boundary Peak, 13,140 ft; southern area is within the Mojave Desert; lowest elevation, Colorado R., at southern tip of state, 479 ft. **Capital:** Carson City. **Chief airports:** Las Vegas, Reno.

Economy. Chief industries: gaming, tourism, mining, manufacturing, government, retailing, warehousing, trucking. **Chief manuf. goods:** gaming machines, cement & concrete, plastics, printing, architectural & structural metals, electricity instruments. **Chief crops:** hay, onions, potatoes, alfalfa, wheat, garlic, mint, barley. **Livestock:** 460,000 cattle/calves, 73,000 sheep/lambs. **Nonfuel minerals:** $11.2 bil; gold, copper, silver, lime, sand and gravel (construction). **Gross state product:** $133.6 bil. **Sales tax:** 6.85%. **Employment distrib.:** 13.4% govt.; 18.9% trade/trans./util.; 3.4% mfg.; 9.5% ed./health; 12.5% prof./bus. serv.; 27.8% leisure/hosp.; 4.7% finance; 5.8% constr./mining/log.; 1.1% info.; 2.9% other serv. **Unemployment:** 11.1%. **Per cap. pers. income:** $37,361. **New private housing:** 9,071 units/$1.3 bil. **Broadband Internet:** 84.8%. **Commercial banks:** 40; deposits: $48.1 bil. **Savings institutions:** 8; deposits: $64.8 bil.

Federal govt. Fed. civ. employees: 12,465; **avg. salary:** $66,348. **Notable fed. facilities:** Nevada Natl. Security Site; Hawthorne Army Depot; Creech AFB; Nellis AFB & Range Complex; Fallon NAS; Natl. Wild Horse & Burro Ctr. at Palomino Valley.

Energy. Electricity use/cost: 897 kWh, $104.10.

State data. Motto: All for our country. **Flower:** Sagebrush. **Bird:** Mountain bluebird. **Trees:** Single-leaf piñon and bristlecone pine. **Song:** "Home Means Nevada." **Entered union:** Oct. 31, 1864; rank: 36th. **State fair** at Las Vegas, mid-Sept.

History. Shoshone, Paiute, Bannock, and Washoe peoples lived in the area at the time of European contact. Nevada was first explored by Spaniards, 1776. In the 1820s, fur traders Peter Skene Ogden and Jedediah Smith separately explored the area. It was acquired by the U.S., 1848, at the end of the Mexican War. A trading post at Mormon Station, now Genoa, was established, 1850. Discovery of the Comstock Lode, rich in gold and silver, 1859, spurred a population boom. Nevada became a territory, 1861, and a state, 1864. Hoover Dam was built, 1931-36. With gambling legal since 1931, a surge in resort casino construction after World War II turned Las Vegas into one of the nation's most popular tourist destinations. An influx of Hispanics and Asians, attracted by service-industry and construction jobs, helped make Nevada the fastest-growing state in the U.S. during 1990-2005, and again in 2007. The recession in recent years has had an equally powerful effect. Nevada had the highest state unemployment and home foreclosure rates in 2011.

Tourist attractions. Legalized gambling, incl. at Lake Tahoe, Reno, Las Vegas, Laughlin, and Elko; Hoover Dam, Lake Mead Natl. Recreation Area, near Boulder City; Great Basin Natl. Park; Valley of Fire State Park; Red Rock Canyon Natl. Conservation Area; Las Vegas Strip, Fremont St., Natl. Atomic Testing Museum, Pinball Hall of Fame, Las Vegas Motor Speedway, in Las Vegas; Natl. Automobile Museum, Reno.

Famous Nevadans. Andre Agassi, Kyle Busch, Walter Van Tilburg Clark, George W. G. Ferris, Sarah Winnemucca Hopkins, Paul Laxalt, Dat So La Lee, John William Mackay, Anne Henrietta Martin, Pat McCarran, Key Pittman, William Morris Stewart.

Tourist information. Commission on Tourism, 401 N. Carson St., Carson City, NV 89701; 1-800-NEVADA-8; www.travelnevada.com

Website. www.nv.gov

New Hampshire (NH)
Granite State

People. Population: 1,320,718; rank: 42. **Pop. change** (2010-12): 0.3%. **Pop. density:** 147.5 per sq mi. **Racial distribution:** 94.4% white; 1.4% black; 2.4% Asian; 0.3% Amer. Ind.; <0.05% Hawaiian/Pacific Islander; two or more races, 1.5%. **Hispanic pop.:** 3.0%.

Geography. Total area: 9,349 sq mi; rank: 46. **Land area:** 8,953 sq mi; rank: 44. **Acres forested:** 4.8 mil. **Location:** New England state bounded on S by Massachusetts, on W by Vermont, on N by Canada, on E by Maine and the Atlantic Ocean. **Climate:** highly varied, due to its nearness to high mountains and ocean. **Topography:** low, rolling coast followed by countless hills and mountains rising out of a central plateau. **Capital:** Concord. **Chief airport:** Manchester.

Economy. Chief industries: tourism, manufacturing, agriculture, trade, mining. **Chief manuf. goods:** navigational instruments, circuit boards, electrical equip., fabricated metal, machinery, medical equip., plastics. **Chief crops:** greenhouse & nursery, apples, sweet corn, hay, Christmas trees, berries, maple syrup. **Livestock:** 33,000 cattle/calves. **Nonfuel minerals:** $157 mil; sand and gravel (construction), stone (crushed), stone (dimension), gemstones (natural). **Commercial fishing:** $23.2 mil. **Chief port:** Portsmouth. **Gross state product:** $64.7 bil. **Sales tax:** none. **Employment distrib.:** 14.6% govt.; 20.9% trade/trans./util.; 10.2% mfg.; 18.2% ed./health; 11% prof./bus. serv.; 10.3% leisure/hosp.; 5.5% finance; 3.9% constr./mining/log.; 1.8% info.; 3.5% other serv. **Unemployment:** 5.5%. **Per cap. pers. income:** $47,058. **New private housing:** 2,296 units/$425.7 mil. **Broadband Internet:** 69.9%. **Commercial banks:** 17; deposits: $21 bil. **Savings institutions:** 24; deposits: $7 bil. **Lottery:** total sales: $254.9 mil; profit: $66.8 mil.

Federal govt. Fed. civ. employees: 4,677; **avg. salary:** $81,538. **Notable fed. facilities:** Army Cold Regions Res. & Engineering Lab.

Energy. Electricity use/cost: 619 kWh, $102.28.

State data. Motto: Live free or die. **Flower:** Purple lilac. **Bird:** Purple finch. **Tree:** White birch. **Song:** "Old New Hampshire." **Ninth** of the original 13 states to ratify the Constitution, June 21, 1788. **State fair:** Hopkinton State Fair at Contoocook, late Aug.-early Sept.

History. The area has been inhabited for about 10,000 years. Algonquian-speaking peoples, including the Pennacook, lived in the region when the Europeans arrived. The first explorers to visit the area were England's Martin Pring, 1603, and France's Samuel de Champlain, 1605. The first settlement was Odiorne's Point (now port of Rye), 1623. Before the American Revolution, New Hampshire residents raided a British fort at Portsmouth, 1774, and drove the royal governor out, 1775. New Hampshire became the first colony to adopt its own constitution, 1776. After statehood, 1788, New Hampshire became a textile manufacturing center. The mill towns declined in the first half of the 20th cent., but tourism and high-tech industries, lured by low taxes, have revived the economy since the 1960s. A state law requires it to hold the first primary of the presidential campaign season.

Tourist attractions. Mt. Washington Cog Railway, Mt. Washington (highest peak in Northeast); Lake Winnipesaukee; Crawford, Franconia, Pinkham Notches (mountain passes), Flume Gorge, Cannon Mountain Aerial Tramway, in White Mountains region; Strawbery Banke Museum, Portsmouth; Canterbury Shaker Village; Saint-Gaudens Natl. Historic Site, Cornish; Mt. Monadnock; Santa's Village, Jefferson.

Famous New Hampshirites. Dan Brown, Salmon P. Chase, Ralph Adams Cram, Mary Baker Eddy, Daniel Chester French, Robert Frost, Horace Greeley, Sarah Josepha Buell Hale, John Irving, Seth Meyers, Bode Miller, Franklin Pierce, Augustus Saint-Gaudens, Adam Sandler, Alan B. Shepard Jr., Sarah Silverman, David H. Souter, Daniel Webster.

Tourist information. Division of Travel & Tourism Development, 172 Pembroke Rd., P.O. Box 1856; Concord, NH 03302; 1-800-FUN-IN-NH; www.visitnh.gov

Website. www.nh.gov

New Jersey (NJ)
Garden State

People. Population: 8,864,590; rank: 11. **Pop. change** (2010-12): 0.8%. **Pop. density:** 1,205.3 per sq mi. **Racial distribution:** 73.8% white; 14.7% black; 9.0% Asian; 0.6% Amer. Ind.; 0.1% Hawaiian/Pacific Islander; two or more races, 1.9%. **Hispanic pop.:** 18.5%.

Geography. Total area: 8,723 sq mi; rank: 47. **Land area:** 7,354 sq mi; rank: 46. **Acres forested:** 2.0 mil. **Location:** Middle Atlantic state bounded on N and E by New York and Atlantic Ocean, on S and W by Delaware and Pennsylvania. **Climate:** moderate, with marked difference between NW and SE extremities. **Topography:** Appalachian Valley in the NW also has highest elevation, High Pt., 1,801 ft; Appalachian Highlands, flat-topped NE-SW mountain ranges; Piedmont Plateau, low plains broken by high ridges (Palisades) rising 400-500 ft; Coastal Plain, covering three-fifths of state in SE, rises from sea level to gentle slopes. **Capital:** Trenton. **Chief airports:** Atlantic City, Newark.

Economy. Chief industries: pharmaceuticals, telecommunications, biotechnology, printing & publishing. **Chief manuf. goods:** petroleum, pharmaceuticals, toiletries, chemicals, plastics, printing, navigational instruments, medical equip., paper prod. **Chief crops:** greenhouse & nursery, blueberries, peaches, corn, hay, tomatoes, bell peppers, cranberries, soybeans, apples. **Livestock:** 31,000 cattle/calves. **Nonfuel minerals:** $292 mil; stone (crushed), sand and gravel (construction), sand and gravel (industrial), greensand marl, peat. **Commercial fishing:** $187.7 mil. **Chief ports:** Newark-Elizabeth, Camden. **Gross state product:** $508.0 bil. **Sales tax:** 7.0%. **Employment distrib.:** 15.9% govt.; 20.9% trade/trans./util.; 6.2% mfg.; 16.2% ed./health; 15.9% prof./bus. serv.; 9% leisure/hosp.; 6.3% finance; 3.4% constr./mining/log.; 1.9% info.; 4.3% other serv. **Unemployment:** 9.5%. **Per cap. pers. income:** $53,628. **New private housing:** 17,939 units/$2.4 bil. **Broadband Internet:** 73.6%. **Commercial banks:** 96; deposits $198.6 bil. **Savings institutions:** 66; deposits $69.9 bil. **Lottery:** total sales: $2.8 bil; profit: $950.0 mil.

Federal govt. Fed. civ. employees: 26,189; **avg. salary:** $82,943. **Notable fed. facilities:** Joint Base McGuire-Dix-Lakehurst; Picatinny Arsenal; FAA William J. Hughes Technical Ctr.

Energy. Electricity use/cost: 709 kWh, $115.04.

State data. Motto: Liberty and prosperity. **Flower:** Purple violet. **Bird:** Eastern goldfinch. **Tree:** Red oak. **Third of the** original 13 states to ratify the Constitution, Dec. 18, 1787. **State fair** at Augusta, early to mid-Aug.

History. The Lenni Lenape (Delaware) peoples lived in the region and had mostly peaceful relations with European colonists, who arrived after the explorers Giovanni da Verrazano, 1524, and Henry Hudson, 1609. The first permanent European settlement was Dutch, at Bergen (now Jersey City), 1660. When the British took New Netherland, 1664, the area between the Delaware and Hudson Rivers was given to Lord John Berkeley and Sir George Carteret. During the American Revolution, New Jersey was the scene of many major battles, including Trenton, 1776; Princeton, 1777; and Monmouth, 1778. New Jersey was the third state to ratify the Constitution, 1787, and the first to approve the Bill of Rights, 1789. In a duel at Weehawken, 1804, Vice Pres. Aaron Burr fatally shot Alexander Hamilton. Canal and railroad building

stimulated the growth of cities and industries in the 19th cent. The 20th cent. arrival of large numbers of African Americans, Italians, Irish, European Jews, Puerto Ricans, South Asians, and other groups made New Jersey one of the most diverse states in the U.S. Construction of resort casinos in Atlantic City from the late 1970s revitalized tourism. Gov. James McGreevey resigned, 2004, after acknowledging an extramarital affair with a man identified as his former homeland security adviser. An estimated 37 people in New Jersey were killed when Hurricane Sandy (by then downgraded to a tropical storm) made landfall Oct. 29-30, 2012.

Tourist attractions. 130 mi of beaches, boardwalks on the Jersey Shore at Atlantic City (with gambling), Seaside Heights, Ocean City, Wildwood; Grover Cleveland Birthplace, Caldwell; Cape May Historic District; Thomas Edison Natl. Historical Park, West Orange; Six Flags Great Adventure, Jackson; Liberty State Park, Liberty Science Ctr., in Jersey City; Pine Barrens wilderness; Princeton Univ., Princeton Battlefield State Park, in Princeton; Morristown Natl. Historical Park; Adventure Aquarium, Battleship *New Jersey*, Walt Whitman House, in Camden.

Famous New Jerseyans. Buzz Aldrin, Jason Alexander, Samuel Alito, Count Basie, Judy Blume, Jon Bon Jovi, Bill Bradley, Aaron Burr, Grover Cleveland, Stephen Crane, Danny DeVito, Thomas Edison, Albert Einstein, James Gandolfini, Allen Ginsberg, Alexander Hamilton, Ed Harris, Whitney Houston, Joyce Kilmer, Jack Nicholson, Shaquille O'Neal, Thomas Paine, Bill Parcells, Dorothy Parker, Joe Pesci, Molly Pitcher, Paul Robeson, Philip Roth, Antonin Scalia, Wally Schirra, H. Norman Schwarzkopf, Frank Sinatra, Bruce Springsteen, Martha Stewart, Meryl Streep, Dave Thomas, John Travolta, Walt Whitman, William Carlos Williams, Woodrow Wilson.

Tourist information. Dept. of State, Division of Travel and Tourism, P.O. Box 460, Trenton, NJ 08625; 1-800-VISITNJ; www.visitnj.org

Website. www.state.nj.us

New Mexico (NM)
Land of Enchantment

People. Population: 2,085,538; rank: 36. **Pop. change** (2010-12): 1.3%. **Pop. density:** 17.2 per sq mi. **Racial distribution:** 83.2% white; 2.4% black; 1.6% Asian; 10.2% Amer. Ind.; 0.2% Hawaiian/Pacific Islander; two or more races, 2.4%. **Hispanic pop.:** 47.0%.

Geography. Total area: 121,590 sq mi; rank: 5. **Land area:** 121,298 sq mi; rank: 5. **Acres forested:** 24.8 mil. **Location:** southwestern state bounded by Colorado on the N; Oklahoma, Texas, and Mexico on the E and S; and Arizona on the W. **Climate:** dry, with temperatures rising or falling 5°F with every 1,000 ft elevation. **Topography:** eastern third, Great Plains; central third, Rocky Mts. (85% of the state is over 4,000-ft elevation); western third, high plateau. **Capital:** Santa Fe. **Chief airport:** Albuquerque.

Economy. Chief industries: government, services, trade. **Chief manuf. goods:** semiconductors, medical equip., navigational/measuring/medical/control instruments, aircraft, chemicals, jewelry. **Chief crops:** hay, pecans, corn, greenhouse & nursery, chiles, onions, cotton, wheat, peanuts. **Livestock:** 1.34 mil cattle/calves, 100,000 sheep/lambs. **Nonfuel minerals:** $1.5 bil; copper, potash, sand and gravel (construction), stone (crushed), molybdenum concentrates. **Gross state product:** $80.6 bil. **Sales tax:** 5.125%. **Employment distrib.:** 24.1% govt.; 16.4% trade/trans./util.; 3.5% mfg.; 15.2% ed./health; 12% prof./bus. serv.; 11% leisure/hosp.; 4.2% finance; 8.2% constr./mining/log.; 1.8% info.; 3.5% other serv. **Unemployment:** 6.9%. **Per cap. pers. income:** $35,079. **New private housing:** 4,672 units/$758.6 mil. **Broadband Internet:** 74.2%. **Commercial banks:** 56; deposits: $24.7 bil. **Savings institutions:** 8; deposits: $1.4 bil. **Lottery:** total sales: $133.8 mil; profit: $41.3 mil.

Federal govt. Fed. civ. employees: 25,515; **avg. salary:** $68,862. **Notable fed. facilities:** Kirtland, Cannon, Holloman AF Bases; Los Alamos Natl. Lab; White Sands Missile Range; Natl. Solar Observatory; Natl. Radio Astronomy Observatory; Sandia Natl. Labs.

Energy. Electricity use/cost: 669 kWh, $73.57.

State data. Motto: Crescit Eundo (It grows as it goes). **Flower:** Yucca. **Bird:** Roadrunner. **Tree:** Piñon. **Songs:** "O, Fair New Mexico"; "Asi Es Nuevo Mexico." **Entered union:**

Jan. 6, 1912; rank: 47th. **State fair** at Albuquerque, mid-Sept.; at Las Cruces, early Oct.; at Roswell, early Oct.

History. Inhabited for more than 10,000 years, the region was home to Sandia, Clovis, Folsom, Mogollon, and Anasazi cultures, followed by the Pueblo people, Anasazi descendants; later, nomadic Navajo and Apache came. Franciscan Marcos de Niza and a former black slave, Estevanico, explored the area, 1539, seeking gold; Coronado followed, 1540. First settlements were near San Juan Pueblo, 1598, and at Santa Fe, 1610. Settlers alternately traded and fought with the Apache, Comanche, and Navajo. Trade on the Santa Fe Trail to Missouri started, 1821. After the Mexican War began, 1846, Gen. Stephen Kearny took Santa Fe without firing a shot, and declared New Mexico part of the U.S. All Hispanic New Mexicans and Pueblo became U.S. citizens by terms of the 1848 treaty ending the war. New Mexico became a territory, 1850, but did not attain statehood until 1912. Pancho Villa raided Columbus, 1916, and U.S. troops were sent to the area. The world's first atomic bomb was exploded at a test site near Alamogordo, 1945. An underground nuclear waste depository opened near Carlsbad, 1999. Spaceport America, a state-owned commercial spaceport, hosted its first test launch in 2006.

Tourist attractions. Carlsbad Caverns Natl. Park (with Lechuguilla Cave, among world's longest caves); Petroglyph Natl. Monument, Sandia Peak Tramway, in Albuquerque; New Mexico History Museum, Museum of Intl. Folk Art, in Santa Fe (oldest U.S. capital); White Sands Natl. Monument (world's largest gypsum dune field); Chaco Culture Natl. Historical Park; Acoma Pueblo, or Sky City, built atop a 367-ft mesa; Taos Art Colony, Taos Ski Valley; Elephant Butte Lake State Park; Shiprock volcanic remnant; Intl. UFO Museum and Research Ctr., Roswell.

Famous New Mexicans. Ben Abruzzo, Maxie Anderson, Jeff Bezos, William Bonney (Billy the Kid), Kit Carson, Bob Foster, Neil Patrick Harris, Tony Hillerman, Peter Hurd, Jean Baptiste Lamy, Nancy Lopez, Bill Mauldin, Georgia O'Keeffe, Bill Richardson, Kim Stanley, Al Unser, Bobby Unser.

Tourist information. New Mexico Dept. of Tourism, 491 Old Santa Fe Trl., Santa Fe, NM 87501; 1-800-733-6396; www.newmexico.com

Website. www.newmexico.gov

New York (NY)
Empire State

People. Population: 19,570,261; rank: 3. **Pop. change** (2010-12): 1.0%. **Pop. density:** 415.3 per sq mi. **Racial distribution:** 71.2% white; 17.5% black; 8.0% Asian; 1.0% Amer. Ind.; 0.1% Hawaiian/Pacific Islander; two or more races, 2.2%. **Hispanic pop.:** 18.2%.

Geography. Total area: 54,555 sq mi; rank: 27. **Land area:** 47,126 sq mi; rank: 30. **Acres forested:** 19.0 mil. **Location:** Middle Atlantic state, bordered by the New England states, Atlantic Ocean on E; New Jersey and Pennsylvania on S; Lakes Ontario and Erie on W; Canada on N. **Climate:** variable; the SE region moderated by the ocean. **Topography:** highest and most rugged mountains in the NE Adirondack upland; St. Lawrence-Champlain lowlands extend from Lake Ontario NE along the Canadian border; Hudson-Mohawk lowland follows rivers N and W, 10-30 mi wide; Atlantic coastal plain in the SE; Appalachian Highlands, covering half the state westward from the Hudson Valley, include the Catskill Mts., Finger Lakes; plateau of Erie-Ontario lowlands. **Capital:** Albany. **Chief airports:** Albany, Buffalo, Islip, New York (2), Rochester, Syracuse, White Plains.

Economy. Chief industries: manufacturing, finance, communications, tourism, transportation, services. **Chief manuf. goods:** pharmaceuticals, photographic chemicals, electronics, automotive parts, toiletries, printing, plastics, apparel. **Chief crops:** greenhouse & nursery, apples, corn, hay, cabbage, onions, soybeans, potatoes, snap beans, grapes, squash, pumpkins, tomatoes, wheat, cucumbers, green peas. **Livestock:** 6.06 mil chickens (excl. broilers), 1.4 mil cattle/calves, 70,000 sheep/lambs. **Nonfuel minerals:** $1.3 bil; stone (crushed), salt, sand and gravel (construction), cement (portland), wollastonite. **Commercial fishing:** $39.3 mil. **Chief ports:** New York, Buffalo, Albany. **Gross state product:** $1.2 tril. **Sales tax:** 4.0%. **Employment distrib.:** 16.4% govt.; 17.1% trade/trans./util.; 5% mfg.; 20.2% ed./health; 13.4% prof./bus. serv.; 9.4% leisure/hosp.; 7.6% finance;

3.6% constr./mining/log.; 2.9% info.; 4.3% other serv. **Unemployment:** 8.5%. **Per cap. pers. income:** $52,095. **New private housing:** 24,872 units/$3.8 bil. **Broadband Internet:** 76%. **Commercial banks:** 161; deposits: $969.3 bil. **Savings institutions:** 67; deposits: $74 bil. **Lottery:** total sales: $8.4 bil; profit: $2.9 bil.

Federal govt. Fed. civ. employees: 67,430; **avg. salary:** $74,801. **Notable fed. facilities:** Ft. Drum; West Point Military Academy; Merchant Marine Academy; NY Fed. Reserve; Griffis AFB (Research Lab), Rome; U.S. Army Watervliet Arsenal; Brookhaven Natl. Lab.; U.S. Mission to the United Nations.

Energy. Electricity use/cost: 611 kWh, $111.59.

State data. Motto: Excelsior (Ever upward). **Flower:** Rose. **Bird:** Bluebird. **Tree:** Sugar maple. **Song:** "I Love New York." **Eleventh** of the original 13 states to ratify the Constitution, July 26, 1788. **State fair** at Syracuse, late Aug.-early Sept.

History. When Europeans arrived, Algonquians including the Mahican, Wappinger, and Lenni Lenape inhabited the region, as did the Iroquoian Mohawk, Oneida, Onondaga, Cayuga, and Seneca tribes, who established the League of the Five Nations. Giovanni da Verrazano entered New York harbor, 1524. In 1609, Henry Hudson visited the river later named for him, and Samuel de Champlain explored the lake that now bears his name. The first permanent settlement was Dutch, near present-day Albany, 1624. New Amsterdam was settled, 1626, at the southern tip of Manhattan island. A British fleet seized New Netherland, 1664. Key battles of the American Revolution included Saratoga, 1777. In the 19th cent., New York City emerged as one of the world's great metropolitan areas, a center for trade, finance, and arts, and a haven for millions of immigrants. Completion of Erie Canal, 1825, established the state as a gateway to the West. The first women's rights convention was held in Seneca Falls, 1848. Although the state backed the Union in the Civil War, an 1863 military draft triggered three days of riots in New York City. Industry declined in the 20th cent., and California and Texas passed New York in population. Attica was the scene of a bloody prison revolt, 1971. Two jet aircraft hijacked by terrorists on Sept. 11, 2001, destroyed the World Trade Center in lower Manhattan. Gov. Eliot Spitzer resigned in Mar. 2008 after 14-months in office; he was alleged to have patronized a prostitution ring. An estimated 65 people in New York state were killed when Hurricane Sandy (by then downgraded to a tropical storm) made landfall Oct. 29-30, 2012.

Tourist attractions. New York City; Adirondack and Catskill Mountains; Watkins Glen State Park; Thousand Islands region; Niagara Falls; Saratoga Race Course, Saratoga Springs; Philipsburg Manor, Old Dutch Church of Sleepy Hollow, in Sleepy Hollow; Washington Irving's Sunnyside, Tarrytown; Corning Museum of Glass; Fenimore Art Museum, Natl. Baseball Hall of Fame and Museum, in Cooperstown; Ft. Ticonderoga; New York State Capitol, Albany; Home of Franklin D. Roosevelt Natl. Historic Site, Hyde Park; Long Island beaches; Sagamore Hill (Theodore Roosevelt's "Summer White House"), Oyster Bay.

Famous New Yorkers. Woody Allen, Susan B. Anthony, James Baldwin, Lucille Ball, Ann Bancroft, L. Frank Baum, Milton Berle, Humphrey Bogart, Barbara Boxer, Mel Brooks, Benjamin Cardozo, De Witt Clinton, James Fenimore Cooper, Peter Cooper, Aaron Copland, Francis Ford Coppola, Tom Cruise, Robert De Niro, George Eastman, Jimmy Fallon, Millard Fillmore, Lou Gehrig, George and Ira Gershwin, Ruth Bader Ginsburg, Rudolph Giuliani, Jackie Gleason, Stephen Jay Gould, Julia Ward Howe, Charles Evans Hughes, Washington Irving, Henry and William James, John Jay, Edward Koch, Fiorello LaGuardia, Herman Melville, Arthur Miller, J. Pierpont Morgan Jr., Eddie Murphy, Joyce Carol Oates, Carroll O'Connor, Rosie O'Donnell, Eugene O'Neill, Jerry Orbach, George Pataki, Colin Powell, Nancy Reagan, John Roberts, John D. Rockefeller, Nelson Rockefeller, Richard Rodgers, Ray Romano, Eleanor Roosevelt, Franklin D. Roosevelt, Theodore Roosevelt, Tim Russert, J. D. Salinger, Caroline Kennedy Schlossberg, Jerry Seinfeld, Al Sharpton, Paul Simon, Alfred E. Smith, Elizabeth Cady Stanton, Barbra Streisand, Donald Trump, William (Boss) Tweed, Martin Van Buren, Luther Vandross, Gore Vidal, Denzel Washington, Edith Wharton, Walt Whitman, Mark Zuckerberg.

Tourist information. Empire State Development, Travel Information Center, 30 South Pearl St., Albany, NY 12245; 1-800-CALLNYS; www.iloveny.com

Website. www.state.ny.us

North Carolina (NC)
Tar Heel State, Old North State

People. Population: 9,752,073; rank: 10. **Pop. change** (2010-12): 2.3%. **Pop. density:** 200.6 per sq mi. **Racial distribution:** 71.9% white; 22% black; 2.5% Asian; 1.5% Amer. Ind.; 0.1% Hawaiian/Pacific Islander; two or more races, 2.0%. **Hispanic pop.:** 8.7%.

Geography. Total area: 53,819 sq mi; rank: 28. **Land area:** 48,618 sq mi; rank: 29. **Acres forested:** 18.6 mil. **Location:** South Atlantic state bounded on N by Virginia, on S by South Carolina, on SW by Georgia, on W by Tennessee, and on E by Atlantic. **Climate:** subtropical in SE, medium-continental in mountain region; tempered by the Gulf Stream and mountains in W. **Topography:** coastal plain and tidewater in two-fifths of state, extending to the fall line of the rivers; Piedmont Plateau in another two-fifths has gentle to rugged hills; southern Appalachian Mts. contain the Blue Ridge and Great Smoky Mts. **Capital:** Raleigh. **Chief airports:** Charlotte, Greensboro, Raleigh.

Economy. Chief industries: manufacturing, agriculture, tourism. **Chief manuf. goods:** transportation, tobacco, pharmaceuticals, toiletries, plastics, animal slaughtering & processing, household furniture, fabric & apparel. **Chief crops:** greenhouse & nursery, tobacco, cotton, soybeans, corn, Christmas trees, sweet potatoes, wheat, peanuts, blueberries, cucumbers, tomatoes, hay, potatoes. **Livestock:** 19.67 mil chickens (excl. broilers), 799.7 mil broilers, 820,000 cattle/calves, 26,000 sheep/lambs, 870,000 hogs/pigs. **Nonfuel minerals:** $911 mil; stone (crushed), phosphate rock, sand and gravel (construction), sand and gravel (industrial), feldspar. **Commercial fishing:** $72.9 mil. **Chief ports:** Morehead City, Wilmington. **Gross state product:** $456.0 bil. **Sales tax:** 4.75%. **Employment distrib.:** 18% govt.; 18.5% trade/trans./util.; 10.8% mfg.; 13.7% ed./health; 13.5% prof./bus. serv.; 11% leisure/hosp.; 5.1% finance; 4.3% constr./mining/log.; 1.7% info.; 3.5% other serv. **Unemployment:** 9.5%. **Per cap. pers. income:** $37,049. **New private housing:** 48,692 units/$7.1 bil. **Broadband Internet:** 76.3%. **Commercial banks:** 91; deposits: $335 bil. **Savings institutions:** 28; deposits: $6.7 bil. **Lottery:** total sales: $1.6 bil; profit: $456.8 mil.

Federal govt. Fed. civ. employees: 45,182; **avg. salary:** $67,838. **Notable fed. facilities:** Ft. Bragg; Camp LeJeune Marine Base, Marine Corps Air Station Cherry Point; NOAA Natl. Climatic Data Ctr.; Natl. Inst. of Environmental Health Sciences, EPA Research and Dev. Labs, all in Research Triangle Park.

Energy. Electricity use/cost: 1,151 kWh, $118.09.

State data. Motto: Esse Quam Videri (To be rather than to seem). **Flower:** Dogwood. **Bird:** Cardinal. **Tree:** Pine. **Song:** "The Old North State." **Twelfth** of the original 13 states to ratify the Constitution, Nov. 21, 1789. **State fair** at Raleigh, mid to late-Oct.; at Fletcher, mid-Sept.

History. Algonquian, Siouan, and Iroquoian peoples lived in the region at the time of European contact. Sir Walter Raleigh tried to found a colony, 1584-87; the "Lost Colony" on Roanoke Island, 1587, disappeared without a trace. Permanent settlers came from Virginia in the mid-17th cent. The province's congress was the first to vote for independence, 1776. In the Revolutionary War, Gen. Charles Cornwallis's forces were defeated at Kings Mountain, 1780, and forced out after Guilford Courthouse, 1781. The state ratified the Constitution, 1789, only after Congress passed the Bill of Rights. North Carolina, where one-third of the population was slaves, seceded from the Union, 1861, and provided more troops to the Confederacy than any other state; it was readmitted, 1868. The Wright brothers made the first powered airplane flight at Kitty Hawk, 1903. Sit-ins at segregated Greensboro lunch counters, 1960, drew national attention to the civil rights movement. Long reliant on tobacco, textiles, and wood products, North Carolina has prospered since the 1960s from advanced technologies in the Raleigh-Durham-Chapel Hill area and banking in Charlotte. The hurricane-prone state was hit hard by Hazel, 1954, Fran, 1996, and Floyd, 1999.

Tourist attractions. Cape Hatteras and Cape Lookout Natl. Seashores; Great Smoky Mountains Natl. Park; Guilford Courthouse Natl. Military Park; Moore's Creek Natl. Battlefield (1776 victory ended British rule in colony); Bennett Place (site of largest troop surrender of Civil War), Durham; Ft. Raleigh Natl. Historic Site, North Carolina Aquarium, on Roanoke Island; Wright Brothers Natl. Mem., Kill Devil Hills; USS *North Carolina*, Wilmington; North Carolina Zoo, Asheboro; North Carolina Symphony, Marbles Kids Museum, North Carolina Museum of Art, North Carolina Museum of Natural Sciences, in Raleigh; Carl Sandburg Home, Flat Rock; Biltmore House and Gardens, North Carolina Arboretum, in Asheville; U.S. Natl. Whitewater Ctr., Discovery Place, in Charlotte; Fort Macon State Park, Atlantic Beach.

Famous North Carolinians. David Brinkley, Shirley Caesar, John Coltrane, Rick Dees, Elizabeth Hanford Dole, Dale Earnhardt Sr., John Edwards, Ava Gardner, Richard Jordan Gatling, Billy Graham, Andy Griffith, O. Henry, Andrew Jackson, Andrew Johnson, Michael Jordan, William Rufus King, Charles Kuralt, Meadowlark Lemon, Dolley Madison, Thelonious Monk, Edward R. Murrow, Richard Petty, James K. Polk, Charlie Rose, Carl Sandburg, Enos Slaughter, Dean Smith, James Taylor, Thomas Wolfe.

Tourist information. North Carolina Division of Tourism, Film and Sports Development, 4324 Mail Service Ctr., Raleigh, NC 27699; 1-800-VISIT-NC, (919) 733-8372; www.visitnc.com

Website. www.nc.gov

North Dakota (ND)
Peace Garden State

People. Population: 699,628; rank: 48. **Pop. change** (2010-12): 4.0%. **Pop. density:** 10.1 per sq mi. **Racial distribution:** 90.1% white; 1.5% black; 1.1% Asian; 5.5% Amer. Ind.; 0.1% Hawaiian/Pacific Islander; two or more races, 1.8%. **Hispanic pop.:** 2.5%.

Geography. Total area: 70,698 sq mi; rank: 19. **Land area:** 69,001 sq mi; rank: 17. **Acres forested:** 0.8 mil. **Location:** West North Central state, situated exactly in the middle of North America, bounded on the N by Canada, on the E by Minnesota, on the S by South Dakota, on the W by Montana. **Climate:** continental, with a wide range of temperatures and moderate rainfall. **Topography:** Central Lowland in the E comprises the flat Red R. Valley and the Rolling Drift Prairie; Missouri Plateau of the Great Plains on the W. **Capital:** Bismarck.

Economy. Chief industries: agriculture, mining, tourism, manufacturing, telecommunications, energy, food processing. **Chief manuf. goods:** machinery, wood prods., motor vehicles & parts, furniture, processed foods. **Chief crops:** wheat, soybeans, corn, sugar beets, barley, dry beans, sunflowers, canola, potatoes, flaxseed, hay, dry peas, lentils, oats. **Livestock:** 1.79 mil cattle/calves, 74,000 sheep/lambs. **Nonfuel minerals:** $97 mil; sand and gravel (construction), lime, stone (crushed), clays (common), sand and gravel (industrial). **Gross state product:** $46.0 bil. **Sales tax:** 5.0%. **Employment distrib.:** 18.5% govt.; 22.4% trade/trans./util.; 5.7% mfg.; 13.1% ed./health; 7.8% prof./bus. serv.; 8.7% leisure/hosp.; 5.1% finance; 13.7% constr./mining/log.; 1.5% info.; 3.5% other serv. **Unemployment:** 3.1%. **Per cap. pers. income:** $51,893. **New private housing:** 10,340 units/$1.4 bil. **Broadband Internet:** 69.1%. **Commercial banks:** 96; deposits: $19.9 bil. **Savings institutions:** 2; deposits: $1.4 bil. **Lottery:** total sales: $26.0 mil; profit: $7.6 mil.

Federal govt. Fed. civ. employees: 6,357; **avg. salary:** $63,553. **Notable fed. facilities:** Minot AFB; Grand Forks AFB; Northern Prairie Wildlife Res. Ctr.; Garrison Dam Natl. Fish Hatchery; Grand Forks Human Nutrition Res. Ctr.

Energy. Electricity use/cost: 1,147 kWh, $98.46.

State data. Motto: Liberty and union, now and forever, one and inseparable. **Flower:** Wild prairie rose. **Bird:** Western meadowlark. **Tree:** American elm. **Song:** "North Dakota Hymn." **Entered union:** Nov. 2, 1889; rank: 39th. **State fair** at Minot, late July.

History. Paleo-Indian peoples hunted in the area at least 11,000 years ago. At the time of European contact, the Ojibwa, Yanktonai and Teton Sioux, Mandan, Arikara, and Hidatsa peoples lived in the region. Pierre de Varennes, sieur de La Vérendrye, was the first French fur trader in the area, 1738, followed by the English at the end of the 18th cent. Lewis and Clark built Ft. Mandan, near present-day Washburn, 1804-05, and wintered there. The first permanent settlement was at Pembina, 1812. Missouri River steamboats reached the area, 1832. Dakota Territory was organized, 1861. The first railroad arrived, 1872. The "bonanza farm" craze of the 1870s-80s led to statehood, 1889. The Nonpartisan League, a farmers' group favoring state ownership of industries, helped elect Lynn Frazier as governor, 1916, but he and others were ousted in a recall

vote, 1921. The predominantly agricultural state has one of the nation's lowest unemployment rates, mostly due to surging oil production since late-2008 in the state's Bakken formation.

Tourist attractions. North Dakota Heritage Ctr., North Dakota State Capitol, in Bismarck; Bonanzaville, West Fargo; Ft. Union Trading Post Natl. Historic Site; Intl. Peace Garden, Dunseith; Elkhorn Ranch site, in Theodore Roosevelt Natl. Park; Ft. Abraham Lincoln State Park and Museum, Mandan; Dakota Dinosaur Museum, Dickinson; Knife River Indian Villages Natl. Historic Site; Scandinavian Heritage Park, Minden.

Famous North Dakotans. Maxwell Anderson, Angie Dickinson, Josh Duhamel, John Bernard Flannagan, Phil Jackson, Louis L'Amour, Peggy Lee, Roger Maris, Eric Sevareid, Vilhjalmur Stefansson, Lawrence Welk.

Tourist information. North Dakota Tourism Division, Century Center, 1600 E. Century Ave., Ste. 2, P.O. Box 2057, Bismarck, ND 58502; 1-800-435-5663; www.ndtourism.com

Website. www.nd.gov

Ohio (OH)
Buckeye State

People. Population: 11,544,225; rank: 7. **Pop. change** (2010-12): 0.1%. **Pop. density:** 282.5 per sq mi. **Racial distribution:** 83.4% white; 12.5% black; 1.8% Asian; 0.3% Amer. Ind.; <0.05% Hawaiian/Pacific Islander; two or more races, 2.0%. **Hispanic pop.:** 3.3%.

Geography. Total area: 44,826 sq mi; rank: 34. **Land area:** 40,861 sq mi; rank: 35. **Acres forested:** 8.1 mil. **Location:** East North Central state bounded on the N by Michigan and Lake Erie; on the E and S by Pennsylvania, West Virginia, and Kentucky; on the W by Indiana. **Climate:** temperate but variable; weather subject to much precipitation. **Topography:** generally rolling plain; Allegheny Plateau in E; Lake Erie Plains extend southward; central plains in the W. **Capital:** Columbus. **Chief airports:** Akron, Cleveland, Columbus, Dayton.

Economy. Chief industries: manufacturing, trade, services. **Chief manuf. goods:** motor vehicles & parts, petroleum, plastics & rubber, iron & steel, aircraft, machinery, fabricated metal, printing. **Chief crops:** corn, soybeans, hay, wheat, grapes, potatoes, tomatoes, apples, strawberries, tobacco. **Livestock:** 35.99 mil chickens (excl. broilers), 63.2 mil broilers, 1.23 mil cattle/calves, 121,000 sheep/lambs, 160,000 hogs/pigs. **Nonfuel minerals:** $1.2 bil; stone (crushed), sand and gravel (construction), salt, lime, cement (portland). **Commercial fishing:** $5.2 mil. **Chief ports:** Cincinnati, Toledo, Conneaut, Cleveland, Ashtabula. **Gross state product:** $509.4 bil. **Sales tax:** 5.5%. **Employment distrib.:** 14.6% govt.; 18.6% trade/trans./util.; 12.7% mfg.; 16.9% ed./health; 12.8% prof./bus. serv.; 10% leisure/hosp.; 5.3% finance; 3.7% constr./mining/log.; 1.4% info.; 3.9% other serv. **Unemployment:** 7.2%. **Per cap. pers. income:** $39,289. **New private housing:** 16,905 units/$2.8 bil. **Broadband Internet:** 72.3%. **Commercial banks:** 172; deposits: $211.5 bil. **Savings institutions:** 92; deposits: $32.4 bil. **Lottery:** total sales: $2.8 bil; profit: $771.0 mil.

Federal govt. Fed. civ. employees: 52,023; **avg. salary:** $76,321. **Notable fed. facilities:** Wright-Patterson AFB; Defense Supply Ctr., Columbus; NASA Glenn Research Ctr.; Lima Army Tank Plant.

Energy. Electricity use/cost: 918 kWh, $104.86.

State data. Motto: With God, all things are possible. **Flower:** Scarlet carnation. **Bird:** Cardinal. **Tree:** Buckeye. **Song:** "Beautiful Ohio." **Entered union:** Mar. 1, 1803; rank: 17th. **State fair** at Columbus, late July-early Aug.

History. Paleo-Indians hunted in the area about 11,000 years ago; the Adena and Hopewell cultures followed. Wyandot, Delaware, Miami, and Shawnee peoples sparsely occupied the area when the first Europeans arrived. René-Robert Cavelier, sieur de La Salle visited the region, 1669. France claimed it, 1682, but ceded it to Britain, 1763. After the American Revolution, Ohio became part of the Northwest Territory, 1787. The first permanent settlement was at Marietta, 1788. Cincinnati was also founded, 1788; Cleveland, 1796. Indian warfare abated with the Treaty of Greenville, 1795. Ohio became a state, 1803. In the War of 1812, Oliver Hazard Perry's victory on Lake Erie and William Henry Harrison's invasion of Canada, 1813, ended British incursions. Columbus, founded 1812, became the state capital, 1816. Before the Civil War, Ohioans aided the Underground Railroad, helping runaway slaves. Agricultural for much of the 19th cent., the

state became an industrial powerhouse in the 20th. Manufacturing jobs dropped by 24%, 1998-2007. No Republican has ever won the presidency without carrying Ohio.

Tourist attractions. Hopewell Culture Natl. Historical Park, Chillicothe; Cuyahoga Valley Natl. Park; Armstrong Air and Space Museum, Wapakoneta; Natl. Museum of the U.S. Air Force, near Dayton; Pro Football Hall of Fame, First Ladies Natl. Historic Site, in Canton; Kings Island amusement park, Mason; Lake Erie Islands, Cedar Point amusement park, in Sandusky; birthplaces, homes of, and memorials to presidents W. H. Harrison, Grant, Hayes, Garfield, B. Harrison, McKinley, Taft, and Harding; Amish Country, particularly in Holmes County; German Village historic neighborhood, Franklin Park Conservatory and Botanical Gardens, in Columbus; Rock and Roll Hall of Fame and Museum, West Side Market, Cleveland Metroparks Zoo, in Cleveland; Cincinnati Museum Center at Union Terminal; Toledo Zoo.

Famous Ohioans. Berenice Abbott, Sherwood Anderson, Neil Armstrong, George Bellows, Halle Berry, Ambrose Bierce, Erma Bombeck, Drew Carey, Hart Crane, George Custer, Clarence Darrow, Paul Laurence Dunbar, Thomas Edison, Clark Gable, John Glenn, Zane Grey, Bob Hope, William Dean Howells, LeBron James, Maya Lin, Toni Morrison, Paul Newman, Jack Nicklaus, Annie Oakley, Jesse Owens, Jack Paar, Pontiac, Eddie Rickenbacker, John D. Rockefeller Sr. and Jr., Roy Rogers, Pete Rose, Arthur Schlesinger Jr., Gen. William Sherman, Steven Spielberg, Gloria Steinem, Harriet Beecher Stowe, Robert A. Taft, William H. Taft, Tecumseh, James Thurber, Ted Turner, Orville and Wilbur Wright.

Tourist information. Division of Travel and Tourism, P.O. Box 1001, Columbus, OH 43216; 1-800-BUCKEYE; www.discoverohio.com

Website. www.ohio.gov

Oklahoma (OK)
Sooner State

People. Population: 3,814,820; rank: 28. **Pop. change** (2010-12): 1.7%. **Pop. density:** 55.6 per sq mi. **Racial distribution:** 75.5% white; 7.6% black; 1.9% Asian; 9.0% Amer. Ind.; 0.2% Hawaiian/Pacific Islander; two or more races, 5.8%. **Hispanic pop.:** 9.3%.

Geography. Total area: 69,899 sq mi; rank: 20. **Land area:** 68,595 sq mi; rank: 19. **Acres forested:** 12.6 mil. **Location:** West South Central state bounded on the N by Colorado and Kansas, on the E by Missouri and Arkansas, on the S and W by Texas and New Mexico. **Climate:** temperate; southern humid belt merging with colder northern continental; humid eastern and dry western zones. **Topography:** high plains predominate in the W, hills and small mountains in the E; the E central region is dominated by the Arkansas R. Basin, and the S by the Red R. Plains. **Capital:** Oklahoma City. **Chief airports:** Oklahoma City, Tulsa.

Economy. Chief industries: manufacturing, mineral and energy exploration and production, agriculture, services. **Chief manuf. goods:** animal slaughtering & processing, petroleum, plastics & rubber, fabricated metals, machinery, motor vehicles & parts. **Chief crops:** wheat, greenhouse & nursery, hay, cotton, corn, soybeans, pecans, sorghum, peanuts. **Livestock:** 4.28 mil chickens (excl. broilers), 211.8 mil broilers, 4.2 mil cattle/calves, 75,000 sheep/lambs, 410,000 hogs/pigs. **Nonfuel minerals:** $651 mil; stone (crushed), cement (portland), sand and gravel (industrial), sand and gravel (construction), iodine. **Chief port:** Catoosa. **Gross state product:** $161.0 bil. **Sales tax:** 4.5%. **Employment distrib.:** 21.8% govt.; 17.9% trade/trans./util.; 8.2% mfg.; 13.7% ed./health; 11.1% prof./bus. serv.; 9.6% leisure/hosp.; 4.9% finance; 7.8% constr./mining/log.; 1.3% info.; 3.5% other serv. **Unemployment:** 5.2%. **Per cap. pers. income:** $39,006. **New private housing:** 11,930 units/$1.9 bil. **Broadband Internet:** 91.2%. **Commercial banks:** 250; deposits: $69 bil. **Savings institutions:** 5; deposits: $5.4 bil. **Lottery:** total sales: $200.0 mil; profit: $70.0 mil.

Federal govt. Fed. civ. employees: 38,861; **avg. salary:** $64,990. **Notable fed. facilities:** Tinker AFB; FAA Mike Monroney Aeronautical Ctr.; Ft. Sill; Altus AFB; McAlester Army Ammunition Plant; Vance AFB; Natl. Severe Storms Lab.

Energy. Electricity use/cost: 1,221 kWh, $115.61.

State data. Motto: Labor Omnia Vincit (Labor conquers all things). **Flower:** Mistletoe. **Bird:** Scissor-tailed flycatcher. **Tree:** Redbud. **Song:** "Oklahoma!" **Entered union:** Nov. 16, 1907;

rank: 46th. **State fair** at Oklahoma City, mid-Sept.; at Tulsa, late Sept.-early Aug.

History. Few Native Americans inhabited the region when the Spanish explorer Coronado arrived, 1541; in the 16th and 17th cent., French traders visited. Part of the Louisiana Purchase, 1803, Oklahoma was known as Indian Country and, from 1834, Indian Territory. It became home to the "Five Civilized Tribes"—Cherokee, Choctaw, Chickasaw, Creek, and Seminole—after the forced removal of Indians from the eastern U.S., 1828-46. The land was also used by Comanche, Osage, and other Plains Indians. As white settlers pressed west, land was opened for homesteading by "runs" and lottery. The first run was in 1889; the most famous run, 1893, was to the Cherokee Outlet. Oklahoma became a state, 1907. In the early 20th cent., oil finds brought wealth to the Tulsa area; the Greenwood section of the city, then known as the "Negro Wall Street," was devastated by a white mob, 1921. Depression and drought drove many "Okies" from the Dust Bowl to California in the 1930s. A truck bomb in Oklahoma City, 1995, destroyed a federal office building, killing 168 people; Timothy McVeigh was executed for the crime, 2001. A tornado in Moore killed 23 people May 20, 2013.

Tourist attractions. Cherokee Heritage Ctr., Tahlequah; Oklahoma City Natl. Memorial and Museum, Natl. Cowboy and Western Heritage Museum, White Water Bay and Frontier City amusement parks, Museum of Osteology, Bricktown neighborhood, in Oklahoma City; Will Rogers Memorial Museums, Claremore and Oologah; Philbrook Museum of Art, Gilcrease Museum, in Tulsa; Wichita Mountains Wildlife Refuge; Woolaroc Museum and Wildlife Preserve, Price Tower Arts Center, in Bartlesville; Sequoyah's Cabin, Sallisaw; Sam Noble Museum of Natural History, Norman.

Famous Oklahomans. Troy Aikman, Carl Albert, Gene Autry, Johnny Bench, William Boyd (Hopalong Cassidy), Garth Brooks, Lon Chaney, Gordon Cooper, Ralph Ellison, John Hope Franklin, James Garner, Vince Gill, Woody Guthrie, Paul Harvey, Ron Howard, Patrick J. Hurley, Ben Johnson, Jeane Kirkpatrick, Louis L'Amour, Shannon Lucid, Wilma Mankiller, Mickey Mantle, Reba McEntire, Wiley Post, Tony Randall, Oral Roberts, Will Rogers, Barry Switzer, Maria Tallchief, Jim Thorpe, Carrie Underwood, J. C. Watts Jr.

Tourist information. Travel and Tourism Division, 120 N. Robinson, 6th Fl., P.O. Box 52002, Oklahoma City, OK 73152-2002; 1-800-652-6552; www.travelok.com

Website. www.ok.gov

Oregon (OR)
Beaver State

People. Population: 3,899,353; rank: 27. **Pop. change** (2010-12): 1.8%. **Pop. density:** 40.6 per sq mi. **Racial distribution:** 88.3% white; 2.0% black; 4.0% Asian; 1.8% Amer. Ind.; 0.4% Hawaiian/Pacific Islander; two or more races, 3.5%. **Hispanic pop.:** 12.2%.

Geography. Total area: 98,379 sq mi; rank: 9. **Land area:** 95,988 sq mi; rank: 10. **Acres forested:** 29.8 mil. **Location:** Pacific state, bounded on N by Washington, on E by Idaho, on S by Nevada and California, on W by the Pacific. **Climate:** mild and humid on coast; continental dryness and extreme temperatures in the interior. **Topography:** Coast Range of rugged mountains; fertile Willamette R. Valley to E and S; Cascade Mt. Range of volcanic peaks E of the valley; plateau E of Cascades, remaining two-thirds of state. **Capital:** Salem. **Chief airport:** Portland.

Economy. Chief industries: manufacturing, services, trade, finance, insurance, real estate, government, construction. **Chief manuf. goods:** wood prods., frozen produce, printing, computers & electronics, transportation equip., industrial machinery. **Chief crops:** greenhouse & nursery, grass seed, hay, wheat, potatoes, Christmas trees, onions, pears, hazelnuts, corn, grapes, cherries, blackberries, blueberries, peppermint, snap beans, apples, hops. **Livestock:** 2.85 mil chickens (excl. broilers), 1.28 mil cattle/calves, 210,000 sheep/lambs. **Nonfuel minerals:** $316 mil; stone (crushed), sand and gravel (construction), cement (portland), diatomite, perlite (crude). **Commercial fishing:** $128.0 mil. **Chief ports:** Portland, Coos Bay. **Gross state product:** $198.7 bil. **Sales tax:** none. **Employment distrib.:** 18% govt.; 19% trade/trans./util.; 10.4% mfg.; 14.5% ed./health; 11.9% prof./bus. serv.; 10.6% leisure/hosp.; 5.5% finance; 4.6% constr./mining/log.; 2% info.; 3.5% other serv. **Unemployment:** 8.7%. **Per**

cap. pers. income: $38,786. **New private housing:** 10,608 units/$2 bil. **Broadband Internet:** 82%. **Commercial banks:** 53; deposits: $64 bil. **Savings institutions:** 8; deposits: $2.2 bil. **Lottery:** total sales: $1.1 bil; profit: $526.6 mil.

Federal govt. Fed. civ. employees: 20,090; **avg. salary:** $70,313. **Notable fed. facilities:** Bonneville Power Admin.

Energy. Electricity use/cost: 991 kWh, $94.51.

State data. Motto: She flies with her own wings. **Flower:** Oregon grape. **Bird:** Western meadowlark. **Tree:** Douglas fir. **Song:** "Oregon, My Oregon." **Entered union:** Feb. 14, 1859; rank: 33rd. **State fair** at Salem, 11 days ending on Labor Day.

History. More than 100 Native American tribes inhabited the area at the time of European contact, including the Chinook, Yakima, Cayuse, Modoc, and Nez Percé. Capt. Robert Gray sighted and sailed into the Columbia R., 1792. Lewis and Clark, traveling overland, wintered at its mouth, 1805-06. Fur traders sent by John Jacob Astor established the Astoria trading post in the Columbia River region, 1811. Settlers arrived in the Willamette Valley, 1834. In 1843, the first large wave of settlers arrived via the Oregon Trail. Oregon became a territory, 1848, and a state, 1859. Early in the 20th cent., the "Oregon System"—political reforms that included initiative, referendum, recall, direct primary, and woman suffrage—was adopted. Originally dominated by forest products, the economy diversified after World War II, with high-tech firms clustering in the "Silicon Forest" area around Portland. Oregonians were the first in the U.S. to pass measures allowing physician-assisted suicide for terminally ill patients, 1994, and establishing an all-mail voting system, 1998.

Tourist attractions. John Day Fossil Beds Natl. Monument; Multnomah Falls, Columbia River Gorge; Timberline Lodge, Mount Hood Natl. Forest; Crater Lake Natl. Park; Oregon Dunes Natl. Recreation Area; Ft. Clatsop (Lewis and Clark Natl. Historical Park), Astoria Column, in Astoria; Oregon Caves Natl. Monument; Intl. Rose Test Garden, Lan Su Chinese Garden, Pittock Mansion, Oregon Museum of Science and Industry, in Portland; Oregon Shakespeare Festival, Ashland; High Desert Museum, Bend; "Spruce Goose" (largest aircraft ever built), Evergreen Aviation and Space Museum, McMinnville; Yaquina Head Outstanding Natural Area, Oregon Coast Aquarium, in Newport.

Famous Oregonians. Ernest Bloch, Bill Bowerman, Ty Burrell, Beverly Cleary, Matt Groening, Ernest Haycox, Chief Joseph, Ken Kesey, Phil Knight, Ursula K. Le Guin, Edwin Markham, Tom McCall, John McLoughlin, Joaquin Miller, Bob Packwood, Linus Pauling, Steve Prefontaine, John "Jack" Reed, Alberto Salazar, Mary Decker Slaney, William Simon U'Ren.

Tourist information. Travel Oregon, 670 Hawthorne SE, Ste. 240, Salem, OR 97301; 1-800-547-7842; www.travel oregon.com

Website. www.oregon.gov

Pennsylvania (PA)
Keystone State

People. Population: 12,763,536; rank: 6. **Pop. change** (2010-12): 0.5%. **Pop. density:** 285.3 per sq mi. **Racial distribution:** 83.5% white; 11.4% black; 3.0% Asian; 0.3% Amer. Ind.; 0.1% Hawaiian/Pacific Islander; two or more races, 1.7%. **Hispanic pop.:** 6.1%.

Geography. Total area: 46,054 sq mi; rank: 33. **Land area:** 44,743 sq mi; rank: 32. **Acres forested:** 16.8 mil. **Location:** Middle Atlantic state, bordered on the E by the Delaware R., on the S by the Mason-Dixon Line, on the W by West Virginia and Ohio, on the N/NE by Lake Erie and New York. **Climate:** continental with wide fluctuations in seasonal temperatures. **Topography:** Allegheny Mts. run SW-NE, with Piedmont and Coast Plain in the SE triangle; Allegheny Front a diagonal spine across the state's center; N and W rugged plateau falls to Lake Erie Lowland. **Capital:** Harrisburg. **Chief airports:** Harrisburg, Philadelphia, Pittsburgh.

Economy. Chief industries: agribusiness, advanced manufacturing, health care, travel & tourism, depository institutions, biotechnology, printing & publishing, research & consulting, trucking & warehousing, transportation by air, engineering & management, legal services. **Chief manuf. goods:** petroleum, pharmaceuticals, plastics, iron & steel, printing, paper & paperboard, confectionery & snacks, animal slaughtering & processing. **Chief crops:** greenhouse & nursery, mushrooms, corn, hay, soybeans, apples, tomatoes, wheat, grapes, peaches, potatoes, strawberries, tobacco.

Livestock: 29.89 mil chickens (excl. broilers), 154.5 mil broilers, 1.61 mil cattle/calves, 86,000 sheep/lambs, 100,000 hogs/pigs. **Nonfuel minerals:** $1.8 bil; stone (crushed), cement (portland), lime, sand and gravel (construction), sand and gravel (industrial). **Commercial fishing:** $51,000. **Chief ports:** Philadelphia, Pittsburgh. **Gross state product:** $600.9 bil. **Sales tax:** 6.0%. **Employment distrib.:** 12.6% govt.; 19% trade/trans./util.; 9.8% mfg.; 20.4% ed./health; 12.8% prof./bus. serv.; 9.4% leisure/hosp.; 5.4% finance; 4.6% constr./mining/log.; 1.5% info.; 4.5% other serv. **Unemployment:** 7.9%. **Per cap. pers. income:** $43,616. **New private housing:** 18,796 units/$3.1 bil. **Broadband Internet:** 78.2%. **Commercial banks:** 160; deposits: $255.4 bil. **Savings institutions:** 81; deposits: $57.1 bil. **Lottery:** total sales: $3.5 bil; profit: $1.1 bil.

Federal govt. Fed. civ. employees: 66,747; **avg. salary:** $69,933. **Notable fed. facilities:** Army War College, Carlisle Barracks; NAVSUP Weapon Systems Support, Mechanicsburg; Philadelphia Mint, Defense Supply Ctr., Naval Surface Warfare Ctr., in Phila.; DLA Distribution Ctr. Susquehanna, New Cumberland; Tobyhanna Army Depot; Letterkenny Army Depot.

Energy. Electricity use/cost: 870 kWh, $115.33.

State data. Motto: Virtue, liberty, and independence. **Flower:** Mountain laurel. **Bird:** Ruffed grouse. **Tree:** Hemlock. **Song:** "Pennsylvania." **Second** of the original 13 states to ratify the Constitution, Dec. 12, 1787. **State fair:** no official state fair; county and community fairs, Mar.-Oct.

History. When Europeans came, Algonquian-speaking Lenni Lenape (Delaware) and Shawnee and the Iroquoian Susquehannocks, Erie, and Seneca occupied the region. Swedish explorers made the first permanent settlement, 1643, on Tinicum Island. The Dutch seized the settlement, 1655, but lost it to the British, 1664. The region was given by Charles II to William Penn, 1681. Philadelphia ("brotherly love") was the capital of the colonies during most of the American Revolution, and of the U.S., 1790-1800; the Declaration of Independence, 1776, and Constitution, 1787, were signed here. Philadelphia was taken by the British, 1777; George Washington's troops encamped at Valley Forge in the bitter winter of 1777-78. Slavery was abolished, 1780. Union victory at the Battle of Gettysburg, July 1-3, 1863, marked a turning point in the Civil War. A dam collapse at Johnstown, 1889, killed at least 2,200 people. From the late 19th to the mid-20th cent., Pittsburgh prospered from coal and steel; later, heavy industry declined, but the city revived as a hub of finance, health care, and research. The Three mile Island nuclear plant near Harrisburg had a near-meltdown, 1979. One of four hijacked planes on Sept. 11, 2001, crashed near Shanksville; a national memorial was designated on the site in 2002.

Tourist attractions. Liberty Bell Ctr. at Independence Natl. Historical Park, Franklin Institute, Philadelphia Museum of Art, in Philadelphia; Valley Forge Natl. Historical Park, King of Prussia; Gettysburg Natl. Military Park; Pennsylvania Dutch Country, Lancaster County; Hersheypark, Hershey; Duquesne Incline, Carnegie Museums of Pittsburgh, Heinz Hall for the Performing Arts, in Pittsburgh; Pocono Mountains; Pine Creek Gorge (Pennsylvania Grand Canyon), Allegheny Natl. Forest; Fallingwater (house designed by Frank Lloyd Wright), Mill Run; Johnstown Flood Natl. Memorial; Steamtown Natl. Historic Site, Scranton; U.S. Brig *Niagara*, Erie Maritime Museum, Presque Isle State Park, in Erie; Oil Region Natl. Heritage Area; Longwood Gardens, Kennett Square.

Famous Pennsylvanians. Marian Anderson, Maxwell Anderson, George Blanda, Kobe Bryant, James Buchanan, Andrew Carnegie, Rachel Carson, Wilt Chamberlain, Noam Chomsky, Perry Como, Bill Cosby, Cyrus H. K. Curtis, Thomas Eakins, Tina Fey, Stephen Foster, Benjamin Franklin, Robert Fulton, Martha Graham, Milton Hershey, Gene Kelly, Grace Kelly (Princess Grace of Monaco), Dan Marino, George C. Marshall, Chris Matthews, John J. McCloy, Margaret Mead, Andrew W. Mellon, Joe Montana, Stan Musial, Joe Namath, John O'Hara, Arnold Palmer, Robert E. Peary, Mike Piazza, Pink (Alecia Beth Moore), Tom Ridge, Mary Roberts Rinehart, Fred Rogers, Betsy Ross, Will Smith, Jimmy Stewart, Taylor Swift, Jim Thorpe, Johnny Unitas, John Updike, Honus Wagner, Andy Warhol, Benjamin West.

Tourist information. Pennsylvania Tourism Office, Department of Community and Economic Development, Commonwealth Keystone Building, 4th Fl., 400 North St., Harrisburg, PA 17120-0225; 1-800-VISITPA; www.visitpa.com

Website. www.pa.gov

Rhode Island (RI)
Little Rhody, Ocean State

People. Population: 1,050,292; rank: 43. **Pop. change** (2010-12): –0.2%. **Pop. density:** 1,015.9 per sq mi. **Racial distribution:** 85.9% white; 7.3% black; 3.2% Asian; 0.9% Amer. Ind.; 0.2% Hawaiian/Pacific Islander; two or more races, 2.5%. **Hispanic pop.:** 13.2%.

Geography. Total area: 1,545 sq mi; rank: 50. **Land area:** 1,034 sq mi; rank: 50. **Acres forested:** 0.4 mil. **Location:** New England state. **Climate:** invigorating and changeable. **Topography:** eastern lowlands of Narragansett Basin; western uplands of flat and rolling hills. **Capital:** Providence. **Chief airport:** Warwick.

Economy. Chief industries: services, manufacturing. **Chief manuf. goods:** plastics, fabricated metals, electrical equip., jewelry. **Chief crops:** greenhouse & nursery, sweet corn, berries, potatoes, apples, hay. **Livestock:** 4,600 cattle/calves. **Nonfuel minerals:** $40.9 mil; stone (crushed), sand and gravel (construction), sand and gravel (industrial), gemstones (natural). **Commercial fishing:** $80.8 mil. **Chief ports:** Providence, Davisville, Newport. **Gross state product:** $51.0 bil. **Sales tax:** 7.0%. **Employment distrib.:** 12.9% govt.; 15.7% trade/trans./util.; 8.6% mfg.; 22.4% ed./health; 12.4% prof./bus. serv.; 11.2% leisure/hosp.; 6.9% finance; 3.2% constr./mining/log.; 2% info.; 4.8% other serv. **Unemployment:** 10.4%. **Per cap. pers. income:** $44,990. **New private housing:** 731 units/$138.4 mil. **Broadband Internet:** 79.9%. **Commercial banks:** 14; deposits $41.8 bil. **Savings institutions:** 12; deposits: $3.1 bil. **Lottery:** total sales: $3.5 bil; profit: $377.7 mil.

Federal govt. Fed. civ. employees: 7,315; **avg. salary:** $84,948. **Notable fed. facilities:** Naval War College; Naval Undersea Warfare Ctr.; EPA Atlantic Ecology Div. Lab.

Energy. Electricity use/cost: 603 kWh, $86.44.

State data. Motto: Hope. **Flower:** Violet. **Bird:** Rhode Island red chicken. **Tree:** Red maple. **Song:** "Rhode Island." **Thirteenth** of original 13 states to ratify the Constitution, May 29, 1790. **State fair:** none; largest fair at Richmond, mid-Aug.

History. When Europeans arrived, Narragansett, Niantic, Nipmuc, and Wampanoag peoples lived in the region. Verrazano visited the area, 1524. The first permanent settlement was founded at Providence, 1636, by Roger Williams, who was exiled from the Massachusetts Bay Colony; Anne Hutchinson, also exiled, settled Portsmouth, 1638. Quaker and Jewish immigrants seeking freedom of worship began arriving, 1650s-60s. The colonists broke the power of the Narragansett in the Great Swamp Fight, 1675, the decisive battle in King Philip's War. The colony was the first to formally renounce all allegiance to King George III, May 4, 1776. Initially opposed to joining the Union, Rhode Island was the last of the 13 colonies to ratify the Constitution, 1790. Trade, textiles, and metal goods dominated the economy in the 19th cent., and Newport became a fashionable resort after the Civil War. The U.S. Navy was the state's largest civilian employer, 1945-73, until the destroyer force was relocated from Newport. A nightclub fire in West Warwick killed 100 people in 2003.

Tourist attractions. Block Island mansions (The Breakers, The Elms, among others), Cliff Walk, Intl. Tennis Hall of Fame and Museum, Touro Synagogue (completed 1763, oldest in U.S.), in Newport; First Baptist Church in America, Rhode Island School of Design Museum of Art, WaterFire art installation, in Providence; Slater Mill Historic Site, Pawtucket; Gilbert Stuart Birthplace and Museum, Saunderstown.

Famous Rhode Islanders. Ambrose Burnside, George M. Cohan, Nelson Eddy, Jabez Gorham, Nathanael Greene, Elisabeth Hasselbeck, Christopher and Oliver La Farge, Cormac McCarthy, John McLaughlin, Matthew C. and Oliver Hazard Perry, Gilbert Stuart, Meredith Vieira.

Tourist information. Rhode Island Tourism Division, 315 Iron Horse Way, Ste. 101, Providence, RI 02908; 1-800-556-2484; www.visitrhodeisland.com

Website. www.ri.gov

South Carolina (SC)
Palmetto State

People. Population: 4,723,723; rank: 24. **Pop. change** (2010-12): 2.1%. **Pop. density:** 157.1 per sq mi. **Racial distribution:** 68.4% white; 28% black; 1.4% Asian; 0.5% Amer.

Ind.; 0.1% Hawaiian/Pacific Islander; two or more races, 1.6%. **Hispanic pop.:** 5.3%.

Geography. Total area: 32,020 sq mi; rank: 40. **Land area:** 30,061 sq mi; rank: 40. **Acres forested:** 13.1 mil. **Location:** South Atlantic state, bordered by North Carolina on the N; Georgia on the SW and W; the Atlantic Ocean on the E, SE, and S. **Climate:** humid subtropical. **Topography:** Blue Ridge province in NW has highest peaks; piedmont lies between the mountains and the fall line; coastal plain covers two-thirds of state. **Capital:** Columbia. **Chief airports:** Charleston, Greer, Myrtle Beach.

Economy. Chief industries: tourism, agriculture, manufacturing. **Chief manuf. goods:** chemicals & synthetics, motor vehicles & parts, plastics, paper & paper prods., turbines, rubber, textiles. **Chief crops:** greenhouse & nursery, tobacco, soybeans, cotton, corn, peaches, wheat, tomatoes, peanuts. **Livestock:** 6.04 mil chickens (excl. broilers), 222.8 mil broilers, 355,000 cattle/calves. **Nonfuel minerals:** $498 mil; cement (portland), stone (crushed), sand and gravel (construction), clays (kaolin), cement (masonry). **Commercial fishing:** $23.9 mil. **Chief ports:** Charleston, Georgetown. **Gross state product:** $176.2 bil. **Sales tax:** 6.0%. **Employment distrib.:** 18.7% govt.; 18.8% trade/trans./util.; 11.6% mfg.; 11.2% ed./health; 12.4% prof./bus. serv.; 12.3% leisure/hosp.; 5.5% finance; 4.4% constr./mining/log.; 1.4% info.; 3.6% other serv. **Unemployment:** 9.1%. **Per cap. pers. income:** $34,266. **New private housing:** 18,708 units/$3.4 bil. **Broadband Internet:** 72.2%. **Commercial banks:** 80; deposits: $66.2 bil. **Savings institutions:** 14; deposits: $1.2 bil. **Lottery:** total sales: $1.1 bil; profit: $297.7 mil.

Federal govt. Fed. civ. employees: 22,520; **avg. salary:** $67,519. **Notable fed. facilities:** Ft. Jackson; Joint Base Charleston; Marine Corps Recruit Depot Parris Island; Shaw AFB; USMC Air Station Beaufort; Savannah River Site.

Energy. Electricity use/cost: 1,221 kWh, $135.01.

State data. Motto: Dum Spiro Spero (While I breathe, I hope). **Flower:** Yellow jessamine. **Bird:** Carolina wren. **Tree:** Palmetto. **Song:** "Carolina." **Eighth** of the original 13 states to ratify the Constitution, May 23, 1788. **State fair** at Columbia, mid-Oct.; at Aiken, mid to late-Oct.

History. When Europeans arrived, Cherokee, Catawba, and Muskogean peoples lived in the area. Spanish and French came in the 16th cent. The first English colonists settled near the Ashley R., 1670, and moved to the site of present-day Charleston, 1680. The colonists seized the government, 1775, and the royal governor fled. The British took Charleston, 1780, but were defeated at Kings Mountain that same year, and at Cowpens, 1781. In the 1830s, South Carolinians, angered by federal protective tariffs, adopted the Nullification Doctrine, holding that a state can void an act of Congress. Plantation agriculture relied on slave labor to cultivate rice and cotton; slaves made up 57% of the population in 1860, when South Carolina was the first state to secede from the Union. Confederate troops fired on and forced the surrender of U.S. troops at Ft. Sumter, in Charleston Harbor, 1861, launching the Civil War. The state was readmitted to the Union, 1868. Strom Thurmond, who ran for president as a segregationist in 1948, later served 48 years in the U.S. Senate (1955-2003). Formerly dependent on textiles, the state has attracted new industries by courting foreign investment.

Tourist attractions. Historic Charleston, Waterfront Park, Charleston Museum (est. 1773, oldest in U.S.), Middleton Place, Magnolia Plantation and Gardens, Drayton Hall, in Charleston; Ft. Sumter Natl. Monument (where first shots of Civil War were fired), in Charleston Harbor; Cypress Gardens, Moncks Corner; Boone Hall Plantation and Gardens, Mt. Pleasant; Brookgreen Gardens, Murrells Inlet; Myrtle Beach; Hilton Head Island; Andrew Jackson State Park, Lancaster; South Carolina State Museum, Riverbanks Zoo, in Columbia.

Famous South Carolinians. Charles F. Bolden Jr., James F. Byrnes, John C. Calhoun, Stephen Colbert, Marian Wright Edelman, Joe Frazier, DuBose Heyward, Ernest F. Hollings, Andrew Jackson, Jesse Jackson, "Shoeless" Joe Jackson, Jasper Johns, Andie MacDowell, Francis Marion, Ronald E. McNair, Charles Pinckney, John Rutledge, Thomas Sumter, Strom Thurmond, John B. Watson.

Tourist information. SC Dept. of Parks, Recreation, & Tourism, 1205 Pendleton St., Columbia, SC 29201; 1-866-224-9339, (803) 734-1700; www.discoversouthcarolina.com **Website.** www.sc.gov

South Dakota (SD)
Coyote State, Mount Rushmore State

People. Population: 833,354; rank: 46. **Pop. change** (2010-12): 2.4%. **Pop. density:** 11.0 per sq mi. **Racial distribution:** 86.2% white; 1.7% black; 1.1% Asian; 8.9% Amer. Ind.; 0.1% Hawaiian/Pacific Islander; two or more races, 2.1%. **Hispanic pop.:** 3.1%.

Geography. Total area: 77,116 sq mi; rank: 17. **Land area:** 75,811 sq mi; rank: 16. **Acres forested:** 1.9 mil. **Location:** West North Central state bounded on the N by North Dakota, on the E by Minnesota and Iowa, on the S by Nebraska, on the W by Wyoming and Montana. **Climate:** characterized by extremes of temperature, persistent winds, low precipitation and humidity. **Topography:** Prairie Plains in the E; rolling hills of the Great Plains in the W; the Black Hills, rising 3,500 ft, in the SW corner. **Capital:** Pierre.

Economy. Chief industries: agriculture, services, manufacturing. **Chief manuf. goods:** animal slaughtering, machinery, semiconductors, surgical appliances. **Chief crops:** corn, soybeans, wheat, hay, sunflowers, sorghum, oats, barley. **Livestock:** 2.79 mil chickens (excl. broilers), 3.85 mil cattle/calves, 275,000 sheep/lambs, 180,000 hogs/pigs. **Nonfuel minerals:** $364 mil; gold, stone (crushed), cement (portland), sand and gravel (construction), lime. **Gross state product:** $42.5 bil. **Sales tax:** 4.0%. **Employment distrib.:** 18.8% govt.; 20.3% trade/trans./util.; 9.9% mfg.; 16.3% ed./health; 6.8% prof./bus. serv.; 11.1% leisure/hosp.; 6.9% finance; 4.9% constr./mining/log.; 1.4% info.; 3.7% other serv. **Unemployment:** 4.4%. **Per cap. pers. income:** $43,659. **New private housing:** 4,178 units/$575.6 mil. **Broadband Internet:** 71.2%. **Commercial banks:** 86; deposits: $312.7 bil. **Savings institutions:** 6; deposits: $2.3 bil. **Lottery:** total sales: $603.2 mil; profit: $100.4 mil.

Federal govt. Fed. civ. employees: 8,610; **avg. salary:** $60,924. **Notable fed. facilities:** Ellsworth AFB.

Energy. Electricity use/cost: 1,035 kWh, $96.78.

State data. Motto: Under God, the people rule. **Flower:** Pasqueflower. **Bird:** Chinese ring-necked pheasant. **Tree:** Black Hills spruce. **Song:** "Hail, South Dakota." **Entered union:** Nov. 2, 1889; rank: 40th. **State fair** at Huron, late Aug.-early Sept.

History. Paleo-Indians hunted in the region at least 11,500 years ago. At the time of first European contact, Mandan, Hidatsa, Arikara, and Sioux lived in the area. The French Vérendrye brothers explored the region, 1742-43. The U.S. acquired the territory in the Louisiana Purchase, 1803, and Meriwether Lewis and William Clark passed through, 1804-06. In 1817 a trading post opened at what would become Ft. Pierre. Dakota Territory was established, 1861. Gold was discovered, 1874, in the Black Hills on Lakota Sioux land; the "Great Dakota Boom" began in 1879. South Dakota became a state, 1889. Massacre of Native Americans at Wounded Knee, in which 200 men, women, and children, and 29 U.S. soldiers were killed, 1890 ended Sioux resistance. Armed supporters of the American Indian Movement, a Native American rights group, occupied the area, leading to a 70-day standoff, 1973. Major economic activities include agribusiness and, since the 1980s, credit card services. Republicans scored a key election victory, 2004, with the defeat of 3-term U.S. Sen. Tom Daschle, a national Democratic leader.

Tourist attractions. Mt. Rushmore Natl. Memorial, Keystone; Harney Peak (tallest E of Rockies); Custer State Park; Crazy Horse Memorial (mtn. carving in progress); Wind Cave Natl. Park, near Hot Springs; Black Hills Natl. Forest; Needles Hwy., part of Peter Norbeck Natl. Scenic Byway; Minuteman Missile Natl. Historic Site; Deadwood (1876 gold rush town); Jewel Cave Natl. Monument, near Custer; Badlands Natl. Park; Great Lakes of South Dakota; Great Plains Zoo and Delbridge Museum of Natural History, Sioux Falls; Corn Palace, Mitchell; Reptile Gardens, Chapel in the Hills, Bear Country USA, in Rapid City.

Famous South Dakotans. Sparky Anderson, Bob Barker, Black Elk, Tom Brokaw, Crazy Horse, Tom Daschle, Myron Floren, Mary Hart, Cheryl Ladd, Ernest O. Lawrence, George McGovern, Russell Means, Billy Mills, Allen H. Neuharth, Pat O'Brien, Sitting Bull.

Tourist information. Department of Tourism and State Development, Capitol Lake Plaza, 711 E. Wells Ave., c/o 500 E. Capitol Ave., Pierre, SD 57501; 1-800-SDAKOTA; www.travelsd.com **Website.** www.sd.gov

Tennessee (TN)
Volunteer State

People. Population: 6,456,243; rank: 17. **Pop. change** (2010-12): 1.7%. **Pop. density:** 156.6 per sq mi. **Racial distribution:** 79.3% white; 17% black; 1.6% Asian; 0.4% Amer. Ind.; 0.1% Hawaiian/Pacific Islander; two or more races, 1.6%. **Hispanic pop.:** 4.8%.

Geography. Total area: 42,144 sq mi; rank: 36. **Land area:** 41,235 sq mi; rank: 34. **Acres forested:** 13.9 mil. **Location:** East South Central state bounded on the N by Kentucky and Virginia; on the E by North Carolina; on the S by Georgia, Alabama, and Mississippi; on the W by Arkansas and Missouri. **Climate:** humid continental to the N; humid subtropical to the S. **Topography:** rugged country in the E; the Great Smoky Mts. of the Unakas; low ridges of the Appalachian Valley; flat Cumberland Plateau; slightly rolling terrain and knobs of the Interior Low Plateau, the largest region; Eastern Gulf Coastal Plain to the W, laced with streams; Mississippi Alluvial Plain, a narrow strip of swamp and floodplain in the extreme W. **Capital:** Nashville. **Chief airports:** Alcoa, Memphis, Nashville.

Economy. Chief industries: manufacturing, trade, services, tourism, finance, insurance, real estate. **Chief manuf. goods:** motor vehicles & parts, computers & electronics, food, chemicals, plastics, printing, appliances, aluminum. **Chief crops:** greenhouse & nursery, soybeans, cotton, corn, tobacco, hay, tomatoes, wheat. **Livestock:** 2.6 mil chickens (excl. broilers), 167.6 mil broilers, 1.83 mil cattle/calves, 33,000 sheep/lambs. **Nonfuel minerals:** $1 bil; stone (crushed), zinc, cement (portland), sand and gravel (industrial), sand and gravel (construction). **Chief ports:** Memphis, Nashville, Chattanooga. **Gross state product:** $277.0 bil. **Sales tax:** 7.0%. **Employment distrib.:** 15.4% govt.; 21% trade/trans./util.; 11.6% mfg.; 14.5% ed./health; 12.7% prof./bus. serv.; 10.6% leisure/hosp.; 5% finance; 4% constr./mining/log.; 1.5% info.; 3.8% other serv. **Unemployment:** 8.0%. **Per cap. pers. income:** $37,678. **New private housing:** 20,147 units/$3.1 bil. **Broadband Internet:** 74.5%. **Commercial banks:** 211; deposits: $114.5 bil. **Savings institutions:** 16; deposits: $3.9 bil. **Lottery:** total sales: $1.3 bil; profit: $323.4 mil.

Federal govt. Fed. civ. employees: 28,648; **avg. salary:** $66,908. **Notable fed. facilities:** Tennessee Valley Authority; Oak Ridge Natl. Lab; Arnold Engineering Development Ctr.; Ft. Campbell; NSA Mid-South, Millington.

Energy. Electricity use/cost: 1,325 kWh, $132.26.

State data. Motto: Agriculture and commerce. **Flower:** Iris. **Bird:** Mockingbird. **Tree:** Tulip poplar. **Songs:** "My Homeland, Tennessee"; "When It's Iris Time in Tennessee"; "My Tennessee"; "Tennessee Waltz"; "Rocky Top"; "Smoky Mountain Rain." **Entered union:** June 1, 1796; rank: 16th. **State fair** at Nashville, early to mid-Sept.; at Jackson, mid-Sept.

History. Inhabited for at least 20,000 years, the region was home to Creek and Yuchi peoples when the first Europeans arrived; the Cherokee moved into the region in the early 18th cent. Spanish explorers visited the area, 1540. English traders crossed the Great Smoky Mtns. from the east, while France's Jacques Marquette and Louis Jolliet sailed down the Mississippi on the west, 1673. The first permanent settlement was of Virginians on the Watauga R., 1769. After the American Revolution, in which Tennesseans fought in eastern campaigns, the region became a territory, 1790, and a state, 1796. Slavery was widespread in western Tennessee, where cotton was the main crop, but much less common in the east. The state seceded, 1861, and saw many Civil War engagements; some 187,000 Tennesseans fought for the Confederacy and 51,000 for the Union. Tennessee was readmitted in 1866, the only former Confederate state not to have a postwar military government. The famous Scopes trial, 1925, questioned the teaching of evolution in public schools. In the 1930s, the Tennessee Valley Authority, a federal program, brought electric power to rural areas. Nashville became the capital of country music, while Memphis fostered the blues and, with Elvis Presley in the 1950s, rock 'n' roll. Martin Luther King Jr. was assassinated in Memphis, 1968. Since the 1970s, auto plants have become major employers, as has Federal Express. Al Gore Jr., U.S. vice pres. (1993-2001), lost his 2000 presidential bid partly because he failed to carry his home state of Tennessee. Record amounts of rainfall flooded parts of Tennessee, including Nashville, in May 2010.

Tourist attractions. Lookout Mountain, Tennessee Aquarium, Ruby Falls, in Chattanooga; Great Smoky Mountains Natl. Park; Lost Sea (largest underground lake in U.S.), Sweetwater; Cherokee Natl. Forest; Cumberland Gap Natl. Historical Park; James K. Polk Ancestral Home, Columbia; American Museum of Science and Energy, Oak Ridge; The Hermitage (home of Pres. Andrew Jackson), Country Music Hall of Fame and Museum, Ryman Auditorium, Belle Meade Plantation, Parthenon replica, Grand Ole Opry, in Nashville; Dollywood theme park, Pigeon Forge; Graceland (home of Elvis Presley), Sun Studio, in Memphis; Alex Haley Museum and Interpretive Ctr., Henning; Casey Jones Village, Jackson; Bristol Motor Speedway.

Famous Tennesseans. Roy Acuff, Kenny Chesney, Davy Crockett, David Farragut, Ernie Ford, Aretha Franklin, Bill Frist, Al Gore Jr., Alex Haley, William C. Handy, Sam Houston, Cordell Hull, Andrew Jackson, Andrew Johnson, Casey Jones, Estes Kefauver, Grace Moore, Dolly Parton, Minnie Pearl, James Polk, Elvis Presley, Wilma Rudolph, Dinah Shore, Bessie Smith, Fred Thompson, Justin Timberlake, Tina Turner, Hank Williams Jr., Alvin York.

Tourist information. Dept. of Tourist Development, Wm. Snodgrass/Tennessee Tower, 312 Rosa L. Parks Ave., 25th Fl., Nashville, TN 37243; 1-800-462-8366; www.tnvacation.com

Website. www.tn.gov

Texas (TX)
Lone Star State

People. Population: 26,059,203; rank: 2. **Pop. change** (2010-12): 3.6%. **Pop. density:** 99.8 per sq mi. **Racial distribution:** 80.6% white; 12.3% black; 4.2% Asian; 1.0% Amer. Ind.; 0.1% Hawaiian/Pacific Islander; two or more races, 1.7%. **Hispanic pop.:** 38.2%.

Geography. Total area: 268,596 sq mi; rank: 2. **Land area:** 261,232 sq mi; rank: 2. **Acres forested:** 62.4 mil. **Location:** southwestern state, bounded on the SE by the Gulf of Mexico; on the SW by Mexico, separated by the Rio Grande; surrounding states are Louisiana, Arkansas, Oklahoma, New Mexico. **Climate:** extremely varied; driest region is the Trans-Pecos; wettest is the NE. **Topography:** Gulf Coast Plain in the S and SE; North Central Plains slope upward with some hills; the Great Plains extend over the Panhandle, are broken by low mountains; the Trans-Pecos is the southern extension of the Rockies. **Capital:** Austin. **Chief airports:** Austin, Dallas, El Paso, Fort Worth, Houston (2), San Antonio.

Economy. Chief industries: manufacturing, trade, oil and gas extraction, services. **Chief manuf. goods:** petroleum, chemicals & resins, computers & electronics, animal slaughtering & processing, plastics, aerospace. **Chief crops:** cotton, greenhouse & nursery, corn, wheat, sorghum, hay, peanuts, onions, rice, pecans, grapefruit. **Livestock:** 24.73 mil chickens (excl. broilers), 602.5 mil broilers, 11.3 mil cattle/calves, 700,000 sheep/lambs, 100,000 hogs/pigs. **Nonfuel minerals:** $3.4 bil; cement (portland), stone (crushed), sand and gravel (construction), sand and gravel (industrial), salt. **Commercial fishing:** $194.0 mil. **Chief ports:** Houston, Galveston, Brownsville, Beaumont, Port Arthur, Corpus Christi, Texas City, Freeport. **Gross state product:** $1.4 tril. **Sales tax:** 6.25%. **Employment distrib.:** 16.4% govt.; 19.8% trade/trans./util.; 7.7% mfg.; 13.4% ed./health; 13% prof./bus. serv.; 10.3% leisure/hosp.; 6% finance; 8.1% constr./mining/log.; 1.8% info.; 3.5% other serv. **Unemployment:** 6.8%. **Per cap. pers. income:** $41,471. **New private housing:** 135,514 units/$19.5 bil. **Broadband Internet:** 85.4%. **Commercial banks:** 596; deposits: $537 bil. **Savings institutions:** 52; deposits: $62 bil. **Lottery:** total sales: $4.2 bil; profit: $1.2 bil.

Federal govt. Fed. civ. employees: 144,299; **avg. salary:** $69,971. **Notable fed. facilities:** Ft. Hood; Ft. Bliss; Sheppard, Dyess, Goodfellow AF Bases; Joint Base San Antonio; NASA Johnson Space Ctr.; Naval Air Training School, Corpus Christi NAS; Red River Army Depot; Western Currency Facility, Ft. Worth.

Energy. Electricity use/cost: 1,262 kWh, $139.81.

State data. Motto: Friendship. **Flower:** Bluebonnet. **Bird:** Mockingbird. **Tree:** Pecan. **Song:** "Texas, Our Texas." **Entered union:** Dec. 29, 1845; rank: 28th. **State fair** at Dallas, late Sept.-mid-Oct.; at Beaumont, late Mar.-early Apr.; at Belton, late Aug.-early Sept.; at Denton, mid-Aug.; at Tyler, late Sept.

History. Humans have lived in the region for at least 12,000 years. Coahuiltecan, Karankawa, Caddo, Jumano, and Tonkawa peoples were in the area when the first

Europeans came; later, Apache, Comanche, Cherokee, and Wichita arrived. Early Spanish explorers included Alonso çlvarez de Pineda, who sailed along the Texas coast, 1519; Cabeza de Vaca, shipwrecked near Galveston along with the former slave Estevanico, 1528; and Coronado, who crossed the Panhandle, 1541. Spaniards made the first settlement at Ysleta, near El Paso, 1682. Americans moved into the land early in the 19th cent. Mexico, of which Texas was a part, won independence from Spain, 1821. Texans rebelled, 1836, losing to Santa Anna at the Alamo, but winning decisively under Sam Houston at San Jacinto. With Houston as president, 1836-38 and 1841-44, the Republic of Texas functioned as a nation until admitted to the Union. With a slave population of 30%, Texas seceded, 1861; mostly unscathed by the Civil War, it was readmitted, 1870. In 1900 a powerful hurricane lashed Galveston, killing at least 8,000. Cotton and cattle were dominant until 1901, when the Spindletop gusher, near Beaumont, launched the petroleum and petrochemical industries. By 2000, the state population ranked second in the U.S. With wealth and population came political power, notably in the presidencies of Lyndon B. Johnson (1963-69), George H. W. Bush (1989-93), and George W. Bush (2001-09). Texas was plagued with drought conditions and wildfires starting in late 2010, with almost 4 mil acres burned and close to 3,000 homes destroyed in the 2011 fire season. A fertilizer plant in the town of West exploded Apr. 17, 2013, killing 15 people.

Tourist attractions. Big Bend and Guadalupe Mountains Natl. Parks; Fort Davis Natl. Historic Site; Six Flags Over Texas, Arlington; SeaWorld San Antonio, Six Flags Fiesta Texas, The Alamo, San Antonio Missions Natl. Historical Park, San Antonio River Walk, in San Antonio; Natl. Cowgirl Museum and Hall of Fame, Kimbell Art Museum, Ft. Worth Zoo, Bureau of Engraving and Printing, in Ft. Worth; Lyndon B. Johnson Natl. Historical Park, Johnson City; LBJ Presidential Library and Museum, Bullock Texas State History Museum, Austin; George Bush Presidential Library and Museum, College Station; Dallas Arboretum and Botanical Garden, Sixth Floor Museum at Dealey Plaza, George W. Bush Presidential Library and Museum, in Dallas; USS *Lexington*, Texas State Aquarium, Padre Island Natl. Seashore, in Corpus Christi.

Famous Texans. Lance Armstrong, Stephen F. Austin, Lloyd Bentsen, James Bowie, Drew Brees, Carol Burnett, George H. W. Bush, George W. Bush, Joan Crawford, J. Frank Dobie, Dwight D. Eisenhower, Morgan Fairchild, Farrah Fawcett, Sam Houston, Howard Hughes, Kay Bailey Hutchison, Molly Ivins, Lyndon B. Johnson, Tommy Lee Jones, Janis Joplin, Barbara Jordan, Beyoncé Knowles, Mary Martin, Matthew McConaughey, Chester Nimitz, Sandra Day O'Connor, H. Ross Perot, Katherine Anne Porter, Dan Rather, Sam Rayburn, Ann Richards, Sissy Spacek, George Strait, Babe Didrikson Zaharias.

Tourist information. Texas Tourism, P.O. Box 141009, Austin, TX 78714; (512) 486-5876, 1-800-452-9292; www.traveltex.com

Website. www.texas.gov

Utah (UT)
Beehive State

People. Population: 2,855,287; rank: 34. **Pop. change** (2010-12): 3.3%. **Pop. density:** 34.7 per sq mi. **Racial distribution:** 91.8% white; 1.3% black; 2.2% Asian; 1.5% Amer. Ind.; 1.0% Hawaiian/Pacific Islander; two or more races, 2.3%. **Hispanic pop.:** 13.3%.

Geography. Total area: 84,897 sq mi; rank: 13. **Land area:** 82,170 sq mi; rank: 12. **Acres forested:** 18.3 mil. **Location:** middle Rocky Mountain state; its SE corner touches Colorado, New Mexico, and Arizona, and is the only spot in the U.S. where 4 states join. **Climate:** arid; ranging from warm desert in SW to alpine in NE. **Topography:** high Colorado Plateau is cut by brilliantly colored canyons of the SE; broad, flat, desertlike Great Basin of the W; the Great Salt Lake and Bonneville Salt Flats to the NW; Middle Rockies in the NE run E-W; valleys and plateaus of the Wasatch Front. **Capital:** Salt Lake City. **Chief airport:** Salt Lake City.

Economy. Chief industries: services, trade, manufacturing, government, transportation, utilities. **Chief manuf. goods:** food, petroleum, nonferrous metal, motor vehicles & parts, aerospace, sporting goods, fabricated metal, computers & electronics. **Chief crops:** hay, greenhouse & nursery, wheat, cherries, onions, apples, barley, peaches, corn.

Livestock: 4.6 mil chickens (excl. broilers), 770,000 cattle/calves, 295,000 sheep/lambs, 75,000 hogs/pigs. **Nonfuel minerals:** $3.5 bil; copper, molybdenum concentrates, gold, potash, magnesium metal. **Gross state product:** $130.5 bil. **Sales tax:** 5.95%. **Employment distrib.:** 17.4% govt.; 19.5% trade/trans./util.; 9.3% mfg.; 12.8% ed./health; 13.6% prof./bus. serv.; 9.6% leisure/hosp.; 5.6% finance; 6.6% constr./mining/log.; 2.8% info.; 2.8% other serv. **Unemployment:** 5.7%. **Per cap. pers. income:** $34,601. **New private housing:** 13,007 units/$2.4 bil. **Broadband Internet:** 81.7%. **Commercial banks:** 59; deposits: $299.2 bil. **Savings institutions:** 7; deposits: $40.4 bil.

Federal govt. Fed. civ. employees: 29,266; **avg. salary:** $64,108. **Notable fed. facilities:** Hill AFB; Tooele Army Depot; Army Dugway Proving Ground.

Energy. Electricity use/cost: 788 kWh, $70.61.

State data. Motto: Industry. **Flower:** Sego lily. **Bird:** (California) sea gull. **Tree:** Blue spruce. **Song:** "Utah, This Is the Place." **Entered union:** Jan. 4, 1896; rank: 45th. **State fair** at Salt Lake City, early Sept.

History. Ute, Gosiute, Southern Paiute, and Navajo peoples lived in the region at the time of European contact. Spanish Franciscans visited the area, 1776; American fur traders followed. Permanent settlement began with the arrival of the Latter-day Saints, or Mormons, 1847; they made the arid land bloom and created a prosperous economy. Organized in 1849, the State of Deseret asked admission to the Union; instead, Congress established Utah Territory, 1850, and Brigham Young was appointed governor. The Union Pacific and Central Pacific railroads met near Promontory Point, May 10, 1869, creating the first transcontinental railroad. Statehood was not achieved until 1896, after a long controversy over the Mormon practices of economic isolationism and polygamy (the church renounced the latter in 1890). The 20th cent. brought expansion in mining, defense-related industries, and, more recently, information technologies. More than two-thirds of Utahans are Mormons; the church has its world headquarters in Salt Lake City. Utah experienced 60% population growth, 1990-2010, and has the highest birthrate and lowest median age of any state in the U.S.

Tourist attractions. Temple Square (site of Mormon Church headquarters), Salt Lake City; Great Salt Lake; Zion, Canyonlands, Bryce Canyon, Arches, and Capitol Reef Natl. Parks; Dinosaur, Rainbow Bridge, Timpanogos Cave, and Natural Bridges Natl. Monuments; Lake Powell; Flaming Gorge Natl. Recreation Area; Utah Olympic Park, Sundance Film Festival, in Park City.

Famous Utahans. Maude Adams, Roseanne Barr, Ezra Taft Benson, John Moses Browning, Butch Cassidy, Marriner S. Eccles, Philo T. Farnsworth, David M. Kennedy, J. Willard Marriott, Merlin Olsen, the Osmonds, Ivy Baker Priest, George W. Romney, Wallace Stegner, Brigham Young, Loretta Young.

Tourist information. Utah Office of Tourism, Council Hall/Capitol Hill, 300 N. State St., Salt Lake City, UT 84114; 1-800-200-1160; www.utah.com

Website. www.utah.gov

Vermont (VT)
Green Mountain State

People. Population: 626,011; rank: 50. **Pop. change** (2010-12): <0.05%. **Pop. density:** 67.9 per sq mi. **Racial distribution:** 95.4% white; 1.1% black; 1.4% Asian; 0.4% Amer. Ind.; <0.05% Hawaiian/Pacific Islander; two or more races, 1.7%. **Hispanic pop.:** 1.6%.

Geography. Total area: 9,616 sq mi; rank: 45. **Land area:** 9,217 sq mi; rank: 43. **Acres forested:** 4.6 mil. **Location:** northern New England state. **Climate:** temperate, with considerable temperature extremes; heavy snowfall in mountains. **Topography:** Green Mts. N-S backbone 20-36 mi wide; avg. altitude 1,000 ft. **Capital:** Montpelier. **Chief airport:** Burlington.

Economy. Chief industries: manufacturing, tourism, agriculture, trade, finance, insurance, real estate, government. **Chief manuf. goods:** dairy, plastics, printing, wood furniture, sporting goods, metalworking machinery. **Chief crops:** greenhouse & nursery, hay, maple syrup, apples, berries, sweet corn. **Livestock:** 225,000 chickens (excl. broilers), 270,000 cattle/calves. **Nonfuel minerals:** $117 mil; stone (crushed), sand and gravel (construction), stone (dimension), talc (crude),

gemstones (natural). **Gross state product:** $27.3 bil. **Sales tax:** 6.0%. **Employment distrib.:** 18.4% govt.; 18.1% trade/trans./util.; 10.6% mfg.; 20.3% ed./health; 8.9% prof./bus. serv.; 10% leisure/hosp.; 4% finance; 4.9% constr./mining/log.; 1.5% info.; 3.3% other serv. **Unemployment:** 5.0%. **Per cap. pers. income:** $42,994. **New private housing:** 1,301 units/$219 mil. **Broadband Internet:** 76.7%. **Commercial banks:** 14; deposits: $7 bil. **Savings institutions:** 10; deposits: $4.7 bil. **Lottery:** total sales: $100.9 mil; profit: $22.3 mil.

Federal govt. Fed. civ. employees: 4,797; **avg. salary:** $69,040. **Notable fed. facilities:** Law Enforcement Support Ctr.

Energy. Electricity use/cost: 573 kWh, $93.19.
State data. Motto: Freedom and unity. **Flower:** Red clover. **Bird:** Hermit thrush. **Tree:** Sugar maple. **Song:** "These Green Mountains." **Entered union:** Mar. 4, 1791; rank: 14th. **State fair** at Rutland, late Aug.-early Sept.

History. Inhabited for 10,000 years or more, the region attracted Abenaki and Mahican peoples before Europeans arrived. Champlain explored the lake that now bears his name, 1609. The first European settlement was on Isle la Motte, in Lake Champlain, 1666. During the American Revolution, Ethan Allen and the Green Mountain Boys captured Ft. Ticonderoga (NY), 1775. Under a constitution that provided for public schools and abolished slavery, settlers declared a republic, 1777. Vermont joined the Union, 1791. Agriculture dominated in the 19th cent. Still mainly rural, the state expanded tourism and manufacturing after World War II, and IBM became the largest private employer. Vermont was the first state to recognize same-sex unions (2000) and to enact equal same-sex marriage rights via legislation (2009).

Tourist attractions. Shelburne Museum; Shelburne Farms; Vermont Marble Museum, Proctor; Bennington Battle Monument; Pres. Calvin Coolidge Homestead, Plymouth; Ben & Jerry's Factory, Waterbury; Stowe, Killington, and Burke ski resorts: Hildene (Robert Todd Lincoln home), Manchester; Marsh-Billings-Rockefeller Natl. Historical Park, Woodstock.

Famous Vermonters. Ethan Allen, Chester A. Arthur, Calvin Coolidge, Howard Dean, John Deere, George Dewey, John Dewey, Stephen A. Douglas, Dorothy Canfield Fisher, James Fisk, James "Jim" Jeffords, Jody Williams.

Tourist information. Vermont Dept. of Tourism and Marketing, Natl. Life Building, 6th Fl., Montpelier, VT 05620; (802) 828-3237, 1-800-VERMONT; www.vermontvacation.com
Website. www.vermont.gov

Virginia (VA)
Old Dominion

People. Population: 8,185,867; rank: 12. **Pop. change** (2010-12): 2.3%. **Pop. density:** 207.3 per sq mi. **Racial distribution:** 71.1% white; 19.7% black; 6.0% Asian; 0.5% Amer. Ind.; 0.1% Hawaiian/Pacific Islander; two or more races, 2.6%. **Hispanic pop.:** 8.4%.

Geography. Total area: 42,775 sq mi; rank: 35. **Land area:** 39,490 sq mi; rank: 36. **Acres forested:** 15.9 mil. **Location:** South Atlantic state bounded by the Atlantic Ocean on the E and surrounded by North Carolina, Tennessee, Kentucky, West Virginia, and Maryland. **Climate:** mild and equable. **Topography:** mountain and valley region in the W, including the Blue Ridge Mts.; rolling Piedmont Plateau; tidewater, or coastal plain, including the eastern shore. **Capital:** Richmond. **Chief airports:** Arlington, Dulles, Highland Springs, Norfolk.

Economy. Chief industries: services, trade, government, manufacturing, tourism, agriculture. **Chief manuf. goods:** beverages & tobacco, transportation equip., animal slaughtering & processing, plastics, textiles, paper & paper prods., printing, pharmaceuticals, furniture, chemicals. **Chief crops:** greenhouse & nursery, soybeans, tomatoes, corn, tobacco, hay, cotton, apples, wheat, peanuts, potatoes. **Livestock:** 3.85 mil chickens (excl. broilers), 240.5 mil broilers, 1.61 mil cattle/calves, 87,000 sheep/lambs. **Nonfuel minerals:** $1.3 bil; zirconium concentrates, sand and gravel (construction), cement (portland), lime, titanium concentrates. **Commercial fishing:** $175.6 mil. **Chief ports:** Norfolk Harbor, Newport News, Richmond, Hopewell. **Gross state product:** $445.9 bil. **Sales tax:** 5.0%. **Employment distrib.:** 19.1% govt.; 16.8% trade/trans./util.; 6.2% mfg.; 12.9% ed./health; 18% prof./bus. serv.; 9.9% leisure/hosp.; 5.2% finance; 5.1% constr./mining/log.; 1.9% info.; 5% other serv. **Unemployment:** 5.9%. **Per

cap. pers. income:** $47,082. **New private housing:** 27,278 units/$4.1 bil. **Broadband Internet:** 75.6%. **Commercial banks:** 138; deposits: $211.3 bil. **Savings institutions:** 11; deposits: $37.5 bil. **Lottery:** total sales: $1.6 bil; profit: $487.1 mil.

Federal govt. Fed. civ. employees: 148,747; **avg. salary:** $86,765. **Notable fed. facilities:** Pentagon; Norfolk Naval Sta., Shipyard, and other Hampton Roads military bases; Ft. Belvoir; Joint Base Langley-Eustis; NASA Langley Res. Ctr.; CIA George Bush Ctr. for Intelligence, Langley; Quantico USMC Base, FBI Academy; Dahlgren Nav. Surface Warfare Ctr. & Lab; USDA Food and Nutrition Serv.; U.S. Geological Survey Natl. Ctr.

Energy. Electricity use/cost: 1,183 kWh, $125.86.
State data. Motto: Sic Semper Tyrannis (Thus always to tyrants). **Flower:** Dogwood. **Bird:** Cardinal. **Tree:** Dogwood. **Song emeritus:** "Carry Me Back to Old Virginia." **Tenth** of the original 13 states to ratify the Constitution, June 25, 1788. **State fair** at Doswell, late Sept.-early Oct.

History. Cherokee and Susquehanna peoples and the Algonquians of the Powhatan Confederacy were in the region when Europeans arrived. English settlers founded Jamestown, 1607. Virginians were indispensable to the founding of the American republic, and 4 of the first 5 U.S. presidents—Washington, Jefferson, Madison, and Monroe—came from there. The conclusive battle of the American Revolution took place at Yorktown, 1781. The state profited from tobacco, cotton, and the slave trade; in 1860, slaves made up nearly one-third of the population. Virginia seceded from the Union, 1861, and Richmond became the capital of the Confederacy, but western counties, loyal to the Union, split off to become West Virginia, 1863. The war ended with Robert E. Lee's surrender to Ulysses S. Grant at Appomattox, 1865, and Virginia was readmitted to the Union, 1870. In the 20th cent., expansion of federal civilian jobs and military facilities transformed the economy. State officials pledged "massive resistance" to racial integration in the mid-1950s, but eventually accommodated. In 1989, L. Douglas Wilder became the first elected black governor in U.S. history. On Sept. 11, 2001, terrorist hijackers crashed a jet into U.S. defense headquarters at the Pentagon, in Arlington.

Tourist attractions. Colonial Williamsburg, Busch Gardens Williamsburg, Jamestown Settlement, in Williamsburg; Yorktown Victory Ctr.; Wolf Trap Natl. Park for the Performing Arts, near Vienna; Arlington Natl. Cemetery; George Washington's Mount Vernon; Thomas Jefferson's Monticello, Charlottesville; Stratford Hall (Robert E. Lee birthplace); Appomattox Court House Natl. Historical Park; Shenandoah Natl. Park; Blue Ridge Natl. Parkway; Virginia Beach; Kings Dominion amusement park, Doswell.

Famous Virginians. Arthur Ashe, Sandra Bullock, Richard E. Byrd, James B. Cabell, Henry Clay, Katie Couric, Gabby Douglas, Jubal Early, Jerry Falwell, William Henry Harrison, Patrick Henry, A. P. Hill, Thomas Jefferson, Joseph E. Johnston, Robert E. Lee, Meriwether Lewis and William Clark, James Madison, John Marshall, George Mason, James Monroe, Sean Parker, George Pickett, Pocahontas, Edgar Allan Poe, John Randolph, Walter Reed, Rev. Pat Robertson, John Smith, J. E. B. Stuart, William Styron, Zachary Taylor, John Tyler, Maggie Walker, Booker T. Washington, George Washington, L. Douglas Wilder, Woodrow Wilson.

Tourist information. Virginia Tourism Corp., 901 E. Byrd St., Richmond, VA 23219; 1-800-VISITVA; www.virginia.org
Website. www.virginia.gov

Washington (WA)
Evergreen State

People. Population: 6,897,012; rank: 13. **Pop. change** (2010-12): 2.6%. **Pop. density:** 103.8 per sq mi. **Racial distribution:** 81.6% white; 3.9% black; 7.7% Asian; 1.8% Amer. Ind.; 0.7% Hawaiian/Pacific Islander; two or more races, 4.3%. **Hispanic pop.:** 11.7%.

Geography. Total area: 71,298 sq mi; rank: 18. **Land area:** 66,456 sq mi; rank: 20. **Acres forested:** 22.4 mil. **Location:** Pacific state bordered by Canada on the N, Idaho on the E, Oregon on the S, and the Pacific Ocean on the W. **Climate:** mild, dominated by the Pacific Ocean and protected by the Cascades. **Topography:** Olympic Mts. on NW peninsula; open land along coast to Columbia R.; flat terrain of Puget Sound Lowland; high peaks of Cascade Mts. to the E; Columbia Basin in central portion; highlands to the NE; mountains

to the SE. **Capital:** Olympia. **Chief airports:** Bellingham, Seattle, Spokane.

Economy. Chief industries: advanced technology, aerospace, biotechnology, intl. trade, forestry, tourism, recycling, agriculture & food processing. **Chief manuf. goods:** aerospace, petroleum, food, paper, milled lumber, plastics, structural metals, computers & electronics. **Chief crops:** apples, potatoes, wheat, hay, cherries, greenhouse & nursery, forest products, pears, grapes, onions, hops, sweet corn, Christmas trees, mint, raspberries. **Livestock:** 8.06 mil chickens (excl. broilers), 1.15 mil cattle/calves, 54,000 sheep/lambs. **Nonfuel minerals:** $689 mil; gold, sand and gravel (construction), stone (crushed), cement (portland), diatomite. **Commercial fishing:** $275.6 mil. **Chief ports:** Seattle, Tacoma, Vancouver, Kelso-Longview, Anacortes. **Gross state product:** $375.7 bil. **Sales tax:** 6.5%. **Employment distrib.:** 18.9% govt.; 18.7% trade/trans./util.; 9.8% mfg.; 13.5% ed./health; 12% prof./bus. serv.; 9.8% leisure/hosp.; 4.9% finance; 5% constr./mining/log.; 3.6% info.; 3.8% other serv. **Unemployment:** 8.2%. **Per cap. pers. income:** $45,413. **New private housing:** 28,118 units/$5.6 bil. **Broadband Internet:** 82%. **Commercial banks:** 86; deposits: $101.6 bil. **Savings institutions:** 17; deposits: $11.7 bil. **Lottery:** total sales: $535.2 mil; profit: $138.0 mil.

Federal govt. Fed. civ. employees: 57,035; **avg. salary:** $72,850. **Notable fed. facilities:** Bonneville Power Admin.; Lewis-McChord Joint Base; Fairchild AFB; DOE Hanford Nuclear Site; Naval Base Kitsap (Bremerton and Bangor); Whidbey Island NAS; Pacific Northwest Natl. Lab.

Energy. Electricity use/cost: 1,068 kWh, $88.41.

State data. Motto: Alki (By and by). **Flower:** Western rhododendron. **Bird:** Willow goldfinch. **Tree:** Western hemlock. **Song:** "Washington, My Home." **Entered union:** Nov. 11, 1889; rank: 42nd. **State fair:** at Monroe, late Aug-early Sept.; at Puyallup, Sept.; at Yakima, late Sept.

History. People of the Clovis culture lived in the region 11,000 years ago. At the time of European contact, Native Americans in the area included Nez Percé, Spokane, Yakima, Cayuse, Okanogan, Walla Walla, and Colville peoples in the interior, and Nooksak, Chinook, Nisqually, Clallam, Makah, Quinault, and Puyallup peoples along the coast. Spain's Bruno de Hezeta sailed the coast, 1775. In 1792, British naval officer George Vancouver mapped the Puget Sound area, and American Capt. Robert Gray sailed up the Columbia R. Fur traders and missionaries arrived in the first half of the 19th cent. Final agreement on the border of Washington and Canada was made with Britain, 1846. Completion in 1883 of a transcontinental rail link between Puget Sound and the eastern U.S. aided immigration, and Washington became a state in 1889. In the 20th cent., cheap hydroelectric power spurred growth in the aluminum and aircraft industries. Founded in 1975, Microsoft became a computer software giant. Mt. St. Helens erupted, 1980. With grunge music, Starbucks coffee, and Amazon.com, Seattle became a national trendsetter in the 1990s. Violent street protests disrupted a World Trade Organization meeting there in 1999. Gary Locke, in office 1997-2005, was the first U.S. governor of Chinese ancestry.

Tourist attractions. Seattle Center, Space Needle, EMP Museum, Museum of Flight, Pike Place Market, Underground Tour, in Seattle; Mount Rainier, Olympic, and North Cascades Natl. Parks; Mount St. Helens Natl. Volcanic Monument; Puget Sound; San Juan Islands; Grand Coulee Dam; Columbia R. Gorge Natl. Scenic Area; Riverfront Park, Spokane; Snoqualmie Falls.

Famous Washingtonians. Paul Allen, Glenn Beck, Raymond Carver, Kurt Cobain, Bing Crosby, William O. Douglas, Bill Gates, Jimi Hendrix, Henry M. Jackson, Gary Larson, Mary McCarthy, Robert Motherwell, Edward R. Murrow, Apolo Ohno, Theodore Roethke, Ann Rule, Hope Solo, Hilary Swank, Julia Sweeney, Adam West, Marcus Whitman, Minoru Yamasaki.

Tourist information. WA State Tourism Office, 128 10th Ave. SW, P.O. Box 42525, Olympia, WA 98504; 1-866-964-8913; www.experiencewa.com

Website. access.wa.gov

West Virginia (WV)
Mountain State

People. Population: 1,855,413; rank: 38. **Pop. change** (2010-12): 0.1%. **Pop. density:** 77.2 per sq mi. **Racial distribution:** 94.0% white; 3.5% black; 0.7% Asian; 0.2% Amer. Ind.; <0.05% Hawaiian/Pacific Islander; two or more races, 1.5%. **Hispanic pop.:** 1.3%.

Geography. Total area: 24,230 sq mi; rank: 41. **Land area:** 24,038 sq mi; rank: 41. **Acres forested:** 12.2 mil. **Location:** South Atlantic state bounded on the N by Pennsylvania, Maryland; on the S, W, and NW by Virginia, Kentucky, Ohio; on the E by Maryland and Virginia. **Climate:** humid continental climate except for marine modification in the lower panhandle. **Topography:** hilly to mountainous; Allegheny Plateau in the W covers two-thirds of state; mountains here are the highest in the state, over 4,000 ft. **Capital:** Charleston.

Economy. Chief industries: manufacturing, services, mining, tourism. **Chief manuf. goods:** chemicals, aluminum, motor vehicle parts, lumber & plywood, primary & fabricated metals. **Chief crops:** hay, apples, corn, peaches, soybeans, tobacco, wheat. **Livestock:** 1.9 mil chickens (excl. broilers), 94 mil broilers, 410,000 cattle/calves, 30,000 sheep/lambs. **Nonfuel minerals:** $341 mil; stone (crushed), cement (portland), lime, sand and gravel (industrial), cement (masonry). **Chief port:** Huntington. **Gross state product:** $69.4 bil. **Sales tax:** 6.0%. **Employment distrib.:** 20.3% govt.; 17.5% trade/trans./util.; 6.3% mfg.; 16.4% ed./health; 8.3% prof./bus. serv.; 9.9% leisure/hosp.; 3.6% finance; 9.4% constr./mining/log.; 1.2% info.; 7.1% other serv. **Unemployment:** 7.3%. **Per cap. pers. income:** $34,477. **New private housing:** 2,718 units/$346.6 mil. **Broadband Internet:** 90%. **Commercial banks:** 77; deposits: $29.5 bil. **Savings institutions:** 5; deposits: $824 mil. **Lottery:** total sales: $1.5 bil; profit: $663.0 mil.

Federal govt. Fed. civ. employees: 16,110; **avg. salary:** $69,735. **Notable fed. facilities:** Natl. Radio Astronomy Observatory, Green Bank; Bureau of Public Debt Bldg.; Alderson Fed. Prison Camp; FBI Criminal Justice Information Services.

Energy. Electricity use/cost: 1,128 kWh, $105.89.

State data. Motto: Montani Semper Liberi (Mountaineers are always free). **Flower:** Big rhododendron. **Bird:** Cardinal. **Tree:** Sugar maple. **Songs:** "The West Virginia Hills"; "This Is My West Virginia"; "West Virginia, My Home, Sweet Home." **Entered union:** June 20, 1863; rank: 35th. **State fair** at Lewisburg, mid-Aug.

History. Sparsely inhabited at the time of European contact, the area was primarily Native American hunting grounds. British explorers Thomas Batts and Robert Fallam reached the New R., 1671. Coal, discovered in 1742, was mined extensively by the mid-19th cent. White settlement led to conflicts with Native Americans, including a major battle in which settlers defeated an Indian confederacy at Point Pleasant, 1774. The region joined the Union as part of Virginia, 1788. Longstanding tensions between the E and W parts of the state came to a head in 1861, when Virginia seceded. Delegates of W counties, meeting at Wheeling, repudiated the act and created a new state, Kanawha, later renamed West Virginia, which was admitted to the Union in 1863. Poverty has been a problem for much of the state's subsequent history. West Virginia continued to rank low in per capita personal income, despite billions of dollars in federal contracts brought to the state by 9-term U.S. Sen. Robert Byrd, who passed away in 2010. Coal mining, though dangerous, continues to be a major industry; nearly 30 miners were killed in a mine explosion in 2010.

Tourist attractions. Harpers Ferry Natl. Historical Park, Appalachian Trail Conservancy and Visitor Ctr., in Harpers Ferry; Clay Center for the Arts and Sciences and Avampato Discovery Museum, Charleston; The Greenbrier resort, White Sulphur Springs; Berkeley Springs State Park; Seneca Rocks State Park; New River Gorge Natl. River; Beckley Exhibition Coal Mine; Monongahela Natl. Forest; Fenton Art Glass Company, Williamstown; Mountain State Forest Festival, Elkins; Mountain State Art & Craft Fair, Ripley; Natl. Radio Astronomy Observatory in Green Bank (with world's largest fully steerable radio telescope); Cass Scenic Railroad State Park.

Famous West Virginians. George Brett, Pearl S. Buck, Robert C. Byrd, Henry Louis Gates Jr., Stonewall Jackson, Don Knotts, Michael Joseph Owens, Brad Paisley, Mary Lou Retton, Walter Reuther, Cyrus Vance, Jerry West, Charles "Chuck" Yeager.

Tourist information. West Virginia Division of Tourism, Capitol Complex, Bldg. 6, Rm. 525, Charleston, WV 25305; 1-800-CALLWVA; www.wvtourism.com

Website. www.wv.gov

Wisconsin (WI)
Badger State

People. Population: 5,726,398; rank: 20. **Pop. change** (2010-12): 0.7%. **Pop. density:** 105.7 per sq mi. **Racial distribution:** 88.2% white; 6.5% black; 2.5% Asian; 1.1% Amer. Ind.; <0.05% Hawaiian/Pacific Islander; two or more races, 1.7%. **Hispanic pop.:** 6.2%.

Geography. Total area: 65,496 sq mi; rank: 23. **Land area:** 54,158 sq mi; rank: 25. **Acres forested:** 17.1 mil. **Location:** East North Central state, bounded on the N by Lake Superior and Upper Michigan, on the E by Lake Michigan, on the S by Illinois, on the W by the St. Croix and Mississippi Rivers. **Climate:** long, cold winters and short, warm summers tempered by the Great Lakes. **Topography:** narrow Lake Superior Lowland plain met by Northern Highland, which slopes gently to the sandy crescent Central Plain; Western Upland in the SW; 3 broad parallel limestone ridges running N-S are separated by wide and shallow lowlands in the SE. **Capital:** Madison. **Chief airports:** Madison, Milwaukee.

Economy. Chief industries: services, manufacturing, trade, government, agriculture, tourism. **Chief manuf. goods:** transportation, dairy, animal slaughtering & processing, paper, printing, plastics, computers & electronics. **Chief crops:** corn, greenhouse & nursery, soybeans, potatoes, cranberries, hay, wheat, snap beans, apples, peas. **Livestock:** 6.7 mil chickens (excl. broilers), 51.7 mil broilers, 3.45 mil cattle/calves, 84,000 sheep/lambs. **Nonfuel minerals:** $660 mil; sand and gravel (industrial), stone (crushed), sand and gravel (construction), lime, stone (dimension). **Commercial fishing:** $5.0 mil. **Chief ports:** Superior, Milwaukee, Green Bay. **Gross state product:** $261.5 bil. **Sales tax:** 5.0%. **Employment distrib.:** 14.8% govt.; 18% trade/trans./util.; 16.3% mfg.; 14.9% ed./health; 10.4% prof./bus. serv.; 9.8% leisure/hosp.; 5.8% finance; 3.6% constr./mining/log.; 1.6% info.; 4.9% other serv. **Unemployment:** 6.9%. **Per cap. pers. income:** $40,537. **New private housing:** 12,041 units/$2 bil. **Broadband Internet:** 83.7%. **Commercial banks:** 260; deposits: $119.6 bil. **Savings institutions:** 35; deposits: $13.2 bil. **Lottery:** total sales: $547.0 mil; profit: $149.9 mil.

Federal govt. Fed. civ. employees: 16,120; **avg. salary:** $66,585. **Notable fed. facilities:** Ft. McCoy; USDA Forest Products Lab.

Energy. Electricity use/cost: 709 kWh, $92.39.

State data. Motto: Forward. **Flower:** Wood violet. **Bird:** Robin. **Tree:** Sugar maple. **Song:** "On, Wisconsin!" **Entered union:** May 29, 1848; rank: 30th. **State fair** at West Allis, early Aug.

History. At the time of European contact, Ojibwa, Menominee, Winnebago, Kickapoo, Sauk, Fox, and Potawatomi peoples inhabited the area. French explorer Jean Nicolet reached Green Bay, 1634; French missionaries and fur traders followed. The British took over, 1763. The U.S. won the land after the American Revolution but did not wield control until forts were established at Green Bay and Prairie du Chien, 1816. Native Americans rebelled against the seizure of tribal lands in the Black Hawk War, 1832, but were defeated and relocated to reservations. Wisconsin became a territory, 1836, and a state, 1848. Some 96,000 soldiers served the Union cause during the Civil War. Many immigrants arrived from Germany, Poland, and Scandinavia. Wisconsin agriculture focused on dairy; Milwaukee became a manufacturing center. As governor, 1901-06, Robert La Follette pushed Progressive reforms such as direct primary voting and consumer protection laws. An era of "McCarthyism" ended when anti-Communist crusader Sen. Joseph McCarthy (WI) was censured by the U.S. Senate, 1954. After weeks of protests in Madison, the Republican-controlled state legislature passed controversial measures in 2011 to restrict collective bargaining by some 170,000 public-sector employees.

Tourist attractions. Wade House, Greenbush; Villa Louis, Prairie du Chien; Circus World Museum, Baraboo; Wisconsin Dells; Old World Wisconsin, Eagle; shoreline and state parks of Door County; Chequamegon-Nicolet Natl. Forest; House on the Rock, Taliesin, in Spring Green; Monona Terrace Community and Convention Ctr., Madison; Milwaukee Art Museum, Pabst Mansion, in Milwaukee.

Famous Wisconsinites. Don Ameche, Carrie Chapman Catt, Willem Dafoe, Edna Ferber, Hamlin Garland, King Camp Gillette, Harry Houdini, Robert La Follette, (Vladzio Valentino) Liberace, Alfred Lunt, Pat O'Brien, Georgia O'Keeffe, Danica Patrick, Les Paul, William H. Rehnquist, John Ringling, Donald K. "Deke" Slayton, Spencer Tracy, Orson Welles, Laura Ingalls Wilder, Thornton Wilder, Frank Lloyd Wright.

Tourist information. Wisconsin Dept. of Tourism, 201 W. Washington Ave., P.O. Box 8690, Madison, WI 53708; 1-800-432-TRIP; www.travelwisconsin.com

Website. www.wisconsin.gov

Wyoming (WY)
Equality State, Cowboy State

People. Population: 576,412; rank: 51. **Pop. change** (2010-12): 2.3%. **Pop. density:** 5.9 per sq mi. **Racial distribution:** 93.1% white; 1.5% black; 0.9% Asian; 2.6% Amer. Ind.; 0.1% Hawaiian/Pacific Islander; two or more races, 1.8%. **Hispanic pop.:** 9.5%.

Geography. Total area: 97,813 sq mi; rank: 10. **Land area:** 97,093 sq mi; rank: 9. **Acres forested:** 10.4 mil. **Location:** Mountain state lying in the high western plateaus of the Great Plains. **Climate:** semidesert conditions throughout; true desert in the Bighorn and Great Divide Basins. **Topography:** eastern Great Plains rise to the foothills of the Rocky Mts.; the Continental Divide crosses the state from the NW to the SE. **Capital:** Cheyenne.

Economy. Chief industries: mineral extraction, oil, natural gas, tourism and recreation, agriculture. **Chief manuf. goods:** petroleum, chemicals, fabricated metal, beet sugar, lumber. **Chief crops:** hay, sugar beets, barley, dry beans, wheat, corn, greenhouse & nursery, oats. **Livestock:** 13,000 chickens (excl. broilers), 1.29 mil cattle/calves, 375,000 sheep/lambs. **Nonfuel minerals:** $2.2 bil; soda ash, clays (bentonite), helium (Grade-A), sand and gravel (construction), cement (portland). **Gross state product:** $38.4 bil. **Sales tax:** 4.0%. **Employment distrib.:** 26% govt.; 18.6% trade/trans./util.; 3.3% mfg.; 9.2% ed./health; 5.9% prof./bus. serv.; 11.3% leisure/hosp.; 3.7% finance; 16.9% constr./mining/log.; 1.3% info.; 3.7% other serv. **Unemployment:** 5.4%. **Per cap. pers. income:** $48,670. **New private housing:** 2,110 units/$439.1 mil. **Broadband Internet:** 65.3%. **Commercial banks:** 43; deposits: $12.5 bil. **Savings institutions:** 3; deposits: $485 mil.

Federal govt. Fed. civ. employees: 5,782; **avg. salary:** $61,289. **Notable fed. facilities:** Warren AFB.

Energy. Electricity use/cost: 903 kWh, $82.28.

State data. Motto: Equal rights. **Flower:** Indian paintbrush. **Bird:** Western meadowlark. **Tree:** Plains cottonwood. **Song:** "Wyoming." **Entered union:** July 10, 1890; rank: 44th. **State fair** at Douglas, mid-Aug.

History. Inhabited for at least 12,000 years, the region supported Shoshone, Crow, Cheyenne, Oglala Sioux, and Arapaho peoples when Europeans arrived. France's Vérendrye brothers were the first Europeans to see the region, 1742-43. John Colter, an American, traversed the Yellowstone area, 1807-08. Trappers and fur traders followed in the 1820s. Forts Laramie and Bridger became important stops on trails to the West Coast. Population grew after the Union Pacific crossed the state, 1867-68. Wyoming became a territory, 1868, and the first to extend full voting rights to women, 1869. Statehood was attained, 1890. Disputes between large landowners and small ranchers culminated in the Johnson County Cattle War, 1892; federal troops were called in to restore order. Nellie Tayloe Ross was the first woman governor to take office in the U.S., 1925. Wyoming, the least populous state, has relied on the energy, tourism, and ranching industries in recent decades. Dick Cheney, Wyoming's representative in the U.S. House, 1979-89, served as U.S. vice pres. (2001-09).

Tourist attractions. Yellowstone Natl. Park (est. 1872, first U.S. national park); Grand Teton Natl. Park; Natl. Elk Refuge, Jackson; Devils Tower Natl. Monument; Ft. Laramie Natl. Historic Site; Oregon Trail ruts, Guernsey; Buffalo Bill Historical Ctr., Cody; Cheyenne Frontier Days.

Famous Wyomingites. James Bridger, Dick Cheney, William F. "Buffalo Bill" Cody, Curt Gowdy, Esther Hobart Morris, Nellie Tayloe Ross.

Tourist information. Wyoming Travel and Tourism, 1520 Etchepare Cir., Cheyenne, WY 82007; 1-800-225-5996; www.wyomingtourism.org

Website. www.wyoming.gov

District of Columbia (DC)

People. Population: 632,323; rank: 49. **Pop. change** (2010-12): 5.1%. **Pop. density:** 10,357.7 per sq mi. **Racial**

distribution: 42.9% white; 50.1% black; 3.8% Asian; 0.6% Amer. Ind.; 0.2% Hawaiian/Pacific Islander; two or more races, 2.5%. **Hispanic pop.:** 9.9%.

Geography. Total area: 68 sq mi; rank: 51. **Land area:** 61 sq mi; rank: 51. **Acres forested:** NA. **Location:** at the confluence of the Potomac and Anacostia Rivers, flanked by Maryland on the N, E, and SE and by Virginia on the SW. **Climate:** hot humid summers, mild winters. **Topography:** low hills rise toward the N away from the Potomac R. and slope to the S; highest elevation, 410 ft, lowest on Potomac R., 1 ft.

Economy. Chief industries: government, legal, publishing, medical, service, tourism. **Gross state product:** $109.8 bil. **Sales tax:** 6.0%. **Employment distrib.:** 33.2% govt.; 3.7% trade/trans./util.; 0.2% mfg.; 16.1% ed./health; 20.5% prof./bus. serv.; 9% leisure/hosp.; 3.7% finance; 1.8% constr./mining/log.; 2.5% info.; 9.4% other serv. **Unemployment:** 8.9%. **Per cap. pers. income:** $74,710. **New private housing:** 3,823 units/$471.5 mil. **Broadband Internet:** 75.7%. **Commercial banks:** 30; deposits: $33 bil. **Savings institutions:** 5; deposits: $182 mil. **Lottery:** total sales: $252.2 mil; profit: $65.5 mil. **Federal govt. Fed. civ. employees:** 162,164; **avg. salary:** $105,996.

Energy. Electricity use/cost: 749 kWh, $100.30.

District data. Motto: Justitia omnibus (Justice for all). **Flower:** American beauty rose. **Tree:** Scarlet oak. **Bird:** Wood thrush.

History. The District of Columbia, coextensive with the city of Washington, is the seat of the U.S. federal government. It lies on the west central edge of Maryland on the Potomac R., opposite Virginia. The Piscataway, an Algonquian-speaking people, were living in the region when Europeans arrived in the 17th cent. Proposals for a "federal town" for the deliberations of the Continental Congress were made in 1783. Authorized by Congress, 1790, Pres. George Washington chose the Potomac site and persuaded landowners to sell their holdings to the government. Its area was originally 100 sq mi taken from the sovereignty of Maryland and Virginia. Virginia's portion south of the Potomac was given back to that state in 1846.

Pres. Washington chose Pierre Charles L'Enfant, a Frenchman, to plan the capital. Surveyor Andrew Ellicott finished the official map and design of the city, assisted by Benjamin Banneker, a black architect and astronomer. Washington laid the cornerstone of the north wing of the Capitol building, 1793, and Pres. John Adams moved to the new national capital, 1800. The City of Washington was incorporated, 1802. British troops invaded, 1814, setting fire to the Capitol, the President's House (as the White House was then called), and other buildings. Pres. Abraham Lincoln ended slavery in the district, 1862. Many African Americans arrived after the Civil War, but racial segregation remained legal until the mid-20th cent. After federal government expansion spurred population growth, 1930-50, an exodus to the suburbs shrank the city's population, 1950-2005.

The 23rd Amendment (1961) granted residents the right to vote for president and vice president. Congress, which has legislative authority over the District under the Constitution, approved legislation in 1970 giving the District one delegate to the House of Representatives, who could vote in committee but not on the floor. Voters approved, 1974, a congressionally drafted charter giving them the right to elect their own mayor and city council. The district won the right to levy taxes, but Congress retained power to veto council actions and approve the city budget. Security measures were dramatically increased after terrorists attacked the U.S. on Sept. 11, 2001. After a 34-year absence, major league baseball returned to the city in 2005.

Tourist attractions. See Attractions in Washington, DC, Capital of the U.S.

Famous Washingtonians. Edward Albee, Michael Chabon, Frederick Douglass, John Foster Dulles, Kevin Durant, Edward Kennedy "Duke" Ellington, Marvin Gaye, Katharine Graham, Goldie Hawn, J. Edgar Hoover, Bill Nye, Pete Sampras, John Philip Sousa.

Tourist information. Destination DC, 901 7th St. NW, 4th Fl., Washington, DC, 20001-3719; 1-800-422-8644; www.washington.org

Website. www.dc.gov

OUTLYING U.S. AREAS

American Samoa (AS)

People. Population (2013 est.): 54,719. **Pop. change** (2010-13): −1.4%. **Pop. density:** 710.6 per sq mi. **Racial distrib.** (2000): 91.6% Pac. Isl.; 2.8% Asian; 1.1% white; 2 or more races, 4.2%. **Languages:** Samoan, English, Tongan.

Geography. Total area: 77 sq mi. **Land area:** 77 sq mi. **Acres forested:** 43,631. **Location:** most southerly of all lands under U.S. sovereign, about 2,300 mi SW of Honolulu. It is an unincorporated territory consisting of 7 small islands of the Samoan group: **Tutuila** (52.59 sq mi), **Aunu'u** (0.59 sq mi); Manu'a group: **Ta'u** (17.57 sq mi), **Olosega** (2.03 sq mi), **Ofu** (2.83 sq mi), and the atolls **Rose** (0.03 sq mi) and **Swains** (1.38 sq mi). **Climate:** marine tropical, avg. temp 82°F with little seasonal variation; avg. annual rainfall about 36 in. **Topography:** volcanic islands, rugged peaks, and limited coastal plains. About 70% of the land is bush and mountains. **Capital:** Pago Pago on Tutuila. **Airport:** Pago Pago.

Economy. Chief industries: tuna fishing and processing, trade, services, tourism. **Chief crops:** giant taro, taro, yams, coconuts, breadfruits, bananas, papayas. **Livestock** (2008): 35,709 chickens, 16,904 hogs/pigs. **Nonfuel minerals:** crushed stone, trap rock. **Commercial fishing** (2008): $9.7 mil. **Unemployment** (2007): 29.8%. **Gross domestic product** (2010): $615.0 mil. **Broadband Internet:** NA. **Commercial banks:** 2; deposits: $189 mil.

Energy. Electricity production (2008): 190 mil kWh.

Fed. civ. employees (Mar. 2013): 117; **avg. salary:** $53,344.

Misc. data. Motto: Samoa Muamua le Atua (In Samoa, God is first). **Flower:** Paogo (Ula-fala). **Plant:** Ava. **Song:** "Amerika Samoa."

History. A tripartite agreement between Great Britain, Germany, and the U.S. in 1899 gave the U.S. sovereignty over the eastern islands of the Samoan group; these islands became American Samoa. Local chiefs ceded Tutuila and Aunu'u to the U.S. in 1900, and the Manu'a group and Rose Island in 1904; Swains Island was annexed in 1925. Samoa (Western), comprising the larger islands of the Samoan group, was a New Zealand mandate and UN Trusteeship until it became independent Jan. 1, 1962 (now called Samoa).

From 1900 to 1951, American Samoa was under the jurisdiction of the U.S. Navy. Since 1951, it has been under the Interior Dept. On Jan. 3, 1978, the first popularly elected Samoan governor and lieutenant governor were inaugurated. Previously, the governor was appointed by the Sec. of the Interior. American Samoa has a bicameral legislature and elects a delegate to the U.S. House of Representatives who has a voice but no vote, except in committees.

Five of the seven islands are volcanoes. Scientists discovered a rapidly growing volcano, Vailulu'u, between Ta'u and Rose in 1975.

The tuna canning industry has been the backbone of the economy since the 1950s, but one of the two canneries closed in 2009. An 8.1 magnitude earthquake in Sept. 2009 triggered a tsunami that severely damaged Tutuila.

American Samoans are of Polynesian origin. They are nationals of the U.S. As of 2010, 109,637 lived in the U.S., including 18,287 in Hawaii and 40,100 in California.

Tourist attractions. Natl. Park of American Samoa; Natl. Marine Sanctuary of American Samoa; Jean P. Haydon Museum.

Tourist information. Office of Tourism, Dept. of Commerce, American Samoa Govt., P.O. Box 1147, Pago Pago, AS 96799; (684) 699-9411; www.amsamoatourism.com

Website. www.americansamoa.gov

Guam (GU)

People. Population (2013 est.): 160,378. **Pop change** (2010-13): 0.6%. **Pop. density:** 756.5 per sq mi. **Racial/ethnic distrib.** (2010 est.): 41.0% Chamorro; 30.6% Filipino; 11.7% other Pac. Isl.; 3.2% white. **Languages:** English, Chamorro, Philippine/other Pacific Island languages.

Geography. Total area: 212 sq mi. **Land area:** 212 sq mi. **Acres forested:** 63,830. **Location:** largest and southernmost of the Mariana Islands in the West Pacific, 3,700 mi W of Hawaii. **Climate:** tropical, with temperatures from 70° to 90°F; rainy July to Nov., avg. annual rainfall, about 80-100 in. **Topography:** coralline limestone plateau in the N; southern chain of low volcanic mountains slope gently to the W, more steeply to coastal cliffs on the E; general elevation, 500 ft;

highest point, Mt. Lamlam, 1,334 ft. **Capital:** Hagåtña. **Chief airport:** Tamuning.

Economy. Chief industries: U.S. military, tourism, construction, shipping, concrete products, printing & publishing. **Chief manuf. goods:** textiles, foods. **Chief crops:** watermelons, cucumbers, eggplant, long beans, bananas, corn. **Livestock** (2007): 533 chickens, 112 cattle, 635 hogs/pigs, 124 goats. **Nonfuel minerals** (2008): $3.8 mil; crushed stone. **Commercial fishing** (2008): $499,095. **Chief port:** Apra Harbor. **Gross domestic product** (2010): $4.6 bil. **Employment distrib.** (Dec. 2012): 30.2% trade/trans; 26.7% serv.; 25.5% govt.; 10.6% constr.; 2.7% mfg.; 0.2% agric. **Unemployment** (2012): 10.7%. **Per capita income** (2010): $12,864. **Broadband Internet:** NA. **Commercial banks:** 6; deposits: $2.2 bil. **Savings institutions:** 1; deposits: $85 mil.

Energy. Electricity production (2009): 1.8 bil kWh.

Federal govt. Fed. employees (Mar. 2013): 2,823; **avg. salary:** $58,732. **Notable fed. facilities:** Andersen AFB.

Misc. data. Motto: Where America's day begins. **Flower:** Puti Tai Nobio (Bougainvillea). **Bird:** Ko'ko (Guam rail). **Tree:** Ifit (Intsia bijuga). **Song:** "Stand Ye Guamanians."

History. Guam was probably settled by voyagers from the Indonesian-Philippine archipelago by 3rd cent. BCE. Pottery, rice cultivation, and megalithic technology show strong East Asian cultural influence. Centralized, village clan-based communities engaged in agriculture and offshore fishing. The estimated population by the early 16th cent. was 50,000–75,000. Ferdinand Magellan arrived in the Marianas Mar. 6, 1521. They were colonized in 1668 by Spanish missionaries, who named them the Mariana Islands in honor of Maria Anna, queen of Spain. When Spain ceded Guam to the U.S., it sold the other Marianas to Germany. Japan obtained a League of Nations mandate over the German islands in 1919; in Dec. 1941 it seized Guam, which was retaken by the U.S. in July-Aug. 1944.

Guam is a self-governing organized unincorporated U.S. territory. The Organic Act of 1950 provided for a governor, elected to a 4-year term, and a 21-member unicameral legislature, elected biennially by the residents, who are American citizens. In 1970, the first governor was elected. In 1972, a U.S. law gave Guam one delegate to the U.S. House of Representatives who has a voice but no vote, except in committees.

Guam's quest to change its status to a U.S. commonwealth began in the late 1970s. The Guam Commission on Self-Determination, created in 1984, developed a draft Commonwealth Act. In 1993, legislation proposing a change of status was submitted to the U.S. Congress. In 1994, the U.S. Congress passed legislation transferring 3,200 acres of land on Guam from federal to local control. The U.S. plans to move 8,000 Marines stationed in Okinawa, Japan, to Guam by 2014.

Tourist attractions. Ritidian Point, Guam Natl. Wildlife Refuge; War in the Pacific Natl. Historical Park; Chamorro Village; Two Lovers Point.

Tourist information. Guam Visitors Bureau, 401 Pale San Vitores Rd., Tumon, Guam 96913; (671) 646-5278; www.visitguam.org

Website. www.guam.gov

Commonwealth of the Northern Mariana Islands (MP)

People. Population (2013 est.): 51,170; **Pop. change** (2010-13): −5.0%. **Pop. density:** 277.8 per sq mi. **Racial/ethnic distrib.** (2000): 56.3% Asian; 36.3% Pac. Isl.; 1.8% white; 0.8% other; 2 or more races/ethnicities, 4.8%. **Languages:** Philippine languages, Chinese, Chamorro, English.

Geography. Total area: 184.2 sq mi. **Land area:** 184.2 sq mi. **Acres forested:** 50,218. **Location:** between Guam and the Tropic of Cancer, the 14 islands of the Northern Marianas form a 300-mi long archipelago. The indigenous population is concentrated on the 3 largest of the 6 inhabited islands: **Saipan,** the seat of government and commerce, **Rota,** and **Tinian.** **Climate:** tropical, with avg. temperature around 82°F, moderated by NE trade winds; avg. annual rainfall, 80-100 in. **Topography:** limestone southern islands with even terraces, coral reefs; volcanic northern isles. **Capital:** Saipan. **Airport:** Saipan.

Economy. Chief industries: banking, construction, fishing, mining, tourism, apparel mfg., retail. **Chief manuf. goods:** apparel, stone, clay and glass prods. **Chief crops:** bananas, cucumbers, sweet potatoes, taro, watermelons.

Livestock (2007): 9,700 chickens, 1,395 cattle, 1,483 hogs/pigs. **Commercial fishing** (2008): $751,388. **Chief port:** Saipan. **Gross domestic product** (2010): $733.0 mil. **Unemployment** (2010): 11.2%. **Broadband Internet:** NA. **Commercial banks:** 3; deposits: $468 mil.

Energy. Electricity production (2009): 60,600 kWh.

Federal govt. Fed. civ. employees (Mar. 2013): 200; **avg. salary:** $51,014.

Misc. data. Flower: Plumeria. **Bird:** Mariana fruit-dove. **Tree:** Flame tree. **Song:** "Gi Talo Gi Halom Tasi" (In the Middle of the Sea).

History. The people of the Northern Marianas are predominantly of Chamorro cultural extraction, although Carolinians and immigrants from other areas of E. Asia and Micronesia have also settled in the islands. English is among the several languages commonly spoken.

The German-controlled Northern Marianas were placed under Japanese control by a League of Nations mandate after World War I. The U.S. captured the islands during World War II. From July 18, 1947, the U.S. had administered the Northern Marianas under a trusteeship agreement with the UN Security Council. In 1975, the residents voted to become a U.S. commonwealth.

The Northern Mariana Islands has been self-governing since 1978, when a constitution drafted and adopted by the people became effective and a popularly elected bicameral legislature (2-year term), with offices of governor (4-year term) and lieut. governor, was inaugurated. Pres. Ronald Reagan proclaimed the Northern Marianas a commonwealth, 1986, and the UN formally ended its trusteeship, 1990. In 2008, U.S. law gave the islands one delegate to the U.S. House of Representatives who has a voice but no vote, except in committees.

Under the 1976 Commonwealth Covenant with the U.S., the islands are exempt from federal immigration and import laws, and minimum wage is lower than on the mainland. The garment-making industry, which has since boomed, has drawn accusations of sweatshop conditions from some critics. Legislation passed in 2007 will raise the minimum wage to the federal rate by 2015.

Tourist attractions. House of Taga; American Memorial Park; Banzai Cliff.

Tourist information. Marianas Visitors Authority, P.O. Box 500861, Saipan, MP 96950; (670) 664-3200; www.mymarianas.com

Website. www.gov.mp

Commonwealth of Puerto Rico (PR)
(Estado Libre Asociado de Puerto Rico)

People. Population (2013 est.): 3,674,209 (about 4.6 mil additional Puerto Ricans reside in the mainland U.S.); **Pop. change** (2010-13): −1.4%. **Pop. density:** 1,073.1 per sq mi. **Racial distribution:** 75.8% white; 12.4% black; 0.2% Asian; 0.5% Amer. Ind.; <0.05% Pac. Isl.; 2 or more races, 3.3%. **Hispanic pop.:** 99.0%. **Languages:** Spanish and English are joint official languages.

Geography. Total area: 5,325 sq mi. **Land area:** 3,424 sq mi. **Acres forested:** 1.2 mil. **Location:** island lying between the Atlantic to the N and the Caribbean to the S; it is easternmost of the West Indies group called the Greater Antilles, of which Cuba, Hispaniola, and Jamaica are the larger islands. **Climate:** mild, with a mean temperature of 77°F. **Topography:** mountainous throughout three-fourths of its rectangular area, surrounded by a broken coastal plain; highest peak, Cerro de Punta, 4,390 ft. **Capital:** San Juan. **Chief airport:** San Juan.

Economy. Chief industries: manufacturing, service, tourism. **Chief manuf. goods:** pharmaceuticals, medical equip., electronics, apparel, food products. **Chief crops:** pumpkins, coffee, watermelons, plantains, yams, oranges, pineapples, sugarcane, bananas. **Livestock** (2007): 1.4 mil chickens, 5.1 mil broilers, 490,817 cattle, 11,137 sheep, 69,892 hogs/pigs. **Nonfuel minerals** (2008): $164 mil; crushed stone, lime, salt, cement (portland), clays (common). **Commercial fishing** (2008): $3.8 mil. **Chief ports:** San Juan, Ponce, Mayaguez. **Gross domestic product** (2012): $101.5 bil. **Employment distrib.:** 27.7% govt.; 18.7% trade/trans./util.; 8.2% mfg.; 13.1% ed./health; 11.8% prof./bus. serv.; 8.2% leisure/hosp.; 5% finance; 3.2% constr./mining/log.; 2.2% info.; 2.0% other serv. **Unemployment** (2012): 14.2%. **Per capita**

pers. income (est. 2009): $14,905. **Broadband Internet:** 87.4%. **Commercial banks:** 9; deposits: $53.5 bil. **Lottery** (2009): total sales: $421.2 mil; profit: $146.9 mil.

Federal govt. Fed. civ. employees (Mar. 2013): 10,849; **avg. salary:** $64,207. **Notable fed. facilities:** PR Natl. Guard Training Area at Camp Santiago; Ft. Buchanan; Intl. Inst. of Tropical Forestry; Vieques Natl. Wildlife Refuge; USGS Caribbean Water Science Ctr.

Energy. Electricity production (2009): 22.7 bil kWh.

Misc. data. Motto: Joannes Est Nomen Eius (John is his name). **Flower:** Maga. **Bird:** Reinita. **Tree:** Ceiba. **Anthem:** La Borinqueña.

History. Puerto Rico (or Borinquen, after the original Arawak Indian name, Boriquen) was visited by Christopher Columbus on his second voyage, Nov. 19, 1493. In 1508, the Spanish arrived.

Sugarcane was introduced, 1515, and slaves were imported three years later. Gold mining petered out, 1570. Spaniards fought off a series of British and Dutch attacks; slavery was abolished, 1873. Under the treaty of Paris, Puerto Rico was ceded to the U.S. after the Spanish-American War, 1898. In 1952 the people voted in favor of Commonwealth status.

The Commonwealth of Puerto Rico is a self-governing part of the U.S. with a primarily Hispanic culture. The island's citizens have virtually the same control over their internal affairs as do the 50 states of the U.S. However, they do not vote in national general elections, only in national primaries.

Puerto Rico is represented in the U.S. House of Representatives by a Resident Commissioner who has a voice but no vote, except in committees.

No federal income tax is collected from residents on income earned from local sources in Puerto Rico. Nevertheless, as part of the U.S. legal system, Puerto Rico is subject to the provisions of the U.S. Constitution; most federal laws apply as they do in the 50 states.

Puerto Rico's famous "Operation Bootstrap," begun in the late 1940s, succeeded in changing the island from the "Poorhouse of the Caribbean" to an area with the highest per capita income in Latin America. This program encouraged manufacturing and development of the tourist trade by selective tax exemption, low-interest loans, and other incentives. Despite the marked success of Puerto Rico's development efforts over an extended period of time, per capita income in Puerto Rico is low in comparison to that of the 50 states.

In plebiscites held in 1967, 1993, and 1998, voters chose to retain Commonwealth status. Protests mounted in the late-1990s over the U.S. Navy's use of Vieques Island for live ammunition training; official military exercises there were terminated, 2003.

Tourist attractions. Museo de Arte de Ponce; San Felipe del Morro and San Cristóbal forts, San Juan Natl. Historic Site, Walled City of Old San Juan, Casa Blanca in San Juan; Arecibo Observatory; Cordillera Central mtn. range; El Yunque Natl. Forest (only tropical rain forest in Natl. Forest system); Cathedral of San Juan Bautista; Porta Coeli (Doorway to Heaven) Church and Religious Art Museum, San Germán; Rio Camuy Cave Park, Camuy; Mosquito Bay.

Cultural facilities and events. Festival Casals classical music concerts, mid-June; Puerto Rico Symphony Orchestra at Music Conservatory; Botanical Garden and Museum of Anthropology, Art, and History at the Univ. of Puerto Rico; Institute of Puerto Rican Culture, at the Dominican Convent.

Famous Puerto Ricans. Julia de Burgos, Marta Casals Istomin, Pablo Casals, José Celso Barbosa, Orlando Cepeda, Roberto Clemente, José de Diego, José Feliciano, Doña Felisa Rincón de Gautier, Luis A. Ferré, José Ferrer, Commodore Diégo E. Hernández, Miguel Hernández Agosto, Rafael Hernández (El Jibarito), Rafael Hernández Colón, Raúl Juliá, René Marqués, Ricky Martin, Concha Meléndez, Rita Moreno, Luis Muñoz Marín, Luis Palés Matos, Joaquin Phoenix, Adm. Horacio Rivero.

Tourist information. The Puerto Rico Tourism Company, La Princesa Bldg. #2, Paseo La Princesa, Old San Juan, PR 00902; (800) 866-7827; www.seepuertorico.com

Website. www.pr.gov (in Spanish)

Virgin Islands (VI)
St. John, St. Croix, St. Thomas

People. Population (2013 est.): 104,737. **Pop. change** (2010-13): −1.6%. **Pop. density:** 775.8 per sq mi. **Racial** distrib.** (2000): 76.2% black; 13.1% white; 1.1% Asian; 6.1% other races; 2 or more races, 3.5%. **Languages:** English (official), Spanish, Creole.

Geography. Total area: 136 sq mi. **Land area:** 135 sq mi. **Acres forested:** 45,163. **Location:** 3 larger and 50 smaller islands and cays in the S and W of the V.I. group (British V.I. colony to the N and E), which is situated 70 mi E of Puerto Rico; located W of Anegada Passage, a major channel connecting the Atlantic Ocean and Caribbean Sea. **Climate:** subtropical; sun tempered by gentle trade winds; humidity is low; avg. temperature, 78°F. **Topography:** St. Thomas is mainly a ridge of hills running E-W, and has little tillable land; St. Croix rises abruptly in the N but slopes to the S to flatlands and lagoons; St. John has steep, lofty hills and valleys with little level tillable land. **Capital:** Charlotte Amalie on St. Thomas. **Chief airports:** Charlotte Amalie, Burlington.

Economy. Chief industries: retail, petroleum, tourism, prof. consulting. **Chief manuf. goods:** rum, stone, glass & clay products, electronics, textiles. **Chief crops:** cucumbers, coconuts, mangoes, tomatoes, bananas. **Livestock** (2007): 699 chickens, 776 cattle, 2,981 sheep, 1,125 hogs/pigs, 2,331 goats. **Nonfuel minerals:** crushed stone, limestone, traprock. **Commercial fishing** (2008): $8.8 mil. **Chief port:** Charlotte Amalie. **Gross domestic product** (2010): $4.5 bil. **Employment distrib.:** 28.4% govt.; 21.2% trade/trans./util.; 2.1% mfg.; 6.2% ed./health; 8.5% prof./bus. serv.; 18.1% leisure/hosp.; 5.7% finance; 4.4% constr./mining/log.; 2.1% info.; 3.4% other serv. **Unemployment** (June 2011): 9.4%. **Per capita pers. income** (2007): $19,787. **Broadband Internet:** 81.6%. **Commercial banks:** 4; deposits: $1.8 bil.

Energy. Electricity production (2009 est.): 872 mil kWh.

Federal govt. Fed. civ. employees (Mar. 2013): 708; **avg. salary:** $59,372.

Misc. data. Motto: United in pride and hope. **Flower:** Yellow cedar. **Bird:** Yellow breast. **Song:** "Virgin Islands March."

History. The islands were visited by Columbus in 1493. Spanish forces, 1555, defeated the Caribes and claimed the territory; by 1596 the native population was annihilated. First permanent settlement in the U.S. territory, 1672, by the Danes; U.S. purchased the islands, 1917, for defense purposes.

The Virgin Islands has a republican form of government, headed by a governor and lieut. governor elected, since 1970, by popular vote for 4-year terms. There is a 15-member unicameral legislature, elected by popular vote for a 2-year term. Residents of the V.I. have been U.S. citizens since 1927. Since 1973 they have elected a delegate to the U.S. House of Representatives, who has a voice but no vote, except in committees.

Tourist attractions. St. Croix Isl.: Salt River Bay Natl. Historic Park and Ecological Preserve, Christiansted Natl. Historic Site. St. John and Hassel Isls.: Virgin Islands Natl. Park. St. Thomas Isl.: Blackbeard's Castle, Coral World Ocean Park, Magens Bay, 99 Steps.

Tourist information. USVI Division of Tourism, P.O. Box 6400, St. Thomas 00804; 1-800-372-USVI; www.visitusvi.com **Website.** ltg.gov.vi

Other Islands

Navassa lies between Haiti and Jamaica, 100 mi S of Guantanamo Bay, Cuba, in the Caribbean; it covers 1,147 acres, and is uninhabited. Claimed 1857, USCG lighthouse built 1917, now inoperative. Natl. Wildlife Refuge since 1999. Administered by the Dept. of Interior.

The 3 coral islands of **Wake Atoll—Wake, Wilkes,** and **Peale**—lie in the Pacific Ocean on a direct route from Hawaii to Hong Kong, about 2,300 mi W of Honolulu and 1,500 mi NE of Guam. The group is 4.5 mi long, 1.5 mi wide. Land area totals 2.5 sq mi. The U.S. annexed Wake Atoll Jan. 17, 1899. Japan occupied Wake 1941-45. Designated a National Historic Landmark in 1985. Wake is owned by the U.S. Air Force, administered by the Dept. of Interior, but used by the Army as a missile launch facility. The population consists of military personnel and contractors. Most infrastructure damaged by super typhoon Ioke in 2006.

The following mostly uninhabited islands are part of the **Pacific/Remote Islands National Wildlife Refuge Complex**, along with Wake Atoll, administered by the Dept. of Interior: **Midway Atoll**, acquired in 1867, has 3 main islands—Sand, Spit, and Eastern—1,250 mi WNW of Honolulu, with an area of about 1,500 acres. Naval activity ended in 1997. Has the world's largest colony of Laysan albatross. **Johnston Atoll**, 800 mi WSW of Honolulu, is two natural and two artificial

islands across 107 sq mi administered by the Navy. Johnston was a nuclear test site in 1958, 1962; the Army disposed of chemical weapons 1990-2000. Cleanup ended in 2005. **King-man Reef** is a barren, coral atoll 932 mi S of Hawaii, annexed 1922. **Palmyra Atoll** is 54 islets over 753 sq mi, 1,052 mi S of

Hawaii; annexed with Hawaii in 1898. Part privately owned by the Nature Conservancy. **Jarvis Island** covers 1,086 acres, 1,300 mi S of Honolulu near the equator. West of Jarvis are **Howland and Baker Islands**, 36 mi apart and about 1,600 mi SW of Honolulu.

Attractions in Washington, DC, Capital of the U.S.

Most attractions are free. All times are subject to change. For more details call the Washington, DC, Convention and Visitors Association at 1-800-422-8644, or visit www.washington.org

Bureau of Engraving and Printing

The **Bureau of Engraving and Printing** of the U.S. Treasury Dept. is the headquarters for the making of U.S. paper money. Public tours are offered Mon.-Fri., 9 AM-2 PM (7 PM in spring and summer), except on federal holidays. 14th and C Sts. SW; (866) 874-2330. **Website:** www.moneyfactory.gov

Capitol

The **United States Capitol** was originally designed by Dr. William Thornton, an amateur architect, who submitted a plan in 1793 that won him $500 and a city lot. Three other architects designed or supervised the construction of the Capitol before its completion.

The present cast iron dome at its greatest exterior height measures 135 ft, 5 in. and is topped by the bronze Statue of Freedom, which stands 19½ ft and weighs 14,985 lbs. On its base are the words E Pluribus Unum (Out of Many, One).

The Capitol is open to the public Mon.-Sat., 8:30 AM-4:30 PM. It is closed Jan. 1, Inauguration Day, Thanksgiving Day, and Dec. 25.

To observe debate while Congress is in session, those living in the U.S. May obtain tickets from their U.S. representative or senator. Visitors from other countries may obtain passes at the Capitol. Between Constitution & Independence Aves., at Pennsylvania Ave.; (202) 225-6827. **Website:** www.visitthecapital.gov

Federal Bureau of Investigation

The **Federal Bureau of Investigation** does not currently offer tours of its headquarters. Visitors to the city may learn about the FBI through exhibits at the Newseum, the National Crime and Punishment Museum, and the International Spy Museum. J. Edgar Hoover Bldg., Pennsylvania Ave., between 9th and 10th Sts. NW; (202) 324-3447. **Website:** www.fbi.gov

Folger Shakespeare Library

The **Folger Shakespeare Library**, on Capitol Hill, is a research institution holding rare books and manuscripts of the Renaissance period and the largest collection of Shakespearean materials in the world. Exhibit may be visited Mon.-Sat., 10 AM-5 PM, and Sun., 12 PM-5 PM, except federal holidays. Building and garden tours are available to groups and the public. 201 E. Capitol St. SE; (202) 544-4600. **Website:** www.folger.edu

Holocaust Memorial Museum

The **U.S. Holocaust Memorial Museum** opened on Apr. 21, 1993. The museum documents the events of the Holocaust through permanent and temporary displays, interactive videos, and special lectures. The permanent exhibition is not recommended for children under age 11.

The museum is open daily, 10 AM-5:20 PM, except Yom Kippur and Dec. 25; extended hrs. Mon.-Thurs. (10 AM-6:20 PM) from early June. Admission is free. Tickets are needed only for the permanent exhibition, Mar. through Aug. A limited number of free tickets are available at the door; advance tickets may be ordered for a small fee at 1-800-400-9373. 100 Raoul Wallenberg Pl. SW; (202) 488-0400. **Website:** www.ushmm.org

Jefferson Memorial

Dedicated Apr. 13, 1943, the **Thomas Jefferson Memorial** stands on the south shore of the Tidal Basin in West Potomac Park. It is a circular stone structure that combines architectural elements of the dome of the Pantheon in Rome and the rotunda designed by Jefferson for the Univ. of Virginia.

The memorial is open daily, 24 hrs., staffed 9:30 AM-11:30 PM. Ohio Dr. SW & E. Basin Dr. SW; (202) 426-6841. **Website:** www.nps.gov/thje/

John F. Kennedy Center

The **John F. Kennedy Center for the Performing Arts** opened Sept. 8, 1971. Designed by Edward Durell Stone, it includes an opera house, a concert hall, several theaters, restaurants, and a library. Free tours are available Mon.-Fri., 10 AM-5 PM and Sat. & Sun., 10 AM-1 PM. 2700 F St. NW; (202) 467-4600; (800) 444-1324. **Website:** www.kennedycenter.org

Martin Luther King Jr. Memorial

Officially dedicated Aug. 28, 2011, the **MLK Jr. Memorial** features a 30-ft figure of Dr. King emerging from a block of granite, the "Stone of Hope." Designed by sculptor Lei Yikin, the 4-acre memorial is located on the Tidal Basin between the Lincoln and Jefferson Memorials.

The memorial is open daily, 24 hrs., staffed 9:30 AM-11:30 PM. 1964 Independence Ave. SW; (202) 426-6841 **Website:** www.nps.gov/mlkm/

Korean War Veterans Memorial

Dedicated on July 27, 1995, the **Korean War Veterans Memorial** honors Americans who served in the war. Situated at the west end of the Mall, the triangular-shaped stone and steel memorial features a multiservice formation of 19 combat-ready troops clad in ponchos with the wind at their back. A granite wall, with images of men and women who served, juts into the Pool of Remembrance.

The memorial is open daily, 24 hrs., staffed 9:30 AM-11:30 PM. French Dr. SW across from Lincoln Memorial; (202) 426-6841. **Website:** www.nps.gov/kowa/

Library of Congress

Established by and for Congress in 1800, the **Library of Congress** extends its services to other government agencies and libraries, scholars, and the general public. It contains more than 134 mil items in some 460 languages.

Most exhibit halls are open to the public Mon.-Fri., 8:30 AM-9:30 PM, and Sat., 8:30 AM-5 PM. Thomas Jefferson Building (Great Hall and Exhibitions) is open Mon.-Sat., 8:30 AM-4:30 PM. A few areas are open on most federal holidays; all are closed Jan. 1, Thanksgiving, and Dec. 25. 101 Independence Ave. SE; (202) 707-8000. **Website:** www.loc.gov

Lincoln Memorial

Designed by Henry Bacon, the **Lincoln Memorial** in West Potomac Park is a large marble hall enclosing a statue of Abraham Lincoln seated on an armchair. The memorial was dedicated May 30, 1922. The statue was designed by Daniel Chester French and sculpted by French and the Piccirilli brothers. The text of the Gettysburg Address is in the south chamber; that of Lincoln's Second Inaugural speech is in the north chamber. Each is engraved on a stone tablet.

The memorial is open daily, 24 hrs., staffed 9:30 AM-11:30 PM, and is wheelchair-accessible. W. Potomac Park at 23rd St. NW; (202) 426-6841. **Website:** www.nps.gov/linc/

National Archives and Records

Original copies of the Declaration of Independence, the Constitution, and the Bill of Rights are on display in the **National Archives** Exhibition Hall. The National Archives also holds other valuable U.S. government records and historic maps, photographs, and manuscripts. Central Research and Microfilm Research Rooms are also available to the public for genealogical research.

Exhibition Hall open daily 10 AM-5:30 PM, except Thanksgiving and Dec. 25. 7th St. and Pennsylvania Ave. NW; (202) 357-5000. **Website:** www.archives.gov

National Gallery of Art

The **National Gallery of Art** was established by Congress, Mar. 24, 1937, and opened Mar. 17, 1941. The original West Building was designed by John Russell Pope. The East Building, opened in 1978, was designed by I. M. Pei. Open daily, Mon.-Sat. 10 AM-5 PM, Sun. 11 AM-6 PM. Closed Jan. 1 and Dec. 25. 4th St. and Constitution Ave NW; (202) 737-4215. **Website:** www.nga.gov

Franklin Delano Roosevelt Memorial

Opened May 2, 1997, the **FDR Memorial** features 9 bronze sculptural ensembles depicting FDR, Eleanor Roosevelt, and events from the Great Depression and World War II. This 7.5-acre memorial is located near the Tidal Basin in a park-like setting and is wheelchair accessible.

Grounds, staffed daily, 9:30 AM-11:30 PM, except Dec. 25. 1850 W. Basin Dr. SW; (202) 426-6841. **Website:** www.nps.gov/fdrm/

Smithsonian Institution

The **Smithsonian Institution**, established in 1846, is the world's largest museum complex. It holds some 137 mil artifacts and specimens in its trust. There are 17 museums and the National Zoo in the DC area. The **Smithsonian Information Center** is located in "the Castle" on the Mall. Also on the Mall are the **National Museum of American History**, the **National Museum of Natural History**, the **National Air and Space Museum**, the **National Museum of the American Indian**, the **Hirshhorn Museum and Sculpture Garden**, the **Arthur M. Sackler & Freer Galleries of Art**, the **National Museum of African Art**, and the **Arts and Industries Building** (currently closed for renovation). Located nearby are the **National Postal Museum**, the **National Museum of American Art**, the **National Portrait Gallery**, and the **Renwick Gallery**. Farther away is the **Anacostia Museum**. The **Air and Space Museum's Udvar-Hazy Center** is near Dulles Airport in Virginia.

Most museums are open daily, except Dec. 25, 10 AM-5:30 PM (later in summer); (202) 633-1000. **Website:** www.si.edu

Vietnam Veterans Memorial

Originally dedicated Nov. 13, 1982, the **Vietnam Veterans Memorial** recognizes the men and women who served in the armed forces in the Vietnam War. The names of more than 58,000 Americans who lost their lives or remain missing are inscribed on a V-shaped black-granite wall, designed by Maya Ying Lin.

Since 1982, two additions have been made to the Memorial. The first, dedicated on Nov. 11, 1984, is the Frederick Hart sculpture *Three Servicemen*. On Nov. 11, 1993, the Vietnam Women's Memorial, designed by Glenna Goodacre, was dedicated, honoring the more than 11,500 women who served in Vietnam.

The memorial is open daily, 24 hrs., staffed 9:30 AM-11:30 PM. Constitution Ave. and Bacon Dr. NW; (202) 426-6841. **Website:** www.nps.gov/vive/

Washington Monument

The **Washington Monument**, dedicated in 1885, is a tapering shaft, or obelisk, of white marble, 555 ft, 5⅛ in. in height and 55 ft, 1½ in. square at base. Eight small windows, 2 on each side, are located at the 500-ft level.

(As of mid-2013, the monument was still closed to the public while damages caused during a Aug. 23, 2011, earthquake, were assessed.) Normally open daily, 9 AM-5 PM (later in summer), except July 4 and Dec. 25. Free timed passes are available; advance passes are available for a small fee. 15th St. and Constitution Ave. NW; (202) 426-6841. **Website:** www.nps.gov/wamo/

White House

The **White House**, the President's residence, stands on 18 acres on the south side of Pennsylvania Ave., between the Treasury and the old Executive Office Building. The walls are of sandstone, quarried at Aquia Creek, VA. The building was first made white with lime-based whitewash in 1798, but the name did not become official until 1901.

Tours of the White House have been canceled during the budget sequester; free self-guided tours for 10 or more normally available Tues.-Thurs., 7:30-11 AM; Fri., 7:30 AM-noon; Sat., 7:30 AM-1 PM. (Tour requests must be made at least 21 days in advance through your member of Congress.) Only the public rooms on the ground floor and state floor may be visited. 1600 Pennsylvania Ave. The White House Visitor Center at 1450 Pennsylvania Ave. is open daily 7:30 AM-4 PM; (202) 456-7041. **Website:** www.whitehouse.gov

National World War II Memorial

The **National WWII Memorial** is dedicated to the approx. 16 mil veterans who served and the more than 400,000 who died in the war. It rests on 7.4 acres of land at the east end of the reflecting pool on the Mall. The memorial opened on Apr. 29, 2004, and was dedicated on May 29.

At the north and south entrances are 43-ft archways, representing the Atlantic and Pacific theaters. Inside the grounds is a large, oval plaza with a wall of 4,000 gold stars; each represents 100 American deaths. Fifty-six pillars ringing the center represent the states, territories, and District of Columbia. There is also a garden enclosed by a stone wall, the Circle of Remembrance.

The memorial is wheelchair-accessible and open daily, 24 hrs., staffed 9:30 AM-11:30 PM. Located on 17th St. between Constitution and Independence Aves.; (202) 426-6841. **Website:** www.nps.gov/nwwm/

Attractions Near Washington, DC

Arlington National Cemetery

Arlington National Cemetery, on the former Custis-Lee estate in Arlington, VA, is the site of the **Tomb of the Unknowns** and is the final resting place of Pres. W. H. Taft and Pres. John F. Kennedy and his wife, Jacqueline Bouvier Kennedy Onassis. An eternal flame burns over the site of Kennedy's grave. Many other famous Americans are buried at Arlington, as well as more than 300,000 U.S. military personnel, from every major war.

North of the National Cemetery stands the **U.S. Marine Corps War Memorial**, also known as Iwo Jima. The memorial is a bronze statue of the raising of the U.S. flag on Mt. Suribachi, Feb. 23, 1945, during World War II, executed by Felix de Weldon from the photograph by Joe Rosenthal.

On the southern side of the Memorial Bridge, near the cemetery entrance, a memorial honoring the women in the military was dedicated Oct. 18, 1997. The **Women in military Service for America Memorial** is a semicircular retaining wall 226 ft long with a central niche 30 ft high.

Open daily, 8 AM-5 PM (8 AM-7 PM, Apr.-Sept.), Arlington, VA; (703) 607-8000; (877) 907-8585. **Website:** www.arlingtoncemetery.org

Mount Vernon

Mount Vernon, George Washington's estate, is on the south bank of the Potomac R., 16 mi from Washington, DC, in northern Virginia. The present house is believed to be an enlargement of one built by Augustine Washington in 1735. His son Lawrence renamed the estate after British Navy Adm. Edward Vernon. George Washington, Lawrence's half brother, inherited it in 1761. The estate has been restored to its 18th-cent. appearance and includes many original furnishings. Washington and his wife, Martha, are buried on the grounds.

Open 365 days, Apr.-Aug. 8 AM-5 PM; Mar., Sept.-Oct. 9 AM-5 PM; Nov.-Feb. 9 AM-4 PM; (703) 780-2000; (800) 429-1520. Admission: adults $17, seniors (62+) $16, children (6-11) $8, age 5 and under free. **Website:** www.mountvernon.org

The Pentagon

The **Pentagon**, headquarters of the Dept. of Defense, is the largest office building in the U.S. It houses more than 23,000 employees in offices occupying 3,705,793 sq ft. The building was severely damaged when struck by a plane Sept. 11, 2001.

Tours available by reservation only, 14 to 90 days in advance. General public must use the Pentagon website or contact their member of Congress to request a tour. Non U.S. citizens must contact their national embassy. Arlington, VA (I-395 S to Boundary Channel Dr. exit); (703) 697-1776. **Website:** pentagontours.osd.mil

100 MOST POPULOUS U.S. CITIES

Sources: Population: Decennial Census and Population Estimates Program, U.S. Census Bureau, U.S. Dept. of Commerce. Population is as of July 1, 2012; population rank is indicated within parentheses. **Pop. density** specifies the number of persons per square mile (sq mi) of land area. Unless otherwise noted, **all other figures** are estimates for 2007-11 from the American Community Survey, U.S. Census Bureau. **Racial distribution** categories are abbreviated here; their full forms are white, black or African American, Asian, American Indian and Alaska Native, Native Hawaiian and Other Pacific Islander, some other race, two or more races. **Hispanic** or Latino persons may be of any race. **Language** includes those spoken at home; languages other than Spanish spoken by less than 5% of the population over age 5 are omitted. **Employment:** Bureau of Labor Statistics, U.S. Dept. of Labor, for 2012. **Per capita income:** Bureau of Economic Analysis, U.S. Dept. of Commerce; figures apply to MSA for 2011. **Educational attainment** is the percentage of persons ages 25 and up who have graduated high school (HS) and those with a bachelor's degree or higher. **Avg. commute** is the time it takes for workers 16 years and over to travel from home to work. "Drive" includes only those who drive to work alone. Forms of transport used by less than 10% are omitted. **Avg. home:** National Association of Realtors®. Figures represent median 2012 sales price of existing single-family homes in the metropolitan area; data not available for all cities. **Avg. rent** is the median gross rent per month. **Mayor** (or other city leader) and **website:** World Almanac research as of mid-2013; subject to change.

Included here are the 100 most populous U.S. cities, according to U.S. Census Bureau estimates released in May 2013. Most data are for the city proper; some, where noted, apply to the Metropolitan Statistical Area (MSA). Inc. = incorporated; est. = established.

Albuquerque, New Mexico

Population: 555,417 (32). **Pop. density:** 2,959. **Pop. change (2010-12):** 1.5%. **Area:** 187.7 sq mi. **Racial distribution:** 69.3% white; 3.2% black; 2.6% Asian; 4.5% Amer. Ind.; 0.1% Pac. Isl.; 16.5% other; 2+ races 3.7%. **Hispanic pop.:** 45.9%. **Foreign born:** 10.7%. **U.S. citizens:** 93.0%. **Language:** 70.1% English only; 24.6% Spanish.
Employment: 238,259 employed; 6.8% unemployed. **Per capita income:** $35,007; change (2010-11): 2.8%. **Below poverty level:** 16.6%; 12.5% of families. **Educational attainment:** 87.7% HS; 32.2% bachelor's. **Avg. commute:** 21.4 min. 79.0% drive; 10.5% carpool. **Housing units:** 237,735; 92.6% occupied. **Home ownership:** 61.2%. **Avg. home:** $170,300; change (2010-12): –4.7%. **Avg. rent:** $738.
Mayor: Richard J. Berry, nonpartisan
History: Founded 1706 by the Spanish; inc. 1890.
Website: www.cabq.gov

Anaheim, California

Population: 343,248 (55). **Pop. density:** 6,888. **Pop. change (2010-12):** 1.8%. **Area:** 49.8 sq mi. **Racial distribution:** 60.2% white; 2.7% black; 14.6% Asian; 0.3% Amer. Ind.; 0.4% Pac. Isl.; 18.9% other; 2+ races 2.9%. **Hispanic pop.:** 53.0%. **Foreign born:** 38.4%. **U.S. citizens:** 77.2%. **Language:** 39.6% English only; 44.2% Spanish.
Employment: 159,926 employed; 9.7% unemployed. **Per capita income:** $44,423; change (2010-11): 3.7%. **Below poverty level:** 14.3%; 11.4% of families. **Educational attainment:** 73.6% HS; 23.4% bachelor's. **Avg. commute:** 26.8 min. 75.0% drive; 13.5% carpool. **Housing units:** 104,663; 94.5% occupied. **Home ownership:** 49.1%. **Avg. home:** $327,470; change (2010-12): 1.3%. **Avg. rent:** $1,314.
Mayor: Tom Tait, nonpartisan
History: Founded 1857; inc. 1870. Home of Disneyland, the Anaheim Ducks, and the Los Angeles Angels.
Website: www.anaheim.net

Anchorage, Alaska

Population: 298,610 (63). **Pop. density:** 175. **Pop. change (2010-12):** 1.8%. **Area:** 1704.7 sq mi. **Racial distribution:** 67.3% white; 5.5% black; 7.7% Asian; 6.5% Amer. Ind.; 1.9% Pac. Isl.; 1.8% other; 2+ races 9.3%. **Hispanic pop.:** 7.5%. **Foreign born:** 9.1%. **U.S. citizens:** 96.0%. **Language:** 83.2% English only; 4.5% Spanish.
Employment: 148,450 employed; 5.4% unemployed. **Per capita income:** $48,810; change (2010-11): 4.3%. **Below poverty level:** 7.8%; 5.4% of families. **Educational attainment:** 92.1% HS; 32.3% bachelor's. **Avg. commute:** 18.6 min. 75.7% drive; 12.9% carpool. **Housing units:** 112,630; 93.2% occupied. **Home ownership:** 61.4%. **Avg. rent:** $1,058.
Mayor: Dan Sullivan, Republican
History: Founded 1914 as a construction camp for railroad; HQ of Alaska Defense Command, WWII. Severely damaged in earthquake, 1964. Current population center of Alaska.
Website: www.muni.org

Arlington, Texas

Population: 375,600 (50). **Pop. density:** 3,917. **Pop. change (2010-12):** 2.5%. **Area:** 95.9 sq mi. **Racial distribution:** 63.2% white; 18.9% black; 7.4% Asian; 0.5% Amer. Ind.; 0.1% Pac. Isl.; 7.6% other; 2+ races 2.4%. **Hispanic pop.:** 27.8%. **Foreign born:** 19.9%. **U.S. citizens:** 86.8%. **Language:** 67.8% English only; 22.3% Spanish.
Employment: 192,944 employed; 6.4% unemployed. **Per capita income:** $43,708; change (2010-11): 4.2%. **Below poverty level:** 15.6%; 12.1% of families. **Educational attainment:** 84.1% HS; 28.9% bachelor's. **Avg. commute:** 25.6 min. 81.0% drive; 12.3% carpool. **Housing units:** 145,298; 91.0% occupied. **Home ownership:** 58.5%. **Avg. home:** $159,300; change (2010-12): 10.8%. **Avg. rent:** $823.
Mayor: Robert N. Cluck, nonpartisan
History: Settled in 1840s; inc. 1884.
Website: www.arlingtontx.gov

Atlanta, Georgia

Population: 443,775 (40). **Pop. density:** 3,333. **Pop. change (2010-12):** 5.0%. **Area:** 133.2 sq mi. **Racial distribution:** 38.9% white; 54.1% black; 3.3% Asian; 0.2% Amer. Ind.; <0.05% Pac. Isl.; 1.8% other; 2+ races 1.7%. **Hispanic pop.:** 5.0%. **Foreign born:** 7.6%. **U.S. citizens:** 94.5%. **Language:** 89.5% English only; 4.9% Spanish.
Employment: 172,885 employed; 11.2% unemployed. **Per capita income:** $39,713; change (2010-11): 4.1%. **Below poverty level:** 23.2%; 19.5% of families. **Educational attainment:** 87.3% HS; 46.1% bachelor's. **Avg. commute:** 25.4 min. 67.3% drive; 11.5% public trans. **Housing units:** 226,275; 79.1% occupied. **Home ownership:** 47.0%. **Avg. home:** $101,400; change (2010-12): –11.7%. **Avg. rent:** $910.
Mayor: Kasim Reed, nonpartisan
History: Founded as Terminus 1837; renamed Atlanta 1845; inc. 1847. Played major role in Civil War; became permanent state capital 1877. Birthplace of civil rights movement. Host to 1996 Centennial Olympic Games.
Website: www.atlantaga.gov

Aurora, Colorado

Population: 339,030 (56). **Pop. density:** 2,191. **Pop. change (2010-12):** 4.0%. **Area:** 154.7 sq mi. **Racial distribution:** 66.8% white; 15.4% black; 4.7% Asian; 1.2% Amer. Ind.; 0.3% Pac. Isl.; 7.4% other; 2+ races 4.1%. **Hispanic pop.:** 28.1%. **Foreign born:** 20.4%. **U.S. citizens:** 85.0%. **Language:** 69.1% English only; 21.2% Spanish.
Employment: 164,516 employed; 8.5% unemployed. **Per capita income:** $48,980; change (2010-11): 4.3%. **Below poverty level:** 16.5%; 13.1% of families. **Educational attainment:** 85.2% HS; 26.1% bachelor's. **Avg. commute:** 28.2 min. 76.6% drive; 11.4% carpool. **Housing units:** 131,848; 91.9% occupied. **Home ownership:** 61.0%. **Avg. home:** $252,400; change (2010-12): 8.6%. **Avg. rent:** $888.
Mayor: Steve Hogan, nonpartisan
History: Founded 1891; originally called Fletcher; renamed Aurora 1907; inc. 1929. Early growth stimulated by presence of military bases; fast-growing trade, technology, and med. science center.
Website: www.auroragov.org

Austin, Texas

Population: 842,592 (11). **Pop. density:** 2,828. **Pop. change (2010-12):** 6.0%. **Area:** 297.9 sq mi. **Racial distribution:** 68.4% white; 8.2% black; 6.1% Asian; 0.5% Amer. Ind.; 0.1% Pac. Isl.; 14.3% other; 2+ races 2.4%. **Hispanic pop.:** 35.3%. **Foreign born:** 19.3%. **U.S. citizens:** 85.1%. **Language:** 66.1% English only; 26.3% Spanish.
Employment: 435,438 employed; 5.4% unemployed. **Per capita income:** $40,455; change (2010-11): 3.9%. **Below poverty level:** 18.5%; 13.0% of families. **Educational attainment:** 85.6% HS; 44.5% bachelor's. **Avg. commute:** 22.8 min. 71.8% drive; 11.4% carpool. **Housing units:** 351,397; 91.9% occupied. **Home ownership:** 45.5%. **Avg. home:** $206,000; change (2010-12): 6.4%. **Avg. rent:** $920.
Mayor: Lee Leffingwell, nonpartisan
History: First permanent settlement 1835; capital of Rep. of Texas 1839; named after Stephen Austin; inc. 1840.
Website: www.austintexas.gov

Bakersfield, California

Population: 358,597 (52). **Pop. density:** 2,522. **Pop. change (2010-12):** 2.7%. **Area:** 142.2 sq mi. **Racial distribution:** 62.9% white; 8.2% black; 5.9% Asian; 1.0% Amer. Ind.; 0.1% Pac. Isl.; 17.4% other; 2+ races 4.5%. **Hispanic pop.:** 44.5%. **Foreign born:** 18.8%. **U.S. citizens:** 88.3%. **Language:** 62.9% English only; 30.4% Spanish.
Employment: 150,855 employed; 9.3% unemployed. **Per capita income:** $31,400; change (2010-11): 5.5%. **Below poverty level:** 18.2%; 14.7% of families. **Educational attainment:** 77.8% HS; 19.8% bachelor's. **Avg. commute:** 22.5 min. 79.2%

drive; 13.9% carpool. **Housing units:** 116,200; 92.2% occupied. **Home ownership:** 59.0%. **Avg. rent:** $937.
Mayor: Harvey L. Hall, nonpartisan
History: Named after Col. Thomas Baker, an early settler; inc. 1898.
Website: www.bakersfieldcity.us

Baltimore, Maryland

Population: 621,342 (26). **Pop. density:** 7,676. **Pop. change (2010-12):** 0.1%. **Area:** 80.9 sq mi. **Racial distribution:** 30.1% white; 63.8% black; 2.3% Asian; 0.4% Amer. Ind.; <0.05% Pac. Isl.; 1.2% other; 2+ races 2.1%. **Hispanic pop.:** 3.9%. **Foreign born:** 7.2%. **U.S. citizens:** 95.7%. **Language:** 91.1% English only; 3.7% Spanish.
Employment: 250,818 employed; 10.2% unemployed. **Per capita income:** $51,126; change (2010-11): 4.9%. **Below poverty level:** 22.4%; 17.7% of families. **Educational attainment:** 78.5% HS; 25.8% bachelor's. **Avg. commute:** 29.6 min. 59.5% drive; 18.4% public trans.; 11.1% carpool. **Housing units:** 296,572; 80.6% occupied. **Home ownership:** 49.5%. **Avg. home:** $206,000; change (2010-12): −16.3%. **Avg. rent:** $889.
Mayor: Stephanie C. Rawlings-Blake, Democrat
History: Founded by Maryland legislature 1729; inc. 1797. War of 1812 British artillery barrage of Ft. McHenry (1814) inspired Francis Scott Key to write "Star-Spangled Banner." Birthplace of America's railroads 1828; rebuilt after fire 1904. Site of National Aquarium.
Website: www.baltimorecity.gov

Baton Rouge, Louisiana

Population: 230,058 (90). **Pop. density:** 2,990. **Pop. change (2010-12):** 0.2%. **Area:** 76.9 sq mi. **Racial distribution:** 40.5% white; 53.7% black; 3.3% Asian; 0.2% Amer. Ind.; <0.05% Pac. Isl.; 0.8% other; 2+ races 1.5%. **Hispanic pop.:** 3.6%. **Foreign born:** 5.4%. **U.S. citizens:** 96.3%. **Language:** 91.5% English only; 3.3% Spanish.
Employment: 101,253 employed; 7.3% unemployed. **Per capita income:** $38,985; change (2010-11): 4.2%. **Below poverty level:** 24.8%; 17.7% of families. **Educational attainment:** 84.3% HS; 32.4% bachelor's. **Avg. commute:** 20.4 min. 78.0% drive; 12.1% carpool. **Housing units:** 99,369; 88.1% occupied. **Home ownership:** 51.7%. **Avg. home:** $164,300; change (2010-12): −3.1%. **Avg. rent:** $757.
Mayor-President: Melvin "Kip" Holden, Democrat
History: Claimed by Spain at time of Louisiana Purchase 1803; est. independence by rebellion 1810; inc. as town 1817. Became state capital 1849; Union-held most of Civil War.
Website: www.brgov.com

Birmingham, Alabama

Population: 212,038 (100). **Pop. density:** 1,452. **Pop. change (2010-12):** −0.1%. **Area:** 146.1 sq mi. **Racial distribution:** 23.2% white; 73.8% black; 0.9% Asian; 0.3% Amer. Ind.; <0.05% Pac. Isl.; 1.3% other; 2+ races 0.5%. **Hispanic pop.:** 2.8%. **Foreign born:** 3.4%. **U.S. citizens:** 97.3%. **Language:** 95.4% English only; 2.8% Spanish.
Employment: 82,581 employed; 8.5% unemployed. **Per capita income:** $40,816; change (2010-11): 4.4%. **Below poverty level:** 27.3%; 22.5% of families. **Educational attainment:** 82.6% HS; 21.3% bachelor's. **Avg. commute:** 21.7 min. 79.5% drive; 13.6% carpool. **Housing units:** 111,858; 80.3% occupied. **Home ownership:** 51.2%. **Avg. home:** $151,100; change (2010-12): 5.7%. **Avg. rent:** $706.
Mayor: William A. Bell, nonpartisan
History: Settled 1871 at the intersection of two major railroads, within proximity of elements needed for iron and steel production.
Website: www.birminghamal.gov

Boise, Idaho

Population: 212,303 (99). **Pop. density:** 2,675. **Pop. change (2010-12):** 2.9%. **Area:** 79.4 sq mi. **Racial distribution:** 90.8% white; 1.4% black; 3.2% Asian; 0.7% Amer. Ind.; 0.3% Pac. Isl.; 1.1% other; 2+ races 2.5%. **Hispanic pop.:** 7.1%. **Foreign born:** 7.5%. **U.S. citizens:** 95.5%. **Language:** 89.7% English only; 4.7% Spanish.
Employment: 103,994 employed; 6.4% unemployed. **Per capita income:** $34,274; change (2010-11): 3.0%. **Below poverty level:** 13.7%; 9.3% of families. **Educational attainment:** 93.2% HS; 36.9% bachelor's. **Avg. commute:** 17.5 min. 78.1% drive. **Housing units:** 91,628; 93.3% occupied. **Home ownership:** 61.5%. **Avg. home:** $138,700; change (2010-12): 1.8%. **Avg. rent:** $761.
Mayor: David H. Bieter, nonpartisan
History: Gold discovered in area, 1862; inc., proclaimed capital of Idaho Terr., 1964; on Oregon Trail.
Website: www.cityofboise.org

Boston, Massachusetts

Population: 636,479 (21). **Pop. density:** 13,184. **Pop. change (2010-12):** 2.6%. **Area:** 48.3 sq mi. **Racial distribution:** 53.6% white; 25.1% black; 9.0% Asian; 0.3% Amer. Ind.; 0.1% Pac. Isl.; 8.1% other; 2+ races 3.7%. **Hispanic pop.:** 17.3%. **Foreign born:** 27.1%. **U.S. citizens:** 84.9%. **Language:** 63.9% English only; 15.5% Spanish.
Employment: 299,620 employed; 6.4% unemployed. **Per capita income:** $57,893; change (2010-11): 4.5%. **Below poverty level:** 21.4%; 16.0% of families. **Educational attainment:** 84.2% HS; 42.8% bachelor's. **Avg. commute:** 28.6 min. 39.1% drive; 33.1% public trans.; 14.9% walk. **Housing units:** 272,007; 91.0% occupied. **Home ownership:** 34.6%. **Avg. home:** $351,200; change (2010-12): −1.7%. **Avg. rent:** $1,238.
Mayor: Thomas M. Menino, Democrat
History: Settled 1630 by John Winthrop; capital of Mass. Bay Colony. Figured strongly in American Revolution, earning distinction as the "Cradle of Liberty"; inc. 1822.
Website: www.cityofboston.gov

Buffalo, New York

Population: 259,384 (73). **Pop. density:** 6,423. **Pop. change (2010-12):** −0.7%. **Area:** 40.4 sq mi. **Racial distribution:** 51.9% white; 37.9% black; 3.0% Asian; 0.6% Amer. Ind.; <0.05% Pac. Isl.; 3.7% other; 2+ races 3.0%. **Hispanic pop.:** 9.1%. **Foreign born:** 7.4%. **U.S. citizens:** 95.7%. **Language:** 85.8% English only; 6.5% Spanish.
Employment: 103,038 employed; 10.9% unemployed. **Per capita income:** $40,121; change (2010-11): 4.5%. **Below poverty level:** 29.9%; 26.1% of families. **Educational attainment:** 81.1% HS; 22.5% bachelor's. **Avg. commute:** 20.0 min. 67.0% drive; 12.7% public trans. **Housing units:** 137,954; 82.2% occupied. **Home ownership:** 42.6%. **Avg. home:** $126,900; change (2010-12): 4.7%. **Avg. rent:** $666.
Mayor: Byron W. Brown, Democrat
History: Settled 1780 by Seneca Indians; raided twice by British in War of 1812. Served as western terminus for Erie Canal; became a center for trade and manufacturing; inc. 1832. A last stop on the Underground Railroad. Key point for Canada-U.S. political, trade, and social relations.
Website: www.ci.buffalo.ny.us

Chandler, Arizona

Population: 245,628 (80). **Pop. density:** 3,813. **Pop. change (2010-12):** 3.8%. **Area:** 64.4 sq mi. **Racial distribution:** 79.7% white; 5.0% black; 7.5% Asian; 1.3% Amer. Ind.; 0.2% Pac. Isl.; 2.9% other; 2+ races 3.5%. **Hispanic pop.:** 22.2%. **Foreign born:** 13.4%. **U.S. citizens:** 92.6%. **Language:** 78.1% English only; 12.9% Spanish.
Employment: 124,653 employed; 5.9% unemployed. **Per capita income:** $36,833; change (2010-11): 4.0%. **Below poverty level:** 7.9%; 5.8% of families. **Educational attainment:** 92.3% HS; 39.6% bachelor's. **Avg. commute:** 24.5 min. 78.3% drive; 11.4% carpool. **Housing units:** 95,202; 90.5% occupied. **Home ownership:** 66.2%. **Avg. home:** $147,600; change (2010-12): 6.0%. **Avg. rent:** $1,064.
Mayor: Jay Tibshraeny, nonpartisan
History: Formed 1912; population doubled in 1990s as "the high-tech oasis of the Silicon Desert."
Website: www.chandleraz.gov

Charlotte, North Carolina

Population: 775,202 (17). **Pop. density:** 2,604. **Pop. change (2010-12):** 4.9%. **Area:** 297.7 sq mi. **Racial distribution:** 53.4% white; 34.4% black; 4.9% Asian; 0.4% Amer. Ind.; 0.1% Pac. Isl.; 4.5% other; 2+ races 2.2%. **Hispanic pop.:** 12.6%. **Foreign born:** 14.7%. **U.S. citizens:** 89.6%. **Language:** 80.9% English only; 11.2% Spanish.
Employment: 358,365 employed; 8.2% unemployed. **Per capita income:** $40,223; change (2010-11): 4.5%. **Below poverty level:** 15.0%; 11.3% of families. **Educational attainment:** 87.9% HS; 39.6% bachelor's. **Avg. commute:** 24.2 min. 76.7% drive; 11.4% carpool. **Housing units:** 317,899; 90.4% occupied. **Home ownership:** 58.7%. **Avg. home:** $156,600; change (2010-12): 9.3%. **Avg. rent:** $850.
Mayor: Anthony R. Foxx, Democrat
History: Settled by Scotch-Irish immigrants 1740s; inc. 1768 and named after Queen Charlotte, wife of English King George III. Scene of first major U.S. gold discovery 1799.
Website: charmeck.org

Chesapeake, Virginia

Population: 228,417 (92). **Pop. density:** 670. **Pop. change (2010-12):** 2.1%. **Area:** 340.8 sq mi. **Racial distribution:** 62.8% white; 29.8% black; 3.0% Asian; 0.4% Amer. Ind.; 0.1% Pac. Isl.; 1.4% other; 2+ races 2.4%. **Hispanic pop.:** 4.2%. **Foreign born:** 4.6%. **U.S. citizens:** 98.0%. **Language:** 93.0% English only; 3.2% Spanish.
Employment: 110,278 employed; 6.0% unemployed. **Per capita income:** $41,976; change (2010-11): 4.6%. **Below poverty level:** 7.4%; 5.8% of families. **Educational attainment:** 89.5% HS; 28.1% bachelor's. **Avg. commute:** 23.9 min. 85.8% drive. **Housing units:** 82,763; 95.3% occupied. **Home ownership:**

74.3%. **Avg. home:** $187,500; change (2010-12): –8.5%. **Avg. rent:** $1,090.
Mayor: Alan P. Krasnoff, Independent
History: Region settled in 1620s with first English colonies on banks of Elizabeth R. Home to Great Dismal Swamp Canal, first envisioned by George Washington in 1763. Battle of Great Bridge fought here Dec. 1775; inc. 1963.
Website: www.cityofchesapeake.net

Chicago, Illinois

Population: 2,714,856 (3). **Pop. density:** 11,926. **Pop. change (2010-12):** 0.6%. **Area:** 227.6 sq mi. **Racial distribution:** 44.9% white; 33.4% black; 5.4% Asian; 0.3% Amer. Ind.; <0.05% Pac. Isl.; 14.2% other; 2+ races 1.8%. **Hispanic pop.:** 28.1%. **Foreign born:** 21.0%. **U.S. citizens:** 87.4%. **Language:** 64.5% English only; 24.3% Spanish.
Employment: 1,144,896 employed; 10.1% unemployed. **Per capita income:** $45,977; change (2010-11): 3.7%. **Below poverty level:** 21.4%; 17.6% of families. **Educational attainment:** 80.2% HS; 32.9% bachelor's. **Avg. commute:** 33.7 min. 50.4% drive; 26.9% public trans. **Housing units:** 1,198,408; 86.0% occupied. **Home ownership:** 47.0%. **Avg. home:** $175,300; change (2010-12): –8.4%. **Avg. rent:** $916.
Mayor: Rahm Emanuel, nonpartisan
History: Site acquired from Indians 1795; significant white settlement began with completion of Erie Canal 1825; chartered as city 1837. Boomed with arrival of railroads and canal to Mississippi R.; one-third of city destroyed by fire 1871.
Website: www.cityofchicago.org

Chula Vista, California

Population: 252,422 (76). **Pop. density:** 5,086. **Pop. change (2010-12):** 3.2%. **Area:** 49.6 sq mi. **Racial distribution:** 64.5% white; 4.5% black; 14.3% Asian; 0.7% Amer. Ind.; 0.6% Pac. Isl.; 10.8% other; 2+ races 4.6%. **Hispanic pop.:** 56.8%. **Foreign born:** 31.4%. **U.S. citizens:** 85.7%. **Language:** 42.3% English only; 46.5% Spanish; 6.5% Tagalog.
Employment: 84,118 employed; 10.4% unemployed. **Per capita income:** $46,800; change (2010-11): 4.1%. **Below poverty level:** 9.7%; 8.0% of families. **Educational attainment:** 81.8% HS; 26.7% bachelor's. **Avg. commute:** 26.5 min. 78.3% drive; 11.6% carpool. **Housing units:** 82,329; 89.4% occupied. **Home ownership:** 59.5%. **Avg. home:** $385,520; change (2010-12): <0.05%. **Avg. rent:** $1,242.
Mayor: Cheryl Cox, nonpartisan
History: Visited by Spanish in 1542; became part of Spanish land grant in 1795; brought into the U.S. during the Mexican War in 1847; inc. 1911. WWII brought aircraft industry and growth.
Website: www.chulavistaca.gov

Cincinnati, Ohio

Population: 296,550 (65). **Pop. density:** 3,805. **Pop. change (2010-12):** –0.1%. **Area:** 77.9 sq mi. **Racial distribution:** 50.7% white; 44.0% black; 1.9% Asian; 0.2% Amer. Ind.; <0.05% Pac. Isl.; 0.9% other; 2+ races 2.4%. **Hispanic pop.:** 2.8%. **Foreign born:** 4.9%. **U.S. citizens:** 96.7%. **Language:** 92.7% English only; 3.0% Spanish.
Employment: 130,269 employed; 7.7% unemployed. **Per capita income:** $40,918; change (2010-11): 4.6%. **Below poverty level:** 27.4%; 21.8% of families. **Educational attainment:** 83.6% HS; 31.0% bachelor's. **Avg. commute:** 22.2 min. 70.8% drive. **Housing units:** 167,914; 78.5% occupied. **Home ownership:** 41.4%. **Avg. home:** $128,300; change (2010-12): 0.2%. **Avg. rent:** $617.
Mayor: Mark Mallory, nonpartisan
History: Founded 1788; named after the Society of Cincinnati, an organization of Revolutionary War officers; chartered as village 1802; inc. 1819.
Website: www.cincinnati-oh.gov

Cleveland, Ohio

Population: 390,928 (48). **Pop. density:** 5,031. **Pop. change (2010-12):** –1.3%. **Area:** 77.7 sq mi. **Racial distribution:** 41.0% white; 52.6% black; 1.6% Asian; 0.3% Amer. Ind.; <0.05% Pac. Isl.; 2.1% other; 2+ races 2.4%. **Hispanic pop.:** 9.4%. **Foreign born:** 4.7%. **U.S. citizens:** 97.6%. **Language:** 88.2% English only; 7.2% Spanish.
Employment: 147,338 employed; 9.5% unemployed. **Per capita income:** $42,365; change (2010-11): 5.6%. **Below poverty level:** 32.6%; 27.9% of families. **Educational attainment:** 76.3% HS; 13.8% bachelor's. **Avg. commute:** 24.1 min. 70.0% drive; 11.8% public trans. **Housing units:** 216,726; 78.3% occupied. **Home ownership:** 46.3%. **Avg. home:** $110,000; change (2010-12): –3.9%. **Avg. rent:** $646.
Mayor: Frank G. Jackson, nonpartisan
History: Surveyed in 1796; given recognition as village 1815; inc. 1836; annexed Ohio City 1854.
Website: www.city.cleveland.oh.us

Colorado Springs, Colorado

Population: 431,834 (41). **Pop. density:** 2,220. **Pop. change (2010-12):** 3.0%. **Area:** 194.5 sq mi. **Racial distribution:** 80.2% white; 6.4% black; 2.7% Asian; 0.8% Amer. Ind.; 0.2% Pac. Isl.; 4.7% other; 2+ races 4.9%. **Hispanic pop.:** 15.9%. **Foreign born:** 7.9%. **U.S. citizens:** 95.7%. **Language:** 87.6% English only; 7.5% Spanish.
Employment: 189,246 employed; 9.2% unemployed. **Per capita income:** $39,994; change (2010-11): 5.3%. **Below poverty level:** 12.7%; 9.3% of families. **Educational attainment:** 92.2% HS; 36.1% bachelor's. **Avg. commute:** 20.7 min. 79.4% drive; 10.1% carpool. **Housing units:** 178,362; 92.0% occupied. **Home ownership:** 61.1%. **Avg. home:** $201,600; change (2010-12): 3.1%. **Avg. rent:** $812.
Mayor: Steve Bach, nonpartisan
History: Founded 1871 at the foot of Pike's Peak; inc. 1872.
Website: www.springsgov.com

Columbus, Ohio

Population: 809,798 (15). **Pop. density:** 3,729. **Pop. change (2010-12):** 2.4%. **Area:** 217.2 sq mi. **Racial distribution:** 62.9% white; 27.8% black; 4.1% Asian; 0.2% Amer. Ind.; <0.05% Pac. Isl.; 1.8% other; 2+ races 3.1%. **Hispanic pop.:** 5.3%. **Foreign born:** 10.3%. **U.S. citizens:** 93.3%. **Language:** 87.1% English only; 4.4% Spanish.
Employment: 401,579 employed; 6.2% unemployed. **Per capita income:** $40,188; change (2010-11): 4.9%. **Below poverty level:** 21.8%; 16.6% of families. **Educational attainment:** 87.7% HS; 32.3% bachelor's. **Avg. commute:** 21.0 min. 80.8% drive. **Housing units:** 371,537; 86.1% occupied. **Home ownership:** 48.6%. **Avg. home:** $136,500; change (2010-12): 0.1%. **Avg. rent:** $776.
Mayor: Michael B. Coleman, Democrat
History: First settlement 1797; laid out as new state capital 1812 with current name; inc. 1834.
Website: www.columbus.gov

Corpus Christi, Texas

Population: 312,195 (60). **Pop. density:** 1,944. **Pop. change (2010-12):** 2.2%. **Area:** 160.6 sq mi. **Racial distribution:** 84.1% white; 4.4% black; 1.7% Asian; 0.3% Amer. Ind.; <0.05% Pac. Isl.; 7.2% other; 2+ races 2.2%. **Hispanic pop.:** 59.2%. **Foreign born:** 7.6%. **U.S. citizens:** 95.5%. **Language:** 61.3% English only; 36.1% Spanish.
Employment: 151,066 employed; 6.0% unemployed. **Per capita income:** $38,609; change (2010-11): 5.3%. **Below poverty level:** 18.5%; 14.5% of families. **Educational attainment:** 80.4% HS; 21.2% bachelor's. **Avg. commute:** 18.9 min. 79.0% drive; 11.4% carpool. **Housing units:** 123,797; 88.7% occupied. **Home ownership:** 59.5%. **Avg. home:** $142,700; change (2010-12): 5.6%. **Avg. rent:** $823.
Mayor: Nelda Martinez, nonpartisan
History: Settled 1839; inc. 1852. One of the largest U.S. ports.
Website: www.cctexas.com

Dallas, Texas

Population: 1,241,162 (9). **Pop. density:** 3,645. **Pop. change (2010-12):** 3.4%. **Area:** 340.5 sq mi. **Racial distribution:** 55.0% white; 24.5% black; 2.8% Asian; 0.4% Amer. Ind.; <0.05% Pac. Isl.; 15.3% other; 2+ races 1.9%. **Hispanic pop.:** 41.9%. **Foreign born:** 24.6%. **U.S. citizens:** 80.5%. **Language:** 57.9% English only; 37.3% Spanish.
Employment: 539,041 employed; 7.3% unemployed. **Per capita income:** $43,708; change (2010-11): 4.2%. **Below poverty level:** 23.0%; 19.6% of families. **Educational attainment:** 73.3% HS; 28.8% bachelor's. **Avg. commute:** 25.1 min. 77.4% drive; 11.5% carpool. **Housing units:** 517,279; 87.5% occupied. **Home ownership:** 45.2%. **Avg. home:** $159,300; change (2010-12): 10.8%. **Avg. rent:** $811.
Mayor: Mike Rawlings, nonpartisan
History: First settled 1841; platted 1846; inc. 1871. Developed as financial and commercial center of Southwest; headquarters of regional Federal Reserve Bank; major center for distribution and high-tech manufacturing.
Website: www.dallascityhall.com

Denver, Colorado

Population: 634,265 (23). **Pop. density:** 4,146. **Pop. change (2010-12):** 5.1%. **Area:** 153.0 sq mi. **Racial distribution:** 73.6% white; 10.2% black; 3.4% Asian; 1.2% Amer. Ind.; 0.1% Pac. Isl.; 8.5% other; 2+ races 3.0%. **Hispanic pop.:** 31.9%. **Foreign born:** 16.4%. **U.S. citizens:** 88.4%. **Language:** 72.4% English only; 21.1% Spanish.
Employment: 301,053 employed; 8.5% unemployed. **Per capita income:** $48,980; change (2010-11): 4.3%. **Below poverty level:** 18.8%; 14.2% of families. **Educational attainment:** 84.7% HS; 41.3% bachelor's. **Avg. commute:** 24.6 min. 69.3% drive; 10.0% carpool. **Housing units:** 283,658; 91.0% occupied. **Home ownership:** 51.7%. **Avg. home:** $252,400; change (2010-12): 8.6%. **Avg. rent:** $832.

Mayor: Michael Hancock, nonpartisan
History: Settled 1858 by gold prospectors and miners; inc. 1861; became territorial capital 1867. Growth spurred by gold and silver boom. Became financial, industrial, cultural center of Rocky Mt. region.
Website: www.denvergov.org

Detroit, Michigan

Population: 701,475 (18). **Pop. density:** 5,056. **Pop. change (2010-12):** −1.4%. **Area:** 138.8 sq mi. **Racial distribution:** 11.3% white; 82.4% black; 1.1% Asian; 0.3% Amer. Ind.; <0.05% Pac. Isl.; 3.1% other; 2+ races 1.8%. **Hispanic pop.:** 6.7%. **Foreign born:** 5.1%. **U.S. citizens:** 96.6%. **Language:** 90.7% English only; 5.8% Spanish.
Employment: 279,960 employed; 18.6% unemployed. **Per capita income:** $40,009; change (2010-11): 6.2%. **Below poverty level:** 36.2%; 31.1% of families. **Educational attainment:** 77.1% HS; 12.2% bachelor's. **Avg. commute:** 26.6 min. 72.0% drive; 11.4% carpool. **Housing units:** 363,281; 72.7% occupied. **Home ownership:** 53.8%. **Avg. home:** $53,800 (2011). **Avg. rent:** $761.
Mayor: Dave Bing, nonpartisan
History: Founded by French 1701; controlled by British 1760; acquired by U.S. 1796. Destroyed by fire 1805; fought over during War of 1812; inc. 1815; capital of state 1837-47. Auto manufacturing began 1890.
Website: www.detroitmi.gov

Durham, North Carolina

Population: 239,358 (83). **Pop. density:** 2,229. **Pop. change (2010-12):** 4.4%. **Area:** 107.4 sq mi. **Racial distribution:** 43.8% white; 40.1% black; 4.8% Asian; 0.2% Amer. Ind.; <0.05% Pac. Isl.; 8.0% other; 2+ races 3.0%. **Hispanic pop.:** 13.4%. **Foreign born:** 14.6%. **U.S. citizens:** 88.8%. **Language:** 80.2% English only; 12.5% Spanish.
Employment: 114,440 employed; 7.0% unemployed. **Per capita income:** $41,785; change (2010-11): 3.0%. **Below poverty level:** 18.6%; 13.1% of families. **Educational attainment:** 86.4% HS; 46.3% bachelor's. **Avg. commute:** 20.9 min. 74.1% drive; 13.6% carpool. **Housing units:** 103,227; 89.6% occupied. **Home ownership:** 50.9%. **Avg. home:** $185,700; change (2010-12): 17.3%. **Avg. rent:** $809.
Mayor: William V. Bell, nonpartisan
History: Inc. 1869. Trinity College moved to Durham in 1892, renamed Duke Univ. in 1924.
Website: durhamnc.gov

El Paso, Texas

Population: 672,538 (19). **Pop. density:** 2,635. **Pop. change (2010-12):** 3.2%. **Area:** 255.2 sq mi. **Racial distribution:** 79.7% white; 3.2% black; 1.2% Asian; 0.5% Amer. Ind.; 0.1% Pac. Isl.; 13.0% other; 2+ races 2.4%. **Hispanic pop.:** 80.2%. **Foreign born:** 25.5%. **U.S. citizens:** 85.6%. **Language:** 27.8% English only; 70.1% Spanish.
Employment: 249,070 employed; 8.6% unemployed. **Per capita income:** $30,088; change (2010-11): 5.0%. **Below poverty level:** 23.3%; 20.1% of families. **Educational attainment:** 74.6% HS; 21.9% bachelor's. **Avg. commute:** 22.0 min. 79.8% drive; 10.9% carpool. **Housing units:** 227,257; 92.6% occupied. **Home ownership:** 61.0%. **Avg. home:** $138,600; change (2010-12): 3.2%. **Avg. rent:** $661.
Mayor: Oscar Leeser, nonpartisan
History: First settled 1598; inc. 1873. Arrival of railroad, 1881, boosted city's population and industries.
Website: home.elpasotexas.gov

Fort Wayne, Indiana

Population: 254,555 (74). **Pop. density:** 2,301. **Pop. change (2010-12):** 0.3%. **Area:** 110.6 sq mi. **Racial distribution:** 75.1% white; 15.5% black; 2.7% Asian; 0.4% Amer. Ind.; <0.05% Pac. Isl.; 3.2% other; 2+ races 3.1%. **Hispanic pop.:** 7.6%. **Foreign born:** 6.6%. **U.S. citizens:** 95.9%. **Language:** 90.4% English only; 5.4% Spanish.
Employment: 111,539 employed; 8.8% unemployed. **Per capita income:** $35,042; change (2010-11): 4.9%. **Below poverty level:** 16.3%; 12.3% of families. **Educational attainment:** 88.1% HS; 25.5% bachelor's. **Avg. commute:** 19.6 min. 85.9% drive. **Housing units:** 114,749; 88.1% occupied. **Home ownership:** 64.6%. **Avg. home:** $106,200; change (2010-12): 9.0%. **Avg. rent:** $638.
Mayor: Tom Henry, Democrat
History: French fort 1680; U.S. fort 1794; settled by 1832; inc. 1840 prior to Wabash-Erie Canal completion in 1843.
Website: www.cityoffortwayne.org

Fort Worth, Texas

Population: 777,992 (16). **Pop. density:** 2,289. **Pop. change (2010-12):** 4.3%. **Area:** 339.8 sq mi. **Racial distribution:** 64.1% white; 18.9% black; 3.5% Asian; 0.7% Amer. Ind.; 0.1% Pac. Isl.; 10.6% other; 2+ races 2.2%. **Hispanic pop.:** 33.6%. **Foreign born:** 17.5%. **U.S. citizens:** 87.4%. **Language:** 68.1% English only; 27.1% Spanish.

Employment: 333,866 employed; 6.7% unemployed. **Per capita income:** $43,708; change (2010-11): 4.2%. **Below poverty level:** 18.1%; 14.5% of families. **Educational attainment:** 79.0% HS; 25.9% bachelor's. **Avg. commute:** 25.6 min. 81.4% drive; 11.3% carpool. **Housing units:** 288,130; 89.4% occupied. **Home ownership:** 59.8%. **Avg. home:** $159,300; change (2010-12): 10.8%. **Avg. rent:** $827.
Mayor: Betsy Price, nonpartisan
History: Established as military post 1849; inc. 1873; oil discovered 1917.
Website: fortworthtexas.gov

Fremont, California

Population: 221,986 (96). **Pop. density:** 2,866. **Pop. change (2010-12):** 3.4%. **Area:** 77.5 sq mi. **Racial distribution:** 33.9% white; 3.3% black; 49.0% Asian; 0.4% Amer. Ind.; 0.6% Pac. Isl.; 7.7% other; 2+ races 5.1%. **Hispanic pop.:** 15.4%. **Foreign born:** 43.1%. **U.S. citizens:** 80.8%. **Language:** 42.6% English only; 10.5% Spanish; 15.7% Chinese; 6.0% Hindi.
Employment: 104,605 employed; 6.5% unemployed. **Per capita income:** $61,395; change (2010-11): 4.8%. **Below poverty level:** 5.4%; 3.4% of families. **Educational attainment:** 90.5% HS; 49.9% bachelor's. **Avg. commute:** 29.1 min. 75.7% drive; 10.5% carpool. **Housing units:** 74,782; 93.1% occupied. **Home ownership:** 64.3%. **Avg. home:** $543,780; change (2010-12): 3.5%. **Avg. rent:** $1,494.
Mayor: Bill Harrison, nonpartisan
History: Area first settled by Spanish 1769; inc. 1956 with consolidation of five communities.
Website: www.fremont.gov

Fresno, California

Population: 505,882 (34). **Pop. density:** 4,519. **Pop. change (2010-12):** 1.8%. **Area:** 112.0 sq mi. **Racial distribution:** 54.0% white; 7.5% black; 12.4% Asian; 0.9% Amer. Ind.; 0.2% Pac. Isl.; 20.6% other; 2+ races 4.4%. **Hispanic pop.:** 46.4%. **Foreign born:** 21.3%. **U.S. citizens:** 86.3%. **Language:** 57.6% English only; 28.9% Spanish.
Employment: 199,014 employed; 14.3% unemployed. **Per capita income:** $31,542; change (2010-11): 3.1%. **Below poverty level:** 25.9%; 20.7% of families. **Educational attainment:** 74.6% HS; 20.1% bachelor's. **Avg. commute:** 21.0 min. 77.6% drive; 11.8% carpool. **Housing units:** 170,495; 91.9% occupied. **Home ownership:** 49.3%. **Avg. rent:** $862.
Mayor: Ashley Swearengin, nonpartisan
History: Founded 1872; inc. 1885.
Website: www.fresno.gov

Garland, Texas

Population: 233,564 (86). **Pop. density:** 4,092. **Pop. change (2010-12):** 2.7%. **Area:** 57.1 sq mi. **Racial distribution:** 47.9% white; 14.4% black; 9.4% Asian; 0.4% Amer. Ind.; 0.1% Pac. Isl.; 22.4% other; 2+ races 5.5%. **Hispanic pop.:** 37.5%. **Foreign born:** 27.0%. **U.S. citizens:** 81.9%. **Language:** 55.8% English only; 32.8% Spanish.
Employment: 108,299 employed; 6.8% unemployed. **Per capita income:** $43,708; change (2010-11): 4.2%. **Below poverty level:** 14.5%; 11.1% of families. **Educational attainment:** 75.9% HS; 21.4% bachelor's. **Avg. commute:** 27.7 min. 78.4% drive; 14.2% carpool. **Housing units:** 78,206; 92.7% occupied. **Home ownership:** 65.3%. **Avg. home:** $159,300; change (2010-12): 10.8%. **Avg. rent:** $923.
Mayor: Douglas Athas, nonpartisan
History: Settled 1850s; inc. 1891.
Website: www.garlandtx.gov

Gilbert, Arizona

Population: 221,140 (97). **Pop. density:** 3,254. **Pop. change (2010-12):** 5.6%. **Area:** 68.0 sq mi. **Racial distribution:** 82.4% white; 3.9% black; 6.1% Asian; 0.6% Amer. Ind.; 0.1% Pac. Isl.; 3.5% other; 2+ races 3.3%. **Hispanic pop.:** 15.2%. **Foreign born:** 9.3%. **U.S. citizens:** 95.6%. **Language:** 83.8% English only; 8.7% Spanish.
Employment: 108,231 employed; 5.3% unemployed. **Per capita income:** $36,833; change (2010-11): 4.0%. **Below poverty level:** 5.8%; 4.8% of families. **Educational attainment:** 95.3% HS; 38.0% bachelor's. **Avg. commute:** 26.9 min. 79.2% drive; 12.3% carpool. **Housing units:** 71,000; 93.5% occupied. **Home ownership:** 74.2%. **Avg. home:** $147,600; change (2010-12): 6.0%. **Avg. rent:** $1,277.
Mayor: John Lewis, nonpartisan
History: Est. 1891; inc. 1920.
Website: www.gilbertaz.gov

Glendale, Arizona

Population: 232,143 (87). **Pop. density:** 3,871. **Pop. change (2010-12):** 2.4%. **Area:** 60.0 sq mi. **Racial distribution:** 75.9% white; 5.9% black; 3.5% Asian; 1.3% Amer. Ind.; 0.1% Pac. Isl.; 9.6% other; 2+ races 3.7%. **Hispanic pop.:** 35.3%. **Foreign**

born: 16.1%. **U.S. citizens:** 89.4%. **Language:** 70.1% English only; 23.6% Spanish.
Employment: 107,851 employed; 7.5% unemployed. **Per capita income:** $36,833; change (2010-11): 4.0%. **Below poverty level:** 17.7%; 13.5% of families. **Educational attainment:** 83.2% HS; 21.4% bachelor's. **Avg. commute:** 26.5 min. 74.9% drive; 14.9% carpool. **Housing units:** 90,439; 88.1% occupied. **Home ownership:** 61.1%. **Avg. home:** $147,600; change (2010-12): 6.0%. **Avg. rent:** $860.
Mayor: Jerry Weiers, nonpartisan
History: Est. 1892; inc. 1910.
Website: www.glendaleaz.com

Greensboro, North Carolina

Population: 277,080 (69). **Pop. density:** 2,190. **Pop. change (2010-12):** 2.5%. **Area:** 126.5 sq mi. **Racial distribution:** 50.5% white; 39.9% black; 3.9% Asian; 0.5% Amer. Ind.; <0.05% Pac. Isl.; 2.9% other; 2+ races 2.2%. **Hispanic pop.:** 7.4%. **Foreign born:** 10.0%. **U.S. citizens:** 93.2%. **Language:** 86.8% English only; 6.8% Spanish.
Employment: 127,107 employed; 9.1% unemployed. **Per capita income:** $35,405; change (2010-11): 3.8%. **Below poverty level:** 18.4%; 12.8% of families. **Educational attainment:** 87.1% HS; 35.0% bachelor's. **Avg. commute:** 19.9 min. 82.0% drive. **Housing units:** 123,483; 88.2% occupied. **Home ownership:** 55.2%. **Avg. home:** $124,800; change (2010-12): –3.9%. **Avg. rent:** $722.
Mayor: Robbie Perkins, nonpartisan
History: Settled 1749; site of 1781 Revolutionary War conflict between Generals Nathanael Greene and Lord Charles Cornwallis; inc. 1807. Origin of civil rights sit-in movement.
Website: www.greensboro-nc.gov

Henderson, Nevada

Population: 265,679 (71). **Pop. density:** 2,466. **Pop. change (2010-12):** 2.9%. **Area:** 107.7 sq mi. **Racial distribution:** 79.0% white; 5.7% black; 7.5% Asian; 0.5% Amer. Ind.; 0.6% Pac. Isl.; 3.4% other; 2+ races 3.3%. **Hispanic pop.:** 14.2%. **Foreign born:** 11.7%. **U.S. citizens:** 95.6%. **Language:** 83.6% English only; 7.8% Spanish.
Employment: 127,872 employed; 10.5% unemployed. **Per capita income:** $35,680; change (2010-11): 2.9%. **Below poverty level:** 8.2%; 5.5% of families. **Educational attainment:** 92.3% HS; 30.4% bachelor's. **Avg. commute:** 22.9 min. 82.1% drive. **Housing units:** 112,826; 88.2% occupied. **Home ownership:** 67.0%. **Avg. home:** $134,100; change (2010-12): –2.8%. **Avg. rent:** $1,193.
Mayor: Andy A. Hafen, nonpartisan
History: Early growth spurred by WWII magnesium mining; inc. 1953.
Website: www.cityofhenderson.com

Hialeah, Florida

Population: 231,941 (88). **Pop. density:** 10,813. **Pop. change (2010-12):** 2.9%. **Area:** 21.5 sq mi. **Racial distribution:** 93.0% white; 2.2% black; 0.5% Asian; 0.1% Amer. Ind.; <0.05% Pac. Isl.; 3.4% other; 2+ races 0.9%. **Hispanic pop.:** 94.9%. **Foreign born:** 73.4%. **U.S. citizens:** 59.9%. **Language:** 6.2% English only; 93.2% Spanish.
Employment: 94,007 employed; 11.7% unemployed. **Per capita income:** $43,072; change (2010-11): 2.9%. **Below poverty level:** 21.6%; 18.8% of families. **Educational attainment:** 67.9% HS; 13.4% bachelor's. **Avg. commute:** 24.2 min. 78.1% drive. **Housing units:** 76,669; 94.7% occupied. **Home ownership:** 51.9%. **Avg. home:** $203,100; change (2010-12): 0.6%. **Avg. rent:** $967.
Mayor: Carlos Hernandez, nonpartisan
History: Founded 1917; inc. 1925. Industrial and residential city NW of Miami; site of Hialeah Park Racetrack.
Website: www.hialeahfl.gov

Honolulu, Hawaii

Population: 345,610 (54). **Pop. density:** 5,711. **Pop. change (2010-12):** 2.0%. **Area:** 60.5 sq mi. **Racial distribution:** 18.4% white; 1.6% black; 55.6% Asian; 0.1% Amer. Ind.; 8.0% Pac. Isl.; 0.6% other; 2+ races 15.6%. **Hispanic pop.:** 5.0%. **Foreign born:** 28.3%. **U.S. citizens:** 86.4%. **Language:** 62.4% English only; 1.5% Spanish; 7.4% Japanese; 7.3% Chinese; 5.3% Tagalog; 8.0% other Pac. Isl. languages.
Employment: 434,339 employed; 5.2% unemployed. **Per capita income:** $46,624; change (2010-11): 5.1%. **Below poverty level:** 11.6%; 7.5% of families. **Educational attainment:** 88.0% HS; 33.6% bachelor's. **Avg. commute:** 22.4 min. 57.6% drive; 13.1% carpool; 12.5% public trans. **Housing units:** 143,602; 88.9% occupied. **Home ownership:** 44.8%. **Avg. home:** $628,800; change (2010-12): 3.5%. **Avg. rent:** $1,185.
Mayor: Kirk Caldwell, nonpartisan
History: Europeans entered harbor 1778; declared capital of kingdom by King Kamehameha III 1850. Pearl Harbor naval base attacked by Japanese Dec. 7, 1941.
Website: www.honolulu.gov

Houston, Texas

Population: 2,160,821 (4). **Pop. density:** 3,604. **Pop. change (2010-12):** 2.8%. **Area:** 599.6 sq mi. **Racial distribution:** 56.1% white; 23.7% black; 6.0% Asian; 0.4% Amer. Ind.; <0.05% Pac. Isl.; 12.3% other; 2+ races 1.4%. **Hispanic pop.:** 43.1%. **Foreign born:** 28.4%. **U.S. citizens:** 79.3%. **Language:** 54.2% English only; 37.4% Spanish.
Employment: 961,342 employed; 6.9% unemployed. **Per capita income:** $47,612; change (2010-11): 5.9%. **Below poverty level:** 21.5%; 18.2% of families. **Educational attainment:** 74.4% HS; 28.4% bachelor's. **Avg. commute:** 25.8 min. 75.0% drive; 13.0% carpool. **Housing units:** 898,502; 85.7% occupied. **Home ownership:** 46.6%. **Avg. home:** $164,800; change (2010-12): 6.3%. **Avg. rent:** $820.
Mayor: Annise D. Parker, Democrat
History: Founded 1836; inc. 1837; capital of Rep. of Texas 1837-39. Developed rapidly after completion of channel to Gulf of Mexico 1914. World center of oil, natural gas technology.
Website: www.houstontx.gov

Indianapolis, Indiana

Population: 834,852 (13). **Pop. density:** 2,310. **Pop. change (2010-12):** 1.6%. **Area:** 361.4 sq mi. **Racial distribution:** 63.7% white; 27.3% black; 2.1% Asian; 0.2% Amer. Ind.; <0.05% Pac. Isl.; 4.1% other; 2+ races 2.7%. **Hispanic pop.:** 8.9%. **Foreign born:** 8.3%. **U.S. citizens:** 93.8%. **Language:** 88.2% English only; 8.0% Spanish.
Employment: 382,848 employed; 8.8% unemployed. **Per capita income:** $40,572; change (2010-11): 4.4%. **Below poverty level:** 18.9%; 14.7% of families. **Educational attainment:** 84.0% HS; 27.1% bachelor's. **Avg. commute:** 22.5 min. 82.2% drive; 10.0% carpool. **Housing units:** 380,298; 85.4% occupied. **Home ownership:** 57.2%. **Avg. home:** $129,600; change (2010-12): 5.1%. **Avg. rent:** $737.
Mayor: Gregory A. Ballard, Republican
History: Settled 1820; became state capital 1825.
Website: www.indy.gov

Irvine, California

Population: 229,985 (91). **Pop. density:** 3,479. **Pop. change (2010-12):** 7.8%. **Area:** 66.1 sq mi. **Racial distribution:** 53.7% white; 1.8% black; 37.5% Asian; 0.4% Amer. Ind.; 0.3% Pac. Isl.; 2.1% other; 2+ races 4.1%. **Hispanic pop.:** 9.4%. **Foreign born:** 34.8%. **U.S. citizens:** 84.9%. **Language:** 56.9% English only; 5.8% Spanish; 9.2% Chinese; 6.6% Korean.
Employment: 79,519 employed; 5.7% unemployed. **Per capita income:** $44,423; change (2010-11): 3.7%. **Below poverty level:** 10.6%; 5.1% of families. **Educational attainment:** 96.4% HS; 65.0% bachelor's. **Avg. commute:** 22.5 min. 77.5% drive. **Housing units:** 79,423; 94.1% occupied. **Home ownership:** 52.7%. **Avg. home:** $327,470; change (2010-12): 1.3%. **Avg. rent:** $1,813.
Mayor: Steven S. Choi, nonpartisan
History: Univ. of CA–Irvine campus announced 1959; planned city developed around campus 1960s; inc. 1971.
Website: www.cityofirvine.org

Irving, Texas

Population: 225,427 (93). **Pop. density:** 3,364. **Pop. change (2010-12):** 3.9%. **Area:** 67.0 sq mi. **Racial distribution:** 58.9% white; 12.1% black; 14.2% Asian; 0.6% Amer. Ind.; 0.1% Pac. Isl.; 11.9% other; 2+ races 2.3%. **Hispanic pop.:** 40.3%. **Foreign born:** 33.1%. **U.S. citizens:** 75.9%. **Language:** 49.2% English only; 35.0% Spanish.
Employment: 114,391 employed; 6.2% unemployed. **Per capita income:** $43,708; change (2010-11): 4.2%. **Below poverty level:** 16.1%; 13.3% of families. **Educational attainment:** 78.9% HS; 33.3% bachelor's. **Avg. commute:** 22.0 min. 79.1% drive; 12.4% carpool. **Housing units:** 90,674; 90.1% occupied. **Home ownership:** 40.3%. **Avg. home:** $159,300; change (2010-12): 10.8%. **Avg. rent:** $869.
Mayor: Beth Van Duyne, nonpartisan
History: Founded 1903; inc. 1914; remained small until 1950s.
Website: www.ci.irving.tx.us

Jacksonville, Florida

Population: 836,507 (12). **Pop. density:** 1,120. **Pop. change (2010-12):** 1.6%. **Area:** 747.0 sq mi. **Racial distribution:** 60.8% white; 30.5% black; 4.2% Asian; 0.3% Amer. Ind.; 0.1% Pac. Isl.; 1.6% other; 2+ races 2.5%. **Hispanic pop.:** 7.5%. **Foreign born:** 9.3%. **U.S. citizens:** 95.5%. **Language:** 86.9% English only; 6.1% Spanish.
Employment: 385,074 employed; 8.6% unemployed. **Per capita income:** $40,709; change (2010-11): 3.7%. **Below poverty level:** 15.2%; 11.3% of families. **Educational attainment:** 87.2% HS; 24.2% bachelor's. **Avg. commute:** 23.5 min. 81.2% drive; 10.6% carpool. **Housing units:** 364,678; 85.5% occupied. **Home ownership:** 63.3%. **Avg. home:** $128,200; change (2010-12): –6.9%. **Avg. rent:** $910.
Mayor: Alvin Brown, Democrat

History: Settled 1816 as Cowford; renamed after Andrew Jackson 1822; inc. 1832; rechartered 1851. Scene of conflicts in Seminole and Civil Wars.
Website: www.coj.net

Jersey City, New Jersey

Population: 254,441 (75). **Pop. density:** 17,199. **Pop. change (2010-12):** 2.4%. **Area:** 14.8 sq mi. **Racial distribution:** 34.5% white; 26.3% black; 23.0% Asian; 0.5% Amer. Ind.; <0.05% Pac. Isl.; 12.9% other; 2+ races 2.7%. **Hispanic pop.:** 28.0%. **Foreign born:** 38.2%. **U.S. citizens:** 79.4%. **Language:** 47.8% English only; 23.8% Spanish; 5.6% Tagalog.
Employment: 105,965 employed; 10.9% unemployed. **Per capita income:** $56,770; change (2010-11): 4.0%. **Below poverty level:** 16.4%; 13.9% of families. **Educational attainment:** 84.0% HS; 40.6% bachelor's. **Avg. commute:** 34.6 min. 46.2% public trans.; 33.1% drive. **Housing units:** 108,750; 87.0% occupied. **Home ownership:** 31.8%. **Avg. home:** $379,300; change (2010-12): -3.7%. **Avg. rent:** $1,127.
Mayor: Steven M. Fulop, nonpartisan
History: Site bought from Indians 1630; chartered as town by British 1668; scene of Revolutionary War conflict 1779; chartered under present name 1838. Important station on Underground Railroad.
Website: www.cityofjerseycity.com

Kansas City, Missouri

Population: 464,310 (37). **Pop. density:** 1,474. **Pop. change (2010-12):** 0.8%. **Area:** 315.0 sq mi. **Racial distribution:** 60.4% white; 29.7% black; 2.3% Asian; 0.4% Amer. Ind.; 0.2% Pac. Isl.; 3.7% other; 2+ races 3.2%. **Hispanic pop.:** 9.9%. **Foreign born:** 7.7%. **U.S. citizens:** 95.2%. **Language:** 88.1% English only; 7.2% Spanish.
Employment: 211,864 employed; 7.4% unemployed. **Per capita income:** $43,062; change (2010-11): 3.9%. **Below poverty level:** 18.2%; 13.8% of families. **Educational attainment:** 86.6% HS; 30.1% bachelor's. **Avg. commute:** 21.5 min. 80.5% drive. **Housing units:** 224,622; 85.6% occupied. **Home ownership:** 57.3%. **Avg. home:** $142,600; change (2010-12): 0.7%. **Avg. rent:** $752.
Mayor: Sly James, nonpartisan
History: Settled by 1838 at confluence of Missouri and Kansas Rivers; inc. 1850.
Website: www.kcmo.org

Laredo, Texas

Population: 244,731 (81). **Pop. density:** 2,753. **Pop. change (2010-12):** 3.2%. **Area:** 88.9 sq mi. **Racial distribution:** 86.7% white; 0.5% black; 0.8% Asian; 0.3% Amer. Ind.; <0.05% Pac. Isl.; 10.6% other; 2+ races 1.1%. **Hispanic pop.:** 95.4%. **Foreign born:** 29.5%. **U.S. citizens:** 78.9%. **Language:** 7.8% English only; 91.4% Spanish.
Employment: 89,391 employed; 6.7% unemployed. **Per capita income:** $24,985; change (2010-11): 5.4%. **Below poverty level:** 29.8%; 25.2% of families. **Educational attainment:** 64.7% HS; 17.7% bachelor's. **Avg. commute:** 20.0 min. 77.3% drive; 14.3% carpool. **Housing units:** 67,800; 92.0% occupied. **Home ownership:** 63.2%. **Avg. rent:** $727.
Mayor: Raul G. Salinas, nonpartisan
History: Founded by Spanish colonists in 1755; part of U.S. from 1848. Fast growth fueled by immigration. Principal port of entry into Mexico.
Website: www.cityoflaredo.com

Las Vegas, Nevada

Population: 596,424 (31). **Pop. density:** 4,391. **Pop. change (2010-12):** 2.1%. **Area:** 135.8 sq mi. **Racial distribution:** 70.3% white; 11.0% black; 5.9% Asian; 0.7% Amer. Ind.; 0.5% Pac. Isl.; 7.1% other; 2+ races 4.3%. **Hispanic pop.:** 31.3%. **Foreign born:** 21.8%. **U.S. citizens:** 85.8%. **Language:** 67.0% English only; 24.7% Spanish.
Employment: 255,192 employed; 11.6% unemployed. **Per capita income:** $35,680; change (2010-11): 2.9%. **Below poverty level:** 14.9%; 11.0% of families. **Educational attainment:** 81.7% HS; 21.5% bachelor's. **Avg. commute:** 25.2 min. 77.3% drive; 11.7% carpool. **Housing units:** 245,767; 86.1% occupied. **Home ownership:** 55.9%. **Avg. home:** $134,100; change (2010-12): -2.8%. **Avg. rent:** $1,016.
Mayor: Carolyn G. Goodman, nonpartisan
History: Occupied by Mormons 1855-57; bought by railroad 1903; inc. 1911. Gambling legalized 1931.
Website: www.lasvegasnevada.gov

Lexington, Kentucky

Population: 305,489 (62). **Pop. density:** 1,077. **Pop. change (2010-12):** 3.0%. **Area:** 283.6 sq mi. **Racial distribution:** 76.5% white; 14.4% black; 3.4% Asian; 0.2% Amer. Ind.; 0.1% Pac. Isl.; 3.2% other; 2+ races 2.3%. **Hispanic pop.:** 6.5%. **Foreign born:** 8.5%. **U.S. citizens:** 93.6%. **Language:** 88.9% English only; 6.0% Spanish.

Employment: 146,362 employed; 6.3% unemployed. **Per capita income:** $37,763; change (2010-11): 4.5%. **Below poverty level:** 17.9%; 11.8% of families. **Educational attainment:** 88.5% HS; 39.3% bachelor's. **Avg. commute:** 19.7 min. 79.8% drive; 10.3% carpool. **Housing units:** 134,069; 91.1% occupied. **Home ownership:** 56.9%. **Avg. home:** $143,200; change (2010-12): <0.05%. **Avg. rent:** $722.
Mayor: Jim Gray, nonpartisan
History: Site founded and named in 1775 after site of the Revolutionary War's opening battle at Lexington, MA; settled 1779; chartered 1782; inc. 1832.
Website: www.lexingtonky.gov

Lincoln, Nebraska

Population: 265,404 (72). **Pop. density:** 2,978. **Pop. change (2010-12):** 2.5%. **Area:** 89.1 sq mi. **Racial distribution:** 88.1% white; 3.8% black; 3.9% Asian; 0.6% Amer. Ind.; 0.1% Pac. Isl.; 0.9% other; 2+ races 2.5%. **Hispanic pop.:** 6.0%. **Foreign born:** 7.4%. **U.S. citizens:** 95.7%. **Language:** 88.6% English only; 4.3% Spanish.
Employment: 145,811 employed; 3.4% unemployed. **Per capita income:** $39,018; change (2010-11): 4.8%. **Below poverty level:** 15.5%; 9.1% of families. **Educational attainment:** 93.1% HS; 36.0% bachelor's. **Avg. commute:** 17.4 min. 81.0% drive. **Housing units:** 109,743; 93.8% occupied. **Home ownership:** 59.2%. **Avg. home:** $139,600; change (2010-12): 4.5%. **Avg. rent:** $689.
Mayor: Chris Beutler, nonpartisan
History: Originally called Lancaster; chosen state capital, 1867, and renamed after Abraham Lincoln; inc. 1869.
Website: lincoln.ne.gov

Long Beach, California

Population: 467,892 (36). **Pop. density:** 9,303. **Pop. change (2010-12):** 1.1%. **Area:** 50.3 sq mi. **Racial distribution:** 49.7% white; 13.5% black; 13.2% Asian; 0.5% Amer. Ind.; 1.0% Pac. Isl.; 16.8% other; 2+ races 5.3%. **Hispanic pop.:** 40.1%. **Foreign born:** 26.8%. **U.S. citizens:** 84.4%. **Language:** 54.8% English only; 31.8% Spanish.
Employment: 208,159 employed; 12.0% unemployed. **Per capita income:** $44,423; change (2010-11): 3.7%. **Below poverty level:** 19.4%; 15.5% of families. **Educational attainment:** 79.0% HS; 28.7% bachelor's. **Avg. commute:** 28.0 min. 72.0% drive; 11.4% carpool. **Housing units:** 176,188; 91.9% occupied. **Home ownership:** 41.4%. **Avg. home:** $327,470; change (2010-12): 1.3%. **Avg. rent:** $1,075.
Mayor: Bob Foster, nonpartisan
History: Settled as early as 1784 by Spanish; by 1884, present site developed on harbor; inc. 1888. Oil discovered 1921.
Website: www.longbeach.gov

Los Angeles, California

Population: 3,857,799 (2). **Pop. density:** 8,231. **Pop. change (2010-12):** 1.6%. **Area:** 468.7 sq mi. **Racial distribution:** 51.9% white; 9.6% black; 11.4% Asian; 0.5% Amer. Ind.; 0.2% Pac. Isl.; 23.3% other; 2+ races 3.1%. **Hispanic pop.:** 48.1%. **Foreign born:** 39.4%. **U.S. citizens:** 76.4%. **Language:** 40.1% English only; 43.0% Spanish.
Employment: 1,680,134 employed; 12.1% unemployed. **Per capita income:** $44,423; change (2010-11): 3.7%. **Below poverty level:** 20.2%; 16.5% of families. **Educational attainment:** 73.9% HS; 30.5% bachelor's. **Avg. commute:** 29.1 min. 67.2% drive; 11.0% public trans.; 10.5% carpool. **Housing units:** 1,412,641; 92.9% occupied. **Home ownership:** 38.4%. **Avg. home:** $327,470; change (2010-12): 1.3%. **Avg. rent:** $1,127.
Mayor: Antonio Villaraigosa, nonpartisan
History: Founded by Spanish 1781; captured by U.S. 1846; inc. 1850; grew rapidly after coming of railroads, 1876 and 1885. Hollywood is a district of Los Angeles.
Website: www.lacity.org

Louisville, Kentucky

Population: 605,110 (27). **Pop. density:** 1,860. **Pop. change (2010-12):** 1.1%. **Area:** 325.2 sq mi. **Racial distribution:** 71.8% white; 22.4% black; 2.1% Asian; 0.2% Amer. Ind.; <0.05% Pac. Isl.; 1.1% other; 2+ races 2.4%. **Hispanic pop.:** 4.3%. **Foreign born:** 6.1%. **U.S. citizens:** 95.9%. **Language:** 92.2% English only; 3.6% Spanish.
Employment: 334,034 employed; 8.6% unemployed. **Per capita income:** $39,037; change (2010-11): 4.4%. **Below poverty level:** 17.5%; 13.7% of families. **Educational attainment:** 86.2% HS; 26.0% bachelor's. **Avg. commute:** 22.0 min. 80.8% drive. **Housing units:** 271,780; 88.6% occupied. **Home ownership:** 63.0%. **Avg. home:** $137,100; change (2010-12): 1.9%. **Avg. rent:** $666.
Mayor: Greg Fischer, Democrat
History: Settled 1778; named for Louis XVI of France; inc. 1828. Base for Union forces in Civil War.
Website: www.louisvilleky.gov

Lubbock, Texas

Population: 236,065 (84). **Pop. density:** 1,928. **Pop. change (2010-12):** 2.3%. **Area:** 122.4 sq mi. **Racial distribution:** 77.8% white; 7.8% black; 2.4% Asian; 0.5% Amer. Ind.; 0.1% Pac. Isl.; 8.3% other; 2+ races 3.2%. **Hispanic pop.:** 32.1%. **Foreign born:** 5.9%. **U.S. citizens:** 96.3%. **Language:** 77.6% English only; 19.1% Spanish.
Employment: 112,848 employed; 5.4% unemployed. **Per capita income:** $34,573; change (2010-11): 1.9%. **Below poverty level:** 20.3%; 12.8% of families. **Educational attainment:** 84.4% HS; 29.4% bachelor's. **Avg. commute:** 15.4 min. 81.9% drive; 10.5% carpool. **Housing units:** 95,928; 90.3% occupied. **Home ownership:** 56.2%. **Avg. rent:** $760.
Mayor: Glen Robertson, nonpartisan
History: Settled 1879; laid out 1891; inc. 1909 through merger of two towns.
Website: www.ci.lubbock.tx.us

Madison, Wisconsin

Population: 240,323 (82). **Pop. density:** 3,130. **Pop. change (2010-12):** 2.8%. **Area:** 76.8 sq mi. **Racial distribution:** 80.8% white; 7.2% black; 7.4% Asian; 0.3% Amer. Ind.; <0.05% Pac. Isl.; 1.4% other; 2+ races 2.9%. **Hispanic pop.:** 6.5%. **Foreign born:** 10.7%. **U.S. citizens:** 93.0%. **Language:** 85.0% English only; 5.5% Spanish.
Employment: 138,673 employed; 4.7% unemployed. **Per capita income:** $45,964; change (2010-11): 4.7%. **Below poverty level:** 18.4%; 8.6% of families. **Educational attainment:** 94.5% HS; 52.9% bachelor's. **Avg. commute:** 19.0 min. 64.1% drive. **Housing units:** 107,598; 92.5% occupied. **Home ownership:** 51.4%. **Avg. home:** $210,600; change (2010-12): −3.3%. **Avg. rent:** $878.
Mayor: Paul R. Soglin, nonpartisan
History: Settled 1832; selected as site for state capital and named after James Madison, 1836; chartered 1856.
Website: www.cityofmadison.com

Memphis, Tennessee

Population: 655,155 (20). **Pop. density:** 2,079. **Pop. change (2010-12):** 1.2%. **Area:** 315.1 sq mi. **Racial distribution:** 31.0% white; 62.6% black; 1.7% Asian; 0.2% Amer. Ind.; <0.05% Pac. Isl.; 2.9% other; 2+ races 1.6%. **Hispanic pop.:** 6.2%. **Foreign born:** 6.2%. **U.S. citizens:** 95.3%. **Language:** 91.2% English only; 5.8% Spanish.
Employment: 260,186 employed; 10.2% unemployed. **Per capita income:** $38,622; change (2010-11): 3.6%. **Below poverty level:** 26.0%; 21.3% of families. **Educational attainment:** 81.9% HS; 23.1% bachelor's. **Avg. commute:** 21.4 min. 79.0% drive; 12.7% carpool. **Housing units:** 294,722; 82.9% occupied. **Home ownership:** 52.7%. **Avg. home:** $117,200; change (2010-12): −2.5%. **Avg. rent:** $786.
Mayor: A. C. Wharton, nonpartisan
History: French, Spanish, and U.S. forts by 1797; settled by 1819; inc. as town 1826, as city 1840; surrendered charter to state, 1879, after yellow fever epidemics; rechartered as city 1893.
Website: www.cityofmemphis.org

Mesa, Arizona

Population: 452,084 (38). **Pop. density:** 3,313. **Pop. change (2010-12):** 2.7%. **Area:** 136.5 sq mi. **Racial distribution:** 83.6% white; 3.1% black; 2.0% Asian; 2.3% Amer. Ind.; 0.3% Pac. Isl.; 6.2% other; 2+ races 2.6%. **Hispanic pop.:** 25.7%. **Foreign born:** 13.4%. **U.S. citizens:** 89.9%. **Language:** 78.2% English only; 18.1% Spanish.
Employment: 207,012 employed; 7.0% unemployed. **Per capita income:** $36,833; change (2010-11): 4.0%. **Below poverty level:** 13.5%; 9.8% of families. **Educational attainment:** 86.4% HS; 23.5% bachelor's. **Avg. commute:** 25.0 min. 75.3% drive; 14.3% carpool. **Housing units:** 196,457; 84.8% occupied. **Home ownership:** 64.0%. **Avg. home:** $147,600; change (2010-12): 6.0%. **Avg. rent:** $876.
Mayor: Scott Smith, nonpartisan
History: Founded by Mormons 1878; inc. 1883. Population boomed fivefold 1960-80.
Website: www.mesaaz.gov

Miami, Florida

Population: 413,892 (44). **Pop. density:** 11,538. **Pop. change (2010-12):** 3.3%. **Area:** 35.9 sq mi. **Racial distribution:** 73.7% white; 20.6% black; 0.8% Asian; 0.1% Amer. Ind.; <0.05% Pac. Isl.; 3.5% other; 2+ races 1.2%. **Hispanic pop.:** 70.6%. **Foreign born:** 58.4%. **U.S. citizens:** 65.8%. **Language:** 22.4% English only; 70.5% Spanish.
Employment: 164,940 employed; 10.3% unemployed. **Per capita income:** $43,072; change (2010-11): 2.9%. **Below poverty level:** 27.7%; 22.8% of families. **Educational attainment:** 68.4% HS; 22.4% bachelor's. **Avg. commute:** 26.6 min. 69.4% drive; 10.9% public trans.; 10.7% carpool. **Housing units:** 185,520; 80.7% occupied. **Home ownership:** 34.7%. **Avg. home:** $203,100; change (2010-12): 0.6%. **Avg. rent:** $910.
Mayor: Tomás Regalado, nonpartisan
History: Site of fort 1836; settlement began 1870; inc. 1896. Land speculation in 1920s added to city's growth, as did Cuban, Central and South American, and Haitian immigration since 1960.
Website: www.miamigov.com

Milwaukee, Wisconsin

Population: 598,916 (30). **Pop. density:** 6,231. **Pop. change (2010-12):** 0.6%. **Area:** 96.1 sq mi. **Racial distribution:** 47.4% white; 39.3% black; 3.5% Asian; 0.7% Amer. Ind.; 0.1% Pac. Isl.; 5.9% other; 2+ races 3.2%. **Hispanic pop.:** 16.8%. **Foreign born:** 9.9%. **U.S. citizens:** 93.1%. **Language:** 80.9% English only; 13.5% Spanish.
Employment: 243,685 employed; 10.1% unemployed. **Per capita income:** $44,610; change (2010-11): 3.8%. **Below poverty level:** 27.0%; 22.6% of families. **Educational attainment:** 80.5% HS; 21.3% bachelor's. **Avg. commute:** 21.7 min. 71.0% drive; 11.9% carpool. **Housing units:** 259,500; 88.7% occupied. **Home ownership:** 45.5%. **Avg. home:** $187,400; change (2010-12): −9.0%. **Avg. rent:** $754.
Mayor: Tom Barrett, Democrat
History: Indian trading post by 1674; settlement began 1835; inc. 1848. Famous beer industry.
Website: city.milwaukee.gov

Minneapolis, Minnesota

Population: 392,880 (47). **Pop. density:** 7,279. **Pop. change (2010-12):** 2.6%. **Area:** 54.0 sq mi. **Racial distribution:** 68.5% white; 17.7% black; 5.5% Asian; 1.9% Amer. Ind.; <0.05% Pac. Isl.; 2.8% other; 2+ races 3.7%. **Hispanic pop.:** 9.6%. **Foreign born:** 14.9%. **U.S. citizens:** 90.5%. **Language:** 80.2% English only; 8.1% Spanish.
Employment: 204,126 employed; 5.5% unemployed. **Per capita income:** $48,657; change (2010-11): 4.6%. **Below poverty level:** 22.3%; 15.8% of families. **Educational attainment:** 88.0% HS; 44.7% bachelor's. **Avg. commute:** 22.1 min. 61.4% drive; 14.0% public trans. **Housing units:** 184,414; 91.2% occupied. **Home ownership:** 50.4%. **Avg. home:** $171,600; change (2010-12): 0.7%. **Avg. rent:** $793.
Mayor: R. T. Rybak, Democrat
History: Site visited by French missionary Louis Hennepin 1680; included in area of military reservations 1819; inc. 1867.
Website: www.ci.minneapolis.mn.us

Nashville, Tennessee

Population: 624,496 (25). **Pop. density:** 1,314. **Pop. change (2010-12):** 3.3%. **Area:** 475.1 sq mi. **Racial distribution:** 62.5% white; 28.6% black; 3.1% Asian; 0.3% Amer. Ind.; <0.05% Pac. Isl.; 3.7% other; 2+ races 1.8%. **Hispanic pop.:** 9.6%. **Foreign born:** 11.9%. **U.S. citizens:** 91.6%. **Language:** 84.3% English only; 8.5% Spanish.
Employment: 312,761 employed; 6.6% unemployed. **Per capita income:** $42,129; change (2010-11): 3.9%. **Below poverty level:** 18.2%; 13.9% of families. **Educational attainment:** 85.1% HS; 33.7% bachelor's. **Avg. commute:** 23.3 min. 79.7% drive; 10.2% carpool. **Housing units:** 271,625; 89.9% occupied. **Home ownership:** 56.2%. **Avg. home:** $151,900; change (2010-12): −1.2%. **Avg. rent:** $795.
Mayor: Karl Dean, nonpartisan
History: Settled 1779; first chartered 1806; became permanent state capital 1843. Home of Grand Ole Opry.
Website: www.nashville.gov

New Orleans, Louisiana

Population: 369,250 (51). **Pop. density:** 2,179. **Pop. change (2010-12):** 6.2%. **Area:** 169.4 sq mi. **Racial distribution:** 33.5% white; 60.1% black; 3.0% Asian; 0.3% Amer. Ind.; 0.1% Pac. Isl.; 1.6% other; 2+ races 1.5%. **Hispanic pop.:** 5.2%. **Foreign born:** 5.8%. **U.S. citizens:** 96.7%. **Language:** 90.3% English only; 4.8% Spanish.
Employment: 139,212 employed; 7.8% unemployed. **Per capita income:** $43,603; change (2010-11): 2.5%. **Below poverty level:** 25.7%; 20.5% of families. **Educational attainment:** 83.9% HS; 32.3% bachelor's. **Avg. commute:** 22.9 min. 68.6% drive; 12.2% carpool. **Housing units:** 179,057; 75.0% occupied. **Home ownership:** 48.3%. **Avg. home:** $156,200; change (2010-12): −2.2%. **Avg. rent:** $924.
Mayor: Mitchell J. Landrieu, Democrat
History: Founded by French 1718; became major seaport on Mississippi R.; acquired by U.S. as part of Louisiana Purchase 1803; inc. 1805. Americans defeated British forces at Battle of New Orleans in 1815.
Website: www.nola.gov

New York, New York

Population: 8,336,697 (1). **Pop. density:** 27,546. **Pop. change (2010-12):** 1.8%. **Area:** 302.6 sq mi. **Racial distribution:** 44.3% white; 25.2% black; 12.7% Asian; 0.4% Amer. Ind.; <0.05% Pac. Isl.; 14.8% other; 2+ races 2.7%. **Hispanic**

pop.: 28.4%. **Foreign born:** 36.8%. **U.S. citizens:** 82.2%. **Language:** 51.5% English only; 24.6% Spanish; 5.5% Chinese.
Employment: 3,632,508 employed; 9.2% unemployed. **Per capita income:** $56,770; change (2010-11): 4.0%. **Below poverty level:** 19.4%; 16.4% of families. **Educational attainment:** 79.3% HS; 33.7% bachelor's. **Avg. commute:** 39.2 min. 55.4% public trans.; 22.8% drive; 10.3% walk. **Housing units:** 3,356,992; 90.9% occupied. **Home ownership:** 32.6%. **Avg. home:** $379,300; change (2010-12): -3.7%. **Avg. rent:** $1,125.
Mayor: Michael R. Bloomberg, Republican
History: Trading post est. 1624; British took control from Dutch, 1664, and named city New York. Briefly U.S. capital; under new charter, 1898, city expanded to include five boroughs: Bronx, Brooklyn, Queens, and Staten Island, as well as Manhattan. Sept. 11, 2001, terrorist attacks destroyed World Trade Center, killed more than 2,750.
Website: www.nyc.gov

Newark, New Jersey

Population: 277,727 (68). **Pop. density:** 11,482. **Pop. change (2010-12):** 0.1%. **Area:** 24.2 sq mi. **Racial distribution:** 27.1% white; 52.5% black; 1.6% Asian; 0.4% Amer. Ind.; <0.05% Pac. Isl.; 12.5% other; 2+ races 5.8%. **Hispanic pop.:** 32.6%. **Foreign born:** 26.6%. **U.S. citizens:** 82.5%. **Language:** 55.3% English only; 29.9% Spanish; 8.5% Portuguese.
Employment: 91,911 employed; 15.0% unemployed. **Per capita income:** $56,770; change (2010-11): 4.0%. **Below poverty level:** 26.1%; 23.5% of families. **Educational attainment:** 69.0% HS; 12.5% bachelor's. **Avg. commute:** 30.9 min. 49.1% drive; 25.3% public trans.; 13.6% carpool. **Housing units:** 109,504; 83.8% occupied. **Home ownership:** 24.9%. **Avg. home:** $379,300; change (2010-12): -3.7%. **Avg. rent:** $941.
Mayor: Cory A. Booker, nonpartisan
History: Settled by Puritans 1666; used as supply base by Washington 1776; inc. as town 1833, as city 1836.
Website: www.ci.newark.nj.us

Norfolk, Virginia

Population: 245,782 (79). **Pop. density:** 4,541. **Pop. change (2010-12):** 1.2%. **Area:** 54.1 sq mi. **Racial distribution:** 48.2% white; 43.4% black; 3.5% Asian; 0.4% Amer. Ind.; 0.2% Pac. Isl.; 1.6% other; 2+ races 2.8%. **Hispanic pop.:** 6.5%. **Foreign born:** 6.8%. **U.S. citizens:** 96.3%. **Language:** 90.5% English only; 4.6% Spanish.
Employment: 95,622 employed; 7.9% unemployed. **Per capita income:** $41,976; change (2010-11): 4.6%. **Below poverty level:** 17.1%; 13.6% of families. **Educational attainment:** 84.8% HS; 24.7% bachelor's. **Avg. commute:** 21.4 min. 69.2% drive; 10.9% carpool. **Housing units:** 95,001; 89.6% occupied. **Home ownership:** 46.4%. **Avg. home:** $187,500; change (2010-12): -8.5%. **Avg. rent:** $888.
Mayor: Paul D. Fraim, nonpartisan
History: Founded 1682; burned by colonists to prevent capture by British during Revolutionary War; rebuilt and inc. as town 1805, as city 1845. Site of world's largest naval base; major East Coast commercial port and cruise terminal.
Website: www.norfolk.gov

North Las Vegas, Nevada

Population: 223,491 (95). **Pop. density:** 2,205. **Pop. change (2010-12):** 2.9%. **Area:** 101.3 sq mi. **Racial distribution:** 57.9% white; 19.9% black; 6.3% Asian; 0.4% Amer. Ind.; 0.8% Pac. Isl.; 10.1% other; 2+ races 4.6%. **Hispanic pop.:** 39.0%. **Foreign born:** 23.0%. **U.S. citizens:** 84.7%. **Language:** 61.0% English only; 32.6% Spanish.
Employment: 83,861 employed; 13.3% unemployed. **Per capita income:** $35,680; change (2010-11): 2.9%. **Below poverty level:** 13.7%; 10.5% of families. **Educational attainment:** 76.4% HS; 14.8% bachelor's. **Avg. commute:** 27.6 min. 81.6% drive; 11.5% carpool. **Housing units:** 73,670; 86.8% occupied. **Home ownership:** 60.6%. **Avg. home:** $134,100; change (2010-12): -2.8%. **Avg. rent:** $1,140.
Mayor: John J. Lee, nonpartisan
History: Inc. 1946.
Website: www.cityofnorthlasvegas.com

Oakland, California

Population: 400,740 (45). **Pop. density:** 7,184. **Pop. change (2010-12):** 2.4%. **Area:** 55.8 sq mi. **Racial distribution:** 39.0% white; 28.1% black; 16.1% Asian; 0.6% Amer. Ind.; 0.5% Pac. Isl.; 11.0% other; 2+ races 4.7%. **Hispanic pop.:** 25.0%. **Foreign born:** 27.5%. **U.S. citizens:** 83.7%. **Language:** 60.4% English only; 21.6% Spanish; 7.5% Chinese.
Employment: 177,834 employed; 13.7% unemployed. **Per capita income:** $61,395; change (2010-11): 4.8%. **Below poverty level:** 19.6%; 16.0% of families. **Educational attainment:** 79.5% HS; 37.2% bachelor's. **Avg. commute:** 27.8 min. 56.6% drive; 17.1% public trans.; 10.5% carpool. **Housing units:** 173,204; 89.2% occupied. **Home ownership:** 41.9%. **Avg. home:** $543,780; change (2010-12): 3.5%. **Avg. rent:** $1,042.
Mayor: Jean Quan, nonpartisan

History: Area settled by Spanish 1820; inc. 1854.
Website: www.oaklandnet.com

Oklahoma City, Oklahoma

Population: 599,199 (29). **Pop. density:** 988. **Pop. change (2010-12):** 2.9%. **Area:** 606.4 sq mi. **Racial distribution:** 66.2% white; 14.5% black; 3.9% Asian; 3.3% Amer. Ind.; 0.1% Pac. Isl.; 5.3% other; 2+ races 6.7%. **Hispanic pop.:** 16.8%. **Foreign born:** 11.9%. **U.S. citizens:** 91.7%. **Language:** 81.5% English only; 13.3% Spanish.
Employment: 258,615 employed; 4.8% unemployed. **Per capita income:** $40,002; change (2010-11): 5.9%. **Below poverty level:** 17.1%; 13.3% of families. **Educational attainment:** 84.8% HS; 27.9% bachelor's. **Avg. commute:** 20.1 min. 81.9% drive; 11.6% carpool. **Housing units:** 255,629; 88.0% occupied. **Home ownership:** 60.6%. **Avg. home:** $145,000; change (2010-12): -0.5%. **Avg. rent:** $699.
Mayor: Mick Cornett, nonpartisan
History: Settled during land rush in Midwest 1889; inc. 1890; became state capital 1910. Oil discovered 1928. Bomb in 1995 terrorist attack destroyed federal office bldg., killed 168 people.
Website: www.okc.gov

Omaha, Nebraska

Population: 421,570 (43). **Pop. density:** 3,317. **Pop. change (2010-12):** 2.5%. **Area:** 127.1 sq mi. **Racial distribution:** 75.7% white; 12.9% black; 2.1% Asian; 0.7% Amer. Ind.; 0.1% Pac. Isl.; 5.0% other; 2+ races 3.4%. **Hispanic pop.:** 12.6%. **Foreign born:** 9.2%. **U.S. citizens:** 93.6%. **Language:** 86.1% English only; 9.7% Spanish.
Employment: 209,029 employed; 4.6% unemployed. **Per capita income:** $44,470; change (2010-11): 4.4%. **Below poverty level:** 15.5%; 11.4% of families. **Educational attainment:** 88.1% HS; 32.1% bachelor's. **Avg. commute:** 17.8 min. 80.3% drive; 11.1% carpool. **Housing units:** 178,311; 91.2% occupied. **Home ownership:** 59.8%. **Avg. home:** $139,200; change (2010-12): 1.4%. **Avg. rent:** $735.
Mayor: Jean Stothert, nonpartisan
History: Founded 1854; inc. 1857. Large food-processing, telecommunications, information-processing center.
Website: www.cityofomaha.org

Orlando, Florida

Population: 249,562 (77). **Pop. density:** 2,437. **Pop. change (2010-12):** 4.5%. **Area:** 102.4 sq mi. **Racial distribution:** 58.4% white; 27.8% black; 3.2% Asian; 0.4% Amer. Ind.; <0.05% Pac. Isl.; 7.9% other; 2+ races 2.3%. **Hispanic pop.:** 24.6%. **Foreign born:** 18.8%. **U.S. citizens:** 88.4%. **Language:** 67.7% English only; 21.4% Spanish.
Employment: 126,360 employed; 8.3% unemployed. **Per capita income:** $35,535; change (2010-11): 3.3%. **Below poverty level:** 17.3%; 14.0% of families. **Educational attainment:** 86.7% HS; 31.9% bachelor's. **Avg. commute:** 24.7 min. 78.7% drive. **Housing units:** 119,343; 82.2% occupied. **Home ownership:** 40.6%. **Avg. home:** $134,000; change (2010-12): -0.5%. **Avg. rent:** $975.
Mayor: Buddy Dyer, nonpartisan
History: Ft. Gatlin built just south of present-day Orlando in 1838; name changed from Jernigan 1856; inc. 1875. Walt Disney World opened in 1971.
Website: www.cityoforlando.net

Philadelphia, Pennsylvania

Population: 1,547,607 (5). **Pop. density:** 11,541. **Pop. change (2010-12):** 1.3%. **Area:** 134.1 sq mi. **Racial distribution:** 41.5% white; 43.6% black; 6.3% Asian; 0.3% Amer. Ind.; <0.05% Pac. Isl.; 6.1% other; 2+ races 2.2%. **Hispanic pop.:** 12.0%. **Foreign born:** 11.6%. **U.S. citizens:** 93.9%. **Language:** 79.0% English only; 9.7% Spanish.
Employment: 585,378 employed; 10.8% unemployed. **Per capita income:** $48,723; change (2010-11): 4.0%. **Below poverty level:** 25.6%; 20.5% of families. **Educational attainment:** 80.0% HS; 22.6% bachelor's. **Avg. commute:** 31.5 min. 50.8% drive; 25.9% public trans. **Housing units:** 669,672; 86.3% occupied. **Home ownership:** 54.9%. **Avg. home:** $213,400; change (2010-12): -0.7%. **Avg. rent:** $850.
Mayor: Michael A. Nutter, Democrat
History: First settled by Swedes 1638; Swedes surrendered to Dutch 1654; settled by English and Scottish Quakers 1678; named Philadelphia 1682; chartered 1701. Continental Congresses convened 1774, 1775; Declaration of Independence signed here 1776; national capital 1790-1800; state capital 1683-1799.
Website: www.phila.gov

Phoenix, Arizona

Population: 1,488,750 (6). **Pop. density:** 2,881. **Pop. change (2010-12):** 2.7%. **Area:** 516.7 sq mi. **Racial distribution:** 77.7% white; 6.3% black; 3.1% Asian; 1.9% Amer. Ind.; 0.2% Pac. Isl.; 8.5% other; 2+ races 2.3%. **Hispanic pop.:** 40.1%. **Foreign born:** 21.5%. **U.S. citizens:** 83.9%. **Language:** 63.2% English only; 30.7% Spanish.

Employment: 672,547 employed; 7.6% unemployed. **Per capita income:** $36,833; change (2010-11): 4.0%. **Below poverty level:** 20.3%; 15.9% of families. **Educational attainment:** 79.7% HS; 25.4% bachelor's. **Avg. commute:** 24.7 min. 74.2% drive; 13.3% carpool. **Housing units:** 598,165; 86.3% occupied. **Home ownership:** 58.5%. **Avg. home:** $147,600; change (2010-12): 6.0%. **Avg. rent:** $860.

Mayor: Greg Stanton, nonpartisan

History: Founded 1867; inc. 1881; became territorial capital 1889.

Website: www.phoenix.gov

Pittsburgh, Pennsylvania

Population: 306,211 (61). **Pop. density:** 5,531. **Pop. change (2010-12):** 0.2%. **Area:** 55.4 sq mi. **Racial distribution:** 66.2% white; 25.8% black; 4.4% Asian; 0.1% Amer. Ind.; <0.05% Pac. Isl.; 0.7% other; 2+ races 2.8%. **Hispanic pop.:** 2.4%. **Foreign born:** 7.1%. **U.S. citizens:** 95.6%. **Language:** 90.0% English only; 2.1% Spanish.

Employment: 144,230 employed; 7.6% unemployed. **Per capita income:** $44,982; change (2010-11): 5.5%. **Below poverty level:** 22.2%; 15.4% of families. **Educational attainment:** 88.8% HS; 34.4% bachelor's. **Avg. commute:** 23.2 min. 53.5% drive; 19.0% public trans.; 11.3% walk; 10.2% carpool. **Housing units:** 159,463; 84.0% occupied. **Home ownership:** 50.6%. **Avg. rent:** $724.

Mayor: Luke Ravenstahl, Democrat

History: Settled around Ft. Pitt 1758; inc. 1816. Became an inland port; by Civil War, already a center for iron production.

Website: www.pghgov.com

Plano, Texas

Population: 272,068 (70). **Pop. density:** 3,801. **Pop. change (2010-12):** 4.2%. **Area:** 71.6 sq mi. **Racial distribution:** 71.5% white; 6.8% black; 16.7% Asian; 0.5% Amer. Ind.; 0.1% Pac. Isl.; 2.2% other; 2+ races 2.3%. **Hispanic pop.:** 14.6%. **Foreign born:** 22.8%. **U.S. citizens:** 87.1%. **Language:** 68.8% English only; 11.8% Spanish.

Employment: 141,548 employed; 6.0% unemployed. **Per capita income:** $43,708; change (2010-11): 4.2%. **Below poverty level:** 7.1%; 5.1% of families. **Educational attainment:** 93.2% HS; 54.0% bachelor's. **Avg. commute:** 25.9 min. 81.8% drive. **Housing units:** 103,353; 94.3% occupied. **Home ownership:** 65.5%. **Avg. home:** $159,300; change (2010-12): 10.8%. **Avg. rent:** $1,012.

Mayor: Harry LaRosiliere, nonpartisan

History: Settled 1846; inc. 1873.

Website: www.plano.gov

Portland, Oregon

Population: 603,106 (28). **Pop. density:** 4,520. **Pop. change (2010-12):** 3.0%. **Area:** 133.4 sq mi. **Racial distribution:** 77.4% white; 6.3% black; 7.2% Asian; 1.0% Amer. Ind.; 0.5% Pac. Isl.; 3.2% other; 2+ races 4.3%. **Hispanic pop.:** 9.2%. **Foreign born:** 13.7%. **U.S. citizens:** 91.8%. **Language:** 81.0% English only; 7.3% Spanish.

Employment: 298,956 employed; 7.6% unemployed. **Per capita income:** $41,302; change (2010-11): 4.9%. **Below poverty level:** 16.8%; 11.7% of families. **Educational attainment:** 89.9% HS; 42.0% bachelor's. **Avg. commute:** 24.3 min. 60.1% drive; 12.1% public trans. **Housing units:** 264,956; 93.5% occupied. **Home ownership:** 54.2%. **Avg. home:** $232,900; change (2010-12): -1.9%. **Avg. rent:** $855.

Mayor: Sam Adams, nonpartisan

History: Settled by pioneers 1845; developed as trading center, aided by California Gold Rush of 1849; chartered 1851.

Website: www.portlandonline.com

Raleigh, North Carolina

Population: 423,179 (42). **Pop. density:** 2,961. **Pop. change (2010-12):** 4.2%. **Area:** 142.9 sq mi. **Racial distribution:** 59.8% white; 29.7% black; 4.4% Asian; 0.3% Amer. Ind.; <0.05% Pac. Isl.; 4.4% other; 2+ races 1.5%. **Hispanic pop.:** 10.8%. **Foreign born:** 14.2%. **U.S. citizens:** 89.9%. **Language:** 82.2% English only; 9.8% Spanish.

Employment: 206,747 employed; 6.9% unemployed. **Per capita income:** $40,631; change (2010-11): 3.7%. **Below poverty level:** 15.1%; 10.7% of families. **Educational attainment:** 90.7% HS; 47.3% bachelor's. **Avg. commute:** 21.4 min. 79.1% drive; 10.0% carpool. **Housing units:** 175,325; 90.3% occupied. **Home ownership:** 54.8%. **Avg. home:** $188,500; change (2010-12): -1.0%. **Avg. rent:** $855.

Mayor: Nancy McFarlane, nonpartisan

History: Named after Sir Walter Raleigh; site chosen for state capital 1788; laid out 1792; inc. 1795. Occupied by Union Gen. William Sherman 1865.

Website: www.raleighnc.gov

Reno, Nevada

Population: 231,027 (89). **Pop. density:** 2,243. **Pop. change (2010-12):** 2.0%. **Area:** 103.0 sq mi. **Racial distribution:** 79.1% white; 3.3% black; 6.2% Asian; 0.9% Amer. Ind.; 0.7% Pac. Isl.; 6.5% other; 2+ races 3.3%. **Hispanic pop.:** 23.6%. **Foreign born:** 17.1%. **U.S. citizens:** 89.6%. **Language:** 75.2% English only; 17.4% Spanish.

Employment: 104,798 employed; 11.0% unemployed. **Per capita income:** $41,718; change (2010-11): 3.6%. **Below poverty level:** 16.1%; 11.6% of families. **Educational attainment:** 85.3% HS; 28.4% bachelor's. **Avg. commute:** 18.8 min. 76.4% drive; 10.5% carpool. **Housing units:** 100,284; 88.5% occupied. **Home ownership:** 48.5%. **Avg. home:** $169,700; change (2010-12): -5.5%. **Avg. rent:** $879.

Mayor: Robert Cashell, nonpartisan

History: Founded 1857; originally named Lakes Crossing; name changed to Reno, after a Union Civil War general, 1868, with arrival of transcontinental railroad.

Website: www.reno.gov

Riverside, California

Population: 313,673 (59). **Pop. density:** 3,866. **Pop. change (2010-12):** 2.6%. **Area:** 81.1 sq mi. **Racial distribution:** 65.1% white; 6.6% black; 6.9% Asian; 0.9% Amer. Ind.; 0.4% Pac. Isl.; 15.6% other; 2+ races 4.6%. **Hispanic pop.:** 49.4%. **Foreign born:** 24.0%. **U.S. citizens:** 85.0%. **Language:** 56.6% English only; 35.6% Spanish.

Employment: 145,595 employed; 12.3% unemployed. **Per capita income:** $29,961; change (2010-11): 2.9%. **Below poverty level:** 15.8%; 10.9% of families. **Educational attainment:** 77.5% HS; 21.9% bachelor's. **Avg. commute:** 28.6 min. 76.4% drive; 12.4% carpool. **Housing units:** 99,331; 90.9% occupied. **Home ownership:** 58.9%. **Avg. home:** $189,300; change (2010-12): 5.6%. **Avg. rent:** $1,115.

Mayor: Rusty Bailey, nonpartisan

History: Founded 1870; inc. 1886. Known for its citrus industry; home of the parent navel orange tree, historic Mission Inn resort.

Website: www.riversideca.gov

Sacramento, California

Population: 475,516 (35). **Pop. density:** 4,856. **Pop. change (2010-12):** 1.7%. **Area:** 97.9 sq mi. **Racial distribution:** 49.3% white; 13.9% black; 19.1% Asian; 1.1% Amer. Ind.; 1.4% Pac. Isl.; 8.9% other; 2+ races 6.3%. **Hispanic pop.:** 26.0%. **Foreign born:** 22.3%. **U.S. citizens:** 88.6%. **Language:** 63.0% English only; 17.3% Spanish.

Employment: 189,052 employed; 12.4% unemployed. **Per capita income:** $40,745; change (2010-11): 3.2%. **Below poverty level:** 18.6%; 14.1% of families. **Educational attainment:** 81.5% HS; 29.2% bachelor's. **Avg. commute:** 23.6 min. 72.5% drive; 13.6% carpool. **Housing units:** 192,452; 91.1% occupied. **Home ownership:** 50.0%. **Avg. home:** $176,800; change (2010-12): -4.0%. **Avg. rent:** $978.

Mayor: Kevin Johnson, nonpartisan

History: Settled 1839; important trading center during California Gold Rush in 1840s; became state capital 1854.

Website: www.cityofsacramento.org

St. Louis, Missouri

Population: 318,172 (58). **Pop. density:** 5,139. **Pop. change (2010-12):** -0.3%. **Area:** 61.9 sq mi. **Racial distribution:** 44.4% white; 49.2% black; 2.6% Asian; 0.2% Amer. Ind.; <0.05% Pac. Isl.; 0.8% other; 2+ races 2.7%. **Hispanic pop.:** 3.4%. **Foreign born:** 6.9%. **U.S. citizens:** 95.3%. **Language:** 90.7% English only; 2.9% Spanish.

Employment: 126,908 employed; 9.3% unemployed. **Per capita income:** $42,864; change (2010-11): 4.6%. **Below poverty level:** 26.0%; 21.0% of families. **Educational attainment:** 81.9% HS; 27.7% bachelor's. **Avg. commute:** 24.3 min. 70.2% drive; 10.8% carpool; 10.0% public trans. **Housing units:** 176,113; 79.3% occupied. **Home ownership:** 46.4%. **Avg. home:** $123,900; change (2010-12): -5.5%. **Avg. rent:** $690.

Mayor: Francis Slay, Democrat

History: Founded 1764 as fur trading post by French; acquired by U.S. 1803; chartered as city 1822; became independent city 1876. Lies on Mississippi R., near confluence with Missouri R.

Website: www.stlouis-mo.gov

St. Paul, Minnesota

Population: 290,770 (66). **Pop. density:** 5,594. **Pop. change (2010-12):** 1.8%. **Area:** 52.0 sq mi. **Racial distribution:** 62.6% white; 15.0% black; 14.7% Asian; 1.1% Amer. Ind.; 0.1% Pac. Isl.; 2.4% other; 2+ races 4.1%. **Hispanic pop.:** 9.8%. **Foreign born:** 17.5%. **U.S. citizens:** 89.9%. **Language:** 74.0% English only; 7.4% Spanish; 8.8% Hmong.

Employment: 138,048 employed; 6.2% unemployed. **Per capita income:** $48,657; change (2010-11): 4.6%. **Below poverty level:** 22.5%; 17.0% of families. **Educational attainment:** 86.2% HS; 37.2% bachelor's. **Avg. commute:** 22.0 min. 68.3% drive; 11.5% carpool. **Housing units:** 120,965; 92.5% occupied. **Home ownership:** 52.2%. **Avg. home:** $171,800; change (2010-12): 0.7%. **Avg. rent:** $778.

Mayor: Chris Coleman, nonpartisan
History: Founded in early 1840s as Pig's Eye Landing; became capital of Minnesota territory 1849; chartered as St. Paul 1854.
Website: www.stpaul.gov

St. Petersburg, Florida

Population: 246,541 (78). **Pop. density:** 3,993. **Pop. change (2010-12):** 0.7%. **Area:** 61.7 sq mi. **Racial distribution:** 69.2% white; 24.1% black; 3.3% Asian; 0.2% Amer. Ind.; 0.1% Pac. Isl.; 1.2% other; 2+ races 2.1%. **Hispanic pop.:** 6.3%. **Foreign born:** 10.2%. **U.S. citizens:** 95.2%. **Language:** 88.3% English only; 4.4% Spanish.
Employment: 110,984 employed; 8.5% unemployed. **Per capita income:** $39,261; change (2010-11): 3.2%. **Below poverty level:** 15.3%; 10.4% of families. **Educational attainment:** 87.5% HS; 27.8% bachelor's. **Avg. commute:** 22.0 min. 80.1% drive. **Housing units:** 128,208; 81.5% occupied. **Home ownership:** 63.2%. **Avg. home:** $133,900; change (2010-12): –0.2%. **Avg. rent:** $898.
Mayor: Bill Foster, nonpartisan
History: Founded 1888; inc. 1903. Site of Salvador Dali Museum.
Website: www.stpete.org

San Antonio, Texas

Population: 1,382,951 (7). **Pop. density:** 3,000. **Pop. change (2010-12):** 3.7%. **Area:** 460.9 sq mi. **Racial distribution:** 73.1% white; 6.8% black; 2.2% Asian; 0.7% Amer. Ind.; 0.1% Pac. Isl.; 14.5% other; 2+ races 2.7%. **Hispanic pop.:** 62.7%. **Foreign born** 13.7%. **U.S. citizens:** 91.3%. **Language:** 53.9% English only; 42.7% Spanish.
Employment: 588,290 employed; 6.5% unemployed. **Per capita income:** $36,781; change (2010-11): 4.5%. **Below poverty level:** 19.2%; 15.1% of families. **Educational attainment:** 79.8% HS; 23.9% bachelor's. **Avg. commute:** 23.5 min. 78.8% drive; 11.4% carpool. **Housing units:** 521,055; 89.9% occupied. **Home ownership:** 57.5%. **Avg. home:** $159,500; change (2010-12): 5.6%. **Avg. rent:** $775.
Mayor: Julián Castro, nonpartisan
History: First Spanish garrison 1718; Battle of the Alamo 1836; city subsequently captured by Texans; inc. 1837; first town meeting in Texas took place here in 1845.
Website: www.sanantonio.gov

San Bernardino, California

Population: 213,295 (98). **Pop. density:** 3,603. **Pop. change (2010-12):** 1.4%. **Area:** 59.2 sq mi. **Racial distribution:** 44.8% white; 14.9% black; 4.4% Asian; 0.9% Amer. Ind.; 0.2% Pac. Isl.; 30.8% other; 2+ races 4.1%. **Hispanic pop.:** 58.8%. **Foreign born:** 23.8%. **U.S. citizens:** 84.0%. **Language:** 52.9% English only; 41.8% Spanish.
Employment: 71,148 employed; 16.0% unemployed. **Per capita income:** $29,961; change (2010-11): 2.9%. **Below poverty level:** 28.6%; 23.4% of families. **Educational attainment:** 68.0% HS; 12.7% bachelor's. **Avg. commute:** 26.9 min. 74.5% drive; 15.9% carpool. **Housing units:** 66,575; 91.0% occupied. **Home ownership:** 51.7%. **Avg. home:** $189,300; change (2010-12): 5.6%. **Avg. rent:** $924.
Mayor: Patrick J. Morris, nonpartisan
History: Named by Spanish Franciscan missionaries 1810; major Mormon settlement in the 1850s, though Mormons were later recalled to Utah; inc. 1854. Population grew in 1860s when gold was discovered nearby; later became transportation hub.
Website: www.ci.san-bernardino.ca.us

San Diego, California

Population: 1,338,348 (8). **Pop. density:** 4,116. **Pop. change (2010-12):** 2.5%. **Area:** 325.2 sq mi. **Racial distribution:** 65.8% white; 6.8% black; 15.8% Asian; 0.5% Amer. Ind.; 0.5% Pac. Isl.; 6.1% other; 2+ races 4.4%. **Hispanic pop.:** 28.2%. **Foreign born** 25.8%. **U.S. citizens:** 86.9%. **Language:** 61.3% English only; 22.1% Spanish.
Employment: 650,129 employed; 8.9% unemployed. **Per capita income:** $46,800; change (2010-11): 4.1%. **Below poverty level:** 14.6%; 9.9% of families. **Educational attainment:** 86.4% HS; 41.0% bachelor's. **Avg. commute:** 22.4 min. 75.3% drive. **Housing units:** 515,019; 92.1% occupied. **Home ownership:** 49.2%. **Avg. home:** $385,520; change (2010-12): <0.05%. **Avg. rent:** $1,294.
Mayor: Bob Filner, nonpartisan
History: Claimed by Spanish 1542; first mission est. 1769; scene of conflict during Mexican-American War 1846; inc. 1850.
Website: www.sandiego.gov

San Francisco, California

Population: 825,863 (14). **Pop. density:** 17,619. **Pop. change (2010-12):** 2.5%. **Area:** 46.9 sq mi. **Racial distribution:** 51.2% white; 6.2% black; 33.5% Asian; 0.5% Amer. Ind.; 0.4% Pac. Isl.; 4.4% other; 2+ races 3.8%. **Hispanic pop.:** 14.9%.

Foreign born: 35.6%. **U.S. citizens:** 86.5%. **Language:** 54.7% English only; 11.6% Spanish; 18.8% Chinese.
Employment: 442,773 employed; 7.3% unemployed. **Per capita income:** $61,395; change (2010-11): 4.8%. **Below poverty level:** 12.3%; 7.6% of families. **Educational attainment:** 85.7% HS; 51.4% bachelor's. **Avg. commute:** 29.5 min. 37.7% drive; 32.7% public trans. **Housing units:** 374,919; 90.3% occupied. **Home ownership:** 37.1%. **Avg. home:** $543,780; change (2010-12): 3.5%. **Avg. rent:** $1,388.
Mayor: Edwin M. Lee, nonpartisan
History: Nearby Farallon Islands sighted by Spanish 1542; city settled by 1776; claimed by U.S. 1846. Became major city during California Gold Rush of 1849; inc. 1850. Devastated by earthquake 1906.
Website: www.sfgov.org

San Jose, California

Population: 982,765 (10). **Pop. density:** 5,567. **Pop. change (2010-12):** 2.9%. **Area:** 176.5 sq mi. **Racial distribution:** 47.6% white; 3.0% black; 32.1% Asian; 0.7% Amer. Ind.; 0.3% Pac. Isl.; 12.0% other; 2+ races 4.2%. **Hispanic pop.:** 33.0%. **Foreign born:** 38.6%. **U.S. citizens:** 81.7%. **Language:** 44.8% English only; 23.7% Spanish; 9.8% Vietnamese; 6.2% Chinese.
Employment: 433,067 employed; 9.4% unemployed. **Per capita income:** $61,028; change (2010-11): 7.6%. **Below poverty level:** 11.1%; 7.9% of families. **Educational attainment:** 82.3% HS; 36.6% bachelor's. **Avg. commute:** 25.3 min. 78.0% drive; 10.6% carpool. **Housing units:** 315,255; 95.5% occupied. **Home ownership:** 59.5%. **Avg. home:** $645,000; change (2010-12): 8.4%. **Avg. rent:** $1,390.
Mayor: Chuck Reed, nonpartisan
History: Founded by Spanish, 1777, between San Francisco and Monterey; state capital 1849-51; inc. 1850.
Website: www.sanjoseca.gov

Santa Ana, California

Population: 330,920 (57). **Pop. density:** 12,135. **Pop. change (2010-12):** 1.8%. **Area:** 27.3 sq mi. **Racial distribution:** 42.1% white; 1.2% black; 10.1% Asian; 0.5% Amer. Ind.; 0.2% Pac. Isl.; 44.4% other; 2+ races 1.6%. **Hispanic pop.:** 78.7%. **Foreign born:** 49.2%. **U.S. citizens:** 65.7%. **Language:** 17.1% English only; 72.7% Spanish; 7.1% Vietnamese.
Employment: 142,854 employed; 12.0% unemployed. **Per capita income:** $44,423; change (2010-11): 3.7%. **Below poverty level:** 19.5%; 16.6% of families. **Educational attainment:** 51.9% HS; 11.7% bachelor's. **Avg. commute:** 24.7 min. 69.1% drive; 18.4% carpool. **Housing units:** 77,262; 95.3% occupied. **Home ownership:** 48.8%. **Avg. home:** $327,470; change (2010-12): 1.3%. **Avg. rent:** $1,269.
Mayor: Miguel Pulido, nonpartisan
History: Founded 1769; inc. 1869.
Website: www.ci.santa-ana.ca.us

Scottsdale, Arizona

Population: 223,514 (94). **Pop. density:** 1,215. **Pop. change (2010-12):** 2.7%. **Area:** 183.9 sq mi. **Racial distribution:** 90.9% white; 1.6% black; 3.3% Asian; 0.9% Amer. Ind.; <0.05% Pac. Isl.; 1.7% other; 2+ races 1.5%. **Hispanic pop.:** 9.0%. **Foreign born** 10.7%. **U.S. citizens:** 94.4%. **Language:** 85.9% English only; 6.7% Spanish.
Employment: 112,679 employed; 5.7% unemployed. **Per capita income:** $36,833; change (2010-11): 4.0%. **Below poverty level:** 7.4%; 4.6% of families. **Educational attainment:** 95.8% HS; 52.2% bachelor's. **Avg. commute:** 22.5 min. 77.1% drive. **Housing units:** 125,662; 80.3% occupied. **Home ownership:** 70.6%. **Avg. home:** $147,600; change (2010-12): 6.0%. **Avg. rent:** $1,122.
Mayor: W. J. Lane, nonpartisan
History: Founded 1888 by Army Chaplain Winfield Scott; inc. 1951; slogan "West's Most Western Town" adopted same year.
Website: www.scottsdaleaz.gov

Seattle, Washington

Population: 634,535 (22). **Pop. density:** 7,559. **Pop. change (2010-12):** 4.0%. **Area:** 83.9 sq mi. **Racial distribution:** 70.6% white; 7.7% black; 14.2% Asian; 0.8% Amer. Ind.; 0.4% Pac. Isl.; 1.7% other; 2+ races 4.6%. **Hispanic pop.:** 6.3%. **Foreign born:** 17.5%. **U.S. citizens:** 91.7%. **Language:** 78.2% English only; 4.7% Spanish.
Employment: 350,188 employed; 6.4% unemployed. **Per capita income:** $50,944; change (2010-11): 4.6%. **Below poverty level:** 13.2%; 6.8% of families. **Educational attainment:** 92.4% HS; 55.8% bachelor's. **Avg. commute:** 25.0 min. 52.9% drive; 18.5% public trans. **Housing units:** 304,164; 92.9% occupied. **Home ownership:** 48.0%. **Avg. home:** $300,400; change (2010-12): 1.6%. **Avg. rent:** $1,003.
Mayor: Mike McGinn, nonpartisan
History: Settled 1851; inc. 1869. Suffered severe fire 1889; played prominent role during Klondike Gold Rush beginning in 1897; growth followed opening of Panama Canal 1914. Center of aircraft industry during WWII.
Website: www.seattle.gov

Stockton, California

Population: 297,984 (64). **Pop. density:** 4,832. **Pop. change (2010-12):** 1.8%. **Area:** 61.7 sq mi. **Racial distribution:** 45.6% white; 12.0% black; 21.8% Asian; 1.1% Amer. Ind.; 0.5% Pac. Isl.; 12.7% other; 2+ races 6.3%. **Hispanic pop.:** 40.0%. **Foreign born:** 26.5%. **U.S. citizens:** 85.1%. **Language:** 54.7% English only; 26.4% Spanish.
Employment: 102,915 employed; 18.3% unemployed. **Per capita income:** $31,013; change (2010-11): 2.5%. **Below poverty level:** 22.1%; 18.0% of families. **Educational attainment:** 73.3% HS; 17.1% bachelor's. **Avg. commute:** 27.0 min. 73.5% drive; 17.7% carpool. **Housing units:** 99,701; 90.1% occupied. **Home ownership:** 53.3%. **Avg. rent:** $936.
Mayor: Anthony Silva, nonpartisan
History: Site purchased 1842; settled 1849; inc. 1850. Chief distribution point for agric. products of San Joaquin Valley.
Website: www.stocktongov.com

Tampa, Florida

Population: 347,645 (53). **Pop. density:** 3,065. **Pop. change (2010-12):** 3.2%. **Area:** 113.4 sq mi. **Racial distribution:** 64.3% white; 26.5% black; 3.3% Asian; 0.8% Amer. Ind.; 0.1% Pac. Isl.; 2.3% other; 2+ races 2.7%. **Hispanic pop.:** 22.8%. **Foreign born:** 14.9%. **U.S. citizens:** 91.6%. **Language:** 75.3% English only; 18.4% Spanish.
Employment: 148,012 employed; 9.2% unemployed. **Per capita income:** $39,261; change (2010-11): 3.2%. **Below poverty level:** 19.2%; 15.4% of families. **Educational attainment:** 84.6% HS; 32.2% bachelor's. **Avg. commute:** 22.7 min. 77.2% drive. **Housing units:** 157,597; 85.1% occupied. **Home ownership:** 53.4%. **Avg. home:** $133,900; change (2010-12): −0.2%. **Avg. rent:** $923.
Mayor: Bob Buckhorn, nonpartisan
History: U.S. army fort on site 1824; inc. 1851. Ybor City, Tampa's Latin Quarter, a Natl. Historical Landmark District.
Website: www.tampagov.net

Toledo, Ohio

Population: 284,012 (67). **Pop. density:** 3,520. **Pop. change (2010-12):** −1.0%. **Area:** 80.7 sq mi. **Racial distribution:** 66.3% white; 27.0% black; 1.2% Asian; 0.3% Amer. Ind.; <0.05% Pac. Isl.; 1.8% other; 2+ races 3.4%. **Hispanic pop.:** 7.0%. **Foreign born:** 3.4%. **U.S. citizens:** 98.1%. **Language:** 93.8% English only; 3.1% Spanish.
Employment: 119,413 employed; 8.6% unemployed. **Per capita income:** $36,338; change (2010-11): 5.1%. **Below poverty level:** 25.6%; 20.7% of families. **Educational attainment:** 84.6% HS; 17.3% bachelor's. **Avg. commute:** 19.1 min. 81.9% drive. **Housing units:** 139,254; 85.7% occupied. **Home ownership:** 57.2%. **Avg. home:** $80,400; change (2010-12): −1.3%. **Avg. rent:** $629.
Mayor: Mike Bell, nonpartisan
History: Site of Ft. Industry 1794; Battle of Ft. Meigs 1812; figured in Toledo War 1835-36 between OH and MI over borders; inc. 1837.
Website: toledo.oh.gov

Tucson, Arizona

Population: 524,295 (33). **Pop. density:** 2,313. **Pop. change (2010-12):** 0.7%. **Area:** 226.7 sq mi. **Racial distribution:** 74.7% white; 4.8% black; 2.7% Asian; 2.5% Amer. Ind.; 0.2% Pac. Isl.; 12.1% other; 2+ races 3.1%. **Hispanic pop.:** 41.3%. **Foreign born:** 15.8%. **U.S. citizens:** 90.0%. **Language:** 66.3% English only; 28.9% Spanish.
Employment: 230,362 employed; 8.0% unemployed. **Per capita income:** $34,961; change (2010-11): 3.2%. **Below poverty level:** 22.6%; 16.5% of families. **Educational attainment:** 83.9% HS; 24.5% bachelor's. **Avg. commute:** 21.6 min. 73.6% drive; 10.8% carpool. **Housing units:** 231,883; 88.4% occupied. **Home ownership:** 52.3%. **Avg. home:** $149,900; change (2010-12): −4.3%. **Avg. rent:** $714.
Mayor: Jonathan Rothschild, Democrat
History: Settled 1775 by Spanish as a presidio; acquired by U.S. in Gadsden Purchase 1853; inc. 1877.
Website: www.tucsonaz.gov

Tulsa, Oklahoma

Population: 393,987 (46). **Pop. density:** 2,002. **Pop. change (2010-12):** 0.4%. **Area:** 196.8 sq mi. **Racial distribution:** 67.3% white; 15.3% black; 2.3% Asian; 4.2% Amer. Ind.; 0.1% Pac. Isl.; 4.3% other; 2+ races 6.5%. **Hispanic pop.:** 13.6%. **Foreign born:** 9.6%. **U.S. citizens:** 93.0%. **Language:** 85.8% English only; 10.5% Spanish.
Employment: 179,547 employed; 5.3% unemployed. **Per capita income:** $42,236; change (2010-11): 6.8%. **Below poverty level:** 19.4%; 15.1% of families. **Educational attainment:** 86.3% HS; 29.5% bachelor's. **Avg. commute:** 18.2 min. 80.0% drive; 11.9% carpool. **Housing units:** 186,215; 88.4% occupied.

Home ownership: 54.4%. **Avg. home:** $136,300; change (2010-12): 3.0%. **Avg. rent:** $697.
Mayor: Dewey F. Bartlett Jr., Republican
History: Settled in 1836 by Creek Indians; modern town founded 1882; inc. 1898; oil discovered early 20th century. Emerging telecommunications hub.
Website: www.cityoftulsa.org

Virginia Beach, Virginia

Population: 447,021 (39). **Pop. density:** 1,795. **Pop. change (2010-12):** 1.8%. **Area:** 249.0 sq mi. **Racial distribution:** 69.0% white; 19.4% black; 6.1% Asian; 0.3% Amer. Ind.; 0.1% Pac. Isl.; 1.2% other; 2+ races 3.9%. **Hispanic pop.:** 6.5%. **Foreign born:** 8.7%. **U.S. citizens:** 96.5%. **Language:** 88.6% English only; 4.0% Spanish.
Employment: 213,920 employed; 5.6% unemployed. **Per capita income:** $41,976; change (2010-11): 4.6%. **Below poverty level:** 7.1%; 5.2% of families. **Educational attainment:** 92.9% HS; 32.3% bachelor's. **Avg. commute:** 22.7 min. 82.2% drive. **Housing units:** 177,278; 92.5% occupied. **Home ownership:** 65.9%. **Avg. home:** $187,500; change (2010-12): −8.5%. **Avg. rent:** $1,191.
Mayor: William D. Sessoms Jr., nonpartisan
History: Area founded by Capt. John Smith 1607; formed by merger with Princess Anne Co. 1963.
Website: www.vbgov.com

Washington, District of Columbia

Population: 632,323 (24). **Pop. density:** 10,358. **Pop. change (2010-12):** 4.5%. **Area:** 61.0 sq mi. **Racial distribution:** 38.9% white; 51.9% black; 3.5% Asian; 0.3% Amer. Ind.; 0.1% Pac. Isl.; 3.4% other; 2+ races 1.9%. **Hispanic pop.:** 9.0%. **Foreign born:** 13.3%. **U.S. citizens:** 91.6%. **Language:** 85.5% English only; 7.1% Spanish.
Employment: 329,270 employed; 8.9% unemployed. **Per capita income:** $59,345; change (2010-11): 3.5%. **Below poverty level:** 18.2%; 13.9% of families. **Educational attainment:** 87.1% HS; 50.5% bachelor's. **Avg. commute:** 29.6 min. 37.5% public trans.; 35.5% drive; 12.0% walk. **Housing units:** 295,510; 88.0% occupied. **Home ownership:** 42.8%. **Avg. home:** $352,000; change (2010-12): 8.2%. **Avg. rent:** $1,135.
Mayor: Vincent C. Gray, Democrat
History: U.S. capital; site on Potomac R. chosen by George Washington, 1790, on land ceded from VA and MD (portion S of Potomac returned to VA 1846.) Congress first met 1800; inc. 1802; sacked by British, War of 1812. 125 killed in Sept. 11, 2001, terrorist attack on the Pentagon.
Website: dc.gov

Wichita, Kansas

Population: 385,577 (49). **Pop. density:** 2,421. **Pop. change (2010-12):** 0.7%. **Area:** 159.3 sq mi. **Racial distribution:** 73.2% white; 10.9% black; 4.8% Asian; 0.9% Amer. Ind.; 0.1% Pac. Isl.; 5.4% other; 2+ races 4.7%. **Hispanic pop.:** 14.5%. **Foreign born:** 9.5%. **U.S. citizens:** 94.2%. **Language:** 84.4% English only; 9.9% Spanish.
Employment: 171,540 employed; 7.5% unemployed. **Per capita income:** $38,568; change (2010-11): 4.4%. **Below poverty level:** 16.0%; 12.1% of families. **Educational attainment:** 86.7% HS; 27.9% bachelor's. **Avg. commute:** 17.3 min. 84.6% drive. **Housing units:** 167,052; 90.1% occupied. **Home ownership:** 62.6%. **Avg. home:** $116,900; change (2010-12): −1.5%. **Avg. rent:** $650.
Mayor: Carl Brewer, nonpartisan
History: Founded 1864; inc. 1871. Established itself as aircraft manufacturing hub between WWI and WWII.
Website: www.wichita.gov

Winston-Salem, North Carolina

Population: 234,349 (85). **Pop. density:** 1,769. **Pop. change (2010-12):** 1.9%. **Area:** 132.4 sq mi. **Racial distribution:** 54.1% white; 34.8% black; 2.0% Asian; 0.2% Amer. Ind.; 0.1% Pac. Isl.; 7.1% other; 2+ races 1.7%. **Hispanic pop.:** 14.0%. **Foreign born:** 11.0%. **U.S. citizens:** 91.5%. **Language:** 83.4% English only; 13.0% Spanish.
Employment: 102,676 employed; 8.6% unemployed. **Per capita income:** $36,416; change (2010-11): 4.5%. **Below poverty level:** 20.6%; 15.7% of families. **Educational attainment:** 85.5% HS; 31.7% bachelor's. **Avg. commute:** 19.3 min. 82.1% drive. **Housing units:** 104,329; 86.5% occupied. **Home ownership:** 58.7%. **Avg. home:** $123,600; change (2010-12): −8.2%. **Avg. rent:** $685.
Mayor: Allen Joines, Democrat
History: Salem founded 1766; Winston founded 1849; became Winston-Salem 1913. The Reynolds Building, completed 1929, used as model for Empire State Building (designed by same architects).
Website: www.cityofws.org

UNITED STATES POPULATION

Census Origins and Methods

A census is conducted in the U.S. every 10 years. The primary purpose is to apportion seats in the House of Representatives. Census data is also used to determine the boundaries of state legislative districts.

The first U.S. census, mandated by Article 1, Section 2 of the Constitution, was conducted in 1790, a little more than a year after George Washington became president. It counted the numbers of free white males ages 16 and over (as a measure of available workers or military personnel), free white males under 16, free white females, all other free persons, and slaves. The data was collected over 18 months, at a cost of about $1 million in today's dollars. The 1790 census counted a total of 3.9 million people, resulting in an increase of 41 seats (from 65 to 106) in the House of Representatives.

As the nation grew, so did the scope of the census. The first inquiries on manufacturing were made in 1810. Questions on "the pursuits, industry, education, and resources of the country" were added to the 1840 census. It took a full 10 years to publish the results of the 1880 and 1890 censuses because of the number of questions asked. Due to those delays, Congress limited the 1900 census to questions on population, manufacturing, agriculture, and mortality.

Today, the secretary of commerce and the Census Bureau are directed by law to take censuses of population, housing, agriculture, irrigation, manufacturing, mineral industries, other businesses (wholesale trade, retail trade, and services), construction, transportation, and governments at stated intervals. They also conduct smaller-scale surveys on behalf of other federal agencies.

U.S. marshals supervised the first nine censuses and reported to the president (1790), to the secretary of state (1800-40), or to the secretary of the interior (1850-70). There was no continuity in personnel from one census to the next. In 1902, Congress authorized a permanent Census Office within the Interior Department. In 1903, the agency was transferred to the new Department of Commerce and Labor. When the department split in 1913, the Bureau of the Census went with the Commerce Department.

The Census Bureau began using statistical sampling techniques in the 1940s, the first modern computer in the 1950s, and enumeration by mail in the 1960s. It introduced these innovations so that it could publish data sooner, at a lower cost, and with less burden on the public. For the 2010 census, the Census Bureau mailed questionnaires to most housing units in the country. Follow-up interviews at nonresponding households were conducted using handheld computers.

The 2010 census asked just 10 questions, making its questionnaire one of the shortest in census history. In previous censuses, about five in six households received a short form while one in six households answered a long-form questionnaire, which asked about details such as ancestry, marital status, and occupation. The American Community Survey (ACS) replaced the need in 2010 for a long-form questionnaire. Implemented nationwide in 2005, the ACS is conducted yearly on a random sample of the population. It gathers demographic, economic, and housing information on communities across the country.

U.S. Population by State and Region, 2000, 2012

Source: Population Estimates Program, Decennial Census, U.S. Census Bureau, U.S. Dept. of Commerce
(ranked by 2012 resident population)

Rank	State	2012[1]	2000[2]	% change, 2000-12	Rank	State	2012[1]	2000[2]	% change, 2000-12
1.	California	38,041,430	33,871,648	12.3%	29.	Connecticut	3,590,347	3,405,565	5.4%
2.	Texas	26,059,203	20,851,820	25.0	30.	Iowa	3,074,186	2,926,324	5.1
3.	New York	19,570,261	18,976,457	3.1	31.	Mississippi	2,984,926	2,844,658	4.9
4.	Florida	19,317,568	15,982,378	20.9	32.	Arkansas	2,949,131	2,673,400	10.3
5.	Illinois	12,875,255	12,419,293	3.7	33.	Kansas	2,885,905	2,688,418	7.3
6.	Pennsylvania	12,763,536	12,281,054	3.9	34.	Utah	2,855,287	2,233,169	27.9
7.	Ohio	11,544,225	11,353,140	1.7	35.	Nevada	2,758,931	1,998,257	38.1
8.	Georgia	9,919,945	8,186,453	21.2	36.	New Mexico	2,085,538	1,819,046	14.7
9.	Michigan	9,883,360	9,938,444	-0.6	37.	Nebraska	1,855,525	1,711,263	8.4
10.	North Carolina	9,752,073	8,049,313	21.2	38.	West Virginia	1,855,413	1,808,344	2.6
11.	New Jersey	8,864,590	8,414,350	5.4	39.	Idaho	1,595,728	1,293,953	23.3
12.	Virginia	8,185,867	7,078,515	15.6	40.	Hawaii	1,392,313	1,211,537	14.9
13.	Washington	6,897,012	5,894,121	17.0	41.	Maine	1,329,192	1,274,923	4.3
14.	Massachusetts	6,646,144	6,349,097	4.7	42.	New Hampshire	1,320,718	1,235,786	6.9
15.	Arizona	6,553,255	5,130,632	27.7	43.	Rhode Island	1,050,292	1,048,319	0.2
16.	Indiana	6,537,334	6,080,485	7.5	44.	Montana	1,005,141	902,195	11.4
17.	Tennessee	6,456,243	5,689,283	13.5	45.	Delaware	917,092	783,600	17.0
18.	Missouri	6,021,988	5,595,211	7.6	46.	South Dakota	833,354	754,844	10.4
19.	Maryland	5,884,563	5,296,486	11.1	47.	Alaska	731,449	626,932	16.7
20.	Wisconsin	5,726,398	5,363,675	6.8	48.	North Dakota	699,628	642,200	8.9
21.	Minnesota	5,379,139	4,919,479	9.3	49.	District of Columbia	632,323	572,059	10.5
22.	Colorado	5,187,582	4,301,261	20.6	50.	Vermont	626,011	608,827	2.8
23.	Alabama	4,822,023	4,447,100	8.4	51.	Wyoming	576,412	493,782	16.7
24.	South Carolina	4,723,723	4,012,012	17.7		**United States**	**313,914,040**	**281,421,906**	**11.5**
25.	Louisiana	4,601,893	4,468,976	3.0		Northeast[3]	55,761,091	53,594,378	4.0
26.	Kentucky	4,380,415	4,041,769	8.4		Midwest[4]	67,316,297	64,392,776	4.5
27.	Oregon	3,899,353	3,421,399	14.0		South[5]	117,257,221	100,236,820	17.0
28.	Oklahoma	3,814,820	3,450,654	10.6		West[6]	73,579,431	63,197,932	16.4

Note: The U.S. resident population consists of individuals whose "usual residence," or where they live and sleep most of the time, is in one of the 50 states or DC. It excludes overseas U.S. military personnel and civilian U.S. citizens living abroad. (1) Estimates are as of July 1. (2) Figures are for Apr. 1 of decennial census year. (3) Incl. the states of the New England (Connecticut, Maine, Massachusetts, New Hampshire, Rhode Island, Vermont) and Middle Atlantic (New Jersey, New York, Pennsylvania) divisions. (4) Incl. the states of the East North Central (Illinois, Indiana, Michigan, Ohio, Wisconsin) and West North Central (Iowa, Kansas, Minnesota, Missouri, Nebraska, North Dakota, South Dakota) divisions. (5) Incl. the states of the South Atlantic (Delaware, DC, Florida, Georgia, Maryland, North Carolina, South Carolina, Virginia, West Virginia), East South Central (Alabama, Kentucky, Mississippi, Tennessee), and West South Central (Arkansas, Louisiana, Oklahoma, Texas) divisions. (6) Incl. the states of the Mountain (Arizona, Colorado, Idaho, Montana, Nevada, New Mexico, Utah, Wyoming) and Pacific (Alaska, California, Hawaii, Oregon, Washington) divisions.

Density of U.S. Population by State, 1930-2010

Source: Decennial Censuses, U.S. Census Bureau, U.S. Dept. of Commerce

(per square mile, land area only)

State	1930	1950	1970	1990	2010	State	1930	1950	1970	1990	2010
AL	52.3	60.5	68.0	79.8	94.4	MT	3.7	4.1	4.8	5.5	6.8
AK	0.1	0.2	0.5	1.0	1.2	NE	17.9	17.3	19.3	20.5	23.8
AZ	3.8	6.6	15.6	32.3	56.3	NV	0.8	1.5	4.5	10.9	24.6
AR	35.6	36.7	37.0	45.2	56.0	NH	52.0	59.6	82.4	123.9	147.0
CA	36.4	68.0	128.1	191.0	239.1	NJ	549.5	657.5	974.7	1,051.1	1,195.5
CO	10.0	12.8	21.3	31.8	48.5	NM	3.5	5.6	8.4	12.5	17.0
CT	331.8	414.5	626.1	678.5	738.1	NY	267.1	314.7	387.0	381.7	411.2
DE	122.3	163.2	281.3	341.9	460.8	NC	65.2	83.5	104.5	136.3	196.1
DC	7,975.1	13,140.3	12,392.0	9,941.3	9,856.5	ND	9.9	9.0	9.0	9.3	9.7
FL	27.4	51.7	126.6	241.3	350.6	OH	162.7	194.5	260.7	265.5	282.3
GA	50.6	59.9	79.8	112.6	168.4	OK	34.9	32.6	37.3	45.9	54.7
HI	57.3	77.8	119.7	172.6	211.8	OR	9.9	15.8	21.8	29.6	39.9
ID	5.4	7.1	8.6	12.2	19.0	PA	215.3	234.6	263.6	265.6	283.9
IL	137.4	156.9	200.2	205.9	231.1	RI	665.0	766.0	915.8	970.6	1,018.1
IN	90.4	109.8	145.0	154.8	181.0	SC	57.8	70.4	86.2	116.0	153.9
IA	44.2	46.9	50.6	49.7	54.5	SD	9.1	8.6	8.8	9.2	10.7
KS	23.0	23.3	27.5	30.3	34.9	TN	63.5	79.8	95.2	118.3	153.9
KY	66.2	74.6	81.5	93.3	109.9	TX	22.3	29.5	42.9	65.0	96.3
LA	48.6	62.1	84.3	97.7	104.9	UT	6.2	8.4	12.9	21.0	33.6
ME	25.9	29.6	32.2	39.8	43.1	VT	39.0	41.0	48.2	61.1	67.9
MD	168.1	241.4	404.1	492.6	594.8	VA	61.3	84.0	117.7	156.7	202.6
MA	544.8	601.3	729.4	771.3	839.4	WA	23.5	35.8	51.3	73.2	101.2
MI	85.6	112.7	157.0	164.4	174.8	WV	71.9	83.4	72.6	74.6	77.1
MN	32.2	37.5	47.8	54.9	66.6	WI	54.3	63.4	81.6	90.3	105.0
MS	42.8	46.4	47.2	54.8	63.2	WY	2.3	3.0	3.4	4.7	5.8
MO	52.8	57.5	68.0	74.4	87.1	U.S.	34.7	42.6	57.5	70.4	87.4

Note: For the sake of comparison, the densities of Alaska and Hawaii in 1930 and 1950 are included though they were not yet states.

U.S. Area and Population, 1790-2010

Source: Decennial Censuses, U.S. Census Bureau, U.S. Dept. of Commerce

Census date	AREA (square miles)			RESIDENT POPULATION		Increase over preceding census	
	Total area[1]	Land area	Water area[1]	Number	Per sq mi of land	Number	%
1790 (Aug. 2)	891,364	864,746	24,065	3,929,214	4.5	—	—
1800 (Aug. 4)	891,364	864,746	24,065	5,308,483	6.1	1,379,269	35.1%
1810 (Aug. 6)	1,722,685	1,681,828	34,175	7,239,881	4.3	1,931,398	36.4
1820 (Aug. 7)	1,792,552	1,749,462	38,544	9,638,453	5.5	2,398,572	33.1
1830 (June 1)	1,792,552	1,749,462	38,544	12,866,020	7.4	3,227,567	33.5
1840 (June 1)	1,792,552	1,749,462	38,544	17,069,453	9.8	4,203,433	32.7
1850 (June 1)	2,991,655	2,940,042	52,705	23,191,876	7.9	6,122,423	35.9
1860 (June 1)	3,021,295	2,969,640	52,747	31,443,321	10.6	8,251,445	35.6
1870 (June 1)	3,612,299	3,540,705	68,082	39,818,449	11.2	8,375,128	26.6
1880 (June 1)	3,612,299	3,540,705	68,082	50,189,209	14.2	10,370,760	26.0
1890 (June 1)	3,612,299	3,540,705	68,082	62,979,766	17.8	12,790,557	25.5
1900 (June 1)	3,618,770	3,547,314	67,901	76,212,168	21.5	13,232,402	21.0
1910 (Apr. 15)	3,618,770	3,547,045	68,170	92,228,496	26.0	16,016,328	21.0
1920 (Jan. 1)	3,618,770	3,546,931	68,284	106,021,537	29.9	13,793,041	15.0
1930 (Apr. 1)	3,618,770	3,554,608	60,607	123,202,624	34.7	17,181,087	16.2
1940 (Apr. 1)	3,618,770	3,554,608	60,607	132,164,569	37.2	8,961,945	7.3
1950 (Apr. 1)	3,618,770	3,552,206	63,005	151,325,798	42.6	19,161,229	14.5
1960 (Apr. 1)	3,618,770	3,540,911	74,212	179,323,175	50.6	27,997,377	18.5
1970 (Apr. 1)	3,618,770	3,536,855	78,444	203,302,031	57.5	23,978,856	13.4
1980 (Apr. 1)	3,618,770	3,539,289	79,481	226,542,199	64.0	23,240,168	11.4
1990 (Apr. 1)	3,717,796	3,536,278	181,518	248,718,302	70.3	22,176,103	9.8
2000 (Apr. 1)	3,794,083	3,537,438	256,645	281,424,603	79.6	32,706,301	13.1
2010 (Apr. 1)	3,796,742	3,531,905	264,837	308,745,538	87.4	27,320,935	9.7

Note: Percent changes are computed on the basis of change in population since the preceding census date, so the period covered is not always exactly 10 years. Population density figures given for various years represent the area within the boundaries of the U.S. under its jurisdiction on the date in question including, in some cases, considerable areas not organized or settled and not actually covered by the census. Area data beginning in 1870 include Alaska; from 1900 on, data include Hawaii. Population figures may reflect corrections made to initial tabulated census counts. (1) Figures for 1790-1980 cover inland water only. Figures for 1990 include inland, coastal, and Great Lakes water. Figures for 2000-10 include additional territorial water.

U.S. Population by Official

Source: Decennial Censuses, U.S. Census Bureau,
(population figures for 1790-1860

State	1790	1800	1810	1820	1830	1840	1850	1860	1870	1880	1890	1900	1910	1920
AL[1]	...	1	9	128	310	591	772	964	996,992	1,262,505	1,513,401	1,828,697	2,138,093	2,348,174
AK	...	...	...	...	...	...	...	...	...	33,426	32,052	63,592	64,356	55,036
AZ[2]	...	...	...	...	...	...	...	...	9,658	40,440	88,243	122,931	204,354	334,162
AR	...	...	1	14	30	98	210	435	484,471	802,525	1,128,211	1,311,564	1,574,449	1,752,204
CA	...	...	...	...	...	...	93	380	560,247	864,694	1,213,398	1,485,053	2,377,549	3,426,861
CO[2]	...	...	...	...	...	...	...	34	39,864	194,327	413,249	539,700	799,024	939,629
CT	238	251	262	275	298	310	371	460	537,454	622,700	746,258	908,420	1,114,756	1,380,631
DE	59	64	73	73	77	78	92	112	125,015	146,608	168,493	184,735	202,322	223,003
DC	...	8	16	23	30	34	52	75	131,700	177,624	230,392	278,718	331,069	437,571
FL	...	...	...	...	35	54	87	140	187,748	269,493	391,422	528,542	752,619	968,470
GA	83	163	252	341	517	691	906	1,057	1,184,109	1,542,180	1,837,353	2,216,331	2,609,121	2,895,832
HI	...	...	...	...	...	...	...	...	...	...	...	154,001	191,909	255,912
ID[3]	...	...	...	...	...	...	...	...	14,999	32,610	88,548	161,772	325,594	431,866
IL	...	...	12	55	157	476	851	1,712	2,539,891	3,077,871	3,826,352	4,821,550	5,638,591	6,485,280
IN	...	6	25	147	343	686	988	1,350	1,680,637	1,978,301	2,192,404	2,516,462	2,700,876	2,930,390
IA	...	...	...	...	...	43	192	675	1,194,020	1,624,615	1,912,297	2,231,853	2,224,771	2,404,021
KS	...	...	...	...	...	...	...	107	364,399	996,096	1,428,108	1,470,495	1,690,949	1,769,257
KY	74	221	407	564	688	780	982	1,156	1,321,011	1,648,690	1,858,635	2,147,174	2,289,905	2,416,630
LA	...	...	77	153	216	352	518	708	726,915	939,946	1,118,588	1,381,625	1,656,388	1,798,509
ME[4]	97	152	229	298	399	502	583	628	626,915	648,936	661,086	694,466	742,371	768,014
MD	320	342	381	407	447	470	583	687	780,894	934,943	1,042,390	1,188,044	1,295,346	1,449,661
MA[4]	379	423	472	523	610	738	995	1,231	1,457,351	1,783,085	2,238,947	2,805,346	3,366,416	3,852,356
MI	...	...	5	9	32	212	398	749	1,184,059	1,636,937	2,093,890	2,420,982	2,810,173	3,668,412
MN	...	...	...	...	...	...	6	172	439,706	780,773	1,310,283	1,751,394	2,075,708	2,387,125
MS[1]	...	8	31	75	137	376	607	791	827,922	1,131,597	1,289,600	1,551,270	1,797,114	1,790,618
MO	...	...	20	67	140	384	682	1,182	1,721,295	2,168,380	2,679,185	3,106,665	3,293,335	3,404,055
MT[3]	...	...	...	...	...	...	...	...	20,595	39,159	142,924	243,329	376,053	548,889
NE	...	...	...	...	...	...	...	29	122,993	452,402	1,062,656	1,066,300	1,192,214	1,296,372
NV[2]	...	...	...	...	...	...	...	7	42,491	62,266	47,355	42,335	81,875	77,407
NH	142	184	214	244	269	285	318	326	318,300	346,991	376,530	411,588	430,572	443,083
NJ	184	211	246	278	321	373	490	672	906,096	1,131,116	1,444,933	1,883,669	2,537,167	3,155,900
NM[2]	...	...	...	...	...	...	62	94	91,874	119,565	160,282	195,310	327,301	360,350
NY	340	589	959	1,373	1,919	2,429	3,097	3,881	4,382,759	5,082,871	6,003,174	7,268,894	9,113,614	10,385,227
NC	394	478	556	639	736	753	869	993	1,071,361	1,399,750	1,617,949	1,893,810	2,206,287	2,559,123
ND[5]	...	...	...	...	...	...	...	...	2,405	36,909	190,983	319,146	577,056	646,872
OH	...	45	231	581	938	1,519	1,980	2,340	2,665,260	3,198,062	3,672,329	4,157,545	4,767,121	5,759,394
OK	...	...	...	...	...	...	...	...	...	...	258,657	790,391	1,657,155	2,028,283
OR[6]	...	...	...	...	...	...	12	52	90,923	174,768	317,704	413,536	672,765	783,389
PA	434	602	810	1,049	1,348	1,724	2,312	2,906	3,521,951	4,282,891	5,258,113	6,302,115	7,665,111	8,720,017
RI	69	69	77	83	97	109	148	175	217,353	276,531	345,506	428,556	542,610	604,397
SC	249	346	415	503	581	594	669	704	705,606	995,577	1,151,149	1,340,316	1,515,400	1,683,724
SD[5]	...	...	...	...	...	...	...	5	11,776	98,268	348,600	401,570	583,888	636,547
TN	36	106	262	423	682	829	1,003	1,110	1,258,520	1,542,359	1,767,518	2,020,616	2,184,789	2,337,885
TX	...	...	...	...	...	...	213	604	818,579	1,591,749	2,235,527	3,048,710	3,896,542	4,663,228
UT	...	...	...	...	...	...	11	40	86,786	143,963	210,779	276,749	373,351	449,396
VT	85	154	218	236	281	292	314	315	330,551	332,286	332,422	343,641	355,956	352,428
VA[7]	692	808	878	938	1,044	1,025	1,120	1,220	1,225,163	1,512,565	1,655,980	1,854,184	2,061,612	2,309,187
WA[3,6]	...	...	...	...	...	...	1	12	23,955	75,116	357,232	518,103	1,141,990	1,356,621
WV[7]	56	79	105	137	177	225	302	377	442,014	618,457	762,794	958,800	1,221,119	1,463,701
WI	...	...	...	...	...	31	305	776	1,054,670	1,315,497	1,693,330	2,069,042	2,333,860	2,632,067
WY[3]	...	...	...	...	...	...	...	...	9,118	20,789	62,555	92,531	145,965	194,402
U.S.[8]	3,929	5,308	7,240	9,638	12,866	17,063	23,192	31,443	38,558,371	50,189,209	62,979,766	76,212,168	92,228,531	106,021,568

Note: Unless otherwise noted, pop. shown is for a state's present-day area. Excl. overseas U.S. military personnel and civilian U.S. citizens living abroad. (1) 1800-10 figures for MS are for those areas of Mississippi Territory now part of present-day AL and MS. (2) 1850 figure for NM incl. parts of New Mexico Territory now part of present-day AZ, NM, CO, and NV; 1860 figure incl. parts taken in formation of Arizona Territory in 1863. (3) 1860 figure for WA incl. pop. in present-day ID and parts of MT and WY. (4) 1790-1810 figures for MA do not incl. district taken to form state of ME in 1820. (5) 1860 figure is for Dakota Territory, which comprised present-day ND and SD; 1870-80 figures are for parts of territory that became the two states in 1889. (6) Parts of Oregon Territory went to Washington Territory in 1853 and 1859. 1850 pop. in those areas are listed under WA, not OR. (7) 1790-1860 figures for VA do not incl. areas taken in creation of WV in 1863. (8) 1830-40 totals incl. persons (5,318 in 1830; 6,100 in 1840) on public ships in service of the U.S. not credited to any state.

Estimated Population of American Colonies, 1630-1780

Source: U.S. Census Bureau, U.S. Dept. of Commerce
(numbers in thousands)

Colony	1630	1650	1670	1690	1700	1720	1740	1750	1770	1780
Total.	4.6	50.4	111.9	210.4	250.9	466.2	905.6	1,170.8	2,148.1	2,780.4
Connecticut	—	4.1	12.6	21.6	26.0	58.8	89.6	111.3	183.9	206.7
Delaware	—	0.2	0.7	1.5	2.5	5.4	19.9	28.7	35.5	45.4
Georgia	—	—	—	—	—	—	2.0	5.2	23.4	56.1
Kentucky[1]	—	—	—	—	—	—	—	—	15.7	45.0
Maine (counties)[2]	0.4	1.0	—	—	—	—	—	—	31.3	49.1
Maryland	—	4.5	13.2	24.0	29.6	66.1	116.1	141.1	202.6	245.5
New Hampshire	0.5	1.3	1.8	4.2	5.0	9.4	23.3	27.5	62.4	87.8
New Jersey	—	—	1.0	8.0	14.0	29.8	51.4	71.4	117.4	139.6
New York	0.4	4.1	5.8	13.9	19.1	36.9	63.7	76.7	162.9	210.5
North Carolina	—	—	3.9	7.6	10.7	21.3	51.8	73.0	197.2	270.1
Pennsylvania	—	—	—	11.4	18.0	31.0	85.6	119.7	240.1	327.3
Plymouth and Massachusetts[2,3]	0.9	15.6	35.3	56.9	55.9	91.0	151.6	188.0	235.3	268.6
Rhode Island	—	0.8	2.2	4.2	5.9	11.7	25.3	33.2	58.2	52.9
South Carolina	—	—	0.2	3.9	5.7	17.0	45.0	64.0	124.2	180.0
Tennessee[4]	—	—	—	—	—	—	—	—	1.0	10.0
Vermont[5]	—	—	—	—	—	—	—	—	—	47.6
Virginia	2.5	18.7	35.3	53.0	58.6	87.8	180.4	231.0	447.0	538.0

Note: With the exception of KY, ME, Plymouth, TN, and VT, colonies shown are the original 13 states. (1) Admitted as state 1792. (2) For 1660-1750, the pop. of ME counties are included with MA. ME was annexed by MA in the 1650s but became a separate state in 1820. (3) Plymouth became part of Prov. of Massachusetts in 1691. (4) Admitted as state 1796. (5) Admitted as state 1791.

Census, 1790-2010

U.S. Dept. of Commerce
only are in thousands)

1930	1940	1950	1960	1970	1980	1990	2000	2010	State
2,646,248	2,832,961	3,061,743	3,266,740	3,444,165	3,893,888	4,040,587	4,447,100	4,779,736	AL
59,278	72,524	128,643	226,167	300,382	401,851	550,043	626,932	710,231	AK
435,573	499,261	749,587	1,302,161	1,770,900	2,718,215	3,665,228	5,130,632	6,392,017	AZ
1,854,482	1,949,387	1,909,511	1,786,272	1,923,295	2,286,435	2,350,725	2,673,400	2,915,918	AR
5,677,251	6,907,387	10,586,223	15,717,204	19,953,134	23,667,902	29,760,021	33,871,648	37,253,956	CA
1,035,791	1,123,296	1,325,089	1,753,947	2,207,259	2,889,964	3,294,394	4,301,261	5,029,196	CO
1,606,903	1,709,242	2,007,280	2,535,234	3,031,709	3,107,576	3,287,116	3,405,565	3,574,097	CT
238,380	266,505	318,085	446,292	548,104	594,338	666,168	783,600	897,934	DE
486,869	663,091	802,178	763,956	756,510	638,333	606,900	572,059	601,723	DC
1,468,211	1,897,414	2,771,305	4,951,560	6,789,443	9,746,324	12,937,926	15,982,378	18,801,310	FL
2,908,506	3,123,723	3,444,578	3,943,116	4,589,575	5,463,105	6,478,216	8,186,453	9,687,653	GA
368,336	422,330	499,794	632,772	768,561	964,691	1,108,229	1,211,537	1,360,301	HI
445,032	524,873	588,637	667,191	712,567	943,935	1,006,749	1,293,953	1,567,582	ID
7,630,654	7,897,241	8,712,176	10,081,158	11,113,976	11,426,518	11,430,602	12,419,293	12,830,632	IL
3,238,503	3,427,796	3,934,224	4,662,498	5,193,669	5,490,224	5,544,159	6,080,485	6,483,802	IN
2,470,939	2,538,268	2,621,073	2,757,537	2,824,376	2,913,808	2,776,755	2,926,324	3,046,355	IA
1,880,999	1,801,028	1,905,299	2,178,611	2,246,578	2,363,679	2,477,574	2,688,418	2,853,118	KS
2,614,589	2,845,627	2,944,806	3,038,156	3,218,706	3,660,777	3,685,296	4,041,769	4,339,367	KY
2,101,593	2,363,880	2,683,516	3,257,022	3,641,306	4,205,900	4,219,973	4,468,976	4,533,372	LA
797,423	847,226	913,774	969,265	992,048	1,124,660	1,227,928	1,274,923	1,328,361	ME
1,631,526	1,821,244	2,343,001	3,100,689	3,922,399	4,216,975	4,781,468	5,296,486	5,773,552	MD
4,249,614	4,316,721	4,690,514	5,148,578	5,689,170	5,737,037	6,016,425	6,349,097	6,547,629	MA
4,842,325	5,256,106	6,371,766	7,823,194	8,875,083	9,262,078	9,295,297	9,938,444	9,883,640	MI
2,563,953	2,792,300	2,982,483	3,413,864	3,804,971	4,075,970	4,375,099	4,919,479	5,303,925	MN
2,009,821	2,183,796	2,178,914	2,178,141	2,216,912	2,520,638	2,573,216	2,844,658	2,967,297	MS
3,629,367	3,784,664	3,954,653	4,319,813	4,676,501	4,916,686	5,117,073	5,595,211	5,988,927	MO
537,606	559,456	591,024	674,767	694,409	786,690	799,065	902,195	989,415	MT
1,377,963	1,315,834	1,325,510	1,411,330	1,483,493	1,569,825	1,578,385	1,711,263	1,826,341	NE
91,058	110,247	160,083	285,278	488,738	800,493	1,201,833	1,998,257	2,700,551	NV
465,293	491,524	533,242	606,921	737,681	920,610	1,109,252	1,235,786	1,316,470	NH
4,041,334	4,160,165	4,835,329	6,066,782	7,168,164	7,364,823	7,730,188	8,414,350	8,791,894	NJ
423,317	531,818	681,187	951,023	1,016,000	1,302,894	1,515,069	1,819,046	2,059,179	NM
12,588,066	13,479,142	14,830,192	16,782,304	18,236,967	17,558,072	17,990,455	18,976,457	19,378,102	NY
3,170,276	3,571,623	4,061,929	4,556,155	5,082,059	5,881,766	6,628,637	8,049,313	9,535,483	NC
680,845	641,935	619,636	632,446	617,761	652,717	638,800	642,200	672,591	ND
6,646,697	6,907,612	7,946,627	9,706,397	10,652,017	10,797,630	10,847,115	11,353,140	11,536,504	OH
2,396,040	2,336,434	2,233,351	2,328,284	2,559,229	3,025,290	3,145,585	3,450,654	3,751,351	OK
953,786	1,089,684	1,521,341	1,768,687	2,091,385	2,633,105	2,842,321	3,421,399	3,831,074	OR
9,631,350	9,900,180	10,498,012	11,319,366	11,793,909	11,863,895	11,881,643	12,281,054	12,702,379	PA
687,497	713,346	791,896	859,488	949,723	947,154	1,003,464	1,048,319	1,052,567	RI
1,738,765	1,899,804	2,117,027	2,382,594	2,500,616	3,121,820	3,486,703	4,012,012	4,625,364	SC
692,849	642,961	652,740	680,514	665,507	690,768	696,004	754,844	814,180	SD
2,616,556	2,915,841	3,291,718	3,567,089	3,923,687	4,591,120	4,877,185	5,689,283	6,346,105	TN
5,824,715	6,414,824	7,711,194	9,579,677	11,196,730	14,229,191	16,986,510	20,851,820	25,145,561	TX
507,847	550,310	688,862	890,627	1,059,273	1,461,037	1,722,850	2,233,169	2,763,885	UT
359,611	359,231	377,747	389,881	444,330	511,456	562,758	608,827	625,741	VT
2,421,851	2,677,773	3,318,680	3,966,949	4,648,494	5,346,818	6,187,358	7,078,515	8,001,024	VA
1,563,396	1,736,191	2,378,963	2,853,214	3,409,169	4,132,156	4,866,692	5,894,121	6,724,540	WA
1,729,205	1,901,974	2,005,552	1,860,421	1,744,237	1,949,644	1,793,477	1,808,344	1,852,994	WV
2,939,006	3,137,587	3,434,575	3,951,777	4,417,731	4,705,767	4,891,769	5,363,675	5,686,986	WI
225,565	250,742	290,529	330,066	332,416	469,557	453,588	493,782	563,626	WY
123,202,660	132,164,569	151,325,798	179,323,175	203,211,926	226,545,805	248,709,873	281,421,906	308,745,538	U.S.

U.S. Center of Population, 1790-2010

Source: Decennial Censuses, Geography Division, U.S. Census Bureau, U.S. Dept. of Commerce

The country's (mean) center of population is the center of population gravity. In other words, it is the point upon which the U.S. would balance if the country were a rigid, weightless plane and its population was distributed thereon, with each individual assuming an equal weight.

Census year	N Lat °	'	"	W Long °	'	"	Approximate location
1790	39	16	30	76	11	12	Kent Co., MD, 23 miles east of Baltimore
1800	39	16	6	76	56	30	Howard Co., MD, 18 miles west of Baltimore
1810	39	11	30	77	37	12	Loudoun Co., VA, 40 miles northwest by west of Washington, DC
1820	39	5	42	78	33	0	Hardy Co., WV[1], 16 miles east of Moorefield
1830	38	57	54	79	16	54	Grant Co., WV[1], 19 miles west-southwest of Moorefield
1840	39	2	0	80	18	0	Upshur Co., WV[1], 16 miles south of Clarksburg
1850	38	59	0	81	19	0	Wirt Co., WV[1], 23 miles southeast of Parkersburg
1860	39	0	24	82	48	48	Pike Co., OH, 20 miles south by east of Chillicothe
1870	39	12	0	83	35	42	Highland Co., OH, 48 miles east by north of Cincinnati
1880	39	4	8	84	39	40	Boone Co., KY, 8 miles west by south of Cincinnati, OH
1890	39	11	56	85	32	53	Decatur Co., IN, 20 miles east of Columbus
1900	39	9	36	85	48	54	Bartholomew Co., IN, 6 miles southeast of Columbus
1910	39	10	12	86	32	20	Monroe Co., IN, in the city of Bloomington
1920	39	10	21	86	43	15	Owen Co., IN, 8 miles south-southeast of Spencer
1930	39	3	45	87	8	6	Greene Co., IN, 3 miles northeast of Linton
1940	38	56	54	87	22	35	Sullivan Co., IN, 2 miles southeast by east of Carlisle
1950	38	50	21	88	9	33	Richland Co., IL, 8 miles north-northwest of Olney
1950[2]	38	48	15	88	22	8	Clay Co., IL, 3 miles northwest of Louisville
1960[2]	38	35	58	89	12	35	Clinton Co., IL, 6.5 miles northwest of Centralia
1970[2]	38	27	47	89	42	22	St. Clair Co., IL, 5 miles east-southeast of Mascoutah
1980[2]	38	8	13	90	34	26	Jefferson Co., MO, 0.25 mile west of DeSoto
1990[2]	37	52	20	91	12	55	Crawford Co., MO, 9.7 miles southeast of Steelville
2000[2]	37	41	49	91	48	34	Phelps Co., MO, 2.8 miles east of Edgar Springs
2010[2]	37	31	3	92	10	23	Texas Co., MO, 2.7 miles northeast of Plato

(1) West Virginia was set off from Virginia on Dec. 31, 1862, and admitted as a state on June 20, 1863. (2) Incl. Alaska and Hawaii.

U.S. Congressional Apportionment by Census Year, 1850-2010
Source: Decennial Censuses, U.S. Census Bureau, U.S. Dept. of Commerce

The U.S. Constitution, in Article 1, Section 2, mandates that the population be counted every 10 years so that the number of representatives can be apportioned among the states. Every state is entitled to at least one House seat. The size of a state's resident population, both citizens and noncitizens, determines if it may send additional representatives to Congress. A congressional apportionment has been made after every decennial census except for that of 1920. Prior to 1870, slaves were counted as only three-fifths of a person in the apportionment population. Apportionments made before the 20th century also excluded some Native Americans and armed forces personnel and federal civilian employees stationed overseas. District of Columbia residents still lack voting representation.

Under the provisions of a law that went into effect Nov. 15, 1941, representatives are apportioned by the method of equal proportions. The apportionment is made so that the average number of people each House member represents has the least possible variation between states.

The first House of Representatives, in 1789, had 65 members as provided by the Constitution. The largest numbers were from Virginia (10), Massachusetts (8), and Pennsylvania (8). As the nation's population grew, the number of representatives was increased, but a 1911 act fixed the total membership of the House at 435. (Alaska and Hawaii each gained one House seat when they became states, temporarily raising the total to 437 representatives until after the 1960 census was conducted.)

State	2010	2000	1990	1970	1950	1900	1850	State	2010	2000	1990	1970	1950	1900	1850
AL	7	7	7	7	9	9	7	NE	3	3	3	3	4	6	NA
AK	1	1	1	1	1	NA	NA	NV	4	3	2	1	1	1	NA
AZ	9	8	6	4	2	NA	NA	NH	2	2	2	2	2	2	3
AR	4	4	4	4	6	7	2	NJ	12	13	13	15	14	10	5
CA	53	53	52	43	30	8	2	NM	3	3	3	2	2	NA	NA
CO	7	7	6	5	4	3	NA	NY	27	29	31	39	43	37	33
CT	5	5	6	6	6	5	4	NC	13	13	12	11	12	10	8
DE	1	1	1	1	1	1	1	ND	1	1	1	1	2	2	NA
FL	27	25	23	15	8	3	1	OH	16	18	19	23	23	21	21
GA	14	13	11	10	10	11	8	OK	5	5	6	6	6	5	NA
HI	2	2	2	2	1	NA	NA	OR	5	5	5	4	4	2	1
ID	2	2	2	2	2	1	NA	PA	18	19	21	25	30	32	25
IL	18	19	20	24	25	25	9	RI	2	2	2	2	2	2	2
IN	9	9	10	11	11	13	11	SC	7	6	6	6	6	7	6
IA	4	5	5	6	8	11	2	SD	1	1	1	2	2	2	NA
KS	4	4	4	5	6	8	NA	TN	9	9	9	8	9	10	10
KY	6	6	6	7	8	11	10	TX	36	32	30	24	22	16	2
LA	6	7	7	8	8	7	4	UT	4	3	3	2	2	1	NA
ME	2	2	2	2	3	4	6	VT	1	1	1	1	1	2	3
MD	8	8	8	8	7	6	6	VA	11	11	11	10	10	10	13
MA	9	10	10	12	14	14	11	WA	10	9	9	7	7	3	NA
MI	14	15	16	19	18	12	4	WV	3	3	3	4	6	5	NA
MN	8	8	8	8	9	9	2	WI	8	8	9	9	10	11	3
MS	4	4	5	5	6	8	5	WY	1	1	1	1	1	1	NA
MO	8	9	9	10	11	16	7	Total	435	435	435	435	437	391	237
MT	1	1	1	2	2	1	NA								

NA = Not applicable.

U.S. Slave and "Free Colored" Population, 1790, 1820, 1860
Source: Decennial Censuses, U.S. Census Bureau, U.S. Dept. of Commerce

	1790 census			1820 census			1860 census		
	Slaves	% slaves[1]	Free colored	Slaves	% slaves[1]	Free colored	Slaves	% slaves[1]	Free colored
Northern states[2]	40,370	2.1%	33,016	18,001	0.3%	92,351	18	0%	225,224
Connecticut	2,759	1.2	2,801	97	0	7,844	0	0	8,627
New Jersey	11,423	6.2	2,762	7,557	2.7	12,460	18	0	25,318
New York	21,324	6.3	4,654	10,088	0.7	29,279	0	0	49,005
Pennsylvania	3,737	0.9	6,537	211	0	30,202	0	0	56,949
Border/disputed states	123,753	27.4	12,056	248,860	22.4	55,794	429,403	20.6	118,652
Delaware	8,887	15.0	3,899	4,509	6.2	12,958	1,798	1.6	19,829
Kansas	—	—	—	—	—	—	2	0	625
Kentucky	11,830	16.2	114	126,732	22.5	2,759	225,483	19.5	10,684
Maryland	103,036	32.2	8,043	107,397	26.4	39,730	87,189	12.7	83,942
Missouri	—	—	—	10,222	15.4	347	114,931	9.7	3,572
Southern states	533,774	35.4	20,301	1,263,780	37.8	74,381	3,521,110	34.3	132,760
Alabama	—	—	—	41,879	32.7	571	435,080	45.1	2,690
Arkansas	—	—	—	1,617	11.3	59	111,115	25.5	144
Florida	—	—	—	—	—	—	61,745	44.0	932
Georgia	29,264	35.5	398	149,654	43.9	1,763	462,198	43.7	3,500
Louisiana	—	—	—	69,064	45.2	10,476	331,726	46.9	18,647
Mississippi	—	—	—	32,814	43.5	458	436,631	55.2	773
North Carolina	100,572	25.5	4,975	205,017	32.1	14,612	331,059	33.4	30,463
South Carolina	107,094	43.0	1,801	258,475	51.4	6,826	402,406	57.2	9,914
Tennessee	3,417	9.5	361	80,107	18.9	2,727	275,719	24.8	7,300
Texas	—	—	—	—	—	—	182,566	30.2	355
Virginia	293,427	39.2	12,766	425,153	39.9	36,889	490,865	30.7	58,042
Total territories[3]	—	—	—	6,377	19.3	4,048	3,229	1.1	11,434
Total states and territories	697,897	17.8	59,466	1,538,125	16.0	233,504	3,953,760	12.6	488,070

Note: "Free colored" was an official Census Bureau designation in these decades. Pop. figures shown here include both blacks and those of mixed-race background. States are grouped roughly by their allegiance in the Civil War. (1) Percentage of total pop., of all races. (2) The following states had free colored pops. that are not listed separately but are included in totals for Northern states (relevant census years in parentheses): California (1860), Illinois (1820, 1860), Indiana (1820, 1860), Iowa (1860), Maine (1820, 1860), Massachusetts (1790, 1820, 1860), Michigan (1820, 1860), Minnesota (1860), New Hampshire (1790, 1820, 1860), Ohio (1820, 1860), Oregon (1860), Rhode Island (1790, 1820, 1860), Vermont (1820, 1860), and Wisconsin (1860). (3) Incl. Colorado (1860), Dakota (1860), District of Columbia (1820, 1860), Nebraska (1860), Nevada (1860), New Mexico (1860), Utah (1860), and Washington (1860).

Largest U.S. Metropolitan Areas by Population, 2000-12

Source: Population Estimates Program, Decennial Censuses, U.S. Census Bureau, U.S. Dept. of Commerce

(ranked by 2012 population; 2012 estimates are as of July 1; 2000 and 2010 decennial census figures are for Apr. 1)

Metropolitan Statistical Areas (MSAs) are defined, or delineated geographically, for federal statistical use by the Office of Management and Budget (OMB) with technical assistance from the Census Bureau. The standards used to define metropolitan areas are revised before each decennial census. Areas are delineated using the most recently issued standards and are updated between census years.

An MSA consists of at least one urbanized area of 50,000 or more inhabitants, plus adjacent territory closely integrated socially and economically with the core as measured by commuting ties. The OMB's most recent definitions, issued in Feb. 2013, designates 381 MSAs in the U.S. About 85% of the population resides in an MSA.

Rank	Metropolitan Statistical Area	Population			Percent change	
		2012	2010	2000	2010-12	2000-12
1.	New York-Newark-Jersey City, NY-NJ-PA	19,831,858	19,567,410	18,944,519	1.4%	4.7%
2.	Los Angeles-Long Beach-Anaheim, CA	13,052,921	12,828,837	12,365,627	1.7	5.6
3.	Chicago-Naperville-Elgin, IL-IN-WI	9,522,434	9,461,105	9,098,316	0.6	4.7
4.	Dallas-Fort Worth-Arlington, TX	6,700,991	6,426,214	5,204,126	4.3	28.8
5.	Houston-The Woodlands-Sugar Land, TX	6,177,035	5,920,416	4,693,161	4.3	31.6
6.	Philadelphia-Camden-Wilmington, PA-NJ-DE-MD	6,018,800	5,965,343	5,687,140	0.9	5.8
7.	Washington-Arlington-Alexandria, DC-VA-MD-WV	5,860,342	5,636,232	4,837,428	4.0	21.1
8.	Miami-Fort Lauderdale-West Palm Beach, FL	5,762,717	5,564,635	5,007,564	3.6	15.1
9.	Atlanta-Sandy Springs-Roswell, GA	5,457,831	5,286,728	4,263,438	3.2	28.0
10.	Boston-Cambridge-Newton, MA-NH	4,640,802	4,552,402	4,391,344	1.9	5.7
11.	San Francisco-Oakland-Hayward, CA	4,455,560	4,335,391	4,123,740	2.8	8.0
12.	Riverside-San Bernardino-Ontario, CA	4,350,096	4,224,851	3,254,821	3.0	33.7
13.	Phoenix-Mesa-Scottsdale, AZ	4,329,534	4,192,887	3,251,876	3.3	33.1
14.	Detroit-Warren-Dearborn, MI	4,292,060	4,296,250	4,452,557	-0.1	-3.6
15.	Seattle-Tacoma-Bellevue, WA	3,552,157	3,439,809	3,043,878	3.3	16.7
16.	Minneapolis-St. Paul-Bloomington, MN-WI	3,422,264	3,348,859	3,031,918	2.2	12.9
17.	San Diego-Carlsbad, CA	3,177,063	3,095,313	2,813,833	2.6	12.9
18.	Tampa-St. Petersburg-Clearwater, FL	2,842,878	2,783,243	2,395,997	2.1	18.7
19.	St. Louis, MO-IL	2,795,794	2,787,701	2,675,343	0.3	4.5
20.	Baltimore-Columbia-Towson, MD	2,753,149	2,710,489	2,552,994	1.6	7.8
21.	Denver-Aurora-Lakewood, CO	2,645,209	2,543,482	2,179,240	4.0	21.4
22.	Pittsburgh, PA	2,360,733	2,356,285	2,431,087	0.2	-2.9
23.	Charlotte-Concord-Gastonia, NC-SC	2,296,569	2,217,012	1,717,372	3.6	33.7
24.	Portland-Vancouver-Hillsboro, OR-WA	2,289,800	2,226,009	1,927,881	2.9	18.8
25.	San Antonio-New Braunfels, TX	2,234,003	2,142,508	1,711,703	4.3	30.5
26.	Orlando-Kissimmee-Sanford, FL	2,223,674	2,134,411	1,644,561	4.2	35.2
27.	Sacramento–Roseville–Arden-Arcade, CA	2,196,482	2,149,127	1,796,857	2.2	22.2
28.	Cincinnati, OH-KY-IN	2,128,603	2,114,580	1,994,830	0.7	6.7
29.	Cleveland-Elyria, OH	2,063,535	2,077,240	2,148,143	-0.7	-3.9
30.	Kansas City, MO-KS	2,038,724	2,009,342	1,811,254	1.5	12.6
31.	Las Vegas-Henderson-Paradise, NV	2,000,759	1,951,269	1,375,765	2.5	45.4
32.	Columbus, OH	1,944,002	1,901,974	1,675,013	2.2	16.1
33.	Indianapolis-Carmel-Anderson, IN	1,928,982	1,887,877	1,658,462	2.2	16.3
34.	San Jose-Sunnyvale-Santa Clara, CA	1,894,388	1,836,911	1,735,819	3.1	9.1
35.	Austin-Round Rock, TX	1,834,303	1,716,289	1,249,763	6.9	46.8
36.	Nashville-Davidson–Murfreesboro–Franklin, TN	1,726,693	1,670,890	1,381,287	3.3	25.0
37.	Virginia Beach-Norfolk-Newport News, VA-NC	1,699,925	1,676,822	1,580,057	1.4	7.6
38.	Providence-Warwick, RI-MA	1,601,374	1,600,852	1,582,997	0.0	1.2
39.	Milwaukee-Waukesha-West Allis, WI	1,566,981	1,555,908	1,500,741	0.7	4.4
40.	Jacksonville, FL	1,377,850	1,345,596	1,122,750	2.4	22.7
41.	Memphis, TN-MS-AR	1,341,690	1,324,829	1,213,230	1.3	10.6
42.	Oklahoma City, OK	1,296,565	1,252,987	1,095,421	3.5	18.4
43.	Louisville-Jefferson County, KY-IN	1,251,351	1,235,708	1,121,109	1.3	11.6
44.	Richmond, VA	1,231,980	1,208,101	1,055,683	2.0	16.7
45.	New Orleans-Metairie, LA	1,227,096	1,189,866	1,337,726	3.1	-8.3
46.	Hartford-West Hartford-East Hartford, CT	1,214,400	1,212,381	1,148,618	0.2	5.7
47.	Raleigh, NC	1,188,564	1,130,490	797,071	5.1	49.1
48.	Birmingham-Hoover, AL	1,136,650	1,128,047	1,052,238	0.8	8.0
49.	Buffalo-Cheektowaga-Niagara Falls, NY	1,134,210	1,135,509	1,170,111	-0.1	-3.1
50.	Salt Lake City, UT	1,123,712	1,087,873	939,122	3.3	19.7
51.	Rochester, NY	1,082,284	1,079,671	1,062,452	0.2	1.9
52.	Grand Rapids-Wyoming, MI	1,005,648	988,938	930,670	1.7	8.1
53.	Tucson, AZ	992,394	980,263	843,746	1.2	17.6
54.	Urban Honolulu, HI	976,372	953,207	876,156	2.4	11.4
55.	Tulsa, OK	951,880	937,478	859,532	1.5	10.7
56.	Fresno, CA	947,895	930,450	799,407	1.9	18.6
57.	Bridgeport-Stamford-Norwalk, CT	933,835	916,829	882,567	1.9	5.8
58.	Worcester, MA-CT	923,762	916,980	860,054	0.7	7.4
59.	Albuquerque, NM	901,700	887,077	729,649	1.6	23.6
60.	Omaha-Council Bluffs, NE-IA	885,624	865,350	767,041	2.3	15.5
61.	Albany-Schenectady-Troy, NY	874,646	870,716	825,875	0.5	5.9
62.	New Haven-Milford, CT	862,813	862,477	824,008	0.0	4.7
63.	Bakersfield, CA	856,158	839,631	661,645	2.0	29.4
64.	Knoxville, TN	848,350	837,571	748,259	1.3	13.4
65.	Greenville-Anderson-Mauldin, SC	842,863	824,112	725,680	2.3	16.1
66.	Oxnard-Thousand Oaks-Ventura, CA	835,981	823,318	753,197	1.5	11.0
67.	El Paso, TX	830,735	804,123	682,966	3.3	21.6
68.	Allentown-Bethlehem-Easton, PA-NJ	827,171	821,173	740,395	0.7	11.7
69.	Baton Rouge, LA	815,298	802,484	705,973	1.6	15.5
70.	McAllen-Edinburg-Mission, TX	806,552	774,769	569,463	4.1	41.6
71.	Dayton, OH	800,972	799,232	805,816	0.2	-0.6
72.	Columbia, SC	784,745	767,598	647,158	2.2	21.3

Largest U.S. Cities by Population, 1850-2012

Source: Population Estimates Program, Decennial Censuses, U.S. Census Bureau, U.S. Dept. of Commerce
(ranked by 2012 population)

Rank City	2012	2000	1990	1980	1970	1950	1900	1850
1. New York, NY	8,336,697	8,008,278	7,322,564	7,071,639	7,895,563	7,891,957	3,437,202	696,115
2. Los Angeles, CA	3,857,799	3,694,820	3,485,398	2,968,528	2,811,801	1,970,358	102,479	1,610
3. Chicago, IL	2,714,856	2,896,016	2,783,726	3,005,072	3,369,357	3,620,962	1,698,575	29,963
4. Houston, TX	2,160,821	1,953,631	1,630,553	1,595,138	1,233,535	596,163	44,633	2,396
5. Philadelphia, PA	1,547,607	1,517,550	1,585,577	1,688,210	1,949,996	2,071,605	1,293,697	121,376
6. Phoenix, AZ	1,488,750	1,321,045	983,403	789,704	584,303	106,818	5,544	...
7. San Antonio, TX	1,382,951	1,144,646	935,933	785,940	654,153	408,442	53,321	3,488
8. San Diego, CA	1,338,348	1,223,400	1,110,549	875,538	697,471	334,387	17,700	...
9. Dallas, TX	1,241,162	1,188,580	1,006,877	904,599	844,401	434,462	42,638	...
10. San Jose, CA	982,765	894,943	782,248	629,400	459,913	95,280	21,500	...
11. Austin, TX	842,592	656,562	465,622	345,890	253,539	132,459	22,258	629
12. Jacksonville, FL	836,507	735,617	635,230	540,920	504,265	204,517	28,429	1,045
13. Indianapolis, IN[1]	834,852	781,870	741,952	700,807	736,856	427,173	169,164	8,091
14. San Francisco, CA	825,863	776,733	723,959	678,974	715,674	775,357	342,782	34,776
15. Columbus, OH	809,798	711,470	632,910	565,021	540,025	375,901	125,560	17,882
16. Fort Worth, TX	777,992	534,694	447,619	385,164	393,455	278,778	26,688	...
17. Charlotte, NC	775,202	540,828	395,934	315,474	241,420	134,042	18,091	1,065
18. Detroit, MI	701,475	951,270	1,027,974	1,203,368	1,514,063	1,849,568	285,704	21,019
19. El Paso, TX	672,538	563,662	515,342	425,259	322,261	130,485	15,906	...
20. Memphis, TN	655,155	650,100	610,337	646,174	623,988	396,000	102,320	8,841
21. Boston, MA	636,479	589,141	574,283	562,994	641,071	801,444	560,892	136,881
22. Seattle, WA	634,535	563,374	516,259	493,846	530,831	467,591	80,671	...
23. Denver, CO	634,265	554,636	467,610	492,686	514,678	415,786	133,859	...
24. Washington, DC	632,323	572,059	606,900	638,432	756,668	802,178	278,718	40,001
25. Nashville-Davidson, TN[1]	624,496	545,524	510,784	455,651	426,029	174,307	80,865	10,165
26. Baltimore, MD	621,342	651,154	736,014	786,741	905,787	949,708	508,957	169,054
27. Louisville-Jefferson Co., KY[1]	605,110	256,231	269,063	298,694	361,706	369,129	204,731	43,194
28. Portland, OR	603,106	529,121	437,319	368,148	379,967	373,628	90,426	...
29. Oklahoma City, OK	599,199	506,132	444,719	404,014	368,164	243,504	10,037	...
30. Milwaukee, WI	598,916	596,974	628,088	636,297	717,372	637,392	285,315	20,061
31. Las Vegas, NV	596,424	478,434	258,295	164,674	125,787	24,624	...	...
32. Albuquerque, NM	555,417	448,607	384,736	332,920	244,501	96,815	6,238	...
33. Tucson, AZ	524,295	486,699	405,390	330,537	262,933	45,454	7,531	...
34. Fresno, CA	505,882	427,652	354,202	217,491	165,655	91,669	12,470	...
35. Sacramento, CA	475,516	407,018	369,365	275,741	257,105	137,572	29,282	6,820
36. Long Beach, CA	467,892	461,522	429,433	361,498	358,879	250,767	2,252	...
37. Kansas City, MO	464,310	441,545	435,146	448,028	507,330	456,622	163,752	...
38. Mesa, AZ	452,084	396,375	288,091	152,404	63,049	16,790	722	...
39. Virginia Beach, VA	447,021	425,257	393,069	262,199	172,106	5,390	...	...
40. Atlanta, GA	443,775	416,474	394,017	425,022	495,039	331,314	89,872	2,572
41. Colorado Springs, CO	431,834	360,890	281,140	215,105	135,517	45,472	21,085	...
42. Raleigh, NC	423,179	276,093	207,951	150,255	122,830	65,679	13,643	4,518
43. Omaha, NE	421,570	390,007	335,795	313,939	346,929	251,117	102,555	...
44. Miami, FL	413,892	362,470	358,548	346,681	334,859	249,276	1,681	...
45. Oakland, CA	400,740	399,484	372,242	339,337	361,561	384,575	66,960	...
46. Tulsa, OK	393,987	393,049	367,302	360,919	330,350	182,740	1,390	...
47. Minneapolis, MN	392,880	382,618	368,383	370,951	434,400	521,718	202,718	...
48. Cleveland, OH	390,928	478,403	505,616	573,822	750,879	914,808	381,768	17,034
49. Wichita, KS	385,577	344,284	304,011	279,838	276,554	168,279	24,671	...
50. Arlington, TX	375,600	332,969	261,721	160,113	90,229	7,692	1,079	...
51. New Orleans, LA	369,250	484,674	496,938	557,927	593,471	570,445	287,104	116,375
52. Bakersfield, CA	358,597	247,057	174,820	105,611	69,515	34,784	4,836	...
53. Tampa, FL	347,645	303,447	280,015	271,577	277,714	124,681	15,839	...
54. Honolulu, HI[2]	345,610	371,657	365,272	365,048	324,871	248,034	39,306	...
55. Anaheim, CA	343,248	328,014	266,406	219,494	166,408	14,556	1,456	...
56. Aurora, CO	339,030	276,393	222,103	158,588	74,974	11,421	202	...
57. Santa Ana, CA	330,920	337,977	293,742	204,023	155,710	45,533	4,933	...
58. St. Louis, MO	318,172	348,189	396,685	452,801	622,236	856,796	575,238	77,860
59. Riverside, CA	313,673	255,166	226,505	170,591	140,089	46,764	7,973	...
60. Corpus Christi, TX	312,195	277,454	257,453	232,134	204,525	108,287	4,703	...
61. Pittsburgh, PA	306,211	334,563	369,879	423,959	520,089	676,806	321,616	46,601
62. Lexington-Fayette, KY	305,489	260,512	225,366	204,165	108,137	55,534	26,369	8,159
63. Anchorage, AK	298,610	260,283	226,338	174,431	48,081	11,254	...	...
64. Stockton, CA	297,984	243,771	210,943	148,283	109,963	70,853	17,506	...
65. Cincinnati, OH	296,550	331,285	364,040	385,409	453,514	503,998	325,902	115,435
66. St. Paul, MN	290,770	287,151	272,235	270,230	309,866	311,349	163,065	1,112
67. Toledo, OH	284,012	313,619	332,943	354,635	383,062	303,616	131,822	3,829
68. Newark, NJ	277,727	273,546	275,221	329,248	381,930	438,776	246,070	38,894
69. Greensboro, NC	277,080	223,891	183,521	155,642	144,076	74,389	10,035	...
70. Plano, TX	272,068	222,030	128,713	72,331	17,872	2,126	1,304	...
71. Henderson, NV	265,679	175,381	64,942	23,376	16,400	5,717	...	...
72. Lincoln, NE	265,404	225,581	191,972	171,932	149,518	98,884	40,169	...
73. Buffalo, NY	259,384	292,648	328,123	357,870	462,768	580,132	352,387	42,261
74. Fort Wayne, IN	254,555	205,727	173,072	172,391	178,269	133,607	45,115	4,282
75. Jersey City, NJ	254,441	240,055	228,537	223,532	260,350	299,017	206,433	6,856
76. Chula Vista, CA	252,422	173,556	135,163	83,927	67,901	31,339	...	...
77. Orlando, FL	249,562	185,951	164,693	128,394	99,006	52,367	2,481	...
78. St. Petersburg, FL	246,541	248,232	238,629	238,647	216,159	96,738	1,575	...
79. Norfolk, VA	245,782	234,403	261,229	266,979	307,951	213,513	46,624	14,326
80. Chandler, AZ	245,628	176,581	89,862	29,673	13,763	3,799	...	...

Rank	City	2012	2000	1990	1980	1970	1950	1900	1850
81.	Laredo, TX	244,731	176,576	122,899	91,449	69,024	51,910	13,429	...
82.	Madison, WI	240,323	208,054	191,262	170,616	171,809	96,056	19,164	1,525
83.	Durham, NC	239,358	187,035	136,611	100,831	95,438	71,311	6,679	...
84.	Lubbock, TX	236,065	199,564	186,206	174,361	149,101	71,747	...	...
85.	Winston-Salem, NC	234,349	185,776	143,485	131,885	133,683	87,811	13,650	...
86.	Garland, TX	233,564	215,768	180,650	138,857	81,437	10,571	819	...
87.	Glendale, AZ	232,143	218,812	148,134	96,988	36,228	8,179	...	...
88.	Hialeah, FL	231,941	226,419	188,004	145,254	102,452	19,676	...	...
89.	Reno, NV	231,027	180,480	134,230	100,756	72,863	32,497	4,500	...
90.	Baton Rouge, LA	230,058	227,818	219,531	220,394	165,921	125,629	11,269	3,905
91.	Irvine, CA	229,985	143,072	110,330	62,134	...	...	...	...
92.	Chesapeake, VA	228,417	199,184	151,976	114,486	89,580	...	...	...
93.	Irving, TX	225,427	191,615	155,037	109,943	97,260	2,621	...	...
94.	Scottsdale, AZ	223,514	202,705	130,069	88,364	67,823	2,032	...	...
95.	North Las Vegas, NV	223,491	115,488	47,707	42,739	46,067	...	...	...
96.	Fremont, CA	221,986	203,413	173,339	131,945	100,869	...	...	...
97.	Gilbert, AZ	221,140	109,697	29,188	5,717	1,971	...	...	...
98.	San Bernardino, CA	213,295	185,401	164,164	117,490	104,251	63,058	6,150	...
99.	Boise City, ID	212,303	185,787	125,738	102,451	74,990	34,393	5,957	...
100.	Birmingham, AL	212,038	242,820	265,968	284,413	300,910	326,037	38,415	...

Note: 2012 population estimates are as of July 1. Decennial census figures for 1950-2010 are for Apr. 1; 1850 and 1900 are for June 1. Cities are incorporated places unless otherwise noted. (1) Consolidated city. Population figures are for the primary incorporated place only, i.e., exclude the populations of semi-independent incorporated places within the consolidated city. For years predating consolidation, city population figures are shown. (2) Census designated place. Although not incorporated, it is recognized as a statistical equivalent by the Census Bureau.

Largest U.S. Counties by Population, 2000, 2012

Source: Population Estimates Program, Decennial Census, U.S. Census Bureau, U.S. Dept. of Commerce
(ranked by 2012 population; 2012 estimates are as of July 1; 2000 decennial census figures are for Apr. 1)

Rank	County	2012	2000	% change	Rank	County	2012	2000	% change
1.	Los Angeles Co., CA..	9,962,789	9,519,338	4.7%	16.	Santa Clara Co., CA..	1,837,504	1,682,585	9.2%
2.	Cook Co., IL......	5,231,351	5,376,741	-2.7	17.	Broward Co., FL.....	1,815,137	1,623,018	11.8
3.	Harris Co., TX......	4,253,700	3,400,578	25.1	18.	Wayne Co., MI.....	1,792,365	2,061,162	-13.0
4.	Maricopa Co., AZ ...	3,942,169	3,072,149	28.3	19.	Bexar Co., TX......	1,785,704	1,392,931	28.2
5.	San Diego Co., CA ..	3,177,063	2,813,833	12.9	20.	New York Co., NY...	1,619,090	1,537,195	5.3
6.	Orange Co., CA	3,090,132	2,846,289	8.6	21.	Alameda Co., CA	1,554,720	1,443,741	7.7
7.	Miami-Dade Co., FL..	2,591,035	2,253,362	15.0	22.	Philadelphia Co., PA	1,547,607	1,517,550	2.0
8.	Kings Co., NY......	2,565,635	2,465,326	4.1	23.	Middlesex Co., MA...	1,537,215	1,465,396	4.9
9.	Dallas Co., TX......	2,453,843	2,218,899	10.6	24.	Suffolk Co., NY.....	1,499,273	1,419,369	5.6
10.	Queens Co., NY.....	2,272,771	2,229,379	1.9	25.	Sacramento Co., CA..	1,450,121	1,223,499	18.5
11.	Riverside Co., CA	2,268,783	1,545,387	46.8	26.	Bronx Co., NY.......	1,408,473	1,332,650	5.7
12.	San Bernardino Co.,				27.	Palm Beach Co., FL..	1,356,545	1,131,184	19.9
	CA..	2,081,313	1,709,434	21.8	28.	Nassau Co., NY	1,349,233	1,334,544	1.1
13.	King Co., WA	2,007,440	1,737,034	15.6	29.	Hillsborough Co., FL..	1,277,746	998,948	27.9
14.	Clark Co., NV	2,000,759	1,375,765	45.4	30.	Cuyahoga Co., OH ...	1,265,111	1,393,978	-9.2
15.	Tarrant Co., TX	1,880,153	1,446,219	30.0					

Note: The 10 smallest counties by estimated 2012 population: (1) Loving Co., TX (pop. 71); (2) Kalawao Co., HI (90); (3) King Co., TX (276); (4) Kenedy Co., TX (431); (5) Arthur Co., NE (486); (6) McPherson Co., NE (509); (7) Petroleum Co., MT (511); (8) Blaine Co., NE (514); (9) Loup Co., NE (589); and (10) Borden Co., TX (616).

Mobility of U.S. Population by Selected Characteristics, 2011-12

Source: Annual Social and Economic Supplement, Current Population Survey (CPS), U.S. Census Bureau, U.S. Dept. of Commerce
(numbers in thousands)

	Total movers	Location of new residence					Total movers	Location of new residence			
		Same county	Diff. county, same state	Diff. state	Abroad			Same county	Diff. county, same state	Diff. state	Abroad
Age						**Marital status**[1]					
1 to 14 years..........	8,358	5,691	1,420	1,040	205	Married, spouse present	9,467	5,472	1,954	1,691	350
15 years and older	28,131	17,801	5,363	4,018	948	Married, spouse absent	716	402	104	123	87
25 years and older	20,280	12,691	3,932	2,997	658	Widowed............	686	415	154	102	16
65 years and older	1,426	823	344	234	25	Divorced............	3,244	2,204	646	347	47
85 years and older	174	102	41	28	2	Separated...........	1,187	838	210	111	28
Income[1]						Never married........	12,830	8,471	2,296	1,643	421
Without income........	4,365	2,718	748	549	350	**Educational attainment**[2]					
Under $5,000 or less ...	2,532	1,576	451	365	140	Not a h.s. graduate	2,898	2,065	430	283	119
$5,000 to $9,999.......	2,711	1,719	487	425	80	High school graduate ...	5,765	3,860	1,130	665	110
$10,000 to $19,999.....	5,056	3,346	940	657	112	Some college or					
$20,000 to $29,999.....	4,235	2,883	765	516	71	associate degree	5,563	3,541	1,177	753	91
$30,000 to $39,999.....	2,994	1,925	626	397	47	Bachelor's degree......	4,041	2,267	815	749	208
$40,000 to $59,999.....	3,033	1,861	663	460	49	Prof. or grad. degree	2,014	958	379	546	131
$60,000 to $74,999.....	1,180	700	254	197	29	**Tenure**					
$75,000 to $99,999.....	905	471	194	209	30	In owner-occupied unit ..	9,701	5,940	2,203	1,337	221
$100,000 and over	1,120	603	234	242	41	In renter-occupied unit[3]..	26,787	17,553	4,580	3,723	933
						Total movers	**36,488**	**23,493**	**6,782**	**5,059**	**1,154**

Note: Total movers consists of persons ages 1 and older who moved to a new residence in the 12 months preceding the administering of the survey. Figures may not add up to totals due to rounding. (1) Ages 15 and older. (2) Ages 25 and older. (3) Includes units occupied without payment of cash rent.

U.S. Foreign-Born Population

Source: Annual Social and Economic Supplements, Current Population Surveys (CPS), U.S. Census Bureau, U.S. Dept. of Commerce

Percentage of Population That Is Foreign-Born, 1900-2011

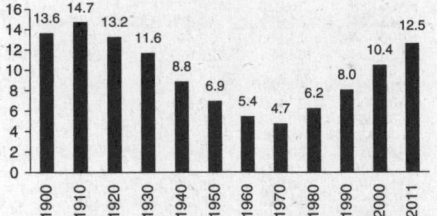

Foreign-Born Population by Region of Birth, 1995-2010

(numbers in thousands)

Region	2010[1] No.	%	2000	1995
Asia.............	10,126	26.9%	7,246	6,121
Under 18.....	760	27.7	657	767
Europe	4,509	12.0	4,355	3,937
Under 18.....	270	9.8	250	232
Latin America....	20,419	54.3	14,477	11,777
Under 18.....	1,453	52.9	1,684	1,481
Other[2].........	2,551	6.8	2,301	2,658
Under 18.....	265	9.6	245	275
All regions....	37,606	100.0	28,379	24,493
Under 18	2,748	100.0	2,837	2,726

(1) Figures are percentage of total foreign-born population or of all foreign-born under 18 years of age. (2) Including those born at sea.

U.S. Foreign-Born Population: Top Countries of Origin, 1880-2012

Source: American Community Survey (ACS), Decennial Censuses, U.S. Census Bureau, U.S. Dept. of Commerce

(numbers in thousands; percentage is of all foreign-born)

1880 Country	No.	%	1920 Country	No.	%	1960 Country	No.	%	2000 Country	No.	%	2012[4] Country	No.	%
Germany	1,967	29.4	Germany	1,686	12.1	Italy	1,257	12.9	Mexico	9,177	29.5	Mexico	11,563	28.3
Ireland	1,855	27.8	Italy	1,610	11.6	Germany	990	10.2	China[2]	1,519	4.9	China[2]	2,292	5.6
UK	918	13.7	U.S.S.R.	1,400	10.1	Canada	953	9.8	Philippines	1,369	4.4	India	1,968	4.8
Canada	717	10.7	Poland	1,140	8.2	UK	765	7.9	India	1,023	3.3	Philippines	1,868	4.6
Sweden	194	2.9	Canada	1,138	8.2	Poland	748	7.7	Vietnam	988	3.2	El Salvador	1,272	3.1
Norway	182	2.7	UK	1,135	8.2	U.S.S.R.	691	7.1	Cuba	873	2.8	Vietnam	1,259	3.1
France	107	1.6	Ireland	1,037	7.5	Mexico	576	5.9	Korea[3]	864	2.8	Cuba	1,114	2.7
China[1]	104	1.6	Sweden	626	4.5	Ireland	339	3.5	Canada	821	2.6	Korea[3]	1,085	2.7
Switzerland	89	1.3	Austria	576	4.1	Austria	305	3.1	El Salvador	817	2.6	Dominican Republic	957	2.3
Czech.	85	1.3	Mexico	486	3.5	Hungary	245	2.5	Germany	707	2.3	Guatemala	859	2.1
Total	**6,680**	**100.0**	**Total**	**13,921**	**100.0**	**Total**	**9,738**	**100.0**	**Total**	**31,108**	**100.0**	**Total**	**40,825**	**100.0**

(1) Includes Taiwan. (2) Includes Hong Kong and Taiwan. (3) Includes North and South Korea. (4) Data based on sample and subject to sampling variability.

Language Spoken at Home by the U.S. Population, 2012

Source: American Community Survey (ACS), U.S. Census Bureau, U.S. Dept. of Commerce

(number of speakers ages 5 and older, by major language group)

Language	Number (thous.)	% of tot. pop.	% English inability[1]	Language	Number (thous.)	% of tot. pop.	% English inability[1]
Total population	294,003.7	100.00%	8.5%	Other Slavic languages	318.3	0.11%	37.7%
Speak only English.........	232,126.5	78.95	NA	Other West Germanic langs. ...	316.1	0.11	23.7
Speak another language	61,877.2	21.05	40.5	Other Indo-European langs.	490.3	0.17	34.8
Spanish				Asian and Pacific Island languages			
Spanish or Spanish Creole....	38,325.2	13.04	42.1	Chinese	2,964.4	1.01	55.5
Other Indo-European languages				Hmong	228.4	0.08	38.1
Armenian	248.3	0.08	43.3	Japanese	446.8	0.15	42.8
French (incl. Patois, Cajun)....	1,350.2	0.46	20.7	Korean	1,131.1	0.38	54.8
French Creole..............	767.1	0.26	43.8	Laotian	156.7	0.05	46.7
German	1,063.2	0.36	16.3	Mon-Khmer, Cambodian......	211.3	0.07	52.4
Greek	306.6	0.10	24.7	Tagalog	1,672.4	0.57	31.6
Gujarati	388.2	0.13	35.7	Thai......................	149.1	0.05	52.9
Hindi.....................	687.9	0.23	20.3	Vietnamese................	1,425.8	0.48	58.5
Italian	701.1	0.24	25.6	Other Asian languages.......	946.4	0.32	31.3
Persian	407.6	0.14	36.0	Other Pacific Island langs.	420.0	0.14	36.4
Polish	574.0	0.20	39.4	All other languages			
Portuguese or Portuguese				African languages...........	948.1	0.32	32.5
Creole	681.9	0.23	37.1	Arabic....................	1,010.7	0.34	37.1
Russian...................	914.2	0.31	46.0	Hebrew	222.1	0.08	16.9
Scandinavian languages	124.0	0.04	9.6	Hungarian.................	78.8	0.03	29.2
Serbo-Croatian	276.1	0.09	38.1	Navajo...................	165.0	0.06	20.0
Urdu	398.4	0.14	28.3	Other Native North American			
Yiddish	157.6	0.05	33.7	languages...............	198.6	0.07	13.3
Other Indic languages	863.4	0.29	39.1	Other and unspecified langs. ...	141.7	0.05	39.3

NA = Not applicable/available. **Note:** Data based on sample and subject to sampling variability. (1) Speakers of other languages were asked how well they spoke English. Respondents who indicated that they spoke English less than very well are given as a percentage of their population. (For example, 43.3% of respondents who use Armenian at home do not speak English very well.)

Persons Granted Legal Permanent Resident Status by State of Residence, 2012
Source: Office of Immigration Statistics, U.S. Dept. of Homeland Security
(ranked by fiscal year 2012 number)

State/territory	Number	State/territory	Number	State/territory	Number	State/territory	Number
Total	1,031,631	Michigan	17,494	Kentucky	5,243	Idaho	2,428
California	196,622	North Carolina	17,487	Kansas	4,980	Delaware	2,208
New York	149,505	Ohio	13,948	Iowa	4,679	Alaska	1,612
Florida	103,047	Colorado	13,327	Oklahoma	4,646	Mississippi	1,583
Texas	95,557	Minnesota	12,999	Louisiana	4,454	South Dakota	1,521
New Jersey	50,790	Connecticut	12,237	Nebraska	4,384	Maine	1,497
Illinois	38,373	Nevada	10,343	South Carolina	3,924	Guam	1,430
Massachusetts	31,392	Tennessee	8,573	Alabama	3,873	North Dakota	1,144
Virginia	28,227	Indiana	8,359	Rhode Island	3,798	Vermont	877
Georgia	26,134	Oregon	7,791	New Mexico	3,714	West Virginia	779
Pennsylvania	25,032	Hawaii	6,764	Puerto Rico	3,106	Montana	503
Maryland	24,971	Missouri	6,635	District of Columbia	2,811	Wyoming	427
Washington	23,060	Wisconsin	6,049	Arkansas	2,795	Other[1]	1,667
Arizona	18,434	Utah	5,932	New Hampshire	2,466		

Note: Applicants for legal permanent resident (LPR) status, or "green cards," may already live in the U.S. They include refugees and asylees, temporary workers, foreign students, family members of U.S. citizens, and undocumented immigrants. Applicants from outside the U.S. enter on a visa and are granted LPR status upon admittance. (1) Includes other U.S. territories and armed forces posts.

Persons Granted Legal Permanent Resident Status by Top Areas of Residence, 2012
Source: Office of Immigration Statistics, U.S. Dept. of Homeland Security
(ranked by fiscal year 2012 number)

Core Based Statistical Area (CBSA)[1]	Number	% of total	Core Based Statistical Area (CBSA)[1]	Number	% of total
Total	1,031,631	100.0%	Austin-Round Rock-San Marcos, TX	5,897	0.6%
New York-Northern New Jersey-Long Island, NY-NJ-PA	179,011	17.4	San Antonio-New Braunfels, TX	5,712	0.6
Los Angeles-Long Beach-Santa Ana, CA	81,508	7.9	El Paso, TX	5,436	0.5
Miami-Fort Lauderdale-Pompano Beach, FL	66,153	6.4	Charlotte-Gastonia-Rock Hill, NC-SC	5,400	0.5
Washington-Arlington-Alexandria, DC-VA-MD-WV	38,518	3.7	Columbus, OH	5,129	0.5
Chicago-Joliet-Naperville, IL-IN-WI	34,898	3.4	Honolulu, HI	5,020	0.5
Houston-Sugar Land-Baytown, TX	31,738	3.1	Providence-New Bedford-Fall River, RI-MA	4,787	0.5
San Francisco-Oakland-Fremont, CA	29,583	2.9	Bridgeport-Stamford-Norwalk, CT	4,640	0.4
Dallas-Fort Worth-Arlington, TX	28,010	2.7	Indianapolis-Carmel, IN	4,336	0.4
Boston-Cambridge-Quincy, MA-NH	25,042	2.4	Nashville-Davidson-Murfreesboro-Franklin, TN	4,285	0.4
Atlanta-Sandy Springs-Marietta, GA	21,289	2.1	Hartford-West Hartford-East Hartford, CT	4,059	0.4
San Diego-Carlsbad-San Marcos, CA	18,893	1.8	Kansas City, MO-KS	3,838	0.4
Philadelphia-Camden Wilmington, PA-NJ-DE-MD	17,903	1.7	Salt Lake City, UT	3,811	0.4
Seattle-Tacoma-Bellevue, WA	17,644	1.7	Raleigh-Cary, NC	3,746	0.4
San Jose-Sunnyvale-Santa Clara, CA	16,937	1.6	McAllen-Edinburg-Mission, TX	3,617	0.4
Riverside-San Bernardino-Ontario, CA	14,547	1.4	St. Louis, MO-IL	3,408	0.3
Phoenix-Mesa-Glendale, AZ	12,805	1.2	Jacksonville, FL	3,365	0.3
Detroit-Warren-Livonia, MI	11,597	1.1	Worcester, MA	3,201	0.3
Minneapolis-St. Paul-Bloomington, MN-WI	10,673	1.0	Cleveland-Elyria-Mentor, OH	3,111	0.3
Orlando-Kissimmee-Sanford, FL	10,229	1.0	Buffalo-Niagara Falls, NY	2,985	0.3
Denver-Aurora-Broomfield, CO	8,967	0.9	Stockton, CA	2,930	0.3
Las Vegas-Paradise, NV	8,785	0.9	Tucson, AZ	2,895	0.3
Tampa-St. Petersburg-Clearwater, FL	8,700	0.8	Fresno, CA	2,894	0.3
Baltimore-Towson, MD	8,608	0.8	San Juan-Caguas-Guaynabo, PR	2,842	0.3
Sacramento-Arden-Arcade-Roseville, CA	7,975	0.8	Oxnard-Thousand Oaks-Ventura, CA	2,792	0.3
Portland-Vancouver-Hillsboro, OR-WA	6,352	0.6	Other CBSAs	201,570	19.5
			Non-CBSA or unknown	13,560	1.3

Note: Applicants for legal permanent resident (LPR) status, or "green cards," may already live in the U.S. They include refugees and asylees, temporary workers, foreign students, family members of U.S. citizens, and undocumented immigrants. Applicants from outside the U.S. enter on a visa and are granted LPR status upon admittance. (1) CBSAs refer collectively to metropolitan and micropolitan statistical areas. These areas are defined for federal statistical use by the Office of Management and Budget with technical assistance from the Census Bureau.

Unauthorized Immigrant Population in the U.S., 2000, 2011
Source: Office of Immigration Statistics, U.S. Dept. of Homeland Security
(ranked by 2011 est. population; as of Jan. of given year)

Country of Birth				State of Residence			
Country	Est. population 2011	2000	% change, 2000-11	State	Est. population 2011	2000	% change, 2000-11
All countries	11,510,000	8,460,000	36%	All states	11,510,000	8,460,000	36%
Mexico	6,800,000	4,680,000	45	California	2,830,000	2,510,000	12
El Salvador	660,000	430,000	55	Texas	1,790,000	1,090,000	64
Guatemala	520,000	290,000	82	Florida	740,000	800,000	-8
Honduras	380,000	160,000	132	New York	630,000	540,000	18
China	280,000	190,000	43	Illinois	550,000	440,000	26
Philippines	270,000	200,000	35	Georgia	440,000	220,000	95
India	240,000	120,000	94	New Jersey	420,000	350,000	19
Korea[1]	230,000	180,000	31	North Carolina	400,000	260,000	53
Ecuador	210,000	110,000	83	Arizona	360,000	330,000	9
Vietnam	170,000	160,000	10	Washington	260,000	170,000	51
Other countries	1,750,000	1,940,000	-10	Other states	3,100,000	1,750,000	77

Note: Unauthorized immigrant population estimates are made using the "residual" method. The estimated size of the legally resident foreign-born population (i.e., legal permanent residents, asylees, refugees, and nonimmigrants) is subtracted from the estimated size of the total foreign-born population. Numbers may not add up to totals because of rounding. (1) Includes North and South Korea.

U.S. Population by Age, Sex, and Household, 2012

Source: American Community Survey (ACS), U.S. Census Bureau, U.S. Dept. of Commerce

	Number	% of tot.		Number	% of tot.
Total population[1]	313,914,040	100.0%	Sex		
Age			Male	154,436,243	49.2%
Under 5 years	19,910,326	6.3	Female	159,477,797	50.8
5 to 14 years	41,258,565	13.1	Total households[2]	115,969,540	100.0%
15 to 17 years	12,541,519	4.0	Family households	76,509,262	66.0
15 to 44 years	126,812,583	40.4	2-person household	33,123,012	28.6
18 years and over	240,203,630	76.5	3-person household	17,319,404	14.9
Male	116,741,774	37.2	4-person household	14,800,235	12.8
Female	123,461,856	39.3	5-or-more person household	11,266,611	9.7
18 to 24 years	31,472,132	10.0	Married-couple family	55,754,450	48.1
25 to 34 years	42,100,846	13.4	Female HH, no husband present	15,176,600	13.1
35 to 44 years	40,698,086	13.0	Male HH, no wife present	5,578,212	4.8
45 to 54 years	44,204,952	14.1	Nonfamily households (total HHs)	39,460,278	34.0
55 to 64 years	38,587,137	12.3	HH living alone	32,256,217	27.8
65 years and over	43,140,477	13.7	HH 65 years and over	11,513,067	9.9
75 years and over	19,135,717	6.1	2-person household	5,903,672	5.1
85 years and over	5,833,401	1.9	3-or-more person household	1,300,389	1.1
Median age (years)	37.4	NA	Average household size	2.64	NA

NA = Not applicable. HH = Householder, or person in whose name a home is owned or rented. **Note:** Data based on sample and subject to sampling variability. (1) Includes population living in group quarters (institutional and noninstitutional, e.g., correctional facilities, university housing). (2) Number of households, not number of household members. Group quarters are not considered households.

Elderly U.S. Population, 1900-2050

Source: Decennial Censuses, Population Projections Program, U.S. Census Bureau, U.S. Dept. of Commerce
(numbers of resident population in thousands)

	65 and over		85 and over			65 and over		85 and over	
Year	Number	% tot. pop.	Number	% tot. pop.	Year	Number	% tot. pop.	Number	% tot. pop.
1900[1]	3,080	4.1%	122	0.2%	2010	40,268	13.0%	5,493	1.8%
1920[1]	4,933	4.7	210	0.2	2015	47,695	14.8	6,306	2.0
1940[1]	9,019	6.8	365	0.3	2020	55,969	16.8	6,693	2.0
1960	16,560	9.2	929	0.5	2030	72,774	20.3	8,946	2.5
1980	25,549	11.3	2,240	1.0	2040	79,719	21.0	14,115	3.7
2000	34,992	12.4	4,240	1.5	2050	83,739	21.0	17,978	4.5

Note: 1900 figures are for June 1; 1920 figures are for Jan. 1; and 1940-2010 figures are for Apr. 1. 2015-50 projections are as of July 1. (1) Excludes Alaska and Hawaii.

U.S. Population Projections by Age, 2015-50

Source: Population Projections Program, U.S. Census Bureau, U.S. Dept. of Commerce
(numbers of resident population in thousands)

	2015		2020		2030		2040		2050	
Age	No.	% distrib.	No.	% distrib.	No.	% distrib.	No.	% distrib.	No.	% distrib.
Total	321,363	100.0%	333,896	100.0%	358,471	100.0%	380,016	100.0%	399,803	100.0%
Under 5 years	21,051	6.6	21,808	6.5	22,252	6.2	23,004	6.1	24,115	6.0
5 to 13 years	36,772	11.4	37,769	11.3	40,366	11.3	41,190	10.8	42,951	10.7
14 to 17 years	16,695	5.2	16,582	5.0	17,730	4.9	18,427	4.8	18,852	4.7
18 to 24 years	30,983	9.6	30,028	9.0	30,605	8.5	33,199	8.7	33,967	8.5
25 to 44 years	84,327	26.2	88,501	26.5	93,878	26.2	96,078	25.3	101,609	25.4
45 to 64 years	83,839	26.1	83,238	24.9	80,865	22.6	88,398	23.3	94,570	23.7
65 years and over	47,695	14.8	55,969	16.8	72,774	20.3	79,719	21.0	83,739	20.9
85 years and over	6,306	2.0	6,693	2.0	8,946	2.5	14,115	3.7	17,978	4.5
100 years and over	78	0.0	106	0.0	168	0.0	230	0.1	442	0.1

Note: Projections are as of July 1 of given year. They are based on assumptions about future births, deaths, and net international migration. Numbers exclude overseas U.S. military personnel and civilian U.S. citizens living abroad.

Disability Status of U.S. Population by Age, 2012

Source: American Community Survey (ACS), U.S. Census Bureau, U.S. Dept. of Commerce
(numbers in thousands)

Disability type	Number	% of pop.	Disability type	Number	% of pop.
Total population	308,896	100.00%	Total population (5 and over)	288,989	100.00%
With a disability[1]	37,633	12.18	With a cognitive difficulty[2]	14,312	4.95
Under 5 years	168	0.05	5 to 17 years	2,154	0.75
Under 18 years	3,018	0.98	18 to 64 years	8,266	2.86
18 to 64 years	19,607	6.35	65 years and over	3,892	1.35
65 years and over	15,008	4.86	With an ambulatory difficulty[3]	20,025	6.93
With a hearing difficulty	10,565	3.42	5 to 17 years	345	0.12
Under 5 years	111	0.04	18 to 64 years	10,005	3.46
Under 18 years	451	0.15	65 years and over	9,675	3.35
18 to 64 years	3,964	1.28	With a self-care difficulty[4]	7,742	2.68
65 years and over	6,150	1.99	5 to 17 years	517	0.18
With a vision difficulty	6,693	2.17	18 to 64 years	3,596	1.24
Under 5 years	104	0.03	65 years and over	3,630	1.26
Under 18 years	534	0.17	Total population (18 and over)	235,319	100.00%
18 to 64 years	3,424	1.11	With an independent living difficulty[5]	13,611	5.78
65 years and over	2,734	0.89	18 to 64 years	6,984	2.97
			65 years and over	6,627	2.82

Note: Data based on sample and subject to sampling variability. Does not include military personnel and civilian institutionalized population (i.e., those under formal supervision or custody in a facility). (1) Defined by the Census Bureau as the "restriction in participation that results from a lack of fit between the individual's functional limitations and the characteristics of the physical and social environment." (2) Concentrating, remembering, or making decisions. (3) Walking or climbing stairs. (4) Dressing or bathing. (5) Doing errands alone, such as visiting a doctor's office or shopping.

Marital Status of the U.S. Population, 1960-2012

Source: Annual Social and Economic Supplements, Current Population Surveys (CPS), U.S. Census Bureau, U.S. Dept. of Commerce
(numbers in millions)

Marital status	Both sexes				Male				Female			
	2012	2000	1980	1960	2012	2000	1980	1960	2012	2000	1980	1960
Total..................	247.6	213.8	171.9	124.9	119.9	103.1	81.9	60.3	127.7	110.7	89.9	64.6
Married[1]..............	131.3	120.2	104.8	84.4	65.3	59.7	51.8	41.8	66.0	60.5	53.0	42.6
Never married.........	77.3	60.0	44.5	27.5	41.0	32.3	24.2	15.3	36.2	27.8	20.2	12.3
Divorced	24.9	19.9	9.9	2.8	10.7	8.6	3.9	1.1	14.2	11.3	6.0	1.7
Widowed	14.1	13.7	12.7	10.2	2.9	2.6	2.0	2.1	11.2	11.1	10.8	8.1
% of total or subset pops.												
Married[1]..............	53.0%	56.2%	61.0%	67.6%	54.5%	57.9%	63.2%	69.3%	51.7%	54.7%	58.9%	65.9%
Never married.........	31.2	28.1	25.9	22.0	34.2	31.3	29.6	25.3	28.4	25.1	22.5	19.0
Divorced	10.1	9.3	5.8	2.3	8.9	8.3	4.8	1.8	11.1	10.2	6.6	2.6
Widowed	5.7	6.4	7.4	8.1	2.4	2.5	2.4	3.5	8.8	10.0	12.0	12.5

Note: Total population for 1980, 2000, and 2012 is persons ages 15 and older and for 1960, persons ages 14 and older. Data is based on sample of occupied households in the civilian noninstitutional population. Figures may not add up to totals due to rounding.
(1) Comprises subcategories Married, spouse present; Married, spouse absent; and Separated.

Living Arrangements of Children in the U.S. by Parental Presence, 1970-2012

Source: Annual Social and Economic Supplements, Current Population Surveys (CPS), U.S. Census Bureau, U.S. Dept. of Commerce

Race and Hispanic origin/year	No. of children (thous.)	Both parents[3]	% of children (within selected population at left) living with—						
			Total[4]	Married spouse absent	Mother only—			Father only	Neither parent
					Divorced	Widowed	Never married		
All children									
2012	73,817	68%	24%	1%	7%	1%	11%	4%	4%
White alone[1]									
1970	58,791	90	8	3	3	2	Z	1	2
1980	52,242	83	14	4	7	2	1	2	2
1990	51,390	79	16	4	8	1	3	3	2
2000	56,455	75	17	NA	NA	NA	NA	4	3
2012	54,259	74	19	1	7	1	7	4	3
Black alone[1]									
1970	9,422	59	30	16	5	4	4	2	10
1980	9,375	42	44	16	11	4	13	28	12
1990	10,018	38	51	12	10	2	27	4	8
2000	11,412	38	49	NA	NA	NA	NA	4	9
2012	11,166	38	51	2	8	1	34	4	7
Hispanic[2]									
1970	4,006	78	NA	NA	NA	NA	NA	NA	NA
1980	5,459	75	20	8	6	2	4	2	4
1990	7,174	67	27	10	7	2	8	3	3
2000	11,613	65	25	NA	NA	NA	NA	4	5
2012	17,570	66	28	2	7	1	13	3	3

NA = Not available. Z = Less than 1%. Note: Children are defined as all persons under 18 years of age excluding those who are a family reference person or spouse. Data based on sample of occupied households in the civilian noninstitutional population. (1) One race only, not in combination with another race. (2) May be of any race. (3) Includes married and unmarried couples. (4) Includes children whose mothers are separated, a subcategory not shown in detail here.

Children in the U.S. by Parental Presence, 2012

Source: Annual Social and Economic Supplement, Current Population Survey (CPS), U.S. Census Bureau, U.S. Dept. of Commerce
(numbers in thousands)

	Number	% of total		Number	% of total
Total children	73,817	100.0%	Living with 1 parent.................	20,916	28.3%
			Mother only.......................	17,991	24.4
Living with 2 parents...............	50,267	68.1	Biological mother	17,756	24.1
Married parents	47,330	64.1	Father only	2,924	4.0
Unmarried parents	2,937	4.0	Biological father	2,810	3.8
Biological mother and father........	45,221	61.3	Living with no parents..............	2,634	3.6
Married parents	42,691	57.8	Grandparents only	1,454	2.0
Biological mother and stepfather	3,016	4.1	Other relatives only	592	0.8
Biological father and stepmother	919	1.2	Nonrelatives only	435	0.6
Biological mother and adoptive father	185	0.3	Other arrangement..............	153	0.2
Biological father and adoptive mother	34	0.0	Living with at least 1 biological parent ..	69,941	94.7
Adoptive mother and father	661	0.9	Living with at least 1 stepparent	4,287	5.8
Other[1]	231	0.3	Living with at least 1 adoptive parent ...	1,126	1.5

Note: Children are defined as all persons under 18 years of age excluding those who are a family reference person or spouse. Data based on sample of occupied households in the civilian noninstitutional population. (1) Includes children living with one adoptive parent and one stepparent, or two stepparents.

Unmarried-Partner Households in the U.S. by Sex of Partners, 2012

Source: American Community Survey (ACS), U.S. Census Bureau, U.S. Dept. of Commerce

Household	Number	% of total	% of cat.	Household	Number	% of total	% of cat.
Total households	115,969,540	100.0%	—	Female HH, female partner	333,646	0.3%	4.8%
Unmarried-partner households...	6,928,231	6.0	100.0%	Male HH, male partner	305,794	0.3	4.4
Male HH, female partner	3,207,495	2.8	46.3	All other households..........	109,041,309	94.0	100.0
Female HH, male partner	3,081,296	2.7	44.5				

HH = Householder, or person in whose name a home is owned or rented. Note: Data based on sample and subject to sampling variability. A household is defined as an occupied housing unit; the household population thus does not include people living in group quarters (e.g., correctional facilities, university housing).

U.S. Population by Sex, Race, Residence, and Median Age, 1790-2010

Source: Decennial Censuses, U.S. Census Bureau, U.S. Dept. of Commerce

(numbers in thousands, unless otherwise noted)

| Census date | SEX | | RACE[2] | | | | RESIDENCE | | MEDIAN AGE (years) | | |
| | Male | Female | White | Black | | Other | Urban[3] | Rural | All races | White[2] | Black[2] |
				Number	% tot. pop						
Conterminous U.S.[1]											
1790 (Aug. 2)	NA	NA	3,172	757	19.3%	NA	202	3,728	NA	NA	NA
1810 (Aug. 6)	NA	NA	5,862	1,378	19.0	NA	525	6,714	NA	16.0	NA
1820 (Aug. 7)	4,897	4,742	7,867	1,772	18.4	NA	693	8,945	16.7	16.6	17.2
1840 (June 1)	8,689	8,381	14,196	2,874	16.8	NA	1,845	15,218	17.8	17.9	17.6
1850 (June 1)	11,838	11,354	19,553	3,639	15.7	NA	3,574	19,617	18.9	19.2	17.4
1860 (June 1)	16,085	15,358	26,923	4,442	14.1	79	6,217	25,227	19.4	19.7	17.5
1870 (June 1)	19,494	19,065	33,589	4,880	12.7	89	9,902	28,656	20.2	20.4	18.5
1880 (June 1)	25,519	24,637	43,403	6,581	13.1	172	14,130	36,059	20.9	21.4	18.0
1890 (June 1)	32,237	30,711	55,101	7,489	11.9	358	22,106	40,874	22.0	22.5	17.8
1900 (June 1)	38,816	37,178	66,809	8,834	11.6	351	30,215	45,997	22.9	23.4	19.4
1910 (Apr. 15)	47,332	44,640	81,732	9,828	10.7	413	42,064	50,164	24.1	24.5	20.8
1920 (Jan. 1)	53,900	51,810	94,821	10,463	9.9	427	54,253	51,768	25.3	25.5	22.3
1930 (Apr. 1)	62,137	60,638	110,287	11,891	9.7	597	69,161	54,042	26.5	26.9	23.5
1940 (Apr. 1)	66,062	65,608	118,215	12,866	9.8	589	74,705	57,459	29.0	29.5	25.3
United States											
1950 (Apr. 1)	74,833	75,864	135,150	15,045	10.0	713	96,847	54,479	30.2	30.8	26.1
1960 (Apr. 1)	88,331	90,992	158,832	18,872	10.5	1,620	125,269	54,054	29.5	30.3	23.5
1970 (Apr. 1)	98,926	104,309	178,098	22,581	11.1	2,557	149,647	53,565	28.1	28.9	22.4
1980 (Apr. 1)	110,053	116,493	194,713	26,683	11.8	5,150	167,051	59,495	30.0	30.9	24.9
1990 (Apr. 1)	121,284	127,507	208,741	30,517	12.3	9,533	187,053	61,656	32.8	33.7	27.9
2000 (Apr. 1)	138,056	143,368	195,577	35,705	12.7	13,716	222,361	59,061	35.3	38.6	30.0
2010 (Apr. 1)	151,781	156,964	196,818	37,686	12.2	18,147	249,253	59,492	37.2	42.0	32.4

NA = Not available. (1) Excludes Alaska and Hawaii. (2) New race categories were introduced in the 2000 census. Race data for 2000 and on are for one race alone, not in combination with one or more other races. "White" does not include people who reported being of Hispanic origin. "Other" comprises Asians, Native Hawaiians and other Pacific Islanders, and American Indians and Alaska Natives. Because of these changes, race data from 2000 on are not comparable to figures from previous years. (3) The Census Bureau's definition of "urban" has changed over time. Figures for 2000 and 2010 include residents of so-called urban areas (50,000 or more inhabitants) and urban clusters (at least 2,500 but fewer than 50,000 inhabitants).

U.S. Population by Race and Hispanic Origin, 2000-10

Source: Decennial Censuses, U.S. Census Bureau, U.S. Dept. of Commerce

| | 2010 | | 2000 | | % change, 2000-10[2] | |
	One race alone	One or more races[1]	One race alone	One or more races[1]	One race alone	One or more races
Total population	299,736,465	308,745,538	274,595,678	281,421,906	9.2%	9.7%
Race						
White........................	223,553,265	231,040,398	211,460,626	216,930,975	5.7	6.5
Black or African American...........	38,929,319	42,020,743	34,658,190	36,419,434	12.3	15.4
American Indian and Alaska Native ...	2,932,248	5,220,579	2,475,956	4,119,301	18.4	26.7
Asian...........................	14,674,252	17,320,856	10,242,998	11,898,828	43.3	45.6
Native Hawaiian and other Pac. Isl. ...	540,013	1,225,195	398,835	874,414	35.4	40.1
Some other race	19,107,368	21,748,084	15,359,073	18,521,486	24.4	17.4
Hispanic origin and race						
Hispanic or Latino, any race	47,435,002	50,477,594	33,081,736	35,305,818	43.4	43.0
Not Hispanic or Latino..............	252,301,463	258,267,944	241,513,942	246,116,088	4.5	4.9
White	196,817,552	201,856,108	194,552,774	198,177,900	1.2	1.9
Black or African American	37,685,848	40,123,525	33,947,837	35,383,751	11.0	13.4
American Indian and Alaska Native..	2,247,098	4,029,675	2,068,883	3,444,700	8.6	17.0
Asian	14,465,124	16,722,710	10,123,169	11,579,494	42.9	44.4
Native Hawaiian and other Pac. Isl.	481,576	1,014,888	353,509	748,149	36.2	35.7
Some other race	604,265	1,033,866	467,770	1,770,645	29.2	–41.6

(1) Alone or in combination with one or more of the other races listed. Numbers may not add up to totals because of individuals reporting more than one race. (2) Columns 5 and 6 provide, respectively, a minimum-maximum range for the percent change in the population of each race.

U.S. Population by Ancestry Reported, 2012

Source: American Community Survey (ACS), U.S. Census Bureau, U.S. Dept. of Commerce

(numbers in thousands; ranked by number)

Ancestry	Number	% of total	Ancestry	Number	% of total	Ancestry	Number	% of total
Total population	313,914	100.0%	Norwegian	4,399	1.4%	French Canadian	1,992	0.6%
German	46,875	14.9	Dutch	4,351	1.4	Arab[4]	1,799	0.6
Irish	34,149	10.9	Swedish	3,981	1.3	Welsh	1,780	0.6
English	25,262	8.0	European	3,947	1.3	Czech	1,508	0.5
American	23,567	7.5	Scotch-Irish[1]	3,118	1.0	Other ancestry not		
Italian	17,343	5.5	Sub-Saharan African[2]	3,009	1.0	shown here	143,407	45.7
Polish	9,501	3.0	Russian	2,896	0.9	Unclassified or not		
French (excl. Basque)	8,475	2.7	West Indian (excl.			reported	38,369	12.2
Scottish	5,380	1.7	Hispanic groups)[3]	2,758	0.9			

Note: Data based on sample and subject to sampling variability. Because respondents could self-identify with more than one ancestry, numbers do not add up to total. (1) People who reported Irish-Scotch ancestry are classified under "Other ancestry not shown here." (2) Incl. Cape Verdean, Ethiopian, Ghanian, Kenyan, Liberian, Nigerian, Senegalese, Sierra Leonean, Somalian, South African, Sudanese, Ugandan, Zimbabwean, African, and other sub-Saharan African. (3) Incl. Bahamian, Barbadian, Belizean, Bermudan, British or Dutch West Indian, Haitian, Jamaican, Trinidadian and Tobagonian, U.S. Virgin Islander, West Indian, and other West Indian. (4) Incl. Egyptian, Iraqi, Jordanian, Lebanese, Moroccan, Palestinian, Syrian, Arab, and other Arab.

U.S. Race and Minority Group Populations by Age, 2012

Source: American Community Survey (ACS), U.S. Census Bureau, U.S. Dept. of Commerce

Race and origin/age	Number	% of race	Race and origin/age	Number	% of race
White (not Hispanic or Latino)	197,243,423	100.0%	Native Hawaiian and other		
Under 5 years	9,967,942	5.1	Pacific Islander	543,198	100.0
Under 18 years	38,761,155	19.7	Under 5 years	44,153	8.1
18 to 64 years	124,314,846	63.0	Under 18 years	152,676	28.1
65 years and over	34,167,422	17.3	18 to 64 years	357,300	65.8
85 years and over	4,887,633	2.5	65 years and over	33,222	6.1
Black or African American	39,623,138	100.0	85 years and over	1,515	0.3
Under 5 years	2,829,618	7.1	Some other race	14,562,678	100.0
Under 18 years	10,540,154	26.6	Under 5 years	1,302,316	8.9
18 to 64 years	25,361,139	64.0	Under 18 years	4,582,259	31.5
65 years and over	3,721,845	9.4	18 to 64 years	9,344,744	64.2
85 years and over	408,206	1.0	65 years and over	635,675	4.4
Asian	15,555,530	100.0	85 years and over	57,393	0.4
Under 5 years	889,274	5.7	Two or more races	9,073,614	100.0
Under 18 years	3,319,395	21.3	Under 5 years	1,381,490	15.2
18 to 64 years	10,635,960	68.4	Under 18 years	4,223,640	46.5
65 years and over	1,600,175	10.3	18 to 64 years	4,410,065	48.6
85 years and over	169,661	1.1	65 years and over	439,019	4.8
American Indian and Alaska Native	2,563,505	100.0	85 years and over	39,539	0.4
Under 5 years	190,031	7.4	Hispanic or Latino	52,961,017	100.0
Under 18 years	722,413	28.2	Under 5 years	5,135,206	9.7
18 to 64 years	1,629,326	63.6	Under 18 years	17,574,025	33.2
65 years and over	211,766	8.3	18 to 64 years	32,251,724	60.9
85 years and over	18,947	0.7	65 years and over	3,135,268	5.9
			85 years and over	324,104	0.6

Note: Data based on sample and subject to sampling variability. Categories are for one race alone, not in combination with any other race, unless otherwise noted.

Educational Attainment of the U.S. Population, 2012

Source: American Community Survey (ACS), U.S. Census Bureau, U.S. Dept. of Commerce

(numbers in thousands; population 25 years of age and over)

Race and origin/highest ed. completed	Number	% of race	Race and origin/highest ed. completed	Number	% of race
White (not Hispanic or Latino)	140,902	100.0%	Native Hawaiian and other Pacific		
Less than high school diploma	11,992	8.5	Islander	324	100.0%
High school graduate[1]	40,482	28.7	Less than high school diploma	47	14.6
Some college or associate's degree	42,627	30.3	High school graduate[1]	115	35.6
Bachelor's degree or higher	45,800	32.5	Some college or associate's degree	114	35.0
Black or African American	24,281	100.0	Bachelor's degree or higher	48	14.8
Less than high school diploma	4,084	16.8	Some other race	8,095	100.0
High school graduate[1]	7,602	31.3	Less than high school diploma	3,362	41.5
Some college or associate's degree	8,047	33.1	High school graduate[1]	2,207	27.3
Bachelor's degree or higher	4,547	18.7	Some college or associate's degree	1,700	21.0
Asian	10,661	100.0	Bachelor's degree or higher	826	10.2
Less than high school diploma	1,529	14.3	Two or more races	3,684	100.0
High school graduate[1]	1,645	15.4	Less than high school diploma	550	14.9
Some college or associate's degree	2,098	19.7	High school graduate[1]	859	23.3
Bachelor's degree or higher	5,389	50.5	Some college or associate's degree	1,286	34.9
American Indian and Alaska Native	1,533	100.0	Bachelor's degree or higher	989	26.8
Less than high school diploma	325	21.2	Hispanic or Latino	28,911	100.0
High school graduate[1]	476	31.1	Less than high school diploma	10,414	36.0
Some college or associate's degree	525	34.2	High school graduate[1]	7,706	26.7
Bachelor's degree or higher	207	13.5	Some college or associate's degree	6,800	23.5
			Bachelor's degree or higher	3,991	13.8

Note: Data based on sample and subject to sampling variability. Categories are for one race alone, not in combination with any other race, unless otherwise noted. (1) Incl. equivalency.

U.S. Population Growth by Race and Hispanic Origin, 1970-2030
Source: Decennial Censuses, Population Projections Program, U.S. Census Bureau, U.S. Dept. of Commerce
(numbers in millions)

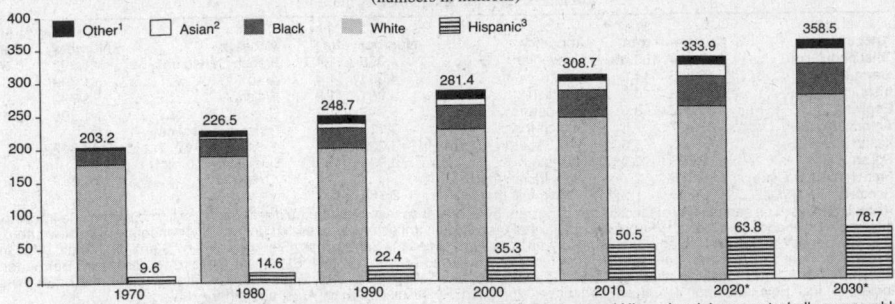

*Projected. **Note:** Because of changes in census questions and methods, data on race and Hispanic origin are not wholly comparable over time. (1) Includes American Indians and Alaska Natives, and other races. For 2000 and on, this category also includes Native Hawaiians and other Pacific Islanders as well as persons reporting two or more races. (2) Figures for 1970-90 include Pacific Islanders. (3) May be of any race.

U.S. Race and Minority Group Percentages by State, 2010
Source: Decennial Census, U.S. Census Bureau, U.S. Dept. of Commerce
(percentage of state or country's total population)

State	One race alone[1] (%)						Two or more races[1] (%)	Hispanic or Latino, any race (%)
	White	Black or African American	Asian	American Indian and Alaska Native	Native Hawaiian and other Pacific Islander	Some other race		
Alabama	67.0%	26.0%	1.1%	0.5%	0.04%	0.08%	1.3%	3.9%
Alaska	64.1	3.1	5.3	14.4	1.02	0.16	6.4	5.5
Arizona	57.8	3.7	2.7	4.0	0.17	0.13	1.8	29.6
Arkansas	74.5	15.3	1.2	0.7	0.19	0.07	1.6	6.4
California	40.1	5.8	12.8	0.4	0.35	0.23	2.6	37.6
Colorado	70.0	3.8	2.7	0.6	0.11	0.15	2.0	20.7
Connecticut	71.2	9.4	3.8	0.2	0.03	0.34	1.7	13.4
Delaware	65.3	20.8	3.2	0.3	0.03	0.17	2.0	8.2
District of Columbia	34.8	50.0	3.5	0.2	0.04	0.24	2.1	9.1
Florida	57.9	15.2	2.4	0.3	0.05	0.26	1.5	22.5
Georgia	55.9	30.0	3.2	0.2	0.05	0.20	1.6	8.8
Hawaii	22.7	1.5	37.7	0.2	9.43	0.14	19.4	8.9
Idaho	84.0	0.6	1.2	1.1	0.14	0.10	1.7	11.2
Illinois	63.7	14.3	4.5	0.1	0.02	0.12	1.4	15.8
Indiana	81.5	9.0	1.6	0.2	0.03	0.13	1.5	6.0
Iowa	88.7	2.9	1.7	0.3	0.06	0.07	1.4	5.0
Kansas	78.2	5.7	2.3	0.8	0.07	0.10	2.3	10.5
Kentucky	86.3	7.7	1.1	0.2	0.05	0.11	1.5	3.1
Louisiana	60.3	31.8	1.5	0.6	0.03	0.15	1.3	4.2
Maine	94.4	1.1	1.0	0.6	0.02	0.08	1.4	1.3
Maryland	54.7	29.0	5.5	0.2	0.04	0.21	2.2	8.2
Massachusetts	76.1	6.0	5.3	0.2	0.02	0.94	1.9	9.6
Michigan	76.6	14.0	2.4	0.6	0.02	0.10	1.9	4.4
Minnesota	83.1	5.1	4.0	1.0	0.04	0.11	1.9	4.7
Mississippi	58.0	36.9	0.9	0.5	0.03	0.06	0.9	2.7
Missouri	81.0	11.5	1.6	0.4	0.10	0.09	1.8	3.5
Montana	87.8	0.4	0.6	6.1	0.06	0.05	2.2	2.9
Nebraska	82.1	4.4	1.7	0.8	0.05	0.12	1.6	9.2
Nevada	54.1	7.7	7.1	0.9	0.57	0.18	2.9	26.5
New Hampshire	92.3	1.0	2.1	0.2	0.02	0.14	1.4	2.8
New Jersey	59.3	12.8	8.2	0.1	0.02	0.31	1.5	17.7
New Mexico	40.5	1.7	1.3	8.5	0.06	0.18	1.4	46.3
New York	58.3	14.4	7.3	0.3	0.03	0.42	1.7	17.6
North Carolina	65.3	21.2	2.2	1.1	0.06	0.16	1.6	8.4
North Dakota	88.9	1.1	1.0	5.3	0.04	0.05	1.5	2.0
Ohio	81.1	12.0	1.7	0.2	0.03	0.13	1.8	3.1
Oklahoma	68.7	7.3	1.7	8.2	0.11	0.08	5.1	8.9
Oregon	78.5	1.7	3.6	1.1	0.33	0.14	2.9	11.7
Pennsylvania	79.5	10.4	2.7	0.1	0.02	0.13	1.4	5.7
Rhode Island	76.4	4.9	2.8	0.4	0.03	0.84	2.2	12.4
South Carolina	64.1	27.7	1.3	0.4	0.05	0.12	1.4	5.1
South Dakota	84.7	1.2	0.9	8.5	0.04	0.06	1.8	2.7
Tennessee	75.6	16.5	1.4	0.3	0.04	0.10	1.4	4.6
Texas	45.3	11.5	3.8	0.3	0.07	0.14	1.3	37.6
Utah	80.4	0.9	2.0	1.0	0.87	0.13	1.8	13.0
Vermont	94.3	0.9	1.3	0.3	0.02	0.09	1.6	1.5
Virginia	64.8	19.0	5.5	0.3	0.06	0.19	2.3	7.9
Washington	72.5	3.4	7.1	1.3	0.58	0.18	3.7	11.2
West Virginia	93.2	3.4	0.7	0.2	0.02	0.06	1.3	1.2
Wisconsin	83.3	6.2	2.3	0.9	0.03	0.07	1.4	5.9
Wyoming	85.9	0.8	0.8	2.1	0.06	0.08	1.5	8.9
United States	**63.7**	**12.2**	**4.7**	**0.7**	**0.16**	**0.20**	**1.9**	**16.3**

(1) Not Hispanic or Latino.

American Indian and Alaska Native Population by State, 2010

Source: Decennial Census, U.S. Census Bureau, U.S. Dept. of Commerce
(ranked by one race alone)

Rank	State	One race alone[1]	More than one race[2]	Rank	State	One race alone[1]	More than one race[2]
1.	California	362,801	360,424	27.	Kansas	28,150	30,980
2.	Oklahoma	321,687	161,073	28.	Missouri	27,376	45,000
3.	Arizona	296,529	56,857	29.	Pennsylvania	26,843	54,249
4.	New Mexico	193,222	26,290	30.	Ohio	25,292	64,832
5.	Texas	170,972	144,292	31.	Arkansas	22,248	25,340
6.	North Carolina	122,110	61,972	32.	Idaho	21,441	14,944
7.	New York	106,906	114,152	33.	Maryland	20,420	38,237
8.	Alaska	104,871	33,441	34.	Tennessee	19,994	34,880
9.	Washington	103,869	95,129	35.	South Carolina	19,524	22,647
10.	South Dakota	71,817	10,256	36.	Massachusetts	18,850	31,855
11.	Florida	71,458	91,104	37.	Indiana	18,462	31,276
12.	Montana	62,555	16,046	38.	Nebraska	18,427	11,389
13.	Michigan	62,007	77,088	39.	Mississippi	15,030	10,880
14.	Minnesota	60,916	40,984	40.	Wyoming	13,336	5,260
15.	Colorado	56,010	51,822	41.	Connecticut	11,256	19,884
16.	Wisconsin	54,526	31,702	42.	Iowa	11,084	13,427
17.	Oregon	53,203	56,020	43.	Kentucky	10,120	21,235
18.	Illinois	43,963	57,488	44.	Maine	8,568	9,914
19.	North Dakota	36,591	6,405	45.	Rhode Island	6,058	8,336
20.	Utah	32,927	17,137	46.	Delaware	4,181	5,718
21.	Georgia	32,151	51,873	47.	Hawaii	4,164	29,306
22.	Nevada	32,062	23,883	48.	West Virginia	3,787	9,527
23.	Louisiana	30,579	24,500	49.	New Hampshire	3,150	7,374
24.	Virginia	29,225	51,699	50.	Vermont	2,207	5,172
25.	New Jersey	29,026	41,690	51.	District of Columbia	2,079	4,442
26.	Alabama	28,218	28,900		United States	2,932,248	2,288,331

(1) Respondents who self-identified as American Indian and Alaska Native (AIAN) alone. (2) Respondents who self-identified as AIAN in combination with one or more other races.

American Indian and Alaska Native Population by Selected Tribal Groupings, 2010

Source: Decennial Census, U.S. Census Bureau, U.S. Dept. of Commerce
(ranked by American Indian and Alaska Native [AIAN] alone, one tribal grouping alone)

Tribal grouping	AIAN alone — One tribal grouping alone[1]	AIAN alone — One or more tribal groupings[2]	AIAN alone or in combination — One or more tribal groupings[3]	Tribal grouping	AIAN alone — One tribal grouping alone[1]	AIAN alone — One or more tribal groupings[2]	AIAN alone or in combination — One or more tribal groupings[3]
Total	2,879,638	2,932,248	5,220,579	Crow	10,332	10,860	15,203
AIAN tribes, not specified	693,709	693,709	1,545,963	Kiowa	9,437	10,355	13,787
Amer. Ind. tribes, specified	1,935,363	2,032,133	3,397,251	Paiute	9,340	10,205	13,767
Navajo	286,731	295,016	332,129	Osage	8,938	10,063	18,576
Cherokee	284,247	300,463	819,105	Yakama	8,786	9,096	11,527
Mexican Amer. Ind.	121,221	123,550	175,494	Menominee	8,374	8,627	11,133
Chippewa	112,757	115,402	170,742	Houma	8,169	8,240	10,768
Sioux	112,176	116,477	170,110	Colville	8,114	8,314	10,549
Choctaw	103,910	110,308	195,764	Arapaho	8,014	8,402	10,861
Apache	63,193	69,694	111,810	Shoshone	7,852	8,462	13,002
Lumbee	62,306	62,957	73,691	Delaware	7,843	8,215	18,264
Pueblo	49,695	52,026	62,540	Yuman	7,727	8,278	10,089
Creek	48,352	52,948	88,332	Ute	7,435	8,220	11,491
Iroquois	40,570	42,461	81,002	Ottawa	7,272	8,048	13,033
Chickasaw	27,973	30,206	52,278	Canadian and French Amer. Ind.	6,433	7,051	14,822
Blackfeet	27,279	31,798	105,304	Cree	2,211	2,950	7,983
Pima	22,040	23,205	26,655	All other tribes	270,141	282,747	429,629
Yaqui	21,679	23,195	32,595	Amer. Ind. tribes, not specified	131,943	132,060	234,320
S. Amer. Ind.	20,901	21,380	47,233	AK Native tribes, specified	98,892	103,086	138,850
Potawatomi	20,412	20,874	33,771	Yup'ik	28,927	29,618	33,889
Tohono O'Odham	19,522	20,247	23,478	Inupiat[4]	24,859	25,736	33,360
Central Amer. Ind.	15,882	16,454	27,844	Alaskan Athabascan	15,623	16,427	22,484
Puget Sound Salish	14,320	14,535	20,260	Tlingit-Haida	15,256	16,115	26,080
Seminole	14,080	16,448	31,971	Aleut	11,920	12,643	19,282
Spanish Amer. Ind.	13,460	13,758	19,951	Tsimshian	2,307	2,547	3,755
Hopi	12,580	14,634	18,327	AK Native tribes, not specified	19,731	19,904	29,933
Comanche	12,284	13,471	23,330				
Cheyenne	11,375	12,493	19,051				

Note: This table measures the number of responses, not respondents. Respondents who self-identified with multiple tribal groupings are counted more than once. A tribal grouping refers to combined individual tribes (e.g., Fort Sill Apache and San Carlos Apache as Apache or King Salmon Tribe and Native Village of Kanatak as Aleut). (1) For example, Navajo or Alaskan Athabascan. (2) As in footnote 1 or in combination with other tribal groupings (e.g., Yakama and Aleut). (3) As in footnotes 1 or 2 or in combination with another race (e.g., Apache, Navajo, and white; or Inupiat, white, and black). (4) Eskimo in previous censuses.

Populations, ZIP, and Area Codes for U.S. Places of 10,000 or More

Source: Decennial Census and Population Estimates Program, U.S. Census Bureau, U.S. Dept. of Commerce; NeuStar Inc.

The following is a list of places of 10,000 or more inhabitants in 2012 according to the U.S. Census Bureau's Population Estimates Program and the results of the 2010 census.

Census designated places (CDPs) are marked with a (c). CDP boundaries are defined by the Census Bureau and may change over time. Unless an exception is noted, the Census Bureau does not include CDPs in its estimates program. This list includes **places that are incorporated** under the laws of their respective states as cities, boroughs, towns, and villages. **Townships are not included.** This list also includes, in *italics*, **minor civil divisions (MCDs)** for Connecticut, Maine, Massachusetts, New Hampshire, Rhode Island, and Vermont. MCDs are not incorporated and not automatically recognized as CDPs, but are often the primary political or administrative divisions of a county.

An asterisk (*) denotes that the ZIP code given is for general delivery; named streets and/or P.O. boxes within the community may use a different one; consult www.usps.com. Telephone **area codes** are given in parentheses. New phone numbers may be assigned a different area code from that of existing phone numbers in the area. These areas of overlay are noted. When two or more area codes are listed for one place, consult local operators for assistance. Area codes based on latest information as of Sept. 2013. — = Not available.

Alabama

Area code (938) overlays area code (256).

ZIP	Place	Area code	2010 population	2012 estimate
*35007	Alabaster	(205)	30,352	30,991
*35950	Albertville	(256)	21,160	21,516
*35010	Alexander City	(256)	14,875	14,728
36201	Anniston	(256)	23,106	22,749
*35611	Athens	(256)	21,897	23,469
36502	Atmore	(251)	10,194	10,121
*36830	Auburn	(334)	53,380	56,908
*35020	Bessemer	(205)	27,456	27,289
*35201	Birmingham	(205)	212,237	212,038
35040	Calera	(205)	11,620	12,472
*35215	Center Point	(205)	16,921	16,961
35043	Chelsea	(205)	10,183	10,801
35055	Cullman	(256)	14,775	14,864
36526	Daphne	(251)	21,570	22,845
*35601	Decatur	(256)	55,683	55,996
*36301	Dothan	(334)	65,496	67,382
36330	Enterprise	(334)	26,562	27,789
*36027	Eufaula	(334)	13,137	12,943
35064	Fairfield	(205)	11,117	11,029
*36532	Fairhope	(251)	15,326	16,479
35630	Florence	(256)	39,319	39,447
*36535	Foley	(251)	14,618	15,402
35214	Forestdale (c)	(205)	10,162	—
*35967	Fort Payne	(256)	14,012	14,104
*35901	Gadsden	(256)	36,856	36,674
35071	Gardendale	(205)	13,893	13,849
36542	Gulf Shores	(251)	9,741	10,118
35640	Hartselle	(256)	14,255	14,489
35080	Helena	(205)	16,793	17,209
*35209	Homewood	(205)	25,167	25,262
*35244	Hoover	(205)	81,619	83,412
*35023	Hueytown	(205)	16,105	15,991
*35801	Huntsville	(256)	180,105	183,739
35210	Irondale	(205)	12,349	12,426
36265	Jacksonville	(256)	12,548	12,430
*35501	Jasper	(205)	14,352	14,235
35094	Leeds	(205)	11,773	11,885
*35758	Madison	(256)	42,938	44,972
36054	Millbrook	(334)	14,640	14,952
*36601	Mobile	(251)	195,111	194,822
*36104	Montgomery	(334)	205,764	205,293
35004	Moody	(205)	11,726	12,150
*35223	Mountain Brook	(205)	20,413	20,369
*35661	Muscle Shoals	(256)	13,146	13,371
*35476	Northport	(205)	23,330	24,088
*36801	Opelika	(334)	26,477	27,825
36203	Oxford	(256)	21,348	21,275
*36360	Ozark	(334)	14,907	14,901
35124	Pelham	(205)	21,352	22,012
*35125	Pell City	(205)	12,695	13,129
*36867	Phenix City	(334)	32,822	36,185
35127	Pleasant Grove	(205)	10,110	10,371
*36067	Prattville	(334)	33,960	34,873
36610	Prichard	(251)	22,659	22,416
36206	Saks (c)	(256)	10,744	—
36571	Saraland	(251)	13,405	13,490
*35768	Scottsboro	(256)	14,770	14,786
*36701	Selma	(334)	20,756	20,251
35150	Sylacauga	(256)	12,749	12,761
*35160	Talladega	(256)	15,676	15,591
36619	Tillman's Corner (c)	(251)	17,398	—
*36081	Troy	(334)	18,033	18,264
35173	Trussville	(205)	19,933	20,178
*35401	Tuscaloosa	(205)	90,468	93,357
*35216	Vestavia Hills	(205)	34,033	34,090

Alaska

Area code 907 applies to the entire state.

ZIP	Place	2010 population	2012 estimate
*99501	Anchorage	291,826	298,610
*99711	Badger (c)	19,482	—
*99708	College (c)	12,964	—
*99701	Fairbanks	31,535	32,312
*99801	Juneau	31,275	32,556
99654	Knik-Fairview (c)	14,923	—

Arizona

ZIP	Place	Area code	2010 population	2012 estimate
85086	Anthem (c)	(623)	21,700	—
*85120	Apache Junction	(480)	35,840	36,613
*85123	Arizona City (c)	(520)	10,475	—
*85323	Avondale	(623)	76,238	78,256
*85326	Buckeye	(623)	50,876	54,542
*86442	Bullhead City	(928)	39,540	39,571
86322	Camp Verde	(928)	10,873	10,925
*85122	Casa Grande	(520)	48,571	49,974
85704	Casas Adobes (c)	(520)	66,795	—
85718	Catalina Foothills (c)	(520)	50,796	—
*85225	Chandler	(480)	236,123	245,628
86323	Chino Valley	(928)	10,817	10,839
85128	Coolidge	(520)	11,825	11,882
86326	Cottonwood	(928)	11,265	11,279
*85607	Douglas	(520)	17,378	17,270
85746	Drexel Heights (c)	(520)	27,749	—
85335	El Mirage	(623)	31,797	32,574
85131	Eloy	(520)	16,631	17,448
*86004	Flagstaff	(928)	65,870	67,468
85132	Florence	(520)	25,536	26,754
85705	Flowing Wells (c)	(520)	16,419	—
*86427	Fort Mohave (c)	(928)	14,364	—
*85367	Fortuna Foothills (c)	(928)	26,265	—
*85268	Fountain Hills	(480)	22,489	23,031
*85299	Gilbert	(480)	208,453	221,140
*85302	Glendale	(623)	226,721	232,143
85118	Gold Canyon (c)	(480)	10,159	—
*85338	Goodyear	(623)	65,275	69,648
*85622	Green Valley (c)	(520)	21,391	—
86401	Kingman	(928)	28,068	28,336
*86403	Lake Havasu City	(928)	52,527	52,819
*85653	Marana	(520)	34,961	36,756
*85139	Maricopa	(520)	43,482	44,803
*85201	Mesa	(480)	439,041	452,084
86401	New Kingman-Butler (c)	(928)	12,134	—
*85087	New River (c)	(623)	14,952	—
*85621	Nogales	(520)	20,837	20,751
*85737	Oro Valley	(520)	41,011	41,388
85253	Paradise Valley	(480)	12,820	13,154
*85541	Payson	(928)	15,301	15,215
*85345	Peoria	(623)	154,065	159,789
*85034	Phoenix	(480)/(602)/(623)	1,445,632	1,488,750
*86301	Prescott	(928)	39,843	40,308
*86314	Prescott Valley	(928)	38,822	39,114
*85142	Queen Creek	(480)	26,361	27,963
85648	Rio Rico (c)	(520)	18,962	—
*85629	Sahuarita	(520)	25,259	26,289
85349	San Luis	(928)	25,505	26,418
*85142	San Tan Valley (c)	(480)	81,321	—
*85251	Scottsdale	(480)	217,385	223,514
86336	Sedona	(928)	10,031	10,037
*85901	Show Low	(928)	10,660	10,724
*85635	Sierra Vista	(520)	43,888	46,351
85650	Sierra Vista Southeast (c)	(520)	14,797	—
85350	Somerton	(928)	14,287	14,854
*85351	Sun City (c)	(623)	37,499	—
*85375	Sun City West (c)	(623)	24,535	—
85248	Sun Lakes (c)	(480)	13,975	—
*85374	Surprise	(623)	117,517	121,287
85749	Tanque Verde (c)	(520)	16,901	—
*85282	Tempe	(480)	161,719	166,842
*85726	Tucson	(520)	520,116	524,295
85735	Tucson Estates (c)	(520)	12,192	—
85641	Vail (c)	(520)	10,208	—
86326	Verde Village (c)	(928)	11,605	—
*85364	Yuma	(928)	93,064	95,429

Arkansas

ZIP	Place	Area code	2010 population	2012 estimate
*71923	Arkadelphia	(870)	10,714	10,796
*72501	Batesville	(870)	10,248	10,427
*72714	Bella Vista	(479)	26,461	27,347
*72015	Benton	(501)	30,681	32,117
72712	Bentonville	(479)	35,301	38,284

ZIP	Place	Area code	2010 population	2012 estimate
*72315	Blytheville	(870)	15,620	15,308
*72022	Bryant	(501)	16,688	18,686
72023	Cabot	(501)	23,776	24,502
*71701	Camden	(870)	12,183	11,836
*72719	Centerton	(479)	9,515	10,170
*72032	Conway	(501)	58,908	62,939
*71730	El Dorado	(870)	18,884	18,491
*72701	Fayetteville	(479)	73,580	76,899
*72335	Forrest City	(870)	15,371	15,220
*72901	Fort Smith	(479)	86,209	87,443
*72601	Harrison	(870)	12,943	13,163
72342	Helena-West Helena	(870)	12,282	11,748
*71801	Hope	(870)	10,095	10,036
*71901	Hot Springs	(501)	35,193	35,478
*71909	Hot Springs Village (c)	(501)	12,807	—
*72076	Jacksonville	(501)	28,364	28,657
*72401	Jonesboro	(870)	67,263	70,187
*72201	Little Rock	(501)	193,524	196,537
*71753	Magnolia	(870)	11,577	11,713
*72104	Malvern	(501)	10,318	10,859
72364	Marion	(870)	12,345	12,288
*72113	Maumelle	(501)	17,163	17,577
*72653	Mountain Home	(870)	12,448	12,298
*72114	North Little Rock	(501)	62,304	64,633
*72450	Paragould	(870)	26,113	27,016
*71601	Pine Bluff	(870)	49,083	47,035
*72756	Rogers	(479)	55,964	58,895
*72801	Russellville	(479)	27,920	28,616
*72143	Searcy	(501)	22,858	23,525
*72120	Sherwood	(501)	29,523	29,824
72761	Siloam Springs	(479)	15,039	15,680
*72764	Springdale	(479)	69,797	73,123
71854	Texarkana	(870)	29,919	30,049
*72956	Van Buren	(479)	22,791	23,006
*72301	West Memphis	(870)	26,245	25,686

California

Area code (442) overlays area code (760). Area code (669) overlays area code (408). Area code (707) overlays area code (714). Area code (747) overlays area code (818).

ZIP	Place	Area code	2010 population	2012 estimate
92301	Adelanto	(760)	31,765	31,239
*01376	Agoura Hills	(818)	20,330	20,657
*94501	Alameda	(510)	73,812	75,041
94507	Alamo (c)	(925)	14,570	—
94706	Albany	(510)	18,539	18,969
*91802	Alhambra	(626)	83,089	84,322
92656	Aliso Viejo	(949)	47,823	49,493
*91901	Alpine (c) (San Diego Co.)	(619)	14,236	—
*91003	Altadena (c)	(626)	42,777	—
95127	Alum Rock (c)	(408)	15,536	—
94589	American Canyon	(707)	19,454	19,933
*92803	Anaheim	(714)	336,265	343,248
96007	Anderson	(530)	9,932	10,058
95843	Antelope (c)	(916)	45,770	—
*94509	Antioch	(925)	102,372	105,508
*92307	Apple Valley	(760)	69,135	70,700
*91006	Arcadia	(626)	56,364	57,497
*95521	Arcata	(707)	17,231	17,726
95825	Arden-Arcade (c)	(916)	92,186	—
*93420	Arroyo Grande	(805)	17,252	17,543
*90701	Artesia	(562)	16,522	16,682
93203	Arvin	(661)	19,304	20,127
94577	Ashland (c)	(510)	21,925	—
*93422	Atascadero	(805)	28,310	28,814
95301	Atwater	(209)	28,168	28,742
*95603	Auburn	(530)	13,330	13,676
93204	Avenal	(559)	15,505	14,846
91706	Avocado Heights (c)	(626)	15,411	—
91702	Azusa	(626)	46,361	47,407
*93302	Bakersfield	(661)	347,483	358,597
91706	Baldwin Park	(626)	75,390	76,419
92220	Banning	(951)	29,603	30,310
*92312	Barstow	(760)	22,639	23,033
94565	Bay Point (c)	(925)	21,349	—
92223	Beaumont	(951)	36,877	39,455
*90201	Bell	(323)	35,477	35,820
*90202	Bell Gardens	(213)/(323)/(562)	42,072	42,757
*90706	Bellflower	(562)	76,616	77,356
94002	Belmont	(650)	25,835	26,491
94510	Benicia	(707)	26,997	27,426
*94704	Berkeley	(510)	112,580	115,403
*90210	Beverly Hills	(213)/(310)/(323)	34,109	34,622
*92314	Big Bear City (c)	(909)	12,304	—
92316	Bloomington (c)	(951)	23,851	—
*92225	Blythe	(760)	20,817	20,590
*91902	Bonita (c)	(619)	12,538	—
92021	Bostonia (c)	(619)	15,379	—
92227	Brawley	(760)	24,953	25,567
*92822	Brea	(562)/(714)	39,282	40,330
*94513	Brentwood	(925)	51,481	53,673

ZIP	Place	Area code	2010 population	2012 estimate
*90622	Buena Park	(714)	80,530	82,155
*91510	Burbank (Los Angeles Co.)	(818)	103,340	104,391
*94010	Burlingame	(650)	28,806	29,660
*91372	Calabasas	(818)	23,058	23,954
*92231	Calexico	(760)	38,572	39,310
*93504	California City	(760)	14,120	13,364
*93010	Camarillo	(805)	65,201	65,968
95682	Cameron Park (c)	(530)	18,228	—
92058	Camp Pendleton South (c)	(760)	10,616	—
*95008	Campbell	(408)	39,349	40,272
92587	Canyon Lake	(951)	10,561	10,861
95010	Capitola	(831)	9,918	10,012
*92008	Carlsbad	(760)	105,328	109,318
*95608	Carmichael (c)	(916)	61,762	—
*93013	Carpinteria	(805)	13,040	13,231
*90745	Carson	(310)	91,714	93,002
92077	Casa de Oro-Mt. Helix (c)	(619)	18,762	—
*91384	Castaic (c)	(661)	19,015	—
*94546	Castro Valley (c)	(510)	61,388	—
*92235	Cathedral City	(760)	51,200	52,655
95307	Ceres	(209)	45,417	45,719
90703	Cerritos	(562)	49,041	49,629
94541	Cherryland (c)	(510)	14,728	—
*95926	Chico	(530)	86,187	87,714
*91708	Chino	(909)	77,983	80,164
91709	Chino Hills	(909)	74,799	76,457
93610	Chowchilla	(559)	18,720	17,925
*91910	Chula Vista	(619)	243,916	252,422
91702	Citrus (c)	(626)	10,866	—
*95621	Citrus Heights	(916)	83,301	84,870
91711	Claremont	(909)	34,926	35,457
94517	Clayton	(925)	10,897	11,318
95422	Clearlake	(707)	15,250	15,029
*93612	Clovis	(559)	95,631	98,632
92236	Coachella	(760)	40,704	42,734
93210	Coalinga	(559)	13,380	16,789
*92324	Colton	(909)	52,154	53,123
90040	Commerce	(323)	12,823	12,954
90221	Compton	(310)	96,455	97,559
*94520	Concord	(925)	122,067	124,711
*93212	Corcoran	(559)	24,813	23,551
92877	Corona	(951)	152,374	158,391
*92118	Coronado	(619)	18,912	23,391
*92628	Costa Mesa	(714)/(949)	109,960	111,918
92679	Coto de Caza (c)	(949)	14,866	—
*91722	Covina	(626)	47,796	48,346
*92325	Crestline (c)	(909)	10,770	—
90201	Cudahy	(323)	23,805	24,021
*90230	Culver City	(310)	38,883	39,313
*95014	Cupertino	(408)	58,302	60,009
90630	Cypress	(714)	47,802	48,779
*94015	Daly City	(415)/(650)	101,123	103,690
*92629	Dana Point	(949)	33,351	34,048
*94526	Danville	(925)	42,039	43,088
95616	Davis	(530)	65,622	65,993
90250	Del Aire (c)	(310)/(323)	10,001	—
*93215	Delano	(661)	53,041	52,426
95315	Delhi (c)	(209)	10,755	—
*92240	Desert Hot Springs	(760)	25,938	27,745
91765	Diamond Bar	(909)	55,544	56,363
*95619	Diamond Springs (c)	(530)	11,037	—
93618	Dinuba	(559)	21,453	22,955
*94514	Discovery Bay (c)	(925)	13,352	—
95620	Dixon	(707)	18,351	18,660
90239	Downey	(562)	111,772	112,873
*91009	Duarte	(626)	21,321	21,657
94568	Dublin	(925)	46,036	48,775
92343	East Hemet (c)	(951)	17,418	—
90022	East Los Angeles (c)	(323)	126,496	—
94303	East Palo Alto	(650)	28,155	28,867
90221	East Rancho Dominguez (c)	(310)/(323)	15,135	—
91775	East San Gabriel (c)	(626)	14,874	—
*91752	Eastvale[1]	(909)/(951)	53,668	54,635
*92020	El Cajon	(619)	99,478	101,435
*92244	El Centro	(760)	42,598	43,107
94530	El Cerrito	(510)	23,549	24,048
95762	El Dorado Hills (c)	(916)	42,108	—
*91734	El Monte	(626)	113,475	115,111
*93446	El Paso de Robles (Paso Robles)	(805)	29,793	30,556
90245	El Segundo	(310)	16,654	16,849
*94803	El Sobrante (c) (Contra Costa Co.)	(510)	12,669	—
92503	El Sobrante (c) (Riverside Co.)	(714)/(909)	12,723	—
*95624	Elk Grove	(916)	153,015	159,038
*94608	Emeryville	(510)	10,080	10,335
*92024	Encinitas	(760)	59,518	60,994
*92025	Escondido	(760)	143,911	147,575
*95501	Eureka	(707)	27,191	26,961
93221	Exeter	(559)	10,334	10,466
95628	Fair Oaks (c)	(916)	30,912	—
94533	Fairfield	(707)	105,321	107,684

ZIP	Place	Area code	2010 population	2012 estimate
94541	Fairview (c)	(510)	10,003	—
*92028	Fallbrook (c)	(760)	30,534	—
93223	Farmersville	(559)	10,588	10,740
*93015	Fillmore	(805)	15,002	15,162
90001	Florence-Graham (c)	(323)	63,387	—
95828	Florin (c)	(916)	47,513	—
95630	Folsom	(916)	72,203	73,384
*92334	Fontana	(909)	196,069	201,812
95841	Foothill Farms (c)	(916)	33,121	—
95540	Fortuna	(707)	11,926	11,836
94404	Foster City	(650)	30,567	32,129
*92728	Fountain Valley	(714)	55,313	56,464
*94537	Fremont	(510)	214,089	221,986
92563	French Valley (c)	(951)	23,067	—
*93706	Fresno	(559)	494,665	505,882
*92834	Fullerton	(714)	135,161	138,574
95632	Galt	(209)	23,647	24,337
95215	Garden Acres (c)	(209)	10,648	—
*92842	Garden Grove	(714)	170,883	174,389
*90247	Gardena	(310)	58,829	59,490
*95020	Gilroy	(408)	48,821	50,660
92509	Glen Avon (c)	(951)	20,199	—
*91209	Glendale	(818)	191,719	194,478
*91741	Glendora	(626)	50,073	50,719
*93116	Goleta	(805)	29,888	30,289
92324	Grand Terrace	(951)	12,040	12,290
95746	Granite Bay (c)	(916)	20,402	—
*95945	Grass Valley	(530)	12,860	12,808
93927	Greenfield	(831)	16,330	16,793
93433	Grover Beach	(805)	13,156	13,342
91745	Hacienda Heights (c)	(626)	54,038	—
94019	Half Moon Bay	(650)	11,324	11,653
*93230	Hanford	(559)	53,967	54,324
90716	Hawaiian Gardens	(562)	14,254	14,393
*90250	Hawthorne	(310)/(323)	84,293	85,681
*94544	Hayward	(510)	144,186	149,392
95448	Healdsburg	(707)	11,254	11,440
92546	Hemet	(951)	78,657	81,046
94547	Hercules	(510)	24,060	24,660
90254	Hermosa Beach	(310)	19,506	19,773
*92340	Hesperia	(760)	90,173	92,062
92346	Highland	(909)	53,104	54,154
94010	Hillsborough	(650)	10,825	11,144
*95023	Hollister	(831)	34,928	36,096
92879	Home Gardens (c)	(909)	11,570	—
*92647	Huntington Beach	(714)	189,992	194,708
90255	Huntington Park	(323)	58,114	58,673
92251	Imperial	(760)	14,758	15,665
*91932	Imperial Beach	(619)	26,324	26,845
*92201	Indio	(760)	76,036	79,302
*90301	Inglewood	(310)/(323)	109,673	111,182
*92619	Irvine	(714)/(949)	212,375	229,985
93117	Isla Vista (c)	(805)	23,096	—
91752	Jurupa Valley[1]	(951)	95,004	97,426
93630	Kerman	(559)	13,544	14,306
93930	King City	(831)	12,874	13,169
93631	Kingsburg	(559)	11,382	11,588
*91011	La Cañada Flintridge	(818)	20,246	20,493
*91214	La Crescenta-Montrose (c)	(818)	19,653	—
*90061	La Habra	(562)/(949)	60,239	61,392
*91941	La Mesa	(619)	57,065	58,160
*90638	La Mirada	(562)/(714)	48,527	49,001
90623	La Palma	(562)/(714)	15,568	15,860
91977	La Presa (c)	(619)	34,169	—
*91747	La Puente	(626)	39,816	40,272
*92253	La Quinta	(760)	37,467	38,783
95401	La Riviera (c)	(916)	10,802	—
91750	La Verne	(909)	31,063	31,348
92694	Ladera Ranch (c)	(949)	22,980	—
94549	Lafayette	(925)	23,893	24,589
*92652	Laguna Beach	(949)	22,723	23,176
*92654	Laguna Hills	(949)	30,344	30,951
*92607	Laguna Niguel	(949)	62,979	64,452
*92654	Laguna Woods	(949)	16,192	16,493
92352	Lake Arrowhead (c)	(909)	12,424	—
*92531	Lake Elsinore	(951)	51,821	55,288
92630	Lake Forest	(949)	77,264	78,853
*93535	Lake Los Angeles (c)	(661)	12,328	—
92530	Lakeland Village (c)	(909)/(951)	11,541	—
92040	Lakeside (c)	(619)	20,648	—
*90714	Lakewood	(562)	80,048	80,833
93241	Lamont (c)	(661)	15,120	—
*93359	Lancaster	(661)	156,633	159,055
*94939	Larkspur	(415)	11,926	12,099
95330	Lathrop	(209)	18,023	19,141
*90260	Lawndale	(310)	32,769	33,122
*91945	Lemon Grove	(619)	25,320	25,961
95824	Lemon Hill (c)	(916)	13,729	—
93245	Lemoore	(559)	24,531	24,738
90304	Lennox (c)	(310)	22,753	—
95648	Lincoln	(916)	42,819	44,390
95901	Linda (c)	(530)	17,773	—
93247	Lindsay	(559)	11,768	12,833
95062	Live Oak (c) (Santa Cruz Co.)	(831)	17,158	—
*94550	Livermore	(925)	80,968	83,547
95334	Livingston	(209)	13,058	13,538
*95240	Lodi	(209)	62,134	63,301
92354	Loma Linda	(951)	23,261	23,600
90717	Lomita	(310)	20,256	20,533
*93436	Lompoc	(805)	42,434	43,260
*90801	Long Beach	(310)/(562)	462,257	467,892
*90720	Los Alamitos	(562)/(949)	11,449	11,668
94022	Los Altos	(650)	28,976	29,929
*90086	Los Angeles	(213)/(310)/(323)	3,792,621	3,857,799
93635	Los Banos	(209)	35,972	36,747
*95030	Los Gatos	(408)	29,413	30,141
*93402	Los Osos (c)	(805)	14,276	—
90262	Lynwood	(213)/(310)/(323)	69,772	70,709
*93638	Madera	(559)	61,416	62,624
95954	Magalia (c)	(530)	11,310	—
*90265	Malibu	(310)	12,645	12,832
*90266	Manhattan Beach	(310)	35,135	35,738
95336	Manteca	(209)	67,096	71,067
93933	Marina	(831)	19,718	20,253
94553	Martinez	(925)	35,824	36,673
95901	Marysville	(530)	12,072	12,152
90270	Maywood	(323)	27,395	27,659
93250	McFarland	(661)	12,707	12,393
95521	McKinleyville (c)	(707)	15,177	—
92570	Mead Valley (c)	(951)	18,510	—
93640	Mendota	(559)	11,014	11,398
92586	Menifee	(951)	77,519	81,474
*94025	Menlo Park	(650)	32,026	32,881
*95340	Merced	(209)	78,958	80,793
94941	Mill Valley	(415)	13,903	14,159
94030	Millbrae	(650)	21,532	22,078
*95035	Milpitas	(408)	66,790	68,800
91752	Mira Loma (c)	(951)	21,930	—
*92690	Mission Viejo	(949)	93,305	95,290
*95350	Modesto	(209)	201,165	203,547
*91017	Monrovia	(626)	36,590	36,955
91763	Montclair	(909)	36,664	37,528
90640	Montebello	(323)	62,500	63,305
*93940	Monterey	(831)	27,810	29,003
*91754	Monterey Park	(323)/(626)/(818)	60,269	60,937
*93021	Moorpark	(805)	34,421	35,088
*94556	Moraga	(925)	16,016	16,511
*92552	Moreno Valley	(951)	193,365	199,552
95037	Morgan Hill	(408)	37,882	39,420
*93442	Morro Bay	(805)	10,234	10,370
94041	Mountain View	(650)	74,066	76,621
*92564	Murrieta	(951)	103,466	106,810
92407	Muscoy (c)	(909)	10,644	—
*94558	Napa	(707)	76,915	78,340
*91950	National City	(619)	58,582	59,387
94560	Newark	(510)	42,573	43,621
95360	Newman	(209)	10,224	10,576
92658	Newport Beach	(949)	85,186	87,068
93444	Nipomo (c)	(805)	16,714	—
91760	Norco	(951)	27,063	27,393
95603	North Auburn (c)	(530)	13,022	—
94025	North Fair Oaks (c)	(650)	14,687	—
95660	North Highlands (c)	(916)	42,694	—
92705	North Tustin (c)	(714)/(949)	24,917	—
*90650	Norwalk	(562)	105,549	106,278
*94947	Novato	(415)	51,904	53,301
*91377	Oak Park (c)	(805)/(818)	13,811	—
95361	Oakdale	(209)	20,675	21,194
*94617	Oakland	(510)	390,724	400,740
94561	Oakley	(925)	35,432	37,278
*92056	Oceanside	(760)	167,086	171,293
93308	Oildale (c)	(661)	32,684	—
95961	Olivehurst (c)	(530)	13,656	—
91761	Ontario	(909)	163,924	167,211
*92863	Orange	(714)	136,416	139,419
95662	Orangevale (c)	(916)	33,960	—
*93457	Orcutt (c)	(805)	28,905	—
94563	Orinda	(925)	17,643	18,342
*95965	Oroville	(530)	15,546	15,566
*93030	Oxnard	(805)	197,899	201,555
93950	Pacific Grove	(831)	15,041	15,407
94044	Pacifica	(650)	37,234	38,189
*92260	Palm Desert	(760)	48,445	50,013
*92262	Palm Springs	(760)	44,552	45,907
*93590	Palmdale	(661)	152,750	155,650
*94303	Palo Alto	(650)	64,403	66,363
90274	Palos Verdes Estates	(310)	13,438	13,606
95969	Paradise	(530)	26,218	26,216
90723	Paramount	(562)	54,098	54,680
95823	Parkway (c)	(916)	14,670	—
93648	Parlier	(559)	14,494	14,777
*91109	Pasadena	(323)/(626)/(818)	137,122	138,547
	Paso Robles. See El Paso de Robles			
95363	Patterson	(209)	20,413	20,659
92509	Pedley (c)	(951)	12,672	—

ZIP	Place	Area code	2010 population	2012 estimate
*92572	Perris	(951)	68,386	71,326
*94952	Petaluma	(707)	57,941	58,921
*92371	Phelan (c)	(760)	14,304	—
*90660	Pico Rivera	(562)	62,942	63,522
*94611	Piedmont	(510)	10,667	10,893
94564	Pinole	(510)	18,390	18,729
94565	Pittsburg	(925)	63,264	65,664
*92871	Placentia	(714)	50,533	51,673
*95667	Placerville	(530)	10,389	10,348
94523	Pleasant Hill	(925)	33,152	33,831
*94566	Pleasanton	(925)	70,285	72,338
*91769	Pomona	(909)	149,058	150,812
*93041	Port Hueneme	(805)	21,723	21,856
*93257	Porterville	(559)	54,165	55,023
*92064	Poway	(858)	47,811	49,071
93907	Prunedale (c)	(831)	17,560	—
*93536	Quartz Hill (c)	(661)	10,912	—
92065	Ramona (c)	(760)	20,292	—
*95670	Rancho Cordova	(916)	64,776	66,997
*91729	Rancho Cucamonga	(909)	165,269	170,746
92270	Rancho Mirage	(760)	17,218	17,667
90275	Rancho Palos Verdes	(310)	41,643	42,323
91941	Rancho San Diego (c)	(619)	21,208	—
92688	Rancho Santa Margarita	(949)	47,853	48,879
96080	Red Bluff	(530)	14,076	14,157
*96049	Redding	(530)	89,861	90,755
*92373	Redlands	(909)	68,747	69,916
*90277	Redondo Beach	(310)	66,748	67,693
*94063	Redwood City	(650)	76,815	79,009
93654	Reedley	(559)	24,194	24,842
*92377	Rialto	(909)	99,171	101,740
*94802	Richmond	(510)	103,701	106,516
*93556	Ridgecrest	(760)	27,616	28,325
95673	Rio Linda (c)	(916)	15,106	—
95366	Ripon	(209)	14,297	14,686
95367	Riverbank	(209)	22,678	23,298
*92502	Riverside	(951)	303,871	313,673
*95677	Rocklin	(916)	56,974	59,030
*94928	Rohnert Park	(707)	40,971	41,232
93560	Rosamond (c)	(661)	18,150	—
93314	Rosedale (c)	(661)	14,058	—
*91770	Rosemead	(626)	53,764	54,393
95826	Rosemont (c)	(916)	22,681	—
*95678	Roseville	(916)	118,788	124,519
90720	Rossmoor (c)	(714)	10,244	—
91748	Rowland Heights (c)	(626)	48,993	—
92519	Rubidoux (c)	(951)	34,280	—
*95814	Sacramento	(916)	466,488	475,516
95368	Salida (c)	(209)	13,722	—
*93907	Salinas	(831)	150,441	154,484
*94960	San Anselmo	(415)	12,336	12,491
*92401	San Bernardino	(909)	209,924	213,295
*94066	San Bruno	(650)	41,114	42,165
*93001	San Buenaventura (Ventura)	(805)	106,433	107,734
*94070	San Carlos	(650)	28,406	29,092
92674	San Clemente	(949)	63,522	64,882
*92138	San Diego	(619)/(858)	1,307,402	1,338,348
92065	San Diego Country Estates (c)	(760)	10,109	—
91773	San Dimas	(909)	33,371	33,737
*91341	San Fernando	(818)	23,645	23,880
*94142	San Francisco	(415)	805,235	825,863
*91778	San Gabriel	(626)	39,718	40,150
*92581	San Jacinto	(951)	44,199	45,384
*95113	San Jose	(408)	945,942	982,765
*92690	San Juan Capistrano	(949)	34,593	35,360
*94577	San Leandro	(510)	84,950	86,890
94580	San Lorenzo (c)	(510)	23,452	—
*93401	San Luis Obispo	(805)	45,119	45,878
*92069	San Marcos	(760)	83,781	86,752
*91108	San Marino	(626)	13,147	13,269
*94402	San Mateo	(650)	97,207	99,670
94806	San Pablo	(510)	29,139	29,720
*94915	San Rafael	(415)	57,713	58,502
94583	San Ramon	(925)	72,148	73,927
93657	Sanger	(559)	24,270	24,567
*92711	Santa Ana	(714)/(949)	324,528	330,920
*93102	Santa Barbara	(805)	88,410	89,639
*95050	Santa Clara	(408)	116,468	119,311
*91380	Santa Clarita	(661)	176,320	179,013
95060	Santa Cruz	(831)	59,946	62,041
90670	Santa Fe Springs	(562)	16,223	16,767
*93454	Santa Maria	(805)	99,553	101,459
*90401	Santa Monica	(310)	89,736	91,812
93060	Santa Paula	(805)	29,321	29,963
*95402	Santa Rosa	(707)	167,815	170,685
*92071	Santee	(619)	53,413	55,343
*95070	Saratoga	(408)	29,926	30,677
*95066	Scotts Valley	(831)	11,580	11,670
90740	Seal Beach	(562)	24,168	24,664
93955	Seaside	(831)	33,025	33,878
93662	Selma	(559)	23,219	23,778
93263	Shafter	(661)	16,988	17,117
*96019	Shasta Lake	(916)	10,164	10,213
*91025	Sierra Madre	(626)	10,917	11,016
*90806	Signal Hill	(562)	11,016	11,185
*93065	Simi Valley	(805)	124,237	125,793
92075	Solana Beach	(858)	12,867	13,154
93960	Soledad	(831)	25,738	26,478
95476	Sonoma	(707)	10,648	10,849
91733	South El Monte	(626)	20,116	20,296
90280	South Gate	(323)/(562)	94,396	95,304
*96151	South Lake Tahoe	(530)	21,403	21,286
*91030	S. Pasadena	(213)/(323)/(626)/(818)	25,619	25,860
*94080	South San Francisco	(650)	63,632	65,547
91744	South San Jose Hills (c)	(626)	20,551	—
90605	South Whittier (c)	(562)	57,156	—
*91977	Spring Valley (c)	(619)	28,205	—
*94309	Stanford (c)	(650)	13,809	—
90680	Stanton	(714)	38,186	38,915
91381	Stevenson Ranch (c)	(661)	17,557	—
*95208	Stockton	(209)	291,707	297,984
*94585	Suisun City	(707)	28,111	28,644
93543	Sun Village (c)	(661)	11,565	—
*94086	Sunnyvale	(408)	140,081	146,197
*96130	Susanville	(530)	17,947	16,616
94941	Tamalpais-Homestead Valley (c)	(415)	10,735	—
*93581	Tehachapi	(661)	14,414	13,784
*92589	Temecula	(951)	100,097	105,208
92883	Temescal Valley (c)	(951)	22,535	—
91780	Temple City	(626)	35,558	36,099
*91359	Thousand Oaks	(805)	126,683	128,412
*90503	Torrance	(310)	145,438	147,027
*95376	Tracy	(209)	82,922	84,669
*96161	Truckee	(916)	16,180	16,156
*93274	Tulare	(559)	59,278	60,933
*95380	Turlock	(209)	68,549	69,733
*92781	Tustin	(714)/(949)	75,540	78,049
92277	Twentynine Palms	(760)	25,048	25,713
*95482	Ukiah	(707)	16,075	15,907
94587	Union City	(510)	69,516	71,763
*91785	Upland	(909)	73,732	75,209
*95687	Vacaville	(707)	92,428	93,899
91744	Valinda (c)	(626)	22,822	—
92343	Valle Vista (c)	(951)	14,578	—
*94590	Vallejo	(707)	115,942	117,796
	Ventura. See San Buenaventura			
*92393	Victorville	(760)	115,903	120,336
90043	View Park-Windsor Hills (c)	(310)	11,075	—
91722	Vincent (c)	(925)	15,922	—
95829	Vineyard (c)	(916)	24,836	—
*93291	Visalia	(559)	124,442	127,081
*92083	Vista	(760)	93,834	96,047
*91788	Walnut	(626)	29,172	30,011
*94596	Walnut Creek	(925)	64,173	65,695
90255	Walnut Park (c)	(213)	15,966	—
93280	Wasco	(661)	25,545	25,495
*95076	Watsonville	(831)	51,199	51,881
90502	West Carson (c)	(310)	21,699	—
*91790	West Covina	(626)	106,098	107,440
90069	West Hollywood	(310)/(323)	34,399	34,781
91746	West Puente Valley (c)	(626)	22,636	—
*95691	West Sacramento	(916)	48,744	49,523
*90606	West Whittier-Los Nietos (c)	(562)	25,540	—
*92685	Westminster	(714)	89,701	91,377
*90047	Westmont (c)	(323)	31,853	—
*90605	Whittier	(562)	85,331	86,177
92595	Wildomar	(951)	32,176	33,192
90222	Willowbrook (c)	(323)	35,983	—
95492	Windsor	(707)	26,801	27,144
92040	Winter Gardens (c)	(619)	20,631	—
95388	Winton (c)	(209)	10,613	—
92504	Woodcrest (c)	(909)/(951)	14,347	—
*95695	Woodland	(530)	55,468	56,271
*92885	Yorba Linda	(714)	64,234	66,735
*95991	Yuba City	(530)	64,925	65,105
92399	Yucaipa	(909)	51,367	52,265
*92286	Yucca Valley	(760)	20,700	21,098

(1) Place was incorporated after the 2010 Census was conducted. Data in the 2010 column is the Census Bureau's estimates base, not the official 2010 population.

Colorado

Area code (720) overlays area code (303).

ZIP	Place	Area code	2010 population	2012 estimate
*80004	Arvada	(303)	106,433	109,745
*80017	Aurora	(303)	325,078	339,030
80221	Berkley (c)	(970)	11,207	—
*80908	Black Forest (c)	(719)	13,116	—
*80302	Boulder	(303)	97,385	101,808
*80601	Brighton	(303)	33,352	34,636
*80020	Broomfield	(303)	55,889	58,298

ZIP	Place	Area code	2010 population	2012 estimate
*81212	Cañon City	(719)	16,400	16,462
80108	Castle Pines[1]	(303)	10,360	10,651
80104	Castle Rock	(303)	48,231	51,348
*80015	Centennial	(303)	100,377	103,743
80111	Cherry Creek (c)	(303)	11,120	—
81222	Cimarron Hills (c)	(719)	16,161	—
81520	Clifton (c)	(970)	19,889	—
*80903	Colorado Springs	(719)	416,427	431,834
80120	Columbine (c)	(303)	24,280	—
80022	Commerce City	(303)	45,913	48,421
80304	Dakota Ridge (c)	(303)	32,005	—
*80202	Denver	(303)	600,158	634,265
*81301	Durango	(970)	16,887	17,216
81632	Edwards (c)	(970)	10,266	—
*80110	Englewood	(303)	30,255	31,177
80516	Erie	(303)	18,135	19,272
80620	Evans	(970)	18,537	19,576
80221	Federal Heights	(303)	11,467	11,794
*80520	Firestone	(303)	10,147	10,903
80913	Fort Carson (c)	(719)	13,813	—
*80525	Fort Collins	(970)	143,986	148,612
*80701	Fort Morgan	(970)	11,315	11,451
80817	Fountain	(719)	25,846	26,891
*81521	Fruita	(970)	12,646	12,696
*80401	Golden	(303)	18,867	19,186
*81501	Grand Junction	(970)	58,566	59,899
*80631	Greeley	(970)	92,889	95,357
*80111	Greenwood Village	(303)	13,925	14,454
80163	Highlands Ranch (c)	(303)	96,713	—
80534	Johnstown	(970)	9,887	11,051
80127	Ken Caryl (c)	(303)	32,438	—
80026	Lafayette	(303)	24,453	25,733
80226	Lakewood	(303)	142,980	145,516
*80126	Littleton	(303)	41,737	43,775
80124	Lone Tree	(303)	10,218	11,852
*80501	Longmont	(303)	86,270	88,669
80027	Louisville	(303)	18,376	19,074
*80538	Loveland	(970)	66,859	70,223
*81401	Montrose	(970)	19,132	18,981
*80233	Northglenn	(303)	35,789	36,891
80134	Parker	(303)	45,297	47,169
*81003	Pueblo	(719)	106,595	107,772
81007	Pueblo West (c)	(719)	29,637	—
80911	Security-Widefield (c)	(719)	32,882	—
80221	Sherrelwood (c)	(303)	18,287	—
*80477	Steamboat Springs	(970)	12,088	12,029
80751	Sterling	(970)	14,777	14,727
80027	Superior	(303)	12,483	12,782
80134	The Pinery (c)	(303)	10,517	—
*80229	Thornton	(303)	118,772	124,140
80229	Welby (c)	(303)	14,846	—
*80030	Westminster	(303)	106,114	109,169
*80033	Wheat Ridge	(303)	30,166	30,717
*80550	Windsor	(970)	18,644	19,751

(1) Place was incorporated after the 2010 Census was conducted. Data in the 2010 column is the Census Bureau's estimates base, not the official 2010 population.

Connecticut
Area code (475) overlays area code (203). See introductory note.

ZIP	Place	Area code	2010 population	2012 estimate
06401	Ansonia	(203)	19,249	19,158
06001	Avon	(860)	18,098	18,283
06037	Berlin	(860)	19,866	20,463
06801	Bethel	(203)	18,584	19,161
06002	Bloomfield	(860)	20,486	20,602
06405	Branford	(203)	28,026	28,024
*06602	Bridgeport	(203)	144,229	146,425
*06010	Bristol	(860)	60,477	60,603
06804	Brookfield	(203)	16,452	16,783
06019	Canton	(860)	10,292	10,351
*06410	Cheshire	(203)	29,261	29,300
06413	Clinton	(860)	13,260	13,196
*06415	Colchester	(860)	16,068	16,187
06238	Coventry	(860)	12,435	12,425
06416	Cromwell	(860)	14,005	14,217
*06810	Danbury	(203)	80,893	82,807
06820	Darien	(203)	20,732	21,114
06418	Derby	(203)	12,902	12,830
*06424	East Hampton	(860)	12,959	12,940
*06108	East Hartford	(860)	51,252	51,272
*06512	East Haven	(203)	29,257	29,190
06333	East Lyme	(860)	19,159	18,892
*06088	East Windsor	(860)	11,162	11,387
06029	Ellington	(860)	15,602	15,779
*06082	Enfield	(860)	44,654	44,660
06825	Fairfield	(203)	59,404	60,450
*06032	Farmington	(860)	25,340	25,529
06033	Glastonbury	(860)	34,427	34,698
*06035	Granby	(860)	11,282	11,316
*06830	Greenwich	(203)	61,171	62,256
06351	Griswold	(860)	11,951	11,986
06340	Groton	(860)	40,115	39,896
06437	Guilford	(203)	22,375	22,403
*06514	Hamden	(203)	60,960	60,863
*06101	Hartford	(860)	124,775	124,893
*06239	Killingly	(860)	17,370	17,269
06339	Ledyard	(860)	15,051	15,077
06443	Madison	(203)	18,269	18,291
*06040	Manchester	(860)	58,241	58,289
*06250	Mansfield	(860)	26,543	25,648
*06450	Meriden	(203)	60,868	60,638
06457	Middletown	(860)	47,648	47,325
*06460	Milford	(203)	51,271	51,488
06468	Monroe	(203)	19,479	19,794
06353	Montville	(860)	19,571	19,686
06770	Naugatuck	(203)	31,862	31,774
*06050	New Britain	(860)	73,206	73,153
*06840	New Canaan	(203)	19,738	20,110
06812	New Fairfield	(203)	13,881	14,112
*06511	New Haven	(203)	129,779	130,741
06320	New London	(860)	27,620	27,707
06776	New Milford	(860)	28,142	27,835
*06101	Newington	(860)	30,562	30,602
06470	Newtown	(203)	27,560	28,042
06471	North Branford	(203)	14,407	14,379
06473	North Haven	(203)	24,093	24,033
*06856	Norwalk	(203)	85,603	87,190
06360	Norwich	(860)	40,493	40,502
06475	Old Saybrook	(860)	10,242	10,238
06477	Orange	(203)	13,956	13,935
06478	Oxford	(203)	12,683	12,819
06374	Plainfield	(860)	15,405	15,267
06062	Plainville	(203)	17,716	17,819
06782	Plymouth	(860)	12,243	12,089
06877	Ridgefield	(203)	24,638	25,045
06067	Rocky Hill	(860)	19,709	19,729
*06483	Seymour	(203)	16,540	16,561
06484	Shelton	(203)	39,559	40,261
*06070	Simsbury	(860)	23,511	23,620
06071	Somers	(860)	11,444	11,451
*06074	South Windsor	(860)	25,709	25,835
06488	Southbury	(203)	19,904	19,877
06489	Southington	(860)	43,069	43,434
*06075	Stafford	(860)	12,087	11,987
*06904	Stamford	(203)	122,643	125,109
06378	Stonington	(860)	18,545	18,556
*06268	Storrs (c)	(860)	15,344	—
*06602	Stratford	(203)	51,384	52,077
*06078	Suffield	(860)	15,735	15,868
06084	Tolland	(860)	15,052	14,964
*06790	Torrington	(860)	36,383	35,808
06611	Trumbull	(203)	36,018	36,514
06066	Vernon	(860)	29,179	29,122
*06492	Wallingford	(203)	45,135	45,179
06492	Wallingford Center (c)	(203)	18,209	—
*06702	Waterbury	(203)	110,366	109,915
*06385	Waterford	(860)	19,517	19,533
06795	Watertown	(860)	22,514	22,261
*06101	West Hartford	(860)	63,268	63,274
06516	West Haven	(203)	55,564	55,404
*06883	Weston	(203)	10,179	10,350
*06880	Westport	(203)	26,391	27,068
*06101	Wethersfield	(860)	26,668	26,710
06226	Willimantic (c)	(860)	17,737	—
06897	Wilton	(203)	18,062	18,617
*06094	Winchester	(860)	11,242	11,071
*06280	Windham	(860)	25,268	25,091
*06095	Windsor	(860)	29,044	29,140
*06096	Windsor Locks	(860)	12,498	12,546
*06716	Wolcott	(203)	16,680	16,724

Delaware
Area code 302 applies to the entire state.

ZIP	Place	2010 population	2012 estimate
19701	Bear (c)	19,371	—
19713	Brookside (c)	14,353	—
*19901	Dover	36,047	37,089
19702	Glasgow (c)	14,303	—
19707	Hockessin (c)	13,527	—
19709	Middletown	18,871	19,483
*19711	Newark	31,454	32,367
19808	Pike Creek Valley (c)	11,217	—
19977	Smyrna	10,023	10,708
*19899	Wilmington	70,851	71,292

District of Columbia
Area code 202 applies to the entire district.

ZIP	Place	2010 population	2012 estimate
*20090	Washington	601,723	632,323

Florida

Area code (321) overlays area code (407). Area code (754) overlays area code (954). Area code (786) overlays area code (305).

ZIP	Place	Area code	2010 population	2012 estimate
*32828	Alafaya (c)	(407)	78,113	—
*32714	Altamonte Springs	(407)	41,496	41,920
33572	Apollo Beach (c)	(813)	14,055	—
*32712	Apopka	(407)	41,542	44,474
*32233	Atlantic Beach	(904)	12,655	12,864
33823	Auburndale	(863)	13,507	13,918
*33160	Aventura	(305)	35,762	36,981
32807	Azalea Park (c)	(407)	12,556	—
*33830	Bartow	(863)	17,298	17,665
34667	Bayonet Point (c)	(727)	23,467	—
33507	Bayshore Gardens (c)	(941)	16,323	—
*33756	Bellair-Meadowbrook Terrace (c)	(904)	13,343	—
33430	Belle Glade	(561)	17,467	17,817
*34420	Belleview (c)	(352)	23,355	—
*33509	Bloomingdale (c)	(813)	22,711	—
*33431	Boca Raton	(561)	84,392	87,836
*34135	Bonita Springs	(239)	43,914	46,340
*33436	Boynton Beach	(561)	68,217	70,101
*34206	Bradenton	(941)	49,546	50,672
33509	Brandon (c)	(813)	103,483	—
32503	Brent (c)	(850)	21,804	—
33142	Brownsville (c)	(305)	15,313	—
34743	Buenaventura Lakes (c)	(407)	26,079	—
32404	Callaway	(850)	14,405	14,484
*33920	Cape Coral	(239)	154,305	161,248
*33618	Carrollwood (c)	(813)	33,365	—
*32707	Casselberry	(407)	26,241	26,449
33558	Cheval (c)	(813)	10,702	—
33624	Citrus Park (c)	(813)	24,252	—
*33758	Clearwater	(727)	107,685	108,732
*34711	Clermont	(352)	28,742	29,421
*32922	Cocoa	(321)	17,140	17,217
*32931	Cocoa Beach	(321)	11,231	11,260
*33097	Coconut Creek	(954)	52,909	55,001
32809	Conway (c)	(407)	13,467	—
*33328	Cooper City	(954)	28,547	32,345
*33114	Coral Gables	(305)	46,780	49,411
*33075	Coral Springs	(954)	121,096	125,287
33157	Coral Terrace (c)	(305)	24,376	—
33015	Country Club (c)	(305)	47,105	—
33196	Country Walk (c)	(305)	15,997	—
*32536	Crestview	(850)	20,978	22,351
33189	Cutler Bay	(305)	40,286	42,221
33919	Cypress Lake (c)	(239)	11,846	—
*33004	Dania Beach	(954)	29,639	30,574
*33329	Davie	(954)	91,992	95,489
*32114	Daytona Beach	(386)	61,005	62,035
*32713	DeBary	(386)	19,320	19,319
*33441	Deerfield Beach	(954)	75,010	77,439
32720	DeLand	(386)	27,031	27,447
*33444	Delray Beach	(561)	60,522	62,357
*32783	Deltona	(407)	85,182	85,442
32541	Destin	(850)	12,305	12,809
32836	Doctor Phillips (c)	(407)	10,981	—
*33178	Doral	(305)	45,704	48,134
*34698	Dunedin	(727)	35,321	35,444
33610	East Lake (c)	(813)	30,962	—
33619	East Lake-Orient Park (c)	(813)	22,753	—
32583	East Milton (c)	(850)	11,074	—
*32132	Edgewater	(386)	20,750	20,803
33614	Egypt Lake-Leto (c)	(813)	35,282	—
34680	Elfers (c)	(727)	13,986	—
*34295	Englewood (c)	(941)	14,863	—
32534	Ensley (c)	(850)	20,602	—
*33928	Estero (c)	(239)	22,612	—
*32726	Eustis	(352)	18,558	18,899
32804	Fairview Shores (c)	(305)	10,239	—
*32034	Fernandina Beach	(904)	11,487	11,705
32514	Ferry Pass (c)	(850)	28,921	—
33547	Fish Hawk (c)	(813)	14,087	—
32003	Fleming Island (c)	(904)	27,126	—
*33034	Florida City	(305)	11,245	11,913
32960	Florida Ridge (c)	(772)	18,164	—
32714	Forest City (c)	(407)	13,854	—
*33310	Fort Lauderdale	(954)	165,521	170,747
*33902	Fort Myers	(239)	62,298	65,725
*34981	Fort Pierce	(772)	41,590	42,645
*32548	Fort Walton Beach	(850)	19,507	20,293
33172	Fountainbleau (c)	(305)	59,764	—
34747	Four Corners (c)	(863)	26,116	—
*32259	Fruit Cove (c)	(904)	29,362	—
34232	Fruitville (c)	(941)	13,224	—
*32602	Gainesville	(352)	124,354	126,047
33534	Gibsonton (c)	(813)	14,234	—
33138	Gladeview (c)	(954)	11,535	—
33143	Glenvar Heights (c)	(305)	16,898	—
34116	Golden Gate (c)	(239)	23,961	—
33055	Golden Glades (c)	(305)	33,145	—
32733	Goldenrod (c)	(407)	12,039	—
32560	Gonzalez (c)	(850)	13,273	—
33170	Goulds (c)	(305)	10,103	—
*33454	Greenacres	(561)	37,573	38,467
33581	Gulf Gate Estates (c)	(941)	10,911	—
*33737	Gulfport	(727)	12,029	12,066
*33844	Haines City	(863)	20,535	21,008
*33009	Hallandale Beach	(305)/(954)	37,113	38,327
*33010	Hialeah	(305)	224,669	231,941
*33016	Hialeah Gardens	(305)	21,744	22,495
33846	Highland City (c)	(863)	10,834	—
*33455	Hobe Sound (c)	(772)	11,521	—
*34690	Holiday (c)	(727)	22,403	—
*32125	Holly Hill	(386)	11,659	11,628
*33022	Hollywood	(954)	140,768	145,236
*33030	Homestead	(305)	60,512	63,190
34447	Homosassa Springs (c)	(352)	13,791	—
34787	Horizon West (c)	(352)	14,000	—
*34667	Hudson (c)	(727)	12,158	—
32837	Hunters Creek (c)	(407)	14,321	—
*34142	Immokalee (c)	(239)	24,154	—
33908	Iona (c)	(239)	15,369	—
33162	Ives Estates (c)	(305)	19,525	—
*32203	Jacksonville	(904)	821,784	836,507
*33250	Jacksonville Beach	(904)	21,362	21,682
33568	Jasmine Estates (c)	(727)	18,989	—
*34957	Jensen Beach (c)	(772)	11,707	—
*33458	Jupiter	(561)	55,156	57,221
33478	Jupiter Farms (c)	(561)	11,994	—
33183	Kendale Lakes (c)	(305)	56,148	—
*33256	Kendall (c)	(305)	75,371	—
33193	Kendall West (c)	(305)	36,154	—
*33149	Key Biscayne	(305)	12,344	12,762
33037	Key Largo (c)	(305)	10,433	—
*33040	Key West	(305)	24,649	25,057
33556	Keystone (c)	(813)	24,039	—
*34744	Kissimmee	(407)	59,682	63,369
*32159	Lady Lake	(352)	13,926	14,098
34786	Lake Butler (c)	(407)	15,400	—
*32055	Lake City	(386)	12,046	12,099
33612	Lake Magdalene (c)	(813)	28,509	—
*32746	Lake Mary	(407)	13,822	14,554
*33853	Lake Wales	(863)	14,225	14,700
*33461	Lake Worth	(561)	34,910	35,786
*33804	Lakeland	(863)	97,422	99,999
33801	Lakeland Highlands (c)	(863)	11,056	—
32073	Lakeside (c)	(904)	30,943	—
34951	Lakewood Park (c)	(772)	11,323	—
*34639	Land O'Lakes (c)	(813)	31,996	—
*33465	Lantana	(561)	10,423	10,627
*33770	Largo	(727)	77,648	77,878
*33313	Lauderdale Lakes	(954)	32,593	33,772
*33313	Lauderhill	(954)	66,887	69,100
33714	Lealman (o)	(727)	19,879	—
*34748	Leesburg	(352)	20,117	20,796
*33936	Lehigh Acres (c)	(239)	86,784	—
*33033	Leisure City (c)	(305)	22,655	—
*33074	Lighthouse Point	(954)	10,344	10,714
32810	Lockhart (c)	(407)	13,060	—
*32750	Longwood	(407)	13,657	13,751
*33549	Lutz (c)	(813)	19,344	—
32444	Lynn Haven (c)	(850)	18,493	18,974
*32751	Maitland	(407)	15,751	16,337
33550	Mango (c)	(813)	11,313	—
*34145	Marco Island	(239)	16,413	16,820
*33093	Margate	(954)	53,284	55,026
32824	Meadow Woods (c)	(407)	25,558	—
*32901	Melbourne	(321)	76,068	77,048
*32953	Merritt Island (c)	(321)	34,743	—
*33101	Miami	(305)	399,457	413,892
*33152	Miami Beach	(305)	87,779	90,588
33023	Miami Gardens	(305)	107,167	110,754
*33014	Miami Lakes	(305)	29,361	30,396
33138	Miami Shores	(305)	10,493	10,609
33266	Miami Springs	(305)	13,809	14,231
32068	Middleburg (c)	(904)	13,008	—
32563	Midway (c)	(850)	16,115	—
*33023	Miramar	(954)	122,041	128,729
*32757	Mount Dora	(352)	12,370	12,655
32526	Myrtle Grove (c)	(850)	15,870	—
*34102	Naples	(239)	19,537	20,115
32566	Navarre (c)	(850)	31,378	—
*34653	New Port Richey	(727)	14,911	14,934
34653	New Port Richey East (c)	(727)	10,036	—
*32168	New Smyrna Beach	(386)	22,464	22,900
*32578	Niceville	(850)	12,749	13,587
*33918	North Fort Myers (c)	(239)	39,407	—
*33068	North Lauderdale	(954)	41,023	42,413
*33261	North Miami	(305)	58,786	60,565
*33160	North Miami Beach	(305)	41,523	42,971
*33408	North Palm Beach	(561)	12,015	12,272
*34287	North Port	(941)	57,357	58,378

ZIP	Place	Area code	2010 population	2012 estimate
33624	Northdale (c)	(813)	22,079	—
33860	Oak Ridge (c)	(407)	22,685	—
33307	Oakland Park	(305)	41,363	42,832
32065	Oakleaf Plantation (c)	(904)	20,315	—
*34478	Ocala	(352)	56,315	56,945
34761	Ocoee	(407)	35,579	38,354
*33163	Ojus (c)	(305)	18,036	—
34677	Oldsmar	(813)	13,591	13,703
*33265	Olympia Heights (c)	(305)	13,488	—
*33054	Opa-Locka	(305)	15,219	15,701
*32763	Orange City	(386)	10,599	10,813
*32802	Orlando	(407)	238,300	249,562
*32174	Ormond Beach	(386)	38,137	38,376
*32765	Oviedo	(407)	33,342	35,291
32571	Pace (c)	(850)	20,039	—
*32177	Palatka	(386)	10,558	10,472
*32905	Palm Bay	(321)	103,190	104,124
*33408	Palm Beach Gardens	(561)	48,452	49,889
*34990	Palm City (c)	(772)	23,120	—
*32135	Palm Coast	(386)	75,180	77,374
*34683	Palm Harbor (c)	(727)	57,439	—
*33601	Palm River-Clair Mel (c)	(813)	21,024	—
*33406	Palm Springs	(561)	18,928	20,342
32082	Palm Valley (c)	(904)	20,019	—
*34221	Palmetto	(941)	12,606	12,852
33157	Palmetto Bay	(305)	23,410	24,180
33157	Palmetto Estates (c)	(305)	13,535	—
*32401	Panama City	(850)	36,484	36,167
*32417	Panama City Beach	(850)	12,018	11,814
*33067	Parkland	(954)	23,962	25,701
*33029	Pembroke Pines	(954)	154,750	160,306
*32502	Pensacola	(850)	51,923	52,340
*32809	Pine Castle (c)	(407)	10,805	—
32858	Pine Hills (c)	(407)	60,076	—
33156	Pinecrest	(305)	18,223	18,887
*33781	Pinellas Park	(727)	49,079	49,686
33168	Pinewood (c)	(305)	16,520	—
*33566	Plant City	(813)	34,721	35,903
*33318	Plantation	(954)	84,955	88,016
*34758	Poinciana (c)	(407)	53,193	—
*33060	Pompano Beach	(954)	99,845	102,984
*33952	Port Charlotte (c)	(941)	54,392	—
*32129	Port Orange	(904)	56,048	56,766
32927	Port St. John (c)	(321)	12,267	—
*34981	Port St. Lucie	(772)	164,603	168,716
34992	Port Salerno (c)	(772)	10,091	—
*33032	Princeton (c)	(305)	22,038	—
*33950	Punta Gorda	(941)	16,641	16,869
33177	Richmond West (c)	(305)	31,973	—
*33569	Riverview (c)	(813)	71,050	—
*33419	Riviera Beach	(561)	32,488	33,129
*32955	Rockledge	(321)	24,926	25,413
*33411	Royal Palm Beach	(561)	34,140	35,162
*33570	Ruskin (c)	(813)	17,208	—
*34695	Safety Harbor	(727)	16,884	16,970
*32084	Saint Augustine	(904)	12,975	13,407
*34769	Saint Cloud	(407)	35,183	39,171
*33733	Saint Petersburg	(727)	244,769	246,541
33912	San Carlos Park (c)	(239)	16,824	—
*32771	Sanford	(407)	53,570	54,651
*34230	Sarasota	(941)	51,917	52,811
33577	Sarasota Springs (c)	(941)	14,395	—
32937	Satellite Beach	(321)	10,109	10,249
*32958	Sebastian	(772)	21,929	22,364
*33870	Sebring	(863)	10,491	10,340
*33770	Seminole	(813)	17,233	17,267
34610	Shady Hills (c)	(727)	11,523	—
33505	South Bradenton (c)	(941)	22,178	—
32121	South Daytona	(386)	12,252	12,235
*33243	South Miami	(305)	11,657	12,028
33157	South Miami Heights (c)	(305)	35,696	—
33595	South Venice (c)	(941)	13,949	—
32824	Southchase (c)	(407)	15,921	—
*34604	Spring Hill (c)	(352)	98,621	—
*34994	Stuart	(772)	15,593	15,841
*33573	Sun City Center (c)	(813)	19,258	—
33160	Sunny Isles Beach	(305)	20,832	21,522
*33325	Sunrise	(954)	84,439	88,843
*33283	Sunset (c)	(305)	16,389	—
33144	Sweetwater	(305)	13,499	20,566
*32301	Tallahassee	(850)	181,376	186,971
*33320	Tamarac	(954)	60,427	62,557
33144	Tamiami (c)	(305)	55,271	—
*33601	Tampa	(813)	335,709	347,645
*34689	Tarpon Springs	(727)	23,484	23,657
32778	Tavares	(352)	13,951	14,248
*33687	Temple Terrace	(813)	24,541	25,189
33412	The Acreage (c)	(561)	38,704	—
33186	The Crossings (c)	(305)	22,758	—
33196	The Hammocks (c)	(305)	51,003	—
*32162	The Villages (c)	(352)	51,442	—
33592	Thonotosassa (c)	(813)	13,014	—
33186	Three Lakes (c)	(305)	15,047	—
*32780	Titusville	(321)	43,761	43,940
32615	Town 'n' Country (c)	(813)	78,442	—
34655	Trinity (c)	(813)	10,907	—
33613	University (c) (Hillsborough Co.)	(813)	41,163	—
32826	University (c) (Orange Co.)	(407)	31,084	—
33165	University Park (c)	(305)	26,995	—
32401	Upper Grand Lagoon (c)	(850)	13,963	—
*33594	Valrico (c)	(813)	35,545	—
*34285	Venice	(941)	20,748	21,054
*32960	Vero Beach	(772)	15,220	15,527
32960	Vero Beach South (c)	(772)	23,092	—
32955	Viera East (c)	(321)	10,757	—
33901	Villas (c)	(239)	11,569	—
32507	Warrington (c)	(850)	14,531	—
32779	Wekiwa Springs (c)	(407)	21,998	—
*33414	Wellington	(561)	56,508	58,679
*33544	Wesley Chapel (c)	(813)	44,092	—
33714	West Lealman (c)	(727)	15,651	—
33138	West Little River (c)	(305)	34,699	—
*32912	West Melbourne	(321)	18,355	19,164
*33416	West Palm Beach	(561)	99,919	101,903
33023	West Park	(954)	14,156	14,609
32505	West Pensacola (c)	(850)	21,339	—
33626	Westchase (c)	(813)	21,747	—
33165	Westchester (c)	(305)	29,862	—
*33326	Weston	(954)	65,333	67,641
33165	Westwood Lakes (c)	(305)	11,838	—
*33305	Wilton Manors	(954)	11,632	11,995
*34787	Winter Garden	(407)	34,568	37,063
*33880	Winter Haven	(863)	33,874	34,975
*32789	Winter Park	(407)	27,852	28,924
*32707	Winter Springs	(407)	33,282	33,540
32092	World Golf Village (c)	(904)	12,310	—
32547	Wright (c)	(850)	23,127	—
*32097	Yulee (c)	(904)	11,491	—
*33540	Zephyrhills	(813)	13,288	13,830

Georgia

Area codes (470) and (678) overlay area code (770). Area code (762) overlays area code (706).

ZIP	Place	Area code	2010 population	2012 estimate
*30101	Acworth	(770)	20,425	21,215
*31706	Albany	(229)	77,434	77,431
*30004	Alpharetta	(770)	57,551	61,981
*31709	Americus	(229)	17,041	16,393
*30603	Athens-Clarke County	(706)	115,452	118,999
*30301	Atlanta	(404)	420,003	443,775
*30903	Augusta-Richmond County	(706)	195,844	197,872
*39818	Bainbridge	(229)	12,697	12,603
30032	Belvedere Park (c)	(404)	15,152	—
*31520	Brunswick	(912)	15,383	15,640
*30518	Buford	(404)	12,225	12,735
*30701	Calhoun	(706)	15,650	15,812
30032	Candler-McAfee (c)	(404)	23,025	—
*30114	Canton	(770)	22,958	23,791
*30117	Carrollton	(770)	24,388	24,958
*30120	Cartersville	(770)	19,731	19,810
*30341	Chamblee	(770)	9,892	15,790
30337	College Park	(404)	13,942	14,649
*31908	Columbus	(706)	189,885	198,413
*30013	Conyers	(404)	15,195	15,408
*31015	Cordele	(229)	11,147	11,297
*30014	Covington	(770)	13,118	13,347
31805	Cusseta-Chattahoochee County	(706)	11,267	13,037
*30132	Dallas	(770)	11,544	12,044
*30720	Dalton	(706)	33,128	33,413
*30030	Decatur	(404)	19,335	19,853
*31533	Douglas	(912)	11,589	11,834
*30134	Douglasville	(404)	30,961	31,269
30333	Druid Hills (c)	(404)	14,568	—
*31021	Dublin	(478)	16,201	16,215
*30096	Duluth	(404)	26,600	27,926
*30338	Dunwoody	(770)	46,267	47,224
30364	East Point	(404)	33,712	35,584
30809	Evans (c)	(706)	29,011	—
30213	Fairburn	(770)	12,950	13,720
*30214	Fayetteville	(404)	15,945	16,206
*30297	Forest Park	(404)	18,468	18,874
*30501	Gainesville	(770)	33,804	34,786
31754	Georgetown (c)	(912)	11,823	—
*30223	Griffin	(770)	23,643	23,389
30813	Grovetown	(706)	11,216	12,210
*31313	Hinesville	(912)	33,437	34,751
*31546	Jesup	(912)	10,214	10,268
30097	Johns Creek	(770)	76,728	82,306
*30144	Kennesaw	(404)	29,783	30,990
31548	Kingsland	(912)	15,946	16,285
*30240	LaGrange	(706)	29,588	30,478
*30045	Lawrenceville	(404)	28,546	29,481
*30047	Lilburn	(404)	11,596	12,266
30122	Lithia Springs (c)	(770)	15,491	—

ZIP	Place	Area code	2010 population	2012 estimate
30052	Loganville	(770)	10,458	10,646
30126	Mableton (c)	(404)	37,115	—
*31201	Macon	(478)	91,351	91,234
*30060	Marietta	(404)	56,579	58,359
30907	Martinez (c)	(706)	35,795	—
30253	McDonough	(770)	22,084	22,599
*31061	Milledgeville	(478)	17,715	19,401
30004	Milton	(770)	32,661	35,015
*30655	Monroe	(770)	13,234	13,349
*31768	Moultrie	(229)	14,268	14,506
30087	Mountain Park (c)	(404)	11,554	—
*30263	Newnan	(770)	33,039	34,174
*30071	Norcross	(770)	9,116	15,632
30319	North Atlanta (c)	(404)	40,456	—
30033	North Decatur (c)	(404)	16,698	—
30033	North Druid Hills (c) . . .	(404)	18,947	—
*30269	Peachtree City	(404)	34,364	34,662
31069	Perry	(478)	13,839	14,730
31322	Pooler	(912)	19,140	20,598
30127	Powder Springs	(404)	13,940	14,253
30074	Redan (c)	(404)	33,015	—
31324	Richmond Hill	(912)	9,281	10,452
*30274	Riverdale	(404)	15,134	15,493
*30161	Rome	(706)	36,303	36,159
*30077	Roswell	(404)	88,346	93,692
31558	Saint Marys	(912)	17,121	17,606
31522	Saint Simons (c)	(912)	12,743	—
30358	Sandy Springs	(404)	93,853	99,419
*31402	Savannah	(912)	136,286	142,022
30079	Scottdale (c)	(404)	10,631	—
*30080	Smyrna	(404)	51,271	52,650
*30078	Snellville	(404)	18,242	19,026
*30458	Statesboro	(912)	28,422	29,779
30281	Stockbridge	(404)	25,636	26,281
30518	Sugar Hill	(404)	18,522	19,681
30024	Suwanee	(770)	15,355	16,253
*31792	Thomasville	(229)	18,413	18,488
*31794	Tifton	(229)	16,350	16,672
30084	Tucker (c)	(404)	27,581	—
30291	Union City	(404)	19,456	20,501
*31603	Valdosta	(229)	54,518	57,597
*30474	Vidalia	(912)	10,473	10,609
30180	Villa Rica	(770)	13,956	14,226
*31088	Warner Robins	(478)	66,588	70,712
*31501	Waycross	(912)	14,649	14,322
31410	Wilmington Island (c) . .	(912)	15,138	—
30680	Winder	(770)	14,099	14,271
*30188	Woodstock	(770)	23,896	25,135

Hawaii

Area code 808 applies to the entire state.

ZIP	Place	2000 population	2010 population
96821	East Honolulu (c)	—	49,914
96706	Ewa Beach (c)	14,650	14,955
96706	Ewa Gentry (c)	4,939	22,690
96701	Halawa (c)	13,891	14,014
96749	Hawaiian Paradise Park (c)	7,051	11,404
96720	Hilo (c)	40,759	43,263
*96820	Honolulu, urban (c)	371,657	345,610[1]
*96732	Kahului (c)	20,146	26,337
96740	Kailua (c) (Hawaii Co.)	9,870	11,975
96734	Kailua (c) (Honolulu Co.)	36,513	38,635
96744	Kaneohe (c)	34,970	34,597
96746	Kapaa (c)	9,472	10,699
*96707	Kapolei (c)	—	15,186
96753	Kihei (c)	16,749	20,881
96761	Lahaina (c)	9,118	11,704
96706	Makakilo (c)	13,156	18,248
96789	Mililani Mauka (c)	—	21,039
96789	Mililani Town (c)	28,608	27,629
96792	Nanakuli (c)	10,814	12,666
96782	Pearl City (c)	30,976	47,698
96797	Royal Kunia (c)	—	14,525
96857	Schofield Barracks (c)	14,428	16,370
*96786	Wahiawa (c)	16,151	17,821
96792	Waianae (c)	10,506	13,177
96793	Wailuku (c)	12,296	15,313
96701	Waimalu (c)	29,371	13,730
96797	Waipahu (c)	33,108	38,216
96797	Waipio (c)	11,672	11,674

(1) 2012 estimate for Urban Honolulu, a census-designated place.

Idaho

Area code 208 applies to the entire state.

ZIP	Place	2010 population	2012 estimate
*83401	Ammon	13,816	14,199
83221	Blackfoot	11,899	11,852
*83707	Boise	205,671	212,303
83318	Burley	10,345	10,425

ZIP	Place	2010 population	2012 estimate
*83605	Caldwell	46,237	47,668
83202	Chubbuck	13,922	14,166
*83814	Coeur d'Alene	44,137	45,579
83616	Eagle	19,908	21,025
*83714	Garden City	10,972	11,251
83835	Hayden	13,294	13,549
*83402	Idaho Falls	56,813	57,899
83338	Jerome	10,890	11,027
*83634	Kuna	15,210	16,189
83501	Lewiston	31,894	32,051
*83642	Meridian	75,092	80,386
*83843	Moscow	23,800	24,499
*83647	Mountain Home	14,206	13,791
*83651	Nampa	81,557	83,930
*83201	Pocatello	54,255	54,777
*83854	Post Falls	27,574	28,651
*83440	Rexburg	25,484	25,732
*83301	Twin Falls	44,125	45,158

Illinois

Area code (224) overlays area code (847). Area code (331) overlays area code (630). Area code (779) overlays area code (815). Area code (872) overlays area code (312).

ZIP	Place	Area code	2010 population	2012 estimate
60101	Addison	(630)	36,942	37,287
*60102	Algonquin	(847)	30,046	30,004
60803	Alsip	(708)	19,277	19,419
62002	Alton	(618)	27,865	27,415
60002	Antioch	(847)	14,430	14,409
*60005	Arlington Heights	(847)	75,101	75,777
*60505	Aurora	(630)	197,899	199,932
*60010	Barrington	(847)	10,327	10,351
*60103	Bartlett	(630)	41,208	41,618
*60510	Batavia	(630)	26,045	26,318
*60083	Beach Park	(847)	13,638	13,789
*62220	Belleville	(618)	44,478	43,765
60104	Bellwood	(708)	19,071	19,137
61008	Belvidere	(815)	25,585	25,371
*60106	Bensenville	(630)	18,352	18,493
60402	Berwyn	(708)	56,657	56,800
*60108	Bloomingdale	(630)	22,018	22,237
*61701	Bloomington	(309)	76,610	77,733
*60406	Blue Island	(708)	23,706	23,816
*60440	Bolingbrook	(630)	73,366	74,039
60914	Bourbonnais	(815)	18,631	18,629
60915	Bradley	(815)	15,895	15,871
60455	Bridgeview	(708)	16,446	16,521
60513	Brookfield	(708)	18,978	19,035
*60089	Buffalo Grove	(847)	41,496	41,715
60459	Burbank	(708)	28,925	29,124
60527	Burr Ridge	(630)	10,559	10,696
62206	Cahokia	(618)	15,241	14,920
60409	Calumet City	(708)	37,042	37,232
*60119	Campton Hills	(630)/(847)	11,131	11,276
61520	Canton	(309)	14,704	14,518
*62901	Carbondale	(618)	25,902	26,241
60188	Carol Stream	(630)	39,711	40,222
60110	Carpentersville	(847)	37,691	38,196
*60013	Cary	(847)	18,271	18,139
62801	Centralia	(618)	13,032	12,858
*61821	Champaign	(217)	81,055	82,517
60410	Channahon	(815)	12,560	12,598
61920	Charleston	(217)	21,838	21,911
62629	Chatham	(217)	11,500	11,946
*60607	Chicago	(312)/(773)	2,695,598	2,714,856
*60411	Chicago Heights	(708)	30,276	30,392
60415	Chicago Ridge	(708)	14,305	14,428
60804	Cicero	(708)	83,891	84,137
62234	Collinsville	(618)	25,579	25,240
60478	Country Club Hills	(708)	16,541	16,854
60435	Crest Hill	(815)	20,837	20,864
60445	Crestwood	(708)	10,950	11,018
*60014	Crystal Lake	(815)	40,743	40,480
*61832	Danville	(217)	33,027	32,649
60561	Darien	(630)	22,086	22,302
*62525	Decatur	(217)	76,122	75,407
60015	Deerfield	(847)	18,225	18,275
60115	DeKalb	(815)	43,862	43,842
*60018	Des Plaines	(847)	58,364	58,840
61021	Dixon	(815)	15,733	15,400
60419	Dolton	(708)	23,153	23,274
*60515	Downers Grove	(630)	47,833	49,399
61244	East Moline	(309)	21,302	21,398
*61611	East Peoria	(309)	23,402	23,445
*62201	East St. Louis	(618)	27,006	26,708
*62025	Edwardsville	(618)	24,293	24,457
62401	Effingham	(217)	12,328	12,554
*60120	Elgin	(847)	108,188	109,927
*60009	Elk Grove Village	(847)	33,127	33,350
60126	Elmhurst	(630)	44,121	45,171
60707	Elmwood Park	(708)	24,883	24,973
*60201	Evanston	(847)	74,486	75,430

ZIP	Place	Area code	2010 population	2012 estimate
60805	Evergreen Park	(708)	19,852	19,929
*62208	Fairview Heights	(618)	17,078	16,996
*60130	Forest Park	(708)	14,167	14,219
60020	Fox Lake	(847)	10,579	10,551
60423	Frankfort	(815)	17,782	18,042
*60131	Franklin Park	(847)	18,333	18,398
61032	Freeport	(815)	25,638	25,185
60030	Gages Lake (c)	(847)	10,198	—
*61401	Galesburg	(309)	32,195	31,745
60134	Geneva	(630)	21,495	21,722
62034	Glen Carbon	(618)	12,934	12,922
*60137	Glen Ellyn	(630)	27,450	27,650
*60139	Glendale Heights	(630)	34,208	34,535
*60025	Glenview	(847)	44,692	45,029
62035	Godfrey	(618)	17,982	17,923
62040	Granite City	(618)	29,849	29,545
60030	Grayslake	(847)	20,957	21,101
60031	Gurnee	(847)	31,295	31,273
60133	Hanover Park	(630)	37,973	38,373
*60426	Harvey	(708)	25,282	25,381
60429	Hazel Crest	(708)	14,100	14,184
62948	Herrin	(618)	12,501	12,696
*60457	Hickory Hills	(708)	14,049	14,145
*60035	Highland Park	(847)	29,763	29,914
*60521	Hinsdale	(630)	16,816	17,126
*60195	Hoffman Estates	(847)	51,895	52,305
*60491	Homer Glen	(708)	24,220	24,363
*60430	Homewood	(708)	19,323	19,418
60142	Huntley	(847)	24,291	24,820
*62650	Jacksonville	(217)	19,446	19,301
*60436	Joliet	(815)	147,433	148,268
60458	Justice	(708)	12,926	13,026
60901	Kankakee	(815)	27,537	27,349
61443	Kewanee	(309)	12,916	12,778
60525	La Grange	(708)	15,550	15,680
60526	La Grange Park	(708)	13,579	13,635
60045	Lake Forest	(847)	19,375	19,349
*60102	Lake in the Hills	(847)	28,965	29,098
*60047	Lake Zurich	(847)	19,631	19,917
60438	Lansing	(708)	28,331	28,479
*60439	Lemont	(630)	16,000	16,377
*60048	Libertyville	(847)	20,315	20,360
62656	Lincoln	(217)	14,504	14,319
*60645	Lincolnwood	(847)	12,590	12,656
60046	Lindenhurst	(847)	14,462	14,475
60532	Lisle	(630)	22,390	22,647
*60441	Lockport	(815)	24,839	25,046
60148	Lombard	(630)	43,165	43,773
*61130	Loves Park	(815)	23,996	23,805
60534	Lyons	(708)	10,729	10,770
*61115	Machesney Park	(815)	23,499	23,280
61455	Macomb	(309)	19,288	19,254
62959	Marion	(618)	17,193	17,315
*60426	Markham	(708)	12,508	12,625
*60443	Matteson	(708)	19,009	19,147
61938	Mattoon	(217)	18,555	18,364
*60153	Maywood	(708)	24,090	24,164
*60050	McHenry	(815)	26,992	26,825
*60160	Melrose Park	(708)	25,411	25,527
60445	Midlothian	(708)	14,819	14,896
60447	Minooka	(815)	10,924	11,099
60448	Mokena	(708)	18,740	19,042
*61265	Moline	(309)	43,483	43,259
60538	Montgomery	(630)	18,438	19,084
60450	Morris	(815)	13,636	13,825
61550	Morton	(309)	16,267	16,415
60053	Morton Grove	(847)	23,270	23,461
60056	Mount Prospect	(847)	54,167	54,505
62864	Mount Vernon	(618)	15,277	15,218
60060	Mundelein	(847)	31,064	31,249
*60540	Naperville	(630)	141,853	143,684
60451	New Lenox	(815)	24,394	24,715
60714	Niles	(847)	29,803	29,962
*61761	Normal	(309)	52,497	53,837
*60634	Norridge	(708)	14,572	14,653
60542	North Aurora	(630)	16,760	17,019
*60064	North Chicago	(847)	32,574	29,667
*60062	Northbrook	(708)	33,170	33,477
60164	Northlake	(708)	12,323	12,370
62269	O'Fallon	(618)	28,281	29,193
60452	Oak Forest	(708)	27,962	28,155
*60303	Oak Lawn	(708)	56,690	56,995
*60303	Oak Park	(708)	51,878	52,015
*60462	Orland Park	(708)	56,767	57,392
60543	Oswego	(630)	30,355	31,672
61350	Ottawa	(815)	18,768	18,563
*60067	Palatine	(847)	68,557	69,144
60463	Palos Heights	(708)	12,515	12,590
60465	Palos Hills	(708)	17,484	17,610
60466	Park Forest	(708)	21,975	22,035
60068	Park Ridge	(847)	37,480	37,721
*61554	Pekin	(309)	34,094	34,084
*61601	Peoria	(309)	115,007	115,687

ZIP	Place	Area code	2010 population	2012 estimate
61354	Peru	(815)	10,295	10,187
*60544	Plainfield	(815)	39,581	40,466
60545	Plano	(630)	10,856	11,053
*61764	Pontiac	(815)	11,931	11,828
60070	Prospect Heights	(847)	16,256	16,367
*62301	Quincy	(217)	40,633	40,798
61866	Rantoul	(217)	12,941	12,937
60471	Richton Park	(708)	13,646	13,741
60305	River Forest	(708)	11,172	11,216
60171	River Grove	(708)	10,227	10,274
60827	Riverdale	(708)	13,549	13,609
*61201	Rock Island	(309)	39,018	38,920
*61125	Rockford	(815)	152,871	150,843
60008	Rolling Meadows	(847)	24,099	24,241
*60446	Romeoville	(815)	39,680	39,752
61073	Roscoe	(815)	10,785	10,720
60172	Roselle	(630)	22,763	22,984
60073	Round Lake	(847)	18,289	18,470
60073	Round Lake Beach	(847)	28,175	28,116
*60174	Saint Charles	(630)	32,974	33,327
60411	Sauk Village	(708)	10,506	10,559
*60194	Schaumburg	(847)	74,227	74,781
*60176	Schiller Park	(847)	11,793	11,858
*62269	Shiloh	(618)	12,651	13,107
*60436	Shorewood	(815)	15,615	16,221
*60077	Skokie	(847)	64,784	65,074
60177	South Elgin	(847)	21,985	22,224
60473	South Holland	(708)	22,030	22,145
*62703	Springfield	(217)	116,250	117,126
61081	Sterling	(815)	15,370	15,243
60107	Streamwood	(630)	39,858	40,238
61364	Streator	(815)	13,710	13,557
60501	Summit	(708)	11,054	11,446
*62221	Swansea	(618)	13,430	13,758
60178	Sycamore	(815)	17,519	17,481
62568	Taylorville	(217)	11,246	11,180
60477	Tinley Park	(708)	56,703	57,144
*61801	Urbana	(217)	41,250	41,581
60061	Vernon Hills	(847)	25,113	25,678
60181	Villa Park	(630)	21,904	22,052
60555	Warrenville	(630)	13,140	13,316
61571	Washington	(309)	15,134	15,410
60084	Wauconda	(847)	13,603	13,753
*60085	Waukegan	(847)	89,078	88,862
*60185	West Chicago	(630)	27,086	27,576
60154	Westchester	(708)	16,718	16,792
60558	Western Springs	(708)	12,975	13,105
60559	Westmont	(630)	24,685	24,898
*60187	Wheaton	(630)	52,894	53,469
60090	Wheeling	(847)	37,648	37,946
60091	Wilmette	(847)	27,087	27,294
60093	Winnetka	(847)	12,187	12,270
*60191	Wood Dale	(630)	13,770	13,911
62095	Wood River	(618)	10,657	10,493
60517	Woodridge	(630)	32,971	33,305
60098	Woodstock	(815)	24,770	25,084
60482	Worth	(708)	10,789	10,844
60560	Yorkville	(630)	16,921	17,495
60099	Zion	(847)	24,413	24,362

Indiana

ZIP	Place	Area code	2010 population	2012 estimate
*46011	Anderson	(765)	56,129	55,554
46706	Auburn	(260)	12,731	12,787
46123	Avon	(317)	12,446	13,306
47421	Bedford	(812)	13,413	13,402
46107	Beech Grove	(317)	14,192	14,340
*47408	Bloomington	(812)	80,405	81,963
46112	Brownsburg	(317)	21,285	22,603
*46032	Carmel	(317)	79,191	83,565
46303	Cedar Lake	(219)	11,560	11,664
46304	Chesterton	(219)	13,068	13,199
*47129	Clarksville	(812)	21,724	21,837
*47201	Columbus	(812)	44,061	45,429
47331	Connersville	(765)	13,481	13,335
*47933	Crawfordsville	(765)	15,915	16,015
*46307	Crown Point	(219)	27,317	28,171
*46311	Dyer	(219)	16,390	16,379
46312	East Chicago	(219)	29,698	29,476
46515	Elkhart	(574)	50,949	51,152
*47708	Evansville	(812)	117,429	120,235
46038	Fishers	(317)	76,794	81,833
*46802	Fort Wayne	(260)	253,691	254,555
*46041	Frankfort	(765)	16,422	16,276
46131	Franklin	(317)	23,712	23,953
*46401	Gary	(219)	80,294	79,170
*46526	Goshen	(574)	31,719	32,064
46530	Granger (c)	(574)	30,465	—
46135	Greencastle	(765)	10,326	10,331
46140	Greenfield	(317)	20,602	21,056
47240	Greensburg	(812)	11,492	11,638

ZIP	Place	Area code	2010 population	2012 estimate
*46142	Greenwood	(317)	49,791	52,652
46319	Griffith	(219)	16,893	16,726
*46320	Hammond	(219)	80,830	79,686
*46322	Highland	(219)	23,727	23,458
46342	Hobart	(219)	29,059	28,735
46750	Huntington	(260)	17,391	17,291
*46206	Indianapolis	(317)	820,445	834,852
*47546	Jasper	(812)	15,038	15,157
*47130	Jeffersonville	(812)	44,953	45,671
*46902	Kokomo	(765)	45,468	56,866
46350	La Porte	(219)	22,053	22,096
*47901	Lafayette	(765)	67,140	67,925
46405	Lake Station	(219)	12,572	12,392
46226	Lawrence	(317)	46,001	46,756
46052	Lebanon	(765)	15,792	15,715
46947	Logansport	(574)	18,396	18,217
47250	Madison	(812)	11,967	12,083
*46952	Marion	(765)	29,948	29,639
46151	Martinsville	(765)	11,828	11,831
*46401	Merrillville	(219)	35,246	35,631
*46360	Michigan City	(219)	31,479	31,150
*46544	Mishawaka	(574)	48,252	48,031
*47302	Muncie	(765)	70,085	70,087
46321	Munster	(219)	23,603	23,413
*47150	New Albany	(812)	36,372	36,462
47362	New Castle	(765)	18,114	17,805
46774	New Haven	(260)	14,794	15,390
*46060	Noblesville	(317)	51,969	55,075
*46970	Peru	(765)	11,417	11,257
46168	Plainfield	(317)	27,631	29,154
46563	Plymouth	(574)	10,033	10,032
46368	Portage	(219)	36,828	36,860
47907	Purdue University (c)	(765)	12,183	—
*47374	Richmond	(765)	36,812	36,599
46373	Saint John	(219)	14,850	15,335
46375	Schererville	(219)	29,243	29,101
47274	Seymour	(812)	17,503	18,520
46176	Shelbyville	(765)	19,191	19,159
*46624	South Bend	(574)	101,168	100,800
46224	Speedway	(317)	11,812	11,930
*47808	Terre Haute	(812)	60,785	61,112
*46383	Valparaiso	(219)	31,730	32,014
47591	Vincennes	(812)	18,423	18,239
*46992	Wabash	(260)	10,666	10,484
*46580	Warsaw	(574)	13,559	13,815
47501	Washington	(812)	11,509	11,739
*46580	West Lafayette	(765)	29,596	30,419
46074	Westfield	(317)	30,068	32,070
46077	Zionsville	(317)	14,160	24,159

Iowa

ZIP	Place	Area code	2010 population	2012 estimate
50009	Altoona	(515)	14,541	15,409
*50010	Ames	(515)	58,965	60,634
*50021	Ankeny	(515)	45,582	49,080
52722	Bettendorf	(563)	33,217	34,255
*50036	Boone	(515)	12,661	12,546
52601	Burlington	(319)	25,663	25,665
51401	Carroll	(712)	10,103	10,017
*50613	Cedar Falls	(319)	39,260	39,993
*52401	Cedar Rapids	(319)	126,326	128,119
*52732	Clinton	(563)	26,885	26,647
50325	Clive	(515)	15,447	16,220
52241	Coralville	(319)	18,907	19,692
*51501	Council Bluffs	(712)	62,230	62,115
*52802	Davenport	(563)	99,685	101,363
*50318	Des Moines	(515)	203,433	206,688
*52001	Dubuque	(563)	57,637	58,155
50501	Fort Dodge	(515)	25,206	24,751
52627	Fort Madison	(319)	11,051	11,019
50125	Indianola	(515)	14,782	14,947
*52240	Iowa City	(319)	67,862	70,133
50131	Johnston	(515)	17,278	18,728
52632	Keokuk	(319)	10,780	10,732
52302	Marion	(319)	34,768	35,843
50158	Marshalltown	(641)	27,552	27,683
*50401	Mason City	(641)	28,079	27,823
52761	Muscatine	(563)	22,886	22,988
50208	Newton	(641)	15,254	15,108
52317	North Liberty	(319)	13,374	14,485
52577	Oskaloosa	(641)	11,463	11,555
52501	Ottumwa	(641)	25,023	24,806
50219	Pella	(641)	10,352	10,397
*51101	Sioux City	(712)	82,684	82,719
51301	Spencer	(712)	11,233	11,192
50588	Storm Lake	(712)	10,600	10,775
*50322	Urbandale	(515)	39,463	41,020
*50701	Waterloo	(319)	68,406	68,297
50263	Waukee	(515)	13,790	15,931
50677	Waverly	(319)	9,874	10,035
*50265	West Des Moines	(515)	56,609	59,296

Kansas

ZIP	Place	Area code	2010 population	2012 estimate
67002	Andover	(316)	11,791	12,099
67005	Arkansas City	(620)	12,415	12,340
66002	Atchison	(913)	11,021	10,953
67037	Derby	(316)	22,158	22,943
*67801	Dodge City	(620)	27,340	28,075
67042	El Dorado	(316)	13,021	12,900
66801	Emporia	(620)	24,916	24,958
*67846	Garden City	(620)	26,658	26,985
*66030	Gardner	(913)	19,123	20,318
67530	Great Bend	(620)	15,995	15,923
*67601	Hays	(785)	20,510	20,993
67060	Haysville	(316)	10,826	10,951
*67501	Hutchinson	(620)	42,080	41,962
*66441	Junction City	(785)	23,353	25,817
*66102	Kansas City	(913)	145,786	147,268
66043	Lansing	(913)	11,265	11,591
*66044	Lawrence	(785)	87,643	89,512
*66048	Leavenworth	(913)	35,251	35,816
66209	Leawood	(913)	31,867	32,539
*66214	Lenexa	(913)	48,190	49,398
*67901	Liberal	(620)	20,525	21,084
*66502	Manhattan	(785)	52,281	56,069
67460	McPherson	(620)	13,155	13,218
*66202	Merriam	(913)	11,003	11,174
*67114	Newton	(316)	19,132	19,189
*66061	Olathe	(913)	125,872	130,045
66067	Ottawa	(785)	12,649	12,575
*66204	Overland Park	(913)	173,372	178,919
67357	Parsons	(620)	10,500	10,327
*66762	Pittsburg	(620)	20,233	20,360
*66208	Prairie Village	(913)	21,447	21,769
*67401	Salina	(785)	47,707	48,045
*66203	Shawnee	(913)	62,209	63,622
*66601	Topeka	(785)	127,473	127,939
*67202	Wichita	(316)	382,368	385,577
67156	Winfield	(620)	12,301	12,365

Kentucky

Area code (364) overlays area code (270) as of Mar. 3, 2014.

ZIP	Place	Area code	2010 population	2012 estimate
*41101	Ashland	(606)	21,684	21,506
40004	Bardstown	(502)	11,700	12,848
*10403	Berea	(859)	13,561	14,148
42101	Bowling Green	(270)	58,067	60,600
41005	Burlington (c)	(859)	15,926	—
*42718	Campbellsville	(270)	9,108	10,759
41011	Covington	(859)	40,640	40,713
40422	Danville	(859)	16,218	16,349
*42701	Elizabethtown	(270)	28,531	29,335
*41018	Erlanger	(859)	18,082	18,359
*41042	Florence	(859)	29,951	31,088
42223	Fort Campbell North (c)	(270)	13,685	—
40121	Fort Knox (c)	(270)	10,124	—
41075	Fort Thomas	(859)	16,325	16,222
*40601	Frankfort	(502)	25,527	27,590
40324	Georgetown	(502)	29,098	30,271
*42141	Glasgow	(270)	14,028	14,095
42420	Henderson	(270)	28,757	28,911
*42240	Hopkinsville	(270)	31,577	32,966
41051	Independence	(859)	24,757	25,664
40269	Jeffersontown	(502)	26,595	26,923
*40342	Lawrenceburg	(502)	10,505	11,042
*40507	Lexington-Fayette	(859)	295,803	305,489
*40232	Louisville-Jefferson Co.[1]	(502)	597,337	605,110
*40252	Lyndon	(502)	11,002	11,170
42431	Madisonville	(270)	19,591	19,798
42066	Mayfield	(270)	10,024	10,115
40965	Middlesborough	(606)	10,334	10,014
42071	Murray	(270)	17,741	17,981
*41071	Newport	(859)	15,273	15,438
*40356	Nicholasville	(859)	28,015	28,400
*42301	Owensboro	(270)	57,265	58,083
*42003	Paducah	(270)	25,024	25,048
*40160	Radcliff	(270)	21,688	23,036
*40475	Richmond	(859)	31,364	32,112
*40207	Saint Matthews	(502)	17,472	17,700
*40066	Shelbyville	(502)	14,045	14,585
40165	Shepherdsville	(502)	11,222	11,463
40256	Shively	(502)	15,264	15,455
*42501	Somerset	(606)	11,196	11,320
*40391	Winchester	(859)	18,368	18,451

(1) Louisville merged with Jefferson County in 2003.

Louisiana

ZIP	Place	Area code	2010 population	2012 estimate
*70510	Abbeville	(337)	12,257	12,382
*71301	Alexandria	(318)	47,723	48,367
70714	Baker	(225)	13,895	13,890
71220	Bastrop	(318)	11,365	11,154

ZIP	Place	Area code	2010 population	2012 estimate
*70821	Baton Rouge	(225)	229,493	230,058
*70360	Bayou Blue (c)	(985)	12,352	—
*70364	Bayou Cane (c)	(985)	19,355	—
*70037	Belle Chase (c)	(504)	12,679	—
*70427	Bogalusa	(985)	12,232	12,044
*71111	Bossier City	(318)	61,315	64,655
70818	Central	(225)	26,864	27,548
*70043	Chalmette (c)	(504)	16,751	—
70433	Claiborne (c)	(985)	11,507	—
*70526	Crowley	(337)	13,265	13,189
*70726	Denham Springs	(225)	10,215	10,129
70634	DeRidder	(337)	10,578	10,758
70047	Destrehan (c)	(985)	11,535	—
70072	Estelle (c)	(504)	16,377	—
70535	Eunice	(337)	10,398	10,379
70810	Gardere (c)	(225)	10,580	—
*70707	Gonzales	(225)	9,781	10,176
*70053	Gretna	(504)	17,736	17,754
*70401	Hammond	(985)	20,019	20,122
*70058	Harvey (c)	(504)	20,348	—
*70360	Houma	(985)	33,727	33,707
70121	Jefferson (c)	(504)	11,193	—
70546	Jennings	(337)	10,383	10,252
*70062	Kenner	(504)	66,702	66,820
*70501	Lafayette	(337)	120,623	122,761
*70601	Lake Charles	(337)	71,993	73,474
*70068	Laplace (c)	(985)	29,872	—
70070	Luling (c)	(985)	12,119	—
*70471	Mandeville	(985)	11,560	12,112
*70072	Marrero (c)	(504)	33,141	—
*70009	Metairie (c)	(504)	138,481	—
*71055	Minden	(318)	13,082	12,992
*71207	Monroe	(318)	48,815	49,156
*70380	Morgan City	(985)	12,404	12,122
70611	Moss Bluff (c)	(337)	11,557	—
*71457	Natchitoches	(318)	18,323	18,299
*70560	New Iberia	(337)	30,617	30,846
*70140	New Orleans	(504)	343,829	369,250
*70570	Opelousas	(337)	16,634	16,554
*71360	Pineville	(318)	14,555	14,557
70769	Prairieville (c)	(225)	26,895	—
70394	Raceland (c)	(985)	10,193	—
70123	River Ridge (c)	(504)	13,494	—
*71270	Ruston	(318)	21,859	21,953
70817	Shenandoah (c)	(318)	18,399	—
*71102	Shreveport	(318)	199,311	201,867
*70458	Slidell	(985)	27,068	27,369
*70663	Sulphur	(337)	20,410	20,157
70056	Terrytown (c)	(504)	23,319	—
*70301	Thibodaux	(985)	14,566	14,546
70056	Timberlane (c)	(504)	10,243	—
70094	Waggaman (c)	(504)	10,015	—
*71291	West Monroe	(318)	13,065	13,082
70058	Woodmere (c)	(504)	12,080	—
70791	Zachary	(225)	14,960	15,565

Maine

Area code 207 applies to the entire state. See introductory note.

ZIP	Place	2010 population	2012 estimate
*04210	Auburn	23,055	22,972
*04330	Augusta	19,136	18,946
*04401	Bangor	33,039	32,817
*04005	Biddeford	21,277	21,309
04011	Brunswick	20,278	20,329
04011	Brunswick (c)	15,175	—
04105	Falmouth	11,185	11,399
04038	Gorham	16,381	16,667
04043	Kennebunk	10,798	10,971
*04240	Lewiston	36,592	36,460
*04473	Orono	10,362	10,585
*04101	Portland	66,194	66,214
04072	Saco	18,482	18,758
04073	Sanford	20,798	20,882
*04074	Scarborough	18,919	19,165
*04106	South Portland	25,002	25,088
*04901	Waterville	15,722	15,855
*04092	Westbrook	17,494	17,606
*04062	Windham	17,001	17,272
03909	York	12,529	12,656

Maryland

Area code (240) overlays area code (301). Area codes (443) and (667) overlay area code (410).

ZIP	Place	Area code	2010 population	2012 estimate
21001	Aberdeen	(410)	14,959	15,018
20607	Accokeek (c)	(301)	10,573	—
*20783	Adelphi (c)	(301)	15,086	—
*21401	Annapolis	(410)	38,394	38,620
21403	Annapolis Neck (c)	(410)	10,950	—
21227	Arbutus (c)	(410)	20,483	—
*21012	Arnold (c)	(410)	23,106	—
*20916	Aspen Hill (c)	(301)	48,759	—
21220	Ballenger Creek (c)	(410)	18,274	—
*21203	Baltimore	(410)	620,961	621,342
*21014	Bel Air	(410)	10,120	10,274
21050	Bel Air North (c)	(410)	30,568	—
21014	Bel Air South (c)	(410)	47,709	—
*20705	Beltsville (c)	(301)	16,772	—
20603	Bensville (c)	(301)	11,923	—
20814	Bethesda (c)	(301)	60,858	—
*20715	Bowie	(301)	54,727	56,129
21225	Brooklyn Park (c)	(410)	14,373	—
20619	California (c)	(301)	11,857	—
20705	Calverton (c)	(301)	17,724	—
*21613	Cambridge	(410)	12,326	12,503
*20748	Camp Springs (c)	(301)	19,096	—
21234	Carney (c)	(410)	29,941	—
*21228	Catonsville (c)	(410)	41,567	—
20657	Chesapeake Ranch Estates (c)	(301)	10,519	—
20782	Chillum (c)	(301)	33,513	—
20871	Clarksburg (c)	(301)	13,766	—
20735	Clinton (c)	(301)	35,970	—
20904	Cloverly (c)	(301)	15,126	—
21030	Cockeysville (c)	(410)	20,776	—
*20914	Colesville (c)	(301)	14,647	—
*20740	College Park	(301)	30,413	31,208
*21045	Columbia (c)	(410)	99,615	—
21114	Crofton (c)	(410)	27,348	—
*21502	Cumberland	(301)	20,859	20,572
20872	Damascus (c)	(301)	15,257	—
21222	Dundalk (c)	(410)	63,597	—
20737	East Riverdale (c)	(301)	15,509	—
*21601	Easton	(410)	15,945	16,598
21040	Edgewood (c)	(410)	25,562	—
21784	Eldersburg (c)	(410)	30,531	—
21075	Elkridge (c)	(410)	15,593	—
*21921	Elkton	(410)	15,443	15,579
21043	Ellicott City (c)	(410)	65,834	—
21221	Essex (c)	(410)	39,262	—
20904	Fairland (c)	(301)	23,681	—
21061	Ferndale (c)	(410)	16,746	—
*20747	Forestville (c)	(301)	12,353	—
20744	Fort Washington (c)	(301)	23,717	—
*21701	Frederick	(301)	65,239	66,382
*20877	Gaithersburg	(301)	59,933	62,794
*20874	Germantown (c)	(301)	86,395	—
20745	Glassmanor (c)	(301)	17,295	—
*21061	Glen Burnie (c)	(410)	67,639	—
20906	Glenmont (c)	(301)	13,529	—
20769	Glenn Dale (c)	(301)	13,466	—
*20770	Greenbelt	(301)	23,068	23,541
*21740	Hagerstown	(301)	39,662	40,638
21740	Halfway (c)	(301)	10,701	—
21078	Havre de Grace	(410)	12,952	13,392
20748	Hillcrest Heights (c)	(301)	16,469	—
*20780	Hyattsville	(301)	17,557	17,865
21043	Ilchester (c)	(410)	23,476	—
21085	Joppatowne (c)	(410)	12,616	—
20902	Kemp Mill (c)	(301)	12,564	—
*20772	Kettering (c)	(301)	12,790	—
*21122	Lake Shore (c)	(410)	19,477	—
20785	Landover (c)	(301)	23,078	—
20787	Langley Park (c)	(301)	18,755	—
20706	Lanham (c)	(301)	10,157	—
20774	Largo (c)	(301)	10,709	—
*20707	Laurel	(301)	25,115	25,554
20653	Lexington Park (c)	(301)	11,626	—
21090	Linthicum (c)	(410)	10,324	—
21207	Lochearn (c)	(410)	25,333	—
20724	Maryland City (c)	(301)	16,093	—
21093	Mays Chapel (c)	(410)	11,420	—
21220	Middle River (c)	(410)	25,191	—
21207	Milford Mill (c)	(410)	29,042	—
*20716	Mitchellville (c)	(301)	10,967	—
*20886	Montgomery Village (c)	(301)	32,032	—
20784	New Carrollton	(301)	12,135	12,383
*20815	North Bethesda (c)	(301)	43,828	—
20878	North Potomac (c)	(301)	24,410	—
21811	Ocean Pines (c)	(410)	11,710	—
21113	Odenton (c)	(410)	37,132	—
*20832	Olney (c)	(301)	33,844	—
21206	Overlea (c)	(410)	12,275	—
21117	Owings Mills (c)	(410)	30,622	—
*20745	Oxon Hill (c)	(301)	17,722	—
21234	Parkville (c)	(410)	30,734	—
21401	Parole (c)	(410)	15,922	—
21122	Pasadena (c)	(410)	24,287	—
21128	Perry Hall (c)	(410)	28,474	—
21282	Pikesville (c)	(410)	30,764	—
*20850	Potomac (c)	(301)	44,965	—
21133	Randallstown (c)	(301)	32,430	—

ZIP	Place	Area code	2010 population	2012 estimate
20855	Redland (c)	(301)	17,242	—
*21136	Reisterstown (c)	(410)	25,968	—
*21122	Riviera Beach (c)	(410)	12,677	—
*20850	Rockville	(301)	61,209	63,244
20772	Rosaryville (c)	(301)	10,697	—
21237	Rosedale (c)	(410)	19,257	—
21221	Rossville (c)	(410)	15,147	—
*21801	Salisbury	(410)	30,343	31,243
20723	Scaggsville (c)	(301)	24,333	—
*20706	Seabrook (c)	(301)	17,287	—
21144	Severn (c)	(410)	44,231	—
21146	Severna Park (c)	(410)	37,634	—
*20907	Silver Spring (c)	(301)	71,452	—
20707	South Laurel (c)	(301)	26,112	—
*20746	Suitland (c)	(301)	25,825	—
21842	Summerfield (c)	(410)	10,898	—
*20913	Takoma Park	(301)	16,715	17,205
*21204	Towson (c)	(410)	55,197	—
20854	Travilah (c)	(301)	12,159	—
*20602	Waldorf (c)	(301)	67,752	—
20743	Walker Mill (c)	(301)	11,302	—
*21157	Westminster	(410)	18,590	18,628
*20902	Wheaton (c)	(301)	48,284	—
20903	White Oak (c)	(301)	17,403	—
21207	Woodlawn (c) (Baltimore Co.)	(410)	37,879	—

Massachusetts

Area code (339) overlays area code (781). Area code (351) overlays area code (978). Area code (774) overlays area code (508). Area code (857) overlays area code (617). See introductory note.

ZIP	Place	Area code	2010 population	2012 estimate
02351	Abington	(781)	15,985	16,060
*01720	Acton	(978)	21,924	22,599
*02743	Acushnet	(508)	10,303	10,326
01001	Agawam	(413)	28,438	28,608
01913	Amesbury	(978)	16,283	16,535
*01002	Amherst	(413)	37,819	39,016
*01002	Amherst Center (c)	(413)	19,065	—
*01810	Andover	(978)	33,201	34,142
*02205	Arlington	(781)	42,844	43,711
01721	Ashland	(508)	16,593	16,993
*01331	Athol	(978)	11,584	11,631
02703	Attleboro	(508)	43,593	43,837
01501	Auburn	(508)	16,188	16,287
*02630	Barnstable	(508)	45,193	44,824
*01730	Bedford	(781)	13,320	13,765
01007	Belchertown	(413)	14,649	14,719
02019	Bellingham	(508)	16,332	16,521
*02478	Belmont	(781)	24,729	25,204
01915	Beverly	(978)	39,502	40,286
*01821	Billerica	(978)	40,243	41,454
*02205	Boston	(617)	617,594	636,479
*02532	Bourne	(508)	19,754	19,806
*02185	Braintree	(781)	35,744	36,249
*02324	Bridgewater	(508)	26,563	26,902
*02303	Brockton	(508)	93,810	94,094
*02446	Brookline	(617)	58,732	59,115
*01803	Burlington	(781)	24,498	25,165
*02139	Cambridge	(617)	105,162	106,471
02021	Canton	(781)	21,561	21,932
*02330	Carver	(508)	11,509	11,521
01507	Charlton	(508)	12,981	13,119
01824	Chelmsford	(978)	33,802	34,545
02150	Chelsea	(617)	35,177	36,828
*01020	Chicopee	(413)	55,298	55,490
01510	Clinton	(978)	13,606	13,668
01742	Concord	(978)	17,668	18,957
01923	Danvers	(978)	26,493	27,020
*02714	Dartmouth	(508)	34,032	34,448
*02026	Dedham	(781)	24,729	24,974
02638	Dennis	(508)	14,207	14,153
01826	Dracut	(978)	29,457	30,220
01571	Dudley	(508)	11,390	11,557
*02332	Duxbury	(781)	15,059	15,172
02333	East Bridgewater	(508)	13,794	13,955
*01028	East Longmeadow	(413)	15,720	15,896
01027	Easthampton	(413)	16,053	16,007
*02334	Easton	(508)	23,112	23,352
02149	Everett	(617)	41,667	42,567
02719	Fairhaven	(508)	15,873	15,900
*02722	Fall River	(508)	88,857	88,945
*02540	Falmouth	(508)	31,531	31,514
01420	Fitchburg	(978)	40,318	40,411
02035	Foxborough	(508)	16,865	17,087
*01701	Framingham	(508)	68,318	70,068
02038	Franklin	(508)	31,635	32,374
*01440	Gardner	(978)	20,228	20,254
*01930	Gloucester	(978)	28,789	29,191
01519	Grafton	(508)	17,765	18,045
*01301	Greenfield	(413)	17,456	17,553

ZIP	Place	Area code	2010 population	2012 estimate
*01450	Groton	(978)	10,646	11,017
*02339	Hanover	(781)	13,879	14,151
*02341	Hanson	(781)	10,209	10,292
02645	Harwich	(508)	12,243	12,263
*01830	Haverhill	(978)	60,879	61,797
*02043	Hingham	(781)	22,157	22,520
02343	Holbrook	(781)	10,791	10,899
01520	Holden	(508)	17,346	17,636
01746	Holliston	(508)	13,547	14,014
*01040	Holyoke	(413)	39,880	40,135
01748	Hopkinton	(508)	14,925	15,478
01749	Hudson	(978)	19,063	19,481
01749	Hudson (c)	(978)	14,907	—
02045	Hull	(781)	10,293	10,302
01938	Ipswich	(978)	13,175	13,545
02364	Kingston	(781)	12,629	12,727
02347	Lakeville	(508)	10,602	10,861
*01842	Lawrence	(978)	76,377	77,326
01524	Leicester	(508)	10,970	11,110
01453	Leominster	(978)	40,759	40,989
*02420	Lexington	(781)	31,394	32,272
*01028	Longmeadow	(413)	15,784	15,835
*01853	Lowell	(978)	106,519	108,522
01056	Ludlow	(413)	21,103	21,195
*01462	Lunenburg	(978)	10,086	10,847
*01901	Lynn	(781)	90,329	91,253
01940	Lynnfield	(781)	11,596	11,805
02148	Malden	(781)	59,450	60,374
*02048	Mansfield	(508)	23,184	23,414
01945	Marblehead	(781)	19,808	20,076
01752	Marlborough	(508)	38,499	39,204
*02050	Marshfield	(781)	25,132	25,436
02649	Mashpee	(508)	14,006	14,005
01754	Maynard	(978)	10,106	10,304
02052	Medfield	(508)	12,024	12,219
*02155	Medford	(781)	56,173	57,033
02053	Medway	(508)	12,752	12,864
02176	Melrose	(781)	26,983	27,435
01844	Methuen	(978)	47,255	48,009
*02346	Middleborough	(508)	23,116	23,395
01757	Milford	(508)	27,999	28,184
01757	Milford (c)	(508)	25,055	—
*01527	Millbury	(508)	13,261	13,305
02186	Milton	(617)	27,003	27,158
*02584	Nantucket	(508)	10,172	10,298
01760	Natick	(508)	33,006	33,760
*02494	Needham	(781)	28,886	29,300
*02740	New Bedford	(508)	95,072	94,929
01950	Newburyport	(978)	17,416	17,654
*02456	Newton	(617)	85,146	86,307
02056	Norfolk	(508)	11,227	11,539
01247	North Adams	(413)	13,708	13,583
01845	North Andover	(978)	28,352	28,422
*02760	North Attleborough	(508)	20,712	28,806
*01864	North Reading	(978)	14,892	15,254
*01060	Northampton	(413)	28,549	28,592
01532	Northborough	(508)	14,155	14,724
01534	Northbridge	(508)	15,707	15,917
*02766	Norton	(508)	19,031	19,310
02061	Norwell	(781)	10,506	10,574
02062	Norwood	(781)	28,602	28,780
01540	Oxford	(508)	13,709	13,771
01069	Palmer	(413)	12,140	12,152
*01960	Peabody	(978)	51,251	51,867
*02359	Pembroke	(781)	17,837	17,959
*01463	Pepperell	(978)	11,497	11,797
*01201	Pittsfield	(413)	44,737	44,168
*02360	Plymouth	(508)	56,468	57,463
*02169	Quincy	(617)	92,271	93,027
02368	Randolph	(781)	32,112	33,226
*02767	Raynham	(508)	13,383	13,504
01867	Reading	(781)	24,747	25,192
02769	Rehoboth	(508)	11,608	11,739
02151	Revere	(781)	51,755	53,179
02370	Rockland	(781)	17,489	17,580
*01970	Salem	(978)	41,340	42,219
*02563	Sandwich	(508)	20,675	20,662
01906	Saugus	(781)	26,628	27,338
*02066	Scituate	(781)	18,133	18,173
02771	Seekonk	(508)	13,722	13,983
02067	Sharon	(781)	17,612	17,826
*01545	Shrewsbury	(508)	35,608	36,077
02725	Somerset	(508)	18,165	18,270
*02143	Somerville	(617)	75,754	77,104
01075	South Hadley	(413)	17,514	17,773
02664	South Yarmouth (c)	(508)	11,092	—
01550	Southbridge	(508)	16,719	16,799
01562	Spencer	(508)	11,688	11,749
*01101	Springfield	(413)	153,060	153,552
02180	Stoneham	(781)	21,437	21,605
02072	Stoughton	(781)	26,962	27,849
01776	Sudbury	(978)	17,659	18,119
01907	Swampscott	(781)	13,787	13,919

ZIP	Place	Area code	2010 population	2012 estimate
02777	Swansea	(508)	15,865	16,010
*02780	Taunton	(508)	55,874	56,055
01876	Tewksbury	(978)	28,961	29,669
01879	Tyngsborough	(978)	11,292	11,953
01569	Uxbridge	(508)	13,457	13,560
01880	Wakefield	(781)	24,932	25,613
02081	Walpole	(508)	24,070	24,562
*02451	Waltham	(781)	60,632	61,918
02571	Wareham	(508)	21,822	22,339
*02471	Watertown	(781)	31,915	32,863
01778	Wayland	(508)	12,994	13,285
01570	Webster	(508)	16,767	16,812
01570	Webster (c)	(508)	11,412	—
02457	Wellesley	(781)	27,982	28,748
*01089	West Springfield	(413)	28,391	28,574
01581	Westborough	(508)	18,272	18,455
*01085	Westfield	(413)	41,094	41,399
01886	Westford	(978)	21,951	22,851
02493	Weston	(781)	11,261	11,737
02790	Westport	(508)	15,532	15,655
02090	Westwood	(781)	14,618	14,768
*02188	Weymouth	(781)	53,743	54,906
02382	Whitman	(781)	14,489	14,609
01095	Wilbraham	(413)	14,219	14,337
01887	Wilmington	(978)	22,325	22,936
01475	Winchendon	(978)	10,300	10,472
01890	Winchester	(781)	21,374	21,869
02152	Winthrop	(617)	17,497	17,940
*01801	Woburn	(781)	38,120	38,949
*01613	Worcester	(508)	181,045	182,669
*02093	Wrentham	(508)	10,955	11,118
*02675	Yarmouth	(508)	23,793	23,703

Michigan

Area code (947) overlays area code (248).

ZIP	Place	Area code	2010 population	2012 estimate
49221	Adrian	(517)	21,133	20,842
*48101	Allen Park	(313)	28,210	27,732
49401	Allendale (c)	(616)	17,579	—
49707	Alpena	(906)	10,483	10,340
*48106	Ann Arbor	(734)	113,934	116,121
*48321	Auburn Hills	(248)	21,412	21,614
*49016	Battle Creek	(269)	52,347	51,911
*48707	Bay City	(906)	34,932	34,521
48505	Beecher (c)	(810)	10,232	—
*49022	Benton Harbor	(269)	10,038	10,040
48072	Berkley	(248)	14,970	15,123
48025	Beverly Hills	(248)	10,267	10,367
49307	Big Rapids	(231)	10,601	10,702
*48012	Birmingham	(248)	20,103	20,437
*48509	Burton	(810)	29,999	29,432
49601	Cadillac	(231)	10,355	10,270
*48017	Clawson	(248)	11,825	11,945
49036	Coldwater	(517)	10,945	10,887
49321	Comstock Park (c)	(616)	10,088	—
49508	Cutlerville (c)	(616)	14,370	—
*48120	Dearborn	(313)	98,153	96,474
*48127	Dearborn Heights	(313)	57,774	56,838
*48231	Detroit	(313)	713,777	701,475
*49506	East Grand Rapids	(616)	10,694	11,001
*48826	East Lansing	(517)	48,579	48,518
48021	Eastpointe	(586)	32,442	32,411
49829	Escanaba	(906)	12,616	12,552
*48333	Farmington	(248)	10,372	10,479
*48333	Farmington Hills	(248)	79,740	80,756
48430	Fenton	(810)	11,756	11,554
48220	Ferndale	(248)	19,900	20,053
*48501	Flint	(810)	102,434	100,515
49506	Forest Hills (c)	(616)	25,867	—
48026	Fraser	(586)	14,480	14,518
*48135	Garden City	(734)	27,692	27,235
49417	Grand Haven	(616)	10,412	10,650
*49501	Grand Rapids	(616)	188,040	190,411
*49418	Grandville	(616)	15,378	15,596
48230	Grosse Pointe Park	(313)	11,555	11,345
*48230	Grosse Pointe Woods	(313)	16,135	15,838
*48212	Hamtramck	(313)	22,423	22,101
48225	Harper Woods	(313)	14,236	13,990
48840	Haslett (c)	(517)	19,220	—
48030	Hazel Park	(248)	16,422	16,588
48203	Highland Park	(313)	11,776	11,629
*49423	Holland	(616)	33,051	33,279
48842	Holt (c)	(517)	23,973	—
48141	Inkster	(313)/(734)	25,369	24,962
48846	Ionia	(616)	11,394	11,422
*49204	Jackson	(517)	33,534	33,411
*49428	Jenison (c)	(616)	16,538	—
*49001	Kalamazoo	(269)	74,262	75,092
*49518	Kentwood	(616)	48,707	49,694
*48901	Lansing	(517)	114,297	113,996
48146	Lincoln Park	(313)	38,144	37,478

ZIP	Place	Area code	2010 population	2012 estimate
*48150	Livonia	(734)	96,942	95,586
48071	Madison Heights	(248)	29,694	29,985
49855	Marquette	(906)	21,355	21,532
48122	Melvindale	(313)	10,715	10,525
*48640	Midland	(906)	41,863	42,020
*48161	Monroe	(734)	20,733	20,535
*48046	Mount Clemens	(586)	16,314	16,303
*48804	Mount Pleasant	(906)	26,016	26,183
*49440	Muskegon	(231)	38,401	37,046
49444	Muskegon Heights	(231)	10,856	10,789
*48047	New Baltimore	(586)	12,084	12,113
*49120	Niles	(269)	11,600	11,502
49505	Northview (c)	(616)	14,541	—
*49441	Norton Shores	(231)	23,994	23,870
*48376	Novi	(248)	55,224	56,912
48237	Oak Park	(248)	29,319	29,594
*48805	Okemos (c)	(517)	21,369	—
*48867	Owosso	(906)	15,194	14,852
*48343	Pontiac	(248)	59,515	60,175
*48061	Port Huron	(810)	30,184	29,684
*49081	Portage	(269)	46,292	47,126
*48192	Riverview	(734)	12,486	12,314
*48308	Rochester	(248)	12,711	12,889
*48306	Rochester Hills	(248)	70,995	72,283
48174	Romulus	(313)/(734)	23,989	23,592
48066	Roseville	(586)	47,299	47,321
*48068	Royal Oak	(248)	57,236	58,410
*48605	Saginaw	(906)	51,508	50,790
*48080	Saint Clair Shores	(313)	59,715	59,749
*49783	Sault Sainte Marie	(906)	14,144	14,194
48178	South Lyon	(248)	11,327	11,500
*48037	Southfield	(248)	71,739	72,507
48195	Southgate	(734)	30,047	29,585
*48311	Sterling Heights	(586)	129,699	130,410
49091	Sturgis	(269)	10,994	10,884
48180	Taylor	(313)/(734)	63,131	62,114
*49684	Traverse City	(231)	14,674	14,911
48183	Trenton	(734)	18,853	18,562
*48099	Troy	(248)	80,980	82,212
49534	Walker	(616)	23,537	24,003
*48090	Warren	(586)	134,056	134,141
48917	Waverly (c)	(517)	23,925	—
48184	Wayne	(734)	17,593	17,310
*48185	Westland	(313)/(734)	84,094	82,883
48393	Wixom	(248)	13,498	13,684
48183	Woodhaven	(734)	12,875	12,701
*48192	Wyandotte	(734)	25,883	25,485
*49509	Wyoming	(616)	72,125	73,371
*48197	Ypsilanti	(734)	19,435	19,621

Minnesota

ZIP	Place	Area code	2010 population	2012 estimate
56007	Albert Lea	(507)	18,016	17,898
56308	Alexandria	(320)	11,070	11,549
*55304	Andover	(763)	30,598	31,200
55303	Anoka	(612)	17,142	17,243
55124	Apple Valley	(952)	49,084	49,978
55912	Austin	(507)	24,718	24,800
*56601	Bemidji	(218)	13,431	13,723
55309	Big Lake	(763)	10,060	10,247
55014	Blaine	(651)	57,186	59,412
55420	Bloomington	(952)	82,893	86,033
*56401	Brainerd	(218)	13,590	13,517
55429	Brooklyn Center	(763)	30,104	30,643
*55443	Brooklyn Park	(763)	75,781	77,752
55313	Buffalo	(763)	15,453	15,724
55337	Burnsville	(651)	60,306	61,130
55316	Champlin	(763)	23,089	23,694
55317	Chanhassen	(952)	22,952	23,840
55318	Chaska	(952)	23,770	24,074
55720	Cloquet	(218)	12,124	12,036
55421	Columbia Heights	(612)	19,496	19,667
*55433	Coon Rapids	(763)	61,476	61,931
55016	Cottage Grove	(651)	34,589	35,181
*55428	Crystal	(763)	22,151	22,524
*55806	Duluth	(218)	86,265	86,211
55121	Eagan	(651)	64,206	64,854
*55005	East Bethel	(763)	11,626	11,596
*55344	Eden Prairie	(612)	60,797	62,258
55424	Edina	(952)	47,941	49,050
55330	Elk River	(763)	22,974	23,273
*56031	Fairmont	(507)	10,666	10,463
55021	Faribault	(507)	23,352	23,394
55024	Farmington	(651)	21,086	21,902
56537	Fergus Falls	(218)	13,138	13,215
55025	Forest Lake	(651)	18,375	18,957
*55432	Fridley	(763)	27,208	27,639
*55427	Golden Valley	(763)	20,371	20,776
*55744	Grand Rapids	(218)	10,869	10,916
*55304	Ham Lake	(763)	15,296	15,552
55033	Hastings	(651)	22,172	22,321

ZIP	Place	Area code	2010 population	2012 estimate
*55746	Hibbing	(218)	16,361	16,287
*55343	Hopkins	(952)	17,591	17,982
55038	Hugo	(651)	13,332	13,834
55350	Hutchinson	(320)	14,178	13,929
*55076	Inver Grove Heights	(651)	33,880	34,198
*55044	Lakeville	(952)	55,954	57,342
*55014	Lino Lakes	(651)	20,216	20,746
*55109	Little Canada	(651)	9,773	10,008
*56001	Mankato	(507)	39,309	40,119
*55311	Maple Grove	(763)	61,567	64,420
*55109	Maplewood	(651)	38,018	39,337
56258	Marshall	(507)	13,680	13,446
*55118	Mendota Heights	(651)	11,071	11,138
*55440	Minneapolis	(612)	382,578	392,880
*55345	Minnetonka	(952)	49,734	51,123
*55362	Monticello	(763)	12,759	12,964
*56560	Moorhead	(218)	38,065	39,039
55112	Mounds View	(763)	12,155	12,407
55112	New Brighton	(651)	21,456	21,867
*54427	New Hope	(763)	20,339	20,728
56073	New Ulm	(507)	13,522	13,265
55056	North Branch	(651)	10,125	10,006
*56002	North Mankato	(507)	13,394	13,369
55109	North Saint Paul	(651)	11,460	11,694
55057	Northfield	(507)	20,007	20,515
*55128	Oakdale	(651)	27,378	27,726
*55330	Otsego	(763)	13,571	14,138
55060	Owatonna	(507)	25,599	25,421
*55446	Plymouth	(763)	70,576	72,928
55372	Prior Lake	(952)	22,796	23,754
55303	Ramsey	(763)	23,668	24,071
55066	Red Wing	(651)	16,459	16,441
55423	Richfield	(612)	35,228	36,087
55422	Robbinsdale	(763)	13,953	14,263
*55901	Rochester	(507)	106,769	108,992
55374	Rogers	(763)	8,597	11,641
55068	Rosemount	(651)	21,874	22,420
*55113	Roseville	(651)	33,660	34,666
*56301	Saint Cloud	(320)	65,842	65,986
*55426	Saint Louis Park	(952)	45,250	46,362
55376	Saint Michael	(763)	16,399	16,765
*55101	Saint Paul	(651)	285,068	290,770
56082	Saint Peter	(507)	11,196	11,427
56377	Sartell	(320)	15,876	16,183
56379	Sauk Rapids	(320)	12,773	12,965
55378	Savage	(952)	26,911	27,959
*55379	Shakopee	(612)	37,076	38,744
55126	Shoreview	(651)	25,043	25,628
55075	South Saint Paul	(651)	20,160	20,404
*55082	Stillwater	(651)	18,225	18,542
*55127	Vadnais Heights	(651)	12,302	12,764
*55087	Waconia	(952)	10,697	11,222
*55118	West Saint Paul	(651)	19,540	19,708
*55110	White Bear Lake	(651)	23,797	24,311
56201	Willmar	(320)	19,610	19,674
*55987	Winona	(507)	27,592	27,944
*55125	Woodbury	(651)	61,961	64,496
56187	Worthington	(507)	12,764	12,870

Mississippi

Area code (769) overlays area code (601).

ZIP	Place	Area code	2010 population	2012 estimate
39520	Bay Saint Louis	(228)	9,260	10,259
*39530	Biloxi	(228)	44,054	44,578
*39042	Brandon	(601)	21,705	22,160
*39601	Brookhaven	(601)	12,513	12,515
39272	Byram	(601)	11,489	11,721
39046	Canton	(601)	13,189	13,218
*38614	Clarksdale	(662)	17,962	17,648
*38732	Cleveland	(662)	12,334	12,206
*39056	Clinton	(601)	25,216	25,752
*39701	Columbus	(662)	23,640	23,452
*38834	Corinth	(662)	14,573	14,784
39553	Gautier	(228)	18,572	18,554
*38701	Greenville	(662)	34,400	33,418
*38930	Greenwood	(662)	15,205	14,954
*38901	Grenada	(662)	13,092	12,956
*39501	Gulfport	(228)	67,793	70,113
*39401	Hattiesburg	(601)	45,989	47,169
38632	Hernando	(662)	14,090	14,763
38637	Horn Lake	(662)	26,066	26,529
*38751	Indianola	(662)	10,683	10,495
*39205	Jackson	(601)	173,514	175,437
*39440	Laurel	(601)	18,540	18,838
39560	Long Beach	(228)	14,792	15,300
*39110	Madison	(601)	24,149	24,841
*39648	McComb	(601)	12,790	12,744
*39302	Meridian	(601)	41,148	40,832
*39563	Moss Point	(228)	13,704	13,687
*39120	Natchez	(601)	15,792	15,590
*39564	Ocean Springs	(228)	17,442	17,461

ZIP	Place	Area code	2010 population	2012 estimate
38654	Olive Branch	(662)	33,484	34,512
38655	Oxford	(662)	18,916	20,088
*39567	Pascagoula	(228)	22,392	22,249
*39288	Pearl	(601)	25,092	26,154
39465	Petal	(601)	10,454	10,795
39466	Picayune	(601)	10,878	10,854
*39157	Ridgeland	(601)	24,047	24,258
38671	Southaven	(662)	48,982	50,374
*39759	Starkville	(662)	23,888	24,360
38801	Tupelo	(662)	34,546	35,490
*39180	Vicksburg	(601)	23,856	23,450
39773	West Point	(662)	11,307	11,203
39194	Yazoo City	(662)	11,403	11,517

Missouri

ZIP	Place	Area code	2010 population	2012 estimate
63123	Affton (c)	(314)	20,307	—
63010	Arnold	(636)	20,808	21,013
*63011	Ballwin	(636)	30,404	30,443
63137	Bellefontaine Neighbors	(314)	10,860	10,828
64012	Belton	(816)	23,116	23,244
*64015	Blue Springs	(816)	52,575	53,014
*65613	Bolivar	(417)	10,325	10,389
65616	Branson	(417)	10,520	10,842
*63044	Bridgeton	(314)	11,550	11,630
*63701	Cape Girardeau	(573)	37,941	38,544
64836	Carthage	(417)	14,378	14,095
63017	Chesterfield	(636)	47,484	47,684
63105	Clayton	(314)	15,939	15,910
65201	Columbia	(573)	108,500	113,225
*63128	Concord (c)	(314)	16,421	—
63126	Crestwood	(314)	11,912	11,926
63141	Creve Coeur	(314)	17,833	17,855
63366	Dardenne Prairie	(636)	11,494	12,017
63025	Eureka	(636)	10,189	10,391
64024	Excelsior Springs	(816)	11,084	11,288
63640	Farmington	(573)	16,240	17,203
63135	Ferguson	(314)	21,203	21,135
63028	Festus	(636)	11,602	11,740
*63033	Florissant	(314)	52,158	52,252
65473	Fort Leonard Wood (c)	(573)	15,061	—
65251	Fulton	(573)	12,790	12,728
*64118	Gladstone	(816)	25,410	25,931
64029	Grain Valley	(816)	12,854	13,030
64030	Grandview	(816)	24,475	24,601
63401	Hannibal	(573)	17,916	17,814
64701	Harrisonville	(816)	10,019	10,008
*63042	Hazelwood	(314)	25,703	25,677
64050	Independence	(816)	116,830	117,270
63755	Jackson	(573)	13,758	14,180
65101	Jefferson City	(573)	43,079	43,183
63136	Jennings	(314)	14,712	14,740
64801	Joplin	(417)	50,150	49,526
*64108	Kansas City	(816)	459,787	464,310
63857	Kennett	(573)	10,932	10,902
63501	Kirksville	(660)	17,505	17,522
63122	Kirkwood	(314)	27,540	27,553
63367	Lake Saint Louis	(636)	14,545	14,687
65536	Lebanon	(417)	14,474	14,543
*64063	Lee's Summit	(816)	91,364	92,468
63125	Lemay (c)	(314)	16,645	—
*64068	Liberty	(816)	29,149	29,811
*63011	Manchester	(636)	18,094	18,165
65340	Marshall	(660)	13,065	13,033
63043	Maryland Heights	(314)	27,472	27,446
64468	Maryville	(660)	11,972	12,015
63129	Mehlville (c)	(314)	28,380	—
65265	Mexico	(573)	11,543	11,551
65270	Moberly	(660)	13,974	13,987
*64850	Neosho	(417)	11,835	12,121
65714	Nixa	(417)	19,022	19,858
63129	Oakville (c)	(314)	36,143	—
63366	O'Fallon	(636)	79,329	81,979
63034	Old Jamestown (c)	(314)	19,184	—
63114	Overland	(314)	16,062	16,006
65721	Ozark	(417)	17,820	18,348
*63901	Poplar Bluff	(573)	17,023	17,169
64083	Raymore	(816)	19,206	19,550
*64133	Raytown	(816)	29,526	29,513
65738	Republic	(417)	14,751	15,371
*65401	Rolla	(573)	19,559	19,789
63074	Saint Ann	(314)	13,020	12,978
*63301	Saint Charles	(636)	65,794	66,463
64501	Saint Joseph	(816)	76,780	77,176
*63166	Saint Louis	(314)	319,294	318,172
63376	Saint Peters	(636)	52,575	54,078
*65301	Sedalia	(660)	21,387	21,476
63801	Sikeston	(573)	16,318	16,330
63138	Spanish Lake (c)	(314)	19,650	—
*65801	Springfield	(417)	159,498	162,191
63011	Town and Country	(314)	10,815	10,866
63379	Troy	(314)	10,540	10,930

ZIP	Place	Area code	2010 population	2012 estimate
63084	Union	(636)	10,204	10,456
63130	University City	(314)	35,371	35,228
64093	Warrensburg	(660)	18,838	19,687
63090	Washington	(636)	13,982	13,918
64870	Webb City	(417)	10,996	10,841
63119	Webster Groves	(314)	22,995	23,055
63385	Wentzville	(636)	29,070	31,216
*65775	West Plains	(417)	11,986	12,270
*63011	Wildwood	(314)	35,517	35,698

Montana
Area code 406 applies to the entire state.

ZIP	Place	2010 population	2012 estimate
*59101	Billings	104,170	106,954
*59718	Bozeman	37,280	38,695
*59701	Butte-Silver Bow	33,525	33,730
*59401	Great Falls	58,505	58,893
*59601	Helena	28,190	29,134
*59901	Kalispell	19,927	20,487
*59801	Missoula	66,788	68,394

Nebraska
Area code (531) overlays area code (402).

ZIP	Place	Area code	2010 population	2012 estimate
68310	Beatrice	(402)	12,459	12,147
*68108	Bellevue	(402)	50,137	52,604
68108	Chalco (c)	(402)	10,994	—
*68601	Columbus	(402)	22,111	22,509
*68025	Fremont	(402)	26,397	26,167
*68802	Grand Island	(308)	48,520	49,989
*68901	Hastings	(402)	24,907	25,058
*68847	Kearney	(308)	30,787	31,790
68128	La Vista	(402)	15,758	17,344
68850	Lexington	(308)	10,230	10,213
*68501	Lincoln	(402)	258,379	265,404
*68701	Norfolk	(402)	24,210	24,332
*69101	North Platte	(308)	24,733	24,592
*68005	Omaha	(402)	408,958	421,570
*68046	Papillion	(402)	18,894	20,785
*69361	Scottsbluff	(308)	15,039	15,062
68776	South Sioux City	(402)	13,353	13,400

Nevada
Area code (725) overlays area code (702) as of June 3, 2014.

ZIP	Place	Area code	2010 population	2012 estimate
*89005	Boulder City	(702)	15,023	15,168
*89701	Carson City	(775)	55,274	54,838
*89801	Elko	(775)	18,297	19,386
89139	Enterprise (c)	(702)	108,481	—
89408	Fernley	(775)	19,368	19,093
89410	Gardnerville Ranchos (c)	(775)	11,312	—
*89015	Henderson	(702)	257,729	265,679
*89125	Las Vegas	(702)	583,756	596,424
*89024	Mesquite	(702)	15,276	16,062
*89030	North Las Vegas	(702)	216,961	223,491
*89041	Pahrump (c)	(775)	36,441	—
89109	Paradise (c)	(702)	223,167	—
*89501	Reno	(775)	225,221	231,027
89441	Spanish Springs (c)	(775)	15,064	—
*89431	Sparks	(775)	90,264	92,183
89815	Spring Creek (c)	(702)	12,361	—
89147	Spring Valley (c)	(702)	178,395	—
89135	Summerlin South (c)	(702)	24,085	—
89433	Sun Valley (c)	(775)	189,372	—
89110	Sunrise Manor (c)	(702)	19,299	—
89122	Whitney (c)	(702)	38,585	—
89101	Winchester (c)	(702)	27,978	—

New Hampshire
Area code 603 applies to the entire state. See introductory note.

ZIP	Place	2010 population	2012 estimate
03031	Amherst	11,201	11,258
03110	Bedford	21,203	21,538
03743	Claremont	13,355	13,077
*03301	Concord	42,695	42,630
*03818	Conway	10,115	10,070
03038	Derry	33,109	33,223
03038	Derry (c)	22,015	—
*03820	Dover	29,987	30,220
03824	Durham	14,638	15,141
03824	Durham (c)	10,345	—
03833	Exeter	14,306	14,429
03045	Goffstown	17,651	17,709
*03842	Hampton	15,430	15,033
03755	Hanover	11,260	11,210
03106	Hooksett	13,451	13,549

ZIP	Place	2010 population	2012 estimate
03051	Hudson	24,467	24,565
*03431	Keene	23,409	23,272
*03246	Laconia	15,951	16,055
*03766	Lebanon	13,151	13,483
03053	Londonderry	24,129	24,269
03053	Londonderry (c)	11,037	—
*03103	Manchester	109,565	110,209
03054	Merrimack	25,494	25,544
03055	Milford	15,115	15,152
*03060	Nashua	86,494	86,933
03076	Pelham	12,897	13,002
*03801	Portsmouth	20,779	21,379
03077	Raymond	10,138	10,220
*03867	Rochester	29,752	29,823
03079	Salem	28,776	28,835
03878	Somersworth	11,766	11,754
03087	Windham	13,592	13,958

New Jersey
Area code (551) overlays area code (201). Area code (848) overlays area code (732). Area code (862) overlays area code (973).

ZIP	Place	Area code	2010 population	2012 estimate
07712	Asbury Park	(732)	16,116	15,865
*08401	Atlantic City	(609)	39,558	39,504
07001	Avenel (c)	(732)	17,011	—
07002	Bayonne	(201)	63,024	64,416
08722	Beachwood	(732)	11,045	11,100
*08031	Bellmawr	(856)	11,583	11,547
07621	Bergenfield	(201)	26,764	27,017
08805	Bound Brook	(732)	10,402	10,702
08807	Bradley Gardens (c)	(908)	14,206	—
08302	Bridgeton	(856)	25,349	25,290
08015	Browns Mills (c)	(609)	11,223	—
*08101	Camden	(856)	77,344	77,250
07008	Carteret	(732)	22,844	24,062
08002	Cherry Hill Mall (c)	(856)	14,171	—
07010	Cliffside Park	(201)	23,594	23,872
*07015	Clifton	(973)	84,136	84,722
08108	Collingswood	(856)	13,926	13,869
07067	Colonia (c)	(732)	17,795	—
*07801	Dover	(973)	18,157	18,307
07628	Dumont	(201)	17,479	17,645
*07019	East Orange	(973)	64,270	64,268
*07724	Eatontown	(732)	12,709	12,431
08043	Echelon (c)	(856)	10,743	—
07020	Edgewater	(201)	11,513	11,972
*07207	Elizabeth	(908)	124,969	126,458
*07407	Elmwood Park	(201)	19,403	19,890
*07631	Englewood	(201)	27,147	27,605
07410	Fair Lawn	(201)/(973)	32,457	32,847
07022	Fairview (Bergen Co.)	(201)	13,835	14,217
07932	Florham Park	(973)	11,696	11,860
08863	Fords (c)	(732)	15,187	—
07024	Fort Lee	(201)	35,345	35,732
07417	Franklin Lakes	(201)	10,590	10,697
08823	Franklin Park (c)	(732)	13,295	—
07728	Freehold	(732)	12,052	12,097
07026	Garfield	(973)	30,487	30,872
08028	Glassboro	(856)	18,579	18,897
07452	Glen Rock	(201)	11,601	11,799
*08030	Gloucester City	(856)	11,456	11,440
08053	Greentree (c)	(856)	11,367	—
07093	Guttenberg	(201)	11,176	11,356
*07602	Hackensack	(201)	43,010	43,845
08033	Haddonfield	(856)	11,593	11,577
08690	Hamilton Square (c)	(609)	12,784	—
08037	Hammonton	(609)	14,791	14,751
07029	Harrison	(973)	13,620	13,874
07604	Hasbrouck Heights	(201)	11,842	11,936
*07506	Hawthorne	(973)	18,791	18,888
08904	Highland Park	(732)	13,982	14,299
*07642	Hillsdale	(201)	10,219	10,346
07030	Hoboken	(201)	50,005	52,034
08753	Holiday City-Berkeley (c)	(732)	12,831	—
07843	Hopatcong	(973)	15,147	14,927
08830	Iselin (c)	(732)	18,695	—
*07303	Jersey City	(201)	247,597	254,441
07734	Keansburg	(732)	10,105	10,013
*07032	Kearny	(201)/(973)	40,684	41,389
07405	Kinnelon	(973)	10,248	10,404
08701	Lakewood (c)	(732)	53,805	—
07035	Lincoln Park	(973)	10,521	10,524
07036	Linden	(732)/(908)	40,499	40,880
08021	Lindenwold	(856)	17,613	17,783
07643	Little Ferry	(201)	10,626	10,730
07644	Lodi	(201)/(973)	24,136	24,360
07740	Long Branch	(732)	30,719	30,646
07940	Madison	(973)	15,845	16,128
08835	Manville	(908)	10,344	10,399
08053	Marlton (c)	(856)	10,133	—
08836	Martinsville (c)	(908)	11,980	—

ZIP	Place	Area code	2010 population	2012 estimate
08619	Mercerville (c)	(609)	13,230	—
08840	Metuchen	(732)	13,574	13,691
08846	Middlesex	(732)	13,635	13,737
08332	Millville	(856)	28,400	28,619
08057	Moorestown-Lenola (c)	(856)	14,217	—
*07960	Morristown	(973)	18,411	18,523
*08901	New Brunswick	(732)	55,181	56,160
07646	New Milford	(201)	16,341	16,504
07974	New Providence	(908)	12,171	12,385
*07102	Newark	(973)	277,140	277,727
07031	North Arlington	(201)	15,392	15,533
*07060	North Plainfield	(908)	21,936	22,013
07436	Oakland	(201)	12,754	12,873
*08050	Ocean Acres (c)	(609)	16,142	—
08226	Ocean City	(609)	11,701	11,527
08857	Old Bridge (c)	(732)	23,753	—
07650	Palisades Park	(201)	19,622	19,936
*07652	Paramus	(201)	26,342	26,532
07055	Passaic	(973)	69,781	70,218
*07510	Paterson	(973)	146,199	145,219
08070	Pennsville (c)	(856)	11,888	—
*08861	Perth Amboy	(732)	50,814	51,744
08865	Phillipsburg	(908)	14,950	14,699
08021	Pine Hill	(856)	10,233	10,571
*07061	Plainfield	(908)	49,808	50,244
*08232	Pleasantville	(609)	20,249	20,750
08742	Point Pleasant	(732)	18,392	18,449
07442	Pompton Lakes	(973)	11,097	11,137
*08540	Princeton	(609)	12,307	12,339
08536	Princeton Meadows (c)	(609)	13,834	—
07065	Rahway	(732)	27,346	27,785
07446	Ramsey	(201)	14,473	14,727
*07701	Red Bank	(732)	12,206	12,187
07657	Ridgefield	(201)	11,032	11,255
07660	Ridgefield Park	(201)	12,729	12,864
*07451	Ridgewood	(201)/(973)	24,958	25,205
07456	Ringwood	(973)	12,228	12,334
07661	River Edge	(201)	11,340	11,464
07751	Robertsville (c)	(732)	11,297	—
07203	Roselle	(908)	21,085	21,299
07204	Roselle Park	(908)	13,297	13,512
07070	Rutherford	(201)	18,061	18,219
*08872	Sayreville	(732)	42,704	43,761
*07094	Secaucus	(201)	16,264	18,351
07078	Short Hills (c)	(973)	13,165	—
08244	Somers Point	(609)	10,795	10,804
*08873	Somerset	(732)	22,083	—
08876	Somerville	(908)	12,098	12,160
07080	South Plainfield	(732)/(908)	23,385	23,669
*08882	South River	(732)	16,008	16,137
08003	Springdale (c)	(856)	14,518	—
*0/901	Summit	(908)	21,457	21,828
07670	Tenafly	(201)	14,488	14,635
*07724	Tinton Falls	(732)	17,892	17,869
*08753	Toms River (c)	(732)	88,791	—
*07512	Totowa	(973)	10,804	10,932
*08650	Trenton	(609)	84,913	84,477
*07087	Union City	(201)	66,455	67,744
07043	Upper Montclair (c)	(973)	11,565	—
08406	Ventnor City	(609)	10,650	10,615
*08360	Vineland	(856)	60,724	60,854
07057	Wallington	(201)/(973)	11,335	11,592
07465	Wanaque	(201)/(973)	11,116	11,148
07728	West Freehold (c)	(732)/(908)	13,613	—
07093	West New York	(201)	49,708	51,464
*07091	Westfield	(732)/(908)	30,316	30,639
*07675	Westwood	(201)	10,908	11,011
08094	Williamstown (c)	(609)/(856)	15,567	—
07095	Woodbridge (c)	(732)/(908)	19,265	—
*08096	Woodbury	(856)	10,174	10,085
*07424	Woodland Park	(973)	11,819	12,428

New Mexico

ZIP	Place	Area code	2010 population	2012 estimate
*88310	Alamogordo	(575)	30,403	31,500
*87101	Albuquerque	(505)	545,852	555,417
*88210	Artesia	(575)	11,301	11,365
*88220	Carlsbad	(575)	26,138	26,697
*88021	Chaparral (c)	(505)	14,631	—
*88101	Clovis	(575)	37,775	39,197
*88030	Deming	(505)	14,855	14,793
*87532	Española	(505)	10,224	10,240
*87401	Farmington	(505)	45,877	45,854
*87301	Gallup	(505)	21,678	22,088
*88240	Hobbs	(575)	34,122	35,007
*88001	Las Cruces	(575)	97,618	101,047
*87701	Las Vegas	(505)	13,753	13,529
87544	Los Alamos (c)	(505)	12,019	—
87031	Los Lunas	(505)	14,835	15,168
*88260	Lovington	(575)	11,009	11,275
87107	North Valley (c)	(505)	11,333	—

ZIP	Place	Area code	2010 population	2012 estimate
*88130	Portales	(575)	12,280	12,723
*87124	Rio Rancho	(505)	87,521	90,818
*88201	Roswell	(575)	48,366	48,477
*87501	Santa Fe	(505)	67,947	69,204
*88061	Silver City	(575)	10,315	10,273
87105	South Valley (c)	(505)	40,976	—
*88063	Sunland Park	(575)	14,106	14,776

New York

Area codes (347) and (929) overlay area code (718). Area codes (646) and (917) overlay area code (212).

ZIP	Place	Area code	2010 population	2012 estimate
*12201	Albany	(518)	97,856	97,904
12010	Amsterdam	(518)	18,620	18,290
*13021	Auburn	(315)	27,687	27,365
11702	Babylon	(631)	12,166	12,174
11510	Baldwin (c)	(516)	24,033	—
*14020	Batavia	(585)	15,465	15,399
11706	Bay Shore (c)	(631)	26,337	—
12508	Beacon	(845)	15,541	15,346
11710	Bellmore (c)	(516)	16,218	—
11714	Bethpage (c)	(516)	16,429	—
*13902	Binghamton	(607)	47,376	46,551
11716	Bohemia (c)	(631)	10,180	—
11717	Brentwood (c)	(631)	60,664	—
14610	Brighton (c)	(585)	36,609	—
*14240	Buffalo	(716)	261,310	259,384
*14424	Canandaigua	(585)	10,545	10,489
11720	Centereach (c)	(631)	31,578	—
11722	Central Islip (c)	(516)	34,450	—
14225	Cheektowaga (c)	(716)	75,178	—
12047	Cohoes	(518)	16,168	16,174
11725	Commack (c)	(631)	36,124	—
11726	Copiague (c)	(631)	22,993	—
11727	Coram (c)	(631)	39,113	—
*14830	Corning	(607)	11,183	11,108
13045	Cortland	(607)	19,204	19,292
11729	Deer Park (c)	(631)	27,745	—
14043	Depew	(716)	15,303	15,216
11746	Dix Hills (c)	(631)	26,892	—
10522	Dobbs Ferry	(914)	10,875	10,988
*14048	Dunkirk	(716)	12,563	12,382
11730	East Islip (c)	(631)	14,475	—
11758	East Massapequa (c)	(516)	19,060	—
11554	East Meadow (c)	(516)	38,132	—
11731	East Northport (c)	(631)	20,217	—
11772	East Patchogue (c)	(631)	22,469	—
10709	Eastchester (c)	(914)	19,554	—
14226	Eggertsville (c)	(716)	15,019	—
*14901	Elmira	(607)	29,200	28,987
11003	Elmont (c)	(516)	33,198	—
11731	Elwood (c)	(631)	11,177	—
*13760	Endicott	(607)	13,392	13,184
13762	Endwell (c)	(607)	11,446	—
13219	Fairmount (c)	(315)	10,224	—
11738	Farmingville (c)	(631)	15,481	—
*11001	Floral Park	(516)	15,863	15,914
13603	Fort Drum (c)	(315)	12,955	—
11768	Fort Salonga (c)	(631)	10,008	—
11010	Franklin Square (c)	(516)	29,320	—
14063	Fredonia	(716)	11,230	11,047
11520	Freeport	(516)	42,860	43,138
13069	Fulton	(315)	11,896	11,776
*11530	Garden City	(516)	22,371	22,546
*14456	Geneva	(315)	13,261	13,210
11542	Glen Cove	(516)	26,964	27,100
12801	Glens Falls	(518)	14,700	14,609
12078	Gloversville	(518)	15,665	15,388
*11022	Great Neck	(516)	9,989	10,066
14616	Greece (c)	(585)	14,519	—
11740	Greenlawn (c)	(631)	13,742	—
11946	Hampton Bays (c)	(631)	13,603	—
10528	Harrison	(914)	27,472	27,785
*11788	Hauppauge (c)	(631)	20,882	—
10927	Haverstraw	(845)	11,910	12,037
*11551	Hempstead	(516)	53,891	54,883
*11802	Hicksville (c)	(516)	41,547	—
11741	Holbrook (c)	(631)	27,195	—
11742	Holtsville (c)	(631)	19,714	—
11743	Huntington (c)	(631)	18,046	—
11746	Huntington Station (c)	(631)	33,029	—
14617	Irondequoit (c)	(585)	51,692	—
11751	Islip (c)	(631)	18,689	—
*14850	Ithaca	(607)	30,014	30,331
*14702	Jamestown	(716)	31,146	30,767
10535	Jefferson Valley-Yorktown (c)	(914)	14,142	—
11753	Jericho (c)	(516)	13,567	—
13790	Johnson City	(607)	15,174	14,937
*14217	Kenmore	(716)	15,423	15,295
11754	Kings Park (c)	(631)	17,282	—

ZIP	Place	Area code	2010 population	2012 estimate
*12401	Kingston	(845)	23,893	23,711
10950	Kiryas Joel	(845)	20,175	21,357
14218	Lackawanna	(716)	18,141	18,006
11755	Lake Grove	(631)	11,163	11,204
11779	Lake Ronkonkoma (c)	(631)	20,155	—
*14086	Lancaster	(716)	10,352	10,280
11756	Levittown (c)	(516)	51,881	—
11757	Lindenhurst	(631)	27,253	27,256
*14094	Lockport	(716)	21,165	20,965
11561	Long Beach	(516)	33,275	33,480
11563	Lynbrook	(516)	19,427	19,509
10543	Mamaroneck	(914)	18,929	19,112
11949	Manorville (c)	(631)	14,314	—
11758	Massapequa (c)	(516)	21,685	—
11762	Massapequa Park	(516)	17,008	17,105
13662	Massena	(315)	10,936	10,837
11950	Mastic (c)	(631)	15,481	—
11951	Mastic Beach[1]	(631)	12,930	14,866
11763	Medford (c)	(631)	24,142	—
11747	Melville (c)	(631)	18,985	—
11566	Merrick (c)	(516)	22,097	—
11953	Middle Island (c)	(631)	10,483	—
*10940	Middletown	(845)	28,086	27,886
11764	Miller Place (c)	(631)	12,339	—
11501	Mineola	(516)	18,799	18,880
10952	Monsey (c)	(845)	18,412	—
10549	Mount Kisco	(914)	10,877	10,994
11766	Mount Sinai (c)	(631)	12,118	—
*10551	Mount Vernon	(914)	67,292	67,896
10954	Nanuet (c)	(845)	17,882	—
11767	Nesconset (c)	(631)	13,387	—
11590	New Cassel (c)	(516)	14,059	—
10956	New City (c)	(845)	33,559	—
*10802	New Rochelle	(914)	77,062	78,388
*10001	New York (212)/	(718)	8,175,133	8,336,697
*12550	Newburgh	(845)	28,866	28,651
*14302	Niagara Falls	(716)	50,193	49,722
11701	North Amityville (c)	(631)	17,862	—
11703	North Babylon (c)	(631)	17,509	—
11706	North Bay Shore (c)	(631)	18,944	—
11710	North Bellmore (c)	(516)	19,941	—
11713	North Bellport (c)	(631)	11,545	—
11757	North Lindenhurst (c)	(631)	11,652	—
11758	North Massapequa (c)	(516)	17,886	—
11566	North Merrick (c)	(516)	12,272	—
11040	North New Hyde Park (c)	(516)	14,899	—
14120	North Tonawanda	(716)	31,568	31,269
11580	North Valley Stream (c)	(516)	16,628	—
11793	North Wantagh (c)	(516)	11,960	—
11572	Oceanside (c)	(516)	32,109	—
13669	Ogdensburg	(315)	11,128	11,083
14760	Olean (585)/	(716)	14,452	14,220
13421	Oneida	(315)	11,393	11,263
13820	Oneonta	(607)	13,901	13,840
10562	Ossining	(914)	25,060	25,266
13126	Oswego	(315)	18,142	18,147
11772	Patchogue	(631)	11,798	11,879
10965	Pearl River (c)	(845)	15,876	—
10566	Peekskill	(914)	23,583	23,835
11803	Plainview (c)	(516)	26,217	—
*12901	Plattsburgh	(518)	19,989	19,750
10573	Port Chester	(914)	28,967	29,247
11050	Port Washington (c)	(516)	15,846	—
*12601	Poughkeepsie	(845)	32,736	30,847
11961	Ridge (c)	(631)	13,336	—
11901	Riverhead (c)	(631)	13,299	—
*14692	Rochester	(585)	210,565	210,532
*11571	Rockville Centre	(516)	24,023	24,109
11778	Rocky Point (c)	(631)	14,014	—
*13440	Rome	(315)	33,725	32,840
11779	Ronkonkoma (c)	(631)	19,082	—
11575	Roosevelt (c)	(516)	16,258	—
12303	Rotterdam (c)	(518)	20,652	—
10580	Rye	(914)	15,720	15,868
11780	Saint James (c)	(631)	13,338	—
13454	Salisbury (c)	(315)	12,093	—
12866	Saratoga Springs	(518)	26,586	26,960
11782	Sayville (c)	(631)	16,853	—
10583	Scarsdale	(914)	17,166	17,471
*12301	Schenectady	(518)	66,135	66,078
11783	Seaford (c)	(516)	15,294	—
11784	Selden (c)	(631)	19,851	—
11733	Setauket-East Setauket (c)	(631)	15,477	—
11967	Shirley (c)	(631)	27,854	—
11787	Smithtown (c)	(631)	26,470	—
11735	South Farmingdale (c)	(516)	14,486	—
10977	Spring Valley	(845)	31,347	32,082
*11790	Stony Brook (c)	(631)	13,740	—
10980	Stony Point (c)	(845)	12,147	—
*10901	Suffern	(845)	10,723	10,851
11791	Syosset (c)	(516)	18,829	—
*13220	Syracuse	(315)	145,170	144,170
10591	Tarrytown	(914)	11,277	11,410

ZIP	Place	Area code	2010 population	2012 estimate
11776	Terryville (c)	(631)	11,849	—
*14150	Tonawanda	(716)	15,130	15,020
*14150	Tonawanda (c)	(716)	58,144	—
*12180	Troy	(518)	50,129	49,946
11553	Uniondale (c)	(516)	24,759	—
*13504	Utica	(315)	62,235	61,822
*11582	Valley Stream	(516)	37,511	37,646
11793	Wantagh (c)	(516)	18,871	—
*13601	Watertown	(315)	27,023	27,900
12189	Watervliet	(518)	10,254	10,244
*11704	West Babylon (c)	(631)	43,213	—
10993	West Haverstraw	(845)	10,165	10,287
11552	West Hempstead (c)	(516)	18,862	—
11795	West Islip (c)	(631)	28,335	—
14224	West Seneca (c)	(716)	44,711	—
*11590	Westbury	(516)	15,146	15,294
*10602	White Plains	(914)	56,853	57,403
11797	Woodbury (c)	(516)	10,686	10,688
11598	Woodmere (c)	(516)	17,121	—
11798	Wyandanch (c)	(631)	11,647	—
*10702	Yonkers	(914)	195,976	198,449

(1) Place was incorporated after the 2010 Census was conducted. Data in the 2010 column is the Census Bureau's estimates base, not the official 2010 population.

North Carolina

Area code (980) overlays area code (704). Area code (984) overlays area code (919).

ZIP	Place	Area code	2010 population	2012 estimate
28315	Albemarle	(910)	15,903	15,932
*27502	Apex	(919)	37,476	40,420
27263	Archdale	(336)	11,415	11,500
*27203	Asheboro	(336)	25,012	25,559
*28802	Asheville	(828)	83,393	85,712
28012	Belmont	(704)	10,076	10,302
*28607	Boone	(828)	17,122	17,774
*27215	Burlington	(336)	49,963	51,306
27510	Carrboro	(919)	19,582	20,433
*27511	Cary	(919)	135,234	145,693
*27514	Chapel Hill	(919)	57,233	58,424
*28204	Charlotte	(704)	731,424	775,202
*27520	Clayton	(919)	16,116	17,031
27012	Clemmons	(336)	18,627	19,108
*28025	Concord	(704)	79,066	81,981
28031	Cornelius	(704)	24,866	26,243
*28036	Davidson	(704)	10,944	11,484
*27701	Durham	(919)	228,330	239,358
*27909	Elizabeth City	(252)	18,683	18,478
*28302	Fayetteville	(910)	200,564	202,103
27526	Fuquay-Varina	(919)	17,937	19,929
27529	Garner	(919)	25,745	26,732
*28052	Gastonia	(704)	71,741	72,723
*27530	Goldsboro	(919)	36,437	37,051
27253	Graham	(336)	14,153	14,248
*27420	Greensboro	(336)	269,666	277,080
*27834	Greenville	(252)	84,554	87,242
28075	Harrisburg	(704)	11,526	11,973
*28532	Havelock	(252)	20,735	20,767
*27536	Henderson	(252)	15,368	15,320
*28739	Hendersonville	(828)	13,137	13,288
*28603	Hickory	(828)	40,010	40,093
*27260	High Point	(336)	104,371	106,586
27540	Holly Springs	(919)	24,661	26,865
28348	Hope Mills	(910)	15,176	15,597
*28070	Huntersville	(704)	46,773	49,344
28079	Indian Trail	(704)	33,518	34,800
*28540	Jacksonville	(910)	70,145	69,220
*28081	Kannapolis	(704)	42,625	43,782
*27284	Kernersville	(336)	23,123	23,452
28086	Kings Mountain	(704)	10,296	10,648
*28502	Kinston	(252)	21,677	21,625
27545	Knightdale	(919)	11,401	12,724
*28352	Laurinburg	(910)	15,962	15,791
28451	Leland	(910)	13,527	15,123
*28645	Lenoir	(828)	18,228	17,999
27023	Lewisville	(336)	12,639	13,050
*27292	Lexington	(336)	18,931	18,936
*28092	Lincolnton	(704)	10,486	10,640
*28358	Lumberton	(910)	21,542	21,768
*28105	Matthews	(704)	27,198	28,699
27302	Mebane	(919)	11,393	12,685
28227	Mint Hill	(704)	22,722	23,956
*28110	Monroe	(704)	32,797	33,640
*28115	Mooresville	(704)	32,711	33,451
*28655	Morganton	(828)	16,918	16,861
27560	Morrisville	(919)	18,576	20,591
*27030	Mount Airy	(336)	10,388	10,436
28120	Mount Holly	(704)	13,656	13,776
28411	Murraysville (c)	(910)	14,215	—
*28562	New Bern	(252)	29,524	30,316

ZIP	Place	Area code	2010 population	2012 estimate
28658	Newton	(828)	12,968	12,975
*28374	Pinehurst	(910)	13,124	15,008
28399	Piney Green (c)	(910)	13,293	—
*27611	Raleigh	(919)	403,892	423,179
*27320	Reidsville	(336)	14,520	14,341
27870	Roanoke Rapids	(252)	15,754	15,692
*27801	Rocky Mount	(252)	57,477	57,136
*28144	Salisbury	(704)	33,662	33,622
*27330	Sanford	(919)	28,094	29,064
*28150	Shelby	(704)	20,323	20,270
27577	Smithfield	(919)	10,966	11,339
*28387	Southern Pines	(910)	12,334	12,736
*28390	Spring Lake	(910)	11,964	13,217
28104	Stallings	(704)	13,831	14,379
*28677	Statesville	(704)	24,532	25,044
27358	Summerfield	(336)	10,232	10,485
27886	Tarboro	(252)	11,415	11,327
*27360	Thomasville	(336)	26,757	26,841
*27587	Wake Forest	(919)	30,117	32,936
28173	Waxhaw	(704)	9,859	10,334
*28402	Wilmington	(910)	106,476	109,922
*27893	Wilson	(252)	49,167	49,610
*27102	Winston-Salem	(336)	229,617	234,349

North Dakota
Area code 701 applies to the entire state.

ZIP	Place	2010 population	2012 estimate
*58501	Bismarck	61,272	64,751
*58601	Dickinson	17,787	19,697
*58102	Fargo	105,549	109,779
*58201	Grand Forks	52,838	53,456
*58401	Jamestown	15,427	15,323
58554	Mandan	18,331	18,978
*58701	Minot	40,888	43,746
58078	West Fargo	25,830	27,478
*58801	Williston	14,716	18,532

Ohio
Area code (234) overlays area code (330). Area code (567) overlays area code (419).

ZIP	Place	Area code	2010 population	2012 estimate
*44309	Akron	(330)	199,110	108,549
*44601	Alliance	(330)	22,322	22,183
44001	Amherst	(440)	12,021	12,038
44805	Ashland	(419)	20,362	20,320
*44004	Ashtabula	(440)	19,124	18,811
45701	Athens	(740)	23,832	23,755
44202	Aurora	(330)	15,548	15,479
44515	Austintown (c)	(330)	29,677	—
44011	Avon	(440)	21,193	21,772
44012	Avon Lake	(440)	22,581	22,816
44203	Barberton	(330)	26,550	26,316
44140	Bay Village	(440)	15,651	15,484
44122	Beachwood	(216)	11,953	11,844
45434	Beavercreek	(937)	45,193	45,780
44146	Bedford	(216)/(440)	13,074	12,907
*44146	Bedford Heights	(216)/(440)	10,751	10,641
43311	Bellefontaine	(937)	13,370	13,197
44017	Berea	(440)	19,093	18,980
43209	Bexley	(614)	13,057	13,252
*45242	Blue Ash	(513)	12,114	12,106
44513	Boardman (c)	(330)	35,376	—
*43402	Bowling Green	(419)	30,028	31,384
44141	Brecksville	(440)	13,656	13,536
45211	Bridgetown (c)	(513)	14,407	—
44147	Broadview Heights	(440)	19,400	19,303
44142	Brook Park	(216)/(440)	19,212	19,003
44144	Brooklyn	(216)	11,169	11,026
44212	Brunswick	(330)	34,255	34,364
44820	Bucyrus	(419)	12,362	12,092
*43725	Cambridge	(740)	10,635	10,555
*44711	Canton	(330)	73,007	72,683
*45822	Celina	(419)	10,400	10,395
*45458	Centerville (Montgomery Co.)	(937)	23,999	23,974
45601	Chillicothe	(740)	21,901	21,735
*45202	Cincinnati	(513)	296,943	296,550
43113	Circleville	(740)	13,314	13,453
45315	Clayton	(937)	13,209	13,216
*44101	Cleveland	(216)	396,815	390,928
*44118	Cleveland Heights	(216)	46,121	45,475
*43216	Columbus	(614)	787,033	809,798
44030	Conneaut	(440)	12,841	12,879
43812	Coshocton	(740)	11,216	11,173
*44222	Cuyahoga Falls	(330)	49,652	49,245
*45401	Dayton	(937)	141,527	141,359
43512	Defiance	(419)	16,494	16,838
43015	Delaware	(740)	34,753	35,925
*45247	Dent (c)	(513)	10,497	—

ZIP	Place	Area code	2010 population	2012 estimate
44622	Dover	(330)	12,826	12,795
*43016	Dublin	(614)/(740)	41,751	42,906
*44112	East Cleveland	(216)	17,843	17,593
43920	East Liverpool	(330)	11,195	11,062
*44095	Eastlake	(440)	18,577	18,459
*44035	Elyria	(440)	54,533	54,086
*45322	Englewood	(937)	13,465	13,463
*44117	Euclid	(216)	48,920	48,281
45324	Fairborn	(937)	32,352	32,599
*45011	Fairfield	(513)	42,510	42,647
44126	Fairview Park	(440)	16,826	16,612
*45839	Findlay	(419)	41,202	41,526
45224	Finneytown (c)	(513)	12,741	—
45240	Forest Park	(513)	18,720	18,682
45230	Forestville (c)	(513)	10,532	—
44830	Fostoria	(419)	13,441	13,282
45005	Franklin	(513)	11,771	11,819
43420	Fremont	(419)	16,734	16,564
43230	Gahanna	(614)	33,248	33,828
44833	Galion	(419)	10,512	10,276
*44125	Garfield Heights	(216)	28,849	28,454
44232	Green	(330)	25,699	25,789
45331	Greenville	(937)	13,227	13,105
43123	Grove City	(614)	35,575	36,832
*45011	Hamilton	(513)	62,477	62,295
45030	Harrison	(513)	9,897	10,103
43056	Heath	(740)	10,310	10,389
43026	Hilliard	(614)/(740)	28,435	30,564
45424	Huber Heights	(937)	38,101	38,129
*44236	Hudson	(330)	22,262	22,323
45638	Ironton	(740)	11,129	11,067
*44240	Kent	(330)	28,904	29,807
*45429	Kettering	(937)	56,163	55,990
44107	Lakewood	(216)	52,131	51,385
43130	Lancaster	(740)	38,780	38,880
45036	Lebanon	(513)	20,033	20,387
*45802	Lima	(419)	38,771	38,339
*44052	Lorain	(440)	64,097	63,707
*45140	Loveland	(513)	12,081	12,198
44124	Lyndhurst	(216)/(440)	14,001	13,821
*44056	Macedonia	(330)	11,188	11,350
*45248	Mack (c)	(513)	11,585	—
*44901	Mansfield	(419)	47,821	47,052
45750	Maple Heights	(216)	23,138	22,840
45750	Marietta	(740)	14,085	14,027
*43302	Marion	(740)	36,837	36,904
*43040	Marysville	(937)	22,094	22,051
45040	Mason	(513)	30,712	31,091
*44646	Massillon	(330)	32,149	32,156
43537	Maumee	(419)	14,286	14,129
44124	Mayfield Heights	(440)	19,155	18,974
*44256	Medina	(330)	26,678	26,533
*44060	Mentor	(440)	47,159	47,023
*45343	Miamisburg	(937)	20,181	20,165
44130	Middleburg Heights	(216)/(440)	15,946	15,806
*45042	Middletown	(513)	48,694	48,702
45211	Monfort Heights (c)	(513)	11,948	—
*45050	Monroe	(513)	12,442	12,844
45242	Montgomery	(513)	10,251	10,292
43050	Mount Vernon	(740)	16,990	16,812
44657	New Franklin	(330)	14,227	14,231
44663	New Philadelphia	(330)	17,288	17,292
43055	Newark	(740)	47,573	47,688
44446	Niles	(330)	19,266	19,020
*44720	North Canton	(330)	17,488	17,404
44070	North Olmsted	(440)	32,718	32,354
*44039	North Ridgeville	(440)	29,465	30,571
44133	North Royalton	(440)	30,444	30,325
45239	Northbrook (c)	(513)	10,668	—
44203	Norton	(330)	12,085	12,030
44857	Norwalk	(419)	17,012	16,931
*45212	Norwood	(513)	19,207	19,086
*43616	Oregon	(419)	20,291	20,221
45056	Oxford	(513)	21,371	21,351
44077	Painesville	(440)	19,563	19,634
*44129	Parma	(216)/(440)	81,601	80,597
44130	Parma Heights	(216)/(440)	20,718	20,468
43062	Pataskala	(740)	14,962	15,091
*43551	Perrysburg	(419)	20,623	21,161
43147	Pickerington	(614)/(740)	18,291	18,692
45356	Piqua	(937)	20,522	20,619
*45662	Portsmouth	(740)	20,226	20,302
43065	Powell	(614)	11,500	11,960
44266	Ravenna	(330)	11,724	11,570
*45215	Reading	(513)	10,385	10,348
43068	Reynoldsburg	(614)/(740)	35,893	36,347
44143	Richmond Heights	(216)/(440)	10,546	10,488
45431	Riverside	(937)	25,201	25,145
44116	Rocky River	(440)	20,213	20,011
44460	Salem	(330)	12,303	12,161
*44870	Sandusky	(419)	25,793	25,493
*44131	Seven Hills	(216)/(440)	11,804	11,724
*44122	Shaker Heights	(216)	28,448	28,039

ZIP	Place	Area code	2010 population	2012 estimate
*45241	Sharonville	(513)	13,560	13,521
*45365	Sidney	(937)	21,229	21,031
44139	Solon	(440)	23,348	23,160
*44121	South Euclid	(216)	22,295	22,012
45066	Springboro	(513)	17,409	17,643
45246	Springdale	(513)	11,223	11,198
*45501	Springfield	(937)	60,608	60,147
*43952	Steubenville	(740)	18,659	18,429
44224	Stow	(330)	34,837	34,674
44241	Streetsboro	(330)	16,028	16,098
*44136	Strongsville	(440)	44,750	44,620
44471	Struthers	(330)	10,713	10,564
43560	Sylvania	(419)	18,965	18,892
44278	Tallmadge	(330)	17,537	17,515
44883	Tiffin	(419)	17,963	17,828
*43601	Toledo	(419)	287,208	284,012
45067	Trenton	(513)	11,869	12,126
*45426	Trotwood	(937)	24,431	24,326
*45373	Troy	(937)	25,058	25,374
44087	Twinsburg	(330)	18,795	18,761
*44122	University Heights	(216)	13,539	13,442
*43221	Upper Arlington	(614)	33,771	34,203
43078	Urbana	(937)	11,793	11,669
45891	Van Wert	(419)	10,846	10,844
45377	Vandalia	(937)	15,246	15,204
*44089	Vermilion	(440)	10,594	10,507
*44281	Wadsworth	(330)	21,567	21,729
*44481	Warren	(330)	41,557	40,723
*44122	Warrensville Heights	(216)	13,542	13,380
43160	Washington Court House	(740)	14,192	14,110
*45449	West Carrollton	(937)	13,143	13,099
*43081	Westerville	(614)	36,120	37,073
44145	Westlake	(440)	32,729	32,487
45239	White Oak (c)	(513)	19,167	—
43213	Whitehall	(614)	18,062	18,403
44092	Wickliffe	(440)	12,750	12,663
*44094	Willoughby	(440)	22,268	22,353
*44095	Willowick	(440)	14,171	14,082
45177	Wilmington	(937)	12,520	12,448
44691	Wooster	(330)	26,119	26,375
43085	Worthington	(614)	13,575	13,757
45385	Xenia	(937)	25,719	25,944
*44501	Youngstown	(330)	66,982	65,405
*43701	Zanesville	(740)	25,487	25,411

Oklahoma

Area code (539) overlays area code (918).

ZIP	Place	Area code	2010 population	2012 estimate
*74820	Ada	(580)	16,810	17,097
*73521	Altus	(580)	19,813	19,681
*73401	Ardmore	(580)	24,283	24,677
*74003	Bartlesville	(918)	35,750	36,245
73008	Bethany	(405)	19,051	19,418
74008	Bixby	(918)	20,884	22,580
*74012	Broken Arrow	(918)	98,850	102,019
*73018	Chickasha	(405)	16,036	16,162
73020	Choctaw	(405)	11,146	11,626
*74017	Claremore	(918)	18,581	18,867
*73115	Del City	(405)	21,332	21,813
*73533	Duncan	(580)	23,431	23,287
*74701	Durant	(580)	15,856	16,425
*73034	Edmond	(405)	81,405	84,885
73036	El Reno	(405)	16,749	17,510
*73644	Elk City	(580)	11,693	12,251
*73701	Enid	(580)	49,379	49,854
*74033	Glenpool	(918)	10,808	11,411
73044	Guthrie	(405)	10,191	10,623
73942	Guymon	(580)	11,442	11,930
74037	Jenks	(918)	16,924	18,059
*73501	Lawton	(580)	96,867	98,376
*74501	McAlester	(918)	18,383	18,303
*74354	Miami	(918)	13,570	13,737
*73140	Midwest City	(405)	54,371	56,080
*73153	Moore	(405)	55,081	57,810
*74401	Muskogee	(918)	39,223	38,981
73064	Mustang	(405)	17,395	18,543
*73069	Norman	(405)	110,925	115,562
*73125	Oklahoma City	(405)	579,999	599,199
74447	Okmulgee	(918)	12,321	12,406
*74055	Owasso	(918)	28,915	31,453
*74601	Ponca City	(580)	25,387	24,974
74063	Sand Springs	(918)	18,906	19,101
*74066	Sapulpa	(918)	20,544	20,793
*74801	Shawnee	(405)	29,857	30,649
*74074	Stillwater	(405)	45,688	46,560
*74464	Tahlequah	(918)	15,753	16,333
*74103	Tulsa	(918)	391,906	393,987
*73112	Warr Acres	(405)	10,043	10,286
73096	Weatherford	(580)	10,833	11,357
*73801	Woodward	(580)	12,051	12,274
*73099	Yukon	(405)	22,709	24,128

Oregon

Area code (458) overlays area code (541). Area code (971) overlays area code (503).

ZIP	Place	Area code	2010 population	2012 estimate
*97321	Albany	(541)	50,158	51,322
*97006	Aloha (c)	(503)	49,425	—
97601	Altamont (c)	(541)	19,257	—
97520	Ashland	(541)	20,078	20,366
*97005	Beaverton	(503)	89,803	92,680
*97701	Bend	(541)	76,639	79,109
97229	Bethany (c)	(503)	20,646	—
97013	Canby	(503)	15,829	15,986
97291	Cedar Mill (c)	(503)	14,546	—
97502	Central Point	(541)	17,169	17,411
97420	Coos Bay	(541)	15,967	15,857
97113	Cornelius	(503)	11,869	12,147
*97333	Corvallis	(541)	54,462	54,998
97338	Dallas	(503)	14,583	14,760
*97009	Damascus	(503)	10,539	10,684
*97440	Eugene	(541)	156,185	157,986
97116	Forest Grove	(503)	21,083	21,961
97301	Four Corners (c)	(503)	15,947	—
97027	Gladstone	(503)	11,497	11,654
*97526	Grants Pass	(541)	34,533	34,805
*97030	Gresham	(503)	105,594	108,956
97015	Happy Valley	(503)	13,903	15,406
97303	Hayesville (c)	(503)	19,936	—
*97838	Hermiston	(541)	16,745	17,111
*97123	Hillsboro	(503)	91,611	95,327
97307	Keizer	(503)	36,478	36,907
*97601	Klamath Falls	(541)	20,840	21,005
97850	La Grande	(541)	13,082	13,048
*97034	Lake Oswego	(503)	36,619	37,243
97355	Lebanon	(541)	15,518	15,740
97741	McMinnville	(541)	32,187	32,535
*97501	Medford	(541)	74,907	76,462
*97269	Milwaukie	(503)	20,291	20,439
97132	Newberg	(503)	22,068	22,396
97365	Newport	(541)	9,989	10,017
97268	Oak Grove (c)	(503)	16,629	—
97006	Oak Hills (c)	(503)	11,333	—
97267	Oatfield (c)	(503)	13,415	—
97914	Ontario	(541)	11,366	11,143
97045	Oregon City	(503)	31,859	32,755
97801	Pendleton	(541)	16,612	16,838
*97208	Portland	(503)	583,776	603,106
97756	Redmond	(541)	26,215	26,924
97470	Roseburg	(541)	21,181	21,884
97051	Saint Helens	(503)	12,883	12,910
*97309	Salem	(503)	154,637	157,429
97140	Sherwood	(503)	18,194	18,771
*97477	Springfield	(541)	59,403	59,869
97058	The Dalles	(541)	13,620	13,783
*97281	Tigard	(503)	48,035	49,774
97060	Troutdale	(503)	15,962	16,425
97062	Tualatin	(503)	26,054	26,716
97068	West Linn	(503)	25,109	25,600
97070	Wilsonville	(503)	19,509	20,489
97071	Woodburn	(503)	24,080	24,223

Pennsylvania

Area code (267) overlays area code (215). Area code (484) overlays area code (610). Area code (878) overlays area code (412). Area code (272) overlays area code (570) as of Oct. 21, 2013.

ZIP	Place	Area code	2010 population	2012 estimate
*18105	Allentown	(610)	118,032	118,974
15101	Allison Park (c)	(412)/(724)	21,552	—
*16603	Altoona	(814)	46,320	46,148
19003	Ardmore (c)	(610)	12,455	—
15234	Baldwin	(412)	19,767	19,801
18603	Berwick	(570)	10,477	10,365
15102	Bethel Park	(412)	32,313	32,374
*18016	Bethlehem	(610)	74,982	75,103
*17815	Bloomsburg	(570)	14,855	14,633
19008	Broomall (c)	(610)	10,789	—
*16001	Butler	(724)	13,757	13,620
*17013	Carlisle	(717)	18,682	18,880
15108	Carnot-Moon (c)	(412)	11,372	—
17201	Chambersburg	(717)	20,268	20,360
*19013	Chester	(610)	33,972	34,031
19320	Coatesville	(610)	13,100	13,134
17109	Colonial Park (c)	(717)	13,229	—
17512	Columbia	(717)	10,400	10,381
19023	Darby	(610)	10,687	10,682
19026	Drexel Hill (c)	(610)	28,043	—
*18512	Dunmore	(570)	14,057	14,069
*18042	Easton	(610)	26,800	26,951
17022	Elizabethtown	(717)	11,545	11,560
*18049	Emmaus	(610)	11,211	11,307
17522	Ephrata	(717)	13,394	13,506
*16501	Erie	(814)	101,786	101,047

ZIP	Place	Area code	2010 population	2012 estimate
16063	Fernway (c)	(724)	12,414	—
15237	Franklin Park	(412)	13,470	13,900
18052	Fullerton (c)	(610)	14,925	—
*15601	Greensburg	(724)	14,892	14,736
*17331	Hanover	(717)	15,289	15,349
*17105	Harrisburg	(717)	49,528	49,279
*18201	Hazleton	(570)	25,340	25,224
16148	Hermitage	(724)	16,220	16,217
17033	Hershey (c)	(717)	14,257	—
19044	Horsham (c)	(215)	14,842	—
*15701	Indiana	(724)	13,975	13,953
15025	Jefferson Hills	(412)	10,619	10,990
*15907	Johnstown	(814)	20,978	20,577
19406	King of Prussia (c)	(610)	19,936	—
18704	Kingston	(570)	13,182	13,131
*17604	Lancaster	(717)	59,322	59,360
19446	Lansdale	(215)	16,269	16,367
19050	Lansdowne	(610)	10,620	10,621
*17042	Lebanon	(717)	25,477	25,554
*19055	Levittown (c)	(215)	52,983	—
15068	Lower Burrell	(724)	11,761	11,642
*15134	McKeesport	(412)	19,731	19,686
*16335	Meadville	(814)	13,388	13,263
*15146	Monroeville	(412)/(724)	28,386	28,386
18936	Montgomeryville (c)	(215)	12,624	—
18707	Mountain Top (c)	(570)	10,982	—
15120	Munhall	(412)	11,406	11,380
*15668	Murraysville	(412)/(724)	20,079	20,219
18634	Nanticoke	(570)	10,465	10,419
*16108	New Castle	(724)	23,273	22,851
*15068	New Kensington	(724)	13,116	12,962
*19403	Norristown	(610)	34,324	34,427
16301	Oil City	(814)	10,557	10,375
*19104	Philadelphia	(215)	1,526,006	1,547,607
*19460	Phoenixville	(610)	16,440	16,518
*15233	Pittsburgh	(412)	305,704	306,211
15239	Plum	(412)	27,126	27,395
*19464	Pottstown	(610)	22,377	22,480
17901	Pottsville	(570)	14,324	14,129
*19612	Reading	(610)	88,082	88,102
15857	Saint Marys	(814)	13,070	12,913
*18505	Scranton	(570)	76,089	75,809
*16146	Sharon	(724)	14,038	13,815
17404	Shiloh (c)	(717)	11,218	—
15129	South Park Twp. (c)	(814)	13,416	—
*16804	State College	(814)	42,034	41,900
15401	Uniontown	(724)	10,372	10,231
15241	Upper Saint Clair (c)	(412)	19,229	—
15301	Washington	(724)	13,663	13,555
*17268	Waynesboro	(717)	10,568	10,633
17315	Weigelstown (c)	(717)	12,875	—
*19380	West Chester	(610)	18,461	18,857
*15122	West Mifflin	(412)	20,313	20,284
18052	Whitehall	(412)	13,944	13,938
*18703	Wilkes-Barre	(570)	41,498	41,243
15221	Wilkinsburg	(412)	15,930	15,906
*17701	Williamsport	(570)	29,381	29,497
19090	Willow Grove (c)	(215)	15,726	—
19610	Wyomissing	(610)	10,461	10,476
19050	Yeadon	(610)	11,443	11,496
*17405	York	(717)	43,718	43,550

Rhode Island

Area code 401 applies to the entire state. See introductory note.

ZIP	Place	2010 population	2012 estimate
02806	Barrington	16,310	16,267
02809	Bristol	22,954	22,323
02830	Burrillville	15,955	16,082
02863	Central Falls	19,376	19,369
02816	Coventry	35,014	34,928
*02905	Cranston	80,387	80,529
02864	Cumberland	33,506	33,861
02818	East Greenwich	13,146	13,094
02914	East Providence	47,037	47,096
02919	Johnston	28,769	28,960
02865	Lincoln	21,105	21,250
02842	Middletown	16,150	16,039
02882	Narragansett	15,868	15,695
02840	Newport	24,672	24,034
02843	Newport East (c)	11,769	—
02852	North Kingstown	26,486	26,194
02908	North Providence	32,078	32,154
02896	North Smithfield	11,967	12,079
*02860	Pawtucket	71,148	71,170
02871	Portsmouth	17,389	17,293
*02904	Providence	178,042	178,432
02857	Scituate	10,329	10,401
02917	Smithfield	21,430	21,448
02879	South Kingstown	30,639	30,345
02878	Tiverton	15,780	15,771
02864	Valley Falls (c)	11,547	—

ZIP	Place	2010 population	2012 estimate
02885	Warren	10,611	10,554
*02886	Warwick	82,672	81,873
02893	West Warwick	29,191	28,861
02891	Westerly	22,787	22,633
02891	Westerly (c)	17,936	—
02895	Woonsocket	41,186	41,032

South Carolina

ZIP	Place	Area code	2010 population	2012 estimate
*29801	Aiken	(803)	29,524	29,884
*29621	Anderson	(864)	26,686	26,708
*29906	Beaufort	(843)	12,361	12,788
29611	Berea (c)	(864)	14,295	—
*29910	Bluffton	(843)	12,530	12,932
29033	Cayce	(803)	12,528	12,679
*29402	Charleston	(843)	120,083	125,583
*29631	Clemson	(864)	13,905	14,089
*29201	Columbia	(803)	129,272	131,686
*29526	Conway	(843)	17,103	18,688
29204	Dentsville (c)	(803)	14,062	—
*29640	Easley	(864)	19,993	20,098
29681	Five Forks (c)	(864)	14,140	—
*29501	Florence	(843)	37,056	37,498
29206	Forest Acres	(803)	10,361	10,489
*29715	Fort Mill	(803)	10,811	11,387
*29341	Gaffney	(864)	12,414	12,449
29605	Gantt (c)	(864)	14,229	—
*29445	Goose Creek	(843)	35,938	38,579
*29602	Greenville	(864)	58,409	60,709
*29646	Greenwood	(864)	23,222	23,324
*29650	Greer	(864)	25,515	26,645
*29406	Hanahan	(843)	17,997	19,157
*29928	Hilton Head Island	(843)	37,099	38,366
29063	Irmo	(803)	11,097	11,500
29456	Ladson (c)	(843)	13,790	—
*29072	Lexington	(803)	17,870	19,141
*29662	Mauldin	(864)	22,889	23,808
*29465	Mount Pleasant	(843)	67,843	71,875
*29575	Myrtle Beach	(803)	27,109	28,292
29108	Newberry	(803)	10,277	10,255
*29841	North Augusta	(803)	21,348	21,873
*29410	North Charleston	(843)	97,471	101,989
*29582	North Myrtle Beach	(843)	13,752	14,472
29073	Oak Grove (c)	(803)	10,291	—
*29115	Orangeburg	(003)	13,964	13,850
29611	Parker (c)	(864)	11,431	—
29935	Port Royal	(843)	10,678	11,265
29020	Red Hill (c)	(843)	13,223	—
*29730	Rock Hill	(803)	66,154	68,094
29417	Saint Andrews (c)	(843)	20,493	—
29210	Seven Oaks (c)	(803)	15,144	—
*29681	Simpsonville	(864)	18,238	19,056
29577	Socastee (c)	(843)	19,952	—
*29306	Spartanburg	(864)	37,013	37,401
*29483	Summerville	(843)	43,392	44,719
*29150	Sumter	(803)	40,524	40,836
29687	Taylors (c)	(864)	21,617	—
*29607	Wade Hampton (c)	(864)	20,622	—
*29169	West Columbia	(803)	14,988	15,631

South Dakota

Area code 605 applies to the entire state.

ZIP	Place	2010 population	2012 estimate
*57401	Aberdeen	26,091	26,791
*57006	Brookings	22,056	22,591
*57350	Huron	12,592	12,867
57301	Mitchell	15,254	15,484
57501	Pierre	13,646	13,914
*57701	Rapid City	67,956	69,854
*57101	Sioux Falls	153,888	159,908
*57783	Spearfish	10,494	10,718
57069	Vermillion	10,571	10,811
57201	Watertown	21,482	21,803
*57078	Yankton	14,454	14,538

Tennessee

ZIP	Place	Area code	2010 population	2012 estimate
38002	Arlington	(901)	11,517	11,686
*37303	Athens	(423)	13,458	13,489
*38184	Bartlett	(901)	54,613	55,945
*37027	Brentwood	(615)	37,060	39,012
*37621	Bristol	(423)	26,702	26,675
*37401	Chattanooga	(423)	167,674	171,279
*37040	Clarksville	(931)	132,929	142,519
*37311	Cleveland	(423)	41,285	42,386
*38017	Collierville	(901)	43,965	46,462
*38401	Columbia	(931)	34,681	34,901

ZIP	Place	Area code	2010 population	2012 estimate
*38501	Cookeville	(931)	30,435	31,010
*38555	Crossville	(931)	10,795	11,115
*37055	Dickson	(615)	14,538	14,858
*38024	Dyersburg	(731)	17,145	17,043
37412	East Ridge	(423)	20,979	21,291
*37643	Elizabethton	(423)	14,176	14,204
*37922	Farragut	(865)	20,676	21,126
*37064	Franklin	(615)	62,487	66,280
37066	Gallatin	(615)	30,278	31,603
*38138	Germantown	(901)	38,844	39,446
*37072	Goodlettsville	(615)	15,921	16,415
*37743	Greeneville	(423)	15,062	15,024
*37075	Hendersonville	(615)	51,372	53,080
*38301	Jackson	(731)	65,211	67,265
*37601	Johnson City	(423)	63,152	64,528
*37662	Kingsport	(423)	48,205	51,501
*37950	Knoxville	(865)	178,874	182,200
*37086	La Vergne	(615)	32,588	33,777
38002	Lakeland	(901)	12,430	12,622
38464	Lawrenceburg	(931)	10,428	10,444
*37087	Lebanon	(615)	26,190	27,710
37091	Lewisburg	(931)	11,100	11,210
37355	Manchester	(931)	10,102	10,224
38237	Martin	(731)	11,473	11,421
37801	Maryville	(865)	27,465	27,914
*37110	McMinnville	(931)	13,605	13,598
*38101	Memphis	(901)	646,889	655,155
37343	Middle Valley (c)	(423)	12,684	—
*38053	Millington	(901)	10,176	10,487
*37813	Morristown	(423)	29,137	29,269
*37122	Mount Juliet	(615)	23,671	26,870
*37130	Murfreesboro	(615)	108,755	114,038
*37202	Nashville-Davidson	(615)	601,222	624,496
*37830	Oak Ridge	(865)	29,330	29,320
38242	Paris	(731)	10,156	10,166
37148	Portland	(615)	11,480	11,840
37415	Red Bank	(423)	11,651	11,817
*37862	Sevierville	(865)	14,807	15,613
37865	Seymour (c)	(865)	10,919	—
*37160	Shelbyville	(931)	20,335	20,598
37167	Smyrna	(615)	39,974	41,705
*37379	Soddy-Daisy	(423)	12,714	12,937
*37174	Spring Hill	(931)	29,036	31,140
37172	Springfield	(615)	16,440	16,574
*37388	Tullahoma	(931)	18,655	18,739
*38261	Union City	(731)	10,895	10,782
37188	White House	(615)	10,255	10,587

Texas

Area codes (281) and (832) overlay area code (713). Area code (430) overlays area code (903). Area code (682) overlays area code (817). Area code (737) overlays area code (512). Area codes (972) and (469) overlay area code (214).

ZIP	Place	Area code	2010 population	2012 estimate
*79604	Abilene	(325)	117,063	118,887
75001	Addison	(214)	13,056	15,179
78516	Alamo	(956)	18,353	18,761
77039	Aldine (c)	(713)	15,869	—
*78332	Alice	(361)	19,104	19,536
*75002	Allen	(214)	84,246	89,640
78574	Alton	(956)	12,341	14,490
*77511	Alvin	(713)	24,236	24,905
*79105	Amarillo	(806)	190,695	195,250
79714	Andrews	(432)	11,088	12,157
*77515	Angleton	(979)	18,862	18,977
*76004	Arlington	(817)	365,438	375,600
77346	Atascocita (c)	(281)	65,844	—
*75751	Athens	(903)	12,710	12,846
*78712	Austin	(512)	790,390	842,592
*76020	Azle	(817)	10,947	11,220
75180	Balch Springs	(214)	23,728	24,866
*77414	Bay City	(979)	17,614	17,476
*77520	Baytown	(713)	71,802	73,238
*77707	Beaumont	(409)	118,296	118,228
*76021	Bedford	(817)	46,979	48,150
*78102	Beeville	(361)	12,863	13,101
*77401	Bellaire	(713)	16,855	17,435
76513	Belton	(254)	18,216	19,409
*76126	Benbrook	(817)	21,234	21,939
*79720	Big Spring	(432)	27,282	27,546
*78006	Boerne	(830)	10,471	11,534
75418	Bonham	(903)	10,127	10,068
*79007	Borger	(806)	13,251	13,077
*77833	Brenham	(979)	15,716	16,136
78520	Brownsville	(956)	175,023	180,097
*76801	Brownwood	(325)	19,288	18,972
78717	Brushy Creek (c)	(903)	21,764	—
*77801	Bryan	(979)	76,201	78,061
76354	Burkburnett	(940)	10,811	10,828
*76028	Burleson	(817)	36,690	38,983
*79015	Canyon	(806)	13,303	13,857

ZIP	Place	Area code	2010 population	2012 estimate
78130	Canyon Lake (c)	(830)	21,262	—
*75006	Carrollton	(214)	119,097	125,409
*75104	Cedar Hill	(214)	45,028	46,461
*78613	Cedar Park	(512)	48,937	57,957
77530	Channelview (c)	(713)	38,289	—
78108	Cibolo	(210)	15,349	17,785
77450	Cinco Ranch (c)	(281)	18,274	—
*76031	Cleburne	(817)	29,337	29,344
77015	Cloverleaf (c)	(713)	22,942	—
77531	Clute	(979)	11,211	11,282
*77840	College Station	(979)	93,857	97,801
76034	Colleyville	(817)	22,807	23,936
*77301	Conroe	(936)	56,207	61,533
78109	Converse	(210)	18,198	19,673
*75019	Coppell	(214)	38,659	40,022
76522	Copperas Cove	(254)	32,032	33,374
*76205	Corinth	(940)	19,935	20,483
*78469	Corpus Christi	(361)	305,215	312,195
*75110	Corsicana	(903)	23,770	23,899
76036	Crowley	(817)	12,838	13,580
*75221	Dallas	(214)	1,197,816	1,241,162
*77536	Deer Park	(713)	32,010	32,995
*78840	Del Rio	(830)	35,591	35,543
*75020	Denison	(903)	22,682	22,665
*76201	Denton	(940)	113,383	121,123
*75115	DeSoto	(214)	49,047	51,102
78537	Donna	(956)	15,798	16,204
79029	Dumas	(806)	14,691	14,989
*75138	Duncanville	(214)	38,524	39,501
*78852	Eagle Pass	(830)	26,248	27,283
*78539	Edinburg	(956)	77,100	81,029
77437	El Campo	(979)	11,602	11,546
*79910	El Paso	(915)	649,121	672,538
75119	Ennis	(214)	18,513	18,653
*76039	Euless	(817)	51,277	52,780
*75381	Farmers Branch	(214)	28,616	29,368
*75022	Flower Mound	(214)	64,669	67,825
76119	Forest Hill	(817)	12,355	12,628
75126	Forney	(214)	14,661	15,877
76544	Fort Hood (c)	(254)	29,589	—
*76161	Fort Worth	(817)	741,206	777,992
77498	Four Corners (c)	(281)	12,382	—
78624	Fredericksburg	(830)	10,530	10,715
*77541	Freeport	(979)	12,049	12,079
77545	Fresno (c)	(281)	19,069	—
77546	Friendswood	(281)	35,805	36,898
*75034	Frisco	(214)	116,989	128,176
*76240	Gainesville	(940)	16,002	16,067
77547	Galena Park	(713)	10,887	11,048
*77550	Galveston	(409)	47,743	47,762
*75040	Garland	(214)	226,876	233,564
*76528	Gatesville	(254)	15,751	15,995
78626	Georgetown	(512)	47,400	52,303
75154	Glenn Heights	(214)	11,278	11,726
*75051	Grand Prairie	(214)	175,396	181,824
*76051	Grapevine	(817)	46,334	48,447
77479	Greatwood (c)	(281)	11,538	—
*75401	Greenville	(903)	25,557	25,834
77619	Groves	(409)	16,144	15,819
*76117	Haltom City	(817)	42,409	43,376
*76548	Harker Heights	(254)	26,700	27,826
*78550	Harlingen	(956)	64,849	65,679
*75652	Henderson	(903)	13,712	13,806
79045	Hereford	(806)	15,370	15,349
*76643	Hewitt	(254)	13,549	13,860
78557	Hidalgo	(956)	11,198	11,711
75067	Highland Village	(214)	15,056	15,593
*79927	Horizon City	(915)	16,735	18,769
*77052	Houston	(713)	2,099,451	2,160,821
*77338	Humble	(713)	15,133	15,392
*77340	Huntsville	(936)	38,548	39,666
76053	Hurst	(817)	37,337	38,194
78634	Hutto	(512)	14,698	18,765
*75015	Irving	(214)	216,290	225,427
77029	Jacinto City	(281)	10,553	10,721
75766	Jacksonville	(903)	14,544	14,747
78729	Jollyville (c)	(512)	16,151	—
*77449	Katy	(713)	14,102	14,661
*76248	Keller	(817)	39,627	41,923
*78028	Kerrville	(830)	22,347	22,455
*75662	Kilgore	(903)	12,975	13,738
*76540	Killeen	(254)	127,921	134,654
*78363	Kingsville	(361)	26,213	26,206
78640	Kyle	(512)	28,016	30,875
78572	La Homa (c)	(956)	11,985	—
77568	La Marque	(409)	14,509	14,873
*77571	La Porte	(713)	33,800	34,469
77566	Lake Jackson	(979)	26,849	27,166
*78734	Lakeway	(512)	11,391	12,459
*75146	Lancaster	(214)	36,361	37,845
*78041	Laredo	(956)	236,091	244,731

ZIP	Place	Area code	2010 population	2012 estimate
*77573	League City	(281)	83,560	88,188
*78641	Leander	(512)	26,521	29,620
*78268	Leon Valley	(210)	10,151	10,676
*79336	Levelland	(806)	13,542	13,632
*75067	Lewisville	(214)	95,290	99,453
75068	Little Elm	(214)	25,898	28,966
*78233	Live Oak	(210)	13,131	14,200
78644	Lockhart	(512)	12,698	12,913
*75606	Longview	(903)	80,455	81,092
*79408	Lubbock	(806)	229,573	236,065
*75901	Lufkin	(936)	35,067	36,009
77657	Lumberton	(409)	11,943	12,061
76063	Mansfield	(817)	56,368	59,317
76063	Marshall	(903)	23,523	24,751
*78501	McAllen	(956)	129,877	134,719
*75070	McKinney	(214)	131,117	143,223
78570	Mercedes	(956)	15,570	16,313
*75149	Mesquite	(214)	139,824	143,195
*79701	Midland	(432)	111,147	119,385
76065	Midlothian	(214)	18,037	19,101
*76067	Mineral Wells	(940)	16,788	16,731
*78572	Mission	(956)	77,058	80,452
77083	Mission Bend (c)	(713)	36,501	—
*77489	Missouri City	(713)	67,358	69,020
*75455	Mount Pleasant	(903)	15,564	16,081
*75094	Murphy	(214)	17,708	18,960
*75961	Nacogdoches	(936)	32,996	34,047
77627	Nederland	(409)	17,547	17,480
*78130	New Braunfels	(830)	57,740	60,761
77479	New Territory (c)	(281)	15,186	—
*76161	North Richland Hills	(817)	63,343	65,290
*79761	Odessa	(432)	99,940	106,102
*77630	Orange	(409)	18,595	18,948
*75801	Palestine	(903)	18,712	18,516
*79065	Pampa	(806)	17,994	18,332
*75460	Paris	(903)	25,171	25,082
*77501	Pasadena	(713)	149,043	152,272
*77581	Pearland	(713)	91,252	96,294
78721	Pecan Grove (c)	(254)	15,963	—
*78660	Pflugerville	(512)	46,936	51,894
78577	Pharr	(956)	70,400	73,138
*79072	Plainview	(806)	22,194	22,230
*75074	Plano	(214)	259,841	272,068
*77640	Port Arthur	(409)	53,818	54,010
77979	Port Lavaca	(361)	12,248	12,300
77651	Port Neches	(409)	13,040	12,833
78374	Portland	(361)	15,099	15,443
75078	Prosper	(972)	9,423	11,729
*78580	Raymondville	(965)	11,284	11,194
*75154	Red Oak	(972)	10,769	11,081
76140	Rendon (c)	(817)	12,552	—
*75080	Richardson	(214)	99,223	103,297
*77469	Richmond	(713)	11,679	11,807
78582	Rio Grande City	(956)	13,834	13,939
76701	Robinson	(254)	10,509	11,068
78380	Robstown	(361)	11,487	11,618
*75087	Rockwall	(214)	37,490	39,957
77471	Rosenberg	(713)	30,618	31,734
*78681	Round Rock	(512)	99,887	106,573
*75088	Rowlett	(214)	56,199	57,703
75048	Sachse	(214)	20,329	21,596
*76179	Saginaw	(817)	19,806	20,877
*76902	San Angelo	(325)	93,200	95,887
*78265	San Antonio	(210)	1,327,407	1,382,951
78586	San Benito	(956)	24,250	24,491
79849	San Elizario (c)	(915)	13,603	—
78589	San Juan	(956)	33,856	35,204
*78666	San Marcos	(512)	44,894	50,001
*77510	Santa Fe	(409)	12,222	12,520
*78154	Schertz	(210)	31,465	34,883
77586	Seabrook	(281)	11,952	12,433
75159	Seagoville	(214)	14,835	15,478
*78155	Seguin	(830)	25,175	26,272
*75090	Sherman	(903)	38,521	39,122
77459	Sienna Plantation (c)	(281)	13,721	—
*79549	Snyder	(325)	11,202	11,400
79927	Socorro	(915)	32,013	32,693
77587	South Houston	(713)	16,983	17,336
76092	Southlake	(817)	26,575	27,706
*77373	Spring (c)	(713)	54,298	—
*77477	Stafford	(713)	17,693	17,962
*76401	Stephenville	(254)	17,123	18,208
*77478	Sugar Land	(713)	78,817	82,480
*75482	Sulphur Springs	(903)	15,449	15,578
79556	Sweetwater	(325)	10,906	10,681
76574	Taylor	(512)	15,191	16,080
*76501	Temple	(254)	66,102	69,148
*75160	Terrell	(214)	15,816	16,143
*75501	Texarkana	(903)	36,411	37,217
*77590	Texas City	(409)	45,099	45,671
*75056	The Colony	(214)	36,328	39,030
77387	The Woodlands (c)	(713)	93,847	—
78260	Timberwood Park (c)	(830)	13,447	—

ZIP	Place	Area code	2010 population	2012 estimate
*77375	Tomball	(713)	10,753	10,964
*75702	Tyler	(903)	96,900	99,323
*78148	Universal City	(830)	18,530	19,155
75205	University Park	(214)	23,068	23,797
*78801	Uvalde	(830)	15,751	16,108
*76384	Vernon	(940)	11,002	10,769
*77901	Victoria	(361)	62,592	64,376
*77662	Vidor	(409)	10,579	10,915
76702	Waco	(254)	124,805	127,018
76148	Watauga	(817)	23,497	24,044
*75165	Waxahachie	(214)	29,621	31,091
*76086	Weatherford	(817)	25,250	26,385
77598	Webster	(281)	10,400	10,881
78728	Wells Branch (c)	(512)	12,120	—
*78596	Weslaco	(956)	35,670	36,846
79764	West Odessa (c)	(432)	22,707	—
77005	West University Place	(713)	14,787	15,221
76108	White Settlement	(817)	16,116	16,565
*76307	Wichita Falls	(940)	104,553	104,552
75098	Wylie	(214)	41,427	44,267

Utah
Area code (385) overlays area code (801).

ZIP	Place	Area code	2010 population	2012 estimate
84003	American Fork	(801)	26,263	27,147
*84010	Bountiful	(801)	42,552	42,898
84302	Brigham City	(435)	17,899	18,149
84720	Cedar City	(435)	28,857	29,118
84062	Cedar Hills	(801)	9,796	10,063
84014	Centerville	(801)	15,335	16,203
*84015	Clearfield	(801)	30,112	30,376
84015	Clinton	(801)	20,426	20,805
84121	Cottonwood Heights	(801)	33,433	34,017
84020	Draper	(801)	42,274	44,103
84043	Eagle Mountain	(801)	21,415	23,212
84025	Farmington	(801)	18,275	20,750
*84032	Heber City	(435)	11,362	12,260
84065	Herriman	(801)	21,785	24,433
84003	Highland	(801)	15,523	16,440
*84117	Holladay	(801)	26,472	26,936
84737	Hurricane	(435)	13,748	14,362
84037	Kaysville	(801)	27,300	28,283
84118	Kearns (c)	(801)	35,731	—
*84041	Layton	(801)	67,311	68,677
84043	Lehi	(801)	47,407	51,173
84042	Lindon	(801)	10,070	10,442
84321	Logan	(435)	48,174	48,879
84044	Magna (c)	(801)	26,505	—
84047	Midvale	(801)	27,964	30,229
84109	Millcreek (c)	(801)	62,139	—
*84157	Murray	(801)	46,746	48,263
*84404	North Ogden	(801)	17,357	17,791
84054	North Salt Lake	(801)	16,322	16,717
*84201	Ogden	(801)	82,825	83,793
*84057	Orem	(801)	88,328	90,749
84651	Payson	(801)	18,294	18,938
84062	Pleasant Grove	(801)	33,509	34,519
*84601	Provo	(801)	112,488	115,919
*84065	Riverton	(801)	38,753	40,398
84067	Roy	(801)	36,884	37,604
84770	Saint George	(435)	72,897	75,561
*84101	Salt Lake City	(801)	186,440	189,314
*84070	Sandy	(801)	87,461	89,344
84043	Saratoga Springs	(801)	17,781	21,137
84095	South Jordan	(801)	50,418	55,934
84403	South Ogden	(801)	16,532	16,738
84165	South Salt Lake	(801)	23,617	24,366
84660	Spanish Fork	(801)	34,691	36,277
84663	Springville	(801)	29,466	30,621
84075	Syracuse	(801)	24,331	25,118
84118	Taylorsville	(801)	58,652	60,227
84074	Tooele	(435)	31,605	32,115
84780	Washington	(435)	18,761	20,888
84401	West Haven	(801)	10,272	11,069
*84084	West Jordan	(801)	103,712	108,383
*84170	West Valley City	(801)	129,480	132,434
84010	Woods Cross	(801)	9,761	10,212

Vermont
Area code 802 applies to the entire state. See introductory note.

ZIP	Place	2010 population	2012 estimate
05201	Bennington	15,764	15,555
*05301	Brattleboro	12,046	11,848
*05401	Burlington	42,417	42,282
05446	Colchester	17,067	17,245
*05451	Essex	19,587	20,057
05468	Milton	10,352	10,526
*05701	Rutland	16,495	16,217
*05403	South Burlington	17,904	18,400

Virginia
Area code (571) overlays area code (703).

ZIP	Place	Area code	2010 population	2012 estimate
*22313	Alexandria	(703)	139,966	146,294
22003	Annandale (c)	(703)	41,008	—
*22210	Arlington (c)	(703)	207,627	—
*20146	Ashburn (c)	(703)	43,511	—
*22041	Bailey's Crossroads (c)	(703)	23,643	—
*24060	Blacksburg	(540)	42,620	42,627
23235	Bon Air (c)	(804)	16,366	—
23112	Brandermill (c)	(804)	13,173	—
*24203	Bristol	(276)	17,835	17,662
20148	Broadlands (c)	(703)	12,313	—
20111	Buckhall (c)	(703)	16,293	—
20109	Bull Run (c)	(703)	14,983	—
*22015	Burke (c)	(703)	41,055	—
22015	Burke Centre (c)	(703)	17,326	—
24069	Cascades (c)	(434)	11,912	—
24018	Cave Spring (c)	(540)	24,922	—
*20120	Centreville (c)	(703)	71,135	—
*20151	Chantilly (c)	(703)	23,039	—
*22906	Charlottesville	(434)	43,475	43,956
22026	Cherry Hill (c)	(703)	16,000	—
*23320	Chesapeake	(757)	222,209	228,417
*23831	Chester (c)	(804)	20,987	—
*24073	Christiansburg	(540)	21,041	21,458
23834	Colonial Heights	(804)	17,411	17,479
20165	Countryside (c)	(703)	10,072	—
*22701	Culpeper	(540)	16,379	16,633
22193	Dale City (c)	(703)	65,969	—
*24541	Danville	(434)	43,055	42,996
20170	Dranesville (c)	(703)	11,921	—
23222	East Highland Park (c)	(804)	14,796	—
22033	Fair Oaks (c)	(703)	30,223	—
*22030	Fairfax	(703)	22,565	23,461
22039	Fairfax Station (c)	(703)	12,030	—
*22046	Falls Church	(703)	12,332	13,229
22308	Fort Hunt (c)	(703)	16,045	—
22310	Franconia (c)	(703)	18,245	—
20171	Franklin Farm (c)	(703)	19,288	—
*22404	Fredericksburg	(540)	24,286	27,307
22630	Front Royal	(540)	14,440	14,666
*20155	Gainesville (c)	(703)	11,481	—
*23060	Glen Allen (c)	(804)	14,774	—
22066	Great Falls (c)	(703)	15,427	—
22306	Groveton (c)	(703)	14,598	—
*23670	Hampton	(757)	137,436	136,836
*22801	Harrisonburg	(540)	48,914	50,981
*20170	Herndon	(703)	23,292	24,268
23075	Highland Springs (c)	(804)	15,711	—
24019	Hollins (c)	(540)	14,673	—
23860	Hopewell	(804)	22,591	22,348
22303	Huntington (c)	(703)	11,267	—
22306	Hybla Valley (c)	(703)	15,801	—
22043	Idylwood (c)	(703)	17,288	—
22038	Kings Park West (c)	(703)	13,390	—
22315	Kingstowne (c)	(703)	15,556	—
22191	Lake Ridge (c)	(540)	41,058	—
23228	Lakeside (c)	(804)	11,849	—
20176	Lansdowne (c)	(703)	11,253	—
23060	Laurel (c)	(804)	16,713	—
*20175	Leesburg	(703)	42,616	45,936
22312	Lincolnia (c)	(703)	22,855	—
20136	Linton Hall (c)	(703)	35,725	—
*22079	Lorton (c)	(703)	18,610	—
20165	Lowes Island (c)	(703)	10,756	—
*24506	Lynchburg	(434)	75,568	77,113
24572	Madison Heights (c)	(434)	11,285	—
*20110	Manassas	(703)	37,821	40,605
20113	Manassas Park	(703)	14,273	15,798
23235	Manchester (c)	(804)	10,804	—
*24112	Martinsville	(276)	13,821	13,733
22191	Marumsco (c)	(703)	35,036	—
*22101	McLean (c)	(703)	48,115	—
20171	McNair (c)	(703)	17,513	—
23234	Meadowbrook (c)	(804)	18,312	—
*23111	Mechanicsville (c)	(804)	36,348	—
*22116	Merrifield (c)	(703)	15,212	—
22026	Montclair (c)	(703)	19,570	—
22121	Mount Vernon (c)	(703)	12,416	—
22191	Neabsco (c)	(703)	12,068	—
22122	Newington (c)	(703)	12,943	—
22153	Newington Forest (c)	(703)	12,442	—
*23607	Newport News	(757)	180,719	180,726
*23501	Norfolk	(757)	242,803	245,782
22124	Oakton (c)	(703)	34,166	—
*23804	Petersburg	(804)	32,420	31,973
23662	Poquoson	(757)	12,150	12,097
*23707	Portsmouth	(757)	95,535	96,470
*24141	Radford	(540)	16,408	16,685
*20190	Reston (c)	(703)	58,404	—
*23232	Richmond	(804)	204,214	210,309
*24022	Roanoke	(540)	97,032	97,469
24281	Rose Hill (c) (Fairfax Co.)	(276)	20,226	—
*24153	Salem	(540)	24,802	24,970
23233	Short Pump (c)	(804)	24,729	—
20152	South Riding (c)	(703)	24,256	—
*22150	Springfield (c)	(703)	30,484	—
*24402	Staunton	(540)	23,746	23,921
*20164	Sterling (c)	(703)	27,822	—
20109	Sudley (c)	(703)	16,203	—
*23434	Suffolk	(757)	84,585	85,181
20164	Sugarland Run (c)	(703)	11,799	—
24502	Timberlake (c)	(434)	12,183	—
23229	Tuckahoe (c)	(804)	44,990	—
22101	Tysons Corner (c)	(703)	19,627	—
*22180	Vienna	(703)	15,687	16,188
*23450	Virginia Beach	(757)	437,994	447,021
23888	Wakefield (c)	(757)	11,275	—
22980	Waynesboro	(540)	21,006	21,107
22042	West Falls Church (c)	(703)	29,207	—
22152	West Springfield (c)	(703)	22,460	—
*23185	Williamsburg	(757)	14,068	15,167
*22601	Winchester	(540)	26,203	26,881
24592	Wolf Trap (c)	(703)	16,131	—
24381	Woodlawn (c) (Fairfax Co.)	(276)	20,804	—

Washington

ZIP	Place	Area code	2010 population	2012 estimate
98520	Aberdeen	(360)	16,896	16,529
*98221	Anacortes	(360)	15,778	15,928
98223	Arlington	(360)	17,926	18,317
98335	Artondale (c)	(253)	12,653	—
*98002	Auburn	(253)	70,180	73,505
98110	Bainbridge Island	(206)	23,025	23,263
98604	Battle Ground	(360)	17,571	18,044
*98009	Bellevue	(425)	122,363	126,439
*98225	Bellingham	(360)	80,885	82,234
*98390	Bonney Lake	(360)	17,374	17,964
*98011	Bothell	(425)	33,505	34,651
98036	Bothell West (c)	(425)	16,607	—
*98337	Bremerton	(360)	37,729	39,251
98178	Bryn Mawr-Skyway (c)	(206)	15,645	—
*98166	Burien	(206)	33,313	49,410
98607	Camas	(360)	19,355	20,490
98531	Centralia	(360)	16,336	16,505
99004	Cheney	(509)	10,590	11,018
98072	Cottage Lake (c)	(206)	22,494	—
98042	Covington	(253)	17,575	18,298
*98198	Des Moines	(206)	29,673	30,449
98031	East Hill-Meridian (c)	(253)/(425)	29,878	—
98056	East Renton Highlands (c)	(425)	11,140	—
98802	East Wenatchee	(509)	13,190	13,439
98204	Eastmont (c)	(425)	20,101	—
*98020	Edmonds	(425)	39,709	40,400
98387	Elk Plain (c)	(253)	14,205	—
*98926	Ellensburg	(509)	18,174	18,348
98022	Enumclaw	(360)	10,669	11,327
*98201	Everett	(425)	103,019	104,655
98058	Fairwood (c) (King Co.)	(253)/(425)	19,102	—
*98002	Federal Way	(253)	89,306	91,933
98248	Ferndale	(360)	11,415	11,998
98597	Five Corners (c)	(360)	18,159	—
98433	Fort Lewis (c)	(253)	11,046	—
98375	Frederickson (c)	(253)	18,719	—
98338	Graham (c)	(253)	23,491	—
98930	Grandview	(509)	10,862	11,012
98665	Hazel Dell (c)	(360)	19,435	—
98011	Inglewood-Finn Hill (c)	(425)	22,707	—
*98027	Issaquah	(425)	30,434	32,633
98626	Kelso	(360)	11,925	11,832
98028	Kenmore	(425)	20,460	21,280
*99336	Kennewick	(509)	73,917	75,971
*98031	Kent	(253)/(425)	92,411	122,999
98033	Kingsgate (c)	(425)	13,065	—
*98003	Kirkland	(425)	48,787	50,697
98029	Klahanie (c)	(425)	10,674	—
*98509	Lacey	(360)	42,393	43,860
98155	Lake Forest Park	(206)	12,598	12,972
98042	Lake Morton-Berrydale (c)	(253)/(425)	10,160	—
98258	Lake Stevens	(425)	28,069	29,104
98391	Lake Tapps (c)	(253)	11,859	—
98002	Lakeland North (c)	(253)	12,942	—
98002	Lakeland South (c)	(253)	11,574	—
*98498	Lakewood	(253)	58,163	58,852
98632	Longview	(360)	36,648	36,458
98264	Lynden	(360)	11,951	12,605
*98046	Lynnwood	(425)	35,836	36,275

ZIP	Place	Area code	2010 population	2012 estimate
98290	Maltby (c)	(360)/(425)	10,830	—
98038	Maple Valley	(425)	22,684	24,171
98012	Martha Lake (c)	(425)	15,473	—
*98270	Marysville	(360)	60,020	62,402
98040	Mercer Island	(206)	22,699	23,661
*98082	Mill Creek	(425)	18,244	18,671
98012	Mill Creek East (c)	(425)	15,709	—
98272	Monroe	(360)	17,304	17,503
98837	Moses Lake	(509)	20,366	21,182
*98273	Mount Vernon	(360)	31,743	32,287
98043	Mountlake Terrace	(425)	19,909	20,198
98275	Mukilteo	(425)	20,254	20,605
*98059	Newcastle	(425)	10,380	10,792
98037	North Lynnwood (c)	(425)	16,574	—
*98277	Oak Harbor	(360)	22,075	22,260
*98501	Olympia	(360)	46,478	47,698
98662	Orchards (c)	(360)	19,556	—
98444	Parkland (c)	(253)	35,803	—
*99301	Pasco	(509)	59,781	65,398
*98362	Port Angeles	(360)	19,038	19,056
*98366	Port Orchard	(360)	11,144	11,680
98390	Prairie Ridge (c)	(360)	11,464	—
*99163	Pullman	(509)	29,799	31,359
*98371	Puyallup	(253)	37,022	38,147
*98052	Redmond	(425)	54,144	56,561
*98058	Renton	(425)	90,927	95,448
*99352	Richland	(509)	48,058	51,440
98686	Salmon Creek (c)	(360)	19,686	—
*98074	Sammamish	(425)	45,780	49,069
*98148	SeaTac	(206)	26,909	27,667
*98101	Seattle	(206)/(425)	608,660	634,535
98284	Sedro-Woolley	(360)	10,540	10,636
*98133	Shoreline	(206)	53,007	54,352
98208	Silver Firs (c)......	(206)/(425)	20,891	—
*98315	Silverdale (c)	(360)	19,204	—
*98065	Snoqualmie	(425)	10,670	11,594
98373	South Hill (c)	(253)	52,431	—
98387	Spanaway (c)	(253)	27,227	—
*99210	Spokane	(509)	208,916	209,525
*99211	Spokane Valley	(509)	89,755	90,641
98944	Sunnyside	(509)	15,858	16,054
*98402	Tacoma	(253)	198,397	202,010
*98138	Tukwila	(206)	19,107	19,611
*98501	Tumwater	(360)	17,371	18,102
98053	Union Hill-Novelty Hill (c)	(425)	18,805	—
*98467	University Place	(253)	31,144	31,502
*98661	Vancouver	(360)	161,791	165,489
*98013	Vashon (c)	(206)	10,624	—
99362	Walla Walla	(509)	31,731	31,864
*98671	Washougal	(360)	14,095	14,584
*98801	Wenatchee	(509)	31,925	32,562
*99353	West Richland	(509)	11,811	12,663
98166	White Center (c)	(206)	13,495	—
*98072	Woodinville	(425)	10,938	11,234
*98903	Yakima	(509)	91,067	93,101

West Virginia

Area code (681) overlays area code (304); both apply to the entire state.

ZIP	Place	2010 population	2012 estimate
*25801	Beckley	17,614	17,606
24701	Bluefield	10,447	10,502
*25301	Charleston	51,400	51,018
*26301	Clarksburg	16,578	16,439
26554	Fairmont	18,704	18,737
*25704	Huntington	49,138	49,160
*25401	Martinsburg	17,227	17,513
*26505	Morgantown	29,660	31,000
*26101	Parkersburg	31,492	31,261
25177	Saint Albans	11,044	10,973
*25303	South Charleston	13,450	13,340
25569	Teays Valley (c)	13,175	—
*26105	Vienna	10,749	10,686
26062	Weirton	19,746	19,503
26003	Wheeling	28,486	28,213

Wisconsin

Area code (534) overlays area code (715).

ZIP	Place	Area code	2010 population	2012 estimate
54301	Allouez	(920)	13,975	13,992
*54911	Appleton	(920)	72,623	73,016
*54304	Ashwaubenon	(920)	16,963	17,101
53913	Baraboo	(608)	12,048	12,046
53916	Beaver Dam	(920)	16,214	16,291
54311	Bellevue	(920)	14,570	14,760
*53511	Beloit	(608)	36,966	36,842
*53045	Brookfield	(262)	37,920	37,977
*53209	Brown Deer	(414)	11,999	12,088
53105	Burlington	(262)	10,464	10,508
53108	Caledonia	(262)	24,705	24,687
53012	Cedarburg	(262)	11,412	11,435
*54729	Chippewa Falls	(715)	13,661	13,676
53110	Cudahy	(414)	18,267	18,340
53115	De Pere	(920)	23,800	24,209
*54703	Eau Claire	(715)	65,883	66,966
53121	Elkhorn	(262)	10,084	10,082
*53711	Fitchburg	(608)	25,260	25,895
*54935	Fond du Lac	(920)	43,021	43,045
53538	Fort Atkinson	(920)	12,368	12,466
53132	Franklin	(414)	35,451	36,083
53022	Germantown	(262)	19,749	19,783
*53209	Glendale	(414)	12,872	12,932
53024	Grafton	(262)	11,459	11,508
*54303	Green Bay	(920)	104,057	104,868
53129	Greendale	(414)	14,046	14,325
*53220	Greenfield	(414)	36,720	37,072
53027	Hartford	(262)	14,223	14,243
*54303	Howard	(920)	17,399	18,500
*54016	Hudson	(715)	12,719	13,026
*53545	Janesville	(608)	63,575	63,588
54130	Kaukauna	(920)	15,462	15,696
*53140	Kenosha	(262)	99,218	100,150
*54601	La Crosse	(608)	51,320	51,647
54140	Little Chute	(920)	10,449	10,428
*53714	Madison	(608)	233,209	240,323
*54220	Manitowoc	(920)	33,736	33,383
54143	Marinette	(715)	10,968	10,862
*54449	Marshfield	(715)	19,118	18,952
54952	Menasha	(920)	17,353	17,522
*53051	Menomonee Falls	(262)	35,626	35,802
54751	Menomonie	(715)	16,264	16,261
*53097	Mequon	(262)	23,132	23,225
*53562	Middleton	(608)	17,442	18,159
*53201	Milwaukee	(414)	594,833	598,916
53566	Monroe	(608)	10,827	10,794
53406	Mount Pleasant	(262)	26,197	26,185
53150	Muskego	(414)	24,135	24,407
*54956	Neenah	(920)	25,501	25,763
*53186	New Berlin	(262)	39,584	39,703
53154	Oak Creek	(414)	34,451	34,908
53066	Oconomowoc	(262)	15,759	15,888
54650	Onalaska	(608)	17,736	18,256
*54901	Oshkosh	(920)	66,083	66,653
53072	Pewaukee	(262)	13,195	13,610
53818	Platteville	(608)	11,224	11,286
*53158	Pleasant Prairie	(262)	19,719	20,027
54467	Plover	(715)	12,123	12,239
53074	Port Washington	(262)	11,250	11,365
53901	Portage	(608)	10,324	10,208
*53401	Racine	(262)	78,860	78,303
*53076	Richfield	(262)	11,300	11,353
54022	River Falls	(715)	15,000	15,182
*53081	Sheboygan	(920)	49,288	48,895
53211	Shorewood	(414)	13,162	13,196
53172	South Milwaukee	(414)	21,156	21,238
*54481	Stevens Point	(715)	26,717	26,748
53589	Stoughton	(608)	12,611	12,927
*54173	Suamico	(920)	11,346	11,631
*53590	Sun Prairie	(608)	29,364	30,403
54880	Superior	(715)	27,244	26,862
53089	Sussex	(262)	10,518	10,633
*54241	Two Rivers	(920)	11,712	11,545
53593	Verona	(608)	10,619	11,212
*53094	Watertown	(920)	23,861	23,957
*53186	Waukesha	(262)	70,718	70,920
53597	Waunakee	(608)	12,097	12,657
53963	Waupun	(920)	11,340	11,295
*54403	Wausau	(715)	39,106	39,160
*53213	Wauwatosa	(414)	46,396	47,068
*53214	West Allis	(414)	60,411	60,732
*53095	West Bend	(262)	31,078	31,540
*54476	Weston	(715)	14,868	14,930
*53217	Whitefish Bay	(414)	14,110	14,137
53190	Whitewater	(262)	14,390	14,505
*54494	Wisconsin Rapids	(715)	18,367	18,217

Wyoming

Area code 307 applies to the entire state.

ZIP	Place	2010 population	2012 estimate
*82609	Casper	55,316	57,813
*82009	Cheyenne	59,466	61,537
*82930	Evanston	12,359	12,262
*82716	Gillette	29,087	31,378
*82935	Green River	12,515	12,801
*82072	Laramie	30,816	31,681
82501	Riverton	10,615	10,971
*82901	Rock Springs	23,036	24,047
82801	Sheridan	17,444	17,698

WORLD HISTORY
Chronology of World History

Note: In this section, the notation BCE (before the common era) is applied to years dating to the traditional BC (before Christ) era, and CE (common era) is applied to AD (anno domini) dates. This notation is now preferred in scientific and academic publications. The traditional Gregorian Calendar system and its dates and years are unaltered except by these labels.

Other abbreviations used in this chapter include the following: KYA = thousand years ago, MYA = million years ago, c. = circa, fl. = flourished, r. = ruled, b. = born, d. = died.

Prehistory: Our Ancestors Emerge
Reviewed by Albert Rolls, Ph.D., June 2013

Evidence of the origins of *Homo sapiens sapiens*, the genus, species, and subspecies to which all living humans belong, comes from a small but increasing number of fossils, from genetic and anatomical studies, and from interpretation of the geological and archaeological records. The latest evidence suggests that humans evolved from apelike primate ancestors that lived in eastern and central Africa 7 to 5 million years ago (MYA). Although all humans living today are members of a single species, the fossil record confirms that our ancestors coexisted with a number of similar species throughout our evolutionary history. Current theories trace the first hominin[1] (upright, bipedal, humanlike primate) to Africa, where several distinct genera appeared 6-4 MYA. They lived in a variety of environments throughout most of the continent, including swampy forest margins, woodlands, and open savannas (usually near lakes or springs). In addition to *Australopithecus afarensis*—better known as "Lucy," a 3.2 MYA Ethiopian specimen found in 1974—these earliest hominins include such recent discoveries as *Sahelanthropus* (c. 6.5 MYA, from Chad), *Ardipithecus* (c. 5 MYA, Kenya), *Kenyanthropus* (c. 3.5 MYA, Kenya), and *Orrorin* (c. 5 MYA, Kenya). Later, between 4 and 3 MYA, these earliest hominins gave rise to at least two groups of savanna/lake-edge adapted "man-apes." Called australopithecines, they are divided into "gracile" and "robust" lineages, both containing a number of species. The robust australopithecines were characterized by enormous molar and premolar teeth; they probably went extinct around 1 MYA or slightly thereafter. Although it is uncertain from which australopithecine species humans descended, the most likely species are usually assigned to the gracile lineage.

Our genus, *Homo*, arose 3-2 MYA, when hominins began to produce primitive stone tools. The oldest tools are dated to c. 2.5 MYA from the Kada Gona site, in Ethiopia, and were used for scraping and cutting meat, sinew, and wood. It is not known whether these early hominins had the ability to speak, but they were social animals, lived in groups of 12-20 individuals, aggregated and dispersed seasonally, had campsites, and subsisted by gathering plants and small animals and by scavenging other kills. A closer ancestor, *Homo ergaster*, appeared in E Africa around 1.9 MYA and was the first to leave the continent, spreading throughout Eurasia by c. 1.8 MYA. *H. ergaster* is sometimes grouped with *H. erectus*, a species first identified in the 1890s on the island of Java. It was capable of hunting large and medium-sized hoofed animals, such as antelopes and horses, learned to make and control fire—by c. 500 thousand years ago (KYA) in Europe, possibly earlier in Africa—and almost certainly had primitive language skills.

After about 350 KYA, Europe provides a particularly rich set of fossil evidence usually assigned to *H. erectus*. By a near-universal consensus, this species gave rise to the Neanderthals, who appeared c. 200 KYA. Neanderthals were humanlike in most respects: they could speak, were proficient hunters of large game, had sophisticated tools and weapons and a developed social organization, and were well adapted to the harsh climates of Ice Age Europe. Recent advances in molecular biology support the theory that Neanderthals were a distinct population or species that in some places coexisted and may have interbred with early modern humans (also called Crô-Magnons). *H. antecessor*, a new species (c. 870 KYA) identified at the Trinchera Dolina site in north-central Spain, might help clarify the relationship between the earliest representatives of *Homo* in western Europe, and the Neanderthals. A similar situation may have occurred in E Asia, where more primitive *Homo* species coexisted with early modern humans after c. 40 KYA, and possibly as recently as 18 KYA, on the island of Flores, in Indonesia.

Genetic evidence indicates that the first *Homo sapiens* originated in E Africa between 200 and 100 KYA. The oldest modern human fossils date to c. 160 KYA and were found at the Herto site in Ethiopia's Middle Awash Valley. The species quickly spread, displacing, extinguishing, outcompeting, and/or genetically swamping the archaic humans it encountered. Modern humans were living in Israel by c. 100 KYA, and in Romania by c. 35 KYA. Migration from Asia to Australia took place as early as 60 KYA. First confirmation for the crossing from Asia to the Americas by the Bering land bridge dates to the end of the last Ice Age, at 14 KYA. However, genetic data suggests that small, isolated groups of hunter-gatherers arrived in the Americas up to 10,000 years earlier, settling in both continents. Their arrival was rapidly followed by the extinction of the indigenous Pleistocene megafauna (e.g., mammoths, mastodonts), due either to overexploitation by humans, an extraterrestrial impact c. 12,900 years ago, or a combination of both.

As human cognitive capacities slowly expanded over the Pleistocene (1.7-0.01 MYA), a variety of behavioral modes—in toolmaking, diet, shelter, social arrangements, and spiritual expression—arose as humans adapted to different geographic and climatic zones. By about 13,000 years ago, sites from all over the world show seasonal migration patterns and efficient exploitation of a wide range of plant and animal foods, some of which were eventually domesticated.

The ability to make fire at will enormously expanded the human food niche. Fire-making possibly began as early as 1 MYA in Africa and is clearly documented throughout Eurasia after c. 500 KYA. Hearths were found in northern Israel by c. 750 KYA, and by 465 KYA in southwestern France. Fire-hardened wooden throwing spears about 3 m long were fashioned by big-game hunters 400 KYA at the Schoeningen lignite mine in Germany. Scraping tools, dated after 750 KYA in Europe, N Africa, the Middle East, and Central Asia, suggest the preparation of hides for clothing. The oldest relatively unambiguous evidence of personal adornment—perforated shell beads—dates to c. 120 KYA at Skhul Cave on Mount Carmel in Israel. Although they were probably invented much earlier, impressions in burnt clay from the Czech Republic document the ability to weave cloth baskets and nets by 28 KYA. By the time Australia was settled, human ancestors had learned to navigate in boats over considerable distances in open water. The earliest-known bone tools were fashioned some 90 KYA at Semliki, in the Congo basin, by fishermen who crafted sophisticated bone harpoons to catch giant catfish.

About 60 KYA, the earliest immigrants to Australia carved and painted designs on rocks. Although the painted caves of Cosquer and Chauvet in southern France have (contested) radiocarbon dates of c. 32 KYA, painting, engraving and bodily decoration flourished in Europe 15 KYA, along with stone and ivory sculpture. More than 200 western European caves show remarkable examples of naturalistic wall painting. A few musical instruments—bone flutes with precisely bored holes—have been found in sites dated after 40 KYA. Over the course of the Upper Pleistocene (c. 130-12 KYA), the number of people who survived to become grandparents slowly increased. With more adults available to provide child care, humans began to develop more complex, multigenerational social systems.

Cave paintings in Lascaux, France, discovered in 1940, have been carbon-dated to 11,000 to 30,000 years before the present.

The reach of social memory increased accordingly. Shortly after 12 KYA, among widely separated foraging communities in both hemispheres, a series of dramatic technological and social changes occurred, marking the Neolithic, or New Stone, Age. As the world climate became drier and warmer, population/resource imbalances ensued, creating the conditions that allowed for increased human interference in the life cycles of certain plants and animals. This interference ultimately resulted in the appearance of domestication economies, initially in the northern Middle East. Domesticated plants and animals encouraged population growth and the appearance of permanent settlements, which in turn reduced birth spacing and spurred more population growth. Agricultural economies increasingly replaced hunting and gathering. Reliance upon domesticated plants and animals, coupled with technological advances like pottery-making, precipitated a dramatic increase in world population and social complexity. Genetic research suggests that mutations related to traits currently found in some human populations, such as Europeans' unusually light skin pigmentation and ability to process lactose, arose after c. 12 KYA.

Sites in the Americas, SE Europe, and the Middle East show roughly contemporaneous (12-6 KYA) evidence of Neolithic domestication economies; similar evidence of E and S Asian, W European, and sub-Saharan African Neolithic adaptations dates to 10-7 KYA. From W Asian sources, farming and the herding of sheep and goats spread rapidly throughout the Mediterranean Basin, perhaps in as short a time interval as 100-200 years. The variety of crops—wheat, barley, rice, maize, squash, beans, and tubers—and a mix of other characteristics suggest that this adaptation occurred independently in as many as 12 or 13 places in both hemispheres. Evidence for fermented beverages likewise coincides with the early Neolithic settled farming lifestyle. Northern Chinese farmers concocted a wine-like drink from rice, honey, and fruit between 9 and 8 KYA. In highland W Asia, in what is today Iran, vintners were fermenting grapes and making wine by c. 7.4 KYA. The plants and animals associated with the Neolithic Revolution provided the basis for all subsequent social and cultural evolution worldwide.

---

(1) Although "hominid" was standard usage several decades ago, "hominin" is now more commonly used in reference to human ancestors because of new developments in the interpretation of primate evolution.

Earliest Civilizations: 4000-1000 BCE

Mesopotamia. If history began with writing, the first chapter opened in Mesopotamia, the Tigris-Euphrates river valley. The Sumerians used clay tablets with pictographs to keep records after 4000 BCE. A **cuneiform** (wedge-shaped) script evolved by 3000 BCE as a full syllabic alphabet. Neighboring peoples adapted the script for their own use.

Sumerian life centered, from 4000 BCE, on large cities (Eridu, Ur, Uruk, Nippur, Kish, and Lagash) organized around temples and priestly bureaucracies, with surrounding plains watered by swift irrigation works and worked with traction plows. Sailboats, wheeled vehicles, potter's wheels, and kilns were used. Copper was smelted and tempered from c. 4000 BCE; bronze was produced not long after. Ores, as well as precious stones and metals, were obtained through long-distance ship and caravan trade. Iron was used from c. 2000 BCE. Improved ironworking, developed partly by the Hittites, became widespread by 1200 BCE.

Sumerian political primacy passed among cities and their kingly dynasties. Semitic-speaking peoples, with cultures derived from the Sumerian, founded a succession of dynasties that ruled in Mesopotamia and neighboring areas for most of 1,800 years. Among them were the **Akkadians** (first under Sargon I, c. 2350 BCE), the Amorites (whose laws, codified by **Hammurabi**, c. 1792-1750 BCE, have biblical parallels), and the Assyrians, with interludes of rule by the Hittites, Kassites, and Mitanni.

Mesopotamian learning, preserved in vast libraries, was practically oriented. Scribes maintained lists of astronomical phenomena, plants, animals, and stones. Medical texts listed ailments and herbal cures. The Sumerians worshipped anthropomorphic gods representing natural forces. Sacrifices were made at **ziggurats**, or huge stepped temples.

The Syria-Palestine area, site of some of the earliest urban remains (Jericho, 7000 BCE) and of the recently uncovered **Ebla** civilization (fl. 2500 BCE), experienced Egyptian cultural and political influence along with Mesopotamian. The **Phoenician** coast was an active commercial center. A phonetic alphabet was invented here before 1600 BCE. It became the ancestor of many other alphabets.

Egypt. Agricultural villages along the Nile R. were united by around 3300 BCE into two kingdoms, Upper and Lower Egypt. They were unified (c. 3100 BCE) under the pharaoh Menes. A bureaucracy supervised construction of canals and monuments (**pyramids** starting 2700 BCE). Control over Nubia to the S was asserted from 2600 BCE. Brilliant **Old Kingdom** period achievements in architecture, sculpture, and painting reached their height during the 3rd and 4th dynasties. **Hieroglyphic writing** appeared by 3200 BCE, recording a sophisticated literature that included religious writings, philosophy, history, and science. An ordered hierarchy of gods, including totemistic animal elements, was served by a powerful priesthood in Memphis. The pharaoh was identified with the falcon god Horus. Other trends included belief in an afterlife and short-lived quasi-monotheistic reforms introduced by the pharaoh **Akhenaton** (c. 1379-1362 BCE), who was married to Nefertiti.

After a period of dominance by Semitic Hyksos from Asia (c. 1700-1550 BCE), the **New Kingdom** established an empire in Syria. Egypt became increasingly embroiled in Asiatic wars and diplomacy. Conquered by Persia in 525 BCE, it eventually faded away as an independent culture.

India. An urban civilization with an as-yet undeciphered writing system stretched across the Indus Valley and along the Arabian Sea c. 3000-1500 BCE. Major sites are Harappa and **Mohenjo-Daro** in Pakistan, well-planned geometric cities with underground sewers and vast granaries. The entire region may have been ruled as a single state. Bronze was used, and arts and crafts were well developed. Religious life apparently took the form of fertility cults. Indus civilization was in decline before the arrival of **Aryan** migrants who arrived from the NW, speaking an Indo-European language. Led by a warrior aristocracy whose legendary deeds are in the **Rig Veda**, the Aryans spread E and S, bringing their sky gods, priestly (Brahman) ritual, and the beginnings of the caste system. Local customs and beliefs were assimilated by the conquerors.

Europe. On Crete, the Bronze Age **Minoan civilization** emerged c. 2500 BCE. A prosperous economy and richly decorative art was supported by seaborne commerce. Mycenae and other cities in mainland Greece and Asia Minor (e.g., **Troy**) preserved elements of the culture until c. 1200 BCE. Cretan Linear A script (c. 2000-1700 BCE) remains undeciphered; Linear B script (c. 1300-1200 BCE) records an early Greek dialect. The possible connection between Mycenaean monumental stonework and the megalithic monuments of W Europe, Iberia, and Malta (c. 4000-1500 BCE) is unclear.

China. Proto-Chinese neolithic cultures had long covered N and SE China when the first large political state was organized in the N by the **Shang dynasty** (c. 1523 BCE). Shang kings

The Great Sphinx of Giza is believed to have been built during Egypt's 4th dynasty (c. 2575-2465 BCE).

called themselves Sons of Heaven, and they presided over a cult of human and animal sacrifice to ancestors and nature gods. The Chou dynasty, starting c. 1027 BCE, expanded the area of the Sons of Heaven's dominion, but feudal states exercised most temporal power. A writing system with 2,000 characters was already in use under the Shang, with **pictographs** later supplemented by phonetic characters. Many of its principles and symbols, despite changes in spoken Chinese, were preserved in later writing systems. Technical advances allowed urban specialists to create fine ceramic and jade products, and bronze casting after 1500 BCE was the most advanced in the world. Bronze artifacts discovered in N Thailand date from 3600 BCE, hundreds of years before similar Middle Eastern finds.

Americas. Olmecs settled (1500 BCE) on the Gulf coast of Mexico and developed the first known civilization in the W Hemisphere. Temple cities and huge stone sculptures date from 1200 BCE. A rudimentary calendar and writing system existed. Olmec religion—centered on a jaguar god—and art forms influenced later Mesoamerican cultures.

Formation of Classical Societies: 1000-400 BCE

Greece. After a period of decline during the Dorian Greek invasions (1200-1000 BCE), the Aegean area developed a unique civilization. Drawing on Mycenaean traditions, Mesopotamian learning (weights and measures, lunisolar calendar, astronomy, musical scales), the Phoenician alphabet (modified for Greek), and Egyptian art, Greek **city-states** saw a rich elaboration of intellectual life. The two great epic poems attributed to **Homer**, the *Iliad* and the *Odyssey*, were probably composed around the 8th cent. BCE. Long-range commerce was aided by metal coinage (introduced by the Lydians in Asia Minor before 700 BCE). Colonies were founded around the Mediterranean (Cumae in Italy in 760 BCE; Massalia in France c. 600 BCE) and Black Sea shores.

Philosophy, starting on Ionian speculation on the nature of matter (Thales, c. 634-546 BCE), continued by other "Pre-Socratics" (e.g., Heraclitus, c. 535-415 BCE; Parmenides, b. c. 515 BCE), reached a high point in Athens in the rationalist idealism of **Plato** (c. 428-347 BCE), a disciple of **Socrates** (c. 469-399 BCE; executed for alleged impiety), and in **Aristotle** (384-322 BCE), a pioneer in many fields, from natural sciences to logic, ethics, and metaphysics. The **arts** were highly valued. Architecture culminated in the **Parthenon** (438 BCE) by Phidias (fl. 490-430 BCE). Poetry (Sappho, c. 610-580 BCE; Pindar, c. 518-438 BCE) and **drama** (Aeschylus, 525-456 BCE; Sophocles, c. 496-406 BCE; Euripides, c. 484-406 BCE) thrived. Male beauty and strength, a chief artistic theme, were celebrated at the national games at Olympia.

Ruled by local tyrants or **oligarchies**, the Greeks were not politically united but managed to resist inclusion in the Persian Empire. Persian king Darius was defeated at Marathon (490 BCE), his son Xerxes at Salamis (480 BCE), and the Persian army at Plataea (479 BCE). Democracy sprouted in Athens as statesman Pericles (495-429 BCE) sought participation in government from all citizens. Local warfare was common; the **Peloponnesian Wars** (431-404 BCE) ended in Sparta's victory over Athens. Greek political power subsequently waned, but Greek cultural forms spread far and wide.

Hebrews. Nomadic Hebrew tribes entered Canaan before 1200 BCE, settling among other Semitic peoples speaking the same language. They brought from the desert a **monotheistic** faith said to have been revealed to Abraham in Canaan c. 1800 BCE and Moses at Mt. Sinai c. 1250 BCE, after the Hebrews' escape from bondage in Egypt. David (r. 1000-961 BCE) and Solomon (r. 961-922 BCE) united them in a kingdom that briefly dominated the area. **Phoenicians** to the N founded Mediterranean colonies (Carthage, c. 814 BCE) and sailed into the Atlantic.

A temple in Jerusalem became the national religious center, with sacrifices performed by a hereditary priesthood. Polytheistic influences, especially of the fertility cult of Baal, were opposed by **prophets** (Elijah, Amos, Isaiah).

Divided into **two kingdoms** after Solomon, the Hebrews were unable to resist the revived Assyrian empire, which conquered Israel, the N kingdom, in 722 BCE. Judah, the S kingdom, was conquered in 586 BCE by the Babylonians under Nebuchadnezzar II. With the fixing of most of the biblical canon by the mid-4th cent. BCE and the emergence of rabbis, Judaism successfully survived the loss of Hebrew autonomy. A Jewish kingdom was revived under the Hasmoneans (168-42 BCE).

China. During the **Eastern Zhou** dynasty (770-256 BCE), Chinese culture spread E to the sea and S to the Yangtze R. Large feudal states on the periphery of the empire contended for preeminence but continued to recognize the Son of Heaven (king), who retained a purely ritual role enriched with courtly music and dance. In the Age of Warring States (403-221 BCE), when the first sections of the **Great Wall** were built, the Ch'in state in the W gained supremacy and finally united all of China. Iron tools entered China c. 500 BCE. Casting techniques were advanced, aiding agriculture. Peasants owned their land and owed civil and military service to nobles. China's cities grew in number and size; barter remained the chief trade medium.

Intellectual ferment among noble scribes and officials produced a classical age of Chinese literature and philosophy. **Confucius** (551-479 BCE) urged a restoration of a supposedly harmonious social order of the past through proper conduct in accordance with one's station and through filial and ceremonial piety. The *Analects* attributed to him are revered throughout E Asia.

Among other thinkers, **Mencius** (d. 289 BCE) added the view that the Mandate of Heaven can be removed from an unjust dynasty. The Legalists sought to curb the supposed natural wickedness of people through new institutions and harsh laws. The Naturalists emphasized the balance of opposites—yin, yang—in the world. **Daoists** sought mystical knowledge through meditation and disengagement.

India. The political and cultural center of India shifted from the Indus to the Ganges River Valley. Buddhism, Jainism, and mystical revisions of orthodox Vedism all developed c. 500-300 BCE. The *Upanishads*, last part of the *Veda*, urged escape from the cycle of rebirth into the physical world. Vedism remained the preserve of the Brahman caste.

In contrast, **Buddhism**, founded by Siddhartha Gautama (c. 563-c. 483 BCE)—Buddha ("Enlightened One")—appealed to merchants in the urban centers and took hold at first (and most lastingly) on the geographic fringes of Indian civilization. The classic Indian epics were composed in this era: the *Ramayana* perhaps c. 300 BCE, the *Mahabharata* over a period starting around 400 BCE.

N India was divided into a large number of monarchies and aristocratic republics, probably derived from tribal groupings, when the Magadha kingdom was formed in Bihar c. 542 BCE. It soon became the dominant power. The **Maurya** dynasty, founded by Chandragupta c. 321 BCE, expanded the kingdom, uniting most of N India in a centralized bureaucratic empire. The third Mauryan king, **Asoka** (reigned c. 274-236 BCE), conquered most of the subcontinent. He converted to Buddhism, inscribed its tenets on pillars throughout India, and downplayed the caste system.

China's Great Wall, first built during the Age of Warring States (403-221 BCE), was rebuilt, extended, and modified over thousands of years to protect China from invaders.

Before its final decline in India, Buddhism developed into a popular worship of heavenly Bodhisattvas ("enlightened beings"), and it produced a refined architecture (the Great Stupa [shrine] at Sanchi, 100 CE) and sculpture (Gandhara reliefs, 1-400 CE).

Persia. Aryan peoples (Persians, Medes) dominated the area of present Iran by the beginning of the 1st millennium BCE. The prophet **Zoroaster** (b. c. 628 BCE) introduced a dualistic religion in which the forces of good (Ahura Mazda, "Lord of Wisdom") and evil (Ahriman) battle for dominance; individuals are judged by their actions and earn damnation or salvation. Zoroaster's hymns (*Gathas*) are included in the *Avesta*, the Zoroastrian scriptures. A version of this faith became the established religion of the Persian Empire.

Africa. Nubia, periodically occupied by Egypt since about 2600 BCE, ruled Egypt c. 750-661 BCE and survived as an independent Egyptianized kingdom (**Kush**; capital Meroe) for 1,000 years. The Iron Age Nok culture flourished c. 500 BCE-200 CE on the Benue Plateau of **Nigeria**.

Americas. The Chavin culture controlled N Peru c. 900 BCE to 200 BCE. Its ceremonial centers, featuring the jaguar god, survived long after. Its architecture, ceramics, and textiles had influenced other Peruvian cultures. **Mayan civilization** began to develop in Central America as early as 1500 BCE.

Great Empires Unite the Classical World: 400 BCE-400 CE

Persia and the Mediterranean. Cyrus, ruler of a small kingdom in Persia from 559 BCE, united the Persians and Medes within 10 years and conquered Asia Minor and Babylonia in another 10. His son Cambyses, followed by **Darius** (r. 522-486 BCE), added vast lands to the E and N as far as the Indus Valley and Central Asia, as well as Egypt and Thrace. The whole empire was ruled by an international bureaucracy and army, with Persians holding the chief positions. The resources and styles of all the subject civilizations were exploited to create a rich syncretic art.

The kingdom of Macedon, which under Philip II dominated the Greek world and Egypt, was passed on to Philip's son **Alexander** in 336 BCE. Within 13 years, Alexander had conquered all the Persian dominions. Imbued by his tutor Aristotle with Greek ideals, Alexander encouraged colonization, and Greek-style cities were founded. After his death in 323 BCE, wars of succession divided the empire into three significant dynasties—the **Antigonids** in Asia Minor and Macedon, the **Ptolemies** in Egypt, and the **Seleucids** in Mesopotamia. In the ensuing 300 years (the **Hellenistic Era**), a cosmopolitan Greek-oriented culture permeated the ancient world from W Europe to the borders of India, absorbing native elites everywhere.

Hellenistic philosophy stressed the private individual's search for happiness. The Cynics followed Diogenes (c. 372-287 BCE), who stressed self-sufficiency and restriction of desires and expressed contempt for luxury and social convention. Zeno (c. 335-c. 263 BCE) and the **Stoics** exalted reason, identified it with virtue, and counseled an ascetic disregard for misfortune. The **Epicureans** tried to build lives of moderate pleasure without political or emotional involvement. Hellenistic arts imitated life realistically, especially in sculpture and literature (comedies of Menander, 342-292 BCE).

The sciences thrived, especially at Alexandria, where the Ptolemies financed a great library and museum. Fields of study included mathematics (**Euclid**'s geometry, c. 300 BCE); astronomy (heliocentric theory of Aristarchus, 310-230 BCE; Julian calendar, 45 BCE; **Ptolemy**'s *Almagest*, c. 150 CE); geography (world map of Eratosthenes, 276-194 BCE); hydraulics (**Archimedes**, 287-212 BCE); medicine (Galen, 130-200 CE); and chemistry. Inventors refined uses for siphons, valves, gears, springs, screws, levers, cams, and pulleys.

A restored Persian empire under the **Parthians** (northern Iranian tribesmen) controlled the eastern Hellenistic world from 250 BCE to 229 CE. The Parthians and the succeeding **Sassanian dynasty** (c. 224-651 CE) fought with Rome periodically. The Sassanians revived Zoroastrianism as a state religion and patronized a nationalistic artistic and scholarly renaissance.

Rome. The city of Rome was founded, according to legend, by Romulus in 753 BCE. Through military expansion and colonization, and by granting citizenship to leading members of conquered tribes, the city annexed all of Italy S of the Po R. in the 100-year period before 268 BCE. The Latin and other Italic tribes were annexed first, followed by the **Etruscans** (founders of a great civilization N of Rome) and Greek colonies in the S. With a large standing army and reserve forces of several hundred thousand, Rome was able to defeat **Carthage** in the three **Punic Wars** (264-241 BCE, 218-201 BCE, 149-146 BCE), despite the invasion of Italy by **Hannibal** (218 BCE), thus gaining Sicily and territory in Spain and N Africa.

Rome exploited local disputes to conquer Greece and Asia Minor in the 2nd cent. BCE and Egypt in the 1st (after the defeat and suicide of **Antony and Cleopatra**, 30 BCE).

The Mediterranean civilized world, up to the disputed Parthian border, was now Roman and remained so for 500 years. Less civilized regions were added to the Empire: Gaul (conquered by **Julius Caesar**, 58-51 BCE), Britain (43 CE), and Dacia NE of the Danube (107 CE).

The original aristocratic republican government, with democratic features added in the 5th and 4th cent. BCE, deteriorated under the pressures of empire and class conflict (**Gracchus** brothers, social reformers, murdered in 133 BCE and 121 BCE; slave revolts in 135 BCE and 73 BCE). After a series of civil wars (Marius vs. Sulla, 88-82 BCE; Caesar vs. **Pompey**, 49-45 BCE; triumvirate vs. Caesar's assassins, 44-43 BCE; Antony vs. Octavian, 32-30 BCE), the empire came under the rule of a deified monarch (first emperor, **Augustus**, 27 BCE-14 CE).

Provincials (nearly all granted citizenship by Caracalla, 212 CE) came to dominate the army and civil service. Traditional **Roman law**, systematized and interpreted by independent jurists, and local self-rule in provincial cities were supplanted by a vast tax-collecting bureaucracy in the 3rd and 4th cent. The legal rights of women, children, and slaves were strengthened.

Roman innovations in **civil engineering** included water mills, windmills, and rotary mills and the use of cement that hardened under water. Monumental architecture (baths, theaters, temples) relied on the arch and the dome. A network of roads (some still standing) stretched 53,000 mi, passing through mountain tunnels as long as 3.5 mi. Aqueducts brought water to cities; underground sewers removed waste.

Roman art and literature were derivative of Greek models. Innovations were made in sculpture (naturalistic busts, equestrian statues), decorative wall painting (as at Pompeii), satire (**Juvenal**, 60-127 CE), history (**Tacitus**, 56-120 CE), and prose romance (**Petronius**, d. 66 CE). Gladiatorial contests dominated public amusements, which were supported by the state.

India. The **Gupta** monarchs reunited N India c. 320 CE. Their peaceful and prosperous reign saw a revival of Hindu religious thought and Brahman power. The old Vedic traditions were combined with devotion to many indigenous deities (who were seen as manifestations of Vedic gods). Caste lines were reinforced, and Buddhist practices gradually disappeared or were integrated with **Hindu** traditions. The art (often erotic), architecture, and literature of the period, patronized by the Gupta court, are considered among India's

Tutored by Aristotle and imbued with Greek ideals, Alexander the Great (356-323 BCE) conquered the Persian Empire and is considered one of the greatest military leaders of all time.

finest achievements (Kalidasa, poet and dramatist, fl. c. 400 CE). Mathematical innovations included the use of zero and decimal numbers. Invasions by White Huns from the NW led to the empire's destruction c. 550 CE. Rich cultures also developed in S India during this period. Emotional Tamil religious poetry contributed to the Hindu revival. The Pallava kingdom controlled much of S India c. 350-880 CE and helped to spread Indian civilization to SE Asia.

China. The Ch'in ruler Shih Huang Ti (r. 221-210 BCE), known as the First Emperor, centralized political authority; standardized the written language, laws, weights, measures, and coinage; and conducted a census. But he tried to destroy most philosophical texts. The **Han** dynasty (202 BCE-220 CE) instituted the Mandarin bureaucracy, which lasted 2,000 years. Local officials were selected by examination in Confucian classics and trained at the imperial university and provincial schools.

The invention of **paper** facilitated this bureaucratic system. Agriculture was promoted, but peasants bore most of the tax burden. Irrigation was improved, water clocks and sundials were used, astronomy and mathematics thrived, and landscape painting was perfected.

With the expansion S and W (to nearly the present borders of today's China), trade was opened with India, SE Asia, and the Middle East over sea and caravan routes. Indian missionaries brought Mahayana Buddhism to China by the 1st cent. CE and spawned a variety of sects. Daoism was revived and merged with popular superstitions. **Daoist and Buddhist monasteries** and convents multiplied in the turbulent centuries after the collapse of the Han dynasty in 220 CE.

Monotheism Spreads: 1-750 CE

Roman Empire. Polytheism was practiced in the Roman Empire, and religions indigenous to particular Middle Eastern nations became international. Roman citizens worshiped **Isis** of Egypt, **Mithras** of Persia, **Demeter** of Greece, and the great mother **Cybele** of Phrygia. Their cults centered on mysteries (secret ceremonies) and the promise of an afterlife, symbolized by the death and rebirth of the god. The Jews of the empire preserved their monotheistic religion, Judaism, the world's oldest (c. 1300 BCE) continuous religion. Its teachings are contained in the Bible (the Old Testament). 1st-cent. CE Judaism embraced several sects, including the **Sadducees**, mostly drawn from the Temple priesthood, who were culturally Hellenized; the **Pharisees**, who upheld the full range of traditional customs and practices as of equal weight to literal scriptural law and elaborated synagogue worship; and the **Essenes**, an ascetic, millenarian sect. Messianic fervor led to repeated, unsuccessful rebellions against Rome (66-70, 135 CE). As a result, the Temple in Jerusalem was destroyed and the population decimated; this event marked the beginning of the Diaspora (living in exile). To preserve the faith, codification of law was begun at the academy of Yavneh. The work continued for some 500 years in Palestine and in Babylonia, ending in the final redaction (c. 600) of the **Talmud**, a huge collection of legal and moral debates, rulings, liturgy, biblical exegesis, and legendary materials.

Christianity. Emerging as a distinct sect by the second half of the 1st cent. CE, Christianity is based on the teachings of **Jesus**, whom believers considered the Savior (Messiah or Christ) and son of God. Missionary activities of the Apostles and such early leaders as **Paul of Tarsus** spread the faith. Intermittent persecution, as in Rome under Nero in 64 CE, on grounds of suspected disloyalty, failed to disrupt Christian communities. Each congregation, generally urban and of plebeian character, was tightly organized under a leader (bishop), elders (presbyters or priests), and assistants (deacons). The four **Gospels** (accounts of the life and teachings of Jesus) and the Acts of the Apostles were written down in the late 1st and early 2nd cent. and circulated along with letters of Paul and other Christian leaders. An authoritative canon of these writings was not fixed until the 4th cent.

A school for priests was established at Alexandria in the 2nd cent. Its teachers (**Origen**, c. 182-251) helped define doctrine and promote the faith in Greek-style philosophical works. Neoplatonism underwent Christian coloration in the writings of Church Fathers such as **Augustine** (354-430). Christian hermits began to associate in monasteries, first in Egypt (St. Pachomius, c. 290-345), then in other E lands, then in the W (**St. Benedict's rule**, 529). Devotion to saints, especially Mary, mother of Jesus, spread. Under **Constantine** (r. 306-37), Christianity became in effect the established religion of the Empire. Pagan temples were expropriated, state funds were used to build churches and support the hierarchy, and laws were adjusted in accordance with Christian ideas. Pagan worship was banned by the end of the 4th cent., and severe restrictions were placed on Judaism.

The newly established church was rocked by doctrinal disputes, often exacerbated by regional rivalries. Chief heresies (as defined by church councils, backed by imperial authority) were **Arianism**, which denied the divinity of Jesus; **Monophysitism**, denying the human nature of Christ; **Donatism**, which regarded as invalid any sacraments administered by sinful clergy; and **Pelagianism**, which denied the necessity of unmerited divine aid (grace) for salvation.

Islam. The earliest Arab civilization emerged by the end of the 2nd millennium BCE in the watered highlands of Yemen. Seaborne and caravan trade in frankincense and myrrh connected the area with the Nile and Fertile Crescent. The Minaean, Sabean (Sheba), and Himyarite states successively held sway. By Muhammad's time (7th cent. CE), the region was a province of Sassanian Persia. In the N, the Nabataean kingdom at Petra and the kingdom of Palmyra were Aramaicized, Romanized, and finally absorbed, as neighboring Judea had been, into the Roman Empire. Nomads shared the central region with a few trading towns and oases. Wars between tribes and raids on communities were common and were celebrated in a poetic tradition that by the 6th cent. helped establish a classic literary Arabic.

About 610, **Muhammad**, a 40-year-old Arab man of Mecca, emerged as a prophet. He proclaimed a revelation from the one true God, calling on contemporaries to abandon idolatry and restore the faith of Abraham. He introduced his religion as **Islam**, meaning "submission" to the one God, Allah, as a continuation of the biblical faith of Abraham, Moses, and Jesus, all respected as prophets in this system. His teachings, recorded in the **Koran** (al-Qur'an in Arabic), in many ways were inclusive of Abrahamic monotheistic ideas known to the Jews and Christians in Arabia. A key aspect of the Abrahamic connection was insistence on justice in society, which led to severe opposition among the aristocrats in Mecca. As conditions worsened for Muhammad and his followers, he decided in 622 to make a *hegira* (flight) to Medina, 200 mi to the N. This event marks the beginning of the Muslim lunar calendar. Hostilities between Mecca and Medina increased, and in 629 Muhammad conquered Mecca. By the time he died in 632, nearly all the Arabian peninsula accepted his political and religious leadership.

After his death the majority of Muslims (later known as **Sunni** Muslims) recognized the leadership of the **caliph** (successor) Abu Bakr (632-34), followed by Umar (634-44), Uthman (644-56), and Ali (656-60). A minority, the **Shiites**, insisted instead on the leadership of Ali, Muhammad's cousin and son-in-law. By 644, **Muslim rule** over Arabia was

The now-typical use of a minaret as the location for the Muslim call to prayer began at the Mosque of Uqba, or Great Mosque of Kairouan, built from 670 CE in present-day Tunisia.

confirmed. Muslim armies had threatened the Byzantine and Persian empires, which were weakened by wars and disaffection among subject peoples (including Coptic and Syriac Christians opposed to the Byzantine Orthodox establishment). Syria, Palestine, Egypt, Iraq, and Persia fell to Muslim armies. The new administration assimilated existing systems in the region; hence the conquered peoples participated in running the empire. The Koran recognized the so-called Peoples of the Book, i.e., Christians, Jews, and Zoroastrians, as tolerated monotheists, and Muslim policy was relatively tolerant to minorities living as "protected" peoples. An expanded tax system, based on conquests of the Persian and Byzantine empires, provided revenue to organize campaigns against neighboring non-Muslim regions.

Under the **Umayyads** (661-750) and **Abbasids** (750-1256), territorial expansion led Muslim armies across N Africa and into Spain (711). Muslim armies in the W were stopped at Tours, France, in 732 by the Frankish ruler **Charles Martel**. Asia Minor, the Indus Valley, and Transoxiana were conquered in the E. The conversion of conquered peoples to Islam was gradual. In many places the official Arabic language supplanted the local tongues. But in the eastern regions the Arab rulers and their armies adopted Persian cultures and language as part of their Muslim identity.

Disputes over succession and pious opposition to injustices in society led to a number of oppositional movements, which led to the factionalization of Muslim community. The **Shiites** supported leadership candidates descended from Muhammad, believing them to be carriers of some kind of divine authority. The **Kharijites** supported an egalitarian system derived from the Koran, opposing and even engaging in battle against those who did not agree with them.

New Peoples Enter World History: 400-900 CE

Barbarian invasions and fall of Rome. Germanic tribes infiltrated S and E from their Baltic homeland during the 1st millennium BCE, reaching S Germany by 100 BCE and the Black Sea by 214 CE. Organized into large federated tribes under elected kings, most resisted Roman domination and raided the empire in times of civil war (Goths took Dacia in 214, raided Thrace in 251-69). Germanic troops and commanders dominated the Roman armies by the end of the 4th cent. **Huns**, invaders from Asia, entered Europe in 372, driving more Germans into the empire. Emperor Valens allowed Visigoths to cross the Danube in 376. Huns under Attila (d. 453) raided Gaul, Italy, and the Balkans.

The western empire, weakened by overtaxation and social stagnation, was overrun in the 5th cent. Gaul was effectively lost in 406-07, Spain in 409, Britain in 410, and Africa in 429-39. Rome was sacked in 410 by Visigoths under Alaric and in 455 by Vandals. The **last western emperor**, Romulus Augustulus, was deposed in 476 by the Germanic chief Odovacar.

Celts. Celtic cultures, which in pre-Roman times covered most of W Europe, were confined almost entirely to the British Isles after the Germanic invasions. **St. Patrick** completed (c. 457-92) the conversion of Ireland and a strong monastic tradition took hold. Irish monastic missionaries in Scotland, England, and on the continent (Columba, c. 521-97; Columbanus, c. 543-615) helped restore Christianity after the Germanic invasions. **Monasteries** became centers of classic and Christian learning and presided over the recording of a Christianized Celtic mythology, elaborated by secular writers and bards. An intricate decorative art style developed, especially in book illumination (Lindisfarne Gospels, c. 700; Book of Kells, 8th cent.).

Successor states. The Visigothic kingdom in Spain (from 419) and much of France (to 507) saw continuation of Roman administration, language, and law (Breviary of Alaric, 506) until its destruction by the Muslims (711). The Vandal kingdom in Africa (from 429) was conquered by the Byzantines in 533. Italy was ruled successively by an Ostrogothic kingdom under Byzantine suzerainty (489-554), direct Byzantine government, and German Lombards (568-774). The Lombards divided the peninsula with the Byzantines and papacy under the dynamic reformer **Pope Gregory the Great** (590-604) and successors.

King Clovis (r. 481-511) united the Franks on both sides of the Rhine and, after his conversion to Christianity, defeated the Arian heretics, Burgundians (after 500), and Visigoths (507) with the support of native clergy and the papacy. Under the **Merovingian** kings, a feudal system emerged: power was fragmented among hierarchies of military landowners. Social stratification, which in late Roman times had acquired legal, hereditary sanction, was reinforced.

The Carolingians (747-987) expanded the kingdom and restored central power. **Charlemagne** (r. 768-814) conquered nearly all the Germanic lands, including Lombard Italy. He was crowned emperor by Pope Leo III in Rome in 800. A centuries-long decline in commerce and arts was reversed under Charlemagne's patronage. He welcomed Jews to his kingdom, which became a center of Jewish learning (Rashi, 1040-1105). He sponsored the Carolingian Renaissance of learning under the Anglo-Latin scholar Alcuin (c. 732-804), who reformed church liturgy.

Byzantine Empire. Under **Diocletian** (r. 284-305) the Roman empire had been divided into two parts to facilitate administration and defense. **Constantine** founded (330) **Constantinople** (at old Byzantium) as a fully Christian city. Commerce and taxation financed a sumptuous, orientalized court, a class of hereditary bureaucratic families, and magnificent urban construction (Hagia Sophia, 532-37). The city's fortifications and naval innovations repelled assaults by Goths, Huns, Slavs, Bulgars, Avars, Arabs, and Scandinavians. Greek replaced Latin as the official language by c. 700. **Byzantine art**, a solemn, sacral, and stylized variation of late classical styles (mosaics at the Church of San Vitale, Ravenna, Italy, 526-48), was a starting point for medieval art in E and W Europe.

Justinian (r. 527-65) briefly reconquered parts of Spain, N Africa, and Italy, codified **Roman law** (Codex Justinianus [529] was medieval Europe's chief legal text), closed the Platonic Academy at Athens, and ordered all pagans to convert. Lombards in Italy and Arabs in Africa retook most of his conquests. The Isaurian dynasty from Anatolia (from 717) and the Macedonian dynasty (867-1054) restored military and commercial power. The Iconoclast controversy (726-843) over the permissibility of images helped alienate the Eastern Church from the papacy.

Abbasid Empire. Baghdad (established 762) became seat of the **Abbasid dynasty** (established 750), while Umayyads continued to rule in Spain. A brilliant cosmopolitan civilization emerged, inaugurating a Muslim-Arab golden age. Arabic was the lingua franca of the empire; intellectual sources from Persian, Sanskrit, Greek, and Syriac were rendered into Arabic. Christians and Jews equally participated in this translation movement, which also involved interaction between Jewish legal thought and Islamic law, as much as between Christian theology and Muslim scholasticism. Persian-style court life, with art and music, flourished at the court of **Harun al-Rashid** (786-809), celebrated in the masterpiece known to English readers as *The Arabian Nights*. The sciences, medicine, and mathematics were pursued at Baghdad, Cordova, and Cairo (c. 969). The culmination of this intellectual synthesis in Islamic civilization came with the scientific and philosophical works of **Avicenna** (Ibn Sina, 980-1037), **Averroes** (Ibn Rushd, 1126-98), and **Maimonides** (1135-1204), a Jew who wrote in Arabic. This intellectual tradition was translated into Latin and opened a new period in Christian thought.

The decentralization of the **Abbasid** empire, from 874, led to the establishment of various Muslim dynasties under different ethnic groups. Persians, Berbers, and Turks ruled different regions, retaining connection with the Abbasid caliph at the religious level. The Abbasid period also saw various religious movements against the orthodox position held by governing authorities. This situation in Muslim religion led to the establishment of different legal, theological, and mystical schools of thought. The most influential mass movement was **Sufism**, which aimed at the reaching out of the average individual in quest of a spiritual path. Al-Ghazali (1058-1111) is credited with reconciling personal Sufism with orthodox Sunni tradition.

Africa. Immigrants from Saba in S Arabia helped set up the **Axum** kingdom in Ethiopia in the 1st cent. (their language, Ge'ez, is preserved by the Ethiopian Church). In the 3rd cent., when the kingdom became Christianized, it defeated Kushite Meroe and expanded its influence into Yemen. Axum was the center of a vast ivory trade and controlled the Red Sea coast until c. 1100. Arab conquest in Egypt cut Axum's political and economic ties with Byzantium.

The pyramid of Kukulkan (El Castillo) at Chichen Itza is one of the preeminent existing examples of Mayan architecture in present-day Mexico.

The Iron Age entered W Africa by the end of the 1st millennium BCE. **Ghana**, the first known sub-Saharan state, ruled in the upper Senegal-Niger region c. 400-1240, controlling the trade of gold from mines in the S to trans-Sahara caravan routes to the N. The **Bantu** peoples, probably of W African origin, began to spread E and S perhaps 2,000 years ago, displacing the Pygmies and Bushmen of central and S Africa during a 1,500-year period.

Japan. The advanced Neolithic Yayoi period, when irrigation, rice farming, and iron and bronze casting techniques were introduced from China or Korea, persisted to c. 400 CE. The myriad Japanese states were then united by the **Yamato** clan, under an emperor who acted as chief priest of the animistic Shinto cult. Japanese political and military intervention by the 6th cent. in Korea, then under strong Chinese influence, quickened a Chinese cultural invasion of Japan, bringing Buddhism, the Chinese language (which long remained a literary and governmental medium), Chinese ideographs, and Buddhist styles in painting, sculpture, literature, and architecture (7th cent., Horyuji temple at Nara). The Taika Reforms (646) tried unsuccessfully to centralize Japan according to Chinese bureaucratic and Buddhist philosophical values.

A nativist reaction against the Buddhist **Nara** period (710-94) ushered in the **Heian** period (794-1185) centered at the new capital, Kyoto. Japanese elegance and simplicity modified Chinese styles in architecture, scroll painting, and literature; the writing system was also simplified. The courtly novel *Tale of Genji* (1010-20) testifies to the enhanced role of women in medieval Japanese literature and culture.

Southeast Asia. The historic peoples of SE Asia began arriving some 2,500 years ago from China and Tibet, displacing scattered aborigines. Their agriculture relied on rice and yams. Indian cultural influences were strongest; literacy and Hindu and Buddhist ideas followed the S India-China trade route. From the S tip of Indochina, the kingdom of **Funan** (1st-7th cent.) traded as far W as Persia. It was absorbed by Chenla, itself conquered by the **Khmer Empire** (600-1300). The Khmers, under Hindu god-kings (Suryavarman II, 1113-c. 1150), built the monumental Angkor Wat temple center for the royal phallic cult. The **Nam-Viet** kingdom in Annam, dominated by China and Chinese culture for 1,000 years, emerged in the 10th cent., growing at the expense of the Khmers, who also lost ground in the NW to the new, highly organized **Thai** kingdom. On Sumatra, the **Srivijaya** Empire controlled vital sea lanes (7th-10th cent.). A Buddhist dynasty, the Sailendras, ruled central **Java** (8th-9th cent.), building at Borobudur one of the largest stupas (dome-shaped Buddhist shrines) in the world.

China. The Sui dynasty (581-618) ushered in a period of commercial, artistic, and scientific achievement in China, which continued under the **Tang** dynasty (618-906). Inventions like the magnetic compass, gunpowder, the abacus, and printing were introduced or perfected. Medical innovations included cataract surgery. The state, from its cosmopolitan capital, Chang-an, supervised foreign trade, which exchanged Chinese silks, porcelains, and art for spices and ivory over Central Asian caravan routes and sea routes reaching Africa. A golden age of poetry bequeathed valuable works to later generations (Tu Fu, 712-70; Li Po, 701-62). Landscape painting flourished.

Commercial and industrial expansion continued under the **Northern Sung** dynasty (960-1126), facilitated by paper money and credit notes. But commerce never achieved full respectability; government monopolies expropriated successful merchants. The population, long stable at 50 million, doubled in 200 years with the introduction of early-ripening rice and the double harvest. In art, native Chinese styles were revived.

Americas. From 300 to 600, a Native American empire stretched from the Valley of Mexico to Guatemala, centering on the huge city **Teotihuacán** (founded 100 BCE). To the S, in Guatemala, a high **Mayan** civilization developed (150-900) around hundreds of rural ceremonial centers. The Mayans improved on Olmec writing and the calendar and pursued astronomy and mathematics. In South America, a widespread pre-Inca culture grew from **Tiahuanacu**, Bolivia, near Lake Titicaca (Gateway of the Sun doorway, c. 700).

Christian Europe Regroups and Expands: 900-1300

Scandinavia. Pagan Danish and Norse (Viking) adventurers, traders, and pirates raided the coasts of the British Isles (Dublin, c. 831), France, and even the Mediterranean for over 200 years beginning in the late 8th cent. Inland settlement in the W was limited to Great Britain (King Canute, 994-1035) and Normandy, settled (911) under Rollo, as a fief of France. Vikings also reached Iceland (874), Greenland (c. 986), and North America (**Leif Ericson** and others, c. 1000). Norse traders (**Varangians**) developed Russian river commerce from the 8th to the 11th cent. and helped set up a state at Kiev in the late 9th cent. Conversion to Christianity occurred in the 10th cent., reaching Sweden 100 years later. In the 11th cent. Norman bands conquered S Italy and Sicily, and Duke **William of Normandy** conquered (1066) England, bringing feudal government and the French language, essential elements in later English civilization.

Central and East Europe. Slavs began to expand from about 150 CE in all directions in Europe. By the 7th cent. they reached as far S as the Adriatic and Aegean seas. In the Balkan Peninsula they dislocated Romanized local populations or assimilated newcomers (Bulgarians, a Turkic people). The first **Slavic states** were Moravia (628) in Central Europe and the Bulgarian state (680) in the Balkans. Byzantine missions of St. Methodius and Cyril (whose Greek-based cyrillic alphabet is still used by some S and E Slavs) converted (863) Moravia.

The Eastern Slavs, part-civilized under the overlordship of the Turkish-Jewish **Khazar** trading empire (7th-10th cent.), gravitated toward Constantinople by the 9th cent. The **Kievan** state adopted (989) Eastern Christianity under Prince Vladimir.

King Boleslav I (992-1025) began **Poland**'s long history of conquest. The Magyars (**Hungarians**), in present-day Hungary since 896, accepted (1001) Latin Christianity.

Germany. The German kingdom that emerged after the breakup of Charlemagne's W Empire remained a confederation of largely autonomous states. Otto I, a Saxon who was king from 936, established the **Holy Roman Empire**—a union of Germany and N Italy—in alliance with Pope John XII, who crowned (962) him emperor; he defeated (955) the Magyars. Imperial power was greatest under the **Hohenstaufens** (1138-1254), despite the growing opposition of the papacy, which ruled central Italy and the Lombard League cities. Frederick II (1194-1250) improved administration and patronized the arts. After his death, German influence was removed from Italy.

Christian Spain. From its N mountain redoubts, Christian rule slowly migrated S through the 11th cent., when Muslim unity collapsed. After the capture (1085) of **Toledo**, the kingdoms of Portugal, Castile, and Aragon undertook repeated crusades of reconquest, finally completed in 1492. Elements of Islamic civilization persisted in recaptured areas, influencing all Western Europe.

Crusades. Pope **Urban II** called for a crusade (1095) to restore Asia Minor to Byzantium and the Holy Land to Christendom. This first crusade captured Jerusalem and led to the foundation of four Frankish states in the Levant. The defeat inflicted upon crusaders at the Battle of Hattin (1187) by **Saladin**

(c. 1137-93), the Kurdish ruler of Egypt and Syria, effectively negated territorial gains. Many crusades followed until 1291. The 4th crusade sacked Constantinople (1204). Other crusades were launched against Christian heretics (Albigensian Crusade, 1229), pagans, and enemies of the papacy.

Economy. The agricultural base of European life benefited from improvements in **plow design** (c. 1000) and by the draining of lowlands and clearing of forests, leading to a rural population increase. Towns grew in N Italy, Flanders, and N Germany (Hanseatic League). Improvements in **loom design** permitted factory textile production. **Guilds** dominated urban trades from the 12th cent. Banking (centered in Italy, 12th-15th cent.) facilitated long-distance trade.

Christianity. The split between the Eastern and Western churches was formalized in 1054. Western and Central Europe was divided into 500 bishoprics under one united hierarchy, but conflicts between secular and church authorities were frequent (German **Investiture Controversy**, 1075-1122). Clerical power was first strengthened through the international monastic reform begun at Cluny in 910. Popular religious enthusiasm often expressed itself in heretical movements (Waldensians

from 1173), but was channeled by the **Dominican** (1215) and **Franciscan** (1223) friars into the religious mainstream.

Arts. Romanesque architecture (9th to mid-12th cent.) expanded on late Roman models, using the rounded arch and massed stone to support enlarged basilicas. Painting and sculpture followed Byzantine models. The literature of **chivalry** was exemplified by the epic (*Chanson de Roland*, c. 1100) and by courtly love poems of the troubadours of Provence and minnesingers of Germany. **Gothic** architecture emerged in France (choir of St. Denis, c. 1140) and spread along with French cultural influence. Rib vaulting and pointed arches were used to combine soaring heights with delicacy, and they freed walls for display of stained glass. Exteriors were covered with painted relief sculpture and embellished with elaborate architectural detail.

Learning. Law, medicine, and philosophy were advanced at independent **universities** (Bologna, Paris, 12th cent.), originally corporations of students and masters. Twelfth-cent. translations of Greek classics, especially by Aristotle, encouraged an analytic approach. Scholastic philosophy, from Anselm (1033-1109) to **Aquinas** (1225-74), attempted to understand revelation through reason.

Apogee of Central Asian Power and the Spread of Islam: 1250-1500

Turks. Turkic peoples, of Central Asian ancestry, were a military threat to the Byzantine and Persian Empires from the 6th cent. After several waves of invasions, during which most of the Turks adopted Islam, the **Seljuk Turks** took (1055) Baghdad. They ruled Persia, Iraq, and, after 1071, Asia Minor, where massive numbers of Turks settled. The empire was divided in the 12th cent. into smaller states ruled by Seljuks, Kurds, and Mamluks (a military caste of former Turk, Kurd, and Circassian slaves), which governed Egypt and the Middle East until the Ottoman era (c. 1290-1922).

Osman I (r. c. 1290-1326) and succeeding sultans united Anatolian Turkish warriors in a militaristic state that waged holy war against Byzantium and Balkan Christians. Most of the Balkans had been subdued and Anatolia united when Constantinople fell (1453). By the mid-16th cent., Hungary, the Middle East, and N Africa had been conquered. The Turkish advance was stopped at Vienna (1529) and at the naval battle of Lepanto (1571) by Spain, Venice, and the papacy.

The **Ottoman state** was governed in accordance with orthodox Muslim law. Greek, Armenian, and Jewish communities were segregated and were ruled by religious leaders responsible for taxation; they dominated trade. Many state offices and most army ranks were filled by slaves, in part through a system of child conscription among Christians.

India. Mahmud of Ghazni (971-1030) led repeated Turkish raids into N India. Turkish power was consolidated in 1206 with the start of the **Sultanate at Delhi**. Centralization of state power under the early Delhi sultans went far beyond traditional Indian practice. Muslim rule of much of the subcontinent lasted until the British conquest 600 years later, though Hinduism remained the majority religion.

Mongols. Genghis Khan (c. 1167-1227) first united the feuding Mongol tribes and built their armies into an effective offensive force around a core of highly mobile cavalry. He and his immediate successors created the largest land empire in history; by 1279 it stretched from the E coast of Asia to the Danube and from the Siberian steppes to the Arabian Sea. East-West trade and contacts were facilitated (Marco Polo, c. 1254-1324). The western Mongols were Islamized by 1295; successor states soon lost their Mongol character by assimilation. They were briefly reunited under the Turk Tamerlane (1336-1405).

Kublai Khan ruled China from his new capital Beijing (established c. 1264). Naval campaigns against Japan (1274, 1281) and Java (1293) were defeated, the latter by the Hindu-Buddhist maritime kingdom of Majapahit. The **Yuan** dynasty used Mongols and other foreigners (including Europeans) in official posts and tolerated the return of Nestorian Christianity

(suppressed 841-45) and the spread of Islam in the S and W. A native reaction expelled the Mongols in 1367-68.

Russia. The Kievan state in Russia, weakened by the decline of Byzantium and the rise of the Catholic Polish-Lithuanian state, was overrun (1238-40) by the Mongols. Only the northern trading republic of Novgorod remained independent. The grand dukes of Moscow emerged as leaders of a coalition of princes that eventually (by 1481) defeated the Mongols. After the fall of Constantinople in 1453, the **Tsars** (Caesars) at Moscow (from Ivan III, r. 1462-1505) set up an independent Russian Orthodox Church. Commerce failed to revive. The isolated Russian state remained agrarian with the peasant class falling into serfdom.

Persia. A revival of Persian literature, making use of the Arab alphabet and literary forms, began in the 10th cent. (epic of Firdausi, 935-1020). An art revival, influenced by Chinese styles introduced after the Mongols came to power in Iran, began in the 13th cent. Persian cultural and political forms, and often the Persian language, were used for centuries by Turkish and Mongol elites from the Balkans to India. Persian mystics from Rumi (1207-73) to Jami (1414-92) promoted **Sufism** in their poetry.

Africa. Two militant Islamic Berber dynasties emerged from the Sahara to carve out empires from the Sahel to central Spain—the **Almoravids** (c. 1050-1140) and the fanatical **Almohads** (c. 1125-1269). The Ghanaian empire was replaced in the upper Niger by Mali (c. 1230-1340), whose Muslim rulers imported Egyptians to help make **Timbuktu** a center of commerce (in gold, leather, and slaves) and learning. The Songhay empire (to 1590) replaced Mali. To the S, forest kingdoms produced refined artworks (Ife terra cotta, **Benin** bronzes).

Other **Muslim states** in Nigeria (Hausas) and Chad originated in the 11th cent. and continued in some form until the 19th-cent. European conquest. Less-developed Bantu kingdoms existed across central Africa.

Some 40 Muslim Arab-Persian trading colonies and city-states were established all along the E African coast from the 10th cent. (Kilwa, Mogadishu). The interchange with Bantu peoples produced the **Swahili** language and culture. Gold, palm oil, and slaves were brought from the interior, stimulating the growth of the Monamatapa kingdom of the Zambezi (15th cent.). The Christian Ethiopian empire (from 13th cent.) continued the traditions of Axum.

Southeast Asia. Islam was introduced into Malaya and the Indonesian islands by Arab, Persian, and Indian traders. Coastal Muslim cities and states (starting before 1300) soon dominated the interior. Chief among these was the **Malacca** state (c. 1400-1511), on the Malay peninsula.

Arts and Statecraft Thrive in Europe; New Asian Empires Rise: 1350-1600

Italy. Distinctive Italian achievements in literature and fine arts during the late Middle Ages (**Dante**, 1265-1321; Giotto, 1276-1337) led to the vigorous new styles of the Renaissance (14th-16th cent.). Patronized by the rulers of the quarreling

petty states of Italy (**Medicis** in Florence and the papacy, c. 1400-1737), the plastic arts perfected realistic techniques, including **perspective** (Masaccio, 1401-28; Leonardo **da Vinci**, 1452-1519). Classical motifs were used in architecture, and

The Magna Carta, granted by England's King John to his rebellious barons in 1215, is considered a foundational document for constitutional liberties.

increased talent and expense were put into secular buildings. The Florentine dialect was refined as a national literary language (**Petrarch**, 1304-74). Greek refugees from the E strengthened the respect of humanist scholars for the classic sources. Soon an international movement aided by the spread of **printing** (Gutenberg, c. 1397-1468), **humanism** was optimistic about the power of human reason (Erasmus of Rotterdam, 1466-1536, More's *Utopia*, 1516) and valued individual effort in the arts and in politics (**Machiavelli**, 1469-1527).

France. The French monarchy, strengthened in its repeated struggles with powerful nobles (Burgundy, Flanders, Aquitaine) by alliances with the growing commercial towns, consolidated bureaucratic control under Philip IV (r. 1285-1314) and extended French influence into Germany and Italy (popes at Avignon, France, 1309-1417). The **Hundred Years War** (1337-1453) ended English dynastic claims in France (battles of Crécy, 1346, and Poitiers, 1356; Joan of Arc executed, 1431). A French Renaissance, dating from royal invasions (1494, 1499) of Italy, was encouraged at the court of Francis I (r. 1515-47), who centralized taxation and law. French vernacular literature consciously asserted its independence (La Pléiade, 1549).

England. The evolution of England's political institutions began with the **Magna Carta** (1215), by which King John guaranteed the privileges of nobles and church against the monarchy and assured jury trial. After the **Wars of the Roses** (1455-85), the **Tudor** dynasty reasserted royal prerogatives (Henry VIII, r. 1509-47), but the trend toward independent departments and ministerial government also continued. English trade (wool exports from c. 1340) was protected by the nation's growing maritime power (**Spanish Armada** destroyed, 1588).
English replaced French and Latin in the late 14th cent. in law and literature (**Chaucer**, c. 1340-1400), and English translation of the Bible began (Wycliffe, 1380s). **Elizabeth I** (r. 1558-1603) presided over a confident flowering of poetry (Spenser, 1552-99), drama (**Shakespeare**, 1564-1616), and music.

German Empire. From among a welter of minor feudal states, church lands, and independent cities, the **Habsburgs** assembled a far-flung territorial domain, based in Austria from 1276. Family members held the title of Holy Roman Emperor from 1438 to the Empire's dissolution in 1806 but failed to centralize its domains, leaving Germany disunited for centuries. Resistance to Turkish expansion brought Hungary under Austrian control from the 16th cent. The Netherlands, Luxembourg, and Burgundy were added in 1477, curbing French expansion.
The Flemish painting tradition of naturalism, technical proficiency, and bourgeois subject matter began in the 15th cent. (Jan van Eyck, c. 1390-1441), the earliest northern manifestation of the Renaissance. Albrecht **Dürer** (1471-1528) typified

the merging of late Gothic and Italian trends in 16th-cent. German art. Imposing civic architecture flourished in the prosperous commercial cities.

Black Death. The bubonic plague reached Europe from the E in 1348, killing up to half the population by 1350 (and recurring periodically in most areas until the early 18th cent.). Labor scarcity forced wages to rise and brought greater freedom to the peasantry, making possible **peasant uprisings** (Jacquerie in France, 1358; Wat Tyler's rebellion in England, 1381).

Spain. Despite the unification of Castile and Aragon in 1479, the two countries retained separate governments, and the nobility, especially in Aragon and Catalonia, retained many privileges. Spanish lands in Italy (Naples, Sicily) and the Netherlands entangled the country in European wars through the mid-17th cent., while explorers, traders, and conquerors built up a Spanish empire in the Americas and the Philippines.
From the late 15th cent., a **golden age** of literature and art produced works of social satire (plays of Lope de Vega, 1562-1635; **Cervantes**, 1547-1616), as well as spiritual intensity (**El Greco**, 1541-1614; **Velázquez**, 1599-1660).

Explorations. Organized European maritime exploration began, seeking to evade the Venice-Ottoman monopoly of eastern trade and to promote Christianity. A key goal was to satisfy a growing taste for Asian goods. Beginning in 1418, expeditions from Portugal explored the W coast of Africa, until Vasco da Gama rounded the Cape of Good Hope in 1497 and reached India. A Portuguese trading empire was consolidated by the seizure of Goa (1510) and Malacca (1551). Japan was reached in 1542. The voyages of Christopher **Columbus** (1492-1504) uncovered a world new to Europeans, which Spain hastened to subdue. Navigation schools in Spain and Portugal, the development of large sailing ships (carracks) mounted with cannons, and the invention (c. 1475) of the rifle aided European penetration.

Mughals and Safavids. E of the Ottoman Empire, two Muslim dynasties ruled unchallenged in the 16th and 17th cent. The Mughal dynasty of India, founded by Persianized Turkish invaders from the NW under Babur, dates from their 1526 conquest of the Delhi Sultanate. The dynasty ruled most of India for more than 200 years, surviving nominally until 1857. **Akbar** (r. 1556-1605) consolidated administration at his glorious court, where the Urdu language (Persian-influenced Hindi) developed. Trade relations with Europe increased. Under Shah Jahan (1629-58), a secularized art fusing Hindu and Muslim elements flourished in miniature painting and in architecture (**Taj Mahal**). **Sikhism** (founded late 15th cent.) combined elements of both faiths. Suppression of Hindus and Shiite Muslims in S India in the late 17th cent. weakened the empire.
Intense devotion to the Shiite sect characterized the Safavids (1502-1736) of Persia and led to hostilities with the Sunni Ottomans for more than a century. The prosperity and the strength of the empire are evidenced by the mosques at its capital city, **Isfahan**. The Safavids enhanced Iranian national consciousness.

China. The **Ming** emperors (1368-1644), the last native dynasty in China, wielded strong personal power. European trade (Portuguese monopoly through Macao from 1557) was strictly controlled. Jesuit scholars and scientists (Matteo Ricci, 1552-1610) introduced some Western science; their writings familiarized the West with China. The arts thrived, especially in the areas of painting and ceramics. Chinese manufacturing boomed, bringing in new profits from world trade.

Japan. After the decline of the first hereditary *shogunate* (chief generalship) at **Kamakura** (1185-1333), fragmentation of power accelerated, as did the consequent social mobility. Under Kamakura and the Ashikaga shogunate (1338-1573), the *daimyos* (lords) and *samurai* (warriors) grew more powerful and promoted a martial ideology. Japanese pirates and traders plied the China coast. Popular Buddhist movements included the nationalist Nichiren sect (from c. 1250) and **Zen** (brought from China, 1191), which stressed meditation and a disciplined aesthetic (tea ceremony, gardening, martial arts, *No* drama).

Change and Expansion in Europe: 1500-1700

Reformation. Theological debate and protests against real and perceived clerical corruption existed in the medieval Christian world, expressed by such dissenters as John **Wycliffe** (c. 1320-84) and his followers (the Lollards) in England, and **Huss** (burned as a heretic, 1415) in Bohemia.

Martin **Luther** (1483-1546) preached that faith alone, without the mediation of clergy or good works, leads to salvation. He attacked the authority of the pope, rejected priestly celibacy, and recommended individual study of the Bible (which he translated into German c. 1525). His 95 Theses (1517) led to

his excommunication (1521). John **Calvin** (1509-64) said that God's elect were predestined for salvation and all others for damnation; good conduct and success were signs of election. Calvin in Geneva and John **Knox** (1505-72) in Scotland established theocratic states.

Henry VIII asserted English national authority and secular power by breaking away (1534) from the Catholic Church, creating what would become the Anglican Church. Monastic property was confiscated, and some Protestant doctrines given official sanction.

Religious wars. A century and a half of religious wars began with a S German peasant uprising (1524), repressed with Luther's support. Radical sects—democratic, pacifist, millenarian—arose (Anabaptists ruled Münster, 1534-35) and were suppressed violently. Civil war in France from 1562 between **Huguenots** (Protestant nobles and merchants) and Catholics ended with the 1598 **Edict of Nantes**, tolerating Protestants (revoked 1685). Habsburg attempts to restore Catholicism in Germany were resisted in 25 years of fighting. The 1555 Peace of Augsburg guarantee of religious independence to local princes and cities was confirmed only after the **Thirty Years' War** (1618-48), when much of Germany was devastated by local and foreign armies (Sweden, France).

A Catholic Reformation, or **Counter-Reformation**, met the Protestant challenge, defining an official theology at the Council of Trent (1545-63). The **Jesuit** order (Society of Jesus), founded in 1534 by Ignatius Loyola (1491-1556), helped reconvert large areas of Poland, Hungary, and S Germany and sent missionaries to the New World, India, and China. The **Inquisition** suppressed heresy in Catholic countries. A revival of religious fervor appeared in devotional literature (Teresa of Avila, 1515-82) and in grandiose **Baroque** art (Bernini, 1598-1680).

Scientific Revolution. The late nominalist thinkers (Ockham, c. 1300-49) of Paris and Oxford challenged Aristotelian orthodoxy, allowing for a freer scientific approach. At the same time, metaphysical values, such as the Neoplatonic faith in an orderly, mathematical cosmos, still motivated and directed inquiry. Nicolaus **Copernicus** (1473-1543) promoted the heliocentric theory, which was confirmed when Johannes **Kepler** (1571-1630) discovered the mathematical laws describing the elliptical orbits of the planets. The traditional Christian-Aristotelian belief that the heavens and the Earth were fundamentally different collapsed when **Galileo Galilei** (1564-1642) discovered moving sunspots, irregular moon topography, and moons around Jupiter, but he faced religious opposition (Galileo's retraction, 1633). He and Sir Isaac **Newton** (1642-1727) developed a mechanics that unified cosmic and earthly phenomena. Newton and Gottfried von **Leibniz** (1646-1716) invented calculus. René **Descartes** (1596-1650), best known for his influential philosophy, also invented analytic geometry.

An explosion of **observational science** included the discovery of blood circulation (Harvey, 1578-1657) and microscopic life (Leeuwenhoek, 1632-1723) and advances in anatomy (Vesalius, 1514-64, dissected corpses) and chemistry (Boyle, 1627-91). Scientific research institutes were founded in Florence (1657), London (**Royal Society**, 1660), and Paris (1666). Inventions proliferated (Savery's steam engine, 1696).

Arts. Mannerist trends of the High Renaissance (**Michelangelo**, 1475-1564) exploited virtuosity, grace, novelty, and exotic subjects and poses. The notion of artistic genius was promoted. Private connoisseurs entered the art market. These trends were elaborated in the 17th cent. **Baroque** era on a grander scale. Dynamic movement in painting and sculpture was emphasized by sharp lighting effects, rich materials (colored marble, gilt), and realistic details. Curved facades, broken lines, rich detail, and ceiling decoration characterized Baroque architecture. Monarchs, princes, and prelates, usually Catholic, used Baroque art to enhance and embellish their authority, as in royal portraits (Velázquez, 1599-1660; Van Dyck, 1599-1641).

National styles emerged. In France, a taste for rectilinear order and serenity (Poussin, 1594-1665), linked to the new rational philosophy, was expressed in classical forms. The influence of **classical values** in French literature (tragedies of **Racine**, 1639-99) gave rise to the "battle of the Ancients and Moderns." New forms included the essay (**Montaigne**, 1533-92) and novel (*Princesse de Clèves*, La Fayette, 1678).

Dutch painting of the 17th cent. was unique in its wide social distribution. The Flemish tradition of undemonstrative realism reached its peak in **Rembrandt** (1606-69) and Jan Vermeer (1632-75).

Economy. European economic expansion, known as the **commercial revolution**, was stimulated by new trade with the East, by New World gold and silver, and by a doubling of population (50 million in 1450, 100 million in 1600). **New business and financial techniques** were developed and refined, such as joint-stock companies, insurance, and letters of credit and exchange. The Bank of Amsterdam (1609) and the Bank of England (1694) broke the old monopoly of private banking families. The rise of a business mentality was typified by the spread of clock towers in cities in the 14th cent. By the mid-15th cent., portable clocks were available; the first watch was invented in 1502.

By 1650, most governments had adopted the **mercantile system**, in which they sought to amass metallic wealth by protecting merchants' foreign and colonial trade monopolies. The rise in prices and the new coin-based economy undermined craft guild and feudal manorial systems. Expanding industries (clothweaving, mining) benefited from technical advances. Coal began to replace wood as the chief fuel; it was used to fuel new 16th-cent. blast furnaces making cast iron.

New World. The **Aztecs** united much of the Mesoamerican area in a militarist empire by 1519 from their capital, Tenochtitlán (pop. 300,000), which was the center of a cult requiring ritual human sacrifice. Most of the civilized areas of South America were ruled by the centralized Inca Empire (1476-1534), stretching 2,000 mi from Ecuador to NW Argentina. Lavish and sophisticated traditions in pottery, weaving, sculpture, and architecture were maintained in both regions.

These empires, beset by revolts, fell in two short campaigns to gold-seeking Spanish forces based in the Antilles and Panama. Hernán **Cortés** took Mexico (1519-21); Francisco **Pizarro**, Peru (1532-35). From these centers, land and sea expeditions claimed most of North and South America for Spain. The indigenous high cultures did not survive the impact of **Christian missionaries** and the new upper class of whites. Although the Spanish administration intermittently concerned itself with their welfare, the population was devastated by European diseases and remained impoverished at most levels. New World silver and such native products as potatoes, tobacco, corn, peanuts, chocolate, and rubber exercised a major economic influence on Europe.

Brazil, which the Portuguese reached in 1500 and settled after 1530, and the Caribbean colonies of several European nations developed a plantation economy where sugarcane, tobacco, cotton, coffee, rice, indigo, and lumber were grown by slaves. From the early 16th to late 19th cent., 10 million Africans were transported to **slavery** in the Americas and Caribbean islands.

Netherlands. The urban, Calvinist N provinces of the Netherlands rebelled (1568) against Habsburg Spain and founded an oligarchic mercantile republic. Their control of the Baltic grain market enabled them to exploit Mediterranean food shortages. Religious refugees—French and Belgian Protestants, Iberian Jews—added to the commercial talent pool. After Spain

Nicolaus Copernicus's theory of heliocentricity (1533) was later proven by Johannes Kepler, but the concept of a moving Earth was too outlandish for many 16th-century thinkers.

absorbed Portugal (1580), the Dutch seized Portuguese possessions and created a vast commercial empire ultimately centered in parts of the Caribbean and in Indonesia. The Dutch also challenged or supplanted Portuguese traders in China and Japan. Revolution in 1640 restored Portuguese independence.

England. Anglicanism became firmly established under **Elizabeth I** after a brief Catholic interlude under "Bloody Mary" (1553-58). But religious and political conflicts led to a rebellion (1642) by Parliament. Forces of the Roundheads (Puritans) defeated the Cavaliers (Royalists); Charles I was beheaded (1649). The new Commonwealth was ruled as a military dictatorship by Oliver **Cromwell**, who also brutally crushed (1649-51) an Irish rebellion. Conflicts within the Puritan camp (democratic Levelers defeated, 1649) aided the Stuart restoration (1660), but Parliament was strengthened and the peaceful **"Glorious Revolution"** (1688) advanced political and religious liberties (writings of **Locke**, 1632-1704). British privateers (Drake, 1540-96) challenged Spanish control of the New World and penetrated Asian trade routes (Madras taken, 1639). North American colonies (Jamestown, 1607; Plymouth, 1620) provided an outlet for private enterprise and religious dissenters from Europe. The British East India company gained growing sway in 18th-cent. India, as Mughal power declined.

France. Emerging from the religious civil wars in 1628, France regained military and commercial great power status (under the ministries of **Richelieu**, Mazarin, and Colbert). Under **Louis XIV** (r. 1643-1715), royal absolutism triumphed over nobles and local *parlements* (defeat of Fronde, 1648-53). Durable colonies were founded in Canada (1608), the Caribbean (1626), and India (1674).

Sweden. Sweden seceded from the Scandinavian Union in 1523. The thinly populated agrarian state (with copper, iron, and timber exports) was united by the Vasa kings, whose conquests by the mid-17th cent. made Sweden the dominant Baltic power. The empire collapsed in the Great Northern War (1700-21).

Poland. After the union with Lithuania in 1447, Poland ruled vast territories from the Baltic to the Black Sea, resisting German and Turkish incursions. Catholic nobles failed to gain the loyalty of their Orthodox Christian subjects in the E; commerce and trades were practiced by German and Jewish immigrants. The bloody 1648-49 Cossack uprising began the kingdom's dismemberment.

Russia. Growing authority of the tsars continued with advancing serfdom. Around 1700, **Peter the Great** imported new Western styles and technologies. Steady territorial expansion created a vast territory touching China, the Ottoman Empire, and east-central Europe.

China. A new dynasty, the **Manchus**, invaded from the NE, seized power in 1644, and expanded Chinese control to its greatest extent in Central and SE Asia. Trade and diplomatic contact with Europe grew, carefully controlled by China. New crops (sweet potato, maize, peanut) allowed economic and population growth (pop. 300 million, in 1800). Traditional arts and literature were pursued with increased sophistication (*Dream of the Red Chamber*, novel, mid-18th cent.).

Japan. Tokugawa Ieyasu, shogun from 1603, finally unified and pacified feudal Japan. Hereditary nobles (daimyos and samurai) monopolized government office and the professions. An urban merchant class grew, literacy spread, and a cultural renaissance occurred (**haiku**, a verse innovation of the poet Basho, 1644-94). Fear of European domination led to persecution of Christian converts from 1597 and to substantial isolation from outside contact from 1640.

Philosophy, Industry, and Revolution: 1700-1800

Science and reason. Greater faith in reason and empirical observation, instead of tradition and religious beliefs, espoused since the Renaissance (Francis Bacon, 1561-1626), was bolstered by scientific discoveries. René **Descartes** (1596-1650) used a rationalistic approach modeled on geometry and introspection to discover "self-evident" truths as a foundation of knowledge. Sir Isaac **Newton** emphasized induction from experimental observation. Baruch de **Spinoza** (1632-77), who called for political and intellectual freedom, developed a systematic rationalistic philosophy in his classic work *Ethics*.

French philosophers assumed leadership of the **Enlightenment** in the 18th cent. Montesquieu (1689-1755) used British history to support his notions of limited government. **Voltaire**'s (1694-1778) diaries and novels of exotic travel illustrated the intellectual trends toward secular ethics and relativism. Jean-Jacques **Rousseau**'s (1712-78) radical concepts of the **social contract** and of the inherent goodness of the common man gave impetus to antimonarchical republicanism. The *Encyclopedia* (1751-72), edited by Diderot and d'Alembert), designed as a monument to reason, was largely devoted to practical technology.

In England, ideals of liberty were connected with empiricist philosophy and science in the followers of John **Locke**. But British empiricism, especially as developed by the skeptical David **Hume** (1711-76), radically reduced the role of reason in philosophy, as did the evolutionary approach to law and politics of Edmund Burke (1729-97) and the utilitarian ethics of Jeremy Bentham (1748-1832). Adam Smith (1723-90) and other economists called for a rationalization of economic activity by removing artificial barriers to a supposedly natural free exchange of goods known as **laissez-faire**.

German writers participated in the new philosophical trends popularized by Christian von Wolff (1679-1754). Immanuel **Kant**'s (1724-1804) transcendental idealism, unifying an empirical epistemology with a priori moral and logical concepts, directed German thought away from skepticism. Italian contributions included work on electricity (Galvani, 1737-98; Volta, 1745-1827), the pioneer historiography of Vico (1668-1744), and writings on penal reform (Beccaria, 1738-94). Benjamin Franklin (1706-90) was celebrated in Europe for his varied achievements.

The growth of the **press** (*Spectator*, 1711-12) and the wide distribution of sentimental **novels** attested to the increase of a large bourgeois public.

Arts. Rococo art, characterized by extravagant decorative effects, asymmetries copied from organic models, and artificial pastoral subjects, was favored by the continental aristocracy for most of the century (Watteau, 1684-1721) and had musical analogies in the ornamentalized polyphony of late Baroque. The **Neoclassical** art after 1750, associated with the new scientific archaeology, was more streamlined and was infused with the supposed moral and geometric rectitude of the Roman Republic (David, 1748-1825). In England, **town planning** on a grand scale began.

Industrial Revolution in England. Agricultural improvements, such as the sowing drill (1701) and livestock breeding, were implemented on the large fields provided by enclosure of common lands by private owners. Profits from agriculture and from colonial and foreign trade (1800 volume, £54 mil) were channeled through hundreds of banks and the **Stock Exchange** (est. 1773) into new industrial processes.

The Newcomen steam pump (1712) aided coal mining. Coal fueled the new efficient steam engines patented by James Watt in 1769, and coke-smelting produced cheap, sturdy iron for machinery by the 1730s. The **flying shuttle** (1733) and **spinning jenny** (c. 1764) were used in the large new cotton textile factories, where women and children were much of the workforce. Goods were transported cheaply over **canals** (2,000 mi; built 1760-1800). By the early 19th cent., industrialization spread in Western Europe and North America.

American Revolution. The British colonies in North America attracted a mass immigration of religious dissenters and poor people throughout the 17th and 18th cent., coming from the British Isles, Germany, the Netherlands, and other countries including imported African slaves. The population reached 3 million non-natives by the 1770s. The indigenous population was greatly reduced by European diseases and by wars with the various colonies. British attempts to control colonial trade and to tax the colonists to pay for the costs of colonial administration and defense clashed with local self-government and eventually provoked the colonies to a successful rebellion.

Central and East Europe. The monarchs of the three states that dominated E Europe—Austria, Prussia, and Russia—expanded royal power and centralized institutions in their kingdoms, which were enlarged by the division (1772-95) of Poland.

The invention of the spinning jenny (1764) revolutionized the cotton industry in the late 18th century, allowing women and children to be put to work in large factories.

Under **Frederick II** (called the Great) (r. 1740-86) Prussia, with its efficient modern army, doubled in size. State monopolies and tariff protection fostered industry, and some legal reforms were introduced. Austria's heterogeneous realms were unified under **Maria Theresa** (r. 1740-80) and **Joseph II** (r. 1780-90). Reforms in education, law, and religion were enacted, and the Austrian serfs were freed (1781). With its defeat in the Seven Years' War in 1763, Austria failed to regain Silesia, which had been seized by Prussia, but it was compensated by expansion to the E and S (Hungary, Slavonia, 1699; Galicia, 1772).

Russia, whose borders continued to expand, adopted some Western bureaucratic and economic policies under **Peter I** (r. 1682-1725) and **Catherine II** (r. 1762-96). Trade and cultural contacts with the West multiplied from the new Baltic Sea capital, **St. Petersburg** (est. 1703).

French Revolution. The growing French middle class lacked political power and resented aristocratic tax privileges, especially in light of the successful American Revolution. Peasants lacked adequate land and were burdened with feudal obligations to nobles. War with Britain led to the loss of French Canada and drained the treasury, finally forcing the king to call the **Estates-General** in 1789 for the first time since 1614, in an atmosphere of food riots (poor crop in 1788).

Aristocratic resistance to absolutism was soon overshadowed by the reformist Third Estate (middle class), which proclaimed itself the **National Constituent Assembly** June 17 and took the "Tennis Court oath" on June 20 to secure a constitution. The storming of the **Bastille** on July 14, 1789, by Parisian artisans was followed by looting and the seizure of aristocratic property throughout France. Assembly reforms included abolition of class and regional privileges, a Declaration of Rights, suffrage by taxpayers (75% of male population), and the **Civil Constitution of the Clergy** providing for election and loyalty oaths for priests. A republic was declared Sept. 22, 1792, in spite of royalist pressure from Austria and Prussia, which had declared war in Apr. (joined by Britain the next year). Louis XVI was beheaded Jan. 21, 1793, and Queen Marie Antoinette was beheaded Oct. 16, 1793.

Royalist uprisings in La Vendée and military reverses led to institution of a **reign of terror** in which tens of thousands of opponents of the Revolution and criminals were executed. Radical reforms in the **Convention** period (Sept. 1793-Oct. 1795) included the abolition of colonial slavery, economic measures to aid the poor, support of public education, and a short-lived de-Christianization.

Division among radicals (execution of Hebert, Danton, and Robespierre, 1794) aided the ascendancy of a moderate **Directory**, which consolidated military victories. **Napoleon Bonaparte** (1769-1821), a popular young general, exploited political divisions and participated in a coup Nov. 9, 1799, making himself first consul (dictator).

India. Sikh and Hindu rebels (Rajputs, Marathas) and Afghans destroyed the power of the Mughals during the 18th cent. After French defeat (1763) in the Seven Years' War, Britain was the primary European trade power in India. Its control of inland **Bengal** and **Bihar** was recognized (1765) by the Mughal shah, who granted the **British East India Co.** (under Clive, 1725-74) the right to collect land revenue there. Despite objections from Parliament (1784 India Act), the company's involvement in local wars and politics led to repeated acquisitions of new territory. The company exported Indian textiles, sugar, and indigo, but industry was discouraged to promote British imports.

Nationalism Gathers Momentum: 1800-40

French ideals and empire spread. Inspired by the ideals of the French Revolution, and supported by the expanding French armies, new republican regimes arose near France: the **Batavian** Republic in the Netherlands (1795-1806), the **Helvetic** Republic in Switzerland (1798-1803), the **Cisalpine** Republic in N Italy (1797-1805), the **Ligurian** Republic in Genoa (1797-1805), and the **Parthenopean** Republic in S Italy (1799). A Roman Republic existed briefly in 1798 after Pope Pius VI was arrested by French troops. In Italy and Germany, new nationalist sentiments were stimulated both in imitation of and in reaction to developments in France (anti-French and anti-Jacobin peasant uprisings in Italy, 1796-99).

From 1804, when Napoleon declared himself emperor, to 1812, a succession of military victories (Austerlitz, 1805; Jena, 1806) extended his control over most of Europe through puppet states (**Confederation of the Rhine** united W German states for the first time and **Grand Duchy of Warsaw** revived Polish national hopes), expansion of the empire, and alliances.

Among the lasting reforms initiated under Napoleon's absolutist reign were establishment of the Bank of France, centralization of tax collection, codification of law along Roman models (Code Napoléon), and reform and extension of secondary and university education. In an 1801 concordat, the papacy recognized the effective autonomy of the French Catholic Church.

Napoleon's continental successes were offset by a British victory under Adm. Horatio Nelson in the **Battle of Trafalgar** (1805). Some 400,000 French soldiers were killed in the Napoleonic Wars, along with about 600,000 foreign troops.

Last gasp of old regimes. The disastrous 1812 invasion of Russia exposed Napoleon's overextension. After Napoleon's 1814 exile at Elba, his armies were defeated (1815) at **Waterloo** by British and Prussian troops.

At the **Congress of Vienna**, the monarchs and princes of Europe redrew their boundaries, to the advantage of Prussia (in Saxony and the Ruhr), Austria (in Illyria and Venetia), and Russia (in Poland and Finland). British conquest of Dutch and French colonies (S Africa, Ceylon, Mauritius) was recognized. France, under the restored Bourbons, retained its expanded 1792 borders. The settlement brought 50 years of international peace to Europe.

But the Congress was unable to check the advance of liberal ideals and of nationalism among the smaller European nations. The 1825 **Decembrist uprising** by liberal officers in Russia was easily suppressed. But an independence movement in **Greece**, stirred by commercial prosperity and a cultural revival, succeeded in expelling Ottoman rule by 1831, with the aid of Britain, France, and Russia.

A constitutional monarchy was secured in France by the **1830 Revolution**; Louis Philippe became king. The revolutionary contagion spread to **Belgium**, which gained its independence (1830) from the Dutch monarchy, and to **Poland**, whose rebellion was defeated (1830-31) by Russia, and to Germany.

Romanticism. A new style in intellectual and artistic life replaced Neoclassicism and Rococo after the mid-18th cent. By the early 19th cent., Romanticism prevailed in Europe.

Rousseau had begun the reaction against rationalism; in education (*Émile*, 1762) he stressed subjective spontaneity over regularized instruction. German writers (Lessing, 1729-81; Herder, 1744-1803) favorably compared the German folk song to classical forms and began a cult of Shakespeare, whose passion and "natural" wisdom was a model for the romantic *Sturm und Drang* (Storm and Stress) movement. **Goethe's** *Sorrows of Young Werther* (1774) set the model for the tragic, passionate genius.

A new interest in **Gothic architecture** in England after 1760 (Walpole, 1717-97) spread through Europe, associated with an aesthetic Christian and mystic revival (**Blake**, 1757-1827). Celtic, Norse, and German mythology and folk tales were

revived or imitated (Grimm's Fairy Tales, 1812-22). The medieval revival (Scott's *Ivanhoe*, 1819) led to a new interest in history, stressing national differences and organic growth (**Carlyle**, 1795-1881; Michelet, 1798-1874), corresponding to theories of natural evolution (Lamarck's *Philosophie Zoologique*, 1809; Lyell's *Geology*, 1830-33). A reaction against classicism characterized the English **romantic poets** (beginning with Wordsworth, 1770-1850). Revolution and war fed an emphasis on freedom and conflict, expressed by both poets (**Byron**, 1788-1824; **Hugo**, 1802-85) and philosophers (**Hegel**, 1770-1831).

Wild gardens replaced the formal French variety, and painters favored rural, stormy, and mountainous landscapes (**Turner**, 1775-1851; **Constable**, 1776-1837). Clothing became freer, with wigs, hoops, and ruffles discarded. Originality and genius were expected in the life and work of inspired artists (Murger's *Scenes From Bohemian Life*, 1847-49). Exotic locales and themes (as in Gothic horror stories) were used in art and literature (Delacroix, 1798-1863; **Poe**, 1809-49). Music exhibited the new dramatic style and a breakdown of classical forms (**Beethoven**, 1770-1827). The use of folk melodies and modes aided the growth of distinct national traditions (Glinka in Russia, 1804-57).

Latin America. François **Toussaint L'Ouverture** led a successful slave revolt in Haiti, which subsequently became the first Caribbean state to achieve independence (1804). The mainland Spanish colonies won their independence (1810-24) under such leaders as Simón **Bolívar** (1783-1830). Brazil became an independent empire (1822) under the Portuguese prince regent. A new class of military officers divided power with large landholders and the church.

United States. Territory under U.S. control nearly doubled in size with the **Louisiana Purchase** (1803). Heavy immigration and exploitation of ample natural resources fueled rapid economic growth. The spread of the franchise, public education, and antislavery sentiment were signs of a widespread democratic ethic.

China. Failure to keep pace with Western arms technology exposed China to greater European influence and hampered efforts to bar imports of opium, which had damaged Chinese society and drained wealth overseas. In the **Opium War** (1839-42), Britain forced China to expand trade opportunities and to cede Hong Kong.

New Complexities: Reforms and Imperialism: 1840-80

Idea of progress. As a result of the cumulative scientific, economic, and political changes of the preceding eras, the idea took hold among literate people in the West that continuing growth and improvement constituted the usual state of human and natural life.

Charles **Darwin**'s statement of the **theory of evolution** and survival of the fittest (*On the Origin of Species*, 1859), defended by intellectuals and scientists against theological objections, was taken as confirmation that progress was the natural direction of life. The controversy helped define popular ideas of the dedicated scientist and of science's increasing control over the world (Foucault's demonstration of Earth's rotation, 1851; **Pasteur**'s germ theory, 1861).

Liberals following Ricardo (1772-1823) in their faith that unrestrained competition would bring continuous economic expansion sought to adjust political life to new social realities and believed that unregulated competition of ideas would yield truth (**Mill**, 1806-73). In England, successive reform bills (1832, 1867, 1884) gave representation to the new industrial towns and extended the franchise to the middle and lower classes and to Catholics, Dissenters, and Jews. On both sides of the Atlantic, reformists tried to improve conditions for the mentally ill (**Dix**, 1802-87), women (Anthony, 1820-1906), and prisoners. Slavery was barred in the British Empire (1833), the U.S. (1865), and Brazil (1888).

Socialist theories based on ideas of human perfectibility or progress were widely disseminated. Utopian socialists such as Saint-Simon (1760-1825) envisaged an orderly, just society directed by a technocratic elite. A model factory town, New Lanark, Scotland, was set up by utopian Robert Owen (1771-1858), and communal experiments were tried in the U.S. (Brook Farm, MA, 1841-47). Bakunin's (1814-76) anarchism represented the opposite extreme of total freedom. Karl **Marx** (1818-83) posited the inevitable triumph of socialism in industrial countries through a dialectical process of class conflict. Effective development of oceanic steamship lines (Cunard Lines, 1840s) and the opening of the **Suez Canal** accelerated shipping and commerce. Telegraph lines (Australia-Europe, 1871) sped communication. International organizations included the General (later Universal) Postal Union (1874) and conferences to limit epidemics like cholera. The initial **Geneva Convention** (1864) regulated treatment of prisoners of war.

Spread of industry. The technical processes and managerial innovations of the English industrial revolution spread to Europe (especially Germany) and the U.S., causing an explosion of industrial production, demand for raw materials, and competition for markets. Inventors, both trained and self-taught, provided means for larger-scale production (Bessemer steel, 1856; sewing machine, 1846). Many inventions were shown at the universal prosperity-themed 1851 London Great Exhibition at the **Crystal Palace**.

Local specialization and long-distance trade were aided by a revolution in transportation and communication. Railroads were first introduced in the 1820s in England and the U.S. Over 150,000 mi of track had been laid worldwide by 1880, with another 100,000 mi laid in the next decade. Steamships were

improved (*Savannah* crossed Atlantic, 1819). The **telegraph**, perfected by 1844 (Morse), connected the Old and New Worlds by cable in 1866 and quickened the pace of international commerce and politics. The first commercial **telephone** exchange went into operation in the U.S. in 1878.

The new class of industrial workers, uprooted from their rural homes, lacked job security and suffered from dangerous overcrowding at work and at home. Many responded by organizing **trade unions** (legalized in England, 1824; France, 1884). The U.S. Knights of Labor had 700,000 members by 1886. The First International (1864-76) tried to unite workers worldwide around a Marxist program. The quasi-Socialist Paris Commune uprising (1871) was violently suppressed. Acts to reduce child labor and regulate conditions were passed (1833-50 in England). Social security measures were introduced by the Bismarck regime (1883-89) in Germany.

Queen Victoria's 63-year rule of the UK (1837-1901) witnessed the rise of a middle class and was marked by conservative morality and intense nationalism.

Revolutions of 1848. Among the causes of the continent-wide revolutions were an international collapse of credit and resulting unemployment, bad harvests in 1845-47, and a cholera epidemic. The new urban proletariat and expanding bourgeoisie demanded greater political roles. Republics were proclaimed in France, Rome, and Venice. Nationalist feelings reached fever pitch in the Habsburg empire, as Hungary declared independence under Kossuth, a Slav Congress demanded equality, and Piedmont tried to drive Austria from Lombardy. A national liberal assembly at Frankfurt called for German unification.

But riots fueled bourgeois fear of socialism (**Marx** and **Engels**, *Communist Manifesto*, 1848), and peasants remained conservative. The old establishment—the Papacy, the Habsburgs with the help of the Tsarist Russian army—was able to rout the revolutionaries by 1849. The French Republic succumbed to a renewed monarchy by 1852 (Emperor Napoleon III).

Great nations unified. Using the "blood and iron" tactics of Bismarck from 1862, Prussia controlled N Germany by 1867 (war with Denmark, 1864; Austria, 1866). After defeating France in 1870 (annexation of Alsace-Lorraine), it won the allegiance of S German states. A new **German Empire** was proclaimed (1871). **Italy**, inspired by Giuseppe Mazzini (1805-72) and Giuseppe Garibaldi (1807-82), was unified by the reformed Piedmont kingdom through uprisings, plebiscites, and war.

The **United States** expanded its area after the 1846-48 Mexican War and defeated (1861-65) a secession attempt by Southern states in the **Civil War**. Canadian provinces were united in an autonomous **Dominion of Canada** (1867). Control in **India** was removed from the East India Co. and centralized under British administration after the 1857-58 Sepoy rebellion, laying the groundwork for the modern Indian state. Queen Victoria was named Empress of India (1876).

Europe dominates Asia. The Ottoman Empire began to weaken in the face of Balkan nationalisms and European imperial incursions in N Africa (**Suez Canal**, 1869). The Ottomans had lost control of most of both regions by 1882. Russia completed its expansion S by 1884 (despite the temporary setback of the **Crimean War** with Turkey, Britain, and France, 1853-56), taking Turkestan, all the Caucasus, and Chinese areas in the E and sponsoring Balkan Slavs against the Turks. A succession of reformist and reactionary regimes presided over a slow modernization (serfs freed, 1861). Persian independence suffered as Russia and British India competed for influence.

China was forced to sign a series of unequal treaties with European powers and Japan. Overpopulation and an inefficient dynasty brought misery and caused rebellions (Taiping, Muslims) leaving tens of millions dead. **Japan** was forced by the U.S. (Commodore Perry's visits, 1853-54) and Europe to end its isolation. The Meiji restoration (1868) gave power to a Westernizing oligarchy, abolishing feudalism and expanding education. Intensified empire-building gave Burma to Britain (1824-85) and Indochina to France (1862-95). Christian missionary activity followed imperial and trade expansion in Asia.

Arts. The official **Beaux Arts** school in Paris set an international style of imposing public buildings (Paris Opera, 1861-74; Vienna Opera, 1861-69) and uplifting statues (Bartholdi's Statue of Liberty, 1884). Realist painting, influenced by photography (Daguerre, 1837), appealed to a new mass audience with social or historical narrative (Wilkie, 1785-1841; Poynter, 1836-1919) or with serious religious, moral, or social messages (pre-Raphaelites, Millet's *Angelus*, 1858), often drawn from ordinary life. The **Impressionists** (Monet, 1840-1926; Pissarro, 1830-1903; Renoir, 1841-1919) rejected the formalism, sentimentality, and precise techniques of academic art in favor of a spontaneous, undetailed rendering of the world through careful representation of the effect of natural light on objects. They were strongly influenced by Asian and African styles.

Realistic **novelists** presented the full panorama of social classes and personalities but retained sentimentality and moral judgment (**Dickens**, 1812-70; **Eliot**, 1819-80; **Tolstoy**, 1828-1910; **Balzac**, 1799-1850).

Veneer of Stability: 1880-1900

Imperialism triumphant. The vast **African** interior, visited by European explorers (Barth, 1821-65; Livingstone, 1813-73), was conquered by the European powers in rapid, competitive thrusts from their coastal bases after 1880, mostly for domestic political and international strategic reasons. W African Muslim kingdoms (Fulani), Arab slave traders (Zanzibar), and Bantu military confederations (Zulu) were alike subdued. Only Christian Ethiopia (defeat of Italy, 1896) and Liberia resisted successfully. France (W Africa) and Britain ("Cape to Cairo," **Boer War**, 1899-1902) were the major beneficiaries. The ideology of "the white man's burden" (Kipling, *Barrack Room Ballads*, 1892) justified the conquests, which in fact reflected Europe's weapons superiority.

W European foreign capital investment soared to nearly $40 bil by 1914, but most was in E Europe (France, Germany), the Americas (Britain), and Europe's colonies. The foundation of the modern interdependent world economy was laid, with cartels dominating raw material trade. Global developments included a new agreement on international patents (1883), the modern Olympics (1896), and the global spread of department stores.

An industrious world. Industrial and technological proficiency characterized the two new great powers—Germany and the U.S. Coal and iron deposits enabled Germany to reach second- or third-place status in iron, steel, and shipbuilding by the 1900s. German electrical and chemical industries were world leaders. The U.S. post-Civil War boom (interrupted by financial panics—1884, 1893, 1896) was shaped by massive immigration from S and E Europe from 1880, government subsidy of railroads, and huge private monopolies (Standard Oil, 1870; U.S. Steel, 1901). The **Spanish-American War**, 1898 (Philippine Insurrection, 1899-1902), and the **Open Door policy** in China (1899) made the U.S. a world power.

England led in **urbanization**, with London the world capital of finance, insurance, and shipping. Sewer systems (Paris, 1850s), electric subways (London, 1890), parks, and bargain department stores helped improve living standards for most of the urban population of the industrial world. Birthrates declined in the West while infant mortality rates plunged (demographic transition, 1880-1920).

Upheavals in Asia. Asian reaction to European economic, military, and religious incursions took the form of imitation of Western techniques and adoption of Western ideas of progress and freedom. The Chinese "self-strengthening" movement of the 1860s and 1870s included rail, port, and arsenal improvements and metal and textile mills. Reformers such as **K'ang Yu-wei** (1858-1927) won liberalizing reforms in 1898, right after the European and Japanese "scramble for concessions."

A universal education system in Japan and importation of foreign industrial, scientific, and military experts aided Japan's rapid modernization after 1868, under the authoritarian Meiji regime. Japan's victory in the **Sino-Japanese War** (1894-95) put Formosa and Korea in its power. Industrialization began in earnest by 1890.

In India, the British alliance with the remaining princely states masked reform sentiment among the Westernized urban elite; higher education had been conducted largely in English for 50 years. The **Indian National Congress**, founded in 1885, demanded a larger government role for Indians.

Fin-de-siècle **sophistication.** Naturalist writers pushed realism to its extreme limits, adopting a quasi-scientific attitude and writing about formerly taboo subjects such as sex, crime, extreme poverty, and corruption (Flaubert, 1821-80; Zola, 1840-1902; Hardy, 1840-1928). Unseen or repressed psychological motivations were explored in the clinical and theoretical works of Sigmund **Freud** (1856-1939) and in works of fiction (**Dostoyevsky**, 1821-81; Henry James, 1843-1916; Schnitzler, 1862-1931).

A contempt for bourgeois life or a desire to shock a complacent audience was shared by the French **symbolist** poets (Verlaine, 1844-96; Rimbaud, 1854-91), by neopagan English writers (Swinburne, 1837-1909), by continental dramatists (**Ibsen**, 1828-1906), and by satirists (**Wilde**, 1854-1900). The German philosopher Friedrich **Nietzsche** (1844-1900) was influential in his elitism and pessimism.

Postimpressionist art neglected long-cherished conventions of representation (**Cézanne**, 1839-1906) and showed a willingness to learn from primitive and non-European art (**Gauguin**, 1848-1903; Japanese prints).

Racism. Gobineau (1816-82) gave a pseudobiological foundation to modern racist theories, which spread in Europe in the latter 19th cent., along with **Social Darwinism**, the belief that societies are and should be organized as a struggle for survival of the fittest. The medieval period was interpreted as an era of natural Germanic rule (Chamberlain, 1855-1927), and notions of racial superiority were associated with German national aspirations (Treitschke, 1834-96). **Anti-Semitism**, with a new racist rationale, became a significant political force in Germany (Anti-Semitic Petition, 1880), Austria (Lueger, 1844-1910), and France (**Dreyfus affair**, 1894-1906).

Imperialism's High Point: 1900-09

Alliances. While the peace of Europe (and its dependencies) continued to hold (1907 **Hague Conference** extended the rules of war and international arbitration procedures), imperial rivalries, protectionist trade practices (in Germany and France), and the escalating arms race (British *Dreadnought* battleship launched; Germany widens Kiel canal, 1906) exacerbated minor disputes (German-French Moroccan "crises," 1905, 1911).

Security was sought through balance-of-power alliances: **Triple Alliance** (Germany, Austria-Hungary, Italy; renewed in 1902 and 1907); Anglo-Japanese Alliance (1902), Franco-Russian Alliance (1899), **Entente Cordiale** (Britain, France, 1904), Anglo-Russian Treaty (1907), German-Ottoman friendship. Global developments included the establishment of an International Court in The Hague, the first transatlantic radio transmission (1901), and the creation of the first international association for European football (1904).

Ottomans decline. The Ottoman government was unable to resist further loss of territory, and earlier reform efforts gave way to greater authoritarianism. Nearly all European lands were lost in 1912 to Serbia, Greece, Montenegro, and Bulgaria. Italy took Libya and the Dodecanese islands the same year. Britain took Kuwait (1899) and the Sinai (1906). The **Young Turk** revolution in 1908 forced the sultan to restore a constitution, and it introduced some social reform and secularization.

British Empire. British trade and cultural influence remained dominant in the empire, but constitutional reforms presaged its eventual dissolution. The colonies of **Australia** were united in 1901 under a self-governing commonwealth. **New Zealand** acquired dominion status in 1907. The old Boer republics joined Cape Colony and Natal in the self-governing Union of **South Africa** in 1910.

The 1909 Indian Councils Act enhanced the role of elected province legislatures in **India**. The Muslim League (founded 1906) sought separate communal representation.

East Asia. Japan exploited its growing industrial power to expand its empire. Victory in the 1904-05 war against Russia (naval battle of Tsushima, 1905) assured Japan's domination of **Korea** (annexed 1910) and Manchuria (Port Arthur taken, 1905).

In China, central authority began to crumble (empress died, 1908). Reforms (Confucian exam system ended 1905, modernization of the army, building of railroads) were inadequate, and secret societies of reformers and nationalists, inspired by the Westernized **Sun Yat-sen** (1866-1925), fomented periodic uprisings in the S.

Siam, whose independence had been guaranteed by Britain and France in 1896, was split into spheres of influence by those countries in 1907.

Russia. The population of the Russian Empire approached 150 million in 1900. Reforms in education, in law, and in local institutions (*zemstvos*) and an industrial boom starting in the 1880s (oil, railroads) created the beginnings of a modern society, despite the autocratic tsarist regime. Liberals (1903 Union of Liberation), Socialists (Social Democrats founded 1898, Bolsheviks split off 1903), and populists (Social Revolutionaries founded 1901) were periodically repressed, and national minorities were persecuted (anti-Jewish pogroms, 1903, 1905-06).

An industrial crisis after 1900 and harvest failures aggravated poverty among urban workers, and the 1904-05 defeat by Japan (which checked Russia's Asian expansion) sparked the **Revolution of 1905-06**. A **Duma** (parliament) was created under Tsar Nicholas II. Agricultural reform (under Stolypin, prime minister, 1906-11) created a large class of land-owning peasants (*kulaks*).

The world shrinks. Developments in transportation and communication and mass population movements helped create an awareness of an interdependent world. Early **automobiles** (Daimler, Benz, 1885) were experimental or were designed as luxuries. Assembly-line mass production (Ford Motor Co., 1903) made the invention practical, and by 1910 nearly 500,000 motor vehicles were registered in the U.S. alone. **Heavier-than-air flights** began in 1903 in the U.S. (Wright brothers' *Flyer*), preceded by glider, balloon, and model plane advances in several countries. Trade was advanced by improvements in **ship design** (gyrocompass, 1910), speed (*Lusitania* crossed Atlantic in five days, 1907), and reach (Panama Canal begun, 1904).

The first transatlantic **radio** telegraphic transmission occurred in 1901, six years after Marconi discovered radio. Radio transmission of human speech had been made in 1900. Telegraphic transmission of photos was achieved in 1904, lending immediacy to news reports. **Phonographs**, popularized by Caruso's recordings (starting 1902), made for quick international spread of musical styles (ragtime). **Motion pictures**, perfected in the 1890s (Dickson, Lumière brothers), became a popular and artistic medium after 1900; newsreels appeared in 1909.

Emigration from crowded European centers soared in the decade: 9 million migrated to the U.S., and millions more went to Siberia, Canada, Argentina, Australia, South Africa, and Algeria. Some 70 million Europeans emigrated in the century before 1914. Several million Chinese, Indians, and Japanese migrated to SE Asia, where their urban skills often enabled them to take a predominant economic role.

Social reform. The social and economic problems of the poor were kept in the public eye by realist fiction writers (Dreiser's *Sister Carrie*, 1900; Gorky's *Lower Depths*, 1902; Sinclair's *The Jungle*, 1906), journalists (U.S. **muckrakers**—Steffens, Tarbell), and artists (Ashcan school). Frequent labor strikes and occasional assassinations by anarchists or radicals (Empress Elizabeth of Austria, 1898; King Umberto I of Italy, 1900; U.S. Pres. McKinley, 1901; Russian Interior Min. Plehve, 1904; Portugal's King Carlos, 1908) added to social tension and fear of revolution. Feminist agitators for the vote surfaced in several countries.

Italian tenor Enrico Caruso was one of the first acclaimed singers to make phonograph records (1902); he became universally famous by means of the new medium.

But democratic reformism responded in part. In Germany, Bernstein's (1850-1932) **revisionist Marxism**, downgrading revolution, was accepted by the powerful Social Democrats and trade unions. The British Fabian Society (the Webbs, Shaw) and the Labour Party (founded 1906) worked for reforms such as social security and union rights (1906), while woman suffragists grew more militant. U.S. **progressives** fought big business (Pure Food and Drug Act, 1906). In France, the 10-hour workday (1904) and separation of church and state (1905) were reform victories, as was universal suffrage in Austria (1907).

Arts. An unprecedented period of experimentation, entered in France, produced several **new painting styles**: Fauvism exploited bold color areas (Matisse, *Woman With Hat*, 1905); expressionism reflected powerful inner emotions (Brücke group, 1905); Cubism combined several views of an object on one flat surface (Picasso, *Demoiselles*, 1906-07); futurism tried to depict speed and motion (Italian Futurist Manifesto, 1910). **Architects** explored new uses of steel structures, with facades either neoclassical (Adler and Sullivan in U.S.), curvilinear Art Nouveau (Gaudi's Casa Mila, 1905-10), or functionally streamlined (Wright's Robie House, 1909).

Music and dance shared the experimental spirit. Ruth St. Denis (1877-1968) and Isadora Duncan (1878-1927) pioneered modern dance, while Sergei Diaghilev in Paris revitalized classic ballet from 1909. Composers explored atonal music (Debussy, 1862-1918) and dissonance (Schoenberg, 1874-1951) or revolutionized classical forms (Stravinsky, 1882-1971), often showing jazz or folk music influences.

War and Revolution: 1910-19

War threatens. Germany under Wilhelm II sought a political and imperial role consonant with its industrial strength, challenging Britain's world supremacy and threatening France, which was still resenting the loss (1871) of Alsace-Lorraine. Austria wanted to curb an expanded Serbia (after 1912) and the threat it posed to its own Slav lands. Russia feared Austrian and German political and economic aims in the Balkans and Turkey.

An accelerated arms race resulted from these circumstances. The German standing army rose to more than 2 million men by 1914. Russia and France had more than a million each, and Austria and the British Empire nearly a million each. Dozens of enormous battleships were built by the powers after 1906.

The **assassination of Austrian Archduke Franz Ferdinand** by a Serbian nationalist, June 28, 1914, was the trigger for war. The system of alliances made the conflict Europe-wide; Germany's invasion of Belgium to outflank France forced Britain to enter the war. Patriotic fervor was nearly unanimous among all classes in most countries.

World War I. German forces were stopped in France in one month. The rival armies dug trench networks. Artillery and improved machine guns prevented either side from any lasting advance despite repeated assaults (600,000 dead at **Verdun**, Feb.-July 1916). Poison gas, used by Germany in 1915, proved ineffective. The entrance of more than 1 million U.S. troops tipped the balance after mid-1917, forcing Germany to sue for peace the next year. The formal armistice was signed on Nov. 11, 1918, and the German emperor abdicated.

In the E, the Russian armies were thrown back (battle of **Tannenberg**, Aug. 20, 1914), and the war grew unpopular in Russia. An allied attempt to relieve Russia through Turkey failed (**Gallipoli**, 1915). The **Russian Revolution** (1917) abolished the monarchy. The new Bolshevik regime signed the capitulatory Brest-Litovsk peace in Mar. 1918. Italy entered the war on the allied side in May 1915 but was pushed back by Oct. 1917. A renewed offensive with Allied aid in Oct.-Nov. 1918 forced Austria to surrender.

The British Navy successfully blockaded Germany, which responded with submarine U-boat attacks; **unrestricted submarine warfare** against neutrals after Jan. 1917 helped bring the U.S. into the war. Other battlefields included Palestine and Mesopotamia, both of which Britain wrested from the Turks in 1917, and the African and Pacific colonies of Germany, most of which fell to Britain, France, Australia, Japan, and South Africa.

Settlement. At the **Paris Peace Conference** (Jan.-June 1919), concluded by the **Treaty of Versailles**, and in subsequent negotiations and local wars (Russian-Polish War, 1920), the **map of Europe** was redrawn with a nod to U.S. Pres. Woodrow Wilson's principle of self-determination. Austria and Hungary were separated, and much of their land was given to Yugoslavia (formerly Serbia), Romania, Italy, and the newly independent Poland and Czechoslovakia. Germany lost territory in the W, N, and E, while Finland and the Baltic states were detached from Russia. The Ottoman Empire ended (1922) and most of its Arab lands went to British-sponsored Arab states or to direct French and British rule. Belgium's sovereignty was recognized.

From 1916, the civilian populations and economies of both sides were mobilized to an unprecedented degree. Hardships intensified among fighting nations in 1917 (French mutiny crushed in May). More than 10 million soldiers died in the war.

A huge **reparations** burden and partial demilitarization were imposed on Germany. Pres. Wilson obtained approval for a League of Nations, but the U.S. Senate refused to allow the U.S. to join.

Russian revolution. Military defeats and high casualties caused a contagious lack of confidence in Tsar Nicholas, who was forced to abdicate Mar. 1917. A liberal provisional government failed to end the war, and massive desertions, riots, and fighting between factions followed. A moderate socialist government under Aleksandr Kerensky was overthrown (Nov. 1917) in a violent coup by the **Bolsheviks** in Petrograd under **Lenin**, who later disbanded the elected Constituent Assembly.

The Bolsheviks brutally suppressed all opposition and ended the war with Germany in Mar. 1918. **Civil war** broke out in the summer between the Red Army (the Bolsheviks and their supporters), and monarchists, anarchists, minority nationalities (Ukrainians, Georgians, Poles), and others. Small U.S., British, French, and Japanese units also opposed the Bolsheviks (1918-19; Japan in Vladivostok to 1922). The civil war, anarchy, and pogroms devastated the country until the 1920 Red Army victory. The **Communist Party** leadership retained absolute power.

Other European revolutions. An unpopular monarchy in **Portugal** was overthrown in 1910. The new republic took severe anticlerical measures in 1911.

After a century of Home Rule agitation, during which **Ireland** was devastated by famine (1 million dead, 1846-47) and emigration, republican militants staged an unsuccessful uprising in Dublin during **Easter 1916**. The execution of the leaders and mass arrests by the British won popular support for the rebels. The **Irish Free State**, comprising all but the six northern counties, achieved dominion status in 1922.

In the aftermath of the world war, radical revolutions were attempted in Germany (**Spartacist** uprising, Jan. 1919), **Hungary** (Kun regime, 1919), and elsewhere. All were suppressed or failed for lack of support.

Chinese revolution. The Manchu Dynasty was overthrown and a republic proclaimed in Oct. 1911. First Pres. Sun Yat-sen resigned in favor of strongman Yuan Shih-k'ai. Sun organized the parliamentarian **Kuomintang** party.

Students launched protests on May 4, 1919, against League of Nations concessions in China to Japan. Nationalist, liberal,

Archduke of Austria Franz Ferdinand was assassinated in Sarajevo in 1914, precipitating the military conflict that escalated into World War I.

and socialist ideas and political groups spread. The **Communist Party** was founded in 1921. A Communist regime took power in Mongolia with Soviet support in 1921.

India restive. Indian objections to British rule erupted in nationalist riots as well as in the nonviolent tactics of Mahatma **Gandhi** (1869-1948). Nearly 400 unarmed demonstrators were shot at **Amritsar** in Apr. 1919. Britain approved limited self-rule that year.

Mexican revolution. Under the long Diaz dictatorship (1877-1911) the economy advanced, but Indian and mestizo lands were confiscated, and concessions to foreigners (mostly

U.S.) damaged the middle class. A **revolution in 1910** led to civil wars and U.S. intervention (1914, 1916-17). Land reform and a more democratic constitution (1917) were achieved.

Sciences. Scientific specialization prevailed by the 20th cent. Advances in knowledge and technological aptitude increased with the geometric rise in the number of practitioners. Physicists challenged common-sense views of causality, observation, and a mechanistic universe, putting science further beyond popular grasp (**Einstein**'s general theory of relativity, 1916; Bohr's quantum mechanics, 1913; Heisenberg's uncertainty principle, 1927).

Aftermath of War: 1920-29

U.S. Easy credit, technological ingenuity, and war-related industrial decline in Europe caused a long economic boom, in which ownership of new products—**autos, phones, radios**—became more democratized. **Prosperity**, an increase in women workers, women's suffrage (19th Amendment ratified, 1920), and drastic change in fashion (**flappers**, mannish bob for women, clean-shaven men) created a wide perception of social change, despite prohibition of alcoholic beverages (1919-33). Union membership and strikes increased. Fear of radicals led to Palmer raids (1919-20) and the Sacco-Vanzetti case (1921-27).

Europe sorts itself out. Germany's liberal **Weimar constitution** (1919) could not guarantee a stable government in the face of rightist violence (Rathenau assassinated, 1922) and Communist refusal to cooperate with Socialists. Reparations and Allied occupation of the Rhineland caused staggering inflation that destroyed middle-class savings, but economic expansion resumed after mid-decade, aided by U.S. loans. A sophisticated, **innovative culture** developed in architecture and design (Bauhaus, 1919-28), film (Lang, *M*, 1931), painting (Grosz), music (Weill, *Threepenny Opera*, 1928), theater (Brecht, *A Man's a Man*, 1926), criticism (Benjamin), philosophy (Jung), and fashion. This culture was considered decadent and socially disruptive by rightists.

England elected its first Labour governments (Jan. 1924, June 1929). A 10-day general strike in support of coal miners failed in May 1926. In **Italy**, strikes, political chaos, and violence by small Fascist bands culminated in the Oct. 1922 Fascist March on Rome, which established **Mussolini**'s dictatorship. Strikes were outlawed (1926), and Italian influence was pressed in the Balkans (Albania made a protectorate, 1926). A conservative dictatorship was also established in **Portugal** in a 1926 military coup.

Czechoslovakia, the only stable democracy to emerge from the war in Central or E Europe, faced opposition from Germans (in the Sudetenland), Ruthenians, and some Slovaks. As the industrial heartland of the old Habsburg empire, it remained fairly prosperous. With French backing, it formed the Little Entente with Yugoslavia (1920) and **Romania** (1921) to block Austrian or Hungarian irredentism. Croats and Slovenes in **Yugoslavia** demanded a state until King Alexander I proclaimed (1929) a royal dictatorship. Poland faced internal nationality problems as well (Germans, Ukrainians, Jews); Pilsudski ruled as dictator from 1926. The Baltic states were threatened by traditionally dominant ethnic Germans and by Soviet-supported Communists.

An economic collapse and famine in **Russia** (1921-22) claimed 5 million lives. The New Economic Policy (1921) allowed land ownership by peasants and some private commerce and industry. **Stalin** was absolute ruler within four years of Lenin's death (1924). He inaugurated a brutal collectivization program (1929-32) and used foreign Communist parties for Soviet state advantage. Industrialization advanced rapidly.

Internationalism. Revulsion against World War I led to pacifist agitation, to the Kellogg-Briand Pact renouncing

aggressive war (1928), and to **naval disarmament** pacts (Washington, 1922; London, 1930). But the League of Nations was able to arbitrate only minor disputes (Greece-Bulgaria, 1925). A number of countries pulled back from global contacts, as with American isolationism and Russia's separation from international capitalism.

Middle East. Mustafa Kemal (**Ataturk**) led **Turkish** nationalists in resisting Italian, French, and Greek military advances (1919-23). The sultanate was abolished (1922), and elaborate reforms were passed, including secularization of law and adoption of the Latin alphabet. Ethnic conflict led to persecution of **Armenians** (more than 1 million dead in 1915, 1 million expelled), Greeks (forced Greek-Turk population exchange, 1923), and Kurds (1925 uprising).

With evacuation of the Turks from **Arab** lands, the puritanical Wahabi dynasty of E Arabia conquered (1919-25) what is now Saudi Arabia. British, French, and Arab dynastic and nationalist maneuvering resulted in the creation of two more Arab monarchies in 1921—Iraq and Transjordan (both under British control)—and two French mandates—Syria and Lebanon. Jewish immigration into British-mandated **Palestine**, inspired by the Zionist movement, was resisted by Arabs, at times violently (1921, 1929 massacres).

Reza Khan ruled **Persia** after his 1921 coup (shah from 1925), centralized control, and created the trappings of a modern secular state.

In 1922, English archaeologist Howard Carter discovered the tomb of the boy pharaoh **Tutankhamen** in the Valley of the Kings in Egypt.

China. The Kuomintang under **Chiang Kai-shek** (1887-1975) subdued the warlords by 1928. The Communists were brutally suppressed after their alliance with the Kuomintang was broken in 1927. Relative peace thereafter allowed for industrial and financial improvements, with some Russian, British, and U.S. cooperation.

Arts. Nearly all bounds of subject matter, style, and attitude were broken in the arts of the period. **Abstract** art first took inspiration from natural forms or narrative themes (Kandinsky from 1911) and then worked free of any representational aims (Malevich's suprematism, 1915-19; Mondrian's geometric style from 1917). The **Dada** movement (from 1916) mocked artistic pretension with absurd collages and constructions. Paradox, illusion, and psychological taboos were exploited by **surrealists** by the late 1920s (Dali, Magritte). Architectural schools celebrated industrial values, whether vigorous abstract constructivism (Tatlin, *Monument to the Third International*, 1919) or the machined, streamlined **Bauhaus** style, which was extended to many design fields (Helvetica typeface).

Prose writers explored revolutionary narrative modes related to dreams (Kafka's *Trial*, 1925), internal monologue (Joyce's *Ulysses*, 1922), and word play (Stein's *Making of Americans*, 1925). Poets and novelists wrote of modern alienation (Eliot's *Waste Land*, 1922) and aimlessness ("The Lost Generation").

Rise of Totalitarians: 1930-39

Depression. A worldwide financial panic and economic depression began with the Oct. 1929 U.S. stock market crash and the May 1931 failure of the Austrian Credit-Anstalt. A credit crunch caused international bankruptcies and **unemployment**: 12 million jobless by 1932 in the U.S., 5.6 million in Germany, 2.7 million in England. Governments responded with **tariff restrictions** (Smoot-Hawley Act, 1930; Ottawa Imperial Conference, 1932), which dried up world trade. Government public works programs were vitiated by deflationary budget balancing.

Germany. Years of agitation by violent extremists were brought to a head by the Depression. Nazi leader Adolf Hitler was named chancellor in Jan. 1933 and given dictatorial power by the Reichstag in Mar. Opposition parties were disbanded, strikes banned, and all aspects of economic, cultural, and religious life were brought under central government and Nazi party control and manipulated by sophisticated propaganda. Severe persecution of Jews began (**Nuremberg Laws**, Sept. 1935). Many Jews, political opponents, and others were sent to concentration camps

Italy's Benito Mussolini and Germany's Adolf Hitler affirmed their full political and military alliance with the Pact of Steel (1939).

(Dachau, 1933), where thousands died or were killed. Public works, renewed conscription (1935), arms production, and a four-year plan (1936) all but ended unemployment.

Hitler's expansionism started with reincorporation of the Saar (1935), occupation of the **Rhineland** (Mar. 1936), and annexation of Austria (Mar. 1938). At **Munich** (Sept. 1938) Britain and France attempted to appease Hitler and avoid war by successfully encouraging Czechoslovakia's surrender of the Sudetenland territory.

Russia. Rapid industrialization was achieved through successive **five-year plans** starting in 1928, using severe labor discipline and mass forced labor. Industry was financed by exploitation of agriculture, which was almost totally collectivized by the early 1930s (*kolkhoz* [collective farm]; *sovkhoz* [state farm], often in newly worked lands). Millions perished in a series of manufactured disasters: extermination (1929-34) of kulaks (peasant landowners), severe famine (1932-33), party purges and show trials (Great Purge, 1936-38), suppression of nationalities, and poor conditions in labor camps. Purges also increased Stalin's power in the Communist party.

Spain. An industrial revolution during World War I created an urban proletariat, which was attracted to socialism and anarchism; Catalan nationalists challenged central authority. The five years after King Alfonso left Spain in Apr. 1931 were dominated by tension between intermittent leftist and anticlerical governments and clericals, monarchists, and other rightists. Anarchist and Communist rebellions were crushed, but a July 1936 extreme right rebellion led by Gen. Francisco **Franco** and aided by Nazi Germany and Fascist Italy succeeded after

a three-year **civil war** (more than 1 million dead in battles and atrocities). The war polarized international public opinion.

Italy. Despite propaganda for the ideal of the Corporate State, few domestic reforms were attempted. An entente with Hungary and Austria (Mar. 1934), a pact with Germany and Japan (Nov. 1937), and intervention by 50,000-75,000 troops in Spain (1936-39) sealed Italy's identification with the fascist bloc (anti-Semitic laws after Mar. 1938). Ethiopia was conquered (1935-36) and Albania annexed (Jan. 1939) in conscious imitation of ancient Rome.

Eastern Europe. Repressive regimes fought for power against an active opposition (liberals, socialists, Communists, peasants, Nazis). Minority groups and Jews were restricted within national boundaries that did not coincide with ethnic population patterns. In the destruction of **Czechoslovakia**, Hungary occupied S Slovakia (Nov. 1938) and Ruthenia (Mar. 1939), and a pro-Nazi regime took power in the rest of Slovakia. Other boundary disputes (e.g., Poland-Lithuania, Yugoslavia-Bulgaria, and Romania-Hungary) doomed attempts to build joint fronts against Germany or Russia. Economic depression was severe.

East Asia. After a period of liberalism in **Japan**, nativist militarists dominated the government with peasant support. Manchuria was seized (Sept. 1931-Feb. 1932), and a puppet state was set up (Manchukuo). Adjacent Jehol (Inner Mongolia) was occupied in 1933. **China** proper was invaded in July 1937; large areas were conquered by Oct. 1938. Hundreds of thousands of rapes, murders, and other atrocities were attributed to the Japanese.

Communist forces left Kuomintang-besieged strongholds in the S of China in a Long March (1934-35) to the N. The Kuomintang-Communist civil war was suspended in Jan. 1937 in the face of threatening Japan.

Democracies. The Roosevelt Administration, in office Mar. 1933, embarked on an extensive program of **New Deal** social reform and economic stimulation, including protection for labor unions (heavy industries organized), Social Security, public works, wage-and-hour laws, and assistance to farmers. Isolationist sentiment (1937 Neutrality Act) prevented U.S. intervention in Europe, but military expenditures were increased in 1939.

French political instability and polarization prevented resolution of economic and international security questions. The **Popular Front** government under Leon Blum (June 1936-Apr. 1938) passed social reforms (40-hour work week) and raised arms spending. National coalition governments, which ruled Britain from Aug. 1931, brought economic recovery but failed to define a consistent international policy until Chamberlain's government (from May 1937), which practiced **appeasement** of Germany and Italy.

India. Twenty years of agitation for autonomy and then for independence (Gandhi's **salt march**, 1930) achieved some constitutional reform (extended provincial powers, 1935) despite Muslim-Hindu strife. Social issues assumed prominence with peasant uprisings (1921), strikes (1928), Gandhi's efforts for untouchables (1932 "fast unto death"), and social and agrarian reform by the provinces after 1937.

Arts. The streamlined, geometric design motifs of Art Deco (from 1925) prevailed through the 1930s. **Abstract art** flourished (Moore sculptures from 1931) alongside a new **realism** related to social and political concerns (Socialist Realism, the official Soviet style from 1934; Mexican muralist Rivera, 1886-1957; and Orozco, 1883-1949), which were also expressed in fiction and poetry (Steinbeck's *Grapes of Wrath*, 1939; Sandburg's *The People, Yes*, 1936). Modern architecture (International Style, 1932) was unchallenged in its use of artificial materials (concrete, glass), lack of decoration, and monumentality (Rockefeller Center, 1929-40). Larger-than-life U.S.-made films captured a worldwide audience (*Gone With the Wind*, *The Wizard of Oz*, both 1939).

War, Hot and Cold: 1940-49

War in Asia-Pacific. Japan occupied Indochina in Sept. 1940, dominated Thailand in Dec. 1941, and attacked Hawaii (**Pearl Harbor**), the Philippines, Hong Kong, and Malaya on Dec. 7, 1941 (precipitating U.S. entrance into the war). Indonesia was attacked in Jan. 1942, and Burma was conquered in Mar. 1942. The Battle of **Midway** (June 1942) turned back the Japanese advance. "Island-hopping" battles (**Guadalcanal**, Aug. 1942-Jan. 1943; **Leyte Gulf**, Oct. 1944; **Iwo Jima**,

Feb.-Mar. 1945; **Okinawa**, Apr. 1945) and massive bombing raids on Japan from June 1944 wore out Japanese defenses. U.S. atom bombs, dropped Aug. 6 and 9 on **Hiroshima** and **Nagasaki**, forced Japan to agree, on Aug. 14, to surrender; formal surrender was on Sept. 2, 1945.

War in Europe. The Nazi-Soviet nonaggression pact (Aug. 1939) freed Germany to attack Poland (Sept. 1939). Britain and France, which had guaranteed Polish independence,

World War II came to an end soon after atomic bombs devastated Hiroshima and Nagasaki, Japan (1945).

declared war on Germany. Russia seized E Poland (Sept. 1939), attacked Finland (Nov. 1939), and took the Baltic states (July 1940). Mobile German forces staged *blitzkrieg* attacks during Apr.-June 1940, conquering neutral Denmark, Norway, and the Low Countries and defeating France; 350,000 British and French troops were evacuated at **Dunkirk,** France (May). The **Battle of Britain** (June-Dec. 1940) denied Germany air superiority. German-Italian campaigns won the Balkans by Apr. 1941. Three million Axis troops **invaded Russia** in June 1941, marching through Ukraine to the Caucasus, and through White Russia and the Baltic republics to Moscow and Leningrad.

Russian winter counterthrusts (1941-42 and 1942-43) stopped the German advance (**Stalingrad,** Sept. 1942-Feb. 1943). Sustaining great casualties, the Russians drove the Axis from all E Europe and the Balkans in the next two years. Invasions of N Africa (Nov. 1942), Italy (Sept. 1943), and **Normandy** (launched on D-Day, June 6, 1944) brought U.S., British, Free French, and allied troops to Germany by spring 1945. In Feb. 1945, the three Allied leaders, Winston **Churchill** (Britain), Joseph **Stalin** (USSR), and Franklin D. **Roosevelt** (U.S.), met in Yalta to discuss strategy and resolve political issues, including the postwar Allied occupation of Germany. Germany surrendered May 7, 1945.

Atrocities. The war brought 20th-cent. cruelty to its peak. The Nazi regime systematically killed an estimated 5-6 million Jews, including some 3 million who died in death camps (e.g., **Auschwitz**). Gypsies, political opponents, people with mental or physical disabilities, and others deemed undesirable were also murdered by the Nazis, as were vast numbers of Slavs.

German bombs killed 70,000 British civilians. More than 100,000 Chinese civilians were killed by Japanese forces in the capture and occupation of Nanking. Severe retaliation by the Soviet army, E European partisans, Free French, and others took a heavy toll. U.S. and British bombing of Germany killed hundreds of thousands, as did U.S. bombing of Japan (80,000-200,000 at Hiroshima alone). Some 45 million people died in the war.

Settlement. The **United Nations** charter was signed in San Francisco on June 26, 1945, by 50 nations. The International Tribunal at **Nuremberg** convicted 22 German leaders for war crimes in Sept. 1946; 23 Japanese leaders were convicted in Nov. 1948. Postwar border changes included large gains in territory for the USSR, losses for Germany, a shift to the W in Polish borders, and minor losses for Italy. Communist regimes, supported by Soviet troops, took power in most of E Europe, including Soviet-occupied Germany (GDR, aka East Germany, proclaimed Oct. 1949). Japan lost all overseas lands. Global developments involved establishing new economic coordinating bodies like the International Monetary Fund (1944) and the Universal Declaration of Human Rights (1948).

Recovery. Basic political and social changes were imposed on Japan and W Germany by the Western allies (Japan constitution adopted, Nov. 1946; W German basic law, May 1949). U.S. **Marshall Plan** aid ($12 bil, 1947-51) spurred W European economic recovery after a period of severe inflation and strikes in Europe and the U.S. The British Labour Party introduced a national health service and nationalized basic industries in 1946.

Cold War. Western fears of further Soviet advances (Cominform formed in Oct. 1947; Czechoslovakia coup, Feb. 1948; Berlin blockade, Apr. 1948-Sept. 1949) led to the formation of **NATO.** Civil War in Greece and Soviet pressure on Turkey led to U.S. aid under the **Truman Doctrine** (Mar. 1947). Other anti-Communist security pacts were the Organization of American States (Apr. 1948) and the SE Asia Treaty Organization (Sept. 1954). A new wave of **Soviet purges** and repression intensified in the last years of Stalin's rule, extending to E Europe (Slansky trial in Czechoslovakia, 1951). Only Yugoslavia resisted Soviet control (expelled by Cominform, June 1948; U.S. aid, June 1949).

China, Korea. Communist forces emerged from World War II strengthened by the Soviet takeover of industrial Manchuria. In four years of fighting, the Kuomintang was driven from the mainland; the People's Republic of China was proclaimed Oct. 1, 1949. Korea was divided by USSR and U.S. occupation forces. Separate republics were proclaimed in the two zones in Aug.-Sept. 1948.

India. India and Pakistan became independent dominions on Aug. 15, 1947. Millions of Hindu and Muslim refugees were created by the partition. Riots (1946-47) took hundreds of thousands of lives. Mahatma **Gandhi** was assassinated in Jan. 1948. Burma became completely independent in Jan. 1948; Ceylon took dominion status in Feb.

Middle East. The UN approved partition of Palestine into Jewish and Arab states. **Israel** was proclaimed a state, May 14, 1948. Arabs rejected partition, but failed to defeat Israel in war (May 1948-July 1949). Immigration from Europe and the Middle East swelled Israel's Jewish population. British and French forces left Lebanon and Syria in 1946. Transjordan occupied most of Arab Palestine.

Southeast Asia. Communists and others fought against restoration of French rule in **Indochina** from 1946; a non-Communist government was recognized by France in Mar. 1949, but fighting continued. Both Indonesia and the Philippines became independent; the former in 1949 after four years of war with Netherlands, the latter in 1946. Philippine economic and military ties with the U.S. remained strong; a Communist-led peasant rising was checked in 1948.

Arts. New York became the center of the world art market; **abstract expressionism** was the chief mode (Pollock from 1943, de Kooning from 1947). Literature and philosophy explored **existentialism** (Camus's *The Stranger*, 1942; Sartre's *Being and Nothingness*, 1943). Non-Western attempts to revive or create regional styles (Senghor's Négritude, Mishima's novels) were responses to global cultural influences. Radio and phonograph records spread American popular music (swing, bebop) around the world.

The Cold War Decade: 1950-59

Decolonization. The relatively peaceful decline of European political and military power in Asia and Africa accelerated in the 1950s. Nearly all of **N Africa** was freed by 1956, but France fought a bitter war to retain Algeria, with its large European minority, until 1962. **Ghana,** independent in

1957, led a parade of new black African nations (more than two dozen by 1962), which altered the political character of the UN. Ethnic disputes often exploded in the new nations after decolonization (UN troops in Cyprus, 1964; **Nigerian civil war,** 1967-70). Leaders of the new states, mostly

Mao Zedong's Great Leap Forward policies caused one of history's worst famines (1958-62), in which tens of millions died.

sharing socialist ideologies, tried to create an Afro-Asian bloc (Bandung Conference, 1955), but Western economic influence and U.S. political ties remained strong (Baghdad Pact, 1955).

Trade. World trade volume soared, in an atmosphere of monetary stability assured by international accords (**Bretton Woods**, 1944). In Europe, economic integration advanced (**European Economic Community**, 1957; European Free Trade Association, 1960). Comecon (1949) coordinated the economies of Soviet-bloc countries. Global developments included transcontinental jet travel (first South Africa to Britain flight, 1952; introduction of term "jet lag," 1965) and the increasing spread of English in global business, sports, and transportation.

U.S. Economic growth produced an abundance of consumer goods (9.3 million motor vehicles sold, 1955). Suburban housing changed life patterns for middle and working classes (Levittown, NY, 1947-51). Pres. Dwight **Eisenhower's** landslide election victories (1952, 1956) reflected consensus politics. A system of alliances and military bases bolstered U.S. influence on all continents. Trade and payments surpluses were balanced by overseas investments and foreign aid ($50 bil, 1950-59).

USSR. In the "thaw" after Stalin's death in 1953, relations with the West improved (evacuation of Vienna, Geneva summit conference, both 1955). Repression of scientific and cultural life eased, and many prisoners were freed culminating in de-Stalinization (1956). **Nikita Khrushchev's** leadership aimed at consumer sector growth, but farm production lagged, despite the virgin lands program (from 1954). Soviet crushing of the 1956 Hungarian revolution, the 1960 U-2 spy plane episode, and other incidents renewed E-W tension and domestic curbs.

Eastern Europe. Resentment of Russian domination and Stalinist repression combined with nationalist, economic, and religious factors to produce periodic violence. E Berlin workers rioted (1953), Polish workers rioted in Poznan (June 1956), and a broad-based **revolution** broke out in **Hungary** (Oct. 1956). All

were suppressed by Soviet force or threats (at least 7,000 dead in Hungary), but Poland was allowed to restore private ownership of farms, and a degree of personal and economic freedom returned to Hungary. Yugoslavia experimented with worker self-management and a market economy.

Korea. The 1945 division of Korea along the 38th parallel left industry in the N, which was organized into a militant regime and armed by the USSR. The S was politically disunited. More than 60,000 N Korean troops invaded the S on June 25, 1950. The U.S., backed by the UN Security Council, sent troops. **UN troops** reached the Chinese border in Nov. Some 200,000 Chinese troops crossed the Yalu R. and drove back UN forces. By spring 1951, battle lines had become stabilized near the original 38th parallel border, but heavy fighting continued. Finally, an armistice was signed on July 27, 1953. U.S. troops remained in the S, and U.S. economic and military aid continued. The war stimulated rapid economic recovery in Japan.

China. Starting in 1952, industry, agriculture, and social institutions were forcibly collectivized. In a massive purge, as many as several million people were executed as Kuomintang supporters or as class and political enemies. The **Great Leap Forward** (1958-60) unsuccessfully tried to force the pace of development by substituting labor for investment.

Indochina. Ho Chi Minh's forces, aided by the USSR and the new Chinese Communist government, fought French and pro-French Vietnamese forces to a standstill and captured the strategic **Dien Bien Phu** camp in May 1954. The Geneva Agreements divided Vietnam in half pending elections (never held) and recognized Laos and Cambodia as independent. The U.S. aided the anti-Communist Republic of Vietnam in the S.

Middle East. Arab revolutions placed leftist, militantly nationalist regimes in power in Egypt (1952) and Iraq (1958). But Arab unity attempts failed (United Arab Republic joined Egypt, Syria, Yemen, 1958-61). Arab refusal to recognize Israel (Arab League economic blockade began Sept. 1951) led to a permanent **state of war**, with repeated incidents (Gaza, 1955). Israel occupied Sinai, and Britain and France took (Oct. 1956) the Suez Canal, but were replaced by the UN Emergency Force. The Mossadegh government in Iran nationalized (May 1951) the British-owned oil industry in May, but was overthrown (Aug. 1953) in a U.S.-aided coup.

Latin America. Argentinian dictator Juan **Perón**, in office 1946, crushed opposition and enforced land reform, some nationalization, welfare state measures, and curbs on the Roman Catholic Church. A Sept. 1955 coup deposed Perón. The 1952 revolution in Bolivia brought land reform, nationalization of tin mines, and improvement in the status of Native Americans, who nevertheless remained poor. The Batista regime in Cuba was overthrown (Jan. 1959) by Fidel **Castro**, who imposed a Communist dictatorship, aligned Cuba with the USSR, and improved education and health care. A U.S.-backed anti-Castro invasion (**Bay of Pigs**, Apr. 1961) was crushed. Self-government advanced in the British Caribbean.

Technology. Large outlays on research and development in the U.S. and the USSR focused on military applications (H-bomb in U.S., 1952; USSR, 1953; Britain, 1957; intercontinental missiles, late 1950s). Soviet launching of the **Sputnik** satellite (Oct. 4, 1957) spurred increases in U.S. science education funds (National Defense Education Act).

Literature and film. Alienation from social and literary conventions reached an extreme in the theater of the absurd (Beckett's *Waiting for Godot*, 1952), the "new novel" (Robbe-Grillet's *Voyeur*, 1955), and avant-garde film (Antonioni's *L'Avventura*, 1960). U.S. beatniks (Kerouac's *On the Road*, 1957) and others rejected the supposed conformism of Americans (Riesman's *The Lonely Crowd*, 1950).

Rising Expectations and New Protests: 1960-69

Global economy. The longest sustained economic boom on record spanned almost the entire decade in the capitalist world; the closely watched GNP figure doubled (1960-70) in the U.S., fueled by Vietnam War-related budget deficits. The **General Agreement on Tariffs and Trade** (1967) stimulated W European prosperity, which spread to peripheral areas (Spain, Italy, E Germany). Japan became a top economic power. Foreign investment aided the industrialization of Brazil. There were limited Soviet economic reform attempts. Outside the Soviet

zone the global economy was marked by the growing role of multinational corporations (3,000 in 1914; 6,000 by 1970). International Non-Government Organizations also multiplied rapidly (Amnesty International, 1961). The United Nations began sponsoring international "Years of Women" (1964).

Reform and radicalization. Pres. John F. Kennedy, inaugurated 1961, emphasized youthful idealism and vigor; his assassination Nov. 22, 1963, was a national trauma. A series of political and social reform movements took root in the U.S. and

American astronauts walked on the moon (1969) just a dozen years after the Soviet Union launched the first human-made satellite into orbit.

other countries. Blacks demonstrated nonviolently and with partial success against segregation and poverty (1963 March on Washington; 1964 **Civil Rights Act**), but some urban areas erupted in extensive riots (Watts, 1965; Detroit, 1967; **Martin Luther King Jr.** assassination, Apr. 4, 1968). New concern for the poor (Harrington's *Other America*, 1963) helped lead to Pres. Lyndon Johnson's **"Great Society"** programs (Medicare, Water Quality Act, Higher Education Act, all 1965). Concern for the **environment** surged (Carson's *Silent Spring*, 1962).

Feminism revived as a cultural and political movement (Friedan's *Feminine Mystique*, 1963; National Organization for Women founded, 1966), and a movement for homosexual rights emerged (Stonewall riot in NYC, 1969). Pope John XXIII called the **Second Vatican Council** (1962-65), which liberalized Roman Catholic liturgy and some other aspects of Catholicism.

Opposition to U.S. involvement in Vietnam, especially among university students (**Moratorium** protest, Nov. 1969), turned violent (Weatherman Chicago riots, Oct. 1969). **New Left** and Marxist theories became popular, and membership in radical groups (Students for a Democratic Society, Black Panthers) increased. Maoist groups, especially in Europe, called for total transformation of society. In France, students sparked a nationwide strike affecting 10 million workers in May-June 1968, but an electoral reaction barred revolutionary change.

China. China's revolutionary militancy under **Mao Zedong** caused disputes with the USSR under "revisionist" Khrushchev, starting in 1960. The two powers exchanged fire in 1969 border disputes. China used force to capture (1962) areas disputed with India. The **"Great Proletarian Cultural Revolution"** tried to impose a utopian egalitarian program in China and spread revolution abroad; political struggle, often violent, convulsed China in 1965-68.

Indochina. Communist-led guerrillas aided by N Vietnam fought from 1960 against the S Vietnam government of Ngo Dinh Diem (killed 1963). The U.S. military role increased after the 1964 **Tonkin Gulf** incident. U.S. forces there peaked at 543,400 in Apr. 1969. Massive numbers of N Vietnamese troops also fought. Laotian and Cambodian neutrality were threatened by Communist insurgencies, with N Vietnamese aid, and U.S. intrigues.

Developing world. A bloc of authoritarian leftist regimes among the newly independent nations emerged in political opposition to the U.S.-led Western alliance and came to dominate the conference of nonaligned nations (Belgrade, 1961; Cairo, 1964; Lusaka, 1970). Soviet political ties and military bases were established in Cuba, Egypt, Algeria, Guinea, and other countries whose leaders were regarded as revolutionary heroes by opposition groups in pro-Western or colonial countries. Some leaders were ousted in coups by pro-Western groups—Dem. Rep. of the Congo's Patrice Lumumba (killed 1961), Ghana's Kwame Nkrumah (exiled 1966), and Indonesia's Sukarno (effectively ousted in 1965 after a Communist coup failed).

Middle East. Arab-Israeli tension erupted into a brief war June 1967. Israel emerged from the war as a major regional power. Military shipments before and after the war increased Soviet influence in much of the Arab world. Most Arab states broke U.S. diplomatic ties, while Communist countries cut their ties to Israel. Intra-Arab disputes continued: Egypt and Saudi Arabia supported rival factions in a bloody Yemen civil war 1962-70; Lebanese troops fought Palestinian commandos 1969.

Eastern Europe. To stop the large-scale exodus of citizens, E German authorities built (Aug. 1961) a fortified **wall across Berlin**. Soviet sway in the Balkans was weakened by Albania's support of China (USSR broke ties in Dec. 1961) and Romania's assertion (1964) of industrial and foreign policy autonomy. Liberalization (spring 1968) in Czechoslovakia was crushed with massive force by troops of five Warsaw Pact countries. W German treaties (1970) with the USSR and Poland facilitated the transfer of German technology and confirmed postwar boundaries.

Arts and styles. The boundary between fine and popular arts was blurred to some extent by Pop Art (Warhol) and rock musicals (*Hair*, 1968). Informality and exaggeration prevailed in fashion (beards, miniskirts). A nonpolitical "counterculture" developed, rejecting traditional bourgeois life goals and personal habits, and use of marijuana and hallucinogens spread (**Woodstock** festival, Aug. 1969). Indian influence was felt in religion (Ram Dass) and fashion, and **The Beatles**, who brought unprecedented sophistication to rock music, became for many a symbol of the decade.

Science. Achievements in space (**humans on the moon**, July 1969) and electronics (lasers, integrated circuits) encouraged a faith in scientific solutions to problems in agriculture ("green revolution"), medicine (heart transplants, 1967), and other areas. Harmful technology, it was believed, could be controlled (1963 Limited Test Ban Treaty, 1968 Nuclear Nonproliferation Treaty).

New Global Balances and Religious Revivals: 1970-79

U.S.: Caution and neoconservatism. A relatively sluggish economy, energy shortages, and environmental problems contributed to a **"limits of growth"** philosophy. Suspicion of science and technology killed or delayed major projects (supersonic transport dropped, 1971) and was fed by the Three Mile Island nuclear reactor accident (Mar. 1979).

There were signs of growing mistrust of government and less support for new policies. School busing and racial quotas were opposed (Bakke decision, June 1978); the Equal Rights Amendment for women languished; civil rights legislation aimed at protecting homosexuals was opposed (Dade County referendum, June 1977).

Completion of Communist forces' takeover of **South Vietnam** (evacuation of U.S. civilians, Apr. 1975), revelations of Central Intelligence Agency misdeeds (Rockefeller Commission report, June 1975), and **Watergate** scandals (Nixon resigned in Aug. 1974) reduced faith in U.S. moral and material capacity to influence world affairs. Revelations of Soviet crimes (Solzhenitsyn's *Gulag Archipelago*, 1974) and Soviet intervention in Africa helped foster a revival of anti-Communist sentiment.

Economy sluggish. The 1960s boom faltered in the 1970s; a severe recession in the U.S. and Europe (1974-75) followed a huge oil price hike (Dec. 1973). Monetary instability (U.S. cut ties to gold in Aug. 1971), the decline of the dollar, and protectionist moves by industrial countries (1977-78) threatened trade. Business investment and spending for research declined. Severe inflation plagued many countries (25% in Britain, 1975; 18% in U.S., 1979).

China readjusts. After the 1976 deaths of Mao Zedong and Zhou Enlai, struggle for the leadership succession was won by pragmatists. A nationwide purge of orthodox Maoists was carried out, and the **Gang of Four**, led by Mao's widow, Chiang Ching, was arrested. The new leaders freed more than 100,000 political prisoners and reduced public adulation of Mao. Political and trade ties were expanded with Japan, Europe, and the U.S. in the late 1970s, as relations worsened with the USSR, Cuba, and Vietnam (four-week invasion by China, 1979). Ideological guidelines in industry, science, education, and the armed forces, which the ruling faction said had caused chaos and decline, were reversed

The Vietnam War, in which an estimated 2 million Vietnamese and 50,000 Americans died, also engulfed Laos and Cambodia.

(bonuses to workers, Dec. 1977; exams for college entrance, Oct. 1977). Severe restrictions on cultural expression were eased.

Europe. European unity moves (EEC-EFTA trade accord, 1972) faltered as economic problems appeared (Britain floated pound, 1972; France floated franc, 1974). Germany and Switzerland curbed guest workers from S Europe. Greece and Turkey quarreled over Cyprus and Aegean oil rights.

All non-Communist Europe was under democratic rule after free elections (June 1976) in **Spain** seven months after the death of Franco. The conservative, colonialist regime in **Portugal** was overthrown in Apr. 1974. In **Greece** the seven-year military dictatorship yielded power in 1974. N Europe, though ruled mostly by Socialists, became more conservative. The **British** Labour government imposed (1975) wage curbs and suspended nationalization schemes. Terrorism in **Germany** (1972 Munich Olympics killings) led to laws curbing some civil liberties. **French** "new philosophers" rejected leftist ideologies, and the Socialist-Communist coalition lost a 1978 election bid.

Religion and politics. The improvement in **Muslim** countries' political fortunes by the 1950s (with the exception of Central Asia under Soviet and Chinese rule) and the growth of Arab oil wealth were followed by a resurgence of traditional religious fervor. Libyan dictator Muammar al-Qaddafi mixed Islamic laws with socialism. The illegal Muslim Brotherhood in **Egypt** was accused of violence, while extreme groups bombed (1977) theaters to protest Western and secular values.

In **Turkey**, the National Salvation Party was the first Islamic group to share (1974) power since secularization in the 1920s. In **Iran**, Ayatollah Ruhollah **Khomeini** led a revolution that deposed the secular shah (Jan. 1979) and created an Islamic republic. Religiously motivated Muslims took part in an insurrection in Saudi Arabia that briefly seized (1979) the Grand Mosque in Mecca. Muslim puritan opposition to **Pakistan** Pres. Zulfikar Ali-Bhutto helped lead to his overthrow in July 1977. Muslim solidarity, however, could not prevent Pakistan's eastern province (**Bangladesh**) from declaring (Dec. 1971) independence after a bloody civil war.

Muslim and Hindu resentment of coerced sterilization in **India** helped defeat the Indira Gandhi government, and a coalition including religious Hindu parties replaced it (Mar. 1977). Muslims in the S **Philippines**, aided by Libya, rebelled against central rule from 1973. The Buddhist Soka Gakkai movement launched (1964) the Komeito party in **Japan**, which became a major opposition party in 1972 and 1976 elections.

Evangelical Protestant groups grew in the U.S. A revival of interest in Orthodox Christianity occurred among **Russian** intellectuals (Solzhenitsyn). The secularist **Israeli** Labor party, after decades of rule, was ousted in 1977 by conservatives led by Menachem Begin; religious militants founded settlements on the disputed West Bank, part of biblically promised Israel. Reform Judaism in U.S. revived many previously discarded traditional practices.

Religious wars raged intermittently in **Northern Ireland** (Catholic vs. Protestant, 1969-97) and **Lebanon** (Christian vs. Muslim, 1975-90), while religious militancy complicated the Israel-Arab dispute (1973 Israel-Arab war). The Camp David Accords in 1978, negotiated by Egyptian Pres. Anwar al-Sadat, Israeli Prime Min. Menachem Begin, and U.S. Pres. Jimmy Carter, facilitated the landmark 1979 **Egypt-Israel peace treaty**, but increased militancy on the West Bank impeded further progress.

Latin America. Repressive conservative regimes strengthened their hold, with a violent coup against the elected (Sept. 1973) Allende government in **Chile**, military coup in **Argentina** (1976), and coups against reformist regimes in **Bolivia** (1971, 1979) and **Peru** (1976). In Central America, increasing liberal and leftist militancy led to the ouster (1979) of the Somoza regime of **Nicaragua** and to civil conflict in **El Salvador**.

Indochina. Communist victories in Vietnam, Cambodia, and Laos by May 1975 led to new turmoil. The Pol Pot regime ordered millions to resettle in rural areas, in a program of forced labor and terrorism that cost more than 1 million lives (1975-79) and caused hundreds of thousands to flee. The Vietnamese invasion of Cambodia (1979) swelled the refugee population and contributed to widespread starvation.

Russian expansion. Soviet influence, checked in some countries (troops ousted by Egypt, 1972), was projected farther afield, often with the use of Cuban troops (Angola, 1975-89; Ethiopia, 1977-88) and aided by a growing navy, a merchant fleet, and international banking ability. Détente with the West—1972 Berlin pact, 1972 strategic arms pact (**SALT**)—gave way to a more antagonistic relationship in the late 1970s, exacerbated by the Soviet invasion (1979) of **Afghanistan**.

Africa. The last remaining European colonies were granted independence (**Spanish Sahara**, 1976; **Djibouti**, 1977), and, after 10 years of civil war, a black government took over (1979) in **Zimbabwe** (Rhodesia); white domination remained in **South Africa**. European involvement in local wars (Russia in **Angola, Ethiopia**; France in **Chad, Zaire, Mauritania**) and the use of tens of thousands of Cuban troops were denounced by some African leaders. Ethnic or tribal clashes made Africa a locus of sustained warfare during the late 1970s.

Arts. Traditional modes of painting, architecture, and music received increased popular and critical attention in the 1970s. These more conservative styles coexisted with modernist works in an atmosphere of increased variety and tolerance.

End of the Cold War and Demand for Democracy: 1980-89

Global developments. International contacts accelerated thanks to new openness in China (1978) and USSR (1985); global consumerism was symbolized by the rapid spread of McDonald's restaurants (Japan, 1971; Russia, 1990).

USSR, Eastern Europe. The late 1980s saw the remaking of the Soviet state and the beginning of the disintegration of the Soviet empire. After the deaths of Gen. Sec. Leonid Brezhnev (1982) and two successors, the harsh treatment of dissent and restriction of emigration, and the Soviet invasion (Dec. 1979) of Afghanistan, Gen. Sec. Mikhail Gorbachev (in office 1985-91) promoted *glasnost* and *perestroika*—economic, political, and social reform. Supported by the Communist Party (July 1988), he signed (Dec. 1987) the INF disarmament treaty. Military withdrawal from Afghanistan was completed in Feb. 1989, and the Soviet people chose (Mar. 1989) part of the new Congress of People's Deputies from competing candidates. By decade's end the **Cold War** appeared to be fading away.

In **Poland**, Solidarity, the labor union founded (1980) by Lech Walesa, was outlawed in 1982 and then legalized in 1988, after years of unrest. Poland's first free election since the Communist takeover brought **Solidarity** victory (June 1989); Tadeusz Mazowiecki, a Walesa adviser, became (Aug. 1989) prime minister in a government with the Communists. In the fall of 1989 the failure of Marxist economies in **Hungary, East Germany, Czechoslovakia, Bulgaria,** and **Romania** brought the collapse of the Communist monopoly and a demand for democracy. In a historic step, the **Berlin Wall** was opened in Nov. 1989.

U.S. The **"Reagan Years"** (1981-88) featured new economic policies via budget and tax cuts, deregulation, "junk bond" financing, leveraged buyouts, and mergers. However, there was a stock market crash (Oct. 1987), and federal budget deficits and the trade deficit increased. Foreign policy showed a **strong anti-Communist stance**, via increased defense spending, aid to anti-Communists in Central America, invasion of

Benazir Bhutto became Pakistan's first woman prime minister (1988) and the first woman ever elected to lead a Muslim nation.

Cuba-threatened Grenada, and championing of the "Star Wars" missile defense program. Four Reagan-Gorbachev summits (1985-88) climaxed in the INF treaty (1987), as the Cold War began to wind down. The **Iran-Contra affair** (Oliver North's testimony, July 1987) was a major political scandal. In 1988, Vice Pres. George H. W. Bush was elected to succeed Ronald Reagan as president.

Middle East. The Middle East remained militarily unstable, with sharp divisions along economic, political, racial, and religious lines. In **Iran**, the Islamic revolution of 1979 created a strong anti-U.S. stance (hostage crisis, Nov. 1979-Jan. 1981). In Sept. 1980, **Iraq** repudiated its border agreement with Iran and began major hostilities that led to an eight-year war in which hundreds of thousands of people were killed.

Libya's support for international terrorism induced the U.S. to close (May 1981) its diplomatic mission there and embargo (Mar. 1982) Libyan oil. The U.S. accused Libyan leader Muammar al-Qaddafi of aiding (Dec. 1985) terrorists. Following attack on a West Berlin disco frequented by U.S. military, U.S. bombed targets in Libya (Apr. 1986).

Israel affirmed (July 1980) all Jerusalem as its capital, destroyed (June 1981) an Iraqi atomic reactor, and invaded Lebanon, citing terrorism from the Palestine Liberation Organization; PLO withdrew after cease-fire. A **Palestinian** uprising began (Dec. 1987) in Israeli-occupied Gaza and spread to the West Bank; troops responded with force, killing 300 by the end of 1988, with 6,000 more in detention camps. Israeli withdrawal from **Lebanon** began in Feb. 1985 and ended in June 1985, as Lebanon continued to be torn by military and political conflict. Artillery duels (Mar.-Apr. 1989) between Christian East Beirut and Muslim West Beirut left 200 dead and 700 wounded.

Latin America. In **Nicaragua**, the leftist Sandinista National Liberation Front, in power after the 1979 civil war, faced problems as a result of Nicaragua's military aid to leftist guerrillas in El Salvador and U.S. backing of antigovernment contras. The CIA admitted (1984) having directed the mining of Nicaraguan ports, and the U.S. sent humanitarian (1985) and military (1986) aid. Profits from **secret arms sales** to Iran were found (1987) diverted to contras. Cease-fire talks between the Sandinista government and contras came in 1988, and elections were held in Nicaragua in Feb. 1990.

In **El Salvador**, a military coup (Oct. 1979) failed to halt extremist terrorism. Archbishop Oscar Romero was assassinated in Mar. 1980; from Jan. to June some 4,000 civilians were killed in the civil unrest. In 1984, newly elected Pres. José Napoleon Duarte worked to stem human rights abuses, but violence continued.

In **Chile**, Gen. Augusto Pinochet yielded the presidency after a democratic election (Dec. 1989), but remained as head of the army. He had ruled the country since 1973, imposing harsh measures against leftists and dissidents.

Africa. The 1980s saw continuing economc decline in virtually all African countries, a result of accelerating desertification, the world economic recession, heavy indebtedness to overseas creditors, rapid population growth, and political instability. Some 60 million Africans faced prolonged hunger in 1981. Much of Africa had one of the worst **droughts** ever in 1983, and by year's end, one-third of the population, or about 150 million, were near **famine**. Live Aid, a marathon rock concert, was presented in July 1985, and the U.S. and Western nations sent aid in Sept. 1985. Wars in Ethiopia and Sudan and military strife in several other nations continued. **HIV/AIDS** took a heavy toll.

Anti-apartheid sentiment gathered force in **South Africa** as demonstrations and violent police response grew. White voters approved (Nov. 1983) the first constitution to give "Coloureds" (people of mixed-race background) and Asians a voice, while still excluding blacks (70% of the population). The U.S. imposed economic sanctions in Aug. 1985, and 11 Western nations followed in Sept. 1985. Pres. P. W. **Botha** was succeeded by F. W. **de Klerk**, in Sept. 1989, who promised "evolutionary" change via negotiation with the black population.

Asia and the Pacific. Benazir **Bhutto** became the first woman to lead a majority-Muslim nation as prime minister of **Pakistan** (Dec. 1988). The "people power" revolt in the **Philippines** ousted Ferdinand **Marcos** (Feb. 1986) after two decades as president; replaced by Corazon **Aquino**.

During the 1980s **China**'s Communist government and paramount leader **Deng Xiaoping** pursued far-reaching changes, expanding commercial and technical ties to the industrialized world and increasing the role of market forces in stimulating urban development. Apr. 1989 brought new demands for political reforms; student demonstrators camped out in **Tiananmen Square**, Beijing, in a massive peaceful protest. Some 100,000 students and workers marched, and at least 20 other cities saw protests. In response, martial law was imposed; army troops crushed the demonstration in and around Tiananmen Square on June 3-4, with death toll estimates of 500-7,000, up to 10,000 dissidents arrested, 31 people tried and executed. The conciliatory Communist Party chief was ousted; the Politburo adopted (July 1989) reforms against official corruption.

Japan's relations with other nations, especially the U.S., were dominated by **trade imbalances** favoring Japan. Western Europe and the U.S. accused Japan of restrictive trade policies.

Europe. With the addition of Greece, Portugal, and Spain, the European Community became a common market of more than 300 million people. Margaret **Thatcher** became the first British prime minister in the 20th cent. to win a third consecutive term (1987). **France** elected (1981) its first socialist president, François **Mitterrand**, who was reelected in 1988. Elections in 1983 brought **Italy** its first socialist premier, Bettino **Craxi**.

International terrorism. With the 1979 **overthrow of the shah** of Iran and with instablity in the Middle East, terrorism became a prominent tactic. In 1979-81, Iranian militants held 52 **U.S. hostages in Iran** for 444 days; in 1983 a TNT-laden suicide terrorist blew up U.S. Marine headquarters in Beirut, killing 241 Americans, and a truck bomb blew up a French paratroop barracks, killing 58. The *Achille Lauro* cruise ship was hijacked in 1985, and an American passenger killed; the U.S. subsequently intercepted the Egyptian plane flying the terrorists to safety. Incidents rose to 700 in 1985, and to 1,000 in 1988. **Assassinated leaders** included Egypt's Pres. Anwar al-Sadat (1981), India's Prime Min. Indira **Gandhi** (1984), and Lebanese Prem. Rashid **Karami** (1987).

New Regional Tensions in the Post-Cold War World: 1990-99

Global developments. Nations in the 1990s made post-Cold War adjustments; a growing awareness of globalization developed with further spread of democracy. Global contacts accelerated with the growth of the Internet (1990). Efforts to deal with global environmental change intensified with tentative agreements in Kyoto, Japan (1997). A milestone protest against global economic trends burst forth in a World Bank meeting in Seattle (1999).

Soviet Empire breakup. The breakup of the Soviet Union into 15 independent states began with declarations of

independence by the Baltic republics of **Lithuania**, **Latvia**, and **Estonia** during an abortive coup against Mikhail **Gorbachev** (Aug. 1991). Other republics soon took the same step. In Dec. 1991, **Russia**, **Ukraine**, and **Belarus** declared the Soviet Union dead; Gorbachev resigned, and the Soviet Parliament went out of existence. The Warsaw Pact and the Council for Mutual Economic Assistance (Comecon) were disbanded. Most of the former Soviet republics joined in a loose confederation called the **Commonwealth of Independent States**. Russia's people suffered severe economic hardship as the nation, under Pres. Boris **Yeltsin**, moved to reboot the economy under a free market system. In Oct. 1993, **anti-Yeltsin forces** occupied the Parliament building and were ousted by the army.

The Muslim republic of **Chechnya** declared independence from the rest of Russia, but this was met with an invasion by Russian troops (Dec. 1994). A cease-fire took hold in 1996, and the Russians withdrew. In 1999 Russia forcibly suppressed Muslim insurgents in Dagestan and entered Chechnya, again fighting separatist rebels there. Yeltsin resigned Dec. 31, 1999, to be replaced by Vladimir **Putin** (elected in his own right, Mar. 2000).

Europe. Yugoslavia broke apart, and hostilities ensued along ethnic and religious lines. **Croatia**, **Slovenia**, and **Macedonia** declared independence (1991), followed by **Bosnia-Herzegovina** (1992). **Serbia** and **Montenegro** remained as the republic of Yugoslavia. Bitter fighting followed, especially in Bosnia, where Serbs reportedly engaged in **"ethnic cleansing"** of the Muslim population; a peace plan (Dayton accord, 1995), brokered by the U.S., was signed by **Bosnia**, **Serbia**, and **Croatia**, with **NATO** responsible for policing its implementation. In spring 1999, NATO conducted a bombing campaign aimed at stopping Yugoslavia from driving out ethnic Albanians from the **Kosovo** region; a peace accord was reached in June under which NATO peacekeeping troops entered Kosovo.

The **two Germanys were reunited** after 45 years (Oct. 1990). The union was greeted with jubilation, but economic stresses followed. West German chancellor Helmut **Kohl**, a Christian Democrat, lost power after 16 years, in Sept. 1998 elections; Gerhard **Schröder**, a Social Democrat, took over. Czechoslovakia broke apart peacefully (Jan. 1993), becoming the **Czech Republic** and **Slovakia**. In **Poland**, Lech **Wałęsa** was elected president (Dec. 1991) but was defeated in his bid for a second term (Nov. 1995).

NATO approved the **Partnership for Peace** Program (Jan. 1994) coordinating the defense of E and Central European countries; Russia joined the program later that year. NATO signed a pact with **Russia** (1997) providing for NATO expansion into the former Soviet-bloc countries; a similar treaty was set up with **Ukraine**. The **Czech Republic**, **Hungary**, and **Poland** became members in Jan. 1999. Efforts toward European unity continued with adoption of a single market (Jan. 1993) and conversion of the European Community to the **European Union** as the Maestricht Treaty took effect (Nov. 1993). Agreement was reached for 11 EU members to participate in Economic and Monetary Union, adopting a common currency (**euro**) in Jan. 1999.

An intraparty revolt forced Margaret **Thatcher** out as prime minister of **Great Britain**, to be succeeded by John **Major** (Nov. 1990); seven years later, Labour was returned to power under Tony **Blair** (May 1997). The divorce of Prince **Charles and Diana**, followed by the death of Diana in a car accident (Aug. 1997), made headlines around the world. Talks on peace in **Northern Ireland** that included participation of Sinn Fein, political arm of the IRA, led to a peace plan, approved in an all-Ireland vote (May 1998). In Dec. 1999, Northern Ireland was granted home rule. In **Scotland** voters overwhelmingly approved establishment of a regional legislature (1997), and in **Wales** voters narrowly approved establishment of a local assembly (1997). In a historic innovation, the Church of England ordained women as priests (1994).

Middle East. In Aug. 1990, **Iraq**'s Saddam Hussein ordered troops to invade **Kuwait**. The UN approved military action (Nov. 1990), and an international military force led by the U.S. bombed Iraq (Jan. 1991) and launched a land attack, crushing the invasion (Feb. 1991). Iraq accepted the terms of a cease-fire (Apr. 1991) and U.S. troops withdrew, but "no-fly" zones were set up over some regions to protect Kurds and Shiite Muslims. The **UN** imposed **sanctions** on Iraq for failure to abide by the cease-fire. Iraq's reported failure to cooperate with UN inspectors seeking to eliminate **"weapons of mass destruction"** led to air strikes by the U.S. and Britain (1998, 2001).

The last Western hostages were freed in **Lebanon**, June 1992. **Israel** and the **PLO** signed a peace accord (Sept. 1993) providing for Palestinian self-government in the West Bank and Gaza Strip. Prime Min. Yitzhak **Rabin** and Foreign Min. Shimon **Peres** of Israel and Yasir **Arafat** of the PLO received the Nobel Peace Prize for their efforts (1994). Six Arab nations relaxed boycott against Israel (1994), and Israel and **Jordan** signed a peace treaty (Oct. 1994). Rabin was assassinated (Nov. 1995) by an Israeli opponent of the peace process. Benjamin **Netanyahu** became prime minister (May 1996). Arafat was elected to the presidency of the Palestinian Authority (Jan. 1996). A Labour government under Ehud **Barak** took power after Israel's May 1999 elections.

Asia and the Pacific. Hong Kong was returned to **China** (July 1997) after 156 years as a British colony, and **Macao** reverted to Chinese sovereignty (Dec. 1999) after over 400 years of Portuguese rule. Both were to retain their legal and economic systems for 50 years. **Jiang** Zemin, general secretary of the Chinese Communist Party, assumed the additional post of president of China (Mar. 1993) and emerged as the key leader after the death of leader **Deng** Xiaoping (Feb. 1997). China released from prison—and exiled—some well-known dissidents but continued to earn criticism for widespread **human rights abuses**. In Nov. 1999 the U.S. and China signed a landmark pact normalizing trade relations. China's annual economic growth approached and even eclipsed 10% during the decade.

After years of prosperity, **Thailand**, **Indonesia**, and **South Korea** in 1997 began to suffer economic reverses that had a worldwide ripple effect. These countries received billion-dollar IMF bailout packages. In **Indonesia**, protests over mismanagement led to the resignation of Pres. Suharto (May 1998) after 32 years of nearly autocratic rule. Abdurraham Wahid was elected (Oct. 1999) in the country's first fully democratic elections. In a referendum (Aug. 1999), **East Timor** voted overwhelmingly for independence from Indonesia; pro-Indonesian militias then rampaged through the territory, but a multinational **peacekeeping force** helped restore order (Sept. 1999). In South Korea, former dissident **Kim** Dae-jung was elected president (Dec. 1997).

In Japan members of a religious cult released the nerve gas sarin on five **Tokyo subway** cars, killing 12 people and injuring more than 5,500 (Mar. 1995). Tamil rebels continued their armed conflict in **Sri Lanka**. In **Afghanistan** the **Taliban**, an extreme Islamic fundamentalist group, gained control of Kabul (Sept. 1996) and, eventually, most of the country. In **North Korea**, longtime dictator Kim Il Sung died (July 1994), to be succeeded by his son, Kim Jong Il. In the same year the country signed an agreement with the U.S. setting a timetable for North Korea to eliminate its **nuclear program**. The country also suffered a severe drought, and widespread starvation was feared.

India was beset by riots following destruction of a mosque by Hindu militants (Dec. 1992); Indian army troops repeatedly clashed with pro-independence demonstrators in the disputed Muslim region of **Kashmir**, exacerbating relations with **Pakistan**. Uneasy relations between India and Pakistan reached a new level when both nations conducted nuclear tests in 1998.

F. W. de Klerk and Nelson Mandela shared the Nobel Peace Prize in 1993 for negotiating the South African transition to nonracial democracy.

Conflict in Pakistan between government and the military led to a bloodless coup (Oct. 1999).

Africa. South Africa's Pres. F. W. **de Klerk** released dissident Nelson **Mandela** from prison (Feb. 1990) after 27 years, and lifted a ban on the black nationalist African National Congress. The white minority government repealed apartheid laws (1990, 1991). Mandela was elected president (Apr. 1994), and a new nonracial constitution became law (Dec. 1996). In **Nigeria,** Gen. Olusegun Obasanjo was elected president (Feb. 1999), to become the country's first civilian leader in 15 years. The decades-long rule of **Mobutu** Sese Seko in **Zaire** came to an end (May 1997) at the hands of rebel forces led by Laurent **Kabila;** an ailing Mobutu fled the country and soon after died. Kabila changed the country's name back to **Democratic Republic of the Congo;** conditions remained unstable.

After the presidents of **Burundi** and **Rwanda** were killed in an airplane crash (Apr. 1994), violence erupted in Rwanda between Hutu and Tutsi factions; hundreds of thousands were slain in genocidal fashion. The conflict spread to refugee camps in neighboring Zaire and Burundi. Factional fighting also erupted in **Somalia** (Jan. 1991). The UN sent a U.S.-led **peacekeeping force,** but it was unsuccessful in restoring order. The UN ended its mission (Mar. 1995) with no durable government in place. **Liberia** endured factional fighting that lasted almost five years and claimed over 150,000 lives; a cease-fire was concluded in Aug. 1995. The World Health Organization reported (1995) that Africa accounted for 70% of **AIDS** cases worldwide.

A 16-year civil war appeared to end in **Angola** (May 1991) when the government signed a peace accord with the rebel UNITA faction. Despite the inauguration of a national unity government (Apr. 1997), insurgents continued to fight. **Namibia** officially became independent in Mar. 1990 after almost 20 years under UN trusteeship. In **Algeria,** the army cancelled a second round of parliamentary elections (Jan. 1992) after the Islamic party won a first round. Ensuing violence by **Islamic fundamentalists** claimed thousands of lives; a peace plan was worked out in 1999.

North America. The **North American Free Trade Agreement** (NAFTA), liberalizing trade between the U.S., Canada, and Mexico, went into effect Jan. 1, 1994. In **Canada,** the Progressive Conservative Party suffered a crushing defeat in general elections (Oct. 1993), and liberal Jean **Chrétien** became prime minister. The map of Canada was altered in Apr. 1999 to create a new territory, **Nunavut,** out of an area that had been part of Northwest Territories.

In the U.S.'s 1992 presidential election, Bill **Clinton** (D) defeated Pres. George H. W. Bush (R), but Republicans gained control of Congress in 1994 midterm elections. Clinton won reelection in 1996; despite scandals, the administration remained popular, aided by economic prosperity. Clinton proposed (Feb. 1998) the first balanced federal budget in nearly 30 years. In Dec. 1998 Clinton was **impeached** by the U.S. House on charges related to the Monica Lewinsky scandal; he was acquitted by the Senate in Feb. 1999.

In **Mexico,** Ernesto Zedillo of the ruling PRI party was elected president (July 1994) after the party's first candidate was assassinated. The country soon faced a crisis affecting the value of the peso, but recovered with the help of a bailout package

from the U.S. A peasant revolt spearheaded by the **Zapatista National Liberation Army** erupted in the state of Chiapas (Jan. 1994) and was suppressed.

Central America and the Caribbean. In **Haiti,** Jean-Bertrand **Aristide** was elected president (Dec. 1990) but was ousted in a military coup after nine months. A delegation headed by former U.S. Pres. Jimmy Carter arranged (Sept. 1994) for the junta to step aside for Aristide, who served until 1996. In **Nicaragua,** Violeta Chamorro defeated Daniel **Ortega** in the presidential election (Feb. 1990), thus ousting the Sandinistas. In **Panama,** U.S. troops invaded and overthrew the government of Manuel **Noriega** (Dec. 1989). Noriega was captured Jan. 1990; convicted and jailed on drug-related charges in U.S. in 1992, and in France in 2010. On Dec. 31, 1999, Panama assumed full control of the **Panama Canal,** in accord with a treaty with the U.S. In **El Salvador** (1992) and **Guatemala** (1996) the governments signed agreements with rebel factions.

South America. Alberto **Fujimori** was elected president of **Peru** in June 1990 and, despite his suppression of the constitution (1992), was reelected in 1995. Peru succeeded in capturing (Sept. 1992) the leader of the Shining Path guerrilla movement. Leftist guerrillas took hostages at an ambassador's residence in Lima (Dec. 1996); one hostage was killed during a government assault rescuing the rest (Apr. 1997). Peronist Pres. Carlos Saúl **Menem** served as **Argentina**'s president for much of the decade (elected 1989, reelected 1995), imposing economic austerity.

Former Chilean Pres. Augusto **Pinochet** continued to head the army until Mar. 1998; he was arrested in London (Oct. 1998) on human rights charges but judged unfit for trial and returned to Chile (Mar. 2000). In **Brazil,** Fernando Henrique **Cardoso** was elected president (Oct. 1994) and reelected in 1998 despite an economic slump; the IMF announced a $42 bil aid package (Nov. 1998). In **Venezuela** two coup attempts were thwarted (1992); coup leader Hugo **Chávez,** a leftist populist, was elected president in Dec. 1998.

Terrorism. The U.S. was a prominent target of terrorism linked to Middle Eastern sources. A bomb exploded in a garage beneath New York City's **World Trade Center,** killing six people (Feb. 1993). Bombs set off outside **U.S. embassies** in Kenya and Tanzania killed over 220 people (Aug. 1998); the U.S. retaliated with missiles fired at alleged terrorist-linked sites in Afghanistan and Sudan. In the U.S.'s deadliest instance of domestic terrorism, 168 people were killed in the bombing of a federal building in **Oklahoma City,** OK (Apr. 1995).

Science and technology. The powerful **Hubble Space Telescope** was launched in Apr. 1990. U.S. space shuttle *Atlantis* docked with the orbiting Russian space station *Mir* (June 1995) in first of several joint missions. In Nov. 1998 the first component for a new **International Space Station** was launched into space from Kazakhstan.

Scottish scientist Ian Wilmut announced (Feb. 1997) the **cloning** of a sheep, nicknamed Dolly—the first mammal successfully cloned from a cell from an adult animal.

Tim Berners-Lee launched the first **World Wide Web** server (1990). User-friendly graphical browsers (Mosaic, 1993; Netscape, 1994) and affordable Internet service providers followed, expanding the reach of the **Internet.**

Globalization and Global Realignments: 2000-09

Terrorism and crime. The first decade of the new century saw new levels of international terrorism. In Oct. 2000, 17 American sailors were killed aboard the **USS Cole** in Aden, **Yemen,** when a small boat exploded alongside it in a terrorist attack. Terrorism reached a new level on **Sept. 11, 2001:** hijackers crashed two jetliners into the twin towers of the **World Trade Center** in New York City and another into the **Pentagon** outside Washington, DC, with a fourth crashing in a Pennsylvania field. The attacks, which destroyed both towers and damaged the Pentagon, killed about 3,000 people. Saudi exile Osama **bin Laden** and his **al-Qaeda** terrorist network, based in **Afghanistan** and backed by the Taliban government there, proved responsible.

Among many other incidents tied to Islamic radicals, a car bomb on the Indonesian island of **Bali** (Oct. 2002) killed about 200. **Commuter trains** were bombed in **Madrid,** Spain, killing 191 (Mar. 2004); elections held a week later ousted Spain's premier. **Subway trains** and a bus were bombed in **London** (July 2005); 56 people died. Eight explosions killed 207 on **commuter trains** in **Mumbai,** India (July 2006); also in Mumbai (Nov. 2008), terrorists launched coordinated attacks on sites

frequented by foreigners, killing some 170. **Chechen** separatist guerrillas were implicated in an attack on a Moscow movie theater (Oct. 2002; over 100 hostages died), bombings in Moscow's subways (Feb. 2004); explosions on two Russian planes (Aug. 2004; 89 died), and the takeover of a school in Beslan (Aug.-Sept. 2004; over 330 died).

Other attacks were reportedly foiled, as in Aug. 2006, when British authorities announced thwarting a plot to detonate **liquid explosives** on transatlantic flights. In Dec. 2009 a Nigerian man—reportedly aided by al-Qaeda in Yemen—attempted to ignite explosives in his underwear, on a Detroit-bound international flight.

Global economic crisis. Rapid economic growth in China, Brazil, India, and other countries, along with more sluggish rates in traditional economic powers, signaled global rebalancing, and efforts at international economic coordination expanded to include rising economies (Group of 20, 2008). A global recession, beginning in late 2007, led to a financial meltdown (Sept. 2008), sending shock waves through industrialized and developing countries. Soaring food and **fuel prices** led to unrest,

including an attempted general strike in **Egypt** and riots in **Haiti** (Apr. 2008). Among many ripple effects around the world, **Iceland**'s banking system collapsed (Oct. 2008), rescued by loans and austerity measures. **Dubai**'s state-controlled investment company Dubai World could not meet payments on $59 bil debt; bailed out (Dec. 2009) by a loan from Abu Dhabi. Spending cuts, pension reforms, tax hikes, and other **austerity** measures spurred wide-scale protests in several European countries.

War in Iraq and Afghanistan. The U.S., with Great Britain, launched an invasion of **Iraq** (Mar. 2003) to oust the regime of Saddam **Hussein**. Troops took control of Baghdad and other cities, and U.S. Pres. George W. **Bush** declared major combat ended by May 1, but insurgents caused continuing casualties. Interim government installed, June 2004. No **weapons of mass destruction**, cited as major grounds for the invasion, were found. Hussein was captured by U.S. troops (Dec. 2003) and convicted and executed by Iraqi authorities for crimes against humanity (Dec. 2006). Despite threats by insurgents, large numbers of Iraqis voted in **elections** for a transitional assembly (Jan. 2005), democratic constitution (Oct. 2005), and parliament (Dec. 2005); negotiations produced a Shiite coalition government under Prime Min. Nouri **al-Maliki** (May 2006). With sectarian and **insurgent violence** intensifying, Bush announced (Jan. 2007) a **"surge"** of additional U.S. troops; military and civilian casualties declined sharply after mid-2007, aided by a cease-fire with Shiite militias and shift in Sunni clan support for al-Qaeda.

In **Afghanistan**, a U.S.-led military coalition ousted the **Taliban**. A transitional government was installed (Dec. 2001), but the Taliban insurgency remained strong. NATO assumed control of multinational forces in Aug. 2003. Afghans elected Hamid **Karzai** (Nov. 2004). The next presidential election (Aug. 2009) was marked by widespread **vote-rigging**; Karzai was reelected after his main opponent withdrew from a runoff, citing transparency issues. From 2007, Taliban and other Islamist militants stepped up activities, often operating from safe havens inside **Pakistan**. The U.S. increased its troop strength in Afghanistan (2009), and expanded use of unmanned aerial vehicles (drones).

Asia. Gen. Pervez **Musharraf**, brought to power in a 1999 coup, assumed **Pakistan**'s presidency (June 2001) and retained office through elections were denounced by protesters. In the wake of the Sept. 11, 2001 terrorist attacks, Pakistan pledged cooperation fighting **Taliban** and **al-Qaeda** militants. **Pakistan** and **India** restored ties (May 2003) and declared a cease-fire in disputed territory (Nov. 2003); relations remained tense. After former Pakistani Prime Min. Benazir **Bhutto** was assassinated (Dec. 2007) at a political rally, her party won parliamentary elections (Feb. 2008), and her widower, Asif Ali **Zardari**, was elected president (Sept. 2008). In May 2009, after a cease-fire collapsed, the government launched a major offensive against Taliban insurgents in the Swat Valley.

The UN Intl. Atomic Energy Agency censured **Iran** (Dec. 2003) for covering up aspects of its **nuclear** program, which it claimed was for peaceful purposes. Iran continued enriching uranium in defiance of IAEA deadlines and tested missiles said to be capable of reaching Israel. Pres. Mahmoud **Ahmadinejad** was declared the landslide winner in June 2009 elections widely perceived to have been rigged. **Protests** by hundreds of thousands were crushed by police and Basij paramilitaries.

Protests in **Kyrgyzstan** (Mar. 2005) against election fraud brought down Pres. Askar Akayev (in a **"tulip revolution"**), leading to the election of Kumanbek **Bakiyev**.

South Korean Pres. Kim Dae-jung and **North Korean** ruler Kim Jong Il agreed to seek peace and reunification at a summit (June 2000), but tensions rose after North Korea admitted conducting a covert **nuclear weapons** development program (Oct. 2002). North Korea withdrew (Jan. 2003) from the Nuclear Nonproliferation Treaty. Multination talks were held in Beijing; North Korea agreed (Feb. 2007) to end its nuclear program in exchange for an aid package but reneged, conducting tests in Apr.-May 2009.

A tsunami in the Indian Ocean (Dec. 2004) devastated parts of Indonesia, Thailand, India, Sri Lanka, and other Asian and African nations, leaving more than 200,000 dead. An earthquake struck the disputed territory of Kashmir and parts of Pakistan and India (Oct. 2005), killing nearly 80,000. With the retirement of **China**'s Pres. Jiang Zemin, **Hu** Jintao was named Communist party chief (Nov. 2002) and president (Mar. 2003). An **earthquake** killed nearly 70,000 in Sichuan province (May 2008). In **Japan**, the Liberal Democrats, in virtually uninterrupted power since the 1950s, were dispatched in parliamentary elections (Aug. 2009).

Myanmar's military junta cracked down on hundreds of thousands of antigovernment protesters (Sept. 2007). More than 80,000 people were killed in a **cyclone** in Myanmar (May 2008); the regime thwarted aid agencies. **Sri Lanka** government forces launched a stepped-up offensive in 2008 against **Tamil guerrillas**, leading them to declare an end (May 2009) to a rebellion that since 1983 had claimed at least 80,000 lives. The military carried out a bloodless coup in **Thailand** (Sept. 2006), ousting Prem. Thaksin Shinawatra; civilian rule was restored after Dec. 2007 elections.

Middle East. The peace process languished as violence between Israelis and Palestinians escalated, with **suicide bombings** by Palestinians and retaliation by Israeli armed forces. Israel launched a major West Bank offensive (Mar. 2002), and withdrew in early May but, after another wave of suicide bombings, reoccupied much of the West Bank. The U.S., Russia, UN, and EU initiated (Apr. 2003) a **"road map"** plan for peace negotiations; little progress was made. After Palestinian leader Yasir Arafat's death (Nov. 2004), Mahmoud Abbas was elected in his place. Israeli Prime Min. Ariel **Sharon** decided in 2005 to pull troops and settlers out of the **Gaza Strip**, angering his own party's right wing. He formed a new party and, after suffering a stroke (Jan. 2006), was succeeded by an ally, Ehud **Olmert**, who led a coalition government following elections (Apr. 2006). The militant Palestinian party **Hamas** won a parliamentary majority over the long-ruling **Fatah** party (Jan. 2006).

Israel launched attacks on **Lebanon** (July 2006) in response to a raid into N Israel by Lebanon-based **Hezbollah** guerrillas; a cease-fire was declared a month later. In reaction to Hamas rocket and mortar attacks, Israel launched an offensive in the **Gaza Strip** (Dec. 2008), which killed an estimated 1,300 Palestinians. Olmert resigned as prime minister (effective Sept. 2008) amid corruption inquiries, and Feb. 2009 elections led to a coalition government headed by former Prime Min. Benjamin **Netanyahu**, a conservative.

Europe. By early 2002 the **euro** was the common currency in 12 EU nations. The EU admitted 10 E European nations (May 2004); two more joined in Jan. 2007. Voters in France and the Netherlands rejected a treaty to establish a new **EU constitution** (May-June 2005). A modified plan, known as the **Treaty of Lisbon**, came into force (Dec. 2009) after Irish voters approved it (Oct. 2009).

One of the deadliest natural disasters in recorded history, a 2004 tsunami killed more than 200,000 people in 11 African and Asian countries.

The conventional military combat phase of the Iraq War (2003-10) was over quickly, but violence stretched on, killing nearly 5,000 coalition troops and an estimated 100,000 Iraqi civilians.

In Oct. 2000, Yugoslav strongman Slobodan **Milosevic** yielded power to Vojislav **Kostunica**, who had declared himself president after a disputed election. Milosevic surrendered to Serbian authorities; he went on trial in the Hague (Feb. 2002) for **war crimes** during 1990s ethnic conflicts in the Balkans but died (Mar. 2006) before a verdict was reached. Former Bosnian Serb leader Radovan **Karadzic** was arraigned on war crimes charges (July 2008). **Kosovo** unilaterally declared independence (Feb. 2008).

Germany elected its first East German and first woman chancellor (Nov. 2005) in Angela **Merkel**, a Christian Democrat. **Rioting** shook France's immigrant communities in 300 cities and towns (Nov. 2005). A Danish newspaper's publication of cartoon **caricatures of Muhammad** sparked violent worldwide protests by Muslims (Jan.-Feb. 2006).

British Prime Min. Tony **Blair** won reelection twice (2001, 2005), becoming the first Labour prime minister to earn three straight terms. He stepped down in June 2007, to be succeeded by fellow Labourite Gordon **Brown**. **France** saw the election (May 2007) of conservative Nicolas **Sarkozy** as president and rejoined NATO's active military command (Apr. 2009) after more than 40 years. Vladimir **Putin**, in power in Russia since 1999, was constitutionally barred from a new presidential term in 2008; his protégé, Dmitri **Medvedev**, was elected (May 2008) and named Putin prime minister. In **Ukraine**, a tainted presidential runoff election (Nov. 2004) led to the country's "orange revolution"; a recount gave power to nationalist Viktor **Yushchenko**.

Africa. Ethiopia and Eritrea signed a **peace treaty** (Dec. 2000). Laurent **Kabila**, president of Dem. Rep. of the Congo, was shot to death (Jan. 2001). Liberian Pres. Charles **Taylor** went into exile (Aug. 2003) as part of a deal to end a 14-year-old civil war; other accords were reached aimed at ending civil wars in **Angola** (Apr. 2002) and Côte d'Ivoire (Jan. 2003). **Libya** agreed (Dec. 2003) to abandon programs pursuing weapons of mass destruction.

A peace agreement in **Dem. Rep. of the Congo** (Apr. 2003) did not end violence there; the nation agreed to work with Rwanda to disarm Hutu rebels (Nov. 2007). In **Sudan** a power-sharing accord between the Muslim-led government and rebels from the Christian south was signed, Jan. 2005, giving the south limited autonomy. Rebellion in the **Darfur** area of western Sudan led to large-scale violence. Arab militias (**janjaweed**), reportedly backed by the government, were accused of displacing over 2 million people in acts bordering on genocide; by Sept. 2009 more than 300,000 people had been killed. The Intl. Criminal Court issued an arrest warrant for Sudanese Pres. Omar Hassan Ahmad al-**Bashir**, for war crimes (Mar. 2009); he remained in power.

Zimbabwean Pres. Robert **Mugabe** pulled his country out of the Commonwealth (Dec. 2003) after the group reaffirmed suspension of **Zimbabwe** for alleged voter fraud. Disputed elections sparked violence in Kenya (Jan. 2008) and Zimbabwe (Apr. 2008). Under Mugabe's rule, unemployment in Zimbabwe topped 90% and hyperinflation left the currency virtually

worthless. **Guinea-Bissau**'s defense chief and then its president were assassinated in turn by rival groups (Mar. 2009).

Americas and the Caribbean. The long-supreme **Institutional Revolutionary Party** lost power in **Mexico** with the election of two successive presidents from a center-right party, Vicente **Fox** and Felipe **Calderón** (July 2000, July 2006). Calderón launched a crackdown on drug trafficking (Dec. 2006); from then through the end of 2010, more than 30,000 people were killed in violence fueled by warring **drug cartels**.

In Jan. 2001, Republican George W. **Bush** was inaugurated as **U.S. president**, after one of the closest elections in U.S. history; he was reelected in Nov. 2004. Democrats claimed the White House with the Nov. 2008 election of Barack **Obama**, the first-ever black U.S. president.

In **Brazil**, reformist candidate Luiz Inácio Lula **da Silva** won a runoff (Oct. 2002) to become president. **Chile** was ruled by Socialist governments under Ricardo Lagos Escobar (from 2000) and Michelle **Bachelet** (from 2006).

In **Venezuela**, Pres. Hugo **Chávez** regained power after a 48-hour coup (Dec. 2002) and consolidated it, in part through a referendum (Feb. 2009) that gave him new authority and eliminated presidential term limits. In **Bolivia**, Evo **Morales**, another leftist populist, won election as president (Dec. 2005) and passage of a new constitution (Jan. 2009) that gave the federal government control over resources and gave new rights to indigenous peoples. In **Honduras**, leftist opposition leader Manuel **Zelaya** was elected president (Nov. 2005) but was ousted by the military (June 2009) after he had sought constitutional changes; Porfirio (Pepe) **Lobo**, a conservative landowner, was elected (Nov. 2009) to succeed him.

Argentina was beset by economic problems; its **default** on IMF loans led (Sept. 2003) to a massive debt-refinancing agreement, but the money was repaid. **Haiti** was wracked by antigovernment protests, leading to the resignation of Jean-Bertrand **Aristide** in Feb. 2004; a UN peacekeeping mission was brought in.

For the first time in 12 years, the Liberal Party handed control of **Canada**'s government to the Conservative Party, led by Prime Min. Stephen **Harper** (Jan. 2006). After 47 years in office, Cuban Pres. Fidel **Castro** ceded administrative powers to his brother, Raúl Castro, to undergo surgery (July 2006); he formally resigned in Feb. 2008.

Religion. Pope **John Paul II** died, Apr. 2005, after 26 years in the papacy; German Cardinal Joseph Ratzinger was elected as his successor, taking the name **Benedict XVI**. During the decade, reports of **sexual abuse** by Catholic priests going back generations and evidence of inaction by church officials emerged.

Science and technology. The U.S. **space shuttle** *Columbia* broke up on reentering Earth's atmosphere (Feb. 2003), killing all seven crew members. NASA landed two rovers, *Spirit* and *Opportunity*, on Mars (Jan. 2004) and resumed the space shuttle program with the July 2005 launch of *Discovery*. The Phoenix *Mars Lander* verified the presence of water ice on **Mars** (June 2008). China also expanded its space program, launching its first manned space flights Oct. 2003.

China, Oct. 2010, unveiled the Tianhe-1A **supercomputer**, said to be the world's fastest. **Internet** penetration and access to technology expanded exponentially, as more than one-fifth of the world's population had regular web access by the decade's end. Online commerce, social networking (Facebook, 2004; Twitter, 2006), and file-sharing services became commonplace.

Environment and health. The **Kyoto Protocol** took effect for 141 ratifying nations, Feb. 2005, requiring industrialized nations to achieve targeted reductions by 2012 in emissions of **greenhouse gases** linked to global warming. A NASA report (Jan. 2010) found that 2000-09 had the **warmest average global temperatures** since modern records began in the 1880s.

The 13th International **AIDS Conference**, held in Durban, South Africa (July 2000), focused on ways of controlling AIDS in developing countries. Worldwide AIDS estimates were revised downward (Nov. 2007) to show new infections had peaked in the late 1990s. An epidemic of **swine flu**, or influenza A (H1N1), broke out in Mexico (Apr. 2009) and spread around the globe, killing more than 18,000.

Searching for Resolutions: 2010-13

Terrorism. Terrorism remained a major global threat. Bombs in Kampala, **Uganda**, killed more than 70 gathered to watch **World Cup soccer** (July 2010). In Norway, an anti-Muslim right-wing extremist killed 77 people in two incidents, July 2011, including a car bombing in Oslo and a shooting spree at

a summer camp. American forces raided Osama **bin Laden**'s compound in Abbottabad, Pakistan, and killed the al-Qaeda leader (May 2011) as his terrorist network appeared to weaken as a result of the 10-year U.S. **War on Terror**. Al-Qaeda nonetheless remained influential. An al-Qaeda-inspired terrorist

killed seven in the French towns of Toulouse and Montauban (Mar. 2012). Two similarly inspired terrorists set off two bombs, killing three and injuring 264, at the finish line of the Boston Marathon (Apr. 2013).

War in Iraq and Afghanistan. Last combat unit withdrew from Iraq, Aug. 2010, and the U.S. military mission formally ended, Dec. 2011. Since the U.S.-led invasion in Mar. 2003, nearly 4,500 U.S. service members had been killed and another 32,000 wounded; tens of thousands of Iraqi civilians and combatants had also lost their lives in the conflict, which cost more than $800 bil.

In Afghanistan, U.S. Pres. Barack Obama outlined plans (June 2011) to withdraw all U.S. forces by the end of 2014 and enable Afghan forces to take over security operations in preparation for the complete withdrawal.

Arab Spring. Economic inequality, religious tensions, and government corruption and repression fueled a wave of discontent that challenged entrenched Arab regimes from NW Africa to the Persian Gulf. Mass protests forced the ouster of Tunisian Pres. Zine al-Abidine **Ben Ali** (Jan. 2011) and Egyptian Pres. Hosni **Mubarak** (Feb. 2011). With NATO military backing, insurgents overthrew Libyan dictator Muammar al-Qaddafi, who was killed (Oct. 2011). Syrian Pres. Bashar al-Assad launched a ferocious offensive against antigovernment protesters, giving rise to a civil war that had killed more than 93,000 by the end of June 2013, the month Pres. **Obama** announced that the U.S. would begin providing arms to opposition forces. Mohammed Morsi, having won Egypt's presidential election (June 2012), was ousted in a military coup (July 2013).

Europe. In response to the **European debt crisis**, the European Union, with help from the IMF, provided loan packages to bail out **Greece** (May 2010) and **Ireland** (Nov. 2010). The **European Central Bank** bailed out **Portugal** (May 2011). The EU provided a bank bailout for **Spain** (June 2012) and reached a bailout agreement with Cyprus (Mar. 2013). Greece received two other bailout pledges (July 2011, Feb. 2012).

Polish Pres. Lech **Kaczynski** and 95 others were killed in a plane crash (Apr. 2010). Bronisław **Komorowski** was elected to replace him (July 2010).

In **Britain**, conservatives were returned to power in a coalition government under David **Cameron** (May 2010). In **France**, the socialist François **Hollande** defeated Nicolas **Sarkozy** to become president (May 2012). The pro-Russian Viktor **Yanukovich** captured **Ukraine**'s presidency in Feb. 2010. Amid accusations of official corruption and voter fraud, Vladimir Putin won a third term as president in **Russia** (Mar. 2012).

Asia and the Pacific. Monsoon rains and **floods** (July-Aug. 2010) inundated nearly one-fifth of **Pakistan**, leaving millions homeless. A devastating earthquake and tsunami (Mar. 2011) struck Japan, killing more than 16,000; a nuclear plant overwhelmed by seawater had meltdowns at three of six nuclear reactors. **India** experienced the largest blackouts in history at the end of July 2012.

In **Kyrgyzstan**, Kumanbek **Bakiyeve** was ousted (Apr. 2010), after clashes between protesters and security forces left at least 85 people dead. Despite ethnic violence (up to 2,000 killed), a referendum was held (June 2010) and new constitution approved. Almazbek **Atambayev** won the first presidential election under the new constitution (Oct. 2011).

North Korea. North Korean dictator Kim Jong Il died (Dec. 2011) and was succeeded by his youngest son, Kim Jong Un, who threatened the U.S. with a preemptive nuclear strike (Mar. 2013). The reformist-minded cleric Hassan **Rouhani** won the June 2013 presidential election in **Iran**, having promised to improve the country's relationship with the West.

Myanmar's military junta was dissolved (Mar. 2011) following the country's first election in 20 years (Nov. 2010), which brought the military-backed USDP party to power; the party led by the pro-democracy dissident Aung San **Suu Kyi** did not participate, but won 43 seats, including one for Suu Kyi, in interim elections (Apr. 2012).

Upon Chinese Pres. **Hu** Jintao's retirement, **Xi** Jinping was named Communist party chief (Nov. 2012) and president (Mar. 2013). Liberal Democrats in **Japan** regained control in Dec. 2012 elections.

In **Australia**, Prime Min. Kevin Rudd was displaced (June 2010) by his deputy, Julia **Gillard**, who became Australia's first female prime minister; Rudd subsequently ousted Gillard and again became prime minister (June 2013).

Africa. Niger's president was ousted in a coup (Feb. 2010). In a referendum on independence held in 2011, southern Sudanese voted overwhelmingly in favor of secession and became the independent nation of **South Sudan** (July 2011).

Low-level soldiers staged a coup in **Mali**, but the military junta quickly ceded power to Dioncounda **Traoré**, who became interim president in Apr. 2012; Ibrahim Boubacar Keita was elected president (Aug. 2013). A military coup in **Guinea-Bissau** halted elections in Apr. 2012; Manuel Serifo **Nhamadjo**, the third-place candidate during the first round of voting, was installed as interim president.

Middle East. Palestinian Authority Pres. Mahmoud Abbas officially applied for full UN membership for an independent Palestinian state, Sept. 2011; **Palestine** was granted nonmember observer state status (Nov. 2012). Israel and the U.S. opposed both moves.

Americas. Haiti was devastated by an **earthquake** (Jan. 2010) that killed more than 200,000.

In **Chile**, conservative billionaire Sebastián **Piñera** won presidential elections (Jan. 2010). More than 500 Chileans were killed in a Feb. 2010 earthquake.

Mexico's **Institutional Revolutionary Party** regained power with the election of Enrique Peña **Nieto** (July 2012). In **Brazil**, Pres. **Lula** da Silva's chosen successor, Dilma **Rousseff**, was elected (Oct. 2010); she faced mass protests (June 2013) after announcing a plan to raise bus fares in the face of growing deficits. In **Venezuela**, Pres. Hugo **Chávez** was reelected (Oct. 2012) but died (Mar. 2013) before he could be inaugurated. Nicolás **Maduro**, Chávez's chosen successor and vice president, was elected to replace him (Apr. 2013).

Religion. Pope **Benedict XVI** resigned after eight years as pope (Feb. 2013) and took the title Pope Emeritus. The Argentinean Cardinal Jorge Mario Bergoglio succeeded him, taking the name **Francis** and becoming the first Latin American and first Jesuit pontiff.

Science and technology. WikiLeaks, a controversial organization formed in 2007, began disseminating secret government documents related to the Iraq and Afghanistan wars (Apr., July 2010). NASA's space shuttle program ended when *Atlantis* landed (July 2011); NASA's rover *Curiosity* landed on Mars (Aug. 2012). China launched its fifth manned space flight (June 2013).

Environment. In Dec. 2012, parties to the Kyoto Protocol adopted an amendment requiring further emission reductions of **greenhouse gases** linked to global warming by 2020.

Kim Jong Un (right) took over North Korea following the 2011 death of his father, dictator Kim Jong Il (left), and continued to escalate the nation's belligerent nuclear and foreign policy.

HISTORICAL FIGURES

Note: Information accurate as of Sept. 2013.

Ancient Greeks and Romans

Greeks

Aeschines, orator, 389-314 BCE
Aeschylus, dramatist, 525-456 BCE
Aesop, fableist, c. 620-c. 560 BCE
Alcibiades, politician, 450-404 BCE
Anacreon, poet, c. 582-c. 485 BCE
Anaxagoras, philosopher, c. 500-428 BCE
Anaximander, philosopher, 611-546 BCE
Anaximenes, philosopher, c. 570-500 BCE
Antiphon, speechwriter, c. 480-411 BCE
Apollonius, mathematician, c. 265-170 BCE
Archimedes, mathematician, 287-212 BCE
Aristophanes, dramatist, c. 448-380 BCE
Aristotle, philosopher, 384-322 BCE
Athenaeus, scholar, fl. c. 200
Callicrates, architect, fl. 5th cent. BCE
Callimachus, poet, c. 305-240 BCE
Cratinus, comic dramatist, 520-421 BCE
Democritus, philosopher, c. 460-370 BCE
Demosthenes, orator, 384-322 BCE
Diodorus, historian, fl. 20 BCE
Diogenes, philosopher, 372-c. 287 BCE
Dionysius, historian, d. c. 7 BCE
Empedocles, philosopher, c. 490-430 BCE
Epicharmus, dramatist, c. 530-440 BCE
Epictetus, philosopher, c. 55-c. 135
Epicurus, philosopher, 341-270 BCE
Eratosthenes, scientist, 276-194 BCE
Euclid, mathematician, fl. c. 300 BCE
Euripides, dramatist, c. 484-406 BCE
Galen, physician, 129-216
Heraclitus, philosopher, c. 540-c. 475 BCE
Herodotus, historian, c. 484-420 BCE

Hesiod, poet, 8th cent. BCE
Hippocrates, physician, c. 460-377 BCE
Homer, poet, fl. c. 8th cent. BCE
Isocrates, orator, 436-338 BCE
Menander, dramatist, 342-292 BCE
Parmenides, philosopher, b. c. 515 BCE
Pericles, statesman, c. 495-429 BCE
Phidias, sculptor, c. 500-435 BCE
Pindar, poet, c. 518-c. 438 BCE
Plato, philosopher, c. 428-347 BCE
Plutarch, biographer, c. 46-120
Polybius, historian, c. 200-c. 118 BCE
Praxiteles, sculptor, 400-330 BCE
Pythagoras, phil., math., c. 580-c. 500 BCE
Sappho, poet, c. 610-c. 580 BCE
Simonides, poet, 556-c. 468 BCE
Socrates, philosopher, 469-399 BCE
Solon, statesman, 640-560 BCE
Sophocles, dramatist, c. 496-406 BCE
Strabo, geographer, c. 63 BCE-24 CE
Thales, philosopher, c. 634-546 BCE
Themistocles, politician, c. 524-c. 460 BCE
Theocritus, poet, c. 310-250 BCE
Theophrastus, phil., c. 372-c. 287 BCE
Thucydides, historian, fl. 5th cent. BCE
Timon, philosopher, c. 320-c. 230 BCE
Xenophon, historian, c. 434-c. 355 BCE
Zeno, philosopher, c. 335-c. 263 BCE

Romans

Ammianus, historian, c. 330-395
Apuleius, satirist, c. 124-c. 170
Boethius, scholar, c. 480-524
Caesar, Julius, leader, 100-44 BCE

Catiline, politician, c. 108-62 BCE
Cato (Elder), statesman, 234-149 BCE
Catullus, poet, c. 84-54 BCE
Cicero, orator, 106-43 BCE
Claudian, poet, c. 370-c. 404
Ennius, poet, 239-170 BCE
Gellius, author, c. 130-c. 165
Horace, poet, 65-8 BCE
Juvenal, satirist, 60-127
Livy, historian, 59 BCE-17 CE
Lucan, poet, 39-65
Lucilius, poet, c. 180-c.102 BCE
Lucretius, poet, c. 99-c. 55 BCE
Martial, epigrammatist, c. 38-c. 103
Nepos, historian, c. 100-c. 25 BCE
Ovid, poet, 43 BCE-17 CE
Persius, satirist, 34-62
Plautus, dramatist, c. 254-c. 184 BCE
Pliny the Elder, scholar, 23-79
Pliny the Younger, author, 62-113
Quintilian, rhetorician, c. 35-c. 97
Sallust, historian, 86-34 BCE
Seneca, philosopher, 4 BCE-65 CE
Silius, poet, c. 25-101
Statius, poet, c. 45-c. 96
Suetonius, biographer, c. 69-c. 122
Tacitus, historian, 56-120
Terence, dramatist, 195/185-c. 159 BCE
Tibullus, poet, c. 55-c. 19 BCE
Vergil, poet, 70-19 BCE
Vitruvius, architect, fl. 1st cent. BCE

Roman Rulers

From Romulus to the end of the Empire in the West. Rulers in the East sat in Constantinople and, for a brief period, in Nicaea, until the capture of Constantinople by the Turks in 1453, when Byzantium was succeeded by the Ottoman Empire.

The Kingdom

BCE
753 Romulus (Quirinus)
715 Numa Pompilius
673 Tullus Hostilius
641 Ancus Marcius
616 L. Tarquinius Priscus
579 Servius Tullius
534 L. Tarquinius Superbus

The Republic

509 Consulate established
509 Quaestorship instituted
498 Dictatorship introduced
494 Plebeian Tribunate created
494 Plebeian Aedileship created
444 Consular Tribunate organized
435 Censorship instituted
366 Praetorship established
366 Curule Aedileship created
362 Military Tribunate elected
326 Proconsulate introduced
311 Naval Duumvirate elected
217 Dictatorship of Fabius Maximus
133 Tribunate of Tiberius Gracchus
123 Tribunate of Gaius Gracchus
82 Dictatorship of Sulla
60 First Triumvirate formed
   (Caesar, Pompeius, Crassus)
47 Dictatorship of Caesar
43 Second Triumvirate formed
   (Octavianus, Antonius, Lepidus)

The Empire

27 Augustus (or Octavian)
CE
14 Tiberius
37 Caligula
41 Claudius
54 Nero
68 Galba
69 Otho; Vitellius; Vespasian,
   established Flavian Dynasty
79 Titus

81 Domitian, end of Flavian Dynasty
96 Nerva
98 Trajan
117 Hadrian
138 Antoninus Pius
161 Marcus Aurelius and Lucius Verus
169 Marcus Aurelius (alone)
180 Commodus
193 Pertinax; Didius Julianus
193 Septimius Severus
211 Caracalla and Geta
212 Caracalla (alone)
217 Macrinus
218 Elagabalus (or Heliogabalus)
222 Alexander Severus
235 Maximinus (the Thracian)
238 Gordian I and Gordian II;
   Pupienus and Balbinus
238 Gordian III
244 Philip (the Arabian)
249 Decius
251 Gallus and Volusianus
253 Aemilian
253 Valerian and Gallienus
258 Gallienus (alone)
268 Claudius II (or Claudius Gothicus)
270 Quintillus
270 Aurelian
275 Tacitus
276 Florian
276 Probus
282 Carus
283 Carinus and Numerian
286 Diocletian and Maximian
305 Galerius and Constantius I
306 Galerius, Maximinus II (or
   Maximinus Daia), Severus
307 Galerius, Maximinus II (Daia),
   Constantine I, Licinius, Maxentius
311 Maximinus II (Daia), Constantine I,
   Licinius, Maxentius
314 Constantine I, Licinius
324 Constantine I (the Great), first
   Christian emperor

337 Constantine II, Constans I,
   Constantius II
340 Constantius II and Constans I
350 Constantius II (alone)
361 Julian (the Apostate)
363 Jovian

West (Rome) and East (Constantinople)

364 Valentinian I (West),
   Valens (East)
367 Valentinian I with Gratian
   (West), Valens (East)
375 Gratian with Valentinian II
   (West), Valens (East)
378 Gratian with Valentinian II
   (West), Theodosius I (East)
383 Valentinian II (West),
   Theodosius I (East)
394 Theodosius I (the Great)
395 Honorius (West), Arcadius (East)
408 Honorius (West),
   Theodosius II (East)
423 Valentinian III (West),
   Theodosius II (East)
450 Valentinian III (West),
   Marcian (East)
455 Maximus (or Magnus Maximus)
   (West), Avitus (West);
   Marcian (East)
456 Avitus (West), Marcian (East)
457 Majorian (West), Leo I (East)
461 Severus II (West), Leo I (East)
467 Anthemius (West), Leo I (East)
472 Olybrius (West), Leo I (East)
473 Glycerius (West), Leo I (East)
474 Julius Nepos (West), Leo II (East)
475 Romulus Augustulus (West),
   Zeno (East)
476 End of Empire in West with
   deposing of Romulus Augustulus
   by Germanic chief Odovacar,
   who proclaimed self king. Odovacar
   murdered by King Theodoric of
   Ostrogoths, 493

Rulers of England and Great Britain

Reign began	Name	Age at death[1]
	England: Saxons and Danes	
829	Egbert, king of Wessex, won allegiance of all English	NA
839	Ethelwulf, son of Egbert, king of Wessex, Sussex, Kent, Essex.	NA
858	Ethelbald, eldest son of Ethelwulf, displaced father in Wessex.	NA
860	Ethelbert, 2nd son of Ethelwulf, united Kent and Wessex.	NA
866	Ethelred I, 3rd son of Ethelwulf, king of Wessex, fought Danes	NA
871	Alfred (the Great), 4th son of Ethelwulf, defeated Danes, fortified London	52
899	Edward (the Elder), son of Alfred, united English, claimed Scotland	55
924	Athelstan (the Glorious), eldest son of Edward, king of Mercia, Wessex	45
940	Edmund, 3rd son of Edward, king of Wessex, Mercia.	25
946	Edred, 4th son of Edward	32
955	Edwy (the Fair), eldest son of Edmund, king of Wessex.	18
959	Edgar (the Peaceful), 2nd son of Edmund, ruled all English.	32
975	Edward (the Martyr), eldest son of Edgar, murdered by stepmother.	17
978; 1014[2]	Ethelred II (the Unready), 2nd son of Edgar, married Emma of Normandy.	48
1016	Edmund II (Ironside), son of Ethelred II, king of London.	27
1016	Canute (the Dane), son of Sweyn, who conquered English territory; gave Wessex to Edmund II; married Emma, Ethelred II's widow.	40
1035	Harold I (Harefoot), illegitimate son of Canute	NA
1040	Hardecanute, son of Canute by Emma, also king of Denmark	24
1042	Edward (the Confessor), son of Ethelred II, canonized 1161	62
1066	Harold II, Edward's brother-in-law, last Saxon king.	44
	England: House of Normandy	
1066	William I (the Conqueror), son of Duke Robert I of Normandy, defeated Harold II at Hastings	60
1087	William II (Rufus), 3rd son of William I, killed by arrow while hunting in possible assassination.	43
1100	Henry I (Beauclerc), youngest son of William I	67
	England: House of Blois	
1135	Stephen, son of Adela, daughter of William I, and Count of Blois	50
	England: House of Plantagenet	
1154	Henry II, son of Geoffrey Plantagenet (Angevin) by Matilda, daughter of Henry I.	56
1189	Richard I (Coeur de Lion), son of Henry II, crusader.	42
1199	John (Lackland), son of Henry II, approved Magna Carta, 1215.	50
1216	Henry III, son of John, acceded at 9, under regency until 1227	65
1272	Edward I (Longshanks), son of Henry III.	68
1307	Edward II, son of Edward I, deposed by Parliament	43
1327	Edward III (of Windsor), son of Edward II	65
1377	Richard II, grandson of Edward III, deposed	33
	England: House of Lancaster	
1399	Henry IV (of Bolingbroke), son of John of Gaunt, duke of Lancaster, son of Edward III	47
1413	Henry V, son of Henry IV, victor over French at Agincourt	34
1422; 1470	Henry VI, son of Henry V, overthrown by Edward IV in 1461 but was returned to throne in 1470. Deposed, died in Tower of London, 1471.	40
	England: House of York	
1461; 1471	Edward IV, great-great-grandson of Edward III, son of duke of York. Acclaimed king by Parliament, 1461. Driven into exile in 1470 but regained throne, 1471.	40
1483	Edward V, son of Edward IV, murdered in Tower of London	13
1483	Richard III, brother of Edward IV, fell in battle at Bosworth Field against Henry Tudor	32
	England: House of Tudor	
1485	Henry VII, son of Edmund Tudor, earl of Richmond, whose father had married Henry V's widow. Descended from Edward III through mother, Margaret Beaufort, via John of Gaunt. Married Elizabeth of York, eldest daughter of Edward IV, to unite Lancaster and York	53
1509	Henry VIII, 2nd son of Henry VII, by Elizabeth	56
1547	Edward VI, son of Henry VIII, by Jane Seymour, his 3rd queen. Ruled under regents, was forced to name Lady Jane Grey his successor. Council of State proclaimed her queen, July 10, 1553. Mary Tudor won Council, was proclaimed queen, July 19. Mary had Jane beheaded for treason, 1554.	16
1553	Mary I, daughter of Henry VIII, by his 1st wife, Catherine of Aragon.	43
1558	Elizabeth I, daughter of Henry VIII, by his 2nd wife, Anne Boleyn	69
	Great Britain: House of Stuart	
1603	James I (James VI of Scotland), son of Mary, Queen of Scots. First to call self king of Great Britain; this became official with Act of Union, 1707.	59
1625	Charles I, only surviving son of James I.	48
	Great Britain: Commonwealth	
1649	Declared upon execution of Charles I	
	Great Britain: Protectorate	
1653	Oliver Cromwell, served on Council of State, executive body of Commonwealth, following overthrow of monarchy. Named Lord Protector upon creation of Protectorate by 1653 Instrument of Government	59
1658	Richard Cromwell, 3rd son of Oliver Cromwell. Resigned as Lord Protector amid civil war, 1659.	86
	Great Britain: House of Stuart (restored)	
1660	Charles II, eldest son of Charles I, Restoration put him back on throne, died without issue	55
1685	James II, 2nd son of Charles I, deposed 1688.	68
1689	William III, son of William, Prince of Orange, by Mary, daughter of Charles I. Offered joint rule of throne with wife by Parliament	51
1689	Mary II, eldest daughter of James II and wife of William III, died 1694	33
1702	Anne, 2nd daughter of James II, sister-in-law of William III, assumed throne on William's death	49
	Great Britain: House of Hanover	
1714	George I, son of Elector of Hanover by Sophia, granddaughter of James I	67
1727	George II, only son of George I, married Caroline of Brandenburg.	77
1760	George III, grandson of George II, married Charlotte of Mecklenburg.	81
1820	George IV, eldest son of George III, prince regent from Feb. 1811	67
1830	William IV, 3rd son of George III, married Adelaide of Saxe-Meiningen	71
1837	Victoria, daughter of Edward, 4th son of George III; married Prince Albert of Saxe-Coburg and Gotha, 1840 . . .	81
	Great Britain: House of Saxe-Coburg and Gotha	
1901	Edward VII, eldest son of Victoria, married Alexandra, Princess of Denmark.	68

Reign began	Great Britain: House of Windsor[3]	Age at death[1]
1910	George V, 2nd son of Edward VII, married Princess Mary of Teck	70
1936	Edward VIII, eldest son of George V, acceded Jan. 20, abdicated Dec. 11.	77
1936	George VI, 2nd son of George V, married Lady Elizabeth Bowes-Lyon	56
1952	Elizabeth II, elder daughter of George VI, acceded Feb. 6	

NA = Age/birth date not certain. (1) Except where noted, year of death is year of accession of succeeding ruler. (2) King Sweyn I of Denmark invaded England in 1013 and declared himself king. Ethelred II reclaimed the throne upon Sweyn's death in 1014. (3) Name adopted by proclamation of George V, July 17, 1917.

Rulers of Scotland

Reign began	Name	Reign began	Name
846	Kenneth I MacAlpin, first Scot to rule both Scots and Picts	1306	Robert I (the Bruce), victor at Bannockburn, 1314. Treaty with England and secured throne, 1328
1005	Malcolm II Mackenneth	1329	David II, only surviving son
1034	Duncan I, first general ruler	1371	Robert II (the Steward), son of Robert I's daughter Marjorie
1040	Macbeth, seized kingdom, slain by Malcolm Canmore		and Walter, steward of Scotland. First of Stewart line
1057	Malcolm III (Canmore), eldest son of Duncan I	1390	Robert III, son
1093	Donald Bane, younger brother	1406	James I, son
1094	Duncan II, eldest son of Malcolm III by first wife	1437	James II, son
1095	Donald Bane (restored)	1460	James III, eldest son
1097	Edgar, 4th son of Malcolm III and Queen Margaret	1488	James IV, eldest son
1107	Alexander I, brother	1513	James V, eldest son
1124	David I, brother of Edgar	1542	Mary (Queen of Scots), daughter, became queen before
1153	Malcolm IV (the Maiden), grandson		she was 1 week old. Married Francis II (d. 1560), son of
1165	William (the Lion), brother		King Henry II of France, 1558. Married her cousin, Henry
1214	Alexander II, son		Stewart, Lord Darnley (d. 1567), 1565. Married James
1249	Alexander III, son		Hepburn, Earl of Bothwell, 1567. Imprisoned by
1286	Margaret (Maid of Norway), granddaughter; died 1290 at age 8. (Interregnum, 1290-92)		Elizabeth I, 1568; beheaded, 1587
		1567	James VI, son of Mary and Lord Darnley, became
1292	John Balliol, proclaimed king of Scotland by Edward I of England. (Interregnum, 1296-1306[1])		James I, king of England, on Elizabeth's death, 1603. Legislative union of Scotland and England not official until Act of Union, 1707

(1) Edward I decreed annexation of Scotland to England, 1296. William Wallace led resistance, 1297-1305.

Prime Ministers of Great Britain
Designations in parentheses describe each government.
Cl. = Coalition; C = Conservative; La. = Labour; Li. = Liberal; P = Peelite; T = Tory; W = Whig

Entered office	Name	Entered office	Name	Entered office	Name
1721	Sir Robert Walpole (W)[1]	1830	Earl Grey (W)	1915	Herbert H. Asquith (Cl.)
1742	Earl of Wilmington (W)	1834	Viscount Melbourne (W)	1916	David Lloyd George (Cl.)
1743	Henry Pelham (W)	1834	Sir Robert Peel (C)	1922	Andrew Bonar Law (C)
1754	Duke of Newcastle (W)	1835	Viscount Melbourne (W)	1923	Stanley Baldwin (C)
1756	Duke of Devonshire (W)	1841	Sir Robert Peel (C)	1924	James Ramsay MacDonald (La.)
1757	Duke of Newcastle (W)	1846	Lord (later Earl) John Russell (W)	1924	Stanley Baldwin (C)
1762	Earl of Bute (T)	1852	Earl of Derby (C)	1929	James Ramsay MacDonald (La.)
1763	George Grenville (W)	1852	Earl of Aberdeen (P)	1931	James Ramsay MacDonald (Cl.)
1765	Marquess of Rockingham (W)	1855	Viscount Palmerston (Li.)	1935	Stanley Baldwin (Cl.)
1766	William Pitt the Elder (Earl of Chatham) (W)	1858	Earl of Derby (C)	1937	Neville Chamberlain (Cl.)
		1859	Viscount Palmerston (Li.)	1940	Winston Churchill (Cl.)
1768	Duke of Grafton (W)	1865	Earl Russell (Li.)	1945	Winston Churchill (C)
1770	Frederick North (Lord North) (T)	1866	Earl of Derby (C)	1945	Clement Attlee (La.)
1782	Marquess of Rockingham (W)	1868	Benjamin Disraeli (C)	1951	Sir Winston Churchill (C)
1782	Earl of Shelburne (W)	1868	William E. Gladstone (Li.)	1955	Sir Anthony Eden (C)
1783	Duke of Portland (Cl.)	1874	Benjamin Disraeli (C)	1957	Harold Macmillan (C)
1783	William Pitt the Younger (T)	1880	William E. Gladstone (Li.)	1963	Sir Alec Douglas-Home (C)
1801	Henry Addington (T)	1885	Marquess of Salisbury (C)	1964	Harold Wilson (La.)
1804	William Pitt the Younger (T)	1886	William E. Gladstone (Li.)	1970	Edward Heath (C)
1806	William Wyndham Grenville, Baron Grenville (W)	1886	Marquess of Salisbury (C)	1974	Harold Wilson (La.)
		1892	William E. Gladstone (Li.)	1976	James Callaghan (La.)
1807	Duke of Portland (T)	1894	Earl of Rosebery (Li.)	1979	Margaret Thatcher (C)
1809	Spencer Perceval (T)	1895	Marquess of Salisbury (C)	1990	John Major (C)
1812	Earl of Liverpool (T)	1902	Arthur J. Balfour (C)	1997	Tony Blair (La.)
1827	George Canning (T)	1905	Sir Henry Campbell-Bannerman (Li.)	2007	Gordon Brown (La.)
1827	Viscount Goderich (T)			2010	David Cameron (Cl.)
1828	Duke of Wellington (T)	1908	Herbert H. Asquith (Li.)		

Note: The Conservative Party was formed in 1834, an outgrowth of the Tory party. (1) Walpole is commonly regarded as the first prime minister of Britain, though the title was not commonly used then and did not become official until 1905.

Prime Ministers of Canada
C = Conservative; Li. = Liberal; PC = Progressive Conservative; U = Unionist

Entered office	Name (party)	Entered office	Name (party)	Entered office	Name (party)
1867	Sir John A. Macdonald (C)	1920	Arthur Meighen (U)	1968	Pierre Elliott Trudeau (Li.)
1873	Alexander Mackenzie (Li.)	1921	W. L. Mackenzie King (Li.)	1979	Joe Clark (PC)
1878	Sir John A. Macdonald (C)	1926[3]	Arthur Meighen (C)	1980	Pierre Elliott Trudeau (Li.)
1891	Sir John J. C. Abbott (C)	1926	W. L. Mackenzie King (Li.)	1984[3]	John Napier Turner (Li.)
1892	Sir John S. D. Thompson (C)	1930	Richard Bedford Bennett (C)	1984	Brian Mulroney (PC)
1894	Sir Mackenzie Bowell (C)	1935	W. L. Mackenzie King (Li.)	1993[4]	Kim Campbell (PC)
1896[1]	Sir Charles Tupper (C)	1948	Louis St. Laurent (Li.)	1993	Jean Chrétien (Li.)
1896	Sir Wilfrid Laurier (Li.)	1957	John G. Diefenbaker (PC)	2003	Paul Martin (Li.)
1911	Sir Robert Laird Borden (C/U)[2]	1963	Lester Bowles Pearson (Li.)	2006	Stephen Harper (C)

(1) May-July. (2) Conservative 1911-17, Unionist 1917-20. (3) June-Sept. (4) June-Oct.

Rulers of France

Caesar to Charlemagne

Julius Caesar subdued the Gauls, native tribes of Gaul (France), 58 to 51 BCE. The Romans ruled 500 years. The Franks, a Teutonic tribe, reached the Somme from the east c. 250 CE. By the 5th cent., the Merovingian Franks ousted the Romans. In 451, with the help of Visigoths, Burgundians, and others, they defeated Attila and the Huns at Châlons-sur-Marne.

Childeric I became leader of the Merovingians, 458. His son Clovis I, crowned 481, founded the dynasty. After defeating the Alemanni (Germans), 496, he was baptized a Christian and made Paris his capital. His line ruled until Childeric III was deposed, 751.

The West Merovingians were called Neustrians, the eastern Austrasians. Pepin of Herstal (687-714), major domus (head of the palace) of Austrasia, took over Neustria as dux (leader) of the Franks. Pepin's son, Charles, called Martel (the Hammer), defeated the Saracens at Tours-Poitiers, 732; was succeeded by his son, Pepin the Short, 741, who deposed Childeric III and ruled as king until 768.

His son, Charlemagne, or Charles the Great (742-814), became king of the Franks, 768, with his brother Carloman (751-71). Charlemagne ruled France, Germany, parts of Italy, Spain, and Austria, and enforced Christianity. Crowned Emperor of the Romans by Pope Leo III in Rome, Dec. 25, 800. Succeeded by son, Louis I (the Pious), 814. At death, 840, Louis left empire to sons Lothair (Roman emperor), Pepin I (king of Aquitaine), Louis II (the German), and Charles II (the Bald, of France). They quarreled and, by the Treaty of Verdun, 843, divided the empire.

The date preceding each entry is year of accession.

Carolingian Dynasty

- **843** Charles I (the Bald), Roman emperor, 875
- **877** Louis II (the Stammerer), son
- **879** Louis III (d. 882) and brother Carloman
- **885** Charles II (the Fat), Roman emperor, 881
- **888** Eudes (Odo), elected by nobles
- **898** Charles III (the Simple), son of Louis II, defeated by Robert
- **922** Robert, brother of Eudes, killed in war
- **923** Rudolph (Raoul), duke of Burgundy
- **936** Louis IV, son of Charles III
- **954** Lothair, son, aged 13, defeated by Capet
- **986** Louis V (the Sluggard), left no heirs

House of Capet

- **987** Hugh Capet, son of Hugh the Great
- **996** Robert II (the Pious), son
- **1031** Henry I, son
- **1060** Philip I (the Fair), son
- **1108** Louis VI (the Fat), son
- **1137** Louis VII (the Younger), son
- **1180** Philip II (Augustus), son, crowned at Reims
- **1223** Louis VIII (the Lion), son
- **1226** Louis IX, son, arbitrated disputes with English King Henry III; led crusades, 1248 (captured in Egypt, 1250) and 1270, when he died of plague in Tunis. Canonized as St. Louis, 1297
- **1270** Philip III (the Hardy), son
- **1285** Philip IV (the Fair), son, king at 17
- **1314** Louis X (the Headstrong), son. His posthumous son, John I, lived and reigned only five days.
- **1316** Philip V (the Tall), brother of Louis X
- **1322** Charles IV (the Fair), brother of Louis X

House of Valois

- **1328** Philip VI (of Valois), grandson of Philip III
- **1350** John II (the Good), son, retired to England
- **1364** Charles V (the Wise), son
- **1380** Charles VI (the Beloved), son
- **1422** Charles VII (the Victorious), son. In 1429, Joan of Arc (Jeanne d'Arc) defeated English at Orleans and Patay and had Charles crowned at Reims, July 17. Joan was captured May 24, 1430, and executed May 30, 1431, at Rouen for heresy. Charles ordered her rehabilitation, effected 1455.
- **1461** Louis XI (the Cruel), son, civil reformer
- **1483** Charles VIII (the Affable), son
- **1498** Louis XII, great-grandson of Charles V
- **1515** Francis I, of Angouleme, nephew, son-in-law. Fought four major wars, was patron of the arts
- **1547** Henry II, son, killed at joust. Husband of Catherine de Médicis and lover of Diane de Poitiers. Catherine was daughter of Lorenzo de Medici. By marriage to Henry II, she became the mother of Francis II, Charles IX, Henry III, and Queen Margaret (Reine Margot), wife of Henry IV (of Navarre).
- **1559** Francis II, son. Betrothed in 1548 at age 4 to Mary, Queen of Scots, aged 6; they were married 1558. Francis died 1560, aged 16. Mary returned to rule Scotland, 1561.
- **1560** Charles IX, brother
- **1574** Henry III, brother, assassinated

House of Bourbon

- **1589** Henry IV (of Navarre), grandson of Queen Margaret of Navarre. Made enemies when he gave tolerance to Protestants by Edict of Nantes, 1598. Married Margaret of Valois, daughter of Henry II and Catherine de Médicis; was divorced. In 1600, he married Marie de Médicis. She became regent upon Henry's assassination, 1610-17, for her son, Louis XIII; she was exiled by Richelieu, 1631.
- **1610** Louis XIII (the Just), son, married Anne of Austria. His chief minister (1622-42), Cardinal Richelieu, determined his policies.
- **1643** Louis XIV (the Sun King), son; was king 72 years. Until 1661, Anne of Austria was regent, with Cardinal Mazarin as chief minister; after that, Louis ruled absolutely. Known for his lavish court and patronage of the arts, he exhausted a prosperous country in wars for thrones and territory.
- **1715** Louis XV (the Beloved), great-grandson. Married a Polish princess, lost Canada to the English. His favorite mistresses, Mme. de Pompadour and Mme. Du Barry, influenced policies. Mme. Pompadour's saying "Après moi, le déluge" (After me, the deluge) often incorrectly attributed to Louis XV
- **1774** Louis XVI, grandson, married Marie Antoinette, daughter of Empress Maria Therese of Austria. King and queen beheaded by Revolution, 1793. Their son, called Louis XVII, died in prison, never ruled

First Republic

- **1792** National Convention of the French Revolution
- **1795** Directory, under Barras and others
- **1799** Consulate, Napoleon Bonaparte, first consul. Elected consul for life, 1802

First Empire

- **1804** Napoleon I (Napoleon Bonaparte), emperor. Josephine (de Beauharnais), empress, 1804-09; Marie Louise, empress, 1810-14. Her son, Francois (1811-32), titular king of Rome, later duke de Reichstadt and Napoleon II, never ruled. Napoleon abdicated 1814; died in exile, 1821.

House of Bourbon (restored)

- **1814** Louis XVIII, brother of Louis XVI, king
- **1824** Charles X, brother, reactionary, deposed by the July Revolution, 1830

House of Orleans

- **1830** Louis-Philippe (the Citizen King)

Second Republic

- **1848** Louis Napoleon Bonaparte, nephew of Napoleon I, president

Second Empire

- **1852** Napoleon III (Louis Napoleon Bonaparte), emperor; Eugenie (de Montijo), empress. Lost Franco-Prussian war, deposed 1870. Son, Prince Imperial (1856-79), died in Zulu War. Eugenie died 1920.

Third Republic: Presidents

- **1871** Thiers, Louis Adolphe (1797-1877)
- **1873** MacMahon, Marshal Patrice M. de (1808-93)
- **1879** Grevy, Paul J. (1807-91)
- **1887** Sadi-Carnot, M. (1837-94), assassinated
- **1894** Casimir-Perier, Jean P. P. (1847-1907)
- **1895** Faure, François Felix (1841-99)
- **1899** Loubet, Emile (1838-1929)
- **1906** Fallieres, C. Armand (1841-1931)
- **1913** Poincare, Raymond (1860-1934)
- **1920** Deschanel, Paul (1856-1922)
- **1920** Millerand, Alexandre (1859-1943)
- **1924** Doumergue, Gaston (1863-1937)
- **1931** Doumer, Paul (1857-1932), assassinated
- **1932** Lebrun, Albert (1871-1950), resigned 1940
- **1940** Vichy govt. under German armistice: Henri Philippe Petain (1856-1951), chief of state, 1940-44. Provisional govt. after liberation: Charles de Gaulle (1890-1970), Oct. 1944-Jan. 21, 1946; Felix Gouin (1884-1977), Jan. 23, 1946; Georges Bidault (1899-1983), June 24, 1946

Fourth Republic: Presidents

- **1947** Auriol, Vincent (1884-1966)
- **1954** Coty, Rene (1882-1962)

Fifth Republic: Presidents

- **1959** de Gaulle, Charles Andre J. M. (1890-1970)
- **1969** Pompidou, Georges (1911-74)
- **1974** Giscard d'Estaing, Valéry (1926-)
- **1981** Mitterrand, François (1916-96)
- **1995** Chirac, Jacques (1932-)
- **2007** Sarkozy, Nicolas (1955-)
- **2012** Hollande, François (1954-)

Rulers of Middle Europe and Germany

Carolingian Dynasty

Charles I (the Great), or Charlemagne, made Roman emperor by pope in Rome, 800. Ruled France, Italy, and Middle Europe; established Ostmark (later Austria). Died 814.

Louis I (Ludwig) (the Pious), son, crowned co-emperor by Charlemagne, 813. Divided empire among sons. Died 840; sons fought for control.

Louis II (the German), son, succeeded to East Francia (Germany), 843-76, with Treaty of Verdun.

Charles III (the Fat), son, inherited Swabia, 876. With brothers' deaths, acquired East Francia and West Francia (France), reuniting empire. Crowned emperor by pope, 881; deposed 887.

Arnulf, nephew, 887-99, took over East Francia; partition of empire.

Louis IV (the Child), son, 900-11, last direct descendant of Charlemagne.

Conrad I, duke of Franconia, first elected German king, 911-18.

Saxon Dynasty; First Reich

Henry I (the Fowler), duke of Saxony, elected king 919-36.

Otto I (the Great), son, 936-73, crowned Holy Roman Emperor by pope, 962.

Otto II, son, 961-83, ruled with Otto I as king, then emperor, 967.

Otto III, son, 983-1002, crowned Holy Roman Emperor, 996.

Henry II (the Saint), great-grandson of Otto the Great, duke of Bavaria, 1002-24. Crowned emperor, 1014.

Salian Dynasty

Conrad II, 1024-39, elected king of Germany.

Henry III (the Black), son, 1039-56, deposed three popes; annexed Burgundy.

Henry IV, son, 1056-1106, with mother, Agnes of Poitou, as regent in early years. He and Pope Gregory VII tried to depose each other. Civil war lasted about 20 years.

Henry V, son, 1106-25, last of Salian Dynasty.

Lothair, duke of Saxony, elected king 1125-37. Crowned emperor in Rome, 1133.

Hohenstaufen Dynasty

Conrad III, duke of Franconia, 1138-52, in Second Crusade.

Frederick I (Barbarossa, Italian for "Redbeard"), nephew, 1152-90.

Henry VI, son, 1190-97, gained kingdom of Sicily through marriage.

Philip of Swabia, brother, 1197-1208. Otto IV, nephew of King Richard I of England, 1198-1215, was elected rival king. Philip's murder, in 1208, led to Otto's win in new election same year. Civil war followed before Otto was deposed, 1215.

Frederick II, son of Henry VI, elected 1212-50. Had earlier succeeded father as king of Sicily; crowned himself king of Jerusalem, 1229, in Sixth Crusade.

Conrad IV, son, 1250-54. Conquered Naples.

(Interregnum, 1254-73. Conradin, son of Conrad IV and last legitimate Hohenstaufen, defeated by Charles of Anjou—brother of King Louis IX of France—and executed, 1268. Rise of electors of German monarch.)

Transition

Rudolf I, of Hapsburg, 1273-91, defeated King Ottocar II of Bohemia, 1278. Bequeathed duchies of Austria and Styria to sons.

Adolf of Nassau, 1292-98, killed in war with Albert I.

Albert I, elder son of Rudolf I, 1298-1308, assassinated.

Henry VII, of Luxemburg, 1308-13. Gained Bohemia, 1310; crowned Holy Roman Emperor, 1312.

Louis IV, of Wittelsbach, 1314-46. Also elected was a son of Albert I, Frederick of Austria, whom Louis defeated in 1322. Rejected need for papal confirmation of elected German king.

Charles IV, of Luxemburg, grandson of Henry VII, 1346-78. Took Brandenburg.

Wenceslaus, son, 1378-1400; deposed.

Rupert, of Wittelsbach, elector palatine, 1400-10.

Sigismund, brother of Wenceslaus, 1410-37.

Hapsburg Dynasty

Albert II, duke of Austria, son-in-law of Sigismund, elected German king, 1438-39; king of Hungary and Holy Roman Emperor.

Frederick III, cousin, 1440-93, fought Turks.

Maximilian I, son, 1493-1519, archduke of Austria.

Charles V, grandson, 1519-58. King of Spain; assumed title of Holy Roman Emperor. Martin Luther, who had been excommunicated by pope, appeared at Diet of Worms, 1521. Charles attempted church reform and conciliation between Catholicism and Protestantism; abdicated.

Ferdinand I, brother, 1558-64; king of Hungary and Bohemia, 1526 (successive leaders through Maria Theresa will rule these lands as well).

Maximilian II, son, 1564-76.

Rudolf II, son, 1576-1612.

Matthias, brother, 1612-19.

Ferdinand II, grandson of Ferdinand I, 1619-37. Bohemian Protestants, unhappy with Ferdinand's support of Catholic Counter-Reformation, crowned Frederick V, elector palatine. Frederick became known as "Winter King" with defeat in battle, 1620; start of Thirty Years' War.

Ferdinand III, son, 1637-57. Treaties signed, 1648, in Peace of Westphalia ended war.

Leopold I, son, 1658-1705.

Joseph I, son, 1705-11.

Charles VI, brother, 1711-40; died without male heir.

Maria Theresa, daughter, 1740-80. Appointed husband, Francis Stephen of Lorraine, co-regent. Dispute over her inheritance led to War of the Austrian Succession. Charles VII, also known as Charles Albert, elected in opposition to Francis, 1742-45. After Charles's death, she obtained election of her husband as Holy Roman Emperor Francis I, 1745-65. Fought Seven Years' War with Frederick II of Prussia.

Hapsburg-Lorraine Dynasty

Joseph II, son, 1765-90, reformer. Ruled jointly with Maria Theresa until her death. Participated in first partition of Poland, with Prussia and Russia.

Leopold II, brother, 1790-92; king of Hungary and Bohemia.

Francis II, son, 1792-1806; king of Hungary and Bohemia. Proclaimed first emperor of Austria, 1804-35. Unsuccessfully fought against Napoleon; forced to abdicate, 1806, as Holy Roman Emperor, last use of title.

Ferdinand, son, 1835-48, emperor of Austria; king of Hungary and Bohemia. Abdicated in favor of nephew after revolution broke out in Vienna.

Austro-Hungarian Monarchy

Francis Joseph I, nephew, 1848-1916, emperor of Austria and king of Hungary. Defeated in Austro-Prussian War, 1866. Formed dual monarchy of Austria-Hungary, 1867. After Serbian nationalist assassinated Francis Joseph's nephew and heir, Archduke Francis Ferdinand, June 28, 1914, Austrian diplomacy precipitated World War I.

Charles I, grandnephew, 1916-18, last emperor of Austria and king of Hungary. Abdicated Nov. 1918; died in exile, 1922.

Second and Third Reichs

William I, brother of Frederick William IV, 1861-88, king of Prussia. Appointed Otto von Bismarck chancellor, 1862. Franco-Prussian War, also known as Franco-German War, 1870-71, unified German states. William proclaimed German emperor, 1871; beginning of Second Reich.

Frederick III, son, 1888.

William II, son, 1888-1918, led Germany into World War I. Abdicated Nov. 1918; died in exile in the Netherlands, 1941.

Germany adopted constitution at Weimar, July 1, 1919, setting up Weimar Republic. Presidents included Friedrich Ebert, 1919-25, and Paul von Hindenburg, 1925-34, field marshal in World War I. Hindenburg appointed Adolf Hitler chancellor, 1933, at beginning of Third Reich. Following Hindenburg's death, Hitler succeeded as Führer and chancellor, 1934-45, with dictatorial powers. Annexed Austria, 1938. Precipitated World War II, 1939-45. Hitler committed suicide, 1945.

Germany After 1945

After World War II, Germany was split between democratic West and Soviet-dominated East. West German chancellors: Konrad Adenauer, 1949-63; Ludwig Erhard, 1963-66; Kurt Georg Kiesinger, 1966-69; Willy Brandt, 1969-74; Helmut Schmidt, 1974-82; Helmut Kohl, 1982-90. East German Communist party leaders: Walter Ulbricht, 1950-71; Erich Honecker, 1971-89; Egon Krenz, 1989.

Germany reunited Oct. 3, 1990. Post-reunification chancellors: Helmut Kohl, 1990-98; Gerhard Schröder, 1998-2005; Angela Merkel, 2005- .

Rulers of Hungary

The first king of Hungary was Stephen I, of the Arpad Dynasty, 1000-38. Feuds followed his death.

Charles I, also known as Charles Robert, became king, 1308-42.

Louis I (the Great), son, 1342-82. Succeeded uncle Casimir III as ruler of Poland, 1370.

Mary, elder daughter, 1382-95, ruled with husband, Sigismund of Luxemburg, 1387-1437, who also became king of Bohemia, Germany and Holy Roman Emperor. Hedwig (Jadwiga), younger daughter of Louis I, became queen of Poland. (See **Rulers of Poland**.)

Albert II, duke of Austria, son-in-law of Sigismund, 1438-39. Also king of Germany and Holy Roman Emperor.

Vladislaus I, 1440-44, king of Poland.

Ladislaus V, posthumous son of Albert II, 1444-57, not crowned until 1453. Janos Hunyadi acted as governor under young king, 1446-52; fought Turks.

Matthias I (Corvinus), son of Janos Hunyadi, 1458-90. Shared title of king of Bohemia. Captured Vienna, 1485; annexed Styria, Carinthia.

Vladislaus II, 1490-1516, king of Bohemia.

Louis II, son, 1516-26. Died in Battle of Mohács against Suleiman (the Magnificent), head of Ottoman Empire.

Ferdinand I, of Austria, brother-in-law, and John I, also known as John Zapolya of Transylvania, elected rival kings. Suleiman claimed part of Hungary for Ottoman Empire. Hungary partitioned. (Refer to **Hapsburg Dynasty** for continuation.)

Rulers of Prussia

Nucleus of Prussia was the margravate of Brandenburg, an electorate of the Holy Roman Empire. Frederick VI, burgrave of Nuremberg, was made elector of Brandenburg, 1415. Rise of Hohenzollern Dynasty in territory that included Brandenburg and duchy of Prussia.

Frederick William (the Great Elector), 1640-88, elector of Brandenburg.

Frederick III, son, 1688-1713, elector of Brandenburg. Crowned Frederick I, king in Prussia, 1701.

Frederick William I, son, 1713-40.

Frederick II (the Great), son, 1740-86; military strategist who expanded Prussia's holdings.

Frederick William II, nephew, 1786-97.

Frederick William III, son, 1797-1840; Napoleonic Wars.

Frederick William IV, son, 1840-61. Revolution of 1848; constitution adopted, 1850. (Refer to **Second and Third Reichs** for continuation.)

Rulers of Poland

House of Piast

Mieszko I, c. 963-92, duke of Poland; Poland Christianized, 966. Expansion under three with name Boleslaus (reigns not consecutive): Boleslaus I (the Brave), son, 992-1025, crowned first king of Poland, 1025; Boleslaus II (the Bold), great-grandson, 1058-79, exiled after killing bishop of Krakow, Stanislaus (who became a patron saint of Poland); Boleslaus III (the Wry-Mouthed), nephew, 1102-38, divided Poland among four sons with oldest also in control of crown. Period of feudal division followed.

A Polish duke, Conrad of Masovia, asked the Teutonic Knights—a German military religious order—to crusade against Prussia, 1226. Teutonic Knights conquered lands; thereafter warred with Poland. Mongols/Tatars invaded Poland, 1241.

Vladislaus I, 1306-33, reunited most Polish territories; crowned king, 1320. Casimir III (the Great), son, 1333-70, developed economy, cultural life, foreign policy. No male heir. Succeeded by Louis I, nephew, 1370-82, who was also Louis I (the Great) of Hungary.

Jadwiga, daughter, 1384-99.

House of Jagiello

Vladislaus Jagiello, grand duke of Lithuania, married Jadwiga, 1386, and ruled jointly as Vladislaus II, 1386-1434. Poland and Lithuania united; Lithuania converted to Christianity. Defeated Teutonic Knights at Grunwald (Tannenberg), 1410.

Vladislaus III, son, 1434-44, also king of Hungary. Fought Turks; killed in Battle of Varna, 1444.

Casimir IV, brother, 1447-92, put son Vladislaus on throne of Bohemia and Hungary. Victorious over Teutonic Knights; signed treaty, 1466, after 13-year war.

John I, son, 1492-1501.

Alexander I, brother, 1501-05.

Sigismund I, brother, 1506-48, patronized sciences and arts; his and son's reign were golden age. Grand Master of Teutonic Order, Albert Hohenzollern, converted to Protestantism; secularized his state and made first duke of Prussia by Sigismund, 1525.

Sigismund II, son, 1548-72; Union of Lublin, 1569, established dual state of Poland and Lithuania. No male heir.

Elective Kings

Henry of Valois, 1573-74, first king elected by nobility. Left Poland to assume crown of France after brother's death. Interregnum.

Stephen Bathory, 1576-86, prince of Transylvania, married Anna, sister of Sigismund II. Fought Russians.

Sigismund III Vasa, nephew of Sigismund II and son of king of Sweden, 1587-1632. Fought to reclaim Swedish crown, which he'd lost because of his Catholicism; battled Russians and Turks.

Vladislaus IV Vasa, son, 1632-48.

John II Casimir Vasa, brother, 1648-68. Fought Cossacks, Swedish, Russians, Turks, Tatars; period of invasions known as "the Deluge."

Michael Korybut Wisniowiecki, 1669-73.

John III Sobieski, 1674-96, freed Vienna from besieging Turks, 1683.

Augustus II (the Strong), 1697-1733, elector of Saxony.

Augustus III, son, 1733-63, elector of Saxony.

Stanislaus II, 1764-95, last king. Encouraged reforms; first modern constitution in Europe, 1791. Poland lost territory to Russia, Austria, and Prussia in three partitions (1772, 1793, 1795). Thaddeus Kosciusko, American-Polish general, attempted unsuccessful insurrection, 1794.

Poland Under Foreign Rule

Grand duchy of Warsaw created by Napoleon I out of Prussian (formerly Polish) territory. Frederick Augustus I, king of Saxony, ruled grand duchy, 1807-15. Defeat of Napoleon led to Congress of Vienna, 1814-15; part of Poland claimed as kingdom by Russia. Polish uprisings against Russia (1830, 1863) and Austria (1846) repressed. Poland regained independence following World War I.

Second Republic

Jozef Pilsudski, 1918-22, head of state. Presidents: Gabriel Narutowicz, 1922, assassinated by extremist; Stanislaus Wojciechowski, 1922-26, resigned after coup d'état by Pilsudski; Ignacy Moscicki, 1926-39, ruled with Pilsudski (d. 1935) and Pilsudski's military colleagues as virtual dictator during what came to be known as Sanacja (meaning "cleansing" or "healing") regime.

Poland Under Foreign Occupation, Influence

After Hitler and Stalin signed nonaggression pact, Germany invaded Poland Sept. 1, 1939; Russia invaded Sept. 17. Polish government-in-exile was in France, then England. Vladislaus Raczkiewicz, 1939-47, president; Gen. Vladislaus Sikorski, 1939-43, and Stanislaus Mikolajczyk, 1943-44, prime ministers. Polish residents were sent to German concentration camps and Soviet labor camps; about 3 million Jewish Poles were killed in the Holocaust. Thousands of Polish prisoners of war, mostly military officers, massacred in Katyn Forest by Soviet secret police, 1940. Soviet-sponsored Polish Committee of National Liberation took formative role in new government, 1945, renamed Polish People's Republic in 1952. Communist Party ruled the country. Brief period of liberalization followed Stalin's death in 1953. Vladislaus Gomulka, 1956-70, and Edward Gierek, 1970-80, led country as first secretary of Polish United Workers' Party.

Election of Cardinal Karol Wojtyla, archbishop of Krakow, as pope (John Paul II) inspired Poles, 1978. Strikes in 1980 prompted creation of Solidarity, an independent trade union headed by Lech Walesa. Solidarity gained control of government in partly free elections, 1985.

Third Republic

Presidents: Lech Walesa, 1990-95; Aleksander Kwasniewski, 1995-2005; Lech Kaczynski, 2005-10, died in plane crash; Bronislaus Komorowski and Grzegorz Schetyna, acting, 2010; Komorowski, 2010- .

Current prime minister: Donald Tusk, 2007- .

Rulers of Denmark, Sweden, Norway

Denmark

Canute (the Great) ruled area that included England, Denmark, and Norway, 1016-35. Valdemar IV Atterdag reunited Denmark, 1361. Margaret I, daughter, married to Haakon VI, king of Norway, 1363. After Valdemar's death, Olaf, Margaret's infant son, made king of Denmark, 1375. He was also crowned king of Norway after death of Haakon, 1380. Following Olaf's death, 1387, Margaret served as regent of Denmark, Norway, and Sweden. She effected the Union of Kalmar of the three kingdoms, 1397. She had her grandnephew, Eric of Pomerania, crowned (she held actual power until her death, 1412).

Succeeding rulers were unable to enforce their claims on Sweden until Christian II, 1512-23, conquered the country, 1520. He was soon deposed; accession of Gustavus I as king of Sweden, 1523, ended Kalmar Union. Denmark continued to dominate Norway until the Napoleonic Wars when Frederick VI, 1808-39, allied with Napoleon I after Danish fleet was attacked by Britain, 1807. By 1814 treaty, Denmark was forced to cede Norway to Sweden.

Succession: House of Oldenborg (began with Christian I, 1448): Christian VIII, 1839-48; Frederick VII, son, 1848-63. House of Glücksborg: Christian IX, 1863-1906; Frederick VIII, son, 1906-12; Christian X, son, 1912-47; Frederick IX, son, 1947-72; Margrethe II, daughter, 1972- .

Sweden

Under King Magnus Ladulas, hereditary nobility established around 1280. Swedish nobles opposed to Albert of Mecklenburg accepted Margaret I, regent of Denmark, as ruler, 1389. Sweden joined Kalmar Union, 1397. After internal unrest, Sweden was conquered anew by Denmark's Christian II, 1520. Execution of Christian's opponents in "Stockholm Bloodbath" led to uprising under Gustavus Vasa, who was elected Swedish king, 1523-60. Gustavus established an independent kingdom with centralized power, state church, and hereditary throne. Gustavus II Adolphus,

1611-32, fought Russia, Poland, Germany and was called the Lion of the North; died in battle.

Later rulers: Christina, daughter, 1632-54, abdicated; Charles X Gustavus, cousin, 1654-60; Charles XI, son, 1660-97; Charles XII, son, 1697-1718; Ulrika Eleonora, sister, 1718-20, abdicated; Frederick I, of Hesse, husband, 1720-51; Adolphus Frederick, 1751-71; Gustavus III, son, 1771-92; Gustavus IV Adolphus, son, 1792-1809, deposed; Charles XIII, uncle, 1809-18. Charles XIV John (born Jean Baptiste Bernadotte, a general under Napoleon I), 1818-44, founded House of Bernadotte.

Succession: Oscar I, son, 1844-59; Charles XV, son, 1859-72; Oscar II, brother, 1872-1907; Gustavus V, son, 1907-50; Gustavus VI Adolf, son, 1950-73; Carl XVI Gustavus, grandson, 1973- .

Norway

Harald I (Fairhair) overcame rivals to become first king of Norway, c. 885-c. 933. Olaf II Haraldsson, 1015-28, Christianized country; became patron saint of Norway. Haakon V Magnusson, 1299-1319, died without male heir. His daughter Ingeborg was married to Erik, a son of the Norwegian king; their son Magnus VII Eriksson became ruler of Norway, 1319-55, and Sweden, 1319-63. Haakon VI Magnusson, son, 1355-80, married Margaret of Denmark. Olaf IV, son, became king of Norway, 1380-87, and Denmark, 1375-87, with mother as regent. Margaret took over rule upon his death, 1387. Union of Kalmar, 1397, united Norway, Denmark, and Sweden.

After Napoleonic Wars, Denmark ceded Norway to Sweden, 1814. A strong nationalist movement forced Sweden to recognize Norway as an independent kingdom under the Swedish kings. Norwegian constitution, adopted 1814, allowed for creation of the Storting (Norwegian parliament), which governed country domestically. In 1905, the union was dissolved. Prince Charles of Denmark elected king of Norway as Haakon VII, 1905-57; founded House of Glücksburg. Succession: Olav V, son, 1957-91; Harald V, son, 1991- .

Rulers of the Netherlands and Belgium

The Netherlands

William I, son of Prince William V of Orange, came to power after French rule ended in the Netherlands, 1813; crowned king with approval of Congress of Vienna, 1815. Started House of Orange-Nassau. Northern Netherlands was known as Holland. Belgians, in southern Netherlands, rebelled against the Dutch and seceded, Oct. 4, 1830. Dutch formally recognized Belgian independence, Apr. 19, 1839. William I abdicated, 1840.

Succession: William II, son, 1840-49; William III, son, 1849-90; Wilhelmina, daughter, 1890-1948, abdicated; Juliana,

daughter, 1948-80, abdicated; Beatrix, daughter, 1980-2013, abdicated; Willem-Alexander, son, 2013- .

Belgium

A national congress elected Prince Leopold of Saxe-Coburg as king. He took the throne July 21, 1831, as Leopold I.

Succession: Leopold II, son, 1865-1909; Albert I, nephew, 1909-34; Leopold III, son, 1934-51, in exile after Germany invaded Belgium, later abdicated; Prince Charles, brother, acted as regent 1944-50; Baudouin I, son of Leopold III, 1951-93; Albert II, brother, 1993-2013; Philippe, son, 2013- .

Rulers of Modern Italy

After the fall of Napoleon in 1814, the Congress of Vienna, 1815, restored Italy as a political patchwork, comprising the Kingdom of Naples and Sicily, the Papal States, and smaller units. Piedmont and Genoa were awarded to Sardinia, ruled by King Victor Emmanuel I of Savoy.

United Italy emerged under the leadership of Camillo Benso, Count di Cavour, prime minister of Sardinia, 1852-61. Giuseppe Mazzini and Giuseppe Garibaldi were both figures in Risorgimento ("resurgence"), period before Italy's unification. Victor Emmanuel I abdicated 1821. Charles Felix, brother, 1821-31, died without issue. Succeeded by Charles Albert, 1831-49; he abdicated upon defeat by the Austrians at Novara. Succeeded by Victor Emmanuel II, son, 1849-61.

In 1859, France forced Austria to cede Lombardy to Sardinia, which gave rights to Savoy and Nice to France. In 1860, Garibaldi led 1,000 volunteers in a campaign, took Sicily, and expelled the king of Naples. In 1860, the House of Savoy annexed Tuscany, Parma, Modena, Romagna, the Two Sicilies, the Marches, and Umbria. Victor Emmanuel assumed the title of king of Italy, Mar. 17, 1861.

In 1866, Victor Emmanuel allied with Prussia in the Austro-Prussian War and, with Prussia's victory, received Venetia. On Sept. 20, 1870, his troops under Gen. Raffaele Cadorna entered Rome and took over the Papal States, ending the temporal power of the Roman Catholic Church.

Succession: Umberto I, son, 1878-1900, assassinated; Victor Emmanuel III, son, 1900-46, abdicated; Umberto II, son, 1946, ruled a month. In 1921, Benito Mussolini formed the Fascist party; he became prime minister, 1922. He entered World War II as an ally of Hitler. He was deposed, 1943.

At a plebiscite, 1946, Italy voted for a republic. Premier Alcide de Gasperi became chief of state; Liberal Enrico de Nicola was elected provisional president by Constituent Assembly. Successive presidents: Luigi Einaudi, 1948-55; Giovanni Gronchi, 1955-62; Antonio Segni, 1962-64; Giuseppe Saragat, 1964-71; Giovanni Leone, 1971-78; Alessandro Pertini, 1978-85; Francesco Cossiga, 1985-92; Oscar Luigi Scalfaro, 1992-99; Carlo Azeglio Ciampi, 1999-2006; Giorgio Napolitano, 2006- .

Rulers of Spain

From 8th to 11th centuries, Spain was dominated by the Moors (Arabs and Berbers). The Christian reconquest established small kingdoms (Asturias, Aragon, Castile, Catalonia, Leon, Navarre, and Valencia). In 1474, Isabella became Queen of Castile and Leon. Her husband, Ferdinand, inherited Aragon, 1479, with Catalonia, Valencia, and the Balearic Islands; became Ferdinand V of Castile. By Isabella's request, Pope Sixtus IV established

the Inquisition, 1478. Last Moorish kingdom, Granada, fell 1492. Columbus opened New World, 1492. Isabella was succeeded by daughter, Juana (the Mad), but Ferdinand ruled until his death.

Charles I, son of Juana, grandson of Ferdinand and Isabella, and of Maximilian I of Hapsburg, later became Holy Roman Emperor Charles V, 1520; abdicated 1556. Philip II, son, 1556-98, inherited only Spanish throne; conquered Portugal, fought

Turks, sent Armada against England. Married to Mary I of England, 1554-58. Succession: Philip III, 1598-1621; Philip IV, 1621-65; Charles II, 1665-1700, left Spain to Philip of Anjou, grandson of Louis XIV, who as Philip V, 1700-46, founded Bourbon dynasty; Ferdinand VI, 1746-59; Charles III, 1759-88; Charles IV, 1788-1808, abdicated.

Napoleon made his brother Joseph king of Spain, 1808, but the Spanish ousted him in 1813. Ferdinand VII, 1808, 1814-33, lost American colonies except for Cuba, Puerto Rico. Maria Christina of the Two Sicilies, wife, was regent until 1843 for Isabella II, daughter, who was deposed by revolution, 1868. Amadeo of Savoy elected king by the Cortes (parliament), 1870; abdicated 1873. First republic, 1873-74. Alfonso XII, son of Isabella, 1875-85. Alfonso XIII, his posthumous son, with mother Maria Christina as regent before he assumed throne, 1902. Spain ceded territory after loss in Spanish-American War, 1898. Alfonso married British princess Victoria Eugenia of Battenberg, 1906. Dictatorship of Primo de Rivera, 1923-30, precipitated revolution of 1931. Alfonso agreed to leave without formal abdication; he died in Rome, 1941. Monarchy abolished; the second republic established with socialist backing. Niceto Alcala Zamora, 1931-36, president. Manuel Azaña elected, 1936.

In July 1936, the military revolted against the Republican government at start of Spanish Civil War. Gen. Francisco Franco entered the country with troops from Spanish Morocco. He became head of Nationalist regime.

A law restoring the monarchy was approved in a 1947 referendum. Juan Carlos, grandson of Alfonso XIII, was designated by Franco and the Cortes. Franco died in office, Nov. 1975; Juan Carlos I proclaimed king.

Rulers of Russia; Leaders of the USSR and Russian Federation

First ruler to consolidate Slavic tribes was Rurik, leader of the Russians who established himself at Novgorod, 862 CE. His successors ruled as dukes of Kiev after 972. In 988, Vladimir was converted and adopted the Byzantine Greek Orthodox service, later modified by Slav influences. Yaroslav, 1019-54, was important organizer and lawgiver; his daughters married kings of Norway, Hungary, and France. Vladimir II Monomakh, grandson, 1113-25, was progenitor of several rulers, but in 1169, Andrew Bogolyubsky overthrew Kiev and began the line known as grand dukes of Vladimir.

Of the grand dukes of Vladimir, Alexander Nevsky, 1246-63, had a son, Daniel, first to be called duke of Muscovy (Moscow), 1263-1303. After Dmitri III Donskoi defeated the Tatars in 1380, they also became grand dukes of all Russia. Tatar independence and considerable territorial expansion were achieved under Ivan III, 1462-1505.

Tsars of Muscovy: Ivan III was referred to in church ritual as tsar. He married Sofia, niece of the last Byzantine emperor. Succession: Basil III, died 1533. Ivan IV (the Terrible), son, crowned 1547 as Tsar of All Russia, ruled until 1584. Feodor I, son, 1584-98, was weak; Boris Godunov had control. The dynasty died. After years of internal strife, the Russians united under 17-year-old Michael Romanov, distantly related to Ivan IV's first wife. He ruled 1613-45, establishing the Romanov line.

Tsars, or emperors, of Russia (Romanovs): Peter I (the Great), 1682-1725. Succession: Catherine, his widow, 1725. Peter II, grandson of Peter I, 1727. Anna, daughter of Ivan V and niece of Peter I, 1730. Ivan VI, great-grandson of Ivan V, 1740, deposed by Elizabeth, daughter of Peter I, 1741. (Ivan VI was later assassinated, 1764.) Peter III, grandson of Peter I, 1761, deposed 1762 for his consort, Catherine II (the Great), former princess of Anhalt Zerbst (Germany). Paul I, son, 1796, killed 1801. Alexander I, son, 1801, defeated Napoleon. Nicholas I, brother, 1825. Alexander II, son, 1855, assassinated 1881. Alexander III, son, 1881. Nicholas II, son, 1894-1917, last tsar of Russia, was forced to abdicate by the March 1917 Revolution, which followed losses to Germany in WWI. The tsar, empress, tsarevich (crown prince), and tsar's four daughters were murdered by the Bolsheviks, July 1918.

Premiers of provisional government: Prince Georgi Lvov, followed by Alexander Kerensky, 1917.

Union of Soviet Socialist Republics

Bolshevik Revolution, Nov. 7, 1917, removed Kerensky from power; council of People's Commissars formed. Lenin (Vladimir Ilyich Ulyanov) became premier, died Jan. 1924. Aleksei Rykov (executed 1938) and V. M. Molotov held the office, but actual ruler was Joseph Stalin (Joseph Vissarionovich Dzhugashvili), general secretary of the Central Committee of the Communist Party. Stalin became president of the Council of Ministers (premier) May 1941; died Mar. 1953. Georgi Malenkov succeeded him; he also briefly served as first secretary of Central Committee before giving up the position to Nikita S. Khrushchev. Malenkov was forced to resign as premier, 1955, and was dropped from Central Committee, 1957. Marshal Nikolai A. Bulganin became premier, 1955, was demoted, and Khrushchev became premier, 1958.

Khrushchev was ousted, 1964; he was replaced by Leonid I. Brezhnev as first secretary of the party and by Aleksei N. Kosygin as premier. Brezhnev also took office as president, 1977; he died 1982. The Central Committee elected former KGB head Yuri V. Andropov president; he died 1984. Konstantin U. Chernenko was chosen by Central Committee as its general secretary. Upon his death in 1985, he was succeeded by Mikhail Gorbachev, who replaced Andrei Gromyko as president in 1988. Gorbachev resigned Dec. 25, 1991, and the Soviet Union officially disbanded the next day. Each of the 15 former Soviet constituent republics became independent.

Post-Soviet Russia

Boris Yeltsin was sworn in July 10, 1991, as Russia's first elected president. With the Dec. 1991 dissolution of the Soviet Union, the Russian Federation became a founding member of the Commonwealth of Independent States. Yeltsin stepped down as president, Dec. 1999, and he named Vladimir Putin interim successor. Presidents: Yeltsin, 1991-99; Putin, 2000-08; Dmitry Medvedev, 2008-12, appointed Putin prime minister; Putin, 2012- .

Leaders in the South American Wars of Liberation

Francisco de Miranda, José de San Martín, and Simón Bolívar led early 19th-cent. struggles of South American nations to free themselves from Spain.

Miranda (1750-1816), a Venezuelan, served with the French in the American Revolution and commanded French Revolutionary forces in the Netherlands. He attempted a revolt in Venezuela in 1806 but failed. In 1810, with British and American backing, he returned and was briefly dictator until the British withdrew their support. In 1812, he was overcome by royalists and taken prisoner. He died in a Spanish prison.

San Martín (1778-1850) was born in Argentina. He served in Spanish campaigns in Europe and Africa, 1789-1811. He first joined the independence movement in Argentina in 1812. In 1817, he invaded Chile over the mountain passes with 4,000 men. He and Gen. Bernardo O'Higgins (1778-1842) defeated the Spaniards at Chacabuco, 1817. O'Higgins was named Liberator and became first director of Chile, 1817-23. In 1821, San Martín occupied Lima and Callao, Peru, and became protector of Peru.

Bolívar (1783-1830) was born into an aristocratic family in Venezuela. He served under Miranda in 1812. In 1813, he captured Caracas, where he was named Liberator. In 1814, he was forced out by civil unrest. In 1817, he was again in control of Venezuela and was named dictator. He organized Nueva Granada with the help of Gen. Francisco de Paula Santander (1792-1840). By joining Nueva Granada, Venezuela, and the area that is now Panama and Ecuador, the republic of Colombia was formed with Bolívar as president. He decisively defeated the Spaniards in the Second Battle of Carabobo, Venezuela, June 24, 1821.

In May 1822, Gen. Antonio Jose de Sucre, Bolívar's lieutenant, took Quito. Bolívar went to Guayaquil to confer with San Martín, who resigned as protector of Peru. With a new army of Colombians and Peruvians, Bolívar defeated the Spaniards in the Battle of Junin, 1824, and cleared Peru.

De Sucre organized Charcas (Upper Peru) as Republica Bolívar (now Bolivia) and acted as president in place of Bolívar, who wrote its constitution. De Sucre defeated the Spanish faction of Peru at Ayacucho, Dec. 19, 1824.

Continued civil strife caused the Colombian federation to break apart. Santander turned against Bolívar, but the latter defeated and banished him. In 1828, Bolívar gave up the presidency. He died from tuberculosis Dec. 17, 1830.

Governments of China

Where dynastic dates overlap, the rulers or events referred to appeared in different areas of China.

Years in power	Government
c. 1994-c. 1766 BCE	Hsia dynasty, first hereditary Chinese dynasty
c. 1766-c. 1027 BCE	Shang dynasty
c. 1027-770 BCE	Western Chou dynasty, capital near present-day Xi'an
770-256 BCE	Eastern Chou dynasty, new capital established at Luoyang
403-221 BCE	Period of the Warring States
221-206 BCE	Ch'in dynasty, quasi-feudal states unified for first time; name of China derived from this dynasty
206 BCE-9 CE	Earlier, or Western Han dynasty, founded by rebel leader Liu Pang; Chinese state expanded under Emperor Wu Ti, 140-87 BCE, who represented zenith of power
9-23	Hsin dynasty, established by courtier Wang Mang, who deposed infant emperor for whom he had been acting as regent
25-220	Later, or Eastern Han dynasty
220-265[1]	Wei dynasty, established by son of Han general Ts'ao Ts'ao
221-263[1]	Shu Han dynasty in SW China
222-280[1]	Wu dynasty in SE China
265-317	Western Chin dynasty, established by Ssu-ma Yen, Wei dynasty general
317-420	Eastern Chin dynasty, established by prince of Ssu-ma family
420-589	Southern dynasties, four short-lived dynasties with capital at Chien-k'ang (present-day Nanjing)
589-618	Sui dynasty, reunified China; first emperor was Yang Chien, military servant who usurped throne of non-Chinese Northern Chou, 581
618-906	T'ang dynasty, founded by Li Yuan, who led rebellion against the Sui. Early rulers included former imperial concubine Empress Wu, 683-705; Hsuan Tsung, 712-56
907-960	Five Dynasties, period of disunion with short-lived dynasties in N, 10 independent states mostly in S
907-1125	Liao dynasty, of Khitan Mongols, capital at Yen-ching (present-day Beijing)
960-1126	Northern Sung dynasty, established by military leader Chao K'uang-yin, capital at Kaifeng
1122-1234	Chin dynasty, of Juchen people of Manchuria; drove Sung out of N China
1127-1279	Southern Sung dynasty, capital at Lin-an (present-day Hangzhou)
1279-1368	Yuan dynasty, of Mongols; Kublai Khan, grandson of Genghis Khan, high point of Mongol power
1368-1644	Ming dynasty, founded by rebel leader Chu Yuan-chang, former Buddhist monk. Country again under Chinese rule, capital in present-day Nanjing, then Beijing after defeat of Mongolian tribes
1644-1912	Manchu, or Ch'ing dynasty, under Manchu rule with capital at Chiang-ning (present-day Nanjing). Power of Chinese empire reached highest point in its 2,000-year history. Last imperial dynasty; Hsuan T'ung, or Pu Yi, last emperor. Sun Yat-sen led revolution, 1911. Republic of China formed, 1912
1912-1949	Rep. of China, Gen. Yüan Shih-k'ai elected first president. Power passed to provincial warlords upon his death, 1916. Gen. Chiang Kai-shek sought to reunify China under Kuomintang (Nationalist party), with new national government at Nanjing, 1928. War with Japan, then civil war, led to Nationalist authority collapse, Communist declaration of People's Rep. of China, 1949

(1) Also known as the period of the Three Kingdoms because of warfare between the Wei, Shu Han, and Wu dynasties.

Leaders of People's Republic of China

Name	Title/position, years in power
Mao Zedong	Chairman, 1949-59; Communist Party of China (CPC) Chairman, 1949-76
Zhou Enlai	Premier, 1949-76; foreign minister, 1949-76
Deng Xiaoping	Deputy Premier, 1952-66, 1973-76; "paramount leader," 1977-97
Liu Shaoqi	Chairman, 1959-68
Hua Guofeng	Premier, 1976-80; CPC Chairman, 1976-81
Hu Yaobang	CPC General Secretary, 1980-87; CPC Chairman 1981-82
Zhao Ziyang	Premier, 1980-87; CPC General Secretary, 1987-89
Li Xiannian	President, 1983-88
Yang Shangkun	President, 1988-93
Li Peng	Premier, 1988-98
Jiang Zemin	CPC General Secretary, 1989-2002; President, 1993-2003
Zhu Rongji	Premier, 1998-2003
Hu Jintao	CPC General Secretary, 2002-12; President, 2003-13
Wen Jiabao	Premier, 2003-13
Xi Jinping	CPC General Secretary, 2012- ; President, 2013-
Li Keqiang	Premier, 2013-

Historical Periods of Japan

Years in power	Period	Founding event
c. 300-592	Yamato	Conquest of Yamato plain
592-710	Asuka	Accession of Empress Suiko
710-794	Nara	Heijo (Nara) completed; capital moved to Nagaoka, 784
794-1185	Heian	Heian (Kyoto) completed
858-1160	Fujiwara	Fujiwara-no-Yoshifusa became regent
1160-1185	Taira	Taira-no-Kiyomoro assumed control; Minamoto-no-Yoritomo victor over Taira, 1185
1192-1333	Kamakura	Yoritomo became shogun
1334-1392	Namboku	Emperor Godaigo restored; established Southern Court at Yoshino, 1336
1392-1573	Muromachi	Unification of Southern and Northern Courts
1467-1600	Sengoku	Onin war began
1573-1603	Momoyama	Oda Nobunaga entered Kyoto, 1568, deposed last Ashikaga shogun, 1573. Tokugawa Ieyasu victor at Sekigahara, 1600
1603-1867	Edo	Ieyasu became shogun
1868-1912	Meiji	Meiji (Mutsuhito) ascended throne in Meiji Restoration; Charter Oath, 1868, led to Westernization
1912-1926	Taisho	Accession of Emperor Taisho (Yoshihito)
1926-1989	Showa	Accession of Emperor Hirohito
1989-	Heisei	Accession of Emperor Akihito

── WORLD EXPLORATION AND GEOGRAPHY ──
Early Explorers of the Western Hemisphere
Reviewed by G. A. Clark, Ph.D., Aug. 2008

In light of recent discoveries, theories about how and when the first people arrived in the Western Hemisphere are being reconsidered. Genetic evidence suggests that beginning around 14,000 years before the present (BP), the earliest immigrants crossed a 1,000-km wide land bridge between Siberia and Alaska in small groups and spread rapidly south through the Americas, arriving at S America's southern tip by c. 10,700 BP. Kennewick Man, found in 1996 in Washington's Columbia River Gorge, dates to 9,600-9,200 BP, and Luzia, dating to 11,500 BP from Brazil, are examples of these early arrivals. Modern Native Americans appear to be descended from peoples indigenous to N and central Asia who arrived in subsequent waves of migration. A growing body of genetic, skeletal, and linguistic evidence documents their migration throughout the Americas.

Archaeologists have confirmed evidence of habitation by 12,900 BP at sites located on the shores of ancient lakes at an elevation of 17,400 ft in Chile's Atacama Desert. There is also growing support for the settlement of Chile's Monte Verde site, dated to c. 12,500 BP, and eight other 13th-millennium sites in Brazil, Chile, and Argentina. One theory on their migration holds that a glacier covered much of N America from c. 20,000 to 13,000 BP, so those who settled in S America might have traveled there in small boats skirting the pack ice along the W coast, or spread from N to S America through an "ice-free corridor" in what today is western Canada. Other theories hold that they arrived before continental glaciation blocked migration from the north, or migrated from Iberia in skin boats. Controversial skeletal evidence from a burial at Santana do Riacho in Brazil (9,460 BP) suggests that some of the early immigrants who came via the land bridge from Siberia may have originated in Africa.

Long before Europeans arrived, the Americas were—for the most part—populated by hunter-gatherers and small-scale horticulturalists. In a few areas (SE U.S., Mesoamerica, coastal Peru and Chile), complex chiefdoms and state-level societies had appeared. Irrigation canals dating to 4,700 BP provide evidence for the origins of large-scale agriculture along the western slopes of Peru's Andes Mountains. The earliest known state in the Americas occupied a 700-sq-mi area spanning four river valleys in coastal Peru between 3,500 and 500 BP.

The Norse (Vikings sailing out of Iceland and Greenland), led by Leif Ericson, are usually credited with having been the first Europeans to reach America, with at least five voyages occurring about 1000 CE to areas they called Helluland, Markland, and Vinland—possibly what are known today as Baffin Island, Labrador, and either Newfoundland or somewhere farther south in New England. L'Anse aux Meadows, on the northern tip of Newfoundland, is the only documented settlement, with evidence of a small village with a church dating to c. 1000 CE. The Norse tried to import farming and herding economies, but these efforts failed after a few centuries, and Greenland and Newfoundland were abandoned by Europeans.

Sustained contact between the hemispheres began with the first voyage of Christopher Columbus (born Cristoforo Colombo, c. 1451, near Genoa, Italy). Columbus made four voyages to the New World while sailing for the Spanish monarchs Ferdinand II and Isabella. He left Palos, Spain, Aug. 3, 1492, with 88 men and landed at San Salvador (Watling Islands, Bahamas), Oct. 12, 1492. His fleet included three vessels, the *Niña, Pinta,* and *Santa María.* He also visited Cuba, Hispaniola, and many smaller Caribbean islands, then populated by the now-extinct Taino Indians. A second expedition left Cadíz, Spain, Sept. 25, 1493, with 17 ships and 1,400 men, reaching the island of Dominica, in the Lesser Antilles, on Nov. 3, 1493. His third voyage took him from Sanlucar, Spain (May 30, 1498, with six ships), to the island of Trinidad and to the adjacent coast of S America, where he made landfall at the mouth of the Orinoco River. A fourth voyage departed Cadíz on May 9, 1502, and reached the E coast of Mexico, Honduras, Panama, and what he christened Santiago (the present-day island of Jamaica). Columbus died in Valladolid, Spain, on May 20, 1506, still convinced he had reached Asia by sailing west.

In N America, John and Sebastian Cabot, Italian explorers sailing for the English crown, reached Newfoundland and possibly Nova Scotia in 1497. John's second voyage (1498), seeking the fabled Northwest Passage, a new trade route to Asia, resulted in the loss of his entire fleet. For most of the 16th cent., exploration of the New World was dominated by the empires of Spain and Portugal.

In 1497 and 1499, Amerigo Vespucci (for whom the Americas are named), an Italian explorer sailing for Spain, passed along the N and E coasts of S America. He was the first to argue that these lands were previously unknown and not part of Asia.

Other early explorations are listed below.

Year	Explorer	Nationality (sponsor, if different)	Area reached or explored
1497-98	Vasco da Gama	Portuguese	Cape of Good Hope (Africa), India
1499	Alonso de Ojeda	Spanish	N South American coast, Venezuela
1500, Feb.	Vicente Yañez Pinzon	Spanish	S American coast, Amazon R.
1500, Apr.	Pedro Álvarez Cabral	Portuguese	Brazil
1501	Rodrigo de Bastidas	Spanish	Central America
1513	Vasco Núñez de Balboa	Spanish	Panama, Pacific Ocean
1513	Juan Ponce de León	Spanish	Florida, Yucatán Peninsula
1515	Juan de Solis	Spanish	Río de la Plata
1519	Alonso de Pineda	Spanish	Mouth of Mississippi R.
1519	Hernán Cortés	Spanish	Mexico
1519-20	Ferdinand Magellan	Portuguese (Spanish)	Straits of Magellan, Tierra del Fuego
1524	Giovanni da Verrazano	Italian (French)	Atlantic coast, incl. New York Harbor
1528	Álvar Núñez Cabeza de Vaca	Spanish	Texas coast and interior
1532	Francisco Pizarro	Spanish	Peru
1534	Jacques Cartier	French	Canada, Gulf of St. Lawrence
1536	Pedro de Mendoza	Spanish	Buenos Aires
1539	Francisco de Ulloa	Spanish	California coast
1539-41	Hernando de Soto	Spanish	Mississippi R., near Memphis, TN
1539	Marcos de Niza	Italian (Spanish)	SW United States
1540	Francisco de Coronado	Spanish	SW United States
1540	Hernando de Alarcón	Spanish	Colorado R.
1540	Garcia Lopez de Cárdenas	Spanish	Colorado, Grand Canyon
1541	Francisco de Orellana	Spanish	Amazon R.
1542	Juan Rodriguez Cabrillo	Portuguese (Spanish)	W Mexico, San Diego Harbor
1565	Pedro Menéndez de Avilés	Spanish	St. Augustine, FL
1576	Sir Martin Frobisher	English	Frobisher Bay, Canada
1577-80	Sir Francis Drake	English	California coast
1582	Antonio de Espejo	Spanish	SW U.S. (New Mexico)
1584	Philip Amadas and Arthur Barlowe (for Raleigh)	English	Virginia
1585-87	Sir Walter Raleigh's men	English	Roanoke Isl., NC
1595	Sir Walter Raleigh	English	Orinoco R.
1603-09	Samuel de Champlain	French	Canadian interior, Lake Champlain
1607	Capt. John Smith	English	Atlantic coast
1609-10	Henry Hudson	English (Dutch)	Hudson R., Hudson Bay
1634	Jean Nicolet	French	Lake Michigan, Wisconsin
1673	Jacques Marquette and Louis Jolliet	French	Mississippi R., south to Arkansas
1682	René-Robert Cavelier, sieur de La Salle	French	Mississippi R., south to Gulf of Mexico
1727-29	Vitus Bering	Danish (Russian)	Bering Strait, Alaska
1789	Sir Alexander Mackenzie	Canadian	NW Canada
1804-06	Meriwether Lewis and William Clark	American	Missouri R., Rocky Mts., Columbia R.

Arctic Exploration

Early Explorers

1587: John Davis (Eng.) traveled Davis Strait to Sanderson's Hope, 72°12´N.

1596: Willem Barents and Jacob van Heemskerck (Dutch) discovered Bear Isl., touched NW tip of Spitsbergen, 79°49´N, rounded Novaya Zemlya, wintered at Ice Haven.

1607: Henry Hudson (Eng.) went north along Greenland's E coast to Cape Hold-with-Hope, 73°30´, then north of Spitsbergen to 80°23´. Explored Hudson's Touches (Jan Mayen).

1616: William Baffin and Robert Bylot (Eng.) traveled Baffin Bay to Smith Sound.

1728: Vitus Bering (Dan./Russ.) sailed through strait (Bering), proving Asia and America are separate.

1733-40: Great Northern Expedition (Russ.) surveyed Siberian Arctic coast.

1741: Vitus Bering (Dan./Russ.) sighted Alaska, named Mount St. Elias. His lieutenant, Aleksei Chirikof, explored coast.

1771: Samuel Hearne (Brit., Hudson's Bay Co.) went overland from Prince of Wales Fort (Churchill) on Hudson Bay to mouth of Coppermine R.

1778: James Cook (Eng.) sailed through Bering Strait to Icy Cape, AK, and North Cape, Siberia.

1789: Alexander Mackenzie (Scot., North West Co.). Montreal to mouth of Mackenzie R.

1806: William Scoresby (Brit.). North of Spitsbergen to 81°30´.

1820-23: Ferdinand von Wrangel (Russ.) surveyed Siberian Arctic coast. His exploration joined James Cook's at North Cape, confirming separation of the continents.

1878-79: Baron Adolf Erik Nordenskiöld (Swed.) was first to navigate the Northeast Passage—an ocean route connecting Europe's North Sea, along the Arctic coast of Asia and through the Bering Sea, to the Pacific Ocean.

1881: The U.S. steamer *Jeannette*, led by Lt. Cmdr. George W. DeLong, was trapped in ice and crushed, June. DeLong and 11 others died; 12 survived.

1888: Fridtjof Nansen (Nor.) crossed Greenland icecap.

1893-96: Nansen in *Fram* drifted from New Siberian Isls. to Spitsbergen; tried polar dash in 1895, reached Franz Josef Land, 86°14´N.

1897: Salomon A. Andrée (Swed.) and two others started in balloon from Spitsbergen, July 11; they drifted across pole to U.S. before disappearing. Their bodies were found, Aug. 6, 1930, on White Isl., 82°57´N, 29°52´E.

1903-06: Roald Amundsen (Nor.) was first to sail whole length of Northwest Passage—ocean route linking the Atlantic Ocean to the Pacific via Canada's marine waterways.

North Pole Exploration

Robert E. Peary (U.S.) explored Greenland's coast, 1891-92; tried for North Pole, 1893. In 1900, he reached northern limit of Greenland and 83°50´N; in 1902, he reached 84°17´N; in 1906, he went from Ellesmere Isl. to 87°06´N. He sailed in the *Roosevelt*, July 1908, to winter off Cape Sheridan, Grant Land. The dash for the North Pole began Mar. 1 from Cape Columbia, Ellesmere Isl. Peary reportedly reached the pole, 90°N, Apr. 6, 1909; more recent research suggests he may have fallen short of his goal by c. 30-60 mi. (Dr. Frederick Cook claimed to have reached the North Pole, in 1908.) The first surface expedition

independently confirmed to have reached the North Pole was that of Ralph Plaisted in 1968 (see below).

Peary had several support groups carrying supplies until the last group turned back at 87°47´N. Peary, Matthew Henson, and four Eskimos (or Inuit) proceeded with dog teams and sleds. They were said to have crossed the pole several times, then built an igloo there and rested before returning south.

1914: Donald MacMillan (U.S.) traveled 200 miles from Axel Heiberg Isl. in search of Peary-named Crocker Land; MacMillan realized Peary had seen a Fata Morgana, mirage whereby pack ice in distance appears to be land.

1915-17: Vilhjalmur Stefansson (Can.) discovered Borden, Brock, Meighen, and Lougheed Isls.

1918-20: Roald Amundsen (Nor.) sailed Northeast Passage.

1925: Amundsen and Lincoln Ellsworth (U.S.) reached 87°44´N in attempt to fly to North Pole from Spitsbergen.

1926: Richard E. Byrd and Floyd Bennett (U.S.) reputedly flew over North Pole, May 9.

Amundsen, Ellsworth, and Umberto Nobile (Ital.) flew over North Pole May 12 in dirigible *Norge*.

1928: Nobile crossed North Pole in airship, May 24; crashed, May 25. Amundsen died attempting rescue.

North Pole Exploration Records

1958: Nuclear-powered submarine USS *Nautilus*, under Cmdr. William R. Anderson, crossed the North Pole beneath the ice, Aug. 3.

1960: In Aug., the nuclear submarine USS *Seadragon* (Cmdr. George P. Steele II) made the first E-W underwater transit through Northwest Passage. Traveling mostly submerged, it made the 850-mi trek from Baffin Bay to the Beaufort Sea in six days.

1968: Ralph Plaisted (U.S.) and three amateur explorers on snowmobiles became first independently confirmed surface expedition to reach North Pole, Apr. 19.

1977: Soviet nuclear icebreaker *Arktika* became first surface ship to reach North Pole, Aug. 16.

1978: On Apr. 30, Naomi Uemura (Jpn.) became first person to reach the North Pole alone, traveling by dog sled in a 54-day, 600-mi trek over the frozen Arctic.

1982: In Apr., Sir Ranulph Fiennes and Charles Burton, Brit. explorers, reached the North Pole and became first to circle the Earth from pole to pole. They had reached the South Pole 16 months earlier. The 52,000-mi trek took three years, involved 23 people, and cost an estimated $18 mil.

1986: Six explorers reached the North Pole assisted only by dogs, May 2. They became first to reach the pole without aerial logistics support since at least 1909. The explorers—Americans Will Steger, Paul Schurke, Ann Bancroft, and Geoff Carroll and Canadians Brent Boddy and Richard Weber—completed the 500-mi journey in 56 days.

1995: Weber and Mikhail Malakhov (Russ.) became first pair to make it to North Pole and back without any mechanical assistance, June 15. The 940-mi trip, made entirely on skis, took 121 days.

2003: Pen Hadow (Brit.) became first to reach North Pole from Canada, solo and without resupply, May 20. The 377-mi journey across the ice took 64 days.

2006: Prince Albert II of Monaco became first royal to reach North Pole, Apr. 16.

Antarctic Exploration

Antarctica has been approached since 1773-75, when Capt. James Cook (Eng.) reached 71°10´S. Many seas and landmarks bear the names of early explorers. Fabian von Bellingshausen (Russ.) discovered Peter I and Alexander I Isls., 1819-21. Nathaniel Palmer (U.S.) traveled throughout Palmer Peninsula, 60°W, 1820. Capt. John Davis (U.S.) made the first known Antarctic landing on Feb. 7, 1821. In 1823, James Weddell (Brit.) found Weddell Sea, 74°15´S, the southernmost point that had been reached.

First to determine existence of the continent of Antarctica was Charles Wilkes (U.S.), who followed the coast for 1,500 mi, 1840. Adelie Coast, 140°E, was found by Dumont d'Urville (Fr.), 1840. Ross Ice Shelf was found by James Clark Ross (Brit.), 1841-42.

1895: Leonard Kristensen (Nor.) landed a party on the coast of Victoria Land. They were first ashore on main continental mass. C. E. Borchgrevink, a member of that party, returned in 1899 with a Brit. expedition, first to winter on Antarctica.

1902-04: Robert Falcon Scott (Brit.) explored Edward VII Peninsula to 82°17´S, 146°33´E from McMurdo Sound.

1908-09: Ernest Shackleton (Brit.) was first to use Manchurian ponies in Antarctic sledging. He reached 88°23´S, discovering route onto plateau by way of Beardmore Glacier and pioneering the way to the pole.

1911: Roald Amundsen (Nor.) with four men and dog teams reached South Pole, Dec. 14.

1912: Scott reached the pole from Ross Isl., Jan. 18, with four companions. None survived. Their bodies and expedition notes were found, Nov. 12.

1928: Sir George Hubert Wilkins (Austral.) was first to use airplane over Antarctica.

1929: Richard E. Byrd (U.S.) established Little America on Bay of Whales. On 1,600-mi airplane flight begun Nov. 28, he crossed South Pole, Nov. 29, with three others.

1934-35: Byrd led second expedition to Little America, explored 450,000 sq mi, wintered alone at 80°08´S.

1934-37: John Rymill (Austral.) led British Graham Land Expedition; discovered Palmer Peninsula was part of mainland.

1935: Lincoln Ellsworth (U.S.) flew south along E Coast of Palmer Peninsula, then crossed continent to Little America, making four landings.

1939-41: U.S. Navy planes discovered about 150,000 sq mi of new land.

1940: Byrd charted most of coast between Ross Sea and Palmer Peninsula.

1946-47: U.S. Navy undertook Operation Highjump, commanded by Byrd, which included 13 ships and 4,000 men. Airplanes photomapped coastline and penetrated beyond pole.

1946-48: Ronne Antarctic Research Expedition Cmdr. Finn Ronne, USNR, determined Antarctic to be only one continent with no strait between Weddell Sea and Ross Sea; explored 250,000 sq mi of land by flights to 79°S.

1955-57: U.S. Navy's Operation Deep Freeze led by Byrd. Supporting U.S. scientific efforts for International Geophysical Year (IGY), the operation established five coastal stations fronting Indian, Pacific, and Atlantic Oceans and three interior stations; explored more than 1 mil sq mi in Wilkes Land.

1957-58: During IGY, July 1957 through Dec. 1958, scientists from 12 countries conducted research within network of some 60 stations on Antarctica.

Dr. Vivian E. Fuchs (Brit.) led 12-person Trans-Antarctic Expedition on first land crossing of Antarctica. Starting from the Weddell Sea, they reached Scott Station, Mar. 2, 1958, after traveling 2,158 mi in 99 days.

1958: A group of five U.S. scientists led by seismologist Edward C. Thiel, moving by tractor from Ellsworth Station on Weddell Sea, identified a mountain range 5,000 ft above the ice sheet and 9,000 ft above sea level. The range, originally

seen by a Navy plane, was named Dufek Massif, for Rear Adm. George Dufek.

1959: Argentina, Australia, Belgium, Chile, France, Japan, New Zealand, Norway, South Africa, USSR, UK, and U.S. signed a treaty suspending territorial claims for 30 years and reserving the continent south of 60°S for research.

1961-62: Scientists discovered Bentley Trench, running from Ross Ice Shelf into Marie Byrd Land, near the end of the Ellsworth Mts., toward Weddell Sea.

1962: U.S. nuclear power plant went online at McMurdo Sound; in operation until 1972.

1963: On Feb. 22, a U.S. plane made the region's longest nonstop flight from McMurdo Station south past the pole to Shackleton Mts., southeast to "Area of Inaccessibility," and back to McMurdo Station, covering 3,600 mi in 10 hours.

1964: New Zealanders mapped the mountain area from Cape Adare west some 400 mi to Pennell Glacier.

1985: Researcher Igor A. Zotikov (Russ.) discovered sediments in Ross Ice Shelf that seem to support continental drift theory. Ocean Drilling Project finds that the ice sheets of E Antarctica are 37 mil years old.

1989: Victoria Murden and Shirley Metz became first women as well as first Americans to reach South Pole overland when they arrived with nine others, Jan. 17.

1991: 24 nations approved a protocol to 1959 Antarctica Treaty, Oct. 4. New conservation provisions include banning oil and other mineral exploration for 50 years.

1994: On Dec. 25, after 50-day trek, Liv Arnesen (Nor.) became first woman to ski alone and unaided to South Pole.

1995: Borge Ousland (Nor.) reached South Pole on skis, Dec. 22, becoming first to reach both N and S Poles solo.

1996-97: Ousland became first to traverse Antarctica alone; reached South Pole Dec. 19, 1996. Traveled 1,675 mi in 64 days, ending Jan. 18, 1997.

2000-01: Ann Bancroft (U.S.) and Arnesen became first women to ski unaided across Antarctica, Feb. 11, 2001. The 1,717-mi journey took 94 days.

2008: Norwegians Christian Eide, Rune Midtgaard, Morten Andvig, and Mads Agerup reached the South Pole unaided in record 24 days, 8 hrs., 50 mins.

Volcanoes

Source: *Volcanoes of the World*, Geoscience Press; Global Volcanism Program, Smithsonian Institution

Eruptions have been documented in about 550 volcanoes. More than half to three-quarters of these historically active volcanoes can be found on the so-called **Ring of Fire**, which runs along the W coast of the Americas from the southern tip of Chile to Alaska, down the E coast of Asia from Kamchatka to Indonesia, and continues from New Guinea to New Zealand. The Ring of Fire marks the boundaries between tectonic plates underlying the Pacific Ocean and those of the surrounding continents. Volcanic activity also occurs along rift zones like Iceland, where plates pull apart, or over hot spots such as Hawaii, where plumes of molten material rise from the mantle to the Earth's crust. The majority of Earth's volcanism takes place at submarine rift zones, on the seafloor. For more information on volcanoes, see the Smithsonian Institution's global volcanism website at www.volcano.si.edu.

Notable Volcanic Eruptions

In approximately 5,700 BC, Mount Mazama, in southern Oregon, erupted violently, ejecting large amounts of ash and pumice and sending out pyroclastic flows (mixture of volcanic debris and gases). The ash spread over the northwestern U.S. and southern Canada. The eruption collapsed the top of the mountain, leaving a caldera about 6 mi across and 1 mi deep. This depression filled with water from rain and snow to form what is now called Crater Lake.

In 79 CE, Mount Vesuvius, a volcano overlooking Naples Bay, became active after several centuries of apparent inactivity. On Aug. 24 of that year, heated mud and ash swept down the mountain, engulfing the cities of Pompeii, Herculaneum, and Stabiae with debris more than 60 ft deep. About 10% of the population of the three towns were killed.

In 1883, an eruption similar to the Mazama eruption occurred on the island of Krakatau. At least 2,000 people died in pyroclastic flows on Aug. 26. The next day, the 2,640-ft peak of the volcano collapsed to 1,000 ft below sea level, sinking most of the island and killing over 3,000. The eruptions and collapse generated a series of tsunamis that killed more than 31,000 people in Java and Sumatra. Ash from the eruption colored sunsets around the world for two years.

Date	Volcano	Deaths (est.)	Date	Volcano	Deaths (est.)
Aug. 24, 79 CE	Mt. Vesuvius, Italy	16,000	May 8, 1902	Mt. Pelée, Martinique	28,000
1586	Kelut, Java, Indon.	10,000	Jan. 30, 1911	Mt. Taal, Philippines	1,400
Dec. 15, 1631	Mt. Vesuvius, Italy	4,000	May 19, 1919	Mt. Kelut, Java, Indon.	5,000
Aug. 12, 1772	Mt. Papandayan, Java, Indon.	3,000	Jan. 17-21, 1951	Mt. Lamington, New Guinea	3,000
June 8, 1783	Laki, Iceland	9,350	May 18, 1980	Mt. St. Helens, U.S.	57
May 21, 1792	Mt. Unzen, Japan	14,500	Mar. 28, 1982	El Chichon, Mexico	1,880
Apr. 10-12, 1815	Mt. Tambora, Sumbawa, Indon.	92,000[1]	Nov. 13, 1985	Nevado del Ruiz, Colombia	23,000
Aug. 26-27, 1883	Krakatau, Indon.	36,000[2]	Aug. 21, 1986	Lake Nyos, Cameroon	1,700
Apr. 24, 1902	Santa María, Guatemala	1,000[3]	June 15, 1991	Mt. Pinatubo, Luzon, Philippines	800[4]

(1) Of these, 10,000 were directly related to the eruption; additional deaths were the result of starvation and disease brought on by the event. (2) Collapse of volcano generated tsunamis, which were responsible for the majority of deaths. (3) An additional 3,000 deaths due to a malaria outbreak are sometimes attributed to the eruption. (4) Of these, about 500 were associated with post-eruption lahars (volcanic mudflows).

Notable Active Volcanoes

Source: Global Volcanism Program, Smithsonian Institution; Volcano Hazards Program, U.S. Geological Survey, U.S. Dept. of the Interior

Active volcanoes display a wide range of activity, including the production of ash plumes and seismic swarms. An eruption may involve the explosive ejection of fragmental material and escape of liquid lava. In this table, the year given indicates a volcano's last known or confirmed eruption, as of June 2013. Volcanoes are listed by height, which does not reflect eruptive magnitude. Submarine volcanoes are not included.

Volcano (latest eruption)	Location	Height (ft)
Africa		
Mt. Cameroon (2000)	Cameroon	13,435
Nyiragongo (2011)	Dem. Rep. of the Congo	11,384
Nyamuragira (2010)	Dem. Rep. of the Congo	10,033
Mt. Oku [Lake Nyos] (1986)	Cameroon	9,878
Ol Doinyo Lengai (2010)	Tanzania	9,718
Fogo (1995)	Cape Verde Isls.	9,281
Piton de la Fournaise (2010)	Réunion Isl., Indian O.	8,635
Karthala (2007)	Comoros	7,746
Nabro (2011)	Eritrea	7,277
Antarctica		
Erebus (2011)	Ross Isl.	12,447
Michael (2006)	Saunders Isl. (UK)	3,248
Asia and Oceania		
Kliuchevskoi (2012)	Kamchatka, Russia	15,863
Kerinci (2009)	Sumatra, Indon.	12,467
Fuji (1708)	Honshu, Japan	12,388
Rinjani (2010)	Lesser Sunda Isl., Indon.	12,224
Tolbachik (2013)	Kamchatka, Russia	12,080
Semeru (2011)	Java, Indon.	12,060
Koryaksky (2009)	Kamchatka, Russia	11,339
Slamet (2009)	Java, Indon.	11,247
Raung (2008)	Java, Indon.	10,932
Shiveluch (2013)	Kamchatka, Russia	10,771
On-take (1980)	Honshu, Japan	10,049
Merapi (2011)	Java, Indon.	9,737
Marapi (2011)	Sumatra, Indon.	9,485
Bezymianny (2012)	Kamchatka, Russia	9,455
Peuet Sague (2000)	Sumatra, Indon.	9,190
Ruapehu (2007)	New Zealand	9,176
Heard (2013)	Australia	9,006
Changbaishan (1903)	China-Korea	9,003
Papandayan (2002)	Java, Indon.	8,743
Asama (2009)	Honshu, Japan	8,425
Dieng (2009)	Java, Indon.	8,415
Mayon (2010)	Luzon, Philippines	8,077
Sinabung (2010)	Sumatra, Indon.	8,071
Kanlaon (2006)	Negros Isl., Philippines	7,989
Niigata-Yake-yama (1998)	Honshu, Japan	7,874
Kizimen (2013)	Kamchatka, Russia	7,795
Alaid (2012)	Kuril Isls., Russia	7,674
Ulawun (2011)	Papua New Guinea	7,657
Tengger Caldera (2011)	Java, Indon.	7,641
Chokai (1974)	Honshu, Japan	7,326
Galunggung (1984)	Java, Indon.	7,113
Azuma (1977)	Honshu, Japan	6,676
Tongariro (Ngauruhoe) (2012)	New Zealand	6,489
Sangeang Api (1999)	Lesser Sunda Isls., Indon.	6,394
Nasu (1963)	Honshu, Japan	6,283
Karkar (1979)	Papua New Guinea	6,033
Gorely (2010)	Kamchatka, Russia	6,001
Bandai (1888)	Honshu, Japan	5,968
Tiatia (2010)	Kuril Isls., Russia	5,968
Chikurachki (2008)	Kuril Isls., Russia	5,958
Manam (2013)	Papua New Guinea	5,928
Kuju (1996)	Kyushu, Japan	5,876
Karangetang (Api Siau) (2011)	Sangihe Isls., Indon.	5,853
Soputan (2012)	Sulawesi, Indon.	5,853
Bagana (2013)	Papua New Guinea	5,741
Kelut (2008)	Java, Indon.	5,679
Adatara (1996)	Honshu, Japan	5,636
Gamalama (2012)	Halmahera, Indon.	5,627
Kirishima (2011)	Kyushu, Japan	5,577
Gamkonora (2007)	Halmahera, Indon.	5,364
Aso (2011)	Kyushu, Japan	5,223
Lokon-Empung (2013)	Sulawesi, Indon.	5,184
Bulusan (2011)	Luzon, Philippines	5,134
Karymsky (2013)	Kamchatka, Russia	5,039
Unzen (1996)	Kyushu, Japan	4,921
Akan (2008)	Hokkaido, Japan	4,918
Aoba (2011)	Vanuatu	4,908
Sarychev Peak (2009)	Kuril Isls., Russia	4,908
Pinatubo (1993)	Luzon, Philippines	4,875
Lopevi (2008)	Vanuatu	4,636
Akita-Yake-yama (1997)	Honshu, Japan	4,482
Dukono (2012)	Halmahera, Indon.	4,380
Ambrym (2013)	Vanuatu	4,377
Langila (2010)	Papua New Guinea	4,363
Ibu (2013)	Halmahera Isl., Indon	4,347
Awu (2004)	Sangihe Isls., Indon.	4,331
Etorofu-Yakeyama (Grozny Group) (2013)	Iturup Isl., Japan/Russia	3,973
Ekarma (2010)	Kuril Isls., Russia	3,839
Ebeko (2010)	Kuril Isls., Russia	3,793

Volcano (latest eruption)	Location	Height (ft)
Central America and Caribbean		
Tacaná (1986)	Guatemala	13,320
Acatenango (1972)	Guatemala	13,044
Santa María (2013)	Guatemala	12,375
Fuego (2013)	Guatemala	12,346
Irazú (1994)	Costa Rica	11,260
Turrialba (2013)	Costa Rica	10,958
Poás (2013)	Costa Rica	8,884
Pacaya (2013)	Guatemala	8,373
Santa Ana (2005)	El Salvador	7,812
San Miguel (2002)	El Salvador	6,988
Rincón de la Vieja (1998)	Costa Rica	6,286
San Cristóbal (2013)	Nicaragua	5,725
Concepción (2011)	Nicaragua	5,577
Arenal (2010)	Costa Rica	5,479
Soufrière Guadeloupe (1977)	Guadeloupe Isl., France	4,813
Pelée (1932)	Martinique, France	4,583
Momotombo (1905)	Nicaragua	4,255
North America		
Pico de Orizaba (1846)	Mexico	18,619
Popocatépetl (2013)	Mexico	17,802
Rainier (1894)	Washington	14,409
Shasta (1786)	California	14,163
Wrangell (2002)	Alaska	14,163
Colima (2011)	Mexico	12,631
Lassen Peak (1917)	California	10,456
Redoubt (2009)	Alaska	10,197
Iliamna (1876)	Alaska	10,016
Shishaldin (2004)	Aleutian Isls., AK	9,373
St. Helens (2008)	Washington	8,363
Pavlof (2013)	Alaska	8,264
Veniaminof (2013)	Alaska	8,225
Katmai (1912)	Alaska	6,716
Makushin (1995)	Aleutian Isls., AK	5,905
Great Sitkin (1974)	Aleutian Isls., AK	5,709
Cleveland (2013)	Aleutian Isls., AK	5,676
Gareloi (1989)	Aleutian Isls., AK	5,161
Korovin (2007)	Aleutian Isls., AK	5,029
Kanaga (1995)	Aleutian Isls., AK	4,287
Akutan (1992)	Aleutian Isls., AK	4,275
Augustine (2006)	Alaska	4,108
South America		
Llullaillaco (1877)	Chile-Argentina	22,109
Guallatiri (1960)	Chile	19,918
Tupungatito (1987)	Chile-Argentina	19,685
Sabancaya (2003)	Peru	19,572
Cotopaxi (1940)	Ecuador	19,393
El Misti (1985)	Peru	19,101
Láscar (2007)	Chile	18,346
Nevado del Huila (2011)	Colombia	17,598
Nevado del Ruiz (2013)	Colombia	17,457
Sangay (2013)	Ecuador	17,159
Irruputuncu (1995)	Chile-Bolivia	16,939
Tungurahua (2013)	Ecuador	16,479
Guagua Pichincha (2009)	Ecuador	15,695
Puracé (1977)	Colombia	15,256
Galeras (2010)	Colombia	14,029
Planchón-Peteroa (2011)	Chile	13,474
Reventador (2013)	Ecuador	11,686
Llaima (2009)	Chile	10,253
Copahue (2000)	Chile-Argentina	9,830
Villarrica (2011)	Chile	9,340
Puyehue-Cordón Caulle (2011)	Chile	7,336
Europe		
Etna (2013)	Italy	10,925
Vesuvius (1944)	Italy	4,203
Stromboli (2011)	Italy	3,031
Santorini (1950)	Greece	1,204
Mid-Atlantic		
Jan Mayen (1985)	N Atlantic O., Norway	7,470
Grímsvötn (2011)	Iceland	5,659
Eyjafjallajökull (2010)	Iceland	5,466
Katla (2011)	Iceland	4,961
Hekla (2000)	Iceland	4,892
Mid-Pacific		
Mauna Loa (1984)	Hawaii, HI	13,681
Haleakala (1750)	Maui, HI	10,023
Kilauea (2013)	Hawaii, HI	4,009

Mountains
North America

Source: U.S. Geological Survey, U.S. Dept. of the Interior; Natural Resources Canada. Survey dates and elevation sources may differ.

Peak, state/prov., country	Height (ft)	Peak, state/prov., country	Height (ft)	Peak, state/prov., country	Height (ft)
McKinley (Denali), AK	20,237	Hunter, AK	14,573	Cameron, CO	14,245
Logan, Yukon, Canada	19,551	Browne Tower, AK	14,530	Shavano, CO	14,236
Pico de Orizaba, Mexico	18,619	Alverstone, AK-YT, U.S.-Can.	14,500	Belford, CO	14,204
St. Elias, AK-YT, U.S.-Can.	18,009	Whitney, CA	14,500	Princeton, CO	14,204
Popocatépetl, Mexico	17,802	University Peak, AK	14,470	Crestone Needle, CO	14,203
Foraker, AK	17,400	Elbert, CO	14,440	Yale, CO	14,203
Iztaccíhuatl, Mexico	17,154	Massive, CO	14,428	Bross, CO	14,179
Lucania, YT, Canada	17,146	Harvard, CO	14,427	Kit Carson, CO	14,171
King, YT, Canada	16,972	Rainier, WA	14,416	El Diente Peak, CO	14,165
Steele, YT, Canada	16,624	Williamson, CA	14,376	Point Success, WA	14,164
Bona, AK	16,500	La Plata Peak, CO	14,368	Shasta, CA	14,163
Blackburn, AK	16,390	Blanca Peak, CO	14,351	Wrangell, AK	14,163
Sanford, AK	16,237	Uncompahgre Peak, CO	14,315	Maroon Peak, CO	14,163
Vancouver, AK-YT, U.S.-Can.	15,699	Crestone Peak, CO	14,300	Tabeguache, CO	14,162
South Buttress, AK	15,885	Lincoln, CO	14,293	Oxford, CO	14,160
Wood, YT, Canada	15,873	Antero, CO	14,276	Sill, CA	14,159
Churchill, AK	15,638	Grays Peak, CO	14,276	Sneffels, CO	14,156
Nevado de Toluca (Xinantécatl), Mexico	15,350	Torreys Peak, CO	14,273	Democrat, CO	14,155
Fairweather, AK-BC, U.S.-Can.	15,299	Castle Peak, CO	14,272	Capitol Peak, CO	14,137
MacAulay, YT, Canada	15,299	Quandary Peak, CO	14,272	Liberty Cap, WA	14,118
Slaggard, YT, Canada	15,299	Evans, CO	14,270	Pikes Peak, CO	14,111
Hubbard, AK-YT, U.S.-Can.	15,016	Longs Peak, CO	14,260	Snowmass, CO	14,098
Bear, AK	14,831	McArthur, YT, Canada	14,253	Russell, CA	14,094
Walsh, YT, Canada	14,780	White Mountain Peak, CA	14,252	Eolus, CO	14,089
East Buttress, AK	14,730	Wilson, CO	14,252	Windom, CO	14,088
Matlalcueyetl, Mexico	14,636	North Palisade, CA	14,248	Columbia, CO	14,080

Note: The highest point in the West Indies is Pico Duarte (10,417 ft), in the Dominican Republic.

Other Notable U.S. Mountains

Peak, state	Height (ft)	Peak, state	Height (ft)	Peak, state	Height (ft)
Gannett Peak, WY	13,810	Adams, WA	12,281	Clingmans Dome, NC-TN	6,643
Grand Teton, WY	13,775	San Gorgonio, CA	11,503	Washington, NH	6,289
Kings, UT	13,534	Hood, OR	11,240	Rogers, VA	5,729
Cloud, WY	13,171	Lassen, CA	10,461	Marcy, NY	5,344
Wheeler, NM	13,166	Granite, CA	10,325	Katahdin, ME	5,269
Boundary, NV	13,146	Guadalupe, TX	8,751	Spruce Knob, WV	4,863
Granite, MT	12,804	Olympus, WA	7,973	Mansfield, VT	4,393
Borah, ID	12,661	Harney, SD	7,244	Black Mountain, KY	4,145
Humphreys, AZ	12,637	Mitchell, NC	6,683		

South America

Peak, country	Height (ft)	Peak, country	Height (ft)	Peak, country	Height (ft)
Aconcagua, Argentina	22,831	Coropuna, Peru	21,083	Solo, Argentina	20,492
Ojos del Salado, Arg.-Chile	22,595	Laudo, Argentina	20,997	Polleras, Argentina	20,456
Bonete, Argentina	22,546	Ancohuma, Bolivia	20,958	Pular, Chile	20,423
Tupungato, Argentina-Chile	22,310	Ausangate, Peru	20,945	Chani, Argentina	20,341
Pissis, Argentina	22,241	Toro, Argentina-Chile	20,932	Aucanquilcha, Chile	20,295
Mercedario, Argentina	22,211	Illampu, Bolivia	20,873	Juncal, Argentina-Chile	20,276
Huascaran, Peru	22,205	Tres Cruces, Argentina-Chile.	20,853	Negro, Argentina	20,184
Llullaillaco, Argentina-Chile	22,109	Huandoy, Peru	20,852	Quela, Argentina	20,128
El Libertador, Argentina	22,047	Parinacota, Bolivia-Chile	20,768	Condoriri, Bolivia	20,095
Cachi, Argentina	22,047	Tortolas, Argentina-Chile	20,745	Palermo, Argentina	20,079
Yerupajá, Peru	21,765	Ampato, Peru	20,702	Solimana, Peru	20,068
Incahuasi, Argentina-Chile	21,720	Chimborazo, Ecuador	20,702	San Juan, Argentina-Chile	20,049
Galan, Argentina	21,654	El Condor, Argentina	20,669	Sierra Nevada, Argentina-Chile	20,023
El Muerto, Argentina-Chile	21,457	Salcantay, Peru	20,574	Antofalla, Argentina	20,013
Sajama, Bolivia	21,391	Huancarhuas, Peru	20,531	Marmolejo, Argentina-Chile	20,013
Nacimiento, Argentina	21,302	Famatina, Argentina	20,505	Chachani, Peru	19,931
Illimani, Bolivia	21,201	Pumasillo, Peru	20,492		

Africa

Peak, country	Height (ft)	Peak, country	Height (ft)	Peak, country	Height (ft)
Kilimanjaro, Tanzania	19,341	Meru, Tanzania	14,977	Guna, Ethiopia	13,881
Kenya, Kenya	17,057	Karisimbi, Congo-Rwanda	14,787	Gughe, Ethiopia	13,780
Margherita Pk., Uganda-Congo	16,763	Elgon, Kenya-Uganda	14,178	Toubkal, Morocco	13,661
Ras Dashan, Ethiopia	15,158	Batu, Ethiopia	14,131	Cameroon, Cameroon	13,435

Australia, New Zealand, SE Asian Islands

Peak, country	Height (ft)	Peak, country	Height (ft)	Peak, country	Height (ft)
Jaya, New Guinea	16,500	Wilhelm, New Guinea	14,793	Cook, New Zealand	12,349
Trikora, New Guinea	15,585	Kinabalu, Malaysia	13,455	Semeru, Java, Indonesia	12,060
Mandala, New Guinea	15,420	Kerinci, Sumatra, Indon.	12,467	Kosciusko, Australia	7,310

Height of Mount Everest

Mt. Everest, the world's highest mountain, was considered 29,002 ft when Edmund Hillary and Tenzing Norgay became the first to scale it, in 1953. That triangulation figure had been accepted since 1850. In 1954, the Surveyor General of the Republic of India set the height at 29,028 ft, plus or minus 10 ft because of snow.

In 1999, a team of climbers sponsored by Boston's Museum of Science and the National Geographic Society measured the height at the summit using satellite-based technology. The new measurement, of 29,035 ft, was accepted by other authorities, including the U.S. National Imagery and Mapping Agency.

As of the end of the 2013 climbing season, which lasts April through May, there have been approximately 6,800 successful ascents to the summit of Everest. About 242 climbers have died in the attempt. Climbers typically ascend Everest on its north (Tibet) or south face (Nepal).

Europe

Peak, country	Height (ft)	Peak, country	Height (ft)	Peak, country	Height (ft)
Alps		Dent D'Herens, Switzerland	13,686	Schalihorn, Switzerland	13,040
		Breithorn, It.-Switzerland	13,665	Scerscen, Switzerland	13,028
Mont Blanc, France-Italy	15,781	Bishorn, Switzerland	13,645	Eiger, Switzerland	13,025
Monte Rosa (highest peak		Jungfrau, Switzerland	13,642	Jagerhorn, Switzerland	13,024
of group), Switzerland	15,203	Ecrins, France	13,461	Rottalhorn, Switzerland	13,022
Dom, Switzerland	14,911	Monch, Switzerland	13,448		
Liskamm, It.-Switzerland	14,852	Pollux, Switzerland	13,422	**Pyrenees**	
Weisshorn, Switzerland	14,780	Schreckhorn, Switzerland	13,379	Aneto, Spain	11,168
Taschhorn, Switzerland	14,733	Ober Gabelhorn, Switzerland	13,330	Posets, Spain	11,073
Matterhorn, It.-Switzerland	14,692	Gran Paradiso, Italy	13,323	Perdido, Spain	11,007
Dent Blanche, Switzerland	14,293	Bernina, It.-Switzerland	13,284	Vignemale, France-Spain	10,820
Nadelhorn, Switzerland	14,196	Fiescherhorn, Switzerland	13,283	Long, Spain	10,479
Grand Combin, Switzerland	14,154	Grunhorn, Switzerland	13,266	Estats, Spain	10,304
Lenzpitze, Switzerland	14,088	Lauteraarhorn, Switzerland	13,261	Montcalm, Spain	10,105
Finsteraarhorn, Switzerland	14,022	Durrenhorn, Switzerland	13,238		
Castor, Switzerland	13,865	Allalinhorn, Switzerland	13,213	**Caucasus (Europe-Asia)**	
Zinalrothorn, Switzerland	13,849	Weissmies, Switzerland	13,199	Elbrus, Russia	18,510
Hohberghorn, Switzerland	13,842	Lagginhorn, Switzerland	13,156	Shkhara, Georgia	17,064
Alphubel, Switzerland	13,799	Zupo, Switzerland	13,120	Dykh Tau, Russia	17,054
Rimpfischhorn, Switzerland	13,776	Fletschhorn, Switzerland	13,110	Kashtan Tau, Russia	16,877
Aletschorn, Switzerland	13,763	Adlerhorn, Switzerland	13,081	Janqi, Georgia	16,565
Strahlhorn, Switzerland	13,747	Gletscherhorn, Switzerland	13,068	Kazbek, Georgia	16,558

Asia (Mainland)

Peak, country/region	Height (ft)	Peak, country/region	Height (ft)	Peak, country/region	Height (ft)
Everest, Nepal-Tibet	29,035	Tirich Mir, Pakistan	25,230	Badrinath, India	23,420
K2 (Godwin Austen), Kashmir	28,251	Makalu II, Nepal-Tibet	25,120	Nunkun, Kashmir	23,410
Kanchenjunga, India-Nepal	28,169	Minya Konka, China	24,900	Lenin Peak, Tajikistan	23,406
Lhotse I (Everest), Nepal-Tibet	27,923	Annapurna III, Nepal	24,786	Pyramid, India-Nepal	23,400
Makalu I, Nepal-Tibet	27,824	Kula Gangri, Bhutan-Tibet	24,784	Api, Nepal	23,399
Lhotse II (Everest), Nepal-Tibet	27,560	Changtse (Everest), Nepal-Tibet	24,780	Pauhunri, India-Tibet	23,385
Dhaulagiri, Nepal	26,795	Muztagh Ata, Xinjiang, China	24,757	Trisul, India	23,360
Manaslu I, Nepal	26,781	Skyang Kangri, Kashmir	24,750	Kangto, India-Tibet	23,260
Cho Oyu, Nepal-Tibet	26,750	Annapurna IV, Nepal	24,688	Nyenchhe Thanglha, Tibet	23,255
Nanga Parbat, Kashmir	26,660	Ismail Samani Peak, Tajikistan	24,590	Trisuli, India	23,210
Annapurna I, Nepal	26,545	Jongsong Peak,		Pumori, Nepal-Tibet	23,190
Gasherbrum, Kashmir	26,470	India-Nepal-China	24,472	Dunagiri, India	23,184
Broad, Kashmir	26,400	Jengish Chokusu, Xinjiang,		Lombo Kangra, Tibet	23,165
Annapurna II, Nepal	26,545	China-Kyrgyzstan	24,406	Saipal, Nepal	23,100
Gosainthan, Nepal-Tibet	26,287	Sia Kangri, Kashmir	24,350	Macha Pucchare, Nepal	22,958
Gyachung Kang, Nepal-Tibet	25,910	Haramosh Peak, Pakistan	24,270	Khan Tengri, Kazakhstan-	
Disteghil Sar, Kashmir	25,868	Istoro Nal, Pakistan	24,240	Kyrgyzstan-Xinjiang, China	22,949
Himalchuli, Nepal	25,801	Kirat Chuli, India-Nepal	24,165	Numbar, Nepal	22,817
Nuptse (Everest), Nepal-Tibet	25,726	Chomo Lhari, Bhutan-Tibet	24,040	Kanjiroba, Nepal	22,580
Masherbrum, Kashmir	25,660	Chamlang, Nepal	24,012	Ama Dablam, Nepal	22,350
Nanda Devi, India	25,645	Kabru, India-Nepal	24,002	Cho Polu, Nepal	22,093
Rakaposhi, Kashmir	25,550	Alung Gangri, Tibet	24,000	Lingtren, Nepal-Tibet	21,972
Kamet, India-Tibet	25,447	Baltoro Kangri, Kashmir	23,990	Khumbutse, Nepal-Tibet	21,785
Namcha Barwa, Tibet	25,445	Mana, India	23,860	Hlako Gangri, Tibet	21,266
Gurla Mandhata, Tibet	25,355	Baruntse, Nepal	23,688	Grosvenor, China	21,190
Ulugh Muztagh, Xinjiang,		Nepal Peak, India-Nepal	23,500	Thagchhab Gangri, Tibet	20,970
China-Tibet	25,340	Amne Machin, China	23,490	Damavand, Iran	18,406
Kungur, Xinjiang, China	25,325	Gauri Sankar, Nepal-Tibet	23,440	Ararat, Turkey	16,854

Antarctica

Peak	Height (ft)	Peak	Height (ft)	Peak	Height (ft)
Vinson Massif	16,066	Minto	13,668	Anne	12,703
Tyree	15,919	Miller	13,650	Press	12,566
Shinn	15,750	Long Gables	13,620	Falla	12,549
Gardner	15,375	Dickerson	13,517	Rucker	12,520
Epperly	15,100	Giovinetto	13,412	Goldthwait	12,510
Kirkpatrick	14,855	Wade	13,400	Morris	12,500
Elizabeth	14,698	Fisher	13,386	Erebus	12,450
Markham	14,290	Fridtjof Nansen	13,350	Campbell	12,434
Bell	14,117	Wexler	13,202	Don Pedro Christophersen	12,355
Mackellar	14,098	Lister	13,200	Lysaght	12,326
Anderson	13,957	Shear	13,100	Huggins	12,247
Bentley	13,934	Odishaw	13,008	Sabine	12,200
Kaplan	13,878	Donaldson	12,894	Astor	12,175
Andrew Jackson	13,750	Ray	12,808	Mohl	12,172
Sidley	13,720	Sellery	12,779	Frankes	12,064
Ostenso	13,710	Waterman	12,730	Jones	12,040

Notable Islands and Their Areas

Figures are for total area in square miles. Boldface figures in parentheses show rank among the world's 10 largest individual islands. Only the largest islands in an island group are shown. Table does not include islands smaller than 10 sq mi in area.

Antarctica

Adelaide	1,400
Alexander	16,700
Berkner	18,500
Roosevelt	2,900

Arctic Ocean

Akimski, Nunavut (NU), Can.	1,159
Amund Ringnes, NU, Can.	2,029
Axel Heiberg, NU, Can.	16,671
Baffin, NU, Can. (5)	195,928
Banks, Northwest Terr. (NT), Can.	27,038
Bathurst, NU, Can.	6,194
Bolshevik, Russia	4,368
Bolshoy Lyakhovsky, Russia	1,776
Borden, NT-NU, Can.	1,079
Bylot, NU, Can.	4,273
Coats, NU, Can.	2,123
Cornwallis, NU, Can.	2,701
Devon, NU, Can.	21,331
Disko, Greenland, Denmark	3,312
Ellef Ringnes, NU, Can.	4,361
Ellesmere, NU, Can. (10)	75,767
Faddayevskiy, Russia	1,930
Franz Josef Land, Russia	8,000
Iturup (Etorofu), Russia	2,596
King William, NU, Can.	5,062
Komsomolets, Russia	3,477
Kotelny, Russia	4,504
Mackenzie King, NT, Can.	1,949
Mansel, NU, Can.	1,228
Melville, NT-NU, Can.	16,274
Milne Land, Greenland, Den.	1,400
New Siberian Isls., Russia	14,500
Novaya Zemlya, Russia (2 isls.)	31,730
Oktyabrskoy, Russia.	5,471
Prince Charles, NT, Can.	3,676
Prince Patrick, NT, Can.	6,119
Prince of Wales, NU, Can.	12,872
Somerset, NU, Can.	9,570
Southampton, NU, Can.	15,913
Svalbard, Norway (tot. group).	23,560
Nordaustlandet	5,410
Spitsbergen	14,546
Traill, Greenland, Denmark	1,300
Victoria, NT-NU, Can. (9)	83,897
Wrangel, Russia	2,800

Atlantic Ocean

Anticosti, QC, Can.	3,068
Ascension, UK	34
Azores, Portugal (tot. group)	868
Faial	67
San Miguel	291
Bahama Isls. (tot. group)	5,382
Andros	2,300
Bermuda Isls., UK (tot. group)	21
Bioko Isl., Equatorial Guinea	785
Block Island, RI, U.S.	21
Canary Isls., Spain (tot. group)	2,807
Fuerteventura	688
Gran Canaria	592
Tenerife	795
Cape Breton, NS, Can.	3,981
Cape Verde	1,557
Caviana, Pará, Brazil	1,918
Channel Isls., UK (tot. group)	75
Guernsey	24
Jersey	45
Falkland Isls., UK (tot. group)	4,700
East Falkland	2,550
West Falkland	1,750
Faroe Isls., Denmark	538
Great Britain, UK (8)	88,407
Greenland, Denmark (1)	836,330
Gurupá, Pará, Brazil	1,878
Hebrides, Scotland, UK	2,744
Iceland	39,699
Ireland (tot. group)	32,589
Irish Republic	27,137
Northern Ireland, UK	5,452
Isle of Man, UK	221
Isle of Wight, England, UK	147
Long Island, NY, U.S.	1,320
Madeira Islands, Portugal	306

Atlantic Ocean (cont.)

Marajo, Brazil	15,444
Martha's Vineyard, MA, U.S.	89
Mount Desert, ME, U.S.	104
Nantucket, MA, U.S.	45
Newfoundland, Canada	42,031
Orkney Isls., Scotland, UK	390
Prince Edward, Canada	2,185
St. Helena, UK	160
Shetland Isls., Scotland, UK.	587
Skye, Scotland, UK	670
South Georgia, UK	1,450
Tierra del Fuego, Chile-Arg.	18,800
Tristan da Cunha, UK	40

Baltic Sea

Aland Isls., Finland	590
Bornholm, Denmark	227
Gotland, Sweden	1,159

Caribbean Sea

Antigua	108
Aruba, Netherlands	75
Barbados	166
Cuba	42,804
Isle of Youth	926
Cayman Isls., UK	100
Curaçao, Netherlands	171
Dominica	290
Guadeloupe, France	687
Hispaniola (Haiti and Dominican Rep.)	29,389
Jamaica	4,244
Martinique, France	436
Puerto Rico, U.S.	3,339
Tobago	116
Trinidad	1,864
Virgin Isls., UK	59
Virgin Isls., U.S.	134

East Indies

Bali, Indonesia	2,171
Bangka, Indonesia	4,375
Borneo, Indonesia-Malaysia-Brunei (3)	280,100
Bougainville, Papua New Guinea	3,880
Buru, Indonesia	3,670
Celebes, Indonesia	69,000
Flores, Indonesia	5,500
Halmahera, Indonesia	6,865
Java (Jawa), Indonesia.	48,900
Madura, Indonesia	2,113
Moluccas, Indonesia.	32,307
New Britain, Papua New Guinea	14,093
New Guinea, Indon.-PNG (2)	306,000
New Ireland, PNG.	3,707
Seram, Indonesia	6,621
Sumatra, Indonesia (6)	165,000
Sumba, Indonesia	4,306
Sumbawa, Indonesia	5,965
Timor, Indon.–Timor-Leste	13,094
Yos Sudarsa, Indonesia	4,500

Indian Ocean

Andaman Isls., India	2,500
Kerguelen, France	2,247
Madagascar (4)	226,658
Mauritius	720
Pemba, Tanzania	380
Réunion, France	970
Seychelles	176
Sri Lanka	25,332
Zanzibar, Tanzania	640

Mediterranean Sea

Balearic Isls., Spain	1,927
Corfu, Greece	229
Corsica, France	3,369
Crete, Greece	3,189
Cyprus	3,572
Elba, Italy	86
Euboea, Greece	1,411
Malta	95
Rhodes, Greece	540
Sardinia, Italy	9,301
Sicily, Italy	9,926

Pacific Ocean

Admiralty, AK, U.S.	1,709
Aleutian Isls., AK, U.S. (tot. group)	6,912
Adak	275
Amchitka	116
Attu	350
Kanaga	142
Kiska	106
Tanaga	195
Umnak	686
Unalaska	1,051
Unimak	1,571
Baranof, AK, U.S.	1,636
Chichagof, AK, U.S.	2,062
Chiloe, Chile	3,241
Christmas, Kiribati	94
Diomede (Big), Russia	11
Easter Isl., Chile	69
Fiji (tot. group)	7,056
Vanua Levu	2,242
Viti Levu	4,109
Galapagos Isls., Ecuador	3,043
Graham Isl., BC, Can.	2,456
Guadalcanal, Solomon Isls.	2,180
Guam, U.S.	210
Hainan, China.	13,000
Hawaiian Isls., HI, U.S. (tot. group)	6,428
Hawaii	4,028
Oahu	597
Hong Kong, China	31
Hoste, Chile	1,590
Japan (tot. group)	145,914
Hokkaido	30,144
Honshu (7)	87,805
Kyushu	14,114
Okinawa	459
Shikoku	7,049
Kangaroo, South Australia	1,680
Kodiak, AK, U.S.	3,485
Kupreanof, AK, U.S.	1,084
Marquesas Isls., France	492
Marshall Islands	70
Melville, N Terr., Australia	2,240
Micronesia	271
New Caledonia, France	6,530
New Zealand (tot. group)	103,363
Chatham Isls.	373
North	43,911
South	58,084
Stewart	649
Northern Mariana Isls., U.S.	179
Nunivak, AK, U.S.	1,600
Palau	188
Philippines (tot. group)	115,831
Leyte	2,787
Luzon	40,680
Mindanao	36,775
Mindoro	3,690
Negros	4,907
Palawan	4,554
Panay	4,446
Samar	5,050
Prince of Wales, AK, U.S.	2,770
Revillagigedo, AK, U.S.	1,134
Riesco, Chile	1,973
St. Lawrence, AK, U.S.	1,780
Sakhalin, Russia	29,500
Samoa Isls. (tot. group)	1,177
American Samoa, U.S.	77
Savaii, Samoa	659
Tutuila, U.S.	55
Upolu, Samoa.	432
Santa Catalina, CA, U.S.	75
Santa Ines, Chile	1,407
Tahiti, France	402
Taiwan (tot. group)	13,892
Jinmen Dao (Quemoy)	56
Tasmania, Australia	26,178
Tonga	290
Vancouver Isl., BC, Can.	12,079
Vanuatu	4,707
Wellington, Chile	2,549

Persian Gulf

Bahrain	293

Notable Deserts of the World

Deserts are defined as regions of the Earth receiving less than 10 in. of precipitation annually, usually in combination with an evaporation rate exceeding precipitation.

In addition to areas listed below, the continent of Antarctica, with an area of about 5.4 mil sq mi (roughly doubled by ice in winter), is generally considered a desert. Annual precipitation averages 8 in. along the coast and far less in the deep interior; however, there is little evaporation.

Arabian (Eastern), 86,000 sq mi in Egypt between the Nile R. and Red Sea, extending S into Sudan
Atacama, 600-mi-long area rich in nitrate and copper deposits in northern Chile
Chihuahuan, 140,000 sq mi in TX, NM, AZ, and Mexico
Dasht-e Kavir, approx. 500 mi long by 200 mi wide in north-central Iran
Dasht-e Lut, approx. 300 mi long by 200 mi wide in south-central Iran
Death Valley, 3,300 sq mi in CA and NV
Gibson, 120,000 sq mi in the interior of western Australia
Gobi, 500,000 sq mi in Mongolia and China
Great Sandy, 150,000 sq mi in western Australia
Great Victoria, 150,000 sq mi in southwestern Australia
Kalahari, 275,000 sq mi in southern Africa
Kara Kum, 115,000 sq mi in Turkmenistan
Kyzyl Kum, 115,000 sq mi in Kazakhstan and Uzbekistan
Libyan, 425,000 sq mi in the Sahara, extending from Libya through southwestern Egypt into Sudan

Mojave, 15,000 sq mi in southern CA
Namib, long narrow area (varies 30-100 mi wide) extending 800 mi along SW coast of Africa
Nubian, 157,000 sq mi in the Sahara in northeastern Sudan
Painted Desert, section of high plateau in northern AZ extending 200 mi SE from Grand Canyon
Patagonia, 300,000 sq mi in southern Argentina
Rub al-Khali (Empty Quarter), 225,000 sq mi in the S Arabian Peninsula
Sahara, 3,500,000 sq mi in N Africa, extending W to the Atlantic. Largest desert in the world
Sonoran, 70,000 sq mi in southwestern AZ and southeastern CA extending into NW Mexico
Syrian, 100,000-sq-mi area extending over much of northern Saudi Arabia, eastern Jordan, southern Syria, and western Iraq
Taklamakan, 140,000 sq mi in Xinjiang Prov., China
Thar (Great Indian), 100,000-sq-mi area extending 400 mi along India-Pakistan border

Areas and Average Depths of Oceans, Seas, and Gulfs

Geographers and mapmakers recognize at least four major bodies of water: the Pacific, Atlantic, Indian, and Arctic Oceans. The Atlantic and Pacific Oceans are considered divided at the equator into the N and S Atlantic and the N and S Pacific. The Arctic Ocean is the name for waters north of the continental landmasses in the region of the Arctic Circle. The International Hydrographic Organization delimited a fifth world ocean in 2000. The Southern Ocean extends from the coast of Antarctica north to 60°S latitude, encompassing portions of the Atlantic, Indian, and Pacific Oceans.

Body of water	Area (sq mi)	Avg. depth (ft)	Body of water	Area (sq mi)	Avg. depth (ft)
Pacific Ocean	60,060,869	14,040	Sea of Japan	391,100	5,468
Atlantic Ocean	29,637,962	11,810	Hudson Bay	281,900	305
Indian Ocean	26,469,609	12,800	East China Sea	256,600	620
Southern Ocean	7,848,295	14,450	Andaman Sea	218,100	3,667
Arctic Ocean	5,427,050	4,300	Black Sea	196,100	3,906
South China Sea	1,148,500	4,802	Red Sea	174,900	1,764
Caribbean Sea	971,400	8,448	North Sea	164,900	308
Mediterranean Sea	969,100	4,926	Baltic Sea	147,500	180
Bering Sea	873,000	4,893	Yellow Sea	113,500	121
Gulf of Mexico	582,100	5,297	Persian Gulf	88,800	328
Sea of Okhotsk	537,500	3,192	Gulf of California	59,100	2,375

Principal Ocean Depths

Source: National Geospatial-Intelligence Agency, U.S. Dept. of Defense

Body of water	Location (lat.)	(long.)	Depth (meters)	(fathoms)	(feet)
Pacific Ocean					
Marianas Trench	11°22′ N	142°36′ E	10,924	5,973	35,840
Tonga Trench	23°16′ S	174°44′ W	10,800	5,906	35,433
Philippine Trench	10°38′ N	126°36′ E	10,057	5,499	32,995
Kermadec Trench	31°53′ S	177°21′ W	10,047	5,494	32,963
Bonin Trench	24°30′ N	143°24′ E	9,994	5,464	32,788
Kuril Trench	44°15′ N	150°34′ E	9,750	5,331	31,988
Izu Trench	31°05′ N	142°10′ E	9,695	5,301	31,808
New Britain Trench	06°19′ S	153°45′ E	8,940	4,888	29,331
Yap Trench	08°33′ N	138°02′ E	8,527	4,663	27,976
Japan Trench	36°08′ N	142°43′ E	8,412	4,600	27,599
Peru-Chile Trench	23°18′ S	71°14′ W	8,064	4,409	26,457
Palau Trench	07°52′ N	134°56′ E	8,054	4,404	26,424
Aleutian Trench	50°51′ N	177°11′ E	7,679	4,199	25,194
New Hebrides Trench	20°36′ S	168°37′ E	7,570	4,139	24,836
North Ryukyu Trench	24°00′ N	126°48′ E	7,181	3,927	23,560
Middle America Trench	14°02′ N	93°39′ W	6,662	3,643	21,857
Atlantic Ocean					
Puerto Rico Trench	19°55′ N	65°27′ W	8,605	4,705	28,232
South Sandwich Trench	55°42′ S	25°56′ W	8,325	4,552	27,313
Romanche Gap	0°13′ S	18°26′ W	7,728	4,226	25,354
Cayman Trench	19°12′ N	80°00′ W	7,535	4,120	24,721
Brazil Basin	09°10′ S	23°02′ W	6,119	3,346	20,076
Indian Ocean					
Java Trench	10°19′ S	109°58′ E	7,125	3,896	23,376
Ob' Trench	09°45′ S	67°18′ E	6,874	3,759	22,553
Diamantina Trench	35°50′ S	105°14′ E	6,602	3,610	21,660
Vema Trench	09°08′ S	67°15′ E	6,402	3,501	21,004
Agulhas Basin	45°20′ S	26°50′ E	6,195	3,387	20,325
Arctic Ocean					
Eurasia Basin	82°23′ N	19°31′ E	5,450	2,980	17,881
Mediterranean Sea					
Ionian Basin	36°32′ N	21°06′ E	5,150	2,816	16,896

Note: Greater depths have been reported in some areas but have not been officially confirmed by research vessels.

Major World Rivers

North American rivers are listed in a separate table.

River	Source or upper limit of length	Outflow	Length (mi)
Africa			
Chari	Bamingui-Bangoran region, Central African Republic	Lake Chad	650
Congo	Junction of Lualaba and Luava Rivers, Congo	Atlantic Ocean	2,720
Cubango (fmr. Okavango)	Central Angola	Okavango Delta	1,000
Gambia	Fouta Djallon, Guinea	Atlantic Ocean	700
Kasai	Central Angola	Congo River	1,100
Limpopo	Junction of Marico and Ngotwane Rivers, South Africa	Indian Ocean	1,100
Lualaba	Southeastern Congo	Congo River	1,100
Niger	Fouta Djallon, Guinea	Gulf of Guinea	2,600
Nile	Luvironza River, Burundi	Mediterranean Sea	4,160
Orange	Maluti Mountains, northern Lesotho	Atlantic Ocean	1,300
Sénégal	Junction of Bafing and Bakoy Rivers, Mali	Atlantic Ocean	1,000
Ubangi	Junction of Uele and Bomu Rivers, Congo	Congo River	700
Zambezi	Northwestern Zambia	Indian Ocean	1,700
Asia			
Amu Darya	Junction of Wakhsh and Panj Rivers, Tajikistan	Aral Sea	1,660
Amur	Junction of Shilka and Argun Rivers, China-Russia	Tartar Strait	1,780
Angara	Lake Baykal, Russia	Yenisei River	1,150
Ayeyarwady (fmr. Irrawaddy)	Junction of Mali and Nmai Rivers, Myanmar	Andaman Sea	1,000
Brahmaputra	Kailas Range, Himalayas, southwestern Tibet	Bay of Bengal	1,800
Chang-Jiang	Tibetan Plateau, southwestern Qinghai, China	East China Sea	3,450
Euphrates	Junction of Kara (Sarasu) and Murat Rivers, Turkey	Shatt al-Arab	1,700
Ganges	Gangotri glacier, Himalayas, India	Bay of Bengal	1,560
Godavari	Western Ghats, Maharashtra, India	Bay of Bengal	900
Hsi (see Xi He)			
Huang-He	Kunlun Mountains, Qinghai, China	Yellow Sea	3,000
Indus	Kailas Range, Himalayas, Tibet	Arabian Sea	1,900
Irtysh	Kazakhstan-Russia	Ob River	2,650
Jordan	Junction of Dan, Banias, and Hazbani streams, Israel	Dead Sea	200
Kolyma	Kolyma and Cherskogo Ranges, Russia	Arctic Ocean	1,500
Krishna	Western Ghats, Maharashtra, India	Bay of Bengal	800
Kura	Northeastern Turkey	Caspian Sea	950
Lena	Western Baikal Range, Russia	Laptev Sea	2,648
Mekong	Eastern Tibetan Plateau, China	South China Sea	2,700
Narmada	Madhya Pradesh, India	Arabian Sea	775
Ob	Junction of Biya and Katun Rivers, Russia	Gulf of Ob	2,300
Salween	Eastern Tibet, China	Gulf of Martaban	1,750
Songhua Jiang	Changbai Mountains, Jilin, China	Amur River	1,150
Sungari (see Songhua Jiang)			
Sutlej	Kailas Range, Himalayas, Tibet	Indus River	900
Syr	Junction of Naryn and Kara Darya Rivers, Uzbekistan	Aral Sea	1,380
Tarim	Junction of Kashi and Yarkant Rivers, China	Lop Nor	1,300
Tigris	Taurus Mountains, Turkey	Shatt al-Arab	1,150
Xi He	Eastern Yunnan, China	South China Sea	1,250
Yamuna	Uttarakhand, India	Ganges River	850
Yangtze (see Chang-Jiang)			
Yellow (see Huang-He)			
Yenisei	Kyzyl, Tuva Republic, Russia	Kara Sea	2,500
Australia			
Darling	Eastern Highlands, NE New South Wales/SE Queensland	Murray River	1,702
Murray	Australian Alps, SE New South Wales	Southern Ocean	1,609
Murrumbidgee	Australian Alps, SE New South Wales	Murray River	1,050
Europe			
Buh, Southern	NW of Khmel'nyts'kyy, Ukraine	Black Sea	532
Buh, Western	ENE of Zolochiv, Ukraine	Wisla River	500
Danube	Brege and Brigach Rivers, Black Forest, southwestern Germany	Black Sea	1,770
Dnieper	W of Sychevka, Smolensk, Russia	Black Sea	1,420
Dniester	Carpathian Mountains, Ukraine	Black Sea	850
Don	SE of Tula, Russia	Sea of Azov	1,200
Drava	Carnic Alps, northern Italy	Danube River	450
Dvina, North	Near Veliki Ustyug, Vologda, Russia	White Sea	465
Dvina, West	Valdai Hills, Russia	Gulf of Riga	635
Ebro	Cantabrian Mountains, northern Spain	Mediterranean Sea	575
Elbe	Giant Mountains, northwestern Czech Republic	North Sea	725
Garonne	Central Pyrenees, Spain	Bay of Biscay	402
Kama	Ural Mountains, N of Kuliga, Russia	Volga River	1,260
Loire	Mt. Gerbier-de-Jonc, Vivrais Mountains, France	Atlantic Ocean	630
Marne	Langres Plateau, northeastern France	Seine River	325
Meuse	Langres Plateau, northeastern France	North Sea	560
Oder	Sudetes Mountains, northeastern Czech Republic	Baltic Sea	562
Oka	S of Orél, Russia	Volga River	925
Pechora	Northern Ural Mountains, Russia	Barents Sea	1,120
Po	Cottian Alps, Piedmont, northwestern Italy	Adriatic Sea	405
Rhine	Swiss Alps	North Sea	820

River	Source or upper limit of length	Outflow	Length (mi)
Rhône	Rhône glacier, northeastern Valais, Switzerland	Mediterranean Sea	505
Seine	Langres Plateau, northern Burgundy, France	English Channel	480
Shannon	Near Cuilcagh Mountain, northwestern Cavan County, Ireland	Atlantic Ocean	240
Tagus	E of Madrid, Spain	Atlantic Ocean	585
Thames	4 headstreams in the Cotswold Hills, Gloucestershire, England, UK	North Sea	210
Tiber	Etruscan Apennines, Italy	Tyrrhenian Sea	251
Tisza	N of Rakhiv, western Ukraine	Danube River	700
Ural	Southern Ural Mountains, northeastern Bashkortostan, Russia	Caspian Sea	1,580
Volga	Valdai Hills, Smolensk, Russia	Caspian Sea	2,290
Weser	Junction of Fulda and Werra Rivers, Germany	North Sea	273
Wisla	W Beskid range, Carpathian Mountains, southwestern Poland	Gulf of Gdansk	665
South America			
Amazon	Junction of Ucayali and Marañón Rivers, Andes Mountains, Peru	Atlantic Ocean	3,900
Araguaía	Serra des Araras, Goiás-Mato Grosso, Brazil	Tocantins River	1,100
Beni	Cordillera Real, La Paz, Bolivia	Madeira River	1,000
Caquetá-Japura	Andes Mountains, southwestern Colombia	Amazon River	1,750
Juruá	Cerros de Canchyuaya, eastern Peru	Amazon River	1,500
Madeira	Junction of Beni and Mamoré Rivers, Bolivia	Amazon River	2,100
Magdalena	Cordillera Central, southwestern Colombia	Caribbean Sea	1,000
Negro	Southeastern Colombia	Amazon River	1,400
Orinoco	Near Mt. Delgado Chalbaud, Guiana Highlands, S Venezuela	Atlantic Ocean	1,600
Paraguay	Central Mato Grosso highlands, Brazil	Paraná River	1,584
Paraná	Junction of Paranaíba and Rio Grande Rivers, SE Brazil	Rio de la Plata	2,485
Pilcomayo	E of Lake Poopó, Bolivia	Paraguay River	1,000
Purus	Andes Mountains, eastern Peru	Amazon River	2,100
Putumayo	Andes Mountains, southern Colombia	Amazon River	1,000
Rio de la Plata	Estuary of Paraná and Uruguay Rivers, Argentina-Uruguay	Atlantic Ocean	170
São Francisco	Serra de Canastra, southwestern Minas Gerais, Brazil	Atlantic Ocean	1,800
Tocantins	South-central Goiás, Brazil	Para River	1,640
Ucayali	Junction of Apurímac and Urubamba Rivers, eastern Peru	Marañón River	1,000
Uruguay	Southern Brazil	Rio de la Plata	1,000
Xingu	Central Mato Grosso, Brazil	Amazon River	1,230

Major Rivers in North America

River	Source or upper limit of length	Outflow	Length (mi)
Alabama	Gilmer County, GA	Mobile River	729
Albany	Lake St. Joseph, ON, Can.	James Bay	610
Allegheny	Potter County, PA.	Ohio River	325
Altamaha-Ocmulgee	Junction of Yellow and South Rivers, Newton Co., GA	Atlantic Ocean	392
Apalachicola-Chattahoochee	Towns County, GA	Gulf of Mexico	524
Arkansas	Lake County, CO	Mississippi River	1,459
Assiniboine	Eastern Saskatchewan, Can.	Red River	450
Attawapiskat	Attawapiskat, ON, Can.	James Bay	465
Back (NT)	Contwoyto Lake, NT, Can.	Chantrey Inlet, Arctic Ocean	605
Big Black	Webster County, MS	Mississippi River	330
Brazos	Junction of Salt and Double Mountain Forks, Stonewall Co., TX.	Gulf of Mexico	1,280
Canadian	Las Animas County, CO.	Arkansas River	906
Cedar (IA)	Dodge County, MN.	Iowa River	329
Cheyenne	Junction of Antelope Creek and Dry Fork, Converse Co., WY	Missouri River	290
Churchill, Labrador	Lake Ashuanipi, NL, Can.	Atlantic Ocean	532
Churchill, Manitoba	Methy Lake, SK, Can.	Hudson Bay	1,000
Cimarron	Colfax County, NM	Arkansas River	600
Colorado (AZ)	Rocky Mountain Natl. Park, CO (90 mi in Mexico)	Gulf of California	1,450
Colorado (TX)	Dawson County, TX	Matagorda Bay	862
Columbia	Columbia Lake, BC, Can.	Pacific Ocean, bet. OR and WA	1,243
Columbia, Upper	Columbia Lake, BC, Can.	Mouth of Snake River	890
Connecticut	Third Connecticut Lake, NH	Long Island Sound, CT	407
Coppermine	Lac de Gras, NT, Can.	Coronation Gulf, Arctic Ocean	525
Cumberland	Letcher County, KY	Ohio River	720
Delaware	Schoharie County, NY	Liston Point, Delaware Bay	390
Fraser	Near Mount Robson (on Continental Divide)	Strait of Georgia	850
Gila	Catron County, NM	Colorado River	649
Green (UT-WY)	Junction of Wells and Trail Creeks, Sublette County, WY	Colorado River	730
Hudson	Henderson Lake, Essex County, NY	Upper New York Bay	306
Illinois	St. Joseph County, IN.	Mississippi River	420
James (ND-SD)	Wells County, ND	Missouri River	710
James (VA)	Junction of Jackson and Cowpasture Rivers, Botetourt Co., VA	Hampton Roads	340
Kanawha-New	Junction of North and South Forks of New River, NC	Ohio River	352
Kentucky	Junction of North and Middle Forks, Lee County, KY	Ohio River	259
Klamath	Lake Ewauna, Klamath Falls, OR	Pacific Ocean	250

River	Source or upper limit of length	Outflow	Length (mi)
Kootenay	Kootenay Lake, BC, Can.	Columbia River	485
Koyukuk	Endicott Mountains, AK	Yukon River	470
Kuskokwim	Alaska Range	Kuskokwim Bay	724
Liard	Southern Yukon, AK	Mackenzie River	693
Little Missouri	Crook County, WY	Missouri River	560
Mackenzie	Great Slave Lake, NT, Can.	Arctic Ocean	1,060
Milk	Junction of North and South Forks, AB, Can.	Missouri River	625
Minnesota	Big Stone Lake, MN	Mississippi River	332
Mississippi	Lake Itasca, Clearwater County, MN	Gulf of Mexico	2,340
Mississippi-Missouri-Red Rock	Source of Red Rock, Beaverhead County, MT	Gulf of Mexico	3,710
Missouri	Junction of Jefferson, Madison, and Gallatin Rivers, Gallatin County, MT	Mississippi River	2,315
Missouri-Red Rock	Source of Red Rock, Beaverhead County, MT	Mississippi River	2,540
Mobile-Alabama-Coosa	Gilmer County, GA	Mobile Bay	774
Nelson	Lake Winnipeg, MB, Can.	Hudson Bay	410
Neosho	Morris County, KS	Arkansas River, OK	460
Niobrara	Niobrara County, WY	Missouri River, NE	431
North Canadian	Union County, NM	Canadian River, OK	800
North Platte	Junction of Grizzly and Little Grizzly Creeks, Jackson Co., CO	Platte River, NE	618
Ohio	Junction of Allegheny and Monongahela Rivers, Pittsburgh, PA	Mississippi River	981
Ohio-Allegheny	Potter County, PA.	Mississippi River	1,310
Osage	East-central Kansas	Missouri River	500
Ottawa	Lake Capimitchigama, QC, Can.	St. Lawrence River	790
Ouachita	Polk County, AR	Black River	605
Peace	Junction of Finlay and Parsnip Rivers, BC, Can.	Slave River	1,210
Pearl	Neshoba County, MS	Gulf of Mexico	411
Pecos	Mora County, NM	Rio Grande	926
Pee Dee-Yadkin	Watauga County, NC	Winyah Bay	435
Pend Oreille-Clark Fork	Near Butte, MT	Columbia River	531
Platte	Junction of North Platte and South Platte Rivers, NE.	Missouri River	310
Porcupine	Ogilvie Mountains, AK	Yukon River, AK	569
Potomac	Garrett County, MD	Chesapeake Bay	383
Powder	Junction of South and Middle Forks, WY	Yellowstone River	375
Red (River of the South)	Curry County, NM.	Atchafalaya River, LA	1,290
Red River of the North	Junction of Otter Tail and Bois de Sioux Rivers, Wilkin, Co., MN	Lake Winnipeg	545
Republican	Junction of North Fork and Arikaree Rivers, NE.	Kansas River	445
Rio Grande	San Juan County, CO.	Gulf of Mexico	1,900
Roanoke	Junction of North Platte and South Forks, Montgomery Co., VA	Albemarle Sound	380
Rock (IL-WI)	Dodge County, WI	Mississippi River	300
Sabine	Junction of South and Caddo Forks, Hunt Co., TX	Sabine Lake	380
Sacramento	Siskiyou County, CA.	Suisun Bay	377
St. Francis	Iron County, MO	Mississippi River	425
St. John	Northwestern Maine	Bay of Fundy	418
St. Lawrence	Lake Ontario, ON-NY	Gulf of St. Lawrence, Atlantic Ocean	800
Saguenay	Lake St. John, QC, Can.	St. Lawrence River	434
Salmon (ID)	Custer County, ID.	Snake River	420
San Joaquin	Junction of South and Middle Forks, Madera Co., CA	Suisun Bay	350
San Juan	Silver Lake, Archuleta County, CO.	Colorado River	360
Santee-Wateree-Catawba	McDowell County, NC	Atlantic Ocean	538
Saskatchewan, North	Rocky Mountains, AB, Can.	Saskatchewan R.	800
Saskatchewan, South	Rocky Mountains, AB, Can.	Saskatchewan R.	865
Savannah	Junction of Seneca and Tugaloo Rivers, Anderson Co., SC	Atlantic Ocean, GA-SC	314
Severn (ON)	Sandy Lake, ON, Can.	Hudson Bay	610
Smoky Hill	Cheyenne County, CO	Kansas River, KS	540
Snake	Teton County, WY	Columbia River, WA	1,038
South Platte	Junction of South and Middle Forks, Park County, CO	Platte River	424
Susitna	Alaska Range	Cook Inlet	313
Susquehanna	Otsego Lake, Otsego County, NY	Chesapeake Bay	447
Tallahatchie	Tippah County, MS.	Yazoo River	301
Tanana	Wrangell Mountains, AK.	Yukon River	659
Tennessee	Junction of French Broad and Holston Rivers, TN	Ohio River	652
Tennessee-French Broad	Courthouse Creek, Transylvania County, NC	Ohio River	886
Tombigbee	Prentiss County, MS.	Mobile River	525
Trinity	N of Dallas, TX	Galveston Bay	360
Wabash	Darke County, OH	Ohio River	512
Washita	Hemphill County, TX.	Red River, OK	500
White (AR-MO)	Madison County, AR.	Mississippi River	722
Willamette	Douglas County, OR.	Columbia River	309
Wind-Bighorn	Junction of Wind and Little Wind Rivers, Fremont Co., WY (source of Wind R. is Togwotee Pass, Teton Co., WY)	Yellowstone River	338
Wisconsin	Lac Vieux Desert, Vilas County, WI	Mississippi River	430
Yellowstone	Park County, WY	Missouri River	682
Yukon	McNeil River, YT, Can.	Bering Sea	1,979

Major Natural Lakes of the World

Source: U.S. Geological Survey, U.S. Dept. of the Interior; Natural Resources Canada

A lake is generally defined as a body of water surrounded by land. By this definition some bodies of water that are called seas, such as the Caspian Sea and the Aral Sea, are really lakes. In the following table, the word "lake" is omitted when it is part of the name.

Name	Continent	Area (sq mi)	Length (mi)	Maximum depth (ft)	Elevation (ft)
Caspian Sea[1]	Asia-Europe	143,244	760	3,363	−92
Superior	North America	31,700	350	1,330	600
Victoria	Africa	26,828	250	270	3,720
Huron	North America	23,000	206	750	579
Michigan	North America	22,300	307	923	579
Aral Sea[1]	Asia	13,000[2]	260	180	125
Tanganyika	Africa	12,700	420	4,823	2,534
Baykal	Asia	12,162	395	5,315	1,493
Great Bear	North America	12,096	192	1,463	512
Nyasa (Malawi)	Africa	11,150	360	2,280	1,550
Great Slave	North America	11,031	298	2,015	513
Erie	North America	9,910	241	210	570
Winnipeg	North America	9,417	266	200	713
Ontario	North America	7,340	193	802	245
Balkhash[1]	Asia	7,115	376	85	1,115
Ladoga	Europe	6,835	124	738	13
Maracaibo	South America	5,217	133	115	sea level
Onega	Europe	3,710	145	328	108
Eyre[1]	Australia	3,600[3]	90	4	−52
Titicaca	South America	3,200	122	922	12,500
Nicaragua	North America	3,100	102	230	102
Athabasca	North America	3,064	208	407	700
Reindeer	North America	2,568	143	720	1,106
Tonle Sap	Asia	2,500[3]	70	45	NA
Turkana (Rudolf)	Africa	2,473	154	240	1,230
Issyk Kul[1]	Asia	2,355	115	2,303	5,279
Torrens[1]	Australia	2,230[3]	130	(3)	92
Vanern	Europe	2,156	91	328	144
Nettilling	North America	2,140	67	(3)	95
Winnipegosis	North America	2,075	141	38	830
Albert	Africa	2,075	100	168	2,030
Nipigon	North America	1,872	72	540	1,050
Gairdner[1]	Australia	1,840[3]	90	(3)	112
Urmia[1]	Asia	1,815	90	49	4,180
Manitoba	North America	1,799	140	21	813
Chad	Africa	500+[4]	175	24	787

NA = Not available. (1) Salt lake. (2) The diversion of feeder rivers since the 1960s has devastated the Aral—once the world's fourth-largest lake (26,000 sq mi). By 2000, the Aral had effectively become three lakes, with the total area shown. (3) Subject to great seasonal variation. (4) Once fourth-largest lake in Africa (about 10,000 sq mi in the 1960s), Chad had shrunk to around 5% of its original size by 2006 as a result of irrigation and long-term drought.

The Great Lakes

Source: National Ocean Service, National Oceanic and Atmospheric Administration, U.S. Dept. of Commerce

The Great Lakes form the world's **largest freshwater body** (in surface area) and with their connecting waterways are the largest inland water transportation unit. Draining the north-central basin of the U.S., they enable shipping to get to the Atlantic via their outlet, the St. Lawrence R.; the Gulf of Mexico can be reached via the Illinois Waterway, between Lake Michigan and the Mississippi R. A third outlet connects with the Hudson R. and then the Atlantic via the New York State Barge Canal System. Illinois Waterway and NYS Barge Canal System traffic is limited to recreational boating and small shipping vessels.

Only Lake Michigan is wholly in the U.S.; the other lakes are shared with Canada. Ships move from the shores of Lake Superior to Whitefish Bay in the east, then through the Soo Locks in Sault Ste. Marie, MI, onto St. Mary's R. and into Lake Huron. To reach the Port of Indiana-Burns Harbor and South Chicago, IL, ships travel west from Lake Huron to Lake Michigan through the Straits of Mackinac. Low water datum is based on the International Great Lakes Datum (1985), with Rimouski, Quebec, as the reference zero point. The distance between Duluth, MN, and Lake Ontario's east end is 1,156 mi.

	Superior	Michigan	Huron	Erie	Ontario
Length (mi)	350	307	206	241	193
Breadth (mi)	160	118	183	57	53
Deepest soundings (ft)	1,333	923	750	210	802
Volume of water (cu mi)	2,935	1,180	850	116	393
Area (sq mi) water surface—U.S.	20,600	22,300	9,100	4,980	3,460
Canada	11,100	NA	13,900	4,930	3,880
Area (sq mi) entire drainage basin—U.S.	16,900	45,600	16,200	18,000	15,200
Canada	32,400	NA	35,500	4,720	12,100
Total area (sq mi), U.S. and Canada	**81,000**	**67,900**	**74,700**	**32,630**	**34,850**
Low water datum above mean water level at Rimouski, QC, avg. level (ft)	601.10	577.50	577.50	569.20	243.30
Latitude, N	46°25′	41°37′	43°00′	41°23′	43°11′
	49°00′	46°06′	46°17′	42°52′	44°15′
Longitude, W	84°22′	84°45′	79°43′	78°51′	76°03′
	92°06′	88°02′	84°45′	83°29′	79°53′
National boundary line (mi)	282.8	NA	260.8	251.5	174.6
U.S. shoreline (mainland only) (mi)	863	1,400	580	431	300

NA = Not applicable.

Notable Waterfalls

Source: National Geographic Society

The Earth has thousands of waterfalls, some of considerable magnitude. Their magnitude is determined not only by height but also by volume of flow, steadiness of flow, crest width, whether the water drops sheerly or over a sloping surface, and whether it descends in one leap or in a succession of leaps. A series of low falls flowing over a considerable distance is known as a cascade. Waterfalls are highly variable and few authoritative figures exist. For more information and some alternative measurements, see the World Waterfall Database at www.worldwaterfalldatabase.com.

Estimated mean annual flow (ft³/sec) of major waterfalls: Niagara, 212,200; Paulo Afonso, 100,000; Iguazú, 61,000; Victoria, 35,400; and Kaieteur, 23,400.

Height is total drop in feet in one or more leaps. If river name is not shown, it is the same as the waterfall. # = more than one leap; * = diminishes greatly seasonally; ** = reduces to a trickle or is dry for part of each year; R. = river; (C) = cascade.

Name, location	Height (ft)
Africa	
Angola	
Ruacana, Cunene R.	406
Lesotho	
Maletsunyane*	630
South Africa	
Augrabies, Orange R.*	480
Tugela#.	2,800
Tanzania-Zambia	
Kalambo*	704
Zimbabwe-Zambia	
Victoria, Zambezi R.*	343
Asia and Oceania	
Australia	
New South Wales	
Wentworth	614
Wollomombi	722
Queensland	
Tully**	984
Wallaman, Stony Creek#	1,137
India	
Sivasamudram	320
Jog, Sharavati R.*	830
Japan	
Kegon, Lake Chuzenji*	350
New Zealand	
Helena	722
Sutherland, Arthur R.#	1,904
Europe	
Austria	
Gastein#	487
Krimml#	1,246
France	
Gavarnie*	1,385
Italy	
Toce (C)	470
Norway	
Mardalsfossen#**	2,154
Skykje**	984
Vetti, Morka-Koldedola R.	900

Name, location	Height (ft)
Sweden	
Handol#	345
Switzerland	
Giessbach (C).	984
Reichenbach#.	820
Staubbach	984
Trümmelbach#	1,312
United Kingdom	
Scotland	
Glomach	370
Wales	
Pistyll Rhaeadr	240
North America	
Canada	
Alberta	
Panther, Nigel Creek	600
British Columbia	
Della#	1,444
Takakkaw, Daly Glacier#	833
Quebec	
Montmorency	276
Canada-United States	
Niagara (American)	194
Niagara (Horseshoe)	187
United States	
Alabama	
Noccalula Falls	90
California	
Feather*	640
Yosemite National Park	
Bridalveil*	620
Illilouette*	370
Nevada, Merced R.*	594
Ribbon**	1,612
Silver Strand, Meadow Brook**	574
Vernal, Merced R.*	317
Yosemite#**	2,425
Colorado	
Seven Falls, S. Cheyenne Creek#	300
Hawaii	
Akaka, Kolekole Stream	420

Name, location	Height (ft)
Idaho	
Shoshone, Snake R.**	212
Kentucky	
Cumberland	68
Maryland	
Great, Potomac R. (C)*	76
Minnesota	
Minnehaha**	53
New Jersey	
Great, Passaic R.	70
New York	
Taughannock*	215
Oregon	
Multnomah#	850
Tennessee	
Fall Creek	256
Washington	
Sluiskin, Paradise R.	300
Snoqualmie**	268
Wisconsin	
Big Manitou, Black R. (C)*	165
Wyoming	
Tower	132
Yellowstone (upper)*	109
Yellowstone (lower)*	308
South America	
Argentina-Brazil	
Iguazú	269
Brazil	
Cachoeira da Fumaça*	1,312
Paulo Afonso, São Francisco R.	275
Colombia	
Tequendama, Bogota R.*	482
Ecuador	
Agoyan, Pastaza R.*	200
Guyana	
Kaieteur, Potaro R.	741
King George VI, Kamarang R.	1,600
Marina, Ipobe R.#	500
Venezuela	
Angel#*	3,212
Cuquenan	2,000

Latitude, Longitude, and Altitude of U.S. and Canadian Cities

Source: U.S. geographic positions and altitudes provided by Geological Survey, U.S. Dept. of the Interior.
Canadian geographic positions and altitudes provided by Natural Resources Canada.

City, state/province	Lat. N °	'	"	Long. W °	'	"	Elev. (ft)
Abilene, TX	32	26	55	99	43	58	1,718
Akron, OH	41	4	53	81	31	9	1,050
Albany, NY	42	39	9	73	45	24	20
Albuquerque, NM	35	5	4	106	39	2	4,955
Alert, NU	82	30	0	62	22	0	100
Allentown, PA	40	36	30	75	29	26	350
Amarillo, TX	35	13	19	101	49	51	3,685
Anchorage, AK	61	13	5	149	54	1	101
Ann Arbor, MI	42	16	15	83	43	35	880
Asheville, NC	35	36	3	82	33	15	2,134
Ashland, KY	38	28	42	82	38	17	558
Atlanta, GA	33	44	56	84	23	17	1,050
Atlantic City, NJ	39	21	51	74	25	24	8
Augusta, GA	33	28	15	81	58	30	414
Augusta, ME	44	18	38	69	46	48	45
Austin, TX	30	16	1	97	44	34	501
Bakersfield, CA	35	22	24	119	1	4	408
Baltimore, MD	39	17	25	76	36	45	100
Bangor, ME	44	48	4	68	46	42	158
Baton Rouge, LA	30	27	2	91	9	16	53
Battle Creek, MI	42	19	16	85	10	47	820
Bay City, MI	43	35	40	83	53	20	595
Beaumont, TX	30	5	9	94	6	6	20
Belleville, ON	44	14	0	77	21	0	320
Bellingham, WA	48	45	35	122	29	13	100
Berkeley, CA	37	52	18	122	16	18	150
Billings, MT	45	47	0	108	30	0	3,124
Biloxi, MS	30	23	45	88	53	7	25
Binghamton, NY	42	5	55	75	55	6	865
Birmingham, AL	33	31	14	86	48	9	600
Bismarck, ND	46	48	30	100	47	0	1,700
Bloomington, IL	40	29	3	88	59	37	829
Boise, ID	43	36	49	116	12	9	2,730
Boston, MA	42	21	30	71	3	37	20
Bowling Green, KY	36	59	25	86	26	37	510
Brandon, MB	49	54	35	99	57	03	1,343
Brantford, ON	43	08	0	80	16	0	815
Brattleboro, VT	42	51	3	72	33	30	240
Bridgeport, CT	41	10	1	73	12	19	10
Brockton, MA	42	5	0	71	1	8	112
Buffalo, NY	42	53	11	78	52	43	585
Burlington, ON	43	23	10	79	50	15	640
Burlington, VT	44	28	33	73	12	45	113
Butte, MT	46	0	14	112	32	2	5,549
Calgary, AB	51	03	0	114	05	0	3,557
Cambridge, MA	42	22	30	71	6	22	30

City, state/province	Lat. N °	'	"	Long. W °	'	"	Elev. (ft)
Canton, OH	40	47	56	81	22	43	1,100
Carson City, NV	39	9	50	119	45	59	4,730
Cedar Rapids, IA	42	0	30	91	38	38	730
Central Islip, NY	40	47	26	73	12	8	88
Champaign, IL	40	6	59	88	14	36	740
Charleston, SC	32	46	35	79	55	52	118
Charleston, WV	38	20	59	81	37	58	606
Charlotte, NC	35	13	37	80	50	36	850
Charlottetown, PE	46	14	25	63	08	05	160
Chattanooga, TN	35	2	44	85	18	35	685
Cheyenne, WY	41	8	24	104	49	11	6,067
Churchill, MB	58	43	30	94	07	0	94
Chicago, IL	41	51	0	87	39	0	596
Cincinnati, OH	39	9	43	84	27	25	683
Cleveland, OH	41	29	58	81	41	44	690
Colorado Springs, CO	38	50	2	104	49	15	6,008
Columbia, MO	38	57	6	92	20	2	758
Columbia, SC	34	0	2	81	2	6	314
Columbus, GA	32	27	39	84	59	16	300
Columbus, OH	39	57	40	82	59	56	800
Concord, NH	43	12	29	71	32	17	288
Corpus Christi, TX	27	48	1	97	23	46	35
Dallas, TX	32	47	0	96	48	0	463
Dawson, YT	64	03	45	139	25	50	1,214
Dayton, OH	39	45	32	84	11	30	750
Daytona Beach, FL	29	12	38	81	1	23	10
Decatur, IL	39	50	25	88	57	17	670
Denver, CO	39	44	21	104	59	3	5,260
Des Moines, IA	41	36	2	93	36	32	803
Detroit, MI	42	19	53	83	2	45	585
Dodge City, KS	37	45	10	100	1	0	2,550
Dubuque, IA	42	30	2	90	39	52	620
Duluth, MN	46	47	0	92	6	23	610
Durham, NC	35	59	38	78	53	56	394
Eau Claire, WI	44	48	41	91	29	54	850
Edmonton, AB	53	33	0	113	28	0	2,200
El Paso, TX	31	45	31	106	29	11	3,695
Elizabeth, NJ	40	39	50	74	12	40	38
Enid, OK	36	23	44	97	52	41	1,246
Erie, PA	42	7	45	80	5	7	650
Eugene, OR	44	3	8	123	5	8	419
Eureka, CA	40	48	8	124	9	45	44
Evansville, IN	37	58	29	87	33	21	388
Fairbanks, AK	64	50	16	147	42	59	440
Fall River, MA	41	42	5	71	9	20	200
Fargo, ND	46	52	38	96	47	22	900
Flagstaff, AZ	35	11	53	111	39	2	6,900
Flint, MI	43	0	45	83	41	15	750
Ft. Smith, AR	35	23	9	94	23	54	446
Ft. Wayne, IN	41	7	50	85	7	44	781
Ft. Worth, TX	32	43	31	97	19	14	670
Fredericton, NB	45	56	43	66	40	0	67
Fresno, CA	36	44	52	119	46	17	296
Gadsden, AL	34	0	51	86	0	24	554
Gainesville, FL	29	39	5	82	19	30	183
Gallup, NM	35	31	41	108	44	31	6,508
Galveston, TX	29	18	4	94	47	51	10
Gary, IN	41	35	36	87	20	47	600
Grand Junction, CO	39	3	50	108	33	0	4,597
Grand Rapids, MI	42	57	48	85	40	5	610
Great Falls, MT	47	30	1	111	18	0	3,334
Green Bay, WI	44	31	9	88	1	11	594
Greensboro, NC	36	4	21	79	47	32	770
Greenville, SC	34	51	9	82	23	39	966
Guelph, ON	43	33	0	80	15	0	1,100
Gulfport, MS	30	22	2	89	5	34	25
Halifax, NS	44	52	0	63	43	0	477
Hamilton, OH	39	23	58	84	33	41	600
Hamilton, ON	43	14	0	79	57	0	780
Harrisburg, PA	40	16	25	76	53	5	320
Hartford, CT	41	45	49	72	41	8	40
Helena, MT	46	35	34	112	2	7	4,090
Hilo, HI	19	43	47	155	5	24	38
Honolulu, HI	21	18	25	157	51	30	18
Houston, TX	29	45	47	95	21	47	40
Huntsville, AL	34	43	49	86	35	10	641
Indianapolis, IN	39	46	6	86	9	29	717
Iowa City, IA	41	39	40	91	31	48	685
Jackson, MI	42	14	45	84	24	5	940
Jackson, MS	32	17	55	90	11	5	294
Jacksonville, FL	30	19	55	81	39	21	12
Jersey City, NJ	40	43	41	74	4	41	83
Johnstown, PA	40	19	36	78	55	20	1,200
Joplin, MO	37	5	3	94	30	47	990
Juneau, AK	58	18	7	134	25	11	50
Kalamazoo, MI	42	17	30	85	35	14	755
Kansas City, KS	39	6	51	94	37	38	750
Kansas City, MO	39	5	59	94	34	42	740

City, state/province	Lat. N °	'	"	Long. W °	'	"	Elev. (ft)
Kenosha, WI	42	35	5	87	49	16	610
Key West, FL	24	33	19	81	46	58	8
Kingston, ON	44	18	0	76	28	0	305
Kitchener, ON	43	27	0	80	29	0	1,040
Knoxville, TN	35	57	38	83	55	15	889
Lafayette, IN	40	25	0	86	52	31	567
Lancaster, PA	40	2	16	76	18	21	368
Lansing, MI	42	43	57	84	33	20	830
Laredo, TX	27	30	22	99	30	26	414
Las Vegas, NV	36	10	30	115	8	11	2,000
Lawrence, MA	42	42	25	71	9	49	50
Lethbridge, AB	49	42	0	112	49	0	3,047
Lexington, KY	37	59	19	84	28	40	955
Lihue, HI	21	58	52	159	22	16	206
Lima, OH	40	44	33	84	6	19	875
Lincoln, NE	40	48	0	96	40	0	1,150
Little Rock, AR	34	44	47	92	17	22	350
London, ON	42	59	0	81	14	0	875
Los Angeles, CA	34	3	8	118	14	34	330
Louisville, KY	38	15	15	85	45	34	462
Lowell, MA	42	38	0	71	19	0	102
Lubbock, TX	33	34	40	101	51	17	3,195
Macon, GA	32	50	26	83	37	57	400
Madison, WI	43	4	23	89	24	4	863
Manchester, NH	42	59	44	71	27	19	175
Marshall, TX	32	32	41	94	22	2	410
Medicine Hat, AB	50	03	0	110	40	0	2,352
Memphis, TN	35	8	58	90	2	56	254
Meriden, CT	41	32	17	72	48	27	190
Miami, FL	25	46	26	80	11	38	11
Milwaukee, WI	43	2	20	87	54	23	634
Minneapolis, MN	44	58	48	93	15	49	815
Minot, ND	48	13	57	101	17	45	1,555
Mobile, AL	30	41	39	88	2	35	16
Moncton, NB	46	06	57	64	48	11	232
Montgomery, AL	32	22	0	86	18	0	250
Montpelier, VT	44	15	36	72	34	33	525
Montréal, QC	45	31	0	73	39	0	221
Moose Jaw, SK	50	24	0	105	32	0	1,892
Muncie, IN	40	11	36	85	23	11	952
Nashville, TN	36	9	57	86	47	4	440
Natchez, MS	31	33	37	91	24	11	230
New Britain, CT	41	39	40	72	46	48	200
New Haven, CT	41	18	29	72	55	43	40
New Orleans, LA	29	57	16	90	4	30	11
New York, NY	40	42	51	74	0	23	55
Newark, NJ	40	44	8	74	10	22	95
Niagara Falls, ON	43	06	0	79	04	0	589
Nome, AK	64	30	4	165	24	23	25
Norfolk, VA	36	50	48	76	17	8	10
North Bay, ON	46	19	0	79	28	0	1,200
Oakland, CA	37	48	16	122	16	11	42
Ogden, UT	41	13	23	111	58	23	4,299
Oklahoma City, OK	35	28	3	97	30	58	1,195
Omaha, NE	41	15	31	95	56	15	1,040
Orlando, FL	28	32	17	81	22	46	106
Ottawa, ON	45	16	0	75	45	0	382
Paducah, KY	37	5	0	88	36	0	345
Pasadena, CA	34	8	52	118	8	37	865
Paterson, NJ	40	55	0	74	10	20	70
Pensacola, FL	30	25	16	87	13	1	32
Peoria, IL	40	41	37	89	35	20	470
Peterborough, ON	44	18	0	78	19	0	628
Philadelphia, PA	39	57	8	75	9	51	40
Phoenix, AZ	33	26	54	112	4	24	1,090
Pierre, SD	44	22	6	100	21	2	1,484
Pittsburgh, PA	40	26	26	79	59	46	770
Pittsfield, MA	42	27	0	73	14	45	1,039
Pocatello, ID	42	52	17	112	26	41	4,464
Pt. Arthur, TX	29	53	55	93	55	43	10
Portland, ME	43	39	41	70	15	21	25
Portland, OR	45	31	25	122	40	30	50
Portsmouth, NH	43	4	18	70	45	47	21
Portsmouth, VA	36	50	7	76	17	55	10
Prince Rupert, BC	54	19	0	130	19	0	116
Providence, RI	41	49	26	71	24	48	80
Provo, UT	40	14	2	111	39	28	4,549
Pueblo, CO	38	15	16	104	36	31	4,662
Québec City, QC	46	49	0	71	13	0	244
Racine, WI	42	43	34	87	46	58	630
Raleigh, NC	35	46	19	78	38	20	350
Rapid City, SD	44	4	50	103	13	50	3,247
Reading, PA	40	20	8	75	55	38	266
Regina, SK	50	27	0	104	37	0	1,894

City, state/province	Lat. N °	'	"	Long. W °	'	"	Elev. (ft)	City, state/province	Lat. N °	'	"	Long. W °	'	"	Elev. (ft)
Reno, NV	39	31	47	119	48	46	4,498	Stockton, CA	37	57	28	121	17	23	15
Richmond, VA	37	33	13	77	27	38	190	Sudbury, ON	46	31	0	80	54	0	1,140
Roanoke, VA	37	16	15	79	56	30	940	Superior, WI	46	43	15	92	6	14	642
Rochester, MN	44	1	18	92	28	11	990	Sydney, NS	46	09	0	60	11	0	203
Rochester, NY	43	9	17	77	36	57	515	Syracuse, NY	43	2	53	76	8	52	400
Rockford, IL	42	16	16	89	5	38	715								
								Tacoma, WA	47	15	11	122	26	35	380
Sacramento, CA	38	34	54	121	29	36	20	Tallahassee, FL	30	26	17	84	16	51	188
Saginaw, MI	43	25	10	83	57	3	595	Tampa, FL	27	56	50	82	27	31	48
St. Catharines, ON	43	10	0	79	15	0	321	Terre Haute, IN	39	28	0	87	24	50	501
St. Cloud, MN	45	33	39	94	9	44	1,040	Texarkana, TX	33	25	30	94	2	51	324
St. John, NB	45	15	33	66	02	20	357	Thunder Bay, ON	48	24	0	89	19	0	653
St. John's, NL	47	34	0	52	44	0	461	Timmins, ON	48	28	0	81	20	0	967
St. Joseph, MO	39	46	7	94	50	47	850	Toledo, OH	41	39	50	83	33	19	615
St. Louis, MO	38	37	38	90	11	52	455	Topeka, KS	39	2	54	95	40	40	1,000
St. Paul, MN	44	56	40	93	5	35	780	Toronto, ON	43	37	39	79	23	46	251
St. Petersburg, FL	27	46	14	82	40	46	44	Trenton, NJ	40	13	1	74	44	36	54
Salem, OR	44	56	35	123	2	2	154	Trois-Rivières, QC	46	21	0	72	33	0	198
Salina, KS	38	50	25	97	36	40	1,225	Troy, NY	42	43	42	73	41	32	35
Salt Lake City, UT	40	45	39	111	53	25	4,266	Tucson, AZ	32	13	18	110	55	33	2,390
San Antonio, TX	29	25	26	98	29	36	650	Tulsa, OK	36	9	14	95	59	33	804
San Bernardino, CA	34	6	30	117	17	20	1,200								
San Diego, CA	32	42	55	117	9	23	40	Urbana, IL	40	6	38	88	12	26	725
San Francisco, CA	37	46	30	122	25	6	63	Utica, NY	43	6	3	75	13	59	415
San Jose, CA	37	20	22	121	53	38	87								
San Juan, PR	18	28	6	66	6	22	8	Vancouver, BC	49	15	0	123	7	0	14
Santa Barbara, CA	34	25	15	119	41	50	50	Victoria, BC	48	26	0	123	22	0	63
Santa Cruz, CA	36	58	27	122	1	47	20								
Santa Fe, NM	35	41	13	105	56	14	6,989	Waco, TX	31	32	57	97	8	47	405
Sarasota, FL	27	20	10	82	31	51	27	Walla Walla, WA	46	3	53	118	20	31	1,000
Saskatoon, SK	52	07	0	106	38	0	1,653	Washington, DC	38	53	42	77	2	12	25
Sault Ste. Marie, ON	46	31	0	84	20	0	630	Waterloo, IA	42	29	34	92	20	34	850
Savannah, GA	32	5	0	81	6	0	42	West Palm Beach, FL	26	42	54	80	3	13	21
Schenectady, NY	42	48	51	73	56	24	245	Wheeling, WV	40	3	50	80	43	16	672
Seattle, WA	47	36	23	122	19	51	350	White Plains, NY	41	2	2	73	45	48	220
Sheboygan, WI	43	45	3	87	42	52	630	Whitehorse, YT	60	43	0	135	03	0	2,305
Sherbrooke, QC	45	24	0	71	54	0	792	Wichita, KS	37	41	32	97	20	14	1,305
Sheridan, WY	44	47	50	106	57	20	3,742	Wilkes-Barre, PA	41	14	45	75	52	54	550
Shreveport, LA	32	31	30	93	45	0	209	Wilmington, DE	39	44	45	75	32	49	100
Sioux City, IA	42	30	0	96	24	0	1,117	Wilmington, NC	34	13	32	77	56	42	50
Sioux Falls, SD	43	32	48	96	43	48	1,442	Windsor, ON	42	18	0	83	01	0	622
South Bend, IN	41	41	0	86	15	0	725	Winnipeg, MB	49	54	39	97	14	36	783
Spartanburg, SC	34	56	58	81	55	56	816	Winston-Salem, NC	36	5	59	80	14	40	912
Spokane, WA	47	39	32	117	25	30	2,000	Worcester, MA	42	15	45	71	48	10	480
Springfield, IL	39	48	6	89	38	37	610								
Springfield, MA	42	6	5	72	35	25	70	Yakima, WA	46	36	8	120	30	17	1,066
Springfield, MO	37	12	55	93	17	53	1,300	Yellowknife, NT	62	27	20	114	21	0	675
Springfield, OH	39	55	27	83	48	32	1,000	Youngstown, OH	41	5	59	80	38	59	861
Stamford, CT	41	3	12	73	32	21	35	Yuma, AZ	32	43	31	114	37	25	160
Steubenville, OH	40	22	11	80	38	3	1,060	Zanesville, OH	39	56	25	82	0	48	710

Latitude and Longitude of World Cities

Source: National Imagery Mapping Agency, U.S. Dept. of Defense

City, country	Lat. °	'	Long. °	'	City, country	Lat. °	'	Long. °	'
Athens, Greece	37	59 N	23	44 E	Moscow, Russia	55	45 N	37	35 E
Bangkok, Thailand	13	45 N	100	31 E	Mumbai (Bombay), India	18	58 N	72	50 E
Beijing, China	39	56 N	116	24 E	New Delhi, India	28	36 N	77	12 E
Berlin, Germany	52	31 N	13	25 E	Panama City, Panama	08	58 N	79	32 W
Bogotá, Colombia	04	36 N	74	05 W	Paris, France	48	52 N	02	20 E
Buenos Aires, Argentina	34	36 S	58	28 W	Quito, Ecuador	00	13 S	78	30 W
Cairo, Egypt	30	03 N	31	15 E	Rio de Janeiro, Brazil	22	43 S	43	13 W
Jakarta, Indonesia	06	10 S	106	48 E	Rome, Italy	41	53 N	12	30 E
Jerusalem, Israel	31	46 N	35	14 E	Santiago, Chile	33	27 S	70	40 W
Johannesburg, South Africa	26	12 S	28	05 E	Seoul, South Korea	37	34 N	127	00 E
Kathmandu, Nepal	27	43 N	85	19 E	Sydney, Australia	33	53 S	151	12 E
Kiev, Ukraine	50	26 N	30	31 E	Tehran, Iran	35	40 N	51	26 E
London, UK (Greenwich)	51	30 N	00	00	Tokyo, Japan	35	42 N	139	46 E
Manila, Philippines	14	35 N	121	00 E	Warsaw, Poland	52	15 N	21	00 E
Mexico City, Mexico	19	24 N	99	09 W	Wellington, New Zealand	41	18 S	174	47 E

Highest and Lowest Continental Altitudes

Source: National Geographic Society

Continent	Highest point	Elev. (ft)	Continent	Lowest point	Ft below sea level
Asia	Mount Everest, Nepal-Tibet	29,035	Antarctica	Bentley Subglacial Trench	8,333[1]
South America	Mount Aconcagua, Argentina	22,834	Asia	Dead Sea, Israel-Jordan	1,348
North America	Mount McKinley, Alaska	20,320	Africa	Lake Assal, Djibouti	512
Africa	Kilimanjaro, Tanzania	19,341	North America	Death Valley, California	282
Europe	Mount Elbrus, Russia	18,510	South America	Valdes Peninsula, Argentina	131
Antarctica	Vinson Massif	16,066	Europe	Caspian Sea, Russia, Azerbaijan	92
Australia	Mount Kosciusko, New South Wales	7,310	Australia	Lake Eyre, South Australia	52

(1) Estimated level of the continental floor. Lower points that have yet to be discovered may exist beneath the ice.

RELIGION

Memberships of Religious Groups in the U.S.

Source: *Yearbook of American & Canadian Churches*, © National Council of Churches U.S.A., or as otherwise indicated Figures are the latest available from the source, and are generally based on reports made by officials of each group. Reporting practices vary from one denomination to another. Many groups keep careful records; others only estimate. Not all groups report annually. Membership figures, for the most part, are inclusive and do not refer solely to full communicants or confirmed members. Groups reporting fewer than 5,000 members or providing no data in recent years are not included.

Religious group (houses of worship)	Members
Adventist Churches	
Advent Christian Ch. (294)	23,629
Seventh-day Adventist Ch. (4,916)	1,060,386
Agnostics	41,889,421[1]
American Evangelical Christian Chs. (192)	17,400
Anglo-Lutheran Catholic Church (19)	11,100
Apostolic Catholic Ch. (29)	7,414
Apostolic Catholic Orthodox Ch. (8)	8,500
Apostolic Christian Churches of America (93)	12,850
Apostolic Episcopal Church (200)	12,000
Apostolic Orthodox Catholic Ch. of N.A. (25)	15,900
Atheists	1,309,897[1]
Baha'i Faith	512,864[1]
Baptist Churches	
Alliance of Baptists (127)	65,000
American Baptist Assn. (1,600)	100,000
American Baptist Chs. in the U.S.A. (5,366)	1,308,054
Baptist Bible Fellowship Intl. (4,000)	110,000
Baptist Missionary Assn. of America (1,272)	137,909
Conservative Baptist Assn. of America (1,200)	200,000
Converge Worldwide (fmr. Baptist Gen. Conf.) (1,100)	16,000
Free Will Baptists, National Assn. of (2,369)	185,798
General Baptists, General Assn. of (1,154)	61,040
Natl. Baptist Convention, U.S.A., Inc. (10,358)	5,197,512
Natl. Baptist Convention of America, Inc.	3,500,000
Natl. Missionary Baptist Conv. of America (280)	449,000[1]
Natl. Primitive Baptist Conv., Inc. (1,565)	600,000[1]
North American Baptist Conference (272)	47,150
Progressive Natl. Baptist Convention, Inc. (1,500)	1,010,000
Regular Baptist Chs., General Assn. of (1,321)	132,700
Separate Baptists in Christ (90)	10,700[1]
Seventh Day Baptist General Conf., USA/Canada (97)	6,300
Southern Baptist Convention (45,727)	16,136,044
Berean Fellowship of Chs. (56)	12,000
Brethren (German Baptists)	
Brethren Ch. (Ashland, OH) (112)	10,227
Church of the Brethren (1,043)	120,041
Buddhists	3,955,046[1]
Calvary Chapel	10,000
Chinese Folk Religionists	108,634[1]
Christian Brethren (Plymouth Brethren) (1,145)	86,000
Christian Church (Disciples of Christ) (3,624)	639,551
Christian Churches and Churches of Christ (5,007)	1,174,000[1]
Christian Congregation, Inc. (1,496)	122,181
Christian and Missionary Alliance (2,042)	436,428
Church of Christ	8,000
Church of Christ (Holiness) U.S.A. (148)	11,468
Church of Christ, Scientist (2,206)	848,000[1]
Church of the Living God (170)	42,000
Church of the Nazarene (5,058)	649,836
Church of the United Brethren in Christ, USA (193)	21,000
Churches of Christ (13,000)	1,639,495
Churches of Christ in Christian Union (230)	11,234
Churches of God	
Church of God (Anderson, IN) (2,187)	249,521
Church of God (Seventh Day; Gen. Conf.), Denver, CO (233)	14,000
Church of God, Mountain Assembly, Inc. (3,390)	7,000
Church of God by Faith, Inc. (149)	35,000
Church of God of Prophecy (1,860)	89,674
Churches of God (Gen. Conf.) (332)	32,560
Community Churches, Intl. Council of (148)	68,300
Congregational Christian Chs., Natl. Assn. of (400)	67,200[1]
Conservative Congregational Christian Conf. (298)	42,296
Eastern Orthodox Churches	
American Carpatho-Russian Orthodox Greek Catholic Ch. (79)	12,660
Antiochian Orthodox Christian Archdiocese of North America (256)	430,000
Armenian Apostolic Ch., Dioceses of America (81)	65,000
Armenian Apostolic Ch. of America (38)	350,000
Coptic Orthodox Ch. (100)	300,000
Greek Orthodox Archdiocese of America (560)	1,500,000
Malankara Orthodox Syrian Ch., Diocese of America (80)	30,000

Religious group (houses of worship)	Members
Mar Thoma Syrian Ch. of India (80)	50,000
Orthodox Ch. in America (750)	131,000
Patriarchal Parishes of the Russian Orthodox Ch. in the U.S.A. (31)	17,000
Russian Orthodox Ch. Outside of Russia (190)	480,000
Serbian Orthodox Ch. in the U.S.A. and Canada (68)	67,000
Syriac-Greek Antiochian Orthodox Catholic Ch. (160)	17,108
Syrian (Syriac) Orthodox Ch. of Antioch (32)	32,500
Ukrainian Orthodox Ch. of the U.S.A. (118)	50,000
Episcopal Church (6,794)	1,951,907
Ethnic religionists	1,084,637[1]
Evangelical Church Alliance	300,000
Evangelical Congregational Church (141)	17,577
Evangelical Covenant Church (783)	114,283
Evangelical Free Church of America (1,475)	356,000
Fellowship of Grace Brethren Churches (260)	36,000[1]
Friends	
Evangelical Friends Intl.–N. Amer. Region (284)	38,428
Friends General Conference (832)	32,000
Friends United Meeting (600)	36,302
Philadelphia Yearly Meeting of the Religious Society of Friends (103)	11,511
Religious Society of Friends (Conservative) (1,200)	104,000
Full Gospel Fellowship of Churches and Ministers Intl. (1,273)	432,632
General Church of the New Jerusalem (37)	7,052
Grace Gospel Fellowship (120)	20,000[1]
Hindus	1,444,775[1]
International Evangelical Church (100)	50,000[1]
Jains	85,356[1]
Jehovah's Witnesses (13,021)	1,184,249
Jews	6.2-6.5 mil[2]
Jewish Reconstructionist Federation (100)	(2)
Union of Orthodox Jewish Congregations of America (1,930)	(2)
Union for Reform Judaism (850)	(2)
United Synagogue of Conservative Judaism (600)	(2)
Latter-day Saints (Mormons)	
Ch. of Jesus Christ of Latter-day Saints (13,601)	6,157,238
Community of Christ (935)	178,328
Liberal Catholic Church–Province of the United States of America (21)	5,800
Lutheran Churches	
American Assn. of Lutheran Chs. (70)	16,000
Apostolic Lutheran Ch. of America (56)	7,300[1]
Ch. of the Lutheran Brethren of America (105)	13,099
Ch. of the Lutheran Confession (87)	8,390
Evangelical Lutheran Ch. in America (9,995)	4,274,855
Evangelical Lutheran Synod (132)	19,384
Free Lutheran Congregations, Assn. of (280)	44,473
Independent Evangelical Lutheran Chs., Assn. of (45)	7,760
Latvian Evangelical Lutheran Ch. in America (60)	10,950
Lutheran Ch.–Missouri Synod (LCMS) (6,158)	2,278,586
Wisconsin Evangelical Lutheran Synod (1,287)	385,321
Mennonite Churches	
Beachy Amish Mennonite Chs. (201)	11,611
Brethren in Christ Church (222)	46,300[1]
Ch. of God in Christ, Mennonite (150)	14,804
Fellowship of Evangelical Chs. (46)	7,754
Hutterian Brethren (150)	17,000[1]
Mennonite Brethren Chs., Gen. Conf. of (464)	111,000[1]
Mennonite Ch. USA (920)	104,684
Old Order Amish Mennonite Ch. (950)	115,000[1]
Old Order (Wisler) Mennonite Ch. (47)	7,100
Methodist Churches	
African Methodist Episcopal Ch. (4,100)	2,500,000
African Methodist Episcopal Zion Ch. (3,393)	1,400,000
Christian Methodist Episcopal Ch. (3,500)	850,000
Evangelical Methodist Ch. (108)	7,348
Free Methodist Ch. U.S.A. (1,051)	75,020
Southern Methodist Ch. (101)	6,000
United Methodist Ch. (33,583)	7,679,850
Wesleyan Ch. (1,715)	139,330
Metropolitan Community Churches, Universal Fellowship of (115)	15,666

Religious group (houses of worship)	Members
Missionary Church (431)	38,206
Moravian Church in America (84)	20,220
Muslims	4,106,065[1,3]
New Apostolic Church of North America, Natl. Org. of the (303)	39,532
New religionists	1,624,154[1]
Old Catholic Orthodox Ch. (11)	11,470
Pentecostal Churches	
Apostolic Faith Mission Ch. of God (16)	6,880
Assemblies of God (12,457)	3,030,944
Bible Fellowship Ch. (65)	7,627
Ch. of God (Cleveland, TN) (6,481)	1,074,047
Ch. of God in Christ (22,401)	8,016,000
Ch. of God of Prophecy (1,860)	89,674
Congregational Holiness Ch. (225)	25,000
Elim Assemblies Fellowship (240)	41,000[1]
Intl. Ch. of the Foursquare Gospel (1,875)	353,995
Intl. Pentecostal Holiness Ch. (2,024)	330,054
Open Bible Churches (275)	45,000
Pentecostal Assemblies of the World, Inc. (2,550)	1,800,000
Pentecostal Ch. of God (1,134)	98,579
Pentecostal Chs. of Christ (45)	5,000
Pentecostal Free Will Baptist Ch., Inc. (200)	20,000[1]
United House of Prayer (161)	1,632,000[1]
United Pentecostal Ch. Intl. (4,358)	646,304
Polish National Catholic Ch. of America (126)	60,000
Presbyterian Churches	
Associate Reformed Presbyterian Ch. (General Synod) (293)	39,639

Religious group (houses of worship)	Members
Cumberland Presbyterian Ch. (657)	72,167
Evangelical Presbyterian Ch. (207)	89,190
Korean Presbyterian Ch. Abroad (302)	55,000
Orthodox Presbyterian Ch. (269)	29,842
Presbyterian Ch. (U.S.A.) (10,560)	2,675,873
Presbyterian Ch. in America (1,737)	341,482
Reformed Presbyterian Ch. of North America	6,799
Reformed Catholic Ch. (100)	57,000
Reformed Churches	
Christian Reformed Ch. in North America (808)	180,502
Netherlands Reformed Congregations (27)	10,493
Protestant Reformed Chs. in America (31)	7,806
Reformed Ch. in America (886)	246,024
United Church of Christ (5,227)	1,058,423
Reformed Episcopal Church (149)	15,573
Roman Catholic Church (17,644)	78,200,000[4]
Romanian Orthodox Church in America (32)	9,700
Romanian Orthodox Episcopate of America (64)	10,635
Salvation Army (1,232)	413,961
Shintoists	62,688[1]
Sikhs	279,346[1]
Spiritists	225,213[1]
Taoists (or Daoists)	12,415[1]
Vineyard USA (554)	181,474
Unitarian Universalist Assn. of Congregations (1,048)	221,367
United Evangelical Churches (294)	78,800[1]
Zoroastrians	17,636[1]

(1) Source: Todd M. Johnson, ed., World Christian Database (Leiden/Boston: Brill, July 2013). (2) About 35% of Jews classify themselves as Reform, 26% as Conservative, 10% as Orthodox, 2% as Reconstructionist, the rest as "just Jewish." Source: Ira M. Sheskin and Arnold Dashefsky, "Jewish Population of the United States, 2013," in Arnold Dashevsky and Ira M. Sheskin (editors), *The American Jewish Year Book* (2013) (Dordrecht: Springer). (3) Other sources vary widely. Pew Research Center estimated 2,595,000 for 2010; Council on Islamic-American Relations estimates a current U.S. Muslim population of 6.7 mil. (4) Source: U.S. Center for Research in the Apostolate. Pew Research Center estimates population at 75,380,000 for 2010.

World Adherents of Religions by Continental Area, 2012

Source: *2013 Encyclopædia Britannica Book of the Year.* All figures are midyear estimates.

Religion (no. of countries)	Africa	Asia	Europe	Latin America	Northern America	Oceania	World
Baha'is (222)	2,246,000	3,516,000	160,000	925,000	587,000	116,000	7,550,000
Buddhists (151)	263,000	496,787,000	1,803,000	775,000	4,549,000	607,000	504,784,000
Chinese folk religionists (120)	137,000	435,455,000	444,000	194,000	797,000	106,000	437,133,000
Christians (232)	519,501,000	358,211,000	581,360,000	556,946,000	275,189,000	28,632,000	2,319,839,000
Roman Catholics (232)	189,983,000	141,740,000	278,115,000	494,205,000	87,732,000	9,075,000	1,200,850,000
Protestants (229)	144,846,000	90,044,000	67,598,000	60,896,000	59,356,000	7,885,000	430,625,000
Independents (221)	109,049,000	136,487,000	10,824,000	40,519,000	58,557,000	1,297,000	356,733,000
Orthodox (137)	45,192,000	18,720,000	204,008,000	1,083,000	7,594,000	1,008,000	277,605,000
Anglicans (162)	53,522,000	876,000	26,435,000	877,000	2,764,000	4,829,000	89,303,000
Marginal (217)	4,245,000	3,230,000	4,136,000	11,757,000	12,098,000	684,000	36,150,000
Unaffiliated (227)	25,444,000	4,160,000	20,603,000	6,266,000	49,333,000	4,341,000	110,147,000
Confucianists (16)	20,400	8,107,000	15,800	490	0	51,000	8,194,690
Ethnoreligionists (146)	92,039,000	148,934,000	1,168,000	3,717,000	1,232,000	383,000	247,473,000
Hindus (127)	3,054,000	959,711,000	1,200,000	776,000	1,897,000	526,000	967,164,000
Jains (19)	98,900	5,227,000	19,300	1,400	103,000	3,000	5,452,600
Jews (140)	135,000	6,307,000	1,928,000	977,000	5,525,000	121,000	14,993,000
Muslims (211)	444,868,000	1,115,159,900	41,949,000	1,556,000	5,091,000	577,000	1,609,200,000
New religionists (119)	117,000	59,227,000	366,000	1,773,000	1,737,000	107,000	63,327,000
Shintoists (8)	0	2,695,000	0	7,900	63,300	0	2,766,200
Sikhs (55)	77,000	23,466,000	572,000	7,300	620,000	51,100	24,793,400
Spiritists (57)	2,700	2,100	145,000	13,527,000	248,000	8,100	13,932,900
Taoists (6)	0	8,526,000	0	0	12,500	4,700	8,543,200
Zoroastrians (27)	1,000	169,000	5,800	0	21,300	2,700	199,800
Other religionists (79)	85,000	225,000	275,000	120,000	690,000	12,000	1,407,000
Nonreligious/agnostic (231)	6,862,000	503,989,000	93,415,100	18,889,910	49,987,900	5,910,400	679,054,310
Atheists (221)	589,000	114,647,000	15,349,000	2,981,000	2,245,000	516,000	136,327,000

Note: Continental areas. These are as per UN demographic terminology; "Asia" is defined to include the former Soviet Central Asian states, while "Europe" includes all of Russia, extending to the Pacific coast. Countries. Figures in parentheses indicate the number of countries where the religion or type of belief has a statistically significant following. Adherents. Totals are based on self-definition, as reported in censuses, polls, and other data. Figures may conflict with estimates elsewhere. Buddhists. 56% Mahayana, 38% Theravada (Hinayana), 6% Tantrayana (Lamaism). Chinese folk religionists. Followers of traditional Chinese religion; may involve worship of local deities, ancestor veneration, Confucian ethics, divination, and Buddhist or Taoist elements, among other beliefs and practices. Christians. Followers of Jesus Christ. Unaffiliated Christians profess Christian beliefs but are not affiliated with a church or sect. Independents belong to sects or groups that consider themselves post-denominational and thus independent from organized Christianity. Marginal Christians belong to churches that profess Christianity but regard themselves as on the margins of the mainstream, including Unitarians, Mormons, Jehovah's Witnesses, and Christian Science adherents. Denominational figures include individuals with more than one denominational affiliation. Confucianists. Followers of Confucius, mostly in China, South Korea, and elsewhere in East/Southeast Asia. Ethnoreligionists. Followers of local, tribal, animistic, or shamanistic religions, generally belonging to a single ethnic group. Hindus. 68% Vaishnavites, 27% Shaivites, 5% other. Jews. Adherents of Judaism. Muslims. 86% Sunni Muslims, 13% Shia Muslims (Shiites), 1% other. New religionists. Followers of Asian new religions, radical new crisis religions, and non-Christian syncretistic mass religions. Other religionists. Including various small religions, quasi-religions, parareligions, mystical systems, religious brotherhoods, and the like.

Episcopal Church Liturgical Colors and Calendar, 2013-17

The most common liturgical colors in the Episcopal Church are **White**—Christmas Day through first Sunday after Epiphany; Maundy Thursday (as an alternative to crimson at the Eucharist); from the Vigil of Easter to the Day of Pentecost (Whitsunday); Trinity Sunday; Feasts of the Lord (except Holy Cross Day); the Confession of St. Peter; the Conversion of St. Paul; St. Joseph; St. Mary Magdalene; St. Mary the Virgin; St. Michael and All Angels; All Saints' Day; St. John the Evangelist; memorials of other saints who were not martyred; Independence Day and Thanksgiving Day; weddings and funerals. **Red**—the Day of Pentecost; Holy Cross Day; feasts of apostles and evangelists (except those previously mentioned); feasts and memorials of martyrs (including Holy Innocents' Day). **Violet**—Advent and Lent. **Crimson** or oxblood (dark red)—Holy Week. **Green**—the seasons after Epiphany and after Pentecost. **Black**—optional alternative for funerals and Good Friday.

The days of fasting are Ash Wednesday and Good Friday. Other days of special devotion (penitence) include the 40 days of Lent. Ember days are days of prayer for the church's ministry. They fall on the Wednesday, Friday, and Saturday after the first Sunday in Lent, the Day of Pentecost, Holy Cross Day, and Dec. 13. Rogation Days, the three days before Ascension Day, are days of prayer for God's blessing on the crops, on commerce and industry, and for the conservation of the Earth's resources.

Holy days and other variables	2013	2014	2015	2016	2017
Golden Number	19	1	2	3	4
Sunday Letter	F	E	D	C/B	A
Sundays after Epiphany	5	8	6	5	8
Ash Wednesday	Feb. 13	Mar. 5	Feb. 18	Feb. 10	Mar. 1
First Sunday in Lent	Feb. 17	Mar. 9	Feb. 22	Feb. 14	Mar. 5
Passion/Palm Sunday	Mar. 24	Apr. 13	Mar. 29	Mar. 20	Apr. 9
Good Friday	Mar. 29	Apr. 18	Apr. 3	Mar. 25	Apr. 14
Easter Day	Mar. 31	Apr. 20	Apr. 5	Mar. 27	Apr. 16
Ascension Day	May 9	May 29	May 14	May 5	May 25
Day of Pentecost	May 19	June 8	May 24	May 15	June 4
Trinity Sunday	May 26	June 15	May 31	May 22	June 11
Numbered Proper of 2 Pentecost	#4	#7	#5	#4	#6
First Sunday of Advent	Dec. 1	Nov. 30	Nov. 29	Nov. 27	Dec. 3

Greek Orthodox Movable Ecclesiastical Dates, 2013-17

Feast days and fasting days are determined annually on the basis of the date of Holy Pascha (Easter). This ecclesiastical cycle begins with the first day of the Triodion and ends with the Sunday of All Saints, a total of 18 weeks.

Holy days and observances	2013	2014	2015	2016	2017
Triodion begins	Feb. 24	Feb. 9	Feb. 1	Feb. 21	Feb. 5
1st Saturday of Souls	Mar. 9	Feb. 22	Feb. 14	Mar. 5	Feb. 18
Meat Fare	Mar. 10	Feb. 23	Feb. 15	Mar. 6	Feb. 19
2nd Saturday of Souls	Mar. 16	Mar. 1	Feb. 21	Mar. 12	Feb. 25
Lent begins	Mar. 18	Mar. 3	Feb. 23	Mar. 14	Feb. 27
St. Theodore—3rd Saturday of Souls	Mar. 23	Mar. 8	Feb. 28	Mar. 19	Mar. 4
Sunday of Orthodoxy	Mar. 24	Mar. 9	Mar. 1	Mar. 20	Mar. 5
Saturday of Lazarus	Apr. 27	Apr. 12	Apr. 4	Apr. 23	Apr. 8
Palm Sunday	Apr. 28	Apr. 13	Apr. 5	Apr. 24	Apr. 9
Holy (Good) Friday	May 3	Apr. 18	Apr. 10	Apr. 29	Apr. 14
Western Easter	Mar. 31	Apr. 20	Apr. 5	Mar. 27	Apr. 16
Orthodox Easter	May 5	Apr. 20	Apr. 12	May 1	Apr. 16
Ascension	June 13	May 29	May 21	June 9	May 25
Saturday of Souls	June 22	June 7	May 30	June 18	June 3
Pentecost	June 23	June 8	May 31	June 19	June 4
All Saints	June 30	June 15	June 7	June 26	June 11
Fast of Holy Apostles (first day)	—	June 16	June 8	June 27	June 12

Islamic Holy Days, 1434-1438 AH (late 2012-17)

The Islamic calendar is a strict lunar calendar reckoned from the year of the Hijra (anno Hegirae, or AH)—Muhammad's flight from Mecca to Medina, in 622 CE. Each year consists of 12 lunar months of 29 or 30 days beginning and ending with each new moon's visible crescent. Common years have 354 days; leap years have 355 days. Some Muslim countries employ a conventionalized calendar with the leap date added to the last month, Dhu'l-Hijja, but for religious purposes the leap date is taken into account by tracking each new moon sighting. Holy days begin at sunset of the day previous to the day cited. The actual dates of holy days may also vary slightly from what is cited below, depending on the locality and the times of actual moon sightings as determined by different authorities.

Day (date)	(1434) 2012-13	(1435) 2013-14	(1436) 2014-15	(1437) 2015-16	(1438) 2016-17
New Year's Day (Muharram 1)	Nov. 15, 2012	Nov. 4, 2013	Oct. 25 2014	Oct. 14, 2015	Oct. 2, 2016
Ashura (Muharram 10)	Nov. 24, 2012	Nov. 13, 2013	Nov. 3, 2014	Oct. 23, 2015	Oct. 12, 2016
Mawlid (Rabi' I 12)	Jan. 24, 2013	Jan. 13, 2014	Jan. 3, 2015	Dec. 23, 2015	Dec. 12, 2016
Ramadan begins (Ramadan 1)	July 9, 2013	June 28, 2014	June 18, 2015	June 6, 2016	May 27, 2017
Eid al-Fitr (Shawwal 1)	Aug. 8, 2013	July 29, 2014	July 17, 2015	July 7, 2016	June 26, 2017
Eid al-Adha (Dhu'l-Hijja 10)	Oct. 15, 2013	Oct. 4, 2014	Sept. 23, 2015	Sept. 11, 2016	Sept. 1, 2017

Jewish Holy Days, 5773-5777 (2012-17)

The Jewish calendar consists of 12 lunar months, alternating between 29 and 30 days. It is lunisolar and adjusts for the solar cycle by adding an extra month (Adar II) in the 3rd, 6th, 8th, 11th, 14th, 17th, and 19th years of a 19-year cycle. The calendar starts on the day of Creation, reckoned in the 2nd-3rd cent. BCE as Tishrei 1, 3,761 years before the common era.

The religious calendar begins with the month Nisan, from which all other months are counted, and the civil calendar with Tishrei. The months are 1) Nisan, 2) Iyar, 3) Sivan, 4) Tammuz, 5) Av (also Abh), 6) Elul, 7) Tishrei, 8) Cheshvan (also Marcheshvan), 9) Kislev, 10) Tevet (also Tebeth), 11) Shevat (also Shebhat), 12) Adar, and 12a) Adar Sheni (II), added in leap years. All holidays listed below begin at sunset of the previous day, and end at sundown on the last day shown.

Holiday	Date on Jewish cal.	(5773) 2012-13	(5774) 2013-14	(5775) 2014-15	(5776) 2015-16	(5777) 2016-17
Rosh Hashanah (New Year)	Tishrei 1	Sept. 17 Mon.	Sept. 5 Thu.	Sept. 25 Thu.	Sept. 14 Mon.	Oct. 3 Mon.
	Tishrei 2	Sept. 18 Tue.	Sept. 6 Fri.	Sept. 26 Fri.	Sept. 15 Tue.	Oct. 4 Tue.
Yom Kippur (Day of Atonement). .	Tishrei 10	Sept. 26 Wed.	Sept. 14 Sat.	Oct. 4 Sat.	Sept. 23 Wed.	Oct. 12 Wed.
Sukkot.....................	Tishrei 15	Oct. 1 Mon.	Sept. 19 Thu.	Oct. 9 Thu.	Sept. 28 Mon.	Oct. 17 Mon.
	Tishrei 21	Oct. 7 Sun.	Sept. 25 Wed.	Oct. 15 Wed.	Oct. 4 Sun.	Oct. 23 Sun.
Shemini Atzeret	Tishrei 22	Oct. 8 Mon.	Sept. 26 Thu.	Oct. 16 Thu.	Oct. 5 Mon.	Oct. 24 Mon.
Simchat Torah	Tishrei 23	Oct. 9 Tue.	Sept. 27 Fri.	Oct. 17 Fri.	Oct. 6 Tue.	Oct. 25 Tue.
Hanukkah..................	Kislev 25	Dec. 9 Sun.	Nov. 28 Thu.	Dec. 17 Wed.	Dec. 7 Mon.	Dec. 25 Sun.
	Tevet 2 or 3	Dec. 16 Sun.	Dec. 5 Thu.	Dec. 24 Wed.	Dec. 14 Mon.	Jan. 1 Sun.
Purim	Adar 14	Feb. 24 Sun.	Mar. 16 Sun.	Mar. 5 Thu.	Mar. 24 Thu.	Mar. 12 Sun.
Pesach (Passover)...........	Nisan 15	Mar. 26 Tue.	Apr. 15 Tue.	Apr. 4 Sat.	Apr. 23 Sat.	Apr. 11 Tue.
	Nisan 22	Apr. 2 Tue.	Apr. 22 Tue.	Apr. 11 Sat.	Apr. 30 Sat.	Apr. 18 Tue.
Shavuot (Pentecost)..........	Sivan 6	May 15 Wed.	June 4 Wed.	May 24 Sun.	June 12 Sun.	May 31 Wed.
	Sivan 7	May 16 Thu.	June 5 Thu.	May 25 Mon.	June 13 Mon.	June 1 Thu.
Fast of the 9th of Av	Av 9	July 16 Tue.	Aug. 5 Tue.	July 26 Sun.*	Aug. 14 Sun.*	Aug. 1 Tue.

*Date changed to avoid Sabbath.

Ash Wednesday and Easter Sunday (Western Churches), 2001-2100

Year	Ash Wed.	Easter Sunday	Year	Ash Wed.	Easter Sunday	Year	Ash Wed.	Easter Sunday	Year	Ash Wed.	Easter Sunday	Year	Ash Wed.	Easter Sunday
2001	Feb. 28	Apr. 15	2021	Feb. 17	Apr. 4	2041	Mar. 6	Apr. 21	2061	Feb. 23	Apr. 10	2081	Feb. 12	Mar. 30
2002	Feb. 13	Mar. 31	2022	Mar. 2	Apr. 17	2042	Feb. 19	Apr. 6	2062	Feb. 8	Mar. 26	2082	Mar. 4	Apr. 19
2003	Mar. 5	Apr. 20	2023	Feb. 22	Apr. 9	2043	Feb. 11	Mar. 29	2063	Feb. 28	Apr. 15	2083	Feb. 17	Apr. 4
2004	Feb. 25	Apr. 11	2024	Feb. 14	Mar. 31	2044	Mar. 2	Apr. 17	2064	Feb. 20	Apr. 6	2084	Feb. 9	Mar. 26
2005	Feb. 9	Mar. 27	2025	Mar. 5	Apr. 20	2045	Feb. 22	Apr. 9	2065	Feb. 11	Mar. 29	2085	Feb. 28	Apr. 15
2006	Mar. 1	Apr. 16	2026	Feb. 18	Apr. 5	2046	Feb. 7	Mar. 25	2066	Feb. 24	Apr. 11	2086	Feb. 13	Mar. 31
2007	Feb. 21	Apr. 8	2027	Feb. 10	Mar. 28	2047	Feb. 27	Apr. 14	2067	Feb. 16	Apr. 3	2087	Mar. 5	Apr. 20
2008	Feb. 6	Mar. 23	2028	Mar. 1	Apr. 16	2048	Feb. 19	Apr. 5	2068	Mar. 7	Apr. 22	2088	Feb. 25	Apr. 11
2009	Feb. 25	Apr. 12	2029	Feb. 14	Apr. 1	2049	Mar. 3	Apr. 18	2069	Feb. 27	Apr. 14	2089	Feb. 16	Apr. 3
2010	Feb. 17	Apr. 4	2030	Mar. 6	Apr. 21	2050	Feb. 23	Apr. 10	2070	Feb. 12	Mar. 30	2090	Mar. 1	Apr. 16
2011	Mar. 9	Apr. 24	2031	Feb. 26	Apr. 13	2051	Feb. 15	Apr. 2	2071	Mar. 4	Apr. 19	2091	Feb. 21	Apr. 8
2012	Feb. 22	Apr. 8	2032	Feb. 11	Mar. 28	2052	Mar. 6	Apr. 21	2072	Feb. 24	Apr. 10	2092	Feb. 13	Mar. 30
2013	Feb. 13	Mar. 31	2033	Mar. 2	Apr. 17	2053	Feb. 19	Apr. 6	2073	Feb. 8	Mar. 26	2093	Feb. 25	Apr. 12
2014	Mar. 5	Apr. 20	2034	Feb. 22	Apr. 9	2054	Feb. 11	Mar. 29	2074	Feb. 28	Apr. 15	2094	Feb. 17	Apr. 4
2015	Feb. 18	Apr. 5	2035	Feb. 7	Mar. 25	2055	Mar. 3	Apr. 18	2075	Feb. 20	Apr. 7	2095	Mar. 9	Apr. 24
2016	Feb. 10	Mar. 27	2036	Feb. 27	Apr. 13	2056	Feb. 16	Apr. 2	2076	Mar. 4	Apr. 19	2096	Feb. 29	Apr. 15
2017	Mar. 1	Apr. 16	2037	Feb. 18	Apr. 5	2057	Mar. 7	Apr. 22	2077	Feb. 24	Apr. 11	2097	Feb. 13	Mar. 31
2018	Feb. 14	Apr. 1	2038	Mar. 10	Apr. 25	2058	Feb. 27	Apr. 14	2078	Feb. 16	Apr. 3	2098	Mar. 5	Apr. 20
2019	Mar. 6	Apr. 21	2039	Feb. 23	Apr. 10	2059	Feb. 12	Mar. 30	2079	Mar. 8	Apr. 23	2099	Feb. 25	Apr. 12
2020	Feb. 26	Apr. 12	2040	Feb. 15	Apr. 1	2060	Mar. 3	Apr. 18	2080	Feb. 21	Apr. 7	2100	Feb. 10	Mar. 28

Papal Transition, 2013

Pope Benedict XVI, born Joseph Ratzinger, Apr. 16, 1927, in Marktl am Inn, Bavaria, Germany, was elected to office by the College of Cardinals on Apr. 19, 2005. On Feb. 11, 2013, the 85-year-old Benedict announced he would resign effective Feb. 28, citing his advanced age and declining health. He was the first pope to resign in almost 600 years. Benedict's tenure encountered turmoil over sexual abuse scandals and leaked Vatican documents giving the impression of a curia (administration) marred by infighting and instances of corruption. Assuming the title of supreme pontiff emeritus, Benedict took up residence in a restored convent near the Vatican.

At the papal conclave that followed, 115 cardinals from 48 countries elected Argentinean Cardinal Jorge Mario Bergoglio as pope on the second day of balloting and fifth ballot, Mar. 13, 2013. He was the first Jesuit and first Latin-American pope, and the first born outside Europe since Syrian-born Gregory III, who died in 741. He took the name Francis, after St. Francis of Assisi (1182-1226), known for his life of voluntary poverty, humility, and devotion to the poor. At 76 years old, Bergoglio was one of the oldest men elected to the post.

Pope Francis was born in Buenos Aires, Argentina, Dec. 17, 1936; his parents were Italian immigrants. After earning a master's degree in chemistry he joined the Society of Jesus (Jesuit order) as a novice in 1958 and was ordained a priest in 1969. He served in various roles, as parish priest, theology professor, college administrator, and provincial (head) of the Jesuit province covering Argentina and Uruguay, and became known for his informal manner, simple lifestyle, and work with the poor. Ordained a bishop in 1992, he was named archbishop of Buenos Aires in 1998 and made a cardinal in 2001. He was said to have placed second in balloting for pope in 2005.

In his early days as pope, Francis made symbolic gestures to illustrate his commitment to the ideals of St. Francis; for example, he chose to live in a simply furnished apartment in the Casa Santa Marta, a Vatican guest house, and take meals there in the refectory rather than stay in the elaborate papal suite overlooking St. Peter's Square. He named a group of eight cardinals to advise him on reforming the curia and appointed a committee to investigate the scandal-ridden Vatican Bank.

Roman Catholic Hierarchy

The Roman Catholic Church is headed by the pope, or bishop of Rome. He is assisted by members of the College of Cardinals.

The Papacy

Roman Catholics consider Peter the Apostle to have been the first bishop of Rome and first in a line of popes extending to the present. He is said to have arrived in Rome c. 42 CE and suffered martyrdom there c. 67; he was later canonized as saint. Popes through history have had both religious and secular roles. In the 2013 *Annuario Pontificio*, the official Church yearbook, the pope was given one primary title, "Bishop of Rome." Other titles listed are "Vicar of Jesus Christ, Successor of the Prince of the Apostles, Supreme Pontiff of the Universal Church, Primate of Italy, Archbishop and metropolitan of the Roman province, Sovereign of Vatican City-State, Servant of the Servants of God."

Chronological List of Past Popes

Source: *Annuario Pontificio*

Table lists year of accession of each pope. * = antipope, an illegitimate claimant to the papal throne.

Year	Pope	Year	Pope	Year	Pope	Year	Pope	Year	Pope
	St. Peter	526	St. Felix IV (III)	872	John VIII	1100	Theodoric*	1417	Martin V
67	St. Linus	530	Boniface II	882	Marinus I	1102	Albert*	1431	Eugene IV
76	St. Anacletus	530	Dioscorus*	884	St. Adrian III	1105	Sylvester IV*	1439	Felix V*
	or Cletus	533	John II	885	Stephen V (VI)	1118	Gelasius II	1447	Nicholas V
88	St. Clement I	535	St. Agapitus I	891	Formosus	1118	Gregory VIII*	1455	Callistus III
97	St. Evaristus	536	St. Silverius, Martyr	896	Boniface VI	1119	Callistus II	1458	Pius II
105	St. Alexander I	537	Vigilius	896	Stephen VI (VII)	1124	Honorius II	1464	Paul II
115	St. Sixtus I	556	Pelagius I	897	Romanus	1124	Celestine II*	1471	Sixtus IV
125	St. Telesphorus	561	John III	897	Theodore II	1130	Innocent II	1484	Innocent VIII
136	St. Hyginus	575	Benedict I	898	John IX	1130	Anacletus II*	1492	Alexander VI
140	St. Pius I	579	Pelagius II	900	Benedict IV	1138	Victor IV*	1503	Pius III
155	St. Anicetus	590	St. Gregory I	903	Leo V	1143	Celestine II	1503	Julius II
166	St. Soter	604	Sabinian	903	Christopher*	1144	Lucius II	1513	Leo X
175	St. Eleutherius	607	Boniface III	904	Sergius III	1145	Bl. Eugene III	1522	Adrian VI
189	St. Victor I	608	St. Boniface IV	911	Anastasius III	1153	Anastasius IV	1523	Clement VII
199	St. Zephyrinus	615	St. Deusdedit	913	Landus	1154	Adrian IV	1534	Paul III
217	St. Callistus I		or Adeodatus	914	John X	1159	Alexander III	1550	Julius III
217	St. Hippolytus*	619	Boniface V	928	Leo VI	1159	Victor IV*	1555	Marcellus II
222	St. Urban I	625	Honorius I	928	Stephen VII (VIII)	1164	Paschal III*	1555	Paul IV
230	St. Pontian	640	Severinus	931	John XI	1168	Callistus III*	1559	Pius IV
235	St. Anterus	640	John IV	936	Leo VII	1179	Innocent III*	1566	St. Pius V
236	St. Fabian	642	Theodore I	939	Stephen VIII (IX)	1181	Lucius III	1572	Gregory XIII
251	St. Cornelius	649	St. Martin I, Martyr	942	Marinus II	1185	Urban III	1585	Sixtus V
251	Novatian*	654	St. Eugene I	946	Agapitus II	1187	Clement III	1590	Urban VII
253	St. Lucius I	657	St. Vitalian	955	John XII	1187	Gregory VIII	1590	Gregory XIV
254	St. Stephen I	672	Adeodatus II	963	Leo VIII	1191	Celestine III	1591	Innocent IX
257	St. Sixtus II	676	Donus	964	Benedict V	1198	Innocent III	1592	Clement VIII
259	St. Dionysius	678	St. Agatho	965	John XIII	1216	Honorius III	1605	Leo XI
269	St. Felix I	682	St. Leo II	973	Benedict VI	1227	Gregory IX	1605	Paul V
275	St. Eutychian	684	St. Benedict II	974	Boniface VII*	1241	Celestine IV	1621	Gregory XV
283	St. Caius	685	John V	974	Benedict VII	1243	Innocent IV	1623	Urban VIII
296	St. Marcellinus	686	Conon	983	John XIV	1254	Alexander IV	1644	Innocent X
308	St. Marcellus I	687	Theodore*	985	John XV	1261	Urban IV	1655	Alexander VII
309	St. Eusebius	687	Paschal*	996	Gregory V	1265	Clement IV	1667	Clement IX
311	St. Melchiades	687	St. Sergius I	997	John XVI*	1271	Bl. Gregory X	1670	Clement X
314	St. Sylvester I	701	John VI	999	Sylvester II	1276	Bl. Innocent V	1676	Bl. Innocent XI
336	St. Marcus	705	John VII	1003	John XVII	1276	Adrian V	1689	Alexander VIII
337	St. Julius I	708	Sisinnius	1004	John XVIII	1276	John XXI	1691	Innocent XII
352	Liberius	708	Constantine	1009	Sergius IV	1277	Nicholas III	1700	Clement XI
355	Felix II*	715	St. Gregory II	1012	Benedict VIII	1281	Martin IV	1721	Innocent XIII
366	St. Damasus I	731	St. Gregory III	1012	Gregory*	1285	Honorius IV	1724	Benedict XIII
366	Ursinus*	741	St. Zachary	1024	John XIX	1288	Nicholas IV	1730	Clement XII
384	St. Siricius	752	Stephen II (III)[1]	1032	Benedict IX	1294	St. Celestine V	1740	Benedict XIV
399	St. Anastasius I	757	St. Paul I	1045	Sylvester III	1294	Boniface VIII	1758	Clement XIII
401	St. Innocent I	767	Constantine*	1045	Benedict IX	1303	Bl. Benedict XI	1769	Clement XIV
417	St. Zosimus	768	Philip*	1045	Gregory VI	1305	Clement V	1775	Pius VI
418	St. Boniface I	768	Stephen III (IV)	1046	Clement II	1316	John XXII	1800	Pius VII
418	Eulalius*	772	Adrian I	1047	Benedict IX	1328	Nicholas V*	1823	Leo XII
422	St. Celestine I	795	St. Leo III	1048	Damasus II	1334	Benedict XII	1829	Pius VIII
432	St. Sixtus III	816	Stephen IV (V)	1049	St. Leo IX	1342	Clement VI	1831	Gregory XVI
440	St. Leo I	817	St. Paschal I	1055	Victor II	1352	Innocent VI	1846	Pius IX
461	St. Hilary	824	Eugene II	1057	Stephen IX (X)	1362	Bl. Urban V	1878	Leo XIII
468	St. Simplicius	827	Valentine	1058	Benedict X*	1370	Gregory XI	1903	St. Pius X
483	St. Felix III (II)	827	Gregory IV	1059	Nicholas II	1378	Urban VI	1914	Benedict XV
492	St. Gelasius I	844	John*	1061	Alexander II	1378	Clement VII*	1922	Pius XI
496	Anastasius II	844	Sergius II	1061	Honorius II*	1389	Boniface IX	1939	Pius XII
498	St. Symmachus	847	St. Leo IV	1073	St. Gregory VII	1394	Benedict XIII*	1958	John XXIII
498	Lawrence* (also in 501-505)	855	Benedict III	1080	Clement III*	1404	Innocent VII	1963	Paul VI
		855	Anastasius*	1086	Bl. Victor III	1406	Gregory XII	1978	John Paul I
514	St. Hormisdas	858	St. Nicholas I	1088	Bl. Urban II	1409	Alexander V*	1978	John Paul II
523	St. John I, Martyr	867	Adrian II	1099	Paschal II	1410	John XXIII*	2005	Benedict XVI

Bl. = Blessed (1) After St. Zachary, a Roman priest named Stephen was elected who died before assuming the papacy. Another Stephen was then elected to succeed Zachary as Stephen II. He is sometimes listed as Stephen III.

College of Cardinals

Members of the Sacred College of Cardinals are chosen by the pope to be his chief assistants and advisers in the administration of the church. Among their duties is the election of the pope.

In its present form, the College of Cardinals dates from the 12th century. The first cardinals, from about the 6th century, were deacons and priests of the leading churches of Rome and were bishops of neighboring dioceses. The title of cardinal was limited to members of the college in 1567. The number of cardinals was set at 70 in 1586. Pope John XXIII began to increase the number in 1959; however, the number eligible to participate in papal elections was limited to 120. Previous limitations were set aside by Pope John Paul II when he created new cardinals. In 1918, the Code of Canon Law specified that all cardinals must be priests. Pope John XXIII in 1962 ruled that cardinals must ordinarily be bishops. In 1971, Pope Paul VI decreed that at age 80, cardinals must retire from curial departments and offices and cannot be summoned to participate in papal elections.

As of Aug. 2013, there were 202 cardinals from 66 countries, of whom 112, from 49 countries, remained eligible to vote.

North American Cardinals

Name	Office	Born	Named cardinal
William W. Baum[1]	Archbishop emeritus of Washington, DC	1926	1976
Raymond L. Burke	Prefect, Supreme Tribunal of the Apostolic Signature	1948	2010
Thomas C. Collins	Archbishop of Toronto, ON, Canada	1947	2012
Daniel N. DiNardo	Archbishop of Galveston-Houston	1949	2007
Timothy M. Dolan	Archbishop of New York	1950	2012
Edward M. Egan[1]	Archbishop emeritus of New York	1932	2001
Francis E. George	Archbishop of Chicago	1937	1998
James M. Harvey	Archpriest of St. Paul Outside-the-Walls	1949	2012
William Henry Keeler[1]	Archbishop emeritus of Baltimore	1931	1994
Bernard F. Law[1]	Archbishop emeritus of Boston	1931	1985
William Levada	Archbishop emeritus of San Francisco	1936	2006
Javier Lozano Barragán[1]	Archbishop emeritus of Zacatecas, Mexico	1933	2003
Roger Mahony	Archbishop emeritus of Los Angeles	1936	1991
Adam Joseph Maida[1]	Archbishop emeritus of Detroit	1930	1994
Theodore McCarrick[1]	Archbishop emeritus of Washington, DC	1930	2001
Edwin F. O'Brien	Grand Master of the Knights of the Holy Sepulcher	1939	2012
Sean O'Malley	Archbishop of Boston	1944	2006
Marc Ouellet	Prefect, Congregation for Bishops	1944	2003
Justin F. Rigali	Archbishop emeritus of Philadelphia	1935	2003
Norberto Rivera Carrera	Archbishop of Mexico City	1942	1998
José Francisco Robles Ortega	Archbishop of Guadalajara, Mexico	1949	2007
Juan Sandoval Íñiguez[2]	Archbishop emeritus of Guadalajara, Mexico	1933	1994
James F. Stafford[1]	Archbishop emeritus of Denver	1932	1998
Edmund C. Szoka[1]	Archbishop emeritus of Detroit	1927	1988
Jean-Claude Turcotte	Archbishop emeritus of Montréal, QC, Canada	1936	1994
Donald W. Wuerl	Archbishop of Washington, DC	1940	2010

(1) Ineligible to take part in conclave of Mar. 2013 because of age. (2) Ineligible to participate in future papal elections because of age.

The Ten Commandments

In the Hebrew Bible (Old Testament) the Ten Commandments (also called the Decalogue, from the Greek meaning "ten words") were revealed by God to Moses on Mt. Sinai. They form the covenant between God and the Israelites and the moral code that is the basis for the Jewish and Christian religions. The Ten Commandments appear in two places in the Old Testament—Exodus 20:1-17 and Deuteronomy 5:6-21.

Most Protestant, Anglican, and Orthodox Christians follow Jewish tradition, as shown here, which considers the introduction ("I am the Lord ...") the first commandment and makes the prohibition against idolatry the second. Roman Catholic and Lutheran traditions combine I and II and split the last commandment into two that separately prohibit coveting of a neighbor's wife and of a neighbor's goods. This arrangement alters the numbering of the other commandments by one.

Following is the text as it appears in Exodus 20:1-17, in the King James version of the Bible [Roman numerals added]:

And God spake all these words, saying,

I. I *am* the LORD thy God, which have brought thee out of the land of Egypt, out of the house of bondage. Thou shalt have no other gods before me.

II. Thou shalt not make unto thee any graven image, or any likeness of *any thing* that *is* in heaven above, or that *is* in the earth beneath, or that *is* in the water under the earth. Thou shalt not bow down thyself to them, nor serve them: for I the LORD thy God *am* a jealous God, visiting the iniquity of the fathers upon the children unto the third and fourth *generation* of them that hate me; and shewing mercy unto thousands of them that love me, and keep my commandments.

III. Thou shalt not take the name of the LORD thy God in vain: for the LORD will not hold him guiltless that taketh his name in vain.

IV. Remember the sabbath day, to keep it holy. Six days shalt thou labour, and do all thy work: but the seventh day *is* the sabbath of the LORD thy God: *in it* thou shalt not do any

work, thou, nor thy son, nor thy daughter, thy manservant, nor thy maidservant, nor thy cattle, nor thy stranger that *is* within thy gates: for *in* six days the LORD made heaven and earth, the sea, and all that in them *is*, and rested the seventh day: wherefore the LORD blessed the sabbath day, and hallowed it.

V. Honour thy father and thy mother: that thy days may be long upon the land which the LORD thy God giveth thee.

VI. Thou shalt not kill.

VII. Thou shalt not commit adultery.

VIII. Thou shalt not steal.

IX. Thou shalt not bear false witness against thy neighbour.

X. Thou shalt not covet thy neighbour's house, thou shalt not covet thy neighbour's wife, nor his manservant, nor his maidservant, nor his ox, nor his ass, nor any thing that *is* thy neighbour's.

Major Christian Denominations:

Brackets indicate some features that tend to

Denomination	Origins	Organization	Authority	Special rites
Baptists	In radical Reformation, objections to infant baptism, demands for church and state separation; John Smyth, English Separatist, in 1609; Roger Williams, 1638, Providence, RI.	Congregational; each local church is autonomous.	Scripture; some Baptists, particularly in the South, interpret the Bible literally.	[Baptism, usually early teen years and after, by total immersion]; Lord's Supper.
Church of Christ (Disciples)	Among evangelical Presbyterians in KY (1804) and PA (1809), in distress over Protestant factionalism and decline of fervor; organized in 1832.	Congregational.	["Where the Scriptures speak, we speak; where the Scriptures are silent, we are silent."]	Adult baptism; Lord's Supper (weekly).
Episcopalians	Henry VIII separated English Catholic Church from Rome, 1534, for political reasons; Protestant Episcopal Church in U.S. founded in 1789.	[Diocesan bishops, in apostolic succession, are elected by parish representatives; the national Church is headed by General Convention and Presiding Bishop; part of the Anglican Communion.]	Scripture as interpreted by tradition, especially 39 Articles (1563); tri-annual convention of bishops, priests, and lay people.	Infant baptism, Eucharist, and other sacraments; sacrament taken to be symbolic, but as having real spiritual effect.
Jehovah's Witnesses	Founded in 1870 in PA by Charles Taze Russell; incorporated as Watch Tower Bible and Tract Society of PA, 1884; name Jehovah's Witnesses adopted in 1931.	A governing body located in NY coordinates worldwide activities; each congregation cared for by a body of elders; each Witness considered a minister.	The Bible.	Baptism by immersion; annual Lord's Meal ceremony.
Latter-day Saints (Mormons)	In a vision of the Father and the Son reported by Joseph Smith (1820s) in NY; Smith also reported receiving new scripture on golden tablets: the Book of Mormon.	Theocratic; 1st Presidency (church president, two counselors), 12 Apostles preside over international church; local congregations headed by lay priesthood leaders.	Revelation to living prophet (church president). The Bible, Book of Mormon, and other revelations to Smith and his successors.	Baptism at age 8; laying on of hands (which confers the gift of the Holy Ghost); Lord's Supper; temple rites: baptism for the dead, marriage for eternity, others.
Lutherans	Begun by Martin Luther in Wittenberg, Germany, in 1517; objection to Catholic doctrine of salvation and sale of indulgences; break complete, 1519.	Varies from congregational to episcopal; in U.S., a combination of regional synods and congregational polities is most common.	Scripture alone; the Book of Concord (1580), which includes the three Ecumenical Creeds, is subscribed to as a correct exposition of Scripture.	Infant baptism; Lord's Supper; Christ's true body and blood present "in, with, and under the bread and wine."
Methodists	Rev. John Wesley began movement in 1738, within Church of England; first U.S. denomination, Baltimore (1784).	Conference and superintendent system; [in United Methodist Church, general superintendents are bishops—not a priestly order, only an office—who are elected for life].	Scripture as interpreted by tradition, reason, and experience.	Baptism of infants or adults; Lord's Supper commanded; other rites: marriage, ordination, solemnization of personal commitments.
Orthodox	Developed in original Christian proselytizing; broke with Rome in 1054 after centuries of doctrinal disputes and diverging traditions.	Synods of bishops in autonomous, usually national, churches elect a patriarch, archbishop, or metropolitan; these men, as a group, are the heads of the church.	Scripture, tradition, and the first seven church councils up to Nicaea II in 787; bishops in council have authority in doctrine and policy.	Seven sacraments: infant baptism and anointing, Eucharist, ordination, penance, marriage, and anointing of the sick.
Pentecostal	In Topeka, KS (1901) and Los Angeles (1906), in reaction to perceived loss of evangelical fervor among Methodists and others.	Originally a movement, not a formal organization, Pentecostalism now has a variety of organized forms and continues also as a movement.	Scripture; individual charismatic leaders, the teachings of the Holy Spirit.	[Spirit baptism, especially as shown in "speaking in tongues"; healing and sometimes exorcism]; adult baptism; Lord's Supper.
Presbyterians	In 16th-cent. Calvinist reformation; differed with Lutherans over sacraments, church government; John Knox founded Scotch Presbyterian church about 1560.	[Highly structured representational system of ministers and lay persons (presbyters) in local, regional, and national bodies (synods).]	Scripture.	Infant baptism; Lord's Supper; bread and wine symbolize Christ's spiritual presence.
Roman Catholics	Traditionally, founded by Jesus who named St. Peter the first vicar; developed in early Christian proselytizing, especially after the conversion of imperial Rome in the 4th cent.	[Hierarchy with supreme power vested in pope elected by cardinals]; councils of bishops advise on matters of doctrine and policy.	[The pope, when speaking for the whole church in matters of faith and morals; and tradition (which is expressed in church councils and in part contained in Scripture).]	Mass; seven sacraments: baptism, reconciliation, Eucharist, confirmation, marriage, ordination, and anointing of the sick (unction).
United Church of Christ	[By ecumenical union, in 1957, of Congregationalists and Evangelical and Reformed, representing both Calvinist and Lutheran traditions.]	Congregational; a General Synod, representative of all congregations, sets general policy.	Scripture.	Infant baptism; Lord's Supper.

How Do They Differ?
distinguish a denomination sharply from others.

Practice	Ethics	Doctrine	Other	Denomination
Worship style varies from staid to evangelistic; extensive missionary activity.	Usually opposed to alcohol and tobacco; some tendency toward a perfectionist ethical standard.	[No creed; true church is of believers only, who are all equal.]	Believing no authority can stand between the believer and God, the Baptists are strong supporters of church and state separation.	**Baptists**
Tries to avoid any rite not considered part of the 1st-cent. church; some congregations may reject instrumental music.	Some tendency toward perfectionism; increasing interest in social action programs.	Simple New Testament faith; avoids any elaboration not firmly based on Scripture.	Highly tolerant in doctrinal and religious matters; strongly supportive of scholarly education.	**Church of Christ (Disciples)**
Formal, based on *Book of Common Prayer*, updated 1979; services range from austerely simple to highly liturgical.	Tolerant, sometimes permissive; some social action programs.	Scripture; the "historic creeds," which include the Apostles, Nicene, and Athanasian, and the *Book of Common Prayer*; ranges from Anglo-Catholic to low church, with Calvinist influences.	Strongly ecumenical, holding talks with many branches of Christendom.	**Episcopalians**
Meetings are held in Kingdom Halls and members' homes for study and worship; [extensive door-to-door visitations].	High moral code; stress on marital fidelity and family values; avoidance of tobacco and blood transfusions.	[God, by his first creation, Christ, will soon destroy all wickedness; 144,000 faithful ones will rule in heaven with Christ over others on a paradise earth.]	Total allegiance proclaimed only to God's kingdom or heavenly government by Christ; main periodical, *The Watchtower*, is printed in 195 languages.	**Jehovah's Witnesses**
Simple service with prayers, hymns, sermon; private temple ceremonies may be more elaborate.	Temperance; strict moral code; [tithing]; a strong work ethic with communal self-reliance; [strong missionary activity]; family emphasis.	Jesus Christ is the Son of God, the Eternal Father. Jesus's atonement saves all humans; those who are obedient to God's laws may become joint-heirs with Christ in God's kingdom.	Mormons believe theirs is the true church of Jesus Christ, restored by God through Joseph Smith. Official name: The Church of Jesus Christ of Latter-day Saints.	**Latter-day Saints (Mormons)**
Relatively simple, formal liturgy with emphasis on the sermon.	Generally conservative in personal and social ethics; doctrine of "two kingdoms" (worldly and holy) supports conservatism in secular affairs.	Salvation by grace alone through faith; Lutheranism has made major contributions to Protestant theology.	Though still somewhat divided along ethnic lines (German, Swedish, etc.), main divisions are between fundamentalists and liberals.	**Lutherans**
Worship style varies widely by denomination, local church, geography.	Originally pietist and perfectionist; always strong social activist elements.	No distinctive theological development; 25 articles abridged from Church of England's 39, not binding.	In 1968, The United Methodist Church was formed by the union of The Methodist Church and The Evangelical United Brethren Church.	**Methodists**
Elaborate liturgy, usually in the vernacular, though extremely traditional; the liturgy is the essence of Orthodoxy; veneration of icons.	Tolerant; little stress on social action; divorce, remarriage permitted in some cases; bishops are celibate; priests need not be.	Emphasis on Christ's resurrection, rather than crucifixion; the Holy Spirit proceeds from God the Father only.	Orthodox Church in America originally under Patriarch of Moscow, was granted autonomy in 1970; Greek Orthodox do not recognize this autonomy.	Orthodox
Loosely structured service with rousing hymns and sermons, culminating in spirit baptism.	Usually, emphasis on perfectionism, with varying degrees of tolerance.	Simple traditional beliefs, usually Protestant, with emphasis on the immediate presence of God in the Holy Spirit.	Once confined to lower-class "holy rollers," Pentecostalism now appears in mainline churches and has established middle-class congregations.	**Pentecostal**
A simple, sober service in which the sermon is central.	Traditionally, a tendency toward strictness, with firm church- and self-discipline; otherwise tolerant.	Emphasizes the sovereignty and justice of God; no longer dogmatic.	Although traces of belief in predestination (that God has foreordained salvation for the "elect") remain, this idea is no longer a central element in Presbyterianism.	**Presbyterians**
Relatively elaborate ritual centered on the Mass; also rosary recitation, novenas, etc.	Traditionally strict but increasingly tolerant in practice; divorce and remarriage not accepted, but annulments sometimes granted; celibate clergy, except in Eastern rite.	Highly elaborated; salvation by merit gained through grace; dogmatic; special veneration of Mary, the mother of Jesus.	Relatively rapid change followed Vatican Council II; Mass now in vernacular; more stress on social action, tolerance, ecumenism.	**Roman Catholics**
Usually simple service with emphasis on the sermon.	Tolerant; some social action emphasis.	Standard Protestant; "Statement of Faith" (1959) is not binding.	Two main churches in the 1957 union represented earlier unions with small groups of almost every Protestant denomination.	**United Church of Christ**

Books of the Bible

Old Testament—Standard Protestant List

Genesis	I Kings	Ecclesiastes	Obadiah			
Exodus	II Kings	Song of Solomon	Jonah			
Leviticus	I Chronicles	Isaiah	Micah			
Numbers	II Chronicles	Jeremiah	Nahum			
Deuteronomy	Ezra	Lamentations	Habakkuk			
Joshua	Nehemiah	Ezekiel	Zephaniah			
Judges	Esther	Daniel	Haggai			
Ruth	Job	Hosea	Zechariah			
I Samuel	Psalms	Joel	Malachi			
II Samuel	Proverbs	Amos				

New Testament List

Matthew	Ephesians	Hebrews
Mark	Philippians	James
Luke	Colossians	I Peter
John	I Thessalonians	II Peter
Acts	II Thessalonians	I John
Romans	I Timothy	II John
I Corinthians	II Timothy	III John
II Corinthians	Titus	Jude
Galatians	Philemon	Revelation

The standard Protestant Old Testament consists of the same 39 books as in the Bible of Judaism, but the latter is organized differently. The Old Testament used by Roman Catholics has 7 additional deuterocanonical books, plus some additional parts of books. The 7 are **Tobit, Judith, Wisdom, Sirach (Ecclesiasticus), Baruch, I Maccabees,** and **II Maccabees.** Both Catholic and Protestant versions of the New Testament have 27 books with the same names.

Figures in the Hebrew Bible (Old Testament)

Aaron: First of Hebrew high priests; brother of Moses and Miriam.

Abel: Second son of Adam and Eve; slain by Cain.

Abraham: Founder of monotheism; patriarch; also called Abram.

Adam: First human according to Genesis.

Amos: Herdsman; prophesized against social injustice and oppression of the poor.

Bathsheba: Seduced by King David; mother of King Solomon.

Cain: First son of Adam and Eve; killed his brother Abel.

Cyrus: Persian ruler; sent Jews home from exile.

Daniel: Cast into lion's den for violating decree of King Darius; saved.

David: Israel's greatest king; shepherd, warrior, musician, psalmist.

Deborah: Prophet and judge; ruled over Israel.

Elijah: Great prophet; was victorious over the priests of the Phoenician god Baal.

Elisha: Prophet; successor to Elijah.

Esther: Jewish wife of the king of Persia; saved Jews from annihilation.

Eve: First woman according to Genesis.

Ezekiel: Visionary; prophesized hope to exiled Jews in Babylon.

Ezra: Great Jewish leader; rededicated worship and Torah law after exile.

Goliath: Giant Philistine warrior; slain by David.

Hannah: Childless; promised child to God; mother to the prophet Samuel.

Hosea: Enacted prophecy; asked God's forgiveness for Israel's unfaithfulness.

Isaac: Son of Abraham and Sarah; saved from sacrificial altar.

Isaiah: Highly educated prophet; avoided war with Assyria; Israel destroyed; Jerusalem survived.

Jacob: Son of Isaac; father of the Twelve Tribes; renamed "Israel" by angel.

Jeremiah: Confronted leaders; urged surrender to Babylon.

Jezebel: Phoenician queen of King Ahab; had Israelite prophets killed.

Job: "Blameless" man; allowed by God to lose family, health, and possessions in a test of his faith.

Jonah: Swallowed by a great fish; prophesied destruction of Nineveh, averted when the people repented.

Jonathan: Son of King Saul; friend of David.

Joseph: Favorite of Jacob; interpreted Pharaoh's dreams; brought Hebrews to Egypt.

Joshua: Successor of Moses; led Hebrews into Canaan.

Josiah: Reformist king; repaired Solomon's Temple; restored worship; reintroduced Passover.

Leah: Matriarch; older sister of Rachel; Jacob's wife.

Micah: Prophet; predicted the end of war and beginning of peace.

Miriam: Prophet and great leader of the Hebrews; sister to Moses and Aaron.

Moses: Most important Hebrew prophet; leader of the Israelites; received the Torah.

Nathan: Prophet; confronted King David over his seduction of Bathsheba.

Nebuchadnezzar: Babylonian king; destroyed Jerusalem.

Nehemiah: Led Jews back to Jerusalem from Babylonian exile.

Noah: Man of great faith who, according to Genesis, saved his family and two of every living thing on Earth from a great flood.

Rachel: Matriarch; younger sister of Leah; Jacob's wife; Joseph's mother.

Rebecca: Matriarch; wife of Isaac; mother of Jacob.

Ruth: Moabite convert; ancestor of David.

Samson: Judge and military leader of Israel; possessed super-human strength.

Samuel: Prophet; anointed Saul king of Israel and later anointed David to succeed him.

Sarah: First matriarch of Israel; wife of Abraham; mother of Isaac.

Saul: First king of Israel; father of Jonathan.

Solomon: King of Israel at its zenith; known for great wisdom.

Zechariah: Prophet; encouraged rebuilding of Solomon's Temple destroyed by Babylonians.

Figures in the New Testament

Andrew: One of the Twelve Apostles; brother of Peter and former fisherman; one of the earlier disciples.

Barabbas: Imprisoned with Jesus; set free by Pilate on Passover.

Barnabas: Disciple of Jesus; closely connected with Paul.

Bartholomew: A lesser-known member of the Twelve Apostles; cheerful and prayed often.

Cornelius: A Roman convert; defended by Peter, allowing Gentiles to become Christians.

Elizabeth: Mother of John the Baptist; relation of the Virgin Mary.

Gabriel: Archangel; appeared to the Virgin Mary to announce that she was to give birth to the Messiah.

Herod: May refer to Herod the Great, who ordered the death of children after Jesus's birth, or to his son, Herod, who had John the Baptist beheaded.

James: May refer to either of two apostles: James, son of Zebedee, brother of John the apostle, or the lesser-known James, son of Alphaeus.

Jesus: Central figure of the Gospels; believed to be the Messiah and son of God; crucified by the Romans.

John (Apostle): Beloved disciple of Jesus; one of the Twelve; possible author of fourth Gospel; brother of James.

John (Baptist): Known as John the Baptist; important prophet and forerunner to Jesus; relation of the Virgin Mary.

Joseph: Husband of the Virgin Mary; descendant of King David.

Judas Iscariot: Betrayer of Jesus; prominent member of the Apostles; committed suicide.

Judas Thaddeus: One of the Twelve; also called Jude to distinguish him from Judas Iscariot.

Lazarus: Brother of the disciples Martha and Mary of Bethany; raised from the dead at their request; possibly the same Lazarus who appears in Jesus's parable of the rich man.

Luke: Traditional author of the Gospel of Luke; possibly a follower of Paul.

Mark: Traditional author of the Gospel of Mark; possibly a disciple of Peter.

Mary, the mother of Jesus: Traditionally believed to be a virgin who conceived without sin; wife of Joseph.

Mary Magdalene: Important female disciple of Jesus; witness to his death and resurrection.

Matthew: One of the Twelve; possible author of the Gospel of Matthew; former tax collector.

Matthias: Often included on lists of the Twelve Apostles as the apostle who replaced Judas Iscariot after his betrayal.

Paul (Saul): Writer of nearly a quarter of the New Testament; a former persecutor of Christians, converted after a vision; played a significant role in spreading Christianity.

Peter: Considered the foremost of the Twelve Apostles; traditionally the first pope and "rock" of the Christian church; author of epistles; also called Simon and Simon Peter.

Philip: One of the Twelve; considered pragmatic and sensible.

Pilate, Pontius: A Roman prefect; played large role in the trial and crucifixion of Jesus.

Simon: One of the Twelve; known as "the Zealot" to distinguish from Simon Peter.

Stephen: Fervently preached that Jesus was the Messiah; stoned to death by angry mob, including Saul; important figure in Saul's conversion.

Thomas: One of the Twelve; known as "Doubting Thomas" because he did not believe Jesus was risen until he could touch him.

Timothy: A disciple closely connected with Paul; recipient of epistles.

Zacharias: Father of John the Baptist; husband of Elizabeth; struck dumb when he doubted his barren wife could become pregnant.

Major Non-Christian Religions

Source: Baha'i reviewed by the Baha'i Community Relations Center; Islam reviewed by Natana Delong-Bas, Lecturer in Islamic Studies, Boston Coll.; Hinduism and Judaism reviewed by Anthony Padovano, PhD, STD, Prof. of Literature & Relig. Studies, Ramapo College, NJ, Adj. Prof. of Theol., Fordham Univ.; Sikhism reviewed by The Sikh Coalition of New York, NY.

Islam

Founded: Muhammad received his first revelation in 610 CE.

Founder: Muhammad (c. 570-632 CE), the Prophet.

Sacred texts: Two texts constitute the Muslim sacred canon, the *Qur'an* (Koran) and the *Hadith*. The Koran provides the foundation for Islamic religion and culture. It is regarded as the final, perfect, and complete word of God as revealed to Muhammad over the course of his life. Received by Muhammad in the Arabic language, it is memorized in Arabic by adherents regardless of their native language. It is divided into 114 chapters of unequal length, the shortest containing only 3 verses, and the longest containing 286 verses. The Koran is the ultimate source of everything Islamic, from metaphysics to theology to sacred history, to ethics and law, to art. The Hadith, which describes Muhammad's actions, attitudes, and teachings, complements the Koran. Due to its long history of oral transmission, the Hadith's lessons are seen as somewhat vulnerable to human error. It does not contain God's unadulterated voice as does the Koran but functions as a powerful spiritual and behavioral code nonetheless.

Organization: Muhammad was both the last prophet and a statesman. Muslim leaders have often assumed both civil and moral functions within Islamic states. Within the larger community, there are cultural and national groups, held together by a common religious law, the *Sharia*. Muslims believe that God is the ultimate lawgiver and that human beings cannot devise laws that oppose divine laws. Still, the Sharia is approached differently in different parts of the Islamic world. Over the centuries, Sunnis have developed four major schools of law: the Hanafi, the Shafi'i, the Hanbali, and the Maliki schools. The Ja'fari school is the most important and well-known Shiite school. Before the 20th century, religious scholars known as the *ulama* held much legal power. Judges (*qadis*) and law-interpreters (*muftis*) are people learned in religious law who lead congregational prayers in mosques and perform other religious duties.

Practice: Five duties (of both men and women), known as the Pillars of Islam, are regarded as cardinal in Islam and as central to the life of the Islamic community. In accordance with Islam's absolute commitment to monotheism, the first duty is the profession of faith (the *Shahadah*): "There is no God but Allah and Muhammad is His Prophet." A Muslim must profess this belief publicly at least once in his or her lifetime; it defines the membership of an individual in the Islamic community. The second duty is that of five daily prayers organized in intervals throughout the day: sunrise, early afternoon, late afternoon, immediately after sunset, and before midnight. During prayer, Muslims face the Kaaba, a small, cube-shaped structure in the courtyard of al-Haram (the "inviolate place"), at the Grand Mosque of Mecca. All five prayers in Islam are congregational and are to be offered in a mosque, but they may be offered individually if one cannot be present with a congregation. Congregational prayer is required only at the early afternoon prayer on Friday for men. The third cardinal duty of a Muslim is to pay alms, or *zakat*, which should be 2.5% of one's total wealth. This was originally the tax levied by Muhammad on the wealthy members of the community, primarily to help the poor. Only when zakat has been paid is the rest of a Muslim's property considered purified and legitimate. The fourth duty is the fast of the lunar month of Ramadan. During the fasting month, one must abstain from eating, drinking, smoking, impure thoughts, and sexual intercourse from dawn until sunset, and feed at least one poor person, if able. The fifth duty is the pilgrimage to the Kaaba, which a Muslim must undertake, with exceptions for poverty and ill health, at least once during his or her lifetime.

Divisions: There are two major groups: the majority Sunni (84% of the worldwide Muslim population) and the minority Shiites (14%). Sects first appeared in Islam at the time of Muhammad's death. The group that came to be known as Sunni accepted Abu Bakr, an early convert, as his successor (caliph), while a smaller number, which became the Shia, believed that Ali ibn Abi Talib, the son-in-law and first cousin of the prophet, should have become his successor (Imam). Imams are believed to interpret the Koran infallibly. **Shiites** fall into three major branches: Fivers, Seveners, and Twelvers, reflecting the number of Imams they recognize. Twelvers believe that the 12th Imam has lived an invisible existence since 874, and will return as the Mahdi (a messiah figure) who will usher in a 1,000-year reign of peace and justice. **Sufism** (mystical dimension of Islam) emphasizes personal relation to God and obedience informed by love of God; it is prevalent among both Sunni and Shiites.

Location: W Africa to Philippines, across a band including E Africa, Central Asia and W China, India, Malaysia, Indonesia. Islam has several million adherents in North America and about 30 mil in Europe.

Beliefs: Strictly monotheistic. God is creator of the universe, omnipotent, omniscient, just, forgiving, and merciful. God revealed the Koran to Muhammad to guide humanity to truth and justice. Those who sincerely "submit" (literal meaning of "Islam") to God attain salvation.

World's Largest Muslim Populations, 2012
Source: Pew Research Center

Rank	Country	Muslim population	% of country's pop.
1.	Indonesia	209,120,000	87.2%
2.	India	176,190,000	14.4
3.	Pakistan	167,410,000	96.4
4.	Bangladesh	133,540,000	89.8
5.	Nigeria	77,300,000	48.8
6.	Egypt	76,990,000	94.9
7.	Iran	73,570,000	99.0+
8.	Turkey	71,330,000	98.0
9.	Algeria	34,730,000	97.9
10.	Morocco	31,940,000	99.0+
11.	Iraq	31,340,000	99.0
12.	Afghanistan	31,330,000	99.0+
13.	Sudan[1]	30,490,000	90.7
14.	Ethiopia	28,680,000	34.6
15.	Uzbekistan	26,550,000	96.7
16.	Saudi Arabia	25,520,000	93.0
17.	China	24,690,000	1.8
18.	Yemen	23,830,000	99.0+
19.	Syria	18,930,000	92.8
20.	Malaysia	18,100,000	63.7

(1) Excluding what is now South Sudan.

Baha'i

Founded: Mid-19th century.

Founder: Mirza Husayn-Ali Nuri (1817-92), later known as Baha'u'llah (Arabic for "Glory of God").

Sacred texts: The writings of Baha'u'llah and of his herald the Bab (Siyyid Ali-Muhammad, 1819-50). The primary text is *Kitab-i-Aqdas* (Most Holy Book).

Organization: The Baha'i administrative system consists of elected nine-member councils at the local, national, and international levels. There are also more than 180 National Spiritual Assemblies and an elected, international governing body known as the Universal House of Justice.

Practice: Prayer, meditation, and fasting are key components of the Baha'i Faith. Work performed in a spirit of service to humanity is considered an important form of worship. The Baha'i Faith has no clergy and minimal ritual and congregational worship.

Divisions: In a religion in which unity is perhaps the central spiritual value, the Baha'i Faith has avoided separating into sects with differentiated theologies and practices.

Location: Worldwide.

Beliefs: God has progressively revealed His will and purpose through a series of Divine manifestations including Jesus, Buddha, Muhammad, Zoroaster, and Baha'u'llah. Baha'u'llah's teachings include the oneness of humanity, the equality of men and women, the harmony of science and religion, the abandonment of all forms of prejudice, and the elimination of extremes of poverty and wealth.

Buddhism

Founded: About 525 BCE, reportedly near Benares, India.

Founder: Gautama Siddhartha (c. 563-483 BCE), the Buddha, who achieved enlightenment through intense meditation.

Sacred texts: The *Tripitaka*, a collection of the Buddha's teachings, rules of monastic life, and philosophical commentaries on the teachings; also a vast body of Buddhist teachings and commentaries, many of which are called *sutras*.

Organization: The basic institution is the *sangha*, or monastic order, through which traditions are passed down. Monastic life tends to be democratic and antiauthoritarian.

Practice: Varies widely according to the sect and ranges from austere meditation to magical chanting and elaborate temple rites. Many practices, such as exorcism of devils, reflect pre-Buddhist beliefs.

Divisions: A variety of sects grouped into three primary branches: Theravada, which emphasizes the importance of pure thought and deed; Mahayana (includes Zen and Soka-gakkai), which ranges from philosophical schools to belief in the saving grace of higher beings or ritual practices and to practical meditative disciplines; and Vajrayana, or Tantrism, a combination of belief in ritual magic and sophisticated philosophy.

Location: Mainly in Asia, from Sri Lanka to Japan.

Beliefs: Life is suffering, and there is no ultimate reality behind it. The cycle of birth and rebirth continues because of desire and attachment to the unreal "self." Meditation and deeds will end the cycle and achieve Nirvana (nothingness, enlightenment).

Hinduism

Founded: About 1500 BCE by Aryans who migrated to India, where their Vedic religion intermixed with the practices and beliefs of the native peoples.

Sacred texts: The *Veda*, including the *Upanishads*, a collection of rituals and commentaries; a vast number of epic stories about gods, heroes, and saints, including the *Bhaga-vadgita*, a part of the *Mahabharata*, and the *Ramayana*.

Organization: None, strictly speaking. Generally, rituals should be performed or assisted by Brahmins, the priestly caste, but in practice, simpler rituals can be performed by anyone. Brahmins are the final judges of ritual purity, the vital element in Hindu life. Temples and religious organizations are usually presided over by Brahmins.

Practice: Primarily passage rites (e.g., initiation, marriage, death) and daily devotions. Of the public rites, the *puja*, a ceremonial dinner for a god, is the most common.

Divisions: There is no concept of orthodoxy in Hinduism, which presents a variety of sects. The three major living traditions are those devoted to the gods Vishnu and Shiva and to the goddess Shakti. Numerous folk beliefs and practices, often in amalgamation with the above groups, exist side by side with philosophical schools.

Location: Mainly India, Nepal, Malaysia, Guyana, Suriname, and Sri Lanka.

Beliefs: There is only one divine principle; the many gods are only aspects of that unity. Life in all its forms is an aspect of the divine, but it appears as a separation from the divine, a meaningless cycle of birth and rebirth (*samsara*) determined by the purity or impurity of past deeds (*karma*). To improve one's karma or escape samsara by pure acts, thought, and/or devotion is the aim of every Hindu.

Judaism

Founded: About 2000 BCE.

Founder: Abraham is regarded as the founding patriarch.

Sacred texts: The five books of Moses (the Torah), the basic source of teachings.

Organization: Originally theocratic, Judaism has evolved into a congregational polity. The basic institution is the local synagogue or temple, operated by the congregation and led by a rabbi of their choice. Chief rabbis in France and Great Britain have authority only over those who accept it; in Israel, the two chief rabbis have civil authority in family law.

Practice: Among traditional practitioners, almost all areas of life are governed by strict discipline. Sabbath and holidays are marked by observances, and attendance at public worship is considered especially important. Chief annual observances are Passover, celebrating liberation of the Israelites from Egypt and marked by the Seder meal in homes, and the 10 days from Rosh Hashanah (New Year) to Yom Kippur (Day of Atonement), a period of penitence.

Divisions: Judaism is an unbroken spectrum from ultra-conservative to ultraliberal, largely reflecting different points of view regarding the binding character of the prohibitions and duties—particularly the dietary and Sabbath observations—traditionally prescribed for the daily life of the Jew.

Location: Mainly in Israel and the U.S.

Beliefs: Strictly monotheistic. God is the creator and ruler of the universe. God established a particular relationship with the Hebrew people: by obeying a divine law God gave them, they would be a special witness to God's mercy and justice. Judaism stresses ethical behavior (and, among the traditional, careful ritual obedience) as true worship of God.

Sikhism

Founded: Late 15th century in South Asia.

Founder: Guru Nanak Dev ji, Sikhism's first Guru.

Sacred texts: The *Guru Granth Sahib* was compiled by the Sikh Gurus and contains their experiences of the Divine. It also contains writing by other saintly figures of different faiths.

Organization: Each Sikh must make her or his own spiritual journey and not depend on clergy. Congregational prayer led by both men and women takes place in local *Gurdwaras*. Harmandir Sahib in Amritsar, Punjab (northern India), is the central place of worship.

Practice: Prayers are required in the morning, evening, and before sleeping. The most important mode of congregational prayer is the singing of hymns from the Guru Granth Sahib. The "Five Ks" are five articles of faith required of all Sikhs: *Kes* (uncut hair), *Kangha* (comb), *Kara* (steel bracelet), *Kirpan* (sword), and *Kaccha* (short pants).

Divisions: The last living Guru, Guru Gobind Singh (1666-1708) crystallized the practices and beliefs of the faith and determined that no future living Guru was needed. Today the religion is guided by joint sovereignty of Guru Granth and Guru Panth. Guru Granth is the Sikh scripture, as the spiritual manifestation of the Guru, while the Guru Panth is the collectivity of all initiated Sikhs worldwide, as the physical manifestation of the Guru.

Location: Many Sikhs have Punjabi backgrounds. The Punjab region was divided between India and Pakistan with the end of British rule.

Beliefs: Sikhism preaches a message of devotion, remembrance of God at all times, truthful living, equality between all human beings, and social justice, while emphatically denouncing superstitions and blind rituals. Sikhism is a monotheistic religion based on revelation.

LANGUAGE

New Words in English

The following words and definitions were provided by Merriam-Webster Inc., publishers of *Merriam-Webster's Collegiate Dictionary, Eleventh Edition*, released in 2003. The words are among those that the Merriam-Webster editors decided had achieved enough currency in English to be added to the latest (2013) printing of the dictionary.

adware: computer software that is provided usually for free but contains advertisements

Amber Alert: a widely publicized bulletin that alerts the public to a recently abducted or missing child

augmented reality: an enhanced version of reality created by the use of technology to overlay digital information on an image of something being viewed through a device (as a smartphone camera); *also:* the technology used to create augmented reality

autofocus: an automatic focusing system (as on a camera)

cachaca: a Brazilian liquor distilled from sugarcane

chemo brain: impaired cognition (as memory loss or lack of concentration) that has been observed in patients who have received chemotherapy

coltan: a dull black ore that consists of a mixture of columbite and tantalite and is a minor source of tantalum

copernicium: a short-lived, artificially produced radioactive element that has 112 protons

fair trade: a movement whose goal is to help producers in developing countries to get a fair price for their products so as to reduce poverty, provide for the ethical treatment of workers and farmers, and promote environmentally sustainable practices

fan fiction: stories involving popular fictional characters that are written by fans and often posted on the Internet

glass closet: the state in which the sexual orientation of a homosexual person is known to many but not publicly acknowledged

human trafficking: organized criminal activity in which human beings are treated as possessions to be controlled and exploited (as by being forced into prostitution or involuntary labor)

kettle chip: a type of potato chip made so as to be thicker and crunchier than the typical potato chip

kettlebell: a round weight with a flat bottom and thick handle on top that is used for exercise and weight training

labradoodle: a dog that is a cross between a Labrador retriever and a poodle

McMansion: a very large house built in usually a suburban neighborhood or development; *especially:* one regarded critically as oversized and ostentatious

microblogging: blogging done with severe space or size constraints typically by posting frequent brief messages about personal activities

mission creep: the gradual broadening of the original objectives of a mission or organization

muscle shirt: a close-fitting usually sleeveless T-shirt

newb: a newcomer; *especially:* a newcomer to cyberspace

plan B: an alternative plan of action for use if the original plan should fail

pole dancing: usually solo dancing performed while using a fixed vertical pole as a prop

quant: an expert at analyzing and managing quantitative data

road rash: mild to severe skin abrasion resulting from a fall (as from a bicycle or motorcycle) which usually involves sliding on a hard rough surface

scratch card: a card (as a lottery ticket) having a small area covered by an opaque coating which may be scraped away to reveal hidden information

sippy cup: a cup that has a detachable lid with a projecting hole designed to help a young child sip liquid from the cup without spilling it

smack talk: disparaging, taunting, or boastful comments especially between opponents trying to intimidate each other

string trimmer: a machine for cutting grass with a rapidly spinning length of monofilament cord

tasting: an occasion for sampling a selection of foods or drinks in order to compare qualities

tostone: a thick slice of green plantain that is fried, flattened, and then fried again

Ultimate Frisbee: a game played on a rectangular field between two seven-player teams in which a plastic disc is advanced by being thrown from player to player and in which a team scores by catching a throw in the opponent's end zone

vog: air pollution caused by volcanic emissions

Words About Words

alliteration: repetition of same, initial consonant sounds of two or more words in sequence or in short intervals. Ex.: "I have stood still and stopped the sound of feet." —Robert Frost, "Acquainted With the Night"

anagram: word or word sequence that is a rearrangement, typically clever, of letters in another word or word sequence. Ex: The Leaning Tower of Pisa = I spot one giant flaw here.

assonance: repetition of same or similar vowel sounds in words located near each other. Ex.: "Green as a dream, and deep as death." —Rupert Brooke, "The Old Vicarage, Grantchester"

back-formation: creation of a word from an existing word, whose forms seem to suggest that the previously existing word derived from the newer word. Ex.: The verb "edit" is a back-formation of the word "editor."

cliché: a saying or expression that has been used so often it has lost its effect. Ex.: work like a dog

euphemism: a mild, indirect expression used instead of a plainer one that might be harsh, unpleasant, or offensive. Ex.: restroom instead of toilet; pass away, or pass, instead of die

hyperbole: exaggeration for emphasis or effect. Ex.: "And fired the shot heard round the world." —Ralph Waldo Emerson, "Concord Hymn"

irony: deliberate use of an expression in which the literal or surface meaning is contrary to a hidden intended, often opposite meaning that can be inferred. Ex.: "Yet Brutus says he was ambitious; / And Brutus is an honorable man." —William Shakespeare, *Julius Caesar*

litotes: intentional understatement made by negating the opposite of what is meant. Ex.: This was no small matter.

metaphor: a stated equivalence between two dissimilar things or a reference to one thing rather than another, so as to imply a comparison. Ex.: "Life is a tale told by an idiot, full of sound and fury, signifying nothing." —William Shakespeare, *Macbeth*

metonymy: substitution of one word for another that it suggests. Ex.: The pen is mightier than the sword.

onomatopoeia: words that imitate the sounds they describe. Ex.: buzz, murmur

oxymoron: expression containing seemingly contradictory words. Ex.: deafening silence

palindrome: word or phrase that reads the same backward and forward. Ex: radar, Hannah, "Madam, I'm Adam."

paradox: a statement that is phrased to seem contradictory, odd, or opposed to common sense or expectation, while being presented as true. Ex.: "What a pity that youth must be wasted on the young." —George Bernard Shaw

personification: treatment of objects or abstractions as if they were persons. Ex.: "Because I could not stop for Death— / He kindly stopped for me." —Emily Dickinson, "Because I Could Not Stop for Death"

simile: a comparison between two dissimilar things using the words "like" or "as." Ex.: "My love is like a red, red rose" —Robert Burns, "A Red, Red Rose"

spoonerism: play on words in which the initial sounds of two or more words are transposed, creating different phrases whose meanings when compared can be humorous. Ex.: blushing crow instead of crushing blow

synecdoche: a form of metonymy; the use of a part for the whole, or the whole for the part. Ex.: All hands on deck!

tautology: useless, often unwitting repetition of the same idea in different wording. Ex.: close proximity. In logic, a proposition that would be self-contradictory to deny. Ex.: All bachelors are male.

National Spelling Bee

The annual Scripps National Spelling Bee competition, conducted by The E.W. Scripps Company and other newspapers since 1941, was instituted by *The Courier-Journal* of Louisville, KY, in 1925. Students under 16 who are not beyond the 8th grade are eligible to compete at the local level for a chance to advance to the national competition in Washington, DC. The 2013 winner was Arvind Mahankali of Bayside Hills, NY. Second place went to Parav Sivakumar of Tower Lakes, IL, and third place to Sriram Hathwar of Painted Post, NY.

Here are the last words given and spelled correctly at the National Spelling Bee in recent years.

1979	maculature	1986	odontalgia	1993	kamikaze	2000	demarche	2007	serrefine
1980	elucubrate	1987	staphylococci	1994	antediluvian	2001	succedaneum	2008	guerdon
1981	sarcophagus	1988	elegiacal	1995	xanthosis	2002	prospicience	2009	Laodicean
1982	psoriasis	1989	spoliator	1996	vivisepulture	2003	pococurante	2010	stromuhr
1983	Purim	1990	fibranne	1997	euonym	2004	autochthonous	2011	cymotrichous
1984	luge	1991	antipyretic	1998	chiaroscurist	2005	appoggiatura	2012	guetapens
1985	milieu	1992	lyceum	1999	logorrhea	2006	Ursprache	2013	knaidel

Commonly Misspelled English Words

a lot	changeable	eligible	inoculate	miscellaneous	personnel	sheriff
accidentally	Cincinnati	embarrass	irresistible	Mississippi	potatoes	sincerely
accommodate	collectible	environment	jewelry	misspelled	precede	success
accumulate	commitment	existence	judgment	mnemonic	prescient	supersede
acknowledgment	committee	fascinating	laboratory	mysterious	privilege	temperament
acquainted	connoisseur	February	leisure	necessary	propaganda	temperature
acquire	conscience	fluorescent	liaison	noticeable	questionnaire	transferred
already	conscious	forty	license	occasionally	raspberry	transsexual
amateur	convenience	gauge	lieutenant	occurrence	receipt	truly
appearance	deceive	government	lightning	omitted	receive	twelfth
appropriate	defendant	grammar	liquefy	opportunity	recommend	vaccinate
assimilate	definitely	harass	maintenance	parallel	rhythm	vacillate
bureau	desirable	humorous	management	patience	ridiculous	vacuum
business	desperate	incidentally	marriage	performance	sacrilegious	vicious
calendar	deterrent	independent	medieval	permanent	seize	Wednesday
Caribbean	doesn't	indispensable	millennium	permissible	separate	weird
cemetery	eighth	innocuous	miniature	perseverance	sergeant	wholly

Foreign Words and Phrases

(A = Arabic; F = French; Ger = German; Gr = Greek; I = Italian; J = Japanese; L = Latin; R = Russian; S = Spanish; Y = Yiddish)

ad hoc (L; ad-HOK): for the end or purpose at hand; impromptu

ad hominem (L; ad-HOH-mee-nem): argument that criticizes an opponent, often unfairly, rather than addressing an issue directly

al fresco (I; ahl-FRAYS-koh): outdoors

anime (J: A-nuh-may): Japanese-style animation

antebellum (L; AHN-teh-BEL-lum): pre-war

aperçu (F; ah-per-SOO): first perception or insight; outline

au courant (F; oh-koo-RAHN): up-to-date, fashionable

belles lettres (F; bel-LET-truh): writing aspiring to artistic merit

bête noire (F; bet-NWAHR): a thing or person viewed with particular dislike or fear

bildungsroman (Ger; BIL-doongs-roh-mahn): novel embodying coming-of-age story

bodega (S; boh-DAY-gah): grocery store

bon vivant (F; bon-vee-VAHN): a person with refined tastes, especially for food and drink

bonhomie (F; boh-noh-MEE): friendliness

bourgeois (F; boo-ZHWAH): middle-class; materialistic

carte blanche (F; kahrt-BLANSH): full discretionary power

cause célèbre (F; kawz-suh-LEB): a notorious incident

cognoscenti (I; kahn-yuh-SHEN-tee): experts; connoisseurs

comme il faut (F; cum-eel-FOH): proper; as it should be

contretemps (F; kon-truh-TAHN): awkward situation

coup de grâce (F; kooh-duh-GRAHS): the decisive final blow

cum laude/magna cum laude/summa cum laude (L; kuhm-LOU-day; MAG-na ... ; SOO-ma ...): with praise or honor/with great praise or honor/with the highest praise or honor

de facto (L; di-FAK-toh): in fact, if not by law

de jure (L; dee-JOOR-ee, day-YOOR-ay): by right or by law

de rigueur (L; duh-ree-GUR): required by convention or etiquette

détente (F; day-TAHNT): an easing of strained relations

deus ex machina (L; DAY-uhs-eks-MAH-keh-nah): person/event that provides a solution unexpectedly or suddenly, espec. (in literature) a contrived solution to a plot

doppelgänger (Ger; DAH-pul-gang-ur): a double or ghostly counterpart of a person

double entendre (F; DOO-blahn-TAHN-druh): expression with a double meaning, one meaning of which is often risqué

e pluribus unum (L; eh-PLOO-ree-boos-OO-noom): out of many, one (U.S. motto)

éminence grise (F; ay-meh-nahns-GREEZ): one who wields power behind the scenes

ennui (F; ah-NOOEE): boredom; world-weariness; annoyance

ersatz (Ger; EHR-zats): artificial; being a (usually inferior) substitute

ex post facto (L; eks-pohst-FAK-toh): retroactive(ly)

fait accompli (F; fayt-uh-kom-PLEE): an accomplished fact

fatwa (A; FAHT-wah): in Islam, a legal or religious decree

faux pas (F; foh-PAH): false step; breach of etiquette

habeas corpus (L; HAY-bee-ahs-KOR-pus): an order for a prisoner to be brought to court to challenge his or her detention

hoi polloi (Gr; hoy-puh-LOY): the masses

impresario (I; im-prah-SAH-ri-oh): manager, promoter, or sponsor of a musical or theatrical program or company

imprimatur (L; im-prah-MAH-toor): approval or official permission to print, espec. by the Roman Catholic church

in loco parentis (L; in-LOH-koh-puh-REN-tis): in place of parent

in medias res (L; in-MAY-dee-oos-rays): into the middle of things

intelligentsia (R; in-te-luh-JEN-see-uh): elite social class made up of intellectuals and educated people

ipso facto (L; ip-soh-FAK-toh): by that fact itself

je ne sais quoi (F; zhuh-nuh-say-KWAH): literally, "I don't know what"; the little something that eludes description

jihad (A; jih-HAHD): Islamic holy war; struggle in devotion to Islam

joie de vivre (F; zhwah-duh-VEEV-ruh): zest for life

leitmotif (Ger; lyt-moh-TEEF): the central theme or idea, particularly in art and literature

mano a mano (S; MAH-noh-ah-MAH-noh): hand to hand; in direct combat

mea culpa (L; MAY-uh-CUL-puh): through my fault

mensch (Y; MENTSCH): an upright, noble, admirable person

modus operandi (L; MOH-duhs-op-uh-RAN-dee): method of operation

mujahedeen (A; moo-jah-ha-DEEN): Islamic holy warrior

noblesse oblige (F; noh-BLES-oh-BLEEZH): the obligation of nobility to help the less fortunate

nolo contendere (L; NOH-loh-kohn-TEN-duh-ree): a plea of no contest to charges, without admitting guilt

non compos mentis (L; non-KOM-puhs-MEN-tis): not of sound mind

non sequitur (L; non-SEH-kwi-tour): a conclusion that does not logically follow from what preceded it

nouveau riche (F; noo-voh-REESH): a newly rich person, espec. one who spends money conspicuously

ombudsman (Swedish; AHM-budz-muhn): person who receives, investigates, and settles complaints

par excellence (F; par-ek-seh-LANS): best of all; incomparable

parvenu (F; par-vuh-NOO): upstart

persona non grata (L; per-SOH-nah-non-GRAH-tah): unwelcome person

pièce de résistance (F; pee-es-duh-ray-ZEES-tonz): the outstanding item in a series or group

prima facie (L; pry-muh-FAY-shee-ee; pry-muh-FAY-shuh): true at first glance; presumptively valid

pro bono (L; proh-BOH-noh): (work) donated for the public good

quid pro quo (L; kwid-proh-KWOH): something given or received for something else

raison d'être (F; RAY-zohnn-DET-ruh): reason for being

savoir faire (F; sav-wahr-FAIR): dexterity in social affairs

schadenfreude (Ger; SHAH-duhn-froy-deh): joy at another's misfortune

semper fidelis (L; SEM-puhr-fee-DAY-lis): always faithful

sobriquet (F; SOH-bri-kay): nickname or informal descriptive name for someone

sotto voce (I; sah-toh-VOH-chee): in a low voice

sui generis (L; soo-ee-JEN-er-is): unique; one of a kind

terra firma (L; TER-uh-FUR-muh): solid ground

troika (R; TROY-kuh): group of three, espec. a ruling group

verboten (Ger; ver-BOH-ten): forbidden

vis-à-vis (F; vee-zuh-VEE): compared with; with regard to

voir dire (F; vwar-DEER): examination by lawyers or judge to determine the suitability of a witness or a prospective juror

zeitgeist (Ger; ZITE-gyste): the general intellectual, moral, and cultural climate of an era

Names for Animal Young

calf: cattle, elephant, hippo, camel, others

cheeper: grouse, partridge, quail

chick: chicken, penguin, other birds

cockerel: rooster

codling, sprag: codfish

colt: horse, zebra (male)

cria: llama, alpaca

cub: lion, bear, shark, fox, others

cygnet: swan

duckling: duck

elver: eel

ephyra: jellyfish

eyas: hawk, others

fawn: deer, antelope

filly: horse, zebra (female)

fingerling, fry: fish generally

fledgling, nestling: birds generally

foal: horse, zebra, others

gosling: goose

heifer: cow

hoglet: hedgehog

joey: kangaroo, opossum, wombat

kid: goat

kit: beaver, rabbit, ferret, wolverine, others

kitten: cat, other small mammals

lamb: sheep

larva: frog, sea urchin, insects generally

parr, smolt, grilse: salmon

piglet, shoat, farrow, suckling: pig

polliwog, tadpole: frog

poult: turkey

puggle: echidna

pullet: hen

pup: dog, fox, seal, rat, others

spat: oyster, other bivalves

spiderling: spider

spike, blinker, tinker: mackerel

squab: pigeon

whelp: dog, tiger, other carnivorous mammals

yearling: cattle, sheep, horse, others

Names for Animal Collectives

alligators: congregation
ants: army, colony, swarm
apes: shrewdness, troop
bats: colony
bears: sleuth, sloth
bees: colony, swarm, hive, grist
birds: flight, volery
boars/swine: singular, sounder
buffalo: gang, obstinacy
butterflies: flutter
buzzards: wake
camels: caravan, flock, train
cats: clowder, cluster, glaring, pounce
cattle: drove
cheetahs: coalition
clams, oysters: bed
cockroaches: intrusion
cranes: sedge, siege

crocodiles: bask, nest, float
crows: murder, horde
dolphins: pod
doves: dule, pitying
ducks: brace, team
eagles: convocation, aerie
ferrets: business
finches: charm
fish: school, shoal
flamingos: stand, flamboyance
foxes: skulk
geese: flock, gaggle, skein
giraffes: corps, herd, tower
goats: tribe, trip
gorillas: band, whoop
grasshoppers: cloud
hares: down, husk, trip
hawks: cast, kettle
hedgehogs: array, prickle
hippopotamuses: bloat

horses: pair, team
hounds: cry, mute, pack
hyenas: cackle
iguanas: mess
jellyfish: smack
kangaroos: mob, troop
larks: exaltation
leopards: leap
lions: pride
locusts: plague, swarm
moles: labor
monkeys: troop
mules: barren, span
nightingales: watch
otters: romp
owls: parliament
oxen: yoke
peacocks: muster
pheasants: nest, nide, bouquet

ponies: string
raccoons: gaze
ravens: unkindness
rhinoceroses: crash
seals: pod
sheep: flock, drove, hurtle
snakes: nest
squirrels: dray, scurry
starlings: flock, murmuration
swans: bevy
tigers: streak
toads: knot
trout: hover
turkeys: rafter
turtles: bale
vultures: committee
whales: gam, herd, pod
woodchucks: fall
woodpeckers: descent
zebras: herd, zeal

Some Common Abbreviations and Acronyms

Acronyms are pronounceable words formed from first letters (or syllables) of other words. Some abbreviations below (e.g., AIDS, NATO) are thus acronyms. Some acronyms are words coined as abbreviations and written in lowercase (e.g., sonar, yuppie). Acronyms do not have periods; usage for other abbreviations varies, but periods have become less common. Capitalization usage may vary from what is shown here. Some acronyms may have other, typically less common, meanings not given here. Italicized words preceding parenthetical definitions below are *Latin* unless otherwise noted.

AA: Alcoholics Anonymous; Associate in Arts; administrative assistant
ABA: American Bar Association
AC: alternating current; air-conditioning
ACLU: American Civil Liberties Union
AD: *anno Domini* (in the year of the Lord)
ADD: attention deficit disorder
AFL-CIO: American Federation of Labor and Congress of Industrial Organizations
AFSCME: American Federation of State, County, and Municipal Employees
AI: artificial intelligence
AIDS: acquired immune deficiency syndrome
ALA: American Library Association
a.m. or **AM:** *ante meridiem* (before noon)
AP: Associated Press
APO: army post office
APR: annual percentage rate
ARM: adjustable rate mortgage
ASCAP: American Society of Composers, Authors, and Publishers
ASCII: American Standard Code for Information Interchange
ATM: automated teller machine
Ave.: Avenue
AWOL: absent without leave
BA: Bachelor of Arts
bbl: barrel(s)
BC: before Christ
BCE: before the Common Era; before the Christian Era
bpd: barrels per day
BS: Bachelor of Science
Btu: British thermal unit(s)
bu: bushel(s)
BYOB: bring your own bottle
C: Celsius, centigrade
c: *circa* (about); copyright
CAT: computerized axial tomography
CD: compact disc
CDC: Centers for Disease Control and Prevention; Community Development Corporation
CE: Common Era; Christian Era
CEO: chief executive officer
cf.: *confer* (compare)
CFO: chief financial officer
CIA: Central Intelligence Agency
CIF: cost, insurance, and freight
COBRA: Consolidated Omnibus Budget Reconciliation Act (health insurance continuation)
COD: cash (or collect) on delivery
COL or **Col.:** Colonel
COLA: cost of living adjustment
COO: chief operating officer

CPA: certified public accountant
CPI: consumer price index
CPL or **Cpl.:** Corporal
CPR: cardiopulmonary resuscitation
CPU: central processing unit
CST: central standard time
CV: curriculum vitae
DA: district attorney
DC: direct current
DD: Doctor of Divinity
DDS: Doctor of Dental Surgery
DEA: Drug Enforcement Agency
DHS: Department of Homeland Security
DMD: Doctor of Dental Medicine
DMZ: demilitarized zone
DNA: deoxyribonucleic acid
DNC: Democratic National Committee
DNR: do not resuscitate
DOA: dead on arrival
DOB: date of birth
dpi: dots per inch
DPT: diphtheria, pertussis, tetanus
DUI: driving under the influence
DVD: digital video disc
DVM: Doctor of Veterinary Medicine
DWI: driving while intoxicated
ed.: edited; edition; editor
EEG: electroencephalogram
e.g.: *exempli gratia* (for example)
EKG: electrocardiogram
EOE: equal opportunity employer
EP: extended play
EPA: Environmental Protection Agency
ERA: Equal Rights Amendment; earned run average
ESL: English as a second language
ESP: extrasensory perception
Esq.: Esquire
EST: eastern standard time
et al.: *et alii* (and others)
etc.: *et cetera* (and so forth)
EU: European Union
F: Fahrenheit
Fannie Mae: Federal National Mortgage Association
FAQ: frequently asked questions
FBI: Federal Bureau of Investigation
FDA: Food and Drug Administration
FDIC: Federal Deposit Insurance Corporation
FEC: Federal Election Commission
FEMA: Federal Emergency Management Agency
ff.: and those following
FICA: Federal Insurance Contributions Act (Social Security)
fl.: *floruit* (flourished), used for historical figures when life dates uncertain

Freddie Mac: Federal Home Loan Mortgage Corporation
FTP: file transfer protocol
FY: fiscal year
FYI: for your information
GATT: General Agreement on Tariffs and Trade
GB: gigabyte(s)
GDP: gross domestic product
GED: general equivalency diploma; General Educational Development (Tests)
GMT: Greenwich mean time
GOP: Grand Old Party (Republican Party)
GPS: Global Positioning System
GUI: graphical user interface
hazmat: HAZardous MATerial
HDTV: high-definition television
HIV: human immunodeficiency virus
HMO: health maintenance organization
HMS: His/Her Majesty's Ship (UK)
Hon.: the Honorable
HOV: high-occupancy vehicle
HRH: Her (His) Royal Highness (UK)
HTML: hypertext markup language
HTTP: hypertext transfer protocol
HUD: Department of Housing and Urban Development
HVAC: heating, ventilating, and air-conditioning
Hz: hertz
ibid.: *ibidem* (in the same place)
ICU: intensive care unit
i.e.: *id est* (that is)
IM: instant messaging
IMF: International Monetary Fund
INS: Immigration and Naturalization Service
IPO: initial public offering
IQ: intelligence quotient
IRA: individual retirement account; Irish Republican Army
IRS: Internal Revenue Service
ISBN: International Standard Book Number
ISP: Internet service provider
IVF: in vitro fertilization
JD: *Juris Doctor* (Doctor of Law)
k: karat
K: kelvin
kWh: kilowatt-hour(s)
laser: Light Amplification by Stimulated Emission of Radiation
LGBT: lesbian, gay, bisexual, and transgender
LLP: limited liability partnership
loc. cit.: *loco citato* (in the place cited)
LSAT: Law School Admission Test

LT or **Lt.:** Lieutenant
MA: Master of Arts
MB: megabyte(s)
MBA: Master of Business Administration
MCAT: Medical College Admission Test
MD: *Medicinae Doctor* (Doctor of Medicine)
MIA: missing in action
modem: MOdulator-DEModulator
MP: member of Parliament (UK)
mph: miles per hour
MRI: magnetic resonance imaging
ms, mss: manuscript(s)
MS: Master of Science; multiple sclerosis
MSG: monosodium glutamate
MST: mountain standard time
MVP: most valuable player
NA: not applicable; not available
NAACP: National Association for the Advancement of Colored People
NAFTA: North American Free Trade Agreement
NASA: National Aeronautics and Space Administration
NATO: North Atlantic Treaty Organization
NB or **n.b.:** *nota bene* (note carefully)
NCAA: National Collegiate Athletic Association
NEA: National Education Association
NIH: National Institutes of Health
NOW: National Organization for Women
NPR: National Public Radio
NRA: National Rifle Association
NSA: National Security Agency
obs.: obsolete
OED: Oxford English Dictionary
OMB: Office of Management and Budget
op: *opus* (work)
OPEC: Organization of Petroleum Exporting Countries
OTC: over-the-counter
p, pp: page(s)

PA: public address
PAC: political action committee
PC: personal computer; politically correct
PDA: Personal Digital Assistant
PETA: People for the Ethical Treatment of Animals
PhD: *Philosophiae Doctor* (Doctor of Philosophy)
PIN: personal identification number
p.m. or **PM:** *post meridiem* (after noon)
POTUS: President of the United States
PPO: preferred provider organization, a type of healthcare provider network
PS: *post scriptum* (postscript)
PST: Pacific standard time
pt: part(s); pint(s); point(s)
PVT or **Pvt.:** Private
QC: Queen's Council (UK)
QED: *quod erat demonstrandum* (which was to be demonstrated)
q.v.: *quod vide* (which see)
radar: RAdio Detecting And Ranging
RAM: random access memory
RCMP: Royal Canadian Mounted Police
REM: rapid eye movement
Rev.: Reverend
rev.: revised; reviewed
RIP: *requiescat in pace* (may he/she rest in peace)
RN: Registered Nurse
RNA: ribonucleic acid
RNC: Republican National Committee
ROM: read only memory
ROTC: Reserve Officers' Training Corps
rpm: revolutions per minute
RSVP: *répondez s'il vous plaît* (Fr.) (please reply)
SARS: severe acute respiratory syndrome
SASE: self-addressed stamped envelope
SEC: Securities and Exchange Commission

SETI: Search for Extraterrestrial Intelligence
SGT or **Sgt.:** Sergeant
SIDS: sudden infant death syndrome
SJ: Society of Jesus (Jesuits)
sonar: SOund NAvigation and Ranging
SPCA: Society for the Prevention of Cruelty to Animals
SSI: Supplementary Security Income
St.: Saint; Street
TB: tuberculosis; terabyte(s)
TBA: to be announced
TBD: to be determined
TEFL: teaching English as a foreign language
TSA: Transportation Security Administration
UFO: unidentified flying object
UPC: Universal Product Code
URL: Universal Resource Locator
USDA: United States Department of Agriculture
USS: United States ship
UTC: coordinated universal time
var.: variant
VAT: value-added tax
VCR: videocassette recorder
viz: *videlicet* (namely)
VP: vice president
W: watt(s)
WHO: World Health Organization
WMD: weapon of mass destruction
WPM: words per minute
WWW: World Wide Web
YMCA: Young Men's Christian Association
YWCA: Young Women's Christian Association
YTD: year to date
yuppie: young urban professional
ZIP: zone improvement plan (U.S. Postal Service)

Top 10 First Names of Americans by Decade or Year of Birth

Source: U.S. Social Security Administration

BOYS

1880-1889	John, William, Charles, George, James, Frank, Joseph, Harry, Henry, Edward
1890-1899	John, William, George, James, Charles, Joseph, Frank, Robert, Harry, Henry
1900-1909	John, William, James, George, Joseph, Charles, Robert, Frank, Edward, Henry
1910-1919	John, William, James, Robert, Joseph, Charles, George, Edward, Frank, Walter
1920-1929	John, Robert, James, William, Charles, George, Joseph, Richard, Edward, Donald
1930-1939	Robert, James, John, William, Richard, Charles, Donald, George, Thomas, Joseph
1940-1949	James, Robert, John, William, Richard, David, Charles, Thomas, Michael, Ronald
1950-1959	Michael, James, Robert, John, David, William, Steven, Richard, Thomas, Mark
1960-1969	Michael, John, David, James, Robert, Mark, Steven, William, Jeffrey, Richard
1970-1979	Michael, Christopher, Jason, David, James, John, Brian, Robert, Steven, William
1980-1989	Michael, Christopher, Matthew, Joshua, David, Daniel, James, John, Robert, Brian
1990-1999	Michael, Christopher, Matthew, Joshua, Nicholas, Jacob, Andrew, Daniel, Brandon, Tyler
2000-2009	Jacob, Michael, Joshua, Matthew, Daniel, Christopher, Andrew, Ethan, Joseph, William
2012	Jacob, Mason, Ethan, Noah, William, Liam, Jayden, Michael, Alexander, Aiden

GIRLS

1880-1889	Mary, Anna, Elizabeth, Catherine, Margaret, Emma, Bertha, Minnie, Florence, Clara
1890-1899	Mary, Anna, Margaret, Helen, Catherine, Elizabeth, Florence, Ruth, Rose, Ethel
1900-1909	Mary, Helen, Margaret, Anna, Ruth, Catherine, Elizabeth, Dorothy, Marie, Mildred
1910-1919	Mary, Helen, Dorothy, Margaret, Ruth, Catherine, Mildred, Anna, Elizabeth, Frances
1920-1929	Mary, Dorothy, Betty, Helen, Margaret, Ruth, Virginia, Catherine, Doris, Frances
1930-1939	Mary, Betty, Barbara, Shirley, Patricia, Dorothy, Joan, Margaret, Carol, Nancy
1940-1949	Mary, Linda, Barbara, Patricia, Carol, Sandra, Nancy, Sharon, Judith, Susan
1950-1959	Deborah, Mary, Linda, Patricia, Susan, Barbara, Karen, Nancy, Donna, Catherine
1960-1969	Lisa, Deborah, Mary, Karen, Michelle, Susan, Kimberly, Lori, Teresa, Linda
1970-1979	Jennifer, Michelle, Amy, Melissa, Kimberly, Lisa, Angela, Heather, Kelly, Sarah
1980-1989	Jessica, Jennifer, Ashley, Sarah, Amanda, Stephanie, Nicole, Melissa, Katherine, Megan
1990-1999	Ashley, Jessica, Sarah, Brittany, Emily, Kaitlyn, Samantha, Megan, Brianna, Katherine
2000-2009	Emily, Madison, Emma, Olivia, Hannah, Abigail, Isabella, Samantha, Elizabeth, Ashley
2012	Sophia, Emma, Isabella, Olivia, Ava, Emily, Abigail, Mia, Madison, Elizabeth

Origins of Popular American Given Names

Source: World Almanac research

Some names are commonly used for either sex but are listed here under the more traditionally associated sex. Some names listed here have variant spellings that are not shown.

Boys

Aiden: Gaelic *Aodhan*, "little fire," from name of Celtic sun god
Alexander: Gr. *Alexandros*, "defender of man"
Andrew: Gr. *andreios*, "manly"
Anthony: Roman *Antonius*, possibly from Gr. *anthos*, "flower"
Benjamin: Heb. *Binyamin*, "son of the right hand"
Brandon: Eng. place name, "gorse-covered hill"
Brian: Irish, perhaps Celtic *Brigonos*, "high" or "noble"
Charles: Ger. *ceorl*, "free man"
Christopher: Gr. *Khristophoros*, "bearing Christ [in one's heart]"
Daniel: Heb. "God is my judge"
David: Heb. *Dodavehu*, perhaps "darling"
Edward: Old Eng. *Eadweard*, "wealth-guard"
Elijah: Heb. "the Lord is my God"
Ethan: Heb. "solid, firm"

Frank: Ger. "Frenchman"
George: Gr. *georgos*, "soil tiller, farmer"
Henry: Ger. *Haimric*, "home-power"
Jack: nickname for or variant of John
Jacob: Heb. *Yaakov*, "God protects" or "supplanter"
James: Late Lat. *Iacomus*, form of Jacob
Jason: Gr. *Iason*, "healer"
Jayden: prob. from Jay (short form for many *J* names) and Hayden (Old Eng. "little hollow")
Jeffrey: Norman Fr., from Ger. *Gaufrid*, "land-peace," or *Gisfrid*, "pledge-peace"
John: Heb. *Yohanan*, "God is gracious"
Jonathan: Heb. "God has given"
José: Heb. and Aramaic *Yose*, variant of Joseph
Joseph: Heb. *Yosef*, "[God] shall add"
Joshua: Heb. *Yoshua*, "God saves"
Liam: Gaelic form of William
Mark: Lat. *Marcus*, perhaps from Mars, Roman god of war

Mason: Fr. "stone worker," related to Old Eng. "work"
Matthew: Heb. *Mattathia*, "gift of God"
Michael: Heb. "who could ever be like God?"
Nathan: Heb. "God has given"; modern short form of Nathaniel or Jonathan
Nicholas: Gr. *Nikolaos*, "victory-people"
Noah: Heb. "rest"
Patrick: Lat. *Patricius*, "belonging to the noble class"
Richard: Ger. "power-hardy"
Robert: Ger. *Hrodberht*, "fame-bright"
Ryan: prob. from Irish surname, Gaelic "king"
Samuel: Heb. *Shemuel*, "God heard"
Sean: Gaelic form of John
Steven: Gr. *stephanos*, "crown" or "garland"
Thomas: Aramaic "twin"
Tyler: Old Eng. *tigeler*, "tile layer"
William: Ger. *Wilhelm*, "will-helmet"

Girls

Abigail: Heb. "my father is joy"
Addison: Eng. "son of Adam"
Alexandra, Sandra: fem. forms of Alexander
Alexis: Gr. "helper" or "defender"
Alyssa: variant of Alicia (Eng., Sp.) or Alice (Eng., Fr.); may mean "noble"
Amanda: 17th-cent. invention from Lat. "lovable"
Amy: Old Fr. *Amee*, "beloved"
Andrea: fem. form of Andrew
Angela: Gr. *angelos*, "messenger [of God]"
Anna: Lat., Gr. form of Hannah; variants include Ann (Eng.), Ana (Sp.), Anne (Eng., Fr., Ger.)
Ashley: Eng. place name, "ash grove"
Aubrey: Fr., orig. from Ger. *Alberic*, "king of elves"
Ava: prob. modern form of Eva, Lat. form of Heb. *Eve*, "to breathe"
Avery: Eng., common place name; may also mean "elf counsel" or "elf ruler"
Barbara: Gr. *barbarus*, "foreign"
Brianna: modern fem. form of Brian
Brittany: place name, Fr. province settled by Britons
Carol: form of Charles
Chloe: Gr. "young shoot," "blooming"
Claire, Clara: Lat. *clarus*, "famous"
Deborah: Heb. "bee"
Donna: Ital. "lady"
Dorothy: Gr. *Dorothea*, "gift of God"
Elizabeth: Heb. *Elisheba*, perhaps "God is my oath" or "God is good fortune"

Ella: prob. variant or nickname for Eleanor or Ellen
Emily: Roman *Aemilia*, possibly from Lat. *aemulus*, "rival"
Emma: Ger. *ermen*, "whole" or "entire"
Frances: fem. form of Francis, from Lat. "a Frenchman"
Grace: Lat. *gratia*, "grace, blessing"
Hailey: Eng. place name, "hay clearing"
Hannah: Heb. "He has favored me"
Heather: Middle Eng. *hathir*, "heather"
Helen: Gr. *Helene*, possibly "sunbeam"
Isabella, Isabel: Lat., Sp. variant of Elizabeth
Jennifer: Cornish form of Welsh *Gwenhwyfar*, "fair-smooth"
Jessica: Shakesp. invention, prob. fem. form of Jesse, Heb. "God exists"
Judith: Heb. "Jewish woman"
Julia: fem. form of Julius, Roman family name, or Lat. "youthful"
Kaitlyn: American spelling of Caitlin, the Irish form of Katherine
Karen: Danish form of Katherine
Katherine: Egyptian *Aikaterine*, later modified to resemble Gr. *katharos*, "pure"
Kelly: Irish Gaelic *Ceallagh*, perhaps "churchwoman" or "bright-headed"
Kimberly: Eng. place name, "Cyneburgh's clearing"
Laura: Lat. *laurus*, "laurel"
Linda: Sp. "pretty" or Ger. "tender"
Lily: for the flower, suggesting purity, innocence
Lisa: nickname for Elizabeth

Madison: Middle Eng. surname, "son of Madeline or Maud"
Margaret: Gr. *margaron*, "pearl"
Maria, Marie, Mary: Lat., Fr., Eng. forms for Heb. *Maryam*, perhaps "seeress" or "wished-for child"
Megan: Welsh form of Margaret
Melissa: Gr. "bee"
Mia: Nordic or Ital., short for Maria and other names
Michelle: Fr. fem. form of Michael
Nancy: medieval Eng. nickname for Agnes (Gr. *hagnos*, "holy"), later also for Ann
Natalie: Fr., from Lat. *natalia*, "birthday [of Christ]"
Nicole: Fr. fem. form of Nicholas
Olivia: Lat. *oliva*, "olive tree"
Patricia: Lat. fem. form of Patrick
Rachel: Heb. "ewe"
Rose, Rosa: for the flower, suggesting beauty
Ruth: Heb., perhaps "companion"
Samantha: colonial American invention, prob. combining Sam from Samuel with *-antha* from Gr. *anthos*, "flower"
Sarah: Heb. "princess"
Sharon: Biblical place name, Heb. "plain"
Sophia: Gr. "wisdom"
Stephanie: Fr. fem. form of Steven
Susan: Eng. form of Heb. *Shoshana*, "lily"
Teresa: Sp., perhaps "woman from Therasia"
Victoria: fem. form of Victor, from Lat. *vincere*, "to conquer"

Eponyms

(words named for people)

boycott: to avoid trade or dealings with, as a protest; after Charles C. Boycott, an English land agent in County Mayo, Ireland, ostracized in 1880 for refusing to reduce rents
derby: a stiff felt hat with a dome-shaped crown and narrow rolled brim; after Edward Stanley, 12th Earl of Derby, who in 1780 founded the Derby horse race, to which these hats are worn
derrick: a type of crane consisting of a boom connected to the base of an upright mast; after Derrick, early 17th-cent. English hangman who used a gallows that operated via cables and pulleys
draconian: harsh or severe; after Draco, statesman who codified the laws in Athens in 621 BCE
gerrymander: to draw an election district in such a way as to favor a political party; after Elbridge Gerry, who created (1812) just such an election district (shaped like a salamander) during his governorship of Massachusetts
guillotine: a machine for beheading; after Joseph Guillotin, French physician who proposed its use in 1789 as more humane than hanging
Luddite: one who opposes new technology; from Ned Ludd, leader of a group of textile workers in England who destroyed machinery in the early 1800s

maudlin: excessively sentimental; from scriptural figure Mary Magdalene, who is often shown weeping in depictions
milquetoast: a timid, unassertive person; after Caspar Milquetoast, comic strip character created by American cartoonist Harold Tucker Webster in 1924
Pollyanna: an overly optimistic person; based on the title character of a 1913 novel by American writer Eleanor Porter
salmonella: group of bacteria that can cause infections when contaminated food or water is consumed; named after Daniel Elmer Salmon, American veterinarian and public health official
sandwich: two or more slices of bread with a filling in-between; after John Montagu, 4th Earl of Sandwich (1718-92), who supposedly ate these at the gaming table
shrapnel: originally, a projectile with lead balls designed to inflict maximum damage in explosions, later pieces of shell casings; from Henry Shrapnel (1761-1842), British artillery officer who designed the projectile
silhouette: an outline image; from Étienne de Silhouette (1709-67), a stingy French finance minister
Zamboni: an ice resurfacing machine; after American inventor Frank Zamboni, who owned an ice skating rink

American Manual Alphabet

In the American Manual Alphabet, each letter of the alphabet is represented by a position of the fingers. This system was originally developed in France by Charles-Michel de l'Épée in the 1700s. Laurent Clerc and Thomas Gallaudet further refined it into the American Manual Alphabet.

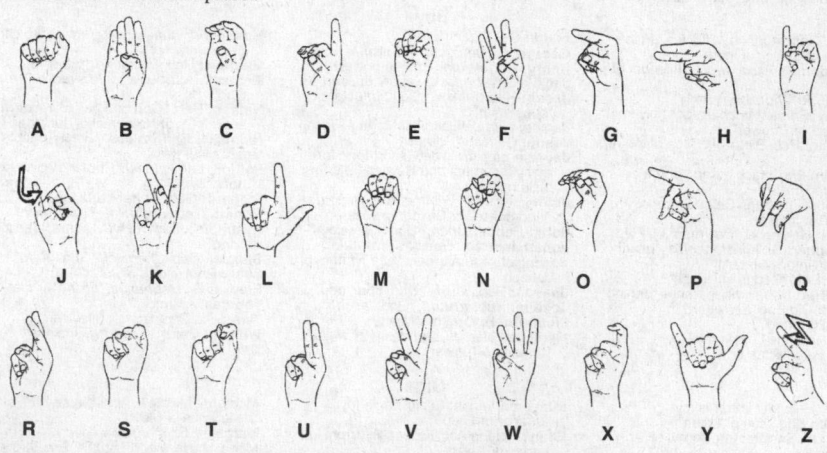

Words and Expressions in Common Languages

English	Arabic	Chinese[1]	French	German	Hebrew	Russian	Spanish
Hello/hi	Salam	Ni hao	Bonjour	Hallo	Shalom	Privet (informal)	Hola
Good morning	Sabah el kheer	Zao shang hao	Bonjour	Guten Morgen	Boker tov	Dobraye utra	Buenos días
Good night	Tosbeho 'ala khair	Wan an	Bonne nuit	Gute Nacht	Layla tov	Spakoynay noci	Buenas noches
Good-bye	Ma'a salama	Zai jian	Au revoir	Auf wiedersehen	Lehitraot	Da svidan'ya	Adiós
Please	Men fadlek	Qing	S'il vous plaît	Bitte	Bevakasha	Pazhalusta	Por favor
Thank you very much	Shokran jazeelan	Xie xie	Merci beaucoup	Danke schön	Toda raba	Spasiba	Muchas gracias
You're welcome	Al' afw	Huan ying	De rien/pas de quoi	Keine Ursache	Bevakasha	Pazhalusta	De nada
How are you?	Kaifa haloka?	Ni hao?	Comment allez-vous?	Wie geht's dir/Ihnen?	Ma shelomkha?	Kak dela?	Cómo estás?
I'm fine	Ana bekhair	Hen hao	Je vais bien	Mir geht's gut	Tov	Harasho	Estoy bien
I'm sorry	Aasef	Bao qian	Je suis désolé	Entschuldigung	Ani mamash mitstaer	Prastite	Lo siento
Excuse me	Alma'derah	Bao qian	Pardon	Darf ich mal vorbei?	Seliha	Izvinite	Perdone
yes	na'am	shi [it is so]	oui	ja	ken	da	si
no	laa	bu [not]	non	nein	lo	nyet	no
one	wahed	yi	un	eins	ehad	adin	uno
two	ithnaan	er	deux	zwei	shenayim	dva	dos
three	thalatha	san	trois	drei	shelosha	tri	tres
four	arba'a	si	quatre	vier	arbaa	chityri	cuatro
five	khamsa	wu	cinq	fünf	hamisha	p'at	cinco

Note: Actual form or usage of some words and expressions may vary depending on dialect, grammar, or circumstances. Transliterations for languages not in Latin alphabet vary. (1) Mandarin.

Language Diversity

Source: *Ethnologue: Languages of the World, 17th Edition*; United Nations Educational, Scientific, and Cultural Organization (UNESCO); World Almanac research

There are an estimated 7,000 individual languages spoken somewhere in the world. But more than 40% of the world's people speak one of the eight most common languages as their native tongue, and more than 75% speak one of the top 85 languages. Some 3,700 languages have fewer than 10,000 native speakers, and about 700 languages have fewer than 100.

Using classifications developed by linguists, about 2,400 languages spoken today are said to be at least threatened or unsustainably losing speakers. In some cases, people of the child-bearing generation still use the language but do not transmit it to their children. In others, only those in the grandparent generation or older use a language, though they may have little occasion to do so. *Ethnologue* classifies 432 languages as nearly extinct and another 188 as dormant—that is, having no speakers with more than a "symbolic proficiency." Some languages disappear when the last native speaker dies.

Some say it should be left up to communities to determine whether a language remains worth using; if not, it should be allowed to die naturally. Others give more value to language preservation in the name of cultural diversity. Some experts have concluded that as languages die out, knowledge of the local environment and physical world is lost. A recent study of the Amesha tribe in the Peruvian Amazon found that as their severely endangered language faded, crop diversity decreased.

UNESCO supports efforts to preserve various endangered languages. In one, experts created a system for writing down words in the Khang language (spoken in parts of northwest Vietnam), which had no written version. In addition, they produced recordings, word lists, grammars, and other materials for use in language classes aimed at reviving and perpetuating the use of Khang.

Principal Languages of the World

Source: Database of *Ethnologue: Languages of the World, 17th Edition.* www.ethnologue.com. M. Paul Lewis, editor.
Copyright © 2013, SIL International. Used by permission.

Languages shown in italics are macrolanguages, or language groups that are equivalent in some ways to individual languages. Each language group consists of many variants, which may be mutually unintelligible; these variants may also appear in the larger table below. Numbers are estimates and count only speakers for whom the language is a first language, or mother tongue.

Languages Spoken by the Most People

Language	Speakers (mil)	Language	Speakers (mil)	Language	Speakers (mil)
Chinese	1,197	Russian	162	Tamil	69
Spanish	406	Japanese	122	French	69
English	335	Javanese	84	Vietnamese	68
Hindi	260	German	84	Korean	66
Arabic	223	*Lahnda*	83	Urdu	63
Portuguese	202	Telugu	74	Italian	61
Bengali	193	Marathi	72		

Languages With at Least 2.5 Million Speakers

Hub country is country of origin, not necessarily where the most speakers reside (e.g., Portugal is the hub country of Portuguese, but more Portuguese speakers live in Brazil). Number of speakers is worldwide total for each language.

Hub country	Language	Countries	Speakers (mil)	Hub country	Language	Countries	Speakers (mil)
Afghanistan	Dari	2	9.6	Ethiopia	Amharic	2	21.8
	Pashto, Southern	4	7.6		*Oromo*	4	17.5
	Uzbek, Southern	2	3.0		Oromo, West Central	1	8.9
Albania	*Albanian*	18	7.4		Tigrigna	3	6.9
	Albanian, Tosk	3	3.1		Oromo, Eastern	1	4.5
Algeria	Arabic, Algerian Spoken	1	28.0		Oromo, Borana-Arsi-Guji	3	3.9
	Kabyle	1	5.6		Sidamo	1	3.0
Angola	Umbundu	1	6.0	Finland	Finnish	3	5.0
	Kimbundu	1	4.0	France	French	51	68.5
Armenia	Armenian	14	5.9	Georgia	Georgian	3	4.2
Austria	Bavarian	4	13.3	Germany	German, Standard	18	83.8
Azerbaijan	Azerbaijani, North	4	7.3		Mainfränkisch	1	4.9
Bangladesh	Bengali	4	193.3	Ghana	Akan	1	8.3
	Rangpuri	2	15.0		Ghanaian Pidgin English	1	5.0
	Chittagonian	1	13.0		Éwé	2	3.1
	Sylheti	2	10.3	Greece	Greek	9	13.1
Belarus	Belarusan	4	7.8	Guinea	*Mandingo*	7	6.5
Bolivia	*Aymara*	4	2.8		Maninkakan, Eastern	3	3.5
	Quechua, South Bolivian	2	2.8		Pular	4	2.9
	Aymara, Central	4	2.6	Haiti	Haitian	2	7.7
Botswana	Tswana	4	4.5	Hungary	Hungarian	9	12.3
Brazil	Hunsrik	1	3.0	India	Hindi	4	260.3
Bulgaria	Bulgarian	8	6.8		Telugu	2	74.0
Burkina Faso	Mòoré	3	5.1		Marathi	1	71.8
	Jula	3	2.6		Tamil	6	68.8
Burundi	Rundi	1	10.2		Oriya	3	50.1
Cambodia	Khmer, Central	2	14.2		Gujarati	6	46.6
China	*Chinese*	33	1,197.4		Bhojpuri	3	39.8
	Chinese, Mandarin	13	847.8		Kannada	1	37.7
	Chinese, Wu	1	77.2		Malayalam	2	33.5
	Chinese, Yue	11	62.2		Maithili	2	32.8
	Chinese, Min Nan	10	46.8		Oriya	1	32.1
	Chinese, Jinyu	1	45.0		Panjabi, Eastern	3	29.5
	Chinese, Xiang	1	36.0		*Marwari*	3	19.7
	Chinese, Hakka	13	30.1		Sambalpuri	1	18.0
	Chinese, Gan	1	20.6		Magahi	1	14.0
	Zhuang	2	14.9		Chhattisgarhi	1	13.3
	Chinese, Min Bei	2	10.3		Assamese	1	12.8
	Chinese, Min Dong	6	9.1		Deccan	1	12.8
	Uyghur	4	8.8		*Rajasthani*	3	12.4
	Hmong	10	7.7		Kanauji	1	9.5
	Chinese, Huizhou	1	4.6		Haryanvi	1	8.0
	Mongolian, Peripheral	2	3.4		Varhadi-Nagpuri	1	7.0
	Chinese, Min Zhong	1	3.1		Santhali	3	6.2
	Bouyei	2	2.6		*Konkani*	4	6.1
	Chinese, Pu-Xian	3	2.6		Marwari	2	5.6
Congo, Dem. Rep. of	Luba-Kasai	1	6.3		Kashmiri	2	5.6
	Kongo	3	5.6		Malvi	1	5.6
	Koongo	3	5.0		Mewari	1	5.1
	Kituba	1	4.2		Lambadi	1	4.2
Croatia	Croatian	9	5.5		*Dogri*	1	4.0
Czech Rep.	Czech	6	9.5		Merwari	1	3.9
Denmark	Danish	3	5.6		Mina	1	3.8
Egypt	Arabic, Egyptian Spoken	1	54.0		Konkani, Goan	2	3.6
	Arabic, Sa'idi Spoken	1	19.0		Bhili	1	3.3

Hub country	Language	Countries	Speakers (mil)
India (cont.)	Sadri	2	3.3
	Awadhi	2	3.1
	Bundeli	1	3.1
	Shekhawati	1	3.0
	Godwari	1	3.0
	Garhwali	1	2.9
	Bagheli	2	2.9
	Indian Sign Language	2	2.7
	Wagdi	1	2.5
Indonesia	Javanese	3	84.3
	Sunda	1	34.0
	Indonesian	1	23.2
	Madura	2	6.8
	Minangkabau	1	5.5
	Betawi	1	5.0
	Bugis	2	5.0
	Banjar	2	3.5
	Aceh	1	3.5
	Bali	1	3.3
	Musi	1	3.1
Iran	*Persian*	29	56.6
	Persian, Iranian	6	47.0
	Azerbaijani	15	24.2
	Azerbaijani, South	4	16.9
	Domari	13	4.0
	Gilaki	1	3.3
	Mazanderani	1	3.3
	Kurdish, Southern	2	3.0
Iraq	*Kurdish*	31	30.0
	Arabic, Mesopotamian Spoken	4	15.1
	Kurdish, Central	2	6.8
	Arabic, North Mesopotamian Spoken	3	6.3
	Arabic, Gulf Spoken	9	3.6
Israel	Hebrew	1	5.3
Italy	Italian	10	61.1
	Napoletano-Calabrese	1	5.7
	Sicilian	1	4.7
	Lombard	2	3.9
	Venetian	4	3.9
Jamaica	Jamaican Creole English	3	3.2
Japan	Japanese	3	122.1
Jordan	Arabic, South Levantine Spoken	3	6.2
Kazakhstan	Kazakh	6	8.1
Kenya	Gikuyu	1	6.6
	Oluluyia	3	5.2
	Kalenjin	3	5.1
	Dholuo	2	4.2
	Kamba	1	3.9
Korea, South	Korean	6	66.4
Kyrgyzstan	Kyrgyz	4	2.9
Laos	Lao	3	3.3
Lesotho	Sotho, Southern	2	6.0
Libya	Arabic, Libyan Spoken	3	4.3
Lithuania	Lithuanian	1	3.1
Madagascar	*Malagasy*	5	16.4
	Malagasy, Plateau	2	7.5
Malawi	Chichewa	4	8.7
	Yao	4	3.1
	Tumbuka	2	2.7
Malaysia	*Malay*	13	59.4
	Malay	3	15.8
	Malay, Kedah	2	2.6
Mali	Bamanankan	2	4.1
Mauritania	Hassaniyya	6	3.3
Mongolia	*Mongolian*	6	5.8
Morocco	Arabic, Moroccan Spoken	2	21.0
	Tachelhit	2	3.9
Mozambique	Makhuwa	1	3.1
Myanmar	Burmese	1	32.0
	Shan	3	3.3
Nepal	*Nepali*	5	14.4
	Nepali	3	14.2
Netherlands	Dutch	7	23.0
Nigeria	Hausa	7	25.0
	Yoruba	2	19.4
	Igbo	1	18.0
	Fulfulde, Nigerian	3	11.5
Nigeria (cont.)	*Kanuri*	6	3.8
	Kanuri, Central	5	3.2
Norway	Norwegian	1	4.7
Pakistan	*Lahnda*	7	82.7
	Urdu	6	63.4
	Panjabi, Western	2	62.6
	Pushto	9	26.9
	Sindhi	3	20.3
	Seraiki	2	14.0
	Pashto, Northern	3	11.4
	Pashto, Central	1	7.9
	Baluchi	8	7.0
	Brahui	3	4.2
	Balochi, Southern	4	3.4
	Pahari-Potwari	1	2.5
Paraguay	*Guarani*	5	4.9
	Guaraní, Paraguayan	1	4.9
Peru	*Quechua*	6	9.1
Philippines	Filipino	1	25.0
	Tagalog	1	24.2
	Cebuano	1	15.8
	Ilocano	1	7.0
	Hiligaynon	1	5.8
	Bikol	1	3.6
	Waray-Waray	1	2.6
	Bikol, Central	1	2.5
Poland	Polish	9	39.0
Portugal	Portuguese	11	202.5
Romania	*Romanian*	6	23.6
	Romany	41	3.0
Russia	Russian	16	161.7
	Tatar	4	5.4
Rwanda	Rwanda	3	7.2
Saudi Arabia	*Arabic*	59	223.0
	Arabic, Najdi Spoken	4	9.7
	Arabic, Hijazi Spoken	2	6.0
Senegal	*Fulah*	20	22.2
	Wolof	2	4.0
	Pulaar	6	3.7
Serbia	*Serbo-Croatian*	28	17.1
	Serbian	10	9.3
	Albanian, Gheg	7	4.2
Slovakia	Slovak	9	5.0
Somalia	Somali	4	16.6
South Africa	Zulu	5	10.3
	Xhosa	2	7.8
	Afrikaans	6	4.9
	Sotho, Northern	1	4.1
	Tsonga	4	3.7
Spain	Spanish	31	405.6
	Catalán	4	7.2
	Galician	2	3.2
Sri Lanka	Sinhala	2	15.6
Sweden	Swedish	3	8.4
Switzerland	German, Swiss	5	6.5
Syria	Arabic, North Levantine Spoken	2	14.4
Tajikistan	Tajiki	4	4.5
Tanzania	*Swahili*	15	15.5
	Swahili	8	15.5
	Sukuma	1	5.4
Thailand	Thai	2	20.4
	Thai, Northeastern	1	15.0
	Thai, Northern	2	6.0
	Thai, Southern	1	4.5
Tunisia	Arabic, Tunisian Spoken	1	9.4
Turkey	Turkish	8	50.7
	Kurdish, Northern	9	20.2
Turkmenistan	Turkmen	4	7.6
Uganda	Ganda	1	4.1
Ukraine	Ukrainian	9	36.0
United Kingdom	English	101	334.8
Uzbekistan	*Uzbek*	14	21.9
	Uzbek, Northern	6	19.0
Vietnam	Vietnamese	3	67.8
Yemen	Arabic, Sanaani Spoken	1	7.6
	Arabic, Ta'izzi-Adeni Spoken	2	7.1
Zambia	Bemba	2	3.6
Zimbabwe	Shona	3	10.8

BUILDINGS, BRIDGES, AND TUNNELS

100 Tallest Buildings in the World

Source: Phorio, phorio.com; Council on Tall Buildings and Urban Habitat (CTBUH), Illinois Inst. of Technology, www.ctbuh.org

Structures under construction and topped out architecturally are denoted by an asterisk (*). Year in parentheses is date of completion or projected completion. Only buildings that are completed or under construction and topped out as of Sept. 2013 are included here. Height is generally measured from the lowest significant open-air pedestrian entrance to the architectural top, including penthouses, spires, and other decorative features that are an integral part of the design. Stories generally counted from street level. NA = Not applicable.

Building	Ht. (ft)	Stories	Building	Ht. (ft)	Stories
Burj Khalifa, Dubai, United Arab Emirates (2010)	2,717	163	Al Yaqoub Tower, Dubai, UAE (2013)	1,076	69
Makkah Royal Clock Tower Hotel, Mecca, Saudi Arabia (2013)	1,972	120	*Wuxi Suning Plaza 1, Wuxi, China (2014)	1,076	68
*One World Trade Center, New York, NY, U.S. (2014)[1]	1,776	104	The Index, Dubai, UAE (2010)	1,070	80
Taipei 101, Taipei, Taiwan (2004)	1,667	101	The Landmark, Abu Dhabi, UAE (2013)	1,063	72
Shanghai World Financial Center, Shanghai, China (2008)	1,614	101	Deji Plaza Phase 2, Nanjing, China (2013)	1,063	62
International Commerce Centre, Hong Kong, China (2010)	1,588	108	Q1, Gold Coast, Australia (2005)	1,058	78
Petronas Tower I, Kuala Lumpur, Malaysia (1998)	1,483	88	Wenzhou Trade Center, Wenzhou, China (2011)	1,056	68
Petronas Tower II, Kuala Lumpur, Malaysia (1998)	1,483	88	Burj Al Arab Hotel, Dubai, UAE (1999)	1,053	56
Zifeng Tower, Nanjing, China (2010)	1,476	66	Nina Tower I, Hong Kong, China (2007)	1,046	80
Willis (formerly Sears) Tower, Chicago, IL, U.S. (1974)	1,451	108	Chrysler Building, New York, NY, U.S. (1930)	1,046	77
Kingkey 100, Shenzhen, China (2011)	1,449	100	New York Times Tower, New York, NY, U.S. (2007)	1,046	52
Guangzhou International Finance Center, Guangzhou, China (2010)	1,439	103	United International Mansion, Chongqing, China (2013)	1,043	67
Trump International Hotel & Tower, Chicago, IL, U.S. (2009)	1,389	98	HHHR Tower, Dubai, UAE (2010)	1,042	72
Jin Mao Tower, Shanghai, China (1999)	1,380	88	Bank of America Plaza, Atlanta, GA, U.S. (1992)	1,039	55
Princess Tower, Dubai, UAE (2012)	1,356	101	*Moi Center Tower A, Shenyang, China (2013)	1,020	75
Al Hamra Tower, Kuwait City, Kuwait (2011)	1,354	80	US Bank Tower, Los Angeles, CA, U.S. (1990)	1,018	73
Two International Finance Centre, Hong Kong, China (2003)	1,352	88	Ocean Heights, Dubai, UAE (2010)	1,017	83
23 Marina, Dubai, UAE (2012)	1,289	90	Menara Telekom Headquarters, Kuala Lumpur, Malaysia (2001)	1,017	59
CITIC Plaza, Guangzhou, China (1997)	1,280	80	Pearl River Tower, Guangzhou, China (2012)	1,015	71
Shun Hing Square, Shenzhen, China (1996)	1,260	69	*Guangzhou Fortune Center, Guangzhou, China (2014)	1,015	68
*World Trade Center Abu Dhabi-The Residences, Abu Dhabi, UAE (2013)	1,251	88	Jumeirah Emirates Towers Hotel, Dubai, UAE (2000)	1,014	56
Empire State Building, New York, NY, U.S. (1931)	1,250	102	*Eurasia, Moscow, Russia (2014)	1,013	72
Elite Residence, Dubai, UAE (2012)	1,248	87	*Burj Rafal, Riyadh, Saudi Arabia (2014)	1,010	68
Central Plaza, Hong Kong, China (1992)	1,227	78	Cayan Tower, Dubai, UAE (2013)	1,008	73
Bank of China Tower, Hong Kong, China (1990)	1,205	72	Franklin Center-North Tower, Chicago, IL, U.S. (1989)	1,007	60
Bank of America Tower, New York, NY, U.S. (2009)	1,200	55	*One57, New York, NY, U.S. (2014)	1,004	79
Almas Tower, Dubai, UAE (2008)	1,181	68	*East Pacific Center Tower A, Shenzhen, China (2013)	1,004	85
The Pinnacle, Guangzhou, China (2012)	1,181	60	The Shard, London, United Kingdom (2013)	1,004	73
JW Marriott Marquis Hotel Dubai Tower 1, Dubai, UAE (2012)	1,166	82	Etihad Towers 2, Abu Dhabi, UAE (2011)	1,002	70
JW Marriott Marquis Hotel Dubai Tower 2, Dubai, UAE (2013)	1,166	82	JPMorganChase Tower, Houston, TX, U.S. (1982)	1,002	75
Emirates Office Tower, Dubai, UAE (2000)	1,163	54	NE Asia Trade Tower, New Songdo City, Incheon, South Korea (2011)	1,001	68
Tuntex Sky Tower, Kaohsiung, Taiwan (1998)	1,140	85	Baiyoke Tower II, Bangkok, Thailand (1997)	997	85
Aon Center, Chicago, IL, U.S. (1973)	1,136	83	*Maoye City-Marriott Hotel, Wuxi, China (2013)	997	68
The Center, Hong Kong, China (1998)	1,135	73	Two Prudential Plaza, Chicago, IL, U.S. (1990)	995	64
John Hancock Center, Chicago, IL, U.S. (1969)	1,128	100	Leatop Plaza, Guangzhou, China (2011)	993	64
*Ahmed Abdul Rahim Al Attar Tower, Dubai, UAE (2014)	1,122	76	Wells Fargo Plaza, Houston, TX, U.S. (1983)	992	71
*Chongqing World Financial Center, Chongqing, China (2014)	1,112	73	Kingdom Centre, Riyadh, Saudi Arabia (2002)	992	41
*Mercury City Tower, Moscow, Russia (2013)	1,112	75	The Address Downtown Dubai, Dubai, UAE (2008)	991	63
Tianjin World Financial Center, Tianjin, China (2011)	1,105	75	*Gate of the Orient, Suzhou, China (2014)	990	68
The Torch, Dubai, UAE (2011)	1,105	79	Capital City Moscow Tower, Moscow, Russia (2010)	990	76
Hanoi Landmark Tower, Hanoi, Vietnam (2012)	1,103	72	*Heung Kong Tower, Shenzhen, China (2014)	987	70
Shanghai Shimao International Plaza, Shanghai, China (2006)	1,094	60	Doosan Haeundae We've the Zenith Tower A, Busan, South Korea (2011)	984	80
Rose Rayhaan by Rotana, Dubai, UAE (2007)	1,093	71	*Torre Costanera, Santiago, Chile (2013)	984	64
*Modern Media Center, Changzhou, China (2013)	1,089	57	*Abeno Harukas, Osaka, Japan (2014)	984	62
Minsheng Bank Building, Wuhan, China (2008)	1,087	68	Arraya Tower, Kuwait City, Kuwait (2009)	984	60
*Ryugyong Hotel, Pyongyang, North Korea (NA)	1,083	105	Aspire Tower, Doha, Qatar (2007)	984	36
China World Tower, Beijing, China (2009)	1,083	74	One Island East, Hong Kong, China (2008)	979	69
Longxi International Hotel, Jiangyin, China (2011)	1,076	72	First Bank Tower, Toronto, ON, Canada (1975)	978	72
			*Four World Trade Center, New York, NY, U.S. (2013)	977	64
			Eureka Tower, Melbourne, Australia (2006)	975	91
			Comcast Center, Philadelphia, PA, U.S. (2008)	974	57
			Landmark Tower, Yokohama, Japan (1993)	972	73

(1) The CTBUH has not yet verified One World Trade Center's height claim as it has not received final drawings from building owner.

Tallest Free-Standing Towers in the World

Source: Phorio, phorio.com; Council on Tall Buildings and Urban Habitat (CTBUH), Illinois Inst. of Technology, www.ctbuh.org
Year is date of completion. As of Sept. 2013.

Tower	Ht. (ft)	Year	Tower	Ht. (ft)	Year
Tokyo Sky Tree, Tokyo, Japan	2,080	2012	Central Radio & TV Tower, Beijing, China	1,288	1992
Canton Tower, Guangzhou, China	1,969	2010	Kiev TV Tower, Kiev, Ukraine	1,263	1974
CN Tower, Toronto, ON, Canada	1,815	1976	Tashkent Tower, Tashkent, Uzbekistan	1,230	1985
Ostankino Tower, Moscow, Russia	1,772	1967	Liberation Tower, Kuwait City, Kuwait	1,220	1996
Oriental Pearl Television Tower, Shanghai, China	1,535	1995	Alma-Ata Tower, Almaty, Kazakhstan	1,217	1982
Milad Tower, Tehran, Iran	1,427	2008	TV Tower, Riga, Latvia	1,208	1987
Manara Kuala Lumpur, Kuala Lumpur, Malaysia	1,379	1996	Berliner Fernsehturm, Berlin, Germany	1,207	1969
Tianjin Radio & TV Tower, Tianjin, China	1,362	1991	Stratosphere Tower, Las Vegas, NV, U.S.	1,149	1996
Henan Province Radio & Television Emission Tower, Zhengzhou, China	1,273	2010	West Pearl Tower, Chengdu, China	1,112	2004
			Macau Tower, Macau, China	1,109	2001
			Europaturm, Frankfurt, Germany	1,106	1979

Tall Buildings in Selected North American Cities

Source: Phorio, phorio.com; Council on Tall Buildings and Urban Habitat (CTBUH), Illinois Inst. of Technology, www.ctbuh.org

List includes freestanding towers and other structures that do not have stories and are not technically considered buildings. Structures still under construction as of Sept. 2013 are denoted by an asterisk (*). Year in parentheses is date of completion or projected completion. Height is generally measured from the lowest significant open-air pedestrian entrance to the architectural top, including penthouses, spires, and other decorative features that are an integral part of the design. Stories generally counted from street level. NA = Not applicable.

Building/structure	Ht. (ft)	Stories
Atlanta, GA		
Bank of America Plaza (incl. spire), 600 Peachtree St. NE (1992)	1,039	55
SunTrust Plaza, 303 Peachtree St. NE (1993)[1]	867	60
One Atlantic Center, 1201 W. Peachtree St. (1987)	820	50
191 Peachtree Tower (1991)	770	50
Westin Peachtree Plaza, 210 Peachtree St. NW (1976)[2]	723	73
Georgia Pacific Tower, 133 Peachtree St. NE (1981)	697	51
Promenade II (incl. spire), 1230 Peachtree St. NE (1989)	691	40
AT&T Building, 675 W. Peachtree St. (1980)	677	47
Sovereign, 3344 Peachtree (2008)	665	48
1180 Peachtree (2006)	657	41
GLG Grand/Four Seasons Hotel, 75 14th St. NE (1992)	609	53
The Mansion on Peachtree, 3376 Peachtree Rd. NE (2008)	580	42
Atlantic, 270 17th St. NW (2009)	577	46
State of Georgia Building, 2 Peachtree St. NW (1967)[3]	556	44
Marriott Marquis, 265 Peachtree Center Ave. NE (1985)	554	52
Viewpoint, 855 Peachtree St. NE (2008)	501	36
(1) 902 ft incl. antenna. (2) 883 ft incl. antenna. (3) 599 ft incl. antenna.		
Austin, TX		
Austonian, 200 Congress Ave. (2010)	683	56
360 Condominiums (incl. spire), 360 Nueces St. (2008)	581	45
Frost Bank Tower, 401 N. Congress Ave. (2004)	516	33
Boston, MA		
Hancock Place, 200 Clarendon St. (1976)	790	62
Prudential Tower, 800 Boylston St. (1964)[1]	750	52
Federal Reserve Bldg., 600 Atlantic Ave. (1978)	604	32
BNY Mellon Center at One Boston Place, 201 Washington St. (1970)	602	41
One International Place, 100 Oliver St. (1987)	600	46
100 Federal St. (1971)	591	37
One Financial Center, 10 Dewey Sq. (1984)	590	46
111 Huntington Ave. (2002)	564	36
Two International Place (1993)	538	35
One Post Office Square (1981)	525	40
1 Federal St. (1975)	520	38
Exchange Place, 53 State St. (1984)	510	39
Sixty State Street (1977)	509	38
1 Beacon St. (1972)	507	36
State Street Financial Center (incl. spire), 1 Lincoln St. (2003)	503	36
28 State St. (1970)	500	40
(1) 836 ft incl. antenna.		
Calgary, AB, Canada		
The Bow, 510 Centre St. (2012)	779	57
Petro Canada Centre West Tower, 150 6th Ave. SW (1984)	705	53
Eighth Avenue Place East Tower, 8th Ave. and 5th St. SW (2011)	696	49
Bankers Hall East Tower, 855 2nd St. SW (1989)	645	50
Bankers Hall West Tower, 888 3rd St. SW (2000)	645	50
Calgary Tower, 101 9th Ave. SW (1967)	626	NA
Centennial Place 1 (incl. spire), 520 3rd Ave. SW (2010)	599	40
*Eighth Avenue Place West Tower, 8th Ave. and 5th St. SW (2014)	581	41
TransCanada Tower, 450 1st St. SW (2001)	581	38
Canterra Tower, 400 3rd Ave. SW (1988)	580	46
Jamieson Place (incl. spires), 302 4th Ave. SW (2009)	568	38
First Canadian Centre, 350 7th Ave. SW (1982)	547	41
Western Canadian Place-North Tower, 707 6th St. SW (1983)	538	41
arriVa Tower 2 (2012)	535	43
Canada Trust, Calgary Eatons Centre, 421 7th Ave. SW (1991)	530	40
Scotia Square, 700 2nd St. SW (1976)	509	41
Nexen Building, 801 7th Ave. SW (1982)	500	37
Charlotte, NC		
Bank of America Corporate Center, 100 N. Tryon St. (1992)	871	60
Duke Energy Center, 534 S. Tryon St. (2010)	786	48

Building/structure	Ht. (ft)	Stories
Hearst Tower, 214 N. Tryon St. (2002)	659	47
One Wells Fargo Center, 301 S. College St. (1988)	588	42
The Vue, 400 W. 5th St. (2010)	574	50
Bank of America Plaza, 101 S. Tryon St. (1974)	503	40
Chicago, IL		
Willis Tower, 233 S. Wacker Dr. (1974)[1]	1,451	108
Trump International Hotel & Tower (incl. spire), 401 N. Wabash Ave. (2009)	1,389	98
Aon Center, 200 E. Randolph St. (1973)	1,136	83
John Hancock Center, 875 N. Michigan Ave. (1969)[2]	1,128	100
Franklin Center-North Tower (incl. spires), 227 W. Monroe St. (1989)	1,007	60
Two Prudential Plaza (incl. spire), 180 N. Stetson Ave. (1990)	995	64
311 S. Wacker Drive (1990)	961	65
900 N. Michigan Ave. (1989)	871	66
Aqua, 225 N. Columbus Dr. (2009)	859	86
Water Tower Place, 845 N. Michigan Ave. (1976)	859	74
Chase Tower, 21 S. Clark St. (1969)	850	60
Park Tower, 800 N. Michigan Ave. (2000)	844	68
The Legacy at Millennium Park, 21-39 S. Wabash (2010)	818	73
300 N. LaSalle (2009)	785	60
3 First National Plaza, 70 W. Madison St. (1981)	767	57
Chicago Title & Trust Center, 161 N. Clark St. (1992)	756	50
Blue Cross Headquarters, 300 E. Randolph St. (2010)	744	54
One Museum Park, 1215 S. Prairie Ave. (2009)	726	62
Olympia Centre, 737 N. Michigan Ave. (1986)	725	63
330 N. Wabash Ave. (1973)	695	52
Waldorf Astoria Chicago, 940 N. Rush St. (2009)	686	60
111 S. Wacker Dr. (2005)	681	51
181 W. Madison St. (1990)	680	50
Hyatt Center, 71 S. Wacker Dr. (2005)	679	48
One Magnificent Mile, 980 N. Michigan Ave. (1983)	673	57
340 on the Park, 340 W. Randolph St. (2007)	672	64
United Bldg., 77 W. Wacker Dr. (1992)	668	49
UBS Tower, 1 N. Wacker Dr. (2001)	652	50
Daley Center, 55 W. Washington St. (1965)	648	32
55 E. Erie St. (2004)	647	56
Lake Point Tower, 505 N. Lake Shore Dr. (1968)	645	70
River East Center, 350 E. Illinois St. (2001)	644	58
Grand Plaza I (incl. spire), 540 N. State St. (2003)	641	57
155 N. Wacker Dr. (2009)	638	45
Leo Burnett Bldg., 35 W. Wacker Dr. (1989)	635	46
The Heritage at Millennium Park, 125 N. Wabash Ave. (2005)	631	57
*111 West Wacker (2014)	630	59
NBC Tower (incl. spire), 455 N. Cityfront Plaza Dr. (1989)	627	37
353 North Clark (2009)	623	44
Millennium Centre, 33 W. Ontario St. (2003)	610	58
Chicago Place, 700 N. Michigan Ave. (1991)	608	49
Board of Trade (incl. statue), 141 W. Jackson Blvd. (1930)	605	44
CNA Plaza, 325 S. Wabash St. (1972)	601	44
One Prudential Plaza, 130 E. Randolph St. (1955)[3]	601	41
Heller International Tower, 500 W. Monroe St. (1992)	600	45
One Madison Plaza, 200 W. Madison St. (1982)	599	44
One Museum Park West, 201 E. Roosevelt Rd. (2010)	595	54
1000 Lake Shore Plaza (1964)	590	55
The Clare at Water Tower, 55 East Pearson St. (2008)	589	52
Citigroup Center, 500 W. Madison St. (1987)	588	42
The Park Monroe, 65 E. Monroe St. (1972)	583	49
Crain Communications Bldg., 150 N. Michigan Ave. (1983)	582	41
North Pier Apts., 474 N. Lake Shore Dr. (1990)	581	61
Citadel Center, 131 S. Dearborn St. (2003)	580	49
The Fordham, 25 E. Superior St. (2003)	574	52
190 S. LaSalle St. (1987)	573	40
One S. Dearborn (2005)	571	39
Onterie Center, 446 E. Ontario St. (1986)	570	58
*435 N. Park Drive (2015)	569	49
Chicago Temple, 77 W. Washington St. (1924)	568	23

Building/structure	Ht. (ft)	Stories
Palmolive Building (incl. beacon), 919 N. Michigan Ave. (1929)	565	37
Marina City I, 300 N. State St. (1964)	562	61
Marina City II, 301 N. Dearborn St. (1964)	562	61
Huron Plaza Apartments, 30 E. Huron St. (1983)	560	56
Boeing International Headquarters, 100 N. Riverside Plz. (1990)	560	36
The Parkshore, 195 N. Harbor Dr. (1991)	556	56
North Harbor Tower, 175 N. Harbor Dr. (1988)	556	55
Civic Opera Building, 20 N. Wacker Dr. (1929)	555	45
Streeter Place, 351 E. Ohio St. (2009)	554	55
Newberry Plaza, 1000 N. State St. (1974)	553	53
Michigan Plaza South, 205 N. Michigan Ave. (1985)	553	46
30 N. LaSalle St. (1975)	553	44
Pittsfield Building, 55 E. Washington St. (1927)	551	38
Harbor Point, 155 N. Harbor Dr. (1975)	550	54
One S. Wacker Dr. (1982)	550	40
Kluczynski Federal Building, 230 S. Dearborn St. (1975)	545	45
Park Millennium, 222 N. Columbus Dr. (2002)	544	57
*AMLI River North, 401 N. Clark St. (2013)	543	49
Franklin Center-South Tower, 125 S. Franklin St. (1992)	538	35
The Pinnacle, 21 E. Huron St. (2004)	535	48
LaSalle National Bank, 135 S. LaSalle St. (1934)	535	45
Park Place Tower, 655 W. Irving Park Rd. (1971)	531	56
One N. LaSalle St. (1930)	530	48
The Elysees, 111 E. Chestnut St. (1973)	529	56
River Plaza, 405 N. Wabash St. (1977)	524	56
35 E. Wacker Drive (1927)	523	40
Kemper Building, 1 E. Wacker Dr. (1962)	522	41
Mather Tower, 75 E. Wacker Dr. (1928)	521	41
Chicago Mercantile Exchange, 30 S. Wacker Dr. (1983)	520	40
Chicago Mercantile Exchange, 10 S. Wacker Dr. (1987)	520	40
The Columbian, 1180 S. Michigan Ave. (2008)	517	47
191 N. Wacker Dr. (2002)	516	37
401 E. Ontario St. (1990)	515	51
One Financial Place, 440 S. LaSalle St. (1985)	515	39
The Streeter, 345 E. Ohio St. (2006)	514	50
Park Tower Condominiums, 5415 N. Sheridan Rd. (1973)	513	54
600 North Lake Shore Drive-South Tower (2009)	513	47
LaSalle-Wacker Building, 221 N. LaSalle St. (1930)	512	41
Harris Bank III, 115 S. LaSalle St. (1974)	510	38
321 N. Clark St. (1987)	510	35
215 West, 215 W. Washington St. (2010)	509	50
400 E. Ohio St. (1982)	505	50
Carbide & Carbon Building, 230 N. Michigan Ave. (1929)	503	37
One Superior Place, 1 W. Superior St. (1999)	502	52
120 N. LaSalle St. (1992)	501	39
10 S. LaSalle St. (1986)	501	37
The Tides, 360 E. South Water St. (2008)	500	51
200 S. Wacker Drive (1981)	500	41

(1) 1,729 ft incl. antenna. (2) 1,499 ft incl. antenna. (3) 912 ft incl. antenna.

Cleveland, OH

Building/structure	Ht. (ft)	Stories
Key Tower (incl. spire), 127 Public Sq. (1991)	947	57
Terminal Tower, 50 Public Sq. (1928)[1]	708	52
200 Public Sq. (1985)	658	46
Tower at Erieview, 1301 E. 9th St. (1964)	529	40

(1) 771 ft incl. flagpole.

Columbus, OH

Building/structure	Ht. (ft)	Stories
James A. Rhodes State Office Tower, 30 E. Broad St. (1973)	624	41
Leveque-Lincoln Tower, 50 W. Broad St. (1927)	555	47
William Green Bldg., 30 W. Spring St. (1990)	530	33
Huntington Center, 41 S. High St. (1983)	512	37
Vern Riffe State Office Tower, 77 S. High St. (1988)	503	37

Dallas, TX

Building/structure	Ht. (ft)	Stories
Bank of America Plaza, 901 Main St. (1985)	921	72
Renaissance Tower (incl. spire), 1201 Elm St. (1974)	886	56
Comerica Bank Tower, 1717 Main St. (1987)	787	60
JP Morgan Chase Tower, 2200 Ross Ave. (1987)	738	55
Fountain Place, 1445 Ross Ave. (1986)	720	58
Trammel Crow Center, 2001 Ross Ave. (1984)	686	50
1700 Pacific Ave. (1983)	655	50
Thanksgiving Tower, 1600 Pacific Ave. (1982)	645	50
Energy Plaza, 1601 Bryan St. (1983)	629	49
Elm Place, 1401 Elm St. (1965)	628	52
Gables Republic Tower (incl. spire), 300 N. Ervay (1954)	602	36
Republic Center Tower II, 325 N. St. Paul (1964)	598	50
One AT&T Plaza, 208 S. Akard St. (1984)	580	37
Ross Tower, 500 N. Akard St. (1984)	579	45
Cityplace Center East, 2711 N. Haskell Ave. (1989)	560	42
*Museum Tower, 2112 Flora St. (2013)	560	42
Reunion Tower, 300 Reunion Blvd. (1976)	560	NA
Sheraton Dallas Hotel Center Tower, 400 Olive St. (1959)	550	42
Mercantile Bldg. (incl. spire), 1700 Main St. (1943)	523	31
Bryan Tower, 2001 Bryan St. (1973)	512	40

Denver, CO

Building/structure	Ht. (ft)	Stories
Republic Plaza, 330 17th St. (1984)	714	56
1801 California Street (1982)	709	52
Wells Fargo Center, 1700 Lincoln Ave. (1983)	698	50
Four Seasons Hotel and Private Residences, 1111 14th St. (2010)	639	45
1999 Broadway (1985)	544	43
707 17th St. (1981)	522	42
555 17th St. (1978)	507	40

Detroit, MI

Building/structure	Ht. (ft)	Stories
Marriott Hotel, Renaissance Center I (1977)[1]	727	70
One Detroit Center, 500 Woodward Ave. (1991)	619	43
Penobscot Building, 633 Griswold Ave. (1928)[2]	565	47
Renaissance Center 100 Tower (1976)	508	39
Renaissance Center 200 Tower (1976)	508	39
Renaissance Center 300 Tower (1976)	508	39
Renaissance Center 400 Tower (1976)	508	39

(1) 755 ft incl. antenna. (2) 665 ft incl. antenna.

Fort Worth, TX

Building/structure	Ht. (ft)	Stories
Burnett Plaza, 801 Cherry St. (1983)	567	40
D.R. Horton Tower, 301 Commerce St. (1984)	547	38
Carter Burgess Plaza, 777 Main St. (1982)	525	40

Hartford, CT

Building/structure	Ht. (ft)	Stories
City Place I, 185 Asylum St. (1980)	535	38
Travelers Tower, 26 Grove St. (1919)	527	24
Goodwin Square, 225 Asylum St. (1990)	522	30

Houston, TX

Building/structure	Ht. (ft)	Stories
JPMorganChase Tower, 600 Travis St. (1982)	1,002	75
Wells Fargo Plaza, 1000 Louisiana St. (1983)	992	71
Williams Tower, 2800 Post Oak Blvd. (1982)	901	64
Bank of America Center, 700 Louisiana St. (1983)	780	56
Texaco Heritage Plaza, 1111 Bagby St. (1987)	762	53
Enterprise Plaza, 1100 Louisiana St. (1980)[1]	756	55
Centerpoint Energy Plaza, 1111 Louisiana St. (1996)	741	47
Continental Center I, 1600 Smith St. (1984)	732	55
Fulbright Tower, 1301 McKinney St. (1982)	725	52
One Shell Plaza, 900 Louisiana St. (1970)[2]	714	50
1400 Smith St. (1983)	691	50
3 Allen Center, 333 Clay St. (1980)	685	50
LyondellBassell Tower, 1221 McKinney St. (1978)	678	47
First City Tower, 1001 Fannin St. (1904)	662	47
BG Group Place, 811 Main St. (2011)	632	46
San Felipe Plaza, 5847 San Felipe Blvd. (1984)	625	45
ExxonMobil Building, 800 Bell Ave. (1962)	606	44
1500 Louisiana St. (2002)	600	40
America General Center, 2929 Allen Pkwy. (1983)	590	42
Two Houston Center, 909 Fannin St. (1974)	579	40
San Jacinto Column, La Porte (1939)	570	NA
Marathon Oil Tower, 5555 San Felipe Blvd. (1983)	562	41
Wedge International Tower, 1415 Louisiana St. (1983)	550	44
KBR Tower, 601 Jefferson St. (1973)	550	40
Pennzoil Place I, 700 Milam St. (1976)	523	36
Pennzoil Place II, 700 Louisiana St. (1976)	523	36
Devon Energy Center, 1200 Smith St. (1978)	521	36
RRI Energy Plaza, 1000 Main St. (2003)	518	36
Total Plaza, 1201 Louisiana St. (1971)	518	35
The Huntington, 2121 Kirby Dr. (1982)	503	34
El Paso Energy Bldg, 1010 Milam St. (1962)	502	33
One Park Place, 1500 McKinney St. (2009)	501	37
Memorial Hermann Tower, 929 Gessner Rd. (2009)	500	35

(1) 782 ft incl. antenna. (2) 999 ft incl. antenna.

Indianapolis, IN

Building/structure	Ht. (ft)	Stories
Chase Tower, 111 Monument Cir. (1990)[1]	701	49
One America Tower, 200 N. Illinois St. (1982)	533	38
One Indiana Square, 200 N. Delaware St. (1970)	504	36

(1) 811 ft incl. antenna.

Jersey City, NJ

Building/structure	Ht. (ft)	Stories
30 Hudson St. (2004)	781	42
101 Hudson St. (1992)	548	42
Trump Plaza I, 88 Morgan St. (2008)	532	55
Newport Tower, 525 Washington Blvd. (1990)	531	37
Exchange Place Center, 10 Exchange Pl. (incl. spire) (1990)	516	32
Hudson Green East Tower, 77 Hudson St. (2009)	509	48
Hudson Green West Tower, 77 Hudson St. (2010)	501	48

Las Vegas, NV

Building/structure	Ht. (ft)	Stories
Stratosphere Tower, 2000 Las Vegas Blvd. S. (1996)	1,149	NA
*Fontainebleau Resort Hotel, 2755 Las Vegas Blvd. S. (2013)	735	63
The Palazzo, 3339 Las Vegas Blvd. S. (2007)	642	53
Encore at Wynn Las Vegas, 3145 Las Vegas Blvd. S. (2008)	631	52
Trump International Hotel and Tower 1, 3128 Las Vegas Blvd. S. (2008)	622	64
Wynn Las Vegas, 3145 Las Vegas Blvd. S. (2005)	613	45
Cosmopolitan Casino Spa Tower, Las Vegas Blvd. and Harmon Ave. (2010)	603	52
Cosmopolitan Beach Resort Tower, Las Vegas Blvd. and Harmon Ave. (2010)	603	50
Aria Resort and Casino, 3730 Las Vegas Blvd. S. (2009)	600	60
Planet Hollywood Towers, 3667 Las Vegas Blvd. S. (2009)	597	50
VDARA, 2551 W. Harmon Ave. (2009)	556	55
Eiffel Tower, Paris Hotel and Casino, 3645 Las Vegas Blvd. S. (1998)	540	NA
Mandarin Oriental Hotel Las Vegas, 3750 Las Vegas Blvd. S. (2009)	539	47
New York, New York Hotel and Casino, 3790 Las Vegas Blvd. S. (1997)	529	48
Palms Place, 4321 W. Flamingo Rd. (2008)	518	50
Bellagio Hotel and Casino, 3600 Las Vegas Blvd. S. (1998)	508	36
Sky Las Vegas, 2780 Las Vegas Blvd. S. (2007)	500	45

Los Angeles, CA

Building/structure	Ht. (ft)	Stories
US Bank Tower, 633 W. 5th St. (1990)	1,018	73
Aon Center, 707 Wilshire Blvd. (1974)	858	62
Two California Plaza, 350 S. Grand Ave. (1992)	750	52
Gas Company Tower, 555 W. 5th St. (1991)	749	52
Bank of America Plaza, 333 South Hope St. (1975)	735	55
777 Tower, 777 S. Figueroa St. (1991)	725	53
Wells Fargo Tower, 333 S. Grand Ave. (1983)	723	54
Figueroa at Wilshire, 601 S. Figueroa St. (1989)	717	52
Paul Hastings Tower, 515 S. Flower St. (1971)	699	52
City National Tower, 555 S. Flower St. (1971)	699	52
L.A. Live Hotel & Condominiums, 900 W. Olympic Blvd. (2010)	667	54
Citigroup Center, 444 S. Flower St. (1979)	625	48
611 Place, 611 W. 6th St. (1967)	620	42
KPMG Tower, 355 S. Grand Ave. (1984)	606	45
One California Plaza, 300 S. Grand Ave. (1985)	578	42
Century Plaza Tower 1, 2029 Century Park East (1973)	571	44
Century Plaza Tower 2, 2049 Century Park East (1973)	571	44
Ernst & Young, LLP Plaza, 725 S. Figueroa St. (1986)	534	41
AIG-SunAmerica Ctr., 1999 Ave. of the Stars (1989)	533	39
TCW Tower, 865 S. Figueroa St. (1990)	517	37
Union Bank Plaza, 445 S. Figueroa St. (1968)	516	40
10 Universal City Plaza (1984)	506	36

Mexico City, Mexico

Building/structure	Ht. (ft)	Stories
*Torre Mitikah, Rio Churubusco 601 (2016)	876	62
*Torre Reforma, Paseo de la Reforma 483 (2015)	800	57
Torre Mayor, Paseo de la Reforma 505 (2003)	738	55
*Torre BBVA Bancomer, Paseo de la Reforma 506 (2014)	738	50
Torre Ejecutiva Pemex, Marina Nacional 329 Col. Huasteca (1984)	693	51
Torre Altus, Paseo de los Laureles 416 (1999)	640	44
Torre Latino Americana (incl. spire), Eje Central Lazaro Cardenas 2 (1956)	597	45
*Peninsula Tower, Av. Santa Fe 1240 (2014)	591	51
World Trade Center, Montecito 38 Col. Napoles (1972)	565	50
*Siroco Elite Residences, Av. Santa Fe 482 (2013)	561	43
*Torre Punta Reforma, Paseo de la Reforma 180 (2014)	558	37
Arcos Torre I, Paseo de los Tamarindos 400 (1997)	529	35
Arcos Torre II, Paseo de los Tamarindos 400 (2008)	529	35

Miami, FL

Building/structure	Ht. (ft)	Stories
Four Seasons Hotel & Tower, 1441 Brickell Ave. (2003)	789	64
Wachovia Financial Center, 200 S. Biscayne Blvd. (1983)	764	55
900 Biscayne Bay, 900 Biscayne Blvd. (2008)	712	65
Marquis, 1100 Biscayne Blvd. (2009)	679	63
Met 2 Office Tower, 200 SE 3rd St. (2010)	655	47
*Brickell CityCentre Office Tower 3 (2016)	634	45
Mint at Riverfront, 90 SW 3rd St. (2009)	631	44
Infinity at Brickell, 60 W. 13th St. (2008)	630	52

Building/structure	Ht. (ft)	Stories
Miami Tower, 100 SE Second St. (1987)	625	47
Marinablue, 888 Biscayne Blvd. (2007)	615	57
Plaza on Brickell Tower I, 901 Brickell Ave. (2007)	610	56
Epic Residences & Hotel, 300 Biscayne Blvd. Way (2009)	601	54
Icon Brickell North Tower, 495 Brickell Ave. (2008)	586	58
Icon Brickell South Tower, 495 Brickell Ave. (2008)	586	58
Ten Museum Park, 1040 Biscayne Blvd. (2007)	585	50
Paramount at Edgewater Square, 2066 N. Bayshore Dr. (2009)	555	47
50 Biscayne Blvd. (2007)	554	55
Quantum on the Bay South Tower, 1900 N. Bayshore Dr. (2008)	554	51
Opera Tower, 1750 N. Bayshore Dr. (2007)	543	56
Everglades on the Bay North Tower, 244 Biscayne Blvd. (2008)	538	49
Everglades on the Bay South Tower, 244 Biscayne Blvd. (2008)	538	49
Quantum on the Bay North Tower, 1900 N. Bayshore Dr. (2008)	536	44
Jade at Brickell Bay, 1331 Brickell Bay Dr. (2004)	528	49
Plaza on Brickell Tower II, 901 Brickell Ave. (2007)	525	48
*Brickell CityCentre Condo Tower 3 (2016)	522	48
Santa Maria, 1643 Brickell Ave. (1997)	520	51
*Brickell CityCentre Condo Tower 2 (2015)	520	45
*Brickell CityCentre Hotel Tower (2015)	516	41
The Ivy, 90-95 SW 3rd St. (2008)	512	45
Stephen P. Clark Center, 111 NW 1st St. (1985)	510	28
*Brickell CityCentre Condo Tower 1 (2015)	503	44
Met 2 Marriott Marquis, 200 SE 3rd St. (2010)	502	41
Wind, 330 S. Miami Ave. (2008)	501	41
*Brickell House, 1300 Brickell Bay Dr. (2014)	500	46
1450 Brickell (2010)	500	34

Minneapolis, MN

Building/structure	Ht. (ft)	Stories
IDS Tower, 80 S. 8th St. (1973)[1]	792	55
Capella Tower, 225 South Sixth (1992)	776	56
Wells Fargo Center, 90 S. 7th St. (1988)	775	56
33 South Sixth Street (1983)	668	52
Campbell Mithun Tower, 222 S. 9th St. (1985)	582	42
US Bank Plaza I, 200 S. 6th St. (1981)	561	40
RBC Plaza, 60 S. 6th St. (1992)	539	40
Fifth Street Towers II, 150 S. 5th St. (1988)	504	36
(1) 910 ft incl. antenna.		

Monterrey, Mexico

Building/structure	Ht. (ft)	Stories
*Pabellon M (2015)	682	47
Torre Avalanz, San Pedro Garza Garcia (2000)	597	43
Centro de Gobierno Plaza Civica (2010)	591	36
Torre Helicon, San Pedro Garza Garcia (2012)	512	33
*LIU East, San Pedro Garza Garcia (2013)	476	34
Torre Commercial America, San Pedro Garza Garcia (1994)	427	35

Montréal, QC, Canada

Building/structure	Ht. (ft)	Stories
1250 Boulevard Rene Levesque (incl. spire) (1992)	743	47
1000 Rue de la Gauchetiere (1992)	673	51
Tour de la Bourse, 800 Place Victoria (1964)	624	47
1 Place Villa Marie (1962)	616	43
La Tour CIBC, 1155 Rene Levesque Blvd. (1962)[1]	604	45
Montréal Tower (1987)	574	NA
Tour McGill College, 1501 McGill College (1992)	519	38
(1) 740 ft incl. antenna.		

New Orleans, LA

Building/structure	Ht. (ft)	Stories
One Shell Square, 701 Poydras St. (1972)	697	51
CapitalOne Center, 201 St. Charles Ave. (1985)	645	53
Plaza Tower, 1001 Howard Ave. (1969)	531	45
Energy Centre, 1100 Poydras St. (1984)	530	39

New York, NY

Building/structure	Ht. (ft)	Stories
*One World Trade Center (incl. spire) (2014)[1]	1,776	104
*432 Park Avenue (2015)	1,397	85
Empire State Building, 350 5th Ave. (1931)[2]	1,250	102
Bank of America (incl. spire), One Bryant Park (2009)	1,200	55
*Three World Trade Center (incl. spires), 175 Greenwich St. (2017)	1,171	80
Chrysler Building (incl. spire), 405 Lexington Ave. (1930)	1,046	77
New York Times Tower (incl. spire), 620 8th Ave. (2007)	1,046	52
*One57, 157 W. 57th St. (2013)	1,005	75
*Four World Trade Ctr., 150 Greenwich St. (2013)	977	64
American International Bldg. (incl. spire), 70 Pine St. (1932)	952	67
The Trump Building, 40 Wall St. (1930)	927	71
Citigroup Center, 153 E. 53rd St. (1977)	915	59
*Hudson Yards South Tower (2015)	895	47
New York by Gehry at Eight Spruce Street (2011)	870	76
Trump World Tower, 845 UN Plaza (2001)	861	72
GE Building, 30 Rockefeller Center (1933)	850	70

Building/structure	Ht. (ft)	Stories
*56 Leonard Street (2016)	821	57
Cityspire Center, 150 W. 56th St. (1989)	814	75
One Chase Manhattan Plaza (1960)	813	60
4 Times Square (1999)[3]	809	48
MetLife Building, 200 Park Ave. (1963)	808	59
Bloomberg Tower, 731 Lexington Ave. (2005)[4]	806	54
Woolworth Building, 233 Broadway (1913)	792	57
1 Worldwide Plaza, 935 8th Ave. (1989)	778	47
Carnegie Hall Tower, 152 W. 57th St. (1991)	757	60
383 Madison Avenue (2001)	755	47
*1717 Broadway (2013)	753	68
AXA Center, 787 7th Ave. (1985)	752	51
One Penn Plaza, 250 W. 34th St. (1972)	750	57
1251 Ave. of the Americas (1971)	750	54
Time Warner Center North Tower, 10 Columbus Circle (2004)	749	55
Time Warner Center South Tower, 10 Columbus Circle (2004)	749	55
Goldman Sachs HQ, 200 Murray St. (2010)	749	44
60 Wall Street (1989)	745	55
One Astor Plaza, 1515 Broadway (1970)	745	54
1 Liberty Plaza, 165 Broadway (1973)	743	54
7 World Trade Center (2006)	743	49
20 Exchange Place (1931)	741	57
Three World Financial Center, 200 Vesey St. (1986)	739	51
1540 Broadway (incl. spire) (1990)	732	42
Times Square Tower, 1459 Broadway (2004)	726	47
Metropolitan Tower, 142 W. 57th St. (1985)	716	68
JPMorganChase World Headquarters, 270 Park Avenue (1960)	707	52
General Motors Bldg., 767 5th Ave. (1968)	705	50
Metropolitan Life Tower, 1 Madison Ave. (1909)	700	50
500 5th Avenue (1931)	697	60
Americas Tower, 1177 Ave. of the Americas (1992)	692	48
Solow Bldg., 9 W. 57th St. (1974)	689	49
HSBC Bank Bldg., 140 Broadway (1967)	688	52
55 Water Street (1972)	687	53
277 Park Avenue (1963)	687	50
1585 Broadway (1989)	685	42
Random House/Park Imperial, 1739 Broadway (2003)	684	52
Four Seasons Hotel, 57 E. 57th St. (1993)	682	52
McGraw-Hill Bldg., 1221 Ave. of the Americas (1972)	674	51
Barclay Tower, 10 Barclay St. (2007)	673	56
Lincoln Bldg., 60 E. 42nd St. (1930)	673	53
Citicorp, 1 Court Square, Queens (1990)	673	50
Paramount Plaza, 1633 Broadway (1970)	670	48
Trump Tower, 725 5th Ave. (1982)	664	58
*Atelier II, 605 W. 42nd St. (2015)	656	61
Bank of New York Building, 1 Wall St. (1932)	654	50
Silver Towers East, 600 W. 42nd St. (2009)	653	58
Silver Towers West, 600 W. 42nd St. (2009)	653	58
599 Lexington Avenue (1986)	653	51
712 5th Avenue (1990)	650	53
Chanin Building, 122 E. 42nd St. (1929)	649	56
245 Park Avenue (1967)	648	47
550 Madison Avenue (1983)	647	37
Two World Financial Center, 225 Liberty St. (1986)	645	44
570 Lexington Avenue (1931)	642	50
1 New York Plaza, 1 Water St. (1969)	640	50
1 MiMA Tower, 440 W. 42nd St. (2011)	638	63
1 Dag Hammarskjold Plaza, 885 2nd Ave. (1972)	637	48
345 Park Avenue (1968)	634	44
400 5th Avenue (2010)	632	58
Mercantile Bldg., 10 E. 40th St. (1929)	632	48
W New York Downtown Hotel & Residences, 123 Washington St. (2010)	631	57
Grace Plaza, 1114 Ave. of the Americas (1972)	630	50
Home Insurance Plaza, 59 Maiden Ln. (1966)	630	44
1095 Avenue of the Americas (1970)	630	40
101 Park Avenue (1982)	629	49
Central Park Place, 301 W. 57th St. (1988)	628	56
888 7th Avenue (1971)	628	45
Burlington House, 1345 Ave. of the Americas (1969)	625	50
Waldorf Astoria, 301 Park Ave. (1931)	625	47
Olympic Tower, 645 5th Ave. (1976)	620	51
425 Fifth Avenue (2003)	618	55
One Madison Park, 20 E. 23rd St. (2010)	621	50
The Epic, 125 W. 31st St. (2007)	615	58
919 3rd Avenue (1970)	615	47
Tower 49, 12 E. 49th St. (1985)	615	44
750 7th Avenue (incl. spire) (1989)	615	35
New York Life, 51 Madison Ave. (1928)	615	33
Eventi, 851 6th Ave. (2010)	614	46
*Baccarat Hotel & Residences, 20 West 53rd St. (2015)	610	46
Credit Lyonnais Building, 1301 Ave. of the Americas (1964)	609	46
The Orion, 350 W. 42nd St. (2006)	604	58
590 Madison Avenue (1983)	603	41
250 W. 55th St. (2013)	602	40
Eleven Times Square, 644 8th Ave. (2011)	601	40
1166 Avenue of the Americas (1974)	600	44
*160 W. 62nd St. (2014)	598	54
Hearst Magazine Tower, 959 8th Ave. (2006)	597	46
*Avalon Willoughby West, 100 Willoughby St. (2015)	596	57
3 Lincoln Center, 160 W. 66th St. (1993)	595	60
Trump Palace, 200 E. 69th St. (1991)	594	54
Celanese Building, 1211 Ave. of the Americas (1973)	592	45
The London NYC, 151 W. 54th St. (1990)	590	54
*388 Bridge St., Brooklyn (2014)	590	51
Thurgood Marshall U.S. Courthouse, 505 Pearl St. (1936)	590	37
The Millenium Hilton Hotel, 55 Church St. (1992)	588	58
Sky House, 11 E. 29th St. (2008)	588	55
Museum Tower Apartments, 21 W. 53rd St. (1985)	588	52
Time-Life Building, 1271 Ave. of the Americas (1959)	587	48
Jacob K. Javits Federal Bldg., 26 Federal Plz. (1967)	587	41
W Times Square, 1567 Broadway (2000)	584	53
Trump International Hotel & Tower, 15 Columbus Circle (1970)	583	44
Stevens Tower, 1185 Ave. of the Americas (1971)	580	42
Municipal Building, 1 Centre St. (1914)	580	34
520 Madison Avenue (1981)	577	43
One World Financial Center, 200 Liberty St. (1985)	577	37
Merchandise Mart, 41 Madison Ave. (1973)	576	42
Park Avenue Plaza, 55 E. 52nd St. (1981)	575	44
Lehman Building, 745 7th Ave. (2001)	575	38
One Financial Square, 33 Old Slip (1987)	575	37
Marriott Marquis Times Square, 1531 Broadway (1985)	574	50
299 Park Avenue (1967)	574	42
5 Times Square, 590 7th Ave. (2002)	574	40
Socony Mobil Building, 150 E. 42nd St. (1956)	572	42
1290 Ave. of the Americas (1963)	571	43
780 3rd Avenue (1983)	570	49
600 3rd Avenue (1971)	570	42
450 Lexington Avenue (1991)	568	38
Paramount Tower, 240 E. 39th St. (1998)	567	51
230 Park Avenue (1928)	565	35
New York Palace Hotel, 455 Madison Ave. (1980)	563	51
Continental Bank Bldg., 30 Broad St. (1932)	562	48
Park Avenue Tower, 65 E. 55th St. (1986)	561	36
Nelson Tower, 450 7th Ave. (1931)	560	46
Sherry-Netherland, 781 5th Ave. (1927)	560	40
623 5th Ave. (1990)	560	36
South Park Tower, 124 W. 60th St. (1986)	558	51
100 UN Plaza, 327 E. 48th St. (1986)	557	52
Continental Can, 633 3rd Ave. (1962)	557	39
3 Park Avenue (1975)	556	42
Continental Center, 180 Maiden Ln. (1983)	555	41
Sperry & Hutchinson Bldg., 330 Madison Ave. (1964)	555	41
Reuters Building, 3 Times Sq. (2001)[5]	555	30
The Belvedere, 10 E. 29th St. (1999)	554	48
Tower 111, 885 6th Ave. (2011)	554	48
Inmont Bldg., 1133 Ave. of the Americas (1970)	552	45
Downtown by Philippe Starck, 15 Broad St. (1927)	551	42
*Hyatt Times Square, 135 W. 45th St. (2013)	550	53
Biltmore Tower, 267 W. 47th St. (2003)	550	51
Unisys Building, 605 3rd Ave. (1963)	550	44
2 Grand Central Tower, 140 E. 45th St. (1982)	550	43
The Tower at 15 Central Park West (2008)	550	35
AT&T Long Lines Building, 33 Thomas St. (1974)	550	29
*50 UN Plaza, 345 E. 46th St. (2015)	548	44
Bankers Trust, 33 E. 48th St. (1971)	547	41
The Corinthian, 330 E. 38th St. (1988)	546	55
Transportation Building, 225 Broadway (1928)	546	44
MillenniumTower, 101 W. 67th St. (1995)	545	54
Equitable Building, 120 Broadway (1915)	545	36
The Galleria, 117 E. 57th St. (1975)	544	56
2 Gold Street (2005)	543	51
220 Riverside Boulevard at Trump Place (2003)	542	49
17 State Street (1988)	542	41
Grand Central Plaza, 622 3rd Ave. (1973)	542	38
New York Telephone, 375 Pearl St. (1976)	540	42
1285 Avenue of the Americas (1960)	540	42
Ritz Tower, 109 E. 57th St. (1925)	540	41
14 Wall Street (1912)	540	29
Tribeca Tower, 105 Duane St. (1990)	537	53
Lefcourt Colonial Building, 295 Madison Ave. (1929)	537	45
300 Madison Avenue (2003)	535	35
1700 Broadway (1969)	533	41

Building/structure	Ht. (ft)	Stories
Westin Hotel New York, 43rd St. and 8th Ave. (2002) ..	532	45
515 Park Avenue (1999)	532	43
DuMont Building, 515 Madison Ave. (1931)	532	42
The Brooklyner, 111 Lawrence St., Brooklyn (2010)	531	52
One East River Place, 525 E. 72nd St. (1989)	530	49
The Metropolis, 150 E. 44th St. (2001)	528	50
William Beaver House, 15 William St. (2010)	528	47
North American Plywood, 800 3rd Ave. (1972)	526	41
Hotel Pierre, 2 E. 61st. St. (1928)	525	44
767 3rd Avenue (1980)	525	39
Citibank, 399 Park Ave. (1961)	524	41
Random House, 825 3rd Ave. (1969).	522	40
Atelier, 625 W. 42nd St. (2007)	521	46
26 Broadway (1924)	520	31
Newsweek Building, 444 Madison Ave. (1931)	518	42
The Downtown Club, 19 West St. (1930)	518	39
Architects and Designers Building, 964 Third Ave. (1969)	518	39
785 8th Avenue (2009)	517	42
High Point Condominium, 250 E. 40th St. (1988) . .	516	49
House of Seagram, 375 Park Ave. (1958)	516	38
Sterling Drug Building, 90 Park Ave. (1964).	515	41
Millennium Towers North, 512 7th Ave. (1930)	513	44
1214 Fifth Avenue (2012)	513	42
Bank of New York, 48 Wall St. (1927)	513	31
The Belaire, 524 E. 72nd St. (1988).	512	50
One Hanson Place, Brooklyn (1929)	512	42
1407 Broadway Realty Corp. (1950)	512	41
International Building, Rockefeller Center, 630 5th Ave. (1935).	512	41
ITT-American, 437 Madison Ave. (1967)	512	40
Continental Building, 1450 Broadway (1931).	511	42
1155 Ave. of the Americas (1984).	511	40
Liberty Plaza, 10 Liberty St. (2004)	510	45
810 7th Avenue (1970)	506	41
The Sheffield Apartments, 325 W. 56th St. (1978)	505	50
United Nations Secretariat Building, 405 E. 42nd St. (1950)	505	39
1 UN Plaza (1975)	505	39
2 UN Plaza (1981)	505	39
2 New York Plaza, 125 Broad St. (1970).	504	40
Johns-Manville Building, 22 E. 40th St. (1931)	503	43
60 Broad Street (1962)	503	39
Lefcourt National Building, 521 5th Ave. (1928) . . .	503	37
1325 Ave. of the Americas (1989).	502	35
Sheraton Centre, 811 7th Ave. (1962).	501	51
World Apparel Center, 1411 Broadway (1969)	501	39
International Gem Tower, 44 W. 47th St. (2013) . . .	501	34
Bristol Plaza, 200 E. 65th St. (1987).	500	50
One Columbus Place Tower I, 400 W. 59th St. (1999)	500	49
One Columbus Place Tower II, 400 W. 59th St. (1999)	500	49
Four World Financial Center, 250 Vesey St. (1986)	500	34

(1) The CTBUH had not yet verified One World Trade Center's height claim as it had not received final drawings from building owner. (2) 1,455 ft incl. antenna. (3) 1,118 ft incl. antenna. (4) 941 ft incl. antenna. (5) 659 ft incl. antenna.

Oklahoma City, OK

Building/structure	Ht. (ft)	Stories
Devon Energy Center, 333 W. Sheridan Ave. (2012)	844	52
Chase Tower, 100 N. Broadway Ave. (1971).	500	36
First National Center (incl. spire), 120 N. Robinson St. (1931)	493	33
City Place, 204 N. Robinson St. (1931)	440	32
Oklahoma Tower, 210 Park Ave. (1982)	434	31

Orlando, FL

Building/structure	Ht. (ft)	Stories
SunTrust Center Tower, 200 S. Orange Ave. (1988)	441	31
Peabody Orlando Expansion Tower (incl. spire), 9801 International Dr. (2010)	428	31
Vue at Lake Eola, 136 E. Robinson St. (2007)	426	35
Orange County Courthouse, 425 N. Orange Ave. (1997)	416	24
Bank of America Center, 390 N. Orange Ave. (1988)	409	28

Philadelphia, PA

Building/structure	Ht. (ft)	Stories
Comcast Center, 1701 JFK Blvd. (2008)	974	57
One Liberty Place (incl. spire), 1650 Market St. (1987)	945	61
Two Liberty Place (incl. spire), 1601 Chestnut St. (1989)	848	58
Mellon Bank Center, 1735 Market St. (1990)	792	54
Three Logan, 1717 Arch St. (1991).	739	55
G. Fred DiBona Jr. Building, 1901 Market St. (1990)	625	45
Commerce Square #1, 2005 Market St. (1990)	572	40
Commerce Square #2, 2001 Market St. (1992)	572	40
City Hall (incl. statue) (1901)	548	7

Building/structure	Ht. (ft)	Stories
Residences at Ritz-Carlton, 1416 S. Penn Square (2009)	518	46
1818 Market St. (1974).	500	40
The St. James, 700 Walnut St. (2004)	498	45
Loews Philadelphia Hotel, 12 S. 12th St. (1932)[1]	492	39

(1) 748 ft incl. antenna.

Pittsburgh, PA

Building/structure	Ht. (ft)	Stories
US Steel Tower, 600 Grant St. (1970).	841	64
One Mellon Bank Center, 500 Grant St. (1983) . . .	725	54
One PPG Place (1984).	635	40
Fifth Avenue Place, 120 5th Ave. (1987).	616	32
One Oxford Centre, 301 Grant St. (1982).	615	46
Gulf Tower, 707 Grant St. (1932)	582	44
*The Tower at PNC Plaza (2015)	564	33
University of Pittsburgh Cathedral of Learning, 4200 5th Ave. (1936)	535	42
3 Mellon Bank Center, 525 Wm. Penn Way (1951)	520	41
K & L Gates Center, 210 6th Ave. (1968)	511	39

Portland, OR

Building/structure	Ht. (ft)	Stories
Wells Fargo Center, 1300 SW 5th Ave. (1973)	546	40
U.S. Bancorp Tower, 111 SW 5th Ave. (1983).	536	42
Koin Center, 222 SW Columbia St. (1984)	509	31

St. Louis, MO

Building/structure	Ht. (ft)	Stories
Gateway Arch (1965)	630	NA
Metropolitan Square Tower, 211 N. Broadway (1988)	593	42
AT&T Center, 900 Pine St. (1984).	588	44
Thomas F. Eagleton Federal Courthouse, 111 S. 10th St. (2000).	557	29

San Francisco, CA

Building/structure	Ht. (ft)	Stories
Sutro Tower (1972)	977	NA
Transamerica Pyramid, 600 Montgomery St. (1972).	853	48
555 California St. (1969).	779	52
345 California Center (1986)	695	48
Millennium Tower, 301 Mission St. (2009)	645	58
One Rincon Hill South Tower, 425 First St. (2008)	605	54
101 California St. (1982).	600	48
50 Fremont Center (1985)	600	43
Chevron Tower, 575 Market St. (1975)	573	40
Four Embarcadero Center, 55 Clay St. (1984)	570	45
One Embarcadero Center, 355 Clay St. (1970) . . .	569	45
44 Montgomery St. (1967)	565	43
Spear Tower, 1 Market St. (1976)	565	42
One Sansome Street (1984).	550	43
*One Rincon Hill North Tower, 425 First St. (2014)	541	45
Shaklee Terrace Bldg., 444 Market St. (1982)	537	38
McKesson Plaza, 1 Post St. (1969)	529	38
First Market Tower, 525 Market St. (1972).	529	38
425 Market St. (1973).	524	38
Telsis Tower, 1 Montgomery St. (1982).	500	38

Seattle, WA

Building/structure	Ht. (ft)	Stories
Columbia Center, 701 5th Ave. (1985)	933	76
1201 Third Avenue Tower, 1201 3rd Ave. (1988)	772	55
Two Union Square, 601 Union St. (1989).	740	56
Seattle Municipal Tower, 700 5th Ave. (1990)	722	57
Safeco Plaza, 1001 4th Ave. (1969)	630	50
City Centre, 1420 5th Ave. (1989).	606	44
Space Needle, 203 6th Ave. (1962)	605	NA
Russell Investments Center, 1301 2nd Ave. (2006)	598	42
Wells Fargo Center, 999 3rd Ave. (1983)	574	47
Bank of America Fifth Avenue Plaza, 800 5th Ave. (1981)	543	42
901 5th Ave. (1973)	536	41
Rainier Tower, 1301 5th Ave. (1977).	514	31
Fourth & Madison Building, 915 4th Ave. (2003) . .	512	40
1918 8th Ave. (2009)	500	36

Sunny Isles Beach, FL

Building/structure	Ht. (ft)	Stories
*Mansions at Acqualina, 17749 Collins Ave. (2015)	643	46
*Porsche Design Tower, 18555 Collins Ave. (2016)	641	57
Jade on the Beach Condominiums, 17001 Collins Ave. (2008)	574	51
Trump Palace, 18101 Collins Ave. (2005)	551	43
Trump Royale, 18201 Collins Ave. (2008).	551	43
Acqualina Ocean Residences, 17875 Collins Ave. (2004)	550	51
Jade Ocean, 17121 Collins Ave. (2009)	543	51

Tampa, FL

Building/structure	Ht. (ft)	Stories
Regions Building, 100 N. Tampa St. (1992)	579	42
Bank of America Plaza, 101 E. Kennedy Blvd. (1986)	577	42
One Tampa City Center, 201 N. Franklin St. (1981)	537	39
SunTrust Financial Center, 401 E. Jackson St. (1992)	525	36

Building/structure	Ht. (ft)	Stories
Toronto, ON, Can.		
CN Tower, 310 Front St. West (1976)	1,815	NA
First Bank Tower, 100 King St. West (1975)[1]	978	72
Trump International Hotel & Tower (incl. spire), 325 Bay St. (2012)	908	63
Scotia Tower, 40 King St. West (1989)	902	68
*Aura at College Park, 388 Yonge St. (2014)	892	78
Brookfield Place (incl. spire), 161 Bay St. (1990) . .	856	53
*Number One Bloor, 1 Bloor St. East (2015)	844	75
Commerce Court West, 199 Bay St. (1973)[2]	784	57
*Ice Condos at York Centre 2, 16 York St. (2014) . .	768	67
*Harbour Plaza Residences East, 90 Harbour St. (2017)	764	66
*Harbour Plaza Residences West, 90 Harbour St. (2017)	735	62
TD Centre-Toronto Dominion Bank Tower, 66 Wellington St. West (1967)	730	56
Bay-Adelaide Center West Tower, 335 Bay St. (2010)	704	52
Living Shangri-La Toronto, 180 University Ave. (2012)	702	65
Ritz-Carlton Hotel and Residences, 185 Wellington St. West (2011)	687	54
BCE Place, Bay-Wellington Tower, 181 Bay St. (1991)	679	49
*L Tower, 1 Front St. (2013)	673	58
*Ice Condos at York Centre 1, 16 York St. (2014) . .	663	57
*Bay-Adelaide Center East Tower, 40 Adelaide St. (2016)	643	44
Four Seasons Private Residences West, 48 Yorkville Ave. (2012)	623	55
RBC Centre, 155 Wellington St. West (2009)	607	42
*U Condominiums II, 50 St. Joseph St. (2014)	604	55
TD Centre-Royal Trust Tower, 77 King St. W. (1969)	600	46
Maple Leaf Square North Tower, 65 Bremmer Blvd. (2010)	595	54
1 King West (2005)	578	51
Success Tower 2, 33 Bay St. (2010)	569	55
Royal Bank Plaza-South Tower, 200 Bay St. (1976)	567	41
Maple Leaf Square South Tower, 55 Bremmer Blvd. (2010)	562	50
*Hullmark Centre I, 4789 Yonge St. (2014)	561	45
44 Charles St. West (1974)	545	51
*Karma, 9 Grenville St. (2015)	544	50
Quantum 2, 2195 Yonge St. (2008)	541	51
Residences @ College Park I, 763 Bay St. (2006)	535	50
Burano, 832 Bay St. (2012)	535	52
Success Tower 1, 18 Harbour St. (2011)	531	44
*X2, 580 Jarvis St. (2014).	529	48
*FIVE, 606 Yonge St. (2014).	528	48
*Southcore Financial Centre Delta Hotel (2014). . .	524	47
*Three Hundred, 300 Front St. West (2013)	518	52
The Uptown, 35 Balmuto St. (2011)	518	48
*Theatre Park, 224 King St. West (2014)	515	47
Festival Tower, 330 King St. West (2011)	514	42
*U Condominiums I, 50 St. Joseph St. (2014)	505	45
TD Waterhouse Tower, 79 Wellington St. W. (1985)	504	39
35 Mariner Terrace (2005)	503	49
*Westlake Village 1 (2014)	503	48
Montage, 20 Fort York Blvd. (2009)	502	48
(1) 1,116 ft incl. antenna. (2) 942 ft incl. antenna.		
Tulsa, OK		
BOK Tower, 1 E. 2nd St. (1975)	667	52
Cityplex Central Tower, 2448 E. 81st St. (1979) . . .	648	60
First Place Tower, 15 E. 5th St. (1973)	516	40
Mid-Continent Tower, 401 S. Boston St. (1984) . . .	513	36

Building/structure	Ht. (ft)	Stories
Vancouver, BC, Canada		
Shangri-La Vancouver, 1120 W. Georgia St. (2009)	659	59
*Trump International Hotel & Tower, 1153 W. Georgia (2016)	616	58
Hotel Georgia, 667 Howe St. (2012)	520	50

Other Tall Buildings in North America

Building/structure	City	Ht. (ft)	Stories
RSA Battle House Tower (incl. spire) (2007)	Mobile, AL.	745	35
Revel Hotel (2012)	Atlantic City, NJ . . .	718	53
Hotel Riu Plaza Guadalajara (2011)	Guadalajara, Mex.	705	44
Great American Tower at Queen City Square (2011)	Cincinnati, OH	665	40
The Tower at First National Center (2002)	Omaha, NE.	634	45
801 Grand (1991)	Des Moines, IA	630	44
One Kansas City Place (incl. spire) (1988)	Kansas City, MO. . .	623	42
Tower of the Americas (1968)	San Antonio, TX . . .	622	NA
Bank of America Tower (1990)	Jacksonville, FL . . .	617	42
AT&T Building (1994)	Nashville, TN	617	33
*Solo District-Altus (2016)	Burnaby, BC, Can.	602	48
U.S. Bank Center (1973). . . .	Milwaukee, WI.	601	42
Town Pavilion (1986)	Kansas City, MO. . .	591	38
Erastus Corning II Tower (1973)	Albany, NY	589	44
Niagara Falls Hilton Phase 2 (2009)	Niagara Falls, ON, Can.	581	58
Absolute World 56 (2012). .	Mississauga, ON, Can.	576	56
Carew Tower (1931)[1]	Cincinnati, OH	574	49
Concourse Corporate Center V (incl. spire) (1988). .	Sandy Springs, GA	570	34
Torre Aura Altitude (2008). .	Zapopan, Mex. . . .	563	44
Blue Diamond Tower (2000)	Miami Beach, FL. . .	559	44
Green Diamond Tower (2000)	Miami Beach, FL. . .	559	44
Washington Monument (1884)	Washington, DC . . .	555	NA
Concourse Corporate Center VI (incl. spire) (1991)	Sandy Springs, GA	553	34
100 E. Wisconsin Ave. (1989)	Milwaukee, WI.	549	37
AEGON Center (1992)	Louisville, KY	549	35
Metropolitan Tower (1986)	Little Rock, AR	546	40
Marriott Rivercenter (incl. spires) (1988)	San Antonio, TX . . .	546	38
RBC Plaza (incl. spire), (2008)	Raleigh, NC	538	32
Modis Tower (1975)	Jacksonville, FL . . .	535	37
Legg Mason Building (1973)	Baltimore, MD.	529	40
One HSBC Center (1970). .	Buffalo, NY	529	38
Vehicle Assembly Building (1965)	Cape Canaveral, FL	526	40
Harrah's Waterfront Tower (2008)	Atlantic City, NJ . . .	525	44
Skylon (1965)	Niagara Falls, ON, Can.	520	NA
Absolute World 50 (2012). .	Mississauga, ON, Can.	518	50
*Sovereign (2014).	Burnaby, BC, Can.	511	45
Bank of America (1924) . . .	Baltimore, MD.	509	37
The Westin Virginia Beach Town Center and Residences (2007).	Virginia Beach, VA	508	38
The Beach Club Tower 2 (2006)	Hallandale Beach, FL	505	50
One American Plaza (1991)	San Diego, CA	500	34
(1) 623 ft incl. antenna.			

Notable North American Bridges

Source: World Almanac research; Office of Bridge Technology, Federal Highway Administration, U.S. Dept. of Transportation Asterisk (*) designates a bridge that carries railroads only. All other bridges carry roads or roads and rail unless otherwise noted. Year is date of completion or projected completion. Span of bridge is the distance between its main supports. As of mid-2013.

Year Bridge	Location	Main span (ft)	Year Bridge	Location	Main span (ft)
Suspension			1970 Pierre Laporte	Quebec City, QC, Can. . .	2,190
1964 Verrazano-Narrows	New York, NY	4,260	1951/Delaware Mem. (twin)	Pennsville, NJ-	
1937 Golden Gate.	San Francisco Bay, CA . .	4,200	68	New Castle, DE.	2,150
1957 Mackinac	Straits of Mackinac, MI . .	3,800	1957 Walt Whitman	Philadelphia, PA	2,000
1931 George Washington	New York, NY-Fort Lee, NJ	3,500	1929 Ambassador.	Detroit, MI-Windsor, ON,	
2007 Tacoma Narrows	Tacoma, WA	2,800		Canada	1,850
1950 Tacoma Narrows	Tacoma, WA	2,800	1961 Throgs Neck	New York, NY	1,801
2003 Al Zampa Memorial (New Carquinez) (westbound) . .	Carquinez Strait, CA	2,388	1926 Benjamin Franklin	Phila., PA-Camden, NJ. . .	1,750
1936 San Francisco-Oakland Bay			1924 Bear Mountain	Hudson R., Peekskill, NY	1,632
San Francisco-Yerba (West Span)[1]	Buena Isl., CA	2,310	1969 Claiborne Pell/Newport . . .	Narragansett Bay, RI	1,600
1939 Bronx-Whitestone.	East R., New York, NY . . .	2,300	1952/William Preston Lane Jr. 73 Memorial (twin).	Sandy Point, MD.	1,600

Year	Bridge	Location	Main span (ft)
1903	Williamsburg	East R., New York, NY	1,600
1883	Brooklyn	East R., New York, NY	1,596
1938	Lions Gate	Vancouver, BC, Canada	1,550
1963	Vincent Thomas	L.A. Harbor, CA	1,500
1930	Mid-Hudson	Poughkeepsie, NY	1,495
1909	Manhattan	East R., New York, NY	1,470
1955	Angus L. Macdonald	Halifax, NS, Canada	1,447
1970	A. Murray MacKay	Halifax, NS, Canada	1,400
1936	Triborough (Harlem R. Lift/Bronx Crossing/ East R. Suspension)	East R., New York, NY	1,380
2013	San Francisco-Oakland Bay (SAS)[2]	San Francisco Bay, CA	1,263

Cantilever

Year	Bridge	Location	Main span (ft)
1917	Quebec	Quebec City, QC, Can.	1,800
1974	Commodore Barry	Chester, PA-Bridgeport, NJ	1,644
1958/ 88	Crescent City Connection (twin)	Mississippi R., New Orleans, LA	1,575
1995	Veterans Memorial	Gramercy, LA	1,460
1968	Baton Rouge	Mississippi R., LA	1,235
1955	Tappan Zee (I-287)	Hudson R., Tarrytown, NY	1,212
1930	Lewis and Clark	Longview, WA-Rainier, OR	1,200
1909	Queensboro	East R., New York, NY	1,182
1958	Carquinez (eastbound)	San Francisco Bay, CA	1,100
1930	Jacques Cartier	Montreal, QC, Canada	1,097
1968	Isaiah D. Hart	Jacksonville, FL	1,088
1956	Richmond-San Rafael (twin)	San Francisco Bay, CA	1,070
1963/ 80	Newburgh-Beacon (twin)	Hudson R., NY	1,000

Simple Truss

Year	Bridge	Location	Main span (ft)
1977	Jennings Randolph	Chester, WV-E. Liverpool, OH.	750
1929	Irvin S. Cobb (U.S. 45)	Ohio R., Brookport, IL-Paducah, KY	716
1923	*Mears Mem., Tanana R.	Nenana, AK	700
1967	Williamstown-Marietta (I-77)	Ohio R., WV-OH	650
1917	*MacArthur	E. St. Louis, IL-St. Louis, MO	647
1992	Discovery	Missouri R., MO	625
1958	*Castleton	Hudson R., NY	598
1938	Easton-Phillipsburg	Delaware R., PA	550
1930	Swindell	Pittsburgh, PA	545
1951	Rankin	Pittsburgh, PA	525
1906	Donora-Webster	Donora-Webster, PA	515

Continuous Truss

Year	Bridge	Location	Main span (ft)
1966	Astoria	Columbia R., OR-WA	1,232
1976	Francis Scott Key	Baltimore, MD	1,200
1981	Ravenswood	Ohio R., Ravenswood, WV	902
1995	Taylor-Southgate, Ohio R.	Cincinnati, OH-Newport, KY	850
1943	Julien Dubuque (U.S. 20)	Mississippi R., IA-IL	845
1966	Charles Braga	Fall River, MA	840
1956	Shawneetown (KY 56) (twin)	Ohio R., IL-KY	825
1953	John E. Mathews	Jacksonville, FL	810
1992	Cooper R.	Charleston, SC	800
1957	Kingston-Rhinecliff	Hudson R., NY	800
1950	Maurice J. Tobin	Boston, MA	800
1940	Gov. Nice Mem.	Newburg, MD-Dahlgren, VA	800
1986	Rochester-Monaca	Rochester-Monaca, PA	780
1973/ 88	Atchafalaya R. (U.S. 190) (twin)	Krotz Springs, LA	780
1990	Glade Creek	Beckley, WV	784
1917	*Sciotoville RR (twin)	Sciotoville, OH-KY	775
1981	Sewickley	Sewickley, PA	750
1974	Carroll C. Cropper (I-275)	Ohio R., IN-KY	750
1940	Glover Cary	Ohio R., Owensboro, KY-IN	750
1984	13th Street	Ohio R., Ashland, KY-OH	740
1959	Monaca-E. Rochester	Monaca-E. Rochester, PA	730
1976	Betsy Ross	Philadelphia, PA	729
2013	Milton-Madison (U.S. 421)	Ohio R., KY-IN	727
1967	Matthew E. Welsh	Ohio R., Mauckport, IN-KY	725
1994	Robert C. Byrd	Huntington, WV	720
1972	LA 1, Atchafalaya R.	Simmesport, LA	720
1962	U.S. 41 Twin, Ohio R.	Evansville, IN-Henderson, KY	720
1970	Vanport	Vanport, PA	715
1962	Champlain	Montreal, QC, Canada	707
1973	Girard Point	Philadelphia, PA	700
1963	John F. Kennedy (I-65)	Ohio R., Louisville, KY-Jeffersonville, IN	700

Plate and Box Girder

Year	Bridge	Location	Main span (ft)
2010	Kanawha R. (I-64)	S. Charleston-Dunbar, WV	760
1977	LA 27, Intracoastal Canal	Gibbstown, LA	750
1976	LA 82, Intracoastal Canal	Forked Isl., LA	750
1967	San Mateo-Hayward	San Francisco Bay, CA	750
1969	San Diego-Coronado (twin)	San Diego Bay, CA	660
1967	B. F. Dickmann (Poplar St.)	Mississippi R., St. Louis, MO-IL	647
1992/94	Acosta (twin)	Jacksonville, FL	630
1973	Loop 610/Sidney Sherman	Houston, TX	630
1981	Douglas	Juneau, AK	620
1981	Glenn Jackson (I-205)	Columbia R., OR-WA	600

Cable-Stayed

Year	Bridge	Location	Main span (ft)
2012	Baluarte Bicentennial	Mexico	1,706
2011	John James Audubon	Pointe Coupee-West Feliciana, LA	1,583
2005	Arthur Ravenel Jr.	Charleston, SC	1,546
2012	Port Mann	Vancouver, BC, Can.	1,542
1986	Alex Fraser	Vancouver, BC, Can.	1,526
2014	New Mississippi R. (I-70)	St. Louis, MO-IL	1,500
2010	U.S. 82, Mississippi R.	Greenville, MS-Lake Village, AR	1,378
1994	Clark	Alton, IL-MO	1,360
1989	Dames Point	Jacksonville, FL	1,300
2003	Sidney Lanier	Brunswick, GA	1,250
1995	Fred Hartman	Houston Ship Channel, Baytown, TX	1,250
2007	Veterans' Glass City Skyway	Maumee R., Toledo, OH	1,225
1983	Hale Boggs Memorial	Luling, LA	1,222
2002	William Natcher, Ohio R.	Owensboro, KY-IN	1,200
1987	Sunshine Skyway	Tampa Bay, FL	1,200
2012	Margaret Hunt Hill	Trinity R., Dallas, TX	1,197
1988	Tampico	Panuco R., Mexico	1,181
2006	Penobscot Narrows	Bucksport, ME	1,161
2003	Bill Emerson Memorial	Cape Girardeau, MO-IL	1,150
1988	Skybridge[3]	Vancouver, BC, Canada	1,115
1991	Talmadge Memorial	Savannah, GA	1,100
2000	Maysville (Wm. H. Harsha)	Savannah, GA	1,050

Steel Arch

Year	Bridge	Location	Main span (ft)
1977	New River Gorge	Fayetteville, WV	1,700
1931	Bayonne (Kill Van Kull)	Bayonne, NJ-NY, NY	1,675
1973	Fremont	Portland, OR	1,255
1964	Port Mann	Vancouver, BC, Can.	1,200
1967	Laviolette	Trois-Rivières, QC, Can.	1,100
1990	Roosevelt Lake	Roosevelt Lake, AZ	1,080
1959	Glen Canyon	Page, AZ	1,028
1962	Lewiston-Queenston	NY-ON, Can.	1,001
1976	Perrine	Twin Falls, ID	993
1916	*Hell Gate	East R., New York, NY	978
1941	Rainbow	Niagara Falls, NY-ON, Can.	950
1997	Second Blue Water	Port Huron, MI-ON, Can.	922
1977	Moundsville	Ohio R., WV	912
1983/ 90	Jefferson Barracks (I-255) (twin)	Mississippi R., IL-MO	910
1973	Hernando DeSoto (I-40) (two spans)	Mississippi R., AR-TN	900
2008	Blennerhassett (U.S. 50)	Parkersburg, WV-OH	878
1936	Henry Hudson	Harlem R., New York, NY	840
1966	Bob Cummings Lincoln Trail	Ohio R., IN-KY	825
1978	I-57, Mississippi R.	Cairo, IL	821
1980	I-65, Mobile R.	Mobile, AL	800
1961	Sherman Minton (I-64)	New Albany, IN-Louisville, KY	800
1978	I-470, Ohio R.	Wheeling, WV	780
1932	West End	Pittsburgh, PA	780
1971	Piscataqua R. (I-95 High Level)	Portsmouth, NH-Kittery, ME	756
1995	Navajo	Marble Canyon, AZ	726

Segmental Concrete

Year	Bridge	Location	Main span (ft)
1997	Confederation[4]	Prince Edward Isl.-NB, Can.	820
1978	Shubenacadie R.	S. Maitland, NS, Can.	790
1982	Jesse H. Jones Mem.	Houston, TX	750
1992	Jamestown-Verrazano	Narragansett Bay, RI	674
2002	Vietnam Veterans Memorial	James R., Richmond, VA	672
1986	Umatilla	Columbia R., OR-WA	660
2007	Benicia-Martinez (new)	Carquinez Strait, CA	659
1978	Stanislaus R.	Parrots Ferry, CA	640
1981	Juneau-Douglas	Gastineau Channel, AK	620
2010	Allegheny R. (I-76) (twin)	Nr. Oakmont, PA	532
1991	Veterans Mem. Centennial	Coeur d'Alene, ID	520

Movable Bridges

Vertical Lift

Year	Bridge	Location	Main span (ft)
1959	*Arthur Kill	New York, NY-Elizabeth, NJ	558
1965	Pennsylvania Railroad	Kirkwood-Mt. Pleas., DE	548
1935	*Cape Cod Canal	Buzzards Bay, MA	544
1896	*Delair	Pennsauken, NJ-Phila., PA	542
1937	Marine Pkwy. Gil Hodges Mem.	Jamaica Bay, New York, NY	540
1931	Burlington-Bristol	Delaware R., NJ-PA	540
1958	Columbia R. Interstate (I-5)	Portland, OR-Vancouver, WA	531
1908	Burlington Northern RR	Portland, OR.	516
1968	Second Narrows	Vancouver, BC, Canada	493
1911	*Armour-Swift-Burlington	Missouri R., Kansas City, MO	428
1945	*Harry S Truman	Kansas City, MO.	427

Bascule

Year	Bridge	Location	Main span (ft)
2006/08	Woodrow Wilson (twin)	Potomac R., VA-MD	366

Year	Bridge	Location	Main span (ft)
1940	Charles Berry Memorial	Lorain, OH	333
1917	Market St./Ch. John Ross	Chattanooga, TN	306
2003	*SW 2nd Avenue	Miami, FL	302
1956/96	1st Ave. S. (Duwamish R.) (twin)	Seattle, WA.	300

Swing

Year	Bridge	Location	Main span (ft)
1927	Santa Fe, Mississippi R.	Ft. Madison, IA	525
1952	George P. Coleman Mem.	Yorktown, VA	500
1991	SW Spokane St.	Seattle, WA.	480
1899	Illinois Central RR	Chicago, IL	479
1914	*Coos Bay RR	Coos Bay, OR.	458
1913	East Haddam (Rt. 82)	East Haddam, CT.	456

Floating Pontoon[5]

Year	Bridge	Location	Main span (ft)
1963	Evergreen Pt. (SR 520)[6]	Seattle, WA.	7,578
1961	Hood Canal (SR 104)	Kitsap Co.-Jefferson Co., WA	7,450
1993	Lacey V. Murrow (I-90)	Seattle, WA.	6,561
1989	Homer M. Hadley (I-90)	Seattle, WA.	5,736

Other Notable North American Bridges[7]

Year	Bridge	Type	Location	Length (ft)
1956/69	Lake Pontchartrain Causeway[8]	Twin concrete trestle	Metairie-Mandeville, LA	126,034
1979	Manchac Swamp	Twin concrete trestle	Manchac, LA	120,384
1972	Atchafalaya Basin (I-10)	Twin concrete trestle	Baton Rouge, LA	93,984
1982	Seven Mile (Overseas Hwy, U.S. 1)	Segmental concrete	Florida Keys	35,867
2002	Croatan Sound	Continuous post-tensioned girder	Manteo, NC	27,000
1993	Choctawhatchee Mid-Bay	Segmental concrete	Destin-Niceville, FL	19,265
1962	International	Arch truss	Sault Ste. Marie, MI-ON, Canada	9,278
2009	Walkway Over the Hudson[9]	Pedestrian	Poughkeepsie-Highland, NY	6,768
1874	Eads, Mississippi R.	Steel arch	St. Louis, MO-IL	6,442
1987	Powder Point	Tropical hardwood	Duxbury, MA	2,200
2010	Mike O'Callaghan-Pat Tillman Mem. (U.S. 93)[10]	Concrete arch	Colorado R., AZ-NV	1,900
1969	Silver Memorial, Ohio R.[11]	Cantilever	Pt. Pleasant, WV-OH	1,964
1994	Natchez Trace Parkway	Concrete arch	Franklin, TN	1,572
1901	Hartland[12]	Covered	St. John R., Hartland, NB, Canada	1,282

(1) Two complete bridges end-to-end, each with a main span of 2,310 ft, which share an anchor point in San Francisco Bay. (2) The San Francisco-Oakland Bay (East Span) cantilever bridge (built 1936; 1,400-ft main span) closed to traffic in Aug. 2013 and is being dismantled with the opening of the Self-Anchored Suspension Span (SAS), the world's longest single-tower, self-anchored suspension bridge. (3) World's longest cable-stayed bridge carrying mass transit only. (4) World's longest bridge crossing ice-covered water, with total length of 8 mi. (5) Length listed is of bridge's floating section. (6) To be replaced by new, wider SR 520 floating pontoon, with expected opening in 2015-16. (7) Length listed is total length of bridge. (8) World's second-longest bridge over water, behind China's Jiaozhou Bay Bridge (26.3 mi). (9) Originally opened in 1889 as a railroad bridge. (10) Longest single-span concrete arch in Western Hemisphere. (11) Replaced Silver Bridge, the collapse of which in 1967 led to the creation of National Bridge Inspection Standards in the U.S. (12) World's longest covered bridge.

Selected Bridge Styles

Bridges support weight through tension (pulling), compression (pushing), or a combination of both. **Suspension** and **cable-stayed** bridges are characterized by cables under tension. While the deck of a suspension bridge hangs from suspenders, that of a cable-stayed bridge ties directly to a bridge tower. The elements of a **truss** form triangles, which distribute the forces of tension and compression. Truss bridges can thus carry more weight than beam bridges. Steel plates can be welded or bolted together to make a **plate girder**, a kind of beam. A common form is the **box girder**.

A bridge can have a **simple** configuration, whereby its load is supported at both ends. If a bridge is **continuous**, its load extends across multiple supports. In a **cantilever** configuration, structural elements (e.g., trusses or girders) supported at one end project out, or cantilever, to carry a span.

Oldest U.S. Bridges in Continuous Use

Built in 1697, the stone-arch Frankford Ave. Bridge (U.S. 13) crosses Pennypack Creek in Philadelphia, PA. It consists of three spans and has a total length of 154 ft. The bridge was constructed as part of the King's Road, which eventually connected Philadelphia to New York.

The oldest covered bridge, completed in 1829, is the double-span, 256-ft-long Bath-Haverhill Bridge, which spans the Ammonoosuc River between the towns of Bath and Haverhill, NH. The bridge was bypassed in 1999. It has since reopened to pedestrian traffic only.

Notable World Bridges

Source: World Almanac research; Laboratory of Bridge Engineering, Aalto Univ. School of Science and Technology
Year is date of completion or projected completion. Span of bridge is the distance between its main supports. As of mid-2013.

Suspension

Year	Bridge	Location	Main span (ft)
1998	Akashi Kaikyo	Japan	6,532
2009	Xihoumen	China	5,413
1998	Storebælt (Great Belt, East Bridge)	Denmark	5,328
2012	Yi Sun-sin (Gwangyang)	South Korea	5,069
2005	Runyang Yangtze R. (south)	China	4,888
2012	Nanjing Fourth Yangtze R.	China	4,652
1981	Humber	England	4,626
1999	Jiangyin Yangtze R.	China	4,544
1997	Tsing Ma	China	4,518
2013	Hardanger	Norway	4,298
2007	Yangluo Yangtze R.	China	4,199
1997	Höga Kusten	Sweden	3,970
2012	Aizhai	China	3,858
2015	Ulsan Grand	South Korea	3,773
2008	Huangpu	China	3,635
1988	Minami Bisan-Seto	Japan	3,609
1988	Fatih Sultan Mehmet (Bosphorus II)	Turkey	3,576
2010	Baling R.	China	3,570
2012	Taizhou Yangtze R.[1]	China	3,543
1973	Bosphorus	Turkey	3,524
1999	Kurushima III	Japan	3,379
1999	Kurushima II	Japan	3,346
1966	Ponte 25 de Abril, Tagus R.	Portugal	3,323
1964	Forth Road	Scotland	3,300

(1) Two consecutive spans of equal length.

Steel Arch

Year	Bridge	Location	Main span (ft)
2009	Chongqing Chaotianmen Yangtze R.	China	1,811
2003	Lupu	China	1,804
1932	Sydney Harbour	Australia	1,650
2005	Wushan Yangtze R.	China	1,614
2016	Chenab (rail)[1]	India	1,539
2007	Xinguang	China	1,404
2007	Caiyuanba	China	1,378
2008	Airport	Japan	1,247
2000	Yajisha	China	1,181
1962	Bridge of the Americas	Panama	1,128
1967	Zdakov	Czech Republic	1,083
1961	Runcorn-Widnes	England	1,082
1935	Birchenough	Zimbabwe	1,080

(1) Will be world's highest arch bridge upon completion.

Year	Bridge	Location	Main span (ft)
	Concrete Arch		
1997	Wanxian	China	1,378
1980	Krk I	Croatia	1,280
1995	Jiangjiehe	China	1,083
1996	Yongjiang	China	1,024
1964	Gladesville	Australia	1,000
1965	Amizade	Brazil-Paraguay	951
2003	Infant Dom Henrique	Portugal	919
1984	Bloukrans	South Africa	892
1963	Arrábida	Portugal	886
1943	Sandö	Sweden	866
	Cantilever		
1890	Forth Rail[1]	Scotland	1,710
1974	Minato	Japan	1,673
1943	Rabindra Setu (Howrah)	India	1,500
	(1) Two spans of equal length.		
	Plate and Box Girder		
2006	Shibanpo	China	1,083
1998	Stolmasundet	Norway	988
1998	Raftsundet	Norway	978
1974	Pres. Costa e Silva (Rio-Niterói)	Brazil	984
1978	Neckar Valley Viaduct, Weitingen	Germany	863
1956	Branko's	Serbia	856
1989	Third	Brazil	853
1966	Zoobrücke	Germany	850
	Cable-Stayed		
2012	Russky Island	Russia	3,622
2008	Sutong Yangtze R.	China	3,570
2009	Stonecutters	China	3,340
2009	Edong	China	3,038
1999	Tatara	Japan	2,920
1995	Normandy	France	2,808
2010	Jingyue Yangtze R.	China	2,677

Year	Bridge	Location	Main span (ft)
2009	Incheon	South Korea	2,625
2012	Zolotoy Rog	Russia	2,418
2009	Shanghai Yangtze R.	China	2,395
2009	Minpu	China	2,323
2005	Third Nanjing Yangtze R.	China	2,126
2001	Second Nanjing Yangtze R.	China	2,060
2000	Third Wuhan Yangtze R. (Baishazhou)	China	2,028
2002	Qingzhou Minjiang R.	China	1,985
1993	Yangpu	China	1,975
1998	Meiko Chuo	Japan	1,936
1997	Xupu	China	1,936
2004	Rion-Antirion	Greece	1,837
1991	Skarnsundet	Norway	1,739
1999	Shantou Queshi	China	1,699
1995	Tsurumi Tsubasa	Japan	1,673
2008	Tianxingzhou Yangtze R.	China	1,654
2002	Jingsha	China	1,640
2000	Øresund	Denmark-Sweden	1,608
1991	Ikuchi	Japan	1,608
1994	Higashi Kobe	Japan	1,591
2011	Geo Geum	South Korea	1,575
1998	Zhanjiang	China	1,575
1997	Ting Kau	China	1,558
1999	Seohae Grand	South Korea	1,542
1989	Yokohama Bay	Japan	1,509
	Other Notable World Bridges[1]		
2011	Danyang-Kunshan Grand[2]	China	538,000
2011	Qingdao Jiaozhou Bay[3]	China	139,000
2007	Hangzhou Bay	China	118,000
2005	Donghai	China	106,627
2013	Jiashao	China	33,136
1978	Demerara Harbour (floating)	Guyana	6,074
1994	Nordhordland (floating)	Norway	4,088

(1) Length listed is total length of bridge. (2) World's longest bridge. (3) World's longest transoceanic bridge. Carries Beijing-Shanghai high-speed rail.

World's Longest Railway Tunnels

Source: World Almanac research

Year is date of opening or projected opening unless otherwise noted. As of mid-2013.

Year	Tunnel	Location	Operating railway	Length (mi)
2016	Gotthard Base (twin)	Switzerland-Italy	Swiss Federal Railways (SBB)	35.4/35.5
1988	Seikan	Japan	Japan Railways Group	33.5
1994	English Channel (Chunnel) (twin)	UK-France	Eurotunnel	31.1
2007	Lötschberg Base (twin)	Switzerland	BLS Lötschbergbahn AG	21.0
2007	Guadarrama (twin)	Spain	Renfe	17.6
2009	Taihang (twin)	China	China's Ministry of Railways	17.3
2005	Hakkoda	Japan	Japan Railways Group	16.4
2015	Guangzhou-Shenzhen-Hong Kong Express Rail Link (XRL), Hong Kong section	Hong Kong, China	MTR Corporation	16.2
2002	Iwate-Ichinohe	Japan	Japan Railways Group	16.0
2012-13[1]	Pajares (twin)	Spain	Renfe	15.5
2014	Iiyama	Japan	Japan Railways Group	13.8
1982	Daishimizu	Japan	Japan Railways Group	13.8
2006	Wushaoling (twin)	China	China's Ministry of Railways	12.5
1906/22	Simplon No. 1 and 2	Switzerland-Italy	BLS Lötschbergbahn AG	12.3
1999	Vereina	Switzerland	Rhätische Bahn (RhB)	11.8
2007	High Speed 1 (Channel Tunnel Rail Link, or CTRL) (twin)	UK-France	London & Continental Railways (LCR)	11.8
1975	Shin-Kanmon (twin)	Japan	Japan Railways Group	11.6
1934	Apennine	Italy	Ferrovie dello Stato (FS)	11.5
2002	Qinling (twin)	China	China's Ministry of Railways	11.5
2006	Vaglia	Italy	Ferrovie dello Stato (FS)	10.4
2014	West Qinling (twin)	China	China's Ministry of Railways	10.3
1972	Rokko	Japan	Japan Railways Group	10.1
1982	Furka Base	Switzerland	Matterhorn Gotthard Railway	9.6
1982	Haruna	Japan	Japan Railways Group	9.6
2019	Ceneri Base (twin)	Switzerland	Swiss Federal Railways (SBB)	9.5/9.6

(1) Tunnels have been dug but are not yet in operation.

Underwater Vehicular Tunnels in North America

Source: World Almanac research

(more than 5,000 ft in length; year is date of opening)

Year	Name	Location	Waterway	Length (ft)
1950	Brooklyn Battery (twin)	New York, NY	East River	9,117
1927	Holland (twin)	New York, NY-Jersey City, NJ	Hudson River	8,558/8,371
1937/45/57	Lincoln (center/north/south tubes)	New York, NY-Weehawken, NJ	Hudson River	8,216/7,482/8,006
1985	Fort McHenry (twin)	Baltimore, MD	Patapsco River	7,920
1957/76	Hampton Roads (twin)	Hampton, VA	Hampton Roads	7,479
1957	Baltimore Harbor (twin)	Baltimore, MD	Baltimore Harbor	7,392
1940	Queens Midtown (twin)	New York, NY	East River	6,414
1934	Sumner	Boston, MA	Boston Harbor	5,653
1964	Thimble Shoal	Northampton Co., VA	Chesapeake Bay	5,552
1964	Chesapeake Channel	Northampton Co., VA	Chesapeake Bay	5,237
1930	Detroit-Windsor	Detroit, MI-Windsor, ON, Canada	Detroit River	5,160
1961	Callahan	Boston, MA	Boston Harbor	5,070

Land Vehicular Tunnels in the U.S.

Source: World Almanac research; Federal Highway Administration, U.S. Dept. of Transportation
(3,200 ft or more in length)

Name	Location	Length (ft)	Name	Location	Length (ft)
Anton Anderson Memorial[1]	Whittier, AK	13,300	Lehigh (twin)	PA Tpke., NE Extension	4,461/ 4,380
Edwin C. Johnson Memorial (eastbound)	I-70, Clear Creek Co.- Summit Co., CO	8,960	Cumberland Gap (twin)	U.S. 25E, KY-TN	4,600
Eisenhower Mem. (westbound)	I-70, Clear Creek Co.- Summit Co., CO	8,939	Blue Mountain (twin)	PA Turnpike	4,339
			Wawona	Yosemite Natl. Pk., CA	4,233
Ted Williams[2]	MA Turnpike, Boston, MA	8,448	Big Walker Mountain (twin)	Bland Co., VA	4,229
Thomas P. O'Neill Jr.	I-93, Boston, MA	7,920	Squirrel Hill	Pittsburgh, PA	4,225
Allegheny (twin)	PA Turnpike	6,070	Tom Lantos/Devil's Slide		
Liberty (twin)	Pittsburgh, PA	5,920	(twin)	San Mateo Co., CA	4,200
Zion-Mount Carmel	Zion Natl. Park, UT	5,808	Hanging Lake (twin)	Glenwood Canyon, CO	4,000
East River Mountain (twin)	I-77, Rocky Gap, VA-Bluefield, WV	5,412	Caldecott (4 tubes)	Oakland, CA	3,771/3,610/ 3,610/3,389
Tuscarora Mountain (twin)	PA Turnpike	5,326	Fort Pitt (twin)	Pittsburgh, PA	3,614
Tetsuo Harano (twin)	H-3 Freeway, HI	5,165	Mount Baker	Seattle, WA	3,456
Kittatinny Mountain (twin)	PA Turnpike	4,727	Dingess	Mingo Co., WV	3,400
			Mall	Washington, DC	3,400

(1) Vehicles and trains take turns using the tunnel's one lane. (2) Total length of tunnel is 8,448 ft, 3,960 ft of which is underwater.

Major U.S. Dams and Reservoirs

Source: 2013 National Inventory of Dams, U.S. Army Corps of Engineers

Highest U.S. Dams

Rank	Dam	River	State	Type	Height Feet	Height Meters	Year completed
1.	Oroville	Feather	California	E	770	235	1968
2.	Hoover	Colorado	Nevada	A-G	730	221	1935
3.	Dworshak	N. Fork Clearwater	Idaho	G	717	219	1973
4.	Glen Canyon	Colorado	Arizona	A	710	216	1963
5.	New Bullards Bar	North Yuba	California	A	645	197	1970
6.	Mossyrock	Cowlitz	Washington	A	606	185	1968
7.	Shasta	Sacramento	California	G	602	183	1945
8.	New Melones	Stanislaus	California	E-R	578	176	1979
9.	Don Pedro	Tuolumne	California	E	568	173	1971
10.	Hungry Horse	S. Fork Flathead	Montana	A	564	172	1952

A = Arch; E = Embankment, earthfill; R = Embankment, rockfill; G = Gravity. **Note:** The height of a dam is the vertical distance between the original streambed or excavated foundation and the dam's crest, parapet wall, or maximum design water level. Tailings and other mining dams (i.e., dams built from the waste generated by mining operations) are not included in this list.

Largest U.S. Embankment Dams

Rank	Dam	River	State	Volume Cubic yards (thousands)	Volume Cubic meters (thousands)	Year completed
1.	Fort Peck	Missouri	Montana	125,628	96,049	1957
2.	Diamond Valley Lake	Domenigoni Valley Creek	California	110,551	84,523	2000
3.	Oahe	Missouri	South Dakota	92,000	70,339	1966
4.	Oroville	Feather	California	80,000	61,164	1968
5.	B. F. Sisk	San Luis Creek	California	77,670	59,383	1967
6.	Garrison	Missouri	North Dakota	66,500	50,843	1953
7.	Scotts Flat	Deer Creek	California	66,300	50,690	1948
8.	Cochiti	Rio Grande	New Mexico	65,000	49,696	1975
9.	Herbert Hoover	North New River Canal	Florida	54,700	41,821	1965
10.	Fort Randall	Missouri	South Dakota	50,200	38,381	1954

Note: An embankment dam is any dam constructed with excavated material, including earth, rocks, and mining or other industrial waste. (In contrast, gravity, arch, and buttress dams are generally made out of concrete or masonry.) The majority of the world's dams are embankment dams. All dams in this list are earthfill, or formed primarily out of layers of compacted earth.

Largest-Capacity U.S. Reservoirs

Rank	Dam	Reservoir	State	Max. reservoir capacity Acre feet (thousands)	Max. reservoir capacity Cubic meters (thousands)	Year completed
1.	Hoover	Lake Mead	Nevada	30,237	37,296,790	1935
2.	Glen Canyon	Lake Powell	Arizona	29,875	36,850,270	1963
3.	Garrison	Lake Sakakawea	North Dakota	24,500	30,220,305	1953
4.	Oahe	Lake Oahe	South Dakota	23,600	29,110,172	1966
5.	Fort Peck	Fort Peck Lake	Montana	19,100	23,559,503	1957
6.	Grand Coulee	Lake Roosevelt	Washington	9,562	11,794,553	1941
7.	Herbert Hoover	Lake Okeechobee	Florida	8,519	10,508,032	1965
8.	Sam Rayburn	Sam Rayburn Lake	Texas	6,520	8,042,302	1965
9.	Wright Patman	Wright Patman Lake	Texas	6,505	8,023,799	1954
10.	Fort Randall	Lake Francis Case	South Dakota	6,300	7,770,936	1954

Note: A reservoir is a body of water created by a dam for storage. This water may serve a single or multiple purposes, such as irrigation, flood reduction, and electricity generation.

Major Dams and Reservoirs of the World
Source: World Register of Dams, Intl. Commission on Large Dams (ICOLD)
Asterisk (*) designates structure is planned or under construction as of mid-2013.

World's Highest Dams

Rank	Dam	Country	Height above lowest formation Meters	Feet
1.	*Rogun	Tajikistan	335	1,099
2.	*Bakhtiari	Iran	315	1,033
3.	Jinping	China	305	1,001
4.	Nurek	Tajikistan	300	984
5.	Xiaowan (Yunnan Gorge)	China	292	958
6.	Grand Dixence	Switzerland	285	935
7.	Xiluodu	China	278	912
8.	Inguri	Georgia	272	892
9.	Vajont	Italy	262	860
10.	Chicoasén	Mexico	261	856
11.	Alvaro Obregon	Mexico	260	853
12.	Tehri	India	260	853
13.	Mauvoisin	Switzerland	250	820
14.	Laxiwa	China	250	820
15.	Deriner	Turkey	249	817

World's Largest Embankment Dams

Rank	Dam	Country	Volume cubic meters (thousands)
1.	Tarbela	Pakistan	129,200
2.	Fort Peck	U.S.	96,049
3.	Diamond Valley Lake	U.S.	84,523
4.	Yacyreta	Argentina/Paraguay	81,000
5.	Tucurui	Brazil	80,865
6.	Ataturk	Turkey	84,500
7.	*Rogun	Tajikistan	75,500
8.	Guri	Venezuela	70,000
9.	Parambikulam	India	69,165
10.	High Island West	China	67,000
11.	Gardiner	Canada	65,440
12.	Mangla	Pakistan	64,991
13.	Afsluitdijk	Netherlands	63,400
14.	Oroville	U.S.	61,164
15.	B. F. Sisk	U.S.	59,378

World's Largest-Capacity Reservoirs

Rank	Dam	Country	Max. capacity cubic meters (millions)
1.	Kariba	Zimbabwe/Zambia	180,600
2.	Bratsk	Russia	169,000
3.	High Aswan	Egypt	162,000
4.	Kpong	Ghana	150,000
5.	Akosombo (Lake Volta)	Ghana	150,000
6.	Daniel-Johnson	Canada	141,851
7.	W. A. C. Bennett	Canada	74,300
8.	Krasnoyarsk	Russia	73,300
9.	Zeya	Russia	68,400
10.	Lajeado	Brazil	64,530
11.	Robert-Bourassa (La Grande 2)	Canada	61,715
12.	La Grande 3	Canada	60,020
13.	Ust-Ilim	Russia	59,300
14.	*Boguchany	Russia	58,200
15.	Kuibyshev	Russia	58,000

World's Largest-Capacity Hydro Plants

Rank	Dam	Country	Rated capacity planned (MW)
1.	San Xia (Three Gorges Dam)	China	18,200
2.	Wangjiahe	China	12,630
3.	Xiluodu	China	12,600
4.	Itaipu	Brazil/Paraguay	12,600
5.	Guri	Venezuela	10,000
6.	Tucuruí	Brazil	8,370
7.	Grand Coulee	U.S.	6,809
8.	Sayano-Shushenskaya	Russia	6,400
9.	Qilinguan	China	6,400
10.	Krasnoyarsk	Russia	6,000
11.	Xiangjiaba	China	6,000
12.	Robert-Bourassa	Canada	5,616
13.	Longtan (Guangxi, Tian'e)	China	5,400
14.	Fengyan	China	5,200
15.	Bratsk	Russia	4,500

Timeline of Selected Architectural Styles and Structures
Asterisk (*) denotes part of a UNESCO World Heritage site.

Style and period	Location; characteristics; significant examples
Mesopotamian c. 3500-539 BCE	City-states of Sumer, Akkad, Babylon, Assyria (modern-day Iraq). Mud-brick rectangular temples on oval platforms with simple corbel vaults, later ziggurats. Painted terra-cotta mosaics and murals; carved reliefs on columns and walls. **Ziggurat of Nanna**, Ur (Muqayyar, Iraq), ordered by Ur-Nammu, c. 2100 BCE **Anu Ziggurat and White Temple**, Uruk (Warka, Iraq), c. 3000 BCE
Egyptian c. 3000-30 BCE	Along Nile R. Mud-brick and limestone tombs and massive, geometric pyramids, post-and-lintel construction. Highly decorative with colorful hieroglyphics, carvings, columns, obelisks, paintings, and sculpture. ***Stepped Pyramid of Pharaoh Zoser** (Saqqara), by Imhotep, c. 2737-2717 BCE ***Great Pyramid of Khufu** (Giza), c. 2250 BCE ***Great Temple of Amon-Ra** (Karnak), c. 1530-300 BCE ***Mortuary Temple of Queen Hatshepsut**, Deir el Bahari (Thebes), by Senenmut, c. 1479-1458 BCE
Three Dynasties c. 2100-221 BCE	China. Single-level mud-brick or mud-smeared timber structures on earthen platforms with thatched roofs. Later, bracketed wooden-framed structures with brick-tiled floors, roofs with overhanging eaves. **City of Erlitou** (Yanshi, China), c. 1900-1500 BCE
Minoan c. 1800-1450 BCE	Crete. Palaces, tombs in monumental style adapted from Mesopotamia and Egypt. Multilevel stone palaces with large central court, no fortifications. Walls made of doors (*polythyron*); stone porticoes and lintels; wooden ceilings and columns; beehive-shaped tombs (*tholi*). **Palace at Knossos** (Heraklion, Crete, Greece), c. 1700 BCE
Mycenaean c. 1600-1100 BCE	Greece. Adapted Minoan style, with large stone masonry, huge walls, and fortified citadels with complex palaces (*megaron*). ***Treasury of Atreus** (Mycenae, Greece), c. 1250 BCE
Olmec c. 1200-400 BCE	Mexico Gulf Coast. Many religious structures, including stone temple-pyramids centered in cities; also large stone sculptures and mosaic pavement with natural and animistic themes. **Great Pyramid** (La Venta, Mexico), c. 800-400 BCE
Mayan c. 900 BCE-900 CE	Central America. Religious structures with plaster-surfaced stone temple-pyramids with stairs containing tombs. Decorative animistic and geometric relief sculptures, lintels, and stone monuments with hieroglyphics. ***Pyramid of the Magician** (Uxmal, Mexico), c. 700-910 CE ***North Acropolis** (Tikal, Guatemala), c. 200 BCE

Style and period	Location; characteristics; significant examples
Greek c. 750-323 BCE	Greek peninsula, Asia Minor, North Africa, western Mediterranean. Religious, civic buildings in monumental style, inspired by Egypt, based on strict rules of form and human proportion; many ornamental details. Marble and limestone structures (including rectangular temples) with pediment, colonnaded porticoes in diverse regional styles, defined by orders of architecture like Ionic, Doric, Corinthian. Most early buildings with timber supports; solid stone in later temples. *Parthenon, Acropolis (Athens, Greece), by Ictinus and Callicrates, 447-436 BCE *Temple of Zeus (Olympia, Greece), by Libon of Elis, mid-5th cent. BCE Mausoleum of Halicarnassus (Bodrum, Turkey), by Pythis, c. 353 BCE (destroyed) *Temple of Apollo Epicurius (Bassae, Greece), by Ictinus, c. 420 BCE
Achaemenid c. 550-334 BCE	Persian Empire (Eastern Mediterranean to Indus R.). Palatial complexes influenced by cultures absorbed by the empire; limestone and mud-brick complexes on raised stone terraces with ornamental stairways, rectangular pillared audience halls with porticoes and corner towers; pleasure gardens (*bāgh*) as focal point of architecture. *Pasargadae (Iran), founded by Cyrus II, after 547 BCE *Persepolis (Iran), founded by Darius I, around 518 BCE
Roman c. 500 BCE-400 CE	Roman Empire. Civic and religious structures with grandiose limestone brick and concrete construction in systematic, practical layout. Adapted Greek orders in many structures, including circular temples and large covered halls (basilica), but emphasized movement with rounded arches and domes, geometric vaults. *Pantheon (Rome, Italy), ordered by Emperor Hadrian, 118-128 CE *Colosseum (Rome, Italy), ordered by Emperor Vespasian, 70-82 CE *Roman Forum (Rome, Italy), 500s BCE-608 CE
Qin and Han c. 221 BCE-220 CE	China. Massive public works, palaces, tombs, and planned cities; systematic layout and design determined by divination techniques (geomancy). Multistoried timber palace complexes with gardens, courtyards laid along a long hall with a south-north axis for weather; decorative roof with overhanging eaves. *The Great Wall (China), ordered by Qin Shi Huang, 220 BCE-c. 1600 CE *Mausoleum of the First Qin Emperor (Xianyang [Xi'an], China), c. 210 BCE
Sassanian 226-651 CE	Iran. Mud-brick, mortared rubble, and stone palaces on platforms. Tall, vaulted entry chambers with one open side (*iwans*). Three-aisled hall chambers covered with rudimentary barrel vaults. Parabolic domes abandoned for square courtyards in later Sassanian period. Palace of Ardashir I (Firuzabad, Iran), c. 224 Taq-i Kisra [Arch of Khosrau] (Ctesiphon, Iraq), c. 260 or c. 550
Byzantine 330-1453	Byzantine Empire, Italy, Russia. Religious structures with masonry construction based on Roman architecture, many salvaged pieces. Centralized cross-in-square layout, with large central dome supported by vaults. Highly decorative, with iconographic frescoes, glass mosaics. *Hagia Sophia (Istanbul, Turkey), by Anthemius and Isidorus, 532-37 *St. Mark's Basilica (Venice, Italy), ordered by Domenico Contarini, 1063-94
Sui and Tang 581-906	China. Includes influences from other cultures; geomancy used to enhance harmony and social status. Rectangular, multistory modular timber structures with interlinking corridors; single-eaved roofs with exposed beams. Daming Palace (Xi'an, China), 634 (destroyed) *Hall of the Great Buddha, Foguang Temple (Mount Wutai), ordered rebuilt by Xuan Zhong, 857
Early Islamic (Umayyad) 692-c. 1000	Syria, Middle East, North Africa, southern Spain. Mosques in adapted Sassanian style. Austere exteriors; simple columned halls with minarets and mihrabs (prayer niches), walled courtyards and gardens, onion domes. Highly decorative interiors with patterned marble, mosaics. Dome of the Rock [Qubbat al-Sakhra] (Jerusalem), ordered by Abd al-Malik, 692 *Great Mosque of Córdoba (Spain), ordered by Abd al-Rahman I, 784-86
Khmer c. 880-1200s	Indochina. Hindu or Buddhist temple complexes, including brick, later sandstone beehive-shaped shrines with arches atop terraced temple "mountains" symbolizing Mount Meru, Hindu and Buddhist center of the universe, where the gods dwell. Concentric layout of structures mimics the cosmos, relating religious narrative in carved reliefs. *Angkor Wat (Cambodia), ordered by Suryavarman II, 12th cent.
Romanesque (Norman) c. 900s-1100s	Western Europe. Churches and monasteries in localized Roman style; many reused material from Roman structures. Austere, heavy, simple masonry construction with thick walls, concealed buttresses, small windows, barrel arches, and vaults. Churches like Roman basilica with arched central nave, lower side aisles, apse, transept formed Latin cross. Monumental art and ornaments with Christian narrative throughout, especially on façade and portals. *Durham Cathedral (England, UK), ordered by Bishop William de Saint-Calais, 1093-1133 *Cathedral, Baptistery, and "Leaning" Tower (Pisa, Italy), by various architects, begun in 1063, tower not completed until 1372
Gothic c. 1100s-1500s	France, Europe. Cathedrals meant to inspire spirituality with design like Roman basilica: pointed arches and spires that reach toward heavens, skeletal masonry, revealed structure like flying buttresses, ribbed vaults to allow better lighting, large stained-glass windows. Abbey Church of Saint-Denis (France), ordered by Abbot Suger, 1136-47 *Cathedral of Notre-Dame (Paris, France), ordered by Bishop Maurice de Sully, 1163-1351 *Chartres Cathedral (France), 1194-1260 *Cologne Cathedral (Cologne, Germany), ordered by Archbishop Konrad von Hochstaden, 1248-1880 *St. Vitus Cathedral (Prague, Czech Republic), by Matthias of Arras, later Peter Parler, 1344-1929
Yüan and Ming 1279-1644	China. Mongol-influenced timber and some brick structures influenced by geomancy. Emphasized monumental mass in low-lying, sprawling structures with simple rectangular pavilions, great halls, elaborate wooden latticework, carved and painted details. *Forbidden City (Beijing, China), ordered by Emperor Yung Lo, 1406-20
Renaissance 1420s-1520s	Italy. The rebirth or rediscovery of ancient Roman design, grounded in a scholarly approach to architecture. Followed rules of proportion in perspective and symmetry, classical orders, and simple but perfected geometric forms; emphasis on human scale. *Pazzi Chapel (Florence, Italy), by Filippo Brunelleschi, 1429-61 *Palazzo Medici-Riccardi (Florence, Italy), by Michelozzo di Bartolomeo, 1444-60 *Tempietto San Pietro (Rome, Italy), by Donato Bramante, 1502-10 *Villa Almerico Capra "La Rotonda" (near Vicenza, Italy), by Andrea Palladio, later Vincenzo Scamozzi, 1566-1610

Style and period	Location; characteristics; significant examples
Mughal 1526-1858	India. Monumental palaces and mosques blending Hindu and Islamic architecture. Sandstone with marble inlay; highly decorative, with semiprecious stones, vegetal and Koranic motifs. Formulaic four-part pleasure gardens (*charbâgh*), exemplified by grounds of Taj Mahal. ***Humayun Tomb** (Delhi, India), by Sayyid Muhammad, 1562-72 ***Taj Mahal** (Agra, India), ordered by Emperor Shah Jahan, 1631-48
Baroque 1630s-1700s	Italy, later Western Europe. Elaborate and theatrical religious and civic structures, focused on dramatic overall effect. Complex geometric shapes and elaborate sculptures meant to be viewed from many angles. **St. Carlo alle Quattro Fontane** (Rome, Italy), by Francesco Borromini, 1638-41 ***Palace of Versailles** (Versailles, France), royal hunting lodge (built 1631-34) expanded under Louis XIV, 1661-1710 **Church of San Lorenzo** (Turin, Italy), by Guarino Guarini, 1666-79 **Church of St. John of Nepomuk "Asamkirche"** (Munich, Germany), by Cosmas Damian and Egid Quirin Asam, 1733-46
Rococo 1690s-1700s	Europe. Mostly interior, simplified but still fanciful Baroque designs; ornate with natural motifs, gold trim, light and creamy colors, asymmetrical designs, and unusual materials. ***Sanssouci Palace** (Potsdam, Germany), by Georg Wenzeslaus von Knobelsdorff, 1745-47
Neoclassicism 1750-1830	Europe, Americas. Civic, commercial, and religious structures; chaste, non-decorative designs in reaction to Baroque excess. Grounded in Enlightenment-era principles and simple, strict adherence to classic (Greek, Roman, Renaissance) forms and details. Palladian style in England, Federal style in U.S. **Chiswick House** (Chiswick, England, UK), by Richard Boyle, 1725-29 ***Monticello** (Charlottesville, VA), by Thomas Jefferson, 1768-1809
Neo-Gothic 1837-1900s	Britain and U.S. Civic, commercial, and religious structures utilizing Gothic forms in new commercial enterprises like railway stations and hotels. Traditional masonry façade disguised modern structural material like iron and glass. ***Westminster Palace** (London, England, UK), by Charles Barry and A.W.N. Pugin, 1840-47 **Hotel fronting St. Pancras Railway Station** (London, England, UK), by George Gilbert Scott, 1865-71
Arts and Crafts 1850s-1930s	England and U.S. Residential structures made of brick and other indigenous materials with pastoral and traditional elements like gabled roofs. Conceived as a reaction against homogenization of style following the Industrial Revolution. **Red House** (Bexley Heath, England, UK), by Philip Webb, 1859 **Tigbourne Court** (Surrey, England, UK), by Edwin Lutyens, 1898
Beaux-Arts 1870s-1930s	France, U.S. Grandiose, highly decorative style, using a mix of classical forms taught at the École des Beaux-Arts (School of Fine Arts) in Paris: columns, wall projections, elaborate rooftops, high-relief decoration. **Boston Public Library** (Boston, MA), by McKim, Mead, and White, 1888-95 **Grand Central Terminal** (New York, NY), Reed & Stem and Warren & Wetmore, 1903-13
Art Nouveau 1884-1905	Europe (esp. Brussels, Belgium, France). Civic and residential structures using industrial products like metal and glass to mimic natural forms; airy, fluid, and ornate. **Hôtel Tassel** (Brussels, Belgium), by Victor Horta, 1892-93 **Entrances to Métro (subway)** (Paris, France), by Hector Guimard, 1900
Prairie 1893-1917	U.S. Mostly residences, some civic buildings in adapted Arts and Crafts style. Inspired by American Midwest and small-town values. Frank Lloyd Wright most notable architect of the style. Buildings centered on chimney, with overhanging eaves and horizontal emphasis, long bands of windows. **Robie House** (Chicago, IL), by Frank Lloyd Wright, 1908-10 **National Farmer's Bank** (Owatonna, MN), by Louis Sullivan, 1906-08
Futurism 1913-14	Italy. Purely theoretical style that produced no actual structures. Emphasized concrete, glass, and steel construction; pure geometric forms and straight lines; and exposed structure and utilities. **La Citta Nuova** (sketches), by Antonio Sant'Elia, 1913
Constructivism 1914-20s	Russia, Europe. Public buildings based on socialist philosophies. Purely utilitarian industrial design, modern materials. **Rusakov Club** (Moscow, Russia), by Konstantin Melnikov, 1927-28
De Stijl 1917-31	Netherlands. Building and fixtures designed as a complete, sculpture-like piece of art; emphasis on primary colors, simple but asymmetrical geometry. Name is Dutch for "The Style." **Schröder House** (Utrecht, Netherlands), by Gerrit Thomas Rietveld, 1923-24
Bauhaus 1919-33	Weimar Republic Germany. Art and design school founded by Walter Gropius with philosophy that the machine is the modern medium. Concrete, glass, and steel construction that united industrial crafts and fine arts with simple geometric forms and colors. **Bauhaus** (Dessau, Germany), by Walter Gropius, 1925-26
International Style 1920s-70s	Asia, Europe, North America. Reinforced concrete and steel structures, mostly commercial buildings with some residences and civic structures. Post-and-slab construction meant walls no longer supported weight so façades could be continuous strip (ribbon) glass "curtain-walls" with modular interiors. Emphasis on simple forms; glass, marble, and stainless steel; minimal decoration. **Philadelphia Savings Fund Society Building** (Philadelphia, PA), by George Howe and William Lescaze, 1926-32 **Villa Savoye** (Poissy, France), by Le Corbusier, 1928-31 **Seagram Building** (New York, NY), by Ludwig Mies Van Der Rohe with Philip Johnson, 1954-58
Art Deco 1925-30s	Europe, U.S. Traditional, symmetric, elegant construction like Beaux-Arts whimsically mixed with modern styles like geometric forms and steel or chrome features. **Chrysler Building** (New York, NY), by William van Alen, 1928-30 **Empire State Building** (New York, NY), by Shreve, Lamb, & Harmon, 1930-31
Postmodernism 1970s-present	Asia, Europe, North America. Playful reaction against generic, mainstream "orthodox modern architecture," according to Robert Venturi. Token references to traditional architectural elements like pediments or gables on houses; aim to present, Venturi wrote, "old clichés in new settings." **Vanna Venturi House** (Philadelphia, PA), by Robert Venturi, 1962 **Public Service Building** (Portland, OR), by Michael Graves, 1980-83

World Population Growth

The global population in ancient times can only be very roughly estimated, but there were perhaps 50 mil people in the world in 1000 BCE. The United Nations (UN) Population Division estimates a figure of 300 mil for 1 CE. This diagram shows estimated population growth since then.

Although different sources may provide varying estimates, they agree that the world's population began growing more rapidly in the 18th and 19th centuries and increased at an even greater rate in the 20th century. According to the UN, the total population reached 1 bil in 1804; rose to 2 bil 123 years later, in 1927; to 3 bil 33 years after that, in 1960; to 4 bil in 1974; to 5 bil in 1987; and to 6 bil in 1999. Its projections indicate that the population will reach 8 bil in 2023-24.

The U.S. Census Bureau put the world population in mid-2013 at about 7.1 bil. It projects that the population will reach 8 bil by 2026.

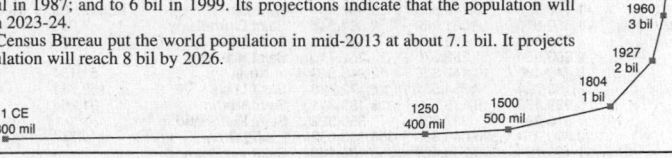

2011 7 bil
1999 6 bil
1987 5 bil
1974 4 bil
1960 3 bil
1927 2 bil
1804 1 bil
1 CE 300 mil
1250 400 mil
1500 500 mil

Area and Population of the World by Continent/Region

Source: International Data Base, International Programs Center, U.S. Census Bureau, U.S. Dept. of Commerce; *The World Factbook*, Central Intelligence Agency (CIA)

Composition of geographical (continental) regions are as defined by the United Nations. Land area figures are from *The World Factbook*. Figures may not add up to totals due to rounding.

Continent/ region	Land area (sq km)	Land area (sq mi)	% of Earth's land	Population (midyear) 1950	1975	2000	2013	% of world total, 2013	2025[1]
Asia..........	31,119,378	12,015,259	21.3	1,437,565,483	2,413,261,390	3,693,908,399	4,265,250,843	60.1	4,713,703,396
Africa........	29,771,296	11,494,762	20.4	229,058,740	416,194,561	803,586,680	1,099,180,700	15.5	1,429,328,419
Europe[2].......	22,168,368	8,559,255	15.2	547,140,324	678,635,710	730,597,984	740,793,786	10.4	742,526,332
N. America	20,407,482	7,879,373	14.0	165,945,185	238,783,486	313,388,332	351,369,733	5.0	389,046,607
Latin America[3]	20,104,280	7,762,306	13.8	165,442,794	320,629,690	517,908,376	602,352,158	8.5	668,600,120
Oceania	8,490,744	3,278,295	5.8	12,476,128	21,114,852	30,420,890	36,270,760	0.5	41,266,804
Antarctica[4]	14,000,000	5,405,430	9.6	NA	NA	NA	NA	NA	NA
World	**146,061,548**	**56,394,679**	**100.0**	**2,557,628,654**	**4,088,619,689**	**6,089,810,661**	**7,095,217,980**	**100.0**	**7,984,471,678**

NA = Not applicable. (1) Projected. (2) Includes all of Russia. (3) Includes the Caribbean. (4) Antarctica has no indigenous inhabitants, though people are present at permanent and seasonal research stations.

Current Population and Projections for Countries and Other Areas

Source: International Data Base, International Programs Center, U.S. Census Bureau, U.S. Dept. of Commerce; *The World Factbook*, Central Intelligence Agency (CIA)

(midyear figures)

Country/area	2013	2025	2050	Country/area	2013	2025	2050
Afghanistan	31,108,077	41,117,073	63,795,418	Cape Verde	531,046	619,168	741,842
Albania	3,011,405	3,104,932	2,824,012	Cayman Islands	53,737	67,661	91,118
Algeria	38,087,812	45,841,317	55,444,735	Central African			
American Samoa	54,719	53,316	49,308	Republic	5,166,510	6,637,613	10,338,863
Andorra	85,293	85,112	74,765	Chad	11,193,452	13,914,726	20,473,601
Angola	18,565,269	25,673,282	45,888,061	Chile	17,216,945	18,764,737	19,688,474
Anguilla	15,754	19,749	26,980	China[1]	1,349,585,838	1,394,638,699	1,303,723,332
Antigua and				Colombia	45,745,783	51,194,904	56,227,630
Barbuda	90,156	103,830	122,930	Comoros	752,288	905,545	1,169,893
Argentina	42,610,981	47,164,630	53,511,279	Congo, Dem. Rep. of	75,507,308	99,162,003	144,805,434
Armenia	2,974,184	3,044,164	2,943,441	Congo Republic	4,492,689	6,161,500	9,598,623
Aruba	109,153	126,130	150,730	Cook Islands	10,447	7,621	5,460
Australia	22,262,501	25,053,669	29,012,740	Costa Rica	4,695,942	5,353,218	6,065,989
Austria	8,221,646	8,189,560	7,520,950	Côte d'Ivoire	22,400,835	27,651,498	37,111,782
Azerbaijan	9,590,159	10,533,598	11,209,644	Croatia	4,475,611	4,374,007	3,864,201
Bahamas, The	319,031	349,116	371,219	Cuba	11,061,886	10,784,894	9,161,479
Bahrain	1,281,332	1,579,899	1,847,072	Curaçao	146,836	153,501	150,128
Bangladesh	163,654,860	197,673,655	250,155,274	Cyprus	1,155,403	1,329,908	1,392,078
Barbados	288,725	297,015	282,041	Czech Republic	10,162,921	9,844,275	8,540,221
Belarus	9,625,888	9,325,020	8,339,664	Denmark	5,556,452	5,697,913	5,575,147
Belgium	10,444,268	10,453,261	9,882,599	Djibouti	792,198	1,016,919	1,395,810
Belize	334,297	411,050	543,690	Dominica	73,286	74,374	64,772
Benin	9,877,292	13,564,964	22,118,545	Dominican Republic	10,219,630	11,702,846	13,690,264
Bermuda	69,467	72,851	69,874	Ecuador	15,439,429	17,867,616	21,102,550
Bhutan	725,296	820,143	951,873	Egypt	85,294,388	103,742,157	137,872,522
Bolivia	10,461,053	12,463,434	16,003,638	El Salvador	6,108,590	6,288,430	6,181,181
Bosnia and				Equatorial Guinea	704,001	935,553	1,428,139
Herzegovina	3,875,723	3,787,402	3,216,039	Eritrea	6,233,682	7,987,458	11,381,250
Botswana	2,127,825	2,425,114	2,871,345	Estonia	1,266,375	1,149,245	861,913
Brazil	201,009,622	218,259,140	232,304,177	Ethiopia	93,877,025	131,260,566	228,066,276
Brunei	415,717	498,756	638,157	Faroe Islands	49,709	53,200	57,112
Bulgaria	6,981,642	6,257,716	4,651,477	Fiji	896,758	956,003	1,013,636
Burkina Faso	17,812,961	25,384,628	47,429,509	Finland	5,266,114	5,251,272	4,819,615
Burundi	10,888,321	15,469,164	27,148,888	France	65,951,611	68,860,292	69,484,481
Cambodia	15,205,539	18,037,946	22,338,891	French Polynesia	277,293	305,484	324,712
Cameroon	20,549,221	25,522,447	34,908,839	Gabon	1,640,286	2,063,339	3,229,741
Canada	34,568,211	37,558,781	41,135,648	Gambia, The	1,883,051	2,369,298	3,210,223

Country/area	2013	2025	2050
Gaza Strip	1,763,387	2,350,255	3,392,849
Georgia	4,555,911	4,341,061	3,784,724
Germany	81,147,265	79,226,209	71,541,906
Ghana	25,199,609	32,610,058	52,415,526
Gibraltar	29,111	29,753	28,423
Greece	10,772,967	10,670,697	10,035,935
Greenland	57,714	57,174	49,356
Grenada	109,590	114,741	114,205
Guam	160,378	176,770	201,610
Guatemala	14,373,472	17,564,073	22,995,434
Guernsey	65,605	67,710	66,521
Guinea	11,176,026	15,240,839	26,407,254
Guinea-Bissau	1,660,870	2,061,262	2,894,545
Guyana	739,903	786,286	888,494
Haiti	9,893,934	11,252,370	13,352,710
Honduras	8,448,465	10,143,828	12,948,839
Hong Kong	7,182,724	7,354,531	6,172,725
Hungary	9,939,470	9,615,020	8,489,811
Iceland	315,281	337,632	350,922
India	1,220,800,359	1,396,046,308	1,656,553,632
Indonesia	251,160,124	276,746,433	300,183,166
Iran	79,853,900	90,481,226	100,044,564
Iraq	31,858,481	40,387,147	56,316,329
Ireland	4,775,982	5,417,947	6,333,836
Isle of Man	86,159	92,606	92,840
Israel	7,707,042	8,984,285	10,828,462
Italy	61,482,297	62,591,055	61,415,852
Jamaica	2,909,714	3,151,611	3,554,571
Japan	127,253,075	123,385,521	107,209,536
Jersey	95,732	104,140	107,581
Jordan	6,482,081	7,945,150	11,243,177
Kazakhstan	17,736,896	19,809,426	22,237,156
Kenya	44,037,656	53,196,255	70,755,460
Kiribati	103,248	117,779	139,738
Korea, North	24,720,407	26,242,210	26,969,396
Korea, South	48,955,203	49,372,307	43,368,983
Kosovo	1,847,708	1,999,461	2,222,619
Kuwait	2,695,316	3,169,497	3,863,453
Kyrgyzstan	5,548,042	6,218,713	7,063,351
Laos	6,695,166	7,971,675	10,068,995
Latvia	2,178,443	1,992,516	1,544,073
Lebanon	4,131,583	4,307,087	4,155,101
Lesotho	1,936,181	1,970,540	1,920,225
Liberia	3,989,703	5,283,774	8,192,118
Libya	6,002,347	7,374,566	8,970,664
Liechtenstein	37,009	40,505	43,610
Lithuania	3,515,858	3,355,985	2,787,516
Luxembourg	514,862	586,296	720,603
Macao	583,003	630,434	620,184
Macedonia	2,087,171	2,119,511	1,990,728
Madagascar	22,599,098	30,182,920	45,807,534
Malawi	16,777,547	22,859,677	37,406,745
Malaysia	29,628,392	34,683,300	42,928,546
Maldives	393,988	388,681	444,429
Mali	15,968,882	22,533,811	38,395,414
Malta	411,277	421,239	395,639
Marshall Islands	69,747	83,203	103,092
Mauritania	3,437,610	4,425,089	6,536,272
Mauritius	1,322,238	1,412,384	1,441,100
Mexico	116,220,947	130,198,692	147,907,650
Micronesia	106,104	98,948	74,483
Moldova	3,619,925	3,176,863	2,261,208
Monaco	30,500	31,706	29,810
Mongolia	3,226,516	3,725,352	4,340,496
Montenegro	653,474	635,537	577,654
Montserrat	5,189	5,529	5,707
Morocco	32,649,130	36,484,418	42,026,448
Mozambique	24,096,669	32,306,018	58,998,457
Myanmar (Burma)	55,167,330	61,747,758	70,673,160
Namibia	2,182,852	2,283,845	2,149,815
Nauru	9,434	10,008	11,995
Nepal	30,430,267	36,622,606	45,984,605
Netherlands	16,805,037	17,572,113	17,906,594
New Caledonia	264,022	307,452	370,511
New Zealand	4,365,113	4,775,930	5,198,992
Nicaragua	5,788,531	6,493,913	7,233,620
Niger	16,899,327	24,618,828	44,221,854
Nigeria	174,507,539	234,362,895	402,425,535
Northern Mariana Islands	51,170	61,985	77,842
Norway	4,722,701	4,916,787	4,966,385
Oman	3,154,134	3,981,057	5,401,957
Pakistan	193,238,868	228,385,138	290,847,790
Palau	21,108	22,102	22,894

Country/area	2013	2025	2050
Panama	3,559,408	4,117,882	4,859,334
Papua New Guinea	6,431,902	7,823,210	10,110,027
Paraguay	6,623,252	7,602,853	8,840,105
Peru	29,849,303	33,283,408	36,943,693
Philippines	105,720,644	128,921,424	171,964,187
Poland	38,383,809	37,349,696	32,084,570
Portugal	10,799,270	10,806,202	9,933,334
Puerto Rico	3,674,209	3,388,348	2,342,328
Qatar	2,042,444	2,562,764	2,558,854
Romania	21,790,479	20,872,127	18,060,354
Russia	142,500,482	140,139,049	129,908,086
Rwanda	12,012,589	16,080,729	27,506,207
Saint Barthélemy	7,298	7,056	6,527
Saint Helena	7,754	7,888	7,296
Saint Kitts and Nevis	51,134	55,405	56,362
Saint Lucia	162,781	168,519	162,356
Saint Martin	31,264	33,048	34,601
Saint Pierre and Miquelon	5,774	5,030	3,516
Saint Vincent and the Grenadines	103,220	100,409	93,507
Samoa	195,476	210,369	245,010
San Marino	32,448	35,203	35,178
São Tomé and Príncipe	186,817	227,395	309,457
Saudi Arabia	26,939,583	31,877,311	40,250,628
Senegal	13,300,410	17,580,816	27,244,158
Serbia	7,243,007	6,845,638	5,869,146
Seychelles	90,846	98,843	100,391
Sierra Leone	5,612,685	7,500,140	13,593,862
Singapore	5,460,302	6,732,999	8,609,518
Sint Maarten	39,689	46,560	53,001
Slovakia	5,488,339	5,458,581	4,943,616
Slovenia	1,992,690	1,907,560	1,596,947
Solomon Islands	597,248	747,001	1,015,731
Somalia	10,251,568	13,274,251	22,626,120
South Africa	48,601,098	48,714,478	49,400,628
South Sudan	11,090,104	16,615,122	26,843,710
Spain	47,370,542	51,415,437	52,490,640
Sri Lanka	21,675,648	23,563,343	25,166,733
Sudan	34,847,910	42,733,103	59,129,521
Suriname	566,846	636,782	717,936
Swaziland	1,403,362	1,585,439	1,834,151
Sweden	9,119,423	9,315,507	9,084,788
Switzerland	7,996,026	8,665,531	9,539,097
Syria	22,457,336	26,536,400	33,657,629
Taiwan	23,299,716	23,642,264	20,834,040
Tajikistan	7,910,041	9,510,130	12,132,365
Tanzania	48,261,942	66,904,889	118,586,412
Thailand	67,448,120	70,643,689	69,611,256
Timor-Leste	1,172,390	1,539,173	2,191,749
Togo	7,154,237	9,741,450	16,583,950
Tonga	106,322	104,648	78,995
Trinidad and Tobago	1,225,225	1,183,838	1,023,741
Tunisia	10,835,873	11,849,537	12,180,271
Turkey	80,694,485	90,498,016	100,955,188
Turkmenistan	5,113,040	5,800,391	6,607,083
Turks and Caicos Islands	47,754	61,293	84,240
Tuvalu	10,698	11,819	13,423
Uganda	34,758,809	50,692,201	93,476,229
Ukraine	44,573,205	41,037,583	33,573,842
United Arab Emirates	5,473,972	7,063,346	8,018,904
United Kingdom	63,395,574	67,243,723	71,153,797
United States	316,668,567	351,352,771	422,554,384
Uruguay	3,324,460	3,431,610	3,495,238
Uzbekistan	28,661,637	31,823,964	35,116,374
Vanuatu	261,565	323,464	432,658
Vatican City	839	NA	NA
Venezuela	28,459,085	33,188,608	40,255,592
Vietnam	92,477,857	102,458,828	111,173,583
Virgin Islands, British	31,912	41,324	59,618
Virgin Islands, U.S.	104,737	95,902	68,933
Wallis and Futuna	15,507	16,023	15,598
West Bank	2,676,740	3,328,248	4,376,251
Western Sahara	538,811	735,697	1,173,350
Yemen	25,408,288	32,650,107	45,780,651
Zambia	14,222,233	20,104,997	38,992,619
Zimbabwe	13,182,908	17,370,260	25,198,196
World[2]	7,095,217,980	7,984,471,678	9,383,147,855

NA = Not available. (1) Not including the populations of Hong Kong and Macao, listed separately in this table. (2) Total projected populations do not include countries for which projections were not available.

Population of the World's Largest Urban Areas

Source: *World Urbanization Prospects*, Dept. of Economic and Social Affairs, UN Population Division; International Data Base, International Programs Center, U.S. Census Bureau, U.S. Dept. of Commerce

Population figures are midyear estimates for urban agglomerations, i.e., whole metropolitan areas comprising an urban center and surrounding settlements of lower density. The UN releases an update every two years. Population counts for 2025 are projections. Data may differ from figures elsewhere in *The World Almanac*.

(ranked by mid-2011 population)

Rank	Urban area, country	Population (thous.)				Rate of change (%)			Pop. of urban area as % of country's 2011 pop.
		1975	2000	2011	2025	1975-2000	2000-11	2011-25	
1.	Tokyo, Japan	26,614.7	34,449.9	37,217.4	38,661.4	29.4%	8.0%	3.9%	29.2%
2.	Delhi, India.	4,426.0	15,732.3	22,653.6	32,935.0	255.5	44.0	45.4	1.9
3.	Mexico City, Mexico	10,689.7	18,021.6	20,445.8	24,580.9	68.6	13.5	20.2	18.0
4.	New York-Newark, NY-NJ, U.S.	15,880.3	17,845.9	20,351.7	23,572.2	12.4	14.0	15.8	6.5
5.	Shanghai, China	5,626.6	13,959.0	20,207.6	28,403.9	148.1	44.8	40.6	1.5
6.	São Paulo, Brazil	9,614.0	17,099.2	19,924.5	23,174.7	77.9	16.5	16.3	10.1
7.	Mumbai (Bombay), India	7,082.0	16,366.8	19,743.6	26,556.9	131.1	20.6	34.5	1.7
8.	Beijing, China	4,827.9	10,162.4	15,594.4	22,632.8	110.5	53.5	45.1	1.2
9.	Dhaka, Bangladesh	2,221.1	10,284.9	15,390.9	22,906.3	363.1	49.6	48.8	9.7
10.	Kolkata (Calcutta), India.	7,887.8	13,058.1	14,402.3	18,711.0	65.5	10.3	29.9	1.2
11.	Karachi, Pakistan.	3,989.2	10,031.1	13,876.3	20,190.3	151.5	38.3	45.5	7.4
12.	Buenos Aires, Argentina	8,744.6	11,847.0	13,527.8	15,524.2	35.5	14.2	14.8	32.4
13.	Los Angeles-Long Beach-Santa Ana, CA, U.S.	8,925.5	11,813.5	13,395.0	15,687.0	32.4	13.4	17.1	4.3
14.	Rio de Janeiro, Brazil.	7,557.4	10,802.8	11,959.7	13,621.3	42.9	10.7	13.9	6.1
15.	Manila, Philippines.	4,999.3	9,958.3	11,861.6	16,277.7	99.2	19.1	37.2	11.6

National Rankings by Population, Area, Population Density, 2013

Source: International Data Base, International Programs Center, U.S. Census Bureau, U.S. Dept. of Commerce; *The World Factbook*, Central Intelligence Agency (CIA)

Population figures are for midyear. The world had an estimated population of 7.1 bil in mid-2013. China was the most populous nation, with nearly one-fifth of the world total. A country's land area does not include inland water. Refer to the Nations chapter for a country's total area. Population density is calculated using land area.

Largest Populations

Rank	Country	Population
1.	China[1].	1,349,585,838
2.	India	1,220,800,359
3.	United States	316,668,567
4.	Indonesia	251,160,124
5.	Brazil.	201,009,622
6.	Pakistan	193,238,868
7.	Nigeria	174,507,539
8.	Bangladesh.	163,654,860
9.	Russia.	142,500,482
10.	Japan	127,253,075

Smallest Populations

Rank	Country	Population
1.	Vatican City.	839
2.	Nauru	9,434
3.	Tuvalu	10,698
4.	Palau	21,108
5.	Monaco.	30,500
6.	San Marino	32,448
7.	Liechtenstein	37,009
8.	Saint Kitts and Nevis.	51,134
9.	Marshall Islands	69,747
10.	Dominica.	73,286

Largest Land Areas

Rank	Country	Area (sq mi)	Area (sq km)
1.	Russia.	6,323,482	16,377,742
2.	China	3,694,959	9,569,901
3.	United States	3,531,905	9,147,593
4.	Canada.	3,511,023	9,093,507
5.	Brazil.	3,266,199	8,459,417
6.	Australia	2,966,153	7,682,300
7.	India	1,147,956	2,973,193
8.	Argentina	1,056,642	2,736,690
9.	Kazakhstan.	1,042,360	2,699,700
10.	Algeria	919,595	2,381,741

Smallest Land Areas

Rank	Country	Area (sq mi)	Area (sq km)
1.	Vatican City.	0.17	0.44
2.	Monaco.	0.77	2
3.	Nauru	8.1	21
4.	Tuvalu	10	26
5.	San Marino	24	61
6.	Liechtenstein	62	160
7.	Marshall Islands	70	181
8.	Saint Kitts and Nevis.	101	261
9.	Maldives	115	298
10.	Malta.	122	316

Most Densely Populated

Rank	Country	Persons per sq mi	Persons per sq km
1.	Monaco.	39,497.3	15,250.0
2.	Singapore	20,585.3	7,948.0
3.	Vatican City.	4,938.6	1,906.8
4.	Bahrain.	4,366.6	1,686.0
5.	Maldives	3,424.2	1,322.1
6.	Malta.	3,370.9	1,301.5
7.	Bangladesh.	3,256.3	1,257.3
8.	Taiwan	1,870.6	722.2
9.	Barbados	1,739.1	671.5
10.	Mauritius.	1,687.0	651.3

Most Sparsely Populated

Rank	Country	Persons per sq mi	Persons per sq km
1.	Mongolia.	5.4	2.1
2.	Namibia	6.9	2.7
3.	Australia	7.5	2.9
4.	Iceland	8.1	3.1
5.	Mauritania.	8.6	3.3
6.	Libya	8.8	3.4
7.	Suriname	9.4	3.6
8.	Botswana	9.7	3.8
9.	Guyana	9.7	3.8
10.	Canada.	9.8	3.8

(1) Does not include mid-2013 population of Hong Kong (7,182,724) and Macao (583,003).

Countries Ranked by Gross Domestic Product and Per Capita GDP, 2012

Source: *The World Factbook*, Central Intelligence Agency (CIA)

Estimates of gross domestic product (GDP)—the value of all final goods and services that a country produced in a year—were made based on purchasing power parity exchange rates. Per capita GDP is calculated using the estimated population size as of July 1 in a given year. Data may differ from estimates made by the U.S. Bureau of Economic Analysis. GDP figures are for 2012 unless otherwise noted.

GDP (in mil)				Per capita GDP			
Highest		**Lowest**		**Highest**		**Lowest**	
1. U.S.	$15,940,000	1. Tuvalu	$38	1. Qatar	$103,900	1. Congo, Dem. Rep. of	$400
2. China[1]	12,610,000	2. Nauru[2]	60	2. Liechtenstein[5]	89,400	2. Somalia[6]	600
3. India	4,761,000	3. Palau[3]	221	3. Luxembourg	81,100	Burundi	600
4. Japan	4,704,000	4. São Tomé and Príncipe	409	4. Monaco[3]	70,700	Zimbabwe	600
5. Germany	3,250,000	5. Marshall Islands	482	5. Singapore	61,400	5. Liberia	700
6. Russia	2,555,000	6. Kiribati	636	6. Norway	55,900	6. Niger	800
7. Brazil	2,394,000	7. Micronesia[4]	766	7. Brunei	55,300	Eritrea	800
8. UK	2,375,000	8. Tonga	801	8. U.S.	50,700	Central African Republic	800
9. France	2,291,000	9. Comoros	887	9. United Arab Emirates	49,800	9. Malawi	900
10. Italy	1,863,000	10. St. Kitts and Nevis	946	10. Switzerland	46,200	10. South Sudan	1,000
11. Mexico	1,788,000	11. Dominica	1,018	11. Canada	43,400	Madagascar	1,000
12. Korea, South	1,640,000	12. Samoa	1,146	12. Australia	43,300	12. Togo	1,100
13. Canada	1,513,000	13. Vanuatu	1,251	13. Austria	43,100	Mali	1,100
14. Spain	1,434,000	14. St. Vincent and the Grenadines	1,312	14. Netherlands	42,900	Guinea	1,100
15. Indonesia	1,237,000	15. San Marino	1,371	15. Ireland	42,600	Afghanistan	1,100
16. Turkey	1,142,000	16. Grenada	1,467	16. Sweden	41,900	16. Mozambique	1,200
17. Iran	1,016,000	17. Antigua and Barbuda	1,605	17. Kuwait	40,500	Ethiopia	1,200
18. Australia	986,700	18. Solomon Islands	1,922	18. Iceland	39,900	Guinea-Bissau	1,200
19. Saudi Arabia	921,700	19. Guinea-Bissau	1,963	19. Germany	39,700	19. Nepal	1,300
20. Taiwan	918,300	20. Cape Verde	2,214	20. Taiwan	39,400	Haiti	1,300
						Comoros	1,300

(1) Does not include Hong Kong, which had an estimated GDP of $375.5 bil in 2012, or Macao, with an estimated GDP of $47.2 bil in 2011. (2) 2005 est. (3) 2011 est. (4) Supplemented by grant aid, averaging perhaps $100 mil annually. (5) 2009 est. (6) 2010 est.

Gold Reserves of Selected Central Banks and Governments, 1975-2012

Source: *International Financial Statistics*, International Monetary Fund (IMF)

(in mil fine troy ounces)

Year end	All countries	Canada	China[1]	France	Germany[2]	India	Italy	Japan	Nether- lands	Russia	Switzer- land	UK	U.S.
1975	1,188.0	22.0	NA	100.9	117.6	7.0	82.5	21.1	54.3	NA	83.2	21.0	274.7
1980	1,152.2	21.0	12.8	81.9	95.2	8.6	66.7	24.2	43.9	NA	83.3	18.8	264.3
1985	1,147.4	20.1	12.7	81.9	95.2	9.4	66.7	24.2	43.9	NA	83.3	19.0	262.7
1990	1,144.2	14.8	12.7	81.9	95.2	10.7	66.7	24.2	43.9	NA	83.3	18.9	261.9
1995	1,114.4	3.4	12.7	81.9	95.2	12.8	66.7	24.2	34.8	9.4	83.3	18.4	261.7
2000	1,066.0	1.2	12.7	97.2	111.5	11.5	78.8	24.5	29.3	12.4	77.8	15.7	261.6
2002	1,045.2	0.6	19.3	97.2	110.8	11.5	78.8	24.6	27.4	12.5	61.6	10.1	262.0
2003	1,027.4	0.1	19.3	97.2	110.6	11.5	78.8	24.6	25.0	12.5	52.5	10.1	261.5
2004	1,010.7	0.1	19.3	96.0	110.4	11.5	78.8	24.6	25.0	12.4	43.5	10.0	261.6
2005	991.4	0.1	19.3	90.9	110.2	11.5	78.8	24.6	22.3	12.4	41.5	10.0	261.6
2006	979.6	0.1	19.3	87.4	110.0	11.5	78.8	24.6	20.6	12.9	41.5	10.0	261.5
2007	963.3	0.1	19.3	83.7	109.9	11.5	78.8	24.6	20.0	14.5	36.8	10.0	261.5
2008	963.9	0.1	19.3	80.1	109.7	11.5	78.8	24.6	19.7	16.7	33.4	10.0	261.5
2009	981.2	0.1	33.9	78.3	109.5	17.9	78.8	24.6	19.7	20.9	33.4	10.0	261.5
2010	992.0	0.1	33.9	78.3	109.3	17.9	78.8	24.6	19.7	25.4	33.4	10.0	261.5
2011	1,003.8	0.1	33.9	78.3	109.2	17.9	78.8	24.6	19.7	28.4	33.4	10.0	261.5
2012	1,019.4	0.1	33.9	78.3	109.0	17.9	78.8	24.6	19.7	30.8	33.4	10.0	261.5

NA = Not available. (1) Figures are for mainland China only and do not include Hong Kong (0.07 mil oz t in 2012) or Macao. (2) West Germany prior to 1991.

Consumer Price Changes in Selected Countries, 1975-2012

Source: International Monetary Fund (IMF); World Development Indicators, The World Bank

(annual average % change)

Country	1975-80	1980-85	1995-96	1997-98	1998-99	1999-2000	2000-01	2004-05	2006-07	2008-09	2009-10	2010-11	2011-12
Canada	8.7%	7.5%	1.6%	1.0%	1.7%	2.7%	2.5%	2.2%	2.1%	0.3%	1.8%	2.9%	1.5%
China[1]	NA	NA	8.3	−0.8	−1.4	0.3	0.7	1.8	4.8	−0.7	3.3	5.4	2.7
France	10.5	9.7	2.0	0.6	0.5	1.7	1.6	1.7	1.5	0.1	1.5	2.1	2.0
Germany	NA	NA	1.4	0.9	0.6	1.5	2.0	1.5	2.3	0.3	1.1	2.1	2.0
Italy	16.4	13.8	4.0	2.0	1.7	2.5	2.8	2.0	1.8	0.8	1.5	2.7	3.0
Japan	6.6	2.8	0.1	0.7	−0.3	−0.7	−0.8	−0.3	0.1	−1.3	−0.7	−0.3	−0.03
Spain	18.6	12.2	3.6	1.8	2.3	3.4	3.6	3.4	2.8	−0.3	1.8	3.2	2.4
Sweden	10.5	9.0	0.5	−0.1	0.5	1.0	2.4	0.5	2.2	−0.5	1.2	3.0	0.9
Switzerland	2.3	4.3	0.8	0.02	0.8	1.5	1.0	1.2	0.7	−0.5	0.7	0.2	−0.7
United Kingdom	NA	NA	2.5	1.6	1.3	0.8	1.2	2.0	2.3	2.2	3.3	4.5	2.8
United States	8.9	5.5	2.9	1.6	2.2	3.4	2.8	3.4	2.9	−0.4	1.6	3.2	2.1

NA = Not available. (1) Figures are for mainland China only and do not include Hong Kong (4.1% in 2011-12) or Macao (6.1% in 2011-12).

Hourly Compensation Costs in Manufacturing in Selected Countries, 1996-2012

Source: International Labor Comparisons Program, U.S. Bureau of Labor Statistics, U.S. Dept. of Labor

For all workers in manufacturing, including part-time and temporary employees. Compensation costs include direct pay (pay for time worked and directly-paid benefits), social insurance expenditures, and labor-related taxes.

(in U.S. dollars)

Country	1996	2000	2003	2006	2009	2012	Country	1996	2000	2003	2006	2009	2012
Argentina	7.43	8.16	3.65	6.63	10.23	18.87	Korea, South	9.54	9.62	11.33	17.37	15.06	20.72
Australia	19.17	16.45	22.65	29.17	33.42	47.68	Mexico	3.05	4.70	5.31	5.88	5.70	6.36
Austria	28.12	21.97	28.38	33.63	42.62	41.53	Netherlands	NA	21.04	29.66	34.37	41.39	39.62
Belgium	32.71	26.14	35.01	42.49	52.27	52.19	New Zealand	12.11	9.00	12.62	15.75	17.47	24.77
Brazil	7.11	4.35	3.23	5.99	8.13	11.20	Norway	NA	24.50	35.59	44.57	53.39	63.36
Canada	18.62	18.33	21.08	28.58	29.40	36.59	Philippines	1.36	1.00	1.03	1.35	1.71	2.10
Czech Republic	3.38	3.40	5.65	8.16	11.42	11.95	Poland	NA	3.41	4.40	6.18	7.72	8.25
Denmark	NA	22.21	31.70	38.23	48.60	48.47	Portugal	7.13	5.94	8.19	9.96	12.34	12.10
Estonia	NA	2.55	4.11	6.53	10.03	10.41	Singapore	11.93	11.71	12.74	13.77	17.54	24.16
Finland	25.01	19.87	28.12	35.19	44.25	42.60	Slovakia	2.73	2.60	4.38	6.56	11.24	11.30
France	27.82	21.37	28.46	33.85	40.37	39.81	Spain	15.48	12.40	17.42	21.80	27.86	26.83
Germany	33.22	25.41	34.00	39.37	45.76	45.79	Sweden	27.15	23.40	31.01	36.55	40.92	49.80
Greece	12.61	9.94	13.72	16.60	22.72	19.41	Switzerland	35.52	26.92	36.79	40.91	50.54	57.79
Hungary	3.11	2.96	5.19	6.85	8.62	8.95	Taiwan	7.10	7.30	6.97	8.05	7.77	9.46
Ireland	16.87	15.76	23.64	30.41	41.21	38.17	United Kingdom	17.78	20.67	25.15	31.23	29.47	31.23
Israel	10.90	12.25	12.47	13.86	17.55	20.14	United States	22.47	24.96	28.57	30.48	34.19	35.67
Italy	21.00	16.64	23.42	28.53	34.32	34.18	OECD countries[1]	NA	16.57	19.92	24.36	27.18	30.53
Japan	23.67	25.02	23.41	24.03	30.03	35.34							

NA = Not available. **Note:** China and India are not shown here because data for those countries are not comparable. (1) The Organisation for Economic Co-operation and Development (OECD) includes Australia, Canada, Israel, Japan, South Korea, Mexico, New Zealand, U.S., and all European countries covered in this table.

Unemployment Rates in Selected Countries, 1970-2012

Source: International Labor Comparisons Program, U.S. Bureau of Labor Statistics, U.S. Dept. of Labor

Year	U.S.	Australia	Canada	France	Germany[1]	Italy	Japan	Netherlands	Spain	Sweden	UK
1970	4.9%	1.7%	5.7%	2.5%	0.5%	3.2%	1.2%	NA	NA	1.5%	NA
1975	8.5	4.9	6.9	3.6	3.4	3.4	1.9	5.1%	NA	1.6	4.5%
1980	7.1	6.1	7.3	5.6	2.8	4.4	2.0	6.0	11.3%	2.0	6.8
1985	7.2	8.3	10.1	9.0	7.2	6.0	2.5	9.6	20.7	2.8	11.4
1990	5.6	6.9	7.7	8.0	5.0	7.0	2.0	7.6	15.2	1.8	7.1
1995	5.6	8.5	8.6	10.2	8.2	11.3	2.9	7.1	20.9	9.1	8.7
1997	4.9	8.5	8.4	10.8	9.9	11.3	3.1	5.6	18.5	10.1	7.0
1999	4.2	6.9	7.0	10.1	8.5	11.0	4.2	3.5	13.7	7.1	6.0
2000	4.0	6.3	6.1	8.6	7.8	10.1	4.4	3.1	12.0	5.8	5.5
2001	4.7	6.8	6.5	7.8	7.9	9.1	4.5	2.5	10.6	5.0	5.1
2002	5.8	6.4	7.0	8.0	8.6	8.6	4.9	3.0	11.5	5.1	5.2
2003	6.0	5.9	6.9	8.6	9.3	8.5	4.6	4.1	11.5	5.8	5.0
2004	5.5	5.4	6.4	9.0	10.3	8.1	4.2	5.0	11.0	6.6	4.8
2005	5.1	5.0	6.0	9.0	11.2	7.8	3.8	5.2	9.2	7.7	4.9
2006	4.6	4.8	5.5	8.9	10.3	6.9	3.6	4.3	8.6	7.0	5.5
2007	4.6	4.4	5.2	8.1	8.7	6.2	3.6	3.5	8.3	6.1	5.4
2008	5.8	4.2	5.3	7.5	7.6	6.8	3.7	3.0	11.4	6.1	5.7
2009	9.3	5.6	7.3	9.2	7.8	7.9	4.8	3.7	18.1	8.3	7.6
2010	9.6	5.2	7.1	9.4	7.1	8.5	4.7	4.5	20.2	8.5	7.9
2011	8.9	5.1	6.5	9.3	5.9	8.5	4.2	4.5	21.8	7.7	8.1
2012	8.1	5.2	6.3	10.0	5.5	10.8	3.9	5.3	25.2	7.9	8.0

NA = Not available. **Note:** Unemployment rates are for the civilian working-age population. Data from other countries have been adjusted to U.S. concepts so that comparisons can be made. Because of changes in survey methodology, some data may not be fully comparable over time. (1) For former West Germany only through 1990; data after 1991 are for unified Germany.

Personal Tax Payments in Selected Countries, 2012

Source: *Taxing Wages*, Organisation for Economic Co-operation and Development (OECD)

Rates are averages for a single person without children at an average earnings level.

(as % of gross wage earnings before taxes, in U.S. dollars with equal purchasing power; ranked by total payment rate)

Country	Total payment rate[1]	Income tax	Employee soc. sec. contribs.	Gross earnings	Country	Total payment rate[1]	Income tax	Employee soc. sec. contribs.	Gross earnings
Belgium	42.8%	28.8%	14.0%	$53,047	Poland	24.6%	6.8%	17.8%	$20,591
Germany	39.9	19.2	20.7	56,058	Spain	23.9	17.5	6.4	36,162
Denmark	38.9	36.2	2.7	49,887	Australia	22.9	22.9	0.0	48,199
Hungary	35.0	16.5	18.5	20,875	Czech Republic	22.8	11.8	11.0	21,793
Austria	34.0	15.9	18.1	48,187	Slovakia	22.8	9.4	13.4	18,511
Slovenia	33.1	11.0	22.1	26,793	United States	22.7	17.1	5.7	47,650
Netherlands	31.9	16.5	15.4	55,640	Canada	22.6	15.2	7.3	38,291
Italy	30.8	21.3	9.5	36,563	Portugal	21.7	10.7	11.0	25,341
Iceland	29.4	28.9	0.5	42,761	Japan	21.2	7.5	13.7	46,086
Finland	29.4	21.8	7.6	44,148	Estonia	19.9	17.1	2.8	19,866
Norway	29.4	21.6	7.8	55,350	Ireland	18.0	14.8	3.2	39,042
France	28.3	14.6	13.7	42,494	Switzerland	16.5	10.3	6.3	61,048
Turkey	27.9	12.9	15.0	25,395	New Zealand	16.4	16.4	0.0	33,528
Luxembourg	27.9	15.5	12.3	54,211	Israel	15.5	7.9	7.6	29,531
Greece	25.4	8.9	16.5	28,846	Korea	13.0	4.8	8.1	47,242
United Kingdom	24.9	15.5	9.5	52,720	Mexico	9.5	8.1	1.4	11,262
Sweden	24.9	17.9	7.0	43,685	Chile	7.0	0.0	7.0	15,666
					Total OECD	25.1	15.3	9.8	38,131

(1) Figures may not add up to totals due to rounding.

Refugees and People in a Refugee-Like Situation, 2012

Source: *UNHCR Global Trends*, United Nations High Commissioner for Refugees (UNHCR)

Refugees are persons who are recognized under the 1951 UN Convention Relating to the Status of Refugees, its 1967 Protocol, or the 1969 OAU (Org. of African Unity) Refugee Convention; those recognized in accordance with the UNHCR Statute; and persons granted or receiving protection. Persons outside of their country or territory of origin who face protection risks—but whose refugee status has not been ascertained—are described as being in a refugee-like situation.

Only countries hosting 50,000 or more refugees and people in a refugee-like situation are shown. Only places originating 5,000 or more refugees and people in a refugee-like situation are shown, in decreasing order. As of year-end.

Place of asylum	Origin of most refugees (excl. asylum seekers with pending cases)	Number
Africa		**2,774,471**
Cameroon	Central African Republic	98,969
Chad	Sudan, Central African Republic	373,695
Congo, Dem. Rep. of	Rwanda, Burundi	65,109
Congo Republic	Dem. Rep. of the Congo, Rwanda	98,455
Ethiopia	Somalia, Eritrea, South Sudan, Sudan	376,393
Kenya	Somalia, Ethiopia, South Sudan, Dem. Rep. of the Congo	564,933
Liberia	Côte d'Ivoire	65,909
Mauritania	Mali, Western Sahara	80,496
Niger	Mali	50,510
Rwanda	Dem. Rep. of the Congo	58,212
South Africa	Somalia, Dem. Rep. of the Congo, Angola, Ethiopia	65,233
South Sudan	Sudan, Dem. Rep. of the Congo, Ethiopia	202,581
Sudan	Eritrea, Chad	152,194
Tanzania	Dem. Rep. of the Congo, Burundi	101,021
Uganda	Dem. Rep. of the Congo, Somalia, Rwanda, South Sudan, Burundi, Sudan	197,877
Americas		**806,550**
Canada	Colombia, China, Sri Lanka, Pakistan, Haiti, Mexico, India	163,756
Ecuador	Colombia	123,824
United States	China, Haiti, Colombia, Ethiopia, Venezuela, Russia, Cameroon, Egypt, El Salvador, Guatemala, Nepal, India	262,030
Venezuela	Colombia	203,644
Asia and Pacific		**3,525,512**
Bangladesh	Myanmar (Burma)	230,697
China (incl. HK, Macao)	Vietnam	301,154
India	China, Sri Lanka, Afghanistan, Myanmar (Burma)	185,656
Malaysia	Myanmar (Burma)	90,185
Nepal	Bhutan, Tibetan	56,264
Pakistan	Afghanistan	1,638,456
Thailand	Myanmar (Burma)	84,479
Europe		**1,799,851**
Austria	Russia, Afghanistan	51,730
France	Sri Lanka, Cambodia, Dem. Rep. of the Congo, Russia, Serbia-Kosovo, Turkey, Vietnam, Laos	217,865
Germany	Serbia-Kosovo, Turkey, Iraq, Russia, Afghanistan, Vietnam, Bosnia and Herzegovina, Iran, Ukraine, Syria, Lebanon, Sri Lanka, Pakistan, Azerbaijan, Macedonia, stateless[1], Dem. Rep. of the Congo	589,737
Italy	Eritrea, Somalia, Afghanistan	64,779
Netherlands	Iraq, Somalia, Afghanistan	74,598
Serbia-Kosovo	Croatia, Bosnia and Herzegovina	66,370
Sweden	Iraq, Somalia, Afghanistan, Eritrea, Syria	92,872
Switzerland	Eritrea	50,747
United Kingdom	Somalia, Zimbabwe, Iran, Eritrea, Afghanistan, Iraq	149,765
Middle East and North Africa		**1,593,857**
Algeria	Western Sahara	94,133
Egypt	Palestinian[2], Syria, Sudan, Somalia, Iraq	109,933
Iran	Afghanistan, Iraq	868,242
Iraq	Syria, Turkey, Palestinian[2]	98,822
Jordan	Syria, Iraq	302,707
Lebanon	Syria, Iraq	133,940
Syria	Iraq	476,506
Turkey	Syria, Iraq	267,063
Yemen	Somalia, Ethiopia	237,182
TOTAL		**10,500,241**

(1) Persons not considered nationals by any state under the operation of its laws. (2) Palestinians under the UNHCR mandate only.

Internally Displaced Persons, 2012

Source: Internal Displacement Monitoring Centre, Norwegian Refugee Council

Internally displaced persons (IDPs) are people who have been forced to flee due to armed conflict or human rights violations but who have not crossed into another country. As such, they are not protected by international refugee law and legally remain under the protection of their home country. Estimates are latest available and may comprise only registered IDPs or those displaced from a certain area of a country.

Country	Number	Country	Number	Country	Number
Afghanistan	493,000+	Haiti	360,000+	Philippines	15,746+
Armenia	<8,400	India	540,000+	Russia	8,500+
Azerbaijan	<600,000	Indonesia	<170,000	Senegal	10,000-40,000
Bosnia and Herzegovina	113,000	Iraq	<2.1 mil	Serbia	225,000
Burundi	78,800	Kenya	300,000	Somalia	1.1 mil
Central African Republic	206,000	Kosovo	17,900	South Sudan	360,000+
Chad	90,000	Kyrgyzstan	67,000	Sri Lanka	93,000+
Colombia[1]	4.9 mil-5.5 mil	Lebanon	44,600+	Sudan	2.5 mil+
Congo, Dem. Rep. of	2.6 mil	Libya	50,000	Syria	4.3 mil+
Congo	<7,800	Mali	353,400	Turkey	954,000-1.2 mil
Côte d'Ivoire	40,000-80,000	Myanmar (Burma)	450,000+	Uganda	30,000
Cyprus	<208,000	Pakistan	758,000+	Uzbekistan	3,400
Eritrea	<10,000	Palestine[2]	144,500	Yemen	299,087
Georgia	<274,000	Peru	150,000	**Total**	**26.4 mil**

Note: The number of IDPs in the following countries was undetermined: Algeria, Angola, Bangladesh, Ethiopia, Guatemala, Israel, Laos, Liberia, Macedonia, Mexico, Nepal, Niger, Nigeria, Rwanda, Thailand, Timor-Leste, Togo, Turkmenistan, and Zimbabwe. (1) Low end of range cumulative since 2000; high end since 1985. (2) Occupied Palestinian Territory.

Estimated HIV Infection and Reported AIDS Cases, 2011

Source: Joint United Nations Programme on HIV/AIDS (UNAIDS)

In 2011, about 2.5 mil people were newly infected with HIV, a lower number than in previous years. Changes in behavior among young adults, intravenous drug users, and other at-risk populations have contributed to that decline, as has increased access to HIV prevention services. About 34 mil people worldwide—more than ever before—were living with HIV/AIDS in 2011. Of those, 69% lived in sub-Saharan Africa. Fifty-four percent of all who were eligible for antiretroviral therapy received it. The number of AIDS-related deaths fell in 2011, to 1.7 mil. Tuberculosis remained the leading cause of death among those living with HIV/AIDS.

Worldwide in 2011, $16.8 bil was spent on the HIV/AIDS epidemic. UNAIDS estimates that between $22 bil and $24 bil would be needed yearly if it is to meet targets it has set for 2015, including the elimination of new infections in children. As of 2012, 45 countries and territories still restricted the right of those living with HIV/AIDS to enter or stay.

Current and New HIV/AIDS Cases and Deaths by Region, 2011

Region	Number living with HIV/AIDS	Percent of world total[1]	New HIV infections	AIDS-related deaths
Sub-Saharan Africa	23,500,000	69.1%	1,800,000	1,200,000
South and South-East Asia	4,000,000	11.8	280,000	250,000
Eastern Europe and Central Asia	1,400,000	4.1	140,000	92,000
Latin America	1,400,000	4.1	83,000	54,000
North America	1,400,000	4.1	51,000	21,000
Western and Central Europe	900,000	2.6	30,000	7,000
East Asia	830,000	2.4	89,000	59,000
Middle East and North Africa	300,000	0.9	37,000	23,000
Caribbean	230,000	0.7	13,000	10,000
Oceania	53,000	0.2	2,900	1,300
World[2]	34,000,000	100.0	2,500,000	1,700,000

(1) Population within a region living with HIV/AIDS as a percentage of population worldwide living with HIV/AIDS. (2) Figures may not add up to totals because of rounding.

Infectious Disease, Sanitation, and Water Quality

Source: *Global Burden of Disease* and *World Health Statistics* publications, World Health Organization (WHO); United Nations Children's Fund (UNICEF)

By year-end 2011, 89% of the world's population had access to improved drinking-water sources, although the service and water quality could be inconsistent. Meanwhile, the UN's Millennium Development Goal (MDG) for access to improved sanitation has yet to be reached. As of the end of 2011, only 64% of all people worldwide could rely on improved sanitation facilities. The population in unserved areas, the majority of which are rural, are at increased risk of contracting a variety of infectious and parasitic diseases such as diarrhea, malaria, and hepatitis A.

Listed below are nations with the highest death rates from infectious and parasitic diseases in 2008 and the lowest access to improved sanitation and water in 2011. Rankings and death rates for G8 countries and China are included for comparison. With the exception of China and Russia, these nations have near-universal (99% or greater) access to improved sanitation and water. In 2011, 65% of China's population had access to improved sanitation, and 92% had access to improved drinking-water sources. In Russia, the figures were 70% and 97%, respectively.

Deaths From Infectious and Parasitic Diseases, 2008

(per 100,000 population; ranked by deaths from infectious and parasitic diseases)

Rank	Country	Infectious and parasitic diseases	Tuberculosis	Diarrheal diseases	All causes
1.	Zimbabwe	931.4	50.6	36.3	1,467.5
2.	Lesotho	793.3	29.4	41.7	1,558.8
3.	Chad	787.3	66.8	210.9	1,716.9
4.	Swaziland	770.4	32.5	48.6	1,504.4
5.	Central African Republic	754.9	46.2	113.5	1,670.5
6.	Sierra Leone	733.7	128.5	156.0	1,502.3
7.	South Africa	727.6	39.3	71.6	1,344.7
8.	Malawi	719.3	23.7	101.5	1,626.7
9.	Mozambique	697.0	39.5	82.2	1,558.7
10.	Congo, Dem. Rep. of	687.4	78.8	187.5	1,606.8
91.	Russia	53.3	18.0	0.3	1,473.7
123.	China	23.4	11.8	1.4	715.7
124.	United States	22.9	0.2	2.3	817.5
130.	Japan	20.8	3.1	1.8	892.5
136.	France	18.8	1.1	2.2	841.8
144.	Germany	16.0	0.5	1.7	1,009.1
149.	Italy	14.0	0.7	0.3	975.7
151.	United Kingdom	13.4	0.7	5.0	960.2
154.	Canada	12.8	0.3	3.2	704.3

Lowest Access to Improved Sanitation Facilities, 2011

Sanitation facilities are considered improved if they are private and not shared with other households, incl. sewer or septic system connections, ventilated improved pit latrines, and composting toilets.

Rank	Country	% of pop. with access
1.	South Sudan	9%
2.	Niger	10
3.	Togo	11
4.	Chad	12
	Tanzania	12
6.	Ghana	13
	Sierra Leone	13
8.	Benin	14
	Madagascar	14
10.	Guinea	18
	Liberia	18
	Burkina Faso	18
	Congo Republic	18
	World	64

Lowest Access to Improved Drinking-Water Sources, 2011

Improved drinking-water sources protect from outside contamination and incl. household connections, public taps or standpipes, dug wells, and rainwater collection.

Rank	Country	% of pop. with access
1.	Somalia	30%
2.	Papua New Guinea	40
3.	Congo, Dem. Rep. of	46
4.	Mozambique	47
5.	Madagascar	48
6.	Ethiopia	49
7.	Mauritania	50
	Chad	50
	Niger	50
10.	Tanzania	53
	World	89

Foreign Development Aid Donors, 2011-12

Source: Development Assistance Committee (DAC), Organisation for Economic Co-operation and Development (OECD)
Listed below is the amount of official development assistance (ODA)—in the form of grants or loans—each DAC member country disbursed in a given year to developing countries. The numbers are net disbursements, or amounts disbursed less repayments on earlier loans. Both bilateral ODA (made directly to an aid recipient) and multilateral ODA (made to an agency like the World Bank) are included.
(ranked by size of ODA as % of 2012 gross national income; 2012 figures are prelim.)

Rank	Donor	ODA as % of GNI 2012	ODA as % of GNI 2011	ODA in mil of current U.S. dollars 2012	ODA in mil of current U.S. dollars 2011	Rank	Donor	ODA as % of GNI 2012	ODA as % of GNI 2011	ODA in mil of current U.S. dollars 2012	ODA in mil of current U.S. dollars 2011
1.	Luxembourg . . .	1.00%	0.97%	$432.14	$409.24	16.	New Zealand . .	0.28%	0.28%	$455.41	$424.15
2.	Sweden.	0.99	1.02	5,242.02	5,603.12	17.	Portugal	0.27	0.31	567.17	707.82
3.	Norway.	0.93	0.96	4,754.15	4,755.59	18.	Iceland	0.22	0.21	25.99	25.57
4.	Denmark.	0.84	0.85	2,718.29	2,931.13	19.	United States . .	0.19	0.20	30,460.37	30,782.77
5.	Netherlands . . .	0.71	0.75	5,523.87	6,343.96	20.	Japan	0.17	0.18	10,493.53	10,831.40
6.	UK.	0.56	0.56	13,659.41	13,832.36	21.	Spain	0.15	0.29	1,947.98	4,173.11
7.	Finland	0.53	0.53	1,319.64	1,406.04	22.	Korea, South. . .	0.14	0.12	1,550.92	1,324.59
8.	Ireland.	0.48	0.51	809.09	913.56	23.	Greece	0.13	0.15	323.93	424.77
9.	Belgium.	0.47	0.54	2,303.47	2,807.41	24.	Italy	0.13	0.20	2,639.23	4,325.97
10.	Switzerland. . . .	0.45	0.45	3,021.93	3,050.87		Total DAC.	0.29	0.31	125,586.48	133,716.45
11.	France.	0.45	0.46	12,000.00	12,997.24		Average country				
12.	Germany.	0.38	0.39	13,108.17	14,092.94		effort	0.43	0.47		
13.	Australia	0.36	0.34	5,439.77	4,982.91		G7 countries[1]	0.26	0.27	88,038.31	92,321.24
14.	Canada	0.32	0.32	5,677.60	5,458.56		EU institutions	NA	NA	17,570.08	17,390.53
15.	Austria	0.28	0.27	1,112.40	1,111.37						

NA = Not applicable/available. (1) Canada, France, Germany, Italy, Japan, the UK, and the U.S.

Recipients of U.S. Official Development Assistance, 2010-11

Source: Development Assistance Committee (DAC), Organisation for Economic Co-operation and Development (OECD)
(net disbursements of total ODA in mil of current U.S. dollars; ranked by 2011 numbers)

Rank	Country	2011	2010	Rank	Country	2011	2010
1.	Afghanistan.	$2,901.22	$2,893.40	11.	Tanzania	$535.18	$457.41
2.	Congo, Dem. Rep. of.	1,293.20	277.85	12.	Colombia	500.64	423.98
3.	Pakistan	1,273.85	1,196.76	13.	Jordan.	448.97	371.62
4.	Iraq	1,264.03	1,622.91	14.	Nigeria	409.23	445.90
5.	Kenya	715.42	565.92	15.	Uganda	397.92	378.13
6.	South Sudan.	707.42	—	16.	Mozambique	387.01	277.91
7.	Ethiopia.	706.66	875.34	17.	Mexico	374.89	205.60
8.	West Bank and Gaza Strip	625.04	720.75	18.	Ghana.	307.90	208.05
9.	Haiti	620.18	1,106.85	19.	Libya	290.25	6.60
10.	South Africa	564.03	529.53	20.	Zambia	276.69	225.12
					All developing countries	27,075.96	26,586.41

Nuclear Powers of the World

As of Aug. 2013, eight countries were acknowledged nuclear powers: the **UK, France, China, India, Pakistan, Russia, North Korea**, and the **U.S. Israel** was suspected of having an arsenal. **Iran** was suspected of developing nuclear weapons. More than 40 nations have the knowledge or technology to produce nuclear weapons. All—except Israel, India, and Pakistan—have signed the Nuclear Non-Proliferation Treaty (NPT). North Korea announced its withdrawal Jan. 10, 2003, following its expulsion of Intl. Atomic Energy Agency (IAEA) inspectors in Dec. 2002.

North Korea conducted its first nuclear test Oct. 9, 2006. After a new round of talks in Feb. 2007, it agreed to close its main nuclear facility and take steps toward disabling its nuclear weapons program in exchange for economic aid and diplomatic recognition. In July, IAEA inspectors confirmed the shutdown of the main reactor at the Yongbyon nuclear facility. But the next round of talks, in Dec. 2008, ended in deadlock. North Korea conducted a second nuclear test May 25, 2009; the state-run media reported a third test took place Feb. 12, 2013. The country announced in Apr. 2013 that it would restart operations at Yongbyon.

Despite UN sanctions dating back to Dec. 2006, Iran has refused to suspend its activities in the enrichment of uranium.

Iran argued that as an NPT signatory, it had a right to pursue the peaceful application of nuclear technology. The IAEA maintained that Iran had withheld information on the extent of its nuclear activities.

In Sept. 2009, the U.S., France, and Britain accused Iran of building a secret uranium enrichment facility near the city of Qom. Iran acknowledged the existence of the facility as a backup to its main enrichment site, at Natanz. Enrichment at the new facility, called Fordow, began in Jan. 2012. Iranian president Hassan Rouhani, elected in June 2013, expressed his willingness to enter new talks. In its Aug. quarterly report, IAEA investigators concluded that while Iran's nuclear stockpile continues to increase, the amount of weapons-grade uranium was below the "red line" invoked by Israeli Prime Min. Benjamin Netanyahu in a 2012 UN speech.

Several countries abandoned their nuclear ambitions. **South Africa** announced in 1993 that it had built seven fission weapons (one was under construction) but had dismantled all of them. In the 1980s, **Argentina** and **Brazil** had active nuclear weapons programs but abandoned them by mutual treaty.

Estimated Numbers of Nuclear Weapons by Country, 1945-2013

Source: *Bulletin of the Atomic Scientists*; Carnegie Endowment for International Peace; Federation of American Scientists (FAS); Natural Resources Defense Council (NRDC); Nuclear Threat Initiative (NTI); Stockholm International Peace Research Institute (SIPRI)

Year	United States	USSR/Russia	United Kingdom	France	China	Israel[1]	India	Pakistan	Total[2]
1945	6	—	—	—	—	—	—	—	6
1950	369	5	—	—	—	—	—	—	374
1960	20,434	1,605	30	—	—	—	—	—	22,069
1970	26,662	11,643	280	36	75	8	—	—	38,696
1980	24,304	30,062	350	250	280	31	—	—	55,246
1990	21,004	37,000	300	505	430	53	—	—	59,239
2000	10,577	21,000	185	470	400	72	—	—	32,632
2010	9,400	12,300	225	300	240	60-80	60-80	70-90	22,400
2013	7,700	8,500	225	300	250	80	90-110	100-120	17,300

(1) Israel is widely presumed to have a nuclear stockpile although it has never confirmed nor denied its nuclear status. (2) Numbers may not add up to total due to rounding and uncertainty over size of stockpiles and operational status of warheads.

Nuclear Arms Treaties and Negotiations: A Historical Overview

Aug. 5, 1963: Partial (Limited) Test Ban Treaty signed by U.S., USSR, and Britain, went into effect Oct. 10, 1963. Prohibits parties from testing or participating in the testing of nuclear weapons in the atmosphere, in outer space, and under water.

July 1, 1968: Nuclear Nonproliferation Treaty (NPT) opened to signatures, went into effect Mar. 5, 1970. With the U.S., USSR, and Great Britain as major signers, the treaty limits the spread of nuclear material for military purposes by agreement not to help non-nuclear nations get or make nuclear weapons. On May 11, 1995, at an NPT review conference, parties to the treaty voted to extend it indefinitely. As of Aug. 2013, 190 countries were party to the treaty, not including North Korea, which withdrew in 2003. Israel, India, and Pakistan were not signatories.

May 26, 1972: The **Strategic Arms Limitation Talks (SALT I)** led to the signing of two agreements by the U.S. and USSR: the **Treaty on the Limitation of Anti-Ballistic Missile Systems** (or **ABM Treaty**) and an interim agreement. These treaties cap the numbers of intercontinental ballistic missile (ICBM) launchers and submarine-launched ballistic missile (SLBM) launchers.

July 3, 1974: Treaty on the Limitation of Underground Nuclear Weapon Tests (or **Threshold Test Ban Treaty**) signed by the U.S. and USSR. Limits underground testing of nuclear weapons to yields of 150 kilotons or less. On May 28, 1976, U.S. and Russia signed the **Peaceful Nuclear Explosions Treaty**, governing explosions outside weapons test sites. Both treaties entered into force Dec. 11, 1990.

June 18, 1979: Strategic Offensive Arms Limitation Treaty (or **SALT II**) signed by the U.S. and USSR. Limited each side to 2,400 missile launchers and heavy bombers; ceiling to apply until Jan. 1, 1985. Treaty also set a sub-ceiling of 1,320 ICBMs and SLBMs with multiple warheads on each side. Following Dec. 1979 Soviet invasion of Afghanistan, Pres. Jimmy Carter withdrew SALT II from Senate consideration for ratification.

Dec. 8, 1987: Intermediate-Range Nuclear Forces (INF) Treaty signed by the U.S. and USSR. Eliminates all U.S. and Soviet intermediate- and shorter-range nuclear missiles from Europe and Asia. Entered into force June 1, 1988.

July 31, 1991: Strategic Arms Reduction Treaty (START I) signed by the USSR and U.S., to reduce strategic offensive arms by about 30% in three phases over seven years. This was the first treaty to mandate reductions by the superpowers.

With the Soviet Union breakup in Dec. 1991, four former republics became independent nations with strategic nuclear weapons: Russia, Ukraine, Kazakhstan, and Belarus. Under the **Lisbon Protocol** of May 1992, Ukraine, Kazakhstan, and Belarus agreed to accede to the NPT as non-nuclear-weapon states, to destroy or transfer their nuclear weapons to Russia, and to ratify START I. START I expired on Dec. 5, 2009.

Jan. 3, 1993: START II signed by the U.S. and Russia, ratified by the two countries on Jan. 26, 1996, and Apr. 14, 2000, respectively. Called for reductions in their long-range nuclear arsenals. Both sides withdrew from the treaty before it went into force.

Sept. 24, 1996: Comprehensive Nuclear-Test-Ban Treaty (CTBT) signed by the U.S. and Russia. The CTBT bans all nuclear explosions. It is intended to prevent the nuclear powers from developing more advanced weapons while limiting the ability of other states to acquire such devices. As of Aug. 2013, the CTBT had been signed by 183 nations. It had been ratified by 159, including France, Russia, and the UK but neither the U.S. nor China. It will enter into force only after ratification by all Annex 2 states—the 44 states with nuclear technology capabilities at the time of the treaty's final negotiations. Only 36 have done so.

Dec. 13, 2001: The U.S. announced its intention to withdraw from the **ABM Treaty** in 180 days, arguing that it hindered the government in protecting itself from "future terrorist or rogue state missile attacks." Russia responded by withdrawing from **START II**, stating that U.S. withdrawal from the ABM Treaty effectively invalidated START II.

May 24, 2002: Strategic Offensive Reductions Treaty (SORT or **Moscow Treaty)** signed by the U.S. and Russia, entered into force June 1, 2003. Committed both countries to cutting nuclear arsenals to 1,700-2,200 warheads each, down from about 6,000, by Dec. 31, 2012. SORT terminated upon entry into force of the New START Treaty.

Apr. 8, 2010: New START Treaty signed by the U.S. and Russia and entered into force on Feb. 5, 2011. It limits each country's arsenal of deployed strategic nuclear warheads to 1,550.

Major International Organizations

African Union (AU), inaugurated July 9, 2002, in Durban, South Africa, following disbanding of the Organization of African Unity. All of Africa's countries, with the exception of Morocco, make up its 54 members. (Morocco had left the OAU after it admitted Western Sahara [Sahrawi Arab Dem. Rep.], a territory claimed by Morocco.) The AU is focused on achieving greater socioeconomic integration and unity among its member states. The AU's founding document authorized the organization to intervene to stop genocide, war crimes, or human rights abuses within individual member nations. **Headquarters:** Addis Ababa, Ethiopia. **Website:** www.au.int

Asia-Pacific Economic Cooperation (APEC), founded Nov. 1989 as a forum to further cooperation on trade and investment between nations of the region and the rest of the world. Its 21 members are Australia, Brunei, Canada, Chile, China, Hong Kong, Indonesia, Japan, Malaysia, Mexico, New Zealand, Papua New Guinea, Peru, Philippines, Russia, Singapore, South Korea, Taiwan, Thailand, the U.S., and Vietnam. **Headquarters:** Singapore. **Website:** www.apec.org

Association of Southeast Asian Nations (ASEAN), formed Aug. 8, 1967, to promote economic, social, and cultural cooperation and development among states of the Southeast Asian region. Its members are Brunei, Cambodia, Indonesia, Laos, Malaysia, Myanmar, Philippines, Singapore, Thailand, and Vietnam. **Headquarters:** Jakarta, Indonesia. **Website:** www. asean.org

Caribbean Community and Common Market (CARICOM), established Aug. 1, 1973. Its aim is to increase cooperation in economics, health, education, culture, science and technology, and tax administration, as well as the coordination of foreign policy. Its 15 members are Antigua and Barbuda, The Bahamas, Barbados, Belize, Dominica, Grenada, Guyana, Haiti, Jamaica, Montserrat, St. Kitts and Nevis, St. Lucia, St. Vincent and the Grenadines, Suriname, and Trinidad and Tobago. Anguilla, Bermuda, British Virgin Islands, Cayman Islands, and Turks and Caicos Islands are associate members. **Headquarters:** Georgetown, Guyana. **Website:** www.caricom.org

The Commonwealth, originally called the British Commonwealth of Nations, then the Commonwealth of Nations, is an association of nations and dependencies that were part of the former British Empire. The British monarch is the symbolic head of the Commonwealth.

There are 54 independent nations in the Commonwealth. Regular members include the UK and 15 other nations recognizing the British monarch, represented by a governor-general, as their head of state, and member countries in good standing with their own heads of state. Zimbabwe was suspended in Mar. 2002, following election and land redistribution controversies; it withdrew from the Commonwealth in 2003. In Sept. 2009, Fiji's military regime was suspended. **Headquarters:** London, UK. **Website:** www.thecommonwealth.org

Commonwealth of Independent States (CIS), an alliance established in Dec. 1991, made up of former Soviet constituent republics. Its members are Armenia, Azerbaijan, Belarus, Kazakhstan, Kyrgyzstan, Moldova, Russia, Tajikistan, Turkmenistan, Ukraine, and Uzbekistan. Georgia withdrew from the organization in Aug. 2009 following fighting with Russia over disputed territory. Policy is set through coordinating bodies such as the Council of the Heads of States and Council of the Heads of Governments. **Headquarters:** Minsk, Belarus. **Website:** www.cis.minsk.by or www.cisstat.com/eng/

European Free Trade Association (EFTA), created May 3, 1960, to promote expansion of free trade. Members entered into free trade agreements with the EU in 1972-73. In 1992, EFTA and EU agreed to create a single market—with free flow of goods, services, capital, and labor—among nations of the two organizations. Its members are Iceland, Liechtenstein, Norway, and Switzerland. **Headquarters:** Geneva, Switzerland. **Website:** www.efta.int

European Union (EU), known as the European Community (EC) until 1994, comprises three organizations with common membership: the European Economic Community (EEC, or Common Market), the European Coal and Steel Community, and the European Atomic Energy Community (Euratom). A merger of the three communities' executives went into effect in 1967. As of Aug. 2013, there were 28 EU members: the 12 original members (Belgium, Denmark, France, Germany, Greece, Ireland, Italy, Luxembourg, Netherlands, Portugal, Spain, and UK), three that entered Jan. 1, 1995 (Austria, Finland, Sweden), 10 that joined on May 1, 2004 (Cyprus, Czech Republic, Estonia, Hungary, Latvia, Lithuania, Malta, Poland, Slovakia, Slovenia), two that joined Jan. 1, 2007 (Bulgaria, Romania), and one that joined July 1, 2013 (Croatia). Iceland, Macedonia, Montenegro, Serbia, and Turkey were candidate countries. Some 70 countries and territories in Africa, the Caribbean, and the Pacific are affiliated under the Lomé Convention. **Headquarters:** Brussels, Belgium. **Website:** europa.eu

The EU aims to integrate the economies, coordinate social developments, and bring about political union of the member states. Effective Dec. 31, 1992, there are no restrictions on the movement of goods, services, capital, workers, and tourists within the EU. There are also common agricultural, fisheries, and nuclear research policies.

Leaders of the member nations (12 at the time) met Dec. 9-11, 1991, in Maastricht, the Netherlands, and signed a treaty. The Maastricht treaty, which went into effect in 1993, committed the organization to launching a common currency; establishing common foreign policies; and taking a leading role in social policy among other issues. The European Central Bank was established in 1998. In 1999, 11 of the then-15 EU countries began using the euro. By 2002, national currencies in those 11 countries and Greece were removed from circulation and replaced with the euro as the only currency of legal tender. EU peacekeeping forces replaced NATO troops in Macedonia, Mar. 31, 2003, the first such mission for the organization. A Treaty Establishing a Constitution for Europe was signed in 2004 by EU members but was never ratified.

Group of Eight (G8), forum of major industrialized countries. France, Germany, Italy, Japan, the UK, and the U.S. first met in 1975 as the Group of Six. Canada joined in 1976 and Russia in 1998. The EU is also represented at summits. Members meet periodically to discuss economic and other issues. The presidency rotates yearly among members.

International Criminal Police Organization (INTERPOL), created 1923 as the International Criminal Police Commission before changing its name in 1956, is the world's largest international police organization. There were 190 member nations as of Aug. 2013. **Headquarters:** Lyon, France. **Website:** www.interpol.int

League of Arab States (Arab League), created Mar. 22, 1945. The League promotes economic, social, political, and military cooperation, mediates disputes, and represents Arab states in certain international negotiations. Its members are Algeria, Bahrain, Comoros, Djibouti, Egypt, Iraq, Jordan, Kuwait, Lebanon, Libya, Mauritania, Morocco, Oman, Palestine (considered an independent state by the League), Qatar, Saudi Arabia, Somalia, Sudan, Syria, Tunisia, United Arab Emirates, and Yemen. **Headquarters:** Cairo, Egypt. **Website:** www.lasportal.org

North Atlantic Treaty Organization (NATO), created by treaty (signed Apr. 4, 1949; in effect Aug. 24, 1949). Its 28 members as of Aug. 2013 are Albania, Belgium, Bulgaria, Canada, Croatia, Czech Republic, Denmark, Estonia, France, Germany, Greece, Hungary, Iceland, Italy, Latvia, Lithuania, Luxembourg, Netherlands, Norway, Poland, Portugal, Romania, Slovakia, Slovenia, Spain, Turkey, UK, and U.S. Several of these states are former Warsaw Pact Eastern European nations.

Members have agreed to settle disputes by peaceful means, to develop their capacity to resist armed attack, to regard an attack on one as an attack on all, and to take necessary action to repel an attack under Article 51 of the UN Charter. **Headquarters:** Brussels, Belgium. **Website:** www.nato.int

The NATO structure consists of the North Atlantic Council (NAC), the Defense Planning Committee, the Military Committee (realigned in June 2003 and consisting of two commands: Allied Command Operations and Allied Command Transformation), the Nuclear Planning Group, and the Canada-U.S. Regional Planning Group. France detached itself from the military command structure in 1966.

With the end of the Cold War in the early 1990s, members put greater stress on political action and on creating a rapid deployment force to react to local crises. By the mid-1990s, 27 nations, including Russia and other former Soviet republics, had joined with NATO in the so-called Partnership for Peace (PfP; drafted Dec. 1993), which provided for limited joint military exercises and peacekeeping missions. NATO has proceeded gradually toward extending full membership to former Eastern bloc nations. Three former Warsaw Pact members, Hungary, Poland, and the Czech Republic, formally became members in 1999. NATO and Russia signed a cooperation pact in 2002, forming a NATO-Russia Council; NATO that same year invited seven former Eastern-bloc nations to join the alliance.

A NATO-led multinational force was deployed to help keep the peace in Bosnia and Herzegovina in 1995. In 1999, another force was deployed in Kosovo. Following the Sept. 2001 terrorist attacks on the U.S., the NATO Council agreed to invoke for the first time Article 5 of the treaty, which stipulates mutual defense of alliance members. NATO assumed control of the International Security Assistance Force in Afghanistan (ISAF), Aug. 2003, marking the first time NATO led a mission outside Europe.

Organization of American States (OAS), formed in Bogotá, Colombia, Apr. 30, 1948. It has a Permanent Council, Inter-American Council for Integral Development, Juridical Committee, and Commission on Human Rights. A general assembly meets annually.

Its 35 members are Antigua and Barbuda, Argentina, The Bahamas, Barbados, Belize, Bolivia, Brazil, Canada, Chile, Colombia, Costa Rica, Cuba, Dominica, Dominican Republic, Ecuador, El Salvador, Grenada, Guatemala, Guyana, Haiti, Honduras, Jamaica, Mexico, Nicaragua, Panama, Paraguay, Peru, St. Kitts and Nevis, St. Lucia, St. Vincent and the Grenadines, Suriname, Trinidad and Tobago, U.S., Uruguay, and Venezuela. **Headquarters:** Washington, DC. **Website:** www.oas.org

Organization for Economic Cooperation and Development (OECD), established Dec. 14, 1960, to promote the economic and social welfare of all its member countries and to stimulate efforts on behalf of developing nations. Its 34 members are Australia, Austria, Belgium, Canada, Chile, Czech Republic, Denmark, Estonia, Finland, France, Germany, Greece, Hungary, Iceland, Ireland, Israel, Italy, Japan, Luxembourg, Mexico, Netherlands, New Zealand, Norway, Poland, Portugal, Slovakia, Slovenia, South Korea, Spain, Sweden, Switzerland, Turkey, UK, and the U.S. **Headquarters:** Paris, France. **Website:** www.oecd.org

Organization of Petroleum Exporting Countries (OPEC), created Sept. 14, 1960, by Iran, Iraq, Kuwait, Saudi Arabia, and Venezuela. This group made up of most but not all the major petroleum exporting nations seeks to stabilize the oil market and set world oil prices by controlling production. In addition to the founding countries, members include Algeria, Angola, Ecuador, Indonesia (suspended membership starting in Jan. 2009), Libya, Nigeria, Qatar, and United Arab Emirates. Gabon is a former member. **Headquarters:** Vienna, Austria. **Website:** www.opec.org

Organization for Security and Cooperation in Europe (OSCE), established in 1972 as the Conference on Security and Cooperation in Europe; current name adopted 1995. The group, formed by NATO and Warsaw Pact members, seeks improved East-West relations through a commitment to nonaggression and human rights, and cooperation in economics, science and technology, cultural exchange, and environmental protection. There were 57 member states as of Aug. 2013, making it the world's largest regional security organization. **Headquarters:** Vienna, Austria. **Website:** www.osce.org

United Nations

The 68th regular session of the United Nations General Assembly opened Sept. 17, 2013, attended by world leaders and other delegates from 193 nations. The UN headquarters is located on 18 acres in New York, NY.

Proposals to establish an organization for maintenance of world peace led to the convening of the United Nations Conference on International Organization in San Francisco, Apr. 25-June 26, 1945, where the UN charter was drawn. It was signed June 26 by 50 nations and on Oct. 15 by Poland. It went into effect Oct. 24, 1945, upon ratification by the permanent members of the Security Council and a majority of the other signatories.

Purposes. To maintain international peace and security; to develop friendly relations among nations; to achieve international cooperation in solving economic, social, cultural, and humanitarian problems and in promoting respect for human rights and basic freedoms; to be a center for harmonizing the actions of nations in attaining these common ends.

Visitors to the UN. The UN headquarters is open every day except New Year's Day, President's Day, Good Friday, Memorial Day, Independence Day, Eid al-Fitr, Labor Day, Eid al-Adha, Thanksgiving, and Christmas. It may also close on short notice when meetings of heads of state and government are held. Because of ongoing renovations, new security procedures went into effect in June 2013. Only visitors with tickets for a guided tour may enter the UN.

Guided one-hour tours are conducted on weekdays. Tickets must be purchased in advance online. Audio tours are no longer offered. Groups of 46 or more can make reservations directly with the UN by emailing unitg@un.org. For safety reasons, children under 5 are years of age not admitted on tours.

United Nations Secretaries General

Took office	Secretary, nation
1946	Trygve Lie, Norway
1953	Dag Hammarskjöld, Sweden
1961	U Thant, Burma (Myanmar)
1972	Kurt Waldheim, Austria

Took office	Secretary, nation
1982	Javier Pérez de Cuéllar, Peru
1992	Boutros Boutros-Ghali, Egypt
1997	Kofi Annan, Ghana
2007	Ban Ki-moon, South Korea

Six Main Organs of the United Nations

The United Nations consists of six principal organs, 15 agencies, and many programs and other bodies. The six principal organs are the General Assembly, the Security Council, the Secretariat, the Economic and Social Council, the International Court of Justice, and the Trusteeship Council.

General Assembly. The General Assembly is composed of representatives of all the member nations. Each nation is entitled to one vote. The General Assembly meets in regular annual sessions and in special session when convoked at the request of the Security Council or a majority of UN members. On important questions a two-thirds majority of members present and voting is required; on other questions a simple majority is sufficient.

The General Assembly must approve the UN budget and apportion expenses among members. A member in arrears can lose its vote if the amount of arrears equals or exceeds the amount of the contributions due for the preceding two full years. **Website:** www.un.org/en/ga/

Security Council. The Security Council consists of 15 members, five with permanent seats. The remaining 10 are elected for two-year terms by the General Assembly.

The permanent members of the Council are China, France, Russia, United Kingdom, and the United States. Nonpermanent members with terms expiring Dec. 31, 2013, are Azerbaijan, Guatemala, Morocco, Pakistan, and Togo; those with terms expiring Dec. 31, 2014, are Argentina, Australia, South Korea, Luxembourg, and Rwanda.

The Security Council has the primary responsibility within the UN for maintaining international peace and security. The Council may investigate any dispute that threatens international peace and security.

Any UN member may participate in Council discussions at its invitation. Decisions on procedural questions are made by an affirmative vote of nine members. On all other matters the affirmative vote of nine members must include the concurring votes of all permanent members (giving them veto power).

The Security Council directs the various peacekeeping forces deployed throughout the world. **Website:** www.un.org/en/sc/

Secretariat. The Secretariat is responsible for the UN's day-to-day operations. It is headed by the secretary-general, who is the chief administrative officer of the UN. This person is appointed by the General Assembly, on the recommendation of the Security Council, for a five-year, renewable term. The secretary-general reports to the General Assembly and may bring to the attention of the Security Council any matter that threatens international peace. As of mid-2012, the Secretariat had an international staff of 42,887. **Website:** www.un.org/en/mainbodies/secretariat/

Economic and Social Council. The Economic and Social Council consists of 54 members elected by the General Assembly to overlapping three-year terms. The council is responsible for economic, social, and environmental matters. It meets with academics, non-governmental organizations, and private-sector representatives throughout the year. A month-long substantive session takes place each July. These sessions are alternately held in New York and Geneva, Switzerland. **Website:** www.un.org/ecosoc/

International Court of Justice (World Court). The International Court of Justice is the principal judicial organ of the UN. The Court has jurisdiction over cases that UN members or parties to the court's statute submit to it. In addition to rendering judgments, the Court gives advisory opinions.

The court's 15 judges are elected to nine-year terms by the General Assembly and the Security Council. No two judges come from the same nation, and they represent the world's principal legal systems. Once elected, the judges no longer act as representatives of a government. The Court remains permanently in session, except during vacations. All questions are decided by a majority. The International Court of Justice sits in The Hague, Netherlands. **Website:** www.icj-cij.org

Trusteeship Council. The Trusteeship Council, made up of the five permanent Security Council members, supervised the administration of UN trust territories. All 11 trust territories have since attained their right to self-determination. The Council formally suspended its work on Nov. 1, 1994, with Palau's independence. **Website:** www.un.org/en/mainbodies/trusteeship/

The text of the **UN Charter** is online at www.un.org/en/documents/charter/index.shtml.

Selected Specialized and UN-Related Agencies

These specialized and related agencies are autonomous, with their own memberships and organs. They have a functional relationship or working agreement with the UN except for UNICEF and UNHCR, which report directly to the General Assembly. The location in parentheses is the primary office or headquarters.

Food and Agriculture Org. (FAO) helps countries modernize farms, forests, and fisheries; improves food distribution; and raises levels of nutrition. (Rome, Italy) **Website:** www.fao.org

International Atomic Energy Agency (IAEA) aims to promote safe, peaceful uses of atomic energy. (Vienna, Austria) **Website:** www.iaea.org

International Civil Aviation Org. (ICAO) promotes international civil aviation standards and regulations. (Montréal, Quebec, Canada) **Website:** www.icao.int

International Fund for Agricultural Development (IFAD) seeks to alleviate poverty in rural areas of developing countries. (Rome, Italy) **Website:** www.ifad.org

International Labor Org. (ILO) aims to promote decent and productive employment practices, the improvement of labor conditions, social security, and vocational training. (Geneva, Switzerland) **Website:** www.ilo.org

International Maritime Org. (IMO) aims to promote cooperation on technical matters affecting international shipping. (London, England, UK) **Website:** www.imo.org

International Monetary Fund (IMF) aims to promote international monetary cooperation, currency stabilization, and the expansion of international trade. (Washington, DC) **Website:** www.imf.org

International Telecommunication Union (ITU) regulates all aspects of global communication, including setting standards for radio, telegraph, telephone, and space radio-communications, and allocating radio frequencies. (Geneva, Switzerland) **Website:** www.itu.int

Office of the United Nations High Commissioner for Refugees (UNHCR) safeguards the rights of and provides essential assistance for refugees. (Geneva, Switzerland) **Website:** www.unhcr.org

United Nations Children's Fund (UNICEF) provides financial aid and development assistance to programs for children and mothers in developing countries. (New York, NY) **Website:** www.unicef.org

United Nations Educational, Scientific, and Cultural Org. (UNESCO) aims to promote collaboration among nations through education, science, and culture. (Paris, France) **Website:** www.unesco.org

United Nations Industrial Development Org. (UNIDO) helps developing and transitional nations pursue sustainable industrial development while promoting international industrial cooperation. (Vienna, Austria) **Website:** www.unido.org

Universal Postal Union (UPU) aims to perfect postal services and promote international collaboration. (Berne, Switzerland) **Website:** www.upu.int

World Bank Group encompasses two development institutions and three affiliates focused on worldwide poverty reduction. The **International Bank for Reconstruction and Development (IBRD)** provides loans and technical assistance for projects in developing member countries and encourages co-financing for projects from other sources. The **International Development Assn. (IDA)** provides funds for development projects on concessionary terms to poorer developing member countries. The **International Finance Corp. (IFC)** promotes private-sector growth in developing member countries; encourages the development of local capital markets; and stimulates the international flow of private capital. The **Multilateral Investment Guarantee Agency (MIGA)** promotes investment in developing countries; guarantees investments to protect investors from noncommercial risks, such as nationalization; and advises governments on attracting private investment. The **International Center for Settlement of Investment Disputes (ICSID)** provides conciliation and arbitration services for disputes between foreign investors and host governments that arise out of an investment. (Washington, DC) **Website:** www.worldbank.org, www.ifc.org, www.miga.org

World Health Org. (WHO) aims for the attainment of the highest possible level of health. (Geneva, Switzerland) **Website:** www.who.int

World Intellectual Property Org. (WIPO) seeks to protect, literary, industrial, scientific, and artistic works through international cooperation. (Geneva, Switzerland) **Website:** www.wipo.int

World Meteorological Org. (WMO) aims to coordinate and improve world meteorological work. (Geneva, Switzerland) **Website:** www.wmo.int

World Tourism Org. (UNWTO) promotes responsible, sustainable, and universally accessible tourism with the aim of fostering economic development and international understanding. (Madrid, Spain) **Website:** www.unwto.org

World Trade Org. (WTO) administers trade agreements and treaties between nations, examines members' trade regimes, keeps track of trade measures and statistics, and attempts to settle disputes. (Geneva, Switzerland) **Website:** www.wto.org

Ongoing UN Peacekeeping Missions, 2013

Source: Dept. of Peacekeeping Operations (DPKO), Dept. of Field Support, Dept. of Management; United Nations Secretariat
Unless otherwise noted, numbers are for peacekeeping operations only, as of July 31, 2013, unless otherwise noted. Year given in graphic is the year each mission started.

Uniformed personnel (troops, police, military observers)	97,369	Total personnel serving in 16 DPKO-led peace operations (15 peacekeeping, 1 political mission)	117,905
Countries contributing uniformed personnel	115	Peacekeeping operations since 1948	68
Civilian personnel (as of June 30, 2013):		Total fatalities in peace operations since 1948	3,136
International	5,032	Est. total cost of operations, 1948 to June 30, 2010	$69 bil
Local	11,693		

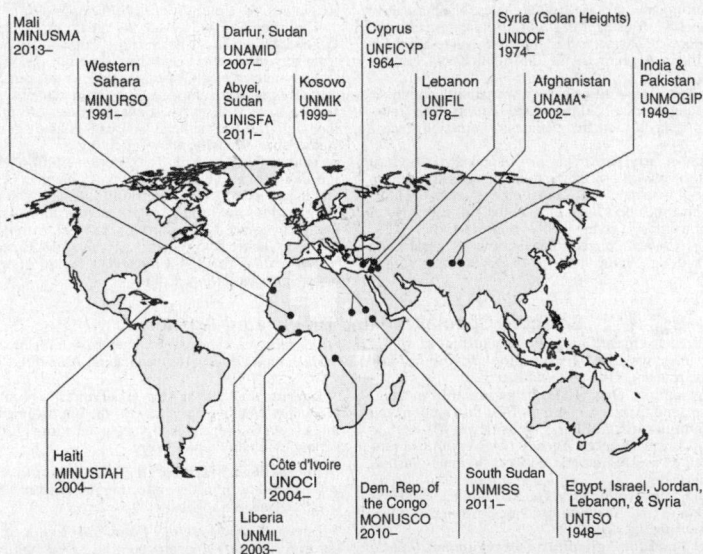

Mali MINUSMA 2013–
Western Sahara MINURSO 1991–
Darfur, Sudan UNAMID 2007–
Abyei, Sudan UNISFA 2011–
Kosovo UNMIK 1999–
Cyprus UNFICYP 1964–
Lebanon UNIFIL 1978–
Syria (Golan Heights) UNDOF 1974–
Afghanistan UNAMA* 2002–
India & Pakistan UNMOGIP 1949–
Haiti MINUSTAH 2004–
Côte d'Ivoire UNOCI 2004–
Liberia UNMIL 2003–
Dem. Rep. of the Congo MONUSCO 2010–
South Sudan UNMISS 2011–
Egypt, Israel, Jordan, Lebanon, & Syria UNTSO 1948–

*Political mission directed and supported by the Dept. of Peacekeeping Operations.

Roster of the United Nations

Listed below are the 193 members of the United Nations, with the years in which they were admitted (as of Aug. 2013). Vatican City, Kosovo, and China (Taiwan)[1] are not members. Taiwan's repeated bids for UN membership have so far been unsuccessful. Vatican City is a permanent observer.

Member	Year	Member	Year	Member	Year	Member	Year
Afghanistan	1946	Dominica	1978	Libya	1955	Saint Vincent and the	
Albania	1955	Dominican Republic	1945	Liechtenstein	1990	Grenadines	1980
Algeria	1962	Ecuador	1945	Lithuania	1991	Samoa	1976
Andorra	1993	Egypt[4]	1945	Luxembourg	1945	San Marino	1992
Angola	1976	El Salvador	1945	Macedonia[2,7]	1993	São Tomé and Príncipe	1975
Antigua and Barbuda	1981	Equatorial Guinea	1968	Madagascar	1960	Saudi Arabia	1945
Argentina	1945	Eritrea	1993	Malawi	1964	Senegal	1960
Armenia	1992	Estonia	1991	Malaysia[8]	1957	Serbia[2,9]	2000
Australia	1945	Ethiopia	1945	Maldives	1965	Seychelles	1976
Austria	1955	Fiji	1970	Mali	1960	Sierra Leone	1961
Azerbaijan	1992	Finland	1955	Malta	1964	Singapore[8]	1965
Bahamas, The	1973	France	1945	Marshall Islands	1991	Slovakia[3]	1993
Bahrain	1971	Gabon	1960	Mauritania	1961	Slovenia[2]	1992
Bangladesh	1974	Gambia, The	1965	Mauritius	1968	Solomon Islands	1978
Barbados	1966	Georgia	1992	Mexico	1945	Somalia	1960
Belarus	1945	Germany[5]	1973	Micronesia	1991	South Africa[11]	1945
Belgium	1945	Ghana	1957	Moldova	1992	South Sudan[12]	2011
Belize	1981	Greece	1945	Monaco	1993	Spain	1955
Benin	1960	Grenada	1974	Mongolia	1961	Sri Lanka	1955
Bhutan	1971	Guatemala	1945	Montenegro[2,9]	2006	Sudan[12]	1956
Bolivia	1945	Guinea	1958	Morocco	1956	Suriname	1975
Bosnia and		Guinea-Bissau	1974	Mozambique	1975	Swaziland	1968
Herzegovina[2]	1992	Guyana	1966	Myanmar (Burma)	1948	Sweden	1946
Botswana	1966	Haiti	1945	Namibia	1990	Switzerland	2002
Brazil	1945	Honduras	1945	Nauru	1999	Syria[3]	1945
Brunei	1984	Hungary	1955	Nepal	1955	Tajikistan	1992
Bulgaria	1955	Iceland	1946	Netherlands	1945	Tanzania[13]	1961
Burkina Faso	1960	India	1945	New Zealand	1945	Thailand	1946
Burundi	1962	Indonesia[6]	1950	Nicaragua	1945	Timor-Leste	2002
Cambodia	1955	Iran	1945	Niger	1960	Togo	1960
Cameroon	1960	Iraq	1945	Nigeria	1960	Tonga	1999
Canada	1945	Ireland	1955	Norway	1945	Trinidad and Tobago	1962
Cape Verde	1975	Israel	1949	Oman	1971	Tunisia	1956
Central African Rep.	1960	Italy	1955	Pakistan	1947	Turkey	1945
Chad	1960	Jamaica	1962	Palau	1994	Turkmenistan	1992
Chile	1945	Japan	1956	Panama	1945	Tuvalu	2000
China[1]	1945	Jordan	1955	Papua New Guinea	1975	Uganda	1962
Colombia	1945	Kazakhstan	1992	Paraguay	1945	Ukraine	1945
Comoros	1975	Kenya	1963	Peru	1945	United Arab Emirates	1971
Congo, Dem. Rep. of	1960	Kiribati	1999	Philippines	1945	United Kingdom	1945
Congo Republic	1960	Korea, North	1991	Poland	1945	United States	1945
Costa Rica	1945	Korea, South	1991	Portugal	1955	Uruguay	1945
Côte d'Ivoire	1960	Kuwait	1963	Qatar	1971	Uzbekistan	1992
Croatia[2]	1992	Kyrgyzstan	1992	Romania	1955	Vanuatu	1981
Cuba	1945	Laos	1955	Russia[10]	1945	Venezuela	1945
Cyprus	1960	Latvia	1991	Rwanda	1962	Vietnam	1977
Czech Republic[3]	1993	Lebanon	1945	Saint Kitts and Nevis	1983	Yemen[14]	1947
Denmark	1945	Lesotho	1966	Saint Lucia	1979	Zambia	1964
Djibouti	1977	Liberia	1945			Zimbabwe	1980

(1) The General Assembly (GA) voted in 1971 to expel the Chinese government in Taiwan and admit the government in Beijing. (2) The Socialist Federal Republic of Yugoslavia was an original UN member. After four of its six republics (Bosnia and Herzegovina, Croatia, Macedonia, and Slovenia) declared independence in 1991-92, the two remaining republics, Montenegro and Serbia, reconstituted as the Federal Republic of Yugoslavia. They sought to take over the former Yugoslavia's UN seat in 1992 but were expelled a few months later by GA vote. The Federal Republic of Yugoslavia was granted membership in 2000. In 2003, the country changed its name to Serbia and Montenegro. (3) Czechoslovakia, an original UN member from 1945 to 1992, was succeeded by both the Czech Republic and Slovakia in 1993. (4) Egypt and Syria were original UN members. In 1958, Egypt and Syria established the United Arab Republic and continued under a single UN membership. In 1961, Syria resumed separate membership without relinquishing independence. (5) The Federal Republic of Germany and the German Democratic Republic became UN members in 1973. In 1990, the two formed one sovereign state. (6) Withdrew from the UN in 1965; rejoined in 1966. (7) Provisionally referred to as The Former Yugoslav Republic of Macedonia within the UN pending settlement of Greece's objection to its constitutional name. (8) The Federation of Malaya joined the UN in 1957. In 1963, it changed its name to Malaysia following the accession of Singapore, Sabah, and Sarawak. Singapore became an independent UN member in 1965. (9) After Montenegro declared independence in 2006, the Republic of Serbia continued Serbia and Montenegro's UN membership. Montenegro was admitted to the UN as the Republic of Montenegro the same month. (10) The USSR was an original UN member. After the USSR's dissolution in 1991, Russia informed the UN it would continue the Soviet Union's membership in the Security Council and all other UN organs with the support of the Commonwealth of Independent States (comprising most of the former Soviet republics). (11) Readmitted in 1994. Its delegation had been suspended from participation in 1974 because of apartheid. (12) The Republic of South Sudan seceded from the Republic of the Sudan in 2011 and was admitted to the UN the same year. (13) Tanganyika was a UN member from 1961 and Zanzibar from 1963. The two countries united in 1964 to form the United Republic of Tanganyika and Zanzibar, which continued a single UN membership. It later changed its name to the United Republic of Tanzania. (14) The Yemen Arab Republic was admitted in 1947; the People's Democratic Republic of Yemen in 1967. In 1990, the two nations formed the Republic of Yemen.

U.S. Representatives to the United Nations, 1946-2013

The U.S. Permanent Representative to the United Nations is head of the U.S. Mission to the UN in New York. He or she is appointed by the president and confirmed by the Senate. This individual holds the rank and status of Ambassador Extraordinary and Plenipotentiary. Year given is the year each took office.

Year	Representative	Year	Representative	Year	Representative	Year	Representative
1946	Edward R. Stettinius Jr.	1968	James Russell Wiggins	1985	Vernon A. Walters	2001	John D. Negroponte
1946	Herschel V. Johnson (act.)	1969	Charles W. Yost	1989	Thomas R. Pickering	2004	John C. Danforth
1947	Warren R. Austin	1971	George H. W. Bush	1992	Edward J. Perkins	2005	Anne W. Patterson (act.)
1953	Henry Cabot Lodge Jr.	1973	John A. Scali	1993	Madeleine K. Albright		
1960	James J. Wadsworth	1975	Daniel P. Moynihan	1997	Bill Richardson	2005	John R. Bolton
1961	Adlai E. Stevenson	1976	William W. Scranton	1998	A. Peter Burleigh (act.)	2006	Alejandro D. Wolff (act.)
1965	Arthur J. Goldberg	1977	Andrew Young	1999	Richard C. Holbrooke	2007	Zalmay M. Khalilzad
1968	George W. Ball	1979	Donald McHenry	2001	James B. Cunningham (act.)	2009	Susan E. Rice
		1981	Jeane J. Kirkpatrick			2013	Samantha Power

International Criminal Court

The International Criminal Court (ICC) was created when 120 nations signed the Rome Statute on July 17, 1998. Its mission is to try individuals accused of genocide, war crimes, or other crimes against humanity, which was undertaken in the past by temporary tribunals. The statute came into force on July 1, 2002. As of mid-Sept. 2013, 122 nations were state parties to the Rome Statute of the ICC. China, Russia, and the U.S. have not yet joined.

The ICC, unlike the World Court, is not part of the UN. It is an independent international agency with its own administration and budget, which is made up of funds from member states and voluntary contributions by other institutions, international groups, individuals, and corporations. It consists of 18 judges elected by member nations. An absolute majority of these 18 judges elect three from among themselves to serve as president, first vice president, and second vice president in three-year, renewable terms. A Registry handles the nonjudicial aspects of administration. The Office of the Prosecutor reviews,

investigates, and, prosecutes cases referred to it by a state or by the UN Security Council.

As of mid-Sept. 2013, 18 cases in eight situations had been brought before the ICC. These situations were in the Central African Republic; Côte d'Ivoire; Dem. Rep. of the Congo; Kenya; Libya; Mali; Darfur, Sudan; and Uganda. On Mar. 14, 2012, the court issued its first-ever conviction when it found the warlord Thomas Lubanga Dyilo guilty of war crimes for his use of child soldiers in the Dem. Rep. of the Congo. Kenya's deputy president went on trial Sept. 10, 2013; Kenyan president Uhuru Kenyatta was set to go on trial in Nov. In protest, Kenya's parliament voted to withdraw from the ICC.

Though jurisdiction is limited to member nations, the ICC is a court of last resort. It may also initiate cases involving non-member nations if it deems the country's authorities have not taken steps to investigate or prosecute a case. The ICC is based in The Hague, Netherlands, though it may sit elsewhere. **Website:** icc-cpi.int

Geneva Conventions

The Geneva Conventions are four international treaties governing the protection of civilians in times of war, the treatment of prisoners of war, and the care of the wounded and sick in the armed forces. The first convention, covering the sick and wounded in war, was concluded in Geneva, Switzerland, in 1864, at a conference convened by the Swiss government at the urging of the International Committee of the Red Cross. The convention was amended and expanded in 1906. In 1929, two more conventions covering the wounded and prisoners of war were signed. Outrage at the treatment of prisoners and civilians during WWII by some belligerents, notably Germany and Japan, prompted the conclusion, on Aug. 12, 1949, of four new conventions. Three of these restated and strengthened the previous conventions. The fourth codified general principles of international law governing the treatment of civilians in wartime.

The 1949 convention for civilians provided for special safeguards for wounded persons, children under 15 years of age,

pregnant women, and the elderly. Discrimination on racial, religious, national, or political grounds was forbidden. Torture, collective punishment, reprisals, unwarranted destruction of property, and forced use of civilians for an occupier's armed forces were also prohibited. Also included was a pledge for the humane treatment, adequate feeding, and delivery of supplies to prisoners. They were not to be forced to disclose more than minimal information. Two additional protocols were adopted in June 1977 dealing with the protection of victims, especially civilians, in international and non-international armed conflicts. (A third protocol, adopted in 2005, created the Red Crystal emblem for use along with the Red Cross and Red Crescent.)

Most countries have formally accepted all or most of the humanitarian conventions as binding. However, there is no permanent international machinery in place to enforce these treaties.

Genocide

Source: Convention on the Prevention and Punishment of the Crime of Genocide, United Nations Treaty Series 277; Rome Statute of the International Criminal Court

The term "genocide" (which combines Greek and Latin roots to mean "murder of a race") was coined by Polish-Jewish lawyer Raphael Lemkin in 1944 to describe the intentional destruction or attempted destruction of a national, ethnic, racial, or religious group, whether in wartime or peacetime. Genocide is defined as killing members of a group, causing serious bodily harm to members of a group, or otherwise attempting to bring about a group's destruction, including efforts to prevent births or transfer children away from a group. Although the legal definition of genocide does not extend to political groups, the term is often used colloquially to refer to large-scale political violence.

The prohibition against genocide is part of customary international law and is codified in the Convention on the Prevention and Punishment of the Crime of Genocide, which entered into force on Jan. 12, 1951. As of Aug. 2013, 142 nations, including

the U.S., were parties to it. Genocide is also prohibited by the domestic laws of many nations.

The first modern trials for genocide were conducted by the Allies after WWII. Although the charter of the Nuremberg Tribunal—the international court set up to try Nazi war criminals—did not use the term genocide, its definition of "crimes against humanity" included persecution on racial or religious grounds. More recently, the UN Security Council created ad hoc tribunals to try those responsible for genocide and other serious crimes in the former Yugoslavia and in Rwanda. The International Criminal Court (ICC) also has jurisdiction to try perpetrators of genocide. In 2005, the Security Council referred the situation in Darfur, Sudan, to the ICC prosecutor. The ICC has since issued two arrest warrants for Sudanese Pres. Omar Hassan al-Bashir on multiple counts of genocide, crimes against humanity, and war crimes.

Examples of Genocides Since 1900

Year	Event	Location	Est. deaths
1915	Extermination of Armenians by the Young Turks	Turkey/Ottoman Empire	1,000,000+
1930s	Intentional infliction of famine on Ukraine	Soviet Union (Ukraine)	6,000,000-7,000,000
1933-45	Attempted destruction of European Jewry (Holocaust)	Europe	6,000,000
1975-79	Khmer Rouge campaign of extermination under Pol Pot[1]	Cambodia	1,500,000-2,000,000
1981-83	Army and paramilitary killings of indigenous Mayan during civil war	Guatemala	200,000+
1988	Anfal Campaign (named by the Iraqi government) against Iraqi Kurds	Iraq	100,000-200,000
1992-95	Ethnic killings during the breakup of Yugoslavia, chiefly Serbs against Bosnian Muslims	Bosnia-Herzegovina, Serbia, Croatia	200,000
1994	Hutu massacre of Tutsis	Rwanda	800,000
2003-present	Rebel group and government-backed Arab militia attacks on non-Arab southern tribes, black population[2]	Darfur region, Sudan	200,000-400,000

Note: Estimates based on historical evidence. The legal definition of "genocide" does not include politically motivated mass killings. Therefore, instances of mass violence against political or class enemies, such as Josef Stalin's purges of some 20 mil Soviets in the 1930s, and Mao Zedong's Cultural Revolution, which killed several mil Chinese, are not included. (1) The mass killings during Cambodia's Khmer Rouge regime are often spoken of as genocide, though many of the murders were politically or class motivated. (2) In 2005, a UN commission concluded that although the "international offenses ... that have been committed in Darfur may be no less serious and heinous than genocide," it did not term the situation there a genocide.

NATIONS OF THE WORLD

As of mid-2013, there were **196 nations** in the world. This number includes three nations that are not United Nations members—Kosovo, Taiwan, and Vatican City (the Holy See). Certain regions and territories can be found under the entry for their governing nation.

Sources: FAOSTAT, Economic and Social Development Dept. and Fisheries and Aquaculture Dept., Food and Agric. Org. of the UN (FAO); *Global Report: UNAIDS Report on the Global AIDS Epidemic*, Joint UN Programme on HIV/AIDS (UNAIDS); Intl. Civil Aviation Org. (ICAO); Intl. Data Base, U.S. Census Bureau; *International Energy Annual*, Energy Information Admin., U.S. Dept. of Energy; *International Financial Statistics*, Intl. Monetary Fund (IMF); ITU World Telecommunication/ICT Indicators Database, Intl. Telecommunication Union; *The Military Balance*, Intl. Inst. for Strategic Studies; *Oil & Gas Journal*, PennWell Corp.; *Statistical Yearbook*, UN Statistics Div.; UN Educational, Scientific, and Cultural Org. (UNESCO); *UNWTO World Tourism Barometer* © World Tourism Org.; U.S. Dept. of State; WardsAuto Group, a div. of Penton; The World Bank; *The World Factbook*, Central Intelligence Agency (CIA); *World Population Prospects* and *World Urbanization Prospects*, Dept. of Economic and Social Affairs, UN Population Div.

Note: Because of rounding or incomplete enumeration, percentages may not add up to 100%. FY = Fiscal year. NA = Not available/applicable. Data are for the following specified years unless otherwise noted. **Population**, **age distrib.**, and **pop. density** figures are mid-2013 est. Percent of total pop. living in **urban** areas, as defined by each country, are mid-2011 ests. **Languages** are ranked with most widely spoken languages listed first. Pop. of **capitals and cities (urban aggl.)** are mid-2011 ests. **Defense budget** is for 2012, **active troops** for 2013. Selected **industries** are ranked by descending value of annual output. **Chief crops** are listed in descending order of importance. **Crude oil reserves** are as of Jan. 1, 2013; countries without this entry lack reserves. **Arable land** is given as percentage of country's land area. **Livestock** and **fish catch** (captured and farmed) are for 2011. **Electricity prod.** indicates net, not gross, generated in 2010. **Labor force** percentages are latest available. **GDP** data, for 2012, are based on purchasing power parity calculations. **Per capita GDP** is calculated using a country's est. pop. size as of July 1 of given year. Value of **imports** and **exports** and trade partners—listed in descending order of importance by percentage of total dollar value—are from 2012. **Tourism** figures are latest available receipts from intl. tourism; countries without this entry had no available data. **Budget** figures, calculated on an exchange rate basis not purchasing power parity terms, are 2012 expenditures. **Total reserves less gold** and **gold** are from 2012. **CPI change** measures the percent change in the consumer price index between 2011 and 2012. The total length of a country's railway network is listed under **Railways. Motor vehicle** statistics, for cars and comm. vehicles in operation based on registrations, are for 2012. **Civil aviation** measures the number of passengers carried a certain distance on scheduled flights operated by airlines registered in a country; they are the latest available. The number of **airports** with paved, usable runways are as of 2013. **TV sets** (in businesses and households) and **radios** (receivers for public broadcast) are latest available figures. Number of fixed **telephone lines** and percentage of pop. accessing the **Internet**, regardless of device used, are for 2012. **Life expect.** is at birth for persons born in 2013. **Natural inc.** measures the difference between the number of **births** and **deaths** in 2013. **Infant mortality** measures the probability of a child dying between birth and exact age 1 in 2013. **HIV rate** is of country's pop. of 15- to 49-year-olds living with HIV in 2011. **Education** figures and **literacy** rates are latest available. Literacy measures the percent of pop. age 15 and older able to read and write simple statements; some countries define as literate those who have completed a certain amount of schooling. **Embassy** addresses are for Wash., DC, area code (202).

See pages 459-74 for full-color maps and flags of all nations.

Afghanistan
Islamic Republic of Afghanistan

People: Population: 31,108,077. **Age distrib.:** <15: 42.6%; 65+: 2.5%. **Pop. density:** 123.5 per sq mi, 47.7 per sq km. **Urban:** 23.5%. **Ethnic groups:** Pashtun 42%, Tajik 27%, Hazara 9%, Uzbek 9%, Aimak 4%, Turkmen 3%, Baloch 2%. **Languages:** Afghan Persian, or Dari, Pashto (both official); Turkic langs. (Uzbek, Turkmen); 30 minor langs. (Balochi, Pashai). **Religions:** Sunni Muslim 80%, Shia Muslim 19%.

Geography: Total area: 251,827 sq mi, 652,230 sq km; **Land area:** 251,827 sq mi, 652,230 sq km. **Location:** In SW Asia, NW of the Indian subcontinent. **Neighbors:** Pakistan on E, S; Iran on W; Turkmenistan, Tajikistan, Uzbekistan on N. NE tip touches China. **Topography:** Landlocked and mountainous, much of it over 4,000 ft above sea level. The Hindu Kush Mts. tower 16,000 ft above Kabul and reach a height of 25,000 ft to the E. Trade with Pakistan flows through the 35-mi-long Khyber Pass. Climate is dry, with extreme temperatures; there are large desert regions. **Capital:** Kabul, 3,096,910.

Government: Type: Islamic republic. **Head of state and gov.:** Pres. Hamid Karzai; b. Dec. 24, 1957; in office: Dec. 7, 2004. **Local divisions:** 34 provinces. **Defense budget:** $2.09 bil. **Active troops:** 190,700.

Economy: Industries: small-scale prod. of bricks, textiles, soap, furniture, shoes, fertilizer, apparel, food prods. **Chief crops:** opium, wheat, fruits, nuts. **Natural resources:** nat. gas, petroleum, coal, copper, chromite, talc, barites, sulfur, lead, zinc, iron ore, salt, prec. and semiprec. stones. **Arable land:** 11.9%. **Livestock:** cattle: 5.5 mil; chickens: 13.4 mil; goats: 7.6 mil; sheep: 14.3 mil. **Fish catch:** 1,000 metric tons. **Electricity prod.:** 986 mil kWh. **Labor force:** agric. 78.6%, industry 5.7%, services 15.7%.

Finance: Monetary unit: Afghani (AFN) (Sept. 2013: 55.58 = $1 U.S.). **GDP:** $34.3 bil; **per capita GDP:** $1,100; **GDP growth:** 10.2%. **Imports:** $6.4 bil; Pakistan 25.8%, U.S. 17.4%, Russia 8.4%, India 5.5%, China 5.4%, Kazakhstan 4.5%, Germany 4.3%. **Exports:** $376 mil; Pakistan 33.1%, India 24.9%, Tajikistan 8.7%, U.S. 5.8%. **Tourism:** $53 mil. **Budget:** $4 bil. **Total reserves less gold:** $6 bil. **Gold:** 703,005 oz t. **CPI change:** 6.8%.

Transport: Motor vehicles: 34.1 vehicles per 1,000 pop. **Civil aviation:** 23 airports. **Chief ports:** Kheyrabad, Shir Khan.

Communications: TV sets: 80 per 1,000 pop. **Radios:** 129 per 1,000 pop. **Telephone lines:** 0.04 per 100 pop. **Internet:** 5.5%.

Health: Life expect.: 48.8 male; 51.5 female. **Births:** 39.1 per 1,000 pop. **Deaths:** 14.4 per 1,000 pop. **Natural inc.:** 2.47%. **Infant mortality:** 119.4 per 1,000 live births. **HIV rate:** <0.1%.

Education: Compulsory: ages 7-15. **Literacy:** 18.2%.

Major intl. organizations: UN (FAO, IBRD, ILO, IMF, WHO), WTO (observer).

Embassy: 2341 Wyoming Ave. NW 20008; 483-6410.

Website: www.president.gov.af

Afghanistan, occupying a favored invasion route since antiquity, has been variously known as Ariana or Bactria (in ancient times) and Khorasan (in the Middle Ages). Foreign empires alternated rule with local emirs and kings until the 18th cent., when a unified kingdom was established. In 1973, a military coup ushered in a republic.

Pro-Soviet leftists took power in a bloody 1978 coup and concluded an economic and military treaty with the USSR. In Dec. 1979 the USSR began a massive airlift into Kabul and backed a new coup, leading to the installation of a more pro-Soviet leader. Soviet forces fanned out over Afghanistan and waged a protracted guerrilla war with Muslim rebels, in which some 15,000 Soviet troops reportedly died.

A UN-mediated agreement was signed Apr. 14, 1988, providing for withdrawal of Soviet troops, a neutral Afghan state, and repatriation of refugees. Afghan rebels rejected the pact. The Soviets completed their troop withdrawal Feb. 15, 1989; fighting between Afghan rebels and government forces ensued. Communist Pres. Najibullah resigned Apr. 16, 1992, as competing guerrilla forces advanced on Kabul. The rebels achieved power Apr. 28, ending 14 years of Soviet-backed regimes. More than 2 mil Afghans had been killed, and 6 mil had left the country since 1979.

Clashes between moderates and Islamic fundamentalist forces followed the rebel victory. Burhanuddin Rabbani, a guerrilla leader, became president June 28, 1992, but fierce fighting continued around Kabul and elsewhere. The Taliban, an insurgent Islamic radical faction, captured Kabul in Sept. 1996. The Taliban executed Najibullah and empowered Islamic religious police to enforce strict Islamic codes of dress and behavior. Rabbani and other ousted leaders fled to the north.

Victories in the northern cities of Mazar-e Sharif, Aug. 8, 1998, and Taloqan, Aug. 8-11, gave the Taliban control over more than 90% of the country. On Aug. 20, U.S. cruise missiles struck SE of Kabul, hitting facilities the U.S. said were terrorist training camps run by Osama bin Laden. The UN imposed sanctions Nov. 14, 1999, when Afghanistan refused to turn over bin Laden to the U.S. for prosecution; a UN ban on military aid to the Taliban took effect Jan. 19, 2001.

After the Sept. 11, 2001, attacks on the World Trade Center and Pentagon, the U.S., blaming bin Laden, demanded that the Taliban surrender him and shut down his al-Qaeda terrorist network. When the Taliban refused, the U.S., with British assistance, began bombing Afghanistan Oct. 7, as part of Operation Enduring Freedom.

Supported by the U.S., the opposition Northern Alliance recaptured Mazar-e Sharif Nov. 9 and took Kabul 4 days later; Taliban forces abandoned Kandahar, their last stronghold, to southern tribesmen Dec. 7. A power-sharing agreement signed by 4 anti-Taliban factions, including the Northern Alliance, provided for an interim government headed by Hamid Karzai, a Pashtun tribal leader. The UN authorized a multinational security force Dec. 20, 2001.

Meeting June 13, 2002, in Kabul, a traditional council (*loya jirga*) chose Karzai to head a new transitional government. The U.S. announced the end of major combat operations in Afghanistan, May 1, 2003, but resistance continued. NATO officially assumed control of peacekeeping forces (ISAF) Aug. 11. A new constitution took effect Jan. 26, 2004.

The most intense fighting in more than 4 years erupted Mar. 2006 with a new wave of suicide bombings, rocket and mortar attacks, and other strikes by Taliban insurgents against military and civilian targets. Erosion of government authority led to an increase in opium growing; the Taliban, local warlords, and some Karzai associates were accused of profiting from the drug trade. A record poppy crop of 8,200 metric tons in 2007 made Afghanistan the source of 93% of

the world's illicit opium; drought, blight, and local suppression efforts cut estimated output to 3,600 metric tons by 2010.

Operating from sanctuaries across the border in Pakistan, Islamist suicide bombers and Taliban insurgents stepped up their activities, 2007-11. Violence escalated in the run-up to the presidential election Aug. 20, 2009; on that day, Taliban attacks, intended to suppress turnout, killed at least 30 people. With Karzai in the lead, a UN-backed commission overseeing the tally ordered a recount, citing "clear and convincing evidence of fraud" at numerous polling stations; a runoff election scheduled for Nov. 7 was canceled when Karzai's lone opponent dropped out of the race. Karzai was sworn in for a second term Nov. 19, despite growing U.S. doubts about his ability to prosecute the war and root out corruption. Weak turnout, allegations of vote-buying, and Taliban attacks marred parliamentary elections Sept. 18, 2010. After a decade-long manhunt, U.S. commandos killed bin Laden shortly after midnight May 2, 2011, in Abbottabad, Pakistan. Insurgents retaliated Aug. 6 by shooting down a Chinook transport helicopter, killing 30 Americans (including 22 Navy SEALs) and 8 Afghans. Other violence included the killing July 12 of Ahmed Wali Karzai, the powerful half-brother of Pres. Karzai; a truck bombing Sept. 11 in Wardak Province that killed 5 Afghan civilians and wounded 77 NATO soldiers; attacks Sept. 13 on the U.S. embassy, NATO headquarters, and other targets in Kabul; and the assassination Sept. 20 of former Pres. Rabbani, a leader in government-backed peace talks with the Taliban.

Between Jan. 2009 and June 2011, the number of U.S. troops in Afghanistan rose from about 36,000 to 101,000, while the number of allied foreign forces under ISAF increased from nearly 32,000 to more than 42,000. The U.S. June 22, 2011, outlined a timetable for ending the war. Ten-thousand U.S. troops left by the end of 2011 and another 23,000 pulled out in 2012; the combined total of 33,000 roughly equaled the "surge" in U.S. troops that Pres. Obama announced in Dec. 2009. Other coalition partners including the UK and France also began troop pullouts. In 2013, U.S. troop commanders in Afghanistan suggested maintaining about 13,600 American troops in the country after 2014.

Intensification of hostilities between coalition forces and insurgents increased casualties. Coalition military fatalities rose from 295 in 2008 to 521 in 2009, 711 in 2010, 566 in 2011, 402 in 2012, and 74 from Jan.-June 2013; of more than 3,309 coalition military deaths since Operation Enduring Freedom began in Oct. 2001, more than 2,235 were from the U.S., 444 from the UK, and nearly 160 from Canada. According to the UN, despite an overall drop of 12% in civilian casualties in 2012, 1,319 Afghan civilians were killed and 2,533 wounded during the first 6 months of 2013; the combined total was 23% higher than the corresponding period in 2012. By Mar. 2013, the U.S. Congress had appropriated about $640 bil for the Afghanistan war and related military activities. "Green-on-blue" attacks, or Afghan security forces attacks on coalition troops, were slightly down in the first half of 2013 to 13% of coalition casualties after increasing to 15% in 2012, which was markedly up from 6% in 2011, 3% in 2010, 2% in 2009, and less than 1% in 2008.

Albania
Republic of Albania

People: Population: 3,011,405. **Age distrib.:** <15: 19.9% 65+: 10.8%. **Pop. density:** 284.7 per sq mi, 109.9 per sq km. **Urban:** 53.4%. **Ethnic groups:** Albanian 95%, Greek 3%, other (Vlach, Roma, Serb, Macedonian, Bulgarian) 2%. **Languages:** Albanian (official), Greek, Vlach, Romani, Slavic dialects. **Religions:** Muslim 70%, Albanian Orthodox 20%, Roman Catholic 10%.

Geography: Total area: 11,100 sq mi, 28,748 sq km; **Land area:** 10,578 sq mi, 27,398 sq km. **Location:** SE Europe, on SE coast of Adriatic Sea. **Neighbors:** Greece on S; Montenegro, Kosovo, Serbia on N; Macedonia on E. **Topography:** Apart from a narrow coastal plain, Albania consists of hills and mountains covered with scrub forest, cut by small E-W rivers. **Capital:** Tirana, 419,215.

Government: Type: Parliamentary democracy. **Head of state:** Pres. Bujar Nishani; b. Sept. 29, 1966; in office: July 24, 2012. **Head of gov.:** Prime Min. Edi Rama; b. July 4, 1964; in office: Sept. 10, 2013. **Local divisions:** 12 counties. **Defense budget:** $226 mil. **Active troops:** 14,250.

Finance: Monetary unit: Lek (ALL) (Sept. 2013: 106.44 = $1 U.S.). **GDP:** $26.5 bil (country has an informal and unreported sector that may be as large as 50% of official GDP); **per capita GDP:** $8,200; **GDP growth:** 1.3%. **Imports:** $4.2 bil; Italy 34.9%, Greece 11.7%, China 7.5%, Turkey 5.6%, Germany 4.3%. **Exports:** $921 mil; Italy 44.2%, Spain 9%, China 6.8%, Greece 4.9%, Turkey 4.7%. **Tourism:** $1.5 bil. **Budget:** $3.5 bil. **Total reserves less gold:** $2.5 bil. **Gold:** 50,607 oz t. **CPI change:** 2%.

Economy: Industries: perfumes and cosmetics, food and tobacco prods., textiles and clothing, lumber. **Chief crops:** wheat, corn, potatoes, vegetables, fruits, sugar beets, grapes. **Natural resources:** petroleum, nat. gas, coal, bauxite, chromite, copper, iron ore, nickel, salt, timber, hydropower. **Crude oil reserves:** 172.4 mil bbls. **Arable land:** 22.7%. **Livestock:** cattle: 492,000; chickens: 6.6 mil; goats: 775,000; pigs: 163,000; sheep: 1.8 mil. **Fish catch:** 7,333 metric tons. **Electricity prod.:** 7.5 bil kWh. **Labor force:** agric. 47.8%, industry 23%, services 29.2%.

Transport: Railways: 211 mi. **Civil aviation:** 105.6 mil pass.-mi; 4 airports. **Chief ports:** Durres, Sarande, Shengjin, Vlore.

Communications: TV sets: 190 per 1,000 pop. **Radios:** 585 per 1,000 pop. **Telephone lines:** 9.7 per 100 pop. **Internet:** 54.7%.

Health: Life expect.: 75.2 male; 80.7 female. **Births:** 12.6 per 1,000 pop. **Deaths:** 6.4 per 1,000 pop. **Natural inc.:** 0.62%. **Infant mortality:** 13.7 per 1,000 live births. **HIV rate:** NA.

Major intl. organizations: UN (FAO, IBRD, ILO, IMF, IMO, WHO), NATO, OSCE, WTO.

Education: Compulsory: ages 6-14. **Literacy:** 96.8%.

Embassy: 2100 S St. NW 20008; 223-4942.

Website: www.km.gov.al

Ancient Illyria was conquered by Romans, Slavs, and Turks (15th cent.); the Turks Islamized the population. Independent Albania was proclaimed in 1912; the republic was formed in 1920. King Zog I ruled 1925-39 until Italy invaded.

Communist partisans took over in 1944 and allied Albania with the USSR but broke with the USSR in 1960 over de-Stalinization. Billions of dollars in Chinese financial assistance was cut off in 1978 when Albania attacked China's policies. Large-scale purges of officials occurred during the 1970s.

Enver Hoxha, the nation's ruler for 4 decades, died Apr. 11, 1985. The new regime introduced some liberalization, including measures in 1990 providing for freedom to travel abroad. Efforts were begun to improve ties with the outside world.

Albania's former Communists were routed in elections Mar. 1992, amid economic collapse and social unrest. Sali Berisha was elected as the first non-Communist president since WWII. Berisha's party claimed a landslide victory in disputed parliamentary elections, May 26 and June 2, 1996. Public protests over the collapse of fraudulent investment schemes in Jan. 1997 led to armed rebellion. The UN Security Council, Mar. 28, authorized a 7,000-member force to restore order. Socialists and their allies won parliamentary elections, June 29 and July 6, and international peacekeepers pulled out by Aug. 11.

During NATO's air war against Yugoslavia, Mar.-June 1999, Albania hosted some 465,000 Kosovar refugees. A pro-Berisha coalition victory in July 3, 2005, elections ended eight years of Socialist rule. Albania became a full member of NATO Apr. 1, 2009; the nation formally applied for EU membership Apr. 28. Following parliamentary elections June 28, 2009, Berisha remained prime min. Albania's candidacy for EU membership was delayed after parliament refused, Aug. 7, 2012, to reform its disciplinary procedures. The EU, Oct. 10, requested further government reforms, so the government announced, Feb. 25, 2013, a referendum to gain the necessary membership approval, for which it received stiff EU criticism. Socialists won June 23 parliamentary elections, and Edi Rama became the new prime min.

Algeria
People's Democratic Republic of Algeria

People: Population: 38,087,812. **Age distrib.:** <15: 28.1% 65+: 5.1%. **Pop. density:** 41.4 per sq mi, 16 per sq km. **Urban:** 73%. **Ethnic groups:** Arab-Berber 99%. **Languages:** Arabic (official), French (lingua franca), Berber dialects. **Religions:** Sunni Muslim (official) 99%, Christian and Jewish 1%.

Geography: Total area: 919,595 sq mi, 2,381,741 sq km; **Land area:** 919,595 sq mi, 2,381,741 sq km. **Location:** In NW Africa, from Medit. Sea into Sahara. **Neighbors:** Morocco, Western Sahara on W; Mauritania, Mali, Niger on S; Libya, Tunisia on E. **Topography:** The Tell, located on the coast, comprises fertile plains 50-100 mi wide with a moderate climate and adequate rain. Two major chains of Atlas Mts., running roughly E-W and reaching 7,000 ft, enclose a dry plateau region. Below lies the Sahara, mostly desert with major mineral resources. **Capital:** Algiers, 2,915,650. **Cities (urban aggl.):** Oran, 783,020.

Government: Type: Republic. **Head of state:** Pres. Abdelaziz Bouteflika; b. Mar. 2, 1937; in office: Apr. 27, 1999. **Head of gov.:** Prime Min. Abdelmakek Sellal; b. Aug. 1, 1948; in office: Sept. 3, 2012. **Local divisions:** 48 provinces. **Defense budget:** $9.37 bil. **Active troops:** 130,000.

Economy: Industries: petroleum, nat. gas, light industries, mining, electrical, petrochemical, food proc. **Chief crops:** wheat, barley, oats, grapes, olives, citrus, fruits. **Natural resources:** petroleum, nat. gas, iron ore, phosphates, uranium, lead, zinc. **Crude oil reserves:** 12.2 bil bbls. **Arable land:** 3.2%. **Livestock:** cattle: 1.8 mil; chickens: 127 mil; goats: 4.4 mil; pigs: 5,200; sheep: 24 mil. **Fish catch:** 104,003 metric tons. **Electricity prod.** 42.8 bil kWh. **Labor force:** agric. 14%, industry 13.4%, constr. and public works 10%, trade 14.6%, govt. 32%, other 16%.

Finance: Monetary unit: Dinar (DZD) (Sept. 2013: 82.53 = $1 U.S.). **GDP:** $277.4 bil; **per capita GDP:** $7,600; **GDP growth:** 2.5%. **Imports:** $48.3 bil; France 17.2%, China 11.5%, Spain 9.4%, Italy 9.1%, Germany 4.6%. **Exports:** $71.8 bil; U.S. 16.1%, Spain 13.9%, Canada 10.4%, Netherlands 8.4%, France 8%, Brazil 5.6%, UK 5.1%. **Tourism:** $209 mil. **Budget:** $84.8 bil. **Total reserves less gold:** $191.3 bil. **Gold:** 5.6 mil oz t. **CPI change:** 8.9%.

Transport: Railways: 2,469 mi. **Motor vehicles:** 115.9 vehicles per 1,000 pop. **Civil aviation:** 2.4 bil pass.-mi; 64 airports. **Chief ports:** Algiers, Annaba, Oran.

Communications: TV sets: 190 per 1,000 pop. **Radios:** 229 per 1,000 pop. **Telephone lines:** 8.8 per 100 pop. **Internet:** 15.2%.

Health: Life expect.: 75.0 male; 77.5 female. **Births:** 24.3 per 1,000 pop. **Deaths:** 4.3 per 1,000 pop. **Natural inc.:** 1.99%. **Infant mortality:** 22.6 per 1,000 live births. **HIV rate:** 0.1%.

Education: Compulsory: ages 6-14. **Literacy:** 72.6%.
Major intl. organizations: UN (FAO, IBRD, ILO, IMF, IMO, WHO), AL, AU, OPEC, WTO (observer).
Embassy: 2118 Kalorama Rd. NW 20008; 265-2800.
Website: www.premier-ministre.gov.dz or www.algerianembassy.org

Earliest known inhabitants were ancestors of Berbers, followed by Phoenicians, Romans, Vandals, and, finally, Arabs. Turkey ruled 1518-1830, when France took control. Large-scale European immigration followed. Arab nationalists launched a guerrilla war, 1954, that more than 400,000 French troops were unable to suppress. After French Pres. Charles de Gaulle came to power, 1958, colonial rule ended, nearly all Europeans left, and Algeria declared independence July 5, 1962. Ahmed Ben Bella ruled until 1965, when an army coup installed Col. Houari Boumedienne, a former guerrilla leader who held power until his death in 1978.

Hundreds died in antigovernment riots protesting economic hardship, Oct. 1988. In 1989, voters approved a new constitution. The government canceled the Jan. 1992 elections and banned all non-religious activities at Algeria's 10,000 mosques. Pres. Mohammed Boudiaf was assassinated June 29, 1992. Over the next 7 years, Muslim fundamentalists attacked high-ranking officials, security forces, foreigners, and others; pro-government death squads also were active.

Liamine Zeroual won the Nov. 16, 1995, presidential election. A new constitution banning Islamic political parties and increasing the president's powers passed in a Nov. 1996 referendum. Abdelaziz Bouteflika, who became president after a flawed Apr. 15, 1999, election, reconciled with rebels and won approval for an amnesty plan in a referendum, Sept. 16. Some 100 people died and thousands were injured in violent protests Apr.-June 2001, chiefly by Algeria's Berber minority. Bouteflika was reelected Apr. 8, 2004; opponents charged fraud.

An earthquake in northern Algeria, May 21, 2003, claimed more than 2,200 lives. Under a reconciliation plan approved by referendum Sept. 2005, the government in Mar. 2006 began freeing Islamists jailed for their role in the 1990s civil war, which left up to 200,000 people dead and 8,000 "disappeared."

Radical Islamists bombed police stations in Oct. 2006 and Feb. 2007. A group known as al-Qaeda in the Islamic Maghreb (AQIM) carried out several suicide bombings throughout 2007, killing more than 100 people. A surge in AQIM violence in Aug. 2008 left more than 100 people dead.

Parliament, Nov. 12, 2008, amended the constitution to abolish presidential term limits, enabling Bouteflika to run for a 3rd term. He claimed more than 90% of the vote in a 2009 election denounced as fraudulent by opposition parties. During Arab Spring uprisings in early 2011, Bouteflika's government suppressed street protests in Algiers, Feb. 12, and used oil revenues to raise salaries of teachers, police, and other discontented civil servants. The country's governing party, the Natl. Liberation Front, strengthened its hold on power in May 10, 2012, parliamentary elections that opposition groups called fraudulent. On Apr. 27, 2013, 76-year-old Bouteflika, who was rarely seen and was suspected of being in poor health, was hospitalized briefly after suffering a transient ischemic attack, or mini-stroke. Though his health continued to suffer as of Aug. 2013, he was said to be considering running for a 4th term in 2014.

AQIM members protesting France's involvement in Mali seized the In Amenas gas facility Jan. 16, 2013, holding about 40 foreign workers hostage for 4 days and demanding the release of about 100 Islamist prisoners being held in Algeria. In the end, 37 hostages, including 3 Americans, had died, as well as some 29 militants at the hands of French-led forces attempting to liberate the facility.

Andorra
Principality of Andorra

People: Population: 85,293. **Age distrib.:** <15: 15.5%; 65+: 13.8%. **Pop. density:** 472 per sq mi, 182.3 per sq km. **Urban:** 87.3%. **Ethnic groups:** Spanish 43%, Andorran 33%, Portuguese 11%, French 7%. **Languages:** Catalan (official), French, Castilian, Portuguese. **Religion:** Roman Catholic (predominant).
Geography: Total area: 181 sq mi, 468 sq km; **Land area:** 181 sq mi, 468 sq km. **Location:** SW Europe, in Pyrenees Mts. **Neighbors:** Spain on S, France on N. **Topography:** High mountains and narrow valleys cover the country. **Capital:** Andorra la Vella, 23,497.
Government: Type: Parliamentary co-principality. **Heads of state:** President of France and Bishop of Urgel (Spain), as co-princes. **Head of gov.:** Antoni Martí Petit; b. 1963; in office: May 12, 2011. **Local divisions:** 7 parishes. **Defense budget:** NA. **Active troops:** No regular military forces. France and Spain responsible for defense.
Economy: Industries: tourism (skiing), banking, tobacco, cattle raising, timber, furniture. **Chief crops:** rye, wheat, barley, oats, vegetables. **Natural resources:** hydropower, mineral water, timber, iron ore, lead. **Arable land:** 5.3%. **Labor force:** agric. 0.4%, industry 4.7%, services 94.9%.
Finance: Monetary unit: Euro (EUR) (Sept. 2013: 0.76 = $1 U.S.). **GDP:** $3.2 bil; **per capita GDP** (2011): $37,200; **GDP growth:** –1.6%. **Imports:** $1.4 bil. **Exports:** $70 mil. **Budget** (2011): $470 mil. **Total reserves less gold:** NA. **CPI change:** NA.
Transport: NA

Communications; TV sets: 440 per 1,000 pop. **Radios:** 243 per 1,000 pop. **Telephone lines:** 44.6 per 100 pop. **Internet:** 86.4%.
Health: Life expect.: 80.5 male; 84.8 female. **Births:** 8.9 per 1,000 pop. **Deaths:** 6.7 per 1,000 pop. **Natural inc.:** 0.22%. **Infant mortality:** 3.7 per 1,000 live births. **HIV rate:** NA.
Education: Compulsory: ages 6-15. **Literacy:** 100%.
Major intl. organizations: UN (FAO, WHO), OSCE, WTO (observer).
Embassy: 2 UN Plaza, 27th Fl., New York, NY 10017; (212) 750-8064.
Website: www.andorra.ad

France and the bishop of Urgel held joint sovereignty over Andorra from 1278 to 1993. Voters chose to adopt a parliamentary system Mar. 14, 1993, although co-princes remain heads of state. Tourism, especially skiing, is the economic mainstay. Andorra attracts more than 9 mil visitors annually. For years, Andorra served as a tax haven, but it began reforms in 2008 and was removed from the list of uncooperative tax havens, May 27, 2009, and added South Korea, Apr. 30, 2012; Poland, June 15, 2012; and Italy, July 25, 2012; to the list of countries with which it has tax information exchange treaties.

Angola
Republic of Angola

People: Population: 18,565,269. **Age distrib.:** <15: 43.5%; 65+: 2.9%. **Pop. density:** 38.6 per sq mi, 14.9 per sq km. **Urban:** 59.2%. **Ethnic groups:** Ovimbundu 37%, Kimbundu 25%, Bakongo 13%, mestico (mixed European and native African) 2%, European 1%. **Languages:** Portuguese (official), Bantu, other African langs. **Religions:** indigenous beliefs 47%, Roman Catholic 38%, Protestant 15%.
Geography: Total area: 481,354 sq mi, 1,246,700 sq km; **Land area:** 481,354 sq mi, 1,246,700 sq km. **Location:** In SW Africa on Atlantic coast. **Neighbors:** Namibia on S, Zambia on E, Dem. Rep. of the Congo on N; Cabinda, an enclave separated from rest of country by short Atlantic coast of Dem. Rep. of the Congo, borders Congo Rep. **Topography:** Mostly plateau 3,000-5,000 ft above sea level, rising from a narrow coastal strip. There is also a temperate highland area in the west-central region, a desert in S, and a tropical rain forest covering Cabinda. **Capital:** Luanda, 5,067,530. **Cities (urban aggl.):** Huambo, 1,097,970.
Government: Type: Republic. **Head of state and gov.:** Pres. José Eduardo dos Santos; b. Aug. 28, 1942; in office: Sept. 21, 1979. **Local divisions:** 18 provinces. **Defense budget:** $4.09 bil. **Active troops:** 107,000.
Economy: Industries: petroleum, diamonds, mining, cement, metal prods., fish and food proc. **Chief crops:** bananas, sugarcane, coffee, sisal, corn, cotton, cassava, tobacco. **Natural resources:** petroleum, diamonds, iron ore, phosphates, copper, feldspar, gold, bauxite, uranium. **Crude oil reserves:** 10.5 bil bbls. **Arable land:** 3.3%. **Livestock:** cattle: 4.6 mil; chickens: 20 mil; goats: 3.9 mil; pigs: 2.1 mil; sheep: 1 mil. **Fish catch:** 262,910 metric tons. **Electricity prod.:** 5.1 bil kWh. **Labor force:** agric. 85%, industry and services 15%.
Finance: Monetary unit: Kwanza (AOA) (Sept. 2013: 96.06 = $1 U.S.). **GDP:** $130.4 bil; **per capita GDP:** $6,500; **GDP growth:** 8.4%. **Imports:** $22.9 bil; China 20.8%, Portugal 19.5%, U.S. 7.7%, South Africa 7.1%, Brazil 5.9%. **Exports:** $69.3 bil; China 45.8%, U.S. 13.7%, India 11%, South Africa 4.1%. **Tourism:** $647 mil. **Budget:** $44.2 bil. **Total reserves less gold:** $33.4 bil. **CPI change:** 10.3%.
Transport: Railways: 1,717 mi. **Motor vehicles:** 7 vehicles per 1,000 pop. **Civil aviation:** 422.5 mil pass.-mi; 31 airports. **Chief ports:** Cabinda, Lobito, Luanda, Namibe.
Communications: TV sets: 140 per 1,000 pop. **Radios:** 81 per 1,000 pop. **Telephone lines:** 1.5 per 100 pop. **Internet:** 16.9%.
Health: Life expect.: 53.8 male; 56.1 female. **Births:** 39.2 per 1,000 pop. **Deaths:** 11.9 per 1,000 pop. **Natural inc.:** 2.73%. **Infant mortality:** 81.8 per 1,000 live births. **HIV rate:** 2.1%.
Education: Compulsory: ages 6-11. **Literacy:** 70.4%.
Major intl. organizations: UN (FAO, IBRD, ILO, IMF, WHO), AU, OPEC, WTO.
Embassy: 2100-2108 16th St. NW 20009; 785-1156.
Website: www.governo.gov.ao or www.angola.org

From the early centuries CE to 1500, Bantu tribes penetrated most of the region. Portuguese came in 1583, allied with the Bakongo kingdom in the north, and developed the slave trade. Large-scale colonization began in the 20th cent., when 400,000 Portuguese immigrated.

A guerrilla war, 1961-75, ended when Portugal granted independence. Fighting then erupted among 3 rival rebel groups—the National Front, based in Zaire (now Dem. Rep. of the Congo); the Soviet-backed Popular Movement for the Liberation of Angola (MPLA); and the National Union for the Total Independence of Angola (UNITA), aided by the U.S. and South Africa. Cuban troops and Soviet aid helped the MPLA win control of most of the country by 1976, although fighting continued through the 1980s. The MPLA government and UNITA signed a peace accord May 1, 1991.

Elections were held, Sept. 1992, but fighting again broke out, as UNITA rejected the results. UNITA signed a new peace treaty with the government, Nov. 20, 1994, but the rebels were slow to demobilize. The UN Security Council voted, Aug. 28, 1997, to impose sanctions on UNITA. The UN ended its mission in Angola, Mar. 1999, as the civil war continued.

The UN estimated that the war with UNITA had claimed some 1 mil lives and left another 2.5 mil people homeless by mid-2001. Government troops killed rebel leader Jonas Savimbi Feb. 22, 2002. UNITA agreed to a truce Apr. 4, 2002, ending the 27-year-long civil war but not fighting between government forces and separatists in oil-rich Cabinda; rebels there agreed to a cease-fire July 2006.

With proven petroleum reserves estimated at more than 9 bil barrels, Angola is among Africa's leading oil producers. Due to mismanagement and corruption, up to $4.2 bil in oil revenues went missing, 1997-2002. The ruling MPLA claimed victory in voting Sept. 2008, in Angola's first parliamentary elections in 16 years. Parliament approved Jan. 21, 2010, a new constitution augmenting the power of MPLA leader José Eduardo dos Santos, Angola's president since 1979. The MPLA won flawed elections, Aug 31, 2012, giving Dos Santos another 5-year term.

Antigua and Barbuda

People: Population: 90,156. **Age distrib.:** <15: 24.7%; 65+: 7.1%. **Pop. density:** 527.1 per sq mi, 203.7 per sq km. **Urban:** 29.8%. **Ethnic groups:** black 91%, mixed 4%, white 2%. **Languages:** English (official), local dialects. **Religions:** Protestant 76% (Anglican 26%, Seventh-Day Adventist 12%, Pentecostal 11%, Moravian 11%, Methodist 8%, Baptist 5%, Church of God 5%), Roman Catholic 10%, other Christian 5%.

Geography: Total area: 171 sq mi, 443 sq km (Antigua, 108 sq mi, 280 sq km; Barbuda, 62 sq mi, 161 sq km); **Land area:** 171 sq mi, 443 sq km. **Location:** E Caribbean. **Neighbors:** St. Kitts and Nevis to W, Guadeloupe (Fr.) to S. **Topography:** These are mostly low-lying and limestone coral islands. Antigua is mostly hilly with an indented coast; Barbuda is a flat island with a large lagoon on W. **Capital:** St. John's, 26,720.

Government: Type: Constitutional monarchy with parliamentary system of govt. **Head of state:** Queen Elizabeth II, rep. by Gov.-Gen. Dame Louise Agnetha Lake-Tack; b. July 26, 1944; in office: July 17, 2007. **Head of gov.:** Prime Min. Baldwin Spencer; b. Oct. 8, 1948; in office: Mar. 24, 2004. **Local divisions:** 6 parishes, 2 dependencies. **Defense budget:** $7 mil. **Active troops:** 180.

Economy: Industries: tourism, constr., light mfg. **Chief crops:** cotton, fruits, vegetables, bananas, coconuts. **Natural resources:** negligible. **Arable land:** 9.1%. **Livestock:** cattle: 14,600; chickens: 150,000; goats: 37,000; pigs: 3,000; sheep: 22,000. **Fish catch:** 2,300 metric tons. **Electricity prod.:** 115 mil kWh. **Labor force:** agric. 7%, industry 11%, services 82%.

Finance: Monetary unit: East Caribbean Dollar (XCD) (Sept. 2013: 2.70 = $1 U.S.). **GDP:** $1.6 bil; **per capita GDP:** $18,300; **GDP growth:** 1.6%. **Imports:** $400 mil. **Exports:** $37.9 mil. **Tourism:** $319 mil. **Budget** (2009): $293.4 mil. **Total reserves less gold:** $162 mil. **CPI change:** 3.4%.

Transport: Civil aviation: 76.4 mil pass.-mi; 2 airports. **Chief port:** Saint John's.

Communications: TV sets: 465 per 1,000 pop. **Radios:** 497 per 1,000 pop. **Telephone lines:** 38.7 per 100 pop. **Internet:** 83.8%.

Health: Life expect.: 73.9 male; 78.1 female. **Births:** 16.1 per 1,000 pop. **Deaths:** 5.7 per 1,000 pop. **Natural inc.:** 1.04%. **Infant mortality:** 13.7 per 1,000 live births. **HIV rate:** NA.

Education: Compulsory: ages 5-15. **Literacy:** 99%.

Major intl. organizations: UN (FAO, IBRD, ILO, IMF, WHO), Caricom, the Commonwealth, OAS, OECS, WTO.

Embassy: 3216 New Mexico Ave. NW 20016; 362-5122.
Website: www.ab.gov.ag

Columbus landed on Antigua in 1493. The British colonized it in 1632. The British-associated state of Antigua and Barbuda achieved independence as Antigua and Barbuda on Nov. 1, 1981. Tourism, which accounts for more than 25% of GDP, was hit hard by the worldwide recession in 2008-10. The economy also suffered after Robert Allen Stanford, a Texas businessman, was charged by U.S. authorities Feb. 17, 2009, with employing his Antigua-based Stanford Intl. Bank to conduct a fraudulent $7 bil investment scheme. He was convicted Mar. 6, 2012.

The WTO ruled Jan. 28, 2013, that Antigua and Barbuda had a right to recoup its losses by offering downloads of such American copyrighted material as movies and TV shows because the U.S. had failed to comply with the WTO's 2004 ruling that the U.S.'s gambling ban that applied to websites sponsored by Antigua and Barbuda violated the nations' trade agreement.

Argentina

Argentine Republic

People: Population: 42,610,981. **Age distrib.:** <15: 25.1%; 65+: 11.3%. **Pop. density:** 40.3 per sq mi, 15.6 per sq km. **Urban:** 92.5%. **Ethnic groups:** white (mostly Spanish and Italian) 97%; mestizo (mixed white and Amerindian), Amerindian, other non-white groups 3%. **Languages:** Spanish (official), Italian, English, German, French, indigenous (Mapudungun, Quechua). **Religions:** nominally Roman Catholic 92%, Protestant 2%, Jewish 2%.

Geography: Total area: 1,073,518 sq mi, 2,780,400 sq km; **Land area:** 1,056,642 sq mi, 2,736,690 sq km. **Location:** Occupies most of southern S America. **Neighbors:** Chile on W; Bolivia, Paraguay on N; Brazil, Uruguay on NE. **Topography:** Mountains in W are the Andean, Central, Misiones, and Southern ranges. Aconcagua (22,831 ft) is the highest peak in the Western Hemisphere. E of the Andes are heavily wooded plains, called the Gran Chaco

in N, and the fertile, treeless Pampas in the central region. Patagonia, in S, is bleak and arid. Rio de la Plata, an estuary in NE, 170 by 140 mi, is mostly freshwater, from 2,485-mi Parana and 1,000-mi Uruguay Rivers. **Capital:** Buenos Aires, 13,527,800. **Cities (urban aggl.):** Córdoba, 1,555,927; Rosario, 1,283,314.

Government: Type: Republic. **Head of state and gov.:** Pres. Cristina Fernández de Kirchner; b. Feb. 19, 1953; in office: Dec. 10, 2007. **Local divisions:** 23 provinces, 1 autonomous city. **Defense budget:** $4.26 bil. **Active troops:** 73,100.

Economy: Industries: food proc., motor vehicles, consumer durables, textiles, chemicals and petrochemicals. **Chief crops:** sunflower seeds, lemons, soybeans, grapes, corn. **Natural resources:** lead, zinc, tin, copper, iron ore, manganese, petroleum, uranium. **Crude oil reserves:** 2.8 bil bbls. **Arable land:** 13.9%. **Livestock:** cattle: 48 mil; chickens: 100 mil; goats: 4.3 mil; pigs: 2.4 mil; sheep: 16.3 mil. **Fish catch:** 795,698 metric tons. **Electricity prod.:** 119.3 bil kWh. **Labor force:** agric. 5%, industry 23%, services 72%.

Finance: Monetary unit: Peso (ARS) (Sept. 2013: 5.70 = $1 U.S.). **GDP:** $755.3 bil; **per capita GDP:** $18,400; **GDP growth:** 1.9%. **Imports:** $65.6 bil; Brazil 26.9%, U.S. 15.4%, China 11.8%, Germany 4.5%. **Exports:** $81.2 bil; Brazil 19.7%, China 7.2%, Chile 5.8%, U.S. 5%. **Tourism:** $4.9 bil. **Budget:** $133.6 bil. **Total reserves less gold:** $39.9 bil. **Gold:** 2 mil oz t. **CPI change:** 10%.

Transport: Railways: 22,970 mi. **Motor vehicles:** 286.8 vehicles per 1,000 pop. **Civil aviation:** 7.3 bil pass.-mi; 161 airports. **Chief ports:** Bahia Blanca, Buenos Aires, La Plata, Punta Colorado.

Communications: TV sets: 325 per 1,000 pop. **Radios:** 681 per 1,000 pop. **Telephone lines:** 24.3 per 100 pop. **Internet:** 55.8%.

Health: Life expect.: 74.1 male; 80.7 female. **Births:** 17.1 per 1,000 pop. **Deaths:** 7.4 per 1,000 pop. **Natural inc.:** 0.98%. **Infant mortality:** 10.2 per 1,000 live births. **HIV rate:** 0.4%.

Education: Compulsory: ages 5-17. **Literacy:** 97.9%.

Major intl. organizations: UN (FAO, IBRD, ILO, IMF, WHO), OAS, WTO.

Embassy: 1600 New Hampshire Ave. NW 20009; 238-6401.
Website: www.argentina.ar

Nomadic Indians roamed the Pampas when Spaniards arrived, 1515-16, led by Juan Díaz de Solís. Nearly all the Indians were killed by the late 19th cent. The colonists won independence, 1816, and a long period of disorder ended in a strong centralized government.

Large-scale Italian, German, and Spanish immigration in the decades after 1880 spurred modernization. Social reforms were enacted in the 1920s, but military coups prevailed, 1930-46, until Gen. Juan Perón was elected president.

Perón, with his wife, Eva Duarte (d. 1952), introduced labor reforms but suppressed speech and press freedoms, closed religious schools, and ran the country into debt. A 1955 coup exiled Perón. A series of military and civilian regimes followed. Perón returned in 1973 and was again elected president. He died 10 months later. His wife Isabel, who had been elected vice president, succeeded him, becoming the first woman head of state in the Western Hemisphere.

A military junta ousted Perón in 1976 amid charges of corruption. Under a continuing state of siege, the army conducted a "dirty war" against guerrillas and leftists. An estimated 30,000 people "disappeared."

Argentine troops seized control of the British-held Falkland Islands (Islas Malvinas) on Apr. 2, 1982. The British imposed an air and sea blockade around the Falklands. Fighting began May 1. British troops landed on East Falkland May 21. Argentine troops surrendered, June 14.

Democratic rule returned in 1983. On Dec. 9, 1985, 5 former junta members were found guilty of murder and human rights abuses during the "dirty war" period. Buenos Aires Mayor Fernando de la Rúa won the presidential election Oct. 24, 1999, but resigned in 2001 after a prolonged recession resulted in a debt of more than $130 bil.

Congress, Jan. 1, 2002, chose a Peronist, Eduardo Alberto Duhalde, to finish de la Rúa's term after 2 weeks of mass protests. Further economic decline and renewed protests led Duhalde, July 2, to schedule an early presidential election for Mar. 2003; another Peronist, Néstor Kirchner, took office May 25, 2003. A new IMF aid deal, approved Sept. 10, 2003, rescued Argentina from default.

The supreme court, June 14, 2005, overturned amnesty laws that had barred prosecution for "dirty war" crimes committed while the military ruled Argentina. Economic growth, 2004-05, allowed Argentina to repay its $9.57 bil debt to the IMF, Jan. 3, 2006.

Cristina Fernández de Kirchner, ran as the Peronist candidate after her husband and was elected president Oct. 28, 2007. Responding to mass protests by farmers, Argentina's senate voted July 2008 to block Kirchner's proposed tax increase on agricultural exports. A candidate slate led by Néstor Kirchner was defeated in legislative elections June 2009, and the Peronists lost control of both houses of congress. Argentina became the first Latin American country to extend full marriage rights to same-sex couples in July 2010.

Néstor Kirchner died Oct. 27, 2010. Cristina Fernández de Kirchner was reelected Oct. 23, 2011. She was the first woman to win reelection in Latin America. An inflation rate of 25% prompted a general strike by farmers, bank workers, and train operators among others on Nov. 20, 2012. Meanwhile, the nation's Jewish population charged the government with anti-Semitism for attempting to ease relations with Iran in Nov. On May 29, 2013, Argentine special prosecutor Alberto Nisman claimed that Iran was plotting to carry out

terrorist attacks throughout Latin America, directly and through the Lebanese militant group Hezbollah.

Former Pres. Carlos Saúl Menem, a senator, was convicted Mar. 8, 2013, of weapons smuggling during his 1989-99 term and was sentenced, June 13, to 7 years in prison. Buenos Aires Archbishop Jorge Mario Bergoglio was elected pope Mar. 13, 2013; he was the first Jesuit pope and the first pope from the Americas. He took the name Francis after advocate for the poor St. Francis of Assisi.

About 12 in. of rain fell in roughly 4 hours the night of Apr. 2, 2013, causing flash flooding, 86 deaths in Greater La Plata and Greater Buenos Aires, and the evacuation of more than 2,500 people.

Armenia
Republic of Armenia

People: Population: 2,974,184. **Age distrib.:** <15: 17.3%; 65+: 9.8%. **Pop. density:** 273.1 per sq mi, 105.5 per sq km. **Urban:** 64.1%. **Ethnic groups:** Armenian 98%, Yezidi (Kurd) 1%. **Languages:** Armenian (official), Yezidi, Russian. **Religions:** Armenian Apostolic 95%, other Christian 4%, Yezidi 1%.

Geography: Total area: 11,484 sq mi, 29,743 sq km; **Land area:** 10,889 sq mi, 28,203 sq km. **Location:** SW Asia. **Neighbors:** Georgia on N, Azerbaijan on E, Iran on S, Turkey on W. **Topography:** Mountainous with many peaks above 10,000 ft. **Capital:** Yerevan, 1,116,380.

Government: Type: Republic. **Head of state:** Pres. Serzh Sargsyan; b. June 30, 1954; in office: Apr. 9, 2008. **Head of gov.:** Prime Min. Tigran Sargsyan; b. Jan. 29, 1960; in office; Apr. 9, 2008. **Local divisions:** 11 provinces. **Defense budget:** $391 mil. **Active troops:** 48,850.

Economy: Industries: diamond proc., metal-cutting machine tools, forging-pressing machines, elec. motors, tires, knitted wear. **Chief crops:** fruits (espec. grapes), vegetables. **Natural resources:** gold, copper, molybdenum, zinc, bauxite. **Arable land:** 15.1%. **Livestock:** cattle: 571,400; chickens: 3.3 mil; goats: 28,891; pigs: 114,800; sheep: 503,624. **Fish catch:** 7,095 metric tons. **Electricity prod.:** 6.3 bil kWh. **Labor force:** agric. 44.2%, industry 16.8%, services 39%.

Finance: Monetary unit: Dram (AMD) (Sept. 2013: 412.19 = $1 U.S.). **GDP:** $20 bil; **per capita GDP:** $5,900; **GDP growth:** 7.2%. **Imports:** $3.6 bil; Russia 24.6%, China 9%, Germany 6.2%, Iran 5.4%, Ukraine 5.4%, Turkey 4.7%. **Exports:** $1.5 bil; Russia 19.9%, Germany 11%, Belgium 9.4%, Bulgaria 8.8%, Iran 7.1%, Canada 6.2%, U.S. 6.1%, Georgia 5.9%, Netherlands 5.2%, Switzerland 5%. **Tourism:** $451 mil. **Budget:** $2.5 bil. **Total reserves less gold:** $1.8 bil. **CPI change:** 2.0%.

Transport: Railways: 540 mi. **Civil aviation:** 667.4 mil pass.-mi; 10 airports.

Communications: TV sets: 293 per 1,000 pop. **Radios:** 270 per 1,000 pop. **Telephone lines:** 18.8 per 100 pop. **Internet:** 39.2%.

Health: Life expect.: 70.1 male; 77.8 female. **Births:** 12.9 per 1,000 pop. **Deaths:** 8.5 per 1,000 pop. **Natural inc.:** 0.44%. **Infant mortality:** 17.6 per 1,000 live births. **HIV rate:** 0.2%.

Education: Compulsory: ages 6-14. **Literacy:** 99.6%.

Major intl. organizations: UN (FAO, IBRD, ILO, IMF, WHO), CIS, OSCE, WTO.

Embassy: 2225 R St. NW 20008; 319-1976.

Website: www.gov.am

Ancient Armenia extended into parts of what are now Turkey and Iran. Present-day Armenia was set up as a Soviet republic Apr. 2, 1921. It joined Georgian and Azerbaijan SSRs Mar. 12, 1922, to form the Transcaucasian SFSR, which became part of the USSR Dec. 30, 1922. Armenia became a constituent republic of the USSR Dec. 5, 1936. An earthquake struck Armenia Dec. 7, 1988; approximately 25,000 were killed.

Armenia declared independence Sept. 23, 1991, and became an independent state when the USSR disbanded Dec. 26, 1991. Nagorno-Karabakh, an enclave in Azerbaijan with an ethnic Armenian majority, seceded from Azerbaijan in 1988. A 1992-94 war that cost 30,000 lives ended in a cease-fire with Armenian forces in control of the enclave. Voters in the breakaway region approved a pro-independence constitution Dec. 10, 2006, that was rejected by the EU and OSCE.

Voters approved, July 5, 1995, a new constitution increasing presidential powers. Pres. Levon Ter-Petrosian won reelection Sept. 22, 1996, amid claims of fraud; he resigned Feb. 3, 1998, in a conflict over Nagorno-Karabakh. Robert Kocharian, a nationalist born in the disputed region, won the presidency Mar. 30, 1998. Gunmen stormed Parliament Oct. 27, 1999, killing Prime Min. Vazgen Sarkissian and 7 others. Kocharian won a second term Mar. 5, 2003, in a runoff vote that opposition groups and Western observers viewed as flawed.

Prime Min. Andranik Margaryan died of a heart attack Mar. 25, 2007, and was replaced by Def. Min. Serzh Sargsyan. He defeated Ter-Petrosian in a Feb. 19, 2008, presidential election criticized as flawed; opposition protests in Yerevan were forcibly suppressed Mar. 1, and a 20-day state of emergency followed. Sargsyan took office Apr. 9, 2008.

Armenia failed to ratify an Oct. 2009 treaty approved by Armenia and Turkey over the 1915-18 killing of more than 1 mil Armenians by Ottoman Turks due to renewed friction between the 2 countries in 2010. Pres. Sargsyan's party won May 6, 2012, parliamentary

elections that the OSCE called "open and peaceful" in spite of lingering shortcomings, and Sargsyan won reelection Feb. 18, 2013, with 59% of the vote. The presidential campaign was marred by violence, when Paruir Airikian, a minor candidate, was shot, Jan. 31, 2013, outside of his home in Yerevan.

Australia
Commonwealth of Australia

People: Population: 22,262,501. **Age distrib.:** <15: 18.1%; 65+: 14.7%. **Pop. density:** 7.5 per sq mi, 2.9 per sq km. **Urban:** 89.2%. **Ethnic groups:** white 92%, Asian 7%, aboriginal and other 1%. **Languages:** English, Chinese, Italian, Greek, Arabic, Vietnamese. **Religions:** Protestant 27% (Anglican 19%, Uniting Church 6%, Presbyterian and Reformed 3%), Catholic 26%, Eastern Orthodox 3%, other Christian 8%, Buddhist 2%, Muslim 2%, none 19%.

Geography: Total area: 2,988,902 sq mi, 7,741,220 sq km; **Land area:** 2,966,153 sq mi, 7,682,300 sq km. **Location:** SE of Asia, Indian O. is W and S, Pacific O. (Coral, Tasman Seas) is E; they meet N of Australia in Timor and Arafura Seas. Tasmania lies 150 mi S of Victoria state, across Bass Strait. **Neighbors:** Nearest are Indonesia, Papua New Guinea on N; Solomons, Fiji, and New Zealand on E. **Topography:** An island continent. The Great Dividing Range along the E coast has Mt. Kosciusko (7,310 ft). The Western Plateau rises to 2,000 ft, with arid areas in the Great Sandy and Great Victoria Deserts. The NW part of Western Australia and Northern Terr. are arid and hot. The NE has heavy rainfall and Cape York Peninsula has jungles. **Capital:** Canberra, 398,757. **Cities (urban aggl.):** Sydney, 4,543,205; Melbourne, 3,961,205; Brisbane, 2,038,565; Perth, 1,649,209; Adelaide, 1,198,271.

Government: Type: Federal parliamentary democracy. **Head of state:** Queen Elizabeth II, rep. by Gov.-Gen. Quentin Bryce; b. Dec. 23, 1942; in office: Sept. 5, 2008. **Head of gov.:** Prime Min. Anthony John Abbott; b. Nov. 4, 1957; in office: Sept. 18, 2013. **Local divisions:** 6 states, 2 territories. **Defense budget:** $25.1 bil. **Active troops:** 57,050.

Economy: Industries: mining, industrial and transp. equip., food proc., chemicals, steel. **Chief crops:** wheat, barley, sugarcane, fruits. **Natural resources:** bauxite, coal, iron ore, copper, tin, gold, silver, uranium, nickel, tungsten, rare earth elements, mineral sands, lead, zinc, diamonds, nat. gas, petroleum. **Crude oil reserves:** 1.4 bil bbls. **Other resources:** Wool (world's leading producer), beef. **Arable land:** 6.2%. **Livestock:** cattle: 28.5 mil; chickens: 90.7 mil; goats: 4.5 mil; pigs: 2.3 mil; sheep: 73.1 mil. **Fish catch:** 236,803 metric tons. **Electricity prod.:** (2011): 225.5 bil kWh. **Labor force:** agric. 3.6%, industry 21.1%, services 75%.

Finance: Monetary unit: Dollar (AUD) (Sept. 2013: 1.09 = $1 U.S.). **GDP:** $986.7 bil; **per capita GDP:** $43,300; **GDP growth:** 3.6%. **Imports:** $239.7 bil; China 18.2%, U.C. 11.6%, Japan 7.8%, Singapore 5.9%, Germany 4.6%, Thailand 4.2%, South Korea 4%. **Exports:** $258.8 bil; China 29.5%, Japan 19.3%, South Korea 8%, India 4.9%. **Tourism:** $31.5 bil. **Budget:** $541 bil. **Total reserves less gold:** $44.9 bil. **Gold:** 2.6 mil oz t. **CPI change:** 1.8%.

Transport: Railways: 23,889 mi. **Motor vehicles:** 725.8 vehicles per 1,000 pop. **Civil aviation:** 62.5 bil pass.-mi; 349 airports. **Chief ports:** Brisbane, Darwin, Fremantle, Geelong, Gladstone, Melbourne, Newcastle, Sydney.

Communications: TV sets: 659 per 1,000 pop. **Radios:** 1,885 per 1,000 pop. **Telephone lines:** 45.7 per 100 pop. **Internet:** 82.3%.

Health: Life expect.: 79.6 male; 84.5 female. **Births:** 12.2 per 1,000 pop. **Deaths:** 7.0 per 1,000 pop. **Natural inc.:** 0.52%. **Infant mortality:** 4.5 per 1,000 live births. **HIV rate:** 0.2%.

Education: Compulsory: ages 5-15. **Literacy:** 99%.

Major intl. organizations: UN and all of its specialized agencies, APEC, the Commonwealth, OECD, WTO.

Embassy: 1601 Massachusetts Ave. NW 20036; 797-3000.

Website: www.australia.gov.au

Australia harbors many plant and animal species not found elsewhere, including kangaroos, koalas, platypuses, dingoes (wild dogs), Tasmanian devils, wombats, and barking and frilled lizards.

Capt. James Cook explored the eastern coast in 1770, when the continent was inhabited by a variety of indigenous peoples. The first European settlers, beginning in 1788, were mostly convicts, soldiers, and government officials. By 1830, Britain had claimed the entire continent, and the immigration of free settlers accelerated. The Commonwealth was proclaimed Jan. 1, 1901. Northern Terr. was granted limited self-rule July 1, 1978.

State/territory, capital	Area (sq mi)	Population (Dec. 2012 est.)
New South Wales, Sydney	309,500	7,348,900
Victoria, Melbourne	87,900	5,679,600
Queensland, Brisbane	666,990	4,610,900
Western Australia, Perth	975,100	2,472,700
South Australia, Adelaide	379,900	1,662,200
Tasmania, Hobart	26,200	512,400
Australian Capital Terr., Canberra	900	379,600
Northern Terr., Darwin	519,800	236,900

Racially discriminatory immigration policies ended in 1973, after 3 mil Europeans (half British) had entered since 1945. Indigenous peoples, 90% of them aborigines, numbered 669,900 in 2011; in the Northern Territory they accounted for nearly 30% of the population. They remain economically disadvantaged.

Australia is among the top exporters of beef, lamb, wool, and wheat. Major mineral deposits have been developed, largely for export.

The Labor Party won a majority in Feb. 1983 general elections and was reelected in 1984, 1987, 1990, and 1993. Conservatives swept into power in Mar. 2, 1996 after an election that focused mainly on economic issues. Incumbent Prime Min. John Howard retained power in the 1998, 2001, and 2004 elections.

Australia led an international peacekeeping force into Timor in Sept. 1999. In a referendum Nov. 6, voters rejected a proposal that would have made Australia a republic.

Australian troops fought in U.S.-led military operations in Afghanistan (2001) and Iraq (2003). Some 2,000 Australian peacekeepers began arriving in the Solomon Isls., July 24, 2003; nearly all were withdrawn by mid-2005. In race riots in Sydney suburbs, Dec. 11-12, 2005, thousands of youths assaulted people of Middle Eastern ancestry, who then retaliated. Australian troops were dispatched, 2006, to suppress disorder in the Solomon Isls. in Apr. and Timor in May. As of 2013, about 3,000 Australian troops were serving overseas, including 1,550 in Afghanistan. With the operation finished in Timor, the last Australian troops there returned home on Mar. 27, 2013. The Dept. of Defence planned to bring most of its forces home from Afghanistan by the end of 2013.

Kevin Rudd led the Labor Party to victory in parliamentary elections Nov. 24, 2007. Quentin Bryce, the nation's first female governor-general, was sworn in Sept. 5, 2008. "Black Saturday" bushfires Feb. 7 in Victoria State claimed 173 lives.

After a series of policy missteps eroded his popularity and alienated his Labor supporters, Rudd was forced out June 24, 2010, by his deputy, Julia Gillard, who became Australia's first female prime minister. Inconclusive parliamentary elections Aug. 21 led to the formation of a minority government headed by Gillard. Downpours from Cyclone Tasha and other storms flooded Queensland in late Dec. 2010 and early Jan. 2011, with three-fourths of the state declared a disaster zone. By late Jan. the flood death toll had reached 35. A carbon tax that will cost companies AUD $23 ($24 USD) for each ton of carbon they produce went into effect July 1, 2012.

Destructive bush fires attributed to a severe heat wave scorched the western and southeastern areas of the country, including populous areas, in the first half of Jan. 2013. They were followed by torrential rainstorms that killed about 6 people and caused some $2.43 bil in damages in the second half of the month.

Prime Min. Gillard, Mar. 20, 2013, officially apologized for Australia's forced adoption policy (in effect late 1950s-70s), in which the state took the babies of single, teenage, or unfit mothers, often under duress, and gave them to childless married couples. After surviving a coup by a faction of her party Mar. 21, Gillard resigned June 26 after being voted out as party leader. Former Prime Min. Rudd, who engineered Gillard's ouster, became premier once again. The conservatives won Sept. 7, 2013, elections, and Tony Abbott, the party leader, became prime min. Sept 16, 2013.

Australian External Territories

Norfolk Isl., area 14 sq mi, pop. (2013 est.) 2,196, was taken over, 1914. The soil is very fertile, suitable for citrus, bananas, and coffee. Many of the inhabitants are descendants of the *Bounty* mutineers, moved to Norfolk 1856 from Pitcairn Isl. Australia offered the island limited home rule in 1978. **Website:** www.info.gov.nf

Coral Sea Isls. territory, area less than 1.2 sq mi, is administered from Norfolk Isl.

Ashmore and Cartier Isls., area 1.9 sq mi, in the Indian O., came under Australian authority 1934 and are administered as part of Northern Territory. **Heard Isl. and McDonald Isls.**, area 159 sq mi, are administered by the Dept. of Science.

Cocos (Keeling) Isls., 27 small coral islands in the Indian O. 1,750 mi NW of Australia. Pop. (2010 est.) 596; area 5 sq mi. The residents voted to become part of Australia, Apr. 1984.

Christmas Isl., area 52 sq mi, pop (2013 est.) 1,513; 230 mi S of Java, was transferred by Britain in 1958. It has phosphate deposits.

Australian Antarctic Territory was claimed by Australia in 1933, including 2,362,000 sq mi of territory S of 60th parallel S lat. and between 160th-45th meridians E long. It does not include Adelie Coast.

Austria
Republic of Austria

People: Population: 8,221,646. **Age distrib.:** <15: 13.7%; 65+: 18.9%. **Pop. density:** 258.3 per sq mi, 99.7 per sq km. **Urban:** 67.7%. **Ethnic groups:** Austrian 91%, fmr. Yugoslav (incl. Croatian, Slovene, Serb, Bosniak) 4%, Turk 2%. **Languages:** German (official), Turkish, Serbian, Croatian (official in Burgenland). **Religions:** Roman Catholic 74%, Protestant 5%, Muslim 4%, none 12%.

Geography: Total area: 32,383 sq mi, 83,871 sq km; **Land area:** 31,832 sq mi, 82,445 sq km. **Location:** In S Central Europe. **Neighbors:** Switzerland, Liechtenstein on W; Germany, Czech Rep. on N; Slovakia, Hungary on E; Slovenia, Italy on S. **Topography:** Austria is primarily mountainous, with the Alps and foothills covering the western and southern provinces. The eastern provinces and Vienna are located in the Danube River Basin. **Capital:** Vienna, 1,720,170.

Government: Type: Federal republic. **Head of state:** Pres. Heinz Fischer; b. Oct. 9, 1938; in office: July 8, 2004. **Head of gov.:** Chancellor Werner Faymann; b. May 4, 1960; in office: Dec. 2, 2008.

Local divisions: 9 states. **Defense budget:** $3.16 bil. **Active troops:** 23,250.

Economy: Industries: constr., machinery, vehicles and parts, food, metals, chemicals, lumber and wood proc., paper and paperboard, communications equip., tourism. **Chief crops:** grains, potatoes, wine, fruit. **Natural resources:** oil, coal, lignite, timber, iron ore, copper, zinc, antimony, magnesite, tungsten, graphite, salt, hydropower. **Crude oil reserves:** 46.7 mil bbls. **Arable land:** 16.5%. **Livestock:** cattle: 2 mil; chickens: 16 mil; goats: 71,768; pigs: 3.1 mil; sheep: 358,415. **Fish catch:** 2,510 metric tons. **Electricity prod.** (2011): 59.5 bil kWh. **Labor force:** agric. 5.5%, industry 26%, services 68.5%.

Finance: Monetary unit: Euro (EUR) (Sept. 2013: 0.76 = $1 U.S.). **GDP:** $364.9 bil; **per capita GDP:** $43,100; **GDP growth:** 0.8%. **Imports:** $163.2 bil; Germany 42.1%, Italy 6.6%, Switzerland 5.1%. **Exports:** $160.1 bil; Germany 31.4%, Italy 7%, France 4.7%, Switzerland 4.5%, U.S. 4.4%. **Tourism:** $18.9 bil. **Budget:** $206.2 bil. **Total reserves less gold:** $12.2 bil. **Gold:** 9 mil oz t. **CPI change:** 2.5%.

Transport: Railways: 3,976 mi. **Motor vehicles:** 609.5 vehicles per 1,000 pop. **Civil aviation:** 9.2 bil pass.-mi; 24 airports. **Chief ports:** Enns, Krems, Linz, Vienna.

Communications: TV sets: 656 per 1,000 pop. **Radios:** 752 per 1,000 pop. **Telephone lines:** 39.6 per 100 pop. **Internet:** 81%.

Health: Life expect.: 77.1 male; 83.1 female. **Births:** 8.7 per 1,000 pop. **Deaths:** 10.3 per 1,000 pop. **Natural inc.:** −0.16%. **Infant mortality:** 4.2 per 1,000 live births. **HIV rate:** 0.4%.

Education: Compulsory: ages 6-14. **Literacy:** 98%.

Major intl. organizations: UN and all of its specialized agencies, EU, OECD, OSCE, WTO.

Embassy: 3524 International Ct. NW 20008; 895-6700.

Website: www.austria.gv.at

Rome conquered Austrian lands from Celtic tribes around 15 BC. In 788 the territory was incorporated into Charlemagne's empire. By 1300, the House of Hapsburg had gained control; they added vast territories in all parts of Europe to their realm in the next few hundred years.

Austrian dominance of Germany was undermined in the 18th cent. and ended by Prussia by 1866. But the Congress of Vienna, 1815, confirmed Austrian control of a large empire in southeast Europe consisting of Germans, Hungarians, Slavs, Italians, and others. The dual Austro-Hungarian monarchy was established in 1867, giving autonomy to Hungary and almost 50 years of peace.

World War I started after the June 28, 1914, assassination of Archduke Franz Ferdinand, the Hapsburg heir, by a Serbian nationalist, destroyed the empire. By 1918 Austria was reduced to a small republic, with the borders it has today.

Nazi Germany, ruled by the Austrian-born Adolf Hitler, annexed Austria Mar. 13, 1938. The republic was reestablished in 1945, under Allied occupation. Full independence and neutrality were restored in 1955. Austria joined the EU Jan. 1, 1995.

The rise of the right-wing, anti-immigrant Austrian Freedom Party challenged the dominance of the Austrian Social Democratic Party in the late 1990s. When Freedom Party members joined the cabinet, Feb. 4, 2000, the EU imposed political sanctions on Austria for 7 months. Social Democrats won parliamentary elections Oct. 2006; they held onto their plurality in elections Sept. 2008, although far-right parties made gains. One of the stronger economies in the eurozone, Austria's unemployment rate was 4.8%, the zone's lowest, as of Aug. 2013.

Azerbaijan
Republic of Azerbaijan

People: Population: 9,590,159. **Age distrib.:** <15: 22.6%; 65+: 6.3%. **Pop. density:** 300.6 per sq mi, 116.1 per sq km. **Urban:** 53.6%. **Ethnic groups:** Azeri 91%, Dagestani 2%, Russian 2%, Armenian 2%. **Languages:** Azerbaijani (Azeri) (official), Lezgi, Russian, Armenian. **Religions:** Muslim 93%, Russian Orthodox 3%, Armenian Orthodox 2%.

Geography: Total area: 33,436 sq mi, 86,600 sq km; **Land area:** 31,903 sq mi, 82,629 sq km. **Location:** SW Asia. **Neighbors:** Russia, Georgia on N; Iran on S; Armenia on W; Caspian Sea on E. **Topography:** The Great Caucasus Mts. in N, Karabakh Upland in W border the Kur-Abas lowland; climate is arid except in the subtropical SE. **Capital:** Baku, 2,122,900.

Government: Type: Republic. **Head of state:** Pres. Ilham Aliyev; b. Dec. 24, 1961; in office: Oct. 31, 2003. **Head of gov.:** Prime Min. Artur Rasizade; b. Feb. 26, 1935; in office: Nov. 4, 2003. **Local division:** 66 rayons, 11 cities. **Defense budget:** $1.77 bil. **Active troops:** 66,950.

Economy: Industries: petroleum and nat. gas, petroleum prods., oil field equip.; steel, iron ore; cement. **Chief crops:** cotton, grain, rice, grapes. **Natural resources:** petroleum, nat. gas, iron ore, nonferrous metals, bauxite. **Crude oil reserves:** 7 bil bbls. **Arable land:** 22.8%. **Livestock:** cattle: 2.4 mil; chickens: 23.2 mil; goats: 627,425; pigs: 6,342; sheep: 7.9 mil. **Fish catch:** 1,578 metric tons. **Electricity prod.:** 17.8 bil kWh. **Labor force:** agric. 38.3%, industry 12.1%, services 49.6%.

Finance: Monetary unit: New Manat (AZN) (Sept. 2013: 0.78 = $1 U.S.). **GDP:** $98.4 bil; **per capita GDP:** $10,700; **GDP growth:** 2.2%. **Imports:** $10.1 bil; Turkey 18.6%, Russia 14.3%, China 7.8%, Germany 7.2%, UK 7.1%, U.S. 5.1%, Ukraine 5%. **Exports:**

$31 bil; Italy 25.9%, France 7.7%, India 6.7%, Indonesia 6.6%, Germany 5.6%, Israel 5.1%. **Tourism:** $2.4 bil. **Budget:** $21.8 bil. **Total reserves less gold:** $11.3 bil. **Gold:** 64 oz t. **CPI change:** 1.1%.

Transport: Railways: 1,813 mi. **Motor vehicles:** 117.8 vehicles per 1,000 pop. **Civil aviation:** 791.6 mil pass.-mi; 30 airports. **Chief port:** Baku.

Communications: TV sets: 216 per 1,000 pop. **Radios:** 214 per 1,000 pop. **Telephone lines:** 18.4 per 100 pop. **Internet:** 54.2%.

Health: Life expect.: 68.7 male; 75.0 female. **Births:** 17.2 per 1,000 pop. **Deaths:** 7.1 per 1,000 pop. **Natural inc.:** 1.01%. **Infant mortality:** 27.7 per 1,000 live births. **HIV rate:** 0.1%.

Education: Compulsory: ages 6-16. **Literacy:** 99.8%.

Major intl. organizations: UN (FAO, IBRD, ILO, IMF, WHO), CIS, OSCE, WTO (observer).

Embassy: 2741 34th St. NW 20008; 337-3500.

Website: www.president.az

Azerbaijan was home to Scythian tribes and part of the Roman Empire. Overrun by Turks in the 11th cent. and conquered by Russia in 1806 and 1813, it joined the USSR Dec. 30, 1922, and became a constituent republic in 1936. Azerbaijan gained independence when the Soviet Union disbanded Dec. 26, 1991.

Nagorno-Karabakh, an enclave with a majority population of ethnic Armenians, seceded from Azerbaijan in 1988, triggering a war between mostly Muslim Azerbaijan and mostly Christian Armenia, 1992-94, in which 30,000 lives were lost (see Armenia).

Voters approved a new constitution expanding presidential powers, Nov. 12, 1995. Pres. Haydar Aliyev, a pro-Russian former Communist, was reelected Oct. 11, 1998, but international monitors called the vote seriously flawed.

The dying Pres. Aliyev named his son Ilham prime min. Aug. 4, 2003. The younger Aliyev won the Oct. 15, 2003, presidential election. International observers called the vote fraudulent. He responded to violent protests Oct. 16 by arresting hundreds of opposition leaders and their supporters. Serious abuses also marred parliamentary elections, Nov. 6, 2005, won by parties loyal to Aliyev. The opening May 25, 2005, of the Baku-Tbilisi-Ceyhan pipeline, providing an outlet for Azerbaijan's vast Caspian oil reserves, transformed the nation's economy.

Pres. Ilham Aliyev won a second term Oct. 15, 2008, but main opposition parties boycotted the election. A constitutional amendment abolishing presidential term limits was approved by referendum Mar. 18, 2009. Azerbaijan is a transit point for U.S. troops and supplies bound for Afghanistan.

Riots erupted Jan. 23-24, 2013, in Ismayilli, about 100 mi NW of Baku. Protestors demanded the resignation of the local governor, claiming he was corrupt and unwilling to address the community's income inequality. Police confronted demonstrators Mar. 10, 2013, in Baku over what protesters alleged to be the hazing of noncombat military recruits, 472 of whom had died under suspicious circumstances, 2003-12.

The Bahamas
Commonwealth of The Bahamas

People: Population: 319,031. **Age distrib.:** <15: 23.6%; 65+: 6.7%. **Pop. density:** 82.5 per sq mi, 31.9 per sq km. **Urban:** 84.3%. **Ethnic groups:** black 85%, white 12%, Asian and Hispanic 3%. **Languages:** English (official), Creole (among Haitian immigrants). **Religions:** Protestant 68% (Baptist 35%, Anglican 15%, Pentecostal 8%, Church of God 5%, Methodist 4%), Roman Catholic 14%, other Christian 15%.

Geography: Total area: 5,359 sq mi, 13,880 sq km; **Land area:** 3,865 sq mi, 10,010 sq km. **Location:** In Atlantic O., E of Florida. **Neighbors:** Nearest are U.S. on W, Cuba on S. **Topography:** Nearly 700 islands (29 inhabited) and over 2,000 islets in the W Atlantic O. extend 760 mi NW to SE. **Capital:** Nassau, 254,000.

Government: Type: Constitutional parliamentary democracy. **Head of state:** Queen Elizabeth II, rep. by Gov.-Gen. Sir Arthur Foulkes; b. May 11, 1928; in office: Apr. 14, 2010. **Head of gov.:** Prime Min. Perry Christie; b. Aug. 21, 1943; in office: May 8, 2012. **Local divisions:** 31 districts. **Defense budget:** $57 mil. **Active troops:** 850.

Economy: Industries: tourism, banking, cement, oil transshipment, salt, rum. **Chief crops:** citrus, vegetables. **Natural resources:** salt, aragonite, timber. **Arable land:** 0.9%. **Livestock:** cattle: 750; chickens: 3 mil; goats: 14,500; pigs: 5,000; sheep: 6,500. **Fish catch:** 10,370 metric tons. **Electricity prod.** 1.9 bil kWh. **Labor force:** agric. 5%, industry 5%, tourism 50%, other services 40%.

Finance: Monetary unit: Dollar (BSD) (Sept. 2013: 1.00 = $1 U.S.). **GDP:** $11.2 bil; **per capita GDP:** $31,900; **GDP growth:** 2.5%. **Imports:** $2.9 bil; U.S. 29.9%, India 20.1%, Singapore 8.7%, South Korea 6.7%, China 5%, Colombia 4.3%, Canada 4.2%. **Exports:** $750 mil; Singapore 23.7%, U.S. 19.5%, Dominican Republic 13.4%, Ecuador 9.8%, Canada 5.4%, Guatemala 4.4%. **Tourism:** $2.4 bil. **Budget** $1.8 bil. **Total reserves less gold:** $846.9 mil. **CPI change:** 2%.

Transport: Motor vehicles: 401.4 vehicles per 1,000 pop. **Civil aviation:** 171.5 mil pass.-mi; 24 airports. **Chief ports:** Freeport, Nassau.

Communications: TV sets: 248 per 1,000 pop. **Radios:** 746 per 1,000 pop. **Telephone lines:** 39 per 100 pop. **Internet:** 71.7%.

Health: Life expect.: 69.3 male; 74.2 female. **Births:** 15.8 per 1,000 pop. **Deaths:** 7.0 per 1,000 pop. **Natural inc.:** 0.89%. **Infant mortality:** 12.9 per 1,000 live births. **HIV rate:** 2.8%.

Education: Compulsory: ages 5-16. **Literacy:** NA.

Major intl. organizations: UN (FAO, IBRD, ILO, IMF, WHO), Caricom, the Commonwealth, OAS, WTO (observer).

Embassy: 2220 Massachusetts Ave. NW 20008; 319-2660.

Website: www.bahamas.gov.bs

Christopher Columbus first set foot in the New World on San Salvador (Watling Isl.) in 1492, when Arawak Indians inhabited the islands. British settlement began in 1647; the islands became a British colony in 1783. Internal self-government was granted in 1964; full independence within the Commonwealth was attained July 10, 1973. International banking and investment management have become major industries alongside tourism. The Progressive Liberal Party's Perry Christie, who was prime min. 2002-07, returned to the post after May 7, 2012, parliamentary elections, which saw the defeat of the Free Natl. Movment as the majority party.

Bahrain
Kingdom of Bahrain

People: Population: 1,281,332. **Age distrib.:** <15: 20%; 65+: 2.6%. **Pop. density:** 4,366.6 per sq mi, 1,686 per sq km. **Urban:** 88.7%. **Ethnic groups:** Bahraini 42%, non-Bahraini 54%. **Languages:** Arabic (official), English, Farsi, Urdu. **Religions:** Muslim (Shia and Sunni) 81%, Christian 9%.

Geography: Total area: 293 sq mi, 760 sq km; **Land area:** 293 sq mi, 760 sq km. **Location:** SW Asia, in Persian Gulf. **Neighbors:** Nearest are Saudi Arabia on W, Qatar on E. **Topography:** Bahrain Island, and several adjacent, smaller islands, are flat, hot, and humid with little rain. **Capital:** Manama, 261,782.

Government: Type: Constitutional monarchy. **Head of state:** King Hamad bin Isa al-Khalifa; b. Jan. 28, 1950; in office: as emir Mar. 6, 1999; as king Feb. 14, 2002. **Head of gov.:** Prime Min. Khalifa bin Sulman al-Khalifa; b. Nov. 24, 1936; in office: 1971. **Local divisions:** 5 governorates. **Defense budget:** $1.02 bil. **Active troops:** 8,200.

Economy: Industries: petroleum proc. and refining, aluminum smelting, iron pelletization, fertilizers, Islamic and offshore banking. **Chief crops:** fruit, vegetables. **Natural resources:** oil, nat. gas, fish, pearls. **Crude oil reserves:** 124.6 mil bbls. **Arable land:** 1.8%. **Livestock:** cattle: 10,000; chickens: 540,000; goats: 19,000; sheep: 40,000. **Fish catch:** 9,918 metric tons. **Electricity prod.:** 12.4 bil kWh. **Labor force:** agric. 1%, industry 79%, services 20%.

Finance: Monetary unit: Dinar (BHD) (Sept. 2013: 0.38 = $1 U.S.). **GDP:** $33.6 bil; **per capita GDP:** $29,200; **GDP growth:** 3.9%. **Imports:** $15.2 bil; Saudi Arabia 26.8%, U.S. 9.7%, China 9.6%, Japan 6.4%, India 4.9%, France 4.7%. **Exports:** $21.4 bil; Saudi Arabia 3%, India 2.2%, UAE 2%, South Korea 1.9%. **Tourism:** $1.04 bil. **Budget:** $8.7 bil. **Total reserves less gold:** $5.2 bil. **Gold:** 150,000 oz t. **CPI change:** 2.8%.

Transport: Motor vehicles: 359.7 vehicles per 1,000 pop. **Civil aviation:** 8.7 bil pass.-mi; 4 airports. **Chief ports:** Mina Salman, Sitrah.

Communications: TV sets: 414 per 1,000 pop. **Radios:** 544 per 1,000 pop. **Telephone lines:** 21.3 per 100 pop. **Internet:** 88%.

Health: Life expect.: 76.3 male; 80.6 female. **Births:** 14.2 per 1,000 pop. **Deaths:** 2.7 per 1,000 pop. **Natural inc.:** 1.15%. **Infant mortality:** 9.9 per 1,000 live births. **HIV rate:** NA.

Education: Compulsory: ages 6-14. **Literacy:** 94.6%.

Major intl. organizations: UN (FAO, IBRD, ILO, IMF, WHO), AL, WTO.

Embassy: 3502 International Dr. NW 20008; 342-1111.

Website: www.bahrain.bh

Long ruled by the Khalifa family, Bahrain was a British protectorate from 1861 to Aug. 15, 1971, when it regained independence. Pearls, shrimp, fruits, and vegetables were the mainstays of the economy until oil was discovered in 1932. Crude oil production has declined since the 1970s, but natural gas output has grown, and international banking has thrived. Shiite dissidents have clashed with the Sunni-led government since 1996.

Emir Hamad bin Isa al-Khalifa proclaimed himself king Feb. 14, 2002. Local elections in May 2002 marked the first time Bahraini women were allowed to vote and run for office. The first female judge was appointed June 6, 2006. The monarchy suppressed Arab Spring demonstrations Feb.-Mar. 2011; to bolster security, a Gulf Cooperation Council force of 1,600, led by Saudi Arabia, entered Bahrain Mar. 14, and the government recruited hundreds of additional former soldiers and police from Pakistan. Protests, however, continued throughout 2012-13. On Feb. 14, 2013, a young protester was shot during a demonstration commemorating the Arab Spring and died from his wounds Feb 21. Two police officers were sentenced to 10 years in prison, Mar. 12, 2013, for fatally beating an antigovernment demonstrator at the start of that movement in Feb. 2011.

Bangladesh
People's Republic of Bangladesh

People: Population: 163,654,860. **Age distrib.:** <15: 33%; 65+: 4.9%. **Pop. density:** 3,256.3 per sq mi, 1,257.3 per sq km. **Urban:** 28.4%. **Ethnic groups:** Bengali 98%. **Languages:** Bangla, or Bengali (official), English. **Religions:** Muslim 89.5%, Hindu 9.6%.

Geography: Total area: 55,598 sq mi, 143,998 sq km; **Land area:** 50,258 sq mi, 130,168 sq km. **Location:** In S Asia, on N bend

of Bay of Bengal. **Neighbors:** India nearly surrounds country on W, N, E; Myanmar on SE. **Topography:** Mostly a low plain cut by the Ganges and Brahmaputra Rivers and their delta. The land is alluvial and marshy along the coast, with hills only in the extreme SE and NE. A tropical monsoon climate prevails, among the rainiest in the world. **Capital:** Dhaka, 15,390,900. **Cities (urban aggl.):** Chittagong, 5,239,095; Khulna, 1,780,566.

Government: Type: Parliamentary democracy. **Head of state:** Pres. Abdul Hamid; b. Jan. 1, 1944; in office: Apr. 24, 2013. **Head of gov.:** Prime Min. Sheikh Hasina; b. Sept. 28, 1947; in office: Jan. 6, 2009. **Local divisions:** 7 divisions. **Defense budget:** $1.49 bil. **Active troops:** 157,050.

Economy: Industries: cotton, garments, paper, leather, fertilizer, iron and steel, cement, petroleum prods., tobacco, drugs and pharmaceuticals, ceramics. **Chief crops:** rice, jute, tea, wheat, sugarcane, potatoes, tobacco, pulses, oilseeds, spices. **Natural resources:** nat. gas, timber, coal. **Crude oil reserves:** 28 mil bbls. **Arable land:** 58.6%. **Livestock:** cattle: 23.1 mil; chickens: 234.7 mil; goats: 53.4 mil; sheep: 1.9 mil. **Fish catch:** 3.1 mil metric tons. **Electricity prod.:** 39.8 bil kWh. **Labor force:** agric. 45%, industry 30%, services 25%.

Finance: Monetary unit: Taka (BDT) (Sept. 2013: 77.83 = $1 U.S.). **GDP:** $311 bil; **per capita GDP:** $2,100; **GDP growth:** 6.1%. **Imports:** $34.6 bil; China 19.5%, India 13.4%, Singapore 4.9%, Malaysia 4.7%, South Korea 4.1%. **Exports:** $26.3 bil; U.S. 16.7%, Germany 12.5%, UK 8.4%, France 5%. **Tourism:** $110 mil. **Budget:** $19.7 bil. **Total reserves less gold:** $12 bil. **Gold:** 434,500 oz t. **CPI change:** 8.7%.

Transport: Railways: 1,629 mi. **Motor vehicles:** 3.6 vehicles per 1,000 pop. **Civil aviation:** 2.7 bil pass.-mi; 16 airports. **Chief ports:** Chittagong, Mongla Port.

Communications: TV sets: 106 per 1,000 pop. **Radios:** 64 per 1,000 pop. **Telephone lines:** 0.6 per 100 pop. **Internet:** 6.3%.

Health: Life expect.: 68.5 male; 72.3 female. **Births:** 22.1 per 1,000 pop. **Deaths:** 5.7 per 1,000 pop. **Natural inc.:** 1.64%. **Infant mortality:** 47.3 per 1,000 live births. **HIV rate:** <0.1%.

Education: Compulsory: ages 6-10. **Literacy:** 57.7%.

Major intl. organizations: UN (FAO, IBRD, ILO, IMF, WHO), the Commonwealth, WTO.

Embassy: 3510 International Dr. NW 20008; 244-0183.

Website: www.bangladesh.gov.bd

Muslim invaders conquered the formerly Hindu area in the 12th cent. British rule lasted from the 18th cent. to 1947, when East Bengal became part of Pakistan.

Opposing domination by West Pakistan, the Awami League, based in the East, won control of the National Assembly in 1971. Assembly sessions were postponed; riots broke out. Pakistani troops attacked, Mar. 25; Bangladesh independence was proclaimed the next day. In the ensuing civil war, 1 mil died and 10 mil fled to India. War between India and Pakistan broke out Dec. 3, 1971. Pakistan surrendered in the East on Dec. 16. Mujibur Rahman, known as Sheikh Mujib, became prime min.; he was killed in a coup Aug. 15, 1975.

Army rivals killed Pres. Ziaur Rahman in an unsuccessful coup attempt, May 1981. Vice Pres. Abdus Sattar assumed the presidency but was ousted in a coup led by army chief of staff Gen. H. M. Ershad, Mar. 1982. Ershad declared Bangladesh an Islamic Republic in 1988; a parliamentary system of government was adopted in 1991. A cyclone struck Apr. 1991, killing over 131,000 people.

Political turmoil led to the resignation, Mar. 1996, of Prime Min. Khaleda Zia, the widow of Ziaur Rahman. Sheikh Mujib's daughter, known as Sheikh Hasina, led the country after the June 1996 election. Khaleda Zia returned to power following parliamentary elections, Oct. 1, 2001. Floods July-Aug. 2004 caused at least 950 deaths. Militant Islamists set off more than 400 small bombs in more than 50 cities and towns, Aug. 17, 2005, killing 3. Another wave of jihadist bombings killed 22, Nov. 29-Dec. 8, 2005. Bangladeshi economist Muhammad Yunus won the 2006 Nobel Peace Prize for using very small loans (microcredit) to help alleviate the nation's severe poverty.

Escalating political violence led Pres. Iajuddin Ahmed to declare a state of emergency Jan. 11, 2007. A military-backed caretaker government filed criminal charges against Khaleda Zia and Sheikh Hasina but failed to force the 2 former prime ministers into exile. Cyclone Sidr struck Nov. 15, 2007, damaging more than 1.5 mil homes and leaving about 3,400 dead.

The Awami League triumphed in parliamentary elections Dec. 2008, and Sheikh Hasina was sworn in as prime min. Jan. 6, 2009, ending 2 years of emergency rule. A mutiny Feb. 25-26, 2009, at the Dhaka headquarters of the Bangladesh Rifles, a border force, left 74 people dead. A fire that raged through a crowded residential area of Dhaka June 3, 2010, killed at least 117. The UN Intl. Tribunal for the Law of the Sea (ITLOS) ruled in favor of Bangladesh in its maritime dispute with Myanmar Mar. 14, 2012, granting its claim to 200 nautical mi in the oil-rich Bay of Bengal and beyond.

The online release of an anti-Muslim film made by an American drew days of violent clashes between protesters and police Sept. 2012 in Dhaka. A garment factory fire Nov. 24, 2012, outside Dhaka killed 112 workers and sparked protests at other factories in the region. Rana Plaza, a building which housed 5 garment factories employing 3,000 people, collapsed Apr. 24, 2013, due to poor construction and unsafe practices, killing more than 1,100 workers in the deadliest garment-factory disaster in world history.

Barbados

People: Population: 288,725. **Age distrib.:** <15: 18.6%; 65+: 10.2%. **Pop. density:** 1,739.1 per sq mi, 671.5 per sq km. **Urban:** 44.4%. **Ethnic groups:** black 93%, white 3%, mixed 3%, East Indian 1%. **Language:** English. **Religions:** Protestant 63%, Roman Catholic 4%, other Christian 7%.

Geography: Total area: 166 sq mi, 430 sq km; **Land area:** 166 sq mi, 430 sq km. **Location:** In Atlantic O., farthest E of West Indies. **Neighbors:** Nearest are St. Lucia and St. Vincent and the Grenadines to the W. **Topography:** The island lies alone in the Atlantic almost completely surrounded by coral reefs. Highest point is Mt. Hillaby (1,115 ft). **Capital:** Bridgetown, 121,657.

Government: Type: Parliamentary democracy. **Head of state:** Queen Elizabeth II, rep. by Gov.-Gen. Sir Elliot Belgrave; b. Mar. 16, 1931; in office: June 1, 2012. **Head of gov.:** Prime Min. Freundel Stuart; b. Apr. 27, 1951; in office: Oct. 23, 2010. **Local divisions:** 11 parishes and Bridgetown. **Defense budget:** $38 mil. **Active troops:** 610.

Economy: Industries: tourism, light mfg., component assembly for export. **Chief crops:** sugarcane, vegetables, cotton. **Natural resources:** petroleum, fish, nat. gas. **Crude oil reserves:** 2.3 mil bbls. **Other resources:** Fish. **Arable land:** 27.9%. **Livestock:** cattle: 10,800; chickens: 3.6 mil; goats: 5,200; pigs: 22,000; sheep: 12,500. **Fish catch:** 1,837 metric tons. **Electricity prod.:** 1 bil kWh. **Labor force:** agric. 10%, industry 15%, services 75%.

Finance: Monetary unit: Dollar (BBD) (Sept. 2013: 2.00 = $1 U.S.). **GDP:** $7.2 bil; **per capita GDP:** $25,800; **GDP growth:** 0%. **Imports:** $1.6 bil; Trinidad and Tobago 37.9%, U.S. 25.7%, China 5.4%. **Exports:** $1 bil; Trinidad and Tobago 21.3%, U.S. 11%, St. Lucia 9.9%, St. Vincent and the Grenadines 6.1%, Antigua and Barbuda 5%, St. Kitts and Nevis 4.7%, Jamaica 4.5%, UK 4.1%, Colombia 4%. **Tourism:** $916 mil. **Budget:** $1.5 bil. **Total reserves less gold:** $839.7 mil. **CPI change:** 4.5%.

Transport: Motor vehicles: 358.3 vehicles per 1,000 pop. **Civil aviation:** 1 airport. **Chief port:** Bridgetown.

Communications: TV sets: 291 per 1,000 pop. **Radios:** 287 per 1,000 pop. **Telephone lines:** 52.5 per 100 pop. **Internet:** 73.3%.

Health: Life expect.: 72.5 male; 77.1 female. **Births:** 12.1 per 1,000 pop. **Deaths:** 8.4 per 1,000 pop. **Natural inc.:** 0.37%. **Infant mortality:** 11.1 per 1,000 live births. **HIV rate:** 0.9%.

Education: Compulsory: ages 5-15. **Literacy:** NA.

Major intl. organizations: UN (FAO, IBRD, ILO, IMF, WHO), Caricom, the Commonwealth, OAS, WTO.

Embassy: 2144 Wyoming Ave. NW 20008; 939-9200.

Website: www.gov.bb

Barbados was probably named by Portuguese sailors in reference to bearded fig trees. An English ship visited in 1605, and British settled on the uninhabited island in 1627. Slaves worked the sugar plantations until slavery was abolished in 1834. Self-rule came gradually, with full independence proclaimed Nov. 30, 1966. Tourism and manufacturing surpassed the sugar trade in economic importance in the 1990s. The country signed an Economic and Technical Agreement with China Aug. 24, 2012, to strengthen the growing ties between the 2 countries.

Airline baggage handler and Barbados native Victor Bourne was convicted and sentenced to life in prison Oct. 2012 after a trial in Brooklyn, NY, for leading a drug-smuggling ring that brought drugs from Barbados to New York in commercial jets.

Belarus
Republic of Belarus

People: Population: 9,625,888. **Age distrib.:** <15: 15.2%; 65+: 14%. **Pop. density:** 122.9 per sq mi, 47.4 per sq km. **Urban:** 75%. **Ethnic groups:** Belarusian 84%, Russian 8%, Polish 3%, Ukrainian 2%. **Languages:** Belarusian, Russian (both official). **Religions:** Eastern Orthodox 80%, other (incl. Roman Catholic, Protestant, Jewish, Muslim) 20%.

Geography: Total area: 80,155 sq mi, 207,600 sq km; **Land area:** 78,340 sq mi, 202,900 sq km. **Location:** E Europe. **Neighbors:** Poland on W; Latvia, Lithuania on N; Russia on E; Ukraine on S. **Topography:** Landlocked country consisting mostly of hilly lowland with significant marsh areas in S. **Capital:** Minsk, 1,861,320.

Government: Type: Republic. **Head of state:** Pres. Aleksandr Lukashenko; b. Aug. 30, 1954; in office: July 20,1994. **Head of gov.:** Prime Min. Mikhail Myasnikovich; b. May 6, 1950; in office: Dec. 28, 2010. **Local divisions:** 6 provinces, 1 municipality. **Defense budget:** $547 mil. **Active troops:** 48,000.

Economy: Industries: metal-cutting machine tools, tractors, trucks, earthmovers, motorcycles. **Chief crops:** grain, potatoes, vegetables, sugar beets, flax. **Natural resources:** timber, peat, oil, nat. gas, granite, dolomitic limestone, marl, chalk, sand, gravel, clay. **Crude oil reserves:** 198 mil bbls. **Arable land:** 27.2%. **Livestock:** cattle: 4.2 mil; chickens: 35.2 mil; goats: 72,300; pigs: 3.9 mil; sheep: 51,800. **Fish catch:** 17,415 metric tons. **Electricity prod.:** 32.8 bil kWh. **Labor force:** agric. 9.4%, industry 45.9%, services 44.7%.

Finance: Monetary unit: Ruble (BYR) (Sept. 2013: 9,049.77 = $1 U.S.). **GDP:** $149.2 bil; **per capita GDP:** $15,900; **GDP growth:** 1.5%. **Imports:** $45 bil; Russia 59.3%, Germany 5.9%, China 5.1%, Ukraine 5%. **Exports:** $45.5 bil; Russia 35.4%, Netherlands 16.5%, Ukraine 12.1%, Latvia 7.1%. **Tourism:** $664 mil. **Budget:** $22 bil. **Total reserves less gold:** $5.8 bil. **Gold:** 1.4 mil oz t. **CPI change:** 59.2%.

Transport: Railways: 3,441 mi. Motor vehicles: 308.2 vehicles per 1,000 pop. Civil aviation: 272.2 mil pass.-mi; 33 airports. Chief port: Mazyr.

Communications: TV sets: 386 per 1,000 pop. Radios: 340 per 1,000 pop. Telephone lines: 46.3 per 100 pop. Internet: 46.9%.

Health: Life expect.: 66.1 male; 77.8 female. Births: 11.0 per 1,000 pop. Deaths: 13.7 per 1,000 pop. Natural inc.: −0.27%. Infant mortality: 3.7 per 1,000 live births. HIV rate: 0.4%.

Education: Compulsory: ages 6-14. Literacy: 99.6%.

Major intl. organizations: UN (FAO, IBRD, ILO, IMF, WHO), CIS, OSCE, WTO (observer).

Embassy: 1619 New Hampshire Ave. NW 20009; 986-1604.

Website: www.president.gov.by

Belarus became a constituent republic of the USSR in 1922. Overrun by German armies in 1941, Belarus was recaptured by Soviet troops in 1944. Following WWII, Belarus increased in area through Soviet annexation of part of NE Poland. Belarus declared independence Aug. 25, 1991, and became independent when the Soviet Union disbanded Dec. 26, 1991.

After a new constitution was adopted, Mar. 15, 1994, Aleksandr Lukashenko was elected president. Russia and Belarus signed a pact, Apr. 2, 1996, linking their political and economic systems. An authoritarian constitution enacted in Nov. gave Pres. Lukashenko vast new powers. Since then, Lukashenko and his supporters have retained power in elections criticized as seriously flawed by Western observers.

The IMF agreed Jan. 2009 to extend $2.5 bil in credits to help Belarus weather the global economic downturn. Belarus agreed July 5 to form a customs union with Russia and Kazakhstan. Lukashenko crushed protests that followed the Dec. 19, 2010, presidential election in which he claimed nearly 80% of the vote; the U.S. and EU imposed sanctions on Lukashenko and other Belarus officials Jan. 31, 2011. New sanctions imposed Feb. 28, 2012, prompted Lukashenko to expel the EU and Polish ambassadors from Belarus and recall its own envoys. In Sept. 23, 2012, parliamentary elections that many observers considered fraudulent, Lukashenko's supporters won every seat.

Belgium
Kingdom of Belgium

People: Population: 10,444,268. Age distrib.: <15: 15.7%; 65+: 18.7%. Pop. density: 893.4 per sq mi, 344.9 per sq km. Urban: 97.5%. Ethnic groups: Fleming 58%, Walloon 31%, mixed or other 11%. Languages: Dutch, French, German (all official). Religions: Roman Catholic 75%, other (incl. Protestant) 25%.

Geography: Total area: 11,787 sq mi, 30,528 sq km; Land area: 11,690 sq mi, 30,278 sq km. Location: In W Europe, on North Sea. Neighbors: France on W and S, Luxembourg on SE, Germany on E, Netherlands on N. Topography: Mostly flat, the country is trisected by the Scheldt and Meuse, major commercial rivers. The land becomes hilly and forested in the SE (Ardennes region). Capital: Brussels, 1,948,880 (figure is for urban aggl.). Cities (urban aggl.): Antwerp, 959,474.

Government: Type: Parliamentary democracy under a constitutional monarchy. Head of state: King Philippe; b. Apr. 15, 1960; in office: Aug. 21, 2013. Head of gov.: Prime Min. Elio Di Rupo; b. July 18, 1951; in office: Dec. 6, 2011. Local divisions: 3 regions. Defense budget: $4.77 bil. Active troops: 32,650.

Economy: Industries: engineering and metal prods., motor vehicle assembly, transp. equip., scientific instruments, processed food and beverages, chemicals, metals, textiles, glass, petroleum. Chief crops: sugar beets, vegetables, fruits, grain, tobacco. Natural resources: constr. materials, silica sand, carbonates. Arable land: 27.3%. Livestock: cattle: 2.5 mil; chickens: 35.4 mil; goats: 35,530; pigs: 6.5 mil; sheep: 113,995. Fish catch: 22,526 metric tons. Electricity prod. (2011): 83.4 bil kWh. Labor force: agric. 2%, industry 25%, services 73%.

Finance: Monetary unit: Euro (EUR) (Sept. 2013: 0.76 = $1 U.S.). GDP: $427.2 bil; per capita GDP: $38,500; GDP growth: −0.2%. Imports: $322 bil; Netherlands 20.9%, Germany 14.2%, France 10.6%, U.S. 6.1%, UK 5.5%, Ireland 4.4%. Exports: $315.4 bil; Germany 18%, France 16.1%, Netherlands 13%, UK 7.3%, U.S. 5.3%, Italy 4.4%. Tourism: $11.4 bil. Budget: $265.5 bil. Total reserves less gold: $18.6 bil. Gold: 7.3 mil oz t. CPI change: 2.8%.

Transport: Railways: 2,009 mi. Motor vehicles: 597.7 vehicles per 1,000 pop. Civil aviation: 4.4 bil pass.-mi; 26 airports. Chief ports: Antwerp (one of the world's busiest), Gent, Liege, Zeebrugge.

Communications: TV sets: 585 per 1,000 pop. Radios: 791 per 1,000 pop. Telephone lines: 42.9 per 100 pop. Internet: 82%.

Health: Life expect.: 76.6 male; 83.1 female. Births: 10.0 per 1,000 pop. Deaths: 10.7 per 1,000 pop. Natural inc.: −0.07%. Infant mortality: 4.2 per 1,000 live births. HIV rate: 0.3%.

Education: Compulsory: ages 6-17. Literacy: 99%.

Major intl. organizations: UN and all of its specialized agencies, EU, NATO, OECD, OSCE, WTO.

Embassy: 3330 Garfield St. NW 20008; 333-6900.

Website: www.belgium.be

Belgium derives its name from the Belgae, the first recorded inhabitants, probably Celts. The land was ruled for 1800 years by conquerors, including Rome, the Franks, Burgundy, Spain, Austria,

and France. After 1815, Belgium was made a part of the Netherlands but became an independent constitutional monarchy in 1830.

King Leopold III surrendered to Germany, May 28, 1940. After WWII, he was forced to abdicate in favor of his son, King Baudouin. Baudouin was succeeded by his brother, Albert II, Aug. 9, 1993.

The Flemings of northern Belgium speak Dutch, while the Walloons in the south speak French. The language difference has been a perennial source of controversy between the 2 groups. Parliament has passed measures aimed at transferring power from the central government to 3 regions—Wallonia, Flanders, and Brussels. Constitutional changes in 1993 made Belgium a federal state.

After elections June 2007, rivalries between Flemings and Walloons led to a 9-month political stalemate. Controversy over the sale of troubled bank Fortis NV to BNP Paribas of France led to the resignation of Prime Min. Yves Leterme, Dec. 2008, and his replacement by former Budget Min. Herman Van Rompuy. Leterme returned to office after Van Rompuy was chosen Nov. 2009, to become EU president. Elections June 2010 led to a prolonged political deadlock that ended when Elio Di Rupo became prime min. Dec. 2011.

A team of thieves Feb. 18, 2013, stole $50 mil in diamonds from a passenger plane at Brussels Airport; 30 people were arrested in the heist in Belgium and Switzerland May 7-8, and its mastermind was arrested in France.

Belize

People: Population: 334,297. Age distrib.: <15: 35.8%; 65+: 3.6%. Pop. density: 38 per sq mi, 14.7 per sq km. Urban: 44.7%. Ethnic groups: mestizo 49%, Creole 25%, Maya 11%, Garifuna 6%. Languages: Spanish, Creole, Mayan dialects, English (official), Garifuna (Carib), German. Religions: Roman Catholic 39%, Pentacostal 8%, Seventh Day Adventist 5%, Anglican 5%, Mennonite 4%, Baptist 4%, Methodist 3%, Nazarene 3%, Jehovah's Witnesses 2%, none 15%.

Geography: Total area: 8,867 sq mi, 22,966 sq km; Land area: 8,805 sq mi, 22,806 sq km. Location: Eastern coast of Central America. Neighbors: Mexico on N, Guatemala on W and S. Topography: Swampy lowlands in N, Maya Mts. in S, coral reefs and cays near coast. Climate is tropical. Capital: Belmopan, 14,472.

Government: Type: Parliamentary democracy. Head of state: Queen Elizabeth II, rep. by Gov.-Gen. Sir Colville Young; b. Nov. 20, 1932; in office: Nov. 17, 1993. Head of gov.: Prime Min. Dean Barrow; b. Mar. 2, 1951; in office: Feb. 8, 2008. Local divisions: 6 districts. Defense budget: $16 mil. Active troops: 1,050.

Economy: Industries: garment prod., food proc., tourism, constr., oil. Chief crops: bananas, cacao, citrus, sugar. Natural resources: timber, fish, hydropower. Crude oil reserves: 6.7 mil bbls. Arable land: 3.3%. Livestock: cattle: 91,200; chickens: 1.5 mil; goats: 185; pigs: 16,800; sheep: 13,100. Fish catch: 268,184 metric tons. Electricity prod.: 524.2 mil kWh. Labor force: agric. 10.2%, industry 18.1%, services 71.7%.

Finance: Monetary unit: Dollar (BZD) (Sept. 2013: 1.99 = $1 U.S.). GDP: $3 bil; per capita GDP: $8,900; GDP growth: 5.3%. Imports: $808.3 mil; U.S. 23.1%, Germany 14.6%, Mexico 11.2%, Cuba 9.1%, Guatemala 5.4%, China 4.5%, Trinidad and Tobago 4.1%. Exports: $548.5 mil; U.S. 30.8%, UK 21.2%, Nigeria 4.8%, Costa Rica 4.1%. Tourism: $299 mil. Budget: $450 mil. Total reserves less gold: $288.9 mil. CPI change: 1.3%.

Transport: Motor vehicles: 98.3 vehicles per 1,000 pop. Civil aviation: 6 airports. Chief ports: Belize City, Big Creek.

Communications: TV sets: 445 per 1,000 pop. Radios: 590 per 1,000 pop. Telephone lines: 7.8 per 100 pop. Internet: 25%.

Health: Life expect.: 66.8 male; 70.1 female. Births: 25.6 per 1,000 pop. Deaths: 5.9 per 1,000 pop. Natural inc.: 1.97%. Infant mortality: 20.8 per 1,000 live births. HIV rate: 2.3%.

Education: Compulsory: ages 5-14. Literacy: 70.3%.

Major intl. organizations: UN (FAO, IBRD, ILO, IMF, WHO), Caricom, the Commonwealth, OAS, WTO.

Embassy: 2535 Massachusetts Ave. NW 20008; 332-9636.

Website: www.belize.gov.bz

Belize (formerly British Honduras) was Britain's last colony on the American mainland; independence was achieved Sept. 21, 1981. Relations with neighboring Guatemala, which claims the southern half of Belize and its islands as its own territory, have improved in recent years. Belize has become a center for drug trafficking between Colombia and the U.S.

Benin
Republic of Benin

People: Population: 9,877,292. Age distrib.: <15: 44.1%; 65+: 2.8%. Pop. density: 231.3 per sq mi, 89.3 per sq km. Urban: 44.9%. Ethnic groups: Fon & related 39%, Adja & related 15%, Yoruba & related 12%, Bariba & related 9%, Peulh & related 7%, Ottamari & related 6%, Yoa-Lokpa & related 4%, Dendi & related 3%. Languages: French (official), Fon, Yoruba, tribal languages. Religions: Catholic 27%, Muslim 24%, Vodoun 17%, Protestant 10%.

Geography: Total area: 43,484 sq mi, 112,622 sq km; Land area: 42,711 sq mi, 110,622 sq km. Location: In W Africa on Gulf of Guinea. Neighbors: Togo on W; Burkina Faso, Niger on N; Nigeria on E. Topography: Most of Benin is flat and covered with dense vegetation. The coast is hot, humid, and rainy. Capital: Porto-Novo (constitutional), 314,496; Cotonou (seat), 923,923.

Government: Type: Republic. **Head of state and gov.:** Pres. Boni Yayi; b. July 1, 1952; in office: Apr. 6, 2006. **Local divisions:** 12 departments. **Defense budget** (2011): $74 mil. **Active troops:** 6,950.

Economy: Industries: textiles, food proc., constr. materials, cement. **Chief crops:** cotton, corn, cassava, yams, beans. **Natural resources:** oil, limestone, marble, timber. **Crude oil reserves:** 8 mil bbls. **Arable land:** 22.9%. **Livestock:** cattle: 2.1 mil; chickens: 17.1 mil; goats: 1.6 mil; pigs: 383,000; sheep: 825,000. **Fish catch:** 39,218 metric tons. **Electricity prod.:** 142.1 mil kWh. **Labor force:** NA.

Finance: Monetary unit: West African CFA Franc (XOF) (Sept. 2013: 498.17 = $1 U.S.). **GDP:** $15.8 bil; **per capita GDP:** $1,700; **GDP growth:** 3.8%. **Imports:** $2.2 bil; China 37.2%, U.S. 8.9%, India 6.7%, France 5.6%, Malaysia 5.3%. **Exports:** $1.6 bil; China 25.4%, India 24.6%, Lebanon 15.6%, Niger 4.8%, Nigeria 4.2%. **Tourism:** $187 mil. **Budget:** $1.7 bil. **Total reserves less gold:** $712.8 mil. **CPI change:** 6.8%.

Transport: Railways: 272 mi. **Motor vehicles:** 3.3 vehicles per 1,000 pop. **Civil aviation:** 80.8 mil pass.-mi; 1 airport. **Chief port:** Cotonou.

Communications: TV sets: 45 per 1,000 pop. **Radios:** 323 per 1,000 pop. **Telephone lines:** 1.7 per 100 pop. **Internet:** 3.8%.

Health: Life expect.: 59.4 male; 62.0 female. **Births:** 37.0 per 1,000 pop. **Deaths:** 8.6 per 1,000 pop. **Natural inc.:** 2.84%. **Infant mortality:** 58.5 per 1,000 live births. **HIV rate:** 1.2%.

Education: Compulsory: ages 6-11. **Literacy:** 28.7%.

Major intl. organizations: UN (FAO, IBRD, ILO, IMF, WHO), AU, WTO.

Embassy: 2124 Kalorama Rd. NW 20008; 232-6656.

Website: www.gouv.bj

The Kingdom of Abomey, rising to power in wars with neighboring kingdoms in the 17th cent., came under French domination in the late 19th cent., and was incorporated into French West Africa by 1904. Under the name Dahomey, the country gained independence Aug. 1, 1960; it became Benin in 1975. In the fifth coup since independence Col. Ahmed Kerekou took power in 1972; 2 years later he declared a socialist state with a Marxist-Leninist philosophy. In Dec. 1989, Kerekou announced Marxism-Leninism would no longer be the state ideology.

In Mar. 1991, Kerekou lost Benin's first free presidential election in 30 years to Nicéphore Soglo. Kerekou defeated Soglo in Mar. 1996 to reclaim the presidency. He won reelection in a runoff Mar. 22, 2001. Boni Yayi, an economist, won a presidential runoff vote, Mar. 19, 2006.

In 2006, Benin signed a 5-year, $307-mil aid deal with the U.S. More than 100,000 people reportedly lost their savings when a fraudulent investment scheme linked to high government officials collapsed in mid-2010. Pres. Yayi won reelection to a second 5-year term Mar. 13, 2011.

Bhutan
Kingdom of Bhutan

People: Population: 725,296. **Age distrib.:** <15: 27.8%; 65+: 5.9%. **Pop. density:** 49.9 per sq mi, 18.9 per sq km. **Urban:** 35.6%. **Ethnic groups:** Bhote 50%, ethnic Nepalese 35%, indigenous or migrant tribes 15%. **Languages:** Sharchhopka, Dzongkha (official), Lhotshamkha. **Religions:** Lamaistic Buddhist 75%, Indian- and Nepalese-influenced Hinduism 25%.

Geography: Total area: 14,824 sq mi, 38,394 sq km; **Land area:** 14,824 sq mi, 38,394 sq km. **Location:** S Asia, in eastern Himalayan Mts. **Neighbors:** India on W (Sikkim) and S, China on N. **Topography:** Very high mountains in the N, fertile valleys in the center, and thick forests in the Duar Plain in the S. **Capital:** Thimphu, 99,337.

Government: Type: Constitutional monarchy. **Head of state:** King Jigme Khesar Namgyal Wangchuk; b. Feb. 21, 1980; in office: Dec. 14, 2006. **Head of gov.:** Prime Min. Tshering Tobgay; b. Sept. 16, 1965; in office: July 29, 2013. **Local divisions:** 20 districts. **Defense budget/active troops:** NA.

Economy: Industries: cement, wood prods., processed fruits, alcoholic beverages, calcium carbide, tourism. **Chief crops:** rice, corn, root crops, citrus. **Natural resources:** timber, hydropower, gypsum, calcium carbonate. **Arable land:** 2.5%. **Livestock:** cattle: 306,190; chickens: 434,580; goats: 43,734; pigs: 21,170; sheep: 12,459. **Fish catch:** 235 metric tons. **Electricity prod.:** 7.2 bil kWh. **Labor force:** agric. 43.7%, industry 39.1%, services 17.2%.

Finance: Monetary unit: Ngultrum (BTN) (Sept. 2013: 65.24 = $1 U.S.). **GDP:** $5 bil; **per capita GDP:** $6,800; **GDP growth:** 9.7%. **Imports:** $1.3 bil. **Exports:** $721.8 mil. **Tourism:** $63 mil. **Budget:** $651.2 mil (nearly one-quarter financed by India's govt.). **Total reserves less gold:** $954.7 mil. **CPI change:** 10.9%.

Transport: Civil aviation: 44.7 mil pass.-mi; 2 airports.

Communications: TV sets: 12 per 1,000 pop. **Radios:** 118 per 1,000 pop. **Telephone lines:** 3.6 per 100 pop. **Internet:** 25.4%.

Health: Life expect.: 67.5 male; 69.4 female. **Births:** 18.4 per 1,000 pop. **Deaths:** 6.9 per 1,000 pop. **Natural inc.:** 1.16%. **Infant mortality:** 40.0 per 1,000 live births. **HIV rate:** 0.3%.

Education: Compulsory: ages NA. **Literacy:** 52.8%.

Major intl. organizations: UN (FAO, IBRD, IMF, WHO), WTO (observer).

Permanent UN mission: 763 United Nations Plz., New York, NY 10017; (212) 490-9660.

Website: www.bhutan.gov.bt

The region came under Tibetan rule in the 16th cent. British influence grew in the 19th cent. A Buddhist monarchy was set up in 1907. After a 1910 treaty, Britain guided Bhutan's external affairs, while the country remained internally self-governing. Upon independence the treaty was revised, 1949, to allow India to assume Britain's role.

Isolated for much of its history, Bhutan has taken steps toward modernization. King Jigme Singye Wangchuk, in power since 1972, stepped down Dec. 14, 2006, in favor of his son, Jigme Khesar Namgyal Wangchuk. Multiparty parliamentary elections took place Mar. 24, 2008, and a new constitution was ratified July 18, making Bhutan a democratic constitutional monarchy. Namgay Peldon became the first woman elected governor in the Mar. 2008 election, and Tashi Chhozom became the first woman appointed to the country's supreme court Aug. 3, 2012. The ruling party was defeated in July 13, 2013, parliamentary elections, with the opposition People's Democratic Party (PDP) winning 32 out of 47 seats.

Bolivia
Plurinational State of Bolivia

People: Population: 10,461,053. **Age distrib.:** <15: 33.8%; 65+: 4.8%. **Pop. density:** 25 per sq mi, 9.7 per sq km. **Urban:** 66.8%. **Ethnic groups:** Quechua 30%, mestizo (mixed white and Amerindian) 30%, Aymara 25%, white 15%. **Languages:** Spanish, Quechua, Aymara (all official). **Religions:** Roman Catholic 95%, Protestant (Evangelical Methodist) 5%.

Geography: Total area: 424,164 sq mi, 1,098,581 sq km; **Land area:** 418,265 sq mi, 1,083,301 sq km. **Location:** In W central South America, in the Andes Mts. (one of 2 landlocked countries in South America). **Neighbors:** Peru and Chile on W, Argentina and Paraguay on S, Brazil on E and N. **Topography:** The great central plateau, at an altitude of 12,000 ft, over 500 mi long, lies between 2 great cordilleras having 3 of the highest peaks in South America. Lake Titicaca, on Peruvian border, is highest lake in world on which steamboats ply (12,506 ft). The E central region has semitropical forests; the llanos, or Amazon-Chaco lowlands are in E. **Capital:** La Paz (admin.), 1,714,530; Sucre (constitutional), 306,597. **Cities (urban aggl.):** Santa Cruz, 1,719,346.

Government: Type: Republic. **Head of state and gov.:** Pres. Juan Evo Morales Ayma; b. Oct. 26, 1959; in office: Jan. 22, 2006. **Local divisions:** 9 departments. **Defense budget:** $336 mil. **Active troops:** 46,100.

Economy: Industries: mining, smelting, petroleum, food and beverages, tobacco, handicrafts, clothing. **Chief crops:** soybeans, coffee, coca, cotton, corn, sugarcane, rice, potatoes. **Natural resources:** tin, nat. gas, petroleum, zinc, tungsten, antimony, silver, iron, lead, gold, timber, hydropower. **Crude oil reserves:** 209.8 mil bbls. **Other resources:** Timber. **Arable land:** 3.5%. **Livestock:** cattle: 8.4 mil; chickens: 195 mil; goats: 2.3 mil; pigs: 2.7 mil; sheep: 8.9 mil. **Fish catch:** 7,643 metric tons. **Electricity prod.:** 6.6 bil kWh. **Labor force:** agric. 32%, industry 20%, services 48%.

Finance: Monetary unit: Boliviano (BOB) (Sept. 2013: 6.91 = $1 U.S.). **GDP:** $56.1 bil; **per capita GDP:** $5,200; **GDP growth:** 5.2%. **Imports:** $7.7 bil; Chile 20.8%, Brazil 19.9%, Argentina 11.7%, U.S. 9.9%, Peru 7.1%, Venezuela 6%, China 4.8%. **Exports:** $10.7 bil; Brazil 40.3%, U.S. 17.7%, Argentina 7.7%, Peru 5.3%. **Tourism:** $532 mil. **Budget:** $12.2 bil. **Total reserves less gold:** $11.7 bil. **Gold:** 1.4 mil oz t. **CPI change:** 4.6%.

Transport: Railways: 2,269 mi. **Motor vehicles:** 51.1 vehicles per 1,000 pop. **Civil aviation:** 1.2 bil pass.-mi; 21 airports. **Chief port:** Puerto Aguirre.

Communications: TV sets: 155 per 1,000 pop. **Radios:** 672 per 1,000 pop. **Telephone lines:** 8.6 per 100 pop. **Internet:** 34.2%.

Health: Life expect.: 65.5 male; 71.1 female. **Births:** 23.8 per 1,000 pop. **Deaths:** 6.7 per 1,000 pop. **Natural inc.:** 1.71%. **Infant mortality:** 39.8 per 1,000 live births. **HIV rate:** 0.3%.

Education: Compulsory: ages 6-13. **Literacy:** 91.2%.

Major intl. organizations: UN (FAO, IBRD, ILO, IMF, WHO), OAS, WTO.

Embassy: 3014 Massachusetts Ave. NW 20008; 483-4410.

Website: www.bolivia.gob.bo

The Incas conquered the region's earlier Indian inhabitants in the 13th cent. Spanish rule began in the 1530s and lasted until Aug. 6, 1825. The country is named after independence fighter Simón Bolívar. In a series of wars, Bolivia lost its Pacific coast to Chile, the oil-bearing Chaco to Paraguay, and rubber-growing areas to Brazil, 1879-1935.

Economic unrest, especially among militant mine workers, has led to continuing political instability. A reformist government under Victor Paz Estenssoro, 1951-64, nationalized tin mines and attempted to improve conditions for the Indian majority but was overthrown by a military junta. A series of coups and countercoups continued until constitutional government was restored in 1982.

U.S. pressure on the government to reduce coca output, the raw material for cocaine, has led to clashes between police and growers and increased anti-U.S. feeling among Bolivians. Gen. Hugo Banzer Suárez, who ruled as a dictator, 1971-78, later governed as president, 1997-2001.

After an inconclusive presidential election June 2002, Congress chose Gonzalo Sánchez de Lozada, a U.S.-educated mining

executive, as head of state. He quit Oct. 17, 2003, after indigenous Bolivians staged a month of antigovernment protests in which over 70 people died. His successor, Vice Pres. Carlos D. Mesa Gisbert, was embroiled in controversies over energy policy.

Juan Evo Morales Ayma, a leftist and coca-farmer advocate, won the presidential election, Dec. 2005. He nationalized the hydrocarbon sector, launched a land-redistribution program to benefit poor farmers, and tightened ties with Venezuela and Cuba. He faced resistance and demands for autonomy from leaders of Bolivia's relatively prosperous lowland provinces. Voters, Jan. 25, 2009, approved a new constitution strengthening the rights of Bolivia's indigenous majority and increasing federal control over the country's natural resources. Morales won a second term Dec. 6, 2009, and his Movement Toward Socialism consolidated its hold over Bolivia's legislature. Morales nationalized a Spanish utility company, May 1, 2012, that served about 74% of the country, and 2 others Dec. 29, 2012.

Bosnia and Herzegovina

People: Population: 3,875,723. **Age distrib.:** <15: 14%; 65+: 12.9%. **Pop. density:** 196.1 per sq mi, 75.7 per sq km. **Urban:** 48.3%. **Ethnic groups:** Bosniak 48%, Serb 37%, Croat 14%. **Languages:** Bosnian, Croatian (both official); Serbian. **Religions:** Muslim 40%, Orthodox 31%, Roman Catholic 15%.

Geography: Total area: 19,767 sq mi, 51,197 sq km; **Land area:** 19,763 sq mi, 51,187 sq km. **Location:** On Balkan Peninsula in SE Europe. **Neighbors:** Serbia, Montenegro on E and SE, Croatia on N and W. **Topography:** Hilly with some mountains. About 36% of the land is forested. **Capital:** Sarajevo, 389,042.

Government: Type: Federal democratic republic. **Heads of state:** Collective presidency with rotating leadership. **Head of gov.:** Prime Min. Vjekoslav Bevanda; b. May 13 1956; in office: Jan. 12, 2012. **Local divisions:** Bosniak-Croat Federation, Serbian-led Republika Srpska, and internationally supervised Brcko district. **Defense budget:** $228 mil. **Active troops:** 10,550.

Economy: Industries: steel, coal, mining, vehicle assembly, textiles, tobacco prods., wooden furniture, ammunition, domestic appliances, oil refining. **Chief crops:** wheat, corn, fruits, vegetables. **Natural resources:** coal, iron ore, bauxite, copper, lead, zinc, chromite, cobalt, manganese, nickel, clay, gypsum, salt, sand, timber, hydropower. **Arable land:** 19.7%. **Livestock:** cattle: 455,258; chickens: 17.3 mil; goats: 65,260; pigs: 576,789; sheep: 1 mil. **Fish catch:** 10,014 metric tons. **Electricity prod.:** 16.5 bil kWh. **Labor force:** agric. 20.5%, industry 32.6%, services 47%.

Finance: Monetary unit: Convertible Marka (BAM) (Sept. 2013: 1.49 = $1 U.S.). **GDP:** $32.4 bil; **per capita GDP:** $8,400; **GDP growth:** –0.7%. **Imports:** $8.8 bil; Croatia 21.1%, Germany 12.5%, Slovenia 12.4%, Italy 9%, Russia 7.3%, Austria 6.1%, Hungary 4.9%, Greece 4.3%. **Exports:** $3.3 bil; Slovenia 17.3%, Croatia 16.5%, Italy 13.6%, Germany 12.8%, Austria 12.7%. **Tourism:** $603 mil. **Budget:** $8.5 bil. **Total reserves less gold:** $4.3 bil. **Gold:** 64,000 oz t. **CPI change:** NA.

Transport: Railways: 373 mi. **Civil aviation:** 69 mil pass.-mi; 7 airports. **Chief ports:** Bosanski Samac, Brcko.

Communications: TV sets: 282 per 1,000 pop. **Radios:** 251 per 1,000 pop. **Telephone lines:** 23.5 per 100 pop. **Internet:** 65.4%.

Health: Life expect.: 73.1 male; 79.3 female. **Births:** 8.9 per 1,000 pop. **Deaths:** 9.5 per 1,000 pop. **Natural inc.:** –0.06%. **Infant mortality:** 6.0 per 1,000 live births. **HIV rate:** NA.

Education: Compulsory: ages 6-14. **Literacy:** 98%.

Major intl. organizations: UN (FAO, IBRD, ILO, IMF, WHO), OSCE, WTO (observer).

Embassy: 2109 E St. NW 20037; 337-1500.

Website: www.fbihvlada.gov.ba

Bosnia was ruled by Croatian kings c. 958 CE, and by Hungary 1000-1200. It became organized c. 1200 and later took control of Herzegovina. The kingdom disintegrated after 1391, with the southern part becoming the independent duchy of Herzegovina. It was conquered by Turks in 1463 and made a Turkish province. The area was placed under control of Austria-Hungary in 1878 and made part of the province of Bosnia and Herzegovina, which was formally annexed to Austria-Hungary, 1908. Bosnia became a province of Yugoslavia in 1918. It was reunited with Herzegovina as a federated republic in the 1946 Yugoslav constitution.

Bosnia and Herzegovina declared sovereignty Oct. 15, 1991. A referendum for independence was passed Feb. 29, 1992. Ethnic Serbs' opposition to the referendum spurred violent clashes and bombings. The U.S. and EU recognized the republic Apr. 7. Fierce 3-way fighting continued between Bosnia's Serbs, Muslims, and Croats. Serb forces massacred thousands of Bosnian Muslims and engaged in ethnic cleansing, expelling Muslims and other non-Serbs from areas under Bosnian Serb control. The capital, Sarajevo, was surrounded and besieged by Bosnian Serb forces. Muslims and Croats in Bosnia began a cease-fire Feb. 23, 1994, and signed an accord, Mar. 18, to create a Muslim-Croat confederation in Bosnia. However, by mid-1994, Bosnian Serbs controlled over 70% of the country.

As fighting continued in 1995, the balance of power shifted toward the Muslim-Croat alliance. Massive NATO air strikes at Bosnian Serb targets beginning Aug. 30 triggered a new round of peace talks, and the siege of Sarajevo was lifted Sept. 15. The new talks produced an agreement to create autonomous regions within Bosnia, with the Serb region (Republika Srpska) constituting 49% of

the country. A Croat-Muslim offensive in Sept. recaptured significant territory, leaving Bosnian Serbs in control of approximately half that percentage.

A Nov. 1995 peace agreement was signed in Paris, Dec. 14, 1995, by leaders of Bosnia, Croatia, and Serbia. Some 60,000 NATO troops (about 20,000 from the U.S.) moved in to police the accord. Meanwhile, a UN tribunal began bringing charges against suspected war criminals. Elections were held Sept. 14, 1996, for a 3-person collective presidency, for seats in a federal parliament, and for regional offices. In Dec. a revamped NATO Stabilization Force (SFOR) of over 30,000 members (more than 8,000 from the U.S.) received an 18-month mandate, which was later extended.

The UN tribunal found Radislav Krstic, a Bosnian Serb general, guilty Aug. 2, 2001, in connection with the genocide of thousands of Muslims at Srebrenica in 1995. An EU peacekeeping force (EUFOR), with 7,000 members, assumed responsibility from SFOR, Dec. 2, 2004. Accused of complicity in the Sarajevo and Srebrenica atrocities, former Bosnian Serb leader Radovan Karadzic was arrested in Serbia, July 21, 2008, and handed over to the UN tribunal at The Hague, Netherlands. He was charged with 10 counts of genocide, war crimes, and crimes against humanity; the prosecution rested its case in May and Karadzic began his defense Oct. 16, 2012. Also extradited to The Hague was Gen. Ratko Mladic, the former Bosnian Serb military commander accused of directing the Srebrenica massacre, who was arrested in Serbia May 26, 2011. He faced 11 counts of war crimes and crimes against humanity, 2 of them for genocide, in a trial that began May 16, 2012. As the security situation in Bosnia improved, EUFOR strength dropped to about 1,600 troops as of Aug. 2012. On Dec. 12, 2012, Mladic's close associate Zdravko Tolimir was convicted of genocide and sentenced to life in prison.

The government's failure to renew a law on personal ID numbers that lapsed in Feb. 2013 prompted protests June 5-6, 2013. The government, June 6, adopted a measure allowing it to issue temporary IDs for 6 months.

Botswana
Republic of Botswana

People: Population: 2,127,825. **Age distrib.:** <15: 33.2%; 65+: 4%. **Pop. density:** 9.7 per sq mi, 3.8 per sq km. **Urban:** 61.7%. **Ethnic groups:** Tswana or Setswana 79%, Kalanga 11%, Basarwa 3%, other (incl. Kgalagadi, white) 7%. **Languages:** Setswana, Kalanga, Sekgalagadi, English (official). **Religions:** Christian 72%, Badimo 6%, none 21%.

Geography: Total area: 224,607 sq mi, 581,730 sq km; **Land area:** 218,816 sq mi, 566,730 sq km. **Location:** In southern Africa. **Neighbors:** Namibia on N and W, South Africa on S, Zimbabwe on NE; Botswana claims border with Zambia on N. **Topography:** The Kalahari Desert, supporting nomadic Bushmen and wildlife, spreads over SW; there are swamplands and farming areas in N, and rolling plains in E where livestock are grazed. **Capital:** Gaborone, 201,709.

Government: Type: Parliamentary republic. **Head of state and gov.:** Pres. Seretse Khama Ian Khama; b. Feb. 27, 1953; in office: Apr. 1, 2008. **Local divisions:** 9 districts, 5 town councils. **Defense budget:** $467 mil. **Active troops:** 9,000.

Economy: Industries: diamonds, copper, nickel, salt, soda ash, potash, coal, iron ore, silver. **Chief crops:** sorghum, maize, millet, beans, sunflowers, groundnuts. **Natural resources:** diamonds, copper, nickel, salt, soda ash, potash, coal, iron ore, silver. **Arable land:** 0.5%. **Livestock:** cattle: 2.8 mil; chickens: 5.5 mil; goats: 2 mil; pigs: 13,000; sheep: 285,000. **Fish catch:** 234 metric tons. **Electricity prod.:** 429.6 mil kWh. **Labor force:** NA.

Finance: Monetary unit: Pula (BWP) (Sept. 2013: 8.66 = $1 U.S.). **GDP:** $32.1 bil; **per capita GDP:** $17,100; **GDP growth:** 3.8%. **Imports:** $6.9 bil. **Exports:** $6.3 bil. **Tourism:** $218 mil. **Budget:** $5.4 bil. **Total reserves less gold:** $7.6 bil. **CPI change:** 7.5%.

Transport: Railways: 552 mi. **Motor vehicles:** 170.2 vehicles per 1,000 pop. **Civil aviation:** 70.2 mil pass.-mi; 10 airports.

Communications: TV sets: 44 per 1,000 pop. **Radios:** 734 per 1,000 pop. **Telephone lines:** 7.8 per 100 pop. **Internet:** 11.5%.

Health: Life expect.: 56.0 male; 52.9 female. **Births:** 21.7 per 1,000 pop. **Deaths:** 12.9 per 1,000 pop. **Natural inc.:** 0.88%. **Infant mortality:** 9.9 per 1,000 live births. **HIV rate:** 23.4%.

Education: Compulsory: ages 6-15. **Literacy:** 85.1%.

Major intl. organizations: UN (FAO, IBRD, ILO, IMF, WHO), AU, the Commonwealth, WTO.

Embassy: 1531-1533 New Hampshire Ave. NW 20036; 244-4990.

Website: www.gov.bw

First inhabited by Bushmen, then Bantus, the region became the British protectorate of Bechuanaland in 1886. The country became fully independent Sept. 30, 1966. Cattle raising and mining (diamonds, copper, nickel) have contributed to economic growth. Pres. Festus Mogae transferred power Apr. 1, 2008, to Seretse Khama Ian Khama, son of Botswana's independence leader and first president (1966-80), Sir Seretse Khama. In power since independence, the Botswana Democratic Party dominated national elections Oct. 16, 2009, and Ian Khama was sworn in for a full term Oct. 20. De Beers, the world's largest diamond producer, moved its diamond-sorting operations from London to Botswana in 2012.

Brazil
Federative Republic of Brazil

People: Population: 201,009,622. **Age distrib.:** <15: 24.2%; 65+: 7.3%. **Pop. density:** 61.5 per sq mi, 23.8 per sq km. **Urban:** 84.6%. **Ethnic groups:** white 54%, mulatto (mixed white and black) 39%, black 6%. **Languages:** Portuguese (official), Spanish, German, Italian, Japanese, English, minor Amerindian langs. **Religions:** Roman Catholic (nominal) 74%, Protestant 15%, Spiritualist 1%, none 7%.

Geography: Total area: 3,287,612 sq mi, 8,514,877 sq km; **Land area:** 3,266,199 sq mi, 8,459,417 sq km. **Location:** Occupies E half of South America. **Neighbors:** French Guiana, Suriname, Guyana, Venezuela on N; Colombia, Peru, Bolivia, Paraguay, on W; Argentina, Uruguay on S. **Topography:** Brazil's Atlantic coastline stretches 4,603 mi. In N is the heavily wooded Amazon basin covering half the country. Its network of rivers is navigable for 15,814 mi. The Amazon itself flows 2,093 mi in Brazil, all navigable. The NE region is semiarid scrubland, heavily settled and poor. The S central region, favored by climate and resources, has almost half of the population. The narrow coastal belt includes most of the major cities. Almost the entire country has a tropical or semitropical climate. **Capital:** Brasília, 3,813,010. **Cities (urban aggl.):** São Paulo, 19,924,458; Rio de Janeiro, 11,959,725; Belo Horizonte, 5,487,376.

Government: Type: Federal republic. **Head of state and gov.:** Pres. Dilma Rousseff; b. Dec. 14, 1947; in office: Jan. 1, 2011. **Local divisions:** 26 states, 1 federal district. **Defense budget:** $35.3 bil. **Active troops:** 318,500.

Economy: Industries: textiles, shoes, chemicals, cement, lumber, iron ore, tin, steel, aircraft, motor vehicles and parts. **Chief crops:** coffee, soybeans, wheat, rice, corn, sugarcane, cocoa, citrus. **Natural resources:** bauxite, gold, iron ore, manganese, nickel, phosphates, platinum, tin, rare earth elements, uranium, petroleum hydropower, timber. **Crude oil reserves:** 13.2 bil bbls. **Arable land:** 8.5%. **Livestock:** cattle: 212.8 mil; chickens: 1.3 bil; goats: 9.4 mil; pigs: 39.3 mil; sheep: 17.7 mil. **Fish catch:** 1.4 mil metric tons. **Electricity prod.:** (2011): 530.6 bil kWh. **Labor force:** agric. 15.7%, industry 13.3%, services 71%.

Finance: Monetary unit: Real (BRL) (Sept. 2013: 2.29 = $1 U.S.). **GDP:** $2.4 tril; **per capita GDP:** $12,100; **GDP growth:** 0.9%. **Imports:** $223.2 bil; China 15.4%, U.S. 14.7%, Argentina 7.4%, Germany 6.4%, South Korea 4.1%. **Exports:** $242.6 bil; China 17%, U.S. 11.1%, Argentina 7.4%, Netherlands 6.2%. **Tourism:** $6.6 bil. **Budget:** $822.1 bil. **Total reserves less gold:** $369.6 bil. **Gold:** 2.2 mil oz t. **CPI change:** 5.4%.

Transport: Railways: 17,733 mi. **Motor vehicles:** 187 vehicles per 1,000 pop. **Civil aviation:** 46 bil pass.-mi; 698 airports. **Chief ports:** Ilha Grande, Paranagua, Rio Grande, Santos, São Sebastião, Tubarão.

Communications: TV sets: 279 per 1,000 pop. **Radios:** 255 per 1,000 pop. **Telephone lines:** 22.3 per 100 pop. **Internet:** 49.8%.

Health: Life expect.: 69.5 male; 76.7 female. **Births:** 15.0 per 1,000 pop. **Deaths:** 6.5 per 1,000 pop. **Natural inc.:** 0.85%. **Infant mortality:** 19.8 per 1,000 live births. **HIV rate:** 0.3%.

Education: Compulsory: ages 6-14. **Literacy:** 90.4%.

Major intl. organizations: UN and most of its specialized agencies, OAS, WTO.

Embassy: 3006 Massachusetts Ave. NW 20008; 238-2700. **Website:** www.brasil.gov.br

Pedro Álvares Cabral, a Portuguese navigator, is generally credited as the first European to reach Brazil, in 1500. The country was thinly settled by various Indian tribes. Only a few survive today, mostly in the Amazon Basin.

In the next centuries, Portuguese colonists gradually pushed inland, bringing along large numbers of African slaves. (Slavery was not abolished until 1888.) The king of Portugal, fleeing Napoleon's army, moved the seat of government to Brazil in 1808. Brazil thereupon became a kingdom under Dom Joao VI. After Joao VI returned to Portugal, his son Pedro proclaimed Brazil's independence, Sept. 7, 1822, and was crowned emperor. The second emperor, Dom Pedro II, was deposed in 1889, and a republic proclaimed, called the United States of Brazil. It was renamed the Federative Republic of Brazil in 1967.

A military junta took control in 1930; Getulio Vargas assumed dictatorial power. The military forced him out in 1945. A democratic regime prevailed 1945-64, during which time the capital was moved from Rio de Janeiro to Brasília. Military-backed governments ruled Brazil for the next 20 years. Censorship was imposed, and the opposition was suppressed.

Brazil became the leading industrial power of Latin America by the 1970s, while agricultural output soared. By the 1990s, Brazil had one of the world's largest economies; income was poorly distributed, however, and more than one in four Brazilians survived on less than $1 a day. Despite protective environmental legislation, development has destroyed much of the Amazon ecosystem.

Democratic presidential elections held in 1985 brought civilian rule back. Fernando Collor de Mello was elected president, Dec. 1989. In Sept. 1992, Collor was impeached for corruption. He resigned as his trial was beginning, and acting Pres. Itamar Franco was officially sworn in. Fernando Henrique Cardoso won Oct. 1994 and 1998 elections; he guided Brazil through a series of financial crises.

A new civil code guaranteeing legal equality for women was enacted Aug. 15, 2001. With Brazil's debt exceeding $260 bil, the IMF approved a $30 bil loan Aug. 2002. Luiz Inácio Lula da Silva, a union leader and reformer, won a presidential runoff, Oct. 2002. Brazil's space program launched its first rocket into space Oct. 23, 2004.

A top aide to Pres. Lula resigned June 16, 2005, amid allegations the ruling party bribed legislators for votes; he and 2 others involved in the scandal were found guilty and sentenced to upwards of 40 years in prison Oct.-Nov. 2012. Despite this and other scandals, Lula won a second presidential term, Oct. 2006. The nation reported huge offshore oil finds in 2007-08. Lula's former chief of staff, Dilma Rousseff, won a runoff election Oct. 31, 2010, and took office as Brazil's first woman president Jan. 1, 2011. Brazilian police raided Rocinha, Rio de Janeiro's largest slum, Nov. 13, 2011, as part of an effort to bring law to the entire city as it prepared to host the soccer World Cup in 2014 and the Olympic Games in 2016. São Paulo's 2012 murder rate was up nearly 40% over the previous year, with more than 70 police officers killed, allegedly by various gangs and criminal organizations.

Unsafe building conditions and a band's careless use of pyrotechnics caused a deadly fire at the Kiss nightclub in Santa Maria Jan. 27, 2013, that killed more than 230 patrons. Brazil's independent Public Ministry announced Apr. 6, 2013, an investigation into former Pres. Lula for buying votes and for channeling funds into the Workers' Party. After 10 months of sporadic demonstrations over planned increases in the cost of public transportation, fares were raised June 1, 2013, and demonstrations began in São Paulo June 6 and quickly spread to Rio de Janeiro and other cities. Protestors turned their attention to other problems, including a lack of public services and government corruption, and protests continued even after fares were lowered June 20. Demonstrators also targeted the $52 mil price tag of Pope Francis's historic visit the week of July 23, 2013.

Brunei
Brunei Darussalam

People: Population: 415,717. **Age distrib.:** <15: 24.6%; 65+: 3.8%. **Pop. density:** 204.5 per sq mi, 79 per sq km. **Urban:** 76%. **Ethnic groups:** Malay 66%, Chinese 11%, indigenous 3%. **Languages:** Malay (official), English, Chinese. **Religions:** Muslim (official) 67%, Buddhist 13%, Christian 10%, other (incl. indigenous beliefs) 10%.

Geography: Total area: 2,226 sq mi, 5,765 sq km; **Land area:** 2,033 sq mi, 5,265 sq km. **Location:** In SE Asia, on the N coast of the island of Borneo; it is surrounded on its landward side by the Malaysian state of Sarawak. **Topography:** Brunei has a narrow coastal plain, with mountains in E, hilly lowlands in W. There are swamps in W and NE. Climate is tropical. **Capital:** Bandar Seri Begawan, 16,381.

Government: Type: Constitutional sultanate. **Head of state and gov.:** Sultan Sir Muda Hassanal Bolkiah Mu'izzadin Waddaulah; b. July 15, 1946; in office: Jan. 1, 1984 (sultan since Oct. 5, 1967). **Local divisions:** 4 districts. **Defense budget:** $405 mil. **Active troops:** 7,000.

Economy: Industries: petroleum, petroleum refining, liquefied nat. gas, constr. **Chief crops:** rice, vegetables, fruits. **Natural resources:** petroleum, nat. gas, timber. **Crude oil reserves:** 1.1 bil bbls. **Arable land:** 0.6%. **Livestock:** cattle: 852; chickens: 15 mil; goats: 7,000; pigs: 1,300; sheep: 4,000. **Fish catch:** 2,630 metric tons. **Electricity prod.:** 3.6 bil kWh. **Labor force:** agric. 4.2%, industry 62.8%, services 33%.

Finance: Monetary unit: Dollar (BND) (Sept. 2013: 1.27 = $1 U.S.). **GDP:** $22 bil; **per capita GDP:** $55,300; **GDP growth:** 1.3%. **Imports** (2011): $3 bil; Singapore 26.3%, China 21.3%, UK 21.3%, Malaysia 11.8%. **Exports** (2011): $12.8 bil; Japan 46.5%, South Korea 15.5%, Australia 9.3%, India 7%, New Zealand 6.7%. **Budget:** $5.1 bil. **Total reserves less gold:** $3.3 bil. **Gold:** 98,470 oz t. **CPI change:** NA.

Transport: Motor vehicles: 450.1 vehicles per 1,000 pop. **Civil aviation:** 2.1 bil pass.-mi; 1 airport. **Chief ports:** Lumut, Muara, Seria.

Communications: TV sets: 629 per 1,000 pop. **Radios:** 300 per 1,000 pop. **Telephone lines:** 17.2 per 100 pop. **Internet:** 60.3%.

Health: Life expect.: 74.3 male; 79.0 female. **Births:** 17.6 per 1,000 pop. **Deaths:** 3.4 per 1,000 pop. **Natural inc.:** 1.42%. **Infant mortality:** 10.8 per 1,000 live births. **HIV rate:** NA.

Education: Compulsory: ages 6-14. **Literacy:** 95.4%.

Major intl. organizations: UN and some of its specialized agencies, APEC, ASEAN, the Commonwealth, WTO.

Embassy: 3520 International Ct. NW 20008; 237-1838. **Website:** www.gov.bn

The Sultanate of Brunei was a powerful state in the early 16th cent., with authority over all of the island of Borneo as well as parts of the Sulu Islands and the Philippines. In 1888, a treaty placed the state under the protection of Great Britain.

Brunei became a fully sovereign and independent state on Jan. 1, 1984. Much of the country's oil wealth has been squandered by members of the royal family. Brunei broke with tradition and fielded female athletes for the first time at the 2012 Summer Olympic Games.

Bulgaria
Republic of Bulgaria

People: Population: 6,981,642. **Age distrib.:** <15: 14.2%; 65+: 18.9%. **Pop. density:** 166.7 per sq mi, 64.4 per sq km. **Urban:** 73.1%. **Ethnic groups:** Bulgarian 77%, Turk 8%, Roma 4%, other (incl. Macedonian, Armenian, Tatar, Circassian) 1%. **Languages:** Bulgarian (official), Turkish, Roma. **Religions:** Eastern Orthodox 60%, Sunni Muslim 7%, other (incl. Catholic, Protestant, Armenian Apostolic Orthodox, Judaism) 2%, none 4%.

Geography: Total area: 42,811 sq mi, 110,879 sq km; **Land area:** 41,888 sq mi, 108,489 sq km. **Location:** SE Europe, in E Balkan Peninsula on Black Sea. **Neighbors:** Romania on N; Serbia, Macedonia on W; Greece, Turkey on S. **Topography:** The Stara Planina (Balkan) Mts. stretch E-W across the center of the country, with the Danubian plain on N, the Rhodope Mts. on SW, and Thracian Plain on SE. **Capital:** Sofia, 1,173,770.

Government: Type: Parliamentary democracy. **Head of state:** Pres. Rosen Plevneliev; b. May 14, 1964; in office: Jan. 22, 2012. **Head of gov.:** Prime Min. Zinaida Zlatanova; b. July 24, 1973; in office: May 29, 2013. **Local divisions:** 28 provinces. **Defense budget:** $657 mil. **Active troops:** 31,300.

Economy: Industries: utilities, food, beverages, tobacco, machinery and equip. **Chief crops:** vegetables, fruits, tobacco, wine, wheat, barley, sunflowers, sugar beets. **Natural resources:** bauxite, copper, lead, zinc, coal, timber. **Crude oil reserves:** 15 mil bbls. **Arable land:** 29.9%. **Livestock:** cattle: 544,456; chickens: 14.1 mil; goats: 356,334; pigs: 664,000; sheep: 1.4 mil. **Fish catch:** 15,150 metric tons. **Electricity prod.:** 43.4 bil kWh. **Labor force:** agric. 7.1%, industry 35.2%, services 57.7%.

Finance: Monetary unit: Lev (BGN) (Sept. 2013: 1.49 = $1 U.S.). **GDP:** $105.5 bil; **per capita GDP:** $14,500; **GDP growth:** 0.8%. **Imports:** $31.5 bil; Russia 20.9%, Germany 11.3%, Italy 6.7%, Romania 6.6%, Greece 6.1%, Turkey 4.6%, Spain 4.5%. **Exports:** $26.8 bil; Germany 10.4%, Turkey 9.1%, Italy 8.7%, Romania 8.2%, Greece 7.3%, France 4%. **Tourism:** $3.7 bil. **Budget:** $18 bil. **Total reserves less gold:** $18.4 bil. **Gold:** 1.3 mil oz t. **CPI change:** 3%.

Transport: Railways: 2,580 mi. **Motor vehicles:** 452.1 vehicles per 1,000 pop. **Civil aviation:** 775.5 mil pass.-mi; 57 airports. **Chief ports:** Burgas, Varna.

Communications: TV sets: 429 per 1,000 pop. **Radios:** 553 per 1,000 pop. **Telephone lines:** 30.4 per 100 pop. **Internet:** 55.1%.

Health: Life expect.: 70.5 male; 77.9 female. **Births:** 9.1 per 1,000 pop. **Deaths:** 14.3 per 1,000 pop. **Natural inc.:** −0.52%. **Infant mortality:** 15.6 per 1,000 live births. **HIV rate:** 0.1%.

Education: Compulsory: ages 7-14. **Literacy:** 98.4%.

Major intl. organizations: UN (FAO, IBRD, ILO, IMF, WHO), EU, NATO, OϽCE, WTO.

Embassy: 1621 22nd St. NW 20008; 387-0174.

Website: www.government.bg

Bulgaria was settled by Slavs in the 6th cent. Turkic Bulgars arrived in the 7th cent., merged with the Slavs, became Christians by the 9th cent., and set up powerful empires in the 10th and 12th cents. Ottomans took over in 1396 and ruled for nearly 500 years.

An 1876 revolt led to an independent kingdom in 1908. Bulgaria expanded after the first Balkan War but lost its Aegean coastline in WWI, when it sided with Germany. Bulgaria joined the Axis in WWII but withdrew in 1944. Communists took power with Soviet aid; the monarchy was abolished Sept. 8, 1946.

On Nov. 10, 1989, Communist Party leader and head of state Todor Zhivkov, resigned after 35 years. In Jan. 1990, Parliament voted to revoke the constitutionally guaranteed dominant role of the Communist Party. A new constitution took effect July 13, 1991.

The anti-Communist Union of Democratic Forces (UDF) won national elections in 1997 but lost in 2001 to the party of the former king, Simeon II. Socialist opposition leader Georgi Parvanov won a presidential runoff vote in 2001 and was reelected, 2006.

Bulgaria became a full member of NATO, Apr. 2, 2004, and entered the EU, Jan. 1, 2007. Boyko Borisov became prime min. after his center-right party won parliamentary elections July 5, 2009. A suicide bomber blew up a bus carrying Israeli tourists, July 18, 2012, leaving 5 Israelis and the Bulgarian bus driver dead. Israel initially blamed Iran for the attack, but an investigation ending Feb. 5, 2013, found the Muslim militant group Hezbollah responsible.

Worsening economic conditions during 2012-13 inspired protests, including instances of self-immolation. They began on Jan 28, 2013, in Blagoevgrad and spread to other cities in Feb., leading Prime Min. Borisov to submit his government's resignation Feb. 20, 2013. No clear winner emerged from May 12 elections. Parliament elected Plamen Oresharski, with no party affiliation, prime min. May 29. Forty days of protests against ineffectual government came to a head July 24 in Sofia, when police clashed violently with demonstrators outside parliament, injuring about 20 unarmed protesters.

Burkina Faso

People: Population: 17,812,961. **Age distrib.:** <15: 45.5%; 65+: 2.5%. **Pop. density:** 168.5 per sq mi, 65.1 per sq km. **Urban:** 26.5%. **Ethnic groups:** Mossi 40%+, other (incl. Gurunsi, Senufo, Lobi, Bobo, Mande, Fulani) approx. 60%. **Languages:** French

(official), native African Sudanic-family langs. **Religions:** Muslim 61%, Catholic 19%, animist 15%, Protestant 4%.

Geography: Total area: 105,869 sq mi, 274,200 sq km; **Land area:** 105,715 sq mi, 273,800 sq km. **Location:** In W Africa, S of the Sahara. **Neighbors:** Mali on NW; Niger on NE; Benin, Togo, Ghana, Côte d'Ivoire on S. **Topography:** Landlocked Burkina Faso is in the savanna region of W Africa. The N is arid, hot, and thinly populated. **Capital:** Ouagadougou, 2,052,530.

Government: Type: Parliamentary republic. **Head of state:** Pres. Blaise Compaoré; b. Feb. 3, 1951; in office: Oct. 15, 1987. **Head of gov.:** Prime Min. Luc Adolphe Tiao; b. June 4, 1954; in office: Apr. 18, 2011. **Local divisions:** 13 regions. **Defense budget** (2011): $132 mil. **Active troops:** 11,200.

Economy: Industries: cotton lint, beverages, agric. proc., soap, cigarettes, textiles, gold. **Chief crops:** cotton, peanuts, shea nuts, sesame, sorghum, millet. **Natural resources:** manganese, limestone, marble, gold, phosphates, pumice, salt. **Arable land:** 20.8%. **Livestock:** cattle: 8.6 mil; chickens: 40 mil; goats: 12.7 mil; pigs: 2.2 mil; sheep: 8.5 mil. **Fish catch:** 15,275 metric tons. **Electricity prod.:** 670 mil kWh. **Labor force:** agric. 90%, industry and services 10%.

Finance: Monetary unit: West African CFA Franc (XOF) (Sept. 2013: 498.17 = $1 U.S.). **GDP:** $24.7 bil; **per capita GDP:** $1,400; **GDP growth:** 8%. **Imports:** $2.7 bil; Côte d'Ivoire 17.8%, France 14.8%, Ghana 5.1%, Togo 4.8%. **Exports:** $2.2 bil; China 26%, Turkey 24.9%, Belgium 5.2%. **Tourism:** $133 mil. **Budget:** $2.3 bil. **Total reserves less gold:** $1 bil. **CPI change:** 3.8%.

Transport: Railways: 386 mi. **Motor vehicles:** 10.9 vehicles per 1,000 pop. **Civil aviation:** 25.5 mil pass.-mi; 2 airports.

Communications: TV sets: 19 per 1,000 pop. **Radios:** 111 per 1,000 pop. **Telephone lines:** 0.8 per 100 pop. **Internet:** 3.7%.

Health: Life expect.: 52.4 male; 56.5 female. **Births:** 42.8 per 1,000 pop. **Deaths:** 12.2 per 1,000 pop. **Natural inc.:** 3.06% **Infant mortality:** 78.3 per 1,000 live births. **HIV rate:** 1.1%.

Education: Compulsory: ages 6-16. **Literacy:** 28.7%.

Major intl. organizations: UN and many of its specialized agencies, AU, WTO.

Embassy: 2340 Massachusetts Ave. NW 20008; 332-5577.

Website: www.primature.gov.bf or burkina-usa.org

The Mossi people entered Burkina Faso in the 11th-13th cents. Their kingdoms ruled until they were defeated by the Mali and Songhai empires.

French control came by 1896, but Upper Volta (renamed Burkina Faso on Aug. 4, 1984) was not established as a separate territory until 1947. Independence came Aug. 5, 1960, and a pro-French government was elected. The military seized power in 1980. A 1987 coup established the current regime, which instituted a multiparty system in the early 1990s. Pres. Blaise Compaoré won reelection, Nov. 13, 2005. The country, among the world's poorest, depends heavily on foreign aid. A severe drought threatened the nation with extreme food insecurity in 2012.

Burma
See Myanmar.

Burundi
Republic of Burundi

People: Population: 10,888,321. **Age distrib.:** <15: 45.6%; 65+: 2.5%. **Pop. density:** 1,098.2 per sq mi, 424 per sq km. **Urban:** 10.9%. **Ethnic groups:** Hutu (Bantu) 85%, Tutsi (Hamitic) 14%, Twa (Pygmy) 1%. **Languages:** Kirundi, French (both official), Swahili. **Religions:** Christian 67% (Roman Catholic 62%, Protestant 5%), indigenous beliefs 23%, Muslim 10%.

Geography: Total area: 10,745 sq mi, 27,830 sq km; **Land area:** 9,915 sq mi, 25,680 sq km. **Location:** In central Africa. **Neighbors:** Rwanda on N, Dem. Rep. of the Congo (formerly Zaire) on W, Tanzania on E and S. **Topography:** Much of the country is grassy highland, with mountains reaching 8,900 ft. The southernmost source of the White Nile is located in Burundi. Lake Tanganyika is the second deepest lake in the world. **Capital:** Bujumbura, 604,732.

Government: Type: Republic. **Head of state and gov.:** Pres. Pierre Nkurunziza; b. Dec. 18, 1963; in office: Aug. 26, 2005. **Local divisions:** 17 provinces. **Defense budget:** $64 mil. **Active troops:** 20,000.

Economy: Industries: light consumer goods, assembly of imported components, public works constr., food proc. **Chief crops:** coffee, cotton, tea, corn, sorghum, sweet potatoes, bananas, cassava. **Natural resources:** nickel, uranium, rare earth oxides, peat, cobalt, copper, platinum, vanadium, hydropower, niobium, tantalum, gold, tin, tungsten, kaolin, limestone. **Arable land:** 35.8%. **Livestock:** cattle: 653,580; chickens: 5.1 mil; goats: 2.3 mil; pigs: 443,908; sheep: 332,463. **Fish catch:** 10,704 metric tons. **Electricity prod.:** 152 mil kWh. **Labor force:** agric. 93.6%, industry 2.3%, services 4.1%.

Finance: Monetary unit: Franc (BIF) (Sept. 2013: 1,534.99 = $1 U.S.). **GDP:** $5.6 bil; **per capita GDP:** $600; **GDP growth:** 4%. **Imports:** $810 mil; Saudi Arabia 16.3%, China 7.9%, Uganda 7.7%, Belgium 7%, Kenya 6.7%, Zambia 6.6%, India 5.5%, Singapore 5.1%. **Exports:** $127.1 mil; Germany 14.8%, Pakistan 9.1%, China

8.7%, Austria 7.5%, Sweden 7.2%, Belgium 5.1%, France 4.7%, Rwanda 4.4%, U.S. 4.1%. **Tourism:** $3 mil. **Budget:** $865.8 mil. **Total reserves less gold:** $307.2 mil. **Gold:** 961 oz t. **CPI change:** 18%.
Transport: Motor vehicles: 5.7 vehicles per 1,000 pop. **Civil aviation:** 1 airport. **Chief port:** Bujumbura.
Communications: TV sets: 36 per 1,000 pop. **Radios:** 166 per 1,000 pop. **Telephone lines** 0.2 per 100 pop. **Internet:** 1.2%.
Health: Life expect.: 57.9 male; 61.5 female. **Births:** 40.0 per 1,000 pop. **Deaths:** 9.1 per 1,000 pop. **Natural inc.:** 3.09%. **Infant mortality:** 58.9 per 1,000 live births. **HIV rate:** 1.3%.
Education: Compulsory: ages NA. **Literacy:** 86.9%.
Major intl. organizations: UN (FAO, IBRD, ILO, IMF, WHO), AU, WTO.
Embassy: 2233 Wisconsin Ave. NW, Ste. 212, 20007; 342-2574.
Website: www.burundi-gov.bi or www.burundiembassydc-usa.org
The pygmy Twa were the first inhabitants, followed by Bantu Hutus, who were conquered in the 16th cent. by the Tutsi (Watusi), probably from Ethiopia. Germany gained control in 1899. Belgium took over in 1916, successively exercising a League of Nations mandate and UN trusteeship over Ruanda-Urundi (now the 2 countries of Rwanda and Burundi). Burundi became independent July 1, 1962.
An unsuccessful Hutu rebellion in 1972-73 left 10,000 Tutsi and 150,000 Hutu dead. Over 100,000 Hutu fled to Tanzania and Zaire (now Dem. Rep. of the Congo). In the 1980s, Burundi's Tutsi-dominated regime pledged itself to ethnic reconciliation and democratic reform. In the nation's first democratic presidential election, June 1993, a Hutu, Melchior Ndadaye, was elected. He was killed in an attempted coup, Oct. 21, 1993. At least 150,000 Burundians died in ethnic conflicts over the next 3 years. Pres. Cyprien Ntaryamira, elected Jan. 1994, was killed with the president of Rwanda in a mysterious plane crash, Apr. 6. The incident sparked massive carnage in Rwanda; violence in Burundi, initially far more limited, intensified in 1995. Ethnic strife continued after a military coup, July 25, 1996. Former South African Pres. Nelson Mandela mediated peace talks from Dec. 1999; most warring groups signed a draft peace treaty in Arusha, Tanzania, Aug. 2000. Two coup attempts were suppressed in 2001. A power-sharing government headed by Pierre Buyoya was sworn in Nov. 1, 2001, but clashes with rebels continued.
Domitien Ndayizeye, a Hutu, became president Apr. 2003. The UN Security Council authorized, May 2004, a peacekeeping force (ONUB) for Burundi. Approval of a power-sharing constitution by referendum, Feb. 28, 2005, paved the way for local and parliamentary elections. Pierre Nkurunziza, former leader of a Hutu rebel group, became president Aug. 2005. ONUB was succeeded, Jan. 1, 2007, by the UN Integrated Office in Burundi (BINUB). Under a reconciliation accord reached Dec. 4, 2008, remaining Hutu rebels began to demobilize. Candidates opposing Nkurunziza dropped out of the June 2010, presidential election, claiming the vote was rigged. The government was accused of ordering extrajudicial killings, 2010-11. A probe into the allegations, criticized for its limited scope, concluded, Aug. 23, 2012, the allegations were untrue.
Pres. Pierre Nkurunziza signed a controversial law, June 4, 2013, that forbids journalists from reporting on issues of national security.

Cambodia
Kingdom of Cambodia

People: Population: 15,205,539. **Age distrib.:** <15: 31.7%; 65+: 3.9%. **Pop. density:** 223.1 per sq mi, 86.1 per sq km. **Urban:** 20%. **Ethnic groups:** Khmer 90%, Vietnamese 5%, Chinese 1%. **Languages:** Khmer (official), French, English. **Religions:** Buddhist (official) 96%, Muslim 2%.
Geography: Total area: 69,898 sq mi, 181,035 sq km; **Land area:** 68,153 sq mi, 176,515 sq km. **Location:** SE Asia, on Indochina Peninsula. **Neighbors:** Thailand on W and N, Laos on NE, Vietnam on E. **Topography:** The central area, formed by the Mekong R. basin and Tonle Sap lake, is level. Hills and mountains are in SE, a long escarpment separates the country from Thailand on NW. 76% of the area is forested. **Capital:** Phnom Penh, 1,549,760.
Government: Type: Multiparty democracy under constitutional monarchy. **Head of state:** King Norodom Sihamoni; b. May 14, 1953; in office: Oct. 29, 2004. **Head of gov.:** Prime Min. Samdech Hun Sen; b. Aug. 5, 1952; in office: Jan. 14, 1985. **Local divisions:** 23 provinces, 1 municipality. **Defense budget:** $346 mil. **Active troops:** 124,300.
Economy: Industries: tourism, garments, constr., rice milling, fishing, wood and wood prods., rubber, cement, gem mining, textiles. **Chief crops:** rice, corn, vegetables, cashews, cassava. **Natural resources:** oil and gas, timber, gems, iron ore, manganese, phosphates, hydropower potential. **Arable land:** 22.7%. **Livestock:** cattle: 3.4 mil; chickens: 17 mil; pigs: 2 mil. **Fish catch:** 562,000 metric tons. **Electricity prod.:** 937.3 mil kWh. **Labor force:** agric. 55.8%, industry 16.9%, services 27.3%.
Finance: Monetary unit: Riel (KHR) (Sept. 2013: 4,092.99 = $1 U.S.). **GDP:** $37.3 bil; **per capita GDP:** $2,400; **GDP growth:** 6.5%. **Imports:** $7.8 bil; Thailand 27.2%, Vietnam 20%, China 19.5%, Singapore 7.1%, Hong Kong 5.9%, South Korea 4.3%. **Exports:** $5.8 bil; U.S. 32.7%, UK 8.4%, Germany 7.7%, Canada 7.7%, Singapore 6.6%, Vietnam 5.8%, Japan 4.7%. **Tourism:** $1.8 bil. **Budget:** 2.8 bil. **Total reserves less gold:** $4.3 bil. **Gold:** 399,832 oz t. **CPI change:** 2.9%.

Transport: Railways: 429 mi (under restoration). **Civil aviation:** 157.2 mil pass.-mi; 6 airports. **Chief ports:** Phnom Penh, Kampong Saom.
Communications: TV sets: 8 per 1,000 pop. **Radios:** 112 per 1,000 pop. **Telephone lines:** 4 per 100 pop. **Internet:** 4.9%.
Health: Life expect.: 61.0 male; 65.9 female. **Births:** 24.9 per 1,000 pop. **Deaths:** 7.9 per 1,000 pop. **Natural inc.:** 1.70%. **Infant mortality:** 52.7 per 1,000 live births. **HIV rate:** 0.6%.
Education: Compulsory ages: NA. **Literacy:** 73.9%.
Major intl. organizations: UN (FAO, IBRD, ILO, IMF, WHO), ASEAN, WTO.
Embassy: 4530 16th St. NW 20011; 726-7742.
Website: www.cambodia.gov.kh
Early kingdoms dating from that of Funan in the 1st cent. CE culminated in the great Khmer empire that flourished from the 9th cent. to the 13th, encompassing present-day Thailand, Cambodia, Laos, and southern Vietnam. The peripheral areas were lost to invading Siamese and Vietnamese. France established a protectorate in 1863. Independence came in 1953.
Prince Norodom Sihanouk, king (1941-55) and head of state from 1960, tried to maintain neutrality during the Vietnam War. The U.S. bombed Cambodia, 1969-73, targeting suspected border sanctuaries of Vietnamese insurgents.
In 1970, pro-U.S. Prem. Lon Nol seized power, demanded removal of 40,000 North Vietnamese troops, and abolished the monarchy. Sihanouk formed a government-in-exile in Beijing, and open war began between the government and Communist Khmer Rouge guerrillas. The U.S. provided heavy military and economic aid.
Khmer Rouge forces captured Phnom Penh Apr. 17, 1975. Cities were depopulated and their residents executed or condemned to forced labor. An estimated 1.7 mil people died in "killing fields" or from other hardships under Khmer Rouge rule, 1975-79.
Severe border fighting broke out with Vietnam in 1978 and developed into a full-fledged Vietnamese invasion. Formation of a Vietnamese-backed government was announced, Jan. 8, 1979, one day after the capture of Phnom Penh. Thousands of refugees fled to Thailand, and widespread starvation was reported. Vietnamese troops remained in Cambodia during the 1980s, meeting resistance from Khmer Rouge guerrillas, especially along the Thai border. Vietnam withdrew nearly all its troops by Sept. 1989.
Following 1993 UN-sponsored elections in Cambodia, 2 leading parties agreed to share power in an interim government. On Sept. 21, the National Assembly adopted a constitution reestablishing a monarchy, and Sihanouk became king. The Khmer Rouge boycotted the elections and opposed the new government. The insurgency had weakened and splintered by 1996.
Co-Prime Min. Hun Sen staged a coup July 5, 1997, ousting his rival, Prince Norodom Ranariddh. Pol Pot, the Khmer Rouge leader during the late 1970s, was denounced by his former comrades at a show trial, July 25, 1997, and sentenced to house arrest; he died Apr. 15, 1998. Sihanouk abdicated because of poor health and was succeeded, Oct. 2004, by his son Norodom Sihamoni.
Hun Sen's party retained power through a series of flawed elections. A UN-backed war crimes tribunal convicted a former prison warden known as Duch July 2010 for overseeing the killing and torture of more than 14,000 inmates under the Khmer Rouge. A panic and stampede on a crowded Phnom Penh bridge Nov. 22, 2010, killed 353 people.
Journalist Mam Sonando was sentenced to 20 years in prison Oct. 2012 for criticizing allegedly corrupt practices by local government officials. Condemnation by the UN and other human rights groups led to his sentence being suspended Mar. 14 and his release. Unsafe working conditions led to 2 factory collapses May 16, 2013, outside of Phnom Penh and in Tream Tbai that killed 4 workers. Protesting workers at a Nike plant in Kampong Speu Province clashed with police May 27, injuring 23 of the roughly 3,000 demonstrators.

Cameroon
Republic of Cameroon

People: Population: 20,549,221. **Age distrib.:** <15: 40%; 65+: 3.4%. **Pop. density:** 112.6 per sq mi, 43.5 per sq km. **Urban:** 52.1%. **Ethnic groups:** Cameroon Highlanders 31%, Equatorial Bantu 19%, Kirdi 11%, Fulani 10%, NW Bantu 8%, E Nigritic 7%, other African 13%. **Languages:** 24 major African lang. groups; English, French (both official). **Religions:** indigenous beliefs 40%, Christian 40%, Muslim 20%.
Geography: Total area: 183,568 sq mi, 475,440 sq km; **Land area:** 182,514 sq mi, 472,710 sq km. **Location:** Between W and central Africa. **Neighbors:** Nigeria on NW; Chad, Central African Republic on E; Congo, Gabon, Equatorial Guinea on S. **Topography:** Low coastal plain with rain forests in S; plateaus in center lead to forested mountains in W, including Mt. Cameroon (13,435 ft); grasslands in N lead to marshes around Lake Chad. **Capital:** Yaoundé, 2,431,680. **Cities (urban aggl.):** Douala, 2,449,071.
Government: Type: Republic. **Head of state:** Pres. Paul Biya; b. Feb. 13, 1933; in office: Nov. 6, 1982. **Head of gov.:** Prime Min. Philemon Yang; b. June 14, 1947; in office: June 30, 2009. **Local divisions:** 10 regions. **Defense budget** (2011): $353 mil. **Active troops:** 14,200.

Economy: Industries: petroleum prod. and refining, aluminum prod., food proc., light consumer goods, textiles, lumber. **Chief crops:** coffee, cocoa, cotton, rubber, bananas, oilseed, grains, cassava. **Natural resources:** petroleum, bauxite, iron ore, timber, hydropower. **Crude oil reserves:** 200 mil bbls. **Arable land:** 13.1%. **Livestock:** cattle: 4.8 mil; chickens: 46 mil; goats: 4.5 mil; pigs: 1.7 mil; sheep: 3.9 mil. **Fish catch:** 140,835 metric tons. **Electricity prod.:** 5.8 bil kWh. **Labor force:** agric. 70%, industry 13%, services 17%.

Finance: Monetary unit: Central African CFA Franc BEAC (XAF) (Sept. 2013: 498.17 = $1 U.S.). **GDP:** $51.6 bil; **per capita GDP:** $2,400; **GDP growth:** 4.7%. **Imports:** $6.6 bil; China 18.9%, France 15%, Nigeria 12.1%, Belgium 5.2%, U.S. 4.4%, India 4.2%. **Exports:** $6 bil; China 14.8%, Netherlands 9.5%, Spain 8.8%, India 8.4%, Portugal 7.9%, Italy 5.9%, U.S. 5.3%. **Tourism:** $159 mil. **Budget:** $5.7 bil. **Total reserves less gold:** $3.4 bil. **CPI change:** 2.9%.

Transport: Railways: 774 mi. **Motor vehicles:** 15.8 vehicles per 1,000 pop. **Civil aviation:** 577.9 mil pass.-mi; 11 airports. **Chief ports:** Douala, Limboh Terminal.

Communications: TV sets: 51 per 1,000 pop. **Radios:** 131 per 1,000 pop. **Telephone lines:** 3.6 per 100 pop. **Internet:** 5.7%.

Health: Life expect.: 54.1 male; 56.0 female. **Births:** 31.9 per 1,000 pop. **Deaths:** 12.1% per 1,000 pop. **Natural inc.:** 2.04%. **Infant mortality:** 58.5 per 1,000 live births. **HIV rate:** 4.6%.

Education: Compulsory: ages 6-11. **Literacy:** 71.3%.

Major intl. organizations: UN (FAO, IBRD, ILO, IMF, WHO), AU, the Commonwealth, WTO.

Embassy: 2349 Massachusetts Ave. NW 20008; 265-8790.

Website: www.spm.gov.cm

Portuguese sailors were the first Europeans to reach Cameroon, in the 15th cent. The European and American slave trade was very active in the area. German control lasted from 1884 to 1916, when France and Britain divided the territory, later receiving League of Nations mandates and UN trusteeships. French Cameroon became independent Jan. 1, 1960; one part of British Cameroon joined Nigeria in 1961 while the other part joined Cameroon. Pres. Paul Biya has retained power since 1982 in a series of elections that were boycotted by opposition parties or disputed as fraudulent. Rising food and fuel costs and discontent with Biya's continued rule sparked antigovernment riots Feb. 23-29, 2008. The legislature, controlled by Biya loyalists, voted Apr. 2008 to abolish presidential term limits introduced in 1996.

More than a dozen French citizens were kidnapped during 2013, allegedly in retaliation for France's intervention in neighboring Mali, and taken to Nigeria by the jihadist group Boko Haram.

Canada

People: Population: 34,568,211. **Age distrib.:** <15: 15.5%; 65+: 16.8%. **Pop. density:** 9.8 per sq mi, 3.8 per sq km. **Urban:** 80.7%. **Ethnic groups:** British Isles origin 28%, French origin 23%, other European 15%, Amerindian 2%, other (mostly Asian, African, Arab) 6%, mixed background 26%. **Languages:** English, French (both official). **Religions:** Roman Catholic 43%, Protestant 23%, other Christian 4%, Muslim 2%, none 16%.

Geography: Total area: 3,855,103 sq mi, 9,984,670 sq km; **Land area:** 3,511,023 sq mi, 9,093,507 sq km. The largest country in land size in the Western Hemisphere. **Topography:** Canada stretches 3,426 mi E-W and extends south from the North Pole to the U.S. border. Its seacoast includes 36,356 mi of mainland and 115,133 mi of islands, including the Arctic islands almost from Greenland to near the Alaskan border. **Climate:** While generally temperate, varies from freezing winter cold to blistering summer heat. **Capital:** Ottawa, 1,207,510 (pop. for Ottawa-Gatineau). **Cities (urban aggl.):** Toronto, 5,572,647; Montréal, 3,855,934; Vancouver, 2,267,301; Calgary, 1,216,477; Edmonton, 1,141,658; Québec City, 755,377.

Government: Type: Democratic constitutional monarchy with federal system of parliamentary govt. **Head of state:** Queen Elizabeth II, rep. by Gov.-Gen. David Johnston; b. June 28, 1941; in office:

Oct. 1, 2010. **Head of gov.:** Prime Min. Stephen Harper; b. Apr. 30, 1959; in office: Feb. 6, 2006. **Local divisions:** 10 provinces, 3 territories. **Defense budget:** $18.4 bil. **Active troops:** 66,000.

Economy: Industries: transp. equip., chemicals, minerals, food prods., wood and paper prods., fish prods., petroleum and nat. gas. **Chief crops:** wheat, barley, oilseed, tobacco, fruits, vegetables. **Natural resources:** iron ore, nickel, zinc, copper, gold, lead, rare earth elements, molybdenum, potash, diamonds, silver, fish, timber, wildlife, coal, petroleum, nat. gas, hydropower. **Crude oil reserves:** 173.1 bil bbls. **Arable land:** 4.7%. **Livestock:** cattle: 12.2 mil; chickens: 164.6 mil; goats: 30,000; pigs: 12.8 mil; sheep: 879,300. **Fish catch:** 1 mil metric tons. **Electricity prod.** (2011): 618.9 bil kWh. **Labor force:** agric. 2%, mfg. 13%, constr. 6%, services 76%, other 3%.

Finance: Monetary unit: Dollar (CAD) (Sept. 2013: 1.04 = $1 U.S.). **GDP:** $1.5 tril; **per capita GDP:** $43,400; **GDP growth:** 1.8%. **Imports:** $474.8 bil; U.S. 50.6%, China 11%, Mexico 5.5%. **Exports:** $462.9 bil; U.S. 74.5%, China 4.3%, UK 4.1%. **Tourism:** $17.4 bil. **Budget:** $749.5 bil. **Total reserves less gold:** $68.4 bil. **Gold:** 109,000 oz t. **CPI change:** 1.5%.

Transport: Railways: 28,926 mi. **Motor vehicles:** 634 vehicles per 1,000 pop. **Civil aviation:** 66.7 bil pass.-mi; 523 airports. **Chief ports:** Fraser River, Halifax, Hamilton, Montréal, Port-Cartier, Québec City, Saint John (New Brunswick), Sept-Isles, Vancouver.

Communications: TV sets: 731 per 1,000 pop. **Radios:** 1,052 per 1,000 pop. **Telephone lines:** 51.9 per 100 pop. **Internet:** 86.8%.

Health: Life expect.: 79.0 male; 84.3 female. **Births:** 10.3 per 1,000 pop. **Deaths:** 8.2 per 1,000 pop. **Natural inc.:** 0.21%. **Infant mortality:** 4.8 per 1,000 live births. **HIV rate:** 0.3%.

Education: Compulsory: ages 6-16. **Literacy:** 99%.

Major intl. organizations: UN and all of its specialized agencies, APEC, the Commonwealth, NAFTA, NATO, OAS, OECD, OSCE, WTO.

Embassy: 501 Pennsylvania Ave. NW 20001; 682-1740.

Website: www.canada.gc.ca

French explorer Jacques Cartier, who reached the Gulf of St. Lawrence in 1534, is generally regarded as Canada's founder. But English seaman John Cabot sighted Newfoundland in 1497, and Vikings are believed to have reached the Atlantic coast centuries before either explorer. The French pioneered Canadian settlement, establishing Quebec City (1608) and Montréal (1642) and declaring New France a colony in 1663.

Britain acquired Acadia (later Nova Scotia) in 1717 and defeated French forces in Canada to gain control of Quebec (1759) and the rest of New France in 1763. The French, through the Quebec Act of 1774, retained rights to their language, religion, and civil law. The British presence in Canada increased during the American Revolution when many colonials, calling themselves United Empire Loyalists, moved north to Canada. Fur traders and explorers led Canadians westward across the continent. Sir Alexander Mackenzie reached the Pacific in 1793 and scrawled on a rock, "From Canada by land."

In Upper and Lower Canada (later called Ontario and Quebec) and in the Maritimes, legislative assemblies were formed in the 18th cent. Upper Canada was involved in the War of 1812, a conflict between Great Britain and the U.S. that ended in a stalemate in 1814.

In 1837 political agitation for more democratic government culminated in rebellions in Upper and Lower Canada and the union of the 2 parts into the colony of Canada in 1839. The union lasted until the 1867 British North America Act (now known as the Constitution Act) launched the Dominion of Canada, consisting of Ontario, Quebec, and the former colonies of Nova Scotia and New Brunswick.

The British North America Act, which was the basis for the country's written constitution, established a federal system of government modeled on the British parliament and cabinet structure under the crown. Canada was proclaimed a self-governing dominion within the British Empire in 1931. The Constitution Act, 1982, gave Canada the right to amend its constitution, thereby severing its last legislative link with Britain.

Canada's Provinces and Territories

Provinces/territories	Joined confed.	Area (sq mi)	Population (2012 est.)	Capital	Premier	Party	In office
Alberta	1905	255,287	3,873,745	Edmonton	Alison Redford	Prog. Cons.	2011
British Columbia	1871	365,948	4,622,573	Victoria	Christy Clark	Liberal	2011
Manitoba	1870	250,947	1,267,003	Winnipeg	Greg Selinger	New Democratic	2009
New Brunswick	1867	28,355	755,950	Fredericton	David Alward	Prog. Cons.	2010
Newfoundland and Labrador	1949	156,649	512,659	St. John's	Kathy Dunderdale	Prog. Cons.	2010
Nova Scotia	1867	21,425	948,695	Halifax	Darrell Dexter	New Democratic	2009
Ontario	1867	412,581	13,505,900	Toronto	Kathleen Wynne	Liberal	2013
Prince Edward Island	1873	2,185	146,105	Charlottetown	Robert Ghiz	Liberal	2007
Québec	1867	594,860	8,054,756	Québec	Pauline Marois	Parti Québécois	2012
Saskatchewan	1905	251,866	1,079,958	Regina	Brad Wall	Saskatchewan	2007
Northwest Territories[1]	1871	503,951	43,349	Yellowknife	Bob McLeod	nonpartisan	2011
Nunavut[1,2]	1999	818,959	33,697	Iqaluit	Eva Aariak	nonpartisan	2008
Yukon[1]	1898	186,661	36,101	Whitehorse	Darrell Pasloski	Yukon	2011

(1) Territories also have federally appointed commissioners to represent federal interests. (2) Territory created in 1999 from eastern portion of Northwest Territories.

Failure in 1990 of the so-called Meech Lake Accord, which would have assured constitutional protection for Quebec's efforts to preserve its French language and culture, sparked a separatist revival in Quebec. Subsequently, the Charlottetown agreement, calling for constitutional changes, such as recognition of Quebec as a "distinct society" within the Canadian confederation, was defeated by a national referendum Oct. 1992.

Canada became the first nation to ratify the North American Free Trade Agreement among Canada, Mexico, and the U.S., June 1993. It took effect Jan. 1, 1994. A Quebec referendum on secession held Oct. 1995 was defeated. On Jan. 7, 1998, the government apologized to indigenous peoples for 150 years of mistreatment and pledged to set up a "healing fund." Nunavut ("Our Land"), carved from Northwest Territories as a homeland for the Inuit, was established Apr. 1, 1999.

Victory by the Liberals in national elections Nov. 27, 2000, made Jean Chrétien the first Canadian prime min. in over 50 years to head a third successive majority government. Canada sent troops and warships to aid the U.S.-led coalition in Afghanistan beginning Oct. 2001; 157 Canadian troops had been killed in Afghanistan by the time Canada's combat mission ended July 7, 2011.

Chrétien retired Dec. 12, 2003, and Paul Martin became prime min. Weakened by a scandal involving improper payments to Quebec firms for sponsorship of cultural and sporting events, the Liberals won only 135 of 308 seats in parliamentary elections June 28, 2004. Martin became head of a minority government. Same-sex marriage (already permitted in 8 of 10 provinces) became legal throughout the country July 2005. Michaëlle Jean, a Haitian-born TV journalist, was installed Sept. 27 as Canada's first black governor-general.

Twelve years of Liberal Party rule ended when Conservatives won 124 seats to the Liberals' 103 in parliamentary elections, Jan. 23, 2006. Conservative leader Stephen Harper took office Feb. 6 as head of a minority government. Police and intelligence officials in the Toronto area, June 2-3, 2006, arrested and charged 17 people with plotting terrorist attacks in Canada. The supreme court, Feb. 23, 2007, unanimously struck down a law under which foreign-born terrorism suspects had been indefinitely detained without charge.

Prime Min. Harper remained the head of a minority government after 2008 elections, as Conservatives increased their plurality to 143 seats. A no-confidence vote Mar. 25, 2011, led to federal elections May 2, in which Harper's Conservatives gained a parliamentary majority of 166 seats. The New Democratic Party with 103 seats became the official opposition, as the Liberals had only 34 seats. While the technology for extracting oil from tar sands, large deposits of which are found in Alberta, has improved, the lack of a pipeline from Alberta to the U.S. has obliged Canada producers to sell oil at discounted prices, thereby losing an estimated $45 mil a day in 2013 and diminishing tax revenue. The figure is disputed by some economists, who argue that Canadian politicians are comparing the price of the oil from the tar sands to higher quality oil produced elsewhere.

In a bid to open up the Canadian oil market to international buyers, the government approved Dec. 7, 2012, a $15-bil takeover of the energy company Nexen by China Natl. Offshore Oil and the acquisition of Progress Energy Resources of Canada by the Malaysian state-owned oil and gas company Petronas.

Cape Verde
Republic of Cape Verde

People: Population: 531,046. **Age distrib.:** <15: 31.2%; 65+: 5.2%. **Pop. density:** 341 per sq mi, 131.7 per sq km. **Urban:** 62.6%. **Ethnic groups:** Creole (mulatto) 71%, African 28%, European 1%. **Languages:** Portuguese (official), Crioulo (blend of Portuguese and W African words). **Religions:** Roman Catholic (infused with indigenous beliefs), Protestant (mostly Church of the Nazarene).

Geography: Total area: 1,557 sq mi, 4,033 sq km; **Land area:** 1,557 sq mi, 4,033 sq km. **Location:** In Atlantic O., off W tip of Africa. **Neighbors:** Nearest are Mauritania, Senegal to E. **Topography:** 15 Cape Verde islands, volcanic in origin (active crater on Fogo). Landscape is eroded and stark, with vegetation mostly in interior valleys. **Capital:** Praia, 132,029.

Government: Type: Republic. **Head of state:** Pres. Jorge Carlos Fonseca; b. Oct. 20, 1950; in office: Sept. 9, 2011. **Head of gov.:** Prime Min. José Maria Neves; b. Mar. 28, 1960; in office: Feb. 1, 2001. **Local divisions:** 22 municipalities. **Defense budget** (2011): $9 mil. **Active troops:** 1,200.

Economy: Industries: food and beverages, fish proc., shoes and garments, salt mining, ship repair. **Chief crops:** bananas, corn, beans, sweet potatoes, sugarcane, coffee, peanuts. **Natural resources:** salt, basalt rock, limestone, kaolin, fish, clay, gypsum. **Arable land:** 11.7%. **Livestock:** cattle: 46,500; chickens: 700,000; goats: 235,000; pigs: 240,000; sheep: 20,550. **Fish catch:** 22,500 metric tons. **Electricity prod.:** 287 mil kWh. **Labor force:** NA.

Finance: Monetary unit: Escudo (CVE) (Sept. 2013: 82.60 = $1 U.S.). **GDP:** $2.2 bil; **per capita GDP:** $4,200; **GDP growth:** 4.3%. **Imports:** $902 mil; Portugal 38%, Netherlands 21.4%, China 7.9%, Spain 7%. **Exports:** $184 mil; Spain 66.6%, Portugal 13.9%, U.S. 5%. **Tourism:** $414 mil. **Budget:** $588.4 mil. **Total reserves less gold:** $375.8 mil. **CPI change:** 2.5%.

Transport: Civil aviation: 755.6 mil pass.-mi; 9 airports. **Chief port:** Porto Grande.
Communications: TV sets: 128 per 1,000 pop. **Radios:** 176 per 1,000 pop. **Telephone lines:** 13.9 per 100 pop. **Internet:** 34.7%.
Health: Life expect.: 69.1 male; 73.6 female. **Births:** 21.0 per 1,000 pop. **Deaths:** 6.2 per 1,000 pop. **Natural inc.:** 1.47%. **Infant mortality:** 25.1 per 1,000 live births. **HIV rate:** 1%.
Education: Compulsory: ages 6-11. **Literacy:** 84.9%.
Major intl. organizations: UN (FAO, IBRD, ILO, IMF, WHO), AU, WTO.
Embassy: 3415 Massachusetts Ave. NW 20007; 965-6820.
Website: www.governo.cv

The first Portuguese colonists landed in 1462; African slaves were brought soon after, and most Cape Verdeans descend from both groups. Cape Verde independence came July 5, 1975. Antonio Mascarenhas Monteiro won the nation's first free presidential election Feb. 17, 1991; he was reelected without opposition 5 years later. After Pres. Pedro Pires retired after serving two 5-year terms, 2001-11, Jorge Carlos Fonseca won a presidential runoff election Aug. 21, 2011. Remittances from Cape Verdean emigrants are a major source of income. Japan announced June 3, 2013, that it would help fund the construction of water and energy projects in Cape Verde.

Central African Republic

People: Population: 5,166,510. **Age distrib.:** <15: 40.7%; 65+: 3.6%. **Pop. density:** 21.5 per sq mi, 8.3 per sq km. **Urban:** 39.1%. **Ethnic groups:** Baya 33%, Banda 27%, Mandjia 13%, Sara 10%, Mboum 7%, M'Baka 4%, Yakoma 4%. **Languages:** French (official), Sangho (lingua franca and national lang.), tribal langs. **Religions:** indigenous beliefs 35%, Protestant 25%, Roman Catholic 25%, Muslim 15%.

Geography: Total area: 240,535 sq mi, 622,984 sq km; **Land area:** 240,535 sq mi, 622,984 sq km. **Location:** In central Africa. **Neighbors:** Chad on N, Cameroon on W, Congo Republic and Dem. Rep. of the Congo on S, Sudan on E. **Topography:** Mostly rolling plateau, average altitude 2,000 ft, with rivers draining S to the Congo and N to Lake Chad. Open, well-watered savanna covers most of area, with an arid area in NE, and tropical rain forest in SW. **Capital:** Bangui, 740,062.

Government: Type: Republic. **Head of state:** Pres. Michel Djotodia; b. 1949; in office: Mar. 24, 2013. **Head of gov.:** Prime Min. Nicolas Tiangaye; b. Dec. 13, 1956; in office: Jan. 17, 2013. **Local divisions:** 14 prefectures, 2 economic prefectures, 1 commune. **Defense budget** (2011): $54 mil. **Active troops:** 2,150.

Economy: Industries: gold and diamond mining, logging, brewing, sugar refining. **Chief crops:** cotton, coffee, tobacco, manioc, yams, millet, corn, bananas. **Natural resources:** diamonds, uranium, timber, gold, oil, hydropower. **Arable land:** 2.9%. **Livestock:** cattle: 4.2 mil; chickens: 6.6 mil; goats: 5.7 mil; pigs: 1 mil; sheep: 386,000. **Fish catch:** 35,170 metric tons. **Electricity prod.:** 160 mil kWh. **Labor force:** NA.

Finance: Monetary unit: Central African CFA Franc BEAC (XAF) (Sept. 2013: 498.17 = $1 U.S.). **GDP:** $4 bil; **per capita GDP:** $800; **GDP growth:** 4.1%. **Imports:** $332.4 mil; Netherlands 19.5%, Cameroon 9.7%, France 9.3%, South Korea 8.7%. **Exports:** $208 mil; Belgium 31.5%, China 27.7%, Dem. Rep. of the Congo 8.6%, Indonesia 5.2%, France 4.5%. **Tourism:** $6 mil. **Budget:** $356.9 mil. **Total reserves less gold:** $157.9 mil. **CPI change:** 5.8%.

Transport: Motor vehicles: 0.9 vehicles per 1,000 pop. **Civil aviation:** 2 airports. **Chief ports:** Bangui, Nola, Nzinga, Salo.
Communications: TV sets: 10 per 1,000 pop. **Radios:** 111 per 1,000 pop. **Telephone lines:** 0.1 per 100 pop. **Internet:** 3%.
Health: Life expect.: 49.6 male; 52.2 female. **Births:** 35.8 per 1,000 pop. **Deaths:** 14.4 per 1,000 pop. **Natural inc.:** 2.14%. **Infant mortality:** 95.0 per 1,000 live births. **HIV rate:** 4.6%.
Education: Compulsory: ages 6-15. **Literacy:** 56.6%.
Major intl. organizations: UN (FAO, IBRD, ILO, IMF, WHO), AU, WTO.
Embassy: 1618 22nd St. NW 20008; 483-7800.
Website: www.centrafricaine.info or www.state.gov/p/af/ci/car/

Various Bantu peoples migrated through the region for centuries before French control was asserted in the late 19th cent., when the region was named Ubangi-Shari. Independence was attained Aug. 13, 1960.

Pres. Jean-Bedel Bokassa, who seized power in a 1965 military coup, proclaimed himself constitutional emperor of the renamed Central African Empire Dec. 1976. Bokassa's rule was characterized by ruthless authoritarianism and human rights violations. He was ousted in a bloodless coup aided by the French government, Sept. 20, 1979. In 1981, Gen. André Kolingba became head of state in another bloodless coup. The government canceled 1992 multiparty legislative and presidential elections because of polling problems. New elections, held in Aug. and Sept. 1993, led to civilian rule under Pres. Ange-Félix Patassé.

France sent in troops to suppress army mutinies in 1996 and 1997. After thwarting several coup attempts, Patassé was ousted Mar. 15, 2003, by rebels under former army chief François Bozizé. Bozizé won a presidential runoff election May 8, 2005, but insurgent activity by Patassé loyalists and others continued in the north. A national peace conference, Dec. 8-20, 2008, enabled the installation of a unity government Jan. 19, 2009. Pres. Bozizé won

reelection Jan. 23, 2011, but was ousted 2 years later when rebel group Seleka, led by Michel Djotodia, seized the capital of Bengui Mar. 24, 2013. Bozizé fled to Cameroon. Djotodia declared himself president, suspended the Constitution, dissolved Parliament, and began a 3-year transitional plan; 78 people died in the coup, including 13 South African troops, and human rights violations were reported. Bozizé supporters clashed with pro-Djotodia fighters in Aug. 21, 2013, resulting in 10 deaths.

Chad
Republic of Chad

People: Population: 11,193,452. **Age distrib.:** <15: 45.2%; 65+: 2.9%. **Pop. density:** 23 per sq mi, 8.9 per sq km. **Urban:** 21.8%. **Ethnic groups:** Sara 28%, Arab 12%, Mayo-Kebbi 12%, Kanem-Bornou 9%, Ouaddai 9%, Hadjarai 7%, Tandjile 7%, Gorane 6%, Fitri-Batha 5%. **Languages:** French, Arabic (both official); Sara; 120+ langs. and dialects. **Religions:** Muslim 53%, Catholic 20%, Protestant 14%, animist 7%, atheist 3%.

Geography: Total area: 495,755, sq mi, 1,284,000 sq km; **Land area:** 486,180 sq mi, 1,259,200 sq km. **Location:** In central N Africa. **Neighbors:** Libya on N; Niger, Nigeria, Cameroon on W; Central African Republic on S; Sudan on E. **Topography:** Wooded savanna, steppe, and desert in the S; part of the Sahara in the N. Southern rivers flow N to Lake Chad, surrounded by marshland. **Capital:** N'Djaména, 1,078,640.

Government: Type: Republic. **Head of state:** Pres. Idriss Déby Itno; b. 1952; in office: Dec. 4, 1990. **Head of gov.:** Prime Min. Djimrangar Dadnadji; b. 1954; in office: Jan. 21, 2013. **Local divisions:** 23 regions. **Defense budget** (2011): $135 mil. **Active troops:** 25,350.

Economy: Industries: oil, cotton textiles, meatpacking, brewing, sodium carbonate, soap, cigarettes, constr. materials. **Chief crops:** cotton, sorghum, millet, peanuts, rice, potatoes, manioc. **Natural resources:** petroleum, uranium, natron, kaolin, fish, gold, limestone, sand and gravel, salt. **Crude oil reserves:** 1.5 bil bbls. **Arable land:** 3.9%. **Livestock:** cattle: 7.7 mil; chickens: 5.6 mil; goats: 6.8 mil; pigs: 31,600; sheep: 3.1 mil. **Fish catch:** 60,000 metric tons. **Electricity prod.:** 98 mil kWh. **Labor force:** agric. 80% (subsistence farming, herding, fishing), industry and services 20%.

Finance: Monetary unit: Central African CFA Franc BEAC (XAF) (Sept. 2013: 498.17 = $1 U.S.). **GDP:** $21 bil; **per capita GDP:** $2,000; **GDP growth:** 5%. **Imports:** $2.6 bil; China 19.8%, Cameroon 19.7%, France 15.8%, Saudi Arabia 5.4%, U.S. 4.1%. **Exports:** $4.1 bil; U.S. 82.5%, China 6.7%. **Budget:** $3 bil. **Total reserves less gold:** $1.2 bil. **CPI change:** 10.2%.

Transport: Civil aviation: 9 airports.

Communications: TV sets: 9 per 1,000 pop. **Radios:** 103 per 1,000 pop. **Telephone lines:** 0.3 per 100 pop. **Internet:** 2.1%.

Health: Life expect.: 48.0 male; 50.2 female. **Births:** 38.0 per 1,000 pop. **Deaths:** 14.9 per 1,000 pop. **Natural inc.:** 2.31%. **Infant mortality:** 91.9 per 1,000 live births. **HIV rate:** 3.1%.

Education: Compulsory: ages 6-15. **Literacy:** 35.4%.

Major intl. organizations: UN (FAO, IBRD, ILO, IMF, WHO), AU, WTO.

Embassy: 2002 R St. NW 20009; 462-4009.

Website: www.state.gov/p/af/ci/cd/

Chad was the site of Paleolithic and Neolithic cultures before the Sahara Desert formed. A succession of kingdoms and Arab slave traders dominated Chad until France took control around 1900. Independence came Aug. 11, 1960. Northern Muslim rebels have fought animist and Christian southern government and French troops from 1966, despite numerous cease-fires and peace pacts.

Rebel forces, led by Hissène Habré, captured the capital and forced Pres. Goukouni Oueddei to flee the country in June 1982. In Dec. 1990, a Libyan-supported insurgent group, the Patriotic Salvation Movement, overthrew Habré. After approval of a new constitution Mar. 1996, Chad's first multiparty presidential election was held in June and July.

Oil began flowing July 15, 2003, through a 665-mi pipeline that allows landlocked Chad to export via Cameroon. Pres. Idriss Déby Itno won a third term, May 3, 2006, in an election boycotted by major opposition groups. Violence along the Sudan border escalated during the year, as Sudanese *janjaweed* militias and Chadian rebels attacked civilians, and Darfur rebels preyed on refugee camps. Between 140 and 700 civilians died in N'Djamena, Feb. 2-5, 2008, as more than 2,000 Chadian rebels stormed the capital and clashed with government troops in a failed coup attempt.

On Jan. 15, 2010, Chad and Sudan signed an accord aimed at normalizing relations and suppressing cross-border activities by rebel groups. Established in 2007, a UN peacekeeping force (MINURCAT) completed its mandate Dec. 31, 2010. In early 2011, camps in E Chad housed some 262,900 refugees, most from Darfur, and camps in S Chad held about 73,500 refugees, most from the Central African Republic. More than 157,000 Chadians were internally displaced. Pres. Déby won reelection Apr. 25, 2011, in a vote boycotted as fraudulent by major opposition groups.

After Islamist groups took over northern Mali and imposed a repressive regime in late 2012, Chad contributed roughly 2,000 soldiers to aid French, Malian, and other African forces in a military intervention. On Apr. 15, 2013, the Chadian government announced

it would begin pulling its troops out of Mali. Former Pres. Hissène Habré, accused of killing and torturing thousands of opponents in the 1980s, was arrested in Senegal June 30, 2013. It remains unclear whether he will face charges there or in Intl. Criminal Court, which had reopened proceedings against him Feb. 8, 2013.

Chile
Republic of Chile

People: Population: 17,216,945. **Age distrib.:** <15: 21%; 65+: 9.7%. **Pop. density:** 60 per sq mi, 23.1 per sq km. **Urban:** 89.2%. **Ethnic groups:** white and white-Amerindian 95%, Mapuche 4%. **Languages:** Spanish (official), Mapudungun, German, English. **Religions:** Roman Catholic 70%, Evangelical 15%, Jehovah's Witnesses 1%, other Christian 1%, none 8%.

Geography: Total area: 291,933 sq mi, 756,102 sq km; **Land area:** 287,187 sq mi, 743,812 sq km. **Location:** Occupies W coast of southern S America. **Neighbors:** Peru on N, Bolivia on NE, Argentina on E. **Topography:** Andes Mts. on E border incl. some of the world's highest peaks; on W is 2,650-mi Pacific coast. Width varies 100-250 mi. In N is Atacama Desert; in center are agricultural regions; in S, forests and grazing lands. **Capital:** Santiago, 6,034,480. **Cities (urban aggl.):** Valparaíso, 882,954.

Government: Type: Republic. **Head of state and gov.:** Pres. Sebastián Piñera Echenique; b. Dec. 1, 1949; in office: Mar. 11, 2010. **Local divisions:** 15 regions. **Defense budget:** $4.31 bil. **Active troops:** 59,050.

Economy: Industries: copper, lithium, other minerals, foodstuffs, fish proc., iron and steel, wood and wood prods., transp. equip., cement, textiles. **Chief crops:** grapes, apples, pears, onions, wheat, corn, oats, peaches, garlic, asparagus, beans. **Natural resources:** copper, timber, iron ore, nitrates, prec. metals, molybdenum, hydropower. **Crude oil reserves:** 150 mil bbls. **Arable land:** 1.8%. **Livestock:** cattle: 3.8 mil; chickens: 47.5 mil; goats: 760,000; pigs: 2.8 mil; sheep: 3.6 mil. **Fish catch:** 4.4 mil metric tons. **Electricity prod.** (2011): 62.9 bil kWh. **Labor force:** agric. 13.2%, industry 23%, services 63.9%.

Finance: Monetary unit: Peso (CLP) (Sept. 2013: 506.46 = $1 U.S.). **GDP:** $325.8 bil; **per capita GDP:** $18,700; **GDP growth:** 5.5%. **Imports:** $74.9 bil; U.S. 21.9%, China 18.2%, Argentina 6.7%, Brazil 6.5%. **Exports:** $78.3 bil; China 23.9%, U.S. 12.2%, Japan 10.6%, South Korea 5.8%, Brazil 5.5%. **Tourism:** $2.2 bil. **Budget:** $57.4 bil. **Total reserves less gold:** $41.6 bil. **Gold:** 7,900 oz t. **CPI change:** 3%.

Transport: Railways: 4,401 mi. **Motor vehicles:** 210.5 vehicles per 1,000 pop. **Civil aviation:** 10.9 bil pass.-mi; 90 airports. **Chief ports:** Coronel, Huasco, Lirquen, Puerto Ventanas, San Antonio, San Vicente, Valparaiso.

Communications: TV sets: 313 per 1,000 pop. **Radios:** 783 per 1,000 pop. **Telephone lines:** 18.8 per 100 pop. **Internet:** 61.4%.

Health: Life expect.: 75.3 male; 81.4 female. **Births:** 14.1 per 1,000 pop. **Deaths:** 5.9 per 1,000 pop. **Natural inc.:** 0.83%. **Infant mortality:** 7.2 per 1,000 live births. **HIV rate:** 0.5%.

Education: Compulsory: ages 6-17. **Literacy:** 98.6%.

Major intl. organizations: UN and all of its specialized agencies, APEC, OAS, OECD, WTO.

Embassy: 1732 Massachusetts Ave. NW 20036; 785-1746.

Website: www.gob.cl

Northern Chile was under Inca rule before the Spanish conquest, 1536-40. The southern Araucanian Indians resisted until the late 19th cent. Independence was gained 1810-18 under José de San Martin and Bernardo O'Higgins; the latter, as supreme director 1817-23, sought social and economic reforms until deposed. Chile defeated Peru and Bolivia in 1836-39 and 1879-84, gaining mineral-rich northern land.

In 1970, Salvador Allende Gossens, a Marxist, became president with a narrow plurality of the popular vote. His government improved conditions for the poor, but property seizures by left-wing extremists, poorly planned socialist economic programs, and a destabilization campaign backed by the U.S. led to political and financial chaos. A military junta seized power Sept. 11, 1973. With the presidential palace under attack, Allende refused to surrender; a 2011 autopsy confirmed police reports that he killed himself. The junta, headed by Gen. Augusto Pinochet Ugarte, implemented plans to privatize the economy and "exterminate Marxism." Repression continued into the 1980s.

In Dec. 1989 voters elected a civilian president, although Pinochet continued to head the army until Mar. 10, 1998. In Mar. 1994, a Chilean human rights group estimated that human rights violations had claimed more than 3,100 lives during Pinochet's rule. Efforts to prosecute him failed when courts in Britain and Chile declared him mentally unfit to stand trial.

Ricardo Lagos Escobar, Chile's first Socialist president since the 1973 coup, took office Mar. 11, 2000. Chile and the U.S. signed a free trade accord June 6, 2003. Verónica Michelle Bachelet Jeria, also a Socialist, won a runoff election Jan. 2006 and took office in Mar. as Chile's first woman president. Pinochet died Dec. 10, 2006.

Billionaire businessman Sebastián Piñera Echenique, a conservative, won a presidential runoff election Jan. 2010 and took office in Mar. In the interim, a powerful earthquake and the tsunami that

followed it Feb. 27, 2010, off the coast of central Chile killed at least 521 people and caused up to $30 bil in property damage. A judge ruled May 16, 2013, that the manslaughter trial of 4 government officials for failing to issue adequate warnings about the approaching tsunami should go forward. Chile successfully rescued 33 miners trapped for 10 weeks 2,300 ft underground after a cave-in at the San José Mine Aug. 5, 2010. A prison fire Dec. 8 in Santiago killed at least 81 inmates. Chile's economy was growing at a 6.6% annual rate in mid-2011, but lagging wages sparked labor protests against the Piñera government that continued into 2012 and spread to the student population. Piñera proposed sweeping tax reform, Apr. 2012, to raise corporate and reduce individual taxes. Student protests continued in 2013, demanding education reform.

Tierra del Fuego is the largest (18,800 sq mi) island in the archipelago of the same name at the southern tip of S America, an area of majestic mountains, tortuous channels, and high winds. It was visited 1520 by Magellan and named Land of Fire because of its many Indian bonfires. Part of the island is in Chile, part in Argentina. Punta Arenas, on a mainland peninsula, is a center of sheep raising and the world's southernmost city (pop. [2012 census] 131,067); Puerto Williams is the southernmost settlement.

China

People's Republic of China
(Statistical data do not include Hong Kong or Macao.)

People: Population: 1,349,585,838. **Age distrib.:** <15: 17.2%; 65+: 9.4%. **Pop. density:** 365.3 per sq mi, 141 per sq km. **Urban:** 50.6%. Hong Kong and Macao). **Ethnic groups:** Han Chinese 92%; Zhuang, Manchu, Hui, Miao, Uighur, Tujia, Yi, Mongol, Tibetan, Buyi, Dong, Yao, Korean, other nationalities 9%. **Languages:** Standard Chinese or Mandarin (Putonghua, based on Beijing dialect), Yue (Cantonese), Wu (Shanghainese), Minbei (Fuzhou), Minnan (Hokkien-Taiwanese), Xiang, Gan, Hakka dialects, minority langs. **Religions:** officially atheist; Daoist (Taoist), Buddhist, Christian, Muslim.

Geography: Total area: 3,705,407 sq mi, 9,596,961 sq km; **Land area:** 3,694,959 sq mi, 9,569,901 sq km. **Location:** Occupies most of the habitable mainland of E Asia. **Neighbors:** Mongolia on N; Russia on NE and NW; Afghanistan, Pakistan, Tajikistan, Kyrgyzstan, Kazakhstan on W; India, Nepal, Bhutan, Myanmar, Laos, Vietnam on S; North Korea on NE. **Topography:** Two-thirds of the vast territory is mountainous or desert; only one-tenth is cultivated. Rolling topography rises to high elevations in the N in the Daxinganlingshanmai separating Manchuria and Mongolia; the Tien Shan in Xinjiang; the Himalayan and Kunlunshanmai in the SW and in Tibet. Length is 1,860 mi from N to S, width E to W is more than 2,000 mi. The eastern half of China is one of the world's best-watered lands. Three great river systems, the Chang (Yangtze), Huang (Yellow), and Xi, provide water for vast farmlands. **Capital:** Beijing, 15,594,400. **Cities (urban aggl.):** Shanghai, 20,207,612; Guangzhou, Guangdong, 10,848,502; Shenzhen, 10,629,684; Chongqing, 9,977,035; Wuhan, 9,157,680; Tianjin, 8,744,365; Dongguan, Guangdong, 7,280,345; Chengdu, 6,670,149; Foshan, 6,485,510; Nanjing, Jiangsu, 5,866,243; Haerbin, 5,687,339; Shenyang, 5,567,968; Hangzhou, 5,448,263.

Government: Type: Communist state. **Head of state:** Pres. Xi Jinping; b. June 1953; in office: Mar. 14, 2013 (gen. sec. of Communist Party since Nov. 15, 2012). **Head of gov.:** Premier Li Keqiang; b. July 1, 1955; in office: Mar. 16, 2013. **Local divisions:** 22 provinces (not incl. Taiwan), 5 autonomous regions, 4 municipalities, plus the special administrative regions of Hong Kong (as of July 1, 1997) and Macao (as of Dec. 20, 1999). **Defense budget:** $102 bil. **Active troops:** 2,285,000.

Economy: Industries: (world leader in gross value of industrial output) mining and ore proc., iron, steel, aluminum, other metals, coal; machine building; armaments; textiles and apparel; petroleum; cement; chemicals; fertilizers; consumer prods. food proc.; transp. equip.; telecom equip. **Chief crops:** world leader in gross value of agric. output; rice, wheat, potatoes, corn, peanuts, tea, millet, barley, apples, cotton, oilseed. **Natural resources:** coal, iron ore, petroleum, nat. gas, mercury, tin, tungsten, antimony, manganese, molybdenum, vanadium, magnetite, aluminum, lead, zinc, rare earth elements, uranium, hydropower potential (world's largest). **Crude oil reserves:** 25.6 bil bbls. **Arable land:** 12%. **Livestock:** cattle: 82.9 mil; chickens: 5.2 bil; goats: 142 mil; pigs: 464.6 mil; sheep: 138.8 mil. **Fish catch:** 66.2 mil metric tons. **Electricity prod.** 3.9 tril kWh. **Labor force:** agric. 34.8%, industry 29.5%, services 35.7%.

Finance: Monetary unit: Yuan Renminbi (CNY) (Sept. 2013: 6.12 = $1 U.S.). **GDP:** $12.6 tril; per capita **GDP:** $9,300; **GDP growth:** 7.8%. **Imports:** $1.7 tril; Japan 9.8%, South Korea 9.2%, U.S. 7.1%, Germany 5.1%, Australia 4.3%. **Exports:** $2.1 tril; U.S. 17.2%, Hong Kong 15.8%, Japan 7.4%, South Korea 4.3%. **Tourism:** $50.0 bil. **Budget:** $2 tril. **Total reserves less gold:** $3.3 tril. **Gold:** 33.9 mil oz t. **CPI change:** 2.7%.

Transport: Railways: 53,438 mi. **Motor vehicles:** 81.5 vehicles per 1,000 pop. **Civil aviation:** 205.2 bil pass.-mi (incl. data for Hong Kong and Macao); 463 airports. **Chief ports:** Dalian, Guangzhou, Ningbo, Qingdao, Qinhuangdao, Shanghai, Shenzhen, Tianjin.

Communications: TV sets: 380 per 1,000 pop. **Radios:** 336 per 1,000 pop. **Telephone lines:** 20.6 per 100 pop. **Internet:** 42.3%.

Health: Life expect.: 73.0 male; 77.3 female. **Births:** 12.3 per 1,000 pop. **Deaths:** 7.3 per 1,000 pop. **Natural inc.:** 0.49%. **Infant mortality:** 15.2 per 1,000 live births. **HIV rate:** <0.1%.

Education: Compulsory: ages 6-14. **Literacy:** 95.1%.

Major intl. organizations: UN (FAO, IBRD, ILO, IMF, WHO), APEC, WTO.

Embassy: 2300 Connecticut Ave. NW 20008; 328-2500.

Website: www.gov.cn

Remains of various humanlike creatures who lived as early as several hundred thousand years ago have been found in many parts of China. Neolithic agricultural settlements dotted the Huang (Yellow) R. basin from about 5000 BCE. Their language, religion, and art were the sources of later Chinese civilization.

Bronze metallurgy reached a peak and Chinese pictographic writing, similar to today's, was in use in the more developed culture of the Shang Dynasty (c. 1500 BCE-c. 1000 BCE), which ruled much of North China.

A succession of dynasties and interdynastic warring kingdoms ruled China for the next 3,000 years. They expanded Chinese political and cultural domination to the south and west, and developed a technologically and culturally advanced society that was unaffected by foreign rule (Mongols in the Yuan Dynasty, 1271-1368, and Manchus in the Ch'ing Dynasty, 1644-1911).

Rebellions in the 19th cent. left tens of millions dead. Russia, Japan, Britain, and other powers exercised political and economic control in large parts of the country. China became a republic Jan. 1, 1912, following the Wuchang Uprising inspired by Dr. Sun Yat-sen, founder of the Kuomintang (Nationalist) party. By 1928, the Kuomintang, led by Chiang Kai-shek, succeeded in nominal reunification of China. About the same time, a bloody purge of Communists from the ranks of the Kuomintang fomented hostilities.

For over 50 years, 1894-1945, China was involved in conflicts with Japan. In 1895, China ceded Korea, Taiwan, and other areas. On Sept. 18, 1931, Japan seized the Northeastern Provinces (Manchuria) and set up a puppet state called Manchukuo. Taking advantage of Chinese dissension, Japan invaded China proper July 7, 1937. On Nov. 20 the retreating Nationalist government moved its capital to Chongqing (Chungking) from Nanking (Nanjing), which Japanese troops then ravaged Dec. 13.

From 1939 the Sino-Japanese War (1937-45) became part of the broader world conflict. After its defeat in World War II, Japan relinquished China. Within China, conflicts involving the Kuomintang, Communists, and other factions resumed. China came under the domination of Communist armies, 1949-50. The Kuomintang government fled to Taiwan, Dec. 8, 1949.

The People's Republic of China was proclaimed in Beijing (Peking) Oct. 1, 1949, under Mao Zedong. China and the USSR signed a 30-year treaty of "friendship, alliance, and mutual assistance," Feb. 15, 1950. The U.S. refused to recognize the new regime. On Nov. 26, 1950, the People's Republic sent armies into Korea against U.S. troops and forced a stalemate in the Korean War.

Frequent drastic changes in policy and violent factionalism 1949-52 interfered with economic development. In 1957, Mao admitted an estimated 800,000 people had been executed 1949-54; opponents claimed much higher figures. The Great Leap Forward, 1958-60, tried to accelerate economic development through intensive labor on huge new rural communes, and through emphasis on ideological purity. The program caused resistance and was largely abandoned.

By the 1960s, relations with the USSR deteriorated, with disagreements on borders, ideology, and leadership of world Communism. The USSR canceled aid accords, and China, with Albania, launched anti-Soviet propaganda drives. The Great Proletarian Cultural Revolution, 1965, an attempt to instruct a new generation in revolutionary principles, resulted in massive purges. Millions of urban teenagers were relocated into the countryside. By 1968 the movement had run its course; many purged officials returned to office in subsequent years, and several ideological reforms were gradually weakened.

On Oct. 25, 1971, the UN General Assembly ousted the Taiwan government from the UN and seated the People's Republic in its place. The U.S. had supported the mainland's admission but opposed Taiwan's expulsion.

U.S. Pres. Richard Nixon visited China Feb. 21-28, 1972, on invitation from Premier Zhou Enlai, ending years of antipathy between the 2 nations. China and the U.S. opened liaison offices in each other's capitals, May-June 1973. The U.S., Dec. 15, 1978, formally recognized the People's Republic of China as the sole legal government of China; diplomatic relations between the 2 nations were established, Jan. 1, 1979.

Mao died Sept. 9, 1976. By 1978, Vice Premier Deng Xiaoping had consolidated power, succeeding Mao as "paramount leader" of China. The new ruling group modified Maoist policies in education, culture, and industry, and sought better ties with non-Communist countries. By the mid-1980s, China had enacted far-reaching economic reforms, deemphasizing centralized planning and incorporating market-oriented incentives.

Some 100,000 students and workers marched in Beijing to demand political reforms, May 4, 1989. As the unrest spread, martial law was imposed, May 20. Troops entered Beijing, June 3-4, and crushed the pro-democracy protests, as tanks and armored personnel carriers rolled through Tiananmen Square. It is estimated

that hundreds died and thousands were injured, and hundreds of students and workers were arrested.

Deng Xiaoping died Feb. 19, 1997, leaving Jiang Zemin in control as president. Hong Kong reverted to Chinese sovereignty July 1, 1997. Portugal returned Macao to China Dec. 20, 1999.

Hu Jintao was named Communist Party general secretary at the 16th party congress, Nov. 2002, and elected president by the 10th National People's Congress, Mar. 2003. With the successful launch and recovery, Oct. 15-16, 2003, of the *Shenzhou 5* spacecraft, China became the third nation (after the U.S. and USSR) to send a man into space.

China's industries, exports, and oil demand have increased rapidly since the 1980s. Reports in 2007 that China had exported hazardous pet products, toothpaste, tires, and toys resulted in the execution, July 10, of Zheng Xiaoyu, the former head of China's food and drug safety agency.

The National People's Congress Mar. 15-16, 2008, reelected Pres. Hu Jintao and Prem. Wen Jiabao. A powerful earthquake rocked Sichuan Province May 12, leaving 69,226 people dead and 17,923 missing. China reportedly spent $43 bil preparing for the Summer Olympics, held in Beijing Aug. 8-24, 2008. China's health ministry reported Sept.-Dec. 2008 that 300,000 babies had been sickened by contaminated milk powder.

Western computer security experts Jan.-Feb. 2010 blamed hackers at 2 Chinese schools for Internet attacks on Google and at least 30 other firms. An earthquake Apr. 14 killed at least 2,200 people in NW China. The government reacted angrily when the Nobel Peace Prize was awarded Oct. 8 to Liu Xiaobo, a human rights activist who had received an 11-year prison sentence in 2009.

China has invested heavily in environmental technologies, especially wind and solar power, but illegal mining and ore processing remain major public-health hazards. Rapid growth during 2009-10 made China the world's second-largest economy, ranking behind the U.S. and ahead of Japan. A June 2011 report by China's central bank alleged that corrupt officials had smuggled more than $120 bil out of the country from the mid-1990s to 2008.

Xi Jinping was chosen Communist Party general secretary and China's new leader, and Li Keqiang the country's prime min. Nov. 15, 2012. Air quality deteriorated to the most dangerous levels on record in Beijing and N China throughout Jan. 2013. The H7N9 strain of bird flu spread Mar.-Apr., infecting about 130, 44 of whom died. In Lushan County, near Ya'an City in Sichuan prov., a magnitude 7.0 earthquake struck on Apr. 20, killing at least 196 people and injuring about 13,000.

The IMF and World Bank lowered their 2013 economic forecasts for China's growth May 2013, after the 2012 economic slowdown spilled into the first half of 2013. China was the largest foreign holder of U.S. debt, with about $1.26 tril in U.S. obligations as of Apr. 2013. A visit-the-elderly law went into effect July 1 to ensure that China's growing elderly population is cared for by their only children, the products of the country's long-standing one-child policy.

Autonomous Regions

Guangxi Zhuang is in SE China, bounded on the N by Guizhou and Hunan provinces, E and S by Guangdong, on the SW by Vietnam, and on the W by Yunnan. It produces rice in the river valleys and has valuable forest products. Pop. (2010): 46,026,629.

Inner Mongolia was organized by the People's Republic in 1947. Its boundaries have undergone frequent changes, reaching its greatest extent in 1956 (and restored in 1979), with an area of 454,600 sq mi, allegedly in order to dilute the minority Mongol population. Chinese settlers outnumber the Mongols more than 10 to 1. Pop. (2010): 24,706,321. Capital: Hohhot.

Ningxia Hui, in north central China, is about 60,000 sq mi. Pop. (2010): 6,301,350. Capital: Yinchuan. The climate is mostly semiarid, with desert areas in the N. The Huang He (Yellow R.) flows across the N, furnishing water for irrigation. Coal is mined in the E. The majority of the population is Han, and the Hui (Chinese Muslims) constitute about one-third of the population. The region experienced a significant population boom, 1950-80, which has now stabilized.

Xinjiang Uighur, in Central Asia, is 635,900 sq mi, pop. (2010): 21,813,334 (75% Uighurs, a Turkic Muslim group, with a heavy Han Chinese increase in recent years). Capital: Urumqi. It is China's richest region in strategic minerals. China has moved to crack down on Uighur separatists, whom Beijing regards as terrorists. A protest march July 5, 2009, by Uighurs in Urumqi led to violent clashes with Han Chinese; at least 197 people (mostly Han) were killed in the riots. Renewed unrest including protests by Han in early Sept. led to the dismissal of the city's top Communist official.

Tibet, 471,700 sq mi, is a thinly populated region of high plateaus and massive mountains, the Himalayas on the S, the Kunluns on the N. High passes connect with India and Nepal; roads lead into China proper. Capital: Lhasa. Average altitude is 15,000 ft. Jiachan, 15,870 ft, is believed to be the highest inhabited town on earth. Agriculture is primitive. Pop. (2010): 3,002,166 (of whom about 500,000 are Chinese). Another 4 mil Tibetans form the majority of the population of vast adjacent areas that have long been incorporated into China.

China ruled all of Tibet from the 18th cent. Independence came in 1911, but China reasserted control in 1951, and a Communist government was installed in 1953. Serfdom was abolished, but all land remained collectivized.

A Tibetan uprising within China in 1956 spread to Lhasa in 1959. The rebellion was crushed by Chinese troops, and Buddhism was almost totally suppressed. The Dalai Lama and 100,000 Tibetans fled to India.

Efforts by Chinese authorities to halt peaceful demonstrations by Tibetan monks led to anti-Chinese riots in Lhasa, Mar. 14, 2008; the Chinese government sent troops into Tibet to crush dissent, sparking international protests.

Hong Kong

Hong Kong (Xianggang), located at the mouth of the Zhu Jiang (Pearl R.) in SE China, 90 mi S of Canton (Guangzhou), was a British dependency from 1842 until July 1, 1997, when it became a Special Administrative Region of China. Its nucleus is Hong Kong Isl., 31 sq mi, occupied by the British in 1841 and formally ceded to them in 1842, on which is located the seat of government. Opposite is Kowloon Peninsula, 3 sq mi, and Stonecutters Isl., added to the territory in 1860. An additional 355 sq mi known as the New Territories, a mainland area and islands, were leased from China, 1898, for 99 years. Area: 426 sq mi (total); 407 sq mi (land); pop. (2013 est.) 7,182,724. **Website:** www.gov.hk

Hong Kong is a major trade and banking center. Per capita GDP, $52,300 (2012 est.), is among the highest in the world. Principal industries are textiles and apparel, tourism, electronics, shipbuilding, iron and steel, fishing, cement, and small manufactures. Tourism receipts in 2012 were $32.1 bil. Hong Kong's spinning mills are among the best in the world. Outside of the public sector, the labor force is engaged in the following sectors: wholesale and retail trade, restaurants, and hotels 40.9%; financing, insurance, and real estate 12.5%; community and social services 16.9%; transport and communications 9.9%; manufacturing 4%; and construction 2.7%.

Hong Kong harbor was long an important British naval station and one of the world's great transshipment ports. The colony often provided refuge for exiles from mainland China. It was occupied by Japan during WWII.

From 1949 to 1962, Hong Kong absorbed more than 1 mil refugees fleeing Communist China. Starting in the 1950s, cheap labor led to a boom in light manufacturing, while liberal tax policies attracted foreign investment; Hong Kong became one of the wealthiest, most productive areas in the Far East.

With the end of the 99-year lease on the New Territories drawing near, Britain and China signed an agreement, Dec. 19, 1984, under which all of Hong Kong was to be returned to China in 1997; under this agreement Hong Kong was to be allowed to keep its capitalist system for 50 years. Following the transfer of government, Hong Kong retained its street names and its currency, the Hong Kong dollar, but without the queen's picture. Official languages remained Chinese (Cantonese dialect) and English.

Hundreds of thousands of Hong Kong residents protested July 1, 2003, a proposed anti-subversion law; the bill was withdrawn Sept. 5. Another mass march, July 1, 2004, protested Beijing's refusal to allow greater freedom. Pro-democracy candidates won a majority of the popular vote in elections, Sept. 12, but failed to gain control of the Legislative Council. After Hong Kong's chief executive, Tung Chee-hwa resigned Mar. 10, 2005, Donald Tsang served the remaining 2 years of Tung's term; he won a full 5-year term Mar. 2007, but left office tarnished by a scandal that involved receiving preferential treatment and favors from wealthy businessmen. Leung Chun-ying, whose close ties to China became an issue during the campaign, was elected Mar. 2012 and took office July 1.

Macao

Macao, area of 11 sq mi, is an enclave, a peninsula and 2 small islands, at the mouth of the Xi (Pearl) R. in China. It was established as a Portuguese trading colony in 1557. In 1849, Portugal claimed sovereignty over the territory; this claim was accepted by China in an 1887 treaty. Portugal granted broad autonomy in 1976. Under a 1987 agreement, Macao reverted to China Dec. 20, 1999. As in the case of Hong Kong, the Chinese government guaranteed Macao it would not interfere in its way of life and capitalist system for a period of 50 years. Tourism is the fastest-growing economic sector. Tourism receipts in 2012 were $43.7 bil. The labor force is occupied in the following areas: gambling 15.1%, restaurants and hotels 15.5%, wholesale and retail trade 12.7%, construction 6.6%, public sector 7.1%, transport and communications 4.3%, manufacturing 3%, and financial services 2.2%. Pop. (2013 est.): 583,003. **Website:** www.gov.mo

Colombia

Republic of Colombia

People: Population: 45,745,783. **Age distrib.:** <15: 25.8%; 65+: 6.5%. **Pop. density:** 114.1 per sq mi, 44 per sq km. **Urban:** 75.3%. **Ethnic groups:** mestizo 58%, white 20%, mulatto 14%, black 4%, mixed black-Amerindian 3%, Amerindian 1%. **Language:** Spanish (official). **Religion:** Roman Catholic 90%.

Geography: Total area: 439,736 sq mi, 1,138,910 sq km; **Land area:** 401,044 sq mi, 1,038,700 sq km. **Location:** At the NW corner of South America. **Neighbors:** Panama on NW, Ecuador and Peru on S, Brazil and Venezuela on E. **Topography:** Three ranges of Andes—Western, Central, and Eastern Cordilleras—run through the country from N to S. The eastern range consists mostly of high tablelands, densely populated. The Magdalena R. rises in the Andes, flows N to Caribbean, through a rich alluvial plain. Sparsely settled plains in E are drained by Orinoco and Amazon systems. **Capital:**

Bogotá, 8,743,500. **Cities (urban aggl.):** Medellín, 3,693,676; Cali, 2,452,560; Barranquilla, 1,899,609; Bucaramanga, 1,119,622.

Government: Type: Republic. **Head of state and gov.:** Pres. Juan Manuel Santos Calderón; b. Aug. 10, 1951; in office: Aug. 7, 2010. **Local divisions:** 32 departments, 1 capital district. **Defense budget:** $6.13 bil. **Active troops:** 281,400.

Economy: Industries: textiles, food proc., oil, clothing and footwear, beverages, chemicals, cement. **Chief crops:** coffee, cut flowers, bananas, rice, tobacco, corn, sugarcane, cocoa beans, oilseed, vegetables. **Natural resources:** petroleum, nat. gas, coal, iron ore, nickel, gold, copper, emeralds, hydropower. **Crude oil reserves:** 2.2 bil bbls. **Arable land:** 1.9%. **Livestock:** cattle: 25.2 mil; chickens: 160 mil; goats: 1.7 mil; pigs: 5.1 mil; sheep: 1.5 mil. **Fish catch:** 169,191 metric tons. **Electricity prod.** 55.3 bil kWh. **Labor force:** agric. 18%, industry 13%, services 68%.

Finance: Monetary unit: Peso (COP) (Sept. 2013: 1,949.29 = $1 U.S.). **GDP:** $511.1 bil. **per capita GDP:** $11,000; **GDP growth:** 4%. **Imports:** $53.8 bil; U.S. 30.2%, China 11.5%, Mexico 10.3%, Brazil 5.2%. **Exports:** $60 bil; U.S. 39.4%, Spain 5.1%, China 4.9%, Netherlands 4.3%. **Tourism:** $2.4 bil. **Budget:** $107.1 bil. **Total reserves less gold:** $36.4 bil. **Gold:** 332,800 oz t. **CPI change:** 3.2%.

Transport: Railways: 543 mi. **Motor vehicles:** 77.4 vehicles per 1,000 pop. **Civil aviation:** 9 bil pass.-mi; 121 airports. **Chief ports:** Barranquilla, Buenaventura, Cartagena, Puerto Bolivar, Santa Marta, Turbo.

Communications: TV sets: 291 per 1,000 pop. **Radios:** 543 per 1,000 pop. **Telephone lines:** 13.2 per 100 pop. **Internet:** 49%.

Health: Life expect.: 71.8 male; 78.4 female. **Births:** 17.0 per 1,000 pop. **Deaths:** 5.3 per 1,000 pop. **Natural inc.:** 1.17%. **Infant mortality:** 15.5 per 1,000 live births. **HIV rate:** 0.5%.

Education: Compulsory: ages 5-14. **Literacy:** 93.6%.

Major intl. organizations: UN (FAO, IBRD, ILO, IMF, WHO), OAS, WTO.

Embassy: 2118 Leroy Pl. NW 20008; 387-8338.

Website: wsp.presidencia.gov.co

Spain subdued the local Indian kingdoms (Funza, Tunja) by the 1530s and ruled Colombia and neighboring areas as New Granada for 300 years. Independence was won by 1819. Venezuela and Ecuador broke away in 1829-30, and Panama withdrew in 1903.

Colombia is plagued by rural and urban violence. "La Violencia" of 1948-58 claimed 200,000 lives; since 1989, political killings, kidnappings, and "disappearances" have victimized many thousands of civilians, and the internally displaced population has been estimated at up to 3 mil or more. Attempts at land and social reform and progress in industrialization have not reduced massive social problems. Government activity against local drug traffickers has sparked retaliation killings of politicians and judges.

Right-wing paramilitaries launched a campaign Dec. 22, 2000, against suspected left-wing guerrillas. A hardliner, Álvaro Uribe Vélez, whose father had been killed by leftist rebels in 1983, won a presidential election May 2002. A wave of guerrilla violence as he took office led Uribe to declare a state of unrest Aug. 12, and police powers were increased as part of a new government offensive. The constitution was amended, Nov. 2004, to allow the president to seek a second consecutive term; Uribe easily won reelection May 2006. Key political figures, including major allies of Uribe, were arrested in 2007 on charges of colluding with paramilitary death squads. Guerrilla strength has waned in recent years. Peace talks began in Norway Oct. 2012 and shifted to Havana, Cuba, where, May 2013, an agreement to provide equal access to rural land for people of all economic levels was reached.

Former Def. Min. Juan Manuel Santos Calderón, a conservative ally of Uribe, won a presidential runoff election June 2010, and took office Aug. 7.

Since 2000, the U.S. has provided more than $8 bil to Colombia, mostly to combat the drug trade. Cocaine production, according to U.S. figures disputed by the UN, has fallen 72% since 2001. On Sept. 22, 2012, Pres. Santos announced the capture of a drug trafficker he considered "the last of the great kingpins."

Pope Francis, May 12, 2013, canonized Colombia's first saint, Laura of St. Catherine of Siena Montoya y Upegui, a 20th-cent. nun and spiritual advisor for the country's indigenous population.

Comoros
Union of the Comoros

People: Population: 752,288. **Age distrib.:** <15: 41.8%; 65+: 3.7%. **Pop. density:** 871.8 per sq mi, 336.6 per sq km. **Urban:** 28%. **Ethnic groups:** Antalote, Cafre, Makoa, Oimatsaha, Sakalava. **Languages:** Arabic, French (both official); Shikomoro (blend of Swahili and Arabic). **Religions:** Sunni Muslim 98%, Roman Catholic 2%.

Geography: Total area: 863 sq mi, 2,235 sq km; **Land area:** 863 sq mi, 2,235 sq km. **Location:** 3 islands—Grande Comore (Njazidja), Anjouan (Nzwani), and Moheli (Mwali)—in the Mozambique Channel between NW Madagascar and SE Africa. **Neighbors:** Nearest are Mozambique on W, Madagascar on E. **Topography:** The islands are of volcanic origin, with an active volcano on Grande Comore. **Capital:** Moroni, 53,819.

Government: Type: Republic. **Head of state and gov.:** Pres. Ikililou Dhoinine; b. Aug. 14, 1962; in office: May 26, 2011. **Local divisions:** 3 islands, 4 municipalities. **Defense budget/active troops:** NA.

Economy: Industries: fishing, tourism, perfume distillation. **Chief crops:** vanilla, cloves, ylang-ylang, copra, coconuts, bananas,

cassava. **Natural resources:** negligible. **Arable land:** 44.1%. **Livestock:** cattle: 50,000; chickens: 520,000; goats: 118,000; sheep: 23,000. **Fish catch:** 25,070 metric tons. **Electricity prod.:** 40 mil kWh. **Labor force:** agric. 80%, industry and services 20%.

Finance: Monetary unit: Franc (KMF) (Sept. 2013: 373.63 = $1 U.S.). **GDP:** $887.4 mil; **per capita GDP:** $1,300; **GDP growth:** 2.5%. **Imports:** $208 mil; Pakistan 16.9%, France 13.9%, UAE 11%, India 8.3%, China 6.5%, Kenya 5.8%, Singapore 5.1%. **Exports:** $19.6 mil; Netherlands 58.8%, Singapore 10.6%, Turkey 9.3%, France 5.6%, India 5%. **Tourism:** $42 mil. **Budget:** $157.7 mil. **Total reserves less gold:** $194.1 mil. **Gold:** 579 oz t. **CPI change:** 1.8%.

Transport: Civil aviation: 4 airports. **Chief ports:** Mayotte, Mutsamudu.

Communications: TV sets: 31 per 1,000 pop. **Radios:** 159 per 1,000 pop. **Telephone lines:** 3.1 per 100 pop. **Internet:** 6%.

Health: Life expect.: 60.9 male; 65.4 female. **Births:** 30.3 per 1,000 pop. **Deaths:** 8.0 per 1,000 pop. **Natural inc.:** 2.23%. **Infant mortality:** 67.1 per 1,000 live births. **HIV rate:** 0.1%.

Education: Compulsory: ages 6-13. **Literacy:** 75.5%.

Major intl. organizations: UN (FAO, IBRD, ILO, IMF, WHO), AL, AU, WTO (observer).

Permanent UN Mission: 866 United Nations Plz., Ste. 418, New York, NY 10017; (212) 750-1637.

Website: www.beit-salam.km

The French acquired the islands from Muslim sultans, 1841-1909. They became a French overseas territory in 1947. In a 1974 referendum, all islands favored independence except Mayotte. The French National Assembly decided to allow each island to decide its own fate. The Comore Chamber of Deputies declared independence July 6, 1975, with Ahmed Abdallah as president. In a 1976 referendum, Mayotte voted to remain French.

A leftist regime that seized power from Abdallah in 1975 was deposed in a pro-French 1978 coup in which he regained the presidency. In Nov. 1989, Pres. Abdallah was assassinated; soon after, a multiparty system was instituted. A Sept. 1995 military coup, assisted by French mercenaries, ousted Pres. Said Mohamed Djohar. French troops invaded, Oct. 4, and forced coup leaders to surrender.

Anjouan and Moheli seceded from the Comoros in 1997. Unrest on Grande Comore culminated in a military coup, Apr. 1999. Anjouans endorsed secession in a disputed vote Jan. 2000. A constitution adopted in a referendum Dec. 2001 that went into effect the following year reunited Anjouan and Moheli with Grande Comore, granting each a semi-autonomous status with their own presidents.

Irregularities marred the Apr. 2002, presidential runoff election, won by Azali Assoumani, who led the 1999 coup. Elections for national and island assemblies took place Mar.-Apr. 2004. Ahmed Abdallah Mohamed Sambi won a presidential runoff vote, May 2006. Each of the 3 islands elected its own president in 2002 and 2007. Col. Mohamed Bacar, who refused to relinquish power after the central government ruled his 2007 election illegal, fled when Comorian and African Union troops took control of the island, Mar. 2008. Sambi's Vice Pres. Ikililou Dhoinine won a presidential runoff election Dec. 2010.

The heaviest rains in decades devastated some of the country's poorest areas Apr. 20-25, 2012, forcing government officials to request $19 mil in aid to facilitate recovery for some 65,000 people who were displaced and affected with water-borne diseases.

Congo
Democratic Republic of the Congo

(Congo, officially Democratic Republic of the Congo, is also known as Congo-Kinshasa. The Republic of the Congo, commonly called Congo Republic, is also known as Congo-Brazzaville.)

People: Population: 75,507,308. **Age distrib.:** <15: 43.5%; 65+: 2.6%. **Pop. density:** 86.3 per sq mi, 33.3 per sq km. **Urban:** 34.3%. **Ethnic groups:** 200+ groups, majority Bantu. Four largest tribes (Mongo, Luba, Kongo [all Bantu], Mangbetu-Azande [Hamitic]) 45%. **Languages:** French (official), Lingala (lingua franca), Kingwana (Kiswahili or Swahili dialect), Kikongo, Tshiluba. **Religions:** Roman Catholic 50%, Protestant 20%, Kimbanguist 10%, Muslim 10%, other (incl. syncretic sects, indigenous beliefs) 10%.

Geography: Total area: 905,355 sq mi, 2,344,858 sq km; **Land area:** 875,312 sq mi, 2,267,048 sq km. **Location:** In central Africa. **Neighbors:** Congo Republic on W; Central African Republic, Sudan on N; Uganda, Rwanda, Burundi, Tanzania on E; Zambia, Angola on S. **Topography:** Congo includes the bulk of the Congo R. basin. The vast central region is a low-lying plateau covered by rain forest. Mountainous terraces in the W, savannas in the S and SE, grasslands toward the N, and the high Ruwenzori Mts. on the E surround the central region. A short strip of territory borders the Atlantic O. **Capital:** Kinshasa, 8,797,730. **Cities (urban aggl.):** Lubumbashi, 1,556,368; Mbuji-Mayi, 1,503,585.

Government: Type: Republic. **Head of state:** Pres. Joseph Kabila; b. June 24, 1971; in office: Jan. 17, 2001. **Head of gov.:** Prime Min. Augustin Matata Ponyo Mapon; b. June 5, 1964; in office: Apr. 18, 2012. **Local divisions:** 10 provinces, 1 city. **Defense budget:** $229 mil. **Active troops:** 134,250.

Economy: Industries: mining, mineral proc., consumer prods., metal prods., processed foods and beverages, timber, cement.

Chief crops: coffee, sugar, palm oil, rubber, tea, cotton, cocoa, quinine, cassava, bananas, plantains, peanuts, root crops, corn, fruits. **Natural resources:** cobalt, copper, niobium, tantalum, petroleum, diamonds, gold, silver, zinc, manganese, tin, uranium, coal, hydropower, timber. **Crude oil reserves:** 180 mil bbls. **Arable land:** 3%. **Livestock:** cattle: 748,000; chickens: 20.5 mil; goats: 4.1 mil; pigs: 1 mil; sheep: 905,000. **Fish catch:** 238,970 metric tons. **Electricity prod.:** 7.8 bil kWh. **Labor force:** NA.

Finance: Monetary unit: Franc (CDF) (Sept. 2013: 923.24 = $1 U.S.). **GDP:** $28 bil; **per capita GDP:** $400; **GDP growth:** 7.1%. **Imports:** $8.2 bil; South Africa 21.4%, China 15.1%, Belgium 7.9%, Zambia 7.5%, Zimbabwe 6.1%, Kenya 5.1%, France 4.9%. **Exports:** $8.9 bil; China 53.4%, Zambia 24.5%, Belgium 5.6%. **Tourism:** $11 mil. **Budget:** $5.5 bil. **Total reserves less gold:** $1.6 bil. **CPI change** (2009-10): 85.1%.

Transport: Railways: 2,490 mi. **Motor vehicles:** 23.4 vehicles per 1,000 pop. **Civil aviation:** 26 airports. **Chief ports:** Boma, Bukavu, Bumba, Goma, Kinshasa, Kisangani, Matadi, Mbandaka.

Communications: TV sets: 5 per 1,000 pop. **Radios:** 379 per 1,000 pop. **Telephone lines:** 0.08 per 100 pop. **Internet:** 1.7%.

Health: Life expect.: 54.7 male; 57.7 female. **Births:** 36.3 per 1,000 pop. **Deaths:** 10.5 per 1,000 pop. **Natural inc.:** 2.58%. **Infant mortality:** 74.9 per 1,000 live births. **HIV rate:** NA.

Education: Compulsory: ages 6-15. **Literacy:** 61.2%.

Major intl. organizations: UN and most of its specialized agencies, AU, WTO.

Embassy: 1726 M St. NW 20036; 234-7690.

Website: www.presidentrdc.cd

The earliest inhabitants of Congo may have been the pygmies, followed by Bantus from the east and Nilotic tribes from the north. The large Bantu Bakongo kingdom ruled much of Congo and Angola when Portuguese explorers visited in the 15th cent.

Leopold II, king of the Belgians, formed an international group to exploit the Congo region in 1876. In 1877, British explorer Henry M. Stanley traveled the Congo, and in 1878 he returned to organize the region and win over the indigenous leaders. The Conference of Berlin, 1884-85, established the Congo Free State with Leopold as king and chief owner. The colony became known as the Belgian Congo in 1908. Millions of Congolese rubber plantation workers were exploited and others died under brutal European rule between 1880 and 1920.

Belgian and Congolese leaders agreed Jan. 27, 1960, that Congo would become independent in June. In the first general elections, May 31, Patrice Lumumba's party won a plurality in the National Assembly. The Republic of the Congo was proclaimed June 30. Europeans and others fled widespread violence. The UN Security Council, Aug. 9, called on Belgium to withdraw its troops and sent a UN contingent. Lumumba was dismissed as premier in Sept. and murdered Jan. 17, 1961 The last UN troops left the Congo June 30, 1964.

In late 1965, Gen. Joseph D. Mobutu was named president. He later changed his name to Mobutu Sese Seko and ruled as a dictator. The country became the Democratic Republic of the Congo (1966) and the Republic of Zaire (1971). Under Mobutu, economic decline and government corruption plagued Zaire. He retained power despite mounting international pressure and internal opposition.

During 1994, Zaire was inundated with refugees from the massive ethnic bloodshed in Rwanda. Ethnic violence spread to eastern Zaire in 1996. In Oct., militant Hutus, who dominated in the refugee camps, fought rebels (mostly Tutsis) in Zaire, precipitating intervention by government troops. As a result of the fighting, Rwandan refugees abandoned the camps; hundreds of thousands returned to Rwanda, while hundreds of thousands more were dispersed throughout eastern Zaire. The rebels, led by Gen. Laurent Kabila—a former Marxist and longtime opponent of Mobutu—began to move west across Zaire. On May 17, 1997, Kabila's troops entered Kinshasa and Mobutu went into exile. The country again became the Democratic Republic of the Congo. Mobutu died Sept. 7 in Morocco.

Kabila, who ruled by decree, alienated UN officials, international aid donors, and former allies. Rebels assisted by Rwanda and Uganda threatened Kinshasa in Aug. 1998 but were turned back with help from Angola, Namibia, and Zimbabwe. Rebel groups agreed to a cease-fire, Aug. 31, 1999, but the truce was widely violated. Kabila was assassinated Jan. 16, 2001, and was succeeded by his son Joseph.

The estimated death toll from the civil war and related causes was 3.3 mil through Nov. 2002. By then, Rwanda and Uganda had agreed to pull out their remaining troops. A power-sharing accord signed Apr. 2, 2003, led to the installation of a new Congolese government in July. A new constitution won legislative approval May 13, 2005. A UN peacekeeping force (MONUC), established in 1999, oversaw July 2006 elections, the nation's first multiparty vote since 1960. Kabila defeated former rebel leader Jean-Pierre Bemba in a presidential runoff election, Oct. 2006.

Hundreds reportedly died in Kinshasa, Mar. 22-23, 2007, in clashes between security forces and a militia loyal to Bemba, who fled to Europe. He was arrested in Belgium May 24, 2008, on war crimes charges; his trial was ongoing at The Hague in 2013. A peace deal with militia groups in eastern Congo, including one led by Tutsi rebel Gen. Laurent Nkunda, was signed Jan. 23, 2008, but Nkunda launched a new offensive Aug. 28; Rwandan authorities arrested him Jan. 2009.

A June 2011 study published by the *American Journal of Public Health* estimated that more than 1,000 women were raped in Congo every day. The Intl. Criminal Court (ICC) convicted Congolese warlord Thomas Lubanga Dyilo Mar. 2012 of war crimes for conscripting child soldiers during the country's civil war.

The MONUC peacekeeping mission, reconstituted and renamed MONUSCO as of July 1, 2010, included 18,587 military personnel on July 31, 2013. Eleven African nations signed a peace plan Feb. 24, 2013, designed to end the violence in the Congo. Rebel leader Bosco Ntaganda turned himself in at the U.S. embassy in Rwanda Mar. 18 to face charges of war crimes and crimes against humanity. A UN-backed "intervention brigade" was announced Mar. 28 with a mandate to respond militarily to rebel violence. A 6-month period of peace was broken May 21 with conflicts between rebels and the Congolese army, but a temporary cease-fire was declared May 23 for a visit by UN Sec. Gen. Ban Ki-moon. Hostilities resumed soon after. A rebel attack on Kamango July 14 caused more than 60,000 refugees to cross into Uganda. Rebel and government fighters took turns initiating attacks throughout Aug.

Congo Republic
Republic of the Congo

(Congo Republic, officially Republic of the Congo, is also known as Congo-Brazzaville. The Democratic Republic of the Congo [formerly Zaire], now commonly called Congo, is also known as Congo-Kinshasa.)

People: Population: 4,492,689. **Age distrib.:** <15: 45.1%; 65+: 2.7%. **Pop. density:** 34.1 per sq mi, 13.2 per sq km. **Urban:** 63.7%. **Ethnic groups:** Kongo 48%, Sangha 20%, Teke 17%, M'Bochi 12%, Europeans and other 3%. **Languages:** French (official); Lingala, Monokutuba (lingua francas); many local langs. and dialects (Kikongo most widespread). **Religions:** Christian 50%, animist 48%, Muslim 2%.

Geography: Total area: 132,047 sq mi, 342,000 sq km; **Land area:** 131,854 sq mi, 341,500 sq km. **Location:** In W central Africa. **Neighbors:** Gabon and Cameroon on W, Central African Republic on N, Dem. Rep. of the Congo on E, Angola on SW. **Topography:** Much of country is covered by thick forests. A coastal plain leads to the fertile Niari Valley. The center is a plateau; the Congo R. basin consists of flood plains in the lower and savanna in the upper portion. **Capital:** Brazzaville, 1,610,760.

Government: Type: Republic. **Head of state and gov.:** Pres. Denis Sassou-Nguesso; b. 1943; in office: Oct. 25, 1997. **Local divisions:** 10 regions, 2 communes. **Defense budget** (2011): $229 mil. **Active troops:** 10,000.

Economy: Industries: petroleum extraction, cement, lumber, brewing, soap, palm oil. **Chief crops:** cassava, sugar, rice, corn, peanuts, vegetables, coffee, cocoa. **Natural resources:** petroleum, timber, potash, lead, zinc, uranium, copper, phosphates, gold, magnesium, nat. gas, hydropower. **Crude oil reserves:** 1.0 bil bbls. **Arable land:** 1.5%. **Livestock:** cattle: 335,000; chickens: 2.7 mil; goats: 323,000; pigs: 92,000; sheep: 122,000. **Fish catch:** 73,301 metric tons. **Electricity prod.:** 547.3 mil kWh. **Labor force:** NA.

Finance: Monetary unit: Central African CFA Franc BEAC (XAF) (Sept. 2013: 498.17 = $1 U.S.). **GDP:** $19.4 bil; **per capita GDP:** $4,700; **GDP growth:** 3.8%. **Imports:** $5.8 bil; France 19.2%, China 13.3%, Brazil 9%, U.S. 6.1%. India 5.7%, Italy 4.8%, Belgium 4.3%. **Exports:** $12.1 bil; China 38.9%, U.S. 12.9%, France 9.5%, Australia 8.8%, Netherlands 6.8%, Spain 5.3%, India 5.3%. **Budget:** $5.9 bil. **Total reserves less gold:** $5.5 bil. **CPI change:** 3.9%.

Transport: Railways: 551 mi. **Motor vehicles:** 16 vehicles per 1,000 pop. **Civil aviation:** 19.3 mil pass.-mi; 8 airports. **Chief ports:** Brazzaville, Djeno, Impfondo, Ouesso, Oyo, Pointe-Noire.

Communications: TV sets: 50 per 1,000 pop. **Radios:** 107 per 1,000 pop. **Telephone lines:** 0.4 per 100 pop. **Internet:** 6.1%.

Health: Life expect.: 54.3 male; 57.0 female. **Births:** 39.6 per 1,000 pop. **Deaths:** 11.0 per 1,000 pop. **Natural inc.:** 2.86% **Infant mortality:** 72.5 per 1,000 live births. **HIV rate:** 3.3%.

Education: Compulsory: ages 6-15. **Literacy:** NA.

Major intl. organizations: UN (FAO, IBRD, ILO, IMF, WHO), AU, WTO.

Embassy: 4891 Colorado Ave. NW 20011; 726-5500.

Website: www.presidence.cg

The Loango kingdom flourished in the 15th cent., as did the Anzico kingdom of the Batekes; by the late 17th cent. they had weakened. By 1885, France established control of the region, then called the Middle Congo. The Republic of the Congo gained independence Aug. 15, 1960.

After trade unions sparked a 1963 coup, the country adopted a Marxist-Leninist stance, with the USSR and China vying for influence. France remained a dominant trade partner and source of technical assistance, and French-owned private enterprise retained a major economic role. In 1970, the country was renamed People's Republic of the Congo. Since the 1980s, oil has dominated the economy.

In 1990, Marxism was renounced and opposition parties were legalized. In 1991 the country's name was changed back to Republic of the Congo, and a new constitution was approved. A democratically elected government came into office in 1992. Factional fighting broke out in Brazzaville, June 1997 and intensified during the summer, devastating the capital. Troops loyal to former Marxist dictator Denis Sassou-Nguesso took control of the city Oct. 15, 1997; he claimed lopsided victories in 2002 and 2009 presidential elections. His party won an absolute majority in the country's National Assembly, Aug. 5, 2012.

Costa Rica
Republic of Costa Rica

People: Population: 4,695,942. **Age distrib.:** <15: 23.8%; 65+: 6.8%. **Pop. density:** 238.2 per sq mi, 92 per sq km. **Urban:** 64.7%. **Ethnic groups:** white (incl. mestizo) 94%, black 3%, Amerindian 1%, Chinese 1%. **Languages:** Spanish (official), English. **Religions:** Roman Catholic 76%, Evangelical 14%, Jehovah's Witnesses 1%, none 3%.

Geography: Total area: 19,730 sq mi, 51,100 sq km; **Land area:** 19,714 sq mi, 51,060 sq km. **Location:** In Central America. **Neighbors:** Nicaragua on N, Panama on S. **Topography:** Lowlands by the Caribbean are tropical. The interior plateau, with an altitude of about 4,000 ft, is temperate. **Capital:** San José, 1,515,140.

Government: Type: Democratic republic. **Head of state and gov.:** Pres. Laura Chinchilla Miranda; b. Mar. 28, 1959; in office: May 8, 2010. **Local divisions:** 7 provinces. **Defense budget:** $343 mil (paramilitary). **Active troops:** No armed forces. 9,800 paramilitary only.

Economy: Industries: microprocessors, food proc., medical equip., textiles and clothing, constr. materials, fertilizer, plastic prods. **Chief crops:** bananas, pineapples, coffee, melons, ornamental plants, sugar, corn, rice, beans, potatoes. **Natural resources:** hydropower. **Arable land:** 4.9%. **Livestock:** cattle: 1.4 mil; chickens: 21 mil; goats: 5,050; pigs: 432,000; sheep: 2,800. **Fish catch:** 48,285 metric tons. **Electricity prod.:** 9.5 bil kWh. **Labor force:** agric. 14%, industry 22%, services 64%.

Finance: Monetary unit: Colon (CRC) (Sept. 2013: 506.45 = $1 U.S.). **GDP:** $59.8 bil; **per capita GDP:** $12,800; **GDP growth:** 5%. **Imports:** $16.8 bil; U.S. 46.2%, Mexico 6.4%, Japan 6.1%, China 5.8%. **Exports:** $11.4 bil; U.S. 30.7%, China 13.2%, Netherlands 10.4%, UK 9%, Mexico 9%. **Tourism:** $2.4 bil. **Budget:** $8.5 bil. **Total reserves less gold:** $6.9 bil. **Gold:** 1,914 oz t. **CPI change:** 4.5%.

Transport: Railways: 173 mi (not in current use). **Motor vehicles:** 180.2 vehicles per 1,000 pop. **Civil aviation:** 1.4 bil pass.-mi; 47 airports. **Chief ports:** Caldera, Puerto Limon.

Communications: TV sets: 250 per 1,000 pop. **Radios:** 222 per 1,000 pop. **Telephone lines:** 21.2 per 100 pop. **Internet:** 47.5%.

Health: Life expect.: 75.4 male; 80.8 female. **Births:** 16.3 per 1,000 pop. **Deaths:** 4.4 per 1,000 pop. **Natural inc.:** 1.18%. **Infant mortality:** 9.0 per 1,000 live births. **HIV rate:** 0.3%.

Education: Compulsory: ages 5-14. **Literacy:** 96.3%.

Major intl. organizations: UN (FAO, IBRD, ILO, IMF, WHO), OAS, WTO.

Embassy: 2114 S St. NW 20008; 234-2945.

Website: www.gobiernofacil.go.cr

Guaymi Indians inhabited the area when Spaniards arrived, 1502. Independence came in 1821. Costa Rica seceded from the Central American Federation in 1838. Since the civil war of 1948-49, there has been little violent social conflict, and free political institutions have been preserved.

Costa Rica, though still a largely agricultural country, has achieved a relatively high standard of living, and land ownership is widespread. Tourism is growing rapidly. Nobel Peace Prize-winner Óscar Arias Sánchez, president 1986-90, won a second term in a close election, Feb. 5, 2006. An election victory Feb. 7, 2010, made ruling party candidate Laura Chinchilla Miranda the nation's first female president.

Côte d'Ivoire
Republic of Côte d'Ivoire

People: Population: 22,400,835. **Age distrib.:** <15: 38.9%; 65+: 3.2%. **Pop. density:** 182.4 per sq mi, 70.4 per sq km. **Urban:** 51.3%. **Ethnic groups:** Akan 42%, Voltaiques or Gur 18%, N Mandes 17%, Krous 11%, S Mandes 10%. **Languages:** French (official), 60 native dialects (Dioula most widely spoken). **Religions:** Muslim 39%, Christian 33%, indigenous 12%, none 17%.

Geography: Total area: 124,504 sq mi, 322,463 sq km; **Land area:** 122,782 sq mi, 318,003 sq km. **Location:** On S coast of W Africa. **Neighbors:** Liberia, Guinea on W; Mali, Burkina Faso on N; Ghana on E. **Topography:** Forests cover the W half of the country, and range from a coastal strip to halfway to the N on the E. A sparse inland plain leads to low mountains in NW. **Capital:** Yamoussoukro (official), 966,394; Abidjan (admin.), 4,287,820.

Government: Type: Republic. **Head of state:** Pres. Alassane Ouattara; b. Jan. 1, 1942; in office: Apr. 11, 2011 (sworn in Dec. 4, 2010). **Head of gov.:** Prime Min. Daniel Kablan Duncan; b. 1943; in office: Nov. 21, 2012. **Local divisions:** 12 districts, 2 autonomous districts. **Defense budget:** $625 mil. **Active troops:** 40,000 (target).

Economy: Industries: foodstuffs, beverages, wood prods., oil refining, gold mining, truck and bus assembly, textiles, fertilizer. **Chief crops:** coffee, cocoa beans, bananas, palm kernels, corn, rice, cassava, sweet potatoes, sugar, cotton, rubber. **Natural resources:** petroleum, nat. gas, diamonds, manganese, iron ore, cobalt, bauxite, copper, gold, nickel, tantalum, silica sand, clay, cocoa beans, coffee, palm oil, hydropower. **Crude oil reserves:** 100 mil bbls. **Arable land:** 9.1%. **Livestock:** cattle: 1.6 mil; chickens: 43.1 mil; goats: 1.3 mil; pigs: 349,739; sheep: 1.7 mil. **Fish catch:** 75,113 metric tons. **Electricity prod.:** 5.7 bil kWh. **Labor force:** agric. 68%.

Finance: Monetary unit: West African CFA Franc (XOF) (Sept. 2013: 498.17 = $1 U.S.). **GDP:** $41 bil; **per capita GDP:** $1,800; **GDP growth:** 9.8%. **Imports:** $8.6 bil; Nigeria 18.6%, France 14.8%, China 9.9%, India 5.2%. **Exports:** $12.3 bil; U.S. 10.1%, Netherlands 9%, Germany 8.7%, Nigeria 7.4%, France 5.8%, Canada 4.4%. **Tourism:** $141 mil. **Budget:** $6.1 bil. **Total reserves less gold:** $3.9 bil. **CPI change:** 1.3%.

Transport: Railways: 410 mi. **Motor vehicles:** 23 vehicles per 1,000 pop. **Civil aviation:** 7 airports. **Chief ports:** Abidjan, Espoir, San-Pédro.

Communications: TV sets: 44 per 1,000 pop. **Radios:** 138 per 1,000 pop. **Telephone lines:** 1.3 per 100 pop. **Internet:** 2.4%.

Health: Life expect.: 56.6 male; 58.8 female. **Births:** 29.8 per 1,000 pop. **Deaths:** 9.8 per 1,000 pop. **Natural inc.:** 2.00%. **Infant mortality:** 61.7 per 1,000 live births. **HIV rate:** 3%.

Education: Compulsory: ages 6-15. **Literacy:** 56.9%.

Major intl. organizations: UN and all of its specialized agencies, AU, WTO.

Embassy: 3421 Massachusetts Ave. NW 20007; 797-0300.

Website: www.gouv.ci

A French protectorate from 1842, Côte d'Ivoire became independent in 1960. The name was officially changed from Ivory Coast, Oct. 1985.

Students and workers protested, Feb. 1990, demanding the ouster of longtime Pres. Félix Houphouët-Boigny. Côte d'Ivoire held its first multiparty presidential election Oct. 1990, which Houphouët-Boigny won. He died Dec. 7, 1993. The National Assembly named as successor Henri Konan Bédié. He was reelected Oct. 1995 but was ousted in a military coup Dec. 24, 1999. The coup leader, Robert Guéi, lost a presidential vote Oct. 2000 but claimed victory anyway. After mass protests, he fled, and Laurent Gbagbo became president. Guéi was killed in Abidjan Sept. 19, 2002.

Agreement on power sharing was reached in Mar. 2003, and Gbagbo and former rebel leaders declared an end to the war July 5. The country remained divided, however. Rebels held the north and government forces controlled the south. Under a new accord reached Mar. 2007, rebel leader Guillaume Soro became prime min.

Both Gbagbo and his main challenger, former Prime Min. Alassane Ouattara, claimed victory after a presidential runoff election Nov. 2010. Gbagbo clung to power, although the UN and much of the international community recognized Ouattara as the legitimate winner. A violent power struggle followed, claiming an estimated 1,500 lives and displacing at least 1 mil people. With support from French and UN forces, Ouattara loyalists captured Gbagbo in Abidjan, Apr. 2011. Human Rights Watch reported June 2 that after taking power, Ouattara's troops killed at least 149 suspected Gbagbo supporters. A UN peacekeeping mission (UNOCI), authorized since 2004, had more than 10,011 military personnel in Côte d'Ivoire in mid-2013. More than 100 prisoners were freed and 5 people died in a raid at a security post west of Abidjan Aug. 16, 2012, blamed on Gbagbo supporters.

A 2012 New Year's Eve post-fireworks stampede killed at least 61 people outside a stadium in Abidjan. Crude roadblocks had been placed across a main road, trapping the crowd of 50,000. Amnesty Intl., Feb. 26, 2013, accused the army and its allies of killing and torturing Gbagbo supporters.

Croatia
Republic of Croatia

People: Population: 4,475,611. **Age distrib.:** <15: 14.6%; 65+: 17.4%. **Pop. density:** 207.1 per sq mi, 80 per sq km. **Urban:** 57.8%. **Ethnic groups:** Croat 90%, Serb 5%, other (incl. Bosniak, Hungarian, Slovene, Czech, Roma) 6%. **Languages:** Croatian (official), Serbian. **Religions:** Roman Catholic 88%, Orthodox 4%, Muslim 1%, none 5%.

Geography: Total area: 21,851 sq mi, 56,594 sq km; **Land area:** 21,612 sq mi, 55,974 sq km. **Location:** SE Europe, on the Balkan Peninsula. **Neighbors:** Slovenia, Hungary on N; Bosnia and Herzegovina, Serbia, Montenegro on E. **Topography:** Flat plains in NE; highlands, low mts. along Adriatic coast. **Capital:** Zagreb, 686,439.

Government: Type: Parliamentary democracy. **Head of state:** Pres. Ivo Josipovic; b. Aug. 28, 1957; in office: Feb. 18, 2010. **Head of gov.:** Prime Min. Zoran Milanovic; b. Oct. 30, 1966; in office: Dec. 23, 2011. **Local divisions:** 20 counties, 1 city with special county status. **Defense budget:** $814 mil. **Active troops:** 18,600.

Economy: Industries: chemicals and plastics, machine tools, fabricated metal, electronics. **Chief crops:** wheat, corn, barley, sugar beets, sunflower seeds, rapeseeds, alfalfa, clover, vegetables, fruits. **Natural resources:** oil, coal, bauxite, iron ore, calcium, gypsum, nat. asphalt, silica, mica, clays, salt, hydropower. **Crude oil reserves:** 71 mil bbls. **Arable land:** 16%. **Livestock:** cattle: 446,000; chickens: 4.2 mil; goats: 70,000; pigs: 1.2 mil; sheep: 639,000. **Fish catch:** 83,839 metric tons. **Electricity prod.:** 13.5 bil kWh. **Labor force:** agric. 2.1%, industry 29%, services 69%.

Finance: Monetary unit: Kuna (HRK) (Sept. 2013: 5.76 = $1 U.S.). **GDP:** $79.7 bil; **per capita GDP:** $18,100; **GDP growth:** –2%. **Imports:** $20.2 bil; Italy 16.7%, Germany 12.9%, Russia 7.6%, China 7.1%, Slovenia 5.9%, Austria 4.5%. **Exports:** $12.4 bil; Italy

14.9%, Bosnia and Herzegovina 13.2%, Germany 10.6%, Slovenia 8.8%, Austria 6.8%. **Tourism:** $8.8 bil. **Budget:** $23.4 bil. **Total reserves less gold:** $14.8 bil. **CPI change:** 3.4%.
Transport: Railways: 1,691 mi. **Motor vehicles:** 377.2 vehicles per 1,000 pop. **Civil aviation:** 715.2 mil pass.-mi; 24 airports. **Chief ports:** Omisalj, Ploce, Rijeka, Sibenik, Split, Vukovar.
Communications: TV sets: 550 per 1,000 pop. **Radios:** 327 per 1,000 pop. **Telephone lines:** 37.4 per 100 pop. **Internet:** 63%.
Health: Life expect.: 72.6 male; 80.0 female. **Births:** 9.5 per 1,000 pop. **Deaths:** 12.1 per 1,000 pop. **Natural inc.:** −0.25%. **Infant mortality:** 6.0 per 1,000 live births. **HIV rate:** <0.1%.
Education: Compulsory: ages 7-14. **Literacy:** 98.9%.
Major intl. organizations: UN (FAO, IBRD, ILO, IMF, WHO), NATO, OSCE, WTO.
Embassy: 2343 Massachusetts Ave. NW 20008; 588-5899.
Website: www.vlada.hr
From the 7th cent. the area was inhabited by Croats, a south Slavic people. It was formed into a kingdom under Tomislav in 924, and joined with Hungary in 1102. The Croats became westernized and separated from Slavs under Austro-Hungarian influence. Croatia united with other Yugoslav areas to proclaim the Kingdom of Serbs, Croats, and Slovenes in 1918. A nominally independent state between 1941 and 1945, it became a constituent republic of Yugoslavia in the 1946 constitution.
On June 25, 1991, Croatia declared independence from Yugoslavia. Fighting began between ethnic Serbs and Croats. The Serbs gained control of some Croatian territory, but Croatian troops recaptured most of the Serb-held territory Aug. 1995. A peace accord was signed in Paris in Dec. The last Serb-held enclave, E Slavonia, was returned to Croatia in 1998. Indicted in 2001 and arrested in 2005, former Croatian Gen. Ante Gotovina was convicted by a UN tribunal Apr. 2011 and sentenced to 24 years in prison for war crimes committed in the mid-1990s. Stipe Mesic, a moderate, won a presidential runoff election in 2000 and was reelected 2005. Croatia became a full NATO member Apr. 1, 2009. Law professor and composer Ivo Josipovic, the nominee of the Social Democratic Party, won a presidential runoff election Jan. 2010 and took office Feb. 18. Croatia joined the EU July 1, 2013.
The convictions of 2 former Croatian generals for war crimes against the Serbs were overturned Nov. 16, 2012. But a former Croatian prime min. received a 10-year sentence for graft on Nov. 20. A UN tribunal convicted 6 other Croats May 29, 2013 for ethnic cleansing of Bosnians during the 1990s, while 2 Serbs were acquitted of war crimes on May 31.

Cuba
Republic of Cuba

People: Population: 11,061,886. **Age distrib.:** <15: 16.6%; 65+: 12.3%. **Pop. density:** 260.9 per sq mi, 100.7 per sq km. **Urban:** 75.2%. **Ethnic groups:** white 65%; mulatto, mestizo 25%; black 10%. **Language:** Spanish (official). **Religion:** Roman Catholic (nominally, prior to Castro assuming power) 85%.
Geography: Total area: 42,803 sq mi, 110,860 sq km; **Land area:** 42,402 sq mi, 109,820 sq km. **Location:** In Caribbean, westernmost of West Indies. **Neighbors:** Bahamas, U.S. to N; Mexico to W; Jamaica to S; Haiti to E. **Topography:** Coastline is about 2,500 mi. The N coast is steep and rocky, the S coast low and marshy. Low hills and fertile valleys cover more than half the country. Sierra Maestra, in E, is the highest of 3 mountain ranges. **Capital:** Havana, 2,116,470.
Government: Type: Communist state. **Head of state and gov.:** Pres. Raúl Castro Ruz; b. June 3, 1931; in office: Feb. 24, 2008 (acting from July 31, 2006). **Local divisions:** 15 provinces, 1 special municipality. **Defense budget:** $99 mil. **Active troops:** 49,000.
Economy: Industries: petroleum, nickel/cobalt, pharmaceuticals, tobacco, constr., steel, cement, agric. machinery. **Chief crops:** sugar, tobacco, citrus, coffee, rice, potatoes, beans. **Natural resources:** cobalt, nickel, iron ore, chromium, copper, salt, timber, silica, petroleum. **Crude oil reserves:** 124 mil bbls. **Arable land:** 33.4%. **Livestock:** cattle: 4.1 mil; chickens: 33.7 mil; goats: 844,300; pigs: 1.5 mil; sheep: 2.1 mil. **Fish catch:** 48,618 metric tons. **Electricity prod.:** 16.4 bil kWh. **Labor force:** agric. 19.7, industry 17.1, services 63.2%.
Finance: Monetary unit: Peso (CUP) (Sept. 2013: 26.50 = $1 U.S.). **GDP:** $121 bil; **per capita GDP** (2010 est.): $10,200; **GDP growth:** 3.1%. **Imports:** $13.7 bil; Venezuela 36.4%, China 10.5%, Spain 8.7%, Brazil 5.1%, U.S. 4.2%. **Exports:** $6 bil; Canada 17.3%, China 16.6%, Venezuela 12.7%, Netherlands 8.8%, Spain 5.8%. **Tourism:** $2.3 bil. **Budget:** $50.5 bil. **Total reserves less gold:** NA. **CPI change:** NA.
Transport: Railways: 5,097 mi. **Motor vehicles:** 40.9 vehicles per 1,000 pop. **Civil aviation:** 1.5 bil pass.-mi; 64 airports. **Chief ports:** Cienfuegos, Guantánamo, Havana, Mariel, Matanzas, Santiago de Cuba.
Communications: TV sets: 213 per 1,000 pop. **Radios:** 276 per 1,000 pop. **Telephone lines:** 10.8 per 100 pop. **Internet:** 25.6%.
Health: Life expect.: 75.8 male; 80.5 female. **Births:** 9.9 per 1,000 pop. **Deaths:** 7.6 per 1,000 pop. **Natural inc.:** 0.23%. **Infant mortality:** 4.8 per 1,000 live births. **HIV rate:** 0.2%.
Education: Compulsory: ages 6-14. **Literacy:** 99.8%.

Major intl. organizations: UN (FAO, ILO, WHO), WTO. Cuba is an OAS member state, but its current govt. has been excluded from formal participation since 1962.
Cuban Interests Section: 2630 16th St. NW 20009; 797-8518.
Website: www.cubagob.cu
Some 50,000 indigenous people lived in Cuba when Columbus reached it in 1492. Its name derives from the Indian Cubanacan. Except for British occupation of Havana, 1762-63, Cuba remained Spanish until 1898. A slave-based sugar plantation economy developed from the 18th cent. Sugar remains a leading export. Spain failed to deliver on rights guaranteed in 1878, prompting a full-scale liberation movement under Jose Martí in 1895.
The Spanish-American War began Apr. 1898 with the sinking of the USS *Maine* in Havana harbor. Spain lost the war and gave up all claims to Cuba. U.S. troops withdrew in 1902, but under 1903 and 1934 agreements, the U.S. continued to lease a site at Guantánamo Bay in the SE as a naval base. U.S. and other foreign investors dominated the economy. In 1952, former Pres. Fulgencio Batista established a dictatorship, which grew increasingly harsh and corrupt. Fidel Castro began a rebellion in 1956; guerrilla fighting intensified in 1958. Batista fled Jan. 1, 1959, and Castro took power, becoming premier Feb. 16.
Government-instituted economic and social changes failed to restore promised liberties. Opponents were imprisoned or executed. Some 700,000 Cubans emigrated in the first years after Castro's takeover, mostly to the U.S. By 1960, all banks and industrial companies had been nationalized, including over $1 bil worth of U.S.-owned properties, mostly without compensation.
In 1961, some 1,400 Cubans, trained and backed by the U.S. Central Intelligence Agency, unsuccessfully tried to overthrow the regime. On Oct. 22, 1962, U.S. Pres. John F. Kennedy ordered a naval blockade around Cuba and demanded that Soviet-installed nuclear missiles be withdrawn. The crisis ended Oct. 28 when Soviet Prem. Nikita S. Khrushchev agreed to withdraw the missiles; the U.S. ended the blockade, pledged not to invade Cuba, and removed its own missiles from Turkey.
In 1977, Cuba and the U.S. agreed to exchange diplomats, without restoring full ties, and to regulate offshore fishing. In 1978 and 1980, the U.S. agreed to accept political prisoners released by Cuba, some of whom were criminals and mental patients. A 1987 agreement provided for 20,000 Cubans to emigrate to the U.S. each year; Cuba agreed to take back some 2,500 jailed in the U.S. since 1980. Cuba's support for left-wing regimes and liberation movements in Central America, Africa, and the Caribbean contributed to poor relations with the U.S.
Cuba's economy, hobbled by U.S. sanctions and dependent on aid from other Communist countries, was shaken by the collapse of the Communist bloc in the late 1980s. Stiffer trade sanctions enacted by the U.S. in 1992 made things worse. Antigovernment demonstrations in Aug. 1994 prompted Castro to loosen emigration restrictions. A new U.S.-Cuba accord in Sept. ended the exodus of "boat people" after more than 30,000 had left Cuba. The U.S. also announced May 1995 it would admit 20,000 Cuban refugees held at Guantánamo but would return additional refugees to Cuba.
The U.S. imposed additional sanctions after Cuba, Feb. 1996, shot down two aircraft operated by anti-Castro exiles. Cuba blamed exile groups for bombings at Havana tourist hotels, July-Sept. 1997. Pope John Paul II visited Cuba, Jan. 21-25, 1998.
On July 31, 2006, the ailing Fidel Castro yielded power to his 75-year-old brother Raúl, who served as acting president until formally succeeding Feb. 24, 2008.
The U.S. in 2009 eased restrictions on remittances and family travel to the island but retained its trade embargo. The Cuban government announced, Sept. 2010, economic restructuring plans involving cutting more than 500,000 workers from the public payroll. A Communist Party conference, Apr. 2011, confirmed Raúl Castro as first secretary and approved economic reforms, including an expansion of private property rights. Pope Benedict XVI visited Cuba, Mar. 26-28, 2012.
The U.S., Jan. 11, 2002, began using its naval base at Guantánamo Bay to detain prisoners captured in Afghanistan. The indefinite detention and aggressive interrogation of Guantánamo prisoners were criticized by human rights groups. U.S. Pres. Barack Obama signed, Jan. 2009, an executive order calling for the closure of the Guantánamo detention center within a year; as of Aug. 2013, however, 164 detainees were still held there. Landmark migration rules were enacted Jan. 14 allowing Cubans to remain overseas—including in the U.S.—longer without forfeiting their Cuban residency.
By Apr. 26, 2013, about 100 prisoners were said to be on a hunger strike at Guantánamo, 19 of whom had been placed on feeding tubes. Pres. Obama announced Apr. 30 his recommitment to closing the base and appointed May 23 a new Pentagon position to oversee the transfer of prisoners, many of them to Yemen.

Cyprus
Republic of Cyprus

People: Population: 1,155,403. **Age distrib.:** <15: 15.8%; 65+: 11%. **Pop. density:** 323.8 per sq mi, 125 per sq km. **Urban:** 70.5%. **Ethnic groups:** Greek 77%, Turkish 18%. **Languages:** Greek, Turkish (both official); English. **Religions:** Greek Orthodox 78%, Muslim 18%, other (incl. Maronite, Armenian Apostolic) 4%.

Geography: Total area: 3,572 sq mi, 9,251 sq km; **Land area:** 3,568 sq mi, 9,241 sq km. **Location:** In eastern Mediterranean Sea, off Turkish coast. **Neighbors:** Nearest are Turkey on N, Syria and Lebanon on E. **Topography:** Two mountain ranges run E-W, separated by a wide, fertile plain. **Capital:** Nicosia (Lefkosia), 252,570.

Government: Type: Republic. **Head of state and gov.:** Pres. Nicos Anastasiades; b. Sept. 27, 1946; in office: Feb. 28, 2013. **Local divisions:** 6 districts. **Defense budget:** $258 mil. **Active troops:** 12,000.

Economy: Industries: tourism, food and beverage proc., cement and gypsum prod., ship repair and refurb., textiles, light chemicals, metal prods. **Chief crops:** citrus, vegetables, barley, grapes, olives, vegetables. **Natural resources:** copper, pyrites, asbestos, gypsum, timber, salt, marble, clay earth pigment. **Arable land:** 9.1%. **Livestock:** cattle: 56,915; chickens: 3.1 mil; goats: 290,334; pigs: 439,236; sheep: 355,944. **Fish catch:** 5,929 metric tons. **Electricity prod.:** 5 bil kWh. **Labor force:** agric. 8.5%, industry 20.5%, services 71%.

Finance: Monetary unit: Euro (EUR) (Sept. 2013: 0.76 = $1 U.S.). **GDP:** $24 bil; **per capita GDP:** $27,500; **GDP growth:** −2.4%. **Imports:** $7.1 bil; Greece 21.5%, Israel 11.9%, Italy 8.3%, UK 7.4%, Germany 7%, Netherlands 6.7%, France 6%, China 4.5%. **Exports:** $2.7 bil; Greece 23.3%, UK 10.1%. **Tourism:** $2.6 bil. **Budget:** $10.9 bil. **Total reserves less gold:** $448.9 mil. **Gold:** 446,000 oz t. **CPI change:** 2.4%.

Transport: Motor vehicles: 614.2 vehicles per 1,000 pop. **Civil aviation:** 2.6 bil pass.-mi; 13 airports. **Chief ports:** Larnaca, Limassol (under govt. control); Famagusta (admin. by Turkish Cypriots).

Communications: TV sets: 358 per 1,000 pop. **Radios:** 505 per 1,000 pop. **Telephone lines:** 33.1 per 100 pop. **Internet:** 61%.

Health: Life expect.: 75.4 male; 81.1 female. **Births:** 11.5 per 1,000 pop. **Deaths:** 6.5 per 1,000 pop. **Natural inc.:** 0.49%. **Infant mortality:** 8.8 per 1,000 live births. **HIV rate:** NA.

Education: Compulsory: ages 6-14. **Literacy:** 98.7%.

Major intl. organizations: UN (FAO, IBRD, ILO, IMF, WHO), the Commonwealth, EU, OSCE, WTO.

Embassy: 2211 R St. NW 20008; 462-5772.

Website: www.cyprus.gov.cy

The Ottoman Empire held Cyprus, 1571-1878, until it yielded control to Britain. Agitation for *enosis* (union) with Greece increased after WWII, with the Turkish minority opposed, and led to violence in 1955-56. In 1959, Britain, Greece, Turkey, and Cypriot leaders approved a plan for an independent republic, with constitutional guarantees for the Turkish minority and permanent division of offices on an ethnic basis.

Archbishop Makarios III was elected president, and full independence became final Aug. 16, 1960. Communal strife led the UN to send a peacekeeping force (UNFICYP) in 1964; its mandate has been repeatedly renewed.

The Cypriot National Guard, led by officers from the Greek army, seized the government July 15, 1974. On July 20, Turkey invaded the island; Greece mobilized its forces but did not intervene. By Aug. 16, Turkish forces had occupied the northeastern 40% of the island.

Turkish Cyprus opened its border with Greek Cyprus Apr. 23, 2003, for the first time since partition. In separate referendums Apr. 2004, 65% of Turkish Cypriot voters accepted a UN-sponsored reunification plan, but 76% of Greek Cypriots rejected it. Still divided, Cyprus became a full member of the EU on May 1. Dimitris Christofias won a 2008 runoff election, becoming the country's first Communist president. A blast July 11, 2011, at a naval base in southern Cyprus killed 13 people; also in mid-2011, exposure to Greece's troubled economy caused the U.S. ratings agency Fitch to downgrade Cyprus's credit rating to junk status, June 2012.

In a runoff election Feb. 24, 2013, the conservative candidate and head of the Democratic Rally party, Nicos Anastasiades, was voted Cyprus's new president. The outline of a Cyprus bailout package was agreed upon Mar. 5, 2013, among the Intl. Monetary Fund, the European Central Bank, and eurozone countries. A proposed tax on bank deposits was among the ideas put forth to meet the conditions of the deal, prompting a minor run on ATMs Mar. 16. Parliament passed part of the bailout Mar. 22 and voted to restructure Laiki Bank, or Cyprus Popular Bank, the nation's most troubled, but changed course Mar. 24, agreeing to close Laiki and abandon the idea of deposit tax. Those with deposits of more than 100,000 euros would instead lose some or all the money above that amount to help finance the restructuring of the banking system.

Turkish Republic of Northern Cyprus

A declaration of independence was announced by Turkish-Cypriot leader Rauf Denktash, Nov. 15, 1983. The state is not internationally recognized, but has trade relations with some countries. Denktash was succeeded as president by Mehmet Ali Talat (2005-10) and Dervis Eroglu, who unseated Talat in the Apr. 18, 2010, election. Area of TRNC: 1,295 sq mi; pop. (2010): 287,856, nearly all Turkish. Capital: Nicosia (Lefkosia). Local divisions: 5 districts. Active troops: 3,500. In Apr. 2013, Turkish Prime Min. Tayyip Erdogan expressed an interest in reuniting Northern Cyprus with Cyprus. Antigovernment protests spread from Turkey into Northern Cyprus June 2013.

Czech Republic

People: Population: 10,162,921. **Age distrib.:** <15: 13.4%; 65+: 17.6%. **Pop. density:** 340.7 per sq mi, 131.6 per sq km. **Urban:** 73.4%. **Ethnic groups:** Czech 64%, Moravian 5%, Slovak 1%. **Languages:** Czech, Slovak. **Religions:** Roman Catholic 27%, Protestant 2%, unaffiliated 59%.

Geography: Total area: 30,451 sq mi, 78,867 sq km; **Land area:** 29,825 sq mi, 77,247 sq km. **Location:** In E central Europe. **Neighbors:** Poland on N, Germany on N and W, Austria on S, Slovakia on E and SE. **Topography:** Bohemia, in W, is a plateau surrounded by mountains; Moravia is hilly. **Capital:** Prague, 1,275,550.

Government: Type: Parliamentary democracy. **Head of state:** Pres. Milos Zeman; b. Sept. 28, 1944; in office: Mar. 8, 2013. **Head of gov.:** Prime Min. Jiri Rusnok; b. Oct. 16, 1960; in office: July 10, 2013. **Local divisions:** 13 regions, 1 capital city. **Defense budget:** $2.17 bil. **Active troops:** 23,650.

Economy: Industries: motor vehicles, metallurgy, machinery and equip., glass, armaments. **Chief crops:** wheat, potatoes, sugar beets, hops, fruit. **Natural resources:** coal, kaolin, clay, graphite, timber. **Crude oil reserves:** 15 mil bbls. **Arable land:** 41%. **Livestock:** cattle: 1.3 mil; chickens: 20.6 mil; goats: 23,263; pigs: 1.7 mil; sheep: 209,052. **Fish catch:** 24,869 metric tons. **Electricity prod.** (2011): 82.2 bil kWh. **Labor force:** agric 3.1%, industry 38.6%, services 58.3%.

Finance: Monetary unit: Koruna (CZK) (Sept. 2013: 19.57 = $1 U.S.). **GDP:** $291.7 bil; **per capita GDP:** $27,600; **GDP growth:** −1.2%. **Imports:** $124.2 bil; Germany 29.5%, Poland 7.7%, Slovakia 7.4%, China 6.3%, Netherlands 5.8%, Russia 5.3%, Austria 4.3%. **Exports:** $131.7 bil; Germany 31.8%, Slovakia 9.1%, Poland 6.1%, France 5.1%, UK 4.9%, Austria 4.7%. **Tourism:** $7 bil. **Budget:** $89.4 bil. **Total reserves less gold:** $44.3 bil. **Gold:** 372,241 oz t. **CPI change:** 3.3%.

Transport: Railways: 5,884 mi. **Motor vehicles:** 525.3 vehicles per 1,000 pop. **Civil aviation:** 3.9 bil pass.-mi; 41 airports. **Chief ports:** Decin, Prague, Usti nad Labem.

Communications: TV sets: 457 per 1,000 pop. **Radios:** 802 per 1,000 pop. **Telephone lines:** 19.9 per 100 pop. **Internet:** 75%.

Health: Life expect.: 74.3 male; 81.0 female. **Births:** 8.6 per 1,000 pop. **Deaths:** 11.0 per 1,000 pop. **Natural inc.:** −0.25%. **Infant mortality:** 3.7 per 1,000 live births. **HIV rate:** <0.1%.

Education: Compulsory: ages 6-14. **Literacy:** 99%.

Major intl. organizations: UN (FAO, IBRD, ILO, IMF, WHO), EU, NATO, OECD, OSCE, WTO.

Embassy: 3900 Spring of Freedom St. NW 20008; 274-9100.

Website: www.czech.cz

Bohemia and Moravia were part of the Great Moravian Empire in the 9th cent. and later became part of the Holy Roman Empire. Under the kings of Bohemia, Prague in the 14th cent. was the cultural center of Central Europe. Bohemia and Hungary became part of Austria-Hungary.

In 1914-18, Thomas G. Masaryk and Eduard Benes formed a provisional government with the support of Slovak leaders, including Milan Stefanik. They proclaimed the Republic of Czechoslovakia Oct. 28, 1918.

By 1938, Nazi Germany had generated disaffection among German-speaking citizens in Sudetenland and demanded its cession. British Prime Min. Neville Chamberlain signed with Hitler at Munich, Sept. 30, 1938, an agreement to the cession, with a guarantee of peace by Hitler and Mussolini. Germany occupied Sudetenland Oct. 1-2. Hitler on Mar. 15, 1939, dissolved Czechoslovakia, made protectorates of Bohemia and Moravia, and supported the autonomy of Slovakia, proclaimed independent Mar. 14, 1939.

Soviet troops with some Czechoslovak contingents entered eastern Czechoslovakia in 1944 and reached Prague in May 1945; Benes returned as president. In May 1946 elections, the Communist Party won 38% of the votes. In Feb. 1948, the Communists seized power in advance of scheduled elections. The country was renamed the Czechoslovak Socialist Republic. A harsh Stalinist period followed; all opposition was suppressed.

In Jan. 1968 a liberalization movement spread through Czechoslovakia. Long-time Stalinist ruler Antonin Novotny was deposed; the democrat Slovak Alexander Dubcek succeeded him. In July, the USSR and 4 Warsaw Pact nations demanded an end to liberalization. On Aug. 20, the Soviet, Polish, East German, Hungarian, and Bulgarian armies invaded Czechoslovakia. Despite demonstrations and riots by students and workers, press censorship was imposed and liberal leaders were ousted. On Apr. 17, 1969, Dubcek resigned as Communist Party leader and was succeeded by Gustav Husak. Censorship was tightened, and the Communist Party expelled a third of its members.

More than 700 leading Czechoslovak intellectuals and former party leaders signed a human rights manifesto in 1977, called Charter 77, prompting a renewed crackdown by the regime.

The police crushed a massive protest in Prague, Nov. 17, 1989. As protesters demanded free elections, the Communist Party leadership resigned Nov. 24; millions went on strike Nov. 27.

On Dec. 10, 1989, the first cabinet in 41 years without a Communist majority took power; Vaclav Havel, playwright and human rights campaigner, was chosen president, Dec. 29. In Mar. 1990 the country was officially renamed the Czech and Slovak Federal Republic. A Slovak-led coalition blocked Havel's bid to win reelection July 1992.

Slovakia declared sovereignty, July 17, 1992. Czech and Slovak leaders agreed, July 23, on a plan for a peaceful division of Czechoslovakia into 2 independent states.

Czechoslovakia split into 2 separate states—the Czech Republic and Slovakia—Jan. 1, 1993. Havel was elected president of the Czech Republic on Jan. 26. The country became a full member of NATO in 1999.

Vaclav Klaus replaced the retiring Havel, 2003. The nation became a full EU member May 1, 2004. Inconclusive parliamentary elections, June 2006, led to a political deadlock, after which a minority center-right government took office Sept. 2006. Center-right parties made a strong showing in May 2010 parliamentary elections. In the country's first direct presidential election, former Social Democrat prime min. Milos Zeman was elected with more than 55% of the vote in a runoff election Jan. 26, 2013.

Heavy rains in early June 2013 caused massive flooding throughout central Europe, crippling Prague, where the Vltava River overflowed its banks, submerging parts of the city. On June 4, the prime min. declared a state of emergency throughout the country, as more than 7,000 residents were evacuated from their homes.

A corruption scandal erupted June 13, 2013, with a police raid on government offices and the arrests of 7 parliamentarians, including the prime minister's closest aide, causing Prime Min. Petr Necas to resign June 17. Pres. Zeman, June 25, appointed his economic advisor, Jiri Rusnok, prime min.

Denmark
Kingdom of Denmark

People: Population: 5,556,452. **Age distrib.:** <15: 17.2%; 65+: 18%. **Pop. density:** 339.1 per sq mi, 130.9 per sq km. **Urban:** 86.9%. **Ethnic groups:** Scandinavian, Inuit, Faroese, German, Turkish, Iranian, Somali. **Languages:** Danish, Faroese, Greenlandic, English (predominant second language). **Religions:** Evangelical Lutheran (official) 95%, other Christian (incl. Protestant, Roman Catholic) 3%, Muslim 2%.

Geography: Total area: 16,639 sq mi, 43,094 sq km; **Land area:** 16,384 sq mi, 42,434 sq km. **Location:** In N Europe, separating North and Baltic seas. **Neighbors:** Germany on S, Norway on NW, Sweden on NE. **Topography:** Consists of the Jutland Peninsula and about 500 islands, 100 inhabited. Land is flat or gently rolling and is almost all in productive use. **Capital:** Copenhagen, 1,206,020.

Government: Type: Constitutional monarchy. **Head of state:** Queen Margrethe II; b. Apr. 16, 1940; in office: Jan. 14, 1972. **Head of gov.:** Prime Min. Helle Thorning-Schmidt; b. Dec. 14, 1966; in office: Oct. 3, 2011. **Local divisions:** 5 regions. **Defense budget:** $4.37 bil. **Active troops:** 16,450.

Economy: Industries: iron, steel, nonferrous metals, chemicals, food proc., machinery and transp. equip., textiles and clothing, electronics, windmills, constr., furniture and other wood prods. **Chief crops:** barley, wheat, potatoes, sugar beets. **Natural resources:** petroleum, nat. gas, fish, salt, limestone, chalk, stone, gravel and sand. **Crude oil reserves:** 805 mil bbls. **Arable land:** 58.9%. **Livestock:** cattle: 1.6 mil; chickens: 14.3 mil; pigs: 12.9 mil; sheep: 143,890. **Fish catch:** 751,230 metric tons. **Electricity prod.** (2011): 33.7 bil kWh. **Labor force:** agric. 2.6%, industry 20.3%, services 77.1%.

Finance: Monetary unit: Krone (DKK) (Sept. 2013: 5.66 = $1 U.S.). **GDP:** $213.6 bil; **per capita GDP:** $38,300; **GDP growth:** –0.6%. **Imports:** $97 bil; Germany 20.8%, Sweden 13.3%, Netherlands 7.4%, China 6.3%, Norway 6.2%, UK 5.6%. **Exports:** $105.1 bil; Germany 15.9%, Sweden 13.5%, UK 9.6%, U.S. 6.6%, Norway 6.3%, Netherlands 4.6%. **Tourism:** $6.2 bil. **Budget:** $188.1 bil. **Total reserves less gold:** $86.1 bil. **Gold:** 2.1 mil oz t. **CPI change:** 2.4%.

Transport: Railways: 1,657 mi. **Motor vehicles:** 488.9 vehicles per 1,000 pop. **Civil aviation:** 5.5 bil pass.-mi; 28 airports. **Chief ports:** Aalborg, Aarhus, Copenhagen, Ensted, Esbjerg, Fredericia, Kalundborg.

Communications: TV sets: 975 per 1,000 pop. **Radios:** 1,399 per 1,000 pop. **Telephone lines:** 43.5 per 100 pop. **Internet:** 93%.

Health: Life expect.: 76.5 male; 81.5 female. **Births:** 10.2 per 1,000 pop. **Deaths:** 10.2 per 1,000 pop. **Natural inc.:** 0%. **Infant mortality:** 4.1 per 1,000 live births. **HIV rate:** 0.2%.

Education: Compulsory: ages 6-15. **Literacy:** 99%.

Major intl. organizations: UN and all of its specialized agencies, EU, NATO, OECD, OSCE, WTO.

Embassy: 3200 Whitehaven St. NW 20008; 234-4300.

Website: www.denmark.dk

Most of the Viking raiders in the early Middle Ages were Danes. The Danish kingdom was a major power until the 17th cent., when it lost its land in southern Sweden. Norway was separated in 1815, and Schleswig-Holstein in 1864. Northern Schleswig was returned in 1920. Denmark was occupied by Nazi Germany, Apr. 1940-May 1945, but Danes helped more than 7,200 Jews escape to safety in Sweden, Sept. 1943.

Voters ratified the Maastricht Treaty, enabling them to join the EU, in May 1993. In Sept. 2000, Danes voted not to adopt the euro.

The Danish newspaper *Jyllands-Posten* published, Sept. 30, 2005, cartoon images of the prophet Muhammad, offensive to Muslims; the caricatures, republished elsewhere, triggered violent protests and a boycott of Danish products in Islamic countries in early 2006. Danish police raids broke up alleged Islamist bomb plots Sept. 2006 and Sept. 2007. A car bomb blast linked to al-Qaeda killed 8 people outside Denmark's embassy in Islamabad, Pakistan, June 2, 2008.

Ten years of center-right government ended Sept. 2011, as a left-wing coalition won parliamentary elections. Helle Thorning-Schmidt, a Social Democrat, became Denmark's first female prime

minister Oct. 3. A bill granting marriage rights to same-sex couples was voted into law, June 7, 2012.

The **Faroe Islands** in the N Atlantic, about 300 mi NW of the Shetlands, and 850 mi from Denmark proper, 18 inhabited, have an area of 540 sq mi and pop. (2013 est.) of 49,709. They are an administrative division of Denmark, self-governing in most matters. Torshavn is the capital. Fish is a primary export (292,519 metric tons in 2006). **Website:** www.us.fo

Greenland (Kalaallit Nunaat)

Greenland, an island between the North Atlantic and the Polar Sea, is separated from the North American continent by Davis Strait and Baffin Bay. Its total area is 836,330 sq mi, 81% of which is ice-capped. Most of the island is a lofty plateau 9,000-10,000 ft in altitude. The average thickness of the cap is 1,000 ft. Scientists point to accelerated melting of Greenland's ice sheet in recent years as evidence of global warming. The population (2013 est.) is 57,714. Under the 1953 Danish constitution the colony became an integral part of the realm with representatives in the Folketing (Danish legislature). The Danish parliament, 1978, approved home rule for Greenland, effective May 1, 1979. With home rule, Greenlandic place names came into official use. The technically correct name for Greenland is now Kalaallit Nunaat; the official name for its capital is Nuuk, rather than Godthab. Fish is the principal export (about 89% of all exports in 2010). Other natural resources include coal, iron ore, lead, zinc, molybdenum, diamonds, gold, and platinum. **Website:** www.nanoq.gl

Djibouti
Republic of Djibouti

People: Population: 792,198. **Age distrib.:** <15: 33.6%; 65+: 3.5%. **Pop. density:** 88.5 per sq mi, 34.2 per sq km. **Urban:** 77.1%. **Ethnic groups:** Somali 60%, Afar 35%, other (incl. French, Arab, Ethiopian, Italian) 5%. **Languages:** French, Arabic (both official); Somali; Afar. **Religions:** Muslim 94%, Christian 6%.

Geography: Total area: 8,958 sq mi, 23,200 sq km; **Land area:** 8,950 sq mi, 23,180 sq km. **Location:** On E coast of Africa, separated from Arabian Peninsula by strategically vital strait of Bab el-Mandeb. **Neighbors:** Ethiopia on W and SW, Eritrea on NW, Somalia on SE. **Topography:** The territory, divided into a low coastal plain, mountains behind, and an interior plateau, is arid, sandy, and desolate. Climate is generally hot and dry. **Capital:** Djibouti, 495,804.

Government: Type: Republic. **Head of state:** Pres. Ismail Omar Guelleh; b. Nov. 27, 1947; in office: May 8, 1999. **Head of gov.:** Prime Min. Abdoulkader Kamil Mohamed; b. 1951; in office: Apr. 1, 2013. **Local divisions:** 6 districts. **Defense budget** (2011): $10 mil. **Active troops:** 10,450.

Economy: Industries: constr., agric. proc. **Chief crops:** fruits, vegetables. **Natural resources:** potential geothermal power, gold, clay, granite, limestone, marble, salt, diatomite, gypsum, pumice, petroleum. **Arable land:** 0.1%. **Livestock:** cattle: 296,000; goats: 512,000; sheep: 468,000. **Fish catch:** 1,667 metric tons. **Electricity prod.:** 325 mil kWh. **Labor force:** NA.

Finance: Monetary unit: Franc (DJF) (Sept. 2013: 179.70 = $1 U.S.). **GDP:** $2.4 bil; **per capita GDP:** $2,700; **GDP growth:** 4.8%. **Imports:** $579.5 mil; China 24.4%, Saudi Arabia 16.1%, India 10.6%, Indonesia 7.3%, Pakistan 4.1%. **Exports:** $87.1 mil; Somalia 78.4%, Egypt 5.3%, UAE 4%, Yemen 4%. **Tourism:** $19 mil. **Budget:** $503 mil. **Total reserves less gold:** $248.6 mil. **CPI change:** 7.9%.

Transport: Railways: 62 mi (part of Addis Ababa-Djibouti railway, under joint control with Ethiopia, but largely inoperable). **Civil aviation:** 3 airports. **Chief port:** Djibouti.

Communications: TV sets: 67 per 1,000 pop. **Radios:** 93 per 1,000 pop. **Telephone lines:** 2 per 100 pop. **Internet:** 8.3%.

Health: Life expect.: 59.5 male; 64.5 female. **Births:** 24.5 per 1,000 pop. **Deaths:** 8.0 per 1,000 pop. **Natural inc.:** 1.4%. **Infant mortality:** 51.8 per 1,000 live births. **HIV rate:** 1.4%.

Education: Compulsory: ages 6-14. **Literacy:** NA.

Major intl. organizations: UN (FAO, IBRD, ILO, IMF, WHO), AL, AU, WTO.

Embassy: 1156 15th St. NW, Ste. 515, 20005; 331-0270.

Website: www.presidence.dj

France gained control of the territory in stages between 1862 and 1900. As French Somaliland, it became an overseas French territory in 1945; in 1967 it was renamed the French Territory of the Afars and the Issas.

Ethiopia and Somalia have renounced their claims to the area, but each has accused the other of trying to gain control. There were clashes between Afars (ethnically related to Ethiopians) and Issas (related to Somalis) in 1976. Immigrants from both countries continued to enter Djibouti until independence on June 27, 1977.

Economic support comes from French aid and Arab countries. A peace accord Dec. 1994 ended a 3-year Afar rebel uprising. Drought in 2007-11 devastated crops and livestock. Protests associated with the Arab Spring broke out in late Jan. 2011 demanding the resignation of Pres. Ismail Omar Guelleh. Authorities suppressed the protests, and Guelleh won a third term in an Apr. 2011 election boycotted by the main opposition. Parliamentary elections, Feb. 22, 2013, in which the ruling coalition won the majority of votes, prompted protests by the opposition Union for National Salvation (USN). Although international observers declared the elections fair, the USN called them flawed and staged protests.

Dominica
Commonwealth of Dominica

People: Population: 73,286. **Age distrib.:** <15: 22.3%; 65+: 10.4%. **Pop. density:** 252.7 per sq mi, 97.6 per sq km. **Urban:** 67.1%. **Ethnic groups:** black 87%, mixed 9%, Carib Amerindian 3%, white 1%. **Languages:** English (official), French patois. **Religions:** Roman Catholic 61%, Protestant 21% (Seventh-Day Adventist 6%, Pentecostal 6%, Baptist 4%, Methodist 4%, Church of God 1%), Jehovah's Witnesses 1%, none 6%.

Geography: Total area: 290 sq mi, 751 sq km; **Land area:** 290 sq mi, 751 sq km. **Location:** In E Caribbean, most northerly Windward Isl. **Neighbors:** Guadeloupe to N, Martinique to S. **Topography:** Mountainous, a central ridge running from N to S, terminating in cliffs; volcanic in origin, with numerous thermal springs; rich deep topsoil on leeward side, red tropical clay on windward coast. **Capital:** Roseau, 13,562.

Government: Type: Parliamentary democracy. **Head of state:** Pres. Eliud Williams; b. Aug. 21, 1948; in office: Sept. 17, 2012. **Head of gov.:** Prime Min. Roosevelt Skerrit; b. June 8, 1972; in office: Jan. 8, 2004. **Local divisions:** 10 parishes. **Defense budget:** NA. **Active troops:** No regular military forces.

Economy: Industries: soap, coconut oil, tourism, copra, furniture, cement blocks, shoes. **Chief crops:** bananas, citrus, mangoes, root crops, coconuts, cocoa. **Natural resources:** timber, hydropower. **Arable land:** 8%. **Livestock:** cattle: 13,500; chickens: 190,000; goats: 9,700; pigs: 5,000; sheep: 7,800. **Fish catch:** 699 metric tons. **Electricity prod.:** 100.5 mil kWh. **Labor force:** agric. 40%, industry 32%, services 28%.

Finance: Monetary unit: East Caribbean Dollar (XCD) (Sept. 2013: 2.70 = $1 U.S.). **GDP:** $1.02 bil; **per capita GDP:** $14,400; **GDP growth:** 0.4%. **Imports:** $218.6 mil; Japan 37.5%, U.S. 14.9%, Trinidad and Tobago 14.2%, China 4.9%, Colombia 4%. **Exports:** $41 mil; Japan 38.2%, Antigua and Barbuda 8.4%, Jamaica 7.4%, Guyana 7.1%, Paraguay 6.1%, Trinidad and Tobago 4.6%. **Tourism:** $110 mil. **Budget:** $185.2 mil. **Total reserves less gold:** $94.6 mil. **CPI change:** 1.4%.

Transport: Civil aviation: 2 airports. **Chief ports:** Portsmouth, Roseau.

Communications: TV sets: 230 per 1,000 pop. **Radios:** 602 per 1,000 pop. **Telephone lines** 21.5 per 100 pop. **Internet:** 55.2%.

Health: Life expect.: 73.4 male; 79.5 female. **Births:** 15.6 per 1,000 pop. **Deaths:** 8.0 per 1,000 pop. **Natural inc.:** 0.76%. **Infant mortality:** 12.0 per 1,000 live births. **HIV rate:** NA.

Education: Compulsory: ages 5-16. **Literacy:** NA.

Major intl. organizations: UN (FAO, IBRD, ILO, IMF, WHO), Caricom, the Commonwealth, OAS, OECS, WTO.

Embassy: 3216 New Mexico Ave. NW 20016; 364-6781.

Website: www.dominica.gov.dm

A British colony since 1805, Dominica was granted self-government in 1967. Independence was achieved Nov. 3, 1978.

Hurricane David struck, Aug. 30, 1979, devastating the island and destroying the banana plantations, Dominica's economic mainstay. Coups were attempted in 1980 and 1981.

Dominica participated in the 1983 U.S.-led invasion of nearby Grenada. Prime Min. Pierre Charles, 49, died of a heart attack Jan. 6, 2004, and was succeeded by Roosevelt Skerrit.

Dominican Republic

People: Population: 10,219,630. **Age distrib.:** <15: 28.5%; 65+: 6.9%. **Pop. density:** 547.8 per sq mi, 211.5 per sq km. **Urban:** 69.7%. **Ethnic groups:** mixed 73%, white 16%, black 11%. **Language:** Spanish (official). **Religion:** Roman Catholic 95%.

Geography: Total area: 18,792 sq mi, 48,670 sq km; **Land area:** 18,656 sq mi, 48,320 sq km. **Location:** In W Indies, sharing isl. of Hispaniola with Haiti. **Neighbors:** Haiti on W, Puerto Rico (U.S.) to E. **Topography:** The Cordillera Central range crosses center of the country, rising to over 10,000 ft, highest in the Caribbean. The Cibao Valley to N is major agricultural area. **Capital:** Santo Domingo, 2,190,990.

Government: Type: Democratic republic. **Head of state and gov.:** Pres. Danila Medina Sánchez; b. Nov. 10, 1951; in office: Aug. 16, 2012. **Local divisions:** 31 provinces, 1 district. **Defense budget:** $238 mil. **Active troops:** 24,500.

Economy: Industries: tourism, sugar proc., mining, textiles, cement, tobacco. **Chief crops:** sugarcane, coffee, cotton, cocoa, tobacco, rice, beans, potatoes, corn, bananas. **Natural resources:** nickel, bauxite, gold, silver. **Arable land:** 16.6%. **Livestock:** cattle: 3 mil; chickens: 102 mil; goats: 230,000; pigs: 630,000; sheep: 245,000. **Fish catch:** 15,948 metric tons. **Electricity prod.** 14.7 bil kWh. **Labor force:** agric. 14.6%, industry 22.3%, services 63.1%.

Finance: Monetary unit: Peso (DOP) (Sept. 2013: 42.62 = $1 U.S.). **GDP:** $100.4 bil; **per capita GDP:** $9,800; **GDP growth:** 3.9%. **Imports:** $17.8 bil; U.S. 42.5%, Venezuela 7.4%, China 6.2%, Mexico 5.2%, Colombia 4.2%. **Exports:** $9.1 bil; U.S. 46.1%, Haiti 17.4%, China 4.2%. **Tourism:** $4.5 bil. **Budget:** $12.1 bil. **Total reserves less gold:** $3.5 bil. **Gold:** 18,296 oz t. **CPI change:** 3.7%.

Transport: Railways: 88 mi. **Motor vehicles:** 140 vehicles per 1,000 pop. **Civil aviation:** 16 airports. **Chief ports:** Puerto Haina, Puerto Plata, Santo Domingo.

Communications: TV sets: 219 per 1,000 pop. **Radios:** 185 per 1,000 pop. **Telephone lines:** 10.5 per 100 pop. **Internet:** 45%.

Health: Life expect.: 75.4 male; 79.9 female. **Births:** 19.2 per 1,000 pop. **Deaths:** 4.5 per 1,000 pop. **Natural inc.:** 1.48%. **Infant mortality:** 20.4 per 1,000 live births. **HIV rate:** 0.7%.

Education: Compulsory: ages 5-13. **Literacy:** 90.1%.

Major intl. organizations: UN (FAO, IBRD, ILO, IMF, WHO), OAS, WTO.

Embassy: 1715 22nd St. NW 20008; 332-6280.

Website: www.presidencia.gov.do

Carib and Arawak Indians inhabited the island of Hispaniola when Columbus landed in 1492. The city of Santo Domingo, founded 1496, is the oldest European settlement in the hemisphere.

France took over the western third of the island in 1697 and Santo Domingo in 1795. Haitian leader Toussaint L'Ouverture seized it, 1801. Spain returned intermittently 1803-21, as several native republics came and went. Haiti ruled again, 1822-44; Spanish occupation occurred 1861-63. U.S. Marines occupied the country 1916-24.

In 1930, Gen. Rafael Leonidas Trujillo Molina was elected president. The brutal Trujillo era ended with his assassination in 1961. Pres. Joaquín Balaguer, appointed by Trujillo in 1960, resigned under pressure in 1962.

Juan Bosch, elected president in the first free elections in 38 years, was overthrown in 1963. On Apr. 24, 1965, Bosch's followers and others, including a few Communists, launched a revolt. Four days later U.S. Marines intervened against pro-Bosch forces. Five South American countries later sent token units as a peacekeeping force. A provisional government supervised a June 1966 election in which Balaguer defeated Bosch. Balaguer remained in office for most of the next 28 years, but his May 1994 reelection was widely denounced as fraudulent. He called for new elections but did not run, and Leonel Fernández Reyna was elected June 1996.

Hurricane Georges, Sept. 22, 1998, claimed more than 200 lives. The leftist candidate, Hipólito Mejía, won a presidential vote in 2000. With the nation reeling from a banking scandal and soaring inflation, Fernández defeated Mejía in a 2004 election. Floods and mudslides in late May killed about 395 people. A fight between rival prison gangs led to a fire, Mar. 7, 2005, in which 136 inmates died. Torrential rains from Tropical Storm Noel, Oct. 28-31, 2007, claimed at least 87 lives. Fernández was reelected in 2008. Danilo Medina Sánchez, Fernández's ally, was elected May 2012 and sworn into office Aug 16.

East Timor
See Timor-Leste.

Ecuador
Republic of Ecuador

People: Population: 15,439,429. **Age distrib.:** <15: 29%; 65+: 6.7%. **Pop. density:** 144.4 per sq mi, 55.8 per sq km. **Urban:** 67.5%. **Ethnic groups:** mestizo (mixed Amerindian and white) 72%, Montubio 7%, Afroecuadorian 7%, Amerindian 7%, white 6%. **Languages:** Spanish (official), indigenous (Quechua, Shuar). **Religion:** Roman Catholic 95%.

Geography: Total area: 109,484 sq mi, 283,561 sq km; **Land area:** 106,889 sq mi, 276,841 sq km. **Location:** In NW S America, on Pacific coast, astride the equator. **Neighbors:** Colombia on N, Peru on E and S. **Topography:** Two ranges of Andes run N and S, splitting country into 3 zones: hot, humid lowlands on coast; temperate highlands between ranges; and rainy, tropical lowlands to E. **Capital:** Quito, 1,622,390. **Cities (urban aggl.):** Guayaquil, 2,286,682.

Government: Type: Republic. **Head of state and gov.:** Pres. Rafael Correa; b. Apr. 6, 1963; in office: Jan. 15, 2007. **Local divisions:** 24 provinces. **Defense budget:** $1.51 bil. **Active troops:** 58,000.

Economy: Industries: petroleum, food proc., textiles, wood prods., chemicals. **Chief crops:** bananas, coffee, cocoa, rice, potatoes, manioc, plantains, sugarcane. **Natural resources:** petroleum, fish, timber, hydropower. **Crude oil reserves:** 8.2 bil bbls. **Arable land:** 4.7%. **Livestock:** cattle: 5.4 mil; chickens: 104 mil; goats: 112,331; pigs: 1.8 mil; sheep: 1.9 mil. **Fish catch:** 817,354 metric tons. **Electricity prod.:** 17.1 bil kWh. **Labor force:** agric. 27.6%, industry 18.8%, services 53.6%.

Finance: Monetary unit: Dollar (USD). **GDP:** $155.8 bil; **per capita GDP:** $10,200; **GDP growth:** 5%. **Imports:** $24.6 bil; U.S. 28%, China 11.2%, Colombia 9.3%, Peru 4.9%. **Exports:** $24.7 bil; U.S. 37%, Chile 8.1%, Peru 7.1%, Colombia 6%, Japan 4.5%, Russia 4.4%. **Tourism:** $1.03 bil. **Budget:** $35.5 bil. **Total reserves less gold:** $1.1 bil. **Gold:** 845,000 oz t. **CPI change:** 5.1%.

Transport: Railways: 600 mi. **Motor vehicles:** 79.9 vehicles per 1,000 pop. **Civil aviation:** 2.5 bil pass.-mi; 104 airports. **Chief ports:** Esmeraldas, Guayaquil, Manta, Puerto Bolivar.

Communications: TV sets: 261 per 1,000 pop. **Radios:** 517 per 1,000 pop. **Telephone lines:** 15.9 per 100 pop. **Internet:** 35.1%.

Health: Life expect.: 73.2 male; 79.3 female. **Births:** 19.2 per 1,000 pop. **Deaths:** 5.0 per 1,000 pop. **Natural inc.:** 1.42%. **Infant mortality:** 18.5 per 1,000 live births. **HIV rate:** 0.4%.

Education: Compulsory: ages 5-14. **Literacy:** 91.6%.
Major intl. organizations: UN (FAO, IBRD, ILO, IMF, WHO), OAS, OPEC, WTO.
Embassy: 2535 15th St. NW 20009; 234-7200.
Website: www.presidencia.gob.ec

The region, which was the northern Inca empire, was conquered by Spain in 1533. Liberation forces defeated the Spanish May 24, 1822, near Quito. Ecuador became part of the Great Colombia Republic but seceded, May 13, 1830.

Ecuadoran indigenous peoples, demanding greater rights, staged protests in the 1990s. A border war with Peru flared Jan. 26-Mar. 1, 1995. Vice Pres. Alberto Dahik resigned and fled Ecuador, Oct. 1995, to avoid arrest on corruption charges. Elected president, July 1996, Abdalá Bucaram—a populist known as El Loco, or "The Crazy One"—imposed stiff price increases and other austerity measures. His rising unpopularity and erratic behavior led the National Congress, Feb. 1997, to dismiss him for "mental incapacity."

Jamil Mahuad Witt won a presidential runoff election July 1998. In Sept. 1998 and Mar. 1999 he imposed emergency measures to cope with a continuing economic crisis. Opposed by Indian groups and military leaders, he was ousted Jan. 2000, and succeeded by Vice Pres. Gustavo Noboa Bejarano. Noboa enacted a plan introduced by Mahuad to replace the sucre with the U.S. dollar as Ecuador's currency. Lucio Gutiérrez Borbúa, a leader in the 2000 coup, won a presidential runoff Nov. 2002. Noboa, under investigation for financial mismanagement, went into exile Aug. 2003.

Gutiérrez imposed economic austerity measures, purged opponents from the supreme court, Dec. 2004, and then dissolved the court, Apr. 15, 2005. With street protests rising, Congress ousted Gutiérrez Apr. 20, and Vice Pres. Alfredo Palacio González became president. The U.S. suspended free-trade talks after Ecuador, May 2006, took over oil assets belonging to U.S.-based Occidental Petroleum.

Rafael Correa, a left-wing economist, won a presidential runoff vote Nov. 2006. After a power struggle with the National Congress, Correa won voter approval, Apr. 2007, to convene an assembly to rewrite the constitution. The revised constitution won overwhelming approval in a national referendum Sept. 2008. Early in his term, when oil revenues were high, he boosted development spending and aid to poor families; later, as oil prices dropped, he restricted imports to prevent an outflow of dollars and, Dec. 2008, allowed Ecuador to default on part of its $10 bil foreign debt.

Correa, reelected Apr. 2009, pressured foreign oil companies in 2010 to renegotiate contracts to increase the government's share of mineral revenues. A confrontation Sept. 30, 2010, between Correa and rebellious police officers led to a shootout between government troops and police: 5 people were killed and at least 38 wounded. An Ecuadoran judge Feb. 14, 2011, ordered Chevron (which had absorbed Texaco in 2001) to pay $9.5 bil to clean up oil pollution from Texaco operations in Ecuador, 1965-92; the plaintiffs and defendants disputed the ruling. Ecuador granted asylum, Aug. 16, 2012, to Julian Assange, the founder of WikiLeaks. Assange had been in Ecuador's embassy since June 19, avoiding extradition to Sweden from Britain. In June 2013, Great Britain and Ecuador agreed to more talks on Assange's possible extradition.

Correa was reelected Feb. 17, 2013, becoming the longest-serving president in the country's history.

The **Galápagos Islands,** pop. (2008 est.) 30,000, about 600 mi to the W, are the home of huge tortoises and other unusual animals. The oil tanker *Jessica* ran aground Jan. 16, 2001, off San Cristóbal Isl., spilling some 185,000 gallons of fuel.

Egypt
Arab Republic of Egypt

People: Population: 85,294,388. **Age distrib.:** <15: 32.3%; 65+: 4.8%. **Pop. density:** 221.9 per sq mi, 85.7 per sq km. **Urban:** 43.5%. **Ethnic groups:** Egyptian 99.6%. **Languages:** Arabic (official), English and French widely understood by educated classes. **Religions:** Muslim (mostly Sunni) 90%, Coptic 9%.

Geography: Total area: 386,662 sq mi, 1,001,450 sq km; **Land area:** 384,345 sq mi, 995,450 sq km. **Location:** NE corner of Africa. **Neighbors:** Libya on W; Sudan on S; Israel, Gaza Strip on E. **Topography:** Almost entirely desolate and barren, with hills and mountains in E and along Nile. The Nile Valley, where most people live, stretches 550 mi. **Capital:** Cairo, 11,169,000. **Cities (urban aggl.):** Alexandria, 4,494,482.

Government: Type: In transition. **Head of state:** Interim Pres. Adly Mansour; b. Dec. 23, 1945; in office: July 4, 2013. **Head of gov.:** Interim Prime Min. Hazem el-Beblawi; b. Oct. 17, 1936; in office: July 9, 2013. **Local divisions:** 27 governorates. **Defense budget:** $4.21 bil. **Active troops:** 438,500.

Economy: Industries: textiles, food proc., tourism, chemicals, pharmaceuticals, hydrocarbons, constr., cement, metals, light manufactures. **Chief crops:** cotton, rice, corn, wheat, beans, fruits, vegetables. **Natural resources:** petroleum, nat. gas, iron ore, phosphates, manganese, limestone, gypsum, talc, asbestos, lead, rare earth elements, zinc. **Crude oil reserves:** 4.4 bil bbls. **Arable land:** 2.9%. **Livestock:** cattle: 4.8 mil; chickens: 108 mil; goats: 4.2 mil; pigs: 10,500; sheep: 5.5 mil. **Fish catch:** 1.4 mil metric tons. **Electricity prod.** 138.7 bil kWh. **Labor force:** agric. 32%, industry 17%, services 51%.

Finance: Monetary unit: Pound (EGP) (Sept. 2013: 6.91 = $1 U.S.). **GDP:** $548.8 bil; **per capita GDP:** $6,700; **GDP growth:** 2.2%. **Imports:** $59.7 bil; China 11.9%, U.S. 8%, Turkey 5.3%, Italy 5.1%, Germany 4.8%, Russia 4.4%, India 4.1%. **Exports:** $26.8 bil; U.S. 8.2%, India 7%, Italy 6.7%, Saudi Arabia 6.3%, Germany 4.4%, France 4.2%. **Tourism:** $9.9 bil. **Budget:** $77.7 bil. **Total reserves less gold:** $11.6 bil. **Gold:** 2.4 mil oz t. **CPI change:** 7.1%.

Transport: Railways: 3,158 mi. **Motor vehicles:** 52.2 vehicles per 1,000 pop. **Civil aviation:** 9.2 bil pass.-mi; 72 airports. **Chief ports:** Alexandria, Ayn Sukhnah, Damietta, El Dekheila, Port Said, Sidi Kurayr, Suez.

Communications: TV sets: 243 per 1,000 pop. **Radios:** 242 per 1,000 pop. **Telephone lines:** 10.2 per 100 pop. **Internet:** 44.1%.

Health: Life expect.: 70.6 male; 75.9 female. **Births:** 23.8 per 1,000 pop. **Deaths:** 4.8 per 1,000 pop. **Natural inc.:** 1.90%. **Infant mortality:** 23.3 per 1,000 live births. **HIV rate:** <0.1%.

Education: Compulsory: ages 6-14. **Literacy:** 73.9%.

Major intl. organizations: UN (FAO, IBRD, ILO, IMF, WHO), AL, AU, WTO.

Embassy: 3521 International Ct. NW 20008; 895-5400.

Website: www.egypt.gov.eg

Archaeological records of ancient Egyptian civilization date back to 4000 BCE. A unified kingdom arose around 3200 BCE and extended south into Nubia and as far north as Syria. A high culture of rulers and priests was built on an economic base of serfdom, fertile soil, and annual flooding of the Nile.

Imperial decline facilitated conquest by Asian invaders (Hyksos, Assyrians). The last native dynasty fell in 341 BCE to the Persians, who were in turn replaced by Greeks (Alexander and the Ptolemies), Romans, Byzantines, and Arabs, who introduced Islam and the Arabic language. The ancient Egyptian language is preserved only in Coptic Christian liturgy.

Egypt was ruled as part of larger Islamic empires for many centuries. Britain intervened in Egypt in 1882 and ruled the country as a protectorate, 1914-22. A 1936 treaty strengthened Egyptian autonomy, but Britain retained bases in Egypt and a condominium over the Sudan. When the state of Israel was proclaimed in 1948, Egypt joined other Arab nations invading Israel and was defeated. In 1951 Egypt abrogated the 1936 treaty; the Sudan became independent in 1956.

A July 1952 uprising overthrew King Farouk and established a republic. Lt. Col. Gamal Abdel Nasser rose to power, becoming premier in 1954 and president in 1956. Nasser soon emerged as the most influential leader in the Arab world; he pushed construction of Egypt's Aswan High Dam, completed in 1970.

After guerrilla raids across its border, Israel invaded Egypt's Sinai Peninsula, Oct. 29, 1956. Egypt rejected a cease-fire demand by Britain and France; on Oct. 31 the 2 nations dropped bombs and on Nov. 5-6 landed forces. Egypt and Israel accepted a UN cease-fire; fighting ended Nov. 7. Subsequently, a UN Emergency Force guarded the border. Full-scale war with Israel broke out again, June 5, 1967; before it ended under a UN cease-fire June 10, Israel had captured Gaza and the Sinai Peninsula and taken control of the E bank of the Suez Canal.

Nasser died Sept. 28, 1970, and was replaced by Vice Pres. Anwar Sadat. In a surprise attack Oct. 6, 1973, Egyptian forces crossed the Suez Canal into the Sinai. (At the same time, Syrian forces attacked Israelis on the Golan Heights.) A USSR military airlift supplied Egypt; the U.S. responded with an airlift to Israel. Israel counterattacked, crossed the canal, and surrounded Suez City. A UN cease-fire took effect Oct. 24. Under an agreement signed Jan. 1974, Israeli forces withdrew from the canal's W bank; limited numbers of Egyptian forces occupied a strip along the E bank. A second accord was signed in 1975, with Israel yielding Sinai oil fields.

Pres. Sadat's surprise visit to Jerusalem, Nov. 1977, opened the prospect of peace with Israel. On Mar. 26, 1979, Egypt and Israel signed a formal peace treaty, ending 30 years of war and establishing diplomatic relations. On Oct. 6, 1981, Muslim extremists within the army assassinated Pres. Sadat, who was succeeded by Hosni Mubarak. Israel returned control of the Sinai to Egypt in Apr. 1982.

Egyptian security forces battled Islamist violence in the 1990s, and Pres. Mubarak escaped assassination in Ethiopia, June 26, 1995; Egypt blamed Sudan for the attack. On Nov. 17, 1997, near Luxor, Muslim extremists killed 58 foreign tourists and 4 Egyptians. Bombs Oct. 7, 2004, in and near Taba (a Sinai tourist site popular with Israelis) killed at least 35 people. Another 88 people were killed in bombings July 23, 2005, at Sharm el Sheikh, a Red Sea resort city.

Pressured by the U.S., Mubarak allowed opposition candidates in the Sept. 2005 presidential election, which he easily won. Suicide bombings at the Sinai resort town of Dahab, Apr. 24, 2006, killed at least 18 people; security forces May 9 killed Nasser Khamis al-Mallahi, leader of the group blamed for the Taba, Sharm el Sheikh, and Dahab attacks. Constitutional amendments expanding presidential powers and barring religiously based political parties were approved Mar. 2007, in a referendum criticized as fraudulent by opposition groups and human rights observers.

Following 18 days of mass protests in which at least 846 people died in clashes between Arab Spring dissidents and Mubarak loyalists, Mubarak surrendered power Feb. 11, 2011. While Islamists and pro-democracy secularists contended for influence, the transitional military regime prepared for elections and charged Mubarak and

associates with corruption and abuse of power. Mubarak was convicted June 2, 2012, and sentenced to life in prison, but the verdict was thrown out on appeal Jan. 13, 2013. The Islamist candidate Mohammed Morsi was declared winner of the presidential election, June 2012. Egypt continued to adhere to the 1979 peace treaty with Israel, but improved ties with Hamas in Gaza and deployed troops to Sinai Aug. 9, 2012, in breach of the treaty, to crack down on Islamist militants. Morsi overhauled the country's military leadership Aug. 12 in what some saw as an attempt to reclaim authority assumed by the military after Mubarak left office. On Oct. 8, 2012, he pardoned select political prisoners detained during the Arab Spring uprising. At least 110 people were injured in violent clashes between Morsi supporters and opponents Oct. 12, and additional conflicts erupted Nov. 23 after Morsi announced an edict interpreted as a power-grab. The proposal of a new Islamist constitution prompted demonstrations throughout Dec.; it passed Dec. 23, 2012.

Violent clashes, Jan. 25, 2013, killed 9 demonstrators and injured more than 400. Protesters firebombed the Muslim Brotherhood headquarters June 30 demanding Morsi's ouster. Six of his cabinet ministers resigned July 1, and the military forced Morsi out of office July 3. Morsi's supporters protested continuously in Cairo and other cities. The military cracked down violently on these encampments Aug. 14, using tanks and live ammunition to drive out demonstrators. More than 600 protesters and at least 40 police officers died in confrontations. Vice Pres. Mohamed ElBaradei, a Nobel Peace Prize-winner, resigned Aug. 14 over what he saw as the government's brutality. The military took over the administration of the country.

The Suez Canal, 103 mi long, links the Mediterranean and Red Seas. It was built by a French corporation 1859-69, but Britain obtained controlling interest in 1875. The last British troops were removed June 13, 1956. On July 26, Egypt nationalized the canal.

El Salvador
Republic of El Salvador

People: Population: 6,108,590. **Age distrib.:** <15: 28.9%; 65+: 6.7%. **Pop. density:** 763.5 per sq mi, 294.8 per sq km. **Urban:** 64.8%. **Ethnic groups:** mestizo 86%, white 13%, Amerindian 1%. **Languages:** Spanish (official), Nahua. **Religions:** Roman Catholic 57%, Protestant 21%, Jehovah's Witnesses 2%, none 17%.
Geography: Total area: 8,124 sq mi, 21,041 sq km; **Land area:** 8,000 sq mi, 20,721 sq km. **Location:** In Central America. **Neighbors:** Guatemala on W, Honduras on N. **Topography:** A hot Pacific coastal plain in S rises to a cooler plateau and valley region, densely populated. The N is mountainous, including many volcanoes. **Capital:** San Salvador, 1,604,650.
Government: Type: Republic. **Head of state and gov.:** Pres. Mauricio Funes; b. Oct. 18, 1959; in office: June 1, 2009. **Local divisions:** 14 departments. **Defense budget:** $144 mil. **Active troops:** 15,300.
Economy: Industries: food proc., beverages, petroleum, chemicals, fertilizer, textiles, furniture, light metals. **Chief crops:** coffee, sugar, corn, rice, beans, oilseed, cotton, sorghum. **Natural resources:** hydropower, geothermal power, petroleum. **Arable land:** 32.1%. **Livestock:** cattle: 1 mil; chickens: 15.5 mil; goats: 15,100; pigs: 440,000; sheep: 5,250. **Fish catch:** 59,165 metric tons. **Electricity prod.:** 6.1 bil kWh. **Labor force:** agric. 21%, industry 20%, services 58%.
Finance: Monetary unit: Colon (SVC) (Sept. 2013: 8.75 = $1 U.S.). **GDP:** $47.1 bil; **per capita GDP:** $7,600; **GDP growth:** 1.6%. **Imports:** $9.9 bil; U.S. 34.4%, Guatemala 10.8%, Mexico 6.8%, Colombia 5.7%, China 5.5%, Germany 4%. **Exports:** $5.4 bil; U.S. 45.8%, Guatemala 14.9%, Honduras 9.6%, Nicaragua 5.8%. **Tourism:** $544 mil. **Budget:** $5.4 bil. **Total reserves less gold:** $2.8 bil. **Gold:** 233,100 oz t. **CPI change:** 1.7%.
Transport: Railways: 176 mi (inoperable because of disuse and costs). **Motor vehicles:** 36.7 vehicles per 1,000 pop. **Civil aviation:** 2.2 bil pass.-mi; 5 airports. **Chief ports:** Acajutla, Puerto Cutuco.
Communications: TV sets: 227 per 1,000 pop. **Radios:** 477 per 1,000 pop. **Telephone lines:** 16.9 per 100 pop. **Internet:** 25.5%.
Health: Life expect.: 70.7 male; 77.4 female. **Births:** 17.1 per 1,000 pop. **Deaths:** 5.7 per 1,000 pop. **Natural inc.:** 1.15%. **Infant mortality:** 19.1 per 1,000 live births. **HIV rate:** 0.6%.
Education: Compulsory: ages 7-15. **Literacy:** 84.5%.
Major intl. organizations: UN (FAO, IBRD, ILO, IMF, WHO), OAS, WTO.
Embassy: 1400 16th St. NW, Ste. 100, 20036; 265-9671.
Website: www.presidencia.gob.sv
El Salvador became independent of Spain in 1821, and of the Central American Federation in 1839. A fight with Honduras in 1969 over the presence of 300,000 Salvadoran workers left 2,000 dead.

A military coup overthrew the government of Pres. Carlos Humberto Romero in 1979, but the ruling military-civilian junta failed to quell a rebellion by leftist insurgents, armed by Cuba and Nicaragua. Extreme right-wing death squads organized to eliminate suspected leftists killed thousands in the 1980s. The Reagan administration staunchly supported the government with military aid.

After taking the lives of some 75,000 people (with thousands more "disappeared"), the 12-year civil war ended Jan. 16, 1992, as the government and leftist rebels signed a formal peace treaty. Rightist legislators in the National Assembly passed a sweeping amnesty Mar. 20, 1993, for civil war atrocities.

Members of the right-wing ARENA party held the presidency from 1989 to 2009. Mauricio Funes, a leftist, won the 2009 presidential election. The right-wing Nationalist Republican Alliance won a majority of congressional seats in Mar. 2012, elections. Remittances from Salvadorans working in the U.S. are a major source of income.

Equatorial Guinea
Republic of Equatorial Guinea

People: Population: 704,001. **Age distrib.:** <15: 41%; 65+: 4.1%. **Pop. density:** 65 per sq mi, 25.1 per sq km. **Urban:** 39.5%. **Ethnic groups:** Fang 86%, Bubi 7%, Mdowe 4%, Annobon 2%, Bujeba 1%. **Languages:** Spanish, French (both official); Fang; Bubi. **Religions:** nominally Christian and predominantly Roman Catholic, pagan practices.
Geography: Total area: 10,831 sq mi, 28,051 sq km; **Land area:** 10,831 sq mi, 28,051 sq km. **Location:** Bioko Isl. off W Africa coast in Gulf of Guinea, and Rio Muni, mainland enclave. **Neighbors:** Gabon on S, Cameroon on E and N. **Topography:** Bioko Isl. consists of 2 volcanic mountains and connecting valley. Rio Muni, with over 90% of the area, has coastal plain and low hills beyond. **Capital:** Malabo, 136,971.
Government: Type: Republic. **Head of state:** Pres. Teodoro Obiang Nguema Mbasogo; b. June 5, 1942; in office: Aug. 3, 1979. **Head of gov.:** Prime Min. Vicente Ehate Tomi; b. 1968; in office: May 22, 2012. **Local divisions:** 7 provinces. **Defense budget:** NA. **Active troops:** 1,320.
Economy: Industries: petroleum, nat. gas, sawmilling. **Chief crops:** coffee, cocoa, rice, yams, cassava, bananas, palm oil nuts. **Natural resources:** petroleum, nat. gas, timber, gold, bauxite, diamonds, tantalum, sand and gravel, clay. **Crude oil reserves:** 1.1 bil bbls. **Arable land:** 4.6%. **Livestock:** cattle: 5,200; chickens: 350,000; goats: 9,200; pigs: 6,500; sheep: 39,000. **Fish catch:** 7,130 metric tons. **Electricity prod.:** 97 mil kWh. **Labor force:** NA.
Finance: Monetary unit: Central African CFA Franc BEAC (XAF) (Sept. 2013: 498.17 = $1 U.S.). **GDP:** $19.6 bil; **per capita GDP:** $26,400 (pop. figures uncertain; per capita GDP might be significantly lower); per capita GDP might be significantly lower); **GDP growth:** 2%. **Imports:** $7.6 bil; Spain 18%, China 17%, U.S. 10.8%, France 7.9%, Côte d'Ivoire 6.7%, Italy 5.8%, Brazil 4.3%. **Exports:** $14.7 bil; Japan 18.8%, France 16.1%, China 11.7%, U.S. 11.3%, Spain 7.1%, Netherlands 7.1%, Italy 5.1%. **Budget:** $6.6 bil. **Total reserves less gold:** $4.4 bil. **CPI change:** 6.1%.
Transport: Civil aviation: 6 airports. **Chief ports:** Bata, Luba, Malabo.
Communications: TV sets: 116 per 1,000 pop. **Radios:** 431 per 1,000 pop. **Telephone lines** 2 per 100 pop. **Internet:** 13.9%.
Health: Life expect.: 62.1 male; 64.2 female. **Births:** 34.4 per 1,000 pop. **Deaths:** 8.6 per 1,000 pop. **Natural inc.:** 2.58%. **Infant mortality:** 73.1 per 1,000 live births. **HIV rate:** 4.7%.
Education: Compulsory: ages 7-12. **Literacy:** 94.2%.
Major intl. organizations: UN (FAO, IBRD, ILO, IMF, WHO), AU, WTO (observer).
Embassy: 2020 16th St. NW 20009; 518-5700.
Website: www.guineaecuatorialpress.com or www.state.gov/p/af/ci/ek/
Fernando Po (now Bioko) Island was reached by Portugal in the late 15th cent. and ceded to Spain in 1778. Independence came Oct. 12, 1968. Riots occurred in 1969 over disputes between the island and the more backward Rio Muni province on the mainland.

Masie Nguema Biyogo, a mainlander, became president for life in 1972. His reign, among the most brutal in Africa, left the nation bankrupt; most of the nation's 7,000 Europeans emigrated. He was ousted in a military coup, Aug. 1979. Teodoro Obiang Nguema Mbasogo, leader of the coup, became president and installed his family members in key government posts. Multiparty presidential elections, held in 1996, 2002, and 2009, were seriously flawed.

Oil sales, especially to the U.S., have boomed in recent years. Foreign investment in the oil sector has been extensive, but poverty remains widespread. Human Rights Watch (HRW) reported in 2012 that the Obiang regime "regularly tortures and arbitrarily detains" suspected dissidents. A referendum on constitutional reforms was overwhelmingly approved Nov. 2011, but HRW reported voter fraud and intimidation. As. of Dec. 2012, Pres. Obiang planned to move the nation's capital to Oyala and finance construction with the sale of oil reserves.

Eritrea
State of Eritrea

People: Population: 6,233,682. **Age distrib.:** <15: 41.3%; 65+: 3.7%. **Pop. density:** 159.9 per sq mi, 61.7 per sq km. **Urban:** 21.3%. **Ethnic groups:** Tigrinya 55%, Tigre 30%, Saho 4%, Kunama 2%, Rashaida 2%, Bilen 2%, other (Afar, Beni Amir, Nera) 5%. **Languages:** Tigrinya, Arabic, English (all official); Tigre; Kunama; Afar; other Cushitic langs. **Religions:** Muslim, Coptic Christian, Roman Catholic, Protestant.
Geography: Total area: 45,406 sq mi, 117,600 sq km; **Land area:** 38,996 sq mi, 101,000 sq km. **Location:** In E Africa, on SW coast of Red Sea. **Neighbors:** Ethiopia on S, Djibouti on SE, Sudan on W. **Topography:** Includes many islands of the Dahlak Archipelago, low coastal plains in S, mountain range with peaks to 9,000 ft in N. **Capital:** Asmara, 711,605.

Government: Type: In transition. **Head of state and gov.:** Pres. Isaias Afewerki; b. Feb. 2, 1946; in office: June 8, 1993. **Local divisions:** 6 regions. **Defense budget:** NA. **Active troops:** 201,750.

Economy: Industries: food proc., beverages, clothing and textiles, light mfg. **Chief crops:** sorghum, lentils, vegetables, corn, cotton, tobacco, sisal. **Natural resources:** gold, potash, zinc, copper, salt, poss. oil and nat. gas, fish. **Arable land:** 6.8%. **Livestock:** cattle: 2.1 mil; chickens: 1.3 mil; goats: 1.8 mil; sheep: 2.3 mil. **Fish catch:** 2,639 metric tons. **Electricity prod.:** 292.5 mil kWh. **Labor force:** agric. 80%, industry and services 20%.

Finance: Monetary unit: Nakfa (ERN) (Sept. 2013: 10.47 = $1 U.S.). **GDP:** $4.5 bil; **per capita GDP:** $800; **GDP growth:** 7%. **Imports:** $1 bil. **Exports:** $434.8 mil. **Budget:** $1.2 bil. **Total reserves less gold:** (2011) $114.8 mil. **CPI change:** NA.

Transport: Railways: 190 mi. **Civil aviation:** 4 airports. **Chief ports:** Assab, Massawa.

Communications: TV sets: 67 per 1,000 pop. **Radios:** 458 per 1,000 pop. **Telephone lines:** 1.1 per 100 pop. **Internet:** 0.8%.

Health: Life expect.: 61.0 male; 65.4 female. **Births:** 31.4 per 1,000 pop. **Deaths:** 7.8 per 1,000 pop. **Natural inc.:** 2.36%. **Infant mortality:** 39.4 per 1,000 live births. **HIV rate:** 0.6%.

Education: Compulsory: ages 7-14. **Literacy:** 68.9%.

Major intl. organizations: UN (FAO, IBRD, ILO, IMF, WHO), AU. **Embassy:** 1708 New Hampshire Ave. NW 20009; 319-1991. **Website:** www.shabait.com

Eritrea was part of the Ethiopian kingdom of Aksum. It was an Italian colony from 1890 to 1941, when it was captured by the British. Following a period of British and UN supervision, Eritrea was awarded to Ethiopia as part of a federation in 1952. Ethiopia annexed Eritrea as a province in 1962. After a 31-year struggle, Eritrea formally declared its independence May 24, 1993. A constitution was ratified in 1997 but not implemented.

A border war with Ethiopia that erupted in June 1998 intensified in May 2000, as Ethiopian troops plunged into western Eritrea; a cease-fire signed June 18 provided for a UN peacekeeping force (UNMEE) to patrol a buffer zone on Eritrean territory. A peace treaty was signed Dec. 12, 2000.

A 2007 UN report accused Eritrea of aiding an Islamic insurgency in Somalia. Citing Eritrean obstruction of UNMEE activities, the UN Security Council ended the peacekeeping mission July 2008. Many thousands have fled repressive conditions in Eritrea, including all 12 players from the national soccer team, who defected to Kenya during a Dec. 2009 tournament. The Eritrean government is suspected of plotting a failed attack against an African Union summit conference Jan. 30-31, 2011, in Addis Ababa, Ethiopia. Four Eritrean athletes sought asylum in the UK during the 2012 Summer Olympics in London. A coup attempt against Pres. Isaias Afwerki failed Jan. 21, 2013, after about 100 members of the army stormed the Ministry of Information and briefly assumed control of the state-run television service before being stopped, presumably by forces loyal to the president.

Estonia
Republic of Estonia

People: Population: 1,266,375. **Age distrib.:** <15: 15.4%; 65+: 18.2%. **Pop. density:** 77.4 per sq mi, 29.9 per sq km. **Urban:** 69.5%. **Ethnic groups:** Estonian 69%, Russian 26%, Ukrainian 2%, Belarusian 1%, Finn 1%. **Languages:** Estonian (official), Russian. **Religions:** Evangelical Lutheran 14%, Orthodox 13%, unaffiliated 34%, none 6%.

Geography: Total area: 17,463 sq mi, 45,228 sq km; **Land area:** 16,366 sq mi, 42,388 sq km. **Location:** E Europe, bordering Baltic Sea and Gulf of Finland. **Neighbors:** Russia on E, Latvia on S. **Topography:** Marshy lowland with numerous lakes and swamps; about 40% forested. Elongated hills show evidence of former glaciation. More than 800 islands on Baltic coast. **Capital:** Tallinn, 400,308.

Government: Type: Parliamentary republic. **Head of state:** Pres. Toomas Hendrik Ilves; b. Dec. 26, 1953; in office: Oct. 9, 2006. **Head of gov.:** Prime Min. Andrus Ansip; b. Oct. 1, 1956; in office: Apr. 13, 2005. **Local divisions:** 15 counties. **Defense budget:** $432 mil. **Active troops:** 5,750.

Economy: Industries: engineering, electronics, wood and wood prods., textiles, information technology, telecom. **Chief crops:** grain, potatoes, vegetables. **Natural resources:** oil shale, peat, rare earth elements, phosphorite, clay, limestone, sand, dolomite, sea mud. **Arable land:** 14.9%. **Livestock:** cattle: 236,300; chickens: 2 mil; goats: 4,100; pigs: 371,700; sheep: 78,600. **Fish catch:** 81,731 metric tons. **Electricity prod.** (2011): 12.2 bil kWh. **Labor force:** agric. 4.2%, industry 20.2%, services 75.6%.

Finance: Monetary unit: Euro (EUR) (Sept. 2013: 0.76 = $1 U.S.). **GDP:** $29.6 bil; **per capita GDP:** $22,100; **GDP growth:** 3.2%. **Imports:** $17.1 bil; Finland 15.1%, Germany 10.7%, Sweden 10.7%, Latvia 10%, Lithuania 9%, Poland 6.6%, China 4.4%, Russia 4.1%. **Exports:** $16.2 bil; Sweden 16.8%, Finland 15.3%, Russia 12.7%, Latvia 9.2%, Lithuania 5.7%, Germany 4.8%. **Tourism:** $1.2 bil. **Budget:** $8.2 bil. **Total reserves less gold:** $287.3 mil. **Gold:** 8,000 oz t. **CPI change:** 3.9%.

Transport: Railways: 743 mi. **Civil aviation:** 223.1 mil pass.-mi; 13 airports. **Chief ports:** Kuivastu, Kunda, Muuga, Sillamae, Tallinn.

Communications: TV sets: 511 per 1,000 pop. **Radios:** 1,200 per 1,000 pop. **Telephone lines:** 33.5 per 100 pop. **Internet:** 79%.

Health: Life expect.: 68.6 male; 79.4 female. **Births:** 10.4 per 1,000 pop. **Deaths:** 13.7 per 1,000 pop. **Natural inc.:** −0.33%. **Infant mortality:** 6.8 per 1,000 live births. **HIV rate:** 1.3%.

Education: Compulsory: ages 7-15. **Literacy:** 99.8%.

Major intl. organizations: UN (FAO, IBRD, ILO, IMF, WHO), EU, NATO, OECD, OSCE, WTO.

Embassy: 2131 Massachusetts Ave. NW 20008; 588-0101.

Website: www.eesti.ee

Estonia, a province of imperial Russia before World War I, was independent between World Wars I and II. The USSR conquered it in 1940 and incorporated it as the Estonian SSR. During an abortive Soviet coup, Estonia, Aug. 20, 1991, declared immediate full independence, which the Soviet Union recognized Sept. 1991. The first free elections in over 50 years were held Sept. 20, 1992. The last occupying Russian troops departed Aug. 31, 1994.

Estonia became a full member of the EU and NATO in 2004. The government accused Russia of orchestrating a cyber attack against Estonia's computer network in Apr.-May 2007. A former high-ranking defense official, Herman Simm, was convicted of treason Feb. 2009, for passing Estonian and NATO security secrets to Russia. Estonia adopted the euro Jan. 1, 2011. On Feb. 20, 2013, it became the first nation to launch a network of fast chargers for electric cars.

Ethiopia
Federal Democratic Republic of Ethiopia

People: Population: 93,877,025. **Age distrib.:** <15: 44.4%; 65+: 2.8%. **Pop. density:** 243.1 per sq mi, 93.9 per sq km. **Urban:** 17%. **Ethnic groups:** Oromo 35%, Amhara 27%, Somali 6%, Tigray 6%, Sidama 4%, Guragie 3%, Welaita 2%, Hadiya 2%, Afar 2%, Gamo 2%, Gedeo 1%. **Languages:** Oromo (official regional), Amharic (official), Somali, Tigrayan (official regional), Sidamo, Wolaytta, Guragiegna, Afar, Hadiyya, Gamo; English and Arabic (both official). **Religions:** Orthodox 44%, Muslim 34%, Protestant 19%, traditional 3%.

Geography: Total area: 426,373 sq mi, 1,104,300 sq km; **Land area:** 386,102 sq mi, 1,000,000 sq km. **Location:** In E Africa. **Neighbors:** Sudan on W; Kenya on S; Somalia, Djibouti on E; Eritrea on N. **Topography:** A high central plateau, 6,000-10,000 ft high, rises to higher mountains near the Great Rift Valley, cutting in from SW. Blue Nile and other rivers cross the plateau, which descends to plains on both W and SE. **Capital:** Addis Ababa, 2,979,100.

Government: Type: Federal republic. **Head of state:** Pres. Girma Wolde-Giorgis; b. Dec. 1924; in office: Oct. 8, 2001. **Head of gov.:** Prime Min. Hailemariam Desalegn; b. July 19, 1965; in office: Sept. 21, 2012. **Local divisions:** 9 states, 2 self-governing administrations. **Defense budget:** $375 mil. **Active troops:** 138,000.

Economy: Industries: food proc., beverages, textiles, leather, chemicals, metals proc., cement. **Chief crops:** cereals, pulses, coffee, oilseed, cotton, sugarcane, potatoes, khat, cut flowers. **Natural resources:** gold, platinum, copper, potash, nat. gas, hydropower. **Crude oil reserves:** 430,000 bbls. **Arable land:** 14.6%. **Livestock:** cattle: 53.4 mil; chickens: 49.3 mil; goats: 22.8 mil; pigs: 32,000; sheep: 25.5 mil. **Fish catch:** 24,066 metric tons. **Electricity prod.:** 4.9 bil kWh. **Labor force:** agric. 85%, industry 5%, services 10%.

Finance: Monetary unit: Birr (ETB) (Sept. 2013: 18.88 − $1 U.S.). **GDP:** $105 bil; **per capita GDP:** $1,200; **GDP growth:** 7%. **Imports:** $9.5 bil; China 13.1%, U.S. 11%, Saudi Arabia 8.2%, India 5.5%. **Exports:** $3.1 bil; China 13%, Germany 10.8%, U.S. 7.9%, Saudi Arabia 7.8%, Belgium 7.7%. **Tourism:** $763 mil. **Budget:** $7.5 bil. **Total reserves less gold** (2009) $1.8 bil. **CPI change:** 22.8%.

Transport: Railways: 423 mi (part of Addis Ababa-Djibouti railway, under joint control with Djibouti, but largely inoperable). **Motor vehicles:** 1.6 vehicles per 1,000 pop. **Civil aviation:** 6.1 bil pass.-mi; 17 airports. **Chief port:** None. A landlocked country, Ethiopia uses ports in Djibouti and Somalia.

Communications: TV sets: 7 per 1,000 pop. **Radios:** 171 per 1,000 pop. **Telephone lines:** 0.9 per 100 pop. **Internet:** 1.5%.

Health: Life expect.: 57.7 male; 62.4 female. **Births:** 38.1 per 1,000 pop. **Deaths:** 8.9 per 1,000 pop. **Natural inc.:** 2.92%. **Infant mortality:** 58.3 per 1,000 live births. **HIV rate:** 1.4%.

Education: Compulsory: ages: NA. **Literacy:** 39.0%.

Major intl. organizations: UN (FAO, IBRD, ILO, IMF, WHO), AU, WTO (observer).

Embassy: 3506 International Dr. NW 20008; 364-1200.

Website: www.ethiopia.gov.et

Ethiopian culture was influenced by Egypt and Greece. Italy invaded the region in 1880, but it maintained its independence until the Italian invasion of 1936. British forces freed the country in 1941.

A series of droughts in the 1970s killed hundreds of thousands. An army mutiny, strikes, and student demonstrations led to the 1974 dethronement of Ethiopia's last emperor, Haile Selassie I, ending his 58-year reign; he died a prisoner of the ruling junta, known as the Dergue, 1975. The junta dissolved parliament, abolished the monarchy, established a socialist state, redistributed land, curbed the influence of the Coptic Church, and violently suppressed opposition.

The regime, torn by bloody coups, faced uprisings by tribal and political groups aided in part by Sudan and Somalia. Ties with the U.S., once a major ally, deteriorated, while cooperation accords were signed with the USSR in 1977. In 1978, Soviet advisers and

Cuban troops helped defeat Somali forces. Ethiopia and Somalia signed a peace agreement in 1988.

A worldwide relief effort began in 1984, as an extended drought precipitated famine; up to 1 mil people died as a result.

The Ethiopian People's Revolutionary Democratic Front (EPRDF), an umbrella group of 6 rebel armies, launched a major push against government forces in 1991, prompting Pres. Mengistu Haile Mariam's resignation. The EPRDF set up a transitional government. Ethiopia's first multiparty general elections were held in 1995.

Eritrea, a province on the Red Sea, declared its independence May 24, 1993. Fighting along the border with Eritrea, which erupted in 1998, intensified in May 2000, as Ethiopian forces entered Eritrean territory; a cease-fire was signed June 18 and a peace treaty Dec. 12. The war displaced 350,000 Ethiopians and cost the country nearly $3 bil.

The ruling EPRDF won parliamentary elections May 2005, but opposition parties made big gains. Police opened fire on antigovernment protesters in Addis Ababa, June 8, killing at least 36; the government arrested some 3,000 dissidents. Police suppression of further protests in the capital, Nov. 1-4, left at least 46 dead. In July 2006, Ethiopia sent troops into Somalia in response to advances by Islamist militias there. Tried in absentia, former Pres. Mengistu was convicted of genocide Dec. 12, 2006. Drought and other food supply disruptions led Ethiopia June 2008 to appeal for $325 mil in emergency aid in 2008 and $175 mil in 2009. Ethiopia withdrew troops from Somalia Jan. 2009. The EPRDF dominated 2010 parliamentary elections, though the opposition contested the results, accusing the EPRDF of voter fraud. When Prime Min. Meles Zenawi died, Aug. 2012, the EPRDF's Hailemariam Desalegn became prime min.

Ethiopia began construction of what will be Africa's largest dam across the Nile, Apr. 2, 2013, receiving sharp criticism from the Egyptian government, which considered the dam a threat to national security and threatened to respond militarily. As of July 2013, Ethiopia housed 240,226 refugees fleeing violence and famine in Somalia.

Fiji
Republic of Fiji

People: Population: 896,758. **Age distrib.:** <15: 28.4%; 65+: 5.6%. **Pop. density:** 127.1 per sq mi, 49.1 per sq km. **Urban:** 52.2%. **Ethnic groups:** Fijian (predominantly Melanesian with Polynesian) 57%, Indian 38%, Rotuman 1%, other (European, other Pacific Islanders, Chinese) 4%. **Languages:** English, Fijian (both official); Hindustani. **Religions:** Protestant 55% (Methodist 35%, Assembly of God 6%, Seventh-Day Adventist 4%), Hindu 28%, Roman Catholic 9%, Muslim 6%.

Geography: Total area: 7,056 sq mi, 18,274 sq km; **Land area:** 7,056 sq mi, 18,274 sq km. **Location:** In western S Pacific O. **Neighbors:** Nearest are Vanuatu to W, Tonga to E. **Topography:** 322 isls. (106 inhabited), many mountainous, with tropical forests and large fertile areas. Viti Levu, the largest isl., has over half the total land area. **Capital:** Suva, 177,316.

Government: Type: In transition. **Head of state:** Pres. Ratu Epeli Nailatikau; b. July 5, 1941; in office: Nov. 5, 2009 (acting from July 30). **Head of gov.:** Interim Prime Min. Vorege (Frank) Bainimarama; b. Apr. 27, 1954; in office: Jan. 5, 2007. **Local divisions:** 4 divisions, 1 dependency. **Defense budget:** $26 mil. **Active troops:** 3,500.

Economy: Industries: tourism, clothing, copra, gold, silver, lumber. **Chief crops:** sugarcane, coconuts, cassava, rice, sweet potatoes, bananas. **Natural resources:** timber, fish, gold, copper, offshore oil potential, hydropower. **Arable land:** 9.2%. **Livestock:** cattle: 312,000; chickens: 3.7 mil; goats: 258,000; pigs: 145,000; sheep: 6,400. **Fish catch:** 42,145 metric tons. **Electricity prod.** 869.1 mil kWh. **Labor force:** agric. 70%, industry and services 30%.

Finance: Monetary unit: Dollar (FJD) (Sept. 2013: 1.90 = $1 U.S.). **GDP:** $4.4 bil; **per capita GDP:** $4,900; **GDP growth:** 2.1%. **Imports:** $1.9 bil; Singapore 32.6%, Australia 15.4%, New Zealand 14.4%, China 10.7%. **Exports:** $991.6 mil; U.S. 13.3%, Australia 12%, Japan 6.3%, Samoa 5.8%, Tonga 5.1%. **Tourism:** $728 mil. **Budget:** $1.2 bil. **Total reserves less gold:** $920 mil. **Gold:** 800 oz t. **CPI change:** 4.3%.

Transport: Railways: 371 mi. **Motor vehicles:** 174.4 vehicles per 1,000 pop. **Civil aviation:** 2.2 bil pass.-mi; 4 airports. **Chief ports:** Lautoka, Levuka, Suva.

Communications: TV sets: 117 per 1,000 pop. **Radios:** 678 per 1,000 pop. **Telephone lines:** 10.1 per 100 pop. **Internet:** 33.7%.

Health: Life expect.: 69.3 male; 74.6 female. **Births:** 20.3 per 1,000 pop. **Deaths:** 6.0 per 1,000 pop. **Natural inc.:** 1.43%. **Infant mortality:** 10.5 per 1,000 live births. **HIV rate:** 0.1%.

Education: Compulsory: ages 6-15. **Literacy:** NA.

Major intl. organizations: UN (FAO, IBRD, ILO, IMF, WHO), WTO. **Embassy:** 2000 M St. NW, Ste. 710, 20036; 466-8320.

Website: www.fiji.gov.fj

A British colony since 1874, Fiji became independent Oct. 10, 1970. Cultural differences between the Indian community (descendants of contract laborers brought to the islands in the 19th cent.) and indigenous Fijians have led to political polarization. More than 100,000 Indians have left Fiji since the mid-1980s.

Military coups have been frequent in recent decades. Fiji's first Indian prime minister, Mahendra Chaudhry, and other government officials were taken captive May 19, 2000, by indigenous Fijian gunmen led by George Speight, culminating in a military takeover,

May 29, led by Frank Bainimarama. Release of the last remaining hostages in July 2000 coincided with the installation of an interim military-backed government. Speight was convicted of treason and sentenced to life in prison in 2002. Prime Min. Laisenia Qarase headed an elected civilian government, 2001-06. He retained his office in parliamentary voting, May 2006, but was ousted in a military coup Dec. 5, and Bainimarama took office as interim prime minister. After a court ruled in 2009 that the 2006 coup was illegal, Pres. Ratu Josefa Iloilo abrogated the constitution, dissolved the judiciary, and reappointed Interim Prime Min. Bainimarama. In July, Bainimarama promised a new constitution by 2013 and legislative elections by 2014; he also named Vice Pres. Ratu Epeli Nailatikau to replace the retiring Pres. Iloilo. In a move applauded by the international community, Bainimarama announced Jan. 1, 2012, the imminent lifting of the state of emergency in place since 2009, which banned public meetings and imposed other limits on civil liberties, but on Jan. 5 he announced new, albeit less severe, civil liberty regulations. Bainimarama accepted a draft constitution released Mar. 22, 2013, and elections were scheduled for Sept. 2014.

Finland
Republic of Finland

People: Population: 5,266,114. **Age distrib.:** <15: 15.8%; 65+: 19.2%. **Pop. density:** 44.9 per sq mi, 17.3 per sq km. **Urban:** 83.7%. **Ethnic groups:** Finn 93%, Swede 6%, Russian 1%. **Languages:** Finnish, Swedish (both official). **Religions:** Lutheran Church of Finland 83%, Orthodox Church 1%, none 15%.

Geography: Total area: 130,559 sq mi, 338,145 sq km; **Land area:** 117,304 sq mi, 303,815 sq km. **Location:** In N Europe. **Neighbors:** Norway on N, Sweden on W, Russia on E. **Topography:** South and central are generally flat with low hills and many lakes. The N has mountainous areas, 3,000-4,000 ft above sea level. **Capital:** Helsinki, 1,133,780.

Government: Type: Republic. **Head of state:** Pres. Sauli Niinistö; b. Aug. 24, 1948; in office: Mar. 1, 2012. **Head of gov.:** Prime Min. Jyrki Katainen; b. Oct. 14, 1971; in office: June 22, 2011. **Local divisions:** 19 regions. **Defense budget:** $3.6 bil. **Active troops:** 22,200.

Economy: Industries: metals and metal prods., electronics, machinery and scientific instruments, shipbuilding, pulp and paper, foodstuffs, chemicals, textiles, clothing. **Chief crops:** barley, wheat, sugar beets, potatoes. **Natural resources:** timber, iron ore, copper, lead, zinc, chromite, nickel, gold, silver, limestone. **Arable land:** 7.4%. **Livestock:** cattle: 914,053; chickens: 5.4 mil; goats: 4,902; pigs: 1.3 mil; sheep: 129,091. **Fish catch:** 165,050 metric tons. **Electricity prod.** (2011): 70.3 bil kWh. **Labor force:** agric. and forestry 4.4%; industry 15.5%; constr. 7.1%; commerce 21.3%; finance, insurance, and business services 13.3%; transp. and communications 9.9%; public services 28.5%.

Finance: Monetary unit: Euro (EUR) (Sept. 2013: 0.76 = $1 U.S.). **GDP:** $200.7 bil; **per capita GDP:** $37,000; **GDP growth:** −0.2%. **Imports:** $73.2 bil; Russia 17.8%, Sweden 14.8%, Germany 13.9%, Netherlands 8%, China 4.4%. **Exports:** $73.4 bil; Sweden 11.1%, Russia 9.9%, Germany 9.4%, Netherlands 6.4%, U.S. 6.1%, UK 5.1%, China 4.6%. **Tourism:** $4.1 bil. **Budget:** $139.8 bil (central govt. budget). **Total reserves less gold:** $8.5 bil. **Gold:** 1.6 mil oz t. **CPI change:** 2.8%.

Transport: Railways: 3,678 mi. **Motor vehicles:** 675.4 vehicles per 1,000 pop. **Civil aviation:** 10.2 bil pass.-mi; 74 airports. **Chief ports:** Helsinki, Kotka, Naantali, Porvoo, Raahe, Rauma.

Communications: TV sets: 679 per 1,000 pop. **Radios:** 1,623 per 1,000 pop. **Telephone lines:** 16.5 per 100 pop. **Internet:** 91%.

Health: Life expect.: 76.1 male; 83.2 female. **Births:** 10.4 per 1,000 pop. **Deaths:** 10.4 per 1,000 pop. **Natural inc.:** −0.01%. **Infant mortality:** 3.4 per 1,000 live births. **HIV rate:** 0.1%.

Education: Compulsory: ages 7-16. **Literacy:** 100%.

Major intl. organizations: UN (FAO, IBRD, ILO, IMF, WHO), EU, OECD, OSCE, WTO.

Embassy: 3301 Massachusetts Ave. NW 20008; 298-5800.

Website: www.government.fi

The early Finns probably migrated from the Ural area at about the beginning of the Christian era. Swedish settlers brought the country into Sweden, 1154 to 1809, when Finland became an autonomous grand duchy of the Russian Empire. Russian exactions created a strong national spirit; on Dec. 6, 1917, Finland declared its independence, and in 1919 it became a republic.

On Nov. 30, 1939, the Soviet Union invaded, and the Finns were forced to cede 16,173 sq mi of territory. After World War II, further cessions were exacted. In 1948, Finland signed a treaty of mutual assistance with the USSR that was renegotiated in Jan. 1992.

Following approval by Finnish voters in a 1994 advisory referendum, Finland entered the EU Jan. 1, 1995. Pres. Tarja Halonen won a second 6-year term in 2006. Former Pres. Martti Ahtisaari was awarded the Nobel Peace Prize, Oct. 10, 2008, for his efforts in mediating international conflicts. Following 2011 parliamentary elections, Jyrki Katainen, leader of the conservative National Coalition Party, became prime minister. The conservative Sauli Niinistö won the 2012 presidential election. Russian military aircraft violated Finnish airspace on May 13, June 11, and June 28, 2013. Russia denied the first 2 incursions but claimed the third was due to bad weather conditions.

Aland, or Ahvenanmaa, constituting an autonomous province, is a group of small islands, 590 sq mi, in the Gulf of Bothnia, 25 mi from Sweden, 15 mi from Finland. Mariehamn is the chief port. **Website:** www.aland.ax

France
French Republic

People: Population: 65,951,611. **Age distrib.:** <15: 18.7%; 65+: 17.9%. **Pop. density:** 266.7 per sq mi, 103 per sq km. **Urban:** 85.8%. **Ethnic groups:** Celtic and Latin with Teutonic, Slavic, N African, Indochinese, Basque minorities. **Languages:** French (official); rapidly declining regional dialects (Provençal, Breton, Alsatian, Corsican, Catalan, Basque, Flemish). **Religions:** Roman Catholic 83%-88%, Muslim 5%-10%, Protestant 2%, Jewish 1%.

Geography: Total area: 248,573 sq mi, 643,801 sq km; **Land area:** 247,270 sq mi, 640,427 sq km. **Location:** In W Europe, between Atlantic O. and Medit. Sea. **Neighbors:** Spain, Andorra, Monaco on S; Italy, Switzerland, Germany on E; Luxembourg, Belgium on N. **Topography:** A wide plain covers more than half of the country, in N and W, drained to W by Seine, Loire, Garonne Rivers. The Massif Central is a mountainous plateau in center. In E are Alps (Mt. Blanc is tallest in W Europe, 15,781 ft), the lower Jura range, and forested Vosges. The Rhone flows from Lake Geneva to Mediterranean. Pyrenees are in SW, on border with Spain. **Capital:** Paris, 10,620,100. **Cities (urban aggl.):** Marseille-Aix-en-Provence, 1,488,596; Lyon, 1,487,507; Lille, 1,042,382.

Government: Type: Republic. **Head of state:** Pres. François Hollande; b. Aug. 12, 1954; in office: May 15, 2012. **Head of gov.:** Prime Min. Jean-Marc Ayrault; b. Jan. 25, 1950; in office: May 16, 2012. **Local divisions:** 22 metropolitan regions, 5 overseas regions. **Defense budget:** $48.1 bil. **Active troops:** 228,850.

Economy: Industries: machinery, chemicals, automobiles, metallurgy, aircraft, electronics, textiles, food proc., tourism. **Chief crops:** wheat, cereals, sugar beets, potatoes, wine grapes. **Natural resources:** coal, iron ore, bauxite, zinc, uranium, antimony, arsenic, potash, feldspar, fluorspar, gypsum, timber, fish. **Crude oil reserves:** 85.2 mil bbls. **Other resources:** Timber, dairy. **Arable land:** 33.5%. **Livestock:** cattle: 19.1 mil; chickens: 150.8 mil; goats: 1.4 mil; pigs: 14 mil; sheep: 7.6 mil. **Fish catch:** 679,879 metric tons. **Electricity prod.** (2011): 530.6 bil kWh. **Labor force:** agric. 3.8%, industry 24.3%, services 71.8%.

Finance: Monetary unit: Euro (EUR); Sept. 2013: 0.76 = $1 U.S.). **GDP:** $2.3 tril; **per capita GDP:** $36,100; **GDP growth:** 0%. **Imports:** $641.3 bil; Germany 19.5%, Belgium 11.3%, Italy 7.6%, Netherlands 7.4%, Spain 6.6%, UK 5.1%, China 4.9%. **Exports:** $567.1 bil; Germany 16.7%, Belgium 7.5%, Italy 7.5%, Spain 6.9%, UK 6.9%, U.S. 5.6%, Netherlands 4.3%. **Tourism:** $53.7 bil. **Budget:** $1.5 tril. **Total reserves less gold:** $54.2 bil. **Gold:** 78.3 mil oz t. **CPI change:** 2%.

Transport: Railways: 18,417 mi. **Motor vehicles:** 581.1 vehicles per 1,000 pop. **Civil aviation:** 94.6 bil pass.-mi (incl. airlines based in territories and dependencies); 294 airports. **Chief ports:** Calais, Dunkerque, Le Havre, Marseille, Nantes, Paris, Rouen.

Communications: TV sets: 861 per 1,000 pop. **Radios:** 043 por 1,000 pop. **Telephone lines:** 61.9 per 100 pop. **Internet:** 83%.

Health: Life expect.: 78.5 male; 84.8 female. **Births:** 12.6 per 1,000 pop. **Deaths:** 9.0 per 1,000 pop. **Natural inc.:** 0.36%. **Infant mortality:** 3.3 per 1,000 live births. **HIV rate:** 0.4%.

Education: Compulsory: ages 6-16. **Literacy:** 99%.

Major intl. organizations: UN and most of its specialized agencies, EU, NATO, OECD, OSCE, WTO.

Embassy: 4101 Reservoir Rd. NW 20007; 944-6195. **Website:** www.gouvernement.fr

Julius Caesar conquered Celtic Gaul 58-51 BCE; Romans ruled for 500 years. Under Charlemagne, Frankish rule extended over much of Europe. After his death, France emerged as one of the successor kingdoms.

The monarchy was overthrown in the French Revolution (1789-93) and succeeded by the First Republic, followed by the First Empire under Napoleon (1804-15), a monarchy (1814-48), the Second Republic (1848-52), the Second Empire (1852-70), the Third Republic (1871-1946), the Fourth Republic (1946-58), and the Fifth Republic (1958 to present).

France suffered severe losses in manpower and wealth in WWI, when it was invaded by Germany. By the Treaty of Versailles, France exacted return of Alsace and Lorraine, provinces seized by Germany in 1871. Germany invaded France again in May 1940, and signed an armistice with a government based in Vichy. After the Allies liberated France in Sept. 1944, Gen. Charles de Gaulle became head of the provisional government, serving until 1946. De Gaulle again became premier in 1958, during a crisis over Algeria, and obtained voter approval for a new constitution, ushering in the Fifth Republic. He then became president.

France withdrew from Indochina in 1954 and from Morocco and Tunisia in 1956. Most of its remaining African territories, including Algeria, were freed 1958-62.

In May 1968, rebellious students in Paris and other centers rioted, battled police, and were joined by workers who launched nationwide strikes. The government awarded pay increases to the strikers May 26. De Gaulle resigned from office in Apr. 1969, after losing a nationwide referendum on constitutional reform. Georges

Pompidou was elected to succeed him. After Pompidou's death, in 1974, Valery Giscard d'Estaing was elected president; he continued his predecessors' conservative policies.

In 1981, France elected François Mitterrand, a Socialist, president. Under Mitterrand the government nationalized 5 major industries and most private banks. After 1986, however, when rightists won a narrow victory in the National Assembly, Mitterrand chose conservative Jacques Chirac as premier. During a 2-year period of "cohabitation," France pursued a privatization program, selling many state-owned companies. During Mitterrand's second 7-year term starting in 1988, he appointed first a Socialist as premier, then a conservative after the center-right won a large majority in 1993 legislative elections.

Chirac won the 1995 presidency in a runoff election. He cut government spending to meet budgetary goals for the introduction of the euro. With unemployment at nearly 13%, leftist parties won a decisive victory in 1997 legislative elections, resulting in a new period of cohabitation, this time between a conservative president and a Socialist prime minister, Lionel Jospin.

Chirac easily won the 2002 presidential election in a runoff, and his center-right allies won parliamentary elections. Parliament gave final approval in 2004 to a law barring the wearing of Islamic head scarves and other religious symbols in public schools.

Displeased with sluggish economic growth, high unemployment, and budget cuts in entitlement programs, voters rejected, 2005, a proposed EU constitution supported by the Chirac government. A state of emergency was declared Nov. 8 after 12 days of riots that began in Paris and spread to some 300 French cities and towns; rioters were mainly young immigrants from N and W Africa. After a wave of mass protests and strikes, Chirac agreed, Apr. 2006, to rescind a law making it easier for employers to fire inexperienced young workers.

The conservative Nicolas Sarkozy won the 2007 presidential runoff election. The French bank Société Générale disclosed Jan. 2008 that it had lost more than $7 bil because of a rogue trader, who in 2010 was sentenced to 3 years in prison and ordered to pay restitution.

Sarkozy responded to the global recession, Dec. 2008, with a $33 bil economic stimulus plan focused on infrastructure development; measures announced Feb. 2009, following labor protests, added $3.3 bil in aid for lower-income people. A French court Jan. 2010, acquitted former Prime Min. Dominique de Villepin of conspiring to smear Sarkozy during the campaign. Sarkozy's policy of shutting Roma (Gypsy) encampments and expelling thousands of Roma to Romania and Bulgaria drew public rebukes from EU allies, Sept. 2010.

France, a founding NATO member, formally returned to the alliance's military command structure Apr. 2009 after 43 years. In Dec. 2012, France withdrew its last combat troops deployed with NATO forces in Afghanistan; about 1,000 remained as of July 2013. France participated in military operations that removed Pres. Laurent Gbagbo from power in Côte d'Ivoire, Apr. 11, 2011, and ousted Libyan leader Muammar al-Qaddafi, Aug. 23.

Former Pres. Chirac was convicted Dec. 2011 of corruption charges stemming from his tenure (1977-95) as mayor of Paris. With France's economy still struggling, the socialist François Hollande won a presidential runoff over incumbent Sarkozy in 2012, while the Socialist Party won an absolute majority in parliamentary elections.

The French entered the conflict between government forces in Mali and Islamist militants Jan. 10, 2013; they quickly overpowered the militants but retained a presence to prevent a resurgence as of Sept. 2013.

Hollande May 18, 2013, signed a bill that legalized same-sex marriage and allowed gay couples to adopt children. Small protests had erupted throughout Apr. as parliament considered the bill, and a large demonstration against it took place May 25.

The island of **Corsica**, in the Mediterranean W of Italy and N of Sardinia, is a territorial collectivity and region of France comprising 2 departments. It elects a total of 2 senators and 3 deputies to the French Parliament. Area: 3,369 sq mi; pop. (2006 census): 294,118. The capital is Ajaccio, birthplace of Napoleon I. Violence by Corsican separatist groups has hurt tourism, a leading industry on the island. Corsicans rejected, 51%-49%, a limited autonomy plan in a referendum July 6, 2003.

French Overseas Departments

French Guiana is on the NE coast of South America with Suriname on the W and Brazil on the E and S. Its area is 35,135 sq mi (total); 34,421 sq mi (land); pop. (2012 est.) 245,000. Guiana sends one senator and 2 deputies to the French Parliament. Guiana is administered by a prefect and has a Council General of 16 elected members; capital is Cayenne.

The famous penal colony, Devil's Island, was phased out between 1938 and 1951. The European Space Agency maintains a satellite-launching center (established by France in 1964) in the city of Kourou.

Immense forests of rich timber cover 88% of the land. Fishing (especially shrimp), forestry, and gold mining are the most important industries. Natural resources include petroleum, kaolin, niobium, tantalum, and clay.

Guadeloupe, in the West Indies' Leeward Islands, consists of 2 large islands, Basse-Terre and Grande-Terre, separated by the Salt

River, plus Marie Galante and the Saintes group to the S and, to the N, Desirade. A French possession since 1635, the department is represented in the French Parliament; administration consists of a prefect (governor) as well as an elected general and regional councils. St. Barthélemy and over half of St. Martin (the Netherlands' portion is called St. Maarten), both formerly part of Guadeloupe, voted for secession in 2003 and became separate overseas territorial collectivities in 2007.

Area of the islands is 525 sq mi; pop. (2011 est., incl. St. Barthélemy and St. Martin) 463,000, mainly descendants of slaves; capital is Basse-Terre on Basse-Terre Island. The land is fertile; sugar, rum, and bananas are exported. Tourism is an important industry.

Martinique, the northernmost of the Windward Islands, in the West Indies, has been a possession since 1635, and a department since Mar. 1946. It is represented in the French Parliament by 2 senators and 4 deputies. The island was the birthplace of Napoleon's first wife, Empress Josephine.

It has an area of 425 sq mi (total); 409 sq mi (land); pop. (2012 est.) 396,000, mostly descendants of slaves. The capital is Fort-de-France. It is a popular tourist stop. The chief exports are rum, bananas, and petroleum products. **Website:** www.region-martinique.mq

Mayotte, claimed by Comoros and administered by France, voted in 1976 to become a territorial collectivity of France. An island NW of Madagascar, area is 144 sq mi, pop. (2012 est.) 216,000. The capital is Mamoudzou. In a Mar. 29, 2009, referendum, 95% of voters endorsed a plan under which Mayotte became an overseas department of France as of Mar. 31, 2011.

Réunion is a volcanic island in the Indian O. about 420 mi E of Madagascar, and has belonged to France since 1665. Area, 972 sq mi (total); 968 sq mi (land); pop. (2012 est.) 857,000, 30% of French extraction. Capital: Saint-Denis. The chief export is sugar. It elects 5 deputies, 3 senators to the French Parliament. **Website:** www. regionreunion.com

French Overseas Territorial Collectivities

French Polynesia, comprises 130 islands widely scattered among 5 archipelagos in the S Pacific; administered by a Council of Ministers (headed by a president). Territorial Assembly and the Council have headquarters at Papeete, on Tahiti, one of the Society Islands (which include the Windward Isls. and Leeward Isls.). Two deputies and a senator are elected to the French Parliament.

Other groups are the Marquesas Islands; the Tuamotu Archipelago; the Gambier Islands; and the Austral, or Tubuai, Islands.

Total area of the islands administered from Tahiti is 1,609 sq mi (total); 1,478 sq mi (land); pop. (2013 est.) 277,293, more than half on Tahiti. Tahiti is mountainous with a productive coastline bearing coconuts, citrus, pineapples, and vanilla. Cultured pearls are also produced.

Tahiti was visited by Capt. James Cook in 1769 and by Capt. Bligh in the *Bounty*, 1788-89. Its beauty impressed Herman Melville, Paul Gauguin, and Charles Darwin. A coalition favoring independence for French Polynesia within 20 years gained control of the territorial assembly after elections May 23, 2004.

St. Pierre and Miquelon became a territorial collectivity in 1985. It consists of 2 groups of rocky islands near the SW coast of Newfoundland, inhabited by fishermen. Fish products are the chief export. The St. Pierre group has an area of 10 sq mi; Miquelon, 83 sq mi. Total pop. (2013 est.) 5,774. Capital: Saint-Pierre. Both Mayotte and St. Pierre and Miquelon elect a deputy and a senator to the French Parliament.

St. Barthélemy and **St. Martin** became overseas territorial collectivities in 2007, with total pop. (2013 est.) of 7,298 and 31,264 respectively.

The territorial collectivity of **Wallis and Futuna** comprises 2 island groups in the SW Pacific S of Tuvalu, N of Fiji, and W of Western Samoa. It became an overseas territory July 29, 1961. The islands have a total area of 55 sq mi and pop. (2013 est.) of 15,507. Alofi, attached to Futuna, is uninhabited. Capital: Mata-Utu. Chief products are copra, coconuts, yams, taro, and bananas. A senator and a deputy are elected to the French Parliament.

Overseas Territory and Special Collectivity

The territory of the **French Southern and Antarctic Lands** comprises Adelie Land, on Antarctica, and island groups in the Indian O. Area: 2,991 sq mi (total); 2,960 sq mi (land).

Adelie, reached 1840, has a 185-mi coastline and tapers 1,240 mi inland to the S Pole. (The U.S. does not recognize national claims in Antarctica.) It has a research station. There are 2 glaciers: Ninnis, 22 mi wide, 99 mi long, and Mentz, 11 mi by 140 mi.

The Indian O. groups are as follows: Kerguelen Archipelago, visited 1772, consists of one large and 300 small islands. The chief is 87 mi long, 74 mi wide, and has Mt. Ross (6,429 ft). Principal research station is Port-aux-Français. There are seals, blue whales, coal, peat, semiprecious stones. Crozet Archipelago, reached 1772, covers 136 sq mi. Eastern Island rises to 6,560 ft. Saint Paul, in southern Indian O., has warm springs with earth at places heating to 120° to 390°F. Amsterdam is nearby; both produce cod and rock

lobster. Military garrisons and meteorological stations are located on the Scattered Isls.

The special collectivity of **New Caledonia** and Dependencies is a group of islands in the Pacific O. about 1,115 mi E of Australia and approx. the same distance NW of New Zealand. Dependencies are the Loyalty Isls., Isle of Pines, Belep Archipelago, and Huon Isls.

The largest island, New Caledonia, is 6,530 sq mi. Total area of the territory is 7,172 sq mi (total); 7,056 sq mi (land); pop. (2013 est.) 264,022. The group was acquired by France in 1853.

The territory is administered by a High Commissioner. There is a popularly elected Territorial Congress. Two deputies and a senator are elected to the French Parliament. Capital: Noumea.

Mining is the chief industry. New Caledonia is one of the world's largest nickel producers. Chrome, iron, cobalt, manganese, silver, gold, lead, and copper are also found. Agric. products include yams, sweet potatoes, potatoes, manioc, corn, and coconuts.

In 1987, New Caledonian voters chose by referendum to remain within the French Republic. There were clashes between French and Melanesians (Kanaks) in 1988. An agreement Apr. 21, 1998, between France and rival New Caledonian factions specified a 15- to 20-year period of "shared sovereignty." The French constitution was amended, July 6, to allow the territory a gradual increase in autonomy; New Caledonian voters approved the plan Nov. 8, 1998, by a 72% majority.

Gabon
Gabonese Republic

People: Population: 1,640,286. **Age distrib.:** <15: 42.1%; 65+: 3.8%. **Pop. density:** 16.5 per sq mi, 6.4 per sq km. **Urban:** 86.2%. **Ethnic groups:** Bantu tribes (incl. Fang, Bapounou, Nzebi, Obamba). **Languages:** French (official), Fang, Myene, Nzebi, Bapounou/Eschira, Bandjabi. **Religions:** Christian 55%-75%, animist.

Geography: Total area: 103,347 sq mi, 267,667 sq km; **Land area:** 99,486 sq mi, 257,667 sq km. **Location:** On Atlantic coast of W central Africa. **Neighbors:** Equatorial Guinea, Cameroon on N; Congo on E and S. **Topography:** Heavily forested, consisting of coastal lowlands; plateaus in N, E, and S; mountains in N, SE, and center. The Ogooue R. system covers most of Gabon. **Capital:** Libreville, 686,356.

Government: Type: Republic. **Head of state:** Pres. Ali Bongo Ondimba; b. Feb. 9, 1959; in office: Oct. 16, 2009. **Head of gov.:** Prime Min. Raymond Ndong Sima; b. Jan. 23, 1955; in office: Feb. 27, 2012. **Local divisions:** 9 provinces. **Defense budget** (2011): $253 mil. **Active troops:** 4,700.

Economy: Industries: petroleum extraction and refining; manganese, gold; chemicals, ship repair, food and beverages. **Chief crops:** cocoa, coffee, sugar, palm oil, rubber. **Natural resources:** petroleum, nat. gas, diamonds, niobium, manganese, uranium, gold, timber, iron ore, hydropower. **Crude oil reserves:** 2 bil bbls. **Arable land:** 1.3%. **Livestock:** cattle: 37,500; chickens: 3.2 mil; goats: 96,000; pigs: 215,000; sheep: 198,000. **Fish catch:** 32,160 metric tons. **Electricity prod.:** 1.8 bil kWh. **Labor force:** agric. 60%, industry 15%, services 25%.

Finance: Monetary unit: Central African CFA Franc BEAC (XAF) (Sept. 2013: 498.17 = $1 U.S.). **GDP:** $25.9 bil; **per capita GDP:** $16,800; **GDP growth:** 6.2%. **Imports:** $3.6 bil; France 28.1%, China 12.6%, U.S. 9.4%, Belgium 5.8%, Cameroon 4.7%. **Exports:** $10.2 bil; Japan 23.9%, U.S. 16.9%, Australia 11.2%, India 7.3%, China 5.4%, Spain 4.1%. **Budget:** $4.6 bil. **Total reserves less gold:** $2.4 bil. **CPI change:** 2.7%.

Transport: Railways: 403 mi. **Civil aviation:** 578.5 mil pass.-mi; 14 airports. **Chief ports:** Gamba, Libreville, Lucinda, Owendo, Port-Gentil.

Communications: TV sets: 161 per 1,000 pop. **Radios:** 217 per 1,000 pop. **Telephone lines:** 1.1 per 100 pop. **Internet:** 8.6%.

Health: Life expect.: 51.6 male; 52.7 female. **Births:** 34.8 per 1,000 pop. **Deaths:** 13.1 per 1,000 pop. **Natural inc.:** 2.17%. **Infant mortality:** 48.0 per 1,000 live births. **HIV rate:** 5%.

Education: Compulsory: ages 6-15. **Literacy:** 89%.

Major intl. organizations: UN (FAO, IBRD, ILO, IMF, WHO), AU, WTO.

Embassy: 2034 20th St. NW 20009; 797-1000.

Website: www.gouvernement.ga or www.state.gov/p/af/ci/gb/

France established control over the region in the second half of the 19th cent. Gabon became independent Aug. 17, 1960. Backed by France, Pres. Albert-Bernard Bongo (later Omar Bongo Ondimba) ruled the country 1967-2009, greatly enriching himself and his family. A multiparty political system was introduced in 1990; a new constitution was enacted in 1991. Bongo's reelection victories in 1993, 1998, and 2003 were faulted by international observers. After he died June 8, 2009, his son Ali Bongo Ondimba, Gabon's defense minister 1999-2009, claimed victory in the disputed 2009 presidential election.

Gabon is one of the most prosperous African countries, thanks to abundant natural resources, foreign private investment, and government development programs. Antigovernment protests in the days before Gabon's independence day celebrations, Aug 17, 2012, were put down with force. Bongo announced Oct. 12, 2012, the country was switching its official language from French to English.

The Gambia
Republic of The Gambia

People: Population: 1,883,051. **Age distrib.:** <15: 39.2%; 65+: 3.2%. **Pop. density:** 487.7 per sq mi, 188.3 per sq km. **Urban:** 57.3%. **Ethnic groups:** Mandinka 42%, Fula 18%, Wolof 16%, Jola 10%, Serahuli 9%. **Languages:** English (official), Mandinka, Wolof, Fula, other indigenous vernaculars. **Religions:** Muslim 90%, Christian 8%, indigenous beliefs 2%.

Geography: Total area: 4,361 sq mi, 11,295 sq km; **Land area:** 3,861 sq mi, 10,000 sq km. **Location:** On Atlantic coast near W tip of Africa. **Neighbors:** Surrounded on 3 sides by Senegal. **Topography:** A narrow strip of land on each side of lower Gambia R. **Capital:** Banjul, 506,277.

Government: Type: Republic. **Head of state and gov.:** Pres. Yahya Jammeh; b. May 25, 1965; in office: Oct. 18, 1996. **Local divisions:** 5 divisions, 1 city. **Defense budget** (2011): $6 mil. **Active troops:** 800.

Economy: Industries: peanuts, fish, and hides proc.; tourism; beverages; agric. machinery assembly. **Chief crops:** rice, millet, sorghum, peanuts, corn, sesame, cassava, palm kernels. **Natural resources:** fish, clay, silica sand, titanium, tin. **Arable land:** 44.5%. **Livestock:** cattle: 398,472; chickens: 900,000; goats: 303,878; pigs: 29,000; sheep: 250,000. **Fish catch:** 45,025 metric tons. **Electricity prod.:** 230 mil kWh. **Labor force:** agric. 75%, industry 19%, services 6%.

Finance: Monetary unit: Dalasi (GMD) (Sept. 2013: 35.32 = $1 U.S.). **GDP:** $3.5 bil; **per capita GDP:** $1,900; **GDP growth:** 3.9%. **Imports:** $360.3 mil; China 27.1%, Senegal 8.4%, Brazil 8%, UK 6.3%, India 6%, Indonesia 4.1% **Exports:** $104.7 mil; China 57.3%, India 18%, France 4.6%, UK 4.1%. **Tourism:** $96 mil. **Budget:** $208.9 mil. **Total reserves less gold:** $236.2 mil. **CPI change:** (2010-11): 4.8%.

Transport: Civil aviation: 1 airport. **Chief port:** Banjul.
Communications: TV Sets: 14 per 1,000 pop. **Radios:** 147 per 1,000 pop. **Telephone lines:** 3.5 per 100 pop. **Internet:** 12.4%.
Health: Life expect.: 61.8 male; 66.5 female. **Births:** 32.6 per 1,000 pop. **Deaths:** 7.4 per 1,000 pop. **Natural inc.:** 2.52%. **Infant mortality:** 67.6 per 1,000 live births. **HIV rate:** 1.5%.
Education: Compulsory: ages 7-12. **Literacy:** 51.1%.
Major intl. organizations: UN (FAO, IBRD, ILO, IMF, WHO), AU, the Commonwealth, WTO.
Embassy: 1156 15th St. NW 20005; 785-1399.
Website: www.gambia.gm

The peoples of The Gambia were at one time associated with the West African empires of Ghana, Mali, and Songhai. The area became Britain's first African possession in 1588.

Independence came Feb. 18, 1965; republic status within the Commonwealth was achieved in 1970. The country suffered from severe famine in the 1970s. Senegambia, a confederation with Senegal, lasted from 1982 to 1989.

On July 22, 1994, after 24 years in power, Pres. Dawda K. Jawara was deposed in a bloodless coup by a military officer, Yahya Jammeh. Jammeh barred political activity, detained potential opponents, and governed by decree. Despite a nominal return to constitutional government in 1996, Jammeh has retained a tight grip on power. Security forces suppressed an alleged coup plot by army officers Mar. 2006. Pres. Jammeh won a fourth 5-year term in 2011. Jammeh announced Aug. 19, 2012, that the 47 death-row inmates would be executed by the middle of Sept. The announcement drew widespread condemnation by intl. civil rights groups, and Jammeh placed a moratorium on executions on Sept 15. With per capita GDP of $1,900 in 2012, The Gambia is one of the world's poorest countries.

Georgia

People: Population: 4,555,911. **Age distrib.:** <15: 15.4%; 65+: 16.2%. **Pop. density:** 169.3 per sq mi, 65.4 per sq km. **Urban:** 52.8%. **Ethnic groups:** Georgian 84%, Azeri 7%, Armenian 6%, Russian 2%. **Languages:** Georgian (official), Russian, Armenian, Azeri, Abkhaz (official in Abkhazia). **Religions:** Orthodox Christian (official) 84%, Muslim 10%, Armenian-Gregorian 4%.

Geography: Total area: 26,911 sq mi, 69,700 sq km; **Land area:** 26,911 sq mi, 69,700 sq km. **Location:** SW Asia, on E coast of Black Sea. **Neighbors:** Russia on N and NE, Turkey and Armenia on S, Azerbaijan on SE. **Topography:** Separated from Russia on NE by main range of Caucasus Mts. **Capital:** Tbilisi, 1,120,690.

Government: Type: Republic. **Head of state:** Pres. Mikhail Saakashvili; b. Dec. 21, 1967; in office: Jan. 25, 2004. **Head of gov.:** Prime Min. Bidzina Ivanishvili; b. Feb. 18, 1956; in office: Oct. 25, 2012. **Local divisions:** 9 regions, 1 city, 2 autonomous republics. **Defense budget:** $391 mil. **Active troops:** 20,650.

Economy: Industries: steel, machine tools, elec. appliances, mining, chemicals, wood prods., wine. **Chief crops:** citrus, grapes, tea, hazelnuts, vegetables. **Natural resources:** timber, hydropower, manganese, iron ore, copper, minor coal and oil deposits. **Crude oil reserves:** 35 mil bbls. **Arable land:** 6%. **Livestock:** cattle: 1 mil; chickens: 6.1 mil; goats: 57,100; pigs: 110,100; sheep: 596,800. **Fish catch:** 27,147 metric tons. **Electricity prod.:** 10 bil kWh. **Labor force:** agric. 55.6%, industry 8.9%, services 35.5%.

Finance: Monetary unit: Lari (GEL) (Sept. 2013: 1.66 = $1 U.S.). **GDP:** $27.1 bil; **per capita GDP:** $6,000; **GDP growth:** 6.5%.

Imports: $6.6 bil; Turkey 13.9%, China 8.2%, Ukraine 8.2%, Russia 7.4%, Azerbaijan 7.1%, U.S. 6%, Germany 5.6%, Bulgaria 4%. **Exports:** $3.3 bil; Azerbaijan 13.8%, U.S. 8.5%, Germany 8.3%, Bulgaria 7.4%, Kazakhstan 7%, Turkey 6.4%, Ukraine 6.3%, Lebanon 5.7%, Canada 4.2%. **Tourism:** $1.4 bil. **Budget:** $4.9 bil. **Total reserves less gold:** $2.9 bil. **CPI change:** −0.9%.

Transport: Railways: 1,002 mi. **Civil aviation:** 369.1 mil pass.-mi; 18 airports. **Chief ports:** Batumi, Poti.
Communications: TV sets: 450 per 1,000 pop. **Radios:** 542 per 1,000 pop. **Telephone lines:** 29.6 per 100 pop. **Internet:** 45.5%.
Health: Life expect.: 74.2 male; 81.2 female. **Births:** 10.7 per 1,000 pop. **Deaths:** 10.2 per 1,000 pop. **Natural inc.:** 0.06%. **Infant mortality:** 14.2 per 1,000 live births. **HIV rate:** 0.2%.
Education: Compulsory: ages 6-14. **Literacy:** 99.7%.
Major intl. organizations: UN (FAO, IBRD, ILO, IMF, WHO), CIS, OSCE, WTO.
Embassy: 2209 Massachusetts Ave. NW 20008; 387-2390.
Website: www.government.gov.ge

The region, which contained the ancient kingdoms of Colchis and Iberia, was Christianized in the 4th cent. and conquered by Arabs in the 8th cent. Annexed by Russia in 1801, Georgia was forcibly incorporated into the USSR in 1922.

Georgia declared independence Apr. 9, 1991, and became an independent country when the Soviet Union disbanded Dec. 26. After a power struggle, former Soviet Foreign Min. Eduard A. Shevardnadze became president. He survived several coup attempts and won reelection in 1995 and 2000. Parliamentary elections Nov. 2, 2003, denounced as fraudulent by opposition groups and international observers, sparked massive antigovernment protests, causing Shevardnadze to resign Nov. 23. Opposition leader Mikhail Saakashvili won the 2004 presidential election. He survived an apparent assassination attempt along with U.S. Pres. George W. Bush in Tbilisi May 10, 2005; suppressed an alleged coup plot Sept. 6, 2006; and cracked down violently on antigovernment protests and imposed a state of emergency, Nov. 7-16, 2007. He called early elections, Jan. 2008, which he won.

Since its independence, secessionist movements in the enclaves of South Ossetia and Abkhazia, supported by Russia, have rejected the Tbilisi government. Open warfare between Georgia and Russia erupted when Saakashvili sent troops Aug. 7, 2008, to suppress insurgent activity in Tskhinvali, the South Ossetian capital. Russia retaliated Aug. 8-9 by dispatching its forces to South Ossetia and Abkhazia and attacking key Georgian cities. A cease-fire signed Aug. 15-16 called for withdrawal of Russian forces from Georgia proper, but allowed thousands of Russian troops to remain in the breakaway regions. On Aug. 26, 2008, Russia formally recognized Ossetia's independence, a step protested by the U.S. and Georgia's other Western allies. International donors Oct. 22 pledged $4.55 bil in reconstruction aid, including about $1.5 bil from EU members and $1 bil from the U.S. Abkhzia's pro-Russian Pres. Sergei Bagapsh died May 2011; his vice president, Aleksandr Ankvab, was elected to succeed him in Aug. Citing voting irregularities, the supreme court invalidated the results of the South Ossetian Nov. 2011 presidential election. Pro-Russian candidate Leonid Tibilov won a runoff election in Apr. 2012. The Georgian Dream coalition, led by Bidzina Ivanishvili, defeated Saakashvili's party in Oct. parliamentary elections; Ivanishvili was sworn in as prime min. in Oct. 2013. Some 10,000 antigay activists led by Orthodox priests attacked a small group of gay rights demonstrators in Tbilisi May 17, 2013, resulting in dozens of injuries.

Germany
Federal Republic of Germany

People: Population: 81,147,265. **Age distrib.:** <15: 13.1%; 65+: 20.9%. **Pop. density:** 602.8 per sq mi, 232.7 per sq km. **Urban:** 73.9%. **Ethnic groups:** German 92%, Turkish 2%, other (incl. Greek, Italian, Polish, Russian, Serbo-Croatian, Spanish) 6%. **Language:** German. **Religions:** Protestant 34%, Roman Catholic 34%, Muslim 4%, unaffiliated or other 28%.

Geography: Total area: 137,847 sq mi, 357,022 sq km; **Land area:** 134,623 sq mi, 348,672 sq km. **Location:** In central Europe. **Neighbors:** Denmark on N; Netherlands, Belgium, Luxembourg, France on W; Switzerland, Austria on S; Czech Rep., Poland on E. **Topography:** Germany is flat in N, hilly in center and W, and mountainous in Bavaria in the S. Chief rivers are Elbe, Weser, Ems, Rhine, and Main, all flowing toward North Sea, and Danube, flowing toward Black Sea. **Capital:** Berlin, 3,462,410. **Cities (urban aggl.):** Hamburg, 1,796,029; Munich, 1,364,324; Cologne, 1,005,901.

Government: Type: Federal republic. **Head of state:** Pres. Joachim Gauck; b. Jan. 24, 1940; in office: Mar. 23, 2012. **Head of gov.:** Chancellor Angela Merkel; b. July 17, 1954; in office: Nov. 22, 2005. **Local divisions:** 16 states. **Defense budget:** $40.4 bil. **Active troops:** 196,000.

Economy: Industries: among the world's largest and most technologically advanced producers of iron, steel, coal, cement, chemicals, machinery, vehicles, machine tools, electronics, food and beverages, shipbuilding, textiles. **Chief crops:** potatoes, wheat, barley, sugar beets, fruit, cabbages. **Natural resources:** lignite, nat. gas, iron ore, copper, nickel, uranium, potash, salt, constr. materials, timber. **Crude oil reserves:** 254.2 mil bbls. **Arable land:** 34.1%. **Livestock:** cattle: 12.6 mil; chickens: 118.6 mil; goats: 160,000; pigs: 26.8 mil; sheep: 2.1 mil. **Fish catch:** 273,024 metric

tons. **Electricity prod.** (2011): 575.6 bil kWh. **Labor force:** agric. 1.6%, industry 24.6%, services 73.8%.

Finance: Monetary unit: Euro (EUR) (Sept. 2013: 0.76 = $1 U.S.). **GDP:** $3.3 tril; **per capita GDP:** $39,700; **GDP growth:** 0.7%. **Imports:**$1.2 tril; Netherlands 14%, France 7.5%, China 6.7%, Belgium 6.4%, Italy 5.5%, UK 4.9%, Austria 4.4%, Russia 4.4%, Czech Republic 4.1%. **Exports:** $1.5 tril; France 10.2%, UK 7%, Netherlands 6.9%, U.S. 6.3%, Austria 5.6%, Italy 5.4%, China 5.1%, Switzerland 4.7%, Belgium 4.3%, Poland 4.1%. **Tourism:** $38.1 bil. **Budget:** $1.5 tril. **Total reserves less gold:** $67.4 bil. **Gold:** 109 mil oz t. **CPI change:** 2%.

Transport: Railways: 26,086 mi. **Motor vehicles:** 572.4 vehicles per 1,000 pop. **Civil aviation:** 127.6 bil pass.-mi; 318 airports. **Chief ports:** Bremen, Bremerhaven, Duisburg, Hamburg, Karlsruhe, Lubeck, Neuss-Dusseldorf, Rostock, Wilhemshaven.

Communications: TV sets: 675 per 1,000 pop. **Radios:** 558 per 1,000 pop. **Telephone lines:** 61.8 per 100 pop. **Internet:** 84%.

Health: Life expect.: 78.0 male; 82.7 female. **Births:** 8.4 per 1,000 pop. **Deaths:** 11.2 per 1,000 pop. **Natural inc.:** −0.28%. **Infant mortality:** 3.5 per 1,000 live births. **HIV rate:** 0.1%.

Education: Compulsory: ages 6-18. **Literacy:** 99%.

Major intl. organizations: UN and all of its specialized agencies, EU, NATO, OECD, OSCE, WTO.

Embassy: 4645 Reservoir Rd. NW 20007; 298-4000.

Website: www.deutschland.de

Julius Caesar defeated Germanic tribes, 55 and 53 BCE, but Roman expansion north of the Rhine was stopped in 9 CE. Charlemagne, ruler of the Franks, consolidated Saxon, Bavarian, Rhenish, Frankish, and other lands; after him the eastern part became the German Empire. The Thirty Years' War, 1618-48, split Germany into small principalities and kingdoms.

Otto von Bismarck, Prussian chancellor, formed the North German Confederation, 1867. In 1870 Bismarck maneuvered Napoleon III into declaring war. After the quick defeat of France, Bismarck formed the German Empire and on Jan. 18, 1871, in Versailles, proclaimed King Wilhelm I of Prussia German emperor (Deutscher kaiser).

The German Empire reached its peak before WWI in 1914, with 208,780 sq mi, plus overseas colonies. After losing the war in 1918, Germany ceded Alsace-Lorraine to France, West Prussia and Posen (Poznan) province to Poland, and part of Schleswig to Denmark. It lost all colonies and the ports of Memel and Danzig.

Republic of Germany, 1919-33, adopted the Weimar constitution; met reparation payments and elected Friedrich Ebert and Gen. Paul von Hindenburg presidents.

Third Reich, 1933-45, Adolf Hitler led the National Socialist German Workers' (Nazi) party after WWI. Pres. von Hindenburg named Hitler chancellor in 1933; on Aug. 3, 1934, the day after Hindenburg's death, the cabinet joined the offices of president and chancellor and made Hitler *fuehrer* (leader). Hitler abolished freedom of speech and assembly, and began a long series of persecutions climaxed by the murder of millions of Jews and others.

He repudiated the Versailles treaty and reparations agreements, remilitarized the Rhineland (1936), and annexed Austria (Anschluss, 1938). At Munich he made an agreement with British Prime Min. Neville Chamberlain, which permitted Germany to annex part of Czechoslovakia. He signed a nonaggression treaty with the USSR, 1939, and declared war on Poland Sept. 1, 1939, precipitating WWII. With total defeat near, Hitler committed suicide in Berlin Apr. 1945. The victorious Allies voided all acts and annexations of Hitler's Reich.

Germany was sectioned into 4 zones of occupation, administered by the Allied Powers (U.S., USSR, UK, and France). The USSR took control of many E German states. The territory E of the so-called Oder-Neisse line was assigned to, and later annexed by, Poland. The USSR annexed Northern East Prussia (now Kaliningrad). Greater Berlin, within but not part of the Soviet zone, was administered by the 4 occupying powers under the Allied Command. In 1948 the USSR withdrew, established its single command in East Berlin, and cut off supplies. The Western Allies utilized a gigantic airlift to bring food to West Berlin, 1948-49.

In 1949, 2 separate German states were established. In May the zones administered by the Western Allies became West Germany; in Oct. the Soviet sector became East Germany. West Berlin was considered a West German enclave, a status the Soviet bloc disputed.

East Germany. The German Democratic Republic (East Germany) was proclaimed in the Soviet sector of Berlin Oct. 7, 1949. It was declared fully sovereign in 1954, but Soviet troops remained.

Coincident with the entrance of West Germany into the European defense community in 1952, the East German government decreed a prohibited zone 3 mi deep along its 600-mi border with West Germany and cut Berlin's telephone system in 2. Berlin was further divided by erection of a fortified wall in 1961, after over 3 mil East Germans had fled to the West. The oppressive Communist regime maintained control through the state security police, known as the Stasi.

By the early 1970s, the economy of East Germany was highly industrialized, and the nation was credited with the highest standard of living among Warsaw Pact countries. Growth slowed in the late 1970s because of shortages of natural resources and labor and huge debt. Comparison with the lifestyle in the West caused many young people to emigrate.

In the late 1980s the government firmly resisted following the USSR's policy of openness (*glasnost*) but was faced with nationwide demonstrations demanding reform. Pres. Erich Honecker, in office since 1976, was forced to resign Oct. 18, 1989. On Nov. 9, the East German government announced its decision to open the border with the West, signaling the end of the Berlin Wall. On Aug. 23, 1990, the East German parliament agreed to reunite with West Germany; this occurred Oct. 3.

West Germany. The Federal Republic of Germany (West Germany) was proclaimed May 23, 1949, in Bonn. The occupying powers, the U.S., Britain, and France, restored civil status, Sept. 21. The Western Allies ended the state of war with Germany in 1951, while the USSR did so in 1955. The powers lifted controls, and the republic became fully independent May 5, 1955.

Dr. Konrad Adenauer, a Christian Democrat, was made chancellor 1949 and was reelected 1953, 1957, 1961. Willy Brandt, heading a coalition of Social Democrats and Free Democrats, became chancellor 1969 and pursued a policy of *Ostpolitik*, or rapprochement with East Germany and the USSR. Brandt resigned May 1974 after a spy scandal. Terrorist acts on German soil in the 1970s included activities of the Baader-Meinhof gang and the murder of Israeli athletes by Palestinian commandos at the Olympic Games in Munich, Sept. 5, 1972.

Helmut Kohl became chancellor in 1982 and led Christian Democrats to victory in 1983 and 1987. In 1990, under Kohl's leadership, West Germany moved rapidly to reunite with East Germany.

Unified Germany. In May 1990, NATO ministers voted to make the united Germany a full member of NATO and barred the new Germany from having its own nuclear, chemical, or biological weapons. The merger of the two Germanys took place Oct. 3, and the first all-German elections since 1932 were held Dec. 2, with West German Chancellor Helmut Kohl confirmed as leader of the unified nation. Eastern Germany received over $1 tril in public and private funds from western Germany between 1990 and 1995. In 1991, Berlin again became Germany's official capital; the Bundestag (parliament) and parts of the federal executive were relocated from Bonn to Berlin in 1999.

Unemployment hit a postwar high of 12.6% in Jan. 1998. The 16-year Kohl era ended with the defeat of the Christian Democrats in parliamentary elections Sept. 27; Gerhard Schröder, of the Social Democratic Party, became chancellor. Germany supplied troops to coalition military operations in Afghanistan (2001).

The Christian Democrats, led by Angela Merkel, won a razor-thin plurality in 2005 parliamentary elections and she became chancellor Nov. 22, heading a "grand coalition" that included the Socialists.

Responding to the global recession, the government passed a 50 bil euro economic stimulus plan in early 2009. Merkel led a center-right coalition to victory in 2009 national elections. Christian Wulff, the Christian Democratic leader of Lower Saxony, became federal president June 2010. After an earthquake and tsunami in Japan caused a nuclear disaster, the Merkel government announced May 2011 that it would close Germany's 17 nuclear power plants by 2022. Merkel and French Pres. Sarkozy led the international response to the European debt crisis involving Greece in late 2009, followed by Ireland, Portugal, Italy, and Spain, which required stern austerity measures in return for aid. But Sarkozy's 2012 ouster and new recessions in several austerity-bound countries cast doubt on Germany's strategy in resolving the eurozone crisis. Merkel's party performed badly in 2012 state parliamentary elections.

A report released Jan 19, 2013, contained information from more than 1,100 people describing themselves as victims of child sexual abuse perpetrated by German Catholic priests over the course of several years. The opposition gained the majority in Germany's upper house of parliament following elections in Lower Saxony Jan. 20, 2013, putting Merkel's reelection later in the year at risk. The Constitutional Court in Karlsruhe, the nation's highest court, affirmed Feb. 19, 2013, gay couples' right to adopt children.

Floods due to heavy rains began afflicting Germany June 3 and caused mass evacuations from cities, including Dresden, Pirna, Magdeburg, and others.

Helgoland, an island of 130 acres in the North Sea, was taken from Denmark by a British Naval Force in 1807 and later ceded to Germany to become part of Schleswig-Holstein province in return for rights in East Africa. The heavily fortified island was surrendered to UK, May 23, 1945, demilitarized in 1947, and returned to West Germany, Mar. 1, 1952. It is a free port.

Ghana
Republic of Ghana

People: Population: 25,199,609. **Age distrib.:** <15: 38.7%; 65+: 4.1%. **Pop. density:** 286.8 per sq mi, 110.8 per sq km. **Urban:** 51.9%. **Ethnic groups:** Akan 48%, Mole-Dagbon 17%, Ewe 14%, Ga-Dangme 7%, Gurma 6%, Guan 4%, Grusi 3%, Mande-Busanga 1%. **Languages:** Asante, Ewe, Fante, Boron, Dagomba, Dangme, Dagarte, Akyem, Ga, Akuapem, English (official). **Religions:** Christian 69% (Pentecostal/Charismatic 24%, Protestant 19%, Catholic 15%), Muslim 16%, traditional 9%, none 6%.

Geography: Total area: 92,098 sq mi, 238,533 sq km; **Land area:** 87,851 sq mi, 227,533 sq km. **Location:** On S coast of W Africa. **Neighbors:** Côte d'Ivoire on W, Burkina Faso on N, Togo on E. **Topography:** Mostly low fertile plains and scrubland, cut by rivers and by the artificial Lake Volta. **Capital:** Accra, 2,573,220. **Cities (urban aggl.):** Kumasi, 2,019,350.

Government: Type: Constitutional democracy. **Head of state and gov.:** Pres. John Dramani Mahama; b. Nov. 29, 1958; in office: July 24, 2012. **Local divisions:** 10 regions. **Defense budget:** $109 mil. **Active troops:** 15,500.

Economy: Industries: mining, lumbering, light mfg., aluminum smelting, food proc., cement, small comm. shipbuilding. **Chief crops:** cocoa, rice, cassava, peanuts, corn, shea nuts, bananas. **Natural resources:** gold, timber, industrial diamonds, bauxite, manganese, fish, rubber, hydropower, petroleum, silver, salt, limestone. **Crude oil reserves:** 660 mil bbls. **Arable land:** 21.1%. **Livestock:** cattle: 1.5 mil; chickens: 52.6 mil; goats: 5.1 mil; pigs: 568,000; sheep: 3.9 mil. **Fish catch:** 352,616 metric tons. **Electricity prod.:** 8.2 bil kWh. **Labor force:** agric. 56%, industry 15%, services 29%.

Finance: Monetary unit: Cedi (GHS) (Sept. 2013: 2.16 = $1 U.S.). **GDP:** $83.7 bil; **per capita GDP:** $3,400; **GDP growth:** 7%. **Imports:** $17.6 bil; China 25.8%, Nigeria 10.9%, U.S. 7%, Netherlands 6.3%, Singapore 4.5%, UK 4.1%, India 4%. **Exports:** $13.7 bil; France 13.3%, Italy 12.1%, Netherlands 8.7%, China 7.2%, Germany 4.2%. **Tourism:** $694 mil. **Budget:** $14.1 bil. **Total reserves less gold:** $5.4 bil. **Gold:** 281,000 oz t. **CPI change:** 9.2%.

Transport: Railways: 588 mi. **Motor vehicles:** 7.5 vehicles per 1,000 pop. **Civil aviation:** 225.6 mil pass.-mi; 7 airports. **Chief ports:** Takoradi, Tema.

Communications: TV sets: 52 per 1,000 pop. **Radios:** 133 per 1,000 pop. **Telephone lines:** 1.1 per 100 pop. **Internet:** 17.1%.

Health: Life expect.: 63.0 male; 67.7 female. **Births:** 31.7 per 1,000 pop. **Deaths:** 7.5 per 1,000 pop. **Natural inc.:** 2.42%. **Infant mortality:** 39.7 per 1,000 live births. **HIV rate:** 1.5%.

Education: Compulsory: ages 4-14. **Literacy:** 71.5%.

Major intl. organizations: UN and all of its specialized agencies, AU, the Commonwealth, WTO.

Embassy: 3512 International Dr. NW 20008; 686-4520.

Website: www.ghana.gov.gh

Named for an African empire along the Niger River, 400-1240 CE, Ghana was ruled by Britain for 113 years as the Gold Coast. The UN in 1956 approved merger with the British Togoland trust territory. Independence came Mar. 6, 1957, and republic status within the Commonwealth in 1960.

Pres. Kwame Nkrumah built hospitals and schools and promoted development projects, including the Volta R. hydroelectric and aluminum plants, but ran the country into debt, jailed opponents, and was accused of corruption. A 1964 referendum gave Nkrumah dictatorial powers and set up a one-party socialist state. A police-army coup overthrew Nkrumah in 1966. Elections were held in 1969, but 4 further coups occurred in 1972, 1978, 1979, and 1981. The 1979 and 1981 coups, led by Flight Lieut. Jerry Rawlings, were followed by suspension of the constitution and banning of political parties. A new constitution, allowing multiparty politics, was approved in Apr. 1992.

In Feb. 1993 more than 1,000 people were killed in ethnic clashes in northern Ghana. Rawlings won the 1996 presidential election. Kofi Annan, a career UN diplomat from Ghana, served as UN sec.-gen., 1997-2006.

Opposition leader John Agyekum Kufuor won a 2000 runoff vote and was sworn in Jan. 7, 2001, marking Ghana's first peaceful transfer of power from one elected president to another. He was reelected in 2004. John Atta Mills, a tax law expert who lost presidential elections in 2000 and 2004, defeated the ruling party candidate, Nana Akufo-Addo, in a 2008 runoff election. A major offshore oil and gas find was announced June 2007; the Jubilee field, estimated to hold recoverable reserves of 1.5 bil barrels, began production Dec. 2010. When Mills died in 2012, Vice-Pres. John Dramani Mahama replaced him. A 9-month-old building in Accra collapsed due to poor construction Nov. 7, 2012, killing 9 people.

Greece
Hellenic Republic

People: Population: 10,772,967. **Age distrib.:** <15: 14.1%; 65+: 20.1%. **Pop. density:** 213.6 per sq mi, 82.5 per sq km. **Urban:** 61.4%. **Ethnic groups:** Greek (citizenship) 93%, other (foreign citizenship) 7%. (Greece does not collect ethnicity data.) **Language:** Greek (official). **Religions:** Greek Orthodox (official) 98%, Muslim 1%.

Geography: Total area: 50,949 sq mi, 131,957 sq km; **Land area:** 50,443 sq mi, 130,647 sq km. **Location:** Occupies S end of Balkan Peninsula in SE Europe. **Neighbors:** Albania, Macedonia, Bulgaria on N; Turkey on E. **Topography:** About three-quarters is nonarable, with mountains in all areas. Pindus Mts. run through the country N-S. The heavily indented coastline is 9,385 mi long. More than 2,000 islands, only 169 inhabited, among them Crete, Rhodes, Milos, Kerkira (Corfu), Chios, Lesbos, Samos, Euboea, Delos, Mykonos. **Capital:** Athens, 3,413,990. **Cities (urban aggl.):** Thessaloniki, 883,017.

Government: Type: Parliamentary republic. **Head of state:** Pres. Karolos Papoulias; b. June 4, 1929; in office: Mar. 12, 2005. **Head of gov.:** Prime Min. Antonis Samaras; b. May 23, 1951; in office: June 20, 2012. **Local divisions:** 13 regions, 1 autonomous monastic state. **Defense budget:** $7.62 bil. **Active troops:** 144,350.

Economy: Industries: tourism, food and tobacco proc., textiles, chemicals, metal prods., mining, petroleum. **Chief crops:** wheat, corn, barley, sugar beets, olives, tomatoes, wine, tobacco, potatoes.

Natural resources: lignite, petroleum, iron ore, bauxite, lead, zinc, nickel, magnesite, marble, salt, hydropower potential. **Crude oil reserves:** 10 mil bbls. **Arable land:** 19.4%. **Livestock:** cattle: 627,000; chickens: 33 mil; goats: 4.8 mil; pigs: 1.1 mil; sheep: 9 mil. **Fish catch:** 213,508 metric tons. **Electricity prod.** (2011): 50.4 bil kWh. **Labor force:** agric. 12.4%, industry 22.4%, services 65.1%.

Finance: Monetary unit: Euro (EUR) (Sept. 2013: 0.76 = $1 U.S.). **GDP:** $281.4 bil; **per capita GDP:** $24,900; **GDP growth:** –6.4%. **Imports:** $53.5 bil; Russia 12.4%, France 7.5%, Italy 7.8%, Saudi Arabia 5.7%, Netherlands 4.7%. **Exports:** $28.3 bil; Turkey 10.8%, Italy 7.7%, Germany 6.4%, Bulgaria 5.6%, Cyprus 5%. **Tourism:** $12.9 bil. **Budget:** $136.4 bil. **Total reserves less gold:** $1.3 bil. **Gold:** 3.6 mil oz t. **CPI change:** 1.5%.

Transport: Railways: 1,583 mi. **Motor vehicles:** 604.9 vehicles per 1,000 pop. **Civil aviation:** 4.7 bil pass.-mi; 68 airports. **Chief ports:** Agioi Theodoroi, Aspropyrgos, Pachi, Piraeus, Thessaloníki.

Communications: TV sets: 556 per 1,000 pop. **Radios:** 464 per 1,000 pop. **Telephone lines:** 47.8 per 100 pop. **Internet:** 56%.

Health: Life expect.: 77.6 male; 82.9 female. **Births:** 8.9 per 1,000 pop. **Deaths:** 10.9 per 1,000 pop. **Natural inc.:** –0.20%. **Infant mortality:** 4.9 per 1,000 live births. **HIV rate:** 0.2%.

Education: Compulsory: ages 5-14. **Literacy:** 97.3%.

Major intl. organizations: UN (FAO, IBRD, ILO, IMF, WHO), EU, NATO, OECD, OSCE, WTO.

Embassy: 2217 Massachusetts Ave. NW 20008; 939-1306.

Website: www.primeminister.gov.gr

The achievements of ancient Greece in art, architecture, science, mathematics, philosophy, drama, literature, and democracy became legacies for succeeding ages. Greece reached the height of its power, particularly in the Athenian city-state, in the 5th cent. BCE. Greece fell under Roman rule in the 2nd and 1st cents. BCE. In the 4th cent. CE, it became part of the Byzantine Empire, and after the fall of Constantinople to the Turks in 1453, part of the Ottoman Empire.

Greece won its war of independence from Turkey 1821-29, and became a kingdom. A republic was established 1924; the monarchy was restored, 1935. In Oct. 1940, Greece rejected an ultimatum from Italy, but the country was defeated and occupied by Germans, Italians, and Bulgarians. By the end of 1944 the invaders withdrew. Communist resistance forces were overcome by Royalist and British troops. A plebiscite restored the monarchy.

Communists waged guerrilla war 1947-49 against the government but were defeated with the aid of the U.S. A period of reconstruction and rapid development followed, mainly with conservative governments under Premier Constantine Karamanlis. The Center Union, led by George Papandreou, won elections in 1963 and 1964, but King Constantine forced Papandreou to resign. A period of political maneuvers ended with Col. George Papadopoulos's military takeover Apr. 1967. King Constantine tried to reverse the consolidation of the harsh dictatorship Dec. 1967, but failed and fled to Italy. Papadopoulos was ousted Nov. 1973.

Greek army officers serving in the Cyprus National Guard staged a coup on the island July 15, 1974. Turkey invaded Cyprus a week later, precipitating the collapse of the Greek junta. Democratic government returned, and in 1975 the monarchy was abolished.

The 1981 electoral victory of the Panhellenic Socialist Movement (Pasok) of Andreas Papandreou substantially changed Greece's internal and external policies. A scandal centered on George Kostokas, a banker and publisher, led to the arrest or investigation of leading Socialists, implicated Papandreou, and contributed to the 1989 defeat of the Socialists at the polls. Papandreou, who was acquitted Jan. 1992 of corruption charges, led the Socialists to a comeback victory in 1993 general elections. Costas Simitis replaced the ailing Papandreou as prime minister, Jan. 1996, and led the Socialists to victory in the Sept. 22 election.

An earthquake shook Athens Sept. 7, 1999, killing at least 143 people and leaving more than 60,000 homeless. The Socialists retained power by a narrow margin in the 2000 elections. Police in 2002 cracked down on the November 17 terrorist movement, blamed for 23 killings since the mid-1970s.

The conservative New Democracy Party won the 2004 parliamentary elections, and Konstantinos (Costas) Karamanlis became prime min. Rampant wildfires, Aug. 2007, left at least 65 people dead and caused over $1.6 bil in damage. On Jan. 23-25, 2008, Karamanlis became the first Greek government leader in 49 years to pay an official visit to Turkey.

Beset by scandals and an ailing economy, Karamanlis called early elections for Oct. 4, 2009, won by Pasok under the leadership of the U.S.-born George A. Papandreou, whose father and grandfather had headed previous Greek governments. The IMF and the 16 eurozone countries agreed in 2010, on a 110 bil euro ($146 bil) loan package to prevent Greece from defaulting; in return, Greek leaders implemented an austerity plan. With default again impending, eurozone leaders agreed July 2011 on another Greek bailout package, for 109 bil euros ($157 bil). The conservative, pro-bailout Antonis Samaras became prime min. of a coalition government, June 2012. The government agreed on a plan for 13.5 bil euro ($23 bil) in budget cuts and austerity measures Sept. 27, touching off a series of often violent protests and nationwide general strikes Oct-Nov. 2012. The measure narrowly survived a vote by the coalition government Nov. 8. The Intl. Monetary Fund, European Central Bank, and eurozone members also agreed to a 43.7 bil euro ($56.7 bil) bailout package Nov. 26.

Grenada

People: Population: 109,590. **Age distrib.:** <15: 24.7%; 65+: 9.2%. **Pop. density:** 825.1 per sq mi, 318.6 per sq km. **Urban:** 39.1%. **Ethnic groups:** black 82%, mixed black and European 13%, European and East Indian 5%. **Languages:** English (official), French patois. **Religions:** Roman Catholic 53%, Anglican 14%, other Protestant 33%.

Geography: Total area: 133 sq mi, 344 sq km; **Land area:** 133 sq mi, 344 sq km. **Location:** In Caribbean, 90 mi N of Venezuela. **Neighbors:** Venezuela, Trinidad and Tobago to S; St. Vincent and the Grenadines to N. **Topography:** Main island is mountainous; country includes Carriacou and Petit Martinique isls. **Capital:** St. George's, 41,054.

Government: Type: Parliamentary democracy. **Head of state:** Queen Elizabeth II, rep. by Gov.-Gen. Cecile La Grenade; b. Dec. 30, 1952; in office: May 7, 2013. **Head of gov.:** Prime Min. Keith Mitchell; b. Nov. 12, 1946; in office: Feb. 20, 2013. **Local divisions:** 6 parishes, 1 dependency. **Defense budget:** NA. **Active troops:** No regular military forces.

Economy: Industries: food and beverages, textiles, light assembly operations, tourism, constr. **Chief crops:** bananas, cocoa, nutmeg, mace, citrus, avocados, root crops, sugarcane, corn, vegetables. **Natural resources:** timber, tropical fruit. **Arable land:** 8.8%. **Livestock:** cattle: 4,450; chickens: 270,000; goats: 7,200; pigs: 3,000; sheep: 13,200. **Fish catch:** 2,322 metric tons. **Electricity prod.** 201.4 mil kWh. **Labor force:** agric. 11%, industry 20%, services 69%.

Finance: Monetary unit: East Caribbean Dollar (XCD) (Sept. 2013: 2.70 = $1 U.S.). **GDP:** $1.5 bil; **per capita GDP:** $13,900; **GDP growth:** −0.8%. **Imports** (2011): $296.3 mil; Trinidad and Tobago 45.9%, U.S. 15.4%, China 4.3%. **Exports:** $36.4 mil; Nigeria 37%, St. Lucia 10.9%, Antigua and Barbuda 7.4%, St. Kitts and Nevis 6.6%, Dominica 6.6%, U.S. 6.1%. **Tourism:** $110 mil. **Budget** (2009): $215.9 mil. **Total reserves less gold:** $119.5 mil. **CPI change:** 2.4%.

Transport: Civil aviation: 3 airports. **Chief port:** Saint George's.

Communications: TV sets: 383 per 1,000 pop. **Radios:** 567 per 1,000 pop. **Telephone lines** 27.1 per 100 pop. **Internet:** 42.1%.

Health: Life expect.: 71.0 male; 76.4 female. **Births:** 16.6 per 1,000 pop. **Deaths:** 8.0 per 1,000 pop. **Natural inc.:** 0.86%. **Infant mortality:** 10.8 per 1,000 live births. **HIV rate:** NA.

Education: Compulsory: ages 5-16. **Literacy:** NA.

Major intl. organizations: UN (FAO, IBRD, ILO, IMF, WHO), Caricom, the Commonwealth, OAS, OECS, WTO.

Embassy: 1701 New Hampshire Ave. NW 20009; 265-2561.

Website: www.gov.gd

Columbus sighted Grenada in 1498. The first European settlers were French, 1650. The island was held alternately by France and England until final British occupation, 1784. Grenada became fully independent Feb. 7, 1974, during a general strike.

On Oct. 14, 1983, a military coup ousted Prime Min. Maurice Bishop, who was put under house arrest, later freed by supporters, rearrested, and executed Oct. 19. U.S. forces, with a token force from 6 area nations, invaded Grenada, Oct. 25. Resistance from the Grenadian army and Cuban advisors was quickly overcome, and U.S. troops left Grenada in June 1985.

Hurricane Ivan slammed into Grenada, Sept. 7, 2004, killing 39 people and damaging an estimated 90% of the buildings on the island. Tillman Thomas of the National Democratic Congress became prime min. after 2008 parliamentary elections. Thomas survived one no-confidence vote May 15, 2012, and avoided another before dissolving parliament Jan. 9, 2013, and calling for new elections. The opposition New National Party won all 15 seats available in general elections Feb. 19, 2013, and Dr. Keith Mitchell was sworn in as prime min. the next day.

Guatemala
Republic of Guatemala

People: Population: 14,373,472. **Age distrib.:** <15: 36.8%; 65+: 4.1%. **Pop. density:** 347.4 per sq mi, 134.1 per sq km. **Urban:** 49.8%. **Ethnic groups:** mestizo (mixed Amerindian-Spanish) and European 59%, K'iche 9%, Kaqchikel 8%, Mam 8%, Q'eqchi 6%, other Mayan 9%. **Languages:** Spanish (official), Amerindian langs. (23 officially recognized). **Religions:** Roman Catholic, Protestant, indigenous Mayan beliefs.

Geography: Total area: 42,042 sq mi, 108,889 sq km; **Land area:** 41,374 sq mi, 107,159 sq km. **Location:** In Central America. **Neighbors:** Mexico on N and W, El Salvador on S, Honduras and Belize on E. **Topography:** The central highland and mountain areas are bordered by the narrow Pacific coast and lowlands and fertile river valleys on the Caribbean. Numerous volcanoes in S, more than half a dozen over 11,000 ft. **Capital:** Guatemala City, 1,168,420.

Government: Type: Constitutional democratic republic. **Head of state and gov.:** Pres. Otto Fernando Perez Molina; b. Dec. 1, 1950; in office: Jan. 14, 2012. **Local divisions:** 22 departments. **Defense budget:** $206 mil.$196 mil. **Active troops:** 17,300.

Economy: Industries: textiles and clothing, furniture, chemicals, petroleum, metals, rubber, tourism. **Chief crops:** sugarcane, corn, bananas, coffee, beans, cardamom. **Natural resources:** petroleum, nickel, rare woods, fish, chicle, hydropower. **Crude oil reserves:**

83.1 mil bbls. **Arable land:** 14%. **Livestock:** cattle: 3.4 mil; chickens: 34 mil; goats: 130,000; pigs: 2.8 mil; sheep: 612,000. **Fish catch:** 41,171 metric tons. **Electricity prod.:** 8.6 bil kWh. **Labor force:** agric. 38%, industry 14%, services 48%.

Finance: Monetary unit: Quetzal (GTQ) (Sept. 2013: 7.99 = $1 U.S.). **GDP:** $80 bil; **per capita GDP:** $5,300; **GDP growth:** 3%. **Imports:** $15.8 bil; U.S. 38.4%, Mexico 11.9%, China 8.3%, El Salvador 5.1%, Colombia 4.2%. **Exports:** $10.1 bil; U.S. 39.2%, El Salvador 11.4%, Honduras 6.8%, Mexico 5.4%, Nicaragua 4%. **Tourism:** $1.4 bil. **Budget:** $7.1 bil. **Total reserves less gold:** $6.3 bil. **Gold:** 221,600 oz t. **CPI change:** 3.8%.

Transport: Railways: 206 mi. **Motor vehicles:** 118.7 vehicles per 1,000 pop. **Civil aviation:** 16 airports. **Chief ports:** Puerto Quetzal, Santo Tomas de Castilla.

Communications: TV sets: 163 per 1,000 pop. **Radios:** 80 per 1,000 pop. **Telephone lines:** 11.5 per 100 pop. **Internet:** 16%.

Health: Life expect.: 69.6 male; 73.5 female. **Births:** 26.0 per 1,000 pop. **Deaths:** 4.9 per 1,000 pop. **Natural inc.:** 2.11%. **Infant mortality:** 24.3 per 1,000 live births. **HIV rate:** 0.8%.

Education: Compulsory: ages 6-15. **Literacy:** 75.9%.

Major intl. organizations: UN (FAO, IBRD, ILO, IMF, WHO), OAS, WTO.

Embassy: 2220 R St. NW 20008; 745-4952.

Website: www.guatemala.gob.gt

A Mayan Indian empire flourished in what is today Guatemala for over 1,000 years before Spaniards came. Guatemala was a Spanish colony 1524-1821. A republic was established in 1839.

The U.S. intervened in Guatemala in 1954 when the Central Intelligence Agency engineered the overthrow of elected Pres. Jacobo Arbenz Guzmán, a left-wing reformer. Since then, the country has experienced a variety of military and civilian governments and periods of insurgency, repression, paramilitary violence, and civil war. After military coups in 1982 and 1983, the nation returned to civilian rule in 1986.

On Sept. 19, 1996, the Guatemalan government and leftist rebels approved a peace accord; the final agreement was signed Dec. 29. During more than 35 years of armed conflict, some 200,000 people were killed or "disappeared" (and are presumed dead); most of these casualties were attributed to the government and its paramilitary allies. U.S. Pres. Bill Clinton, on a Mar. 1999 visit to Guatemala, apologized for aid the U.S. had given to forces which he said "engaged in violence and widespread repression."

Drought and weak export prices during 2001-02 worsened the plight of Guatemala's poor, who comprise 80% of the population. Floods and mudslides from Tropical Storm Stan, Oct. 2005, killed at least 669 people; another 844 were missing and presumed dead.

After a campaign marred by violence, Álvaro Colom Caballeros, a businessman who pledged to fight poverty, won a 2007 presidential runoff election and took office Jan. 2008. Floods and landslides from Tropical Storm Agatha, which hit Guatemala May 29, 2010, killed more than 170 people. With Pres. Colom and his relatives constitutionally barred from running in the Sept. 2011 presidential election, his wife, Sandra Torres de Colom, declared her candidacy Mar. 8 and filed for divorce 3 days later, saying she was "getting married to the Guatemalan people." Her bid was blocked by the courts. Former Gen. Otto Pérez Molina won a runoff election Nov. 6 and took office, Jan. 2012. Gen. Efraín Ríos Montt, dictator for 17 months, 1982-83, was found guilty of genocide and sentenced to 80 years in prison May 10, 2013, but the Constitutional Court overturned his conviction May 20 and ruled that part of his trial had to be repeated. Former Pres. Alfonso Portillo was extradited to the U.S. May 24 to be tried for money laundering. Drug trafficking, arms smuggling, police corruption, and one of the world's highest homicide rates pose threats to national stability.

Guinea
Republic of Guinea

People: Population: 11,176,026. **Age distrib.:** <15: 42.2%; 65+: 3.6%. **Pop. density:** 117.8 per sq mi, 45.5 per sq km. **Urban:** 35.4%. **Ethnic groups:** Peuhl 40%, Malinke 30%, Soussou 20%, smaller ethnic groups 10%. **Languages:** French (official), ethnic group-specific langs. **Religions:** Muslim 85%, Christian 8%, indigenous beliefs 7%.

Geography: Total area: 94,926 sq mi, 245,857 sq km; **Land area:** 94,872 sq mi, 245,717 sq km. **Location:** On Atlantic coast of W Africa. **Neighbors:** Guinea-Bissau, Senegal, Mali on N; Côte d'Ivoire on E; Liberia, Sierra Leone on S. **Topography:** A narrow coastal belt leads to mountainous middle region, source of the Gambia, Senegal, and Niger rivers. Upper Guinea, farther inland, is cooler upland. The SE is forested. **Capital:** Conakry, 1,786,300.

Government: Type: Republic. **Head of state:** Pres. Alpha Condé; b. Mar. 4, 1938; in office: Dec. 21, 2010. **Head of gov.:** Prime Min. Mohamed Said Fofana; b. 1952; in office: Dec. 24, 2010. **Local divisions:** 7 regions, 1 governate. **Defense budget** (2011): $42 mil. **Active troops:** 9,700.

Economy: Industries: bauxite, gold, diamonds, iron; alumina refining; light mfg.; agric. proc. **Chief crops:** rice, coffee, pineapples, palm kernels, cassava, bananas, sweet potatoes. **Natural resources:** bauxite, iron ore, diamonds, gold, uranium, hydropower, fish, salt. **Arable land:** 11.6%. **Livestock:** cattle: 4.7 mil; chickens: 15.1 mil; goats: 1.8 mil; pigs: 91,000; sheep: 1.4 mil. **Fish catch:**

115,020 metric tons. **Electricity prod.:** 969 mil kWh. **Labor force:** agric. 76%, industry and services 24%.
Finance: Monetary unit: Franc (GNF) (Sept. 2013: 7,020.99 = $1 U.S.). **GDP:** $12.4 bil; **per capita GDP:** $1,100; **GDP growth:** 3.9%. **Imports:** $2.6 bil; China 14%, Netherlands 7.6%. **Exports:** $1.3 bil; India 10.3%, Spain 9.2%, Chile 9%, U.S. 6.9%, Germany 6.1%, Ireland 6%, Ukraine 5.5%, France 4.8%. **Tourism:** $2 mil. **Budget:** $1.6 bil. **Total reserves less gold** (2011): $103.2 mil. **Gold** (2011): 7,107 oz t. **CPI change:** 15.2%.
Transport: Railways: 736 mi. **Civil aviation:** 4 airports. **Chief ports:** Conakry, Kamsar.
Communications: TV sets: 18 per 1,000 pop. **Radios:** 81 per 1,000 pop. **Telephone lines:** 0.2 per 100 pop. **Internet:** 1.5%.
Health: Life expect.: 57.6 male; 60.7 female. **Births:** 36.3 per 1,000 pop. **Deaths:** 9.9 per 1,000 pop. **Natural inc.:** 2.64%. **Infant mortality:** 57.1 per 1,000 live births. **HIV rate:** 1.4%.
Education: Compulsory: ages 7-16. **Literacy:** 25.3%.
Major intl. organizations: UN and most of its specialized agencies, AU, WTO.
Embassy: 2112 Leroy Pl. NW 20008; 906-4300.
Website: www.state.gov/p/af/ci/gv/
Guinea, a French colony, attained independence Oct. 2, 1958. Sékou Touré, Guinea's first president (1958-84), turned to Communist nations for support and set up a one-party state. Thousands of opponents were jailed and tortured, and many were killed in the 1970s after an unsuccessful Portuguese invasion.
The military took control in a bloodless coup after the Mar. 1984 death of Touré. A new constitution was approved in 1991, but movement toward democracy was slow. Gen. Lansana Conté, the incumbent, won long-awaited presidential election in Dec. 1993, which outside monitors called flawed. Conté suppressed an army mutiny in Conakry, Feb. 2-3, 1996, and won reelection in 1998. Fighting in early 2001 along the border with Liberia and Sierra Leone created a refugee crisis in Guinea; voluntary repatriation of more than 51,000 Liberian refugees was largely completed in 2007.
Major opposition parties boycotted the 2003 presidential election, in which the ailing Conté won 95.6% of the vote. More than 120 died in Jan.-Feb. 2007 strikes and protests that pressured Conté to name a new prime min. from a union-leader approved list; protests followed his ouster by Conté in May 2008. After Conté's death Dec. 22, a military junta took power, calling itself the National Council for Democracy and Development. More than 150 people were reportedly killed Sept. 28, 2009, when Guinean troops fired into a crowd of about 50,000 antigovernment protesters in Conakry. After an assassination attempt Dec. 3, 2009, by a former aide left Pres. Moussa Dadis Camara seriously wounded, Vice Pres. Sékouba Konaté became interim head of state. Presidential elections June-Nov. 2010 brought a civilian government headed by Alpha Condé to power Dec. 21. He survived an assassination attempt, July 19, 2011, but was criticized for postponing elections. Election delays continued, prompting frequent demonstrations in Conakry and resulting in the deaths of 4 protesters Sept. 27, 2011, and 50 deaths in spring 2013. Elections were scheduled to be held Sept. 24, 2013.

Guinea-Bissau
Republic of Guinea-Bissau

People: Population: 1,660,870. **Age distrib.:** <15: 40%; 65+: 3.2%. **Pop. density:** 153 per sq mi, 59.1 per sq km. **Urban:** 43.9%. **Ethnic groups:** African 99% (incl. Balanta 30%, Fula 20%, Manjaca 14%, Mandinga 13%, Papel 7%). **Languages:** Portuguese (official), Crioulo, African langs. **Religions:** Muslim 50%, indigenous beliefs 40%, Christian 10%.
Geography: Total area: 13,948 sq mi, 36,125 sq km; **Land area:** 10,857 sq mi, 28,120 sq km. **Location:** On Atlantic coast of W Africa. **Neighbors:** Senegal on N, Guinea on E and S. **Topography:** A swampy coastal plain covers most of country; to E is a low savanna region. **Capital:** Bissau, 422,811.
Government: Type: Republic. **Head of state:** Pres. Manuel Serifo Nhamadjo; b. 1958; in office: May 11, 2012. **Head of gov.:** Prime Min. Rui Duarte Barros; in office: May 16, 2012. **Local divisions:** 9 regions. **Defense budget:** $25 mil. **Active troops:** 4,450.
Economy: Industries: agric. prods. proc., beer, soft drinks. **Chief crops:** rice, corn, beans, cassava, cashew nuts, peanuts, palm kernels, cotton. **Natural resources:** fish, timber, phosphates, bauxite, clay, granite, limestone, unexploited deposits of petroleum. **Arable land:** 10.7%. **Livestock:** cattle: 650,000; chickens: 1.7 mil; goats: 731,716; pigs: 462,025; sheep: 460,000. **Fish catch:** 6,750 metric tons. **Electricity prod.:** 67 mil kWh. **Labor force:** agric. 82%, industry and services 18%.
Finance: Monetary unit: West African CFA Franc (XOF) (Sept. 2013: 498.17 = $1 U.S.). **GDP:** $2 bil; **per capita GDP:** $1,200; **GDP growth:** –1.5%. **Imports:** $237 mil; Portugal 27.8%, Senegal 16.8%, U.S. 7.1%, China 4.8%, Cuba 4.2%. **Exports:** $139.8 mil; India 56%, Nigeria 28.4%, Togo 6.6%. **Tourism:** $13 mil. **Budget:** $153.4 mil. **Total reserves less gold:** $164.6 mil. **CPI change:** 2.1%.
Transport: Civil aviation: 2 airports. **Chief ports:** Bissau, Buba, Cacheu, Farim.
Communications: TV sets: 39 per 1,000 pop. **Radios:** 41 per 1,000 pop. **Telephone lines** 0.3 per 100 pop. **Internet:** 2.9%.

Health: Life expect.: 47.5 male; 51.5 female. **Births:** 34.3 per 1,000 pop. **Deaths:** 14.8 per 1,000 pop. **Natural inc.:** 1.95%. **Infant mortality:** 92.7 per 1,000 live births. **HIV rate:** 2.5%.
Education: Compulsory: ages 6-11. **Literacy:** 55.3%.
Major intl. organizations: UN (FAO, IBRD, ILO, IMF, WHO), AU, WTO.
Permanent UN Mission: 800 Second Ave., Ste. 400F, New York, NY 10017; (917) 770-5598.
Website: www.state.gov/p/af/ci/pu/
Portuguese mariners explored the area in the mid-15th cent.; the slave trade flourished in the 17th and 18th cents., and colonization began in the 19th. Independence came Sept. 10, 1974, ending 13 years of guerrilla warfare against the Portuguese regime.
A Nov. 1980 coup gave army chief João Bernardo Vieira absolute power. Vieira eventually initiated political liberalization; multiparty elections were held in 1994. A 1998 army uprising triggered a civil war, with Senegal and Guinea aiding the Vieira regime. After a peace accord signed Nov. 2 broke down, rebel troops ousted Vieira on May 7, 1999.
Civilian rule returned with 1999-2000 elections, but top military officers staged a coup Sept. 14, 2003. Vieira won a presidential runoff election, July 24, 2005, and returned to power Oct. 1. Gen. Batista Tagme Na Waie, the nation's defense chief, was killed by a bomb Mar. 1, 2009; less than a day later, a group of soldiers murdered Vieira in his presidential palace. Political violence continued as the 2009 presidential election approached; the ruling party candidate, Malam Bacai Sanhá, won a runoff vote July 26. He died Jan. 9, 2012. A military coup Apr. 12 derailed a runoff election scheduled for Apr. 29. The military appointed Manuel Serifo Nhamadjo to serve as pres. of a transitional government. Drug trafficking increased substantially in the country with the support of the military, and the U.S. arrested and indicted Rear Adm. Jose Americo Bubo Na Tchuto and 4 other men on drug charges Apr. 5, 2013.

Guyana
Cooperative Republic of Guyana

People: Population: 739,903. **Age distrib.:** <15: 30.2%; 65+: 5.1%. **Pop. density:** 9.7 per sq mi, 3.8 per sq km. **Urban:** 28.4%. **Ethnic groups:** East Indian 44%, black (African) 30%, mixed 17%, Amerindian 9%. **Languages:** English, Amerindian dialects, Creole, Caribbean Hindustani, Urdu. **Religions:** Protestant 31% (Pentecostal 17%, Anglican 7%, Seventh-Day Adventist 5%, Methodist 2%), Hindu 28%, Roman Catholic 8%, Muslim 7%, Anglican 7%, Seventh-Day Adventist 5%, Methodist 2%, Jehovah's Witnesses 1%, other Christian 18%, none 4%.
Geography: Total area: 83,000 sq mi, 214,969 sq km; **Land area:** 76,004 sq mi, 196,849 sq km. **Location:** On N coast of S America. **Neighbors:** Venezuela on W, Brazil on S, Suriname on E. **Topography:** Dense tropical forests cover much of land, although flat coastal area up to 40 mi wide, where 90% of the population lives, provides rich alluvial soil for agriculture. A grassy savanna divides the 2 zones. **Capital:** Georgetown, 127,150.
Government: Type: Republic. **Head of state:** Pres. Donald Rabrindranath Ramotar; b. Oct. 22, 1950; in office: Dec. 3, 2011. **Head of gov.:** Prime Min. Samuel Hinds; b. Dec. 27, 1943; in office: Dec. 19, 1997. **Local divisions:** 10 regions. **Defense budget:** $31 mil. **Active troops:** 1,100.
Economy: Industries: bauxite, rice milling, timber, textiles, gold mining. **Chief crops:** sugarcane, rice, edible oils. **Natural resources:** bauxite, gold, diamonds, timber, shrimp, fish. **Arable land:** 2.1%. **Livestock:** cattle: 112,800; chickens: 22 mil; goats: 81,000; pigs: 13,650; sheep: 131,000. **Fish catch:** 43,448 metric tons. **Electricity prod.:** 700 mil kWh. **Labor force:** NA.
Finance: Monetary unit: Dollar (GYD) (Sept. 2013: 202.95 = $1 U.S.). **GDP:** $6.3 bil; **per capita GDP:** $8,100; **GDP growth:** 3.3%. **Imports:** $2.1 bil; Trinidad and Tobago 23.2%, U.S. 21.3%, China 11.8%, Cuba 6.4%, Suriname 4.3%. **Exports:** $1.3 bil; U.S. 29.7%, Canada 27.8%, UK 5.9%, Trinidad and Tobago 4.2%, Jamaica 4.1%. **Tourism:** $80 mil. **Budget:** $806.4 mil. **Total reserves less gold:** $864 mil. **CPI change:** 2.4%.
Transport: Motor vehicles: 71.3 vehicles per 1,000 pop. **Civil aviation:** 11 airports. **Chief port:** Georgetown.
Communications: TV sets: 167 per 1,000 pop. **Radios:** 571 per 1,000 pop. **Telephone lines:** 20.4 per 100 pop. **Internet:** 34.3%.
Health: Life expect.: 63.8 male; 71.7 female. **Births:** 16.3 per 1,000 pop. **Deaths:** 7.2 per 1,000 pop. **Natural inc.:** 0.91%. **Infant mortality:** 34.5 per 1,000 live births. **HIV rate:** 1.1%.
Education: Compulsory: ages 6-14. **Literacy:** 85%.
Major intl. organizations: UN (FAO, IBRD, ILO, IMF, WHO), Caricom, the Commonwealth, OAS, WTO.
Embassy: 2490 Tracy Pl. NW 20008; 265-6900.
Website: www.gina.gov.gy
Guyana became a Dutch possession in the 17th cent., but sovereignty passed to Britain in 1815. Indentured servants from India soon outnumbered African slaves. Guyana became independent May 26, 1966.
The Port Kaituma ambush of U.S. Rep. Leo J. Ryan and others investigating mistreatment of American followers of the Rev. Jim Jones's People's Temple cult triggered a mass suicide-execution of 911 cultists at Jonestown in the jungle, Nov. 18, 1978.

The People's National Congress, the party in power since Guyana became independent, was voted out of office with the election of Cheddi Jagan in Oct. 1992. When Pres. Jagan died Mar. 6, 1997, Prime Min. Samuel Hinds succeeded him. Jagan's widow, Janet, became prime min. Mar. 17. She won the presidency in a disputed election Dec. 15. She resigned because of ill health Aug. 1999 and was succeeded by Bharrat Jagdeo, then 35, who became the youngest head of state in the Americas. He won reelection in 2001 and 2006.

Floods from torrential rains, Jan. 2005, affected about 40% of the population. Gunmen in Georgetown killed Agric. Min. Satyadeow Sawh and 2 members of his family, Apr. 22, 2006. Donald Ramotar, the candidate of Jagdeo's party, was elected president in 2011. On June 12, 2013, Guyana was among 38 countries that met a UN challenge to reduce hunger in their countries by half.

Haiti
Republic of Haiti

People: Population: 9,893,934. **Age distrib.:** <15: 34.6%; 65+: 4.1%. **Pop. density:** 929.8 per sq mi, 359 per sq km. **Urban:** 53.4%. **Ethnic groups:** black 95%, mulatto and white 5%. **Languages:** French, Creole (both official). **Religions:** Roman Catholic 80%, Protestant 16% (Baptist 10%, Pentecostal 4%); roughly half of pop. practices voodoo.

Geography: Total area: 10,714 sq mi, 27,750 sq km; **Land area:** 10,641 sq mi, 27,560 sq km. **Location:** In Caribbean, occupies W third of isl. of Hispaniola. **Neighbors:** Dominican Republic on E, Cuba to W. **Topography:** About two-thirds is mountainous. Much of rest is semiarid. Coastal areas are warm and moist. **Capital:** Port-au-Prince, 2,207,110.

Government: Type: Republic. **Head of state: Pres.** Michel Martelly; b. Feb. 12, 1961; in office: May 14, 2011. **Head of gov.:** Prime Min. Laurent Lamothe; b. Aug. 14, 1972; in office: May 16, 2012. **Local divisions:** 10 departments. **Defense budget:** NA. **Active troops:** No active armed forces. UN mission MINUSTAH in country since 2004.

Economy: Industries: textiles, sugar refining, flour milling, cement, light assembly of imported parts. **Chief crops:** coffee, mangoes, cocoa, sugarcane, rice, corn, sorghum. **Natural resources:** bauxite, copper, calcium carbonate, gold, marble, hydropower. **Arable land:** 36.3%. **Livestock:** cattle: 1.5 mil; chickens: 5.6 mil; goats: 1.9 mil; pigs: 1 mil; sheep: 153,500. **Fish catch:** 17,130 metric tons. **Electricity prod.:** 560.4 mil kWh. **Labor force:** agric 38.1%, industry 11.5%, services 50.4%.

Finance: Monetary unit: Gourde (HTG) (Sept. 2013: 43.35 = $1 U.S.). **GDP:** $13.2 bil; **per capita GDP:** $1,300; **GDP growth:** 2.8%. **Imports:** $2.6 bil; Dominican Republic 35.9%, U.S. 24.7%, Netherlands Antilles 9.8%, China 6.6%. **Exports:** $785 mil; U.S. 81.5%. **Tourism:** $162 mil. **Budget:** $2.3 bil. **Total reserves less gold:** $1.3 bil. **Gold:** 1,308 oz t. **CPI change:** 6.3%.

Transport: Motor vehicles: 8 vehicles per 1,000 pop. **Civil aviation:** 4 airports. **Chief ports:** Cap-Haïtien, Gonaïves Jacmel, Port-au-Prince.

Communications: TV sets: 104 per 1,000 pop. **Radios:** 170 per 1,000 pop. **Telephone lines** 0.5 per 100 pop. **Internet:** 10.9%.

Health: Life expect.: 61.5 male; 64.3 female. **Births:** 23.4 per 1,000 pop. **Deaths:** 8.0 per 1,000 pop. **Natural inc.:** 1.54%. **Infant mortality:** 50.9 per 1,000 live births. **HIV rate:** 1.8%.

Education: Compulsory: ages 6-11. **Literacy:** 48.7%.

Major intl. organizations: UN and most of its specialized agencies, Caricom, OAS, WTO.

Embassy: 2311 Massachusetts Ave. NW 20008; 332-4090.

Website: primature.gouv.ht or www.haiti.org

Haiti, visited by Columbus in 1492 and a French colony from 1697, attained its independence, 1804, following a rebellion led by former slave Toussaint L'Ouverture. After a period of political violence, the U.S. occupied the country 1915-34.

François Duvalier, known as Papa Doc, was elected president in 1957; in 1964 he was named president for life. Upon his death in 1971, he was succeeded by his son, Jean Claude Duvalier, known as Baby Doc. Following weeks of unrest, Jean Claude fled Haiti aboard a U.S. Air Force jet Feb. 7, 1986. His departure ended the Duvalier family's brutal 28-year dictatorship, but political violence, government corruption, poverty, AIDS and other health problems, and deteriorating environmental quality have continued to plague Haiti.

Jean-Bertrand Aristide was elected president in 1990, but the military arrested and expelled him from the country in Sept. 1991. The U.S. Coast Guard intercepted some 35,000 Haitian refugees as they tried to enter the U.S., 1991-92. Most were returned to Haiti. There was a new upsurge of refugees starting in late 1993.

The UN authorized in 1994 an invasion of Haiti by a multinational force. With U.S. troops already en route, a full-scale invasion was averted, Sept. 18, when military leaders agreed to step down. Aristide returned to Haiti and was restored to office Oct. 15. A UN peacekeeping force exercised responsibility in Haiti from 1995 to 1997. Aristide transferred power to his elected successor, René Préval, in 1996.

At least 140 people died and over 160,000 were left homeless when Hurricane Georges struck Haiti Sept. 22, 1998. Aristide won the 2000 presidency in an election boycotted by opposition groups.

An armed uprising in early 2004 and pressure from France and the U.S. toppled Aristide, who went into exile Feb. 29. A U.S.-led contingent, sent in after the upheaval, yielded authority June 1 to a UN stabilization force (MINUSTAH).

Flooding in late May 2004 killed more than 1,000 people, and more than 2,400 were killed in Tropical Storm Jeanne in Sept. Préval was reelected in 2006. Skyrocketing prices for food imports sparked riots and mass protests in Apr. 2008. A succession of hurricanes and tropical storms (Fay, Gustav, Hanna, Ike), Aug.-Sept. 2008, left more than 550 Haitians dead and up to 1 mil homeless. A school collapse near Port-au-Prince Nov. 7, 2008, killed 91 students and teachers.

An earthquake Jan. 12, 2010, near Port-au-Prince caused cataclysmic damage. More than 220,000 people (including nearly 100 UN peacekeepers) were killed, at least 300,000 were injured, and many more were left homeless. With the central government paralyzed and the presidential palace and parliament building in ruins, the U.S. and other countries mounted a massive relief effort. Nearly 600,000 Haitians were still living in displacement camps 18 months later.

After the first round of presidential balloting Nov. 28, 2010, Michel Martelly, an entertainer popularly known as Sweet Micky, was declared ineligible for the second round. Violent protests by his supporters, allegations of electoral fraud from international observers, and diplomatic pressure from the U.S. and other donor countries gained him a place in the runoff Mar. 20, 2011, which he won. Parliament twice blocked his nominee for prime min. before approving his third choice, Garry Conille, a physician and development expert. Conille resigned Feb. 2012, and was replaced by Laurent Lamothe in May. MINUSTAH uniformed personnel numbered about 9,000 in mid-2013. Poor living and sanitation conditions gave rise to cholera in areas affected by the 2010 earthquake. As of 2013, more than 8,000 had died, and more than 600,000 had been ill with the disease.

Honduras
Republic of Honduras

People: Population: 8,448,465. **Age distrib.:** <15: 35.5%; 65+: 3.9%. **Pop. density:** 195.6 per sq mi, 75.5 per sq km. **Urban:** 52.2%. **Ethnic groups:** mestizo (mixed Amerindian and European) 90%, Amerindian 7%, black 2%, white 1%. **Languages:** Spanish (official), Amerindian dialects. **Religions:** Roman Catholic 97%, Protestant 3%.

Geography: Total area: 43,278 sq mi, 112,090 sq km; **Land area:** 43,201 sq mi, 111,890 sq km. **Location:** In Central America. **Neighbors:** Guatemala on W; El Salvador, Nicaragua on S. **Topography:** Caribbean coast is 500 mi long. Pacific coast, on Gulf of Fonseca, is 40 mi long. Country is mountainous, with wide fertile valleys and rich forests. **Capital:** Tegucigalpa, 1,088,470.

Government: Type: Democratic constitutional republic. **Head of state and gov.:** Pres. Porfirio (Pepe) Lobo; b. Dec. 22, 1947; in office: Jan. 27, 2010. **Local divisions:** 18 departments. **Defense budget:** $150 mil. **Active troops:** 12,000.

Economy: Industries: sugar, coffee, woven and knit apparel, wood prods., cigars. **Chief crops:** bananas, coffee, citrus, corn, African palm. **Natural resources:** timber, gold, silver, copper, lead, zinc, iron ore, antimony, coal, fish, hydropower. **Arable land:** 9.1%. **Livestock:** cattle: 2.7 mil; chickens: 39.5 mil; goats: 25,000; pigs: 478,000; sheep: 16,000. **Fish catch:** 46,122 metric tons. **Electricity prod.:** 6.5 bil kWh. **Labor force:** agric. 39.2%, industry 20.9%, services 39.8%.

Finance: Monetary unit: Lempira (HNL) (Sept. 2013: 20.39 = $1 U.S.). **GDP:** $38.4 bil; **per capita GDP:** $4,700; **GDP growth:** 3.3%. **Imports:** $11.2 bil; U.S. 44.3%, Guatemala 8.5%, China 6%, El Salvador 5.6%, Mexico 5.5%. **Exports:** $7.9 bil; U.S. 40%, Germany 9.7%, El Salvador 6%, Belgium 5.9%, Guatemala 4.5%, Nicaragua 4.1%. **Tourism:** $661 mil. **Budget:** $4.2 bil. **Total reserves less gold:** $2.5 bil. **Gold:** 21,400 oz t. **CPI change:** 5.2%.

Transport: Railways: 47 mi. **Motor vehicles:** 16.8 vehicles per 1,000 pop. **Civil aviation:** 13 airports. **Chief ports:** La Ceiba, Puerto Cortes, San Lorenzo, Tela.

Communications: TV sets: 176 per 1,000 pop. **Radios:** 1,698 per 1,000 pop. **Telephone lines:** 7.7 per 100 pop. **Internet:** 18.1%.

Health: Life expect.: 69.1 male; 72.6 female. **Births:** 24.2 per 1,000 pop. **Deaths:** 5.1 per 1,000 pop. **Natural inc.:** 1.91%. **Infant mortality:** 19.3 per 1,000 live births. **HIV rate:** 0.5%-0.9%.

Education: Compulsory: ages 6-11. **Literacy:** 85.1%.

Major intl. organizations: UN (FAO, IBRD, ILO, IMF, WHO), OAS, WTO.

Embassy: 3007 Tilden St. NW 20008; 966-7702.

Website: honduras.usembassy.gov

Mayan civilization flourished in Honduras in the 1st millennium CE. Columbus arrived in 1502. Honduras became independent after freeing itself from Spain, 1821, and from the Fed. of Central America, 1838.

The army ousted Gen. Oswaldo Lopez Arellano, president for most of the period 1963-75 by virtue of one election and 2 coups, in 1975 over charges of pervasive bribery by United Brands Co. of the U.S. An elected civilian government took power in 1982. Some 3,200 U.S. troops were sent to Honduras after Nicaraguan forces violated the Honduran border Mar. 1988.

Already one of the poorest countries in the Western Hemisphere, Honduras was devastated in late Oct. 1998 by Hurricane Mitch, which killed at least 5,600 people and caused more than $850 mil in damage to crops and livestock.

Ricardo Maduro, a businessman who pledged to crack down on crime, won the 2001 presidency. He was succeeded by Manuel Zelaya Rosales of the opposition Liberal Party, who won the 2005 presidential election. Seeking constitutional changes in his final year in office that may have allowed him to run for a second term, Zelaya lost a political struggle with the Honduran congress and supreme court; the military ousted him June 2009. Porfirio (Pepe) Lobo, a conservative landowner, defeated Liberal Party nominee Elvin Santos in the 2009 presidential election, and took office Jan. 27, 2010, resolving the constitutional crisis. Honduras has diversified its economy, once dominated by banana and coffee exports, by expanding its textile industry, yet drug smuggling out of the country remains a problem.

Hungary

People: Population: 9,939,470. **Age distrib.:** <15: 14.8%; 65+: 17.5%. **Pop. density:** 287.3 per sq mi, 110.9 per sq km. **Urban:** 69.5%. **Ethnic groups:** Hungarian 92%, Roma 2%. **Language:** Hungarian. **Religions:** Roman Catholic 52%, Calvinist 16%, Lutheran 3%, Greek Catholic 3%, unaffiliated 15%.

Geography: Total area: 35,918 sq mi, 93,028 sq km; **Land area:** 34,598 sq mi, 89,608 sq km. **Location:** In E central Europe. **Neighbors:** Slovakia, Ukraine on N; Austria on W; Slovenia, Serbia, Croatia on S; Romania on E. **Topography:** Danube R. forms Slovak border in NW, then swings S to bisect the country. Eastern half of Hungary is mainly a great fertile plain, the Alfold; the W and N are hilly. **Capital:** Budapest, 1,736,720.

Government: Type: Parliamentary democracy. **Head of state:** Pres. János Áder; b. May 9, 1959; in office: May 10, 2012. **Head of gov.:** Prime Min. Viktor Orbán; b. May 31, 1963; in office: May 29, 2010. **Local divisions:** 19 counties, 23 urban counties, 1 capital city. **Defense budget:** $1.03 bil. **Active troops:** 26,500.

Economy: Industries: mining, metallurgy, constr. materials, processed foods, textiles, chemicals (espec. pharmaceuticals), motor vehicles. **Chief crops:** wheat, corn, sunflower seeds, potatoes, sugar beets. **Natural resources:** bauxite, coal, nat. gas. **Crude oil reserves:** 27.3 mil bbls. **Arable land:** 48.5%. **Livestock:** cattle: 682,000; chickens: 31.8 mil; goats: 75,000; pigs: 3.2 mil; sheep: 1.2 mil. **Fish catch:** 22,632 metric tons. **Electricity prod.** 35.5 bil kWh. **Labor force:** agric. 7.1%, industry 29.7%, services 63.2%.

Finance: Monetary unit: Forint (HUF) (Sept. 2013: 227.77 = $1 U.S.). **GDP:** $198.8 bil; **per capita GDP:** $20,000; **GDP growth:** −1.7%. **Imports:** $07.4 bil; Germany 25.1%, Russia 0.0%, China 7.4%, Austria 7.1%, Slovakia 5.6%, Poland 4.8%, Italy 4.5%, Netherlands 4.2%. **Exports:** $90.2 bil; Germany 25.6%, Romania 6.2%, Slovakia 6.1%, Austria 6%, Italy 4.8%, France 4.8%, UK 4.2%. **Tourism:** $4.8 bil. **Budget:** $61 bil. **Total reserves less gold:** $44.5 bil. **Gold:** 98,900 oz t. **CPI change:** 5.7%.

Transport: Railways: 5,006 mi. **Motor vehicles:** 343.2 vehicles per 1,000 pop. **Civil aviation:** 2.4 bil pass.-mi; 20 airports. **Chief ports:** Baja, Budapest, Csepel, Dunaujvaros, Gyor-Gonyu, Mohacs. **Communications: TV sets:** 572 per 1,000 pop. **Radios:** 473 per 1,000 pop. **Telephone lines:** 29.8 per 100 pop. **Internet:** 72%.

Health: Life expect.: 71.5 male; 79.2 female. **Births:** 9.4 per 1,000 pop. **Deaths:** 12.7 per 1,000 pop. **Natural inc.:** −0.33%. **Infant mortality:** 5.2 per 1,000 live births. **HIV rate:** 0.1%.

Education: Compulsory: ages 7-16. **Literacy:** 99%.

Major intl. organizations: UN (FAO, IBRD, ILO, IMF, WHO), EU, NATO, OECD, OSCE, WTO.

Embassy: 3910 Shoemaker St. NW 20008; 362-6730.

Website: www.hungary.hu

Earliest settlers, chiefly Slav and Germanic, were overrun by Magyars from the east. Stephen I (997-1038) was made king by Pope Sylvester II in 1000 CE. The country suffered repeated Turkish invasions in the 15th-17th cents. After the Turks were defeated, 1686-97, Austria dominated, but Hungary obtained concessions, and regained internal independence in 1867 under a dual monarchy with the emperor of Austria. Defeated with the Central Powers in 1918, Hungary lost Transylvania to Romania, Croatia and Bacska to Yugoslavia, and Slovakia and Carpatho-Ruthenia to Czechoslovakia. All had large Hungarian minorities. A republic under Michael Karolyi and a Bolshevist revolt under Bela Kun were followed by a vote for a monarchy in 1920 with Adm. Nicholas Horthy as regent.

Hungary joined Germany in WWII and was allowed to annex most of its lost territories. Russian troops captured the country, 1944-45. By terms of an armistice with the Allied powers Hungary agreed to give up territory acquired by the 1938 dismemberment of Czechoslovakia and to return to its borders of 1937.

A republic was declared Feb. 1, 1946. In 1947 a hard-line Communist, pro-Soviet government was installed. Demonstrations against Communist rule developed into open revolt in 1956. Soviet forces launched a massive attack Nov. 4 against Budapest. About 200,000 persons fled the country. Thousands were arrested and executed.

Hungarian troops participated in the 1968 Warsaw Pact invasion of Czechoslovakia. Major economic reforms were launched early in 1968, switching from a central planning system to one based on market forces and profit.

In 1989 Parliament legalized freedom of assembly and association as Hungary shifted away from Communism. In Oct. the Communist Party was formally dissolved. The last Soviet troops left June 19, 1991. Hungary became a full member of NATO in 1999 and of the EU in 2004.

The IMF, EU, and World Bank agreed Oct. 2008 to extend $25.1 bil to rescue Hungary's economy, which was battered by the global financial crisis. With the nation still reeling from recession, the center-right Fidesz party ousted the Socialists in 2010 parliamentary elections. Parliament, dominated by Fidesz, approved Apr. 2011 a fiscally and socially conservative constitution that drew EU criticism; the law went into force Jan. 1, 2012. A hunger strike began outside the Hungarian Parliament in Budapest Sept. 4, 2012, to protest changes in the voting requirements; it was joined Sept. 9 by former Prime Min. Ferenc Gyurcsany. Heavy rains in early June 2013 caused the Danube River to overflow its banks in Budapest. Although a state of emergency was declared June 4, flood waters never reached the top of the city's 9.3-m-high flood walls.

Iceland
Republic of Iceland

People: Population: 315,281. **Age distrib.:** <15: 19.8%; 65+: 13.2%. **Pop. density:** 8.1 per sq mi, 3.1 per sq km. **Urban:** 93.7%. **Ethnic groups:** homogeneous mixture of Norse and Celt descendants 94%, pop. of foreign origin 6%. **Languages:** Icelandic, English, Nordic langs., German. **Religions:** Lutheran Church of Iceland (official) 81%, Roman Catholic 3%, Reykjavik Free Church 2%, Hafnarfjorour Free Church 2%.

Geography: Total area: 39,769 sq mi, 103,000 sq km; **Land area:** 38,707 sq mi, 100,250 sq km. **Location:** Isl. at N end of Atlantic O. **Neighbors:** Nearest is Greenland (Den.) to W. **Topography:** Recent volcanic origin. Three-quarters of surface is wasteland: glaciers, lakes, a lava desert. There are geysers and hot springs, and the climate is moderated by the Gulf Stream. **Capital:** Reykjavík, 206,297.

Government: Type: Constitutional republic. **Head of state:** Pres. Olafur Ragnar Grímsson; b. May 14, 1943; in office: Aug. 1, 1996. **Head of gov.:** Prime Min. Sigmundur David Gunnlaugsson; b. Mar. 12, 1975; in office: May 23, 2013. **Local divisions:** 8 regions. **Defense budget:** NA. **Active troops:** No regular military forces. Operates coast guard; relies on NATO allies for air defense.

Economy: Industries: fish proc., aluminum smelting, ferrosilicon prod., geothermal power, hydropower, tourism. **Chief crops:** potatoes, green vegetables. **Natural resources:** fish, hydropower, geothermal power, diatomite. **Arable land:** 1.2%. **Livestock:** cattle: 72,773; chickens: 370,000; goats: 818; pigs: 34,300; sheep: 475,068. **Fish catch:** 1.2 mil metric tons. **Electricity prod.** 16.9 bil kWh. **Labor force:** agric. 4.8%, industry 22.2%, services 73%.

Finance: Monetary unit: Krona (ISK) (Sept. 2013: 121.35 = $1 U.S.). **GDP:** $13 bil; **per capita GDP:** $39,900; **GDP growth:** 1.6%. **Imports:** $4.4 bil; Norway 16.6%, U.S. 10.1%, Germany 9.2%, China 7.1%, Brazil 6.6%, Netherlands 5.7%, Denmark 5.6%, UK 4.7%. **Exports:** $5 bil; Netherlands 30.1%, Germany 12.9%, UK 9.8%, Norway 5%, U.S. 4.5%, France 4.4%. **Tourism:** $845 mil. **Budget:** $6.1 bil. **Total reserves less gold:** $4.1 bil. **Gold:** 63,800 oz t. **CPI change:** 5.2%.

Transport: Motor vehicles: 766.3 vehicles per 1,000 pop. **Civil aviation:** 2.3 bil pass.-mi; 7 airports. **Chief ports:** Grundartangi, Hafnarfjordur, Reykjavik.

Communications: TV sets: 505 per 1,000 pop. **Radios:** 1,077 per 1,000 pop. **Telephone lines:** 57.6 per 100 pop. **Internet:** 96%.

Health: Life expect.: 78.9 male; 83.4 female. **Births:** 13.2 per 1,000 pop. **Deaths:** 7.1 per 1,000 pop. **Natural inc.:** 0.61%. **Infant mortality:** 3.2 per 1,000 live births. **HIV rate:** 0.3%.

Education: Compulsory: ages 6-16. **Literacy:** 99%.

Major intl. organizations: UN (FAO, IBRD, ILO, IMF, WHO), EFTA, NATO, OECD, OSCE, WTO.

Embassy: 1156 15th St. NW, Ste. 1200, 20005; 265-6653.

Website: www.iceland.is

Iceland was an independent republic from 930 to 1262, when it joined with Norway. Its language has maintained its purity for 1,000 years. The Althing, or assembly, established in 930, is the world's oldest surviving parliament. Danish rule lasted 1380-1918; the last ties with the Danish crown were severed in 1941.

A 55-year U.S. military presence in Iceland ended with the closure of the Keflavík naval air station in Sept. 2006. Iceland's banking system and currency collapsed amid the global financial crisis in Oct. 2008. More than $10 bil in loans from the IMF and European governments restored financial stability; austerity measures were imposed, and the nation entered a deep recession. Political unrest sparked by soaring inflation and unemployment led to the Feb. 2009 installation of a center-left government, which swept to victory in Apr. 25 elections. Parliament July 16 approved a plan for Iceland to seek EU membership. A major eruption Apr. 14, 2010, of the Eyjafjallajökull volcano disrupted European air traffic, affecting about 10 mil passengers and 100,000 flights during the next 6 days. The economy has stabilized under the new government; unemployment rates fell to 4.8% July 2012. The governing coalition Jan. 14, 2013, tabled discussions about EU membership ahead of Apr. 28, 2013, parliamentary elections, in which the center-left government was voted out in favor of center-right parties.

India
Republic of India

People: Population: 1,220,800,359. **Age distrib.:** <15: 28.9%; 65+: 5.7%. **Pop. density:** 1,063.5 per sq mi, 410.6 per sq km. **Urban:** 31.3%. **Ethnic groups:** Indo-Aryan 72%, Dravidian 25%, Mongoloid and other 3%. **Languages:** Hindi (most widely spoken and primary tongue); 14 other official langs. (Bengali, Telugu, Marathi, Tamil, Urdu, Gujarati, Malayalam, Kannada, Oriya, Punjabi, Assamese, Kashmiri, Sindhi, Sanskrit); English (crucial for natl., political, commercial communication); Hindustani (popular variant of Hindi/Urdu widely spoken throughout N). **Religions:** Hindu 81%, Muslim 13%, Christian 2%, Sikh 2%.

Geography: Total area: 1,269,219 sq mi, 3,287,263 sq km; **Land area:** 1,147,956 sq mi, 2,973,193 sq km. **Location:** Occupies most of Indian subcontinent in S Asia. **Neighbors:** Pakistan on W; China, Nepal, Bhutan on N; Myanmar, Bangladesh on E. **Topography:** The Himalaya Mts., highest in world, stretch across India's northern borders. Below, the Ganges Plain is wide, fertile, and among the world's most densely populated regions. Area below includes Deccan Peninsula. Close to one quarter of area is forested. The climate varies from tropical heat in S to near-Arctic cold in N. Rajasthan Desert is NW; NE Assam Hills get 400 in. of rain a year. **Capital:** New Delhi, 22,653,600 (figure for Delhi urban aggl.). **Cities (urban aggl.):** Mumbai (Bombay), 19,743,613; Kolkata (Calcutta), 14,402,345; Chennai (Madras), 8,784,447; Bangalore, 8,614,328; Hyderabad, 7,837,054; Ahmadabad, 6,424,953; Pune, 5,100,205.

Government: Type: Federal republic. **Head of state:** Pres. Pranab Mukherjee; b. Dec. 11, 1935; in office: July 22, 2012. **Head of gov.:** Prime Min. Manmohan Singh; b. Sept. 26, 1932; in office: May 22, 2004. **Local divisions:** 28 states, 7 union territories. **Defense budget:** $38.5 bil. **Active troops:** 1,325,000.

Economy: Industries: textiles, chemicals, food proc., steel, transp. equip., cement, mining, petroleum, machinery, software, pharmaceuticals. **Chief crops:** rice, wheat, oilseed, cotton, jute, tea, sugarcane, lentils, onions, potatoes. **Natural resources:** coal (world's fourth-largest reserves), iron ore, manganese, mica, bauxite, rare earth elements, titanium ore, chromite, nat. gas, diamonds, petroleum, limestone. **Crude oil reserves:** 5.5 bil bbls. **Arable land:** 52.9%. **Livestock:** cattle: 210.8 mil; chickens: 942 mil; goats: 157 mil; pigs: 9.5 mil; sheep: 74.5 mil. **Fish catch:** 8.9 mil metric tons. **Electricity prod.** (2011): 985.4 bil kWh. **Labor force:** agric. 53%, industry 19%, services 28%.

Finance: Monetary unit: Rupee (INR) (Sept. 2013: 65.24 = $1 U.S.). **GDP:** $4.8 tril; **per capita GDP:** $3,900; **GDP growth:** 6.5%. **Imports:** $500.4 bil; China 11%, UAE 7.7%, Saudi Arabia 6.7%, Switzerland 5.9%, U.S. 4.9%. **Exports:** $298.4 bil, U.S. 12.7%, UAE 12.3%, China 5%, Singapore 5%, Hong Kong 4.1%. **Tourism:** $18 bil. **Budget:** $267.7 bil. **Total reserves less gold:** $270.6 bil. **Gold:** 17.9 mil oz t. **CPI change:** 9.3%.

Transport: Railways: 39,752 mi. **Motor vehicles:** 24.4 vehicles per 1,000 pop. **Civil aviation:** 53.3 bil pass.-mi; 253 airports. **Chief ports:** Chennai, Jawaharal Nehru, Kandla, Kolkata, Mumbai, Sikka, Vishakhapatnam.

Communications: TV sets: 137 per 1,000 pop. **Radios:** 120 per 1,000 pop. **Telephone lines:** 2.5 per 100 pop. **Internet:** 12.6%.

Health: Life expect.: 66.4 male; 68.7 female. **Births:** 20.2 per 1,000 pop. **Deaths:** 7.4 per 1,000 pop. **Natural inc.:** 1.29%. **Infant mortality:** 44.6 per 1,000 live births. **HIV rate:** NA.

Education: Compulsory: ages 6-14. **Literacy:** 62.8%.

Major intl. organizations: UN (FAO, IBRD, ILO, IMF, WHO), the Commonwealth, WTO.

Embassy: 2107 Massachusetts Ave. NW 20008; 939-7000.

Website: www.india.gov.in

India has one of the oldest civilizations in the world. Excavations trace the Indus Valley civilization back for at least 5,000 years. Paintings in the mountain caves of Ajanta, richly carved temples, the Taj Mahal in Agra, and the Kutab Minar in Delhi are among treasured relics of the past.

Aryan tribes, speaking Sanskrit, invaded from the northwest around 1500 BCE. Asoka ruled most of the Indian subcontinent in the 3rd cent. BCE and established Buddhism. But Hinduism revived and eventually predominated. Under the Guptas, 4th-6th cent. CE, science, literature, and the arts enjoyed a golden age. Arab invaders established a Muslim foothold in the west in the 8th cent., and Turkish Muslims gained control of North India by 1200. The Mughal emperors ruled 1526-1857.

Vasco da Gama established Portuguese trading posts 1498-1503. The Dutch followed. The British East India Co. sent Capt. William Hawkins, 1609, to get concessions from the Mughal emperor for spices and textiles. Operating as the East India Co., the British gained control of most of India. The British parliament assumed political direction; under Lord Bentinck, 1828-35, rule by rajahs was curbed. After the Sepoy troops mutinied, 1857-58, the British supported the native rulers.

Nationalism grew after WWI. The Indian National Congress and the Muslim League demanded constitutional reform. A leader emerged in Mohandas K. Gandhi (called Mahatma, or Great Soul) (b. Oct. 2, 1869), who was assassinated Jan. 30, 1948. He advocated self-rule, nonviolence, and an end to caste discrimination against "untouchables." In 1930 he launched a program of civil disobedience, boycotting British goods and rejecting taxes without representation.

In 1935, Britain gave India a constitution providing a bicameral federal congress. Muhammad Ali Jinnah, head of the Muslim League, sought creation of a Muslim nation, Pakistan.

The British government partitioned British India into the dominions of India and Pakistan. India became a member of the UN in 1945, a self-governing member of the Commonwealth in 1947, and a democratic republic, Jan. 26, 1950. More than 12 mil Hindu and Muslim refugees crossed the India-Pakistan borders in 1947; about 200,000 were killed in communal fighting.

After Pakistan troops began attacks on Bengali separatists in East Pakistan, Mar. 25, 1971, some 10 mil refugees fled to India. India and Pakistan went to war Dec. 3, 1971, on both the east and west fronts. Pakistan troops in the east surrendered Dec. 16; Pakistan agreed to a cease-fire in the west Dec. 17.

Indira Gandhi, India's prime minister since Jan. 1966, invoked emergency powers in June 1975. Thousands of opponents were arrested and press censorship imposed. These and other actions, including population control through forced vasectomies, were widely resented. Opposition parties, united in the Janata coalition, won the 1977 elections.

Gandhi became prime minister for the second time in 1980. She was assassinated by 2 of her Sikh bodyguards Oct. 31, 1984, in response to the government suppression in June 1984 of a Sikh uprising in Punjab, which included an assault on the Golden Temple at Amritsar, the holiest Sikh shrine. Widespread rioting followed the assassination; thousands of Sikhs were killed and some 50,000 left homeless. Rajiv, Indira Gandhi's son, replaced her as prime minister. A gas leak at a Union Carbide chemical plant in Bhopal, Dec. 1984, eventually killed some 14,000 people.

Many died in religious, ethnic, and political conflicts during the late 1980s and early '90s. To suppress the Sikh insurgency in Punjab, Indian government troops attacked the Golden Temple again in 1988. Rajiv Gandhi was swept from office in 1989 amid charges of incompetence and corruption and assassinated May 21, 1991, while campaigning to regain power. Nationwide riots followed the destruction of a 16th-cent. mosque by Hindu militants in Dec. 1992. Ethnic clashes in Assam, in NW India, killed thousands in Feb. 1993. Bombs jolted Mumbai and Kolkata, Mar. 12-19, killing over 300.

India's first president from the lowest caste, K. R. Narayanan, took office July 1997. India conducted a series of nuclear tests in mid-May 1998, raising tensions with Pakistan. A cyclone hit the state of Orissa, East India, on Oct. 29, 1999, leaving some 10,000 people dead. A powerful earthquake in Gujarat state, Jan. 26, 2001, claimed more than 20,000 lives.

India blamed Pakistani-sponsored terrorist groups for an Oct. 1, 2001, suicide attack on the state legislature in Jammu and Kashmir (see below), in which at least 40 people died, and a Dec. 13 assault on the Indian parliament in New Delhi that left 13 people dead. Hindu-Muslim clashes in Gujarat Feb.-Mar. 2002 claimed more than 700 lives. A. P. J. Abdul Kalam, a Muslim scientist who spearheaded India's nuclear weapons program, became president July 25.

Led by Rajiv Gandhi's Italian-born widow, Sonia, the Congress Party won the most seats in 2004 parliamentary elections. When Hindu nationalists objected to her candidacy, she chose not to become prime minister, and Manmohan Singh, a Sikh economist, took office instead.

The Indian Ocean tsunami of Dec. 26, 2004, left more than 10,700 people dead, some 5,600 missing, and over 647,000 displaced. Islamic extremists were suspected in 7 bombings in Mumbai, July 11, 2006, that killed more than 200 on commuter trains. Pratibha Patil took office July 2007, as India's first female president. Monsoon floods, July-Sept. 2007, killed more than 2,600 people. The next year, monsoon floods killed more than 2,200. At least 224 died in a stampede Sept. 30, 2008, at a Hindu temple in Jodhpur. The unmanned Chandrayaan-1, India's first lunar survey mission, was launched into space Oct. 22, 2008.

Ten Pakistanis linked to the militant group Lashkar-e-Taiba stormed luxury hotels, a railway station, a Jewish center, and other sites in Mumbai, Nov. 26, 2008; by the time Indian army commandos took control 3 days later, the attackers had slaughtered 163 people. Nine of the terrorists were also killed. Convicted of murder and of waging war against India, the lone surviving gunman, Ajmal Kasab, received a death sentence in 2010, and was executed by hanging Nov. 20, 2012.

In 2009 parliamentary elections, Prime Min. Manmohan Singh's United Progressive Alliance, headed by the Congress party, gained a resounding victory. A triple bombing in Mumbai July 13, 2011, killed 26 people and injured about 140; 11 were killed when a bomb exploded Sept. 7 outside the High Court in New Delhi. Electricity blackouts July 30-31, 2012, left 670 mil people without power.

Several rapes in New Delhi in Nov.-Dec. 2012 prompted outrage and large protests for their mishandling by police and government inaction. Tougher laws against sexual violence were passed Feb. 4, 2013, that included the death penalty for some cases.

A building collapse in a Mumbai suburb Apr. 5 killed 72 and injured 70, many of them construction workers, who were working without the proper permits. Flooding caused by torrential rains in Uttarakhand killed 23 people June 17 as roads and buildings were swept away.

Development of high-tech industries has propelled rapid economic growth since the 1990s; nearly 200 mil people have emerged from extreme poverty, although distribution of wealth remains highly uneven.

Sikkim, bordered by Tibet, Bhutan, and Nepal, formerly British protected, became a protectorate of India in 1950. Area: 2,740 sq mi; pop. (2011 census): 607,688; capital: Gangtok. In Sept. 1974, India's parliament voted to make Sikkim an associate Indian state, absorbing it into India.

Kashmir is a predominantly Muslim region in the NW that borders India, Pakistan, Afghanistan, and China. Originally a Hindu kingdom, Muslim rule began in 1341; after almost 200 years under the Mughals, the area was incorporated into British India in 1846. Fighting broke out in the region between India and Pakistan in 1947 following independence from Britain. A cease-fire was negotiated by the UN Jan. 1, 1949; it gave Pakistan control of one-third of the area as Azad Kashmir, in the W and NW, and India the remaining two-thirds, as the Indian state of Jammu and Kashmir. Area: 85,806 sq mi; pop. (2011 census): 12,548,926; capitals: Srinagar (summer) and Jammu (winter). Fighting in the area resumed during the 1965 and 1971 wars with Pakistan. China occupied about 14,000 sq mi in the Ladakh district after a war with India in 1962.

In the 1990s, India's decision to impose central government rule triggered clashes between Indian army troops and separatist fighters. India charged Pakistan with aiding the separatists; fighting was especially heavy in May-June 1999.

A cease-fire between Indian and Pakistani troops along the line of control took effect Nov. 2003, but fighting between Indian forces and Islamic militants continued. Estimates of conflict-related deaths since 1989 range from 40,000 to over 80,000. A powerful earthquake Oct. 8, 2005, killed about 80,000 and left up to 3 mil homeless in Pakistani-held Kashmir and northern Pakistan. Fighting between militants and security forces rose in 2013 and with it the number of security personnel deaths.

France, 1952-54, peacefully yielded to India its 5 colonies, former French India: Pondicherry, Karikal, Mahe, and Yanaon were merged to become Pondicherry, now **Puducherry**, area 185 sq mi; pop. (2011 census): 1,244,464. The colony of Chandernagor was incorporated into the state of **West Bengal**.

Indonesia
Republic of Indonesia

People: Population: 251,160,124. **Age distrib.:** <15: 26.6%; 65+: 6.4%. **Pop. density:** 359.1 per sq mi, 138.6 per sq km. **Urban:** 50.7%. **Ethnic groups:** Javanese 41%, Sundanese 15%, Madurese 3%, Minangkabau 3%, Betawi 2%, Bugis 2%, Banten 2%, Banjar 2%. **Languages:** Bahasa Indonesia (official; modified form of Malay), English, Dutch, local dialects (Javanese most widely spoken). **Religions:** Muslim 86%, Protestant 6%, Roman Catholic 3%, Hindu 2%.

Geography: Total area: 735,358 sq mi, 1,904,569 sq km; **Land area:** 699,451 sq mi, 1,811,569 sq km. **Location:** Archipelago SE of Asian mainland along the Equator. **Neighbors:** Malaysia on N, Papua New Guinea on E, Timor-Leste on S. **Topography:** Indonesia comprises over 13,500 islands (6,000 inhabited), including Java (one of the most densely populated areas in the world with over 2,000 persons per sq mi), Sumatra, Kalimantan (most of Borneo), Sulawesi (Celebes), and West Irian (Irian Jaya, the W half of New Guinea). Also: Bangka, Billiton, Madura, Bali, Timor. The mountains and plateaus on the major islands have a cooler climate than the tropical lowlands. **Capital:** Jakarta, 9,769,010. **Cities (urban aggl.):** Surabaya, 2,787,165; Bandung, 2,429,144; Medan, 2,117,531; Semarang, 1,573,420; Palembang, 1,454,884; Ujung Pandang, 1,386,855; Batam, 1,034,429.

Government: Type: Republic. **Head of state and gov.:** Pres. Susilo Bambang Yudhoyono; b. Sept. 9, 1949; in office: Oct. 20, 2004. **Local divisions:** 31 provinces, 1 autonomous province, 1 special region, 1 capital district. **Defense budget:** $7.74 bil. **Active troops:** 395,500.

Economy: Industries: petroleum and nat. gas, textiles, automotive, elec. appliances, apparel, footwear, mining, cement, medical instruments and appliances, handicrafts, chemical fertilizers, plywood, proc. food, jewelry, tourism. **Chief crops:** rubber, palm oil, forest prods., cocoa, coffee, medicinal herbs. **Natural resources:** petroleum, tin, nat. gas, nickel, timber, bauxite, copper, coal, gold, silver. **Crude oil reserves:** 4 bil bbls. **Arable land:** 13%. **Livestock:** cattle: 14.8 mil; chickens: 1.4 bil; goats: 17.5 mil; pigs: 7.8 mil; sheep: 11.4 mil. **Fish catch:** 13.7 mil metric tons. **Electricity prod.** 161.1 bil kWh. **Labor force:** agric. 38.9, industry 22.2%, services 47.9%.

Finance: Monetary unit: Rupiah (IDR) (Sept. 2013: 11,563.30 = $1 U.S.). **GDP:** $1.2 tril; **per capita GDP:** $5,100; **GDP growth:** 6.2%. **Imports:** $178.5 bil; China 15.3%, Singapore 13.6%, Japan 11.9%, Malaysia 6.4%, South Korea 6.2%, U.S. 6.1%, Thailand 6%. **Exports:** $187 bil; Japan 15.9%, China 11.4%, Singapore 9%, South Korea 7.9%, U.S. 7.8%, India 6.6%, Malaysia 5.9%. **Tourism:** $8.3 bil. **Budget:** $180.9 bil. **Total reserves less gold:** $108.8 bil. **Gold:** 2.4 mil oz t. **CPI change:** 4.3%.

Transport: Railways: 3,133 mi. **Motor vehicles:** 72.4 vehicles per 1,000 pop. **Civil aviation:** 19.8 bil pass.-mi; 186 airports. **Chief ports:** Banjarmasin, Belawan, Kotabaru, Krueg Geukueh, Palembang, Panjang, Sungai Pakning, Tanjung Perak, Tanjung Priok.

Communications: TV sets: 161 per 1,000 pop. **Radios:** 157 per 1,000 pop. **Telephone lines:** 15.5 per 100 pop. **Internet:** 15.4%.

Health: Life expect.: 69.3 male; 74.6 female. **Births:** 17.4 per 1,000 pop. **Deaths:** 6.3 per 1,000 pop. **Natural inc.:** 1.11%. **Infant mortality:** 26.1 per 1,000 live births. **HIV rate:** 0.3%.

Education: Compulsory: ages 7-15. **Literacy:** 92.8%.

Major intl. organizations: UN and all of its specialized agencies, APEC, ASEAN, WTO.

Embassy: 2020 Massachusetts Ave. NW 20036; 775-5200.

Website: www.indonesia.go.id

Hindu and Buddhist civilization from India reached Indonesia nearly 2,000 years ago, taking root especially in Java. Islam spread along the maritime trade routes in the 15th cent., and became predominant by the 16th cent. The Dutch replaced the Portuguese as the area's most important European trade power in the 17th cent., securing territorial control over Java by 1750. The outer islands were subdued in the early 20th cent.

Following Japanese occupation, 1942-45, nationalists led by Sukarno and Hatta declared independence. The Netherlands ceded sovereignty in 1949. A republic was declared, Aug. 17, 1950, with Sukarno as president. West Irian, on New Guinea, remained under Dutch control but was transferred by the UN to Indonesia in 1963.

Sukarno suspended parliament in 1960 and was named president for life in 1963. He made close alliances with Communist governments. In Sept. 1965 an attempted coup was successfully put down, but Sukarno was forced to cede power to the army, led by Gen. Suharto, who became acting president in 1967 and ruled Indonesia for the next 31 years. The regime blamed the coup on the Communist Party; more than 300,000 alleged Communists were killed in army-initiated massacres.

Parliament reelected Suharto to a seventh consecutive 5-year term in 1998, as a severe economic downturn focused public anger on nepotism, cronyism, and corruption in the Suharto regime. Price increases in May sparked mass protests and then mob violence in Jakarta and other cities, claiming some 500 lives. Suharto resigned May 21 and was succeeded by his vice president, Bacharuddin Jusuf Habibie. Abdurrahman Wahid, leader of Indonesia's largest Muslim organization, was elected president in 1999. In Aug. 2000, under pressure from the legislature, he agreed to share power with Vice Pres. Megawati Sukarnoputri, the daughter of the late Pres. Sukarno. Charging Wahid with incompetence and corruption, the legislature ousted him July 23, 2001, and Megawati became Indonesia's first woman president.

Clashes between Muslims and Christians in the Maluku (Molucca) Isls., 1999-2002, claimed about 5,000 lives. Ethnic violence in Kalimantan, Borneo, killed more than 400 in Feb. 2001. East Timor, a former Portuguese colony that Indonesia invaded in Dec. 1975 and controlled until Oct. 1999, became a fully independent country May 20, 2002, as Timor-Leste. Separatists in Aceh, NW Sumatra, fought against government troops during the 1980s and '90s; peace accords were announced in Dec. 2002. The deal unraveled, July 2005, and the last of 24,000 Indonesian troops pulled out of Aceh, Dec. 29, 2005.

Investigators blamed the Islamic terrorist group Jemaah Islamiyah, an al-Qaeda affiliate, for bombings that killed 202 people, mostly foreign tourists, at nightclubs in Bali, Oct. 12, 2002, and 12 people at a Marriott hotel in Jakarta, Aug. 5, 2003. A car bomb attack outside the Australian embassy in Jakarta, Sept. 9, 2004, killed 9 people. Susilo Bambang Yudhoyono, a retired general, defeated Megawati in a 2004 direct presidential runoff vote.

A massive earthquake off northwest Sumatra, Dec. 26, 2004, triggered tsunamis that wreaked havoc in the Indian Ocean region. The death toll in Indonesia alone exceeded 125,000, not counting almost 40,000 missing. Another large quake off northwest Sumatra, Mar. 28, 2005, left at least 1,300 dead. On Java in 2006, an earthquake May 27 killed 5,800; a tsunami July 17 claimed at least 650 lives.

Faced with falling oil production, Indonesia left OPEC in 2008. Pres. Yudhoyono won a second 5-year term July 8, 2009. Suicide bombings at 2 Jakarta hotels July 17 left 9 people dead. Police confirmed Sept. 17 that Noordin Muhammad Top, suspected of plotting the Jakarta attacks and other terrorist bombings, had been killed in a shootout.

Padang, Sumatra, was hit Sept. 30, 2009, by a powerful earthquake, which also triggered mudslides in the region; at least 1,115 people were killed. On Oct. 25, 2010, a 7.7-magnitude earthquake in the Mentawai Islands, off Sumatra's western coast, triggered a tsunami that killed at least 500 people; that same day, Mt. Merapi, a volcano near Yogyakarta in central Java, began a series of major eruptions that claimed at least 228 lives and displaced 430,500.

Eight-thousand miners at Freeport's Grasberg copper and gold mines on Batam went on strike Sept. 2011, demanding higher wages; they won a 37% pay raise and ended the strike Dec. 17. Close to 100 Indonesian refugees died when their boat sank off the coast of Java June 22, 2012.

Iran
Islamic Republic of Iran

People: Population: 79,853,900. **Age distrib.:** <15: 23.8%; 65+: 5.1%. **Pop. density:** 135 per sq mi, 52.1 per sq km. **Urban:** 69.1%. **Ethnic groups:** Persian 61%, Azeri 16%, Kurd 10%, Lur 6%, Baloch 2%, Arab 2%, Turkmen and Turkic tribes 2%. **Languages:** Persian (official), Azeri Turkic and Turkic dialects, Kurdish, Gilaki and Mazandarani, Luri, Balochi, Arabic. **Religions:** Muslim (official) 98% (Shia 89%, Sunni 9%), other (incl. Zoroastrian, Jewish, Christian, Baha'i) 2%.

Geography: Total area: 636,372 sq mi, 1,648,195 sq km; **Land area:** 591,352 sq mi, 1,531,595 sq km. **Location:** Between the Middle East and S Asia. **Neighbors:** Turkey, Iraq on W; Armenia, Azerbaijan, Turkmenistan on N; Afghanistan, Pakistan on E. **Topography:** Interior highlands and plains surrounded by high mountains, up to 18,000 ft. Large salt deserts cover much of area, but there are many oases and forest areas. Most of population inhabits N and NW. **Capital:** Tehran, 7,304,150. **Cities (urban aggl.):** Mashhad, 2,713,344; Esfahan, 1,780,640; Karaj, 1,635,215; Tabriz, 1,509,091; Shiraz, 1,321,380; Ahvaz, 1,082,148; Qom, 1,064,658.

Government: Type: Theocratic republic. **Religious head:** Ayatollah Sayyed Ali Khamenei; b. July 17, 1939; in office: June 4, 1989. **Head of state and gov.:** Pres. Hassan Rouhani; b. Nov. 12, 1948; in office: Aug. 4, 2013. **Local divisions:** 31 provinces. **Defense budget:** $23.9 bil. **Active troops:** 523,000.

Economy: Industries: petroleum, petrochemicals, fertilizers, caustic soda, textiles, cement and other constr. materials, food proc. (sugar refining and vegetable oil proc.), metal fabrication, armaments. **Chief crops:** wheat, rice, other grains, sugar beets, sugarcane, fruits, nuts, cotton. **Natural resources:** petroleum, nat. gas, coal, chromium, copper, iron ore, lead, manganese, zinc, sulfur. **Crude oil reserves:** 154.6 bil bbls. **Arable land:** 10.8%. **Livestock:** cattle: 8.6 mil; chickens: 900 mil; goats: 23.5 mil; sheep: 49 mil. **Fish catch:** 735,079 metric tons. **Electricity prod.** 219.5 bil kWh. **Labor force:** agric. 25%, industry 31%, services 45%.

Finance: Monetary unit: Rial (IRR) (Sept. 2013: 12,285.01 = $1 U.S.). **GDP:** $1.02 tril; **per capita GDP:** $13,300; **GDP growth:** –1.9%. **Imports:** $67 bil; UAE 32.2%, China 13.8%, Turkey 11.8%, South Korea 7.4%. **Exports:** $65.3 bil; China 22.1%, India 11.9%, Turkey 10.6%, South Korea 7.6%, Japan 7.1%. **Tourism:** $2.4 bil. **Budget (2011):** $92.6 bil. **Total reserves less gold:** NA. **CPI change:** 27.3%.

Transport: Railways: 5,246 mi. **Motor vehicles:** 53.1 vehicles per 1,000 pop. **Civil aviation:** 8 bil pass.-mi; 140 airports. **Chief ports:** Assaluyeh, Bandar Abbas, Bandar-e-Eman Khomeyni.

Communications: TV sets: 170 per 1,000 pop. **Radios:** 734 per 1,000 pop. **Telephone lines:** 38 per 100 pop. **Internet:** 26%.

Health: Life expect.: 69.1 male; 72.2 female. **Births:** 18.4 per 1,000 pop. **Deaths:** 5.9 per 1,000 pop. **Natural inc.:** 1.25%. **Infant mortality:** 40.0 per 1,000 live births. **HIV rate:** 0.2%.

Education: Compulsory: ages 6-13. **Literacy:** 85%.

Major intl. organizations: UN (FAO, IBRD, ILO, IMF, WHO), OPEC, WTO (observer).

Iranian Interests Section: 2209 Wisconsin Ave. NW 20007; 965-4990.

Website: www.president.ir

Ancestors of inhabitants of Iran, formerly known as Persia, came from the east during the second millennium BCE; they were an Indo-European group related to the Aryans of India. In 549 BCE, Cyrus the Great united the Medes and Persians in the Persian Empire; he conquered Babylonia in 538 BCE, and restored Jerusalem to the Jews. Alexander the Great conquered Persia in 333 BCE, but Persians regained independence in the next century under the Parthians, themselves succeeded by Sassanian Persians in 226 CE. Arabs brought Islam to Persia in the 7th cent., replacing the indigenous Zoroastrian faith. After Persian political and cultural autonomy was reasserted in the 9th cent., arts and sciences flourished.

Turks and Mongols ruled Persia in turn from the 11th cent. to 1502, when Ismael I established the Iranian Safavid dynasty and made Shiite Islam the official religion. The dynasty lasted until 1722. The British and Russian empires vied for influence in the 19th cent.; Britain severed Afghanistan from Iran in 1857.

Reza Khan, a military officer, became prime min., 1923, and shah in 1925. He began modernization, curbed foreign influence, and officially changed the country's name from Persia to Iran in 1935. Fearing the shah's Axis sympathies, British and Soviet troops forced him to abdicate, 1941; he was succeeded by his son, Mohammad Reza Pahlavi. The U.S. Central Intelligence Agency had a major role in the ouster, 1953, of Prime Min. Muhammad Mossadegh, who had nationalized the oil industry.

With U.S. backing, the shah brought economic and social change to Iran (White Revolution), but repression of opposition groups grew severe. Violent protests in 1978 eventually forced the shah to depart, Jan. 16, 1979. Shiite leader Ayatollah Ruhollah Khomeini, exiled by the shah in 1963, returned to Tehran, Feb. 1. Pro-Khomeini forces defeated government troops, Feb 11. Khomeini established an Islamic theocracy.

Iranian militants seized the U.S. embassy in Tehran Nov. 4, 1979, and took hostages, including 62 Americans. Despite international condemnations and U.S. efforts, including an abortive Apr. 1980 rescue attempt, the crisis continued. The U.S. broke diplomatic

relations with Iran, Apr. 7. The shah died in Egypt, July 27. The hostage drama ended Jan. 20, 1981, when an accord, involving the release of frozen Iranian assets, was reached.

A dispute over the Shatt al-Arab waterway between Iran and Iraq led to a long and costly war between the 2 countries, 1980-88, killing hundreds of thousands of people. In Nov. 1986 it became known that the U.S., which had generally sided with Iraq during the war, had secretly shipped arms to Iran to gain that country's help in obtaining the release of U.S. hostages held in Lebanon. The revelation sparked a major scandal in the U.S. A U.S. Navy warship shot down an Iranian airliner, July 3, 1988, after mistaking it for an F-14 fighter jet; all 290 aboard died.

An earthquake struck northern Iran June 21, 1990, killing more than 45,000 and leaving 400,000 homeless. Some 1 mil Kurdish refugees fled from Iraq to Iran following the Persian Gulf War of 1991. To curb Iran's alleged support for international terrorism, the U.S. in 1996 authorized sanctions on foreign companies that invested there.

Mohammad Khatami, a moderate Shiite Muslim cleric, was elected president in 1997. During the next 3 years, hard-line Islamists clashed, sometimes violently, with reformers, who won a majority in 2000 parliamentary elections. Inviting rapprochement with Iran, the U.S. eased some sanctions Mar. 18. Khatami was reelected in 2001 but continued to face resistance from religious conservatives.

The U.S.-led war in Iraq, beginning Mar. 2003, contributed to a new period of instability in Iran. An earthquake Dec. 26 in Bam, SE Iran, killed about 26,000 people. After the Guardian Council, dominated by religious conservatives, disqualified some 2,400 reformist candidates, hard-liners won legislative elections Feb. 20, 2004.

The religiously conservative mayor of Tehran, Mahmoud Ahmadinejad, defeated former Pres. Hashemi Rafsanjani in a 2005 runoff election. The Bush administration accused Iran of seeking to build nuclear weapons, aiding Shiite militias in Iraq, and supplying rockets to Hezbollah fighters in Lebanon for use against Israel.

Seeking to halt Iran's uranium-enrichment program, the UN Security Council imposed sanctions, Dec. 2006, and toughened them, Mar. 2007. After the Guardian Council disqualified about 1,700 reformist candidates, conservative allies of Ahmadinejad won parliamentary elections Mar.-Apr. 2008. Further talks on nuclear enrichment ended in deadlock July 20, and the U.S. imposed additional sanctions Sept. 10.

After a hard-fought campaign, Ahmadinejad won the 2009 presidential election. His main opponent, former Prime Min. Mir Hussein Moussavi claimed the official count, which gave Ahmadinejad more than 62% of the total vote, was fraudulent. Huge protests by Moussavi supporters in Tehran and other major cities were crushed. Tensions with the U.S. and European governments were heightened in late Sept. 2009 by disclosures that Iran had been secretly enriching uranium at an underground site near Qom, and by Iranian tests of medium-range missiles capable of reaching Israel or U.S. and European bases in the Persian Gulf region. Iran agreed in Oct. to allow international inspection of the Qom site and other nuclear safeguards.

The UN and U.S. toughened sanctions, June-July 2010, but did not object when loading of uranium fuel began in Aug. at Iran's Russian-built Bushehr nuclear power plant. Iran blamed Israel, the U.S., and other Western powers for carrying out cyberattacks against the country's nuclear facilities and for assassinating Iranian scientists. In Dec. 2010, the U.S. announced new sanctions targeting companies linked to Iran's nuclear program. The Bushehr plant began generating electricity for the national power grid in Sept. 2011. Iran further advanced its nuclear program, announcing Jan. 2012, that it was enriching uranium at its underground Fordo nuclear facility; more international sanctions followed. Iran sentenced, Jan. 2012, Amir Mirzaei Hekmati, an American citizen and former Marine arrested in Aug. 2011, to death for being a spy, a charge the U.S. government denied. Despite sanctions against Iran, the U.S. pledged humanitarian aid to the country after it was hit by 3 earthquakes Aug. 11-14, 2012, which killed more than 300 people and left thousands homeless.

Iran supported the Syrian government with military aid, 2012-13, in its civil war. The moderate cleric Hassan Rouhani was elected president June 14, 2013, and took office Aug. 4. Rouhani and U.S. Pres. Barack Obama spoke on the telephone Sept. 27—the first time since 1979 that leaders of the two nations directly communicated.

Iraq
Republic of Iraq

People: Population: 31,858,481. **Age distrib.:** <15: 37.2%; 65+: 3.2%. **Pop. density:** 188.7 per sq mi, 72.8 per sq km. **Urban:** 66.5%. **Ethnic groups:** Arab 75%-80%; Kurdish 15%-20%; Turkoman, Assyrian, other 5%. **Languages:** Arabic (official), Kurdish (official in Kurdish regions), Turkmen, Assyrian (Neo-Aramaic), Armenian. **Religions:** Muslim 97% (Shia 60%-65%, Sunni 32%-37%), Christian or other 3%.

Geography: Total area: 169,235 sq mi, 438,317 sq km; **Land area:** 168,868 sq mi, 437,367 sq km. **Location:** In Middle East, occupying most of historic Mesopotamia. **Neighbors:** Jordan, Syria on W; Turkey on N; Iran on E; Kuwait, Saudi Arabia on S. **Topography:**

Mostly an alluvial plain, including the Tigris and Euphrates rivers, descending from mountains in N to desert in SW. Persian Gulf region is marshland. **Capital:** Baghdad, 6,035,580. **Cities (urban aggl.):** Mosul, 1,493,527; Erbil, 1,038,978; Basra, 942,170.

Government: Type: In transition. **Head of state:** Pres. Jalal Talabani; b. Nov. 12, 1933; in office: Apr. 7, 2005. **Head of gov.:** Prime Min. Nouri Kamel al-Maliki; b. June 20, 1950; in office: May 20, 2006. **Local divisions:** 18 governorates, 1 region (Kurdistan Regional Govt.). **Defense budget:** $14.7 bil. **Active troops:** 271,400.

Economy: Industries: petroleum, chemicals, textiles, leather, constr. materials, food proc., fertilizer, metal fabrication/proc. **Chief crops:** wheat, barley, rice, vegetables, dates, cotton. **Natural resources:** petroleum, nat. gas, phosphates, sulfur. **Arable land:** 9.2%. **Crude oil reserves:** 141.4 bil bbls. **Livestock:** cattle: 1.6 mil; chickens: 38 mil; goats: 1.6 mil; sheep: 8.2 mil. **Fish catch:** 51,841 metric tons. **Electricity prod.:** 47.4 bil kWh. **Labor force:** agric. 21.6%, industry 18.7%, services 59.8%.

Finance: Monetary unit: Dinar (IQD) (Sept. 2013: 1,163.49 = $1 U.S.). **GDP:** $242.5 bil; **per capita GDP:** $7,200; **GDP growth:** 8.4%. **Imports:** $56.9 bil; Turkey 27.8%, Syria 15.9%, China 12.6%, U.S. 5.2%, South Korea 4.8%. **Exports:** $93.9 bil; U.S. 21.4%, India 21.1%, China 13.8%, South Korea 11.2%, Canada 4.8%, Italy 4.5%, Spain 4.3%. **Tourism:** $1.5 bil. **Budget:** $88.3 bil. **Total reserves less gold:** $68.7 bil. **Gold:** 957,717 oz t. **CPI change** (2010-11): 5.8%.

Transport: Railways: 1,412 mi. **Motor vehicles:** 53.1 vehicles per 1,000 pop. **Civil aviation:** 72 airports. **Chief ports:** Al Basrah, Khawr az Zubayr, Umm Qasr.

Communications: TV sets: 82 per 1,000 pop. **Radios:** 211 per 1,000 pop. **Telephone lines:** 5.6 per 100 pop. **Internet:** 7.1%.

Health: Life expect.: 69.7 male; 72.7 female. **Births:** 27.5 per 1,000 pop. **Deaths:** 4.7 per 1,000 pop. **Natural inc.:** 2.29%. **Infant mortality:** 38.9 per 1,000 live births. **HIV rate:** NA.

Education: Compulsory: ages 6-11. **Literacy:** 78.5%.

Major intl. organizations: UN (FAO, IBRD, ILO, IMF, WHO), AL, OPEC, WTO (observer).

Iraqi Interests Section: 1801 P St. NW 20036; 483-7500.

Website: www.cabinet.iq

The Tigris-Euphrates valley, formerly called Mesopotamia, was the site of one of the earliest civilizations in the world. Mesopotamia ceased to be a separate entity after Persian, Greek, and Arab conquests. The Arabs founded Baghdad, from where the caliph ruled a vast Islamic empire in the 8th and 9th cents. Mongol and Turkish conquests led to a decline in the region's population, economy, cultural life, and irrigation system.

Britain secured a League of Nations mandate over Iraq after WWI. Independence under a king came in 1932. Rebellious army officers killed King Faisal II, July 1958 and established a leftist, pan-Arab republic, which pursued close ties with the USSR. The Baath Arab Socialist Party increasingly dominated successive regimes. A Baath leader, Saddam Hussein, became president in 1979. After purging his enemies, he ruled as a dictator for more than 2 decades, repressing Iraq's Kurds and Shiites and launching disastrous wars against 2 neighboring nations, Iran and Kuwait. Hussein sought weapons of mass destruction; Israeli planes destroyed a nuclear reactor near Baghdad in 1981, claiming it could be used to produce nuclear weapons.

After skirmishing intermittently for 10 months over the sovereignty of the disputed Shatt al-Arab waterway dividing the 2 countries, Iraq and Iran entered into open warfare on Sept. 22, 1980. Iran repulsed early Iraqi advances, producing a long and costly stalemate; hundreds of thousands of Iraqis lost their lives during the 8-year conflict. Hussein used poison gas against Iraqi Kurds in 1988, killing more than 5,000 people in Halabja, the first mass use of poison gas against civilians since the Holocaust.

Iraq invaded Kuwait in 1990. Backed by the UN, a U.S.-led coalition launched air and missile attacks on Iraq, Jan. 16, 1991, and began a ground attack to retake Kuwait Feb. 23. Iraqi forces showed little resistance and were defeated in 4 days. Some 175,000 Iraqis were taken prisoner, and Iraqi casualties were estimated at over 85,000. As part of the cease-fire agreement, Iraq agreed to scrap all poison gas and germ weapons and allow UN observers to inspect the sites. UN trade sanctions would remain in effect until Iraq complied with all terms.

Iraqi cooperation with UN weapons inspection teams was intermittent throughout the 1990s. Standoffs over inspections led to diplomatic crises 1997-98, culminating in intensive U.S. and British aerial bombardment of Iraqi military targets, Dec. 16-19, 1998. After 2 years of sporadic activity, U.S. and British warplanes struck sites near Baghdad mid-Feb. 2001.

Despite opposition from some countries, including France, Germany, and Russia, a U.S.-led coalition invaded Iraq Mar. 19, 2003. By Apr. 6 the British controlled Basra and other areas in the south, and the U.S. entered Baghdad Apr. 7. Hussein disappeared, the Iraqi government collapsed, and most of Iraq's armed forces dissolved into the civilian population. On May 1, Pres. Bush declared the end of major combat. Searches failed to find chemical, biological, or nuclear weapons that the U.S. and other countries claimed Iraq had stockpiled.

The U.S.-led Coalition Provisional Authority was unable to maintain order in the weeks following Hussein's fall. Reconstruction efforts were hampered by guerrilla attacks from Baath remnants,

Islamic extremists, and others. Bombings at UN headquarters in Baghdad, Aug. 19 and Sept. 22, 2003, led the UN to scale back its presence in Iraq. Coalition forces succeeded in neutralizing many leaders of the former regime. U.S. troops killed 2 of Hussein's sons, Uday and Qusay, July 22, 2003, in Mosul. Saddam Hussein was captured in an underground hideout mid-Dec. 2003; tried and convicted for committing crimes against humanity in the 1980s, he was executed Dec. 30, 2006.

Photographs released in Apr. 2004 showed instances of physical abuse and sexual humiliation of Iraqi inmates by U.S. military personnel at Baghdad's Abu Ghraib prison in 2003. The images sparked widespread condemnation and U.S. criminal proceedings against some individuals.

On June 28, 2004, U.S. authorities transferred sovereignty to a transitional Iraqi government. Despite insurgent threats, an estimated 8 mil people in Iraq, mostly Shiites and Kurds, cast ballots Jan. 30, 2005, for a 275-member transitional national assembly. The assembly elected Jalal al-Talabani, a Kurd, as president; Ibrahim al-Jaafari, a Shiite, became prime min. Insurgents launched new waves of attacks. Rumors of a suicide bomber set off a stampede by Shiite pilgrims in northern Baghdad Aug. 31, killing close to 1,000 people. The U.S. blamed Jordanian militant Abu Musab al-Zarqawi, leader of al-Qaeda in Iraq, for directing a series of kidnappings, beheadings, and suicide bombings. He was killed by a U.S. air strike, June 2006.

A new government elected in legislative elections Dec. 15, 2005, was installed May 20, 2006, headed by Shiite member Nouri Kamel al-Maliki. Meanwhile, the Feb. 22 bombing that destroyed the dome of Samarra's Golden Mosque, a Shiite shrine, intensified sectarian violence between Sunnis and Shiites, much of it in Baghdad. The Iraqi civilian death toll averaged more than 2,800 per month in 2006.

A "surge" engineered by U.S. Lt. Gen. David H. Petraeus in Jan. 2007 elevated U.S. troop strength from 132,000 in Jan. to 171,000 in Oct. U.S. troop deaths in 2007 totaled 899 (the highest for any year since the war began), but military and civilian casualties dropped steadily from mid-2007 through 2008. Contributing to the reduction in violence were a cease-fire by Shiite militias and a shift by Sunni clan leaders against al-Qaeda in Iraq.

A Nov. 2008, status-of-forces agreement called for the U.S. to withdraw its troops from Iraqi cities and towns by June 30, 2009, and for all U.S. forces to leave Iraq by Dec. 31, 2011. Legislative elections in 2010 brought gains by the Iraqi coalition headed by former Prime Min. Iyad Allawi, a Shiite who had campaigned as a secularist to win widespread Sunni support. On Aug. 31, Pres. Barack Obama formally declared an end to the U.S. combat role, and Operation Iraqi Freedom was succeeded by Operation New Dawn. More than 9 months of political deadlock ended when Prime Min. Maliki was sworn in for a second term Dec. 21, heading a unity government that included Shiite, Sunni, and Kurdish factions. Civilian casualties declined to about 200 per month during 2010.

U.S. troops completed their withdrawal from Iraq Dec. 15, 2011. From Mar. 2003 through Dec. 2011, operations in Iraq cost the lives of more than 4,486 U.S. service members; another 32,000 were wounded. British troop losses totaled 179; other allies, 139. More than 115,000 Iraqi civilians and over 10,000 police and security forces were killed. U.S. budgeted costs of the Iraq war exceeded $820 bil for the 2003-12 period.

Tensions manifested between Sunnis and Shiites after the U.S. departure. The Sunni-backed Iraqiya began a 6-week boycott of parliament Dec. 17, 2011, and accused Prime Min. Maliki of not sharing power. Maliki issued an arrest warrant for Sunni Vice Pres. Tariq al-Hashemi, Dec. 19, for terrorism. The Sunni insurgent group al-Qaeda in Iraq has been blamed for ongoing violence; in periodic assaults throughout 2012, 4,573 civilians were killed. Attacks accelerated Jan.-June 2013; more than 1,000 died in sectarian violence in May alone, making it the deadliest month in Iraq since 2008.

As a concession to the Sunni population, the Shiite-led government Jan. 14, 2013, released 300 Sunni prisoners it had detained for antigovernment activities.

Ireland

People: Population: 4,775,982. **Age distrib.:** <15: 21.4%; 65+: 12.1%. **Pop. density:** 179.6 per sq mi, 69.3 per sq km. **Urban:** 62.2%. **Ethnic groups:** Irish 87%, other white 8%, Asian 1%, black 1%, mixed 1%. **Languages:** English (official; generally used), Irish (Gaelic or Gaeilge) (official; spoken mainly on W coast). **Religions:** Roman Catholic 87%, Church of Ireland 3%, other Christian 2%, none 4%.

Geography: Total area: 27,133 sq mi, 70,273 sq km; **Land area:** 26,596 sq mi, 68,883 sq km. **Location:** In Atlantic O. just W of Great Britain. **Neighbors:** United Kingdom (Northern Ireland) on E. **Topography:** Consists of a central plateau surrounded by isolated groups of hills and mountains. Coastline is heavily indented by the Atlantic O. **Capital:** Dublin, 1,120,870.

Government: Type: Parliamentary republic. **Head of state:** Pres. Michael D. Higgins; b. Apr. 18, 1941; in office: Nov. 11, 2011. **Head of gov.:** Prime Min. Enda Kenny; b. Apr. 24, 1951; in office: Mar. 9, 2011. **Local divisions:** 29 counties, 5 cities. **Defense budget:** $1.13 bil. **Active troops:** 8,900.

Economy: Industries: pharmaceuticals, chemicals, computer hardware and software, food prods., beverages and brewing,

medical devices. **Chief crops:** barley, potatoes, wheat. **Natural resources:** nat. gas, peat, copper, lead, zinc, silver, barite, gypsum, limestone, dolomite. **Arable land:** 15.4%. **Livestock:** cattle: 6.5 mil; chickens: 14 mil; goats: 11,400; pigs: 1.5 mil; sheep: 4.7 mil. **Fish catch:** 287,720 metric tons. **Electricity prod.** (2011): 26 bil kWh. **Labor force:** agric. 5%, industry 19%, services 76%.

Finance: Monetary unit: Euro (EUR) (Sept. 2013: 0.76 = $1 U.S.). **GDP:** $195.4 bil; **per capita GDP:** $42,600; **GDP growth:** 0.9%. **Imports:** $64.3 bil; UK 40%, U.S. 13.2%, Germany 7.6%, Netherlands 5.6%. **Exports:** $119 bil; U.S. 18%, UK 17.4%, Belgium 15.6%, Germany 8.4%, Switzerland 5.8%, France 5%. **Tourism:** $4.1 bil. **Budget:** $88.5 bil. **Total reserves less gold:** $1.4 bil. **Gold:** 193,000 oz t. **CPI change:** 1.7%.

Transport: Railways: 2,011 mi. **Motor vehicles:** 487.9 vehicles per 1,000 pop. **Civil aviation:** 54.4 bil pass.-mi; 16 airports. **Chief ports:** Cork, Dublin, Shannon Foynes, Waterford.

Communications: TV sets: 715 per 1,000 pop. **Radios:** 695 per 1,000 pop. **Telephone lines:** 43.8 per 100 pop. **Internet:** 79%.

Health: Life expect.: 78.2 male; 82.8 female. **Births:** 15.5 per 1,000 pop. **Deaths:** 6.4 per 1,000 pop. **Natural inc.:** 0.91% live births. **Infant mortality:** 3.8 per 1,000 live births. **HIV rate:** 0.3%.

Education: Compulsory: ages 6-15. **Literacy:** 99%.

Major intl. organizations: UN (FAO, IBRD, ILO, IMF, WHO), EU, OECD, OSCE, WTO.

Embassy: 2234 Massachusetts Ave. NW 20008; 462-3939.

Website: www.gov.ie

Celtic tribes invaded the islands about the 4th cent. BCE; their Gaelic culture and literature flourished in the 5th cent. CE, the same century in which St. Patrick converted the Irish to Christianity. Invasions by Norsemen began in the 8th cent., ending with defeat of the Danes by the Irish King Brian Boru in 1014. English invasions started in the 12th cent. For over 700 years the Anglo-Irish struggle continued with bitter rebellions and savage repressions.

The Easter Monday Rebellion in 1916 failed but was followed by guerrilla warfare and harsh reprisals by British troops called the "Black and Tans." The Dail Eireann (Irish parliament) reaffirmed independence in Jan. 1919. The British offered dominion status to Ulster (6 counties) and southern Ireland (26 counties) Dec. 1921. The constitution of the Irish Free State, a British dominion, was adopted Dec. 11, 1922. Northern Ireland remained part of the United Kingdom (see United Kingdom—Northern Ireland).

A new constitution adopted by plebiscite came into operation Dec. 29, 1937. It declared the name of the state Eire in the Irish language (Ireland in the English) and declared it a sovereign democratic state. On Dec. 21, 1948, the country was declared a republic rather than a dominion and withdrew from the Commonwealth. The British Parliament recognized both actions, 1949, but the 6 northeastern counties remained in the UK.

Irish governments have favored peaceful unification of all Ireland and cooperated with Britain against terrorist groups. After negotiators in Northern Ireland approved a peace settlement on Good Friday, Apr. 10, 1998, voters in the Irish Republic endorsed the accord, on May 22, and the Irish gave up their constitution's territorial claims on the north.

Expansion of educational opportunities and foreign investment in high-tech industries in the 1990s boosted Ireland's prosperity. Ireland's first woman president, Mary Robinson, resigned Sept. 1997, to become UN high commissioner for human rights, 1997-2002. She was succeeded as president by Mary McAleese, a law professor from Northern Ireland and the first northerner to hold the office. Implicated in a corruption inquiry, Prime Min. Bertie Ahern announced his resignation Apr. 2008 after 11 years in power; the Dail Eireann May 7 chose Finance Min. Brian Cowen to succeed him.

In an Oct. 2009 referendum, Irish voters approved the Lisbon Treaty, a plan to revamp the EU. Responding to a growing scandal over abusive Catholic clergy, Pope Benedict XVI issued a public apology to victims and their families Mar. 2010 and launched an official church investigation May 31 of Irish dioceses, seminaries, and religious orders.

To aid Ireland's ailing banks and prevent deficit after a 2008-10 financial crisis, finance ministers from EU member countries approved Nov. 2010 an 85 bil euro ($115 bil) emergency loan package that obligated Ireland to impose unpopular austerity measures. Fianna Fáil, the party that had dominated Irish politics since the 1930s, suffered a crushing defeat in Feb. 2011 elections, and Enda Kenny, leader of the opposition Fine Gael and a critic of the bailout, became prime minister. Ireland voted May 31, 2012, to ratify the 2012 European Fiscal Compact, which 25 of the 27 EU countries had signed Mar. 2, 2012. Debate errupted over Ireland's abortion ban after an Indian woman having a miscarriage was denied a potentially life-saving abortion and died Oct. 28, 2012, prompting an inquiry. Lawmakers voted July 11, 2013, to legalize abortion when a woman's pregnancy is thought to jeopardize her life; Pres. Michael D. Higgins signed the landmark bill into law July 31.

Israel

State of Israel

People: Population: 7,707,042. **Age distrib.:** <15: 27.3%; 65+: 10.5%. **Pop. density:** 981.9 per sq mi, 379.1 per sq km. **Urban:** 91.9%. **Ethnic groups:** Jewish 76% (Israel-born 67%, Europe/

American-born 23%, Africa-born 6%, Asia-born 4%), non-Jewish (mostly Arab) 24%. **Languages:** Hebrew, Arabic (both official); English (most common foreign lang.). **Religions:** Jewish 76%, Muslim 17%, Christian 2%, Druze 2%.

Geography: Total area: 8,019 sq mi, 20,770 sq km; **Land area:** 7,849 sq mi, 20,330 sq km. **Location:** Middle East, on E end of Mediterranean Sea. **Neighbors:** Lebanon on N; Syria, West Bank, Jordan on E; Gaza Strip, Egypt on W. **Topography:** The Mediterranean coastal plain is fertile and well-watered. In the center is the Judean Plateau. A triangular-shaped semi-desert region, the Negev, extends from S of Beersheba to an apex at head of Gulf of Aqaba. The E border drops sharply into the Jordan Rift Valley, including Lake Tiberias (Sea of Galilee) and the Dead Sea, which is 1,348 ft below sea level, lowest point on Earth's surface. **Capital:** Jerusalem, 790,719. **Cities (urban aggl.):** Tel Aviv-Jaffa, 3,381,429; Haifa, 1,053,937.

Government: Type: Parliamentary democracy. **Head of state:** Pres. Shimon Peres; b. Aug. 1923; in office: July 15, 2007. **Head of gov.:** Prime Min. Benjamin Netanyahu; b. Oct. 21, 1949; in office; Mar. 31, 2009. **Local divisions:** 6 districts. **Defense budget:** $16.3 bil. **Active troops:** 176,500.

Economy: Industries: high-tech prods. (incl. aviation, communications computer-aided design and manufactures, medical electronics, fiber optics), wood and paper prods., potash and phosphates, food, beverages, tobacco. **Chief crops:** citrus, vegetables, cotton. **Natural resources:** timber, potash, copper ore, nat. gas, phosphate rock, magnesium bromide, clays, sand. **Crude oil reserves:** 11.5 mil bbls. **Arable land:** 14%. **Livestock:** cattle: 432,000; chickens: 40.7 mil; goats: 107,000; pigs: 224,000; sheep: 486,000. **Fish catch:** 22,757 metric tons. **Electricity prod.** (2011): 55.8 bil kWh. **Labor force:** agric. 2%, industry 16%, services 82%.

Finance: Monetary unit: Shekel (ILS) (Sept. 2013: 3.65 = $1 U.S.). **GDP:** $252.8 bil; **per capita GDP:** $32,800; **GDP growth:** 3.1%. **Imports:** $71.4 bil; U.S. 12.9%, China 7.3%, Germany 6.3%, Switzerland 5.5%, Belgium 4.8%. **Exports:** $61.5 bil; U.S. 27.8%, Hong Kong 7.7%, UK 5.7%, Belgium 4.6%, China 4.3%. **Tourism:** $5.5 bil. **Budget:** $73.7 bil. **Total reserves less gold:** $75.9 bil. **CPI change:** 1.7%.

Transport: Railways: 606 mi. **Motor vehicles:** 347.4 vehicles per 1,000 pop. **Civil aviation:** 10.7 bil pass.-mi; 29 airports. **Chief ports:** Ashdod, Elat, Hadera, Haifa.

Communications: TV sets: 340 per 1,000 pop. **Radios:** 540 per 1,000 pop. **Telephone lines:** 46.7 per 100 pop. **Internet:** 73.4%.

Health: Life expect.: 79.0 male; 83.5 female. **Births:** 18.7 per 1,000 pop. **Deaths:** 5.5 per 1,000 pop. **Natural inc.:** 1.32%. **Infant mortality:** 4.0 per 1,000 live births. **HIV rate:** 0.2%.

Education: Compulsory: ages 5-15. **Literacy:** 91.8%.

Major intl. organizations: UN (FAO, IBRD, ILO, IMF, WHO), OECD, WTO.

Embassy: 3514 International Dr. NW 20008; 364-5500.

Website: www.gov.il

Occupying the southwest corner of the ancient Fertile Crescent, Israel contains some of the oldest known evidence of agriculture and of primitive town life. The Hebrews probably arrived early in the 2nd millennium BCE. Under King David and his successors (c. 1000 BCE-597 BCE), Judaism was developed and secured. After conquest by Babylonians, Persians, and Greeks, an independent Jewish kingdom was revived, 168 BCE, but Rome took over in the next century, suppressed Jewish revolts in 70 CE and 135 CE, and renamed Judea Palestine, after the earlier coastal inhabitants, the Philistines.

Arab invaders conquered Palestine in 636. The Arabic language and Islam prevailed within a few centuries, but a Jewish minority remained. The land was ruled from the 11th cent. as a part of non-Arab empires by Seljuks, Mamluks, and Ottomans (with a Crusader interval, 1098-1291).

After 4 centuries of Ottoman rule, the land was taken in 1917 by Britain, which pledged in the Balfour Declaration to support a Jewish homeland there. In 1920 a British Palestine Mandate was recognized; in 1922 the land east of the Jordan was detached.

Jewish immigration, begun in the late 19th cent., swelled in the 1930s with refugees from Nazi Germany; heavy Arab immigration from Syria and Lebanon also occurred. Arab opposition to Jewish immigration turned violent in 1920, 1921, 1929, and 1936. The UN General Assembly voted in 1947 to partition Palestine into an Arab and a Jewish state. Britain withdrew in May 1948.

Israel was declared independent May 14, 1948; Arabs rejected partition. Egypt, Jordan, Syria, Lebanon, Iraq, and Saudi Arabia invaded but failed to destroy the Jewish state, which gained territory. Separate armistices with the Arab nations were signed in 1949; Jordan occupied the West Bank, Egypt occupied Gaza. Neither granted Palestinian autonomy.

After persistent terrorist raids, Israel invaded Egypt's Sinai, Oct. 29, 1956, aided briefly by British and French forces. A UN cease-fire was arranged Nov. 6.

An uneasy truce between Israel and the Arab countries lasted until 1967, when Egypt reoccupied the Gaza Strip and closed the Gulf of Aqaba to Israeli shipping. In a 6-day war that started June 5, the Israelis took the Gaza Strip, occupied the Sinai Peninsula to the Suez Canal, and captured East Jerusalem, Syria's Golan Heights, and Jordan's West Bank. Together, the West Bank and Gaza comprise the Palestinian territories, now represented by the Palestinian Authority.

Egypt and Syria attacked Israel, Oct. 6, 1973 (Yom Kippur, the most solemn day in the Jewish calendar). Israel counterattacked,

driving the Syrians back, and crossed the Suez Canal. A cease-fire took effect Oct. 24 and a UN peacekeeping force arrived. Under a 1974 disengagement agreement, Israel withdrew from the canal's west bank. Israeli forces raided Entebbe, Uganda, in 1976 and rescued 103 hostages who had been seized by Arab and German terrorists.

Israel's prime ministers, including David Ben-Gurion, Golda Meir, and Yitzhak Rabin, pursued a moderate socialist program, 1948-77. In 1977, the conservative opposition, led by Menachem Begin, was voted into office for the first time. Egypt's Pres. Anwar al-Sadat visited Jerusalem in 1977, and on Mar. 26, 1979, Egypt and Israel signed a formal peace treaty, ending 30 years of war. Israel returned the Sinai to Egypt in 1982.

On June 7, 1981, Israeli jets destroyed an Iraqi atomic reactor near Baghdad that, Israel claimed, would have enabled Iraq to manufacture nuclear weapons. Israeli forces invaded Lebanon, June 6, 1982, to destroy Palestine Liberation Organization (PLO) strongholds. After massive Israeli bombing of West Beirut, the PLO agreed to evacuate the city. Israeli troops entered West Beirut after newly elected Lebanese Pres. Bashir Gemayel was assassinated on Sept. 14. Israel drew widespread condemnation when Lebanese Christian forces, Sept. 16, entered 2 West Beirut refugee camps and slaughtered hundreds of Palestinians.

In 1989, violence escalated over the Israeli military occupation of the West Bank and Gaza Strip. In a series of uprisings known as the first intifada, Palestinian protesters defied Israeli troops, who forcibly retaliated. During the Persian Gulf War, 1991, Iraq fired Scud missiles at Israel. The Labor Party of Yitzhak Rabin won parliamentary elections in 1992.

Ongoing peace talks led to historic agreements between Israel and the PLO, Sept. 1993. The PLO recognized Israel's right to exist; Israel recognized the PLO as the Palestinians' representative. The 2 sides then signed, Sept. 13, an agreement for limited Palestinian self-rule in the West Bank and Gaza. Israel and Jordan signed, July 25, 1994, in Washington, DC, a declaration ending their 46-year state of war.

Arab and Jewish extremists repeatedly challenged the peace process. On Nov. 4, 1995, an Orthodox Jewish Israeli assassinated Rabin as he left a peace rally in Tel Aviv. Support for Rabin's successor, Shimon Peres, was shaken by a series of suicide bombings and rocket attacks against Israel by Islamic militants. Emphasizing security issues, the candidate of the conservative Likud bloc, Benjamin Netanyahu, was elected prime minister on May 29, 1996.

Under an interim accord brokered by Pres. Bill Clinton and signed by Netanyahu and PLO leader Yasir Arafat at the White House, Oct. 23, 1998, Israel yielded more West Bank territory to the Palestinians, in exchange for new security guarantees. Full implementation did not begin until Sept. 1999. In the interim, Netanyahu lost to the Labor candidate, Ehud Barak, in the May 1999, election.

Israel pulled virtually all its troops out of southern Lebanon in May 2000. Marathon summit talks in the U.S. between Barak and Arafat, July 11-25, failed. A second intifada began in late Sept. in Israel and the Palestinian territories. Barak called new elections for prime minister but lost Feb. 2001 to Ariel Sharon, a hardliner. The bloodshed intensified during the summer, as Palestinian suicide bombers attacked Israeli civilians, and Israel struck at Palestinian-controlled territory attempting to assassinate suspected terrorists.

Israel launched a major West Bank offensive Mar. 29, 2002, 2 days after a suicide bomber killed 26 Israeli Jews at a Passover celebration in Netanya. Fighting was particularly fierce at the Jenin refugee camp, where 23 Israeli troops and at least 50 Palestinians were killed. A U.S.-sponsored "road map" to Middle East peace, unveiled Apr. 2003, made little headway, as violence flared between Israel and Hamas militants in Gaza.

Sharon's decision to pull all Israeli settlers and troops out of Gaza, approved by the cabinet Feb. 2005, led Israeli politics to be realigned. When right-wing Likud members opposed the plan, Sharon and Deputy Prime Min. Ehud Olmert broke with them and formed the centrist Kadima Party. Sharon suffered a massive stroke Jan. 4, 2006. With Sharon incapacitated, Olmert became prime minister, led Kadima to victory in Mar. elections, and formed a broad coalition government.

Clashes in mid-2006 along the Gaza and Lebanon borders rapidly escalated into full-scale war. Israeli air and ground forces hit hard in Gaza, but the fiercest fighting raged on the northern front. By Aug. 14, when a UN-sponsored cease-fire took hold, the estimated death toll from the war included nearly 1,150 Lebanese, almost 200 Gaza Palestinians, and 150 Israelis. Olmert, criticized for leadership failures during the 2006 war and targeted in multiple corruption inquiries, announced his resignation July 30, 2008. (After a 4-year trial, he was acquitted of 2 counts of bribery but convicted of a lesser count of breach of public trust July 10, 2012.) Foreign Min. Tzipi Livni won a hard-fought party primary Sept. 17. Unable to form a stable government, she called early elections for Feb. 2009. After a campaign overshadowed by a 3-week war between Israel and Hamas in Gaza, both Kadima and Likud fell far short of a majority. On Mar. 31, Netanyahu became prime min. for a second time.

Israel's relations with allies were strained when senior Hamas commander Mahmoud al-Mabhouh was killed Jan. 2010 in Dubai, allegedly by agents of the Israeli spy agency Mossad who entered the UAE carrying false European and Australian passports. Further criticism greeted the Israeli government after its Mar. 2010

announcement that it would proceed to build 1,600 homes in Ramat Shlomo (a Jewish settlement in mostly Arab East Jerusalem), and later in the spring, when Israeli commandos killed 9 pro-Palestinian activists in clashes May 31 on board the *Mavi Marmara*, part of a flotilla that was seeking to break Israel's blockade of Gaza.

Arab Spring uprisings in 2011, which toppled the Mubarak government in neighboring Egypt and shook other Middle Eastern regimes, unsettled Israeli policy in the region. Egyptian militants Aug. 18, 2011, killed 8 Israelis (6 civilians, 2 soldiers), and Israel killed at least 7 of the attackers, 3 Egyptian security officers, and, according to some reports, several civilians across the border. Israel evacuated its diplomats from Egypt after thousands of protesters stormed the Israeli embassy in Cairo Sept. 9. Mass protests within Israel July-Sept. 2011 focused on social and economic inequality and the rising cost of living.

Tensions between Iran and Israel have grown over Iran's nuclear program, which Israel sees as an existential threat. Prime Min. Netanyahu met in the U.S. with Pres. Barack Obama Mar. 2012; both nations pledged to use force against Iran if necessary, though the U.S. urged continued diplomacy and tighter sanctions.

The Israeli military Oct. 6, 2012, shot down a Hezbollah drone that had crossed into the country's airspace. Israel also clashed with Palestinians in Gaza Oct.-Nov., with both sides suffering casualties. In retaliation for the Gaza attacks, the hacker collective Anonymous launched cyberattacks on Israel before a cease-fire was declared Nov. 21.

Netanyahu's right-wing Likud-Yisrael Beitenu political bloc narrowly won Jan. 22, 2013, parliamentary elections. Netanyahu assembled a new coalition government Mar. 15. Clashes in Gaza resumed Apr. 3, after Gaza fired missiles into Israeli territory in support of hunger-striking detainees held in Israeli prisons.

Palestinian Territories

The Palestinian territories comprise the Gaza Strip, often called Gaza, and the West Bank, both occupied by Israel in 1967. Since 1996 the Palestinian Authority has been responsible for civil government in the territories. Elected president Jan. 20, 1996, PLO leader Yasir Arafat headed the Palestinian Authority until his death Nov. 11, 2004. Mahmoud Abbas (also called Abu Mazen), who had succeeded Arafat as PLO chairman and leader of the Fatah faction, was elected president Jan. 2005. A victory by Hamas militants in Jan. 2006 legislative elections led to a power struggle with Abbas, who favored a negotiated settlement with Israel. In bitter fighting, Hamas ousted Fatah from Gaza, June 2007, but Abbas retained power in the West Bank. From Sept. 2000, when the second intifada began, through the end of 2008, the Israeli-Palestinian conflict claimed the lives of nearly 1,060 Israelis and at least 4,900 Palestinians; nearly 600 Palestinians were killed by other Palestinians in factional fighting. Fatah and Hamas reached a reconciliation agreement Apr. 27, 2011, and announced Feb. 6, 2012, that Abbas would lead an interim unity government. In a 2011 speech to the UN General Assembly, Abbas sought full UN membership of an independent Palestinian state; the U.S. and Israel opposed the request.

The **Gaza Strip** extends northeast from the Sinai Peninsula for 25 mi, with the Mediterranean Sea to the west and Israel to the east. The Palestinian Authority is responsible for civil government. Nearly all the inhabitants are Palestinian Arabs, more than 35% of whom live in refugee camps. Pop. (2013 est.): 1,763,387; area: 139 sq mi.

Israel captured Gaza from Egypt in the 1967 war. It remained under Israeli occupation until May 1994, when the Israeli Defense Forces withdrew. Agreements between Israel and the PLO in 1993 and 1994 provided for interim self-rule in Gaza, but Israel retained control over security. Israel forcibly evacuated all 9,000 Jewish settlers from Gaza by Aug. 22, 2005, and the last remaining Israeli soldiers pulled out Sept. 12. Israel established a fortified barrier on its Gaza border to block Palestinian infiltrators.

After the Hamas takeover, Israel declared Gaza a "hostile entity," Sept. 19, 2007, and intensified military and economic pressures. Hamas thwarted an Israeli blockade, Jan. 2008, blowing up part of the border wall between Gaza and Egypt. Retaliating for Hamas rocket and mortar attacks, Israel launched an aerial assault and ground offensive in Gaza, Dec. 2008-Jan. 2009. A UN report issued in 2009 found evidence of war crimes committed by both sides. After the *Mavi Marmara* incident, Israel June 2010 eased some restrictions on the flow of goods to Gaza. Egypt lifted the blockade along its Gaza border May 28, 2011.

A ceasefire signed June 23, 2012, did not hold. Members of the Israeli Air Force, Oct. 31, 2012, assassinated Hamas's military chief, Ahmed al-Jabari, in the Gaza Strip. Hackers calling themselves #OpIsrael launched millions of cyberattacks on Israeli government agencies and businesses Nov. 14, 2012, in response to Israeli airstrikes, disrupting some online operations and taking many websites offline.

The **West Bank** is located west of the Jordan R. and Dead Sea, bounded by Jordan on the east and by Israel on the north, west, and south. The Palestinian Authority administers several major cities, but Israel retains control over much land, including Jewish settlements. Area: 2,263 sq mi; pop. (2013 est.): 2,676,740.

Israel captured the West Bank from Jordan in the 1967 war. An accord between Israel and the PLO expanding Palestinian self-rule

in the West Bank was signed Sept. 28, 1995. Later agreements gave Palestinians full or shared control of 40% of West Bank territory.

In June 2002 the Israeli government began building a controversial security barrier in the West Bank to restrict Palestinian access to Israel and reduce infiltration by suicide bombers. In a nonbinding ruling, July 9, 2004, the World Court said the barrier violated international law. Israel has continued to allow the expansion of Jewish settlements on the West Bank, despite U.S. government calls for a settlement freeze; by mid-2011, an estimated 320,000 Jewish settlers were living in the West Bank (not including East Jerusalem, which Israel annexed in 1967). Resignations by prime ministers of the Palestinian Authority Apr. 13 and June 23, 2013, raised concern in the region.

Italy
Italian Republic

People: Population: 61,482,297. **Age distrib.:** <15: 13.8%; 65+: 20.8%. **Pop. density:** 541.4 per sq mi, 209 per sq km. **Urban:** 68.4%. **Ethnic groups:** Italian (incl. small clusters of German-, French-, and Slovene-Italians in N; Albanian- and Greek-Italians in S). **Languages:** Italian (official), German, French, Slovene. **Religions:** Christian 80% (predominantly Roman Catholic), atheists and agnostics 20%.

Geography: Total area: 116,348 sq mi, 301,340 sq km; **Land area:** 113,568 sq mi, 294,140 sq km. **Location:** In S Europe, jutting into Mediterranean Sea. **Neighbors:** France on W; Switzerland, Austria on N; Slovenia on E; San Marino, Vatican City. **Topography:** Occupies long boot-shaped peninsula, extending SE from the Alps into Mediterranean, with islands of Sicily and Sardinia offshore. The alluvial Po Valley drains most of N. Rest of the country is rugged and mountainous, except for intermittent coastal plains, like the Campania, S of Rome. Apennine Mts. run down through center of peninsula. **Capital:** Rome, 3,298,300. **Cities (urban aggl.):** Milan, 2,909,180; Naples, 2,372,526; Turin, 1,612,882.

Government: Type: Republic. **Head of state:** Pres. Giorgio Napolitano; b. June 29, 1925; in office: May 15, 2006. **Head of gov.:** Prime Min. Enrico Letta; b. Aug. 20, 1966; in office: Apr. 17, 2013. **Local divisions:** 20 regions (5 autonomous). **Defense budget:** $23.6 bil. **Active troops:** 181,450.

Economy: Industries: tourism, machinery, iron and steel, chemicals, food proc., textiles, motor vehicles, clothing, footwear, ceramics. **Chief crops:** fruits, vegetables, grapes, potatoes, sugar beets, soybeans, grain, olives. **Natural resources:** coal, mercury, zinc, potash, marble, barite, asbestos, pumice, fluorspar, feldspar, pyrite (sulfur), nat. gas and crude oil reserves, fish. **Crude oil reserves:** 521.3 mil bbls. **Arable land:** 23.1%. **Livestock:** cattle: 5.8 mil; chickens: 138 mil; goats: 1 mil; pigs: 9.3 mil; sheep: 7.9 mil. **Fish catch:** 378,029 metric tons. **Electricity prod.** (2011): 283.5 bil kWh. **Labor force:** agric. 3.9%, industry 28.3%, services 67.8%.

Finance: Monetary unit: Euro (EUR) (Sept. 2013: 0.76 = $1 U.S.). **GDP:** $1.9 tril; **per capita GDP:** $30,600; **GDP growth:** −2.4%. **Imports:** $453.5 bil; Germany 15.7%, France 8.9%, China 7%, Netherlands 5.8%, Spain 4.8%, Belgium 4.1%. **Exports:** $478.9 bil; Germany 12.8%, France 11.3%, U.S. 6.6%, Switzerland 5.8%, UK 5%, Spain 4.8%. **Tourism:** $41.2 bil. **Budget:** $1 tril. **Total reserves less gold:** $50.5 bil. **Gold:** 78.8 mil oz t. **CPI change:** 3%.

Transport: Railways: 12,586 mi. **Motor vehicles:** 686.6 vehicles per 1,000 pop. **Civil aviation:** 24.7 bil pass.-mi; 98 airports. **Chief ports:** Augusta, Cagliari, Genoa, Livorno, Sarroch, Taranto, Trieste, Venice.

Communications: TV sets: 492 per 1,000 pop. **Radios:** 878 per 1,000 pop. **Telephone lines:** 35.5 per 100 pop. **Internet:** 58%.

Health: Life expect.: 79.3 male; 84.7 female. **Births:** 8.9 per 1,000 pop. **Deaths:** 10.0 per 1,000 pop. **Natural inc.:** −0.11%. **Infant mortality:** 3.3 per 1,000 live births. **HIV rate:** 0.4%.

Education: Compulsory: ages 6-15. **Literacy:** 99%.

Major intl. organizations: UN and all of its specialized agencies, EU, NATO, OECD, OSCE, WTO.

Embassy: 3000 Whitehaven St. NW 20008; 612-4400.

Website: www.quirinale.it

Rome emerged as the major power in Italy after 500 BCE, dominating the Etruscans to the north and Greeks to the south. Under the Empire, which lasted until the 5th cent. CE, Rome ruled most of Western Europe, the Balkans, the Middle East, and North Africa. After Rome fell, Italy became a patchwork of kingdoms, principalities, and city-states until reunified, 1870.

The Fascist leader Benito Mussolini came to power, 1922, and aligned Italy with Nazi Germany in WWII. After Fascism was overthrown in 1943, Italy declared war on Germany and Japan and contributed to the Allied victory. It surrendered conquered lands and lost its colonies. Mussolini was killed by partisans Apr. 28, 1945. Victor Emmanuel III abdicated May 9, 1946; his son Humbert II was king until June 10, when Italy became a republic after a referendum, June 2-3. In the postwar decades, Italy had a succession of short-lived governments.

Christian Democratic leader and former prime min. Aldo Moro was abducted and murdered in 1978 by Red Brigade terrorists. The wave of left-wing political violence, including other kidnappings and assassinations, continued into the 1980s.

Political scandals marred the early 1990s, but in Mar. 1994 voting, under reformed election rules, right-wing parties won a majority,

dislodging Italy's long-powerful Christian Democratic Party. Italy led a 7,000-member peacekeeping force in Albania, Apr.-Aug. 1997, and contributed 2,000 troops to the NATO-led security force (KFOR) that entered Kosovo in June 1999.

Supporters of Silvio Berlusconi, a multibillionaire media magnate, won the 2001 parliamentary elections. Berlusconi, a close U.S. ally, backed American-led military operations in Afghanistan (2001) and Iraq (2003). As of mid-2013, 3,034 Italian troops were serving with the NATO mission in Afghanistan.

A coalition of center-left parties led by Romano Prodi scored a narrow win over Berlusconi in 2008 parliamentary voting; Berlusconi returned at the head of a center-right coalition. An earthquake in the Abruzzo region of central Italy Apr. 6, 2009, battered the town of L'Aquila, killing more than 300 people. Sluggish economic growth and rising public debt (equal to about 120% of annual GDP in mid-2011) raised investors' concerns about Italy's financial stability. Berlusconi resigned Nov. 12, 2011, and Mario Monti, an economist, succeeded him Nov. 16. Italy's economic problems worsened and its public debt reached nearly 2 tril euros ($2.5 tril) by Aug. 30, 2012. Monti announced Dec. 8, 2012, that he would resign the premiership and elections Feb. 25, 2013, initially produced a deadlock. A coalition government was announced Apr. 27, 2013, with Enrico Letta as prime minister.

The luxury cruise ship *Costa Concordia* ran into a reef off the coast of Italy Jan. 13, 2012, killing 32 people. A Milan court found Berlusconi guilty of paying for sex with a teenager and using his office to cover it up, for which he received a 7-year sentence and a lifetime ban from holding public office, June 24, 2013.

Sicily, 9,927 sq mi, pop. (2012 est.) 5,043,000, is an island 180 by 120 mi, seat of a region that embraces the island of Pantelleria, 32 sq mi, and the Lipari group, 44 sq mi, including 2 active volcanoes: Vulcano (1,637 ft) and Stromboli (3,031 ft). From prehistoric times Sicily has been settled by various peoples; a Greek state had its capital at Syracuse. Rome took Sicily from Carthage 215 BCE. Mt. Etna, an 11,053-ft active volcano, is its tallest peak.

Sardinia, 9,301 sq mi, pop. (2010 est.) 1,675,411, lies in the Mediterranean, 115 mi W of Italy and 7½ mi S of Corsica. It is 160 mi long, 68 mi wide, and mountainous, with mining of coal, zinc, lead, copper. In 1720, Sardinia was added to the possessions of the Dukes of Savoy in Piedmont and Savoy to form the Kingdom of Sardinia. Giuseppe Garibaldi is buried on the nearby isle of Caprera.

Elba, 86 sq mi, lies 6 mi W of Tuscany. Napoleon I lived in exile on Elba 1814-15.

Jamaica

People: Population: 2,909,714. **Age distrib.:** <15: 29%; 65+: 7.7%. **Pop. density:** 695.8 per sq mi, 268.6 per sq km. **Urban:** 52%. **Ethnic groups:** black 91%, mixed 6%. **Languages:** English, English patois. **Religions:** Protestant 63%, Roman Catholic 3%, none 21%.

Geography: Total area: 4,244 sq mi, 10,991 sq km; **Land area:** 4,182 sq mi, 10,831 sq km. **Location:** In W Indies. **Neighbors:** Nearest are Cuba to N, Haiti to E. **Topography:** Four-fifths of country covered by mountains. **Capital:** Kingston, 571,110.

Government: Type: Constitutional parliamentary democracy. **Head of state:** Queen Elizabeth II, rep. by Sir Patrick Allen; b. Feb. 7, 1951; in office: Feb. 26, 2009. **Head of gov.:** Prime Min. Portia Simpson-Miller; b. Dec. 12, 1945; in office: Jan. 5, 2012. **Local divisions:** 14 parishes. **Defense budget:** $124 mil. **Active troops:** 2,830.

Economy: Industries: tourism, bauxite/alumina, agric. proc., light manufactures, rum, cement, metal, paper, chem. prods., telecom. **Chief crops:** sugarcane, bananas, coffee, citrus, yams. **Natural resources:** bauxite, gypsum, limestone. **Arable land:** 11.1%. **Livestock:** cattle: 168,000; chickens: 13 mil; goats: 500,000; pigs: 200,000; sheep: 1,400. **Fish catch:** 16,250 metric tons. **Electricity prod.:** 4 bil kWh. **Labor force:** agric. 17%, industry 19%, services 64%.

Finance: Monetary unit: Dollar (JMD) (Sept. 2013: 101.55 = $1 U.S.). **GDP:** $25.6 bil; **per capita GDP:** $9,300; **GDP growth:** 0.1%. **Imports:** $5.9 bil; U.S. 30.1%, Venezuela 14.8%, Trinidad and Tobago 14.4%, China 11.9%. **Exports:** $1.7 bil; U.S. 38.7%, Russia 8.1%, Canada 7.8%, Slovenia 5.6%. **Tourism:** $2 bil. **Budget:** $4.5 bil. **Total reserves less gold:** $2 bil. **CPI change:** 6.9%.

Transport: Motor vehicles: 61.6 vehicles per 1,000 pop. **Civil aviation:** 1.8 bil pass.-mi; 11 airports. **Chief ports:** Kingston, Montego Bay, Port Antonio, Port Esquivel, Port Kaiser, Port Rhoades (Discovery Bay), Rocky Point.

Communications: TV sets: 382 per 1,000 pop. **Radios:** 23 per 1,000 pop. **Telephone lines:** 9.6 per 100 pop. **Internet:** 46.5%.

Health: Life expect.: 71.8 male; 75.2 female. **Births:** 18.7 per 1,000 pop. **Deaths:** 6.6 per 1,000 pop. **Natural inc.:** 1.20%. **Infant mortality:** 14.0 per 1,000 live births. **HIV rate:** 1.8%.

Education: Compulsory: ages 6-11. **Literacy:** 87%.

Major intl. organizations: UN (FAO, IBRD, ILO, IMF, WHO), Caricom, the Commonwealth, OAS, WTO.

Embassy: 1520 New Hampshire Ave. NW 20036; 452-0660.

Website: www.jis.gov.jm

Jamaica was discovered by Columbus, 1494, and ruled by Spain (under whom Arawak Indians died out) until seized by Britain, 1655. Jamaica won independence Aug. 6, 1962. The island's rich musical innovations include ska and reggae. Rastafarianism is an influential religious movement.

In 1974 Jamaica sought an increase in taxes paid by U.S. and Canadian bauxite mines. The socialist government acquired 50% ownership of the companies' Jamaican interests in 1976, and was reelected that year. Rudimentary welfare state measures were passed. Relations with the U.S. improved in the 1980s when Jamaican politics entered a more conservative phase. Violence between government forces and West Kingston slum residents claimed at least 20 lives July 7-10, 2001.

At least 17 died when Hurricane Ivan hit southern Jamaica in Sept. 2004. Portia Simpson-Miller, leader of the People's National Party, became Jamaica's first female prime min., Mar. 30, 2006. The opposition Jamaica Labour Party (JLP) won the parliamentary elections of Sept. 3, 2007. While trying to arrest an alleged gang leader, Christopher (Dudus) Coke, police and soldiers clashed with residents in the Tivoli Gardens section of Kingston in May 2010, leaving 76 people dead. Coke surrendered June 22, 2010, and was extradited to the U.S.; he pleaded guilty to racketeering charges in 2011. Prime Min. Bruce Golding resigned Oct. 23, 2011. The People's National Party won a landslide victory Dec. 2011; Portia Simpson-Miller again became prime min. Jan. 2012.

Japan

People: Population: 127,253,075. **Age distrib.:** <15: 13.4%; 65+: 24.8%. **Pop. density:** 904.2 per sq mi, 349.1 per sq km. **Urban:** 91.3%. **Ethnic groups:** Japanese 98.5%, Korean 0.5%. **Language:** Japanese. **Religions:** Shintoism 84%, Buddhism 71% (many people observe both); Christian 2%.

Geography: Total area: 145,914 sq mi, 377,915 sq km; **Land area:** 140,728 sq mi, 364,485 sq km. **Location:** Archipelago off E coast of Asia. **Neighbors:** Russia to N, S. Korea to W. **Topography:** Consists of 4 main islands: Honshu ("mainland"), 87,805 sq mi; Hokkaido, 30,144 sq mi; Kyushu, 14,114 sq mi; and Shikoku, 7,049 sq mi. The coast, deeply indented, measures 16,654 mi. The northern islands are continuation of the Sakhalin Mts. The Kunlun range of China continues into southern islands, the ranges meeting in Japanese Alps. In a vast transverse fissure crossing Honshu E-W rises a group of volcanoes, mostly extinct or inactive, including Mt. Fuji (Fujiyama) (12,388 ft) near Tokyo. **Capital:** Tokyo, 37,217,400. **Cities (urban aggl.):** Osaka-Kobe, 11,494,433; Nagoya, 3,328,296; Fukuoka-Kitakyushu, 2,868,051; Sapporo, 2,741,771; Sendai, 2,427,794; Hiroshima, 2,119,150; Kyoto, 1,804,215.

Government: Type: Parliamentary govt. with constitutional monarchy. **Head of state:** Emperor Akihito; b. Dec. 23, 1933; in office: Jan. 7, 1989. **Head of gov.:** Prime Min. Shinzo Abe; b. Sept. 21, 1954; in office: Dec. 26, 2012. **Local divisions:** 47 prefectures. **Defense budget:** $59.4 bil. **Active troops:** 247,450.

Economy: Industries: among world's largest and technologically advanced producers of motor vehicles, electronic equip., machine tools, steel and nonferrous metals, ships, chemicals, textiles, processed foods. **Chief crops:** rice, sugar beets, vegetables, fruit. **Natural resources:** negligible mineral resources, fish. **Crude oil reserves:** 44.1 mil bbls. **Arable land:** 11.7%. **Livestock:** cattle: 4.2 mil; chickens: 175.9 mil; goats: 15,500; pigs: 9.8 mil; sheep: 12,500. **Fish catch:** 4.8 mil metric tons. **Electricity prod.** (2011): 1.1 tril kWh. **Labor force:** agric. 3.9%, industry 26.2%, services 69.8%.

Finance: Monetary unit: Yen (JPY) (Sept. 2013: 99.03 = $1 U.S.). **GDP:** $4.7 tril; **per capita GDP:** $36,900; **GDP growth:** 2%. **Imports:** $830.6 bil; China 21.3%, U.S. 8.8%, Australia 6.4%, Saudi Arabia 6.2%, UAE 5%, South Korea 4.6%, Qatar 4%. **Exports:** $773.9 bil; China 18%, U.S. 17.7%, South Korea 7.7%, Thailand 5.5%, Hong Kong 5.1%. **Tourism:** $14.6 bil. **Budget:** $2.6 tril. **Total reserves less gold:** $1.2 tril. **Gold:** 24.6 mil oz t. **CPI change:** −0.03%.

Transport: Railways: 16,890 mi. **Motor vehicles:** 584.8 vehicles per 1,000 pop. **Civil aviation:** 79.4 bil pass.-mi; 142 airports. **Chief ports:** Chiba, Kawasaki, Kobe, Mizushima, Moji, Nagoya, Osaka, Tokyo, Tomakomai, Yokohama.

Communications: TV sets: 842 per 1,000 pop. **Radios:** 955 per 1,000 pop. **Telephone lines:** 50.8 per 100 pop. **Internet:** 79.1%.

Health: Life expect.: 80.9 male; 87.7 female. **Births:** 8.2 per 1,000 pop. **Deaths:** 9.3 per 1,000 pop. **Natural inc.:** −0.10%. **Infant mortality:** 2.2 per 1,000 live births. **HIV rate:** <0.1%.

Education: Compulsory: ages 6-14. **Literacy:** 99%.

Major intl. organizations: UN and all its specialized agencies, APEC, OECD, WTO.

Embassy: 2520 Massachusetts Ave. NW 20008; 238-6700. **Website:** www.kantei.go.jp

According to Japanese legend, the empire was founded by Emperor Jimmu, 660 BCE, but earliest records of a unified Japan date from 1,000 years later. Chinese influence was strong in the formation of Japanese civilization. Buddhism was introduced before the 6th cent. CE.

A feudal system, with locally powerful noble families and their samurai warrior retainers, dominated from 1192. Central power was held by successive families of shoguns (military dictators), 1192-1867, until recovered by Emperor Meiji, 1868. The Portuguese and Dutch had minor trade with Japan in the 16th and 17th cents.; U.S. Commodore Matthew C. Perry opened the country to U.S. trade in a treaty ratified 1854. Industrialization began in the late 19th cent. Military conflicts won Taiwan from China, 1894-95, and the southern half of Sakhalin from Russia, 1904-05. Japan annexed Korea, 1910.

In WWI Japan ousted Germany from Shandong in China and took over German Pacific islands. Japan took Manchuria in 1931 and launched full-scale war in China in 1937. Japan attacked Pearl Harbor Dec. 7, 1941, launching a war with the U.S. The U.S. dropped atomic bombs on Hiroshima, Aug. 6, and Nagasaki, Aug. 9, 1945. Japan surrendered Aug. 14.

In a new constitution adopted May 3, 1947, Japan renounced the right to wage war; the emperor renounced claims to divinity; and the Diet became the sole lawmaking authority. The U.S. and 48 other non-Communist nations signed a peace treaty and the U.S. a bilateral defense agreement with Japan, in San Francisco 1951, restoring Japan's sovereignty as of Apr. 28, 1952.

Rebuilding after WWII, Japan emerged as one of the most powerful economies in the world. Japan's controversial import policies allowed it to accumulate huge trade surpluses.

In 1968, the U.S. returned control of the Bonin Isls., Volcano Isls. (including Iwo Jima), and Marcus Isls to Japan. In 1972, the U.S. returned Okinawa, the other Ryukyu Isls., and the Daito Isls., but the U.S. continued to maintain military bases on Okinawa. An agreement reached in 2012, would reduce the number of U.S. Marines stationed on Okinawa from 19,000 to 10,000.

The Liberal Democratic Party (LDP) governed Japan from the mid-1950s through early 1990s. In 1994, Tomiichi Murayama became Japan's first Socialist premier since 1947-48. An earthquake in the Kobe area in Jan. 1995 claimed more than 5,000 lives. With the country mired in a lengthy recession, the LDP regained power in 1996 and led Japan until 2009.

For the first time since WWII, Japan sent troops to an overseas warzone, when about 600 noncombat troops served in Iraq Feb. 2004-July 2006. The 2008-09 global recession hit Japan hard, prompting a series of economic stimulus plans; the largest, unveiled Apr. 2009, called for more than $150 bil in spending and tax measures. The LDP suffered a crushing defeat in 2009 parliamentary elections, and Yukio Hatoyama of the opposition Democratic Party of Japan (DPJ) became prime min. His public support soon plummeted, and he was replaced June 2010 by former finance min. Naoto Kan.

A magnitude 9.0 earthquake and tsunami in the Pacific Ocean off Japan's east coast Mar. 11, 2011, killed more than 15,800 people with another 2,671 still listed as missing (as of Mar. 2013). Inundated by the tsunami, the Fukushima Daiichi nuclear power plant experienced meltdowns at 3 of the plant's 6 nuclear reactors, spewing radiation over a large area. Criticized for his response to the catastrophe, Prime Min. Naoto Kan submitted his resignation Aug. 26, 2011, and was succeeded by Finance Min. Yoshihiko Noda. Following Fukushima Daiichi meltdowns, Japan began shutting down nuclear reactors and promised to keep them closed until each passed stress tests. The last of the reactors was shut down May 2012, and the first was restarted July 1. Revised nuclear safety guidelines were announced in June 2013.

Prime Min. Noda resigned Dec. 26, 2012, after Dec. 16 elections swept LDP candidates into office, and former Prime Min. Shinzo Abe became prime minister. The ruling Liberal Democrats won reelection in July 21, 2013, securing both houses of parliament for another 3 years.

Jordan
Hashemite Kingdom of Jordan

People: Population: 6,482,081. **Age distrib.:** <15: 34.6%; 65+: 5.1%. **Pop. density:** 189.1 per sq mi, 73 per sq km. **Urban:** 82.7%. **Ethnic groups:** Arab 98%, Circassian 1%, Armenian 1%. **Languages:** Arabic (official), English widely understood among upper and middle classes. **Religions:** Sunni Muslim (official) 92%, Christian 6% (majority Greek Orthodox).

Geography: Total area: 34,495 sq mi, 89,342 sq km; **Land area:** 34,287 sq mi, 88,802 sq km. **Location:** In Middle East. **Neighbors:** Israel, West Bank on W; Saudi Arabia on S; Iraq on E; Syria on N. **Topography:** About 88% is arid. Fertile areas are in W. Only port is on short Aqaba Gulf coast. Country shares Dead Sea (1,348 ft below sea level) with Israel. **Capital:** Amman, 1,178,650.

Government: Type: Constitutional monarchy. **Head of state:** King Abdullah II; b. Jan. 30, 1962; in office: Feb. 7, 1999. **Head of gov.:** Prime Min. Abdullah Ensour; b. 1939; in office: Oct. 11, 2012. **Local divisions:** 12 governorates. **Defense budget:** $1.45 bil. **Active troops:** 100,500.

Economy: Industries: clothing, fertilizers, potash, phosphate mining, pharmaceuticals, petroleum refining, cement, inorganic chemicals, light mfg., tourism. **Chief crops:** citrus, tomatoes, cucumbers, olives, strawberries, stone fruits. **Natural resources:** phosphates, potash, shale oil. **Crude oil reserves:** 1 mil bbls. **Arable land:** 2%. **Livestock:** cattle: 67,600; chickens: 26 mil; goats: 752,230; sheep: 2.3 mil. **Fish catch:** 1,075 metric tons. **Electricity prod.:** 13.9 bil kWh. **Labor force:** agric. 2.7%, industry 20%, services 77.4%.

Finance: Monetary unit: Dinar (JOD) (Sept. 2013: 0.71 = $1 U.S.). **GDP:** $39.3 bil; **per capita GDP:** $6,100; **GDP growth:** 2.8%. **Imports:** $18.4 bil; Saudi Arabia 23.6%, China 9.4%, U.S. 6.7%, Italy 4.7%, Turkey 4.6%. **Exports:** $7.9 bil; U.S. 16.6%, Iraq 15.1%, Saudi Arabia 11%, India 10.5%, Indonesia 4.2%. **Tourism:** $3.5 bil. **Budget:** $9.7 bil. **Total reserves less gold:** $8.1 bil. **Gold:** 445,363 oz t. **CPI change:** 4.8%.

Transport: Railways: 315 mi. **Motor vehicles:** 157 vehicles per 1,000 pop. **Civil aviation:** 4 bil pass.-mi; 16 airports. **Chief port:** Al Aqabah.

Communications: TV sets: 207 per 1,000 pop. **Radios:** 361 per 1,000 pop. **Telephone lines:** 6.7 per 100 pop. **Internet:** 41%.

Health: Life expect.: 78.9 male; 81.8 female. **Births:** 26.2 per 1,000 pop. **Deaths:** 2.8 per 1,000 pop. **Natural inc.:** 2.34%. **Infant mortality:** 15.3 per 1,000 live births. **HIV rate:** NA.

Education: Compulsory: ages 6-15. **Literacy:** 95.9%.

Major intl. organizations: UN (FAO, IBRD, ILO, IMF, WHO), AL, WTO.

Embassy: 3504 International Dr. NW 20008; 966-2664.

Website: www.kinghussein.gov.jo

From ancient times to 1922 the lands to the east of the Jordan R. were culturally and politically united with the lands to the W. Arabs conquered the area in the 7th cent.; the Ottomans took control in the 16th. Britain's 1920 Palestine Mandate covered both sides of the Jordan. In 1921, Abdullah, son of the ruler of Hejaz in Arabia, was installed by Britain as emir of an autonomous Transjordan, covering two-thirds of Palestine. An independent kingdom was proclaimed, 1946.

During the 1948 Arab-Israeli war, the West Bank and East Jerusalem were added to the kingdom, which changed its name to Jordan. These territories were lost to Israel in 1967, which swelled the number of Arab refugees on the East Bank.

Jordan and Israel officially agreed, July 25, 1994, to end their state of war; a peace treaty was signed Oct. 26. King Hussein died Feb. 7, 1999, ending a nearly 47-year reign; his eldest son assumed the throne as Abdullah II. According to government estimates, at least 450,000 refugees from the Iraq war were living in Jordan at the beginning of 2011. Abdullah II responded to 3 weeks of Arab Spring protests by replacing his prime min. in early Feb 2011. Low-level protests persisted, and he appointed 2 more prime mins. over the next 15 months.

King Abdullah dissolved parliament Oct. 5, 2012, and protesters called for an end to the king's rule. Elections at the end of Jan. 23, 2013, brought several candidates accused of vote-buying into office. UNHCR projected Sept. 3, 2013, that more than 430,000 Syrian refugees would be living in Jordan by the end of 2013.

Kazakhstan
Republic of Kazakhstan

People: Population: 17,736,896. **Age distrib.:** <15: 24.7%; 65+: 6.8%. **Pop. density:** 17 per sq mi, 6.6 per sq km. **Urban:** 53.6%. **Ethnic groups:** Kazakh (Qazaq) 63%, Russian 24%, Uzbek 3%, Ukrainian 2%, Uighur 1%, Tatar 1%, German 1%. **Languages:** Kazakh (Qazaq; state lang.), Russian (official; used in everyday business). **Religions:** Muslim 47%, Russian Orthodox 44%, Protestant 2%.

Geography: Total area: 1,052,090 sq mi, 2,724,900 sq km; **Land area:** 1,042,360 sq mi, 2,699,700 sq km. **Location:** In Central Asia. **Neighbors:** Russia on N; China on E; Kyrgyzstan, Uzbekistan, Turkmenistan on S; Caspian Sea on W. **Topography:** Extends from lower reaches of Volga in Europe to Altay Mts. on Chinese border. **Capital:** Astana, 664,086. **Cities (urban aggl.):** Almaty, 1,426,277.

Government: Type: Republic. **Head of state:** Pres. Nursultan A. Nazarbayev; b. July 6, 1940; in office: Apr. 24, 1990. **Head of gov.:** Prime Min. Serik Akhmetov; b. June 25, 1958; in office: Sept. 24, 2012. **Local divisions:** 14 provinces, 3 cities. **Defense budget:** $2.27 bil. **Active troops:** 39,000.

Economy: Industries: oil, coal, iron ore, manganese, chromite, lead, zinc, copper, titanium, bauxite, gold, silver, phosphates, sulfur, uranium, iron and steel, tractors and other agric. machinery, elec. motors, constr. materials. **Chief crops:** grain (mostly spring wheat, barley), potatoes, vegetables. **Natural resources:** petroleum, nat. gas, coal, iron ore, manganese, chrome ore, nickel, cobalt, copper, molybdenum, lead, zinc, bauxite, gold, uranium. **Crude oil reserves:** 30 bil bbls. **Arable land:** 8.9%. **Livestock:** cattle: 6.2 mil; chickens: 32.5 mil; goats: 2.9 mil; pigs: 1.3 mil; sheep: 15.1 mil. **Fish catch:** 43,250 metric tons. **Electricity prod.** 78.1 bil kWh. **Labor force:** agric. 25.8%, industry 11.9%, services 62.3%.

Finance: Monetary unit: Tenge (KZT) (Sept. 2013: 153.09 = $1 U.S.). **GDP:** $235.6 bil; **per capita GDP:** $14,100; **GDP growth:** 5%. **Imports:** $47.9 bil; Russia 31.6%, China 26.6%, Germany 6%, Ukraine 4.4%. **Exports:** $93.1 bil; China 21%, Russia 9.9%, France 9.3%, Germany 6.9%, Italy 5%, Canada 4.8%, Ukraine 4.7%, Romania 4.1%. **Tourism:** $1.3 bil. **Budget:** $45 bil. **Total reserves less gold:** $22.1 bil. **Gold:** 3.7 mil oz t. **CPI change:** 5.1%.

Transport: Railways: 9,370 mi. **Civil aviation:** 1.6 bil pass.-mi; 63 airports. **Chief ports:** Aqtau, Atyrau, Oskemen.

Communications: TV sets: 497 per 1,000 pop. **Radios:** 215 per 1,000 pop. **Telephone lines:** 26.5 per 100 pop. **Internet:** 53.3%.

Health: Life expect.: 64.7 male; 74.9 female. **Births:** 20.0 per 1,000 pop. **Deaths:** 8.4 per 1,000 pop. **Natural inc.:** 1.16%. **Infant mortality:** 22.3 per 1,000 live births. **HIV rate:** 0.2%.

Education: Compulsory: ages 7-17. **Literacy:** 99.7%.

Major intl. organizations: UN (FAO, IBRD, ILO, IMF, WHO), CIS, OSCE, WTO (observer).

Embassy: 1401 16th St. NW 20036; 232-5488.

Website: www.government.kz

The region came under the Mongols' rule in the 13th cent. and gradually came under Russian rule, 1730-1853. It was admitted to the USSR as a constituent republic in 1936.

Kazakhstan's Dec. 16, 1991, declaration of independence became reality when the Soviet Union dissolved Dec. 26, 1991. The Communist Party chief, Nursultan Nazarbayev, was elected president unopposed. He encouraged Western investment in the oil industry, boosting the economy. Dissent was suppressed, and much of the nation's oil wealth was controlled by Nazarbayev's family and aides.

Kazakhstan agreed, Feb. 1994, to dismantle nuclear missiles. Private land ownership was legalized Dec. 1995. Astana (formerly Akmola) became the nation's new capital, June 9, 1998. Reelected in 1999 and 2005, Pres. Nazarbayev was authorized to run for an unlimited number of terms under a constitutional amendment passed by parliament May 2007; he claimed more than 95% of the vote in the 2011 presidential election, deemed flawed by international election monitors. Nazarbayev's Nur Otan party won 81% of the vote in 2012 parliamentary elections, also faulted despite its introduction of 2 new parties into the formerly one-party parliament. The opposition party leader Vladimir Kozlov was sentenced to more than 7 years in prison Oct. 8, 2012, for trying to overthrow the government, a charge he denied.

Kenya
Republic of Kenya

People: Population: 44,037,656. **Age distrib.:** <15: 42.4%; 65+: 2.7%. **Pop. density:** 200.4 per sq mi, 77.4 per sq km. **Urban:** 24%. **Ethnic groups:** Kikuyu 22%, Luhya 14%, Luo 13%, Kalenjin 12%, Kamba 11%, Kisii 6%, Meru 6%, other African 15%, non-African 1%. **Languages:** English, Kiswahili (both official); numerous indigenous langs. **Religions:** Protestant 45%, Roman Catholic 33%, Muslim 10%, indigenous beliefs 10%.

Geography: Total area: 224,081 sq mi, 580,367 sq km; **Land area:** 219,746 sq mi, 569,140 sq km. **Location:** E Africa, on coast of Indian O. **Neighbors:** Uganda on W, Tanzania on S, Somalia on E, Ethiopia on N, Sudan on NW. **Topography:** The northern three-fifths of Kenya is arid. To S, a low coastal area and a plateau varying 3,000-10,000 ft. The Great Rift Valley enters the country N-S, flanked by high mountains. **Capital:** Nairobi, 3,363,130. **Cities (urban aggl.):** Mombasa, 971,523.

Government: Type: Republic. **Head of state and gov.:** Pres. Uhuru Kenyatta; b. Oct. 1961; in office: Apr. 9, 2013. **Local divisions:** 47 counties. **Defense budget:** $940 mil. **Active troops:** 24,120.

Economy: Industries: small-scale consumer goods (plastic, furniture, batteries, textiles, clothing, soap, cigarettes, flour), agric. prods., horticulture, oil refining, aluminum, steel, lead, cement. **Chief crops:** tea, coffee, corn, wheat, sugarcane, fruit, vegetables. **Natural resources:** limestone, soda ash, salt, gems, fluorspar, zinc, diatomite, gypsum, wildlife, hydropower. **Arable land:** 9.7%. **Livestock:** cattle: 18.2 mil; chickens: 39.8 mil; goats: 28.9 mil; pigs: 348,200; sheep: 17.8 mil. **Fish catch:** 203,736 metric tons. **Electricity prod.:** 7.3 bil kWh. **Labor force:** agric. 75%, industry and services 25%.

Finance: Monetary unit: Shilling (KES) (Sept. 2013: 87.45 = $1 U.S.). **GDP:** $77.1 bil; **per capita GDP:** $1,800; **GDP growth:** 4.7%. **Imports:** $15.1 bil; India 20.7%, China 15.3%, UAE 9.5%, Saudi Arabia 6.7%. **Exports:** $6.3 bil; Uganda 10.5%, Tanzania 10.2%, Netherlands 7.1%, UK 6.7%, U.S. 5.8%, Egypt 5.2%, Dem. Rep. of the Congo 4.5%. **Tourism:** $901 mil. **Budget:** $9.5 bil. **Total reserves less gold:** $5.7 bil. **Gold:** 500 oz t. **CPI change:** 9.4%.

Transport: Railways: 1,284 mi. **Motor vehicles:** 25.4 vehicles per 1,000 pop. **Civil aviation:** 4.9 bil pass.-mi; 16 airports. **Chief ports:** Kisumu, Mombasa.

Communications: TV sets: 46 per 1,000 pop. **Radios:** 89 per 1,000 pop. **Telephone lines:** 0.6 per 100 pop. **Internet:** 32.1%.

Health: Life expect.: 61.8 male; 64.8 female. **Births:** 30.1 per 1,000 pop. **Deaths:** 7.1 per 1,000 pop. **Natural inc.:** 2.30%. **Infant mortality:** 42.2 per 1,000 live births. **HIV rate:** 6.2%.

Education: Compulsory: ages 6-13. **Literacy:** 72.2%.

Major intl. organizations: UN and all of its specialized agencies, AU, the Commonwealth, WTO.

Embassy: 2249 R St. NW 20008; 387-6101.

Website: www.statehousekenya.go.ke

Arab colonies exported spices and slaves from the Kenya coast as early as the 8th cent. Britain obtained control in the 19th cent. Kenya won independence Dec. 12, 1963, 4 years after the end of the violent Mau Mau uprising. Jomo Kenyatta, the country's leader since independence, died Aug. 22, 1978. He was succeeded by his vice president, Daniel arap Moi.

During the first half of the 1990s, Kenya suffered widespread unemployment and high inflation. Tribal clashes in the western provinces claimed thousands of lives and left tens of thousands homeless. Pres. Moi won a 3rd term in Dec. 1992 elections, which were marred by violence and fraud. He was reelected Dec. 1997 in an election plagued by irregularities. A truck bomb explosion at the U.S. embassy in Nairobi, Aug. 7, 1998, killed more than 200 people and injured about 5,000. The U.S. blamed the attack and a near-simultaneous embassy bombing in Tanzania on al-Qaeda.

Constitutionally barred from seeking another term, Pres. Moi was succeeded Dec. 2002, by Mwai Kibaki, the candidate of the opposition Democratic Party. After a disputed election Dec. 2007, that drew criticism from European and Kenyan monitors, Kenya's Electoral Commission declared Kibaki the winner over challenger Raila Odinga. Weeks of factional violence followed, leaving some 1,500 people dead and 600,000 displaced. Under a Feb. 28, 2008, power-sharing deal mediated by former UN Sec. Gen. Kofi Annan, Kibaki remained president and Odinga took the newly created post of prime minister. A new constitution curtailing presidential powers, establishing a senate, and reforming regional government won approval in an Aug. 2010 referendum. The Intl. Criminal Court Jan. 2012, charged 4 with crimes against humanity for their roles in the postelection violence. Two of those charged, Deputy Prime Min. Uhuru Kenyatta and former Education Min. William Ruto, were candidates in the Mar. 4, 2013, presidential election, in which Kenyatta was declared the winner Mar. 10 amid accusations of vote-rigging. His trial was set for Nov. 2013. More than 600,000 Somali refugees were living in Kenya as of June 2013. More than 60 died when Somali Islamist group al-Shabab attacked a Nairobi mall, Sept. 21-24, 2013.

Kiribati
Republic of Kiribati

People: Population: 103,248. **Age distrib.:** <15: 32.3%; 65+: 3.9%. **Pop. density:** 329.7 per sq mi, 127.3 per sq km. **Urban:** 43.9%. **Ethnic groups:** Micronesian 99%. **Languages:** I-Kiribati, English (official). **Religions:** Roman Catholic 55%, Protestant 36%, Mormon 3%, Baha'i 2%, Seventh-Day Adventist 2%.

Geography: Total area: 313 sq mi, 811 sq km; **Land area:** 313 sq mi, 811 sq km. **Location:** 33 Micronesian islands (the Gilbert, Line, and Phoenix groups) in mid-Pacific scattered in a 2-mil sq mi chain around the point where the International Date Line formerly cut the Equator. In 1997 the Date Line was moved to follow Kiribati's E border. **Neighbors:** Nearest are Nauru to SW, Tuvalu and Tokelau Isls. to S. **Topography:** Except Banaba (Ocean) Isl., all are low-lying, with soil of coral sand and rock fragments, subject to erratic rainfall. **Capital:** Bairiki, 44,385 (figure for South Tarawa Isl.).

Government: Type: Republic. **Head of state and gov.:** Pres. Anote Tong; b. June 11, 1952; in office: July 10, 2003. **Local divisions:** 3 units. **Defense budget:** NA. **Active troops:** No regular military forces. Australia and New Zealand provide defense assistance.

Economy: Industries: fishing, handicrafts. **Chief crops:** copra, taro, breadfruit, sweet potatoes, vegetables. **Natural resources:** phosphate (production discontinued in 1979). **Arable land:** 2.5%. **Livestock:** chickens: 570,000; pigs: 12,600. **Fish catch:** 69,633 metric tons. **Electricity prod.:** 25 mil kWh. **Labor force:** agric. 2.7%, industry 32%, services 65.3%.

Finance: Monetary unit: Dollar (AUD) (Sept. 2013: 1.09 = $1 U.S.). **GDP:** $636.3 mil; **per capita GDP:** $6,100; **GDP growth:** 2.5%. **Imports** (2010): $80.1 mil. **Exports** (2010): $7.1 mil. **Budget** (2010): $107.1 mil. **Total reserves less gold:** NA. **CPI change:** NA.

Transport: Civil aviation: 4 airports. **Chief ports:** Betio, English Harbor.

Communications: TV sets: 41 per 1,000 pop. **Radios:** 830 per 1,000 pop. **Telephone lines:** 8.8 per 100 pop. **Internet:** 10.7%.

Health: Life expect.: 62.7 male; 67.6 female. **Births:** 22.2 per 1,000 pop. **Deaths:** 7.2 per 1,000 pop. **Natural inc.:** 1.49%. **Infant mortality:** 36.5 per 1,000 live births. **HIV rate:** NA.

Education: Compulsory: ages 6-14. **Literacy:** NA.

Major intl. organizations: UN (FAO, IBRD, ILO, IMF, WHO), the Commonwealth.

Honorary Consulate: 95 Nakolo Pl., Rm. 265, Honolulu, HI 96819; (808) 834-6775.

Website: www.parliament.gov.ki

A British protectorate since 1892, the Gilbert and Ellice Islands colony was completed with the inclusion of the Phoenix Islands, 1937. Tarawa Atoll was the scene of some of the bloodiest fighting in the Pacific during WWII.

Self-rule was granted 1971; the Ellice Islands separated from the colony in 1975 and became independent Tuvalu, 1978. Kiribati (pronounced *Kiribass*) independence was attained July 12, 1979. Under a treaty of friendship the U.S. relinquished its claims to several Line and Phoenix islands. Kiribati was admitted to the UN in 1999. Pres. Anote Tong won reelection Oct. 2007. Kiribati's land area is shrinking as a result of rising sea levels, and Tong announced Mar. 7, 2012, negotiations with Fiji to buy 5,000 acres of land on which the nation's population could relocate. Researchers announced May 29, 2013, that sonar off the coast of Kiribati may have located the airplane of downed pilot Amelia Earhart, who disappeared in the South Pacific July 2, 1937.

Korea, North
Democratic People's Republic of Korea

People: Population: 24,720,407. **Age distrib.:** <15: 21.7%; 65+: 9.5%. **Pop. density:** 531.7 per sq mi, 205.3 per sq km. **Urban:** 60.3%. **Ethnic group:** racially homogeneous; small Chinese community and few ethnic Japanese. **Language:** Korean. **Religions:** traditionally Buddhist and Confucianist, some Christian and syncretic Chondogyo; autonomous religious activities almost nonexistent.

Geography: Total area: 46,540 sq mi, 120,538 sq km; **Land area:** 46,490 sq mi, 120,408 sq km. **Location:** In northern E Asia. **Neighbors:** China and Russia on N, S. Korea on S. **Topography:** Mountains and hills cover nearly entire country, with narrow valleys and small plains in between. N and E coasts are most rugged areas. **Capital:** P'yongyang, 2,842,570.

Government: Type: Communist state. **Head of state:** Kim Jong Un; b. Jan. 8, 1983; officially assumed post Dec. 17, 2011. **Head of gov.:** Prem. Pak Pong Ju; b. 1939; in office: Apr. 2, 2013. **Local divisions:** 9 provinces, 2 municipalities. **Defense budget:** NA. **Active troops:** 1,190,000.

Economy: Industries: military prods.; machine building, elec. power, chemicals; mining, metallurgy; textiles, food proc. **Chief crops:** rice, corn, potatoes, soybeans. **Natural resources:** coal, lead, tungsten, zinc, graphite, magnesite, iron ore, copper, gold, pyrites, salt, fluorspar, hydropower. **Arable land:** 19.1%. **Livestock:** cattle: 580,000; chickens: 17.5 mil; goats: 3.6 mil; pigs: 2.2 mil; sheep: 167,000. **Fish catch:** 713,350 metric tons. **Electricity prod.:** 21 bil kWh. **Labor force:** agric. 35%, industry and services 65%.

Finance: Monetary unit: Won (KPW) (Sept. 2013: 131.24 = $1 U.S.). **GDP** (2011): $40 bil; **per capita GDP** (2011): $1,800; **GDP growth** (2011): 0.8%. **Imports** (2011): $4.3 bil; (2011) China 61.6%, South Korea 20%, European Union 4%. **Exports** (2011): $4.7 bil; (2011) China 67.2%, South Korea 19.4%, India 3.6%. **Budget** (2007): $3.3 bil. **Total reserves less gold:** NA. **CPI change:** NA.

Transport: Railways: 3,257 mi. **Civil aviation:** 25.5 mil pass.-mi; 39 airports. **Chief ports:** Chongjin, Haeju, Hungnam, Nampo, Senbong, Sonbong, Songnim, Wonsan.

Communications: TV sets: 172 per 1,000 pop. **Radios:** 157 per 1,000 pop. **Telephone lines:** 4.8 per 100 pop. **Internet:** NA.

Health: Life expect.: 65.7 male; 73.6 female. **Births:** 14.5 per 1,000 pop. **Deaths:** 9.2 per 1,000 pop. **Natural inc.:** 0.53%. **Infant mortality:** 25.3 per 1,000 live births. **HIV rate:** NA.

Education: Compulsory: ages 6-16. **Literacy:** 100%.

Major intl. organizations: UN (FAO, WHO).

Permanent UN mission: 820 Second Ave., 13th Fl., New York, NY 10017; (212) 972-3105.

Website: www.korea-dpr.com

The Democratic People's Republic of Korea was founded May 1, 1948, in the zone occupied by Russia after WWII. Its armies tried to conquer the south, 1950. After 3 years of fighting, a cease-fire was proclaimed.

For the next 4 decades, a hard-line Communist regime headed by Kim Il Sung kept tight control over the nation's political, economic, and cultural life. The nation used its abundant mineral and hydroelectric resources to develop its military strength and heavy industry. By the early 1990s, North Korea was widely believed to be developing nuclear weapons. The U.S. and North Korea signed an agreement, Oct. 21, 1994, providing for phased dismantling of North Korea's nuclear development program in return for U.S. energy aid and improved ties with the U.S.

Kim Il Sung died July 8, 1994. He was succeeded by his son, Kim Jong Il. Defections by high officials, a deteriorating economy, and severe food shortages plagued North Korea in the late 1990s. A first-ever summit conference in P'yongyang between North and South Korean leaders, June 13-15, 2000, marked an improvement in relations between the 2 nations. North Korea and Japan agreed to normalize relations in a Sept. 2002 summit.

Pres. George W. Bush, in a speech Jan. 31, 2002, declared North Korea, along with Iraq and Iran, part of an "axis of evil." In Oct. 2002, North Korea admitted to pursuing a secret nuclear weapons program, in violation of past agreements. The U.S. insisted that North Korea end its nuclear weapons program, while P'yongyang demanded a nonaggression treaty and economic aid from the U.S. During 2003-09, as 6-nation talks sponsored by China sought to resolve the nuclear dispute, North Korea followed a zigzag course, alternately stopping and resuming its nuclear program in order to win concessions from the U.S.

In Apr.-May 2009, North Korea suspended participation in the 6-nation talks, expelled IAEA inspectors, tested multiple missiles, and exploded a nuclear device underground. The UN Security Council June 12 toughened sanctions on North Korean. Tensions between North and South Korea increased after the Mar. 26, 2010, sinking of the South Korean warship *Cheonan* killed 46 sailors; a South Korean panel including international investigators concluded May 20 that the *Cheonan* had been torpedoed by a North Korean submarine. Visits to P'yongyang by former presidents Bill Clinton, Aug. 2009, and Jimmy Carter, Aug. 2010, gained the release of several detained Americans. A North Korean artillery barrage killed 2 South Korean marines and 2 civilians on Yeonpyeong Isl. Nov. 23, 2010. Kim Jong Il died Dec. 17, 2011, and was succeeded by his son Kim Jong Un.

Kim Jong Un frequently threatened the U.S. and South Korea in rhetoric and action. North Korea launched a satellite into space Dec. 12, 2012, demonstrating its rocket capabilities; conducted several short- and long-range missile tests Dec. 2012-Mar. 2013; conducted a nuclear test Feb. 10, 2013; and threatened to launch a nuclear strike against the U.S., Mar. 7 after additional sanctions were levied against it in response to its nuclear test. North Korea also negated, Mar. 11, 2013, the cease-fire agreement with the South that ended the Korean War and claimed Mar. 29 that a state of war existed between the 2 countries but proposed peace talks with the U.S. by June 17, an offer it reaffirmed June 22.

Korea, South
Republic of Korea

People: Population: 48,955,203. **Age distrib.:** <15: 14.6%; 65+: 12.3%. **Pop. density:** 1,308.2 per sq mi, 505.1 per sq km. **Urban:** 83.2%. **Ethnic group:** homogeneous, except for some Chinese. **Languages:** Korean, English (widely taught in school). **Religions:** Christian 26% (Protestant 20%, Roman Catholic 7%), Buddhist 23%, none 49%.

Geography: Total area: 38,502 sq mi, 99,720 sq km; **Land area:** 37,421 sq mi, 96,920 sq km. **Location:** In northern E Asia. **Neighbors:** North Korea on N. **Topography:** Mountainous, with a rugged E coast. W and S coasts are deeply indented, with many islands and harbors. **Capital:** Seoul, 9,735,860; Sejong City (planned). **Cities (urban aggl.):** Busan, 3,372,181; Incheon, 2,622,113; Daegu, 2,446,516; Daejon, 1,538,091; Gwangju, 1,502,963; Suweon, 1,159,232; Ulsan, 1,100,053.

Government: Type: Republic. **Head of state:** Pres. Park Geun Hye; b. Feb. 2, 1952; in office: Feb. 25, 2013. **Head of gov.:** Prime Min. Chung Hongwon; b. Oct. 9, 1944; in office: Feb. 26, 2013. **Local divisions:** 9 provinces, 8 cities. **Defense budget:** $29 bil. **Active troops:** 655,000.

Economy: Industries: electronics, telecom, auto prod., chemicals, shipbuilding, steel. **Chief crops:** rice, root crops, barley, vegetables, fruit. **Natural resources:** coal, tungsten, graphite, molybdenum, lead, hydropower potential. **Arable land:** 15.4%. **Livestock:** cattle: 3.4 mil; chickens: 154 mil; goats: 245,000; pigs: 8.2 mil; sheep: 3,400. **Fish catch:** 3.3 mil metric tons. **Electricity prod.** (2011): 485.1 bil kWh. **Labor force:** agric. 6.2%, industry 23.8%, services 70%.

Finance: Monetary unit: Won (KRW) (Sept. 2013: 1,089.72 = $1 U.S.). **GDP:** $1.6 tril; **per capita GDP:** $32,800; **GDP growth:** 2%. **Imports:** $514.2 bil; (2011) China 16.5%, Japan 13%, U.S. 8.5%, Saudi Arabia 7.1%, Australia 5%. **Exports:** $552.6 bil; (2011) China 24.4%, U.S. 10.1%, Japan 7.1%. **Tourism:** $14.2 bil. **Budget:** $260.1 bil. **Total reserves less gold:** $323.2 bil. **Gold:** 2.7 mil oz t. **CPI change:** 2.2%.

Transport: Railways: 2,101 mi. **Motor vehicles:** 386.2 vehicles per 1,000 pop. **Civil aviation:** 51.1 bil pass.-mi; 71 airports. **Chief ports:** Busan, Incheon, Pohang, Ulsan, Yeosu.

Communications: TV sets: 424 per 1,000 pop. **Radios:** 1,037 per 1,000 pop. **Telephone lines:** 61.9 per 100 pop. **Internet:** 84.1%.

Health: Life expect.: 76.4 male; 82.9 female. **Births:** 8.3 per 1,000 pop. **Deaths:** 6.5 per 1,000 pop. **Natural inc.:** 0.18%. **Infant mortality:** 4.0 per 1,000 live births. **HIV rate:** <0.1%.

Education: Compulsory: ages 6-14. **Literacy:** NA.

Major intl. organizations: UN (FAO, IBRD, ILO, IMF, WHO), APEC, OECD, WTO.

Embassy: 2320 Massachusetts Ave. NW 20008; 939-5663.

Website: www.korea.net

Korea, once called the Hermit Kingdom, has a recorded history since the 1st cent. BCE. It was united in a kingdom under the Silla Dynasty, 668 CE. It was at times associated with the Chinese empire; the treaty that concluded the Sino-Japanese war of 1894-95 recognized Korea's complete independence. In 1910 Japan forcibly annexed Korea as Chosun.

At the Potsdam conference, July 1945, the 38th parallel was designated as the line dividing Soviet and U.S. occupation zones. Russian troops entered Korea Aug. 10, 1945; U.S. troops entered Sept. 8.

The South Koreans formed the Republic of Korea in May 1948 with Seoul as the capital. Dr. Syngman Rhee was chosen president. A separate, Communist regime was formed in the north; its army attacked the south on June 1950, initiating the Korean War. UN troops, under U.S. command, supported South Korea in the war, which ended in an armistice (July 1953) leaving Korea divided by a demilitarized zone (DMZ) along the 38th parallel.

Rhee's authoritarian rule became increasingly unpopular, and a movement spearheaded by college students forced his resignation Apr. 26, 1960. In an army coup May 16, 1961, Gen. Park Chung Hee became chairman of a ruling junta. He was elected president, 1963; a 1972 referendum allowed him to be reelected for an unlimited series of 6-year terms. Park was assassinated by the chief of the Korean CIA, Oct. 26, 1979.

In May 1980, Gen. Chun Doo Hwan, head of military intelligence, ordered the brutal suppression of pro-democracy demonstrations in Kwangju. On July 1, 1987, following weeks of sometimes violent antigovernment protests, Chun agreed to democratic reforms. In Dec., Roh Tae Woo, a longtime ally of Chun's, was elected president. In 1990, the nation's 3 largest political parties merged; some 100,000 students protested the merger as undemocratic.

Pres. Kim Young Sam took office in 1993. Convicted of mutiny, treason, and corruption, Chun was sentenced to death by a Seoul court, Aug. 26, 1996, for his role in the 1979 coup and 1980 Kwangju massacre; Roh received a 225-year prison sentence.

The 1997 collapse of the Hanbo steel firm triggered a series of corruption scandals. With currency and stock values plummeting, the nation averted default by agreeing, Dec. 4, on a $57-bil bailout from the IMF. Kim Dae Jung, a longtime dissident, won the presidential election Dec. 18. Chun and Roh were released and pardoned Dec. 22.

At a summit meeting in P'yongyang, June 13-15, 2000, Pres. Kim Dae Jung and North Korean leader Kim Jong Il agreed to work for reconciliation and eventual reunification of their 2 countries. On Oct. 13, 2000, Kim Dae Jung was named the winner of the Nobel Peace Prize. Roh Moo Hyun won the 2002 presidential election.

A subway fire in Taegu, Feb. 18, 2003, killed 198 people; the arsonist received a life term, and 8 subway officials received prison sentences for negligence. Typhoon Maemi battered Pusan and other areas Sept. 12-13, 2003, leaving about 130 people dead.

The National Assembly, Mar. 12, 2004, impeached Pres. Roh Moo Hyun for violating political neutrality and urging voters to support the Uri Party; the Constitutional Court May 14 restored Roh to office. The IAEA Sept. 2 said South Korea had acknowledged having secretly processed a small amount of uranium to near weapons-grade level in 2000, violating the Nuclear Non-Proliferation Treaty and a bilateral accord with N. Korea.

Ban Ki-Moon, South Korea's foreign minister, 2004-06, became UN sec.-gen. Jan. 1, 2007. Lee Myung Bak, a former construction executive and Seoul mayor, won the presidential election Dec. 19. Former Pres. Roh Moo Hyun, under investigation for corruption, committed suicide May 23, 2009.

As of mid-2013, South Korea had 350 troops serving in Afghanistan, and the U.S. had about 28,500 troops stationed in South Korea. Tensions between South Korea and Japan came to the fore after Pres. Lee Myung-bak, Aug. 10, visited Dokdo, a group of small islands that South Korea administers but Japan claims. Conservative Park Geun Hye became South Korea's first female president in Dec. 19, 2012, presidential elections but accusations of fraud began to be made Jan. 1, 2013.

North Korean threats of war against the South persisted throughout late 2012 and early 2013, when the North tested several short- and long-range missiles. On Mar. 11, North Korea declared a negation of the cease-fire agreement with the South that had ended the Korean War and claimed Mar. 29 that a state of war existed between the 2 countries. The North signalled a willingness to resume high-level talks on the future of its nuclear program June 16.

Kosovo
Republic of Kosovo

People: Population: 1,847,708. **Age distrib.:** <15: 26.7%; 65+: 6.9%. **Pop. density:** 439.6 per sq mi, 169.7 per sq km. **Urban:** NA. **Ethnic groups:** Albanian 92%, other (incl. Serb, Bosniak, Gorani, Roma, Turk, Ashkali, Egyptian) 8%. **Languages:** Albanian, Serbian (both official); Bosnian; Turkish; Roma. **Religions:** Muslim, Serbian Orthodox, Roman Catholic.

Geography: Total area: 4,203 sq mi, 10,887 sq km. **Land area:** 4,203 sq mi, 10,887 sq km. **Location:** SE Europe between Serbia and Macedonia. **Neighbors:** Serbia on N, Montenegro on NW, Albania on SW, Macedonia on SE. **Topography:** Low flood basins surrounded by several high mountain ranges. **Capital:** Pristina.

Government: Type: Republic. **Head of state:** Pres. Atifete Jahjaga; b. Apr. 20, 1975; in office: Apr. 7, 2011. **Head of gov.:** Prime Min. Hashim Thaçi; b. Apr. 24, 1968; in office: Jan. 9, 2008. **Local divisions:** 37 municipalities. **Defense budget/active troops:** NA.

Economy: Industries: mineral mining, constr. materials, base metals, leather, machinery, appliances, foodstuffs and beverages, textiles. **Chief crops:** wheat, corn, berries, potatoes, peppers, fruit. **Natural resources:** nickel, lead, zinc, magnesium, lignite, kaolin, chrome, bauxite. **Arable land:** NA. **Labor force:** agric. 23.6%.

Finance: Monetary unit: Euro (EUR) (Sept. 2013: 0.76 = $1 U.S.). **GDP:** $13.6 bil; **per capita GDP:** NA; **GDP growth:** 2.1%. **Imports** (2011): $3.3 bil. **Exports** (2011): $419 mil. **Budget** (2011): $2.1 bil. **Total reserves less gold:** $1.1 bil. **CPI change:** NA.

Transport: Railways: 267 mi. **Civil aviation:** 3 airports.

Communications: NA.

Health: Life expect.: 68.7 male; 73.0 female. **Births:** 17.7 per 1,000 pop. **Deaths:** 7.0 per 1,000 pop. **Natural inc.:** 1.07%. **Infant mortality:** 39.3 per 1,000 live births. **HIV rate:** NA.

Education: NA. **Literacy:** NA.

Major intl. organizations: UN (IBRD, IMF).

Embassy: 900 19th St. NW, Ste. 400, 20006; 380-3581.

Website: www.rks-gov.net

Kosovo was part of the Roman and Byzantine empires before Serbs, a Slavic people, took control in the Middle Ages. After Ottoman Turks defeated Serb forces, 1389, Kosovo's population became predominantly Muslim and Kosovar (ethnic Albanian). Serbia regained control in the First Balkan War (1912-13). Kosovo entered the Kingdom of Serbs, Croats, and Slovenes as part of Serbia after World War I and became an autonomous province of Serbia, a constituent republic of Yugoslavia, after World War II.

Revoking provincial autonomy, Serbia began ruling Kosovo by force in 1989. Albanian secessionists proclaimed an independent Republic of Kosovo in July 1990. As Yugoslavia collapsed, the republics of Serbia (incl. Kosovo) and Montenegro proclaimed a new Federal Republic of Yugoslavia, 1992, under Pres. Slobodan Milosevic. Guerrilla attacks by the Kosovo Liberation Army in 1997 brought a ferocious counteroffensive by Serbian authorities.

Fearful that the Serbs were employing "ethnic cleansing" tactics, as they had in Bosnia, the U.S. and its NATO allies pressured the Yugoslav government to end hostilities. When Milosevic refused, NATO launched an air war against Yugoslavia, Mar.-June 1999; the Serbs retaliated by terrorizing the Kosovars. Hundreds of thousands fled, mostly to Albania and Macedonia. A 50,000-member multinational force (KFOR) entered Kosovo in June, and most refugees returned by Sept. 1, 1999.

From June 1999, Kosovo was administered by a UN mission (UNMIK). Kosovo declared independence, Feb. 17, 2008, and while the U.S. and most European allies immediately recognized the new country, Serbia and Russia refused. In a nonbinding ruling, the World Court held July 22, 2010, that Kosovo's independence declaration was legal. As of June 2013, KFOR had about 5,000 troops in Kosovo. Kosovo and Serbia entered negotiations meant to normalize their relations Mar. 8, 2011. On Apr. 19, 2013, the 2 countries arrived at a power-sharing agreement between the northern Kosovo regions with a Serb majority and the Kosovo central government led by ethnic Albanians.

Kuwait
State of Kuwait

People: Population: 2,695,316. **Age distrib.:** <15: 25.6%; 65+: 2.1%. **Pop. density:** 391.8 per sq mi, 151.3 per sq km. **Urban:** 98.3%. **Ethnic groups:** Kuwaiti 45%, other Arab 35%, South Asian 9%, Iranian 4%. **Languages:** Arabic (official), English (widely spoken). **Religions:** Muslim (official) 85% (Sunni 70%, Shia 30%), other (incl. Christian, Hindu, Parsi) 15%.

Geography: Total area: 6,880 sq mi, 17,818 sq km; **Land area:** 6,880 sq mi, 17,818 sq km. **Location:** In Middle East, at N end of Persian Gulf. **Neighbors:** Iraq on N, Saudi Arabia on S. **Topography:** Flat, very dry, and extremely hot. **Capital:** Kuwait City, 2,406,410.

Government: Type: Constitutional emirate. **Head of state:** Emir Sheikh Sabah al-Ahmad al-Jabir as-Sabah; b. June 6, 1929; in office: Jan. 29, 2006. **Head of gov.:** Prime Min. Sheikh Jaber al-Mubarak al-Hamad al-Sabah; b. Jan. 5, 1942; in office: Nov. 30, 2011. **Local divisions:** 6 governorates. **Defense budget:** $4.62 bil. **Active troops:** 15,500.

Economy: Industries: petroleum, petrochemicals, cement, shipbuilding and repair, water desalination, food proc., constr. materials. **Chief crops:** fish. **Natural resources:** petroleum, fish, shrimp, nat. gas. **Crude oil reserves:** 104 bil bbls. (half of Neutral Zone reserves). **Arable land:** 0.6%. **Livestock:** cattle: 35,000; chickens: 32 mil; goats: 178,703; sheep: 470,000. **Fish catch:** 4,860 metric tons. **Electricity prod.** 53.6 bil kWh. **Labor force:** NA.

Finance: Monetary unit: Dinar (KWD) (Sept. 2013: 0.29 = $1 U.S.). **GDP:** $153.4 bil; **per capita GDP:** $40,500; **GDP growth:** 5.1%. **Imports:** $22.8 bil; U.S. 11.8%, China 9.2%, Saudi Arabia 8.3%, Japan 8.2%, South Korea 7%, Germany 5.1%, Italy 4.7%, India 4.6%, UAE 4.2%. **Exports:** $121 bil; South Korea 16%, India 15.7%, Japan 13.4%, U.S. 11.7%, China 9.2%, Singapore 4.2%. **Tourism:** $425 mil. **Budget:** $58.1 bil. **Total reserves less gold:** $28.9 bil. **Gold:** 2.5 mil oz t. **CPI change:** 2.9%.

Transport: Motor vehicles: 628 vehicles per 1,000 pop. **Civil aviation:** 4.8 bil pass.-mi; 4 airports. **Chief ports:** Ash Shuayhah, Ash Shuwaykh, Az Zawr, Mina Abd Allah, Mina al Ahmadi.

Communications: TV sets: 399 per 1,000 pop. **Radios:** 572 per 1,000 pop. **Telephone lines** 17.6 per 100 pop. **Internet:** 79.2%.

Health: Life expect.: 76.2 male; 78.8 female. **Births:** 20.6 per 1,000 pop. **Deaths:** 2.1 per 1,000 pop. **Natural inc.:** 1.85% **Infant mortality:** 7.7 per 1,000 live births. **HIV rate:** NA.

Education: Compulsory: ages 6-14. **Literacy:** 93.9%.

Major intl. organizations: UN (FAO, IBRD, ILO, IMF, WHO), AL, OPEC, WTO.

Embassy: 2940 Tilden St. NW 20008; 966-0702.

Website: www.da.gov.kw

Kuwait is ruled by the Sabah dynasty, founded 1759. Britain ran foreign relations and defense from 1899 until independence in 1961. Nearly half the population is non-Kuwaiti, including many Palestinians, and cannot vote.

Oil is the fiscal mainstay, providing most of Kuwait's income. Oil pays for free medical care, education, and social security. There are no taxes, except customs duties.

Kuwait was attacked and overrun by Iraqi forces Aug. 1990. In Operation Desert Storm a U.S.-led coalition, with authorization from the UN Security Council, began bombing Iraq and Iraqi forces in Kuwait, Jan. 1991, then launched a ground assault Feb. 23. By Feb. 27, Iraqi forces were routed and Kuwait liberated.

Political rights were extended to women, May 16, 2005; the first female cabinet member was appointed June 12. Kuwait enacted a $5.2 bil program Mar. 2009 to bail out banks and investment companies battered by the global financial crisis. The moderate Jaber al-Mubarak al-Hamad al-Sabah was reappointed prime min. July 2012, after resigning in response to a June 2012 ruling of the Constitutional Court that declared unconstitutional the Feb. 2011 elections that had brought him to power. Al-Sabah dissolved parliament Oct. 7, 2012, and called for new elections, but the opposition-led boycott resulted in just a 39% turnout for a Dec. 2 vote. The Constitutional Court dissolved parliament again June 16, 2013, and in elections held July 27 some liberal and marginalized tribal groups won seats, though the majority of seats were won by lawmakers who support Kuwait's ruling family.

Kyrgyzstan
Kyrgyz Republic

People: Population: 5,548,042. **Age distrib.:** <15: 29.7%; 65+: 4.9%. **Pop. density:** 74.9 per sq mi, 28.9 per sq km. **Urban:** 35.3%. **Ethnic groups:** Kyrgyz 65%, Uzbek 14%, Russian 13%, Dungan

1%, Ukrainian 1%, Uighur 1%. **Languages:** Kyrgyz (official), Uzbek, Russian (official), Dungun. **Religions:** Muslim 75%, Russian Orthodox 20%.

Geography: Total area: 77,202 sq mi, 199,951 sq km; **Land area:** 74,055 sq mi, 191,801 sq km. **Location:** In Central Asia. **Neigh-bors:** Kazakhstan on N, China on E, Uzbekistan on W, Tajikistan on S. **Topography:** Landlocked country nearly covered by Tien Shan and Pamir Mts.; avg. elevation 9,020 ft. A large lake, Issyk-Kul, in NE is 1 mi above sea level. **Capital:** Bishkek, 838,606.

Government: Type: Republic. **Head of state:** Pres. Almazbek Sharshenovich Atambayev; b. Sept. 17, 1956; in office: Dec. 1, 2011. **Head of gov.:** Prime Min. Jantoro Satybaldiev; b. Jan. 6, 1956; in office: Sept. 5, 2012. **Local divisions:** 7 provinces, 1 city. **Defense budget:** $105 mil. **Active troops:** 10,900.

Economy: Industries: small machinery, textiles, food proc., cement, shoes, sawn logs, refrigerators, furniture, elec. motors. **Chief crops:** tobacco, cotton, potatoes, vegetables, grapes, fruits and berries. **Natural resources:** hydropower, gold, rare earth metals, coal, oil, nat. gas, nepheline, mercury, bismuth, lead, zinc. **Crude oil reserves:** 40 mil bbls. **Arable land:** 6.7%. **Livestock:** cattle: 1.3 mil; chickens: 4.5 mil; goats: 1 mil; pigs: 59,202; sheep: 4.3 mil. **Fish catch:** 422 metric tons. **Electricity prod.:** 11.2 bil kWh. **Labor force:** agric. 48%, industry 12.5%, services 39.5%.

Finance: Monetary unit: Som (KGS) (Sept. 2013: 48.82 = $1 U.S.). **GDP:** $13.5 bil; **per capita GDP:** $2,400; **GDP growth:** –0.9%. **Imports:** $5 bil; China 55.9%, Russia 17.7%, Kazakhstan 6.4%. **Exports:** $2 bil; Uzbekistan 28.8%, Kazakhstan 22%, Russia 14.6%, China 7%, UAE 6.3%, Afghanistan 5.7%. **Tourism:** $698 mil. **Budget:** $2.1 bil. **Total reserves less gold:** $1.9 bil. **Gold:** 98,273 oz t. **CPI change:** 2.7%.

Transport: Railways: 292 mi. **Civil aviation:** 361.6 mil pass.-mi; 18 airports. **Chief port:** Balykchy.

Communications: TV sets: 224 per 1,000 pop. **Radios:** 110 per 1,000 pop. **Telephone lines:** 9 per 100 pop. **Internet:** 21.7%.

Health: Life expect.: 65.6 male; 74.2 female. **Births:** 23.7 per 1,000 pop. **Deaths:** 6.8 per 1,000 pop. **Natural inc.:** 1.68%. **Infant mortality:** 29.7 per 1,000 live births. **HIV rate:** 0.4%.

Education: Compulsory: ages 7-15. **Literacy:** 99.2%.

Major intl. organizations: UN (FAO, IBRD, ILO, WHO), CIS, OSCE, WTO.

Embassy: 2360 Massachusetts Ave. NW 20008; 338-5141.

Website: www.president.kg

The region was inhabited around the 13th cent. by the Kyrgyz. It was annexed to Russia, 1864, and became a constituent republic of the USSR in 1936. Kyrgyzstan declared independence Aug. 31, 1991. It became an independent state when the USSR disbanded Dec. 26, 1991.

In power since 1990, Pres. Askar Akayev won a third 5-year term in the 2000 election. Fraud by Akayev loyalists in parliamentary elections Feb.-Mar. 2005 sparked protests. Akayev fled the country, Mar. 24, and formally resigned, Apr. 4. His interim successor, former Prime Min. Kurmanbek Bakiyev, a leader of the "tulip revolution," won the 2005 presidential vote and was reelected 2009, when monitors reported numerous irregularities. He was ousted by opposition parties Apr. 7, 2010, after clashes between protesters and government security forces left at least 85 people dead; an interim government was led by former Foreign Min. Roza Otunbayeva.

Fighting in mid-June between majority Kyrgyz and minority Uzbeks in the southern cities of Osh and Jalalabad claimed up to 2,000 lives. A June 2010 referendum on a new constitution received overwhelming approval. Oct. elections brought 5 parties to the parliament, and Omurbek Babanov became prime min. of a coalition government. Almazbek Atambayev won the 2011 presidential election. Babanov's coalition broke up Aug. 2012; a new coalition was formed Sept. 3, 2 days after Babanov resigned, and Jantoro Satybaldiev was sworn in as prime min. on Sept. 5. Three members of the opposition were convicted Mar. 30, 2013, of inciting crowds to assault government offices during an Oct. 2012 demonstration supporting the nationalizing of a gold mine. Violent demonstrations to nationalize the country's gold mines continued throughout the spring.

Laos
Lao People's Democratic Republic

People: Population: 6,695,166. **Age distrib.:** <15: 35.5%; 65+: 3.7%. **Pop. density:** 75.1 per sq mi, 29 per sq km. **Urban:** 34.3%. **Ethnic groups:** Lao 55%, Khmou 11%, Hmong 8%, other (100+ minor ethnic groups) 26%. **Languages:** Lao (official), French, English, various ethnic langs. **Religions:** Buddhist 67%, Christian 2%.

Geography: Total area: 91,429 sq mi, 236,800 sq km; **Land area:** 89,112 sq mi, 230,800 sq km. **Location:** In Indochina Peninsula in SE Asia. **Neighbors:** Myanmar, China on N; Vietnam on E; Cambodia on S; Thailand on W. **Topography:** Landlocked, dominated by jungle. High mountains along E border are source of the E-W rivers slicing across the country to the Mekong R., which defines most of W border. **Capital:** Vientiane, 810,054.

Government: Type: Communist state. **Head of state:** Pres. Choummaly Sayasone; b. Mar. 6, 1936; in office: June 8, 2006. **Head of gov.:** Prime Min. Thongsing Thammavong; b. 1944; in office: Dec. 23, 2010. **Local divisions:** 16 provinces, 1 capital city. **Defense budget:** $22 mil. **Active troops:** 29,100.

Economy: Industries: mining, timber, elec. power, agric. proc., rubber, constr., garments, cement, tourism. **Chief crops:** sweet potatoes, vegetables, corn, coffee, sugarcane, tobacco, cotton, tea, peanuts, rice, cassava. **Natural resources:** timber, hydropower, gypsum, tin, gold, gems. **Arable land:** 6.1%. **Livestock:** cattle: 1.5 mil; chickens: 26.9 mil; goats: 430,900; pigs: 2.7 mil. **Fish catch:** 116,900 metric tons. **Electricity prod.:** 3.6 bil kWh. **Labor force:** agric. 75.1%.

Finance: Monetary unit: Kip (LAK) (Sept. 2013: 7,865.36 = $1 U.S.). **GDP:** $19.5 bil; **per capita GDP:** $3,100; **GDP growth:** 8.3%. **Imports:** $2.7 bil; Thailand 63.2%, China 16.5%, Vietnam 5.6%. **Exports:** $2 bil; Thailand 32.8%, China 20.7%, Vietnam 14%. **Tourism:** $506 mil. **Budget:** $2.2 bil. **Total reserves less gold** (2011) $741.2 mil. **Gold** (2011): 285,429 oz t. **CPI change:** 4.3%.

Transport: Civil aviation: 82.6 mil pass.-mi; 8 airports.

Communications: TV sets: 57 per 1,000 pop. **Radios:** 148 per 1,000 pop. **Telephone lines:** 1.8 per 100 pop. **Internet:** 10.7%.

Health: Life expect.: 61.2 male; 65.2 female. **Births:** 25.2 per 1,000 pop. **Deaths:** 7.9 per 1,000 pop. **Natural inc.:** 1.74%. **Infant mortality:** 56.1 per 1,000 live births. **HIV rate:** 0.3%.

Education: Compulsory: ages 6-10. **Literacy:** 72.7%.

Major intl. organizations: UN (FAO, IBRD, ILO, IMF, WHO), ASEAN, WTO (observer).

Embassy: 2222 S St. NW 20008; 332-6416.

Website: www.na.gov.la

Laos became a French protectorate in 1893, but regained independence as a constitutional monarchy July 19, 1949. Conflicts among neutralist, Communist, and conservative factions created a chaotic political situation. Armed conflict increased after 1960.

The 3 factions formed a coalition government in June 1962 with neutralist Prince Souvanna Phouma as premier. A 14-nation conference in Geneva signed agreements, 1962, guaranteeing independence. By 1964 the Pathet Lao had withdrawn from the coalition, and, with aid from North Vietnamese troops, renewed sporadic attacks. U.S. planes bombed the Ho Chi Minh trail, a supply line from North Vietnam to Communist forces in Laos and South Vietnam.

In 1970 the U.S. stepped up air support and military aid. After Pathet Lao military gains, Souvanna Phouma, May 1975, ordered government troops to cease fighting; the Pathet Lao took control. The Lao People's Democratic Republic was proclaimed Dec. 3, 1975.

From the mid-1970s through the 1980s, Laos relied on Vietnam for military and financial aid. After easing its finance laws in 1988, Laos attracted substantial foreign investment from Thailand, China, Vietnam, the U.S., and other nations. Laos was admitted to ASEAN in 1997. The U.S. Congress approved normalization of trade with Laos in 2004. To spur further investment, Laos opened its first stock exchange Jan. 11, 2011, in Vientiane. Ground was broken Nov. 7, 2012, on a controversial hydroelectric dam on the Mekong River, despite environmentalists' concern that it will harm the area's wildlife and natural resources. The government had authorized several more dams to be built on the river in the coming years.

Latvia
Republic of Latvia

People: Population: 2,178,443. **Age distrib.:** <15: 14%; 65+: 17.1%. **Pop. density:** 90.6 per sq mi, 35 per sq km. **Urban:** 67.7%. **Ethnic groups:** Latvian 59%, Russian 28%, Belarusian 4%, Ukrainian 3%, Polish 2%, Lithuanian 1%. **Languages:** Latvian (official), Russian, Lithuanian. **Religions:** Lutheran 20%, Orthodox 15%.

Geography: Total area: 24,938 sq mi, 64,589 sq km; **Land area:** 24,034 sq mi, 62,249 sq km. **Location:** E Europe, on Baltic Sea. **Neighbors:** Estonia on N; Lithuania, Belarus on S; Russia on E. **Topography:** Lowland with numerous lakes, marshes, and peat bogs. Principal river, W. Dvina (Daugava), rises in Russia. Glacial hills in E. **Capital:** Riga, 701,135.

Government: Type: Parliamentary democracy. **Head of state:** Pres. Andris Berzins; b. Dec. 10, 1944; in office: July 8, 2011. **Head of gov.:** Prime Min. Valdis Dombrovskis; b. Aug. 5, 1971; in office: Mar. 12, 2009. **Local divisions:** 110 municipalities, 9 cities. **Defense budget:** $257 mil. **Active troops:** 5,350.

Economy: Industries: processed foods, processed wood prods., textiles, processed metals, pharmaceuticals, railroad cars, synthetic fibers, electronics. **Chief crops:** grain, rapeseed, potatoes, vegetables. **Natural resources:** peat, limestone, dolomite, amber, hydropower, timber. **Arable land:** 18.6%. **Livestock:** cattle: 379,500; chickens: 4.2 mil; goats: 13,500; pigs: 389,700; sheep: 76,800. **Fish catch:** 155,876 metric tons. **Electricity prod.:** 6.4 bil kWh. **Labor force:** agric. 8.8%, industry 24%, services 67.2%.

Finance: Monetary unit: Lat (LVL) (Sept. 2013: 0.53 = $1 U.S.). **GDP:** $37.9 bil; **per capita GDP:** $18,600; **GDP growth:** 5.6%. **Imports:** $16.1 bil; Lithuania 18.9%, Germany 11.5%, Russia 9.3%, Poland 8.1%, Estonia 7.5%, Italy 4.6%, Finland 4.4%. **Exports:** $12.5 bil; Russia 18.3%, Lithuania 15%, Estonia 12%, Germany 7.2%, Poland 5.6%, Sweden 4.8%. **Tourism:** $745 mil. **Budget:** $9.7 bil. **Total reserves less gold:** $7.1 bil. **Gold:** 248,700 oz t. **CPI change:** 2.3%.

Transport: Railways: 1,391 mi. **Motor vehicles:** 319.2 vehicles per 1,000 pop. **Civil aviation:** 904.7 mil pass.-mi; 18 airports. **Chief ports:** Riga, Ventspils.

Communications: TV sets: 855 per 1,000 pop. **Radios:** 700 per 1,000 pop. **Telephone lines:** 22.4 per 100 pop. **Internet:** 74%.

Health: Life expect.: 68.1 male; 78.5 female. **Births:** 9.9 per 1,000 pop. **Deaths:** 13.6 per 1,000 pop. **Natural inc.:** −0.37%. **Infant mortality:** 8.1 per 1,000 live births. **HIV rate:** 0.7%.

Education: Compulsory: ages 7-15. **Literacy:** 99.8%.

Major intl. organizations: UN (FAO, IBRD, ILO, IMF, WHO), EU, NATO, OSCE, WTO.

Embassy: 2306 Massachusetts Ave. NW 20008; 328-2840.

Website: www.li.lv

Prior to 1918, Latvia was occupied by the Russians and Germans. It was an independent republic, 1918-39. The Aug. 1939 Soviet-German agreement assigned Latvia to the Soviet sphere of influence. It was officially absorbed by the USSR in 1940. It was overrun by the German army in 1941, but retaken in 1945.

During an abortive Soviet coup, Latvia declared independence, Aug. 21, 1991. The last Russian troops in Latvia withdrew by Aug. 31, 1994. Responding to international pressure, Latvian voters, 1998, eased citizenship laws that had discriminated against some 500,000 ethnic Russians. Latvia joined the EU and NATO in 2004.

Hit hard by recession, Latvia reached agreement Dec. 2008 on a $10.4 bil emergency loan from the EU, IMF, World Bank, and Nordic countries. Angered by the prolonged economic downturn and the growing influence of wealthy oligarchs over Latvian politics, voters in a July 2011 referendum approved a proposal to dissolve parliament. Prime Min. Valdis Dombrovskis's Unity Party came in third in Sept. 2011 elections, but Dombrovskis remained prime min. Latvia repaid its IMF loan Dec. 21, 2012, and made acceptable progress on repaying its EU loan by mid-2013. It was approved for membership in the eurozone June 25, 2013, and officially accepted July 9. Its membership will begin Jan. 1, 2014.

Lebanon
Lebanese Republic

People: Population: 4,131,583. **Age distrib.:** <15: 22.1%; 65+: 9.4%. **Pop. density:** 1,046 per sq mi, 403.9 per sq km. **Urban:** 87.2%. **Ethnic groups:** Arab 95%, Armenian 4%; many Christian Lebanese do not identify as Arab and prefer to be called Phoenician. **Languages:** Arabic (official), French, English, Armenian. **Religions:** Muslim 60%, Christian 39%.

Geography: Total area: 4,015 sq mi, 10,400 sq km; **Land area:** 3,950 sq mi, 10,230 sq km. **Location:** In Middle East, on E end of Mediterranean Sea. **Neighbors:** Syria on E, Israel on S. **Topography:** There is a narrow coastal strip, and 2 mountain ranges running N-S enclosing the fertile Beqaa Valley. The Litani R. runs S through the valley, turning W to empty into Mediterranean. **Capital:** Beirut, 2,022,350.

Government: Type: Republic. **Head of state:** Pres. Michel Suleiman; b. Nov. 21, 1948; in office: May 25, 2008. **Head of gov.:** Prime Min. Tammam Salam; b. 1945; in office: Apr. 6, 2013. **Local divisions:** 6 governorates. **Defense budget:** $1.15 bil. **Active troops:** 60,000.

Economy: Industries: banking, tourism, food proc., wine, jewelry, cement, textiles, mineral and chem. prods., wood and furniture prods. **Chief crops:** citrus, grapes, tomatoes, apples, vegetables, potatoes, olives, tobacco. **Natural resources:** limestone, iron ore, salt, water (surplus in a water-deficit region). **Arable land:** 10.9%. **Livestock:** cattle: 65,000; chickens: 38 mil; goats: 400,000; pigs: 7,650; sheep: 255,000. **Fish catch:** 5,091 metric tons. **Electricity prod.:** 14.8 bil kWh. **Labor force:** NA.

Finance: Monetary unit: Pound (LBP) (Sept. 2013: 1,511.49 = $1 U.S.). **GDP:** $64.2 bil; **per capita GDP:** $16,000; **GDP growth:** 1.5%. **Imports:** $20.4 bil; U.S. 11.2%, China 8.3%, Italy 7.8%, France 7.4%, Germany 5.4%, Turkey 4.7%, Egypt 4.1%, Greece 4.1%. **Exports:** $5.7 bil; South Africa 16.9%, Switzerland 10.7%, UAE 8.7%, Saudi Arabia 8.5%, Syria 6.4%, Iraq 4.4%. **Tourism:** $6.9 bil. **Budget:** $13.3 bil. **Total reserves less gold:** $37.2 bil. **Gold:** 9.2 mil oz t. **CPI change** (2009-10): 4%.

Transport: Railways: 249 mi (unusable because of damage from fighting). **Motor vehicles:** 142.7 vehicles per 1,000 pop. **Civil aviation:** 1.7 bil pass.-mi; 5 airports. **Chief ports:** Beirut, Tripoli.

Communications: TV sets: 387 per 1,000 pop. **Radios:** 75 per 1,000 pop. **Telephone lines:** 20.5 per 100 pop. **Internet:** 61.2%.

Health: Life expect.: 73.9 male; 77.1 female. **Births:** 14.8 per 1,000 pop. **Deaths:** 6.7 per 1,000 pop. **Natural inc.:** 0.81%. **Infant mortality:** 14.8 per 1,000 live births. **HIV rate:** 0.1%.

Education: Compulsory: ages 6-14. **Literacy:** 89.6%.

Major intl. organizations: UN (FAO, IBRD, ILO, IMF, WHO), AL, WTO (observer).

Embassy: 2560 28th St. NW 20008; 939-6300.

Website: www.presidency.gov.lb

Formed from 5 former Turkish Empire districts, Lebanon became independent Sept. 1, 1920, administered under French mandate 1920-41. French troops withdrew in 1946.

Under the 1943 National Covenant, all public positions were divided among the various religious communities, with Christians in the majority. By the 1970s, Muslims became the majority and demanded a larger political and economic role.

U.S. Marines intervened, May-Oct. 1958, during a Syrian-aided revolt. Continued raids against Israeli civilians, 1970-75, brought Israeli retaliation in southern Lebanon.

An estimated 60,000 were killed in a 1975-76 civil war. Palestinian units and leftist Muslims fought against Maronite militia (the Phalange) and other Christians. Several Arab countries provided support to various factions, while Israel aided Christian forces. Syria, which intervened in 1976 to fight Palestinian groups, largely policed a cease-fire.

Israeli forces invaded Lebanon June 6, 1982, attacking strongholds of the Palestine Liberation Organization (PLO). Israeli and Syrian forces engaged in the Bekaa Valley. On Aug. 21, the PLO evacuated W Beirut after massive Israeli bombings. Israeli troops entered W Beirut following the Sept. 14 assassination of newly elected Lebanese Pres. Bashir Gemayel. On Sept. 16, 1982, Lebanese Christian troops entered the Sabra and Shatila refugee camps and massacred hundreds of Palestinian civilians. An agreement May 17, 1983, between Lebanon, Israel, and the U.S. (but not Syria) provided for the withdrawal of Israeli troops; at least 30,000 Syrian troops remained in Lebanon, and Israel held onto a "security zone" in the south.

In 1983, some 50 people were killed in an explosion at the U.S. embassy, Apr. 18; 241 U.S. service members and 58 French soldiers died in separate Islamist suicide attacks, Oct. 23. The 1980s witnessed kidnappings of U.S., British, French, and Soviet citizens by Islamic militants. All hostages were released by 1992.

A treaty signed May 22, 1991, between Lebanon and Syria recognized Lebanon as a separate state for the first time since 1943.

Israeli forces conducted air raids and artillery strikes against guerrilla bases and villages in southern Lebanon, causing over 200,000 to flee their homes July 25-29, 1993. Some 500,000 civilians fled in Apr. 1996 when Israel struck suspected guerrilla bases in the south. The economy revived in the 1990s, but Syria continued to dominate Lebanon's political affairs. Israel withdrew virtually all its troops from S Lebanon by May 2000, leaving Hezbollah, an Iranian-backed guerrilla group, in control of much of the region.

Rafik al-Hariri, a former prime min. (1992-98, 2000-04), was killed by a truck bomb, Feb. 14, 2005. Many Lebanese blamed Syria. As anti-Syrian protests mounted, Syrian troops left Lebanon (some intelligence agents may have remained). An anti-Syrian bloc won May and June parliamentary elections. A new cabinet, installed July 2005, was headed by Fouad Siniora and included a Hezbollah member.

A Hezbollah rocket attack and border raid, July 2006, in which 3 Israeli soldiers were killed and 2 captured, triggered a massive escalation of hostilities. Hezbollah, led by Sheikh Hassan Nasrallah, bombarded northern Israel with nearly 4,000 rockets, while Israeli air and ground forces assaulted suspected Hezbollah strongholds in southern Lebanon and southern Beirut. By Aug. 14, 2006, when a UN-sponsored cease-fire took hold, the war dead included nearly 1,150 Lebanese. To enforce the truce, thousands of Lebanese troops moved into southern Lebanon, and the small UN force already in Lebanon (UNIFIL) was expanded.

At an international conference in Paris, Jan. 2007, donor countries pledged more than $7.6 bil in reconstruction aid. After more than 3 months of fighting in which over 400 people died, Lebanese forces Sept. 2 defeated Islamic militants at the Nahr al-Bared Palestinian refugee camp north of Tripoli. A 2008 power-sharing accord between the Siniora government and Hezbollah eased factional violence and paved the way for Army Chief Gen. Michel Suleiman to become president, ending an 18-month stalemate.

A pro-Western coalition, the March 14 Movement, led by Saad Hariri (son of the slain former prime min.), won a parliamentary majority in 2009 elections. A 5-month impasse ended with the installation of Prime Min. Hariri and his cabinet (including Hezbollah) in Nov. After that government collapsed in Jan. 2011, a 5-month deadlock culminated in the installation June 13 of a cabinet dominated by Hezbollah and headed by Prime Min. Najib Mikati, a telecommunications billionaire. UNIFIL had 10,819 uniformed personnel in Lebanon in mid-2013. The Syrian civil war spilled over into Lebanon in 2012, most dramatically in Tripoli, where Sunni Muslims and Alawite Muslims took part in firefights Aug. 21-26, 2012, that left at least 17 dead. A deadly bombing also linked to the Syrian civil war took place in Beirut in Oct. 19, killing the anti-Syrian Gen. Wissam al-Hassan and prompting Lebanese citizens to demonstrate for a new government. Hezbollah gave military aid to Syria, escalating the conflict on the border and suffering its own casualties. In Apr. 2013, Israel shot down a Hezbollah drone in its airspace. Radical Sunnis fought with the Lebanese Army June 23-24 in growing sectarian violence. As of Sept. 2013, the UNHCR projected there would be 300,000 Syrian refugees in Lebanon by Dec. 2013.

Lesotho
Kingdom of Lesotho

People: Population: 1,936,181. **Age distrib.: <15:** 33.1%; **65+:** 5.4%. **Pop. density:** 165.2 per sq mi, 63.8 per sq km. **Urban:** 27.6%. **Ethnic groups:** Sotho 99.7%. **Languages:** Sesotho, English (both official); Zulu; Xhosa. **Religions:** Christian 80%, indigenous beliefs 20%.

Geography: Total area: 11,720 sq mi, 30,355 sq km; **Land area:** 11,720 sq mi, 30,355 sq km. **Location:** In southern Africa. **Neighbors:** Completely surrounded by South Africa. **Topography:** Landlocked and mountainous, altitudes from 5,000 to 11,000 ft. **Capital:** Maseru, 238,553.

Government: Type: Parliamentary constitutional monarchy. **Head of state:** King Letsie III; b. July 17, 1963; in office: Feb. 7, 1996. **Head of gov.:** Prime Min. Thomas Motsoahae Thabane; b. 1939; in office: June 8, 2012. **Local divisions:** 10 districts. **Defense budget:** $78 mil. **Active troops:** 2,000.

Economy: Industries: food, beverages, textiles, apparel assembly, handicrafts, constr., tourism. **Chief crops:** corn, wheat, pulses, sorghum, barley. **Natural resources:** water, diamonds, sand, clay, building stone. **Arable land:** 10.1%. **Livestock:** cattle: 650,000; chickens: 485,000; goats: 845,000; pigs: 80,000; sheep: 1.2 mil. **Fish catch:** 345 metric tons. **Electricity prod.:** 200 mil kWh. **Labor force:** agric. 86% (subsistence), industry and services 14%. Approx. 35% of active wage earners work in South Africa.

Finance: Monetary unit: Loti (LSL) (Sept. 2013: 10.02 = $1 U.S.). **GDP:** $4.1 bil; **per capita GDP:** $2,200; **GDP growth:** 4%. **Imports:** $2.4 bil. **Exports:** $1 bil. **Tourism:** $26 mil. **Budget:** $1.5 bil. **Total reserves less gold:** NA. **CPI change:** 6.1%.

Transport: Civil aviation: 3 airports.

Communications: TV sets: 44 per 1,000 pop. **Radios:** 121 per 1,000 pop. **Telephone lines:** 1.9 per 100 pop. **Internet:** 4.6%.

Health: Life expect.: 52.2 male; 52.4 female. **Births:** 26.3 per 1,000 pop. **Deaths:** 15.0 per 1,000 pop. **Natural inc.:** 1.13%. **Infant mortality:** 51.9 per 1,000 live births. **HIV rate:** 23.3%.

Education: Compulsory ages: NA. **Literacy:** 75.8%.

Major intl. organizations: UN (FAO, IBRD, ILO, IMF, WHO), AU, the Commonwealth, WTO.

Embassy: 2511 Massachusetts Ave. NW 20008; 797-5533.
Website: www.gov.ls

Lesotho (once called Basutoland) became a British protectorate in 1868 when Chief Moshesh sought protection against the Boers. Independence came Oct. 4, 1966. Most of Lesotho's GNP is provided by citizens working in South Africa. Livestock raising is a major industry; diamonds are the chief export.

In Mar. 1990, King Moshoeshoe was exiled by the military government. Letsie III became king Nov. 12. In Mar. 1993, Ntsu Mokhehle, a civilian, was elected prime minister, ending 23 years of military rule. After a series of violent disturbances, the king dismissed the Mokhehle government Aug. 17, 1994; constitutional rule was restored Sept. 14.

Letsie abdicated and Moshoeshoe was reinstated Jan. 25, 1995. Moshoeshoe died in an automobile accident, Jan. 15, 1996. Letsie was reinstated Feb. 7. South Africa and Botswana sent troops Sept. 1998 to help suppress violent antigovernment protests. After parliamentary elections May 26, 2012, the left-leaning Thomas Motsoahae Thabane became the first new prime min. since 1998.

Cultivation of marijuana for smuggling to South Africa is a significant source of income.

Liberia
Republic of Liberia

People: Population: 3,989,703. **Age distrib.: <15:** 43.6%; **65+:** 3%. **Pop. density:** 107.3 per sq mi, 41.4 per sq km. **Urban:** 48.2%. **Ethnic groups:** Kpelle 20%, Bassa 13%, Grebo 10%, Gio 8%, Mano 8%, Kru 6%, Lorma 5%, Kissi 5%, Gola 4%. **Languages:** English (official), about 20 ethnic langs. **Religions:** Christian 86%, Muslim 12%.

Geography: Total area: 43,000 sq mi, 111,369 sq km; **Land area:** 37,189 sq mi, 96,320 sq km. **Location:** On SW coast of W Africa. **Neighbors:** Sierra Leone on W, Guinea on N, Côte d'Ivoire on E. **Topography:** Marshy Atlantic coastline rises to low mountains and plateaus in forested interior; 6 major rivers flow in parallel courses to the ocean. **Capital:** Monrovia, 750,376.

Government: Type: Republic. **Head of state and gov.:** Pres. Ellen Johnson-Sirleaf; b. Oct. 29, 1938; in office: Jan. 16, 2006. **Local divisions:** 15 counties. **Defense budget** (2011): $16 mil. **Active troops:** 2,050.

Economy: Industries: rubber and palm oil proc., timber, diamonds. **Chief crops:** rubber, coffee, cocoa, rice, cassava, palm oil, sugarcane, bananas. **Natural resources:** iron ore, timber, diamonds, gold, hydropower. **Arable land:** 4.7%. **Livestock:** cattle: 39,800; chickens: 7.1 mil; goats: 340,000; pigs: 288,000; sheep: 268,000. **Fish catch:** 8,020 metric tons. **Electricity prod.:** 335 mil kWh. **Labor force:** agric. 70%, industry 8%, services 22%.

Finance: Monetary unit: Dollar (LRD) (Sept. 2013: 78.80 = $1 U.S.). **GDP:** $2.7 bil; **per capita GDP:** $700; **GDP growth:** 8.3%. **Imports:** $3 bil; South Korea 26.4%, China 24.1%, Singapore 23%, Japan 15.9%. **Exports:** $774.8 mil; China 24.2%, U.S. 15.4%, Spain 11.1%, Thailand 4.5%, Côte d'Ivoire 4.4%, Malaysia 4.1%, France 4%. **Tourism:** $232 mil. **Budget:** $522.3 mil. **Total reserves less gold:** $497.2 mil. **CPI change:** 6.8%.

Transport: Railways: 267 mi. **Motor vehicles:** 14.4 vehicles per 1,000 pop. **Civil aviation:** 2 airports. **Chief ports:** Buchanan, Monrovia.

Communications: TV sets: 26 per 1,000 pop. **Radios:** 318 per 1,000 pop. **Telephone lines:** 0.0002 per 100 pop. **Internet:** 3.8%.

Health: Life expect.: 56.2 male; 59.5 female. **Births:** 35.8 per 1,000 pop. **Deaths:** 10.1 per 1,000 pop. **Natural inc.:** 2.56%. **Infant mortality:** 70.9 per 1,000 live births. **HIV rate:** 1%.

Education: Compulsory ages: 6-11. **Literacy:** 42.9%.

Major intl. organizations: UN and most of its specialized agencies, AU, WTO (observer).

Embassy: 5201 16th St. NW 20011; 723-0437.
Website: www.emansion.gov.lr

Liberia was founded in 1822 by freed black slaves from the U.S. who settled at Monrovia with the aid of colonization societies. It became a republic July 26, 1847, with a constitution modeled on that of the U.S. Descendants of freed slaves dominated politics for much of the 19th and 20th cents.

Under Pres. William V. S. Tubman, Liberia was a founding member of the UN in 1945. Tubman died in 1971 and was succeeded by his vice president, William R. Tolbert Jr. Charging rampant corruption, an Army Redemption Council of enlisted men staged a bloody predawn coup, Apr. 12, 1980, killing Pres. Tolbert and installing Sgt. Samuel Doe, an indigenous African, as head of state. In 1985, Doe was chosen president in a disputed election.

A civil war began Dec. 1989. In Sept. 1990, Pres. Doe was executed. Despite the introduction of a multinational peacekeeping force, the conflict intensified. Factional fighting devastated Monrovia in Apr. 1996. Ruth Perry became modern Africa's first female head of state Sept. 3, 1996, leading a transitional government. By then, the civil war had claimed more than 150,000 lives.

Former rebel leader Charles Taylor was elected president July 1997, in Liberia's first national election in 12 years. The UN imposed sanctions in 2001, to punish Liberia for aiding the Revolutionary United Front (RUF) insurgency in Sierra Leone. Taylor declared a state of emergency Feb. 8, 2002, after Liberian rebels launched raids near Monrovia.

A UN-sponsored war crimes tribunal indicted Taylor June 2003, for his role in the Sierra Leone conflict. With rebels again threatening Monrovia, Taylor resigned Aug. 11 and went into exile. The UN authorized a 15,000-member peacekeeping force (UNMIL) Sept. 19 to help stabilize the nation. A businessman, Charles Gyude Bryant, was sworn in Oct. 14 to head a power-sharing interim government. Ellen Johnson-Sirleaf won presidential elections in 2005 and 2011, and shared the 2011 Nobel Peace Prize with 2 other women. Captured in 2006 while trying to flee Nigeria, Charles Taylor went to trial at The Hague in 2007. After several delays, he was convicted of 11 counts of aiding and abetting war crimes and crimes against humanity in 2012, and sentenced to 50 years in prison May 30.

The UN Security Council passed a resolution Sept. 17, 2012, reducing the UN presence to about 4,000 forces by July 2015. Tens of thousands of refugees fleeing violence in Côte d'Ivoire were unable to be repatriated in 2013 due to continuing violence on the border with Liberia. UNMIL had 7,332 uniformed personnel in Liberia in July 2013.

Libya

People: Population: 6,002,347. **Age distrib.:** <15: 27.3%; 65+: 3.9%. **Pop. density:** 8.8 per sq mi, 3.4 per sq km. **Urban:** 77.7%. **Ethnic groups:** Berber and Arab 97%, other (incl. Greek, Maltese, Italian, Egyptian, Pakistani, Turk, Indian, Tunisian) 3%. **Languages:** Arabic (official), Italian, English, Berber. **Religion:** Sunni Muslim (official) 97%.

Geography: Total area: 679,362 sq mi, 1,759,540 sq km; **Land area:** 679,362 sq mi, 1,759,540 sq km. **Location:** On Mediterranean coast of N Africa. **Neighbors:** Tunisia, Algeria on W; Niger, Chad on S; Sudan, Egypt on E. **Topography:** Desert and semidesert regions cover 92% of land, with low mountains in N, higher mountains in S, and a narrow coastal zone. **Capital:** Tripoli (Tarabulus), 1,126,950.

Government: Type: In transition. **Head of state:** General National Congress Pres. Nouri Abusahmain; in office: June 25, 2013. **Head of gov.:** Interim Prime Min. Ali Zeidan; b. Dec. 15, 1950; in office: Nov. 14, 2012. **Local divisions:** 22 districts. **Defense budget:** $2.97 bil. **Active troops:** NA.

Economy: Industries: petroleum, petrochemicals, aluminum, iron and steel, food proc., textiles, handicrafts, cement. **Chief crops:** wheat, barley, olives, dates, citrus, vegetables, peanuts, soybeans. **Natural resources:** petroleum, nat. gas, gypsum. **Crude oil reserves:** 48 bil bbls. **Arable land:** 1%. **Livestock:** cattle: 197,000; chickens: 34 mil; goats: 2.6 mil; sheep: 7.1 mil. **Fish catch:** 30,244 metric tons. **Electricity prod.:** 29.7 bil kWh. **Labor force:** agric. 17%, industry 23%, services 59%.

Finance: Monetary unit: Dinar (LYD) (Sept. 2013: 1.28 = $1 U.S.). **GDP:** $78.6 bil; **per capita GDP:** $12,300; **GDP growth:** 104.5%. **Imports:** $18.1 bil; China 13.7%, Turkey 12.3%, Italy 8.7%, Tunisia 7.3%, South Korea 6.2%, Greece 5.4%, Germany 4.9%. **Exports:** $52.1 bil; Italy 23.5%, Germany 12.5%, China 11.3%, France 9.7%, Spain 7.6%, UK 4.7%, U.S. 4.5%. **Tourism:** $60 mil. **Budget:** $35.1 bil. **Total reserves less gold:** $118.4 bil. **Gold:** 3.8 mil oz t. **CPI change** 6.1%.

Transport: Motor vehicles: 416.3 vehicles per 1,000 pop. **Civil aviation:** 945.1 mil pass.-mi; 68 airports. **Chief ports:** Az Zawiyah, Marsa al Burayqah, Ra's Lanuf, Tripoli.

Communications: TV sets: 147 per 1,000 pop. **Radios:** 270 per 1,000 pop. **Telephone lines:** 12.6 per 100 pop. **Internet:** 19.9%.

Health: Life expect.: 74.2 male; 77.6 female. **Births:** 18.7 per 1,000 pop. **Deaths:** 3.6 per 1,000 pop. **Natural inc.:** 1.52%. **Infant mortality:** 12.3 per 1,000 live births. **HIV rate:** NA.

Education: Compulsory: ages 6-14. **Literacy:** 89.5%.

Major intl. organizations: UN (FAO, IBRD, ILO, IMF, WHO), AL, AU, OPEC, WTO (observer).

Embassy: 2600 Virginia Ave. NW, Ste. 705, 20037; 944-9601.
Website: www.libyausaembassy.com

First settled by Berbers, Libya was ruled in succession by Carthage, Rome, the Vandals, and the Ottomans. Italy ruled from 1912, and Britain and France after WWII. Libya became an independent constitutional monarchy Jan. 2, 1952. In 1969 a junta led by Col. Muammar al-Qaddafi seized power.

Under Qaddafi's dictatorship, dissent was suppressed and wars were waged with Egypt and Chad. During the 1980s, Libya was accused of promoting terrorism, such as the Apr. 5, 1986, bombing of a West Berlin nightclub, which killed 3, including a U.S. serviceman. The U.S. responded by attacking what it called "terrorist-related targets" in Libya, Apr. 14, including Qaddafi's barracks.

Libyan agents were accused of planting bombs that blew up Pan Am Flight 103 over Lockerbie, Scotland, killing 270 people Dec. 21, 1988, and UTA Flight 772 over Niger, killing 170 people Sept. 19, 1989. The UN imposed sanctions in 1992 for Libya's failure to cooperate in the Lockerbie and UTA cases.

Libya agreed in 2003 to renounce terrorism and settle compensation cases for the families of the Lockerbie and UTA bombing victims. The UN lifted sanctions in Sept., and in Dec., Libya renounced nuclear, chemical, and biological weapons and long-range missiles. The U.S. ended most economic sanctions Apr. 2004 and restored full diplomatic relations May 2006. Abdel Basset Ali al-Megrahi, a former Libyan agent sentenced to life in prison in 2001 for his role in the Lockerbie bombing, was freed by Scottish authorities on humanitarian grounds Aug. 20, 2009; he received a jubilant welcome in Libya.

Arab Spring rebels fought with Qaddafi's forces throughout the spring, but with diplomatic backing from the Arab League and the UN Security Council, NATO forces imposed an arms embargo and no-fly zone against Qaddafi. With aid from NATO, the rebels took control of Tripoli Aug. 23, 2011, and began governing through the Libyan Interim National Council. Rebels killed Qaddafi Oct. 20, 2011. The moderate National Forces Alliance, led by former interim prime min. Mahmoud Jibril, won July 7, 2012, elections. Ansar al-Shariah terrorists attacked the U.S. Consulate in Benghazi Sept. 11, killing Ambassador J. Christopher Stephens and 3 other diplomats. The General National Congress elected Mustafa Abu Shagour prime min. Sept. 12, but he was voted out Oct. 7; the Congress elected independent human rights lawyer Ali Zeidan as the interim prime min. Oct. 14.

Italy closed its consulate, Jan 15, 2013, after its consul was fired upon as he drove through Benghazi Jan. 13. A car bomb destroyed half of the French embassy in Tripoli Apr. 23, severely injuring 2 French guards. Britain announced May 10 a temporary staff reduction at its embassy in Tripoli due to security concerns, the same day that bombs were detonated outside of 2 police stations in Benghazi. Members of the Libyan Shield militia fired on protesters outside their headquarters in Benghazi, June 8, killing at least 12 people.

Liechtenstein
Principality of Liechtenstein

People: Population: 37,009. **Age distrib.:** <15: 15.9%; 65+: 15.4%. **Pop. density:** 599.1 per sq mi, 231.3 per sq km. **Urban:** 14.4%. **Ethnic groups:** Liechtensteiner 66%. **Languages:** German (official), Alemannic dialect. **Religions:** Roman Catholic (official) 76%, Protestant 7%.

Geography: Total area: 62 sq mi, 160 sq km; **Land area:** 62 sq mi, 160 sq km. **Location:** Central Europe, in Alps. **Neighbors:** Switzerland on W, Austria on E. **Topography:** Rhine Valley occupies one-third of country, Alps cover the rest. **Capital:** Vaduz, 5,225.

Government: Type: Hereditary constitutional monarchy. **Head of state:** Prince Hans-Adam II; b. Feb. 14, 1945; in office: Nov. 13, 1989. **Head of gov.:** Prime Min. Adrian Hasler; b. Feb. 11, 1964; in office: Mar. 27, 2013. **Local divisions:** 11 communes. **Defense budget:** NA. **Active troops:** No regular military forces. Natl. Police maintains relations with neighboring forces.

Economy: Industries: electronics, metal mfg., dental prods., ceramics, pharmaceuticals, food prods., precision instruments, tourism, optical instruments. **Chief crops:** wheat, barley, corn, potatoes. **Natural resources:** hydroelectric potential. **Arable land:** 21.9%. **Livestock:** cattle: 6,200; goats: 465; pigs: 1,850; sheep: 4,200. **Labor force:** agric. 0.8%, industry 39.4%, services 59.9%.

Finance: Monetary unit: Franc (CHF) (Sept. 2013: 0.94 = $1 U.S.). **GDP (2009):** $3.2 bil; **per capita GDP** (2009 est.): $89,400; **GDP growth** (2009): −0.5%. **Imports** (2011): $2.2 bil. **Exports** (2011): $3.8 bil. (Trade data excl. trade with Switzerland.) **Budget** (2011): $1.4 bil. **Total reserves less gold:** NA. **CPI change:** NA.

Transport: Railways: 6 mi.

Communications: TV sets: 500 per 1,000 pop. **Radios:** 662 per 1,000 pop. **Telephone lines:** 54.7 per 100 pop. **Internet:** 89.4%.

Health: Life expect.: 79.5 male; 84.3 female. **Births:** 10.7 per 1,000 pop. **Deaths:** 6.9 per 1,000 pop. **Natural inc.:** 0.38%. **Infant mortality:** 4.4 per 1,000 live births. **HIV rate:** NA.

Education: Compulsory: ages 6-14. **Literacy:** 100%.

Major intl. organizations: EFTA, OSCE, WTO.

Embassy: 2900 K St. NW, Ste. 602B, 20007; 331-0590.
Website: www.liechtenstein.li

Liechtenstein became sovereign in 1806. It is united with Switzerland by a customs and monetary union. Nearly half of all workers commute daily from Austria, Switzerland, and Germany.

On Aug. 15, 2004, Prince Hans-Adam II assigned day-to-day responsibilities for running the country to his son, Crown Prince Alois. Long regarded as a tax haven, Liechtenstein has recently agreed to ease banking secrecy laws that had impeded international tax fraud investigations. A referendum to abolish the prince's power to veto referendums was defeated July 1, 2012.

Lithuania
Republic of Lithuania

People: Population: 3,515,858. **Age distrib.:** <15: 13.6%; 65+: 16.8%. **Pop. density:** 145.3 per sq mi, 56.1 per sq km. **Urban:** 67.1%. **Ethnic groups:** Lithuanian 84%, Polish 6%, Russian 5%, Belarusian 1%. **Languages:** Lithuanian (official), Russian, Polish. **Religions:** Roman Catholic 79%, Russian Orthodox 4%, Protestant (incl. Lutheran, Evangelical Christian Baptist) 2%, none 10%.

Geography: Total area: 25,212 sq mi, 65,300 sq km; **Land area:** 24,201 sq mi, 62,680 sq km. **Location:** In E Europe, on SE coast of Baltic. **Neighbors:** Latvia on N; Belarus on E, S; Poland, Russia on W. **Topography:** Lowland with hills in W and S; fertile soil; many small lakes and rivers, with marshes espec. in N and W. **Capital:** Vilnius, 545,607.

Government: Type: Parliamentary democracy. **Head of state:** Pres. Dalia Grybauskaite; b. Mar. 1, 1956; in office: July 12, 2009. **Head of gov.:** Prime Min. Algirdas Butkevicius; b. Nov. 19, 1958; in office: Dec. 7, 2012. **Local divisions:** 10 counties. **Defense budget:** $319 mil. **Active troops:** 11,800.

Economy: Industries: metal-cutting machine tools, elec. motors, TVs, refrigerators and freezers, petroleum refining, shipbuilding, furniture making, textiles, food proc. **Chief crops:** grain, potatoes, sugar beets, flax, vegetables. **Natural resources:** peat, amber. **Crude oil reserves:** 12 mil bbls. **Arable land:** 34.9%. **Livestock:** cattle: 748,000; chickens: 9.2 mil; goats: 16,000; pigs: 929,400; sheep: 58,500. **Fish catch:** 141,837 metric tons. **Electricity prod.:** 4.2 bil kWh. **Labor force:** agric. 7.9%, industry 19.6%, services 72.5%.

Finance: Monetary unit: Litas (LTL) (Sept. 2013: 2.62 = $1 U.S.). **GDP:** $66.1 bil; **per capita GDP:** $22,000; **GDP growth:** 3.6%. **Imports:** $32 bil; Russia 32.5%, Germany 9.8%, Poland 9.8%, Latvia 6.1%, Netherlands 5.5%. **Exports:** $29.6 bil; Russia 19%, Latvia 11%, Estonia 7.9%, Germany 7.9%, UK 6.4%, Poland 6.1%, Netherlands 5.9%, Belarus 4.5%. **Tourism:** $1.3 bil. **Budget:** $14.5 bil. **Total reserves less gold:** $8.2 bil. **Gold:** 187,000 oz t. **CPI change:** 3.1%.

Transport: Railways: 1,098 mi. **Motor vehicles:** 535.2 vehicles per 1,000 pop. **Civil aviation:** 577.9 mil pass.-mi; 22 airports. **Chief port:** Klaipeda.

Communications: TV sets: 518 per 1,000 pop. **Radios:** 525 per 1,000 pop. **Telephone lines:** 20.3 per 100 pop. **Internet:** 68%.

Health: Life expect.: 71.0 male; 80.8 female. **Births:** 9.4 per 1,000 pop. **Deaths:** 11.5 per 1,000 pop. **Natural inc.:** −0.21%. **Infant mortality:** 6.1 per 1,000 live births. **HIV rate:** 0.1%.

Education: Compulsory: ages 7-15. **Literacy:** 99.7%.

Major intl. organizations: UN (FAO, IBRD, ILO, IMF, WHO), EU, NATO, OSCE, WTO.

Embassy: 4590 MacArthur Blvd. NW, Ste. 200, 20007; 234-5860. **Website:** www.lrvk.lt

Lithuania, briefly occupied by the German army, 1914-18, was annexed by the Soviet Union until 1919. In 1939 it rejoined the Soviet sphere of influence and was annexed by the USSR Aug. 3, 1940.

Lithuania declared its independence from the Soviet Union Mar. 11, 1990; its independence was ratified by the Soviet Union Sept. 1991. The country became a full member of NATO and the EU in 2004. A plummeting economy spurred popular discontent and brought a rightward shift in parliamentary and presidential elections, 2008-09. The center-left Social Democrats won 2012 parliamentary elections, held Oct. 14 and 28, marking a shift from the conservative government that led the country the previous 4 years. In mid-2013, Lithuania had 244 troops serving with the NATO mission (ISAF) in Afghanistan.

Luxembourg
Grand Duchy of Luxembourg

People: Population: 514,862. **Age distrib.:** <15: 18%; 65+: 15.2%. **Pop. density:** 515.7 per sq mi, 199.1 per sq km. **Urban:** 85.4%. **Ethnic groups:** Luxembourger 63%, Portuguese 13%, French 5%, Italian 4%, German 2%, other EU 7%. **Languages:** Luxembourgish (national), German, French (both administrative). **Religions:** Roman Catholic 87%, other (incl. Protestant, Jewish, Muslim) 13%.

Geography: Total area: 998 sq mi, 2,586 sq km; **Land area:** 998 sq mi, 2,586 sq km. **Location:** In W Europe. **Neighbors:** Belgium on W, France on S, Germany on E. **Topography:** Heavy forests (Ardennes) cover N. S is a low, open plateau. **Capital:** Luxembourg, 94,478.

Government: Type: Constitutional monarchy. **Head of state:** Grand Duke Henri; b. Apr. 16, 1955; in office: Oct. 7, 2000. **Head of gov.:** Prime Min. Jean-Claude Juncker; b. Dec. 9, 1954; in office: Jan. 20, 1995. **Local divisions:** 3 districts. **Defense budget:** $258 mil. **Active troops:** 900.

Economy: Industries: banking and financial services, iron and steel, information tech., telecom, cargo transp., food proc., chemicals, metal prods., engineering, tires, glass, aluminum, tourism. **Chief crops:** grapes, barley, oats, potatoes, wheat, fruits. **Natural resources:** iron ore (no longer exploited). **Arable land:** 23.9%. **Livestock:** cattle: 192,535; chickens: 102,000; goats: 5,821; pigs: 89,158; sheep: 8,951. **Electricity prod.** (2011): 2.1 bil kWh. **Labor force:** agric. 2.2%, industry 17.2%, services 80.6%.

Finance: Monetary unit: Euro (EUR) (Sept. 2013: 0.76 = $1 U.S.). **GDP:** $42.9 bil; **per capita GDP:** $81,100; **GDP growth:** 0.1%. **Imports:** $23.3 bil; Belgium 30.9%, Germany 23.4%, France 10.4%, U.S. 8.2%, China 7.2%, Netherlands 5.1%. **Exports:** $13.2 bil; Germany 21.6%, France 15.5%, Belgium 14.5%, UK 5.8%, Italy 5.6%, Switzerland 4.7%. **Tourism:** $4.5 bil. **Budget:** $24.4 bil. **Total reserves less gold:** $871 mil. **Gold:** 72,000 oz t. **CPI change:** 2.7%.

Transport: Railways: 171 mi. **Motor vehicles:** 781.1 vehicles per 1,000 pop. **Civil aviation:** 255.4 mil pass.-mi; 1 airport. **Chief port:** Mertert.

Communications: TV sets: 605 per 1,000 pop. **Radios:** 683 per 1,000 pop. **Telephone lines:** 51 per 100 pop. **Internet:** 92%.

Health: Life expect.: 76.6 male; 83.3 female. **Births:** 11.7 per 1,000 pop. **Deaths:** 8.5 per 1,000 pop. **Natural inc.:** 0.32%. **Infant mortality:** 4.3 per 1,000 live births. **HIV rate:** 0.3%.

Education: Compulsory: ages 6-15. **Literacy:** 100%.

Major intl. organizations: UN (FAO, IBRD, ILO, IMF, WHO), EU, NATO, OECD, OSCE, WTO.

Embassy: 2200 Massachusetts Ave. NW 20008; 265-4171. **Website:** www.gouvernement.lu

Luxembourg, founded about 963, was ruled by Burgundy, Spain, Austria, and France from 1448 to 1815. It left the Germanic Confederation in 1866. Overrun by Germany in 2 world wars, Luxembourg ended its neutrality in 1948, when a customs union with Belgium and the Netherlands was adopted.

Luxembourg was one of the 6 founding members (1951) of what became the European Union. Prime Min. Jean-Claude Juncker is the EU's longest-serving head of government. Luxembourg became a nonpermanent member of the UN Security Council for the 2013-14 term in Jan. 1, 2013.

Macedonia
Former Yugoslav Republic of Macedonia

People: Population: 2,087,171. **Age distrib.:** <15: 17.9%; 65+: 12.1%. **Pop. density:** 212.5 per sq mi, 82.1 per sq km. **Urban:** 59.3%. **Ethnic groups:** Macedonian 64%, Albanian 25%, Turkish 4%, Roma 3%, Serb 2%. **Languages:** Macedonian, Albanian (both official); Turkish; Roma; Serbian. **Religions:** Macedonian Orthodox 65%, Muslim 33%.

Geography: Total area: 9,928 sq mi, 25,713 sq km; **Land area:** 9,820 sq mi, 25,433 sq km. **Location:** In SE Europe. **Neighbors:** Bulgaria on E, Greece on S, Albania on W, Serbia on N. **Topography:** Macedonia is a landlocked, mostly mountainous country, with deep river valleys, 3 large lakes; country is bisected by Vardar R. **Capital:** Skopje, 499,026.

Government: Type: Parliamentary democracy. **Head of state:** Pres. Gjorge Ivanov; b. May 2, 1960; in office: May 12, 2009. **Head of gov.:** Prime Min. Nikola Gruevski; b. Aug. 31, 1970; in office: Aug. 27, 2006. **Local divisions:** 71 municipalities. **Defense budget:** $132 mil. **Active troops:** 8,000.

Economy: Industries: food proc., beverages, textiles, chemicals, iron, steel, cement, energy, pharmaceuticals. **Chief crops:** grapes, tobacco, vegetables, fruits. **Natural resources:** iron ore, copper, lead, zinc, chromite, manganese, nickel, tungsten, gold, silver, asbestos, gypsum, timber. **Arable land:** 16.4%. **Livestock:** cattle: 265,299; chickens: 1.9 mil; goats: 72,778; pigs: 196,570; sheep: 766,631. **Fish catch:** 1,636 metric tons. **Electricity prod.:** 6.9 bil kWh. **Labor force:** agric. 16.7%, industry 26%, services 57.3%.

Finance: Monetary unit: Denar (MKD) (Sept. 2013: 46.90 = $1 U.S.). **GDP:** $22.2 bil (figure might not reflect country's large informal sector); **per capita GDP:** $10,800; **GDP growth:** −0.3%. **Imports:** $6.2 bil; Greece 17.7%, Germany 11.5%, UK 9.3%, Bulgaria 8.7%, Italy 5%, Turkey 4.8%. **Exports:** $4.1 bil; Germany 25.5%, Italy 6.1%, Bulgaria 5.2%, Greece 4.5%. **Tourism:** $233 mil. **Budget:** $3.3 bil. **Total reserves less gold:** $2.5 bil. **Gold:** 218,332 oz t. **CPI change:** 3.3%.

Transport: Railways: 434 mi. **Civil aviation:** 54.1 mil pass.-mi; 8 airports.

Communications: TV sets: 296 per 1,000 pop. **Radios:** 207 per 1,000 pop. **Telephone lines:** 19.7 per 100 pop. **Internet:** 63.1%.

Health: Life expect.: 73.0 male; 78.3 female. **Births:** 11.7 per 1,000 pop. **Deaths:** 9.0 per 1,000 pop. **Natural inc.:** 0.27%. **Infant mortality:** 8.1 per 1,000 live births. **HIV rate:** NA.

Education: Compulsory: ages 6-14. **Literacy:** 97.4%.
Major intl. organizations: UN (FAO, IBRD, ILO, IMF, WHO) OSCE, WTO.
Embassy: 2129 Wyoming Ave. NW 20008; 667-0501.
Website: www.vlada.mk

Muslim Turks ruled Macedonia from 1389 to 1912. In 1913, the area was incorporated into Serbia, which in 1918 became part of the Kingdom of Serbs, Croats, and Slovenes (later Yugoslavia). In 1946, Macedonia became a constituent republic of Yugoslavia.

Macedonia declared its independence Sept. 8, 1991, and was admitted to the UN in 1993. Greece, which objected to Macedonia's use of what it considered a Hellenic name and symbols, imposed a trade blockade on the landlocked nation; the 2 countries agreed to normalize relations Sept. 13, 1995.

By the end of NATO's air war against Yugoslavia, Mar.-June 1999, Macedonia had a Kosovar refugee population of more than 250,000; over 90% had been repatriated by Sept. 1. Boris Trajkovski, candidate of the ruling center-right coalition, won a presidential run-off vote Nov. 14.

Ethnic Albanian guerrillas launched an offensive Mar. 2001 in NW Macedonia. An accord signed Aug. 13 paved the way for the introduction of a NATO peacekeeping force. A law broadening the rights of ethnic Albanians was enacted Jan. 2002. A 320-member EU force replaced the NATO peacekeepers, Mar.-Dec. 2003.

After Trajkovski died in a plane crash Feb. 26, 2004, Prime Min. Branko Crvenkovski won a presidential runoff vote Apr. 28. Prime Min. Nikola Gruevski's governing coalition retained power after 2008 and 2011 parliamentary elections. Gjorge Ivanov won a presidential runoff vote Apr. 5, 2009, and took office May 12. Greece has blocked Macedonia's bid to join NATO because of the dispute over Macedonia's name.

Madagascar
Republic of Madagascar

People: Population: 22,599,098. **Age distrib.:** <15: 41.1%; 65+: 3.1%. **Pop. density:** 100.6 per sq mi, 38.9 per sq km. **Urban:** 32.6%. **Ethnic groups:** Malayo-Indonesian (Merina and related Betsileo), Cotiers (mixed African, Malayo-Indonesian, and Arab), French, Indian, Creole, Comoran. **Languages:** French, Malagasy (both official); English. **Religions:** indigenous beliefs 52%, Christian 41%, Muslim 7%.

Geography: Total area: 226,658 sq mi, 587,041 sq km; **Land area:** 224,534 sq mi, 581,540 sq km. **Location:** In Indian O., off SE coast of Africa. **Neighbors:** Comoro Isls. to NW, Mozambique to W. **Topography:** Humid coastal strip in E, fertile valleys in mountainous center plateau region, and a wider coastal strip on W. **Capital:** Antananarivo, 1,986,710.

Government: Type: In transition. **Head of state:** Pres. Andry Rajoelina; b. May 30, 1974; in office: Mar. 17, 2009. **Head of gov.:** Prime Min. Jean Omer Beriziky; in office: Nov. 2, 2011. **Local divisions:** 6 provinces. **Defense budget (2011):** $72 mil. **Active troops:** 13,500.

Economy: Industries: meat proc., seafood, soap, breweries, tanneries, sugar, textiles, glassware, cement, auto assembly, paper, petroleum, tourism. **Chief crops:** coffee, vanilla, sugarcane, cloves, cocoa, rice, cassava, beans, bananas, peanuts. **Natural resources:** graphite, chromite, coal, bauxite, rare earth elements, salt, quartz, tar sands, semiprec. stones, mica, fish, hydropower. **Arable land:** 6%. **Livestock:** cattle: 10 mil; chickens: 27 mil; goats: 1.3 mil; pigs: 1.4 mil; sheep: 735,000. **Fish catch:** 137,603 metric tons. **Electricity prod.:** 1.2 bil kWh. **Labor force:** NA.

Finance: Monetary unit: Ariary (MGA) (Sept. 2013: 2,207.94 = $1 U.S.). **GDP:** $21.8 bil. **per capita GDP:** $1,000; **GDP growth:** 1.9%. **Imports:** $2.8 bil; China 17.2%, France 12.1%, South Africa 5.3%, Bahrain 5.1%, India 5%, Mauritius 4.7%, Kuwait 4.4%. **Exports:** $640.7 mil; France 23.1%, China 6.5%, U.S. 6.5%, Singapore 5.8%, Canada 5.4%, India 5.3%, Germany 5.3%, Indonesia 5.2%, South Africa 4.4%. **Tourism:** $321 mil. **Budget:** $1.9 bil. **Total reserves less gold:** $1.2 bil. **CPI change:** 6.4%.

Transport: Railways: 531 mi. **Motor vehicles:** 11.8 vehicles per 1,000 pop. **Civil aviation:** 508.9 mil pass.-mi; 26 airports. **Chief ports:** Antsiranana, Mahajanga, Toamasina, Toliara.

Communications: TV sets: 37 per 1,000 pop. **Radios:** 268 per 1,000 pop. **Telephone lines:** 7 per 100 pop. **Internet:** 2.1%.

Health: Life expect.: 63.5 male; 66.3 female. **Births:** 33.6 per 1,000 pop. **Deaths:** 7.1 per 1,000 pop. **Natural inc.:** 2.65%. **Infant mortality:** 46.1 per 1,000 live births. **HIV rate:** 0.3%.

Education: Compulsory: ages 6-10. **Literacy:** 64.5%.
Major intl. organizations: UN (FAO, IBRD, ILO, IMF, WHO), AU, WTO.
Embassy: 2374 Massachusetts Ave. NW 20008; 265-5525.
Website: www.madagascar-presidency.gov.mg

Madagascar was settled 2,000 years ago by Malayan-Indonesian people, whose descendants still predominate. A unified kingdom ruled in the 18th and 19th cent. The island became a French protectorate, 1885, and a colony, 1896. Independence came June 26, 1960.

Discontent with inflation and French domination led to a coup in 1972. The new regime nationalized French-owned financial interests, closed French bases and a U.S. space-tracking station, and obtained Chinese aid. The government conducted a program of arrests, expulsion of foreigners, and repression of strikes in 1979.

In 1990, Madagascar ended a ban on multiparty politics that had existed since 1975. Albert Zafy won the 1993 presidential election, ending the 17-year rule of Adm. Didier Ratsiraka, but was impeached and removed from office in 1996. A cholera epidemic, then cyclones in Feb. and Apr. 2000, claimed 1,600 lives.

Marc Ravalomanana won a contentious presidential election over Ratsiraka Dec. 2001 and was reelected in 2006. Cyclone Ivan hit Feb. 17, 2008, killing at least 83 people and leaving 145,000 homeless. A power struggle between Ravalomanana and the military-backed Andry Rajoelina culminated in Ravalomanana's installation as head of a transitional regime, Mar. 17, 2009. The African Union suspended Madagascar and pushed for a power-sharing arrangement, but accords signed in Aug. and Nov. 2009 were abrogated by Rajoelina. The transitional government suppressed a coup attempt launched by dissident military officers Nov. 17, 2010, the same day voters approved a new constitution that would allow Rajoelina to hold power indefinitely. Rajoelina initially promised new elections in May 2013, which were postponed twice. Elections were scheduled to be held Oct. 25, 2013.

Malawi
Republic of Malawi

People: Population: 16,777,547. **Age distrib.:** <15: 44.7%; 65+: 2.7%. **Pop. density:** 461.9 per sq mi, 178.3 per sq km. **Urban:** 15.7%. **Ethnic groups:** Chewa 33%, Lomwe 18%, Yao 14%, Ngoni 12%, Tumbuka 9%, Nyanja 6%, Sena 4%, Tonga 2%, Ngonde 1%. **Languages:** Chichewa (official), Chinyanja, Chiyao, Chitumbuka, Chisena, Chilomwe, Chitonga. **Religions:** Christian 83%, Muslim 13%, none 3%.

Geography: Total area: 45,747 sq mi, 118,484 sq km; **Land area:** 36,324 sq mi, 94,080 sq km. **Location:** In SE Africa. **Neighbors:** Zambia on W, Mozambique on S and E, Tanzania on N. **Topography:** Malawi stretches 560 mi N-S along Lake Malawi (Lake Nyasa), most of which belongs to Malawi. High plateaus and mountains line the Rift Valley the length of the nation. **Capital:** Lilongwe, 771,503.

Government: Type: Multiparty democracy. **Head of state and gov.:** Pres. Joyce Banda; b. Apr. 12, 1950; in office: Apr. 7, 2012. **Local divisions:** 28 districts. **Defense budget:** $34 mil. **Active troops:** 5,300.

Economy: Industries: tobacco, tea, sugar, sawmill prods., cement, consumer goods. **Chief crops:** tobacco, sugarcane, cotton, tea, corn, potatoes, cassava, sorghum, pulses, groundnuts. **Natural resources:** limestone, hydropower, uranium, coal, bauxite. **Arable land:** 38.2%. **Livestock:** cattle: 1.1 mil; chickens: 16.5 mil; goats: 4.4 mil; pigs: 2.2 mil; sheep: 228,649. **Fish catch:** 85,848 metric tons. **Electricity prod.:** 2 bil kWh. **Labor force:** agric. 90%, industry and services 10%.

Finance: Monetary unit: Kwacha (MWK) (Sept. 2013: 334.70 = $1 U.S.). **GDP:** $14.5 bil; **per capita GDP:** $900; **GDP growth:** 1.9%. **Imports:** $1.9 bil; South Africa 26.5%, China 16.2%, Zambia 9.1%, India 8.5%, Tanzania 5.5%, U.S. 4.1%. **Exports:** $1.2 bil; Canada 9.8%, Zimbabwe 9.5%, Germany 6.7%, South Africa 6.3%, Russia 6%, U.S. 5.7%, Egypt 5.3%. **Tourism:** $34 mil. **Budget:** $1.4 bil. **Total reserves less gold:** $223.2 mil. **Gold:** 12,875 oz t. **CPI change:** 21.3%.

Transport: Railways: 495 mi. **Motor vehicles:** 2 vehicles per 1,000 pop. **Civil aviation:** 124.3 mil pass.-mi; 7 airports. **Chief ports:** Chilumba, Chipoka, Monkey Bay, Nkhata Bay, Nkhotakota.

Communications: TV sets: 11 per 1,000 pop. **Radios:** 3 per 1,000 pop. **Telephone lines:** 1.4 per 100 pop. **Internet:** 4.4%.

Health: Life expect.: 52.0 male; 53.6 female. **Births:** 40.0 per 1,000 pop. **Deaths:** 12.5 per 1,000 pop. **Natural inc.:** 2.74%. **Infant mortality:** 77.0 per 1,000 live births. **HIV rate:** 10%.

Education: Compulsory: ages 6-13. **Literacy:** 61.3%.
Major intl. organizations: UN (FAO, IBRD, ILO, IMF, WHO), AU, the Commonwealth, WTO.
Embassy: 1029 Vermont Ave. NW, Ste. 1000, 20005; 721-0270.
Website: www.malawi.gov.mw

Bantus came to the land in the 16th cent., Arab slavers in the 19th. The area became the British protectorate Nyasaland in 1891. It became independent July 6, 1964, and a republic in 1966.

After 3 decades as a one-party state under Pres. Hastings Kamuzu Banda, Malawi adopted a new constitution and, in multiparty elections held May 17, 1994, chose a new leader, Bakili Muluzi.

Bingu wa Mutharika, candidate of the ruling United Democratic Front, won a disputed 2004 presidential election. In an ongoing power struggle, an effort by his former political allies to impeach him was halted by Malawi's Constitutional Court, Oct. 2005. Mutharika won reelection May 2009. Clashes between police and antigovernment protesters July 2011 left at least 19 people dead. Joyce Banda became Malawi's first female pres. after the death of Bingu wa Mutharika Apr. 5, 2012. Her government suspended laws against homosexuality Nov. 5, 2012, but the suspension was lifted 3 days later.

Malaysia

People: Population: 29,628,392. **Age distrib.:** <15: 29.1%; 65+: 5.3%. **Pop. density:** 233.5 per sq mi, 90.1 per sq km. **Urban:** 72.8%. **Ethnic groups:** Malay 50%, Chinese 24%, indigenous 11%, Indian 7%. **Languages:** Bahasa Malaysia (official), English, Chinese, Tamil, Telugu, Malayalam, Panjabi, Thai. **Religions:** Muslim (official) 60%; Buddhist 19%; Christian 9%; Hindu 6%; Confucianism, Taoism, other traditional Chinese religions 3%.

Geography: Total area: 127,355 sq mi, 329,847 sq km; **Land area:** 126,895 sq mi, 328,657 sq km. **Location:** On SE tip of Asia, plus N coast of the island of Borneo. **Neighbors:** Thailand, Brunei on N; Indonesia on S. **Topography:** Most of W is covered by tropical jungle, including the central mountain range that runs N-S through the peninsula. W coast is marshy, the E coast, sandy. In E is a wide, swampy coastal plain, with interior jungles and mountains. **Capital:** Kuala Lumpur (financial), 1,555,910; Putrajaya (admin.). **Cities (urban aggl.):** Klang, 1,189,777; Johore Bahru, 1,045,005.

Government: Type: Constitutional monarchy. **Head of state:** Paramount Ruler Tuanku Abdul Halim Mu'adzam Shah; b. Nov. 28, 1927; in office: Apr. 11, 2012. **Head of gov.:** Prime Min. Najib Razak; b. July 23, 1953; in office: Apr. 3, 2009. **Local divisions:** 13 states, 1 federal territory. **Defense budget:** $4.45 bil. **Active troops:** 109,000.

Economy: Industries: rubber and palm oil proc., petroleum and nat. gas, light mfg., pharmaceuticals, medical tech., electronics, timber proc., logging. **Chief crops:** palm oil, rubber, cocoa, rice, pepper. **Natural resources:** tin, petroleum, timber, copper, iron ore, nat. gas, bauxite. **Crude oil reserves:** 4 bil bbls. **Arable land:** 5.5%. **Livestock:** cattle 925,000; chickens 230 mil; goats 545,000; pigs 1.7 mil; sheep 125,000. **Fish catch:** 1.9 mil metric tons. **Electricity prod.** 118.2 bil kWh. **Labor force:** agric. 11.1%, industry 36%, services 53.5%.

Finance: Monetary unit: Ringgit (MYR) (Sept. 2013: 3.33 = $1 U.S.). **GDP:** $506.7 bil; **per capita GDP:** $17,200; **GDP growth:** 5.6%. **Imports:** $181.6 bil; China 15.1%, Singapore 13.3%, Japan 10.3%, U.S. 8.1%, Thailand 6%, Indonesia 5.1%, South Korea 4.1%. **Exports:** $247 bil; Singapore 13.6%, China 12.6%, Japan 11.8%, U.S. 8.7%, Thailand 5.4%, Hong Kong 4.3%, India 4.2%, Australia 4.1%. **Tourism:** $20.3 bil. **Budget:** $80.9 bil. **Total reserves less gold:** $137.8 bil. **Gold:** 1.2 mil oz t. **CPI change:** 1.7%.

Transport: Railways: 1,149 mi. **Motor vehicles:** 377.1 vehicles per 1,000 pop. **Civil aviation:** 28.3 bil pass.-mi; 39 airports. **Chief ports:** Bintulu, George Town (Penang), Johor Bahru, Port Kelang, Tanjung Pelepas.

Communications: TV sets: 224 per 1,000 pop. **Radios:** 425 per 1,000 pop. **Telephone lines:** 15.7 per 100 pop. **Internet:** 65.8%.

Health: Life expect.: 71.5 male, 77.2 female. **Births:** 20.4 per 1,000 pop. **Deaths:** 5.0 per 1,000 pop. **Natural inc.:** 1.54%. **Infant mortality:** 14.1 per 1,000 live births. **HIV rate:** 0.4%.

Education: Compulsory: ages 6-11. **Literacy:** 93.1%.

Major intl. organizations: UN (FAO, IBRD, ILO, IMF, WHO), APEC, ASEAN, the Commonwealth, WTO.

Embassy: 3516 International Ct. NW 20008; 572-9700.

Website: www.malaysia.gov.my

European traders appeared in the 16th cent.; Britain established control in 1867. Malaysia was created Sept. 16, 1963. It included Malaya (which gained independence in 1957 after the suppression of Communist rebels), plus the formerly British Singapore, Sabah (N Borneo), and Sarawak (NW Borneo). Singapore was separated in 1965 in order to end tensions between Chinese—the majority in Singapore—and Malays in control of the Malaysian government. A monarch is elected by a council of hereditary rulers of the Malayan states every 5 years.

Abundant natural resources have bolstered prosperity, and foreign investment has aided industrialization and trade. Work on a federal administrative center at Putrajaya, south of Kuala Lumpur, was completed in 1999; it is linked by rail with Kuala Lumpur's city center and international airport and with Cyberjaya, a hub for high-tech manufacturing and research.

Mahathir bin Mohamad dominated Malaysian politics as prime minister, 1981-2003. His successor, Abdullah Ahmad Badawi, took office Oct. 31, 2003, and led his National Front coalition to a resounding win in 2004 parliamentary elections. The Indian Ocean tsunami of Dec. 26, 2004, left at least 68 people dead in Malaysia. Recession and scandals plagued Malaysia as National Front leader Najib Razak took over the premiership in 2009. Tuanku Abdul Halim Mu'adzam Shah was chosen in 2011 to serve as the paramount ruler for a second 5-year term, more than 40 years after his first (1970-75). Protests demanding electoral reform in Kuala Lumpur turned violent in Apr. 2012.

Malaysian police, Feb. 14, 2013, confronted a group of Filipino militiamen on the island of Borneo who claimed a right to the land going back to the 18th cent. Clashes between Malaysian forces and Filipino gunmen killed at least 60 Filipinos and 9 Malaysian officers by Mar. 12. Area residents were resettled until hostilities ceased. In a close election May 5, the governing coalition was returned to power, in an election that the opposition deemed fraudulent.

Maldives
Republic of Maldives

People: Population: 393,988. **Age distrib.:** <15: 21.1%; 65+: 4.2%. **Pop. density:** 3,424.2 per sq mi, 1,322.1 per sq km. **Urban:** 41.2%. **Ethnic groups:** South Indian, Sinhalese, Arab. **Languages:** Dhivehi (official), English (spoken by most govt. officials). **Religion:** Sunni Muslim (official).

Geography: Total area: 115 sq mi, 298 sq km; **Land area:** 115 sq mi, 298 sq km. **Location:** In Indian O., SW of India. **Neighbors:** Nearest is India on N. **Topography:** 19 atolls with 1,190 islands, 198 inhabited. None of the islands are over 5 sq mi in area, and all are nearly flat. **Capital:** Male, 131,777.

Government: Type: Republic. **Head of state and gov.:** Pres. Mohamed Waheed Hassan Maniku; b. Jan. 3, 1953; in office: Feb. 7, 2012. **Local divisions:** 7 provinces, 1 municipality. **Defense budget/active troops:** NA.

Economy: Industries: tourism, fish proc., shipping, boat building, coconut proc., woven mats, rope, handicrafts, coral and sand mining. **Chief crops:** coconuts, corn, sweet potatoes. **Natural resources:** fish. **Arable land:** 10%. **Fish catch:** 120,836 metric tons. **Electricity prod.:** 301.1 mil kWh. **Labor force:** agric. 11%, industry 23%, services 65%.

Finance: Monetary unit: Rufiyaa (MVR) (Sept. 2013: 15.29 = $1 U.S.). **GDP:** $3.1 bil; **per capita GDP:** $9,400; **GDP growth:** 3.5%. **Imports:** $1.4 bil; Singapore 21.4%, UAE 20.3%, India 9.5%, Malaysia 7.5%, China 5.9%, Thailand 5.6%, Sri Lanka 5.1%. **Exports:** $283 mil; France 18.6%, Thailand 15.5%, UK 11.2%, Sri Lanka 10%, U.S. 9.2%, Italy 8%, Germany 6.3%. **Tourism:** $1.9 bil. **Budget** $917 mil. **Total reserves less gold:** $318.3 mil. **CPI change:** 11.3%.

Transport: Civil aviation: 28 mil pass.-mi; 7 airports. **Chief port:** Male.

Communications: TV sets: 131 per 1,000 pop. **Radios:** 131 per 1,000 pop. **Telephone lines:** 7.1 per 100 pop. **Internet:** 38.9%.

Health: Life expect.: 72.7 male; 77.3 female. **Births:** 15.4 per 1,000 pop. **Deaths:** 3.8 per 1,000 pop. **Natural inc.:** 1.16%. **Infant mortality:** 25.5 per 1,000 live births. **HIV rate:** <0.1%.

Education: Compulsory: ages 6-12. **Literacy:** 98.4%.

Major intl. organizations: UN (FAO, IBRD, IMF, WHO), the Commonwealth, WTO.

Embassy: 800 2nd Ave., Ste. 400E, New York, NY 10017; (212) 599-6194.

Website: www.presidencymaldives.gov.mv

A British protectorate since 1887, the nation achieved independence July 26, 1965; long a sultanate, the Maldives became a republic in 1968. Tourism and fishing are the most important sectors of the economy. Rising sea levels threaten the country, which comprises at least 1,200 small, low-lying coral islands.

The Indian Ocean tsunami of Dec. 26, 2004, killed at least 82 people and displaced more than 21,600 in the Maldives. Pres. Maumoon Abdul Gayoom, in office 1978-2008, lost a 2008 runoff vote to pro-democracy leader and former political prisoner Mohamed (Anni) Nasheed. Following protests over the arrest of a judge, Nasheed resigned Feb. 2012, and Vice Pres. Mohamed Waheed Hassan Maniku took office. Nasheed later claimed that he resigned at gunpoint, but an international-backed commission ruled, Aug. 29, that it was voluntary. Nasheed was arrested Oct. 8 for failing to appear in court to face charges that he illegally ordered the arrest of a judge. He ran for president Sept. 7, 2013, and won 45% of the vote, which was not enough to avoid a runoff. The Supreme Court canceled the runoff Sept. 24. New elections were scheduled to be held Nov. 9, 2013.

Mali
Republic of Mali

People: Population: 15,968,882. **Age distrib.:** <15: 47.7%; 65+: 3%. **Pop. density:** 33.9 per sq mi, 13.1 per sq km. **Urban:** 34.9%. **Ethnic groups:** Mande (Bambara, Malinke, Soninke) 50%, Peul 17%, Voltaic 12%, Songhai 6%, Tuareg and Moor 10%. **Languages:** French (official), Bambara, numerous African langs. **Religions:** Muslim 90%, Christian 1%, indigenous beliefs 9%.

Geography: Total area: 478,841 sq mi, 1,240,192 sq km; **Land area:** 471,118 sq mi, 1,220,190 sq km. **Location:** In interior of W Africa. **Neighbors:** Mauritania, Senegal on W; Guinea, Côte d'Ivoire, Burkina Faso on S; Niger on E; Algeria on N. **Topography:** Landlocked grassy plain in upper basins of the Senegal and Niger rivers, extending N into the Sahara. **Capital:** Bamako, 2,036,520.

Government: Type: Republic. **Head of state:** Pres. Ibrahim Boubacar Keita; b. Jan. 29, 1945; in office: Sept. 4, 2013. **Head of gov.:** Prime Min. Oumar Tatum Ly; b. 1963; in office: Sept. 5, 2013. **Local divisions:** 8 regions, 1 district. **Defense budget** (2011): $227 mil. **Active troops:** 7,350.

Economy: Industries: food proc., constr., phosphate and gold mining. **Chief crops:** cotton, millet, rice, corn, vegetables, peanuts. **Natural resources:** gold, phosphates, kaolin, salt, limestone, uranium, gypsum, granite, hydropower. **Arable land:** 5.6%. **Livestock:** cattle: 9.4 mil; chickens: 36.8 mil; goats: 17.3 mil; pigs: 75,914; sheep: 12.5 mil. **Fish catch:** 110,217 metric tons. **Electricity prod.:** 520 mil kWh. **Labor force:** agric. 80%, industry and services 20%.

Finance: Monetary unit: West African CFA Franc (XOF) (Sept. 2013: 498.17 = $1 U.S.). **GDP:** $18.3 bil; **per capita GDP:** $1,100; **GDP growth:** –1.2%. **Imports:** $2.8 bil; France 10.9%, Senegal 9.7%, China 8.4%, Côte d'Ivoire 8%. **Exports:** $2.8 bil; China 53.7%, Malaysia 11.2%, Indonesia 5.4%, India 4.1%. **Tourism:** $227 mil. **Budget:** $1.9 bil. **Total reserves less gold:** $1.3 bil. **CPI change:** 5.4%.

Transport: Railways: 368 mi. **Motor vehicles:** 1.6 vehicles per 1,000 pop. **Civil aviation:** 8 airports. **Chief port:** Koulikoro.

Communications: TV sets: 49 per 1,000 pop. **Radios:** 132 per 1,000 pop. **Telephone lines:** 0.7 per 100 pop. **Internet:** 2.2%.

Health: Life expect.: 52.8 male; 56.4 female. **Births:** 46.1 per 1,000 pop. **Deaths:** 13.6 per 1,000 pop. **Natural inc.:** 3.25%. **Infant mortality:** 106.5 per 1,000 live births. **HIV rate:** 1.1%.

Education: Compulsory: ages 7-15. **Literacy:** 33.4%.

Major intl. organizations: UN and most of its specialized agencies, AU, WTO.

Embassy: 2130 R St. NW 20008; 332-2249.

Website: www.primature.gov.ml

Until the 15th cent. the area was part of the great Mali Empire. Timbuktu (Tombouctou) was a center of Islamic study. French rule was secured, 1898. The Sudanese Rep. and Senegal became independent as the Mali Federation in 1960, but Senegal withdrew, and the Sudanese Rep. was renamed Mali.

A coup toppled a socialist regime led, 1960-68, by Pres. Modibo Keita. Famine struck in 1973-74, killing as many as 100,000 people. Drought conditions returned in the 1980s.

The military, Mar. 1991, overthrew Pres. Moussa Traoré, who had ruled since 1968. Oumar Konare, a coup leader, was elected president, 1992. The government and a Tuareg rebel group signed a peace accord in 1994. Twice condemned to death for crimes committed in office, Traoré had his sentences commuted to life imprisonment in 1997 and 1999; he was pardoned in 2002.

Amadou Toumani Touré, who led the 1991 coup, was elected president in 2002 and reelected 2007. Mali's first female prime min., Cissé Mariam Kaïdama Sidibé, took office in 2011. Amadou Sanogo, an army captain, staged a coup Mar. 2012 and brokered a deal to transfer power Apr. 12 to an interim government led by Pres. Dioncounda Traoré and Prime Min. Cheick Modibo Diarra. The coup enabled Islamic rebels to seize control of the country's north. Diarra resigned Dec. 11 under pressure from rebel soldiers, who stopped him from fleeing to France. France entered the fight against Islamist rebels Jan. 10, 2013, and West African regional forces joined them Jan 17. On Feb. 19, forces from Chad killed the regional al-Qaeda leader during fighting in the north. The UN Stabilization Mission in Mali (MINUSMA) was approved Apr. 25, and the international community May 16 pledged about $4.2 bil to help rebuild the country. Rebels signed a peace deal June 18 to reintegrate the northern territory. Ibrahim Boubacar Keita was elected president Aug. 11.

Malta
Republic of Malta

People: Population: 411,277. **Age distrib.:** <15: 15.3%; 65+: 17.2%. **Pop. density:** 3,370.9 per sq mi, 1,301.5 per sq km. **Urban:** 94.8%. **Ethnic groups:** Maltese (descendants of ancient Carthaginians and Phoenicians with strong Italian, other Mediterranean elements). **Languages:** Maltese, English (both official). **Religion:** Roman Catholic (official) 98%.

Geography: Total area: 122 sq mi, 316 sq km; **Land area:** 122 sq mi, 316 sq km. **Location:** In center of Mediterranean Sea. **Neighbors:** Nearest is Italy on N. **Topography:** Isl. of Malta is 95 sq mi; other islands in the group: Gozo, 26 sq mi; Comino, 1 sq mi. Coastline is heavily indented. Low hills cover the interior. **Capital:** Valletta, 198,256.

Government: Type: Republic. **Head of state:** Pres. George Abela; b. Apr. 22, 1948; in office: Apr. 4, 2009. **Head of gov.:** Prime Min. Joseph Muscat; b. Jan. 22, 1974; in office: Mar. 11, 2013. **Local divisions:** 68 localities. **Defense budget:** $52 mil. **Active troops:** 1,950.

Economy: Industries: tourism, electronics, shipbuilding and repair, constr., food and beverages, pharmaceuticals, footwear, clothing, tobacco, aviation services. **Chief crops:** potatoes, cauliflower, grapes, wheat, barley, tomatoes, citrus, cut flowers, green peppers. **Natural resources:** limestone, salt. **Arable land:** 28.1%. **Livestock:** cattle: 15,074; chickens: 920,000; goats: 4,938; pigs: 46,287; sheep: 11,887. **Fish catch:** 4,076 metric tons. **Electricity prod.:** 2 bil kWh. **Labor force:** agric. 1.5%, industry 24.7%, services 73.9%.

Finance: Monetary unit: Euro (EUR) (Sept. 2013: 0.76 = $1 U.S.). **GDP:** $11.5 bil; **per capita GDP:** $27,500; **GDP growth:** 0.8%. **Imports:** $5.4 bil; Italy 39.6%, France 6.9%, UK 6.9%, Germany 5.3%. **Exports:** $4 bil; Germany 14.6%, France 9.9%, Italy 6.8%, Libya 5.5%, UK 5%. **Tourism:** $1.3 bil. **Budget:** $3.8 bil. **Total reserves less gold:** $688.3 mil. **Gold:** 10,000 oz t. **CPI change:** 2.4%.

Transport: Motor vehicles: 724.7 vehicles per 1,000 pop. **Civil aviation:** 2 bil pass.-mi; 1 airport. **Chief ports:** Marsaxlokk (Malta Freeport), Valletta.

Communications: TV sets: 554 per 1,000 pop. **Radios:** 664 per 1,000 pop. **Telephone lines:** 54.8 per 100 pop. **Internet:** 70%.

Health: Life expect.: 77.7 male; 82.4 female. **Births:** 10.3 per 1,000 pop. **Deaths:** 8.8 per 1,000 pop. **Natural inc.:** 0.14%. **Infant mortality:** 3.6 per 1,000 live births. **HIV rate:** 0.1%.

Education: Compulsory: ages 5-15. **Literacy:** 92.4%.

Major intl. organizations: UN (FAO, IBRD, ILO, IMF, WHO), the Commonwealth, EU, OSCE, WTO.

Embassy: 2017 Connecticut Ave. NW 20008; 462-3611.

Website: www.gov.mt

Malta was ruled by Phoenicians, Romans, Arabs, Normans, the Knights of Malta, France, and Britain (since 1814). It became independent Sept. 21, 1964. Malta became a republic in 1974. The withdrawal of the last British sailors, Apr. 1, 1979, ended 179 years of British military presence on the island.

From 1971 to 1987 and again from 1996 to 1998, Malta was governed by the socialist Labour Party; the Nationalist Party, which pressed for Malta's entry into the EU, held office 1987-96 and won parliamentary elections in 1998, 2003, and 2008. Malta became a full member of the EU May 1, 2004.

Marshall Islands
Republic of the Marshall Islands

People: Population: 69,747. **Age distrib.:** <15: 37.2%; 65+: 3.3%. **Pop. density:** 998 per sq mi, 385.3 per sq km. **Urban:** 71.8%. **Ethnic groups:** Marshallese 92%, mixed Marshallese 6%. **Languages:** Marshallese, English (both official). **Religions:** Protestant 55%, Assembly of God 26%, Roman Catholic 8%, Bukot nan Jesus 3%, Mormon 2%, other Christian 4%, none 2%.

Geography: Total area: 70 sq mi, 181 sq km; **Land area:** 70 sq mi, 181 sq km. **Location:** In N Pacific O.; composed of two 800-mi-long parallel chains of coral atolls. **Neighbors:** Nearest are Micronesia to W, Nauru and Kiribati to S. **Topography:** Marshall Islands are low coral limestone and sand islands. **Capital:** Majuro, 31,018.

Government: Type: Constitutional govt. in free association with the U.S. **Head of state and gov.:** Pres. Christopher J. Loeak; b. Nov. 11, 1952; in office: Jan. 17, 2012. **Local divisions:** 24 municipalities. **Defense budget:** NA. **Active troops:** No regular military forces. U.S. responsible for defense.

Economy: Industries: copra, tuna proc., tourism, craft items. **Chief crops:** coconuts, tomatoes, melons, taro, breadfruit, fruits. **Natural resources:** coconut prods., marine prods., deep-seabed minerals. **Arable land:** 11.1%. **Fish catch:** 93,244 metric tons. **Labor force:** agric. 11%, industry 16.3%, services 72.7%.

Finance: Monetary unit: Dollar (USD). **GDP** (2008 est.): $481.8 mil; **per capita GDP:** $8,800; **GDP growth:** 1.9%. **Imports** (2011): $118.7 mil. **Exports** (2011): $50.1 mil. **Tourism:** $3 mil. **Budget:** (FY09) $104.7 mil. **Total reserves less gold:** NA. **CPI change:** NA.

Transport: Civil aviation: 0.6 mil pass.-mi; 4 airports. **Chief port:** Majuro.

Communications: Telephone lines: (2004): 10.6 per 100 pop. **Internet:** 10%.

Health: Life expect.: 70.2 male; 74.6 female. **Births:** 27.2 per 1,000 pop. **Deaths:** 4.3 per 1,000 pop. **Natural inc.:** 2.29%. **Infant mortality:** 22.2 per 1,000 live births. **HIV rate:** NA.

Education: Compulsory: ages 6-13. **Literacy:** NA.

Major intl. organizations: UN (FAO, IBRD, IMF, WHO).

Embassy: 2433 Massachusetts Ave. NW 20008; 234-5414.

Website: www.rmigovernment.org

The Marshall Islands were a German possession until WWI and were administered by Japan between the World Wars. After WWII, they were administered by the U.S. as part of the UN Trust Territory of the Pacific Islands. During 1946-58, Bikini and Enewetak Atolls were used as test sites for U.S. nuclear weapons, including the hydrogen bomb.

The Compact of Free Association, ratified by the U.S. in 1986, gave the islands their independence. In the compact, the U.S. agreed to provide financial aid to the islands, maintain their defense, and compensate victims of nuclear testing; it was renewed Dec. 2003. The Marshall Islands joined the UN in 1991. Amata Kabua, the islands' first and only president since 1979, died Dec. 19, 1996. His cousin Imata Kabua, elected president Jan. 1997, was succeeded by Kessai Note in 2000; Litokwa Tomeing, 2008; Jurelang Zedkaia, 2009; and Christopher J. Loeak, 2012. Severe drought conditions in spring 2013 prompted U.S. Pres. Obama to sign a disaster declaration June 21 for the Marshall Islands, making the country eligible for U.S. federal relief funds.

Mauritania
Islamic Republic of Mauritania

People: Population: 3,437,610. **Age distrib.:** <15: 39.8%; 65+: 3.5%. **Pop. density:** 8.6 per sq mi, 3.3 per sq km. **Urban:** 41.5%. **Ethnic groups:** mixed Moor/black 40%, Moor 30%, black 30%. **Languages:** Arabic (official and national); Pulaar, Soninke, Wolof (all national); French; Hassaniya. **Religion:** Muslim (official) 100%.

Geography: Total area: 397,955 sq mi, 1,030,700 sq km; **Land area:** 397,955 sq mi, 1,030,700 sq km. **Location:** In NW Africa. **Neighbors:** Western Sahara on N; Algeria, Mali on E; Senegal on S. **Topography:** Fertile Senegal R. valley in the S gives way to a wide

central region of sandy plains and scrub trees. N is arid and extends into the Sahara. **Capital:** Nouakchott, 786,226.

Government: Type: Military junta. **Head of state:** Pres. Mohamed Ould Abdel Aziz; b. Dec. 20, 1956; in office: Aug. 5. 2009. **Head of gov.:** Prime Min. Moulaye Ould Mohamed Laghdaf; b. 1957; in office: Aug. 14, 2008. **Local divisions:** 13 regions. **Defense budget:** NA. **Active troops:** 15,850.

Economy: Industries: fish proc.; oil prod.; iron ore, gold, copper mining. **Chief crops:** dates, millet, sorghum, rice, corn. **Natural resources:** iron ore, gypsum, copper, phosphate, diamonds, gold, oil, fish. **Crude oil reserves:** 20 mil bbls. **Arable land:** 0.4%. **Livestock:** cattle: 1.7 mil; chickens: 4.4 mil; goats: 5.6 mil; sheep: 8.9 mil. **Fish catch:** 372,011 metric tons. **Electricity prod.:** 701 mil kWh. **Labor force:** agric. 50%, industry 10%, services 40%.

Finance: Monetary unit: Ouguiya (MRO) (Sept. 2013: 293.50 = $1 U.S.). **GDP:** $7.8 bil; **per capita GDP:** $2,200; **GDP growth:** 6.4%. **Imports:** $2.9 bil; China 12.9%, Netherlands 10.5%, U.S. 7.8%, France 7.7%, Brazil 5.6%, Germany 5.5%, Spain 5.1%, Belgium 4.7%. **Exports:** $2.7 bil; China 48.6%, Italy 7.5%, Japan 7%, Côte d'Ivoire 6.7%, France 4.7%, Spain 4.1%. **Budget:** $1.3 bil. **Total reserves less gold:** $949.5 mil. **Gold:** 11,500 oz t. **CPI change:** 4.9%.

Transport: Railways: 452 mi. **Motor vehicles:** 7.3 vehicles per 1,000 pop. **Civil aviation:** 39.8 mil pass.-mi; 9 airports. **Chief ports:** Nouadhibou, Nouakchott.

Communications: TV sets: 46 per 1,000 pop. **Radios:** 384 per 1,000 pop. **Telephone lines:** 1.8 per 100 pop. **Internet:** 5.4%.

Health: Life expect.: 59.7 male; 64.2 female. **Births:** 32.3 per 1,000 pop. **Deaths:** 8.5 per 1,000 pop. **Natural inc.:** 2.38%. **Infant mortality:** 57.5 per 1,000 live births. **HIV rate:** 1.1%.

Education: Compulsory: ages 6-15. **Literacy:** 58.6%.

Major intl. organizations: UN (FAO, IBRD, ILO, IMF, WHO), AL, AU, WTO.

Embassy: 2129 Leroy Pl. NW 20008; 232-5700.

Website: www.mauritania.mr

A French protectorate from 1903, Mauritania became independent Nov. 28, 1960. It annexed the south of former Spanish Sahara (now Western Sahara) in 1976 but renounced its claim to the region after signing a peace treaty with the Saharan guerrillas of the Polisario Front, 1979.

Maaouiya Ould Sid Ahmed Taya took power in a military coup in 1984. Taya, a U.S. ally, was toppled in a bloodless coup in 2005. During Jan.-June 2006, up to 10,000 people tried to emigrate in handmade boats from Mauritania to Spain's Canary Islands; more than 1,700 died. Civilian rule was restored, 2006-07, but a 2008 military coup toppled the elected government. The coup leader, Gen. Mohamed Ould Abdel Aziz, won a disputed presidential election in 2009. Security concerns, including a rising threat from al-Qaeda in the Islamic Maghreb, led the U.S. Peace Corps to remove its volunteers from Mauritania in Aug. 2009.

Major oil finds have recently been developed. Although slavery has been repeatedly abolished, most recently in 1981, thousands of Mauritanians continued to live under conditions of servitude; legislation mandating prison terms for slaveholders was enacted in 2007. Parliamentary elections scheduled for Mar. 31, 2012, were canceled due to conflicts between Pres. Aziz and opposition parties. Aziz was slightly injured when a military patrol that did not recognize his convoy accidentally fired upon his car Oct. 13, 2012.

Mauritius
Republic of Mauritius

People: Population: 1,322,238. **Age distrib.:** <15: 21.3%; 65+: 8%. **Pop. density:** 1,687 per sq mi, 651.3 per sq km. **Urban:** 41.8%. **Ethnic groups:** Indo-Mauritian 68%, Creole 27%, Sino-Mauritian 3%, Franco-Mauritian 2%. **Languages:** Creole, Bhojpuri, French, English (official). **Religions:** Hindu 48%, Roman Catholic 24%, Muslim 17%, other Christian 9%.

Geography: Total area: 788 sq mi, 2,040 sq km. **Land area:** 784 sq mi, 2,030 sq km. **Location:** In Indian O., 500 mi E of Madagascar. **Neighbors:** Nearest is Madagascar to W. **Topography:** A volcanic island nearly surrounded by coral reefs. A central plateau is encircled by mountain peaks. **Capital:** Port Louis, 150,697.

Government: Type: Parliamentary democracy. **Head of state:** Pres. Rajkeswur Kailash Purryag; b. Dec. 12, 1947; in office: July 21, 2012. **Head of gov.:** Prime Min. Navinchandra Ramgoolam; b. July 14, 1947; in office: July 5, 2005. **Local divisions:** 9 districts, 3 dependencies. **Defense budget:** $74 mil. **Active troops:** No standing armed forces. Special Mobile Force and coast guard provide security.

Economy: Industries: food proc. (largely sugar milling), textiles, clothing, mining, chemicals, metal prods. **Chief crops:** sugarcane, tea, corn, potatoes, bananas, pulses. **Natural resources:** fish. **Arable land:** 38.4%. **Livestock:** cattle: 6,596; chickens: 14.3 mil; goats: 28,176; pigs: 23,285; sheep: 20,500. **Fish catch:** 5,506 metric tons. **Electricity prod.:** 2.5 bil kWh. **Labor force:** agric. and fishing 9%; constr. and industry 30%; transp. and communication 7%; trade, restaurants, hotels 22%; finance 6%; other services 25%.

Finance: Monetary unit: Rupee (MUR) (Sept. 2013: 31.30 = $1 U.S.). **GDP:** $20.5 bil; **per capita GDP:** $15,800; **GDP growth:** 3.3%. **Imports:** $5.1 bil; India 23.7%, China 15.3%, France 8.9%,

South Africa 6.3%. **Exports:** $2.7 bil; UK 18.7%, France 16.4%, U.S. 10.4%, South Africa 9.7%, Spain 7.6%, Italy 7.1%, Madagascar 6.7%. **Tourism:** $1.5 bil. **Budget:** $2.7 bil. **Total reserves less gold:** $2.8 bil. **Gold:** 125,780 oz t. **CPI change:** 3.9%.

Transport: Motor vehicles: 145.4 vehicles per 1,000 pop. **Civil aviation:** 3.5 bil pass.-mi; 2 airports. **Chief port:** Port Louis.

Communications: TV sets: 370 per 1,000 pop. **Radios:** 78 per 1,000 pop. **Telephone lines:** 26.6 per 100 pop. **Internet:** 41.4%.

Health: Life expect.: 71.5 male; 78.6 female. **Births:** 13.6 per 1,000 pop. **Deaths:** 6.8 per 1,000 pop. **Natural inc.:** 0.68%. **Infant mortality:** 10.9 per 1,000 live births. **HIV rate:** 1%.

Education: Compulsory: ages 5-16. **Literacy:** 88.8%.

Major intl. organizations: UN and all of its specialized agencies, AU, the Commonwealth, WTO.

Embassy: 4301 Connecticut Ave. NW, Ste. 441, 20008; 244-1491.

Website: www.gov.mu

Mauritius was uninhabited when settled in 1638 by the Dutch, who introduced sugarcane. France took over in 1721, bringing African slaves. Britain ruled from 1810 to Mar. 12, 1968, bringing Indian workers for the sugar plantations.

Mauritius formally severed its association with the British crown Mar. 12, 1992. Since 2006, Mauritius has topped the Ibrahim Index of African Governance as the best-governed African country.

Mexico
United Mexican States

People: Population: 116,220,947. **Age distrib.:** <15: 27.4%; 65+: 6.9%. **Pop. density:** 154.8 per sq mi, 59.8 per sq km. **Urban:** 78.1%. **Ethnic groups:** mestizo (Amerindian-Spanish) 60%, Amerindian or predominantly Amerindian 30%, white 9%. **Languages:** Spanish, indigenous langs. (incl. various Mayan, Nahuatl, and others). **Religions:** Roman Catholic 77%, Protestant 5%, none 3%.

Geography: Total area: 758,449 sq mi, 1,964,375 sq km; **Land area:** 750,561 sq mi, 1,943,945 sq km. **Location:** In southern N America. **Neighbors:** U.S. on N, Guatemala and Belize on S. **Topography:** The Sierra Madre Occidental Mts. run NW-SE near the W coast; the Sierra Madre Oriental Mts. run near Gulf of Mexico. They join S of Mexico City. Between the 2 ranges lies the dry central plateau (5,000-8,000 ft) rising toward the S, with temperate vegetation. Coastal lowlands are tropical. About 45% of land is arid. **Capital:** Mexico City, 20,445,800. **Cities (urban aggl.):** Guadalajara, 4,524,669; Monterrey, 4,213,328; Puebla, 2,334,514; Tijuana, 1,819,831; Toluca de Lerdo, 1,747,849; León de las Aldamas, 1,652,641; Ciudad Juárez, 1,337,558; Torreón, 1,241,961; Querétaro, 1,143,102; San Luis Potosí, 1,061,040; Mórida, 1,040,229.

Government: Type: Federal republic. **Head of state and gov.:** Enrique Peña Nieto; b. July 20, 1966; in office: Dec. 1, 2012. **Local divisions:** 31 states, 1 federal district. **Defense budget:** $5.11 bil. **Active troops:** 270,250.

Economy: Industries: food and beverages, tobacco, chemicals, iron and steel, petroleum, mining, textiles, clothing, motor vehicles, consumer durables, tourism. **Chief crops:** corn, wheat, soybeans, rice, beans, cotton, coffee, fruit, tomatoes. **Natural resources:** petroleum, silver, copper, gold, lead, zinc, nat. gas, timber. **Crude oil reserves:** 10.3 bil bbls. **Arable land:** 13.1%. **Livestock:** cattle: 32.9 mil; chickens: 510.1 mil; goats: 9 mil; pigs: 15.5 mil; sheep: 8.2 mil. **Fish catch:** 1.7 mil metric tons. **Electricity prod.:** (2011) 257.9 bil kWh. **Labor force:** agric. 13.7%, industry 23.4%, services 62.9%.

Finance: Monetary unit: Peso (MXN) (Sept. 2013: 13.18 = $1 U.S.). **GDP:** $1.8 tril; **per capita GDP:** $15,600; **GDP growth:** 3.9%. **Imports:** $370.8 bil; U.S. 50.5%, China 15.5%, Japan 4.8%. **Exports:** $370.9 bil; U.S. 78%. **Tourism:** $12.7 bil. **Budget:** $297.7 bil. **Total reserves less gold:** $160.4 bil. **Gold:** 4 mil oz t. **CPI change:** 4.1%.

Transport: Railways: 10,666 mi. **Motor vehicles:** 285.7 vehicles per 1,000 pop. **Civil aviation:** 17.4 bil pass.-mi; 243 airports. **Chief ports:** Altamira, Coatzacoalcos, Lazaro Cardenas, Manzanillo, Salina Cruz, Veracruz.

Communications: TV sets: 274 per 1,000 pop. **Radios:** 324 per 1,000 pop. **Telephone lines:** 14.7 per 100 pop. **Internet:** 38.4%.

Health: Life expect.: 74.0 male; 79.8 female. **Births:** 18.6 per 1,000 pop. **Deaths:** 4.9 per 1,000 pop. **Natural inc.:** 1.37%. **Infant mortality:** 16.3 per 1,000 live births. **HIV rate:** 0.2%.

Education: Compulsory: ages 4-14. **Literacy:** 93.5%.

Major intl. organizations: UN (FAO, IBRD, ILO, IMF, WHO), APEC, NAFTA, OAS, OECD, WTO.

Embassy: 1911 Pennsylvania Ave. NW 20006; 728-1600.

Website: www.presidencia.gob.mx

Mexico was the site of advanced civilizations. The Mayans, an agricultural people, moved up from Yucatan, built huge stone pyramids and invented a calendar. The Toltecs were overcome by the Aztecs, who founded Tenochtitlan 1325 CE, now Mexico City. Hernán Cortés, Spanish conquistador, destroyed the Aztec empire, 1519-21. After 3 centuries of Spanish rule the people revolted, under Fr. Miguel Hidalgo y Costilla, 1810, Fr. Morelos y Pavón, 1812, and Gen. Agustín Iturbide, who made himself emperor as Agustín I, 1822. A republic was declared in 1823.

Mexican territory extended into the present American SW and California. Texas established a republic in 1836, and Mexico lost lands north of the Rio Grande during the U.S.-Mexican War, 1846-48.

The French supported an Austrian archduke on the Mexican throne as Maximilian I, 1864-67. He was deposed in an uprising led by Benito Juárez. Dictatorial rule by Porfirio Díaz, president 1877-80, 1884-1911, led to a period of rebellion and factional fighting. A new constitutionin 1917 brought reform.

The Institutional Revolutionary Party (PRI) dominated politics from 1929 until the late 1990s. Radical opposition, including some guerrilla activity, was contained by strong measures. Some gains in agriculture, industry, and social services were achieved, but much of the work force remained jobless or underemployed. Although prospects brightened with the discovery of vast oil reserves, inflation and a drop in world oil prices aggravated Mexico's economic problems in the 1980s. Mexico signed the North American Free Trade Agreement (NAFTA) with the U.S. and Canada in 1992; it took effect Jan. 1, 1994.

After guerrillas of the Zapatista National Liberation Army (EZLN) rebelled Jan. 1994, a tentative peace accord was reached Mar. 2. The presidential candidate of the governing PRI, Luis Donaldo Colosio Murrieta, was assassinated at a political rally in Tijuana, Mar. 23. The new PRI candidate, Ernesto Zedillo Ponce de León, won election Aug. 21 and was inaugurated Dec. 1, 1994.

An austerity plan and pledges of aid from the U.S. saved Mexico's currency from collapse in early 1995. Popular Revolutionary Army guerrillas launched coordinated attacks on government targets in Aug. 1996. In 1997 elections, the PRI lost a congressional majority for the first time since 1929.

In the 2000, presidential election, the PRI lost for the first time in over 7 decades; the winner, Vicente Fox Quesada of the National Action Party (PAN), took office Dec. 12000.

The PAN candidate, conservative Felipe Calderón Hinojosa, won the 2006 presidential election. Claiming vote fraud, the leftist candidate Andrés López Obrador and his supporters held massive protests, but Calderón was declared the winner. Despite a government crackdown on drug cartels, drug-related violence intensified, including an arson attack on a Monterrey casino Aug. 25, 2011, that killed 52 people, mostly women. The cumulative death toll in the drug war exceeded 47,500, Dec. 2006-Sept. 2012. Enrique Peña Nieto (PRI) won 2012 presidential elections. His opponent, López Obrador, challenged the results, but the Federal Electoral Tribunal dismissed his case. The headquarters of a state-owned oil company in Mexico City exploded Jan. 31, 2013, killing 37 people and injuring 121. Named tropical-storm systems Manuel and Ingrid struck opposite coasts of Mexico in mid-Sept. 2013, killing more than 100.

Micronesia
Federated States of Micronesia

People: Population: 106,104. **Age distrib.:** <15: 32.4%; 65+: 3.2%. **Pop. density:** 391.5 per sq mi, 151.1 per sq km. **Urban:** 22.6%. **Ethnic groups:** Chuukese 49%, Pohnpeian 24%, Kosraean 6%, Yapese 5%, Yap outer islands 5%, Asian 2%, Polynesian 2%. **Languages:** English (official and common), Chuukese, Kosrean, Pohnpeian, Yapese, Ulithian, Woleaian, Nukuoro, Kapingamarangi. **Religions:** Roman Catholic 53%, Protestant 42%.

Geography: Total area: 271 sq mi, 702 sq km; **Land area:** 271 sq mi, 702 sq km. **Location:** Consists of 607 islands in W Pacific O. **Topography:** Includes both high mountainous islands and low coral atolls; volcanic outcroppings on Pohnpei, Kosrae, and Truk. Climate is tropical. **Capital:** Palikir, 6,696.

Government: Type: Constitutional govt. in free association with U.S. **Head of state and gov.:** Pres. Emanuel (Manny) Mori; b. Dec. 25, 1948; in office: May 11, 2007. **Local divisions:** 4 states. **Defense budget:** NA. **Active troops:** No regular military forces. U.S. responsible for defense.

Economy: Industries: tourism, constr., fish proc., specialized aquaculture, craft items. **Chief crops:** black pepper, tropical fruits and vegetables, coconuts, bananas, cassava, kava, citrus, betel nuts, sweet potatoes. **Natural resources:** timber, marine prods., deep-seabed minerals, phosphate. **Arable land:** 2.9%. **Livestock:** cattle: 14,000; chickens: 190,000; goats: 4,100; pigs: 33,000. **Fish catch:** 36,269 metric tons. **Labor force:** agric. 0.9%, industry 20.6%, services 78.5% (two-thirds are govt. employees).

Finance: Monetary unit: Dollar (USD). **GDP:** $766.4 mil (supplemented by grant aid, averaging perhaps $100 mil annually); **per capita GDP:** $7,500; **GDP growth:** 1.4%. **Imports** (2004): $132.7 mil. **Exports** (2009): $24.9 mil. **Tourism:** $26 mil. **Budget** (FY10/11) $102 mil. **Total reserves less gold:** $76.8 mil. **CPI change:** NA.

Transport: Civil aviation: 6 airports. **Chief port:** Colonia.

Communications: TV sets: 27 per 1,000 pop. **Radios:** 47 per 1,000 pop. **Telephone lines** 7.5 per 100 pop. **Internet:** 26%.

Health: Life expect.: 70.1 male; 74.2 female. **Births:** 21.4 per 1,000 pop. **Deaths:** 4.3 per 1,000 pop. **Natural inc.:** 1.72%. **Infant mortality:** 22.7 per 1,000 live births. **HIV rate:** NA.

Education: Compulsory: ages 6-13. **Literacy:** NA.

Major intl. organizations: UN (FAO, IBRD, IMF, WHO). **Embassy:** 1725 N St. NW 20036; 223-4383. **Website:** micronesia.fm

Micronesia, formerly known as the Caroline Islands, was ruled successively by Spain, Germany, Japan, and the U.S. The nation gained independence under a compact of free association with the U.S., Nov. 1986, and was admitted to the UN in 1991. Micronesian officials have repeatedly warned of the dangers to their country of rising sea levels linked to global climate change.

Moldova
Republic of Moldova

People: Population: 3,619,925. **Age distrib.:** <15: 17.6%; 65+: 10.7%. **Pop. density:** 285 per sq mi, 110.1 per sq km. **Urban:** 47.7%. **Ethnic groups:** Moldovan/Romanian 78%, Ukrainian 8%, Russian 6%, Gagauz 4%, Bulgarian 2%. **Languages:** Moldovan (official; virtually same as Romanian), Russian, Gagauz. **Religions:** Eastern Orthodox 98%, Jewish 1.5%.

Geography: Total area: 13,070 sq mi, 33,851 sq km; **Land area:** 12,699 sq mi, 32,891 sq km. **Location:** In E Europe. **Neighbors:** Romania on W; Ukraine on N, E, and S. **Topography:** Country is landlocked; mainly hilly plains, with steppelands in S near Black Sea. **Capital:** Chişinău, 676,787.

Government: Type: Republic. **Head of state and gov.:** Pres. Nicolae Timofti; b. Dec. 22, 1948; in office: Mar. 23, 2012. **Local divisions:** 32 raions; 3 municipalities, 2 territorial units. **Defense budget:** $17 mil. **Active troops:** 5,350.

Economy: Industries: sugar, vegetable oil, food proc., agric. machinery, foundry equip, refrigerators and freezers. **Chief crops:** vegetables, fruits, grapes, grain, sugar beets, sunflower seeds, tobacco. **Natural resources:** lignite, phosphorites, gypsum, limestone. **Arable land:** 55.1%. **Livestock:** cattle: 215,951; chickens: 34 mil; goats: 117,585; pigs: 0.5 mil; sheep: 787,885. **Fish catch:** 9,350 metric tons. **Electricity prod.:** 3.3 bil kWh. **Labor force:** agric. 27.5%, industry 13.1%, services 59.4%.

Finance: Monetary unit: Leu (MDL) (Sept. 2013: 12.83 = $1 U.S.). **GDP:** $12.4 bil; **per capita GDP:** $3,500; **GDP growth:** -0.8%. **Imports:** $5.2 bil; Ukraine 20.9%, Romania 16.1%, Germany 9.4%, Russia 7.9%, Italy 5.7%, Belarus 5.3%, Turkey 4.7%, Poland 4.4%. **Exports:** $2.2 bil; Russia 20.9%, Romania 19.8%, Italy 11.6%, Ukraine 6.6%, Turkey 6%, Germany 4.7%. **Tourism:** $213 mil. **Budget:** $2.9 bil. **Total reserves less gold:** $2.5 bil. **Gold:** 2,383 oz t. **CPI change:** 4.7%.

Transport: Railways: 739 mi. **Civil aviation:** 330.6 mil pass.-mi; 5 airports.

Communications: TV sets: 310 per 1,000 pop. **Radios:** 39 per 1,000 pop. **Telephone lines** 34.3 per 100 pop. **Internet:** 43.4%.

Health: Life expect.: 66.0 male; 73.9 female. **Births:** 12.4 per 1,000 pop. **Deaths:** 12.6 per 1,000 pop. **Natural inc.:** -0.02%. **Infant mortality:** 13.3 per 1,000 live births. **HIV rate:** 0.5%.

Education: Compulsory: ages 6-15. **Literacy:** 99%.

Major intl. organizations: UN (FAO, IBRD, ILO, IMF, WHO), CIS, OSCE, WTO.

Embassy: 2101 S St. NW 20008; 667-1130.

Website: www.moldova.md

In 1918, Romania annexed all of Bessarabia that Russia had acquired from Turkey in 1812 by the Treaty of Bucharest. In 1924, the Soviet Union established the Moldavian Autonomous Soviet Socialist Republic on the eastern bank of the Dniester. It was merged with the Romanian-speaking districts of Bessarabia in 1940 to form the Moldavian SSR.

During WWII, Romania, allied with Germany, occupied the area. It was recaptured by the USSR in 1944. Moldova declared independence Aug. 27, 1991. It became an independent state when the USSR disbanded Dec. 26, 1991.

Fighting erupted Mar. 1992 in the Trans-Dniester region between Moldovan security forces and Slavic separatists—ethnic Russians and ethnic Ukrainians—who feared Moldova's merging with neighboring Romania. In a 1994 plebiscite, voters in Moldova supported independence, without unification with Romania.

Defying the Moldovan government, voters in the breakaway Trans-Dniester region held legislative elections and approved a separatist constitution in 1995. A peace accord with Trans-Dniester separatists was signed in Moscow in 1997. In a 2006 referendum, Trans-Dniester voters overwhelmingly supported independence from Moldova and eventual union with Russia. The Communists gained legislative majorities in 2001 and 2005 but were outpolled by a fragile coalition of pro-Western parties in 2009 and 2010. When a deadlocked parliament failed to agree on a president, a constitutional referendum providing for direct presidential elections was held Sept. 5, 2010. Although 88% of voters supported it, the measure failed to pass because of insufficient turnout. The pro-Western Nicolae Timofti became president in 2012. Parliament passed a no-confidence motion against Prime Min. Vlad Filat Mar. 5, 2013, forcing his resignation. Iurie Leanca was chosen the new prime min. May 31, and June 26 announced that he supported Timofti's plan for EU integration.

Monaco
Principality of Monaco

People: Population: 30,500. **Age distrib.:** <15: 11.9%; 65+: 28.7%. **Pop. density:** 39,497.3 per sq mi, 15,250 per sq km. **Urban:** 100%. **Ethnic groups:** French 47%, Monegasque 16%, Italian 16%. **Languages:** French (official), English, Italian, Monegasque. **Religion:** Roman Catholic (official) 90%.

Geography: Total area: 0.77 sq mi, 2 sq km; **Land area:** 0.77 sq mi, 2 sq km. **Location:** On NW Mediterranean coast. **Neighbors:** France to W, N, E. **Topography:** Monaco-Ville sits atop a high promontory, the rest of the principality rises from the port up the hillside. **Capital:** Monaco, 35,427.

Government: Type: Constitutional monarchy. **Head of state:** Prince Albert II; b. Mar. 14, 1958; in office: Apr. 6, 2005. **Head of gov.:** Min. of State Michel Roger; b. Mar. 9, 1949; in office: Mar. 29, 2010. **Local divisions:** 4 quarters. **Defense budget:** NA. **Active troops:** No regular military forces. France responsible for defense.

Economy: Industries: tourism, constr., small-scale industrial and consumer prods. **Chief crops:** none. **Natural resources:** none. **Arable land:** none. **Fish catch:** 1 metric ton. **Labor force:** NA.

Finance: Monetary unit: Euro (EUR) (Sept. 2013: 0.76 = $1 U.S.). **GDP** (2011): $5.7 bil; **per capita GDP** (2011): $70,700; **GDP growth** (2011): 5.1%. **Imports** (2011): $848.9 mil. **Exports** (2011): $865.6 mil. (Full customs integration with France. Also participates in EU market system through customs union with France.) **Budget** (2011): $1.2 bil. **Total reserves less gold:** NA. **CPI change:** NA.

Transport: Civil aviation: 1.9 mil pass.-mi. **Chief port:** Monaco. **Communications:** TV sets: 758 per 1,000 pop. **Telephone lines:** 125.5 per 100 pop. **Internet:** 87%.

Health: Life expect.: 85.7 male; 93.7 female. **Births:** 6.8 per 1,000 pop. **Deaths:** 8.8 per 1,000 pop. **Natural inc.:** −0.20%. **Infant mortality:** 1.8 per 1,000 live births. **HIV rate:** NA.

Education: Compulsory: ages 6-15. **Literacy:** 99%.

Major intl. organizations: UN (FAO, WHO), OSCE.

Embassy: 2314 Wyoming Ave. NW 20008; 234-1530.

Website: www.gouv.mc

An independent principality for over 300 years, Monaco has belonged to the House of Grimaldi since 1297, except during the French Revolution. It was placed under the protectorate of Sardinia in 1815, and under France, 1861. The Prince of Monaco was an absolute ruler until the 1911 constitution. Monaco was admitted to the UN in 1993.

Monaco is noted for its mild climate, magnificent scenery, and elegant casinos. Prince Rainier III, who ruled Monaco from 1949 and turned it into one of Europe's top tourist spots, died in 2005 and was succeeded by his son, Albert II.

Mongolia

People: Population: 3,226,516. **Age distrib.:** <15: 26.9%; 65+: 4%. **Pop. density:** 5.4 per sq mi, 2.1 per sq km. **Urban:** 68.5%. **Ethnic groups:** Mongol (mostly Khalkha) 95%, Turkic (mostly Kazakh) 5%. **Languages:** Khalkha Mongol, Turkic, Russian. **Religions:** Buddhist Lamaist 50%, Shamanist and Christian 6%, Muslim 4%, none 40%.

Geography: Total area: 603,909 sq mi, 1,564,116 sq km; **Land area:** 599,831 sq mi, 1,553,556 sq km. **Location:** In E Central Asia. **Neighbors:** Russia on N, China on E, W, and S. **Topography:** Mostly a high plateau with mountains, salt lakes, and vast grasslands. Arid lands in S are part of the Gobi Desert. **Capital:** Ulaanbaatar, 1,183,910.

Government: Type: Parliamentary. **Head of state:** Pres. Tsakhiagiin Elbegdorj; b. Mar. 30, 1963; in office: June 18, 2009. **Head of gov.:** Prime. Min. Norov Altankhuyag; b. Jan. 20, 1958; in office: Aug. 9, 2012. **Local divisions:** 21 provinces, 1 municipality. **Defense budget:** $87 mil. **Active troops:** 10,000.

Economy: Industries: constr. and constr. materials, mining, oil, food and beverages, animal prods. proc., cashmere and natural fiber mfg. **Chief crops:** wheat, barley, vegetables, forage crops. **Natural resources:** oil, coal, copper, molybdenum, tungsten, phosphates, tin, nickel, zinc, fluorspar, gold, silver, iron. **Arable land:** 0.4%. **Livestock:** cattle: 2.3 mil; chickens: 597,000; goats: 15.9 mil; pigs: 30,397; sheep: 15.7 mil. **Fish catch:** 80 metric tons. **Electricity prod.** 4.2 bil kWh. **Labor force:** agric. 33%, industry 10.6%, services 56.4%.

Finance: Monetary unit: Tughrik (MNT) (Sept. 2013: 1,647.50 = $1 U.S.). **GDP:** $15.4 bil; **per capita GDP:** $5,500; **GDP growth:** 12.3%. **Imports:** $6.7 bil; China 37.6%, Russia 25.7%, U.S. 9.4%, South Korea 6.1%, Japan 4.9%. **Exports:** $4.4 bil; China 88.9%, Canada 4.1%. **Tourism:** $233 mil. **Budget:** $4.1 bil. **Total reserves less gold:** $3.9 bil. **Gold:** 117,718 oz t. **CPI change:** 15%.

Transport: Railways: 1,186 mi (partly owned by Russian State Railway). **Civil aviation:** 379 mil pass.-mi; 15 airports.

Communications: TV sets: 88 per 1,000 pop. **Radios:** 328 per 1,000 pop. **Telephone lines:** 6.2 per 100 pop. **Internet:** 16.4%.

Health: Life expect.: 66.5 male; 71.6 female. **Births:** 20.3 per 1,000 pop. **Deaths:** 6.0 per 1,000 pop. **Natural inc.:** 1.44%. **Infant mortality:** 34.8 per 1,000 live births. **HIV rate:** <0.1%.

Education: Compulsory: ages 6-14. **Literacy:** 97.4%.

Major intl. organizations: UN (FAO, IBRD, ILO, IMF, WHO), WTO.

Embassy: 2833 M St. NW 20007; 333-7117.

Website: www.pmis.gov.mn

One of the world's oldest countries, Mongolia reached the zenith of its power in the 13th cent. when Genghis Khan and his successors conquered all of China and extended their influence as far west as Hungary and Poland. In later centuries, the empire dissolved and Mongolia became a province of China.

With the advent of the 1911 Chinese revolution, Mongolia, with Russian backing, declared its independence. A Communist regime was established in 1921. In 1990, the Mongolian Communist Party yielded its monopoly on power. A new constitution took effect in 1992.

Mongolia sent more than 100 troops to U.S.-led operations in Afghanistan (2001); as of June 2013, 46 remained. Riots followed 2008 parliamentary elections, won by the ruling Mongolian People's Revolutionary Party (MPRP). In 2009 presidential voting, former Prime Min. Tsakhiagiin Elbergdorj (1998, 2004-06), the Democratic Party candidate, defeated the MPRP's incumbent Pres. Nambaryn Enkhbayar. A 2012 legislative election gave the Democratic Party the most seats in parliament, and Norov Altankhuyag became prime min. Aug. 9. Exploitation of vast mineral resources is expected to boost Mongolia's GDP at annual rates of more than 13% from 2013 to 2015. Elbergdorj was reelected June 27, 2013.

Montenegro

People: Population: 653,474. **Age distrib.:** <15: 15.3%; 65+: 13.8%. **Pop. density:** 125.8 per sq mi, 48.6 per sq km. **Urban:** 63.3%. **Ethnic groups:** Montenegrin 43%, Serbian 32%, Bosniak 8%, Albanian 5%, other (Muslim, Croat, Roma) 12%. **Languages:** Serbian, Montenegrin (official), Bosnian, Albanian. **Religions:** Orthodox 74%, Muslim 18%, Catholic 4%, atheist 1%.

Geography: Total area: 5,333 sq mi, 13,812 sq km; **Land area:** 5,194 sq mi, 13,452 sq km. **Location:** On Balkan Peninsula in SE Europe. **Neighbors:** Bosnia and Herzegovina on N and W; Serbia on E; Albania on SE; Adriatic Sea on SW; Croatia on W. **Topography:** Most terrain is rugged and mountainous, with few arable regions, mostly along the Zeta R.; narrow coastline is highly indented. **Capital:** Podgorica, 156,418.

Government: Type: Republic. **Head of state:** Pres. Filip Vujanovic; b. Sept. 1, 1954; in office: May 22, 2003. **Head of gov.:** Prime. Min. Milo Djukanovic; b. Feb. 15, 1962; in office: Dec. 4, 2012. **Local divisions:** 21 municipalities. **Defense budget:** $52 mil. **Active troops:** 2,080.

Economy: Industries: steelmaking, aluminum, agric. proc., consumer goods, tourism. **Chief crops:** tobacco, potatoes, citrus, olives, grapes. **Natural resources:** bauxite, hydroelectricity. **Arable land:** 12.8%. **Livestock:** cattle: 87,183; chickens: 470,050; pigs: 21,398; sheep: 208,771. **Fish catch:** 2,308 metric tons. **Electricity prod.:** 3.9 bil kWh. **Labor force:** agric. 6.3%, industry 20.9%, services 72.8%.

Finance: Monetary unit: Euro (EUR) (Sept. 2013: 0.76 = $1 U.S.). **GDP:** $7.5 bil; **per capita GDP:** $12,000; **GDP growth:** 0%. **Imports:** $2.4 bil; Serbia 29.3%, Greece 8.7%, China 7.1%. **Exports:** $489.2 mil; Croatia 22.7%, Serbia 22.7%, Slovenia 7.8%. **Tourism:** $826 mil. **Budget:** $1.6 bil. **Total reserves less gold:** $458.7 mil. **CPI change:** (2010-11): 3.2%.

Transport: Railways: 155 mi. **Civil aviation:** 5 airports. **Chief port:** Bar.

Communications: Telephone lines (2010): 26.8 per 100 pop. **Telephone lines:** 25.8 per 100 pop. **Internet:** 56.8%.

Health: Life expect.: 75.1 male; 81.3 female. **Births:** 10.8 per 1,000 pop. **Deaths:** 9.2 per 1,000 pop. **Natural inc.:** 0.16%. **Infant mortality:** 9.1 per 1,000 live births. **HIV rate:** NA.

Education: Compulsory: ages 6-14. **Literacy:** 98.5%.

Major intl. organizations: UN (FAO, ILO, WHO), OSCE, WTO (observer).

Embassy: 1610 New Hampshire Ave. NW 20009; 234-6108.

Website: www.gov.me

Part of the medieval Serbian Kingdom, Montenegro preserved its autonomy for centuries because of its mountainous terrain. After WWI, it was part of the Kingdom of Serbs, Croats, and Slovenes, later renamed Yugoslavia. Italian forces occupied parts of Montenegro during WWII. In 1945, with the establishment of a federal Yugoslavia under Communist rule, Montenegro became one of 6 constituent republics.

In Apr. 1992, after 4 other republics had declared independence, Montenegro and Serbia reconstituted themselves as the Federal Republic of Yugoslavia. Because of its ties with Serbia, Montenegro was a target of NATO air strikes during the Kosovo war, Mar.-June 1999. The republic sought closer ties with the West, however, and worked to reduce its political and economic dependence on Serbia. A 2006 referendum on independence passed with barely more than the 55% majority required. Montenegro declared independence June 3, 2006, and was admitted as a UN member June 28. It applied in 2008, to join the EU. In early parliamentary elections held Oct. 14, 2012, Milo Djukanovic's governing coalition won the right to stay in power.

Morocco
Kingdom of Morocco

People: Population: 32,649,130. **Age distrib.:** <15: 27.1%; 65+: 6.3%. **Pop. density:** 189.5 per sq mi, 73.2 per sq km. **Urban:** 57%. **Ethnic groups:** Arab-Berber 99%. **Languages:** Arabic (official), Berber dialects, French (lang. of business, govt., diplomacy). **Religions:** Muslim (official) 99%, Christian 1%.

Geography: Total area: 172,414 sq mi, 446,550 sq km; **Land area:** 172,317 sq mi, 446,300 sq km. **Location:** On NW coast of Africa. **Neighbors:** Western Sahara on S, Algeria on E, Spain on N. **Topography:** Consists of 5 natural regions: mountain ranges (Riff in the N, Middle Atlas, Upper Atlas, and Anti-Atlas); rich plains in W; alluvial plains in SW; well-cultivated plateaus in the center; a pre-Sahara arid zone extending from SE. **Capital:** Rabat, 1,842,850. **Cities (urban aggl.):** Casablanca (Dar-el-Beida), 3,046,040; Fès, 1,087,516.

Government: Type: Constitutional monarchy. **Head of state:** King Mohammed VI; b. Aug. 21, 1963; in office: July 23, 1999. **Head of gov.:** Prime Min. Abdelilah Benkirane; b. Apr. 4, 1954; in office: Nov. 29, 2011. **Local divisions:** 15 regions (not incl. territory in Western Sahara). **Defense budget:** $3.37 bil. **Active troops:** 195,800.

Economy: Industries: phosphate rock mining and proc., food proc., leather goods, textiles, constr., energy, tourism. **Chief crops:** barley, wheat, citrus, grapes, vegetables, olives. **Natural resources:** phosphates, iron ore, manganese, lead, zinc, fish, salt. **Crude oil reserves:** 680,000 bbls. **Arable land:** 17.8%. **Livestock:** cattle: 3 mil; chickens: 175 mil; goats: 6 mil; pigs: 8,250; sheep: 18.7 mil. **Fish catch:** 966,108 metric tons. **Electricity prod.:** 21.1 bil kWh. **Labor force:** agric. 44.6%, industry 19.8%, services 35.5%.

Finance: Monetary unit: Dirham (MAD) (Sept. 2013: 8.47 = $1 U.S.). **GDP:** $174 bil; **per capita GDP:** $5,400; **GDP growth:** 3%. **Imports:** $42.5 bil; Spain 13.1%, France 12.1%, China 6.9%, U.S. 6.8%, Saudi Arabia 6.2%, Italy 5.1%, Russia 5% Germany 4.9%. **Exports:** $21.8 bil; France 21%, Spain 17.3%, Brazil 5.4%, India 4.9%, U.S. 4.6%. **Tourism:** $6.7 bil. **Budget:** $33.3 bil. **Total reserves less gold:** $16.4 bil. **Gold:** 708,800 oz t. **CPI change:** 1.3%.

Transport: Railways: 1,284 mi. **Motor vehicles:** 100.5 vehicles per 1,000 pop. **Civil aviation:** 6 bil pass.-mi; 31 airports. **Chief ports:** Casablanca, Jorf Lasfar, Mohammedia, Safi, Tangier.

Communications: TV sets: 174 per 1,000 pop. **Radios:** 246 per 1,000 pop. **Telephone lines:** 10.1 per 100 pop. **Internet:** 55%.

Health: Life expect.: 73.3 male; 79.5 female. **Births:** 18.7 per 1,000 pop. **Deaths:** 4.8 per 1,000 pop. **Natural inc.:** 1.40%. **Infant mortality:** 25.5 per 1,000 live births. **HIV rate:** 0.2%.

Education: Compulsory: ages 6-14. **Literacy:** 67.1%.

Major intl. organizations: UN (FAO, IBRD, ILO, IMF, WHO), AL, WTO.

Embassy: 1601 21st St. NW 20009; 462-7979.

Website: www.maroc.ma

Berbers were the region's original inhabitants, followed by Carthaginians and Romans. Arabs conquered it in 683. In the 11th and 12th cents., a Berber empire ruled all NW Africa and most of Spain from Morocco.

Part of Morocco came under Spanish rule in the 19th cent.; France controlled the rest in the early 20th. Tribal uprisings lasted from 1911 to 1933. Independence was achieved Mar. 2, 1956. Tangier, an internationalized seaport, was incorporated into Morocco, 1956. Ifni, a Spanish enclave, was ceded in 1969. Morocco annexed the disputed territory of Western Sahara during the second half of the 1970s.

King Hassan II assumed the throne in 1961, reigning until his death in 1999; he was succeeded by his eldest son. A bicameral legislature was established in 1997.

Five terrorist attacks in Casablanca May 16, 2003, left 45 people dead, including 12 suicide bombers; the government blamed Salafia Jihadia, an al-Qaeda-linked group. An earthquake Feb. 24, 2004, killed at least 629 people near al-Hoceima, northern coastal Morocco. Following a series of suicide bombings in 2007, the government stepped up its campaign against militant Islamists. Following Arab Spring street demonstrations Feb.-Mar. 2011, the monarchy implemented modest constitutional reforms. Throughout 2011, Moroccans staged protests of what they saw as social injustices, including persistent unemployment, unjust detentions, and lack of free speech. The moderate Islamist Justice and Development Party won a plurality in Nov. 25, 2011 parliamentary elections, and Abdelilah Benkirane was named prime min.

Western Sahara

Western Sahara, formerly the protectorate of Spanish Sahara, is bounded on the N by Morocco, the NE by Algeria, the E and S by Mauritania, and the W by the Atlantic O. Phosphates are the major resource. Pop. (2013 est.): 538,811; area: 102,703 sq mi; capital: Laayoune (El Aaiún).

Spain withdrew in Feb. 1976. On Apr. 14, 1976, Morocco annexed over 70,000 sq mi, with the remainder annexed by Mauritania. The Polisario Front guerrilla movement, which proclaimed the region independent Feb. 27, launched attacks with Algerian support. After Mauritania signed a treaty with Polisario Aug. 5, 1979, Morocco occupied Mauritania's portion of Western Sahara.

After years of bitter fighting, Morocco controlled the main urban areas, but Polisario guerrillas moved freely in the vast, sparsely populated deserts. The 2 sides implemented a cease-fire in 1991, when a UN peacekeeping force (MINURSO) was established with a mandate to prepare for a referendum on self-determination as early as 1992; in mid-2013, MINURSO had about 237 personnel in Western Sahara, but a referendum had still not been held.

Mozambique
Republic of Mozambique

People: Population: 24,096,669. **Age distrib.:** <15: 45.5%; 65+: 2.9%. **Pop. density:** 79.4 per sq mi, 30.6 per sq km. **Urban:** 31.2%. **Ethnic groups:** African (incl. Makhuwa, Tsonga, Lomwe, Sena) 99.7%. **Languages:** Emakhuwa, Portuguese (official), Xichangana, Cisena, Elomwe, Echuwabo, other Mozambican langs. **Religions:** Catholic 28%, Protestant 28% (Zionist Christian 16%, Evangelical Pentecostal 11%), Muslim 18%, none 19%.

Geography: Total area: 308,642 sq mi, 799,380 sq km; **Land area:** 303,623 sq mi, 786,380 sq km. **Location:** On SE coast of Africa. **Neighbors:** Tanzania on N; Malawi, Zambia, Zimbabwe on W; South Africa, Swaziland on S. **Topography:** Coastal lowlands comprise nearly half the country with plateaus rising in steps to the mountains along W border. **Capital:** Maputo, 1,150,030. **Cities (urban aggl.):** Matola, 793,486.

Government: Type: Republic. **Head of state:** Pres. Armando Guebuza; b. Jan. 20, 1943; in office: Feb. 2, 2005. **Head of gov.:** Prime Min. Alberto Clementino Vaquina; in office: Oct. 8, 2012. **Local divisions:** 10 provinces, 1 city. **Defense budget** (2011): $70 mil. **Active troops:** 11,200.

Economy: Industries: aluminum, petroleum prods., chemicals, textiles, cement, glass, asbestos, tobacco, food, beverages. **Chief crops:** cotton, cashew nuts, sugarcane, tea, cassava, corn, coconuts, sisal, citrus and tropical fruits, potatoes, sunflowers. **Natural resources:** coal, titanium, nat. gas, hydropower, tantalum, graphite. **Arable land:** 6.6%. **Livestock:** cattle: 1.3 mil; chickens: 24 mil; goats: 4 mil; pigs: 1.4 mil; sheep: 220,000. **Fish catch:** 189,831 metric tons. **Electricity prod.:** 16.5 bil kWh. **Labor force:** agric. 81%, industry 6%, services 13%.

Finance: Monetary unit: Metical (MZN) (Sept. 2013: 29.72 = $1 U.S.). **GDP:** $26.7 bil; **per capita GDP:** $1,200; **GDP growth:** 7.5%. **Imports:** $6.2 bil; South Africa 30.7%, China 12.2%, India 11.4%, U.S. 5.1%, Portugal 4.8%, Australia 4.4%. **Exports:** $3.5 bil; South Africa 30.9%, Belgium 12.8%, China 9%, Italy 7.8%, Spain 6.2%, India 5.6%. **Tourism:** $250 mil. **Budget:** $4.9 bil. **Total reserves less gold:** $2.8 bil. **Gold:** 115,189 oz t. **CPI change:** 1.1%.

Transport: Railways: 2,975 mi. **Motor vehicles:** 3.1 vehicles per 1,000 pop. **Civil aviation:** 343 mil pass.-mi; 21 airports. **Chief ports:** Beira, Maputo, Nacala.

Communications: TV sets: 21 per 1,000 pop. **Radios:** 63 per 1,000 pop. **Telephone lines:** 0.4 per 100 pop. **Internet:** 4.8%.

Health: Life expect.: 51.5 male; 53.1 female. **Births:** 39.1 per 1,000 pop. **Deaths:** 12.6 per 1,000 pop. **Natural inc.:** 2.65%. **Infant mortality:** 74.6 per 1,000 live births. **HIV rate:** 11.3%.

Education: Compulsory: ages 6-12. **Literacy:** 50.6%.

Major intl. organizations: UN (FAO, IBRD, ILO, IMF, WHO), AU, the Commonwealth, WTO.

Embassy: 1525 New Hampshire Ave. NW 20036; 293-7146.

Website: www.mozambique.mz

The first Portuguese post on the Mozambique coast was established in 1505 on the trade route to the East. Mozambique became independent June 25, 1975, after a 10-year war against the Portuguese. The 1974 revolution in Portugal paved the way for an orderly transfer of power to Frelimo (Front for the Liberation of Mozambique).

The Frelimo government, headed by Pres. Samora Machel, a former guerrilla commander, gradually transitioned to a Communist system. Most of the country's whites emigrated. In the 1980s, severe drought and civil war caused famine and heavy loss of life. Pres. Machel was killed in a plane crash just inside the South African border, Oct. 19, 1986. Frelimo formally abandoned Marxist-Leninism in 1989, and a new constitution, effective Nov. 30, 1990, established multiparty elections and a free-market economy.

A 1992 peace agreement ended hostilities between the government and the Mozambique National Resistance (MNR). Repatriation of 1.7 mil Mozambican refugees ended June 1995. In Mar. 1999 the heaviest floods in 4 decades left nearly 200,000 people stranded. Worse flooding in Feb.-Mar. 2000 claimed more than 600 lives and devastated the economy.

Frelimo retained its hold under Pres. Joaquim Chissano (in office 1986-2005) and his successor, Pres. Armando Guebuza, elected in 2004. Flooding of the Zambezi River Basin, followed by Cyclone Favio, killed at least 45 people in Feb. 2007. Another flood crisis, Jan.-Mar. 2008, claimed some 700 lives and displaced 650,000 people. Despite robust economic growth during 2000-11, poverty remained widespread. Guebuza won reelection in 2009. According to Aug. 2012 estimates, 70 tril cu ft of crude oil reserves were discovered off Mozambique, 2011-12. Italian oil company Eni reported Dec. 5, 2012, that it had found about 6 tril cu ft of natural gas off the coast, bringing the total amount of natural gas Eni had found in the area up to 68 tril cu ft, worth as much as $15 bil.

SCIENCE & TECHNOLOGY

The Big Boom A meteoroid 59 ft in diameter streaked over Chelyabinsk, Russia, Feb. 15, 2013. The resulting shock wave shattered windows and injured more than 1,000 people.

Unearthing the Past On the basis of DNA and other evidence, skeletal remains found under a parking lot in Leicester, England, were identified Feb. 4, 2013, as belonging to King Richard III (1452-85).

Ear Pioneers Scientists at Cornell Univ. announced Feb. 20, 2013, that they had learned to recreate a human ear using 3-D printing and injections of living cells.

A Lot Like Earth NASA researchers, analyzing data from the Kepler spacecraft, identified Apr. 18, 2013, the most Earth-like planets yet discovered, 1,200 light-years from Earth.

A Better View The ALMA radio telescope array—the world's largest ground-based telescope—was officially opened in Chile's Atacama Desert Mar. 13, 2013.

Introducing the Olinguito The Smithsonian Institution announced Aug. 15, 2013, that it had identified the olinguito as a new mammalian carnivore species—the first to be discovered in the Americas in 35 years.

SPORTS

High Tide   Alabama toppled Notre Dame in a lopsided BCS Championship win Jan. 7, 2013.

Total Dominance   LeBron James and the Miami Heat overpowered the San Antonio Spurs June 20, 2013, to win their second consecutive NBA championship.

Improbable Comeback   After a lockout-shortened season, the Chicago Blackhawks scored twice in less than two minutes to win the Stanley Cup Finals June 24, 2013.

Blackout Bowl   Joe Flacco and the Baltimore Ravens Feb. 3, 2013, defeated the San Francisco 49ers in Super Bowl XLVII despite a 35-min. power failure in New Orleans's Superdome.

Homegrown Champion Andy Murray became the first British man to win Wimbledon in 77 years July 7, 2013, in London, England.

Pretty Good Day Head coach Rick Pitino and the Louisville Cardinals defeated the Michigan Wolverines to win the men's NCAA basketball championship Apr. 8, 2013, hours after Pitino learned he had been elected to the Hall of Fame.

Sweet Seventeen Serena Williams defeated Victoria Azarenka Sept. 8, 2013, at the U.S. Open for her 17th Grand Slam title.

Not Bad for a Freshman Connecticut forward Breanna Stewart led the Huskies in their NCAA tournament championship win over the Louisville Cardinals Apr. 9, 2013, and was named the Final Four's most outstanding player.

SPORTS

Judgment Day Alex Rodriguez and 12 more MLB players, including several other All-Stars, received suspensions Aug. 5, 2013, for their use of banned performance-enhancing drugs.

Ahead of the Crowd Usain Bolt continued to outsprint the field at the 2013 IAAF World Championships in Moscow in Aug. 2013.

Need for Speed Jimmie Johnson held off Dale Earnhardt Jr. on the last lap to win the Daytona 500 Feb. 24, 2013.

Achieving Goals U.S. forward Abby Wambach (top) scored her 160th career goal in international competition June 21, 2013—the most of any man or woman in soccer.

Third Time's the Charm? The Portland Thorns won the first-ever National Women's Soccer League Championship over the Western New York Flash Aug. 31, 2013; the new league was the third attempt to establish a professional soccer league for women in the U.S.

PEOPLE

Meet the Parents Prince William and Catherine, the Duke and Duchess of Cambridge, introduced Prince George, born July 22, 2013; he was third in line in the succession for the British throne.

Papal Transition Pope Benedict XVI (right) resigned effective Feb. 28, 2013, and was replaced as leader of the Roman Catholic Church by Pope Francis, the first Latin American pontiff, Mar. 13, 2013.

Serious Charges South African Olympic sprinter Oscar Pistorius (left) was accused of murder in the death of his girlfriend, Reeva Steenkamp, Feb. 14, 2013. New England Patriots tight end Aaron Hernandez was arrested June 26, 2013, and charged with first-degree murder in the shooting death of a friend, Odin Lloyd.

Groundbreaker Veteran NBA center Jason Collins Apr. 29, 2013, became the first active athlete in the four major U.S. pro sports leagues to come out publicly as gay.

End of an Era Michael Bloomberg (left), mayor of New York City since Jan. 1, 2002, was in the waning days of his third term in 2013; Public Advocate Bill de Blasio hoped to succeed him on election day Nov. 5, 2013.

ARTS

Winners' Toast Daniel Day-Lewis, Jennifer Lawrence, Anne Hathaway, and Christoph Waltz were honored with the major acting Oscars at the Academy Awards Feb. 24, 2013.

Different Strokes English folk rock band Mumford & Sons won Album of the Year for *Babel* at the Grammy Awards Feb. 10, 2013.

Awfully Fond Giant rubber ducks, the work of Dutch artist Florentijn Hofman, delighted viewers around the world, appearing in Hong Kong in May 2013 and Pittsburgh in Sept. 2013.

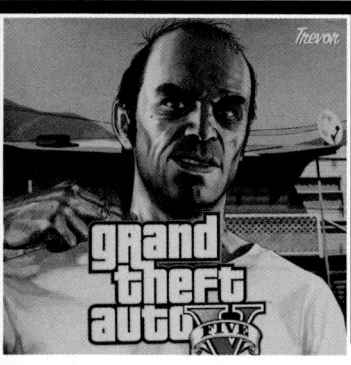

Bad All Over Just a week before the critically acclaimed show aired its final episode Sept. 29, 2013, the cast of *Breaking Bad* celebrated their Emmy win for outstanding drama series.

Record Setter *Grand Theft Auto V*, released Sept. 17, 2013, shattered video game sales records, topping $1 bil in sales in only three days.

FAREWELLS

CHINUA ACHEBE
NOV. 16, 1930-MAR. 21, 2013

JOYCE BROTHERS
OCT. 20, 1927-MAY 13, 2013

DAVE BRUBECK
DEC. 6, 1920-DEC. 5, 2012

TOM CLANCY
APR. 12, 1947 OCT. 1, 2013

ROGER EBERT
JUNE 18, 1942-APR. 4, 2013

ANNETTE FUNICELLO
OCT. 22, 1942-APR. 8, 2013

JAMES GANDOLFINI
SEPT. 18, 1961-JUNE 19, 2013

LARRY HAGMAN
SEPT. 21, 1931-NOV. 23, 2012

RICHIE HAVENS
JAN. 21, 1941-APR. 22, 2013

SEAMUS HEANEY
APR. 13, 1939-AUG. 30, 2013

DANIEL INOUYE
SEPT. 7, 1924-DEC. 17, 2012

DEACON JONES
DEC. 9, 1938-JUNE 3, 2013

FAREWELLS

GEORGE JONES
SEPT. 12, 1931-APR. 26, 2013

ED KOCH
DEC. 12, 1924-FEB. 1, 2013

ELMORE LEONARD
OCT. 11, 1925-AUG. 20, 2013

CORY MONTEITH
MAY 11, 1982-JULY 13, 2013

STAN MUSIAL
NOV. 21, 1920-JAN. 19, 2013

RAVI SHANKAR
APR. 7, 1920-DEC. 11, 2012

JEAN STAPLETON
JAN. 19, 1923-MAY 31, 2013

PAT SUMMERALL
MAY 10, 1930-APR. 16, 2013

MARGARET THATCHER
OCT. 13, 1925-APR. 8, 2013

ABIGAIL VAN BUREN
(PAULINE PHILLIPS) JULY 4, 1918-JAN. 16, 2013

ESTHER WILLIAMS
AUG. 8, 1921-JUNE 6, 2013

JONATHAN WINTERS
NOV. 11, 1925-APR. 11, 2013

Myanmar
(Burma)
Union of Myanmar

People: Population: 55,167,330. **Age distrib.:** <15: 26.7%; 65+: 5.2%. **Pop. density:** 218.6 per sq mi, 84.4 per sq km. **Urban:** 32.6%. **Ethnic groups:** Burman 68%, Shan 9%, Karen 7%, Rakhine 4%, Chinese 3%, Indian 2%, Mon 2%. **Languages:** Burmese (official), ethnic minority langs. **Religions:** Buddhist 89%, Christian 4%, Muslim 4%, animist 1%.

Geography: Total area: 261,228 sq mi, 676,578 sq km; **Land area:** 252,321 sq mi, 653,508 sq km. **Location:** Between S and SE Asia, on Bay of Bengal. **Neighbors:** Bangladesh, India on W; China, Laos, Thailand on E. **Topography:** Mountains surround Myanmar on W, N, and E, and dense forests cover much of the nation. N-S rivers provide habitable valleys, especially the Irrawaddy, navigable for 900 mi. Country has a tropical monsoon climate. **Capital:** Nay Pyi Taw, 1,059,530. **Cities (urban aggl.):** Yangon, 4,456,592; Mandalay, 1,063,103.

Government: Type: Parliamentary govt. took power in Mar. 2011. **Head of state and gov.:** Pres. Thein Sein; b. Apr. 20, 1945; in office: Mar. 30, 2011. **Local divisions:** 7 states, 7 divisions. **Defense budget:** $2.27 bil. **Active troops:** 406,000.

Economy: Industries: agric. proc.; wood and wood prods.; copper, tin, tungsten, iron; cement, constr. materials; pharmaceuticals. **Chief crops:** rice, pulses, beans, sesame, groundnuts, sugarcane. **Natural resources:** petroleum, timber, tin, antimony, zinc, copper, tungsten, lead, coal, marble, limestone, prec. stones, nat. gas, hydropower. **Crude oil reserves:** 50 mil bbls. **Arable land:** 16.5%. **Livestock:** cattle: 14.1 mil; chickens: 176.8 mil; goats: 3.9 mil; pigs: 10.5 mil; sheep: 854,383. **Fish catch:** 4.2 mil metric tons. **Electricity prod.:** 7.3 bil kWh. **Labor force:** agric. 70%, industry 7%, services 23%.

Finance: Monetary unit: Kyat (MMK) (Sept. 2013: 970.00 = $1 U.S.). **GDP:** $90.9 bil; **per capita GDP:** $1,400; **GDP growth:** 6.3%. **Imports:** $7.5 bil; China 37%, Thailand 20.2%, Singapore 8.7%, South Korea 8.7%, Japan 8.2%, Malaysia 4.6%. **Exports:** $8.2 bil; Thailand 40.5%, India 14.7%, China 14.2%, Japan 7.4% (official export figure grossly underestimated due to value of timber, gems, narcotics, rice, and other products smuggled to Thailand, China, Bangladesh). **Tourism:** $281 mil. **Budget:** $4.5 bil. **Total reserves less gold:** $7 bil. **Gold:** 233,700 oz t. **CPI change:** 1.5%.

Transport: Railways: 3,126 mi. **Motor vehicles:** 0.6 vehicles per 1,000 pop. **Civil aviation:** 913.4 mil pass.-mi; 36 airports. **Chief ports:** Moulmein, Rangoon (Yangon), Sittwe.

Communications: TV sets: 7 per 1,000 pop. **Radios:** 200 per 1,000 pop. **Telephone lines:** 1.1 per 1 000 pop. **Internet:** 1.1%.

Health: Life expect.: 63.2 male; 68.1 female. **Births:** 18.9 per 1,000 pop. **Deaths:** 8.1 per 1,000 pop. **Natural inc.:** 1.08%. **Infant mortality:** 46.3 per 1,000 live births. **HIV rate:** 0.6%.

Education: Compulsory: ages 5-9. **Literacy:** 92.7%.

Major intl. organizations: UN (FAO, IBRD, ILO, IMF, WHO), ASEAN, WTO.

Embassy: 2300 S St. NW 20008; 332-3344.

Website: www.mofa.gov.mm

The Burmese arrived from Tibet before the 9th cent., displacing earlier cultures, and a Buddhist monarchy was established by the 11th cent. Burma was conquered by China's Mongol dynasty in 1272, then ruled by Shans as a Chinese tributary until the 16th cent. Britain subjugated Burma in three wars, 1824-84, and ruled the country as part of India until 1937, when Burma became self-governing. Full independence was achieved Jan. 4, 1948.

Gen. Ne Win dominated politics from 1962 to 1988, first as military ruler, then as constitutional president, advancing policies that increased economic socialization and international isolation. In 1987, the UN granted Burma, once the richest nation in SE Asia, less-developed status. Ne Win resigned July 1988, following anti-government riots. In Sept., the military seized power, under Gen. Saw Maung. In 1989 the country's name was changed to Myanmar.

Although the main opposition party won a decisive victory in 1990 multiparty elections, the military refused to surrender power. A key opposition leader, Aung San Suu Kyi, was held under house arrest, 1989-95, 2000-02, and 2003-10. The regime's poor human rights record and continued harassment of Suu Kyi and her supporters led to U.S.-imposed sanctions. The Dec. 26, 2004, Indian Ocean tsunami killed at least 61 people in Myanmar.

In late Sept. 2007, thousands of Buddhist monks led mass protests in Yangon; security forces cracked down by raiding monasteries, arresting monks, and firing on demonstrators. On Sept. 25, the U.S. announced tougher sanctions. Cyclone Nargis, May 2-3, 2008, left at least 84,537 people dead, with an estimated 53,836 missing.

After the military dominated Nov. 2010 parliamentary elections, the ruling council was dissolved and an initially nominal civilian government returned, Mar. 30, 2011. Suu Kyi's National League for Democracy (NLD) won 43 of 45 parliamentary seats in an Apr. 1, 2012, election, and Suu Kyi traveled to Oslo, Norway, to accept the Nobel Peace Prize, which she was awarded in absentia in 1991. The EU, Apr. 23, and U.S., May 17, suspended most sanctions against Myanmar. Myanmar's government announced Aug. 28, 2012, the removal of more than 2,000 names from the country's notorious blacklist of those banned from entering or leaving the country. More than 1,000 political prisoners were granted amnesty between Sept. 2012 and Apr. 2013.

Violence between Buddhists and Muslims in the west at the end of Oct. 2012 killed 89 and destroyed more than 2,000 homes; about 30,000 Muslims became refugeees. Riots in the central part of the country in Mar. 2013 killed at least 43 and displaced another 13,000 Muslims.

Namibia
Republic of Namibia

People: Population: 2,182,852. **Age distrib.:** <15: 32.6%; 65+: 4.3%. **Pop. density:** 6.9 per sq mi, 2.7 per sq km. **Urban:** 38.4%. **Ethnic groups:** black 88%, white 6%, mixed 7%; about 50% of pop. belong to Ovambo tribe. **Languages:** English (official), Afrikaans (common), German, indigenous langs. (incl. Oshivambo, Herero, Nama). **Religions:** Christian 80%-90%, indigenous beliefs 10%-20%.

Geography: Total area: 318,261 sq mi, 824,292 sq km; **Land area:** 317,874 sq mi, 823,290 sq km. **Location:** In southern Africa on coast of Atlantic O. **Neighbors:** Angola on N; Botswana, Zambia on E; South Africa on S. **Topography:** Three distinct regions incl. Namib Desert along the Atlantic, a mountainous central plateau with woodland savanna, and Kalahari Desert in E. True forests found in NE. There are 4 rivers but little other surface water. **Capital:** Windhoek, 380,103.

Government: Type: Republic. **Head of state:** Pres. Hifikepunye Pohamba; b. Aug. 18, 1935; in office: Mar. 21, 2005. **Head of gov.:** Prime Min. Hage Geingob; b. Aug. 3, 1941; in office: Dec. 4, 2012. **Local divisions:** 13 regions. **Defense budget:** $381 mil. **Active troops:** 9,200.

Economy: Industries: meatpacking, fish proc., dairy prods., pasta and beverages, mining. **Chief crops:** millet, sorghum, peanuts, grapes. **Natural resources:** diamonds, copper, uranium, gold, silver, lead, tin, lithium, cadmium, tungsten, zinc, salt, hydropower, fish. **Arable land:** 1%. **Livestock:** cattle: 2.4 mil; chickens: 5.3 mil; goats: 2.2 mil; pigs: 70,000; sheep: 2.9 mil. **Fish catch:** 414,504 metric tons. **Electricity prod.:** 1.4 bil kWh. **Labor force:** agric. 16.3%, industry 22.4%, services 61.3% (formal sector only). About half of population unemployed. About two-thirds of rural population rely on subsistence agric.

Finance: Monetary unit: Dollar (NAD) (Sept. 2013: 10.02 = $1 U.S.). **GDP:** $17 bil; **per capita GDP:** $7,900; **GDP growth:** 4%. **Imports:** $5.6 bil. **Exports:** $4.3 bil. **Tourism:** $485 mil. **Budget:** $4.9 bil. **Total reserves less gold:** $1.7 bil. **CPI change:** 6.5%.

Transport: Railways: 1,632 mi. **Motor vehicles:** 110.1 vehicles per 1,000 pop. **Civil aviation:** 1 bil pass.-mi; 19 airports. **Chief ports:** Ludoritz, Walvis Bay

Communications: TV sets: 78 per 1,000 pop. **Radios:** 62 per 1,000 pop. **Telephone lines:** 7.2 per 100 pop. **Internet:** 12.9%.

Health: Life expect.: 52.4 male; 51.7 female. **Births:** 20.7 per 1,000 pop. **Deaths:** 13.3 per 1,000 pop. **Natural inc.:** 0.74%. **Infant mortality:** 45.6 per 1,000 live births. **HIV rate:** 13.4%.

Education: Compulsory: ages 7-16. **Literacy:** 76.5%.

Major intl. organizations: UN (FAO, IBRD, ILO, IMF, WHO), AU, the Commonwealth, WTO.

Embassy: 1605 New Hampshire Ave. NW 20009; 986-0540.

Website: www.grnnet.gov.na

Namibia was declared a German protectorate in 1890 and officially called South-West Africa. South Africa seized the territory in 1915 during WWI; the League of Nations gave South Africa a mandate over the territory in 1920. In 1966, the Marxist South-West Africa People's Organization (SWAPO) launched a guerrilla war for independence. The UN General Assembly named the area Namibia in 1968.

After many years of guerrilla warfare, South Africa, Angola, and Cuba signed a U.S.-mediated agreement Dec. 22, 1988, to end South African administration of Namibia and provide for a cease-fire and transition to independence, in accordance with a 1978 UN plan. A separate accord between Cuba and Angola provided for a phased withdrawal of Cuban troops from Namibia. A constitution providing for multiparty government was adopted Feb. 9, 1990, and Namibia gained independence Mar. 21.

Walvis Bay, the principal deepwater port, had been turned over to South African administration in 1922. It remained in South African hands after independence, but South Africa turned control of the port back to Namibia, as of Mar. 1, 1994. Separatist violence flared in the Caprivi Strip in the late 1990s. In 2009, severe flooding in northern Namibia claimed more than 100 lives. SWAPO, the leading political group since independence, dominated the general election held Nov. 27-28, 2009.

Nauru
Republic of Nauru

People: Population: 9,434. **Age distrib.:** <15: 32.5%; 65+: 1.8%. **Pop. density:** 1,163.5 per sq mi, 449.2 per sq km. **Urban:** 100%. **Ethnic groups:** Nauruan 58%, other Pacific Islander 26%, Chinese 8%, European 8%. **Languages:** Nauruan (official), English (widely understood, used for most govt. and commercial purposes). **Religions:** Protestant 46% (Nauru Congregational 35%, Nauru Independent Church 10%), Roman Catholic 33%, none 5%.

Geography: Total area: 8.1 sq mi, 21 sq km; **Land area:** 8.1 sq mi, 21 sq km. **Location:** In W Pacific O. just S of Equator. **Neighbors:** Nearest is Kiribati to E. **Topography:** Mostly a plateau bearing

high-grade phosphate deposits, surrounded by a sandy shore and coral reef in concentric rings. **Capital:** Yaren district (admin.).

Government: Type: Republic. **Head of state and gov.:** Pres. Baron Waqa; b. Dec. 31, 1959; in office: June 11, 2013. **Local divisions:** 14 districts. **Defense budget:** NA. **Active troops:** No regular military forces. Australia responsible for defense.

Economy: Industries: phosphate mining, offshore banking, coconut prods. **Chief crops:** coconuts. **Natural resources:** phosphates, fish. **Arable land:** none. **Livestock:** chickens: 5,000; pigs: 3,000. **Fish catch:** 590 metric tons. **Electricity prod.:** 35 mil kWh. **Labor force:** mining phosphates, public administration, education, transportation.

Finance: Monetary unit: Dollar (AUD) (Sept. 2013: 1.09 = $1 U.S.). **GDP** (2005): $60 mil; **per capita GDP** (2005): $5,000; **GDP growth:** NA. **Imports** (2004): $20 mil. **Exports** (2005): $64,000. **Budget** (2005): $13.5 mil. **Total reserves less gold:** NA. **CPI change:** NA.

Transport: Civil aviation: 220 mil pass.-mi; 1 airport. **Chief port:** Nauru.

Communications: TV sets: 1 per 1,000 pop. **Radios:** 618 per 1,000 pop. **Telephone lines** (2009): 18.6 per 100 pop. **Internet** (2011): 54%.

Health: Life expect.: 62.0 male; 69.5 female. **Births:** 26.4 per 1,000 pop. **Deaths:** 5.9 per 1,000 pop. **Natural inc.:** 2.05%. **Infant mortality:** 8.4 per 1,000 live births. **HIV rate:** NA.

Education: Compulsory: ages 6-16. **Literacy:** NA.

Major intl. organizations: UN (FAO, WHO), the Commonwealth. **Permanent UN mission:** 800 2nd Ave., Ste. 400A, New York, NY 10017; (212) 937-0074.

Website: www.mofa.gov.nr
The British discovered the island in 1798, but it was annexed to the German Empire in 1886. After WWI, Australia administered Nauru under a League of Nations mandate. During WWII the Japanese occupied the island. In 1947 Nauru was made a UN trust territory, administered by Australia. It became an independent republic Jan. 31, 1968, and was admitted to the UN Sept. 14, 1999.

Phosphate exports provided Nauru with per capita revenues that were among the highest in the Third World. Phosphate reserves, however, are nearly depleted, and environmental damage from stripmining has been severe. Lax banking practices have made Nauru a haven for money laundering. Financial reforms saved Nauru from bankruptcy in 2004. A Nov. 20, 2012, Amnesty Intl. report found inhumane living conditions for the 387 men being kept at Australia's detention center on Nauru. Rising seas linked to global climate change have eroded the nation's coastline.

Nepal
Federal Democratic Republic of Nepal

People: Population: 30,430,267. **Age distrib.:** <15: 32.6%; 65+: 4.5%. **Pop. density:** 549.8 per sq mi, 212.3 per sq km. **Urban:** 17%. **Ethnic groups:** Chhettri 16%, Brahman-Hill 13%, Magar 7%, Tharu 7%, Tamang 6%, Newar 5%, Muslim 4%, Kami 4%, Yadav 4%. **Languages:** Nepali (official), Maithali, Bhojpuri, Tharu (Dagaura/Rana), Tamang, Newar, Magar, Awadhi, English (spoken by many in govt. and business). **Religions:** Hindu 81%, Buddhist 11%, Muslim 4%, Kirant 4%.

Geography: Total area: 56,827 sq mi, 147,181 sq km; **Land area:** 55,348 sq mi, 143,351 sq km. **Location:** Astride the Himalaya Mts. **Neighbors:** China on N, India on S. **Topography:** The Himalayas stretch across the N, the hill country with its fertile valleys extends across the center. S border region is part of the flat, subtropical Ganges Plain. **Capital:** Kathmandu, 1,014,570.

Government: Type: Federal democratic republic. **Head of state:** Pres. Ram Baran Yadav; b. Feb. 4, 1948; in office: July 23, 2008. **Head of gov.:** Prime Min. Khil Raj Regmi; b. May 31, 1949; in office: Mar. 14, 2013. **Local divisions:** 14 zones. **Defense budget:** $238 mil. **Active troops:** 95,750.

Economy: Industries: tourism, carpets, textiles; small rice, jute, sugar, and oilseed mills; cigarettes, cement, and brick prod. **Chief crops:** pulses, rice, corn, wheat, sugarcane, jute, root crops. **Natural resources:** quartz, water, timber, hydropower, lignite, copper, cobalt, iron ore. **Arable land:** 16.4%. **Livestock:** cattle: 7.2 mil; chickens: 39.5 mil; goats: 9.2 mil; pigs: 1.1 mil; sheep: 805,070. **Fish catch:** 52,450 metric tons. **Electricity prod.:** 3.2 bil kWh. **Labor force:** agric. 75%, industry 7%, services 18%.

Finance: Monetary unit: Rupee (NPR) (Sept. 2013: 105.60 = $1 U.S.). **GDP:** $41.2 bil; **per capita GDP:** $1,300; **GDP growth:** 4.6%. **Imports:** $5.9 bil; India 51%, China 34.5%. **Exports:** $1.1 bil; India 55.7%, U.S. 10.1%, Germany 4.4%. **Tourism:** $352 mil. **Budget** (FY11/12): $4.7 bil. **Total reserves less gold:** $4.3 bil. **Gold:** 768,133 oz t. **CPI change:** 9.5%.

Transport: Railways: 34 mi. **Civil aviation:** 533.1 mil pass.-mi; 11 airports.

Communications: TV sets: 21 per 1,000 pop. **Radios:** 37 per 1,000 pop. **Telephone lines:** 2.7 per 100 pop. **Internet:** 11.1%.

Health: Life expect.: 65.6 male; 68.2 female. **Births:** 21.5 per 1,000 pop. **Deaths:** 6.7 per 1,000 pop. **Natural inc.:** 1.48%. **Infant mortality:** 41.8 per 1,000 live births. **HIV rate:** 0.3%.

Education: NA. **Literacy:** 57.4%.

Major intl. organizations: UN (FAO, IBRD, ILO, IMF, WHO), WTO. **Embassy:** 2131 Leroy Pl. NW 20008; 667-4550.

Website: www.nepalgov.gov.np

Nepal was originally a group of petty principalities, with one, the Gurkhas, becoming dominant about 1769. In 1951 King Tribhubana Bir Bikram, member of the Shah family, ended the system of rule by hereditary premiers of the Ranas family, who had kept the kings virtual prisoners, and established a cabinet system of government. Polygamy, child marriage, and the caste system were officially abolished in 1963. Political parties were legalized in 1990.

Nine members of Nepal's royal family, including King Birendra and Queen Aishwarya, died in a June 1, 2001, massacre. The killings were blamed on a 10th family member, Crown Prince Dipendra, who reportedly shot himself that night and died 3 days later, allowing Birendra's brother Gyanendra Bir Bikram Shah Dev to take the throne.

Citing the government's failure to stop a Maoist insurgency, King Gyanendra assumed absolute authority, Feb. 1, 2005. After weeks of pro-democracy demonstrations, in which police killed at least 12 protesters, the king agreed, Apr. 24, 2006, to reinstate parliament, which had not met for four years. A new government, led by Prime Min. Girija Prasad Koirala, signed a peace accord with Maoist rebels Nov. 21 ending a decade-long civil war that claimed 13,000 lives.

Under a draft constitution that made Koirala acting head of state, Maoists joined an interim parliament Jan. 2007 and entered the cabinet Apr. 1. A constituent assembly voted May 2008 to abolish the monarchy and make Nepal a republic. After months of political wrangling, Maoist leader Pushpa Kamal Dahal, popularly known as Prachanda, became prime min. Aug. 18. On May 3, 2009, Prachanda moved to fire Nepal's army chief, who had refused orders to integrate some 19,000 former Maoist rebels into the armed forces; when Pres. Ram Baran Yadav countermanded the firing, Prachanda resigned May 4. After two more short-lived governments, the Maoist Baburam Bhattarai became prime min. Aug. 29, 2011. Bhattarai dissolved the legislature May 27, 2012, when a deadline passed for agreeing on a new constitution. Absent a plan for supervising new elections, Nepal's Supreme Court Chief Justice Khil Raj Regmi was sworn in as interim-government leader Mar. 14, 2013.

Netherlands
Kingdom of the Netherlands

People: Population: 16,805,037. **Age distrib.:** <15: 17.1%; 65+: 17.1%. **Pop. density:** 1,284.2 per sq mi, 495.8 per sq km. **Urban:** 83.2%. **Ethnic groups:** Dutch 81%, EU 5%, Indonesian 2%, Turkish 2%, Surinamese 2%, Moroccan 2%. **Languages:** Dutch, Frisian (both official). **Religions:** Roman Catholic 30%, Protestant 20% (Dutch Reformed 11%, Calvinist 6%), Muslim 6%, none 42%.

Geography: Total area: 16,040 sq mi, 41,543 sq km; **Land area:** 13,086 sq mi, 33,893 sq km. **Location:** In NW Europe on North Sea. **Neighbors:** Germany on E, Belgium on S. **Topography:** Land is flat, an average alt. of 37 ft above sea level, with much below sea level reclaimed and protected by some 1,500 mi of dikes. Since 1920 the government has been draining the IJsselmeer, formerly the Zuiderzee. **Capital:** Amsterdam, 1,055,610; s-Gravenhage (The Hague) (seat), 635,023. **Cities (urban aggl.):** Rotterdam, 1,013,700.

Government: Type: Constitutional monarchy. **Head of state:** King Willem-Alexander; b. Apr. 27, 1967; in office: Apr. 30, 2013. **Head of gov.:** Prime Min. Mark Rutte; b. Feb. 14, 1967; in office: Oct. 14, 2010. **Local divisions:** 12 provinces. **Defense budget:** $10.4 bil. **Active troops:** 37,400.

Economy: Industries: agroindustries, metal and engineering prods., elec. machinery and equip., chemicals, petroleum, constr., microelectronics, fishing. **Chief crops:** grains, potatoes, sugar beets, fruits, vegetables. **Natural resources:** nat. gas, petroleum, peat, limestone, salt, sand and gravel. **Crude oil reserves:** 243.9 mil bbls. **Arable land:** 30.9%. **Livestock:** cattle: 3.9 mil; chickens: 96.9 mil; goats: 380,350; pigs: 12.4 mil; sheep: 1.1 mil. **Fish catch:** 412,608 metric tons. **Electricity prod.** (2011): 106.7 bil kWh. **Labor force:** agric. 2%, industry 18%, services 80%.

Finance: Monetary unit: Euro (EUR) (Sept. 2013: 0.76 = $1 U.S.). **GDP:** $718.6 bil; **per capita GDP:** $42,900; **GDP growth:** –0.9%. **Imports:** $474.8 bil; Germany 13.9%, China 12%, Belgium 8.4%, UK 6.7%, Russia 6.4%, U.S. 6.1%. **Exports:** $538.5 bil; Germany 26.3%, Belgium 14.1%, France 8.8%, UK 8%, Italy 4.5%. **Tourism:** $13.9 bil. **Budget:** $388.8 bil. **Total reserves less gold:** $22.1 bil. **Gold:** 19.7 mil oz t. **CPI change:** 2.4%.

Transport: Railways: 1,799 mi. **Motor vehicles:** 550.7 vehicles per 1,000 pop. **Civil aviation:** 56 bil pass.-mi (incl. airlines based in territories and dependencies); 23 airports. **Chief ports:** Amsterdam, Ijmuiden, Moerdijk, Rotterdam, Terneuzen, Vlissingen.

Communications: TV sets: 767 per 1,000 pop. **Radios:** 978 per 1,000 pop. **Telephone lines:** 42.4 per 100 pop. **Internet:** 93%.

Health: Life expect.: 78.9 male; 83.2 female. **Births:** 10.9 per 1,000 pop. **Deaths:** 8.5 per 1,000 pop. **Natural inc.:** 0.24%. **Infant mortality:** 3.7 per 1,000 live births. **HIV rate:** 0.2%.

Education: Compulsory: ages 5-17. **Literacy:** 99%.

Major intl. organizations: UN and all of its specialized agencies, EU, NATO, OECD, OSCE, WTO.

Embassy: 4200 Linnean Ave. NW 20008; 877-DUTCHHELP.

Website: www.government.nl

Julius Caesar conquered the region in 55 BCE, when it was inhabited by Celtic and Germanic tribes. After the empire of Charlemagne fell apart, the Netherlands (Holland, Belgium, Flanders) split among counts, dukes, and bishops, passed to Burgundy and thence to

Spain. William the Silent, prince of Orange, led a confederation of the northern provinces, called Estates, in the Union of Utrecht, 1579; in 1581 they repudiated allegiance to Spain. The rise of the Dutch republic to naval, economic, and artistic eminence came in the 17th cent.

After a period of French hegemony, 1795-1813, the Congress of Vienna in 1815 formed a kingdom of the Netherlands, including Belgium, under William I. In 1830, the Belgians seceded and formed a separate kingdom.

The Netherlands maintained its neutrality in WWI, but was invaded and occupied by Germany, 1940-45. In 1949, after several years of fighting, the Netherlands granted independence to Indonesia.

The murder May 6, 2002, of right-wing populist leader Pim Fortuyn, 9 days before legislative elections, marked the first political assassination in modern Dutch history. The killing of filmmaker Theo van Gogh, Nov. 2, 2004, by an Islamic extremist shocked many Dutch. On Apr. 30, 2009, the national Queen's Day holiday, an attempted assassination of Queen Beatrix and other royal family members resulted in the deaths of 5 bystanders and the would-be assassin. The anti-Islamic, right-wing Freedom Party, headed by Geert Wilders, gained in parliamentary elections June 2010. Prime Min. Mark Rutte and his cabinet resigned Apr. 23, 2012, after failing to pass a budget in line with EU requirements. Rutte's government nonetheless remained in a caretaker capacity, and his pro-business Liberal party won a majority of seats in parliamentary elections held Sept. 2012. Queen Beatrix, 75, abdicated the throne to her son, Willem-Alexander, Apr. 30, 2013, changing her title to princess as her son became the first Dutch king in 123 years.

Dutch Dependencies

The Netherlands Antilles consists of two island groups in the West Indies. **Curaçao** and **Bonaire** are near the coast of Venezuela; **Sint Eustatius, Saba,** and the southern part of **Sint Maarten** are southeast of Puerto Rico. The northern two-thirds of St. Maarten was formerly part of French Guadeloupe and is now an overseas territorial collectivity; the French call the island Saint Martin. Total area of the two groups is 371 sq mi, incl. Bonaire (111), Curaçao (171), St. Eustatius (8), Saba (5), St. Maarten (13). St. Maarten suffered extensive damage from Hurricane Luis, Sept. 1995. Pop. (2013 est.): Curaçao, 146,836; Sint Maarten, 39,689. Willemstad, on Curaçao, is the capital. The principal industry is the refining of crude oil from Venezuela. Tourism and shipbuilding are other important industries. Constitutional changes effective Oct. 10, 2010, dissolved the Netherlands Antilles as a political entity and elevated Curaçao and St. Maarten to the status of autonomous countries within the Kingdom of the Netherlands. Bonaire, St. Eustatius, and Saba were classified as special municipalities.

Aruba, about 26 mi west of Curaçao, was separated from the Netherlands Antilles on Jan. 1, 1986; it is an autonomous component of the Netherlands, with a status similar to Curaçao and St. Maarten. Area: 69 sq mi; pop. (2013 est.) 109,153; capital: Oranjestad. Chief industries are oil refining and tourism. Tourism receipts in 2012 were $1.4 bil. **Website:** www.kabga.aw

New Zealand

People: Population: 4,365,113. **Age distrib.:** <15: 20.1%; 65+: 14%. **Pop. density:** 42.2 per sq mi, 16.3 per sq km. **Urban:** 86.2%. **Ethnic groups:** European 57%, Asian 8%, Maori 7%, Pacific Islander 5%, mixed 10%. **Languages:** English, Maori (both official); Samoan; French; Hindi; Yue; Northern Chinese; NZ sign language (official). **Religions:** Protestant 39% (Anglican 14%; Presbyterian, Congregational, Reformed 10%; Christian [no denomination specified] 5%; Methodist 3%; Pentecostal 2%; other Christian 4%); Roman Catholic 13%, Maori Christian 2%, Hindu 2%, none 32%.

Geography: Total area: 103,363 sq mi, 267,710 sq km; **Land area:** 103,363 sq mi, 267,710 sq km. **Location:** In SW Pacific O. **Neighbors:** Nearest are Australia on W, Fiji and Tonga on N. **Topography:** The 2 main islands (North and South Isls.) are hilly and mountainous. The E coasts consist of fertile plains, especially the broad Canterbury Plains on South Isl. A volcanic plateau is in center of North Isl. South Isl. has glaciers and 15 peaks over 10,000 ft. **Capital:** Wellington, 410,410. **Cities (urban aggl.):** Auckland, 1,451,955.

Government: Type: Parliamentary democracy. **Head of state:** Queen Elizabeth II, rep. by Gov.-Gen. Sir Jeremiah "Jerry" Mateparae; b. Nov. 14, 1954; in office: Aug. 31, 2011. **Head of gov.:** Prime Min. John Key; b. Aug. 9, 1961; in office: Nov. 19, 2008. **Local divisions:** 16 regions, 1 territory. **Defense budget:** $2.32 bil. **Active troops:** 8,550.

Economy: Industries: food proc., wood and paper prods., textiles, machinery, transp. equip., banking and insurance, tourism, mining. **Chief crops:** dairy prods., wheat, barley, potatoes, pulses, fruits, vegetables. **Natural resources:** nat. gas, iron ore, sand, coal, timber, hydropower, gold, limestone. **Crude oil reserve:** 81.4 mil bbls. **Arable land:** 1.8%. **Livestock:** cattle: 10 mil; chickens: 13.8 mil; goats: 85,970; pigs: 326,788; sheep: 31.1 mil. **Fish catch:** 545,289 metric tons. **Electricity prod.** (2011): 43.5 bil kWh. **Labor force:** agric. 7%, industry 19%, services 74%.

Finance: Monetary unit: Dollar (NZD) (Sept. 2013: 1.25 = $1 U.S.). **GDP:** $134.2 bil; **per capita GDP:** $30,200; **GDP growth:** 2.5%. **Imports:** $37.2 bil; China 16.4%, Australia 15.2%, U.S. 9.3%, Japan 6.5%, Singapore 4.8%, Germany 4.4%. **Exports:** $37.9 bil; Australia 21%, China 15%, U.S. 9.2%, Japan 7%. **Tourism:**

$5.5 bil. **Budget:** $73.3 bil. **Total reserves less gold:** $17.6 bil. **CPI change:** 0.9%.

Transport: Railways: 2,565 mi. **Motor vehicles:** 726.4 vehicles per 1,000 pop. **Civil aviation:** 16.1 bil pass.-mi; 39 airports. **Chief ports:** Auckland, Lyttelton, Manukau Harbor, Marsden Point, Tauranga, Wellington.

Communications: TV sets: 615 per 1,000 pop. **Radios:** 1,006 per 1,000 pop. **Telephone lines:** 42.1 per 100 pop. **Internet:** 89.5%.

Health: Life expect.: 78.8 male; 82.9 female. **Births:** 13.5 per 1,000 pop. **Deaths:** 7.3 per 1,000 pop. **Natural inc.:** 0.62%. **Infant mortality:** 4.7 per 1,000 live births. **HIV rate:** 0.1%.

Education: Compulsory: ages 5-16. **Literacy:** 99%.

Major intl. organizations: UN (FAO, IBRD, ILO, IMF, WHO), APEC, the Commonwealth, OECD, WTO.

Embassy: 37 Observatory Cir. NW 20008; 328-4800.

Website: newzealand.govt.nz

The Maori, a Polynesian group from the eastern Pacific, reached New Zealand before and during the 14th cent. The first European to sight New Zealand was Dutch navigator Abel Janszoon Tasman. The Maori refused to allow him to land. British Capt. James Cook explored the coasts, 1769-70.

British sovereignty was proclaimed and Maori land rights were recognized in the Treaty of Waitangi, 1840, with organized settlement beginning in the same year. Representative institutions were granted in 1853. The Maori Wars, or New Zealand Wars, ended in 1870 with British victory. The colony became a dominion in 1907 and gained full independence in 1947. It is a member of the Commonwealth. Seven of 122 members of the House of Representatives are directly elected from Maori constituencies, as well as other districts.

A progressive tradition in politics dates back to the 19th cent., when New Zealand was known for social experimentation. Much of the nation's economy has been deregulated since the 1980s. Jenny Shipley of the National Party became the nation's first female prime min., Dec. 8, 1997. The Labour Party, led by Helen Clark, won general elections, Nov. 27, 1999, and July 27, 2002. New Zealand supplied small troop contingents to coalition forces in Iraq and Afghanistan.

Prostitution was legalized June 2003. In July, New Zealand contributed troops to the Australian-led force in the Solomon Islands. A measure establishing a supreme court and ending appeals to the UK Privy Council passed Oct. 14. A major settlement of Maori land claims dating from the 19th cent. was signed June 25, 2008.

A South Island earthquake Sept. 3, 2010, caused property damage estimated at $2.7 bil. An explosion Nov. 19 at the Pike River coal mine on South Island killed 29 men. Another Christchurch quake, Feb. 22, 2011, killed 181 people and caused damage estimated at $11 bil to the central business district. Prime Min. John Key's handling of these disasters bolstered the National Party's popularity, and it was returned to power in elections Nov. 26, 2011. New Zealand became the 13th nation to legalize same-sex marriage in a 77-44 Parliamentary vote Apr. 17, 2013.

New Zealand comprises North Island, 43,911 sq mi; South Island, 58,084 sq mi; Stewart Island, 649 sq mi; Chatham Isls., 373 sq mi; and several groups of smaller islands.

In 1965, the **Cook Islands** (area: 91 sq mi; 2013 est. pop.: 10,447), halfway between New Zealand and Hawaii, became self-governing. New Zealand retains responsibility for defense and foreign affairs. **Niue** attained the same status in 1974; it lies 400 mi W (area: 100 sq mi; 2013 est. pop.: 1,229). Cyclone Heta devastated Niue Jan. 6, 2004. **Tokelau** (area: 4 sq mi; 2013 est. pop.: 1,353) comprises three atolls 300 mi N of Samoa. Two referendums on Tokelau self-government, held Feb. 13-15, 2006, and Oct. 20-24, 2007, failed to gain the required two-third majority. **Ross Dependency,** administered by New Zealand since 1923, comprises 160,000 sq mi of Antarctic territory.

Nicaragua
Republic of Nicaragua

People: Population: 5,788,531. **Age distrib.:** <15: 30%; 65+: 4.7%. **Pop. density:** 124.9 per sq mi, 48.2 per sq km. **Urban:** 57.5%. **Ethnic groups:** mestizo (mixed Amerindian and white) 69%, white 17%, black 9%, Amerindian 5%. **Languages:** Spanish (official), Miskito, English and indigenous langs. on Atlantic coast). **Religions:** Roman Catholic 59%, Protestant 23% (Evangelical 22%, Moravian 2%), none 16%.

Geography: Total area: 50,336 sq mi, 130,370 sq km; **Land area:** 46,328 sq mi, 119,990 sq km. **Location:** In Central America. **Neighbors:** Honduras on N, Costa Rica on S. **Topography:** Both Caribbean and Pacific coasts are over 200 mi long. Cordillera Mts., with many volcanic peaks, run NW-SE through middle of the country. Between this and a volcanic range to the E lie Lakes Managua and Nicaragua. **Capital:** Managua, 969,698.

Government: Type: Republic. **Head of state and gov.:** Pres. Daniel Ortega Saavedra; b. Nov. 11, 1945; in office: Jan. 10, 2007. **Local divisions:** 15 departments, 2 autonomous regions. **Defense budget:** $66 mil. **Active troops:** 12,000.

Economy: Industries: food proc., chemicals, machinery and metal prods., knit and woven apparel, petroleum refining and distrib., beverages, footwear, wood. **Chief crops:** coffee, bananas, sugarcane, cotton, rice, corn, tobacco, sesame, soya, beans. **Natural resources:** gold, silver, copper, tungsten, lead, zinc, timber, fish.

Arable land: 15.8%. **Livestock:** cattle: 3.8 mil; chickens: 19.5 mil; goats: 7,500; pigs: 495,000; sheep: 6,350. **Fish catch:** 46,686 metric tons. **Electricity prod.:** 3.3 bil kWh. **Labor force:** agric. 28%, industry 19%, services 53%.

Finance: Monetary unit: Cordoba (NIO) (Sept. 2013: 25.00 = $1 U.S.). **GDP:** $27.1 bil; **per capita GDP:** $4,500; **GDP growth:** 5.2%. **Imports:** $6.5 bil; U.S. 18.8%, Venezuela 14.4%, Mexico 12.5%, Costa Rica 8.8%, China 7.8%, Guatemala 7.6%, El Salvador 5.1%. **Exports:** $4.2 bil; U.S. 54%, Canada 8.4%, Venezuela 7.4%, El Salvador 4.5%. **Tourism:** $422 mil. **Budget:** $2.8 bil. **Total reserves less gold:** $1.9 bil. **CPI change:** 7.2%.

Transport: Motor vehicles: 76.4 vehicles per 1,000 pop. **Civil aviation:** 12 airports. **Chief ports:** Bluefields, Corinto.

Communications: TV sets: 129 per 1,000 pop. **Radios:** 273 per 1,000 pop. **Telephone lines:** 5.4 per 100 pop. **Internet:** 13.5%.

Health: Life expect.: 70.3 male; 74.7 female. **Births:** 18.8 per 1,000 pop. **Deaths:** 5.1 per 1,000 pop. **Natural inc.:** 1.37%. **Infant mortality:** 21.1 per 1,000 live births. **HIV rate:** 0.2%.

Education: Compulsory: ages 6-11. **Literacy:** 78%.

Major intl. organizations: UN and most of its specialized agencies, OAS, WTO.

Embassy: 1627 New Hampshire Ave. NW 20009; 939-6570.

Website: www.presidencia.gob.ni

Nicaragua, inhabited by various Indian tribes, was conquered by Spain in 1552. After gaining independence from Spain, 1821, Nicaragua was united for a short period with Mexico, then with the United Provinces of Central America, finally becoming an independent republic, 1838. U.S. Marines occupied the country at times in the early 20th cent., the last time from 1926 to 1933.

Gen. Anastasio Somoza Debayle held the presidency 1967-72, 1974-79. Martial law was imposed in Dec. 1974, after officials were kidnapped by Marxist Sandinista guerrillas. Nationwide antigovernment strikes touched off a civil war, 1978, which ended when Somoza fled Nicaragua and the Sandinistas took control of Managua, July 1979. Somoza was assassinated in Paraguay, Sept. 17, 1980.

Relations with the U.S. were strained as a result of Nicaragua's aid to leftist guerrillas in El Salvador and U.S. backing of anti-Sandinista contra guerrilla groups. In 1983 the contras launched a major offensive; the Sandinistas imposed rule by decree. In 1985 the U.S. House rejected Pres. Reagan's request for military aid to the contras. The subsequent diversion of funds to the contras from the proceeds of a secret arms sale to Iran caused a major scandal in the U.S.

In a stunning upset, Violeta Barrios de Chamorro defeated Sandinista leader Daniel Ortega Saavedra in national elections, Feb. 25, 1990. The conservative Arnoldo Alemán Lacayo defeated Ortega in the Oct. 1996 presidential election. Up to 2,000 people died Oct. 30, 1998, in a mudslide caused by rains from Hurricane Mitch.

Drought and a drop in coffee prices precipitated an economic crisis in 2001. Enrique Bolaños Geyer, a conservative businessman, won the presidency that year. Convicted Dec. 7, 2003, on corruption charges, former Pres. Alemán received a $10 mil fine and a 20-year sentence, which he was allowed to serve under house arrest. Ortega won the Nov. 2006 presidential election, then irritated the U.S. by cultivating ties with Venezuela and Iran, which offered Nicaragua financial assistance. He was reelected Nov. 6, 2011. Nicaragua was one of those countries to offer American whistleblower Edward Snowden asylum in July 2013.

Niger
Republic of Niger

People: Population: 16,899,327. **Age distrib.:** <15: 50%; 65+: 2.6%. **Pop. density:** 34.6 per sq mi, 13.3 per sq km. **Urban:** 17.8%. **Ethnic groups:** Haoussa 55%, Djerma Sonrai 21%, Tuareg 9%, Peuhl 9%, Kanouri Manga 5%. **Languages:** French (official), Hausa, Djerma. **Religions:** Muslim 80%, other (incl. indigenous beliefs, Christian) 20%.

Geography: Total area: 489,191 sq mi, 1,267,000 sq km; **Land area:** 489,076 sq mi, 1,266,700 sq km. **Location:** In interior of N Africa. **Neighbors:** Libya, Algeria on N; Mali, Burkina Faso on W; Benin, Nigeria on S; Chad on E. **Topography:** Mostly arid desert and mountains. A narrow savanna in S and Niger R. basin in the SW contain most of the population. **Capital:** Niamey, 1,297,160.

Government: Type: Republic. **Head of state:** Pres. Mahamadou Issoufou; b. 1952; in office: Apr. 7, 2011. **Head of gov.:** Prime Min. Brigi Rafini; b. Apr. 7, 1953; in office: Apr. 7, 2011. **Local divisions:** 8 regions, 1 capital district. **Defense budget** (2011): $50 mil. **Active troops:** 5,300.

Economy: Industries: uranium mining, cement, brick, soap, textiles, food proc., chemicals, slaughterhouses. **Chief crops:** cowpeas, cotton, peanuts, millet, sorghum, cassava, rice. **Natural resources:** uranium, coal, iron ore, tin, phosphates, gold, molybdenum, gypsum, salt, petroleum. **Arable land:** 11.8%. **Livestock:** cattle: 9.6 mil; chickens: 17.3 mil; goats: 13.2 mil; pigs: 41,000; sheep: 10 mil. **Fish catch:** 53,258 metric tons. **Electricity prod.:** 250 mil kWh. **Labor force:** agric. 90%, industry 6%, services 4%.

Finance: Monetary unit: West African CFA Franc (XOF) (Sept. 2013: 498.17 = $1 U.S.). **GDP:** $13.3 bil; **per capita GDP:** $800; **GDP growth:** 11.2%. **Imports:** $2.3 bil; France 14.2%, China 11.1%, French Polynesia 9.9%, Nigeria 9.7%, Togo 5.5%. **Exports:** $1.4 bil; Nigeria 41%, U.S. 17%, India 14.1%, Italy 8.5%, China 7.7%, Ghana 5.7%. **Tourism:** $96 mil. **Budget:** $1.9 bil. **Total reserves less gold:** $1 bil. **CPI change:** 0.5%.

Transport: Motor vehicles: 9.2 vehicles per 1,000 pop. **Civil aviation:** 10 airports.

Communications: TV sets: 12 per 1,000 pop. **Radios:** 235 per 1,000 pop. **Telephone lines:** 0.6 per 100 pop. **Internet:** 1.4%.

Health: Life expect.: 53.2 male; 55.6 female. **Births:** 46.8 per 1,000 pop. **Deaths:** 13.1 per 1,000 pop. **Natural inc.:** 3.38%. **Infant mortality:** 88.0 per 1,000 live births. **HIV rate:** 0.8%.

Education: Compulsory: ages 7-12. **Literacy:** 28.7%.

Major intl. organizations: UN (FAO, IBRD, ILO, IMF, WHO), AU, WTO

Embassy: 2204 R St. NW 20008; 483-4224.

Website: www.gouv.ne

Niger was part of ancient and medieval African empires. European explorers reached the area in the late 18th cent. The French colony of Niger was established 1900-22 after the defeat of Tuareg fighters, who had invaded the area from the north a century before. The country became independent Aug. 3, 1960.

In 1993, Niger held its first free and open elections since independence; an opposition leader, Mahamane Ousmane, won the presidency. A peace accord Apr. 24, 1995, ended a Tuareg rebellion that began in 1990. A coup, Jan. 27, 1996, followed by a disputed presidential election in July, left the military in control of Niger. On Apr. 9, 1999, Gen. Ibrahim Bare Mainassara, Niger's president since 1996, was assassinated, apparently by members of his security team. Elections were held Oct. 17 and Nov. 24, 1999, under a new constitution, approved by referendum July 18, that restored civilian rule.

One of the world's poorest countries, Niger experienced severe food shortages in 2005 after locusts and drought ruined the grain harvest. Popularly elected in 1999 and 2004, Pres. Mamadou Tandja invoked emergency powers in 2009, seeking to remain in office for a third 5-year term. He was overthrown by a military junta Feb. 18, 2010. Civilian rule returned following Jan.-Mar. 2011 elections. Increased terrorist activity in countries surrounding Niger led the U.S. and EU to send anti-terrorist experts to train Niger's forces to fight al-Qaeda-affiliated militants in 2012. Floods in late 2012 killed about 100 people and ruined crops. The first terrorist attacks in Niger occurred May 23, 2013, as two separate bombings by jihadists in the towns of Agadez and Arlit killed 21 soldiers and 5 of the bombers.

Nigeria
Federal Republic of Nigeria

People: Population: 174,507,539. **Age distrib.:** <15: 43.8%; 65+: 3%. **Pop. density:** 496.3 per sq mi, 191.6 per sq km. **Urban:** 49.6%. **Ethnic groups:** 250+ ethnic groups: Hausa and Fulani 29%, Yoruba 21%, Igbo (Ibo) 18%, Ijaw 10%, Kanuri 4%, Ibibio 4%, and Tiv 3% are most populous, politically influential groups. **Languages:** English (official), Hausa, Yoruba, Igbo (Ibo), Fulani, 500+ indigenous langs. **Religions:** Muslim 50%, Christian 40%, indigenous beliefs 10%.

Geography: Total area: 356,669 sq mi, 923,768 sq km; **Land area:** 351,649 sq mi, 910,768 sq km. **Location:** On S coast of W Africa. **Neighbors:** Benin on W, Niger on N, Chad and Cameroon on E. **Topography:** 4 E-W regions divide Nigeria: a coastal mangrove swamp 10-60 mi wide, a tropical rain forest 50-100 mi wide, a plateau of savanna and open woodland, and semi-desert in N. **Capital:** Abuja, 2,152,770. **Cities (urban aggl.):** Lagos, 11,223,041; Kano, 3,374,598; Ibadan, 2,948,530; Port Harcourt, 1,894,164; Kaduna, 1,523,505; Benin City, 1,358,874; Ogbomosho, 1,074,953.

Government: Type: Federal republic. **Head of state and gov.:** Pres. Goodluck Jonathan; b. Nov. 20, 1957; in office: May 6, 2010 (acting from Feb. 9). **Local divisions:** 36 states, 1 capital territory. **Defense budget:** $2.04 bil. **Active troops:** 80,000.

Economy: Industries: crude oil, coal, tin, columbite; rubber prods., wood; hides and skins, textiles, cement and other constr. materials, food prods. **Chief crops:** cocoa, peanuts, cotton, palm oil, corn, rice, sorghum, millet, cassava, yams, rubber. **Natural resources:** nat. gas, petroleum, tin, iron ore, coal, limestone, niobium, lead, zinc. **Crude oil reserves:** 37.2 bil bbls. **Arable land:** 39.5%. **Livestock:** cattle: 18.9 mil; chickens: 202 mil; goats: 57.3 mil; pigs: 7.7 mil; sheep: 38 mil. **Fish catch:** 856,614 metric tons. **Electricity prod.:** 24.9 bil kWh. **Labor force:** agric. 70%, industry 10%, services 20%.

Finance: Monetary unit: Naira (NGN) (Sept. 2013: 163.70 = $1 U.S.). **GDP:** $455.5 bil; **per capita GDP:** $2,800; **GDP growth:** 6.3%. **Imports:** $54.6 bil; China 18.2%, U.S. 10%, India 5.5%. **Exports:** $92.2 bil; U.S. 16.8%, India 12.1%, Netherlands 8.6%, Spain 7.8%, Brazil 7.6%, UK 5.1%, Germany 4.9%, Japan 4.1%, France 4.1%. **Tourism:** $622 mil. **Budget:** $27.9 bil. **Total reserves less gold:** $46.4 bil. **Gold:** 687,000 oz t. **CPI change:** 12.2%.

Transport: Railways: 2,178 mi. **Motor vehicles:** 7.8 vehicles per 1,000 pop. **Civil aviation:** 1.2 bil pass.-mi; 40 airports. **Chief ports:** Calabar, Lagos.

Communications: TV sets: 67 per 1,000 pop. **Radios:** 602 per 1,000 pop. **Telephone lines:** 0.3 per 100 pop. **Internet:** 32.9%.

Health: Life expect.: 49.4 male; 55.8 female. **Births:** 38.8 per 1,000 pop. **Deaths:** 13.2 per 1,000 pop. **Natural inc.:** 2.56%. **Infant mortality:** 73.0 per 1,000 live births. **HIV rate:** 3.7%.

Education: Compulsory: ages 6-14. **Literacy:** 51.1%.

Major intl. organizations: UN (FAO, IBRD, ILO, IMF, WHO), AU, the Commonwealth, OPEC, WTO.

Embassy: 3519 International Ct. NW 20008; 986-8400.

Website: www.nigeria.gov.ng

Early cultures in Nigeria date back to at least 700 BCE. From the 12th to the 14th cent., more advanced cultures developed in the Yoruba area, at Ife, and in the north, where Muslim influence prevailed. Portuguese and British slavers appeared in the 15th-16th cent. Britain seized Lagos, 1861, and gradually extended control inland until 1900. Nigeria became independent Oct. 1, 1960, and a republic Oct. 1, 1963.

On May 30, 1967, the Eastern Region seceded, proclaiming itself the Republic of Biafra, plunging the country into civil war. Casualties were estimated at over 1 mil, including many Biafrans (mostly Ibos) who died of starvation despite international relief efforts. The secessionists capitulated Jan. 12, 1970.

Nigeria emerged as one of the world's leading oil exporters in the 1970s, but much of the revenue has been squandered through corruption and mismanagement. Oil spills have polluted much of the Niger Delta region, and rebel activities there have been extensive.

After 13 years of military rule, the nation made a peaceful return to civilian government Oct. 1979. Military rule resumed Dec. 31, 1983; a second coup came in 1985. Headed by Gen. Ibrahim Babangida, the military regime held elections June 12, 1993, but annulled the vote June 23 when it appeared that Moshood Abiola would win. Riots followed and many were killed. Babangida resigned and appointed a civilian to head an interim government, Aug. 26, but that government was ousted Nov. 17 in a coup led by Gen. Sani Abacha. On June 11, 1994, Abiola declared himself president; he was jailed June 23.

Abacha's brutal rule ended June 8, 1998, when he died of an apparent heart attack. Abiola died in prison July 7 as Abacha's successor, Gen. Abdulsalam Abubakar, was reportedly preparing to free him. Abiola's death sparked riots in Lagos and other cities; on July 20, Abubakar promised elections and a return to civilian rule. Olusegun Obasanjo won the presidential vote Feb. 27, 1999, Nigeria's first civilian government in 15 years.

An oil pipeline explosion in southern Nigeria, Oct. 17, 1998, killed at least 700 people who were scavenging for fuel. The imposition of strict Islamic law in northern states led to clashes, Jan.-Mar. 2000, in which at least 800 people died. Fighting between Muslims and Christians Sept. 7-12 and Oct. 13-14, 2001, claimed an estimated 600 lives; another 200 people died when soldiers went on a rampage in SE Nigeria Oct. 22-24.

At least 1,000 people were killed Jan. 27, 2002, when an army weapons depot in Lagos exploded. Controversy over Nigeria's plans to host a Miss World pageant sparked sectarian riots in Kaduna, Nov. 20-24, 2002, leaving more than 200 people dead. Christian militia members massacred about 630 Muslims at Yelwa, central Nigeria, May 2, 2004. Obasanjo's chosen successor, Umaru Musa Yar'Adua, won a presidential election, Apr. 21, 2007, marred by violence and described as "not credible" by international monitors. After prolonged illness, Yar'Adua died May 5, 2010, and was succeeded by Vice Pres. Goodluck Jonathan, a southern Christian. After he won reelection Apr. 16, 2011, over Muhammadu Buhari, a northern-based Muslim, riots in 12 northern provinces left more than 800 people dead. Boko Haram, a radical Islamist sect in NE Nigeria, aims to transform Nigeria into an Islamist state and has been blamed for more than 3,600 deaths since 2009. Religiously motivated killings conducted by both soldiers and members of Boko Haram continued at schools and colleges, at mosques, and on city streets throughout 2012-13. When Islamists gained control of a number of towns, Pres. Jonathan declared a state of emergency in the northeast May 14, 2013, but the violence continued.

Norway
Kingdom of Norway

People: Population: 4,722,701. **Age distrib.:** <15: 17.5%; 65+: 16.8%. **Pop. density:** 40.2 per sq mi, 15.5 per sq km. **Urban:** 79.4%. **Ethnic groups:** Norwegian (incl. Sami) 94%, other European 4%. **Languages:** Bokmal Norwegian, Nynorsk Norwegian (both official); Sami (official in 6 municipalities). **Religions:** Church of Norway (Evangelical Lutheran official) 86%, other Christian 2%, Muslim 2%.
Geography: Total area: 125,021 sq mi, 323,802 sq km; **Land area:** 117,484 sq mi, 304,282 sq km. **Location:** W part of Scandinavian peninsula in NW Europe (extends farther N than any European land). **Neighbors:** Sweden, Finland, Russia on E. **Topography:** Highly indented coast is lined with tens of thousands of islands. Mountains and plateaus cover most of the country, which is only 25% forested. **Capital:** Oslo, 915,386.
Government: Type: Constitutional monarchy. **Head of state:** King Harald V; b. Feb. 21, 1937; in office: Jan. 17, 1991. **Head of gov.:** Prime Min. Jens Stoltenberg; b. Mar. 16, 1959; in office: Oct. 17, 2005. **Local divisions:** 19 counties. **Defense budget:** $6.85 bil. **Active troops:** 24,450.
Economy: Industries: petroleum and gas, food proc., shipbuilding, pulp and paper prods., metals, chemicals, timber, mining, textiles, fishing. **Chief crops:** barley, wheat, potatoes. **Natural resources:** petroleum, nat. gas, iron ore, copper, lead, zinc, titanium, pyrites, nickel, fish, timber, hydropower. **Crude oil reserves:** 5.4 bil bbls. **Arable land:** 2.7%. **Livestock:** cattle: 864,139; chickens: 3.9 mil; goats: 67,232; pigs: 854,334; sheep: 2.3 mil. **Fish catch:** 3.6 mil metric tons. **Electricity prod.** (2011): 125.2 bil kWh. **Labor force:** agric. 2.9%, industry 21.1%, services 76%.
Finance: Monetary unit: Krone (NOK) (Sept. 2013: 6.08 = $1 U.S.). **GDP:** $281.7 bil; **per capita GDP:** $55,900; **GDP growth:** 3%.

Imports: $86.7 bil; Sweden 13.6%, Germany 12.4%, China 9.3%, Denmark 6.3%, UK 6.1%, U.S. 5.4%. **Exports:** $158.8 bil; UK 25.6%, Germany 12.6%, Netherlands 12%, France 6.7%, Sweden 6.3%, U.S. 5%. **Tourism:** $5.4 bil. **Budget:** $216.5 bil. **Total reserves less gold:** $51.9 bil. **CPI change:** 0.7%.
Transport: Railways: 2,590 mi. **Motor vehicles:** 638.2 vehicles per 1,000 pop. **Civil aviation:** 5.5 bil pass.-mi; 67 airports. **Chief ports:** Bergen, Haugesund, Maaloy, Mongstad, Narvik, Sture.
Communications: TV sets: 1,554 per 1,000 pop. **Radios:** 913 per 1,000 pop. **Telephone lines:** 29.5 per 100 pop. **Internet:** 95%.
Health: Life expect.: 77.8 male; 83.3 female. **Births:** 10.8 per 1,000 pop. **Deaths:** 9.2 per 1,000 pop. **Natural inc.:** 0.16%. **Infant mortality:** 3.5 per 1,000 live births. **HIV rate:** 0.1%.
Education: Compulsory: ages 6-16. **Literacy:** 100%.
Major intl. organizations: UN and all of its specialized agencies, EFTA, NATO, OECD, OSCE, WTO.
Embassy: 2720 34th St. NW 20008; 333-6000.
Website: www.norway.no

The first ruler of Norway was Harald the Fairhaired, who came to power in 872 CE. Between 800 and 1000, Norway's Vikings raided and occupied widely dispersed parts of Europe. The country was united with Denmark, 1381-1814, and with Sweden, 1814-1905. In 1905, the country became independent with Prince Charles of Denmark as king.

Norway remained neutral during WWI. Germany attacked Norway Apr. 9, 1940, and held it until liberation May 8, 1945. The country abandoned its neutrality after the war and joined NATO. In a referendum Nov. 28, 1994, Norwegian voters rejected European Union membership.

Abundant hydroelectric resources provide the base for industrialization, giving Norway one of the highest living standards in the world. The country is a leading producer and exporter of crude oil, with extensive reserves in the North Sea.

A center-left bloc headed by Labor Party leader Jens Stoltenberg won parliamentary elections Sept. 2005 and remained in power after elections Sept. 2009. A right-wing extremist, Anders Behring Breivik, confessed to killing 8 people with a car bomb near government buildings in central Oslo and murdering another 69 at an island camp sponsored by the Labor Party's youth wing July 22, 2011. He was declared sane and sentenced Aug. 24, 2012, to 21 years in prison, the maximum sentence in Norway. As of mid-2013, 166 Norwegian soldiers were serving with the NATO command in Afghanistan. Parliament voted June 18, 2013, to make military service compulsory for women as well as men; it was the first NATO country to do so.

Svalbard is a group of mountainous islands in the Arctic O., area 23,956 sq mi, pop. (2013 est.) 2,637. The largest, Spitsbergen (formerly called West Spitsbergen), 15,060 sq mi, seat of the governor, is about 370 mi N of Norway. By a treaty signed in Paris, 1920, major European powers recognized the sovereignty of Norway, which incorporated it in 1925.

Jan Mayen, area 146 sq mi, is a volcanic island located about 565 mi W-NW of Norway; it was annexed in 1929.

Oman
Sultanate of Oman

People: Population: 3,154,134. **Age distrib.:** <15: 30.6%; 65+: 3.2%. **Pop. density:** 26.4 per sq mi, 10.2 per sq km. **Urban:** 73.4%. **Ethnic groups:** Arab, Baluchi, South Asian (Indian, Pakistani, Sri Lankan, Bangladeshi), African. **Languages:** Arabic (official), English, Baluchi, Urdu, Indian dialects. **Religions:** Ibadhi Muslim (official) 75%, other (incl. Sunni Muslim, Shia Muslim, Hindu) 25%.
Geography: Total area: 119,499 sq mi, 309,500 sq km; **Land area:** 119,499 sq mi, 309,500 sq km. **Location:** On SE coast of Arabian peninsula. **Neighbors:** United Arab Emirates, Saudi Arabia, Yemen on W. **Topography:** A narrow coastal plain up to 10 mi wide, a range of barren mountains reaching 9,900 ft, and a wide, stony, mostly waterless plateau, avg. alt. 1,000 ft. Also, an exclave at the tip of the Musandam peninsula controls access to the Persian Gulf. **Capital:** Muscat, 743,029.
Government: Type: Monarchy. **Head of state and gov.:** Sultan Qaboos bin Said al-Said; b. Nov. 18, 1940; in office: July 23, 1970 (also prime min. since 1972). **Local divisions:** 11 governorates. **Defense budget:** $6.72 bil. **Active troops:** 42,600.
Economy: Industries: crude oil prod. and refining, nat. and liquefied nat. gas prod., constr., cement, copper, steel, chemicals, optic fiber. **Chief crops:** dates, limes, bananas, alfalfa, vegetables. **Natural resources:** petroleum, copper, asbestos, marble, limestone, chromium, gypsum, nat. gas. **Crude oil reserves:** 5.5 bil bbls. **Arable land:** 0.1%. **Livestock:** cattle: 339,500; chickens: 4.5 mil; goats: 1.8 mil; sheep: 396,400. **Fish catch:** 158,723 metric tons. **Electricity prod.:** 18.6 bil kWh. **Labor force:** NA.
Finance: Monetary unit: Rial (OMR) (Sept. 2013: 0.38 = $1 U.S.). **GDP:** $91.5 bil; **per capita GDP:** $29,600; **GDP growth:** 5%. **Imports:** $26.5 bil; UAE 23.6%, Japan 12.6%, India 8.5%, China 6.4%, U.S. 6.1%. **Exports:** $52 bil; China 31.9%, Japan 12.9%, UAE 10.1%, South Korea 10%, Thailand 4.4%, Singapore 4.4%. **Tourism:** $923 mil. **Budget:** $28 bil. **Total reserves less gold:** $14.4 bil. **Gold:** 618 oz t. **CPI change:** 2.9%.
Transport: Motor vehicles: 175.4 vehicles per 1,000 pop. **Civil aviation:** 2.7 bil pass.-mi; 13 airports. **Chief ports:** Mina' Qabus, Salalah, Suhar.

Communications: TV sets: 620 per 1,000 pop. **Radios:** 72 per 1,000 pop. **Telephone lines:** 10.5 per 100 pop. **Internet:** 60%.

Health: Life expect.: 72.8 male; 76.7 female. **Births:** 24.4 per 1,000 pop. **Deaths:** 3.4 per 1,000 pop. **Natural inc.:** 2.10%. **Infant mortality:** 14.5 per 1,000 live births. **HIV rate:** NA.

Education: NA. **Literacy:** 86.9%.

Major intl. organizations: UN (FAO, IBRD, ILO, IMF, WHO), AL, WTO.

Embassy: 2535 Belmont Rd. NW 20008; 387-1980.

Website: www.omanet.om

Oman was originally called Muscat and Oman. A long history of rule by other lands, including Portugal in the 16th cent., ended with the ouster of the Persians in 1744. By the early 19th cent., Muscat and Oman controlled much of the Persian and Pakistani coasts.

British influence was confirmed in a 1951 treaty, and Britain helped suppress an uprising by traditionally rebellious interior tribes against control by Muscat in the 1950s.

On July 23, 1970, Sultan Said bin Taimur was overthrown by his son, Sultan Qabus bin Said, who changed the nation's name to Sultanate of Oman. Petroleum and natural gas are major sources of income. Oman has strong military and economic ties to the U.S. but also has favorable relations with Iran. Sultan Qabus shuffled his cabinet after Arab Spring protests Feb. 2011 and expanded the powers of the Majlis al-Shura, the lower house of parliament, Oct. 20, 2011.

Pakistan
Islamic Republic of Pakistan

People: Population: 193,238,868. **Age distrib.:** <15: 34%; 65+: 4.3%. **Pop. density:** 649.2 per sq mi, 250.7 per sq km. **Urban:** 36.2%. **Ethnic groups:** Punjabi 45%, Pashtun (Pathan) 15%, Sindhi 14%, Sariaki 8%, Muhajir 8%, Balochi 4%. **Languages:** Punjabi, Sindhi, Siraiki, Pashtu, Urdu (official), Balochi, Hindko, Brahui, English (official; lingua franca of elite and in most govt. ministries), Burushaski. **Religions:** Muslim (official) 96% (Sunni 85-90%, Shia 10-15%), other (incl. Christian, Hindu) 4%.

Geography: Total area: 307,374 sq mi, 796,095 sq km; **Land area:** 297,637 sq mi, 770,875 sq km. **Location:** In W part of South Asia. **Neighbors:** Iran on W, Afghanistan and China on N, India on E. **Topography:** The Indus R. rises in the Hindu Kush and Himalaya Mts. in the N (highest is K2, or Godwin Austen, which at 28,251 ft is the 2nd highest in world), then flows over 1,000 mi through a fertile valley and empties into Arabian Sea. Thar Desert, Eastern Plains flank Indus Valley. **Capital:** Islamabad, 918,854. **Cities (urban aggl.):** Karachi, 13,876,254; Lahore, 7,565,722; Faisalabad, 3,038,200; Rawalpindi, 2,164,316; Multan, 1,774,636; Gujranwala, 1,767,370; Hyderabad, 1,700,769; Peshawar, 1,522,703.

Government: Type: Federal republic. **Head of state:** Pres. Mamnoon Hussain; b. 1940; in office: Sept. 9, 2013. **Head of gov.:** Prime Min. Nawaz Sharif; b. Dec. 25, 1949; in office: June 5, 2013. **Local divisions:** 4 provinces, 1 territory, 1 capital territory, plus federally administered tribal areas. **Defense budget:** $5.78 bil. **Active troops:** 642,000.

Economy: Industries: textiles and apparel, food proc., pharmaceuticals, constr. materials, paper prods., fertilizer, shrimp. **Chief crops:** cotton, wheat, rice, sugarcane, fruits, vegetables. **Natural resources:** nat. gas, limited petroleum, poor quality coal, iron ore, copper, salt, limestone. **Crude oil reserves:** 247.5 mil bbls. **Arable land:** 26.9%. **Livestock:** cattle: 35.6 mil; chickens: 349 mil; goats: 61.5 mil; sheep: 28.1 mil. **Fish catch:** 594,935 metric tons. **Electricity prod.:** 89.6 bil kWh. **Labor force:** agric. 45.1%, industry 20.7%, services 34.2%.

Finance: Monetary unit: Rupee (PKR) (Sept. 2013: 104.70 = $1 U.S.). **GDP:** $523.9 bil; **per capita GDP:** $2,900; **GDP growth:** 3.7%. **Imports:** $39.8 bil; China 19.8%, Saudi Arabia 12%, UAE 11.9%, Kuwait 6.2%. **Exports:** $24.6 bil; U.S. 13.3%, China 10.9%, UAE 8.6%, Afghanistan 8.5%. **Tourism:** $341 mil. **Budget:** $42.2 bil. **Total reserves less gold:** $10.2 bil. **Gold:** 2.1 mil oz t. **CPI change:** 9.7%.

Transport: Railways: 4,841 mi. **Motor vehicles:** 13.6 vehicles per 1,000 pop. **Civil aviation:** 8.1 bil pass.-mi; 108 airports. **Chief ports:** Karachi, Port Muhammad Bin Qasim.

Communications: TV sets: 81 per 1,000 pop. **Radios:** 83 per 1,000 pop. **Telephone lines:** 3.2 per 100 pop. **Internet:** 10%.

Health: Life expect.: 64.8 male; 68.7 female. **Births:** 23.8 per 1,000 pop. **Deaths:** 6.7 per 1,000 pop. **Natural inc.:** 1.71%. **Infant mortality:** 59.4 per 1,000 live births. **HIV rate:** 0.1%.

Education: Compulsory: ages 5-9. **Literacy:** 54.9%.

Major intl. organizations: UN (FAO, IBRD, ILO, IMF, WHO), the Commonwealth, WTO.

Embassy: 3517 International Ct. NW 20008; 243-6500.

Website: www.pakistan.gov.pk

Pakistan shares the 5,000-year history of the India-Pakistan subcontinent. At present-day Harappa and Mohenjo Daro, the Indus Valley civilization, with large cities and elaborate irrigation systems, flourished c. 4,000-2,500 BCE. Aryan invaders from the northwest conquered the region around 1,500 BCE, forging the Vedic civilization that dominated the region for over a thousand years. The first Arab invasion, 712 CE, introduced Islam. Present-day Pakistan and India were part of the Mughal empire from 1526 to 1857. Muslim power faded by the end of the 19th cent. as the British gained control.

Muhammad Ali Jinnah (1876-1948) was the principal architect of Pakistan. When the British withdrew Aug. 14, 1947, India's Islamic majority acquired self-government as Pakistan, with dominion status in the Commonwealth. Pakistan was divided into West Pakistan and East Pakistan, nearly 1,000 mi apart on opposite sides of India. Kashmir, a predominantly Muslim region divided between Pakistan and India, has remained a source of conflict between the two countries.

Rioting and strikes broke out in the East after Pakistan's government, Mar. 1, 1971, postponed the constituent assembly, dominated by supporters of regional autonomy for East Pakistan. Armed conflict between East and West lasted from Mar. to Dec. 1971, with India siding with Easterners, who proclaimed the independent nation of Bangladesh. Thousands were killed and some 10 mil Easterners fled to India. Full-scale war erupted between India and Pakistan, but Pakistan troops in the East surrendered Dec. 16; Pakistan agreed to a cease-fire in the West Dec. 17. On July 3, 1972, Pakistan and India signed a pact agreeing to troop withdrawals and peaceful conflict resolution.

Dec. 1970 elections brought Zulfikar Ali Bhutto to the presidency Dec. 20, 1971. Bhutto was overthrown in a military coup July 1977. Convicted of complicity in a 1974 political murder, he was executed Apr. 4, 1979. Millions of Afghan refugees flooded into Pakistan after the USSR invaded Afghanistan Dec. 1979; during 2002-10, some 3.6 mil refugees were repatriated, but 1.7 mil remained.

Pres. Mohammad Zia ul-Haq was killed when his plane exploded in Aug. 1988. Following Nov. elections, Benazir Bhutto, daughter of Zulfikar Ali Bhutto, was named prime min., becoming the first woman leader of a Muslim nation. She was accused of corruption and dismissed by the president, Aug. 1990. Bhutto returned to power Oct. 1993 but was dismissed Nov. 1996 amid further corruption charges. Responding to India's nuclear weapons tests, Pakistan conducted its own tests in 1998; the U.S. imposed economic sanctions on both countries.

Prime Min. Nawaz Sharif fired, Oct. 1999, army chief Gen. Pervez Musharraf, whose supporters staged a bloodless coup. Musharraf assumed the presidency June 20, 2001. Following the Sept. 11, 2001, terrorist attacks on the U.S., Pres. Musharraf pledged cooperation with the U.S. in fighting Taliban and al-Qaeda militants within Pakistan and in neighboring Afghanistan. In return, the U.S. waived its 1998 sanctions and offered Pakistan financial aid and debt relief. A referendum Apr. 30, 2002, extended Musharraf's rule for 5 years; many observers called the vote rigged.

Musharraf Feb. 5, 2004, pardoned Pakistan's top nuclear scientist, Abdul Qadeer Khan, who admitted to selling atomic secrets to Iran, Libya, and North Korea. An earthquake that rocked Pakistan and the Pakistani-held region of Kashmir Oct. 8, 2005, killed about 80,000 people.

Musharraf's grip weakened in 2007, as his efforts to oust Pakistan's chief justice sparked mass pro-democracy demonstrations. He retained the presidency in an electoral-college vote Oct. 6, 2007, after his main opponents boycotted the election. More than 140 people died Oct. 18 when suicide bombers struck a convoy carrying Benazir Bhutto from the Karachi airport after she spent more than eight years in exile. Musharraf imposed emergency rule Nov. 3 and suspended the constitution while Pakistan's supreme court debated the constitutionality of his reelection. Musharraf gave up his army post Nov. 25, was sworn in as civilian president the next day, and lifted emergency rule Dec. 16. Bhutto was assassinated Dec. 27, 2007, after a rally in Rawalpindi.

Headed by Bhutto's widower, Asif Ali Zardari, the Pakistan Peoples Party led in parliamentary elections Feb. 18, 2008. Musharraf resigned Aug. 18 under threat of impeachment, and Zardari became president Sept. 9. Amid deteriorating security, U.S. and Pakistani forces clashed with the Taliban near the Afghan border, and Islamists executed new suicide attacks. The government announced Feb. 16, 2009, a truce conceding de facto control of the strategic Swat Valley to the Taliban, but in May, government forces launched an offensive that reclaimed most of the region; the fighting displaced nearly 2 mil civilians. Catastrophic floods and monsoon rains, July-Aug. 2010, inundated one-fifth of Pakistan, leaving more than 1,750 people dead and displacing up to 20 mil.

From 2003 to Sept. 2013, terrorist attacks, sectarian clashes, and armed conflict between insurgents and government forces killed more than 17,000 civilians. Extremists targeted proponents of religious tolerance, assassinating Punjab's provincial gov. Salman Taseer Jan. 4, 2011, and Shahbaz Bhatti, the only Christian in the federal cabinet, Mar. 2.

A decade-long international manhunt came to an end shortly after midnight May 2, 2011, when U.S. commandos killed al-Qaeda leader Osama bin Laden at his fortified compound in Abbottabad. The raid, carried out by helicopter from Jalalabad, Afghanistan, was launched without prior warning to Pakistani authorities. The operation led to tensions between the U.S. and Pakistan, which grew worse after a U.S. airstrike killed 24 Pakistani soldiers Nov. 2011. In response, Pakistan closed ground supply routes into Afghanistan until July 3, 2012.

Volunteers attempting to administer the polio vaccine to children were attacked and at least 9 were killed, causing vaccinations to be halted Dec. 20, 2012. In the worst industrial accident in Pakistan's history, nearly 300 died in a fire that consumed a factory complex in Karachi Sept. 12, 2012; about 25 died in a simultaneous fire at a shoe factory in Lahore. Workers at both places had been trapped by blocked exits. On Oct. 9, 15-year-old Malala Yousafzai, who advocated for education rights for girls in Pakistan, was shot by the Taliban, sparking worldwide outrage. After treatment at a British hospital, she addressed a UN youth conference July 12, 2013.

Musharraf returned to Pakistan Mar. 24, 2013, to attempt a political comeback but was arrested Apr. 19 on charges related to his confrontation with the nation's top judges while he was in office and his threatening of Benazir Bhutto in 2007. He was permanently barred from Pakistani politics May 1 and indicted for Bhutto's assassination Aug. 20. Amid accusations of vote rigging, former Prime Min. Nawaz Sharif was returned to office with May 11 elections. Mamnoon Hussain won the presidential election July 30, 2013, and took office Sept. 8.

Palau
Republic of Palau

People: Population: 21,108. **Age distrib.:** <15: 20.7%; 65+: 6.8%. **Pop. density:** 119.1 per sq mi, 46 per sq km. **Urban:** 84.2%. **Ethnic groups:** Palauan (Micronesian with Malayan and Melanesian) 70%, Filipino 15%, Chinese 5%, other Asian 2%, white 2%, Carolinian 1%, other Micronesian 1%. **Languages:** Palauan (official on most islands), Filipino, English (official), Chinese, Carolinian, Japanese, other Asian langs. **Religions:** Roman Catholic 42%, Protestant 23%, Modekngei 9%, Seventh-Day Adventist 5%, unspecified or none 16%.

Geography: Total area: 177 sq mi, 459 sq km; **Land area:** 177 sq mi, 459 sq km. **Location:** Archipelago (26 islands, more than 300 islets) in W Pacific O., about 530 mi SE of the Philippines. **Neighbors:** Micronesia to E, Indonesia to S. **Topography:** A mountainous main island and low coral atolls, usually fringed with large barrier reefs. **Capital:** Melekeok, 638.

Government: Type: Constitutional govt. in free association with the U.S. **Head of state and gov.:** Pres. Tommy Remengesau; b. Feb. 29, 1956; in office: Jan. 17, 2013. **Local divisions:** 16 states. **Defense budget:** NA. **Active troops:** No regular military forces. U.S. responsible for defense.

Economy: Industries: tourism, craft items, constr., garment making. **Chief crops:** coconuts, copra, cassava, sweet potatoes. **Natural resources:** forests, minerals (espec. gold), marine prods., deep-seabed minerals. **Arable land:** 2.2%. **Fish catch:** 1,024 metric tons. **Labor force:** agric. 20%.

Finance: Monetary unit: Dollar (USD). **GDP** (2011): $221 mil (incl. U.S. subsidy); **per capita GDP** (2011): $10,500; **GDP growth** (2011): 5.8%. **Imports** (2010): $113.4 mil. **Exports** (2010): $12.3 mil. **Tourism:** $164 mil. **Budget** (2010): $94.3 mil. **Total reserves less gold:** NA. **CPI change:** NA.

Transport: Civil aviation: 1 airport. **Chief port:** Koror.

Communications: TV sets: 98 per 1,000 pop. **Telephone lines:** 35.1 per 100 pop. **Internet** (2004): 27%.

Health: Life expect.: 69.2 male; 76.7 female. **Births:** 10.9 per 1,000 pop. **Deaths:** 7.9 per 1,000 pop. **Natural inc.:** 0.30%. **Infant mortality:** 11.8 per 1,000 live births. **HIV rate:** NA.

Education: Compulsory: ages 6-14. **Literacy:** 91.9%.

Major intl. organizations: UN (FAO, IBRD, ILO, IMF, WHO).

Embassy: 1700 Pennsylvania Ave. NW, Ste. 400, 20006; 452-6814.

Website: www.palaugov.net

Spain acquired the Palau Islands, 1886, and sold them to Germany, 1899. Japan seized them in 1914. American forces occupied the islands in 1944; in 1947, they became part of the U.S.-administered UN Trust Territory of the Pacific Islands. In 1981 Palau became an autonomous republic. The republic ratified a compact of free association with the U.S. in 1993 and became an independent nation, Oct. 1, 1994. On Nov. 1, 2009, the government of Pres. Johnson Toribiong accepted resettlement of six Uighur (Chinese Muslim) detainees who had been held by the U.S. at Guantánamo Bay, Cuba, since 2001. Threatened by climate change, the island nation is pushing the UN court to connect the issue of climate change to international laws forbidding nations to act in ways within their own territories that damage other nations.

Panama
Republic of Panama

People: Population: 3,559,408. **Age distrib.:** <15: 27.7%; 65+: 7.6%. **Pop. density:** 124 per sq mi, 47.9 per sq km. **Urban:** 75.3%. **Ethnic groups:** mestizo (mixed Amerindian and white) 70%, Amerindian and mixed (West Indian) 14%, white 10%, Amerindian 6%. **Languages:** Spanish (official), English. **Religions:** Roman Catholic 85%, Protestant 15%.

Geography: Total area: 29,120 sq mi, 75,420 sq km; **Land area:** 28,703 sq mi, 74,340 sq km. **Location:** In Central America. **Neighbors:** Costa Rica on W, Colombia on E. **Topography:** 2 mountain ranges run the length of the isthmus. Tropical rain forests cover the Caribbean coast and E Panama. **Capital:** Panama City, 1,426,110.

Government: Type: Constitutional democracy. **Head of state and gov.:** Pres. Ricardo Martinelli Berrocal; b. Mar. 11, 1952; in office: July 1, 2009. **Local divisions:** 9 provinces, 3 indigenous territories. **Defense budget:** $548 mil. **Active troops:** No armed forces. 12,000 paramilitary only.

Economy: Industries: constr., brewing, cement and other constr. materials, sugar milling. **Chief crops:** bananas, rice, corn, coffee, sugarcane, vegetables. **Natural resources:** copper, mahogany forests, shrimp, hydropower. **Arable land:** 7.3%. **Livestock:** cattle: 1.7 mil; chickens: 18.7 mil; goats: 322,122. **Fish catch:** 164,689 metric tons. **Electricity prod.:** 7.3 bil kWh. **Labor force:** agric. 17%, industry 18.6%, services 64.4%.

Finance: Monetary unit: Balboa (PAB) (Sept. 2013: 1.00 = $1 U.S.). **GDP:** $58 bil; **per capita GDP:** $15,900; **GDP growth:** 10.7%. **Imports:** $24.7 bil; U.S. 23.6%, China 6.4%, Costa Rica 4.6%, Mexico 4.4%. **Exports:** $18.9 bil; South Korea 15.7%, U.S. 14.9%, Japan 8.3%, Honduras 7.8%, Indonesia 5.9%, Thailand 5.3% (Imports and exports incl. the Colón Free Zone.). **Tourism:** $2.3 bil. **Budget:** $9.8 bil. **Total reserves incl. gold:** $2.5 bil. **CPI change:** 5.7%.

Transport: Railways: 47 mi. **Motor vehicles:** 147 vehicles per 1,000 pop. **Civil aviation:** 5.2 bil pass.-mi; 57 airports. **Chief ports:** Balboa, Colon, Cristobal.

Communications: TV sets: 219 per 1,000 pop. **Radios:** 293 per 1,000 pop. **Telephone lines:** 17.7 per 100 pop. **Internet:** 45.2%.

Health: Life expect.: 75.4 male; 81.0 female. **Births:** 18.9 per 1,000 pop. **Deaths:** 4.7 per 1,000 pop. **Natural inc.:** 1.42%. **Infant mortality:** 11.0 per 1,000 live births. **HIV rate:** 0.8%.

Education: Compulsory: ages 6-14. **Literacy:** 94.1%.

Major intl. organizations: UN (FAO, IBRD, ILO, IMF, WHO), OAS, WTO.

Embassy: 2862 McGill Ter. NW 20008; 483-1407.

Website: www.presidencia.gob.pa

The coast of Panama was sighted by Rodrigo de Bastidas, sailing with Columbus for Spain in 1501, and was visited by Columbus in 1502. Vasco Núñez de Balboa crossed the isthmus and "discovered" the Pacific Ocean, Sept. 13, 1513. Spanish colonies were ravaged by Francis Drake, 1572-95, and Henry Morgan, 1668-71. Morgan destroyed the old city of Panama, which was founded in 1519. Freed from Spain, Panama joined Colombia in 1821.

Panama declared independence from Colombia Nov. 3, 1903, and granted use, occupation, and control of the Canal Zone to the U.S. Feb. 26, 1904. A 1978 treaty provided for a gradual takeover by Panama of the canal, and withdrawal of U.S. troops, to be completed before the end of the century.

Pres. Eric Arturo Delvalle was ousted by the National Assembly, Feb. 26, 1988, after he tried to fire the head of the Panama Defense Forces, Gen. Manuel Antonio Noriega, who was under U.S. federal indictment on drug charges. U.S. troops invaded Panama Dec. 20, 1989, and Noriega surrendered Jan. 3, 1990.

The U.S. handed over control of the Panama Canal to Panama Dec. 31, 1999. A $5.3-bil plan to widen the canal was approved by national referendum Oct. 22, 2006. Ricardo Martinelli Berrocal, a conservative, was elected president May 3, 2009, and took office July 1. After two decades in a U.S. prison, Noriega was extradited to France Apr. 26, 2010, where he was convicted of money laundering July 7 and received a 7-year sentence. France extradited him to Panama, Dec. 11, 2011, to serve a 20-year sentence for human rights violations he had committed as president. A North Korean vessel traveling from Cuba smuggling antiquated weapons was impounded July 16, 2013, by Panamanian authorities.

Papua New Guinea
Independent State of Papua New Guinea

People: Population: 6,431,902. **Age distrib.:** <15: 35.5%; 65+: 3.8%. **Pop. density:** 36.0 per sq mi, 14.2 per sq km. **Urban:** 12.5%. **Ethnic groups:** Melanesian, Papuan, Negrito, Micronesian, Polynesian. **Languages:** Tok Pisin, English, Hiri Motu (all official); some 836 indigenous langs. (most spoken by fewer than 1,000). **Religions:** Protestant 69% (Evangelical Lutheran 20%, United Church 12%, Seventh-Day Adventist 10%, Pentecostal 9%, Evangelical Alliance 5%, Anglican 3%, Baptist 3%), Roman Catholic 27%.

Geography: Total area: 178,704 sq mi, 462,840 sq km; **Land area:** 174,850 sq mi, 452,860 sq km. **Location:** SE Asia, occupying E half of island of New Guinea and about 600 nearby islands. **Neighbors:** Indonesia on W, Australia on S. **Topography:** Thickly forested mts. cover much of center of country, with lowlands along the coasts. Included are some islands of Bismarck and Solomon groups, such as Admiralty Isls., New Ireland, New Britain, and Bougainville. **Capital:** Port Moresby, 342,904.

Government: Type: Constitutional parliamentary democracy. **Head of state:** Queen Elizabeth II, rep. by Gov.-Gen. Sir Michael Ogio; b. July 7, 1942; in office: Feb. 25, 2011 (acting from Dec. 20, 2010). **Head of gov.:** Prime Min. Peter O'Neill; b. Feb. 13, 1965; in office: Aug. 2, 2011. **Local divisions:** 20 provinces, 1 autonomous region, 1 district. **Defense budget:** $103 mil. **Active troops:** 3,100.

Economy: Industries: copra crushing, palm oil proc., plywood prod., wood chip prod., mining, crude oil prod., petroleum refining. **Chief crops:** coffee, cocoa, copra, palm kernels, tea, sugar, rubber, sweet potatoes. **Natural resources:** gold, copper, silver, nat. gas, timber, oil, fisheries. **Crude oil reserves:** 154.3 mil bbls. **Arable land:** 0.7%. **Livestock:** cattle: 94,000; chickens: 3.8 mil; goats: 3,000; pigs: 1.8 mil; sheep: 7,000. **Fish catch:** 186,848 metric tons. **Electricity prod.:** 3.4 bil kWh. **Labor force:** agric. 85%.

Finance: Monetary unit: Kina (PGK) (Sept. 2013: 2.42 = $1 U.S.). **GDP:** $19.4 bil; **per capita GDP:** $2,800; **GDP growth:** 9.1%. **Imports:** $4.4 bil; Australia 36.3%, Singapore 13.8%, Malaysia 8.4%, China 7.9%, Japan 5.8%, U.S. 4.8%. **Exports:** $5.6 bil; Australia 29%, Japan 9.6%, China 4.8%. **Tourism:** $3 mil. **Budget:** $4.8 bil. **Total reserves less gold:** $3.9 bil. **Gold:** 63,000 oz t. **CPI change:** 2.2%.

Transport: Motor vehicles: 21.4 vehicles per 1,000 pop. **Civil aviation:** 452.4 mil pass.-mi; 21 airports. **Chief ports:** Kimbe, Lae, Madang, Rabaul, Wewak.

Communications: TV sets: 24 per 1,000 pop. **Radios:** 191 per 1,000 pop. **Telephone lines:** 1.9 per 100 pop. **Internet:** 2.3%.

Health: Life expect.: 64.4 male; 69.0 female. **Births:** 25.4 per 1,000 pop. **Deaths:** 6.5 per 1,000 pop. **Natural inc.:** 1.89%. **Infant mortality:** 40.8 per 1,000 live births. **HIV rate:** 0.7%.

Education: NA. **Literacy:** 62.4%.

Major intl. organizations: UN (FAO, IBRD, ILO, IMF, WHO), APEC, the Commonwealth, WTO.

Embassy: 1779 Massachusetts Ave. NW, Ste. 805, 20036; 745-3680.

Website: www.pm.gov.pg

Human remains have been found in the interior of New Guinea dating back at least 10,000 years and possibly much earlier. European colonization began in the 19th cent., when the Dutch took control of the island's western half (now part of Indonesia). The southern half of eastern New Guinea was claimed by Britain in 1884 and transferred to Australia in 1905. Germany claimed the northern half in 1884, but Australia captured it in WWI, receiving a League of Nations mandate and later a UN trusteeship. The two territories were administered jointly after 1949; gained self-government Dec. 1, 1973; and became independent Sept. 16, 1975.

Secessionist rebels clashed with government forces on Bougainville 1988-97, claiming some 20,000 lives. A tsunami killed at least 3,000 July 17, 1998. A Bougainville autonomy agreement was signed Aug. 30, 2001. Sir Michael Somare, the nation's first prime min. (1975-80, 1982-85), regained the office in 2002 and was reelected by parliament Aug. 13, 2007. The elderly Somare took indefinite medical leave Apr. 2011; parliament, Aug. 2, elected Peter O'Neill as permanent replacement. The supreme court ruled that election illegal Dec. 12, 2011, and ordered Somare returned to office. O'Neill refused to step aside, beginning a chaotic period in which two prime ministers, two cabinets, and two governors-general claimed legitimacy. The crisis came to an end after elections Aug. 3, 2012, from which O'Neill emerged as the prime min. The country's Sorcery Act was repealed May 29, 2013, and the death penalty reinstated in cases of rape, robbery and murder.

The country has extensive energy resources; a proposed pipeline would transport natural gas to Queensland, Australia.

Paraguay
Republic of Paraguay

People: Population: 6,623,252. **Age distrib.:** <15: 26.8%; 65+: 6.4%. **Pop. density:** 43.2 per sq mi, 16.7 per sq km. **Urban:** 61.9%.

Ethnic groups: mestizo (mixed Spanish and Amerindian) 95%.

Languages: Spanish, Guaraní (both official). **Religions:** Roman Catholic 90%, Protestant 6%.

Geography: Total area: 157,048 sq mi, 406,752 sq km; **Land area:** 153,399 sq mi, 397,302 sq km. **Location:** Landlocked country in central S America. **Neighbors:** Bolivia on N, Argentina on S, Brazil on E. **Topography:** Paraguay R. bisects the country. To E are fertile plains, wooded slopes, grasslands. To W is the Gran Chaco plain, with marshes and scrub trees. Extreme W is arid. **Capital:** Asunción, 2,139,490.

Government: Type: Constitutional republic. **Head of state and gov.:** Pres. Horacio Cartes; b. July 5, 1956; in office: Aug. 15, 2013. **Local divisions:** 17 departments, 1 capital city. **Defense budget:** $330 mil. **Active troops:** 10,650.

Economy: Industries: sugar, cement, textiles, beverages, wood prods., steel. **Chief crops:** cotton, sugarcane, soybeans, corn, wheat, tobacco, cassava, fruits, vegetables. **Natural resources:** hydropower, timber, iron ore, manganese, limestone. **Arable land:** 9.8%. **Livestock:** cattle: 12.4 mil; chickens: 22 mil; goats: 136,500; pigs: 1.2 mil; sheep: 410,000. **Fish catch:** 21,929 metric tons. **Electricity prod.:** 53.5 bil kWh. **Labor force:** agric. 26.5%, industry 18.5%, services 55%.

Finance: Monetary unit: Guarani (PYG) (Sept. 2013: 4,464.88 = $1 U.S.). **GDP:** $41.6 bil; **per capita GDP:** $6,200; **GDP growth:** –1.2%. **Imports:** $11.2 bil; Brazil 24.1%, China 19.4%, Argentina 19.2%, U.S. 11.4%. **Exports:** $9.7 bil; Uruguay 18.3%, Argentina 16.3%, Brazil 16.2%, Russia 11.8%. **Tourism:** $239 mil. **Budget:** $5.1 bil. **Total reserves less gold:** $4.6 bil. **Gold:** 263,425 oz t. **CPI change:** 3.7%.

Transport: Railways: 22 mi. **Motor vehicles:** 77.1 vehicles per 1,000 pop. **Civil aviation:** 311.9 mil pass.-mi; 15 airports. **Chief ports:** Asunción, Encarnación, San Antonio, Villeta.

Communications: TV sets: 262 per 1,000 pop. **Radios:** 182 per 1,000 pop. **Telephone lines:** 5.6 per 100 pop. **Internet:** 27.1%.

Health: Life expect.: 74.0 male; 79.4 female. **Births:** 17.0 per 1,000 pop. **Deaths:** 4.6 per 1,000 pop. **Natural inc.:** 1.23%. **Infant mortality:** 21.5 per 1,000 live births. **HIV rate:** 0.3%.

Education: Compulsory: ages 6-14. **Literacy:** 93.9%.

Major intl. organizations: UN (FAO, IBRD, ILO, IMF, WHO), OAS, WTO.

Embassy: 2400 Massachusetts Ave. NW 20008; 483-6960.

Website: www.embaparusa.gov.py

Guaraní Indians preceded Europeans in Paraguay, which was visited by Sebastian Cabot in 1527 and became a Spanish possession in 1535. Paraguay gained independence from Spain in 1811. It lost half its population and much of its territory to Brazil, Uruguay, and Argentina in the War of the Triple Alliance, 1865-70. Large areas were won from Bolivia in the Chaco War, 1932-35. Gen. Alfredo Stroessner held the presidency 1954-89, until his ouster in a military coup.

Power struggles ensued between civilian and military leaders, 1993-97. The assassination of Vice Pres. Luis María Argaña, Mar. 23, 1999, was widely attributed to Pres. Raúl Cubas Grau and triggered protests and an impeachment vote; Cubas resigned Mar. 28 and was succeeded by Senate leader Luis Angel González Macchi. An attempted military coup was suppressed May 18, 2000.

Mass protests over the depressed economy led to the proclamation of a state of emergency July 15, 2002. Nicanor Duarte Frutos of the conservative Colorado Party won the presidency, Apr. 27, 2003.

Paraguayan authorities blamed a leftist group, Patria Libre, for the Sept. 2004 kidnapping and subsequent murder of Cecilia Cubas, daughter of former Pres. Cubas. Fernando Lugo, a former Catholic cleric known as the "bishop of the poor," won a presidential election Apr. 20, 2008, ending over 6 decades of Colorado rule. On June 22, 2012, Lugo was removed from office after his handling of a dispute between landless peasants and police left 17 dead June 15. Federico Franco, Lugo's vice president, was sworn into office. Colorado candidate Horacio Cartes, a former tobacco magnate with a checkered past, was elected president Apr. 21, 2013.

Peru
Republic of Peru

People: Population: 29,849,303. **Age distrib.:** <15: 27.6%; 65+: 6.7%. **Pop. density:** 60.4 per sq mi, 23.3 per sq km. **Urban:** 77.3%.

Ethnic groups: Amerindian 45%; mestizo (mixed Amerindian and white) 37%; white 15%; black, Japanese, Chinese, and other 3%.

Languages: Spanish, Quechua, Aymara (all official); Ashaninka; other native langs. (incl. large number of minor Amazonian langs.).

Religions: Roman Catholic 81%, Evangelical 13%.

Geography: Total area: 496,225 sq mi, 1,285,216 sq km; **Land area:** 494,209 sq mi, 1,279,996 sq km. **Location:** On Pacific coast of S America. **Neighbors:** Ecuador, Colombia on N; Brazil, Bolivia on E; Chile on S. **Topography:** An arid coastal strip, 10-100 mi wide, supports much of the population thanks to widespread irrigation. The Andes cover 27% of land area. The uplands are well-watered, as are the eastern slopes reaching the Amazon Basin, which covers half the country. **Capital:** Lima, 9,129,790. **Cities (urban aggl.):** Arequipa, 803,902.

Government: Type: Constitutional republic. **Head of state and gov:** Pres. Ollanta Humala Tasso; b. June 27, 1962; in office: July 28, 2011. **Local divisions:** 25 regions, 1 province. **Defense budget:** $2.43 bil. **Active troops:** 115,000.

Economy: Industries: mining and refining of minerals; steel, metal fabrication; petroleum extraction and refining, nat. gas and nat. gas liquefaction; fishing and fish proc., cement, glass, textiles, clothing, food proc. **Chief crops:** asparagus, coffee, cocoa, cotton, sugarcane, rice, potatoes, corn, plantains, grapes, oranges and other fruits, coca, tomatoes, mangoes, barley, medicinal plants. **Natural resources:** copper, silver, gold, petroleum, timber, fish, iron ore, coal, phosphate, potash, hydropower, nat. gas. **Crude oil reserves:** 579.2 mil bbls. **Arable land:** 2.9%. **Livestock:** cattle: 5.7 mil; chickens: 128 mil; goats: 1.9 mil; pigs: 3.3 mil; sheep: 14.1 mil. **Fish catch:** 8.3 mil metric tons. **Electricity prod.:** 33.3 bil kWh. **Labor force:** agric. 0.7%, industry 23.8%, services 75.5%.

Finance: Monetary unit: Nuevo Sol (PEN) (Sept. 2013: 2.81 = $1 U.S.). **GDP:** $332 bil; **per capita GDP:** $10,900; **GDP growth:** 6.3%. **Imports:** $41.1 bil; U.S. 24.4%, China 13.9%, Brazil 6.3%, Argentina 5.4%, Chile 4.7%, Ecuador 4.5%, Colombia 4.2%. **Exports:** $45.6 bil; China 19.7%, U.S. 15.5%, Canada 9.4%, Japan 6.5%, Spain 5.2%, Chile 4.8%. **Tourism:** $2.7 bil. **Budget:** $57.9 bil. **Total reserves less gold:** $62.3 bil. **Gold:** 1.1 mil oz t. **CPI change:** 3.7%.

Transport: Railways: 1,185 mi. **Motor vehicles:** 58.8 vehicles per 1,000 pop. **Civil aviation:** 5.8 bil pass.-mi; 59 airports. **Chief ports:** Callao, Iquitos, Matarani, Paita, Pucallpa, Yurimaguas.

Communications: TV sets: 201 per 1,000 pop. **Radios:** 269 per 1,000 pop. **Telephone lines:** 11.5 per 100 pop. **Internet:** 38.2%.

Health: Life expect.: 71.0 male; 75.1 female. **Births:** 18.9 per 1,000 pop. **Deaths:** 6.0 per 1,000 pop. **Natural inc.:** 1.29%. **Infant mortality:** 20.9 per 1,000 live births. **HIV rate:** 0.4%.

Education: Compulsory: ages 5-16. **Literacy:** 89.6%.

Major intl. organizations: UN and all of its specialized agencies, APEC, OAS, WTO.

Embassy: 1700 Massachusetts Ave. NW 20036; 833-9860.

Website: www.peru.gob.pe

The powerful Inca Empire had its seat at Cuzco in the Andes and covered much of S America. A civil war had weakened the empire when Spaniard Francisco Pizarro began raiding Peru for its wealth, 1532. In 1533 he executed the Inca ruler, Atahualpa, and enslaved the people.

José de San Martin, captured Lima from the Spanish in 1821; Simón Bolívar routed Spanish forces in 1824, and for much of the 19th cent., the country was governed by military leaders. Chile defeated Peru in the War of the Pacific, 1879-83. Right-wing groups allied with the military and the leftist APRA party vied for power in the first half of the 20th cent.

Peru returned to democratic leadership in 1980 but was plagued by economic problems and by leftist Shining Path (Sendero Luminoso) guerrillas. Conflict between guerrillas and government troops, 1980-2000, killed more than 69,000 people, mostly Andean Indians.

Elected president in June 1990, Alberto Fujimori, the son of Japanese immigrants, dissolved the National Congress, suspended parts of the constitution, and initiated press censorship, Apr. 1992.

The leader of Shining Path was captured Sept. 12. Fujimori won reelection in 1995 and 2000, but his repressive antiterrorism tactics drew international criticism.

Scandals involving top aide and intelligence chief, Vladimino Montesinos, led Fujimori to resign Nov. 20, 2000; instead of accepting his resignation, Congress ousted him as "morally unfit." Montesinos was captured in Venezuela June 23, 2001; extradited to Peru, he was convicted in a series of criminal trials. Fujimori was arrested in Chile, Nov. 7, 2005, and extradited to Peru, Sept. 22, 2007. He was convicted in three separate proceedings, 2007-09, on charges that included complicity in a paramilitary death squad's killing at least 25 people, 1991-92.

Alan García, whose first term as president, 1985-90, ended with the country facing hyperinflation and guerrilla war, won a presidential runoff election June 4, 2006. An earthquake rocked SW coastal Peru, Aug. 15, 2007, killing more than 500 people. In a presidential runoff election June 5, 2011, Ollanta Humala Tasso, a leftist former military officer, defeated Peruvian legislator Keiko Fujimori Higuchi, the daughter of jailed former Pres. Fujimori.

Philippines
Republic of the Philippines

People: Population: 105,720,644. **Age distrib.:** <15: 34%; 65+: 4.4%. **Pop. density:** 918.3 per sq mi, 354.6 per sq km. **Urban:** 48.8%. **Ethnic groups:** Tagalog 28%, Cebuano 13%, Ilocano 9%, Bisaya/Binisaya 8%, Hiligaynon Ilonggo 8%, Bikol 6%, Waray 3%. **Languages:** Filipino, English (both official); 8 major dialects. **Religions:** Roman Catholic 81%, Muslim 5%, Evangelical 3%, Iglesia ni Kristo 2%, Aglipayan 2%, other Christian 5%.

Geography: Total area: 115,831 sq mi, 300,000 sq km; **Land area:** 115,124 sq mi, 298,170 sq km. **Location:** An archipelago off SE coast of Asia. **Neighbors:** Nearest are Malaysia, Indonesia on S; Taiwan on N. **Topography:** The country consists of some 7,100 islands stretching 1,100 mi N-S. About 95% of area and population are on 11 largest islands, which are mountainous, except for the heavily indented coastlines and central plain on Luzon. **Capital:** Manila, 11,861,600. **Cities (urban aggl.):** Davao, 1,564,651.

Government: Type: Republic. **Head of state and gov.:** Pres. Benigno (NoyNoy) Aquino III; b. Feb. 8, 1960; in office: June 30, 2010. **Local divisions:** 80 provinces, 39 chartered cities. **Defense budget:** $2.59 bil. **Active troops:** 125,000.

Economy: Industries: electronics assembly, garments, footwear, pharmaceuticals, chemicals, wood prods., food proc., petroleum refining, fishing. **Chief crops:** sugarcane, coconuts, rice, corn, bananas, cassava, pineapples, mangoes. **Natural resources:** timber, petroleum, nickel, cobalt, silver, gold, salt, copper. **Crude oil reserves:** 138.5 mil bbls. **Arable land:** 18.1%. **Livestock:** cattle: 2.5 mil; chickens: 162.8 mil; goats: 3.9 mil; pigs: 12.3 mil; sheep: 30,000. **Fish catch:** 5 mil metric tons. **Electricity prod.:** 64.6 bil kWh. **Labor force:** agric. 32%, industry 15%, services 53%.

Finance: Monetary unit: Peso (PHP) (Sept. 2013: 44.37 = $1 U.S.). **GDP:** $431.3 bil; **per capita GDP:** $4,500; **GDP growth:** 6.6%. **Imports:** $61.5 bil; U.S. 11.5%, China 10.8%, Japan 10.4%, South Korea 7.3%, Singapore 7.1%, Thailand 5.6%, Saudi Arabia 5.6%, Indonesia 4.4%, Malaysia 4%. **Exports:** $46.3 bil; Japan 19%, U.S. 14.2%, China 11.8%, Singapore 9.4%, Hong Kong 9.2%, South Korea 5.5%, Thailand 4.7%. **Tourism:** $4 bil. **Budget:** $42.1 bil. **Total reserves less gold:** $73.5 bil. **Gold:** 6.2 mil oz t. **CPI change:** 3.2%.

Transport: Railways: 618 mi. **Motor vehicles:** 18.4 vehicles per 1,000 pop. **Civil aviation:** 11.3 bil pass.-mi; 89 airports. **Chief ports:** Batangas, Cagayan de Oro, Cebu, Davao, Liman, Manila.

Communications: TV sets: 194 per 1,000 pop. **Radios:** 735 per 1,000 pop. **Telephone lines:** 4.1 per 100 pop. **Internet:** 36.2%.

Health: Life expect.: 69.3 male; 75.3 female. **Births:** 24.6 per 1,000 pop. **Deaths:** 5.0 per 1,000 pop. **Natural inc.:** 1.97%. **Infant mortality:** 18.2 per 1,000 live births. **HIV rate:** <0.1%.

Education: Compulsory: ages 6-11. **Literacy:** 95.4%.

Major intl. organizations: UN (FAO, IBRD, ILO, IMF, WHO), APEC, ASEAN, WTO.

Embassy: 1600 Massachusetts Ave. NW 20036; 467-9300.

Website: www.gov.ph

Originally inhabited by Malay peoples, the archipelago was visited by Magellan, 1521. The Spanish founded Manila, 1571. Spain ceded the islands, named for King Philip II of Spain, to the U.S. for $20 mil, 1898, following the Spanish-American War. U.S. troops suppressed a guerrilla uprising in a brutal war, 1899-1905. Japan attacked the Philippines Dec. 8, 1941, and occupied the islands during WWII. Independence was proclaimed, July 4, 1946. A republic was established.

The repressive and corrupt regime of Pres. Ferdinand Marcos and his wife, Imelda, ruled the Philippines 1965-86. The assassination of prominent opposition leader Benigno S. Aquino Jr., Aug. 21, 1983, sparked calls for Marcos's resignation. Marcos defeated Corazon Aquino, widow of the slain opposition leader, Feb. 16, 1986, in an allegedly fraudulent election. Mass protests and international pressure forced Marcos to flee the country Feb. 25, and Aquino became president.

Her government was plagued by a weak economy, widespread poverty, Communist and Muslim insurgencies, and lukewarm military support. Rebel troops attempting a coup Dec. 1, 1989, were defeated by government forces and U.S. air support. Fidel Ramos

won the May 1992 presidential election. The U.S. vacated the Subic Bay Naval Station in late 1992, ending its long military presence. Some Muslim separatist guerrillas refused to abide by a ceasefire agreement signed Jan. 30, 1994, so a new treaty providing for expansion and development of an autonomous Muslim region on Mindanao was signed Sept. 2, 1996, formally ending a rebellion that had claimed more than 120,000 lives since 1972.

Joseph (Erap) Estrada, a former movie actor, won the presidential election, May 11, 1998, but was impeached on bribery and corruption charges Nov. 13, 2000. Vice Pres. Gloria Macapagal Arroyo became president Jan. 20, 2001.

As part of the war on terror, the U.S. assisted Filipino troops in combating Abu Sayyaf, an Islamic guerrilla group. Pres. Arroyo won reelection May 10, 2004. Flooding and mudslides from tropical storms, Nov.-Dec. 2004, killed at least 1,060 people. Former Pres. Estrada was convicted, Sept. 12, 2007, of taking more than $85 mil in bribes and kickbacks while in office; Pres. Arroyo pardoned him Oct. 25. Typhoon Fengshen, June 21-22, 2008, left at least 557 people dead and destroyed more than 90,000 homes; at least 700 more people died when the ferry Princess of the Stars capsized and ran aground in the storm. Tropical storms Sept.-Oct. 2009 claimed more than 900 lives and affected over 9 mil people. Benigno (NoyNoy) Aquino III, the son of former Pres. Aquino (who died Aug. 1, 2009), defeated Estrada in the May 10, 2010, presidential election and was sworn in June 30.

Former Pres. Arroyo, who was serving in Congress, was arrested Oct. 4, 2012, on corruption charges. The government, Oct. 15, signed a peace deal with the Muslim rebels on Mindanao; violence had persisted after the 1996 accord. Typhoon Bopha, or Pablo, and its 130-mph winds caused flash floods and landslides that killed more than 450 in the south, and displaced about 400,000, Dec. 4, 2012.

Congress voted, Dec. 17, 2012, to provide contraception to the country's poorest women, despite objections from many of the nation's Catholics; the Supreme Court suspended the law Mar. 19, 2013. Malaysian forces and about 200 armed Filipinos began clashing over a centuries-old territorial dispute in late Feb., resulting in some 60 deaths before most combatants fled around Mar. 25. Allies of Pres. Aquino took a majority of Senate seats in May 14, 2013, elections.

Poland
Republic of Poland

People: Population: 38,383,809. **Age distrib.:** <15: 14.6%; 65+: 14.5%. **Pop. density:** 326.7 per sq mi, 126.2 per sq km. **Urban:** 60.9%. **Ethnic groups:** Polish 97%. **Language:** Polish (official). **Religions:** Roman Catholic 90%, Eastern Orthodox 1%.

Geography: Total area: 120,728 sq mi, 312,685 sq km; **Land area:** 117,474 sq mi, 304,255 sq km. **Location:** On Baltic Sea in E central Europe. **Neighbors:** Germany on W; Czech Rep., Slovakia on S; Lithuania, Belarus, Ukraine on E; Russia on N. **Topography:** Mostly lowlands forming part of the Northern European Plain. The Carpathian Mts. along S border rise to 8,200 ft. **Capital:** Warsaw, 1,723,260. **Cities (urban aggl.):** Kraków, 756,047.

Government: Type: Republic. **Head of state:** Pres. Bronislaw Komorowski; b. June 4, 1952; in office: Aug. 6, 2010. **Head of gov.:** Prime Min. Donald Tusk; b. Apr. 22, 1957; in office: Nov. 16, 2007. **Local divisions:** 16 provinces. **Defense budget:** $8.62 bil. **Active troops:** 96,000.

Economy: Industries: machine building, iron and steel, coal mining, chemicals, shipbuilding, food proc., glass, beverages, textiles. **Chief crops:** potatoes, fruits, vegetables, wheat. **Natural resources:** coal, sulfur, copper, nat. gas, silver, lead, salt, amber. **Crude oil reserves:** 156.5 mil bbls. **Arable land:** 36.5%. **Livestock:** cattle: 5.8 mil; chickens: 127.5 mil; goats: 111,824; pigs: 13.5 mil; sheep: 250,966. **Fish catch:** 221,338 metric tons. **Electricity prod.** (2011): 153.4 bil kWh. **Labor force:** agric. 12.9%, industry 30.2%, services 57%.

Finance: Monetary unit: Zloty (PLN) (Sept. 2013: 3.25 = $1 U.S.). **GDP:** $814.1 bil; **per capita GDP:** $20,900; **GDP growth:** 2%. **Imports:** $195.4 bil; Germany 27.3%, Russia 12.2%, Netherlands 5.9%, China 5.4%, Italy 5.2%, Czech Republic 4.3%, France 4.2%. **Exports:** $188.5 bil; Germany 26%, UK 7%, Czech Republic 6.5%, France 6%, Russia 5.2%, Italy 5%, Netherlands 4.6%. **Tourism:** $10.9 bil. **Budget:** $97.7 bil. **Total reserves less gold:** $103.4 bil. **Gold:** 3.3 mil oz t. **CPI change:** 3.7%.

Transport: Railways: 12,072 mi. **Motor vehicles:** 573.3 vehicles per 1,000 pop. **Civil aviation:** 4.5 bil pass.-mi; 87 airports. **Chief ports:** Gdansk, Gdynia, Swinoujscie, Szczecin.

Communications: TV sets: 408 per 1,000 pop. **Radios:** 297 per 1,000 pop. **Telephone lines:** 16 per 100 pop. **Internet:** 65%.

Health: Life expect.: 72.5 male; 80.6 female. **Births:** 9.9 per 1,000 pop. **Deaths:** 10.3 per 1,000 pop. **Natural inc.:** -0.04%. **Infant mortality:** 6.3 per 1,000 live births. **HIV rate:** 0.1%.

Education: Compulsory: ages 7-15. **Literacy:** 99.7%.

Major intl. organizations: UN (FAO, IBRD, ILO, IMF, WHO), EU, NATO, OECD, OSCE, WTO.

Embassy: 2640 16th St. NW 20009; 234-3800.

Website: www.poland.gov.pl

Slavic tribes in the area were converted to Latin Christianity in the 10th cent. Poland was a great power from the 14th to the 17th cent. In three partitions (1772, 1793, 1795) it was apportioned among

Prussia, Russia, and Austria. Overrun by the Austro-German armies in WWI, it declared its independence on Nov. 11, 1918, and was recognized as independent by the Treaty of Versailles, June 28, 1919. Large territories to the east were taken in a war with Russia, 1921.

Germany and the USSR invaded Poland Sept. 1939 and divided the country. During the war, Nazis killed some 6 mil Polish citizens, half of them Jews. In compensation for territory ceded to the USSR when the war ended, Poland received German territory comprising Silesia, Pomerania, West Prussia, and part of East Prussia. Communists, who aligned themselves with the USSR, dominated the 1947 election.

In 12 years of rule by Stalinists, large estates were abolished, industries nationalized, schools secularized, and Roman Catholic prelates jailed. Farm production fell off. Harsh working conditions caused a riot in Poznan, June 28-29, 1956. A new Politburo, committed to a more independent Polish Communism, was named Oct. 1956, with Wladyslaw Gomulka as first secretary of the party. Collectivization of farms was ended. Gomulka agreed to permit religious liberty and religious publications, provided the church kept out of politics.

In Dec. 1970 workers in port cities rioted because of price rises and new incentive wage rules. On Dec. 20 Gomulka resigned as party leader; he was succeeded by Edward Gierek. The rules were dropped and price rises revoked.

Independent trade union Solidarity grew in popularity and strength throughout the 1980s, organizing strikes and making bold demands. Led by Lech Walesa, who had been arrested along with other Solidarity leaders Dec. 13, 1981, Solidarity helped to win political and economic reforms, including free elections, in an Apr. 5, 1989, accord. Candidates endorsed by Solidarity swept the parliamentary elections, June 4. Lech Walesa became president Dec. 22, 1990.

A radical economic program designed to transform the economy into a free-market system led to inflation, unemployment, and a return to the political left in 1993 parliamentary elections. A former Communist, Aleksander Kwasniewski, defeated Walesa in the 1995 presidential election and was reelected 5 years later. A new constitution was approved by referendum May 25, 1997. Poland became a full member of NATO, Mar. 12, 1999, and entered the European Union May 1, 2004.

Lech Kaczynski, the conservative mayor of Warsaw, won a presidential runoff election Oct. 23, 2005. In July 2006 he appointed his identical twin brother Jaroslaw as prime min. Poland's governing coalition fell apart in 2007, and the center-right Civic Platform party, led by Donald Tusk, won parliamentary elections Oct. 21. Pres. Lech Kaczynski, his wife Maria, and many senior Polish government officials were among the 96 passengers and crew members killed in a plane crash Apr. 10, 2010, near Smolensk, in western Russia. Parliament Speaker Bronislaw Komorowski, an ally of Prime Min. Tusk, became acting president after the crash; he won a full term July 4 by defeating Kaczynski's brother Jaroslaw in a runoff election.

Nearly 1,741 Polish troops were serving in Afghanistan as of mid-2013. An epidemic of rubella, or German measles, swept through Poland in 2013, affecting more than 36,000 people through Aug.

Portugal
Portuguese Republic

People: Population: 10,799,270. **Age distrib.:** <15: 16%; 65+: 18.4%. **Pop. density:** 305.8 per sq mi, 118.1 per sq km. **Urban:** 61.1%. **Ethnic groups:** homogeneous Mediterranean stock. **Languages:** Portuguese, Mirandese (both official). **Religions:** Roman Catholic 85%, other Christian 2%, none 4%.

Geography: Total area: 35,556 sq mi, 92,090 sq km; **Land area:** 35,317 sq mi, 91,470 sq km. **Location:** At SW extreme of Europe. **Neighbors:** Spain on N, E. **Topography:** Portugal N of Tajus R., which bisects country NE-SW, is mountainous, cool and rainy. To the S there are drier, rolling plains, and a warm climate. **Capital:** Lisbon, 2,843,410. **Cities (urban aggl.):** Porto, 1,366,940.

Government: Type: Republic. **Head of state:** Pres. Aníbal Cavaco Silva; b. July 15, 1939; in office: Mar. 9, 2006. **Head of gov.:** Prime Min. Pedro Passos Coelho; b. July 24,1964; in office: June 21, 2011. **Local divisions:** 18 districts, 2 autonomous regions. **Defense budget:** $2.6 bil. **Active troops:** 42,600.

Economy: Industries: textiles, clothing, footwear, wood and cork, paper, chemicals, auto-parts mfg., base metals, dairy prods., wine and other foods, porcelain and ceramics, glassware, tech., telecom. **Chief crops:** grain, potatoes, tomatoes, olives, grapes. **Natural resources:** fish, forests (cork), iron ore, copper, zinc, tin, tungsten, silver, gold, uranium, marble, clay, gypsum, salt, hydropower. **Arable land:** 12%. **Livestock:** cattle: 1.5 mil; chickens: 40 mil; goats: 412,700; pigs: 2 mil; sheep: 2.2 mil. **Fish catch:** 225,318 metric tons. **Electricity prod.** (2011): 49.9 bil kWh. **Labor force:** agric. 11.7%, industry 28.5%, services 59.8%.

Finance: Monetary unit: Euro (EUR) (Sept. 2013: 0.76 = $1 U.S.). **GDP:** $250.6 bil; **per capita GDP:** $23,800; **GDP growth:** −3.2%. **Imports:** $69.5 bil; Spain 32%, Germany 11.5%, France 6.6%, Italy 5.3%, Netherlands 4.9%. **Exports:** $58.2 bil; Spain 22.7%, Germany 12.4%, France 11.9%, Angola 6.5%, UK 5.3%, Netherlands 4.2%. **Tourism:** $11.1 bil. **Budget:** $100.8 bil. **Total reserves less gold:** $2.2 bil. **Gold:** 12.3 mil oz t. **CPI change:** 2.8%.

Transport: Railways: 2,062 mi. **Motor vehicles:** 538.6 vehicles per 1,000 pop. **Civil aviation:** 14.2 bil pass.-mi; 43 airports. **Chief ports:** Leixoes, Lisbon, Setubal, Sines.

Communications: TV sets: 425 per 1,000 pop. **Radios:** 299 per 1,000 pop. **Telephone lines:** 42.6 per 100 pop. **Internet:** 64%.

Health: Life expect.: 75.6 male; 82.3 female. **Births:** 9.6 per 1,000 pop. **Deaths:** 10.9 per 1,000 pop. **Natural inc.:** −0.13%. **Infant mortality:** 4.5 per 1,000 live births. **HIV rate:** 0.7%.

Education: Compulsory: ages 6-14. **Literacy:** 95.4%.

Major intl. organizations: UN (FAO, IBRD, ILO, IMF, WHO), EU, NATO, OECD, OSCE, WTO.

Embassy: 2012 Massachusetts Ave. NW 20036; 350-5400.

Website: www.portugal.gov.pt

Portugal, an independent state since the 12th cent., was a kingdom until a 1910 revolution drove out King Manoel II and a republic was proclaimed. Beginning in 1932, Prime Min. Antonio de Oliveira Salazar headed a repressive government. Illness forced his retirement in Sept. 1968.

On Apr. 25, 1974, a military junta led by Gen. Antonio de Spinola seized the government; Spinola became president. The new government granted independence to Guinea-Bissau, Mozambique, Cape Verde Islands, Angola, and São Tomé and Príncipe. Portugal returned Macao to China on Dec. 20, 1999.

With the economy lagging, Socialists led by Jóse Sócrates, gained a parliamentary majority in 2005 and held onto a plurality in 2009. The conservative Aníbal Cavaco Silva, a former prime min. (1985-95), won the Jan. 2006 presidential election and was reelected 5 years later. After Portugal was given a $116-bil bailout package from international lenders to avert default, the center-right Social Democratic Party, headed by Pedro Passos Coelho, won parliamentary elections June 2011. Austerity cuts caused widespread protests in Nov. 2012; the Constitutional Court ruled Apr. 5, 2013 that many of the cuts were illegal. The EU agreed to extend Portugal's loan repayment period Apr. 12.

Azores Isls., in the Atlantic, 740 mi W of Portugal, have an area of 868 sq mi and a pop. (2011 est.) of 246,102. A 1951 agreement gave the U.S. rights to use defense facilities in the Azores. The Madeira Isls., 350 mi off the NW coast of Africa, have an area of 306 sq mi and a pop. (2011 est.) of 267,785. Both groups were offered partial autonomy in 1976.

Qatar
State of Qatar

People: Population: 2,042,444. **Age distrib.:** <15: 12.5%; 65+: 0.8%. **Pop. density:** 456.6 per sq mi, 176.3 per sq km. **Urban:** 98.8%. **Ethnic groups:** Arab 40%, Indian 18%, Pakistani 18%, Iranian 10%. **Languages:** Arabic (official), English (commonly used as second lang.). **Religions:** Muslim 78%, Christian 9%.

Geography: Total area: 4,473 sq mi, 11,586 sq km; **Land area:** 4,473 sq mi, 11,586 sq km. **Location:** Middle East, occupying peninsula on W coast of Persian Gulf. **Neighbors:** Saudi Arabia on S. **Topography:** Mostly flat desert with some limestone ridges; vegetation of any kind is scarce. **Capital:** Ad-Dawhah (Doha), 567,051.

Government: Type: Emirate (monarchy). **Head of state:** Emir Sheikh Tamim bin Hamad al-Thani; b. July 3, 1980; in office: June 25, 2013. **Head of gov.:** Prime Min. Sheikh Abdullah bin Nasser bin Khalifa al-Thani; in office: June 26, 2013. **Local divisions:** 7 municipalities. **Defense budget:** NA. **Active troops:** 11,800.

Economy: Industries: liquefied nat. gas, crude oil prod. and refining, ammonia, fertilizers, petrochemicals, steel reinforcing bars, cement, commercial ship repair. **Chief crops:** fruits, vegetables. **Natural resources:** petroleum, nat. gas, fish. **Crude oil reserves:** 25.4 bil bbls. **Arable land:** 1.2%. **Livestock:** cattle: 10,063; chickens: 8 mil; goats: 190,008; sheep: 241,385. **Fish catch:** 13,021 metric tons. **Electricity prod.:** 22.3 bil kWh. **Labor force:** NA.

Finance: Monetary unit: Riyal (QAR) (Sept. 2013: 3.64 = $1 U.S.). **GDP:** $191 bil; **per capita GDP:** $103,900; **GDP growth:** 6.6%. **Imports:** $30.8 bil; U.S. 14.2%, UAE 11%, Saudi Arabia 8.3%, UK 6.4%, Japan 6%, China 4.8%, Germany 4.7%, Italy 4.4%, France 4.4%. **Exports:** $133.7 bil; Japan 26.6%, South Korea 19%, India 12%, Singapore 5.7%, China 5.4%. **Tourism:** $2.9 bil. **Budget:** $49.3 bil. **Total reserves less gold:** $32.5 bil. **Gold:** 399,100 oz t. **CPI change:** 1.9%.

Transport: Motor vehicles: 165.5 vehicles per 1,000 pop. **Civil aviation:** 25.1 bil pass.-mi; 4 airports. **Chief ports:** Doha, Mesaieed, Ra's Laffan.

Communications: TV sets: 405 per 1,000 pop. **Radios:** 468 per 1,000 pop. **Telephone lines:** 16.9 per 100 pop. **Internet:** 88.1%.

Health: Life expect.: 76.3 male; 80.3 female. **Births:** 10.1 per 1,000 pop. **Deaths:** 1.5 per 1,000 pop. **Natural inc.:** 0.85% **Infant mortality:** 6.6 per 1,000 live births. **HIV rate:** NA.

Education: Compulsory: ages 6-17. **Literacy:** 96.3%.

Major intl. organizations: UN (FAO, IBRD, ILO, IMF, WHO), AL, OPEC, WTO.

Embassy: 2555 M St. NW 20037; 274-1600.

Website: portal.www.gov.qa

Qatar was under Bahrain's control until the Ottoman Turks took power, 1872 to 1915. In a treaty signed 1916, Qatar gave Great Britain responsibility for its defense and foreign relations. After Britain announced it would remove its military forces from the Persian Gulf area by the end of 1971, Qatar unsuccessfully sought a federation with other British-protected states in the area. Qatar thus declared itself independent, Sept. 1, 1971. Crown Prince Hamad bin Khalifa al-Thani ousted his father, Emir Khalifa bin Hamad al-Thani, June 27, 1995. In municipal elections held Mar. 8, 1999, women participated for the first time as candidates and voters.

Qatar, one of the world's leading exporters of liquefied natural gas, has experienced rapid economic growth in recent years. Military ties with the U.S. have been expanding; Camp As-Sayliyah, a base near Doha, served as a command center for the U.S.-led invasion of Iraq, Mar. 2003. The influential Arab news network Al-Jazeera is based in Qatar. Qatar will host the World Cup soccer tournament in 2022. Sheikh Hamad bin Khalifa al-Thani, abdicated in favor of his son, Sheik Tamim bin Hamad al-Thani, June 25, 2013.

Romania

People: Population: 21,790,479. **Age distrib.:** <15: 14.7%; 65+: 15.1%. **Pop. density:** 245.5 per sq mi, 94.8 per sq km. **Urban:** 52.8%. **Ethnic groups:** Romanian 90%, Hungarian 7%, Roma 3%. **Languages:** Romanian (official), Hungarian, Romany. **Religions:** Eastern Orthodox 87%, Protestant 8%, Roman Catholic 5%.

Geography: Total area: 92,043 sq mi, 238,391 sq km; **Land area:** 88,761 sq mi, 229,891 sq km. **Location:** SE Europe, on the Black Sea. **Neighbors:** Moldova on E, Ukraine on N, Hungary and Serbia on W, Bulgaria on S. **Topography:** The Carpathian Mts. encase the N central Transylvanian plateau. There are wide plains S and E of the mountains, through which flow the lower reaches of the rivers of Danube system. **Capital:** Bucharest, 1,936,600.

Government: Type: Republic. **Head of state:** Pres. Traian Basescu; b. Nov. 4, 1951; in office: Dec. 20, 2004. **Head of gov.:** Prime Min. Victor-Viorel Ponta; b. Sept. 20, 1972; in office: May 7, 2012. **Local divisions:** 41 counties, 1 municipality. **Defense budget:** $2.16 bil. **Active troops:** 71,400.

Economy: Industries: elec. machinery and equip., textiles and footwear, light machinery, auto assembly, mining, timber, constr. materials. **Chief crops:** wheat, corn, barley, sugar beets, sunflower seeds, potatoes, grapes. **Natural resources:** petroleum (reserves declining), timber, nat. gas, coal, iron ore, salt, hydropower. **Crude oil reserves:** 600 mil bbls. **Arable land:** 39.1%. **Livestock:** cattle: 2 mil; chickens: 80.8 mil; goats: 1.2 mil; pigs: 5.4 mil; sheep: 8.4 mil. **Fish catch:** 11,594 metric tons. **Electricity prod.:** 57.7 bil kWh. **Labor force:** agric. 31.6%, industry 21.1%, services 47.3%.

Finance: Monetary unit: New Leu (RON) (Sept. 2013: 3.40 = $1 U.S.). **GDP:** $277.9 bil; **per capita GDP:** $13,000; **GDP growth:** 0.3%. **Imports:** $67.5 bil; Germany 17.5%, Italy 11%, Hungary 9.1%, France 5.7%, Russia 4.4%, Poland 4.3%, Austria 4.2%, Kazakhstan 4.1%. **Exports:** $58.1 bil; Germany 18.9%, Italy 12.3%, France 7.1%, Turkey 5.5%, Hungary 5.5%. **Tourism:** $1.5 bil. **Budget:** $60 bil. **Total reserves less gold:** $41.2 bil. **Gold:** 3.3 mil oz t. **CPI change:** 3.3%.

Transport: Railways: 6,701 mi. **Motor vehicles:** 240.2 vehicles per 1,000 pop. **Civil aviation:** 2.5 bil pass.-mi; 26 airports. **Chief ports:** Braila, Constanta, Galati, Mancanulul, Mldla, Tulcea.

Communications: TV sets: 885 per 1,000 pop. **Radios:** 143 per 1,000 pop. **Telephone lines:** 21.9 per 100 pop. **Internet:** 50%.

Health: Life expect.: 71.0 male; 78.1 female. **Births:** 9.4 per 1,000 pop. **Deaths:** 11.9 per 1,000 pop. **Natural inc.:** −0.25%. **Infant mortality:** 10.4 per 1,000 live births. **HIV rate:** 0.1%.

Education: Compulsory: ages 7-16. **Literacy:** 97.7%.

Major intl. organizations: UN (FAO, IBRD, ILO, IMF, WHO), NATO, OSCE, WTO.

Embassy: 1607 23rd St. NW 20008; 332-4846.

Website: www.gov.ro

Romania's earliest known people merged with invading Proto-Thracians, preceding by centuries the Dacians. Rome occupied the Dacian kingdom, 106-271 CE; people and language were Romanized. The Turkey-dominated principalities of Wallachia and Moldavia were united in 1859, became Romania in 1861, and gained recognition as an independent kingdom, 1881.

After WWI, Romania acquired Bessarabia, Bukovina, Transylvania, and Banat. In 1940 it ceded Bessarabia and Northern Bukovina to the USSR, part of southern Dobrudja to Bulgaria, and northern Transylvania to Hungary. In 1941, Prem. Marshal Ion Antonescu led Romania in support of Germany against the USSR. He was overthrown in 1944, and Romania joined the Allies. After occupation by Soviet troops, a People's Republic was proclaimed, Dec. 30, 1947.

On Aug. 22, 1965, a new constitution proclaimed Romania a socialist republic. The domestic policies of Pres. Nicolae Ceausescu were repressive. All industry was state-owned, and state farms and cooperatives owned almost all arable land. Ceausescu's security forces fired on antigovernment demonstrators, Dec. 1989, killing hundreds, but when the army sided with the protesters, his regime fell. Charged with genocide and abuse of power, Ceausescu and his wife were executed Dec. 25, 1989.

A new constitution providing for a multiparty system took effect Dec. 8, 1991. Many of Romania's state-owned companies were privatized in 1996. Romania became a full NATO member in 2004 and entered the European Union Jan. 1, 2007. The IMF and other donors agreed to provide a $27 bil loan Mar. 25, 2009, to rescue the country from the global recession. Romania, a firm U.S. ally, pulled its remaining troops out of Iraq July 2009. About 1,800 Romanian soldiers were serving with NATO-led forces in Afghanistan in mid-2012. After Victor-Viorel Ponta became prime min. May 7, 2012, he accused Pres. Traian Basescu of abusing his authority, and parliament voted to impeach Basescu July 6, 2012, making Crin Antonescu acting pres. More than 87% of voters called for impeachment in a referendum July 29, 2012. The country's Supreme Court overturned the result in Aug., deeming it unconstitutional because less than 50% of eligible voters had participated.

Russia
Russian Federation

People: Population: 142,500,482. **Age distrib.:** <15: 16%; 65+: 13.1%. **Pop. density:** 22.5 per sq mi, 8.7 per sq km. **Urban:** 73.8%. **Ethnic groups:** Russian 80%, Tatar 4%, Ukrainian 2%, Bashkir 1%, Chuvash 1%. **Languages:** Russian (official), many minority langs. **Religions:** Russian Orthodox 15%-20%, Muslim 10%-15%, other Christian 2%.

Geography: Total area: 6,601,668 sq mi, 17,098,242 sq km; **Land area:** 6,323,482 sq mi, 16,377,742 sq km, more than 76% of total area of the former USSR and the largest country in the world. **Location:** Stretches from E Europe across N Asia to the Pacific O. **Neighbors:** Finland, Norway, Estonia, Latvia, Belarus, Ukraine on W; Georgia, Azerbaijan, Kazakhstan, China, Mongolia, N. Korea on S; Kaliningrad exclave bordered by Poland on the S, Lithuania on the N and E. **Topography:** Every type of climate except distinctly tropical. The European portion is a low plain, grassy in S, wooded in N, with Ural Mts. on E, and Caucasus Mts. on S. Urals stretch N-S for 2,500 mi. The Asiatic portion is a vast plain, with mountains on S and in E; tundra covers extreme N with forest belt below; plains, marshes are in W, desert in SW. **Capital:** Moscow, 11,620,600. **Cities (urban aggl.):** Saint Petersburg, 4,865,720; Novosibirsk, 1,478,053; Yekaterinburg, 1,355,296; Nizhniy Novgorod, 1,245,351; Samara, 1,165,506; Omsk, 1,155,804; Kazan, 1,147,068; Chelyabinsk, 1,135,042; Rostov-on-Don, 1,091,669; Ufa, 1,064,087; Volgograd, 1,021,950.

Government: Type: Federation. **Head of state:** Pres. Vladimir Putin; b. Oct. 7, 1952; in office: May 7, 2012. **Head of gov.:** Prime Min. Dmitri Medvedev; b. Sept. 14, 1965; in office: May 8, 2012. **Local divisions:** 46 provinces, 21 republics, 4 autonomous okrugs, 9 krays, 2 federal cities, 1 autonomous oblast. **Defense budget:** $59.9 bil. **Active troops:** 845,000.

Economy: Industries: mining and extractive industries producing coal, oil, gas, chemicals, metals; machine building; defense (incl. radar, missile prod.); transp. equip.; communications equip.; agric. machinery, constr. equip.; elec. power generating and transmitting equip.; medical and scientific instruments; consumer durables, textiles. **Chief crops:** grain, sugar beets, sunflower seeds, vegetables, fruits. **Natural resources:** oil, nat. gas, coal, minerals, rare earth elements, timber (climate, terrain, and distance are obstacles to exploitation of resources). **Crude oil reserves:** 80 bil bbls. **Arable land:** 7.4%. **Livestock:** cattle: 20 mil; chickens: 406 mil; goats: 2.1 mil; pigs: 17.2 mil; sheep: 19.8 mil. **Fish catch:** 4.4 mil metric tons. **Electricity prod.** (2011): 996.3 bil kWh. **Labor force:** agric. 7.9%, industry 27.4%, services 64.7%.

Finance: Monetary unit: Ruble (RUB) (Sept. 2013: 33.29 = $1 U.S.). **GDP:** $2.6 tril; **per capita GDP:** $18,000; **GDP growth:** 3.4%. **Imports:** $334.7 bil; China 15.5%, Germany 9.5%, Ukraine 5.5%. **Exports:** $529.6 bil; Netherlands 14.4%, China 6.4%, Italy 5.3%, Germany 4.5%. **Tourism:** $11.2 bil. **Budget:** $418 bil. **Total reserves less gold:** $486.6 bil. **Gold:** 30.8 mil oz t. **CPI change:** 5.1%.

Transport: Railways: 54,157 mi. **Motor vehicles:** 318.4 vehicles per 1,000 pop. **Civil aviation:** 52.1 bil pass.-mi; 594 airports. **Chief ports:** Kaliningrad, Kavkaz, Nakhodka, Novoroseiysk, Primorsk, Saint Petersburg, Vostochny.

Communications: TV sets: 546 per 1,000 pop. **Radios:** 416 per 1,000 pop. **Telephone lines:** 30.1 per 100 pop. **Internet:** 53.3%.

Health: Life expect.: 64.0 male; 76.0 female. **Births:** 12.1 per 1,000 pop. **Deaths:** 14.0 per 1,000 pop. **Natural inc.:** −0.19%. **Infant mortality:** 7.2 per 1,000 live births. **HIV rate:** 0.8%-1.4%.

Education: Compulsory: ages 6-15. **Literacy:** 99.7%.

Major intl. organizations: UN (FAO, IBRD, ILO, IMF, WHO), APEC, CIS, OSCE, WTO (observer).

Embassy: 2650 Wisconsin Ave. NW 20007; 298-5700.

Website: www.government.ru or kremlin.ru

Slavic tribes began migrating into Russia from the W in the 5th cent. The first Russian state, centered in Novgorod and Kiev, was founded by Scandinavian chieftains in the 9th cent. In the 13th cent., Mongols overran the country. It recovered under the grand dukes and princes of Muscovy, or Moscow, and by 1480 freed itself from the Mongols. Ivan the Terrible was proclaimed Tsar, 1547. Peter the Great (1682-1725) extended the domain and, in 1721, founded the Russian empire. Western ideas and the beginnings of modernization spread through the empire in the 19th and early 20th cent.

Military reverses in the 1905 war with Japan and in WWI led to the breakdown of the Tsarist regime. The 1917 Revolution began in Mar. with a series of sporadic strikes for higher wages by factory workers. A provisional democratic government under Prince Georgi Lvov was established but a second provisional government, under Alexander Kerensky, followed in May. Vladimir Ilyich Lenin, Nov. 7, overthrew the Kerensky government and the freely elected Constituent Assembly in a Communist coup.

Soviet Union. Lenin's death Jan. 21, 1924, led to an internal power struggle won by Joseph Stalin. His brutal tactics, including purge trials, mass executions, and exile of many to work camps, resulted in millions of deaths.

Despite a Germany-USSR non-aggression pact signed in Aug. 1939, Germany invaded the Soviet Union, June 1941. Russian winter counterthrusts, 1941-42 and 1942-43, and resistance to the siege of Leningrad (now St. Petersburg) stopped the German advance. Russians drove the Germans from Eastern Europe and the Balkans in the next two years.

After WWII, Communists took over in countries throughout the region, extending the Soviet sphere of influence. The USSR and the U.S., the world's leading nuclear superpowers, became Cold War rivals. After Stalin died, Mar. 5, 1953, Nikita Khrushchev gained power and denounced Stalin, 1956, beginning "de-Stalinization."

Under Khrushchev the open antagonism of Poles and Hungarians toward Moscow's domination was suppressed in 1956. He aided the Cuban revolution under Fidel Castro but withdrew Soviet missiles from Cuba during a confrontation with U.S. Pres. Kennedy, Sept.-Oct. 1962. Khrushchev was deposed, Oct. 1964, and replaced by Leonid I. Brezhnev. In Aug. 1968, Soviet forces invaded Czechoslovakia, crushing liberalization there.

Massive Soviet military aid to North Vietnam in the late 1960s and early 1970s helped assure Communist victories throughout Indochina. In Dec. 1979, Soviet forces entered Afghanistan to support a pro-Soviet regime against U.S.-supported Muslim resistance fighters. In Apr. 1988, the Soviets agreed to withdraw their troops, ending a futile 8-year war.

Mikhail Gorbachev was chosen Communist Party gen. sec., Mar. 1985. In 1987 he initiated a program of political and economic reforms through openness (glasnost) and restructuring (perestroika). Gorbachev faced economic problems as well as ethnic and nationalist unrest in the republics. A coup by Communist hardliners Aug. 1991 was foiled with help from Russian Republic Pres. Boris Yeltsin. On Aug. 24, Gorbachev resigned as leader of the Communist Party. Several republics declared their independence, including Russia, Ukraine, and Kazakhstan. On Aug. 29, the Soviet Parliament voted to suspend all activities of the Communist Party.

The Soviet Union officially broke up Dec. 26, 1991, ending the 74-year domination of the Communist Party.

Russian Federation. Under Pres. Yeltsin, Russia took steps toward privatization, which caused inflation and a severe economic downturn. In June 1992, Yeltsin and U.S. Pres. George H. W. Bush agreed to massive arms reductions. Yeltsin prevailed in a power struggle with the Congress of People's Deputies, which was dominated by former Communists, and in a referendum Dec. 12, 1993, a new constitution was approved. Russian troops fought rebels in the breakaway republic of Chechnya Dec. 1994-Aug. 1996, when a peace accord temporarily ended the conflict. On May 27, 1997, Yeltsin signed a founding act, increasing cooperation with NATO and paving the way for NATO to admit Eastern European nations.

Russia's economic crisis deepened in the late 1990s, heightening tensions between parliament and Pres. Yeltsin, who had been reelected in 1996. An Aug. 1999 operation to suppress Islamic rebels in Dagestan reignited the war in neighboring Chechnya, where Russia launched a full-scale assault. Yeltsin unexpectedly resigned Dec. 31, 1999, naming Prime Min. Vladimir Putin as his interim successor. Putin won presidential elections Mar. 2000. Putin's allies won legislative elections, Dec. 2003, and the president was reelected Mar. 2004; international election monitors cited flaws on both occasions.

A bomb in Grozny, May 9, 2004, killed Chechnya's pro-Moscow president, Akhmad Kadyrov. In another terrorist act linked to the Chechnya conflict, two passenger planes exploded in midair after taking off from Moscow Aug. 24, killing 90 people. Chechen rebels, Sept. 1, 2004, seized control of a school in Beslan, North Ossetia, taking more than 1,100 hostages. Russian troops stormed the school Sept. 3; more than 330 people died, including 186 children. Putin cited the terrorist threat Sept. 13 in proposing a government overhaul that tightened his control over parliament and regional officeholders. Russian forces killed Chechen rebel leader Aslan Maskhadov, Mar. 8, 2005, and Chechen guerrilla leader Shamil Basayev, organizer of the terrorist attack at Beslan, July 10, 2006.

Constitutionally barred from seeking another term, Pres. Putin backed his protégé Dmitri Medvedev, who won the presidential election Mar. 2, 2008. After taking office May 7 Medvedev named Putin as prime min. A long-simmering conflict with Georgia erupted into open warfare Aug. 7-16. Russia dispatched troops to support secessionists in the enclaves of South Ossetia and Abkhazia and launched assaults on strategic Georgian cities; a cease-fire left thousands of Russian troops in the breakaway regions, which Pres. Medvedev recognized as independent, Aug. 26, 2008.

An economic boom fueled by oil and gas sales stalled in late 2008. The global financial crisis and a drop in oil prices led to turmoil in Russian financial markets, for which the government put together a $130-bil emergency rescue plan. As the crisis deepened, the government loaned banks $37 bil Oct. 7 and began buying shares to prop up the Russian stock exchange.

Russia declared, Apr. 16, 2009, that it had ended counterterrorism operations in Chechnya; from June through Aug., there was an upsurge of insurgent violence in Chechnya and neighboring Dagestan and Ingushetia. Female suicide bombers from Dagestan struck two Moscow subway stations Mar. 29, 2010, killing 40 people. A bombing at a Moscow airport Jan. 24, 2011, killed 37.

With U.S.-Russia relations strained since the 2008 Georgia war, Medvedev and Pres. Barack Obama Apr. 8, 2010, signed a nuclear arms reduction treaty known as New START, which was ratified by the U.S. Senate Dec. 22. Medvedev announced Sept. 24, 2011, that Putin would run for president in elections Mar. 2012, with Medvedev then serving as his prime min. In Dec. 2011 parliamentary elections, Putin's party, United Russia, failed to garner 50% of the vote. Tens of thousands marched through Moscow, Dec 10 and Dec. 24, calling for Putin's resignation. About 120,000 people protested in Moscow during a sanctioned event, Feb. 4, 2012. Unsanctioned protests followed, including the performance of a "punk prayer" at Christ the Savior Cathedral in Moscow, Feb. 21, by members of an anti-Putin punk collective called Pussy Riot. Putin nonetheless won 64% of the vote in the Mar. 4, 2012, election, though there were again claims of fraud. Three members of Pussy Riot were jailed in Mar. 2012. They were convicted of hooliganism and sentenced to two years in jail Aug. 17, 2012, despite international criticism. Putin signed a bill Dec. 28 preventing U.S. citizens from adopting Russian children, a move seen as retaliation for a U.S. law taking action against human rights abuses in Russia.

The Russian Space Agency announced Jan. 15, 2013, plans to send an unmanned craft to the moon in 2015. Putin signed a law banning "homosexual propaganda" June 30, making it illegal to advocate publicly for gay rights. The Putin administration disregarded U.S. wishes and granted temporary asylum to National Security Admin. whistleblower Edward Snowden Aug. 1. As the U.S. threatened to use force in Syria in response to its use of chemical weapons, Russia Sept. 9 proposed that Syrian chemical weapons be placed under international control. Russian-U.S. negotiators reached an agreement requiring Syria to relinquish its chemical weapons; the agreement was reinforced by a UN Security Council resolution Sept. 27.

Sochi, Russia, was scheduled to host the 2014 Winter Olympic Games Feb. 7-23, 2014.

Rwanda
Republic of Rwanda

People: Population: 12,012,589. **Age distrib.:** <15: 42.3%; 65+: 2.5%. **Pop. density:** 1,261.2 per sq mi, 487 per sq km. **Urban:** 19.1%. **Ethnic groups:** Hutu (Bantu) 84%, Tutsi (Hamitic) 15%, Twa (Pygmy) 1%. **Languages:** Kinyarwanda (universal Bantu vernacular), French, English (all official); Swahili (used in commercial centers). **Religions:** Roman Catholic 57%, Protestant 26%, Adventist 11%, Muslim 5%, none 2%.

Geography: Total area: 10,169 sq mi, 26,338 sq km; **Land area:** 9,524 sq mi, 24,668 sq km. **Location:** In E central Africa. **Neighbors:** Uganda on N, Dem. Rep. of the Congo on W, Burundi on S, Tanzania on E. **Topography:** Grassy uplands and hills cover most of country, with chain of volcanoes in the NW. The source of the Nile R. is in headwaters of the Kagera (Akagera) R., SW of Kigali. **Capital:** Kigali, 1,003,570.

Government: Type: Republic. **Head of state:** Pres. Paul Kagame; b. Oct. 23, 1957; in office: Apr. 22, 2000 (de facto from Mar. 24). **Head of gov.:** Prime Min. Pierre Damien Habumuremyi; b. Feb. 21, 1961; in office: Oct. 7, 2011. **Local divisions:** 4 provinces, 1 city. **Defense budget:** $73 mil. **Active troops:** 33,000.

Economy: Industries: cement, agric. prods., small-scale beverages, soap, furniture, shoes, plastic goods, textiles, cigarettes. **Chief crops:** coffee, tea, pyrethrum (insecticide made from chrysanthemums), bananas, beans, sorghum, potatoes. **Natural resources:** gold, tin ore, tungsten ore, methane, hydropower. **Arable land:** 49.5%. **Livestock:** cattle: 1.1 mil; chickens: 4.4 mil; goats: 3 mil; pigs: 706,472; sheep: 829,000. **Fish catch:** 17,788 metric tons. **Electricity prod.:** 280.2 mil kWh. **Labor force:** agric. 90%, industry and services 10%.

Finance: Monetary unit: Franc (RWF) (Sept. 2013: 653.45 = $1 U.S.). **GDP:** $15.7 bil; **per capita GDP:** $1,500; **GDP growth:** 7.7%. **Imports:** $1.6 bil; Kenya 18.4%, Uganda 16.6%, UAE 8.3%, China 6.9%, India 5.4%, Tanzania 5.4%, Belgium 4.3%. **Exports:** $451.3 mil; Kenya 32.6%, Dem. Rep. of the Congo 13.1%, China 11.7%, Malaysia 10.4%, U.S. 5.6%, Swaziland 5.2%, Pakistan 4.1%. **Tourism:** $282 mil. **Budget:** $1.9 bil. **Total reserves less gold:** $847.8 mil. **CPI change:** 6.3%.

Transport: Civil aviation: 4 airports. **Chief ports:** Cyangugu, Gisenyi, Kibuye.

Communications: TV sets: 8 per 1,000 pop. **Radios:** 854 per 1,000 pop. **Telephone lines:** 0.4 per 100 pop. **Internet:** 8%.

Health: Life expect.: 57.3 male; 60.4 female. **Births:** 35.5 per 1,000 pop. **Deaths:** 9.4 per 1,000 pop. **Natural inc.:** 2.61%. **Infant mortality:** 61.0 per 1,000 live births. **HIV rate:** 2.9%.

Education: Compulsory: ages 7-15. **Literacy:** 65.9%.

Major intl. organizations: UN (FAO, IBRD, ILO, IMF, WHO), AU, the Commonwealth, WTO.

Embassy: 1714 New Hampshire Ave. NW 20009; 232-2882. **Website:** www.gov.rw

For centuries, the Tutsi dominated the Hutu majority. A civil war broke out in 1959 and Tutsi power was ended. Many Tutsi went into exile. Rwanda, which had been part of the Belgian UN trusteeship of Rwanda-Urundi, became independent July 1, 1962.

A large-scale massacre of Tutsi occurred in 1963. Hutu rivalries led to a bloodless coup July 1973 in which Hutu army officer Juvénal Habyarimana took power. After another invasion and coup attempt by Tutsi exiles in 1990, a multiparty democracy was established.

Renewed ethnic strife led to an Aug. 1993 peace accord between the government and rebels of the Tutsi-led Rwandan Patriotic Front (RPF). But after Habyarimana and Burundi Pres. Cyprien Ntaryamira were killed Apr. 6, 1994, in a suspicious plane crash, violence broke out. More than 1 mil may have died in massacres, mostly of Tutsi by Hutu militias, and in civil warfare as the RPF sought power. About 2 mil Tutsi and Hutu fled to camps in Zaire (now Dem. Rep. of the Congo) and other countries; many died of disease. French troops under a UN mandate moved into SW Rwanda June 23 to establish a safe zone. The RPF claimed victory, installing a government led by a moderate Hutu president in July. French troops pulled out Aug. 22. A UN peacekeeping mission ended Mar. 8, 1996. More than 1 mil refugees, mostly Hutu, returned to Rwanda in Nov.-Dec. 1996.

Firing squads Apr. 24, 1998, executed 22 people convicted of genocide. Former Prime Min. Jean Kambanda pleaded guilty May 1 before the UN tribunal and received a life sentence Sept. 4, 1998. RPF leader Maj. Gen. Paul Kagame became Rwanda's first Tutsi president Apr. 22, 2000.

Rwandans approved a new constitution, May 26, 2003; reelected Pres. Kagame, Aug. 25; and chose a new parliament, Sept. 29-30. Former Pres. Bizimungu was sentenced to 15 years for embezzlement, June 2004, but was pardoned by Kagame and released, Apr. 6, 2007. Rwanda cut diplomatic ties with France Nov. 24, 2006, after a French judge linked Kagame and his close aides to the 1994 deaths of Habyarimana and Ntaryamira. The country restored relations with France, Nov. 2009, when Rwanda joined the Commonwealth.

Accused of being one of the architects of the 1994 genocide, Col. Theoneste Bagosora was convicted and sentenced to life in prison by the UN tribunal Dec. 18, 2008. A Rwandan court handed out a life sentence, Jan. 20, 2009, to former Justice Min. Agnes Ntamabyariro for her role in inciting the massacres. Up to 4,000 Rwandan troops fought that month alongside Congolese forces against Hutu militias in E Dem. Rep. of the Congo. After a campaign criticized as repressive by human rights groups, Pres. Kagame won reelection Aug. 9, 2010.

Rwanda's steady economic growth has been accompanied by U.S. funding for military training and the control of HIV/AIDS and malaria. An Oct. 17, 2012, UN report found that the Rwanda military was backing M23 rebel troops in the Dem. Rep of the Congo. The U.S. announced in Oct. 2013 that it was sanctioning Rwanda for its continued support of M23 by withholding military funding.

Saint Kitts and Nevis
Federation of Saint Kitts and Nevis

People: Population: 51,134. **Age distrib.:** <15: 21.9%; 65+: 7.8%. **Pop. density:** 507.4 per sq mi, 195.9 per sq km. **Urban:** 32%. **Ethnic group:** predominantly black; some British, Portuguese, Lebanese. **Language:** English (official). **Religions:** Anglican, other Protestant, Roman Catholic.

Geography: Total area: 101 sq mi, 261 sq km; **Land area:** 101 sq mi, 261 sq km. **Location:** In N part of the Leeward group of Lesser Antilles in E Caribbean Sea. **Neighbors:** Antigua and Barbuda to E. **Topography:** St. Kitts has forested volcanic slopes; Nevis rises from beaches to central peak. Climate is tropical moderated by sea breezes. **Capital:** Basseterre, 12,496.

Government: Type: Parliamentary democracy. **Head of state:** Queen Elizabeth II, rep. by Gov.-Gen. Sir Edmund Lawrence; in office: Jan. 2, 2013. **Head of gov.:** Prime Min. Denzil Douglas; b. Jan. 14, 1953; in office: July 6, 1995. **Local divisions:** 14 parishes. **Defense budget/active troops:** NA.

Economy: Industries: tourism, cotton, salt, copra, clothing, footwear, beverages. **Chief crops:** sugarcane, rice, yams, vegetables, bananas. **Arable land:** 19.2%. **Livestock:** cattle: 3,500; chickens: 80,000; goats: 9,000; pigs: 7,000; sheep: 7,000. **Fish catch:** 31,002 metric tons. **Electricity prod.:** 135 mil kWh. **Labor force:** NA.

Finance: Monetary unit: East Caribbean Dollar (XCD) (Sept. 2013: 2.70 = $1 U.S.). **GDP:** $946.3 mil; **per capita GDP:** $16,500; **GDP growth:** -0.9%. **Imports:** $339.6 mil; Algeria 59.9%, U.S. 12%, Trinidad and Tobago 8.3%. **Exports:** $57 mil; U.S. 55.3%, Canada 9.6%, Bangladesh 6.2%. **Tourism:** $94 mil. **Budget:** $222.2 mil. **Total reserves less gold:** $263.5 mil. **CPI change:** 1.4%.

Transport: Railways: 31 mi. **Civil aviation:** 2 airports. **Chief ports:** Basseterre, Charlestown.

Communications: TV sets: 312 per 1,000 pop. **Radios:** 697 per 1,000 pop. **Telephone lines:** 37.2 per 100 pop. **Internet:** 79.3%.

Health: Life expect.: 72.7 male; 77.5 female. **Births:** 13.8 per 1,000 pop. **Deaths:** 7.1 per 1,000 pop. **Natural inc.:** 0.67%. **Infant mortality:** 9.2 per 1,000 live births. **HIV rate:** NA.

Education: Compulsory: ages 5-16. **Literacy:** NA.

Major intl. organizations: UN (FAO, IBRD, ILO, IMF, WHO), Caricom, the Commonwealth, OAS, OECS, WTO.

Embassy: 3216 New Mexico Ave. NW 20016; 686-2636.

Website: www.gov.kn

St. Kitts (formerly St. Christopher; known by indigenous peoples as Liamuiga) and Nevis were reached and named by Columbus in 1493. They were settled by Britain in 1623, but ownership was disputed with France until 1713. They were part of the Leeward Islands Federation, 1871-1956, and the Federation of the West Indies, 1958-62. The colony achieved self-government as an Associated State of the UK in 1967, becoming independent, Sept. 19, 1983, and the smallest independent nation in the Western Hemisphere. A secession referendum on Nevis, Aug. 10, 1998, fell short of the two-thirds majority required.

Saint Lucia

People: Population: 162,781. **Age distrib.:** <15: 21.6%; 65+: 10.2%. **Pop. density:** 695.7 per sq mi, 268.6 per sq km. **Urban:** 17.5%. **Ethnic groups:** black 83%, mixed 12%, East Indian 2%. **Languages:** English (official), French patois. **Religions:** Roman Catholic 68%, Protestant 18% (Seventh-Day Adventist 9%, Pentecostal 6%, Anglican 2%, Evangelical 2%), other Christian 5%, Rastafarian 2%, none 5%.

Geography: Total area: 238 sq mi, 616 sq km; **Land area:** 234 sq mi, 606 sq km. **Location:** In E Caribbean, 2nd largest of Windward Isls. **Neighbors:** Martinique to N, St. Vincent to S. **Topography:** Mountainous, volcanic in origin; Soufrière Volcanic Centre in S. Wooded mountains run N-S to Mt. Gimie (3,145 ft) with streams through fertile valleys. **Capital:** Castries, 20,645.

Government: Type: Parliamentary democracy. **Head of state:** Queen Elizabeth II, rep. by Gov.-Gen. Dame Calliopa Pearlette Louisy; b. June 8, 1946; in office: Sept. 17, 1997. **Head of gov.:** Prime Min. Kenny Davis Anthony; b. Jan. 8, 1951; in office: Nov. 30, 2011. **Local divisions:** 11 quarters. **Defense budget:** NA. **Active troops:** No regular military forces.

Economy: Industries: tourism, clothing, electronic components assembly, beverages, corrugated cardboard boxes, lime proc., coconut proc. **Chief crops:** bananas, coconuts, vegetables, citrus, root crops, cocoa. **Natural resources:** forests, beaches, pumice, mineral springs, geothermal potential. **Arable land:** 4.9%. **Livestock:** cattle: 11,000; chickens: 450,000; goats: 9,500; pigs: 20,000; sheep: 10,000. **Fish catch:** 1,975 metric tons. **Electricity prod.:** 358 mil kWh. **Labor force:** agric. 21.7%, industry 24.7%, services 53.6%.

Finance: Monetary unit: East Caribbean Dollar (XCD) (Sept. 2013: 2.70 = $1 U.S.). **GDP:** $2.2 bil; **per capita GDP:** $13,300; **GDP growth:** -0.4%. **Imports:** $552.3 mil; Brazil 55%, U.S. 18.3%, Trinidad and Tobago 9.5%. **Exports:** $203.3 mil; U.S. 13.1%, Peru 10.1%, UK 9.7%, Antigua and Barbuda 9.7%, Dominica 9.4%, France 8.5%, Barbados 8.5%, Trinidad and Tobago 7.9%, Grenada 6.4%. **Tourism:** $335 mil. **Budget (2011):** $222.2 mil. **Total reserves less gold:** $232 mil. **CPI change:** 4.2%.

Transport: Civil aviation: 2 airports. **Chief ports:** Castries, Culde-Sac, Vieux-Fort.

Communications: TV sets: 341 per 1,000 pop. **Radios:** 1,091 per 1,000 pop. **Telephone lines:** 20.7 per 100 pop. **Internet:** 48.6%.

Health: Life expect.: 74.5 male; 80.1 female. **Births:** 14.2 per 1,000 pop. **Deaths:** 7.2 per 1,000 pop. **Natural inc.:** 0.70%. **Infant mortality:** 12.1 per 1,000 live births. **HIV rate:** NA.

Education: Compulsory: ages 5-14. **Literacy:** NA.

Major intl. organizations: UN (FAO, IBRD, ILO, IMF, WHO), Caricom, the Commonwealth, OAS, OECS, WTO.

Embassy: 3216 New Mexico Ave. NW 20016; 364-6792.

Website: www.stlucia.gov.lc

St. Lucia was ceded to Britain by France with the Treaty of Paris, 1814. Self-government was granted with the West Indies Act, 1967. Independence was attained Feb. 22, 1979.

Saint Vincent and the Grenadines

People: Population: 103,220. **Age distrib.:** <15: 23.4%; 65+: 8.4%. **Pop. density:** 687.2 per sq mi, 265.3 per sq km. **Urban:** 49.3%. **Ethnic groups:** black 66%, mixed 19%, East Indian 6%, European 4%, Carib Amerindian 2%. **Languages:** English, French patois. **Religions:** Protestant 75% (Anglican 47%, Methodist 28%), Roman Catholic 13%, other (incl. Hindu, Seventh-Day Adventist, other Protestant) 12%.

Geography: Total area: 150 sq mi, 389 sq km; **Land area:** 150 sq mi, 389 sq km. **Location:** In E Caribbean; St. Vincent (133 sq mi) and the northern islets of the Grenadines form a part of Windward chain. **Neighbors:** St. Lucia to N, Barbados to E, Grenada to S. **Topography:** St. Vincent is volcanic, with a ridge of thickly wooded mountains running its length. **Capital:** Kingstown, 30,863.

Government: Type: Parliamentary democracy. **Head of state:** Queen Elizabeth II, rep. by Sir Frederick Ballantyne; b. July 5, 1936; in office: Sept. 2, 2002. **Head of gov.:** Prime Min. Ralph Gonsalves; b. Aug. 8, 1946; in office: Mar. 29, 2001. **Local divisions:** 6 parishes. **Defense budget:** NA. **Active troops:** No regular military forces.

Economy: Industries: tourism, food proc., cement, furniture, clothing, starch. **Chief crops:** bananas, coconuts, sweet potatoes, spices. **Natural resources:** hydropower. **Arable land:** 12.8%. **Livestock:** cattle: 5,100; chickens: 270,000; goats: 8,500; pigs: 6,300; sheep: 12,500. **Fish catch:** 76,578 metric tons. **Electricity prod.:** 136 mil kWh. **Labor force:** agric. 26%, industry 17%, services 57%.

Finance: Monetary unit: East Caribbean Dollar (XCD) (Sept. 2013: 2.70 = $1 U.S.). **GDP:** $1.3 bil; **per capita GDP:** $12,000; **GDP growth:** 0.5%. **Imports:** $295.3 mil; Singapore 27%, Trinidad and Tobago 24.1%, U.S. 18.3%, China 5.4%, Barbados 5.3%. **Exports:** $47.1 mil; Trinidad and Tobago 15.2%, St. Lucia 13.5%, Turkey 12.1%, Barbados 11.2%, Dominica 8.9%, Grenada 8.5%, Antigua and Barbuda 7.6%. **Tourism:** $93 mil. **Budget:** $185.2 mil. **Total reserves less gold:** $111 mil. **CPI change:** 2.6%.

Transport: Civil aviation: 5 airports. **Chief port:** Kingstown.

Communications: TV sets: 341 per 1,000 pop. **Radios:** 1,025 per 1,000 pop. **Telephone lines:** 17.7 per 100 pop. **Internet:** 47.5%.

Health: Life expect.: 72.7 male; 76.6 female. **Births:** 14.1 per 1,000 pop. **Deaths:** 7.1 per 1,000 pop. **Natural inc.:** 0.71%. **Infant mortality:** 13.5 per 1,000 live births. **HIV rate:** NA.

Education: Compulsory: ages 5-15. **Literacy:** NA.

Major intl. organizations: UN (FAO, IBRD, ILO, IMF, WHO), Caricom, the Commonwealth, OAS, OECS, WTO.

Embassy: 3216 New Mexico Ave. NW 20016; 364-6730.

Website: www.gov.vc

Columbus landed on St. Vincent on Jan. 22, 1498 (St. Vincent's Day). Britain and France both laid claim to the island in the 17th and 18th cent.; the Treaty of Versailles, 1783, ceded it to Britain. Associated State status was granted 1969; independence was attained Oct. 27, 1979.

Samoa
Independent State of Samoa

People: Population: 195,476. **Age distrib.:** <15: 34%; 65+: 5.4%. **Pop. density:** 179.5 per sq mi, 69.3 per sq km. **Urban:** 19.9%. **Ethnic groups:** Samoan 93%, Euronesians (mixed European,

Polynesian) 7%. **Languages:** Samoan (Polynesian) (official), English. **Religions:** Protestant 60% (Congregationalist 35%, Methodist 15%, Assembly of God 7%, Seventh-Day Adventist 4%), Roman Catholic 20%, Mormon 13%, other Christian 5%.

Geography: Total area: 1,093 sq mi, 2,831 sq km; **Land area:** 1,089 sq mi, 2,821 sq km. **Location:** In S Pacific O. **Neighbors:** Nearest are Fiji to SW, Tonga to S. **Topography:** Main islands, Savaii (659 sq mi) and Upolu (432 sq mi), both ruggedly mountainous, and small islands Manono and Apolima. **Capital:** Apia, 36,513.

Government: Type: Parliamentary democracy. **Head of state:** Tuiatua Tupua Tamasese Efi; b. Mar. 1, 1938; in office: June 20, 2007. **Head of gov.:** Prime Min. Tuilaepa Sailele Malielegaoi; b. Apr. 14, 1945; in office: Nov. 23, 1998. **Local divisions:** 11 districts. **Defense budget:** NA. **Active troops:** No regular military forces. Informal defense ties with New Zealand.

Economy: Industries: food proc., building materials, auto parts. **Chief crops:** coconuts, bananas, taro, yams, coffee, cocoa. **Natural resources:** hardwood forests, fish, hydropower. **Arable land:** 2.8%. **Livestock:** cattle: 30,000; chickens: 620,000; pigs: 204,000. **Fish catch:** 11,805 metric tons. **Electricity prod.:** 120.2 mil kWh. **Labor force:** agric. 65%.

Finance: Monetary unit: Tala (WST) (Sept. 2013: 2.35 = $1 U.S.). **GDP:** $1.1 bil; **per capita GDP:** $6,300; **GDP growth:** 1.2%. **Imports:** (2011) $318.7 mil; Fiji 19%, New Zealand 18.8%, Singapore 18.2%, China 15.5%, Australia 5.8%, U.S. 5.3%. **Exports:** (2011) $11.4 mil; American Samoa 50.4%, Australia 22.6%. **Tourism:** $148 mil. **Budget:** $263.9 mil. **Total reserves less gold:** $168.7 mil. **CPI change:** 2%.

Transport: Civil aviation: 224.9 mil pass.-mi; 1 airport. **Chief port:** Apia.

Communications: TV sets: 122 per 1,000 pop. **Radios:** 312 per 1,000 pop. **Telephone lines** (2005): 10.8 per 100 pop. **Internet:** 12.9%.

Health: Life expect.: 70.1 male; 76.0 female. **Births:** 21.7 per 1,000 pop. **Deaths:** 5.3 per 1,000 pop. **Natural inc.:** 1.64%. **Infant mortality:** 21.0 per 1,000 live births. **HIV rate:** NA.

Education: Compulsory: ages 5-12. **Literacy:** 98.8%.

Major intl. organizations: UN (FAO, IBRD, ILO, IMF, WHO), the Commonwealth, WTO.

Embassy: 800 Second Ave., Ste. 400J, New York, NY 10017; (212) 599-6196.

Website: www.govt.ws

Samoa (formerly known as Western Samoa to distinguish it from American Samoa, a U.S. territory) was a German colony, 1899 to 1914, when New Zealand landed troops and took over. It became a New Zealand mandate under the League of Nations and, in 1945, a New Zealand UN Trusteeship.

An elected local government took office in Oct. 1959, and the country became fully independent Jan. 1, 1962. Malietoa Tanumafili II, Samoa's head of state since independence, was succeeded by Tuiatua Tupua Tamasese Efi. At the end of the day on Dec. 29, 2011, Samoa moved west of the Intl. Date Line to simplify trade with Australia and New Zealand. Samoa is now 3 hours ahead of eastern Australia rather than 21 hours behind.

San Marino
Republic of San Marino

People: Population: 32,448. **Age distrib.:** <15: 16.2%; 65+: 18.5%. **Pop. density:** 1,377.7 per sq mi, 531.9 per sq km. **Urban:** 94.1%. **Ethnic groups:** Sammarinese, Italian. **Language:** Italian. **Religion:** Roman Catholic.

Geography: Total area: 24 sq mi, 61 sq km; **Land area:** 24 sq mi, 61 sq km. **Location:** In N central Italy near Adriatic coast. **Neighbors:** Completely surrounded by Italy. **Topography:** The country lies on slopes of Mt. Titano. **Capital:** San Marino, 4,280.

Government: Type: Republic. **Heads of state:** Two captains regent, elected by parliament from among its members, to 6-month term. **Head of gov.:** Sec. of State for Foreign and Political Affairs Pasquale Valentini; b. July 19, 1953; in office: Dec. 5, 2012. **Local divisions** 9 municipalities. **Defense budget:** NA. **Active troops:** No regular military forces. Italy responsible for defense.

Economy: Industries: tourism, banking, textiles, electronics, ceramics, cement, wine. **Chief crops:** wheat, grapes, corn, olives. **Natural resources:** building stone. **Arable land:** 16.7%. **Labor force:** agric. 0.1%, industry 34.4%, services 65.5%.

Finance: Monetary unit: Euro (EUR) (Sept. 2013: 0.76 = $1 U.S.). **GDP:** $1.4 bil; **per capita GDP** (2009): $36,200; **GDP growth:** –4%. **Imports** (2011): $2.6 bil. **Exports** (2011): $3.8 bil. **Budget** (2011): $694.7 mil. **Total reserves less gold:** $385 mil. **CPI change:** NA.

Transport: NA.

Communications: TV sets: 792 per 1,000 pop. **Radios:** 1,322 per 1,000 pop. **Telephone lines:** 58.5 per 100 pop. **Internet:** 50.9%.

Health: Life expect.: 80.6 male; 85.9 female. **Births:** 8.8 per 1,000 pop. **Deaths:** 8.2 per 1,000 pop. **Natural inc.:** 0.06%. **Infant mortality:** 4.6 per 1,000 live births. **HIV rate:** NA.

Education: Compulsory: ages 6-15. **Literacy:** NA.

Major intl. organizations: UN (FAO, IBRD, ILO, IMF, WHO), OSCE.

Honorary Consulate: 1899 L St. NW, Ste. 500, 20036; 223-3517. **Website:** www.visitsanmarino.com or www.sanmarino.sm

San Marino claims to be the world's oldest republic, having been founded in the 4th cent. It has had a treaty of friendship with Italy since 1862. A Communist-led coalition ruled 1947-57; a similar coalition ruled 1978-86. The Pact for San Marino, a center-right coalition, won parliamentary elections Nov. 9, 2008.

São Tomé and Príncipe
Democratic Republic of São Tomé and Príncipe

People: Population: 186,817. **Age distrib.:** <15: 44%; 65+: 3%. **Pop. density:** 501.9 per sq mi, 193.8 per sq km. **Urban:** 62.7%. **Ethnic groups:** mestico, angolares (descendants of Angolan slaves), forros (descendants of freed slaves), servicais (contract laborers fr. Angola, Mozambique, Cape Verde), tongas (children of servicais born in country), Europeans (primarily Portuguese). **Language:** Portuguese (official). **Religions:** Catholic 70%, Evangelical 3%, New Apostolic 2%, Adventist 2%, none 19%.

Geography: Total area: 372 sq mi, 964 sq km; **Land area:** 372 sq mi, 964 sq km. **Location:** In Gulf of Guinea about 125 mi off W central Africa. **Neighbors:** Gabon, Equatorial Guinea to E. **Topography:** São Tomé and Príncipe Islands, part of an extinct volcano chain, are both covered by lush forests and croplands. **Capital:** São Tomé, 63,952.

Government: Type: Republic. **Head of state:** Pres. Manuel Pinto da Costa; b. Aug. 5, 1937; in office: Sept. 3, 2011. **Head of gov.:** Prime Min. Gabriel Arcanjo Ferreira da Costa; in office: Dec. 10, 2012. **Local divisions:** 2 provinces. **Defense budget/active troops:** NA.

Economy: Industries: light constr., textiles, soap, beer, fish proc., timber. **Chief crops:** cocoa, coconuts, palm kernels, copra, cinnamon, pepper, coffee, bananas, papayas, beans. **Natural resources:** fish, hydropower. **Arable land:** 9.1%. **Livestock:** cattle: 5,100; chickens: 440,000; goats: 5,600; pigs: 2,900; sheep: 3,200. **Fish catch:** 3,900 metric tons. **Electricity prod.:** 30 mil kWh. **Labor force:** Pop. mainly engaged in subsistence agric. and fishing; shortage of skilled workers.

Finance: Monetary unit: Dobra (STD) (Sept. 2013: 18,675.00 = $1 U.S.). **GDP:** $408.6 mil; **per capita GDP:** $2,400; **GDP growth:** 4%. **Imports:** $121.6 mil; Portugal 63%, Gabon 6%. **Exports:** $11.7 mil; Netherlands 32.7%, Belgium 21.4%, Spain 10.8%, Nigeria 5.7%, U.S. 5%. **Tourism:** $15 mil. **Budget:** $131.8 mil. **Total reserves less gold:** $51.6 mil. **CPI change:** 10.4%.

Transport: Civil aviation: 12.4 mil pass.-mi; 2 airports. **Chief port:** São Tomé.

Communications: TV sets: 127 per 1,000 pop. **Radios:** 106 per 1,000 pop. **Telephone lines:** 4.7 per 100 pop. **Internet:** 21.6%.

Health: Life expect.: 62.6 male; 65.1 female. **Births:** 36.1 per 1,000 pop. **Deaths:** 7.7 per 1,000 pop. **Natural inc.:** 2.84%. **Infant mortality:** 50.5 per 1,000 live births. **HIV rate:** 1%.

Education: Compulsory: ages 6-16. **Literacy:** 69.5%.

Major intl. organizations: UN (FAO, IBRD, ILO, IMF, WHO), AU, WTO (observer).

Permanent UN mission: 460 Park Ave., 11th Fl., New York, NY 10022; (212) 317-0533.

Website: www.gov.st

The Portuguese discovered the islands in 1471 and brought the first settlers—convicts and exiled Jews. Sugar planting was replaced by the slave trade as the chief economic activity until coffee and cocoa were introduced in the 19th cent.

Portugal agreed, 1974, to turn the colony over to the Gabon-based Movement for the Liberation of São Tomé and Príncipe; its East German-trained leader, Manuel Pinto da Costa, became its first president. Independence came July 12, 1975. Democratic reforms were instituted in 1987. In 1991, Miguel Trovoada won the first free presidential election. A military coup that ousted Trovoada Aug. 15, 1995, was reversed a week later after Angolan mediation. Trovoada defeated Pinto da Costa in a presidential runoff election July 21, 1996.

Fradique de Menezes, a wealthy cocoa exporter, beat Pinto da Costa in July 29, 2001, presidential elections. The government was ousted in a military coup July 16, 2003, but was restored to power a week later and reelected July 30, 2006. After the opposition Independent Democratic Action party won parliamentary elections Aug. 1, 2010, Patrice Trovoada (son of the former president) was chosen to head the new government. Pinto da Costa returned to power after a presidential runoff vote Aug. 7, 2011. The National Assembly elected Gabriel Arcanjo Ferreira da Costa prime min. Dec. 2012. The country, long one of the world's poorest, has sought to develop oil deposits in the Gulf of Guinea.

Saudi Arabia
Kingdom of Saudi Arabia

People: Population: 26,939,583. **Age distrib.:** <15: 28.2%; 65+: 3.1%. **Pop. density:** 32.5 per sq mi, 12.5 per sq km. **Urban:** 82.3%. **Ethnic groups:** Arab 90%, Afro-Asian 10%. **Language:** Arabic (official). **Religion:** Muslim (official) 100%.

Geography: Total area: 830,000 sq mi, 2,149,690 sq km; **Land area:** 830,000 sq mi, 2,149,690 sq km. **Location:** Occupies most of Arabian Peninsula in Mid-East. **Neighbors:** Kuwait, Iraq, Jordan on N; Yemen, Oman on S; United Arab Emirates, Qatar on E. **Topography:** Bordered by Red Sea on W. The highlands in W, up to 9,000 ft, slope as arid, barren desert to the Persian Gulf on E. **Capital:** Riyadh, 5,450,820. **Cities (urban aggl.):** Jiddah, 3,578,315; Mecca, 1,590,505; Medina, 1,142,292.

Government: Type: Monarchy. **Head of state and gov.:** King Abdullah bin Abdul Aziz; b. Aug. 1, 1924; in office: Aug. 1, 2005. **Local divisions:** 13 provinces. **Defense budget:** NA. **Active troops:** 233,500.

Economy: Industries: crude oil prod., petroleum refining, basic petrochemicals, ammonia, industrial gases, caustic soda, cement, fertilizer, plastics, metals, commercial ship repair, commercial

aircraft repair, constr. **Chief crops:** wheat, barley, tomatoes, melons, dates, citrus. **Natural resources:** petroleum, nat. gas, iron ore, gold, copper. **Crude oil reserves:** 267.9 bil bbls (incl. half of Neutral Zone reserves). **Arable land:** 1.4%. **Livestock:** cattle: 400,000; chickens: 147 mil; goats: 3.2 mil; sheep: 7.3 mil. **Fish catch:** 91,236 metric tons. **Electricity prod.** (2011): 239.2 bil kWh. **Labor force:** agric. 6.7%, industry 21.4%, services 71.9%.

Finance: Monetary unit: Riyal (SAR) (Sept. 2013: 3.75 = $1 U.S.). **GDP:** $921.7 bil; **per capita GDP:** $31,800; **GDP growth:** 6.8%. **Imports:** $136.8 bil; China 13.5%, U.S. 13.2%, South Korea 6.7%, Germany 6.5%, India 6.3%, Japan 6%. **Exports:** $395 bil; U.S. 14.3%, China 13.7%, Japan 13.7%, South Korea 9.9%, India 8.2%, Singapore 4.3%. **Tourism:** $7.4 bil. **Budget:** $234.8 bil. **Total reserves less gold:** $656.5 bil. **Gold:** 10.4 mil oz t. **CPI change:** 2.9%.

Transport: Railways: 856 mi. **Motor vehicles:** 220.4 vehicles per 1,000 pop. **Civil aviation:** 18 bil pass.-mi; 82 airports. **Chief ports:** Ad Dammam, Al Jubayl, Jeddah, Yanbu al Bahr.

Communications: TV sets: 275 per 1,000 pop. **Radios:** 317 per 1,000 pop. **Telephone lines:** 16.7 per 100 pop. **Internet:** 54%.

Health: Life expect.: 72.6 male; 76.7 female. **Births:** 19.0 per 1,000 pop. **Deaths:** 3.3 per 1,000 pop. **Natural inc.:** 1.57%. **Infant mortality:** 15.1 per 1,000 live births. **HIV rate:** NA.

Education: Compulsory: ages 6-11. **Literacy:** 87.2%.

Major intl. organizations: UN (FAO, IBRD, ILO, IMF, WHO), AL, OPEC, WTO.

Embassy: 601 New Hampshire Ave. NW 20037; 342-3800.

Website: www.saudi.gov.sa

Before Muhammad, Arabia was divided among numerous warring tribes and small kingdoms. Muhammad united it in the early 7th cent. His successors conquered the entire Near East and North Africa, bringing Islam and the Arabic language. But Arabia soon returned to its former status.

Nejd, in central Arabia, long an independent state and center of the Wahhabi sect, fell under Turkish rule in the 18th cent. Ibn Saud, founder of the Saudi dynasty, overthrew the Turks, 1913. He captured Hasa, a Turkish province in eastern Arabia, also 1913; the Hejaz region in western Arabia, 1925; and most of Asir, in SW Arabia, by 1926. The discovery of oil in the 1930s transformed the nation.

The Hejaz contains the holy cities of Islam—Medina, where the Mosque of the Prophet enshrines the tomb of Muhammad, and Mecca, his birthplace. An estimated 3 mil Muslims make pilgrimage to Mecca annually.

Ibn Saud reigned until his death, Nov. 1953. Subsequent kings have been his sons. The king exercises authority with a Council of Ministers. The Islamic religious code is the law of the land. Alcohol and public entertainments are restricted; women have an inferior legal status.

Saudi Arabia has often allied itself with and purchased arms from the U.S. and other Western nations. Saudi units, nevertheless, fought against Western ally Israel in the 1948 and 1973 Arab-Israeli wars. Beginning with the 1967 Arab-Israeli war, Saudi Arabia gave large annual financial gifts to Egypt, Syria, Jordan, and Palestinian groups.

King Faisal played a leading role in the 1973-74 Arab oil embargo against the U.S. and other nations. Crown Prince Khalid was proclaimed king, Mar. 25, 1975, after the assassination of Faisal. Fahd became king, June 13, 1982, following Khalid's death.

After Iraq invaded Kuwait, Aug. 2, 1990, Saudi Arabia accepted the Kuwait royal family and over 400,000 Kuwaiti refugees. Western and Arab troops also deployed on Saudi soil before and during the 1991 Persian Gulf War.

When 15 of the 19 al-Qaeda hijackers who carried out the Sept. 11, 2001, attacks on the U.S. were found to be Saudi, some in the U.S. blamed the Saudi government for allowing Muslim extremism to flourish in Saudi Arabia. Policy differences over the Israeli-Palestinian dispute and Iraq (where Saudi jihadists supported the Sunni cause) were further irritants. The U.S. completed a pullout of its combat forces from Saudi Arabia, Sept. 2003.

Alarmed at guerrilla attacks that killed more than 100 people, mostly foreigners, in Saudi Arabia, 2003-04, the Saudis worked with the U.S. to increase antiterrorist activities. Islamist candidates on a "golden list" circulated by conservative clerics fared well in Feb.-Apr. 2005, municipal council elections, the country's first since 1963; women were barred from voting. King Fahd died Aug. 1, 2005, and was succeeded by his half-brother, Abdullah.

Hoping to contain the wave of 2011 Arab Spring uprisings that had challenged or toppled other entrenched regimes in North Africa and the Middle East, a Saudi-led Gulf Cooperation Council force suppressed protests in Bahrain Mar. 14. The Saudis also tried to aid monarchies in Jordan and Morocco, and sent $4 bil to assist Egypt's military council after Pres. Hosni Mubarak was ousted. King Abdullah announced Sept. 25, 2011, that women would have the right to vote and run for office by 2015 and allowed the nation's women athletes to compete in the 2012 Olympics for the first time. King Abdullah also decreed Jan. 11, 2013, that women would be permitted to hold 30 of the 150 seats on the government's Shura council, serving among the king's advisors. Saudi Arabia supplied weapons to members of the anti-government rebels in Syria's civil war.

Senegal
Republic of Senegal

People: Population: 13,300,410. **Age distrib.:** <15: 42.7%; 65+: 2.9%. **Pop. density:** 178.9 per sq mi, 69.1 per sq km. **Urban:** 42.5%. **Ethnic groups:** Wolof 43%, Pular 24%, Serer 15%, Jola 4%, Mandinka 3%, Soninke 1%, European and Lebanese 1%. **Languages:**

French (official), Wolof, Pulaar, Jola, Mandinka. **Religions:** Muslim 94%, Christian 5% (mostly Roman Catholic), indigenous beliefs 1%.

Geography: Total area: 75,955 sq mi, 196,722 sq km; **Land area:** 74,336 sq mi, 192,530 sq km. **Location:** At W extreme of Africa. **Neighbors:** Mauritania on N, Mali on E, Guinea and Guinea-Bissau on S; surrounds The Gambia on three sides. **Topography:** Low rolling plains cover most of Senegal, rising somewhat in SE. Swamp and jungles are in SW. **Capital:** Dakar, 3,035,470.

Government: Type: Republic. **Head of state:** Pres. Macky Sall; b. Dec. 11, 1961; in office: Apr. 2, 2012. **Head of gov.:** Prime Min. Aminata Touré; b. Oct. 12, 1962; in office: Sept. 3, 2013. **Local divisions:** 14 regions. **Defense budget** (2010): $210 mil. **Active troops:** 13,600.

Economy: Industries: agric. and fish proc., phosphate mining, fertilizer prod., petroleum refining, mining, constr. materials, ship constr. and repair. **Chief crops:** peanuts, millet, corn, sorghum, rice, cotton, tomatoes, green vegetables. **Natural resources:** fish, phosphates, iron ore. **Arable land:** 20%. **Livestock:** cattle: 3.3 mil; chickens: 44.2 mil; goats: 4.9 mil; pigs: 364,325; sheep: 5.5 mil. **Fish catch:** 427,468 metric tons. **Electricity prod.:** 2.8 bil kWh. **Labor force:** agric. 77.5%, industry and services 22.5%.

Finance: Monetary unit: West African CFA Franc (XOF) (Sept. 2013: 498.11 = $1 U.S.). **GDP:** $27 bil; **per capita GDP:** $2,100; **GDP growth:** 3.5%. **Imports:** $5.7 bil; France 16.2%, Nigeria 12.9%, India 6.3%, China 6.3%, UK 4.6%. **Exports:** $2.4 bil; Mali 14.4%, Switzerland 14.1%, India 11.9%, France 4.7%, Guinea 4.2%. **Tourism:** $484 mil. **Budget:** $4.2 bil. **Total reserves less gold:** $2.1 bil. **CPI change:** 1.4%.

Transport: Railways: 563 mi. **Civil aviation:** 612.1 mil pass.-mi; 9 airports. **Chief port:** Dakar.

Communications: TV sets: 44 per 1,000 pop. **Radios:** 536 per 1,000 pop. **Telephone lines:** 2.6 per 100 pop. **Internet:** 19.2%.

Health: Life expect.: 58.6 male; 62.6 female. **Births:** 35.6 per 1,000 pop. **Deaths:** 8.9 per 1,000 pop. **Natural inc.:** 2.68%. **Infant mortality:** 53.9 per 1,000 live births. **HIV rate:** 0.7%.

Education: Compulsory: ages 7-16. **Literacy:** 49.7%.

Major intl. organizations: UN and all of its specialized agencies, AU, WTO.

Embassy: 2112 Wyoming Ave. NW 20008; 234-0540.

Website: www.gouv.sn

Portuguese settlers arrived in the 15th cent., but French control grew from the 17th cent. The last independent Muslim state was subdued in 1893. Senegal became an independent republic Aug. 20, 1960, but French political and economic influence remained strong. Senegambia, a loose confederation of Senegal and The Gambia, was established in 1982 but dissolved seven years later.

Forty years of Socialist Party rule ended when Abdoulaye Wade, leader of the Senegalese Democratic Party, won a presidential run-off election, Mar. 19, 2000. A Senegalese ferry capsized off the coast of The Gambia Sept. 26, 2002, killing at least 1,863 people. A peace accord signed Dec. 30, 2004, with separatists in Cassamance Province, S Senegal, sought to end a 22-year insurgency. Pres. Wade was reelected Feb. 25, 2007, but lost his bid for a third term Mar. 26, 2012, to Macky Sall, his former prime min. Former Chad Pres. Hissòne Habré, accused of killing and torturing thousands in the 1980s, was arrested June 30, 2013, in Senegal, where authorities planned to try him for genocide and crimes against humanity.

Serbia
Republic of Serbia

People: Population: 7,243,007. **Age distrib.:** <15: 14.8%; 65+: 16.9%. **Pop. density:** 242.1 per sq mi, 93.5 per sq km. **Urban:** 56.4% (incl. Kosovo). **Ethnic groups:** Serb 83%, Hungarian 4%, Bosniak 2%, Romany 1%, Yugoslav 1%. **Languages:** Serbian (official), Hungarian, Bosniak, Romany. **Religions:** Serbian Orthodox 85%, Catholic 6%, Muslim 3%, Protestant 1%.

Geography: Total area: 29,913 sq mi, 77,474 sq km; **Land area:** 29,913 sq mi, 77,474 sq km. **Location:** On Balkan Peninsula in SE Europe. **Neighbors:** Croatia, Bosnia and Herzegovina on W; Hungary on N; Romania, Bulgaria on E; Montenegro, Albania, Macedonia on S. **Topography:** Terrain varies widely, with fertile plains drained by Danube and other rivers in N, limestone basins in E, and ancient mountains and hills in SE. **Capital:** Belgrade, 1,135,080.

Government: Type: Republic. **Head of state:** Pres. Tomislav Nikolić; b. Feb. 15, 1952; in office: May 31, 2012. **Head of gov.:** Prime Min. Ivica Dačić; b. Jan. 1, 1956; in office: July 27, 2012. **Local divisions:** 122 municipalities, 23 cities. **Defense budget:** $819 mil. **Active troops:** 28,150.

Economy: Industries: base metals, furniture, food proc., machinery, chemicals, sugar, tires, clothes, pharmaceuticals. **Chief crops:** wheat, maize, sugar beets, sunflowers, raspberries. **Natural resources:** oil, gas, coal, iron ore, copper, zinc, antimony, chromite, gold, silver, magnesium, pyrite, limestone, marble, salt. **Crude oil reserves:** 77.5 mil bbls. **Arable land:** 37.7%. **Livestock:** cattle: 936,570; chickens: 70 mil; goats: 129,720; pigs: 3.3 mil; sheep: 1.5 mil. **Fish catch:** 13,013 metric tons. **Electricity prod.:** 35.4 bil kWh. **Labor force:** agric. 21.9%, industry 19.5%, services 58.6%.

Finance: Monetary unit: Dinar (RSD) (Sept. 2013: 87.13 = $1 U.S.). **GDP:** $80 bil; **per capita GDP:** $10,600; **GDP growth:** –1.8%. **Imports:** $18.4 bil. **Exports:** $11.3 bil. **Tourism:** $906 mil. **Budget:** $18.4 bil (consolidated budget, incl. both central and local govts.). **Total reserves less gold:** $13.6 bil. **Gold:** 491,660 oz t. **CPI change:** 7.3%.

Transport: Railways: 2,100 mi. **Civil aviation:** 588.4 mil pass.-mi; 10 airports.

Communications: TV sets: 248 per 1,000 pop. **Telephone lines:** 30.2 per 100 pop. **Internet:** 48.1%.

Health: Life expect.: 71.9 male; 77.8 female. **Births:** 9.2 per 1,000 pop. **Deaths:** 13.8 per 1,000 pop. **Natural inc.:** −0.46%. **Infant mortality:** 6.3 per 1,000 live births. **HIV rate:** 0.1%.

Education: Compulsory: ages 7-14. **Literacy:** 98%.

Major intl. organizations: UN (FAO, IBRD, ILO, IMF, WHO), OSCE, WTO (observer).

Embassy: 2134 Kalorama Rd. NW 20008; 332-0333.

Website: www.srbija.gov.rs

Serbia was a vassal principality of Turkey from 1389 to 1878, when the Treaty of Berlin established it as an independent kingdom. After the Balkan wars, Serbia annexed Old Serbia and Macedonia, 1913.

When the Austro-Hungarian empire collapsed after WWI, the Kingdom of Serbs, Croats, and Slovenes—Yugoslavia after 1929—was formed from the provinces of Croatia, Dalmatia, Bosnia, Herzegovina, Slovenia, Vojvodina, and the independent state of Montenegro.

After Nazi Germany's occupation 1941-45, Yugoslavia became a federal republic, headed by Josip Broz, a Communist, known as Marshal Tito. He rejected Stalin's dictatorship and accepted economic and military aid from the West. After Tito died in 1980, Yugoslavia held together for a decade before breaking apart. During 1991-95, Serbia, under Pres. Slobodan Milosevic, supported ethnic Serb fighters in Croatia and in Bosnia and Herzegovina, which had declared independence. The republics of Serbia and Montenegro proclaimed a new Federal Republic of Yugoslavia, Apr. 17, 1992. The UN imposed sanctions on the newly reconstituted Yugoslavia to end the bloodshed in Bosnia.

A peace agreement was reached in 1995. A UN-backed war crimes tribunal began in May 1996 to try suspects from the former Yugoslavia. Mass protests erupted when Milosevic refused to accept opposition victories in local elections, Nov. 17; non-Communist governments took office in Belgrade and other cities, Feb. 1997. Barred from running for a third term as Serbian president, Milosevic had himself inaugurated as president of Yugoslavia, July 23, 1997.

Serbian efforts to suppress a secessionist movement in Kosovo led in Mar.-June 1999 to a war with the U.S. and its NATO allies; they accused Milosevic of pursuing a policy of ethnic cleansing against the predominantly Muslim Kosovars (ethnic Albanians). NATO stationed a multinational force in Kosovo, which was placed under UN administration.

Milosevic initially refused to accept defeat to opposition leader Vojislav Kostunica in a 2000 presidential election but resigned Oct. 6 after mass demonstrations. Kostunica was sworn in the next day. Charged with corruption and abuse of power, Milosevic surrendered to Serbian authorities Apr. 1, 2001. He was extradited June 28 to The Hague, where a UN tribunal had indicted him for war crimes. His trial began Feb. 12, 2002. He was found dead in prison Mar. 11, 2006, before a verdict was reached.

A pact to reconstitute Yugoslavia as a new union of Serbia and Montenegro took effect Feb. 4, 2003. Zoran Djindjic, premier of the Republic of Serbia, was assassinated Mar. 12 in Belgrade, triggering a roundup of more than 4,500 people associated with organized crime and the Milosevic regime. Serbia's union with Montenegro disintegrated in 2006. Montenegrins voted for separation in a referendum May 21 and became an independent republic June 3.

Kosovo declared independence from Serbia Feb. 17, 2008, but Serbia and Russia refused to recognize the new country. Following parliamentary elections in Serbia May 11, a pro-Western government under Mirko Cvetkovic took office July 7. To meet a requirement for EU membership, Serbia arrested, in 2008, former Bosnian Serb leader Radovan Karadzic, who was extradited to the International Criminal Court in The Hague on charges of genocide and crimes against humanity. Serbia's parliament passed a resolution Mar. 31, 2010, apologizing for the 1995 massacre of thousands of Muslims by Bosnian Serbs at Srebrenica. In a further effort to deal with wartime atrocities, Serbian prosecutors, Sept. 2010, indicted 9 former members of the Jackals paramilitary unit for allegedly killing 43 ethnic Albanian civilians during the 1999 Kosovo conflict. Ratko Mladic, the former Bosnian Serb military commander accused of directing the 1995 massacre of 8,000 Bosnian Muslims in Srebrenica, was arrested in Serbia May 2011, and sent to The Hague. He has been on trial since 2012. Serbia attained EU candidate status, Mar. 1, 2012. Tomislav Nikolic, an advocate for EU membership, was elected president May 20, while Ivica Dacic, once a spokesman for Milosevic, became prime min. of a coalition government, July 27, 2012. Zdravko Tolimir, a former commander in the Bosnian Serb Army, was convicted of genocide Dec. 12 for his role in the July 1995 killings of thousands of prisoners near Srebrenica. After reaching an EU-brokered power-sharing deal with Kosovo Apr. 19, 2013, Serbia awaited the start of EU membership negotiations. Two Milosevic aides were acquitted of war crimes May 30, 2013.

Vojvodina (8,304 sq mi) is a nominally autonomous province in northern Serbia with a pop. (2011 est.) of 1,916,889, mostly Serbian. The capital is Novi Sad.

Seychelles
Republic of Seychelles

People: Population: 90,846. **Age distrib.:** <15: 21.2%; 65+: 7.3%. **Pop. density:** 517.1 per sq mi, 199.7 per sq km. **Urban:**
53.6%. **Ethnic groups:** mixed French, African, Indian, Chinese, Arab. **Languages:** Creole, English (official). **Religions:** Roman Catholic 82%, Protestant 8% (Anglican 6%, Seventh-Day Adventist 1%), other Christian 3%, Hindu 2%, Muslim 1%.

Geography: Total area: 176 sq mi, 455 sq km; **Land area:** 176 sq mi, 455 sq km. **Location:** In Indian O. 700 mi NE of Madagascar. **Neighbors:** Nearest are Madagascar on SW, Somalia on NW. **Topography:** A group of 86 islands, about half of them composed of coral, the other half granite, the latter predominantly mountainous. **Capital:** Victoria, 26,609.

Government: Type: Republic. **Head of state and gov.:** Pres. James Michel, b. Aug. 18, 1944; in office: Apr. 14, 2004. **Local divisions:** 25 districts. **Defense budget** (2011): $24 mil. **Active troops:** 420.

Economy: Industries: fishing, tourism, coconuts and vanilla proc., coir (coconut fiber) rope, boat building, printing, furniture. **Chief crops:** coconuts, cinnamon, vanilla, sweet potatoes, cassava, copra, bananas. **Natural resources:** fish, cinnamon trees. **Arable land:** 2.2%. **Livestock:** cattle: 660; chickens: 350,000; goats: 5,400; pigs: 6,000. **Fish catch:** 75,358 metric tons. **Electricity prod.:** 283 mil kWh. **Labor force:** agric. 3%, industry 23%, services 74%.

Finance: Monetary unit: Rupee (SCR) (Sept. 2013: 12.02 = $1 U.S.). **GDP:** $2.4 bil; **per capita GDP:** $25,600; **GDP growth:** 2.8%. **Imports:** $889.6 mil; Saudi Arabia 23.2%, Spain 11.9%, France 5.8%. **Exports:** $493.3 mil; France 27.8%, UK 17.7%, Japan 15.3%, Italy 10.7%. **Tourism:** $305 mil. **Budget:** $415.4 mil. **Total reserves less gold:** $318.7 mil. **CPI change:** 7.1%.

Transport: Civil aviation: 887.3 mil pass.-mi; 7 airports. **Chief port:** Victoria.

Communications: TV sets: 278 per 1,000 pop. **Radios:** 278 per 1,000 pop. **Telephone lines:** 33.1 per 100 pop. **Internet:** 47.1%.

Health: Life expect.: 69.4 male; 78.8 female. **Births:** 14.9 per 1,000 pop. **Deaths:** 6.9 per 1,000 pop. **Natural inc.:** 0.80%. **Infant mortality:** 11.1 per 1,000 live births. **HIV rate:** NA.

Education: Compulsory: ages 6-15. **Literacy:** 91.8%.

Major intl. organizations: UN (FAO, IBRD, ILO, IMF, WHO), AU, the Commonwealth, WTO (observer).

Embassy: 800 Second Ave., Ste. 400C, New York, NY 10017; (212) 972-1785.

Website: www.egov.sc

The islands were occupied by France in 1768 and seized by Britain in 1794. Ruled as part of Mauritius from 1814, Seychelles became a separate colony in 1903 and declared independence June 29, 1976. The first president was ousted in a coup a year later by socialist leader France Albert René. A new constitution, approved June 1993, provided for a multiparty state. After nearly 27 years in power, Pres. René resigned Apr. 14, 2004, and Vice Pres. James Michel succeeded him. Michel won a 5-year term in elections July 28-30, 2006, and was reelected May 19-21, 2011.

Sierra Leone
Republic of Sierra Leone

People: Population: 5,612,685. **Age distrib.:** <15: 41.9%; 65+: 3.7%. **Pop. density:** 203 per sq mi, 78.4 per sq km. **Urban:** 39.2%. **Ethnic groups:** Temne 35%, Mende 31%, Limba 8%, Kono 5%, Kriole (descendants of freed Jamaican slaves) 2%, Mandingo 2%, Loko 2%, other (incl. Liberian refugees and small numbers of Europeans, Lebanese, Pakistanis, Indians) 15%. **Languages:** English (official), Mende (principal vernacular in S), Temne (principal vernacular in N), Krio (English-based Creole, a lingua franca). **Religions:** Muslim 60%, indigenous beliefs 30%, Christian 10%.

Geography: Total area: 27,699 sq mi, 71,740 sq km; **Land area:** 27,653 sq mi, 71,620 sq km. **Location:** On W coast of W Africa. **Neighbors:** Guinea on N and E, Liberia on S. **Topography:** The heavily-indented, 210-mi coastline has mangrove swamps. Behind are wooded hills, rising to a plateau and mountains in E. **Capital:** Freetown, 940,683.

Government: Type: Constitutional democracy. **Head of state and gov.:** Pres. Ernest Bai Koroma; b. Oct. 2, 1953; in office: Sept. 17, 2007. **Local divisions:** 3 provinces, 1 area. **Defense budget:** $13 mil. **Active troops:** 10,500.

Economy: Industries: diamond mining, small-scale mfg. (beverages, textiles), petroleum refining, small commercial ship repair. **Chief crops:** rice, coffee, cocoa, palm kernels, palm oil, peanuts. **Natural resources:** diamonds, titanium ore, bauxite, iron ore, gold, chromite. **Arable land:** 15.4%. **Livestock:** cattle: 568,700; chickens: 10.4 mil; goats: 883,300; pigs: 52,100; sheep: 750,200. **Fish catch:** 199,045 metric tons. **Electricity prod.:** 145 mil kWh. **Labor force:** NA.

Finance: Monetary unit: Leone (SLL) (Sept. 2013: 4,327.88 = $1 U.S.). **GDP:** $8.4 bil; **per capita GDP:** $1,400; **GDP growth:** 19.8%. **Imports:** $1.5 bil; China 16.3%, India 10.1%, South Africa 7.1%, U.S. 6.6%, UK 6.6%, Côte d'Ivoire 4.6%, Belgium 4.1%. **Exports:** $1.1 bil; China 50.5%, Belgium 18%, Japan 7.6%, Turkey 4.8%. **Tourism:** $44 mil. **Budget:** $728.5 mil. **Total reserves less gold:** $478 mil. **CPI change:** 12.9%.

Transport: Motor vehicles: 4.3 vehicles per 1,000 pop. **Civil aviation:** 66.5 mil pass.-mi; 1 airport. **Chief ports:** Freetown, Pepel.

Communications: TV sets: 13 per 1,000 pop. **Radios:** 132 per 1,000 pop. **Telephone lines** 0.3 per 100 pop. **Internet:** 1.3%.

Health: Life expect.: 54.5 male; 59.6 female. **Births:** 37.8 per 1,000 pop. **Deaths:** 11.3 per 1,000 pop. **Natural inc.:** 2.65%. **Infant mortality:** 75.0 per 1,000 live births. **HIV rate:** 1.6%.
Education: Compulsory: ages 6-11. **Literacy:** 43.3%.
Major intl. organizations: UN (FAO, IBRD, ILO, IMF, WHO), AU, the Commonwealth, WTO.
Embassy: 1701 19th St. NW 20009; 939-9261.
Website: www.statehouse.gov.sl
The British founded Freetown, 1787, as a haven for freed slaves. Full independence arrived Apr. 27, 1961. A one-party state was established by referendum in 1978.

Mutinous soldiers ousted Pres. Joseph Momoh, Apr. 30, 1992. A coup, Jan. 16, 1996, paved the way for multiparty elections and a return to civilian rule. A peace accord, signed Nov. 30 with the Revolutionary United Front (RUF), brought a temporary halt to a civil war that had claimed over 10,000 lives in five years.

A coup on May 25, 1997, was met with international opposition. Nigeria's restored Pres. Ahmad Tejan Kabbah to power on Mar. 10, 1998, but RUF rebels mounted a guerrilla counteroffensive, killing thousands of civilians and mutilating thousands more. A power-sharing agreement between the Kabbah government and the RUF, July 1999, was maintained by a UN mission (UNAMSIL). The accord collapsed in early May 2000, as RUF guerrillas took more than 500 UN peacekeepers hostage. Rebel leader Foday Sankoh was captured in Freetown, May 17. The hostages were freed by the end of May, and 233 more UN personnel behind rebel lines were rescued July 15.

A UN-sponsored disarmament program in 2001 reduced the level of violence. The Sierra Leone Special Court was created in 2002 to try war crimes that had occurred after Nov. 1996. Government and rebel leaders declared an official end to the war Jan. 18; more than 50,000 people had died in the conflict. Kabbah won the May 14 presidential election.

Sankoh, an indicted war criminal, died in UN custody, July 29, 2003. Opposition leader Ernest Bai Koroma won a presidential runoff vote, Sept. 8, 2007. Three former RUF leaders were convicted of war crimes, Feb. 25, 2009. A cholera epidemic swept through the country in 2012 and was declared a national emergency in Aug.; more than 19,000 cases were reported in Sierra Leone in the first 9 months of the year, killing at least 274. Koroma won reelection Nov. 17, 2012, as 87.3% of the electorate turned out to vote.

Singapore
Republic of Singapore

People: Population: 5,460,302. **Age distrib.:** <15: 13.6%; 65+: 8.1%. **Pop. density:** 20,585.3 per sq mi, 7,948 per sq km. **Urban:** 100%. **Ethnic groups:** Chinese 77%, Malay 14%, Indian 8%. **Languages:** Mandarin, English, Malay (all official); Hokkien; Cantonese; Teochew; Tamil (official); other Chinese dialects. **Religions:** Buddhist 43%, Muslim 15%, Taoist 9%, Catholic 5%, Hindu 4%, other Christian 10%, none 15%.
Geography: Total area: 269 sq mi, 697 sq km; **Land area:** 265 sq mi, 687 sq km. **Location:** Off tip of Malayan Peninsula in SE Asia. **Neighbors:** Nearest are Malaysia on N, Indonesia on S. **Topography:** A flat, formerly swampy island with 40 nearby islets. **Capital:** Singapore, 5,187,930.
Government: Type: Parliamentary republic. **Head of state:** Pres. Tony Tan Keng Yam; b. Feb. 7, 1940; in office: Sept. 1, 2011. **Head of gov.:** Prime Min. Lee Hsien Loong; b. Feb. 10, 1952; in office: Aug. 12, 2004. **Defense budget:** $9.68 bil. **Active troops:** 72,500.
Economy: Industries: electronics, chemicals, financial services, oil drilling equip., petroleum refining, rubber proc. and rubber prods., processed food and beverages, ship repair, offshore platform constr. **Chief crops:** orchids, vegetables. **Natural resources:** fish. **Arable land:** 0.9%. **Livestock:** cattle: 200; chickens: 3.3 mil; goats: 670; pigs: 270,000. **Fish catch:** 5,590 metric tons. **Electricity prod.:** 43.8 bil kWh. **Labor force:** agric. 0.1%, industry 19.6%, services 80.3%.
Finance: Monetary unit: Dollar (SGD) (Sept. 2013: 1.27 = $1 U.S.). **GDP:** $331.9 bil; **per capita GDP:** $61,400; **GDP growth:** 1.3%. **Imports:** $374.9 bil; Malaysia 10.6%, China 10.3%, U.S. 10.2%, South Korea 6.8%, Japan 6.2%, Indonesia 5.3%, Saudi Arabia 4.5%, UAE 4.1%. **Exports:** $435.8 bil; Malaysia 12.2%, Hong Kong 10.9%, China 10.7%, Indonesia 10.5%, U.S. 5.5%, Japan 4.6%, Australia 4.2%, South Korea 4%. **Tourism:** $19.3 bil. **Budget:** $37.8 bil (incl. both operational and development expenditures). **Total reserves less gold:** $259.1 bil. **Gold:** 4.1 mil oz t. **CPI change:** 4.5%.
Transport: Motor vehicles: 151.5 vehicles per 1,000 pop. **Civil aviation:** 52.5 bil pass.-mi; 9 airports. **Chief port:** Singapore.
Communications: TV sets: 213 per 1,000 pop. **Radios:** 689 per 1,000 pop. **Telephone lines:** 37.8 per 100 pop. **Internet:** 74.2%.
Health: Life expect.: 81.7 male; 86.6 female. **Births:** 7.9 per 1,000 pop. **Deaths:** 3.4 per 1,000 pop. **Natural inc.:** 0.45%. **Infant mortality:** 2.6 per 1,000 live births. **HIV rate:** 0.1%.
Education: Compulsory: ages 6-11. **Literacy:** 95.9%.
Major intl. organizations: UN (IBRD, ILO, IMF, WHO), APEC, ASEAN, the Commonwealth, WTO.
Embassy: 3501 International Pl. NW 20008; 537-3100.
Website: www.gov.sg

Founded in 1819 by Sir Thomas Stamford Raffles, Singapore was a British colony until 1959, when it became autonomous within the Commonwealth. On Sept. 16, 1963, it joined with Malaya, Sarawak, and Sabah to form the Federation of Malaysia. Tensions between Malayans, dominant in the federation, and ethnic Chinese, dominant in Singapore, led to an accord under which Singapore became a separate nation, Aug. 9, 1965.

Singapore is one of the world's largest ports and a major manufacturing, banking, and commerce center with high standards in health, education, and housing. A free trade pact with the U.S. took effect Jan. 1, 2004.

Singapore has had only three prime mins.: Lee Kuan Yew, 1959-90; Goh Chok Tong, 1990-2004; and Lee Kuan Yew's son, Lee Hsien Loong, who took office, Aug. 12, 2004. The government, dominated by the People's Action Party (PAP), has taken strong actions to keep order and suppress dissent. Singapore's export-dependent economy was hit hard by the 2008 global downturn but rebounded during 2009-11. Air pollution hit record levels in June 2013 due to the persistent burning of fields by farmers in Indonesia, prompting official warnings for people to remain indoors.

Slovakia
Slovak Republic

People: Population: 5,488,339. **Age distrib.:** <15: 15.5%; 65+: 13.4%. **Pop. density:** 295.5 per sq mi, 114.1 per sq km. **Urban:** 54.7%. **Ethnic groups:** Slovak 86%, Hungarian 10%, Roma 2%, Ruthenian/Ukrainian 1%. **Languages:** Slovak (official), Hungarian, Roma, Ukrainian. **Religions:** Roman Catholic 69%, Protestant 11%, Greek Catholic 4%, none 13%.
Geography: Total area: 18,933 sq mi, 49,035 sq km; **Land area:** 18,573 sq mi, 48,105 sq km. **Location:** In E central Europe. **Neighbors:** Poland on N, Hungary on S, Austria and Czech Rep. on W, Ukraine on E. **Topography:** Carpathian Mts. in N, fertile Danube plain in S. **Capital:** Bratislava, 433,540.
Government: Type: Parliamentary democracy. **Head of state:** Pres. Ivan Gasparovic; b. Mar. 27, 1941; in office: June 15, 2004. **Head of gov.:** Prime Min. Robert Fico; b. Sept. 15, 1964; in office: Apr. 4, 2012. **Local divisions:** 8 regions. **Defense budget:** $1.01 bil. **Active troops:** 15,850.
Economy: Industries: metal and metal prods.; food and beverages; electricity, gas, coke, oil, nuclear fuel; chemicals and manmade fibers; machinery; paper and printing. **Chief crops:** grains, potatoes, sugar beets, hops, fruits. **Natural resources:** brown coal and lignite, iron ore, copper and manganese ore, salt. **Crude oil reserves:** 9 mil bbls. **Arable land:** 28.9%. **Livestock:** cattle: 467,125; chickens: 12.7 mil; goats: 35,292; pigs: 687,260; sheep: 394,175. **Fish catch:** 2,749 metric tons. **Electricity prod. (2011):** 24.4 bil kWh. **Labor force:** agric. 3.5%, industry 27%, services 69.4%.
Finance: Monetary unit: Euro (EUR) (Sept. 2013: 0.76 = $1 U.S.). **GDP:** $134.1 bil; **per capita GDP:** $24,600; **GDP growth:** 2%. **Imports:** $76 bil; Germany 18.5%, Czech Republic 17.9%, Russia 9.9%, Austria 7.7%, Hungary 7.2%, Poland 6%, South Korea 4.3%. **Exports:** $80.7 bil; Germany 22.4%, Czech Republic 14.6%, Poland 8.6%, Hungary 7.8%, Austria 7.1%, France 5.6%, Italy 4.9%, UK 4.1%. **Tourism:** $2.3 bil. **Budget:** $34.4 bil. **Total reserves less gold:** $818.4 mil. **Gold:** 1 mil oz t. **CPI change:** 3.6%.
Transport: Railways: 2,251 mi. **Motor vehicles:** 380.4 vehicles per 1,000 pop. **Civil aviation:** 2.1 bil pass.-mi; 21 airports. **Chief ports:** Bratislava, Komarno.
Communications: TV sets: 437 per 1,000 pop. **Radios:** 964 per 1,000 pop. **Telephone lines:** 17.8 per 100 pop. **Internet:** 80%.
Health: Life expect.: 72.4 male; 80.3 female. **Births:** 10.3 per 1,000 pop. **Deaths:** 9.7 per 1,000 pop. **Natural inc.:** 0.06%. **Infant mortality:** 6.4 per 1,000 live births. **HIV rate:** <0.1%.
Education: Compulsory: ages 6-14. **Literacy:** NA.
Major intl. organizations: UN (FAO, IBRD, ILO, IMF, WHO), EU, NATO, OECD, OSCE, WTO.
Embassy: 3523 International Ct. NW 20008; 237-1054.
Website: www.government.gov.sk

Slovakia was originally settled by Illyrian, Celtic, and Germanic tribes and was incorporated into Great Moravia in the 9th cent. It became part of Hungary in the 11th cent. Overrun by Czech Hussites in the 15th cent., it was restored to Hungarian rule in 1526. The Slovaks disassociated themselves from Hungary after WWI and joined the Czechs of Bohemia to form the Republic of Czechoslovakia, Oct. 28, 1918.

Germany invaded Czechoslovakia, 1939, and declared Slovakia independent. Slovakia rejoined Czechoslovakia in 1945. Czechoslovakia split into two separate states—the Czech Republic and Slovakia—on Jan. 1, 1993.

Slovakia joined the EU and NATO in 2004. The country adopted the euro currency Jan. 1, 2009, but its economy, previously one of Europe's fastest growing, was battered in the global recession. Pres. Ivan Gasparovic won a second 5-year term in a runoff election Apr. 2009. A coalition of right-leaning parties led by Iveta Radicová, who became Slovakia's first female prime min., took power after June 2010 parliamentary elections. That coalition fell apart, and in early elections, Mar. 10, 2012, Robert Fico's social-democratic party, Smer (Direction), won 83 seats, the first time in Slovakia's post-communist history that a single party held the majority. Fico became prime min. Apr. 4, 2012.

Slovenia
Republic of Slovenia

People: Population: 1,992,690. **Age distrib.:** <15: 13.4%; 65+: 17.5%. **Pop. density:** 256.1 per sq mi, 98.9 per sq km. **Urban:** 49.9%. **Ethnic groups:** Slovene 83%, Serb 2%, Croat 2%, Bosniak 1%. **Languages:** Slovenian (official); Serbo-Croatian; Italian, Hungarian (both official in some municipalities). **Religions:** Catholic 58%, Muslim 2%, Orthodox 2%, none 10%.
Geography: Total area: 7,827 sq mi, 20,273 sq km; **Land area:** 7,780 sq mi, 20,151 sq km. **Location:** In SE Europe. **Neighbors:** Italy on W, Austria on N, Hungary on NE, Croatia on SE, S. **Topography:** Mostly hilly; 42% forested. **Capital:** Ljubljana, 272,897.
Government: Type: Parliamentary republic. **Head of state:** Pres. Borut Pahor; b. Nov. 2, 1963; in office: Dec. 22, 2012. **Head of gov.:** Prime Min. Alenka Bratusek; b. Mar. 31, 1970; in office: Mar. 20, 2013. **Local divisions:** 200 municipalities, 11 urban municipalities. **Defense budget:** $567 mil. **Active troops:** 7,600.
Economy: Industries: ferrous metallurgy and aluminum prods., lead and zinc smelting, electronics (incl. military), automobiles, elec. power equip., wood prods., textiles, chemicals, machine tools. **Chief crops:** potatoes, hops, wheat, sugar beets, corn, grapes. **Natural resources:** lignite coal, lead, zinc, building stone, hydropower, forests. **Arable land:** 8.4%. **Livestock:** cattle: 470,151; chickens: 2.5 mil; goats: 26,197; pigs: 395,593; sheep: 129,788. **Fish catch:** 2,299 metric tons. **Electricity prod.** (2011): 15.2 bil kWh. **Labor force:** agric. 2.2%, industry 35%, services 62.8%.
Finance: Monetary unit: Euro (EUR) (Sept. 2013: 0.76 = $1 U.S.). **GDP:** $58.9 bil; **per capita GDP:** $28,700; **GDP growth:** −2.3%. **Imports:** $28 bil; Italy 16.3%, Germany 16.2%, Austria 10.4%, Croatia 4.8%, Hungary 4%. **Exports:** $27.6 bil; Germany 20%, Italy 12%, Austria 7.9%, Croatia 6.2%, France 4.8%, Russia 4.6%. **Tourism:** $2.6 bil. **Budget:** $23.1 bil. **Total reserves less gold:** $782.2 mil. **Gold:** 102,000 oz t. **CPI change:** 2.6%.
Transport: Railways: 763 mi. **Motor vehicles:** 576.7 vehicles per 1,000 pop. **Civil aviation:** 541.8 mil pass.-mi; 7 airports. **Chief port:** Koper.
Communications: TV sets: 371 per 1,000 pop. **Radios:** 409 per 1,000 pop. **Telephone lines:** 40.4 per 100 pop. **Internet:** 70%.
Health: Life expect.: 74.0 male; 81.5 female. **Births:** 8.7 per 1,000 pop. **Deaths:** 11.1 per 1,000 pop. **Natural inc.:** −0.25%. **Infant mortality:** 4.1 per 1,000 live births. **HIV rate:** 0.1%.
Education: Compulsory: ages 6-14. **Literacy:** 99.7%.
Major intl. organizations: UN (FAO, IBRD, ILO, IMF, WHO), EU, NATO, OECD, OSCE, WTO.
Embassy: 2410 California St. NW 20008; 386-6601.
Website: e-uprava.gov.si
   The Slovenes settled in their current territory during the 6th to the 8th cent. They fell under German domination in the 9th cent. Modern Slovenian political history began after 1848 when the Slovenes, divided among several Austrian provinces, began their struggle for unification. In 1918 a majority of Slovenes became part of the Kingdom of Serbs, Croats, and Slovenes, later renamed Yugoslavia.
   Slovenia declared independence June 25, 1991; joined the UN May 22, 1992; and attained full membership in the EU and NATO in 2004. Slovenia adopted the euro currency Jan. 1, 2007. On Mar. 5, 2008, it became the first former Yugoslav republic to recognize Kosovo's independence from Serbia. A center-left coalition took office following Sept. 2008 legislative elections. Janez Jansa's Positive Slovenia party won a majority of parliamentary seats in Dec. 2011, forming a five-party coalition government that allowed Jansa to become prime min. Jan. 28, 2012.

Solomon Islands

People: Population: 597,248. **Age distrib.:** <15: 36.8%; 65+: 4%. **Pop. density:** 55.3 per sq mi, 21.3 per sq km. **Urban:** 20.5%. **Ethnic groups:** Melanesian 95%, Polynesian 3%, Micronesian 1%. **Languages:** Melanesian pidgin (lingua franca in much of country), English (official but spoken by only 1%-2% of pop.), 120 indigenous langs. **Religions:** Protestant 74% (Church of Melanesia 33%, South Seas Evangelical 17%, Seventh-Day Adventist 11%, United Church 10%, Christian Fellowship Church 2%), Roman Catholic 19%, other Christian 4%.
Geography: Total area: 11,157 sq mi, 28,896 sq km; **Land area:** 10,805 sq mi, 27,986 sq km. **Location:** Melanesian Archipelago in W Pacific O. **Neighbors:** Nearest is Papua New Guinea to W. **Topography:** 10 large volcanic, rugged islands; 4 groups of smaller ones. **Capital:** Honiara, 67,610.
Government: Type: Parliamentary democracy. **Head of state:** Queen Elizabeth II, rep. by Gov.-Gen. Sir Frank Ofagioro Kabui; in office; July 7, 2009. **Head of gov.:** Prime Min. Gordon Darcy Lilo; b. Aug. 28, 1965; in office: Nov. 16, 2011. **Local divisions:** 9 provinces, 1 capital territory. **Defense budget:** NA. **Active troops:** No regular military forces.
Economy: Industries: fish (tuna), mining, timber. **Chief crops:** cocoa, coconuts, palm kernels, rice, potatoes, vegetables, fruit. **Natural resources:** fish, forests, gold, bauxite, phosphates, lead, zinc, nickel. **Arable land:** 0.6%. **Livestock:** cattle: 14,500; chickens: 235,000; pigs: 53,500. **Fish catch:** 58,943 metric tons. **Electricity prod.:** 82 mil kWh. **Labor force:** agric. 75%, industry 5%, services 20%.

Finance: Monetary unit: Dollar (SBD) (Sept. 2013: 7.28 = $1 U.S.). **GDP:** $1.9 bil; **per capita GDP:** $3,400; **GDP growth:** 5.5%. **Imports:** (2010) $360.3 mil; Singapore 26.6%, Australia 25.1%, China 7%, New Zealand 4.8%, Malaysia 4.7%. **Exports:** (2010) $226.5 mil; China 47.9%, Australia 16.6%. **Tourism:** $73 mil. **Budget:** $326.3 mil. **Total reserves less gold:** $469.5 mil. **Gold:** 17,682 oz t. **CPI change:** 2.6%.
Transport: Civil aviation: 49.7 mil pass.-mi; 1 airport. **Chief ports:** Honiara, Viru Harbor.
Communications: TV sets: 12 per 1,000 pop. **Radios:** 65 per 1,000 pop. **Telephone lines:** 1.4 per 100 pop. **Internet:** 7%.
Health: Life expect.: 72.1 male; 77.4 female. **Births:** 26.9 per 1,000 pop. **Deaths:** 3.9 per 1,000 pop. **Natural inc.:** 2.30%. **Infant mortality:** 16.7 per 1,000 live births. **HIV rate:** NA.
Education: NA. **Literacy:** NA.
Major intl. organizations: UN (FAO, IBRD, ILO, IMF, WHO), the Commonwealth, WTO.
Embassy: 800 Second Ave., Ste. 400L, New York, NY 10017; (212) 599-6192.
Website: www.pmc.gov.sb
   The Solomon Isls. were sighted 1568 by an expedition from Peru. Britain established a protectorate in the 1890s over most of the group, inhabited by Melanesians. The islands saw major WWII battles. They achieved self-government, Jan. 2, 1976, and formal independence, July 7, 1978.
   A coup attempt, June 5, 2000, sparked factional fighting in Honiara. To restore order after 3 years of lawlessness, a 2,225-member intervention force, led by Australia and authorized by the Pacific Isls. Forum, provided security 2003-05.
   Following Apr. 2006 elections, parliament's choice of Snyder Rini as prime min. led to two days of rioting in Honiara over alleged influence-buying by the ethnic Chinese business community. Rini resigned Apr. 26, 2006, rather than face a no-confidence vote. Prime Min. Danny Philip, who was elected Aug. 25, 2010, dismissed finance min. Gordon Darcy Lilo and was forced to resign when a number of MPs abandoned the government in protest. The parliament then elected Lilo prime min., Nov. 16, 2011. A magnitude-8.0 earthquake in the South Pacific caused a tsunami Feb. 6, 2013, that killed at least 9 people and destroyed about 100 homes in the town of Lata.

Somalia
Federal Republic of Somalia

People: Population: 10,251,568. **Age distrib.:** <15: 44.3%; 65+: 2.3%. **Pop. density:** 42.3 per sq mi, 16.3 per sq km. **Urban:** 37.7%. **Ethnic groups:** Somali 85%, Bantu and other non-Somali 15%. **Languages:** Somali, Arabic (both official); Italian; English. **Religion:** Sunni Muslim (official).
Geography: Total area: 246,201 sq mi, 637,657 sq km; **Land area:** 242,216 sq mi, 627,337 sq km. **Location:** Occupies eastern horn of Africa. **Neighbors:** Djibouti, Ethiopia, Kenya on W. **Topography:** The coastline extends for 1,700 mi. Hills cover the N; center and S are flat. **Capital:** Mogadishu, 1,554,260.
Government: Type: In transition. **Head of state:** Pres. Hassan Sheikh Mohamud; b. Nov. 29, 1955; in office: Sept. 16, 2012. **Head of gov.:** Prime Min. Abdi Farrah Shirdon Said; b. 1959; in office: Oct. 17, 2012. **Local divisions:** 18 regions. **Defense budget:** NA. **Active troops:** African Union and EU missions have trained some forces. Some allied militias accompany Somali Natl. Govt. Forces.
Economy: Industries: few light industries incl. sugar refining, textiles, wireless communication. **Chief crops:** bananas, sorghum, corn, coconuts, rice, sugarcane, mangoes, sesame seeds, beans. **Natural resources:** uranium, largely unexploited reserves of iron ore, tin, gypsum, bauxite, copper, salt, nat. gas, likely oil reserves. **Arable land:** 1.8%. **Livestock:** cattle: 4.9 mil; chickens: 3.4 mil; goats: 11.5 mil; pigs: 3,800; sheep: 12.3 mil. **Fish catch:** 30,000 metric tons. **Electricity prod.:** 310 mil kWh. **Labor force:** agric. 71%, industry and services 29%.
Finance: Monetary unit: Shilling (SOS) (Sept. 2013: 1,287.98 = $1 U.S.). **GDP** (2010): $5.9 bil; **per capita GDP** (2010): $600; **GDP growth** (2010): 2.6%. **Imports** (2010): $1.3 bil; Djibouti 27.4%, India 12%, Kenya 7.2%, Pakistan 6.5%, China 6.1%, Egypt 5%, Oman 4.6%, UAE 4.5%, Yemen 4.4%. **Exports:** $515.8 mil; UAE 50.8%, Yemen 19%, Oman 12.8%. **Budget:** NA. **Total reserves less gold:** NA. **CPI change:** NA.
Transport: Civil aviation: 6 airports. **Chief ports:** Berbera, Kismaayo.
Communications: TV sets: 26 per 1,000 pop. **Radios:** 242 per 1,000 pop. **Telephone lines:** 1 per 100 pop. **Internet:** 1.4%.
Health: Life expect.: 49.2 male; 53.2 female. **Births:** 41.5 per 1,000 pop. **Deaths:** 14.2 per 1,000 pop. **Natural inc.:** 2.72%. **Infant mortality:** 101.9 per 1,000 live births. **HIV rate:** 0.7%.
Education: NA. **Literacy:** NA.
Major intl. organizations: UN (FAO, IBRD, ILO, IMF, WHO), AL, AU.
Permanent UN mission: 425 E. 61st St., Ste. 702, New York, NY, 10021; (212) 688-9410. (Embassy ceased operation in U.S. in 1991.)
Website: www.state.gov/p/af/ci/so/
   British Somaliland (present-day North Somalia) was formed in the 19th cent., as was Italian Somaliland (now central and South Somalia). Italy lost its African colonies in WWII. British Somaliland gained independence, June 26, 1960, and by prearrangement, merged, July 1, with the UN Trust Territory of Somalia to create the independent Somali Republic.

On Oct. 15, 1969, Somalia's first civilian president, Abdirashid Ali Sharmarke, was assassinated. Six days later, Maj. Gen. Muhammad Siad Barre led a military coup. In 1970, he declared the country a socialist state—the Somali Democratic Republic.

Somalia has laid claim to Ogaden, the huge eastern region of Ethiopia, peopled mostly by Somalis. Some 11,000 Cuban troops with Soviet arms defeated Somali army troops and ethnic Somali rebels in Ethiopia, 1978. As many as 1.5 mil refugees entered Somalia. Guerrilla fighting in Ogaden continued until 1988, when a peace agreement was reached with Ethiopia.

Fighting in Mogadishu led Siad Barre to flee the capital, Jan. 1991. Fighting between rival factions caused 40,000 casualties, 1991-92, and by mid-1992 the civil war, drought, and banditry combined to produce a famine that threatened some 1.5 mil people.

U.S. troops and the UN worked to safeguard food delivery, 1991-93, resulting in significant U.S. and other casualties; a failed mission Oct. 3-4, 1993, left 18 U.S. troops and more than 500 Somalis dead. The U.S. withdrew its peacekeeping forces Mar. 25, 1994.

When the last UN troops pulled out, Mar. 3, 1995, armed factions controlled different regions. A joint police force in the capital could not stop the continued violence and food shortages. A peace deal Jan. 29, 2004, led to the Aug. 22 inauguration of a transitional parliament, Somalia's first legislature in 13 years. Meeting in Nairobi, Kenya, the parliament chose Abdullahi Yusuf Ahmed as president; he was sworn in Oct. 14.

Because Mogadishu was held by his rivals, Pres. Yusuf moved, July 26, 2005, to make his transitional capital at Jowhar; an interim parliament convened Feb. 26, 2006, at Baidoa. On June 5, an Islamist militia took over Mogadishu, defeating U.S.-backed secular warlords. The Islamists, calling themselves the Supreme Islamic Courts Council, held much of the central and southern regions. Pres. Yusuf escaped assassination, Sept. 18, 2006.

With aid from Ethiopian troops, transitional govt. forces recaptured Mogadishu in Dec. 2006. The UN Security Council authorized, Feb. 20, 2007, an African Union peacekeeping mission to Somalia (AMISOM). An upsurge of fighting in Mogadishu, Feb.-Apr., killed hundreds of people and caused 350,000 to flee. Bombings and kidnappings escalated in 2007-08, as a series of cease-fires failed; the increasing violence forced international aid workers to pull out, worsening a humanitarian crisis. Many of the attacks on transitional authorities and their allies were blamed on al-Shabaab, an al-Qaeda ally.

After Pres. Yusuf resigned Dec. 29, 2008, the transitional parliament, meeting in Djibouti Jan. 31, 2009, elected a moderate Islamist, Sheikh Sharif Sheikh Ahmed. Meanwhile, pirates carried out more than 200 attacks off the Horn of Africa in 2009. Pirates and Islamist insurgents continued to disrupt famine relief efforts in 2010-11, threatening an estimated 3.7 mil Somalis. Pressured by the 9,000-member AMISOM force, al-Shabaab pulled out of Mogadishu, Aug. 6, 2011, but continued to control much of southern Somalia. Despite continuing violence, Somali leaders met in Feb. 2012 for a second Somali national consultative constitutional conference in Garowe, Somalia, and signed Feb. 18 the Garowe II Principles, which established the conditions to install the caretaker government sworn in Aug. 20. The new parliament elected activist-professor Hassan Sheik Mohamud president Sept. 10. He survived an assassination attempt Sept. 12 and was sworn in Sept. 16, 2012. Pres. Mohamud appointed Abdi Farah Shirdon Saaid to a 4-year term as prime min. on Oct. 6. An overcrowded boat capsized off the coast Dec. 20, 2012, killing 55 of the 60 passengers.

South Africa
Republic of South Africa

People: Population: 48,601,098. **Age distrib.:** <15: 28.3%; 65+: 6.1%. **Pop. density:** 103.6 per sq mi, 40 per sq km. **Urban:** 62%. **Ethnic groups:** black African 79%, white 10%, colored 9%, Indian/Asian 3%. **Languages:** IsiZulu, IsiXhosa, Afrikaans, Sepedi, English, Setswana, Sesotho, Xitsonga, siSwati, Tshivenda, isiNdebele (all official). **Religions:** Protestant 37% (Zionist Christian 11%, Pentecostal/Charismatic 8%, Methodist 7%, Dutch Reformed 7%, Anglican 4%), Catholic 7%, Muslim 2%, other Christian 36%, none 15%.

Geography: Total area: 470,693 sq mi, 1,219,090 sq km; **Land area:** 468,909 sq mi, 1,214,470 sq km. **Location:** At southern extreme of Africa. **Neighbors:** Namibia, Botswana, Zimbabwe on N; Mozambique, Swaziland on E; surrounds Lesotho. **Topography:** Large interior plateau reaches close to the country's 1,739-mi coastline. There are few major rivers or lakes. Rainfall is sparse in W, more plentiful in E. **Capital:** Pretoria (admin.), 1,500,960; Cape Town (legislative), 3,562,470; Bloemfontein (judicial), 467,778. **Cities (urban aggl.):** Johannesburg, 3,843,760; Ekurhuleni (East Rand), 3,356,754; Durban, 3,012,423; Vereeniging, 1,200,177; Port Elizabeth, 1,118,923.

Government: Type: Republic. **Head of state and gov.:** Pres. Jacob Zuma; b. Apr. 12, 1942; in office: May 9, 2009. **Local divisions:** 9 provinces. **Defense budget:** $4.62 bil. **Active troops:** 62,100.

Economy: Industries: mining (world's largest producer of platinum, gold, chromium), auto assembly, metalworking, machinery, textiles, iron and steel, chemicals, fertilizer, foodstuffs. **Chief crops:** corn, wheat, sugarcane, fruits, vegetables. **Natural resources:** gold, chromium, antimony, coal, iron ore, manganese, nickel, phosphates, tin, rare earth elements, uranium, gem diamonds, platinum,

copper, vanadium, salt, nat. gas. **Crude oil reserves:** 15 mil bbls. **Arable land:** 9.9%. **Livestock:** cattle: 13.7 mil; chickens: 190 mil; goats: 6.2 mil; pigs: 1.6 mil; sheep: 24.3 mil. **Fish catch:** 545,298 metric tons. **Electricity prod.:** 241.9 bil kWh. **Labor force:** agric. 9%, industry 26%, services 65%.

Finance: Monetary unit: Rand (ZAR) (Sept. 2013: 10.02 = $1 U.S.). **GDP:** $592 bil; **per capita GDP:** $11,600; **GDP growth:** 2.5%. **Imports:** $105 bil; China 14.9%, Germany 10.1%, U.S. 7.3%, Saudi Arabia 7.2%, India 4.6%, Japan 4.5%. **Exports:** $100.7 bil; China 14.5%, U.S. 7.9%, Japan 5.7%, Germany 5.5%, India 4.5%, UK 4.1%. **Tourism:** $10 bil. **Budget:** $117.8 bil. **Total reserves less gold:** $44 bil. **Gold:** 4 mil oz t. **CPI change:** 5.4%.

Transport: Railways: 12,547 mi. **Motor vehicles:** 183.2 vehicles per 1,000 pop. **Civil aviation:** 16.7 bil pass.-mi; 144 airports. **Chief ports:** Cape Town, Durban, Port Elizabeth, Richards Bay, Saldanha Bay.

Communications: TV sets: 195 per 1,000 pop. **Radios:** 443 per 1,000 pop. **Telephone lines:** 7.9 per 100 pop. **Internet:** 41%.

Health: Life expect.: 50.4 male; 48.5 female. **Births:** 19.1 per 1,000 pop. **Deaths:** 17.4 per 1,000 pop. **Natural inc.:** 0.18%. **Infant mortality:** 42.2 per 1,000 live births. **HIV rate:** 17.3%.

Education: Compulsory: ages 7-15. **Literacy:** 93%.

Major intl. organizations: UN (FAO, IBRD, ILO, IMF, WHO), AU, the Commonwealth, WTO.

Embassy: 3051 Massachusetts Ave. NW 20008; 232-4400.
Website: www.gov.za

Bushmen and KhoiKhoi were the original inhabitants. Bantus, including Zulu, Xhosa, Swazi, and Sotho, occupied the area from northeastern to southern South Africa before the 17th cent.

The Dutch settled the Cape of Good Hope area, beginning in the 17th cent. Britain seized the Cape,1806. Many Dutch trekked north and founded two republics, Transvaal and Orange Free State. Diamonds were discovered, 1867, and gold, 1886. The Dutch (Boers) resented encroachments by the British and others; the Anglo-Boer War followed, 1899-1902. Britain won and created, May 31, 1910, the Union of South Africa, incorporating two British colonies (Cape and Natal) with Transvaal and Orange Free State. After a referendum, the Union became the Republic of South Africa, May 31, 1961, and withdrew from the Commonwealth.

Daniel Malan's National Party election in 1948 made the policy of separate development of the races, or apartheid, official. Under apartheid, blacks were severely restricted to certain occupations and paid less than whites for similar work. Only whites could vote or run for public office. Persons of Asian indian ancestry and those of mixed race ("coloureds") had limited political rights. Acts passed in 1959 created several Bantu nations, or Bantustans.

Protests against apartheid were suppressed. At Sharpeville on Mar. 21, 1960, government troops killed 69 black protesters. At least 600 persons, mostly Bantus, were killed in 1976 anti-apartheid riots. In 1986, Nobel Peace Prize winner Bishop Desmond Tutu called for Western nations to apply sanctions against South Africa to force an end to apartheid. Pres. P. W. Botha offered blacks an advisory role in government starting in Apr. On May 19, South Africa attacked three neighboring countries—Zimbabwe, Botswana, Zambia—striking at guerrilla strongholds of the anti-apartheid African National Congress (ANC). A nationwide state of emergency was declared June 12, giving almost unlimited power to the security forces.

Some 2 mil South African black workers staged a strike, June 6-8, 1988. Pres. Botha, head of the government since 1978, resigned Aug. 14, 1989, and was replaced by F. W. de Klerk. In 1990 the government lifted its ban on the ANC. Anti-apartheid leader Nelson Mandela was freed Feb. 11 after more than 27 years in prison. In Feb. 1991, Pres. de Klerk pledged to end apartheid laws.

In 1993 negotiators agreed on basic principles for a new democratic constitution. South Africa's partially self-governing black territories, or "homelands," were incorporated into a national system of 9 provinces. The ANC won elections Apr. 26-29, 1994, making Mandela president. The Inkatha Freedom Party won control of the legislature in a mainly Zulu province. By then, fighting between the ANC and Inkatha (aided, during the apartheid era, by South African defense forces) had killed more than 14,000 people in the Zulu region.

In 1995, Mandela appointed a truth commission, led by Desmond Tutu, to document human rights abuses under apartheid. A post-apartheid constitution became law Dec. 10, 1996. The ANC won elections, June 2, 1999, and ANC leader Thabo Mbeki became president. South Africa, Nov. 30, 2006, became the first African country to legalize same-sex marriage.

After Mbeki's former deputy president, Jacob Zuma, defeated him in a power struggle for the ANC leadership, Mbeki resigned his presidency, Sept. 21, 2008. Corruption charges against Zuma were dropped Apr. 6, 2009, and he became president after Apr. 22, 2009, elections. Thousands of miners struck for better wages at Lonmin platinum mine near Marikana, NW of Johannesburg, Aug. 10, 2012, and strikes spread to mines owned by Anglo American Platinum, the world's largest platinum producer, the week of Sept. 10. Protests at Lonmin left at least 10 dead, including two guards and two police officers, before police officers opened fire on protesters Aug. 16, killing 34 and wounding 78. A strike-ending wage agreement was reached at Lonmin Sept. 18, but demonstrations continued at Anglo American Platinum, resulting in 12,000 miners being fired there Oct. 5 (reversed Oct. 27). The Lonmin disputes resumed May 14, 2013, with another wildcat strike.

South Sudan
Republic of South Sudan

People: Population: 11,090,104. **Age distrib.:** <15: 46.2%; 65+: 2.1%. **Pop. density:** 44.6 per sq mi, 17.2 per sq km. **Urban:** 18%. **Ethnic groups:** Dinka, Kakwa, Bari, Azande, Shilluk, Kuku, Murle, Mandari, Didinga, Ndogo, Bviri, Lndi, Anuak, Bongo, Lango, Dungotona, Acholi. **Languages:** English, Arabic (incl. Juba, Sudanese variants) (both official); regional langs. (incl. Dinka, Nuer, Bari, Zande, Shilluk). **Religions:** animist, Christian.

Geography: Total area: 248,777 sq mi, 644,329 sq km. **Location:** In NE Africa. **Neighbors:** Sudan on N, Uganda and Kenya on S, Ethiopia on E. **Topography:** The White Nile R. flows N through the center of the country. The river feeds the Sudd, a swampy area occupying more than 15% of the country's center; it is one of the world's largest wetlands. **Capital:** Juba, 268,597.

Government: Type: Republic. **Head of state and gov.:** Pres. Salva Kiir Mayardit; b. 1951; in office: July 9, 2011. **Local divisions:** 10 states. **Defense budget:** $537 mil. **Active troops:** 210,000.

Economy: Chief crops: sorghum, maize, rice, millet, wheat, gum arabic, sugarcane, fruits, sweet potatoes, sunflower, cotton, sesame, cassava, beans, peanuts. **Natural resources:** hydropower, gold, diamonds, petroleum, hardwoods, limestone, iron ore, copper, chromium ore, zinc, tungsten, mica, silver. **Labor force:** Vast majority of pop. relies on subsistence agriculture.

Finance: Monetary unit: Pound (SSP) (June 2013: 2.97 = $1 U.S.). **GDP:** $10.6 bil; **per capita GDP:** $1,000; **GDP growth:** –53%. **Budget:** NA. **Total reserves less gold:** NA. **CPI change:** NA.

Transport: Railways: 147 mi (reported to be in disrepair). **Civil aviation:** 3 airports.

Health: Life expect.: 58.6 male; 61.5 female. **Births:** 38.5 per 1,000 pop. **Deaths:** 8.7 per 1,000 pop. **Natural inc.:** 2.98%. **Infant mortality:** 70.0 per 1,000 live births. **HIV rate:** 3.1%.

Major intl. organizations: UN.

Embassy: 1233 20th St. NW, Ste. 602, 20036; 293-7940.

Website: www.goss.org

South Sudan was a region of the Republic of the Sudan when that country became independent in 1956. Northerners (mostly Arab Muslims) dominated, while southerners (mostly black Africans who practiced Christianity or traditional religions) were marginalized. Southern Anya Nya rebels waged war against the north, 1955-72, until an agreement reached in Addis Ababa, Ethiopia, offered regional self-government for the south. Oil was discovered in the south in 1978.

Civil war broke out again in 1983, with southern rebels led by the Sudan People's Liberation Movement (SPLM). Fighting and related famine cost an estimated 2 mil lives and displaced millions of southerners. A peace accord was signed in 2005. A power-sharing agreement offered autonomy for southern Sudan and allowed for an independence referendum.

Almost 99% of southern Sudanese who voted in the referendum, Jan 9-15, 2011, supported secession. The UN Security Council, July 8, authorized 7,900 peacekeepers to the area. South Sudan attained full independence July 9, 2011, and was admitted to the UN, July 14. A 4-year interim deal on the division of oil revenues was reached Aug. 4 and another deal Sept. 27 on the transport of oil from the south through the north. South Sudan clashed with Sudanese rebels on its northern border and faced challenges of poverty, underdevelopment, and factional conflict.

Violence within South Sudan continued in 2013. A battle within its borders, Mar. 28, led to the death of 163 people, mostly South Sudanese rebels, who the government believed were being aided by Sudan, and 5 UN peacekeeping forces caught in the violence, Apr. 9. Unhappy with the direction and pace of economic development, Pres. Salva Kiir fired his entire cabinet and chief negotiator July 23.

Spain
Kingdom of Spain

People: Population: 47,370,542. **Age distrib.:** <15: 15.4%; 65+: 17.5%. **Pop. density:** 245.9 per sq mi, 94.9 per sq km. **Urban:** 77.4%. **Ethnic groups:** mixed Mediterranean and Nordic. **Languages:** Castilian Spanish (official); Catalan, Galician, Basque (all official regionally). **Religion:** Roman Catholic 94%.

Geography: Total area: 195,124 sq mi, 505,370 sq km; **Land area:** 192,657 sq mi, 498,980 sq km. **Location:** In SW Europe. **Neighbors:** Portugal on W; France, Andorra on N; Morocco on S. **Topography:** The interior is a high, arid plateau broken by mountain ranges and river valleys. The NW is heavily watered, the S has lowlands and a Medit. climate. **Capital:** Madrid, 6,574,450. **Cities (urban aggl.):** Barcelona, 5,569,950.

Government: Type: Parliamentary monarchy. **Head of state:** King Juan Carlos I de Borbon y Borbon; b. Jan. 5, 1938; in office: Nov. 22, 1975. **Head of gov.:** Prime Min. Mariano Rajoy; b. Mar. 27, 1955; in office: Dec. 20, 2011. **Local divisions:** 17 autonomous communities, 2 autonomous cities. **Defense budget:** $11.8 bil. **Active troops:** 135,500.

Economy: Industries: textiles and apparel (incl. footwear), food and beverages, metals and metal manufactures, chemicals, shipbuilding, automobiles, machine tools, tourism, clay and refractory prods., footwear, pharmaceuticals. **Chief crops:** grain, vegetables, olives, wine grapes, sugar beets, citrus. **Natural resources:** coal, lignite, iron ore, copper, lead, zinc, uranium, tungsten, mercury, pyrites, magnesite, fluorspar, gypsum, sepiolite, kaolin, potash, hydropower. **Crude oil reserves:** 150 mil bbls. **Arable land:** 25.1%. **Livestock:** cattle: 5.9 mil; chickens: 138 mil; goats: 2.9 mil; pigs: 25.6 mil; sheep: 17 mil. **Fish catch:** 1.3 mil metric tons. **Electricity prod.:** (2011): 276.8 bil kWh. **Labor force:** agric. 4.2%, industry 24%, services 71.7%.

Finance: Monetary unit: Euro (EUR) (Sept. 2013: 0.76 = $1 U.S.). **GDP:** $1.4 tril; **per capita GDP:** $31,100; **GDP growth:** –1.4%. **Imports:** $323.7 bil; Germany 11.8%, France 11.5%, Italy 6.7%, China 5.6%, Netherlands 5.4%, UK 4.1%. **Exports:** $291.7 bil; France 16.8%, Germany 10.8%, Italy 7.7%, Portugal 7.1%, UK 6.5%. **Tourism:** $55.9 bil. **Budget:** $634.6 bil. **Total reserves less gold:** $35.5 bil. **Gold:** 9.1 mil oz t. **CPI change:** 2.4%.

Transport: Railways: 9,503 mi. **Motor vehicles:** 584.2 vehicles per 1,000 pop. **Civil aviation:** 49.8 bil pass.-mi; 99 airports. **Chief ports:** Algeciras, Barcelona, Bilbao, Cartagena, Huelva, Tarragona, Valencia.

Communications: TV sets: 556 per 1,000 pop. **Radios:** 327 per 1,000 pop. **Telephone lines:** 41.1 per 100 pop. **Internet:** 72%.

Health: Life expect.: 78.4 male; 84.6 female. **Births:** 10.1 per 1,000 pop. **Deaths:** 8.9 per 1,000 pop. **Natural inc.:** 0.12%. **Infant mortality:** 3.4 per 1,000 live births. **HIV rate:** 0.4%.

Education: Compulsory: ages 6-16. **Literacy:** 97.7%.

Major intl. organizations: UN and all of its specialized agencies, EU, NATO, OECD, OSCE, WTO.

Embassy: 2375 Pennsylvania Ave. NW 20037; 452-0100.

Website: www.lamoncloa.gob.es

Settled by Iberians, Basques, and Celts, Spain was successively ruled (wholly or in part) by Carthage, Rome, and the Visigoths. Muslims invaded Iberia from N Africa in 711. Reconquest of the peninsula by Christians from the N laid the foundations of modern Spain. In 1469 the kingdoms of Aragon and Castile were united by the marriage of Ferdinand II and Isabella I. Moorish rule ended with the fall of Granada, 1492, the year Spain's large Jewish community was expelled.

Spain established a colonial empire after Columbus's 1492 "discovery" of America. Cortés conquered Mexico, and Pizarro conquered Peru. Spain also controlled the Netherlands and parts of Italy and Germany. Spain lost its American colonies in the early 19th cent. and Cuba, the Philippines, and Puerto Rico during the Spanish-American War, 1898.

Primo de Rivera became dictator, 1923. King Alfonso XIII revoked the dictatorship, 1930, but was forced into exile in 1931. A republic was proclaimed, which disestablished the church, curtailed its privileges, and secularized education. A Popular Front of socialists, Communists, republicans, and anarchists governed 1936-39.

Army officers under Francisco Franco revolted, 1936. Some 500,000 to 1 mil died before the war's end, Mar. 28, 1939. Franco was named caudillo, leader of the nation. Spain was officially neutral in WWII, but its cordial relations with fascist countries prompted its exclusion from the UN until 1955.

After Franco's death, Nov. 20, 1975, Prince Juan Carlos became king. In free elections, June 1977, moderates and democratic socialists won the most votes. The king thwarted a 1981 coup attempt by right-wing military officers. The Socialist Workers' Party, under Felipe González Márquez, won four consecutive general elections between 1982 and 1993 but lost to a coalition of conservative and regional parties, 1996. Conservative Prime Min. José María Aznar, who won a parliamentary majority in the 2000 election, openly supported the U.S.-led invasion of Iraq, Mar. 2003, against Spanish public opinion.

Islamic extremists bombed four commuter trains in central Madrid, Mar. 11, 2004, killing 191 people. The opposition Socialist Workers' Party won elections three days later, and Socialist leader José Luis Rodríguez Zapatero, who became prime min. Apr. 17, removed all 1,300 Spanish troops from Iraq. Spain legalized same-sex marriage in 2005.

Prime Min. Zapatero won a second term in 2008. Spain's banking, building, and tourism industries suffered during the worldwide financial crisis; in May 2010, as the budget deficit mounted and unemployment surged above 20%, the government introduced austerity measures to reassure international lenders. Mariano Rajoy's conservative Popular Party won elections Nov. 2011, and Rajoy became prime min. Dec. 20. Spain received a $125.5-bil EU bailout for its ailing banks in 2012; the request was approved on the condition that Spain establish a "bad bank" for troubled assets.

Huge crowds demonstrated in Barcelona for Catalonian independence Sept. 11, 2012, and two of the region's biggest political parties agreed to an alliance Dec. 18 to push for a 2014 referendum on independence. Spain's unemployment rate surpassed 25% in Oct. 2012. An investigation into Luis Bárcenas, former national treasurer of the Popular Party, widened to include accusations of illegal financing among other members of the Popular Party, including Prime Min. Rajoy, Jan. 15, 2013, but Rajoy resisted resigning in the face of the allegations. A deadly train derailment in Galicia killed 79 July 24; the driver was charged with manslaughter and reckless operation of the train.

Catalonia and the Basque country were granted autonomy, Jan. 1980, following overwhelming approval in home-rule referendums. But Basque extremists pushed for independence. The Basque separatist group ETA carried out bombings that have killed about 830 since 1968. ETA declared a permanent cease-fire effective

Mar. 24, 2006, after which the Spanish govt. agreed to formal peace talks. Negotiations broke down after ETA exploded a car bomb at the Madrid airport, Dec. 30, 2006, killing two; Basque militants formally rescinded the truce, June 5, 2007, but reinstated it Sept. 5, 2010. In Catalonia, voters approved a plan for expanded home-rule, June 18, 2006.

The Balearic Isls. in the W Mediterranean, 1,927 sq mi, are a province of Spain; they include Majorca (Mallorca; capital Palma de Mallorca), Minorca, Cabrera, Ibiza, and Formentera. The Canary Isls., 2,807 sq mi, in the Atlantic W of Morocco, form two provinces, and include the islands of Tenerife, Palma, Gomera, Hierro, Grand Canary, Fuerteventura, and Lanzarote; Las Palmas and Santa Cruz are thriving ports. More than 1,700 people died trying to get from Mauritania to the Canary Isls. in rickety boats, Jan.-June 2006.

Ceuta and Melilla, small Spanish enclaves on Morocco's Mediterranean coast, gained limited autonomy in Sept. 1994. Spain has sought the return of Gibraltar, in British hands since 1704.

Sri Lanka
Democratic Socialist Republic of Sri Lanka

People: Population: 21,675,648. **Age distrib.:** <15: 24.8%; 65+: 8.4%. **Pop. density:** 868.6 per sq mi, 335.4 per sq km. **Urban:** 15.1%. **Ethnic groups:** Sinhalese 74%, Sri Lankan Moors 7%, Indian Tamil 5%, Sri Lankan Tamil 4%. **Languages:** Sinhala (official and national), Tamil (national), English (commonly used in govt). **Religions:** Buddhist (official) 69%, Muslim 8%, Hindu 7%, Christian 6%.

Geography: Total area: 25,332 sq mi, 65,610 sq km; **Land area:** 24,954 sq mi, 64,630 sq km. **Location:** In Indian O. off SE coast of India. **Neighbors:** India on NW. **Topography:** Coastal area and N half are flat; S central area is hilly and mountainous. **Capital:** Sri Jayewardenepura Kotte (admin., legis.), 125,515; Colombo (commercial), 693,470.

Government: Type: Republic. **Head of state:** Pres. Mahinda Rajapaksa; b. Nov. 18, 1945; in office: Nov. 19, 2005. **Head of gov.:** Prime Min. Dissanayake Mudiyanselage (Di Mu) Jayaratne; b. June 7, 1931; in office: Apr. 21, 2010. **Local divisions:** 9 provinces. **Defense budget:** $1.46 bil. **Active troops:** 160,900.

Economy: Industries: rubber, tea, coconuts, tobacco and other agric. commodities proc.; telecom, insurance, banking; tourism, shipping; clothing, textiles; cement, petroleum refining. **Chief crops:** rice, sugarcane, grains, pulses, oilseed, spices, vegetables, fruit, tea, rubber, coconuts. **Natural resources:** limestone, graphite, mineral sands, gems, phosphates, clay, hydropower. **Arable land:** 19.1%. **Livestock:** cattle: 1.2 mil; chickens: 14.2 mil; goats: 375,275; pigs: 82,030; sheep: 8,260. **Fish catch:** 445,101 metric tons. **Electricity prod.:** 10.4 bil kWh. **Labor force:** agric. 31.8%, industry 25.8%, services 42.4%.

Finance: Monetary unit: Rupee (LKR) (Sept. 2013: 133.02 = $1 U.S.). **GDP:** $128.4 bil; **per capita GDP:** $6,200; **GDP growth:** 6.4%. **Imports:** $17.3 bil; India 21.3%, China 16.5%, Singapore 8.6%, Iran 7.7%, UAE 4.4%, Malaysia 4.3%. **Exports:** $9.8 bil; U.S. 22.6%, UK 9.8%, India 6.4%, Belgium 5.2%, Germany 4.8%, Italy 4.3%. **Tourism:** $1.04 bil. **Budget:** $11.6 bil. **Total reserves less gold:** $6.4 bil. **Gold:** 437,990 oz t. **CPI change:** 6.8%.

Transport: Railways: 900 mi. **Motor vehicles:** 44.5 vehicles per 1,000 pop. **Civil aviation:** 4.8 bil pass.-mi; 15 airports. **Chief port:** Colombo.

Communications: TV sets: 118 per 1,000 pop. **Radios:** 200 per 1,000 pop. **Telephone lines:** 16.3 per 100 pop. **Internet:** 18.3%.

Health: Life expect.: 72.6 male; 79.8 female. **Births:** 16.6 per 1,000 pop. **Deaths:** 6.0 per 1,000 pop. **Natural inc.:** 1.06%. **Infant mortality:** 9.2 per 1,000 live births. **HIV rate:** <0.1%.

Education: Compulsory: ages 5-13. **Literacy:** 91.2%.

Major intl. organizations: UN (FAO, IBRD, ILO, IMF, WHO), the Commonwealth, WTO.

Embassy: 2148 Wyoming Ave. NW 20008; 483-4025.

Website: www.priu.gov.lk

The island was known to the ancient world as Taprobane (Greek for copper-colored) and later as Serendip (from Arabic). Colonists from N India subdued the indigenous Veddahs about 543 BCE; their descendants, the Buddhist Sinhalese, still form most of the population. Hindu descendants of Tamil immigrants from S India account for about one-fifth of the population.

Parts were occupied by the Portuguese in 1505 and the Dutch in 1658. The British seized the island in 1796. It became an independent member of the Commonwealth as Ceylon in 1948 before changing its name to Sri Lanka May 22, 1972.

Prime Min. Solomon W. R. D. Bandaranaike was assassinated Sept. 25, 1959. His widow, Sirimavo Bandaranaike, served as prime min. 1960-65, 1970-77, 1994-2000. In the 1970s, thousands of ultra-leftists were executed, while massive land reform and nationalization of foreign-owned plantations took place.

Tensions between Sinhalese and Tamil separatists erupted in the early 1980s and turned into a 20-year civil war that killed more than 60,000; another 20,000, mostly young Tamils, "disappeared" while in government custody.

Pres. Ranasinghe Premadasa was assassinated May 1, 1993, by a Tamil rebel. Mrs. Bandaranaike's daughter, Chandrika Bandaranaike Kumaratunga, became prime min. after Aug. 1994 general elections. Elected president Nov. 9, Kumaratunga appointed her

mother prime min. Kumaratunga, who was injured in a suicide bomb attack at a campaign rally Dec. 18, 1999, won a second 6-year term three days later. In failing health, Mrs. Bandaranaike resigned Aug. 10 and died Oct. 10, 2000. A truce intended to bring an end to the civil war was signed Feb. 22, 2002. More than 31,000 died in the Dec. 26, 2004, Indian Ocean tsunami.

Prime Min. Mahinda Rajapaksa of the United People's Freedom Alliance won the 2005 presidential election. Thousands died during three years of fighting among government forces, paramilitary groups, and Tamil rebels beginning in Dec. 2005. About 7,000 noncombatants were killed Jan. 20-May 7, 2009. Tamil leader Vellupillai Prabhakaran was killed May 18-19, 2009, and Pres. Rajapaksa formally declared victory. He won reelection Jan. 26, 2010. Parliament voted Jan. 11. 2013, to impeach the nation's chief justice, Shirani Bandaranayake; Rajapaksa dismissed her Jan. 13 in what many saw as a politically motivated move.

Sudan
Republic of the Sudan

(Pre-2012 data and communications statistics include South Sudan, which became independent July 9, 2011.)

People: Population: 34,847,910. **Age distrib.:** <15: 41.4%; 65+: 3.3%. **Pop. density:** 48.5 per sq mi, 18.7 per sq km. **Urban:** 33.2%. **Ethnic groups:** Sudanese Arab 70%, Fur, Beja, Nuba, Fallata. **Languages:** Arabic, English (both official); Nubian; Ta Bedawie; Fur. **Religions:** Sunni Muslim, small Christian minority.

Geography: Total area: 718,723 sq mi, 1,861,484 sq km; **Land area:** NA. **Location:** At E end of Sahara desert zone. **Neighbors:** Egypt on N; Libya, Chad, Central African Republic on W; Dem. Rep. of the Congo, South Sudan, Uganda, Kenya on S; Ethiopia, Eritrea on E. **Topography:** The N consists of Libyan Desert in W, and the mountainous Nubia Desert in E, with narrow Nile Valley between. Center contains large, fertile, rainy areas with fields, pastures, and forests. The S has rich soil, heavy rain. **Capital:** Khartoum, 4,632,310.

Government: Type: Federal republic with strong military influence. **Head of state and gov.:** Pres. Gen. Omar Hassan Ahmad al-Bashir; b. Jan. 1, 1944; in office: Oct. 16, 1993 (de facto since June 30, 1989). **Local divisions:** 17 states. **Defense budget:** NA. **Active troops:** 244,300.

Economy: Industries: oil, cotton ginning, textiles, cement, edible oils, sugar, soap distilling, shoes, petroleum refining, pharmaceuticals, armaments. **Chief crops:** cotton, groundnuts, sorghum, millet, wheat, gum arabic, sugarcane, cassava, mangoes, papayas, bananas, sweet potatoes, sesame. **Natural resources:** petroleum; small reserves of iron ore, copper, chromium ore, zinc, tungsten, mica, silver, gold; hydropower. **Crude oil reserves:** 5 bil bbls. **Arable land:** 7.9%. **Livestock:** cattle: 29.6 mil; chickens: 45 mil; goats: 30.6 mil; sheep: 39.3 mil. **Fish catch:** 73,208 metric tons. **Electricity prod.:** 8.1 bil kWh. **Labor force:** agric. 80%, industry 7%, services 13%.

Finance: Monetary unit: Pound (SDG) (Sept. 2013: 4.40 = $1 U.S.). **GDP:** $86.7 bil; **per capita GDP:** $2,600; **GDP growth:** −4.4%. **Imports:** $6.2 bil; Macao 18%, India 8.8%, Saudi Arabia 7.9%, Egypt 6.7%, UAE 5.2%. **Exports:** $4.6 bil; UAE 63.2%, Saudi Arabia 9.2%, Ethiopia 5.3%. **Tourism:** $185 mil. **Budget:** $7.6 bil. **Total reserves less gold:** $192.6 mil. **CPI change** 37.4%.

Transport: Railways: 3,715 mi. **Motor vehicles:** 2.9 vehicles per 1,000 pop. **Civil aviation:** 690.3 mil; pass.-mi; 16 airports. **Chief port:** Port Sudan.

Communications: TV sets: 370 per 1,000 pop. **Radios:** 172 per 1,000 pop. **Telephone lines:** 0.9 per 100 pop. **Internet:** 21%.

Health: Life expect.: 60.9 male; 65.1 female. **Births:** 30.8 per 1,000 pop. **Deaths:** 8.1 per 1,000 pop. **Natural inc.:** 2.28%. **Infant mortality:** 54.2 per 1,000 live births. **HIV rate:** 0.4%.

Education: NA. **Literacy:** 71.9%.

Major intl. organizations: UN (FAO, IBRD, ILO, IMF, WHO), AL, AU, WTO (observer).

Embassy: 2210 Massachusetts Ave. NW 20008; 338-8565.

Website: www.presidency.gov.sd or www.state.gov/p/af/ci/su/

Northern Sudan, ancient Nubia, was settled by Egyptians in antiquity. The population was converted to Coptic Christianity in the 6th cent. Arab conquests brought Islam to the area in the 15th cent. In the 1820s, Egypt took over Sudan, defeating the last of the earlier empires, including the Fung. In the 1880s, Muhammad Ahmad, who called himself the Mahdi (leader of the faithful), and his followers, the dervishes, led a revolution. An Anglo-Egyptian force crushed the Mahdi's successors, 1898.

Sudan gained independence Jan. 1, 1956. In 1969, a Revolutionary Council took power, led by authoritarian Pres. Gaafar al-Nimeiry. He was overthrown, Apr. 6, 1985. Sudan held its first democratic parliamentary elections in 18 years in 1986. Brig. Omar Hassan Ahmad al-Bashir staged a bloodless military coup, toppling the elected government, June 30, 1989. He became president in 1993.

During 1955-72 and 1983-2005, rebels in the south (primarily Christians and followers of traditional religions) rebelled against government domination by mostly Arab-Muslim northern Sudan. War and related famine cost an estimated 2 mil lives. An accord ended the rebellion Jan. 9, 2005.

A rebellion in the Darfur region of western Sudan caused a new crisis, 2003-11. Marauding Arab militias, the *janjaweed*, reportedly

acting in collusion with Sudanese government troops, looted and burned homes in Darfur and killed many African villagers. More than 7,000 African Union peacekeepers were ineffectual. Rebel and militia activities in Sudan and Chad led to border clashes and further attacks on civilians. By Sept. 2009, the Darfur war had killed about 300,000 people and displaced another 2.7 mil. A joint UN-African Union force of up to 26,000 peacekeepers (UNMIS) was deployed in Aug. 2007, followed by UNMISS upon South Sudan's independence, July 2011.

The Intl. Criminal Court in The Hague, Netherlands, issued two arrest warrants for Pres. Bashir—one in 2009 for war crimes and other crimes against humanity in Darfur, and another in 2010 for genocide, the first time it had ever accused a head of state of genocide. Bashir defied the calls for his arrest, and in Apr. 2010 won a new 5-year term in elections after his main challengers dropped out, alleging fraud.

After southern Sudanese voted overwhelmingly for secession, Jan. 9-15, 2011, South Sudan attained full independence July 9. Border disputes between Sudan and South Sudan ensued, though a 4-year interim deal on the division of oil revenues was reached Aug. 6, 2012, and an agreement was signed Sept. 27 to ship oil from the south through Sudan. A gold mine collapsed Apr. 29, 2013, in the Darfur region, killing about 60 miners.

Suriname
Republic of Suriname

People: Population: 566,846. **Age distrib.:** <15: 26.8%; 65+: 5.6%. **Pop. density:** 9.4 per sq mi, 3.6 per sq km. **Urban:** 69.7%. **Ethnic groups:** Hindustani (known locally as East Indian) 37%, Creole 31%, Javanese 15%, Maroon (descendants of escaped slaves) 10%, Amerindian 2%, Chinese 2%, white 1%. **Languages:** Dutch (official), English (widely spoken), Sranang Tongo (Surinamese), Caribbean Hindustani, Javanese. **Religions:** Hindu 27%, Protestant 25% (predominantly Moravian), Roman Catholic 23%, Muslim 20%, indigenous beliefs 5%.

Geography: Total area: 63,251 sq mi, 163,820 sq km; **Land area:** 60,232 sq mi, 156,000 sq km. **Location:** On N shore of S America. **Neighbors:** Guyana on W, Brazil on S, French Guiana on E. **Topography:** A flat Atlantic coast, where dikes permit agriculture. Inland is forest belt. To S, largely unexplored hills cover 75% of country. **Capital:** Paramaribo, 277,802.

Government: Type: Constitutional democracy. **Head of state and gov.:** Pres. Désiré (Dési) Delano Bouterse; b. Oct. 13, 1945; in office: Aug. 12, 2010. **Local divisions:** 10 districts. **Defense budget** (2010): $41 mil. **Active troops:** 1,840.

Economy: Industries: mining, alumina prod., oil, lumber, food proc., fishing. **Chief crops:** rice, bananas, palm kernels, coconuts, plantains, peanuts. **Natural resources:** timber, hydropower, fish, kaolin, shrimp, bauxite, gold; small amounts of nickel, copper, platinum, iron ore. **Crude oil reserves:** 76.8 mil bbls. **Arable land:** 0.4%. **Livestock:** cattle: 55,245; chickens: 6.9 mil; goats: 5,813; pigs: 34,327; sheep: 7,510. **Fish catch:** 34,456 metric tons. **Electricity prod.:** 1.6 bil kWh. **Labor force:** agric. 8%, industry 14%, services 78%.

Finance: Monetary unit: Dollar (SRD) (Sept. 2013: 3.27 = $1 U.S.). **GDP:** $6.9 bil; **per capita GDP:** $12,600; **GDP growth:** 4.5%. **Imports:** $1.8 bil; U.S. 25.8%, Netherlands 15.8%, China 9.8%, UAE 7.9%, Antigua and Barbuda 7.3%, Netherlands Antilles 5.4%, Japan 4.2%. **Exports:** $2.6 bil; U.S. 26.1%, Belgium 17.6%, UAE 12.1%, Canada 10.4%, Guyana 6.5%, France 5.6%, Barbados 4.7%. **Tourism:** $61 mil. **Budget** (2010): $939.7 mil. **Total reserves less gold:** $885.1 mil. **Gold:** 74,373 oz t. **CPI change:** 5%.

Transport: Motor vehicles: 218.2 vehicles per 1,000 pop. **Civil aviation:** 1.1 mil pass.-mi; 6 airports. **Chief ports:** Paramaribo, Wageningen.

Communications: TV sets: 266 per 1,000 pop. **Radios:** 711 per 1,000 pop. **Telephone lines:** 15.5 per 100 pop. **Internet:** 34.7%.

Health: Life expect.: 69.1 male; 73.9 female. **Births:** 17.1 per 1,000 pop. **Deaths:** 6.2 per 1,000 pop. **Natural inc.:** 1.10%. **Infant mortality:** 28.0 per 1,000 live births. **HIV rate:** 1%.

Education: Compulsory: ages 7-12. **Literacy:** 94.7%.

Major intl. organizations: UN (FAO, IBRD, ILO, IMF, WHO), Caricom, OAS, WTO.

Embassy: 4301 Connecticut Ave. NW, Ste. 460, 20008; 244-7488.

Website: www.gov.sr or www.surinameembassy.org

The Netherlands acquired Suriname in 1667 from Britain, in exchange for New Netherlands (New York). The 1954 Dutch constitution raised the colony to a level of equality with the Netherlands and the Netherlands Antilles. Independence was granted Nov. 25, 1975. Some 40% of the population (mostly E Indians, who opposed independence) immigrated to the Netherlands in the months before independence.

Désiré (Dési) Bouterse, who masterminded coups in 1982 and 1990, was elected president by parliament, July 19, 2010; as he took office Aug. 12, he was facing trial in Suriname on charges of having executed 15 political opponents in 1982, and he had been convicted in absentia in the Netherlands, 1999, for drug trafficking. The U.S. State Dept. has labeled Suriname a transshipment point for cocaine trafficking. To repair its reputation, Suriname signed the UN-supported Container Control Programme (CCP), Aug. 23, 2012, to insure the better inspection of shipping containers in its ports. Suriname deposited a demand for reparations with the Dutch embassy, July 28, 2013, for the legacy of the slave trade, which it claimed had left the country with lingering socioeconomic problems.

Swaziland
Kingdom of Swaziland

People: Population: 1,403,362. **Age distrib.:** <15: 36.9%; 65+: 3.7%. **Pop. density:** 211.3 per sq mi, 81.6 per sq km. **Urban:** 21.2%. **Ethnic groups:** African 97%, European 3%. **Languages:** English (used in govt.), siSwati (both official). **Religions:** Zionist 40%, Roman Catholic 20%, Muslim 10%, other (incl. Anglican, Baha'i, Methodist, Mormon, Jewish) 30%.

Geography: Total area: 6,704 sq mi, 17,364 sq km; **Land area:** 6,643 sq mi, 17,204 sq km. **Location:** In southern Africa, near Indian O. coast. **Neighbors:** South Africa on N, W, S; Mozambique on E. **Topography:** Descends W-E in broad belts, becoming more arid in low veld region, then rising to plateau in E. **Capital:** Mbabane (admin.), 65,536; Lobamba (legislative).

Government: Type: Monarchy. **Head of state:** King Mswati III; b. Apr. 19, 1968; in office: Apr. 25, 1986. **Head of gov.:** Prime Min. Barnabas Sibusiso Dlamini; b. May 15, 1942; in office: Oct. 23, 2008. **Local divisions:** 4 districts. **Defense budget/active troops:** NA.

Economy: Industries: coal, wood pulp, sugar, soft drink concentrates, textiles and apparel. **Chief crops:** sugarcane, cotton, corn, tobacco, rice, citrus, pineapples, sorghum, peanuts. **Natural resources:** asbestos, coal, clay, cassiterite, hydropower, forests, small gold and diamond deposits, quarry stone, talc. **Arable land:** 10.2%. **Livestock:** cattle: 625,000; chickens: 3.6 mil; goats: 270,000; pigs: 33,500; sheep: 35,000. **Fish catch:** 290 metric tons. **Electricity prod.:** 496 mil kWh. **Labor force:** agric. 70%.

Finance: Monetary unit: Lilangeni (SZL) (Sept. 2013: 10.02 = $1 U.S.). **GDP:** $6.3 bil; **per capita GDP:** $5,900; **GDP growth:** –1.5%. **Imports:** $2.2 bil. **Exports:** $2 bil. **Tourism:** $51 mil. **Budget:** $1.4 bil. **Total reserves less gold:** $741 mil. **CPI change:** 9.4%.

Transport: Railways: 187 mi. **Civil aviation:** 2 airports.

Communications: TV sets: 37 per 1,000 pop. **Radios:** 362 per 1,000 pop. **Telephone lines:** 4 per 100 pop. **Internet:** 20.8%.

Health: Life expect.: 50.4 male; 49.6 female. **Births:** 25.7 per 1,000 pop. **Deaths:** 14.0 per 1,000 pop. **Natural inc.:** 1.17%. **Infant mortality:** 57.2 per 1,000 live births. **HIV rate:** 26%.

Education: Compulsory: ages 6-12. **Literacy:** 87.8%.

Major intl. organizations: UN (FAO, IBRD, ILO, IMF, WHO), the Commonwealth, WTO.

Embassy: 1712 New Hampshire Ave. NW 20009; 234-5002.

Website: www.gov.sz

The royal house of Swaziland, one of Africa's last ruling dynasties, traces back about 400 years. The Zulus drove the Swazis, a Bantu people, to Swaziland from lands to the N, 1820. Britain and Transvaal (later part of South Africa) later guaranteed their autonomy, and Britain assumed control after 1903. Independence came Sept. 6, 1968. In 1973, the king repealed the constitution and assumed full powers.

A new constitution banning political parties took effect Oct. 13, 1978. Under a revised constitution effective Feb. 8, 2006, nonpartisan parliamentary elections were held Sept. 19, 2008. An attempt to unite various Swazi pro-democracy groups under the banner of the People's United Democratic Movement (PUDEMO) in 2012 failed. The AIDS crisis and the huge gap between rich and poor have fueled student and labor unrest in recent years, but the UN reported July 30, 2013, that AIDS-related deaths in Swaziland had fallen drastically due to the use of antiretroviral therapy. Parliamentary elections were again held Sept. 20, 2013, but the monarch retained absolute power.

Sweden
Kingdom of Sweden

People: Population: 9,119,423. **Age distrib.:** <15: 15.4%; 65+: 20.5%. **Pop. density:** 57.6 per sq mi, 22.2 per sq km. **Urban:** 85.2%. **Ethnic groups:** indigenous Swedes, Finns, Sami; foreign-born or immigrant Finns, Yugoslavs, Danes, Norwegians, Greeks, Turks. **Languages:** Swedish (official), small Sami- and Finnish-speaking minorities. **Religions:** Lutheran 87%, other (incl. Roman Catholic, Orthodox, Baptist, Muslim, Jewish, Buddhist) 13%.

Geography: Total area: 173,860 sq mi, 450,295 sq km; **Land area:** 158,431 sq mi, 410,335 sq km. **Location:** On Scandinavian Peninsula in N Europe. **Neighbors:** Norway on W, Denmark on S (across Kattegat), Finland on E. **Topography:** Mountains along NW border cover 25% of Sweden; flat or rolling terrain covers central and southern areas, which include several large lakes. **Capital:** Stockholm, 1,385,200.

Government: Type: Constitutional monarchy. **Head of state:** King Carl XVI Gustaf; b. Apr. 30, 1946; in office: Sept. 19, 1973. **Head of gov.:** Prime Min. Fredrik Reinfeldt; b. Aug. 4, 1965; in office: Oct. 5, 2006. **Local divisions:** 21 counties. **Defense budget:** $5.79 bil. **Active troops:** 20,500.

Economy: Industries: iron and steel, precision equip. (bearings, radio and phone parts, armaments), wood pulp and paper prods., processed foods, motor vehicles. **Chief crops:** barley, wheat, sugar

beets. **Natural resources:** iron ore, copper, lead, zinc, gold, silver, tungsten, uranium, arsenic, feldspar, timber, hydropower. **Arable land:** 6.4%. **Livestock:** cattle: 1.5 mil; chickens: 8.2 mil; pigs: 1.5 mil; sheep: 622,711. **Fish catch:** 194,762 metric tons. **Electricity prod.** (2011): 148.7 bil kWh. **Labor force:** agric. 1.1%, industry 28.2%, services 70.7%.

Finance: Monetary unit: Krona (SEK) (Sept. 2013: 6.64 = $1 U.S.). **GDP:** $399.4 bil; **per capita GDP:** $41,900; **GDP growth:** 1.2%. **Imports:** $163.6 bil; Germany 17.4%, Denmark 8.5%, Norway 8.4%, UK 6.5%, Netherlands 6.4%, Russia 5.6%, Finland 5.1%, China 4.9%, France 4.2%. **Exports:** $178.5 bil; Norway 10.4%, Germany 10.3%, UK 8.1%, Denmark 6.7%, Finland 6.7%, Netherlands 5.5%, U.S. 5.5%, Belgium 5%, France 4.8%. **Tourism:** $15.4 bil. **Budget:** $271.5 bil. **Total reserves less gold:** $45.5 bil. **Gold:** 4 mil oz t. **CPI change:** 0.9%.

Transport: Railways: 7,228 mi. **Motor vehicles:** 552.5 vehicles per 1,000 pop. **Civil aviation:** 5.6 bil pass.-mi; 149 airports. **Chief ports:** Brofjorden, Göteborg, Helsingborg, Karlshamn, Lulea, Malmö, Stockholm, Trelleborg, Visby.

Communications: TV sets: 551 per 1,000 pop. **Radios:** 931 per 1,000 pop. **Telephone lines:** 45.5 per 100 pop. **Internet:** 94%.

Health: Life expect.: 79.0 male; 83.8 female. **Births:** 10.3 per 1,000 pop. **Deaths:** 10.2 per 1,000 pop. **Natural inc.:** 0.01%. **Infant mortality:** 2.7 per 1,000 live births. **HIV rate:** 0.2%.

Education: Compulsory: ages 7-16. **Literacy:** 99%.

Major intl. organizations: UN and all of its specialized agencies, EU, OECD, OSCE, WTO.

Embassy: 2900 K St. NW 20007; 467-2600.

Website: www.sweden.se

The Swedes have lived in present-day Sweden for at least 5,000 years, longer than nearly any other European people have lived in their present-day homelands. Gothic tribes from Sweden played a major role in the disintegration of the Roman Empire. Other Swedes helped create the first Russian state in the 9th cent.

The Swedes were Christianized from the 11th cent., and a strong centralized monarchy developed. The Riksdag, the first European parliament to represent all classes of society, was first called in 1435.

A revolt led by Gustavus I in 1521-23 freed Sweden from Danish rule (dating from 1397); he built up the government and military and established the Lutheran Church. In the 17th cent. Sweden was a major European power, gaining most of the Baltic seacoast. The Napoleonic wars, 1799-1815, in which Sweden acquired Norway (it became independent 1905), were the last in which Sweden participated. Armed neutrality was maintained in both world wars.

Social Democrats have governed Sweden for most of the period since World War II. Prime Min. Olof Palme was shot to death in Stockholm, Feb. 28, 1986, and Christer Pettersson was found guilty in 1988. He was sentenced to life in prison, but his conviction was overturned on appeal in 1989 for lack of evidence.

Swedish voters approved EU membership in Nov. 1994, and Sweden entered the EU, Jan. 1, 1995.

A center-right alliance led by Fredrik Reinfeldt defeated the Social Democrats in Sept. 2006 elections. Parliament voted Apr. 1, 2009, to legalize same-sex marriage. The 2008-09 global recession led to a decline in Swedish exports, especially cars and trucks, but the economy began recovering in mid-2009. Reinfeldt's center-right bloc won a renewed mandate in Sept. 2010 parliamentary elections. Several nights of riots in poor, immigrant Stockholm neighborhoods starting May 20, 2013, were touched off by the police shooting of a machete-wielding elderly man.

Switzerland
Swiss Confederation

People: Population: 7,996,026. **Age distrib.:** <15: 15.2%; 65+: 17.3%. **Pop. density:** 517.8 per sq mi, 199.9 per sq km. **Urban:** 73.7%. **Ethnic groups:** German 65%, French 18%, Italian 10%, Romansch 1%. **Languages:** German, French, Italian (all official); Serbo-Croatian; Albanian; Portuguese; Spanish; English; Romansch (official). **Religions:** Roman Catholic 42%, Protestant 35%, Muslim 4%, Orthodox 2%, none 11%.

Geography: Total area: 15,937 sq mi, 41,277 sq km; **Land area:** 15,443 sq mi, 39,997 sq km. **Location:** In Alps Mts. in central Europe. **Neighbors:** France on W; Italy on S; Liechtenstein, Austria on E; Germany on N. **Topography:** The Alps cover 60% of land area; the Jura, near France, 10%. Running in-between, NE-SW, are midlands, 30%. **Capital:** Bern, 353,462. **Cities (urban aggl.):** Zürich, 1,194,176.

Government: Type: Federal republic in structure (formally a confederation). **Head of state and gov.:** President chosen on rotating basis from among 7-member Federal Council for 1-year term. Pres. Ueli Maurer, b. Dec. 1, 1950; in office: Jan. 1, 2013. **Local divisions:** 26 cantons. **Defense budget:** $4.76 bil. **Active troops:** 23,100.

Economy: Industries: machinery, chemicals, watches, textiles, precision instruments, tourism, banking, insurance. **Chief crops:** grains, fruits, vegetables. **Natural resources:** hydropower potential, timber, salt. **Arable land:** 10.1%. **Livestock:** cattle: 1.6 mil; chickens: 9.4 mil; goats: 86,255; pigs: 1.6 mil; sheep: 424,018. **Fish catch:** 2,919 metric tons. **Electricity prod.** (2011): 60.2 bil kWh. **Labor force:** agric. 3.4%, industry 23.4%, services 73.2%.

Finance: Monetary unit: Franc (CHF) (Sept. 2013: 0.94 = $1 U.S.). **GDP:** $369.4 bil; **per capita GDP:** $46,200; **GDP growth:**

1%. **Imports:** $287.7 bil; Germany 29.7%, Italy 10.2%, France 8.4%, U.S. 5.6%, China 5.6%, Austria 4.2%. **Exports:** $333.4 bil; Germany 19.8%, U.S. 11.1%, Italy 7.2%, France 7.1%, UK 5.4%. **Tourism:** $16.6 bil. **Budget:** $212.9 bil (incl. federal, cantonal, and municipal accts.). **Total reserves less gold:** $475.7 bil. **Gold:** 33.4 mil oz t. **CPI change:** −0.7%.

Transport: Railways: 3,030 mi. **Motor vehicles:** 589.9 vehicles per 1,000 pop. **Civil aviation:** 18.4 bil pass.-mi; 40 airports. **Chief port:** Basel.

Communications: TV sets: 594 per 1,000 pop. **Radios:** 1,004 per 1,000 pop. **Telephone lines:** 56.7 per 100 pop. **Internet:** 85.2%.

Health: Life expect.: 80.0 male; 84.7 female. **Births:** 10.5 per 1,000 pop. **Deaths:** 8.1 per 1,000 pop. **Natural inc.:** 0.24%. **Infant mortality:** 3.8 per 1,000 live births. **HIV rate:** 0.4%.

Education: Compulsory: ages 7-15. **Literacy:** 99%.

Major intl. organizations: UN and most of its specialized agencies, EFTA, OECD, OSCE, WTO.

Embassy: 2900 Cathedral Ave. NW 20008; 745-7900.

Website: www.ch.ch

Switzerland, the former Roman province of Helvetia, traces its modern history to 1291, when three cantons created a defensive league. Other cantons were subsequently admitted to the Swiss Confederation, which obtained its independence from the Holy Roman Empire through the Peace of Westphalia (1648). The cantons were joined under a federal constitution in 1848.

Switzerland has maintained an armed neutrality since 1815 and has not been involved in a foreign war since 1515. It is the seat of many UN and other international agencies but only became a full UN member on Sept. 10, 2002.

Switzerland is a world banking center. The government announced, Mar. 1997, a $4.7 bil fund to compensate victims of the Nazi Holocaust and other catastrophes. Swiss banks agreed Aug. 12, 1998, to pay $1.25 bil in reparations. A June 2002 referendum decriminalized abortion. Two more referendums in 2005 harmonized travel, asylum, law enforcement, and labor policies with the EU; more rights for same-sex couples were also endorsed June 5.

The Swiss government bailed out the troubled banking giant UBS during the international financial crisis in Oct. 2008. U.S. tax authorities pressured UBS Jan. 2009 to close some 19,000 hidden offshore accounts and to disclose in Aug. data on accounts for over 4,400 U.S. clients. In a Nov. 2009 referendum reflecting rising anti-Muslim sentiment, voters approved a constitutional ban on construction of new minarets on mosques. In Sept. 2011, Switzerland capped its currency at 1.20 Swiss francs per euro, a strategy that seemed to have enabled the economy to grow in 2012. Two multiple-casualty shootings occurred in Jan.-Feb. 2013, prompting many to express the need for further gun control.

Syria
Syrian Arab Republic

People: Population: 22,457,336. **Age distrib.:** <15: 33.9%; 65+: 3.9%. **Pop. density:** 316.7 per sq mi, 122.3 per sq km. **Urban:** 56.1%. **Ethnic groups:** Arab 90%; Kurds, Armenians, and other 10%. **Languages:** Arabic (official), Kurdish, Armenian, Aramaic, Circassian (widely understood). **Religions:** Sunni Muslim 74% (Islam official), other Muslim (incl. Alawite, Druze) 16%, Christian 10%.

Geography: Total area: 71,498 sq mi, 185,180 sq km; **Land area:** 70,900 sq mi, 183,630 sq km. **Location:** Middle East, at E end of Medit. Sea. **Neighbors:** Lebanon, Israel on W; Jordan on S; Iraq on E; Turkey on N. **Topography:** A short Medit. coastline stretches E and S with fertile lowlands and plains, alternating with mountains and large desert areas. **Capital:** Dimashq (Damascus), 2,649,860. **Cities (urban aggl.):** Halab (Aleppo), 3,163,759; Hims (Homs), 1,369,287.

Government: Type: Republic under authoritarian regime. **Head of state:** Pres. Bashar al-Assad; b. Sept. 11, 1965; in office: July 17, 2000. **Head of gov.:** Prime Min. Wael al-Halqi; in office: Aug. 9, 2012. **Local divisions:** 14 provinces. **Defense budget:** $3.52 bil. **Active troops:** 178,000.

Economy: Industries: petroleum, textiles, food proc., beverages, tobacco, phosphate rock mining, cement. **Chief crops:** wheat, barley, cotton, lentils, chickpeas, olives, sugar beets. **Natural resources:** petroleum, phosphates, chrome and manganese ores, asphalt, iron ore, rock salt, marble, gypsum, hydropower. **Crude oil reserves:** 2.5 bil bbls. **Arable land:** 25.1%. **Livestock:** cattle: 1.2 mil; chickens: 26.2 mil; goats: 2.3 mil; sheep: 18.1 mil. **Fish catch:** 12,900 metric tons. **Electricity prod.:** 43.8 bil kWh. **Labor force:** agric. 17%, industry 16%, services 67%.

Finance: Monetary unit: Pound (SYP) (Sept. 2013: 112.95 = $1 U.S.). **GDP** (2011): $107.6 bil; **per capita GDP** (2011): $5,100; **GDP growth:** NA. **Imports:** $10.8 bil; Saudi Arabia 21.2%, UAE 10.4%, Iran 7.7%, China 7%, Iraq 6.3%, Ukraine 6.3%, Egypt 4.3%. **Exports:** $3.9 bil; Iraq 55.9%, Saudi Arabia 9.3%, Kuwait 6.1%, UAE 5.3%, Lebanon 4.2%. **Tourism:** $6.2 bil. **Budget:** $12.6 bil. **Total reserves less gold** (2010): $19.5 bil. **Gold** (2010): 830,000 oz t. **CPI change:** 36.7%.

Transport: Railways: 1,275 mi. **Motor vehicles:** 78 vehicles per 1,000 pop. **Civil aviation:** 1.6 bil pass.-mi; 29 airports. **Chief ports:** Baniyas, Latakia, Tartus.

Communications: TV sets: 192 per 1,000 pop. **Radios:** 267 per 1,000 pop. **Telephone lines:** 20.9 per 100 pop. **Internet:** 24.3%.

Health: Life expect.: 72.7 male; 77.7 female. **Births:** 23.0 per 1,000 pop. **Deaths:** 3.7 per 1,000 pop. **Natural inc.:** 1.93%. **Infant mortality:** 14.6 per 1,000 live births. **HIV rate:** NA.
Education: Compulsory: ages 6-14. **Literacy:** 84.1%.
Major intl. organizations: UN (FAO, IBRD, ILO, IMF, WHO), AL, WTO (observer).
Embassy: 2215 Wyoming Ave. NW 20008; 232-6313.
Website: parliament.sy

Syria was the center of the Seleucid Empire but later was absorbed into the Roman and Arab empires. Ottoman rule prevailed for four cents., until the end of WWI.

The state of Syria was formed from former Turkish districts, separated by the Treaty of Sevres, 1920, and divided into the states of Syria and Greater Lebanon. Both were administered under a French League of Nations mandate, 1920-41. The occupying French proclaimed Syria a republic Sept. 16, 1941; independence came Apr. 17, 1946. Syria joined the Arab invasion of Israel in 1948.

Syria belonged to the United Arab Republic from Feb. 1958 to Sept. 1961. The Socialist Baath party seized power Mar. 1963 and became the only legal party. The Alawite minority has dominated the government.

In the June 1967 Arab-Israeli war, Israel seized and occupied the Golan Heights, from which Syria had shelled Israeli settlements. On Oct. 6, 1973, Syria and Egypt attacked Israel but failed to recapture the Golan Heights. Syrian troops entered Lebanon in 1976, during the Lebanese civil war, and remained a strong presence in the country. They fought Palestinian guerrillas and, later, Christian militiamen. Syria sided with Iran during the Iran-Iraq war, 1980-88.

Thousands died in the city of Hama Feb. 1982 when government forces crushed a Muslim Brotherhood uprising. Following Israel's invasion of Lebanon, June 6, 1982, Israeli planes destroyed 17 Syrian antiaircraft missile batteries in the Bekaa Valley, June 9, and some 25 Syrian planes. Israel and Syria agreed to a cease-fire June 11. Syria's alleged role in promoting international terrorism led to strained relations with the U.S. and Great Britain.

Syria condemned the Aug. 1990 Iraqi invasion of Kuwait and sent troops to help Allied forces in the Gulf War. In 1991, Syria participated with Israel in a U.S.-backed Arab-Israeli peace conference, but little progress was made.

Hafez al-Assad, president of Syria since 1971, died June 10, 2000, and was succeeded by his son Bashar al-Assad. Following the U.S.-led invasion of Iraq, Mar. 2003, hundreds of thousands of Iraqi refugees flooded into Syria. The U.S. pressured Syria to rein in extremists and deny safe haven to fugitive Iraqi leaders. Israeli planes hit an alleged terrorist camp near Damascus Oct. 4, 2003. The U.S. imposed limited sanctions on Syria, May 11, 2004.

Syria denied responsibility for a truck bomb that killed former Lebanese Prime Min. Rafik al-Hariri in Beirut in Feb. 2005. Syria aided Hezbollah fighters in their conflict with Israel and gave about 180,000 Lebanese temporary refuge when Israeli armed forces targeted Hezbollah in Lebanon, July-Aug. 2006.

Syrian voters confirmed Pres. Bashar al-Assad for another 7-year term, May 2007. On Sept. 6, Israel bombed a secret site in N Syria where the Israelis believed Syria and North Korea were developing a nuclear facility; both countries denied the claim. The Assad regime used troops and tanks to enforce control during the Arab Spring demonstrations in Mar. 2011, but the conflict escalated into outright rebellion. The Intl. Committee of the Red Cross declared the conflict a civil war, July 15, 2012, enacting the rules of war under the Geneva Convention. Armed opposition forces achieved a level of unity, though no single group emerged as a viable alternative to Assad. The Natl. Coalition for Syrian Revolutionary and Opposition Forces, consisting of 90% of Syrian opposition groups, replaced the two-year-old Syrian National Council (SNC), Nov. 11, 2012. Sheikh Ahmed Moaz al-Khatib as its president, it quickly gained international support.

NATO, Dec. 4, agreed to deploy Patriot missiles along the Syrian-Turkish border to protect Turkey from being drawn into the Syrian conflict. On Jan. 30, 2013, Israel bombed a convoy in Damascus allegedly carrying missiles to Hezbollah forces in Lebanon, which backed Assad. Although rebel leaders agreed to peace talks in Feb., they and the Assad regime continued their attacks throughout 2013, killing both armed and unarmed civilians. The U.S. announced Feb. 28 that it would send more than $60 mil in humanitarian aid to Syrian rebels. International intelligence communities announced in May that there was increasing evidence that Assad had already used chemical and biological weapons against his own people during the conflict. Fears that Syria was shipping weapons to Hezbollah prompted an Israeli airstrike on a warehouse at Damascus Intl. Airport May 2-3. The EU May 28 lifted an arms embargo prohibiting weapons shipments to rebel fighters. Findings that Assad was using chemical weapons led to U.S. Pres. Barack Obama's June 13 decision to supply military support to the rebels. The Natl. Coalition selected a new president, June 6, in hope that he would rally the rebels, who had been losing ground to the Assad regime. A chemical attack on an opposition-controlled Damascus suburb Aug. 21, 2013, killed more than 1,400. Assad and the rebels accused each other of the attack. In early Sept., Pres. Obama pressed Congress to approve punative military strikes but agreed to negotiate with Russia over its Sept. 9 proposal that Syrian chemical weapons be placed under international control. Russian-U.S. negotiators reached an agreement requiring Syria to relinquish its chemical weapons; the agreement was reinforced by a UN Security Council resolution Sept. 27.

The civilian death toll, according to the UN, was more than 100,000 as of Aug. 2013. The UNHCR announced Sept. 3, 2013, that the number of Syrian refugees had passed the 2 mil mark, at least 1 mil of whom were children. Another 4.25 mil were displaced within Syria.

Taiwan

People: Population: 23,299,716. **Age distrib.:** <15: 14.3%; 65+: 11.6%. **Pop. density:** 1,870.6 per sq mi, 722.2 per sq km. **Urban:** NA. **Ethnic groups:** Taiwanese (incl. Hakka) 84%, mainland Chinese 14%, indigenous 2%. **Languages:** Mandarin Chinese (official), Taiwanese (Min), Hakka dialects. **Religions:** mixture of Buddhist and Taoist 93%, Christian 5%.

Geography: Total area: 13,892 sq mi, 35,980 sq km; **Land area:** 12,456 sq mi, 32,260 sq km. **Location:** Off SE coast of China, between E and S China Seas. **Neighbors:** Nearest is China to NW. **Topography:** A mountain range forms backbone of island. The eastern half is very steep and craggy; western slope is flat, fertile, and well cultivated. **Capital:** Taipei, 2,657,180. **Cities (urban aggl.):** Kaohsiung, 1,516,443; Taichung, 1,156,696.

Government: Type: Multiparty democracy. **Head of state:** Pres. Ma Ying-jeou; b. July 13, 1950; in office: May 20, 2008. **Head of gov.:** Prem. Jiang Yi-huah; b. 1960; in office: Feb. 18, 2013. **Local divisions:** 14 counties, 3 municipalities, 5 special municipalities. **Defense budget:** $10.3 bil. **Active troops:** 290,000.

Economy: Industries: electronics, communications and info. tech. prods., petroleum refining, armaments, chemicals, textiles, iron and steel, machinery, cement, food proc., vehicles, consumer prods., pharmaceuticals. **Chief crops:** rice, vegetables, fruit, tea, flowers. **Natural resources:** small deposits of coal, nat. gas, limestone, marble, asbestos. **Crude oil reserves:** 2.4 mil bbls. **Arable land:** 24%. **Livestock:** cattle: 136,152; chickens: 99 mil; goats: 190,440; pigs: 6.2 mil; sheep: 200. **Fish catch:** 1.2 mil metric tons. **Electricity prod.:** 226.8 bil kWh. **Labor force:** agric. 5%, industry 36.2%, services 58.8%.

Finance: Monetary unit: New Dollar (TWD) (Sept. 2013: 29.78 = $1 U.S.). **GDP:** $918.3 bil; **per capita GDP:** $39,400; **GDP growth:** 1.3%. **Imports:** $268.8 bil; Japan 17.6%, China 16.1%, U.S. 9.5%. **Exports:** $299.8 bil; China 27.1%, Hong Kong 13.2%, U.S. 10.3%, Japan 6.4%, Singapore 4.4%. **Tourism:** $11.7 bil. **Budget:** $64.6 bil. **Total reserves less gold:** NA. **CPI change:** NA.

Transport: Railways: 982 mi. **Motor vehicles:** 307.6 vehicles per 1,000 pop. **Civil aviation:** 35 airports. **Chief ports:** Chilung, Hualian, Kaohsiung, Taichung.

Communications: TV sets: 444 per 1,000 pop. **Radios:** 178 per 1,000 pop. **Telephone lines:** 68.7 per 100 pop. **Internet:** 76%.

Health: Life expect.: 76.6 male; 83.1 female. **Births:** 8.6 per 1,000 pop. **Deaths:** 6.8 per 1,000 pop. **Natural inc.:** 0.18%. **Infant mortality:** 4.6 per 1,000 live births. **HIV rate:** NA.

Education: Compulsory: ages 6-18. **Literacy:** 96.1%.
Major intl. organizations: APEC, WTO.
Taipei Economic and Cultural Representative Office: 4201 Wisconsin Ave. NW 20016; 895-1800.
Website: www.taiwan.gov.tw

Large-scale Chinese immigration began in the 17th cent. The island came under mainland control after an interval of Dutch rule, 1620-62. Japan ruled Taiwan (also called Formosa), 1895-1945. The Kuomintang (Chinese nationalist govt.) fled to Taiwan in 1949 and established the Republic of China under Chiang Kai-shek, who ruled until his death in 1975. The U.S. provided military aid to deter a Communist invasion.

In 1971, the UN expelled Taiwan from its seat and recognized the mainland government. The U.S. recognized the People's Republic of China, Dec. 15, 1978, and severed ties with Taiwan. However, the U.S. and Taiwan have continued a strong trading relationship and maintain contact via quasi-official agencies.

Land reform, government planning, U.S. aid and investment, and free universal education brought advances in industry, agriculture, and living standards. In 1987 martial law was lifted after 38 years, and in 1991 the 43 years of emergency rule ended. Taiwan held its first direct presidential election Mar. 23, 1996. An earthquake on Sept. 21, 1999, killed more than 2,300 people.

Five decades of Nationalist Party rule ended when Chen Shui-bian, leader of the pro-independence Democratic Progressive Party, won the Mar. 2000 presidential election. Chen was wounded in an apparent assassination attempt Mar. 19, 2004, one day before he won a second term as president. Promising increased cooperation with China, Taipei Mayor Ma Ying-jeou won the presidential election, Mar. 22, 2008.

Former Pres. Chen Shui-bian was convicted of corruption and sentenced to life in prison, Sept. 11, 2009. He survived a suicide attempt June 3, 2013. Flooding and mudslides from Typhoon Morakot, Aug. 7-9, 2009, left at least 700 people dead or missing; criticism of the government's disaster response led to a cabinet shake-up a month later. Former Pres. Lee Teng-hui, who introduced democratic reforms 1988-2000, was indicted June 30, 2011, for allegedly embezzling $7.8 mil while in office. The death of a Taiwanese fisherman shot by the Philippine Coast Guard May 9, 2013, prompted a dispute between the two countries. Taiwan lifted sanctions against the Philippines Aug. 9 after the Philippines issued an official apology and agreed to financially compensate the fisherman's family.

Since 1949, the People's Republic has considered Taiwan a rebel province of the mainland; until 1991, Taiwan claimed to be the sole

government of both. In 2003, China replaced the U.S. as Taiwan's leading trade partner. China has warned of military action should Taiwan move toward independence.

The Penghu Isls. (Pescadores), 49 sq mi, pop. (2011 est.) 96,597, lie between Taiwan and the mainland. Kinmen, fmr. Quemoy, pop. (2011 est.) 99,691, and Matsu, pop. (2011 est.) 10,106, lie just off the mainland.

Tajikistan
Republic of Tajikistan

People: Population: 7,910,041. **Age distrib.:** <15: 33.4%; 65+: 3.2%. **Pop. density:** 144.8 per sq mi, 55.9 per sq km. **Urban:** 26.5%. **Ethnic groups:** Tajik 80%, Uzbek 15%, Russian 1%, Kyrgyz 1%. **Languages:** Tajik (official), Russian (widely used in govt. and business). **Religions:** Sunni Muslim 85%, Shia Muslim 5%.

Geography: Total area: 55,251 sq mi, 143,100 sq km; **Land area:** 54,637 sq mi, 141,510 sq km. **Location:** Central Asia. **Neighbors:** Uzbekistan on N and W, Kyrgyzstan on N, China on E, Afghanistan on S. **Topography:** Mountainous region that contains the Pamirs, Trans-Alai mountain system. **Capital:** Dushanbe, 738,883.

Government: Type: Republic. **Head of state:** Pres. Imomali Rakhmon; b. Oct. 5, 1952; in office: Nov. 6, 1994. **Head of gov.:** Prime Min. Akil Akilov; b. Feb. 2, 1944; in office: Dec. 20, 1999. **Local divisions:** 2 provinces, 1 autonomous province, 1 capital region. **Defense budget:** $164 mil. **Active troops:** 8,800.

Economy: Industries: aluminum, cement, vegetable oil. **Chief crops:** cotton, grain, fruits, grapes, vegetables. **Natural resources:** hydropower, petroleum, uranium, mercury, brown coal, lead, zinc, antimony, tungsten, silver, gold. **Crude oil reserves:** 12 mil bbls. **Arable land:** 6.1%. **Livestock:** cattle: 1.9 mil; chickens: 4.7 mil; goats: 1.7 mil; pigs: 525; sheep: 2.7 mil. **Fish catch:** 697 metric tons. **Electricity prod.:** 16.2 bil kWh. **Labor force:** agric. 47.9%, industry 10.9%, services 41.2%.

Finance: Monetary unit: Somoni (TJS) (Sept. 2013: 4.77 = $1 U.S.). **GDP:** $18 bil; **per capita GDP:** $2,300; **GDP growth:** 7.5%. **Imports:** $4 bil; China 42.3%, Russia 16.2%, Kazakhstan 10.1%, Turkey 5.7%, Iran 4.2%. **Exports:** $1.8 bil; Turkey 30.5%, China 9.6%, Iran 7.7%, Afghanistan 6.5%, Kazakhstan 4.9%, Russia 4.3%. **Budget:** $2 bil. **Total reserves less gold:** $297.9 mil. **Gold:** 200,000 oz t. **CPI change:** 5.8%.

Transport: Railways: 423 mi. **Civil aviation:** 1.1 bil pass.-mi; 17 airports.

Communications: TV sets: 386 per 1,000 pop. **Radios:** 398 per 1,000 pop. **Telephone lines:** 5.6 per 100 pop. **Internet:** 14.5%.

Health: Life expect.: 63.6 male; 70.0 female. **Births:** 25.5 per 1,000 pop. **Deaths:** 6.4 per 1,000 pop. **Natural inc.:** 1.91%. **Infant mortality:** 36.2 per 1,000 live births. **HIV rate:** 0.3%.

Education: Compulsory: ages 7-15. **Literacy:** 99.7%.

Major International Organizations: UN (FAO, IBRD, ILO, IMF, WHO), CIS, OSCE, WTO (observer).

Embassy: 1005 New Hampshire Ave. NW 20037; 223-6090.

Website: www.parlament.tj

Societies were settled in the region from about 3000 BCE. Invaders have included Iranians, Arabs (who converted the population to Islam), Mongols, Uzbeks, Afghans, and Russians. The USSR gained control 1918-25, making the region a part of the Uzbek SSR until the Tajik SSR was proclaimed, 1929.

Tajikistan declared independence Sept. 9, 1991. Factional fighting led to the installation of a pro-Communist regime, Jan. 1993. A new constitution establishing a presidential system was approved by referendum in 1994.

An estimated 55,000 died in clashes between Muslim rebels and loyalist troops (supported by Russia) by mid-1997, despite a series of peace accords. Constitutional changes including legalization of Islamic political parties were approved by referendum in 1999. Pres. Imomali Rakhmonov won a Nov. 2009 election called a farce by human-rights observers. Voter-approved constitutional changes in 2003 gave Rakhmonov the right to serve as president until 2020. Leading opposition groups boycotted the Nov. 2006 election again won by Rakhmonov. He changed his name to Rakhmon in 2007 after a decree banned Slavic name endings and other Soviet-era practices.

Poverty and corruption are widespread. Much of the nation's income is supplied by international donors and by remittances from young Tajiks working in Russia and Kazakhstan. After rebels murdered a Tajik general in the semiautonomous province of Gorno-Badakhshan July 21, 2012, the army attacked and killed about 30 militants July 24; 17 government troops died. A former warlord surrendered Aug. 13, 2012, in exchange for troop withdrawal from the region.

Tanzania
United Republic of Tanzania

People: Population: 48,261,942. **Age distrib.:** <15: 44.8%; 65+: 2.9%. **Pop. density:** 141.1 per sq mi, 54.5 per sq km. **Urban:** 26.7%. **Ethnic groups:** African 99% (Bantu 95%). **Languages:** Kiswahili/Swahili, English (primary lang. of commerce, admin., higher ed.) (both official); Arabic (widely spoken in Zanzibar); local langs. **Religions:** Christian 30%, Muslim 35%, indigenous beliefs 35%; 99%+ Muslim on Zanzibar.

Geography: Total area: 365,755 sq mi, 947,300 sq km; **Land area:** 342,009 sq mi, 885,800 sq km. **Location:** On coast of E Africa. **Neighbors:** Kenya, Uganda on N; Rwanda, Burundi, Congo on W; Zambia, Malawi, Mozambique on S. **Topography:** Hot, arid central plateau surrounded by lake region in W, temperate highlands in N and S, the coastal plains. Mt. Kilimanjaro (19,341 ft) is highest in Africa. **Capital:** Dodoma, 226,139 (planned new capital: legis. and National Assembly currently meet here); Dar es Salaam, 3,588,180 (exec. branch).

Government: Type: Republic. **Head of state and gov.:** Pres. Jakaya Mrisho Kikwete; b. Oct. 7, 1950; in office: Dec. 21, 2005. **Local divisions:** 30 regions. **Defense budget:** $260 mil. **Active troops:** 27,000.

Economy: Industries: agric. proc.; diamond, gold, iron mining; salt, soda ash; cement, oil refining, shoes, apparel. **Chief crops:** coffee, sisal, tea, cotton, pyrethrum (insecticide made from chrysanthemums), cashews, tobacco, cloves, corn, wheat. **Natural resources:** hydropower, tin, phosphates, iron ore, coal, diamonds, gems, gold, nat. gas, nickel. **Arable land:** 13.1%. **Livestock:** cattle: 21.3 mil; chickens: 34 mil; goats: 15.2 mil; pigs: 500,000; sheep: 6.4 mil. **Fish catch:** 350,802 metric tons. **Electricity prod.:** 4.3 bil kWh. **Labor force:** agric. 80%, industry and services 20%.

Finance: Monetary unit: Shilling (TZS) (Sept. 2013: 1,615.48 = $1 U.S.). **GDP:** $75.1 bil; **per capita GDP:** $1,600; **GDP growth:** 6.9%. **Imports:** $10.3 bil; China 21.1%, India 16.1%, Kenya 6.6%, South Africa 5.6%, UAE 4.8%. **Exports:** $6 bil; India 14.1%, China 11%, Japan 6.1%, Germany 5%, UAE 4.9%. **Tourism:** $1.6 bil. **Budget:** $6.7 bil. **Total reserves less gold:** $4.1 bil. **CPI change:** 16%.

Transport: Railways: 2,292 mi. **Motor vehicles:** 1.8 vehicles per 1,000 pop. **Civil aviation:** 245.4 mil pass.-mi; 10 airports. **Chief ports:** Dar es Salaam, Zanzibar.

Communications: TV sets: 41 per 1,000 pop. **Radios:** 352 per 1,000 pop. **Telephone lines:** 0.4 per 100 pop. **Internet:** 13.1%.

Health: Life expect.: 59.5 male; 62.1 female. **Births:** 37.3 per 1,000 pop. **Deaths:** 8.4 per 1,000 pop. **Natural inc.:** 2.88%. **Infant mortality:** 45.1 per 1,000 live births. **HIV rate:** 5.8%.

Education: Compulsory: ages 7-13. **Literacy:** 67.8%.

Major intl. organizations: UN and all of its specialized agencies, AU, the Commonwealth, WTO.

Embassy: 2139 R St. NW 20008; 939-6125.

Website: www.tanzania.go.tz

The Republic of Tanganyika in E Africa and the island Republic of Zanzibar, off Tanganyika's coast, both of which had recently gained independence, joined to form the United Republic of Tanzania, Apr. 26, 1964. Zanzibar retains internal self-government.

Until resigning as president in 1985, Julius K. Nyerere, a former Tanganyikan independence leader, dominated Tanzania's single-party government, which emphasized government planning and economic control. A multiparty system was established in 1992, and the economy was privatized in the 1990s.

A bomb at the U.S. embassy in Dar es Salaam, Aug. 7, 1998, killed 11 people and injured at least 70 others. The U.S. blamed the attack and a near-simultaneous embassy bombing in Kenya on Islamic terrorists associated with Osama bin Laden.

President since 1995, Benjamin Mkapa was reelected in 2000. Jakaya Mrisho Kikwete of the ruling Chama Cha Mapinduzi (Party of the Revolution) won the Dec. 2005, presidential election; he was reelected to a second 5-year term Oct. 2010. Discovery of offshore natural gas in 2011-12 increased the country's total recoverable gas reserves to as much as 28.7 tril cubic ft.

Tanganyika. Arab colonization and slaving began in the 8th cent.; Portuguese sailors explored the coast around 1500. Other Europeans followed.

In 1885 Germany established German East Africa, of which Tanganyika formed the bulk. Under Britain, it became a League of Nations mandate and after 1946, a UN trust territory. It became independent, Dec. 9, 1961, and a republic within the Commonwealth a year later.

Zanzibar, the Isle of Cloves, lies 23 mi off mainland Tanzania; area 640 sq mi and pop. (2002) 622,459. The island of **Pemba,** 25 mi to the NE, area 380 sq mi and pop. (2002) 362,166 is included in the administration. Ethnic groups in Zanzibar include Arabs and Africans. Zanzibar and Pemba produce most of the world's supply of cloves and clove oil.

Zanzibar was for centuries the center for Arab slave traders. Portugal ruled the region for two centuries until ousted by Arabs around 1700. Zanzibar became a British Protectorate in 1890; independence came Dec. 10, 1963. Revolutionary forces overthrew the Sultan, Jan. 12, 1964. The new government ousted Western diplomats and newsmen, slaughtered thousands of Arabs, and nationalized farms. Union with Tanganyika followed.

Thailand
Kingdom of Thailand

People: Population: 67,448,120. **Age distrib.:** <15: 19.2%; 65+: 9.8%. **Pop. density:** 341.9 per sq mi, 132 per sq km. **Urban:** 34.1%. **Ethnic groups:** Thai 75%, Chinese 14%. **Languages:** Thai, English (secondary lang. of elite), ethnic and regional dialects. **Religions:** Buddhist (official) 95%, Muslim 5%.

Geography: Total area: 198,117 sq mi, 513,120 sq km; **Land area:** 197,256 sq mi, 510,890 sq km. **Location:** On Indochinese

and Malayan peninsulas in SE Asia. **Neighbors:** Myanmar on W and N, Laos on N, Cambodia on E, Malaysia on S. **Topography:** A plateau dominates NE third of Thailand, dropping to the fertile alluvial valley of Chao Phraya R. in center. Forested mountains are in N, with narrow fertile valleys. The S peninsula region is covered by rain forests. **Capital:** Krung Thep (Bangkok), 8,426,080. **Cities (urban aggl.):** Samut Prakan, 1,211,568.

Government: Type: Constitutional monarchy. **Head of state:** King Bhumibol Adulyadej; b. Dec. 5, 1927; in office: June 9, 1946. **Head of gov.:** Prime Min. Yingluck Shinawatra; b. June 21, 1967; in office: Aug. 8, 2011. **Local divisions:** 77 provinces. **Defense budget:** $5.5 bil. **Active troops:** 360,850.

Economy: Industries: tourism, textiles and garments, agric. proc., beverages, tobacco, cement, light mfg. (jewelry, elec. appliances, computers and parts, integrated circuits, furniture); world's second-largest tungsten producer and third-largest tin producer. **Chief crops:** rice, cassava, rubber, corn, sugarcane, coconuts, soybeans. **Natural resources:** tin, rubber, nat. gas, tungsten, tantalum, timber, lead, fish, gypsum, lignite, fluorite. **Crude oil reserves:** 453.3 mil bbls. **Arable land:** 30.8%. **Livestock:** cattle: 6.7 mil; chickens: 240.7 mil; goats: 427,567; pigs: 7.7 mil; sheep: 51,735. **Fish catch:** 2.9 mil metric tons. **Electricity prod.:** 145.3 bil kWh. **Labor force:** agric. 38.2%, industry 13.6%, services 48.2%.

Finance: Monetary unit: Baht (THB) (Sept. 2013: 32.20 = $1 U.S.). **GDP:** $662.6 bil; **per capita GDP:** $10,300; **GDP growth:** 6.4%. **Imports:** $217.8 bil; Japan 20%, China 14.9%, UAE 6.3%, Malaysia 5.3%, U.S. 5.3%. **Exports:** $226.2 bil; China 11.7%, Japan 10.2%, U.S. 9.9%, Hong Kong 5.7%, Malaysia 5.4%, Indonesia 4.9%, Singapore 4.7%, Australia 4.3%. **Tourism:** $30.1 bil. **Budget:** $88 bil. **Total reserves less gold:** $173.3 bil. **Gold:** 4.9 mil oz t. **CPI change:** 3%.

Transport: Railways: 2,530 mi. **Motor vehicles:** 191.8 vehicles per 1,000 pop. **Civil aviation:** 33.2 bil pass.-mi; 63 airports. **Chief ports:** Bangkok, Laem Chabang, Map Ta Phut, Prachuap Port, Si Racha.

Communication: TV sets: 285 per 1,000 pop. **Radios:** 229 per 1,000 pop. **Telephone lines:** 9.1 per 100 pop. **Internet:** 26.5%.

Health: Life expect.: 71.7 male; 76.6 female. **Births:** 12.7 per 1,000 pop. **Deaths:** 7.5 per 1,000 pop. **Natural inc.:** 0.52%. **Infant mortality:** 15.4 per 1,000 live births. **HIV rate:** 1.2%.

Education: Compulsory: ages 6-14. **Literacy:** 93.5%.

Major intl. organizations: UN (FAO, IBRD, ILO, IMF, WHO), APEC, ASEAN, WTO.

Embassy: 1024 Wisconsin Ave. NW, Ste. 401, 20007; 944-3600. **Website:** www.thaigov.go.th

Thais began migrating from southern China during the 11th cent. and established a unified Thai kingdom, 1350. Known as Siam until 1939, Thailand is the only country in SE Asia never colonized by Europeans. King Mongkut and his son King Chulalongkorn, ruling successively from 1851 to 1910, modernized the country and signed trade treaties with Britain and France. A bloodless revolution in 1932 limited the monarchy. Thailand was an ally of Japan during WWII and of the U.S. during the postwar period. For decades, the military had a dominant role in governing the country.

An economic downturn forced Thailand to seek more than $15 bil in emergency international loans, Aug. 1997. A new constitution won legislative approval Sept. 27. By the end of the 1990s, according to UN estimates, more than 750,000 people in Thailand had HIV/AIDS; a nationwide prevention campaign has reduced the number of new infections.

Following elections in Jan. 2001, Thaksin Shinawatra became prime min. The Indian Ocean tsunami of Dec. 26, 2004, left more than 5,400 people dead in Thailand.

Feb. 2005 elections gave Thaksin's party a huge parliamentary majority. Facing rising opposition and accused of benefiting improperly from the sale of his family's telecom business, Thaksin called snap elections for Apr. 2006, three years ahead of schedule; the vote, which major parties boycotted, was later ruled unconstitutional. A military junta took power in a bloodless coup Sept. 19.

Thaksin supporters won Dec. 2007 elections, and Samak Sundaravej became prime min. after civilian rule was restored Jan. 22, 2008. After a series of antigovernment protests paralyzed Bangkok, Prime Min. Samak imposed emergency rule Sept. 2; Thailand's Constitutional Court ousted him a week later, ostensibly for getting paid to host TV cooking shows while he held public office. Thaksin's brother-in-law Somchai Wongsawat became prime min. Sept. 18, but a Constitutional Court ruling, Dec. 2, barred him from politics and dissolved his People Power Party because of electoral fraud.

Mass protests by Thaksin supporters, known as Red Shirts, led the government to declare a state of emergency in Bangkok, Apr. 12-24, 2009. Meanwhile, about 60,000 security forces in southern Thailand suppressed a Muslim insurgency; from Jan. 2004 to Sept. 2009, more than 3,500 people, mostly civilians, died in the fighting.

On Feb. 26, 2010, Thailand's Supreme Court ordered the seizure of about $1.4 bil of Thaksin's family assets. Thaksin supporters staged mass rallies in Bangkok, and on Apr. 7 a group of Red Shirts stormed the parliament building, leading the government to impose emergency rule in the capital. After the Red Shirts began to build a fortified compound in the heart of Bangkok's business district, a crackdown by Thai security forces May 14-19, 2010, left more than 90 people dead and some 470 injured. After parliamentary elections July 3, 2011, Thaksin's sister, Yingluck Shinawatra,

became Thailand's first female prime min. Monsoon season brought floods beginning July 25, 2011, covered two-thirds of the country by Oct. 12, and did not fully recede until Jan. 16, 2012, costing the country an estimated $45.7 bil. Former Prime Min. Abhisit Vejjajiva was charged Dec. 6, 2012, with murder for his crackdown on antigovernment protesters in May 2010. Insurgents in the southern region continued to attack government forces in 2013, suffering about 16 deaths in Feb.

Timor-Leste
(East Timor)

Democratic Republic of Timor-Leste

People: Population: 1,172,390. **Age distrib.:** <15: 42.7%; 65+: 3.6%. **Pop. density:** 204.1 per sq mi, 78.8 per sq km. **Urban:** 28.3%. **Ethnic groups:** Austronesian (Malayo-Polynesian), Papuan, small Chinese minority. **Languages:** Tetum, Portuguese (both official); Indonesian; English; about 16 indigenous langs. (incl. Tetum, Galole, Mambae, Kemak). **Religions:** Roman Catholic 98%, Muslim 1%, Protestant 1%.

Geography: Total area: 5,743 sq mi, 14,874 sq km. **Land area:** 5,743 sq mi, 14,874 sq km. **Location:** E half of Timor Isl. in SW Pacific O. **Neighbors:** Indonesia (West Timor) on W. **Topography:** Terrain is rugged, rising to 9,721 ft at Mt. Ramelau. **Capital:** Dili, 180,224.

Government: Type: Republic. **Head of state:** Pres. Taur Matan Ruak; b. Oct. 10, 1956; in office: May 20, 2012. **Head of gov.:** Prime Min. Kay Rala Xanana Gusmão; b. June 20, 1946; in office: Aug. 8, 2007. **Local divisions:** 13 districts. **Defense budget:** $64 mil. **Active troops:** 1,330.

Economy: Industries: printing, soap mfg., handicrafts, woven cloth. **Chief crops:** coffee, rice, corn, cassava, sweet potatoes, soybeans. **Natural resources:** gold, petroleum, nat. gas, manganese, marble. **Arable land:** 10.1%. **Livestock:** cattle: 155,000; chickens: 750,000; goats: 147,000; pigs: 420,000; sheep: 45,000. **Fish catch:** 4,681 metric tons. **Labor force:** agric. 64%, industry 10%, services 26%.

Finance: Monetary unit: Dollar (USD). **GDP:** $11.2 bil; **per capita GDP:** $10,000; **GDP growth:** 10%. **Imports** (2011): $689 mil. **Exports** (2011): $34.1 mil. **Tourism:** $21 mil. **Budget:** $1.6 bil. **Total reserves less gold:** $883.6 mil. **CPI change:** 11.8%.

Transport: Civil aviation: 2 airports. **Chief port:** Dili.

Communication: Telephone lines: 0.3 per 100 pop. **Internet:** 0.9%.

Health: Life expect.: 65.6 male; 68.7 female. **Births:** 34.9 per 1,000 pop. **Deaths:** 6.3 per 1,000 pop. **Natural inc.:** 2.86%. **Infant mortality:** 40.1 per 1,000 live births. **HIV rate:** NA.

Education: Compulsory: ages 6-14. **Literacy:** 58.3%.

Major intl. organizations: UN (FAO, IBRD, ILO, IMF, WHO).

Embassy: 4201 Connecticut Ave. NW 20008; 966-3202. **Website:** www.timor-leste.gov.tl

The collapse of Portuguese rule in East Timor led to factional fighting, Aug. 1975, and an invasion by Indonesia in Dec. Indonesia annexed East Timor as a 27th province in 1976. In over two decades, some 200,000 Timorese died due to civil war, famine, and persecution by Indonesian authorities. In a referendum held Aug. 1999 under UN auspices, Timorese voted overwhelmingly for independence but were then terrorized by pro-Indonesian militias. An international peacekeeping force entered in Sept.; a UN interim administration formally took command Oct. 26, 1999.

Pro-independence forces won elections for a constituent assembly Aug. 2001. Xanana Gusmão, a former guerrilla leader, won the presidential election Apr. 2002. As Timor-Leste, the territory became independent May 20 and entered the UN Sept. 27. Australia and other nations sent peacekeepers to suppress a wave of gang violence in Dili May 2006.

José Ramos-Horta, a Nobel laureate, won a presidential runoff vote May 2007. After inconclusive parliamentary elections June 30, Ramos-Horta ended a political deadlock by choosing Gusmão as prime min. The Gusmão-supported independent candidate, Taur Matan Ruak, became president in a May 2012 runoff election. Gusmão's party won a majority of seats in the July parliamentary election, and he became prime min. of a coalition government in Aug. The UN peacekeeping mission ended Dec. 31, 2012. Much of the nation's struggling economy is expected to be supported by a petroleum and gas fund from offshore oil and gas fields, worth about $11.7 bil in June 2013.

Togo
Togolese Republic

People: Population: 7,154,237. **Age distrib.:** <15: 40.8%; 65+: 3.2%. **Pop. density:** 340.7 per sq mi, 131.5 per sq km. **Urban:** 38%. **Ethnic groups:** African (37 tribes; Ewe, Mina, Kabre largest) 99%. **Languages:** French (official, lang. of commerce), Ewe and Mina (in S), Kabye and Dagomba (in N). **Religions:** indigenous beliefs 51%, Christian 29%, Muslim 20%.

Geography: Total area: 21,925 sq mi, 56,785 sq km; **Land area:** 20,998 sq mi, 54,385 sq km. **Location:** On S coast of W Africa. **Neighbors:** Ghana on W, Burkina Faso on N, Benin on E. **Topography:** A range of hills running SW-NE splits Togo into 2 savanna plains regions. **Capital:** Lomé, 1,523,930.

Government: Type: Republic. **Head of state:** Pres. Faure Gnassingbé; b. June 6, 1966; in office: May 4, 2005. **Head of gov.:** Prime Min. Kwesi Ahoomey-Zunu; b. Dec. 1, 1958; in office: July 23, 2012. **Local divisions:** 5 regions. **Defense budget** (2011): $59 mil. **Active troops:** 8,550.

Economy: Industries: phosphate mining, agric. proc., cement, handicrafts, textiles, beverages. **Chief crops:** coffee, cocoa, cotton, yams, cassava, corn, beans, rice, millet, sorghum. **Natural resources:** phosphates, limestone, marble. **Arable land:** 46.1%. **Livestock:** cattle: 311,334; chickens: 22 mil; goats: 2 mil; pigs: 569,000; sheep: 2.1 mil. **Fish catch:** 24,142 metric tons. **Electricity prod.:** 127.1 mil kWh. **Labor force:** agric. 65%, industry 5%, services 30%.

Finance: Monetary unit: Pa'anga (TOP) (Sept. 2013: 1.87 = $1 U.S.). **GDP:** $7 bil; **per capita GDP:** $1,100; **GDP growth:** 5%. **Imports:** $1.5 bil; China 41.2%, Netherlands 8%, France 5.5%, UK 5.4%. **Exports:** $987.1 mil; India 13.7%, Lebanon 10.5%, Burkina Faso 8%, Benin 7.9%, Niger 6%, China 5.8%, Netherlands 4.9%, Ghana 4.6%. **Tourism:** $79 mil. **Budget:** $906.1 mil. **Total reserves less gold:** $441.6 mil. **CPI change:** 2.6%.

Transport: Railways: 353 mi. **Motor vehicles:** 24.2 vehicles per 1,000 pop. **Civil aviation:** 2 airports. **Chief ports:** Kpeme, Lomé.

Communications: TV sets: 26 per 1,000 pop. **Radios:** 669 per 1,000 pop. **Telephone lines:** 3.6 per 100 pop. **Internet:** 4%.

Health: Life expect.: 61.1 male; 66.2 female. **Births:** 34.9 per 1,000 pop. **Deaths:** 7.6 per 1,000 pop. **Natural inc.:** 2.73%. **Infant mortality:** 48.3 per 1,000 live births. **HIV rate:** 3.4%.

Education: Compulsory: ages 6-15. **Literacy:** 60.4%.

Major intl. organizations: UN (FAO, IBRD, ILO, IMF, WHO), AU, WTO.

Embassy: 2208 Massachusetts Ave. NW 20008; 234-4212.

Website: www.gouv.tg or www.state.gov/p/af/ci/to/

Togoland was administered by Germany and then by France and Britain. The French sector became the republic of Togo Apr. 27, 1960. In office since 1967, Pres. Gnassingbé Eyadéma was Africa's longest-serving head of state until his death Feb. 5, 2005. His son, Faure Gnassingbé, was installed as president, but African leaders pressured Togo to hold an election, which Gnassingbé won Apr. 24. Opposition parties disputed the result, and protests led to violent clashes in Lomé.

After a shootout at his home Apr. 12, 2009, former Defense Min. Kpatcha Gnassingbé, the president's brother, sought refuge Apr. 15 at the U.S. embassy in Lomé; denied asylum, he was arrested by Togolese authorities and accused of plotting a coup. Pres. Gnassingbé won reelection Mar. 4, 2010, to a second 5-year term. Weeks of antigovernment protest led Prime Min. Gilbert Fossoun Houngbo to resign, July 13, 2012, and a new government was formed under Prime Min. Kwesi Seleagodzi Ahoomey-Zunu. Legislative elections were held July 25, 2013, with the ruling party maintaining its majority and the opposition claiming voting irregularities.

Tonga
Kingdom of Tonga

People: Population: 106,322. **Age distrib.:** <15: 36.2%; 65+: 6.2%. **Pop. density:** 384.1 per sq mi, 148.3 per sq km. **Urban:** 23.4%. **Ethnic groups:** Polynesian, European. **Languages:** Tongan, English (both official). **Religions:** Christian (mostly Free Wesleyan Church).

Geography: Total area: 288 sq mi, 747 sq km; **Land area:** 277 sq mi, 717 sq km. **Location:** In western S Pacific O. **Neighbors:** Nearest are Fiji to W, Samoa to NE. **Topography:** Comprises 170 volcanic and coral islands, 36 inhabited. **Capital:** Nuku'alofa, 24,500.

Government: Type: Constitutional monarchy. **Head of state:** King Tupou VI, b. July 12, 1959; in office: Mar. 18, 2012. **Head of gov.:** Prime Min. Tu'ivakano; b. Jan. 15, 1952; in office: Dec, 22, 2010. **Local divisions:** 5 island divisions. **Defense budget/active troops:** NA.

Economy: Industries: tourism, constr., fishing. **Chief crops:** squash, coconuts, copra, bananas, vanilla beans, cocoa, coffee, ginger, black pepper. **Natural resources:** fish. **Arable land:** 22.2%. **Livestock:** cattle: 11,300; chickens: 330,000; goats: 12,600; pigs: 81,200. **Fish catch:** 2,105 metric tons. **Electricity prod.:** 41 mil kWh. **Labor force:** agric. 31.8%, industry 30.6%, services 37.6%.

Finance: Monetary unit: West African CFA Franc (XOF) (Sept. 2013: 498.17 = $1 U.S.). **GDP:** $801 mil; **per capita GDP:** $7,700; **GDP growth:** 1.4%. **Imports:** $121.9 mil; Fiji 38%, New Zealand 23.5%, U.S. 10.1%, China 9.9%. **Exports:** $8.4 mil; South Korea 17.8%, U.S. 16.4%, New Zealand 15.1%, Fiji 10.9%, Japan 9.2%, Samoa 9.1%, American Samoa 5.8%, Australia 5%. **Tourism:** $28 mil. **Budget:** $116.3 mil. **Total reserves less gold:** $152.4 mil. **CPI change:** 1.2%.

Transport: Civil aviation: 11.8 mil pass.-mi; 1 airport. **Chief ports:** Neiafu, Nuku'alofa, Pangai.

Communications: TV sets: 49 per 1,000 pop. **Radios:** 662 per 1,000 pop. **Telephone lines:** 28.6 per 100 pop. **Internet:** 34.9%.

Health: Life expect.: 74.2 male; 77.1 female. **Births:** 24.1 per 1,000 pop. **Deaths:** 4.9 per 1,000 pop. **Natural inc.:** 1.93%. **Infant mortality:** 12.8 per 1,000 live births. **HIV rate:** NA.

Education: Compulsory: ages 6-14. **Literacy:** 99%.

Major intl. organizations: UN (FAO, IBRD, ILO, IMF, WHO), the Commonwealth, WTO.

Embassy: 250 E. 51st St., New York, NY 10022; (917) 369-1025.

Website: pmo.gov.to

The Dutch first visited the islands in the early 17th cent. A series of civil wars ended, 1845, with establishment of the Tupou dynasty. In 1900, Tonga became a British protectorate. Tonga gained independence June 1970 and joined the Commonwealth. It joined the UN in 1999. George Tupou VI became king Mar. 18, 2012, following the death of his brother, George Tupou V, who had reigned since 2006 and had introduced democratic reforms. Elections in Nov. 2010 gave the country its first democratically elected parliament, taking the monarch's executive powers and reducing his role to that of an advisor.

Trinidad and Tobago
Republic of Trinidad and Tobago

People: Population: 1,225,225. **Age distrib.:** <15: 19.5%; 65+: 9.1%. **Pop. density:** 618.8 per sq mi, 238.9 per sq km. **Urban:** 13.7%. **Ethnic groups:** Indian (South Asian) 40%, African 38%, mixed 21%. **Languages:** English (official), Caribbean Hindustani, French, Spanish, Chinese. **Religions:** Roman Catholic 26%, Protestant 26% (Anglican 8%, Baptist 7%, Pentecostal 7%, Seventh-Day Adventist 4%), Hindu 23%, Muslim 6%, other Christian 6%, none 2%.

Geography: Total area: 1,980 sq mi, 5,128 sq km; **Land area:** 1,980 sq mi, 5,128 sq km. **Location:** In Caribbean, off E coast of Venezuela. **Neighbors:** Nearest is Venezuela to SW. **Topography:** Three low mountain ranges cross Trinidad E-W, with a well-watered plain between N and central ranges. Parts of E and W coasts are swamps. Tobago, 116 sq mi, lies 20 mi NE. **Capital:** Port of Spain, 65,839.

Government: Type: Parliamentary democracy. **Head of state:** Pres. Anthony Carmona; b. Mar. 7, 1953; in office: Mar. 18, 2013. **Head of gov.:** Prime Min. Kamla Persad-Bissessar; b. Apr. 22, 1952; in office: May 26, 2010. **Local divisions:** 9 regions, 3 boroughs, 2 cities, 1 ward. **Defense budget:** $446 mil. **Active troops:** 4,050.

Economy: Industries: petroleum and petroleum prods., liquefied nat. gas, methanol, ammonia, urea, steel prods., beverages, food proc. **Chief crops:** cocoa, rice, citrus, coffee, vegetables. **Natural resources:** petroleum, nat. gas, asphalt. **Crude oil reserves:** 728.3 mil bbls. **Arable land:** 4.9%. **Livestock:** cattle: 33,000; chickens: 34 mil; goats: 63,000; pigs: 49,000; sheep: 3,800. **Fish catch:** 13,906 metric tons. **Electricity prod.:** 8 bil kWh. **Labor force:** agric. 3.8%; mfg., mining, and quarrying 12.8%; constr. and utilities 20.4%; services 62.9%.

Finance: Monetary unit: Dollar (TTD) (Sept. 2013: 6.42 = $1 U.S.). **GDP:** $27.1 bil; **per capita GDP:** $20,400; **GDP growth:** 0.4%. **Imports:** $8.3 bil; U.S. 30.8%, Colombia 13.9%, Brazil 7.6%, Gabon 5%, Canada 4.1%. **Exports:** $13.6 bil; U.S. 40.3%, Argentina 6.9%, Chile 6.8%, Jamaica 4.9%, Spain 4.3%. **Tourism:** $472 mil. **Budget:** $7.9 bil. **Total reserves less gold:** $9.8 bil. **Gold:** 61,752 oz t. **CPI change:** 9.3%.

Transport: Motor vehicles: 303.2 vehicles per 1,000 pop. **Civil aviation:** 1.9 bil pass.-mi; 2 airports. **Chief ports:** Point Lisas, Port of Spain, Scarborough.

Communications: TV sets: 355 per 1,000 pop. **Radios:** 535 per 1,000 pop. **Telephone lines:** 21.2 per 100 pop. **Internet:** 59.5%.

Health: Life expect.: 69.1 male; 74.9 female. **Births:** 14.1 per 1,000 pop. **Deaths:** 8.4 per 1,000 pop. **Natural inc.:** 0.57%. **Infant mortality:** 25.7 per 1,000 live births. **HIV rate:** 1.5%.

Education: Compulsory: ages 6-11. **Literacy:** 98.8%.

Major intl. organizations: UN (FAO, IBRD, ILO, IMF, WHO), Caricom, the Commonwealth, OAS, WTO.

Embassy: 1708 Massachusetts Ave. NW 20036; 467-6490.

Website: www.ttconnect.gov.tt

Columbus sighted Trinidad in 1498. A British possession since 1802, Trinidad and Tobago won independence Aug. 31, 1962. It became a republic in 1976.

The nation, among the most prosperous in the Caribbean, refines and exports Middle Eastern oil. Oil production increased after offshore finds.

In July 1990, some 120 Muslim extremists captured the Parliament building and TV station and took about 50 hostages, including Prime Min. Arthur N. R. Robinson, who was beaten, shot in the legs, and tied to explosives. After a 6-day siege, the rebels surrendered.

Basdeo Panday, in office 1995-2001, was the nation's first prime min. of East Indian ancestry. The country's first female prime min., Kamla Persad-Bissessar, leader of the People's Partnership coalition, took office May 26, 2010. Anthony Carmona ran for president unopposed and won the office Feb. 15, 2013.

Tunisia
Tunisian Republic

People: Population: 10,835,873. **Age distrib.:** <15: 23%; 65+: 7.7%. **Pop. density:** 180.6 per sq mi, 69.7 per sq km. **Urban:** 66.3%. **Ethnic groups:** Arab 98%, European 1%, Jewish and other 1%. **Languages:** Arabic (official), French (used in commerce), Berber (Tamazight). **Religions:** Muslim (official) 98%, Christian 1%, Jewish and other 1%.

Geography: Total area: 63,170 sq mi, 163,610 sq km; **Land area:** 59,985 sq mi, 155,360 sq km. **Location:** On N coast of Africa. **Neighbors:** Algeria on W, Libya on E. **Topography:** The N is

wooded and fertile. The central coastal plains are given to grazing and orchards. The S is arid, approaching Sahara Desert. **Capital:** Tunis, 790,205.

Government: Type: Republic. **Head of state:** Moncef Marzouki; b. July 7, 1945; in office: Dec. 13, 2011 (interim). **Head of gov.:** Prime Min. Ali Larayedh; b. Aug. 15, 1955; in office: Feb. 27, 2013. **Local divisions:** 24 governorates. **Defense budget:** NA. **Active troops:** 35,800.

Economy: Industries: petroleum, mining, tourism, textiles, footwear, agribusiness, beverages. **Chief crops:** olives, olive oil, grain, tomatoes, citrus, sugar beets, dates, almonds. **Natural resources:** petroleum, phosphates, iron ore, lead, zinc, salt. **Crude oil reserves:** 425 mil bbls. **Arable land:** 18.3%. **Livestock:** cattle: 655,730; chickens: 77 mil; goats: 1.3 mil; pigs: 5,500; sheep: 7 mil. **Fish catch:** 110,945 metric tons. **Electricity prod.:** 15.1 bil kWh. **Labor force:** agric. 18.3%, industry 31.9%, services 49.8%.

Finance: Monetary unit: Dinar (TND) (Sept. 2013: 1.66 = $1 U.S.). **GDP:** $107.1 bil; **per capita GDP:** $9,900; **GDP growth:** 3.6%. **Imports:** $23.3 bil; France 20.2%, Italy 16.9%, Germany 7.5%, China 6.1%, Spain 5.4%. **Exports:** $17 bil; France 26.3%, Italy 16%, Germany 9.4%, Libya 7.9%, U.S. 4.3%. **Tourism:** $2.2 bil. **Budget:** $13.1 bil. **Total reserves less gold** $8.4 bil. **Gold:** 216,700 oz t. **CPI change:** 5.5%.

Transport: Railways: 1,345 mi. **Motor vehicles:** 122.1 vehicles per 1,000 pop. **Civil aviation:** 2 bil pass.-mi; 15 airports. **Chief ports:** Bizerte, Gabes, Rades, Sfax, Skhira.

Communications: TV sets: 225 per 1,000 pop. **Radios:** 158 per 1,000 pop. **Telephone lines:** 10.3 per 100 pop. **Internet:** 41.4%.

Health: Life expect.: 73.4 male; 77.7 female. **Births:** 17.1 per 1,000 pop. **Deaths:** 5.9 per 1,000 pop. **Natural inc.:** 1.12%. **Infant mortality:** 24.1 per 1,000 live births. **HIV rate:** <0.1%.

Education: Compulsory: ages 6-16. **Literacy:** 79.1%.

Major intl. organizations: UN (FAO, IBRD, ILO, IMF, WHO), AL, AU, WTO.

Embassy: 1515 Massachusetts Ave. NW 20005; 862-1850.

Website: www.tunisie.gov.tn

Site of ancient Carthage and a former Barbary state under the suzerainty of Turkey, Tunisia became a protectorate of France, May 12, 1881. The nation became independent Mar. 20, 1956, and ended the monarchy the following year. Habib Bourguiba, an independence leader, served as president until 1987, when he was deposed by his prime min., Zine al-Abidine Ben Ali, who then won five presidential elections, 1989-2009, all tightly controlled.

Arab Spring protests, which began Dec. 2010 in the town of Sidi Bouzid, ousted Ben Ali, Jan. 14, 2011, and parliament speaker Fouad Mebazaa became interim president. Subsequent protests also forced the removal of Prime Min. Mohamed Ghannouchi. Moncef Marzouki of the secular center-left Congress for the Republic party was appointed interim president and took office Dec. 13, 2011, but real power lay with Prime Min. Hamadi Jebali, an Islamist leader of the moderate Ennahda party, which won Oct. 2011 elections. Opposition leader Chokri Belaid was shot to death outside his home Feb. 6, 2013, allegedly by a hard-line Islamist, touching off protests across the country. Prime Min. Jebali resigned Feb. 19 after failing to institute promised reforms. The Islamist-dominated Assembly voted Ali Laarayedh his replacement. Another opposition leader, Mohamed Brahmi, was assassinated July 25, prompting several days of protest. On July 29, 65 members of the Assembly withdrew, and the prime min. announced elections would be held Dec. 17.

Turkey
Republic of Turkey

People: Population: 80,694,485. **Age distrib.:** <15: 25.9%; 65+: 6.6%. **Pop. density:** 271.6 per sq mi, 104.8 per sq km. **Urban:** 71.5%. **Ethnic groups:** Turkish 70%-75%, Kurdish 18%. **Languages:** Turkish (official), Kurdish, other minority langs. **Religion:** Muslim (mostly Sunni) 99.8%.

Geography: Total area: 302,535 sq mi, 783,562 sq km; **Land area:** 297,157 sq mi, 769,632 sq km. **Location:** Occupies Asia Minor, stretches into continental Europe; borders on Medit. and Black Seas. **Neighbors:** Bulgaria, Greece on W; Georgia, Armenia on N; Iran on E; Iraq, Syria on S. **Topography:** Central Turkey has wide plateaus with hot, dry summers and cold winters. High mountains ring the interior on all but W, with more than 20 peaks over 10,000 ft. Rolling plains are in W; mild, fertile coastal plains are in S, W. **Capital:** Ankara, 4,193,850. **Cities (urban aggl.):** Istanbul, 11,253,297; Izmir, 2,927,468; Bursa, 1,712,985; Adana, 1,467,504; Gaziantep, 1,197,537; Konya, 1,056,582.

Government: Type: Republican parliamentary democracy. **Head of state:** Pres. Abdullah Gül; b. Oct. 29, 1950; in office: Aug. 28, 2007. **Head of gov.:** Prime Min. Recep Tayyip Erdogan; b. Feb. 26, 1954; in office: Mar. 14, 2003. **Local divisions:** 81 provinces. **Defense budget:** $17 bil. **Active troops:** 510,600.

Economy: Industries: textiles, food proc., autos, electronics, mining, steel, petroleum, constr., lumber, paper. **Chief crops:** tobacco, cotton, grain, olives, sugar beets, hazelnuts, pulses, citrus. **Natural resources:** coal, iron ore, copper, chromium, antimony, mercury, gold, barite, borate, strontium, emery, feldspar, limestone, magnesite, marble, perlite, pumice, pyrites (sulfur), clay, hydropower. **Crude oil reserves:** 270.4 mil bbls. **Arable land:** 26.7%. **Livestock:** cattle: 11.4 mil; chickens: 234.9 mil; goats: 6.3 mil; pigs:

1,558; sheep: 23.1 mil. **Fish catch:** 703,654 metric tons. **Electricity prod.** (2011): 217.7 bil kWh. **Labor force:** agric. 25.5%, industry 26.2%, services 48.4%.

Finance: Monetary unit: Lira (TRY) (Sept. 2013: 2.04 = $1 U.S.). **GDP:** $1.1 tril; **per capita GDP:** $15,200; **GDP growth:** 2.6%. **Imports:** $228.9 bil; Russia 11.3%, Germany 9%, China 9%, U.S. 6%, Italy 5.6%, Iran 5.1%. **Exports:** $163.4 bil; Germany 8.6%, Iraq 7.1%, Iran 6.5%, UK 5.7%, UAE 5.4%, Russia 4.4%, Italy 4.2%, France 4.1%. **Tourism:** $25.7 bil. **Budget:** $200.7 bil. **Total reserves less gold:** $99.9 bil. **Gold:** 11.6 mil oz t. **CPI change:** 8.9%.

Transport: Railways: 5,405 mi. **Motor vehicles:** 160.8 vehicles per 1,000 pop. **Civil aviation:** 30.8 bil pass.-mi; 91 airports. **Chief ports:** Aliaga, Diliskelesi, Eregli, Izmir, Izmit.

Communications: TV sets: 428 per 1,000 pop. **Radios:** 283 per 1,000 pop. **Telephone lines:** 18.6 per 100 pop. **Internet:** 45.1%.

Health: Life expect.: 71.1 male; 75.1 female. **Births:** 17.2 per 1,000 pop. **Deaths:** 6.1 per 1,000 pop. **Natural inc.:** 1.11%. **Infant mortality:** 22.2 per 1,000 live births. **HIV rate:** <0.1%.

Education: Compulsory: ages 6-13. **Literacy:** 94.1%.

Major intl. organizations: UN (FAO, IBRD, ILO, IMF, WHO), NATO, OECD, OSCE, WTO.

Embassy: 2525 Massachusetts Ave. NW 20008; 612-6700.

Website: www.tccb.gov.tr

Ancient inhabitants of Turkey were among the world's first agriculturalists. Such civilizations as the Hittite, Phrygian, and Lydian flourished in Asiatic Turkey (Asia Minor), as did much of Greek civilization. After the fall of Rome in the 5th cent., Constantinople (now Istanbul) was the capital of the Byzantine Empire for 1,000 years. It fell in 1453 to Ottoman Turks, who ruled a vast empire for over 400 years.

Just before WWI, Turkey, or the Ottoman Empire, ruled what is now Syria, Lebanon, Iraq, Jordan, Israel, Saudi Arabia, Yemen, and islands in the Aegean Sea. Turkey joined Germany and Austria in WWI, and its defeat resulted in the loss of territory and the fall of the sultanate. A secular republic was established Oct. 29, 1923. The first pres., Mustafa Kemal (later Kemal Ataturk), led Turkey until his death in 1938.

Turkey kept neutral during most of WWII. The country became a full member of NATO in 1952 and remained a Western ally despite domestic political instability. Military coups overthrew civilian governments in 1960 and 1980. Turkey invaded nearby Cyprus July 20, 1974, to prevent that country from uniting with Greece, and Cyprus was divided into Greek and Turkish zones.

In recent decades, Kurdish separatists and Islamic militants have challenged Turkish governments. Turkey joined the U.S.-led force that ousted Iraq from Kuwait, 1991. Millions of Kurdish refugees fled to Turkey's border after the war. Turkish offensives against the Kurds caused heavy casualties among guerrillas and civilians. Kurdish militants raided Turkish diplomatic missions in some 25 Western European cities, June 24, 1993.

Tansu Ciller became Turkey's first woman prime minister, July 5, 1993. The Islamic Welfare Party gained strength in the 1990s, and in June 1996, a coalition with Ciller's True Path Party was formed. The pro-Islamic government resigned June 18, 1997, under pressure from the military, which stepped up its campaign against Islamic fundamentalism in 1998.

Kurdish rebel leader Abdullah Öcalan was captured Feb. 15, 1999; convicted of terrorism June 29, he was sentenced to death. His organization, the Kurdistan Workers' Party, announced in 1999 that it would abandon its 14-year-old insurgency.

Earthquakes in Apr. and Nov. 1999 killed over 17,000 people. The death penalty was abolished in 2002, and Öcalan's sentence was commuted to life in prison Oct. 3. The Islamic Justice and Development Party (AKP) led by Recep Tayyip Erdogan won elections Nov. 3.

During the U.S.-led invasion of Iraq, Mar.-Apr. 2003, Turkey refused to allow coalition forces to launch attacks on N Iraq from Turkish soil. Suicide bombings by Islamic extremists, Nov. 15-20, 2003, killed 58 people and wounded more than 750 in Istanbul.

After Erdogan's party scored a landslide win in 2007 national elections, parliament chose an Islamic politician, Abdullah Gül, as president. Secularists failed to ban the ruling AKP in Turkey's Constitutional Court in 2008, but the party's public funding was halved and it was warned against exerting Islamic influence on state institutions. Turkish voters in 2010 gave resounding approval to constitutional changes favored by the Islamic government, including a provision that would expand membership of the Constitutional Court.

The AKP gained a third consecutive general election victory in June 2011, while dozens of military officers were detained for allegedly plotting to seize power. After the nation's four top military commanders resigned en masse, July 29, 2011, Pres Gül appointed their replacements Aug. 4, breaking with the tradition of the military promoting its own leaders.

Turkey has long sought full membership in the European Union, but the EU has deferred talks on accession until economic, human rights, and immigration issues are resolved. Turkey's ties with Islamic countries have soured relations with Israel, a former ally.

Throughout the 2011-13 Syrian crisis, Turkey became a haven for refugees, the Syrian Free Army, and the opposition group the Syrian Natl. Council. After a Syrian mortar shell landed in Turkey, killing 5 civilians, Turkey attacked targets within Syria Oct. 3, 2012. Parliament, Oct. 4, approved further military action against Syria.

Turkey claimed to have found components for Russian weapons on board a Syrian passenger plane that it intercepted Oct. 10, 2012, and banned all Syrian aircraft from flying through Turkish air space Oct. 14. Turkey's NATO allies decided Dec. 4 to send Patriot anti-aircraft missiles to Turkey for its defense. A suicide bomber outside the U.S. embassy in Ankara Feb. 1, 2013, killed himself and a Turkish security guard. Istanbul police revealed Apr. 11 an al-Qaeda plot to target the U.S. embassy, as well as other locations in Turkey.

Police tried to suppress May 31, 2013, protests in Istanbul's Taksim Square over plans to replace Gezi Park, but demonstrations spread and became protests against Prime Min. Erdogan. Erdogan blamed extremists for the protests' escalation and held peaceful discussions with protesters. But force was used, June 15, to clear Gezi Park, resulting in scores of injuries. Arrests began June 19 in Istanbul and Ankara, and protests began to die down at the beginning of July. A court order halted the development plan July 4, 2013.

Turkmenistan

People: Population: 5,113,040. **Age distrib.:** <15: 26.7%; 65+: 4.2%. **Pop. density:** 28.2 per sq mi, 10.9 per sq km. **Urban:** 48.7%. **Ethnic groups:** Turkmen 85%, Uzbek 5%, Russian 4%. **Languages:** Turkmen (official), Russian, Uzbek. **Religions:** Muslim 89%, Eastern Orthodox 9%.

Geography: Total area: 188,456 sq mi, 488,100 sq km; **Land area:** 181,441 sq mi, 469,930 sq km. **Location:** Central Asia bordering Caspian Sea. **Neighbors:** Kazakhstan on N; Uzbekistan on N and E; Afghanistan, Iran on S. **Topography:** The Kara Kum Desert occupies 80% of the area. Bordered on W by Caspian Sea. **Capital:** Ashgabat, 683,260.

Government: Type: Republic with authoritarian rule. **Head of state and gov.:** Pres. Gurbanguly Berdymukhammedov; b. June 29, 1957; in office: Feb. 14, 2007 (acting from Dec. 21, 2006). **Local divisions:** 5 provinces. **Defense budget** (2011): $210 mil. **Active troops:** 22,000.

Economy: Industries: nat. gas, oil, petroleum prods., textiles, food proc. **Chief crops:** cotton, grain, melons. **Natural resources:** petroleum, nat. gas, sulfur, salt. **Crude oil reserves:** 600 mil bbls. **Arable land:** 4%. **Livestock:** cattle: 2.2 mil; chickens 15.5 mil; goats: 2.8 mil; pigs: 30,000; sheep: 13.7 mil. **Fish catch:** 15,017 metric tons. **Electricity prod.:** 15.7 bil kWh. **Labor force:** agric. 48.2%, industry 14%, services 37.8%.

Finance: Monetary unit: Manat (TMT) (Sept. 2013: 2.85 = $1 U.S.). **GDP:** $49.8 bil; **per capita GDP:** $8,900; **GDP growth:** 11%. **Imports:** $10.2 bil; China 20.1%, Turkey 17.5%, Russia 13%, UAE 6.9%, Germany 4.8%, UK 4.4%. **Exports:** $15.4 bil; China 66%, Ukraine 7%, Italy 4.5%. **Budget:** $26.9 bil. **Total reserves less gold:** NA. **CPI change:** NA.

Transport: Railways: 1,852 mi. **Civil aviation:** 1.2 bil pass.-mi; 21 airports. **Chief port:** Turkmenbasy.

Communications: TV sets: 190 per 1,000 pop. **Radios:** 155 per 1,000 pop. **Telephone lines:** 11.1 per 100 pop. **Internet:** 7%.

Health: Life expect.: 66.2 male; 72.3 female. **Births:** 19.5 per 1,000 pop. **Deaths:** 6.2 per 1,000 pop. **Natural inc.:** 1.34%. **Infant mortality:** 39.5 per 1,000 live births. **HIV rate:** NA.

Education: Compulsory: ages 7-16. **Literacy:** 99.6%.

Major intl. organizations: UN (FAO, IBRD, ILO, IMF, WHO), CIS, OSCE.

Embassy: 2207 Massachusetts Ave. NW 20008; 588-1500.

Website: www.turkmenistan.gov.tm

The region has been inhabited by Turkic tribes since the 10th cent. It became part of Russian Turkestan in 1881, and a constituent republic of the USSR in 1925. Turkmenistan declared independence Oct. 27, 1991, and became an independent state when the USSR disbanded Dec. 26, 1991.

Extensive oil and gas reserves place Turkmenistan in a favorable economic position. Political power centered around the former Communist Party apparatus and authoritarian leadership. Gurbanguly Berdymukhammedov won the Feb. 2007 presidential election, considered fraudulent by international observers. In a small gesture toward democracy, the country's one party system officially ended Aug. 21, 2012, permitting a second political party, the Party of Industrialists and Entrepreneurs of Turkmenistan, to be founded.

Tuvalu

People: Population: 10,698. **Age distrib.:** <15: 29.8%; 65+: 5.3%. **Pop. density:** 1,065.7 per sq mi, 411.5 per sq km. **Urban:** 50.6%. **Ethnic groups:** Polynesian 96%, Micronesian 4%. **Languages:** Tuvaluan, English (both official); Samoan; Kiribati. **Religions:** Protestant 98% (Church of Tuvalu [Congregationalist] 97%, Seventh-Day Adventist 1%), Baha'i 1%.

Geography: Total area: 10 sq mi, 26 sq km; **Land area:** 10 sq mi, 26 sq km. **Location:** 9 islands forming NW-SE chain 360 mi long in SW Pacific O. **Neighbors:** Nearest are Kiribati to N, Fiji to S. **Topography:** The islands are all low-lying atolls, nowhere rising more than 15 ft above sea level, composed of coral reefs. **Capital:** Funafuti, 4,979.

Government: Type: Parliamentary democracy. **Head of state:** Queen Elizabeth II, rep. by Gov.-Gen. Sir Iakoba Italeli; b. 1936; in office: Apr. 16, 2010. **Head of gov.:** Prime Min. Enele Sopoaga; b. Feb. 10, 1956; in office: Aug. 5, 2013. **Defense budget:** NA. **Active troops:** No regular military forces.

Economy: Industries: fishing, tourism, copra. **Chief crops:** coconuts. **Natural resources:** fish. **Arable land:** none. **Livestock:** chickens: 45,000; pigs: 13,600. **Fish catch:** 8,311 metric tons. **Labor force:** Pop. makes living mainly through exploitation of the sea, reefs, and atolls and from wages sent home by those abroad (mostly phosphate industry workers and sailors).

Finance: Monetary unit: Dollar (TVD) (Sept. 2013: 1.09 = $1 U.S.). **GDP:** $37.6 mil; **per capita GDP:** $3,400; **GDP growth:** 1.2%. **Imports** (2010): $16.5 mil. **Exports** (2010): $600,000. **Budget** (2006): $23.1 mil. **Total reserves less gold:** NA. **CPI change:** NA.

Transport: Civil aviation: 1 airport (unpaved runway). **Chief port:** Funafuti.

Communications: TV sets: 9 per 1,000 pop. **Telephone lines:** 14.7 per 100 pop. **Internet:** 35%.

Health: Life expect.: 63.4 male; 67.7 female. **Births:** 23.6 per 1,000 pop. **Deaths:** 9.0 per 1,000 pop. **Natural inc.:** 1.46%. **Infant mortality:** 32.6 per 1,000 live births. **HIV rate:** NA.

Education: Compulsory: ages 7-14. **Literacy:** NA.

Major intl. organizations: UN (FAO, ILO, WHO), the Commonwealth.

Permanent UN Mission: 800 Second Ave., Ste. 400D, New York, NY 10017; (212) 490-0534.

Website: www.state.gov/p/eap/ci/tv/

The Ellice Islands separated from the British Gilbert and Ellice Islands Colony in 1975 and became Tuvalu; independence came Oct. 1, 1978. In 2000, Tuvalu joined the United Nations. A major drought since Nov. 2010 obliged the government to declare a state of emergency Sept. 28, 2011. Rising sea levels due to climate change are threatening to submerge the tiny island nation. Prime Min. Willy Telavi received a no-confidence vote from parliament Aug. 2, 2013, and was ousted in favor of Enele Sopoaga.

Uganda
Republic of Uganda

People: Population: 34,758,809. **Age distrib.:** <15: 48.9%; 65+: 2.1%. **Pop. density:** 456.7 per sq mi, 176.4 per sq km. **Urban:** 15.6%. **Ethnic groups:** Baganda 17%, Banyakole 10%, Basoga 8%, Bakiga 7%, Iteso 6%, Langi 6%, Acholi 5%, Bagisu 5%, Lugbara 4%, Bunyoro 3%. **Languages:** English (official), Ganda or Luganda, other Niger-Congo langs., Nilo-Saharan langs., Swahili, Arabic. **Religions:** Roman Catholic 42%, Protestant 42% (Anglican 36%, Pentecostal 5%, Seventh-Day Adventist 2%), Muslim 12%.

Geography: Total area: 93,065 sq mi, 241,038 sq km; **Land area:** 76,101 sq mi, 197,100 sq km. **Location:** In E Central Africa. **Neighbors:** Sudan on N, Dem. Rep. of the Congo on W, Rwanda and Tanzania on S, Kenya on E. **Topography:** Most of Uganda is a high plateau 3,000-6,000 ft high, with Ruwenzori Range in W (Mt. Margherita, 16,763 ft), volcanoes in SW; NE is arid, W and SW rainy. Lakes Victoria, Edward, Albert form much of borders. **Capital:** Kampala, 1,659,480.

Government: Type: Republic. **Head of state and gov.:** Pres. Yoweri Kaguta Museveni; b. Aug. 15, 1944; in office: Jan. 29, 1986. **Local divisions:** 111 districts, 1 capital city. **Defense budget:** $211 mil. **Active troops:** 45,000.

Economy: Industries: sugar, brewing, tobacco, cotton textiles, cement, steel prod. **Chief crops:** coffee, tea, cotton, tobacco, cassava, potatoes, corn, millet, pulses, cut flowers. **Natural resources:** copper, cobalt, hydropower, limestone, salt, gold. **Crude oil reserves:** 2.5 bil bbls. **Arable land:** 33.8%. **Livestock:** cattle: 8.1 mil; chickens: 34.7 mil; goats: 9.3 mil; pigs: 2.4 mil; sheep: 1.9 mil. **Fish catch:** 523,128 metric tons. **Electricity prod.:** 2.4 bil kWh. **Labor force:** agric. 82%, industry 5%, services 13%.

Finance: Monetary unit: Shilling (UGX) (Sept. 2013: 2,583.78 = $1 U.S.). **GDP:** $51.3 bil; **per capita GDP:** $1,400; **GDP growth:** 2.6%. **Imports:** $5.2 bil; Kenya 16.6%, UAE 14.5%, China 12.3%, India 11.3%, South Africa 4.2%. **Exports:** $2.8 bil; Kenya 12.8%, Rwanda 10.7%, UAE 9.9%, Dem. Rep. of the Congo 9.7%, Netherlands 5.7%, Germany 5.2%, Italy 4.1%. **Tourism:** $1.1 bil. **Budget:** $3.7 bil. **Total reserves less gold:** $3.2 bil. **CPI change:** 14%.

Transport: Railways: 773 mi. **Motor vehicles:** 9.8 vehicles per 1,000 pop. **Civil aviation:** 213.8 mil pass.-mi; 5 airports. **Chief ports:** Entebbe, Jinja, Port Bell.

Communications: TV sets: 22 per 1,000 pop. **Radios:** 888 per 1,000 pop. **Telephone lines:** 0.9 per 100 pop. **Internet:** 14.7%.

Health: Life expect.: 52.7 male; 55.4 female. **Births:** 45.4 per 1,000 pop. **Deaths:** 11.3 per 1,000 pop. **Natural inc.:** 3.41%. **Infant mortality:** 62.5 per 1,000 live births. **HIV rate:** 7.2%.

Education: Compulsory: ages 6-12. **Literacy:** 73.2%.

Major intl. organizations: UN (FAO, IBRD, ILO, IMF, WHO), AU, the Commonwealth, WTO.

Embassy: 5911 16th St. NW 20011; 726-7100.

Website: www.statehouse.go.ug

Britain obtained a protectorate over Uganda in 1894. The country became independent Oct. 9, 1962, and a republic within the Commonwealth a year later. In 1967, the traditional kingdoms, including the powerful Buganda state, were abolished.

Gen. Idi Amin seized power from Prime Min. Milton Obote in 1971. During his 8-year dictatorship, he was responsible for the deaths of up to 300,000 of his opponents. In 1972 he expelled nearly all of Uganda's 45,000 Asians. Tanzanian troops and Ugandan exiles and rebels ousted Amin, Apr. 11, 1979.

Obote, president from Dec. 1980, was ousted in a military coup July 1985. Guerrilla war and rampant human rights abuses plagued Uganda under Obote's regime.

Conditions improved after Yoweri Museveni took power in Jan. 1986. In 1993 the Buganda and other traditional monarchies were restored for ceremonial purposes. Uganda helped Laurent Kabila seize power in the Dem. Rep. of the Congo (formerly Zaire) in 1997 but sent troops in 1998 to aid insurgents seeking his ouster. A withdrawal accord was signed Sept. 2002.

Pres. Museveni won reelection in 2001 and 2006; opponents disputed the latter result, citing allegedly trumped-up charges of treason, terrorism, and rape lodged against Museveni's main rival, Kizza Besigye. Museveni again defeated Besigye in a 2011 presidential election that European observers considered flawed.

An insurgency in N Uganda has killed more than 100,000 people and forced about 2 mil to flee. The rebel Lord's Resistance Army (LRA) has fought the Museveni govt. since 1986 and has abducted some 30,000 children to serve as soldiers and sex slaves. Peace talks brokered by Sudan began July 2006; as talks continued through 2007, the violence diminished. A cease-fire accord was signed Feb. 23, 2008, but Ugandan and Congolese troops (with U.S. aid) launched a new offensive against the LRA in late 2008. Suicide bombings July 11, 2010, killed 76 people watching a World Cup soccer match on outdoor video screens in Kampala. Rising food and fuel prices spurred antigovernment protests in 2011. Al-Shabaab, a Somali al-Qaeda-linked Islamist group, claimed responsibility. An Ebola outbreak in summer 2012 took 176 lives before doctors gained control.

An online campaign to capture the LRA's leader, Joseph Kony, was boosted by the film Kony 2012, which gained over 100 mil views by Mar. 2012. On Apr. 3, 2013, the U.S. offered a $5 mil reward for information leading to his capture. More than 60,000 refugees from the conflict in the Rep. of Congo arrived by July 15, threatening Uganda with a humanitarian crisis.

Ukraine

People: Population: 44,573,205. **Age distrib.:** <15: 13.9%; 65+: 15.6%. **Pop. density:** 199.3 per sq mi, 76.9 per sq km. **Urban:** 68.9%. **Ethnic groups:** Ukrainian 78%, Russian 17%. **Languages:** Ukrainian (official), Russian. **Religions:** Ukrainian Orthodox (Kiev patriarchate) 50%, Ukrainian Orthodox (Moscow patriarchate) 26%, Ukrainian Greek Catholic 8%, Ukrainian Autocephalous Orthodox 7%, Roman Catholic 2%, Protestant 2%.

Geography: Total area: 233,032 sq mi, 603,550 sq km; **Land area:** 223,681 sq mi, 579,330 sq km. **Location:** In E Europe. **Neighbors:** Belarus on N; Russia on NE and E; Moldova, Romania on SW; Hungary, Slovakia, Poland on W. **Topography:** Part of the E European plain. Mountainous areas include the Carpathians in the SW and Crimean chain in the S. Arable black soil constitutes a large part of the country. **Capital:** Kiev, 2,829,300. **Cities (urban aggl.):** Kharkiv, 1,450,522; Odesa, 1,009,979.

Government: Type: Republic. **Head of state:** Pres. Viktor Yanukovych; b. July 9, 1950; in office: Feb. 25, 2010. **Head of gov.:** Prime Min. Mykola Azarov; b. Dec. 17, 1947; in office: Mar. 11, 2010. **Local divisions:** 24 provinces, 2 municipalities, 1 autonomous republic. **Defense budget:** $2.05 bil. **Active troops:** 129,950.

Economy: Industries: coal, elec. power, metals, machinery and transp. equip., chemicals, food proc. **Chief crops:** grain, sugar beets, sunflower seeds, vegetables. **Natural resources:** iron ore, coal, manganese, nat. gas, petroleum, salt, sulfur, graphite, titanium, magnesium, kaolin, nickel, mercury, timber. **Crude oil reserves:** 395 mil bbls. **Arable land:** 56.1%. **Livestock:** cattle: 4.5 mil; chickens: 183.6 mil; goats: 631,200; pigs: 8 mil; sheep: 1.1 mil. **Fish catch:** 203,637 metric tons. **Electricity prod.:** 176.3 bil kWh. **Labor force:** agric. 5.6%, industry 26%, services 68.4%.

Finance: Monetary unit: Hryvna (UAH) (Sept. 2013: 8.16 = $1 U.S.). **GDP:** $340.7 bil; **per capita GDP:** $7,500; **GDP growth:** 0.2%. **Imports:** $90.3 bil; Russia 19.4%, China 10.2%, Germany 9.6%, Belarus 7.8%, Poland 7.1%. **Exports:** $69.8 bil; Russia 23.7%, Turkey 6%, China 4.1%. **Tourism:** $4.8 bil. **Budget:** $63.4 bil (planned and consolidated). **Total reserves less gold:** $22.7 bil. **Gold:** 1.1 mil oz t. **CPI change:** 0.6%.

Transport: Railways: 13,474 mi. **Motor vehicles:** 221.7 vehicles per 1,000 pop. **Civil aviation:** 3.7 bil pass.-mi; 108 airports. **Chief ports:** Feodosiya, Illichivsk, Mariupol, Mykolayiv, Odesa, Yuzhnyy.

Communications: TV sets: 433 per 1,000 pop. **Radios:** 283 per 1,000 pop. **Telephone lines:** 27.1 per 100 pop. **Internet:** 33.7%.

Health: Life expect.: 63.4 male; 74.8 female. **Births:** 9.5 per 1,000 pop. **Deaths:** 15.8 per 1,000 pop. **Natural inc.:** −0.62%. **Infant mortality:** 8.2 per 1,000 live births. **HIV rate:** 0.8%.

Education: Compulsory: ages 6-16. **Literacy:** 99.7%.

Major intl. organizations: UN (FAO, IBRD, ILO, IMF, WHO), CIS, OSCE, WTO.

Embassy: 3350 M St. NW 20007; 333-0606.

Website: www.kmu.gov.ua

Ukrainians' Slavic ancestors inhabited the region well before the 1st cent. CE. In the 9th cent., the princes of Kiev established a strong state called Kievan Rus, which included much of present-day Ukraine. Internal conflicts led to the disintegration of the Ukrainian state by the 13th cent. Mongol rule was supplanted by Poland and Lithuania in the 14th and 15th cent. The N Black Sea coast and Crimea came under Turkish control in 1478. Ukrainian Cossacks,

starting in the late 16th cent., rebelled against the occupiers of Ukraine: Russia, Poland, and Turkey.

An independent Ukrainian National Republic was proclaimed on Jan. 22, 1918. But in 1921, Ukraine's neighbors occupied and divided Ukrainian territory. In 1922, Ukraine became a constituent republic of the USSR. In 1932-33, the Soviet government engineered a famine in eastern Ukraine, and 6-7 mil Ukrainians died. During WWII the Ukrainian nationalist underground fought Nazi and Soviet forces. Over 5 mil Ukrainians died in the war. The reoccupation of Ukraine by Soviet troops in 1944 brought a renewed wave of repression.

The world's worst nuclear power plant disaster occurred in Chernobyl, Ukraine, in Apr. 1986; many thousands were killed or disabled as a result of the radiation leak. The plant was shut down in 2000.

Ukrainian independence was restored, Dec. 1991, with the Soviet Union's dissolution. In the post-Soviet period Ukraine's economy deteriorated. Following a 1994 accord with Russia and the U.S., Ukraine's large nuclear arsenal was transferred to Russia for destruction.

President since 1994, Leonid Kuchma attempted to engineer the 2004 election of his handpicked successor, the Russian-backed Prime Min. Viktor Yanukovych. The main challenger, former Prime Min. Viktor Yushchenko, continued to campaign though he had been poisoned with dioxin. When Yanukovych was declared the winner in Nov., Yushchenko supporters, calling the election fraudulent, staged massive protests (the Orange Revolution), and the vote was annulled. An election rerun Dec. 26 gave Yushchenko the victory. Yushchenko's Our Ukraine party fared poorly in Mar. 2006 parliamentary elections, and Yanukovych returned as prime min. in Aug., initiating a year-long political struggle.

Following Sept. 2007 elections, Yulia Tymoshenko, a former Orange Revolution ally of Yushchenko, became prime min. in Dec. 2007 but lost the presidency to Yanukovych in Feb. 2010. The installation of a pro-Russian government in Ukraine led to a rapid improvement in relations with Moscow. In what her supporters and some international observers viewed as a politically motivated prosecution, Tymoshenko went on trial June 2011, for abusing her powers as prime min. She was convicted and sentenced to seven years in jail in Oct. and faced tax-evasion and embezzlement charges. In protest, the EU halted agreements with the Ukraine. Ignoring international pressure, Yanukovych refused to secure Tymoshenko's release. Yanukovych's governing party won parliamentary elections Oct. 28, 2012. The European Court of Human Rights ruled Apr. 30, 2013, that Tymoshenko's arrest was illegal, but Ukraine did not have to free her based on that decision.

United Arab Emirates

People: Population: 5,473,972. **Age distrib.:** <15: 20.6%; 65+: 1%. **Pop. density:** 169.6 per sq mi, 65.5 per sq km. **Urban:** 84.4%. **Ethnic groups:** Emirati 19%, other Arab and Iranian 23%, South Asian 50%, other expatriates (incl. Westerners and E Asians) 8%. (Less than 20% are UAE citizens.) **Languages:** Arabic (official), Persian, English, Hindi, Urdu. **Religions:** Muslim (official) 96% (Shia 16%), other (incl. Christian, Hindu) 4%.

Geography: Total area: 32,278 sq mi, 83,600 sq km; **Land area:** 32,278 sq mi, 83,600 sq km. **Location:** Middle East, on S shore of the Persian Gulf. **Neighbors:** Saudi Arabia on W and S, Oman on E. **Topography:** A barren, flat coastal plain gives way to uninhabited sand dunes on S. Hajar Mts. in E. **Capital:** Abu Dhabi, 942,193. **Cities (urban aggl.):** Dubai, 1,978,377.

Government: Type: Federation of emirates. **Head of state:** Pres. Sheikh Khalifa ibn Zaid an-Nahayan; b. 1948; in office: Nov. 3, 2004. **Head of gov.:** Prime Min. Sheikh Muhammad ibn Rashid al-Maktum; b. 1949; in office: Jan. 5, 2006. **Local divisions:** 7 emirates: Abu Dhabi, Ajman, Dubai, Fujaira, Ras al-Khaimah, Sharjah, Umm al-Qaiwain. **Defense budget** (2011): $9.32 bil. **Active troops:** 51,000.

Economy: Industries: petroleum and petrochemicals, fishing, aluminum, cement, fertilizers, commercial ship repair, constr. materials. **Chief crops:** dates, vegetables, watermelons. **Natural resources:** petroleum, nat. gas. **Crude oil reserves:** 97.8 bil bbls. **Arable land:** 0.6%. **Livestock:** cattle: 105,177; chickens: 21 mil; goats: 1.9 mil; sheep: 1.4 mil. **Fish catch:** 75,319 metric tons. **Electricity prod.:** 91.9 bil kWh. **Labor force:** agric. 7%, industry 15%, services 78%.

Finance: Monetary unit: Dirham (AED) (Sept. 2013: 3.67 = $1 U.S.). **GDP:** $275.8 bil; **per capita GDP:** $49,800; **GDP growth:** 3.9%. **Imports:** $220.3 bil; India 17%, China 13.8%, U.S. 10.5%, Germany 5.2%, Japan 4.2%. **Exports:** $300.9 bil; Japan 15.6%, India 13.4%, Iran 10.5%, Thailand 5.6%, Singapore 5.5%, South Korea 5.3%. **Tourism:** $9.2 bil. **Budget:** $114.2 bil. **Total reserves less gold:** $47 bil. **CPI change:** NA.

Transport: Motor vehicles: 388.6 vehicles per 1,000 pop. **Civil aviation:** 89.4 bil pass.-mi; 25 airports. **Chief ports:** Al Fujayrah, Khawr Fakkan, Mina' Jabal Ali, Mina' Rashid, Mina' Saqr.

Communications: TV sets: 197 per 1,000 pop. **Radios:** 1,455 per 1,000 pop. **Telephone lines:** 24.3 per 100 pop. **Internet:** 85%.

Health: Life expect.: 74.3 male; 79.6 female. **Births:** 15.7 per 1,000 pop. **Deaths:** 2.0 per 1,000 pop. **Natural inc.:** 1.36%. **Infant mortality:** 11.3 per 1,000 live births. **HIV rate:** NA.

Education: Compulsory: ages 6-14. **Literacy:** 90%.

Major intl. organizations: UN (FAO, IBRD, ILO, IMF, WHO), AL, OPEC, WTO.
Embassy: 3522 International Ct. NW, Ste. 400, 20008; 243-2400.
Website: www.government.ae
The 7 "Trucial Sheikdoms" gave Britain control of defense and foreign relations in the 19th cent. They merged to become an independent state Dec. 2, 1971. Oil revenues have made the UAE one of the world's wealthiest countries. Foreigners make up more than 80% of the population and nearly all the private work force.

International banking, investment, and construction boomed during the late 1990s and early 2000s; holdings of Abu Dhabi's largest government-sponsored investment fund were estimated at $550 bil in Oct. 2008. But Dubai, hurt by the global recession, accepted up to $9.5 bil in government loans to help the state-controlled investment company, Dubai World, avoid default. On July 2, 2013, 68 members of the Islamist group Islah were convicted of conspiring to overthrow the government; another 36 were acquitted. The UAE and two other Middle Eastern monarchies together donated, July 9-10, $12 bil to Egypt after the country overthrew the Islamist Pres. Mohammed Morsi.

United Kingdom
United Kingdom of Great Britain and Northern Ireland

People: Population: 63,395,574. **Age distrib.:** <15: 17.3%; 65+: 17.3%. **Pop. density:** 678.7 per sq mi, 262 per sq km. **Urban:** 79.6%. **Ethnic groups:** white 92% (English 84%, Scottish 9%, Welsh 5%, Northern Irish 3%), black 2%, Indian 2%, Pakistani 1%, mixed 1%. **Languages:** English; Scots, Scottish Gaelic, Welsh, Irish, Cornish (all recognized regional langs.). **Religions:** Christian 72%, Muslim 3%, unspecified/none 23%.
Geography: Total area: 94,058 sq mi, 243,610 sq km; **Land area:** 93,410 sq mi, 241,930 sq km. **Location:** Off NW coast of Europe, across English Channel, Strait of Dover, North Sea. **Neighbors:** Ireland to W, France to SE. **Topography:** England is mostly rolling land, rising to Uplands of southern Scotland. Lowlands are in center of Scotland, granite highlands are in N. Coast is heavily indented, especially on W. British Isles have milder climate than N Europe due to Gulf Stream and ample rainfall. Severn, 220 mi, and Thames, 215 mi, are longest rivers. **Capital:** London, 9,005,300. **Cities (urban aggl.):** Birmingham, 2,271,900; Manchester, 2,212,558; West Yorkshire, 1,624,543; Glasgow, 1,137,321.
Government: Type: Constitutional monarchy. **Head of state:** Queen Elizabeth II; b. Apr. 21, 1926; in office: Feb. 6, 1952. **Head of gov.:** Prime Min. David Cameron, b. Oct. 0, 1066; in office: May 11, 2010. **Local divisions:** 232 local authorities (England: 152; Wales: 22; Scotland: 32; Northern Ireland: 26). **Defense budget:** $60.8 bil. **Active troops:** 165,650.
Economy: Industries: machine tools, elec. power equip., automation equip., railroad equip., shipbuilding, aircraft, motor vehicles and parts, electronics and communications equip., metals, chemicals, coal, petroleum, paper and paper prods. **Chief crops:** cereals, oilseed, potatoes, vegetables. **Natural resources:** coal, petroleum, nat. gas, iron ore, lead, zinc, gold, tin, limestone, salt, clay, chalk, gypsum, potash, silica sand, slate. **Crude oil reserves:** 3.1 bil bbls. **Arable land:** 25.1%. **Livestock:** cattle: 9.9 mil; chickens: 151 mil; goats: 85,000; pigs: 4.4 mil; sheep: 31.6 mil. **Fish catch:** 782,252 metric tons. **Electricity prod.** (2011): 342.1 bil kWh. **Labor force:** agric. 1.4%; industry 18.2%, services 80.4%.
Finance: Monetary unit: Pound (GBP) (Sept. 2013: 0.64 = $1 U.S.). **GDP:** $2.4 tril; **per capita GDP:** $37,500; **GDP growth:** 0.2%. **Imports:** $642.6 bil; Germany 12.5%, China 8.1%, Netherlands 7.3%, U.S. 6.8%, France 5.3%, Belgium 4.4%. **Exports:** $474.6 bil; Germany 11.5%, U.S. 10.6%, Netherlands 8.9%, France 7.4%, Ireland 6%, Belgium 5.1%. **Tourism:** $36.4 bil. **Budget:** $1.2 tril. **Total reserves less gold:** $88.6 bil. **Gold:** 10 mil oz t. **CPI change:** 2.8%.
Transport: Railways: 10,224 mi. **Motor vehicles:** 567.2 vehicles per 1,000 pop. **Civil aviation:** 143.3 bil pass.-mi; 271 airports. **Chief ports:** Dover, Felixstowe, Immingham, Liverpool, London, Southampton, Teesport.
Communications: TV sets: 1,105 per 1,000 pop. **Radios:** 2,059 per 1,000 pop. **Telephone lines:** 52.6 per 100 pop. **Internet:** 87%.
Health: Life expect.: 78.2 male; 82.5 female. **Births:** 12.3 per 1,000 pop. **Deaths:** 9.3 per 1,000 pop. **Natural inc.:** 0.29%. **Infant mortality:** 4.5 per 1,000 live births. **HIV rate:** 0.3%.
Education: Compulsory: ages 5-16. **Literacy:** 99%.
Major intl. organizations: UN and all of its specialized agencies, the Commonwealth, EU, NATO, OECD, OSCE, WTO.
Embassy: 3100 Massachusetts Ave. NW 20008; 588-6500.
Website: www.gov.uk
The United Kingdom of Great Britain and Northern Ireland comprises England, Wales, Scotland, and Northern Ireland.

Queen and Royal Family. The ruling sovereign is Elizabeth II of the House of Windsor elder daughter of King George VI. She succeeded to the throne Feb. 6, 1952, and was crowned June 2, 1953. She was married Nov. 20, 1947, to Lt. Philip Mountbatten (b. June 10, 1921), former Prince of Greece. He was created Duke of Edinburgh, and given the title H.R.H., Nov. 19, 1947; he was named Prince of the United Kingdom and Northern Ireland Feb. 22, 1957.

Prince Charles Philip Arthur George (b. Nov. 14, 1948) is the Prince of Wales and heir apparent. His first son, William Philip Arthur Louis (b. June 21, 1982), is second in line to the throne; William's son, George Alexander Louis (b. July 22, 2013) is third in line.

Parliament is the UK's legislative body, with certain powers over dependent units. It consists of two houses. The House of Commons has 650 members, elected by direct ballot and divided as follows: England, 533; Wales, 40; Scotland, 59; Northern Ireland, 18. Following a drastic reduction in 1999 in the number of hereditary peerages, the House of Lords (Mar. 2013) comprised 761 members: 89 hereditary peers, 647 life peers, and 25 archbishops and bishops of the Church of England.

Resources and Industries. Great Britain's major occupations are manufacturing and trade. Metals and metal-using industries contribute more than 50% of exports. Of about 60 mil acres of land in England, Wales, and Scotland, 46 mil are farmed (of which 17 mil are arable) the rest pastures. Large oil and gas fields have been found in the North Sea. Commercial oil production began in 1975. There are large deposits of coal.

Britain imports all of its cotton, rubber, sulphur, about 80% of its wool, half of its food and iron ore, and some paper, tobacco, chemicals. Manufactured goods made from these basic materials have been exported since the industrial age began. Main exports are machinery, chemicals, textiles, clothing, autos and trucks, iron and steel, locomotives, ships, jet aircraft, farm machinery, drugs, radio, TV, radar and navigation equipment, scientific instruments, arms, whisky.

Religion and Education. The Church of England is Protestant Episcopal. The queen is its temporal head, with rights of appointments to archbishoprics, bishoprics, and other offices. There are two provinces, Canterbury and York, each headed by an archbishop. Westminster Abbey (1050-1760) is the site of coronations and the tombs of Elizabeth I, Mary, Queen of Scots, kings, poets, and of the Unknown Warrior. The most celebrated British universities are Oxford and Cambridge, each dating to the 13th cent. There are about 160 other universities and degree-granting institutions of higher learning.

History. Recent research indicates that Britain was separated from the European continent at least 200,000 years ago by a catastrophic flood that created the English Channel. Migrants across the Channel included the Celts, who arrived 2,500 to 3,000 years ago. Their language survives in Welsh and Gaelic enclaves.

England was part of the Roman Empire 43-410 CE, after which waves of Jutes, Angles, and Saxons arrived from German lands, followed by Danish raiders from the 8th through 11th cent. French-speaking Normans invaded in 1066, uniting the country with their dominions in France.

Opposition by nobles to royal authority forced King John to agree to the Magna Carta in 1215, a guarantee of rights and the rule of law. In the ensuing decades, the foundations of the parliamentary system were laid.

English dynastic claims to large parts of France led to the Hundred Years War, 1338-1453, an unsuccessful campaign. A long civil war, the War of the Roses, lasted 1455-85, and ended with the establishment of the Tudor monarchy. The economy prospered over long periods of domestic peace unmatched in continental Europe. The Church of England separated from the authority of the pope, 1534.

During the reign of Queen Elizabeth I, 1558-1603, England became a major naval power, leading to the founding of colonies in the new world and the expansion of trade with Europe and the Orient. Scotland and England shared a single monarch after James VI of Scotland was crowned James I of England in 1603.

A struggle between Parliament and the Stuart kings led to a civil war, 1642-49, and the establishment of a republic under the Puritan Oliver Cromwell. The monarchy was restored in 1660, but the Glorious Revolution of 1688 confirmed the sovereignty of Parliament: a Bill of Rights was granted 1689. Scotland was united with England after the ratification of the Articles of Union of Scotland and England, May 1707.

Technological and entrepreneurial innovations led to the Industrial Revolution in the 18th cent. The 13 N American colonies were lost but replaced by growing empires in Canada and India. Britain's role in the defeat of Napoleon, 1815, strengthened its position as the leading world power.

The extension of the voting rights in 1832, 1867, and 1884; the formation of trade unions; and the development of universal public education were among the social changes that accompanied the spread of industrialization and urbanization in the 19th cent. Large parts of Africa and Asia were added to the empire during the reign of Queen Victoria, 1837-1901.

Though victorious in WWI, Britain suffered huge casualties and economic dislocation. Ireland became independent in 1921, and independence movements became active in India and other colonies. The country suffered major bombing damage in WWII but rallied behind Prime Min. Winston Churchill and held off Germany until Allied victory was achieved, 1945.

Industrial growth continued in the postwar period, but Britain lost its leadership position to other powers. Labour governments passed socialist programs nationalizing some basic industries and expanding social security. Prime Min. Margaret Thatcher's Conservative

governments, 1979-90, revived the role of private enterprise. Her Conservative successor, John Major, held power 1990-97. The UK sent military forces to the Persian Gulf War, 1991. The Channel Tunnel linking Britain to the Continent was opened May 6, 1994.

The 1997 victory by the Labour Party made Tony Blair, 43, Britain's youngest prime min. since 1812. Diana, Princess of Wales, died in a car crash in Paris, Aug. 31. Britain played a leading role in the NATO air war against Yugoslavia, Mar.-June 1999, and contributed 12,000 troops to the multinational Kosovo security force.

After the Sept. 11 attacks on the U.S., Britain took an important role in the U.S.-led war against terrorism. The UK participated in the bombing of Afghanistan that began Oct. 7, 2001; 7,700 UK troops were serving in Afghanistan as of Sept. 2013, with about 444 fatalities since the war started. Blair, who won a landslide election victory June 2001, committed British troops to the U.S.-led invasion of Iraq, Mar.-Apr. 2003, despite dissent within his own cabinet. UK forces, which numbered 46,000 at the height of combat operations, almost entirely pulled out by mid-2009; 179 had died.

In May 2005 elections, Blair became the first Labour prime min. to win 3 consecutive terms. Suicide bombings on 3 London underground trains and a bus, July 7, 2005, left 56 people dead and hundreds injured; police identified the bombers as 4 British Muslim men (3 of Pakistani origin).

Blair was succeeded by Gordon Brown June 2007. Failed car bombings in London, June 29, 2007, and at Glasgow Airport in Scotland, June 30, led to the arrest of 7 mostly foreign-born medical workers. Responding Oct. 13, 2008, to the worldwide financial crisis, Prime Min. Brown initiated a plan to partially nationalize three of Britain's largest banks and support them with a capital infusion of up to $63 bil.

In the wake of Britain's deepest recession since WWII, voters rejected Brown and the Labour Party in May 2010 parliamentary elections. Conservatives and Liberal Democrats formed the first coalition government in 70 years, with Conservative leader David Cameron becoming prime min. and Liberal Democratic leader Nick Clegg deputy prime min. Cameron responded to the country's fiscal crisis with austerity measures meant to rein in the country's debt and named several new cabinet appointments Sept. 4, 2012, in an effort to reinvigorate economic reform. The government reported Oct. 25, 2012, that London's hosting of the Olympics, July 27-Aug. 12, 2012, had helped the economy to recover from its double-dip recession during the third quarter of 2012.

Justin Welby was installed Feb. 4, 2013, as the new Archbishop of Canterbury, the head of the Church of England. Prime Min. Cameron survived a May 15 parliamentary vote criticizing his handling of whether or not the UK should remain part of the EU; most of the 130 lawmakers who voted against him were from his party. A 25-year-old off-duty British soldier was attacked and killed in London, May 22, by two machete-wielding Muslim activists from Nigeria. After the two men were shot by police and hospitalized, 8 others were arrested in connection with the attack. Parliament voted in favor of same-sex marriage July 16, 2013, and Queen Elizabeth approved the measure the next day. Prince William and his wife Catherine gave birth July 22 to a baby boy, who was third in line to the throne.

Wales

The Principality of Wales in western Britain has an area of 8,019 sq mi and a population (2011 est.) of 3,060,000. Cardiff is the capital, pop. (2010 est., city proper) 341,054.

Less than 20% of Wales residents speak English and Welsh; about 32,000 speak Welsh solely. A 1979 referendum rejected, 4-1, the creation of an elected Welsh assembly; a similar proposal passed by a thin margin on Sept. 18, 1997. Elections for the 60-seat assembly were held in 1997, 2003, 2007, and 2011.

Early Anglo-Saxon invaders drove Celtic peoples into the mountains of Wales, where they developed a distinct nationality. Members of the ruling house of Gwynedd in the 13th cent. fought England but were crushed, 1283. Edward of Caernarvon, son of Edward I of England, was created Prince of Wales, 1301.

Scotland

Scotland, now united with England and Wales in Great Britain, occupies the northern 37% of the main British island, and the Hebrides, Orkney, Shetland, and smaller islands. Length 275 mi, breadth approx. 150 mi, area 30,414 sq mi, pop. (2010 est.) 5,222,100.

The Lowlands, a belt of land approx. 60 mi wide from the Firth of Clyde to the Firth of Forth, divide the farming region of the Southern Uplands from the granite Highlands of the N; they contain 75% of the population and most of the industry. The Highlands, famous for hunting and fishing, have been opened to industry by many hydroelectric power stations.

Edinburgh, pop. (2010 est., city proper) 486,120, is the capital. Glasgow, pop. (2010 est., city proper) 592,820, is Britain's greatest industrial center. It is a shipbuilding complex on the Clyde and an ocean port. Aberdeen, pop. (2010 est.) 217,120, NE of Edinburgh, is a major port, center of granite industry, fish-processing, and North Sea oil exploration. Dundee, pop. (2010 est.) 144,290, NE of Edinburgh, is an industrial and fish-processing center. About 90,000 persons speak Gaelic as well as English.

History. Scotland was called Caledonia by the Romans who battled early Celtic tribes and occupied southern areas from the 1st to

the 4th cent. Missionaries from Britain introduced Christianity in the 4th cent.; St. Columba, an Irish monk, converted most of Scotland in the 6th cent.

The Kingdom of Scotland was founded in 1018. William Wallace and Robert Bruce both defeated English armies 1297 and 1314, respectively. In 1603, James VI of Scotland, son of Mary, Queen of Scots, succeeded to the English throne as James I, and effected the Union of the Crowns. In 1707 Scotland received representation in the British Parliament, resulting from the union of formerly separate Parliaments. Its executive in the British cabinet is the sec. of state for Scotland. The growing Scottish National Party urges independence. A 1997 proposal to create a regional legislature with limited taxing authority passed by a landslide. Elections for the 129-seat parliament were held 1999, 2003, 2007, and 2011; in the 2011 vote, Scottish Nationalist candidates won a majority. A referendum on independence was scheduled for 2014.

Memorials of Robert Burns, Sir Walter Scott, John Knox, and Mary, Queen of Scots, draw many tourists, as do the beauties of the Trossachs, Loch Katrine, Loch Lomond, and abbey ruins.

Industries. Engineering products are the most important industry, with growing emphasis on office machinery, autos, electronics, and other consumer goods. Oil has been discovered offshore in the North Sea, stimulating onshore support industries.

Scotland produces fine woolens, worsteds, tweeds, silks, fine linens, and jute. It is known for its special breeds of cattle and sheep. Fisheries have large hauls of herring, cod, and whiting. Whisky is a major export.

The Hebrides are a group of about 500 islands, 100 inhabited, off the W coast. The **Inner Hebrides** include Skye, Mull, and Iona, the last famous for the arrival of St. Columba, 563 CE. The **Outer Hebrides** include Lewis and Harris. Industries include sheep raising and weaving. The **Orkney Isls.**, c. 90, are to the NE. The capital is Kirkwall, on Pomona Isl. Fish curing, sheep raising, and weaving are occupations. NE of the Orkneys are the 200 **Shetland Isls.**, 24 inhabited, home of Shetland ponies. The Orkneys and Shetlands are centers for the North Sea oil industry.

Northern Ireland

Northern Ireland was constituted in 1920 from 6 of the 9 counties of Ulster, the NE corner of Ireland. Area 5,452 sq mi, pop. (2011 est.) 1,810,900. Capital and chief industrial center, Belfast, pop. (2010 est., city proper) 268,745.

Industries. Shipbuilding, including large tankers, has long been an important industry, centered in Belfast, the largest port. Linen is manufactured, along with apparel, rope, and twine. Growing diversification has added engineering products, synthetic fibers, and electronics. There are large numbers of cattle, hogs, and sheep. Potatoes, poultry, and dairy foods are also produced.

Government and History. An act of the British Parliament, 1920, divided Northern from Southern Ireland, each with a parliament and government. When Ireland became a dominion, 1921, and later a republic, Northern Ireland chose to remain a part of the UK. It elects 18 members to the House of Commons.

During 1968-69, Roman Catholics, a minority comprising about one-third of the population, claimed discrimination against them in voting rights, housing, and employment. Violence and terrorism intensified, involving branches of the Irish Republican Army (IRA; outlawed in the Irish Republic), Protestant groups, police, and British troops. Between 1969 and 2001, more than 3,500 were killed in sectarian violence in Northern Ireland, Ireland, England, and elsewhere. For most of this period, the Northern Ireland parliament was suspended, and Britain imposed direct rule.

A settlement reached on Good Friday, Apr. 10, 1998, and approved May 22 by voters in Northern Ireland and the Irish Republic, restored home rule and election of a 108-member assembly with safeguards for minority rights. Both Ireland and Great Britain agreed to relinquish constitutional claims on Northern Ireland. Elections to the assembly were held June 25. IRA dissidents seeking to derail the agreement detonated a bomb at Omagh Aug. 15 that killed 29 people and injured over 330.

London transferred authority to a Northern Ireland power-sharing government in 1999. Delays in IRA disarmament led to several suspensions of self-government. The IRA July 2005 renounced violence and ordered all units to disarm. The British responded by reducing their military presence in the region. On Sept. 26, an international monitoring group reported that the IRA had apparently scrapped its entire arsenal. The Northern Ireland legislature, suspended for 3½ years, reconvened May 15, 2006. Elections were held in 2007 and 2011. More than 6 weeks of violence erupted after Belfast's city government decided, Dec 3, 2012, to limit the flying of the Union Jack at the City Council building, provoking pro-British unionists, who clashed with Catholic republicans. More than 100 police and scores of protesters were injured.

Religion and Education. Northern Ireland is about 58% Protestant, 42% Roman Catholic. Education is compulsory between the ages of 5 and 16 years. Website: www.northernireland.gov.uk

Channel Islands

The Channel Islands, area 75 sq mi, off the NW coast of France, the only parts of the one-time Dukedom of Normandy belonging to England, are Jersey, Guernsey and the dependencies of

Guernsey—Alderney, Brechou, Great Sark, Little Sark, Herm, Jethou, and Lihou. **Jersey,** area 45 sq mi, pop. (2013 est.) 95,732, and **Guernsey,** area 30 sq mi, pop. (2013 est.) 65,605, have separate legal existences and lieutenant governors named by the Crown. The islands were the only British soil occupied by German troops in WWII. **Websites:** www.gov.je (Jersey); www.gov.gg (Guernsey)

Isle of Man

The Isle of Man, area 221 sq mi, pop. (2013 est.) 86,159, is in the Irish Sea, 20 mi from Scotland, 30 mi from Cumberland. It is rich in lead and iron. The island has its own laws and a lieutenant governor appointed by the Crown. The Tynwald (legislature) consists of the Legislative Council, partly elected, and House of Keys, elected. Capital: Douglas. Farming, tourism, and fishing (kippers, scallops) are chief occupations. Man is famous for the Manx tailless cat. **Website:** www.gov.im

Gibraltar

A dependency on the S coast of Spain, Gibraltar guards the entrance to the Mediterranean. The Rock of Gibraltar has been in British possession since 1704. It is 2.5 mi long, 0.75 of a mi wide, and 1,396 ft in height, with a total area of 2.5 sq mi; a narrow isthmus connects it with the mainland. Pop. (2013 est.) 29,111.

Gibraltar has historically been an object of contention between Britain and Spain. In 1967, residents voted almost unanimously to remain under British rule. A new constitution, May 30, 1969, increased Gibraltarian control of domestic affairs (the UK continues to handle defense and internal security matters). The border, closed by Spain in 1969, was fully reopened in Feb. 1985. A UN General Assembly resolution requested Britain to end Gibraltar's colonial status by Oct. 1, 1996. Gibraltar voters rejected a plan for the UK and Spain to share sovereignty, Nov. 7, 2002. Residents approved a new constitution Nov. 30, 2006. Nevertheless, tensions flared again between the two countries in Aug. 2013 over the question of territorial control. **Website:** www.gibraltar.gov.gi

British West Indies

Swinging in a vast arc from the coast of Venezuela NE, then N and NW toward Puerto Rico are the Leeward Isls., forming a coral and volcanic barrier sheltering the Caribbean from the open Atlantic. Many of the islands are self-governing British possessions. Universal suffrage was instituted 1951-54; ministerial systems were set up 1956-60.

The **Leeward Isls.** still associated with the UK are **Montserrat,** area 39 sq mi, pop. (2013 est.) 5,189, capital Plymouth; the **British Virgin Isls.,** 58 sq mi, pop. (2013 est.) 31,912, capital Road Town; and **Anguilla,** the most northerly of Leeward Isls., 35 sq mi, pop. (2013 est.) 15,754, capital The Valley. Montserrat has been devastated by the Soufrière Hills volcano, which began erupting July 18, 1995.

The three **Cayman Isls.,** a dependency, lie S of Cuba, NW of Jamaica. Pop. (2013 est.) 53,737, most of it on Grand Cayman. It is a free port; in the 1970s Grand Cayman became a tax-free refuge for foreign funds and branches of many Western banks were opened there. Total area 102 sq mi, capital George Town.

The **Turks and Caicos Isls.** are a dependency at the SE end of the Bahama Islands. Of about 30 islands, only 6 are inhabited; area 366 sq mi, pop. (2013 est.) 47,754; capital Grand Turk. Salt, shellfish, and conch shells are the main exports.

Bermuda

Bermuda is a British dependency governed by a royal governor and an assembly, dating from 1620, the oldest legislative body among British dependencies. Capital is Hamilton. It is a group of about 150 small islands of coral formation, 21 inhabited, comprising 21 sq mi in the western Atlantic, 580 mi E of N. Carolina. Pop. (2013 est.) 69,467 (about 54% of African descent). Pop. density is high.

Tourism is the major industry; tourism receipts in 2012 were $441 mil. Bermuda is also a haven for the offshore insurance industry. Exports include petroleum products, medicine. In a referendum Aug. 15, 1995, voters rejected independence by nearly a 3-to-1 majority. Hurricane Fabian, the most potent storm to reach Bermuda in 50 years, struck Sept. 5, 2003; four people were missing and presumed dead, and damage was estimated at over $300 mil. **Website:** www.gov.bm

South Atlantic Territories

The **Falkland Isls.,** a dependency, lie 300 mi E of the Strait of Magellan at the southern end of S America.

The Falklands, or Islas Malvinas, include 2 large islands and about 200 smaller ones, area 4,700 sq mi, pop. (2008 est.) 3,140, capital Stanley. The licensing of foreign fishing vessels has become the major source of revenue. Sheep-grazing is a main industry; wool is the principal export. There are indications of large oil and gas deposits. The islands are also claimed by Argentina, though 97% of inhabitants are of British origin. Argentina invaded the islands Apr. 2, 1982. The British responded by sending a task force to the area, landing their main force on the Falklands, May 21, and forcing an Argentine surrender at Port Stanley, June 14. A pact resuming

commercial air service with Argentina was signed July 14, 1999. **Website:** www.falklands.gov.fk

British Antarctic Territory, S of 60° S lat., formerly a dependency of the Falkland Isls., was made a separate colony in 1962 and includes the South Shetland Isls., the South Orkneys, and the Antarctic Peninsula. A chain of meteorological stations is maintained.

South Georgia and the **South Sandwich Isls.,** formerly administered by the Falklands Isls., became a separate dependency in 1985. Total area of 1,507 sq mi. South Georgia, with no permanent population, is about 800 mi SE of the Falklands; the South Sandwich Isls. are uninhabited, about 470 mi SE of South Georgia.

St. Helena, an island 1,200 mi off the W coast of Africa and 1,800 mi E of S America, 47 sq mi and pop. (2013 est.) 7,754. Flax, lace, and rope-making are the chief industries. After Napoleon Bonaparte was defeated at Waterloo the Allies exiled him to St. Helena, where he lived from Oct. 16, 1815, to his death, May 5, 1821. Capital is Jamestown. **Website:** www.sainthelena.gov.sh

Tristan da Cunha is the principal island in a group of islands of volcanic origin, total area 38 sq mi, halfway between the Cape of Good Hope and S America. A volcanic peak 6,760 ft high erupted in 1961. The 262 inhabitants were removed to England, but most returned in 1963. The islands are dependencies of St. Helena. Pop. (2010 est.): 265.

Ascension is an island of volcanic origin, 34 sq mi in area, 700 mi NW of St. Helena, through which it is administered. It is a communications relay center for Britain, and has a U.S. satellite tracking center. Pop. (2010) was 884, half of them communications workers. The island is noted for sea turtles. **Website:** www.ascension-island.gov.ac

British Indian Ocean Territory

Formed Nov. 1965, embracing islands formerly dependencies of Mauritius or Seychelles: the Chagos Archipelago (including Diego Garcia), Aldabra, Farquhar, and Des Roches. The latter three were transferred to Seychelles, which became independent in 1976. Total area 21,004 sq mi, land area 23 sq mi. No permanent civilian population remains; the UK and the U.S. maintain a military presence.

Pacific Ocean Territories

Pitcairn Isl. is in the Pacific, halfway between S America and Australia. The island was discovered in 1767 by Philip Carteret but was not inhabited until 23 years later when the mutineers of the *Bounty* landed there. The 2012 pop. was 48. It is administered by a British High Commissioner in New Zealand and a local Council. The uninhabited islands of Henderson, Ducie, and Oeno are in the Pitcairn group, area 18 sq mi. **Website:** www.government.pn

United States
United States of America

People: Population: 316,668,567. 50 states and DC. (Note: U.S. pop. figures may differ elsewhere in *The World Almanac.*) **Age distrib.:** <15: 20%; 65+: 13.9%. **Pop. density:** 89.7 per sq mi, 34.6 per sq km. **Urban:** 82.4%. **Ethnic groups:** white 80%, black 13%, Asian 4%, Amerindian and Alaska native 1%. (Hispanic, any race 15%.) **Languages:** English, Spanish, other Indo-European, Asian and Pacific island. **Religions:** Protestant 51%, Roman Catholic 24%, Mormon 2%, Jewish 2%, other Christian 2%, unaffiliated 12%, none 4%.

Geography: Total area: 3,794,100 sq mi, 9,826,675 sq km; **Land area:** 3,537,455 sq mi, 9,161,966 sq km. (Area is for 50 states and DC only.) **Topography:** Vast central plain, mountains in W, hills and low mountains in E. **Capital:** Washington, DC, 4,705,070.

Government: Type: Constitution-based federal republic; strong democratic tradition. **Head of state and gov.:** Pres. Barack Obama; b. Aug. 4, 1961; in office: Jan. 20, 2009. **Local divisions:** 50 states, 1 district. **Defense budget:** $676.7 bil. **Active troops:** 1,520,100.

Economy: Industries: second largest industrial output in world; petroleum, steel, motor vehicles, aerospace, telecom, chemicals, electronics, food proc., consumer goods, lumber, mining. **Chief crops:** wheat, corn, other grains, fruits, vegetables, cotton. **Natural resources:** coal, copper, lead, molybdenum, phosphates, rare earth elements, uranium, bauxite, gold, iron, mercury, nickel, potash, silver, tungsten, zinc, petroleum, nat. gas, timber. **Crude oil reserves** (2012): 26.5 bil bbls. **Arable land:** 17.5%. **Livestock:** cattle: 92.7 mil; chickens: 2.1 bil; goats: 3 mil; pigs: 66.4 mil; sheep: 5.5 mil. **Fish catch:** 5.6 mil metric tons. **Electricity prod.** (2011): 4.1 tril kWh. **Labor force** (excl. unemployed): farming, forestry, fishing 0.7%; mfg., extraction, transp., crafts 20.3%; managerial, professional, technical 37.3%; sales and office 24.2%; other services 17.6%.

Finance: Monetary unit: Dollar (USD). **GDP:** $15.9 tril; **per capita GDP:** $50,700; **GDP growth:** 2.2%. **Imports:** $2.3 tril; China 19%, Canada 14.1%, Mexico 12%, Japan 6.4%, Germany 4.7%. **Exports:** $1.6 tril; Canada 18.9%, Mexico 14%, China 7.2%, Japan 4.5%. **Tourism:** $126.2 bil. **Budget:** $3.5 tril (excl. social benefits of approx. $2.3 tril). **Total reserves less gold:** $139.1 bil. **Gold:** 261.5 mil oz t. **CPI change:** 2.1%.

Transport: Railways: 139,679 mi. **Motor vehicles:** 801.3 vehicles per 1,000 pop. **Civil aviation:** 762.8 bil pass.-mi (incl. airlines based in territories and dependencies); 5,054 airports.

Communications: TV sets: 844 per 1,000 pop. **Radios:** 145 per 1,000 pop. **Telephone lines:** 44 per 100 pop. **Internet:** 81%.

Health: Life expect.: 76.2 male; 81.2 female. **Births:** 13.7 per 1,000 pop. **Deaths:** 8.4 per 1,000 pop. **Natural inc.:** 0.53%. **Infant mortality:** 5.9 per 1,000 live births. **HIV rate:** 0.6%.

Education: Compulsory: ages 6-17. **Literacy:** 99%.

Major intl. organizations: UN (FAO, IBRD, ILO, IMF, WHO), APEC, NAFTA, NATO, OAS, OECD, OSCE, WTO.

Website: www.usa.gov

See also U.S. History chapter; Chronology of the Year's Events.

Uruguay
Oriental Republic of Uruguay

People: Population: 3,324,460. **Age distrib.:** <15: 21.4%; 65+: 13.9%. **Pop. density:** 49.2 per sq mi, 19 per sq km. **Urban:** 92.5%. **Ethnic groups:** white 88%, mestizo 8%, black 4%. **Languages:** Spanish (official), Portunol, Brazilero. **Religions:** Roman Catholic 47%, non-Catholic Christian 11%, nondenominational 23%, atheist or agnostic 17%.

Geography: Total area: 68,037 sq mi, 176,215 sq km; **Land area:** 67,574 sq mi, 175,015 sq km. **Location:** In southern S America, on Atlantic O. **Neighbors:** Argentina on W, Brazil on N. **Topography:** Rolling, grassy plains and hills, well-watered by rivers flowing W to Uruguay R. **Capital:** Montevideo, 1,671,570.

Government: Type: Constitutional republic. **Head of state and gov.:** Pres. José (Pepe) Mujica; b. May 20, 1935; in office: Mar. 1, 2010. **Local divisions:** 19 departments. **Defense budget:** $447 mil. **Active troops:** 24,650.

Economy: Industries: food proc., elec. machinery, transp. equip., petroleum prods., textiles, chemicals, beverages. **Chief crops:** soybeans, rice, wheat. **Natural resources:** hydropower, minor minerals, fish. **Arable land:** 10.3%. **Livestock:** cattle: 11.8 mil; chickens: 17.5 mil; goats: 17,000; pigs: 220,000; sheep: 7.5 mil. **Fish catch:** 89,081 metric tons. **Electricity prod.:** 10.7 bil kWh. **Labor force:** agric. 13%, industry 14%, services 73%.

Finance: Monetary unit: Peso (UYU) (Sept. 2013: 22.48 = $1 U.S.). **GDP:** $54.7 bil; **per capita GDP:** $16,200; **GDP growth:** 3.8%. **Imports:** $12.2 bil; China 16.1%, Argentina 15.8%, Brazil 14.6%, U.S. 8.9%, Paraguay 7.6%. **Exports:** $9.9 bil; Brazil 18.5%, China 17.9%, Argentina 6.8%, Germany 4.3%. **Tourism:** $2.1 bil. **Budget:** $15.6 bil. **Total reserves less gold:** $13.6 bil. **Gold:** 8,263 oz t. **CPI change:** 8.1%.

Transport: Railways: 1,020 mi. **Motor vehicles:** 225.1 vehicles per 1,000 pop. **Civil aviation:** 610.2 mil pass.-mi; 11 airports. **Chief port:** Montevideo.

Communications: TV sets: 381 per 1,000 pop. **Radios:** 603 per 1,000 pop. **Telephone lines:** 29.8 per 100 pop. **Internet:** 55.1%.

Health: Life expect.: 73.5 male; 79.9 female. **Births:** 13.3 per 1,000 pop. **Deaths:** 9.5 per 1,000 pop. **Natural inc.:** 0.38%. **Infant mortality:** 9.2 per 1,000 live births. **HIV rate:** 0.6%.

Education: Compulsory: ages 4-17. **Literacy:** 98.1%.

Major intl. organizations: UN (FAO, IBRD, ILO, IMF, WHO), OAS, WTO.

Embassy: 1913 I St. NW 20006; 331-1313.

Website: portal.gub.uy

Spanish settlers began to supplant the indigenous Charrua Indians in 1624. Portuguese from Brazil arrived later, but Uruguay was attached to the Spanish Viceroyalty of Rio de la Plata in the 18th cent. Rebels fought against Spain beginning in 1810, with independence declared Aug. 25, 1825. To suppress Tupamaro guerrilla activities, a repressive military regime took power in 1973. Constitutional government was restored in 1985.

Uruguay's standard of living remains one of the highest in S America, and political and labor conditions now rank among the freest. José (Pepe) Mujica, a former guerrilla who transformed his Marxist Tupamaro movement into a mainstream political party, won a presidential runoff election Nov. 2009 and took office Mar. 1, 2010. Legislation legalizing same-sex marriage was signed into law May 3, 2013.

Uzbekistan
Republic of Uzbekistan

People: Population: 28,661,637. **Age distrib.:** <15: 25.3%; 65+: 4.7%. **Pop. density:** 174.5 per sq mi, 67.4 per sq km. **Urban:** 36.2%. **Ethnic groups:** Uzbek 80%, Russian 6%, Tajik 5%, Kazakh 3%, Karakalpak 3%, Tatar 2%. **Languages:** Uzbek (official), Russian, Tajik. **Religions:** Muslim (mostly Sunni) 88%, Eastern Orthodox 9%.

Geography: Total area: 172,742 sq mi, 447,400 sq km; **Land area:** 164,248 sq mi, 425,400 sq km. **Location:** Central Asia. **Neighbors:** Kazakhstan on N and W; Kyrgyzstan, Tajikistan on E; Afghanistan, Turkmenistan on S. **Topography:** Mostly plains and desert. **Capital:** Tashkent, 2,226,580.

Government: Type: Republic with authoritarian presidential rule. **Head of state:** Pres. Islam A. Karimov; b. Jan. 30, 1938; in office: Mar. 24, 1990. **Head of gov.:** Prime Min. Shavkat Mirziyaev; b. 1957;

in office: Dec. 11, 2003. **Local divisions:** 12 provinces, 1 autonomous republic, 1 city. **Defense budget** (2010): $1.42 bil. **Active troops:** 48,000.

Economy: Industries: textiles, food proc., machine building, metallurgy, mining, hydrocarbon extraction, chemicals. **Chief crops:** cotton, vegetables, fruits, grain. **Natural resources:** nat. gas, petroleum, coal, gold, uranium, silver, copper, lead, zinc, tungsten, molybdenum. **Crude oil reserves:** 594 mil bbls. **Arable land:** 10.1%. **Livestock:** cattle: 9.1 mil; chickens: 37.3 mil; goats: 2.4 mil; pigs: 94,000; sheep: 12.9 mil. **Fish catch:** 10,700 metric tons. **Electricity prod.:** 49.1 bil kWh. **Labor force:** agric. 25.9%, industry 13.2%, services 60.9%.

Finance: Monetary unit: Som (UZS) (Sept. 2013: 2,129.70 = $1 U.S.). **GDP:** $106.4 bil; **per capita GDP:** $3,600; **GDP growth:** 8.2%. **Imports:** $15.5 bil; Russia 20.6%, China 16.5%, South Korea 16.3%, Kazakhstan 12.8%, Germany 4.6%, Turkey 4.2%. **Exports:** $16.7 bil; China 18.5%, Kazakhstan 14.6%, Turkey 13.8%, Russia 12.8%, Ukraine 12.5%, Bangladesh 8.9%. **Tourism:** $121 mil. **Budget:** $16.9 bil. **Total reserves less gold:** NA. **CPI change:** NA.

Transport: Railways: 2,265 mi. **Motor vehicles:** 69.1 vehicles per 1,000 pop. **Civil aviation:** 3 bil pass.-mi; 33 airports. **Chief port:** Termiz.

Communications: TV sets: 226 per 1,000 pop. **Radios:** 456 per 1,000 pop. **Telephone lines:** 7 per 100 pop. **Internet:** 36.5%.

Health: Life expect.: 70.0 male; 76.3 female. **Births:** 17.2 per 1,000 pop. **Deaths:** 5.3 per 1,000 pop. **Natural inc.:** 1.19%. **Infant mortality:** 20.5 per 1,000 live births. **HIV rate:** NA.

Education: Compulsory: ages 7-18. **Literacy:** 99.4%.

Major intl. organizations: UN (FAO, IBRD, ILO, IMF, WHO), CIS, OSCE, WTO (observer).

Embassy: 1746 Massachusetts Ave. NW 20036; 887-5300.

Website: www.gov.uz

The region was overrun by the Mongols under Genghis Khan in 1220. In the 14th cent., Uzbekistan became the center of a native Timurid empire. In later centuries Muslim feudal states emerged. Russian military conquest began in the 19th cent. Uzbek SSR became a Soviet republic in 1925.

Uzbekistan gained independence when the Soviet Union disbanded Dec. 26, 1991, and has been led by the authoritarian government of a former Communist, Islam A. Karimov.

Attacks by Islamic militants, Mar.-July 2004, killed more than 50 people. In June 2004, Russia's OAO Lukoil signed a $1 bil deal to develop Uzbekistan's natural gas fields. Militants bombed the U.S. and Israeli embassies in Tashkent, July 30.

After armed dissidents at Andizhan, east Uzbekistan, attacked government buildings and freed hundreds of prisoners, May 2005, Uzbek security forces killed many rebels and unarmed demonstrators. Karimov then launched a general crackdown on human rights activists. Irritated by U.S. human rights pressures, Karimov ordered the U.S. to vacate an airbase used to support operations in Afghanistan; the U.S. pullout was completed Nov. 21. Meeting in Moscow a week earlier, Karimov and Russian Pres. Vladimir Putin signed a military cooperation agreement.

Karimov remained in office following the formal expiration of his presidential term Jan. 22, 2007; despite a 2-term limit under the constitution, he ran for a third term Dec. 23 and won with an 88.1% majority. Sanctions imposed by the EU on Uzbek officials after the 2005 Andizhan shootings were lifted Oct. 13, 2008.

When Pakistan closed its supply route to Afghanistan in Nov. 2011-July 2012, much of the non-lethal cargo that was moved into the warzone through the Northern Distribution Network came through Uzbekistan.

Vanuatu
Republic of Vanuatu

People: Population: 261,565. **Age distrib.:** <15: 37.9%; 65+: 3.6%. **Pop. density:** 55.6 per sq mi, 21.5 per sq km. **Urban:** 24.9%. **Ethnic groups:** Ni-Vanuatu 99%. **Languages:** local langs. (100+); pidgin (Bislama), English, French (all official). **Religions:** Protestant 56% (Presbyterian 31%, Anglican 13%, Seventh-Day Adventist 11%), Roman Catholic 13%, indigenous beliefs 6%, other Christian 14%.

Geography: Total area: 4,706 sq mi, 12,189 sq km; **Land area:** 4,706 sq mi, 12,189 sq km. **Location:** SW Pacific, 1,200 mi NE of Brisbane, Australia. **Neighbors:** Fiji to E, Solomon Isls. to NW. **Topography:** Dense forest with narrow coastal strips of cultivated land. **Capital:** Port Vila, 47,061.

Government: Type: Parliamentary republic. **Head of state:** Pres. Iolu Johnson Abil; b. 1942; in office: Sept. 2, 2009. **Head of gov.:** Prime Min. Moana Carcasses Kalosil; b. Jan. 12, 1959; in office: Mar. 23, 2013. **Local divisions:** 6 provinces. **Defense budget:** NA. **Active troops:** No regular military forces.

Economy: Industries: food and fish freezing, wood proc., meat canning. **Chief crops:** copra, coconuts, cocoa, coffee, taro, yams, fruits, vegetables. **Natural resources:** manganese, hardwood forests, fish. **Arable land:** 1.6%. **Livestock:** cattle: 160,000; chickens: 810,000; goats: 20,000; pigs: 92,000. **Fish catch:** 56,379 metric tons. **Electricity prod.:** 55 mil kWh. **Labor force:** agric. 65%, industry 5%, services 30%.

Finance: Monetary unit: Vatu (VUV) (Sept. 2013: 96.05 = $1 U.S.). **GDP:** $1.3 bil; **per capita GDP:** $5,000; **GDP growth:** 2.7%. **Imports:** $316.4 mil; China 19.9%, Singapore 18.6%, U.S. 14.8%, Japan 11.4%, Australia 10.3%, Fiji 5.7%, New Zealand 4.7%. **Exports:** $55.9 mil; Thailand 59.9%, Japan 20.9%. **Tourism:** $226 mil. **Budget:** $181 mil. **Total reserves less gold** (2011): $173.8 mil. **CPI change:** 1.4%.

Transport: Motor vehicles: 58.2 vehicles per 1,000 pop. **Civil aviation:** 141.1 mil pass.-mi; 3 airports. **Chief port:** Port-Vila.

Communications: TV sets: 13 per 1,000 pop. **Radios:** 344 per 1,000 pop. **Telephone lines** 2.3 per 100 pop. **Internet:** 10.6%.

Health: Life expect.: 70.8 male; 74.0 female. **Births:** 26.4 per 1,000 pop. **Deaths:** 4.2 per 1,000 pop. **Natural inc.:** 2.22%. **Infant mortality:** 17.2 per 1,000 live births. **HIV rate:** NA.

Education: NA. **Literacy:** 83.2%.

Major intl. organizations: UN (FAO, IBRD, ILO, IMF, WHO), the Commonwealth, WTO.

Permanent UN mission: 800 Second Ave., Ste. 400B, New York, NY 10017; (212) 661-4323.

Website: www.governmentofvanuatu.gov.vu

The Anglo-French condominium of the New Hebrides, administered jointly by France and Great Britain since 1906, became the independent Republic of Vanuatu on July 30, 1980. Vanuatu is located in the Ring of Fire, a zone with frequent earthquakes and volcanic eruptions. The nation joined the World Trade Organization Aug. 24, 2012. Prime Min. Sato Kilman resigned Mar. 21, 2013. He had faced a no-confidence vote in parliament for his failure to curb corruption, among other issues. He was replaced by Moana Carcasses, Mar. 23, 2013.

Vatican City
The Holy See (Vatican City State)

People: Population: 839. **Pop. density:** 4,938.6 per sq mi, 1,906.8 per sq km. **Urban:** 100%. **Ethnic groups:** Italian, Swiss, other. **Languages:** Italian, Latin, French, various others. **Religion:** Roman Catholic.

Geography: Total area: 0.17 sq mi, 0.44 sq km; **Land area:** 0.17 sq mi, 0.44 sq km. **Location:** In Rome, Italy. **Neighbors:** Completely surrounded by Italy. **Capital:** Vatican City, 459.

Defense budget: NA. **Active troops:** Italy responsible for defense.

Economy: Industries: printing; coins, medals, postage stamps prod., mosaics and staff uniforms; worldwide banking and financial activities. **Labor force:** Essentially services with small amount of industry; nearly all dignitaries, priests, nuns, guards, and approx. 3,000 lay workers live outside the Vatican.

Finance: Monetary unit: Euro (EUR) (Sept. 2013: 0.76 = $1 U.S.). **GDP:** NA; **per capita GDP:** NA; **GDP growth:** NA. **Budget** (2011): $326.4 mil. **Total reserves less gold:** NA. **CPI change:** NA.

Apostolic Nunciature: 3339 Massachusetts Ave. NW 20008; 333-7121.

Website: www.vatican.va

The popes for many centuries, with brief interruptions, held temporal sovereignty over mid-Italy (the so-called Papal States), comprising an area of some 16,000 sq mi, with a population in the 19th cent. of more than 3 mil. This territory was incorporated in the new Kingdom of Italy (1861), the sovereignty of the pope being confined to the palaces of the Vatican and the Lateran in Rome and the villa of Castel Gandolfo, by an Italian law, May 13, 1871.

A Treaty of Conciliation, a concordat, and a financial convention were signed Feb. 11, 1929, by Cardinal Gasparri and Premier Mussolini. The documents established the independent state of Vatican City and gave the Roman Catholic Church special status in Italy. The treaty (Lateran Agreement) was incorporated into Italy's Constitution (Article 7) in 1947. Italy and the Vatican signed an agreement in 1984 eliminating Roman Catholicism as the state religion and ending required religious education in Italian schools.

Vatican City includes the Basilica of Saint Peter, the Vatican Palace and Museum covering over 13 acres, the Vatican gardens, and neighboring buildings between Viale Vaticano and the church. Thirteen buildings in Rome, outside the boundaries, which house congregations or officers necessary for the administration of the Holy See, enjoy extraterritorial rights.

The legal system is based on the code of canon law, the apostolic constitutions, and laws especially promulgated for Vatican City by the pope. The Secretariat of State represents the Holy See in its diplomatic relations.

Citing health problems, Pope Benedict XVI, elected sovereign of the State of Vatican City since Apr. 19, 2005, announced he would resign Feb. 11, 2013, the first pontiff to do so since 1415. He became Pope Emeritus Feb. 28. After a 2-day conclave, Cardinal Jorge Mario Bergoglio, from Argentina, was elected Mar. 13, taking the name of Francis. Pope Francis became the first Latin American and the first Jesuit pope.

Venezuela
Bolivarian Republic of Venezuela

People: Population: 28,459,085. **Age distrib.:** <15: 28.6%; 65+: 5.8%. **Pop. density:** 83.6 per sq mi, 32.3 per sq km. **Urban:** 93.5%.

Ethnic groups: Spanish, Italian, Portuguese, Arab, German, African, indigenous. **Languages:** Spanish (official), many indigenous dialects. **Religions:** Roman Catholic (nominally) 96%, Protestant 2%.

Geography: Total area: 352,144 sq mi, 912,050 sq km; **Land area:** 340,561 sq mi, 882,050 sq km. **Location:** On Carib. coast of S America. **Neighbors:** Colombia on W, Brazil on S, Guyana on E. **Topography:** Flat coastal plain and Orinoco Delta are bordered by Andes Mts. and hills. Plains, called llanos, extend between mountains and Orinoco. Guiana Highlands and plains are S of Orinoco, which stretches 1,600 mi and drains 80% of country. **Capital:** Caracas, 3,241,580. **Cities (urban aggl.):** Maracaibo, 2,309,537; Valencia, 1,865,721; Barquisimeto, 1,245,226; Maracay, 1,114,872.

Government: Federal republic. **Head of state and gov.:** Pres. Nicolás Maduro Moros; b. Nov. 23, 1962; in office: Mar. 8, 2013. **Local divisions:** 23 states, 1 federal district, 1 federal dependency (72 islands). **Defense budget:** $6.09 bil. **Active troops:** 115,000.

Economy: Industries: petroleum, constr. materials, food proc., textiles, iron ore mining, steel, aluminum, motor vehicle assembly, chem. prods. **Chief crops:** corn, sorghum, sugarcane, rice, bananas, vegetables, coffee. **Natural resources:** petroleum, nat. gas, iron ore, gold, bauxite, hydropower, diamonds. **Crude oil reserves:** 297.6 bil bbls. **Arable land:** 2.9%. **Livestock:** cattle: 17.4 mil; chickens: 118 mil; goats: 1.5 mil; pigs: 3.5 mil; sheep: 580,000. **Fish catch:** 248,400 metric tons. **Electricity prod.** (2011): 123.3 bil kWh. **Labor force:** agric. 7.3%, industry 21.8%, services 70.9%.

Finance: Monetary unit: Bolivar (VEF) (Sept. 2013: 6.29 = $1 U.S.). **GDP:** $408.5 bil; **per capita GDP:** $13,800; **GDP growth:** 5.5%. **Imports:** $59.3 bil; U.S. 31.2%, China 16.5%, Brazil 8.9%. **Exports:** $97.3 bil; U.S. 39.3%, China 14.4%, India 12%, Netherlands Antilles 7.6%, Cuba 4.5%. **Tourism:** $844 mil. **Budget:** $165.3 bil. **Total reserves less gold:** $9.9 bil. **Gold:** 11.8 mil oz t. **CPI change:** 21.1%.

Transport: Railways: 501 mi. **Motor vehicles:** 119.1 vehicles per 1,000 pop. **Civil aviation:** 1.6 bil pass.-mi; 127 airports. **Chief ports:** La Guaira, Maracaibo, Puerto Cabello, Punta Cardon.

Communications: TV sets: 208 per 1,000 pop. **Radios:** 291 per 1,000 pop. **Telephone lines:** 25.6 per 100 pop. **Internet:** 44%.

Health: Life expect.: 71.1 male; 77.5 female. **Births:** 19.7 per 1,000 pop. **Deaths:** 5.2 per 1,000 pop. **Natural inc.:** 1.44%. **Infant mortality:** 19.8 per 1,000 live births. **HIV rate:** 0.5%.

Education: Compulsory: ages 3-16. **Literacy:** 95.5%.

Major intl. organizations: UN (FAO, IBRD, ILO, IMF, WHO), OAS, OPEC, WTO.

Embassy: 1099 30th St. NW 20007; 342-2214.

Website: www.presidencia.gob.ve or venezuela-us.org

Columbus first set foot on the South American continent on the peninsula of Paria, Aug. 1498. Alonso de Ojeda, 1499, called the land Venezuela, or Little Venice, because the Indians had houses on stilts. Spanish colonialists dominated Venezuela until Simón Bolívar's victory near Carabobo in June 1821. The republic was formed after secession from the Colombian Federation in 1830. Military strongmen ruled Venezuela for much of its history. Since 1959, the country has had democratically elected governments.

Oil accounts for more than 75% of export earnings and about half of government revenues. The government, Jan. 1, 1976, nationalized the oil industry. Attempts to reduce dependence on the hydrocarbon sector have met with limited success. The country has large reserves of natural gas.

Two attempted coups were thwarted by loyalist troops in Feb. and Nov. 1992. Pres. Carlos Andrés Pérez was removed from office on corruption charges, May 1993, and convicted, May 1996, of mismanaging a $17 mil secret government fund.

A 1992 coup leader, Hugo Chávez, who ran as a populist, was elected president Dec. 1998. That month, voters approved a new constitution greatly increasing his powers.

Popular among the poor, Chávez alienated middle- and upper-class Venezuelans with economic and political reforms, and his foreign policy antagonized the U.S. Gunfire erupted at a mass protest Apr. 11, 2002, in Caracas, killing at least 17 people. Chávez was forced to relinquish power, but when an interim government suspended democratic institutions, Chávez loyalists rebelled; the coup fell apart, and the president reclaimed his office Apr. 14. Chávez opponents organized strikes and recall efforts, 2003-04, but failed to oust him.

Chávez countered U.S. attempts to isolate him diplomatically and militarily by solidifying ties with Latin American leftist leaders and with Iran and Russia. With the economy surging, he won Dec. 2006, presidential election. On Jan. 31, 2007, the legislature granted him the power to rule by decree. Venezuelan voters approved constitutional changes abolishing presidential term limits Feb. 15, 2009. Chávez traveled repeatedly to Cuba for cancer treatments 2011-12 and won a tough reelection challenge Oct. 7, 2012. He died Mar. 5, 2013, before he could be sworn in. Vice Pres. Nicolás Maduro Moros became interim president Mar. 8 and won a narrow victory in Apr. 14, 2013, elections. Seven people died in violence that erupted as supporters of the opposition candidate, Henrique Capriles Radonski, demonstrated in Caracas, calling for a recount. A ballot review confirmed the results June 11. Capriles tried to challenge the outcome in court, but his case was rejected Aug. 7, and he was fined for insulting the government and for claiming judicial bias.

Vietnam
Socialist Republic of Vietnam

People: Population: 92,477,857. **Age distrib.:** <15: 24.6%; 65+: 5.6%. **Pop. density:** 772.5 per sq mi, 298.2 per sq km. **Urban:** 31%. **Ethnic groups:** Kinh (Viet) 86%, Tay 2%, Thai 2%, Muong 2%, Khmer 2%, Mong 1%, Nung 1%. **Languages:** Vietnamese (official), English (increasingly favored as second lang.), French, Chinese, Khmer, mountain area langs. (Mon-Khmer, Malayo-Polynesian). **Religions:** Buddhist 9%, Catholic 7%, Hoa Hao 2%, Cao Dai 1%, none 81%.

Geography: Total area: 127,881 sq mi, 331,210 sq km; **Land area:** 119,719 sq mi, 310,070 sq km. **Location:** SE Asia, on E coast of Indochinese Peninsula. **Neighbors:** China on N; Laos, Cambodia on W. **Topography:** Long and narrow, with 1,400-mi coast. About 22% of country is readily arable, including densely settled Red R. Valley in N, narrow coastal plains in center, and the wide, often marshy Mekong R. Delta in S. The rest consists of semi-arid plateaus and barren mountains, with some stretches of tropical rain forest. **Capital:** Hà Noi, 2,955,130. **Cities (urban aggl.):** Ho Chi Minh City, 6,405,447; Can Tho, 1,004,067.

Government: Type: Communist state. **Head of state:** Pres. Truong Tan Sang; b. Jan. 21, 1949; in office: July 25, 2011. **Head of gov.:** Prime Min. Nguyen Tan Dung; b. Nov. 17, 1949; in office: June 27, 2006. **Local divisions:** 58 provinces, 5 municipalities. **Defense budget:** $3.33 bil. **Active troops:** 482,000.

Economy: Industries: food proc., garments, shoes, machine-building, mining, coal, steel, cement, chemical fertilizer. **Chief crops:** paddy rice, coffee, rubber, cotton, tea, pepper, soybeans, cashews, sugarcane, peanuts, bananas. **Natural resources:** phosphates, coal, manganese, rare earth elements, bauxite, chromate, offshore oil and gas deposits, timber, hydropower. **Crude oil reserves:** 4.4 bil bbls. **Arable land:** 21%. **Livestock:** cattle: 5.4 mil; chickens: 225.8 mil; goats: 1.3 mil; pigs: 27.1 mil. **Fish catch:** 5.6 mil metric tons. **Electricity prod.:** 90.6 bil kWh. **Labor force:** agric. 48%, industry 21%, services 31%.

Finance: Monetary unit: Dong (VND) (Sept. 2013: 21,123.79 = $1 U.S.). **GDP:** $325.9 bil; **per capita GDP:** $3,600; **GDP growth:** 5%. **Imports:** $114.3 bil; China 27.2%, South Korea 12.7%, Japan 8.5%, Singapore 8.3%, Thailand 5.3%, Hong Kong 5.2%. **Exports:** $114.3 bil; U.S. 17%, China 12.9%, Japan 12%, South Korea 4.6%, Germany 4.4%, Malaysia 4.2%. **Tourism:** $6.6 bil. **Budget:** $47.8 bil. **Total reserves less gold:** $25.6 bil. **CPI change:** 9.1%.

Transport: Railways: 1,635 mi. **Motor vehicles:** 4 vehicles per 1,000 pop. **Civil aviation:** 10.2 bil pass.-mi; 38 airports. **Chief ports:** Cam Pha Port, Da Nang, Hai Phong, Ho Chi Minh City, Phu My, Quy Nhon.

Communications: TV sets: 208 per 1,000 pop. **Radios:** 109 per 1,000 pop. **Telephone lines:** 11.4 per 100 pop. **Internet:** 39.5%.

Health: Life expect.: 70.2 male; 75.4 female. **Births:** 16.6 per 1,000 pop. **Deaths:** 5.9 per 1,000 pop. **Natural inc.:** 1.06%. **Infant mortality:** 19.6 per 1,000 live births. **HIV rate:** 0.5%.

Education: Compulsory: ages 6-14. **Literacy:** 93.4%.

Major intl. organizations: UN (FAO, IBRD, ILO, IMF, WHO), APEC, ASEAN, WTO.

Embassy: 1233 20th St. NW, Ste. 400, 20036; 861-0737.

Website: www.na.gov.vn

Settled by Viets from central China, Vietnam was held by China, 111 BCE-939 CE, and was a vassal state during subsequent periods. Conquest by France began in 1858 and ended in 1884 with the protectorates of Tonkin and Annam in the N and the colony of Cochin-China in the S.

Japan occupied Vietnam in 1940. Several groups formed the Vietminh (Independence) League, headed by Communist guerrilla leader Ho Chi Minh. In Aug. 1945, the Vietminh forced out Bao Dai, former emperor of Annam and head of a Japan-sponsored regime. France, seeking to reestablish colonial control, unsuccessfully battled Communist and nationalist forces, 1946-54.

Separate states formed in N. and S. Vietnam, with Communists under Ho Chi Minh (backed by Russia and China) controlling N. Vietnam and a non-Communist government (backed by the U.S.) controlling S. Vietnam. N. Vietnam aided Vietcong guerrillas who sought to take over S. Vietnam. U.S. troops defended S. Vietnam against forces in N. Vietnam and border areas of Laos and Cambodia. Casualties of the war were as follows—combat deaths: U.S. 47,369; S. Vietnam more than 200,000; other allied forces, 5,225. Total U.S. fatalities numbered more than 58,000. Vietnamese civilian casualties were more than 1 mil. The war displaced more than 6.5 mil in S. Vietnam.

A never-implemented cease-fire agreement was signed in Paris Jan. 27, 1973, by the U.S., N. and S. Vietnam, and the Vietcong. S. Vietnam surrendered Apr. 30, 1975. N. Vietnam assumed control. The country was officially reunited July 2, 1976.

Among the unstable conditions that persisted in the region, heavy fighting with Cambodia took place, 1977-80. China cut off economic aid when 140,000 ethnic Chinese fled discrimination in Vietnam. Reacting to Vietnam's 1979 invasion of Cambodia, China attacked four Vietnamese border provinces, Feb. 1979.

Vietnam announced reforms aimed at reducing central control of the economy in 1987. Citing Hanoi's cooperation in returning remains of U.S. soldiers killed in the Vietnam War, the U.S. ended, Feb. 1994, a 19-year U.S. embargo on trade with Vietnam. The U.S. extended full diplomatic recognition to Vietnam July 11, 1995. The U.S. has become Vietnam's top export market, with total annual trade over $20 bil between the two countries. In Aug. 2012, the U.S. began cleaning up the herbicide Agent Orange, which it had used to clear forests during the Vietnam War. Vietnamese courts convicted 14 activists Jan. 9, 2013, of conspiring to overthrow the government as dissent continued to be suppressed.

Yemen
Republic of Yemen

People: Population: 25,408,288. **Age distrib.:** <15: 42%; 65+: 2.6%. **Pop. density:** 124.6 per sq mi, 48.1 per sq km. **Urban:** 32.3%. **Ethnic groups:** predominantly Arab; Afro-Arab, S Asian, European. **Language:** Arabic (official). **Religion:** Muslim (official, incl. Sunni, Shia).

Geography: Total area: 203,850 sq mi, 527,968 sq km; **Land area:** 203,850 sq mi, 527,968 sq km. **Location:** Middle East, on S coast of the Arabian Peninsula. **Neighbors:** Saudi Arabia on N, Oman on E. **Topography:** A sandy coastal strip leads to well-watered fertile mountains in interior. **Capital:** Sana'a', 2,418,680. **Cities (urban aggl.):** Aden, 783,608.

Government: Type: Republic. **Head of state:** Pres. Abd al-Rab Mansur al-Hadi; b. Sept. 9, 1950; in office: Feb. 25, 2012. **Head of gov.:** Prime Min. Muhammad Salim Ba Sindwah; b. 1935; in office: Nov. 27, 2011. **Local divisions:** 20 governorates, 1 municipality. **Defense budget:** $1.63 bil. **Active troops:** 66,700.

Economy: Industries: crude oil prod. and petroleum refining, small-scale prod. of cotton textiles and leather goods, food proc., handicrafts. **Chief crops:** grains, fruits, vegetables, pulses, khat, coffee, cotton. **Natural resources:** petroleum; fish; rock salt; marble; small deposits of coal, gold, lead, nickel, copper. **Crude oil reserves:** 3 bil bbls. **Arable land:** 2.2%. **Livestock:** cattle: 1.7 mil; chickens: 60 mil; goats: 9.1 mil; sheep: 9.4 mil. **Fish catch:** 157,261 metric tons. **Electricity prod.:** 7.3 bil kWh. **Labor force:** Most people employed in agric. and herding; services, constr., industry, and commerce account for less than one-fourth of labor force.

Finance: Monetary unit: Rial (YER) (Sept. 2013: 214.90 = $1 U.S.). **GDP:** $60.1 bil; **per capita GDP:** $2,300; **GDP growth:** 0.1%. **Imports:** $8.9 bil; China 15.7%, UAE 14.4%, India 9.7%, Saudi Arabia 6.8%, Kuwait 5.1%. **Exports:** $7.6 bil; China 37.3%, Thailand 15.8%, South Korea 11.4%, India 9.9%, UAE 5.3%. **Tourism:** $783 mil. **Budget:** $11.2 bil. **Total reserves less gold:** $6.1 bil. **Gold:** 50,000 oz t. **CPI change:** 17.3%.

Transport: Motor vehicles: 27.9 vehicles per 1,000 pop. **Civil aviation:** 1.9 bil pass.-mi; 17 airports. **Chief ports:** Aden, Al Hudaydah, Al Mukalla.

Communications: TV sets: 344 per 1,000 pop. **Radios:** 64 per 1,000 pop. **Telephone lines:** 4.3 per 100 pop. **Internet:** 17.4%.

Health: Life expect.: 62.4 male; 66.7 female. **Births:** 31.6 per 1,000 pop. **Deaths:** 6.6 per 1,000 pop. **Natural inc.:** 2.50%. **Infant mortality:** 51.9 per 1,000 live births. **HIV rate:** 0.2%.

Education: Compulsory: ages 6-14. **Literacy:** 65.3%.

Major intl. organizations: UN (FAO, IBRD, ILO, IMF, WHO), AL, WTO (observer).

Embassy: 2319 Wyoming Ave. NW 20008; 965-4760.

Website: www.yemen.gov.ye or www.yemenembassy.org

Yemen's territory once was part of the ancient biblical Kingdom of Sheba, or Saba. Yemen became independent in 1918, after centuries of Ottoman Turkish rule.

Imam Yahya ibn Muhammad ruled, 1904-48, and after his assassination was succeeded by his son, Imam Ahmed, 1948-62. Army officers headed by Brig. Gen. Abdullah al-Salal declared the country the Yemen Arab Republic, Sept. 1962. Ahmed's heir, the Imam Mohamad al-Badr, fled to the mountains where tribesmen joined royalist forces, aided by the Saudi monarchy. Fighting between royalists and republicans killed about 150,000 people until hostilities ended in 1970.

South Yemen, formed from the British colony of Aden and the British protectorate of South Arabia, became independent Nov. 1967. A Marxist state and a Soviet ally, it took the name People's Democratic Republic of Yemen in 1970. More than 300,000 Yemenis fled from the S to the N after independence, contributing to two decades of hostility between the two states.

The two countries were formally united May 21, 1990, but regional clan-based rivalries led to full-scale civil war in 1994. Secessionists declared a breakaway state in South Yemen, May 21, 1994, but northern troops captured the former southern capital of Aden in July. A new constitution was approved Sept. 28.

Yemen, the ancestral home of Osama bin Laden, has been caught in a crossfire between the U.S. and Islamic extremists. While on a refueling stop in Aden, Oct. 12, 2000, the destroyer U.S.S. Cole was bombed, killing 17 Americans and injuring more than three dozen; the U.S. government blamed the attack on terrorists associated with bin Laden.

Clashes beginning in June 2004 between Yemeni government forces and Shiite rebels led by an anti-U.S. cleric, Hussein al-Houthi, left more than 200 people dead. The government announced Sept. 10 that Yemeni troops had killed al-Houthi. Incumbent Pres. Ali Abdullah Saleh was reelected Sept. 2006.

During 2007-10, Shiite rebels in the northwest, secessionists in the south, al-Qaeda militants in the east, and pirates in coastal waters challenged Yemeni government authority. Emboldened by the success of Arab Spring protests in Tunisia and Egypt in early

2011, mass demonstrations in Yemeni cities demanded Pres. Saleh's resignation. The U.S. and Gulf Arab nations also pressed him to depart. Saleh was severely wounded June 3 in a rocket attack on the presidential compound in Sana'a.' Vice Pres. Abd al-Rab Mansur al-Hadi served as acting president June 4-Sept. 23, 2011, while Saleh received extended medical treatment in Saudi Arabia. After a 2-year manhunt, Anwar al-Awlaki, an American citizen and radical Muslim cleric linked to several plots against the U.S., was killed Sept. 30, 2011, by a U.S. missile in northern Yemen. Saleh ceded power Nov. 23, 2011, remaining in office in name only. Hadi served as acting president. He officially became president in uncontested Feb. 2012 elections but has since failed to stabilize the country, allowing al-Qaeda to strengthen its foothold. Islamic militants, including those in al-Qaeda, staged suicide bombings and other terrorist attacks throughout 2012 and 2013. As the U.S. continued to take out al-Qaeda operatives and key leaders, Pres. Hadi, Sept. 29, 2012, lauded the effectiveness of U.S. drone strikes in the country during a visit to Washington, DC.

Zambia
Republic of Zambia

People: Population: 14,222,233. **Age distrib.:** <15: 46.2%; 65+: 2.4%. **Pop. density:** 49.6 per sq mi, 19.1 per sq km. **Urban:** 39.2%. **Ethnic groups:** African (incl. Bemba, Tonga, Chewa, Lozi, Nsenga, Tumbuka, Ngoni, Lala, Kaonde, Lunda) 99.5%. **Languages:** 11 Bantu langs. (incl. Bemba, Nyanja, Tonga, Lozi, Chewa, Nsenga, Tumbuka, Lunda, Kaonde, Lala, Luvale [some official]); English (official). **Religions:** Christian 50%-75%, Muslim and Hindu 24%-49%, indigenous beliefs 1%.
Geography: Total area: 290,587 sq mi, 752,618 sq km; **Land area:** 287,028 sq mi, 743,398 sq km. **Location:** In S central Africa. **Neighbors:** Congo on N; Tanzania, Malawi, Mozambique on E; Zimbabwe, Namibia on S; Angola on W. **Topography:** Mostly high plateau covered with thick forests and drained by several important rivers, including the Zambezi. **Capital:** Lusaka, 1,802,470.
Government: Type: Republic. **Head of state and gov.:** Pres. Michael Sata; b. 1937; in office: Sept. 23, 2011. **Local divisions:** 10 provinces. **Defense budget:** $326 mil. **Active troops:** 15,100.
Economy: Industries: copper mining and proc., constr., foodstuffs, beverages, chemicals, textiles, fertilizer, horticulture. **Chief crops:** corn, sorghum, rice, peanuts, sunflower seeds, vegetables, flowers, tobacco, cotton, sugarcane, cassava, coffee. **Natural resources:** copper, cobalt, zinc, lead, coal, emeralds, gold, silver, uranium, hydropower. **Arable land:** 4.6%. **Livestock:** cattle: 3 mil; chickens: 36 mil; goats: 2.3 mil; pigs: 718,000; sheep: 225,000. **Fish catch:** 79,894 metric tons. **Electricity prod.:** 11.2 bil kWh. **Labor force:** agric. 85%, industry 6%, services 9%.
Finance: Monetary unit: Kwacha (ZMW) (Sept. 2013: 5.35 = $1 U.S.). **GDP:** $24.4 bil; **per capita GDP:** $1,700; **GDP growth:** 7.3%. **Imports:** $7.4 bil; South Africa 36.2%, Dem. Rep. of the Congo 21.3%, China 10.1%, Kuwait 5.7%. **Exports:** $8.6 bil; China 42.2%, South Africa 7.2%, Dem. Rep. of the Congo 7.2%, South Korea 5.3%, India 4.5%, Egypt 4.5%, UAE 4.4%. **Tourism:** $146 mil. **Budget:** $5.3 bil. **Total reserves less gold:** $3 bil. **CPI change:** 6.6%.
Transport: Railways: 1,340 mi (incl. part of Tanzania-Zambia Railway Authority). **Motor vehicles:** 21.3 vehicles per 1,000 pop. **Civil aviation:** 12.4 mil pass.-mi; 8 airports. **Chief port:** Mpulungu.
Communications: TV sets: 64 per 1,000 pop. **Radios:** 145 per 1,000 pop. **Telephone lines:** 0.6 per 100 pop. **Internet:** 13.5%.
Health: Life expect.: 49.9 male; 53.1 female. **Births:** 42.8 per 1,000 pop. **Deaths:** 13.2 per 1,000 pop. **Natural inc.:** 2.96%. **Infant mortality:** 68.6 per 1,000 live births. **HIV rate:** 12.5%.
Education: Compulsory: ages 7-13. **Literacy:** 61.4%.
Major intl. organizations: UN (FAO, IBRD, ILO, IMF, WHO), AU, the Commonwealth, WTO.
Embassy: 2419 Massachusetts Ave. NW 20008; 265-9717.
Website: www.statehouse.gov.zm
Ruled by the British as Northern Rhodesia, the country became the independent republic of Zambia within the Commonwealth Oct. 24, 1964. Independence leader Kenneth Kaunda governed as president, 1964-91. A Zambian government corporation in 1970 took over 51% of two foreign-owned copper-mining companies. Privately held land and other enterprises were nationalized in 1975. In the 1980s and 1990s, lowered copper prices hurt the economy and severe drought caused famine.
Food riots erupted in June 1990. Oct. 1991 elections brought an end to Kaunda's one-party rule. The new government sought to sell state enterprises, including the copper industry. Pres. Frederick Chiluba won reelection Nov. 1996. A coup attempt was suppressed Oct. 1997.
Unable to change the constitution to allow himself a third term, Chiluba endorsed Levy Patrick Mwanawasa, who won a disputed election Dec. 2001. Food shortages threatened more than 2 mil Zambians in 2002; the government refused to distribute shipments of U.S. grain because it was genetically modified. In a hard-fought 2006 election, Mwanawasa won a second term. Accused of embezzling state funds as president, Chiluba was ordered to pay $58 mil by a British court, June 2007; he was acquitted by a Zambian court, Aug. 2009, of misusing $500,000 in public money.
Pres. Mwanawasa suffered a stroke June 29, 2008, and died Aug. 19. Vice Pres. Rupiah Banda became acting pres. He won the

presidency by a narrow margin in the Oct. 2008 election but lost to opposition leader Michael Sata Sept. 2011.
The country has made progress in treating HIV/AIDS, which afflicts nearly 1 mil adults in Zambia. But that progress was compromised, as of Aug. 2013, by a shortage of antiretroviral drugs to treat the disease, forcing the government to institute a rationing system Aug. 21.

Zimbabwe
Republic of Zimbabwe

People: Population: 13,182,908. **Age distrib.:** <15: 39.4%; 65+: 3.6%. **Pop. density:** 88.3 per sq mi, 34.1 per sq km. **Urban:** 38.6%. **Ethnic groups:** African 98% (Shona 82%, Ndebele 14%), mixed and Asian 1%. **Languages:** English (official), Shona, Sindebele, minor tribal dialects. **Religions:** syncretic (Christian and indigenous beliefs) 50%, Christian 25%, indigenous beliefs 24%, Muslim and other 1%.
Geography: Total area: 150,872 sq mi, 390,757 sq km; **Land area:** 149,362 sq mi, 386,847 sq km. **Location:** In southern Africa. **Neighbors:** Zambia on N, Botswana on W, South Africa on S, Mozambique on E. **Topography:** High plateau country, rising to mountains on E border, sloping down on other borders. **Capital:** Harare, 1,541,570.
Government: Type: In transition. **Head of state and gov.:** Pres. Robert Gabriel Mugabe; b. Feb. 21, 1924; in office: Dec. 31, 1987. **Local divisions:** 8 provinces, 2 cities. **Defense budget:** $318 mil. **Active troops:** 29,000.
Economy: Industries: mining, steel, wood prods., cement, chemicals, fertilizer, clothing and footwear, foodstuffs. **Chief crops:** corn, cotton, tobacco, wheat, coffee, sugarcane, peanuts. **Natural resources:** coal, chromium ore, asbestos, gold, nickel, copper, iron ore, vanadium, lithium, tin, platinum group metals. **Arable land:** 10.6%. **Livestock:** cattle: 5.1 mil; chickens: 34 mil; goats: 2.7 mil; pigs: 640,000; sheep: 365,000. **Fish catch:** 18,102 metric tons. **Electricity prod.:** 7.8 bil kWh. **Labor force:** agric. 66%, industry 10%, services 24%.
Finance: Monetary unit: Dollar (ZWD) (Sept. 2013: 361.90 = $1 U.S.). **GDP:** $7.4 bil; **per capita GDP:** $600; **GDP growth:** 4.4%. **Imports:** $4.6 bil; South Africa 51.2%, China 9.7%. **Exports:** $3.3 bil; China 20.4%, South Africa 14.9%, Dem. Rep. of the Congo 12.9%, Botswana 11.5%, Italy 4.4%. **Tourism:** $749 mil. **Budget:** NA. **Total reserves less gold:** $574.4 mil. **Gold:** 688 oz t. **CPI change:** NA.
Transport: Railways: 2,129 mi. **Motor vehicles:** 39.9 vehicles per 1,000 pop. **Civil aviation:** 436.8 mil pass.-mi; 17 airports. **Chief ports:** Binga, Kariba.
Communications: TV sets: 71 per 1,000 pop. **Radios:** 135 per 1,000 pop. **Telephone lines:** 2.3 per 100 pop. **Internet:** 17.1%.
Health: Life expect.: 53.8 male; 53.9 female. **Births:** 32.4 per 1,000 pop. **Deaths:** 11.4 per 1,000 pop. **Natural inc.:** 2.10%. **Infant mortality:** 27.3 per 1,000 live births. **HIV rate:** 14.9%.
Education: Compulsory: ages 6-12. **Literacy:** 83.6%.
Major intl. organizations: UN (FAO, IBRD, ILO, IMF, WHO), AU, WTO.
Embassy: 1608 New Hampshire Ave. NW 20009; 332-7100.
Website: www.zim.gov.zw
Britain took over the area as Southern Rhodesia in 1923 from the British South Africa Co. (which, under Cecil Rhodes, had conquered it by 1897) and granted internal self-government. A 1961 constitution restricted voting to keep whites in power.
On Nov. 11, 1965, Prime Min. Ian D. Smith unilaterally declared independence. Britain termed the act illegal and demanded that the country (known as Rhodesia until 1980) enfranchise the black African majority. The UN imposed sanctions and, in May 1968, a trade embargo, as black nationalists launched guerrilla attacks.
After the country held its first universal-franchise election, Apr. 21, 1979, all parties accepted a cease-fire, Dec. 5. The country changed its name to Zimbabwe upon independence, Apr. 18, 1980. Robert Mugabe, the nation's first prime min., became executive president in 1987.
From the late 1990s, Mugabe's rule became increasingly repressive. A land redistribution campaign triggered violent attacks in Apr. 2000 against some white farmers. (Whites made up less than 1% of the population but held 70% of the land.) Mugabe, relying on fraud and intimidation, international observers claimed, won the Mar. 9-11, 2002, presidential election. The EU, the U.S., and the Commonwealth imposed sanctions on the Mugabe regime. In May 2005, Mugabe launched Operation Murambatsvina ("Drive out rubbish"), razing shanty dwellings and illegal street markets in urban areas and leaving some 700,000 people homeless. During 2006-08, inflation soared to a yearly rate of more than 100,000%.
Mugabe clung to power after a widely discredited 2008 presidential election and runoff. A power-sharing deal was reached Sept. 2008, and opposition leader Morgan Tsvangirai was sworn in as prime min., Feb. 2009. Opposition groups, Jan. 18, 2013, condemned an increasing crackdown on Mugabe's critics. A referendum on a new constitution that technically curbs presidential powers but eliminated the prime min. passed overwhelmingly, Mar. 16, 2013. In the July 31 presidential elections, Mugabe was once again declared winner, with 61% of the vote, despite the challenger's cries of fraud.

SPORTS

Sports Highlights, 2013

Alabama trounced Notre Dame in the **BCS National Championship Game**, 42-14, in Miami Gardens, FL, Jan. 7. The victory was the second consecutive national football title for the Crimson Tide, and the seventh straight championship by a team from the Southeastern Conference.

The Baltimore Ravens withstood a late scoring spree by the San Francisco 49ers to win **Super Bowl XLVII**, 34-31, at the Mercedes-Benz Superdome in New Orleans, Feb. 3. A 34-min. power outage during the 3rd quarter allowed San Francisco to regroup after falling behind by 22 points, but the 49ers never closed the gap. The contest marked the first time brothers faced each other in a Super Bowl as opposing head coaches: Baltimore's John Harbaugh defeated his younger brother Jim. Ravens quarterback Joe Flacco passed for 287 yards and three touchdowns to win MVP honors.

Top-seeded Louisville won its third **NCAA men's basketball championship** Apr. 8, defeating Michigan 82-76 in the final at Atlanta's Georgia Dome. The victory made the Cardinals' Rick Pitino the first head coach to win NCAA titles with two different schools: he won the 1996 title while coaching at cross-state rival Kentucky. Louisville's Luke Hancock scored 22 points in the final and became the first bench player to win the most outstanding player award. Louisville's women's team was not as successful in the finals of the **NCAA women's basketball championship**. The Univ. of Connecticut dismantled the Cardinals, 93-60, at the New Orleans Arena, Apr. 9. It was the eighth championship for Huskies' head coach Geno Auriemma, tying him with Tennessee's Pat Summitt for the most women's national titles. UConn freshman Breanna Stewart won the most outstanding player award on the strength of her 23 points in the final.

Adam Scott became the first Australian to win golf's **Masters Championship**, Apr. 14, in Augusta, GA, defeating Argentina's Angel Cabrera in a sudden-death playoff. Guan Tianlang, a 14-year-old from China, became the youngest player ever to qualify for the Masters. Justin Rose became the first Englishman in 43 years to win the **U.S. Open**, June 16, at Merion Golf Club in Ardmore, PA. American Phil Mickelson returned the favor July 21 by capturing the **British Open** at Muirfield Golf Links in Gullane, Scotland, UK. It was the first British Open and fifth major victory for the 43-year-old lefty. Jason Dufner won his first major by taking the **PGA Championship** Aug. 11 at Oak Hill Country Club in Rochester, NY.

For the 35th consecutive year, there was no Triple Crown winner. Orb captured the **Kentucky Derby** at Churchill Downs in Louisville, KY, May 4, marking the first Derby victory ever for Hall-of-Fame trainer Shug McGaughey. Oxbow won the **Preakness Stakes** at Pimlico Race Course in Baltimore, MD, May 18; Palace Malice, a 15-1 longshot, came from behind to take the **Belmont Stakes** at Belmont Park in Elmont, NY, June 8.

The Miami Heat won their second consecutive **NBA Championship** June 20 in Miami, defeating the San Antonio Spurs in seven games. The Heat were on the brink of elimination in Game 6, trailing by five points with 28 seconds remaining, but Ray Allen's three-pointer forced overtime. Miami won, 100-103, and the following contest, 95-88, two nights later. The Heat's LeBron James was named the most valuable player of both the regular season and the playoffs for the second straight year.

The Chicago Blackhawks scored twice against the Boston Bruins in the final minute of Game 6, June 24 in Boston, to win their second **Stanley Cup** championship in four years. Forward Patrick Kane won the Conn Smythe Trophy as MVP of the playoffs, in which he had nine goals and 10 assists. A 113-day lockout by NHL owners shortened the season to 48 games. When play finally began Jan. 19, the Blackhawks played their first 24 games without losing during regulation.

Chris Froome, a Briton born in Kenya, captured the 100th **Tour de France** July 21. It was the second straight Tour win by a British cyclist, following Bradley Wiggins's triumph in 2012. U.S. cyclist Lance Armstrong, who was stripped of his seven Tour de France titles in Oct. 2012, admitted Jan. 17, 2013, that he had used performance-enhancing drugs (PEDs) throughout his cycling career.

Victoria Azarenka of Belarus and Novak Djokovic of Serbia successfully defended their **Australian Open** titles in Melbourne. Azarenka came back to defeat Li Na of China in three sets at Rod Laver Arena, Jan. 26. The next night, Djokovic outlasted the UK's Andy Murray in four sets, becoming the first man since Roy Emerson (1963-67) to win three consecutive Australian championships. At the **French Open** June 8 at Roland Garros in Paris, American Serena Williams defeated Russia's Maria Sharapova in straight sets. It was Williams's first French Open crown in over a decade. The next day, Spain's Rafael Nadal bested his countryman, David Ferrer, in straight sets, becoming the first man to win the same Grand Slam tournament eight times. Murray ended 77 years of futility by British men at **Wimbledon**, when he defeated Djokovic July 7 in the final at the All England Club in London. The day before, France's Marion Bartoli, the number 15 seed, defeated the number 23 seed, Sabine Lisicki of Germany, in straight sets. Williams and Nadal matched their French Open performances at the **U.S. Open** in Flushing Meadows, NY. Williams bested Azarenka Sept. 8 to win her fifth U.S. Open and 17th Grand Slam title. Nadal downed Djokovic in four sets Sept. 9 for his second U.S. Open and 13th Grand Slam championship.

Major League Baseball continued to struggle with the long shadow of PEDs. In Jan., no player won election to the Baseball Hall of Fame, even though career home run leader Barry Bonds and seven-time Cy Young Award-winner Roger Clemens were on the ballot for the first time. Voters seemed to assert their belief that PEDs had tainted the accomplishments of dozens who played during the 1990s and 2000s.

Despite more stringent testing and harsher penalties, PED use persisted, as evidenced by revelations that a Miami clinic had supplied banned substances to more than a dozen major leaguers. Among them were Milwaukee's Ryan Braun, who had dodged a suspension a year earlier on a technicality, and NY Yankee slugger Alex Rodriguez, who in 2009 admitted to using steroids between 2001 and 2003, but not since. Braun ultimately accepted a 65-game suspension, and 12 other players agreed to 50-game bans. But Rodriguez continued to play while appealing his unprecedented 211-game suspension.

Happier stories unfolded on the field. The Pittsburgh Pirates posted their first winning season in 21 years, made the playoffs as a wild card team, then defeated the Cincinnati Reds in the wild card game to advance to the National League Division Series. The equally low-budget Tampa Bay Rays survived a one-game playoff against the Texas Rangers, then shut out the Cleveland Indians in the wild card game to reach the American League Division Series. They joined the Boston Red Sox, who led the AL in victories just one year removed from a 69-win season in 2012, and the Detroit Tigers and Oakland Athletics. The Atlanta Braves and L.A. Dodgers easily won the NL's Eastern and Western divisions, respectively, while the St. Louis Cardinals notched the NL's best record to win the Central division.

WORLD ALMANAC EDITORS' PICKS: MEMORABLE MOMENTS OF THE WINTER OLYMPIC GAMES

The Black Sea resort town of Sochi, Russia, hosts the XXII Olympic Winter Games Feb. 7-23, 2014 (followed by the XI Paralympic Winter Games a month later). A memorable Olympic moment doesn't have to involve superlative athletic achievement, though it helps. The following moments from recent Winter Olympics stand out in our memories.

1. The Miracle on Ice
Lake Placid, NY, 1980

This David-beats-Goliath battle played out amid escalating Cold War tensions. The Soviet Union team, composed of members of the Red Army specifically recruited to play hockey, had completely dominated the amateur game, winning gold in the four previous Olympiads. The U.S. team consisted almost entirely of collegians. When the two teams squared off in an exhibition a week before the Games, the Soviets battered the U.S. 10-3. But when they met again Feb. 22, 1980, in the round-robin medal round, the U.S. came from behind to win 4-3, prompting announcer Al Michaels's famous line: "Do you believe in miracles? Yes!" That was not the gold medal game, however. Had the U.S. failed to beat Finland two days later, the upset victory would be just a footnote in the record books.

2. Tonya and Nancy
Lillehammer, Norway, 1994

The women's figure skating competition got an extra dose of drama on Jan. 6, 1994, when a man wielding a metal baton struck gold-medal hopeful Nancy Kerrigan across the right knee as she left a practice session the day before the U.S. Figure Skating Championships. Kerrigan's injury sidelined her, and Tonya Harding won the competition, which served as the Olympic team qualifier. Harding's bodyguard and her ex-husband were later charged with planning the attack. Harding had to sue the U.S. Olympic Committee to retain her spot on the team after admitting she knew about the assault after it had occurred. Kerrigan recovered from her injury in time to win a silver medal in Lillehammer, coming up just short against Ukraine's Oksana Baiul. Harding finished 8th.

3. Fourth Time's the Charm
Lillehammer, Norway, 1994

After a solid performance—but no medals—in Sarajevo in 1984, Dan Jansen was a heavy favorite in the 500-m and 1,000-m speed-skating events in Calgary in 1988. But his sister Jane, who had inspired him to take up the sport, died of leukemia Feb. 14, 1988, hours before he took the ice for the 500-m. He fell during that race, and again in the 1,000-m four days later. His performance at Albertville in 1992 was no less disappointing: he finished fourth in the 500-m (Feb. 15, 1992) and 26th in the 1,000-m. Between Olympiads, Jansen continued to set world records. But at Lillehammer, he stumbled during the 500-m, placing 8th. In his last chance to medal, he slipped near the finish line of the 1,000-m on Feb. 18, 1994. But he righted himself and finally won gold, setting a world record to boot. He carried his nine-month-old daughter, Jane, named for his sister, on his victory lap.

4. The Ice Storm
Salt Lake City, UT, 2002

Canadian pairs figure skaters Jamie Salé and David Pelletier were convinced they had won the gold medal Feb. 11, 2002, after their closest competitors, Russia's Elena Berezhnaya and Anton Sikharulidze, had a minor misstep during their long program. But when the judges gave the gold to the Russians, the crowd booed, U.S. broadcasters openly questioned the decision, and the Intl. Skating Union launched an investigation. It was soon reported that French judge Marie-Reine Le Gougne had been coerced into ranking the Russian pair first in exchange for the Russian judge's pledge to do likewise for a French duo in the ice dancing competition. While Le Gougne maintained her innocence, she and the head of the French ice skating federation were suspended for three years in Apr. Salé and Pelletier were awarded a second gold on Feb. 17.

5. Heiden Sweeps
Lake Placid, NY, 1980

If not for the Miracle on Ice, the 1980 Winter Games (Feb. 13-24) might be remembered as the Eric Heiden Olympics. The 21-year-old native of Madison, WI, focused America's attention on speed skating like no one ever before by winning gold—and setting an Olympic record—in all five speed-skating events. The closest races were the 500-m, which he won by only 0.34 sec., and the the 5,000-m, which he won by 0.99 sec. Heiden was the first athlete ever to win five individual gold medals in a single Olympics and is widely regarded as one of the greatest speed skaters of all time.

6. Battle of the Brians
Calgary, Alberta, Canada, 1988

The men stole center stage during the figure skating competition as Canada's Brian Orser and Brian Boitano of the U.S. went head-to-head for Olympic gold. Boitano won the world championship in 1986 while Orser, the silver medalist at the 1984 Games in Sarajevo, was world champion in 1987. The two entered the free skate program Feb. 20, 1988, essentially tied for first place. Boitano skated eight triple jumps, including two triple axels. Orser made one minor mistake in a slightly less ambitious program, which was the difference that gave Boitano the gold.

7. Jamaican Bobsledders, Seriously!?
Calgary, Alberta, Canada, 1988

Eyebrows were raised when Jamaica (a Caribbean island nation without snow) fielded its first-ever team of athletes for the Winter Olympics. Despite a general lack of experience, the Jamaican bobsled team had enthusiasm and underdog appeal. But in Calgary, the 4-man team crashed its sled Feb. 28, 1988, and failed to finish the course. The Jamaicans' high point came in the 1994 Lillehammer Games, where they came in 14th out of 30 (ahead of both U.S. teams), but they didn't qualify for the 2006 or 2010 Games. Still, their adventures inspired a movie, Cool Runnings, and a bobsled ride at Rainforest Adventures theme park in Ocho Rios, Jamaica.

8. (Future) Most-Decorated Winter Olympian
Lillehammer, Norway, 1994

Bjoern Daehlie, the anchorman of the host country's 4x10-km Nordic (cross-country) skiing relay team, was in position to win his third gold medal of the Lillehammer Games, matching the three he had won two years earlier in Albertville. Daehlie and Italy's Silvio Fauner skied neck-and-neck over the final 2 km Feb. 22 before Fauner made his move, crossing the finish line first by 0.4 sec. At the 1998 Games in Nagano, Daehlie won three gold medals. One was for the 4x10-km relay, in which Daehlie skied the third leg for Norway; teammate Thomas Alsgaard held off Fauner in the anchor leg, allowing Norway to beat Italy by 0.2 sec. With eight golds and four silvers in three different Olympiads, Daehlie became the most-decorated Winter Olympian of all time.

9. You Can't Hurt the Herminator
Nagano, Japan, 1998

Hermann Maier's crash during the downhill competition Feb. 13, 1998, was the stuff of "agony of defeat" highlight reels. "The Herminator" lost control coming around a turn, landed on his head, and cartwheeled through two fences. But the Austrian walked away with nothing more than bruises. Three days later he took home gold in the super-G, defeating teammate Hans Knauss and Switzerland's Didier Cuche, who tied for silver. Three days after that, he took gold yet again in the giant slalom. Maier was unable to defend his titles four years later because of a motorcycle crash that almost cost him his right leg. But he returned to competition in 2003 and in 2006 took silver in the super-G and bronze in the giant slalom at the Turin Games.

10. Bonnie Blair Wins in Bunches
Lillehammer, Norway, 1994

Born into a family of speed skaters, Bonnie Blair outshone them all in a career that spanned four Winter Games beginning in 1984. Four years later, thanks in part to the Blair Bunch—a group of friends and family that traveled with her to Calgary—Blair raced to a gold medal in the 500-m and a bronze in the 1,000-m. The Bunch grew in 1992 to about 45 well-wishers, who cheered her on to gold in both events in Albertville. Blair became the first woman speed skater to win the 500-m twice. And her support network swelled to more than 60 at the 1994 Lillehammer Games, where she repeated the feat (Feb. 19 and 23). Her five gold and one bronze medal make her the most decorated American woman in Winter Olympics history.

OLYMPIC GAMES

General Olympic Information

The modern Olympic Games, first held in Athens, Greece, in 1896, were the result of efforts by Baron Pierre de Coubertin, a French educator, to promote interest in education and culture and to foster better international understanding through love of athletics. His inspiration was the ancient Greek Olympic Games, most notable of the four Panhellenic celebrations. The games were combined patriotic, religious, and athletic festivals held every four years. The first such recorded festival was held in 776 BCE, when the Greeks began to keep their calendar by "Olympiads," or four-year spans between the games.

Coubertin enlisted 14 nations to send athletes to the first modern Olympics. Now athletes from more than 200 nations and territories compete in the Summer Olympics. The Winter Olympic Games, started in 1924, draws competitors from about 80 countries and territories.

Symbol: Five rings or circles, linked to represent the sporting friendship of all peoples. They also symbolize five geographic areas—Europe, Asia, Africa, Australia, and America. Each ring is a different color—blue, yellow, black, green, and red—which, with the color white, represent the colors of the world's flags.

Flag: The five-ring symbol on a plain white background.

Creed: "The most important thing in the Olympic Games is not to win but to take part, just as the most important thing in life is not the triumph but the struggle. The essential thing is not to have conquered but to have fought well."

Motto: "Citius, Altius, Fortius." Latin meaning "swifter, higher, stronger."

Oath: "In the name of all the competitors I promise that we shall take part in these Olympic Games, respecting and abiding by the rules which govern them, committing ourselves to a sport without doping and without drugs, in the true spirit of sportsmanship, for the glory of sport and the honor of our teams."

Flame: The modern version of the flame was adopted in 1936. The torch used to kindle it is first lit by the sun's rays in Olympia, Greece, then carried to the site of the Games by relays of runners. Ships and planes are used when necessary.

Winter Olympic Games Sites, 1924-2018

1924 Chamonix, France	1956 Cortina d'Ampezzo, Italy	1980 Lake Placid, NY, U.S.	2006 Turin, Italy
1928 St. Moritz, Switzerland	1960 Squaw Valley, CA, U.S.	1984 Sarajevo, Yugoslavia	2010 Vancouver, BC, Canada
1932 Lake Placid, NY, U.S.	1964 Innsbruck, Austria	1988 Calgary, AB, Canada	2014 Sochi, Russia
1936 Garmisch-Partenkirchen, Germany	1968 Grenoble, France	1992 Albertville, France	2018 PyeongChang, South Korea
1948 St. Moritz, Switzerland	1972 Sapporo, Japan	1994 Lillehammer, Norway	
1952 Oslo, Norway	1976 Innsbruck, Austria	1998 Nagano, Japan	
		2002 Salt Lake City, UT, U.S.	

Summer Olympic Games Sites, 1896-2020

1896 Athens, Greece	1928 Amsterdam, Netherlands	1968 Mexico City, Mexico	1996 Atlanta, GA, U.S.
1900 Paris, France	1932 Los Angeles, CA, U.S.	1972 Munich, W. Germany	2000 Sydney, Australia
1904 St. Louis, MO, U.S.	1936 Berlin, Germany	1976 Montreal, QC, Canada	2004 Athens, Greece
1906 Athens, Greece*	1948 London, England, UK	1980 Moscow, USSR	2008 Beijing, China
1908 London, England, UK	1952 Helsinki, Finland	1984 Los Angeles, CA, U.S.	2012 London, England, UK
1912 Stockholm, Sweden	1956 Melbourne, Australia	1988 Seoul, South Korea	2016 Rio de Janeiro, Brazil
1920 Antwerp, Belgium	1960 Rome, Italy	1992 Barcelona, Spain	2020 Tokyo, Japan
1924 Paris, France	1964 Tokyo, Japan		

*Games not recognized by International Olympic Committee. **Note:** Games VI (1916), XII (1940), and XIII (1944) were not celebrated.

2012 Summer Olympic Games

London, England, UK, July 27-Aug. 12, 2012

London welcomed more than 11,000 athletes from 204 nations and territories at the Summer Olympic Games, July 27-Aug. 12, 2012. The XXX Summer Olympiad marked the first time in history that each nation or territory's delegation included women athletes.

The United States was ahead of all countries with 46 gold medals and 104 overall. Michael Phelps, who starred at the 2008 Beijing Olympics, led a U.S. swim team that dominated with 16 gold medals and 31 overall. Phelps topped all athletes at the Summer Games with six medals and became the all-time most decorated Olympian with 22 career medals. Fellow U.S. swimmers Missy Franklin, Ryan Lochte, and Allison Schmitt each collected five medals. A team of NBA stars carried the U.S. to basketball gold, topping Spain, 107-100, in the men's final. The U.S. women's basketball team extended its Olympic winning streak to 41 games with an 86-50 gold medal win over France. In women's soccer, Carli Lloyd scored both goals as the U.S. defeated Japan, 2-1, to capture the gold medal, avenging the U.S. loss to Japan in the 2011 World Cup final. For the first time since 1996, the U.S. women won the gymnastics team all-around gold, and Americans Gabby Douglas and Aly Raisman captured individual gold medals.

London hosted the Olympic Games for the third time and Britain's competitors recorded the country's best performance in over a century. British athletes won 65 medals overall, including 12 in cycling competitions. Among the British gold medalists were track-and-field stars Mo Farah (men's 5,000-m and 10,000-m) and Jessica Ennis (heptathlon), while Andy Murray earned tennis gold when he defeated Switzerland's Roger Federer in the final in straight sets. Jamaica's Usain Bolt, another star from Beijing 2008, electrified the London games. Bolt won gold in both the men's 100-m and 200-m sprints, as he did in Beijing, and was part of the team that won the 4x100-m relay in world-record time (36.84 sec.). South Africa's Oscar Pistorius became the first double-amputee to compete in the Olympics, reaching the semifinals in the men's 400-m race and running in the 4x400-m relay.

2012 Summer Olympic Games Final Medal Standings

Country	G	S	B	T	Country	G	S	B	T	Country	G	S	B	T
United States	46	29	29	104	Canada	1	5	12	18	Azerbaijan	2	2	6	10
China	38	27	23	88	Hungary	8	4	5	17	Poland	2	2	6	10
Russia	24	26	32	82	Spain	3	10	4	17	Romania	2	5	2	9
Great Britain	29	17	19	65	Brazil	3	5	9	17	Denmark	2	4	3	9
Germany	11	19	14	44	Cuba	5	3	6	14	Sweden	1	4	3	8
Japan	7	14	17	38	Kazakhstan	7	1	5	13	Colombia	1	3	4	8
Australia	7	16	12	35	New Zealand	6	2	5	13	Ethiopia	3	1	3	7
France	11	11	12	34	Iran	4	5	3	12	Georgia	1	3	3	7
South Korea	13	8	7	28	Jamaica	4	4	4	12	Mexico	1	3	3	7
Italy	8	9	11	28	Belarus	2	5	5	12	North Korea	4	0	2	6
Netherlands	6	6	8	20	Kenya	2	4	5	11	South Africa	3	2	1	6
Ukraine	6	5	9	20	Czech Republic	4	3	3	10	Croatia	3	1	2	6

Country	G	S	B	T	Country	G	S	B	T	Country	G	S	B	T
India	0	2	4	6	Finland	0	1	2	3	Grenada	1	0	0	1
Turkey	2	2	1	5	Dominican Republic	1	1	0	2	Uganda	1	0	0	1
Lithuania	2	1	2	5	Latvia	1	0	1	2	Venezuela	1	0	0	1
Ireland	1	1	3	5	Egypt	0	2	0	2	Botswana	0	1	0	1
Mongolia	0	2	3	5	Bulgaria	0	1	1	2	Cyprus	0	1	0	1
Switzerland	2	2	0	4	Estonia	0	1	1	2	Gabon	0	1	0	1
Norway	2	1	1	4	Indonesia	0	1	1	2	Guatemala	0	1	0	1
Argentina	1	1	2	4	Malaysia	0	1	1	2	Montenegro	0	1	0	1
Serbia	1	1	2	4	Puerto Rico	0	1	1	2	Portugal	0	1	0	1
Slovenia	1	1	2	4	Taiwan	0	1	1	2	Afghanistan	0	0	1	1
Trinidad and Tobago	1	0	3	4	Greece	0	0	2	2	Bahrain	0	0	1	1
Uzbekistan	1	0	3	4	Moldova	0	0	2	2	Hong Kong	0	0	1	1
Slovakia	0	1	3	4	Qatar	0	0	2	2	Kuwait	0	0	1	1
Tunisia	1	1	1	3	Singapore	0	0	2	2	Morocco	0	0	1	1
Thailand	0	2	1	3	Algeria	1	0	0	1	Saudi Arabia	0	0	1	1
Armenia	0	1	2	3	The Bahamas	1	0	0	1	Tajikistan	0	0	1	1
Belgium	0	1	2	3										

Summer Olympic Games Champions, 1896-2012

*Olympic record; (w) wind-aided; times are shown in minute:sec

The 1980 games were boycotted by 62 nations, including the U.S. The 1984 games were boycotted by the USSR and most Eastern bloc nations. East and West Germany competed separately, 1968-88. The 1992 Unified Team consisted of 12 former Soviet republics. The 1992 Independent Olympic Participants (IOP) were from Serbia, Montenegro, and Macedonia.

Not all sports are listed here, and many events are omitted, even within listed sports, particularly if the event has not been held in more recent Games. Point systems for scoring events have changed many times. Points shown are those under the point system in use at the time.

Baseball (Men)

1992	Cuba, Taiwan, Japan		2000	United States, Cuba, S. Korea	2008	S. Korea, Cuba, United States
1996	Cuba, Japan, United States		2004	Cuba, Australia, Japan		

Boxing—Men

Weight class limits have changed many times since the first Olympic boxing events were held in 1904. The limits shown were used in the 2012 Olympic Games.

Lt. Flyweight (49 kg/108 lbs)
1968 Francisco Rodriguez, Venezuela
1972 Gyorgy Gedo, Hungary
1976 Jorge Hernandez, Cuba
1980 Shamil Sabyrov, USSR
1984 Paul Gonzalez, United States
1988 Ivailo Hristov, Bulgaria
1992 Rogelio Marcelo, Cuba
1996 Daniel Petrov, Bulgaria
2000 Brahim Asloum, France
2004 Yan Bhartelemy Varela, Cuba
2008 Zou Shiming, China
2012 Zou Shiming, China

Flyweight (52 kg/114 lbs)
1904 George Finnegan, United States
1920 Frank Di Gennara, United States
1924 Fidel LaBarba, United States
1928 Antal Kocsis, Hungary
1932 Istvan Enekes, Hungary
1936 Willi Kaiser, Germany
1948 Pascual Perez, Argentina
1952 Nathan Brooks, United States
1956 Terence Spinks, Great Britain
1960 Gyula Török, Hungary
1964 Fernando Atzori, Italy
1968 Ricardo Delgado, Mexico
1972 Georgi Kostadinov, Bulgaria
1976 Leo Randolph, United States
1980 Peter Lesov, Bulgaria
1984 Steve McCrory, United States
1988 Kim Kwang Sun, S. Korea
1992 Choi Chol-Su, N. Korea
1996 Maikro Romero, Cuba
2000 Wijan Ponlid, Thailand
2004 Yuriorkis Gamboa Toledano, Cuba
2008 Somjit Jongjohor, Thailand
2012 Robeisy Ramírez, Cuba

Bantamweight (56 kg/123 lbs)
1904 Oliver Kirk, United States
1908 A. Henry Thomas, Great Britain
1920 Clarence Walker, South Africa
1924 William Smith, South Africa
1928 Vittorio Tamagnini, Italy
1932 Horace Gwynne, Canada
1936 Ulderico Sergo, Italy
1948 Tibor Csik, Hungary
1952 Pentti Hamalainen, Finland
1956 Wolfgang Behrendt, E. Germany
1960 Oleg Grigoryev, USSR
1964 Takao Sakurai, Japan

Bantamweight (56 kg/123 lbs)
1968 Valery Sokolov, USSR
1972 Orlando Martinez, Cuba
1976 Yong-Jo Gu, N. Korea
1980 Juan Hernandez, Cuba
1984 Maurizio Stecca, Italy
1988 Kennedy McKinney, United States
1992 Joel Casamayor, Cuba
1996 Istvan Kovacs, Hungary
2000 Guillermo Rigondeaux, Cuba
2004 Guillermo Rigondeaux, Cuba
2008 Badar-Uugan Enkhbat, Mongolia
2012 Luke Campbell, Great Britain

Featherweight (57 kg/125 lbs)
1904 Oliver Kirk, United States
1908 Richard Gunn, Great Britain
1920 Paul Fritsch, France
1924 John Fields, United States
1928 Lambertus van Klaveren, Netherlands
1932 Carmelo Robledo, Argentina
1936 Oscar Casanovas, Argentina
1948 Ernesto Formenti, Italy
1952 Jan Zachara, Czechoslovakia
1956 Vladimir Safronov, USSR
1960 Francesco Musso, Italy
1964 Stanislav Stephashkin, USSR
1968 Antonio Roldan, Mexico
1972 Boris Kousnetsov, USSR
1976 Angel Herrera, Cuba
1980 Rudi Fink, E. Germany
1984 Meldrick Taylor, United States
1988 Giovanni Parisi, Italy
1992 Andreas Tews, Germany
1996 Somluck Kamsing, Thailand
2000 Bekzat Sattarkhanov, Kazakhstan
2004 Alexei Tichtchenko, Russia
2008 Vasyl Lomachenko, Ukraine

Lightweight (60 kg/132 lbs)
1904 Harry Spanger, United States
1908 Frederick Grace, Great Britain
1920 Samuel Mosberg, United States
1924 Hans Nielsen, Denmark
1928 Carlo Orlandi, Italy
1932 Lawrence Stevens, South Africa
1936 Imre Harangi, Hungary
1948 Gerald Dreyer, South Africa
1952 Aureliano Bolognesi, Italy

Lightweight (60 kg/132 lbs)
1956 Richard McTaggart, Great Britain
1960 Kazimierz Pazdzior, Poland
1964 Jozef Grudzien, Poland
1968 Ronald Harris, United States
1972 Jan Szczepanski, Poland
1976 Howard Davis, United States
1980 Angel Herrera, Cuba
1984 Pernell Whitaker, United States
1988 Andreas Zülow, E. Germany
1992 Oscar De La Hoya, United States
1996 Hocine Soltani, Algeria
2000 Mario Kindelan, Cuba
2004 Mario Kindelan, Cuba
2008 Alexey Tishchenko, Russia
2012 Vasyl Lomachenko, Ukraine

Lt. Welterweight (64 kg/141 lbs)
1952 Charles Adkins, United States
1956 Vladimir Yengibaryan, USSR
1960 Bohumil Nemecek, Czechoslovakia
1964 Jerzy Kulej, Poland
1968 Jerzy Kulej, Poland
1972 Ray Seales, United States
1976 Ray Leonard, United States
1980 Patrizio Oliva, Italy
1984 Jerry Page, United States
1988 Viatcheslav Janovski, USSR
1992 Hector Vinent, Cuba
1996 Hector Vinent, Cuba
2000 Mahamadkadyz Abdullaev, Uzbekistan
2004 Manus Boonjumnong, Thailand
2008 Felix Diaz, Dominican Republic
2012 Rosniel Iglesias, Cuba

Welterweight (69 kg/152 lbs)
1904 Albert Young, United States
1920 Albert Schneider, Canada
1924 Jean Delarge, Belgium
1928 Edward Morgan, New Zealand
1932 Edward Flynn, United States
1936 Sten Suvio, Finland
1948 Julius Torma, Czechoslovakia
1952 Zygmunt Chychia, Poland
1956 Nicolae Linca, Romania
1960 Giovanni Benvenuti, Italy
1964 Marian Kasprzyk, Poland
1968 Manfred Wolke, E. Germany
1972 Emilio Correa, Cuba

Welterweight (69 kg/152 lbs)

1976	Jochen Bachfeld, E. Germany
1980	Andres Aldama, Cuba
1984	Mark Breland, United States
1988	Robert Wangila, Kenya
1992	Michael Carruth, Ireland
1996	Oleg Saitov, Russia
2000	Oleg Saitov, Russia
2004	Artayev Bakhtiyar, Kazakhstan
2008	Bakhyt Sarsekbayev, Kazakhstan
2012	Serik Sapiyev, Kazakhstan

Lt. Middleweight (71 kg/156 lbs)

1952	Laszlo Papp, Hungary
1956	Laszlo Papp, Hungary
1960	Wilbert McClure, United States
1964	Boris Lagutin, USSR
1968	Boris Lagutin, USSR
1972	Dieter Kottysch, W. Germany
1976	Jerzy Rybicki, Poland
1980	Armando Martinez, Cuba
1984	Frank Tate, United States
1988	Park Si Hun, S. Korea
1992	Juan Lemus, Cuba
1996	David Reid, United States
2000	Yermakhan Ibraimov, Kazakhstan

Middleweight (75 kg/165 lbs)

1904	Charles Mayer, United States
1908	John Douglas, Great Britain
1920	Harry Mallin, Great Britain
1924	Harry Mallin, Great Britain
1928	Piero Toscani, Italy
1932	Carmen Barth, United States
1936	Jean Despeaux, France
1948	Laszlo Papp, Hungary
1952	Floyd Patterson, United States
1956	Gennady Schatkov, USSR
1960	Edward Crook, United States

Middleweight (75 kg/165 lbs)

1964	Valery Popenchenko, USSR
1968	Christopher Finnegan, Great Britain
1972	Vyacheslav Lemechev, USSR
1976	Michael Spinks, United States
1980	Jose Gomez, Cuba
1984	Joon-Sup Shin, S. Korea
1988	Henry Maske, E. Germany
1992	Ariel Hernandez, Cuba
1996	Ariel Hernandez, Cuba
2000	Jorge Gutierrez, Cuba
2004	Gaydarbek Gaydarbekov, Russia
2008	James Degale, Great Britain
2012	Ryota Murata, Japan

Lt. Heavyweight (81 kg/178 lbs)

1920	Edward Eagan, United States
1924	Harry Mitchell, Great Britain
1928	Victor Avendaño, Argentina
1932	David Carstens, South Africa
1936	Roger Michelot, France
1948	George Hunter, South Africa
1952	Norvel Lee, United States
1956	James Boyd, United States
1960	Cassius Clay, United States
1964	Cosimo Pinto, Italy
1968	Dan Poznyak, USSR
1972	Mate Parlov, Yugoslavia
1976	Leon Spinks, United States
1980	Slobodan Kacar, Yugoslavia
1984	Anton Josipovic, Yugoslavia
1988	Andrew Maynard, United States
1992	Torsten May, Germany
1996	Vassili Jirov, Kazakhstan
2000	Alexander Lebziak, Russia
2004	Andre Ward, United States
2008	Zhang Xiaoping, China
2012	Yegor Mekhontsev, Russia

Heavyweight (91 kg/201 lbs)

1984	Henry Tillman, United States
1988	Ray Mercer, United States
1992	Felix Savon, Cuba
1996	Felix Savon, Cuba
2000	Felix Savon, Cuba
2004	Odlanier Solis Fonte, Cuba
2008	Rakhim Chakhkiev, Russia
2012	Oleksandr Usik, Ukraine

Super Heavyweight (91+ kg/201+ lbs)
(known as heavyweight, 1904-80)

1904	Samuel Berger, United States
1908	Albert Oldham, Great Britain
1920	Ronald Rawson, Great Britain
1924	Otto von Porat, Norway
1928	Arturo Rodriguez Jurado, Argentina
1932	Santiago Lovell, Argentina
1936	Herbert Runge, Germany
1948	Rafael Iglesias, Argentina
1952	H. Edward Sanders, United States
1956	T. Peter Rademacher, United States
1960	Franco De Piccoli, Italy
1964	Joe Frazier, United States
1968	George Foreman, United States
1972	Teofilo Stevenson, Cuba
1976	Teofilo Stevenson, Cuba
1980	Teofilo Stevenson, Cuba
1984	Tyrell Biggs, United States
1988	Lennox Lewis, Canada
1992	Roberto Balado, Cuba
1996	Vladimir Klitchko, Ukraine
2000	Audley Harrison, Great Britain
2004	Alexander Povetkin, Russia
2008	Roberto Cammarelle, Italy
2012	Anthony Joshua, Great Britain

Boxing—Women

Flyweight (51 kg/112 lbs)

2012	Nicola Adams, Great Britain

Lightweight (60 kg/132 lbs)

2012	Katie Taylor, Ireland

Middleweight (75 kg/165 lbs)

2012	Claressa Shields, United States

Gymnastics—Men

Floor Exercise

1932	István Pelle, Hungary
1936	Georges Miez, Switzerland
1948	Ferenc Pataki, Hungary
1952	William Thoresson, Sweden
1956	Valentin Muratov, USSR
1960	Nobuyuki Aihara, Japan
1964	Franco Menichelli, Italy
1968	Sawao Kato, Japan
1972	Nikolay Andrianov, USSR
1976	Nikolay Andrianov, USSR
1980	Roland Brückner, E. Germany
1984	Li Ning, China
1988	Serguei Kharikov, USSR
1992	Xiaoshuang Li, China
1996	Ioannis Melissanidis, Greece
2000	Igors Vihrovs, Latvia
2004	Kyle Shewfelt, Canada
2008	Zou Kai, China
2012	Zou Kai, China

Horizontal Bar

1896	Hermann Weingärtner, Germany
1904	Anton Heida, United States; Edward Hennig, United States (tie)
1924	Leon Stukelj, Yugoslavia
1928	Georges Miez, Switzerland
1932	Dallas Denver Bixler, United States
1936	Aleksanteri Saarvala, Finland
1948	Josef Stadler, Switzerland
1952	Jakob "Jack" Günthard, Switzerland
1956	Takashi Ono, Japan
1960	Takashi Ono, Japan
1964	Boris Shakhlin, USSR
1968	Mikhail Voronin, USSR; Akinori Nakayama, Japan (tie)
1972	Mitsuo Tsukahara, Japan
1976	Mitsuo Tsukahara, Japan
1980	Stoyan Deltchev, Bulgaria

Horizontal Bar

1984	Shinji Morisue, Japan
1988	Valeri Lioukine, USSR; Vladimir Artemov, USSR (tie)
1992	Trent Dimas, United States
1996	Andreas Wecker, Germany
2000	Alexei Nemov, Russia
2004	Igor Cassina, Italy
2008	Zou Kai, China
2012	Epke Zonderland, Netherlands

Individual All-Around

1900	Gustave Sandras, France
1904	Julius Lenhart, United States
1908	G. Alberto Braglia, Italy
1912	G. Alberto Braglia, Italy
1920	Giorgio Zampori, Italy
1924	Leon Stukelj, Yugoslavia
1928	Georges Miez, Switzerland
1932	Romeo Neri, Italy
1936	Karl-Alfred Schwarzmann, Germany
1948	Veikko Huhtanen, Finland
1952	Viktor Ivanovich Chukarin, USSR
1956	Viktor Ivanovich Chukarin, USSR
1960	Boris Shakhlin, USSR
1964	Yukio Endo, Japan
1968	Sawao Kato, Japan
1972	Sawao Kato, Japan
1976	Nikolay Andrianov, USSR
1980	Aleksandr Dityatin, USSR
1984	Koji Gushiken, Japan
1988	Vladimir Artemov, USSR
1992	Vitaly Scherbo, Unified Team (Belarus)
1996	Li Xiaoshuang, China
2000	Alexei Nemov, Russia
2004	Paul Hamm, United States
2008	Yang Wei, China
2012	Kohei Uchimura, Japan

Parallel Bars

1896	Alfred Flatow, Germany
1904	George Eyser, United States
1924	August Güttinger, Switzerland
1928	Ladislav Vacha, Czechoslovakia
1932	Romeo Neri, Italy
1936	Konrad Frey, Germany
1948	Michael Reusch, Switzerland
1952	Hans Eugster, Switzerland
1956	Viktor Ivanovich Chukarin, USSR
1960	Boris Shakhlin, USSR
1964	Yukio Endo, Japan
1968	Akinori Nakayama, Japan
1972	Sawao Kato, Japan
1976	Sawao Kato, Japan
1980	Aleksandr Tkachev, USSR
1984	Bart Conner, United States
1988	Vladimir Artemov, USSR
1992	Vitaly Scherbo, Unified Team (Belarus)
1996	Roustam Sharipov, Ukraine
2000	Li Xiaopeng, China
2004	Valeri Goncharov, Ukraine
2008	Li Xiaopeng, China
2012	Feng Zhe, China

Pommel Horse

1896	Louis Zutter, Switzerland
1904	Anton Heida, United States
1924	Josef Wilhelm, Switzerland
1928	Hermann Hänggi, Switzerland
1932	István Pelle, Hungary
1936	Konrad Frey, Germany
1948	Heikki Savolainen, Finland; Paavo Johannes Aaltonen, Finland; Veikko Huhtanen, Finland (tie)
1952	Viktor Ivanovich Chukarin, USSR

Pommel Horse

1956 Boris Shakhlin, USSR
1960 Eugen Georg Oskar Ekman, Finland; Boris Shakhlin, USSR (tie)
1964 Miroslav Cerar, Yugoslavia
1968 Miroslav Cerar, Yugoslavia
1972 Viktor Klimenko, USSR
1976 Zoltan Magyar, Hungary
1980 Zoltan Magyar, Hungary
1984 Li Ning, China; Peter Glen Vidmar, United States (tie)
1988 Zsolt Borkai, Hungary; Dmitri Bilozerchev, USSR; Lubomir Geraskov, Bulgaria (tie)
1992 Pae Gil-Su, N. Korea; Vitaly Scherbo, Unified Team (Belarus) (tie)
1996 Li Donghua, Switzerland
2000 Marius Daniel Urzica, Romania
2004 Teng Haibin, China
2008 Xiao Qin, China
2012 Krisztián Berki, Hungary

Rings

1896 Ioannis Mitropoulos, Greece
1904 Hermann Glass, United States
1924 Francesco Martino, Italy
1928 Leon Stukelj, Yugoslavia
1932 George Julius Gulack, United States
1936 Alois Hudec, Czechoslovakia
1948 Karl Frei, Switzerland
1952 Grant Shaginyan, USSR
1956 Albert Azaryan, USSR
1960 Albert Azaryan, USSR
1964 Takuji Hayata, Japan
1968 Akinori Nakayama, Japan
1972 Akinori Nakayama, Japan
1976 Nikolay Andrianov, USSR
1980 Aleksandr Dityatin, USSR
1984 Li Ning, China; Koji Gushiken, Japan (tie)
1988 Holger Behrendt, E. Germany; Dmitri Bilozerchev, USSR (tie)
1992 Vitaly Scherbo, Unified Team (Belarus)
1996 Juri Chechi, Italy
2000 Szilveszter Csollany, Hungary
2004 Dimosthenis Tampakos, Greece
2008 Chen Yibing, China
2012 Arthur Zanetti, Brazil

Team Competition

1904 United States, United States, United States
1908 Sweden, Norway, Finland
1912 Italy, Hungary, Great Britain
1920 Italy, Belgium, France
1924 Italy, France, Switzerland
1928 Switzerland, Czechoslovakia, Yugoslavia
1932 Italy, United States, Finland
1936 Germany, Switzerland, Finland
1948 Finland, Switzerland, Hungary
1952 USSR, Switzerland, Finland
1956 USSR, Japan, Finland
1960 Japan, USSR, Italy
1964 Japan, USSR, Unified Team of Germany
1968 Japan, USSR, E. Germany
1972 Japan, USSR, E. Germany
1976 Japan, USSR, E. Germany
1980 USSR, E. Germany, Hungary
1984 United States, China, Japan
1988 USSR, E. Germany, Japan
1992 Unified Team, China, Japan
1996 Russia, China, Ukraine
2000 China, Ukraine, Russia
2004 Japan, United States, Romania
2008 China, Japan, United States
2012 China, Japan, Great Britain

Vault

1896 Carl Schumann, Germany
1904 George Eyser, United States; Anton Heida, United States (tie)
1924 Frank Kriz, United States
1928 Eugen Mack, Switzerland
1932 Savino Guglielmetti, Italy
1936 Karl-Alfred Schwarzmann, Germany
1948 Paavo Johannes Aaltonen, Finland
1952 Viktor Ivanovich Chukarin, USSR
1956 Helmut Bantz, Unified Team of Germany; Valentin Muratov, USSR (tie)
1960 Takashi Ono, Japan; Boris Shakhlin, USSR (tie)
1964 Haruhiro Yamashita, Japan
1968 Mikhail Voronin, USSR
1972 Klaus Köste, E. Germany
1976 Nikolay Andrianov, USSR
1980 Nikolay Andrianov, USSR
1984 Lou Yun, China
1988 Lou Yun, China
1992 Vitaly Scherbo, Unified Team (Belarus)
1996 Alexei Nemov, Russia
2000 Gervasio Deferr, Spain
2004 Gervasio Deferr, Spain
2008 Leszek Blanik, Poland
2012 Yang Hak-Seon, South Korea

Gymnastics—Women

Balance Beam

1952 Nina Bocharova, USSR
1956 Agnes Keleti, Hungary
1960 Eva Vechtova-Bosakova, Czechoslovakia
1964 Vera Caslavska, Czechoslovakia
1968 Natalya Kuchinskaya, USSR
1972 Olga Korbut, USSR
1976 Nadia Comaneci, Romania
1980 Nadia Comaneci, Romania
1984 Ecaterina Szabo, Romania; Simona Pauca, Romania (tie)
1988 Daniela Silivas, Romania
1992 Tatiana Lyssenko, Unified Team (Ukraine)
1996 Shannon Miller, United States
2000 Liu Xuan, China
2004 Catalina Ponor, Romania
2008 Shawn Johnson, United States
2012 Deng Linlin, China

Floor Exercise

1952 Agnes Keleti, Hungary
1956 Agnes Keleti, Hungary; Larisa Latynina, USSR (tie)
1960 Larisa Latynina, USSR
1964 Larisa Latynina, USSR
1968 Vera Caslavska, Czechoslovakia; Larisa Petrik, USSR (tie)
1972 Olga Korbut, USSR
1976 Nelli Kim, USSR
1980 Nelli Kim, USSR; Nadia Comaneci, Romania (tie)
1984 Ecaterina Szabo, Romania
1988 Daniela Silivas, Romania
1992 Lavinia Corina Milosovici, Romania
1996 Lilia Podkopayeva, Ukraine
2000 Elena Zamolodchikova, Russia
2004 Catalina Ponor, Romania
2008 Sandra Izbasa, Romania
2012 Aly Raisman, United States

Individual All-Around

1952 Mariya Gorokhovskaya, USSR
1956 Larisa Latynina, USSR
1960 Larisa Latynina, USSR
1964 Vera Caslavska, Czechoslovakia
1968 Vera Caslavska, Czechoslovakia
1972 Lyudmila Turischeva, USSR
1976 Nadia Comaneci, Romania
1980 Elena Davydova, USSR
1984 Mary-Lou Retton, United States
1988 Elena Shushunova, USSR
1992 Tatiana Goutsou, Unified Team (Ukraine)
1996 Lilia Podkopayeva, Ukraine
2000 Simona Amanar, Romania
2004 Carly Patterson, United States
2008 Nastia Liukin, United States
2012 Gabby Douglas, United States

Team Competition

1928 Netherlands, Italy, Great Britain
1936 Germany, Czechoslovakia, Hungary
1948 Czechoslovakia, Hungary, United States
1952 USSR, Hungary, Czechoslovakia
1956 USSR, Hungary, Romania
1960 USSR, Czechoslovakia, Romania
1964 USSR, Czechoslovakia, Japan
1968 USSR, Czechoslovakia, E. Germany
1972 USSR, E. Germany, Hungary
1976 USSR, Romania, E. Germany
1980 USSR, Romania, E. Germany
1984 Romania, United States, China
1988 USSR, Romania, E. Germany
1992 Unified Team, Romania, United States
1996 United States, Russia, Romania
2000 Romania, Russia, United States
2004 Romania, United States, Russia
2008 China, United States, Romania
2012 United States, Russia, Romania

Uneven Bars

1952 Margit Korondi, Hungary
1956 Agnes Keleti, Hungary
1960 Polina Astakhova, USSR
1964 Polina Astakhova, USSR
1968 Vera Caslavska, Czechoslovakia
1972 Karin Janz, E. Germany
1976 Nadia Comaneci, Romania
1980 Maxi Gnauck, E. Germany
1984 Julianne McNamara, United States; Yan-Hong Ma, China (tie)
1988 Daniela Silivas, Romania
1992 Lu Li, China
1996 Svetlana Khorkina, Russia
2000 Svetlana Khorkina, Russia
2004 Emilie LePennec, France
2008 He Kexin, China
2012 Aliya Mustafina, Russia

Vault

1952 Ekaterina Kalinchuk, USSR
1956 Larisa Latynina, USSR
1960 Margarita Nikolaeva, USSR
1964 Vera Caslavska, Czechoslovakia
1968 Vera Caslavska, Czechoslovakia
1972 Karin Janz, E. Germany
1976 Nelli Kim, USSR
1980 Natalia Shaposhnikova, USSR
1984 Ecaterina Szabo, Romania
1988 Svetlana Boginskaya, USSR
1992 Henrietta Onodi, Hungary; Lavinia Corina Milosovici, Romania (tie)
1996 Simona Amanar, Romania
2000 Elena Zamolodchikova, Russia
2004 Monica Rosu, Romania
2008 Hong Un Jong, N. Korea
2012 Sandra Izbaşa, Romania

Soccer

Men	Men	Men
1900 Great Britain, France, Belgium	1960 Yugoslavia, Denmark, Hungary	1996 Nigeria, Argentina, Brazil
1904 Canada, United States, United States	1964 Hungary, Czechoslovakia,	2000 Cameroon, Spain, Chile
1908 Great Britain, Denmark, Netherlands	Unified Team of Germany	2004 Argentina, Paraguay, Italy
1912 Great Britain, Denmark, Netherlands	1968 Hungary, Bulgaria, Japan	2008 Argentina, Nigeria, Brazil
1920 Belgium, Spain, Netherlands	1972 Poland; Hungary; USSR,	2012 Mexico, Brazil, South Korea
1924 Uruguay, Switzerland, Sweden	E. Germany (tie for bronze)	**Women**
1928 Uruguay, Argentina, Italy	1976 E. Germany, Poland, USSR	1996 United States, China, Norway
1936 Italy, Austria, Norway	1980 Czechoslovakia, E. Germany, USSR	2000 Norway, United States, Germany
1948 Sweden, Yugoslavia, Denmark	1984 France, Brazil, Yugoslavia	2004 United States, Brazil, Germany
1952 Hungary, Yugoslavia, Sweden	1988 USSR, Brazil, W. Germany	2008 United States, Brazil, Germany
1956 USSR, Yugoslavia, Bulgaria	1992 Spain, Poland, Ghana	2012 United States, Japan, Canada

Swimming and Diving—Men

	50-Meter Freestyle	Time		400-Meter Freestyle	Time
1988	Matt Biondi, United States	0:22.14	1996	Danyon Loader, New Zealand	3:47.97
1992	Aleksandr Popov, Unified Team	0:21.91	2000	Ian Thorpe, Australia	3:40.59
1996	Aleksandr Popov, Russia	0:22.13	2004	Ian Thorpe, Australia	3:43.10
2000	Anthony Ervin, United States	0:21.98	2008	Park Taehwan, S. Korea	3:41.86
	Gary Hall Jr., United States (tie)	0:21.98	2012	Sun Yang, China	3:40.14*
2004	Gary Hall Jr., United States	0:21.93		**1,500-Meter Freestyle**	**Time**
2008	Cesar Cielo Filho, Brazil	0:21.30*	1908	Henry Taylor, Great Britain	22:48.4
2012	Florent Manaudou, France	0:21.34	1912	George Hodgson, Canada	22:00.0
	100-Meter Freestyle	**Time**	1920	Norman Ross, United States	22:23.2
1896	Alfred Hajos, Hungary	1:22.2	1924	Johnny Charlton, Australia	20:06.6
1904	Zoltan de Halmay, Hungary (100 yds)	1:02.8	1928	Arne Borg, Sweden	19:51.8
1908	Charles Daniels, United States	1:05.6	1932	Kusuo Kitamura, Japan	19:12.4
1912	Duke P. Kahanamoku, United States	1:03.4	1936	Noboru Terada, Japan	19:13.7
1920	Duke P. Kahanamoku, United States	1:01.4	1948	James McLane, United States	19:18.5
1924	Johnny Weissmuller, United States	0:59.0	1952	Ford Konno, United States	18:30.3
1928	Johnny Weissmuller, United States	0:58.6	1956	Murray Rose, Australia	17:58.9
1932	Yasuji Miyazaki, Japan	0:58.2	1960	Jon Konrads, Australia	17:19.6
1936	Ferenc Csik, Hungary	0:57.6	1964	Robert Windle, Australia	17:01.7
1948	Wally Ris, United States	0:57.3	1968	Mike Burton, United States	16:38.9
1952	Clark Scholes, United States	0:57.4	1972	Mike Burton, United States	15:52.58
1956	Jon Henricks, Australia	0:55.4	1976	Brian Goodell, United States	15:02.40
1960	John Devitt, Australia	0:55.2	1980	Vladimir Salnikov, USSR	14:58.27
1964	Don Schollander, United States	0:53.4	1984	Michael O'Brien, United States	15:05.20
1968	Mike Wenden, Australia	0:52.2	1988	Vladimir Salnikov, USSR	15:00.40
1972	Mark Spitz, United States	0:51.22	1992	Kieren Perkins, Australia	14:43.48
1976	Jim Montgomery, United States	0:49.99	1996	Kieren Perkins, Australia	14:56.40
1980	Jorg Woithe, E. Germany	0:50.40	2000	Grant Hackett, Australia	14:48.33
1984	Ambrose "Rowdy" Gaines, United States	0:49.80	2004	Grant Hackett, Australia	14:43.40
1988	Matt Biondi, United States	0:48.63	2008	Oussama Mellouli, Tunisia	14:40.84
1992	Aleksandr Popov, Unified Team	0:49.02	2012	Sun Yang, China	14:31.02*
1996	Aleksandr Popov, Russia	0:48.74		**100-Meter Backstroke**	**Time**
2000	Pieter van den Hoogenband, Netherlands	0:48.30	1904	Walter Brack, Germany (100 yds)	1:16.8
2004	Pieter van den Hoogenband, Netherlands	0:48.17	1908	Arno Bieberstein, Germany	1:24.6
2008	Alain Bernard, France	0:47.21	1912	Harry Hebner, United States	1:21.2
2012	Nathan Adrian, United States	0:47.52	1920	Warren Kealoha, United States	1:15.2
	200-Meter Freestyle	**Time**	1924	Warren Kealoha, United States	1:13.2
1968	Mike Wenden, Australia	1:55.2	1928	George Kojac, United States	1:08.2
1972	Mark Spitz, United States	1:52.78	1932	Masaji Kiyokawa, Japan	1:08.6
1976	Bruce Furniss, United States	1:50.29	1936	Adolph Kiefer, United States	1:05.9
1980	Sergei Kopliakov, USSR	1:49.81	1948	Allen Stack, United States	1:06.4
1984	Michael Gross, W. Germany	1:47.44	1952	Yoshi Oyakawa, United States	1:05.4
1988	Duncan Armstrong, Australia	1:47.25	1956	David Thiele, Australia	1:02.2
1992	Yevgeny Sadovyi, Unified Team	1:46.70	1960	David Thiele, Australia	1:01.9
1996	Danyon Loader, New Zealand	1:47.63	1968	Roland Matthes, E. Germany	0:58.7
2000	Pieter van den Hoogenband, Netherlands	1:45.35	1972	Roland Matthes, E. Germany	0:56.58
2004	Ian Thorpe, Australia	1:44.71	1976	John Naber, United States	0:55.49
2008	Michael Phelps, United States	1:42.96*	1980	Bengt Baron, Sweden	0:56.33
2012	Yannick Agnel, France	1:43.14	1984	Rick Carey, United States	0:55.79
	400-Meter Freestyle	**Time**	1988	Daichi Suzuki, Japan	0:55.05
1904	C. M. Daniels, United States (440 yds)	6:16.2	1992	Mark Tewksbury, Canada	0:53.98
1908	Henry Taylor, Great Britain	5:36.8	1996	Jeff Rouse, United States	0:54.10
1912	George Hodgson, Canada	5:24.4	2000	Lenny Krayzelburg, United States	0:53.72
1920	Norman Ross, United States	5:26.8	2004	Aaron Peirsol, United States	0:54.06
1924	Johnny Weissmuller, United States	5:04.2	2008	Aaron Peirsol, United States	0:52.54
1928	Albert Zorilla, Argentina	5:01.6	2012	Matt Grevers, United States	0:52.16*
1932	Clarence Crabbe, United States	4:48.4		**200-Meter Backstroke**	**Time**
1936	Jack Medica, United States	4:44.5	1964	Jed Graef, United States	2:10.3
1948	William Smith, United States	4:41.0	1968	Roland Matthes, E. Germany	2:09.6
1952	Jean Boiteux, France	4:30.7	1972	Roland Matthes, E. Germany	2:02.82
1956	Murray Rose, Australia	4:27.3	1976	John Naber, United States	1:59.19
1960	Murray Rose, Australia	4:18.3	1980	Sandor Wladar, Hungary	2:01.93
1964	Don Schollander, United States	4:12.2	1984	Rick Carey, United States	2:00.23
1968	Mike Burton, United States	4:09.0	1988	Igor Polianski, USSR	1:59.37
1972	Brad Cooper, Australia	4:00.27	1992	Martin Lopez-Zubero, Spain	1:58.47
1976	Brian Goodell, United States	3:51.93	1996	Brad Bridgewater, United States	1:58.54
1980	Vladimir Salnikov, USSR	3:51.31	2000	Lenny Krayzelburg, United States	1:56.76
1984	George DiCarlo, United States	3:51.23	2004	Aaron Peirsol, United States	1:54.95
1988	Ewe Dassler, E. Germany	3:46.95	2008	Ryan Lochte, United States	1:53.94
1992	Yevgeny Sadovyi, Unified Team	3:45.00	2012	Tyler Clary, United States	1:53.41*

100-Meter Breaststroke

		Time
1968	Don McKenzie, United States.	1:07.79
1972	Nobutaka Taguchi, Japan.	1:04.94
1976	John Hencken, United States.	1:03.11
1980	Duncan Goodhew, Great Britain.	1:03.44
1984	Steve Lundquist, United States.	1:01.65
1988	Adrian Moorhouse, Great Britain	1:02.04
1992	Nelson Diebel, United States.	1:01.50
1996	Fred Deburghgraeve, Belgium.	1:00.60
2000	Domenico Fioravanti, Italy.	1:00.46
2004	Kosuke Kitajima, Japan.	1:00.08
2008	Kosuke Kitajima, Japan.	0:58.91
2012	Cameron van der Burgh, South Africa	0:58.46*

200-Meter Breaststroke

		Time
1908	Frederick Holman, Great Britain.	3:09.2
1912	Walter Bathe, Germany.	3:01.8
1920	Haken Malmroth, Sweden.	3:04.4
1924	Robert Skelton, United States.	2:56.6
1928	Yoshiyuki Tsuruta, Japan.	2:48.8
1932	Yoshiyuki Tsuruta, Japan.	2:45.4
1936	Tetsuo Hamuro, Japan.	2:41.5
1948	Joseph Verdeur, United States.	2:39.3
1952	John Davies, Australia.	2:34.4
1956	Masura Furukawa, Japan.	2:34.7
1960	William Mulliken, United States.	2:37.4
1964	Ian O'Brien, Australia.	2:27.8
1968	Felipe Munoz, Mexico.	2:28.7
1972	John Hencken, United States.	2:21.55
1976	David Wilkie, Great Britain.	2:15.11
1980	Robertas Zhulpa, USSR.	2:15.85
1984	Victor Davis, Canada.	2:13.34
1988	Jozsef Szabo, Hungary.	2:13.52
1992	Mike Barrowman, United States.	2:10.16
1996	Norbert Rozsa, Hungary.	2:12.57
2000	Domenico Fioravanti, Italy.	2:10.87
2004	Kosuke Kitajima, Japan.	2:09.44
2008	Kosuke Kitajima, Japan.	2:07.64
2012	Dániel Gyurta, Hungary.	2:07.28*

100-Meter Butterfly

		Time
1968	Doug Russell, United States.	0:55.9
1972	Mark Spitz, United States.	0:54.27
1976	Matt Vogel, United States.	0:54.35
1980	Par Arvidsson, Sweden.	0:54.92
1984	Michael Gross, W. Germany.	0:53.08
1988	Anthony Nesty, Suriname.	0:53.00
1992	Pablo Morales, United States.	0:53.32
1996	Denis Pankratov, Russia.	0:52.27
2000	Lars Froelander, Sweden.	0:52.00
2004	Michael Phelps, United States.	0:51.25
2008	Michael Phelps, United States.	0:50.58*
2012	Michael Phelps, United States.	0:51.21

200-Meter Butterfly

		Time
1956	William Yorzyk, United States.	2:19.3
1960	Michael Troy, United States.	2:12.8
1964	Kevin J. Berry, Australia.	2:06.6
1968	Carl Robie, United States.	2:08.7
1972	Mark Spitz, United States.	2:00.70
1976	Mike Bruner, United States.	1:59.23
1980	Sergei Fesenko, USSR.	1:59.76
1984	Jon Sieben, Australia.	1:57.04
1988	Michael Gross, W. Germany.	1:56.94
1992	Mel Stewart, United States.	1:56.26
1996	Denis Pankratov, Russia.	1:56.51
2000	Tom Malchow, United States.	1:55.35
2004	Michael Phelps, United States.	1:54.04
2008	Michael Phelps, United States.	1:52.03*
2012	Chad le Clos, South Africa.	1:52.96

200-Meter Individual Medley

		Time
1968	Charles Hickcox, United States.	2:12.0
1972	Gunnar Larsson, Sweden.	2:07.17
1984	Alex Baumann, Canada.	2:01.42
1988	Tamas Darnyi, Hungary.	2:00.17
1992	Tamas Darnyi, Hungary.	2:00.76
1996	Attila Czene, Hungary.	1:59.91
2000	Massimiliano Rosolino, Italy.	1:58.98
2004	Michael Phelps, United States.	1:57.14
2008	Michael Phelps, United States.	1:54.23*
2012	Michael Phelps, United States.	1:54.27

400-Meter Individual Medley

		Time
1964	Dick Roth, United States.	4:45.4
1968	Charles Hickcox, United States.	4:48.4
1972	Gunnar Larsson, Sweden.	4:31.98
1976	Rod Strachan, United States.	4:23.68
1980	Aleksandr Sidorenko, USSR.	4:22.89
1984	Alex Baumann, Canada.	4:17.41
1988	Tamas Darnyi, Hungary.	4:14.75
1992	Tamas Darnyi, Hungary.	4:14.23

400-Meter Individual Medley

		Time
1996	Tom Dolan, United States.	4:14.90
2000	Tom Dolan, United States.	4:11.76
2004	Michael Phelps, United States.	4:08.26
2008	Michael Phelps, United States.	4:03.84*
2012	Ryan Lochte, United States.	4:05.18

4x100-Meter Freestyle Relay

		Time
1964	United States.	3:31.2
1968	United States.	3:31.7
1972	United States.	3:26.42
1984	United States.	3:19.03
1988	United States.	3:16.53
1992	United States.	3:16.74
1996	United States.	3:15.41
2000	Australia.	3:13.67
2004	South Africa.	3:13.17
2008	United States.	3:08.24*
2012	France.	3:09.93

4x200-Meter Freestyle Relay

		Time
1908	Great Britain.	10:55.6
1912	Australasia.	10:11.6
1920	United States.	10:04.4
1924	United States.	9:53.4
1928	United States.	9:36.2
1932	Japan.	8:58.4
1936	Japan.	8:51.5
1948	United States.	8:46.0
1952	United States.	8:31.1
1956	Australia.	8:23.6
1960	United States.	8:10.2
1964	United States.	7:52.1
1968	United States.	7:52.33
1972	United States.	7:35.78
1976	United States.	7:23.22
1980	USSR.	7:23.50
1984	United States.	7:15.69
1988	United States.	7:12.51
1992	Unified Team.	7:11.95
1996	United States.	7:14.84
2000	Australia.	7:07.05
2004	United States.	7:07.33
2008	United States.	6:58.56*
2012	United States.	6:59.70

4x100-Meter Medley Relay

		Time
1960	United States.	4:05.4
1964	United States.	3:58.4
1968	United States.	3:54.9
1972	United States.	3:48.16
1976	United States.	3:42.22
1980	Australia.	3:45.70
1984	United States.	3:39.30
1988	United States.	3:36.93
1992	United States.	3:36.93
1996	United States.	3:34.84
2000	United States.	3:33.73
2004	United States.	3:30.68
2008	United States.	3:29.34*
2012	United States.	3:29.35

10-Kilometer Marathon

		Time
2008	Maarten van der Weijden, Netherlands	1:51:51.6
2012	Oussama Mellouli, Tunisia.	1:49:55.1

Platform Diving

		Points
1904	Dr. G. E. Sheldon, United States.	112.75
1908	Hjalmar Johansson, Sweden.	183.75
1912	Erik Adlerz, Sweden.	73.94
1920	Clarence Pinkston, United States.	100.67
1924	Albert White, United States.	97.46
1928	Pete Desjardins, United States.	98.74
1932	Harold Smith, United States.	124.80
1936	Marshall Wayne, United States.	113.58
1948	Sammy Lee, United States.	130.05
1952	Sammy Lee, United States.	156.28
1956	Joaquin Capilla, Mexico.	152.44
1960	Robert Webster, United States.	165.56
1964	Robert Webster, United States.	148.58
1968	Klaus Dibiasi, Italy.	164.18
1972	Klaus Dibiasi, Italy.	504.12
1976	Klaus Dibiasi, Italy.	600.51
1980	Falk Hoffmann, E. Germany.	835.65
1984	Greg Louganis, United States.	710.91
1988	Greg Louganis, United States.	638.61
1992	Sun Shuwei, China.	677.31
1996	Dmitri Sautin, Russia.	692.34
2000	Tian Liang, China.	724.53
2004	Hu Jia, China.	748.08
2008	Matthew Mitcham, Australia.	537.95
2012	David Boudia, United States.	568.65

Springboard Diving	Points
1908 Albert Zurner, Germany	85.50
1912 Paul Guenther, Germany	79.23
1920 Louis Kuehn, United States	675.40
1924 Albert White, United States	97.46
1928 Pete Desjardins, United States	185.04
1932 Michael Galitzen, United States	161.38
1936 Richard Degener, United States	163.57
1948 Bruce Harlan, United States	163.64
1952 David Browning, United States	205.29
1956 Robert Clotworthy, United States	159.56
1960 Gary Tobian, United States	170.00
1964 Kenneth Sitzberger, United States	159.90
1968 Bernie Wrightson, United States	170.15
1972 Vladimir Vasin, USSR	594.09
1976 Phil Boggs, United States	619.52
1980 Aleksandr Portnov, USSR	905.02
1984 Greg Louganis, United States	754.41

Springboard Diving	Points
1988 Greg Louganis, United States	730.80
1992 Mark Lenzi, United States	676.53
1996 Xiong Ni, China	701.46
2000 Xiong Ni, China	708.72
2004 Peng Bo, China	787.30
2008 He Chong, China	572.90
2012 Ilya Zakharov, Russia	555.90

Synchronized Platform	Points
2004 Tian Liang and Yang Jinghui, China	383.88
2008 Lin Yue and Huo Liang, China	468.18
2012 Cao Yuan and Zhang Yanquan, China	486.78

Synchronized Springboard	Points
2004 Nikolaos Siranidis and Thomas Bimis, Greece	353.34
2008 Wang Feng and Qin Kai, China	469.08
2012 Luo Yutong and Qin Kai, China	477.00

Swimming and Diving—Women

50-Meter Freestyle	Time
1988 Kristin Otto, E. Germany	0:25.49
1992 Yang Wenyi, China	0:24.76
1996 Amy Van Dyken, United States	0:24.87
2000 Inge de Bruijn, Netherlands	0:24.32
2004 Inge de Bruijn, Netherlands	0:24.58
2008 Britta Steffen, Germany	0:24.06
2012 Ranomi Kromowidjojo, Netherlands	0:24.05*

100-Meter Freestyle	Time
1912 Fanny Durack, Australia	1:22.2
1920 Ethelda Bleibtrey, United States	1:13.6
1924 Ethel Lackie, United States	1:12.4
1928 Albina Osipowich, United States	1:11.0
1932 Helene Madison, United States	1:06.8
1936 Hendrika Mastenbroek, Holland	1:05.9
1948 Greta Andersen, Denmark	1:06.3
1952 Katalin Szoke, Hungary	1:06.8
1956 Dawn Fraser, Australia	1:02.0
1960 Dawn Fraser, Australia	1:01.2
1964 Dawn Fraser, Australia	0:59.5
1968 Jan Henne, United States	1:00.0
1972 Sandra Neilson, United States	0:58.59
1976 Kornelia Ender, E. Germany	0:55.65
1980 Barbara Krause, E. Germany	0:54.79
1984 Carrie Steinseifer, United States	0:55.92
Nancy Hogshead, United States (tie)	0:55.92
1988 Kristin Otto, E. Germany	0:54.93
1992 Zhuang Yong, China	0:54.64
1996 Li Jingyi, China	0:54.50
2000 Inge de Bruijn, Netherlands	0:53.83
2004 Jodie Henry, Australia	0:53.84
2008 Britta Steffen, Germany	0:53.12
2012 Ranomi Kromowidjojo, Netherlands	0:53.00*

200-Meter Freestyle	Time
1968 Debbie Meyer, United States	2:10.5
1972 Shane Gould, Australia	2:03.56
1976 Kornelia Ender, E. Germany	1:59.26
1980 Barbara Krause, E. Germany	1:58.33
1984 Mary Wayte, United States	1:59.23
1988 Heike Friedrich, E. Germany	1:57.65
1992 Nicole Haislett, United States	1:57.90
1996 Claudia Poll, Costa Rica	1:58.16
2000 Susan O'Neill, Australia	1:58.24
2004 Camelia Potec, Romania	1:58.03
2008 Federica Pellegrini, Italy	1:54.82
2012 Allison Schmitt, United States	1:53.61*

400-Meter Freestyle	Time
1924 Martha Norelius, United States	6:02.2
1928 Martha Norelius, United States	5:42.8
1932 Helene Madison, United States	5:28.5
1936 Hendrika Mastenbroek, Netherlands	5:26.4
1948 Ann Curtis, United States	5:17.8
1952 Valerie Gyenge, Hungary	5:12.1
1956 Lorraine Crapp, Australia	4:54.6
1960 Susan Chris von Saltza, United States	4:50.6
1964 Virginia Duenkel, United States	4:43.3
1968 Debbie Meyer, United States	4:31.8
1972 Shane Gould, Australia	4:19.44
1976 Petra Thuemer, E. Germany	4:09.89
1980 Ines Diers, E. Germany	4:08.76
1984 Tiffany Cohen, United States	4:07.10
1988 Janet Evans, United States	4:03.85

400-Meter Freestyle	Time
1992 Dagmar Hase, Germany	4:07.18
1996 Michelle Smith, Ireland	4:07.25
2000 Brooke Bennett, United States	4:05.80
2004 Laure Manaudou, France	4:05.34
2008 Rebecca Adlington, Great Britain	4:03.22
2012 Camille Muffat, France	4:01.45*

800-Meter Freestyle	Time
1968 Debbie Meyer, United States	9:24.0
1972 Keena Rothhammer, United States	8:53.68
1976 Petra Thuemer, E. Germany	8:37.14
1980 Michelle Ford, Australia	8:28.90
1984 Tiffany Cohen, United States	8:24.95
1988 Janet Evans, United States	8:20.20
1992 Janet Evans, United States	8:25.52
1996 Brooke Bennett, United States	8:27.89
2000 Brooke Bennett, United States	8:19.67
2004 Ai Shibata, Japan	8:24.54
2008 Rebecca Adlington, Great Britain	8:14.10*
2012 Katie Ledecky, United States	8:14.63

100-Meter Backstroke	Time
1924 Sybil Bauer, United States	1:23.2
1928 Marie Braun, Netherlands	1:22.0
1932 Eleanor Holm, United States	1:19.4
1936 Dina Senff, Netherlands	1:18.9
1948 Karen Harup, Denmark	1:14.4
1952 Joan Harrison, South Africa	1:14.3
1956 Judy Grinham, Great Britain	1:12.9
1960 Lynn Burke, United States	1:09.3
1964 Cathy Ferguson, United States	1:07.7
1968 Kaye Hall, United States	1:06.2
1972 Melissa Belote, United States	1:05.78
1976 Ulrike Richter, E. Germany	1:01.83
1980 Rica Reinisch, E. Germany	1:00.86
1984 Theresa Andrews, United States	1:02.55
1988 Kristin Otto, E. Germany	1:00.89
1992 Krisztina Egerszegi, Hungary	1:00.68
1996 Beth Botsford, United States	1:01.19
2000 Diana Mocanu, Romania	1:00.21
2004 Natalie Coughlin, United States	1:00.37
2008 Natalie Coughlin, United States	0:58.96
2012 Missy Franklin, United States	0:58.33

200-Meter Backstroke	Time
1968 Pokey Watson, United States	2:24.8
1972 Melissa Belote, United States	2:19.19
1976 Ulrike Richter, E. Germany	2:13.43
1980 Rica Reinisch, E. Germany	2:11.77
1984 Jolanda De Rover, Netherlands	2:12.38
1988 Krisztina Egerszegi, Hungary	2:09.29
1992 Krisztina Egerszegi, Hungary	2:07.06
1996 Krisztina Egerszegi, Hungary	2:07.83
2000 Diana Mocanu, Romania	2:08.16
2004 Kirsty Coventry, Zimbabwe	2:09.19
2008 Kirsty Coventry, Zimbabwe	2:05.24
2012 Missy Franklin, United States	2:04.06*

100-Meter Breaststroke	Time
1968 Djurdjica Bjedov, Yugoslavia	1:15.8
1972 Cathy Carr, United States	1:13.58
1976 Hannelore Anke, E. Germany	1:11.16
1980 Ute Geweniger, E. Germany	1:10.22
1984 Petra Van Staveren, Netherlands	1:09.88

100-Meter Breaststroke

Year	Champion	Time
1988	Tania Dangalakova, Bulgaria	1:07.95
1992	Elena Roudkovskaia, Unified Team	1:08.00
1996	Penny Heyns, South Africa	1:07.73
2000	Megan Quann, United States	1:07.05
2004	Luo Xuejuan, China	1:06.64
2008	Leisel Jones, Australia	1:05.17*
2012	Rūta Meilutytė, Lithuania	1:05.47

200-Meter Breaststroke

Year	Champion	Time
1924	Lucy Morton, Great Britain	3:33.2
1928	Hilde Schrader, Germany	3:12.6
1932	Clare Dennis, Australia	3:06.3
1936	Hideko Maehata, Japan	3:03.6
1948	Nelly Van Vliet, Netherlands	2:57.2
1952	Eva Szekely, Hungary	2:51.7
1956	Ursula Happe, Germany	2:53.1
1960	Anita Lonsbrough, Great Britain	2:49.5
1964	Galina Prozumenschikova, USSR	2:46.4
1968	Sharon Wichman, United States	2:44.4
1972	Beverly Whitfield, Australia	2:41.71
1976	Marina Koshevaia, USSR	2:33.35
1980	Lina Kachushite, USSR	2:29.54
1984	Anne Ottenbrite, Canada	2:30.38
1988	Silke Hoerner, E. Germany	2:26.71
1992	Kyoko Iwasaki, Japan	2:26.65
1996	Penny Heyns, South Africa	2:25.41
2000	Agnes Kovacs, Hungary	2:24.35
2004	Amanda Beard, United States	2:23.37
2008	Rebecca Soni, United States	2:20.22
2012	Rebecca Soni, United States	2:19.59*

100-Meter Butterfly

Year	Champion	Time
1956	Shelley Mann, United States	1:11.0
1960	Carolyn Schuler, United States	1:09.5
1964	Sharon Stouder, United States	1:04.7
1968	Lynn McClements, Australia	1:05.5
1972	Mayumi Aoki, Japan	1:03.34
1976	Kornelia Ender, E. Germany	1:00.13
1980	Caren Metschuck, E. Germany	1:00.42
1984	Mary T. Meagher, United States	0:59.26
1988	Kristin Otto, E. Germany	0:59.00
1992	Qian Hong, China	0:58.62
1996	Amy Van Dyken, United States	0:59.13
2000	Inge de Bruijn, Netherlands	0:56.61
2004	Petria Thomas, Australia	0:57.72
2008	Lisbeth Trickett, Australia	0:56.73
2012	Dana Vollmer, United States	0:55.98*

200-Meter Butterfly

Year	Champion	Time
1968	Ada Kok, Netherlands	2:24.7
1972	Karen Moe, United States	2:15.57
1976	Andrea Pollack, E. Germany	2:11.41
1980	Ines Geissler, E. Germany	2:10.44
1984	Mary T. Meagher, United States	2:06.90
1988	Kathleen Nord, E. Germany	2:09.51
1992	Summer Sanders, United States	2:08.67
1996	Susan O'Neill, Australia	2:07.76
2000	Misty Hyman, United States	2:05.88
2004	Otylia Jedrzejczak, Poland	2:06.05
2008	Liu Zige, China	2:04.18
2012	Jiao Liuyang, China	2:04.06*

200-Meter Individual Medley

Year	Champion	Time
1968	Claudia Kolb, United States	2:24.7
1972	Shane Gould, Australia	2:23.07
1984	Tracy Caulkins, United States	2:12.64
1988	Daniela Hunger, E. Germany	2:12.59
1992	Lin Li, China	2:11.65
1996	Michelle Smith, Ireland	2:13.93
2000	Yana Klochkova, Ukraine	2:10.68
2004	Yana Klochkova, Ukraine	2:11.14
2008	Stephanie Rice, Australia	2:08.45
2012	Ye Shiwen, China	2:07.57*

400-Meter Individual Medley

Year	Champion	Time
1964	Donna de Varona, United States	5:18.7
1968	Claudia Kolb, United States	5:08.5
1972	Gail Neall, Australia	5:02.97
1976	Ulrike Tauber, E. Germany	4:42.77
1980	Petra Schneider, E. Germany	4:36.29
1984	Tracy Caulkins, United States	4:39.24
1988	Janet Evans, United States	4:37.76
1992	Krisztina Egerszegi, Hungary	4:36.54
1996	Michelle Smith, Ireland	4:39.18
2000	Yana Klochkova, Ukraine	4:33.59
2004	Yana Klochkova, Ukraine	4:34.83
2008	Stephanie Rice, Australia	4:29.45
2012	Ye Shiwen, China	4:28.43*

4x100-Meter Freestyle Relay

Year	Champion	Time
1912	Great Britain	5:52.8
1920	United States	5:11.6
1924	United States	4:58.8
1928	United States	4:47.6
1932	United States	4:38.0
1936	Netherlands	4:36.0
1948	United States	4:29.2
1952	Hungary	4:24.4
1956	Australia	4:17.1
1960	United States	4:08.9
1964	United States	4:03.8
1968	United States	4:02.5
1972	United States	3:55.19
1976	United States	3:44.82
1980	East Germany	3:42.71
1984	United States	3:43.43
1988	East Germany	3:40.63
1992	United States	3:39.46
1996	United States	3:39.29
2000	United States	3:36.61
2004	Australia	3:35.94
2008	Netherlands	3:33.76
2012	Australia	3:33.15*

4x200-Meter Freestyle Relay

Year	Champion	Time
1996	United States	7:59.87
2000	United States	7:57.80
2004	United States	7:53.42
2008	Australia	7:44.31
2012	United States	7:42.92*

4x100-Meter Medley Relay

Year	Champion	Time
1960	United States	4:41.1
1964	United States	4:33.9
1968	United States	4:28.3
1972	United States	4:20.75
1976	East Germany	4:07.95
1980	East Germany	4:06.67
1984	United States	4:08.34
1988	East Germany	4:03.74
1992	United States	4:02.54
1996	United States	4:02.88
2000	United States	3:58.30
2004	Australia	3:57.32
2008	Australia	3:52.69
2012	United States	3:52.05*

10-Kilometer Marathon

Year	Champion	Time
2008	Larisa Ilchenko, Russia	1:59:27.7
2012	Éva Risztov, Hungary	1:57:38.2

Platform Diving

Year	Champion	Points
1912	Greta Johansson, Sweden	39.90
1920	Stefani Fryland-Clausen, Denmark	34.60
1924	Caroline Smith, United States	33.20
1928	Elizabeth B. Pinkston, United States	31.60
1932	Dorothy Poynton, United States	40.26
1936	Dorothy Poynton Hill, United States	33.93
1948	Victoria M. Draves, United States	68.87
1952	Patricia McCormick, United States	79.37
1956	Patricia McCormick, United States	84.85
1960	Ingrid Kramer, Germany	91.28
1964	Lesley Bush, United States	99.80
1968	Milena Duchkova, Czechoslovakia	109.59
1972	Ulrika Knape, Sweden	390.00
1976	Elena Vaytsekhouskaya, USSR	406.59
1980	Martina Jaschke, E. Germany	596.25
1984	Zhou Jihong, China	435.51
1988	Xu Yanmei, China	445.20
1992	Fu Mingxia, China	461.43
1996	Fu Mingxia, China	521.58
2000	Laura Wilkinson, United States	543.75
2004	Chantelle Newbery, Australia	590.31
2008	Chen Ruolin, China	447.70
2012	Chen Ruolin, China	422.30

Springboard Diving

Year	Champion	Points
1920	Aileen Riggin, United States	539.90
1924	Elizabeth Becker, United States	474.50
1928	Helen Meany, United States	78.62
1932	Georgia Coleman United States	87.52
1936	Marjorie Gestring, United States	89.27
1948	Victoria M. Draves, United States	108.74
1952	Patricia McCormick, United States	147.30
1956	Patricia McCormick, United States	142.36
1960	Ingrid Kramer, Germany	155.81
1964	Ingrid Engel-Kramer, Germany	145.00
1968	Sue Gossick, United States	150.77
1972	Micki King, United States	450.03
1976	Jenni Chandler, United States	506.19
1980	Irina Kalinina, USSR	725.91

Springboard Diving	Points
1984 Sylvie Bernier, Canada	530.70
1988 Gao Min, China	580.23
1992 Gao Min, China	572.40
1996 Fu Mingxia, China	547.68
2000 Fu Mingxia, China	609.42
2004 Guo Jingjing, China	633.15
2008 Guo Jingjing, China	415.35
2012 Wu Minxia, China	414.00

Synchronized Platform	Points
2004 Lao Lishi and Li Ting, China	352.14
2008 Wang Xin and Chen Ruolin, China	363.54
2012 Chen Ruolin and Wang Hao, China	368.40

Synchronized Springboard	Points
2004 Wu Minxia and Guo Jingjing, China	336.90
2008 Guo Jingjing and Wu Minxia, China	343.50
2012 He Zi and Wu Minxia, China	346.20

Tennis

Men's Singles

1896	John Boland, Great Britain
1900	Hugh Lawrence Doherty, Great Britain
1904	Beals Coleman Wright, United States
1908	Josiah George Ritchie, Great Britain
1912	Charles Lyndhurst Winslow, South Africa
1920	Louis Raymond, South Africa
1924	Vincent Richards, United States
1988	Miloslav Mecir, Czechoslovakia
1992	Marc Rosset, Switzerland
1996	Andre Agassi, United States
2000	Eugueni Kafelnikov, Russia
2004	Nicolas Massu, Chile
2008	Rafael Nadal, Spain
2012	Andy Murray, Great Britain

Men's Doubles

1896	John Boland, Great Britain & Friedrick Traun, Germany
1900	Hugh Lawrence Doherty & Reginald Frank Doherty, Great Britain
1904	Edgar Welch Leonard & Beals Coleman Wright, United States
1908	George Whiteside Hillyard & Reginald Frank Doherty, Great Britain
1912	Harry Austin Kitson & Charles Lyndhurst Winslow, South Africa
1920	Oswald Graham Noel Turnbull & Maxwell Woosnam, Great Britain
1924	Vincent Richards & Francis Townsend Hunter, United States
1988	Kenneth Flach & Robert A. Seguso, United States
1992	Boris Becker & Michael Stich, Germany
1996	Mark Woodforde & Todd Woodbridge, Australia
2000	Sebastien Lareau & Daniel Nestor, Canada

Men's Doubles

2004	Fernando Gonzales & Nicolas Massu, Chile
2008	Roger Federer & Stanislas Wawrinka, Switzerland
2012	Mike Bryan & Bob Bryan, United States

Women's Singles

1900	Charlotte Cooper, Great Britain
1908	Dorothy Katherine Chambers, Great Britain
1912	Marguerite Broquedis, France
1920	Suzanne Lenglen, France
1924	Helen Wills, United States
1988	Steffi Graf, W. Germany
1992	Jennifer Capriati, United States
1996	Lindsay Davenport, United States
2000	Venus Williams, United States
2004	Justine Henin-Hardenne, Belgium
2008	Elena Dementieva, Russia
2012	Serena Williams, United States

Women's Doubles

1920	Winifred Margaret McNair & Kathleen McKane, Great Britain
1924	Hazel Virginia Wightman & Helen Wills, United States
1988	Pam Shriver & Zina Garrison, United States
1992	Gigi Fernandez & Mary Joe Fernandez, United States
1996	Gigi Fernandez & Mary Joe Fernandez, United States
2000	Venus Williams & Serena Williams, United States
2004	Ting Li & Tian Tian Sun, China
2008	Serena Williams & Venus Williams, United States
2012	Serena Williams & Venus Williams, United States

Mixed Doubles

2012	Victoria Azarenka & Max Mirnyi, Belarus

Track and Field—Men

100-Meter Run	Time
1896 Thomas Burke, United States	0:12.0
1900 Francis Jarvis, United States	0:11.0
1904 Archie Hahn, United States	0:11.0
1908 Reginald Walker, South Africa	0:10.8
1912 Ralph Craig, United States	0:10.8
1920 Charles Paddock, United States	0:10.8
1924 Harold Abrahams, Great Britain	0:10.6
1928 Percy Williams, Canada	0:10.8
1932 Eddie Tolan, United States	0:10.3
1936 Jesse Owens, United States	0:10.3
1948 Harrison Dillard, United States	0:10.3
1952 Lindy Remigino, United States	0:10.4
1956 Bobby Morrow, United States	0:10.5
1960 Armin Hary, Germany	0:10.2
1964 Bob Hayes, United States	0:10.0
1968 Jim Hines, United States	0:09.95
1972 Valery Borzov, USSR	0:10.14
1976 Hasely Crawford, Trinidad	0:10.06
1980 Allan Wells, Great Britain	0:10.25
1984 Carl Lewis, United States	0:09.99
1988 Carl Lewis, United States	0:09.92
1992 Linford Christie, Great Britain	0:09.96
1996 Donovan Bailey, Canada	0:09.84
2000 Maurice Greene, United States	0:09.87
2004 Justin Gatlin, United States	0:09.85
2008 Usain Bolt, Jamaica	0:09.69
2012 Usain Bolt, Jamaica	0:09.63*

200-Meter Run	Time
1900 Walter Tewksbury, United States	0:22.2
1904 Archie Hahn, United States	0:21.6
1908 Robert Kerr, Canada	0:22.6
1912 Ralph Craig, United States	0:21.7
1920 Allan Woodring, United States	0:22.0
1924 Jackson Scholz, United States	0:21.6
1928 Percy Williams, Canada	0:21.8
1932 Eddie Tolan, United States	0:21.2
1936 Jesse Owens, United States	0:20.7
1948 Mel Patton, United States	0:21.1
1952 Andrew Stanfield, United States	0:20.7
1956 Bobby Morrow, United States	0:20.6
1960 Livio Berruti, Italy	0:20.5
1964 Henry Carr, United States	0:20.3
1968 Tommie Smith, United States	0:19.83
1972 Valery Borzov, USSR	0:20.00

200-Meter Run	Time
1976 Donald Quarrie, Jamaica	0:20.23
1980 Pietro Mennea, Italy	0:20.19
1984 Carl Lewis, United States	0:19.80
1988 Joe DeLoach, United States	0:19.75
1992 Mike Marsh, United States	0:20.01
1996 Michael Johnson, United States	0:19.32
2000 Konstantinos Kenteris, Greece	0:20.09
2004 Shawn Crawford, United States	0:19.79
2008 Usain Bolt, Jamaica	0:19.30*
2012 Usain Bolt, Jamaica	0:19.32

400-Meter Run	Time
1896 Thomas Burke, United States	0:54.2
1900 Maxwell Long, United States	0:49.4
1904 Harry Hillman, United States	0:49.2
1908 Wyndham Halswelle, Gr. Brit. (walkover)	0:50.0
1912 Charles Reidpath, United States	0:48.2
1920 Bevil Rudd, South Africa	0:49.6
1924 Eric Liddell, Great Britain	0:47.6
1928 Ray Barbuti, United States	0:47.8
1932 William Carr, United States	0:46.2
1936 Archie Williams, United States	0:46.5
1948 Arthur Wint, Jamaica	0:46.2
1952 George Rhoden, Jamaica	0:45.9
1956 Charles Jenkins, United States	0:46.7
1960 Otis Davis, United States	0:44.9
1964 Michael Larrabee, United States	0:45.1
1968 Lee Evans, United States	0:43.86
1972 Vincent Matthews, United States	0:44.66
1976 Alberto Juantorena, Cuba	0:44.26
1980 Viktor Markin, USSR	0:44.60
1984 Alonzo Babers, United States	0:44.27
1988 Steve Lewis, United States	0:43.87
1992 Quincy Watts, United States	0:43.50
1996 Michael Johnson, United States	0:43.49*
2000 Michael Johnson, United States	0:43.84
2004 Jeremy Wariner, United States	0:44.00
2008 LaShawn Merritt, United States	0:43.75
2012 Kirani James, Grenada	0:43.94

800-Meter Run	Time
1896 Edwin Flack, Australia	2:11.0
1900 Alfred Tysoe, Great Britain	2:01.2
1904 James Lightbody, United States	1:56.0

800-Meter Run

		Time
1908	Mel Sheppard, United States	1:52.8
1912	James "Ted" Meredith, United States	1:51.9
1920	Albert Hill, Great Britain	1:53.4
1924	Douglas Lowe, Great Britain	1:52.4
1928	Douglas Lowe, Great Britain	1:51.8
1932	Thomas Hampson, Great Britain	1:49.8
1936	John Woodruff, United States	1:52.9
1948	Mal Whitfield, United States	1:49.2
1952	Mal Whitfield, United States	1:49.2
1956	Tom Courtney, United States	1:47.7
1960	Peter Snell, New Zealand	1:46.3
1964	Peter Snell, New Zealand	1:45.1
1968	Ralph Doubell, Australia	1:44.3
1972	Dave Wottle, United States	1:45.9
1976	Alberto Juantorena, Cuba	1:43.50
1980	Steve Ovett, Great Britain	1:45.40
1984	Joaquim Cruz, Brazil	1:43.00
1988	Paul Ereng, Kenya	1:43.45
1992	William Tanui, Kenya	1:43.66
1996	Vebjørn Rodal, Norway	1:42.58
2000	Nils Schumann, Germany	1:45.08
2004	Yuriy Borzakovskiy, Russia	1:44.45
2008	Wilfred Bungei, Kenya	1:44.65
2012	David Lekuta Rudisha, Kenya	1:40.91*

1,500-Meter Run

		Time
1896	Edwin Flack, Australia	4:33.2
1900	Charles Bennett, Great Britain	4:06.2
1904	James Lightbody, United States	4:05.4
1908	Mel Sheppard, United States	4:03.4
1912	Arnold Jackson, Great Britain	3:56.8
1920	Albert Hill, Great Britain	4:01.8
1924	Paavo Nurmi, Finland	3:53.6
1928	Harry Larva, Finland	3:53.2
1932	Luigi Beccali, Italy	3:51.2
1936	Jack Lovelock, New Zealand	3:47.8
1948	Henry Eriksson, Sweden	3:49.8
1952	Joseph Barthel, Luxembourg	3:45.2
1956	Ron Delany, Ireland	3:41.2
1960	Herb Elliott, Australia	3:35.6
1964	Peter Snell, New Zealand	3:38.1
1968	Kipchoge Keino, Kenya	3:34.91
1972	Pekka Vasala, Finland	3:36.33
1976	John Walker, New Zealand	3:39.17
1980	Sebastian Coe, Great Britain	3:38.4
1984	Sebastian Coe, Great Britain	3:32.53
1988	Peter Rono, Kenya	3:35.96
1992	Fermin Cacho Ruiz, Spain	3:40.12
1996	Noureddine Morceli, Algeria	3:35.78
2000	Noah Ngeny, Kenya	3:32.07*
2004	Hicham El Guerrouj, Morocco	3:34.18
2008	Ashel Kiprop, Kenya[1]	3:33.11
2012	Taoufik Makhlouti, Algeria	3:34.08

(1) The Intl. Olympic Committee stripped Rashid Ramzi, Bahrain, of the gold medal in Nov. 2009 after he failed a doping test; the medal was reallocated in Dec. 2011.

3,000-Meter Steeplechase

		Time
1920	Percy Hodge, Great Britain	10:00.4
1924	Ville Ritola, Finland	9:33.6
1928	Toivo Loukola, Finland	9:21.8
1932	Volmari Iso-Hollo, Finland (about 3,450 m; extra lap by error)	10:33.4
1936	Volmari Iso-Hollo, Finland	9:03.8
1948	Tore Sjöstrand, Sweden	9:04.6
1952	Horace Ashenfelter, United States	8:45.4
1956	Chris Brasher, Great Britain	8:41.2
1960	Zdzisław Krzyszkowiak, Poland	8:34.2
1964	Gaston Roelants, Belgium	8:30.8
1968	Amos Biwott, Kenya	8:51.0
1972	Kipchoge Keino, Kenya	8:23.64
1976	Anders Garderud, Sweden	8:08.02
1980	Bronislaw Malinowski, Poland	8:09.7
1984	Julius Korir, Kenya	8:11.80
1988	Julius Kariuki, Kenya	8:05.51*
1992	Matthew Birir, Kenya	8:08.84
1996	Joseph Keter, Kenya	8:07.12
2000	Reuben Kosgei, Kenya	8:21.43
2004	Ezekiel Kemboi, Kenya	8:05.81
2008	Brimin Kiprop Kirpruto, Kenya	8:10.34
2012	Ezekiel Kemboi, Kenya	8:18.56

5,000-Meter Run

		Time
1912	Hannes Kolehmainen, Finland	14:36.6
1920	Joseph Guillemot, France	14:55.6
1924	Paavo Nurmi, Finland	14:31.2
1928	Ville Ritola, Finland	14:38.0
1932	Lauri Lehtinen, Finland	14:30.0
1936	Gunnar Höckert, Finland	14:22.2
1948	Gaston Reiff, Belgium	14:17.6
1952	Emil Zatopek, Czechoslovakia	14:06.6
1956	Vladimir Kuts, USSR	13:39.6
1960	Murray Halberg, New Zealand	13:43.4

5,000-Meter Run

		Time
1964	Bob Schul, United States	13:48.8
1968	Mohamed Gammoudi, Tunisia	14:05.0
1972	Lasse Viren, Finland	13:26.4
1976	Lasse Viren, Finland	13:24.76
1980	Miruts Yifter, Ethiopia	13:20.91
1984	Said Aouita, Morocco	13:05.59
1988	John Ngugi, Kenya	13:11.70
1992	Dieter Baumann, Germany	13:12.52
1996	Venuste Niyongabo, Burundi	13:07.96
2000	Millon Wolde, Ethiopia	13:35.49
2004	Hicham El Guerrouj, Morocco	13:14.39
2008	Kenenisa Bekele, Ethiopia	12:57.82*
2012	Mo Farah, Great Britain	13:41.66

10,000-Meter Run

		Time
1912	Hannes Kolehmainen, Finland	31:20.8
1920	Paavo Nurmi, Finland	31:45.8
1924	Ville Ritola, Finland	30:23.2
1928	Paavo Nurmi, Finland	30:18.8
1932	Janusz Kusocinski, Poland	30:11.4
1936	Ilmari Salminen, Finland	30:15.4
1948	Emil Zatopek, Czechoslovakia	29:59.6
1952	Emil Zatopek, Czechoslovakia	29:17.0
1956	Vladimir Kuts, USSR	28:45.6
1960	Pyotr Bolotnikov, USSR	28:32.2
1964	Billy Mills, United States	28:24.4
1968	Naftali Temu, Kenya	29:27.4
1972	Lasse Viren, Finland	27:38.4
1976	Lasse Viren, Finland	27:40.38
1980	Miruts Yifter, Ethiopia	27:42.7
1984	Alberto Cova, Italy	27:47.54
1988	Brahim Boutayeb, Morocco	27:21.46
1992	Khalid Skah, Morocco	27:46.70
1996	Haile Gebrselassie, Ethiopia	27:07.34
2000	Haile Gebrselassie, Ethiopia	27:18.20
2004	Kenenisa Bekele, Ethiopia	27:05.10
2008	Kenenisa Bekele, Ethiopia	27:01.17*
2012	Mo Farah, Great Britain	27:30.42

Marathon

		Time
1896	Spyridon Louis, Greece	2:58:50
1900	Michel Theato, France	2:59:45.0
1904	Thomas Hicks, United States	3:28:53.0
1908	John Hayes, United States	2:55:18.4
1912	Kenneth McArthur, South Africa	2:36:54.8
1920	Hannes Kolehmainen, Finland	2:32:35.8
1924	Albin Stenroos, Finland	2:41:22.6
1928	Boughera El Ouafi, France	2:32:57
1932	Juan Zabala, Argentina	2:31:36
1936	Kee-chung Sohn, Japan[1]	2:29:19.2
1948	Delfo Cabrera, Argentina	2:34:51.6
1952	Emil Zatopek, Czechoslovakia	2:23:03.2
1956	Alain Mimoun, France	2:25:00.0
1960	Abebe Bikila, Ethiopia	2:15:16.2
1964	Abebe Bikila, Ethiopia	2:12:11.2
1968	Mamo Wolde, Ethiopia	2:20:26.4
1972	Frank Shorter, United States	2:12:19.8
1976	Waldemar Cierpinski, E. Germany	2:09:55.0
1980	Waldemar Cierpinski, E. Germany	2:11:03.0
1984	Carlos Lopes, Portugal	2:09:21
1988	Gelindo Bordin, Italy	2:10:32
1992	Hwang Young-Cho, S. Korea	2:13:23
1996	Josia Thugwane, South Africa	2:12:36
2000	Gezahegne Abera, Ethiopia	2:10:11
2004	Stefano Baldini, Italy	2:10:55
2008	Samuel Kamau Wansiru, Kenya	2:06:32*
2012	Stephen Kiprotich, Uganda	2:08:01

(1) Korean runner who competed under Japanese name Kitei Son.

4x100-Meter Relay

		Time
1912	Great Britain	0:42.4
1920	United States	0:42.2
1924	United States	0:41.0
1928	United States	0:41.0
1932	United States	0:40.0
1936	United States	0:39.8
1948	United States	0:40.6
1952	United States	0:40.1
1956	United States	0:39.5
1960	Germany (U.S. disqualified)	0:39.5
1964	United States	0:39.0
1968	United States	0:38.24
1972	United States	0:38.19
1976	United States	0:38.33
1980	USSR	0:38.26
1984	United States	0:37.83
1988	USSR (U.S. disqualified)	0:38.19
1992	United States	0:37.40
1996	Canada	0:37.69
2000	United States	0:37.61
2004	Great Britain	0:38.07
2008	Jamaica	0:37.10
2012	Jamaica	0:36.84*

4x400-Meter Relay

		Time
1908	United States	3:29.4
1912	United States	3:16.6
1920	Great Britain	3:22.2
1924	United States	3:16.0
1928	United States	3:14.2
1932	United States	3:08.2
1936	Great Britain	3:09.0
1948	United States	3:10.4
1952	Jamaica	3:03.9
1956	United States	3:04.8
1960	United States	3:02.2
1964	United States	3:00.7
1968	United States	2:56.16
1972	Kenya	2:59.8
1976	United States	2:58.65
1980	USSR	3:01.1
1984	United States	2:57.91
1988	United States	2:56.16
1992	United States	2:55.74
1996	United States	2:55.99
2000	Nigeria[1]	2:58.68
2004	United States	2:55.91
2008	United States	2:55.39*
2012	The Bahamas	2:56.72

(1) The Intl. Olympic Committee stripped the U.S. team of their gold medals in Aug. 2008 after one of the team's members, Antonio Pettigrew, admitted to doping; the medal was reallocated to the second-place Nigerian team in July 2012.

20-Kilometer Walk

		Time
1956	Leonid Spirin, USSR	1:31:27.4
1960	Vladimir Golubnichy, USSR	1:34:07.2
1964	Kenneth Matthews, Great Britain	1:29:34.0
1968	Vladimir Golubnichy, USSR	1:33:58.4
1972	Peter Frenkel, E. Germany	1:26:42.4
1976	Daniel Bautista, Mexico	1:24:40.6
1980	Maurizio Damilano, Italy	1:23:35.5
1984	Ernesto Canto, Mexico	1:23:13
1988	Jozef Pribilinec, Czechoslovakia	1:19.57
1992	Daniel Plaza Montero, Spain	1:21:45
1996	Jefferson Perez, Ecuador	1:20:07
2000	Robert Korzeniowski, Poland	1:18:59
2004	Ivano Brugnetti, Italy	1:19:40
2008	Valeriy Borchin, Russia	1:19:01
2012	Chen Ding, China	1:18.46*

50-Kilometer Walk

		Time
1932	Thomas "Tommy" Green, Great Britain	4:50.10
1936	Harold Whitlock, Great Britain	4:30:41.4
1948	John Ljunggren, Sweden	4:41.52
1952	Giuseppe Dordoni, Italy	4:28:07.8
1956	Norman Read, New Zealand	4:30:42.8
1960	Donald Thompson, Great Britain	4:25:30
1964	Abdon Pamich, Italy	4:11:12.4
1968	Christoph Höhne, E. Germany	4:20:13.6
1972	Bernd Kannenberg, W. Germany	3:56:11.6
1980	Hartwig Gauder, E. Germany	3:49:24.0
1984	Raul Gonzalez, Mexico	3:47:26
1988	Vyacheslav Ivanenko, USSR	3:38.29
1992	Andrei Perlov, Unified Team	3:50:13
1996	Robert Korzeniowski, Poland	3:43:30
2000	Robert Korzeniowski, Poland	3:42:22
2004	Robert Korzeniowski, Poland	3:38:46
2008	Alex Schwazer, Italy	3:37:09
2012	Sergey Kirdyapkin, Russia	3:35:59*

110-Meter Hurdles

		Time
1896	Thomas Curtis, United States	0:17.6
1900	Alvin Kraenzlein, United States	0:15.4
1904	Frederick Schule, United States	0:16.0
1908	Forrest Smithson, United States	0:15.0
1912	Frederick Kelly, United States	0:15.1
1920	Earl Thomson, Canada	0:14.8
1924	Daniel Kinsey, United States	0:15.0
1928	Sydney Atkinson, South Africa	0:14.8
1932	George Saling, United States	0:14.6
1936	Forrest Towns, United States	0:14.2
1948	William Porter, United States	0:13.9
1952	Harrison Dillard, United States	0:13.7
1956	Lee Calhoun, United States	0:13.5
1960	Lee Calhoun, United States	0:13.8
1964	Hayes Jones, United States	0:13.6
1968	Willie Davenport, United States	0:13.33
1972	Rod Milburn, United States	0:13.24
1976	Guy Drut, France	0:13.30
1980	Thomas Munkelt, E. Germany	0:13.39
1984	Roger Kingdom, United States	0:13.20
1988	Roger Kingdom, United States	0:12.98
1992	Mark McKoy, Canada	0:13.12
1996	Allen Johnson, United States	0:12.95
2000	Anier Garcia, Cuba	0:13.00
2004	Liu Xiang, China	0:12.91*
2008	Dayron Robles, Cuba	0:12.93
2012	Aries Merritt, United States	0:12.92

400-Meter Hurdles

		Time
1900	Walter Tewksbury, United States	0:57.6
1904	Harry Hillman, United States	0:53.0
1908	Charles Bacon, United States	0:55.0
1920	Frank Loomis, United States	0:54.0
1924	F. Morgan Taylor, United States	0:52.6
1928	Lord Burghley, Great Britain	0:53.4
1932	Bob Tisdall, Ireland	0:51.7
1936	Glenn Hardin, United States	0:52.4
1948	Roy Cochran, United States	0:51.1
1952	Charles Moore, United States	0:50.8
1956	Glenn Davis, United States	0:50.1
1960	Glenn Davis, United States	0:49.3
1964	Rex Cawley, United States	0:49.6
1968	David Hemery, Great Britain	0:48.12
1972	John Akii-Bua, Uganda	0:47.82
1976	Edwin Moses, United States	0:47.64
1980	Volker Beck, E. Germany	0:48.70
1984	Edwin Moses, United States	0:47.75
1988	Andre Phillips, United States	0:47.19
1992	Kevin Young, United States	0:46.78
1996	Derrick Adkins, United States	0:47.54
2000	Angelo Taylor, United States	0:47.50
2004	Félix Sánchez, Dominican Republic	0:47.63
2008	Angelo Taylor, United States	0:47.25
2012	Félix Sánchez, Dominican Republic	0:47.63

Note: Event not held in 1912.

Discus Throw

		Dist.	
1896	Robert Garrett, United States	29.15m	(95' 7")
1900	Rudolf Bauer, Hungary	36.04m	(118' 3")
1904	Martin Sheridan, United States	39.28m	(128' 10")
1908	Martin Sheridan, United States	40.89m	(134' 1")
1912	Armas Taipale, Finland	45.21m	(148' 3")
1920	Elmer Niklander, Finland	44.68m	(146' 7")
1924	Clarence "Bud" Houser, U.S.	46.15m	(151' 4")
1928	Clarence "Bud" Houser, U.S.	47.32m	(155' 3")
1932	John Anderson, United States	49.49m	(162' 4")
1936	Ken Carpenter, United States	50.48m	(165' 7")
1948	Adolfo Consolini, Italy	52.78m	(173' 2")
1952	Sim Iness, United States	55.03m	(180' 6")
1956	Al Oerter, United States	56.36m	(184' 11")
1960	Al Oerter, United States	59.18m	(194' 2")
1964	Al Oerter, United States	61.00m	(200' 1")
1968	Al Oerter, United States	64.78m	(212' 6")
1972	Ludvik Danek, Czechoslovakia	64.40m	(211' 3")
1976	Mac Wilkins, United States	67.50m	(221' 5")
1980	Viktor Rashchupkin, USSR	66.64m	(218' 8")
1984	Rolf Dannenberg, W. Germany	66.60m	(218' 6")
1988	Jürgen Schult, E. Germany	68.82m	(225' 9")
1992	Romas Ubartas, Lithuania	65.12m	(213' 8")
1996	Lars Riedel, Germany	69.40m	(227' 8")
2000	Virgilijus Alekna, Lithuania	69.30m	(227' 4")
2004	Virgilijus Alekna, Lithuania	69.89m	(228' 9¾")*
2008	Gerd Kanter, Estonia	68.82m	(225' 9½")
2012	Robert Harting, Germany	68.27m	(224')

Hammer Throw

		Dist.	
1900	John Flanagan, United States	49.73m	(163' 1")
1904	John Flanagan, United States	51.23m	(168' 1")
1908	John Flanagan, United States	51.92m	(170' 4")
1912	Matt McGrath, United States	54.74m	(179' 7")
1920	Pat Ryan, United States	52.875m	(173' 5¾")
1924	Fred Tootell, United States	53.295m	(174' 10")
1928	Patrick O'Callaghan, Ireland	51.39m	(168' 7")
1932	Patrick O'Callaghan, Ireland	53.92m	(176' 11")
1936	Karl Hein, Germany	56.49m	(185' 4")
1948	Imre Németh, Hungary	56.07m	(183' 11½")
1952	József Csérmák, Hungary	60.34m	(197' 11")
1956	Harold Connolly, United States	63.19m	(207' 3")
1960	Vasily Rudenkov, USSR	67.10m	(202' 0")
1964	Romuald Klim, USSR	69.74m	(228' 10")
1968	Gyula Zsivótzky, Hungary	73.36m	(240' 8")
1972	Anatoly Bondarchuk, USSR	75.50m	(247' 8")
1976	Yuri Sedykh, USSR	77.52m	(254' 4")
1980	Yuri Sedykh, USSR	81.80m	(268' 4")
1984	Juha Tiainen, Finland	78.08m	(256' 2")
1988	Sergei Litvinov, USSR	84.80m	(278' 2")*
1992	Andrey Abduvaliyev, Unified Team.	82.54m	(270' 9")
1996	Balázs Kiss, Hungary	81.24m	(266' 6")
2000	Szymon Ziolkowski, Poland	80.02m	(262' 6")
2004	Koji Murofushi, Japan	82.91m	(272')
2008	Primoz Kozmus, Slovenia	82.02m	(269' 1")
2012	Krisztián Pars, Hungary	80.59m	(264' 5")

High Jump

		Height	
1896	Ellery Clark, United States	1.81m	(5' 11¼")
1900	Irving Baxter, United States	1.90m	(6' 2¾")
1904	Samuel Jones, United States	1.80m	(5' 11")
1908	Harry Porter, United States	1.90m	(6' 2¾")
1912	Alma Richards, United States	1.93m	(6' 4")
1920	Richmond Landon, United States	1.94m	(6' 4¼")
1924	Harold Osborn, United States	1.98m	(6' 6")

High Jump

Year	Athlete	Height	
1928	Robert "Bob" King, United States...	1.94m	(6' 4¼")
1932	Duncan McNaughton, Canada......	1.97m	(6' 5½")
1936	Cornelius Johnson, United States ...	2.03m	(6' 8")
1948	John Winter, Australia	1.98m	(6' 6")
1952	Walter Davis, United States........	2.04m	(6' 8¼")
1956	Charles Dumas, United States......	2.12m	(6' 11½")
1960	Robert Shavlakadze, USSR........	2.16m	(7' 1")
1964	Valery Brumel, USSR.............	2.18m	(7' 1¾")
1968	Dick Fosbury, United States	2.24m	(7' 4¼")
1972	Jüri Tarmak, USSR	2.23m	(7' 3¾")
1976	Jacek Wszola, Poland	2.25m	(7' 4½")
1980	Gerd Wessig, E. Germany.........	2.36m	(7' 8¾")
1984	Dietmar Mögenburg, W. Germany...	2.35m	(7' 8½")
1988	Gennadi Avdeyenko, USSR........	2.38m	(7' 9¾")
1992	Javier Sotomayor, Cuba...........	2.34m	(7' 8")
1996	Charles Austin, United States	2.39m	(7' 10")*
2000	Sergey Kliugin, Russia............	2.35m	(7' 8½")
2004	Stefan Holm, Sweden.............	2.36m	(7' 8¾")
2008	Andrey Silnov, Russia	2.36m	(7' 8¾")
2012	Ivan Ukhov, Russia	2.38m	(7' 9¾")

Javelin Throw

Year	Athlete	Dist.	
1908	Eric Lemming, Sweden............	54.82m	(179' 10")
1912	Eric Lemming, Sweden............	60.64m	(198' 11")
1920	Jonni Myyrä, Finland	65.78m	(215' 9¾")
1924	Jonni Myyrä, Finland	62.96m	(206' 7")
1928	Erik Lundkvist, Sweden	66.60m	(218' 6")
1932	Matti Järvinen, Finland	72.71m	(238' 6½")
1936	Gerhard Stöck, Germany	71.84m	(235' 8")
1948	Kaj Tapio Rautavaara, Finland	69.77m	(228' 11")
1952	Cy Young, United States	73.78m	(242' 1")
1956	Egil Danielsen, Norway	85.71m	(281' 2½")
1960	Viktor Tsybulenko, USSR..........	84.64m	(277' 8")
1964	Pauli Nevala, Finland	82.66m	(271' 2")
1968	Janis Lusis, USSR	90.10m	(295' 7")
1972	Klaus Wolfermann, W. Germany	90.48m	(296' 10")
1976	Miklós Németh, Hungary	94.58m	(310' 4")
1980	Dainis Kula, USSR	91.20m	(299' 2")
1984	Arto Härkönen, Finland............	86.76m	(284' 8")
1988	Tapio Korjus, Finland	84.28m	(276' 6")
1992	Jan Zelezny, Czechoslovakia.......	89.66m	(294' 2")
1996	Jan Zelezny, Czech Republic.......	88.16m	(289' 3")
2000	Jan Zelezny, Czech Republic.......	90.17m	(295' 9½")
2004	Andreas Thorkildsen, Norway	86.50m	(283' 10")
2008	Andreas Thorkildsen, Norway	90.67m	(297' 1¾")
2012	Keshorn Walcott, Trinidad and Tobago	84.58m	(277' 6")

Note: New records were kept after javelin was modified in 1986.

Long Jump

Year	Athlete	Dist.	
1896	Ellery Clark, United States	6.35m	(20' 10")
1900	Alvin Kraenzlein, United States	7.18m	(23' 6¾")
1904	Meyer Prinstein, United States	7.34m	(24' 1")
1908	Frank Irons, United States	7.48m	(24' 6½")
1912	Albert Gutterson, United States	7.60m	(24' 11¼")
1920	William Petersson, Sweden	7.15m	(23' 5½")
1924	William DeHart Hubbard, U.S.	7.45m	(24' 5¼")
1928	Ed Hamm, United States	7.73m	(25' 4½")
1932	Edward Gordon, United States	7.64m	(25' ¾")
1936	Jesse Owens, United States	8.06m	(26' 5½")
1948	Willie Steele, United States	7.82m	(25' 8")
1952	Jerome Biffle, United States	7.57m	(24' 10")
1956	Gregory Bell, United States	7.83m	(25' 8¼")
1960	Ralph Boston, United States	8.12m	(26' 7¾")
1964	Lynn Davies, Great Britain	8.07m	(26' 5¾")
1968	Bob Beamon, United States	8.90m	(29' 2½")*
1972	Randy Williams, United States	8.24m	(27' ½")
1976	Arnie Robinson, United States	8.35m	(27' 4¾")
1980	Lutz Dombrowski, E. Germany.....	8.54m	(28' ¼")
1984	Carl Lewis, United States	8.54m	(28' ¼")
1988	Carl Lewis, United States	8.72m	(28' 7½")
1992	Carl Lewis, United States	8.67m	(28' 5½")
1996	Carl Lewis, United States	8.50m	(27' 10¾")
2000	Ivan Pedroso, Cuba	8.55m	(28' ¾")
2004	Dwight Phillips, United States......	8.59m	(28' 2¼")
2008	Irving Jahir Saladino Aranda, Panama	8.34m	(27' 4¼")
2012	Greg Rutherford, Great Britain	8.31m	(27' 3¼")

Pole Vault

Year	Athlete	Height	
1896	William Welles Hoyt, United States .	3.30m	(10' 10")
1900	Irving Baxter, United States	3.30m	(10' 10")
1904	Charles Dvorak, United States	3.50m	(11' 6")
1908	Edward Cooke, United States	3.71m	(12' 2")
	Alfred Gilbert, United States (tie) ..	3.71m	(12' 2")
1912	Harry Stoddard Babcock, United States	3.95m	(12' 11½")
1920	Frank Foss, United States	4.09m	(13' 5")
1924	Lee Barnes, United States	3.95m	(12' 11½")
1928	Sabin Carr, United States	4.20m	(13' 9¼")
1932	Bill Miller, United States	4.31m	(14' 1¾")
1936	Earle Meadows, United States	4.35m	(14' 3¼")
1948	Guinn Smith, United States	4.30m	(14' 1¼")

Pole Vault

Year	Athlete	Height	
1952	Robert Richards, United States	4.55m	(14' 11¼")
1956	Robert Richards, United States	4.56m	(14' 11½")
1960	Don Bragg, United States..........	4.70m	(15' 5")
1964	Fred Hansen, United States........	5.10m	(16' 8¾")
1968	Bob Seagren, United States........	5.40m	(17' 8½")
1972	Wolfgang Nordwig, E. Germany.....	5.50m	(18' ½")
1976	Tadeusz Slusarski, Poland.........	5.50m	(18' ½")
1980	Wladyslaw Kozakiewicz, Poland	5.78m	(18' 11½")
1984	Pierre Quinon, France	5.75m	(18' 10¼")
1988	Sergei Bubka, USSR	5.90m	(19' 4¼")
1992	Maksim Tarasov, Unified Team	5.80m	(19' ¼")
1996	Jean Galfione, France	5.92m	(19' 5")
2000	Nick Hysong, United States........	5.90m	(19' 4¼")
2004	Timothy Mack, United States	5.95m	(19' 6¼")
2008	Steve Hooker, Australia	5.96m	(19' 6¾")
2012	Renaud Lavillenie, France	5.97m	(19' 7")*

Shot Put

Year	Athlete	Dist.	
1896	Robert Garrett, United States.......	11.22m	(36' 9¾")
1900	Richard Sheldon, United States	14.10m	(46' 3¼")
1904	Ralph Rose, United States.........	14.81m	(48' 7")
1908	Ralph Rose, United States.........	14.21m	(46' 7½")
1912	Pat McDonald, United States	15.34m	(50' 4")
1920	Ville Pörhölä, Finland	14.81m	(48' 7¼")
1924	Clarence "Bud" Houser, United States	14.99m	(49' 2¼")
1928	John Kuck, United States	15.87m	(52' ¾")
1932	Leo Sexton, United States	16.00m	(52' 6")
1936	Hans Woellke, Germany...........	16.20m	(53' 1¾")
1948	Wilbur Thompson, United States ...	17.12m	(56' 2")
1952	W. Parry O'Brien, United States	17.41m	(57' 1½")
1956	W. Parry O'Brien, United States	18.57m	(60' 11¼")
1960	Bill Nieder, United States	19.68m	(64' 6¾")
1964	Dallas Long, United States	20.33m	(66' 8½")
1968	Randy Matson, United States......	20.54m	(67' 4¾")
1972	Wladyslaw Komar, Poland	21.18m	(69' 6")
1976	Udo Beyer, E. Germany	21.05m	(69' ¾")
1980	Vladimir Kiselyov, USSR	21.35m	(70' ½")
1984	Alessandro Andrei, Italy	21.26m	(69' 9")
1988	Ulf Timmermann, E. Germany	22.47m	(73' 8¾")*
1992	Michael Stulce, United States	21.70m	(71' 2½")
1996	Randy Barnes, United States	21.62m	(70' 11¼")
2000	Arsi Harju, Finland	21.29m	(69' 10¼")
2004	Adam Nelson, United States[1]	21.16m	(69' 5¼")
2008	Tomasz Majewski, Poland	21.51m	(70' 6¾")
2012	Tomasz Majewski, Poland	21.89m	(71' 9¾")

(1) The Intl. Olympic Committee stripped Yuriy Bilonog, Ukraine, of the gold medal in Dec. 2012 after he failed a doping test; the medal was reallocated in May 2013.

Triple Jump

Year	Athlete	Dist.	
1896	James Connolly, United States	13.71m	(44' 11¾")
1900	Meyer Prinstein, United States	14.47m	(47' 5¾")
1904	Meyer Prinstein, United States	14.35m	(47' 1")
1908	Tim Ahearne, Gr. Brit.-Ireland	14.92m	(48' 11½")
1912	Gustaf Lindblom, Sweden	14.76m	(48' 5")
1920	Vilho Tuulos, Finland	14.505m	(47' 7")
1924	Anthony Winter, Australia..........	15.525m	(50' 11¼")
1928	Mikio Oda, Japan	15.21m	(49' 11")
1932	Chuhei Nambu, Japan	15.72m	(51' 7")
1936	Naoto Tajima, Japan	16.00m	(52' 6")
1948	Arne Ahman, Sweden............	15.40m	(50' 6¼")
1952	Adhemar Ferreira da Silva, Brazil...	16.22m	(53' 2¾")
1956	Adhemar Ferreira da Silva, Brazil...	16.35m	(53' 7¾")
1960	Jozef Schmidt, Poland	16.81m	(55' 1½")
1964	Jozef Schmidt, Poland	16.85m	(55' 3½")
1968	Viktor Saneyev, USSR	17.39m	(57' ¾")
1972	Viktor Saneyev, USSR	17.35m	(56' 11¼")
1976	Viktor Saneyev, USSR	17.29m	(56' 8¾")
1980	Jaak Uudmäe, USSR	17.35m	(56' 11")
1984	Al Joyner, United States...........	17.26m	(56' 7½")
1988	Khristo Markov, Bulgaria	17.61m	(57' 9½")
1992	Mike Conley, United States	18.17m	(59' 7½")(w)
1996	Kenny Harrison, United States	18.09m	(59' 4¼")*
2000	Jonathan Edwards, Britain	17.71m	(58' 1¼")
2004	Christian Olsson, Sweden	17.79m	(58' 4½")
2008	Nelson Evora, Portugal............	17.67m	(57' 11¾")
2012	Christian Taylor, United States.....	17.81m	(58' 5¼")

Decathlon

Year	Athlete	Points
1904	Thomas F. Kiely, Ireland...........	6,036
1912	Jim Thorpe, United States[1]........	8,412.995
1920	Helge Lovland, Norway	6,804.355
1924	Harold Osborn, United States......	7,710.775
1928	Paavo Yrjölä, Finland	8,053.29
1932	James Bausch, United States	8,462.23
1936	Glenn Morris, United States	7,900
1948	Robert Mathias, United States	7,139
1952	Robert Mathias, United States	7,887
1956	Milton Campbell, United States	7,937
1960	Rafer Johnson, United States	8,392
1964	Willi Holdorf, Germany............	7,887

	Decathlon	Points
1968	Bill Toomey, United States	8,193
1972	Nikolai Avilov, USSR	8,454
1976	Bruce Jenner, United States	8,618
1980	Daley Thompson, Great Britain	8,495
1984	Daley Thompson, Great Britain[2]	8,797
1988	Christian Schenk, E. Germany	8,488
1992	Robert Zmelik, Czechoslovakia	8,611
1996	Dan O'Brien, United States	8,824
2000	Erki Nool, Estonia	8,641

	Decathlon	Points
2004	Roman Sebrle, Czech Republic	8,893*
2008	Bryan Clay, United States	8,791
2012	Ashton Eaton, United States	8,869

Note: Event not held in 1908. (1) Thorpe had been stripped of his medal for playing pro baseball prior to the Olympics. The Intl. Olympic Committee in 1982 posthumously restored his decathlon and pentathlon gold medals. (2) Scoring change effective Apr. 1985; Thompson's readjusted score was a then-world record 8,847 pts.

Track and Field—Women

	100-Meter Run	Time
1928	Elizabeth Robinson, United States	0:12.2
1932	Stella Walsh, Poland[1]	0:11.9
1936	Helen Stephens, United States	0:11.5
1948	Fanny Blankers-Koen, Netherlands	0:11.9
1952	Marjorie Jackson, Australia	0:11.5
1956	Betty Cuthbert, Australia	0:11.5
1960	Wilma Rudolph, United States	0:11.0
1964	Wyomia Tyus, United States	0:11.4
1968	Wyomia Tyus, United States	0:11.08
1972	Renate Stecher, E. Germany	0:11.07
1976	Annegret Richter, W. Germany	0:11.08
1980	Lyudmila Kondratyeva, USSR	0:11.06
1984	Evelyn Ashford, United States	0:10:97
1988	Florence Griffith-Joyner, United States	0:10.54*
1992	Gail Devers, United States	0:10.82
1996	Gail Devers, United States	0:10.94
2000	No winner[2]	NA
2004	Yuliya Nesterenko, Belarus	0:10.93
2008	Shelly-Ann Fraser, Jamaica	0:10.78
2012	Shelly-Ann Fraser-Pryce, Jamaica	0:10.75

(1) Born Stanislawa Walasiewicz. Postmortem testing revealed Walsh possessed both male and female chromosomes. She was raised and lived as a female. (2) Marion Jones, U.S., was stripped of her gold medal in 2007 due to doping; the Intl. Olympic Committee declined to award the medal to the runner-up, who was also suspected of using performance-enhancing drugs.

	200-Meter Run	Time
1948	Fanny Blankers-Koen, Netherlands	0:24.4
1952	Marjorie Jackson, Australia	0:23.7
1956	Betty Cuthbert, Australia	0:23.4
1960	Wilma Rudolph, United States	0:24.0
1964	Edith McGuire, United States	0:23.0
1968	Irena Szewinska, Poland	0:22.5
1972	Renate Stecher, E. Germany	0:22.40
1976	Bärbel Eckert, E. Germany	0:22.37
1980	Bärbel Wöckel, E. Germany	0:22.03
1984	Valerie Brisco-Hooks, United States	0:21.81
1988	Florence Griffith-Joyner, United States	0:21.34*
1992	Gwen Torrence, United States	0:21.81
1996	Marie-Jose Perec, France	0:22.12
2000	Pauline Davis-Thompson, The Bahamas[1]	0:22.27
2004	Veronica Campbell, Jamaica	0:22.05
2008	Veronica Campbell-Brown, Jamaica	0:21.74
2012	Allyson Felix, United States	0:21.88

(1) Originally won by Marion Jones, U.S., who was stripped of the gold in 2007 due to doping.

	400-Meter Run	Time
1964	Betty Cuthbert, Australia	0:52.0
1968	Colette Besson, France	0:52.0
1972	Monika Zehrt, E. Germany	0:51.08
1976	Irena Szewinska, Poland	0:49.29
1980	Marita Koch, E. Germany	0:48.88
1984	Valerie Brisco-Hooks, United States	0:48.83
1988	Olga Bryzgina, USSR	0:48.65
1992	Marie-Jose Perec, France	0:48.83
1996	Marie-Jose Perec, France	0:48.25*
2000	Cathy Freeman, Australia	0:49.11
2004	Tonique Williams-Darling, The Bahamas	0:49.41
2008	Christine Ohuruogu, Great Britain	0:49.62
2012	Sanya Richards-Ross, United States	0:49.55

	800-Meter Run	Time
1928	Lina Radke, Germany	2:16.8
1960	Lyudmila Shevtsova, USSR	2:04.3
1964	Ann Packer, Great Britain	2:01.1
1968	Madeline Manning, United States	2:00.9
1972	Hildegard Falck, W. Germany	1:58.55
1976	Tatyana Kazankina, USSR	1:54.94
1980	Nadezhda Olizarenko, USSR	1:53.43*
1984	Doina Melinte, Romania	1:57.60
1988	Sigrun Wodars, E. Germany	1:56.10
1992	Ellen Van Langen, Netherlands	1:55.54
1996	Svetlana Masterkova, Russia	1:57.73
2000	Maria Mutola, Mozambique	1:56.15

	800-Meter Run	Time
2004	Kelly Holmes, Great Britain	1:56.38
2008	Pamela Jelimo, Kenya	1:54.87
2012	Mariya Savinova, Russia	1:56.19

	1,500-Meter Run	Time
1972	Lyudmila Bragina, USSR	4:01.04
1976	Tatyana Kazankina, USSR	4:05.48
1980	Tatyana Kazankina, USSR	3:56.06
1984	Gabriella Dorio, Italy	4:03.25
1988	Paula Ivan, Romania	3:53.96*
1992	Hassiba Boulmerka, Algeria	3:55.30
1996	Svetlana Masterkova, Russia	4:00.83
2000	Nouria Merah-Benida, Algeria	4:05.10
2004	Kelly Holmes, Great Britain	3:57.90
2008	Nancy Jebet Langat, Kenya	4:00.23
2012	Asli Cakir Alptekin, Turkey	4:10.23

	3,000-Meter Run	Time
1984	Maricica Puica, Romania	8:35.96
1988	Tatyana Samolenko, USSR	8:26.53*
1992	Elena Romanova, Unified Team	8:46.04

	3,000-Meter Steeplechase	Time
2008	Gulnara Galkina-Samitova, Russia	8:58.81*
2012	Yuliya Zaripova, Russia	9:06.72

	5,000-Meter Run	Time
1996	Wang Junxia, China	14:59.88
2000	Gabriela Szabo, Romania	14:40.79*
2004	Meseret Defar, Ethiopia	14:45.65
2008	Tirunesh Dibaba, Ethiopia	15:41.40
2012	Meseret Defar, Ethiopia	15:04.25

	10,000-Meter Run	Time
1988	Olga Boldarenko, USSR	31:05.21
1992	Derartu Tulu, Ethiopia	31:06.02
1996	Fernanda Ribeiro, Portugal	31:01.63
2000	Derartu Tulu, Ethiopia	30:17.49
2004	Xing Huina, China	30:24.36
2008	Tirunesh Dibaba, Ethiopia	29:54.66*
2012	Tirunesh Dibaba, Ethiopia	30:20.75

	Marathon	Time
1984	Joan Benoit, United States	2:24:52
1988	Rosa Mota, Portugal	2:25:40
1992	Valentina Yegorova, Unified Team	2:32:41
1996	Fatuma Roba, Ethiopia	2:26:05
2000	Naoko Takahashi, Japan	2:23:14
2004	Mizuki Noguchi, Japan	2:26:20
2008	Constantina Tomescu, Romania	2:26:44
2012	Tiki Gelana, Ethiopia	2:23:07*

	4x100-Meter Relay	Time
1928	Canada	0:48.4
1932	United States	0:46.9
1936	United States	0:46.9
1948	Netherlands	0:47.5
1952	United States	0:45.9
1956	Australia	0:44.5
1960	United States	0:44.5
1964	Poland	0:43.6
1968	United States	0:42.8
1972	West Germany	0:42.81
1976	East Germany	0:42.55
1980	East Germany	0:41.60
1984	United States	0:41.65
1988	United States	0:41.98
1992	United States	0:42.11
1996	United States	0:41.95
2000	The Bahamas	0:41.95
2004	Jamaica	0:41.73
2008	Russia	0:42.31
2012	United States	0:40.82*

	4x400-Meter Relay	Time
1972	East Germany	3:23.0
1976	East Germany	3:19.23

4x400-Meter Relay

Year	Athlete	Time
1980	USSR	3:20.2
1984	United States	3:18.29
1988	USSR	3:15.18*
1992	Unified Team	3:20.20
1996	United States	3:20.91
2000	United States[1]	3:22.62
2004	United States[2]	3:19.01
2008	United States	3:18.54
2012	United States	3:16.87

(1) Due to team member Marion Jones's doping, the U.S. was stripped of the victory in 2008, but Jones's teammates won an appeal in 2010 to have their medals restored. (2) U.S. team member Crystal Cox was stripped of her gold medal in 2012 due to doping.

20-Kilometer Walk

Year	Athlete	Time
2000	Wang Liping, China	1:29:05
2004	Athanasia Tsoumeleka, Greece	1:29:12
2008	Olga Kaniskina, Russia	1:26:31
2012	Elena Lashmanova, Russia	1:25:02*

100-Meter Hurdles

Year	Athlete	Time
1972	Annelie Ehrhardt, E. Germany	0:12.59
1976	Johanna Schaller, E. Germany	0:12.77
1980	Vera Komisova, USSR	0:12.56
1984	Benita Fitzgerald-Brown, United States	0:12.84
1988	Yordanka Donkova, Bulgaria	0:12.38
1992	Paraskevi Patoulidou, Greece	0:12.64
1996	Ludmila Engquist, Sweden	0:12.58
2000	Olga Shishigina, Kazakhstan	0:12.65
2004	Joanna Hayes, United States	0:12.37
2008	Dawn Harper, United States	0:12.54
2012	Sally Pearson, Australia	0:12.35*

400-Meter Hurdles

Year	Athlete	Time
1984	Nawal El Moutawakel, Morocco	0:54.61
1988	Debra Flintoff-King, Australia	0:53.17
1992	Sally Gunnell, Great Britain	0:53.23
1996	Deon Hemmings, Jamaica	0:52.82
2000	Irina Privalova, Russia	0:53.02
2004	Faní Halkia, Greece	0:52.82
2008	Melaine Walker, Jamaica	0:52.64*
2012	Natalya Antyukh, Russia	0:52.70

Discus Throw

Year	Athlete	Dist.	
1928	Halina Konopacka, Poland	39.62m	(130' 0")
1932	Lillian Copeland, United States	40.58m	(133' 2")
1936	Gisela Mauermayer, Germany	47.63m	(156' 3")
1948	Micheline Ostermeyer, France	41.92m	(137' 6")
1952	Nina Ponomareva, USSR	51.42m	(168' 8")
1956	Olga Fikotová, Czechoslovakia	53.69m	(176' 1¾")
1960	Nina Ponomareva, USSR	55.10m	(180' 9")
1964	Tamara Press, USSR	57.27m	(187' 10¾")
1968	Lia Manoliu, Romania	58.28m	(191' 2")
1972	Faina Melnik, USSR	66.62m	(218' 7")
1976	Evelin Jahl, E. Germany	69.00m	(226' 4")
1980	Evelin Jahl, E. Germany	69.96m	(229' 6")
1984	Ria Stalman, Netherlands	65.36m	(214' 5")
1988	Martina Hellmann, E. Germany	72.30m	(237' 2")*
1992	Maritza Martén, Cuba	70.06m	(229' 10")
1996	Ilke Wyludda, Germany	69.66m	(228' 6")
2000	Ellina Zvereva, Belarus	68.40m	(224' 5")
2004	Natalya Sadova, Russia	67.02m	(219' 8¾")
2008	Stephanie Brown Trafton, United States	64.74m	(212' 4¾")
2012	Sandra Perković, Croatia	69.11m	(226' 9")

Hammer Throw

Year	Athlete	Dist.	
2000	Kamila Skolimowska, Poland	71.16m	(233' 5¾")
2004	Olga Kuzenkova, Russia	75.02m	(246' 1")
2008	Aksana Miankova, Belarus	76.34m	(250' 5½")*
2012	Tatyana Lysenko, Russia	78.18m	(256' 6")

High Jump

Year	Athlete	Height	
1928	Ethel Catherwood, Canada	1.59m	(5' 2½")
1932	Jean Shiley, United States	1.67m	(5' 5½")
1936	Ibolya Csák, Hungary	1.60m	(5' 3")
1948	Alice Coachman, United States	1.68m	(5' 6")
1952	Esther Brand, South Africa	1.67m	(5' 5¾")
1956	Mildred McDaniel, United States	1.76m	(5' 9¼")
1960	Iolanda Balas, Romania	1.85m	(6' ¾")
1964	Iolanda Balas, Romania	1.90m	(6' 2¾")
1968	Miloslava Rezková, Czech.	1.82m	(5' 11½")
1972	Ulrike Meyfarth, W. Germany	1.92m	(6' 3½")
1976	Rosemarie Ackermann, E. Germany	1.93m	(6' 4")
1980	Sara Simeoni, Italy	1.97m	(6' 5½")
1984	Ulrike Meyfarth, W. Germany	2.02m	(6' 7½")
1988	Louise Ritter, United States	2.03m	(6' 8")
1992	Heike Henkel, Germany	2.02m	(6' 7½")

High Jump

Year	Athlete	Height	
1996	Stefka Kostadinova, Bulgaria	2.05m	(6' 8¾")
2000	Yelena Yelesina, Russia	2.01m	(6' 7")
2004	Yelena Slesarenko, Russia	2.06m	(6' 9")*
2008	Tia Hellebaut, Belgium	2.05m	(6' 8¾")
2012	Anna Chicherova, Russia	2.05m	(6' 8¾")

Javelin Throw

Year	Athlete	Dist.	
1932	"Babe" Didrikson, United States	43.68m	(143' 4")
1936	Tilly Fleischer, Germany	45.18m	(148' 3")
1948	Herma Bauma, Austria	45.57m	(149' 6")
1952	Dana Zátopková, Czechoslovakia	50.47m	(165' 7")
1956	Inese Jaunzeme, USSR	53.86m	(176' 8")
1960	Elvira Ozolina, USSR	55.98m	(183' 8")
1964	Mihaela Penes, Romania	60.54m	(198' 7")
1968	Angéla Németh, Hungary	60.36m	(198' 0")
1972	Ruth Fuchs, E. Germany	63.88m	(209' 7")
1976	Ruth Fuchs, E. Germany	65.94m	(216' 4")
1980	Maria Colón, Cuba	68.40m	(224' 5")
1984	Tessa Sanderson, Great Britain	69.56m	(228' 2")
1988	Petra Felke, E. Germany	74.68m	(245' 0")
1992	Silke Renk, Germany	68.34m	(224' 2")
1996	Heli Rantanen, Finland	67.94m	(222' 11")
2000	Trine Hattestad, Norway	68.91m	(226' 1")
2004	Osleidys Menendez, Cuba	71.53m	(234' 8")*
2008	Barbora Špotáková, Czech Republic	71.42m	(234' ¾")
2012	Barbora Špotáková, Czech Republic	69.55m	(228' 2¼")

Note: New records were kept after javelin was modified in 1999.

Long Jump

Year	Athlete	Dist.	
1948	Olga Gyarmati, Hungary	5.69m	(18' 8")
1952	Yvette Williams, New Zealand	6.24m	(20' 5¼")
1956	Elzbieta Krzesinska, Poland	6.35m	(20' 10")
1960	Vera Krepkina, USSR	6.37m	(20' 10¾")
1964	Mary Rand, Great Britain	6.76m	(22' 2¼")
1968	Viorica Viscopoleanu, Romania	6.82m	(22' 4½")
1972	Heidemarie Rosendahl, W. Ger.	6.78m	(22' 3")
1976	Angela Voigt, E. Germany	6.72m	(22' ¾")
1980	Tatyana Kolpakova, USSR	7.06m	(23' 2")
1984	Anisoara Cusmir-Stanciu, Rom.	6.96m	(22' 10")
1988	Jackie Joyner-Kersee, United States	7.40m	(24' 3½")*
1992	Heike Drechsler, Germany	7.14m	(23' 5¼")
1996	Chioma Ajunwa, Nigeria	7.12m	(23' 4¼")
2000	Heike Drechsler, Germany	6.99m	(22' 11¼")
2004	Tatyana Lebedeva, Russia	7.07m	(23' 2½")
2008	Maurren Higa Maggi, Brazil	7.04m	(23' 1¼")
2012	Brittney Reese, United States	7.12m	(23' 4¼")

Pole Vault

Year	Athlete	Height	
2000	Stacy Dragila, United States	4.60m	(15' 1")
2004	Elena Isinbaeva, Russia	4.91m	(16' 1¼')
2008	Elena Isinbaeva, Russia	5.05m	(16' 6¾")
2012	Jennifer Suhr, United States	4.75m	(15' 7")

Shot Put

Year	Athlete	Dist.	
1948	Micheline Ostermeyer, France	13.75m	(45' 1½")
1952	Galina Zybina, USSR	15.28m	(50' 1½")
1956	Tamara Tyshkevich, USSR	16.59m	(54' 5¼")
1960	Tamara Press, USSR	17.32m	(56' 10")
1964	Tamara Press, USSR	18.14m	(59' 6¼")
1968	Margitta Gummel, E. Germany	19.61m	(64' 4")
1972	Nadezhda Chizhova, USSR	21.03m	(69' 0")
1976	Ivanka Khristova, Bulgaria	21.16m	(69' 5¼")
1980	Ilona Slupianek, E. Germany	22.41m	(73' 6¼")*
1984	Claudia Losch, W. Germany	20.48m	(67' 2")
1988	Natalya Lisovskaya, USSR	22.24m	(72' 11¾")
1992	Svetlana Krivelyova, Unified Team	21.06m	(69' 1¼")
1996	Astrid Kumbernuss, Germany	20.56m	(67' 5½")
2000	Yanina Karolchik, Belarus	20.56m	(67' 5½")
2004	Yumileidi Cumbá, Cuba	19.59m	(64' 3¼")
2008	Valerie Vili, New Zealand	20.56m	(67' 5½")
2012	Valerie Adams, New Zealand	20.70m	(67' 11")

Triple Jump

Year	Athlete	Dist.	
1996	Inessa Kravets, Ukraine	15.33m	(50' 3½")
2000	Tereza Marinova, Bulgaria	15.20m	(49' 10½")
2004	Francoise Mbango Etone, Cameroon	15.30m	(50' 2¼")
2008	Francoise Mbango Etone, Cameroon	15.39m	(50' 6")*
2012	Olga Rypakova, Kazakhstan	14.98m	(49' 1¾")

Heptathlon

Year	Athlete	Points
1984	Glynis Nunn, Australia	6,390
1988	Jackie Joyner-Kersee, United States	7,291*
1992	Jackie Joyner-Kersee, United States	7,044
1996	Ghada Shouaa, Syria	6,780
2000	Denise Lewis, Great Britain	6,584
2004	Carolina Kluft, Sweden	6,952
2008	Nataliia Dobrynska, Ukraine	6,733
2012	Jessica Ennis, Great Britain	6,955

2010 Winter Olympic Games
Vancouver, BC, Canada, Feb. 12-28, 2010

More than 2,600 athletes from 82 nations met in Vancouver, BC, Canada, to compete in 86 events in the XXI Olympic Winter Games Feb. 12-28, 2010. Host nation Canada set the record for most gold medals won by a nation at a single Winter Olympics, with 14. Two of Canada's gold medals came in women's and men's hockey, the latter determined by a climactic 3-2 overtime win over the U.S. The U.S. led the overall medal count with 37. Opening ceremonies held Feb. 12 were subdued by the death of luger Nodar Kumaritashvili of Georgia, who was killed during a training run earlier that day.

Despite a well-publicized injury, U.S. alpine skier Lindsey Vonn became the first American woman to win an Olympic gold medal in the downhill event Feb. 17; Vonn also won the bronze medal in the super-G event Feb. 20. U.S. snowboarder Shaun White won his second men's halfpipe gold Feb. 17. Figure skater Evan Lysacek Feb. 18 won the first U.S. gold medal in the men's event since 1988, defeating defending Olympic champion Yevgeny Plushenko of Russia. The women's figure skating gold was awarded to South Korean Kim Yu-Na. Speedskater Apolo Ohno won one silver and two bronze medals, setting a record for a U.S. Winter Olympian with a career total of eight. One new medal event, ski cross, debuted at the Vancouver games, with the event's first gold medals awarded to Switzerland's Michael Schmid and Canada's Ashleigh McIvor.

2010 Winter Olympic Games Final Medal Standings

Country	Gold	Silver	Bronze	Total	Country	Gold	Silver	Bronze	Total
United States	9	15	13	37	Italy	1	1	3	5
Germany	10	13	7	30	Japan	0	3	2	5
Canada	14	7	5	26	Finland	0	1	4	5
Norway	9	8	6	23	Australia	2	1	0	3
Austria	4	6	6	16	Belarus	1	1	1	3
Russia	3	5	7	15	Slovakia	1	1	1	3
South Korea	6	6	2	14	Croatia	0	2	1	3
China	5	2	4	11	Slovenia	0	2	1	3
Sweden	5	2	4	11	Latvia	0	2	0	2
France	2	3	6	11	Great Britain	1	0	0	1
Switzerland	6	0	3	9	Estonia	0	1	0	1
Netherlands	4	1	3	8	Kazakhstan	0	1	0	1
Czech Republic	2	0	4	6	**Total**	**86**	**87**	**85**	**258**
Poland	1	3	2	6					

Winter Olympic Games Champions, 1924-2010

In 1992, the Unified Team represented the former Soviet republics of Russia, Ukraine, Belarus, Kazakhstan, and Uzbekistan.

Alpine Skiing

Men's Downhill

		Time
1948	Henri Oreiller, France	2:55.0
1952	Zeno Colo, Italy	2:30.8
1956	Toni Sailer, Austria	2:52.2
1960	Jean Vuarnet, France	2:06.0
1964	Egon Zimmermann, Austria	2:18.16
1968	Jean-Claude Killy, France	1:59.85
1972	Bernhard Russi, Switzerland	1:51.43
1976	Franz Klammer, Austria	1:45.73
1980	Leonhard Stock, Austria	1:45.50
1984	Bill Johnson, United States	1:45.49
1988	Pirmin Zurbriggen, Switzerland	1:59.63
1992	Patrick Ortlieb, Austria	1:50.37
1994	Tommy Moe, United States	1:45.75
1998	Jean-Luc Cretier, France	1:50.11
2002	Fritz Strobl, Austria	1:39.13
2006	Antoine Deneriaz, France	1:48.80
2010	Didier Defago, Switzerland	1:54.31

Men's Giant Slalom

		Time
1952	Stein Eriksen, Norway	2:25.0
1956	Toni Sailer, Austria	3:00.1
1960	Roger Staub, Switzerland	1:48.3
1964	Francois Bonlieu, France	1:46.71
1968	Jean-Claude Killy, France	3:29.28
1972	Gustavo Thoeni, Italy	3:09.62
1976	Heini Hemmi, Switzerland	3:26.97
1980	Ingemar Stenmark, Sweden	2:40.74
1984	Max Julen, Switzerland	2:41.18
1988	Alberto Tomba, Italy	2:06.37
1992	Alberto Tomba, Italy	2:06.98
1994	Markus Wasmeier, Germany	2:52.46
1998	Hermann Maier, Austria	2:38.51
2002	Stephan Eberharter, Austria	2:23.28
2006	Benjamin Raich, Austria	2:35.00
2010	Carlo Janka, Switzerland	2:37.83

Men's Slalom

		Time
1948	Edi Reinalter, Switzerland	2:10.3
1952	Othmar Schneider, Austria	2:00.0
1956	Toni Sailer, Austria	3:14.7
1960	Ernst Hinterseer, Austria	2:08.9
1964	Josef Stiegler, Austria	2:11.13
1968	Jean-Claude Killy, France	1:39.73
1972	Francisco Fernandez-Ochoa, Spain	1:49.27
1976	Piero Gros, Italy	2:03.29

Men's Slalom

		Time
1980	Ingemar Stenmark, Sweden	1:44.26
1984	Phil Mahre, United States	1:39.41
1988	Alberto Tomba, Italy	1:39.47
1992	Finn Christian Jagge, Norway	1:44.39
1994	Thomas Stangassinger, Austria	2:02.02
1998	Hans-Petter Buraas, Norway	1:49.31
2002	Jean-Pierre Vidal, France	1:41.06
2006	Benjamin Raich, Austria	1:43.14
2010	Giuliano Razzoli, Italy	1:39.32

Men's Super Combined

		Time
1936	Franz-Pfnuer, Germany	99.25 (pts.)
1948	Henri Oreiller, France	3.27 (pts.)
1988	Hubert Strolz, Austria	36.55 (pts.)
1992	Josef Polig, Italy	14.58 (pts.)
1994	Lasse Kjus, Norway	3:17.53
1998	Mario Reiter, Austria	3:08.06
2002	Kjetil Andre Aamodt, Norway	3:17.56
2006	Ted Ligety, United States	3:09.35
2010	Bode Miller, United States	2:44.92

Note: In 2010, a one-day super combined event replaced the traditional two-day combined event.

Men's Super Giant Slalom

		Time
1988	Franck Piccard, France	1:39.66
1992	Kjetil Andre Aamodt, Norway	1:13.04
1994	Markus Wasmeier, Germany	1:32.53
1998	Hermann Maier, Austria	1:34.82
2002	Kjetil Andre Aamodt, Norway	1:21.58
2006	Kjetil Andre Aamodt, Norway	1:30.65
2010	Aksel Lund Svindal, Norway	1:30.34

Women's Downhill

		Time
1948	Hedi Schlunegger, Switzerland	2:28.3
1952	Trude Beiser-Jochum, Austria	1:47.1
1956	Madeleine Berthod, Switzerland	1:40.7
1960	Heidi Biebl, Germany	1:37.6
1964	Christl Haas, Austria	1:55.39
1968	Olga Pall, Austria	1:40.87
1972	Marie-Theres Nadig, Switzerland	1:36.68
1976	Rosi Mittermaier, W. Germany	1:46.16
1980	Annemarie Moser-Proell, Austria	1:37.52
1984	Michela Figini, Switzerland	1:13.36
1988	Marina Kiehl, W. Germany	1:25.86
1992	Kerrin Lee-Gartner, Canada	1:52.55
1994	Katja Seizinger, Germany	1:35.93
1998	Katja Seizinger, Germany	1:28.89
2002	Carole Montillet, France	1:39.56

Women's Downhill

		Time
2006	Michaela Dorfmeister, Austria	1:56.49
2010	Lindsey Vonn, United States	1:44.19

Women's Giant Slalom[1]

		Time
1952	Andrea Mead Lawrence, United States	2:06.8
1956	Ossi Reichert, Germany	1:56.5
1960	Yvonne Ruegg, Switzerland	1:39.9
1964	Marielle Goitschel, France	1:52.24
1968	Nancy Greene, Canada	1:51.97
1972	Marie-Theres Nadig, Switzerland	1:29.90
1976	Kathy Kreiner, Canada	1:29.13
1980	Hanni Wenzel, Liechtenstein	2:41.66
1984	Debbie Armstrong, United States	2:20.98
1988	Vreni Schneider, Switzerland	2:06.49
1992	Pernilla Wiberg, Sweden	2:12.74
1994	Deborah Compagnoni, Italy	2:30.97
1998	Deborah Compagnoni, Italy	2:50.59
2002	Janica Kostelic, Croatia	2:30.01
2006	Julia Mancuso, United States	2:09.19
2010	Viktoria Rebensburg, Germany	2:27.11

(1) Beginning in 1980, the event time combined two runs.

Women's Slalom

		Time
1948	Gretchen Fraser, United States	1:57.2
1952	Andrea Mead Lawrence, United States	2:10.6
1956	Renee Colliard, Switzerland	1:52.3
1960	Anne Heggtveit, Canada	1:49.6
1964	Christine Goitschel, France	1:29.86
1968	Marielle Goitschel, France	1:25.86
1972	Barbara Ann Cochran, United States	1:31.24
1976	Rosi Mittermaier, W. Germany	1:30.54
1980	Hanni Wenzel, Liechtenstein	1:25.09
1984	Paoletta Magoni, Italy	1:36.47
1988	Vreni Schneider, Switzerland	1:36.69
1992	Petra Kronberger, Austria	1:32.68
1994	Vreni Schneider, Switzerland	1:56.01
1998	Hilde Gerg, Germany	1:32.40
2002	Janica Kostelic, Croatia	1:46.10
2006	Anja Paerson, Sweden	1:29.04
2010	Maria Riesch, Germany	1:42.89

Women's Super Combined

		Time
1936	Christl Cranz, Germany	97.06 (pts.)
1948	Trude Beiser-Jochum, Austria	6.58 (pts.)
1988	Anita Wachter, Austria	29.25 (pts.)
1992	Petra Kronberger, Austria	2.55 (pts.)
1994	Pernilla Wiberg, Sweden	3:05.16
1998	Katja Seizinger, Germany	2:40.74
2002	Janica Kostelic, Croatia	2:43.28
2006	Janica Kostelic, Croatia	2:51.08
2010	Maria Riesch, Germany	2:09.14

Note: In 2010, a one-day super combined event replaced the traditional two-day combined event.

Women's Super Giant Slalom

		Time
1988	Sigrid Wolf, Austria	1:19.03
1992	Deborah Compagnoni, Italy	1:21.22
1994	Diann Roffe (Steinrotter), United States	1:22.15
1998	Picabo Street, United States	1:18.02
2002	Daniela Ceccarelli, Italy	1:13.59
2006	Michaela Dorfmeister, Austria	1:32.47
2010	Andrea Fischbacher, Austria	1:20.14

Biathlon

Men's 10-Kilometer Sprint

		Time
1980	Frank Ullrich, E. Germany	32:10.69
1984	Eirik Kvalfoss, Norway	30:53.80
1988	Frank-Peter Roetsch, E. Germany	25:08.10
1992	Mark Kirchner, Germany	26:02.30
1994	Serguei Tchepikov, Russia	28:07.00
1998	Ole Einar Bjoerndalen, Norway	27:16.20
2002	Ole Einar Bjoerndalen, Norway	24:51.30
2006	Sven Fischer, Germany	26:11.6
2010	Vincent Jay, France	24:07.8

Men's 12.5-Kilometer Pursuit

		Time
2002	Ole Einar Bjoerndalen, Norway	32:34.6
2006	Vincent Defrasne, France	35:20.2
2010	Bjorn Ferry, Sweden	33:38.4

Men's 15-Kilometer Mass Start

		Time
2006	Michael Greis, Germany	47:20.0
2010	Evgeny Ustyugov, Russia	35.35.7

Men's 20-Kilometer Individual

		Time
1960	Klas Lestander, Sweden	1:33:21.6
1964	Vladimir Melanin, USSR	1:20:26.8
1968	Magnar Solberg, Norway	1:13:45.9
1972	Magnar Solberg, Norway	1:15:55.50
1976	Nikolai Kruglov, USSR	1:14:12.26
1980	Anatoly Aljabiev, USSR	1:08:16.31
1984	Peter Angerer, W. Germany	1:11:52.7
1988	Frank-Peter Roetsch, E. Germany	0:56:33.33
1992	Yevgeny Redkine, Unified Team	0:57:34.4
1994	Serguei Tarasov, Russia	0:57:25.3
1998	Halvard Hanevold, Norway	0:56:16.4
2002	Ole Einar Bjoerndalen, Norway	0:51:03.03
2006	Michael Greis, Germany	0:54:23.0
2010	Emil Hegle Svendsen, Norway	0:48:22.5

Men's 4x7.5-Kilometer Relay

		Time
1968	USSR, Norway, Sweden (40 km)	2:13:02.4
1972	USSR, Finland, E. Germany (40 km)	1:51:44.92
1976	USSR, Finland, E. Germany (40 km)	1:57:55.64
1980	USSR, E. Germany, W. Germany	1:34:03.27
1984	USSR, Norway, W. Germany	1:38:51.70
1988	USSR, W. Germany, Italy	1:22:30.00
1992	Germany, Unified Team, Sweden	1:24:43.50
1994	Germany, Russia, France	1:30:22.1
1998	Germany, Norway, Russia	1:19:43.3
2002	Norway, Germany, France	1:23:42.3
2006	Germany, Russia, France	1:21:51.5
2010	Norway, Austria, Russia	1:21:38.1

Women's 7.5-Kilometer Sprint

		Time
1992	Anfissa Restsova, Unified Team	24:29.2
1994	Myriam Bedard, Canada	26:08.8
1998	Galina Koukleva, Russia	23:08.0
2002	Kati Wilhelm, Germany	20:41.4
2006	Florence Baverel-Robert, France	22:31.4
2010	Anastazia Kuzmina, Slovakia	19:55.6

Women's 10-Kilometer Pursuit

		Time
2002	Olga Pyleva, Russia	31:07.7
2006	Kati Wilhelm, Germany	36:43.6
2010	Magdalena Neuner, Germany	30:16.0

Women's 12.5-Kilometer Mass Start

		Time
2006	Anna Carin Olofsson, Sweden	40:36.5
2010	Magdalena Neuner, Germany	35:19.6

Women's 15-Kilometer Individual

		Time
1992	Antje Misersky, Germany	51:47.2
1994	Myriam Bedard, Canada	52:06.6
1998	Ekaterina Dafovska, Bulgaria	54:52.0
2002	Andrea Henkel, Germany	47:30.0
2006	Svetlana Ishmouratova, Russia	49:24.1
2010	Tora Berger, Norway	40:52.8

Women's 4x6-Kilometer Relay

		Time
1992	France, Germany, Unified Team (22.5 km)	1:15:55.6
1994	Russia, Germany, France (30 km)	1:47:19.5
1998	Germany, Russia, Norway (30 km)	1:40:13.6
2002	Germany, Norway, Russia (30 km)	1:27:55.0
2006	Russia, Germany, France	1:16:12.5
2010	Russia, France, Germany	1:09:36.3

Bobsledding

(Driver in parentheses.)

2-Man Bobsled

		Time
1932	United States (Hubert Stevens)	8:14.74
1936	United States (Ivan Brown)	5:29.29
1948	Switzerland (Felix Endrich)	5:29.20
1952	Germany (Andreas Ostler)	5:24.54
1956	Italy (Dalla Costa)	5:30.14
1964	Great Britain (Anthony Nash)	4:21.90
1968	Italy (Eugenio Monti)	4:41.54
1972	W. Germany (Wolfgang Zimmerer)	4:57.07
1976	E. Germany (Meinhard Nehmer)	3:44.42
1980	Switzerland (Erich Schaerer)	4:09.36
1984	E. Germany (Wolfgang Hoppe)	3:25.56
1988	USSR (Janis Kipours)	3:54.19
1992	Switzerland (Gustav Weber)	4:03.26
1994	Switzerland (Gustav Weber)	3:30.81
1998	Canada (Pierre Lueders)	3:37.24
	Italy (Guenther Huber) (tie)	3:37.24
2002	Germany II (Christoph Langen)	3:10.11
2006	Germany (Andre Lange)	3:43.38
2010	Germany (Andre Lange)	3:26.65

4-Man Bobsled

		Time
1924	Switzerland (Eduard Scherrer)	5:45.54
1928	United States (William Fiske) (5-man)	3:20.50
1932	United States (William Fiske)	7:53.68
1936	Switzerland (Pierre Musy)	5:19.85
1948	United States (Francis Tyler)	5:20.10

4-Man Bobsled	Time
1952 Germany (Andreas Ostler)	5:07.84
1956 Switzerland (Franz Kapus)	5:10.44
1964 Canada (Victor Emery)	4:14.46
1968 Italy (Eugenio Monti) (2 races)	2:17.39
1972 Switzerland (Jean Wicki)	4:43.07
1976 E. Germany (Meinhard Nehmer)	3:40.43
1980 E. Germany (Meinhard Nehmer)	3:59.92
1984 E. Germany (Wolfgang Hoppe)	3:20.22
1988 Switzerland (Ekkehard Fasser)	3:47.51
1992 Austria (Ingo Appelt)	3:53.90
1994 Germany (Wolfgang Hoppe)	3:27.28
1998 Germany II (Christoph Langen)	2:39.41
2002 Germany II (Andre Lange)	3:07.51
2006 Germany (Andre Lange)	3:40.42
2010 United States (Steven Holcomb)	3:24.46

2-Woman Bobsled	Time
2002 United States II (Jill Bakken)	1:37.76
2006 Germany (Sandra Kiriasis)	3:49.98
2010 Canada (Kaillie Humphries)	3:32.28

Cross-Country Skiing

Men's Individual Sprint Classic	Time
2002 Tor Arne Hetland, Norway (1.5 km)	2:56.9
2006 Bjoern Lind, Sweden (1.3 km)	2:26.5
2010 Nikita Kriukov, Russia	3:36.3

Men's 10 Kilometers	Time
1992 Vegard Ulvang, Norway	27:36.0
1994 Bjoern Daehlie, Norway	24:20.1
1998 Bjoern Daehlie, Norway	27:24.5
2002 Thomas Alsgaard, Norway	49:48.9
Frode Estil, Norway (tie)[1]	49:48.9

(1) Both awarded gold after Johann Muehlegg of Spain was stripped of gold for a drug offense.

Men's 15-Kilometer Free	Time
1924 Thorleif Haug, Norway	1:14:31
1928 Johan Grottumsbraaten, Norway	1:37:01
1932 Sven Utterstrom, Sweden	1:23:07
1936 Erik-August Larsson, Sweden	1:14:38
1948 Martin Lundstrom, Sweden	1:13:50
1952 Hallgeir Brenden, Norway	1:01:34
1956 Hallgeir Brenden, Norway	0:49:39.0
1960 Haakon Brusveen, Norway	0:51:55.5
1964 Eero Maentyranta, Finland	0:50:54.1
1968 Harald Groenningen, Norway	0:47:54.2
1972 Sven-Ake Lundback, Sweden	0:45:28.24
1976 Nikolai Balukov, USSR	0:43:58.47
1980 Thomas Wassberg, Sweden	0:41:57.63
1984 Gunde Svan, Sweden	0:41:25.6
1988 Mikhail Deviatiarov, USSR	0:41:18.9
1992 Bjoern Daehlie, Norway	0:38:01.9
1994 Bjoern Daehlie, Norway	0:35:48.8
1998 Thomas Alsgaard, Norway	1:07:01.7
2002 Andrus Veerpalu, Estonia	0:37:07.4
2006 Andrus Veerpalu, Estonia	0:38:01.3
2010 Dario Cologna, Switzerland	0:33:36.3

Note: Approx. 18-km course 1924-52.

Men's 30-Kilometer Pursuit	Time
1956 Veikko Hakulinen, Finland	1:44:06.0
1964 Eero Maentyranta, Finland	1:30:50.7
1968 Franco Nones, Italy	1:35:39.2
1972 Vyacheslav Vedenine, USSR	1:36:31.15
1976 Sergei Saveliev, USSR	1:30:29.38
1980 Nikolai Zimyatov, USSR	1:27:02.80
1984 Nikolai Zimyatov, USSR	1:28:56.3
1988 Aleksei Prokourorov, USSR	1:24:26.3
1992 Vegard Ulvang, Norway	1:22:27.8
1994 Thomas Alsgaard, Norway	1:12:26.4
1998 Mika Myllylae, Finland	1:33:55.8
2002 Christian Hoffmann, Austria[1]	1:11:31.0
2006 Eugeni Dementiev, Russia	1:17:00.8
2010 Marcus Hellner, Sweden	1:15:11.4

(1) Awarded gold after Johann Muehlegg of Spain was stripped of gold for a drug offense.

Men's 50-Kilometer Mass Start Classic	Time
1924 Thorleif Haug, Norway	3:44:32.0
1928 Per Erik Hedlund, Sweden	4:52:03.0
1932 Veli Saarinen, Finland	4:28:00.0
1936 Elis Wiklund, Sweden	3:30:11.0
1948 Nils Karlsson, Sweden	3:47:48.0
1952 Veikko Hakulinen, Finland	3:33:33.0
1956 Sixten Jernberg, Sweden	2:50:27.0
1960 Kalevi Hamalainen, Finland	2:59:06.3
1964 Sixten Jernberg, Sweden	2:43:52.6

Men's 50-Kilometer Mass Start Classic	Time
1968 Ole Ellefsaeter, Norway	2:28:45.8
1972 Paal Tyldum, Norway	2:43:14.75
1976 Ivar Formo, Norway	2:37:30.05
1980 Nikolai Zimyatov, USSR	2:27:24.60
1984 Thomas Wassberg, Sweden	2:15:55.8
1988 Gunde Svan, Sweden	2:04:30.9
1992 Bjoern Daehlie, Norway	2:03:41.5
1994 Vladimir Smirnov, Kazakhstan	2:07:20.3
1998 Bjoern Daehlie, Norway	2:05:08.2
2002 Mikhail Ivanov, Russia	2:06:20.8
2006 Giorgio di Centa, Italy	2:06:11.8
2010 Petter Northug, Norway	2:05:35.5

Men's 4x10-Kilometer Relay	Time
1936 Finland, Norway, Sweden	2:41:33.0
1948 Sweden, Finland, Norway	2:32:08.0
1952 Finland, Norway, Sweden	2:20:16.0
1956 USSR, Finland, Sweden	2:15:30.0
1960 Finland, Norway, USSR	2:18:45.6
1964 Sweden, Finland, USSR	2:18:34.6
1968 Norway, Sweden, Finland	2:08:33.5
1972 USSR, Norway, Switzerland	2:04:47.94
1976 Finland, Norway, USSR	2:07:59.72
1980 USSR, Norway, Finland	1:57:03.46
1984 Sweden, USSR, Finland	1:55:06.30
1988 Sweden, USSR, Czechoslovakia	1:43:58.60
1992 Norway, Italy, Finland	1:39:26.00
1994 Italy, Norway, Finland	1:41:15.00
1998 Norway, Italy, Finland	1:40:55.70
2002 Norway, Italy, Germany	1:32:45.5
2006 Italy, Germany, Sweden	1:43:45.7
2010 Sweden, Norway, Czech Republic	1:45:05.4

Men's Team Sprint	Time
2006 Bjoern Lind & Thobias Fredriksson, Sweden	17:02.9
2010 Oeystein Pettersen & Petter Northug, Norway	19:01.0

Women's Individual Sprint Classic	Time
2002 Julia Tchepalova, Russia (1.5 km)	3:10.6
2006 Chandra Crawford, Canada (1.1 km)	2:12.3
2010 Marit Bjoergen, Norway	3:39.2

Women's 5 Kilometers	Time
1964 Claudia Boyarskikh, USSR	17:50.5
1968 Toini Gustafsson, Sweden	16:45.2
1972 Galina Koulacova, USSR	17:00.50
1976 Helena Takalo, Finland	15:48.69
1980 Raisa Smetanina, USSR	15:06.92
1984 Marja-Liisa Haemaelainen, Finland	17:04.0
1988 Marjo Matikainen, Finland	15:04.0
1992 Marjut Lukkarinen, Finland	14:13.8
1994 Ljubov Egorova, Russia	14:08.8
1998 Larissa Lazutina, Russia	17:37.9
2002 Beckie Scott, Canada[1]	25:09.9

(1) Awarded gold after Olga Danilova of Russia was stripped of gold and Larissa Lazutina of Russia was stripped of silver for drug offenses.

Women's 10-Kilometer Free	Time
1952 Lydia Wideman, Finland	41:40.0
1956 Lyubov Kosyreva, USSR	38:11.0
1960 Maria Gusakova, USSR	39:46.6
1964 Claudia Boyarskikh, USSR	40:24.3
1968 Toini Gustafsson, Sweden	36:46.5
1972 Galina Koulacova, USSR	34:17.82
1976 Raisa Smetanina, USSR	30:13.41
1980 Barbara Petzold, E. Germany	30:31.54
1984 Marja-Liisa Haemaelainen, Finland	31:44.2
1988 Vida Ventsene, USSR	30:08.3
1992 Lyubov Egorova, Unified Team	25:53.7
1994 Lyubov Egorova, Russia	27:30.1
1998 Larissa Lazutina, Russia	46:06.9
2002 Bente Skari, Norway	28:05.6
2006 Kristina Smigun, Estonia	27:51.4
2010 Charlotte Kalla, Sweden	24:58.4

Women's 15-Kilometer Pursuit	Time
1992 Lyubov Egorova, Unified Team	42:20.8
1994 Manuela Di Centa, Italy	39:44.5
1998 Olga Danilova, Russia	46:55.4
2002 Stefania Belmondo, Italy	39:54.4
2006 Kristina Smigun, Estonia	42:48.7
2010 Marit Bjoergen, Norway	39:58.1

Women's 30-Kilometer Mass Start Classic	Time
1992 Stefania Belmondo, Italy	1:22:30.1
1994 Manuela Di Centa, Italy	1:25:41.6
1998 Julija Tchepalova, Russia	1:22:01.5

Women's 30-Kilometer Mass Start Classic	**Time**
2002 Gabriella Paruzzi, Italy	1:30:57.1
2006 Katerina Neumannova, Czech Republic	1:22:25.4
2010 Justyna Kowalczyk, Poland	1:30:33.7

Women's 4x5-Kilometer Relay	**Time**
1956 Finland, USSR, Sweden (15 km)	1:09:01.0
1960 Sweden, USSR, Finland (15 km)	1:04:21.4
1964 USSR, Sweden, Finland (15 km)	0:59:20.2
1968 Norway, Sweden, USSR (15 km)	0:57:30.0
1972 USSR, Finland, Norway (15 km)	0:48:46.15
1976 USSR, Finland, E. Germany	1:07:49.75
1980 E. Germany, USSR, Norway	1:02:11.1
1984 Norway, Czechoslovakia, Finland	1:06:49.7
1988 USSR, Norway, Finland	0:59:51.1
1992 United Team, Norway, Italy	0:59:34.8
1994 Russia, Norway, Italy	0:57:12.5
1998 Russia, Norway, Italy	0:55:13.5
2002 Germany, Norway, Switzerland	0:49:30.6
2006 Russia, Germany, Italy	0:54:47.7
2010 Norway, Germany, Finland	0:55:19.5

Women's Team Sprint	**Time**
2006 Lina Andersson & Anna Dahlberg, Sweden	16:36.9
2010 Evi Sachenbacher-Stehle & Claudia Nystad, Germany	18:03.7

Curling

Men
1998 Switzerland, Canada, Norway
2002 Norway, Canada, Switzerland
2006 Canada, Finland, United States
2010 Canada, Norway, Switzerland

Women
1998 Canada, Denmark, Sweden
2002 Britain, Switzerland, Canada
2006 Sweden, Switzerland, Canada
2010 Sweden, Canada, China

Figure Skating

Men's Singles
1908[1] Ulrich Salchow, Sweden
1920[1] Gillis Grafstrom, Sweden
1924 Gillis Grafstrom, Sweden
1928 Gillis Grafstrom, Sweden
1932 Karl Schaefer, Austria
1936 Karl Schaefer, Austria
1948 Richard Button, United States
1952 Richard Button, United States
1956 Hayes Alan Jenkins, United States
1960 David W. Jenkins, United States
1964 Manfred Schnelldorfer, Germany
1968 Wolfgang Schwartz, Austria
1972 Ondrej Nepela, Czechoslovakia
1976 John Curry, Great Britain
1980 Robin Cousins, Great Britain
1984 Scott Hamilton, United States
1988 Brian Boitano, United States
1992 Viktor Petrenko, Unified Team
1994 Aleksei Urmanov, Russia
1998 Ilya Kulik, Russia
2002 Alexei Yagudin, Russia
2006 Yevgeny Plushenko, Russia
2010 Evan Lysacek, United States
(1) Event held during Summer Olympic Games.

Women's Singles
1908[1] Madge Syers, Great Britain
1920[1] Magda Julin-Mauroy, Sweden
1924 Herma von Szabo-Planck, Austria
1928 Sonja Henie, Norway
1932 Sonja Henie, Norway
1936 Sonja Henie, Norway
1948 Barbara Ann Scott, Canada
1952 Jeanette Altwegg, Great Britain
1956 Tenley Albright, United States
1960 Carol Heiss, United States
1964 Sjoukje Dijkstra, Netherlands
1968 Peggy Fleming, United States
1972 Beatrix Schuba, Austria
1976 Dorothy Hamill, United States
1980 Anett Poetzsch, E. Germany
1984 Katarina Witt, E. Germany
1988 Katarina Witt, E. Germany
1992 Kristi Yamaguchi, United States

Women's Singles
1994 Oksana Baiul, Ukraine
1998 Tara Lipinski, United States
2002 Sarah Hughes, United States
2006 Shizuka Arakawa, Japan
2010 Kim Yu-Na, South Korea
(1) Event held during Summer Olympic Games.

Pairs
1908[1] Anna Hubler & Heinrich Burger, Germany
1920[1] Ludovika & Walter Jakobsson, Finland
1924 Helene Engelman & Alfred Berger, Austria
1928 Andree Joly & Pierre Brunet, France
1932 Andree Joly & Pierre Brunet, France
1936 Maxi Herber & Ernst Baier, Germany
1948 Micheline Lannoy & Pierre Baugniet, Belgium
1952 Ria & Paul Falk, Germany
1956 Elisabeth Schwartz & Kurt Oppelt, Austria
1964 Ludmila Beloussova & Oleg Protopopov, USSR
1968 Ludmila Beloussova & Oleg Protopopov, USSR
1972 Irina Rodnina & Alexei Ulanov, USSR
1976 Irina Rodnina & Aleksandr Zaitzev, USSR
1980 Irina Rodnina & Aleksandr Zaitzev, USSR
1984 Elena Valova & Oleg Vassiliev, USSR
1988 Ekaterina Gordeeva & Sergei Grinkov, USSR
1992 Natalia Mishkutienok & Artur Dimitriev, Unified Team
1994 Ekaterina Gordeeva & Sergei Grinkov, Russia
1998 Oksana Kazakova & Artur Dmitriev, Russia
2002 Elena Berezhnaya & Anton Sikharulidze, Russia;
     Jamie Sale & David Pelletier, Canada (tie)
2006 Tatyana Totmianina & Maxim Marinin, Russia
2010 Shen Xue & Zhao Hongbo, China
(1) Event held during Summer Olympic Games.

Ice Dancing
1976 Ludmila Pakhomova & Aleksandr Gorschkov, USSR
1980 Natalya Linichuk & Gennadi Karponosov, USSR
1984 Jayne Torvill & Christopher Dean, Great Britain
1988 Natalia Bestemianova & Andrei Bukin, USSR
1992 Marina Klimova & Sergei Ponomarenko, Unified Team
1994 Pasha Grishuk & Evgeny Platov, Russia
1998 Pasha Grishuk & Evgeny Platov, Russia
2002 Marina Anissina & Gwendal Peizerat, France
2006 Tatyana Navka & Roman Kostomarov, Russia
2010 Tessa Virtue & Scott Moir, Canada

Freestyle Skiing

Men's Aerials	**Points**
1994 Andreas Schoenbaechler, Switzerland	234.67
1998 Eric Bergoust, United States	255.64
2002 Ales Valenta, Czech Republic	257.02
2006 Xiaopeng Han, China	250.77
2010 Alexei Grishin, Belarus	248.41

Men's Moguls	**Points**
1992 Edgar Grospiron, France	25.81
1994 Jean-Luc Brassard, Canada	27.24
1998 Jonny Moseley, United States	26.93
2002 Janne Lahtela, Finland	27.97
2006 Dale Begg-Smith, Australia	26.77
2010 Alexandre Bilodeau, Canada	26.75

Men's Ski Cross
2010 Michael Schmid, Switzerland

Women's Aerials	**Points**
1994 Lina Tcherjazova, Uzbekistan	166.84
1998 Nikki Stone, United States	193.00
2002 Alisa Camplin, Australia	193.47
2006 Evelyne Leu, Switzerland	202.55
2010 Lydia Lassila, Australia	214.74

Women's Moguls	**Points**
1992 Donna Weinbrecht, United States	23.69
1994 Stine Lise Hattestad, Norway	25.97
1998 Tae Satoya, Japan	25.06
2002 Kari Traa, Norway	25.94
2006 Jennifer Heil, Canada	26.50
2010 Hannah Kearney, United States	26.63

Women's Ski Cross
2010 Ashleigh McIvor, Canada

Ice Hockey

Men
1920[1] Canada, United States, Czechoslovakia
1924 Canada, United States, Great Britain
1928 Canada, Sweden, Switzerland

Men

Year	
1932	Canada, United States, Germany
1936	Great Britain, Canada, United States
1948	Canada, Czechoslovakia, Switzerland
1952	Canada, United States, Sweden
1956	USSR, United States, Canada
1960	United States, Canada, USSR
1964	USSR, Sweden, Czechoslovakia
1968	USSR, Czechoslovakia, Canada
1972	USSR, United States, Czechoslovakia
1976	USSR, Czechoslovakia, W. Germany
1980	United States, USSR, Sweden
1984	USSR, Czechoslovakia, Sweden
1988	USSR, Finland, Sweden
1992	Unified Team, Canada, Czechoslovakia
1994	Sweden, Canada, Finland
1998	Czech Republic, Russia, Finland
2002	Canada, United States, Russia
2006	Sweden, Finland, Czech Republic
2010	Canada, United States, Finland

Women

Year	
1998	United States, Canada, Finland
2002	Canada, United States, Sweden
2006	Canada, Sweden, United States
2010	Canada, United States, Finland

(1) Event held during Summer Olympic Games.

Luge

	Men's Singles	Time
1964	Thomas Keohler, E. Germany	3:27.77
1968	Manfred Schmid, Austria	2:52.48
1972	Wolfgang Scheidel, E. Germany	3:27.58
1976	Detlef Guenther, E. Germany	3:27.688
1980	Bernhard Glass, E. Germany	2:54.796
1984	Paul Hildgartner, Italy	3:04.258
1988	Jens Mueller, E. Germany	3:05.548
1992	Georg Hackl, Germany	3:02.363
1994	Georg Hackl, Germany	3:21.571
1998	Georg Hackl, Germany	3:18.436
2002	Armin Zoeggeler, Italy	2:57.941
2006	Armin Zoeggeler, Italy	3:26.088
2010	Felix Loch, Germany	3:13.085

	Men's Doubles	Time
1964	Austria	1:41.62
1968	E. Germany	1:35.85
1972	Italy, E. Germany (tie)	1:28.35
1976	E. Germany	1:25.604
1980	E. Germany	1:19.331
1984	W. Germany	1:23.620
1988	E. Germany	1:31.940
1992	Germany	1:32.053
1994	Italy	1:36.720
1998	Germany	1:41.105
2002	Germany	1:26.082
2006	Austria	1:34.497
2010	Austria	1:22.705

	Women's Singles	Time
1964	Ortun Enderlein, Germany	3:24.67
1968	Erica Lechner, Italy	2:28.66
1972	Anna M. Muller, E. Germany	2:59.18
1976	Margit Schumann, E. Germany	2:50.621
1980	Vera Zozulya, USSR	2:36.537
1984	Steffi Martin, E. Germany	2:46.570
1988	Steffi Walter, E. Germany	3:03.973
1992	Doris Neuner, Austria	3:06.696
1994	Gerda Weissensteiner, Italy	3:15.517
1998	Silke Kraushaar, Germany	3:23.779
2002	Sylke Otto, Germany	2:52.464
2006	Sylke Otto, Germany	3:07.979
2010	Tatjana Huefner, Germany	2:46.524

Nordic Combined

Men's 7.5-Kilometer Nordic Combined

2002	Samppa Lajunen, Finland	
2006	Felix Gottwald, Austria	

Men's 15-Kilometer Nordic Combined

1924	Thorleif Haug, Norway	

Men's 15-Kilometer Nordic Combined

1928	Johan Grottumsbraaten, Norway
1932	Johan Grottumsbraaten, Norway
1936	Oddbjorn Hagen, Norway
1948	Heikki Hasu, Finland
1952	Simon Slattvik, Norway
1956	Sverre Stenersen, Norway
1960	Georg Thoma, W. Germany
1964	Tormod Knutsen, Norway
1968	Franz Keller, W. Germany
1972	Ulrich Wehling, E. Germany
1976	Ulrich Wehling, E. Germany
1980	Ulrich Wehling, E. Germany
1984	Tom Sandberg, Norway
1988	Hippolyt Kempf, Switzerland
1992	Fabrice Guy, France
1994	Fred Barre Lundberg, Norway
1998	Bjarte Engen Vik, Norway
2002	Samppa Lajunen, Finland
2006	Georg Hettich, Germany

Men's 10-Kilometer Large Hill

2010	Bill Demong, United States

Men's 10-Kilometer Normal Hill

2010	Jason Lamy Chappuis, France

4x5-Kilometer Relay

1988	W. Germany, Switzerland, Austria
1992	Japan, Norway, Austria
1994	Japan, Norway, Switzerland
1998	Norway, Finland, France
2002	Finland, Germany, Austria
2006	Austria, Germany, Finland
2010	Austria, United States, Germany

Skeleton

	Men	Time
1928	Jennison Heaton, United States	3:01.8
1948	Nino Bibbia, Italy	5:23.2
2002	Jim Shea, United States	1:41.96
2006	Duff Gibson, Canada	1:55.88
2010	Jon Montgomery, Canada	3:29.73

	Women	Time
2002	Tristan Gale, United States	1:45.11
2006	Maya Pedersen, Switzerland	1:59.83
2010	Amy Williams, Great Britain	3:35.64

Ski Jumping

	Normal Hill	Points
1964	Veikko Kankkonen, Finland	229.9
1968	Jiri Raska, Czechoslovakia	216.5
1972	Yukio Kasaya, Japan	244.2
1976	Hans-Georg Aschenbach, E. Germany	252.0
1980	Toni Innauer, Austria	266.3
1984	Jens Weissflog, E. Germany	215.2
1988	Matti Nykaenen, Finland	230.5
1992	Ernst Vettori, Austria	222.8
1994	Espen Bredesen, Norway	282.0
1998	Jani Soininen, Finland	234.5
2002	Simon Ammann, Switzerland	269.0
2006	Lars Bystoel, Norway	266.5
2010	Simon Ammann, Switzerland	276.5

	Large Hill	Points
1924	Jacob Tullin Thams, Norway	18.960
1928	Alfred Andersen, Norway	19.208
1932	Birger Ruud, Norway	228.1
1936	Birger Ruud, Norway	232.0
1948	Petter Hugsted, Norway	228.1
1952	Arnfinn Bergmann, Norway	226.0
1956	Antti Hyvarinen, Finland	227.0
1960	Helmut Recknagel, E. Germany	227.2
1964	Toralf Engan, Norway	230.7
1968	Vladimir Beloussov, USSR	231.3
1972	Wojciech Fortuna, Poland	219.9
1976	Karl Schnabl, Austria	234.8
1980	Jouko Tormanen, Finland	271.0
1984	Matti Nykaenen, Finland	231.2
1988	Matti Nykaenen, Finland	224.0

Large Hill		Points
1992	Toni Nieminen, Finland.	239.5
1994	Jens Weissflog, Germany.	274.5
1998	Kazuyoshi Funaki, Japan.	272.3
2002	Simon Ammann, Switzerland.	281.4
2006	Thomas Morgenstern, Austria	276.9
2010	Simon Ammann, Switzerland.	283.6

Team Large Hill		Points
1988	Finland, Yugoslavia, Norway	634.4
1992	Finland, Austria, Czechoslovakia	644.4
1994	Germany, Japan, Austria	970.1
1998	Japan, Germany, Austria	933.0
2002	Germany, Finland, Slovenia	974.1
2006	Austria, Finland, Norway.	984.0
2010	Austria, Germany, Norway	1,107.9

Snowboarding

Men's Halfpipe		Points
1998	Gian Simmen, Switzerland	85.2
2002	Ross Powers, United States	46.1
2006	Shaun White, United States	46.8
2010	Shaun White, United States	48.4

Men's Parallel Giant Slalom

1998	Ross Rebagliati, Canada
2002	Philipp Schoch, Switzerland
2006	Philipp Schoch, Switzerland
2010	Jasey Jay Anderson, Canada

Note: In 2002, the Giant Slalom became the Parallel Giant Slalom.

Men's Snowboard Cross

2006	Seth Wescott, United States
2010	Seth Wescott, United States

Women's Halfpipe		Points
1998	Nicola Thost, Germany.	74.6
2002	Kelly Clark, United States.	47.9
2006	Hannah Teter, United States	46.4
2010	Torah Bright, Australia	45.0

Women's Parallel Giant Slalom

1998	Karine Ruby, France
2002	Isabelle Blanc, France
2006	Daniela Meuli, Switzerland
2010	Nicolien Sauerbreij, Netherlands

Note: In 2002, the Giant Slalom became the Parallel Giant Slalom.

Women's Snowboard Cross

2006	Tanja Frieden, Switzerland
2010	Maelle Ricker, Canada

Speed Skating

*Olympic record

Men's 500 Meters		Time
1924	Charles Jewtraw, United States	0:44.0
1928	Thunberg, Finland; Evensen, Norway (tie)	0:43.4
1932	John A. Shea, United States.	0:43.4
1936	Ivar Ballangrud, Norway.	0:43.4
1948	Finn Helgesen, Norway	0:43.1
1952	Kenneth Henry, United States	0:43.2
1956	Evgeniy Grishin, USSR.	0:40.2
1960	Evgeniy Grishin, USSR.	0:40.2
1964	Terry McDermott, United States.	0:40.1
1968	Erhard Keller, W. Germany.	0:40.3
1972	Erhard Keller, W. Germany.	0:39.44
1976	Evgeny Kulikov, USSR.	0:39.17
1980	Eric Heiden, United States	0:38.03
1984	Sergei Fokichev, USSR	0:38.19
1988	Uwe-Jens Mey, E. Germany.	0:36.45
1992	Uwe-Jens Mey, Germany.	0:37.14
1994	Aleksandr Golubev, Russia	0:36.33
1998	Hiroyasu Shimizu, Japan.	0:35.59
2002	Casey FitzRandolph, United States	0:34.42*
2006	Joey Cheek, United States.	0:34.82
2010	Mo Tae-Bum, S. Korea	0:34.906

Men's 1,000 Meters		Time
1976	Peter Mueller, United States.	1:19.32
1980	Eric Heiden, United States.	1:15.18
1984	Gaetan Boucher, Canada.	1:15.80

Men's 1,000 Meters		Time
1988	Nikolai Guiliaev, USSR.	1:13.03
1992	Olaf Zinke, Germany	1:14.85
1994	Dan Jansen, United States.	1:12.43
1998	Ids Postma, Netherlands	1:10.64
2002	Gerard van Velde, Netherlands	1:07.18*
2006	Shani Davis, United States.	1:08.89
2010	Shani Davis, United States.	1:08.94

Men's 1,500 Meters		Time
1924	Clas Thunberg, Finland	2:20.8
1928	Clas Thunberg, Finland	2:21.1
1932	John A. Shea, United States.	2:57.5
1936	Charles Mathiesen, Norway.	2:19.2
1948	Sverre Farstad, Norway	2:17.6
1952	Hjalmar Andersen, Norway.	2:20.4
1956	Y. Grishin, USSR; Y. Mikhailov, USSR (tie)	2:08.6
1960	R. Aas, Norway; Y. Grishin, USSR (tie)	2:10.4
1964	Ants Anston, USSR	2:10.3
1968	Cornelis Verkerk, Netherlands	2:03.4
1972	Ard Schenk, Netherlands	2:02.96
1976	Jan Egil Storholt, Norway.	1:59.38
1980	Eric Heiden, United States	1:55.44
1984	Gaetan Boucher, Canada.	1:58.36
1988	Andre Hoffmann, E. Germany.	1:52.06
1992	Johann Koss, Norway.	1:54.81
1994	Johann Koss, Norway.	1:51.29
1998	Aadne Sondral, Norway.	1:47.87
2002	Derek Parra, United States	1:43.95*
2006	Enrico Fabris, Italy	1:45.97
2010	Mark Tuitert, Netherlands.	1:45.57

Men's 5,000 Meters		Time
1924	Clas Thunberg, Finland	8:39.0
1928	Ivar Ballangrud, Norway.	8:50.5
1932	Irving Jaffee, United States	9:40.8
1936	Ivar Ballangrud, Norway.	8:19.6
1948	Reidar Liaklev, Norway.	8:29.4
1952	Hjalmar Andersen, Norway	8:10.6
1956	Boris Shilkov, USSR.	7:48.7
1960	Viktor Kosichkin, USSR	7:51.3
1964	Knut Johannesen, Norway.	7:38.4
1968	F. Anton Maier, Norway.	7:22.4
1972	Ard Schenk, Netherlands	7:23.61
1976	Sten Stensen, Norway	7:24.48
1980	Eric Heiden, United States.	7:02.29
1984	Tomas Gustafson, Sweden	7:12.28
1988	Tomas Gustafson, Sweden	6:44.63
1992	Geir Karlstad, Norway	6:59.97
1994	Johann Koss, Norway	6:34.96
1998	Gianni Romme, Netherlands	6:22.20
2002	Jochem Uytdehaage, Netherlands.	6:14.66
2006	Chad Hedrick, United States	6:14.68
2010	Sven Kramer, Netherlands.	6:14.60*

Men's 10,000 Meters		Time
1924	Julius Skutnabb, Finland	18:04.8
1928	Event not held because of thawing of ice	
1932	Irving Jaffee, United States	19:13.6
1936	Ivar Ballangrud, Norway.	17:24.3
1948	Ake Seyffarth, Sweden.	17:26.3
1952	Hjalmar Andersen, Norway.	16:45.8
1956	Sigvard Ericsson, Sweden.	16:35.9
1960	Knut Johannesen, Norway.	15:46.6
1964	Jonny Nilsson, Sweden	15:50.1
1968	Jonny Hoeglin, Sweden.	15:23.6
1972	Ard Schenk, Netherlands.	15:01.35
1976	Piet Kleine, Netherlands	14:50.59
1980	Eric Heiden, United States.	14:28.13
1984	Igor Malkov, USSR.	14:39.90
1988	Tomas Gustafson, Sweden	13:48.20
1992	Bart Veldkamp, Netherlands	14:12.12
1994	Johann Koss, Norway	13:30.55
1998	Gianni Romme, Netherlands	13:15.33
2002	Jochem Uytdehaage, Netherlands.	12:58.92
2006	Bob de Jong, Netherlands.	13:01.57
2010	Lee Seung-Hoon, S. Korea	12:58.55*

Men's Team Pursuit		Time
2006	Italy, Canada, Netherlands	3:44.46
2010	Canada, United States, Netherlands.	3:41.37

Women's 500 Meters	Time
1960 Helga Haase, Germany	0:45.9
1964 Lydia Skoblikova, USSR	0:45.0
1968 Ludmila Titova, USSR	0:46.1
1972 Anne Henning, United States	0:43.33
1976 Sheila Young, United States	0:42.76
1980 Karin Enke, E. Germany	0:41.78
1984 Christa Rothenburger, E. Germany	0:41.02
1988 Bonnie Blair, United States	0:39.10
1992 Bonnie Blair, United States	0:40.33
1994 Bonnie Blair, United States	0:39.25
1998 Catriona Le May-Doan, Canada	0:38.21
2002 Catriona Le May Doan, Canada	0:37.30*
2006 Svetlana Zhurova, Russia	0:38.23
2010 Lee Sang-Hwa, S. Korea	0:37.850

Women's 1,000 Meters	Time
1960 Klara Guseva, USSR	1:34.1
1964 Lydia Skoblikova, USSR	1:33.2
1968 Carolina Geijssen, Netherlands	1:32.6
1972 Monika Pflug, W. Germany	1:31.40
1976 Tatiana Averina, USSR	1:28.43
1980 Natalya Petruseva, USSR	1:24.10
1984 Karin Enke, E. Germany	1:21.61
1988 Christa Rothenburger, E. Germany	1:17.65
1992 Bonnie Blair, United States	1:21.90
1994 Bonnie Blair, United States	1:18.74
1998 Marianne Timmer, Netherlands	1:16.51
2002 Chris Witty, United States	1:13.83*
2006 Marianne Timmer, Netherlands	1:16.05
2010 Christine Nesbitt, Canada	1:16.56

Women's 1,500 Meters	Time
1960 Lydia Skoblikova, USSR	2:52.2
1964 Lydia Skoblikova, USSR	2:22.6
1968 Kaija Mustonen, Finland	2:22.4
1972 Dianne Holum, United States	2:20.85
1976 Galina Stepanskaya, USSR	2:16.58
1980 Anne Borckink, Netherlands	2:10.95
1984 Karin Enke, E. Germany	2:03.42
1988 Yvonne van Gennip, Netherlands	2:00.68
1992 Jacqueline Boerner, Germany	2:05.87
1994 Emese Hunyady, Austria	2:02.19
1998 Marianne Timmer, Netherlands	1:57.58
2002 Anni Friesinger, Germany	1:54.02*
2006 Cindy Klassen, Canada	1:55.27
2010 Ireen Wust, Netherlands	1:56.89

Women's 3,000 Meters	Time
1960 Lydia Skoblikova, USSR	5:14.3
1964 Lydia Skoblikova, USSR	5:14.9
1968 Johanna Schut, Netherlands	4:56.2
1972 Christina Baas-Kaiser, Netherlands	4:52.14
1976 Tatiana Averina, USSR	4:45.19
1980 Bjoerg Eva Jensen, Norway	4:32.13
1984 Andrea Schoene, E. Germany	4:24.79
1988 Yvonne van Gennip, Netherlands	4:11.94
1992 Gunda Niemann, Germany	4:19.90
1994 Svetlana Bazhanova, Russia	4:17.43
1998 Gunda Niemann-Stirnemann, Germany	4:07.29
2002 Claudia Pechstein, Germany	3:57.70*
2006 Ireen Wust, Netherlands	4:02.43
2010 Martina Sablikova, Czech Republic	4:02.53

Women's 5,000 Meters	Time
1988 Yvonne van Gennip, Netherlands	7:14.13
1992 Gunda Niemann, Germany	7:31.57
1994 Claudia Pechstein, Germany	7:14.37
1998 Claudia Pechstein, Germany	6:59.61
2002 Claudia Pechstein, Germany	6:46.91*
2006 Clara Hughes, Canada	6:59.07
2010 Martina Sablikova, Czech Republic	6:50.91

Women's Team Pursuit	Time
2006 Germany, Canada, Russia	3:01.25
2010 Germany, Japan, Poland	3:02.82

Speed Skating (Short Track)
*Olympic record

Men's 500 Meters	Time
1998 Takafumi Nishitani, Japan	0:42.862
2002 Marc Gagnon, Canada	0:41.802
2006 Apolo Anton Ohno, United States	0:41.935
2010 Charles Hamelin, Canada	0:40.981

Men's 1,000 Meters	Time
1992 Kim Ki-Hoon, S. Korea	1:30.76
1994 Kim Ki-Hoon, S. Korea	1:34.57
1998 Dong-Sung Kim, S. Korea	1:32.375
2002 Steven Bradbury, Australia	1:29.109
2006 Hyun-Soo Ahn, S. Korea	1:26.739
2010 Lee Jung-Su, S. Korea	1:23.747*

Men's 1,500 Meters	Time
2002 Apolo Anton Ohno, United States	2:18.541
2006 Hyun-Soo Ahn, S. Korea	2:25.341
2010 Lee Jung-Su, S. Korea	2:17.611

Men's 5,000-Meter Relay	Time
1992 S. Korea, Canada, Japan	7:14.02
1994 Italy, United States, Australia	7:11.74
1998 Canada, S. Korea, China	7:06.075
2002 Canada, Italy, China	6:51.579
2006 S. Korea, Canada, United States	6:43.376*
2010 Canada, S. Korea, United States	6:44.224

Women's 500 Meters	Time
1992 Cathy Turner, United States	0:47.04
1994 Cathy Turner, United States	0:45.98
1998 Annie Perreault, Canada	0:46.568
2002 Yang Yang (A), China	0:44.187
2006 Wang Meng, China	0:44.345
2010 Wang Meng, China	0:43.048

Women's 1,000 Meters	Time
1998 Chun Lee-Kyung, S. Korea	1:42.776
2002 Yang Yang (A), China	1:36.391
2006 Sun-Yu Jin, S. Korea	1:32.859
2010 Wang Meng, China	1:29.213

Women's 1,500 Meters	Time
2002 Gi-Hyun Ko, S. Korea	2:31.581
2006 Sun-Yu Jin, S. Korea	2:23.494
2010 Zhou Yang, China	2:16.993*

Women's 3,000-Meter Relay	Time
1992 Canada, United States, Unified Team	4:36.62
1994 S. Korea, Canada, United States	4:26.64
1998 S. Korea, China, Canada	4:16.26
2002 S. Korea, China, Canada	4:12.793
2006 S. Korea, Canada, Italy	4:17.040
2010 China, Canada, United States	4:06.610*

Paralympic Games

The first Olympic Games for athletes with disabilities were held in Rome after the 1960 Summer Olympics; use of the name "paralympic" began with the 1964 games in Tokyo. The Paralympics are held by the Olympic host country in the same year and usually the same city and venue or venues. A goal of the Paralympics is to provide elite competition for athletes with functional disabilities that prevent their involvement in the Olympics. In 1976, the first Winter Paralympics were held in Ornskoldsvik, Sweden.

More than 4,250 athletes from a record 164 countries met at the XIV Paralympic Summer Games, held Aug. 29-Sept. 9, 2012, in London, England, UK. A total of 503 gold medals were awarded in 20 sports. China claimed 231 medals, nearly twice as many as host country Great Britain, which collected 120 medals. Russia finished third with 102 medals, just ahead of the U.S., in fourth with 98.

The XI Paralympic Winter Games were scheduled to be held Mar. 7-16, 2014, in Sochi, Russia. The X Paralympic Winter Games were in Mar. 12-21, 2010, in Vancouver, BC, Canada. More than 500 athletes from 44 nations competed in five sports. Russia dominated the total medal count with 38, while Germany won the most gold medals, with 13.

COLLEGE BASKETBALL

2013 Men's NCAA Tournament: Louisville Tops Michigan

The Louisville Cardinals defeated the Univ. of Michigan Wolverines, 82-76, in Atlanta, GA, to claim the NCAA Men's Division I national basketball title Apr. 8, 2013. Luke Hancock led the top-seeded Cardinals with 22 points and was named the Final Four's most outstanding player. Head coach Rick Pitino, who was voted into the Naismith Memorial Basketball Hall of Fame earlier that day, became the first coach ever to claim NCAA championships with two different schools; he also won the title with Kentucky in 1996.

NCAA Division I Basketball Champions, 1943-2013

Year	Champion	Winning coach	Final opponent	Score	Most outstanding player	Site
1943	Wyoming	Everett Shelton	Georgetown	46-34	Ken Sailors, Wyoming	New York, NY
1944	Utah	Vadal Peterson	Dartmouth	42-40[1]	Arnold Ferrin, Utah	New York, NY
1945	Oklahoma St.[2]	Henry Iba	NYU	49-45	Bob Kurland, Oklahoma St.	New York, NY
1946	Oklahoma St.[2]	Henry Iba	North Carolina	43-40	Bob Kurland, Oklahoma St.	New York, NY
1947	Holy Cross	Alvin Julian	Oklahoma	58-47	George Kaftan, Holy Cross	New York, NY
1948	Kentucky	Adolph Rupp	Baylor	58-42	Alex Groza, Kentucky	New York, NY
1949	Kentucky	Adolph Rupp	Oklahoma St.	46-36	Alex Groza, Kentucky	Seattle, WA
1950	CCNY	Nat Holman	Bradley	71-68	Irwin Dambrot, CCNY	New York, NY
1951	Kentucky	Adolph Rupp	Kansas St.	68-58	Bill Spivey, Kentucky	Minneapolis, MN
1952	Kansas	Forrest Allen	St. John's (NY)	80-63	Clyde Lovellette, Kansas	Seattle, WA
1953	Indiana	Branch McCracken	Kansas	69-68	B. H. Born, Kansas	Kansas City, MO
1954	La Salle	Kenneth Loeffler	Bradley	92-76	Tom Gola, La Salle	Kansas City, MO
1955	San Francisco	Phil Woolpert	La Salle	77-63	Bill Russell, San Francisco	Kansas City, MO
1956	San Francisco	Phil Woolpert	Iowa	83-71	Hal Lear, Temple	Evanston, IL
1957	North Carolina	Frank McGuire	Kansas	54-53[1]	Wilt Chamberlain, Kansas	Kansas City, MO
1958	Kentucky	Adolph Rupp	Seattle	84-72	Elgin Baylor, Seattle	Louisville, KY
1959	California	Pete Newell	West Virginia	71-70	Jerry West, West Virginia	Louisville, KY
1960	Ohio St.	Fred Taylor	California	75-55	Jerry Lucas, Ohio St.	San Francisco, CA
1961	Cincinnati	Edwin Jucker	Ohio St.	70-65[1]	Jerry Lucas, Ohio St.	Kansas City, MO
1962	Cincinnati	Edwin Jucker	Ohio St.	71-59	Paul Hogue, Cincinnati	Louisville, KY
1963	Loyola (IL)	George Ireland	Cincinnati	60-58[1]	Art Heyman, Duke	Louisville, KY
1964	UCLA	John Wooden	Duke	98-83	Walt Hazzard, UCLA	Kansas City, MO
1965	UCLA	John Wooden	Michigan	91-80	Bill Bradley, Princeton	Portland, OR
1966	Texas-El Paso[3]	Don Haskins	Kentucky	72-65	Jerry Chambers, Utah	College Park, MD
1967	UCLA	John Wooden	Dayton	79-64	Lew Alcindor[4], UCLA	Louisville, KY
1968	UCLA	John Wooden	North Carolina	78-55	Lew Alcindor[4], UCLA	Los Angeles, CA
1969	UCLA	John Wooden	Purdue	92-72	Lew Alcindor[4], UCLA	Louisville, KY
1970	UCLA	John Wooden	Jacksonville	80-69	Sidney Wicks, UCLA	College Park, MD
1971	UCLA	John Wooden	Villanova*	68-62	Howard Porter, Villanova*	Houston, TX
1972	UCLA	John Wooden	Florida St.	81-76	Bill Walton, UCLA	Los Angeles, CA
1973	UCLA	John Wooden	Memphis[5]	87-66	Bill Walton, UCLA	St. Louis, MO
1974	North Carolina St.	Norm Sloan	Marquette	76-64	David Thompson, NC St.	Greensboro, NC
1975	UCLA	John Wooden	Kentucky	92-85	Richard Washington, UCLA	San Diego, CA
1976	Indiana	Bob Knight	Michigan	86-68	Kent Benson, Indiana	Philadelphia, PA
1977	Marquette	Al McGuire	North Carolina	67-59	Butch Lee, Marquette	Atlanta, GA
1978	Kentucky	Joe Hall	Duke	94-88	Jack Givens, Kentucky	St. Louis, MO
1979	Michigan St.	Jud Heathcote	Indiana St.	75-64	Magic Johnson, Michigan St.	Salt Lake City, UT
1980	Louisville	Denny Crum	UCLA*	59-54	Darrell Griffith, Louisville	Indianapolis, IN
1981	Indiana	Bob Knight	North Carolina	63-50	Isiah Thomas, Indiana	Philadelphia, PA
1982	North Carolina	Dean Smith	Georgetown	63-62	James Worthy, N. Carolina	New Orleans, LA
1983	North Carolina St.	Jim Valvano	Houston	54-52	Hakeem Olajuwon, Houston	Albuquerque, NM
1984	Georgetown	John Thompson	Houston	84-75	Patrick Ewing, Georgetown	Seattle, WA
1985	Villanova	Rollie Massimino	Georgetown	66-64	Ed Pinckney, Villanova	Lexington, KY
1986	Louisville	Denny Crum	Duke	72-69	Pervis Ellison, Louisville	Dallas, TX
1987	Indiana	Bob Knight	Syracuse	74-73	Keith Smart, Indiana	New Orleans, LA
1988	Kansas	Larry Brown	Oklahoma	83-79	Danny Manning, Kansas	Kansas City, MO
1989	Michigan	Steve Fisher	Seton Hall	80-79[1]	Glen Rice, Michigan	Seattle, WA
1990	UNLV	Jerry Tarkanian	Duke	103-73	Anderson Hunt, UNLV	Denver, CO
1991	Duke	Mike Krzyzewski	Kansas	72-65	Christian Laettner, Duke	Indianapolis, IN
1992	Duke	Mike Krzyzewski	Michigan	71-51	Bobby Hurley, Duke	Minneapolis, MN
1993	North Carolina	Dean Smith	Michigan	77-71	Donald Williams, N. Carolina	New Orleans, LA
1994	Arkansas	Nolan Richardson	Duke	76-72	Corliss Williamson, Arkansas	Charlotte, NC
1995	UCLA	Jim Harrick	Arkansas	89-78	Ed O'Bannon, UCLA	Seattle, WA
1996	Kentucky	Rick Pitino	Syracuse	76-67	Tony Delk, Kentucky	E. Rutherford, NJ
1997	Arizona	Lute Olson	Kentucky	84-79[1]	Miles Simon, Arizona	Indianapolis, IN
1998	Kentucky	Tubby Smith	Utah	78-69	Jeff Sheppard, Kentucky	San Antonio, TX
1999	Connecticut	Jim Calhoun	Duke	77-74	Richard Hamilton, Connecticut	St. Petersburg, FL
2000	Michigan St.	Tom Izzo	Florida	89-76	Mateen Cleaves, Michigan St.	Indianapolis, IN
2001	Duke	Mike Krzyzewski	Arizona	82-72	Shane Battier, Duke	Minneapolis, MN
2002	Maryland	Gary Williams	Indiana	64-52	Juan Dixon, Maryland	Atlanta, GA
2003	Syracuse	Jim Boeheim	Kansas	81-78	Carmelo Anthony, Syracuse	New Orleans, LA
2004	Connecticut	Jim Calhoun	Georgia Tech	82-73	Emeka Okafor, Connecticut	San Antonio, TX
2005	North Carolina	Roy Williams	Illinois	75-70	Sean May, N. Carolina	St. Louis, MO
2006	Florida	Billy Donovan	UCLA	73-57	Joakim Noah, Florida	Indianapolis, IN
2007	Florida	Billy Donovan	Ohio St.	84-75	Corey Brewer, Florida	Atlanta, GA
2008	Kansas	Bill Self	Memphis	75-68[1]	Mario Chalmers, Kansas	San Antonio, TX
2009	North Carolina	Roy Williams	Michigan St.	89-72	Wayne Ellington, N. Carolina	Detroit, MI
2010	Duke	Mike Krzyzewski	Butler	61-59	Kyle Singler, Duke	Indianapolis, IN
2011	Connecticut	Jim Calhoun	Butler	53-41	Kemba Walker, Connecticut	Houston, TX
2012	Kentucky	John Calipari	Kansas	67-59	Anthony Davis, Kentucky	New Orleans, LA
2013	Louisville	Rick Pitino	Michigan	82-76	Luke Hancock, Louisville	Atlanta, GA

*Declared ineligible after the tournament. (1) Overtime. (2) Then known as Oklahoma A&M. (3) Then known as Texas Western. (4) Changed name to Kareem Abdul-Jabbar in 1971. (5) Then known as Memphis State.

2013 Men's NCAA Basketball Tournament

MIDWEST REGIONALS

(1) Louisville 79
(16) North Carolina A&T 48 — Louisville 82
(8) Colorado St. 84
(9) Missouri 72 — Colorado St. 56
Louisville 77

(5) Oklahoma St. 55
(12) Oregon 68 — Oregon 74
(4) St. Louis 64
(13) New Mexico St. 44 — St. Louis 57
Oregon 69
Louisville 85

(6) Memphis 54
(11) St. Mary's (CA) 52 — Memphis 48
(3) Michigan St. 65
(14) Valparaiso 54 — Michigan St. 70
Michigan St. 61
Louisville 72

(7) Creighton 67
(10) Cincinnati 63 — Creighton 50
(2) Duke 73
(15) Albany 61 — Duke 66
Duke 71
Duke 63

WEST REGIONALS

(1) Gonzaga 64
(16) Southern 58 — Gonzaga 70
(8) Pittsburgh 55
(9) Wichita St. 73 — Wichita St. 76
Wichita St. 72

(5) Wisconsin 46
(12) Mississippi 57 — Mississippi 74
(4) Kansas St. 61
(13) La Salle 63 — La Salle 76
La Salle 58
Wichita St. 70

(6) Arizona 81
(11) Belmont 64 — Arizona 74
(3) New Mexico 62
(14) Harvard 68 — Harvard 51
Arizona 70
Wichita St. 68

(7) Notre Dame 58
(10) Iowa St. 76 — Iowa St. 75
(2) Ohio St. 95
(15) Iona 70 — Ohio St. 78
Ohio St. 73
Ohio St. 66

SOUTH REGIONALS

(1) Kansas 64
(16) W. Kentucky 57 — Kansas 70
(8) North Carolina 78
(9) Villanova 71 — North Carolina 58
Kansas 85

(5) VCU 88
(12) Akron 42 — VCU 53
(4) Michigan 71
(13) S. Dakota St. 56 — Michigan 78
Michigan 87
Michigan 79

(6) UCLA 63
(11) Minnesota 83 — Minnesota 64
(3) Florida 79
(14) Northwestern St. 47 — Florida 78
Florida 62
Michigan 61

(7) San Diego St. 70
(10) Oklahoma 55 — San Diego St. 71
(2) Georgetown 68
(15) Florida-Gulf Coast 78 — Florida-Gulf Coast 81
FL-Gulf Coast 50
Florida 59

EAST REGIONALS

(1) Indiana 83
(16) James Madison 62 — Indiana 58
(8) NC State 72
(9) Temple 76 — Temple 52
Indiana 50

(5) UNLV 61
(12) California 64 — California 60
(4) Syracuse 81
(13) Montana 34 — Syracuse 66
Syracuse 61
Syracuse 55

(6) Butler 68
(11) Bucknell 56 — Butler 72
(3) Marquette 59
(14) Davidson 58 — Marquette 74
Marquette 71
Syracuse 56

(7) Illinois 57
(10) Colorado 49 — Illinois 59
(2) Miami (FL) 78
(15) Pacific 49 — Miami (FL) 63
Miami (FL) 61
Marquette 39

Louisville 82
Michigan 76

All-Time Winningest Division I College Basketball Teams

Team	Yrs	Won	Lost	Pct.	Team	Yrs	Won	Lost	Pct.	Team	Yrs	Won	Lost	Pct.
Kentucky	110	2,111	661	0.762	W. Kentucky	94	1,675	844	0.665	Utah	105	1,685	936	0.643
N. Carolina	103	2,090	745	0.737	Louisville	99	1,697	869	0.661	VCU	43	818	455	0.643
Kansas	115	2,101	812	0.721	St. John's (NY)	106	1,754	931	0.653	Murray State	88	1,501	835	0.643
UNLV	55	1,158	466	0.713	Illinois	108	1,690	910	0.650	Connecticut	110	1,589	888	0.642
Duke	108	2,001	840	0.704	Notre Dame	108	1,748	949	0.648	Indiana	113	1,719	966	0.640
Syracuse	112	1,874	832	0.693	Temple	117	1,814	992	0.646	Arkansas	90	1,556	880	0.639
UCLA	94	1,753	779	0.692	Arizona	108	1,645	900	0.646	Weber State	51	945	535	0.639

Note: Through 2012-13 season; winningest teams by percentage.

National Invitation Tournament Champions, 1938-2013

The National Invitation Tournament (NIT), first played in 1938, is the oldest U.S. basketball tournament. The first National Collegiate Athletic Association (NCAA) national championship tournament was played one year later. In Aug. 2005, the NCAA agreed to purchase the NIT from the five New York City-area colleges that had run the NIT.

Year	Champion	Year	Champion	Year	Champion	Year	Champion	Year	Champion
1938	Temple	1954	Holy Cross	1969	Temple	1984	Michigan	1999	California
1939	Long Island Univ.	1955	Duquesne	1970	Marquette	1985	UCLA	2000	Wake Forest
1940	Colorado	1956	Louisville	1971	North Carolina	1986	Ohio State	2001	Tulsa
1941	Long Island Univ.	1957	Bradley	1972	Maryland	1987	Southern Miss.	2002	Memphis
1942	West Virginia	1958	Xavier (OH)	1973	Virginia Tech	1988	Connecticut	2003	St. John's (NY)
1943	St. John's (NY)	1959	St. John's (NY)	1974	Purdue	1989	St. John's (NY)	2004	Michigan
1944	St. John's (NY)	1960	Bradley	1975	Princeton	1990	Vanderbilt	2005	South Carolina
1945	DePaul	1961	Providence	1976	Kentucky	1991	Stanford	2006	South Carolina
1946	Kentucky	1962	Dayton	1977	St. Bonaventure	1992	Virginia	2007	West Virginia
1947	Utah	1963	Providence	1978	Texas	1993	Minnesota	2008	Ohio State
1948	St. Louis	1964	Bradley	1979	Indiana	1994	Villanova	2009	Penn State
1949	San Francisco	1965	St. John's (NY)	1980	Virginia	1995	Virginia Tech	2010	Dayton
1950	CCNY	1966	Brigham Young	1981	Tulsa	1996	Nebraska	2011	Wichita State
1951	Brigham Young	1967	Southern Illinois	1982	Bradley	1997	Michigan	2012	Stanford
1952	La Salle	1968	Dayton	1983	Fresno State	1998	Minnesota	2013	Baylor
1953	Seton Hall								

John R. Wooden Award, 1977-2013

Awarded to the nation's outstanding men's college basketball player by the Los Angeles Athletic Club since 1977; awarded under the same name to women since 2004.

Year	Player, school	Year	Player, school	Year	Player, school
1977	Marques Johnson, UCLA	1993	Calbert Cheaney, Indiana	2006	(M) J. J. Redick, Duke
1978	Phil Ford, North Carolina	1994	Glenn Robinson, Purdue		(W) Seimone Augustus, LSU
1979	Larry Bird, Indiana State	1995	Ed O'Bannon, UCLA	2007	(M) Kevin Durant, Texas
1980	Darrell Griffith, Louisville	1996	Marcus Camby, Massachusetts		(W) Candace Parker, Tennessee
1981	Danny Ainge, Brigham Young	1997	Tim Duncan, Wake Forest	2008	(M) Tyler Hansbrough, N. Carolina
1982	Ralph Sampson, Virginia	1998	Antawn Jamison, North Carolina		(W) Candace Parker, Tennessee
1983	Ralph Sampson, Virginia	1999	Elton Brand, Duke	2009	(M) Blake Griffin, Oklahoma
1984	Michael Jordan, North Carolina	2000	Kenyon Martin, Cincinnati		(W) Maya Moore, Connecticut
1985	Chris Mullin, St. John's (NY)	2001	Shane Battier, Duke	2010	(M) Evan Turner, Ohio State
1986	Walter Berry, St. John's (NY)	2002	Jay Williams, Duke		(W) Tina Charles, Connecticut
1987	David Robinson, Navy	2003	T. J. Ford, Texas	2011	(M) Jimmer Fredette, Brigham Young
1988	Danny Manning, Kansas	2004	(M) Jameer Nelson, St. Joseph's		(W) Maya Moore, Connecticut
1989	Sean Elliott, Arizona		(W) Alana Beard, Duke	2012	(M) Anthony Davis, Kentucky
1990	Lionel Simmons, La Salle	2005	(M) Andrew Bogut, Utah		(W) Brittney Griner, Baylor
1991	Larry Johnson, UNLV		(W) Seimone Augustus, LSU	2013	(M) Trey Burke, Michigan
1992	Christian Laettner, Duke				(W) Brittney Griner, Baylor

Most Coaching Victories in the NCAA Basketball Tournament

Coach, school(s), first/latest appearance	Wins	Tournaments	Championships
Mike Krzyzewski, Duke, 1984/2013	82	29	4
Dean Smith, North Carolina, 1967/1997	65	27	2
Roy Williams; Kansas, North Carolina; 1990/2013	62	23	2
Jim Boeheim, Syracuse, 1977/2013	52	30	1
Jim Calhoun; Northeastern, Connecticut; 1981/2012	49	22	3
Rick Pitino; Boston, Providence, Kentucky, Louisville; 1983/2013	48	18	2
John Wooden, UCLA, 1950/1975	47	16	10
Lute Olson; Iowa, Arizona; 1979/2007	46	27	1
Bob Knight; Indiana, Texas Tech; 1973/2007	45	28	3
Denny Crum, Louisville, 1972/2000	42	23	2

Note: Through 2013 tournament. Coaches active in 2012-13 season in bold. Some records adjusted for vacated victories.

Wade Trophy, 1978-2013

Awarded by the National Assn. for Girls and Women in Sport and the Women's Basketball Coaches Assn. (WBCA) for character, leadership, and player performance.

Year	Player, school	Year	Player, school	Year	Player, school
1978	Carol Blazejowski, Montclair St.	1990	Jennifer Azzi, Stanford	2002	Sue Bird, Connecticut
1979	Nancy Lieberman, Old Dominion	1991	Daedra Charles, Tennessee	2003	Diana Taurasi, Connecticut
1980	Nancy Lieberman, Old Dominion	1992	Susan Robinson, Penn St.	2004	Alana Beard, Duke
1981	Lynette Woodard, Kansas	1993	Karen Jennings, Nebraska	2005	Seimone Augustus, LSU
1982	Pam Kelly, Louisiana Tech	1994	Carol Ann Shudlick, Minnesota	2006	Seimone Augustus, LSU
1983	LaTaunya Pollard, Long Beach St.	1995	Rebecca Lobo, Connecticut	2007	Candace Parker, Tennessee
1984	Janice Lawrence, Louisiana Tech	1996	Jennifer Rizzotti, Connecticut	2008	Candice Wiggins, Stanford
1985	Cheryl Miller, USC	1997	DeLisha Milton, Florida	2009	Maya Moore, Connecticut
1986	Kamie Ethridge, Texas	1998	Ticha Penicheiro, Old Dominion	2010	Maya Moore, Connecticut
1987	Shelly Pennefeather, Villanova	1999	Stephanie White-McCarty, Purdue	2011	Maya Moore, Connecticut
1988	Teresa Weatherspoon, Louisiana Tech	2000	Edwina Brown, Texas	2012	Brittney Griner, Baylor
1989	Clarissa Davis, Texas	2001	Jackie Stiles, SW Missouri St.	2013	Brittney Griner, Baylor

2013 Women's NCAA Basketball Tournament

OKLAHOMA REGIONAL

(1) Baylor 82
(16) Prairie View 40
Baylor 85

(8) Florida St. 60
(9) Princeton 44
Florida St. 47

Baylor 81

(5) Louisville 74
(12) Mid. Tennessee St. 49
Louisville 76

(4) Purdue 77
(13) Liberty 43
Purdue 63

Louisville 82

Louisville 86

(6) Oklahoma 78
(11) Central Mich. 73
Oklahoma 85

(3) UCLA 66
(14) Stetson 49
UCLA 72

Oklahoma 59

Louisville 64

(7) Syracuse 56
(10) Creighton 61
Creighton 52

(2) Tennessee 83
(15) Oral Roberts 62
Tennessee 68

Tennessee 74

Tennessee 78

SPOKANE REGIONAL

(1) Stanford 72
(16) Tulsa 56
Stanford 73

(8) Michigan 60
(9) Villanova 52
Michigan 40

Stanford 59

(5) Iowa St. 72
(12) Gonzaga 60
Iowa St. 60

(4) Georgia 70
(13) Montana 50
Georgia 65

Georgia 61

Georgia 62

California 57

(6) LSU 75
(11) WI-Green Bay 71
LSU 71

(3) Penn St. 85
(14) Cal Poly 55
Penn St. 66

LSU 63

(7) Texas Tech 70
(10) South Florida 71
South Florida 78

(2) California 90
(15) Fresno St. 76
California 82

California 73

California 65

Louisville 60
Connecticut 93

NORFOLK REGIONAL

(1) Notre Dame 97
(16) Tennessee-Martin 64
Notre Dame 74

(8) Miami (FL) 53
(9) Iowa 69
Iowa 47

Notre Dame 93

(5) Colorado 52
(12) Kansas 67
Kansas 75

(4) South Carolina 74
(13) South Dakota St. 52
South Carolina 69

Kansas 63

Notre Dame 87

(6) Nebraska 73
(11) Chattanooga 59
Nebraska 74

(3) Texas A&M 71
(14) Wichita St. 45
Texas A&M 63

Nebraska 45

Notre Dame 65

(7) Oklahoma St. 73
(10) DePaul 56
Oklahoma St. 59

(2) Duke 67
(15) Hampton 51
Duke 68

Duke 53

Duke 76

BRIDGEPORT REGIONAL

(1) Connecticut 105
(16) Idaho 37
Connecticut 77

(8) Vanderbilt 60
(9) St. Joseph's 54
Vanderbilt 44

Connecticut 76

(5) Michigan St. 55
(12) Marist 47
Michigan St. 49

(4) Maryland 72
(13) Quinnipiac 52
Maryland 74

Maryland 50

Connecticut 83

Connecticut 83

(6) Delaware 66
(11) West Virginia 53
Delaware 78

(3) North Carolina 59
(14) Albany 54
North Carolina 69

Delaware 62

(7) Dayton 96
(10) St. John's (NY) 90
Dayton 70

(2) Kentucky 61
(15) Navy 41
Kentucky 84

Kentucky 69

Kentucky 53

2013 Women's NCAA Tournament: UConn Conquers Again

The Univ. of Connecticut Huskies Apr. 9, 2013, defeated the Louisville Cardinals in a 93-60 blowout in New Orleans, LA, to claim the Women's Division I basketball title. UConn's eighth national title win tied an NCAA record. All of the titles were credited to head coach Geno Auriemma, who has never lost a national title game. Freshman standout Breanna Stewart scored 23 points and 9 rebounds; she was named the Final Four's most outstanding player.

NCAA Division I Women's Basketball Champions, 1982-2013

Year	Champion	Winning coach	Final opponent	Score	Most outstanding player	Site
1982	Louisiana Tech	Sonja Hogg	Cheyney	76-62	Janice Lawrence, LA Tech	Norfolk, VA
1983	USC	Linda Sharp	Louisiana Tech	69-67	Cheryl Miller, USC	Norfolk, VA
1984	USC	Linda Sharp	Tennessee	72-61	Cheryl Miller, USC	Los Angeles, CA
1985	Old Dominion	Marianne Stanley	Georgia	70-65	Tracy Claxton, Old Dominion	Austin, TX
1986	Texas	Jody Conradt	USC	97-81	Clarissa Davis, Texas	Lexington, KY
1987	Tennessee	Pat Summitt	Louisiana Tech	67-44	Tonya Edwards, Tennessee	Austin, TX
1988	Louisiana Tech	Leon Barmore	Auburn	56-54	Erica Westbrooks, LA. Tech	Tacoma, WA
1989	Tennessee	Pat Summitt	Auburn	76-60	Bridgette Gordon, Tennessee	Tacoma, WA
1990	Stanford	Tara VanDerveer	Auburn	88-81	Jennifer Azzi, Stanford	Knoxville, TN
1991	Tennessee	Pat Summitt	Virginia	70-67 (OT)	Dawn Staley, Virginia	New Orleans, LA
1992	Stanford	Tara VanDerveer	W. Kentucky	78-62	Molly Goodenbour, Stanford	Los Angeles, CA
1993	Texas Tech	Marsha Sharp	Ohio St.	84-82	Sheryl Swoopes, Texas Tech	Atlanta, GA
1994	North Carolina	Sylvia Hatchell	Louisiana Tech	60-59	Charlotte Smith, North Carolina	Richmond, VA
1995	Connecticut	Geno Auriemma	Tennessee	70-64	Rebecca Lobo, Connecticut	Minneapolis, MN
1996	Tennessee	Pat Summitt	Georgia	83-65	Michelle Marciniak, Tennessee	Charlotte, NC
1997	Tennessee	Pat Summitt	Old Dominion	68-59	Chamique Holdsclaw, Tennessee	Cincinnati, OH
1998	Tennessee	Pat Summitt	Louisiana Tech	93-75	Chamique Holdsclaw, Tennessee	Kansas City, MO
1999	Purdue	Carolyn Peck	Duke	62-45	Ukari Figgs, Purdue	San Jose, CA
2000	Connecticut	Geno Auriemma	Tennessee	71-52	Shea Ralph, Connecticut	Philadelphia, PA
2001	Notre Dame	Muffet McGraw	Purdue	68-66	Ruth Riley, Notre Dame	St. Louis, MO
2002	Connecticut	Geno Auriemma	Oklahoma	82-70	Swin Cash, Connecticut	San Antonio, TX
2003	Connecticut	Geno Auriemma	Tennessee	73-68	Diana Taurasi, Connecticut	Atlanta, GA
2004	Connecticut	Geno Auriemma	Tennessee	70-61	Diana Taurasi, Connecticut	New Orleans, LA
2005	Baylor	Kim Mulkey-Robertson	Michigan State	84-62	Sophia Young, Baylor	Indianapolis, IN
2006	Maryland	Brenda Frese	Duke	78-75 (OT)	Laura Harper, Maryland	Boston, MA
2007	Tennessee	Pat Summitt	Rutgers	59-46	Candace Parker, Tennessee	Cleveland, OH
2008	Tennessee	Pat Summitt	Stanford	64-48	Candace Parker, Tennessee	Tampa Bay, FL
2009	Connecticut	Geno Auriemma	Louisville	76-54	Tina Charles, Connecticut	St. Louis, MO
2010	Connecticut	Geno Auriemma	Stanford	53-47	Maya Moore, Connecticut	San Antonio, TX
2011	Texas A&M	Gary Blair	Notre Dame	76-70	Danielle Adams, Texas A&M	Indianapolis, IN
2012	Baylor	Kim Mulkey	Notre Dame	80-61	Brittney Griner, Baylor	Denver, CO
2013	Connecticut	Geno Auriemma	Louisville	93-60	Breanna Stewart, Connecticut	New Orleans, LA

COLLEGE FOOTBALL

2012 BCS Championship: Crimson Tide Overwhelms Notre Dame

The Univ. of Alabama Crimson Tide crushed the top-ranked Notre Dame Fighting Irish, 42-14, to win the Bowl Championship Series (BCS) national title game Jan. 7, 2013, in Miami Gardens, FL. With the blowout win, SEC Conference powerhouse 'Bama claimed its second consecutive title game—its third in four years—and record ninth national title.

National College Football Champions, 1936-2012

The official champion, as determined by the Bowl Championship Series (BCS) National Championship game (BCS No. 1 vs. BCS No. 2), is listed starting with 2006. For years preceding 2006, the unofficial champion, as selected by the AP poll of writers and USA Today/ESPN (until 1991), UPI; 1991-96, USA Today/CNN) poll of coaches, is listed. Where the polls disagreed, both teams are listed with AP winner first. The AP poll started in 1936, the UPI poll in 1950.

Year	Champion(s)	Year	Champion(s)	Year	Champion(s)	Year	Champion(s)	Year	Champion(s)
1936	Minnesota	1952	Michigan St.	1968	Ohio St.	1983	Miami (FL)	1998	Tennessee
1937	Pittsburgh	1953	Maryland	1969	Texas	1984	Brigham Young	1999	Florida St.
1938	Texas Christian	1954	Ohio St./UCLA	1970	Nebraska/Texas	1985	Oklahoma	2000	Oklahoma
1939	Texas A&M	1955	Oklahoma	1971	Nebraska	1986	Penn St.	2001	Miami (FL)
1940	Minnesota	1956	Oklahoma	1972	USC	1987	Miami (FL)	2002	Ohio St.
1941	Minnesota	1957	Auburn/Ohio St.	1973	Notre Dame/Alabama	1988	Notre Dame	2003	LSU/USC
1942	Ohio St.	1958	LSU	1974	Oklahoma/USC	1989	Miami (FL)	2004	Vacated[1]
1943	Notre Dame	1959	Syracuse	1975	Oklahoma	1990	Colorado/GA Tech	2005	Texas
1944	Army	1960	Minnesota	1976	Pittsburgh	1991	Miami (FL)/Washington	2006	Florida
1945	Army	1961	Alabama	1977	Notre Dame	1992	Alabama	2007	LSU
1946	Notre Dame	1962	USC	1978	Alabama/USC	1993	Florida St.	2008	Florida
1947	Notre Dame	1963	Texas	1979	Alabama	1994	Nebraska	2009	Alabama
1948	Michigan	1964	Alabama	1980	Georgia	1995	Nebraska	2010	Auburn
1949	Notre Dame	1965	Alabama/Mich. St.	1981	Clemson	1996	Florida	2011	Alabama
1950	Oklahoma	1966	Notre Dame	1982	Penn St.	1997	Mich./Nebraska	2012	Alabama
1951	Tennessee	1967	USC						

(1) The BCS's Presidential Oversight Committee vacated USC's 2004 championship due to rules violations.

2012 Final Standings

Bowl Championship Series		Associated Press Poll		USA Today Poll	
Rank, team	Rank, team	Rank, team	Rank, team	Rank, team	Rank, team
1. Notre Dame	14. Clemson	1. Alabama	14. LSU	1. Alabama	14. Boise State
2. Alabama	15. Northern Illinois	2. Oregon	15. Oklahoma	2. Oregon	15. Oklahoma
3. Florida	16. Nebraska	3. Ohio State	16. Utah State	3. Notre Dame	16. Northwestern
4. Oregon	17. UCLA	4. Notre Dame	17. Northwestern	4. Oregon	17. Utah State
5. Kansas State	18. Michigan	5. Georgia	18. Boise State	5. Texas A&M	18. Texas
6. Stanford	19. Boise State	6. Texas A&M	19. Texas	6. Stanford	19. Oregon State
7. Georgia	20. Northwestern	7. Stanford	20. Oregon State	7. South Carolina	20. Vanderbilt
8. LSU	21. Louisville	8. South Carolina	21. San Jose State	8. Florida State	21. San Jose State
9. Texas A&M	22. Utah State	9. Florida	22. Northern Illinois	9. Clemson	22. Cincinnati
10. South Carolina	23. Texas	10. Florida State	23. Vanderbilt	10. Florida	23. Nebraska
11. Oklahoma	24. San Jose State	11. Clemson	24. Michigan	11. Kansas State	24. Northern Illinois
12. Florida State	25. Kent State	12. Kansas State	25. Nebraska	12. LSU	25. Tulsa
13. Oregon State		13. Louisville		13. Louisville	

Note: BCS ranking is as of Dec. 2, 2012, prior to bowl games. Final AP and USA Today polls are as of Jan. 8, 2013 (after all bowl games).

Annual Results of Major Bowl Games

Dates indicate years the game was played; bowl games are generally played in late Dec. or early Jan.

Rose Bowl Results, 1935-2013

Year	Result	Year	Result	Year	Result
1935	Alabama 29, Stanford 13	1962	Minnesota 21, UCLA 3	1988	Michigan St. 20, USC 17
1936	Stanford 7, SMU 0	1963	USC 42, Wisconsin 37	1989	Michigan 22, USC 14
1937	Pittsburgh 21, Washington 0	1964	Illinois 17, Washington 7	1990	USC 17, Michigan 10
1938	California 13, Alabama 0	1965	Michigan 34, Oregon St. 7	1991	Washington 46, Iowa 34
1939	USC 7, Duke 3	1966	UCLA 14, Michigan St. 12	1992	Washington 34, Michigan 14
1940	USC 14, Tennessee 0	1967	Purdue 14, USC 13	1993	Michigan 38, Washington 31
1941	Stanford 21, Nebraska 13	1968	USC 14, Indiana 3	1994	Wisconsin 21, UCLA 16
1942	Oregon St. 20, Duke 16	1969	Ohio St. 27, USC 16	1995	Penn St. 38, Oregon 20
1943	Georgia 9, UCLA 0	1970	USC 10, Michigan 3	1996	USC 41, Northwestern 32
1944	USC 29, Washington 0	1971	Stanford 27, Ohio St. 17	1997	Ohio St. 20, Arizona St. 17
1945	USC 25, Tennessee 0	1972	Stanford 13, Michigan 12	1998	Michigan 21, Washington St. 16
1946	Alabama 34, USC 14	1973	USC 42, Ohio St. 17	1999	Wisconsin 38, UCLA 31
1947	Illinois 45, UCLA 14	1974	Ohio St. 42, USC 21	2000	Wisconsin 17, Stanford 9
1948	Michigan 49, USC 0	1975	USC 18, Ohio St. 17	2001	Washington 34, Purdue 24
1949	Northwestern 20, California 14	1976	UCLA 23, Ohio St. 10	2002	Miami (FL) 37, Nebraska 14
1950	Ohio St. 17, California 14	1977	USC 14, Michigan 6	2003	Oklahoma 34, Washington St. 14
1951	Michigan 14, California 6	1978	Washington 27, Michigan 20	2004	USC 28, Michigan 14
1952	Illinois 40, Stanford 7	1979	USC 17, Michigan 10	2005	Texas 38, Michigan 37
1953	USC 7, Wisconsin 0	1980	USC 17, Ohio St. 16	2006	Texas 41, USC 38
1954	Michigan St. 28, UCLA 20	1981	Michigan 23, Washington 6	2007	USC 32, Michigan 18
1955	Ohio St. 20, USC 7	1982	Washington 28, Iowa 0	2008	USC 49, Illinois 17
1956	Michigan St. 17, UCLA 14	1983	UCLA 24, Michigan 14	2009	USC 38, Penn St. 24
1957	Iowa 35, Oregon St. 19	1984	UCLA 45, Illinois 9	2010	Ohio St. 26, Oregon 17
1958	Ohio St. 10, Oregon 7	1985	USC 20, Ohio St. 17	2011	TCU 21, Wisconsin 19
1959	Iowa 38, California 12	1986	UCLA 45, Iowa 28	2012	Oregon 45, Wisconsin 38
1960	Washington 44, Wisconsin 8	1987	Arizona St. 22, Michigan 15	2013	Stanford 20, Wisconsin 14
1961	Washington 17, Minnesota 7				

Orange Bowl Results, 1935-2013

Year	Result	Year	Result	Year	Result
1935	(Jan.) Bucknell 26, Miami (FL) 0	1962	LSU 25, Colorado 7	1988	Miami (FL) 20, Oklahoma 14
1936	Catholic U. 20, Mississippi 19	1963	Alabama 17, Oklahoma 0	1989	Miami (FL) 23, Nebraska 3
1937	Duquesne 13, Mississippi St. 12	1964	Nebraska 13, Auburn 7	1990	Notre Dame 21, Colorado 6
1938	Auburn 6, Michigan St. 0	1965	Texas 21, Alabama 17	1991	Colorado 10, Notre Dame 9
1939	Tennessee 17, Oklahoma 0	1966	Alabama 39, Nebraska 28	1992	Miami (FL) 22, Nebraska 0
1940	Georgia Tech 21, Missouri 7	1967	Florida 27, Georgia Tech 12	1993	Florida St. 27, Nebraska 14
1941	Mississippi St. 14, Georgetown 7	1968	Oklahoma 26, Tennessee 24	1994	Florida St. 18, Nebraska 16
1942	Georgia 40, TCU 26	1969	Penn St. 15, Kansas 14	1995	Nebraska 24, Miami (FL) 17
1943	Alabama 37, Boston College 21	1970	Penn St. 10, Missouri 3	1996	Florida St. 31, Notre Dame 26
1944	LSU 19, Texas A&M 14	1971	Nebraska 17, LSU 12	1996	(Dec.) Nebraska 41, Virginia Tech 21
1945	Tulsa 26, Georgia Tech 12	1972	Nebraska 38, Alabama 6	1998	Nebraska 42, Tennessee 17
1946	Miami (FL) 13, Holy Cross 6	1973	Nebraska 40, Notre Dame 6	1999	Florida 31, Syracuse 10
1947	Rice 8, Tennessee 0	1974	Penn St. 16, LSU 9	2000	Michigan 35, Alabama 34 (OT)
1948	Georgia Tech 20, Kansas 14	1975	Notre Dame 13, Alabama 11	2001	Oklahoma 13, Florida St. 2
1949	Texas 41, Georgia 28	1976	Oklahoma 14, Michigan 6	2002	Florida 56, Maryland 23
1950	Santa Clara 21, Kentucky 13	1977	Ohio St. 27, Colorado 10	2003	USC 38, Iowa 17
1951	Clemson 15, Miami (FL) 14	1978	Arkansas 31, Oklahoma 6	2004	Miami (FL) 16, Florida St. 14
1952	Georgia Tech 17, Baylor 14	1979	Oklahoma 31, Nebraska 24	2005	USC 55, Oklahoma 19
1953	Alabama 61, Syracuse 6	1980	Oklahoma 24, Florida St. 7	2006	Penn St. 26, Florida St. 23 (3 OT)[1]
1954	Oklahoma 7, Maryland 0	1981	Oklahoma 18, Florida St. 17	2007	Louisville 24, Wake Forest 13
1955	Duke 34, Nebraska 7	1982	Clemson 22, Nebraska 15	2008	Kansas 24, Virginia Tech 21
1956	Oklahoma 20, Maryland 6	1983	Nebraska 21, LSU 20	2009	Virginia Tech 20, Cincinnati 7
1957	Colorado 27, Clemson 21	1984	Miami (FL) 31, Nebraska 30	2010	Iowa 24, Georgia Tech 14
1958	Oklahoma 48, Duke 21	1985	Washington 28, Oklahoma 17	2011	Stanford 40, Virginia Tech 12
1959	Oklahoma 21, Syracuse 6	1986	Oklahoma 25, Penn St. 10	2012	West Virginia 70, Clemson 33
1960	Georgia 14, Missouri 0	1987	Oklahoma 42, Arkansas 8	2013	Florida St. 31, Northern Illinois 10
1961	Missouri 21, Navy 14				

(1) The NCAA vacated all of Penn State's 1998-2011 victories July 23, 2012, due to a child sexual abuse scandal at the school.

Sugar Bowl Results, 1935-2013

Year	Result	Year	Result	Year	Result
1935	(Jan.) Tulane 20, Temple 14	1962	Alabama 10, Arkansas 3	1988	Syracuse 16, Auburn 16
1936	TCU 3, LSU 2	1963	Mississippi 17, Arkansas 13	1989	Florida St. 13, Auburn 7
1937	Santa Clara 21, LSU 14	1964	Alabama 12, Mississippi 7	1990	Miami (FL) 33, Alabama 25
1938	Santa Clara 6, LSU 0	1965	LSU 13, Syracuse 10	1991	Tennessee 23, Virginia 22
1939	TCU 15, Carnegie Tech 7	1966	Missouri 20, Florida 18	1992	Notre Dame 39, Florida 28
1940	Texas A&M 14, Tulane 13	1967	Alabama 34, Nebraska 7	1993	Alabama 34, Miami (FL) 13
1941	Boston College 19, Tennessee 13	1968	LSU 20, Wyoming 13	1994	Florida 41, West Virginia 7
1942	Fordham 2, Missouri 0	1969	Arkansas 16, Georgia 2	1995	(Dec.) Virginia Tech 28, Texas 10
1943	Tennessee 14, Tulsa 7	1970	Mississippi 27, Arkansas 22	1997	Florida 52, Florida St. 20
1944	Georgia Tech 20, Tulsa 18	1971	Tennessee 34, Air Force 13	1998	Florida St. 31, Ohio St. 14
1945	Duke 29, Alabama 26	1972	Oklahoma 40, Auburn 22	1999	Ohio St. 24, Texas A&M 14
1946	Oklahoma A&M 33, St. Mary's 13	1972	(Dec.) Oklahoma 14, Penn St. 0	2000	Florida St. 46, Virginia Tech 29
1947	Georgia 20, N. Carolina 10	1973	(Dec.) Notre Dame 24, Alabama 23	2001	Miami (FL) 37, Florida 20
1948	Texas 27, Alabama 7	1974	(Dec.) Nebraska 13, Florida 10	2002	LSU 47, Illinois 34
1949	Oklahoma 14, N. Carolina 6	1975	(Dec.) Alabama 13, Penn St. 6	2003	Georgia 26, Florida St. 13
1950	Oklahoma 35, LSU 0	1977	Pittsburgh 27, Georgia 3	2004	LSU 21, Oklahoma 14
1951	Kentucky 13, Oklahoma 7	1978	Alabama 35, Ohio St. 6	2005	Auburn 16, Virginia Tech 13
1952	Maryland 28, Tennessee 13	1979	Alabama 14, Penn St. 7	2006	West Virginia 38, Georgia 35
1953	Georgia Tech 24, Mississippi 7	1980	Alabama 24, Arkansas 9	2007	LSU 41, Notre Dame 14
1954	Georgia Tech 42, West Virginia 19	1981	Georgia 17, Notre Dame 10	2008	Georgia 41, Hawaii 10
1955	Navy 21, Mississippi 0	1982	Pittsburgh 24, Georgia 20	2009	Utah 31, Alabama 17
1956	Georgia Tech 7, Pittsburgh 0	1983	Penn St. 27, Georgia 23	2010	Florida 51, Cincinnati 24
1957	Baylor 13, Tennessee 7	1984	Auburn 9, Michigan 7	2011	Ohio St. 31, Arkansas 26
1958	Mississippi 39, Texas 7	1985	Nebraska 28, LSU 10	2012	Michigan 23, Virginia Tech 20
1959	LSU 7, Clemson 0	1986	Tennessee 35, Miami (FL) 7	2013	Louisville 33, Florida 23
1960	Mississippi 21, LSU 0	1987	Nebraska 30, LSU 15		
1961	Mississippi 14, Rice 6				

Other Bowl Results, Dec. 2012-Jan. 2013

Alamo Bowl, San Antonio, TX: Texas 31, Oregon St. 27
Armed Forces Bowl, Ft. Worth, TX: Rice 33, Air Force 14
BBVA Compass Bowl, Birmingham, AL: Mississippi 38, Pittsburgh 17
Beef 'O' Brady's Bowl, St. Petersburg, FL: Central Florida 38, Ball St. 17
Belk Bowl, Charlotte, NC: Cincinnati 48, Duke 34
Buffalo Wild Wings Bowl, Phoenix, AZ: Michigan St. 17, TCU 16
Capital One Bowl, Orlando, FL: Georgia 45, Nebraska 31
Chick-fil-A Bowl, Atlanta, GA: Clemson 25, LSU 24
Cotton Bowl, Dallas, TX: Texas A&M 41, Oklahoma 13
Famous Idaho Potato Bowl, Boise, ID: Utah St. 41, Toledo 15
Fiesta Bowl, Glendale, AZ: Oregon 35, Kansas St. 17

Gator Bowl, Jacksonville, FL: Northwestern 34, Mississippi St. 20
GoDaddy.com Bowl, Mobile, AL: Arkansas St. 17, Kent St. 13
Hawaii Bowl, Honolulu, HI: SMU 43, Fresno St. 10
Heart of Dallas Bowl, Dallas, TX: Oklahoma St. 58, Purdue 14
Holiday Bowl, San Diego, CA: Baylor 49, UCLA 26
Independence Bowl, Shreveport, LA: Ohio 45, LA-Monroe 14
Kraft Fight Hunger Bowl, San Francisco, CA: Arizona St. 62, Navy 28
Liberty Bowl, Memphis, TN: Tulsa 31, Iowa St. 17
Little Caesars Bowl, Detroit, MI: Central Michigan 24, Western Kentucky 21
MAACO Las Vegas Bowl, Las Vegas, NV: Boise St. 28, Washington 26
Meineke Car Care Bowl of Texas, Houston, TX: Texas Tech 34, Minnesota 31

Military Bowl, Washington, DC: San Jose St. 29, Bowling Green 20
Music City Bowl, Nashville, TN: Vanderbilt 38, North Carolina St. 24
New Mexico Bowl, Albuquerque, NM: Arizona 49, Nevada 48
New Orleans Bowl, New Orleans, LA: LA-Lafayette 43, Eastern Carolina 34
Outback Bowl, Tampa, FL: South Carolina 33, Michigan 28
Pinstripe Bowl, Bronx, NY: Syracuse 38, West Virginia 14
Poinsettia Bowl, San Diego, CA: Brigham Young 23, San Diego St. 6
Russell Athletic Bowl, Orlando, FL: Virginia Tech 13, Rutgers 10
Sun Bowl, El Paso, TX: Georgia Tech 21, USC 7

All-Time NCAA Bowl Subdivision (FBS) Statistical Leaders

Career Rushing Yards

Player, team	Yrs	Carries	Yds	Avg
Ron Dayne, Wisconsin	1996-99	1,115	6,397	5.74
Ricky Williams, Texas	1995-98	1,011	6,279	6.21
Tony Dorsett, Pittsburgh	1973-76	1,074	6,082	5.66
DeAngelo Williams, Memphis	2002-05	969	6,026	6.22
Charles White, USC	1976-79	1,023	5,598	5.47

Career Passing Yards

Player, team	Yrs	Comp/att	Yds
Case Keenum, Houston	2007-11	1,546/2,229	19,217
Timmy Chang, Hawaii	2000-04	1,388/2,436	17,072
Landry Jones, Oklahoma	2009-12	1,388/2,183	16,646
Graham Harrell, Texas Tech	2005-08	1,403/2,010	15,793
Ty Detmer, BYU	1988-91	958/1,530	15,031

Career Rushing Yards/Game (min. 2,500 yds)

Player, team	Yrs	Carries	Yds	Avg/game
Ed Marinaro, Cornell	1969-71	918	4,715	174.6
O. J. Simpson, USC	1967-68	621	3,214	164.4
Herschel Walker, Georgia	1980-82	994	5,259	159.4
Garrett Wolfe, N. Illinois	2004-06	807	5,164	156.5
LeShon Johnson, N. Illinois	1992-93	592	3,314	150.6

Career Receiving Yards

Player, team	Yrs	Rec	Yds	Avg
Trevor Insley, Nevada	1996-99	298	5,005	16.8
Ryan Broyles, Oklahoma	2008-11	349	4,586	13.1
Marcus Harris, Wyoming	1993-96	259	4,518	17.4
Rashaun Woods, Oklahoma St.	2000-03	293	4,414	15.1
Ryan Yarborough, Wyoming	1990-93	229	4,357	19.0

Note: As of end of 2012 season. Prior to 2002, postseason games were not included in NCAA final football statistics or records. All postseason games were included for the 2002 season and thereafter. Career rushing yards per game rankings do not include active players.

All-Time Bowl Subdivision (FBS) Team Won-Lost Records

Team	Yrs	W	L	T	Tot.	Pct.	Team	Yrs	W	L	T	Tot.	Pct.
Michigan	133	903	315	36	1,254	0.734	Penn St.[2]	126	715	365	41	1,121	0.656
Notre Dame	124	865	301	42	1,208	0.733	LSU	119	743	393	47	1,183	0.648
Boise St. (1996)	45	388	148	2	538	0.723	Georgia	119	759	402	54	1,215	0.647
Oklahoma	118	831	310	53	1,194	0.718	Miami (FL)	87	581	331	19	931	0.634
Texas	120	867	334	33	1,234	0.716	Florida	106	680	387	40	1,107	0.632
Ohio St.[1]	123	825	316	53	1,194	0.713	Auburn	120	714	414	47	1,175	0.628
Alabama[1]	118	827	321	43	1,191	0.712	Miami (OH)	124	668	410	44	1,122	0.615
USC[1]	120	779	313	54	1,146	0.703	Arizona St.	100	569	361	24	954	0.609
Nebraska	123	856	353	40	1,249	0.701	Washington	123	671	424	50	1,145	0.608
Tennessee	116	799	354	53	1,206	0.684	Virginia Tech	119	696	441	46	1,183	0.608
Florida St.[1]	66	485	237	17	739	0.668							

Note: As of end of 2012 season. Includes records as senior college only. Bowl and playoff games are included, and each tie game is computed as half won and half lost. Teams started with years in parentheses indicates reclassification to Bowl Subdivision (FBS), formerly Division I-A. The year in parentheses is the first year of FBS membership. Tiebreaker rule began with 1996 season. (1) Record adjusted by action of the NCAA Committee on Infractions. (2) Does not include 111 Penn St. 1998-2011 victories, which the NCAA vacated July 23, 2012.

Heisman Trophy Winners, 1935-2012

Awarded annually to the nation's outstanding college football player by the Downtown Athletic Club.

Year	Winner, school, position	Year	Winner, school, position	Year	Winner, school, position
1935	Jay Berwanger, Chicago, HB	1961	Ernest Davis, Syracuse, HB	1987	Tim Brown, Notre Dame, WR
1936	Larry Kelley, Yale, E	1962	Terry Baker, Oregon St., QB	1988	Barry Sanders, Oklahoma St., RB
1937	Clinton Frank, Yale, HB	1963	Roger Staubach, Navy, QB	1989	Andre Ware, Houston, QB
1938	David O'Brien, Texas Christian, QB	1964	John Huarte, Notre Dame, QB	1990	Ty Detmer, BYU, QB
1939	Nile Kinnick, Iowa, HB	1965	Mike Garrett, USC, HB	1991	Desmond Howard, Michigan, WR
1940	Tom Harmon, Michigan, HB	1966	Steve Spurrier, Florida, QB	1992	Gino Torretta, Miami (FL), QB
1941	Bruce Smith, Minnesota, HB	1967	Gary Beban, UCLA, QB	1993	Charlie Ward, Florida St., QB
1942	Frank Sinkwich, Georgia, HB	1968	O. J. Simpson, USC, RB	1994	Rashaan Salaam, Colorado, RB
1943	Angelo Bertelli, Notre Dame, QB	1969	Steve Owens, Oklahoma, RB	1995	Eddie George, Ohio St., RB
1944	Leslie Horvath, Ohio St., QB	1970	Jim Plunkett, Stanford, QB	1996	Danny Wuerffel, Florida, QB
1945	Felix Blanchard, Army, FB	1971	Pat Sullivan, Auburn, QB	1997	Charles Woodson, Michigan, CB
1946	Glenn Davis, Army, HB	1972	Johnny Rodgers, Nebraska, RB-WR	1998	Ricky Williams, Texas, RB
1947	John Lujack, Notre Dame, QB	1973	John Cappelletti, Penn St., RB	1999	Ron Dayne, Wisconsin, RB
1948	Doak Walker, SMU, HB	1974	Archie Griffin, Ohio St., RB	2000	Chris Weinke, Florida St., QB
1949	Leon Hart, Notre Dame, E	1975	Archie Griffin, Ohio St., RB	2001	Eric Crouch, Nebraska, QB
1950	Vic Janowicz, Ohio St., HB	1976	Tony Dorsett, Pittsburgh, RB	2002	Carson Palmer, USC, QB
1951	Richard Kazmaier, Princeton, HB	1977	Earl Campbell, Texas, RB	2003	Jason White, Oklahoma, QB
1952	Billy Vessels, Oklahoma, HB	1978	Billy Sims, Oklahoma, RB	2004	Matt Leinart, USC, QB
1953	John Lattner, Notre Dame, HB	1979	Charles White, USC, RB	2005	Reggie Bush, USC, RB[1]
1954	Alan Ameche, Wisconsin, FB	1980	George Rogers, S. Carolina, RB	2006	Troy Smith, Ohio State, QB
1955	Howard Cassady, Ohio St., HB	1981	Marcus Allen, USC, RB	2007	Tim Tebow, Florida, QB
1956	Paul Hornung, Notre Dame, QB	1982	Herschel Walker, Georgia, RB	2008	Sam Bradford, Oklahoma, QB
1957	John Crow, Texas A&M, HB	1983	Mike Rozier, Nebraska, RB	2009	Mark Ingram, Alabama, RB
1958	Pete Dawkins, Army, HB	1984	Doug Flutie, Boston College, QB	2010	Cam Newton, Auburn, QB
1959	Billy Cannon, LSU, HB	1985	Bo Jackson, Auburn, RB	2011	Robert Griffin III, Baylor, QB
1960	Joe Bellino, Navy, HB	1986	Vinny Testaverde, Miami (FL), QB	2012	Johnny Manziel, Texas A&M, QB

(1) Bush forfeited the trophy voluntarily Sept. 14, 2010, following revelations of NCAA rules violations while Bush was at USC.

All-Time Bowl Subdivision (FBS) Coaching Victories

Bobby Bowden	377	Bo Schembechler	234	Jim Sweeney	200	Johnny Majors	185
Glenn "Pop" Warner	336	**Chris Ault**	233	Dana X. Bible	198	Darrell Royal	184
Paul "Bear" Bryant	323	Hayden Fry	232	Fielding Yost	198	Dick Tomey	183
Amos Alonzo Stagg	314	Jim Tressel	229	**Dennis Franchione**	197	Gil Dobie	181
Joe Paterno	298[1]	**Steve Spurrier**	208	Dan McGugin	197	Jackie Sherrill	180
Frank Beamer	258	Jess Neely	207	Howard Jones	194	Carl Snavely	180
LaVell Edwards	257	Warren Woodson	203	John Cooper	192	Jerry Claiborne	179
Tom Osborne	255	Don Nehlen	202	John Vaught	190	Carmen Cozza	179
Lou Holtz	249	Eddie Anderson	201	George Welsh	189	Dennis Erickson	179
Woody Hayes	238	Vince Dooley	201	John Heisman	186	Ben Schwartzwalder	178
Mack Brown	236						

Note: Coaches active in 2012 shown in bold. Total victories through Jan. 8, 2013, including bowl games; coaches must have at least 10 seasons coaching Bowl Championship Series (BCS) schools to be eligible. (1) Does not include Paterno's 111 victories at Penn St., 1998-2011, which were vacated by the NCAA July 23, 2012, because of a child sexual abuse scandal at the school.

College Football Coach of the Year, 1935-2012

The Coach of the Year has been selected by the American Football Coaches Assn. (AFCA) since 1935 as well as the Football Writers Assn. of America (FWAA) since 1957. When polls disagree, both winners are indicated.

1935 Lynn Waldorf, Northwestern	1965 Tommy Prothro, UCLA (AFCA);	1989 Bill McCartney, Colorado
1936 Dick Harlow, Harvard	Duffy Daugherty, Mich. St. (FWAA)	1990 Bobby Ross, Georgia Tech
1937 Edward Mylin, Lafayette	1966 Tom Cahill, Army	1991 Don James, Washington
1938 Bill Kern, Carnegie Tech	1967 John Pont, Indiana	1992 Gene Stallings, Alabama
1939 Eddie Anderson, Iowa	1968 Joe Paterno, Penn St. (AFCA);	1993 Barry Alvarez, Wisconsin (AFCA);
1940 Clark Shaughnessy, Stanford	Woody Hayes, Ohio St. (FWAA)	Terry Bowden, Auburn (FWAA)
1941 Frank Leahy, Notre Dame	1969 Bo Schembechler, Michigan	1994 Tom Osborne, Nebraska (AFCA);
1942 Bill Alexander, Georgia Tech	1970 Charles McClendon, LSU &	Rich Brooks, Oregon (FWAA)
1943 Amos Alonzo Stagg, Pacific (CA)	Darrell Royal, Texas (AFCA);	1995 Gary Barnett, Northwestern
1944 Carroll Widdoes, Ohio St.	Alex Agase, Northwestern (FWAA)	1996 Bruce Snyder, Arizona St.
1945 Bo McMillin, Indiana	1971 Paul "Bear" Bryant, Alabama (AFCA);	1997 Mike Price, Washington St.
1946 Earl "Red" Blaik, Army	Bob Devaney, Nebraska (FWAA)	1998 Phillip Fulmer, Tennessee
1947 Fritz Crisler, Michigan	1972 John McKay, USC	1999 Frank Beamer, Virginia Tech
1948 Bennie Oosterbaan, Michigan	1973 Paul "Bear" Bryant, Alabama (AFCA);	2000 Bob Stoops, Oklahoma
1949 Bud Wilkinson, Oklahoma	Johnny Majors, Pittsburgh (FWAA)	2001 Larry Coker, Miami (FL) &
1950 Charlie Caldwell, Princeton	1974 Grant Teaff, Baylor	Ralph Friedgen, Maryland (AFCA);
1951 Chuck Taylor, Stanford	1975 Frank Kush, Arizona St. (AFCA);	Ralph Friedgen, Maryland (FWAA)
1952 Biggie Munn, Michigan St.	Woody Hayes, Ohio St. (FWAA)	2002 Jim Tressel, Ohio St.
1953 Jim Tatum, Maryland	1976 Johnny Majors, Pittsburgh	2003 Pete Carroll, USC (AFCA);
1954 Henry "Red" Sanders, UCLA	1977 Don James, Washington (AFCA);	Nick Saban, LSU (FWAA)
1955 Duffy Daugherty, Michigan St.	Lou Holtz, Arkansas (FWAA)	2004 Tommy Tuberville, Auburn (AFCA);
1956 Bowden Wyatt, Tennessee	1978 Joe Paterno, Penn St.	Urban Meyer, Utah (FWAA)
1957 Woody Hayes, Ohio St.	1979 Earle Bruce, Ohio St.	2005 Joe Paterno, Penn St. (AFCA);
1958 Paul Dietzel, LSU	1980 Vince Dooley, Georgia	Charlie Weis, Notre Dame (FWAA)
1959 Ben Schwartzwalder, Syracuse	1981 Danny Ford, Clemson	2006 Jim Grobe, Wake Forest (AFCA);
1960 Murray Warmath, Minnesota	1982 Joe Paterno, Penn St.	Greg Schiano, Rutgers (FWAA)
1961 Paul "Bear" Bryant, Alabama (AFCA);	1983 Ken Hatfield, Air Force (AFCA);	2007 Mark Mangino, Kansas
Darrell Royal, Texas (FWAA)	Howard Schnellenberger,	2008 Kyle Whittingham, Utah (AFCA);
1962 John McKay, USC	Miami (FL) (FWAA)	Nick Saban, Alabama (FWAA)
1963 Darrell Royal, Texas	1984 LaVell Edwards, Brigham Young	2009 Gary Patterson, TCU
1964 Ara Parseghian, Notre Dame &	1985 Fisher De Berry, Air Force	2010 Chip Kelly, Oregon
Frank Broyles, Arkansas (AFCA);	1986 Joe Paterno, Penn St.	2011 Les Miles, LSU (AFCA);
Ara Parseghian, Notre Dame	1987 Dick MacPherson, Syracuse	Mike Gundy, Oklahoma St. (FWAA)
(FWAA)	1988 Don Nehlen, W. Virginia (AFCA);	2012 Brian Kelly, Notre Dame
	Lou Holtz, Notre Dame (FWAA)	

NCAA Div. I-A (FBS) Football Conference Champions, 1990-2012

Atlantic Coast
1990 Georgia Tech
1991 Clemson
1992 Florida St.
1993 Florida St.
1994 Florida St.
1995 Virginia, Florida St.
1996 Florida St.
1997 Florida St.
1998 Florida St.,
   Georgia Tech
1999 Florida St.
2000 Florida St.
2001 Maryland
2002 Florida St.
2003 Florida St.
2004 Virginia Tech
2005 Florida St.
2006 Wake Forest
2007 Virginia Tech
2008 Virginia Tech
2009 Georgia Tech
2010 Virginia Tech
2011 Clemson
2012 Florida St.

Big East
1991 Miami (FL),
   Syracuse
1992 Miami (FL)
1993 West Virginia
1994 Miami (FL)
1995 Virginia Tech,
   Miami (FL)
1996 Virginia Tech,
   Miami (FL),
   Syracuse
1997 Syracuse
1998 Syracuse
1999 Virginia Tech
2000 Miami (FL)
2001 Miami (FL)
2002 Miami (FL)
2003 Miami (FL),
   West Virginia
2004 Boston Coll.,
   Pittsburgh,
   Syracuse, West
   Virginia
2005 West Virginia
2006 Louisville
2007 Connecticut,
   West Virginia
2008 Cincinnati
2009 Cincinnati
2010 Connecticut,
   Pittsburgh,
   West Virginia
2011 Cincinnati,
   Louisville,
   West Virginia
2012 Cincinnati,
   Louisville, Rutgers,
   Syracuse

Big Ten
1990 Iowa, Illinois, Mich.,
   Michigan St.
1991 Michigan
1992 Michigan
1993 Ohio St., Wisconsin
1994 Penn St.
1995 Northwestern
1996 Northwestern,
   Ohio St.
1997 Michigan

1998 Michigan, Ohio St.,
   Wisconsin
1999 Wisconsin
2000 Michigan,
   Northwestern,
   Purdue
2001 Illinois
2002 Iowa, Ohio St.
2003 Michigan
2004 Iowa, Michigan
2005 Ohio St., Penn St.[1]
2006 Ohio St.
2007 Ohio St.
2008 Ohio St., Penn St.[1]
2009 Ohio St.
2010 Michigan St.,
   Ohio St., Wisconsin
2011 Wisconsin
2012 Wisconsin

Big 12
1996 Texas
1997 Nebraska
1998 Texas A&M
1999 Nebraska
2000 Oklahoma
2001 Colorado
2002 Oklahoma
2003 Kansas St.
2004 Oklahoma
2005 Texas
2006 Oklahoma
2007 Oklahoma
2008 Oklahoma
2009 Texas
2010 Oklahoma
2011 Oklahoma St.
2012 Kansas St.

Conference USA
1996 Houston,
   Southern Miss.
1997 Southern Miss.
1998 Tulane
1999 Southern Miss.
2000 Louisville
2001 Louisville
2002 Cincinnati, TCU
2003 Southern Miss.
2004 Louisville
2005 Tulsa
2006 Houston
2007 Central Florida
2008 East Carolina
2009 East Carolina
2010 Central Florida
2011 Southern Miss.
2012 Tulsa

Mid-American
1990 Central Michigan
1991 Bowling Green
1992 Bowling Green
1993 Ball St.
1994 Central Michigan
1995 Toledo
1996 Ball St.
1997 Marshall
1998 Marshall
1999 Marshall
2000 Marshall
2001 Toledo
2002 Marshall
2003 Miami (OH)
2004 Toledo
2005 Akron
2006 Central Michigan

2007 Central Michigan
2008 Buffalo
2009 Central Michigan
2010 Miami (OH)
2011 Northern Illinois
2012 Northern Illinois

Mountain West
1999 BYU, Colorado St.,
   Utah
2000 Colorado St.
2001 BYU
2002 Colorado St.
2003 Utah
2004 Utah
2005 TCU
2006 BYU, TCU
2007 BYU
2008 Utah
2009 TCU
2010 TCU
2011 TCU
2012 Boise St., Fresno
   St., San Diego St.

Pac-12
1990 Washington
1991 Washington
1992 Stanford,
   Washington
1993 Arizona, UCLA,
   USC
1994 Oregon
1995 USC, Washington
1996 Arizona St.
1997 UCLA,
   Washington St.
1998 UCLA
1999 Stanford

2000 Oregon, Oregon St., Washington
2001 Oregon
2002 USC, Washington St.
2003 USC
2004 USC
2005 USC
2006 California, USC
2007 Arizona St., USC
2008 USC
2009 Oregon
2010 Oregon
2011 Oregon
2012 Stanford

Southeastern
1990 Tennessee
1991 Florida
1992 Alabama
1993 Florida
1994 Florida
1995 Florida
1996 Florida
1997 Tennessee
1998 Tennessee
1999 Alabama
2000 Florida
2001 LSU
2002 Georgia
2003 LSU
2004 Auburn
2005 Georgia
2006 Florida
2007 LSU
2008 Florida
2009 Alabama
2010 Auburn
2011 LSU
2012 Alabama

Sun Belt
2001 Mid. Tenn. St., North Texas
2002 North Texas
2003 North Texas
2004 North Texas
2005 Arkansas St., LA-Lafayette, LA-Monroe
2006 Mid. Tenn. St., Troy
2007 Florida Atlantic, Troy
2008 Troy
2009 Troy
2010 Florida Intl., Troy
2011 Arkansas St.
2012 Arkansas St.

Western Athletic
1990 BYU
1991 BYU
1992 BYU, Fresno St., Hawaii
1993 BYU, Fresno St., Wyoming
1994 Colorado St.
1995 Air Force, BYU, Colorado St., Utah
1996 BYU
1997 Colorado St.
1998 Air Force
1999 Fresno St., Hawaii, TCU
2000 TCU, UTEP
2001 Louisiana Tech
2002 Boise St.
2003 Boise St.
2004 Boise St.
2005 Boise St., Nevada
2006 Boise St.
2007 Hawaii
2008 Boise St.
2009 Boise St.
2010 Boise St., Hawaii, Nevada
2011 Louisiana Tech
2012 Utah St.

(1) On July 23, 2012, the NCAA vacated all of Penn State's football victories between 1998 and 2011.

NCAA Div. I-AA (FCS) Football Conference Champions, 1990-2012

Big Sky
1990 Nevada
1991 Nevada
1992 Eastern Wash., Idaho
1993 Montana
1994 Boise St.
1995 Montana
1996 Montana
1997 Eastern Wash.
1998 Montana
1999 Montana
2000 Montana
2001 Montana
2002 Idaho St., Montana, Montana St.
2003 Montana, Montana St., N. Arizona
2004 Eastern Wash., Montana
2005 Eastern Wash., Montana, Montana St.
2006 Montana
2007 Montana
2008 Montana, Weber St.
2009 Montana
2010 Eastern Wash., Montana St.
2011 Montana, Montana St.
2012 Eastern Wash., Montana St., Cal. Poly.

Big South
2002 Gardner-Webb
2003 Gardner-Webb
2004 Coastal Carolina
2005 Charleston Southern, Coastal Carolina
2006 Coastal Carolina
2007 Liberty
2008 Liberty
2009 Liberty, Stony Brook
2010 Coastal Carolina, Liberty, Stony Brook
2011 Stony Brook
2012 Coastal Carolina, Liberty, Stony Brook

Colonial Athletic
2007 Massachusetts, Richmond
2008 James Madison
2009 Richmond, Villanova
2010 Delaware, William & Mary
2011 Towson
2012 New Hampshire, Richmond, Villanova, Towson

Ivy League
1990 Cornell, Dartmouth
1991 Dartmouth
1992 Dartmouth, Princeton
1993 Pennsylvania
1994 Pennsylvania
1995 Princeton
1996 Dartmouth
1997 Harvard
1998 Pennsylvania
1999 Brown, Yale
2000 Pennsylvania
2001 Harvard
2002 Pennsylvania
2003 Pennsylvania
2004 Harvard
2005 Brown
2006 Princeton, Yale
2007 Harvard
2008 Harvard, Brown
2009 Pennsylvania
2010 Pennsylvania
2011 Harvard
2012 Pennsylvania

Mid-Eastern Athletic
1990 Florida A&M
1991 North Carolina A&T
1992 North Carolina A&T
1993 Howard
1994 South Carolina St.
1995 Florida A&M
1996 Florida A&M
1997 Hampton
1998 Florida A&M, Hampton
1999 North Carolina A&T
2000 Florida A&M
2001 Florida A&M
2002 Bethune-Cookman
2003 North Carolina A&T
2004 Hampton, South Carolina St.
2005 Hampton
2006 Hampton
2007 Delaware St.
2008 South Carolina St.
2009 South Carolina St.
2010 Bethune-Cookman, Florida A&M, South Carolina St.
2011 Norfolk St.
2012 Bethune-Cookman

Missouri Valley
1990 Northern Iowa
1991 Northern Iowa
1992 Northern Iowa
1993 Northern Iowa
1994 Northern Iowa
1995 Eastern Illinois, Northern Iowa
1996 Northern Iowa
1997 Western Illinois
1998 Western Illinois
1999 Illinois St.
2000 Western Illinois
2001 Northern Iowa
2002 W. Illinois, W. Kentucky
2003 N. Iowa, S. Illinois
2004 Southern Illinois
2005 N. Iowa, S. Illinois, Youngstown St.
2006 Youngstown St.
2007 Northern Iowa
2008 N. Iowa, S. Illinois
2009 Southern Illinois
2010 Northern Iowa
2011 North Dakota St., Northern Iowa
2012 North Dakota St.

Northeast
1996 Monmouth, Robert Morris
1997 Robert Morris
1998 Monmouth, Robert Morris
1999 Robert Morris
2000 Robert Morris
2001 Sacred Heart
2002 Albany
2003 Albany, Monmouth
2004 Central Conn. St., Monmouth
2005 Central Conn. St., Stony Brook
2006 Monmouth
2007 Albany
2008 Albany
2009 Central Conn. St.
2010 Central Conn. St., Robert Morris
2011 Albany, Duquesne
2012 Albany, Wagner

Ohio Valley
1990 Eastern Kentucky, Mid. Tenn. St.
1991 Eastern Kentucky
1992 Mid. Tenn. St.
1993 Eastern Kentucky
1994 Eastern Kentucky
1995 Murray St.
1996 Murray St.
1997 Eastern Kentucky
1998 Tennessee St.
1999 Tennessee St.
2000 Western Kentucky
2001 Eastern Illinois
2002 Eastern Illinois, Murray St.
2003 Jacksonville St.
2004 Jacksonville St.
2005 Eastern Illinois
2006 Eastern Illinois, Tenn.-Martin
2007 Eastern Kentucky
2008 Eastern Illinois
2009 Eastern Illinois
2010 SE Missouri St.
2011 Eastern Kentucky, Jacksonville St., Tennessee Tech
2012 Eastern Illinois

Patriot
1990 Holy Cross
1991 Holy Cross
1992 Lafayette
1993 Lehigh
1994 Lafayette
1995 Lehigh
1996 Bucknell
1997 Colgate
1998 Lehigh
1999 Colgate, Lehigh
2000 Lehigh
2001 Lehigh
2002 Colgate, Fordham
2003 Colgate
2004 Lafayette, Lehigh
2005 Colgate, Lafayette
2006 Colgate, Lafayette, Lehigh
2007 Fordham
2008 Colgate
2009 Holy Cross
2010 Lehigh
2011 Lehigh
2012 Colgate

Pioneer
1993 Dayton
1994 Butler, Dayton
1995 Drake
1996 Dayton
1997 Dayton
1998 Drake
1999 Dayton
2000 Dayton, Drake, Valparaiso
2001 Dayton
2002 Dayton
2003 Valparaiso
2004 Drake
2005 San Diego
2006 San Diego
2007 Dayton, San Diego
2008 Jacksonville
2009 Butler, Dayton
2010 Dayton, Jacksonville
2011 Drake, San Diego
2012 Butler, Drake, San Diego

Southern
1990 Furman
1991 Appalachian St.
1992 Citadel
1993 Georgia Southern
1994 Marshall
1995 Appalachian St.
1996 Marshall
1997 Georgia Southern
1998 Georgia Southern
1999 Appalachian St., Furman, Georgia Southern
2000 Furman, Southern
2001 Furman, Southern
2002 Georgia Southern
2003 Wofford
2004 Furman, Georgia Southern
2005 Appalachian St.
2006 Appalachian St.
2007 Appalachian St., Wofford
2008 Appalachian St.
2009 Appalachian St.
2010 Appalachian St., Wofford
2011 Georgia Southern
2012 Appalachian St., Georgia Southern, Wofford

Southland
1990 LA-Monroe
1991 McNeese St.
1992 LA-Monroe
1993 McNeese St.
1994 North Texas
1995 McNeese St.
1996 Troy St.
1997 McNeese St., Northwestern St.
1998 Northwestern St.
1999 Stephen F. Austin, Troy
2000 Troy
2001 McNeese St., Sam Houston St.
2002 McNeese St.
2003 McNeese St.
2004 Northwestern St., Sam Houston St.
2005 Nicholls St., Texas St.
2006 McNeese St.
2007 McNeese St.
2008 Texas St.
2009 McNeese St., Stephen F. Austin
2010 Stephen F. Austin
2011 Sam Houston St.
2012 Central Arkansas, Sam Houston St.

Southwestern Athletic
1990 Jackson St.
1991 Alabama St.
1992 Alcorn St.
1993 Southern
1994 Alcorn St., Grambling St.
1995 Jackson St.
1996 Jackson St.
1997 Southern
1998 Southern
1999 Southern
2000 Grambling St.
2001 Grambling St.
2002 Grambling St.
2003 Southern
2004 Alabama St.
2005 Grambling St.
2006 Alabama A&M
2007 Jackson St.
2008 Grambling St.
2009 Prairie View A&M
2010 Texas Southern
2011 Grambling St.
2012 Arkansas-Pine Bluff

Note: Missouri Valley Conference was known as Gateway Football Conference, 1992-2007, and as Gateway Collegiate Athletic Conference, 1985-91.

Selected NCAA Division I Teams
(Conferences and coaches listed are as of Aug. 2013)

Team	Nickname	Team colors	Conference	Basketball coach	Football coach
Air Force	Falcons	Blue & silver	Mountain West	Dave Pilipovich	Troy Calhoun
Akron	Zips	Blue & gold	Mid-American	Keith Dambrot	Terry Bowden
Alabama	Crimson Tide	Crimson & white	Southeastern	Anthony Grant	Nick Saban
Appalachian State*	Mountaineers	Black & gold	Southern	Jason Capel	Scott Satterfield
Arizona	Wildcats	Cardinal & navy	Pac-12	Sean Miller	Rich Rodriguez
Arizona State	Sun Devils	Maroon & gold	Pac-12	Herb Sendek	Todd Graham
Arkansas	Razorbacks	Cardinal & white	Southeastern	Mike Anderson	Bret Bielema
Arkansas State	Red Wolves	Scarlet & black	Sun Belt	John Brady	Bryan Harsin
Army	Black Knights	Black, gold, & gray	Independent#	Zach Spiker	Rich Ellerson
Auburn	Tigers	Burnt orange & navy blue	Southeastern	Tony Barbee	Gus Malzahn
Ball State	Cardinals	Cardinal & white	Mid-American	James Whitford	Pete Lembo
Baylor	Bears	Green & gold	Big 12	Scott Drew	Art Briles
Boise State	Broncos	Blue & orange	Mountain West	Leon Rice	Chris Petersen
Boston College	Eagles	Maroon & gold	Atlantic Coast	Steve Donahue	Steve Addazio
Bowling Green	Falcons	Orange & brown	Mid-American	Louis Orr	Dave Clawson
Brigham Young (BYU)	Cougars	Dark blue & white	Independent#	Dave Rose	Bronco Mendenhall
Brown*	Bears	Brown, red, & white	Ivy League	Mike Martin	Phil Estes
California	Golden Bears	Blue & gold	Pac-12	Mike Montgomery	Sonny Dykes
Central Michigan	Chippewas	Maroon & gold	Mid-American	Keno Davis	Dan Enos
Cincinnati	Bearcats	Red & black	American Athletic	Mick Cronin	Tommy Tuberville
Citadel*	Bulldogs	Citadel blue & white	Southern	Chuck Driesell	Kevin Higgins
Clemson	Tigers	Burnt orange & regalia	Atlantic Coast	Brad Brownell	Dabo Swinney
Colgate*	Raiders	Maroon & white	Patriot League	Matt Langel	Dick Biddle
Colorado	Buffaloes	Silver, gold, & black	Pac-12	Tad Boyle	Mike MacIntyre
Colorado State	Rams	Green & gold	Mountain West	Larry Eustachy	Jim McElwain
Columbia*	Lions	Columbia blue & white	Ivy League	Kyle Smith	Pete Mangurian
Connecticut	Huskies	Blue & white	American Athletic	Kevin Ollie	Paul Pasqualoni
Cornell*	Big Red	Carnelian red & white	Ivy League	Bill Courtney	David Archer
Dartmouth*	Big Green	Dartmouth green & white	Ivy League	Paul Cormier	Buddy Teevens
Delaware*	Fightin' Blue Hens	Blue & gold	Colonial Athletic	Monté Ross	Dave Brock
Duke	Blue Devils	Duke blue & white	Atlantic Coast	Mike Krzyzewski	David Cutcliffe
East Carolina	Pirates	Purple & gold	Conference USA	Jeff Lebo	Ruffin McNeill
Eastern Illinois*	Panthers	Blue & gray	Ohio Valley	Jay Spoonhour	Dino Babers
Eastern Kentucky*	Colonels	Maroon & white	Ohio Valley	Jeff Neubauer	Dean Hood
Eastern Michigan	Eagles	Green & white	Mid-American	Rob Murphy	Ron English
Eastern Washington*	Eagles	Red & white	Big Sky	Jim Hayford	Beau Baldwin
Florida	Gators	Orange & blue	Southeastern	Billy Donovan	Will Muschamp
Florida A&M*	Rattlers	Orange & green	Mid-Eastern Athletic	Clemon Johnson	Earl Holmes
Florida State	Seminoles	Garnet & gold	Atlantic Coast	Leonard Hamilton	Jimbo Fisher
Fresno State	Bulldogs	Red & blue	Mountain West	Rodney Terry	Tim DeRuyter
Furman*	Paladins	Purple & white	Southern	Niko Medved	Bruce Fowler
Georgia	Bulldogs	Red & black	Southeastern	Mark Fox	Mark Richt
Georgia Southern*	Eagles	Blue & white	Southern	Mark Byington	Jeff Monken
Georgia Tech	Yellow Jackets	Old gold & white	Atlantic Coast	Brian Gregory	Paul Johnson
Harvard*	Crimson	Crimson, black, & white	Ivy League	Tommy Amaker	Tim Murphy
Hawaii	Rainbows	Green, black, white, silver	Mountain West#	Gib Arnold	Norm Chow
Holy Cross*	Crusaders	Royal purple	Patriot League	Milan Brown	Tom Gilmore
Houston	Cougars	Scarlet & white	Conference USA	James Dickey	Tony Levine
Howard*	Bison	Blue & white	Mid-Eastern Athletic	Kevin Nickelberry	Gary Harrell
Idaho	Vandals	Silver & vandal gold	Western Athletic	Don Verlin	Paul Petrino
Illinois	Fighting Illini	Orange & blue	Big Ten	John Groce	Tim Beckman
Illinois State*	Redbirds	Red & white	Missouri Valley	Dan Muller	Brock Spack
Indiana	Hoosiers	Cream & crimson	Big Ten	Tom Crean	Kevin Wilson
Indiana State*	Sycamores	Royal blue & white	Missouri Valley	Greg Lansing	Mike Sanford
Iowa	Hawkeyes	Gold & black	Big Ten	Fran McCaffery	Kirk Ferentz
Iowa State	Cyclones	Cardinal & gold	Big 12	Fred Hoiberg	Paul Rhoads
Jackson State*	Tigers	Blue & white	Southwestern Athletic	Wayne Brent	Rick Comegy
James Madison*	Dukes	Purple & gold	Colonial Athletic	Matt Brady	Mickey Matthews
Kansas	Jayhawks	Crimson & blue	Big 12	Bill Self	Charlie Weis
Kansas State	Wildcats	Purple & white	Big 12	Bruce Weber	Bill Snyder
Kent State	Golden Flashes	Navy blue & gold	Mid-American	Rob Senderoff	Paul Haynes
Kentucky	Wildcats	Blue & white	Southeastern	John Calipari	Mark Stoops
Lafayette*	Leopards	Maroon & white	Patriot League	Fran O'Hanlon	Frank Tavani
Lehigh*	Mountain Hawks	Brown & white	Patriot League	Brett Reed	Andy Coen
Liberty*	Flames	Red, white, & blue	Big South	Dale Layer	Turner Gill
Louisiana State (LSU)	Fighting Tigers	Purple & gold	Southeastern	Johnny Jones	Les Miles
Louisiana Tech	Bulldogs	Red & blue	Western Athletic	Michael White	Skip Holtz
Louisiana-Lafayette	Ragin' Cajuns	Vermilion & white	Sun Belt	Bob Marlin	Mark Hudspeth
Louisiana-Monroe	Warhawks	Maroon & gold	Sun Belt	Keith Richard	Todd Berry
Louisville	Cardinals	Red & black	American Athletic	Rick Pitino	Charlie Strong
Maine*	Black Bears	Blue & white	Colonial Athletic#	Ted Woodward	Jack Cosgrove
Marshall	Thundering Herd	Green & white	Conference USA	Tom Herrion	Doc Holliday
Maryland	Terrapins	Red, white, black, gold	Atlantic Coast	Mark Turgeon	Randy Edsall
Massachusetts*	Minutemen	Maroon & white	Mid-American#	Derek Kellogg	Charley Molnar
Memphis	Tigers	Blue & gray	Conference USA	Josh Pastner	Justin Fuente
Miami (Florida)	Hurricanes	Orange & green	Atlantic Coast	Jim Larranaga	Al Golden
Miami (Ohio)	RedHawks	Red & white	Mid-American	John Cooper	Don Treadwell
Michigan	Wolverines	Maize & blue	Big Ten	John Beilein	Brady Hoke
Michigan State	Spartans	Green & white	Big Ten	Tom Izzo	Mark Dantonio
Mid. Tennessee State	Blue Raiders	Royal blue & white	Sun Belt	Kermit Davis	Rick Stockstill
Minnesota	Golden Gophers	Maroon & gold	Big Ten	Richard Pitino	Jerry Kill
Mississippi	Rebels	Cardinal red & navy blue	Southeastern	Andy Kennedy	Hugh Freeze
Mississippi State	Bulldogs	Maroon & white	Southeastern	Rick Ray	Dan Mullen
Missouri	Tigers	Old gold & black	Southeastern	Frank Haith	Gary Pinkel

Team	Nickname	Team colors	Conference	Basketball coach	Football coach
Montana*	Grizzlies	Maroon & silver	Big Sky	Wayne Tinkle	Mick Delaney
Montana State*	Bobcats	Blue & gold	Big Sky	Brad Huse	Rob Ash
Morgan State*	Bears	Blue & orange	Mid-Eastern Athletic	Todd Bozeman	Donald Hill-Eley
Murray State*	Racers	Navy & gold	Ohio Valley	Steve Prohm	Chris Hatcher
Navy	Midshipmen	Navy blue & gold	Independent#	Ed DeChellis	Ken Niumatalolo
Nebraska	Cornhuskers	Scarlet & cream	Big Ten	Tim Miles	Bo Pelini
Nevada	Wolf Pack	Silver & blue	Mountain West	David Carter	Brian Polian
Nevada-Las Vegas (UNLV)	Rebels	Scarlet & gray	Mountain West	Dave Rice	Bobby Hauck
New Hampshire*	Wildcats	Blue & white	Colonial Athletic#	Bill Herrion	Sean McDonnell
New Mexico	Lobos	Cherry & silver	Mountain West	Craig Neal	Bob Davie
New Mexico State	Aggies	Crimson & white	Western Athletic	Marvin Menzies	Doug Martin
Nicholls State*	Colonels	Red & gray	Southland	J. P. Piper	Charlie Stubbs
North Carolina	Tar Heels	Carolina blue & white	Atlantic Coast	Roy Williams	Larry Fedora
North Carolina State	Wolfpack	Red & white	Atlantic Coast	Mark Gottfried	Dave Doeren
North Texas	Mean Green	Green & white	Sun Belt	Tony Benford	Dan McCarney
Northern Illinois	Huskies	Cardinal & black	Mid-American	Mark Montgomery	Rod Carey
Northern Iowa*	Panthers	Purple & old gold	Missouri Valley	Ben Jacobson	Mark Farley
Northwestern	Wildcats	Purple & white	Big Ten	Chris Collins	Pat Fitzgerald
Northwestern State*	Demons	Purple, white, & orange	Southland	Mike McConathy	Jay Thomas
Notre Dame	Fighting Irish	Blue & gold	Independent#	Mike Brey	Brian Kelly
Ohio	Bobcats	Hunter green & white	Mid-American	Jim Christian	Frank Solich
Ohio State	Buckeyes	Scarlet & gray	Big Ten	Thad Matta	Urban Meyer
Oklahoma	Sooners	Crimson & cream	Big 12	Lon Kruger	Bob Stoops
Oklahoma State	Cowboys	Orange & black	Big 12	Travis Ford	Mike Gundy
Oregon	Ducks	Green & yellow	Pac-12	Dana Altman	Mark Helfrich
Oregon State	Beavers	Orange & black	Pac-12	Craig Robinson	Mike Riley
Penn State	Nittany Lions	Blue & white	Big Ten	Patrick Chambers	Bill O'Brien
Pennsylvania*	Quakers	Red & blue	Ivy League	Jerome Allen	Al Bagnoli
Pittsburgh	Panthers	Gold & blue	American Athletic	Jamie Dixon	Paul Chryst
Princeton*	Tigers	Orange & black	Ivy League	Mitch Henderson	Bob Surace
Purdue	Boilermakers	Old gold & black	Big Ten	Matt Painter	Darrell Hazell
Rhode Island*	Rams	Keaney blue, dark blue, white	Colonial Athletic#	Dan Hurley	Joe Trainer
Rice	Owls	Blue & gray	Conference USA	Ben Braun	David Bailiff
Richmond*	Spiders	Red & blue	Colonial Athletic#	Chris Mooney	Danny Rocco
Rutgers	Scarlet Knights	Scarlet	American Athletic	Eddie Jordan	Kyle Flood
Sam Houston State*	Bearkats	Orange & white	Southland	Jason Hooten	Willie Fritz
San Diego State	Aztecs	Scarlet & black	Mountain West	Steve Fisher	Rocky Long
San Jose State	Spartans	Gold, white, & blue	Western Athletic	Dave Wojcik	Ron Caragher
South Carolina	Gamecocks	Garnet & black	Southeastern	Frank Martin	Steve Spurrier
South Carolina State*	Bulldogs	Garnet & blue	Mid-Eastern Athletic	Murray Garvin	Oliver Pough
South Florida	Bulls	Green & gold	American Athletic	Stan Heath	Willie Taggart
Southeast Missouri State*	Redhawks	Red, black, & white	Ohio Valley	Dickey Nutt	Tony Samuel
Southern California (USC)	Trojans	Cardinal & gold	Pac-12	Andy Enfield	Lane Kiffin
Southern Illinois*	Salukis	Maroon & white	Missouri Valley	Barry Hinson	Dale Lennon
Southern Methodist (SMU)	Mustangs	Red & blue	Conference USA	Larry Brown	June Jones
Southern Mississippi	Golden Eagles	Black & gold	Conference USA	Donnie Tyndall	Todd Monken
Stanford	Cardinal	Cardinal & white	Pac-12	Johnny Dawkins	David Shaw
Stephen F. Austin*	Lumberjacks	Purple & white	Southland	Brad Underwood	J. C. Harper
Syracuse	Orange	Orange	American Athletic	Jim Boeheim	Scott Shafer
Temple	Owls	Cherry & white	American Athletic#	Fran Dunphy	Matt Rhule
Tennessee	Volunteers	Orange & white	Southeastern	Cuonzo Martin	Butch Jones
Tennessee State*	Tigers	Reflex blue & white	Ohio Valley	Travis Williams	Rod Reed
Tennessee Tech*	Golden Eagles	Purple & gold	Ohio Valley	Steve Payne	Watson Brown
Texas	Longhorns	Burnt orange & white	Big 12	Rick Barnes	Mack Brown
Texas A&M	Aggies	Maroon & white	Southeastern	Billy Kennedy	Kevin Sumlin
Texas Christian (TCU)	Horned Frogs	Purple & white	Big 12	Trent Johnson	Gary Patterson
Texas Southern*	Tigers	Maroon & gray	Southwestern Athletic	Mike Davis	Darrell Asberry
Texas State*	Bobcats	Maroon & gold	Sun Belt	Danny Kaspar	Dennis Franchione
Texas Tech	Red Raiders	Scarlet & black	Big 12	Tubby Smith	Kliff Kingsbury
Toledo	Rockets	Midnight blue & gold	Mid-American	Tod Kowalczyk	Matt Campbell
Troy	Trojans	Cardinal, silver, & black	Sun Belt	Phil Cunningham	Larry Blakeney
Tulane	Green Wave	Olive green & sky blue	Conference USA	Ed Conroy	Curtis Johnson
Tulsa	Golden Hurricane	Old gold, royal blue, & crimson	Conference USA	Danny Manning	Bill Blankenship
UCLA	Bruins	Blue & gold	Pac-12	Steve Alford	Jim Mora
Utah	Utes	Crimson & white	Pac-12	Larry Krystkowiak	Kyle Whittingham
Utah State	Aggies	Navy blue & white	Western Athletic	Stew Morrill	Matt Wells
UTEP (Texas-El Paso)	Miners	Dark blue, orange, & silver	Conference USA	Tim Floyd	Sean Kugler
Vanderbilt	Commodores	Black & gold	Southeastern	Kevin Stallings	James Franklin
Villanova*	Wildcats	Blue & white	Colonial Athletic#	Jay Wright	Andy Talley
Virginia	Cavaliers	Orange & blue	Atlantic Coast	Tony Bennett	Mike London
Virginia Tech	Hokies	Burnt orange & Chicago maroon	Atlantic Coast	James Johnson	Frank Beamer
Wake Forest	Demon Deacons	Old gold & black	Atlantic Coast	Jeff Bzdelik	Jim Grobe
Washington	Huskies	Purple & gold	Pac-12	Lorenzo Romar	Steve Sarkisian
Washington State	Cougars	Crimson & gray	Pac-12	Ken Bone	Mike Leach
Weber State*	Wildcats	Royal purple & white	Big Sky	Randy Rahe	Jody Sears
West Virginia	Mountaineers	Old gold & blue	Big 12	Bob Huggins	Dana Holgorsen
Western Illinois*	Leathernecks	Purple & gold	Missouri Valley#	Jim Molinari	Bob Nielson
Western Kentucky	Hilltoppers	Red & white	Sun Belt	Ray Harper	Bobby Petrino
Western Michigan	Broncos	Brown & gold	Mid-American	Steve Hawkins	Bill Cubit
William & Mary*	Tribe	Green, gold, & silver	Colonial Athletic	Tony Shaver	Jimmye Laycock
Wisconsin	Badgers	Cardinal & white	Big Ten	Bo Ryan	Gary Andersen
Wyoming	Cowboys	Brown & gold	Mountain West	Larry Shyatt	Dave Christensen
Yale*	Bulldogs, Elis	Yale blue & white	Ivy League	James Jones	Tony Reno
Youngstown State*	Penguins	Red & white	Missouri Valley#	Jerry Slocum	Eric Wolford

* = Football Championship Subdivision (FCS) team (formerly known as I-AA). # = Team competes in conference listed in football but not in basketball.

NCAA Men's Baseball Division I Champions, 1947-2013

Year	Champion	Year	Champion	Year	Champion	Year	Champion	Year	Champion
1947	California	1961	USC	1975	Texas	1988	Stanford	2001	Miami (FL)
1948	USC	1962	Michigan	1976	Arizona	1989	Wichita St.	2002	Texas
1949	Texas	1963	USC	1977	Arizona St.	1990	Georgia	2003	Rice
1950	Texas	1964	Minnesota	1978	USC	1991	LSU	2004	Cal. St.-Fullerton
1951	Oklahoma	1965	Arizona St.	1979	Cal. St.-Fullerton	1992	Pepperdine	2005	Texas
1952	Holy Cross	1966	Ohio St.	1980	Arizona	1993	LSU	2006	Oregon St.
1953	Michigan	1967	Arizona St.	1981	Arizona St.	1994	Oklahoma	2007	Oregon St.
1954	Missouri	1968	USC	1982	Miami (FL)	1995	Cal. St.-Fullerton	2008	Fresno St.
1955	Wake Forest	1969	Arizona St.	1983	Texas	1996	LSU	2009	LSU
1956	Minnesota	1970	USC	1984	Cal. St.-Fullerton	1997	LSU	2010	South Carolina
1957	California	1971	USC	1985	Miami (FL)	1998	USC	2011	South Carolina
1958	USC	1972	USC	1986	Arizona	1999	Miami (FL)	2012	Arizona
1959	Oklahoma St.	1973	USC	1987	Stanford	2000	LSU	2013	UCLA
1960	Minnesota	1974	USC						

NCAA Women's Softball Division I Champions, 1982-2013

Year	Champion	Year	Champion	Year	Champion	Year	Champion	Year	Champion
1982	UCLA	1989	UCLA	1996	Arizona	2002	California	2008	Arizona St.
1983	Texas A&M	1990	UCLA	1997	Arizona	2003	UCLA	2009	Washington
1984	UCLA	1991	Arizona	1998	Fresno St.	2004	UCLA	2010	UCLA
1985	UCLA	1992	UCLA	1999	UCLA	2005	Michigan	2011	Arizona St.
1986	Cal. St.-Fullerton	1993	Arizona	2000	Oklahoma	2006	Arizona	2012	Alabama
1987	Texas A&M	1994	Arizona	2001	Arizona	2007	Arizona	2013	Oklahoma
1988	UCLA	1995	UCLA						

NCAA Men's Hockey Division I Champions, 1948-2013

Year	Champion	Year	Champion	Year	Champion	Year	Champion	Year	Champion
1948	Michigan	1962	Michigan Tech	1975	Michigan Tech	1988	Lake Superior St.	2001	Boston College
1949	Boston College	1963	North Dakota	1976	Minnesota	1989	Harvard	2002	Minnesota
1950	Colorado College	1964	Michigan	1977	Wisconsin	1990	Wisconsin	2003	Minnesota
1951	Michigan	1965	Michigan Tech	1978	Boston Univ.	1991	North Michigan	2004	Denver
1952	Michigan	1966	Michigan St.	1979	Minnesota	1992	Lake Superior St.	2005	Denver
1953	Michigan	1967	Cornell	1980	North Dakota	1993	Maine	2006	Wisconsin
1954	Rensselaer	1968	Denver	1981	Wisconsin	1994	Lake Superior St.	2007	Michigan St.
1955	Michigan	1969	Denver	1982	North Dakota	1995	Boston Univ.	2008	Boston College
1956	Michigan	1970	Cornell	1983	Wisconsin	1996	Michigan	2009	Boston Univ.
1957	Colorado College	1971	Boston Univ.	1984	Bowling Green	1997	North Dakota	2010	Boston College
1958	Denver	1972	Boston Univ.	1985	Rensselaer	1998	Michigan	2011	Minnesota-Duluth
1959	North Dakota	1973	Wisconsin	1986	Michigan St.	1999	Maine	2012	Boston College
1960	Denver	1974	Minnesota	1987	North Dakota	2000	North Dakota	2013	Yale
1961	Denver								

NCAA Women's Hockey Champions, 2001-13

Year	Champion	Year	Champion	Year	Champion	Year	Champion	Year	Champion
2001	Minnesota-Duluth	2004	Minnesota	2007	Wisconsin	2010	Minnesota-Duluth	2012	Minnesota
2002	Minnesota-Duluth	2005	Minnesota	2008	Minnesota-Duluth	2011	Wisconsin	2013	Minnesota
2003	Minnesota-Duluth	2006	Wisconsin	2009	Wisconsin				

NCAA Division I Lacrosse Champions, 1982-2013

Year[1]	Men	Women	Year[1]	Men	Women	Year[1]	Men	Women
1982	North Carolina	Massachusetts	1993	Syracuse	Virginia	2004	Syracuse	Virginia
1983	Syracuse	Delaware	1994	Princeton	Princeton	2005	Johns Hopkins	Northwestern
1984	Johns Hopkins	Temple	1995	Syracuse	Maryland	2006	Virginia	Northwestern
1985	Johns Hopkins	New Hampshire	1996	Princeton	Maryland	2007	Johns Hopkins	Northwestern
1986	North Carolina	Maryland	1997	Princeton	Maryland	2008	Syracuse	Northwestern
1987	Johns Hopkins	Penn St.	1998	Princeton	Maryland	2009	Syracuse	Northwestern
1988	Syracuse	Temple	1999	Virginia	Maryland	2010	Duke	Maryland
1989	Syracuse	Penn St.	2000	Syracuse	Maryland	2011	Virginia	Northwestern
1990	Vacated	Harvard	2001	Princeton	Maryland	2012	Loyola (MD)	Northwestern
1991	North Carolina	Virginia	2002	Syracuse	Princeton	2013	Duke	North Carolina
1992	Princeton	Maryland	2003	Virginia	Princeton			

(1) NCAA Championships began in 1971 for men, in 1982 for women.

NCAA Division I Soccer Champions, 1982-2012

Year[1]	Men	Women	Year[1]	Men	Women	Year[1]	Men	Women
1982	Indiana	North Carolina	1992	Virginia	North Carolina	2003	Indiana	North Carolina
1983	Indiana	North Carolina	1993	Virginia	North Carolina	2004	Indiana	Notre Dame
1984	Clemson	North Carolina	1994	Virginia	North Carolina	2005	Maryland	Portland
1985	UCLA	George Mason	1995	Wisconsin	Notre Dame	2006	UC Santa Barbara	North Carolina
1986	Duke	North Carolina	1996	St. John's (NY)	North Carolina	2007	Wake Forest	USC
1987	Clemson	North Carolina	1997	UCLA	North Carolina	2008	Maryland	North Carolina
1988	Indiana	North Carolina	1998	Indiana	Florida	2009	Virginia	North Carolina
1989	Santa Clara;	North Carolina	1999	Indiana	North Carolina	2010	Akron	Notre Dame
	Virginia (tie)		2000	Connecticut	North Carolina	2011	North Carolina	Stanford
1990	UCLA	North Carolina	2001	North Carolina	Santa Clara	2012	Indiana	North Carolina
1991	Virginia	North Carolina	2002	UCLA	Portland			

(1) NCAA Championships began in 1959 for men, in 1982 for women.

NCAA Division I Wrestling Champions, 1964-2013

Year	Champion	Year	Champion	Year	Champion	Year	Champion	Year	Champion
1964	Oklahoma St.	1974	Oklahoma	1984	Iowa	1994	Oklahoma St.	2004	Oklahoma St.
1965	Iowa St.	1975	Iowa	1985	Iowa	1995	Iowa	2005	Oklahoma St.
1966	Oklahoma St.	1976	Iowa	1986	Iowa	1996	Iowa	2006	Oklahoma St.
1967	Michigan St.	1977	Iowa St.	1987	Iowa St.	1997	Iowa	2007	Minnesota
1968	Oklahoma St.	1978	Iowa	1988	Arizona St.	1998	Iowa	2008	Iowa
1969	Iowa St.	1979	Iowa	1989	Oklahoma St.	1999	Iowa	2009	Iowa
1970	Iowa St.	1980	Iowa	1990	Oklahoma St.	2000	Iowa	2010	Iowa
1971	Oklahoma St.	1981	Iowa	1991	Iowa	2001	Minnesota	2011	Penn St.
1972	Iowa St.	1982	Iowa	1992	Iowa	2002	Minnesota	2012	Penn St.
1973	Iowa St.	1983	Iowa	1993	Iowa	2003	Oklahoma St.	2013	Penn St.

FOOTBALL

NFL 2012: Bountygate, Rookie QBs, and Veteran Stars

A bounty scandal and replacement referees blemished an exciting 2012 National Football League season that included the emergence of rookie star quarterbacks and impressive veteran performances. In what became known as Bountygate, a league investigation uncovered a program that involved payments to New Orleans Saints players who inflicted injuries on opposing players during the 2009, 2010, and 2011 seasons. On Mar. 21, 2012, NFL commissioner Roger Goodell suspended Saints head coach Sean Payton for the entire 2012 season; former defensive coordinator Gregg Williams received an indefinite suspension. (Payton was reinstated in Jan. 2013 ahead of Super Bowl XLVII while Williams was reinstated for the 2013 season.)

A labor lockout forced the use of replacement referees through the first three weeks of the 2012 season. Complaints mounted about bad calls, incorrect rule interpretations, and misplaced spotting. The league reached an agreement with its regular officiating crews Sept. 27, 2012, and the referees' association approved a new eight-year contract Sept. 29.

Fans turned their attention to the five rookie quarterbacks who started in Week 1, three of whom led teams to the playoffs. Andrew Luck, the top pick in the 2012 NFL Draft, threw an NFL rookie-record 4,374 passing yards and led the Indianapolis Colts to 11 wins and an AFC Wild Card berth after the team's 2-14 season in 2011. Robert Griffin III led the resurgent Washington Redskins to an NFC East Division crown following a 3-6 start. Griffin rushed for 815 yards—a record for rookie QBs—and passed for 3,200 yards before reinjuring his right knee in an NFC Wild Card playoff loss to Seattle and fellow rookie QB Russell Wilson.

The NFL postseason featured an outstanding run by Baltimore QB Joe Flacco that culminated in the Ravens' 34-31 victory over the San Francisco 49ers in Super Bowl XLVII on Feb. 3, 2013, at the Mercedes-Benz Superdome in New Orleans, LA. Flacco threw a total of 11 TD passes without an interception in playoff wins over Indianapolis, Denver, New England, and San Francisco. Colin Kaepernick led the 49ers to the NFC West Division crown after taking over for injured QB Alex Smith in midseason.

The NFL mourned the loss of former All-Pro linebacker Junior Seau, who committed suicide on May 2, 2012, in his California home. Posthumous testing revealed that the 43-year-old Seau had chronic traumatic encephalopathy (CTE), a degenerative brain disease found in athletes with a history of multiple head trauma. Days before the 2013 season began, the NFL announced Aug. 29, 2013, that it had agreed to a $765 mil settlement in a suit filed by thousands of former players, who claimed the league hid information about the long-term effects of concussions and repeated blows to the head.

NFL Final Standings, 2012

(playoff seeding in parentheses)

AMERICAN FOOTBALL CONFERENCE

East Division	W	L	T	Pct	Pts	Opp	Div
New England (2)...	12	4	0	.750	557	331	6-0
Miami............	7	9	0	.438	288	317	2-4
NY Jets..........	6	10	0	.375	281	375	2-4
Buffalo..........	6	10	0	.375	344	435	2-4
North Division							
Baltimore (4)......	10	6	0	.625	398	344	4-2
*Cincinnati (6).....	10	6	0	.625	391	320	3-3
Pittsburgh........	8	8	0	.500	336	314	3-3
Cleveland.........	5	11	0	.313	302	368	2-4
South Division							
Houston (3).......	12	4	0	.750	416	331	5-1
*Indianapolis (5)...	11	5	0	.688	357	387	4-2
Tennessee........	6	10	0	.375	330	471	1-5
Jacksonville......	2	14	0	.125	255	444	2-4
West Division							
Denver (1)........	13	3	0	.813	481	289	6-0
San Diego........	7	9	0	.438	350	350	4-2
Oakland..........	4	12	0	.250	290	443	2-4
Kansas City......	2	14	0	.125	211	425	0-6

*Wild card qualifier for playoffs. **Note:** New England finished ahead of Houston based on head-to-head win percentage; Baltimore was ahead of Cincinnati based on divison win percentage.

NATIONAL FOOTBALL CONFERENCE

East Division	W	L	T	Pct	Pts	Opp	Div
Washington (4).....	10	6	0	.625	436	388	5-1
NY Giants.........	9	7	0	.563	429	344	3-3
Dallas............	8	8	0	.500	376	400	3-3
Philadelphia.......	4	12	0	.250	280	444	1-5
North Division							
Green Bay (3).....	11	5	0	.688	433	336	5-1
*Minnesota (6).....	10	6	0	.625	379	348	4-2
Chicago..........	10	6	0	.625	375	277	3-3
Detroit............	4	12	0	.250	372	437	0-6
South Division							
Atlanta (1)........	13	3	0	.813	419	299	3-3
Carolina..........	7	9	0	.438	357	363	3-3
New Orleans.......	7	9	0	.438	461	454	3-3
Tampa Bay........	7	9	0	.438	389	394	3-3
West Division							
San Francisco (2)...	11	4	1	.719	397	273	3-2-1
*Seattle (5)........	11	5	0	.688	412	245	3-3
St. Louis..........	7	8	1	.469	299	348	4-1-1
Arizona...........	5	11	0	.313	250	357	1-5

*Wild card qualifier for playoffs. **Note:** Minnesota finished ahead of Chicago in the NFC North based on win percentage in division games.

2012 Playoffs

AFC Wild Card Games: Houston 19, Cincinnati 13; Baltimore 24, Indianapolis 9
NFC Wild Card Games: Green Bay 24, Minnesota 10; Seattle 24, Washington 14
AFC Divisional Playoff Games: Baltimore 38, Denver 35 (2 OT); New England 41, Houston 28

NFC Divisional Playoff Games: San Francisco 45, Green Bay 31; Atlanta 30, Seattle 28
AFC Championship Game: Baltimore 28, New England 13
NFC Championship Game: San Francisco 28, Atlanta 24
Super Bowl XLVII: Baltimore 34, San Francisco 31

NFL Individual Leaders: American Football Conference, 2012

(* = rookie)

					PASSING						
Player, team	Att	Comp	Pct comp	Yds	Yds/Att	Long	TD	Pct TD	Int	Rating
Peyton Manning, Denver.............	583	400	68.6	4,659	8.0	71T	37	6.3	11	105.8
Tom Brady, New England..............	637	401	63.0	4,827	7.6	83T	34	5.3	8	98.7
Ben Roethlisberger, Pittsburgh..........	449	284	63.3	3,265	7.3	82T	26	5.8	8	97.0
Matt Schaub, Houston...............	544	350	64.3	4,008	7.4	60T	22	4.0	12	90.7
Philip Rivers, San Diego..............	527	338	64.1	3,606	6.8	80T	26	4.9	15	88.6
Joe Flacco, Baltimore...............	531	317	59.7	3,817	7.2	61T	22	4.1	10	87.7
Andy Dalton, Cincinnati..............	528	329	62.3	3,669	7.0	59T	27	5.1	16	87.4
Carson Palmer, Oakland..............	565	345	61.1	4,018	7.1	64T	22	3.9	14	85.3

Player, team	Att	Comp	Pct comp	Yds	Yds/Att	Long	TD	Pct TD	Int	Rating
Ryan Fitzpatrick, Buffalo	505	306	60.6	3,400	6.7	68T	24	4.8	16	83.3
Blaine Gabbert, Jacksonville	278	162	58.3	1,662	6.0	80T	9	3.2	6	77.4
*Andrew Luck, Indianapolis	627	339	54.1	4,374	7.0	70T	23	3.7	18	76.5
*Ryan Tannehill, Miami	484	282	58.3	3,294	6.8	80T	12	2.5	13	76.1
Jake Locker, Tennessee	314	177	56.4	2,176	6.9	71T	10	3.2	11	74.0
*Brandon Weeden, Cleveland	517	297	57.4	3,385	6.6	71T	14	2.7	17	72.6
Chad Henne, Miami	308	166	53.9	2,084	6.8	81T	11	3.6	11	72.2
Mark Sanchez, NY Jets	453	246	54.3	2,883	6.4	66	13	2.9	18	66.9
Matt Cassel, Kansas City	277	161	58.1	1,796	6.5	46	6	2.2	12	66.7

RUSHING YARDS

Player, team	Yds	Att	Avg	Long	TD
Jamaal Charles, Kansas City	1,509	285	5.3	91T	5
Arian Foster, Houston	1,424	351	4.1	46	15
Stevan Ridley, New England	1,263	290	4.4	41	12
C.J. Spiller, Buffalo	1,244	207	6.0	62	6
Chris Johnson, Tennessee	1,243	276	4.5	94T	6
Ray Rice, Baltimore	1,143	257	4.4	46	9
BenJarvus Green-Ellis, Cincinnati	1,094	278	3.9	48	6
Shonn Greene, NY Jets	1,063	276	3.9	36	8
Reggie Bush, Miami	986	227	4.3	65T	6
*Trent Richardson, Cleveland	950	267	3.6	32T	11

RECEPTIONS

Player, team	Rec	Yds	Avg	Long	TD
Wes Welker, New England	118	1,354	11.5	59	6
Andre Johnson, Houston	112	1,598	14.3	60T	4
Reggie Wayne, Indianapolis	106	1,355	12.8	33	5
A.J. Green, Cincinnati	97	1,350	13.9	73T	11
Demaryius Thomas, Denver	94	1,434	15.3	71T	10
Eric Decker, Denver	85	1,064	12.5	55	13
Steve Johnson, Buffalo	79	1,046	13.2	63	6
Brandon Myers, Oakland	79	806	10.2	29	4
Brian Hartline, Miami	74	1,083	14.6	80T	1
Brandon Lloyd, New England	74	911	12.3	53	4

INTERCEPTIONS

Player, team	No.	Yds	Avg	Long	TD
Jairus Byrd, Buffalo	5	81	16.2	45	0
Devin McCourty, New England	5	53	10.6	34	0
Darius Butler, Indianapolis	4	101	25.3	51	2
Cary Williams, Baltimore	4	90	22.5	63T	1
*Tavon Wilson, New England	4	87	21.8	45	0
Ed Reed, Baltimore	4	78	19.5	34T	1
Kareem Jackson, Houston	4	71	17.8	63T	1
Bryan Scott, Buffalo	4	66	16.5	32	1
Michael Griffin, Tennessee	4	59	14.8	33	0
Jason McCourty, Tennessee	4	29	7.3	28	0
Reshad Jones, Miami	4	28	7.0	15	0
Derek Cox, Jacksonville	4	18	4.5	16	0

SCORING—KICKERS

Player, team	PAT	FG	Long	Pts
Stephen Gostkowski, New England	66/66	29/35	53	153
Shayne Graham, Houston	45/45	31/38	51	138
Matt Prater, Denver	55/55	26/32	53	133
*Justin Tucker, Baltimore	42/42	30/33	56	132
Sebastian Janikowski, Oakland	25/25	31/34	57	118
Shaun Suisham, Pittsburgh	34/34	28/31	52	118

SCORING—NON-KICKERS

Player, team (position)	TD	Rush	Rec	2-Pt	Pts
Arian Foster, Houston (RB)	17	15	2	0	102
Eric Decker, Denver (WR)	13	0	13	0	78
*Trent Richardson, Cleveland (RB)	12	11	1	0	72
Stevan Ridley, New England (RB)	12	12	0	0	72
A.J. Green, Cincinnati (WR)	11	0	11	0	66
Rob Gronkowski, New England (TE)	11	0	11	0	66

KICKOFF RETURNS

Player, team	No.	Yds	Avg	Long	TD
Jacoby Jones, Baltimore	38	1,167	30.7	108T	2
Joe McKnight, NY Jets	39	1,072	27.5	100T	1
Josh Cribbs, Cleveland	43	1,178	27.4	74	0
Marcus Thigpen, Miami	38	1,040	27.4	96T	1
*Chris Rainey, Pittsburgh	39	1,035	26.5	68	0
Trindon Holliday, Hou.-Den.	21	552	26.3	105T	1

PUNTING

Player, team	No.	Yds	Long	Avg
Brandon Fields, Miami	74	3,715	67	50.2
Mike Scifres, San Diego	81	3,914	66	48.3
Pat McAfee, Indianapolis	73	3,520	64	48.2
*Bryan Anger, Jacksonville	91	4,353	73	47.8
Brett Kern, Tennessee	81	3,855	71	47.6
Shane Lechler, Oakland	81	3,826	68	47.2
Donnie Jones, Houston	88	4,150	66	47.2

PUNT RETURNS

Player, team	No.	Yds	Avg	Long	TD
Leodis McKelvin, Buffalo	23	431	18.7	88T	2
Darius Reynaud, Tennessee	31	410	13.2	81T	2
Marcus Thigpen, Miami	26	316	12.2	72T	1
*Keshawn Martin, Houston	22	267	12.1	71	0
Josh Cribbs, Cleveland	38	457	12.0	60	0
Adam Jones, Cincinnati	26	301	11.6	81T	1

SACKS

Player, team	No.
J.J. Watt, Houston	20.5
Von Miller, Denver	18.5
Cameron Wake, Miami	15.0
Geno Atkins, Cincinnati	12.5
Michael Johnson, Cincinnati	11.5
Elvis Dumervil, Denver	11.0
Mario Williams, Buffalo	10.5
Justin Houston, Kansas City	10.0
Shaun Phillips, San Diego	9.5
Tamba Hali, Kansas City	9.0
Paul Kruger, Baltimore	9.0

NFL Individual Leaders: National Football Conference, 2012

(* = rookie)

PASSING

Player, team	Att	Comp	Pct comp	Yds	Yds/Att	Long	TD	Pct TD	Int	Rating
Aaron Rodgers, Green Bay	552	371	67.2	4,295	7.8	73	39	7.1	8	108.0
*Robert Griffin III, Washington	393	258	65.6	3,200	8.1	88T	20	5.1	5	102.4
*Russell Wilson, Seattle	393	252	64.1	3,118	7.9	67	26	6.6	10	100.0
Matt Ryan, Atlanta	615	422	68.6	4,719	7.7	80T	32	5.2	14	99.1
Drew Brees, New Orleans	670	422	63.0	5,177	7.7	80T	43	6.4	19	96.3
Tony Romo, Dallas	648	425	65.6	4,903	7.6	85T	28	7.6	19	90.5
Eli Manning, NY Giants	536	321	59.9	3,948	7.4	80T	26	4.9	15	87.2
Cam Newton, Carolina	485	280	57.7	3,869	8.0	82	19	3.9	12	86.2
Sam Bradford, St. Louis	551	328	59.5	3,702	6.7	80T	21	3.8	13	82.6
Josh Freeman, Tampa Bay	558	306	54.8	4,065	7.3	95	27	4.8	17	81.6
Jay Cutler, Chicago	434	255	58.8	3,033	7.0	60T	19	4.4	14	81.3
Christian Ponder, Minnesota	483	300	62.1	2,935	6.1	65	18	3.7	12	81.2

RUSHING YARDS

Player, team	Yds	Att	Avg	Long	TD	Player, team	Yds	Att	Avg	Long	TD
Adrian Peterson, Minnesota	2,097	348	6.0	82T	12	Matt Forte, Chicago	1,094	248	4.4	46	5
*Alfred Morris, Washington	1,613	335	4.8	39T	13	Steven Jackson, St. Louis	1,042	257	4.1	46	4
Marshawn Lynch, Seattle	1,590	315	5.0	77T	11	Ahmad Bradshaw, NY Giants	1,015	221	4.6	37	6
*Doug Martin, Tampa Bay	1,454	319	4.6	70T	11	LeSean McCoy, Philadelphia	840	200	4.2	34	2
Frank Gore, San Francisco	1,214	258	4.7	37	8	*Robert Griffin III, Washington	815	120	6.8	76T	7

RECEPTIONS

Player, team	Rec	Yds	Avg	Long	TD
Calvin Johnson, Detroit	122	1,964	16.1	53	5
Brandon Marshall, Chicago	118	1,508	12.8	56	11
Jason Witten, Dallas	110	1,039	9.4	36	3
Tony Gonzalez, Atlanta	93	930	10.0	25	8
Dez Bryant, Dallas	92	1,382	15.0	85T	12
Roddy White, Atlanta	92	1,351	14.7	59	7
Victor Cruz, NY Giants	86	1,092	12.7	80T	10
Michael Crabtree, San Francisco	85	1,105	13.0	49T	9
Jimmy Graham, New Orleans	85	982	11.6	46	9
Marques Colston, New Orleans	83	1,154	13.9	60	10

INTERCEPTIONS

Player, team	No.	Yds	Avg	Long	TD
Tim Jennings, Chicago	9	105	11.7	31	1
Stevie Brown, NY Giants	8	307	38.4	70	0
Richard Sherman, Seattle	8	57	7.1	29	1
Patrick Peterson, Arizona	7	64	9.1	31	0
*Casey Hayward, Green Bay	6	81	13.5	24	0
Thomas DeCoud, Atlanta	6	42	7.0	24	0
Asante Samuel, Atlanta	5	110	22.0	79T	1
London Fletcher, Washington	5	29	5.8	10	0

SCORING—KICKERS

Player, team	PAT	FG	Long	Pts
Lawrence Tynes, NY Giants	46/46	33/39	50	145
Matt Bryant, Atlanta	44/44	33/38	55	143
*Blair Walsh, Minnesota	36/36	35/38	56	141
Jason Hanson, Detroit	38/38	32/36	53	134
David Akers, San Francisco	44/44	29/42	63	131
Dan Bailey, Dallas	37/37	29/31	51	124

SCORING—NON-KICKERS

Player, team (position)	TD	Rush	Rec	2-Pt	Pts
James Jones, Green Bay (WR)	14	0	14	0	84
Adrian Peterson, Minnesota (RB)	13	12	1	1	80
*Alfred Morris, Washington (RB)	13	13	0	0	78
Dez Bryant, Dallas (WR)	12	0	12	1	74
Marshawn Lynch, Seattle (RB)	12	11	1	0	72
*Doug Martin, Tampa Bay (RB)	12	11	1	0	72

KICKOFF RETURNS

Player, team	No.	Yds	Avg	Long	TD
Leon Washington, Seattle	27	784	29.0	98T	1
*David Wilson, NY Giants	57	1,533	26.9	97T	1
*Travaris Cadet, New Orleans	26	690	26.5	75	0
Devin Hester, Chicago	24	621	25.9	40	0
Jacquizz Rodgers, Atlanta	23	592	25.7	77	0
Randall Cobb, Green Bay	38	964	25.4	46	0

PUNTING

Player, team	No.	Yds	Long	Avg
Thomas Morstead, New Orleans	74	3,707	70	50.1
Andy Lee, San Francisco	67	3,226	66	48.1
Steve Weatherford, NY Giants	58	2,757	68	47.5
Matt Bosher, Atlanta	60	2,847	63	47.5
Mat McBriar, Philadelphia	55	2,560	66	46.5
Dave Zastudil, Arizona	112	5,209	70	46.5

PUNT RETURNS

Player, team	No.	Yds	Avg	Long	TD
Dwayne Harris, Dallas	22	354	16.1	78T	1
*Damaris Johnson, Philadelphia	26	291	11.2	98T	1
Ted Ginn, San Francisco	32	326	10.2	38	0
Roscoe Parrish, Tampa Bay	30	298	9.9	39	0
Randall Cobb, Green Bay	31	292	9.4	75T	1
Stefan Logan, Detroit	33	300	9.1	48	0

SACKS

Player, team	No.
Aldon Smith, San Francisco	19.5
Clay Matthews, Green Bay	13.0
Charles Johnson, Carolina	12.5
Jared Allen, Minnesota	12.0
Chris Clemons, Seattle	11.5
Chris Long, St. Louis	11.5
Julius Peppers, Chicago	11.5
DeMarcus Ware, Dallas	11.5
Greg Hardy, Carolina	11.0
Anthony Spencer, Dallas	11.0
Robert Quinn, St. Louis	10.5
John Abraham, Atlanta	10.0
Cliff Avril, Detroit	9.5
Michael Bennett, Tampa Bay	9.0
Daryl Washington, Arizona	9.0

Super Bowl XLVII: Baltimore 34, San Francisco 31

The Baltimore Ravens defeated the San Francisco 49ers in Super Bowl XLVII on Feb. 3, 2013, in New Orleans, LA. Ravens head coach John Harbaugh led Baltimore to its second Super Bowl win in franchise history and handed the 49ers, coached by his brother, Jim, their first Super Bowl defeat.

Baltimore QB Joe Flacco tossed three first-half touchdown passes, including a 56-yarder to Jacoby Jones, as the Ravens took a 21-6 halftime lead. Jones then opened the second half with a 108-yard kickoff return that extended the advantage to 28-6. Shortly thereafter, most of the lights and scoreboards in the Mercedes-Benz Superdome went out. The game was delayed for about 34 minutes. The Niners found new life when the lights returned, and the 49ers posted 17 consecutive third-quarter points, cutting the Ravens' lead to 28-23, but the comeback fizzled and the Ravens held on to preserve their win.

Flacco's solid first-half and 287 total passing yards earned him the Super Bowl MVP award, while Kaepernick passed for 302 yards and rushed for 62 in a losing effort. Super Bowl XLVII was the longest Super Bowl in history at 4 hours, 14 minutes. The game was also the last for Baltimore linebacker Ray Lewis, who earlier announced he would retire at the end of the season following a 17-year career.

Quarters

Team	1	2	3	4	Final
Baltimore	7	14	7	6	34
San Francisco	3	3	17	8	31

Scoring

Baltimore: Anquan Boldin, 13-yard pass from Joe Flacco (Justin Tucker PAT)
San Francisco: David Akers, 36-yard field goal
Baltimore: Dennis Pitta, 1-yard pass from Joe Flacco (Justin Tucker PAT)
Baltimore: Jacoby Jones, 56-yard pass from Joe Flacco (Justin Tucker PAT)
San Francisco: David Akers, 27-yard field goal
Baltimore: Jacoby Jones, 108-yard kickoff return (Justin Tucker PAT)
San Francisco: Michael Crabtree, 31-yard pass from Colin Kaepernick (David Akers PAT)
San Francisco: Frank Gore, 6-yard run (David Akers PAT)
San Francisco: David Akers, 34-yard field goal
Baltimore: Justin Tucker, 19-yard field goal
San Francisco: Colin Kaepernick, 15-yard run (2-point conversion failed)
Baltimore: Justin Tucker, 38-yard field goal
San Francisco: Sam Koch ran out of end zone for safety

Individual statistics

Rushing
Baltimore: Rice, 20-59; Pierce, 12-33; Tucker, 1-8; Leach, 1-1; Koch, 1-minus-8.
San Francisco: Gore, 19-110; Kaepernick, 7-62; James, 3-10.

Passing
Baltimore: Flacco, 22-33, 287 yards, 3 TD, 0 int.
San Francisco: Kaepernick, 16-28, 302 yards, 1 TD, 1 int.

Receiving
Baltimore: Boldin, 6-104; J. Jones, 1-56; Dickson, 2-37; T. Smith, 2-35; Pitta, 4-26; Rice, 4-19; Leach, 3-10.
San Francisco: Crabtree, 5-109; V. Davis, 6-104; Walker, 3-48; Moss, 2-41.

Team statistics	Ravens	49ers
First downs	21	23
Total net yards	367	468
Rushes-yards	35-93	29-182
Passing yards, net	274	286
Punt returns-yards	2-28	1-32
Kickoff returns-yards	5-206	4-106
Interception returns-yards	1-6	0-0
Field goals made-attempts	2-2	3-3
Att-comp-int	33-22-0	28-16-1
Sacked-yards lost	2-13	3-16
Punts-average	3-47.0	3-53.0
Fumbles-lost	2-1	1-1
Penalties-yards	2-20	5-33
Time of possession	32:23	27:37

Total attendance: 71,024   **Game length:** 4:14

Super Bowl Sites, 2013-15

No.	Site	Date	No.	Site	Date
XLVII	Mercedes-Benz Superdome, New Orleans, LA..................	Feb. 3, 2013	XLIX	Univ. of Phoenix Stadium, Glendale, AZ...	Feb. 2015
XLVIII	MetLife Stadium, East Rutherford, NJ	Feb. 2, 2014	L	Levi's Stadium, Santa Clara, CA.........	Feb. 2016

Super Bowl Results, 1967-2013

No.	Year	Winner	Opponent	Winning coach	Site
I	1967	*Green Bay Packers, 35	Kansas City Chiefs, 10	Vince Lombardi	Memorial Coliseum, Los Angeles, CA
II	1968	Green Bay Packers, 33	*Oakland Raiders, 14	Vince Lombardi	Orange Bowl, Miami, FL
III	1969	*NY Jets, 16	Baltimore Colts, 7	Weeb Ewbank	Orange Bowl, Miami, FL
IV	1970	Kansas City Chiefs, 23	*Minnesota Vikings, 7	Hank Stram	Tulane Stadium, New Orleans, LA
V	1971	Baltimore Colts, 16	*Dallas Cowboys, 13	Don McCafferty	Orange Bowl, Miami, FL
VI	1972	Dallas Cowboys, 24	*Miami Dolphins, 3	Tom Landry	Tulane Stadium, New Orleans, LA
VII	1973	*Miami Dolphins, 14	Washington Redskins, 7	Don Shula	Memorial Coliseum, Los Angeles, CA
VIII	1974	*Miami Dolphins, 24	Minnesota Vikings, 7	Don Shula	Rice Stadium, Houston, TX
IX	1975	*Pittsburgh Steelers, 16	Minnesota Vikings, 6	Chuck Noll	Tulane Stadium, New Orleans, LA
X	1976	Pittsburgh Steelers, 21	*Dallas Cowboys, 17	Chuck Noll	Orange Bowl, Miami, FL
XI	1977	*Oakland Raiders, 32	Minnesota Vikings, 14	John Madden	Rose Bowl, Pasadena, CA
XII	1978	*Dallas Cowboys, 27	Denver Broncos, 10	Tom Landry	Superdome, New Orleans, LA
XIII	1979	Pittsburgh Steelers, 35	*Dallas Cowboys, 31	Chuck Noll	Orange Bowl, Miami, FL
XIV	1980	Pittsburgh Steelers, 31	*L.A. Rams, 19	Chuck Noll	Rose Bowl, Pasadena, CA
XV	1981	Oakland Raiders, 27	*Philadelphia Eagles, 10	Tom Flores	Superdome, New Orleans, LA
XVI	1982	*San Francisco 49ers, 26	Cincinnati Bengals, 21	Bill Walsh	Silverdome, Pontiac, MI
XVII	1983	Washington Redskins, 27	*Miami Dolphins, 17	Joe Gibbs	Rose Bowl, Pasadena, CA
XVIII	1984	*L.A. Raiders, 38	Washington Redskins, 9	Tom Flores	Tampa Stadium, Tampa, FL
XIX	1985	*San Francisco 49ers, 38	Miami Dolphins, 16	Bill Walsh	Stanford Stadium, Stanford, CA
XX	1986	*Chicago Bears, 46	New England Patriots, 10	Mike Ditka	Superdome, New Orleans, LA
XXI	1987	NY Giants, 39	*Denver Broncos, 20	Bill Parcells	Rose Bowl, Pasadena, CA
XXII	1988	*Washington Redskins, 42	Denver Broncos, 10	Joe Gibbs	Jack Murphy Stadium, San Diego, CA
XXIII	1989	*San Francisco 49ers, 20	Cincinnati Bengals, 16	Bill Walsh	Joe Robbie Stadium, Miami, FL
XXIV	1990	San Francisco 49ers, 55	*Denver Broncos, 10	George Seifert	Superdome, New Orleans, LA
XXV	1991	NY Giants, 20	*Buffalo Bills, 19	Bill Parcells	Tampa Stadium, Tampa, FL
XXVI	1992	*Washington Redskins, 37	Buffalo Bills, 24	Joe Gibbs	Metrodome, Minneapolis, MN
XXVII	1993	Dallas Cowboys, 52	*Buffalo Bills, 17	Jimmy Johnson	Rose Bowl, Pasadena, CA
XXVIII	1994	*Dallas Cowboys, 30	Buffalo Bills, 13	Jimmy Johnson	Georgia Dome, Atlanta, GA
XXIX	1995	*San Francisco 49ers, 49	San Diego Chargers, 26	George Seifert	Joe Robbie Stadium, Miami, FL
XXX	1996	*Dallas Cowboys, 27	Pittsburgh Steelers, 17	Barry Switzer	Sun Devil Stadium, Tempe, AZ
XXXI	1997	Green Bay Packers, 35	*New England Patriots, 21	Mike Holmgren	Superdome, New Orleans, LA
XXXII	1998	Denver Broncos, 31	*Green Bay Packers, 24	Mike Shanahan	Qualcomm Stadium, San Diego, CA
XXXIII	1999	Denver Broncos, 34	*Atlanta Falcons, 19	Mike Shanahan	Pro Player Stadium, Miami, FL
XXXIV	2000	*St. Louis Rams, 23	Tennessee Titans, 16	Dick Vermeil	Georgia Dome, Atlanta, GA
XXXV	2001	Baltimore Ravens, 34	*NY Giants, 7	Brian Billick	Raymond James Stadium, Tampa, FL
XXXVI	2002	New England Patriots, 20	*St. Louis Rams, 17	Bill Belichick	Superdome, New Orleans, LA
XXXVII	2003	*Tampa Bay Buccaneers, 48	Oakland Raiders, 21	Jon Gruden	Qualcomm Stadium, San Diego, CA
XXXVIII	2004	New England Patriots, 32	*Carolina Panthers, 29	Bill Belichick	Reliant Stadium, Houston, TX
XXXIX	2005	New England Patriots, 24	*Philadelphia Eagles, 21	Bill Belichick	Alltel Stadium, Jacksonville, FL
XL	2006	Pittsburgh Steelers, 21	*Seattle Seahawks, 10	Bill Cowher	Ford Field, Detroit, MI
XLI	2007	Indianapolis Colts, 29	*Chicago Bears, 17	Tony Dungy	Dolphin Stadium, Miami, FL
XLII	2008	*NY Giants, 17	New England Patriots, 14	Tom Coughlin	Univ. of Phoenix Stadium, Glendale, AZ
XLIII	2009	Pittsburgh Steelers, 27	*Arizona Cardinals, 23	Mike Tomlin	Raymond James Stadium, Tampa, FL
XLIV	2010	*New Orleans Saints, 31	Indianapolis Colts, 17	Sean Payton	Sun Life Stadium, Miami Gardens, FL
XLV	2011	*Green Bay Packers, 31	Pittsburgh Steelers, 25	Mike McCarthy	Cowboys Stadium, Arlington, TX
XLVI	2012	NY Giants, 21	*New England Patriots, 17	Tom Coughlin	Lucas Oil Stadium, Indianapolis, IN
XLVII	2013	*Baltimore Ravens, 34	San Francisco 49ers, 31	John Harbaugh	Mercedes-Benz Superdome, New Orleans, LA

*Team that won the coin toss. All teams that won the toss elected to receive, except the 2009 Cardinals, 2011 Packers, 2012 Patriots, and 2013 Ravens, who deferred their choice to receive in the second half.

Super Bowl MVPs, 1967-2013

Year	Most valuable player, team	Year	Most valuable player, team	Year	Most valuable player, team
1967	Bart Starr, Green Bay	1983	John Riggins, Washington	1999	John Elway, Denver
1968	Bart Starr, Green Bay	1984	Marcus Allen, L.A. Raiders	2000	Kurt Warner, St. Louis
1969	Joe Namath, NY Jets	1985	Joe Montana, San Francisco	2001	Ray Lewis, Baltimore
1970	Len Dawson, Kansas City	1986	Richard Dent, Chicago	2002	Tom Brady, New England
1971	Chuck Howley, Dallas	1987	Phil Simms, NY Giants	2003	Dexter Jackson, Tampa Bay
1972	Roger Staubach, Dallas	1988	Doug Williams, Washington	2004	Tom Brady, New England
1973	Jake Scott, Miami	1989	Jerry Rice, San Francisco	2005	Deion Branch, New England
1974	Larry Csonka, Miami	1990	Joe Montana, San Francisco	2006	Hines Ward, Pittsburgh
1975	Franco Harris, Pittsburgh	1991	Ottis Anderson, NY Giants	2007	Peyton Manning, Indianapolis
1976	Lynn Swann, Pittsburgh	1992	Mark Rypien, Washington	2008	Eli Manning, NY Giants
1977	Fred Biletnikoff, Oakland	1993	Troy Aikman, Dallas	2009	Santonio Holmes, Pittsburgh
1978	Randy White, Harvey Martin, Dallas	1994	Emmitt Smith, Dallas	2010	Drew Brees, New Orleans
1979	Terry Bradshaw, Pittsburgh	1995	Steve Young, San Francisco	2011	Aaron Rodgers, Green Bay
1980	Terry Bradshaw, Pittsburgh	1996	Larry Brown, Dallas	2012	Eli Manning, NY Giants
1981	Jim Plunkett, Oakland	1997	Desmond Howard, Green Bay	2013	Joe Flacco, Baltimore
1982	Joe Montana, San Francisco	1998	Terrell Davis, Denver		

Super Bowl Single-Game Statistical Leaders

Passing Yards

Player, team	Year	Att/comp	Yds	TD
Kurt Warner, St. Louis	2000	45/24	414	2
Kurt Warner, Arizona	2009	43/31	377	3
Kurt Warner, St. Louis	2002	44/28	365	1
Donovon McNabb, Philadelphia	2005	51/30	357	3
Joe Montana, San Francisco	1989	36/23	357	2

Passing Touchdowns

Player, team	Year	Att/comp	Yds	TD
Steve Young, San Francisco	1995	36/24	325	6
Joe Montana, San Francisco	1990	29/22	297	5
Troy Aikman, Dallas	1993	30/22	273	4
Doug Williams, Washington	1988	29/18	340	
Terry Bradshaw, Pittsburgh	1979	30/17	318	

Receiving Yards

Player, team	Year	Rec	Yds	TD
Jerry Rice, San Francisco	1989	11	215	1
Ricky Sanders, Washington	1988	9	193	2
Isaac Bruce, St. Louis	2000	6	162	1

Scoring

Player, team	Year	Pts	
Terrell Davis, Denver	1998	18	3 TDs
Jerry Rice, San Francisco	1995		3 TDs
Ricky Watters, San Francisco	1995		3 TDs
Jerry Rice, San Francisco	1990		3 TDs
Roger Craig, San Francisco	1985		3 TDs
Don Chandler, Green Bay	1968	15	4 FGs, 3 PATs
Kevin Butler, Chicago Bears	1986	14	3 FGs, 5 PATs
Ray Wersching, San Francisco	1982		4 FGs, 2 PATs

Rushing Yards

Player, team	Year	Att	Yds	TD
Timmy Smith, Washington	1988	22	204	2
Marcus Allen, L.A. Raiders	1984	20	191	2
John Riggins, Washington	1983	38	166	1

First-Round Selections in the 2013 NFL Draft

Held Apr. 25-27, 2013.

Team	Player	Pos.	College
1. Kansas City	Eric Fisher	OT	Central Michigan
2. Jacksonville	Luke Joeckel	OT	Texas A&M
3. Miami[1]	Dion Jordan	DE	Oregon
4. Philadelphia	Lane Johnson	OT	Oklahoma
5. Detroit	Ezekiel "Ziggy" Ansah	DE	Brigham Young
6. Cleveland	Barkevious Mingo	DE	LSU
7. Arizona	Jonathan Cooper	OG	N. Carolina
8. St. Louis[2]	Tavon Austin	WR	West Virginia
9. NY Jets	Dee Milliner	CB	Alabama
10. Tennessee	Chance Warmack	G	Alabama
11. San Diego	D.J. Fluker	OT	Alabama
12. Oakland[3]	D.J. Hayden	CB	Houston
13. NY Jets[4]	Sheldon Richardson	DT	Missouri
14. Carolina	Star Lotulelei	DT	Utah
15. New Orleans	Kenny Vaccaro	S	Texas
16. Buffalo[5]	E.J. Manuel	QB	Florida St.
17. Pittsburgh	Jarvis Jones	LB	Georgia
18. San Francisco[6]	Eric Reid	S	LSU
19. NY Giants	Justin Pugh	OT	Syracuse
20. Chicago	Kyle Long	OG	Oregon
21. Cincinnati	Tyler Eifert	TE	Notre Dame
22. Atlanta[7]	Desmond Trufant	CB	Washington
23. Minnesota	Sharrif Floyd	DT	Florida
24. Indianapolis	Bjoern Werner	DE	Florida St.
25. Minnesota[8]	Xavier Rhodes	CB	Florida St.
26. Green Bay	Datone Jones	DE	UCLA
27. Houston	DeAndre Hopkins	WR	Clemson
28. Denver	Sylvester Williams	DT	N. Carolina
29. Minnesota[9]	Cordarrelle Patterson	WR	Tennessee
30. St. Louis[10]	Alec Ogletree	LB	Georgia
31. Dallas[11]	Travis Frederick	C	Wisconsin
32. Baltimore	Matt Elam	DB	Florida

(1) From Oakland. (2) From Buffalo. (3) From Miami. (4) From Tampa Bay. (5) From St. Louis. (6) From Dallas. (7) From Washington through St. Louis. (8) From Seattle. (9) From New England. (10) From Atlanta. (11) From San Francisco.

Number One NFL Draft Choices, 1936-2013

Year	Team	Player, pos., college
1936	Philadelphia	Jay Berwanger, HB, Chicago
1937	Philadelphia	Sam Francis, FB, Nebraska
1938	Cleveland Rams	Corbett Davis, FB, Indiana
1939	Chicago Cards	Ki Aldrich, C, TCU
1940	Chicago Cards	George Cafego, HB, Tennessee
1941	Chicago Bears	Tom Harmon, HB, Michigan
1942	Pittsburgh	Bill Dudley, HB, Virginia
1943	Detroit	Frank Sinkwich, HB, Georgia
1944	Boston Yanks	Angelo Bertelli, QB, Notre Dame
1945	Chicago Cards	Charley Trippi, HB, Georgia
1946	Boston Yanks	Frank Dancewicz, QB, Notre Dame
1947	Chicago Bears	Bob Fenimore, HB, Oklahoma St.
1948	Washington	Harry Gilmer, QB, Alabama
1949	Philadelphia	Chuck Bednarik, C/LB, Pennsylvania
1950	Detroit	Leon Hart, E, Notre Dame
1951	NY Giants	Kyle Rote, HB, SMU
1952	L.A. Rams	Bill Wade, QB, Vanderbilt
1953	San Francisco	Harry Babcock, E, Georgia
1954	Cleveland	Bobby Garrett, QB, Stanford
1955	Baltimore Colts	George Shaw, QB, Oregon
1956	Pittsburgh	Gary Glick, DB, Colorado State
1957	Green Bay	Paul Hornung, QB, Notre Dame
1958	Chicago Cards	King Hill, QB, Rice
1959	Green Bay	Randy Duncan, QB, Iowa
1960	L.A. Rams	Billy Cannon, HB, LSU
1961	Minnesota	Tommy Mason, HB, Tulane
1962	Washington	Ernie Davis, HB, Syracuse
1963	L.A. Rams	Terry Baker, QB, Oregon St.
1964	San Francisco	Dave Parks, E, Texas Tech
1965	NY Giants	Tucker Frederickson, RB, Auburn
1966	Atlanta	Tommy Nobis, LB, Texas
1967	Baltimore Colts	Bubba Smith, DE, Michigan St.
1968	Minnesota	Ron Yary, OT, USC
1969	Buffalo	O.J. Simpson, RB, USC
1970	Pittsburgh	Terry Bradshaw, QB, LA Tech
1971	New England	Jim Plunkett, QB, Stanford
1972	Buffalo	Walt Patulski, DE, Notre Dame
1973	Houston	John Matuszak, DE, Tampa
1974	Dallas	Ed "Too Tall" Jones, DE, Tenn. St.
1975	Atlanta	Steve Bartkowski, QB, California
1976	Tampa Bay	Lee Roy Selmon, DE, Oklahoma
1977	Tampa Bay	Ricky Bell, RB, USC
1978	Houston	Earl Campbell, RB, Texas
1979	Buffalo	Tom Cousineau, LB, Ohio St.
1980	Detroit	Billy Sims, RB, Oklahoma
1981	New Orleans	George Rogers, RB, S. Carolina
1982	New England	Kenneth Sims, DT, Texas
1983	Baltimore Colts	John Elway, QB, Stanford
1984	New England	Irving Fryar, WR, Nebraska
1985	Buffalo	Bruce Smith, DE, Virginia Tech
1986	Tampa Bay	Bo Jackson, RB, Auburn
1987	Tampa Bay	Vinny Testaverde, QB, Miami (FL)
1988	Atlanta	Aundray Bruce, LB, Auburn
1989	Dallas	Troy Aikman, QB, UCLA
1990	Indianapolis	Jeff George, QB, Illinois
1991	Dallas	Russell Maryland, DL, Miami (FL)
1992	Indianapolis	Steve Emtman, DL, Washington
1993	New England	Drew Bledsoe, QB, Washington St.
1994	Cincinnati	Dan Wilkinson, DT, Ohio St.
1995	Cincinnati	Ki-Jana Carter, RB, Penn State
1996	NY Jets	Keyshawn Johnson, WR, USC
1997	St. Louis	Orlando Pace, OT, Ohio St.
1998	Indianapolis	Peyton Manning, QB, Tennessee
1999	Cleveland	Tim Couch, QB, Kentucky
2000	Cleveland	Courtney Brown, DE, Penn State
2001	Atlanta	Michael Vick, QB, Virginia Tech
2002	Houston	David Carr, QB, Fresno St.
2003	Cincinnati	Carson Palmer, QB, USC
2004	San Diego	Eli Manning, QB, Mississippi
2005	San Francisco	Alex D. Smith, QB, Utah
2006	Houston	Mario Williams, DE, NC State
2007	Oakland	JaMarcus Russell, QB, LSU
2008	Miami	Jake Long, OT, Michigan
2009	Detroit	Matthew Stafford, QB, Georgia
2010	St. Louis	Sam Bradford, QB, Oklahoma
2011	Carolina	Cam Newton, QB, Auburn
2012	Indianapolis	Andrew Luck, QB, Stanford
2013	Kansas City	Eric Fisher, OT, Central Michigan

American Football League Champions, 1960-69

Year	Eastern (W-L-T)	Western (W-L-T)	Championship
1960	Houston Oilers (10-4-0)	L.A. Chargers (10-4-0)	Houston 24, L.A. 16
1961	Houston Oilers (10-3-1)	San Diego Chargers (12-2-0)	Houston 10, San Diego 3
1962	Houston Oilers (11-3-0)	Dallas Texans (11-3-0)	Dallas 20, Houston 17 (2 OT)
1963	Boston Patriots (7-6-1)[1]	San Diego Chargers (11-3-0)	San Diego 51, Boston 10
1964	Buffalo Bills (12-2-0)	San Diego Chargers (8-5-1)	Buffalo 20, San Diego 7
1965	Buffalo Bills (10-3-1)	San Diego Chargers (9-2-3)	Buffalo 23, San Diego 0
1966	Buffalo Bills (9-4-1)	Kansas City Chiefs (11-2-1)	Kansas City 31, Buffalo 7
1967	Houston Oilers (9-4-1)	Oakland Raiders (13-1-0)	Oakland 40, Houston 7
1968	NY Jets (11-3-0)	Oakland Raiders (12-2-0)[2]	NY Jets 27, Oakland 23
1969	NY Jets (10-4-0)	Oakland Raiders (12-1-1)	Kansas City 17, Oakland 7[3]

(1) Defeated Buffalo Bills in divisional playoff. (2) Defeated Kansas City Chiefs in divisional playoff. (3) Kansas City Chiefs defeated NY Jets, and Oakland Raiders defeated Houston Oilers in divisional playoffs.

National Football League Champions, 1933-69

Year	East (W-L-T)	West (W-L-T)	Championship
1933	NY Giants (11-3-0)	Chicago Bears (10-2-1)	Chicago Bears 23, NY Giants 21
1934	NY Giants (8-5-0)	Chicago Bears (13-0-0)	NY Giants 30, Chicago Bears 13
1935	NY Giants (9-3-0)	Detroit Lions (7-3-2)	Detroit 26, NY Giants 7
1936	Boston Redskins (7-5-0)	Green Bay Packers (10-1-1)	Green Bay 21, Boston 6
1937	Washington Redskins (8-3-0)	Chicago Bears (9-1-1)	Washington 28, Chicago Bears 21
1938	NY Giants (8-2-1)	Green Bay Packers (8-3-0)	NY Giants 23, Green Bay 17
1939	NY Giants (9-1-1)	Green Bay Packers (9-2-0)	Green Bay 27, NY Giants 0
1940	Washington Redskins (9-2-0)	Chicago Bears (8-3-0)	Chicago Bears 73, Washington 0
1941	NY Giants (8-3-0)	Chicago Bears (10-1-0)[1]	Chicago Bears 37, NY Giants 9
1942	Washington Redskins (10-1-0)	Chicago Bears (11-0-0)	Washington 14, Chicago Bears 6
1943	Washington Redskins (6-3-1)[1]	Chicago Bears (8-1-1)	Chicago Bears, 41, Washington 21
1944	NY Giants (8-1-1)	Green Bay Packers (8-2-0)	Green Bay 14, NY Giants 7
1945	Washington Redskins (8-2-0)	Cleveland Rams (9-1-0)	Cleveland Rams 15, Washington 14
1946	NY Giants (7-3-1)	Chicago Bears (8-2-1)	Chicago Bears 24, NY Giants 14
1947	Philadelphia Eagles (8-4-0)[1]	Chicago Cardinals (9-3-0)	Chicago Cardinals 28, Philadelphia 21
1948	Philadelphia Eagles (9-2-1)	Chicago Cardinals (11-1-0)	Philadelphia 7, Chicago Cardinals 0
1949	Philadelphia Eagles (11-1-0)	L.A. Rams (8-2-2)	Philadelphia 14, L.A. Rams 0
1950	Cleveland Browns (10-2-0)[1]	L.A. Rams (9-3-0)[1]	Cleveland 30, L.A. Rams 28
1951	Cleveland Browns (11-1-0)	L.A. Rams (8-4-0)	L.A. Rams 24, Cleveland Browns 17
1952	Cleveland Browns (8-4-0)	Detroit Lions (9-3-0)[1]	Detroit 17, Cleveland Browns 7
1953	Cleveland Browns (11-1-0)	Detroit Lions (10-2-0)	Detroit 17, Cleveland Browns 16
1954	Cleveland Browns (9-3-0)	Detroit Lions (9-2-1)	Cleveland Browns 56, Detroit 10
1955	Cleveland Browns (9-2-1)	L.A. Rams (8-3-1)	Cleveland Browns 38, L.A. Rams 14
1956	NY Giants (8-3-1)	Chicago Bears (9-2-1)	NY Giants 47, Chicago Bears 7
1957	Cleveland Browns (9-2-1)	Detroit Lions (8-4-0)[1]	Detroit 59, Cleveland Browns 14
1958	NY Giants (9-3-0)[1]	Baltimore Colts (9-3-0)	Baltimore 23, NY Giants 17[2]
1959	NY Giants (10-2-0)	Baltimore Colts (9-3-0)	Baltimore 31, NY Giants 16
1960	Philadelphia Eagles (10-2-0)	Green Bay Packers (8-4-0)	Philadelphia 17, Green Bay 13
1961	NY Giants (10-3-1)	Green Bay Packers (11-3-0)	Green Bay 37, NY Giants 0
1962	NY Giants (12-2-0)	Green Bay Packers (13-1-0)	Green Bay 16, NY Giants 7
1963	NY Giants (11-3-0)	Chicago Bears (11-1-2)	Chicago 14, NY Giants 10
1964	Cleveland Browns (10-3-1)	Baltimore Colts (12-2-0)	Cleveland Browns 27, Baltimore 0
1965	Cleveland Browns (11-3-0)	Green Bay Packers (10-3-1)[1]	Green Bay 23, Cleveland Browns 12
1966	Dallas Cowboys (10-3-1)	Green Bay Packers (12-2-0)	Green Bay 34, Dallas 27
1967	Dallas Cowboys (9-5-0)	Green Bay Packers (9-4-1)	Green Bay 21, Dallas 17
1968	Cleveland Browns (10-4-0)	Baltimore Colts (13-1-0)	Baltimore 34, Cleveland Browns 0
1969	Cleveland Browns (10-3-1)	Minnesota Vikings (12-2-0)	Minnesota 27, Cleveland Browns 7

Note: Conference title games preceded NFL Championship from 1967-69. (1) Won divisional or conference playoff. (2) Won at 8:15 of sudden death overtime period.

NFL Divisional Champions and Wild Cards, 1970-95

The American Football League and National Football League officially merged in 1966. At the beginning of the 1970 season, the two leagues became the AFC and NFC conferences in the new NFL. Regular-season (W-L-T) records are in parentheses.

AMERICAN FOOTBALL CONFERENCE

Year	Eastern	Central	Western	Wild card
1970	Baltimore Colts (11-2-1)	Cincinnati Bengals (8-6-0)	Oakland Raiders (8-4-2)	Miami Dolphins (10-4-0)
1971	Miami Dolphins (10-3-1)	Cleveland Browns (9-5-0)	Kansas City Chiefs (10-3-1)	Baltimore Colts (10-4-0)
1972	Miami Dolphins (14-0-0)	Pittsburgh Steelers (11-3-0)	Oakland Raiders (10-3-1)	Cleveland Browns (10-4-0)
1973	Miami Dolphins (12-2-0)	Cincinnati Bengals (10-4-0)	Oakland Raiders (9-4-1)	Pittsburgh Steelers (10-4-0)
1974	Miami Dolphins (11-3-0)	Pittsburgh Steelers (10-3-1)	Oakland Raiders (12-2-0)	Buffalo Bills (9-5-0)
1975	Baltimore Colts (10-4-0)	Pittsburgh Steelers (12-2-0)	Oakland Raiders (11-3-0)	Cincinnati Bengals (11-3-0)
1976	Baltimore Colts (11-3-0)	Pittsburgh Steelers (10-4-0)	Oakland Raiders (13-1-0)	New England Patriots (11-3-0)
1977	Baltimore Colts (10-4-0)	Pittsburgh Steelers (9-5-0)	Denver Broncos (12-2-0)	Oakland Raiders (11-3-0)
1978	New England Patriots (11-5-0)	Pittsburgh Steelers (14-2-0)	Denver Broncos (10-6-0)	Houston Oilers (10-6-0) Miami Dolphins (11-5-0)
1979	Miami Dolphins (10-6-0)	Pittsburgh Steelers (12-4-0)	San Diego Chargers (12-4-0)	Houston Oilers (11-5-0) Denver Broncos (10-6-0)
1980	Buffalo Bills (11-5-0)	Cleveland Browns (11-5-0)	San Diego Chargers (11-5-0)	Houston Oilers (11-5-0) Oakland Raiders (11-5-0)
1981	Miami Dolphins (11-4-1)	Cincinnati Bengals (12-4-0)	San Diego Chargers (10-6-0)	Buffalo Bills (10-6-0) NY Jets (10-5-1)
1982	Strike abbreviated season. See note.			
1983	Miami Dolphins (12-4-0)	Pittsburgh Steelers (10-6-0)	L.A. Raiders (12-4-0)	Denver Broncos (9-7-0) Seattle Seahawks (9-7-0)
1984	Miami Dolphins (14-2-0)	Pittsburgh Steelers (9-7-0)	Denver Broncos (13-3-0)	L.A. Raiders (11-5-0) Seattle Seahawks (12-4-0)

AMERICAN FOOTBALL CONFERENCE

Year	Eastern	Central	Western	Wild card
1985	Miami Dolphins (12-4-0)	Cleveland Browns (8-8-0)	L.A. Raiders (12-4-0)	New England Patriots (11-5-0) NY Jets (11-5-0)
1986	New England Patriots (11-5-0)	Cleveland Browns (12-4-0)	Denver Broncos (11-5-0)	Kansas City Chiefs (10-6-0) NY Jets (10-6-0)
1987	Indianapolis Colts (9-6-0)	Cleveland Browns (10-5-0)	Denver Broncos (10-4-1)	Houston Oilers (9-6-0) Seattle Seahawks (9-6-0)
1988	Buffalo Bills (12-4-0)	Cincinnati Bengals (12-4-0)	Seattle Seahawks (9-7-0)	Cleveland Browns (10-6-0) Houston Oilers (10-6-0)
1989	Buffalo Bills (9-7-0)	Cleveland Browns (9-6-1)	Denver Broncos (11-5-0)	Houston Oilers (9-7-0) Pittsburgh Steelers (9-7-0)
1990	Buffalo Bills (13-3-0)	Cincinnati Bengals (9-7-0)	L.A. Raiders (12-4-0)	Houston Oilers (9-7-0) Kansas City Chiefs (11-5-0) Miami Dolphins (12-4-0)
1991	Buffalo Bills (13-3-0)	Houston Oilers (11-5-0)	Denver Broncos (12-4-0)	Kansas City Chiefs (11-5-0) L.A. Raiders (9-7-0) NY Jets (8-8-0)
1992	Miami Dolphins (11-5-0)	Pittsburgh Steelers (11-5-0)	San Diego Chargers (11-5-0)	Buffalo Bills (11-5-0) Houston Oilers (10-6-0) Kansas City Chiefs (10-6-0)
1993	Buffalo Bills (12-4-0)	Houston Oilers (12-4-0)	Kansas City Chiefs (11-5-0)	Denver Broncos (9-7-0) L.A. Raiders (10-6-0) Pittsburgh Steelers (9-7-0)
1994	Miami Dolphins (10-6-0)	Pittsburgh Steelers (12-4-0)	San Diego Chargers (11-5-0)	Cleveland Browns (11-5-0) Kansas City Chiefs (9-7-0) New England Patriots (10-6-0)
1995	Buffalo Bills (10-6-0)	Pittsburgh Steelers (11-5-0)	Kansas City Chiefs (13-3-0)	Miami Dolphins (9-7-0) Indianapolis Colts (9-7-0) San Diego Chargers (9-7-0)

NATIONAL FOOTBALL CONFERENCE

Year	Eastern	Central	Western	Wild card
1970	Dallas Cowboys (10-4-0)	Minnesota Vikings (12-2-0)	San Francisco 49ers (10-3-1)	Detroit Lions (10-4-0)
1971	Dallas Cowboys (11-3-0)	Minnesota Vikings (11-3-0)	San Francisco 49ers (9-5-0)	Washington Redskins (9-4-1)
1972	Washington Redskins (11-3-0)	Green Bay Packers (10-4-0)	San Francisco 49ers (8-5-1)	Dallas Cowboys (10-4-0)
1973	Dallas Cowboys (10-4-0)	Minnesota Vikings (12-2-0)	L.A. Rams (12-2-0)	Washington Redskins (10-4-0)
1974	St. Louis Cardinals (10-4-0)	Minnesota Vikings (10-4-0)	L.A. Rams (10-4-0)	Washington Redskins (10-4-0)
1975	St. Louis Cardinals (11-3-0)	Minnesota Vikings (12-2-0)	L.A. Rams (12-2-0)	Dallas Cowboys (10-4-0)
1976	Dallas Cowboys (11-3-0)	Minnesota Vikings (11-2-1)	L.A. Rams (10-3-1)	Washington Redskins (10-4-0)
1977	Dallas Cowboys (12-2-0)	Minnesota Vikings (9-5-0)	L.A. Rams (10-4-0)	Chicago Bears (9-5-0)
1978	Dallas Cowboys (12-4-0)	Minnesota Vikings (8-7-1)	L.A. Rams (12-4-0)	Atlanta Falcons (9-7-0) Philadelphia Eagles (9-7-0)
1979	Dallas Cowboys (11-5-0)	Tampa Bay Buccaneers (10-6-0)	L.A. Rams (9-7-0)	Chicago Bears (10-6-0) Philadelphia Eagles (11-5-0)
1980	Philadelphia Eagles (12-4-0)	Minnesota Vikings (9-7-0)	Atlanta Falcons (12-4-0)	Dallas Cowboys (12-4-0) L.A. Rams (11-5-0)
1981	Dallas Cowboys (12-4-0)	Tampa Bay Buccaneers (9-7-0)	San Francisco 49ers (13-3-0)	NY Giants (9-7-0) Philadelphia Eagles (10-6-0)
1982	Strike abbreviated season. See note.			
1983	Washington Redskins (14-2-0)	Detroit Lions (9-7-0)	San Francisco 49ers (10-6-0)	Dallas Cowboys (12-4-0) L.A. Rams (9-7-0)
1984	Washington Redskins (11-5-0)	Chicago Bears (10-6-0)	San Francisco 49ers (15-1-0)	L.A. Rams (10-6-0) NY Giants (9-7-0)
1985	Dallas Cowboys (10-6-0)	Chicago Bears (15-1-0)	L.A. Rams (11-5-0)	NY Giants (10-6-0) San Francisco 49ers (10-6-0)
1986	NY Giants (14-2-0)	Chicago Bears (14-2-0)	San Francisco 49ers (10-5-1)	L.A. Rams (10-6-0) Washington Redskins (12-4-0)
1987	Washington Redskins (11-4-0)	Chicago Bears (11-4-0)	San Francisco 49ers (13-2-0)	Minnesota Vikings (8-7-0) New Orleans Saints (12-3-0)
1988	Philadelphia Eagles (10-6-0)	Chicago Bears (12-4-0)	San Francisco 49ers (10-6-0)	L.A. Rams (10-6-0) Minnesota Vikings (11-5-0)
1989	NY Giants (12-4-0)	Minnesota Vikings (10-6-0)	San Francisco 49ers (14-2-0)	L.A. Rams (11-5-0) Philadelphia Eagles (11-5-0)
1990	NY Giants (13-3-0)	Chicago Bears (11-5-0)	San Francisco 49ers (14-2-0)	New Orleans Saints (8-8-0) Philadelphia Eagles (10-6-0) Washington Redskins (10-6-0)
1991	Washington Redskins (14-2-0)	Detroit Lions (12-4-0)	New Orleans Saints (11-5-0)	Atlanta Falcons (10-6-0) Chicago Bears (11-5-0) Dallas Cowboys (11-5-0)
1992	Dallas Cowboys (13-3-0)	Minnesota Vikings (11-5-0)	San Francisco 49ers (14-2-0)	New Orleans Saints (12-4-0) Philadelphia Eagles (11-5-0) Washington Redskins (9-7-0)
1993	Dallas Cowboys (12-4-0)	Detroit Lions (10-6-0)	San Francisco 49ers (10-6-0)	Green Bay Packers (9-7-0) Minnesota Vikings (9-7-0) NY Giants (11-5-0)
1994	Dallas Cowboys (12-4-0)	Minnesota Vikings (10-6-0)	San Francisco 49ers (13-3-0)	Chicago Bears (9-7-0) Detroit Lions (9-7-0) Green Bay Packers (9-7-0)
1995	Dallas Cowboys (12-4-0)	Green Bay Packers (11-5-0)	San Francisco 49ers (11-5-0)	Philadelphia Eagles (10-6-0) Detroit Lions (9-7-0) Atlanta Falcons (9-7-0)

Note: A strike shortened the 1982 season from 16 to 9 games. The top eight teams in each conference played in a tournament to determine the conference champion.

NFL Playoff Results, 1996-2012

Year	Conference	Division	Winner (W-L-T)	Playoffs[1]	Year
1996	American	Eastern	New England Patriots (11-5-0)	Jacksonville* 30, Denver 27	1996
		Central	Pittsburgh Steelers (10-6-0)	New England 28, Pittsburgh 3	
		Western	Denver Broncos (13-3-0)	New England 20, Jacksonville* 6	
	National	Eastern	Dallas Cowboys (10-6-0)	Green Bay 35, San Francisco* 14	
		Central	Green Bay Packers (13-3-0)	Carolina 26, Dallas 17	
		Western	Carolina Panthers (12-4-0)	Green Bay 30, Carolina 13	
1997	American	Eastern	New England Patriots (10-6-0)	Pittsburgh 7, New England 6	1997
		Central	Pittsburgh Steelers (11-5-0)	Denver* 14, Kansas City 10	
		Western	Kansas City Chiefs (13-3-0)	Denver* 24, Pittsburgh 21	
	National	Eastern	NY Giants (10-5-1)	San Francisco 38, Minnesota* 22	
		Central	Green Bay Packers (13-3-0)	Green Bay 21, Tampa Bay* 7	
		Western	San Francisco 49ers (13-3-0)	Green Bay 23, San Francisco 10	
1998	American	Eastern	NY Jets (12-4-0)	Denver 38, Miami* 3	1998
		Central	Jacksonville Jaguars (11-5-0)	NY Jets 34, Jacksonville 24	
		Western	Denver Broncos (14-2-0)	Denver 23, NY Jets 10	
	National	Eastern	Dallas Cowboys (10-6-0)	Atlanta 20, San Francisco* 18	
		Central	Minnesota Vikings (15-1-0)	Minnesota 41, Arizona* 21	
		Western	Atlanta Falcons (14-2-0)	Atlanta 30, Minnesota 27 (OT)	
1999	American	Eastern	Indianapolis Colts (13-3-0)	Jacksonville 62, Miami* 7	1999
		Central	Jacksonville Jaguars (14-2-0)	Tennessee* 19, Indianapolis 16	
		Western	Seattle Seahawks (9-7-0)	Tennessee* 33, Jacksonville 14	
	National	Eastern	Washington Redskins (10-6-0)	Tampa Bay 14, Washington 13	
		Central	Tampa Bay Buccaneers (11-5-0)	St. Louis 49, Minnesota* 37	
		Western	St. Louis Rams (13-3-0)	St. Louis 11, Tampa Bay 6	
2000	American	Eastern	Miami Dolphins (11-5-0)	Oakland 27, Miami 0	2000
		Central	Tennessee Titans (13-3-0)	Baltimore* 24, Tennessee 10	
		Western	Oakland Raiders (12-4-0)	Baltimore* 16, Oakland 3	
	National	Eastern	NY Giants (12-4-0)	Minnesota 34, New Orleans 16	
		Central	Minnesota Vikings (11-5-0)	NY Giants 20, Philadelphia* 10	
		Western	New Orleans Saints (10-6-0)	NY Giants 41, Minnesota 0	
2001	American	Eastern	New England Patriots (11-5-0)	New England 16, Oakland 13 (OT)	2001
		Central	Pittsburgh Steelers (13-3-0)	Pittsburgh 27, Baltimore* 10	
		Western	Oakland Raiders (10-6-0)	New England 24, Pittsburgh 17	
	National	Eastern	Philadelphia Eagles (11-5-0)	Philadelphia 33, Chicago 19	
		Central	Chicago Bears (13-3-0)	St. Louis 45, Green Bay* 17	
		Western	St. Louis Rams (14-2-0)	St. Louis 29, Philadelphia 24	
2002	American	East	NY Jets (9-7-0)		2002
		North	Pittsburgh Steelers (10-5-1)	Oakland 30, NY Jets 10	
		South	Tennessee Titans (11-5-0)	Tennessee 34, Pittsburgh 31	
		West	Oakland Raiders (11-5-0)	Oakland 41, Tennessee 24	
	National	East	Philadelphia Eagles (12-4-0)		
		North	Green Bay Packers (12-4-0)	Philadelphia 20, Atlanta* 6	
		South	Tampa Bay Buccaneers (12-4-0)	Tampa Bay 31, San Francisco 6	
		West	San Francisco 49ers (10-6-0)	Tampa Bay 27, Philadelphia 10	
2003	American	East	New England Patriots (14-2-0)		2003
		North	Baltimore Ravens (10-6-0)	Indianapolis 38, Kansas City 31	
		South	Indianapolis Colts (12-4-0)	New England 17, Tennessee* 14	
		West	Kansas City Chiefs (13-3-0)	New England 24, Indianapolis 14	
	National	East	Philadelphia Eagles (12-4-0)		
		North	Green Bay Packers (10-6-0)	Carolina 29, St. Louis 23 (2 OT)	
		South	Carolina Panthers (11-5-0)	Philadelphia 20, Green Bay 17	
		West	St. Louis Rams (12-4-0)	Carolina 14, Philadelphia 3	
2004	American	East	New England Patriots (14-2-0)		2004
		North	Pittsburgh Steelers (15-1-0)	Pittsburgh 20, NY Jets* 17 (OT)	
		South	Indianapolis Colts (12-4-0)	New England 20, Indianapolis 3	
		West	San Diego Chargers (12-4-0)	New England 41, Pittsburgh 27	
	National	East	Philadelphia Eagles (13-3-0)		
		North	Green Bay Packers (10-6-0)	Atlanta 47, St. Louis* 17	
		South	Atlanta Falcons (11-5-0)	Philadelphia 27, Minnesota* 14	
		West	Seattle Seahawks (9-7-0)	Philadelphia 27, Atlanta 10	
2005	American	East	New England Patriots (10-6-0)		2005
		North	Cincinnati Bengals (11-5-0)	Denver 27, New England 13	
		South	Indianapolis Colts (14-2-0)	Pittsburgh* 21, Indianapolis 18	
		West	Denver Broncos (13-3-0)	Pittsburgh* 34, Denver 17	
	National	East	NY Giants (11-5-0)		
		North	Chicago Bears (11-5-0)	Seattle 20, Washington* 10	
		South	Tampa Bay Buccaneers (11-5-0)	Carolina* 29, Chicago 21	
		West	Seattle Seahawks (13-3-0)	Seattle 34, Carolina* 14	

Year	Conference	Division	Winner (W-L-T)	Playoffs[1]	Year
2006	American	East	New England Patriots (12-4-0)		2006
		North	Baltimore Ravens (13-3-0)	Indianapolis 15, Baltimore 6	
		South	Indianapolis Colts (12-4-0)	New England 24, San Diego 21	
		West	San Diego Chargers (14-2-0)	Indianapolis 38, New England 34	
	National	East	Philadelphia Eagles (10-6-0)		
		North	Chicago Bears (13-3-0)	New Orleans 27, Philadelphia 24	
		South	New Orleans Saints (10-6-0)	Chicago 27, Seattle 24 (OT)	
		West	Seattle Seahawks (9-7-0)	Chicago 39, New Orleans 14	
2007	American	East	New England Patriots (16-0-0)		2007
		North	Pittsburgh Steelers (10-6-0)	New England 31, Jacksonville* 20	
		South	Indianapolis Colts (13-3-0)	San Diego 28, Indianapolis 24	
		West	San Diego Chargers (11-5-0)	New England 21, San Diego 12	
	National	East	Dallas Cowboys (13-3-0)		
		North	Green Bay Packers (13-3-0)	Green Bay 42, Seattle 20	
		South	Tampa Bay Buccaneers (9-7-0)	NY Giants* 21, Dallas 17	
		West	Seattle Seahawks (10-6-0)	NY Giants* 23, Green Bay 20 (OT)	
2008	American	East	Miami Dolphins (11-5-0)		2008
		North	Pittsburgh Steelers (12-4-0)	Baltimore* 13, Tennessee 10	
		South	Tennessee Titans (13-3-0)	Pittsburgh 35, San Diego 24	
		West	San Diego Chargers (8-8-0)	Pittsburgh 23, Baltimore* 14	
	National	East	NY Giants (12-4-0)		
		North	Minnesota Vikings (10-6-0)	Arizona 33, Carolina 13	
		South	Carolina Panthers (12-4-0)	Philadelphia* 23, NY Giants 11	
		West	Arizona Cardinals (9-7-0)	Arizona 32, Philadelphia* 25	
2009	American	East	New England Patriots (10-6-0)		2009
		North	Cincinnati Bengals (10-6-0)	Indianapolis 20, Baltimore* 3	
		South	Indianapolis Colts (14-2-0)	NY Jets* 17, San Diego 14	
		West	San Diego Chargers (13-3-0)	Indianapolis 30, NY Jets* 17	
	National	East	Dallas Cowboys (11-5-0)		
		North	Minnesota Vikings (12-4-0)	New Orleans 45, Arizona 14	
		South	New Orleans Saints (13-3-0)	Minnesota 34, Dallas 3	
		West	Arizona Cardinals (10-6-0)	New Orleans 31, Minnesota 28 (OT)	
2010	American	East	New England Patriots (14-2-0)		2010
		North	Pittsburgh Steelers (12-4-0)	Pittsburgh 31, Baltimore* 24	
		South	Indianapolis Colts (10-6-0)	NY Jets* 28, New England 21	
		West	Kansas City Chiefs (10-6-0)	Pittsburgh 24, NY Jets* 19	
	National	East	Philadelphia Eagles (10-6-0)		
		North	Chicago Bears (11-5-0)	Green Bay* 48, Atlanta 21	
		South	Atlanta Falcons (13-3-0)	Chicago 35, Seattle 24	
		West	Seattle Seahawks (7-9-0)	Green Bay* 21, Chicago 14	
2011	American	East	New England Patriots (13-3-0)		2011
		North	Baltimore Ravens (12-4-0)	New England 45, Denver 10	
		South	Houston Texans (10-6-0)	Baltimore 20, Houston 13	
		West	Denver Broncos (8-8-0)	New England 23, Baltimore 20	
	National	East	NY Giants (9-7-0)		
		North	Green Bay Packers (15-1-0)	San Francisco 36, New Orleans 32	
		South	New Orleans (13-3-0)	NY Giants 37, Green Bay 20	
		West	San Francisco (13-3-0)	NY Giants 20, San Francisco 17 (OT)	
2012	American	East	New England Patriots (12-4-0)		2012
		North	Baltimore Ravens (10-6-0)	Baltimore 38, Denver 35 (2 OT)	
		South	Houston Texans (12-4-0)	New England 41, Houston 28	
		West	Denver Broncos (13-3-0)	Baltimore 28, New England 13	
	National	East	Washington Redskins (10-6-0)		
		North	Green Bay Packers (11-5-0)	San Francisco 45, Green Bay 31	
		South	Atlanta Falcons (13-3-0)	Atlanta 30, Seattle* 28	
		West	San Francisco 49ers (11-4-1)	San Francisco 28, Atlanta 24	

*Wild card team. (1) Only the final two conference playoff rounds are shown.

American Football Conference Leaders, 1960-2012

(American Football League, 1960-69)

Passing (based on QB rating points)						Receptions			
Player, team	Att	Comp	Yds	TD	Year	Player, team	Rec	Yds	TD
Jack Kemp, L.A. Chargers	406	211	3,018	20	1960	Lionel Taylor, Denver	92	1,235	12
George Blanda, Houston	362	187	3,330	36	1961	Lionel Taylor, Denver	100	1,176	4
Len Dawson, Dallas Texans	310	189	2,759	29	1962	Lionel Taylor, Denver	77	908	4
Tobin Rote, San Diego	286	170	2,510	20	1963	Lionel Taylor, Denver	78	1,101	10
Len Dawson, Kansas City	354	199	2,879	30	1964	Charley Hennigan, Houston	101	1,546	8
John Hadl, San Diego	348	174	2,798	20	1965	Lionel Taylor, Denver	85	1,131	6
Len Dawson, Kansas City	284	159	2,527	26	1966	Lance Alworth, San Diego	73	1,383	13
Daryle Lamonica, Oakland	425	220	3,228	30	1967	George Sauer, NY Jets	75	1,189	6
Len Dawson, Kansas City	224	131	2,109	17	1968	Lance Alworth, San Diego	68	1,312	10
Greg Cook, Cincinnati	197	106	1,854	15	1969	Lance Alworth, San Diego	64	1,003	4
Daryle Lamonica, Oakland	356	179	2,516	22	1970	Marlin Briscoe, Buffalo	57	1,036	8
Bob Griese, Miami	263	145	2,089	19	1971	Fred Biletnikoff, Oakland	61	929	9

Passing (based on QB rating points)

Player, team	Att	Comp	Yds	TD	Year
Earl Morrall, Miami	150	83	1,360	11	1972
Ken Stabler, Oakland	260	163	1,997	14	1973
Ken Anderson, Cincinnati	328	213	2,667	18	1974
Ken Anderson, Cincinnati	377	228	3,169	21	1975
Ken Stabler, Oakland	291	194	2,737	27	1976
Bob Griese, Miami	307	180	2,252	22	1977
Terry Bradshaw, Pittsburgh	368	207	2,915	28	1978
Dan Fouts, San Diego	530	332	4,082	24	1979
Brian Sipe, Cleveland	554	337	4,132	30	1980
Ken Anderson, Cincinnati	479	300	3,754	29	1981
Ken Anderson, Cincinnati	309	218	2,495	12	1982
Dan Marino, Miami	296	173	2,210	20	1983
Dan Marino, Miami	564	362	5,084	48	1984
Ken O'Brien, NY Jets	488	297	3,888	25	1985
Dan Marino, Miami	623	378	4,746	44	1986
Bernie Kosar, Cleveland	389	241	3,033	22	1987
Boomer Esiason, Cincinnati	388	223	3,572	28	1988
Boomer Esiason, Cincinnati	455	258	3,525	28	1989
Jim Kelly, Buffalo	346	219	2,829	24	1990
Jim Kelly, Buffalo	474	304	3,844	33	1991
Warren Moon, Houston	346	224	2,521	18	1992
John Elway, Denver	551	348	4,030	25	1993
Dan Marino, Miami	615	385	4,453	30	1994
Jim Harbaugh, Indianapolis	314	200	2,575	17	1995
John Elway, Denver	466	287	3,328	26	1996
Mark Brunell, Jacksonville	435	264	3,281	18	1997
Vinny Testaverde, NY Jets	421	259	3,256	29	1998
Peyton Manning, Indianapolis	533	331	4,135	26	1999
Brian Griese, Denver	336	216	2,688	19	2000
Rich Gannon, Oakland	549	361	3,828	27	2001
Chad Pennington, NY Jets	399	275	3,120	22	2002
Steve McNair, Tennessee	400	250	3,215	24	2003
Peyton Manning, Indianapolis	497	336	4,557	49	2004
Peyton Manning, Indianapolis	453	305	3,747	28	2005
Peyton Manning, Indianapolis	557	362	4,397	31	2006
Tom Brady, New England	578	398	4,806	50	2007
Philip Rivers, San Diego	478	312	4,009	34	2008
Philip Rivers, San Diego	486	317	4,254	28	2009
Tom Brady, New England	492	324	3,900	36	2010
Tom Brady, New England	611	401	5,235	39	2011
Peyton Manning, Denver	583	400	4,659	37	2012

Receptions

Year	Player, team	Rec	Yds	TD
1972	Fred Biletnikoff, Oakland	58	802	7
1973	Fred Willis, Houston	57	371	1
1974	Lydell Mitchell, Baltimore Colts	72	544	2
1975	Reggie Rucker, Cleveland	60	770	3
	Lydell Mitchell, Baltimore Colts	60	554	4
1976	MacArthur Lane, Kansas City	66	686	1
1977	Lydell Mitchell, Baltimore Colts	71	620	4
1978	Steve Largent, Seattle	71	1,168	8
1979	Joe Washington, Baltimore Colts	82	750	3
1980	Kellen Winslow, San Diego	89	1,290	9
1981	Kellen Winslow, San Diego	88	1,075	10
1982	Kellen Winslow, San Diego	54	721	6
1983	Todd Christensen, L.A. Raiders	92	1,247	12
1984	Ozzie Newsome, Cleveland	89	1,001	5
1985	Lionel James, San Diego	86	1,027	6
1986	Todd Christensen, L.A. Raiders	95	1,153	8
1987	Al Toon, NY Jets	68	976	5
1988	Al Toon, NY Jets	93	1,067	5
1989	Andre Reed, Buffalo	88	1,312	9
1990	Haywood Jeffires, Houston	74	1,048	8
	Drew Hill, Houston	74	1,019	5
1991	Haywood Jeffires, Houston	100	1,181	7
1992	Haywood Jeffires, Houston	90	913	9
1993	Reggie Langhorne, Indianapolis	85	1,038	3
1994	Ben Coates, New England	96	1,174	7
1995	Carl Pickens, Cincinnati	99	1,234	17
1996	Carl Pickens, Cincinnati	100	1,180	12
1997	Tim Brown, Oakland	104	1,408	5
1998	O. J. McDuffie, Miami	90	1,050	7
1999	Jimmy Smith, Jacksonville	116	1,636	6
2000	Marvin Harrison, Indianapolis	102	1,413	14
2001	Rod Smith, Denver	113	1,343	11
2002	Marvin Harrison, Indianapolis	143	1,722	11
2003	LaDainian Tomlinson, San Diego	100	725	4
2004	Tony Gonzalez, Kansas City	102	1,258	7
2005	Chad Johnson, Cincinnati	97	1,432	9
2006	Andre Johnson, Houston	103	1,147	5
2007	Wes Welker, New England	112	1,175	8
2008	Andre Johnson, Houston	115	1,575	8
2009	Wes Walker, New England	123	1,348	4
2010	Reggie Wayne, Indianapolis	111	1,355	6
2011	Wes Welker, New England	122	1,569	9
2012	Wes Welker, New England	118	1,354	6

Scoring

Player, team	TD	XPM	FGM	Pts	Year
Gene Mingo, Denver	6	33	18	123	1960
Gino Cappelletti, Boston	8	48	17	147	1961
Gene Mingo, Denver	4	32	27	137	1962
Gino Cappelletti, Boston	2	35	22	113	1963
Gino Cappelletti, Boston	7	36	25	155	1964
Gino Cappelletti, Boston	9	27	17	132	1965
Gino Cappelletti, Boston	6	35	16	119	1966
George Blanda, Oakland	0	56	20	116	1967
Jim Turner, NY Jets	0	43	34	145	1968
Jim Turner, NY Jets	0	33	32	129	1969
Jan Stenerud, Kansas City	0	26	30	116	1970
Garo Yepremian, Miami	0	33	28	117	1971
Bobby Howfield, NY Jets	0	40	27	121	1972
Roy Gerela, Pittsburgh	0	36	29	123	1973
Roy Gerela, Pittsburgh	0	33	20	93	1974
O. J. Simpson, Buffalo	23	0	0	138	1975
Toni Linhart, Baltimore Colts	0	49	20	109	1976
Errol Mann, Oakland	0	39	20	99	1977
Pat Leahy, NY Jets	0	41	22	107	1978
John Smith, New England	0	46	23	115	1979
John Smith, New England	0	51	26	129	1980
Jim Breech, Cincinnati	0	49	22	115	1981
Nick Lowery, Kansas City	0	37	26	115	
Marcus Allen, L.A. Raiders	14	0	0	84	1982
Gary Anderson, Pittsburgh	0	38	27	119	1983
Gary Anderson, Pittsburgh	0	45	24	117	1984
Gary Anderson, Pittsburgh	0	40	33	139	1985
Tony Franklin, New England	0	44	32	140	1986
Jim Breech, Cincinnati	0	25	24	97	1987
Scott Norwood, Buffalo	0	33	32	129	1988
David Treadwell, Denver	0	39	27	120	1989
Nick Lowery, Kansas City	0	37	34	139	1990
Pete Stoyanovich, Miami	0	28	31	121	1991
Pete Stoyanovich, Miami	0	34	30	124	1992
Jeff Jaeger, L.A. Raiders	0	27	35	132	1993
John Carney, San Diego	0	33	34	135	1994
Norm Johnson, Pittsburgh	0	39	34	141	1995
Cary Blanchard, Indianapolis	0	27	36	135	1996
Mike Hollis, Jacksonville	0	41	31	134	1997

Rushing

Year	Player, team	Yds	Att	TD
1960	Abner Haynes, Dallas Texans	875	156	9
1961	Billy Cannon, Houston	948	200	6
1962	Cookie Gilchrist, Buffalo	1,096	214	13
1963	Clem Daniels, Oakland	1,099	215	3
1964	Cookie Gilchrist, Buffalo	981	230	6
1965	Paul Lowe, San Diego	1,121	222	7
1966	Jim Nance, Boston	1,458	299	11
1967	Jim Nance, Boston	1,216	269	7
1968	Paul Robinson, Cincinnati	1,023	238	8
1969	Dickie Post, San Diego	873	182	6
1970	Floyd Little, Denver	901	209	3
1971	Floyd Little, Denver	1,133	284	6
1972	O. J. Simpson, Buffalo	1,251	292	6
1973	O. J. Simpson, Buffalo	2,003	332	12
1974	Otis Armstrong, Denver	1,407	263	9
1975	O. J. Simpson, Buffalo	1,817	329	16
1976	O. J. Simpson, Buffalo	1,503	290	8
1977	Mark van Eeghen, Oakland	1,273	324	7
1978	Earl Campbell, Houston	1,450	302	13
1979	Earl Campbell, Houston	1,697	368	19
1980	Earl Campbell, Houston	1,934	373	13
1981	Earl Campbell, Houston	1,376	361	10
1982	Freeman McNeil, NY Jets	786	151	6
1983	Curt Warner, Seattle	1,449	335	13
1984	Earnest Jackson, San Diego	1,179	296	8
1985	Marcus Allen, L.A. Raiders	1,759	380	11
1986	Curt Warner, Seattle	1,481	319	13
1987	Eric Dickerson, L.A. Rams-Ind.	1,288*	283	6
1988	Eric Dickerson, Indianapolis	1,659	388	14
1989	Christian Okoye, Kansas City	1,480	370	12
1990	Thurman Thomas, Buffalo	1,297	271	11
1991	Thurman Thomas, Buffalo	1,407	288	7
1992	Barry Foster, Pittsburgh	1,690	390	11
1993	Thurman Thomas, Buffalo	1,315	355	6
1994	Chris Warren, Seattle	1,545	333	9
1995	Curtis Martin, New England	1,487	368	14
1996	Terrell Davis, Denver	1,538	345	13
1997	Terrell Davis, Denver	1,750	369	15

Scoring

Player, team	TD	XPM	FGM	Pts	Year
Steve Christie, Buffalo	0	41	33	140	1998
Mike Vanderjagt, Indianapolis	0	43	34	145	1999
Matt Stover, Baltimore	0	30	35	135	2000
Mike Vanderjagt, Indianapolis	0	41	28	125	2001
Priest Holmes, Kansas City	24	0	0	144	2002
Priest Holmes, Kansas City	27	0	0	162	2003
Adam Vinatieri, New England	0	48	31	141	2004
Shayne Graham, Cincinnati	0	47	28	131	2005
LaDainian Tomlinson, San Diego	31	0	0	186	2006
Randy Moss, New England	23	0	0	138	2007
Stephen Gostkowski, New England	0	40	36	148	2008
Nate Kaeding, San Diego	0	50	32	146	2009
Sebastian Janikowski, Oakland	0	43	33	142	2010
Stephen Gostkowski, New England	0	59	28	143	2011
Stephen Gostkowski, New England	0	66	29	153	2012

Rushing

Year	Player, team	Yds	Att	TD
1998	Terrell Davis, Denver	2,008	392	21
1999	Edgerrin James, Indianapolis	1,553	369	13
2000	Edgerrin James, Indianapolis	1,709	387	13
2001	Priest Holmes, Kansas City	1,555	327	8
2002	Ricky Williams, Miami	1,853	383	16
2003	Jamal Lewis, Baltimore	2,066	387	14
2004	Curtis Martin, NY Jets	1,697	371	12
2005	Larry Johnson, Kansas City	1,750	336	20
2006	LaDainian Tomlinson, San Diego	1,815	348	28
2007	LaDainian Tomlinson, San Diego	1,474	315	15
2008	Thomas Jones, NY Jets	1,312	290	13
2009	Chris Johnson, Tennessee	2,006	358	14
2010	Arian Foster, Houston	1,616	327	16
2011	Maurice Jones-Drew, Jacksonville	1,606	343	8
2012	Jamaal Charles, Kansas City	1,509	285	5

*Includes 277 yards after being traded to NFC; 1,011 yards led AFC.

National Football Conference Leaders, 1960-2012

(National Football League, 1960-69)

Passing (based on QB rating points)

Player, team	Att	Comp	Yds	TD	Year
Milt Plum, Cleveland	250	151	2,297	21	1960
Milt Plum, Cleveland	302	177	2,416	18	1961
Bart Starr, Green Bay	285	178	2,438	12	1962
Y. A. Tittle, NY Giants	367	221	3,145	36	1963
Bart Starr, Green Bay	272	163	2,144	15	1964
Rudy Bukich, Chicago	312	176	2,641	20	1965
Bart Starr, Green Bay	251	156	2,257	14	1966
Sonny Jurgensen, Washington	508	288	3,747	31	1967
Earl Morrall, Baltimore Colts	317	182	2,909	26	1968
Sonny Jurgensen, Washington	442	274	3,102	22	1969
John Brodie, San Francisco	378	223	2,941	24	1970
Roger Staubach, Dallas	211	126	1,882	15	1971
Norm Snead, NY Giants	325	196	2,307	17	1972
Roger Staubach, Dallas	286	179	2,428	23	1973
Sonny Jurgensen, Washington	167	107	1,185	11	1974
Fran Tarkenton, Minnesota	425	273	2,994	25	1975
James Harris, L.A. Rams	158	91	1,460	8	1976
Roger Staubach, Dallas	361	210	2,620	18	1977
Roger Staubach, Dallas	413	231	3,190	25	1978
Roger Staubach, Dallas	461	267	3,586	27	1979
Ron Jaworski, Philadelphia	451	257	3,529	27	1980
Joe Montana, San Francisco	488	311	3,565	19	1981
Joe Theismann, Washington	252	161	2,033	13	1982
Steve Bartkowski, Atlanta	432	274	3,167	22	1983
Joe Montana, San Francisco	432	279	3,630	28	1984
Joe Montana, San Francisco	494	303	3,653	27	1985
Tommy Kramer, Minnesota	372	208	3,000	24	1986
Joe Montana, San Francisco	398	266	3,054	31	1987
Wade Wilson, Minnesota	332	204	2,746	15	1988
Joe Montana, San Francisco	386	271	3,521	26	1989
Phil Simms, NY Giants	311	184	2,284	15	1990
Steve Young, San Francisco	279	180	2,517	17	1991
Steve Young, San Francisco	402	268	3,465	25	1992
Steve Young, San Francisco	462	314	4,023	29	1993
Steve Young, San Francisco	461	324	3,969	35	1994
Brett Favre, Green Bay	570	359	4,413	38	1995
Steve Young, San Francisco	316	214	2,410	14	1996
Steve Young, San Francisco	356	241	3,029	19	1997
Randall Cunningham, Minnesota	425	259	3,704	34	1998
Kurt Warner, St. Louis	499	325	4,353	41	1999
Trent Green, St. Louis	240	145	2,063	16	2000
Kurt Warner, St. Louis	546	375	4,830	36	2001
Brad Johnson, Tampa Bay	451	281	3,049	22	2002
Daunte Culpepper, Minnesota	454	295	3,479	25	2003
Daunte Culpepper, Minnesota	548	379	4,717	39	2004
Matt Hasselbeck, Seattle	449	294	3,459	24	2005
Drew Brees, New Orleans	554	356	4,418	26	2006
Tony Romo, Dallas	520	335	4,211	36	2007
Kurt Warner, Arizona	598	401	4,583	30	2008
Drew Brees, New Orleans	514	363	4,388	34	2009
Aaron Rodgers, Green Bay	475	312	3,922	28	2010
Aaron Rodgers, Green Bay	502	343	4,643	45	2011
Aaron Rodgers, Green Bay	552	371	4,295	39	2012

Receptions

Year	Player, team	Rec	Yds	TD
1960	Raymond Berry, Baltimore Colts	74	1,298	10
1961	Jim Phillips, L.A. Rams	78	1,092	5
1962	Bobby Mitchell, Washington	72	1,384	11
1963	Bobby Joe Conrad, St. Louis Cardinals	73	967	10
1964	Johnny Morris, Chicago	93	1,200	10
1965	Dave Parks, San Francisco	80	1,344	12
1966	Charley Taylor, Washington	72	1,119	12
1967	Charley Taylor, Washington	70	990	9
1968	Clifton McNeil, San Francisco	71	994	7
1969	Dan Abramowicz, New Orleans	73	1,015	7
1970	Dick Gordon, Chicago	71	1,026	13
1971	Bob Tucker, NY Giants	59	791	4
1972	Harold Jackson, Philadelphia	62	1,048	4
1973	Harold Carmichael, Philadelphia	67	1,116	9
1974	Charles Young, Philadelphia	63	696	3
1975	Chuck Foreman, Minnesota	73	691	9
1976	Drew Pearson, Dallas	58	806	6
1977	Ahmad Rashad, Minnesota	51	681	2
1978	Rickey Young, Minnesota	88	704	5
1979	Ahmad Rashad, Minnesota	80	1,156	9
1980	Earl Cooper, San Francisco	83	567	4
1981	Dwight Clark, San Francisco	85	1,105	4
1982	Dwight Clark, San Francisco	60	913	5
1983	Roy Green, St. Louis Cardinals	78	1,227	14
	Charlie Brown, Washington	78	1,225	8
	Earnest Gray, NY Giants	78	1,139	5
1984	Art Monk, Washington	106	1,372	7
1985	Roger Craig, San Francisco	92	1,016	6
1986	Jerry Rice, San Francisco	86	1,570	15
1987	J. T. Smith, St. Louis Cardinals	91	1,117	8
1988	Henry Ellard, L.A. Rams	86	1,414	10
1989	Sterling Sharpe, Green Bay	90	1,423	12
1990	Jerry Rice, San Francisco	100	1,502	13
1991	Michael Irvin, Dallas	93	1,523	8
1992	Sterling Sharpe, Green Bay	108	1,461	13
1993	Sterling Sharpe, Green Bay	112	1,274	11
1994	Cris Carter, Minnesota	122	1,256	7
1995	Herman Moore, Detroit	123	1,686	14
1996	Jerry Rice, San Francisco	108	1,254	8
1997	Herman Moore, Detroit	104	1,293	8
1998	Frank Sanders, Arizona	89	1,145	3
1999	Muhsin Muhammad, Carolina	96	1,253	8
2000	Muhsin Muhammad, Carolina	102	1,183	6
2001	Keyshawn Johnson, Tampa Bay	106	1,266	1
2002	Randy Moss, Minnesota	106	1,347	7
2003	Torry Holt, St. Louis	117	1,696	12
2004	Joe Horn, New Orleans	94	1,399	11
	Torry Holt, St. Louis	94	1,372	10
2005	Steve Smith, Carolina	103	1,563	12
	Larry Fitzgerald, Arizona	103	1,409	10
2006	Mike Furrey, Detroit	98	1,086	6
2007	Larry Fitzgerald, Arizona	100	1,409	10
2008	Larry Fitzgerald, Arizona	96	1,431	12
2009	Steve Smith, NY Giants	107	1,220	7
2010	Roddy White, Atlanta	115	1,389	10
2011	Roddy White, Atlanta	100	1,296	8
2012	Calvin Johnson, Detroit	122	1,964	5

	Scoring						Rushing		
Player, team	TD	XPM	FGM	Pts	Year	Player, team	Yds	Att	TD
Paul Hornung, Green Bay	15	41	15	176	1960	Jim Brown, Cleveland	1,257	215	9
Paul Hornung, Green Bay	10	41	15	146	1961	Jim Brown, Cleveland	1,408	305	8
Jim Taylor, Green Bay	19	0	0	114	1962	Jim Taylor, Green Bay	1,474	272	19
Don Chandler, NY Giants	0	52	18	106	1963	Jim Brown, Cleveland	1,863	291	12
Lenny Moore, Baltimore Colts	20	0	0	120	1964	Jim Brown, Cleveland	1,446	280	7
Gale Sayers, Chicago	22	0	0	132	1965	Jim Brown, Cleveland	1,544	289	17
Bruce Gossett, L.A. Rams	0	29	28	113	1966	Gale Sayers, Chicago	1,231	229	8
Jim Bakken, St. Louis Cardinals	0	36	27	117	1967	Leroy Kelly, Cleveland	1,205	235	11
Leroy Kelly, Cleveland	20	0	0	120	1968	Leroy Kelly, Cleveland	1,239	248	16
Fred Cox, Minnesota	0	43	26	121	1969	Gale Sayers, Chicago	1,032	236	8
Fred Cox, Minnesota	0	35	30	125	1970	Larry Brown, Washington	1,125	237	5
Curt Knight, Washington	0	27	29	114	1971	John Brockington, Green Bay	1,105	216	4
Chester Marcol, Green Bay	0	29	33	128	1972	Larry Brown, Washington	1,216	285	8
David Ray, L.A. Rams	0	40	30	130	1973	John Brockington, Green Bay	1,144	265	3
Chester Marcol, Green Bay	0	19	25	94	1974	Lawrence McCutcheon, L.A. Rams	1,109	236	3
Chuck Foreman, Minnesota	22	0	0	132	1975	Jim Otis, St. Louis Cardinals	1,076	269	5
Mark Moseley, Washington	0	31	22	97	1976	Walter Payton, Chicago	1,390	311	13
Walter Payton, Chicago	16	0	0	96	1977	Walter Payton, Chicago	1,852	339	14
Frank Corral, L.A. Rams	0	31	29	118	1978	Walter Payton, Chicago	1,395	333	11
Mark Moseley, Washington	0	39	25	114	1979	Walter Payton, Chicago	1,610	369	14
Ed Murray, Detroit	0	35	27	116	1980	Walter Payton, Chicago	1,460	317	6
Ed Murray, Detroit	0	46	25	121	1981	George Rogers, New Orleans	1,674	378	13
Rafael Septien, Dallas	0	40	27	121					
Wendell Tyler, L.A. Rams	13	0	0	78	1982	Tony Dorsett, Dallas	745	177	5
Mark Moseley, Washington	0	62	33	161	1983	Eric Dickerson, L.A. Rams	1,808	390	18
Ray Wersching, San Francisco	0	56	25	131	1984	Eric Dickerson, L.A. Rams	2,105	379	14
Kevin Butler, Chicago	0	51	31	144	1985	Gerald Riggs, Atlanta	1,719	397	10
Kevin Butler, Chicago	0	36	28	120	1986	Eric Dickerson, L.A. Rams	1,821	404	11
Jerry Rice, San Francisco	23	0	0	138	1987	Charles White, L.A. Rams	1,374	324	11
Mike Cofer, San Francisco	0	40	27	121	1988	Herschel Walker, Dallas	1,514	361	5
Mike Cofer, San Francisco	0	49	29	136	1989	Barry Sanders, Detroit	1,470	280	14
Chip Lohmiller, Washington	0	41	30	131	1990	Barry Sanders, Detroit	1,304	255	13
Chip Lohmiller, Washington	0	56	31	149	1991	Emmitt Smith, Dallas	1,563	365	12
Morten Andersen, New Orleans	0	33	29	120	1992	Emmitt Smith, Dallas	1,713	373	18
Chip Lohmiller, Washington	0	30	30	120					
Jason Hanson, Detroit	0	28	34	130	1993	Emmitt Smith, Dallas	1,486	283	9
Fuad Reveiz, Minnesota	0	30	34	132	1994	Barry Sanders, Detroit	1,883	331	7
Emmitt Smith, Dallas	22	0	0	132					
Emmitt Smith, Dallas	25	0	0	150	1995	Emmitt Smith, Dallas	1,773	377	25
John Kasay, Carolina	0	34	37	145	1996	Barry Sanders, Detroit	1,553	307	11
Richie Cunningham, Dallas	0	24	34	126	1997	Barry Sanders, Detroit	2,053	335	11
Gary Anderson, Minnesota	0	59	35	164	1998	Jamal Anderson, Atlanta	1,846	410	14
Jeff Wilkins, St. Louis	0	64	20	124	1999	Stephen Davis, Washington	1,405	290	17
Marshall Faulk, St. Louis	26	0	0	160	2000	Robert Smith, Minnesota	1,521	295	7
Marshall Faulk, St. Louis	21	0	0	128	2001	Stephen Davis, Washington	1,432	356	5
Jay Feely, Atlanta	0	42	32	138	2002	Deuce McAllister, New Orleans	1,388	325	13
Jeff Wilkins, St. Louis	0	46	39	163	2003	Ahman Green, Green Bay	1,883	355	15
David Akers, Philadelphia	0	41	27	122	2004	Shaun Alexander, Seattle	1,696	353	16
Shaun Alexander, Seattle	28	0	0	168	2005	Shaun Alexander, Seattle	1,880	370	27
Robbie Gould, Chicago	0	47	32	143	2006	Frank Gore, San Francisco	1,695	312	8
Mason Crosby, Green Bay	0	48	31	141	2007	Adrian Peterson, Minnesota	1,341	238	12
David Akers, Philadelphia	0	45	33	144	2008	Adrian Peterson, Minnesota	1,760	363	10
David Akers, Philadelphia	0	43	32	139	2009	Steven Jackson, St. Louis	1,416	324	4
David Akers, Philadelphia	0	47	32	143	2010	Michael Turner, Atlanta	1,371	334	12
David Akers, San Francisco	0	34	44	166	2011	Michael Turner, Atlanta	1,340	301	11
Lawrence Tynes, NY Giants	0	46	33	145	2012	Adrian Peterson, Minnesota	2,097	348	12

NFL MVP and Rookies of the Year, 1957-2012

The Most Valuable Player, Offensive Rookie of the Year, and Defensive Rookie of the Year are a few of the many awards given out annually by the Associated Press according to the results of balloting by a nationwide panel of media. Many other organizations give out annual awards honoring the NFL's best players.

Year	NFL Most Valuable Player Award	Offensive Rookie of the Year	Defensive Rookie of the Year
1957	Jim Brown, Cleveland	NA	NA
1958	Jim Brown, Cleveland	NA	NA
1959	Charley Conerly, NY Giants	NA	NA
1960	Norm Van Brocklin, Philadelphia	NA	NA
1961	Paul Hornung, Green Bay	NA	NA
1962	Jim Taylor, Green Bay	NA	NA
1963	Y. A. Tittle, NY Giants	NA	NA
1964	Johnny Unitas, Baltimore	NA	NA
1965	Jim Brown, Cleveland	NA	NA
1966	Bart Starr, Green Bay	NA	NA

Year	NFL Most Valuable Player Award	Offensive Rookie of the Year	Defensive Rookie of the Year
1967	Johnny Unitas, Baltimore	Mel Farr, Detroit	Lem Barney, Detroit
1968	Earl Morrall, Baltimore	Earl McCullouch, Detroit	Claude Humphrey, Atlanta
1969	Roman Gabriel, Los Angeles	Calvin Hill, Dallas	Joe Greene, Pittsburgh
1970	John Brodie, San Francisco	Dennis Shaw, Buffalo	Bruce Taylor, San Francisco
1971	Alan Page, Minnesota	John Brockington, Green Bay	Isiah Robertson, Los Angeles
1972	Larry Brown, Washington	Franco Harris, Pittsburgh	Willie Buchanon, Green Bay
1973	O. J. Simpson, Buffalo	Chuck Foreman, Minnesota	Wally Chambers, Chicago
1974	Ken Stabler, Oakland	Don Woods, San Diego	Jack Lambert, Pittsburgh
1975	Fran Tarkenton, Minnesota	Mike Thomas, Washington	Robert Brazile, Houston
1976	Bert Jones, Baltimore	Sammy White, Minnesota	Mike Haynes, New England
1977	Walter Payton, Chicago	Tony Dorsett, Dallas	A. J. Duhe, Miami
1978	Terry Bradshaw, Pittsburgh	Earl Campbell, Houston	Al Baker, Detroit
1979	Earl Campbell, Houston	Ottis Anderson, St. Louis	Jim Haslett, Buffalo
1980	Brian Sipe, Cleveland	Billy Sims, Detroit	Buddy Curry, Atlanta; Al Richardson, Atlanta
1981	Ken Anderson, Cincinnati	George Rogers, New Orleans	Lawrence Taylor, NY Giants
1982	Mark Moseley, Washington	Marcus Allen, Los Angeles	Chip Banks, Cleveland
1983	Joe Theismann, Washington	Eric Dickerson, Los Angeles	Vernon Maxwell, Baltimore
1984	Dan Marino, Miami	Louis Lipps, Pittsburgh	Bill Maas, Kansas City
1985	Marcus Allen, Los Angeles	Eddie Brown, Cincinnati	Duane Bickett, Indianapolis
1986	Lawrence Taylor, NY Giants	Rueben Mayes, New Orleans	Leslie O'Neal, San Diego
1987	John Elway, Denver	Troy Stradford, Miami	Shane Conlan, Buffalo
1988	Boomer Esiason, Cincinnati	John Stephens, New England	Erik McMillan, NY Jets
1989	Joe Montana, San Francisco	Barry Sanders, Detroit	Derrick Thomas, Kansas City
1990	Joe Montana, San Francisco	Emmitt Smith, Dallas	Mark Carrier, Chicago
1991	Thurman Thomas, Buffalo	Leonard Russell, New England	Mike Croel, Denver
1992	Steve Young, San Francisco	Carl Pickens, Cincinnati	Dale Carter, Kansas City
1993	Emmitt Smith, Dallas	Jerome Bettis, Los Angeles	Dana Stubblefield, San Francisco
1994	Steve Young, San Francisco	Marshall Faulk, Indianapolis	Tim Bowens, Miami
1995	Brett Favre, Green Bay	Curtis Martin, New England	Hugh Douglas, NY Jets
1996	Brett Favre, Green Bay	Eddie George, Houston	Simeon Rice, Arizona
1997	Brett Favre, Green Bay; Barry Sanders, Detroit	Warrick Dunn, Tampa Bay	Peter Boulware, Baltimore
1998	Terrell Davis, Denver	Randy Moss, Minnesota	Charles Woodson, Oakland
1999	Kurt Warner, St. Louis	Edgerrin James, Indianapolis	Jevon Kearse, Tennessee
2000	Marshall Faulk, St. Louis	Mike Anderson, Denver	Brian Urlacher, Chicago
2001	Kurt Warner, St. Louis	Anthony Thomas, Chicago	Kendrell Bell, Pittsburgh
2002	Rich Gannon, Oakland	Clinton Portis, Denver	Julius Peppers, Carolina
2003	Peyton Manning, Indianapolis; Steve McNair, Tennessee	Anquan Boldin, Arizona	Terrell Suggs, Baltimore
2004	Peyton Manning, Indianapolis	Ben Roethlisberger, Pittsburgh	Jonathan Vilma, NY Jets
2005	Shaun Alexander, Seattle	Cadillac Williams, Tampa Bay	Shawne Merriman, San Diego
2006	LaDainian Tomlinson, San Diego	Vince Young, Tennessee	DeMeco Ryans, Houston
2007	Tom Brady, New England	Adrian Peterson, Minnesota	Patrick Willis, San Francisco
2008	Peyton Manning, Indianapolis	Matt Ryan, Atlanta	Jerod Mayo, New England
2009	Peyton Manning, Indianapolis	Percy Harvin, Minnesota	Brian Cushing, Houston
2010	Tom Brady, New England	Sam Bradford, St. Louis	Ndamukong Suh, Detroit
2011	Aaron Rodgers, Green Bay	Cam Newton, Carolina	Von Miller, Denver
2012	Adrian Peterson, Minnesota	Robert Griffin III, Washington	Luke Kuechly, Carolina

All-Time Professional (NFL and AFL) Football Records

(at end of 2012 season; * = active in 2012; (a) includes AFL statistics; ** = 2-pt conversions scored)

Leading Lifetime Scorers

Player	Yrs	TD	PAT	FG	Total
Morten Andersen	25	0	849	565	2,544
Gary Anderson	23	0	820	538	2,434
Jason Hanson*	21	0	665	495	2,150
John Carney	23	0	628	478	2,062
Matt Stover	19	0	591	471	2,004
George Blanda (a)	26	9	943	335	2,002
Jason Elam	17	0	675	436	1,983
John Kasay	20	0	587	461	1,970
Adam Vinatieri*	17	0	626**	413	1,867
Norm Johnson	18	0	638	366	1,736
Nick Lowery	18	0	562	383	1,711
Jan Stenerud (a)	19	0	580	373	1,699
Ryan Longwell	15	0	604	361	1,687
David Akers*	15	0	521	367	1,622
Eddie Murray	19	0	538	352	1,594
Al Del Greco	17	0	543	347	1,584

Leading Lifetime Touchdown Scorers

Player	Yrs	Rush	Rec	Ret	TD
Jerry Rice	20	10	197	1	208
Emmitt Smith	15	164	11	0	175
LaDainian Tomlinson	11	145	17	0	162
Randy Moss*	14	0	156	1	157
Terrell Owens	15	3	153	0	156
Marcus Allen	16	123	21	1	145
Marshall Faulk	12	100	36	0	136
Cris Carter	16	0	130	1	131
Marvin Harrison	13	0	128	0	128
Jim Brown	9	106	20	0	126
Walter Payton	13	110	15	0	125
John Riggins	14	104	12	0	116
Lenny Moore	12	63	48	2	113
Shaun Alexander	9	100	12	0	112
Barry Sanders	10	99	10	0	109
Tim Brown	17	1	100	4	105
Don Hutson	11	3	99	3	105

Points, season: 186, LaDainian Tomlinson, San Diego, 2006 (31 TDs).
Points, game: 40, Ernie Nevers, Chicago Cardinals vs. Chicago Bears, Nov. 28, 1929 (6 TDs, 4 PATs).
Touchdowns, season: 31, LaDainian Tomlinson, San Diego, 2006.
Touchdowns, game: 6; Ernie Nevers, Chicago Cardinals vs. Chicago Bears, Nov. 28, 1929 (6 rushing);
   Dub Jones, Cleveland Browns vs. Chicago Bears, Nov. 25, 1951 (4 rushing, 2 pass receptions);
   Gale Sayers, Chicago Bears vs. San Francisco, Dec. 12, 1965 (4 rushing, 1 pass reception, 1 punt return).
Points after TD, season: 74, Stephen Gostkowski, New England, 2007.
Consecutive points after TD: 422, Matt Stover, Baltimore Ravens-Indianapolis, 1996-2009.
Field goals, career: 565, Morten Andersen, New Orleans-Atlanta-NY Giants-Kansas City-Minnesota-Atlanta, 1982-2007.
Field goals, season: 44, David Akers, San Francisco, 2011.
Field goals, game: 8, Rob Bironas, Tennessee vs. Houston, Oct. 21, 2007.
Longest field goal: 63 yards; Tom Dempsey, New Orleans vs. Detroit, Nov. 8, 1970; Jason Elam, Denver vs. Jacksonville, Oct. 25, 1998; Sebastian Janikowski, Oakland vs. Denver, Sept. 12, 2011; David Akers, San Francisco vs. Green Bay, Sept. 9, 2012.

Defensive Records

Interceptions, career: 81, Paul Krause, Washington-Minnesota, 1964-79.
Interceptions, season: 14, Dick "Night Train" Lane, L.A. Rams, 1952.
Touchdowns, career: 12, Rod Woodson, Pittsburgh-San Francisco-Baltimore Ravens-Oakland, 1987-2003.
Touchdowns, season: 4; Ken Houston, Houston, 1971; Jim Kearney, Kansas City, 1972; Eric Allen, Philadelphia, 1993.
Sacks, career (since 1982): 200.0, Bruce Smith, Buffalo-Washington, 1985-2003.
Sacks, season (since 1982): 22.5, Michael Strahan, NY Giants, 2001.

Leading Lifetime Rushers
(ranked by rushing yards; * = active in 2012)

Player	Yrs	Att	Yds	Avg	Long	TD	Player	Yrs	Att	Yds	Avg	Long	TD
Emmitt Smith	15	4,409	18,355	4.2	75T	164	Edgerrin James	11	3,028	12,246	4.0	72	80
Walter Payton	13	3,838	16,726	4.4	76	110	Marcus Allen	16	3,022	12,243	4.1	61T	123
Barry Sanders	10	3,062	15,269	5.0	85	99	Franco Harris	13	2,949	12,120	4.1	75T	91
Curtis Martin	11	3,518	14,101	4.0	70T	90	Thurman Thomas	13	2,877	12,074	4.2	80T	65
LaDainian Tomlinson	11	3,174	13,684	4.3	85T	145	Fred Taylor	13	2,534	11,695	4.6	80T	66
Jerome Bettis	13	3,479	13,662	3.9	71T	91	John Riggins	14	2,916	11,352	3.9	66T	104
Eric Dickerson	11	2,996	13,259	4.4	85T	90	Corey Dillon	10	2,618	11,241	4.3	96T	82
Tony Dorsett	12	2,936	12,739	4.3	99T	77	O. J. Simpson	11	2,404	11,236	4.7	94T	61
Jim Brown	9	2,359	12,312	5.2	80T	106	Warrick Dunn	12	2,669	10,967	4.1	90T	49
Marshall Faulk	12	2,836	12,279	4.3	71T	100	Ricky Watters	10	2,622	10,643	4.1	57	78

Yards gained, season: 2,105, Eric Dickerson, L.A. Rams, 1984.
Yards gained, game: 296, Adrian Peterson, Minnesota vs. San Diego, Nov. 4, 2007.
Rushing TDs, career: 164, Emmitt Smith, Dallas-Arizona, 1990-2004.
Rushing TDs, season: 28, LaDainian Tomlinson, San Diego, 2006.
Rushing TDs, game: 6, Ernie Nevers, Chicago Cardinals vs. Chicago Bears, Nov. 28, 1929.
Rushing attempts, game: 45, Jamie Morris, Washington vs. Cincinnati, Dec. 17, 1988 (OT).
Longest run from scrimmage: 99 yards (TD), Tony Dorsett, Dallas vs. Minnesota, Jan. 3, 1983.

Leading Lifetime Receivers
(ranked by number of receptions; * = active in 2012)

Player	Yrs	No.	Yds	Avg	Long	TD	Player	Yrs	No.	Yds	Avg	Long	TD
Jerry Rice	20	1,549	22,895	14.8	96T	197	Andre Reed	16	951	13,198	13.9	83T	87
Tony Gonzalez*	16	1,242	14,268	11.5	73T	103	Derrick Mason	15	943	12,061	12.8	79T	66
Marvin Harrison	13	1,102	14,580	13.2	80T	128	Art Monk	16	940	12,721	13.5	79T	68
Cris Carter	16	1,101	13,899	12.6	80T	130	Torry Holt	11	920	13,382	14.5	85T	74
Tim Brown	17	1,094	14,934	13.7	80T	100	Keenan McCardell	16	883	11,373	12.9	76T	63
Terrell Owens	15	1,078	15,934	14.8	98T	153	Jimmy Smith	12	862	12,287	14.3	75	67
Isaac Bruce	16	1,024	15,208	14.9	80T	91	Muhsin Muhammad	14	860	11,438	13.3	72T	62
Hines Ward	14	1,000	12,083	12.1	85T	85	Irving Fryar	17	851	12,785	15.0	80T	84
Randy Moss*	14	982	15,292	15.6	82T	156	Rod Smith	12	849	11,389	13.4	85T	68
Reggie Wayne*	12	968	13,063	13.5	71T	78	Larry Centers	14	827	6,797	8.2	54	28

Yards gained, career: 22,895, Jerry Rice, San Francisco-Oakland-Seattle, 1985-2004.
Yards gained, season: 1,964, Calvin Johnson, Detroit, 2012.
Yards gained, game: 336, Willie "Flipper" Anderson, L.A. Rams vs. New Orleans, Nov. 26, 1989 (OT).
Pass receptions, season: 143, Marvin Harrison, Indianapolis, 2002.
Pass receptions, game: 21, Brandon Marshall, Denver vs. Indianapolis, Dec. 13, 2009.
Touchdown receptions, career: 197, Jerry Rice, San Francisco-Oakland-Seattle, 1985-2004.
Touchdown receptions, season: 23, Randy Moss, New England, 2007.
Touchdown receptions, game: 5; Bob Shaw, Chicago Cardinals vs. Baltimore Colts, Oct. 2, 1950; Kellen Winslow, San Diego vs. Oakland, Nov. 22, 1981; Jerry Rice, San Francisco vs. Atlanta, Oct. 14, 1990.

Leading Lifetime Passers
(minimum 1,500 attempts; ranked by quarterback rating points; * = active in 2012)

Player	Yrs	Att	Comp	Yds	TD	Int	Pts[1]	Player	Yrs	Att	Comp	Yds	TD	Int	Pts[1]
Aaron Rodgers*	8	2,665	1,752	21,661	171	46	104.9	Matt Schaub*	9	2,823	1,816	21,944	120	70	91.9
Steve Young	15	4,149	2,667	33,124	232	107	96.8	Matt Ryan*	5	2,637	1,654	18,957	127	60	90.9
Tom Brady*	13	5,958	3,798	44,806	334	123	96.6	Chad Pennington	11	2,471	1,632	17,823	102	64	90.1
Peyton Manning*	14	7,793	5,082	59,487	436	209	95.7	Daunte Culpepper	11	3,199	2,016	24,153	149	106	87.8
Tony Romo*	9	3,240	2,097	25,737	177	91	95.6	Jeff Garcia	11	3,676	2,264	25,537	161	83	87.5
Philip Rivers*	9	3,564	2,268	27,891	189	93	94.5	Dan Marino	17	8,358	4,967	61,361	420	252	86.4
Drew Brees*	12	6,149	4,035	45,919	324	165	94.5	Joe Flacco*	5	2,489	1,507	17,633	102	56	86.3
Kurt Warner	12	4,070	2,666	32,344	208	128	93.7	Carson Palmer*	11	4,110	2,568	29,465	189	130	86.2
Ben Roethlisberger*	9	3,762	2,374	29,844	191	108	92.7	Trent Green	11	3,740	2,266	28,475	162	114	86.0
Joe Montana	15	5,391	3,409	40,551	273	139	92.3	Brett Favre	20	10,169	6,300	71,838	508	336	86.0

(1) Rating points based on performances in the following categories: percentage of completions, percentage of touchdown passes, percentage of interceptions, and average gain per pass attempt.

Yards gained, career: 71,838, Brett Favre, Atlanta-Green Bay-NY Jets-Minnesota, 1991-2010.
Yards gained, season: 5,476, Drew Brees, New Orleans, 2011.
Yards gained, game: 554, Norm Van Brocklin, L.A. Rams vs. NY Yanks, Sept. 28, 1951 (27 completions in 41 attempts).
Touchdowns passing, career: 508, Brett Favre, Atlanta-Green Bay-NY Jets-Minnesota, 1991-2010.
Touchdowns passing, season: 50, Tom Brady, New England, 2007.
Touchdowns passing, game: 7; Sid Luckman, Chicago Bears vs. NY Giants, Nov. 14, 1943; Adrian Burk, Philadelphia vs. Washington, Oct. 17, 1954; George Blanda, Houston vs. NY Titans, Nov. 19, 1961; Y. A. Tittle, NY Giants vs. Washington, Oct. 28, 1962; Joe Kapp, Minnesota vs. Baltimore Colts, Sept. 28, 1969.
Passes completed, career: 6,300, Brett Favre, Atlanta-Green Bay-NY Jets-Minnesota, 1991-2010.
Passes completed, season: 468, Drew Brees, New Orleans, 2011.
Passes completed, game: 45, Drew Bledsoe, New England vs. Minnesota, Nov. 13, 1994 (OT).

National Football League Franchise Origins

(Team: founding year, league. Home stadium location; subsequent history.)

Arizona Cardinals: 1920, American Professional Football Association (APFA)[1]. Chicago, 1920-59; St. Louis, 1960-87; Tempe, AZ, 1988-2005; Glendale, AZ, 2006-present.
Atlanta Falcons: 1966, NFL. Atlanta, 1966-present.
Baltimore Ravens: 1996, NFL. Baltimore, 1996-present.
Buffalo Bills: 1960, American Football League (AFL)[2]. Buffalo, 1960-72; Orchard Park, NY, 1973-present.
Carolina Panthers: 1995, NFL. Clemson, SC, 1995; Charlotte, NC, 1996-present.
Chicago Bears: 1920, APFA. Decatur, IL, 1920; Chicago, 1921-present.
Cincinnati Bengals: 1968, AFL. Cincinnati, 1968-present.
Cleveland Browns: 1946, All-America Football Conference (AAFC)[3]. Cleveland, 1946-95; 1999-present.
Dallas Cowboys: 1960, NFL. Dallas, 1960-70; Irving, TX, 1971-2008; Arlington, TX, 2009-present.
Denver Broncos: 1960, AFL. Denver, 1960-present.
Detroit Lions: 1930, NFL. Portsmouth, OH, 1930-33; Detroit, 1934-74; Pontiac, MI, 1975-2001; Detroit, 2002-present.
Green Bay Packers: 1921, APFA. Green Bay, WI, 1921-present.
Houston Texans: 2002, NFL. Houston, 2002-present.
Indianapolis Colts: 1953, NFL. Baltimore, 1953-83; Indianapolis, 1984-present.
Jacksonville Jaguars: 1995, NFL. Jacksonville, FL, 1995-present.
Kansas City Chiefs: 1960, AFL. Dallas, 1960-62; Kansas City, MO, 1963-present.
Miami Dolphins: 1966, AFL. Miami, 1966-2002; Miami Gardens, FL, 2003-present.

Minnesota Vikings: 1961, NFL. Bloomington, MN, 1961-81; Minneapolis, 1982-present.
New England Patriots: 1960, AFL. Boston, 1960-70; Foxborough, MA, 1971-present.
New Orleans Saints: 1967, NFL. New Orleans, 1967-2004; Baton Rouge and San Antonio, 2005; New Orleans, 2006-present.
NY Giants: 1925, NFL. New York, NY, 1925-73, 1975; New Haven, CT, 1973-74; E. Rutherford, NJ, 1976-present.
NY Jets: 1960, AFL. New York, NY, 1960-83; E. Rutherford, NJ, 1984-present.
Oakland Raiders: 1960, AFL. San Francisco, 1960-61; Oakland, CA, 1962-81; Los Angeles, 1982-94; Oakland, CA, 1995-present.
Philadelphia Eagles: 1933, NFL. Philadelphia, 1933-present.
Pittsburgh Steelers: 1933, NFL. Pittsburgh, 1933-present.
St. Louis Rams: 1937, NFL. Cleveland, 1936-45; Los Angeles, 1946-79; Anaheim, CA, 1980-94; St. Louis, 1995-present.
San Diego Chargers: 1960, AFL. Los Angeles, 1960; San Diego, 1961-present.
Seattle Seahawks: 1976, NFL. Seattle, 1976-present.
San Francisco 49ers: 1946, AAFC. San Francisco, 1946-present.
Tampa Bay Buccaneers: 1976, NFL. Tampa, 1976-present.
Tennessee Titans: 1960, AFL. Houston, 1969-96; Memphis, 1997; Nashville, 1998-present.
Washington Redskins: 1932, NFL. Boston, 1932-36; Washington, DC, 1937-96; Landover, MD, 1997-present.

(1) The American Professional Football Association (APFA) was formed in 1920 to standardize the rules of professional football. In 1922, the name was changed to the National Football League (NFL). (2) The most successful of four leagues called the American Football League or AFL (1926; 1936-37; 1940-41; 1960-69). Congress approved an NFL/AFL merger in 1966. Baltimore, Cleveland, and Pittsburgh agreed to join the 10 incoming AFL teams to form the American Football Conference. The NFL began play in 1970 with 26 teams. (3) The All-America Football Conference, 1946-49. In 1950, three of its teams joined the NFL (Baltimore, Cleveland, and San Francisco). The Baltimore franchise failed, but the NFL awarded the city a second one, also called the Colts, in 1953.

NFL Stadiums, 2012

(**A** = A-Turf Titan, **D** = DD Grassmaster (grass), **F** = FieldTurf, **G** = Grass, **N** = Natural grass, **S** = Synthetic, **SM** = Sportexe Momentum, **SS** = Sportfield Softtop)

Team: stadium, location, surface (year built)	Capacity[1]	Team: stadium, location, surface (year built)	Capacity[1]
Bears: Soldier Field[2], Chicago, IL, N (1924)	61,500	**Giants:** MetLife Stadium[7], E. Rutherford, NJ, F (2010)	82,500
Bengals: Paul Brown Stadium, Cincinnati, OH, S (2000)	65,515	**Jaguars:** EverBank Field[8], Jacksonville, FL, G (1995)	67,246
Bills: Ralph Wilson Stadium, Orchard Park, NY, A (1973)	73,967	**Jets:** MetLife Stadium[7], E. Rutherford, NJ, F (2010)	82,500
Broncos: Sports Authority Field at Mile High[3], Denver, CO, D (2001)	76,125	**Lions:** Ford Field, Detroit, MI, F (2002)	64,500
Browns: Cleveland Browns Stadium, Cleveland, OH, G (1999)	73,300	**Packers:** Lambeau Field[9], Green Bay, WI, D (1957)	73,094
Buccaneers: Raymond James Stadium, Tampa, FL, G (1998)	65,908	**Panthers:** Bank of America Stadium[10], Charlotte, NC, G (1996)	73,504
Cardinals: University of Phoenix Stadium, Glendale, AZ, G (2006)	65,000	**Patriots:** Gillette Stadium, Foxborough, MA, F (2002)	68,756
Chargers: Qualcomm Stadium[4], San Diego, CA, G (1967)	70,000	**Raiders:** O.co Coliseum[11], Oakland, CA, G (1966)	63,132
Chiefs: Arrowhead Stadium, Kansas City, MO, G (1972; fully renovated 2010)	76,416	**Rams:** Edward Jones Dome[12], St. Louis, MO, F (1995)	66,000
Colts: Lucas Oil Stadium, Indianapolis, IN, F (2008)	63,000	**Ravens:** M&T Bank Stadium[13], Baltimore, MD, SM (1998)	71,008
Cowboys: Cowboys Stadium, Arlington, TX, SS (2009)	100,000	**Redskins:** FedExField[14], Landover, MD, N (1997)	85,000
Dolphins: Sun Life Stadium[5], Miami Gardens, FL, G (1987)	75,192	**Saints:** Mercedes-Benz Superdome[15], New Orleans, LA, S (1975)	73,000
Eagles: Lincoln Financial Field, Philadelphia, PA, N (2003)	69,144	**Seahawks:** CenturyLink Field[16], Seattle, WA, F (2002)	67,000
Falcons: Georgia Dome, Atlanta, GA, F (1992)	71,228	**Steelers:** Heinz Field, Pittsburgh, PA, N (2001)	65,500
49ers: Candlestick Park[6], San Francisco, CA, N (1960)	69,732	**Texans:** Reliant Stadium, Houston, TX, G (2002)	71,054
		Titans: LP Field[17], Nashville, TN, N (1999)	69,143
		Vikings: Mall of America Field at Hubert H. Humphrey Metrodome[18], Minneapolis, MN, SM (1982)	63,731

(1) As of the start of the 2012 season. (2) Renovation in 2002 replaced interior of stadium. (3) Formerly INVESCO Field at Mile High (2001-11). (4) Formerly San Diego Stadium (1967-80); San Diego Jack Murphy Stadium (1981-97). (5) Formerly Joe Robbie Stadium (1987-96); Pro Player Stadium (1996-2005); Land Shark Stadium (2009). (6) Formerly Candlestick Park (1960-94); 3Com Park at Candlestick Point (1995-2004). (7) Formerly New Meadowlands Stadium (2010-11). (8) Formerly ALLTEL Stadium (1997-2007); Jacksonville Municipal Stadium (1946-97, 2007-09). (9) Formerly City Stadium (1957-65). Renovation completed in 2003 added 11,625 seats. (10) Formerly Ericsson Stadium (1998-2003). (11) Formerly Oakland-Alameda County Coliseum (1966-98); Network Associates Coliseum (1998-2004); McAfee Stadium (2004-08); Oakland Coliseum (2008-11). (12) Formerly Trans World Dome (1995-2001). (13) Formerly PSINet Stadium (1998-2002); Ravens Stadium (2002-03). (14) Formerly Jack Kent Cooke Stadium (1997-99). (15) Formerly Louisiana Superdome (1975-2011). (16) Formerly Seahawks Stadium (2002-04); Qwest Field (2004-11). (17) Formerly Adelphia Coliseum (1999-2002). (18) Formerly Hubert H. Humphrey Metrodome (1982-2009).

Pro Football Hall of Fame, Canton, OH

(Asterisk indicates member elected in Feb. 2013 and inducted Aug. 3, 2013.)

Herb Adderley
Troy Aikman
George Allen
*Larry Allen
Marcus Allen
Lance Alworth
Doug Atkins
Morris "Red" Badgro
Lem Barney
Cliff Battles
Sammy Baugh
Chuck Bednarik
Bert Bell
Bobby Bell
Raymond Berry
Elvin Bethea
Charles Bidwill
Fred Biletnikoff
George Blanda
Mel Blount
Terry Bradshaw
Bob Brown
Jim Brown
Paul Brown
Roosevelt Brown
Willie Brown
Buck Buchanan
Nick Buoniconti
Dick Butkus
Jack Butler
Earl Campbell
Tony Canadeo
Joe Carr
Harry Carson
*Cris Carter
Dave Casper
Guy Chamberlin
Jack Christiansen
Earl "Dutch" Clark
George Connor
Jim Conzelman
Lou Creekmur
Larry Csonka
*Curley Culp
Al Davis
Willie Davis
Dermontti Dawson
Len Dawson
Fred Dean
Joe DeLamielleure
Richard Dent
Eric Dickerson
Dan Dierdorf
Mike Ditka
Chris Doleman
Art Donovan

Tony Dorsett
John "Paddy" Driscoll
Bill Dudley
Glen "Turk" Edwards
Carl Eller
John Elway
Weeb Ewbank
Marshall Faulk
Tom Fears
Jim Finks
Ray Flaherty
Len Ford
Dr. Daniel Fortmann
Dan Fouts
Benny Friedman
Frank Gatski
Bill George
Joe Gibbs
Frank Gifford
Sid Gillman
Otto Graham
Red Grange
Bud Grant
Darrell Green
Joe Greene
Forrest Gregg
Bob Griese
Russ Grimm
Lou Groza
Joe Guyon
George Halas
Jack Ham
Dan Hampton
Chris Hanburger
John Hannah
Bob Hayes
Mike Haynes
Mel Hein
Ted Hendricks
Wilbur "Pete" Henry
Arnold Herber
Bill Hewitt
Gene Hickerson
Clarke Hinkle
Elroy "Crazylegs" Hirsch
Paul Hornung
Ken Houston
Cal Hubbard
Sam Huff
Lamar Hunt
Don Hutson
Michael Irvin
Rickey Jackson
Jimmy Johnson
John Henry Johnson
Charlie Joiner

David "Deacon" Jones
Stan Jones
Henry Jordan
Sonny Jurgensen
Jim Kelly
Leroy Kelly
Cortez Kennedy
Walt Kiesling
Frank "Bruiser" Kinard
Paul Krause
Earl "Curly" Lambeau
Jack Lambert
Tom Landry
Dick "Night Train" Lane
Jim Langer
Willie Lanier
Steve Largent
Yale Lary
Dante Lavelli
Bobby Layne
Dick LeBeau
Alphonse "Tuffy" Leemans
Marv Levy
Bob Lilly
Floyd Little
Larry Little
James Lofton
Vince Lombardi
Howie Long
Ronnie Lott
Sid Luckman
Roy "Link" Lyman
Tom Mack
John Mackey
John Madden
Tim Mara
Wellington Mara
Gino Marchetti
Dan Marino
Curtis Martin
George Preston Marshall
Bruce Mathews
Ollie Matson
Don Maynard
George McAfee
Mike McCormack
Randall McDaniel
Tommy McDonald
Hugh McElhenny
Johnny "Blood" McNally
Mike Michalske
Wayne Millner
Bobby Mitchell
Ron Mix

Art Monk
Joe Montana
Warren Moon
Lenny Moore
Marion Motley
Mike Munchak
Anthony Munoz
George Musso
Bronko Nagurski
Joe Namath
Earle "Greasy" Neale
Ernie Nevers
Ozzie Newsome
Ray Nitschke
Chuck Noll
Leo Nomellini
*Jonathan Ogden
Merlin Olsen
Jim Otto
Steve Owen
Alan Page
*Bill Parcells
Clarence "Ace" Parker
Jim Parker
Walter Payton
Joe Perry
Pete Pihos
Fritz Pollard
John Randle
Hugh "Shorty" Ray
Dan Reeves
Mel Renfro
Jerry Rice
Les Richter
John Riggins
Jim Ringo
Willie Roaf
*Dave Robinson
Andy Robustelli
Art Rooney
Dan Rooney
Pete Rozelle
Ed Sabol
Bob St. Clair
Barry Sanders
Charlie Sanders
Deion Sanders
*Warren Sapp
Gale Sayers
Joe Schmidt
Tex Schramm
Lee Roy Selmon
Shannon Sharpe
Billy Shaw
Art Shell
Don Shula

O. J. Simpson
Mike Singletary
Jackie Slater
Bruce Smith
Emmitt Smith
Jackie Smith
John Stallworth
Bart Starr
Roger Staubach
Ernie Stautner
Jan Stenerud
Dwight Stephenson
Hank Stram
Ken Strong
Joe Stydahar
Lynn Swann
Fran Tarkenton
Charley Taylor
Jim Taylor
Lawrence "LT" Taylor
Derrick Thomas
Emmitt Thomas
Thurman Thomas
Jim Thorpe
Andre Tippett
Y. A. Tittle
George Trafton
Charley Trippi
Emlen Tunnell
Clyde "Bulldog" Turner
Johnny Unitas
Gene Upshaw
Norm Van Brocklin
Steve Van Buren
Doak Walker
Bill Walsh
Paul Warfield
Bob Waterfield
Mike Webster
Randy White
Reggie White
Dave Wilcox
Bill Willis
Larry Wilson
Ralph Wilson Jr.
Kellen Winslow
Alex Wojciechowicz
Willie Wood
Rod Woodson
Rayfield Wright
Ron Yary
Steve Young
Jack Youngblood
Gary Zimmerman

All-Time NFL Coaching Victories

(at end of 2012 season; ranked by overall career wins; * = active in 2012)

Coach	Team	Yrs	Regular Season				Overall			
			W	L	T	Pct	W	L	T	Pct
Don Shula	Colts, Dolphins	33	328	156	6	.677	347	173	6	.666
George Halas	Bears	40	318	148	31	.682	324	151	31	.682
Tom Landry	Cowboys	29	250	162	6	.607	270	178	6	.603
Earl "Curly" Lambeau	Packers, Chicago Cardinals, Redskins	33	226	132	22	.631	229	134	22	.631
Chuck Noll	Steelers	23	193	148	1	.566	209	156	1	.572
Marty Schottenheimer	Browns, Chiefs, Redskins, Chargers	21	200	126	1	.613	205	139	1	.596
Bill Belichick*	Browns, Patriots	18	187	101	0	.649	205	109	0	.653
Dan Reeves	Broncos, Giants, Falcons	23	190	165	2	.535	201	174	2	.536
Chuck Knox	Rams, Bills, Seahawks	22	186	147	1	.558	193	158	1	.550
Bill Parcells	Giants, Packers, Jets, Cowboys	19	172	130	1	.569	183	138	1	.570
Mike Shanahan*	Raiders, Broncos, Redskins	19	167	125	0	.572	175	131	0	.572
Mike Holmgren	Packers, Seahawks	17	161	111	0	.592	174	122	0	.588
Joe Gibbs	Redskins	16	154	94	0	.621	171	101	0	.629
Paul Brown	Browns, Bengals	21	166	100	6	.624	170	108	6	.612
Bud Grant	Vikings	18	158	96	5	.621	168	108	5	.608
Tom Coughlin*	Jaguars, Giants	17	151	121	0	.555	162	128	0	.559
Bill Cowher	Steelers	15	149	90	1	.623	161	99	1	.619
Jeff Fisher*	Oilers, Titans, Rams	18	149	129	0	.536	154	135	0	.533
Marv Levy	Chiefs, Bills	17	143	112	0	.561	154	120	0	.562
Steve Owen	Giants	23	151	100	17	.602	153	108	17	.586

BASEBALL

Playoff Results, 2013

American League

American League Wild Card Game: Tampa Bay defeated Cleveland, 4-0.

American League Division Series (ALDS): Boston defeated Tampa Bay, 3 games to 1; Detroit defeated Oakland, 3 games to 2.

American League Championship Series (ALCS): Boston defeated Detroit, 4 games to 2.

National League

National League Wild Card Game: Pittsburgh defeated Cincinnati, 6-2.

National League Division Series (NLDS): St. Louis defeated Pittsburgh, 3 games to 2; Los Angeles defeated Atlanta, 3 games to 1.

National League Championship Series (NLCS): St. Louis defeated Los Angeles, 4 games to 2.

World Series, 2013

Boston Defeats St. Louis, 4 Games to 2

David Ortiz and Jon Lester led the Boston Red Sox to their third World Series victory in 10 years, topping the St. Louis Cardinals in six games. Ortiz was named Series MVP after batting .688 (11-for-16) with two homers, six RBI, and eight walks. It was the highest average in a single World Series (min. 15 plate appearances) since Billy Hatcher batted .750 for Cincinnati in 1990. Lester won Games 1 and 5, allowing just one run with 15 strikeouts in the two starts. Ortiz and Mike Napoli each had three RBI in the Sox's 8-1, Game 1 win Oct. 23 at Fenway Park in Boston. Napoli smacked a three-run double in the first inning that came after a missed call at second base. With runners at first and second, Ortiz bounced to Matt Carpenter, whose flip to shortstop Pete Kozma was dropped but second-base umpire Dana DeMuth called the runner (Dustin Pedroia) out. The other umpires overruled the call and Pedroia returned to second to load the bases for Napoli.

Another bizarre play ended St. Louis's 5-4 Game 3 win at Busch Stadium on Oct. 26, when Cardinals pinch-hitter Allen Craig scored the game-winning run in the ninth after umpires ruled that Red Sox third baseman Will Middlebrooks, after diving in a failed attempt to catch an errant throw by catcher Jarrod Saltalamacchia, had obstructed Craig's path toward home. The win gave St. Louis a 2-1 series lead, after rookie Michael Wacha had won his fourth consecutive postseason start in Game 2, a 4-2 Cardinal victory at Fenway Oct. 24. Boston tied the series in Game 4 with a 4-2 victory in St. Louis on Oct. 27, thanks to Jonny Gomes's three-run homer in the sixth. Boston closer Koji Uehara picked off St. Louis pinch-runner Kolten Wong at first base for the final out, ending a World Series game with a pickoff for the first time. Lester won his second game of the series in Game 5 Oct. 28, scattering four hits while Uehara got the last four outs to earn his second save in Boston's 3-1 win. Shane Victorino had four RBI in Boston's 6-1 series-clinching victory in Game 6 Oct. 30 at Fenway.

Game 1

Oct. 23 at Fenway Park, Boston, MA

	1	2	3	4	5	6	7	8	9	R	H	E
St. Louis Cardinals	0	0	0	0	0	0	0	0	1	1	7	3
Boston Red Sox	3	2	0	0	0	0	2	1	X	8	8	1

Winning pitcher: Jon Lester
Losing pitcher: Adam Wainwright
Attendance: 38,345

Game 2

Oct. 24 at Fenway Park, Boston, MA

	1	2	3	4	5	6	7	8	9	R	H	E
St. Louis Cardinals	0	0	0	1	0	0	3	0	0	4	7	1
Boston Red Sox	0	0	0	0	0	2	0	0	0	2	4	2

Winning pitcher: Michael Wacha
Losing pitcher: John Lackey
Save: Trevor Rosenthal
Attendance: 38,436

Game 3

Oct. 26 at Busch Stadium, St. Louis, MO

	1	2	3	4	5	6	7	8	9	R	H	E
Boston Red Sox	0	0	0	0	1	1	0	2	0	4	6	2
St. Louis Cardinals	2	0	0	0	0	0	2	0	1	5	12	0

Winning pitcher: Trevor Rosenthal
Losing pitcher: Brandon Workman
Attendance: 47,432

Game 4

Oct. 27 at Busch Stadium, St. Louis, MO

	1	2	3	4	5	6	7	8	9	R	H	E
Boston Red Sox	0	0	0	0	1	3	0	0	0	4	6	2
St. Louis Cardinals	0	0	1	0	0	0	1	0	0	2	6	0

Winning pitcher: Felix Doubront
Losing pitcher: Lance Lynn
Save: Koji Uehara
Attendance: 47,469

Game 5

Oct. 28 at Busch Stadium, St. Louis, MO

	1	2	3	4	5	6	7	8	9	R	H	E
Boston Red Sox	1	0	0	0	0	0	2	0	0	3	9	0
St. Louis Cardinals	0	0	0	1	0	0	0	0	0	1	4	0

Winning pitcher: Jon Lester
Losing pitcher: Adam Wainwright
Save: Koji Uehara
Attendance: 47,436

Game 6

Oct. 30 at Fenway Park, Boston, MA

	1	2	3	4	5	6	7	8	9	R	H	E
St. Louis Cardinals	0	0	0	0	0	0	1	0	0	1	9	1
Boston Red Sox	0	0	3	3	0	0	0	0	X	6	8	1

Winning pitcher: John Lackey
Losing pitcher: Michael Wacha
Attendance: 38,447

Major League Baseball, 2013: PED Scandals Return

The controversy over performance-enhancing drugs (PEDs) cast a long shadow on the 2013 season. MLB commissioner Bud Selig announced the suspension of Milwaukee Brewers outfielder Ryan Braun July 22, 2013, for the remainder of the season due to violations of the league's PED policy. Braun, the 2011 NL MVP whose suspension for a failed drug test in 2011 was overturned on appeal, served a 65-game ban. Selig suspended 13 more players Aug. 5, 2013, for their connection to the Biogenesis anti-aging clinic in Florida, which allegedly supplied PEDs in violation of the league's drug policy. Most players, including 2013 All-Stars Nelson Cruz, Jhonny Peralta, and Everth Cabrera, received and accepted 50-game suspensions. Alex Rodriguez, a three-time AL MVP, received a 211-game suspension, which he appealed. Allowed to play pending the outcome of the appeal, Rodriguez made his season debut Aug. 5 following offseason hip surgery. His appeal hearing began Sept. 30.

On the field, St. Louis (97-65) earned the NL's best record with solid offense (NL-high 783 runs scored) and pitching (19-game winner Adam Wainwright), claiming the NL Central title. Atlanta (96-66) won the NL East for the first time in eight years, and Pittsburgh (94-68) earned an NL Wild Card berth for their first trip to the postseason and first winning season since 1992. Clayton Kershaw's MLB-best 1.83 ERA and the emergence of rookie Yasiel Puig (.319 batting average) helped the L.A. Dodgers capture the NL West title. The Dodgers were in last place in the West on June 21 but won 42 of their next 50 games. It was MLB's best 50-game stretch since the Cardinals went 42-8 in 1942.

First-year manager John Farrell guided Boston to a 28-win improvement (97-65) from the 2012 season and the AL East title. Oakland won 96 games and took the AL West title for the second year in a row. AL Central-winning Detroit's right-hander Max Scherzer led the majors with 21 wins. Detroit's Miguel Cabrera followed his Triple Crown-winning season by topping the majors with a .348 batting average in 2013, but finished second in both home runs (44) and RBI (137) to Baltimore first baseman Chris Davis, who set a single-season franchise record with 53 homers and an MLB-high 138 RBI. Under former Red Sox manager Terry Francona, Cleveland won their last 10 games to snag a Wild Card slot and went to the playoffs for the first time since 2007. In Houston's first AL season, the team posted a last-in-league 51 wins, 111 losses.

Cincinnati right-hander Homer Bailey pitched the second no-hitter of his career July 2, striking out nine in San Francisco. The Giants' Tim Lincecum no-hit the Padres, 9-0, on July 13 in San Diego, and Miami's Henderson Alvarez threw a 1-0 no-hitter against visiting Detroit when Giancarlo Stanton scored the game-winning run on a wild pitch in the bottom of the ninth in the teams' last game Sept. 29.

Player retirements in 2013 included NY Yankees relief pitcher Mariano Rivera, who recorded 44 saves to increase his major-league record total to 652 and ends his career with a 0.70 ERA in 96 postseason appearances. Rivera's teammate Andy Pettitte (career 256-153 record) also announced his retirement, along with Colorado's Todd Helton, who spent his entire 17-year career with the Rockies and holds franchise records in hits (2,519), home runs (369), and RBI (1,406). Selig officially announced that he will step down as commissioner after the 2014 season.

National League Final Standings, 2013

(* = wild card)

Eastern Division

Team	W	L	PCT	GB	Home	Road	vs. East	vs. Central	vs. West	vs. AL
Atlanta	96	66	.593	—	56-25	40-41	47-29	19-14	19-14	11-9
Washington	86	76	.531	10	47-34	39-42	43-33	15-19	17-15	11-9
NY Mets	74	88	.457	22	33-48	41-40	34-42	12-21	17-16	11-9
Philadelphia	73	89	.451	23	43-38	30-51	37-39	12-21	17-16	7-13
Miami	62	100	.383	34	36-45	26-55	29-47	9-23	15-19	9-11

Central Division

Team	W	L	PCT	GB	Home	Road	vs. East	vs. Central	vs. West	vs. AL
St. Louis	97	65	.599	—	54-27	43-38	23-10	46-30	18-15	10-10
Pittsburgh*	94	68	.580	3	50-31	44-37	20-14	45-31	14-18	15-5
Cincinnati*	90	72	.556	7	49-31	41-41	20-13	40-36	19-14	11-9
Milwaukee	74	88	.457	23	37-44	37-44	21-12	34-42	13-20	6-14
Chicago Cubs	66	96	.407	31	31-50	35-46	14-18	25-51	14-20	13-7

Western Division

Team	W	L	PCT	GB	Home	Road	vs. East	vs. Central	vs. West	vs. AL
L.A. Dodgers	92	70	.568	—	47-34	45-36	22-11	21-12	37-39	12-8
Arizona	81	81	.500	11	45-36	36-45	14-18	20-14	36-40	11-9
San Francisco	76	86	.469	16	42-40	34-46	15-17	11-23	44-32	6-14
San Diego	76	86	.469	16	45-36	31-50	16-17	17-16	35-41	8-12
Colorado	74	88	.457	18	45-36	29-52	13-22	18-13	38-38	5-15

American League Final Standings, 2013

(* = wild card)

Eastern Division

Team	W	L	PCT	GB	Home	Road	vs. East	vs. Central	vs. West	vs. NL
Boston	97	65	.599	—	53-28	44-37	44-32	19-15	20-12	14-6
Tampa Bay*	92	71	.564	5.5	51-30	41-41	43-33	19-14	18-16	12-8
NY Yankees	85	77	.525	12	46-35	39-42	37-39	22-11	17-16	9-11
Baltimore	85	77	.525	12	46-35	39-42	36-40	17-16	21-12	11-9
Toronto	74	88	.457	23	40-41	34-47	30-46	16-16	17-17	11-9

Central Division

Team	W	L	PCT	GB	Home	Road	vs. East	vs. Central	vs. West	vs. NL
Detroit	93	69	.574	—	51-30	42-39	17-15	47-29	17-17	12-8
Cleveland*	92	70	.568	1	51-30	41-40	12-21	44-32	25-8	11-9
Kansas City	86	76	.531	7	44-37	42-39	19-15	44-32	14-18	9-11
Minnesota	66	96	.407	27	32-49	34-47	10-23	29-47	19-14	8-12
Chicago White Sox	63	99	.389	30	37-44	26-55	14-19	26-50	15-18	8-12

Western Division

Team	W	L	PCT	GB	Home	Road	vs. East	vs. Central	vs. West	vs. NL
Oakland	96	66	.593	—	52-29	44-37	17-15	22-12	44-32	13-7
Texas	91	72	.558	5.5	46-36	45-36	15-20	13-19	53-23	10-10
L.A. Angels	78	84	.481	18	39-42	39-42	18-16	18-14	32-44	10-10
Seattle	71	91	.438	25	36-45	35-46	14-18	13-21	36-40	8-12
Houston	51	111	.315	45	24-57	27-54	9-24	9-24	25-51	8-12

Note: Tampa Bay defeated Texas in a one-game tiebreaker to earn the second AL wild-card playoff berth.

National League Statistics, 2013

Individual statistics. Players recording fewer than 150 at-bats (batters) or fewer than 70 innings or 10 saves (pitchers) are not listed here. * = changed teams within NL during season; entry includes statistics for more than one team. # = changed teams to or from AL during season; entry includes only NL statistics. Team Batting and Team Pitching include players not shown separately.

Team Batting

Team	AVG	AB	R	H	HR	RBI
Colorado Rockies	.270	5,599	706	1,511	159	673
St. Louis Cardinals	.269	5,557	783	1,494	125	745
Los Angeles Dodgers	.264	5,491	649	1,447	138	618
San Francisco Giants	.260	5,552	629	1,446	107	596
Arizona Diamondbacks	.259	5,676	685	1,468	130	647
Milwaukee Brewers	.252	5,474	640	1,381	157	610
Washington Nationals	.251	5,436	656	1,365	161	621
Cincinnati Reds	.249	5,499	698	1,370	155	664
Atlanta Braves	.249	5,441	688	1,354	181	656
Philadelphia Phillies	.248	5,456	610	1,355	140	578
Pittsburgh Pirates	.245	5,486	634	1,346	161	603
San Diego Padres	.245	5,517	618	1,349	146	578
Chicago Cubs	.238	5,498	602	1,307	172	576
New York Mets	.237	5,559	619	1,318	130	593
Miami Marlins	.231	5,449	513	1,257	95	485

Team Pitching

Team	ERA	IP	H	BB	SO	SV
Atlanta Braves	3.18	1,450.1	1,326	409	1,232	53
Los Angeles Dodgers	3.25	1,450.1	1,321	460	1,292	46
Pittsburgh Pirates	3.26	1,470.2	1,299	515	1,261	55
Cincinnati Reds	3.38	1,473.2	1,294	435	1,296	43
St. Louis Cardinals	3.42	1,459.2	1,366	451	1,254	44
Washington Nationals	3.59	1,445.2	1,367	405	1,236	47
Miami Marlins	3.71	1,460	1,376	526	1,177	36
New York Mets	3.77	1,476.2	1,442	458	1,209	40
Milwaukee Brewers	3.84	1,442.2	1,401	466	1,125	40
Arizona Diamondbacks	3.92	1,495	1,460	485	1,218	38
San Diego Padres	3.98	1,455	1,407	525	1,171	40
Chicago Cubs	4.00	1,448	1,332	540	1,184	39
San Francisco Giants	4.00	1,447.1	1,380	521	1,256	41
Philadelphia Phillies	4.32	1,436.1	1,465	506	1,199	32
Colorado Rockies	4.44	1,436	1,545	517	1,064	35

Arizona Diamondbacks

Batters	AVG	AB	R	H	HR	RBI	SO	SB
Paul Goldschmidt	.302	602	103	182	36	125	145	15
Wil Nieves	.297	195	16	58	1	22	32	0
Aaron Hill	.291	327	45	95	11	41	48	1
Martin Prado	.282	609	70	172	14	82	53	3
Eric Chavez	.281	228	28	64	9	44	45	1
Cody Ross	.278	317	33	88	8	38	50	3
A.J. Pollock	.269	443	64	119	8	38	82	12
Gerardo Parra	.268	601	79	161	10	48	100	10
Didi Gregorius	.252	357	47	90	7	28	65	0
Adam Eaton	.252	250	40	63	3	22	44	5
Cliff Pennington	.242	269	25	65	1	18	54	2
Miguel Montero	.230	413	44	95	11	42	110	0
Jason Kubel#	.220	241	21	53	9	32	62	0

Pitchers	ERA	W	L	IP	H	BB	SO	SV
Brad Ziegler	2.22	8	1	73	61	22	44	13
Josh Collmenter	3.13	5	5	92	79	33	85	0
Patrick Corbin	3.41	14	8	208.1	189	54	178	0
Wade Miley	3.55	10	10	202.2	201	66	147	0
Trevor Cahill	3.99	8	10	146.2	143	65	102	0
Heath Bell	4.11	5	2	65.2	74	16	72	15
Randall Delgado	4.26	5	7	116.1	116	23	79	0
Brandon McCarthy	4.53	5	11	135	161	21	76	0
Ian Kennedy*	4.91	7	10	181.1	180	73	163	0

Manager: Kirk Gibson

Chicago Cubs

Batters	AVG	AB	R	H	HR	RBI	SO	SB
Dioner Navarro	.300	240	31	72	13	34	36	0
Junior Lake	.284	236	26	67	6	16	68	4
Welington Castillo	.274	380	41	104	8	32	97	2
Ryan Sweeney	.266	192	19	51	6	19	31	1
Alfonso Soriano#	.254	362	47	92	17	51	89	10
Nate Schierholtz	.251	462	56	116	21	68	94	6
David DeJesus*#	.247	287	39	71	6	27	56	3
Starlin Castro	.245	666	59	163	10	44	129	9
Anthony Rizzo	.233	606	71	141	23	80	127	6
Luis Valbuena	.218	331	34	72	12	37	63	1
Darwin Barney	.208	501	49	104	7	41	64	4
Scott Hairston*	.191	157	18	30	10	26	44	2
Cody Ransom*	.189	169	21	32	9	20	62	0

Pitchers	ERA	W	L	IP	H	BB	SO	SV
Travis Wood	3.11	9	12	200	163	66	144	0
Matt Garza#	3.17	6	1	71	61	20	62	0
Scott Feldman#.	3.46	7	6	91	79	25	67	0
Kevin Gregg	3.48	2	6	62	53	32	56	33
Carlos Villanueva	4.06	7	8	128.2	117	40	103	0
Jeff Samardzija	4.34	8	13	213.2	210	78	214	0
Edwin Jackson	4.98	8	18	175.1	197	59	135	0

Manager: Dale Sveum

Atlanta Braves

Batters	AVG	AB	R	H	HR	RBI	SO	SB
Chris Johnson	.321	514	54	165	12	68	116	0
Freddie Freeman	.319	551	89	176	23	109	121	1
Justin Upton	.263	558	94	147	27	70	161	8
Brian McCann	.256	356	43	91	20	57	66	0
Jason Heyward	.254	382	67	97	14	38	73	2
Andrelton Simmons	.248	606	76	150	17	59	55	6
Jordan Schafer	.247	231	32	57	3	21	73	22
Evan Gattis	.243	354	44	86	21	65	81	0
Juan Francisco*	.227	348	36	79	18	48	138	0
B.J. Upton	.184	391	30	72	9	26	151	12
Dan Uggla	.179	448	60	80	22	55	171	2

Pitchers	ERA	W	L	IP	H	BB	SO	SV
Craig Kimbrel	1.21	4	3	67	39	20	98	50
Anthony Varvaro	2.82	3	1	73.1	68	25	43	1
Kris Medlen	3.11	15	12	197	194	47	157	0
Alex Wood	3.13	3	3	77.2	76	27	77	0
Julio Teheran	3.20	14	8	185.2	173	45	170	0
Mike Minor	3.21	13	9	204.2	177	46	181	0
Tim Hudson	3.97	8	7	131.1	120	36	95	0
Paul Maholm	4.41	10	11	153	169	47	105	0

Manager: Fredi González

Cincinnati Reds

Batters	AVG	AB	R	H	HR	RBI	SO	SB
Joey Votto	.305	581	101	177	24	73	138	6
Shin-Soo Choo	.285	569	107	162	21	54	133	20
Jay Bruce	.262	626	89	164	30	109	185	7
Brandon Phillips	.261	606	80	158	18	103	98	5
Derrick Robinson	.255	192	21	49	0	8	44	4
Zack Cozart	.254	567	74	144	12	63	102	0
Xavier Paul	.244	209	24	51	7	32	53	0
Devin Mesoraco	.238	323	31	77	9	42	61	0
Chris Heisey	.237	224	29	53	9	23	51	3
Todd Frazier	.234	531	63	124	19	73	125	6
Ryan Hanigan	.198	222	17	44	2	21	27	0

Pitchers	ERA	W	L	IP	H	BB	SO	SV
Aroldis Chapman	2.54	4	5	63.2	37	29	112	38
Alfredo Simon	2.87	6	4	87.2	68	26	63	1
Tony Cingrani	2.92	7	4	104.2	72	43	120	0
Mat Latos	3.16	14	7	210.2	197	58	187	0
Mike Leake	3.37	14	7	192.1	193	48	122	0
Homer Bailey	3.49	11	12	209	181	54	199	0
Bronson Arroyo	3.79	14	12	202	199	34	124	0

Manager: Dusty Baker

Colorado Rockies

Batters	AVG	AB	R	H	HR	RBI	SO	SB
Michael Cuddyer...	.331	489	74	162	20	84	100	10
Troy Tulowitzki.....	.312	446	72	139	25	82	85	1
Charlie Blackmon..	.309	246	35	76	6	22	49	7
Carlos Gonzalez...	.302	391	72	118	26	70	118	21
Wilin Rosario	.292	449	63	131	21	79	109	4
Jonathan Herrera..	.292	195	16	57	1	16	24	3
DJ LeMahieu	.280	404	39	113	2	28	67	18
Nolan Arenado	.267	486	49	130	10	52	72	2
Dexter Fowler	.263	415	71	109	12	42	105	19
Corey Dickerson...	.263	194	32	51	5	17	41	2
Todd Helton	.249	397	41	99	15	61	87	0
Eric Young Jr.*....	.249	539	70	134	2	32	100	46
Yorvit Torrealba...	.240	179	10	43	0	16	24	0
Jordan Pacheco ...	.239	247	23	59	1	22	38	0
Josh Rutledge.....	.235	285	45	67	7	19	62	12

Pitchers	ERA	W	L	IP	H	BB	SO	SV
Rex Brothers......	1.74	2	1	67.1	51	36	76	19
Adam Ottavino	2.64	1	3	78.1	73	31	78	0
Tyler Chatwood ...	3.15	8	5	111.1	118	41	66	0
Jhoulys Chacin....	3.47	14	10	197.1	188	61	126	0
Jorge De La Rosa..	3.49	16	6	167.2	170	62	112	0
Wilton Lopez......	4.06	3	4	75.1	88	18	48	0
Rafael Betancourt..	4.08	2	5	28.2	26	11	27	16
Matt Belisle.......	4.32	5	7	73	76	15	62	0
Juan Nicasio......	5.14	9	9	157.2	168	64	119	0
Jeff Francis.......	6.27	3	5	70.1	89	24	63	0

Manager: Walt Weiss

Los Angeles Dodgers

Batters	AVG	AB	R	H	HR	RBI	SO	SB
Hanley Ramirez ...	.345	304	62	105	20	57	52	10
Yasiel Puig	.319	382	66	122	19	42	97	11
Adrian Gonzalez...	.293	583	69	171	22	100	98	1
Carl Crawford	.283	435	62	123	6	31	66	15
Michael Young*....	.279	519	52	145	8	46	83	1
Juan Uribe	.278	388	47	108	12	50	81	5
Andre Ethier	.272	482	54	131	12	52	95	4
Mark Ellis	.270	433	46	117	6	48	74	4
Matt Kemp	.270	263	35	71	6	33	76	9
Skip Schumaker ...	.263	319	31	84	2	30	54	2
Nick Punto	.255	294	34	75	2	21	67	3
A.J. Ellis	.238	390	43	93	10	52	78	0
Tim Federowicz ...	.231	160	12	37	4	16	56	0
Jerry Hairston Jr. ..	.211	204	17	43	2	22	22	0

Pitchers	ERA	W	L	IP	H	BB	SO	SV
Clayton Kershaw...	1.83	16	9	236	164	52	232	0
Kenley Jansen	1.88	4	3	76.2	48	18	111	28
Zack Greinke	2.63	15	4	177.2	152	46	148	0
Hyun-Jin Ryu	3.00	14	8	192	182	49	154	0
Ricky Nolasco*....	3.70	13	11	199.1	195	46	165	0
Chris Capuano	4.26	4	7	105.2	125	24	81	0
Brandon League....	5.30	6	4	54.1	69	15	28	14
Edinson Volquez*..	5.71	9	12	170.1	193	77	142	0

Manager: Don Mattingly

Miami Marlins

Batters	AVG	AB	R	H	HR	RBI	SO	SB
Christian Yelich	.288	240	34	69	4	16	66	10
Marcell Ozuna	.265	275	31	73	3	32	57	5
Placido Polanco ...	.260	377	33	98	1	23	31	2
Ed Lucas.........	.256	351	43	90	4	28	78	1
Chris Coghlan	.256	195	10	50	1	10	43	2
Giancarlo Stanton ..	.249	425	62	106	24	62	140	1
Donovan Solano...	.249	361	33	90	3	34	57	3
Juan Pierre	.247	308	36	76	1	8	27	23
Logan Morrison ...	.242	293	32	71	6	36	56	0
Greg Dobbs	.228	237	21	54	2	22	40	1
Adeiny Hechavarria	.227	543	30	123	3	42	96	11
Justin Ruggiano ...	.222	424	49	94	18	50	114	15
Derek Dietrich ...	.214	215	32	46	9	23	56	1
Rob Brantly.......	.211	223	11	47	1	18	53	0
Jeff Mathis	.181	232	14	42	5	29	76	0

Pitchers	ERA	W	L	IP	H	BB	SO	SV
Jose Fernandez	2.19	12	6	172.2	111	58	187	0
Steve Cishek.......	2.33	4	6	69.2	53	22	74	34
Ryan Webb........	2.91	2	6	80.1	70	27	54	0
A.J. Ramos........	3.15	3	4	80	58	43	86	0
Nathan Eovaldi....	3.39	4	6	106.1	100	40	78	0
Henderson Alvarez .	3.59	5	6	102.2	90	27	57	0
Ricky Nolasco*....	3.70	13	11	199.1	195	46	165	0
Jacob Turner......	3.74	3	8	118	116	54	77	0
Kevin Slowey	4.11	3	6	92	106	18	76	0
Tom Koehler	4.41	5	10	143	140	54	92	0

Manager: Mike Redmond

Milwaukee Brewers

Batters	AVG	AB	R	H	HR	RBI	SO	SB
Scooter Gennett	.324	213	29	69	6	21	42	2
Ryan Braun........	.298	225	30	67	9	38	56	4
Jean Segura.......	.294	588	74	173	12	49	84	44
Norichika Aoki.....	.286	597	80	171	8	37	40	20
Carlos Gomez......	.284	536	80	152	24	73	146	40
Aramis Ramirez	.283	304	43	86	12	49	55	0
Jonathan Lucroy	.280	521	59	146	18	82	69	9
Jeff Bianchi.......	.237	236	22	56	1	25	46	4
Juan Francisco*....	.227	348	36	79	18	48	138	0
Yuniesky Betancourt	.212	391	35	83	13	46	71	0
Logan Schafer	.211	298	29	63	4	33	60	7
Rickie Weeks	.209	350	40	73	10	24	105	7
Martin Maldonado...	.169	183	13	31	4	22	53	0

Pitchers	ERA	W	L	IP	H	BB	SO	SV
Francisco Rodriguez#	1.09	1	1	24.2	17	9	26	10
Brandon Kintzler....	2.69	3	3	77	66	16	58	0
Jim Henderson	2.70	5	5	60	44	24	75	28
Kyle Lohse	3.35	11	10	198.2	196	36	125	0
Marco Estrada	3.87	7	4	128	109	29	118	0
Tom Gorzelanny	3.90	3	6	85.1	77	31	83	0
Alfredo Figaro	4.14	3	3	74	77	15	54	1
Yovani Gallardo.....	4.18	12	10	180.2	180	66	144	0
Wily Peralta......	4.37	11	15	183.1	187	73	129	0

Manager: Ron Roenicke

New York Mets

Batters	AVG	AB	R	H	HR	RBI	SO	SB
David Wright	.307	430	63	132	18	58	79	17
Marlon Byrd*.......	.291	532	75	155	24	88	144	2
Daniel Murphy	.286	658	92	188	13	78	95	23
Justin Turner	.280	200	12	56	2	16	34	0
Josh Satin........	.279	190	23	53	3	17	56	1
Eric Young Jr.*....	.249	539	70	134	2	32	100	46
Juan Lagares	.242	392	35	95	4	34	96	6
Andrew Brown	.227	150	16	34	7	24	44	1
Lucas Duda	.223	318	42	71	15	33	102	0
John Buck*.......	.222	392	39	87	15	62	104	2
Omar Quintanilla....	.222	315	28	70	2	21	70	2
Ike Davis...........	.205	317	37	65	9	33	101	4
Ruben Tejada	.202	208	20	42	0	10	24	2

Pitchers	ERA	W	L	IP	H	BB	SO	SV
Bobby Parnell	2.16	5	5	50	38	12	44	22
Matt Harvey	2.27	9	5	178.1	135	31	191	0
LaTroy Hawkins ...	2.93	3	2	70.2	71	10	55	13
Zack Wheeler	3.42	7	5	100	90	46	84	0
Carlos Torres	3.44	4	6	86.1	79	17	75	0
Dillon Gee	3.62	12	11	199	208	47	142	0
Jon Niese	3.71	8	8	143	158	48	105	0
Jeremy Hefner	4.34	4	8	130.2	132	37	99	0
Shaun Marcum	5.29	1	10	78.1	85	21	60	0

Manager: Terry Collins

Philadelphia Phillies

Batters	AVG	AB	R	H	HR	RBI	SO	SB
Ben Revere.........	.305	315	37	96	0	17	36	22
Chase Utley	.284	476	73	135	18	69	79	8
Michael Young*.....	.279	519	52	145	8	46	83	1
Domonic Brown	.272	496	65	135	27	83	97	8
Carlos Ruiz........	.268	310	30	83	5	37	39	1
Ryan Howard	.266	286	34	76	11	43	95	0
Delmon Young#.....	.261	272	22	71	8	31	69	0
Jimmy Rollins	.252	600	65	151	6	39	93	22
Darin Ruf	.247	251	36	62	14	30	91	0
Cody Asche	.235	162	18	38	5	22	43	1
Kevin Frandsen.....	.234	252	27	59	5	26	29	1
Freddy Galvis......	.234	205	13	48	6	19	45	1
John Mayberry Jr....	.227	353	47	80	11	39	90	5
Erik Kratz	.213	197	21	42	9	26	45	0
Roger Bernadina*...	.181	227	26	41	4	11	65	4

Pitchers	ERA	W	L	IP	H	BB	SO	SV
Cliff Lee	2.87	14	8	222.2	193	32	222	0
Jonathan Papelbon..	2.92	5	1	61.2	59	11	57	29
Cole Hamels......	3.60	8	14	220	205	50	202	0
Jonathan Pettibone..	4.04	5	4	100.1	109	38	66	0
Kyle Kendrick	4.70	10	13	182	207	47	110	0
John Lannan	5.33	3	6	74.1	86	27	38	0

Managers: Charlie Manuel, Ryne Sandberg

Pittsburgh Pirates

Batters	AVG	AB	R	H	HR	RBI	SO	SB
Andrew McCutchen..	.317	583	97	185	21	84	101	27
Marlon Byrd*.......	.291	532	75	155	24	88	144	2
Jordy Mercer.......	.285	333	33	95	8	27	62	3
Jose Tabata.......	.282	308	35	87	6	33	45	3
Starling Marte......	.280	510	83	143	12	35	138	41
Gaby Sanchez	.254	264	29	67	7	36	51	1
Neil Walker	.251	478	62	120	16	53	85	1
Pedro Alvarez	.233	558	70	130	36	100	186	2
Garrett Jones......	.233	403	41	94	15	51	101	2
Russell Martin.....	.226	438	51	99	15	55	108	9
John Buck⁴........	.222	392	39	87	16	62	104	2
Travis Snider.....	.215	261	28	56	5	25	75	2
Clint Barmes	.211	304	22	64	5	23	70	0

Pitchers	ERA	W	L	IP	H	BB	SO	SV
Mark Melancon.....	1.39	3	2	71	60	8	70	16
Justin Wilson......	2.08	6	1	73.2	50	28	59	0
Tony Watson	2.39	3	1	71.2	51	12	54	2
Jason Grilli	2.70	0	2	50	40	13	74	33
Vin Mazzaro......	2.81	8	2	73.2	68	21	46	1
Francisco Liriano ...	3.02	16	8	161	134	63	163	0
Gerrit Cole	3.22	10	7	117.1	109	28	100	0
Charlie Morton.....	3.26	7	4	116	113	36	85	0
A.J. Burnett........	3.30	10	11	191	165	67	209	0
Jeanmar Gomez	3.35	3	0	80.2	65	28	53	0
Jeff Locke	3.52	10	7	166.1	146	84	125	0

Manager: Clint Hurdle

St. Louis Cardinals

Batters	AVG	AB	R	H	HR	RBI	SO	SB
Yadier Molina	.319	505	68	161	12	80	55	3
Matt Carpenter	.318	626	126	199	11	78	98	3
Allen Craig	.315	508	71	160	13	97	100	2
Matt Holliday	.300	520	103	156	22	94	86	6
Carlos Beltran......	.296	554	79	164	24	84	90	2
Matt Adams......	.284	296	46	84	17	51	80	0
Jon Jay............	.276	548	75	151	7	67	103	10
David Freese.......	.262	462	53	121	9	60	106	1
Daniel Descalso ...	.238	328	43	78	5	43	56	6
Pete Kozma	.217	410	44	89	1	35	91	3

Pitchers	ERA	W	L	IP	H	BB	SO	SV
Trevor Rosenthal...	2.63	2	4	75.1	63	20	108	3
Joe Kelly	2.69	10	5	124	124	44	79	0
Edward Mujica	2.78	2	1	64.2	60	5	46	37
Adam Wainwright...	2.94	19	9	241.2	223	35	219	0
Shelby Miller	3.06	15	9	173.1	152	57	169	0
Lance Lynn........	3.97	15	10	201.2	189	76	198	0
Jake Westbrook ...	4.63	7	8	116.2	132	50	44	0

Manager: Mike Matheny

San Diego Padres

Batters	AVG	AB	R	H	HR	RBI	SO	SB
Everth Cabrera	.283	381	54	108	4	31	69	37
Yonder Alonso.....	.281	334	34	94	6	45	47	6
Chris Denorfia.....	.279	473	67	132	10	47	84	11
Carlos Quentin	.275	276	42	76	13	44	55	0
Will Venable	.268	481	64	129	22	53	118	22
Chase Headley	.250	520	59	130	13	50	142	8
Jedd Gyorko	.249	486	62	121	23	63	123	1
Kyle Blanks.......	.243	280	31	68	8	35	85	1
Alexi Amarista.....	.236	368	35	87	5	32	57	4
Nick Hundley	.233	373	35	87	13	44	98	1
Jesus Guzman	.226	288	33	65	9	35	79	3
Logan Forsythe....	.214	220	22	47	6	19	54	6
Mark Kotsay......	.194	155	8	30	1	12	25	0
Cody Ransom*....	.189	169	21	32	9	20	62	0

Pitchers	ERA	W	L	IP	H	BB	SO	SV
Huston Street	2.70	2	5	56.2	44	14	46	33
Andrew Cashner...	3.09	10	9	175	151	47	128	0
Tyson Ross.......	3.17	3	8	125	100	44	119	0
Eric Stults.......	3.93	11	13	203.2	219	40	131	0
Jason Marquis	4.05	9	5	117.2	111	68	72	0
Ian Kennedy*.....	4.91	7	10	181.1	180	73	163	0
Edinson Volquez*..	5.71	9	12	170.1	193	77	142	0

Manager: Bud Black

San Francisco Giants

Batters	AVG	AB	R	H	HR	RBI	SO	SB
Marco Scutaro	.297	488	57	145	2	31	34	2
Buster Posey	.294	520	61	153	15	72	70	2
Brandon Belt......	.289	509	76	147	17	67	125	5
Hunter Pence	.283	629	91	178	27	99	115	22
Angel Pagan	.282	280	44	79	5	30	36	9
Pablo Sandoval....	.278	525	52	146	14	79	79	0
Joaquin Arias	.271	225	17	61	1	19	33	1
Gregor Blanco	.265	452	50	120	3	41	95	14
Andres Torres	.250	272	33	68	2	21	61	4
Brandon Crawford..	.248	499	52	124	9	43	96	1

Pitchers	ERA	W	L	IP	H	BB	SO	SV
Sergio Romo......	2.54	5	8	60.1	53	12	58	38
Madison Bumgarner.	2.77	13	9	201.1	146	62	199	0
Chad Gaudin	3.06	5	2	97	81	40	88	0
Matt Cain	4.00	8	10	184.1	158	55	158	0
Tim Lincecum.....	4.37	10	14	197.2	184	76	193	0
Ryan Vogelsong ...	5.73	4	6	103.2	124	38	67	0
Barry Zito	5.74	5	11	133.1	173	54	86	0

Manager: Bruce Bochy

Washington Nationals

Batters	AVG	AB	R	H	HR	RBI	SO	SB
Jayson Werth	.318	462	84	147	25	82	101	10
Ian Desmond	.280	600	77	168	20	80	145	21
Denard Span	.279	610	75	170	4	47	77	20
Ryan Zimmerman..	.275	568	84	156	26	79	133	6
Bryce Harper	.274	424	71	116	20	58	94	11
Wilson Ramos	.272	287	29	78	16	59	42	0
Anthony Rendon...	.265	351	40	93	7	35	69	1
Steve Lombardozzi....	.259	290	25	75	2	22	34	4
David DeJesus* #..	.247	287	39	71	6	27	56	3
Adam LaRoche	.237	511	70	121	20	62	131	4
Kurt Suzuki#.......	.222	252	19	56	3	25	32	2
Tyler Moore	.222	167	16	37	4	21	58	0
Scott Hairston*	.191	157	18	30	10	26	44	2
Roger Bernadina*..	.181	227	26	41	4	11	65	4
Danny Espinosa....	.158	158	11	25	3	12	47	1

Pitchers	ERA	W	L	IP	H	BB	SO	SV
Tyler Clippard......	2.41	6	3	71	37	24	73	0
Craig Stammen	2.76	7	6	81.2	78	27	79	0
Stephen Strasburg	3.00	8	9	183	136	56	191	0
Rafael Soriano	3.11	3	3	66.2	65	17	51	43
Jordan Zimmermann	3.25	19	9	213.1	192	40	161	0
Gio Gonzalez	3.36	11	8	195.2	169	76	192	0
Ross Detwiler	4.04	2	7	71.1	92	14	39	0
Dan Haren	4.67	10	14	169.2	179	31	151	1

Manager: Davey Johnson

American League Statistics, 2013

Individual statistics. Players recording fewer than 150 at-bats (batters) or fewer than 70 innings or 10 saves (pitchers) are not listed here. * = changed teams within AL during season; entry includes statistics for more than one team. # = changed teams to or from NL during season; entry includes only AL statistics. Team Batting and Team Pitching include players not shown separately.

Team Batting

Team	AVG	AB	R	H	HR	RBI
Detroit Tigers	.283	5,735	796	1,625	176	767
Boston Red Sox	.277	5,651	853	1,566	178	819
Los Angeles Angels	.264	5,588	733	1,476	164	696
Texas Rangers	.262	5,585	730	1,465	176	691
Kansas City Royals	.260	5,549	648	1,443	112	620
Baltimore Orioles	.260	5,620	745	1,460	212	719
Tampa Bay Rays	.257	5,538	700	1,421	165	670
Cleveland Indians	.255	5,465	745	1,391	171	711
Oakland Athletics	.254	5,521	767	1,403	186	725
Toronto Blue Jays	.252	5,537	712	1,398	185	669
Chicago White Sox	.249	5,563	598	1,385	148	574
New York Yankees	.242	5,449	650	1,321	144	614
Minnesota Twins	.242	5,564	614	1,346	151	590
Houston Astros	.240	5,457	610	1,307	148	566
Seattle Mariners	.237	5,558	624	1,318	188	597

Team Pitching

Team	ERA	IP	H	BB	SO	SV
Kansas City Royals	3.45	1,448.1	1,366	469	1,208	52
Oakland Athletics	3.56	1,452	1,339	428	1,183	46
Detroit Tigers	3.61	1,462.2	1,369	462	1,428	39
Texas Rangers	3.62	1,463.1	1,370	498	1,309	46
Tampa Bay Rays	3.74	1,464	1,315	482	1,310	42
Boston Red Sox	3.79	1,454	1,366	524	1,294	33
Cleveland Indians	3.82	1,441.1	1,359	554	1,379	38
New York Yankees	3.94	1,447.1	1,452	437	1,233	49
Chicago White Sox	3.98	1,455	1,424	509	1,249	40
Baltimore Orioles	4.20	1,453	1,438	473	1,169	57
Los Angeles Angels	4.23	1,457.2	1,475	533	1,200	41
Toronto Blue Jays	4.25	1,452	1,451	500	1,208	39
Seattle Mariners	4.31	1,465	1,467	478	1,297	43
Minnesota Twins	4.55	1,450.1	1,591	458	985	40
Houston Astros	4.79	1,440	1,530	616	1,084	32

Baltimore Orioles

Batters	AVG	AB	R	H	HR	RBI	SO	SB
Danny Valencia	.304	161	20	49	8	23	33	0
Chris Davis	.286	584	103	167	53	138	199	4
Adam Jones	.285	653	100	186	33	108	136	14
Manny Machado	.283	667	88	189	14	71	113	6
L.J. Hoes*	.282	170	24	48	1	10	35	7
Nick Markakis	.271	634	89	172	10	59	76	1
J.J. Hardy	.263	601	66	158	25	76	73	2
Nate McLouth	.258	531	76	137	12	36	86	30
Brian Roberts	.249	265	33	66	8	39	44	3
Matt Wieters	.235	523	59	123	22	79	104	2
Michael Morse*	.215	312	34	67	13	27	87	0
Ryan Flaherty	.224	246	28	55	10	27	62	2

Pitchers	ERA	W	L	IP	H	BB	SO	SV
Tommy Hunter	2.81	6	5	86.1	71	14	68	4
Jim Johnson	2.94	3	8	70.1	72	18	56	50
Chris Tillman	3.71	16	7	206.1	184	68	179	0
Miguel Gonzalez	3.78	11	8	171.1	157	53	120	0
Wei-Yin Chen	4.07	7	7	137	142	39	104	0
Bud Norris*	4.18	10	12	176.2	196	67	147	0
T.J. McFarland	4.22	4	1	74.2	83	28	58	0
Scott Feldman#	4.27	5	6	90.2	80	31	65	0
Jason Hammel	4.97	7	8	139.1	155	48	96	1

Manager: Buck Showalter

Boston Red Sox

Batters	AVG	AB	R	H	HR	RBI	SO	SB
David Ortiz	.309	518	84	160	30	103	88	4
Daniel Nava	.303	458	77	139	12	66	93	0
Jose Iglesias*	.303	350	39	106	3	29	60	5
Dustin Pedroia	.301	641	91	193	9	84	75	17
Jacoby Ellsbury	.298	577	92	172	9	53	92	52
Mike Carp	.296	216	34	64	9	43	67	1
Shane Victorino	.294	477	82	140	15	61	75	21
Jarrod Saltalamacchia	.273	425	68	116	14	65	139	4
Mike Napoli	.259	498	79	129	23	92	187	1
Stephen Drew	.253	442	57	112	13	67	124	6
Jonny Gomes	.247	312	49	77	13	52	89	1
Will Middlebrooks	.227	348	41	79	17	49	98	3

Pitchers	ERA	W	L	IP	H	BB	SO	SV
Koji Uehara	1.09	4	1	74.1	33	9	101	21
Clay Buchholz	1.74	12	1	108.1	75	36	96	0
John Lackey	3.52	10	13	189.1	179	40	161	0
Jon Lester	3.75	15	8	213.1	209	67	177	0
Jake Peavy*	4.17	12	5	144.2	130	36	121	0
Felix Doubront	4.32	11	6	162.1	161	71	139	0
Ryan Dempster	4.57	8	9	171.1	170	79	157	0

Manager: John Farrell

Chicago White Sox

Batters	AVG	AB	R	H	HR	RBI	SO	SB
Alexei Ramirez	.284	637	68	181	6	48	68	30
Avisail Garcia*	.283	244	31	69	7	31	59	3
Alex Rios*	.278	616	83	171	18	81	108	42
Gordon Beckham	.267	371	46	99	5	24	56	5
Dayan Viciedo	.265	441	43	117	14	56	98	0
Alejandro De Aza	.264	607	84	160	17	62	147	20
Jeff Keppinger	.253	423	38	107	4	40	41	0
Conor Gillaspie	.245	408	46	100	13	40	79	0
Paul Konerko	.244	467	41	114	12	54	74	0
Jordan Danks	.231	160	15	37	5	12	57	7
Adam Dunn	.219	525	60	115	34	86	189	1
Josh Phegley	.206	204	14	42	4	22	41	2
Tyler Flowers	.195	256	24	50	10	24	94	0

Pitchers	ERA	W	L	IP	H	BB	SO	SV
Chris Sale	3.07	11	14	214.1	184	46	226	0
Jose Quintana	3.51	9	7	200	188	56	164	0
Hector Santiago	3.56	4	9	149	137	72	137	0
Addison Reed	3.79	5	4	71.1	56	23	72	40
Nate Jones	4.15	4	5	78	69	26	89	0
Jake Peavy*	4.17	12	5	144.2	130	36	121	0
John Danks	4.75	4	14	138.1	151	27	89	0
Dylan Axelrod	5.68	4	11	128.1	170	43	73	0

Manager: Robin Ventura

Cleveland Indians

Batters	AVG	AB	R	H	HR	RBI	SO	SB
Yan Gomes	.294	293	45	86	11	38	67	2
Michael Brantley	.284	556	66	158	10	73	67	17
Jason Kipnis	.284	564	86	160	17	84	143	30
Ryan Raburn	.272	243	40	66	16	55	67	0
Carlos Santana	.268	541	75	145	20	74	110	3
Michael Bourn	.263	525	75	138	6	50	132	23
Mike Aviles	.252	361	54	91	9	46	41	8
Nick Swisher	.246	549	74	135	22	63	138	1
Asdrubal Cabrera	.242	508	66	123	14	64	114	9
Drew Stubbs	.233	430	59	100	10	45	141	17
Lonnie Chisenhall	.225	289	30	65	11	36	56	1
Mark Reynolds*	.220	445	55	98	21	67	154	3
Jason Giambi	.183	186	21	34	9	31	56	0

Pitchers	ERA	W	L	IP	H	BB	SO	SV
Cody Allen	2.43	6	1	70.1	62	26	88	2
Bryan Shaw	3.24	7	3	75	60	28	73	1
Ubaldo Jimenez	3.30	13	9	182.2	163	80	194	0
Justin Masterson	3.45	14	10	193	156	76	195	0
Zach McAllister	3.75	9	9	134.1	134	49	101	0
Corey Kluber	3.85	11	5	147.1	153	33	136	0
Scott Kazmir	4.04	10	9	158	162	47	162	0
Chris Perez	4.33	5	3	54	56	21	54	25

Manager: Terry Francona

Detroit Tigers

Batters	AVG	AB	R	H	HR	RBI	SO	SB
Miguel Cabrera	.348	555	103	193	44	137	94	3
Omar Infante	.318	453	54	144	10	51	44	5
Torii Hunter	.304	606	90	184	17	84	113	3
Jhonny Peralta	.303	409	50	124	11	55	98	3
Jose Iglesias*	.303	350	39	106	3	29	60	5
Victor Martinez	.301	605	68	182	14	83	62	0
Brayan Pena	.297	229	19	68	4	22	26	0
Avisail Garcia*	.283	244	31	69	7	31	59	3
Prince Fielder	.279	624	82	174	25	106	117	1
Austin Jackson	.272	552	99	150	12	49	129	8
Andy Dirks	.256	438	60	112	9	37	84	7
Matt Tuiasosopo	.244	164	26	40	7	30	57	0
Alex Avila	.227	330	39	75	11	47	112	0
Ramon Santiago	.224	205	27	46	1	14	32	0
Don Kelly	.222	216	33	48	6	23	28	2

Pitchers	ERA	W	L	IP	H	BB	SO	SV
Joaquin Benoit	2.01	4	1	67	47	22	73	24
Drew Smyly	2.37	6	0	76	62	17	81	2
Anibal Sanchez	2.57	14	8	182	156	54	202	0
Max Scherzer	2.90	21	3	214.1	152	56	240	0
Jose Veras*	3.02	0	5	62.2	45	22	60	21
Justin Verlander	3.46	13	12	218.1	212	75	217	0
Doug Fister	3.67	14	9	208.2	229	44	159	0
Rick Porcello	4.32	13	8	177	185	42	142	0

Manager: Jim Leyland

Houston Astros

Batters	AVG	AB	R	H	HR	RBI	SO	SB
Jose Altuve	.283	626	64	177	5	52	85	35
L.J. Hoes*	.282	170	24	48	1	10	35	7
Jason Castro	.276	435	63	120	18	56	130	2
Robbie Grossman	.268	257	29	69	4	21	70	6
Justin Maxwell*	.252	234	35	59	7	25	78	6
J.D. Martinez	.250	296	24	74	7	36	82	2
Jonathan Villar	.243	210	26	51	1	8	71	18
Matt Dominguez	.241	543	56	131	21	77	96	0
Brandon Barnes	.240	408	46	98	8	41	127	11
Carlos Corporan	.225	191	16	43	7	20	60	0
Chris Carter	.223	506	64	113	29	82	212	2
Brett Wallace	.221	262	35	58	13	36	104	1
Marwin Gonzalez	.221	204	22	45	4	14	37	6
Trevor Crowe	.218	165	18	36	1	13	39	6
Carlos Pena*	.207	280	38	58	8	25	92	1

Pitchers	ERA	W	L	IP	H	BB	SO	SV
Brett Oberholtzer	2.76	4	5	71.2	66	13	45	0
Jose Veras*	3.02	0	5	62.2	45	22	60	21
Bud Norris*	4.18	10	12	176.2	196	67	147	0
Erik Bedard	4.59	4	12	151	149	75	138	1
Dallas Keuchel	5.15	6	10	153.2	184	52	123	0
Brad Peacock	5.18	5	6	83.1	78	37	77	0
Paul Clemens	5.40	4	7	73.1	82	26	49	0
Jordan Lyles	5.59	7	9	141.2	165	49	93	1
Lucas Harrell	5.86	6	17	153.2	174	88	89	0

Manager: Bo Porter

Kansas City Royals

Batters	AVG	AB	R	H	HR	RBI	SO	SB
Eric Hosmer	.302	623	86	188	17	79	100	11
Salvador Perez	.292	496	48	145	13	79	63	0
Billy Butler	.289	582	62	168	15	82	102	0
Miguel Tejada	.288	156	15	45	3	20	25	1
David Lough	.286	315	35	90	5	33	52	5
Alex Gordon	.265	633	90	168	20	81	141	11
Jarrod Dyson	.258	213	30	55	2	17	45	34
Justin Maxwell*	.252	234	35	59	7	25	78	6
Lorenzo Cain	.251	399	54	100	4	46	90	14
Emilio Bonifacio*	.243	420	54	102	3	31	103	28
Alcides Escobar	.234	607	57	142	4	52	84	22
Mike Moustakas	.233	472	42	110	12	42	83	2
Chris Getz	.220	209	29	46	1	18	24	16
Jamey Carroll*	.211	227	26	48	0	11	39	2
Jeff Francoeur#	.208	183	19	38	3	13	49	2
Carlos Pena*	.207	280	38	58	8	25	92	1
Elliot Johnson#	.179	162	19	29	2	9	49	14

Pitchers	ERA	W	L	IP	H	BB	SO	SV
Greg Holland	1.21	2	1	67	40	18	103	47
Luke Hochevar	1.92	5	2	70.1	41	17	82	2
James Shields	3.15	13	9	228.2	215	68	196	0
Ervin Santana	3.24	9	10	211	190	51	161	0
Bruce Chen	3.27	9	4	121	107	36	78	0
Jeremy Guthrie	4.04	15	12	211.2	236	59	111	0
Wade Davis	5.32	8	11	135.1	169	58	114	0
Luis Mendoza	5.36	2	6	94	106	43	54	0

Manager: Ned Yost

Los Angeles Angels

Batters	AVG	AB	R	H	HR	RBI	SO	SB
Mike Trout	.323	589	109	190	27	97	136	33
Howie Kendrick	.297	478	55	142	13	54	89	6
J.B. Shuck	.293	437	60	128	2	39	54	8
Kole Calhoun	.282	195	29	55	8	32	41	2
Peter Bourjos	.274	175	26	48	3	12	43	6
Erick Aybar	.271	550	68	149	6	54	59	12
Albert Pujols	.258	391	49	101	17	64	55	1
Alberto Callaspo*	.258	453	52	117	10	58	47	0
Josh Hamilton	.250	576	73	144	21	79	158	4
Hank Conger	.249	233	23	58	7	21	61	0
Mark Trumbo	.234	620	85	145	34	100	184	5
Chris Iannetta	.225	325	40	73	11	39	100	0

Pitchers	ERA	W	L	IP	H	BB	SO	SV
Dane De La Rosa	2.86	6	1	72.1	56	28	65	2
Jered Weaver	3.27	11	8	154.1	139	37	117	0
C.J. Wilson	3.39	17	7	212.1	200	85	188	0
Ernesto Frieri	3.80	2	4	68.2	55	30	98	37
Jason Vargas	4.02	9	8	150	162	46	109	0
Garrett Richards	4.16	7	8	145	151	44	101	1
Jerome Williams	4.57	9	10	169.1	181	55	107	0
Tommy Hanson	5.42	4	3	73	93	30	56	0
Joe Blanton	6.04	2	14	132.2	180	34	108	0

Manager: Mike Scioscia

Minnesota Twins

Batters	AVG	AB	R	H	HR	RBI	SO	SB
Joe Mauer	.324	445	62	144	11	47	89	0
Justin Morneau#	.259	495	56	128	17	74	98	0
Trevor Plouffe	.254	477	44	121	14	52	112	2
Oswaldo Arcia	.251	351	34	88	14	43	117	1
Ryan Doumit	.247	485	49	120	14	55	99	1
Brian Dozier	.244	558	72	136	18	66	120	14
Eduardo Escobar	.236	165	23	39	3	10	34	0
Chris Parmelee	.228	294	21	67	8	24	81	1
Pedro Florimon	.221	403	44	89	9	44	115	15
Clete Thomas	.214	290	39	62	4	13	92	1
Jamey Carroll*	.211	227	26	48	0	11	39	2
Josh Willingham	.208	389	42	81	14	48	128	1
Chris Herrmann	.204	157	16	32	4	18	49	0
Chris Colabello	.194	160	14	31	7	17	58	0
Aaron Hicks	.192	281	37	54	8	27	84	9

Pitchers	ERA	W	L	IP	H	BB	SO	SV
Glen Perkins	2.30	2	0	62.2	43	15	77	36
Anthony Swarzak	2.91	3	2	96	89	22	69	0
Samuel Deduno	3.83	8	8	108	105	41	67	0
Ryan Pressly	3.87	3	3	76.2	71	27	49	0
Kevin Correia	4.18	9	13	185.1	218	45	101	0
Mike Pelfrey	5.19	5	13	152.2	184	53	101	0
Scott Diamond	5.43	6	13	131	163	36	52	0

Manager: Ron Gardenhire

New York Yankees

Batters	AVG	AB	R	H	HR	RBI	SO	SB
Robinson Cano	.314	605	81	190	27	107	85	7
Brett Gardner	.273	539	81	147	8	52	127	24
Ichiro Suzuki	.262	520	57	136	7	35	63	20
Eduardo Nunez	.260	304	38	79	3	28	51	10
Alfonso Soriano#	.256	219	37	56	17	50	67	8
Alex Rodriguez	.244	156	21	38	7	19	43	4
Lyle Overbay	.240	445	43	107	14	59	111	2
Jayson Nix	.236	267	32	63	3	24	80	13
Vernon Wells	.233	424	45	99	11	50	73	7
Curtis Granderson	.229	214	31	49	7	15	69	8
Mark Reynolds*	.220	445	55	98	21	67	154	3
Chris Stewart	.211	294	28	62	4	25	49	4
Travis Hafner	.202	262	31	53	12	37	73	1
Brendan Ryan*	.197	319	30	63	4	22	73	4

Pitchers	ERA	W	L	IP	H	BB	SO	SV
Mariano Rivera	2.11	6	2	64	58	9	54	44
Ivan Nova	3.10	9	6	139.1	135	44	116	0
Hiroki Kuroda	3.31	11	13	201.1	191	43	150	0
Adam Warren	3.39	3	2	77	80	30	64	1
Andy Pettitte	3.74	11	11	185.1	198	48	128	0
CC Sabathia	4.78	14	13	211	224	65	175	0
David Phelps	4.98	6	5	86.2	88	35	79	0
Phil Hughes	5.19	4	14	145.2	170	42	121	0

Manager: Joe Girardi

Oakland Athletics

Batters	AVG	AB	R	H	HR	RBI	SO	SB
Josh Donaldson . . .	.301	579	89	174	24	93	110	5
Jed Lowrie	.290	603	80	175	15	75	91	1
Nate Freiman	.274	190	10	52	4	24	31	0
John Jaso	.271	207	31	56	3	21	45	2
Eric Sogard	.266	368	45	98	2	35	51	10
Coco Crisp	.261	513	93	134	22	66	65	21
Alberto Callaspo* . .	.258	453	52	117	10	58	47	0
Brandon Moss	.256	446	73	114	30	87	140	4
Seth Smith	.253	368	49	93	8	40	94	0
Derek Norris	.246	264	41	65	9	30	71	5
Yoenis Cespedes . .	.240	529	74	127	26	80	137	7
Josh Reddick	.226	385	54	87	12	56	86	9
Chris Young	.200	335	46	67	12	40	93	10

Pitchers	ERA	W	L	IP	H	BB	SO	SV
Grant Balfour	2.59	1	3	62.2	48	27	72	38
Bartolo Colon	2.65	18	6	190.1	193	29	117	0
A.J. Griffin	3.83	14	10	200	171	54	171	0
Dan Straily	3.96	10	8	152.1	132	57	124	0
Jarrod Parker	3.97	12	8	197	178	63	134	0
Tommy Milone	4.14	12	9	156.1	160	39	126	0

Manager: Bob Melvin

Seattle Mariners

Batters	AVG	AB	R	H	HR	RBI	SO	SB
Kendrys Morales . . .	.277	602	64	167	23	80	114	0
Endy Chavez	.267	266	22	71	2	14	31	1
Brad Miller	.265	306	41	81	8	36	52	5
Kyle Seager	.260	615	79	160	22	69	122	9
Dustin Ackley	.253	384	40	97	4	31	72	2
Raul Ibanez	.242	454	54	110	29	65	128	0
Justin Smoak	.238	454	53	108	20	50	119	0
Michael Saunders . .	.236	406	59	96	12	46	118	13
Michael Morse*	.215	312	34	67	13	27	87	0
Nick Franklin	.225	369	38	83	12	45	113	6
Mike Zunino	.214	173	22	37	5	14	49	1
Jason Bay	.204	206	30	42	11	20	62	3
Brendan Ryan*	.197	319	30	63	4	22	73	4

Pitchers	ERA	W	L	IP	H	BB	SO	SV
Hisashi Iwakuma . .	2.66	14	6	219.2	179	42	185	0
Felix Hernandez . . .	3.04	12	10	204.1	185	46	216	0
Tom Wilhelmsen . . .	4.12	0	3	59	45	33	45	24
Danny Farquhar . . .	4.20	0	3	55.2	44	22	79	16
Erasmo Ramirez . . .	4.98	5	3	72.1	79	26	57	0
Joe Saunders	5.26	11	16	183	232	61	107	0
Aaron Harang#	5.76	5	11	120.1	133	28	87	0
Brandon Maurer . . .	6.30	5	8	90	114	27	70	0

Manager: Eric Wedge

Tampa Bay Rays

Batters	AVG	AB	R	H	HR	RBI	SO	SB
James Loney	.299	549	54	164	13	75	77	3
Wil Myers	.293	335	50	98	13	53	91	5
Ben Zobrist	.275	612	77	168	12	71	91	11
Evan Longoria	.269	614	91	165	32	88	162	1
Yunel Escobar	.256	508	61	130	9	56	73	4
Desmond Jennings .	.252	527	82	133	14	54	115	20
Jose Lobaton	.249	277	33	69	7	32	65	0
Ryan Roberts	.247	162	15	40	5	17	39	0
Sean Rodriguez . . .	.246	195	21	48	5	23	59	1

Batters	AVG	AB	R	H	HR	RBI	SO	SB
Luke Scott	.241	253	27	61	9	40	63	1
Kelly Johnson	.235	366	41	86	16	52	99	7
Matt Joyce	.235	413	61	97	18	47	87	7
Jose Molina	.233	283	26	66	2	18	63	2
Sam Fuld	.199	176	25	35	2	17	28	8

Pitchers	ERA	W	L	IP	H	BB	SO	SV
Alex Cobb	2.76	11	3	143.1	120	45	134	0
Jamey Wright	3.09	2	2	70	61	23	65	0
Chris Archer	3.22	9	7	128.2	107	38	101	0
Matt Moore	3.29	17	4	150.1	119	76	143	0
David Price	3.33	10	8	186.2	178	27	151	0
Fernando Rodney . .	3.38	5	4	66.2	53	36	82	37
Joel Peralta	3.41	3	8	71.1	47	34	74	1
Roberto Hernandez .	4.89	6	13	151	164	38	113	1
Jeremy Hellickson . .	5.17	12	10	174	185	50	135	0

Manager: Joe Maddon

Texas Rangers

Batters	AVG	AB	R	H	HR	RBI	SO	SB
Adrian Beltre	.315	631	88	199	30	92	78	1
Craig Gentry	.280	246	39	69	2	22	46	24
Jeff Baker	.279	154	21	43	11	21	48	1
Alex Rios*	.278	616	83	171	18	81	108	42
Ian Kinsler	.277	545	85	151	13	72	59	15
A.J. Pierzynski	.272	503	48	137	17	70	76	1
Elvis Andrus	.271	620	91	168	4	67	97	42
Nelson Cruz	.266	413	49	110	27	76	109	5
Leonys Martin	.260	457	66	119	8	49	104	36
Geovany Soto	.245	163	20	40	9	22	60	1
Lance Berkman	.242	256	27	62	6	34	52	0
Jurickson Profar . . .	.234	286	30	67	6	26	63	2
Mitch Moreland	.232	462	60	107	23	60	117	0
David Murphy	.220	436	51	96	13	45	59	1

Pitchers	ERA	W	L	IP	H	BB	SO	SV
Joe Nathan	1.39	6	2	64.2	36	22	73	43
Tanner Scheppers . .	1.88	6	2	76.2	58	24	59	1
Yu Darvish	2.83	13	9	209.2	145	80	277	0
Alexi Ogando	3.11	7	4	104.1	87	41	72	0
Derek Holland	3.42	10	9	213	210	64	189	0
Martin Perez	3.62	10	6	124.1	129	37	84	0
Matt Garza#	4.38	4	5	84.1	89	22	74	0
Nick Tepesch	4.84	4	6	93	100	27	76	0
Justin Grimm#	6.37	7	7	89	116	31	68	0

Manager: Ron Washington

Toronto Blue Jays

Batters	AVG	AB	R	H	HR	RBI	SO	SB
Jose Reyes	.296	382	58	113	10	37	47	15
Adam Lind	.288	465	67	134	23	67	103	1
Melky Cabrera	.279	344	39	96	3	30	47	2
Colby Rasmus	.276	417	57	115	22	66	135	0
Edwin Encarnacion .	.272	530	90	144	36	104	62	7
Rajai Davis	.260	331	49	86	6	24	67	45
Jose Bautista	.259	452	82	117	28	73	84	7
Brett Lawrie	.254	401	41	102	11	46	68	9
Emilio Bonifacio* . . .	.243	420	54	102	3	31	103	28
Maicer Izturis	.236	365	33	86	5	32	38	1
Mark DeRosa	.235	204	23	48	7	36	49	0
Munenori Kawasaki	.229	240	27	55	1	24	41	7
J.P. Arencibia	.194	474	45	92	21	55	148	0

Pitchers	ERA	W	L	IP	H	BB	SO	SV
Casey Janssen	2.56	4	1	52.2	39	13	50	34
Mark Buehrle	4.15	12	10	203.2	223	51	139	0
R.A. Dickey	4.21	14	13	224.2	207	71	177	0
Todd Redmond	4.32	4	3	77	70	23	76	0
J.A. Happ	4.56	5	7	92.2	91	45	77	0
Esmil Rogers	4.77	5	9	137.2	152	44	96	0
Josh Johnson	6.20	2	8	81.1	105	30	83	0

Manager: John Gibbons

Major League Leaders, 2013

National League

Batting Average: Michael Cuddyer, Colorado, .331; Chris Johnson, Atlanta, .321; Freddie Freeman, Atlanta, .319; Yadier Molina, St. Louis, .319; Jayson Werth, Washington, .318; Matt Carpenter, St. Louis, .318.

Runs Scored: Matt Carpenter, St. Louis, 126; Shin-Soo Choo, Cincinnati, 107; Matt Holliday, St. Louis, 103; Paul Goldschmidt, Arizona, 103; Joey Votto, Cincinnati, 101.

Runs Batted In: Paul Goldschmidt, Arizona, 125; Jay Bruce, Cincinnati, 109; Freddie Freeman, Atlanta, 109; Brandon Phillips, Cincinnati, 103; Adrian Gonzalez, L.A. Dodgers, 100; Pedro Alvarez, Pittsburgh, 100.

Hits: Matt Carpenter, St. Louis, 199; Daniel Murphy, NY Mets, 188; Andrew McCutchen, Pittsburgh, 185; Paul Goldschmidt, Arizona, 182; Hunter Pence, San Francisco, 178.

Doubles: Matt Carpenter, St. Louis, 55; Yadier Molina, St. Louis, 44; Jay Bruce, Cincinnati, 43; Gerardo Parra, Arizona, 43; Anthony Rizzo, Chicago Cubs, 40.

Triples: Denard Span, Washington, 11; Carlos Gomez, Milwaukee, 10; Starling Marte, Pittsburgh, 10; Jean Segura, Milwaukee, 10; Will Venable, San Diego, 8; Adeiny Hechavarria, Miami, 8.

Home Runs: Pedro Alvarez, Pittsburgh, 36; Paul Goldschmidt, Arizona, 36; Jay Bruce, Cincinnati, 30; Hunter Pence, San Francisco, 27; Justin Upton, Atlanta, 27; Domonic Brown, Philadelphia, 27.

Stolen Bases: Eric Young Jr., NY Mets/Colorado, 46; Jean Segura, Milwaukee, 44; Starling Marte, Pittsburgh, 41; Carlos Gomez, Milwaukee, 40; Everth Cabrera, San Diego, 37.

Wins: Adam Wainwright, St. Louis, 19; Jordan Zimmermann, Washington, 19; Jorge De La Rosa, Colorado, 16; Francisco Liriano, Pittsburgh, 16; Clayton Kershaw, L.A. Dodgers, 16.

Earned Run Average: Clayton Kershaw, L.A. Dodgers, 1.83; Jose Fernandez, Miami, 2.19; Matt Harvey, NY Mets, 2.27; Zack Greinke, L.A. Dodgers, 2.63; Madison Bumgarner, San Francisco, 2.77.

Strikeouts: Clayton Kershaw, L.A. Dodgers, 232; Cliff Lee, Philadelphia, 222; Adam Wainwright, St. Louis, 219; Jeff Samardzija, Chicago Cubs, 214; A.J. Burnett, Pittsburgh, 209.

Saves: Craig Kimbrel, Atlanta, 50; Rafael Soriano, Washington, 43; Sergio Romo, San Francisco, 38; Aroldis Chapman, Cincinnati, 38; Edward Mujica, St. Louis, 37.

American League

Batting Average: Miguel Cabrera, Detroit, .348; Joe Mauer, Minnesota, .324; Mike Trout, L.A. Angels, .323; Adrian Beltre, Texas, .315; Robinson Cano, NY Yankees, .314.

Runs Scored: Mike Trout, L.A. Angels, 109; Miguel Cabrera, Detroit, 103; Chris Davis, Baltimore, 103; Adam Jones, Baltimore, 100; Austin Jackson, Detroit, 99.

Runs Batted In: Chris Davis, Baltimore, 138; Miguel Cabrera, Detroit, 137; Adam Jones, Baltimore, 108; Robinson Cano, NY Yankees, 107; Prince Fielder, Detroit, 106.

Hits: Adrian Beltre, Texas, 199; Miguel Cabrera, Detroit, 193; Dustin Pedroia, Boston, 193; Robinson Cano, NY Yankees, 190; Mike Trout, L.A. Angels, 190.

Doubles: Manny Machado, Baltimore, 51; Jed Lowrie, Oakland, 45; Dustin Pedroia, Boston, 42; Chris Davis, Baltimore, 42; Robinson Cano, NY Yankees, 41.

Triples: Brett Gardner, NY Yankees, 10; Mike Trout, L.A. Angels, 9; Stephen Drew, Boston, 8; Jacoby Ellsbury, Boston, 8; Austin Jackson, Detroit, 7.

Home Runs: Chris Davis, Baltimore, 53; Miguel Cabrera, Detroit, 44; Edwin Encarnacion, Toronto, 36; Adam Dunn, Chicago White Sox, 34; Mark Trumbo, L.A. Angels, 34.

Stolen Bases: Jacoby Ellsbury, Boston, 52; Rajai Davis, Toronto, 45; Alex Rios, Chicago White Sox/Texas, 42; Elvis Andrus, Texas, 42; Leonys Martin, Texas, 36.

Wins: Max Scherzer, Detroit, 21; Bartolo Colon, Oakland, 18; C.J. Wilson, L.A. Angels, 17; Matt Moore, Tampa Bay, 17; Chris Tillman, Baltimore, 16.

Earned Run Average: Anibal Sanchez, Detroit, 2.57; Bartolo Colon, Oakland, 2.65; Hisashi Iwakuma, Seattle, 2.66; Yu Darvish, Texas, 2.83; Max Scherzer, Detroit, 2.90.

Strikeouts: Yu Darvish, Texas, 277; Max Scherzer, Detroit, 240; Chris Sale, Chicago White Sox, 226; Justin Verlander, Detroit, 217; Felix Hernandez, Seattle, 216.

Saves: Jim Johnson, Baltimore, 50; Greg Holland, Kansas City, 47; Mariano Rivera, NY Yankees, 44; Joe Nathan, Texas, 43; Addison Reed, Chicago White Sox, 40.

All-Time Major League Single-Season Leaders

Source: www.mlb.com; * = Active in 2013 season; records for "modern" era beginning in 1901.

Home Runs

Barry Bonds (2001)	73
Mark McGwire (1998)	70
Sammy Sosa (1998)	66
Mark McGwire (1999)	65
Sammy Sosa (2001)	64

Runs Scored

Babe Ruth (1921)	177
Lou Gehrig (1936)	167
Lou Gehrig (1931)	163
Babe Ruth (1928)	163
Chuck Klein (1930)	158
Babe Ruth (1920, 1927)	158

Hits

Ichiro Suzuki* (2004)	262
George Sisler (1920)	257
Lefty O'Doul (1929)	254
Bill Terry (1930)	254
Al Simmons (1925)	253
Rogers Hornsby (1922)	250
Chuck Klein (1930)	250

Runs Batted In

Hack Wilson (1930)	191
Lou Gehrig (1931)	184
Hank Greenberg (1937)	183
Jimmie Foxx (1938)	175
Lou Gehrig (1927)	175

Batting Average

Rogers Hornsby (1924)	.424
Napoleon Lajoie (1901)	.421
George Sisler (1922)	.420
Ty Cobb (1911)	.420
Ty Cobb (1912)	.410

Stolen Bases

Rickey Henderson (1982)	130
Lou Brock (1974)	118
Vince Coleman (1985)	110
Vince Coleman (1987)	109
Rickey Henderson (1983)	108

Walks (Batter)

Barry Bonds (2004)	232
Barry Bonds (2002)	198
Barry Bonds (2001)	177
Babe Ruth (1923)	170
Mark McGwire (1998)	162
Ted Williams (1947, 1949)	162

Strikeouts (Batter)

Mark Reynolds* (2009)	223
Adam Dunn* (2012)	222
Chris Carter* (2013)	212
Mark Reynolds* (2010)	211
Drew Stubbs* (2011)	205

Earned Run Average

Dutch Leonard (1914)	0.96
Mordecai "Three Finger" Brown (1906)	1.04
Bob Gibson (1968)	1.12
Christy Mathewson (1909)	1.14
Walter Johnson (1913)	1.14

Wins

Jack Chesbro (1904)	41
Ed Walsh (1908)	40
Christy Mathewson (1908)	37
Walter Johnson (1913)	36
Joe McGinnity (1904)	35

Strikeouts

Nolan Ryan (1973)	383
Sandy Koufax (1965)	382
Randy Johnson (2001)	372
Nolan Ryan (1974)	367
Randy Johnson (1999)	364

Saves

Francisco Rodriguez* (2008)	62
Bobby Thigpen (1990)	57
Eric Gagne (2003)	55
John Smoltz (2002)	55
Trevor Hoffman (1998)	53
Randy Myers (1993)	53
Mariano Rivera* (2004)	53

All-Time Major League Leaders

Source: www.mlb.com; * = active in 2013 season; career records for players in "modern" era beginning in 1901 may include statistics from preceding years.

Games		At Bats		Runs Batted In		Runs	
Pete Rose	3,562	Pete Rose	14,053	Hank Aaron	2,297	Rickey Henderson	2,295
Carl Yastrzemski	3,308	Hank Aaron	12,364	Babe Ruth	2,213	Ty Cobb	2,246
Hank Aaron	3,298	Carl Yastrzemski	11,988	Barry Bonds	1,996	Barry Bonds	2,227
Rickey Henderson	3,081	Cal Ripken Jr.	11,551	Lou Gehrig	1,995	Hank Aaron	2,174
Ty Cobb	3,035	Ty Cobb	11,429	Alex Rodriguez*	1,969	Babe Ruth	2,174
Eddie Murray	3,026	Eddie Murray	11,336	Stan Musial	1,951	Pete Rose	2,165
Stan Musial	3,026	Robin Yount	11,008	Ty Cobb	1,938	Willie Mays	2,062
Cal Ripken Jr.	3,001	Dave Winfield	11,003	Jimmie Foxx	1,922	Stan Musial	1,949
Willie Mays	2,992	Stan Musial	10,972	Eddie Murray	1,917	Alex Rodriguez*	1,919
Barry Bonds	2,986	Rickey Henderson	10,961	Willie Mays	1,903	Lou Gehrig	1,888

Stolen Bases		Triples		Batting Average		Walks (Batter)	
Rickey Henderson	1,406	Sam Crawford	309	Ty Cobb	.367	Barry Bonds	2,558
Lou Brock	938	Ty Cobb	297	Rogers Hornsby	.358	Rickey Henderson	2,190
Billy Hamilton	912	Honus Wagner	252	Joe Jackson	.356	Babe Ruth	2,062
Ty Cobb	892	Jake Beckley	243	Ed Delahanty	.346	Ted Williams	2,019
Tim Raines	808	Roger Connor	233	Tris Speaker	.345	Joe Morgan	1,865
Vince Coleman	752	Tris Speaker	222	Ted Williams	.344	Carl Yastrzemski	1,845
Eddie Collins	745	Fred Clarke	220	Billy Hamilton	.344	Jim Thome	1,747
Arlie Latham	739	Dan Brouthers	205	Dan Brouthers	.342	Mickey Mantle	1,733
Max Carey	738	Joe Kelley	194	Babe Ruth	.342	Mel Ott	1,708
Honus Wagner	722	Paul Waner	191	Harry Heilmann	.342	Frank Thomas	1,667

Strikeouts		Saves		Shutouts		Losses	
Nolan Ryan	5,714	Mariano Rivera*	652	Walter Johnson	110	Cy Young	316
Randy Johnson	4,875	Trevor Hoffman	601	Grover Alexander	90	Nolan Ryan	292
Roger Clemens	4,672	Lee Smith	478	Christy Mathewson	79	Walter Johnson	279
Steve Carlton	4,136	John Franco	424	Cy Young	76	Phil Niekro	274
Bert Blyleven	3,701	Billy Wagner	422	Eddie Plank	69	Gaylord Perry	265
Tom Seaver	3,640	Dennis Eckersley	390	Warren Spahn	63	Don Sutton	256
Don Sutton	3,574	Jeff Reardon	367	Nolan Ryan	61	Jack Powell	254
Gaylord Perry	3,534	Troy Percival	358	Tom Seaver	61	Eppa Rixey	251
Walter Johnson	3,508	Randy Myers	347	Bert Blyleven	60	Bert Blyleven	250
Greg Maddux	3,371	Joe Nathan*	341	Don Sutton	58	Robin Roberts	245
		Rollie Fingers	341			Warren Spahn	245

All-Time Home Run Leaders

Source: www.mlb.com; * = active in 2013 season

Player	HR	Player	HR	Player	HR	Player	HR
Barry Bonds	762	Mike Schmidt	548	Stan Musial	475	Andruw Jones	434
Hank Aaron	755	Mickey Mantle	536	Willie Stargell	475	Paul Konerko*	434
Babe Ruth	714	Jimmie Foxx	534	Carlos Delgado	473	David Ortiz*	431
Willie Mays	660	Willie McCovey	521	Chipper Jones	468	Cal Ripken Jr.	431
Alex Rodriguez*	654	Frank Thomas	521	Dave Winfield	465	Mike Piazza	427
Ken Griffey Jr.	630	Ted Williams	521	Jose Canseco	462	Billy Williams	426
Jim Thome	612	Ernie Banks	512	Carl Yastrzemski	452	Darrell Evans	414
Sammy Sosa	609	Eddie Mathews	512	Jeff Bagwell	449	Duke Snider	407
Frank Robinson	586	Mel Ott	511	Vladimir Guerrero	449	Alfonso Soriano*	406
Mark McGwire	583	Gary Sheffield	509	Dave Kingman	442	Andres Galarraga	399
Harmon Killebrew	573	Eddie Murray	504	Adam Dunn*	440	Al Kaline	399
Rafael Palmeiro	569	Lou Gehrig	493	Andre Dawson	438	Dale Murphy	398
Reggie Jackson	563	Fred McGriff	493	Jason Giambi*	438	Joe Carter	396
Manny Ramirez	555	Albert Pujols*	492	Juan Gonzalez	434	Jim Edmonds	393

Players With 3,000 Major League Hits

Source: www.mlb.com; * = active in 2013 season

Player	Hits	Player	Hits	Player	Hits	Player	Hits
Pete Rose	4,256	Paul Molitor	3,319	George Brett	3,154	Rod Carew	3,053
Ty Cobb	4,191	Derek Jeter*	3,316	Paul Waner	3,152	Lou Brock	3,023
Hank Aaron	3,771	Eddie Collins	3,314	Robin Yount	3,142	Rafael Palmeiro	3,020
Stan Musial	3,630	Willie Mays	3,283	Tony Gwynn	3,141	Cap Anson	3,011
Tris Speaker	3,515	Eddie Murray	3,255	Dave Winfield	3,110	Wade Boggs	3,010
Honus Wagner	3,430	Napoleon Lajoie	3,252	Craig Biggio	3,060	Al Kaline	3,007
Carl Yastrzemski	3,419	Cal Ripken Jr.	3,184	Rickey Henderson	3,055	Roberto Clemente	3,000

50 Home Run Club

Only Barry Bonds and Mark McGwire hit 70 or more home runs in a season. Five players—including Babe Ruth and Roger Maris—hit 60 or more, a feat Sammy Sosa accomplished for the third time in 2001.

HR	Player, team	Year	HR	Player, team	Year
73	Barry Bonds, San Francisco Giants	2001	54	Alex Rodriguez, NY Yankees	2007
70	Mark McGwire, St. Louis Cardinals	1998	54	Babe Ruth, NY Yankees	1920
66	Sammy Sosa, Chicago Cubs	1998	54	Babe Ruth, NY Yankees	1928
65	Mark McGwire, St. Louis Cardinals	1999	53	Chris Davis, Baltimore Orioles	2013
64	Sammy Sosa, Chicago Cubs	2001	52	George Foster, Cincinnati Reds	1977
63	Sammy Sosa, Chicago Cubs	1999	52	Mickey Mantle, NY Yankees	1956
61	Roger Maris, NY Yankees	1961	52	Willie Mays, San Francisco Giants	1965
60	Babe Ruth, NY Yankees	1927	52	Mark McGwire, Oakland A's	1996
59	Babe Ruth, NY Yankees	1921	52	Alex Rodriguez, Texas Rangers	2001
58	Jimmie Foxx, Philadelphia Athletics	1932	52	Jim Thome, Cleveland Indians	2002
58	Hank Greenberg, Detroit Tigers	1938	51	Cecil Fielder, Detroit Tigers	1990
58	Ryan Howard, Philadelphia Phillies	2006	51	Andruw Jones, Atlanta Braves	2005
58	Mark McGwire, Oakland A's/St. Louis Cardinals	1997	51	Ralph Kiner, Pittsburgh Pirates	1947
57	Luis Gonzalez, Arizona Diamondbacks	2001	51	Willie Mays, NY Giants	1955
57	Alex Rodriguez, Texas Rangers	2002	51	Johnny Mize, NY Giants	1947
56	Ken Griffey Jr., Seattle Mariners	1997	50	Brady Anderson, Baltimore Orioles	1996
56	Ken Griffey Jr., Seattle Mariners	1998	50	Albert Belle, Cleveland Indians	1995
56	Hack Wilson, Chicago Cubs	1930	50	Prince Fielder, Milwaukee Brewers	2007
54	Jose Bautista, Toronto Blue Jays	2010	50	Jimmie Foxx, Boston Red Sox	1938
54	Ralph Kiner, Pittsburgh Pirates	1949	50	Sammy Sosa, Chicago Cubs	2000
54	Mickey Mantle, NY Yankees	1961	50	Greg Vaughn, San Diego Padres	1998
54	David Ortiz, Boston Red Sox	2006			

Pitchers With 300 Major League Wins

Source: www.mlb.com

Pitcher	Wins	Pitcher	Wins	Pitcher	Wins	Pitcher	Wins
Cy Young	511	Kid Nichols	361	Eddie Plank	326	Charley Radbourn	309
Walter Johnson	417	Greg Maddux	355	Nolan Ryan	324	Mickey Welch	307
Grover Alexander	373	Roger Clemens	354	Don Sutton	324	Tom Glavine	305
Christy Mathewson	373	Tim Keefe	342	Phil Niekro	318	Randy Johnson	303
Warren Spahn	363	Steve Carlton	329	Gaylord Perry	314	Lefty Grove	300
Pud Galvin	361	John Clarkson	328	Tom Seaver	311	Early Wynn	300

Official Major League Perfect Games Since 1901

Date	Pitcher	Teams	Date	Pitcher	Teams
5/5/1904	Cy Young	Boston 3 vs. Phil. 0 (AL)	9/16/1988	Tom Browning	Cincinnati 1 vs. L.A. 0 (NL)
10/2/1908	Addie Joss	Clev. 1 vs. Chicago 0 (AL)	5/17/1998	David Wells	NY 4 vs. Minn. 0 (AL)
4/30/1922	Charlie Robertson	Chicago 2 vs. Detroit 0 (AL)	7/18/1999	David Cone	NY 6 vs. Montréal 0 (AL)
10/8/1956	Don Larsen	NY 2 (AL) vs. Brooklyn 0* (NL)	5/18/2004	Randy Johnson	Arizona 2 vs. Atlanta 0 (NL)
6/21/1964	Jim Bunning	Phil. 6 vs. NY 0 (NL)	7/23/2009	Mark Buehrle	Chicago 5 vs. Tampa Bay 0 (AL)
9/9/1965	Sandy Koufax	L.A. 1 vs. Chicago 0 (NL)	5/9/2010	Dallas Braden	Oakland 4 vs. Tampa Bay 0 (AL)
5/8/1968	Jim "Catfish" Hunter	Oakland 4 vs. Minn. 0 (AL)	5/29/2010	Roy Halladay	Phil. 1 vs. Florida 0 (NL)
5/15/1981	Len Barker	Clev. 3 vs. Toronto 0 (AL)	4/21/2012	Philip Humber	Chicago 4 vs. Seattle 0 (AL)
9/30/1984	Mike Witt	California 1 vs. Texas 0 (AL)	6/13/2012	Matt Cain	S.F. 10 vs. Houston 0 (NL)
7/28/1991	Dennis Martinez	Montréal 2 vs. L.A. 0 (NL)	8/15/2012	Felix Hernandez	Seattle 1 vs. Tampa Bay 0 (AL)
7/28/1994	Kenny Rogers	Texas 4 vs. California 0 (AL)			

* = World Series game. **Note:** Two pre-1901 National League pitchers are also credited with perfect games. Within one week in 1880, Lee Richmond (June 12, Worcester 1, Cleveland 0) and John "Monte" Ward (June 17, Providence 5, Buffalo 0) each threw a perfect game.

Most Career Major League No-Hitters

No.	Pitcher	No.	Pitcher
7	Nolan Ryan	2	Homer Bailey, Mark Buehrle, Jim Bunning, Steve Busby, Carl Erskine, Bob Forsch,
4	Sandy Koufax		Pud Galvin, Roy Halladay, Ken Holtzman, Randy Johnson, Addie Joss, Dutch
3	Larry Corcoran,		Leonard, Jim Maloney, Christy Mathewson, Hideo Nomo, Allie Reynolds, Frank Smith,
	Bob Feller,		Warren Spahn, Bill Stoneman, Virgil Trucks, Johnny Vander Meer, Justin Verlander,
	Cy Young		Ed Walsh, Don Wilson

Home Run Leaders, by Season, 1901-2013

* = All-time single-season record for league since beginning of "modern" era in 1901.

	National League			American League	
Year	Player, team	HR	Year	Player, team	HR
1901	Sam Crawford, Cincinnati	16	1901	Napoleon Lajoie, Philadelphia	14
1902	Thomas Leach, Pittsburgh	6	1902	Socks Seybold, Philadelphia	16
1903	James Sheckard, Brooklyn	9	1903	Buck Freeman, Boston	13
1904	Harry Lumley, Brooklyn	9	1904	Harry Davis, Philadelphia	10
1905	Fred Odwell, Cincinnati	9	1905	Harry Davis, Philadelphia	8
1906	Timothy Jordan, Brooklyn	12	1906	Harry Davis, Philadelphia	12
1907	David Brain, Boston	10	1907	Harry Davis, Philadelphia	8
1908	Timothy Jordan, Brooklyn	12	1908	Sam Crawford, Detroit	7
1909	Red Murray, New York	7	1909	Ty Cobb, Detroit	9
1910	Fred Beck, Boston; Frank Schulte, Chicago	10	1910	Jake Stahl, Boston	10
1911	Frank Schulte, Chicago	21	1911	J. Franklin Baker, Philadelphia	11
1912	Henry Zimmerman, Chicago	14	1912	J. Franklin Baker, Phil.; Tris Speaker, Boston	10
1913	Gavvy Cravath, Philadelphia	19	1913	J. Franklin Baker, Philadelphia	12
1914	Gavvy Cravath, Philadelphia	19	1914	J. Franklin Baker, Philadelphia	9
1915	Gavvy Cravath, Philadelphia	24	1915	Robert Roth, Chicago-Cleveland	7

Year	National League — Player, team	HR	Year	American League — Player, team	HR
1916	Dave Robertson, NY; Fred "Cy" Williams, Chi.	12	1916	Wally Pipp, New York	12
1917	Gavvy Cravath, Phil.; Dave Robertson, NY	12	1917	Wally Pipp, New York	9
1918	Gavvy Cravath, Philadelphia	8	1918	Babe Ruth, Boston; Tilly Walker, Philadelphia	11
1919	Gavvy Cravath, Philadelphia	12	1919	Babe Ruth, Boston	29
1920	Cy Williams, Philadelphia	15	1920	Babe Ruth, New York	54
1921	George Kelly, New York	23	1921	Babe Ruth, New York	59
1922	Rogers Hornsby, St. Louis	42	1922	Ken Williams, St. Louis	39
1923	Cy Williams, Philadelphia	41	1923	Babe Ruth, New York	41
1924	Jacques Fournier, Brooklyn	27	1924	Babe Ruth, New York	46
1925	Rogers Hornsby, St. Louis	39	1925	Bob Meusel, New York	33
1926	Hack Wilson, Chicago	21	1926	Babe Ruth, New York	47
1927	Hack Wilson, Chicago; Cy Williams, Philadelphia	30	1927	Babe Ruth, New York	60
1928	Hack Wilson, Chicago; Jim Bottomley, St. Louis	31	1928	Babe Ruth, New York	54
1929	Chuck Klein, Philadelphia	43	1929	Babe Ruth, New York	46
1930	Hack Wilson, Chicago	56	1930	Babe Ruth, New York	49
1931	Chuck Klein, Philadelphia	31	1931	Lou Gehrig, New York; Babe Ruth, New York	46
1932	Chuck Klein, Philadelphia; Mel Ott, New York	38	1932	Jimmie Foxx, Philadelphia	58
1933	Chuck Klein, Philadelphia	28	1933	Jimmie Foxx, Philadelphia	48
1934	Rip Collins, St. Louis; Mel Ott, New York	35	1934	Lou Gehrig, New York	49
1935	Walter Berger, Boston	34	1935	Jimmie Foxx, Phil.; Hank Greenberg, Detroit	36
1936	Mel Ott, New York	33	1936	Lou Gehrig, New York	49
1937	Joe Medwick, St. Louis; Mel Ott, New York	31	1937	Joe DiMaggio, New York	46
1938	Mel Ott, New York	36	1938	Hank Greenberg, Detroit	58
1939	John Mize, St. Louis	28	1939	Jimmie Foxx, Boston	35
1940	John Mize, St. Louis	43	1940	Hank Greenberg, Detroit	41
1941	Dolph Camilli, Brooklyn	34	1941	Ted Williams, Boston	37
1942	Mel Ott, New York	30	1942	Ted Williams, Boston	36
1943	Bill Nicholson, Chicago	29	1943	Rudy York, Detroit	34
1944	Bill Nicholson, Chicago	33	1944	Nick Etten, New York	22
1945	Tommy Holmes, Boston	28	1945	Vern Stephens, St. Louis	24
1946	Ralph Kiner, Pittsburgh	23	1946	Hank Greenberg, Detroit	44
1947	Ralph Kiner, Pittsburgh; John Mize, New York	51	1947	Ted Williams, Boston	32
1948	Ralph Kiner, Pittsburgh; John Mize, New York	40	1948	Joe DiMaggio, New York	39
1949	Ralph Kiner, Pittsburgh	54	1949	Ted Williams, Boston	43
1950	Ralph Kiner, Pittsburgh	47	1950	Al Rosen, Cleveland	37
1951	Ralph Kiner, Pittsburgh	42	1951	Gus Zernial, Chicago-Philadelphia	33
1952	Ralph Kiner, Pittsburgh; Hank Sauer, Chicago	37	1952	Larry Doby, Cleveland	32
1953	Ed Mathews, Milwaukee	47	1953	Al Rosen, Cleveland	43
1954	Ted Kluszewski, Cincinnati	49	1954	Larry Doby, Cleveland	32
1955	Willie Mays, New York	51	1955	Mickey Mantle, New York	37
1956	Duke Snider, Brooklyn	43	1956	Mickey Mantle, New York	52
1957	Hank Aaron, Milwaukee	44	1957	Roy Sievers, Washington	42
1958	Ernie Banks, Chicago	47	1958	Mickey Mantle, New York	42
1959	Ed Mathews, Milwaukee	46	1959	Rocky Colavito, Clev.; Harmon Killebrew, Wash.	42
1960	Ernie Banks, Chicago	41	1960	Mickey Mantle, New York	40
1961	Orlando Cepeda, San Francisco	46	1961	Roger Maris, New York	61*
1962	Willie Mays, San Francisco	49	1962	Harmon Killebrew, Minnesota	48
1963	Hank Aaron, Milwaukee; Willie McCovey, S.F.	44	1963	Harmon Killebrew, Minnesota	45
1964	Willie Mays, San Francisco	47	1964	Harmon Killebrew, Minnesota	49
1965	Willie Mays, San Francisco	52	1965	Tony Conigliaro, Boston	32
1966	Hank Aaron, Atlanta	44	1966	Frank Robinson, Baltimore	49
1967	Hank Aaron, Atlanta	39	1967	Harmon Killebrew, Minn.; Carl Yastrzemski, Boston	44
1968	Willie McCovey, San Francisco	36	1968	Frank Howard, Washington	44
1969	Willie McCovey, San Francisco	45	1969	Harmon Killebrew, Minnesota	49
1970	Johnny Bench, Cincinnati	45	1970	Frank Howard, Washington	44
1971	Willie Stargell, Pittsburgh	48	1971	Bill Melton, Chicago	33
1972	Johnny Bench, Cincinnati	40	1972	Dick Allen, Chicago	37
1973	Willie Stargell, Pittsburgh	44	1973	Reggie Jackson, Oakland	32
1974	Mike Schmidt, Philadelphia	36	1974	Dick Allen, Chicago	32
1975	Mike Schmidt, Philadelphia	38	1975	Reggie Jackson, Oak.; George Scott, Milw.	36
1976	Mike Schmidt, Philadelphia	38	1976	Graig Nettles, New York	32
1977	George Foster, Cincinnati	52	1977	Jim Rice, Boston	39
1978	George Foster, Cincinnati	40	1978	Jim Rice, Boston	46
1979	Dave Kingman, Chicago	48	1979	Gorman Thomas, Milwaukee	45
1980	Mike Schmidt, Philadelphia	48	1980	Reggie Jackson, New York; Ben Oglivie, Milw.	41
1981	Mike Schmidt, Philadelphia	31	1981	Tony Armas, Oakland; Dwight Evans, Boston; Bobby Grich, Cal.; Eddie Murray, Baltimore	22
1982	Dave Kingman, New York	37	1982	Gorman Thomas, Milw.; Reggie Jackson, Cal.	39
1983	Mike Schmidt, Philadelphia	40	1983	Jim Rice, Boston	39
1984	Dale Murphy, Atlanta; Mike Schmidt, Philadelphia	36	1984	Tony Armas, Boston	43
1985	Dale Murphy, Atlanta	37	1985	Darrell Evans, Detroit	40
1986	Mike Schmidt, Philadelphia	37	1986	Jesse Barfield, Toronto	40
1987	Andre Dawson, Chicago	49	1987	Mark McGwire, Oakland	49
1988	Darryl Strawberry, New York	39	1988	Jose Canseco, Oakland	42
1989	Kevin Mitchell, San Francisco	47	1989	Fred McGriff, Toronto	36
1990	Ryne Sandberg, Chicago	40	1990	Cecil Fielder, Detroit	51
1991	Howard Johnson, New York	38	1991	Jose Canseco, Oakland; Cecil Fielder, Detroit	44
1992	Fred McGriff, San Diego	35	1992	Juan Gonzalez, Texas	43
1993	Barry Bonds, San Francisco	46	1993	Juan Gonzalez, Texas	46
1994	Matt Williams, San Francisco	43	1994	Ken Griffey Jr., Seattle	40
1995	Dante Bichette, Colorado	40	1995	Albert Belle, Cleveland	50
1996	Andres Galarraga, Colorado	47	1996	Mark McGwire, Oakland	52
1997[1]	Larry Walker, Colorado	49	1997[1]	Ken Griffey Jr., Seattle	56
1998	Mark McGwire, St. Louis	70	1998	Ken Griffey Jr., Seattle	56
1999	Mark McGwire, St. Louis	65	1999	Ken Griffey Jr., Seattle	48
2000	Sammy Sosa, Chicago	50	2000	Troy Glaus, Anaheim	47
2001	Barry Bonds, San Francisco	73*	2001	Alex Rodriguez, Texas	52
2002	Sammy Sosa, Chicago	49	2002	Alex Rodriguez, Texas	57

	National League				American League	
Year	Player, team	HR		Year	Player, team	HR
2003	Jim Thome, Philadelphia	47		2003	Alex Rodriguez, Texas	47
2004	Adrian Beltre, Los Angeles	48		2004	Manny Ramirez, Boston	43
2005	Andruw Jones, Atlanta	51		2005	Alex Rodriguez, New York	48
2006	Ryan Howard, Philadelphia	58		2006	David Ortiz, Boston	54
2007	Prince Fielder, Milwaukee	50		2007	Alex Rodriguez, New York	54
2008	Ryan Howard, Philadelphia	48		2008	Miguel Cabrera, Detroit	37
2009	Albert Pujols, St. Louis	47		2009	Carlos Pena, Tampa Bay; Mark Teixeira, New York	39
2010	Albert Pujols, St. Louis	42		2010	Jose Bautista, Toronto	54
2011	Matt Kemp, Los Angeles	39		2011	Jose Bautista, Toronto	43
2012	Ryan Braun, Milwaukee	41		2012	Miguel Cabrera, Detroit	44
2013	Pedro Alvarez, Pitt.; Paul Goldschmidt, Arizona	36		2013	Chris Davis, Baltimore	53

(1) In 1997, Mark McGwire hit 58 home runs, 34 with the Oakland Athletics (AL) and 24 with the St. Louis Cardinals (NL).

Runs Batted In Leaders, by Season, 1907-2013

* = All-time single-season record for league since beginning of "modern" era in 1901.

	National League				American League	
Year	Player, team	RBI		Year	Player, team	RBI
1907	Sherwood Magee, Philadelphia	85		1907	Ty Cobb, Detroit	119
1908	Honus Wagner, Pittsburgh	109		1908	Ty Cobb, Detroit	108
1909	Honus Wagner, Pittsburgh	100		1909	Ty Cobb, Detroit	107
1910	Sherwood Magee, Philadelphia	123		1910	Sam Crawford, Detroit	120
1911	Frank Schulte, Chicago; Chief Wilson, Pittsburgh	107		1911	Ty Cobb, Detroit	127
1912	Honus Wagner, Pittsburgh	102		1912	J. Franklin Baker, Philadelphia	130
1913	Gavvy Cravath, Philadelphia	128		1913	J. Franklin Baker, Philadelphia	117
1914	Sherwood Magee, Philadelphia	103		1914	Sam Crawford, Detroit	104
1915	Gavvy Cravath, Philadelphia	115		1915	Sam Crawford, Detroit; Robert Veach, Detroit	112
1916	Henry Zimmerman, Chicago-New York	83		1916	Del Pratt, St. Louis	103
1917	Henry Zimmerman, New York	102		1917	Robert Veach, Detroit	103
1918	Sherwood Magee, Philadelphia	76		1918	Robert Veach, Detroit	78
1919	Hi Myers, Boston	73		1919	Babe Ruth, Boston	114
1920	George Kelly, NY; Rogers Hornsby, St. Louis	94		1920	Babe Ruth, New York	137
1921	Rogers Hornsby, St. Louis	126		1921	Babe Ruth, New York	171
1922	Rogers Hornsby, St. Louis	152		1922	Ken Williams, St. Louis	155
1923	Emil Meusel, New York	125		1923	Babe Ruth, New York	131
1924	George Kelly, New York	136		1924	Goose Goslin, Washington	129
1925	Rogers Hornsby, St. Louis	143		1925	Bob Meusel, New York	138
1926	Jim Bottomley, St. Louis	120		1926	Babe Ruth, New York	146
1927	Paul Waner, Pittsburgh	131		1927	Lou Gehrig, New York	175
1928	Jim Bottomley, St. Louis	136		1928	Babe Ruth, New York; Lou Gehrig, New York	142
1929	Hack Wilson, Chicago	159		1929	Al Simmons, Philadelphia	157
1930	Hack Wilson, Chicago	191*		1930	Lou Gehrig, New York	174
1931	Chuck Klein, Philadelphia	121		1931	Lou Gehrig, New York	184*
1932	Don Hurst, Philadelphia	143		1932	Jimmie Foxx, Philadelphia	169
1933	Chuck Klein, Philadelphia	120		1933	Jimmie Foxx, Philadelphia	163
1934	Mel Ott, New York	135		1934	Lou Gehrig, New York	165
1935	Walter Berger, Boston	130		1935	Hank Greenberg, Detroit	170
1936	Joe Medwick, St. Louis	138		1936	Hal Trosky, Cleveland	162
1937	Joe Medwick, St. Louis	154		1937	Hank Greenberg, Detroit	183
1938	Joe Medwick, St. Louis	122		1938	Jimmie Foxx, Boston	175
1939	Frank McCormick, Cincinnati	128		1939	Ted Williams, Boston	145
1940	John Mize, St. Louis	137		1940	Hank Greenberg, Detroit	150
1941	Dolph Camilli, Brooklyn	120		1941	Joe DiMaggio, New York	125
1942	John Mize, New York	110		1942	Ted Williams, Boston	137
1943	Bill Nicholson, Chicago	128		1943	Rudy York, Detroit	118
1944	Bill Nicholson, Chicago	122		1944	Vern Stephens, St. Louis	109
1945	Dixie Walker, Brooklyn	124		1945	Nick Etten, New York	111
1946	Enos Slaughter, St. Louis	130		1946	Hank Greenberg, Detroit	127
1947	John Mize, New York	138		1947	Ted Williams, Boston	114
1948	Stan Musial, St. Louis	131		1948	Joe DiMaggio, New York	155
1949	Ralph Kiner, Pittsburgh	127		1949	Ted Williams, Boston; Vern Stephens, Boston	159
1950	Del Ennis, Philadelphia	126		1950	Walt Dropo, Boston; Vern Stephens, Boston	144
1951	Monte Irvin, New York	121		1951	Gus Zernial, Chicago-Philadelphia	129
1952	Hank Sauer, Chicago	121		1952	Al Rosen, Cleveland	105
1953	Roy Campanella, Brooklyn	142		1953	Al Rosen, Cleveland	145
1954	Ted Kluszewski, Cincinnati	141		1954	Larry Doby, Cleveland	126
1955	Duke Snider, Brooklyn	136		1955	Ray Boone, Detroit; Jackie Jensen, Boston	116
1956	Stan Musial, St. Louis	109		1956	Mickey Mantle, New York	130
1957	Hank Aaron, Milwaukee	132		1957	Roy Sievers, Washington	114
1958	Ernie Banks, Chicago	129		1958	Jackie Jensen, Boston	122
1959	Ernie Banks, Chicago	143		1959	Jackie Jensen, Boston	112
1960	Hank Aaron, Milwaukee	126		1960	Roger Maris, New York	112
1961	Orlando Cepeda, San Francisco	142		1961	Roger Maris, New York; Jim Gentile, Baltimore	141
1962	Tommy Davis, Los Angeles	153		1962	Harmon Killebrew, Minnesota	126
1963	Hank Aaron, Milwaukee	130		1963	Dick Stuart, Boston	118
1964	Ken Boyer, St. Louis	119		1964	Brooks Robinson, Baltimore	118
1965	Deron Johnson, Cincinnati	130		1965	Rocky Colavito, Cleveland	108
1966	Hank Aaron, Atlanta	127		1966	Frank Robinson, Baltimore	122
1967	Orlando Cepeda, St. Louis	111		1967	Carl Yastrzemski, Boston	121
1968	Willie McCovey, San Francisco	105		1968	Ken Harrelson, Boston	109
1969	Willie McCovey, San Francisco	126		1969	Harmon Killebrew, Minnesota	140
1970	Johnny Bench, Cincinnati	148		1970	Frank Howard, Washington	126
1971	Joe Torre, St. Louis	137		1971	Harmon Killebrew, Minnesota	119
1972	Johnny Bench, Cincinnati	125		1972	Dick Allen, Chicago	113
1973	Willie Stargell, Pittsburgh	119		1973	Reggie Jackson, Oakland	117
1974	Johnny Bench, Cincinnati	129		1974	Jeff Burroughs, Texas	118
1975	Greg Luzinski, Philadelphia	120		1975	George Scott, Milwaukee	109

National League			American League		
Year	**Player, team**	**RBI**	**Year**	**Player, team**	**RBI**
1976	George Foster, Cincinnati	121	1976	Lee May, Baltimore	109
1977	George Foster, Cincinnati	149	1977	Larry Hisle, Minnesota	119
1978	George Foster, Cincinnati	120	1978	Jim Rice, Boston	139
1979	Dave Winfield, San Diego	118	1979	Don Baylor, California	139
1980	Mike Schmidt, Philadelphia	121	1980	Cecil Cooper, Milwaukee	122
1981	Mike Schmidt, Philadelphia	91	1981	Eddie Murray, Baltimore	78
1982	Dale Murphy, Atlanta; Al Oliver, Montréal	109	1982	Hal McRae, Kansas City	133
1983	Dale Murphy, Atlanta	121	1983	Cecil Cooper, Milwaukee; Jim Rice, Boston	126
1984	Gary Carter, Montréal; Mike Schmidt, Phil.	106	1984	Tony Armas, Boston	123
1985	Dave Parker, Cincinnati	125	1985	Don Mattingly, New York	145
1986	Mike Schmidt, Philadelphia	119	1986	Joe Carter, Cleveland	121
1987	Andre Dawson, Chicago	137	1987	George Bell, Toronto	134
1988	Will Clark, San Francisco	109	1988	Jose Canseco, Oakland	124
1989	Kevin Mitchell, San Francisco	125	1989	Ruben Sierra, Texas	119
1990	Matt Williams, San Francisco	122	1990	Cecil Fielder, Detroit	132
1991	Howard Johnson, New York	117	1991	Cecil Fielder, Detroit	133
1992	Darren Daulton, Philadelphia	109	1992	Cecil Fielder, Detroit	124
1993	Barry Bonds, San Francisco	123	1993	Albert Belle, Cleveland	129
1994	Jeff Bagwell, Houston	116	1994	Kirby Puckett, Minnesota	112
1995	Dante Bichette, Colorado	128	1995	Albert Belle, Cleveland; Mo Vaughn, Boston	126
1996	Andres Galarraga, Colorado	150	1996	Albert Belle, Cleveland	148
1997	Andres Galarraga, Colorado	140	1997	Ken Griffey Jr., Seattle	147
1998	Sammy Sosa, Chicago	158	1998	Juan Gonzalez, Texas	157
1999	Mark McGwire, St. Louis	147	1999	Manny Ramirez, Cleveland	165
2000	Todd Helton, Colorado	147	2000	Edgar Martinez, Seattle	145
2001	Sammy Sosa, Chicago	160	2001	Bret Boone, Seattle	141
2002	Lance Berkman, Houston	128	2002	Alex Rodriguez, Texas	142
2003	Preston Wilson, Colorado	141	2003	Carlos Delgado, Toronto	145
2004	Vinny Castilla, Colorado	131	2004	Miguel Tejada, Baltimore	150
2005	Andruw Jones, Atlanta	128	2005	David Ortiz, Boston	148
2006	Ryan Howard, Philadelphia	149	2006	David Ortiz, Boston	137
2007	Matt Holliday, Colorado	137	2007	Alex Rodriguez, New York	156
2008	Ryan Howard, Philadelphia	146	2008	Josh Hamilton, Texas	130
2009	Prince Fielder, Milwaukee; Ryan Howard, Phil.	141	2009	Mark Teixeira, New York	122
2010	Albert Pujols, St. Louis	118	2010	Miguel Cabrera, Detroit	126
2011	Matt Kemp, Los Angeles	126	2011	Curtis Granderson, New York	119
2012	Chase Headley, San Diego	115	2012	Miguel Cabrera, Detroit	139
2013	Paul Goldschmidt, Arizona	125	2013	Chris Davis, Baltimore	138

Batting Champions, by Season, 1901-2013

* = All-time single-season record for league since beginning of "modern" era in 1901.

National League			American League		
Year	**Player, team**	**AVG**	**Year**	**Player, team**	**AVG**
1901	Jesse C. Burkett, St. Louis	.376	1901[1]	Napoleon Lajoie, Philadelphia	.426*
1902	Clarence Beaumont, Pittsburgh	.357	1902	Ed Delahanty, Washington	.376
1903	Honus Wagner, Pittsburgh	.355	1903	Napoleon Lajoie, Cleveland	.357
1904	Honus Wagner, Pittsburgh	.349	1904	Napoleon Lajoie, Cleveland	.382
1905	James Seymour, Cincinnati	.377	1905	Elmer Flick, Cleveland	.306
1906	Honus Wagner, Pittsburgh	.339	1906	George Stone, St. Louis	.358
1907	Honus Wagner, Pittsburgh	.350	1907	Ty Cobb, Detroit	.350
1908	Honus Wagner, Pittsburgh	.354	1908	Ty Cobb, Detroit	.324
1909	Honus Wagner, Pittsburgh	.339	1909	Ty Cobb, Detroit	.377
1910	Sherwood Magee, Philadelphia	.331	1910[2]	Ty Cobb, Detroit	.385
1911	Honus Wagner, Pittsburgh	.334	1911	Ty Cobb, Detroit	.420
1912	Henry Zimmerman, Chicago	.372	1912	Ty Cobb, Detroit	.410
1913	Jacob Daubert, Brooklyn	.350	1913	Ty Cobb, Detroit	.390
1914	Jacob Daubert, Brooklyn	.329	1914	Ty Cobb, Detroit	.368
1915	Larry Doyle, New York	.320	1915	Ty Cobb, Detroit	.369
1916	Hal Chase, Cincinnati	.339	1916	Tris Speaker, Cleveland	.386
1917	Edd Roush, Cincinnati	.341	1917	Ty Cobb, Detroit	.383
1918	Zach Wheat, Brooklyn	.335	1918	Ty Cobb, Detroit	.382
1919	Edd Roush, Cincinnati	.321	1919	Ty Cobb, Detroit	.384
1920	Rogers Hornsby, St. Louis	.370	1920	George Sisler, St. Louis	.407
1921	Rogers Hornsby, St. Louis	.397	1921	Harry Heilmann, Detroit	.394
1922	Rogers Hornsby, St. Louis	.401	1922	George Sisler, St. Louis	.420
1923	Rogers Hornsby, St. Louis	.384	1923	Harry Heilmann, Detroit	.403
1924	Rogers Hornsby, St. Louis	.424*	1924	Babe Ruth, New York	.378
1925	Rogers Hornsby, St. Louis	.403	1925	Harry Heilmann, Detroit	.393
1926	Eugene Hargrave, Cincinnati	.353	1926	Henry Manush, Detroit	.378
1927	Paul Waner, Pittsburgh	.380	1927	Harry Heilmann, Detroit	.398
1928	Rogers Hornsby, Boston	.387	1928	Goose Goslin, Washington	.379
1929	Lefty O'Doul, Philadelphia	.398	1929	Lew Fonseca, Cleveland	.369
1930	Bill Terry, New York	.401	1930	Al Simmons, Philadelphia	.381
1931	Chick Hafey, St. Louis	.349	1931	Al Simmons, Philadelphia	.390
1932	Lefty O'Doul, Brooklyn	.368	1932	Dale Alexander, Detroit-Boston	.367
1933	Chuck Klein, Philadelphia	.368	1933	Jimmie Foxx, Philadelphia	.356
1934	Paul Waner, Pittsburgh	.362	1934	Lou Gehrig, New York	.363
1935	Arky Vaughan, Pittsburgh	.385	1935	Buddy Myer, Washington	.349
1936	Paul Waner, Pittsburgh	.373	1936	Luke Appling, Chicago	.388
1937	Joe Medwick, St. Louis	.374	1937	Charlie Gehringer, Detroit	.371
1938	Ernie Lombardi, Cincinnati	.342	1938	Jimmie Foxx, Boston	.349
1939	John Mize, St. Louis	.349	1939	Joe DiMaggio, New York	.381
1940	Debs Garms, Pittsburgh	.355	1940	Joe DiMaggio, New York	.352
1941	Pete Reiser, Brooklyn	.343	1941	Ted Williams, Boston	.406
1942	Ernie Lombardi, Boston	.330	1942	Ted Williams, Boston	.356
1943	Stan Musial, St. Louis	.357	1943	Luke Appling, Chicago	.328

	National League				American League	
Year	Player, team	AVG		Year	Player, team	AVG
1944	Dixie Walker, Brooklyn	.357		1944	Lou Boudreau, Cleveland	.327
1945	Phil Cavarretta, Chicago	.355		1945	George Stirnweiss, New York	.309
1946	Stan Musial, St. Louis	.365		1946	Mickey Vernon, Washington	.353
1947	Harry Walker, St. Louis-Phil.	.363		1947	Ted Williams, Boston	.343
1948	Stan Musial, St. Louis	.376		1948	Ted Williams, Boston	.369
1949	Jackie Robinson, Brooklyn	.342		1949	George Kell, Detroit	.343
1950	Stan Musial, St. Louis	.346		1950	Billy Goodman, Boston	.354
1951	Stan Musial, St. Louis	.355		1951	Ferris Fain, Philadelphia	.344
1952	Stan Musial, St. Louis	.336		1952	Ferris Fain, Philadelphia	.327
1953	Carl Furillo, Brooklyn	.344		1953	Mickey Vernon, Washington	.337
1954	Willie Mays, New York	.345		1954	Roberto Avila, Cleveland	.341
1955	Richie Ashburn, Philadelphia	.338		1955	Al Kaline, Detroit	.340
1956	Hank Aaron, Milwaukee	.328		1956	Mickey Mantle, New York	.353
1957	Stan Musial, St. Louis	.351		1957	Ted Williams, Boston	.388
1958	Richie Ashburn, Philadelphia	.350		1958	Ted Williams, Boston	.328
1959	Hank Aaron, Milwaukee	.355		1959	Harvey Kuenn, Detroit	.353
1960	Dick Groat, Pittsburgh	.325		1960	Pete Runnels, Boston	.320
1961	Roberto Clemente, Pittsburgh	.351		1961	Norm Cash, Detroit	.361
1962	Tommy Davis, Los Angeles	.346		1962	Pete Runnels, Boston	.326
1963	Tommy Davis, Los Angeles	.326		1963	Carl Yastrzemski, Boston	.321
1964	Roberto Clemente, Pittsburgh	.339		1964	Tony Oliva, Minnesota	.323
1965	Roberto Clemente, Pittsburgh	.329		1965	Tony Oliva, Minnesota	.321
1966	Matty Alou, Pittsburgh	.342		1966	Frank Robinson, Baltimore	.316
1967	Roberto Clemente, Pittsburgh	.357		1967	Carl Yastrzemski, Boston	.326
1968	Pete Rose, Cincinnati	.335		1968	Carl Yastrzemski, Boston	.301
1969	Pete Rose, Cincinnati	.348		1969	Rod Carew, Minnesota	.332
1970	Rico Carty, Atlanta	.366		1970	Alex Johnson, California	.329
1971	Joe Torre, St. Louis	.363		1971	Tony Oliva, Minnesota	.337
1972	Billy Williams, Chicago	.333		1972	Rod Carew, Minnesota	.318
1973	Pete Rose, Cincinnati	.338		1973	Rod Carew, Minnesota	.350
1974	Ralph Garr, Atlanta	.353		1974	Rod Carew, Minnesota	.364
1975	Bill Madlock, Chicago	.354		1975	Rod Carew, Minnesota	.359
1976	Bill Madlock, Chicago	.339		1976	George Brett, Kansas City	.333
1977	Dave Parker, Pittsburgh	.338		1977	Rod Carew, Minnesota	.388
1978	Dave Parker, Pittsburgh	.334		1978	Rod Carew, Minnesota	.333
1979	Keith Hernandez, St. Louis	.344		1979	Fred Lynn, Boston	.333
1980	Bill Buckner, Chicago	.324		1980	George Brett, Kansas City	.390
1981	Bill Madlock, Pittsburgh	.341		1981	Carney Lansford, Boston	.336
1982	Al Oliver, Montréal	.331		1982	Willie Wilson, Kansas City	.332
1983	Bill Madlock, Pittsburgh	.323		1983	Wade Boggs, Boston	.361
1984	Tony Gwynn, San Diego	.351		1984	Don Mattingly, New York	.343
1985	Willie McGee, St. Louis	.353		1985	Wade Boggs, Boston	.368
1986	Tim Raines, Montréal	.334		1986	Wade Boggs, Boston	.357
1987	Tony Gwynn, San Diego	.370		1987	Wade Boggs, Boston	.363
1988	Tony Gwynn, San Diego	.313		1988	Wade Boggs, Boston	.366
1989	Tony Gwynn, San Diego	.336		1989	Kirby Puckett, Minnesota	.339
1990	Willie McGee, St. Louis	.335		1990	George Brett, Kansas City	.329
1991	Terry Pendleton, Atlanta	.319		1991	Julio Franco, Texas	.341
1992	Gary Sheffield, San Diego	.330		1992	Edgar Martinez, Seattle	.343
1993	Andres Galarraga, Colorado	.370		1993	John Olerud, Toronto	.363
1994	Tony Gwynn, San Diego	.394		1994	Paul O'Neill, New York	.359
1995	Tony Gwynn, San Diego	.368		1995	Edgar Martinez, Seattle	.356
1996	Tony Gwynn, San Diego	.353		1996	Alex Rodriguez, Seattle	.358
1997	Tony Gwynn, San Diego	.372		1997	Frank Thomas, Chicago	.347
1998	Larry Walker, Colorado	.363		1998	Bernie Williams, New York	.339
1999	Larry Walker, Colorado	.379		1999	Nomar Garciaparra, Boston	.357
2000	Todd Helton, Colorado	.372		2000	Nomar Garciaparra, Boston	.372
2001	Larry Walker, Colorado	.350		2001	Ichiro Suzuki, Seattle	.350
2002	Barry Bonds, San Francisco	.370		2002	Manny Ramirez, Boston	.349
2003	Albert Pujols, St. Louis	.359		2003	Bill Mueller, Boston	.326
2004	Barry Bonds, San Francisco	.362		2004	Ichiro Suzuki, Seattle	.372
2005	Derrek Lee, Chicago	.335		2005	Michael Young, Texas	.331
2006	Freddy Sanchez, Pittsburgh	.344		2006	Joe Mauer, Minnesota	.347
2007	Matt Holliday, Colorado	.340		2007	Magglio Ordonez, Detroit	.363
2008	Chipper Jones, Atlanta	.364		2008	Joe Mauer, Minnesota	.328
2009	Hanley Ramirez, Florida	.342		2009	Joe Mauer, Minnesota	.365
2010	Carlos Gonzalez, Colorado	.336		2010	Josh Hamilton, Texas	.359
2011	Jose Reyes, New York	.377		2011	Miguel Cabrera, Detroit	.344
2012	Buster Posey, San Francisco	.336		2012	Miguel Cabrera, Detroit	.330
2013	Michael Cuddyer, Colorado	.331		2013	Miguel Cabrera, Detroit	.348

(1) Napoleon Lajoie's 1901 batting average varies in historical records from .421 to .426. (2) Some baseball researchers have concluded that Ty Cobb actually hit .382 in 1910 while Napoleon Lajoie, Cleveland, hit .383.

Earned Run Average Leaders, by Season, 1977-2013

	National League					American League			
Year	Pitcher, team	G	IP	ERA	Year	Pitcher, team	G	IP	ERA
1977	John Candelaria, Pittsburgh	33	230.2	2.34	1977	Frank Tanana, California	31	241.1	2.54
1978	Craig Swan, New York	29	207.1	2.43	1978	Ron Guidry, New York	35	273.2	1.74
1979	J. R. Richard, Houston	38	292.1	2.71	1979	Ron Guidry, New York	33	236.1	2.78
1980	Don Sutton, Los Angeles	32	212.1	2.20	1980	Rudy May, New York	41	175.1	2.46
1981	Nolan Ryan, Houston	21	149	1.69	1981	Sammy Stewart, Baltimore	29	112.1	2.32
1982	Steve Rogers, Montréal	35	277	2.40	1982	Rick Sutcliffe, Cleveland	34	216	2.96
1983	Atlee Hammaker, San Francisco	23	172.1	2.25	1983	Rick Honeycutt, Texas	25	174.2	2.42
1984	Alejandro Pena, Los Angeles	28	199.1	2.48	1984	Mike Boddicker, Baltimore	34	261.1	2.79
1985	Dwight Gooden, New York	35	276.2	1.53	1985	Dave Stieb, Toronto	36	265	2.48
1986	Mike Scott, Houston	37	275.1	2.22	1986	Roger Clemens, Boston	33	254	2.48
1987	Nolan Ryan, Houston	34	211.2	2.76	1987	Jimmy Key, Toronto	36	261	2.76

	National League					American League			
Year	Pitcher, team	G	IP	ERA	Year	Pitcher, team	G	IP	ERA
1988	Joe Magrane, St. Louis	24	165.1	2.18	1988	Allan Anderson, Minnesota	30	202.1	2.45
1989	Scott Garrelts, San Francisco	30	193.1	2.28	1989	Bret Saberhagen, Kansas City	36	262.1	2.16
1990	Danny Darwin, Houston	48	162.2	2.21	1990	Roger Clemens, Boston	31	228.1	1.93
1991	Dennis Martinez, Montréal	31	222	2.39	1991	Roger Clemens, Boston	35	271.1	2.62
1992	Bill Swift, San Francisco	30	164.2	2.08	1992	Roger Clemens, Boston	32	246.2	2.41
1993	Greg Maddux, Atlanta	36	267	2.36	1993	Kevin Appier, Kansas City	34	238.2	2.56
1994	Greg Maddux, Atlanta	25	202	1.56	1994	Steve Ontiveros, Oakland	27	115.1	2.65
1995	Greg Maddux, Atlanta	28	209.2	1.63	1995	Randy Johnson, Seattle	30	214.1	2.48
1996	Kevin Brown, Florida	32	233	1.89	1996	Juan Guzman, Toronto	27	187.2	2.93
1997	Pedro Martinez, Montréal	31	241.1	1.90	1997	Roger Clemens, Toronto	34	264	2.05
1998	Greg Maddux, Atlanta	34	251	2.22	1998	Roger Clemens, Toronto	33	234.2	2.65
1999	Randy Johnson, Arizona	35	271.2	2.48	1999	Pedro Martinez, Boston	31	213.1	2.07
2000	Kevin Brown, Los Angeles	33	230	2.58	2000	Pedro Martinez, Boston	29	217	1.74
2001	Randy Johnson, Arizona	35	249.2	2.49	2001	Freddy Garcia, Seattle	34	238.2	3.05
2002	Randy Johnson, Arizona	35	260	2.32	2002	Pedro Martinez, Boston	30	199.1	2.26
2003	Jason Schmidt, San Francisco	29	207.2	2.34	2003	Pedro Martinez, Boston	29	186.2	2.22
2004	Jake Peavy, San Diego	27	166.1	2.27	2004	Johan Santana, Minnesota	34	228	2.61
2005	Roger Clemens, Houston	32	211.1	1.87	2005	Kevin Millwood, Cleveland	30	192	2.86
2006	Roy Oswalt, Houston	33	220.2	2.98	2006	Johan Santana, Minnesota	34	233.2	2.77
2007	Jake Peavy, San Diego	34	223.1	2.54	2007	John Lackey, Los Angeles	33	224	3.01
2008	Johan Santana, New York	34	234.1	2.53	2008	Cliff Lee, Cleveland	31	223.1	2.54
2009	Chris Carpenter, St. Louis	28	192.2	2.24	2009	Zack Greinke, Kansas City	33	229.1	2.16
2010	Josh Johnson, Florida	28	183.2	2.30	2010	Felix Hernandez, Seattle	34	249.2	2.27
2011	Clayton Kershaw, Los Angeles	33	233.1	2.28	2011	Justin Verlander, Detroit	34	251	2.40
2012	Clayton Kershaw, Los Angeles	33	227.2	2.53	2012	David Price, Tampa Bay	31	211	2.56
2013	Clayton Kershaw, Los Angeles	33	236	1.83	2013	Anibal Sanchez, Detroit	29	182	2.57

Note: ERA is computed by multiplying earned runs allowed by 9, then dividing by innings pitched.

Strikeout Leaders, by Season, 1901-2013

* = All-time single-season record for league since beginning of "modern" era in 1901.

	National League			American League	
Year	Pitcher, team	SO	Year	Pitcher, team	SO
1901	Noodles Hahn, Cincinnati	239	1901	Cy Young, Boston	158
1902	Vic Willis, Boston	225	1902	Rube Waddell, Philadelphia	210
1903	Christy Mathewson, New York	267	1903	Rube Waddell, Philadelphia	302
1904	Christy Mathewson, New York	212	1904	Rube Waddell, Philadelphia	349
1905	Christy Mathewson, New York	206	1905	Rube Waddell, Philadelphia	287
1906	Fred Beebe, Chicago-St. Louis	171	1906	Rube Waddell, Philadelphia	196
1907	Christy Mathewson, New York	178	1907	Rube Waddell, Philadelphia	232
1908	Christy Mathewson, New York	259	1908	Ed Walsh, Chicago	269
1909	Orval Overall, Chicago	205	1909	Frank Smith, Chicago	177
1910	Earl Moore, Philadelphia	185	1910	Walter Johnson, Washington	313
1911	Rube Marquard, New York	237	1911	Ed Walsh, Chicago	255
1912	Grover Alexander, Philadelphia	195	1912	Walter Johnson, Washington	303
1913	Tom Seaton, Philadelphia	168	1913	Walter Johnson, Washington	243
1914	Grover Alexander, Philadelphia	214	1914	Walter Johnson, Washington	225
1915	Grover Alexander, Philadelphia	241	1915	Walter Johnson, Washington	203
1916	Grover Alexander, Philadelphia	167	1916	Walter Johnson, Washington	228
1917	Grover Alexander, Philadelphia	200	1917	Walter Johnson, Washington	188
1918	Hippo Vaughn, Chicago	148	1918	Walter Johnson, Washington	162
1919	Hippo Vaughn, Chicago	141	1919	Walter Johnson, Washington	147
1920	Grover Alexander, Chicago	173	1920	Stan Coveleski, Cleveland	133
1921	Burleigh Grimes, Brooklyn	136	1921	Walter Johnson, Washington	143
1922	Dazzy Vance, Brooklyn	134	1922	Urban Shocker, St. Louis	149
1923	Dazzy Vance, Brooklyn	197	1923	Walter Johnson, Washington	130
1924	Dazzy Vance, Brooklyn	262	1924	Walter Johnson, Washington	158
1925	Dazzy Vance, Brooklyn	221	1925	Lefty Grove, Philadelphia	116
1926	Dazzy Vance, Brooklyn	140	1926	Lefty Grove, Philadelphia	194
1927	Dazzy Vance, Brooklyn	184	1927	Lefty Grove, Philadelphia	174
1928	Dazzy Vance, Brooklyn	200	1928	Lefty Grove, Philadelphia	183
1929	Pat Malone, Chicago	166	1929	Lefty Grove, Philadelphia	170
1930	Bill Hallahan, St. Louis	177	1930	Lefty Grove, Philadelphia	209
1931	Bill Hallahan, St. Louis	159	1931	Lefty Grove, Philadelphia	175
1932	Dizzy Dean, St. Louis	191	1932	Red Ruffing, New York	190
1933	Dizzy Dean, St. Louis	199	1933	Lefty Gomez, New York	163
1934	Dizzy Dean, St. Louis	195	1934	Lefty Gomez, New York	158
1935	Dizzy Dean, St. Louis	190	1935	Tommy Bridges, Detroit	163
1936	Van Lingle Mungo, Brooklyn	238	1936	Tommy Bridges, Detroit	175
1937	Carl Hubbell, New York	159	1937	Lefty Gomez, New York	194
1938	Clay Bryant, Chicago	135	1938	Bob Feller, Cleveland	240
1939	Claude Passeau, Philadelphia-Chicago;		1939	Bob Feller, Cleveland	246
	Bucky Walters, Cincinnati	137			
1940	Kirby Higbe, Philadelphia	137	1940	Bob Feller, Cleveland	261
1941	John Vander Meer, Cincinnati	202	1941	Bob Feller, Cleveland	260
1942	John Vander Meer, Cincinnati	186	1942	Tex Hughson, Boston;	
				Bobo Newsom, Washington	113
1943	John Vander Meer, Cincinnati	174	1943	Allie Reynolds, Cleveland	151
1944	Bill Voiselle, New York	161	1944	Hal Newhouser, Detroit	187
1945	Preacher Roe, Pittsburgh	148	1945	Hal Newhouser, Detroit	212
1946	Johnny Schmitz, Cincinnati	135	1946	Bob Feller, Cleveland	348
1947	Ewell Blackwell, Cincinnati	193	1947	Bob Feller, Cleveland	196
1948	Harry Brecheen, St. Louis	149	1948	Bob Feller, Cleveland	164
1949	Warren Spahn, Boston	151	1949	Virgil Trucks, Detroit	153
1950	Warren Spahn, Boston	191	1950	Bob Lemon, Cleveland	170
1951	Warren Spahn, Boston;		1951	Vic Raschi, New York	164
	Don Newcombe, Brooklyn	164			
1952	Warren Spahn, Boston	183	1952	Allie Reynolds, New York	160
1953	Robin Roberts, Philadelphia	198	1953	Billy Pierce, Chicago	186

National League			American League		
Year	Pitcher, team	SO	Year	Pitcher, team	SO
1954	Robin Roberts, Philadelphia	185	1954	Bob Turley, Baltimore	185
1955	Sam Jones, Chicago	198	1955	Herb Score, Cleveland	245
1956	Sam Jones, Chicago	176	1956	Herb Score, Cleveland	263
1957	Jack Sanford, Philadelphia	188	1957	Early Wynn, Cleveland	184
1958	Sam Jones, St. Louis	225	1958	Early Wynn, Chicago	179
1959	Don Drysdale, Los Angeles	242	1959	Jim Bunning, Detroit	201
1960	Don Drysdale, Los Angeles	246	1960	Jim Bunning, Detroit	201
1961	Sandy Koufax, Los Angeles	269	1961	Camilo Pascual, Minnesota	221
1962	Don Drysdale, Los Angeles	232	1962	Camilo Pascual, Minnesota	206
1963	Sandy Koufax, Los Angeles	306	1963	Camilo Pascual, Minnesota	202
1964	Bob Veale, Pittsburgh	250	1964	Al Downing, New York	217
1965	Sandy Koufax, Los Angeles	382*	1965	Sam McDowell, Cleveland	325
1966	Sandy Koufax, Los Angeles	317	1966	Sam McDowell, Cleveland	225
1967	Jim Bunning, Philadelphia	253	1967	Jim Lonborg, Boston	246
1968	Bob Gibson, St. Louis	268	1968	Sam McDowell, Cleveland	283
1969	Ferguson Jenkins, Chicago	273	1969	Sam McDowell, Cleveland	279
1970	Tom Seaver, New York	283	1970	Sam McDowell, Cleveland	304
1971	Tom Seaver, New York	289	1971	Mickey Lolich, Detroit	308
1972	Steve Carlton, Philadelphia	310	1972	Nolan Ryan, California	329
1973	Tom Seaver, New York	251	1973	Nolan Ryan, California	383*
1974	Steve Carlton, Philadelphia	240	1974	Nolan Ryan, California	367
1975	Tom Seaver, New York	243	1975	Frank Tanana, California	269
1976	Tom Seaver, New York	235	1976	Nolan Ryan, California	327
1977	Phil Niekro, Atlanta	262	1977	Nolan Ryan, California	341
1978	J. R. Richard, Houston	303	1978	Nolan Ryan, California	260
1979	J. R. Richard, Houston	313	1979	Nolan Ryan, California	223
1980	Steve Carlton, Philadelphia	286	1980	Len Barker, Cleveland	187
1981	Fernando Valenzuela, Los Angeles	180	1981	Len Barker, Cleveland	127
1982	Steve Carlton, Philadelphia	286	1982	Floyd Bannister, Seattle	209
1983	Steve Carlton, Philadelphia	275	1983	Jack Morris, Detroit	232
1984	Dwight Gooden, New York	276	1984	Mark Langston, Seattle	204
1985	Dwight Gooden, New York	268	1985	Bert Blyleven, Cleveland-Minnesota	206
1986	Mike Scott, Houston	306	1986	Mark Langston, Seattle	245
1987	Nolan Ryan, Houston	270	1987	Mark Langston, Seattle	262
1988	Nolan Ryan, Houston	228	1988	Roger Clemens, Boston	291
1989	Jose DeLeon, St. Louis	201	1989	Nolan Ryan, Texas	301
1990	David Cone, New York	233	1990	Nolan Ryan, Texas	232
1991	David Cone, New York	241	1991	Roger Clemens, Boston	241
1992	John Smoltz, Atlanta	215	1992	Randy Johnson, Seattle	241
1993	Jose Rijo, Cincinnati	227	1993	Randy Johnson, Seattle	308
1994	Andy Benes, San Diego	189	1994	Randy Johnson, Seattle	204
1995	Hideo Nomo, Los Angeles	236	1995	Randy Johnson, Seattle	294
1996	John Smoltz, Atlanta	276	1996	Roger Clemens, Boston	257
1997	Curt Schilling, Philadelphia	319	1997	Roger Clemens, Toronto	292
1998	Curt Schilling, Philadelphia	300	1998	Roger Clemens, Toronto	271
1999	Randy Johnson, Arizona	364	1999	Pedro Martinez, Boston	313
2000	Randy Johnson, Arizona	347	2000	Pedro Martinez, Boston	284
2001	Randy Johnson, Arizona	372	2001	Hideo Nomo, Boston	220
2002	Randy Johnson, Arizona	334	2002	Pedro Martinez, Boston	239
2003	Kerry Wood, Chicago	266	2003	Esteban Loaiza, Chicago	207
2004	Randy Johnson, Arizona	290	2004	Johan Santana, Minnesota	265
2005	Jake Peavy, San Diego	216	2005	Johan Santana, Minnesota	238
2006	Aaron Harang, Cincinnati	216	2006	Johan Santana, Minnesota	245
2007	Jake Peavy, San Diego	240	2007	Scott Kazmir, Tampa Bay	239
2008	Tim Lincecum, San Francisco	265	2008	A. J. Burnett, Toronto	231
2009	Tim Lincecum, San Francisco	261	2009	Justin Verlander, Detroit	269
2010	Tim Lincecum, San Francisco	231	2010	Jered Weaver, Los Angeles	233
2011	Clayton Kershaw, Los Angeles	248	2011	Justin Verlander, Detroit	250
2012	R. A. Dickey, New York	230	2012	Justin Verlander, Detroit	239
2013	Clayton Kershaw, Los Angeles	232	2013	Yu Darvish, Texas	277

Victory Leaders, by Season, 1901-2013

* = All-time single-season record for league since beginning of "modern" era in 1901.

National League			American League		
Year	Pitcher, team	Wins	Year	Pitcher, team	Wins
1901	Bill Donovan, Brooklyn	25	1901	Cy Young, Boston	33
1902	Jack Chesbro, Pittsburgh	28	1902	Cy Young, Boston	32
1903	Joe McGinnity, New York	31	1903	Cy Young, Boston	28*
1904	Joe McGinnity, New York	35	1904	Jack Chesbro, New York	41*
1905	Christy Mathewson, New York	31	1905	Rube Waddell, Philadelphia	27
1906	Joe McGinnity, New York	27	1906	Al Orth, New York	27
1907	Christy Mathewson, New York	24	1907	Addie Joss, Cleveland; Doc White, Chicago	27
1908	Christy Mathewson, New York	37*	1908	Ed Walsh, Chicago	40
1909	Mordecai Brown, Chicago	27	1909	George Mullin, Detroit	29
1910	Christy Mathewson, New York	27	1910	Jack Coombs, Philadelphia	31
1911	Grover Alexander, Chicago	28	1911	Jack Coombs, Philadelphia	28
1912	Larry Cheney, Chicago; Rube Marquard, New York	26	1912	Joe Wood, Boston	34
1913	Tom Seaton, Philadelphia	27	1913	Walter Johnson, Washington	36
1914	Grover Alexander, Philadelphia	27	1914	Walter Johnson, Washington	28
1915	Grover Alexander, Philadelphia	31	1915	Walter Johnson, Washington	27
1916	Grover Alexander, Philadelphia	33	1916	Walter Johnson, Washington	25
1917	Grover Alexander, Philadelphia	30	1917	Eddie Cicotte, Chicago	28
1918	Hippo Vaughn, Chicago	22	1918	Walter Johnson, Washington	23
1919	Jesse Barnes, New York	25	1919	Eddie Cicotte, Chicago	29
1920	Grover Alexander, Philadelphia	27	1920	Jim Bagby, Cleveland	31
1921	Wilbur Cooper, Pitt.; Burleigh Grimes, Brooklyn	22	1921	Carl Mays, New York; Urban Shocker, St. Louis	27
1922	Eppa Rixey, Cincinnati	25	1922	Eddie Rommel, Philadelphia	27
1923	Dolf Luque, Cincinnati	27	1923	George Uhle, Cleveland	26

	National League			American League	
Year	Pitcher, team	Wins	Year	Pitcher, team	Wins
1924	Dazzy Vance, Brooklyn	28	1924	Walter Johnson, Washington	23
1925	Dazzy Vance, Brooklyn	22	1925	Ted Lyons, Chicago; Eddie Rommel, Philadelphia	21
1926	Pete Donohue, Cincinnati; Remy Kremer, Pitt.; Lee Meadows, Pitt.; Flint Rhem, St. Louis	20	1926	George Uhle, Cleveland	27
1927	Charlie Root, Chicago	26	1927	Waite Hoyt, New York; Ted Lyons, Chicago	22
1928	Burleigh Grimes, Pittsburgh; Larry Benton, NY	25	1928	Lefty Grove, Philadelphia; George Pipgras, NY	24
1929	Pat Malone, Chicago	22	1929	George Earnshaw, Philadelphia	24
1930	Pat Malone, Chicago; Remy Kremer, Pitt.	20	1930	Lefty Grove, Philadelphia	28
1931	Jumbo Elliott, Phil.; Bill Hallahan, St. Louis; Heinie Meine, Pittsburgh	19	1931	Lefty Grove, Philadelphia	31
1932	Lon Warneke, Chicago	22	1932	Alvin Crowder, Washington	26
1933	Carl Hubbell, New York	23	1933	Alvin Crowder, Wash.; Lefty Grove, Phila.	24
1934	Dizzy Dean, St. Louis	30	1934	Lefty Gomez, New York	26
1935	Dizzy Dean, St. Louis	28	1935	Wes Ferrell, Boston	25
1936	Carl Hubbell, New York	26	1936	Tommy Bridges, Detroit	23
1937	Carl Hubbell, New York	22	1937	Lefty Gomez, New York	21
1938	Bill Lee, Chicago	22	1938	Red Ruffing, New York	21
1939	Bucky Walters, Cincinnati	27	1939	Bob Feller, Cleveland	24
1940	Bucky Walters, Cincinnati	22	1940	Bob Feller, Cleveland	27
1941	Kirby Higbe, Brooklyn; Whit Wyatt, Brooklyn	22	1941	Bob Feller, Cleveland	25
1942	Mort Cooper, St. Louis	22	1942	Tex Hughson, Boston	22
1943	Mort Cooper, St. Louis; Elmer Riddle, Cincinnati; Rip Sewell, Pittsburgh	21	1943	Spurgeon "Spud" Chandler, New York; Dizzy Trout, Detroit	20
1944	Bucky Walters, Cincinnati	23	1944	Hal Newhouser, Detroit	29
1945	Red Barrett, Boston-St. Louis	23	1945	Hal Newhouser, Detroit	25
1946	Howie Pollet, St. Louis	21	1946	Bob Feller, Cleveland; Hal Newhouser, Detroit	26
1947	Ewell Blackwell, Cincinnati	22	1947	Bob Feller, Cleveland	20
1948	Johnny Sain, Boston	24	1948	Hal Newhouser, Detroit	21
1949	Warren Spahn, Boston	21	1949	Mel Parnell, Boston	25
1950	Warren Spahn, Boston	21	1950	Bob Lemon, Cleveland	23
1951	Larry Jansen, New York; Sal Maglie, New York	23	1951	Bob Feller, Cleveland	22
1952	Robin Roberts, Philadelphia	28	1952	Bobby Shantz, Philadelphia	24
1953	Robin Roberts, Phil.; Warren Spahn, Milwaukee	23	1953	Bob Porterfield, Washington	22
1954	Robin Roberts, Philadelphia	23	1954	Bob Lemon, Cleveland; Early Wynn, Cleveland	23
1955	Robin Roberts, Philadelphia	23	1955	Whitey Ford, New York; Bob Lemon, Cleveland; Frank Sullivan, Boston	18
1956	Don Newcombe, Brooklyn	27	1956	Frank Lary, Detroit	21
1957	Warren Spahn, Milwaukee	21	1957	Jim Bunning, Detroit; Billy Pierce, Chicago	20
1958	Bob Friend, Pitt.; Warren Spahn, Milwaukee	22	1958	Bob Turley, New York	21
1959	Lew Burdette, Warren Spahn, Milwaukee; Sam Jones, NY Giants	21	1959	Early Wynn, Chicago	22
1960	Ernie Broglio, St. Louis; Warren Spahn, Milwaukee	21	1960	Chuck Estrada, Baltimore; Jim Perry, Cleveland	18
1961	Joey Jay, Cincinnati; Warren Spahn, Milwaukee	21	1961	Whitey Ford, New York	25
1962	Don Drysdale, Los Angeles	25	1962	Ralph Terry, New York	23
1963	Sandy Koufax, L.A.; Juan Marichal, San Francisco	25	1963	Whitey Ford, New York	24
1964	Larry Jackson, Chicago	24	1964	Dean Chance, Los Angeles; Gary Peters, Chicago	20
1965	Sandy Koufax, Los Angeles	26	1965	Jim "Mudcat" Grant, Minnesota	21
1966	Sandy Koufax, Los Angeles	27	1966	Jim Kaat, Minnesota	25
1967	Mike McCormick, San Francisco	22	1967	Jim Lonborg, Boston; Earl Wilson, Detroit	22
1968	Juan Marichal, San Francisco	26	1968	Denny McLain, Detroit	31
1969	Tom Seaver, New York	25	1969	Denny McLain, Detroit	24
1970	Bob Gibson, St. Louis; Gaylord Perry, San Francisco	23	1970	Mike Cuellar, Dave McNally, Baltimore; Jim Perry, Minnesota	24
1971	Ferguson Jenkins, Chicago	24	1971	Mickey Lolich, Detroit	25
1972	Steve Carlton, Philadelphia	27	1972	Gaylord Perry, Cleveland; Wilbur Wood, Chicago	24
1973	Ron Bryant, San Francisco	24	1973	Wilbur Wood, Chicago	24
1974	Andy Messersmith, L.A.; Phil Niekro, Atlanta	20	1974	Jim "Catfish" Hunter, Oak.; Ferguson Jenkins, Tex.	25
1975	Tom Seaver, New York	22	1975	Jim "Catfish" Hunter, NY; Jim Palmer, Baltimore	23
1976	Randy Jones, San Diego	22	1976	Jim Palmer, Baltimore	22
1977	Steve Carlton, Philadelphia	23	1977	Dave Goltz, Minnesota; Dennis Leonard, Kansas City; Jim Palmer, Baltimore	20
1978	Gaylord Perry, San Diego	21	1978	Ron Guidry, New York	25
1979	Joe Niekro, Houston; Phil Niekro, Atlanta	21	1979	Mike Flanagan, Baltimore	23
1980	Steve Carlton, Philadelphia	24	1980	Steve Stone, Baltimore	25
1981	Tom Seaver, Cincinnati	14	1981	Dennis Martinez, Balt.; Steve McCatty, Oakland; Jack Morris, Detroit; Pete Vuckovich, Milwaukee	14
1982	Steve Carlton, Philadelphia	23	1982	LaMarr Hoyt, Chicago	19
1983	John Denny, Philadelphia	19	1983	LaMarr Hoyt, Chicago	24
1984	Joaquin Andujar, St. Louis	20	1984	Mike Boddicker, Baltimore	20
1985	Dwight Gooden, New York	24	1985	Ron Guidry, New York	22
1986	Fernando Valenzuela, Los Angeles	21	1986	Roger Clemens, Boston	24
1987	Rick Sutcliffe, Chicago	18	1987	Roger Clemens, Boston; Dave Stewart, Oakland	20
1988	Orel Hershiser, L.A.; Danny Jackson, Cincinnati	23	1988	Frank Viola, Minnesota	24
1989	Mike Scott, Houston	20	1989	Bret Saberhagen, Kansas City	23
1990	Doug Drabek, Pittsburgh	22	1990	Bob Welch, Oakland	27
1991	Tom Glavine, Atlanta; John Smiley, Pittsburgh	20	1991	Scott Erickson, Minnesota; Bill Gullickson, Detroit	20
1992	Tom Glavine, Atlanta; Greg Maddux, Chicago	20	1992	Kevin Brown, Texas; Jack Morris, Toronto	21
1993	John Burkett, San Francisco; Tom Glavine, Atlanta	22	1993	Jack McDowell, Chicago	22
1994	Ken Hill, Montréal; Greg Maddux, Atlanta	16	1994	Jimmy Key, New York	17
1995	Greg Maddux, Atlanta	19	1995	Mike Mussina, Baltimore	19
1996	John Smoltz, Atlanta	24	1996	Andy Pettitte, New York	21
1997	Denny Neagle, Atlanta	20	1997	Roger Clemens, Toronto	21
1998	Tom Glavine, Atlanta	20	1998	Roger Clemens, Toronto; David Cone, New York; Rick Helling, Texas	20
1999	Mike Hampton, Houston	22	1999	Pedro Martinez, Boston	23
2000	Tom Glavine, Atlanta	21	2000	Tim Hudson, Oakland; David Wells, Toronto	20
2001	Matt Morris, St. Louis; Curt Schilling, Arizona	22	2001	Mark Mulder, Oakland	21
2002	Randy Johnson, Arizona	24	2002	Barry Zito, Oakland	23
2003	Russ Ortiz, Atlanta	21	2003	Roy Halladay, Toronto	22
2004	Roy Oswalt, Houston	20	2004	Curt Schilling, Boston	21
2005	Dontrelle Willis, Florida	22	2005	Bartolo Colon, Los Angeles	21

National League			American League		
Year	Pitcher, team	Wins	Year	Pitcher, team	Wins
2006	Aaron Harang, Cincinnati; Derek Lowe, L.A.; Brad Penny, L.A.; John Smoltz, Atlanta; Brandon Webb, Arizona; Carlos Zambrano, Chicago	16	2006	Johan Santana, Minnesota; Chien-Ming Wang, New York	19
2007	Jake Peavy, San Diego	19	2007	Josh Beckett, Boston	20
2008	Brandon Webb, Arizona	22	2008	Cliff Lee, Cleveland	22
2009	Adam Wainwright, St. Louis	19	2009	Felix Hernandez, Seattle; CC Sabathia, New York; Justin Verlander, Detroit	19
2010	Roy Halladay, Philadelphia	21	2010	CC Sabathia, New York	21
2011	Ian Kennedy, Arizona; Clayton Kershaw, L.A.	21	2011	Justin Verlander, Detroit	24
2012	Gio Gonzalez, Washington	21	2012	David Price, Tampa Bay; Jered Weaver, L.A.	20
2013	Adam Wainwright, St. Louis; Jordan Zimmermann, Washington	19	2013	Max Scherzer, Detroit	21

Cy Young Award Winners, 1956-2012

Year	Pitcher, team	Year	Pitcher, team	Year	Pitcher, team
1956	Don Newcombe, Brooklyn	1979	(NL) Bruce Sutter, Chicago	1996	(NL) John Smoltz, Atlanta
1957	Warren Spahn, Milwaukee		(AL) Mike Flanagan, Baltimore		(AL) Pat Hentgen, Toronto
1958	Bob Turley, NY	1980	(NL) Steve Carlton, Philadelphia	1997	(NL) Pedro Martinez, Montréal
1959	Early Wynn, Chicago		(AL) Steve Stone, Baltimore		(AL) Roger Clemens, Toronto
1960	Vernon Law, Pittsburgh	1981	(NL) Fernando Valenzuela, L.A.	1998	(NL) Tom Glavine, Atlanta
1961	Whitey Ford, NY		(AL) Rollie Fingers, Milwaukee		(AL) Roger Clemens, Toronto
1962	Don Drysdale, L.A.	1982	(NL) Steve Carlton, Philadelphia	1999	(NL) Randy Johnson, Arizona
1963	Sandy Koufax, L.A.		(AL) Pete Vuckovich, Milwaukee		(AL) Pedro Martinez, Boston
1964	Dean Chance, L.A.	1983	(NL) John Denny, Philadelphia	2000	(NL) Randy Johnson, Arizona
1965	Sandy Koufax, L.A.		(AL) LaMarr Hoyt, Chicago		(AL) Pedro Martinez, Boston
1966	Sandy Koufax, L.A.	1984	(NL) Rick Sutcliffe, Chicago	2001	(NL) Randy Johnson, Arizona
1967	(NL) Mike McCormick, S.F.		(AL) Willie Hernandez, Detroit		(AL) Roger Clemens, NY
	(AL) Jim Lonborg, Boston	1985	(NL) Dwight Gooden, NY	2002	(NL) Randy Johnson, Arizona
1968	(NL) Bob Gibson, St. Louis		(AL) Bret Saberhagen, Kansas City		(AL) Barry Zito, Oakland
	(AL) Denny McLain, Detroit	1986	(NL) Mike Scott, Houston	2003	(NL) Eric Gagne, L.A.
1969	(NL) Tom Seaver, NY		(AL) Roger Clemens, Boston		(AL) Roy Halladay, Toronto
	(AL) (tie) Denny McLain, Detroit; Mike Cuellar, Baltimore	1987	(NL) Steve Bedrosian, Philadelphia	2004	(NL) Roger Clemens, Houston
1970	(NL) Bob Gibson, St. Louis		(AL) Roger Clemens, Boston		(AL) Johan Santana, Minnesota
	(AL) Jim Perry, Minnesota	1988	(NL) Orel Hershiser, L.A.	2005	(NL) Chris Carpenter, St. Louis
1971	(NL) Ferguson Jenkins, Chicago		(AL) Frank Viola, Minnesota		(AL) Bartolo Colon, L.A.
	(AL) Vida Blue, Oakland	1989	(NL) Mark Davis, San Diego	2006	(NL) Brandon Webb, Arizona
1972	(NL) Steve Carlton, Philadelphia		(AL) Bret Saberhagen, Kansas City		(AL) Johan Santana, Minnesota
	(AL) Gaylord Perry, Cleveland	1990	(NL) Doug Drabek, Pittsburgh	2007	(NL) Jake Peavy, San Diego
1973	(NL) Tom Seaver, NY		(AL) Bob Welch, Oakland		(AL) CC Sabathia, Cleveland
	(AL) Jim Palmer, Baltimore	1991	(NL) Tom Glavine, Atlanta	2008	(NL) Tim Lincecum, S.F.
1974	(NL) Mike Marshall, L.A.		(AL) Roger Clemens, Boston		(AL) Cliff Lee, Cleveland
	(AL) Jim "Catfish" Hunter, Oakland	1992	(NL) Greg Maddux, Chicago	2009	(NL) Tim Lincecum, S.F.
1975	(NL) Tom Seaver, NY		(AL) Dennis Eckersley, Oakland		(AL) Zack Greinke, Kansas City
	(AL) Jim Palmer, Baltimore	1993	(NL) Greg Maddux, Atlanta	2010	(NL) Roy Halladay, Philadelphia
1976	(NL) Randy Jones, San Diego		(AL) Jack McDowell, Chicago		(AL) Felix Hernandez, Seattle
	(AL) Jim Palmer, Baltimore	1994	(NL) Greg Maddux, Atlanta	2011	(NL) Clayton Kershaw, L.A.
1977	(NL) Steve Carlton, Philadelphia		(AL) David Cone, Kansas City		(AL) Justin Verlander, Detroit
	(AL) Sparky Lyle, NY	1995	(NL) Greg Maddux, Atlanta	2012	(NL) R. A. Dickey, NY
1978	(NL) Gaylord Perry, San Diego		(AL) Randy Johnson, Seattle		(AL) David Price, Tampa Bay
	(AL) Ron Guidry, NY				

Most Valuable Players, 1931-2012

As selected by the Baseball Writers' Assn. of America. Prior to 1931, MVP honors were named by various sources.

National League

Year	Player, team	Year	Player, team	Year	Player, team
1931	Frank Frisch, St. Louis	1959	Ernie Banks, Chicago	1986	Mike Schmidt, Philadelphia
1932	Chuck Klein, Philadelphia	1960	Dick Groat, Pittsburgh	1987	Andre Dawson, Chicago
1933	Carl Hubbell, New York	1961	Frank Robinson, Cincinnati	1988	Kirk Gibson, Los Angeles
1934	Dizzy Dean, St. Louis	1962	Maury Wills, Los Angeles	1989	Kevin Mitchell, San Francisco
1935	Gabby Hartnett, Chicago	1963	Sandy Koufax, Los Angeles	1990	Barry Bonds, Pittsburgh
1936	Carl Hubbell, New York	1964	Ken Boyer, St. Louis	1991	Terry Pendleton, Atlanta
1937	Joe Medwick, St. Louis	1965	Willie Mays, San Francisco	1992	Barry Bonds, Pittsburgh
1938	Ernie Lombardi, Cincinnati	1966	Roberto Clemente, Pittsburgh	1993	Barry Bonds, San Francisco
1939	Bucky Walters, Cincinnati	1967	Orlando Cepeda, St. Louis	1994	Jeff Bagwell, Houston
1940	Frank McCormick, Cincinnati	1968	Bob Gibson, St. Louis	1995	Barry Larkin, Cincinnati
1941	Dolph Camilli, Brooklyn	1969	Willie McCovey, San Francisco	1996	Ken Caminiti, San Diego
1942	Mort Cooper, St. Louis	1970	Johnny Bench, Cincinnati	1997	Larry Walker, Colorado
1943	Stan Musial, St. Louis	1971	Joe Torre, St. Louis	1998	Sammy Sosa, Chicago
1944	Martin Marion, St. Louis	1972	Johnny Bench, Cincinnati	1999	Chipper Jones, Atlanta
1945	Phil Cavarretta, Chicago	1973	Pete Rose, Cincinnati	2000	Jeff Kent, San Francisco
1946	Stan Musial, St. Louis	1974	Steve Garvey, Los Angeles	2001	Barry Bonds, San Francisco
1947	Bob Elliott, Boston	1975	Joe Morgan, Cincinnati	2002	Barry Bonds, San Francisco
1948	Stan Musial, St. Louis	1976	Joe Morgan, Cincinnati	2003	Barry Bonds, San Francisco
1949	Jackie Robinson, Brooklyn	1977	George Foster, Cincinnati	2004	Barry Bonds, San Francisco
1950	Jim Konstanty, Philadelphia	1978	Dave Parker, Pittsburgh	2005	Albert Pujols, St. Louis
1951	Roy Campanella, Brooklyn	1979	(tie) Keith Hernandez, St. Louis; Willie Stargell, Pittsburgh	2006	Ryan Howard, Philadelphia
1952	Hank Sauer, Chicago			2007	Jimmy Rollins, Philadelphia
1953	Roy Campanella, Brooklyn	1980	Mike Schmidt, Philadelphia	2008	Albert Pujols, St. Louis
1954	Willie Mays, New York	1981	Mike Schmidt, Philadelphia	2009	Albert Pujols, St. Louis
1955	Roy Campanella, Brooklyn	1982	Dale Murphy, Atlanta	2010	Joey Votto, Cincinnati
1956	Don Newcombe, Brooklyn	1983	Dale Murphy, Atlanta	2011	Ryan Braun, Milwaukee
1957	Hank Aaron, Milwaukee	1984	Ryne Sandberg, Chicago	2012	Buster Posey, San Francisco
1958	Ernie Banks, Chicago	1985	Willie McGee, St. Louis		

American League

Year	Player, team	Year	Player, team	Year	Player, team
1931	Lefty Grove, Philadelphia	1958	Jackie Jensen, Boston	1986	Roger Clemens, Boston
1932	Jimmie Foxx, Philadelphia	1959	Nellie Fox, Chicago	1987	George Bell, Toronto
1933	Jimmie Foxx, Philadelphia	1960	Roger Maris, New York	1988	Jose Canseco, Oakland
1934	Mickey Cochrane, Detroit	1961	Roger Maris, New York	1989	Robin Yount, Milwaukee
1935	Hank Greenberg, Detroit	1962	Mickey Mantle, New York	1990	Rickey Henderson, Oakland
1936	Lou Gehrig, New York	1963	Elston Howard, New York	1991	Cal Ripken Jr., Baltimore
1937	Charlie Gehringer, Detroit	1964	Brooks Robinson, Baltimore	1992	Dennis Eckersley, Oakland
1938	Jimmie Foxx, Boston	1965	Zoilo Versalles, Minnesota	1993	Frank Thomas, Chicago
1939	Joe DiMaggio, New York	1966	Frank Robinson, Baltimore	1994	Frank Thomas, Chicago
1940	Hank Greenberg, Detroit	1967	Carl Yastrzemski, Boston	1995	Mo Vaughn, Boston
1941	Joe DiMaggio, New York	1968	Denny McLain, Detroit	1996	Juan Gonzalez, Texas
1942	Joe Gordon, New York	1969	Harmon Killebrew, Minnesota	1997	Ken Griffey Jr., Seattle
1943	Spurgeon "Spud" Chandler, New York	1970	John "Boog" Powell, Baltimore	1998	Juan Gonzalez, Texas
		1971	Vida Blue, Oakland	1999	Ivan Rodriguez, Texas
1944	Hal Newhouser, Detroit	1972	Dick Allen, Chicago	2000	Jason Giambi, Oakland
1945	Hal Newhouser, Detroit	1973	Reggie Jackson, Oakland	2001	Ichiro Suzuki, Seattle
1946	Ted Williams, Boston	1974	Jeff Burroughs, Texas	2002	Miguel Tejada, Oakland
1947	Joe DiMaggio, New York	1975	Fred Lynn, Boston	2003	Alex Rodriguez, Texas
1948	Lou Boudreau, Cleveland	1976	Thurman Munson, New York	2004	Vladimir Guerrero, Anaheim
1949	Ted Williams, Boston	1977	Rod Carew, Minnesota	2005	Alex Rodriguez, New York
1950	Phil Rizzuto, New York	1978	Jim Rice, Boston	2006	Justin Morneau, Minnesota
1951	Yogi Berra, New York	1979	Don Baylor, California	2007	Alex Rodriguez, New York
1952	Bobby Shantz, Philadelphia	1980	George Brett, Kansas City	2008	Dustin Pedroia, Boston
1953	Al Rosen, Cleveland	1981	Rollie Fingers, Milwaukee	2009	Joe Mauer, Minnesota
1954	Yogi Berra, New York	1982	Robin Yount, Milwaukee	2010	Josh Hamilton, Texas
1955	Yogi Berra, New York	1983	Cal Ripken Jr., Baltimore	2011	Justin Verlander, Detroit
1956	Mickey Mantle, New York	1984	Willie Hernandez, Detroit	2012	Miguel Cabrera, Detroit
1957	Mickey Mantle, New York	1985	Don Mattingly, New York		

Rookie of the Year, 1949-2012

(as selected by the Baseball Writers' Assn. of America)

1947: Jackie Robinson, Brooklyn, 1B (combined selection); 1948: Alvin Dark, Boston (NL), SS (combined selection).

National League

Year	Player, team, position	Year	Player, team, position	Year	Player, team, position
1949	Don Newcombe, Brooklyn, P	1971	Earl Williams, Atlanta, C	1992	Eric Karros, L.A., 1B
1950	Sam Jethroe, Boston, OF	1972	Jon Matlack, NY, P	1993	Mike Piazza, L.A., C
1951	Willie Mays, NY, OF	1973	Gary Matthews, San Francisco, OF	1994	Raul Mondesi, L.A., OF
1952	Joe Black, Brooklyn, P	1974	Bake McBride, St. Louis, OF	1995	Hideo Nomo, L.A., P
1953	Jim Gilliam, Brooklyn, 2B	1975	John Montefusco, San Francisco, P	1996	Todd Hollandsworth, L.A., OF
1954	Wally Moon, St. Louis, OF	1976	(tie) Butch Metzger, San Diego, P;	1997	Scott Rolen, Philadelphia, 3B
1955	Bill Virdon, St. Louis, OF		Pat Zachry, Cincinnati, P	1998	Kerry Wood, Chicago, P
1956	Frank Robinson, Cincinnati, OF	1977	Andre Dawson, Montréal, OF	1999	Scott Williamson, Cincinnati, P
1957	Jack Sanford, Philadelphia, P	1978	Bob Horner, Atlanta, 3B	2000	Rafael Furcal, Atlanta, SS
1958	Orlando Cepeda, San Francisco, 1B	1979	Rick Sutcliffe, L.A., P	2001	Albert Pujols, St. Louis, OF
1959	Willie McCovey, San Francisco, 1B	1980	Steve Howe, L.A., P	2002	Jason Jennings, Colorado, P
1960	Frank Howard, L.A., OF	1981	Fernando Valenzuela, L.A., P	2003	Dontrelle Willis, Florida, P
1961	Billy Williams, Chicago, OF	1982	Steve Sax, L.A., 2B	2004	Jason Bay, Pittsburgh, OF
1962	Ken Hubbs, Chicago, 2B	1983	Darryl Strawberry, NY, OF	2005	Ryan Howard, Philadelphia, 1B
1963	Pete Rose, Cincinnati, 2B	1984	Dwight Gooden, NY, P	2006	Hanley Ramirez, Florida, SS
1964	Richie Allen, Philadelphia, 3B	1985	Vince Coleman, St. Louis, OF	2007	Ryan Braun, Milwaukee, OF
1965	Jim Lefebvre, L.A., 2B	1986	Todd Worrell, St. Louis, P	2008	Geovany Soto, Chicago, C
1966	Tommy Helms, Cincinnati, 2B	1987	Benito Santiago, San Diego, C	2009	Chris Coghlan, Florida, OF
1967	Tom Seaver, NY, P	1988	Chris Sabo, Cincinnati, 3B	2010	Buster Posey, San Francisco, C
1968	Johnny Bench, Cincinnati, C	1989	Jerome Walton, Chicago, OF	2011	Craig Kimbrel, Atlanta, P
1969	Ted Sizemore, L.A., 2B	1990	Dave Justice, Atlanta, 1B	2012	Bryce Harper, Washington, OF
1970	Carl Morton, Montréal, P	1991	Jeff Bagwell, Houston, 1B		

American League

Year	Player, team, position	Year	Player, team, position	Year	Player, team, position
1949	Roy Sievers, St. Louis, OF	1971	Chris Chambliss, Cleveland, 1B	1992	Pat Listach, Milwaukee, SS
1950	Walt Dropo, Boston, 1B	1972	Carlton Fisk, Boston, C	1993	Tim Salmon, California, OF
1951	Gil McDougald, NY, 3B	1973	Al Bumbry, Baltimore, OF	1994	Bob Hamelin, Kansas City, DH
1952	Harry Byrd, Philadelphia, P	1974	Mike Hargrove, Texas, 1B	1995	Marty Cordova, Minnesota, OF
1953	Harvey Kuenn, Detroit, SS	1975	Fred Lynn, Boston, OF	1996	Derek Jeter, NY, SS
1954	Bob Grim, NY, P	1976	Mark Fidrych, Detroit, P	1997	Nomar Garciaparra, Boston, SS
1955	Herb Score, Cleveland, P	1977	Eddie Murray, Baltimore, DH	1998	Ben Grieve, Oakland, OF
1956	Luis Aparicio, Chicago, SS	1978	Lou Whitaker, Detroit, 2B	1999	Carlos Beltran, Kansas City, OF
1957	Tony Kubek, NY, IF-OF	1979	(tie) John Castino, Minnesota, 3B;	2000	Kazuhiro Sasaki, Seattle, P
1958	Albie Pearson, Washington, OF		Alfredo Griffin, Toronto, SS	2001	Ichiro Suzuki, Seattle, OF
1959	Bob Allison, Washington, OF	1980	Joe Charboneau, Cleveland, OF	2002	Eric Hinske, Toronto, 3B
1960	Ron Hansen, Baltimore, SS	1981	Dave Righetti, NY, P	2003	Angel Berroa, Kansas City, SS
1961	Don Schwall, Boston, P	1982	Cal Ripken Jr., Baltimore, SS	2004	Bobby Crosby, Oakland, SS
1962	Tom Tresh, NY, IF-OF	1983	Ron Kittle, Chicago, OF	2005	Huston Street, Oakland, P
1963	Gary Peters, Chicago, P	1984	Alvin Davis, Seattle, 1B	2006	Justin Verlander, Detroit, P
1964	Tony Oliva, Minnesota, OF	1985	Ozzie Guillen, Chicago, SS	2007	Dustin Pedroia, Boston, 2B
1965	Curt Blefary, Baltimore, OF	1986	Jose Canseco, Oakland, OF	2008	Evan Longoria, Tampa Bay, 3B
1966	Tommie Agee, Chicago, OF	1987	Mark McGwire, Oakland, 1B	2009	Andrew Bailey, Oakland, P
1967	Rod Carew, Minnesota, 2B	1988	Walt Weiss, Oakland, SS	2010	Neftali Feliz, Texas, P
1968	Stan Bahnsen, NY, P	1989	Gregg Olson, Baltimore, P	2011	Jeremy Hellickson, Tampa Bay, P
1969	Lou Piniella, Kansas City, OF	1990	Sandy Alomar Jr., Cleveland, C	2012	Mike Trout, L.A., OF
1970	Thurman Munson, NY, C	1991	Chuck Knoblauch, Minnesota, 2B		

Major League Pennant Winners, 1901-75

	National League						American League			
Year	Winner	W	L	PCT	Manager	Year	Winner	W	L	PCT	Manager
1901	Pittsburgh	90	49	.647	Clarke	1901	Chicago	83	53	.610	Griffith
1902	Pittsburgh	103	36	.741	Clarke	1902	Philadelphia	83	53	.610	Mack
1903	Pittsburgh	91	49	.650	Clarke	1903	Boston	91	47	.659	Collins
1904	New York	106	47	.693	McGraw	1904	Boston	95	59	.617	Collins
1905	New York	105	48	.686	McGraw	1905	Philadelphia	92	56	.622	Mack
1906	Chicago	116	36	.763	Chance	1906	Chicago	93	58	.616	Jones
1907	Chicago	107	45	.704	Chance	1907	Detroit	92	58	.613	Jennings
1908	Chicago	99	55	.643	Chance	1908	Detroit	90	63	.588	Jennings
1909	Pittsburgh	110	42	.724	Clarke	1909	Detroit	98	54	.645	Jennings
1910	Chicago	104	50	.675	Chance	1910	Philadelphia	102	48	.680	Mack
1911	New York	99	54	.647	McGraw	1911	Philadelphia	101	50	.669	Mack
1912	New York	103	48	.682	McGraw	1912	Boston	105	47	.691	Stahl
1913	New York	101	51	.664	McGraw	1913	Philadelphia	96	57	.627	Mack
1914	Boston	94	59	.614	Stallings	1914	Philadelphia	99	53	.651	Mack
1915	Philadelphia	90	62	.592	Moran	1915	Boston	101	50	.669	Carrigan
1916	Brooklyn	94	60	.610	Robinson	1916	Boston	91	63	.591	Carrigan
1917	New York	98	56	.636	McGraw	1917	Chicago	100	54	.649	Rowland
1918	Chicago	84	45	.651	Mitchell	1918	Boston	75	51	.595	Barrow
1919	Cincinnati	96	44	.686	Moran	1919	Chicago	88	52	.629	Gleason
1920	Brooklyn	93	61	.604	Robinson	1920	Cleveland	98	56	.636	Speaker
1921	New York	94	59	.614	McGraw	1921	New York	98	55	.641	Huggins
1922	New York	93	61	.604	McGraw	1922	New York	94	60	.610	Huggins
1923	New York	95	58	.621	McGraw	1923	New York	98	54	.645	Huggins
1924	New York	93	60	.608	McGraw	1924	Washington	92	62	.597	Harris
1925	Pittsburgh	95	58	.621	McKechnie	1925	Washington	96	55	.636	Harris
1926	St. Louis	89	65	.578	Hornsby	1926	New York	91	63	.591	Huggins
1927	Pittsburgh	94	60	.610	Bush	1927	New York	110	44	.714	Huggins
1928	St. Louis	95	59	.617	McKechnie	1928	New York	101	53	.656	Huggins
1929	Chicago	98	54	.645	McCarthy	1929	Philadelphia	104	46	.693	Mack
1930	St. Louis	92	62	.597	Street	1930	Philadelphia	102	52	.662	Mack
1931	St. Louis	101	53	.656	Street	1931	Philadelphia	107	45	.704	Mack
1932	Chicago	90	64	.584	Hornsby, Grimm	1932	New York	107	47	.695	McCarthy
1933	New York	91	61	.599	Terry	1933	Washington	99	53	.651	Cronin
1934	St. Louis	95	58	.621	Frisch	1934	Detroit	101	53	.656	Cochrane
1935	Chicago	100	54	.649	Grimm	1935	Detroit	93	58	.616	Cochrane
1936	New York	92	62	.597	Terry	1936	New York	102	51	.667	McCarthy
1937	New York	95	57	.625	Terry	1937	New York	102	52	.662	McCarthy
1938	Chicago	89	63	.586	Grimm, Hartnett	1938	New York	99	53	.651	McCarthy
1939	Cincinnati	97	57	.630	McKechnie	1939	New York	106	45	.702	McCarthy
1940	Cincinnati	100	53	.654	McKechnie	1940	Detroit	90	64	.584	Baker
1941	Brooklyn	100	54	.649	Durocher	1941	New York	101	53	.656	McCarthy
1942	St. Louis	106	48	.688	Southworth	1942	New York	103	51	.669	McCarthy
1943	St. Louis	105	49	.682	Southworth	1943	New York	98	56	.636	McCarthy
1944	St. Louis	105	49	.682	Southworth	1944	St. Louis	89	65	.578	Sewell
1945	Chicago	98	56	.636	Grimm	1945	Detroit	88	65	.575	O'Neill
1946	St. Louis	98	58	.628	Dyer	1946	Boston	104	50	.675	Cronin
1947	Brooklyn	94	60	.610	Shotton	1947	New York	97	57	.630	Harris
1948	Boston	91	62	.595	Southworth	1948	Cleveland	97	58	.626	Boudreau
1949	Brooklyn	97	57	.630	Shotton	1949	New York	97	57	.630	Stengel
1950	Philadelphia	91	63	.591	Sawyer	1950	New York	98	56	.636	Stengel
1951	New York	98	59	.624	Durocher	1951	New York	98	56	.636	Stengel
1952	Brooklyn	96	57	.627	Dressen	1952	New York	95	59	.617	Stengel
1953	Brooklyn	105	49	.682	Dressen	1953	New York	99	52	.656	Stengel
1954	New York	97	57	.630	Durocher	1954	Cleveland	111	43	.721	Lopez
1955	Brooklyn	98	55	.641	Alston	1955	New York	96	58	.623	Stengel
1956	Brooklyn	93	61	.604	Alston	1956	New York	97	57	.630	Stengel
1957	Milwaukee	95	59	.617	Haney	1957	New York	98	56	.636	Stengel
1958	Milwaukee	92	62	.597	Haney	1958	New York	92	62	.597	Stengel
1959	Los Angeles	88	68	.564	Alston	1959	Chicago	94	60	.610	Lopez
1960	Pittsburgh	95	59	.617	Murtaugh	1960	New York	97	57	.630	Stengel
1961	Cincinnati	93	61	.604	Hutchinson	1961	New York	109	53	.673	Houk
1962	San Francisco	103	62	.624	Dark	1962	New York	96	66	.593	Houk
1963	Los Angeles	99	63	.611	Alston	1963	New York	104	57	.646	Houk
1964	St. Louis	93	69	.574	Keane	1964	New York	99	63	.611	Berra
1965	Los Angeles	97	65	.599	Alston	1965	Minnesota	102	60	.630	Mele
1966	Los Angeles	95	67	.586	Alston	1966	Baltimore	97	63	.606	Bauer
1967	St. Louis	101	60	.627	Schoendienst	1967	Boston	92	70	.568	Williams
1968	St. Louis	97	65	.599	Schoendienst	1968	Detroit	103	59	.636	Smith
1969	NY Mets	100	62	.617	Hodges	1969	Baltimore	109	53	.673	Weaver
1970	Cincinnati	102	60	.630	Anderson	1970	Baltimore	108	54	.667	Weaver
1971	Pittsburgh	97	65	.599	Murtaugh	1971	Baltimore	101	57	.639	Weaver
1972	Cincinnati	95	59	.617	Anderson	1972	Oakland	93	62	.600	Williams
1973	NY Mets	82	79	.509	Berra	1973	Oakland	94	68	.580	Williams
1974	Los Angeles	102	60	.630	Alston	1974	Oakland	90	72	.556	Dark
1975	Cincinnati	108	54	.667	Anderson	1975	Boston	95	65	.594	Johnson

Major League Pennant Winners, 1976-2013

National League

	East					West				Pennant
Year	Winner	W	L	PCT	Manager	Winner	W	L	PCT	Manager	winner
1976	Philadelphia	101	61	.623	Ozark	Cincinnati	102	60	.630	Anderson	Cincinnati
1977	Philadelphia	101	61	.623	Ozark	Los Angeles	98	64	.605	Lasorda	Los Angeles
1978	Philadelphia	90	72	.556	Ozark	Los Angeles	95	67	.586	Lasorda	Los Angeles
1979	Pittsburgh	98	64	.605	Tanner	Cincinnati	90	71	.559	McNamara	Pittsburgh

National League

Year	Winner (East)	W	L	PCT	Manager	Winner (West)	W	L	PCT	Manager	Pennant winner
1980	Philadelphia	91	71	.562	Green	Houston	93	70	.571	Virdon	Philadelphia
1981(a)	Philadelphia	34	21	.618	Green	Los Angeles	36	21	.632	Lasorda	(c)
1981(b)	Montréal	30	23	.566	Williams, Fanning	Houston	33	20	.623	Virdon	Los Angeles
1982	St. Louis	92	70	.568	Herzog	Atlanta	89	73	.549	Torre	St. Louis
1983	Philadelphia	90	72	.556	Corrales, Owens	Los Angeles	91	71	.562	Lasorda	Philadelphia
1984	Chicago	96	65	.596	Frey	San Diego	92	70	.568	Williams	San Diego
1985	St. Louis	101	61	.623	Herzog	Los Angeles	95	67	.586	Lasorda	St. Louis
1986	NY Mets	108	54	.667	Johnson	Houston	96	66	.593	Lanier	New York
1987	St. Louis	95	67	.586	Herzog	San Francisco	90	72	.556	Craig	St. Louis
1988	NY Mets	100	60	.625	Johnson	Los Angeles	94	67	.584	Lasorda	Los Angeles
1989	Chicago	93	69	.571	Zimmer	San Francisco	92	70	.568	Craig	San Francisco
1990	Pittsburgh	95	67	.586	Leyland	Cincinnati	91	71	.562	Piniella	Cincinnati
1991	Pittsburgh	98	64	.605	Leyland	Atlanta	94	68	.580	Cox	Atlanta
1992	Pittsburgh	96	66	.593	Leyland	Atlanta	98	64	.605	Cox	Atlanta
1993	Philadelphia	97	65	.599	Fregosi	Atlanta	104	58	.642	Cox	Philadelphia

Year	Division	Winner	W	L	PCT	Manager	Playoffs	Pennant winner
1994(d)	East	Montréal	74	40	.649	Alou	—	—
	Central	Cincinnati	66	48	.579	Johnson		
	West	Los Angeles	58	56	.509	Lasorda		
1995	East	Atlanta	90	54	.625	Cox	Atlanta 3, Colorado* 1	Atlanta
	Central	Cincinnati	85	59	.590	Johnson	Cincinnati 3, Los Angeles 0	
	West	Los Angeles	78	66	.542	Lasorda	Atlanta 4, Cincinnati 0	
1996	East	Atlanta	96	66	.593	Cox	Atlanta 3, Los Angeles* 0	Atlanta
	Central	St. Louis	88	74	.543	La Russa	St. Louis 3, San Diego 0	
	West	San Diego	91	71	.562	Bochy	Atlanta 4, St. Louis 3	
1997	East	Atlanta	101	61	.623	Cox	Atlanta 3, Houston 0	Florida*
	Central	Houston	84	78	.519	Dierker	Florida* 3, San Francisco 0	(Leyland)
	West	San Francisco	90	72	.556	Baker	Florida* 4, Atlanta 2	
1998	East	Atlanta	106	56	.654	Cox	Atlanta 3, Chicago* 0	San Diego
	Central	Houston	102	60	.630	Dierker	San Diego 3, Houston 1	
	West	San Diego	98	64	.605	Bochy	San Diego 4, Atlanta 2	
1999	East	Atlanta	103	59	.636	Cox	Atlanta 3, Houston 1	Atlanta
	Central	Houston	97	65	.599	Dierker, Galante	New York* 3, Arizona 1	
	West	Arizona	100	62	.617	Showalter	Atlanta 4, New York* 2	
2000	East	Atlanta	95	67	.586	Cox	St. Louis 3, Atlanta 0	New York*
	Central	St. Louis	95	67	.586	La Russa	New York* 3, San Francisco 1	(Valentine)
	West	San Francisco	97	65	.599	Baker	New York* 4, St. Louis 1	
2001	East	Atlanta	88	74	.543	Cox	Atlanta 3, Houston 0	Arizona
	Central	Houston	93	69	.574	Dierker	Arizona 3, St. Louis* 2	
	West	Arizona	92	70	.568	Brenly	Arizona 4, Atlanta 1	
2002	East	Atlanta	101	59	.631	Cox	St. Louis 3, Arizona 0	San Francisco*
	Central	St. Louis	97	65	.599	La Russa	San Francisco* 3, Atlanta 2	(Baker)
	West	Arizona	98	64	.605	Brenly	San Francisco* 4, St. Louis 1	
2003	East	Atlanta	101	61	.623	Cox	Chicago 3, Atlanta 2	Florida*
	Central	Chicago	88	74	.543	Baker	Florida* 3, San Francisco 1	(McKeon)
	West	San Francisco	100	61	.621	Alou	Florida* 4, Chicago 3	
2004	East	Atlanta	96	66	.593	Cox	Houston* 3, Atlanta 2	St. Louis
	Central	St. Louis	105	57	.648	La Russa	St. Louis 3, Los Angeles 1	
	West	Los Angeles	93	69	.574	Tracy	St. Louis 4, Houston* 3	
2005	East	Atlanta	90	72	.556	Cox	St. Louis 3, San Diego 0	Houston*
	Central	St. Louis	100	62	.617	La Russa	Houston* 3, Atlanta 1	(Garner)
	West	San Diego	82	80	.506	Bochy	Houston* 4, St. Louis 2	
2006	East	New York	97	65	.599	Randolph	New York 3, Los Angeles* 0	St. Louis
	Central	St. Louis	83	78	.516	La Russa	St. Louis 3, San Diego 1	
	West	San Diego	88	74	.543	Bochy	St. Louis 4, New York 3	
2007	East	Philadelphia	89	73	.549	Manuel	Colorado* 3, Philadelphia 0	Colorado*
	Central	Chicago	85	77	.525	Piniella	Arizona 3, Chicago 0	(Hurdle)
	West	Arizona	90	72	.556	Melvin	Colorado* 4, Arizona 0	
2008	East	Philadelphia	92	70	.568	Manuel	Philadelphia 3, Milwaukee* 1	Philadelphia
	Central	Chicago	97	64	.602	Piniella	Los Angeles 3, Chicago 0	
	West	Los Angeles	84	78	.519	Torre	Philadelphia 4, Los Angeles 1	
2009	East	Philadelphia	93	69	.574	Manuel	Philadelphia 3, Colorado* 1	Philadelphia
	Central	St. Louis	91	71	.562	La Russa	Los Angeles 3, St. Louis 0	
	West	Los Angeles	95	67	.586	Torre	Philadelphia 4, Los Angeles 1	
2010	East	Philadelphia	97	65	.599	Manuel	San Francisco 3, Atlanta* 1	San Francisco
	Central	Cincinnati	91	71	.562	Baker	Philadelphia 3, Cincinnati 0	
	West	San Francisco	92	70	.568	Bochy	San Francisco 4, Philadelphia 2	
2011	East	Philadelphia	102	60	.630	Manuel	Milwaukee 3, Arizona 2	St. Louis*
	Central	Milwaukee	96	66	.593	Roenicke	St. Louis* 3, Philadelphia 2	(La Russa)
	West	Arizona	94	68	.580	Gibson	St. Louis* 4, Milwaukee 2	
2012	East	Washington	98	64	.605	Johnson	#St. Louis* 6, Atlanta* 3	San Francisco
	Central	Cincinnati	97	65	.599	Baker	St. Louis* 3, Washington 2	
	West	San Francisco	94	68	.580	Bochy	San Francisco 3, Cincinnati 2	
							San Francisco 4, St. Louis* 3	
2013	East	Atlanta	96	66	.593	González	#Pittsburgh* 6, Cincinnati* 2	St. Louis
	Central	St. Louis	97	65	.599	Matheny	St. Louis 3, Pittsburgh* 2	
	West	Los Angeles	92	70	.568	Mattingly	Los Angeles 3, Atlanta 1	
							St. Louis 4, Los Angeles 2	

American League

Year	Winner (East)	W	L	PCT	Manager	Winner (West)	W	L	PCT	Manager	Pennant winner
1976	New York	97	62	.610	Martin	Kansas City	90	72	.556	Herzog	New York
1977	New York	100	62	.617	Martin	Kansas City	102	60	.630	Herzog	New York
1978	New York	100	63	.613	Martin, Lemon	Kansas City	92	70	.568	Herzog	New York
1979	Baltimore	102	57	.642	Weaver	California	88	74	.543	Fregosi	Baltimore

Year	East Winner	W	L	PCT	Manager	West Winner	W	L	PCT	Manager	Pennant winner
1980	New York	103	59	.636	Howser	Kansas City	97	65	.599	Frey	Kansas City
1981(a)	New York	34	22	.607	Michael	Oakland	37	23	.617	Martin	(c)
1981(b)	Milwaukee	31	22	.585	Rodgers	Kansas City	30	23	.566	Frey, Howser	New York
1982	Milwaukee	95	67	.586	Rodgers, Kuenn	California	93	69	.574	Mauch	Milwaukee
1983	Baltimore	98	64	.605	Altobelli	Chicago	99	63	.611	La Russa	Baltimore
1984	Detroit	104	58	.642	Anderson	Kansas City	84	78	.519	Howser	Detroit
1985	Toronto	99	62	.615	Cox	Kansas City	91	71	.562	Howser	Kansas City
1986	Boston	95	66	.590	McNamara	California	92	70	.568	Mauch	Boston
1987	Detroit	98	64	.605	Anderson	Minnesota	85	77	.525	Kelly	Minnesota
1988	Boston	89	73	.549	McNamara, Morgan	Oakland	104	58	.642	La Russa	Oakland
1989	Toronto	89	73	.549	Williams, Gaston	Oakland	99	63	.611	La Russa	Oakland
1990	Boston	88	74	.543	Morgan	Oakland	103	59	.636	La Russa	Oakland
1991	Toronto	91	71	.562	Gaston	Minnesota	95	67	.586	Kelly	Minnesota
1992	Toronto	96	66	.593	Gaston	Oakland	96	66	.593	La Russa	Toronto
1993	Toronto	95	67	.586	Gaston	Chicago	94	68	.580	Lamont	Toronto

Year	Division	Winner	W	L	PCT	Manager	Playoffs	Pennant winner
1994(d)	East	New York	70	43	.619	Showalter	—	—
	Central	Chicago	67	46	.593	Lamont		
	West	Texas	52	62	.456	Kennedy		
1995	East	Boston	86	58	.597	Kennedy	Cleveland 3, Boston 0	Cleveland
	Central	Cleveland	100	44	.694	Hargrove	Seattle 3, New York* 2	
	West	Seattle	79	66	.545	Piniella	Cleveland 4, Seattle 2	
1996	East	New York	92	70	.568	Torre	Baltimore* 3, Cleveland 1	New York
	Central	Cleveland	99	62	.615	Hargrove	New York 3, Texas 1	
	West	Texas	90	72	.556	Oates	New York 4, Baltimore* 1	
1997	East	Baltimore	98	64	.605	Johnson	Baltimore 3, Seattle 1	Cleveland
	Central	Cleveland	86	75	.534	Hargrove	Cleveland 3, New York* 2	
	West	Seattle	90	72	.556	Piniella	Cleveland 4, Baltimore 2	
1998	East	New York	114	48	.704	Torre	New York 3, Texas 0	New York
	Central	Cleveland	89	73	.549	Hargrove	Cleveland 3, Boston* 1	
	West	Texas	88	74	.543	Oates	New York 4, Cleveland 2	
1999	East	New York	98	64	.605	Torre	New York 3, Texas 0	New York
	Central	Cleveland	97	65	.599	Hargrove	Boston* 3, Cleveland 2	
	West	Texas	95	67	.586	Oates	New York 4, Boston* 1	
2000	East	New York	87	74	.540	Torre	New York 3, Oakland 2	New York
	Central	Chicago	95	67	.586	Manuel	Seattle* 3, Chicago 0	
	West	Oakland	91	70	.565	Howe	New York 4, Seattle* 2	
2001	East	New York	95	65	.594	Torre	Seattle 3, Cleveland 2	New York
	Central	Cleveland	91	71	.562	Manuel	New York 3, Oakland* 2	
	West	Seattle	116	46	.716	Piniella	New York 4, Seattle 1	
2002	East	New York	103	58	.640	Torre	Anaheim* 3, New York 1	Anaheim*
	Central	Minnesota	94	67	.584	Gardenhire	Minnesota 3, Oakland 2	(Scioscia)
	West	Oakland	103	59	.636	Howe	Anaheim* 4, Minnesota 1	
2003	East	New York	101	61	.623	Torre	New York 3, Minnesota 1	New York
	Central	Minnesota	90	72	.556	Gardenhire	Boston* 3, Oakland 2	
	West	Oakland	96	66	.593	Macha	New York 4, Boston* 3	
2004	East	New York	101	61	.623	Torre	New York 3, Minnesota 1	Boston*
	Central	Minnesota	92	70	.568	Gardenhire	Boston* 3, Anaheim 0	(Francona)
	West	Anaheim	92	70	.568	Scioscia	Boston* 4, New York 3	
2005	East	New York	95	67	.586	Torre	Chicago 3, Boston* 0	Chicago
	Central	Chicago	99	63	.611	Guillen	Los Angeles 3, New York 2	
	West	Los Angeles	95	67	.586	Scioscia	Chicago 4, Los Angeles 1	
2006	East	New York	97	65	.599	Torre	Oakland 3, Minnesota 0	Detroit*
	Central	Minnesota	96	66	.593	Gardenhire	Detroit* 3, New York 1	(Leyland)
	West	Oakland	93	69	.574	Macha	Detroit* 4, Oakland 0	
2007	East	Boston	96	66	.593	Francona	Boston 3, Los Angeles 0	Boston
	Central	Cleveland	96	66	.593	Wedge	Cleveland 3, New York* 1	
	West	Los Angeles	94	68	.580	Scioscia	Boston 4, Cleveland 3	
2008	East	Tampa Bay	97	65	.599	Maddon	Tampa Bay 3, Chicago 1	Tampa Bay
	Central	Chicago	89	74	.546	Guillen	Boston* 3, Los Angeles 1	
	West	Los Angeles	100	62	.617	Scioscia	Tampa Bay 4, Boston* 3	
2009	East	New York	103	59	.636	Girardi	New York 3, Minnesota 0	New York
	Central	Minnesota	87	76	.534	Gardenhire	Los Angeles 3, Boston* 0	
	West	Los Angeles	97	65	.599	Scioscia	New York 4, Los Angeles 2	
2010	East	Tampa Bay	96	66	.593	Maddon	New York* 3, Minnesota 0	Texas
	Central	Minnesota	94	68	.580	Gardenhire	Texas 3, Tampa Bay 2	
	West	Texas	90	72	.556	Washington	Texas 4, New York* 2	
2011	East	New York	97	65	.599	Girardi	Detroit 3, New York 2	Texas
	Central	Detroit	95	67	.586	Leyland	Texas 3, Tampa Bay* 1	
	West	Texas	96	66	.593	Washington	Texas 4, Detroit 2	
2012	East	New York	95	67	.586	Girardi	#Baltimore* 5, Texas* 1	Detroit
	Central	Detroit	88	74	.543	Leyland	New York 3, Baltimore* 2	
	West	Oakland	94	68	.580	Melvin	Detroit 3, Oakland 2 / Detroit 4, New York 0	
2013	East	Boston	97	65	.599	Farrell	#Tampa Bay* 4, Cleveland* 0	Boston
	Central	Detroit	93	69	.574	Leyland	Boston 3, Tampa Bay* 1	
	West	Oakland	96	66	.593	Melvin	Detroit 3, Oakland 2 / Boston 4, Detroit 2	

*Wild card team. If pennant winner is wild card team, manager's name is given in parentheses. #Single-game wild card playoff (debuted in 2012). (a) First half. (b) Second half. (c) Montréal, L.A., NY Yankees, and Oakland won the divisional playoffs. (d) In Aug. 1994, a players' strike began that caused the cancellation of the remainder of the season, the playoffs, and the World Series. Teams listed as division "winners" for 1994 were leading their divisions at the time of the strike.

World Series Results, 1903-2013

1903 Boston AL 5, Pittsburgh NL 3	1940 Cincinnati NL 4, Detroit AL 3	1977 New York AL 4, Los Angeles NL 2
1904 No series	1941 New York AL 4, Brooklyn NL 1	1978 New York AL 4, Los Angeles NL 2
1905 New York NL 4, Philadelphia AL 1	1942 St. Louis NL 4, New York AL 1	1979 Pittsburgh NL 4, Baltimore AL 3
1906 Chicago AL 4, Chicago NL 2	1943 New York AL 4, St. Louis NL 1	1980 Philadelphia NL 4, Kansas City AL 2
1907 Chicago NL 4, Detroit AL 0, 1 tie	1944 St. Louis NL 4, St. Louis AL 2	1981 Los Angeles NL 4, New York AL 2
1908 Chicago NL 4, Detroit AL 1	1945 Detroit AL 4, Chicago NL 3	1982 St. Louis NL 4, Milwaukee AL 3
1909 Pittsburgh NL 4, Detroit AL 3	1946 St. Louis NL 4, Boston AL 3	1983 Baltimore AL 4, Philadelphia NL 1
1910 Philadelphia AL 4, Chicago NL 1	1947 New York AL 4, Brooklyn NL 3	1984 Detroit AL 4, San Diego NL 1
1911 Philadelphia AL 4, New York NL 2	1948 Cleveland AL 4, Boston NL 2	1985 Kansas City AL 4, St. Louis NL 3
1912 Boston AL 4, New York NL 3, 1 tie	1949 New York AL 4, Brooklyn NL 1	1986 New York NL 4, Boston AL 3
1913 Philadelphia AL 4, New York NL 1	1950 New York AL 4, Philadelphia NL 0	1987 Minnesota AL 4, St. Louis NL 3
1914 Boston NL 4, Philadelphia AL 0	1951 New York AL 4, New York NL 2	1988 Los Angeles NL 4, Oakland AL 1
1915 Boston AL 4, Philadelphia NL 1	1952 New York AL 4, Brooklyn NL 3	1989 Oakland AL 4, San Francisco NL 0
1916 Boston AL 4, Brooklyn NL 1	1953 New York AL 4, Brooklyn NL 2	1990 Cincinnati NL 4, Oakland AL 0
1917 Chicago AL 4, New York NL 2	1954 New York NL 4, Cleveland AL 0	1991 Minnesota AL 4, Atlanta NL 3
1918 Boston AL 4, Chicago NL 2	1955 Brooklyn NL 4, New York AL 3	1992 Toronto AL 4, Atlanta NL 2
1919 Cincinnati NL 5, Chicago AL 3	1956 New York AL 4, Brooklyn NL 3	1993 Toronto AL 4, Philadelphia NL 2
1920 Cleveland AL 5, Brooklyn NL 2	1957 Milwaukee NL 4, New York AL 3	1994 No series due to strike
1921 New York NL 5, New York AL 3	1958 New York AL 4, Milwaukee NL 3	1995 Atlanta NL 4, Cleveland AL 2
1922 New York NL 4, New York AL 0, 1 tie	1959 Los Angeles NL 4, Chicago AL 2	1996 New York AL 4, Atlanta NL 2
1923 New York AL 4, New York NL 2	1960 Pittsburgh NL 4, New York AL 3	1997 Florida NL 4, Cleveland AL 3
1924 Washington AL 4, New York NL 3	1961 New York AL 4, Cincinnati NL 1	1998 New York AL 4, San Diego NL 0
1925 Pittsburgh NL 4, Washington AL 3	1962 New York AL 4, San Francisco NL 3	1999 New York AL 4, Atlanta NL 0
1926 St. Louis NL 4, New York AL 3	1963 Los Angeles NL 4, New York AL 0	2000 New York AL 4, New York NL 1
1927 New York AL 4, Pittsburgh NL 0	1964 St. Louis NL 4, New York AL 3	2001 Arizona NL 4, New York AL 3
1928 New York AL 4, St. Louis NL 0	1965 Los Angeles NL 4, Minnesota AL 3	2002 Anaheim AL 4, San Francisco NL 3
1929 Philadelphia AL 4, Chicago NL 1	1966 Baltimore AL 4, Los Angeles NL 0	2003 Florida NL 4, New York AL 2
1930 Philadelphia AL 4, St. Louis NL 2	1967 St. Louis NL 4, Boston AL 3	2004 Boston AL 4, St. Louis NL 0
1931 St. Louis NL 4, Philadelphia AL 3	1968 Detroit AL 4, St. Louis NL 3	2005 Chicago AL 4, Houston NL 0
1932 New York AL 4, Chicago NL 0	1969 New York NL 4, Baltimore AL 1	2006 St. Louis NL 4, Detroit AL 1
1933 New York NL 4, Washington AL 1	1970 Baltimore AL 4, Cincinnati NL 1	2007 Boston AL 4, Colorado NL 0
1934 St. Louis NL 4, Detroit AL 3	1971 Pittsburgh NL 4, Baltimore AL 3	2008 Philadelphia NL 4, Tampa Bay AL 1
1935 Detroit AL 4, Chicago NL 2	1972 Oakland AL 4, Cincinnati NL 3	2009 New York AL 4, Philadelphia NL 2
1936 New York AL 4, New York NL 2	1973 Oakland AL 4, New York NL 3	2010 San Francisco NL 4, Texas AL 1
1937 New York AL 4, New York NL 1	1974 Oakland AL 4, Los Angeles NL 1	2011 St. Louis NL 4, Texas AL 3
1938 New York AL 4, Chicago NL 0	1975 Cincinnati NL 4, Boston AL 3	2012 San Francisco NL 4, Detroit AL 0
1939 New York AL 4, Cincinnati NL 0	1976 Cincinnati NL 4, New York AL 0	2013 Boston AL 4, St. Louis NL 2

World Series Most Valuable Player, 1955-2013

Year	Player, position, team	Year	Player, position, team	Year	Player, position, team
1955	Johnny Podres, P, Brooklyn	1976	Johnny Bench, C, Cincinnati	1995	Tom Glavine, P, Atlanta
1956	Don Larsen, P, NY (AL)	1977	Reggie Jackson, OF, NY (AL)	1996	John Wetteland, P, NY (AL)
1957	Lew Burdette, P, Milwaukee (NL)	1978	Bucky Dent, SS, NY (AL)	1997	Livan Hernandez, P, Florida
1958	Bob Turley, P, NY (AL)	1979	Willie Stargell, 1B, Pittsburgh	1998	Scott Brosius, 3B, NY (AL)
1959	Larry Sherry, P, Los Angeles (NL)	1980	Mike Schmidt, 3B, Philadelphia	1999	Mariano Rivera, P, NY (AL)
1960[1]	Bobby Richardson, 2B, NY (AL)	1981	Ron Cey, 3B, Los Angeles (NL);	2000	Derek Jeter, SS, NY (AL)
1961	Whitey Ford, P, NY (AL)		Pedro Guerrero, OF, Los Angeles;	2001	Curt Schilling, P, Arizona;
1962	Ralph Terry, P, NY (AL)		Steve Yeager, C, Los Angeles		Randy Johnson, P, Arizona
1963	Sandy Koufax, P, Los Angeles (NL)	1982	Darrell Porter, C, St. Louis	2002	Troy Glaus, 3B, Anaheim
1964	Bob Gibson, P, St. Louis	1983	Rick Dempsey, C, Baltimore	2003	Josh Beckett, P, Florida
1965	Sandy Koufax, P, Los Angeles (NL)	1984	Alan Trammell, SS, Detroit	2004	Manny Ramirez, OF, Boston
1966	Frank Robinson, OF, Baltimore	1985	Bret Saberhagen, P, Kansas City	2005	Jermaine Dye, OF, Chicago (AL)
1967	Bob Gibson, P, St. Louis	1986	Ray Knight, 3B, NY (NL)	2006	David Eckstein, SS, St. Louis
1968	Mickey Lolich, P, Detroit	1987	Frank Viola, P, Minnesota	2007	Mike Lowell, 3B, Boston
1969	Donn Clendenon, 1B, NY (NL)	1988	Orel Hershiser, P, Los Angeles (NL)	2008	Cole Hamels, P, Philadelphia
1970	Brooks Robinson, 3B, Baltimore	1989	Dave Stewart, P, Oakland	2009	Hideki Matsui, DH, NY (AL)
1971	Roberto Clemente, OF, Pittsburgh	1990	Jose Rijo, P, Cincinnati	2010	Edgar Renteria, SS, San Francisco
1972	Gene Tenace, C, Oakland	1991	Jack Morris, P, Minnesota	2011	David Freese, 3B, St. Louis
1973	Reggie Jackson, OF, Oakland	1992	Pat Borders, C, Toronto	2012	Pablo Sandoval, 3B, San Francisco
1974	Rollie Fingers, P, Oakland	1993	Paul Molitor, DH, Toronto	2013	David Ortiz, DH, Boston
1975	Pete Rose, 3B, Cincinnati	1994	No series due to strike		

(1) Richardson won the MVP although Pittsburgh beat New York.

World Series Won-Lost Records, by Franchise

Since beginning of "modern" era in 1901. Figures represent overall Series wins, not individual games.

Team	Wins	Losses	Team	Wins	Losses
New York Yankees	27	13	Toronto Blue Jays	2	0
St. Louis Cardinals	11	8	New York Mets	2	2
Philadelphia/Kansas City/Oakland A's	9	5	Cleveland Indians	2	3
Boston Red Sox	8	4	Philadelphia Phillies	2	5
New York/San Francisco Giants	7	12	Chicago Cubs	2	8
Brooklyn/Los Angeles Dodgers	6	12	L.A./California/Anaheim/L.A. Angels	1	0
Pittsburgh Pirates	5	2	Arizona Diamondbacks	1	0
Cincinnati Reds	5	4	Kansas City Royals	1	1
Detroit Tigers	4	7	Houston Astros	0	1
Chicago White Sox	3	2	Seattle Pilots/Milwaukee Brewers	0	1
Washington Senators/Minnesota Twins	3	3	Tampa Bay Rays	0	1
St. Louis Browns/Baltimore Orioles	3	4	Colorado Rockies	0	1
Boston/Milwaukee/Atlanta Braves	3	6	San Diego Padres	0	2
Florida Marlins	2	0	Texas Rangers	0	2

All-Time World Series Career Leaders
(through 2013)

Batting Leaders

Batter (min. 50 PA)	H	AB	AVG	Batter (min. 50 PA)	H	AB	AVG
1. David Ortiz	20	44	.455	6. Lou Brock	34	87	.391
2. Johnny "Pepper" Martin	23	55	.418	7. Marquis Grissom	30	77	.390
3. Paul Molitor	23	55	.418	8. Thurman Munson	25	67	.373
4. Lance Berkman	16	39	.410	9. George Brett	19	51	.373
5. Hal McRae	18	45	.400	10. Hank Aaron	20	55	.364

Games Played

Yogi Berra	75
Mickey Mantle	65
Elston Howard	54
Hank Bauer	53
Gil McDougald	53
Phil Rizzuto	52
Joe DiMaggio	51
Frankie Frisch	50
Pee Wee Reese	44
Roger Maris	41
Babe Ruth	41

Runs Batted In

Mickey Mantle	40
Yogi Berra	39
Lou Gehrig	35
Babe Ruth	33
Joe DiMaggio	30
Bill Skowron	29
Duke Snider	26
Hank Bauer	24
Bill Dickey	24
Reggie Jackson	24
Gil McDougald	24

Hits

Yogi Berra	71
Mickey Mantle	59
Frankie Frisch	58
Joe DiMaggio	54
Derek Jeter	50
Hank Bauer	46
Pee Wee Reese	46
Gil McDougald	45
Phil Rizzuto	45
Lou Gehrig	43

Home Runs

Mickey Mantle	18
Babe Ruth	15
Yogi Berra	12
Duke Snider	11
Lou Gehrig	10
Reggie Jackson	10
Joe DiMaggio	8
Frank Robinson	8
Bill Skowron	8
Hank Bauer	7
Goose Goslin	7
Gil McDougald	7
Chase Utley	7

Runs

Mickey Mantle	42
Yogi Berra	41
Babe Ruth	37
Derek Jeter	32
Lou Gehrig	30
Joe DiMaggio	27
Roger Maris	26
Elston Howard	25
Gil McDougald	23
Jackie Robinson	22

Stolen Bases

Lou Brock	14
Eddie Collins	14
Frank Chance	10
Dave Lopes	10
Phil Rizzuto	10
Frankie Frisch	9
Kenny Lofton	9
Honus Wagner	9
Johnny Evers	8
Roberto Alomar	7
Rickey Henderson	7
Pepper Martin	7
Joe Morgan	7
Joe Tinker	7

Pitching Leaders

Games Pitched

Mariano Rivera	24
Whitey Ford	22
Mike Stanton	20
Rollie Fingers	16
Jeff Nelson	16
Allie Reynolds	15
Bob Turley	15
Clay Carroll	14
Clem Labine	13
Andy Pettitte	13
Mark Wohlers	13
Waite Hoyt	12
Catfish Hunter	12
Art Nehf	12

Wins

Whitey Ford	10
Bob Gibson	7
Allie Reynolds	7
Red Ruffing	7
Chief Bender	6
Lefty Gomez	6
Waite Hoyt	6
Three Finger Brown	5
Jack Coombs	5
Catfish Hunter	5
Christy Mathewson	5
Herb Pennock	5
Andy Pettitte	5
Vic Raschi	5

Strikeouts

Whitey Ford	94
Bob Gibson	92
Allie Reynolds	62
Sandy Koufax	61
Red Ruffing	61
Chief Bender	59
George Earnshaw	56
Andy Pettitte	56
John Smoltz	52
Roger Clemens	49
Waite Hoyt	49
Christy Mathewson	48
Bob Turley	46

Saves

Mariano Rivera	11
Rollie Fingers	6
Johnny Murphy	4
Robb Nen	4
Allie Reynolds	4
John Wetteland	4
Roy Face	3
Neftali Feliz	3
Firpo Marberry	3
Will McEnaney	3
Tug McGraw	3
Jonathan Papelbon	3
Herb Pennock	3
Troy Percival	3
Sergio Romo	3
Kent Tekulve	3
Todd Worrell	3

All-Star Baseball Games, 1933-2013

Year	Winner, score	Host team	Year	Winner, score	Host team	Year	Winner, score	Host team
1933*	American, 4-2	Chicago (AL)	1960*	National, 6-0	New York (AL)	1986	American, 3-2	Houston
1934*	American, 9-7	New York (NL)	1961*	National, 5-4[3]	San Francisco	1987	National, 2-0[5]	Oakland
1935*	American, 4-1	Cleveland	1961*	Called—rain, 1-1	Boston	1988	American, 2-1	Cincinnati
1936*	National, 4-3	Boston (NL)	1962*	National, 3-1[3]	Washington	1989	American, 5-3	California
1937*	American, 8-3	Washington	1962*	American, 9-4	Chicago (NL)	1990	American, 2-0	Chicago (NL)
1938*	National, 4-1	Cincinnati	1963*	National, 5-3	Cleveland	1991	American, 4-2	Toronto
1939*	American, 3-1	New York (AL)	1964*	National, 7-4	New York (NL)	1992	American, 13-6	San Diego
1940*	National, 4-0	St. Louis (NL)	1965*	National, 6-5	Minnesota	1993	American, 9-3	Baltimore
1941*	American, 7-5	Detroit	1966*	National, 2-1[3]	St. Louis	1994	National, 8-7[3]	Pittsburgh
1942*	American, 3-1	New York (NL)	1967*	National, 2-1[4]	California	1995	National, 3-2	Texas
1943*	American, 5-3	Philadelphia (AL)	1968*	National, 1-0	Houston	1996	National, 6-0	Philadelphia
1944*	National, 7-1	Pittsburgh	1969*	National, 9-3	Washington	1997	American, 3-1	Cleveland
1945	Not played		1970*	National, 5-4[2]	Cincinnati	1998	American, 13-8	Colorado
1946*	American, 12-0	Boston (AL)	1971*	American, 6-4	Detroit	1999	American, 4-1	Boston
1947*	American, 2-1	Chicago (NL)	1972*	National, 4-3[3]	Atlanta	2000	American, 6-3	Atlanta
1948*	American, 5-2	St. Louis (AL)	1973*	National, 7-1	Kansas City	2001	American, 4-1	Seattle
1949*	American, 11-7	Brooklyn	1974*	National, 7-2	Pittsburgh	2002	Tie, 7-7[6]	Milwaukee
1950*	National, 4-3[1]	Chicago (AL)	1975	National, 6-3	Milwaukee	2003	American, 7-6[7]	Chicago (AL)
1951*	National, 8-3	Detroit	1976	National, 7-1	Philadelphia	2004	American, 9-4	Houston
1952*	National, 3-2	Philadelphia (NL)	1977	National, 7-5	New York (AL)	2005	American, 7-5	Detroit
1953*	National, 5-1	Cincinnati	1978	National, 7-3	San Diego	2006	American, 3-2	Pittsburgh
1954*	American, 11-9	Cleveland	1979	National, 7-6	Seattle	2007	American, 5-4	San Francisco
1955*	National, 6-5[2]	Milwaukee	1980	National, 4-2	Los Angeles (NL)	2008	American, 4-3[4]	New York (AL)
1956*	National, 7-3	Washington	1981	National, 5-4	Cleveland	2009	American, 4-3	St. Louis
1957*	American, 6-5	St. Louis	1982	National, 4-1	Montréal	2010	National, 3-1	Los Angeles (AL)
1958*	American, 4-3	Baltimore	1983	American, 13-3	Chicago (AL)	2011	National, 5-1	Arizona
1959*	National, 5-4	Pittsburgh	1984	National, 3-1	San Francisco	2012	National, 8-0	Kansas City
1959*	American, 5-3	Los Angeles (NL)	1985	National, 6-1	Minnesota	2013	American, 3-0	New York (NL)
1960*	National, 5-3	Kansas City						

*Day game. Note: Two all-star games played 1959-62 to help increase players' pension fund. (1) 14 innings. (2) 12 innings. (3) 10 innings. (4) 15 innings. (5) 13 innings. (6) Commissioner's decision—game called in 11th inning when both teams ran out of pitchers. (7) Under rule change beginning in 2003, league winning All-Star game earned World Series home-field advantage.

Baseball Stadiums

Team	Stadium (year opened)	Surface	LF	Center	RF	Seating capacity[1]
Arizona Diamondbacks	Chase Field (1998)	Grass	330	407	335	48,635
Atlanta Braves	Turner Field (1997)	Grass	335	400	330	49,586
Chicago Cubs	Wrigley Field (1914)	Grass	355	400	353	41,019
Cincinnati Reds	Great American Ball Park (2003)	Grass	328	404	325	42,319
Colorado Rockies	Coors Field (1995)	Grass	347	415	350	50,480
Los Angeles Dodgers	Dodger Stadium (1962)	Grass	330	395	330	56,000
Miami Marlins	Marlins Park (2012)	Grass	344	420	335	37,442
Milwaukee Brewers	Miller Park (2001)	Grass	344	400	345	41,900
New York Mets	Citi Field (2009)	Grass	335	408	330	41,922
Philadelphia Phillies	Citizens Bank Park (2004)	Grass	329	401	330	43,651
Pittsburgh Pirates	PNC Park at North Shore (2001)	Grass	325	399	320	38,362
St. Louis Cardinals	Busch Stadium (2006)	Grass	336	400	335	43,975
San Diego Padres	Petco Park (2004)	Grass	336	396	322	42,524
San Francisco Giants	AT&T Park (2000)	Grass	339	399	309	41,915
Washington Nationals	Nationals Park (2008)	Grass	336	402	335	41,418
Baltimore Orioles	Oriole Park at Camden Yards (1992)	Grass	333	400	318	45,971
Boston Red Sox	Fenway Park (1912)	Grass	310	390	302	37,071[2]
Chicago White Sox	U.S. Cellular Field (1991)	Grass	330	400	335	40,615
Cleveland Indians	Progressive Field (1994)	Grass	325	405	325	42,241
Detroit Tigers	Comerica Park (2000)	Grass	345	420	330	41,255
Houston Astros	Minute Maid Park (2000)	Grass	315	435	326	40,963
Kansas City Royals	Kauffman Stadium (1973)	Grass	330	410	330	37,903
Los Angeles Angels	Angel Stadium of Anaheim (1966)	Grass	365	400	365	45,483
Minnesota Twins	Target Field (2010)	Grass	339	404	328	39,021
New York Yankees	Yankee Stadium (2009)	Grass	318	408	314	50,291
Oakland Athletics	O.co Coliseum (1968)	Grass	330	400	330	35,067
Seattle Mariners	Safeco Field (1999)	Grass	331	401	326	47,476
Tampa Bay Rays	Tropicana Field (1990)	Astroturf	315	404	322	34,078
Texas Rangers	Rangers Ballpark in Arlington (1994)	Grass	332	400	325	48,114
Toronto Blue Jays	Rogers Centre (1989)	Astroturf	328	400	328	49,282

(1) As of 2013 season. (2) For day games; night game capacity is 37,499.

Major League Franchise Shifts and Additions

1953: Boston Braves (NL) became Milwaukee Braves.
1954: St. Louis Browns (AL) became Baltimore Orioles.
1955: Philadelphia Athletics (AL) became Kansas City Athletics.
1958: New York Giants (NL) became San Francisco Giants.
1958: Brooklyn Dodgers (NL) became L.A. Dodgers.
1961: Washington Senators (AL) became Minnesota Twins.
1961: L.A. Angels enfranchised by the AL.
1961: Washington Senators enfranchised by the AL, replacing the former Washington club, whose franchise moved to Minneapolis-St. Paul.
1962: Houston Colt .45's enfranchised by the NL.
1962: New York Mets enfranchised by the NL.
1966: Milwaukee Braves (NL) became Atlanta Braves.
1968: Kansas City Athletics (AL) became Oakland Athletics.

1969: Kansas City Royals and Seattle Pilots enfranchised by the AL; Montréal Expos and San Diego Padres enfranchised by the NL.
1970: Seattle Pilots (AL) became Milwaukee Brewers.
1971: Washington Senators (AL) became Texas Rangers (Dallas-Fort Worth area).
1977: Toronto Blue Jays and Seattle Mariners enfranchised by the AL.
1993: Colorado Rockies (Denver) and Florida Marlins (Miami) enfranchised by the NL.
1998: Tampa Bay Devil Rays began play in the AL; Arizona Diamondbacks (Phoenix) began play in the NL (both teams enfranchised in 1995). Milwaukee Brewers moved from the AL to the NL.
2005: Montréal Expos (NL) became Washington Nationals.
2013: Houston Astros moved from the NL to the AL.

Little League World Series, 1947-2013

The Little League World Series is played annually in Williamsport, PA.

Year	Winning team; opponent	Score	Year	Winning team; opponent	Score
1947	Williamsport, PA; Lock Haven, PA	16-7	1981	Taiwan; Tampa, FL	4-2
1948	Lock Haven, PA; St. Petersburg, FL	6-5	1982	Kirkland, WA; Taiwan	6-0
1949	Hammonton, NJ; Pensacola, FL	5-0	1983	Marietta, GA; Dominican Republic	3-1
1950	Houston, TX; Bridgeport, CT	2-1	1984	South Korea; Altamonte Springs, FL	6-2
1951	Stamford, CT; Austin, TX	3-0	1985	South Korea; Mexico	7-1
1952	Norwalk, CT; Monongahela, PA	4-3	1986	Taiwan; Tucson, AZ	12-0
1953	Birmingham, AL; Schenectady, NY	1-0	1987	Taiwan; Irvine, CA	21-1
1954	Schenectady, NY; Colton, CA	7-5	1988	Taiwan; Pearl City, HI	10-0
1955	Morrisville, PA; Merchantville, NJ	4-3	1989	Trumbull, CT; Chinese Taipei	5-2
1956	Roswell, NM; Delaware, NJ	3-1	1990	Taiwan; Shippensburg, PA	9-0
1957	Mexico; La Mesa, CA	4-0	1991	Taiwan; Danville, CA	11-0
1958	Mexico; Kankakee, IL	10-1	1992	Long Beach, CA; Philippines	6-0[1]
1959	Hamtramck, MI; Auburn, CA	12-0	1993	Long Beach, CA; Panama	3-2
1960	Levittown, PA; Ft. Worth, TX	5-0	1994	Venezuela; Northridge, CA	4-3
1961	El Cajon, CA; El Campo, TX	4-2	1995	Taiwan; Spring, TX	17-3
1962	San Jose, CA; Kankakee, IL	3-0	1996	Taiwan; Cranston, RI	13-3
1963	Granada Hills, CA; Stratford, CT	2-1	1997	Mexico; Mission Viejo, CA	5-4
1964	Staten Island, NY; Mexico	4-0	1998	Toms River, NJ; Japan	12-9
1965	Windsor Locks, CT; Ontario, Canada	3-1	1999	Japan; Phenix City, AL	5-0
1966	Houston, TX; W. New York, NJ	8-2	2000	Venezuela; Bellaire, TX	3-2
1967	Tokyo; Chicago, IL	4-1	2001	Japan; Apopka, FL	2-1
1968	Osaka, Japan; Richmond, VA	1-0	2002	Louisville, KY; Japan	1-0
1969	Taiwan; Santa Clara, CA	5-0	2003	Tokyo, Japan; East Boynton Beach, FL	10-1
1970	Wayne, NJ; Campbell, CA	2-0	2004	Curaçao; Conejo Valley of Thousand Oaks, CA	5-2
1971	Taiwan; Gary, IN	12-3	2005	Ewa Beach, HI; Curaçao, Neth. Antilles	7-6
1972	Taiwan; Hammond, IN	6-0	2006	Columbus, GA; Kawaguchi City, Japan	2-1
1973	Taiwan; Tucson, AZ	12-0	2007	Macon, GA; Tokyo, Japan	3-2
1974	Taiwan; Red Bluff, CA	12-1	2008	Waipahu, HI; Mexico	12-3
1975	Lakewood, NJ; Tampa, FL	4-3	2009	Chula Vista, CA; Taiwan	6-3
1976	Tokyo, Japan; Campbell, CA	10-3	2010	Tokyo, Japan; Waipahu, HI	4-1
1977	Taiwan; El Cajon, CA	7-2	2011	Huntington Beach, CA; Hamamatsu, Japan	2-1
1978	Taiwan; Danville, CA	11-1	2012	Tokyo, Japan; Goodlettsville, TN	12-2
1979	Taiwan; Campbell, CA	2-1	2013	Tokyo, Japan; Chula Vista, CA	6-4
1980	Taiwan; Tampa, FL	4-3			

(1) Philippines won 15-4 but was disqualified for using ineligible players. Long Beach was awarded title by forfeit 6-0 (1 run per inning).

Manager of the Year, 1983-2012

1983	(NL) Tommy Lasorda, L.A.	1993	(NL) Dusty Baker, San Francisco	2003	(NL) Jack McKeon, Florida
	(AL) Tony La Russa, Chicago		(AL) Gene Lamont, Chicago		(AL) Tony Pena, Kansas City
1984	(NL) Jim Frey, Chicago	1994	(NL) Felipe Alou, Montréal	2004	(NL) Bobby Cox, Atlanta
	(AL) Sparky Anderson, Detroit		(AL) Buck Showalter, NY		(AL) Buck Showalter, Texas
1985	(NL) Whitey Herzog, St. Louis	1995	(NL) Don Baylor, Colorado	2005	(NL) Bobby Cox, Atlanta
	(AL) Bobby Cox, Toronto		(AL) Lou Piniella, Seattle		(AL) Ozzie Guillen, Chicago
1986	(NL) Hal Lanier, Houston	1996	(NL) Bruce Bochy, San Diego	2006	(NL) Joe Girardi, Florida
	(AL) John McNamara, Boston		(AL) (tie) Joe Torre, NY;		(AL) Jim Leyland, Detroit
1987	(NL) Buck Rodgers, Montréal		Johnny Oates, Texas	2007	(NL) Bob Melvin, Arizona
	(AL) Sparky Anderson, Detroit	1997	(NL) Dusty Baker, San Francisco		(AL) Eric Wedge, Cleveland
1988	(NL) Tommy Lasorda, L.A.		(AL) Davey Johnson, Baltimore	2008	(NL) Lou Piniella, Chicago
	(AL) Tony La Russa, Oakland	1998	(NL) Larry Dierker, Houston		(AL) Joe Maddon, Tampa Bay
1989	(NL) Don Zimmer, Chicago		(AL) Joe Torre, NY	2009	(NL) Jim Tracy, Colorado
	(AL) Frank Robinson, Baltimore	1999	(NL) Jack McKeon, Cincinnati		(AL) Mike Scioscia, L.A.
1990	(NL) Jim Leyland, Pittsburgh		(AL) Jimy Williams, Boston	2010	(NL) Bud Black, San Diego
	(AL) Jeff Torborg, Chicago	2000	(NL) Dusty Baker, San Francisco		(AL) Ron Gardenhire, Minnesota
1991	(NL) Bobby Cox, Atlanta		(AL) Jerry Manuel, Chicago	2011	(NL) Kirk Gibson, Arizona
	(AL) Tom Kelly, Minnesota	2001	(NL) Larry Bowa, Philadelphia		(AL) Joe Maddon, Tampa Bay
1992	(NL) Jim Leyland, Pittsburgh		(AL) Lou Piniella, Seattle	2012	(NL) Davey Johnson, Washington
	(AL) Tony La Russa, Oakland	2002	(NL) Tony La Russa, St. Louis		(AL) Bob Melvin, Oakland
			(AL) Mike Scioscia, Anaheim		

National Baseball Hall of Fame and Museum, Cooperstown, NY

Player must generally be retired for five complete seasons before being eligible. Babe Ruth (1936), Lou Gehrig (1939), Joe DiMaggio (1955), and Roberto Clemente (1973) were inducted in fewer than five years. # = Players chosen in first year of eligibility or under special circumstances earlier. * = 2013 inductee.

#Aaron, Hank	Crawford, Sam	Heilmann, Harry	#Mays, Willie	Selee, Frank
Alexander, Grover	Cronin, Joe	#Henderson, Rickey	Mazeroski, Bill	Sewell, Joe
Cleveland "Old Pete"	Cummings, W. A.	Herman, Billy	McCarthy, Joe	Simmons, Al
Alomar, Roberto	"Candy"	Herzog, Whitey	McCarthy, Thomas	Sisler, George
Alston, Walt	Cuyler, Hazen "Kiki"	Hill, Pete	#McCovey, Willie	Slaughter, Enos
Anderson, George	Dandridge, Ray	Hooper, Harry	McGinnity, Joe	Smith, Hilton
Anson, Cap	Davis, George	Hornsby, Rogers	McGowan, Bill	#Smith, Ozzie
Aparicio, Luis	Dawson, Andre	Hoyt, Waite	McGraw, John	Snider, Duke
Appling, Luke	Day, Leon	Hubbard, Cal	McKechnie, Bill	Southworth, Billy
Ashburn, Richie	Dean, Jay Hanna "Dizzy"	Hubbell, Carl	McPhee, John "Bid"	#Spahn, Warren
Averill, Earl	Delahanty, Ed	Huggins, Miller	Medwick, Joe	Spalding, Albert
Baker, Frank "Home Run"	Dickey, Bill	Hulbert, William	Mendez, Jose	Speaker, Tris
Bancroft, Dave	Dihigo, Martín	Hunter, James "Catfish"	Miller, Jon	#Stargell, Willie
#Banks, Ernie	#DiMaggio, Joe	Irvin, Monte	Mize, Johnny	Stearnes, Norman
Barlick, Al	#Doby, Larry	#Jackson, Reggie	#Molitor, Paul	"Turkey"
Barrow, Edward G.	Doerr, Bobby	Jackson, Travis	#Morgan, Joe	Stengel, Casey
Beckley, Jake	Dreyfuss, Barney	Jenkins, Ferguson	#Murray, Eddie	Sutter, Bruce
Bell, James "Cool Papa"	Drysdale, Don	Jennings, Hugh	#Musial, Stan	Suttles, George "Mule"
#Bench, Johnny	Duffy, Hugh	Johnson, Byron "Ban"	Newhouser, Hal	Sutton, Don
Bender, Charles "Chief"	Durocher, Leo	Johnson, Walter[1]	Nichols, Kid	Taylor, Ben
Berra, Lawrence "Yogi"	#Eckersley, Dennis	Johnson, William "Judy"	Niekro, Phil	Terry, Bill
Blyleven, Bert	Evans, Billy	Joss, Addie	*O'Day, Hank	Thompson, Sam
#Boggs, Wade	Evers, John	#Kaline, Al	O'Malley, Walter	Tinker, Joe
Bottomley, Jim	Ewing, Buck	Keefe, Timothy	O'Rourke, James	Torriente, Cristobal
Boudreau, Lou	Faber, Urban "Red"	Keeler, William	Ott, Mel	Traynor, Harold J. "Pie"
Bresnahan, Roger	#Feller, Bob	Kell, George	Paige, Satchel	Vance, Arthur "Dazzy"
#Brett, George	Ferrell, Rick	Kelley, Joe	#Palmer, Jim	Vaughan, Joseph "Arky"
#Brock, Lou	Fingers, Rollie	Kelly, George	Pennock, Herb	Veeck, Bill
Brouthers, Dan	Fisk, Carlton	Kelly, King	Perez, Tony	Waddell, Rube
Brown, Mordecai	Flick, Elmer H.	Killebrew, Harmon	Perry, Gaylord	Wagner, Honus[1]
Brown, Ray	Ford, Whitey	Kiner, Ralph	Peters, Nick	Wallace, Roderick
Brown, Willard	Foster, Andrew "Rube"	Klein, Chuck	Plank, Ed	"Bobby"
Bulkeley, Morgan C.	Foster, Bill	Klem, Bill	Pompez, Alex	Walsh, Ed
Bunning, Jim	Fox, Nellie	#Koufax, Sandy	Posey, Cum(berland)	Waner, Lloyd
Burkett, Jesse C.	Foxx, Jimmie	Kubek, Tony	#Puckett, Kirby	Waner, Paul
Campanella, Roy	Frick, Ford	Kuhn, Bowie	Radbourn, Charlie	Ward, John
#Carew, Rod	Frisch, Frank	Lajoie, Napoleon	Reese, Pee Wee	Weaver, Earl
Carey, Max	Galvin, James "Pud"	Landis, Kenesaw M.	Rice, Jim	Weiss, George
#Carlton, Steve	#Gehrig, Lou	Larkin, Barry	Rice, Sam	Welch, Mickey
Carter, Gary	Gehringer, Charles	Lasorda, Tom	Rickey, Branch	Wells, Willie
Cartwright, Alexander	#Gibson, Bob	Lazzeri, Tony	#Ripken, Cal, Jr.	Wheat, Zach
Cepeda, Orlando	Gibson, Josh	Lemon, Bob	Rixey, Eppa	*White, Deacon
Chadwick, Henry	Giles, Warren	Leonard, Buck	Rizzuto, Phil "Scooter"	White, Sol
Chance, Frank	Gillick, Pat	Lindstrom, Fred	Roberts, Robin	Wilhelm, Hoyt
Chandler, Albert "Happy"	Gomez, Lefty	Lloyd, Pop	#Robinson, Brooks	Wilkinson, J. L.
Charleston, Oscar	Gordon, Joe	Lombardi, Ernie	#Robinson, Frank	Williams, Billy
Chesbro, John	Goslin, Leon "Goose"	Lopez, Al	#Robinson, Jackie	Williams, Dick
Chylak, Nestor	Gossage, Rich	Lyons, Ted	Robinson, Wilbert	Williams, Joe
Clarke, Fred	Grant, Frank	Mack, Connie	Rogan, Joe "Bullet"	"Smokey Joe"
Clarkson, John	Greenberg, Hank	Mackey, James "Biz"	Roush, Edd	#Williams, Ted
#Clemente, Roberto	Griffith, Clark	MacPhail, Larry	Ruffing, Red	Willis, Vic
Cobb, Ty[1]	Grimes, Burleigh	MacPhail, Lee	*Ruppert, Jacob	Wilson, Hack
Cochrane, Mickey	Grove, Lefty	Madden, Bill	Rusie, Amos	Wilson, Jud
Collins, Eddie	#Gwynn, Tony	Manley, Effa	#Ruth, Babe[1]	#Winfield, Dave
Collins, James	Hafey, Charles "Chick"	#Mantle, Mickey	#Ryan, Nolan	Wright, George
Combs, Earle	Haines, Jesse	Manush, Henry	Sandberg, Ryne	Wright, Harry
Comiskey, Charles A.	Hamilton, Bill	Maranville, Walter	Santo, Ron	Wynn, Early
Conlan, John "Jocko"	Hanlon, Ned	"Rabbit"	Santop, Louis	#Yastrzemski, Carl
Connolly, Thomas H.	Harridge, Will	Marichal, Juan	Schalk, Ray	Yawkey, Tom
Connor, Roger	Harris, Bucky	Marquard, Rube	#Schmidt, Mike	Young, Cy
Cooper, Andy	Hartnett, Gabby	Mathews, Eddie	Schoendienst, Red	Youngs, Ross
Coveleski, Stan	Harvey, Doug	Mathewson, Christy[1]	#Seaver, Tom	#Yount, Robin

(1) Player inducted in 1936, the year the Hall of Fame began.

BASKETBALL

King James and Miami Heat Reign for Second Straight Title in 2013

The Miami Heat won their second consecutive NBA championship with a 95-88 victory over the San Antonio Spurs in Game 7 at AmericanAirlines Arena in Miami, FL, on June 20, 2013. Two nights earlier, LeBron James scored a triple-double (32 points, 10 rebounds, and 11 assists) in a tense 103-100 overtime win in Game 6 in Miami to force a Game 7. He was named the NBA Finals MVP for the second straight year.

Oklahoma City (60-22) earned the top playoff seed in the West behind the offense of Kevin Durant and Russell Westbrook but could not overcome Westbrook's knee injury in the Thunder's first-round playoff series with Houston. Westbrook underwent knee surgery and the Thunder fell in the second round to Memphis. The Grizzlies won a franchise-record 56 games but were swept by San Antonio in the Western Conference finals.

New York's Carmelo Anthony won the NBA scoring title (28.7 ppg) and led the Knicks to their first division title since 1994. After 35 seasons in New Jersey, the Nets moved to the Barclays Center in Brooklyn, NY. They reached the playoffs for the time since 2007. Denver's George Karl won NBA Coach of the Year honors after guiding the Nuggets to a 57-25 season but was fired June 6, 2013, with one year left on his contract.

The eventful 2012-13 season began with NBA Commissioner David Stern's announcement in Oct. 2012 that he planned to step down in Feb. 2014. The New Orleans Hornets announced Jan. 24, 2013, that they would officially change their nickname and be known as the Pelicans at the end of the season. Twelve-year-veteran center Jason Collins announced Apr. 29 that he is gay; he was the first active player among the four major U.S. professional sports leagues to come out publicly. In May, the NBA rejected a bid to buy the Sacramento Kings and move the franchise to Seattle. The team was purchased May 31 by another group and will remain in Sacramento.

Final Standings, 2012-13

(playoff seeding in parentheses)

Eastern Conference

Atlantic Division	W	L	PCT	GB
New York Knicks (2)	54	28	.659	—
Brooklyn Nets (4)	49	33	.598	5
Boston Celtics (7)	41	40	.506	12.5
Philadelphia 76ers	34	48	.415	20
Toronto Raptors	34	48	.415	20

Central Division	W	L	PCT	GB
Indiana Pacers (3)	49	32	.605	—
Chicago Bulls (5)	45	37	.549	4.5
Milwaukee Bucks (8)	38	44	.463	11.5
Detroit Pistons	29	53	.354	20.5
Cleveland Cavaliers	24	58	.293	25.5

Southeast Division	W	L	PCT	GB
Miami Heat (1)	66	16	.805	—
Atlanta Hawks (6)	44	38	.537	22
Washington Wizards	29	53	.354	37
Charlotte Bobcats	21	61	.256	45
Orlando Magic	20	62	.244	46

Western Conference

Northwest Division	W	L	PCT	GB
Oklahoma City Thunder (1)	60	22	.732	—
Denver Nuggets (3)	57	25	.695	3
Utah Jazz	43	39	.524	17
Portland Trail Blazers	33	49	.402	27
Minnesota Timberwolves	31	51	.378	29

Pacific Division	W	L	PCT	GB
L.A. Clippers (4)	56	26	.683	—
Golden State Warriors (6)	47	35	.573	9
L.A. Lakers (7)	45	37	.549	11
Sacramento Kings	28	54	.341	28
Phoenix Suns	25	57	.305	31

Southwest Division	W	L	PCT	GB
San Antonio Spurs (2)	58	24	.707	—
Memphis Grizzlies (5)	56	26	.683	2
Houston Rockets (8)	45	37	.549	13
Dallas Mavericks	41	41	.500	17
New Orleans Hornets	27	55	.329	31

Note: Boston and Indiana played only 81 regular season games; the NBA canceled their scheduled Apr. 15 matchup at Boston's TD Garden due to the Boston Marathon bombing. The L.A. Lakers earned the no. 7 seed in the West over Houston due to a better conference record.

NBA Playoff Results, 2013

Eastern Conference

Miami defeated Milwaukee, 4 games to 0
Chicago defeated Brooklyn, 4 games to 3
Indiana defeated Atlanta, 4 games to 2
New York defeated Boston, 4 games to 2
Miami defeated Chicago, 4 games to 1
Indiana defeated New York, 4 games to 2
Miami defeated Indiana, 4 games to 3

Western Conference

Oklahoma City defeated Houston, 4 games to 2
Memphis defeated L.A. Clippers, 4 games to 2
Golden State defeated Denver, 4 games to 2
San Antonio defeated L.A. Lakers, 4 games to 0
Memphis defeated Oklahoma City, 4 games to 1
San Antonio defeated Golden State, 4 games to 2
San Antonio defeated Memphis, 4 games to 0

NBA Championship

Miami defeated San Antonio, 4 games to 3 (88-92, 103-84, 77-113, 109-93, 104-114, 103-100 [OT], 95-88)

NBA Regular Season Individual Highs, 2012-13

Minutes, game: 60, DeMar DeRozan, Toronto v. Utah, Nov. 12 (3 OT)

Points, game: 54, Stephen Curry, Golden State v. New York, Feb. 27

Field goals, game: 19; Al Jefferson, Utah v. Minnesota, Apr. 12; Dwyane Wade, Miami v. Sacramento, Feb. 26

Field goal attempts, game: 41, Kobe Bryant, L.A. Lakers v. Golden State, Dec. 22

3-pointers, game: 11; Stephen Curry, Golden State v. New York, Feb. 27; Deron Williams, Brooklyn v. Washington, Mar. 8

3-point attempts, game: 16, Deron Williams, Brooklyn v. Washington, Mar. 8

Free throws, game: 25, Dwight Howard, L.A. Lakers v. Orlando, Mar. 12

Free throw attempts, game: 39, Dwight Howard, L.A. Lakers v. Orlando, Mar. 12

Rebounds, game: 29, Nikola Vucevic, Orlando v. Miami, Dec. 31

Assists, game: 20; Rajon Rondo, Boston v. Philadelphia, Nov. 9; Rajon Rondo, Boston v. Toronto, Nov. 17

Steals, game: 8; Ricky Rubio, Minnesota v. Milwaukee, Apr. 3; Kemba Walker, Charlotte v. Dallas, Nov. 10

Blocks, game: 11; Joakim Noah, Chicago v. Philadelphia, Feb. 28; Roy Hibbert, Indiana v. New Orleans, Nov. 21

Minutes played, season: 3,167, Damian Lillard, Portland

Off. rebounds, season: 310, Zach Randolph, Memphis

Def. rebounds, season: 694, Dwight Howard, L.A. Lakers

Personal fouls, season: 301, Amir Johnson, Toronto

NBA Finals MVP, 1969-2013

Year	Player, team	Year	Player, team	Year	Player, team
1969	Jerry West, L.A. Lakers	1984	Larry Bird, Boston	1999	Tim Duncan, San Antonio
1970	Willis Reed, New York	1985	Kareem Abdul-Jabbar,	2000	Shaquille O'Neal, L.A. Lakers
1971	Lew Alcindor (Kareem Abdul-		L.A. Lakers	2001	Shaquille O'Neal, L.A. Lakers
	Jabbar), Milwaukee	1986	Larry Bird, Boston	2002	Shaquille O'Neal, L.A. Lakers
1972	Wilt Chamberlain, L.A. Lakers	1987	Magic Johnson, L.A. Lakers	2003	Tim Duncan, San Antonio
1973	Willis Reed, New York	1988	James Worthy, L.A. Lakers	2004	Chauncey Billups, Detroit
1974	John Havlicek, Boston	1989	Joe Dumars, Detroit	2005	Tim Duncan, San Antonio
1975	Rick Barry, Golden State	1990	Isiah Thomas, Detroit	2006	Dwyane Wade, Miami
1976	JoJo White, Boston	1991	Michael Jordan, Chicago	2007	Tony Parker, San Antonio
1977	Bill Walton, Portland	1992	Michael Jordan, Chicago	2008	Paul Pierce, Boston
1978	Wes Unseld, Washington	1993	Michael Jordan, Chicago	2009	Kobe Bryant, L.A. Lakers
1979	Dennis Johnson, Seattle	1994	Hakeem Olajuwon, Houston	2010	Kobe Bryant, L.A. Lakers
1980	Magic Johnson, L.A. Lakers	1995	Hakeem Olajuwon, Houston	2011	Dirk Nowitzki, Dallas
1981	Cedric Maxwell, Boston	1996	Michael Jordan, Chicago	2012	LeBron James, Miami
1982	Magic Johnson, L.A. Lakers	1997	Michael Jordan, Chicago	2013	LeBron James, Miami
1983	Moses Malone, Philadelphia	1998	Michael Jordan, Chicago		

NBA Finals All-Time Statistical Leaders

(At the end of the 2013 NBA Finals. * = Active in 2012-13 season. Minimum 10 games played.)

Scoring average leader	GP	FG	FT	PTS	AVG	Scoring average leader	GP	FG	FT	PTS	AVG
Rick Barry	10	138	87	363	36.3	Hakeem Olajuwon	17	187	91	467	27.5
Michael Jordan	35	438	258	1,176	33.6	Elgin Baylor	44	442	227	1,161	26.4
Jerry West	55	612	455	1,677	30.5	*Dwyane Wade	24	224	157	617	25.7
Shaquille O'Neal	30	349	185	865	28.8	Julius Erving	22	216	128	561	25.5
Bob Pettit	25	241	227	709	28.4	*Kobe Bryant	37	333	223	937	25.3

Games played		Rebounds		Assists	
Bill Russell	70	Bill Russell	1,718	Magic Johnson	584
Sam Jones	64	Wilt Chamberlain	862	Bob Cousy	400
Kareem Abdul-Jabbar	56	Elgin Baylor	593	Bill Russell	315
Jerry West	55	Kareem Abdul-Jabbar	507	Jerry West	306
Tom Heinsohn	52	Tom Heinsohn	473	Dennis Johnson	228

NBA Scoring Leaders, 1947-2013

Year	Player, team	PTS	AVG	Year	Player, team	PTS	AVG
1947	Joe Fulks, Philadelphia	1,389	23.2	1980	George Gervin, San Antonio	2,585	33.1
1948	Max Zaslofsky, Chicago	1,007	21.0	1981	Adrian Dantley, Utah	2,452	30.7
1949	George Mikan, Minneapolis	1,698	28.3	1982	George Gervin, San Antonio	2,551	32.3
1950	George Mikan, Minneapolis	1,865	27.4	1983	Alex English, Denver	2,326	28.4
1951	George Mikan, Minneapolis	1,932	28.4	1984	Adrian Dantley, Utah	2,418	30.6
1952	Paul Arizin, Philadelphia	1,674	25.4	1985	Bernard King, New York	1,809	32.9
1953	Neil Johnston, Philadelphia	1,564	22.3	1986	Dominique Wilkins, Atlanta	2,366	30.3
1954	Neil Johnston, Philadelphia	1,759	24.4	1987	Michael Jordan, Chicago	3,041	37.1
1955	Neil Johnston, Philadelphia	1,631	22.7	1988	Michael Jordan, Chicago	2,868	35.0
1956	Bob Pettit, St. Louis	1,849	25.7	1989	Michael Jordan, Chicago	2,633	32.5
1957	Paul Arizin, Philadelphia	1,817	25.6	1990	Michael Jordan, Chicago	2,753	33.6
1958	George Yardley, Detroit	2,001	27.8	1991	Michael Jordan, Chicago	2,580	31.5
1959	Bob Pettit, St. Louis	2,105	29.2	1992	Michael Jordan, Chicago	2,404	30.1
1960	Wilt Chamberlain, Philadelphia	2,707	37.9	1993	Michael Jordan, Chicago	2,541	32.6
1961	Wilt Chamberlain, Philadelphia	3,033	38.4	1994	David Robinson, San Antonio	2,383	29.8
1962	Wilt Chamberlain, Philadelphia	4,029	50.4	1995	Shaquille O'Neal, Orlando	2,315	29.3
1963	Wilt Chamberlain, San Francisco	3,586	44.8	1996	Michael Jordan, Chicago	2,465	30.4
1964	Wilt Chamberlain, San Francisco	2,948	36.5	1997	Michael Jordan, Chicago	2,431	29.6
1965	Wilt Chamberlain, San Francisco-Phil.	2,534	34.7	1998	Michael Jordan, Chicago	2,357	28.7
1966	Wilt Chamberlain, San Francisco	2,649	33.5	1999	Allen Iverson, Philadelphia	1,284	26.8
1967	Rick Barry, San Francisco	2,775	35.6	2000	Shaquille O'Neal, L.A. Lakers	2,344	29.7
1968	Dave Bing, Detroit	2,142	27.1	2001	Allen Iverson, Philadelphia	2,207	31.1
1969	Elvin Hayes, San Diego	2,327	28.4	2002	Allen Iverson, Philadelphia	1,883	31.4
1970	Jerry West, L.A. Lakers	2,309	31.2	2003	Tracy McGrady, Orlando	2,407	32.1
1971	Lew Alcindor (Kareem Abdul-Jabbar),			2004	Tracy McGrady, Orlando	1,878	28.0
	Milwaukee	2,596	31.7	2005	Allen Iverson, Philadelphia	2,302	30.7
1972	Kareem Abdul-Jabbar, Milwaukee	2,822	34.8	2006	Kobe Bryant, L.A. Lakers	2,832	35.4
1973	Nate Archibald, Kansas City-Omaha	2,719	34.0	2007	Kobe Bryant, L.A. Lakers	2,430	31.6
1974	Bob McAdoo, Buffalo	2,261	30.6	2008	LeBron James, Cleveland	2,250	30.0
1975	Bob McAdoo, Buffalo	2,831	34.5	2009	Dwyane Wade, Miami	2,386	30.2
1976	Bob McAdoo, Buffalo	2,427	31.1	2010	Kevin Durant, Oklahoma City	2,472	30.1
1977	Pete Maravich, New Orleans	2,273	31.1	2011	Kevin Durant, Oklahoma City	2,161	27.7
1978	George Gervin, San Antonio	2,232	27.2	2012	Kevin Durant, Oklahoma City	1,850	28.0
1979	George Gervin, San Antonio	2,365	29.6	2013	Carmelo Anthony, New York	1,920	28.7

NBA Most Valuable Player, 1956-2013

Year	Player, team	Year	Player, team	Year	Player, team
1956	Bob Pettit, St. Louis	1963	Bill Russell, Boston	1970	Willis Reed, New York
1957	Bob Cousy, Boston	1964	Oscar Robertson, Cincinnati	1971	Lew Alcindor (Abdul-Jabbar), Milw.
1958	Bill Russell, Boston	1965	Bill Russell, Boston	1972	Kareem Abdul-Jabbar, Milwaukee
1959	Bob Pettit, St. Louis	1966	Wilt Chamberlain, Philadelphia	1973	Dave Cowens, Boston
1960	Wilt Chamberlain, Philadelphia	1967	Wilt Chamberlain, Philadelphia	1974	Kareem Abdul-Jabbar, Milwaukee
1961	Bill Russell, Boston	1968	Wilt Chamberlain, Philadelphia	1975	Bob McAdoo, Buffalo
1962	Bill Russell, Boston	1969	Wes Unseld, Baltimore	1976	Kareem Abdul-Jabbar, L.A. Lakers

Year	Player, team	Year	Player, team	Year	Player, team
1977	Kareem Abdul-Jabbar, L.A. Lakers	1990	Magic Johnson, L.A. Lakers	2002	Tim Duncan, San Antonio
1978	Bill Walton, Portland	1991	Michael Jordan, Chicago	2003	Tim Duncan, San Antonio
1979	Moses Malone, Houston	1992	Michael Jordan, Chicago	2004	Kevin Garnett, Minnesota
1980	Kareem Abdul-Jabbar, L.A. Lakers	1993	Charles Barkley, Phoenix	2005	Steve Nash, Phoenix
1981	Julius Erving, Philadelphia	1994	Hakeem Olajuwon, Houston	2006	Steve Nash, Phoenix
1982	Moses Malone, Houston	1995	David Robinson, San Antonio	2007	Dirk Nowitzki, Dallas
1983	Moses Malone, Philadelphia	1996	Michael Jordan, Chicago	2008	Kobe Bryant, L.A. Lakers
1984	Larry Bird, Boston	1997	Karl Malone, Utah	2009	LeBron James, Cleveland
1985	Larry Bird, Boston	1998	Michael Jordan, Chicago	2010	LeBron James, Cleveland
1986	Larry Bird, Boston	1999	Karl Malone, Utah	2011	Derrick Rose, Chicago
1987	Magic Johnson, L.A. Lakers	2000	Shaquille O'Neal, L.A. Lakers	2012	LeBron James, Miami
1988	Michael Jordan, Chicago	2001	Allen Iverson, Philadelphia	2013	LeBron James, Miami
1989	Magic Johnson, L.A. Lakers				

NBA Champions, 1947-2013

Year	Eastern champion	Regular season Western champion		Champion	Playoffs Winning coach	Opponent
1947	Washington Capitols	Chicago Stags		Philadelphia	Ed Gottlieb	Chicago
1948	Philadelphia Warriors	St. Louis Bombers		Baltimore	Buddy Jeannette	Philadelphia
1949	Washington Capitols	Rochester		Minneapolis	John Kundla	Washington
1950[1]	Syracuse	Indianapolis		Minneapolis	John Kundla	Syracuse
1951	Philadelphia Warriors	Minneapolis		Rochester	Lester Harrison	New York
1952	Syracuse	Rochester		Minneapolis	John Kundla	New York
1953	New York	Minneapolis		Minneapolis	John Kundla	New York
1954	New York	Minneapolis		Minneapolis	John Kundla	Syracuse
1955	Syracuse	Ft. Wayne		Syracuse	Al Cervi	Ft. Wayne
1956	Philadelphia Warriors	Ft. Wayne		Philadelphia	George Senesky	Ft. Wayne
1957	Boston	St. Louis		Boston	Red Auerbach	St. Louis
1958	Boston	St. Louis		St. Louis	Alex Hannum	Boston
1959	Boston	St. Louis		Boston	Red Auerbach	Minneapolis
1960	Boston	St. Louis		Boston	Red Auerbach	St. Louis
1961	Boston	St. Louis		Boston	Red Auerbach	St. Louis
1962	Boston	L.A. Lakers		Boston	Red Auerbach	L.A. Lakers
1963	Boston	L.A. Lakers		Boston	Red Auerbach	L.A. Lakers
1964	Boston	San Francisco		Boston	Red Auerbach	San Francisco
1965	Boston	L.A. Lakers		Boston	Red Auerbach	L.A. Lakers
1966	Philadelphia	L.A. Lakers		Boston	Red Auerbach	L.A. Lakers
1967	Philadelphia	San Francisco		Philadelphia	Alex Hannum	San Francisco
1968	Philadelphia	St. Louis		Boston	Bill Russell	L.A. Lakers
1969	Baltimore	L.A. Lakers		Boston	Bill Russell	L.A. Lakers
1970	New York	Atlanta		New York	Red Holzman	L.A. Lakers

Year	Atlantic	Central	Midwest	Pacific	Champion	Winning coach	Opponent
1971	New York	Baltimore	Milwaukee	L.A. Lakers	Milwaukee	Larry Costello	Baltimore
1972	Boston	Baltimore	Milwaukee	L.A. Lakers	L.A. Lakers	Bill Sharman	New York
1973	Boston	Baltimore	Milwaukee	L.A. Lakers	New York	Red Holzman	L.A. Lakers
1974	Boston	Capital	Milwaukee	L.A. Lakers	Boston	Tom Heinsohn	Milwaukee
1975	Boston	Washington	Chicago	Golden State	Golden State	Al Attles	Washington
1976	Boston	Cleveland	Milwaukee	Golden State	Boston	Tom Heinsohn	Phoenix
1977	Philadelphia	Houston	Denver	L.A. Lakers	Portland	Jack Ramsay	Philadelphia
1978	Philadelphia	San Antonio	Denver	Portland	Washington	Dick Motta	Seattle
1979	Washington	San Antonio	Kansas City	Seattle	Seattle	Len Wilkens	Washington
1980	Boston	Atlanta	Milwaukee	L.A. Lakers	L.A. Lakers	Paul Westhead	Philadelphia
1981	Boston	Milwaukee	San Antonio	Phoenix	Boston	Bill Fitch	Houston
1982	Boston	Milwaukee	San Antonio	L.A. Lakers	L.A. Lakers	Pat Riley	Philadelphia
1983	Philadelphia	Milwaukee	San Antonio	L.A. Lakers	Philadelphia	Billy Cunningham	L.A. Lakers
1984	Boston	Milwaukee	Utah	L.A. Lakers	Boston	K. C. Jones	L.A. Lakers
1985	Boston	Milwaukee	Denver	L.A. Lakers	L.A. Lakers	Pat Riley	Boston
1986	Boston	Milwaukee	Houston	L.A. Lakers	Boston	K. C. Jones	Houston
1987	Boston	Atlanta	Dallas	L.A. Lakers	L.A. Lakers	Pat Riley	Boston
1988	Boston	Detroit	Denver	L.A. Lakers	L.A. Lakers	Pat Riley	Detroit
1989	New York	Detroit	Utah	L.A. Lakers	Detroit	Chuck Daly	L.A. Lakers
1990	Philadelphia	Detroit	San Antonio	L.A. Lakers	Detroit	Chuck Daly	Portland
1991	Boston	Chicago	San Antonio	Portland	Chicago	Phil Jackson	L.A. Lakers
1992	Boston	Chicago	Utah	Portland	Chicago	Phil Jackson	Portland
1993	New York	Chicago	Houston	Phoenix	Chicago	Phil Jackson	Phoenix
1994	New York	Atlanta	Houston	Seattle	Houston	Rudy Tomjanovich	New York
1995	Orlando	Indiana	San Antonio	Phoenix	Houston	Rudy Tomjanovich	Orlando
1996	Orlando	Chicago	San Antonio	Seattle	Chicago	Phil Jackson	Seattle
1997	Miami	Chicago	Utah	Seattle	Chicago	Phil Jackson	Utah
1998	Miami	Chicago	Utah	L.A. Lakers	Chicago	Phil Jackson	Utah
1999	Miami	Indiana	San Antonio	Portland	San Antonio	Gregg Popovich	New York
2000	Miami	Indiana	Utah	L.A. Lakers	L.A. Lakers	Phil Jackson	Indiana
2001	Philadelphia	Milwaukee	San Antonio	L.A. Lakers	L.A. Lakers	Phil Jackson	Philadelphia
2002	New Jersey	Detroit	San Antonio	Sacramento	L.A. Lakers	Phil Jackson	New Jersey
2003	New Jersey	Detroit	San Antonio	Sacramento	San Antonio	Gregg Popovich	New Jersey
2004	New Jersey	Indiana	Minnesota	L.A. Lakers	Detroit	Larry Brown	L.A. Lakers

Year	Atlantic	Central	Southeast	Northwest	Pacific	Southwest	Champion	Winning coach	Opponent
2005	Boston	Detroit	Miami	Seattle	Phoenix	San Antonio	San Antonio	Gregg Popovich	Detroit
2006	New Jersey	Detroit	Miami	Denver	Phoenix	San Antonio	Miami	Pat Riley	Dallas
2007	Toronto	Detroit	Miami	Utah	Phoenix	Dallas	San Antonio	Gregg Popovich	Cleveland
2008	Boston	Detroit	Orlando	Utah	L.A. Lakers	New Orleans	Boston	Glenn "Doc" Rivers	L.A. Lakers
2009	Boston	Cleveland	Orlando	Denver	L.A. Lakers	San Antonio	L.A. Lakers	Phil Jackson	Orlando
2010	Boston	Cleveland	Orlando	Denver	L.A. Lakers	Dallas	L.A. Lakers	Phil Jackson	Boston
2011	Boston	Chicago	Miami	OK City	L.A. Lakers	San Antonio	Dallas	Rick Carlisle	Miami
2012	Boston	Chicago	Miami	OK City	L.A. Lakers	San Antonio	Miami	Erik Spoelstra	OK City
2013	New York	Indiana	Miami	OK City	L.A. Clippers	San Antonio	Miami	Erik Spoelstra	San Antonio

(1) The newly formed NBA combined the 11-team BAA (Basketball Assn. of Amer.) and six NBL (Natl. Basketball League) teams in the 1949-50 season and had three divisions for one year. The Minneapolis Lakers were co-champions of the soon-defunct Central Division.

All-NBA and All-Defensive Teams, 2012-13

All-NBA Team

First Team	Second Team	Position
LeBron James, Miami	Carmelo Anthony, New York	Forward
Kevin Durant, Oklahoma City	Blake Griffin, L.A. Clippers	Forward
Tim Duncan, San Antonio	Marc Gasol, Memphis	Center
Kobe Bryant, L.A. Lakers	Tony Parker, San Antonio	Guard
Chris Paul, L.A. Clippers	Russell Westbrook, Oklahoma City	Guard

All-Defensive Team

First Team	Second Team
LeBron James, Miami	Tim Duncan, San Antonio
Serge Ibaka, Oklahoma City	Paul George, Indiana
Tyson Chandler, New York; Joakim Noah, Chicago (tie)	Marc Gasol, Memphis
Tony Allen, Memphis	Avery Bradley, Boston
Chris Paul, L.A. Clippers	Mike Conley, Memphis

NBA Statistical Leaders, 2012-13

Scoring Average
(Minimum 70 games or 1,400 points)

Player, team	GP	FG	FT	PTS	AVG
Carmelo Anthony, New York	67	669	425	1,920	28.7
Kevin Durant, Oklahoma City	81	731	679	2,280	28.1
Kobe Bryant, L.A. Lakers	78	738	525	2,133	27.3
LeBron James, Miami	76	765	403	2,036	26.8
James Harden, Houston	78	585	674	2,023	25.9
Russell Westbrook, Oklahoma City	82	673	460	1,903	23.2
Stephen Curry, Golden State	78	626	262	1,786	22.9
Dwyane Wade, Miami	69	569	308	1,463	21.2
LaMarcus Aldridge, Portland	74	638	282	1,560	21.1
Brook Lopez, Brooklyn	74	570	297	1,437	19.4

Rebounds per Game
(Minimum 70 games or 800 rebounds)

Player, team	GP	OFF	DEF	TOT	AVG
Dwight Howard, L.A. Lakers	76	251	694	945	12.4
Nikola Vucevic, Orlando	77	273	644	917	11.9
Omer Asik, Houston	82	275	681	956	11.7
Zach Randolph, Memphis	76	310	544	854	11.2
David Lee, Golden State	79	218	668	886	11.2
Reggie Evans, Brooklyn	80	260	628	888	11.1
J.J. Hickson, Portland	80	266	562	828	10.4
Al Horford, Atlanta	74	195	562	757	10.2
DeMarcus Cousins, Sacramento	75	222	524	746	9.9
Carlos Boozer, Chicago	79	175	596	771	9.8

3-Point Field Goal Percentage
(Minimum 55 3-point field goals made)

Player, team	3-FGM	3-FGA	PCT
Jose Calderon, Toronto-Detroit	130	282	.461
Kyle Korver, Atlanta	189	414	.457
Stephen Curry, Golden State	272	600	.453
Ersan Ilyasova, Milwaukee	95	214	.444
Steve Nash, L.A. Lakers	57	130	.438
Shane Battier, Miami	136	316	.430
Danny Green, San Antonio	177	413	.429
Mike Dunleavy, Milwaukee	128	299	.428
Willie Green, L.A. Clippers	71	166	.428
Kevin Martin, Oklahoma City	158	371	.426

Assists per Game
(Minimum 70 games or 400 assists)

Player, team	GP	AST	APG
Rajon Rondo, Boston	38	420	11.1
Chris Paul, L.A. Clippers	70	678	9.7
Greivis Vasquez, New Orleans	78	704	9.0
Jrue Holiday, Philadelphia	78	625	8.0
Deron Williams, Brooklyn	78	604	7.7
Tony Parker, San Antonio	66	499	7.6
Russell Westbrook, Oklahoma City	82	607	7.4
Goran Dragic, Phoenix	77	569	7.4
Jameer Nelson, Orlando	56	413	7.4
Ricky Rubio, Minnesota	57	418	7.3
LeBron James, Miami	76	551	7.3

Field Goal Percentage
(Minimum 300 field goals made)

Player, team	FGM	FGA	PCT
DeAndre Jordan, L.A. Clippers	314	488	.643
Dwight Howard, L.A. Lakers	470	813	.578
JaVale McGee, Denver	303	527	.575
Serge Ibaka, Oklahoma City	446	778	.573
LeBron James, Miami	765	1,354	.565
J.J. Hickson, Portland	418	744	.562
Tiago Splitter, San Antonio	315	563	.560
Amir Johnson, Toronto	336	606	.554
Kenneth Faried, Denver	380	689	.552
Al Horford, Atlanta	576	1,060	.543

Steals per Game
(Minimum 70 games or 125 steals)

Player, team	GP	STL	AVG
Chris Paul, L.A. Clippers	70	169	2.41
Ricky Rubio, Minnesota	57	137	2.40
Mike Conley, Memphis	80	174	2.18
Monta Ellis, Milwaukee	82	169	2.06
Kemba Walker, Charlotte	82	160	1.95
Dwyane Wade, Miami	69	128	1.86
James Harden, Houston	78	142	1.82
Paul George, Indiana	79	143	1.81
Russell Westbrook, Oklahoma City	82	145	1.77
Thaddeus Young, Philadelphia	76	133	1.75

Free Throw Percentage
(Minimum 125 free throws made)

Player, team	FTM	FTA	PCT
Kevin Durant, Oklahoma City	679	750	.905
Stephen Curry, Golden State	262	291	.900
J.J. Redick, Orlando-Milwaukee	171	190	.900
Kevin Martin, Oklahoma City	219	246	.890
Ray Allen, Miami	140	158	.886
Chris Paul, L.A. Clippers	286	323	.885
Isaiah Thomas, Sacramento	253	287	.882
Jeff Teague, Atlanta	199	226	.881
Darren Collison, Dallas	242	275	.880
Jamal Crawford, L.A. Clippers	216	248	.871

Blocked Shots per Game
(Minimum 70 games or 100 blocked shots)

Player, team	GP	BLK	AVG
Serge Ibaka, Oklahoma City	80	242	3.03
Larry Sanders, Milwaukee	71	201	2.83
Tim Duncan, San Antonio	69	183	2.65
Roy Hibbert, Indiana	79	206	2.61
Dwight Howard, L.A. Lakers	76	186	2.45
Joakim Noah, Chicago	66	141	2.14
Brook Lopez, Brooklyn	74	154	2.08
JaVale McGee, Denver	79	157	1.99
Josh Smith, Atlanta	76	136	1.79
Bismack Biyombo, Charlotte	80	143	1.79

NBA Defensive Player of the Year, 1983-2013

Year	Player, team	Year	Player, team	Year	Player, team
1983	Sidney Moncrief, Milwaukee	1994	Hakeem Olajuwon, Houston	2004	Ron Artest, Indiana
1984	Sidney Moncrief, Milwaukee	1995	Dikembe Mutombo, Denver	2005	Ben Wallace, Detroit
1985	Mark Eaton, Utah	1996	Gary Payton, Seattle	2006	Ben Wallace, Detroit
1986	Alvin Robertson, San Antonio	1997	Dikembe Mutombo, Atlanta	2007	Marcus Camby, Denver
1987	Michael Cooper, L.A. Lakers	1998	Dikembe Mutombo, Atlanta	2008	Kevin Garnett, Boston
1988	Michael Jordan, Chicago	1999	Alonzo Mourning, Miami	2009	Dwight Howard, Orlando
1989	Mark Eaton, Utah	2000	Alonzo Mourning, Miami	2010	Dwight Howard, Orlando
1990	Dennis Rodman, Detroit	2001	Dikembe Mutombo, Philadelphia-Atlanta	2011	Dwight Howard, Orlando
1991	Dennis Rodman, Detroit			2012	Tyson Chandler, New York
1992	David Robinson, San Antonio	2002	Ben Wallace, Detroit	2013	Marc Gasol, Memphis
1993	Hakeem Olajuwon, Houston	2003	Ben Wallace, Detroit		

NBA Rookie of the Year, 1953-2013

Year	Player, team	Year	Player, team	Year	Player, team
1953	Don Meineke, Ft. Wayne	1973	Bob McAdoo, Buffalo	1995	Grant Hill, Detroit;
1954	Ray Felix, Baltimore	1974	Ernie DiGregorio, Buffalo		Jason Kidd, Dallas
1955	Bob Pettit, Milwaukee	1975	Keith Wilkes, Golden State	1996	Damon Stoudamire, Toronto
1956	Maurice Stokes, Rochester	1976	Alvan Adams, Phoenix	1997	Allen Iverson, Philadelphia
1957	Tom Heinsohn, Boston	1977	Adrian Dantley, Buffalo	1998	Tim Duncan, San Antonio
1958	Woody Sauldsberry, Philadelphia	1978	Walter Davis, Phoenix	1999	Vince Carter, Toronto
1959	Elgin Baylor, Minneapolis	1979	Phil Ford, Kansas City	2000	Elton Brand, Chicago;
1960	Wilt Chamberlain, Philadelphia	1980	Larry Bird, Boston		Steve Francis, Houston
1961	Oscar Robertson, Cincinnati	1981	Darrell Griffith, Utah	2001	Mike Miller, Orlando
1962	Walt Bellamy, Chicago	1982	Buck Williams, New Jersey	2002	Pau Gasol, Memphis
1963	Terry Dischinger, Chicago	1983	Terry Cummings, San Diego	2003	Amar'e Stoudemire, Phoenix
1964	Jerry Lucas, Cincinnati	1984	Ralph Sampson, Houston	2004	LeBron James, Cleveland
1965	Willis Reed, New York	1985	Michael Jordan, Chicago	2005	Emeka Okafor, Charlotte
1966	Rick Barry, San Francisco	1986	Patrick Ewing, New York	2006	Chris Paul, New Or./OK City
1967	Dave Bing, Detroit	1987	Chuck Person, Indiana	2007	Brandon Roy, Portland
1968	Earl Monroe, Baltimore	1988	Mark Jackson, New York	2008	Kevin Durant, Seattle
1969	Wes Unseld, Baltimore	1989	Mitch Richmond, Golden State	2009	Derrick Rose, Chicago
1970	Lew Alcindor (Abdul-Jabbar), Milwaukee	1990	David Robinson, San Antonio	2010	Tyreke Evans, Sacramento
		1991	Derrick Coleman, New Jersey	2011	Blake Griffin, L.A. Clippers
1971	Dave Cowens, Boston;	1992	Larry Johnson, Charlotte	2012	Kyrie Irving, Cleveland
	Geoff Petrie, Portland	1993	Shaquille O'Neal, Orlando	2013	Damian Lillard, Portland
1972	Sidney Wicks, Portland	1994	Chris Webber, Golden State		

NBA Sixth Man Award, 1983-2013

Year	Player, team	Year	Player, team	Year	Player, team
1983	Bobby Jones, Philadelphia	1994	Dell Curry, Charlotte	2004	Antawn Jamison, Dallas
1984	Kevin McHale, Boston	1995	Anthony Mason, New York	2005	Ben Gordon, Chicago
1985	Kevin McHale, Boston	1996	Toni Kukoc, Chicago	2006	Mike Miller, Memphis
1986	Bill Walton, Boston	1997	John Starks, New York	2007	Leandro Barbosa, Phoenix
1987	Ricky Pierce, Milwaukee	1998	Danny Manning, Phoenix	2008	Manu Ginobili, San Antonio
1988	Roy Tarpley, Dallas	1999	Darrell Armstrong, Orlando	2009	Jason Terry, Dallas
1989	Eddie Johnson, Phoenix	2000	Rodney Rogers, Phoenix	2010	Jamal Crawford, Atlanta
1990	Ricky Pierce, Milwaukee	2001	Aaron McKie, Philadelphia	2011	Lamar Odom, L.A. Lakers
1991	Detlef Schrempf, Indiana	2002	Corliss Williamson, Detroit	2012	James Harden, Oklahoma City
1992	Detlef Schrempf, Indiana	2003	Bobby Jackson, Sacramento	2013	J.R. Smith, New York
1993	Clifford Robinson, Portland				

NBA Player Draft First-Round Picks, 2013
(June 27, 2013)

Team	Player, position, school/team	Team	Player, position, school/team
1. Cleveland	Anthony Bennett, Forward, UNLV	17. Atlanta	Dennis Schroeder, Guard, Phantoms Braunschweig (Germany)
2. Orlando	Victor Oladipo, Guard, Indiana	18. Atlanta[7]	Shane Larkin, Guard, Miami (FL)[8]
3. Washington	Otto Porter, Forward, Georgetown	19. Cleveland[9]	Sergey Karasev, Forward, BC Triumph Lyubertsy (Russia)
4. Charlotte	Cody Zeller, Center, Indiana	20. Chicago	Tony Snell, Guard, New Mexico
5. Phoenix	Alex Len, Center, Maryland	21. Utah[10]	Gorgui Dieng, Center, Louisville[11]
6. New Orleans . . .	Nerlens Noel, Center, Kentucky	22. Brooklyn	Mason Plumlee, Forward, Duke
7. Sacramento . . .	Ben McLemore, Guard, Kansas	23. Indiana	Solomon Hill, Forward, Arizona
8. Detroit	Kentavious Caldwell-Pope, Guard, Georgia	24. New York	Tim Hardaway Jr., Guard, Michigan
9. Minnesota	Trey Burke, Guard, Michigan[1]	25. L.A. Clippers	Reggie Bullock, Guard, North Carolina
10. Portland[2]	C. J. McCollum, Guard, Lehigh	26. Minnesota[12]	Andre Roberson, Forward, Colorado[13]
11. Philadelphia . . .	Michael Carter-Williams, Guard, Syracuse	27. Denver	Rudy Gobert, Forward, Cholet Basket (France)[14]
12. Oklahoma City[3]	Steven Adams, Center, Pittsburgh		
13. Dallas	Kelly Olynyk, Center, Gonzaga[4]	28. San Antonio	Livio Jean-Charles, Forward, Asvel Lyon-Villeurbanne (France)
14. Utah	Shabazz Muhammad, Guard, UCLA[5]	29. Oklahoma City	Archie Goodwin, Guard, Kentucky[15]
15. Milwaukee	Giannis Antetokounmpo, Forward, Filathlitikos AO (Greece)	30. Phoenix[16]	Nemanja Nedovic, Guard, Lietuvos Rytas (Lithuania)[17]
16. Boston	Lucas Nogueira, Center, Estudiantes (Spain)[6]		

(1) Rights traded to Utah. (2) From Charlotte. (3) From Toronto via Houston. (4) Rights traded to Boston. (5) Rights traded to Minnesota. (6) Rights traded to Atlanta. (7) From Houston via Brooklyn. (8) Rights traded to Dallas. (9) From L.A. Lakers. (10) From Golden State via Brooklyn. (11) Rights traded to Minnesota. (12) From Memphis via Houston. (13) Rights traded to Oklahoma City. (14) Rights traded to Utah. (15) Rights traded to Phoenix. (16) From Miami via L.A. Lakers and Cleveland. (17) Rights traded to Golden State.

Number-One First-Round NBA Draft Picks, 1966-2013

Year	Team	Player, school/team	Year	Team	Player, school/team
1966	New York	Cazzie Russell, Michigan	1983	Houston	Ralph Sampson, Virginia
1967	Detroit	Jimmy Walker, Providence	1984	Houston	Hakeem Olajuwon, Houston
1968	San Diego	Elvin Hayes, Houston	1985	New York	Patrick Ewing, Georgetown
1969	Milwaukee	Lew Alcindor (Kareem Abdul-Jabbar), UCLA	1986	Cleveland	Brad Daugherty, North Carolina
			1987	San Antonio	David Robinson, Navy
1970	Detroit	Bob Lanier, St. Bonaventure	1988	L.A. Clippers	Danny Manning, Kansas
1971	Cleveland	Austin Carr, Notre Dame	1989	Sacramento	Pervis Ellison, Louisville
1972	Portland	LaRue Martin, Loyola-Chicago	1990	New Jersey	Derrick Coleman, Syracuse
1973	Philadelphia	Doug Collins, Illinois State	1991	Charlotte	Larry Johnson, UNLV
1974	Portland	Bill Walton, UCLA	1992	Orlando	Shaquille O'Neal, LSU
1975	Atlanta	David Thompson[1], NC State	1993	Orlando	Chris Webber[2], Michigan
1976	Houston	John Lucas, Maryland	1994	Milwaukee	Glenn Robinson, Purdue
1977	Milwaukee	Kent Benson, Indiana	1995	Golden State	Joe Smith, Maryland
1978	Portland	Mychal Thompson, Minnesota	1996	Philadelphia	Allen Iverson, Georgetown
1979	L.A. Lakers	Earvin "Magic" Johnson, Michigan State	1997	San Antonio	Tim Duncan, Wake Forest
1980	Golden State	Joe Barry Carroll, Purdue	1998	L.A. Clippers	Michael Olowokandi, Pacific (CA)
1981	Dallas	Mark Aguirre, DePaul	1999	Chicago	Elton Brand, Duke
1982	L.A. Lakers	James Worthy, North Carolina	2000	New Jersey	Kenyon Martin, Cincinnati

Year	Team	Player, school/team	Year	Team	Player, school/team
2001	Washington	Kwame Brown, Glynn Academy (HS)	2007	Portland	Greg Oden, Ohio State
2002	Houston	Yao Ming, Shanghai Sharks (China)	2008	Chicago	Derrick Rose, Memphis
2003	Cleveland	LeBron James, St. Vincent-St. Mary (HS)	2009	L.A. Clippers	Blake Griffin, Oklahoma
2004	Orlando	Dwight Howard, Southwest Atlanta Christian Academy (HS)	2010	Washington	John Wall, Kentucky
2005	Milwaukee	Andrew Bogut, Utah	2011	Cleveland	Kyrie Irving, Duke
2006	Toronto	Andrea Bargnani, Benetton Treviso (Italy)	2012	New Orleans	Anthony Davis, Kentucky
			2013	Cleveland	Anthony Bennett, UNLV

HS = High school. (1) Signed with Denver of the American Basketball Association (ABA). (2) Traded to Golden State for rights to Anfernee Hardaway and three future first-round draft choices.

All-Time NBA Statistical Leaders

(At the end of the 2012-13 season. * = Active in 2012-13 season.)

Scoring Average
(Minimum 400 games or 10,000 points)

	GP	PTS	AVG
Michael Jordan	1,072	32,292	30.1
Wilt Chamberlain	1,045	31,419	30.1
*LeBron James	765	21,081	27.6
Elgin Baylor	846	23,149	27.4
Jerry West	932	25,192	27.0
Allen Iverson	914	24,368	26.7
*Kevin Durant	461	12,258	26.6
Bob Pettit	792	20,880	26.4
George Gervin	791	20,708	26.2
Oscar Robertson	1,040	26,710	25.7

Field Goal Percentage
(Minimum 2,000 field goals made)

	FGM	FGA	PCT
Artis Gilmore	5,732	9,570	.599
*Tyson Chandler	2,542	4,356	.584
Shaquille O'Neal	11,330	19,457	.582
Mark West	2,528	4,356	.580
*Dwight Howard	4,504	7,801	.577
Darryl Dawkins	3,477	6,079	.572
Steve Johnson	2,841	4,965	.572
James Donaldson	3,105	5,442	.571
Bo Outlaw	2,005	3,534	.567
Jeff Ruland	2,105	3,734	.564

Free Throw Percentage
(Minimum 1,200 free throws made)

	FTM	FTA	PCT
*Steve Nash	3,038	3,360	.904
Mark Price	2,135	2,362	.904
Rick Barry	3,818	4,243	.900
Peja Stojakovic	2,237	2,500	.895
*Ray Allen	4,293	4,804	.894
*Chauncey Billups	4,486	5,017	.894
Calvin Murphy	3,445	3,864	.892
Scott Skiles	1,548	1,741	.889
Reggie Miller	6,237	7,026	.888
Larry Bird	3,960	4,471	.886

3-Point Field Goal Percentage
(Minimum 250 3-point field goals made)

	3-FGM	3-FGA	PCT
Steve Kerr	726	1,599	.454
*Stephen Curry	644	1,443	.446
Hubert Davis	728	1,651	.441
Drazen Petrovic	255	583	.437
Jason Kapono	457	1,054	.434
*Steve Novak	496	1,146	.433
Tim Legler	260	603	.431
*Steve Nash	1,677	3,915	.428
B.J. Armstrong	436	1,026	.425
*Anthony Morrow	458	1,080	.424
*Danny Green	292	688	.424

Minutes Played

Kareem Abdul-Jabbar	57,446
Karl Malone	54,852
*Jason Kidd	50,110
Elvin Hayes	50,000
Wilt Chamberlain	47,859
*Kevin Garnett	47,801
John Stockton	47,764
Reggie Miller	47,619
Gary Payton	47,117
John Havlicek	46,471

Field Goals Attempted

Kareem Abdul-Jabbar	28,307
Karl Malone	26,210
Michael Jordan	24,537
*Kobe Bryant	24,301
Elvin Hayes	24,272
John Havlicek	23,930
Wilt Chamberlain	23,497
Dominique Wilkins	21,589
Alex English	21,036
Hakeem Olajuwon	20,991

Points

Kareem Abdul-Jabbar	38,387
Karl Malone	36,928
Michael Jordan	32,292
*Kobe Bryant	31,617
Wilt Chamberlain	31,419
Shaquille O'Neal	28,596
Moses Malone	27,409
Elvin Hayes	27,313
Hakeem Olajuwon	26,946
Oscar Robertson	26,710

Games Played

Robert Parish	1,611
Kareem Abdul-Jabbar	1,560
John Stockton	1,504
Karl Malone	1,476
Kevin Willis	1,424
*Jason Kidd	1,391
Reggie Miller	1,389
Clifford Robinson	1,380
Gary Payton	1,335
Moses Malone	1,329

Field Goals Made

Kareem Abdul-Jabbar	15,837
Karl Malone	13,528
Wilt Chamberlain	12,681
Michael Jordan	12,192
Shaquille O'Neal	11,330
*Kobe Bryant	11,024
Elvin Hayes	10,976
Hakeem Olajuwon	10,749
Alex English	10,659
John Havlicek	10,513

Rebounds

Wilt Chamberlain	23,924
Bill Russell	21,620
Kareem Abdul-Jabbar	17,440
Elvin Hayes	16,279
Moses Malone	16,212
Karl Malone	14,968
Robert Parish	14,715
Nate Thurmond	14,464
Walt Bellamy	14,241
*Kevin Garnett	13,843

Personal Fouls

Kareem Abdul-Jabbar	4,657
Karl Malone	4,578
Robert Parish	4,443
Charles Oakley	4,421
Hakeem Olajuwon	4,383
Buck Williams	4,267
Elvin Hayes	4,193
Clifford Robinson	4,175
Kevin Willis	4,172
Shaquille O'Neal	4,146
Otis Thorpe	4,146

3-Point Field Goals Attempted

*Ray Allen	7,120
Reggie Miller	6,486
*Jason Kidd	5,701
*Jason Terry	5,037
*Paul Pierce	4,928
*Kobe Bryant	4,879
*Chauncey Billups	4,677
*Rashard Lewis	4,491
*Vince Carter	4,417
Peja Stojakovic	4,392
*Jamal Crawford	4,385

Assists

John Stockton	15,806
*Jason Kidd	12,091
Mark Jackson	10,334
*Steve Nash	10,249
Magic Johnson	10,141
Oscar Robertson	9,887
Isiah Thomas	9,061
Gary Payton	8,966
Rod Strickland	7,987
*Andre Miller	7,956

Blocks

Hakeem Olajuwon	3,830
Dikembe Mutombo	3,289
Kareem Abdul-Jabbar	3,189
Mark Eaton	3,064
David Robinson	2,954
Patrick Ewing	2,894
Shaquille O'Neal	2,732
*Tim Duncan	2,652
Tree Rollins	2,542
Robert Parish	2,361

3-Point Field Goals Made

*Ray Allen	2,857
Reggie Miller	2,560
*Jason Kidd	1,988
*Jason Terry	1,911
*Paul Pierce	1,823
*Chauncey Billups	1,816
Peja Stojakovic	1,760
*Rashard Lewis	1,741
Dale Ellis	1,719
*Steve Nash	1,677

Steals

John Stockton	3,265
*Jason Kidd	2,684
Michael Jordan	2,514
Gary Payton	2,445
Maurice Cheeks	2,310
Scottie Pippen	2,307
Clyde Drexler	2,207
Hakeem Olajuwon	2,162
Alvin Robertson	2,112
Karl Malone	2,085

NBA Coach of the Year, 1963-2013

Year	Coach, team	Year	Coach, team	Year	Coach, team
1963	Harry Gallatin, St. Louis	1980	Bill Fitch, Boston	1997	Pat Riley, Miami
1964	Alex Hannum, San Francisco	1981	Jack McKinney, Indiana	1998	Larry Bird, Indiana
1965	Red Auerbach, Boston	1982	Gene Shue, Washington	1999	Mike Dunleavy, Portland
1966	Dolph Schayes, Philadelphia	1983	Don Nelson, Milwaukee	2000	Glenn "Doc" Rivers, Orlando
1967	Johnny Kerr, Chicago	1984	Frank Layden, Utah	2001	Larry Brown, Philadelphia
1968	Richie Guerin, St. Louis	1985	Don Nelson, Milwaukee	2002	Rick Carlisle, Detroit
1969	Gene Shue, Baltimore	1986	Mike Fratello, Atlanta	2003	Gregg Popovich, San Antonio
1970	Red Holzman, New York	1987	Mike Schuler, Portland	2004	Hubie Brown, Memphis
1971	Dick Motta, Chicago	1988	Doug Moe, Denver	2005	Mike D'Antoni, Phoenix
1972	Bill Sharman, L.A. Lakers	1989	Cotton Fitzsimmons, Phoenix	2006	Avery Johnson, Dallas
1973	Tom Heinsohn, Boston	1990	Pat Riley, L.A. Lakers	2007	Sam Mitchell, Toronto
1974	Ray Scott, Detroit	1991	Don Chaney, Houston	2008	Byron Scott, New Orleans
1975	Phil Johnson, Kansas City-Omaha	1992	Don Nelson, Golden State	2009	Mike Brown, Cleveland
1976	Bill Fitch, Cleveland	1993	Pat Riley, New York	2010	Scott Brooks, Oklahoma City
1977	Tom Nissalke, Houston	1994	Lenny Wilkens, Atlanta	2011	Tom Thibodeau, Chicago
1978	Hubie Brown, Atlanta	1995	Del Harris, L.A. Lakers	2012	Gregg Popovich, San Antonio
1979	Cotton Fitzsimmons, Kansas City	1996	Phil Jackson, Chicago	2013	George Karl, Denver

National Basketball Association Franchise Origins

Team, founding year (in NBA, BAA, or ABA), location, and subsequent history. Neutral sites and arena sites in the same metropolitan area not listed separately.

Atlanta Hawks: 1949, NBA, as Tri-Cities Blackhawks, 1949-51, Moline, IL. Milwaukee Hawks, 1951-55; St. Louis Hawks, 1955-68; Atlanta Hawks, 1968-present.

Boston Celtics: 1946, BAA, Boston, 1946-present.

Brooklyn Nets: 1967, ABA, as New Jersey Americans, 1967-68, Teaneck, NJ. New York Nets, 1968-77; New Jersey Nets, 1977-2012; Brooklyn Nets, 2012-present.

Charlotte Bobcats: 2004, NBA, Charlotte, NC, 2004-present.

Chicago Bulls: 1966, NBA, Chicago, 1966-present.

Cleveland Cavaliers: 1970, NBA, Cleveland, OH, 1970-present.

Dallas Mavericks: 1980, NBA, Dallas, TX, 1980-present.

Denver Nuggets: 1967, ABA, as Denver Rockets, 1967-74, Denver, CO. Denver Nuggets, 1974-present.

Detroit Pistons: 1948, BAA, as Ft. Wayne Pistons, 1948-57, Ft. Wayne, IN. Detroit Pistons, 1957-present.

Golden State Warriors: 1946, BAA, as Philadelphia Warriors, 1946-62, Philadelphia, PA. San Francisco Warriors, 1962-71; Golden State Warriors, 1971-present.

Houston Rockets: 1967, NBA, as San Diego Rockets, 1967-71, San Diego, CA. Houston Rockets, 1971-present.

Indiana Pacers: 1967, ABA, Indianapolis, IN, 1974-present.

L.A. Clippers: 1970, NBA, as Buffalo Braves, 1970-78, Buffalo, NY. San Diego Clippers, 1978-84; L.A. Clippers, 1984-present.

L.A. Lakers: 1948, BAA, as Minneapolis Lakers, 1948-60, Minneapolis, MN. L.A. Lakers, 1960-present.

Memphis Grizzlies: 1995, NBA, as Vancouver Grizzlies, 1995-2001, Vancouver, BC, Canada. Memphis Grizzlies, 2001-present.

Miami Heat: 1988, NBA, Miami, FL, 1988-present.

Milwaukee Bucks: 1968, NBA, Milwaukee, WI, 1968-present.

Minnesota Timberwolves: 1989, NBA, Minneapolis, MN, 1989-present.

New Orleans Pelicans: 1988, NBA, as Charlotte Hornets, 1988-2002, Charlotte, NC. New Orleans Hornets, 2002-13 (Hornets played most home games in Oklahoma City, 2005-07, as city repaired Hurricane Katrina damage); New Orleans Pelicans, 2013-present.

New York Knicks: 1946, BAA, New York, 1946-present.

Oklahoma City Thunder: 1967, NBA, as Seattle SuperSonics, 1967-2008, Seattle, WA. Oklahoma City Thunder, 2008-present.

Orlando Magic: 1989, NBA, Orlando, FL, 1989-present.

Philadelphia 76ers: 1949, NBA, as Syracuse Nationals, 1949-63, Syracuse, NY. Philadelphia 76ers, 1963-present.

Phoenix Suns: 1968, NBA, Phoenix, AZ, 1968-present.

Portland Trail Blazers: 1970, NBA, Portland, OR, 1970-present.

Sacramento Kings: 1948, BAA, as Rochester Royals, 1948-57, Rochester, NY. Cincinnati Royals, 1957-72; Kansas City/Omaha Kings, 1972-75; Kansas City Kings, 1975-85; Sacramento Kings, 1985-present.

San Antonio Spurs: ABA, as Dallas Chaparrals, 1967-73, Dallas, TX. San Antonio Spurs, 1973-present.

Toronto Raptors: 1995, NBA, Toronto, ON, Canada, 1995-present.

Utah Jazz: 1974, NBA, as New Orleans Jazz, 1974-79, New Orleans, LA. Utah Jazz, 1979-present.

Washington Wizards: 1961, NBA, as Chicago Packers, 1961-62, Chicago, IL. Chicago Zephyrs, 1962-63; Baltimore Bullets, 1963-73; Capital Bullets, 1973-74, Landover, MD; Washington Bullets, 1974-97; Washington Wizards, 1997-present.

NBA Home Courts

Team	Name (year built)	Capacity[1]	Team	Name (year built)	Capacity[1]
Atlanta	Philips Arena (1999)	18,371	Golden State	ORACLE Arena[7] (1966)	19,596
Boston	TD Garden[2] (1995)	18,624	Houston	Toyota Center (2003)	18,023
Brooklyn	Barclays Center (2012)	17,732	Indiana	Bankers Life Fieldhouse[8] (1999)	18,165
Charlotte	Time Warner Cable Arena (2005)	19,077	L.A. Clippers	STAPLES Center (1999)	19,060
Chicago	United Center (1994)	20,917	L.A. Lakers	STAPLES Center (1999)	18,997
Cleveland	Quicken Loans Arena (1994)	20,562	Memphis	FedExForum (2004)	18,119
Dallas	American Airlines Center (2001)	19,200	Miami	AmericanAirlines Arena (1999)	19,600
Denver	Pepsi Center (1999)	19,155	Milwaukee	BMO Harris Bradley Center[9] (1988)	18,717
Detroit	The Palace of Auburn Hills (1988)	22,076	Minnesota	Target Center (1990)	19,356
New Orleans[3]	New Orleans Arena (1999)	17,188	Portland	The Rose Garden (1995)	19,980
New York	Madison Square Garden (IV) (1968)	19,763	Sacramento	Sleep Train Arena[10] (1988)	17,317
Oklahoma City	Chesapeake Energy Arena[4] (2002)	18,203	San Antonio	AT&T Center[11] (2002)	18,581
Orlando	Amway Center (2010)	18,846	Toronto	Air Canada Centre (1999)	19,800
Philadelphia	Wells Fargo Center[5] (1996)	20,328	Utah	EnergySolutions Arena[12] (1991)	19,911
Phoenix	US Airways Center[6] (1992)	18,422	Washington	Verizon Center[13] (1997)	20,290

(1) At the end of the 2012-13 season. (2) Fleet Center, 1995-2005. (3) Because of damage to New Orleans Arena due to Hurricane Katrina, the Hornets played 35 games in the Ford Center in Oklahoma City, OK, 3 games in New Orleans Arena, and 3 games at other locations during the 2005-06 season. In 2006-07, New Orleans played 35 games at the Ford Center and 6 games in New Orleans Arena. (4) Ford Center (2002-11). (5) CoreStates Center, 1996-98; First Union Center (1998-2003). (6) America West Arena, 1992-2006. (7) Oakland Coliseum Arena, 1966-96; Arena in Oakland, 1997-2006. (8) Conseco Fieldhouse, 1999-2011. (9) Bradley Center, 1988-2012. (10) ARCO Arena, 1988-2011; Power Balance Pavilion, 2011-12. (11) SBC Center, 2002-06. (12) Delta Center, 1991-2006. (13) MCI Center, 1997-2006.

All-Time NBA Regular Season Coaching Victories

(At the end of the 2012-13 season, ranked by wins. * = Active in 2012-13 season.)

Coach	W	L	PCT	Coach	W	L	PCT	Coach	W	L	PCT
Don Nelson	1,335	1,063	.557	Bill Fitch	944	1,106	.460	John MacLeod	707	657	.518
Lenny Wilkens	1,332	1,155	.536	Red Auerbach	938	479	.662	Red Holzman	696	604	.535
Jerry Sloan	1,221	803	.603	Dick Motta	935	1,017	.479	Mike Fratello	667	548	.549
Pat Riley	1,210	694	.636	*Gregg Popovich	905	423	.681	Chuck Daly	638	437	.593
Phil Jackson	1,155	485	.704	Jack Ramsay	864	783	.525	Flip Saunders	638	526	.548
*George Karl	1,131	756	.599	Cotton Fitzsimmons	832	775	.518	Doug Moe	628	529	.543
Larry Brown	1,098	904	.548	Gene Shue	784	861	.477	Mike Dunleavy	613	716	.461
*Rick Adelman	1,002	707	.586								

Naismith Memorial Basketball Hall of Fame

(Located in Springfield, MA. * = 2013 inductee. ** = Enshrined as both a player and coach.)

Players

Abdul-Jabbar, Kareem
Archibald, Nate
Arizin, Paul
Barkley, Charles
Barlow, Thomas
Barry, Rick
Baylor, Elgin
Beckman, John
Bellamy, Walt
Belov, Sergei
Bing, Dave
Bird, Larry
Blazejowski, Carol
Borgmann, Bennie
Bradley, Bill
Brennan, Joseph
*Brown, Roger
Cervi, Al
Chamberlain, Wilt
Cooper, Charles
Cooper, Cynthia
Cosic, Kresimir
Cousy, Bob
Cowens, Dave
Crawford, Joan
Cunningham, Billy
Curry, Denise
Dalipagic, Drazen
Daniels, Mel
Dantley, Adrian
Davies, Bob
DeBernardi, Forrest
DeBusschere, Dave
Dehnert, Henry "Dutch"
Donovan, Anne
Drexler, Clyde
Dumars, Joe
Edwards, Teresa
Endacott, Paul
English, Alex
Erving, Julius
Ewing, Patrick
Foster, Bud
Frazier, Walt
Friedman, Max
Fulks, Joe
Gale, Lauren
Gallatin, Harry
Gates, William "Pop"
Gervin, George
Gilmore, Artis
Gola, Tom
Goodrich, Gail
Greer, Hal
Gruenig, Robert "Ace"
*Guerin, Richard
Hagan, Cliff
Hanson, Victor
Harris-Stewart, Lusia

Havlicek, John
Hawkins, Cornelius "Connie"
Hayes, Elvin
Haynes, Marques
Heinsohn, Tom
Holman, Nat
Houbregs, Bob
Howell, Bailey
Hyatt, Chuck
Issel, Dan
Jeannette, Harry "Buddy"
Johnson, Dennis
Johnson, Earvin "Magic"
Johnson, Gus
Johnson, William
Johnston, Neil
Jones, K. C.
Jones, Sam
Jordan, Michael
*King, Bernard
Krause, Ed "Moose"
Kurland, Bob
Lanier, Bob
Lapchick, Joe
Lieberman, Nancy
Lovellette, Clyde
Lucas, Jerry
Luisetti, Angelo "Hank"
Macauley, Ed
Malone, Karl
Malone, Moses
Maravich, Pete
Marcari, Hortencia
Martin, Slater
McAdoo, Bob
McClain, Katrina
McCracken, Emmett "Branch"
McCracken, Jack
McDermott, Bobby
McGuire, Dick
McHale, Kevin
Meneghin, Dino
Meyers, Ann
Mikan, George
Mikkelsen, Vern
Miller, Cheryl
Miller, Reggie
Monroe, Earl
Mullin, Chris
Murphy, Calvin
Murphy, Charles "Stretch"
Olajuwon, Hakeem
Page, Harlan "Pat"
Parish, Robert
*Payton, Gary
Pereira, Maciel "Ubiratan"
Petrovic, Drazen

Pettit, Bob
Phillip, Andy
Pippen, Scottie
Pollard, Jim
Ramsey, Frank
Reed, Willis
Risen, Arnie
Robertson, Oscar
Robinson, David
Rodman, Dennis
Roosma, John
Russell, Bill
Russell, John "Honey"
Sabonis, Arvydas
Sanders, Tom "Satch"
Sampson, Ralph
Schayes, Adolph
Schmidt, Ernest
*Schmidt, Oscar
Schommer, John
Sedran, Barney
Semjonova, Uljana
*Sharman, Bill
*Staley, Dawn
Steinmetz, Chris
Stockton, John
Stokes, Maurice
Tatum, Reece "Goose"
Thomas, Isiah
Thompson, David
Thompson, John
Thurmond, Nate
Twyman, Jack
Unseld, Wes
Vandivier, Robert "Fuzzy"
Wachter, Ed
Walker, Chet
Walton, Bill
Wanzer, Bobby
West, Jerry
White, Nera
**Wilkens, Lenny
Wilkes, Jamaal
Wilkins, Dominique
Woodard, Lynette
**Wooden, John
Worthy, James
Yardley, George

Coaches

Alexeeva, Lidia
Allen, Forrest C. "Phog"
Anderson, Harold
Auerbach, Arnold "Red"
Auriemma, Geno
Barmore, Leon
Barry, Justin "Sam"
Blood, Ernest
Boeheim, Jim

Brown, Larry
Calhoun, Jim
Cann, Howard
Carlson, Clifford
Carnesecca, Lou
Carnevale, Ben
Carril, Pete
Case, Everett
Chancellor, Van
Chaney, John
Conradt, Jody
Crum, Denzil "Denny"
Daly, Chuck
Dean, Everett
Diaz-Miguel, Antonio
Diddle, Edgar
Drake, Bruce
Ferrandiz, Pedro
Gaines, Clarence
Gamba, Sandro
Gardner, James "Jack"
Gill, Amory "Slats"
Gomelsky, Aleksandr
Gunter, Sue
Hannum, Alex
Harshman, Marv
Haskins, Don
*Hatchell, Sylvia
Hickey, Edgar
Hobson, Howard
Holzman, William "Red"
Hurley, Bob, Sr.
Iba, Hank
Jackson, Phil
Julian, Alvin
Keaney, Frank
Keogan, George
Knight, Bob
Krzyzewski, Mike
Kundla, John
Lambert, Ward
*Lewis, Guy V.
Litwack, Harry
Loeffler, Kenneth
Lonborg, Arthur "Dutch"
Magee, Herb
McCutchan, Arad
McGuire, Al
McGuire, Frank
McLendon, John
Meanwell, Dr. Walter
Meyer, Ray
Miller, Ralph
Moore, Billie
Nelson, Don
Newell, Pete
Nikolic, Aleksandar
Novosel, Mirko

Olson, Robert "Lute"
*Pitino, Rick
Ramsay, John "Jack"
Riley, Pat
Rubini, Cesare
Rupp, Adolph
Rush, Cathy
Sachs, Leonard
**Sharman, Bill
Shelton, Everett
Sloan, Jerry
Smith, Dean
Stringer, C. Vivian
Summitt, Pat
*Tarkanian, Jerry
Taylor, Fred
Thompson, John R.
VanDerveer, Tara
Wade, Margaret
Watts, Stan
**Wilkens, Lenny
Williams, Roy
Winter, Tex
**Wooden, John
Woolpert, Phil
Wootten, Morgan
Yow, Kay

Teams

1960 USA Men's Olympic Team
1992 USA Men's Olympic "Dream Team"
All American Red Heads
Buffalo Germans First Team
Harlem Globetrotters
New York Renaissance
Original Celtics
Texas Western

Referees

Enright, James
Hepbron, George
Hoyt, George
Kennedy, Matthew
Leith, Lloyd
Mihalik, Zigmund "Red"
Nichols, Hank
Nucatola, John
Quigley, Ernest
Rudolph, Marvin "Mendy"
Shirley, J. Dallas
Strom, Earl
Tobey, David
Walsh, David

Contributors

Abbott, Senda Berenson

Barksdale, Don
Bee, Clair
Biasone, Danny
Brown, Hubert "Hubie"
Brown, Walter
Bunn, John
Buss, Jerry
Colangelo, Jerry
Davidson, Bill
Douglas, Bob
Duer, Al
Embry, Wayne
Fagan, Cliff
Fisher, Harry
Fleisher, Larry
Gavitt, David
Gottlieb, Edward
*Granik, Russ
Gulick, Dr. Luther
Harrison, Lester
Hearn, Francis "Chick"
*Henderson, E. B.
Hepp, Dr. Ferenc
Hickox, Edward
Hinkle, Tony
Irish, Edward "Ned"
Jones, R. William
Kennedy, Walter
Knight, Phil
Lemon, Meadowlark
Liston, Emil
Lloyd, Earl
Mokray, Bill
Morgan, Ralph
Morgenweck, Frank
Naismith, Dr. James
Newton, C. M.
O'Brien, John
O'Brien, Larry
Olsen, Harold
Podoloff, Maurice
Porter, Henry V.
Reid, William
Ripley, Elmer
St. John, Lynn
Saperstein, Abe
Schabinger, Arthur
Stagg, Alonzo
Stankovic, Boris
Steitz, Edward
Taylor, Chuck
Teague, Bertha
Tower, Oswald
Trester, Arthur
Wells, Clifford
Wilke, Lou
Zollner, Fred

Lynx Win 2013 WNBA Title; Thompson Retires

The Minnesota Lynx went undefeated in the 2013 postseason to win the WNBA championship for the second time in three years. Maya Moore scored 23 points in an 86-77 victory over the Atlanta Dream in the decisive Game 3 Oct. 10, 2013, at the Gwinnett Center in Duluth, GA. Moore, who averaged 18.5 points in leading Minnesota to a league-best 26-8 record, was voted WNBA Finals MVP.

The WNBA bid farewell in 2013 to 17-year veteran Tina Thompson, the first player ever drafted into the WNBA in 1997. Thompson was the only player to compete in all 17 WNBA seasons and is the league's career record-holder in points and minutes played. Tulsa Shock guard Riquna Williams broke the WNBA single-game record with 51 points in Tulsa's 98-65 win over the San Antonio Silver Stars on Sept. 8, 2013.

WNBA Final Standings, 2013

(playoff seeding in parentheses; conference winner automatically gets top seed)

Eastern Conference	W	L	PCT	GB	Western Conference	W	L	PCT	GB
Chicago Sky (1)	24	10	.706	—	Minnesota Lynx (1)	26	8	.765	—
Atlanta Dream (2)	17	17	.500	7	Los Angeles Sparks (2)	24	10	.706	2
Washington Mystics (3)	17	17	.500	7	Phoenix Mercury (3)	19	15	.559	7
Indiana Fever (4)	16	18	.471	8	Seattle Storm (4)	17	17	.500	9
New York Liberty	11	23	.324	13	San Antonio Silver Stars	12	22	.353	14
Connecticut Sun	10	24	.294	14	Tulsa Shock	11	23	.324	15

Note: Atlanta was seeded over Washington based on head-to-head win percentage.

WNBA Playoffs, 2013

Eastern Conference	Western Conference
(4) Indiana defeated (1) Chicago, 2 games to 0	(1) Minnesota defeated (4) Seattle, 2 games to 0
(2) Atlanta defeated (3) Washington, 2 games to 1	(3) Phoenix defeated (2) Los Angeles, 2 games to 1
(2) Atlanta defeated (4) Indiana, 2 games to 0	(1) Minnesota defeated (3) Phoenix, 2 games to 0

WNBA Championship, 2013

Minnesota defeated Atlanta, 3 games to 0 (84-59, 88-63, 86-77), in the best-of-five series.

All-WNBA Teams, 2013

First team	Position	Second team	Position
Maya Moore, Minnesota	Forward	Tamika Catchings, Indiana	Forward
Candace Parker, Los Angeles	Forward	Elena Delle Donne, Chicago	Forward
Sylvia Fowles, Chicago	Center	Tina Charles, Connecticut	Center
Diana Taurasi, Phoenix	Guard	Angel McCoughtry, Atlanta	Guard
Lindsay Whalen, Minnesota	Guard	Seimone Augustus, Minnesota	Guard

WNBA Statistical Leaders, 2013

Minutes played: 1,119, DeWanna Bonner, Phoenix
Total points: 711, Angel McCoughtry, Atlanta
Points per game: 21.5, Angel McCoughtry, Atlanta
Field goal pct.: .586, Sylvia Fowles, Chicago
3-point field goal pct.: .453, Maya Moore, Minnesota
Free throw pct.: .929, Elena Delle Donne, Chicago

Rebounds: 369, Sylvia Fowles, Chicago
Assists: 197, Diana Taurasi, Phoenix; Lindsay Whalen, Minnesota
Steals: 89, Angel McCoughtry, Atlanta
Blocked shots: 81, Brittney Griner, Phoenix

WNBA Champions, 1997-2013

Year	Regular Season Eastern Conference	Western Conference	Champion	Playoffs Winning coach	Opponent
1997	Houston Comets	Phoenix Mercury	Houston	Van Chancellor	New York
1998	Cleveland Rockers	Houston Comets	Houston	Van Chancellor	Phoenix
1999	New York Liberty	Houston Comets	Houston	Van Chancellor	New York
2000	New York Liberty	Los Angeles Sparks	Houston	Van Chancellor	New York
2001	Cleveland Rockers	Los Angeles Sparks	Los Angeles	Michael Cooper	Charlotte
2002	New York Liberty	Los Angeles Sparks	Los Angeles	Michael Cooper	New York
2003	Detroit Shock	Los Angeles Sparks	Detroit	Bill Laimbeer	Los Angeles
2004	Connecticut Sun	Los Angeles Sparks	Seattle	Anne Donovan	Connecticut
2005	Connecticut Sun	Sacramento Monarchs	Sacramento	John Whisenant	Connecticut
2006	Connecticut Sun	Los Angeles Sparks	Detroit	Bill Laimbeer	Sacramento
2007	Detroit Shock	Phoenix Mercury	Phoenix	Paul Westhead	Detroit
2008	Detroit Shock	San Antonio Silver Stars	Detroit	Bill Laimbeer	San Antonio
2009	Indiana Fever	Phoenix Mercury	Phoenix	Corey Gaines	Indiana
2010	Washington Mystics	Seattle Storm	Seattle	Brian Agler	Atlanta
2011	Indiana Fever	Minnesota Lynx	Minnesota	Cheryl Reeve	Atlanta
2012	Connecticut Sun	Minnesota Lynx	Indiana	Lin Dunn	Minnesota
2013	Chicago Sky	Minnesota Lynx	Minnesota	Cheryl Reeve	Atlanta

WNBA Finals MVP, 1997-2013

Year	Player, team	Year	Player, team	Year	Player, team
1997	Cynthia Cooper, Houston	2003	Ruth Riley, Detroit	2009	Diana Taurasi, Phoenix
1998	Cynthia Cooper, Houston	2004	Betty Lennox, Seattle	2010	Lauren Jackson, Seattle
1999	Cynthia Cooper, Houston	2005	Yolanda Griffith, Sacramento	2011	Seimone Augustus, Minnesota
2000	Cynthia Cooper, Houston	2006	Deanna Nolan, Detroit	2012	Tamika Catchings, Indiana
2001	Lisa Leslie, Los Angeles	2007	Cappie Pondexter, Phoenix	2013	Maya Moore, Minnesota
2002	Lisa Leslie, Los Angeles	2008	Katie Smith, Detroit		

WNBA Most Valuable Player, 1997-2013

Year	Player, team	Year	Player, team	Year	Player, team
1997	Cynthia Cooper, Houston	2003	Lauren Jackson, Seattle	2009	Diana Taurasi, Phoenix
1998	Cynthia Cooper, Houston	2004	Lisa Leslie, Los Angeles	2010	Lauren Jackson, Seattle
1999	Yolanda Griffith, Sacramento	2005	Sheryl Swoopes, Houston	2011	Tamika Catchings, Indiana
2000	Sheryl Swoopes, Houston	2006	Lisa Leslie, Los Angeles	2012	Tina Charles, Connecticut
2001	Lisa Leslie, Los Angeles	2007	Lauren Jackson, Seattle	2013	Candace Parker, Los Angeles
2002	Sheryl Swoopes, Houston	2008	Candace Parker, Los Angeles		

WNBA Rookie of the Year, 1997-2013

Year	Player, team	Year	Player, team	Year	Player, team
1997	No award	2003	Cheryl Ford, Detroit	2009	Angel McCoughtry, Atlanta
1998	Tracy Reid, Charlotte	2004	Diana Taurasi, Phoenix	2010	Tina Charles, Connecticut
1999	Chamique Holdsclaw, Washington	2005	Temeka Johnson, Washington	2011	Maya Moore, Minnesota
2000	Betty Lennox, Minnesota	2006	Seimone Augustus, Minnesota	2012	Nneka Ogwumike, Los Angeles
2001	Jackie Stiles, Portland	2007	Armintie Price, Chicago	2013	Elena Delle Donne, Chicago
2002	Tamika Catchings, Indiana	2008	Candace Parker, Los Angeles		

WNBA Scoring Leaders, 1997-2013

(average points per game; 24 games or 480 point minimum in 2013; prior season minimums vary)

Year	Leader, team	PTS	AVG	Year	Leader, team	PTS	AVG
1997	Cynthia Cooper, Houston	621	22.2	2006	Diana Taurasi, Phoenix	860	25.3
1998	Cynthia Cooper, Houston	680	22.7	2007	Lauren Jackson, Seattle	739	23.8
1999	Cynthia Cooper, Houston	686	22.1	2008	Diana Taurasi, Phoenix	820	24.1
2000	Sheryl Swoopes, Houston	643	20.7	2009	Diana Taurasi, Phoenix	631	20.4
2001	Katie Smith, Minnesota	739	23.1	2010	Diana Taurasi, Phoenix	702	22.6
2002	Chamique Holdsclaw, Washington	397	19.9	2011	Diana Taurasi, Phoenix	692	21.6
2003	Lauren Jackson, Seattle	698	21.2	2012	Angel McCoughtry, Atlanta	514	21.4
2004	Lauren Jackson, Seattle	634	20.5	2013	Angel McCoughtry, Atlanta	711	21.5
2005	Sheryl Swoopes, Houston	614	18.6				

WNBA Rebounding Leaders, 1997-2013

(average rebounds per game; 24 games minimum in 2013; prior season minimums vary)

Year	Leader, team	REB	RPG	Year	Leader, team	REB	RPG
1997	Lisa Leslie, Los Angeles	266	9.5	2006	Cheryl Ford, Detroit	363	11.3
1998	Lisa Leslie, Los Angeles	285	10.2	2007	Lauren Jackson, Seattle	300	9.7
1999	Yolanda Griffith, Sacramento	329	11.3	2008	Candace Parker, Los Angeles	313	9.5
2000	Natalie Williams, Utah	336	11.6	2009	Candace Parker, Los Angeles	244	9.8
2001	Yolanda Griffith, Sacramento	357	11.2	2010	Tina Charles, Connecticut	398	11.7
2002	Chamique Holdsclaw, Washington	232	11.6	2011	Tina Charles, Connecticut	374	11.0
2003	Chamique Holdsclaw, Washington	294	10.9	2012	Tina Charles, Connecticut	345	10.5
2004	Lisa Leslie, Los Angeles	336	9.9	2013	Sylvia Fowles, Chicago	369	11.5
2005	Cheryl Ford, Detroit	322	9.8				

WNBA Assist Leaders, 1997-2013

(average assists per game; 24 games minimum in 2013; prior season minimums vary)

Year	Leader, team	AST	APG	Year	Leader, team	AST	APG
1997	Teresa Weatherspoon, New York	172	6.1	2006	Nikki Teasley, Washington	183	5.4
1998	Ticha Penicheiro, Sacramento	224	7.5	2007	Becky Hammon, San Antonio	140	5.0
1999	Ticha Penicheiro, Sacramento	226	7.1	2008	Lindsay Whalen, Connecticut	166	5.4
2000	Ticha Penicheiro, Sacramento	236	7.9	2009	Sue Bird, Seattle	179	5.8
2001	Ticha Penicheiro, Sacramento	172	7.5	2010	Ticha Penicheiro, Los Angeles	220	6.9
2002	Ticha Penicheiro, Sacramento	192	8.0	2011	Lindsay Whalen, Minnesota	199	5.9
2003	Ticha Penicheiro, Sacramento	229	6.7	2012	Lindsay Whalen, Minnesota	178	5.4
2004	Nikki Teasley, Los Angeles	207	6.1	2013	Danielle Robinson, San Antonio	168	6.7
2005	Sue Bird, Seattle	176	5.9				

All-Time WNBA Statistical Leaders

(At the end of the 2013 season.)

Scoring Average
(minimum 100 games)

Player	G	PTS	PPG	Player	G	PTS	PPG
Cynthia Cooper	124	2,601	21.0	Seimone Augustus	224	4,188	18.7
Diana Taurasi	301	6,186	20.6	Candace Parker	149	2,587	17.4
Angel McCoughtry	158	3,088	19.5	Lisa Leslie	363	6,263	17.3
Cappie Pondexter	261	5,005	19.2	Tina Charles	130	2,243	17.3
Lauren Jackson	317	6,007	18.9	Chamique Holdsclaw	279	4,716	16.9

Points

Tina Thompson	7,488
Katie Smith	6,452
Tamika Catchings	6,296
Lisa Leslie	6,263
Diana Taurasi	6,186
Lauren Jackson	6,007
Becky Hammon	5,577
DeLisha Milton-Jones	5,415
Katie Douglas	5,142
Tangela Smith	5,048

Rebounds

Lisa Leslie	3,307
Tina Thompson	3,070
Taj McWilliams-Franklin	3,013
Tamika Catchings	2,838
DeLisha Milton-Jones	2,492
Michelle Snow	2,479
Lauren Jackson	2,447
Yolanda Griffith	2,444
Rebekkah Brunson	2,380
Tangela Smith	2,335

Assists

Ticha Penicheiro	2,599
Sue Bird	1,935
Lindsay Whalen	1,722
Becky Hammon	1,573
Shannon Johnson	1,424
Teresa Weatherspoon	1,338
Dawn Staley	1,337
Tamika Catchings	1,325
Diana Taurasi	1,263
Katie Smith	1,258

3-Point Field Goals Made

Katie Smith	906
Becky Hammon	782
Diana Taurasi	749
Tina Thompson	748
Katie Douglas	663
Sue Bird	600
Nicole Powell	567
Tamika Catchings	539
Kara Lawson	529
Lauren Jackson	436

Steals

Tamika Catchings	930
Ticha Penicheiro	764
Sheryl Swoopes	657
DeLisha Milton-Jones	603
Katie Douglas	593
Taj McWilliams-Franklin	580
Tully Bevilaqua	573
Yolanda Griffith	529
Sue Bird	497
Jia Perkins	495

Blocked Shots

Margo Dydek	877
Lisa Leslie	822
Lauren Jackson	586
Tangela Smith	557
Tammy Sutton-Brown	555
Ruth Riley	505
Taj McWilliams-Franklin	443
Michelle Snow	403
Tina Thompson	372
Tamika Catchings	338

HOCKEY

Chicago Wins Second Cup Since 2010 in Shortened NHL Season

The Chicago Blackhawks excelled from start to finish in the abbreviated 2012-13 National Hockey League season. The team began the season 21-0-3 and ended its year by defeating the Boston Bruins in the Stanley Cup Final, four games to two. Just 17 sec. after Bryan Bickell scored to tie Game 6 at 2-2 in TD Garden in Boston June 24, 2013, Dave Bolland scored the Cup-winning goal with less than 59 seconds left in regulation to give Chicago a 3-2 win. Chicago right wing Patrick Kane won the Conn Smythe Trophy as playoff MVP, totaling nine goals in 23 playoff games.

NHL teams played a 48-game regular season that began Jan. 19, 2013, due to a lockout that forced the cancellation of 510 games. Chicago (36-7-5) won the NHL Presidents' Trophy with a league-best 77 points, five better than the Pittsburgh Penguins, which recorded 15 straight wins Mar. 2-30, the second-longest winning streak in NHL history.

Tampa Bay Lightning forward Martin St. Louis topped the NHL in 2013 with 60 points and Washington's Alex Ovechkin led the league with 32 goals. Ovechkin tallied 56 points, tied for third with Pittsburgh's Sidney Crosby, who missed the final 12 games of the regular season after suffering a broken jaw against the NY Islanders Mar. 30, 2013.

The NHL announced Mar. 14, 2013, a league realignment for the 2013-14 season that will include an unbalanced two-conference, four-division plan. The new setup moves the Detroit Red Wings and Columbus Blue Jackets to the Eastern Conference and the Winnipeg Jets to the West.

Final NHL Standings, 2012-13

Playoff seeding in parentheses; division winners automatically seeded 1, 2, or 3. Standings were determined by total points, then by the greater number of games won, excluding games won in a shootout. This figure is reflected in the ROW column (regulation + OT wins). Teams tied at the end of regulation time are each awarded one point. An additional point is awarded to the overtime or shootout winner.

Eastern Conference

Atlantic Division	W	L	OT	GF	GA	PTS	ROW
Pittsburgh Penguins (1)...	36	12	0	165	119	72	33
New York Rangers (6)..	26	18	4	130	112	56	22
New York Islanders (8)...	24	17	7	139	139	55	20
Philadelphia Flyers	23	22	3	133	141	49	22
New Jersey Devils.......	19	19	10	112	129	48	17

Northeast Division	W	L	OT	GF	GA	PTS	ROW
Montréal Canadiens (2)...	29	14	5	149	126	63	26
Boston Bruins (4).......	28	14	6	131	109	62	24
Toronto Maple Leafs (5)..	26	17	5	145	133	57	26
Ottawa Senators (7)	25	17	6	116	104	56	21
Buffalo Sabres.......	21	21	6	125	143	48	14

Southeast Division	W	L	OT	GF	GA	PTS	ROW
Washington Capitals (3)...	27	18	3	149	130	57	24
Winnipeg Jets..........	24	21	3	128	144	51	22
Carolina Hurricanes	19	25	4	128	160	42	18
Tampa Bay Lightning	18	26	4	148	150	40	17
Florida Panthers	15	27	6	112	171	36	12

Western Conference

Central Division	W	L	OT	GF	GA	PTS	ROW
Chicago Blackhawks (1)...	36	7	5	155	102	77	30
St. Louis Blues (4)........	29	17	2	129	115	60	24
Detroit Red Wings (7)...	24	16	8	124	115	56	22
Columbus Blue Jackets ..	24	17	7	120	119	55	19
Nashville Predators......	16	23	9	111	139	41	14

Northwest Division	W	L	OT	GF	GA	PTS	ROW
Vancouver Canucks (3)...	26	15	7	127	121	59	21
Minnesota Wild (8)......	26	19	3	122	127	55	22
Edmonton Oilers	19	22	7	125	134	45	17
Calgary Flames.........	19	25	4	128	160	42	19
Colorado Avalanche	16	25	7	116	152	39	14

Pacific Division	W	L	OT	GF	GA	PTS	ROW
Anaheim Ducks (2).......	30	12	6	140	118	66	24
Los Angeles Kings (5)...	27	16	5	133	118	59	25
San Jose Sharks (6).......	25	16	7	124	116	57	17
Phoenix Coyotes.........	21	18	9	125	131	51	17
Dallas Stars............	22	22	4	130	142	48	20

Stanley Cup Playoff Results, 2013

Eastern Conference
Pittsburgh defeated NY Islanders, 4-2
Ottawa defeated Montréal, 4-1
NY Rangers defeated Washington, 4-3
Boston defeated Toronto, 4-3
Pittsburgh defeated Ottawa, 4-1
Boston defeated NY Rangers, 4-1
Boston defeated Pittsburgh, 4-0

Western Conference
Chicago defeated Minnesota, 4-1
Detroit defeated Anaheim, 4-3
San Jose defeated Vancouver, 4-0
Los Angeles defeated St. Louis, 4-2
Chicago defeated Detroit, 4-3
Los Angeles defeated San Jose, 4-3
Chicago defeated Los Angeles, 4-1

Stanley Cup Final
Chicago defeated Boston, 4-2 (4-3 [3 OT], 1-2 [OT], 0-2, 6-5 [OT], 3-1, 3-2)

Stanley Cup Champions, 1927-2013

Year	Champion	Coach	Final opponent	Year	Champion	Coach	Final opponent
1927	Ottawa..........	Dave Gill	Boston	1952	Detroit..........	Tommy Ivan	Montréal
1928	NY Rangers	Lester Patrick ..	Montréal Maroons	1953	Montréal........	Dick Irvin......	Boston
				1954	Detroit..........	Tommy Ivan	Montréal
1929	Boston..........	Cy Denneny	NY Rangers	1955	Detroit..........	Jimmy Skinner ..	Montréal
1930	Montréal Canadiens	Cecil Hart	Boston	1956	Montréal........	Toe Blake.......	Detroit
1931	Montréal Canadiens	Cecil Hart	Chicago	1957	Montréal........	Toe Blake.......	Boston
1932	Toronto.........	Dick Irvin	NY Rangers	1958	Montréal........	Toe Blake.......	Boston
1933	NY Rangers......	Lester Patrick ...	Toronto	1959	Montréal........	Toe Blake.......	Toronto
1934	Chicago.........	Tommy Gorman ...	Detroit	1960	Montréal........	Toe Blake.......	Toronto
1935	Montréal Maroons	Tommy Gorman ...	Toronto	1961	Chicago.........	Rudy Pilous	Detroit
1936	Detroit..........	Jack Adams.......	Toronto	1962	Toronto.........	Punch Imlach ...	Chicago
1937	Detroit..........	Jack Adams.......	NY Rangers	1963	Toronto.........	Punch Imlach ...	Detroit
1938	Chicago.........	Bill Stewart	Toronto	1964	Toronto.........	Punch Imlach ...	Detroit
1939	Boston..........	Art Ross	Toronto	1965	Montréal........	Toe Blake.......	Chicago
1940	NY Rangers......	Frank Boucher ..	Toronto	1966	Montréal........	Toe Blake.......	Detroit
1941	Boston..........	Cooney Weiland ..	Detroit	1967	Toronto.........	Punch Imlach ...	Montréal
1942	Toronto.........	Hap Day	Detroit	1968	Montréal........	Toe Blake.......	St. Louis
1943	Detroit..........	Jack Adams.......	Boston	1969	Montréal........	Claude Ruel	St. Louis
1944	Montréal........	Dick Irvin	Chicago	1970	Boston..........	Harry Sinden....	St. Louis
1945	Toronto.........	Hap Day	Detroit	1971	Montréal........	Al MacNeil......	Chicago
1946	Montréal........	Dick Irvin	Boston	1972	Boston..........	Tom Johnson ...	NY Rangers
1947	Toronto.........	Hap Day	Montréal	1973	Montréal........	Scotty Bowman ..	Chicago
1948	Toronto.........	Hap Day	Detroit	1974	Philadelphia	Fred Shero	Boston
1949	Toronto.........	Hap Day	Detroit	1975	Philadelphia	Fred Shero	Buffalo
1950	Detroit..........	Tommy Ivan	NY Rangers	1976	Montréal........	Scotty Bowman ..	Philadelphia
1951	Toronto.........	Joe Primeau	Montréal	1977	Montréal........	Scotty Bowman....	Boston

Year	Champion	Coach	Final opponent	Year	Champion	Coach	Final opponent
1978	Montréal	Scotty Bowman	Boston	1996	Colorado	Marc Crawford	Florida
1979	Montréal	Scotty Bowman	NY Rangers	1997	Detroit	Scotty Bowman	Philadelphia
1980	NY Islanders	Al Arbour	Philadelphia	1998	Detroit	Scotty Bowman	Washington
1981	NY Islanders	Al Arbour	Minnesota	1999	Dallas	Ken Hitchcock	Buffalo
1982	NY Islanders	Al Arbour	Vancouver	2000	New Jersey	Larry Robinson	Dallas
1983	NY Islanders	Al Arbour	Edmonton	2001	Colorado	Bob Hartley	New Jersey
1984	Edmonton	Glen Sather	NY Islanders	2002	Detroit	Scotty Bowman	Carolina
1985	Edmonton	Glen Sather	Philadelphia	2003	New Jersey	Pat Burns	Anaheim
1986	Montréal	Jean Perron	Calgary	2004	Tampa Bay	John Tortorella	Calgary
1987	Edmonton	Glen Sather	Philadelphia	2005	No competition (labor dispute; season cancelled)		
1988	Edmonton	Glen Sather	Boston	2006	Carolina	Peter Laviolette	Edmonton
1989	Calgary	Terry Crisp	Montréal	2007	Anaheim	Randy Carlyle	Ottawa
1990	Edmonton	John Muckler	Boston	2008	Detroit	Mike Babcock	Pittsburgh
1991	Pittsburgh	Bob Johnson	Minnesota	2009	Pittsburgh	Dan Bylsma	Detroit
1992	Pittsburgh	Scotty Bowman	Chicago	2010	Chicago	Joel Quenneville	Philadelphia
1993	Montréal	Jacques Demers	Los Angeles	2011	Boston	Claude Julien	Vancouver
1994	NY Rangers	Mike Keenan	Vancouver	2012	Los Angeles	Darryl Sutter	New Jersey
1995	New Jersey	Jacques Lemaire	Detroit	2013	Chicago	Joel Quenneville	Boston

Most NHL Goals in a Season

Player	Team	Season	Goals	Player	Team	Season	Goals
Wayne Gretzky	Edmonton	1981-82	92	Jari Kurri	Edmonton	1984-85	71
Wayne Gretzky	Edmonton	1983-84	87	Mario Lemieux	Pittsburgh	1987-88	70
Brett Hull	St. Louis	1990-91	86	Bernie Nicholls	Los Angeles	1988-89	70
Mario Lemieux	Pittsburgh	1988-89	85	Brett Hull	St. Louis	1991-92	70
Phil Esposito	Boston	1970-71	76	Mike Bossy	NY Islanders	1978-79	69
Alexander Mogilny	Buffalo	1992-93	76	Mario Lemieux	Pittsburgh	1992-93	69
Teemu Selanne	Winnipeg	1992-93	76	Mario Lemieux	Pittsburgh	1995-96	69
Wayne Gretzky	Edmonton	1984-85	73	Phil Esposito	Boston	1973-74	68
Brett Hull	St. Louis	1989-90	72	Mike Bossy	NY Islanders	1980-81	68
Wayne Gretzky	Edmonton	1982-83	71	Jari Kurri	Edmonton	1985-86	68

All-Time Regular Season Leading Scorers

(Through end of 2012-13 season. * = active in 2012-13 season.)

Player	Goals	Assists	Points	Player	Goals	Assists	Points	Player	Goals	Assists	Points
Wayne Gretzky	894	1,963	2,857	*Jaromir Jagr	681	1,007	1,688	*Teemu Selanne	675	755	1,430
Mark Messier	694	1,193	1,887	Joe Sakic	625	1,016	1,641	Bryan Trottier	524	901	1,425
Gordie Howe	801	1,049	1,850	Phil Esposito	717	873	1,590	Adam Oates	341	1,079	1,420
Ron Francis	549	1,249	1,798	Ray Bourque	410	1,169	1,579	Doug Gilmour	450	964	1,414
Marcel Dionne	731	1,040	1,771	Mark Recchi	577	956	1,533	Dale Hawerchuk	518	891	1,409
Steve Yzerman	692	1,063	1,755	Paul Coffey	396	1,135	1,531	Jari Kurri	601	797	1,398
Mario Lemieux	690	1,033	1,723	Stan Mikita	541	926	1,467	Luc Robitaille	668	726	1,394

Hart Memorial Trophy (MVP), 1927-2013

Year	Player, team	Year	Player, team	Year	Player, team
1927	Herb Gardiner, Montréal Canadiens	1956	Jean Beliveau, Montréal	1984	Wayne Gretzky, Edmonton
1928	Howie Morenz, Montréal Canadiens	1957	Gordie Howe, Detroit	1985	Wayne Gretzky, Edmonton
1929	Roy Worters, NY Americans	1958	Gordie Howe, Detroit	1986	Wayne Gretzky, Edmonton
1930	Nels Stewart, Montréal Maroons	1959	Andy Bathgate, NY Rangers	1987	Wayne Gretzky, Edmonton
1931	Howie Morenz, Montréal Canadiens	1960	Gordie Howe, Detroit	1988	Mario Lemieux, Pittsburgh
1932	Howie Morenz, Montréal Canadiens	1961	Bernie Geoffrion, Montréal	1989	Wayne Gretzky, Los Angeles
1933	Eddie Shore, Boston	1962	Jacques Plante, Montréal	1990	Mark Messier, Edmonton
1934	Aurel Joliat, Montréal Canadiens	1963	Gordie Howe, Detroit	1991	Brett Hull, St. Louis
1935	Eddie Shore, Boston	1964	Jean Beliveau, Montréal	1992	Mark Messier, NY Rangers
1936	Eddie Shore, Boston	1965	Bobby Hull, Chicago	1993	Mario Lemieux, Pittsburgh
1937	Babe Siebert, Montréal Canadiens	1966	Bobby Hull, Chicago	1994	Sergei Fedorov, Detroit
1938	Eddie Shore, Boston	1967	Stan Mikita, Chicago	1995	Eric Lindros, Philadelphia
1939	Toe Blake, Montréal	1968	Stan Mikita, Chicago	1996	Mario Lemieux, Pittsburgh
1940	Ebbie Goodfellow, Detroit	1969	Phil Esposito, Boston	1997	Dominik Hasek, Buffalo
1941	Bill Cowley, Boston	1970	Bobby Orr, Boston	1998	Dominik Hasek, Buffalo
1942	Tom Anderson, Brooklyn Americans	1971	Bobby Orr, Boston	1999	Jaromir Jagr, Pittsburgh
1943	Bill Cowley, Boston	1972	Bobby Orr, Boston	2000	Chris Pronger, St. Louis
1944	Babe Pratt, Toronto	1973	Bobby Clarke, Philadelphia	2001	Joe Sakic, Colorado
1945	Elmer Lach, Montréal	1974	Phil Esposito, Boston	2002	Jose Theodore, Montréal
1946	Max Bentley, Chicago	1975	Bobby Clarke, Philadelphia	2003	Peter Forsberg, Colorado
1947	Maurice Richard, Montréal	1976	Bobby Clarke, Philadelphia	2004	Martin St. Louis, Tampa Bay
1948	Buddy O'Connor, NY Rangers	1977	Guy Lafleur, Montréal	2006	Joe Thornton, San Jose
1949	Sid Abel, Detroit	1978	Guy Lafleur, Montréal	2007	Sidney Crosby, Pittsburgh
1950	Chuck Rayner, NY Rangers	1979	Bryan Trottier, NY Islanders	2008	Alexander Ovechkin, Washington
1951	Milt Schmidt, Boston	1980	Wayne Gretzky, Edmonton	2009	Alexander Ovechkin, Washington
1952	Gordie Howe, Detroit	1981	Wayne Gretzky, Edmonton	2010	Henrik Sedin, Vancouver
1953	Gordie Howe, Detroit	1982	Wayne Gretzky, Edmonton	2011	Corey Perry, Anaheim
1954	Al Rollins, Chicago	1983	Wayne Gretzky, Edmonton	2012	Evgeni Malkin, Pittsburgh
1955	Ted Kennedy, Toronto			2013	Alexander Ovechkin, Washington

Conn Smythe Trophy (MVP in Playoffs), 1965-2013

Year	Player, team	Year	Player, team	Year	Player, team
1965	Jean Beliveau, Montréal	1976	Reggie Leach, Philadelphia	1987	Ron Hextall, Philadelphia
1966	Roger Crozier, Detroit	1977	Guy Lafleur, Montréal	1988	Wayne Gretzky, Edmonton
1967	Dave Keon, Toronto	1978	Larry Robinson, Montréal	1989	Al MacInnis, Calgary
1968	Glenn Hall, St. Louis	1979	Bob Gainey, Montréal	1990	Bill Ranford, Edmonton
1969	Serge Savard, Montréal	1980	Bryan Trottier, NY Islanders	1991	Mario Lemieux, Pittsburgh
1970	Bobby Orr, Boston	1981	Butch Goring, NY Islanders	1992	Mario Lemieux, Pittsburgh
1971	Ken Dryden, Montréal	1982	Mike Bossy, NY Islanders	1993	Patrick Roy, Montréal
1972	Bobby Orr, Boston	1983	Billy Smith, NY Islanders	1994	Brian Leetch, NY Rangers
1973	Yvan Cournoyer, Montréal	1984	Mark Messier, Edmonton	1995	Claude Lemieux, New Jersey
1974	Bernie Parent, Philadelphia	1985	Wayne Gretzky, Edmonton	1996	Joe Sakic, Colorado
1975	Bernie Parent, Philadelphia	1986	Patrick Roy, Montréal	1997	Mike Vernon, Detroit

Year	Player, team	Year	Player, team	Year	Player, team
1998	Steve Yzerman, Detroit	2003	Jean-Sebastien Giguere, Anaheim	2009	Evgeni Malkin, Pittsburgh
1999	Joe Nieuwendyk, Dallas	2004	Brad Richards, Tampa Bay	2010	Jonathan Toews, Chicago
2000	Scott Stevens, New Jersey	2006	Cam Ward, Carolina	2011	Tim Thomas, Boston
2001	Patrick Roy, Colorado	2007	Scott Niedermayer, Anaheim	2012	Jonathan Quick, Los Angeles
2002	Nicklas Lidstrom, Detroit	2008	Henrik Zetterberg, Detroit	2013	Patrick Kane, Chicago

Calder Memorial Trophy (Rookie of the Year), 1933-2013

Year	Player, team	Year	Player, team	Year	Player, team
1933	Carl Voss, Detroit	1960	Bill Hay, Chicago	1987	Luc Robitaille, Los Angeles
1934	Russ Blinco, Montréal Maroons	1961	Dave Keon, Toronto	1988	Joe Nieuwendyk, Calgary
1935	Dave Schriner, NY Americans	1962	Bobby Rousseau, Montréal	1989	Brian Leetch, NY Rangers
1936	Mike Karakas, Chicago	1963	Kent Douglas, Toronto	1990	Sergei Makarov, Calgary
1937	Syl Apps, Toronto	1964	Jacques Laperrière, Montréal	1991	Ed Belfour, Chicago
1938	Cully Dahlstrom, Chicago	1965	Roger Crozier, Detroit	1992	Pavel Bure, Vancouver
1939	Frank Brimsek, Boston	1966	Brit Selby, Toronto	1993	Teemu Selanne, Winnipeg
1940	Kilby MacDonald, NY Rangers	1967	Bobby Orr, Boston	1994	Martin Brodeur, New Jersey
1941	John Quilty, Montréal	1968	Derek Sanderson, Boston	1995	Peter Forsberg, Quebec
1942	Grant Warwick, NY Rangers	1969	Danny Grant, Minnesota	1996	Daniel Alfredsson, Ottawa
1943	Gaye Stewart, Toronto	1970	Tony Esposito, Chicago	1997	Bryan Berard, NY Islanders
1944	Gus Bodnar, Toronto	1971	Gilbert Perreault, Buffalo	1998	Sergei Samsonov, Boston
1945	Frank McCool, Toronto	1972	Ken Dryden, Montréal	1999	Chris Drury, Colorado
1946	Edgar Laprade, NY Rangers	1973	Steve Vickers, NY Rangers	2000	Scott Gomez, New Jersey
1947	Howie Meeker, Toronto	1974	Denis Potvin, NY Islanders	2001	Evgeni Nabokov, San Jose
1948	Jim McFadden, Detroit	1975	Eric Vail, Atlanta	2002	Dany Heatley, Atlanta
1949	Pentti Lund, NY Rangers	1976	Bryan Trottier, NY Islanders	2003	Barret Jackman, St. Louis
1950	Jack Gelineau, Boston	1977	Willi Plett, Atlanta	2004	Andrew Raycroft, Boston
1951	Terry Sawchuk, Detroit	1978	Mike Bossy, NY Islanders	2006	Alexander Ovechkin, Washington
1952	Bernie Geoffrion, Montréal	1979	Bobby Smith, Minnesota	2007	Evgeni Malkin, Pittsburgh
1953	Gump Worsley, NY Rangers	1980	Ray Bourque, Boston	2008	Patrick Kane, Chicago
1954	Camille Henry, NY Rangers	1981	Peter Stastny, Quebec	2009	Steve Mason, Columbus
1955	Ed Litzenberger, Chicago	1982	Dale Hawerchuk, Winnipeg	2010	Tyler Myers, Buffalo
1956	Glenn Hall, Detroit	1983	Steve Larmer, Chicago	2011	Jeff Skinner, Carolina
1957	Larry Regan, Boston	1984	Tom Barrasso, Buffalo	2012	Gabriel Landeskog, Colorado
1958	Frank Mahovlich, Toronto	1985	Mario Lemieux, Pittsburgh	2013	Jonathan Huberdeau, Florida
1959	Ralph Backstrom, Montréal	1986	Gary Suter, Calgary		

Lady Byng Memorial Trophy (Most Gentlemanly Player), 1925-2013

Year	Player, team	Year	Player, team	Year	Player, team
1925	Frank Nighbor, Ottawa	1955	Sid Smith, Toronto	1984	Mike Bossy, NY Islanders
1926	Frank Nighbor, Ottawa	1956	Earl Reibel, Detroit	1985	Jari Kurri, Edmonton
1927	Billy Burch, NY Americans	1957	Andy Hebenton, NY Rangers	1986	Mike Bossy, NY Islanders
1928	Frank Boucher, NY Rangers	1958	Camille Henry, NY Rangers	1987	Joe Mullen, Calgary
1929	Frank Boucher, NY Rangers	1959	Alex Delvecchio, Detroit	1988	Mats Naslund, Montréal
1930	Frank Boucher, NY Rangers	1960	Don McKenney, Boston	1989	Joe Mullen, Calgary
1931	Frank Boucher, NY Rangers	1961	Red Kelly, Toronto	1990	Brett Hull, St. Louis
1932	Joe Primeau, Toronto	1962	Dave Keon, Toronto	1991	Wayne Gretzky, Los Angeles
1933	Frank Boucher, NY Rangers	1963	Dave Keon, Toronto	1992	Wayne Gretzky, Los Angeles
1934	Frank Boucher, NY Rangers	1964	Ken Wharram, Chicago	1993	Pierre Turgeon, NY Islanders
1935	Frank Boucher, NY Rangers	1965	Bobby Hull, Chicago	1994	Wayne Gretzky, Los Angeles
1936	Doc Romnes, Chicago	1966	Alex Delvecchio, Detroit	1995	Ron Francis, Pittsburgh
1937	Marty Barry, Detroit	1967	Stan Mikita, Chicago	1996	Paul Kariya, Anaheim
1938	Gordie Drillon, Toronto	1968	Stan Mikita, Chicago	1997	Paul Kariya, Anaheim
1939	Clint Smith, NY Rangers	1969	Alex Delvecchio, Detroit	1998	Ron Francis, Pittsburgh
1940	Bobby Bauer, Boston	1970	Phil Goyette, St. Louis	1999	Wayne Gretzky, NY Rangers
1941	Bobby Bauer, Boston	1971	John Bucyk, Boston	2000	Pavol Demitra, St. Louis
1942	Syl Apps, Toronto	1972	Jean Ratelle, NY Rangers	2001	Joe Sakic, Colorado
1943	Max Bentley, Chicago	1973	Gil Perreault, Buffalo	2002	Ron Francis, Carolina
1944	Clint Smith, Chicago	1974	John Bucyk, Boston	2003	Alexander Mogilny, Toronto
1945	Bill Mosienko, Chicago	1975	Marcel Dionne, Detroit	2004	Brad Richards, Tampa Bay
1946	Toe Blake, Montréal	1976	Jean Ratelle, NYR-Boston	2006	Pavel Datsyuk, Detroit
1947	Bobby Bauer, Boston	1977	Marcel Dionne, Los Angeles	2007	Pavel Datsyuk, Detroit
1948	Buddy O'Connor, NY Rangers	1978	Butch Goring, Los Angeles	2008	Pavel Datsyuk, Detroit
1949	Bill Quackenbush, Detroit	1979	Bob MacMillan, Atlanta	2009	Pavel Datsyuk, Detroit
1950	Edgar Laprade, NY Rangers	1980	Wayne Gretzky, Edmonton	2010	Martin St. Louis, Tampa Bay
1951	Red Kelly, Detroit	1981	Rick Kehoe, Pittsburgh	2011	Martin St. Louis, Tampa Bay
1952	Sid Smith, Toronto	1982	Rick Middleton, Boston	2012	Brian Campbell, Florida
1953	Red Kelly, Detroit	1983	Mike Bossy, NY Islanders	2013	Martin St. Louis, Tampa Bay
1954	Red Kelly, Detroit				

James Norris Memorial Trophy (Outstanding Defenseman), 1954-2013

Year	Player, team	Year	Player, team	Year	Player, team
1954	Red Kelly, Detroit	1974	Bobby Orr, Boston	1993	Chris Chelios, Chicago
1955	Doug Harvey, Montréal	1975	Bobby Orr, Boston	1994	Ray Bourque, Boston
1956	Doug Harvey, Montréal	1976	Denis Potvin, NY Islanders	1995	Paul Coffey, Detroit
1957	Doug Harvey, Montréal	1977	Larry Robinson, Montréal	1996	Chris Chelios, Chicago
1958	Doug Harvey, Montréal	1978	Denis Potvin, NY Islanders	1997	Brian Leetch, NY Rangers
1959	Tom Johnson, Montréal	1979	Denis Potvin, NY Islanders	1998	Rob Blake, Los Angeles
1960	Doug Harvey, Montréal	1980	Larry Robinson, Montréal	1999	Al MacInnis, St. Louis
1961	Doug Harvey, Montréal	1981	Randy Carlyle, Pittsburgh	2000	Chris Pronger, St. Louis
1962	Doug Harvey, NY Rangers	1982	Doug Wilson, Chicago	2001	Nicklas Lidstrom, Detroit
1963	Pierre Pilote, Chicago	1983	Rod Langway, Washington	2002	Nicklas Lidstrom, Detroit
1964	Pierre Pilote, Chicago	1984	Rod Langway, Washington	2003	Nicklas Lidstrom, Detroit
1965	Pierre Pilote, Chicago	1985	Paul Coffey, Edmonton	2004	Scott Niedermayer, New Jersey
1966	Jacques Laperrière, Montréal	1986	Paul Coffey, Edmonton	2006	Nicklas Lidstrom, Detroit
1967	Harry Howell, NY Rangers	1987	Ray Bourque, Boston	2007	Nicklas Lidstrom, Detroit
1968	Bobby Orr, Boston	1988	Ray Bourque, Boston	2008	Nicklas Lidstrom, Detroit
1969	Bobby Orr, Boston	1989	Chris Chelios, Montréal	2009	Zdeno Chara, Boston
1970	Bobby Orr, Boston	1990	Ray Bourque, Boston	2010	Duncan Keith, Chicago
1971	Bobby Orr, Boston	1991	Ray Bourque, Boston	2011	Nicklas Lidstrom, Detroit
1972	Bobby Orr, Boston	1992	Brian Leetch, NY Rangers	2012	Erik Karlsson, Ottawa
1973	Bobby Orr, Boston			2013	P. K. Subban, Montréal

Art Ross Trophy (Leading Points Scorer), 1947-2013

Year	Player, team	Year	Player, team	Year	Player, team
1947	Max Bentley, Chicago	1969	Phil Esposito, Boston	1991	Wayne Gretzky, Los Angeles
1948	Elmer Lach, Montréal	1970	Bobby Orr, Boston	1992	Mario Lemieux, Pittsburgh
1949	Roy Conacher, Chicago	1971	Phil Esposito, Boston	1993	Mario Lemieux, Pittsburgh
1950	Ted Lindsay, Detroit	1972	Phil Esposito, Boston	1994	Wayne Gretzky, Los Angeles
1951	Gordie Howe, Detroit	1973	Phil Esposito, Boston	1995	Jaromir Jagr, Pittsburgh
1952	Gordie Howe, Detroit	1974	Phil Esposito, Boston	1996	Mario Lemieux, Pittsburgh
1953	Gordie Howe, Detroit	1975	Bobby Orr, Boston	1997	Mario Lemieux, Pittsburgh
1954	Gordie Howe, Detroit	1976	Guy Lafleur, Montréal	1998	Jaromir Jagr, Pittsburgh
1955	Bernie Geoffrion, Montréal	1977	Guy Lafleur, Montréal	1999	Jaromir Jagr, Pittsburgh
1956	Jean Beliveau, Montréal	1978	Guy Lafleur, Montréal	2000	Jaromir Jagr, Pittsburgh
1957	Gordie Howe, Detroit	1979	Bryan Trottier, NY Islanders	2001	Jaromir Jagr, Pittsburgh
1958	Dickie Moore, Montréal	1980	Marcel Dionne, Los Angeles	2002	Jarome Iginla, Calgary
1959	Dickie Moore, Montréal	1981	Wayne Gretzky, Edmonton	2003	Peter Forsberg, Colorado
1960	Bobby Hull, Chicago	1982	Wayne Gretzky, Edmonton	2004	Martin St. Louis, Tampa Bay
1961	Bernie Geoffrion, Montréal	1983	Wayne Gretzky, Edmonton	2006	Joe Thornton, San Jose
1962	Bobby Hull, Chicago	1984	Wayne Gretzky, Edmonton	2007	Sidney Crosby, Pittsburgh
1963	Gordie Howe, Detroit	1985	Wayne Gretzky, Edmonton	2008	Alexander Ovechkin, Washington
1964	Stan Mikita, Chicago	1986	Wayne Gretzky, Edmonton	2009	Evgeni Malkin, Pittsburgh
1965	Stan Mikita, Chicago	1987	Wayne Gretzky, Edmonton	2010	Henrik Sedin, Vancouver
1966	Bobby Hull, Chicago	1988	Mario Lemieux, Pittsburgh	2011	Daniel Sedin, Vancouver
1967	Stan Mikita, Chicago	1989	Mario Lemieux, Pittsburgh	2012	Evgeni Malkin, Pittsburgh
1968	Stan Mikita, Chicago	1990	Wayne Gretzky, Los Angeles	2013	Martin St. Louis, Tampa Bay

Vezina Trophy (Outstanding Goalie), 1927-2013

Before 1982, awarded to the goalie or goalies who played a minimum of 25 games for the team that allowed the fewest goals; since 1982, awarded to the most outstanding goalie, as determined by a vote of NHL general managers.

Year	Player, team	Year	Player, team	Year	Player, team
1927	George Hainsworth, Montréal Canadiens	1954	Harry Lumley, Toronto	1983	Pete Peeters, Boston
1928	George Hainsworth, Montréal Canadiens	1955	Terry Sawchuk, Detroit	1984	Tom Barrasso, Buffalo
		1956	Jacques Plante, Montréal	1985	Pelle Lindbergh, Philadelphia
1929	George Hainsworth, Montréal Canadiens	1957	Jacques Plante, Montréal	1986	John Vanbiesbrouck, NY Rangers
		1958	Jacques Plante, Montréal	1987	Ron Hextall, Philadelphia
1930	Tiny Thompson, Boston	1959	Jacques Plante, Montréal	1988	Grant Fuhr, Edmonton
1931	Roy Worters, NY Americans	1960	Jacques Plante, Montréal	1989	Patrick Roy, Montréal
1932	Charlie Gardiner, Chicago	1961	Johnny Bower, Toronto	1990	Patrick Roy, Montréal
1933	Tiny Thompson, Boston	1962	Jacques Plante, Montréal	1991	Ed Belfour, Chicago
1934	Charlie Gardiner, Chicago	1963	Glenn Hall, Chicago	1992	Patrick Roy, Montréal
1935	Lorne Chabot, Chicago	1964	Charlie Hodge, Montréal	1993	Ed Belfour, Chicago
1936	Tiny Thompson, Boston	1965	Sawchuk, Bower; Toronto	1994	Dominik Hasek, Buffalo
1937	Normie Smith, Detroit	1966	Worsley, Hodge; Montréal	1995	Dominik Hasek, Buffalo
1938	Tiny Thompson, Boston	1967	Hall, DeJordy; Chicago	1996	Jim Carey, Washington
1939	Frank Brimsek, Boston	1968	Worsley, Vachon; Montréal	1997	Dominik Hasek, Buffalo
1940	Dave Kerr, NY Rangers	1969	Hall, Plante; St. Louis	1998	Dominik Hasek, Buffalo
1941	Turk Broda, Toronto	1970	Tony Esposito, Chicago	1999	Dominik Hasek, Buffalo
1942	Frank Brimsek, Boston	1971	Giacomin, Villemure; NY Rangers	2000	Olaf Kolzig, Washington
1943	Johnny Mowers, Detroit	1972	Esposito, Smith; Chicago	2001	Dominik Hasek, Buffalo
1944	Bill Durnan, Montréal	1973	Ken Dryden, Montréal	2002	Jose Theodore, Montréal
1945	Bill Durnan, Montréal	1974	Bernie Parent, Philadelphia;	2003	Martin Brodeur, New Jersey
1946	Bill Durnan, Montréal		Tony Esposito, Chicago	2004	Martin Brodeur, New Jersey
1947	Bill Durnan, Montréal	1975	Bernie Parent, Philadelphia	2006	Miikka Kiprusoff, Calgary
1948	Turk Broda, Toronto	1976	Ken Dryden, Montréal	2007	Martin Brodeur, New Jersey
1949	Bill Durnan, Montréal	1977	Dryden, Larocque; Montréal	2008	Martin Brodeur, New Jersey
1950	Bill Durnan, Montréal	1978	Dryden, Larocque; Montréal	2009	Tim Thomas, Boston
1951	Al Rollins, Toronto	1979	Dryden, Larocque; Montréal	2010	Ryan Miller, Buffalo
1952	Terry Sawchuk, Detroit	1980	Sauve, Edwards; Buffalo	2011	Tim Thomas, Boston
1953	Terry Sawchuk, Detroit	1981	Sevigny, Larocque, Herron; Montréal	2012	Henrik Lundqvist, NY Rangers
		1982	Bill Smith, NY Islanders	2013	Sergei Bobrovsky, Columbus

NHL Home Ice

Team	Name (year built)	Capacity[1]	Team	Name (year built)	Capacity[1]
Anaheim	Honda Center[2] (1993)	17,174	New Jersey	Prudential Center (2007)	17,625
Boston	TD Garden[3] (1995)	17,565	NY Islanders	Nassau Veterans Memorial Coliseum (1972)	16,234
Buffalo	First Niagara Center[4] (1996)	19,070			
Calgary	Scotiabank Saddledome[5] (1983)	19,289	NY Rangers	Madison Square Garden (1968)	18,200
Carolina	PNC Arena[6] (1999)	18,680	Ottawa	Scotiabank Place[11] (1996)	19,153
Chicago	United Center (1994)	19,717	Philadelphia	Wells Fargo Center[12] (1996)	19,538
Colorado	Pepsi Center (1999)	18,007	Phoenix	Jobing.com Arena[13] (2003)	17,125
Columbus	Nationwide Arena (2000)	18,144	Pittsburgh	CONSOL Energy Center (2010)	18,387
Dallas	American Airlines Center (2001)	18,532	St. Louis	Scottrade Center[14] (1994)	19,150
Detroit	Joe Louis Arena (1979)	20,066	San Jose	SAP Center at San Jose[15] (1993)	17,562
Edmonton	Rexall Place[7] (1974)	16,839	Tampa Bay	Tampa Bay Times Forum[16] (1996)	19,204
Florida	BB&T Center[8] (1998)	17,040	Toronto	Air Canada Centre (1999)	18,819
Los Angeles	STAPLES Center (1999)	18,118	Vancouver	Rogers Arena[17] (1995)	18,910
Minnesota	Xcel Energy Center (2000)	18,064	Washington	Verizon Center[18] (1997)	18,506
Montréal	Le Centre Bell[9] (1996)	21,273	Winnipeg	MTS Centre (2004)	15,004
Nashville	Bridgestone Arena[10] (1997)	17,113			

(1) At the end of the 2012-13 season. (2) Arrowhead Pond of Anaheim, 1993-2006. (3) FleetCenter, 1995-2005; TD Banknorth Garden, 2005-09. (4) Marine Midland Arena, 1996-99; HSBC Arena, 1999-2011. (5) Olympic Saddledome, 1983-96; Canadian Airlines Saddledome, 1996-2000; Pengrowth Saddledome, 2000-10. (6) Raleigh Entertainment and Sports Arena, 1999-2002; RBC Center, 2002-11. (7) Northlands Col., 1974-79; Edmonton Col., 1979-98; Skyreach Centre, 1998-2003. (8) National Car Rental Center, 1998-2002; Office Depot Center, 2002-05; BankAtlantic Center, 2005-12. (9) Le Centre Molson, 1996-2002. (10) Nashville Arena, 1997-99; Gaylord Entertainment Center, 1999-2007; Sommet Center, 2007-10. (11) Corel Centre, 1996-2006. (12) CoreStates Center, 1996-98; First Union Center, 1998-2003; Wachovia Center, 2003-10. (13) Glendale Arena, 2003-06. (14) Kiel Center, 1994-2000; Savvis Center, 2000-06. (15) San Jose Arena, 1993-2001; Compaq Center, 2001-02; HP Pavilion, 2002-13. (16) Ice Palace, 1996-2002; St. Pete Times Forum, 2002-12. (17) General Motors Place, 1995-2010. (18) MCI Center, 1997-2006.

Hockey Hall of Fame
(Located in Toronto, ON, Canada. * = 2013 inductee.)

Players

Abel, Sid
Adams, Jack
Anderson, Glenn
Apps, Syl
Armstrong, George
Bailey, Irvine "Ace"
Bain, Dan
Baker, Hobey
Barber, Bill
Barry, Marty
Bathgate, Andy
Bauer, Bobby
Belfour, Ed
Beliveau, Jean
Benedict, Clint
Bentley, Doug
Bentley, Max
Blake, Hector "Toe"
Boivin, Leo
Boon, Dickie
Bossy, Mike
Bouchard, Butch
Boucher, Frank
Boucher, George
Bourque, Ray
Bower, Johnny
Bowie, Russell "Dubbie"
Brimsek, Frank
Broadbent, Harry L. "Punch"
Broda, Turk
Bucyk, John
Burch, Billy
Bure, Pavel
Cameron, Harry
Cheevers, Gerry
*Chelios, Chris
Ciccarelli, Dino
Clancy, King
Clapper, Aubrey "Dit"
Clarke, Bobby
Cleghorn, Sprague
Coffey, Paul
Colville, Neil
Conacher, Charlie
Conacher, Lionel
Conacher, Roy
Connell, Alex
Cook, Bill
Cook, Frederick "Bun"
Coulter, Art
Cournoyer, Yvan
Cowley, Bill
Crawford, Rusty
Darragh, Jack
Davidson, Scotty
Day, Clarence "Hap"
Delvecchio, Alex
Denneny, Cy
Dionne, Marcel
Drillon, Gordie
Drinkwater, Graham
Dryden, Ken
Duff, Terrance "Dick"
Dumart, Woody
Dunderdale, Tommy
Durnan, Bill
Dutton, Mervyn "Red"
Dye, Babe
Esposito, Phil
Esposito, Tony
Farrel, Arthur
Federko, Bernie
Fetisov, Viacheslav
Flaman, Fernie
Foyston, Frank

Francis, Ron
Fredrickson, Frank
Fuhr, Grant
Gadsby, Bill
Gainey, Bob
Gardiner, Chuck
Gardiner, Herb
Gardiner, Jimmy
Gartner, Mike
Geoffrion, Bernie
Gerard, Eddie
Giacomin, Eddie
Gilbert, Rod
Gillies, Clark
Gilmour, Billy
Gilmour, Doug
Goheen, Frank "Moose"
Goodfellow, Ebbie
Goulet, Michel
Granato, Cammi
Grant, Mike
Green, Wilfred "Shorty"
Gretzky, Wayne
Griffis, Si
Hainsworth, George
Hall, Glenn
Hall, Joe
Harvey, Doug
Hawerchuk, Dale
Hay, George
*Heaney, Geraldine
Hern, Riley
Hextall, Bryan
Holmes, Hap
Hooper, Tom
Horner, Red
Horton, Tim
Howe, Gordie
Howe, Mark
Howe, Syd
Howell, Harry
Hull, Bobby
Hull, Brett
Hutton, John "Bouse"
Hyland, Harry
Irvin, Dick
Jackson, Harvey "Busher"
James, Angela
Johnson, Ching
Johnson, Ernie
Johnson, Tom
Joliat, Aurel
Keats, Duke
Kelly, Red
Kennedy, Ted
Keon, Dave
Kharlamov, Valeri
Kurri, Jari
Lach, Elmer
Lafleur, Guy
LaFontaine, Pat
Lalonde, Newsy
Langway, Rod
Laperrière, Jacques
Lapointe, Guy
Laprade, Edgar
Larionov, Igor
Laviolette, Jack
Leetch, Brian
Lehman, Hughie
Lemaire, Jacques
Lemieux, Mario
LeSueur, Percy
Lewis, Herbie
Lindsay, Ted
Lumley, Harry
MacInnis, Al
MacKay, Mickey

Mahovlich, Frank
Malone, Joe
Mantha, Sylvio
Marshall, Jack
Maxwell, Fred
McDonald, Lanny
McGee, Frank
McGimsie, Billy
McNamara, George
Messier, Mark
Mikita, Stan
Moore, Dickie
Moran, Paddy
Morenz, Howie
Mosienko, Bill
Mullen, Joe
Murphy, Larry
Neely, Cam
*Niedermayer, Scott
Nieuwendyk, Joe
Nighbor, Frank
Noble, Reg
Oates, Adam
O'Connor, Buddy
Oliver, Harry
Olmstead, Bert
Orr, Bobby
Parent, Bernie
Park, Brad
Patrick, Lester
Patrick, Lynn
Perreault, Gilbert
Phillips, Tom
Pilote, Pierre
Pitre, Didier
Plante, Jacques
Potvin, Denis
Pratt, Babe
Primeau, Joe
Pronovost, Marcel
Pulford, Bob
Pulford, Harvey
Quackenbush, Bill
Rankin, Frank
Ratelle, Jean
Rayner, Chuck
Reardon, Kenny
Richard, Henri
Richard, Maurice
Richardson, George
Roberts, Gordie
Robinson, Larry
Robitaille, Luc
Ross, Art
Roy, Patrick
Russel, Blair
Russell, Ernie
Ruttan, Jack
Sakic, Joe
Salming, Börje
Savard, Denis
Savard, Serge
Sawchuk, Terry
Scanlan, Fred
Schmidt, Milt
Schriner, Sweeney
Seibert, Earl
Seibert, Oliver
*Shanahan, Brendan
Shore, Eddie
Shutt, Steve
Siebert, Babe
Simpson, Joe "Bullet"
Sittler, Darryl
Smith, Alf
Smith, Billy
Smith, Clint

Smith, Hooley
Smith, Tommy
Stanley, Allan
Stanley, Barney
Stastny, Peter
Stevens, Ronald Scott
Stewart, Jack
Stewart, Nels
Stuart, Bruce
Stuart, Hod
Sundin, Mats
Taylor, Frederick "Cyclone"
Thompson, Cecil "Tiny"
Tretiak, Vladislav
Trihey, Harry
Trottier, Bryan
Ullman, Norm
Vezina, Georges
Walker, Jack
Walsh, Marty
Watson, Harry "Moose"
Watson, Harry Percival
Weiland, Cooney
Westwick, Harry
Whitcroft, Fred
Wilson, Gordon Allan "Phat"
Worsley, Gump
Worters, Roy
Yzerman, Steve

Builders

Adams, Charles
Adams, Weston
Ahearn, Frank
Ahearn, John "Bunny"
Allan, Sir Montagu
Allen, Keith
Arbour, Al
Ballard, Harold
Bauer, Father David
Bickell, J. P.
Bowman, Scotty
Brooks, Herbert
Brown, George
Brown, Walter
Buckland, Frank
Bush, Walter, Jr.
Butterfield, Jack
Calder, Frank
Campbell, Angus
Campbell, Clarence
Cattarinich, Joseph
Chynoweth, Ed
Costello, Murray
Dandurand, Leo
Devellano, Jim
Dilio, Frank
Dudley, George
Dunn, James
Fletcher, Cliff
Francis, Emile
Gibson, Jack
Gorman, Tommy
Gregory, Jim
Griffiths, Frank
Hanley, Bill
Hay, Charles
Hendy, Jim
Hewitt, Foster
Hewitt, William
Hotchkiss, Harley
Hume, Fred
Ilitch, Mike
Imlach, Harry "Punch"
Ivan, Tommy
Jennings, William

Johnson, Bob
Juckes, Gordon
Kilpatrick, John
Kilrea, Brian
Knox, Seymour
Lamoriello, Lou
Leader, Al
LeBel, Robert
Lockhart, Thomas
Loicq, Paul
Mariucci, John
Mathers, Frank
McLaughlin, Frederic
Milford, Jake
Molson, Sen. Hartland
Morrison, Ian "Scotty"
Murray, Athol "Père"
Neilson, Roger
Nelson, Francis
Norris, Bruce
Norris, James
Norris, James, Sr.
Northey, William
O'Brien, J. Ambrose
O'Neill, Brian Francis
Page, Frederick
Patrick, Craig
Patrick, Frank
Pickard, Allan
Pilous, Rudy
Poile, Bud
Pollock, Sam
Raymond, Sen. Donat
Robertson, John Ross
Robinson, Claude
Ross, Phillip
Sabetzki, Gunther
Sather, Glen
Seaman, Daryl "Doc"
Selke, Frank
*Shero, Fred
Sinden, Harry
Smith, Frank
Smythe, Conn
Snider, Ed
Stanley, Lord (of Preston)
Sutherland, Capt. James T.
Tarasov, Anatoli
Torrey, Bill
Turner, Lloyd
Tutt, William
Voss, Carl
Waghorne, Fred
Wirtz, Arthur
Wirtz, Bill
Ziegler, John A., Jr.

Referees and Linesmen

Armstrong, Neil
Ashley, John
Chadwick, Bill
D'Amico, John
Elliott, Edwin "Chaucer"
Hayes, George
Hewiston, Bobby
Ion, Mickey
Pavelich, Matt
Rodden, Mike
Scapinello, Ray
Smeaton, Cooper
Storey, Red
Udvari, Frank
Van Hellemond, Andy

SOCCER

Galaxy Defeats Dynamo for 2012 MLS Championship

The L.A. Galaxy won their second straight Major League Soccer (MLS) Cup title in a rematch against the Houston Dynamo Dec. 1, 2012, at the Home Depot Center in Carson, CA. Omar Gonzalez scored a game-tying goal in the 60th minute, and Landon Donovan scored shortly after on a penalty kick as the Galaxy won, 3-1. The championship was the last MLS game for the Galaxy's international star David Beckham, who joined the club in 2007.

Houston defeated DC United in the Eastern Conference finals to reach its second straight MLS Cup final, while the Galaxy disposed of the Seattle Sounders in the Western Conference playoffs.

The San Jose Earthquakes won the 2012 Supporters' Shield with the league's best record (19-6-9 and 66 points) but fell to the Galaxy in the Western Conference semifinals. San Jose head coach Frank Yallop earned MLS Coach of the Year and Earthquakes forward Chris Wondolowski, whose 27 goals tied the league's single-season record, won the 2012 MLS Most Valuable Player award.

The MLS All-Star team defeated the English Premier League's Chelsea, 3-2, at the MLS All-Star Game July 25, 2012, at PPL Park in Chester, PA. All-Star Game MVP Chris Pontius of DC United tied the game in the 73rd minute and assisted on Eddie Johnson's game-winner.

Major League Soccer (MLS) Cup, 1996-2012

Year	Winner	Final opponent	Score	Site	MVP
1996	DC United	Los Angeles Galaxy	3-2 (OT)	Foxborough, MA	Marco Etcheverry
1997	DC United	Colorado Rapids	2-1	Washington, DC	Jaime Moreno
1998	Chicago Fire	DC United	2-0	Pasadena, CA	Peter Nowak
1999	DC United	Los Angeles Galaxy	2-0	Foxborough, MA	Ben Olsen
2000	Kansas City Wizards	Chicago Fire	1-0	Washington, DC	Tony Meola
2001	San Jose Earthquakes	Los Angeles Galaxy	2-1 (OT)	Columbus, OH	Dwayne De Rosario
2002	Los Angeles Galaxy	New England Revolution	1-0 (OT)	Foxborough, MA	Carlos Ruiz
2003	San Jose Earthquakes	Chicago Fire	4-2	Carson, CA	Landon Donovan
2004	DC United	Kansas City Wizards	3-2	Carson, CA	Alecko Eskandarian
2005	Los Angeles Galaxy	New England Revolution	1-0 (OT)	Frisco, TX	Guillermo Ramírez
2006	Houston Dynamo	New England Revolution	1-1 (4-3)*	Frisco, TX	Brian Ching
2007	Houston Dynamo	New England Revolution	2-1	Washington, DC	Dwayne De Rosario
2008	Columbus Crew	New York Red Bulls	3-1	Carson, CA	Guillermo Barros Schelotto
2009	Real Salt Lake	Los Angeles Galaxy	1-1 (5-4)*	Seattle, WA	Nick Rimando
2010	Colorado Rapids	FC Dallas	2-1 (OT)	Toronto, ON, Canada	Conor Casey
2011	Los Angeles Galaxy	Houston Dynamo	1-0	Carson, CA	Landon Donovan
2012	Los Angeles Galaxy	Houston Dynamo	3-1	Carson, CA	Omar Gonzalez

* = Match decided in penalty kicks (shootout score in parentheses). OT = Overtime.

Major League Soccer Final Standings, 2012

(Does not include playoff games.)

Eastern Conference	W	L	T	PTS	GF	GA	GD	Western Conference	W	L	T	PTS	GF	GA	GD
Sporting Kansas City	18	7	9	63	42	27	15	San Jose							
DC United	17	10	7	58	53	43	10	Earthquakes	19	6	9	66	72	43	29
New York Red Bulls	16	9	9	57	57	46	11	Real Salt Lake	17	11	6	57	46	35	11
Chicago Fire	17	11	6	57	46	41	5	Seattle Sounders FC	15	8	11	56	51	33	18
Houston Dynamo	14	9	11	53	48	41	7	L.A. Galaxy	16	12	6	54	59	47	12
Columbus Crew	15	12	7	52	44	44	0	Vancouver							
Montréal Impact	12	16	6	42	45	51	–6	Whitecaps FC	11	13	10	43	35	41	–6
Philadelphia Union	10	18	6	36	37	45	–8	FC Dallas	9	13	12	39	42	47	–5
New England								Colorado Rapids	11	19	4	37	44	50	–6
Revolution	9	17	8	35	39	44	–5	Portland Timbers	8	16	10	34	34	56	–22
Toronto FC	5	21	8	23	36	62	–26	Chivas USA	7	18	9	30	24	58	–34

Major League Soccer Scoring Leaders, 2012

Player	Club	GP	Goals	Player	Club	GP	Goals
Chris Wondolowski	San Jose	32	27	Eddie Johnson	Seattle	28	14
Kenny Cooper	New York	33	18	Fredy Montero	Seattle	33	13
Alvaro Saborio	Salt Lake	31	17	Alan Gordon	San Jose	23	13
Robbie Keane	Los Angeles	28	16	Chris Pontius	DC	31	12
Thierry Henry	New York	25	15	Will Bruin	Houston	32	12

Selected European Soccer League Champions, 1950-2013

Season	England: Premier League[1]	Spain: La Liga	Italy: Serie A	Germany: Bundesliga[2]
1949-50	Portsmouth FC	Atlético Madrid	Juventus	VfB Stuttgart
1950-51	Tottenham Hotspur	Atlético Madrid	AC Milan	Kaiserslautern
1951-52	Manchester United	FC Barcelona	Juventus	VfB Stuttgart
1952-53	Arsenal	FC Barcelona	Inter Milan	Kaiserslautern
1953-54	Wolverhampton Wanderers	Real Madrid	Inter Milan	Hannoverscher SV 96
1954-55	Chelsea	Real Madrid	AC Milan	Rot-Weiss Essen
1955-56	Manchester United	Athletic Bilbao	Fiorentina	Borussia Dortmund
1956-57	Manchester United	Real Madrid	AC Milan	Borussia Dortmund
1957-58	Wolverhampton Wanderers	Real Madrid	Juventus	Schalke 04
1958-59	Wolverhampton Wanderers	FC Barcelona	AC Milan	Eintracht Frankfurt
1959-60	Burnley FC	FC Barcelona	Juventus	Hamburg SV
1960-61	Tottenham Hotspur	Real Madrid	Juventus	FC Nuremberg
1961-62	Ipswich Town	Real Madrid	AC Milan	FC Cologne
1962-63	Everton	Real Madrid	Inter Milan	Borussia Dortmund
1963-64	Liverpool	Real Madrid	Bologna	FC Cologne
1964-65	Manchester United	Real Madrid	Inter Milan	Werder Bremen
1965-66	Liverpool	Atlético Madrid	Inter Milan	TSV 1860 Munich
1966-67	Manchester United	Real Madrid	Juventus	Eintracht Braunschweig

Season	England: Premier League[1]	Spain: La Liga	Italy: Serie A	Germany: Bundesliga[2]
1967-68	Manchester City	Real Madrid	AC Milan	FC Nuremberg
1968-69	Leeds United	Real Madrid	Fiorentina	Bayern Munich
1969-70	Everton	Atlético Madrid	Cagliari	Borussia Mönchengladbach
1970-71	Arsenal	Valencia	Inter Milan	Borussia Mönchengladbach
1971-72	Derby County	Real Madrid	Juventus	Bayern Munich
1972-73	Liverpool	Atlético Madrid	Juventus	Bayern Munich
1973-74	Leeds United	FC Barcelona	Lazio	Bayern Munich
1974-75	Derby County	Real Madrid	Juventus	Borussia Mönchengladbach
1975-76	Liverpool	Real Madrid	Torino	Borussia Mönchengladbach
1976-77	Liverpool	Atlético Madrid	Juventus	Borussia Mönchengladbach
1977-78	Nottingham Forest	Real Madrid	Juventus	FC Cologne
1978-79	Liverpool	Real Madrid	AC Milan	Hamburg SV
1979-80	Liverpool	Real Madrid	Inter Milan	Bayern Munich
1980-81	Aston Villa	Real Sociedad	Juventus	Bayern Munich
1981-82	Liverpool	Real Sociedad	Juventus	Hamburg SV
1982-83	Liverpool	Athletic Bilbao	AS Roma	Hamburg SV
1983-84	Liverpool	Athletic Bilbao	Juventus	VfB Stuttgart
1984-85	Everton	FC Barcelona	Verona	Bayern Munich
1985-86	Liverpool	Real Madrid	Juventus	Bayern Munich
1986-87	Everton	Real Madrid	Napoli	Bayern Munich
1987-88	Liverpool	Real Madrid	AC Milan	Werder Bremen
1988-89	Arsenal	Real Madrid	Inter Milan	Bayern Munich
1989-90	Liverpool	Real Madrid	Napoli	Bayern Munich
1990-91	Arsenal	FC Barcelona	Sampdoria	FC Kaiserslautern
1991-92	Leeds United	FC Barcelona	AC Milan	VfB Stuttgart
1992-93	Manchester United	FC Barcelona	AC Milan	Werder Bremen
1993-94	Manchester United	FC Barcelona	AC Milan	Bayern Munich
1994-95	Blackburn Rovers	Real Madrid	Juventus	Borussia Dortmund
1995-96	Manchester United	Atlético Madrid	AC Milan	Borussia Dortmund
1996-97	Manchester United	Real Madrid	Juventus	Bayern Munich
1997-98	Arsenal	FC Barcelona	Juventus	FC Kaiserslautern
1998-99	Manchester United	FC Barcelona	AC Milan	Bayern Munich
1999-2000	Manchester United	Deportivo Coruña	Lazio	Bayern Munich
2000-01	Manchester United	Real Madrid	AS Roma	Bayern Munich
2001-02	Arsenal	Valencia	Juventus	Borussia Dortmund
2002-03	Manchester United	Real Madrid	Juventus	Bayern Munich
2003-04	Arsenal	Valencia	AC Milan	Werder Bremen
2004-05	Chelsea	FC Barcelona	None[3]	Bayern Munich
2005-06	Chelsea	FC Barcelona	Inter Milan[3]	Bayern Munich
2006-07	Manchester United	Real Madrid	Inter Milan	VfB Stuttgart
2007-08	Manchester United	Real Madrid	Inter Milan	Bayern Munich
2008-09	Manchester United	FC Barcelona	Inter Milan	VfL Wolfsburg
2009-10	Chelsea	FC Barcelona	Inter Milan	Bayern Munich
2010-11	Manchester United	FC Barcelona	AC Milan	Borussia Dortmund
2011-12	Manchester City	Real Madrid	Juventus	Borussia Dortmund
2012-13	Manchester United	FC Barcelona	Juventus	Bayern Munich

(1) Football League champions are listed prior to 1992-93 season, when the Premier League formed. (2) Regional champions are listed prior to 1963-64 season, when National Bundesliga formed. (3) Juventus was stripped of two titles in 2006 because of match-fixing.

UEFA Champions League, 1956-2013

Year	Winner	Final opponent	Score	Year	Winner	Final opponent	Score
1956	Real Madrid	Reims	4-3	1985	Juventus	Liverpool	1-0
1957	Real Madrid	Fiorentina	2-0	1986	Steaua	Barcelona	0-0 (2-0)*
1958	Real Madrid	AC Milan	3-2#	1987	Porto	Bayern Munich	2-1
1959	Real Madrid	Reims	2-0	1988	PSV	Benfica	0-0 (6-5)*
1960	Real Madrid	Eintracht	7-3	1989	AC Milan	Steaua	4-0
1961	Benfica	Barcelona	3-2	1990	AC Milan	Benfica	1-0
1962	Benfica	Real Madrid	5-3	1991	Crvena Zvezda	Marseille	0-0 (5-3)*
1963	AC Milan	Benfica	2-1	1992	Barcelona	Sampdoria	1-0#
1964	Inter Milan	Real Madrid	3-1	1993	Marseille	AC Milan	1-0
1965	Inter Milan	Benfica	1-0	1994	AC Milan	Barcelona	4-0
1966	Real Madrid	Partizan	2-1	1995	Ajax	AC Milan	1-0
1967	Celtic	Inter Milan	2-1	1996	Juventus	Ajax	1-1 (4-2)*
1968	Manchester United	Benfica	4-1#	1997	Borussia Dortmund	Juventus	3-1
1969	AC Milan	Ajax	4-1	1998	Real Madrid	Juventus	1-0
1970	Feyenoord	Celtic	2-1#	1999	Manchester United	Bayern Munich	2-1
1971	Ajax	Panathinaikos	2-0	2000	Real Madrid	Valencia	3-0
1972	Ajax	Inter Milan	2-0	2001	Bayern Munich	Valencia	1-1 (5-4)*
1973	Ajax	Juventus	1-0	2002	Real Madrid	Leverkusen	2-1
1974	Bayern Munich	Atlético Madrid	5-1[1]	2003	AC Milan	Juventus	0-0 (3-2)*
1975	Bayern Munich	Leeds	2-0	2004	Porto	Monaco	3-0
1976	Bayern Munich	St-Étienne	1-0	2005	Liverpool	AC Milan	3-3 (3-2)*
1977	Liverpool	Mönchengladbach	3-1	2006	Barcelona	Arsenal	2-1
1978	Liverpool	Club Brugge	1-0	2007	AC Milan	Liverpool	2-1
1979	Nottingham Forest	Malmö	1-0	2008	Manchester United	Chelsea	1-1 (6-5)*
1980	Nottingham Forest	Hamburg	1-0	2009	Barcelona	Manchester United	2-0
1981	Liverpool	Real Madrid	1-0	2010	Inter Milan	Bayern Munich	2-0
1982	Aston Villa	Bayern Munich	1-0	2011	Barcelona	Manchester United	3-1
1983	Hamburg	Juventus	1-0	2012	Chelsea	Bayern Munich	1-1 (4-3)*
1984	Liverpool	AS Roma	1-1 (4-2)*	2013	Bayern Munich	Borussia Dortmund	2-1

* = Match decided in penalty kicks (shootout score in parentheses). # = Match decided in extra time. (1) Aggregate score. First game 1-1; second, 4-0.

UEFA European Football Championships, 1960-2012

The final rounds of the 2012 UEFA European Championships were jointly hosted by Poland and Ukraine and opened June 8, 2012, in Warsaw and Wroclawa, Poland, with the final match at Olympic Stadium in Kiev, Ukraine, on July 1, 2012.

Year	Winner	Final opponent	Score	Site	Year	Winner	Final opponent	Score	Site
1960	USSR	Yugoslavia	2-1#	France	1988	Netherlands	USSR	2-0	W. Germany
1964	Spain	USSR	2-1	Spain	1992	Denmark	Germany	2-0	Sweden
1968	Italy	Yugoslavia	2-0	Italy	1996	Germany	Czech Rep.	2-1#	England
1972	W. Germany	USSR	3-0	Belgium	2000	France	Italy	2-1#	Belgium/Neth.
1976	Czechoslovakia	W. Germany	2-2 (5-3)*	Yugoslavia	2004	Greece	Portugal	1-0	Portugal
1980	W. Germany	Belgium	2-1	Italy	2008	Spain	Germany	1-0	Austria/Switz.
1984	France	Spain	2-0	France	2012	Spain	Italy	4-0	Poland/Ukr.

* = Match decided in penalty kicks (shootout score in parentheses). # = Match decided in extra time.

National Women's Soccer League Debuts

The Portland Thorns won the inaugural championship of the National Women's Soccer League (NWSL), which began its first regular season in Apr. 2013. Portland midfielder Tobin Heath scored a first-half goal and was named NWSL Championship Game MVP in Portland's 2-0 victory over the Western New York Flash Aug. 31, 2013, at Sahlen's Stadium in Rochester, NY. Teams played 22 games each in the regular season. Western NY topped the standings with 38 points. Western NY was among five teams (including Boston, Chicago, Sky Blue FC [NJ], and Washington [DC]) that had played in the Women's Professional Soccer league, which folded in 2012 after three seasons. FC Kansas City midfielder Lauren Holiday led the league in goals (12) and assists (9) and was voted NWSL regular season MVP.

Japan Beats U.S. to Claim 2011 Women's World Cup Championship

Japan earned a stunning championship win at the 2011 Women's World Cup, defeating the United States, 3-1, on penalty kicks July 17, 2011, in Frankfurt, Germany. Japan's Homare Sawa scored the game-tying goal in extra time, after the U.S.'s Abby Wambach scored on a header for a 2-1 lead in the 104th minute. Sawa, playing in her fifth World Cup tournament, won both the Golden Ball as the best player of the tournament and the Golden Boot with a tournament-leading five goals.

The U.S. enjoyed a dramatic quarterfinal triumph July 10, 2011, beating Brazil, 5-3, on penalty kicks in Dresden. The U.S. team then advanced to its first World Cup Final since 1999 with a 3-1 win over France in Mönchengladbach on July 13.

Women's World Cup, 1991-2011

Year	Winner	Final opponent	Score	Site	Year	Winner	Final opponent	Score	Site
1991	U.S.	Norway	2-1	China	2003	Germany	Sweden	2-1#	Carson, CA
1995	Norway	Germany	2-0	Sweden	2007	Germany	Brazil	2-0	China
1999	U.S.	China	0-0 (5-4)*	Pasadena, CA	2011	Japan	U.S.	2-2 (3-1)*	Germany

* = Match decided in penalty kicks (shootout score in parentheses). # = Match decided in extra time.

Spain Defeats the Netherlands for 2010 Men's World Cup Title

Amid the drone of vuvuzelas, Spain earned its first-ever FIFA World Cup soccer championship with a 1-0 victory over the Netherlands July 11, 2010, in Johannesburg, South Africa. Andrés Iniesta scored in the 116th minute as Spain became the first country to be crowned World Cup champion after losing its first tournament match. Spain goalkeeper Iker Casillas allowed just two goals and was named winner of the Golden Glove award as the tournament's top goaltender.

Men's World Cup, 1930-2010

Year	Winner	Final opponent	Score	Site	Year	Winner	Final opponent	Score	Site
1930	Uruguay	Argentina	4-2	Uruguay	1978	Argentina	Netherlands	3-1#	Argentina
1934	Italy	Czechoslovakia	2-1#	Italy	1982	Italy	W. Germany	3-1	Spain
1938	Italy	Hungary	4-2	France	1986	Argentina	W. Germany	3-2	Mexico
1950	Uruguay	Brazil	2-1	Brazil	1990	W. Germany	Argentina	1-0	Italy
1954	W. Germany	Hungary	3-2	Switzerland	1994	Brazil	Italy	0-0 (3-2)*	U.S.
1958	Brazil	Sweden	5-2	Sweden	1998	France	Brazil	3-0	France
1962	Brazil	Czechoslovakia	3-1	Chile	2002	Brazil	Germany	2-0	Japan/S. Korea
1966	England	W. Germany	4-2#	England	2006	Italy	France	1-1 (5-3)*	Germany
1970	Brazil	Italy	4-1	Mexico	2010	Spain	Netherlands	1-0#	South Africa
1974	W. Germany	Netherlands	2-1	W. Germany					

* = Match decided in penalty kicks (shootout score in parentheses). # = Match decided in extra time.

FIFA Confederations Cup, 2013

Brazil won its third straight Confederations Cup title with a 3-0 victory over Spain June 30, 2013, at Maracanã Stadium in Rio de Janeiro, Brazil. Fred scored twice in the championship and Neymar, who won the Golden Ball as the tournament's top player, added his fourth goal of the tournament in the 44th minute. Throughout the tournament, anti-government protesters battled with police near many of the host stadiums, but the tournament schedule was not affected. Brazil advanced to the championship game with a 2-1 victory over Uruguay June 26 on a goal by Paulinho in the 86th minute at Mineirão Stadium in Belo Horizonte. Spain and Italy played to a 0-0 draw in the semifinals June 27 at Castelão Stadium in Fortaleza, but Spain advanced with a 7-6 win on penalty kicks.

FIFA Confederations Cup, 1997-2013

Year	Winner	Final opponent	Score	Third place	Fourth place	Site
1997	Brazil	Australia	6-0	Czech Republic	Uruguay	Saudi Arabia
1999	Mexico	Brazil	4-3	U.S.	Saudi Arabia	Mexico
2001	France	Japan	1-0	Australia	Brazil	S. Korea/Japan
2003	France	Cameroon	1-0	Turkey	Colombia	France
2005	Brazil	Argentina	4-1	Germany	Mexico	Germany
2009	Brazil	U.S.	3-2	Spain	South Africa	South Africa
2013	Brazil	Spain	3-0	Italy	Uruguay	Brazil

GOLF

Men's All-Time Major Professional Championship Leaders

Through Sept. 2013. * = Active PGA player in 2013. (a) = Amateur.

Player	Masters	U.S. Open	British Open	PGA	Total
Jack Nicklaus	1963, '65-'66, '72, '75, '86	1962, '67, '72, '80	1966, '70, '78	1963, '71, '73, '75, '80	18
Tiger Woods*	1997, 2001-02, '05	2000, '02, '08	2000, '05-'06	1999-2000, '06-'07	14
Walter Hagen	—	1914, '19	1922, '24, '28-'29	1921, '24-'27	11
Ben Hogan	1951, '53	1948, '50-'51, '53	1953	1946, '48	9
Gary Player	1961, '74, '78	1965	1959, '68, '74	1962, '72	9
Tom Watson	1977, '81	1982	1975, '77, '80, '82-'83	—	8
Bobby Jones (a)	—	1923, '26, '29-'30	1926-27, '30	—	7
Arnold Palmer	1958, '60, '62, '64	1960	1961-62	—	7
Gene Sarazen	1935	1922, '32	1932	1922-23, '33	7
Sam Snead	1949, '52, '54	—	1946	1942, '49, '51	7
Harry Vardon	—	1900	1896, '98-'99, 1903, '11, '14	—	7
Nick Faldo	1989-90, '96	—	1987, '90, '92	—	6
Lee Trevino	—	1968, '71	1971-72	1974, '84	6

Professional Golfers' Association Leading Money Winners, 1946-2012

Year	Player	Earnings	Year	Player	Earnings	Year	Player	Earnings
1946	Ben Hogan	$42,556	1969	Frank Beard	$164,707	1991	Corey Pavin	$979,430
1947	Jimmy Demaret	27,936	1970	Lee Trevino	157,037	1992	Fred Couples	1,344,188
1948	Ben Hogan	32,112	1971	Jack Nicklaus	244,490	1993	Nick Price	1,478,557
1949	Sam Snead	31,593	1972	Jack Nicklaus	320,542	1994	Nick Price	1,499,927
1950	Sam Snead	35,758	1973	Jack Nicklaus	308,362	1995	Greg Norman	1,654,959
1951	Lloyd Mangrum	26,088	1974	Johnny Miller	353,201	1996	Tom Lehman	1,780,159
1952	Julius Boros	37,032	1975	Jack Nicklaus	298,149	1997	Tiger Woods	2,066,833
1953	Lew Worsham	34,002	1976	Jack Nicklaus	266,438	1998	David Duval	2,591,031
1954	Bob Toski	65,819	1977	Tom Watson	310,653	1999	Tiger Woods	6,616,585
1955	Julius Boros	63,121	1978	Tom Watson	362,429	2000	Tiger Woods	9,188,321
1956	Ted Kroll	72,835	1979	Tom Watson	462,636	2001	Tiger Woods	5,687,777
1957	Dick Mayer	65,835	1980	Tom Watson	530,808	2002	Tiger Woods	6,912,625
1958	Arnold Palmer	42,607	1981	Tom Kite	375,699	2003	Vijay Singh	7,573,907
1959	Art Wall Jr.	53,167	1982	Craig Stadler	446,462	2004	Vijay Singh	10,905,166
1960	Arnold Palmer	75,262	1983	Hal Sutton	426,668	2005	Tiger Woods	10,628,024
1961	Gary Player	64,540	1984	Tom Watson	476,260	2006	Tiger Woods	9,941,563
1962	Arnold Palmer	81,448	1985	Curtis Strange	542,321	2007	Tiger Woods	10,867,052
1963	Arnold Palmer	128,230	1986	Greg Norman	653,296	2008	Vijay Singh	6,601,094
1964	Jack Nicklaus	113,284	1987	Curtis Strange	925,941	2009	Tiger Woods	10,508,163
1965	Jack Nicklaus	140,752	1988	Curtis Strange	1,147,644	2010	Matt Kuchar	4,910,477
1966	Billy Casper	121,944	1989	Tom Kite	1,395,278	2011	Luke Donald	6,683,214
1967	Jack Nicklaus	188,998	1990	Greg Norman	1,165,477	2012	Rory McIlroy	8,047,952
1968	Billy Casper	205,168						

Masters Golf Tournament Winners, 1940-2013

First contested in 1934 as Augusta National Invitation Tournament (name changed in 1939); not played, 1943-45.

Year	Winner	Year	Winner	Year	Winner	Year	Winner	Year	Winner
1940	Jimmy Demaret	1958	Arnold Palmer	1973	Tommy Aaron	1988	Sandy Lyle	2000	Vijay Singh
1941	Craig Wood	1959	Art Wall Jr.	1974	Gary Player	1989	Nick Faldo	2001	Tiger Woods
1942	Byron Nelson	1960	Arnold Palmer	1975	Jack Nicklaus	1990	Nick Faldo	2002	Tiger Woods
1946	Herman Keiser	1961	Gary Player	1976	Ray Floyd	1991	Ian Woosnam	2003	Mike Weir
1947	Jimmy Demaret	1962	Arnold Palmer	1977	Tom Watson	1992	Fred Couples	2004	Phil Mickelson
1948	Claude Harmon	1963	Jack Nicklaus	1978	Gary Player	1993	Bernhard Langer	2005	Tiger Woods
1949	Sam Snead	1964	Arnold Palmer	1979	Fuzzy Zoeller	1994	José María Olazábal	2006	Phil Mickelson
1950	Jimmy Demaret	1965	Jack Nicklaus	1980	Seve Ballesteros	1995	Ben Crenshaw	2007	Zach Johnson
1951	Ben Hogan	1966	Jack Nicklaus	1981	Tom Watson	1996	Nick Faldo	2008	Trevor Immelman
1952	Sam Snead	1967	Gay Brewer Jr.	1982	Craig Stadler	1997	Tiger Woods	2009	Angel Cabrera
1953	Ben Hogan	1968	Bob Goalby	1983	Seve Ballesteros	1998	Mark O'Meara	2010	Phil Mickelson
1954	Sam Snead	1969	George Archer	1984	Ben Crenshaw	1999	José María Olazábal	2011	Charl Schwartzel
1955	Cary Middlecoff	1970	Billy Casper	1985	Bernhard Langer			2012	Bubba Watson
1956	Jack Burke	1971	Charles Coody	1986	Jack Nicklaus			2013	Adam Scott
1957	Doug Ford	1972	Jack Nicklaus	1987	Larry Mize				

U.S. Open Winners, 1940-2013

First contested in 1895; not played, 1942-45.

Year	Winner	Year	Winner	Year	Winner	Year	Winner	Year	Winner
1940	Lawson Little	1958	Tommy Bolt	1972	Jack Nicklaus	1986	Ray Floyd	2000	Tiger Woods
1941	Craig Wood	1959	Billy Casper	1973	Johnny Miller	1987	Scott Simpson	2001	Retief Goosen
1946	Lloyd Mangrum	1960	Arnold Palmer	1974	Hale Irwin	1988	Curtis Strange	2002	Tiger Woods
1947	Lew Worsham	1961	Gene Littler	1975	Lou Graham	1989	Curtis Strange	2003	Jim Furyk
1948	Ben Hogan	1962	Jack Nicklaus	1976	Jerry Pate	1990	Hale Irwin	2004	Retief Goosen
1949	Cary Middlecoff	1963	Julius Boros	1977	Hubert Green	1991	Payne Stewart	2005	Michael Campbell
1950	Ben Hogan	1964	Ken Venturi	1978	Andy North	1992	Tom Kite	2006	Geoff Ogilvy
1951	Ben Hogan	1965	Gary Player	1979	Hale Irwin	1993	Lee Janzen	2007	Angel Cabrera
1952	Julius Boros	1966	Billy Casper	1980	Jack Nicklaus	1994	Ernie Els	2008	Tiger Woods
1953	Ben Hogan	1967	Jack Nicklaus	1981	David Graham	1995	Corey Pavin	2009	Lucas Glover
1954	Ed Furgol	1968	Lee Trevino	1982	Tom Watson	1996	Steve Jones	2010	Graeme McDowell
1955	Jack Fleck	1969	Orville Moody	1983	Larry Nelson	1997	Ernie Els	2011	Rory McIlroy
1956	Cary Middlecoff	1970	Tony Jacklin	1984	Fuzzy Zoeller	1998	Lee Janzen	2012	Webb Simpson
1957	Dick Mayer	1971	Lee Trevino	1985	Andy North	1999	Payne Stewart	2013	Justin Rose

British Open Winners, 1946-2013
First contested in 1860; not played, 1940-45.

Year	Winner	Year	Winner	Year	Winner	Year	Winner	Year	Winner
1946	Sam Snead	1960	Kel Nagle	1973	Tom Weiskopf	1987	Nick Faldo	2001	David Duval
1947	Fred Daly	1961	Arnold Palmer	1974	Gary Player	1988	Seve Ballesteros	2002	Ernie Els
1948	Henry Cotton	1962	Arnold Palmer	1975	Tom Watson	1989	Mark Calcavecchia	2003	Ben Curtis
1949	Bobby Locke	1963	Bob Charles	1976	Johnny Miller	1990	Nick Faldo	2004	Todd Hamilton
1950	Bobby Locke	1964	Tony Lema	1977	Tom Watson	1991	Ian Baker-Finch	2005	Tiger Woods
1951	Max Faulkner	1965	Peter Thomson	1978	Jack Nicklaus	1992	Nick Faldo	2006	Tiger Woods
1952	Bobby Locke	1966	Jack Nicklaus	1979	Seve Ballesteros	1993	Greg Norman	2007	Padraig Harrington
1953	Ben Hogan	1967	Roberto de Vicenzo	1980	Tom Watson	1994	Nick Price	2008	Padraig Harrington
1954	Peter Thomson			1981	Bill Rogers	1995	John Daly	2009	Stewart Cink
1955	Peter Thomson	1968	Gary Player	1982	Tom Watson	1996	Tom Lehman	2010	Louis Oosthuizen
1956	Peter Thomson	1969	Tony Jacklin	1983	Tom Watson	1997	Justin Leonard	2011	Darren Clarke
1957	Bobby Locke	1970	Jack Nicklaus	1984	Seve Ballesteros	1998	Mark O'Meara	2012	Ernie Els
1958	Peter Thomson	1971	Lee Trevino	1985	Sandy Lyle	1999	Paul Lawrie	2013	Phil Mickelson
1959	Gary Player	1972	Lee Trevino	1986	Greg Norman	2000	Tiger Woods		

PGA Championship Winners, 1940-2013
First contested in 1916; not played, 1943.

Year	Winner	Year	Winner	Year	Winner	Year	Winner	Year	Winner
1940	Byron Nelson	1956	Jack Burke	1971	Jack Nicklaus	1986	Bob Tway	2001	David Toms
1941	Victor Ghezzi	1957	Lionel Hebert	1972	Gary Player	1987	Larry Nelson	2002	Rich Beem
1942	Sam Snead	1958	Dow Finsterwald	1973	Jack Nicklaus	1988	Jeff Sluman	2003	Shaun Micheel
1944	Bob Hamilton	1959	Bob Rosburg	1974	Lee Trevino	1989	Payne Stewart	2004	Vijay Singh
1945	Byron Nelson	1960	Jay Hebert	1975	Jack Nicklaus	1990	Wayne Grady	2005	Phil Mickelson
1946	Ben Hogan	1961	Jerry Barber	1976	Dave Stockton	1991	John Daly	2006	Tiger Woods
1947	Jim Ferrier	1962	Gary Player	1977	Lanny Wadkins	1992	Nick Price	2007	Tiger Woods
1948	Ben Hogan	1963	Jack Nicklaus	1978	John Mahaffey	1993	Paul Azinger	2008	Padraig Harrington
1949	Sam Snead	1964	Bob Nichols	1979	David Graham	1994	Nick Price	2009	Y.E.Yang
1950	Chandler Harper	1965	Dave Marr	1980	Jack Nicklaus	1995	Steve Elkington	2010	Martin Kaymer
1951	Sam Snead	1966	Al Geiberger	1981	Larry Nelson	1996	Mark Brooks	2011	Keegan Bradley
1952	James Turnesa	1967	Don January	1982	Ray Floyd	1997	Davis Love III	2012	Rory McIlroy
1953	Walter Burkemo	1968	Julius Boros	1983	Hal Sutton	1998	Vijay Singh	2013	Jason Dufner
1954	Melvin Harbert	1969	Ray Floyd	1984	Lee Trevino	1999	Tiger Woods		
1955	Doug Ford	1970	Dave Stockton	1985	Hubert Green	2000	Tiger Woods		

FedEx Cup, 2007-13
The FedEx Cup, a season-long, $10-mil competition with points awarded by finishing rank in each tournament, divides the PGA Tour into a regular season lasting 33 weeks, combined with a 4-week playoff that ends with the Tour Championship at East Lake Golf Club in Atlanta, GA.

Year	Winner	Year	Winner	Year	Winner	Year	Winner	Year	Winner
2007	Tiger Woods	2009	Tiger Woods	2011	Bill Haas	2012	Brandt Snedeker	2013	Henrik Stenson
2008	Vijay Singh	2010	Jim Furyk						

Women's All-Time Major Professional Championship Leaders
Through Oct. 2013. * = Active in 2013 LPGA season.

Player	Kraft Nabisco[1]	LPGA	U.S. Women's Open	Women's British Open[2]	Titleholders[3]	Western Open[4]	Total
Patty Berg	—		1946		1937-39, '48, '53, '55, '57	1941, '43, '48, '51, '55, '57-'58	15
Mickey Wright	—	1958, '60-'61, '63	1958-59, '61, '64	—	1961-62	1962-63, '66	13
Louise Suggs	—	1957	1949, '52	—	1946, '54, '56, '59	1946-47, '49, '53	11
Annika Sorenstam*	2001-02, '05	2003-05	1995-96, 2006	2003	—	—	10
Babe Zaharias	—	—	1948, '50, '54	—	1947, '50, '52	1940, '44-'45, '50	10
Betsy Rawls	—	1959, '69	1951, '53, '57, '60	—	—	1952, '59	8
Juli Inkster*	1984, '89	1999-2000	1999, 2002	1984	—	—	7
Karrie Webb*	2000, '06	2001	2000-01	1999, 2002	—	—	7
Pat Bradley	1986	1986	1981	1980, '85-'86	—	—	6
Betsy King	1987, '90, '97	1992	1989-90	—	—	—	6
Patty Sheehan	1996	1983-84, '93	1992, '94	—	—	—	6
Kathy Whitworth	—	1967, '71, '75	—	—	1965-66	1967	6

(1) Formerly the Nabisco Dinah Shore (1982-99) and the Nabisco Championship (2000-01); designated major in 1983. (2) In 2001, the British Open replaced the du Maurier Classic as the LPGA's fourth major; wins in column prior to 2001 are for the Peter Jackson (1979-82) or du Maurier (1983-2000) Classic. (3) Titleholders Championship was a major, 1937-72. (4) Western Open was a major, 1930-67.

Ladies Professional Golf Association Leading Money Winners, 1954-2012

Year	Player	Earnings	Year	Player	Earnings	Year	Player	Earnings
1954	Patty Berg	$16,011	1974	JoAnne Carner	$87,094	1994	Laura Davies	$687,201
1955	Patty Berg	16,492	1975	Sandra Palmer	76,374	1995	Annika Sorenstam	666,533
1956	Marlene Hagge	20,235	1976	Judy Rankin	150,734	1996	Karrie Webb	1,002,000
1957	Patty Berg	16,272	1977	Judy Rankin	122,890	1997	Annika Sorenstam	1,236,789
1958	Beverly Hanson	12,639	1978	Nancy Lopez	189,814	1998	Annika Sorenstam	1,092,748
1959	Betsy Rawls	26,774	1979	Nancy Lopez	197,489	1999	Karrie Webb	1,591,959
1960	Louise Suggs	16,892	1980	Beth Daniel	231,000	2000	Karrie Webb	1,876,853
1961	Mickey Wright	22,236	1981	Beth Daniel	206,998	2001	Annika Sorenstam	2,105,868
1962	Mickey Wright	21,641	1982	JoAnne Carner	310,400	2002	Annika Sorenstam	2,863,904
1963	Mickey Wright	31,269	1983	JoAnne Carner	291,404	2003	Annika Sorenstam	2,029,506
1964	Mickey Wright	29,800	1984	Betsy King	266,771	2004	Annika Sorenstam	2,544,707
1965	Kathy Whitworth	28,658	1985	Nancy Lopez	416,472	2005	Annika Sorenstam	2,588,240
1966	Kathy Whitworth	33,517	1986	Pat Bradley	492,021	2006	Lorena Ochoa	2,592,872
1967	Kathy Whitworth	32,937	1987	Ayako Okamoto	466,034	2007	Lorena Ochoa	4,364,994
1968	Kathy Whitworth	48,379	1988	Sherri Turner	350,851	2008	Lorena Ochoa	2,763,193
1969	Carol Mann	49,152	1989	Betsy King	654,132	2009	Jiyai Shin	1,807,334
1970	Kathy Whitworth	30,235	1990	Beth Daniel	863,578	2010	Na Yeon Choi	1,871,166
1971	Kathy Whitworth	41,181	1991	Pat Bradley	763,118	2011	Yani Tseng	2,921,713
1972	Kathy Whitworth	65,063	1992	Dottie Mochrie	693,335	2012	Inbee Park	2,287,080
1973	Kathy Whitworth	82,864	1993	Betsy King	595,992			

Kraft Nabisco Championship Winners, 1983-2013

Formerly the Colgate Dinah Shore (1972-81), the Nabisco Dinah Shore (1982-99), and the Nabisco Championship (2000-01). Designated as a major championship in 1983.

Year	Winner	Year	Winner	Year	Winner	Year	Winner	Year	Winner
1983	Amy Alcott	1990	Betsy King	1997	Betsy King	2003	Patricia Meunier-Lebouc	2008	Lorena Ochoa
1984	Juli Inkster	1991	Amy Alcott	1998	Pat Hurst			2009	Brittany Lincicome
1985	Alice Miller	1992	Dottie Pepper	1999	Dottie Pepper	2004	Grace Park	2010	Yani Tseng
1986	Pat Bradley	1993	Helen Alfredsson	2000	Karrie Webb	2005	Annika Sorenstam	2011	Stacy Lewis
1987	Betsy King	1994	Donna Andrews	2001	Annika Sorenstam	2006	Karrie Webb	2012	Sun Young Yoo
1988	Amy Alcott	1995	Nanci Bowen	2002	Annika Sorenstam	2007	Morgan Pressel	2013	Inbee Park
1989	Juli Inkster	1996	Patty Sheehan						

LPGA Championship Winners, 1955-2013

Year	Winner	Year	Winner	Year	Winner	Year	Winner	Year	Winner
1955	Beverly Hanson	1967	Kathy Whitworth	1979	Donna Caponi	1991	Meg Mallon	2003	Annika Sorenstam
1956	Marlene Hagge	1968	Sandra Post	1980	Sally Little	1992	Betsy King	2004	Annika Sorenstam
1957	Louise Suggs	1969	Betsy Rawls	1981	Donna Caponi	1993	Patty Sheehan	2005	Annika Sorenstam
1958	Mickey Wright	1970	Shirley Englehorn	1982	Jan Stephenson	1994	Laura Davies	2006	Se Ri Pak
1959	Betsy Rawls	1971	Kathy Whitworth	1983	Patty Sheehan	1995	Kelly Robbins	2007	Suzann Pettersen
1960	Mickey Wright	1972	Kathy Ahern	1984	Patty Sheehan	1996	Laura Davies	2008	Yani Tseng
1961	Mickey Wright	1973	Mary Mills	1985	Nancy Lopez	1997	Christa Johnson	2009	Anna Nordqvist
1962	Judy Kimball	1974	Sandra Haynie	1986	Pat Bradley	1998	Se Ri Pak	2010	Cristie Kerr
1963	Mickey Wright	1975	Kathy Whitworth	1987	Jane Geddes	1999	Juli Inkster	2011	Yani Tseng
1964	Mary Mills	1976	Betty Burfeindt	1988	Sherri Turner	2000	Juli Inkster	2012	Shanshan Feng
1965	Sandra Haynie	1977	Chako Higuchi	1989	Nancy Lopez	2001	Karrie Webb	2013	Inbee Park
1966	Gloria Ehret	1978	Nancy Lopez	1990	Beth Daniel	2002	Se Ri Pak		

U.S. Women's Open Winners, 1946-2013

Year	Winner	Year	Winner	Year	Winner	Year	Winner	Year	Winner
1946	Patty Berg	1961	Mickey Wright	1973	Susie Maxwell Berning	1986	Jane Geddes	2000	Karrie Webb
1947	Betty Jameson	1962	Murle Lindstrom			1987	Laura Davies	2001	Karrie Webb
1948	Babe Zaharias	1963	Mary Mills	1974	Sandra Haynie	1988	Liselotte Neumann	2002	Juli Inkster
1949	Louise Suggs	1964	Mickey Wright	1975	Sandra Palmer	1989	Betsy King	2003	Hilary Lunke
1950	Babe Zaharias	1965	Carol Mann	1976	JoAnne Carner	1990	Betsy King	2004	Meg Mallon
1951	Betsy Rawls	1966	Sandra Spuzich	1977	Hollis Stacy	1991	Meg Mallon	2005	Birdie Kim
1952	Louise Suggs	1967	Catherine Lacoste (amateur)	1978	Hollis Stacy	1992	Patty Sheehan	2006	Annika Sorenstam
1953	Betsy Rawls			1979	Jerilyn Britz	1993	Lauri Merten	2007	Cristie Kerr
1954	Babe Zaharias	1968	Susie Maxwell Berning	1980	Amy Alcott	1994	Patty Sheehan	2008	Inbee Park
1955	Fay Crocker			1981	Pat Bradley	1995	Annika Sorenstam	2009	Eun-Hee Ji
1956	Kathy Cornelius	1969	Donna Caponi	1982	Janet Alex	1996	Annika Sorenstam	2010	Paula Creamer
1957	Betsy Rawls	1970	Donna Caponi	1983	Jan Stephenson	1997	Alison Nicholas	2011	So Yeon Ryu
1958	Mickey Wright	1971	JoAnne Carner	1984	Hollis Stacy	1998	Se Ri Pak	2012	Na Yeon Choi
1959	Mickey Wright	1972	Susie Maxwell Berning	1985	Kathy Baker	1999	Juli Inkster	2013	Inbee Park
1960	Betsy Rawls								

Women's British Open Winners, 1979-2013

First held as the Ladies' British Open in 1976; became the LPGA's fourth major championship in 2001, replacing the du Maurier Classic. Winners listed are for the Peter Jackson (1979-82) and du Maurier (1983-2000) Classic.

Year	Winner	Year	Winner	Year	Winner	Year	Winner	Year	Winner
1979	Amy Alcott	1986	Pat Bradley	1993	Brandie Burton	2000	Meg Mallon	2007	Lorena Ochoa
1980	Pat Bradley	1987	Jody Rosenthal	1994	Martha Nause	2001	Se Ri Pak	2008	Jiyai Shin
1981	Jan Stephenson	1988	Sally Little	1995	Jenny Lidback	2002	Karrie Webb	2009	Catriona Matthew
1982	Sandra Haynie	1989	Tammie Green	1996	Laura Davies	2003	Annika Sorenstam	2010	Yani Tseng
1983	Hollis Stacy	1990	Cathy Johnston	1997	Colleen Walker	2004	Karen Stupples	2011	Yani Tseng
1984	Juli Inkster	1991	Nancy Scranton	1998	Brandie Burton	2005	Jeong Jang	2012	Jiyai Shin
1985	Pat Bradley	1992	Sherri Steinhauer	1999	Karrie Webb	2006	Sherri Steinhauer	2013	Stacy Lewis

Evian Championship

The Evian Championship began in 1994 as the Evian Masters on the Ladies European Tour, and has been co-sanctioned by the LPGA Tour since 2000. It became an LPGA major tournament for the first time in 2013 and was won by Suzann Pettersen.

Ryder Cup, 1927-2012

The Ryder Cup began in 1927 as a biennial team competition between pro male golfers from the U.S. and Great Britain. The British team was expanded in 1973 to include players from Ireland and in 1979 to golfers from the rest of Europe. The Ryder Cup moved to even years after it was postponed following the terrorist attacks of Sept. 11, 2001.

Year	Winner, score	Year	Winner, score	Year	Winner, score	Year	Winner, score
1927	U.S., 9½-2½	1953	U.S., 6½-5½	1973	U.S., 19-13	1993	U.S., 15-13
1929	Britain-Ireland, 7-5	1955	U.S., 8-4	1975	U.S., 21-11	1995	Europe, 14½-13½
1931	U.S., 9-3	1957	Britain-Ireland, 7½-4½	1977	U.S., 12½-7½	1997	Europe, 14½-13½
1933	Britain, 6½-5½	1959	U.S., 8½-3½	1979	U.S., 17-11	1999	U.S., 14½-13½
1935	U.S., 9-3	1961	U.S., 14½-9½	1981	U.S., 18½-9½	2002	Europe, 15½-12½
1937	U.S., 8-4	1963	U.S., 23-9	1983	U.S., 14½-13½	2004	Europe, 18½-9½
1939-45	Not played	1965	U.S., 19½-12½	1985	Europe, 16½-11½	2006	Europe, 18½-9½
1947	U.S., 11-1	1967	U.S., 23½-8½	1987	Europe, 15-13	2008	U.S., 16½-11½
1949	U.S., 7-5	1969	Draw, 16-16	1989	Draw, 14-14	2010	Europe, 14½-13½
1951	U.S., 9½-2½	1971	U.S., 18½-13½	1991	U.S., 14½-13½	2012	Europe, 14½-13½

Solheim Cup, 1990-2013

The Solheim Cup began in 1990 as a biennial team competition between pro women golfers from the U.S. and Europe. Competition moved to odd years beginning in 2003 to alternate with the Ryder Cup.

Year	Winner, score	Year	Winner, score	Year	Winner, score	Year	Winner, score
1990	U.S., 11½-4½	1998	U.S., 16-12	2003	Europe, 17½-10½	2009	U.S., 16-12
1992	Europe, 11½-6½	2000	Europe, 14½-11½	2005	U.S., 15½-12½	2011	Europe, 15-13
1994	U.S., 13-7	2002	U.S., 15½-12½	2007	U.S., 16-12	2013	Europe, 18-10
1996	U.S., 17-11						

TENNIS

Australian Open Champions, 1969-2013

First contested 1905 for men, 1922 for women. Became an open championship in 1969. Two tournaments held in 1977, in Jan. and Dec. No tournament held in 1986.

Men's Singles

Year	Champion	Final opponent
1969	Rod Laver	Andrés Gimeno
1970	Arthur Ashe	Dick Crealy
1971	Ken Rosewall	Arthur Ashe
1972	Ken Rosewall	Mal Anderson
1973	John Newcombe	Onny Parun
1974	Jimmy Connors	Phil Dent
1975	John Newcombe	Jimmy Connors
1976	Mark Edmondson	John Newcombe
1977	Roscoe Tanner	Guillermo Vilas
	Vitas Gerulaitis	John Lloyd
1978	Guillermo Vilas	John Marks
1979	Guillermo Vilas	John Sadri
1980	Brian Teacher	Kim Warwick
1981	Johan Kriek	Steve Denton
1982	Johan Kriek	Steve Denton
1983	Mats Wilander	Ivan Lendl
1984	Mats Wilander	Kevin Curren
1985	Stefan Edberg	Mats Wilander
1987	Stefan Edberg	Pat Cash
1988	Mats Wilander	Pat Cash
1989	Ivan Lendl	Miloslav Mecir
1990	Ivan Lendl	Stefan Edberg
1991	Boris Becker	Ivan Lendl
1992	Jim Courier	Stefan Edberg
1993	Jim Courier	Stefan Edberg
1994	Pete Sampras	Todd Martin
1995	Andre Agassi	Pete Sampras
1996	Boris Becker	Michael Chang
1997	Pete Sampras	Carlos Moya
1998	Petr Korda	Marcelo Rios
1999	Yevgeny Kafelnikov	Thomas Enqvist
2000	Andre Agassi	Yevgeny Kafelnikov
2001	Andre Agassi	Arnaud Clement
2002	Thomas Johansson	Marat Safin
2003	Andre Agassi	Rainer Schuettler
2004	Roger Federer	Marat Safin
2005	Marat Safin	Lleyton Hewitt
2006	Roger Federer	Marcos Baghdatis
2007	Roger Federer	Fernando Gonzalez
2008	Novak Djokovic	Jo-Wilfried Tsonga
2009	Rafael Nadal	Roger Federer
2010	Roger Federer	Andy Murray
2011	Novak Djokovic	Andy Murray
2012	Novak Djokovic	Rafael Nadal
2013	Novak Djokovic	Andy Murray

Women's Singles

Year	Champion	Final opponent
1969	Margaret Smith Court	Billie Jean King
1970	Margaret Smith Court	Kerry Melville Reid
1971	Margaret Smith Court	Evonne Goolagong
1972	Virginia Wade	Evonne Goolagong
1973	Margaret Smith Court	Evonne Goolagong
1974	Evonne Goolagong	Chris Evert
1975	Evonne Goolagong	Martina Navratilova
1976	Evonne Goolagong Cawley	Renata Tomanova
1977	Kerry Reid	Dianne Balestrat
	Evonne Goolagong Cawley	Helen Gourlay
1978	Chris O'Neill	Betsy Nagelsen
1979	Barbara Jordan	Sharon Walsh
1980	Hana Mandlikova	Wendy Turnbull
1981	Martina Navratilova	Chris Evert Lloyd
1982	Chris Evert Lloyd	Martina Navratilova
1983	Martina Navratilova	Kathy Jordan
1984	Chris Evert Lloyd	Helena Sukova
1985	Martina Navratilova	Chris Evert Lloyd
1987	Hana Mandlikova	Martina Navratilova
1988	Steffi Graf	Chris Evert
1989	Steffi Graf	Helena Sukova
1990	Steffi Graf	Mary Joe Fernandez
1991	Monica Seles	Jana Novotna
1992	Monica Seles	Mary Joe Fernandez
1993	Monica Seles	Steffi Graf
1994	Steffi Graf	Arantxa Sánchez Vicario
1995	Mary Pierce	Arantxa Sánchez Vicario
1996	Monica Seles	Anke Huber
1997	Martina Hingis	Mary Pierce
1998	Martina Hingis	Conchita Martínez
1999	Martina Hingis	Amelie Mauresmo
2000	Lindsay Davenport	Martina Hingis
2001	Jennifer Capriati	Martina Hingis
2002	Jennifer Capriati	Martina Hingis
2003	Serena Williams	Venus Williams
2004	Justine Henin	Kim Clijsters
2005	Serena Williams	Lindsay Davenport
2006	Amelie Mauresmo	Justine Henin
2007	Serena Williams	Maria Sharapova
2008	Maria Sharapova	Ana Ivanovic
2009	Serena Williams	Dinara Safina
2010	Serena Williams	Justine Henin
2011	Kim Clijsters	Li Na
2012	Victoria Azarenka	Maria Sharapova
2013	Victoria Azarenka	Li Na

French Open (Roland Garros) Champions, 1968-2013

First contested 1891 for men, 1897 for women. Became an open championship in 1968.

Men's Singles

Year	Champion	Final opponent
1968	Ken Rosewall	Rod Laver
1969	Rod Laver	Ken Rosewall
1970	Jan Kodes	Zeljko Franulovic
1971	Jan Kodes	Ilie Nastase
1972	Andrés Gimeno	Patrick Proisy
1973	Ilie Nastase	Nikki Pilic
1974	Björn Borg	Manuel Orantes
1975	Björn Borg	Guillermo Vilas
1976	Adriano Panatta	Harold Solomon
1977	Guillermo Vilas	Brian Gottfried
1978	Björn Borg	Guillermo Vilas
1979	Björn Borg	Victor Pecci
1980	Björn Borg	Vitas Gerulaitis
1981	Björn Borg	Ivan Lendl
1982	Mats Wilander	Guillermo Vilas
1983	Yannick Noah	Mats Wilander
1984	Ivan Lendl	John McEnroe
1985	Mats Wilander	Ivan Lendl
1986	Ivan Lendl	Mikael Pernfors
1987	Ivan Lendl	Mats Wilander
1988	Mats Wilander	Henri Leconte
1989	Michael Chang	Stefan Edberg
1990	Andres Gomez	Andre Agassi
1991	Jim Courier	Andre Agassi
1992	Jim Courier	Petr Korda
1993	Sergi Bruguera	Jim Courier
1994	Sergi Bruguera	Alberto Berasategui
1995	Thomas Muster	Michael Chang
1996	Yevgeny Kafelnikov	Michael Stich
1997	Gustavo Kuerten	Sergi Bruguera
1998	Carlos Moya	Alex Corretja
1999	Andre Agassi	Andrei Medvedev
2000	Gustavo Kuerten	Magnus Norman
2001	Gustavo Kuerten	Alex Corretja
2002	Albert Costa	Juan Carlos Ferrero
2003	Juan Carlos Ferrero	Martin Verkerk
2004	Gaston Gaudio	Guillermo Coria
2005	Rafael Nadal	Mariano Puerta
2006	Rafael Nadal	Roger Federer
2007	Rafael Nadal	Roger Federer
2008	Rafael Nadal	Roger Federer
2009	Roger Federer	Robin Soderling
2010	Rafael Nadal	Robin Soderling
2011	Rafael Nadal	Roger Federer
2012	Rafael Nadal	Novak Djokovic
2013	Rafael Nadal	David Ferrer

Women's Singles

Year	Champion	Final opponent
1968	Nancy Richey	Ann Jones
1969	Margaret Smith Court	Ann Jones
1970	Margaret Smith Court	Helga Niessen
1971	Evonne Goolagong	Helen Gourlay
1972	Billie Jean King	Evonne Goolagong
1973	Margaret Smith Court	Chris Evert
1974	Chris Evert	Olga Morozova
1975	Chris Evert	Martina Navratilova
1976	Sue Barker	Renata Tomanova
1977	Mima Jausovec	Florenta Mihai
1978	Virginia Ruzici	Mima Jausovec
1979	Chris Evert Lloyd	Wendy Turnbull
1980	Chris Evert Lloyd	Virginia Ruzici
1981	Hana Mandlikova	Sylvia Hanika
1982	Martina Navratilova	Andrea Jaeger
1983	Chris Evert Lloyd	Mima Jausovec

Year	Champion	Final opponent	Year	Champion	Final opponent
1984	Martina Navratilova	Chris Evert Lloyd	1999	Steffi Graf	Martina Hingis
1985	Chris Evert Lloyd	Martina Navratilova	2000	Mary Pierce	Conchita Martínez
1986	Chris Evert Lloyd	Martina Navratilova	2001	Jennifer Capriati	Kim Clijsters
1987	Steffi Graf	Martina Navratilova	2002	Serena Williams	Venus Williams
1988	Steffi Graf	Natalia Zvereva	2003	Justine Henin	Kim Clijsters
1989	Arantxa Sánchez Vicario	Steffi Graf	2004	Anastasia Myskina	Elena Dementieva
1990	Monica Seles	Steffi Graf	2005	Justine Henin	Mary Pierce
1991	Monica Seles	Arantxa Sánchez Vicario	2006	Justine Henin	Svetlana Kuznetsova
1992	Monica Seles	Steffi Graf	2007	Justine Henin	Ana Ivanovic
1993	Steffi Graf	Mary Joe Fernandez	2008	Ana Ivanovic	Dinara Safina
1994	Arantxa Sánchez Vicario	Mary Pierce	2009	Svetlana Kuznetsova	Dinara Safina
1995	Steffi Graf	Arantxa Sánchez Vicario	2010	Francesca Schiavone	Samantha Stosur
1996	Steffi Graf	Arantxa Sánchez Vicario	2011	Li Na	Francesca Schiavone
1997	Iva Majoli	Martina Hingis	2012	Maria Sharapova	Sara Errani
1998	Arantxa Sánchez Vicario	Monica Seles	2013	Serena Williams	Maria Sharapova

Wimbledon Champions, 1925-2013

First contested 1877 for men, 1884 for women. Became an open championship in 1968. Not held 1940-45.

Men's Singles

Year	Champion	Final opponent
1925	René Lacoste	Jean Borotra
1926	Jean Borotra	Howard Kinsey
1927	Henri Cochet	Jean Borotra
1928	René Lacoste	Henri Cochet
1929	Henri Cochet	Jean Borotra
1930	Bill Tilden	Wilmer Allison
1931	Sidney B. Wood	Francis X. Shields
1932	Ellsworth Vines	Henry Austin
1933	Jack Crawford	Ellsworth Vines
1934	Fred Perry	Jack Crawford
1935	Fred Perry	Gottfried von Cramm
1936	Fred Perry	Gottfried von Cramm
1937	Donald Budge	Gottfried von Cramm
1938	Donald Budge	Henry Austin
1939	Bobby Riggs	Elwood Cooke
1946	Yvon Petra	Geoff E. Brown
1947	Jack Kramer	Tom P. Brown
1948	Bob Falkenburg	John Bromwich
1949	Ted Schroeder	Jaroslav Drobny
1950	Budge Patty	Frank Sedgman
1951	Dick Savitt	Ken McGregor
1952	Frank Sedgman	Jaroslav Drobny
1953	Vic Seixas	Kurt Nielsen
1954	Jaroslav Drobny	Ken Rosewall
1955	Tony Trabert	Kurt Nielsen
1956	Lew Hoad	Ken Rosewall
1957	Lew Hoad	Ashley Cooper
1958	Ashley Cooper	Neale Fraser
1959	Alex Olmedo	Rod Laver
1960	Neale Fraser	Rod Laver
1961	Rod Laver	Chuck McKinley
1962	Rod Laver	Martin Mulligan
1963	Chuck McKinley	Fred Stolle
1964	Roy Emerson	Fred Stolle
1965	Roy Emerson	Fred Stolle
1966	Manuel Santana	Dennis Ralston
1967	John Newcombe	Wilhelm Bungert
1968	Rod Laver	Tony Roche
1969	Rod Laver	John Newcombe
1970	John Newcombe	Ken Rosewall
1971	John Newcombe	Stan Smith
1972	Stan Smith	Ilie Nastase
1973	Jan Kodes	Alex Metreveli
1974	Jimmy Connors	Ken Rosewall
1975	Arthur Ashe	Jimmy Connors
1976	Björn Borg	Ilie Nastase
1977	Björn Borg	Jimmy Connors
1978	Björn Borg	Jimmy Connors
1979	Björn Borg	Roscoe Tanner
1980	Björn Borg	John McEnroe
1981	John McEnroe	Björn Borg
1982	Jimmy Connors	John McEnroe
1983	John McEnroe	Chris Lewis
1984	John McEnroe	Jimmy Connors
1985	Boris Becker	Kevin Curren
1986	Boris Becker	Ivan Lendl
1987	Pat Cash	Ivan Lendl
1988	Stefan Edberg	Boris Becker
1989	Boris Becker	Stefan Edberg
1990	Stefan Edberg	Boris Becker
1991	Michael Stich	Boris Becker
1992	Andre Agassi	Goran Ivanisevic
1993	Pete Sampras	Jim Courier
1994	Pete Sampras	Goran Ivanisevic
1995	Pete Sampras	Boris Becker
1996	Richard Krajicek	MaliVai "Mai" Washington
1997	Pete Sampras	Cedric Pioline
1998	Pete Sampras	Goran Ivanisevic
1999	Pete Sampras	Andre Agassi
2000	Pete Sampras	Patrick Rafter
2001	Goran Ivanisevic	Patrick Rafter
2002	Lleyton Hewitt	David Nalbandian
2003	Roger Federer	Mark Philippoussis
2004	Roger Federer	Andy Roddick
2005	Roger Federer	Andy Roddick
2006	Roger Federer	Rafael Nadal
2007	Roger Federer	Rafael Nadal
2008	Rafael Nadal	Roger Federer
2009	Roger Federer	Andy Roddick
2010	Rafael Nadal	Tomas Berdych
2011	Novak Djokovic	Rafael Nadal
2012	Roger Federer	Andy Murray
2013	Andy Murray	Novak Djokovic

Women's Singles

Year	Champion	Final opponent
1925	Suzanne Lenglen	Joan Fry
1926	Kathleen McKane Godfree	Lili de Alvarez
1927	Helen Wills	Lili de Alvarez
1928	Helen Wills	Lili de Alvarez
1929	Helen Wills	Helen Jacobs
1930	Helen Wills Moody	Elizabeth Ryan
1931	Cilly Aussem	Hilde Krahwinkel
1932	Helen Wills Moody	Helen Jacobs
1933	Helen Wills Moody	Dorothy Round
1934	Dorothy Round	Helen Jacobs
1935	Helen Wills Moody	Helen Jacobs
1936	Helen Jacobs	Hilde Krahwinkel Sperling
1937	Dorothy Round	Jadwiga Jedrzejowska
1938	Helen Wills Moody	Helen Jacobs
1939	Alice Marble	Kay Stammers
1946	Pauline Betz	Louise Brough
1947	Margaret Osborne	Doris Hart
1948	Louise Brough	Doris Hart
1949	Louise Brough	Margaret Osborne duPont
1950	Louise Brough	Margaret Osborne duPont
1951	Doris Hart	Shirley Fry
1952	Maureen Connolly	Louise Brough
1953	Maureen Connolly	Doris Hart
1954	Maureen Connolly	Louise Brough
1955	Louise Brough	Beverly Fleitz
1956	Shirley Fry	Angela Buxton
1957	Althea Gibson	Darlene Hard
1958	Althea Gibson	Angela Mortimer
1959	Maria Bueno	Darlene Hard
1960	Maria Bueno	Sandra Reynolds
1961	Angela Mortimer	Christine Truman
1962	Karen Hantze-Susman	Vera Sukova
1963	Margaret Smith	Billie Jean Moffitt
1964	Maria Bueno	Margaret Smith
1965	Margaret Smith	Maria Bueno
1966	Billie Jean King	Maria Bueno
1967	Billie Jean King	Ann Haydon Jones
1968	Billie Jean King	Judy Tegart
1969	Ann Haydon Jones	Billie Jean King
1970	Margaret Smith Court	Billie Jean King
1971	Evonne Goolagong	Margaret Smith Court
1972	Billie Jean King	Evonne Goolagong
1973	Billie Jean King	Chris Evert
1974	Chris Evert	Olga Morozova
1975	Billie Jean King	Evonne Goolagong Cawley

Year	Champion	Final opponent	Year	Champion	Final opponent
1976	Chris Evert	Evonne Goolagong Cawley	1994	Conchita Martínez	Martina Navratilova
1977	Virginia Wade	Betty Stove	1995	Steffi Graf	Arantxa Sánchez Vicario
1978	Martina Navratilova	Chris Evert	1996	Steffi Graf	Arantxa Sánchez Vicario
1979	Martina Navratilova	Chris Evert Lloyd	1997	Martina Hingis	Jana Novotna
1980	Evonne Goolagong Cawley	Chris Evert Lloyd	1998	Jana Novotna	Nathalie Tauziat
1981	Chris Evert Lloyd	Hana Mandlikova	1999	Lindsay Davenport	Steffi Graf
1982	Martina Navratilova	Chris Evert Lloyd	2000	Venus Williams	Lindsay Davenport
1983	Martina Navratilova	Andrea Jaeger	2001	Venus Williams	Justine Henin
1984	Martina Navratilova	Chris Evert Lloyd	2002	Serena Williams	Venus Williams
1985	Martina Navratilova	Chris Evert Lloyd	2003	Serena Williams	Venus Williams
1986	Martina Navratilova	Hana Mandlikova	2004	Maria Sharapova	Serena Williams
1987	Martina Navratilova	Steffi Graf	2005	Venus Williams	Lindsay Davenport
1988	Steffi Graf	Martina Navratilova	2006	Amelie Mauresmo	Justine Henin
1989	Steffi Graf	Martina Navratilova	2007	Venus Williams	Marion Bartoli
1990	Martina Navratilova	Zina Garrison	2008	Venus Williams	Serena Williams
1991	Steffi Graf	Gabriela Sabatini	2009	Serena Williams	Venus Williams
1992	Steffi Graf	Monica Seles	2010	Serena Williams	Vera Zvonareva
1993	Steffi Graf	Jana Novotna	2011	Petra Kvitova	Maria Sharapova
			2012	Serena Williams	Agnieszka Radwanska
			2013	Marion Bartoli	Sabine Lisicki

U.S. Open Champions, 1925-2013

First contested 1881 for men, 1887 for women. The former U.S. National Championship became an open championship in 1968.

Men's Singles

Year	Champion	Final opponent	Year	Champion	Final opponent
1925	Bill Tilden	William Johnston	1987	Ivan Lendl	Mats Wilander
1926	René Lacoste	Jean Borotra	1988	Mats Wilander	Ivan Lendl
1927	René Lacoste	Bill Tilden	1989	Boris Becker	Ivan Lendl
1928	Henri Cochet	Francis Hunter	1990	Pete Sampras	Andre Agassi
1929	Bill Tilden	Francis Hunter	1991	Stefan Edberg	Jim Courier
1930	John Doeg	Francis Shields	1992	Stefan Edberg	Pete Sampras
1931	Ellsworth Vines	George Lott	1993	Pete Sampras	Cedric Pioline
1932	Ellsworth Vines	Henri Cochet	1994	Andre Agassi	Michael Stich
1933	Fred Perry	John Crawford	1995	Pete Sampras	Andre Agassi
1934	Fred Perry	Wilmer Allison	1996	Pete Sampras	Michael Chang
1935	Wilmer Allison	Sidney Wood	1997	Patrick Rafter	Greg Rusedski
1936	Fred Perry	Don Budge	1998	Patrick Rafter	Mark Philippoussis
1937	Don Budge	Gottfried von Cramm	1999	Andre Agassi	Todd Martin
1938	Don Budge	C. Gene Mako	2000	Marat Safin	Pete Sampras
1939	Bobby Riggs	S. Welby Van Horn	2001	Lleyton Hewitt	Pete Sampras
1940	Don McNeill	Bobby Riggs	2002	Pete Sampras	Andre Agassi
1941	Bobby Riggs	F. L. Kovacs	2003	Andy Roddick	Juan Carlos Ferrero
1942	F. R. Schroeder Jr.	Frank Parker	2004	Roger Federer	Lleyton Hewitt
1943	Joseph Hunt	Jack Kramer	2005	Roger Federer	Andre Agassi
1944	Frank Parker	William Talbert	2006	Roger Federer	Andy Roddick
1945	Frank Parker	William Talbert	2007	Roger Federer	Novak Djokovic
1946	Jack Kramer	Thomas Brown Jr.	2008	Roger Federer	Andy Murray
1947	Jack Kramer	Frank Parker	2009	Juan Martin del Potro	Roger Federer
1948	Pancho Gonzales	Eric Sturgess	2010	Rafael Nadal	Novak Djokovic
1949	Pancho Gonzales	F. R. Schroeder Jr.	2011	Novak Djokovic	Rafael Nadal
1950	Arthur Larsen	Herbert Flam	2012	Andy Murray	Novak Djokovic
1951	Frank Sedgman	E. Victor Seixas Jr.	2013	Rafael Nadal	Novak Djokovic
1952	Frank Sedgman	Gardnar Mulloy			
1953	Tony Trabert	E. Victor Seixas Jr.			

Women's Singles

Year	Champion	Final opponent
1954	E. Victor Seixas Jr.	Rex Hartwig
1955	Tony Trabert	Ken Rosewall
1956	Ken Rosewall	Lewis Hoad
1957	Malcolm Anderson	Ashley Cooper
1958	Ashley Cooper	Malcolm Anderson
1959	Neale A. Fraser	Alejandro Olmedo
1960	Neale A. Fraser	Rod Laver
1961	Roy Emerson	Rod Laver
1962	Rod Laver	Roy Emerson
1963	Rafael Osuna	F. A. Froehling III
1964	Roy Emerson	Fred Stolle
1965	Manuel Santana	Cliff Drysdale
1966	Fred Stolle	John Newcombe
1967	John Newcombe	Clark Graebner
1968	Arthur Ashe	Tom Okker
1969	Rod Laver	Tony Roche
1970	Ken Rosewall	Tony Roche
1971	Stan Smith	Jan Kodes
1972	Ilie Nastase	Arthur Ashe
1973	John Newcombe	Jan Kodes
1974	Jimmy Connors	Ken Rosewall
1975	Manuel Orantes	Jimmy Connors
1976	Jimmy Connors	Björn Borg
1977	Guillermo Vilas	Jimmy Connors
1978	Jimmy Connors	Björn Borg
1979	John McEnroe	Vitas Gerulaitis
1980	John McEnroe	Björn Borg
1981	John McEnroe	Björn Borg
1982	Jimmy Connors	Ivan Lendl
1983	Jimmy Connors	Ivan Lendl
1984	John McEnroe	Ivan Lendl
1985	Ivan Lendl	John McEnroe
1986	Ivan Lendl	Miloslav Mecir

Year	Champion	Final opponent
1925	Helen Willis	Kathleen McKane
1926	Molla B. Mallory	Elizabeth Ryan
1927	Helen Wills	Betty Nuthall
1928	Helen Wills	Helen Jacobs
1929	Helen Wills	Phoebe Holcroft-Watson
1930	Betty Nuthall	L. A. Harper
1931	Helen Wills Moody	E. B. Whittingstall
1932	Helen Jacobs	Carolin A. Babcock
1933	Helen Jacobs	Helen Wills Moody
1934	Helen Jacobs	Sarah H. Palfrey
1935	Helen Jacobs	Sarah Palfrey Fabyan
1936	Alice Marble	Helen Jacobs
1937	Anita Lizana	Jadwiga Jedrzejowska
1938	Alice Marble	Nancye Wynne
1939	Alice Marble	Helen Jacobs
1940	Alice Marble	Helen Jacobs
1941	Sarah Palfrey Cooke	Pauline Betz
1942	Pauline Betz	Louise Brough
1943	Pauline Betz	Louise Brough
1944	Pauline Betz	Margaret Osborne
1945	Sarah Palfrey Cooke	Pauline Betz
1946	Pauline Betz	Patricia Canning
1947	Louise Brough	Margaret Osborne
1948	Margaret Osborne duPont	Louise Brough
1949	Margaret Osborne duPont	Doris Hart
1950	Margaret Osborne duPont	Doris Hart
1951	Maureen Connolly	Shirley Fry
1952	Maureen Connolly	Doris Hart
1953	Maureen Connolly	Doris Hart
1954	Doris Hart	Louise Brough
1955	Doris Hart	Patricia Ward
1956	Shirley Fry	Althea Gibson
1957	Althea Gibson	Louise Brough

Year	Champion	Final opponent	Year	Champion	Final opponent
1958	Althea Gibson	Darlene Hard	1985	Hana Mandlikova	Martina Navratilova
1959	Maria Bueno	Christine Truman	1986	Martina Navratilova	Helena Sukova
1960	Darlene Hard	Maria Bueno	1987	Martina Navratilova	Steffi Graf
1961	Darlene Hard	Ann Haydon	1988	Steffi Graf	Gabriela Sabatini
1962	Margaret Smith	Darlene Hard	1989	Steffi Graf	Martina Navratilova
1963	Maria Bueno	Margaret Smith	1990	Gabriela Sabatini	Steffi Graf
1964	Maria Bueno	Carole Graebner	1991	Monica Seles	Martina Navratilova
1965	Margaret Smith	Billie Jean Moffitt	1992	Monica Seles	Arantxa Sánchez Vicario
1966	Maria Bueno	Nancy Richey	1993	Steffi Graf	Helena Sukova
1967	Billie Jean King	Ann Haydon Jones	1994	Arantxa Sánchez Vicario	Steffi Graf
1968	Virginia Wade	Billie Jean King	1995	Steffi Graf	Monica Seles
1969	Margaret Smith Court	Nancy Richey	1996	Steffi Graf	Monica Seles
1970	Margaret Smith Court	Rosemary Casals	1997	Martina Hingis	Venus Williams
1971	Billie Jean King	Rosemary Casals	1998	Lindsay Davenport	Martina Hingis
1972	Billie Jean King	Kerry Melville	1999	Serena Williams	Martina Hingis
1973	Margaret Smith Court	Evonne Goolagong	2000	Venus Williams	Lindsay Davenport
1974	Billie Jean King	Evonne Goolagong	2001	Venus Williams	Serena Williams
1975	Chris Evert	Evonne Goolagong Cawley	2002	Serena Williams	Venus Williams
			2003	Justine Henin	Kim Clijsters
1976	Chris Evert	Evonne Goolagong Cawley	2004	Svetlana Kuznetsova	Elena Dementieva
			2005	Kim Clijsters	Mary Pierce
1977	Chris Evert	Wendy Turnbull	2006	Maria Sharapova	Justine Henin
1978	Chris Evert	Pam Shriver	2007	Justine Henin	Svetlana Kuznetsova
1979	Tracy Austin	Chris Evert Lloyd	2008	Serena Williams	Jelena Jankovic
1980	Chris Evert Lloyd	Hana Mandlikova	2009	Kim Clijsters	Caroline Wozniacki
1981	Tracy Austin	Martina Navratilova	2010	Kim Clijsters	Vera Zvonareva
1982	Chris Evert Lloyd	Hana Mandlikova	2011	Samantha Stosur	Serena Williams
1983	Martina Navratilova	Chris Evert Lloyd	2012	Serena Williams	Victoria Azarenka
1984	Martina Navratilova	Chris Evert Lloyd	2013	Serena Williams	Victoria Azarenka

Davis Cup, 1950-2012

The Davis Cup began in 1900 as a competition between the U.S. and Great Britain and later expanded to include other countries.

Year	Result	Year	Result	Year	Result
1950	Australia 4, U.S. 1	1971	U.S. 3, Romania 2	1992	U.S. 3, Switzerland 1
1951	Australia 3, U.S. 2	1972	U.S. 3, Romania 2	1993	Germany 4, Australia 1
1952	Australia 4, U.S. 1	1973	Australia 5, U.S. 0	1994	Sweden 4, Russia 1
1953	Australia 3, U.S. 2	1974	South Africa (default by India)	1995	U.S. 3, Russia 2
1954	U.S. 3, Australia 2	1975	Sweden 3, Czechoslovakia 2	1996	France 3, Sweden 2
1955	Australia 5, U.S. 0	1976	Italy 4, Chile 1	1997	Sweden 5, U.S. 0
1956	Australia 5, U.S. 0	1977	Australia 3, Italy 1	1998	Sweden 4, Italy 1
1957	Australia 3, U.S. 2	1978	U.S. 4, Great Britain 1	1999	Australia 3, France 2
1958	U.S. 3, Australia 2	1979	U.S. 5, Italy 0	2000	Spain 3, Australia 1
1959	Australia 3, U.S. 2	1980	Czechoslovakia 4, Italy 1	2001	France 3, Australia 2
1960	Australia 4, Italy 1	1981	U.S. 3, Argentina 1	2002	Russia 3, France 2
1961	Australia 5, Italy 0	1982	U.S. 4, France, 1	2003	Australia 3, Spain 1
1962	Australia 5, Mexico 0	1983	Australia 3, Sweden 2	2004	Spain 3, U.S. 2
1963	U.S. 3, Australia 2	1984	Sweden 4, U.S. 1	2005	Croatia 3, Slovakia 2
1964	Australia 3, U.S. 2	1985	Sweden 3, W. Germany 2	2006	Russia 3, Argentina 2
1965	Australia 4, Spain 1	1986	Australia 3, Sweden 2	2007	U.S. 4, Russia 1
1966	Australia 4, India 1	1987	Sweden 5, India 0	2008	Spain 3, Argentina 1
1967	Australia 4, Spain 1	1988	W. Germany 4, Sweden 1	2009	Spain 5, Czech Republic 0
1968	U.S. 4, Australia 1	1989	W. Germany 3, Sweden 2	2010	Serbia 3, France 2
1969	U.S. 5, Romania 0	1990	U.S. 3, Australia 2	2011	Spain 3, Argentina 1
1970	U.S. 5, W. Germany 0	1991	France 3, U.S. 1	2012	Czech Republic 3, Spain 2

Note: The challenge round format, which guaranteed the previous year's winner a spot in the finals at home, was eliminated in 1972.

All-Time Grand Slam Singles Titles Leaders

Men	Australian Open	French Open[1]	Wimbledon	U.S. Open	Total
Roger Federer	2004, '06-'07, '10	2009	2003-07, '09, '12	2004-08	17
Pete Sampras	1994, '97	—	1993-95, 1997-2000	1990, '93, '95-'96, 2002	14
Rafael Nadal	2009	2005-08, '10-'13	2008, '10	2010, '13	13
Roy Emerson	1961, '63-'67	1963, '67	1964-65	1961, '64	12
Björn Borg	—	1974-75, '78-'81	1976-80	—	11
Rod Laver	1960, '62, '69	1962, '69	1961-62, '68-'69	1962, '69	11
Bill Tilden	—	—	1920-21, '30	1920-25, '29	10
Andre Agassi	1995, 2000, '01, '03	1999	1992	1994, '99	8
Jimmy Connors	1974	—	1974, '82	1974, '76, '78, '82-'83	8
Ivan Lendl	1989-90	1984, '86-'87	—	1985-87	8
Fred Perry	1934	1935	1934-36	1933-34, '36	8
Ken Rosewall	1953, '55, '71-'72	1953, '68	—	1956, '70	8

Women	Australian Open	French Open[1]	Wimbledon	U.S. Open	Total
Margaret Smith Court	1960-66, '69-'71, '73	1962, '64, '69-'70, '73	1963, '65, '70	1962, '65, '69-'70, '73	24
Steffi Graf	1988-90, '94	1987-88, '93, '95-'96, '99	1988-89, '91-'93, '95-'96	1988-89, '93, '95-'96	22
Helen Wills Moody	—	1928-30, '32	1927-30, '32-'33, '35, '38	1923-25, '27-'29, '31	19
Chris Evert	1982, '84	1974-75, '79-'80, '83, '85-'86	1974, '76, '81	1975-78, '80, '82	18
Martina Navratilova	1981, '83, '85	1982, '84	1978-79, '82-'87, '90	1983-84, '86-'87	18
Serena Williams	2003, '05, '07, '09-'10	2002, '13	2002-03, '09-'10, '12	1999, 2002, '08, '12-'13	17
Billie Jean King	1968	1972	1966-68, '72-'73, '75	1967, '71-'72, '74	12
Suzanne Lenglen	—	1920-23, '25-'26	1919-23, '25	—	12
Maureen Connolly	1953	1953-54	1952-54	1951-53	9
Monica Seles	1991-93, '96	1990-92	—	1991-92	9

Note: Players active in 2013 are in bold. (1) Prior to 1925, French Open entry was limited to members of French clubs.

AUTO RACING

Indianapolis 500 Winners, 1911-2013

At Indianapolis Motor Speedway in Indianapolis, IN. Not held 1917-18, 1942-45. * = Race record.

Year	Driver(s), car[1]	Avg. mph	Year	Driver(s), car[1]	Avg. mph
1911	Ray Harroun, Marmon	74.602	1966	Graham Hill, Lola-Ford	144.317
1912	Joe Dawson, National	78.719	1967	A. J. Foyt, Coyote-Ford	151.207
1913	Jules Goux, Peugeot	75.933	1968	Bobby Unser, Eagle-Offy	152.882
1914	Rene Thomas, Delage	82.474	1969	Mario Andretti, Hawk-Ford	156.867
1915	Ralph DePalma, Mercedes	89.840	1970	Al Unser, P.J. Colt-Ford	155.749
1916	Dario Resta, Peugeot	84.001	1971	Al Unser, P.J. Colt-Ford	157.735
1919	Howdy Wilcox, Peugeot	88.050	1972	Mark Donohue, McLaren-Offy	162.962
1920	Gaston Chevrolet, Frontenac	88.618	1973	Gordon Johncock, Eagle-Offy	159.036
1921	Tommy Milton, Frontenac	89.621	1974	Johnny Rutherford, McLaren-Offy	158.589
1922	Jimmy Murphy, Duesenberg-Miller	94.484	1975	Bobby Unser, Eagle-Offy	149.213
1923	Tommy Milton, Miller	90.954	1976	Johnny Rutherford, McLaren-Offy	148.725
1924	L. L. Corum/Joe Boyer, Duesenberg	98.234	1977	A. J. Foyt, Coyote-Foyt	161.331
1925	Peter DePaolo, Duesenberg	101.127	1978	Al Unser, Lola-Cosworth	161.363
1926	Frank Lockhart, Miller	95.904	1979	Rick Mears, Penske-Cosworth	158.899
1927	George Souders, Duesenberg	97.545	1980	Johnny Rutherford, Chaparral-Cosworth	142.862
1928	Louie Meyer, Miller	99.482	1981	Bobby Unser, Penske-Cosworth	139.084
1929	Ray Keech, Miller	97.585	1982	Gordon Johncock, Wildcat-Cosworth	162.029
1930	Billy Arnold, Summers-Miller	100.448	1983	Tom Sneva, March-Cosworth	162.117
1931	Louis Schneider, Stevens-Miller	96.629	1984	Rick Mears, March-Cosworth	163.612
1932	Fred Frame, Wetteroth-Miller	104.144	1985	Danny Sullivan, March-Cosworth	152.982
1933	Louie Meyer, Miller	104.162	1986	Bobby Rahal, March-Cosworth	170.722
1934	Bill Cummings, Miller	104.863	1987	Al Unser, March-Cosworth	162.175
1935	Kelly Petillo, Wetteroth-Offy	106.240	1988	Rick Mears, Penske-Chevy Indy V8	144.809
1936	Louie Meyer, Stevens-Miller	109.069	1989	Emerson Fittipaldi, Penske-Chevy Indy V8	167.581
1937	Wilbur Shaw, Shaw-Offy	113.580	1990	Arie Luyendyk, Lola-Chevy Indy V8	185.981
1938	Floyd Roberts, Wetteroth-Miller	117.200	1991	Rick Mears, Penske-Chevy Indy V8	176.457
1939	Wilbur Shaw, Maserati	115.035	1992	Al Unser Jr., Galmer-Chevy Indy V8A	134.477
1940	Wilbur Shaw, Maserati	114.277	1993	Emerson Fittipaldi, Penske-Chevy Indy V8C	157.207
1941	Floyd Davis/Mauri Rose, Wetteroth-Offy	115.117	1994	Al Unser Jr., Penske-Mercedes Benz	160.872
1946	George Robson, Adams-Sparks	114.820	1995	Jacques Villeneuve, Reynard-Ford Cosworth XB	153.616
1947	Mauri Rose, Deidt-Offy	116.338	1996	Buddy Lazier, Reynard-Ford Cosworth XB	147.956
1948	Mauri Rose, Deidt-Offy	119.814	1997	Arie Luyendyk, G Force-Aurora	145.827
1949	Bill Holland, Deidt-Offy	121.327	1998	Eddie Cheever, Dallara-Aurora	145.155
1950	Johnnie Parsons, Kurtis-Offy	124.002	1999	Kenny Brack, Dallara-Aurora	153.176
1951	Lee Wallard, Kurtis-Offy	126.244	2000	Juan Montoya, G Force-Oldsmobile	167.607
1952	Troy Ruttman, Kuzma-Offy	128.922	2001	Helio Castroneves, Dallara-Oldsmobile	141.574
1953	Bill Vukovich, KK500A-Offy	127.740	2002	Helio Castroneves, Dallara-Chevrolet	166.499
1954	Bill Vukovich, KK500A-Offy	130.840	2003	Gil de Ferran, G Force-Toyota	156.291
1955	Bob Sweikert, KK500C-Offy	128.213	2004	Buddy Rice, G Force-Honda	138.518
1956	Pat Flaherty, Watson-Offy	128.490	2005	Dan Wheldon, Dallara-Honda	157.603
1957	Sam Hanks, Salih-Offy	135.601	2006	Sam Hornish Jr., Dallara-Honda	157.085
1958	Jimmy Bryan, Salih-Offy	133.791	2007	Dario Franchitti, Dallara-Honda	151.774
1959	Rodger Ward, Watson-Offy	135.857	2008	Scott Dixon, Dallara-Honda	143.567
1960	Jim Rathmann, Watson-Offy	138.767	2009	Helio Castroneves, Dallara-Honda	150.318
1961	A. J. Foyt, Trevis-Offy	139.130	2010	Dario Franchitti, Dallara-Honda	161.623
1962	Rodger Ward, Watson-Offy	140.293	2011	Dan Wheldon, Dallara-Honda	170.265
1963	Parnelli Jones, Watson-Offy	143.137	2012	Dario Franchitti, Dallara-Honda	167.734
1964	A. J. Foyt, Watson-Offy	147.350	2013	Tony Kanaan, Dallara-Chevrolet	187.433*
1965	Jim Clark, Lotus-Ford	150.686			

Note: The race was less than 500 mi in the following years: 1916 (300 mi), 1926 (400 mi), 1950 (345 mi), 1973 (332.5 mi), 1975 (435 mi), 1976 (255 mi), 2004 (450 mi), 2007 (415 mi). [1] Chassis-engine.

IndyCar Series Champions, 1996-2013

A breakaway group of Championship Auto Racing Teams (CART) drivers began the Indy Racing League (IRL) in 1994; it awarded its first championship in 1996. Known as IndyCar Series since 2003, IRL announced it would officially change its name to IndyCar as of Jan. 1, 2011. Merged with Champ Car World Series, 2008.

Year	Driver	Year	Driver	Year	Driver	Year	Driver	Year	Driver
1996	Scott Sharp; Buzz Calkins (tie)	1999	Greg Ray	2003	Scott Dixon	2007	Dario Franchitti	2011	Dario Franchitti
		2000	Buddy Lazier	2004	Tony Kanaan	2008	Scott Dixon	2012	Ryan Hunter-Reay
1997	Tony Stewart	2001	Sam Hornish Jr.	2005	Dan Wheldon	2009	Dario Franchitti	2013	Scott Dixon
1998	Kenny Brack	2002	Sam Hornish Jr.	2006	Sam Hornish Jr.	2010	Dario Franchitti		

Champ Car World Series Winners, 1959-2007

U.S. Auto Club champions, 1959-78; Championship Auto Racing Teams (CART) champions, 1979-2003; Champ Car World Series champions, 2004-07. The Vanderbilt Cup became the series championship trophy in 2000. Merged with Indy Racing League, 2008.

Year	Driver	Year	Driver	Year	Driver	Year	Driver	Year	Driver
1959	Rodger Ward	1969	Mario Andretti	1979	Rick Mears	1989	Emerson Fittipaldi	1999	Juan Montoya
1960	A. J. Foyt	1970	Al Unser	1980	Johnny Rutherford	1990	Al Unser Jr.	2000	Gil de Ferran
1961	A. J. Foyt	1971	Joe Leonard	1981	Rick Mears	1991	Michael Andretti	2001	Gil de Ferran
1962	Rodger Ward	1972	Joe Leonard	1982	Rick Mears	1992	Bobby Rahal	2002	Cristiano da Matta
1963	A. J. Foyt	1973	Roger McCluskey	1983	Al Unser	1993	Nigel Mansell	2003	Paul Tracy
1964	A. J. Foyt	1974	Bobby Unser	1984	Mario Andretti	1994	Al Unser Jr.	2004	Sébastien Bourdais
1965	Mario Andretti	1975	A. J. Foyt	1985	Al Unser	1995	Jacques Villeneuve	2005	Sébastien Bourdais
1966	Mario Andretti	1976	Gordon Johncock	1986	Bobby Rahal	1996	Jimmy Vasser	2006	Sébastien Bourdais
1967	A. J. Foyt	1977	Tom Sneva	1987	Bobby Rahal	1997	Alex Zanardi	2007	Sébastien Bourdais
1968	Bobby Unser	1978	Tom Sneva	1988	Danny Sullivan	1998	Alex Zanardi		

NASCAR Sprint Cup Champions, 1949-2012

Known as Strictly Stock, 1949; Grand National, 1950-70; Winston Cup, 1971-2003; and Sprint Cup, 2004-present.

Year	Driver	Year	Driver	Year	Driver	Year	Driver	Year	Driver
1949	Red Byron	1962	Joe Weatherly	1975	Richard Petty	1988	Bill Elliott	2001	Jeff Gordon
1950	Bill Rexford	1963	Joe Weatherly	1976	Cale Yarborough	1989	Rusty Wallace	2002	Tony Stewart
1951	Herb Thomas	1964	Richard Petty	1977	Cale Yarborough	1990	Dale Earnhardt	2003	Matt Kenseth
1952	Tim Flock	1965	Ned Jarrett	1978	Cale Yarborough	1991	Dale Earnhardt	2004	Kurt Busch
1953	Herb Thomas	1966	David Pearson	1979	Richard Petty	1992	Alan Kulwicki	2005	Tony Stewart
1954	Lee Petty	1967	Richard Petty	1980	Dale Earnhardt	1993	Dale Earnhardt	2006	Jimmie Johnson
1955	Tim Flock	1968	David Pearson	1981	Darrell Waltrip	1994	Dale Earnhardt	2007	Jimmie Johnson
1956	Buck Baker	1969	David Pearson	1982	Darrell Waltrip	1995	Jeff Gordon	2008	Jimmie Johnson
1957	Buck Baker	1970	Bobby Isaac	1983	Bobby Allison	1996	Terry Labonte	2009	Jimmie Johnson
1958	Lee Petty	1971	Richard Petty	1984	Terry Labonte	1997	Jeff Gordon	2010	Jimmie Johnson
1959	Lee Petty	1972	Richard Petty	1985	Darrell Waltrip	1998	Jeff Gordon	2011	Tony Stewart
1960	Rex White	1973	Benny Parsons	1986	Dale Earnhardt	1999	Dale Jarrett	2012	Brad Keselowski
1961	Ned Jarrett	1974	Richard Petty	1987	Dale Earnhardt	2000	Bobby Labonte		

NASCAR Sprint Cup Rookie of the Year, 1958-2012

Year	Driver	Year	Driver	Year	Driver	Year	Driver	Year	Driver
1958	Shorty Rollins	1969	Dick Brooks	1980	Jody Riley	1991	Bobby Hamilton	2002	Ryan Newman
1959	Richard Petty	1970	Bill Dennis	1981	Ron Bouchard	1992	Jimmy Hensley	2003	Jamie McMurray
1960	David Pearson	1971	Walter Ballard	1982	Geoff Bodine	1993	Jeff Gordon	2004	Kasey Kahne
1961	Woodie Wilson	1972	Larry Smith	1983	Sterling Marlin	1994	Jeff Burton	2005	Kyle Busch
1962	Tom Cox	1973	Lennie Pond	1984	Rusty Wallace	1995	Ricky Craven	2006	Denny Hamlin
1963	Billy Wade	1974	Earl Ross	1985	Ken Schrader	1996	Johnny Benson	2007	Juan Montoya
1964	Doug Cooper	1975	Bruce Hill	1986	Alan Kulwicki	1997	Mike Skinner	2008	Regan Smith
1965	Sam McQuagg	1976	Skip Manning	1987	Davey Allison	1998	Kenny Irwin	2009	Joey Logano
1966	James Hylton	1977	Ricky Rudd	1988	Ken Bouchard	1999	Tony Stewart	2010	Kevin Conway
1967	Donnie Allison	1978	Ronnie Thomas	1989	Dick Trickle	2000	Matt Kenseth	2011	Andy Lally
1968	Pete Hamilton	1979	Dale Earnhardt	1990	Rob Moroso	2001	Kevin Harvick	2012	Stephen Leicht

Daytona 500 Winners, 1959-2013

At Daytona International Speedway in Daytona Beach, FL.

Year	Driver, car	Avg. mph	Year	Driver, car	Avg. mph	Year	Driver, car	Avg. mph
1959	Lee Petty, Oldsmobile	135.521	1978	Bobby Allison, Ford	159.730	1997	Jeff Gordon, Chevrolet	148.295
1960	Junior Johnson, Chevrolet	124.740	1979	Richard Petty, Oldsmobile	143.977	1998	Dale Earnhardt, Chevrolet	172.712
1961	Marvin Panch, Pontiac	149.601	1980	Buddy Baker, Oldsmobile	177.602	1999	Jeff Gordon, Chevrolet	161.551
1962	Fireball Roberts, Pontiac	152.529	1981	Richard Petty, Buick	169.651	2000	Dale Jarrett, Ford	155.669
1963	Tiny Lund, Ford	151.566	1982	Bobby Allison, Buick	153.991	2001	Michael Waltrip, Chevrolet	161.783
1964	Richard Petty, Plymouth	154.334	1983	Cale Yarborough, Pontiac	155.979	2002	Ward Burton, Dodge	142.971
1965	Fred Lorenzen, Ford	141.539	1984	Cale Yarborough,		2003	Michael Waltrip, Chevrolet	133.870
1966	Richard Petty, Plymouth	160.627		Chevrolet	150.994	2004	Dale Earnhardt Jr.,	
1967	Mario Andretti, Ford	146.926	1985	Bill Elliott, Ford	172.265		Chevrolet	156.345
1968	Cale Yarborough, Mercury	143.251	1986	Geoff Bodine, Chevrolet	148.124	2005	Jeff Gordon, Chevrolet	135.173
1969	LeeRoy Yarbrough, Ford	157.950	1987	Bill Elliott, Ford	176.263	2006	Jimmie Johnson, Chevrolet	142.667
1970	Pete Hamilton, Plymouth	149.601	1988	Bobby Allison, Buick	137.531	2007	Kevin Harvick, Chevrolet	149.335
1971	Richard Petty, Plymouth	144.456	1989	Darrell Waltrip, Chevrolet	148.466	2008	Ryan Newman, Dodge	152.672
1972	A. J. Foyt, Mercury	161.550	1990	Derrike Cope, Chevrolet	165.761	2009	Matt Kenseth, Ford	132.816
1973	Richard Petty, Dodge	157.205	1991	Ernie Irvan, Chevrolet	148.148	2010	Jamie McMurray,	
1974	Richard Petty, Dodge	140.894	1992	Davey Allison, Ford	160.256		Chevrolet	137.284
1975	Benny Parsons, Chevrolet	153.649	1993	Dale Jarrett, Chevrolet	154.972	2011	Trevor Bayne, Ford	130.326
1976	David Pearson, Mercury	152.181	1994	Sterling Marlin, Chevrolet	156.931	2012	Matt Kenseth, Ford	140.256
1977	Cale Yarborough,		1995	Sterling Marlin, Chevrolet	141.710	2013	Jimmie Johnson,	
	Chevrolet	153.218	1996	Dale Jarrett, Ford	154.308		Chevrolet	159.250

Note: The race was less than 500 mi in the following years: 1965 (322.5 mi), 1966 (495 mi), 1974 (450 mi), and 2003 (272.5 mi).

Coca-Cola 600 Winners, 1960-2013

At Charlotte Motor Speedway in Concord, NC. Known as the World 600, 1960-85. * = Rain-shortened.

Year	Driver, car	Avg. mph	Year	Driver, car	Avg. mph	Year	Driver, car	Avg. mph
1960	Joe Lee Johnson,		1978	Darrell Waltrip, Chevrolet	138.355	1997	Jeff Gordon, Chevrolet	136.745*
	Chevrolet	107.735	1979	Darrell Waltrip, Chevrolet	136.674	1998	Jeff Gordon, Chevrolet	136.424
1961	David Pearson, Pontiac	111.633	1980	Benny Parsons,		1999	Jeff Burton, Ford	151.367
1962	Nelson Stacy, Ford	125.552		Chevrolet	119.265	2000	Matt Kenseth, Ford	142.640
1963	Fred Lorenzen, Ford	132.418	1981	Bobby Allison, Buick	129.326	2001	Jeff Burton, Ford	138.107
1964	Jim Paschal, Plymouth	125.772	1982	Neil Bonnett, Ford	130.058	2002	Mark Martin, Ford	137.729
1965	Fred Lorenzen, Ford	121.772	1983	Neil Bonnett, Chevrolet	140.707	2003	Jimmie Johnson,	
1966	Marvin Panch, Plymouth	135.042	1984	Bobby Allison, Buick	129.233		Chevrolet	126.198*
1967	Jim Paschal, Plymouth	135.832	1985	Darrell Waltrip, Chevrolet	141.807	2004	Jimmie Johnson,	
1968	Buddy Baker, Dodge	104.207*	1986	Dale Earnhardt, Chevrolet	140.406		Chevrolet	142.763
1969	LeeRoy Yarbrough,		1987	Kyle Petty, Ford	131.483	2005	Jimmie Johnson,	
	Mercury	134.361	1988	Darrell Waltrip, Chevrolet	124.460		Chevrolet	114.698
1970	Donnie Allison, Ford	129.680	1989	Darrell Waltrip, Chevrolet	144.077	2006	Kasey Kahne, Dodge	128.840
1971	Bobby Allison, Mercury	140.422	1990	Rusty Wallace, Pontiac	137.650	2007	Casey Mears, Chevrolet	130.222
1972	Buddy Baker, Dodge	142.255	1991	Davey Allison, Ford	138.951	2008	Kasey Kahne, Dodge	135.722
1973	Buddy Baker, Dodge	134.890	1992	Dale Earnhardt, Chevrolet	132.980	2009	David Reutimann, Toyota	120.899*
1974	David Pearson, Mercury	135.720	1993	Dale Earnhardt, Chevrolet	145.504	2010	Kurt Busch, Dodge	144.966
1975	Richard Petty, Dodge	145.327	1994	Jeff Gordon, Chevrolet	139.445	2011	Kevin Harvick, Chevrolet	132.414
1976	David Pearson, Mercury	137.352	1995	Bobby Labonte, Chevrolet	151.952	2012	Kasey Kahne, Chevrolet	155.687
1977	Richard Petty, Dodge	137.676	1996	Dale Jarrett, Ford	147.581	2013	Kevin Harvick, Chevrolet	130.521

Brickyard 400 Winners, 1994-2013

At Indianapolis Motor Speedway in Indianapolis, IN.

Year	Driver, car	Avg. mph	Year	Driver, car	Avg. mph	Year	Driver, car	Avg. mph
1994	Jeff Gordon, Chevrolet	131.977	2001	Jeff Gordon, Chevrolet	130.790	2008	Jimmie Johnson, Chevrolet	115.117
1995	Dale Earnhardt, Chevrolet	155.206	2002	Bill Elliott, Dodge	125.033	2009	Jimmie Johnson, Chevrolet	145.882
1996	Dale Jarrett, Ford	139.508	2003	Kevin Harvick, Chevrolet	134.554	2010	Jamie McMurray, Chevrolet	136.054
1997	Ricky Rudd, Ford	130.814	2004	Jeff Gordon, Chevrolet	115.037	2011	Paul Menard, Chevrolet	140.762
1998	Jeff Gordon, Chevrolet	126.772	2005	Tony Stewart, Chevrolet	118.782	2012	Jimmie Johnson, Chevrolet	137.680
1999	Dale Jarrett, Ford	148.194	2006	Jimmie Johnson, Chevrolet	137.182	2013	Ryan Newman, Chevrolet	153.485
2000	Bobby Labonte, Pontiac	155.912	2007	Tony Stewart, Chevrolet	117.379			

Irwin Tools Night Race Winners, 1961-2013

At Bristol Motor Speedway in Bristol, TN. Known as the Volunteer 500, 1961-75, '78-'79; Volunteer 400, 1976-77; Busch 500, 1980-90; Bud 500, 1991-93; Goody's 500, 1994-99; goracing.com 500, 2000; and Sharpie 500, 2001-09. * = Rain-shortened.

Year	Driver, car	Avg. mph	Year	Driver, car	Avg. mph	Year	Driver, car	Avg. mph
1961	Jack Smith, Pontiac	68.373	1979	Darrell Waltrip, Chevrolet	91.493	1997	Dale Jarrett, Ford	80.013
1962	Bobby Johns, Pontiac	73.397	1980	Cale Yarborough, Chevrolet	86.973	1998	Mark Martin, Ford	86.949
1963	Fred Lorenzen, Ford	74.844	1981	Darrell Waltrip, Buick	84.723	1999	Dale Earnhardt, Chevrolet	91.276
1964	Fred Lorenzen, Ford	78.044	1982	Darrell Waltrip, Buick	94.318	2000	Rusty Wallace, Ford	85.394
1965	Ned Jarrett, Ford	61.826	1983	Darrell Waltrip, Chevrolet	89.430*	2001	Tony Stewart, Pontiac	85.106
1966	Paul Goldsmith, Plymouth	77.963	1984	Terry Labonte, Chevrolet	85.365	2002	Jeff Gordon, Chevrolet	77.097
1967	Richard Petty, Plymouth	78.705	1985	Dale Earnhardt, Chevrolet	81.388	2003	Kurt Busch, Ford	77.421
1968	David Pearson, Ford	76.310	1986	Darrell Waltrip, Chevrolet	86.934	2004	Dale Earnhardt Jr., Chevrolet	88.538
1969	David Pearson, Ford	79.737	1987	Dale Earnhardt, Chevrolet	90.373		
1970	Bobby Allison, Dodge	84.880	1988	Dale Earnhardt, Chevrolet	78.775	2005	Matt Kenseth, Ford	84.678
1971	Charlie Glotzbach, Chevrolet	101.074	1989	Darrell Waltrip, Chevrolet	85.554	2006	Matt Kenseth, Ford	90.025
			1990	Ernie Irvan, Chevrolet	91.782	2007	Carl Edwards, Ford	89.006
1972	Bobby Allison, Chevrolet	92.735	1991	Alan Kulwicki, Ford	82.028	2008	Carl Edwards, Ford	91.581
1973	Benny Parsons, Chevrolet	91.342	1992	Darrell Waltrip, Chevrolet	91.198	2009	Kyle Busch, Toyota	84.820
1974	Cale Yarborough, Chevrolet	75.430	1993	Mark Martin, Ford	88.172	2010	Kyle Busch, Toyota	99.071
1975	Richard Petty, Dodge	97.016	1994	Rusty Wallace, Ford	91.363	2011	Brad Keselowski, Dodge	96.753
1976	Cale Yarborough, Chevrolet	99.175	1995	Terry Labonte, Chevrolet	81.979	2012	Denny Hamlin, Toyota	84.402
1977	Cale Yarborough, Chevrolet	79.726	1996	Rusty Wallace, Ford	91.267	2013	Matt Kenseth, Toyota	90.279
1978	Cale Yarborough, Olds.	88.628						

NASCAR Sprint All-Star Race Winners, 1985-2013

At Charlotte Motor Speedway in Concord, NC. Known as The Winston, 1985-93, 1997-2003; The Winston Select, 1994-96; and Nextel All-Star Challenge, 2004-07.

Year	Driver, car	Year	Driver, car	Year	Driver, car
1985	Darrell Waltrip, Chevrolet	1995	Jeff Gordon, Chevrolet	2005	Mark Martin, Ford
1986	Bill Elliott, Ford	1996	Michael Waltrip, Ford	2006	Jimmie Johnson, Chevrolet
1987	Dale Earnhardt, Chevrolet	1997	Jeff Gordon, Chevrolet	2007	Kevin Harvick, Chevrolet
1988	Terry Labonte, Chevrolet	1998	Mark Martin, Ford	2008	Kasey Kahne, Dodge
1989	Rusty Wallace, Pontiac	1999	Terry Labonte, Chevrolet	2009	Tony Stewart, Chevrolet
1990	Dale Earnhardt, Chevrolet	2000	Dale Earnhardt Jr., Chevrolet	2010	Kurt Busch, Dodge
1991	Davey Allison, Ford	2001	Jeff Gordon, Chevrolet	2011	Carl Edwards, Ford
1992	Davey Allison, Ford	2002	Ryan Newman, Ford	2012	Jimmie Johnson, Chevrolet
1993	Dale Earnhardt, Chevrolet	2003	Jimmie Johnson, Chevrolet	2013	Jimmie Johnson, Chevrolet
1994	Geoffrey Bodine, Ford	2004	Matt Kenseth, Ford		

Formula One World Drivers' Champions, 1950-2013

Year	Driver, country	Year	Driver, country	Year	Driver, country
1950	Giuseppe "Nino" Farina, Italy	1972	Emerson Fittipaldi, Brazil	1993	Alain Prost, France
1951	Juan Manuel Fangio, Argentina	1073	Jackie Stewart, Scotland, UK	1994	Michael Schumacher, Germany
1952	Alberto Ascari, Italy	1974	Emerson Fittipaldi, Brazil	1995	Michael Schumacher, Germany
1953	Alberto Ascari, Italy	1975	Niki Lauda, Austria	1996	Damon Hill, England, UK
1954	Juan Manuel Fangio, Argentina	1976	James Hunt, England, UK	1997	Jacques Villeneuve, Canada
1955	Juan Manuel Fangio, Argentina	1977	Niki Lauda, Austria	1998	Mika Hakkinen, Finland
1956	Juan Manuel Fangio, Argentina	1978	Mario Andretti, United States	1999	Mika Hakkinen, Finland
1957	Juan Manuel Fangio, Argentina	1979	Jody Scheckter, South Africa	2000	Michael Schumacher, Germany
1958	Mike Hawthorn, England, UK	1980	Alan Jones, Australia	2001	Michael Schumacher, Germany
1959	Jack Brabham, Australia	1981	Nelson Piquet, Brazil	2002	Michael Schumacher, Germany
1960	Jack Brabham, Australia	1982	Keke Rosberg, Finland	2003	Michael Schumacher, Germany
1961	Phil Hill, United States	1983	Nelson Piquet, Brazil	2004	Michael Schumacher, Germany
1962	Graham Hill, England, UK	1984	Niki Lauda, Austria	2005	Fernando Alonso, Spain
1963	Jim Clark, Scotland, UK	1985	Alain Prost, France	2006	Fernando Alonso, Spain
1964	John Surtees, England, UK	1986	Alain Prost, France	2007	Kimi Raikkonen, Finland
1965	Jim Clark, Scotland, UK	1987	Nelson Piquet, Brazil	2008	Lewis Hamilton, England, UK
1966	Jack Brabham, Australia	1988	Ayrton Senna, Brazil	2009	Jenson Button, England, UK
1967	Denis Hulme, New Zealand	1989	Alain Prost, France	2010	Sebastian Vettel, Germany
1968	Graham Hill, England, UK	1990	Ayrton Senna, Brazil	2011	Sebastian Vettel, Germany
1969	Jackie Stewart, Scotland, UK	1991	Ayrton Senna, Brazil	2012	Sebastian Vettel, Germany
1970	Jochen Rindt, Austria	1992	Nigel Mansell, England, UK	2013	Sebastian Vettel, Germany
1971	Jackie Stewart, Scotland, UK				

24 Hours of Le Mans Race, 2013

Audi won its fourth consecutive 24 Hours of Le Mans on a rain-soaked track in France June 23, 2013, but the race was marred by its first fatality in more than two decades. The No. 2 Audi completed 348 laps at Circuit de la Sarthe in Le Mans, France, one lap ahead of the Toyota No. 8 team. Denmark's Tom Kristensen led the team that drove the No. 2 Audi Sport R18 e-tron quattro hybrid to victory in the 81st running of the race for his record 9th Le Mans win; his team members were Great Britain's Allan McNish and France's Loic Duval. Allan Simonsen, a 34-year-old driver from Denmark, crashed into the barriers just minutes into the race and later died from his injuries.

BOXING

There are many boxing governing bodies, including the World Boxing Assn. (WBA; known as the National Boxing Assn. [NBA] until 1962), World Boxing Council (WBC), International Boxing Fed. (IBF), World Boxing Org., U.S. Boxing Assn., N. American Boxing Fed., and European Boxing Union. All have their own champions and divisions.

Boxing Champions by Class

Class (weight limit)	WBA Champion	WBC Champion	IBF Champion
Heavyweight (none)	Wladimir Klitschko, Ukraine[1] Alexander Povetkin, Russia[2]	Vitali Klitschko, Ukraine	Wladimir Klitschko, Ukraine
Cruiserweight (200 lbs)	Guillermo Jones, Panama	Krzysztof Wlodarczyk, Poland	Yoan Pablo Hernandez, Germany
Light Heavyweight (175 lbs)	Beibut Shumenov, Kazakhstan	Adonis Stevenson, Canada	Bernard Hopkins, U.S.
Super Middleweight (168 lbs)	Andre Ward, U.S.[1] Carl Froch, UK[2] Stanyslav Kashtanov, Ukraine[3]	Sakio Bika, Australia	Carl Froch, UK
Middleweight (160 lbs)	Gennady Golovkin, Kazakhstan[2] Martin Murray, UK[3]	Sergio Martinez, Argentina	Darren Barker, UK
Super Welterweight/ Jr. Middleweight (154 lbs)	Floyd Mayweather Jr., U.S.[1] Ersilandy Lara, Cuba[3]	Floyd Mayweather Jr., U.S.	Carlos Molina, U.S.
Welterweight (147 lbs)	Adrien Broner, U.S.[2] Keith Thurman, U.S.[3]	Floyd Mayweather Jr., U.S.	Devon Alexander, U.S.
Super Lightweight/ Jr. Welterweight (140 lbs)	Danny Garcia, U.S.[1] Khabib Allakhverdiev, Russia[2]	Danny Garcia, U.S.	Lamont Peterson, U.S.
Lightweight (135 lbs)	Richard Abril, Cuba[2] Yuriorkis Gamboa, Cuba[3]	Adrien Broner, U.S.[2] Omar Figueroa, U.S.[3]	Miguel Vazquez, Mexico
Super Featherweight/ Jr. Lightweight (130 lbs)	Takashi Uchiyama, Japan	Takashi Miura, Japan	Argenis Mendez, Dominican Republic
Featherweight (126 lbs)	Chris John, Indonesia[1] Nicholas Walters, Jamaica[2] Jesus Andres Cuellar, Argentina[3]	Jhonny Gonzalez, Mexico	Evgeny Gradovich, Russia
Super Bantamweight/ Jr. Featherweight (122 lbs)	Guillermo Rigondeaux, Cuba[2] Nehomar Cermeño, Venezuela[3]	Leo Santa Cruz, Mexico	Kiko Martinez, Spain
Bantamweight (118 lbs)	Anselmo Moreno, Panama[1] Koki Kameda, Japan[2]	Shinsuke Yamanaka, Japan	Jamie McDonnell, UK
Super Flyweight/ Jr. Bantamweight (115 lbs)	Liborio Solis, Venezuela[2] Denkaosan Kaovichit, Thailand[3]	Srisaket Sor Rungvisai, Thailand	Daiki Kameda, Japan
Flyweight (112 lbs)	Juan Estrada, Mexico[1] Juan Carlos Reveco, Argentina[2] Koki Eto, Japan[3]	Akira Yaegashi, Japan	Moruti Mthalane, South Africa
Jr. Flyweight (108 lbs)	Roman Gonzalez, Nicaragua[1] Kazuto Ioka, Japan[2] Alberto Rossell, Peru[3]	Adrian Hernandez, Mexico	Johnriel Casimero, Philippines
Strawweight/ Mini Flyweight (105 lbs)	Ryo Miyazaki, Japan	Xiong Zhao Zhong, China	Katsunari Takayama, Japan

Note: As of Sept. 24, 2013. (1) Super champion. (2) Regular champion. (3) Interim champion.

Ring Champions by Years

* = Abandoned/relinquished the title or was stripped of it. IBF champions listed only for heavyweight division. International Boxing Hall of Fame inductees in *italics*.

Heavyweights

1882-92	*John L. Sullivan*[1]	1978	Leon Spinks (WBA/WBC*)[5];	1994-95	Oliver McCall (WBC);
1892-97	*James J. Corbett*[2]		Ken Norton (WBC)		*George Foreman* (WBA*/IBF*)
1897-99	*Bob Fitzsimmons*	1978-79	*Muhammad Ali* (WBA*)[5]	1995	Frans Botha (IBF*)
1899-1905	*James J. Jeffries**[3]	1978-83	*Larry Holmes* (WBC*)[6]	1995-96	Bruce Seldon (WBA);
1905-06	Marvin Hart	1979-80	John Tate (WBA)		Frank Bruno (WBC)
1906-08	*Tommy Burns*	1980-82	Mike Weaver (WBA)	1996	*Mike Tyson* (WBA/WBC*)
1908-15	*Jack Johnson*	1982-83	Michael Dokes (WBA)	1996-97	Michael Moorer (IBF)
1915-19	*Jess Willard*	1983-84	Gerrie Coetzee (WBA)	1996-99	Evander Holyfield (WBA/IBF)
1919-26	*Jack Dempsey*	1983-85	*Larry Holmes* (IBF)[6]	1997-2001	*Lennox Lewis* (WBC)
1926-28	*Gene Tunney**	1984	Tim Witherspoon (WBC)	1999-2001	*Lennox Lewis* (WBA*/WBC/IBF)
1928-30	Vacant	1984-85	Greg Page (WBA)	2000-01	Evander Holyfield (WBA)
1930-32	*Max Schmeling*	1984-86	Pinklon Thomas (WBC)	2001	Hasim Rahman (WBC/IBF)
1932-33	*Jack Sharkey*	1985-86	Tony Tubbs (WBA)	2001-02	*Lennox Lewis* (IBF*)
1933-34	Primo Carnera	1985-87	*Michael Spinks* (IBF*)	2001-03	John Ruiz (WBA)
1934-35	*Max Baer*	1986	Tim Witherspoon (WBA);	2001-04	*Lennox Lewis* (WBC)
1935-37	*James J. Braddock*		Trevor Berbick (WBC)	2002-06	Chris Byrd (IBF)
1937-49	*Joe Louis**	1986-87	*Mike Tyson* (WBC); James	2003	Roy Jones Jr. (WBA*)
1949-51	*Ezzard Charles*		"Bonecrusher" Smith (WBA)	2004-05	John Ruiz (WBA)[7];
1951-52	*Joe Walcott*	1987	Tony Tucker (IBF)		Vitali Klitschko (WBC*)
1952-56	*Rocky Marciano**	1987-90	*Mike Tyson* (WBA/WBC/IBF)	2005-06	Hasim Rahman (WBC)
1956-59	*Floyd Patterson*	1990	James "Buster" Douglas	2005-07	Nicolay Valuev (WBA)
1959-60	*Ingemar Johansson*		(WBA/WBC/IBF)	2006-08	Oleg Maskaev (WBC)
1960-62	*Floyd Patterson*	1990-92	Evander Holyfield	2006-	Wladimir Klitschko (IBF)
1962-64	*Sonny Liston*		(WBA/WBC/IBF)	2007-08	Ruslan Chagaev (WBA)
1964-67	*Cassius Clay*	1992-93	Riddick Bowe (WBA/WBC*/IBF)	2008	Samuel Peter (WBC)
	(Muhammad Ali)[4]	1992-94	*Lennox Lewis* (WBC)	2008-09	Nikolai Valuev (WBA)
1970-73	*Joe Frazier*	1993-94	Evander Holyfield (WBA/IBF)	2008-	Vitali Klitschko (WBC)
1973-74	*George Foreman*	1994	Michael Moorer (WBA/IBF)	2009-11	David Haye (WBA)
1974-78	*Muhammad Ali*			2011-	Wladimir Klitschko (WBA)

(1) London Prize Ring (bare-knuckle champion). (2) First Marquis of Queensberry champion. (3) Jeffries vacated title (1905) and designated Marvin Hart and Jack Root as logical contenders. Hart def. Root in 12 rounds (1905); in turn was def. by Tommy Burns (1906), who claimed the title. Jack Johnson def. Burns (1908) and was recognized as champ. Johnson won the title by defeating Jeffries in the latter's attempted comeback (1910). (4) Title declared vacant by the WBA and others in 1967 after Ali refused military induction for religious reasons during the Vietnam War. Joe Frazier recognized as champ by six states, Mexico, and S. America. Jimmy Ellis declared champ by the WBA. Frazier KOd Ellis, Feb. 16, 1970. (5) After Spinks def. Ali, the WBC recognized Ken Norton as champ. Ali def. Spinks in 1978 rematch for WBA title and retired in 1979. (6) Relinquished the WBC title in Dec. 1983 to fight as champ of the new IBF. (7) James Toney def. Ruiz Apr. 30, 2005, to claim the title, but it was rescinded when Toney tested positive for steroids.

Light Heavyweights

Year	Champion	Year	Champion	Year	Champion
1903	Jack Root; George Gardner	1974-78	Victor Galindez (WBA)	1992-97	Virgil Hill (WBA)
1903-05	Bob Fitzsimmons	1977-78	Miguel Cuello (WBC)	1994-95	Mike McCallum (WBC)
1905-12	Philadelphia Jack O'Brien*	1978	Mate Parlov (WBC)	1995-96	Fabrice Tiozzo (WBC*)
1912-16	Jack Dillon	1978-79	Mike Rossman (WBA);	1996-97	Roy Jones Jr. (WBC)
1916-20	Battling Levinsky		Marvin Johnson (WBC)	1997	Montell Griffin (WBC);
1920-22	Georges Carpentier	1979-81	Matthew Saad Muhammad		Roy Jones Jr. (WBC);
1922-23	Battling Siki		(WBC)		Darius Michalczewski (WBA*)
1923-25	Mike McTigue	1979-80	Marvin Johnson (WBA)	1997-98	Lou Del Valle (WBA)
1925-26	Paul Berlenbach	1980-81	Eddie Mustafa Muhammad	1998-2003	Roy Jones Jr. (WBA*/WBC*)
1926-27	Jack Delaney*		(WBA)	2003	Mehdi Sahnoune (WBA);
1927-29	Tommy Loughran*	1981-85	Michael Spinks (WBA)		Antonio Tarver (WBC)
1930-34	Maxie Rosenbloom	1981-83	Dwight Muhammed-Qawi	2003-04	Roy Jones Jr. (WBA/WBC*)
1934-35	Bob Olin		Braxton (WBC)	2004	Antonio Tarver (WBA/WBC*)
1935-39	John Henry Lewis*	1983-85	Michael Spinks (WBC*)	2004-06	Fabrice Tiozzo (WBA)
1939	Melio Bettina	1985-86	J. B. Williamson (WBC)	2005-07	Tomasz Adamek (WBC)
1939-41	Billy Conn*	1986-87	Marvin Johnson (WBA);	2006-07	Silvio Branco (WBA)
1941	Anton Christoforidis		Dennis Andries (WBC)	2007-08	Chad Dawson (WBC)
	(won NBA title)	1987	Leslie Stewart (WBA)	2007	Stipe Drews (WBA);
1941-48	Gus Lesnevich; Freddie Mills	1987-91	Virgil Hill (WBA)		Danny Green (WBA)
1948-50	Freddie Mills	1987	Thomas Hearns (WBC*)	2008	Hugo Hernan Garay (WBA);
1950-52	Joey Maxim	1987-88	Don Lalonde (WBC)		Adrian Diaconu (WBC)
1952-62	Archie Moore	1988	Sugar Ray Leonard (WBC*)	2009-10	Gabriel Campillo (WBA)
1962-63	Harold Johnson	1989	Dennis Andries (WBC)	2009-11	Jean Pascal (WBC)
1963-65	Willie Pastrano	1989-90	Jeff Harding (WBC)	2010-	Beibut Shumenov (WBA)
1965-66	Jose Torres	1990-91	Dennis Andries (WBC)	2011-12	Bernard Hopkins (WBC)
1966-68	Dick Tiger	1991-94	Jeff Harding (WBC)	2012-13	Chad Dawson (WBC)
1968-74	Bob Foster*	1991-92	Thomas Hearns (WBA)	2013-	Adonis Stevenson (WBC)
1974-77	John Conteh (WBC)	1992	Iran Barkley (WBA*)		

Middleweights

Year	Champion	Year	Champion	Year	Champion
1884-91	Jack "Nonpareil" Dempsey	1958	"Sugar" Ray Robinson	1990-93	Julian Jackson (WBC)
1891-97	Bob Fitzsimmons*	1959	Gene Fullmer (NBA);	1992-93	Reggie Johnson (WBA)
1897-1907	Tommy Ryan*		"Sugar" Ray Robinson (NY)	1993-95	Gerald McClellan (WBC*)
1907-08	Stanley Ketchel; Billy Papke	1960	Gene Fullmer (NBA);	1993-94	John David Jackson (WBA)
1908-10	Stanley Ketchel		Paul Pender (NY/MA)	1994-97	Jorge Castro (WBA)
1911-13	Vacant	1961	Gene Fullmer (NBA);	1995	Julian Jackson (WBC)
1913	Frank Klaus; George Chip		Terry Downes (NY/MA/Europe)	1995-96	Quincy Taylor (WBC);
1914-17	Al McCoy	1962	Gene Fullmer;		Shinji Takehara (WBA)
1917-20	Mike O'Dowd		Dick Tiger (NBA);	1996-98	Keith Holmes (WBC)
1920-23	Johnny Wilson		Paul Pender (NY/MA*)	1996-97	William Joppy (WBA)
1923-26	Harry Greb	1963	Dick Tiger (universal)	1997	Julio Cesar Green (WBA)
1926-31	Theodore "Tiger" Flowers;	1963-65	Joey Giardello	1998-2001	William Joppy (WBA)
	Mickey Walker	1965-66	Dick Tiger	1998-99	Hassine Cherifi (WBC)
1931-32	William "Gorilla" Jones (NBA)	1966-67	Emile Griffith	1999-2001	Keith Holmes (WBC)
1932-37	Marcel Thil	1967	Nino Benvenuti	2001	Felix Trinidad (WBA)
1938	Al Hostak (NBA);	1967-68	Emile Griffith	2001-05	Bernard Hopkins (WBC/WBA)
	Solly Krieger (NBA)	1968-70	Nino Benvenuti	2005-06	Jermain Taylor (WBA)
1939-40	Al Hostak (NBA)	1970-77	Carlos Monzon*	2005-07	Jermain Taylor (WBC)
1941-47	Tony Zale	1977-78	Rodrigo Valdez	2006-07	Javier Castillejo (WBA)[1]
1947-48	Rocky Graziano	1978-79	Hugo Corro	2007-09	Felix Sturm (WBA)
1948	Tony Zale; Marcel Cerdan	1979-80	Vito Antuofermo	2007-10	Kelly Pavlik (WBC)
1949-51	Jake LaMotta	1980	Alan Minter	2009-11	Sebastian Zbik (WBC)
1951	"Sugar" Ray Robinson;	1980-87	"Marvelous" Marvin Hagler	2010	Sergio Martinez (WBC)
	Randy Turpin;	1987	Sugar Ray Leonard (WBC*)	2011-12	Julio Cesar Chavez Jr. (WBC)
	"Sugar" Ray Robinson*	1987-89	Sumbu Kalambay (WBA)	2012	Daniel Geale (WBA*)
1953-55	Carl "Bobo" Olson	1987-88	Thomas Hearns (WBC)	2012-	Sergio Martinez (WBC)
1955-57	"Sugar" Ray Robinson	1988-89	Iran Barkley (WBC)	2012-	Gennady Golovkin (WBA)
1957	Gene Fullmer;	1989-90	Roberto Duran (WBC*)	2013	Darren Barker (IBF)
	"Sugar" Ray Robinson	1989-91	Mike McCallum (WBA)		
1957-58	Carmen Basilio				

(1) Castillejo lost title to Mariano Carrera Dec. 2, 2006, but regained it Feb. 23, 2007, after Carrera tested positive for steroids.

Welterweights

Year	Champion	Year	Champion	Year	Champion
1892-94	"Mysterious" Billy Smith	1935-38	Barney Ross	1975-76	John Stracey (WBC);
1894-96	Tommy Ryan	1938-40	Henry Armstrong		Angel Espada (WBA)
1896	Kid McCoy*	1940-41	Fritzie Zivic	1976-79	Carlos Palomino (WBC)
1900	Rube Ferns; Matty Matthews	1941-46	Fred Cochrane	1976-80	Jose "Pipino" Cuevas (WBA)
1901	Rube Ferns	1946	Marty Servo*	1979	Wilfred Benitez (WBC)
1901-04	Joe Walcott	1946-51	Ray Robinson*[1]	1979-80	Sugar Ray Leonard (WBC)
1904-06	Dixie Kid; Joe Walcott;	1951	Johnny Bratton (NBA)	1980	Roberto Duran (WBC)
	William "Honey" Mellody	1951-54	Kid Gavilan	1980-81	Thomas Hearns (WBA)
1907-11	Mike Sullivan	1954-55	Johnny Saxton	1980-82	Sugar Ray Leonard*
1911-15	Vacant	1955	Tony De Marco	1983-85	Donald Curry (WBA);
1915-19	Ted Lewis	1955-56	Carmen Basilio		Milton McCrory (WBC)
1919-22	Jack Britton	1956	Johnny Saxton	1985-86	Donald Curry (WBC)
1922-26	Mickey Walker	1956-57	Carmen Basilio*	1986-87	Lloyd Honeyghan (WBC)
1926	Pete Latzo	1958	Virgil Akins	1987	Mark Breland (WBA)
1927-29	Joe Dundee	1958-60	Don Jordan	1987-88	Marlon Starling (WBA);
1929	Jackie Fields	1960-61	Benny Paret		Jorge Vaca (WBC)
1930	Jack Thompson;	1961	Emile Griffith	1988-89	Thomas Hearns (WBA);
	Tommy Freeman	1961-62	Benny Paret		Lloyd Honeyghan (WBC)
1931	Tommy Freeman;	1962-63	Emile Griffith	1989-90	Marlon Starling (WBC);
	Jack Thompson;	1963	Luis Rodriguez		Mark Breland (WBA)
	Lou Brouillard	1963-66	Emile Griffith*	1990-91	Maurice Blocker (WBC);
1932	Jackie Fields	1966-69	Curtis Cokes		Aaron Davis (WBA)
1933	Young Corbett III;	1969-70	Jose Napoles	1991	Simon Brown (WBC)
	Jimmy McLarnin	1970-71	Billy Backus	1991-92	Meldrick Taylor (WBA)
1934	Barney Ross;	1971-75	Jose Napoles	1991-93	Buddy McGirt (WBC)
	Jimmy McLarnin			1992-94	Crisanto Espana (WBA)

1993-97	Pernell Whitaker (WBC)	2002-03	Vernon Forrest (WBC)	2008	Antonio Margarito (WBA)
1994-98	Ike Quartey (WBA*)	2003	Ricardo Mayorga (WBA/WBC)	2008-11	Andre Berto (WBC)
1997-99	Oscar De La Hoya (WBC*)	2003-05	Cory Spinks (WBA/WBC)	2009	Shane Mosley (WBA)
1998	James Page (WBA*)	2005-06	Zab Judah (WBA/WBC)	2009-12	Vyacheslav Senchenko (WBA)
1999-00	Felix Trinidad (WBC*)	2006	Ricky Hatton (WBA);	2011-12	Victor Ortiz (WBC)
2000	Oscar De La Hoya (WBC*)		Carlos Baldomir (WBC)	2011-	Floyd Mayweather Jr. (WBC)
2000-02	Shane Mosley (WBC)	2006-08	Floyd Mayweather Jr. (WBC);	2012-13	Paulie Malignaggi (WBA)
2001-02	Andrew Lewis (WBA)		Miguel Cotto (WBA)	2013-	Adrien Broner (WBA)
2002	Ricardo Mayorga (WBA)				

(1) Robinson gained the title by defeating Tommy Bell in an elimination agreed to by the New York Commission and the National Boxing Association. Both claimed Robinson waived his title when he won the middleweight crown from LaMotta in 1951.

Lightweights

1896-99	Kid Lavigne	1968-69	Teo Cruz	1992-96	Miguel Angel Gonzalez (WBC*)
1899-02	Frank Erne	1969-70	Mando Ramos	1992-93	Tony Lopez (WBA)
1902-08	Joe Gans	1970	Ismael Laguna	1993	Dingaan Thobela (WBA)
1908-10	Oscar "Battling" Nelson	1970-72	Ken Buchanan (WBA)	1993-98	Orzubek Nazarov (WBA)
1910-12	Ad Wolgast	1971-72	Pedro Carrasco (WBC)	1996-97	Jean-Baptiste Mendy (WBC)
1912-14	Willie Ritchie	1972-79	Roberto Duran (WBA*)	1997-98	Steve Johnston (WBC)
1914-17	Freddie Welsh	1972	Mando Ramos (WBC);	1998-99	Jean-Baptiste Mendy (WBA);
1917-25	Benny Leonard*		Chango Carmona (WBC)		Cesar Bazan (WBC)
1925	Jimmy Goodrich;	1972-74	Rodolfo Gonzalez (WBC)	1999	Julian Lorcy (WBA);
	Rocky Kansas	1974-76	Ishimatsu Suzuki (WBC)		Stefano Zoff (WBC)
1926-30	Sammy Mandell	1976-78	Esteban De Jesus (WBC)	1999-2000	Gilberto Serrano (WBA);
1930	Al Singer; Tony Canzoneri	1979-81	Jim Watt (WBC)		Steve Johnston (WBC)
1930-33	Tony Canzoneri	1979-80	Ernesto Espana (WBA)	2000-01	Takanori Hatakeyama (WBA)
1933-35	Barney Ross*	1980-81	Hilmer Kenty (WBA)	2000-02	Jose Luis Castillo (WBC)
1935-36	Tony Canzoneri	1981	Sean O'Grady (WBA);	2001	Julien Lorcy (WBA)
1936-38	Lou Ambers		Claude Noel (WBA)	2001-02	Raul Balbi (WBA)
1938	Henry Armstrong	1981-83	Alexis Arguello (WBC*)	2002-03	Leonard Dorin (WBA)
1939	Lou Ambers	1981-82	Arturo Frias (WBA)	2002-04	Floyd Mayweather Jr. (WBC)
1940	Lew Jenkins	1982-84	Ray Mancini (WBA)	2004	Lakva Sim (WBA)
1941-43	Sammy Angott	1983-84	Edwin Rosario (WBC)	2004-05	Jose Luis Castillo (WBC)
1944	Sammy Angott (NBA);	1984-86	Livingstone Bramble (WBA)	2004-08	Juan Diaz (WBA)
	J. Zurita (NBA)	1984-85	Jose Luis Ramirez (WBC)	2005-06	Diego Corrales (WBC)
1945-51	Ike Williams	1985-86	Hector "Macho" Camacho	2006	Joel Casamayor (WBC)
	(NBA; later universal)		(WBC)	2006-08	David Diaz (WBC)
1951-52	James Carter	1986-87	Edwin Rosario (WBA)	2008	Nate Campbell (WBA);
1952	Lauro Salas; James Carter	1987-88	Julio Cesar Chavez (WBA);		Manny Pacquiao (WBC)
1953-54	James Carter		Jose Luis Ramirez (WBC)	2009-12	Juan Manuel Marquez
1954	Paddy De Marco; James Carter	1988-89	Julio Cesar Chavez		(WBA*)
1955	James Carter; Bud Smith		(WBA/WBC)	2009-10	Edwin Valero (WBC)
1956	Bud Smith; Joe Brown	1989-90	Edwin Rosario (WBA);	2010-11	Humberto Soto (WBC*)
1956-62	Joe Brown		Pernell Whitaker (WBC)	2011-12	Antonio DeMarco (WBC)
1962-65	Carlos Ortiz	1990	Juan Nazario (WBA)	2012-	Adrien Broner (WBC)
1965	Ismael Laguna	1990-92	Pernell Whitaker*	2013-	Richard Abril (WBA)
1965-68	Carlos Ortiz	1992	Joey Gamache (WBA)		

Featherweights

1892-1900	George Dixon (disputed)	1969-70	Johnny Famechon (WBC)	1993	Goyo Vargas (WBC)
1900-01	Terry McGovern;	1970	Vicente Salvidar (WBC)	1993-95	Kevin Kelley (WBC)
	Young Corbett II*	1970-72	Kuniaki Shibata (WBC)	1993-96	Eloy Rojas (WBA)
1901-12	Abe Attell	1971-72	Antonio Gomez (WBA)	1995	Alejandro Gonzalez (WBC);
1912-23	Johnny Kilbane	1972	Clemente Sanchez (WBC*)		Manuel Medina (WBC)
1923	Eugene Criqui;	1972-74	Ernesto Marcel (WBA*)	1995-99	Luisito Espinosa (WBC)
	Johnny Dundee	1972-73	Jose Legra (WBC)	1996-97	Wilfredo Vasquez (WBA*)
1923-25	Johnny Dundee*	1973-74	Eder Jofre (WBC*)	1998	Freddie Norwood (WBA)
1925-27	Kid Kaplan*	1974	Ruben Olivares (WBA)	1998-99	Antonio Cermeno (WBA)
1927-28	Benny Bass; Tony Canzoneri	1974-75	Bobby Chacon (WBC)	1999	Cesar Soto (WBC);
1928-29	Andre Routis	1974-76	Alexis Arguello (WBA*)		Naseem Hamed (WBC*);
1929-32	Battling Battalino*	1975	Ruben Olivares (WBC)		Freddie Norwood (WBA)
1932-34	Tommy Paul (NBA)	1975-76	David Kotey (WBC)	2000-01	Guty Espadas (WBC)
1933-36	Freddie Miller	1976-80	Danny "Little Red"	2000-03	Derrick Gainer (WBA)
1936-37	Petey Sarron		Lopez (WBC)	2001-04	Erik Morales (WBC)[1]
1937-38	Henry Armstrong*	1977	Rafael Ortega (WBA)	2003-06	Juan Manuel Marquez (WBA)
1938-40	Joey Archibald	1977-78	Cecilio Lastra (WBA)	2004-06	In-Jin Chi (WBC)
1940-41	Harry Jeffra	1978-85	Eusebio Pedroza (WBA)	2006-	Chris John (WBA)
1942-48	Willie Pep	1980-82	Salvador Sanchez (WBC)	2006	Takashi Koshimoto (WBC);
1948-49	Sandy Saddler	1982-84	Juan LaPorte (WBC)		Rodolfo Lopez (WBC)
1949-50	Willie Pep	1984	Wilfredo Gomez (WBC)	2006-07	In-Jin Chi (WBC)
1950-57	Sandy Saddler*	1984-88	Azumah Nelson (WBC)	2007-08	Jorge Linares (WBC)
1957-59	Hogan "Kid" Bassey	1985-86	Barry McGuigan (WBA)	2008	Oscar Larios (WBC)
1959-63	Davey Moore	1986-87	Steve Cruz (WBA)	2009-10	Elio Rojas (WBC)
1963-64	Ultiminio "Sugar" Ramos	1987-91	Antonio Esparragoza (WBA)	2010-11	Hozumi Hasegawa (WBC)
1964-67	Vicente Saldivar*	1988-90	Jeff Fenech (WBC*)	2011-12	Jhonny Gonzalez (WBC)
1968	Raul Rojas (WBA)	1990-91	Marcos Villasana (WBC)	2012-13	Daniel Ponce de León (WBC)
1968-69	Jose Legra (WBC)	1991-93	Park Yung Kyun (WBA);	2013	Abner Mares (WBC)
1968-71	Shozo Saijyo (WBA)		Paul Hodkinson (WBC)	2013-	Jhonny Gonzalez (WBC)

(1) Marco Antonio Barrera won unan. decision over Morales, June 22, 2002, but refused WBC title. Morales regained WBC title with unan. decision over Paulie Ayala, Nov. 16, 2002. Morales moved up to Jr. Lightweight div. in 2004.

International Boxing Hall of Fame Inductees, 2013

Source: International Boxing Hall of Fame, 1 Hall of Fame Dr., Canastota, NY 13032. www.ibhof.com

Modern	Arturo Gatti, 40-9 (31 KO)	Virgil Hill, 50-7 (23 KO)	Myung-Woo Yuh, 38-1 (14 KO)
Old-Timer	Wesley Ramey, 158-26-11 (9 KO)	Jeff Smith, 149-31-5 (52 KO)	
Pioneer	Joe Cobum		
Non-participant	Arturo Hernandez, manager	Mills Lane, referee	Jimmy Lennon Jr., ring announcer
Observer	Ted Carroll, cartoonist	Colin Hart, journalist	

Title-Changing Heavyweight Championship Bouts, 1889-2013

1889: July 8, John L. Sullivan def. Jake Kilrain, 75, Richburg, MS.

1892: Sept. 7, James J. Corbett def. John L. Sullivan, 21, New Orleans.

1897: Mar. 17, Bob Fitzsimmons def. James J. Corbett, 14, Carson City, NV.

1899: June 9, James J. Jeffries def. Bob Fitzsimmons, 11, Coney Island, NY. (Jeffries retired as champion in 1905.)

1905: July 3, Marvin Hart KOd Jack Root, 12, Reno, NV. (James J. Jeffries refereed, gave title to Hart. Jack O'Brien also claimed the title.)

1906: Feb. 23, Tommy Burns def. Marvin Hart, 20, Los Angeles.

1908: Dec. 26, Jack Johnson KOd Tommy Burns, 14, Sydney, Australia. (Police halted contest.)

1915: Apr. 5, Jess Willard KOd Jack Johnson, 26, Havana, Cuba.

1919: July 4, Jack Dempsey KOd Jess Willard, Toledo, OH (Willard failed to answer bell for 4th round).

1926: Sept. 23, Gene Tunney def. Jack Dempsey, 10, Philadelphia. (Tunney retired as champion in 1928.)

1930: June 12, Max Schmeling def. Jack Sharkey, 4, New York City. (Resulted in the election of a successor to Gene Tunney.)

1932: June 21, Jack Sharkey def. Max Schmeling, 15, NYC.

1933: June 29, Primo Carnera KOd Jack Sharkey, 6, NYC.

1934: June 14, Max Baer KOd Primo Carnera, 11, NYC.

1935: June 13, James J. Braddock def. Max Baer, 15, NYC.

1937: June 22, Joe Louis KOd James J. Braddock, 8, Chicago. (Louis retired as champion in 1949.)

1949: June 22, Ezzard Charles def. Joe Walcott, 15, Chicago; NBA recognition only.

1951: July 18, Joe Walcott KOd Ezzard Charles, 7, Pittsburgh.

1952: Sept. 23, Rocky Marciano KOd Joe Walcott, 13, Philadelphia. (Marciano retired as champion in 1956.)

1956: Nov. 30, Floyd Patterson KOd Archie Moore, 5, Chicago.

1959: June 26, Ingemar Johansson KOd Floyd Patterson, 3, NYC.

1960: June 20, Floyd Patterson KOd Ingemar Johansson, 5, NYC.

1962: Sept. 25, Sonny Liston KOd Floyd Patterson, 1, Chicago.

1964: Feb. 25, Cassius Clay (Muhammad Ali) KOd Sonny Liston, 7, Miami Beach, FL. (In 1967, Ali was stripped of his title by the WBA and others for refusing military service.)

1970: Feb. 16, Joe Frazier KOd Jimmy Ellis, 5, NYC. (Frazier def. Ali In 15 rounds, Mar. 8, 1971, in NYC.)

1973: Jan. 22, George Foreman KOd Joe Frazier, 2, Jamaica.

1974: Oct. 30, Muhammad Ali KOd George Foreman, 8, Kinshasa, Zaire (billed as the "Rumble in the Jungle").

1978: Feb. 15, Leon Spinks def. Muhammad Ali, 15, Las Vegas (WBC recognized Ken Norton as champion after Spinks refused to fight him before his rematch with Ali); June 9, (WBC) Larry Holmes def. Ken Norton, 15, Las Vegas; Sept. 15, (WBA) Muhammad Ali def. Leon Spinks, 15, New Orleans. (Ali retired as champion in 1979.)

1979: Oct. 20, (WBA) John Tate def. Gerrie Coetzee, 15, Pretoria, South Africa.

1980: Mar. 31, (WBA) Mike Weaver KOd John Tate, 15, Knoxville, TN.

1982: Dec. 10, (WBA) Michael Dokes KOd Mike Weaver, 1, Las Vegas.

1983: Sept. 23, (WBA) Gerrie Coetzee KOd Michael Dokes, 10, Richfield, OH; in Dec., Larry Holmes relinquished the WBC title and was named champion of the newly formed IBF.

1984: Mar. 9, (WBC) Tim Witherspoon def. Greg Page, 12, Las Vegas; Aug. 31, (WBC) Pinklon Thomas def. Tim Witherspoon, 12, Las Vegas; Dec. 2, (WBA) Greg Page KOd Gerrie Coetzee, 8, Sun City, Bophuthatswana, South Africa.

1985: Apr. 29, (WBA) Tony Tubbs def. Greg Page, 15, Buffalo, NY; Sept. 21, (IBF) Michael Spinks def. Larry Holmes, 15, Las Vegas (Spinks relinquished title in Feb. 1987).

1986: Jan. 17, (WBA) Tim Witherspoon def. Tony Tubbs, 15, Atlanta, GA; Mar. 22, (WBC) Trevor Berbick def. Pinklon Thomas, 12, Miami; Nov. 22, (WBC) Mike Tyson KOd Trevor Berbick, 2, Las Vegas; Dec. 12, (WBA) James "Bonecrusher" Smith KOd Tim Witherspoon, 1, NYC.

1987: Mar. 7, (WBA) Mike Tyson def. James "Bonecrusher" Smith, 12, Las Vegas; May 30, (IBF) Tony Tucker KOd James "Buster" Douglas, 10, Las Vegas; Aug. 1, (IBF) Mike Tyson def. Tony Tucker, 12, Las Vegas. (Tyson became undisputed champion.)

1990: Feb. 11, (WBA/WBC/IBF) James "Buster" Douglas KOd Mike Tyson, 10, Tokyo, Japan; Oct. 25, (WBA/WBC/IBF) Evander Holyfield KOd James "Buster" Douglas, 3, Las Vegas.

1992: Nov. 13, (WBA/WBC/IBF) Riddick Bowe def. Evander Holyfield, 12, Las Vegas; in Dec., Lennox Lewis was named WBC champion after Bowe relinquished the WBC title rather than fight Lewis.

1993: Nov. 6, (WBA/IBF) Evander Holyfield def. Riddick Bowe, 12, Las Vegas.

1994: Apr. 22, (WBA/IBF) Michael Moorer def. Evander Holyfield, 12, Las Vegas; Sept. 24, (WBC) Oliver McCall KOd Lennox Lewis, 2, London, Eng.; Nov. 5, (WBA/IBF) George Foreman KOd Michael Moorer, 10, Las Vegas.

1995: In Mar., George Foreman was stripped of his WBA title for refusing to fight challenger Tony Tucker; in June, Foreman relinquished his IBF title rather than submit to a rematch with Axel Schulz; Sept. 2, (WBC) Frank Bruno def. Oliver McCall, 12, London, Eng.; Dec. 9, (IBF) Frans Botha def. Axel Schulz, 12, Las Vegas (Botha was subsequently stripped of title after testing positive for a steroid).

1996: Mar. 16, (WBC) Mike Tyson KOd Frank Bruno, 3, Las Vegas; June 22, (IBF) Michael Moorer def. Axel Schulz, 12, Dortmund, Germany; Sept. 7, (WBA) Mike Tyson KOd Bruce Seldon, 1, Las Vegas (Tyson was subsequently stripped of WBC title after refusing to fight Lennox Lewis); Nov. 9, (WBA) Evander Holyfield KOd Mike Tyson, 11, Las Vegas.

1997: Feb. 7, (WBC) Lennox Lewis KOd Oliver McCall, 5, Las Vegas; Nov. 8, (IBF) Evander Holyfield def. Michael Moorer, 8, Las Vegas.

1999: Nov. 13, (IBF) Lennox Lewis def. Evander Holyfield, 12, Las Vegas. (Lewis became undisputed champion.)

2000: In Apr., Lennox Lewis was stripped of his WBA title; Aug. 12, (WBA) Evander Holyfield def. John Ruiz, 12, Las Vegas.

2001: Mar. 3, (WBA) John Ruiz def. Evander Holyfield, 12, Las Vegas; Apr. 21, (WBC/IBF) Hasim Rahman KOd Lennox Lewis, 5, Brakpan, South Africa; Nov. 17, (WBC/IBF) Lennox Lewis KOd Hasim Rahman, 4, Las Vegas.

2002: In Sept., Lennox Lewis relinquished his IBF title; Dec. 14, (IBF) Chris Byrd def. Evander Holyfield, 12, Atlantic City, NJ.

2003: Mar. 1, (WBA) Roy Jones Jr. def. John Ruiz, 12, Las Vegas.

2004: Feb. 20, (WBA) John Ruiz gained title when Roy Jones Jr. relinquished it; Apr. 24, (WBC) Vitali Klitschko TKOd Corrie Sanders, 8, Los Angeles, to win title vacated by retirement of Lennox Lewis in Feb.

2005: Apr. 30, (WBA) James Toney def. John Ruiz, 12, NYC (title was returned to Ruiz after Toney tested positive for steroids); Nov. 9, (WBC) Hasim Rahman gained title when Vitali Klitschko retired; Dec. 17, (WBA) Nikolai Valuev def. John Ruiz, 12, Berlin, Germany.

2006: Apr. 22, (IBF) Wladimir Klitschko TKOd Chris Byrd, 7, Mannheim, Germany; Aug. 12, (WBC) Oleg Maskaev TKOd Hasim Rahman, 12, Las Vegas.

2007: Apr. 14, (WBA) Ruslan Chagaev def. Nikolai Valuev, 12, Stuttgart, Germany.

2008: Mar. 8, (WBC) Samuel Peter TKOd Oleg Maskaev, 6, Cancun, Mexico; Aug. 30, (WBA) Nikolai Valuev def. John Ruiz, 12, Berlin, Germany; Oct. 11, (WBC) Vitali Klitschko TKOd Samuel Peter, 8, Berlin, Germany.

2009: Nov. 7, (WBA) David Haye def. Nikolai Valuev, 12, Nuremberg, Germany.

2011: July 2, (WBA) Wladimir Klitschko def. David Haye, 12, Hamburg, Germany.

THOROUGHBRED RACING

Triple Crown Winners

The Kentucky Derby, Preakness Stakes, and Belmont Stakes make up the Triple Crown. Since 1920, colts have carried 126 lbs in Triple Crown events; fillies, 121 lbs.

Year	Horse	Jockey	Trainer	Year	Horse	Jockey	Trainer
1919	Sir Barton	J. Loftus	H. G. Bedwell	1946	Assault	W. Mehrtens	M. Hirsch
1930	Gallant Fox	E. Sande	J. Fitzsimmons	1948	Citation	E. Arcaro	H. A. Jones
1935	Omaha	W. Sanders	J. Fitzsimmons	1973	Secretariat	R. Turcotte	L. Laurin
1937	War Admiral	C. Kurtsinger	G. Conway	1977	Seattle Slew	J. Cruguet	W. H. Turner Jr.
1941	Whirlaway	E. Arcaro	B. A. Jones	1978	Affirmed	S. Cauthen	L. S. Barrera
1943	Count Fleet	J. Longden	G. D. Cameron				

Kentucky Derby, 1875-2013

Churchill Downs, Louisville, KY; inaug. 1875. Distance: 1-1/4 mi; 1-1/2 mi until 1896. 3-year-olds. Best time: 1:59 2/5, Secretariat (1973); 2013 time: 2:02.89.

Year	Winner	Jockey	Year	Winner	Jockey	Year	Winner	Jockey
1875	Aristides	O. Lewis	1922	Morvich	A. Johnson	1968	Dancer's Image[2]	R. Ussery
1876	Vagrant	R. Swim	1923	Zev	E. Sande	1969	Majestic Prince	W. Hartack
1877	Baden Baden	W. Walker	1924	Black Gold	J. D. Mooney	1970	Dust Commander	M. Manganello
1878	Day Star	J. Carter	1925	Flying Ebony	E. Sande	1971	Canonero II	G. Avila
1879	Lord Murphy	C. Schauer	1926	Bubbling Over	A. Johnson	1972	Riva Ridge	R. Turcotte
1880	Fonso	G. Lewis	1927	Whiskery	L. McAtee	1973	Secretariat	R. Turcotte
1881	Hindoo	J. McLaughlin	1928	Reigh Count	C. Lang	1974	Cannonade	A. Cordero
1882	Apollo	B. Hurd	1929	Clyde Van Dusen	L. McAtee	1975	Foolish Pleasure	J. Vasquez
1883	Leonatus	W. Donohue	1930	Gallant Fox	E. Sande	1976	Bold Forbes	A. Cordero
1884	Buchanan	I. Murphy	1931	Twenty Grand	C. Kurtsinger	1977	Seattle Slew	J. Cruguet
1885	Joe Cotton	E. Henderson	1932	Burgoo King	E. James	1978	Affirmed	S. Cauthen
1886	Ben Ali	P. Duffy	1933	Brokers Tip	D. Meade	1979	Spectacular Bid	R. Franklin
1887	Montrose	I. Lewis	1934	Cavalcade	M. Garner	1980	Genuine Risk[1]	J. Vasquez
1888	Macbeth II	G. Covington	1935	Omaha	W. Saunders	1981	Pleasant Colony	J. Velasquez
1889	Spokane	T. Kiley	1936	Bold Venture	I. Hanford	1982	Gato del Sol	E. Delahoussaye
1890	Riley	I. Murphy	1937	War Admiral	C. Kurtsinger	1983	Sunny's Halo	E. Delahoussaye
1891	Kingman	I. Murphy	1938	Lawrin	E. Arcaro	1984	Swale	L. Pincay
1892	Azra	A. Clayton	1939	Johnstown	J. Stout	1985	Spend a Buck	A. Cordero
1893	Lookout	E. Kunze	1940	Gallahadion	C. Bierman	1986	Ferdinand	W. Shoemaker
1894	Chant	F. Goodale	1941	Whirlaway	E. Arcaro	1987	Alysheba	C. McCarron
1895	Halma	J. Perkins	1942	Shut Out	W. Wright	1988	Winning Colors[1]	G. Stevens
1896	Ben Brush	W. Simms	1943	Count Fleet	J. Longden	1989	Sunday Silence	P. Valenzuela
1897	Typhoon II	F. Garner	1944	Pensive	C. McCreary	1990	Unbridled	C. Perret
1898	Plaudit	W. Simms	1945	Hoop Jr.	E. Arcaro	1991	Strike the Gold	C. Antley
1899	Manuel	F. Taral	1946	Assault	W. Mehrtens	1992	Lil E. Tee	P. Day
1900	Lieut. Gibson	J. Boland	1947	Jet Pilot	E. Guerin	1993	Sea Hero	J. Bailey
1901	His Eminence	J. Winkfield	1948	Citation	E. Arcaro	1994	Go for Gin	C. McCarron
1902	Alan-a-Dale	J. Winkfield	1949	Ponder	S. Brooks	1995	Thunder Gulch	G. Stevens
1903	Judge Himes	H. Booker	1950	Middleground	W. Boland	1996	Grindstone	J. Bailey
1904	Elwood	F. Prior	1951	Count Turf	C. McCreary	1997	Silver Charm	G. Stevens
1905	Agile	J. Martin	1952	Hill Gail	E. Arcaro	1998	Real Quiet	K. Desormeaux
1906	Sir Huon	R. Troxler	1953	Dark Star	H. Moreno	1999	Charismatic	C. Antley
1907	Pink Star	A. Minder	1954	Determine	R. York	2000	Fusaichi Pegasus	K. Desormeaux
1908	Stone Street	A. Pickens	1955	Swaps	W. Shoemaker	2001	Monarchos	J. Chavez
1909	Wintergreen	V. Powers	1956	Needles	D. Erb	2002	War Emblem	V. Espinoza
1910	Donau	F. Herbert	1957	Iron Liege	W. Hartack	2003	Funny Cide	J. Santos
1911	Meridian	G. Archibald	1958	Tim Tam	I. Valenzuela	2004	Smarty Jones	S. Elliot
1912	Worth	C. Shilling	1959	Tomy Lee	W. Shoemaker	2005	Giacomo	M. Smith
1913	Donerail	R. Goose	1960	Venetian Way	W. Hartack	2006	Barbaro	E. Prado
1914	Old Rosebud	J. McCabe	1961	Carry Back	J. Sellers	2007	Street Sense	C. Borel
1915	Regret[1]	J. Notter	1962	Decidedly	W. Hartack	2008	Big Brown	K. Desormeaux
1916	George Smith	J. Loftus	1963	Chateaugay	B. Baeza	2009	Mine That Bird	C. Borel
1917	Omar Khayyam	C. Borel	1964	Northern Dancer	W. Hartack	2010	Super Saver	C. Borel
1918	Exterminator	W. Knapp	1965	Lucky Debonair	W. Shoemaker	2011	Animal Kingdom	J. Velazquez
1919	Sir Barton	J. Loftus	1966	Kauai King	D. Brumfield	2012	I'll Have Another	M. Gutierrez
1920	Paul Jones	T. Rice	1967	Proud Clarion	R. Ussery	2013	Orb	J. Rosario
1921	Behave Yourself	C. Thompson						

Only two jockeys have won the Kentucky Derby five times: Eddie Arcaro (1938, 1941, 1945, 1948, 1952) and Bill Hartack (1957, 1960, 1962, 1964, 1969). Willie Shoemaker won four times (1955, 1959, 1965, 1986). Six jockeys won three times: Isaac Murphy (1884, 1890, 1891); Earle Sande (1923, 1925, 1930); Angel Cordero (1974, 1976, 1985); Gary Stevens (1988, 1995, 1997); Kent Desormeaux (1998, 2000, 2008); and Calvin Borel (2007, 2009, 2010). (1) Regret, Genuine Risk, and Winning Colors are the only fillies to have won the Derby. (2) Disqualified from purse money after tests disclosed that the horse had run with a painkilling drug, phenylbutazone, in his system. All wagers were paid on Dancer's Image. Forward Pass was awarded first place money.

Fastest Winning Times for the Kentucky Derby

Until 2001, Kentucky Derby times were measured in fifths of a second.

Time	Horse	Jockey	Year	Time	Horse	Jockey	Year
1 min., 59 2/5 s.	Secretariat	Ron Turcotte	1973	2 min., 1.19 s.	Funny Cide	Jose Santos	2003
1 min., 59.97 s.	Monarchos	Jorge Chavez	2001	2 min., 1 1/5 s.	Thunder Gulch	Gary Stevens	1995
2 min.	Northern Dancer	Bill Hartack	1964		Affirmed	Steve Cauthen	1978
2 min., 1/5 s.	Spend a Buck	Angel Cordero Jr.	1985		Lucky Debonair	Bill Shoemaker	1965
2 min., 2/5 s.	Decidedly	Bill Hartack	1962	2 min., 1 2/5 s.	Whirlaway	Eddie Arcaro	1941
2 min., 3/5 s.	Proud Clarion	Robert Ussery	1967		Barbaro	Edgar Prado	2006
2 min., 1 s.	Fusaichi Pegasus	Kent Desormeaux	2000	2 min., 1 3/5 s.	Bold Forbes	Angel Cordero Jr.	1976
	Grindstone	Jerry Bailey	1996		Hill Gail	Eddie Arcaro	1952
2 min., 1.13 s.	War Emblem	Victor Espinoza	2002		Middleground	William Boland	1950

Preakness Stakes, 1873-2013

Pimlico Race Course, Baltimore, MD; inaug. 1873. Distance: 1-3/16 mi. 3-year-olds. * = Horses ran in two divisions. Best time: 1:53, Secretariat (1973); 2013 time: 1:57.54.

Year	Winner	Jockey	Year	Winner	Jockey	Year	Winner	Jockey
1873	Survivor	G. Barbee	1922	Pillory	L. Morris	1969	Majestic Prince	W. Hartack
1874	Culpepper	M. Donohue	1923	Vigil	B. Marinelli	1970	Personality	E. Belmonte
1875	Tom Ochiltree	L. Hughes	1924	Nellie Morse	J. Merimee	1971	Canonero II.	G. Avila
1876	Shirley	G. Barbee	1925	Coventry	C. Kummer	1972	Bee Bee Bee	E. Nelson
1877	Cloverbrook	C. Holloway	1926	Display	J. Malben	1973	Secretariat	R. Turcotte
1878	Duke of Magenta	C. Holloway	1927	Bostonian	A. Abel	1974	Little Current	M. Rivera
1879	Harold	L. Hughes	1928	Victorian	R. Workman	1975	Master Derby	D. McHargue
1880	Grenada	L. Hughes	1929	Dr. Freeland	L. Schaefer	1976	Elocutionist	J. Lively
1881	Saunterer	W. Costello	1930	Gallant Fox	E. Sande	1977	Seattle Slew	J. Cruguet
1882	Vanguard	W. Costello	1931	Mate	G. Ellis	1978	Affirmed	S. Cauthen
1883	Jacobus	G. Barbee	1932	Burgoo King	E. James	1979	Spectacular Bid	R. Franklin
1884	Knight of Ellerslie	S. Fisher	1933	Head Play	C. Kurtsinger	1980	Codex	A. Cordero
1885	Tecumseh	J. McLaughlin	1934	High Quest	J. Jones	1981	Pleasant Colony	J. Velasquez
1886	The Bard	S. Fisher	1935	Omaha	W. Saunders	1982	Aloma's Ruler	J. Kaenel
1887	Dunboyne	W. Donohue	1936	Bold Venture	G. Woolf	1983	Deputed	
1888	Refund	F. Littlefield	1937	War Admiral	C. Kurtsinger		Testamony	D. Miller
1889	Buddhist	G. Anderson	1938	Dauber	M. Peters	1984	Gate Dancer	A. Cordero
1890	Montague	W. Martin	1939	Challedon	G. Seabo	1985	Tank's Prospect	P. Day
1894	Assignee	F. Taral	1940	Bimelech	F. A. Smith	1986	Snow Chief	A. Solis
1895	Belmar	F. Taral	1941	Whirlaway	E. Arcaro	1987	Alysheba	C. McCarron
1896	Margrave	H. Griffin	1942	Alsab	B. James	1988	Risen Star	E. Delahoussaye
1897	Paul Kauvar	C. Thorpe	1943	Count Fleet	J. Longden	1989	Sunday Silence	P. Valenzuela
1898	Sly Fox	W. Simms	1944	Pensive	C. McCreary	1990	Summer Squall	P. Day
1899	Half Time	R. Clawson	1945	Polynesian	W. D. Wright	1991	Hansel	J. Bailey
1900	Hindus	H. Spencer	1946	Assault	W. Mehrtens	1992	Pine Bluff	C. McCarron
1901	The Parader	F. Landry	1947	Faultless	D. Dodson	1993	Prairie Bayou	M. Smith
1902	Old England	L. Jackson	1948	Citation	E. Arcaro	1994	Tabasco Cat	P. Day
1903	Flocarline	W. Gannon	1949	Capot	T. Atkinson	1995	Timber Country	P. Day
1904	Bryn Mawr	E. Hildebrand	1950	Hill Prince	E. Arcaro	1996	Louis Quatorze	P. Day
1905	Cairngorm	W. Davis	1951	Bold	E. Arcaro	1997	Silver Charm	G. Stevens
1906	Whimsical	W. Miller	1952	Blue Man	C. McCreary	1998	Real Quiet	K. Desormeaux
1907	Don Enrique	G. Mountain	1953	Native Dancer	E. Guerin	1999	Charismatic	C. Antley
1908	Royal Tourist	E. Dugan	1954	Hasty Road	J. Adams	2000	Red Bullet	J. Bailey
1909	Effendi	W. Doyle	1955	Nashua	E. Arcaro	2001	Point Given	G. Stevens
1910	Layminster	R. Estep	1956	Fabius	W. Hartack	2002	War Emblem	V. Espinoza
1911	Watervale	E. Dugan	1957	Bold Ruler	E. Arcaro	2003	Funny Cide	J. Santos
1912	Colonel Holloway	C. Turner	1958	Tim Tam	I. Valenzuela	2004	Smarty Jones	S. Elliot
1913	Buskin	J. Butwell	1959	Royal Orbit	W. Harmatz	2005	Afleet Alex	J. Rose
1914	Holiday	A. Schuttinger	1960	Bally Ache	R. Ussery	2006	Bernardini	J. Castellano
1915	Rhine Maiden	D. Hoffman	1961	Carry Back	J. Sellers	2007	Curlin	R. Albarado
1916	Damrosch	L. McAtee	1962	Greek Money	J. L. Rotz	2008	Big Brown	K. Desormeaux
1917	Kalitan	E. Haynes	1963	Candy Spots	W. Shoemaker	2009	Rachel Alexandra	C. Borel
1918*	War Cloud	J. Loftus	1964	Northern Dancer	W. Hartack	2010	Lookin At Lucky	M. Garcia
	Jack Hare Jr.	C. Peak	1965	Tom Rolfe	R. Turcotte	2011	Shackleford	J. Castanon
1919	Sir Barton	J. Loftus	1966	Kauai King	D. Brumfield	2012	I'll Have Another	M. Gutierrez
1920	Man o' War	C. Kummer	1967	Damascus	W. Shoemaker	2013	Oxbow	G. Stevens
1921	Broomspun	F. Coltiletti	1968	Forward Pass	I. Valenzuela			

Belmont Stakes, 1867-2013

Belmont Park, Elmont, NY; inaug. 1867. Distance: 1-1/2 mi. 3-year-olds. Best time: 2:24, Secretariat (1973); 2013 time: 2:30.70.

Year	Winner	Jockey	Year	Winner	Jockey	Year	Winner	Jockey
1867	Ruthless	J. Gilpatrick	1900	Ildrim	N. Turner	1935	Omaha	W. Saunders
1868	General Duke	R. Swim	1901	Commando	H. Spencer	1936	Granville	J. Stout
1869	Fenian	C. Miller	1902	Masterman	J. Bullman	1937	War Admiral	C. Kurtsinger
1870	Kingfisher	W. Dick	1903	Africander	J. Bullman	1938	Pasteurized	J. Stout
1871	Harry Bassett	W. Miller	1904	Delhi	G. Odom	1939	Johnstown	J. Stout
1872	Joe Daniels	J. Rowe	1905	Tanya	E. Hildebrand	1940	Bimelech	F. A. Smith
1873	Springbok	J. Rowe	1906	Burgomaster	L. Lyne	1941	Whirlaway	E. Arcaro
1874	Saxon	G. Barbee	1907	Peter Pan	G. Mountain	1942	Shut Out	E. Arcaro
1875	Calvin	R. Swim	1908	Colin	J. Notter	1943	Count Fleet	J. Longden
1876	Algerine	W. Donohue	1909	Joe Madden	E. Dugan	1944	Bounding Home	G. L. Smith
1877	Cloverbrook	C. Holloway	1910	Sweep	J. Butwell	1945	Pavot	E. Arcaro
1878	Duke of Magenta	L. Hughes	1913	Prince Eugene	R. Troxler	1946	Assault	W. Mehrtens
1879	Spendthrift	S. Evans	1914	Luke McLuke	M. Buxton	1947	Phalanx	R. Donoso
1880	Grenada	L. Hughes	1915	The Finn	G. Byrne	1948	Citation	E. Arcaro
1881	Saunterer	T. Costello	1916	Friar Rock	E. Haynes	1949	Capot	T. Atkinson
1882	Forester	J. McLaughlin	1917	Hourless	J. Butwell	1950	Middleground	W. Boland
1883	George Kinney	J. McLaughlin	1918	Johren	F. Robinson	1951	Counterpoint	D. Gorman
1884	Panique	J. McLaughlin	1919	Sir Barton	J. Loftus	1952	One Count	E. Arcaro
1885	Tyrant	P. Duffy	1920	Man o' War	C. Kummer	1953	Native Dancer	E. Guerin
1886	Inspector B.	J. McLaughlin	1921	Grey Lag	E. Sande	1954	High Gun	E. Guerin
1887	Hanover	J. McLaughlin	1922	Pillory	C. H. Miller	1955	Nashua	E. Arcaro
1888	Sir Dixon	J. McLaughlin	1923	Zev	E. Sande	1956	Needles	D. Erb
1889	Eric	W. Hayward	1924	Mad Play	E. Sande	1957	Gallant Man	W. Shoemaker
1890	Burlington	S. Barnes	1925	American Flag	A. Johnson	1958	Cavan	P. Anderson
1891	Foxford	E. Garrison	1926	Crusader	A. Johnson	1959	Sword Dancer	W. Shoemaker
1892	Patron	W. Hayward	1927	Chance Shot	E. Sande	1960	Celtic Ash	W. Hartack
1893	Comanche	W. Simms	1928	Vito	C. Kummer	1961	Sherluck	B. Baeza
1894	Henry of Navarre	W. Simms	1929	Blue Larkspur	M. Garner	1962	Jaipur	W. Shoemaker
1895	Belmar	F. Taral	1930	Gallant Fox	E. Sande	1963	Chateaugay	B. Baeza
1896	Hastings	H. Griffin	1931	Twenty Grand	C. Kurtsinger	1964	Quadrangle	M. Ycaza
1897	Scottish Chieftain	J. Scherrer	1932	Faireno	T. Malley	1965	Hail to All	J. Sellers
1898	Bowling Brook	F. Littlefield	1933	Hurryoff	M. Garner	1966	Amberoid	W. Boland
1899	Jean Bereaud	R. R. Clawson	1934	Peace Chance	W. D. Wright	1967	Damascus	W. Shoemaker

Year	Winner	Jockey	Year	Winner	Jockey	Year	Winner	Jockey
1968	Stage Door Johnny	H. Gustines	1984	Swale	L. Pincay	1999	Lemon Drop Kid	J. Santos
1969	Arts and Letters	B. Baeza	1985	Creme Fraiche	E. Maple	2000	Commendable	P. Day
1970	High Echelon	J. L. Rotz	1986	Danzig Connection	M. McCarron	2001	Point Given	G. Stevens
1971	Pass Catcher	W. Blum	1987	Bet Twice	C. Perret	2002	Sarava	E. Prado
1972	Riva Ridge	R. Turcotte	1988	Risen Star	E. Delahoussaye	2003	Empire Maker	J. Bailey
1973	Secretariat	R. Turcotte	1989	Easy Goer	P. Day	2004	Birdstone	E. Prado
1974	Little Current	M. Rivera	1990	Go and Go	M. Kinane	2005	Afleet Alex	J. Rose
1975	Avatar	W. Shoemaker	1991	Hansel	J. Bailey	2006	Jazil	F. Jara
1976	Bold Forbes	A. Cordero	1992	A.P. Indy.	E. Delahoussaye	2007	Rags to Riches.	J. Velazquez
1977	Seattle Slew	J. Cruguet	1993	Colonial Affair	J. Krone	2008	Da' Tara	A. Garcia
1978	Affirmed	S. Cauthen	1994	Tabasco Cat	P. Day	2009	Summer Bird	K. Desormeaux
1979	Coastal	R. Hernandez	1995	Thunder Gulch	G. Stevens	2010	Drosselmeyer	M. Smith
1980	Temperence Hill	E. Maple	1996	Editor's Note	R. Douglas	2011	Ruler On Ice	J. Valdivia Jr.
1981	Summing	G. Martens	1997	Touch Gold	C. McCarron	2012	Union Rags	J. Velazquez
1982	Conquistador Cielo	L. Pincay	1998	Victory Gallop	G. Stevens	2013	Palace Malice	M. Smith
1983	Caveat	L. Pincay						

Annual Leading Jockey by Earnings, 1957-2012

Total purses earned by all horses that jockey raced in year listed; does not reflect what jockey earned.

Year	Jockey	Earnings	Year	Jockey	Earnings	Year	Jockey	Earnings
1957	Bill Hartack	$3,060,501	1976	Angel Cordero Jr.	$4,709,500	1995	Jerry D. Bailey	$16,311,876
1958	Willie Shoemaker	2,961,693	1977	Steve Cauthen	6,151,750	1996	Jerry D. Bailey	19,465,376
1959	Willie Shoemaker	2,843,133	1978	Darrel McHargue	6,029,885	1997	Jerry D. Bailey	18,320,743
1960	Willie Shoemaker	2,123,961	1979	Laffit Pincay Jr.	8,193,535	1998	Gary Stevens	19,622,855
1961	Willie Shoemaker	2,690,819	1980	Chris McCarron	7,663,300	1999	Pat Day	18,092,845
1962	Willie Shoemaker	2,916,844	1981	Chris McCarron	8,397,604	2000	Pat Day	17,479,838
1963	Willie Shoemaker	2,526,925	1982	Angel Cordero Jr.	9,483,590	2001	Jerry D. Bailey	22,597,720
1964	Willie Shoemaker	2,649,553	1983	Angel Cordero Jr.	10,116,697	2002	Jerry D. Bailey	19,271,814
1965	Braulio Baeza	2,582,702	1984	Chris McCarron	12,045,813	2003	Jerry D. Bailey	23,354,960
1966	Braulio Baeza	2,951,022	1985	Laffit Pincay Jr.	13,353,299	2004	John R. Velazquez	22,220,261
1967	Braulio Baeza	3,088,888	1986	Jose Santos	11,329,297	2005	John R. Velazquez	20,799,923
1968	Braulio Baeza	2,835,108	1987	Jose Santos	12,375,433	2006	Garrett K. Gomez	20,122,592
1969	Jorge Velasquez	2,542,315	1988	Jose Santos	14,877,298	2007	Garrett K. Gomez	22,800,074
1970	Laffit Pincay Jr.	2,626,526	1989	Jose Santos	13,838,389	2008	Garrett K. Gomez	23,344,351
1971	Laffit Pincay Jr.	3,784,377	1990	Gary Stevens	13,881,198	2009	Garrett K. Gomez	18,536,105
1972	Laffit Pincay Jr.	3,225,827	1991	Chris McCarron	14,441,083	2010	Ramon A. Dominguez	16,911,880
1973	Laffit Pincay Jr.	4,093,492	1992	Kent Desormeaux	14,193,006	2011	Ramon A. Dominguez	20,267,032
1974	Laffit Pincay Jr.	4,251,060	1993	Mike Smith	14,024,815	2012	Ramon A. Dominguez	25,584,852
1975	Braulio Baeza	3,695,198	1994	Mike Smith	15,979,820			

Breeders' Cup World Thoroughbred Championships, 1984-2013

The Breeders' Cup began in 1984 and through 2006, consisted of seven races at one track on one day. In 2007, it expanded to two days, and three new races debuted: Filly and Mare Sprint, Juvenile Turf, and Dirt. In 2008, a "Ladies' Day" for fillies and several more races debuted: Turf Sprint, Marathon, and Juvenile Fillies Turf. In 2011, the Juvenile Sprint debuted, won in 2011 by Secret Circle (jockey: R. Bejarano) and in 2012 by Hightail (R. Maragh); it was not held in 2013.

Classic
Distance: 1-1/4 mi.

Year	Horse	Jockey	Year	Horse	Jockey	Year	Horse	Jockey
1984	Wild Again	P. Day	1994	Concern	J. Bailey	2004	Ghostzapper	J. Castellano
1985	Proud Truth.	J. Velasquez	1995	Cigar	J. Bailey	2005	Saint Liam	J. Bailey
1986	Skywalker	L. Pincay Jr.	1996	Alphabet Soup	C. McCarron	2006	Invasor	F. Jara
1987	Ferdinand	W. Shoemaker	1997	Skip Away	M. Smith	2007	Curlin	R. Albarado
1988	Alysheba	C. McCarron	1998	Awesome Again	P. Day	2008	Raven's Pass	F. Dettori
1989	Sunday Silence	C. McCarron	1999	Cat Thief	P. Day	2009	Zenyatta	M. Smith
1990	Unbridled	P. Day	2000	Tiznow	C. McCarron	2010	Blame	G. Gomez
1991	Black Tie Affair	J. Bailey	2001	Tiznow	C. McCarron	2011	Drosselmeyer	M. Smith
1992	A.P. Indy	E. Delahoussaye	2002	Volponi	J. Santos	2012	Fort Larned	B. Hernandez
1993	Arcangues	J. Bailey	2003	Pleasantly Perfect	A. Solis	2013	Mucho Macho Man	G. Stevens

Juvenile
Distance: 1 mi, 1984-85, 1987; 1-1/16 mi, 1986 and since 1988.

Year	Horse	Jockey	Year	Horse	Jockey	Year	Horse	Jockey
1984	Chief's Crown	D. MacBeth	1994	Timber Country.	P. Day	2004	Wilko.	F. Dettori
1985	Tasso	L. Pincay Jr.	1995	Unbridled's Song	M. Smith	2005	Stevie Wonderboy	G. Gomez
1986	Capote	L. Pincay Jr.	1996	Boston Harbor	J. Bailey	2006	Street Sense	C. Borel
1987	Success Express	J. Santos	1997	Favorite Trick	P. Day	2007	War Pass	C. Velasquez
1988	Is It True	L. Pincay Jr.	1998	Answer Lively	J. Bailey	2008	Midshipman	G. Gomez
1989	Rhythm	C. Perret	1999	Anees	G. Stevens	2009	Vale of York	A. Ajtebi
1990	Fly So Free	J. Santos	2000	Macho Uno	J. Bailey	2010	Uncle Mo	J. Velazquez
1991	Arazi	P. Valenzuela	2001	Johannesburg.	M. Kinane	2011	Hansen	R. Dominguez
1992	Gilded Time	C. McCarron	2002	Vindication	M. Smith	2012	Shanghai Bobby	R. Napravnik
1993	Brocco	G. Stevens	2003	Action This Day	D. Flores	2013	New Year's Day	M. Garcia

Juvenile Fillies
Distance: 1 mi, 1984-85, 1987; 1-1/16 mi, 1986 and since 1988. Outstandingly won the 1984 race by disqualification.

Year	Horse	Jockey	Year	Horse	Jockey	Year	Horse	Jockey
1984	Outstandingly	W. Guerra	1994	Flanders	P. Day	2004	Sweet Catomine	C. Nakatani
1985	Twilight Ridge	J. Velasquez	1995	My Flag.	J. Bailey	2005	Folklore.	E. Prado
1986	Brave Raj	P. Valenzuela	1996	Storm Song	C. Perret	2006	Dreaming of Anna	R. Douglas
1987	Epitome	P. Day	1997	Countess Diana	S. Sellers	2007	Indian Blessing	G. Gomez
1988	Open Mind	A. Cordero Jr.	1998	Silverbulletday	G. Stevens	2008	Stardom Bound.	M. Smith
1989	Go for Wand	R. Romero	1999	Cash Run	J. Bailey	2009	She Be Wild	J. Leparoux
1990	Meadow Star	J. Santos	2000	Caressing	J. Velazquez	2010	Awesome Feather	J. Sanchez
1991	Pleasant Stage	E. Delahoussaye	2001	Tempera	D. Flores	2011	My Miss Aurelia	C. Nakatani
1992	Eliza	P. Valenzuela	2002	Storm Flag Flying	J. Velazquez	2012	Beholder.	G. Gomez
1993	Phone Chatter	L. Pincay Jr.	2003	Halfbridled	J. Krone	2013	Ria Antonia	J. Castellano

Sprint
Distance: 6 furlongs.

Year	Horse	Jockey	Year	Horse	Jockey	Year	Horse	Jockey
1984	Eillo	C. Perret	1994	Cherokee Run	M. Smith	2004	Speightstown	J. Velazquez
1985	Precisionist	C. McCarron	1995	Desert Stormer	K. Desormeaux	2005	Silver Train	E. Prado
1986	Smile	J. Vasquez	1996	Lit de Justice	C. Nakatani	2006	Thor's Echo	C. Nakatani
1987	Very Subtle	P. Valenzuela	1997	Elmhurst	C. Nakatani	2007	Midnight Lute	G. Gomez
1988	Gulch	A. Cordero Jr.	1998	Reraise	C. Nakatani	2008	Midnight Lute	G. Gomez
1989	Dancing Spree	A. Cordero Jr.	1999	Artax	J. Chaves	2009	Dancing in Silks	J. Rosario
1990	Safely Kept	C. Perret	2000	Kona Gold	A. Solis	2010	Big Drama	E. Coa
1991	Sheikh Albadou	P. Eddery	2001	Squirtle Squirt	J. Bailey	2011	Amazombie	M. Smith
1992	Thirty Slews	E. Delahoussaye	2002	Orientate	J. Bailey	2012	Trinniberg	W. Martinez
1993	Cardmania	E. Delahoussaye	2003	Cajun Beat	C. Velasquez	2013	Secret Circle	M. Garcia

Mile

Year	Horse	Jockey	Year	Horse	Jockey	Year	Horse	Jockey
1984	Royal Heroine	F. Toro	1994	Barathea	L. Dettori	2004	Singletary	D. Flores
1985	Cozzene	W. Guerra	1995	Ridgewood Pearl	J. Murtagh	2005	Artie Schiller	G. Gomez
1986	Last Tycoon	Y. St.-Martin	1996	Da Hoss	G. Stevens	2006	Miesque's Approval	E. Castro
1987	Miesque	F. Head	1997	Spinning World	C. Asmussan	2007	Kip Deville	C. Velasquez
1988	Miesque	F. Head	1998	Da Hoss	J. Velazquez	2008	Goldikova	O. Peslier
1989	Steinlen	J. Santos	1999	Silic	C. Nakatani	2009	Goldikova	O. Peslier
1990	Royal Academy	L. Piggott	2000	War Chant	G. Stevens	2010	Goldikova	O. Peslier
1991	Opening Verse	P. Valenzuela	2001	Val Royal	J. Valdivia Jr.	2011	Court Vision	R. Albarado
1992	Lure	M. Smith	2002	Domedriver	T. Thulliez	2012	Wise Dan	J. Velazquez
1993	Lure	M. Smith	2003	Six Perfections	J. Bailey	2013	Wise Dan	J. Lezcano

Filly and Mare Turf
Distance: 1-3/8 mi, 1999-2000, 2004, 2006-07; 1-1/4 mi, 2001-03, 2005, and since 2008.

Year	Horse	Jockey	Year	Horse	Jockey	Year	Horse	Jockey
1999	Soaring Softly	J. Bailey	2004	Ouija Board	K. Fallon	2009	Midday	T. Queally
2000	Perfect Sting	J. Bailey	2005	Intercontinental	R. Bejarano	2010	Shared Account	E. Prado
2001	Banks Hill	O. Peslier	2006	Ouija Board	F. Dettori	2011	Perfect Shirl	J. Velazquez
2002	Starine	J. Velazquez	2007	Lahudood	A. Garcia	2012	Zagora	J. Castellano
2003	Islington	K. Fallon	2008	Forever Together	J. Leparoux	2013	Dank	R. Moore

Distaff
Distance: 1-1/4 mi, 1984-87; 1-1/8 mi since 1988. Race known as Ladies' Classic, 2008-12.

Year	Horse	Jockey	Year	Horse	Jockey	Year	Horse	Jockey
1984	Princess Rooney	E. Delahoussaye	1994	One Dreamer	G. Stevens	2004	Ashado	J. Velazquez
1985	Life's Magic	A. Cordero Jr.	1995	Inside Information	M. Smith	2005	Pleasant Home	C. Velasquez
1986	Lady's Secret	P. Day	1996	Jewel Princess	C. Nakatani	2006	Round Pond	E. Prado
1987	Sacahuista	R. Romero	1997	Ajina	M. Smith	2007	Ginger Punch	R. Bejarano
1988	Personal Ensign	R. Romero	1998	Escena	G. Stevens	2008	Zenyatta	M. Smith
1989	Bayakoa	I. Pincay Jr.	1999	Beautiful Pleasure	J. Chaves	2009	Life Is Sweet	G. Gomez
1990	Bayakoa	L. Pincay Jr.	2000	Spain	V. Espinoza	2010	Unrivaled Belle	K. Desormeaux
1991	Dance Smartly	P. Day	2001	Unbridled Elaine	P. Day	2011	Royal Delta	J. Lezcano
1992	Paseana	C. McCarron	2002	Azeri	M. Smith	2012	Royal Delta	M. Smith
1993	Hollywood Wildcat	E. Delahoussaye	2003	Adoration	P. Valenzuela	2013	Beholder	G. Stevens

Turf
Distance: 1-1/2 mi.

Year	Horse	Jockey	Year	Horse	Jockey	Year	Horse	Jockey
1984	Lashkari	Y. St.-Martin	1994	Tikkanen	M. Smith	2004	Better Talk Now	R. Dominguez
1985	Pebbles	P. Eddery	1995	Northern Spur	C. McCarron	2005	Shirocco	C. Soumillon
1986	Manila	J. Santos	1996	Pilsudski	W. Swinburn	2006	Red Rocks	F. Dettori
1987	Theatrical	P. Day	1997	Chief Bearhart	J. Santos	2007	English Channel	J. Velasquez
1988	Great Communicator	R. Sibille	1998	Buck's Boy	S. Sellers	2008	Conduit	R. Moore
1989	Prized	E. Delahoussaye	1999	Daylami	L. Dettori	2009	Conduit	R. Moore
1990	In the Wings	G. Stevens	2000	Kalanisi	J. Murtagh	2010	Dangerous Midge	F. Dettori
1991	Miss Alleged	E. Legrix	2001	Fantastic Light	L. Dettori	2011	St Nicholas Abbey	J. O'Brien
1992	Fraise	P. Valenzuela	2002	High Chaparral	M. Kinane	2012	Little Mike	R. Dominguez
1993	Kotashaan	K. Desormeaux	2003	(tie) High Chaparral	M. Kinane	2013	Magician	R. Moore
				Johar	A. Solis			

Filly and Mare Sprint
Distance: 6 furlongs, 2007; 7 furlongs since 2008.

Year	Horse	Jockey	Year	Horse	Jockey	Year	Horse	Jockey
2007	Maryfield	E. Trujillo	2010	Dubai Majesty	J. Theriot	2012	Groupie Doll	R. Maragh
2008	Ventura	G. Gomez	2011	Musical Romance	J. Leyva	2013	Groupie Doll	R. Maragh
2009	Informed Decision	J. Leparoux						

Juvenile Turf
Distance: 1 mi.

Year	Horse	Jockey	Year	Horse	Jockey	Year	Horse	Jockey
2007	Nownownow	J. Leparoux	2010	Pluck	G. Gomez	2012	George Vancouver	R. Moore
2008	Donativum	F. Dettori	2011	Wrote	R. Moore	2013	Outstrip	M. Smith
2009	Pounced	F. Dettori						

Dirt Mile

Year	Horse	Jockey	Year	Horse	Jockey	Year	Horse	Jockey
2007	Corinthian	K. Desormeaux	2010	Dakota Phone	J. Rosario	2012	Tapizar	C. Nakatani
2008	Albertus Maximus	G. Gomez	2011	Caleb's Posse	R. Maragh	2013	Goldencents	R. Bejarano
2009	Furthest Land	J. Leparoux						

Turf Sprint
Distance: 6-1/2 furlongs, 2008-09, and since 2012; 5 furlongs, 2010-11.

Year	Horse	Jockey	Year	Horse	Jockey	Year	Horse	Jockey
2008	Desert Code	R. Migliore	2010	Chamberlain Bridge	J. Theriot	2012	Mizdirection	M. Smith
2009	California Flag	J. Talamo	2011	Regally Ready	C. Nakatani	2013	Mizdirection	M. Smith

Marathon
Distance: 1-1/2 mi., 2008; 1-3/4 mi. since 2009.

Year	Horse	Jockey	Year	Horse	Jockey	Year	Horse	Jockey
2008	Muhannak	P. Smullen	2010	Eldaafer	J. Velazquez	2012	Calidoscopio	A. Gryder
2009	Man of Iron	J. Murtagh	2011	Afleet Again	C. Velasquez	2013	London Bridge	M. Smith

Juvenile Fillies Turf
Distance: 1 mi.

Year	Horse	Jockey	Year	Horse	Jockey	Year	Horse	Jockey
2008	Maram	J. Lezcano	2010	More Than Real	G. Gomez	2012	Flotilla	C. Lemaire
2009	Tapitsfly	R. Albarado	2011	Stephanie's Kitten	J. Velazquez	2013	Chriselliam	R. Hughes

Eclipse Awards

The Eclipse Awards, honoring the Horse of the Year and other champions of the sport, began in 1971 and are sponsored by the *Daily Racing Form*, the National Thoroughbred Racing Association, and the National Turf Writers Assn. Prior to 1971, the *DRF* (1936-70) and the NTRA (1950-70) issued separate selections for Horse of the Year.

Eclipse Awards, 2012

Horse of the Year: Wise Dan
2-year-old male: Shanghai Bobby
2-year-old female: Beholder
3-year-old male: I'll Have Another
3-year-old female: Questing
Older male (4+ years old): Wise Dan

Older female (4+ years old): Royal Delta
Male sprinter: Trinniberg
Female sprinter: Groupie Doll
Male turf horse: Wise Dan
Female turf horse: Zagora

Steeplechase horse: Pierrot Lunaire
Trainer: Dale Romans
Jockey: Ramon Dominguez
Apprentice jockey: Jose Montano
Breeder: Darley
Owner: Godolphin Racing

Horse of the Year, 1936-2012

Year	Horse	Year	Horse	Year	Horse	Year	Horse
1936	Granville	1956	Swaps	1973	Secretariat	1993	Kotashaan
1937	War Admiral	1957	Bold Ruler (DRF); Dedicate (TRA)	1974	Forego	1994	Holy Bull
1938	Seabiscuit			1975	Forego	1995	Cigar
1939	Challedon	1958	Round Table	1976	Forego	1996	Cigar
1940	Challedon	1959	Sword Dancer	1977	Seattle Slew	1997	Favorite Trick
1941	Whirlaway	1960	Kelso	1978	Affirmed	1998	Skip Away
1942	Whirlaway	1961	Kelso	1979	Affirmed	1999	Charismatic
1943	Count Fleet	1962	Kelso	1980	Spectacular Bid	2000	Tiznow
1944	Twilight Tear	1963	Kelso	1981	John Henry	2001	Point Given
1945	Busher	1964	Kelso	1982	Conquistador Cielo	2002	Azeri
1946	Assault	1965	Roman Brother (DRF); Moccasin (TRA)	1983	All Along	2003	Mineshaft
1947	Armed			1984	John Henry	2004	Ghostzapper
1948	Citation	1966	Buckpasser	1985	Spend a Buck	2005	Saint Liam
1949	Capot	1967	Damascus	1986	Lady's Secret	2006	Invasor
1950	Hill Prince	1968	Dr. Fager	1987	Ferdinand	2007	Curlin
1951	Counterpoint	1969	Arts and Letters	1988	Alysheba	2008	Curlin
1952	One Count (DRF); Native Dancer (TRA)	1970	Fort Marcy (DRF); Personality (TRA)	1989	Sunday Silence	2009	Rachel Alexandra
				1990	Criminal Type	2010	Zenyatta
1953	Tom Fool	1971	Ack Ack	1991	Black Tie Affair	2011	Havre de Grace
1954	Native Dancer	1972	Secretariat	1992	A.P. Indy	2012	Wise Dan
1955	Nashua						

HARNESS RACING
Harness Horse of the Year, 1947-2012
Chosen by the U.S. Trotting Assn. and the U.S. Harness Writers Assn.

Year	Horse	Year	Horse	Year	Horse	Year	Horse
1947	Victory Song	1964	Bret Hanover	1981	Fan Hanover	1997	Malabar Man
1948	Rodney	1965	Bret Hanover	1982	Cam Fella	1998	Moni Maker
1949	Good Time	1966	Bret Hanover	1983	Cam Fella	1999	Moni Maker
1950	Proximity	1967	Nevele Pride	1984	Fancy Crown	2000	Gallo Blue Chip
1951	Pronto Don	1968	Nevele Pride	1985	Nihilator	2001	Bunny Lake
1952	Good Time	1969	Nevele Pride	1986	Forrest Skipper	2002	Real Desire
1953	Hi Lo's Forbes	1970	Fresh Yankee	1987	Mack Lobell	2003	No Pan Intended
1954	Stenographer	1971	Albatross	1988	Mack Lobell	2004	Rainbow Blue
1955	Scott Frost	1972	Albatross	1989	Matt's Scooter	2005	Rocknroll Hanover
1956	Scott Frost	1973	Sir Dalrae	1990	Beach Towel	2006	Glidemaster
1957	Torpid	1974	Delmonica Hanover	1991	Precious Bunny	2007	Donato Hanover
1958	Emily's Pride	1975	Savoir	1992	Artsplace	2008	Somebeachsomewhere
1959	Bye Bye Byrd	1976	Keystone Ore	1993	Staying Together	2009	Muscle Hill
1960	Adios Butler	1977	Green Speed	1994	Cam's Card Shark	2010	Rock N Roll Heaven
1961	Adios Butler	1978	Abercrombie	1995	CR Kay Suzie	2011	San Pail
1962	Su Mac Lad	1979	Niatross	1996	Continental Victory	2012	Chapter Seven
1963	Speedy Scot	1980	Niatross				

The Hambletonian (3-year-old trotters), 1965-2013

Year	Horse	Driver	Year	Horse	Driver
1965	Egyptian Candor	Del Cameron	1977	Green Speed	Bill Haughton
1966	Kerry Way	Frank Ervin	1978	Speedy Somolli	Howard Beissinger
1967	Speedy Streak	Del Cameron	1979	Legend Hanover	George Sholty
1968	Nevele Pride	Stanley Dancer	1980	Burgomeister	Bill Haughton
1969	Lindy's Pride	Howard Beissinger	1981	Shiaway St. Pat	Ray Remmen
1970	Timothy T	John Simpson Sr.	1982	Speed Bowl	Tommy Haughton
1971	Speedy Crown	Howard Beissinger	1983	Duenna	Stanley Dancer
1972	Super Bowl	Stanley Dancer	1984	Historic Freight	Ben Webster
1973	Flirth	Ralph Baldwin	1985	Prakas	Bill O'Donnell
1974	Christopher T	Bill Haughton	1986	Nuclear Kosmos	Ulf Thoresen
1975	Bonefish	Stanley Dancer	1987	Mack Lobell	John Campbell
1976	Steve Lobell	Bill Haughton	1988	Armbro Goal	John Campbell

Year	Horse	Driver	Year	Horse	Driver
1989	Park Avenue Joe	Ron Waples	2002	Chip Chip Hooray	Eric Ledford
1990	Harmonious	John Campbell	2003	Amigo Hall	Mike Lachance
1991	Giant Victory	Jack Moiseyev	2004	Windsong's Legacy	Trond Smedshammer
1992	Alf Palema	Mickey McNicholl	2005	Vivid Photo	Roger Hammer
1993	American Winner	Ron Pierce	2006	Glidemaster	John Campbell
1994	Victory Dream	Michel Lachance	2007	Donato Hanover	Ron Pierce
1995	Tagliabue	John Campbell	2008	Deweycheatumnhowe	Ray Schnittker
1996	Continental Victory	Michel Lachance	2009	Muscle Hill	Brian Sears
1997	Malabar Man	Malvern Burroughs	2010	Muscle Massive	Ron Pierce
1998	Muscles Yankee	John Campbell	2011	Broad Bahn	George Brennan
1999	Self Possessed	Mike Lachance	2012	Market Share	Tim Tetrick
2000	Yankee Paco	Trevor Ritchie	2013	Royalty For Life	Brian Sears
2001	Scarlet Knight	Stefan Melander			

BOWLING
Professional Bowlers Association (PBA)
PBA Tournament of Champions, 1965-2013

Year	Winner	Year	Winner	Year	Winner	Year	Winner
1965	Billy Hardwick	1977	Mike Berlin	1989	Del Ballard Jr.	2002	Jason Couch
1966	Wayne Zahn	1978	Earl Anthony	1990	Dave Ferraro	2003	Patrick Healey Jr.
1967	Jim Stefanich	1979	George Pappas	1991	David Ozio	2005	Steve Jaros
1968	Dave Davis	1980	Wayne Webb	1992	Marc McDowell	2006	Chris Barnes
1969	Jim Godman	1981	Steve Cook	1993	George Branham III	2007	Tommy Jones
1970	Don Johnson	1982	Mike Durbin	1994	Norm Duke	2008	Michael Haugen Jr.
1971	Johnny Petraglia	1983	Joe Berardi	1996	Dave D'Entremont	2009	Patrick Allen
1972	Mike Durbin	1984	Mike Durbin	1997	John Gant	2010	Kelly Kulick
1973	Jim Godman	1985	Mark Williams	1998	Bryan Goebel	2011	Mika Koivuniemi
1974	Earl Anthony	1986	Marshall Holman	1999	Jason Couch	2012	Sean Rash
1975	Dave Davis	1987	Pete Weber	2000	Jason Couch	2013	Pete Weber
1976	Marshall Holman	1988	Mark Williams				

Note: No tournament held in 2001 or 2004.

PBA Hall of Fame Performance Inductees

Bill Allen	Paul Colwell	Billy Hardwick	George Pappas	Brian Voss
Earl Anthony	Steve Cook	Marshall Holman	Randy Pedersen	Wayne Webb
Mike Aulby	Jason Couch	Tommy Hudson	Johnny Petraglia	Dick Weber
Del Ballard Jr.	Dave Davis	Dave Husted	Dick Ritger	Pete Weber
Joe Berardi	Gary Dickinson	Don Johnson	Mark Roth	Billy Welu
Ray Bluth	Norm Duke	Doug Kent	Carmen Salvino	Mark Williams
Parker Bohn III	Mike Durbin	Larry Laub	Harry Smith	Walter Ray Williams Jr.
Roy Buckley	Buzz Fazio	Amleto Monacelli	Dave Soutar	Danny Wiseman
Nelson Burton Jr.	Dave Ferraro	David Ozio	Jim Stefanich	Wayne Zahn
Don Carter	Jim Godman			

PBA Leading Money Winners, 1962-2013
Total winnings from tournaments only. After 2000, year shown is year the PBA season ended.

Year	Bowler	Amount	Year	Bowler	Amount	Year	Bowler	Amount
1962	Don Carter	$49,972	1979	Mark Roth	$124,517	1996	Walter Ray Williams Jr.	$241,330
1963	Dick Weber	46,333	1980	Wayne Webb	116,700	1997	Walter Ray Williams Jr.	240,544
1964	Bob Strampe	33,592	1981	Earl Anthony	164,735	1998	Walter Ray Williams Jr.	238,225
1965	Dick Weber	47,674	1982	Earl Anthony	134,760	1999	Parker Bohn III	240,912
1966	Wayne Zahn	54,720	1983	Earl Anthony	135,605	2000	Norm Duke	143,325
1967	Dave Davis	54,165	1984	Mark Roth	158,712	2002	Parker Bohn III	245,200
1968	Jim Stefanich	67,377	1985	Mike Aulby	201,200	2003	Walter Ray Williams Jr.	419,700
1969	Billy Hardwick	64,160	1986	Walter Ray Williams Jr.	145,550	2004	Mika Koivuniemi	238,590
1970	Mike McGrath	52,049	1987	Pete Weber	175,491	2005	Patrick Allen	350,740
1971	Johnny Petraglia	85,065	1988	Brian Voss	225,485	2006	Tommy Jones	301,700
1972	Don Johnson	56,648	1989	Mike Aulby	298,237	2007	Doug Kent	200,530
1973	Don McCune	69,000	1990	Amleto Monacelli	204,775	2008	Norm Duke	176,855
1974	Earl Anthony	99,585	1991	David Ozio	225,585	2009	Norm Duke	199,130
1975	Earl Anthony	107,585	1992	Marc McDowell	174,215	2010	Walter Ray Williams Jr.	152,670
1976	Earl Anthony	110,833	1993	Walter Ray Williams Jr.	296,370	2011	Mika Koivuniemi	333,040
1977	Mark Roth	105,583	1994	Norm Duke	273,753	2012	Sean Rash	140,250
1978	Mark Roth	134,500	1995	Mike Aulby	219,792	2013	Jason Belmonte	169,386

Leading PBA Averages by Year, 1962-2013

Year	Bowler	Average	Year	Bowler	Average	Year	Bowler	Average
1962	Don Carter	212.84	1979	Mark Roth	221.66	1996	Walter Ray Williams Jr.	225.37
1963	Billy Hardwick	210.34	1980	Earl Anthony	218.53	1997	Walter Ray Williams Jr.	222.00
1964	Ray Bluth	210.51	1981	Mark Roth	216.69	1998	Walter Ray Williams Jr.	226.13
1965	Dick Weber	211.89	1982	Marshall Holman	212.84	1999	Parker Bohn III	228.04
1966	Wayne Zahn	208.66	1983	Earl Anthony	216.64	2000	Chris Barnes	220.93
1967	Wayne Zahn	212.34	1984	Marshall Holman	213.91	2002	Parker Bohn III	221.54
1968	Jim Stefanich	211.89	1985	Mark Baker	213.71	2003	Walter Ray Williams Jr.	224.94
1969	Bill Hardwick	212.95	1986	John Gant	214.37	2004	Mika Koivuniemi	222.73
1970	Nelson Burton Jr.	214.90	1987	Marshall Holman	216.80	2005	Walter Ray Williams Jr.	227.07
1971	Don Johnson	213.97	1988	Mark Roth	218.03	2006	Norm Duke	224.29
1972	Don Johnson	215.29	1989	Pete Weber	215.43	2007	Norm Duke	228.47
1973	Earl Anthony	215.79	1990	Amleto Monacelli	218.15	2008	Walter Ray Williams Jr.	228.34
1974	Earl Anthony	219.39	1991	Norm Duke	218.20	2009	Wes Malott	222.98
1975	Earl Anthony	219.06	1992	Dave Ferraro	219.70	2010	Walter Ray Williams Jr.	222.92
1976	Mark Roth	215.97	1993	Walter Ray Williams Jr.	222.98	2011	Mika Koivuniemi	222.50
1977	Mark Roth	218.17	1994	Norm Duke	222.83	2012	Sean Rash	228.13
1978	Mark Roth	219.83	1995	Mike Aulby	225.49	2013	Wes Malott	229.50

United States Bowling Congress (USBC)

Formed Jan. 1, 2005, from a merger of the American Bowling Congress (ABC), Women's International Bowling Congress, the Young American Bowling Alliance, and USA Bowling. Before 2006, certified games and champions are for ABC only.

Men's Career 300 Games
(as of July 31, 2013)

Rank	Bowler, hometown	Games
1.	Andrew Neuer, Lewisburg, PA	149
2.	Fero Williams, Falkfield, OH	145
3.	Jim Hosier, Wayne, NJ	137
4.	Gordon Childers, Benton, AR	133
5.	Chris Hayward, Toledo, OH	123
6.	Jim Tomek, Camp Hill, PA.	121
7.	Stephen Aiello, North Haledon, NJ	120
8.	Frank Massengale Jr., Hixson, TN	114
9.	John Delp III, Sinking Spring, PA	113
10.	Tam Wasson, Murphy, TX.	112

Women's Career 300 Games
(as of July 31, 2013)

Rank	Bowler, hometown	Games
1.	Altramese Webb, Detroit, MI.	43
2.	Teri Haefke, Austintown, OH.	42
3.	Tammy Jones, Decatur, IL	39
4.	Jodi Musto, Schenectady, NY.	38
5.	Shannon Pluhowsky, Dayton, OH.	37
6.	Tish Johnson, Colorado Springs, CO	36
7.	Jodi Woessner, Oregon, OH.	34
8.	Alisia Kellow, Louisville, KY	31
	Marianne DiRupo, Succasunna, NJ	31
	Barb Staub, Cedar Rapids, IA	31

USBC Masters Tournament Champions, 1980-2013

Year	Winner, hometown	Year	Winner, hometown	Year	Winner, hometown
1980	Neil Burton, St. Louis, MO	1992	Ken Johnson, N. Richmond Hills, TX	2004	Walter Ray Williams Jr., FL (Jan.);
1981	Randy Lightfoot, St. Charles, MO	1993	Norm Duke, Oklahoma City, OK		Danny Wiseman, MD (Oct.)
1982	Joe Berardi, Brooklyn, NY	1994	Steve Fehr, Cincinnati, OH	2005	Mike Scroggins, Amarillo, TX
1983	Mike Lastowski, Havre de Grace, MD	1995	Mike Aulby, Indianapolis, IN	2006	Doug Kent, Newark, NY
1984	Earl Anthony, Dublin, CA	1996	Ernie Schlegel, Vancouver, WA	2007	Sean Rash, Wichita, KS
1985	Steve Wunderlich, St. Louis, MO	1997	Jason Queen, Decatur, IL	2008	No tournament
1986	Mark Fahy, Chicago, IL	1998	Mike Aulby, Indianapolis, IN	2009	John Nolen, Waterford, MI
1987	Rick Steelsmith, Wichita, KS	1999	Brian Boghosian, Middletown, CT	2010	Walter Ray Williams Jr., Ocala, FL
1988	Del Ballard Jr., Richardson, TX	2000	Mika Koivuniemi, Finland	2011	Tom Hess, Urbandale, IA
1989	Mike Aulby, Indianapolis, IN	2001	Parker Bohn III, Jackson, NJ	2012	Mike Fagan, Dallas, TX
1990	Chris Warren, Dallas, TX	2002	Brett Wolfe, Reno, NV	2013	Jason Belmonte, Australia
1991	Doug Kent, Canandaigua, NY	2003	Bryon Smith, Roseburg, OR		

USBC Open Champions, 2013

Regular Singles: Zeke Bayt, Westerville, OH
Regular Doubles: Brian Burkhardt, St. Louis, MO, and Rick Gatlin, Eureka, MO

Regular All-Events: John Szczerbinski, North Tonawanda, NY
Regular Team: Lodge Lanes Too, Orlando, FL
Team All-Events: Junior Team USA Support 1, Mansfield, TX

USBC Queens and Women's Champions, 2012

According to the new format introduced in 2010, USBC women's champions are selected from an all-handicap format with three divisions: Diamond (180 and higher with handicap based on 100% of 220), Ruby (150-179 with handicap based on 100% of 180), and Sapphire (149 and below with handicap based on 100% of 150). Overall champions (scratch) also are crowned.

USBC Queens: Diana Zavjalova, Latvia
Scratch Singles: Jeanette Adams, Rancho Cordova, CA
Scratch Doubles: Kristie Leong, Daly City, CA, and Kaleena Henning, Lincoln, NE
Scratch All-Events: Rocio Restrepo, Canton, OH
Scratch Team: Eagle's Edge Pro Shop, Prospect Heights, IL

Diamond Singles: Christine Gill, Lakewood, CO
Diamond Doubles: Kristie Leong, Daly City, CA, and Kaleena Henning, Lincoln, NE
Diamond All-Events: Christine Gill, Lakewood, CO
Diamond Team: Fox Bowl, Bartlett, IL

World Chess Champions, 1886-2012

Source: U.S. Chess Federation, International Chess Federation (FIDE)
Official world champions since the title was first used, as of Nov. 1, 2013.

Years	Champion, country	Years	Champion, country
1886-94	Wilhelm Steinitz, Austria	1972-75	Bobby Fischer, U.S.[2]
1894-1921	Emanuel Lasker, Germany	1975-85	Anatoly Karpov, USSR
1921-27	Jose R. Capablanca, Cuba	1985-2000	Garry Kasparov, USSR/Russia[3]
1927-35	Alexander Alekhine, France	1993-99	Anatoly Karpov, Russia (FIDE)[3]
1935-37	Max Euwe, Netherlands	1999-2000	Alexander Khalifman, Russia (FIDE)
1937-46	Alexander Alekhine, France[1]	2000-02	Viswanathan Anand, India (FIDE)
1948-57	Mikhail Botvinnik, USSR	2000-06	Vladimir Kramnik, Russia (classical)[4,5]
1957-58	Vassily Smyslov, USSR	2002-04	Ruslan Ponomariov, Ukraine (FIDE)
1958-59	Mikhail Botvinnik, USSR	2004-05	Rustam Kasimdzhanov, Uzbekistan (FIDE)
1960-61	Mikhail Tal, USSR	2005-06	Veselin Topalov, Bulgaria (FIDE)
1961-63	Mikhail Botvinnik, USSR	2006-07	Vladimir Kramnik, Russia[5]
1963-69	Tigran Petrosian, USSR	2007-	Viswanathan Anand, India
1969-72	Boris Spassky, USSR		

(1) After Alekhine died in 1946, the title was vacant until 1948, when Botvinnik won the first world championship event sanctioned by FIDE. (2) Defaulted championship after refusing to accept FIDE rules for a championship match, Apr. 1975. (3) Garry Kasparov (USSR/Russia) broke with FIDE, Feb. 26, 1993. FIDE stripped Kasparov of his FIDE title Mar. 23. Kasparov defeated Nigel Short (UK) in a world championship match played Sept.-Oct. 1993 under the auspices of the Professional Chess Association (PCA), a new organization the two had founded. FIDE held a championship match between Anatoly Karpov (Russia) and Jan Timman (Netherlands), which Karpov won in Nov. 1993. The PCA folded in 1995, but Kasparov was still considered the "classical" world champion. (4) In Nov. 2000, Kramnik defeated Garry Kasparov (Russia) for the classical world championship title in London. (5) Kramnik, the classical world champion since 2000, and Veselin Topalov, FIDE champion since 2005, met at a world chess championship match in Elista, Russia, to compete for a unified championship, which Kramnik won Oct. 13, 2006.

U.S. and World Figure Skating Champions, 1952-2013

U.S. Champions			World Champions	
Men, country	**Women, country**	**Year**	**Men, country**	**Women, country**
Dick Button	Tenley Albright	1952	Dick Button, U.S.	Jacqueline du Bief, France
Hayes Jenkins	Tenley Albright	1953	Hayes Jenkins, U.S.	Tenley Albright, U.S.
Hayes Jenkins	Tenley Albright	1954	Hayes Jenkins, U.S.	Gundi Busch, W. Germany
Hayes Jenkins	Tenley Albright	1955	Hayes Jenkins, U.S.	Tenley Albright, U.S.
Hayes Jenkins	Tenley Albright	1956	Hayes Jenkins, U.S.	Carol Heiss, U.S.
Dave Jenkins	Carol Heiss	1957	Dave Jenkins, U.S.	Carol Heiss, U.S.
Dave Jenkins	Carol Heiss	1958	Dave Jenkins, U.S.	Carol Heiss, U.S.
Dave Jenkins	Carol Heiss	1959	Dave Jenkins, U.S.	Carol Heiss, U.S.
Dave Jenkins	Carol Heiss	1960	Alain Giletti, France	Carol Heiss, U.S.
Bradley Lord	Laurence Owen	1961	Competition canceled[1]	Competition canceled[1]
Monty Hoyt	Barbara Roles Pursley	1962	Don Jackson, Canada	Sjoukje Dijkstra, Netherlands
Tommy Litz	Lorraine Hanlon	1963	Don McPherson, Canada	Sjoukje Dijkstra, Netherlands
Scott Allen	Peggy Fleming	1964	Manfred Schnelldorfer, W. Germany	Sjoukje Dijkstra, Netherlands
Gary Visconti	Peggy Fleming	1965	Alain Calmat, France	Petra Burka, Canada
Scott Allen	Peggy Fleming	1966	Emmerich Danzer, Austria	Peggy Fleming, U.S.
Gary Visconti	Peggy Fleming	1967	Emmerich Danzer, Austria	Peggy Fleming, U.S.
Tim Wood	Peggy Fleming	1968	Emmerich Danzer, Austria	Peggy Fleming, U.S.
Tim Wood	Janet Lynn	1969	Tim Wood, U.S.	Gabriele Seyfert, E. Germany
Tim Wood	Janet Lynn	1970	Tim Wood, U.S.	Gabriele Seyfert, E. Germany
John Misha Petkevich	Janet Lynn	1971	Ondrej Nepela, Czechoslovakia	Beatrix Schuba, Austria
Ken Shelley	Janet Lynn	1972	Ondrej Nepela, Czechoslovakia	Beatrix Schuba, Austria
Gordon McKellen Jr.	Janet Lynn	1973	Ondrej Nepela, Czechoslovakia	Karen Magnussen, Canada
Gordon McKellen Jr.	Dorothy Hamill	1974	Jan Hoffmann, E. Germany	Christine Errath, E. Germany
Gordon McKellen Jr.	Dorothy Hamill	1975	Sergei Volkov, USSR	Dianne de Leeuw, Netherlands
Terry Kubicka	Dorothy Hamill	1976	John Curry, UK	Dorothy Hamill, U.S.
Charles Tickner	Linda Fratianne	1977	Vladimir Kovalev, USSR	Linda Fratianne, U.S.
Charles Tickner	Linda Fratianne	1978	Charles Tickner, U.S.	Anett Poetzsch, E. Germany
Charles Tickner	Linda Fratianne	1979	Vladimir Kovalev, USSR	Linda Fratianne, U.S.
Charles Tickner	Linda Fratianne	1980	Jan Hoffmann, E. Germany	Anett Poetzsch, E. Germany
Scott Hamilton	Elaine Zayak	1981	Scott Hamilton, U.S.	Denise Biellmann, Switzerland
Scott Hamilton	Rosalynn Sumners	1982	Scott Hamilton, U.S.	Elaine Zayak, U.S.
Scott Hamilton	Rosalynn Sumners	1983	Scott Hamilton, U.S.	Rosalynn Sumners, U.S.
Scott Hamilton	Rosalynn Sumners	1984	Scott Hamilton, U.S.	Katarina Witt, E. Germany
Brian Boitano	Tiffany Chin	1985	Aleksandr Fadeev, USSR	Katarina Witt, E. Germany
Brian Boitano	Debi Thomas	1986	Brian Boitano, U.S.	Debi Thomas, U.S.
Brian Boitano	Jill Trenary	1987	Brian Orser, Canada	Katarina Witt, E. Germany
Brian Boitano	Debi Thomas	1988	Brian Boitano, U.S.	Katarina Witt, E. Germany
Christopher Bowman	Jill Trenary	1989	Kurt Browning, Canada	Midori Ito, Japan
Todd Eldredge	Jill Trenary	1990	Kurt Browning, Canada	Jill Trenary, U.S.
Todd Eldredge	Tonya Harding	1991	Kurt Browning, Canada	Kristi Yamaguchi, U.S.
Christopher Bowman	Kristi Yamaguchi	1992	Viktor Petrenko, Ukraine	Kristi Yamaguchi, U.S.
Scott Davis	Nancy Kerrigan	1993	Kurt Browning, Canada	Oksana Baiul, Ukraine
Scott Davis	Vacant[2]	1994	Elvis Stojko, Canada	Yuka Sato, Japan
Todd Eldredge	Nicole Bobek	1995	Elvis Stojko, Canada	Chen Lu, China
Rudy Galindo	Michelle Kwan	1996	Todd Eldredge, U.S.	Michelle Kwan, U.S.
Todd Eldredge	Tara Lipinski	1997	Elvis Stojko, Canada	Tara Lipinski, U.S.
Todd Eldredge	Michelle Kwan	1998	Alexei Yagudin, Russia	Michelle Kwan, U.S.
Michael Weiss	Michelle Kwan	1999	Alexei Yagudin, Russia	Maria Butyrskaya, Russia
Michael Weiss	Michelle Kwan	2000	Alexei Yagudin, Russia	Michelle Kwan, U.S.
Timothy Goebel	Michelle Kwan	2001	Yevgeny Plushenko, Russia	Michelle Kwan, U.S.
Todd Eldredge	Michelle Kwan	2002	Alexei Yagudin, Russia	Irina Slutskaya, Russia
Michael Weiss	Michelle Kwan	2003	Yevgeny Plushenko, Russia	Michelle Kwan, U.S.
Johnny Weir	Michelle Kwan	2004	Yevgeny Plushenko, Russia	Shizuka Arakawa, Japan
Johnny Weir	Michelle Kwan	2005	Stephane Lambiel, Switzerland	Irina Slutskaya, Russia
Johnny Weir	Sasha Cohen	2006	Stephane Lambiel, Switzerland	Kimmie Meissner, U.S.
Evan Lysacek	Kimmie Meissner	2007	Brian Joubert, France	Miki Ando, Japan
Evan Lysacek	Mirai Nagasu	2008	Jeffrey Buttle, Canada	Mao Asada, Japan
Jeremy Abbott	Alissa Czisny	2009	Evan Lysacek, U.S.	Yuna Kim, South Korea
Jeremy Abbott	Rachael Flatt	2010	Daisuke Takahashi, Japan	Mao Asada, Japan
Ryan Bradley	Alissa Czisny	2011	Patrick Chan, Canada	Miki Ando, Japan
Jeremy Abbott	Ashley Wagner	2012	Patrick Chan, Canada	Carolina Kostner, Italy
Max Aaron	Ashley Wagner	2013	Patrick Chan, Canada	Yuna Kim, South Korea

(1) Competition canceled after 18-member U.S. team died in plane crash en route. (2) Tonya Harding was stripped of the title for her involvement in an attack on rival Nancy Kerrigan.

Alpine Skiing Men's World Cup Champions, 1967-2013

Year	Champion, country	Year	Champion, country	Year	Champion, country
1967	Jean Claude Killy, France	1983	Phil Mahre, U.S.	1999	Lasse Kjus, Norway
1968	Jean Claude Killy, France	1984	Pirmin Zurbriggen, Switzerland	2000	Hermann Maier, Austria
1969	Karl Schranz, Austria	1985	Marc Girardelli, Luxembourg	2001	Hermann Maier, Austria
1970	Karl Schranz, Austria	1986	Marc Girardelli, Luxembourg	2002	Stephan Eberharter, Austria
1971	Gustavo Thoeni, Italy	1987	Pirmin Zurbriggen, Switzerland	2003	Stephan Eberharter, Austria
1972	Gustavo Thoeni, Italy	1988	Pirmin Zurbriggen, Switzerland	2004	Hermann Maier, Austria
1973	Gustavo Thoeni, Italy	1989	Marc Girardelli, Luxembourg	2005	Bode Miller, U.S.
1974	Piero Gros, Italy	1990	Pirmin Zurbriggen, Switzerland	2006	Benjamin Raich, Austria
1975	Gustavo Thoeni, Italy	1991	Marc Girardelli, Luxembourg	2007	Aksel Lund Svindal, Norway
1976	Ingemar Stenmark, Sweden	1992	Paul Accola, Switzerland	2008	Bode Miller, U.S.
1977	Ingemar Stenmark, Sweden	1993	Marc Girardelli, Luxembourg	2009	Aksel Lund Svindal, Norway
1978	Ingemar Stenmark, Sweden	1994	Kjetil Andre Aamodt, Norway	2010	Carlo Janka, Switzerland
1979	Peter Luescher, Switzerland	1995	Alberto Tomba, Italy	2011	Ivica Kostelic, Croatia
1980	Andreas Wenzel, Liechtenstein	1996	Lasse Kjus, Norway	2012	Marcel Hirscher, Austria
1981	Phil Mahre, U.S.	1997	Luc Alphand, France	2013	Marcel Hirscher, Austria
1982	Phil Mahre, U.S.	1998	Hermann Maier, Austria		

Alpine Skiing Women's World Cup Champions, 1967-2013

Year	Champion, country	Year	Champion, country	Year	Champion, country
1967	Nancy Greene, Canada	1983	Tamara McKinney, U.S.	1999	Alexandra Meissnitzer, Austria
1968	Nancy Greene, Canada	1984	Erika Hess, Switzerland	2000	Renate Goetschl, Austria
1969	Gertrud Gabl, Austria	1985	Michela Figini, Switzerland	2001	Janica Kostelic, Croatia
1970	Michele Jacot, France	1986	Maria Walliser, Switzerland	2002	Michaela Dorfmeister, Austria
1971	Annemarie Proell, Austria	1987	Maria Walliser, Switzerland	2003	Janica Kostelic, Croatia
1972	Annemarie Proell, Austria	1988	Michela Figini, Switzerland	2004	Anja Paerson, Sweden
1973	Annemarie Proell, Austria	1989	Vreni Schneider, Switzerland	2005	Anja Paerson, Sweden
1974	Annemarie Proell, Austria	1990	Petra Kronberger, Austria	2006	Janica Kostelic, Croatia
1975	Annemarie Proell, Austria	1991	Petra Kronberger, Austria	2007	Nicole Hosp, Austria
1976	Rose Mittermaier, W. Germany	1992	Petra Kronberger, Austria	2008	Lindsey Vonn, U.S.
1977	Lise-Marie Morerod, Switzerland	1993	Anita Wachter, Austria	2009	Lindsey Vonn, U.S.
1978	Hanni Wenzel, Liechtenstein	1994	Vreni Schneider, Switzerland	2010	Lindsey Vonn, U.S.
1979	Annemarie Proell Moser, Austria	1995	Vreni Schneider, Switzerland	2011	Maria Höfl-Riesch, Germany
1980	Hanni Wenzel, Liechtenstein	1996	Katja Seizinger, Germany	2012	Lindsey Vonn, U.S.
1981	Marie-Theres Nadig, Switzerland	1997	Pernilla Wiberg, Sweden	2013	Tina Maze, Slovenia
1982	Erika Hess, Switzerland	1998	Katja Seizinger, Germany		

Tour de France, 2013

The UK's Chris Froome July 21, 2013, became the first African-born rider ever to win the Tour de France in the 100th edition of cycling's premier race. Froome, who was born in Kenya, had placed second to Bradley Wiggins in the 2012 Tour. The first stage of the 2,115-mi (3,404-km) Tour de France began June 29 in Porto-Vecchio on the island of Corsica. The final and 21st stage concluded on the streets of Paris, where Froome claimed victory in 83:56.40, followed by Colombia's Nairo Quintana, 4:20 behind, and Spain's Joaquín Rodríguez, 5:04 behind. Quintana won the polka-dot and white jerseys, as the best climber and best rider under age 25 in the Tour de France. Slovakian Peter Sagan won the green jersey as the points leader.

Cycling continued to be plagued with high-profile doping scandals. Lance Armstrong, a seven-time winner of the Tour de France, was stripped of his Tour titles in Oct. 2012. In Jan. 2013, Armstrong publicly admitted to doping for the first time. The 2010 Tour champion, Alberto Contador of Spain, returned to the Tour for the first time following a two-year doping sanction after the Court of Arbitration for Sport found him guilty of doping Feb. 6, 2012, and stripped him of his 2010 Tour win. He placed fourth in the 2013 Tour.

The Tour de France is scheduled to be held July 5-27, 2014. Its 2,272-mi (3,656-km) route will take cyclists from Leeds, England, UK, to Paris in 21 stages (9 flat, 5 hill, 6 mountain, 1 individual time trial).

Tour de France Winners, 1903-2013

The Tour de France was first held in 1903. Sixty cyclists began the 1,509-mi (2,428-km) race, at Montgeron, a suburb of Paris, and 21 cyclists finished the six-stage race 17 days later in Paris.

(Not held, 1915-18; 1940-46.)

Year	Winner, country	Year	Winner, country	Year	Winner, country
1903	Maurice Garin, France	1948	Gino Bartali, Italy	1981	Bernard Hinault, France
1904	Henri Cornet, France	1949	Fausto Coppi, Italy	1982	Bernard Hinault, France
1905	Louis Trousselier, France	1950	Ferdi Kübler, Switzerland	1983	Laurent Fignon, France
1906	René Pottier, France	1951	Hugo Koblet, Switzerland	1984	Laurent Fignon, France
1907	Lucien Petit-Breton, France	1952	Fausto Coppi, Italy	1985	Bernard Hinault, France
1908	Lucien Petit-Breton, France	1953	Louison Bobet, France	1986	Greg LeMond, U.S.
1909	François Faber, Luxembourg	1954	Louison Bobet, France	1987	Stephen Roche, Ireland
1910	Octave Lapize, France	1955	Louison Bobet, France	1988	Pedro Delgado, Spain
1911	Gustave Garrigou, France	1956	Roger Walkowiak, France	1989	Greg LeMond, U.S.
1912	Odile Defraye, Belgium	1957	Jacques Anquetil, France	1990	Greg LeMond, U.S.
1913	Philippe Thys, Belgium	1958	Charly Gaul, Luxembourg	1991	Miguel Indurain, Spain
1914	Philippe Thys, Belgium	1959	Federico Bahamontes, Spain	1992	Miguel Indurain, Spain
1919	Firmin Lambot, Belgium	1960	Gastone Nencini, Italy	1993	Miguel Indurain, Spain
1920	Philippe Thys, Belgium	1961	Jacques Anquetil, France	1994	Miguel Indurain, Spain
1921	Léon Scieur, Belgium	1962	Jacques Anquetil, France	1995	Miguel Indurain, Spain
1922	Firmin Lambot, Belgium	1963	Jacques Anquetil, France	1996	Bjarne Riis, Denmark
1923	Henri Pélissier, France	1964	Jacques Anquetil, France	1997	Jan Ullrich, Germany
1924	Ottavio Bottecchia, Italy	1965	Felice Gimondi, Italy	1998	Marco Pantani, Italy
1925	Ottavio Bottecchia, Italy	1966	Lucien Aimar, France	1999	Vacant[1]
1926	Lucien Buysse, Belgium	1967	Roger Pingeon, France	2000	Vacant[1]
1927	Nicolas Frantz, Luxembourg	1968	Jan Janssen, Netherlands	2001	Vacant[1]
1928	Nicolas Frantz, Luxembourg	1969	Eddy Merckx, Belgium	2002	Vacant[1]
1929	Maurice Dewaele, Belgium	1970	Eddy Merckx, Belgium	2003	Vacant[1]
1930	André Leducq, France	1971	Eddy Merckx, Belgium	2004	Vacant[1]
1931	Antonin Magne, France	1972	Eddy Merckx, Belgium	2005	Vacant[1]
1932	André Leducq, France	1973	Luis Ocana, Spain	2006	Óscar Pereiro, Spain[2]
1933	Georges Speicher, France	1974	Eddy Merckx, Belgium	2007	Alberto Contador, Spain
1934	Antonin Magne, France	1975	Bernard Thévenet, France	2008	Carlos Sastre, Spain
1935	Romain Maes, Belgium	1976	Lucien Van Impe, Belgium	2009	Alberto Contador, Spain
1936	Sylvère Maes, Belgium	1977	Bernard Thévenet, France	2010	Andy Schleck, Luxembourg[3]
1937	Roger Lapépie, France	1978	Bernard Hinault, France	2011	Cadel Evans, Australia
1938	Gino Bartali, Italy	1979	Bernard Hinault, France	2012	Bradley LeMond, UK
1939	Sylvère Maes, Belgium	1980	Joop Zoetemelk, Netherlands	2013	Chris Froome, UK
1947	Jean Robic, France				

(1) Lance Armstrong, U.S., was stripped of his seven Tour titles Oct. 22, 2012, in accordance with World Anti-Doping Code; Armstrong had dropped his fight against doping charges Aug. 23, 2012. (2) Floyd Landis, U.S., was stripped of the 2006 title, Sept. 20, 2007, for doping. Landis lost a final appeal of the ruling June 30, 2008. (3) Alberto Contador, Spain, was stripped of the 2010 title, Feb. 6, 2012, for doping.

World Swimming Records

Long course (50 m), as of Oct. 2013. All times in minutes:seconds.

Men's Records

Freestyle

Distance	Record	Holder	Nationality	Location	Date
50 meters	0:20.91	César Cielo Filho	Brazil	São Paulo, Brazil	Dec. 18, 2009
100 meters	0:46.91	César Cielo Filho	Brazil	Rome, Italy	July 30, 2009
200 meters	1:42.00	Paul Biedermann	Germany	Rome, Italy	July 28, 2009
400 meters	3:40.07	Paul Biedermann	Germany	Rome, Italy	July 26, 2009
800 meters	7:32.12	Zhang Lin	China	Rome, Italy	July 29, 2009
1,500 meters	14:31.02	Yang Sun	China	London, England, UK	Aug. 4, 2012

Backstroke

Distance	Record	Holder	Nationality	Location	Date
50 meters	0:24.04	Liam Tancock	UK	Rome, Italy	Aug. 2, 2009
100 meters	0:51.94	Aaron Peirsol	U.S.	Indianapolis, IN	July 8, 2009
200 meters	1:51.92	Aaron Peirsol	U.S.	Rome, Italy	July 31, 2009

Breaststroke

Distance	Record	Holder	Nationality	Location	Date
50 meters	0:26.67	Cameron van der Burgh	South Africa	Rome, Italy	July 29, 2009
100 meters	0:58.46	Cameron van der Burgh	South Africa	London, England, UK	July 29, 2012
200 meters	2:07.01	Akihiro Yamaguchi	Japan	Gifu, Japan	Sept. 15, 2012

Butterfly

Distance	Record	Holder	Nationality	Location	Date
50 meters	0:22.43	Rafael Muñoz	Spain	Malaga, Spain	Apr. 5, 2009
100 meters	0:49.82	Michael Phelps	U.S.	Rome, Italy	Aug. 1, 2009
200 meters	1:51.51	Michael Phelps	U.S.	Rome, Italy	July 29, 2009

Individual medley

Distance	Record	Holder	Nationality	Location	Date
200 meters	1:54.00	Ryan Lochte	U.S.	Shanghai, China	July 28, 2011
400 meters	4:03.84	Michael Phelps	U.S.	Beijing, China	Aug. 10, 2008

Freestyle relay

Distance	Record	Holder	Nationality	Location	Date
400 m (4×100)	3:08.24	Phelps, Weber-Gale, Jones, Lezak	U.S.	Beijing, China	Aug. 11, 2008
800 m (4×200)	6:58.55	Phelps, Berens, Walters, Lochte	U.S.	Rome, Italy	July 31, 2009

Medley relay

Distance	Record	Holder	Nationality	Location	Date
400 m (4×100)	3:27.28	Peirsol, Shanteau, Phelps, Walters	U.S.	Rome, Italy	Aug. 2, 2009

Women's Records

Freestyle

Distance	Record	Holder	Nationality	Location	Date
50 meters	0:23.73	Britta Steffen	Germany	Rome, Italy	Aug. 2, 2009
100 meters	0:52.07	Britta Steffen	Germany	Rome, Italy	July 31, 2009
200 meters	1:52.98	Federica Pellegrini	Italy	Rome, Italy	July 29, 2009
400 meters	3:59.15	Federica Pellegrini	Italy	Rome, Italy	July 26, 2009
800 meters	8:13.86	Katie Ledecky	U.S.	Barcelona, Spain	Aug. 3, 2013
1,500 meters	15:36.53	Katie Ledecky	U.S.	Barcelona, Spain	July 30, 2013

Backstroke

Distance	Record	Holder	Nationality	Location	Date
50 meters	0:27.06	Zhao Jing	China	Rome, Italy	July 30, 2009
100 meters	0:58.12	Gemma Spofforth	UK	Rome, Italy	July 28, 2009
200 meters	2:04.06	Missy Franklin	U.S.	London, England, UK	Aug. 3, 2012

Breaststroke

Distance	Record	Holder	Nationality	Location	Date
50 meters	0:29.48	Ruta Meilutyte	Lithuania	Barcelona, Spain	Aug. 3, 2013
100 meters	1:04.35	Ruta Meilutyte	Lithuania	Barcelona, Spain	July 29, 2013
200 meters	2:19.11	Rikke Moller Pedersen	Denmark	Barcelona, Spain	Aug. 1, 2013

Butterfly

Distance	Record	Holder	Nationality	Location	Date
50 meters	0:25.07	Therese Alshammar	Sweden	Rome, Italy	July 31, 2009
100 meters	0:55.98	Dana Vollmer	U.S.	London, England, UK	July 29, 2012
200 meters	2:01.81	Liu Zige	China	Jinan, China	Oct. 21, 2009

Individual medley

Distance	Record	Holder	Nationality	Location	Date
200 meters	2:06.15	Ariana Kukors	U.S.	Rome, Italy	July 27, 2009
400 meters	4:28.43	Ye Shiwen	China	London, England, UK	July 28, 2012

Freestyle relay

Distance	Record	Holder	Nationality	Location	Date
400 m (4×100)	3:31.72	Dekker, Kromowidjojo, Heemskerk, Veldhuis	Netherlands	Rome, Italy	July 26, 2009
800 m (4×200)	7:42.08	Yang, Zhu, Liu, Pang	China	Rome, Italy	July 30, 2009

Medley relay

Distance	Record	Holder	Nationality	Location	Date
400 m (4×100)	3:52.05	Franklin, Soni, Vollmer, Schmitt	U.S.	London, England, UK	Aug. 4, 2012

World Track and Field Outdoor Records

The International Association of Athletics Federations (IAAF), the world body of track and field, recognizes only records in metric distances, except for the mile. * = Record pending ratification. As of Oct. 2013.

Men's Records

Running

Event	Record	Holder	Nationality	Location	Date
100 meters	9.58 s.	Usain Bolt	Jamaica	Berlin, Germany	Aug. 16, 2009
200 meters	19.19 s.	Usain Bolt	Jamaica	Berlin, Germany	Aug. 20, 2009
400 meters	43.18 s.	Michael Johnson	U.S.	Seville, Spain	Aug. 26, 1999
800 meters	1 min., 40.91 s.	David Lekuta Rudisha	Kenya	London, England, UK	Aug. 9, 2012
1,000 meters	2 min., 11.96 s.	Noah Ngeny	Kenya	Rieti, Italy	Sept. 5, 1999
1,500 meters	3 min., 26.00 s.	Hicham El Guerrouj	Morocco	Rome, Italy	July 14, 1998
1 mile	3 min., 43.13 s.	Hicham El Guerrouj	Morocco	Rome, Italy	July 7, 1999
2,000 meters	4 min., 44.79 s.	Hicham El Guerrouj	Morocco	Berlin, Germany	Sept. 7, 1999
3,000 meters	7 min., 20.67 s.	Daniel Komen	Kenya	Rieti, Italy	Sept. 1, 1996
3,000-meter stpl.	7 min., 53.63 s.	Saif Saaeed Shaheen	Qatar	Brussels, Belgium	Sept. 3, 2004
5,000 meters	12 min., 37.35 s.	Kenenisa Bekele	Ethiopia	Hengelo, Netherlands	May 31, 2004
10,000 meters	26 min., 17.53 s.	Kenenisa Bekele	Ethiopia	Brussels, Belgium	Aug. 26, 2005
20,000 meters	56 min., 26.00 s.	Haile Gebrselassie	Ethiopia	Ostrava, Czech Rep.	June 27, 2007
25,000 meters	1 hr., 12 min., 25.4 s.	Moses Cheruiyot Mosop	Kenya	Eugene, OR	June 3, 2011
Marathon	2 hr., 3 min., 23 s.*	Wilson Kipsang	Kenya	Berlin, Germany	Sept. 29, 2013
110-meter hurdles	12.80 s.	Aries Merritt	U.S.	Brussels, Belgium	Sept. 7, 2012
400-meter hurdles	46.78 s.	Kevin Young	U.S.	Barcelona, Spain	Aug. 6, 1992
400 m (4x100)	36.84 s.	(Carter, Frater, Blake, Bolt)	Jamaica	London, England, UK	Aug. 11, 2012
800 m (4×200)	1 min., 18.68 s.	(Marsh, Burrell, Heard, Lewis)	U.S.	Walnut, CA	Apr. 17, 1994
1,600 m (4×400)	2 min., 54.29 s.[1]	(Valmon, Watts, Reynolds, Johnson)	U.S.	Stuttgart, Germany	Aug. 22, 1993
3,200 m (4×800)	7 min., 2.43 s.	(Mutua, Yiampoy, Kombich, Bungei)	Kenya	Brussels, Belgium	Aug. 25, 2006

(1) IAAF voted in Aug. 2008 to revoke a world record set by the U.S. team in 1998; one of the team's members, Antonio Pettigrew, admitted to doping in May 2008.

Field Events

Event	Record	Holder	Nationality	Location	Date
High jump	2.45 m (8' ½")	Javier Sotomayor	Cuba	Salamanca, Spain	July 27, 1993
Long jump	8.95 m (29' 4½")	Mike Powell	U.S.	Tokyo, Japan	Aug. 30, 1991
Triple jump	18.29 m (60' ¼")	Jonathan Edwards	UK	Göteborg, Sweden	Aug. 7, 1995
Pole vault	6.14 m (20' 1¾")	Sergey Bubka	Ukraine	Sestriere, Italy	July 31, 1994
Discus	74.08 m (243' 0")	Jürgen Schult	E. Germany	Neubrandenburg, E. Germany	June 6, 1986
Hammer	86.74 m (284' 7")	Yuriy Sedykh	USSR	Stuttgart, W. Germany	Aug. 30, 1986
Javelin	98.48 m (323' 1")	Jan Zelezny	Czech Rep.	Stuttgart, W. Germany	May 25, 1996
Shot put	23.12 m (75' 10¼")	Randy Barnes	U.S.	Westwood, CA	May 20, 1990
Decathlon	9,039 pts.	Ashton Eaton	U.S.	Eugene, OR	June 23, 2012

Women's Records

Running

Event	Record	Holder	Nationality	Location	Date
100 meters	10.49 s.	Florence Griffith-Joyner	U.S.	Indianapolis, IN	July 16, 1988
200 meters	21.34 s.	Florence Griffith-Joyner	U.S.	Seoul, S. Korea	Sept. 29, 1988
400 meters	47.60 s.	Marita Koch	E. Germany	Canberra, Australia	Oct. 6, 1985
800 meters	1 min., 53.28 s.	Jarmila Kratochvílová	Czechoslovakia	Munich, W. Germany	July 26, 1983
1,000 meters	2 min., 28.98 s.	Svetlana Masterkova	Russia	Brussels, Belgium	Aug. 23, 1996
1,500 meters	3 min., 50.46 s.	Qu Yunxia	China	Beijing, China	Sept. 11, 1993
1 mile	4 min., 12.56 s.	Svetlana Masterkova	Russia	Zürich, Switzerland	Aug. 14, 1996
2,000 meters	5 min., 25.36 s.	Sonia O'Sullivan	Ireland	Edinburgh, Scotland, UK	July 8, 1994
3,000 meters	8 min., 6.11 s.	Wang Junxia	China	Beijing, China	Sept. 13, 1993
3,000-meter stpl.	8 min., 58.81 s.	Gulnara Galkina-Samitova	Russia	Beijing, China	Aug. 17, 2008
5,000 meters	14 min., 11.15 s.	Tirunesh Dibaba	Ethiopia	Oslo, Norway	June 6, 2008
10,000 meters	29 min., 31.78 s.	Wang Junxia	China	Beijing, China	Sept. 8, 1993
20,000 meters	1 hr., 5 min., 26.6 s.	Tegla Loroupe	Kenya	Borgholzhausen, Germany	Sept. 3, 2000
30,000 meters	1 hr., 45 min., 50.0 s.	Tegla Loroupe	Kenya	Warstein, Germany	June 6, 2003
Marathon	2 hr., 15 min., 25.0 s.	Paula Radcliffe	UK	London, England, UK	Apr. 13, 2003
100-meter hurdles	12.21 s.	Yordanka Donkova	Bulgaria	Stara Zagora, Bulgaria	Aug. 20, 1988
400-meter hurdles	52.34 s.	Yuliya Pechenkina	Russia	Tula, Russia	Aug. 8, 2003
400 m (4×100)	40.82 s.	(Madison, Felix, Knight, Jeter)	U.S.	London, England, UK	Aug. 10, 2012
800 m (4×200)	1 min., 27.46 s.	(Jenkins, Colander, Perry, Jones)	U.S.	Philadelphia, PA	Apr. 29, 2000
1,600 m (4×400)	3 min., 15.17 s.	(Ledovskaya, Nazarova, Pinigina, Bryzgina)	USSR	Seoul, S. Korea	Oct. 1, 1988
3,200 m (4×800)	7 min., 50.17 s.	(Olizarenko, Gurina, Borisova, Podyalovskaya)	USSR	Moscow, USSR	Aug. 5, 1984

Field Events

Event	Record	Holder	Nationality	Location	Date
High jump	2.09 m (6' 10¼")	Stefka Kostadinova	Bulgaria	Rome, Italy	Aug. 30, 1987
Long jump	7.52 m (24' 8¼")	Galina Chistyakova	USSR	Leningrad, Russia	June 11, 1988
Triple jump	15.50 m (50' 10¼")	Inessa Kravets	Ukraine	Göteborg, Sweden	Aug. 10, 1995
Pole vault	5.06 m (16' 7¾")	Yelena Isinbaeva	Russia	Zürich, Switzerland	Aug. 28, 2009
Discus	76.80 m (252' 0")	Gabriele Reinsch	E. Germany	Neubrandenburg, E. Germany	July 9, 1988
Hammer	79.42 m (260' 4½")	Betty Heidler	Germany	Halle, Germany	May 21, 2011
Javelin	72.28 m (237' 1¾")	Barbora Spotáková	Czech Rep.	Stuttgart, Germany	Sept. 13, 2008
Shot put	22.63 m (74' 3")	Natalya Lisovskaya	USSR	Moscow, Russia	June 7, 1987
Heptathlon	7,291 pts.	Jackie Joyner-Kersee	U.S.	Seoul, S. Korea	Sept. 24, 1988

Iditarod Trail Sled Dog Race, 2013

Mitch Seavey won the 41st annual Iditarod Trail Sled Dog Race from Anchorage to Nome, AK, Mar. 13, 2013, capturing the $50,400 prize and a new pick-up truck. The 53-year-old Seavey finished the 1,131-mi course along the southern route to Nome in 9 days, 7 hr., 39 min., and 56 sec. to become the oldest champion in Iditarod history. The 2014 race was scheduled to begin Mar. 1 in Anchorage and follow the 1,112-mi northern route to Nome.

Westminster Kennel Club Best-In-Show Dogs, 1990-2013

Year	Best-in-Show winner	Breed	Owner(s)
1990	Ch. Wendessa Crown Prince	Pekingese	Ed Jenner
1991	Ch. Whisperwind on a Carousel	Poodle	Joan and Frederick Hartsock
1992	Ch. Registry's Lonesome Dove	Fox Terrier	Marion and Sam Lawrence
1993	Ch. Salilyn's Condor	English Springer Spaniel	Donna and Roger Herzig
1994	Ch. Chidley Willum	Norwich Terrier	Ruth Cooper, Patricia Lussier
1995	Ch. Gaelforce Post Script	Scottish Terrier	Dr. Vandra Huber, Dr. Joe Kinnarney
1996	Ch. Clussexx Country Sunrise	Clumber Spaniel	Judith and Richard Zaleski
1997	Ch. Parsifal Di Casa Netzer	Standard Schnauzer	Rita Holloway, Gabrio Del Torre
1998	Ch. Fairewood Frolic	Norwich Terrier	Sandina Kennels
1999	Ch. Loteki Supernatural Being	Papillon	John Oulton
2000	Ch. Salilyn 'N Erin's Shameless	English Springer Spaniel	Carl Blain, Fran Sunseri, Julia Gasow
2001	Ch. Special Times Just Right	Bichon Frise	Cecilia Ruggles, E. McDonald, F. Werneck
2002	Ch. Surrey Spice Girl	Poodle (Miniature)	Ron L. and Barbara Scott
2003	Ch. Torum's Scarf Michael	Kerry Blue Terrier	Marilu Hanson
2004	Ch. Darbydale's All Rise Pouchcove	Newfoundland	Peggy Helming, Carol A. Bernard Bergmann
2005	Ch. Kan-Point's VJK Autumn Roses	German Shorthaired Pointer	Linda & Richard Stark, Carol Cronk, Valerie Nunes-Atkinson
2006	Ch. Rocky Top's Sundance Kid	Bull Terrier (colored)	Barbara Bishop, W. F. Poole, N. Shepherd, R. P. Poole
2007	Ch. Felicity's Diamond Jim	English Springer Spaniel	Teresa and Allen Patton, Ruth Dehmel, D. Hadsall
2008	Ch. K-Run's Park Me In First	Beagle (15 in.)	Caroline Dowell, Eddie Dziuk, Jon Woodring, Kathy Weichert
2009	Ch. Clussexx Three D Grinchy Glee	Sussex Spaniel	Cecilia Ruggles, Beth Dowd, Scott Sommer
2010	Ch. Roundtown Mercedes Of Maryscot	Scottish Terrier	Amelia Musser
2011	Ch. Foxcliffe Hickory Wind	Scottish Deerhound	Sally Sweatt, Cecilia L. Dove, R. Scott Dove
2012	Ch. Palacegarden Malachy	Pekingese	Iris Love, S. Middlebrooks, D. Fitzpatrick
2013	Ch. Banana Joe V Tani Kazari	Affenpinscher	Zoila Truesdale, Mieke Cooymans

MARATHONS

World Marathon Majors

Five of the world's leading marathons (Berlin, Boston, Chicago, London, and New York) agreed Jan. 23, 2006, to form a series called the World Marathon Majors. Tokyo joined the series in 2013. Marathon runners are awarded points relative to their finish in each race in the series and in Olympic and the Intl. Assn. of Athletics Federations World Championships marathons. The male and female runners with the most points at the end of each two-year cycle win $500,000. The 2010-11 World Marathon Majors series winners were Emmanuel Mutai, Kenya, and Liliya Shobukhova, Russia. The winners of the 2011-12 series were Kenyans Geoffrey Mutai and Mary Keitany.

Boston Marathon Winners, 1972-2013

All times in hour:minute:second format. * = Course record.

Men's winner, country	Time	Year	Women's winner, country	Time
Olavi Suomalainen, Finland	2:15:39	1972	Nina Kuscsik, U.S.	3:10:26
Jon Anderson, U.S.	2:16:03	1973	Jacqueline Hansen, U.S.	3:05:59
Neil Cusack, Ireland	2:13:39	1974	Michiko Gorman, U.S.	2:47:11
Bill Rodgers, U.S.	2:09:55	1975	Liane Winter, West Germany	2:42:24
Jack Fultz, U.S.	2:20:19	1976	Kim Merritt, U.S.	2:47:10
Jerome Drayton, Canada	2:14:46	1977	Michiko Gorman, U.S.	2:48:33
Bill Rodgers, U.S.	2:10:13	1978	Gayle S. Barron, U.S.	2:44:52
Bill Rodgers, U.S.	2:09:27	1979	Joan Benoit, U.S.	2:35:15
Bill Rodgers, U.S.	2:12:11	1980	Jacqueline Gareau, Canada	2:34:28
Toshihiko Seko, Japan	2:09:26	1981	Allison Roe, New Zealand	2:26:46
Alberto Salazar, U.S.	2:08:52	1982	Charlotte Teske, West Germany	2:29:33
Greg Meyer, U.S.	2:09:00	1983	Joan Benoit, U.S.	2:22:43
Geoff Smith, England, UK	2:10:34	1984	Lorraine Moller, New Zealand	2:29:28
Geoff Smith, England, UK	2:14:05	1985	Lisa Larsen Weidenbach, U.S.	2:34:06
Robert de Castella, Australia	2:07:51	1986	Ingrid Kristiansen, Norway	2:24:55
Toshihiko Seko, Japan	2:11:50	1987	Rosa Mota, Portugal	2:25:21
Ibrahim Hussein, Kenya	2:08:43	1988	Rosa Mota, Portugal	2:24:30
Abebe Mekonnen, Ethiopia	2:09:06	1989	Ingrid Kristiansen, Norway	2:24:33
Gelindo Bordin, Italy	2:08:19	1990	Rosa Mota, Portugal	2:25:24
Ibrahim Hussein, Kenya	2:11:06	1991	Wanda Panfil, Poland	2:24:18
Ibrahim Hussein, Kenya	2:08:14	1992	Olga Markova, Russia	2:23:43
Cosmas Ndeti, Kenya	2:09:33	1993	Olga Markova, Russia	2:25:27
Cosmas Ndeti, Kenya	2:07:15	1994	Uta Pippig, Germany	2:21:45
Cosmas Ndeti, Kenya	2:09:22	1995	Uta Pippig, Germany	2:25:11
Moses Tanui, Kenya	2:09:15	1996	Uta Pippig, Germany	2:27:12
Lameck Aguta, Kenya	2:10:34	1997	Fatuma Roba, Ethiopia	2:26:23
Moses Tanui, Kenya	2:07:34	1998	Fatuma Roba, Ethiopia	2:23:21
Joseh Chebet, Kenya	2:09:52	1999	Fatuma Roba, Ethiopia	2:23:25
Elijah Lagat, Kenya	2:09:47	2000	Catherine Nderoba, Kenya	2:26:11
Lee Bong-ju, South Korea	2:09:43	2001	Catherine Nderoba, Kenya	2:23:53
Rodgers Rop, Kenya	2:09:02	2002	Margaret Okayo, Kenya	2:20:43*
Robert Kipkoech Cheruiyot, Kenya	2:10:11	2003	Svetlana Zakharova, Russia	2:25:20
Timothy Cherigat, Kenya	2:10:37	2004	Catherine Nderoba, Kenya	2:24:27
Hailu Negussie, Ethiopia	2:11:45	2005	Catherine Nderoba, Kenya	2:25:13
Robert Kipkoech Cheruiyot, Kenya	2:07:14	2006	Rita Jeptoo, Kenya	2:23:38
Robert Kipkoech Cheruiyot, Kenya	2:14:13	2007	Lidiya Grigoryeva, Russia	2:29:18
Robert Kipkoech Cheruiyot, Kenya	2:07:46	2008	Dire Tune, Ethiopia	2:25:25
Deriba Merga, Ethiopia	2:08:42	2009	Salina Kosgei, Kenya	2:32:16
Robert Kiprono Cheruiyot, Kenya	2:05:52	2010	Teyba Erkesso, Ethiopia	2:26:11
Geoffrey Mutai, Kenya	2:03:02*	2011	Caroline Kilel, Kenya	2:22:36
Wesley Korir, Kenya	2:12:40	2012	Sharon Cherop, Kenya	2:31:50
Lelisa Desisa, Ethiopia	2:10:22	2013	Rita Jeptoo, Kenya	2:26:25

Boston Marathon Winners, 1897-1971

The first Boston Marathon was held in 1897. Women were officially accepted into the race in 1972.

Year	Winner, state/country	Time
1897	John J. McDermott, New York	2:55:10
1898	Ronald J. MacDonald, Canada	2:42:00
1899	Lawrence Brignolia, Massachusetts	2:54:38
1900	John Caffery, Canada	2:39:44
1901	John Caffery, Canada	2:29:23
1902	Sammy Mellor, New York	2:43:12
1903	John Lorden, Massachusetts	2:41:29
1904	Michael Spring, New York	2:38:04
1905	Frederick Lorz, New York	2:38:25
1906	Tim Ford, Massachusetts	2:45:45
1907	Thomas Longboat, Canada	2:24:24
1908	Thomas Morrissey, New York	2:25:43
1909	Henri Renaud, New Hampshire	2:53:36
1910	Fred Cameron, Canada	2:28:52
1911	Clarence DeMar, Massachusetts	2:21:39
1912	Michael Ryan, New York	2:21:18
1913	Fritz Carlson, Minnesota	2:25:14
1914	James Duffy, Canada	2:25:14
1915	Edouard Fabre, Canada	2:31:41
1916	Arthur Roth, Massachusetts	2:27:16
1917	Bill Kennedy, New York	2:28:37
1918	Military relay, Camp Devens	2:29:53
1919	Carl Linder, Massachusetts	2:29:13
1920	Peter Trivoulides, New York	2:29:31
1921	Frank Zuna, New York	2:18:57
1922	Clarence DeMar, Massachusetts	2:18:10
1923	Clarence DeMar, Massachusetts	2:23:47
1924	Clarence DeMar, Massachusetts	2:29:40
1925	Charles Mellor, Illinois	2:33:00
1926	John C. Miles, Canada	2:25:40
1927	Clarence DeMar, Massachusetts	2:40:22
1928	Clarence DeMar, Massachusetts	2:37:07
1929	John C. Miles, Canada	2:33:08
1930	Clarence DeMar, Massachusetts	2:34:48
1931	James P. Henigan, Massachusetts	2:46:45
1932	Paul DeBruyn, Germany	2:33:36
1933	Leslie S. Pawson, Rhode Island	2:31:01
1934	Dave Komonen, Canada	2:32:53
1935	John A. Kelley, Massachusetts	2:32:07
1936	Ellison M. Brown, Rhode Island	2:33:40
1937	Walter Young, Canada	2:33:20
1938	Leslie S. Pawson, Rhode Island	2:35:34
1939	Ellison M. Brown, Rhode Island	2:28:51
1940	Gerard Cote, Canada	2:28:28
1941	Leslie S. Pawson, Rhode Island	2:30:38
1942	Joe Smith, Massachusetts	2:26:51
1943	Gerard Cote, Canada	2:28:25
1944	Gerard Cote, Canada	2:31:50
1945	John A. Kelley, Massachusetts	2:30:40
1946	Stylianos Kyriakides, Greece	2:29:27
1947	Yun Bok Suh, Korea	2:25:39
1948	Gerard Cote, Canada	2:31:02
1949	Karl Leandersson, Sweden	2:31:50
1950	Kee Yong Ham, Korea	2:32:39
1951	Shigeki Tanaka, Japan	2:27:45
1952	Doroteo Flores, Guatamela	2:31:53
1953	Keizo Yamada, Japan	2:18:51
1954	Veikko Karvonen, Finland	2:20:39
1955	Hideo Hamamura, Japan	2:18:22
1956	Antti Viskari, Finland	2:14:14
1957	John J. Kelley, Connecticut	2:20:05
1958	Franjo Mihalic, Yugoslavia	2:25:54
1959	Eino Oksanen, Finland	2:22:42
1960	Paavo Kotila, Finland	2:20:54
1961	Eino Oksanen, Finland	2:23:39
1962	Eino Oksanen, Finland	2:23:48
1963	Aurele Vandendriessche, Belgium	2:18:58
1964	Aurele Vandendriessche, Belgium	2:19:59
1965	Morio Shigematsu, Japan	2:16:33
1966	Kenji Kemihara, Japan	2:17:11
1967	David McKenzie, New Zealand	2:15:45
1968	Amby Burfoot, Connecticut	2:22:17
1969	Yoshiaki Unetani, Japan	2:13:49
1970	Ron Hill, England, UK	2:10:30
1971	Alvaro Mejia, Colombia	2:18:45

New York City Marathon Winners, 1970-2013

All times in hour:minute:second format. * = Course record.

Men's winner, country	Time	Year	Women's winner, country	Time
Gary Muhrcke, U.S.	2:31:38	1970	No finisher	—
Norman Higgins, U.S.	2:22:54	1971	Beth Bonner, U.S.	2:55:22
Sheldon Karlin, U.S.	2:27:52	1972	Nina Kuscsik, U.S.	3:08:41
Tom Fleming, U.S.	2:19:25	1973	Nina Kuscsik, U.S.	2:57:07
Norbert Sander, U.S.	2:26:30	1974	Katherine Switzer, U.S.	3:07:29
Tom Fleming, U.S.	2:19:27	1975	Kim Merritt, U.S.	2:46:14
Bill Rodgers, U.S.	2:10:10	1976	Miki Gorman, U.S.	2:39:11
Bill Rodgers, U.S.	2:11:28	1977	Miki Gorman, U.S.	2:43:10
Bill Rodgers, U.S.	2:12:12	1978	Grete Waitz, Norway	2:32:30
Bill Rodgers, U.S.	2:11:42	1979	Grete Waitz, Norway	2:27:33
Alberto Salazar, U.S.	2:09:41	1980	Grete Waitz, Norway	2:25:42
Alberto Salazar, U.S.	2:08:13	1981	Allison Roe, New Zealand	2:25:29
Alberto Salazar, U.S.	2:09:29	1982	Grete Waitz, Norway	2:27:14
Rod Dixon, New Zealand	2:08:59	1983	Grete Waitz, Norway	2:27:00
Orlando Pizzolato, Italy	2:14:53	1984	Grete Waitz, Norway	2:29:30
Orlando Pizzolato, Italy	2:11:34	1985	Grete Waitz, Norway	2:28:34
Gianni Poli, Italy	2:11:06	1986	Grete Waitz, Norway	2:28:06
Ibrahim Hussein, Kenya	2:11:01	1987	Priscilla Welch, England, UK	2:30:17
Steve Jones, Wales, UK	2:08:20	1988	Grete Waitz, Norway	2:28:07
Juma Ikangaa, Tanzania	2:08:01	1989	Ingrid Kristiansen, Norway	2:25:30
Douglas Wakiihuri, Kenya	2:12:39	1990	Wanda Panfil, Poland	2:30:45
Salvador Garcia, Mexico	2:09:28	1991	Liz McColgan, Scotland, UK	2:27:32
Willie Mtolo, South Africa	2:09:29	1992	Lisa Ondieki, Australia	2:24:40
Andres Espinosa, Mexico	2:10:04	1993	Uta Pippig, Germany	2:26:24
German Silva, Mexico	2:11:21	1994	Tegla Loroupe, Kenya	2:27:37
German Silva, Mexico	2:11:00	1995	Tegla Loroupe, Kenya	2:28:06
Giacomo Leone, Italy	2:09:54	1996	Anuta Catuna, Romania	2:28:43
John Kagwe, Kenya	2:08:12	1997	F. Rochat-Moser, Switzerland	2:28:43
John Kagwe, Kenya	2:08:45	1998	Franca Fiacconi, Italy	2:25:17
Joseph Chebet, Kenya	2:09:14	1999	Adriana Fernandez, Mexico	2:25:06
Abdelkader El Mouaziz, Morocco	2:10:09	2000	Ludmila Petrova, Russia	2:25:45
Tesfaye Jifar, Ethiopia	2:07:43	2001	Margaret Okayo, Kenya	2:24:21
Rodgers Rop, Kenya	2:08:07	2002	Joyce Chepchumba, Kenya	2:25:56
Martin Lel, Kenya	2:10:30	2003	Margaret Okayo, Kenya	2:22:31*
Hendrik Ramaala, South Africa	2:09:28	2004	Paula Radcliffe, England, UK	2:23:10
Paul Tergat, Kenya	2:09:30	2005	Jelena Prokopcuka, Latvia	2:24:41
Marilson Gomes dos Santos, Brazil	2:09:58	2006	Jelena Prokopcuka, Latvia	2:25:05
Martin Lel, Kenya	2:09:04	2007	Paula Radcliffe, England, UK	2:23:09
Marilson Gomes dos Santos, Brazil	2:08:43	2008	Paula Radcliffe, England, UK	2:23:56
Meb Keflezighi, U.S.	2:09:15	2009	Derartu Tulu, Ethiopia	2:28:52
Gebre Gebrmariam, Ethiopia	2:08:14	2010	Edna Kiplagat, Kenya	2:28:20
Geoffrey Mutai, Kenya	2:05:06*	2011	Firehiwot Dado, Ethiopia	2:23:15
Geoffrey Mutai, Kenya	2:08:24	2013	Priscah Jeptoo, Kenya	2:25:07

Note: The 2012 race was canceled as New York recovered from Hurricane Sandy.

Other Marathon Results, 2013

Tokyo Marathon: Feb. 24. Men: Dennis Kimetto, Kenya, 2:06:50.
Women: Aberu Kebede, Ethiopia, 2:25:34.
Los Angeles Marathon: Mar. 17. Men: Erick Mose, Kenya,
2:09:43. Women: Aleksandra Duliba, Belarus, 2:26:07.
Paris Marathon: Apr. 7. Men: Peter Some, Kenya, 2:05:38.
Women: Boru Tadese, Ethiopia, 2:21:06.
Rotterdam Marathon: Apr. 14. Men: Tilahun Regassa, Ethiopia,
2:05:38. Women: Jemima Jelagat, Kenya, 2:23:27.

London Marathon: Apr. 21. Men: Tsegaye Kebede, Ethiopia,
2:06:04. Women: Priscah Jeptoo, Kenya, 2:20:15.
Berlin Marathon: Sept. 29. Men: Wilson Kipsang, Kenya,
2:03:23. Women: Florence Kiplagat, Kenya, 2:21:13.
Chicago Marathon: Oct. 13. Men: Dennis Kimetto, Kenya,
2:03:45. Women: Rita Jeptoo, Kenya, 2:19:57.

Ironman Triathlon World Championships, 1978-2013

All times in hour:minute:second format. * = Course record. The Ironman Triathlon World Championship—a 2.4-mi ocean swim, 112-mi bike ride, and 26.2-mi run—is held annually in Kailua-Kona, HI.

Men's winner, country	Time	Year	Women's winner, country	Time
Gordon Haller, U.S.	11:46:58	1978	No finisher	—
Tom Warren, U.S.	11:15:56	1979	Lyn Lemaire, U.S.	12:55:00
Dave Scott, U.S.	9:24:33	1980	Robin Beck, U.S.	11:21:24
John Howard, U.S.	9:38:29	1981	Linda Sweeney, U.S.	12:00:32
Dave Scott, U.S.	9:08:23	1982	Julie Leach, U.S.	10:54:08
Dave Scott, U.S.	9:05:57	1983	Sylviane Puntous, Canada	10:43:36
Dave Scott, U.S.	8:54:20	1984	Sylvanie Puntous, Canada	10:25:13
Scott Tinley, U.S.	8:50:54	1985	Joanne Ernst, U.S.	10:25:22
Dave Scott, U.S.	8:28:37	1986	Paula Newby-Fraser, Zimbabwe	9:49:14
Dave Scott, U.S.	8:34:13	1987	Erin Baker, New Zealand	9:35:25
Scott Molina, U.S.	8:31:00	1988	Paula Newby-Fraser, Zimbabwe	9:01:01
Mark Allen, U.S.	8:09:15	1989	Paula Newby-Fraser, Zimbabwe	9:00:56
Mark Allen, U.S.	8:28:17	1990	Erin Baker, New Zealand	9:13:42
Mark Allen, U.S.	8:18:32	1991	Paula Newby-Fraser, Zimbabwe	9:07:52
Mark Allen, U.S.	8:09:08	1992	Paula Newby-Fraser, Zimbabwe	8:55:28
Mark Allen, U.S.	8:07:45	1993	Paula Newby-Fraser, Zimbabwe	8:58:23
Greg Welch, Australia	8:20:27	1994	Paula Newby-Fraser, Zimbabwe	9:20:14
Mark Allen, U.S.	8:20:34	1995	Karen Smyers, U.S.	9:16:46
Luc Van Lierde, Belgium	8:04:08	1996	Paula Newby-Fraser, Zimbabwe	9:06:49
Thomas Hellriegel, Germany	8:33:01	1997	Heather Fuhr, Canada	9:31:43
Peter Reid, Canada	8:24:20	1998	Natascha Badmann, Switzerland	9:24:16
Luc Van Lierde, Belgium	8:17:17	1999	Lori Bowden, U.S.	9:13:02
Peter Reid, Canada	8:21:01	2000	Natascha Badmann, Switzerland	9:26:16
Timothy Deboom, U.S.	8:31:18	2001	Natascha Badmann, Switzerland	9:28:37
Timothy Deboom, U.S.	8:29:56	2002	Natascha Badmann, Switzerland	9:07:54
Peter Reid, Canada	8:22:35	2003	Lori Bowden, Canada	9:11:55
Normann Stadler, Germany	8:33:29	2004	Natascha Badmann, Switzerland[1]	9:50:04
Faris al-Sultan, Germany	8:14:17	2005	Natascha Badmann, Switzerland	9:09:30
Normann Stadler, Germany	8:11:56	2006	Michellie Jones, U.S.	9:18:31
Chris McCormack, Australia	8:15:34	2007	Chrissie Wellington, UK	9:08:45
Craig Alexander, Australia	8:17:45	2008	Chrissie Wellington, UK	9:06:23
Craig Alexander, Australia	8:20:21	2009	Chrissie Wellington, UK	8:54:02
Chris McCormack, Australia	0:10:37	2010	Mirinda Carfrae, Australia	8:58:36
Craig Alexander, Australia	8:03:56*	2011	Chrissie Wellington, UK	8:55:08
Pete Jacobs, Australia	8:18:37	2012	Leanda Cave, U.S.	9:15:54
Frederik Van Lierde, Belgium	8:12:29	2013	Mirinda Carfrae, Australia	8:52:14*

(1) First-place finisher Nina Kraft, Germany, admitted to using performance-enhancing drugs and was disqualified, Nov. 15, 2004.

James E. Sullivan Memorial Trophy Winners, 1930-2012

The James E. Sullivan Memorial Trophy, named after the former president of the Amateur Athletic Union (AAU) and inaugurated in 1930, is awarded annually by the AAU to the athlete who "by his or her performance, example, and influence as an amateur, has done the most during the year to advance the cause of sportsmanship."

Year Winner	Sport	Year Winner	Sport	Year Winner	Sport
1930 Bobby Jones	Golf	1962 James Beatty	Track	1991 Mike Powell	Track
1931 Barney Berlinger	Track	1963 John Pennel	Track	1992 Bonnie Blair	Speed skating
1932 Jim Bausch	Track	1964 Don Schollander	Swimming		
1933 Glenn Cunningham	Track	1965 Bill Bradley	Basketball	1993 Charlie Ward	Football, basketball
1934 Bill Bonthron	Track	1966 Jim Ryun	Track		
1935 Lawson Little	Golf	1967 Randy Matson	Track	1994 Dan Jansen	Speed skating
1936 Glenn Morris	Track	1968 Debbie Meyer	Swimming		
1937 Don Budge	Tennis	1969 Bill Toomey	Track	1995 Bruce Baumgartner	Wrestling
1938 Don Lash	Track	1970 John Kinsella	Swimming	1996 Michael Johnson	Track
1939 Joe Burk	Rowing	1971 Mark Spitz	Swimming	1997 Peyton Manning	Football
1940 Greg Rice	Track	1972 Frank Shorter	Track	1998 Chamique Holdsclaw	Basketball
1941 Leslie MacMitchell	Track	1973 Bill Walton	Basketball	1999 Coco Miller and	
1942 Cornelius Warmerdam	Track	1974 Rick Wohlhutter	Track	Kelly Miller	Basketball
1943 Gilbert Dodds	Track	1975 Tim Shaw	Swimming	2000 Rulon Gardner	Wrestling
1944 Ann Curtis	Swimming	1976 Bruce Jenner	Track	2001 Michelle Kwan	Figure skating
1945 Doc Blanchard	Football	1977 John Naber	Swimming		
1946 Arnold Tucker	Football	1978 Tracy Caulkins	Swimming	2002 Sarah Hughes	Figure skating
1947 John Kelly Jr.	Rowing	1979 Kurt Thomas	Gymnastics		
1948 Robert Mathias	Track	1980 Eric Heiden	Speed skating	2003 Michael Phelps	Swimming
1949 Dick Button	Skating			2004 Paul Hamm	Gymnastics
1950 Fred Wilt	Track	1981 Carl Lewis	Track	2005 J. J. Redick	Basketball
1951 Rev. Robert Richards	Track	1982 Mary Decker	Track	2006 Jessica Long	Swimming (paralympics)
1952 Horace Ashenfelter	Track	1983 Edwin Moses	Track		
1953 Dr. Sammy Lee	Diving	1984 Greg Louganis	Diving	2007 Tim Tebow	Football
1954 Mal Whitfield	Track	1985 Joan Benoit		2008 Shawn Johnson	Gymnastics
1955 Harrison Dillard	Track	Samuelson	Marathon	2009 Amy Palmiero-	
1956 Patricia McCormick	Diving	1986 Jackie Joyner-Kersee	Track	Winters	Ultra-marathon
1957 Bobby Joe Morrow	Track	1987 Jim Abbott	Baseball		
1958 Glenn Davis	Track	1988 Florence Griffith Joyner	Track	2010 Evan Lysacek	Figure skating
1959 Parry O'Brien	Track	1989 Janet Evans	Swimming		
1960 Rafer Johnson	Track	1990 John Smith	Wrestling	2011 Andrew Rodriguez	Football
1961 Wilma Rudolph Ward	Track			2012 Missy Franklin	Swimming

America's Cup Yacht Race, 1851-2013

Competition for the America's Cup grew out of a yachting race during the London Exposition of 1851. The race covered an approximately 60-mi course around the Isle of Wight. The prize was a cup donated by the Royal Yacht Squadron of England. It became known as the America's Cup after the New York Yacht Club won the race with the ship *America*. Prior to 1983, all yachts are American unless otherwise noted.

Year	Result	Year	Result
1851	America	1962	Weatherly defeated Gretel, Australia (4-1)
1870	Magic defeated Cambria, England (1-0)	1964	Constellation defeated Sovereign, England (4-0)
1871	Columbia (first three races) and Sappho (last two races)	1967	Intrepid defeated Dame Pattie, Australia (4-0)
	defeated Livonia, England (4-1)	1970	Intrepid defeated Gretel II, Australia (4-1)
1876	Madeline defeated Countess of Dufferin, Canada (2-0)	1974	Courageous defeated Southern Cross, Australia (4-0)
1881	Mischief defeated Atalanta, Canada (2-0)	1977	Courageous defeated Australia, Australia (4-0)
1885	Puritan defeated Genesta, England (2-0)	1980	Freedom defeated Australia, Australia (4-1)
1886	Mayflower defeated Galatea, England (2-0)	1983	Australia II, Australia, defeated Liberty, U.S. (4-3)
1887	Volunteer defeated Thistle, Scotland (2-0)	1987	Stars & Stripes, U.S., defeated Kookaburra III, Aust. (4-0)
1893	Vigilant defeated Valkyrie II, England (3-0)	1988	Stars & Stripes, U.S., defeated New Zealand, NZ (2-0)
1895	Defender defeated Valkyrie III, England (3-0)	1992	America[3], U.S., defeated Il Moro di Venezia, Italy (4-1)
1899	Columbia defeated Shamrock, England (3-0)	1995	Black Magic 1, NZ, defeated Young America, U.S. (5-0)
1901	Columbia defeated Shamrock II, England (3-0)	2000	New Zealand, NZ, defeated Luna Rossa, Italy (5-0)
1903	Reliance defeated Shamrock III, England (3-0)	2003	Alinghi, Switzerland, defeated Team New Zealand, NZ (5-0)
1920	Resolute defeated Shamrock IV, England (3-2)	2007	Alinghi, Switzerland, defeated Emirates Team New
1930	Enterprise defeated Shamrock V, England (4-0)		Zealand, NZ (5-2)
1934	Rainbow defeated Endeavour, England (4-2)	2010	USA-17, U.S., defeated Alinghi 5, Switzerland (2-0)
1937	Ranger defeated Endeavour II, England (4-0)	2013	Oracle, U.S., defeated Emirates Team New Zealand, NZ
1958	Columbia defeated Sceptre, England (4-0)		(9-8)

Rifle and Pistol Championships, 2013

Source: National Rifle Association (NRA)

NRA Bianchi Cup National Action Pistol Championship

Action Pistol: Doug Koenig, Hamburg, PA, 1920-183X
Woman Action Pistol: Jessie Duff, Horn Lake, MS, 1893-142X

Junior Action Pistol: Tiffany Piper, Auckland, New Zealand, 1885-143X

National Outdoor Rifle and Pistol Championships

Pistol: Brian H. Zins, Girard, OH, 2634-126X
Civilian Pistol: Brian H. Zins, Girard, OH, 2634-126X
Woman Pistol: Kimberly Hobart, New Philadelphia, OH, 2501-64X
Smallbore Rifle Prone: SSG Michael D. McPhail, USA, Phenix City, AL, 4798-385X
Civilian Smallbore Rifle Prone: Reya L. Kempley, Farmington, NY, 4792-381X
Woman Smallbore Rifle Prone: Katie L. Bridges, Kingsland, TX, 4791-351X
Smallbore Rifle NRA 3-Position: SPC Joseph C. Hall, USA, Box Springs, GA, 2383-171X
Civilian Smallbore Rifle NRA 3-Position: Tarl Kempley, Carson City, NV, 2374-152X

Woman Smallbore Rifle NRA 3-Position: Amy G. Fister, Lenhartsville, PA, 2374-140X
High Power Rifle: SSG Brandon Keith Green, USA, Box Springs, GA, 2384-126X
Civilian High Power Rifle: Carl Bernosky, Ashland, PA, 2384-126X
Woman High Power Rifle: MSG Julia Watson, USMC, Provo, UT, 2360-103X
High Power Rifle Long Range: SSG Tyrel Cooper, USA, Ft. Benning, GA, 1243-64X
Woman High Power Rifle Long Range: Shirley J. McGee, Brooksville, KS, 1238-65X

National Indoor Rifle and Pistol Championships

Smallbore Rifle Conventional Position: John Husk, Eighty Four, PA, 796-68X
Woman Smallbore Rifle Conventional Position: Dacotah Faught, Amenia, ND, 794-60X
Smallbore Rifle NRA Metric Position: Danny Lowe, Tumwater, WA, 1159
Woman Smallbore Rifle NRA Metric Position: Lauren Phillips, Seabeck, WA, 1141
International Smallbore Rifle: Ryan Anderson, Wasilla, AK, 1166
Woman International Smallbore Rifle: Michelle Bohren, Taylor, MI, 1152
Air Rifle: Dustin Chesebro, Laramie, WY, 592

Woman Air Rifle: Jaycee Carter, Live Oak, CA, 587
Conventional Pistol: John Zurek, Tucson, AZ, 891-42X
Woman Conventional Pistol: Brenda Martin Silva, Snowflake, AZ, 873-29X
International Free Pistol: John Zurek, Tucson, AZ, 551
Woman International Free Pistol: Brenda Martin Silva, Snowflake, AZ, 530
International Standard Pistol: John Zurek, Tucson, AZ, 571
Woman International Standard Pistol: Brenda Martin Silva, Snowflake, AZ, 547
Air Pistol: John Zurek, Tucson, AZ, 585
Woman Air Pistol: Sandra Uptagrafft, Phenix City, AL, 570

Pro Rodeo Cowboys Association All-Around Champions, 1977-2012

Year	Winner, hometown	Earnings	Year	Winner, hometown	Earnings
1977	Tom Ferguson, Miami, OK	$76,730	1995	Joe Beaver, Huntsville, TX	$141,753
1978	Tom Ferguson, Miami, OK	103,734	1996	Joe Beaver, Huntsville, TX	166,103
1979	Tom Ferguson, Miami, OK	96,272	1997	Dan Mortensen, Manhattan, MT	184,559
1980	Paul Tierney, Rapid City, SD	105,568	1998	Ty Murray, Stephenville, TX	264,673
1981	Jimmie Cooper, Monument, NM	105,862	1999	Fred Whitfield, Hockley, TX	217,819
1982	Chris Lybbert, Coyote, CA	123,709	2000	Joe Beaver, Huntsville, TX	225,396
1983	Roy Cooper, Durant, OK	153,391	2001	Cody Ohl, Stephensville, TX	296,419
1984	Dee Pickett, Caldwell, ID	122,618	2002	Trevor Brazile, Anson, TX	273,997
1985	Lewis Feild, Elk Ridge, UT	130,347	2003	Trevor Brazile, Anson, TX	294,839
1986	Lewis Feild, Elk Ridge, UT	166,042	2004	Trevor Brazile, Decatur, TX	253,170
1987	Lewis Feild, Elk Ridge, UT	144,335	2005	Ryan Jarrett, Summerville, GA	263,665
1988	Dave Appleton, Arlington, TX	121,546	2006	Trevor Brazile, Decatur, TX	329,924
1989	Ty Murray, Odessa, TX	134,806	2007	Trevor Brazile, Decatur, TX	425,115
1990	Ty Murray, Stephenville, TX	213,772	2008	Trevor Brazile, Decatur, TX	419,868
1991	Ty Murray, Stephenville, TX	244,230	2009	Trevor Brazile, Decatur, TX	346,779
1992	Ty Murray, Stephenville, TX	225,992	2010	Trevor Brazile, Decatur, TX	507,921
1993	Ty Murray, Stephenville, TX	297,896	2011	Trevor Brazile, Decatur, TX	337,601
1994	Ty Murray, Stephenville, TX	246,170	2012	Trevor Brazile, Decatur, TX	298,626

GENERAL INDEX

Note: Page numbers in boldface indicate key reference. Page numbers in italics indicate photo or illustration captions.

QUICK REFERENCE INDEX

For complete index, see pages 979-1007.